Bradford's Crossword Key Dictionary

Bradford's Crossword Key Dictionary

PETER COLLIN PUBLISHING

Editors

S.M.H. Collin

P.H. Collin

Forword by

Anne R. Bradford

First published in Great Britain 2000

Reprinted 2001

by Peter Collin Publishing Ltd

32-34 Great Peter Street, London, SW1P 2DB - UK

British Library Cataloguing in Publication Data

A catalogue record for this book is available from the British Library

ISBN 1-901659-40-2

Computer processing and typesetting by PCP

Printed by WS Bookwell, Juva, Finland

For details of our complete range of titles, visit our website:

www.petercollin.com

PREFACE

This dictionary lists over 480,000 words, with four to fifteen letters, each organised into chapters according to the length of the word, then sorted according to each letter position within the word (see the section below).

The words within this dictionary have been selected from the wide range of dictionaries that we publish - over 20 specialist and general English dictionaries - to ensure that the terms cover all aspects of English that might be used by the person setting the puzzle.

We created this dictionary as a companion volume to the *Bradford's Crossword Solver's Dictionary* (published by Peter Collin Publishing, ISBN 1-901659-03-8). The *Crossword Solver* provides possible answers to cryptic crossword clues, based on years of research of the key words within crossword clues - by crossword expert, Anne Bradford. This *Crossword Key Dictionary* can be used to help solve cryptic crosswords, but is also very useful for any type of crossword, word puzzle or game.

HOW TO USE THIS DICTIONARY

This dictionary lists words in two ways: firstly, the words are organized into chapters by length (the number of letters that they contain). Within each of these chapters, the words are then sorted alphabetically according to letter in each position.

For example, all the four-letter words are listed four times: alphabetically by the first letter in each word, then by the second letter, then the third, then the fourth.

This repeated listing makes it very easy to find the group of words that fits the space in your crossword puzzle or word game.

Here is the way to find a word that is eight letters long, with 'c' as the fifth letter and 'c' as the last letter:

Word required: □□□□ C □□ C

1. Turn to the chapter for eight-letter words (p327)

2. Turn to the section that lists eight-letter words organised by fifth letter (p405)

3. Look down the list till you find words with 'C' (column 5 of p407)

4. Within this group, look for the words that have the letter 'C' as thelast letter.

You have now found the following words as possible solutions:

ANARCHIC, DICYCLIC, DIDACTIC, ECLECTIC, EIDECTIC, GALACTIC

SOLVING CROSSWORDS & PUZZLES

Simple 'quick' or 'concise' crosswords come in two forms. The familiar one is that used by many newspapers, with clues consisting of synonyms or descriptions, perhaps a single word. In tackling these the technique is to look for a fairly obvious answer, then find other answers which intersect at a mutual letter. From then on the format is not unlike a jigsaw puzzle, with leads of one or two letters into other answers, until the grid is complete. Occasionally there may be an isolated word, perhaps of five or six letters of which two have been found, the rest with no further means of checking, and it is then that the *Crossword Key* can be so useful. Grid styles can vary, using either blocks or bars to separate the answers, and there may be an arrow indicating the direction of the answer, but the basic practice is the same.

The other type of plain puzzle may have a theme requiring specialist or general knowledge and these are often favoured by specialist or in-house magazines; they may involve further research at a library for the solver determined to finish them.

Cryptic crosswords are a more advanced form of the simple ones, from which they have developed, and while they are more satisfying to solve they do require a certain talent for word play and a liking for puns. The setters of these puzzles take delight in using words with more than one meaning, in the hope of misleading the solver. Classic examples of this are the use of such words as - 'flower', not in a botanical sense, but to be read as 'flow-er' e.g a river; 'wicked', not evil but wick-ed, i.e. something with a wick, such as a candle; 'serviceman' can mean a minister of the church, and not a soldier; 'remember' may be intended as 'R.E-member', i.e. a sapper; 'potter' may be a snooker-player; 'quarterdeck' can be not part of a ship but one of the four suits in a pack (deck) of playing-cards; 'early' may refer to an earl; 'bearing' may indicate a compass point, N.S.W, or E; 'army' can be anything with arms, especially an octopus; and 'pupil' can be related to an eye rather than to a school.

Cryptic clues contain more than one part. There will be a definition of the answer required, referred to in crossword circles as the 'light' (sometimes you see it), and also a subsidiary indication which can be made up in a number of ways. In its simplest form the clue may consist of two straight definitions, e.g. 'Clog dance' giving the answer 'ball' because 'clog' as a verb can be to 'ball' and of course 'dance' as a noun may also be a 'ball'. A clue of this type may even have three straight definitions as in 'Crab, grouse and beef?' all leading to 'complain'.

The next simplest cryptic uses an anagram of the light for its subsidiary and there will be an anagram indicator somewhere in the clue. There are hundreds of words which can act as anagram indicators, since anything meaning 'change around', 'alter', 'otherwise', etc. can serve, and a clever setter will find one that fits neatly into the clue. 'Freed tangled bow' is an example, leading to 'defer' (bow), 'freed' being an anagram of 'defer' and 'tangled' the anagram indicator. Note that the clue gives a mental picture of a bow (ribbon or shoe lace) rather than bow (obeisance). The astute solver will look out for a likely word or phrase which fits the number of letters in the light, e.g. 'Expected at a wide gathering' (7) has a convenient 7-letter group which can be rearranged to make the answer 'awaited', 'gathering' being the anagram indicator this time.

First or last letters of words in the clue can be used as the subsidiary using various indicators such as 'head of', 'minimum of', 'top of', 'leaders of', 'introduction to', 'initially', etc, as in 'Honestly paid, declaration's up to you, initially' (Duty). The same system applies for last letters in words, indicated by 'ends', 'tails', 'rears', 'last of', etc. as in 'Last of red may lose colour' (Dye).

The commonest cryptic clue splits the light into two or three parts, either as a sequence or with one part wrapped around the other(s). 'Don's piecework with a logic circuit" (Tutor) is made up of 'Don' (tutor), the definition, 'piecework' (tut) and 'logic circuit' (OR). In 'See accepts archdeacon calmly' (Evenly) 'calmly' is the definition, 'See' is "Ely' (popular with crossword setters) and 'archdeacon' is abbreviated to 'ven'.

When such subsidiary parts are used they may be anagrammatized, reversed, or otherwise adapted. Thus 'Splendid barmaid upset by the French' (Admirable) has 'barmaid' 'upset' (anagram indicator) followed by 'le' ('the' in French). Abbreviations frequently appear, N,S,W,E as 'points'; 'TT' indicated by 'sober' or 'dry'; 0 used for 'nil', 'nought', 'nothing', or 'zero'. In the clue 'Flashy car? Shouldn't leave outside, these nights' (Starry) the 'flashy car' is a Rolls (RR) and 'shouldn't leave' is 'stay', which is 'outside' RR. 'These nights' is an indirect definition, often referred to as '& lit' inasmuch as the entire clue can lead to the required light. 'Tin-opener gets food out of this can' (Metal) is formed by 'T' the 'opener' of the word 'tin', surrounded by 'meal' ('food').

Hidden words may be used as a subsidiary form, indicators being 'bottled in', 'part of, 'found in', etc, e.g. 'American entertains Heather' (Erica, the botanical name for heather) or 'Fish found in pond or a swamp?' (Doras) which could be both hidden and '& lit'. The hidden light may also be reversed, shown by 'back in', 'taken aback', etc. in across clues and by 'taken up' in down clues.

Further play on words can be 'overdrawn', 'bankrupt', or such, implying 'in the red', where the 'red' will be split to go around another word. Hence 'Retained bankrupt minister' (Reserved) has 'Retained' as the definition, whilst 'minister' (serve) is in the 'red'. Similarly, use of 'retired' may indicate 'in bed', e.g. 'Nothing to occupy retirement, dear?' (Beloved) is made up by 'love' (nothing) in 'bed'. 'A follower' can refer to the letter 'b' (follows 'a'); 'a legend' may, in fact, indicate something at the end of a leg viz., foot or ankle (leg-end); 'untrained' may indicate 'BR' to be removed from a word in the clue, hence 'Untrained brute gets truck' (Ute -an accepted abbreviation for a utility truck).

A word which sounds like another may be indicated by 'reportedly', 'say', 'we hear', etc; 'revolutionary' may mean the answer is to be reversed to form the light, but can also be an anagram indicator as well as a popular use for 'red' or 'Che'.Some reference to Cockneys or Londoners can indicate a missing 'ti', and 'starving', hungry', famished', etc, can mean an 'o' is to be included i.e., 'nothing inside' (empty).

Solvers may find that they enter the only seemingly possible word which fits, without a full idea of why such is the answer, though it meets the definition. Practice will eventually bring enlightenment, and if completing the puzzle has brought satisfaction, does it really matter?

When confidence begins to build up and normal cryptics no longer hold terrors, the solver might cast an eye on some of the more elaborate crosswords to be found in weekend newspapers. These usually have an added gimmick explained in a preamble which may alarm the unwary, particularly if it indicates that a number of the lights are unclued. One type is referred to as 'Theme and Variation' there being perhaps three linked theme words, each of which may have two variations of its own, and all these are without clues, but the other lights give sufficient letters to allow for a logical deduction.

Another may use 'Misprints', where the definition is printed with a misprint although the clue still reads soundly. In this type of puzzle the corrected letters of the misprints when taken in clue order lead to a quotation or message, and the latter, in turn, may require the solver to make further amendments.

'Printer's Devilry' puzzles use not a clue, but a sentence which has involved the required light, but this word has then been removed and the remaining words closed up to form a new sentence, often rearranging the spacing. The classic example, often quoted, is 'I came across a flat Atlantic, rowing' in which the light 'stare' has been removed from the original version 'I came across a flat at last, aren't I crowing!'. Comparison of these two sentences will show the re-spacing, involving the formation of new words, and note that there is no definition of 'stare' in either. This type of clue is rarely used in entirety in a puzzle, but tends to be mixed with ordinary cryptic clues, and only the slightly surrealistic air of the 'Printer's Devilry' gives help in identification.

'Definition and Letter Mixtures' have a normal definition but the subsidiary includes a mixture of the letters in the light in place of a subsidiary cryptic part, and these mixtures tend to either start at the beginning of a word, or end at the end of one, e.g. 'This man doesn't settle' (Nomad).

'Letters Latent' require a letter to be omitted from the light wherever it occurs. The clue will have a normal definition, but the subsidiary will be a cryptic reference to what remains after the letter(s) have been removed, and only this residue is entered in the grid. As with 'Misprints' the latent letters taken in clue order are used to make a quotation or message e.g. 'Defence I held improperly' ((S)hield) where the latent letter is 's', and Tlield' would be entered in the grid.

'Carte Blanche' puzzles offer a totally blank grid and the solver is required to work out how the lights are to be entered, putting in blocks or bars accordingly. The grid is generally symmetrical through 180 degrees, and it is thus possible to fill in both halves of the grid as one goes along, but, as can be appreciated, it is necessary to get the majority of the lights before starting to fill them in.

Codes can also appear, the most famous being the 'Playfair'. In this type of puzzle a word or phrase has been selected by the setter, in which there are no repeated letters, then a 5 x 5 letter grid is made up starting with the chosen word or phrase and continuing with the remaining letters of the alphabet in order, ignoring 'J' unless it is needed for the keyword when 'Q' is dropped instead. For example, if 'Previously' is the keyword the grid would be:-

```
PREVI
OUSLY
ABCDF
GHKMN
QTUWZ
```

Certain lights in the puzzle (usually six and always containing an even number of letters) have to be coded before entry by splitting them into pairs of letters, e.g ac-um-en. Each pair is coded by finding the letters in the grid and if they are on the same line, the letter to the right of each is taken, if in the same column the letter below each is taken (if the last letter in a line or column is involved the solver takes the one at the beginning). Where the two letters are diagonally placed the solver takes the diagonally opposite letters, keeping the same direction, so for 'acumen' the code would be AC= BF; UM= LH (not HL); EN= IK, so the letters to be entered in the grid would be BFLHIK. In solving the remainder of the crossword sufficient pairings come to light to enable the solver to experiment with possible layouts and find the keyword(s).

Practice makes perfect. Have fun!

Anne R. Bradford.

4:1

AALU
AARU
ABAC
ABAS
ABBA
ABBE
ABED
ABEL
ABER
ABET
ABIB
ABLE
ABLY
ABRI
ABSE
ABUS
ABUT
ABYE
ABZU
ACAS
ACCT
AC/DC
ACER
ACES
ACHE
ACHT
ACID
ACIS
ACME
ACNE
ACOL
ACRE
ACRI
ACRO
ACTA
ACTS
ADAD
ADAM
ADAR
ADAW
ADEN
ADES
ADIT
ADUR
ADZE
AEON
AERO
AESC
AFAR
AFFY
AFRO
AGAG
AGAR
AGED
AGEE
AGEN
AGES
AGHA
AGIN
AGIO
AGIS
AGLU
AGMA
AGNI
AGOG
AGON
AGRA
AGUE
AHAB
AHEM
AHOY
AIDA
AIDE
AIDS
AÎNÉ
AINT
AINU
AIRE
AIRN
AIRS
AIRT
AIRY
AITU
AJAR
AJAX
AJEE
AKEE
AKIN
ALAI
ALAN
ALAR
ALAS
ALAY
ALBE
ALBI
ALEC
ALEW
ALEX
ALFA
ALGA
ALIA
ALIF
ALKY
ALLO
ALLY
ALMA
ALMS
ALOD
ALOE
ALOW
ALPH
ALPS
ALSO
ALTA
ALTE
ALTO
ALUM
ALVA
AMAH
AMBO
AMEN
AMES
AMID
AMIE
AMIN
AMIR
AMIS
AMLA
AMMO
AMOK
AMOS
AMOY
AMUN
AMUR
AMYL
ANAK
ANAL
ANAN
ANAS
ANCE
ANDA
ANEW
ANFO
ANIL
ANKH
ANNA
ANNE
ANNO
ANOA
ANON
ANTA
ANTE
ANTI
ANTS
ANUS
APAY
APEX
APIA
APIS
APSE
AQUA
ARAB
ARAK
ARAL
ARAM
ARAN
ARAR
ARCH
ARCO
AREA
AREG
ARES
ARET
AREW
ARGO
ARIA
ARID
ARIL
ARIS
ARLY
ARMS
ARMY
ARNA
ARNE
ARNO
ARRU
ARRY
ARSE
ARTA
ARTS
ARTY
ARUM
ARUN
ARVO
ARYL
ASAP
ASAR
ASAS
ASCH
ASHE
ASHY
ASIA
ASKE
ASKR
ASTI
ASUR
ATAP
ATAR
ATEN
ATLI
ATOC
ATOK
ATOM
ATOP
ATTO
ATTU
ATUA
ATUM
AUDE
AUDI
AULA
AULD
AUNE
AUNT
AURA
AUTO
AVAL
AVER
AVES
AVID
AVON
AVOW
AWAY
AWDL
AWED
AWOL
AWRY
AXIL
AXIS
AXLE
AXON
AYAH
AYER
AYES
AYIN
AYMÉ
AYRE
AZAN
AZOV
BAAL
BAAS
BABA
BABE
BABI
BABU
BABY
BACA
BACH
BACK
BADE
BAEL
BAFF
BAFT
BAGS
BAHT
BAIL
BAIT
BAJU
BAKE
BAKU
BALA
BALD
BALE
BALI
BALK
BALL
BALM
BALT
BALU
BANC
BAND
BANE
BANG
BANI
BANK
BANT
BAPU
BARB
BARD
BARE
BARF
BARI
BARK
BARM
BARN
BARP
BARS
BART
BASE
BASH
BASK
BASS
BAST
BATE
BATH
BATS
BATT
BAUD
BAUK
BAUR
BAWD
BAWL
BAWN
BAWR
BAYE
BAYS
BAYT
BCOM
BEAD
BEAK
BEAM
BEAN
BEAR
BEAT
BEAU
BECK
BEDE
BEDS
BEDU
BEEB
BEEF
BEEN
BEEP
BEER
BEES
BEET
BEGO
BEIN
BELL
BELT
BEMA
BEND
BENE
BENJ
BENN
BENT
BENZ
BERE
BERG
BERK
BERM
BERN
BESS
BEST
BETA
BETE
BÊTE
BETH
BEVY
BHEL
BIAS
BIBB
BICE
BIDE
BIEN
BIER
BIFF
BIGA
BIGG
BIKE
BILE
BILK
BILL
BIMM
BIND
BINE
BING
BINK
BINT
BIRD
BIRK
BIRL
BIRO
BIRR
BISE
BISH
BISK
BISP
BITE
BITO
BITS
BITT
BLAB
BLAD
BLAE
BLAG
BLAH
BLAT
BLAY
BLEB
BLED
BLEE
BLET
BLEW
BLEY
BLIN
BLIP
BLOB
BLOC
BLOT
BLOW
BLUB
BLUE
BLUR
BLUT
BOAK
BOAR
BOAT
BOAZ
BOBA
BOCK
BODE
BODY
BOER
BOFF
BOGY
BOIL
BOKE
BOKO
BOLD
BOLE
BOLL
BOLO
BOLT
BOMA
BOMB
BONA
BOND
BONE
BONG
BONK
BONN
BONY
BOOB
BOOK
BOOL
BOOM
BOON
BOOR
BOOT
BORA
BORD
BORE
BORN
BORO
BORS
BOSH
BOSS
BOTE
BOTH
BOTS
BOTT
BOUK
BOUN
BOUT
BOWL
BOWR
BOYG
BOYO
BOYS
BOZO
BRAD
BRAE
BRAG
BRAK
BRAM
BRAN
BRAS
BRAT
BRAW
BRAY
BRED
BREE
BREN
BRER
BREW
BRIE
BRIG
BRIM
BRIO
BRIS
BRIT
BRIX
BRNO
BROD
BROG
BRON
BROO
BROS
BROW
BRUM
BRUT
BUAT
BUBA
BUBO
BUCK
BUDD
BUDE
BUDO
BUFF
BUFO
BUGS
BUHL
BUIK
BUKE
BULB
BULK
BULL
BUMF
BUMP
BUNA
BUND
BUNG
BUNK
BUNT
BUOY
BURD
BURG
BURK
BURL
BURN
BURP
BURR
BURT
BURY
BUSH
BUSK
BUSS
BUST
BUSY
BUTE
BUTT
BUZZ
BYKE
BYNG
BYRD

BYRE
BYTE
CABA
CADE
CADI
CAEN
CAFÉ
CAGE
CAIN
CAKE
CALC
CALF
CALK
CALL
CALM
CALP
CALX
CAMA
CAME
CAMP
CANA
CANE
CANN
CANS
CANT
CAPA
CAPE
CAPH
CAPO
CAPT
CARD
CARE
CARK
CARL
CARP
CARR
CART
CARY
CASA
CASE
CASH
CASK
CAST
CATE
CATO
CATS
CAUK
CAUL
CAUM
CAUP
CAVE
CAVY
CAWK
CCTV
CEDE
CEDI
CEIL
CELL
CELT
CENS
CENT
CERE
CERO
CERT
CESS
CETE
CEYX
CFAF
CHAD
CHAI
CHAL
CHAM
CHAN
CHAP
CHAR
CHAT
CHAW
CHAY
CHEF
CHER
CHEW
CHIC
CHIK
CHIL
CHIN
CHIP
CHIT
CHOC
CHON
CHOP
CHOU
CHOW
CHOY
CHUB
CHUG
CHUM
CHUT
CIAO
CIEL
CIGS
CILL
CINE
CION
CIRÉ
CIRL
CIST
CITE
CITO
CITS
CITY
CIVE
CLAD
CLAG
CLAM
CLAN
CLAP
CLAT
CLAW
CLAY
CLEF
CLEG
CLEM
CLEW
CLIO
CLIP
CLOD
CLOG
CLOP
CLOS
CLOT
CLOU
CLOW
CLOY
CLUB
CLUE
COAL
COAT
COAX
COBB
COBH
COCA
COCH
COCK
COCO
CODA
CODE
CODY
COED
COFF
COIF
COIL
COIN
COIR
COIT
COKE
COLA
COLD
COLE
COLL
COLT
COMA
COMB
COME
COMM
COMO
COMP
CONE
CONK
CONN
CONS
CONT
CONY
COOF
COOK
COOL
COOM
COON
COOP
COOT
COPE
COPS
COPY
CORD
CORE
CORF
CORK
CORM
CORN
CORY
COSE
COSH
COSS
COST
COSY
COTE
COTH
COTT
COTY
COUE
COUP
COUR
COVE
COWL
COWP
COWS
COZE
COZY
CPRS
CRAB
CRAG
CRAM
CRAN
CRAP
CRAW
CRAX
CRAY
CRED
CREE
CREW
CRIB
CRIT
CROP
CROW
CRUD
CRUE
CRUX
CRYO
CUBA
CUBE
CUBS
CUFF
CUIF
CUIT
CULL
CULM
CULT
CUMA
CUNT
CUPS
CURB
CURD
CURE
CURK
CURL
CURN
CURR
CURT
CUSH
CUSK
CUSP
CUSS
CUTE
CUYP
CYAN
CYMA
CYME
CYST
CYTE
CZAR
DABS
DACE
DADA
DADD
DADO
DAFF
DAFT
DAGO
DAHL
DAIL
DAIS
DAKS
DALE
DALI
DAME
DAMN
DAMP
DANE
DANG
DANK
DARD
DARE
DARG
DARI
DARK
DARN
DART
DASH
DATA
DATE
DATO
DAUB
DAUD
DAUR
DAUT
DAVY
DAWD
DAWK
DAWN
DAWT
DAYS
DAZE
DBLE
DEAD
DEAF
DEAL
DEAN
DEAR
DEAW
DEBT
DECA
DECK
DECO
DEED
DEEK
DEEM
DEEN
DEEP
DEER
DEEV
DEFT
DEFY
DEIL
DEKE
DELE
DELF
DELI
DELL
DEME
DEMI
DEMO
DEMY
DENE
DENT
DENY
DEPT
DERE
DERM
DERN
DERO
DERV
DESK
DEVA
DEVI
DEWY
DHAK
DHAL
DHOW
DIAL
DIAS
DIAZ
DIBS
DICE
DICH
DICK
DICY
DIDO
DIEB
DIED
DIES
DIET
DIEU
DIGS
DIKA
DIKE
DILL
DIMA
DIME
DINE
DING
DINK
DINT
DIOR
DIRE
DIRK
DIRL
DIRT
DISA
DISC
DISH
DISK
DISS
DITA
DITE
DITT
DIVA
DIVE
DIXY
DOAB
DOAT
DOCK
DODO
DOEK
DOER
DOES
DOFF
DOGE
DOGS
DOGY
DOHA
DOIT
DOJO
DOLE
DOLL
DOLT
DOME
DONA
DONE
DONG
DONT
DOOB
DOOK
DOOL
DOOM
DOON
DOOR
DOPA
DOPE
DORA
DORÉ
DORM
DORP
DORR
DORT
DORY
DOSE
DOSH
DOSS
DOTE
DOTH
DOTS
DOUC
DOUP
DOUR
DOUT
DOVE
DOWF
DOWN
DOWT
DOXY
DOZE
DOZY
DRAB
DRAD
DRAG
DRAM
DRAT
DRAW
DRAY
DREE
DREG
DREW
DREY
DRIB
DRIP
DROP
DROW
DRUB
DRUG
DRUM
DUAD
DUAL
DUAN
DUAR
DUBS
DUCE
DUCK
DUCT
DUDE
DUDS
DUEL
DUES
DUET
DUFF
DUKE
DULE
DULL
DULY
DUMA
DUMB
DUMP
DUNE
DUNG
DUNK
DUNS
DUNT
DUPE
DURA
DURE
DURN
DURO
DUSE
DUSH
DUSK
DUST
DUTY
DYAD
DYAK
DYER
DYKE
DYNE
EACH
EALE
EARD
EARL
EARN
EARP
EARS
EASE
EAST
EASY
EATS
EBBW
EBOR
EBRO
ECAD
ECCE
ECCO
ECHE
ECHO
ECHT
ECRU
EDAL
EDAM
EDDA
EDDO
EDDY
EDEN
EDER
EDGE
EDGY
EDIT
EDOM
EECH
EELS
EERY
EFIK
EGAD
EGAL
EGER
EGGS
EGIS
EGMA
EHEU
EIGG
EILD
EINE
EIRE
EKKA
ELAM

ELAN
ELAT
ELBA
ELBE
ELIA
ELIS
ELKS
ELLA
ELLE
ELMO
ELOI
ELSA
ELSE
ELUL
EMEU
EMIR
EMIT
EMMA
EMMY
EMYS
ENDS
ENEW
ENID
ENNA
ENOL
ENOS
ENOW
ENSI
ENVY
EOAN
EOKA
EORL
EPEE
EPHA
EPIC
EPOS
ERAT
ERGO
ERIA
ERIC
ERIE
ERIK
ERIN
ERIS
ERNE
EROS
ERSE
ERTÉ
ERYX
ESAU
ESKY
ESLA
ESME
ESNE
ESPY
ESSE
ESTE
ESTH
ETCH
ETEN
ETHE
ETNA
ETON
ETTA
ETTY
ETUI
EUGE
EUGH
EUOI
EURE
EURO
EVAN
EVEN
EVER
EVET
EVIL
EVOE
EWER
EWES
EXAM
EXES
EXIT
EXON
EXOR
EXPO
EXUL
EYAS
EYER
EYES
EYNE
EYOT
EYRA
EYRE
EYRY
EZRA
FACE
FACT
FADE
FADO
FAFF
FAHD
FAIL
FAIN
FAIR
FAIX
FAKE
FALA
FALL
FALX
FAME
FAND
FANE
FANG
FANK
FANS
FARD
FARE
FARM
FARO
FARR
FART
FASH
FASO
FAST
FATE
FATS
FAUN
FAWN
FAZE
FEAL
FEAR
FEAT
FECK
FEED
FEEL
FEER
FEET
FEGS
FEIS
FELL
FELT
FEME
FEND
FENI
FENT
FEOD
FERE
FERM
FERN
FEST
FETA
FETE
FETT
FEUD
FEZE
FIAT
FICO
FIDE
FIDO
FIEF
FIFA
FIFE
FIGO
FIJI
FIKE
FIKY
FILE
FILL
FILM
FILO
FILS
FIND
FINE
FINK
FINN
FINO
FIRE
FIRK
FIRM
FIRN
FISC
FISH
FISK
FIST
FITT
FITZ
FIVE
FIZZ
FLAB
FLAG
FLAK
FLAM
FLAN
FLAP
FLAT
FLAW
FLAX
FLAY
FLEA
FLED
FLEE
FLEG
FLEW
FLEX
FLEY
FLIC
FLIP
FLIT
FLIX
FLOE
FLOG
FLOP
FLOR
FLOW
FLOX
FLUB
FLUE
FLUX
FOAL
FOAM
FOCH
FOEN
FOGG
FOGY
FOIL
FOIN
FOLD
FOLK
FOND
FONE
FONS
FONT
FOOD
FOOL
FOON
FOOT
FORB
FORD
FORE
FORK
FORM
FORT
FOSS
FOUD
FOUG
FOUL
FOUR
FOWL
FOXY
FOZY
FRAB
FRAE
FRAG
FRAP
FRAU
FRAY
FREE
FRET
FRIG
FRIT
FROE
FROG
FROM
FROW
FUEL
FUFF
FUJI
FULL
FUME
FUND
FUNG
FUNK
FUNS
FURL
FURR
FURY
FUSE
FUSS
FUST
FUZE
FUZZ
FYKE
FYRD
GABY
GADE
GADI
GAEA
GAEL
GAFF
GAGA
GAGE
GAIA
GAID
GAIN
GAIR
GAIT
GAJO
GALA
GALE
GALL
GAMB
GAME
GAMP
GAMY
GANG
GANT
GAOL
GAPE
GAPO
GARB
GARE
GART
GARY
GASH
GASP
GAST
GATE
GATH
GATT
GAUD
GAUL
GAUM
GAUP
GAUR
GAVE
GAWD
GAWK
GAWP
GAZA
GAZE
GCSE
GDAY
GEAL
GEAN
GEAR
GEAT
GECK
GEED
GEEK
GEEP
GEEZ
GEIT
GELD
GELT
GEMS
GENE
GENS
GENT
GENU
GERE
GERM
GEST
GETA
GETT
GEUM
GHAN
GHAT
GHEE
GIBE
GIDE
GIER
GIFT
GIGA
GIGI
GILA
GILD
GILL
GILT
GIMP
GING
GINK
GIRD
GIRL
GIRN
GIRO
GIRR
GIRT
GISM
GIST
GITE
GIVE
GIZZ
GLAD
GLAM
GLEE
GLEG
GLEI
GLEN
GLEY
GLIA
GLIB
GLID
GLIM
GLIT
GLOB
GLOM
GLOP
GLOW
GLUE
GLUM
GLUT
GNAR
GNAT
GNAW
GOAD
GOAF
GOAL
GOAT
GOBI
GOBO
GOBY
GODS
GOEL
GOER
GOES
GOEY
GOFF
GOGO
GOLD
GOLE
GOLF
GONE
GONG
GONK
GOOD
GOOF
GOOG
GOOK
GOOL
GOON
GOOP
GOOR
GORE
GORM
GORP
GORY
GOSH
GOSS
GOTA
GOTH
GOUK
GOUT
GOWF
GOWK
GOWL
GOWN
GOYA
GRAB
GRAF
GRAM
GRAN
GRAS
GRAT
GRAY
GREE
GREW
GREY
GRID
GRIG
GRIM
GRIN
GRIP
GRIS
GRIT
GROG
GROT
GROW
GRUB
GRUE
GRUG
GRUM
GRUS
GSOH
GUAM
GUAN
GUAR
GUFF
GUGA
GUID
GULA
GULE
GULF
GULL
GULP
GUMP
GUNK
GUNN
GUNS
GUNZ
GURL
GURN
GURU
GUSH
GUST
GUTS
GUYS
GWYN
GYAL
GYBE
GYMP
GYNT
GYRE
GYRO
GYTE
GYVE
HAAF
HAAL
HAAR
HABU
HACK
HADE
HADJ
HAEM
HAET
HAFF
HAFT
HAGG
HAGH
HAHA
HAIG
HAIK
HAIL
HAIN
HAIR
HAIT
HAKA
HAKE
HALE
HALF
HALL
HALM
HALO
HALS
HALT
HAME
HAMS
HAND
HANG
HANK
HANS
HANT
HAPI
HARD
HARE
HARK
HARL
HARM
HARN
HARO

HARP
HART
HARZ
HASE
HASH
HASK
HASP
HATE
HATH
HAUD
HAUL
HAUT
HAVE
HAWK
HAWM
HAZE
HAZY
HEAD
HEAL
HEAP
HEAR
HEAT
HEBE
HECH
HECK
HECT
HEED
HEEL
HEEP
HEFT
HEIL
HEIR
HELA
HELD
HELE
HELL
HELM
HELP
HEME
HEMI
HEMP
HEND
HENT
HEPT
HERA
HERB
HERD
HERE
HERL
HERM
HERN
HERO
HERR
HERS
HERY
HERZ
HESP
HESS
HEST
HETE
HETH
HICK
HIDE
HIGH
HIKE
HILL
HILO
HILT
HINC
HIND
HING
HINT
HIPT
HIRE
HISH
HISS
HIST
HIVE
HMSO
HOAR
HOAX
HOBO
HOCK
HOGG
HOGH
HOKE
HOKI
HOLD
HOLE
HOLI
HOLM
HOLT
HOLY
HOMA
HOME
HOMO
HOND
HONE
HONG
HONI
HONK
HOOD
HOOF
HOOK
HOON
HOOP
HOOT
HOPE
HOPI
HOPS
HORE
HORN
HORS
HOSE
HOSS
HOST
HOTE
HOUR
HOUT
HOVA
HOVE
HOWE
HOWK
HOWL
HUCK
HUER
HUEY
HUFF
HUGE
HUGH
HUGO
HUHU
HUIA
HULA
HULE
HULK
HULL
HUMA
HUME
HUMF
HUMP
HUNG
HUNK
HUNT
HUON
HURL
HURT
HUSH
HUSK
HUSO
HUSS
HWYL
HYDE
HYKE
HYLA
HYLE
HYMN
HYPE
HYPO
IAGO
IAMB
IBEX
IBID
IBIS
ICED
ICEL
ICKY
ICON
IDEA
IDÉE
IDEM
IDES
IDLE
IDLY
IDOL
IFFY
IFOR
IGAD
IGBO
IGOR
IKAT
IKON
ILEX
ILIA
ILKA
ILLE
ILLY
IMAM
IMPI
INBY
INCA
INCH
INDY
INES
INFO
INGE
INGO
INKY
INLY
INNS
INRI
INRO
INST
INTI
INTO
IONA
IOTA
IOWA
IPOH
IPSE
IRAN
IRAQ
IRAS
IRID
IRIS
IRON
IRUS
ISAR
ISER
ISIS
ISLE
ISMY
ISNT
ITCH
ITEM
ITYS
IVAN
IVES
IVOR
IVRY
IWIS
IYNX
IZAR
JAAP
JACK
JADE
JAGG
JAGS
JAIL
JAIN
JAKE
JAMB
JANE
JANN
JAPE
JARK
JARL
JARP
JASS
JATO
JAUP
JAVA
JAWI
JAWS
JAZZ
JEAT
JEEL
JEEP
JEER
JEFF
JEHU
JELL
JENA
JERK
JESS
JEST
JETÉ
JEWS
JIAO
JIBE
JILL
JILT
JIMP
JINK
JINX
JIRD
JISM
JIVE
JIZZ
JOAN
JOBE
JOCK
JOCO
JODO
JOEL
JOEY
JOHN
JOIN
JOKE
JOLE
JOLL
JOLO
JOLT
JOMO
JOOK
JOSE
JOSH
JOSS
JOTA
JOUK
JOVE
JOWL
JUAN
JUBA
JUBE
JUDE
JUDO
JUDY
JUJU
JUKE
JULY
JUMA
JUMP
JUNE
JUNG
JUNK
JUNO
JURA
JURE
JURY
JUST
JUTE
JYNX
KADE
KADI
KAGO
KAID
KAIE
KAIF
KAIL
KAIM
KAIN
KAKI
KALE
KALI
KAMA
KAME
KAMI
KANA
KANE
KANG
KANO
KANS
KANT
KAON
KAPH
KARA
KARD
KARL
KART
KATA
KATE
KATI
KAVA
KAYO
KEAN
KECK
KEEK
KEEL
KEEN
KEEP
KEIR
KELL
KELP
KELT
KEMB
KEMP
KENO
KENT
KEPI
KEPT
KERB
KERF
KERN
KESH
KEST
KETA
KEYS
KHAN
KHAT
KHOR
KHUD
KIBE
KICK
KIDD
KIEL
KIER
KIEV
KIKE
KILL
KILN
KILO
KILP
KILT
KINA
KIND
KINE
KING
KINK
KINO
KIPE
KIPP
KIRI
KIRK
KIRN
KISH
KISS
KIST
KITE
KITH
KIVA
KIWI
KLEE
KNAG
KNAP
KNAR
KNEE
KNEW
KNIT
KNOB
KNOP
KNOT
KNOW
KNOX
KNUB
KNUR
KNUT
KOAN
KOBE
KOBO
KOEL
KOFF
KOHL
KOKO
KOLA
KOLO
KOND
KONG
KONK
KOOK
KORA
KORE
KOSS
KOTO
KRAB
KRIS
KROO
KSAR
KUDU
KUKU
KUNA
KURD
KURI
KURU
KWAI
KWIC
KYAT
KYLE
KYPE
KYTE
LACE
LACK
LACY
LADA
LADE
LADY
LAER
LAHN
LAIC
LAID
LAIK
LAIN
LAIR
LAIS
LAKE
LAKH
LALO
LAMA
LAMB
LAME
LAMP
LANA
LAND
LANE
LANG
LANK
LANT
LANX
LAON
LAOS
LAPP
LARD
LARE
LARK
LARN
LASH
LASS
LAST
LATE
LATH
LATS
LAUD
LAUF
LAVA
LAVE
LAWN
LAZE
LAZY
LEAD
LEAF
LEAK
LEAL
LEAM
LEAN
LEAP
LEAR
LEAT
LECH
LEDA
LEEK
LEEP
LEER
LEES
LEET
LEFT
LEGO
LEGS
LEHR
LEIR
LELY
LEME
LEND
LENG
LENO
LENS
LENT
LERP
LESS
LEST
LETO
LETS
LETT
LEVA
LEVE
LEVI
LEVY
LEWD
LIAM
LIAR

LIAS
LIBS
LICE
LICH
LICK
LIDE
LIDO
LIED
LIEF
LIEN
LIES
LIEU
LIFE
LIFT
LIKE
LILL
LILO
LILT
LILY
LIMA
LIMB
LIME
LIMN
LIMO
LIMP
LIMY
LIND
LINE
LING
LINK
LINN
LINO
LINT
LION
LIPS
LIRA
LIRK
LISA
LISK
LISP
LIST
LITE
LITH
LIVE
LIVY
LIZA
LLYR
LNER
LOAD
LOAF
LOAM
LOAN
LOBE
LOBO
LOCH
LOCK
LOCO
LODE
LOFT
LOGE
LOGO
LOGS
LOGY
LOID
LOIN
LOIR
LOIS
LOKE
LOKI
LOLA
LOLL
LOMA
LOME
LONE
LONG
LOOF
LOOK
LOOM
LOON
LOOP
LOOR
LOOS
LOOT
LOPE
LORD
LORE
LORI
LORN
LORY
LOSE
LOSH
LOSS
LOST
LOTE
LOTH
LOTI
LOTO
LOTS
LOUD
LOUP
LOUR
LOUT
LOVE
LOWE
LUAU
LUBA
LUCE
LUCK
LUCY
LUDD
LUDO
LUES
LUEZ
LUFF
LUGE
LUGH
LUGS
LUIT
LUKE
LULL
LULU
LUMP
LUNA
LUNE
LUNG
LUNT
LURE
LURK
LUSH
LUSK
LUST
LUTE
LUTZ
LUXE
LWEI
LYAM
LYCH
LYLE
LYLY
LYME
LYNX
LYON
LYRA
LYRE
LYSE
LYTE
MAAM
MAAR
MAAS
MAAT
MACE
MACH
MACK
MADE
MAGE
MAGG
MAGI
MAHU
MAIA
MAID
MAIK
MAIL
MAIM
MAIN
MAKE
MAKO
MALE
MALI
MALL
MALM
MALO
MALT
MAMA
MAME
MANA
MANE
MANG
MANI
MANN
MANO
MANS
MANU
MANX
MANY
MAPS
MARA
MARC
MARE
MARG
MARI
MARK
MARL
MARM
MARO
MARS
MART
MARY
MASA
MASE
MASH
MASK
MASS
MAST
MASU
MATE
MATH
MATT
MATY
MAUD
MAUL
MAUT
MAWK
MAWR
MAXI
MAYA
MAYO
MAZE
MEAD
MEAL
MEAN
MEAT
MEDE
MEED
MEEK
MEER
MEET
MEGA
MEIN
MEIR
MELA
MELD
MELL
MELT
MEMO
MEND
MENE
MENG
MENT
MENU
MEOW
MERE
MERI
MERK
MERL
MERU
MESA
MESE
MESH
MESO
MESS
META
METE
MEVE
MEWL
MEWS
MEZE
MICA
MICE
MICK
MICO
MIDI
MIEN
MIFF
MIKE
MILD
MILE
MILK
MILL
MILO
MILT
MIME
MIMI
MINA
MIND
MINE
MING
MINI
MINK
MINO
MINT
MINX
MIRA
MIRE
MIRK
MIRO
MIRV
MISC
MISE
MISO
MISS
MIST
MITE
MITT
MOAN
MOAT
MOBY
MOCH
MOCK
MODE
MODO
MODS
MOHR
MOHS
MOIL
MOIT
MOJO
MOKE
MOKI
MOKO
MOLA
MOLD
MOLE
MOLL
MOLT
MOLY
MOME
MONA
MONG
MONK
MONO
MONS
MONY
MOOD
MOOG
MOOI
MOOL
MOON
MOOP
MOOR
MOOT
MOPE
MOPP
MORE
MORI
MORN
MORO
MORS
MORT
MOSS
MOST
MOTE
MOTH
MOTT
MOTU
MOUE
MOUL
MOUP
MOVE
MOVY
MOWA
MOXA
MOYA
MOYL
MOZE
MOZZ
MUCH
MUCK
MUFF
MUID
MUIL
MUIR
MULE
MULL
MUMP
MUNG
MUON
MURE
MURK
MURL
MUSA
MUSE
MUSH
MUSK
MUSO
MUSS
MUST
MUTE
MUTI
MUTT
MYAL
MYTH
MZEE
NAAM
NAAN
NABK
NADA
NAFF
NAGA
NAIA
NAIK
NAIL
NAIN
NAIR
NAJA
NALA
NAME
NANA
NAND
NANO
NAOS
NAPE
NARC
NARD
NARE
NARK
NARY
NASA
NASH
NASO
NATO
NAVE
NAVY
NAZE
NAZI
NEAL
NEAP
NEAR
NEAT
NEBO
NECK
NEED
NEEM
NEEP
NEIF
NEIL
NELL
NEMO
NENE
NEON
NERD
NERK
NERO
NESH
NESS
NEST
NETE
NETS
NETT
NEUK
NEVA
NEVE
NEWS
NEWT
NEXT
NIBS
NICE
NICK
NIDE
NIEF
NIFE
NIFF
NIGH
NIKE
NILE
NILL
NINA
NINE
NINO
NIPA
NIRL
NISI
NITH
NIXY
NOAH
NOCK
NODE
NOEL
NOES
NOGO
NOIL
NOLE
NOLL
NOLO
NOMA
NOME
NONE
NONG
NONO
NOOK
NOON
NOOP
NOPE
NORE
NORI
NORK
NORM
NORN
NOSE
NOSH
NOSY
NOTE
NOTT
NOUN
NOUP
NOUS
NOUT
NOVA
NOVO
NOWL
NOWT
NOWY
NUDD
NUDE
NUER
NUKE
NULL
NUMA
NUMB
NUNC
NURD
NURL
NURR
NUTS
NUUK
NYAS
NYET
NYOS
OAHU
OAKS
OAKY
OARS
OAST
OATH
OATS
OBAN
OBEY
OBIA
OBIT
OBOE
OBOL
OCHE
OCTA
ODAL
ODDS
ODER
ODIN
ODOR
ODSO
ODYL
OETA
OFAY
OFFA
OGAM
OGEE
OGEN
OGLE
OGPU
OGRE
OHIO

OILS
OILY
OINK
OINT
OISE
OKAY
OKRA
OKRO
OKTA
OLAF
OLDS
OLEA
OLEO
OLID
OLIM
OLIO
OLLA
OLPE
OMAN
OMAR
OMBU
OMEN
OMER
OMIT
OMNI
ONCE
ONER
ONE'S
ONGO
ONLY
ONST
ONTO
ONUS
ONYX
OONS
OONT
OOPS
OORT
OOSE
OOZE
OOZY
OPAH
OPAL
OPEC
OPEL
OPEN
OPIE
OPPO
OPUS
ORAL
ORAN
ORBY
ORCA
ORFE
ORFF
ORGE
ORGY
ORLE
ORLY
ORNE
ORRA
ORTS
ORYX
OSLO
OSSA
OTHO
OTIC
OTIS
OTTO
OTUS
OUCH
OUDS
OULK
OUMA
OUPA
OUPH
OURS
OUST
OUZO
OVAL
OVEL
OVEN
OVER
OVID
OVRA
OVUM
OWED
OWEN
OWLS
OWLY
OWNS
OWRE
OXEN
OXER
OXON
OXUS
OYER
OYEZ
PAAL
PACA
PACE
PACK
PACO
PACT
PAGE
PAID
PAIK
PAIL
PAIN
PAIR
PAIS
PALE
PALI
PALK
PALL
PALM
PALP
PAND
PANE
PANG
PANT
PAPA
PARA
PARD
PARE
PARK
PARP
PARR
PART
PASE
PASH
PASS
PAST
PATE
PATH
PATU
PAUA
PAUL
PAVE
PAVO
PAWA
PAWK
PAWL
PAWN
PAYE
PEAG
PEAK
PEAL
PEAN
PEAR
PEAS
PEAT
PEBA
PECH
PECK
PEEK
PEEL
PEEN
PEEP
PEER
PEGH
PEIN
PEKE
PELA
PELE
PELF
PELL
PELT
PEND
PENE
PENH
PENI
PENK
PENN
PENT
PEON
PEPO
PÈRE
PERI
PERK
PERM
PERN
PERT
PERU
PESO
PEST
PHEW
PHIL
PHIZ
PHOH
PHOT
PHUT
PIAF
PICA
PICE
PICK
PICT
PIED
PIER
PIES
PIET
PIGS
PIKA
PIKE
PILE
PILI
PILL
PIMP
PINA
PINE
PING
PINK
PINS
PINT
PION
PIPA
PIPE
PIPI
PIRL
PIRN
PIRO
PISE
PISH
PISO
PISS
PITA
PITH
PITT
PITY
PIUM
PIUS
PIXY
PIZE
PLAN
PLAP
PLAT
PLAY
PLEA
PLEB
PLED
PLEW
PLIÉ
PLIM
PLOD
PLOP
PLOT
PLOW
PLOY
PLUE
PLUG
PLUM
PLUS
PNYX
POCK
PODS
POEM
POET
POGO
POKE
POKY
POLE
POLK
POLL
POLO
POLT
POLY
POME
POMP
POND
PONE
PONG
PONK
PONS
PONT
PONY
POOD
POOF
POOH
POOK
POOL
POON
POOP
POOR
POOT
POPE
PORE
PORK
PORN
PORT
POSE
POSH
POSS
POST
POSY
POTE
POTS
POTT
POUF
POUK
POUR
POUT
POWN
POXY
PRAD
PRAM
PRAT
PRAU
PRAY
PREE
PREP
PREY
PRIG
PRIM
PRIX
PROA
PROD
PROF
PROG
PROM
PROO
PROP
PROW
PRUH
PSBR
PTAH
PUCA
PUCE
PUCK
PUDU
PUER
PUFF
PUGH
PUJA
PUKE
PULA
PULE
PULI
PULL
PULP
PULU
PULY
PUMA
PUMP
PUMY
PUNA
PUNG
PUNK
PUNT
PUNY
PUPA
PURE
PURI
PURL
PURR
PUSH
PUSS
PUTT
PUTZ
PYAT
PYET
PYOT
PYRE
PYRO
QADI
QING
QOPH
QUAD
QUAG
QUAT
QUAY
QUEP
QUEY
QUID
QUIM
QUIN
QUIP
QUIT
QUIZ
QUOD
QUOP
RABI
RACA
RACE
RACK
RACY
RADA
RAFF
RAFT
RAGA
RAGE
RAGG
RAGI
RAGS
RAHU
RAID
RAIK
RAIL
RAIN
RAIT
RAKE
RAKI
RAKU
RAKY
RALE
RAMA
RAMI
RAMP
RANA
RAND
RANG
RANI
RANK
RANT
RAPE
RAPT
RARE
RASC
RASE
RASH
RASP
RAST
RATA
RATE
RATH
RATS
RATU
RAUN
RAVE
RAWN
RAYS
RAZE
RAZZ
READ
REAK
REAL
REAM
REAN
REAP
REAR
RECD
RECK
REDD
REDE
REDO
REED
REEF
REEK
REEL
REEN
REFT
REIF
REIK
REIN
REIS
REJA
REKE
RELY
REME
REMS
REND
RENE
RENO
RENT
RENY
REPP
REPS
RESH
REST
RETE
RETT
REVD
RHEA
RHUS
RHYS
RIAL
RIBS
RICA
RICE
RICH
RICK
RICO
RIDE
RIEL
RIEM
RIEN
RIFE
RIFF
RIFT
RIGA
RIGG
RIGI
RILE
RILL
RIMA
RIME
RIMU
RIND
RINE
RING
RINK
RINT
RIOT
RIPE
RIPP
RIPS
RISE
RISK
RISP
RISS
RITA
RITE
RITT
RITZ
RIVA
RIVE
RIVO
RIZA
ROAD
ROAM
ROAN
ROAR
ROBE
ROCA
ROCH
ROCK
RODE
ROIL
ROIN
ROJI
ROKE
ROLE
ROLF
ROLL
ROME
ROMP
RONE
RONG
RONT
ROOD
ROOF
ROOK
ROOM
ROON
ROOP
ROOT
ROPE
ROPY
RORE
RORO

RORT
RORY
ROSE
ROSS
ROSY
ROTA
ROTE
ROTI
ROTL
ROUD
ROUÉ
ROUL
ROUM
ROUP
ROUT
ROUX
ROVE
ROWE
ROWT
RSVP
RUBE
RUBY
RUCK
RUDD
RUDE
RUFF
RUGA
RUHR
RUIN
RUKH
RULE
RULY
RUME
RUMI
RUMP
RUND
RUNE
RUNG
RUNS
RUNT
RURP
RURU
RUSA
RUSE
RUSH
RUSK
RUST
RUTA
RUTE
RUTH
RYAL
RYAN
RYFE
RYND
RYOT
RYVE
SABA
SACK
SADE
SAFE
SAGA
SAGE
SAGO
SAIC
SAID
SAIL
SAIM
SAIN
SAIR
SAKE
SAKI
SALE
SALK
SALP
SALT
SAMA
SAME
SAMI
SAMP
SAND
SANE
SANG
SANK
SANS
SANT
SARD
SARI
SARK
SASA
SASH
SASS
SATE
SATI
SATS
SAUL
SAUT
SAVE
SAWN
SAXE
SAYE
SCAB
SCAD
SCAG
SCAM
SCAN
SCAR
SCAT
SCAW
SCOG
SCOP
SCOT
SCOW
SCRY
SCUD
SCUG
SCUL
SCUM
SCUR
SCUT
SCYE
SEAL
SEAM
SEAN
SEAR
SEAS
SEAT
SECH
SECT
SEED
SEEK
SEEL
SEEM
SEEN
SEEP
SEER
SEGO
SEIF
SEIL
SEIR
SEJM
SEKT
SELE
SELF
SELL
SEMI
SENA
SEND
SENS
SENT
SEPS
SEPT
SERA
SERB
SERE
SERF
SERK
SESE
SESS
SETA
SETT
SEUL
SEVE
SEWN
SEXT
SEXY
SHAD
SHAG
SHAH
SHAM
SHAN
SHAP
SHAW
SHAY
SHEA
SHED
SHEM
SHET
SHIE
SHIM
SHIN
SHIP
SHIT
SHIV
SHOA
SHOD
SHOE
SHOG
SHOO
SHOP
SHOT
SHOW
SHRI
SHUL
SHUN
SHUT
SIAL
SIAM
SIAN
SIBB
SICE
SICH
SICK
SIDA
SIDE
SIEN
SIFT
SIGH
SIGN
SIJO
SIKA
SIKE
SIKH
SILD
SILE
SILK
SILL
SILO
SILT
SIMA
SIMI
SIMP
SIND
SINE
SING
SINK
SINO
SION
SIPE
SIRE
SIRI
SISS
SIST
SITE
SITU
SIUM
SIVA
SIZE
SKAG
SKAT
SKAW
SKED
SKEG
SKEN
SKEO
SKEP
SKER
SKET
SKEW
SKIA
SKID
SKIM
SKIN
SKIO
SKIP
SKIT
SKOL
SKRY
SKUA
SKUG
SKYE
SKYR
SLAB
SLAE
SLAG
SLAM
SLAP
SLAT
SLAV
SLAW
SLAY
SLED
SLEE
SLEW
SLEY
SLID
SLIM
SLIP
SLIT
SLOB
SLOE
SLOG
SLOP
SLOT
SLOW
SLUB
SLUE
SLUG
SLUM
SLUR
SLUT
SMEE
SMEW
SMIT
SMOG
SMUG
SMUR
SMUT
SNAG
SNAP
SNEB
SNED
SNEE
SNIB
SNIG
SNIP
SNIT
SNOB
SNOD
SNOG
SNOT
SNOW
SNUB
SNUG
SNYE
SOAK
SOAP
SOAR
SOAY
SOCA
SOCK
SODA
SOFA
SOFI
SOFT
SOHO
SOIL
SOJA
SOLA
SOLD
SOLE
SOLO
SOMA
SOME
SONE
SONG
SOOK
SOOL
SOOM
SOON
SOOP
SOOT
SOPH
SORA
SORB
SORD
SORE
SORN
SORT
SOSS
SOUK
SOUL
SOUM
SOUP
SOUR
SOWM
SOWP
SOYA
SPAE
SPAG
SPAM
SPAN
SPAR
SPAT
SPAW
SPAY
SPEC
SPED
SPEE
SPET
SPEW
SPEY
SPIC
SPIF
SPIK
SPIN
SPIT
SPIV
SPOT
SPRY
SPUD
SPUE
SPUN
SPUR
STAB
STAG
STAN
STAP
STAR
STAW
STAY
STED
STEM
STEN
STEP
STET
STEW
STEY
STIE
STIM
STIR
STOA
STOB
STOL
STOP
STOT
STOW
STUB
STUD
STUM
STUN
STUR
STYE
STYX
SUCH
SUCK
SUDD
SUDS
SUER
SUET
SUEY
SUEZ
SUFI
SUIT
SULK
SULU
SUMO
SUMP
SUMS
SUNG
SUNK
SUNN
SURA
SURD
SURE
SURF
SUSA
SUSS
SUSU
SUVA
SWAB
SWAD
SWAG
SWAM
SWAN
SWAP
SWAT
SWAY
SWEE
SWEY
SWIG
SWIM
SWIZ
SWOB
SWOP
SWOT
SWUM
SYCE
SYEN
SYKE
SYNC
SYND
SYNE
SYPE
TAAL
TABI
TABU
TACE
TACH
TACK
TACO
TACT
TAEL
TAFF
TAFT
TAHA
TAHR
TAIG
TAIL
TAIN
TAIT
TAKA
TAKE
TALA
TALC
TALE
TALK
TALL
TAME
TAMP
TANA
TANE
TANG
TANH
TANK
TAPA
TAPE
TAPS
TAPU
TARA
TARE
TARN
TARO
TART
TASH
TASK
TASS
TATA
TATE
TATH
TATI
TATT
TATU
TAUT
TAWA
TAWS
TAWT
TAXA
TAXI
TEAK
TEAL
TEAM
TEAN
TEAR
TEAT
TECH
TEDY
TEEM
TEEN
TEER
TEES
TEFF
TEGG
TEHR
TEIL
TELA
TELE
TELL
TEME
TEMP
TEND
TENE
TENG
TENT
TERA
TERF
TERM
TERN
TERR
TESS

TEST
TETE
TETH
TEXT
THAE
THAI
THAN
THAR
THAT
THAW
THEA
THEE
THEM
THEN
THEW
THEY
THIN
THIR
THIS
THON
THOR
THOS
THOU
THRU
THUD
THUG
THUN
THUS
TICE
TICH
TICK
TIDE
TIDY
TIED
TIER
TIFF
TIFT
TIGE
TIKA
TIKE
TIKI
TILE
TILL
TILT
TIME
TINA
TIND
TINE
TING
TINK
TINT
TINY
TIPI
TIPU
TIRE
TIRL
TIRO
TIRR
TITE
TITI
TITO

TOAD
TOBY
TOCO
TODD
TODO
TODY
TOEA
TOEY
TOFF
TOFT
TOFU
TOGA
TOGE
TOGO
TOGS
TOHO
TOIL
TOJO
TOKE
TOKO
TOLA
TOLD
TOLE
TOLL
TOLT
TOLU
TOMB
TOME
TONE
TONG
TONK
TONS
TONY
TOOK
TOOL
TOOM
TOON
TOOT
TOPE
TOPI
TOPS
TORC
TORE
TORN
TORR
TORT
TORY
TOSA
TOSE
TOSH
TOSS
TOST
TOTE
TOTO
TOUK
TOUN
TOUR
TOUT
TOVE
TOWN
TOWT

TOYS
TOZE
TRAD
TRAM
TRAP
TRAY
TREE
TREK
TRET
TREW
TREY
TREZ
TRIE
TRIG
TRIM
TRIN
TRIO
TRIP
TROD
TROG
TRON
TROP
TROT
TROU
TROW
TROY
TRUE
TRUG
TRYE
TSAR
TSHI
TUAN
TUBA
TUBE
TUCK
TUES
TUFA
TUFF
TUFT
TULE
TULI
TULL
TUMP
TUMS
TUNA
TUND
TUNE
TUNG
TUPI
TURD
TURF
TURK
TURM
TURN
TUSH
TUSK
TUTU
TUZZ
TWAE
TWAL
TWAT

TWAY
TWEE
TWIG
TWIN
TWIT
TYKE
TYMP
TYNE
TYPE
TYPO
TYRE
TYRO
TYTE
TZAR
UBER
UCCA
UDAD
UDAL
UFFA
UGLI
UGLY
UIST
ULAD
ULAN
ULEX
ULNA
UMBO
UMPH
UNAU
UNBE
UNCE
UNCO
UNDE
UNDO
UNIO
UNIT
UNTO
UPAS
UPGO
UPON
UPSY
URAL
URAO
URDÉ
URDU
URDY
UREA
URGE
URIC
URIM
URSA
URUS
URVA
USAK
USED
USER
USES
USSR
UTAH
UTAS
UTIS

UVEA
VAAL
VACH
VADE
VAIL
VAIN
VAIR
VALE
VALI
VAMP
VANE
VANG
VARA
VARE
VARY
VASE
VAST
VATU
VAUD
VAUT
VAYU
VEAL
VEDA
VEEP
VEER
VEGA
VEHM
VEIL
VEIN
VELA
VELE
VELL
VENA
VEND
VENN
VENT
VERA
VERB
VERS
VERT
VERY
VEST
VETO
VETS
VIAL
VIBS
VICE
VIDE
VIED
VIEL
VIES
VIEW
VIGO
VILE
VILL
VIMY
VINA
VINE
VINO
VINT
VIOL

VIRL
VISA
VISE
VITA
VITE
VIVA
VIVE
VIVO
VLEI
VOAR
VOCE
VOID
VOLA
VOLE
VOLT
VOTE
VRIL
VTOL
VULN
WACK
WADD
WADE
WADI
WADY
WAFD
WAFF
WAFT
WAGE
WAIF
WAIL
WAIN
WAIT
WAKA
WAKE
WAKF
WALD
WALE
WALI
WALK
WALL
WALY
WAME
WAND
WANE
WANG
WANK
WANT
WARB
WARD
WARE
WARK
WARM
WARN
WARP
WART
WARY
WASE
WASH
WASP
WAST
WATE

WATT
WAUL
WAUR
WAVE
WAVY
WAWA
WAWL
WAXY
WAYS
WEAK
WEAL
WEAN
WEAR
WEBB
WEED
WEEK
WEEL
WEEM
WEEN
WEEP
WEET
WEFT
WEGG
WEID
WEIR
WEKA
WELD
WELK
WELL
WELT
WEMB
WEND
WENT
WEPT
WERE
WERT
WEST
WEVE
WHAM
WHAP
WHAT
WHAU
WHEE
WHEN
WHET
WHEW
WHEY
WHID
WHIG
WHIM
WHIN
WHIP
WHIR
WHIT
WHIZ
WHOA
WHOM
WHOP
WHOT
WICE
WICK

WIDE
WIEL
WIEN
WIFE
WILD
WILE
WILI
WILL
WILT
WILY
WIMP
WIND
WINE
WING
WINK
WINN
WINO
WIPE
WIRE
WIRY
WISE
WISH
WISP
WIST
WITE
WITH
WITS
WIVE
WOAD
WOCK
WOKE
WOLD
WOLF
WOMB
WONG
WONT
WOOD
WOOF
WOOL
WOON
WOOT
WORD
WORE
WORK
WORM
WORN
WORT
WOVE
WOWF
WRAP
WREN
WRIT
WULL
WURM
WUSS
WYND
WYNN
WYTE
XEMA
XERO
XIAN

XMAS
XOSA
XYST
YACK
YAFF
YAGI
YALE
YALU
YAMA
YANG
YANK
YAPP
YARD
YARE
YARN
YARR
YATE
YAUD
YAUP
YAWL
YAWN
YAWP
YAWS
YAWY
YBET
YEAD
YEAH
YEAR
YEDE
YEED
YEGG
YELD
YELL
YELP
YELT
YERK
YESK
YEST
YETI
YETT
YEUK
YEVE
YGOE
YIKE
YILL
YIPS
YIRD
YIRK
YIRR
YITE
YLEM
YLKE
YMIR
YMPE
YOCK
YODH
YOGA
YOGH
YOGI
YOKE
YOLK

YOMP
YOND
YONI
YOOF
YOOP
YORE
YORK
YOUD
YOUK
YOUR
YOWE
YOWL
YOYO
YUAN
YUCA
YUCK
YUEN
YUFT
YUGA
YUKE
YUKO
YULE
YUMP
YUNX
YWIS
ZACK
ZAMA
ZANY
ZARF
ZATI
ZBUD
ZEAL
ZEBU
ZEIN
ZENO
ZERO
ZEST
ZETA
ZEUS
ZEZE
ZIFF
ZILA
ZIMB
ZINC
ZING
ZION
ZITI
ZIZZ
ZOBO
ZOBU
ZOEA
ZOIC
ZOID
ZOLA
ZOMO
ZONA
ZONE
ZOOM
ZOOT
ZORI
ZOUK
ZULU
ZUNI
ZUPA
ZURF
ZYME

4:2

AALU
AARU
BAAL
BAAS
BABA
BABE
BABI
BABU
BABY
BACA
BACH
BACK
BADE
BAEL
BAFF
BAFT
BAGS
BAHT
BAIL
BAIT
BAJU
BAKE
BAKU
BALA
BALD
BALE
BALI
BALK
BALL
BALM
BALT
BALU
BANC
BAND
BANE
BANG
BANI
BANK
BANT
BAPU
BARB
BARD
BARE
BARF
BARI
BARK
BARM
BARN
BARP
BARS
BART
BASE
BASH
BASK
BASS
BAST
BATE
BATH
BATS
BATT
BAUD
BAUK
BAUR
BAWD
BAWL
BAWN
BAWR
BAYE
BAYS
BAYT
CABA
CADE
CADI
CAEN
CAFÉ
CAGE
CAIN
CAKE
CALC
CALF
CALK
CALL
CALM
CALP
CALX
CAMA
CAME
CAMP
CANA
CANE
CANN
CANS
CANT
CAPA
CAPE
CAPH
CAPO
CAPT
CARD
CARE
CARK
CARL
CARP
CARR
CART
CARY
CASA
CASE
CASH
CASK
CAST
CATE
CATO
CATS
CAUK
CAUL
CAUM
CAUP
CAVE
CAVY
CAWK
DABS
DACE
DADA
DADD
DADO
DAFF
DAFT
DAGO
DAHL
DAIL
DAIS
DAKS
DALE
DALI
DAME
DAMN
DAMP
DANE
DANG
DANK
DARD
DARE
DARG
DARI
DARK
DARN
DART
DASH
DATA
DATE
DATO
DAUB
DAUD
DAUR
DAUT
DAVY
DAWD
DAWK
DAWN
DAWT
DAYS
DAZE
EACH
EALE
EARD
EARL
EARN
EARP
EARS
EASE
EAST
EASY
EATS
FACE
FACT
FADE
FADO
FAFF
FAHD
FAIL
FAIN
FAIR
FAIX
FAKE
FALA
FALL
FALX
FAME
FAND
FANE
FANG
FANK
FANS
FARD
FARE
FARM
FARO
FARR
FART
FASH
FASO
FAST
FATE
FATS
FAUN
FAWN
FAZE
GABY
GADE
GADI
GAEA
GAEL
GAFF
GAGA
GAGE
GAIA
GAID
GAIN
GAIR
GAIT
GAJO
GALA
GALE
GALL
GAMB
GAME
GAMP
GAMY
GANG
GANT
GAOL
GAPE
GAPO
GARB
GARE
GART
GARY
GASH
GASP
GAST
GATE
GATH
GATT
GAUD
GAUL
GAUM
GAUP
GAUR
GAVE
GAWD
GAWK
GAWP
GAZA
GAZE
HAAF
HAAL
HAAR
HABU
HACK
HADE
HADJ
HAEM
HAET
HAFF
HAFT
HAGG
HAGH
HAHA
HAIG
HAIK
HAIL
HAIN
HAIR
HAIT
HAKA
HAKE
HALE
HALF
HALL
HALM
HALO
HALS
HALT
HAME
HAMS
HAND
HANG
HANK
HANS
HANT
HAPI
HARD
HARE
HARK
HARL
HARM
HARN
HARO
HARP
HART
HARZ
HASE
HASH
HASK
HASP
HATE
HATH
HAUD
HAUL
HAUT
HAVE
HAWK
HAWM
HAZE
HAZY
IAGO
IAMB
JAAP
JACK
JADE
JAGG
JAGS
JAIL
JAIN
JAKE
JAMB
JANE
JANN
JAPE
JARK
JARL
JARP
JASS
JATO
JAUP
JAVA
JAWI
JAWS
JAZZ
KADE
KADI
KAGO
KAID
KAIE
KAIF
KAIL
KAIM
KAIN
KAKI
KALE
KALI
KAMA
KAME
KAMI
KANA
KANE
KANG
KANO
KANS
KANT
KAON
KAPH
KARA
KARD
KARL
KART
KATA
KATE
KATI
KAVA
KAYO
LACE
LACK
LACY
LADA
LADE
LADY
LAER
LAHN
LAIC
LAID
LAIK
LAIN
LAIR
LAIS
LAKE
LAKH
LALO
LAMA
LAMB
LAME
LAMP
LANA
LAND
LANE
LANG
LANK
LANT
LANX
LAON
LAOS
LAPP
LARD
LARE
LARK
LARN
LASH
LASS
LAST
LATE
LATH
LATS
LAUD
LAUF
LAVA
LAVE
LAWN
LAZE
LAZY
MAAM
MAAR
MAAS
MAAT
MACE
MACH
MACK
MADE
MAGE
MAGG
MAGI
MAHU
MAIA
MAID
MAIK
MAIL
MAIM
MAIN
MAKE
MAKO
MALE
MALI
MALL
MALM
MALO
MALT
MAMA
MAME
MANA
MANE
MANG
MANI
MANN
MANO
MANS
MANU
MANX
MANY
MAPS
MARA
MARC
MARE
MARG
MARI
MARK
MARL
MARM
MARO
MARS
MART
MARY
MASA
MASE
MASH
MASK
MASS
MAST
MASU
MATE

MATH
MATT
MATY
MAUD
MAUL
MAUT
MAWK
MAWR
MAXI
MAYA
MAYO
MAZE
NAAM
NAAN
NABK
NADA
NAFF
NAGA
NAIA
NAIK
NAIL
NAIN
NAIR
NAJA
NALA
NAME
NANA
NAND
NANO
NAOS
NAPE
NARC
NARD
NARE
NARK
NARY
NASA
NASH
NASO
NATO
NAVE
NAVY
NAZE
NAZI
OAHU
OAKS
OAKY
OARS
OAST
OATH
OATS
PAAL
PACA
PACE
PACK
PACO
PACT
PAGE
PAID
PAIK
PAIL
PAIN
PAIR
PAIS
PALE
PALI
PALK
PALL
PALM
PALP
PAND
PANE
PANG
PANT
PAPA
PARA
PARD
PARE
PARK
PARP
PARR
PART
PASE
PASH
PASS
PAST
PATE
PATH
PATU
PAUA
PAUL
PAVE
PAVO
PAWA
PAWK
PAWL
PAWN
PAYE
QADI
RABI
RACA
RACE
RACK
RACY
RADA
RAFF
RAFT
RAGA
RAGE
RAGG
RAGI
RAGS
RAHU
RAID
RAIK
RAIL
RAIN
RAIT
RAKE
RAKI
RAKU
RAKY
RALE
RAMA
RAMI
RAMP
RANA
RAND
RANG
RANI
RANK
RANT
RAPE
RAPT
RARE
RASC
RASE
RASH
RASP
RAST
RATA
RATE
RATH
RATS
RATU
RAUN
RAVE
RAWN
RAYS
RAZE
RAZZ
SABA
SACK
SADE
SAFE
SAGA
SAGE
SAGO
SAIC
SAID
SAIL
SAIM
SAIN
SAIR
SAKE
SAKI
SALE
SALK
SALP
SALT
SAMA
SAME
SAMI
SAMP
SAND
SANE
SANG
SANK
SANS
SANT
SARD
SARI
SARK
SASA
SASH
SASS
SATE
SATI
SATS
SAUL
SAUT
SAVE
SAWN
SAXE
SAYE
TAAL
TABI
TABU
TACE
TACH
TACK
TACO
TACT
TAEL
TAFF
TAFT
TAHA
TAHR
TAIG
TAIL
TAIN
TAIT
TAKA
TAKE
TALA
TALC
TALE
TALK
TALL
TAME
TAMP
TANA
TANE
TANG
TANH
TANK
TAPA
TAPE
TAPS
TAPU
TARA
TARE
TARN
TARO
TART
TASH
TASK
TASS
TATA
TATE
TATH
TATI
TATT
TATU
TAUT
TAWA
TAWS
TAWT
TAXA
TAXI
VAAL
VACH
VADE
VAIL
VAIN
VAIR
VALE
VALI
VAMP
VANE
VANG
VARA
VARE
VARY
VASE
VAST
VATU
VAUD
VAUT
VAYU
WACK
WADD
WADE
WADI
WADY
WAFD
WAFF
WAFT
WAGE
WAIF
WAIL
WAIN
WAIT
WAKA
WAKE
WAKF
WALD
WALE
WALI
WALK
WALL
WALY
WAME
WAND
WANE
WANG
WANK
WANT
WARB
WARD
WARE
WARK
WARM
WARN
WARP
WART
WARY
WASE
WASH
WASP
WAST
WATE
WATT
WAUL
WAUR
WAVE
WAVY
WAWA
WAWL
WAXY
WAYS
YACK
YAFF
YAGI
YALE
YALU
YAMA
YANG
YANK
YAPP
YARD
YARE
YARN
YARR
YATE
YAUD
YAUP
YAWL
YAWN
YAWP
YAWS
YAWY
ZACK
ZAMA
ZANY
ZARF
ZATI
ABAC
ABAS
ABBA
ABBE
ABED
ABEL
ABER
ABET
ABIB
ABLE
ABLY
ABRI
ABSE
ABUS
ABUT
ABYE
ABZU
DBLE
EBBW
EBOR
EBRO
IBEX
IBID
IBIS
OBAN
OBEY
OBIA
OBIT
OBOE
OBOL
UBER
YBET
ZBUD
ACAS
ACCT
AC/DC
ACER
ACES
ACHE
ACHT
ACID
ACIS
ACME
ACNE
ACOL
ACRE
ACRI
ACRO
ACTA
ACTS
BCOM
CCTV
ECAD
ECCE
ECCO
ECHE
ECHO
ECHT
ECRU
GCSE
ICED
ICEL
ICKY
ICON
OCHE
OCTA
SCAB
SCAD
SCAG
SCAM
SCAN
SCAR
SCAT
SCAW
SCOG
SCOP
SCOT
SCOW
SCRY
SCUD
SCUG
SCUL
SCUM
SCUR
SCUT
SCYE
UCCA
ADAD
ADAM
ADAR
ADAW
ADEN
ADES
ADIT
ADUR
ADZE
EDAL
EDAM
EDDA
EDDO
EDDY
EDEN
EDER
EDGE
EDGY
EDIT
EDOM
GDAY
IDEA
IDÉE
IDEM
IDES
IDLE
IDLY
IDOL
ODAL
ODDS
ODER
ODIN
ODOR
ODSO
ODYL
UDAD
UDAL
AEON
AERO
AESC
BEAD
BEAK
BEAM
BEAN
BEAR
BEAT
BEAU
BECK
BEDE
BEDS
BEDU
BEEB
BEEF
BEEN
BEEP
BEER
BEES
BEET
BEGO
BEIN
BELL
BELT
BEMA
BEND
BENE
BENJ
BENN
BENT
BENZ
BERE
BERG
BERK
BERM
BERN
BESS
BEST
BETA
BETE
BETH
BEVY
CEDE
CEDI
CEIL
CELL
CELT
CENS
CENT
CERE
CERO
CERT
CESS
CETE
CEYX
DEAD
DEAF
DEAL
DEAN
DEAR
DEAW
DEBT
DECA
DECK
DECO
DEED
DEEK
DEEM
DEEN
DEEP
DEER
DEEV
DEFT
DEFY
DEIL
DEKE
DELE

DELF
DELI
DELL
DEME
DEMI
DEMO
DEMY
DENE
DENT
DENY
DEPT
DERE
DERM
DERN
DERO
DERV
DESK
DEVA
DEVI
DEWY
EECH
EELS
EERY
FEAL
FEAR
FEAT
FECK
FEED
FEEL
FEER
FEET
FEGS
FEIS
FELL
FELT
FEME
FEND
FENI
FENT
FEOD
FERE
FERM
FERN
FEST
FETA
FETE
FETT
FEUD
FEZE
GEAL
GEAN
GEAR
GEAT
GECK
GEED
GEEK
GEEP
GEEZ
GEIT
GELD
GELT
GEMS
GENE
GENS
GENT
GENU
GERE
GERM
GEST
GETA
GETT
GEUM
HEAD
HEAL
HEAP
HEAR
HEAT
HEBE
HECH
HECK
HECT
HEED
HEEL
HEEP
HEFT
HEIL
HEIR
HELA
HELD
HELE
HELL
HELM
HELP
HEME
HEMI
HEMP
HEND
HENT
HEPT
HERA
HERB
HERD
HERE
HERL
HERM
HERN
HERO
HERR
HERS
HERY
HERZ
HESP
HESS
HEST
HETE
HETH
JEAT
JEEL
JEEP
JEER
JEFF
JEHU
JELL
JENA
JERK
JESS
JEST
JETÉ
JEWS
KEAN
KECK
KEEK
KEEL
KEEN
KEEP
KEIR
KELL
KELP
KELT
KEMB
KEMP
KENO
KENT
KEPI
KEPT
KERB
KERF
KERN
KESH
KEST
KETA
KEYS
LEAD
LEAF
LEAK
LEAL
LEAM
LEAN
LEAP
LEAR
LEAT
LECH
LEDA
LEEK
LEEP
LEER
LEES
LEET
LEFT
LEGO
LEGS
LEHR
LEIR
LELY
LEME
LEND
LENG
LENO
LENS
LENT
LERP
LESS
LEST
LETO
LETS
LETT
LEVA
LEVE
LEVI
LEVY
LEWD
MEAD
MEAL
MEAN
MEAT
MEDE
MEED
MEEK
MEER
MEET
MEGA
MEIN
MEIR
MELA
MELD
MELL
MELT
MEMO
MEND
MENE
MENG
MENT
MENU
MEOW
MERE
MERI
MERK
MERL
MERU
MESA
MESE
MESH
MESO
MESS
META
METE
MEVE
MEWL
MEWS
MEZE
NEAL
NEAP
NEAR
NEAT
NEBO
NECK
NEED
NEEM
NEEP
NEIF
NEIL
NELL
NEMO
NENE
NEON
NERD
NERK
NERO
NESH
NESS
NEST
NETE
NETS
NETT
NEUK
NEVA
NEVE
NEWS
NEWT
NEXT
OETA
PEAG
PEAK
PEAL
PEAN
PEAR
PEAS
PEAT
PEBA
PECH
PECK
PEEK
PEEL
PEEN
PEEP
PEER
PEGH
PEIN
PEKE
PELA
PELE
PELF
PELL
PELT
PEND
PENE
PENH
PENI
PENK
PENN
PENT
PEON
PEPO
PERI
PERK
PERM
PERN
PERT
PERU
PESO
PEST
READ
REAK
REAL
REAM
REAN
REAP
REAR
RECD
RECK
REDD
REDE
REDO
REED
REEF
REEK
REEL
REEN
REFT
REIF
REIK
REIN
REIS
REJA
REKE
RELY
REME
REMS
REND
RENE
RENO
RENT
RENY
REPP
REPS
RESH
REST
RETE
RETT
REVD
SEAL
SEAM
SEAN
SEAR
SEAS
SEAT
SECH
SECT
SEED
SEEK
SEEL
SEEM
SEEN
SEEP
SEER
SEGO
SEIF
SEIL
SEIR
SEJM
SEKT
SELE
SELF
SELL
SEMI
SENA
SEND
SENS
SENT
SEPS
SEPT
SERA
SERB
SERE
SERF
SERK
SESE
SESS
SETA
SETT
SEUL
SEVE
SEWN
SEXT
SEXY
TEAK
TEAL
TEAM
TEAN
TEAR
TEAT
TECH
TEDY
TEEM
TEEN
TEER
TEES
TEFF
TEGG
TEHR
TEIL
TELA
TELE
TELL
TEME
TEMP
TEND
TENE
TENG
TENT
TERA
TERF
TERM
TERN
TERR
TESS
TEST
TETE
TETH
TEXT
VEAL
VEDA
VEEP
VEER
VEGA
VEHM
VEIL
VEIN
VELA
VELE
VELL
VENA
VEND
VENN
VENT
VERA
VERB
VERS
VERT
VERY
VEST
VETO
VETS
WEAK
WEAL
WEAN
WEAR
WEBB
WEED
WEEK
WEEL
WEEM
WEEN
WEEP
WEET
WEFT
WEGG
WEID
WEIR
WEKA
WELD
WELK
WELL
WELT
WEMB
WEND
WENT
WEPT
WERE
WERT
WEST
WEVE
XEMA
XERO
YEAD
YEAH
YEAR
YEDE
YEED
YEGG
YELD
YELL
YELP
YELT
YERK
YESK
YEST
YETI
YETT
YEUK
YEVE
ZEAL
ZEBU
ZEIN
ZENO
ZERO
ZEST
ZETA
ZEUS
ZEZE
PÈRE
BÊTE
AFAR
AFFY
AFRO
CFAF
EFIK
IFFY
IFOR
OFAY
OFFA
UFFA
AGAG
AGAR
AGED
AGEE
AGEN
AGES
AGHA
AGIN
AGIO
AGIS
AGLU
AGMA
AGNI
AGOG
AGON
AGRA
AGUE
EGAD
EGAL
EGER
EGGS
EGIS
EGMA
IGAD
IGBO
IGOR
OGAM
OGEE
OGEN
OGLE
OGPU
OGRE
UGLI
UGLY
YGOE
AHAB
AHEM

AHOY
BHEL
CHAD
CHAI
CHAL
CHAM
CHAN
CHAP
CHAR
CHAT
CHAW
CHAY
CHEF
CHER
CHEW
CHIC
CHIK
CHIL
CHIN
CHIP
CHIT
CHOC
CHON
CHOP
CHOU
CHOW
CHOY
CHUB
CHUG
CHUM
CHUT
DHAK
DHAL
DHOW
EHEU
GHAN
GHAT
GHEE
KHAN
KHAT
KHOR
KHUD
OHIO
PHEW
PHIL
PHIZ
PHOH
PHOT
PHUT
RHEA
RHUS
RHYS
SHAD
SHAG
SHAH
SHAM
SHAN
SHAP
SHAW
SHAY
SHEA

SHED
SHEM
SHET
SHIE
SHIM
SHIN
SHIP
SHIT
SHIV
SHOA
SHOD
SHOE
SHOG
SHOO
SHOP
SHOT
SHOW
SHRI
SHUL
SHUN
SHUT
THAE
THAI
THAN
THAR
THAT
THAW
THEA
THEE
THEM
THEN
THEW
THEY
THIN
THIR
THIS
THON
THOR
THOS
THOU
THRU
THUD
THUG
THUN
THUS
WHAM
WHAP
WHAT
WHAU
WHEE
WHEN
WHET
WHEW
WHEY
WHID
WHIG
WHIM
WHIN
WHIP
WHIR
WHIT

WHIZ
WHOA
WHOM
WHOP
WHOT
AIDA
AIDE
AIDS
AINT
AINU
AIRE
AIRN
AIRS
AIRT
AIRY
AITU
BIAS
BIBB
BICE
BIDE
BIEN
BIER
BIFF
BIGA
BIGG
BIKE
BILE
BILK
BILL
BIMM
BIND
BINE
BING
BINK
BINT
BIRD
BIRK
BIRL
BIRO
BIRR
BISE
BISH
BISK
BISP
BITE
BITO
BITS
BITT
CIAO
CIEL
CIGS
CILL
CINE
CION
CIRÉ
CIRL
CIST
CITE
CITO
CITS
CITY

CIVE
DIAL
DIAS
DIAZ
DIBS
DICE
DICH
DICK
DICY
DIDO
DIEB
DIED
DIES
DIET
DIEU
DIGS
DIKA
DIKE
DILL
DIMA
DIME
DINE
DING
DINK
DINT
DIOR
DIRE
DIRK
DIRL
DIRT
DISA
DISC
DISH
DISK
DISS
DITA
DITE
DITT
DIVA
DIVE
DIXY
EIGG
EILD
EINE
EIRE
FIAT
FICO
FIDE
FIDO
FIEF
FIFA
FIFE
FIGO
FIJI
FIKE
FIKY
FILE
FILL
FILM
FILO
FILS

FIND
FINE
FINK
FINN
FINO
FIRE
FIRK
FIRM
FIRN
FISC
FISH
FISK
FIST
FITT
FITZ
FIVE
FIZZ
GIBE
GIDE
GIER
GIFT
GIGA
GIGI
GILA
GILD
GILL
GILT
GIMP
GING
GINK
GIRD
GIRL
GIRN
GIRO
GIRR
GIRT
GISM
GIST
GITE
GIVE
GIZZ
HICK
HIDE
HIGH
HIKE
HILL
HILO
HILT
HINC
HIND
HING
HINT
HIPT
HIRE
HISH
HISS
HIST
HIVE
JIAO
JIBE
JILL

JILT
JIMP
JINK
JINX
JIRD
JISM
JIVE
JIZZ
KIBE
KICK
KIDD
KIEL
KIER
KIEV
KIKE
KILL
KILN
KILO
KILP
KILT
KINA
KIND
KINE
KING
KINK
KINO
KIPE
KIPP
KIRI
KIRK
KIRN
KISH
KISS
KIST
KITE
KITH
KIVA
KIWI
LIAM
LIAR
LIAS
LIBS
LICE
LICH
LICK
LIDE
LIDO
LIED
LIEF
LIEN
LIES
LIEU
LIFE
LIFT
LIKE
LILL
LILO
LILT
LILY
LIMA
LIMB

LIME
LIMN
LIMO
LIMP
LIMY
LIND
LINE
LING
LINK
LINN
LINO
LINT
LION
LIPS
LIRA
LIRK
LISA
LISK
LISP
LIST
LITE
LITH
LIVE
LIVY
LIZA
MICA
MICE
MICK
MICO
MIDI
MIEN
MIFF
MIKE
MILD
MILE
MILK
MILL
MILO
MILT
MIME
MIMI
MINA
MIND
MINE
MING
MINI
MINK
MINO
MINT
MINX
MIRA
MIRE
MIRK
MIRO
MIRV
MISC
MISE
MISO
MISS
MIST
MITE

MITT
NIBS
NICE
NICK
NIDE
NIEF
NIFE
NIFF
NIGH
NIKE
NILE
NILL
NINA
NINE
NINO
NIPA
NIRL
NISI
NITH
NIXY
OILS
OILY
OINK
OINT
OISE
PIAF
PICA
PICE
PICK
PICT
PIED
PIER
PIES
PIET
PIGS
PIKA
PIKE
PILE
PILI
PILL
PIMP
PINA
PINE
PING
PINK
PINS
PINT
PION
PIPA
PIPE
PIPI
PIRL
PIRN
PIRO
PISE
PISH
PISO
PISS
PITA
PITH
PITT

PITY
PIUM
PIUS
PIXY
PIZE
QING
RIAL
RIBS
RICA
RICE
RICH
RICK
RICO
RIDE
RIEL
RIEM
RIEN
RIFE
RIFF
RIFT
RIGA
RIGG
RIGI
RILE
RILL
RIMA
RIME
RIMU
RIND
RINE
RING
RINK
RINT
RIOT
RIPE
RIPP
RIPS
RISE
RISK
RISP
RISS
RITA
RITE
RITT
RITZ
RIVA
RIVE
RIVO
RIZA
SIAL
SIAM
SIAN
SIBB
SICE
SICH
SICK
SIDA
SIDE
SIEN
SIFT
SIGH

SIGN
SIJO
SIKA
SIKE
SIKH
SILD
SILE
SILK
SILL
SILO
SILT
SIMA
SIMI
SIMP
SIND
SINE
SING
SINK
SINO
SION
SIPE
SIRE
SIRI
SISS
SIST
SITE
SITU
SIUM
SIVA
SIZE
TICE
TICH
TICK
TIDE
TIDY
TIED
TIER
TIFF
TIFT
TIGE
TIKA
TIKE
TIKI
TILE
TILL
TILT
TIME
TINA
TIND
TINE
TING
TINK
TINT
TINY
TIPI
TIPU
TIRE
TIRL
TIRO
TIRR
TITE

TITI
TITO
UIST
VIAL
VIBS
VICE
VIDE
VIED
VIEL
VIES
VIEW
VIGO
VILE
VILL
VIMY
VINA
VINE
VINO
VINT
VIOL
VIRL
VISA
VISE
VITA
VITE
VIVA
VIVE
VIVO
WICE
WICK
WIDE
WIEL
WIEN
WIFE
WILD
WILE
WILI
WILL
WILT
WILY
WIMP
WIND
WINE
WING
WINK
WINN
WINO
WIPE
WIRE
WIRY
WISE
WISH
WISP
WIST
WITE
WITH
WITS
WIVE
XIAN
YIKE
YILL

YIPS
YIRD
YIRK
YIRR
YITE
ZIFF
ZILA
ZIMB
ZINC
ZING
ZION
ZITI
ZIZZ
AÎNÉ
AJAR
AJAX
AJEE
AKEE
AKIN
EKKA
IKAT
IKON
OKAY
OKRA
OKRO
OKTA
SKAG
SKAT
SKAW
SKED
SKEG
SKEN
SKEO
SKEP
SKER
SKET
SKEW
SKIA
SKID
SKIM
SKIN
SKIO
SKIP
SKIT
SKOL
SKRY
SKUA
SKUG
SKYE
SKYR
ALAI
ALAN
ALAR
ALAS
ALAY
ALBE
ALBI
ALEC
ALEW
ALEX
ALFA

ALGA
ALIA
ALIF
ALKY
ALLO
ALLY
ALMA
ALMS
ALOD
ALOE
ALOW
ALPH
ALPS
ALSO
ALTA
ALTE
ALTO
ALUM
ALVA
BLAB
BLAD
BLAE
BLAG
BLAH
BLAT
BLAY
BLEB
BLED
BLEE
BLET
BLEW
BLEY
BLIN
BLIP
BLOB
BLOC
BLOT
BLOW
BLUB
BLUE
BLUR
BLUT
CLAD
CLAG
CLAM
CLAN
CLAP
CLAT
CLAW
CLAY
CLEF
CLEG
CLEM
CLEW
CLIO
CLIP
CLOD
CLOG
CLOP
CLOS
CLOT

CLOU
CLOW
CLOY
CLUB
CLUE
ELAM
ELAN
ELAT
ELBA
ELBE
ELIA
ELIS
ELKS
ELLA
ELLE
ELMO
ELOI
ELSA
ELSE
ELUL
FLAB
FLAG
FLAK
FLAM
FLAN
FLAP
FLAT
FLAW
FLAX
FLAY
FLEA
FLED
FLEE
FLEG
FLEW
FLEX
FLEY
FLIC
FLIP
FLIT
FLIX
FLOE
FLOG
FLOP
FLOR
FLOW
FLOX
FLUB
FLUE
FLUX
GLAD
GLAM
GLEE
GLEG
GLEI
GLEN
GLEY
GLIA
GLIB
GLID
GLIM

GLIT
GLOB
GLOM
GLOP
GLOW
GLUE
GLUM
GLUT
ILEX
ILIA
ILKA
ILLE
ILLY
KLEE
LLYR
OLAF
OLDS
OLEA
OLEO
OLID
OLIM
OLIO
OLLA
OLPE
PLAN
PLAP
PLAT
PLAY
PLEA
PLEB
PLED
PLEW
PLIÉ
PLIM
PLOD
PLOP
PLOT
PLOW
PLOY
PLUE
PLUG
PLUM
PLUS
SLAB
SLAE
SLAG
SLAM
SLAP
SLAT
SLAV
SLAW
SLAY
SLED
SLEE
SLEW
SLEY
SLID
SLIM
SLIP
SLIT
SLOB

SLOE
SLOG
SLOP
SLOT
SLOW
SLUB
SLUE
SLUG
SLUM
SLUR
SLUT
ULAD
ULAN
ULEX
ULNA
VLEI
YLEM
YLKE
AMAH
AMBO
AMEN
AMES
AMID
AMIE
AMIN
AMIR
AMIS
AMLA
AMMO
AMOK
AMOS
AMOY
AMUN
AMUR
AMYL
EMEU
EMIR
EMIT
EMMA
EMMY
EMYS
HMSO
IMAM
IMPI
OMAN
OMAR
OMBU
OMEN
OMER
OMIT
OMNI
SMEE
SMEW
SMIT
SMOG
SMUG
SMUR
SMUT
UMBO
UMPH
XMAS

YMIR
YMPE
ANAK
ANAL
ANAN
ANAS
ANCE
ANDA
ANEW
ANFO
ANIL
ANKH
ANNA
ANNE
ANNO
ANOA
ANON
ANTA
ANTE
ANTI
ANTS
ANUS
ENDS
ENEW
ENID
ENNA
ENOL
ENOS
ENOW
ENSI
ENVY
GNAR
GNAT
GNAW
INBY
INCA
INCH
INDY
INES
INFO
INGE
INGO
INKY
INLY
INNS
INRI
INRO
INST
INTI
INTO
KNAG
KNAP
KNAR
KNEE
KNEW
KNIT
KNOB
KNOP
KNOT
KNOW
KNOX

KNUB
KNUR
KNUT
LNER
ONCE
ONER
ONE'S
ONGO
ONLY
ONST
ONTO
ONUS
ONYX
PNYX
SNAG
SNAP
SNEB
SNED
SNEE
SNIB
SNIG
SNIP
SNIT
SNOB
SNOD
SNOG
SNOT
SNOW
SNUB
SNUG
SNYE
UNAU
UNBE
UNCE
UNCO
UNDE
UNDO
UNIO
UNIT
UNTO
BOAK
BOAR
BOAT
BOAZ
BOBA
BOCK
BODE
BODY
BOER
BOFF
BOGY
BOIL
BOKE
BOKO
BOLD
BOLE
BOLL
BOLO
BOLT
BOMA
BOMB

BONA
BOND
BONE
BONG
BONK
BONN
BONY
BOOB
BOOK
BOOL
BOOM
BOON
BOOR
BOOT
BORA
BORD
BORE
BORN
BORO
BORS
BOSH
BOSS
BOTE
BOTH
BOTS
BOTT
BOUK
BOUN
BOUT
BOWL
BOWR
BOYG
BOYO
BOYS
BOZO
COAL
COAT
COAX
COBB
COBH
COCA
COCH
COCK
COCO
CODA
CODE
CODY
COED
COFF
COIF
COIL
COIN
COIR
COIT
COKE
COLA
COLD
COLE
COLL
COLT
COMA

COMB
COME
COMM
COMO
COMP
CONE
CONK
CONN
CONS
CONT
CONY
COOF
COOK
COOL
COOM
COON
COOP
COOT
COPE
COPS
COPY
CORD
CORE
CORF
CORK
CORM
CORN
CORY
COSE
COSH
COSS
COST
COSY
COTE
COTH
COTT
COTY
COUE
COUP
COUR
COVE
COWL
COWP
COWS
COZE
COZY
DOAB
DOAT
DOCK
DODO
DOEK
DOER
DOES
DOFF
DOGE
DOGS
DOGY
DOHA
DOIT
DOJO
DOLE

DOLL
DOLT
DOME
DONA
DONE
DONG
DONT
DOOB
DOOK
DOOL
DOOM
DOON
DOOR
DOPA
DOPE
DORA
DORÉ
DORM
DORP
DORR
DORT
DORY
DOSE
DOSH
DOSS
DOTE
DOTH
DOTS
DOUC
DOUP
DOUR
DOUT
DOVE
DOWF
DOWN
DOWT
DOXY
DOZE
DOZY
EOAN
EOKA
EORL
FOAL
FOAM
FOCH
FOEN
FOGG
FOGY
FOIL
FOIN
FOLD
FOLK
FOND
FONE
FONS
FONT
FOOD
FOOL
FOON
FOOT
FORB

FORD
FORE
FORK
FORM
FORT
FOSS
FOUD
FOUG
FOUL
FOUR
FOWL
FOXY
FOZY
GOAD
GOAF
GOAL
GOAT
GOBI
GOBO
GOBY
GODS
GOEL
GOER
GOES
GOEY
GOFF
GOGO
GOLD
GOLE
GOLF
GONE
GONG
GONK
GOOD
GOOF
GOOG
GOOK
GOOL
GOON
GOOP
GOOR
GORE
GORM
GORP
GORY
GOSH
GOSS
GOTA
GOTH
GOUK
GOUT
GOWF
GOWK
GOWL
GOWN
GOYA
HOAR
HOAX
HOBO
HOCK
HOGG

HOGH
HOKE
HOKI
HOLD
HOLE
HOLI
HOLM
HOLT
HOLY
HOMA
HOME
HOMO
HOND
HONE
HONG
HONI
HONK
HOOD
HOOF
HOOK
HOON
HOOP
HOOT
HOPE
HOPI
HOPS
HORE
HORN
HORS
HOSE
HOSS
HOST
HOTE
HOUR
HOUT
HOVA
HOVE
HOWE
HOWK
HOWL
IONA
IOTA
IOWA
JOAN
JOBE
JOCK
JOCO
JODO
JOEL
JOEY
JOHN
JOIN
JOKE
JOLE
JOLL
JOLO
JOLT
JOMO
JOOK
JOSE
JOSH

JOSS
JOTA
JOUK
JOVE
JOWL
KOAN
KOBE
KOBO
KOEL
KOFF
KOHL
KOKO
KOLA
KOLO
KOND
KONG
KONK
KOOK
KORA
KORE
KOSS
KOTO
LOAD
LOAF
LOAM
LOAN
LOBE
LOBO
LOCH
LOCK
LOCO
LODE
LOFT
LOGE
LOGO
LOGS
LOGY
LOID
LOIN
LOIR
LOIS
LOKE
LOKI
LOLA
LOLL
LOMA
LOME
LONE
LONG
LOOF
LOOK
LOOM
LOON
LOOP
LOOR
LOOS
LOOT
LOPE
LORD
LORE
LORI

LORN
LORY
LOSE
LOSH
LOSS
LOST
LOTE
LOTH
LOTI
LOTO
LOTS
LOUD
LOUP
LOUR
LOUT
LOVE
LOWE
MOAN
MOAT
MOBY
MOCH
MOCK
MODE
MODO
MODS
MOHR
MOHS
MOIL
MOIT
MOJO
MOKE
MOKI
MOKO
MOLA
MOLD
MOLE
MOLL
MOLT
MOLY
MOME
MONA
MONG
MONK
MONO
MONS
MONY
MOOD
MOOG
MOOI
MOOL
MOON
MOOP
MOOR
MOOT
MOPE
MOPP
MORE
MORI
MORN
MORO
MORS

MORT
MOSS
MOST
MOTE
MOTH
MOTT
MOTU
MOUE
MOUL
MOUP
MOVE
MOVY
MOWA
MOXA
MOYA
MOYL
MOZE
MOZZ
NOAH
NOCK
NODE
NOEL
NOES
NOGO
NOIL
NOLE
NOLL
NOLO
NOMA
NOME
NONE
NONG
NONO
NOOK
NOON
NOOP
NOPE
NORE
NORI
NORK
NORM
NORN
NOSE
NOSH
NOSY
NOTE
NOTT
NOUN
NOUP
NOUS
NOUT
NOVA
NOVO
NOWL
NOWT
NOWY
OONS
OONT
OOPS
OORT
OOSE

OOZE
OOZY
POCK
PODS
POEM
POET
POGO
POKE
POKY
POLE
POLK
POLL
POLO
POLT
POLY
POME
POMP
POND
PONE
PONG
PONK
PONS
PONT
PONY
POOD
POOF
POOH
POOK
POOL
POON
POOP
POOR
POOT
POPE
PORE
PORK
PORN
PORT
POSE
POSH
POSS
POST
POSY
POTE
POTS
POTT
POUF
POUK
POUR
POUT
POWN
POXY
QOPH
ROAD
ROAM
ROAN
ROAR
ROBE
ROCA
ROCH
ROCK

RODE
ROIL
ROIN
ROJI
ROKE
ROLE
ROLF
ROLL
ROME
ROMP
RONE
RONG
RONT
ROOD
ROOF
ROOK
ROOM
ROON
ROOP
ROOT
ROPE
ROPY
RORE
RORO
RORT
RORY
ROSE
ROSS
ROSY
ROTA
ROTE
ROTI
ROTL
ROUD
ROUÉ
ROUL
ROUM
ROUP
ROUT
ROUX
ROVE
ROWE
ROWT
SOAK
SOAP
SOAR
SOAY
SOCA
SOCK
SODA
SOFA
SOFI
SOFT
SOHO
SOIL
SOJA
SOLA
SOLD
SOLE
SOLO
SOMA
SOME
SONE
SONG
SOOK
SOOL
SOOM
SOON
SOOP
SOOT
SOPH
SORA
SORB
SORD
SORE
SORN
SORT
SOSS
SOUK
SOUL
SOUM
SOUP
SOUR
SOWM
SOWP
SOYA
TOAD
TOBY
TOCO
TODD
TODO
TODY
TOEA
TOEY
TOFF
TOFT
TOFU
TOGA
TOGE
TOGO
TOGS
TOHO
TOIL
TOJO
TOKE
TOKO
TOLA
TOLD
TOLE
TOLL
TOLT
TOLU
TOMB
TOME
TONE
TONG
TONK
TONS
TONY
TOOK
TOOL
TOOM
TOON
TOOT
TOPE
TOPI
TOPS
TORC
TORE
TORN
TORR
TORT
TORY
TOSA
TOSE
TOSH
TOSS
TOST
TOTE
TOTO
TOUK
TOUN
TOUR
TOUT
TOVE
TOWN
TOWT
TOYS
TOZE
VOAR
VOCE
VOID
VOLA
VOLE
VOLT
VOTE
WOAD
WOCK
WOKE
WOLD
WOLF
WOMB
WONG
WONT
WOOD
WOOF
WOOL
WOON
WOOT
WORD
WORE
WORK
WORM
WORN
WORT
WOVE
WOWF
XOSA
YOCK
YODH
YOGA
YOGH
YOGI
YOKE
YOLK
YOMP
YOND
YONI
YOOF
YOOP
YORE
YORK
YOUD
YOUK
YOUR
YOWE
YOWL
YOYO
ZOBO
ZOBU
ZOEA
ZOIC
ZOID
ZOLA
ZOMO
ZONA
ZONE
ZOOM
ZOOT
ZORI
ZOUK
APAY
APEX
APIA
APIS
APSE
CPRS
EPEE
EPHA
EPIC
EPOS
IPOH
IPSE
OPAH
OPAL
OPEC
OPEL
OPEN
OPIE
OPPO
OPUS
SPAE
SPAG
SPAM
SPAN
SPAR
SPAT
SPAW
SPAY
SPEC
SPED
SPEE
SPET
SPEW
SPEY
SPIC
SPIF
SPIK
SPIN
SPIT
SPIV
SPOT
SPRY
SPUD
SPUE
SPUN
SPUR
UPAS
UPGO
UPON
UPSY
AQUA
ARAB
ARAK
ARAL
ARAM
ARAN
ARAR
ARCH
ARCO
AREA
AREG
ARES
ARET
AREW
ARGO
ARIA
ARID
ARIL
ARIS
ARLY
ARMS
ARMY
ARNA
ARNE
ARNO
ARRU
ARRY
ARSE
ARTA
ARTS
ARTY
ARUM
ARUN
ARVO
ARYL
BRAD
BRAE
BRAG
BRAK
BRAM
BRAN
BRAS
BRAT
BRAW
BRAY
BRED
BREE
BREN
BRER
BREW
BRIE
BRIG
BRIM
BRIO
BRIS
BRIT
BRIX
BRNO
BROD
BROG
BRON
BROO
BROS
BROW
BRUM
BRUT
CRAB
CRAG
CRAM
CRAN
CRAP
CRAW
CRAX
CRAY
CRED
CREE
CREW
CRIB
CRIT
CROP
CROW
CRUD
CRUE
CRUX
CRYO
DRAB
DRAD
DRAG
DRAM
DRAT
DRAW
DRAY
DREE
DREG
DREW
DREY
DRIB
DRIP
DROP
DROW
DRUB
DRUG
DRUM
ERAT
ERGO
ERIA
ERIC
ERIE
ERIK
ERIN
ERIS
ERNE
EROS
ERSE
ERTÉ
ERYX
FRAB
FRAE
FRAG
FRAP
FRAU
FRAY
FREE
FRET
FRIG
FRIT
FROE
FROG
FROM
FROW
GRAB
GRAF
GRAM
GRAN
GRAS
GRAT
GRAY
GREE
GREW
GREY
GRID
GRIG
GRIM
GRIN
GRIP
GRIS
GRIT
GROG
GROT
GROW
GRUB
GRUE
GRUG
GRUM
GRUS
IRAN
IRAQ
IRAS
IRID
IRIS
IRON
IRUS
KRAB
KRIS
KROO
ORAL
ORAN
ORBY
ORCA
ORFE
ORFF
ORGE
ORGY
ORLE
ORLY
ORNE
ORRA
ORTS
ORYX
PRAD
PRAM
PRAT
PRAU
PRAY
PREE
PREP
PREY
PRIG
PRIM
PRIX
PROA
PROD
PROF
PROG
PROM
PROO
PROP
PROW
PRUH
TRAD
TRAM
TRAP
TRAY
TREE
TREK
TRET
TREW
TREY
TREZ
TRIE
TRIG
TRIM
TRIN
TRIO
TRIP
TROD
TROG
TRON
TROP
TROT
TROU
TROW
TROY
TRUE
TRUG
TRYE
URAL
URAO
URDÉ
URDU
URDY
UREA
URGE
URIC
URIM
URSA
URUS
URVA
VRIL
WRAP
WREN
WRIT
ASAP
ASAR
ASAS
ASCH
ASHE
ASHY
ASIA
ASKE
ASKR
ASTI
ASUR
ESAU
ESKY
ESLA
ESME
ESNE
ESPY
ESSE
ESTE
ESTH
GSOH
ISAR
ISER
ISIS
ISLE
ISMY
ISNT
KSAR
OSLO
OSSA
PSBR
RSVP
TSAR
TSHI
USAK
USED
USER
USES
USSR
ATAP
ATAR
ATEN
ATLI
ATOC
ATOK
ATOM

ATOP ATTO ATTU ATUA ATUM ETCH ETEN ETHE ETNA ETON ETTA ETTY ETUI ITCH ITEM ITYS OTHO OTIC OTIS OTTO OTUS PTAH STAB STAG STAN STAP STAR STAW STAY STED STEM STEN STEP STET STEW STEY STIE STIM STIR STOA STOB STOL STOP STOT STOW STUB STUD STUM STUN STUR STYE STYX UTAH UTAS UTIS VTOL AUDE AUDI AULA AULD AUNE

AUNT AURA AUTO BUAT BUBA BUBO BUCK BUDD BUDE BUDO BUFF BUFO BUGS BUHL BUIK BUKE BULB BULK BULL BUMF BUMP BUNA BUND BUNG BUNK BUNT BUOY BURD BURG BURK BURL BURN BURP BURR BURT BURY BUSH BUSK BUSS BUST BUSY BUTE BUTT BUZZ CUBA CUBE CUBS CUFF CUIF CUIT CULL CULM CULT CUMA CUNT CUPS CURB CURD CURE CURK CURL

CURN CURR CURT CUSH CUSK CUSP CUSS CUTE CUYP DUAD DUAL DUAN DUAR DUBS DUCE DUCK DUCT DUDE DUDS DUEL DUES DUET DUFF DUKE DULE DULL DULY DUMA DUMB DUMP DUNE DUNG DUNK DUNS DUNT DUPE DURA DURE DURN DURO DUSE DUSH DUSK DUST DUTY EUGE EUGH EUOI EURE EURO FUEL FUFF FUJI FULL FUME FUND FUNG FUNK FUNS FURL FURR

FURY FUSE FUSS FUST FUZE FUZZ GUAM GUAN GUAR GUFF GUGA GUID GULA GULE GULF GULL GULP GUMP GUNK GUNN GUNS GUNZ GURL GURN GURU GUSH GUST GUTS GUYS HUCK HUER HUEY HUFF HUGE HUGH HUGO HUHU HUIA HULA HULE HULK HULL HUMA HUME HUMF HUMP HUNG HUNK HUNT HUON HURL HURT HUSH HUSK HUSO HUSS JUAN JUBA JUBE JUDE JUDO

JUDY JUJU JUKE JULY JUMA JUMP JUNE JUNG JUNK JUNO JURA JURE JURY JUST JUTE KUDU KUKU KUNA KURD KURI KURU LUAU LUBA LUCE LUCK LUCY LUDD LUDO LUES LUEZ LUFF LUGE LUGH LUGS LUIT LUKE LULL LULU LUMP LUNA LUNE LUNG LUNT LURE LURK LUSH LUSK LUST LUTE LUTZ LUXE MUCH MUCK MUFF MUID MUIL MUIR MULE MULL MUMP MUNG

MUON MURE MURK MURL MUSA MUSE MUSH MUSK MUSO MUSS MUST MUTE MUTI MUTT NUDD NUDE NUER NUKE NULL NUMA NUMB NUNC NURD NURL NURR NUTS NUUK OUCH OUDS OULK OUMA OUPA OUPH OURS OUST OUZO PUCA PUCE PUCK PUDU PUER PUFF PUGH PUJA PUKE PULA PULE PULI PULL PULP PULU PULY PUMA PUMP PUMY PUNA PUNG PUNK PUNT PUNY PUPA

PURE PURI PURL PURR PUSH PUSS PUTT PUTZ QUAD QUAG QUAT QUAY QUEP QUEY QUID QUIM QUIN QUIP QUIT QUIZ QUOD QUOP RUBE RUBY RUCK RUDD RUDE RUFF RUGA RUHR RUIN RUKH RULE RULY RUME RUMI RUMP RUND RUNE RUNG RUNS RUNT RURP RURU RUSA RUSE RUSH RUSK RUST RUTA RUTE RUTH SUCH SUCK SUDD SUDS SUER SUET SUEY SUEZ SUFI

SUIT SULK SULU SUMO SUMP SUMS SUNG SUNK SUNN SURA SURD SURE SURF SUSA SUSS SUSU SUVA TUAN TUBA TUBE TUCK TUES TUFA TUFF TUFT TULE TULI TULL TUMP TUMS TUNA TUND TUNE TUNG TUPI TURD TURF TURK TURM TURN TUSH TUSK TUTU TUZZ VULN WULL WURM WUSS YUAN YUCA YUCK YUEN YUFT YUGA YUKE YUKO YULE YUMP YUNX ZULU ZUNI

ZUPA ZURF AVAL AVER AVES AVID AVON AVOW EVAN EVEN EVER EVET EVIL EVOE IVAN IVES IVOR IVRY OVAL OVEL OVEN OVER OVID OVRA OVUM UVEA AWAY AWDL AWED AWOL AWRY EWER EWES GWYN HWYL IWIS KWAI KWIC LWEI OWED OWEN OWLS OWLY OWNS OWRE SWAB SWAD SWAG SWAM SWAN SWAP SWAT SWAY SWEE SWEY SWIG SWIM SWIZ SWOB SWOP SWOT

SWUM
TWAE
TWAL
TWAT
TWAY
TWEE
TWIG
TWIN
TWIT
YWIS
AXIL
AXIS
AXLE
AXON
EXAM
EXES
EXIT
EXON
EXOR
EXPO
EXUL
OXEN
OXER
OXON
OXUS
AYAH
AYER
AYES
AYIN
AYMÉ
AYRE
BYKE
BYNG
BYRD
BYRE
BYTE
CYAN
CYMA
CYME
CYST
CYTE
DYAD
DYAK
DYER
DYKE
DYNE
EYAS
EYER
EYES
EYNE
EYOT
EYRA
EYRE
EYRY
FYKE
FYRD
GYAL
GYBE
GYMP
GYNT
GYRE
GYRO
GYTE
GYVE
HYDE
HYKE
HYLA
HYLE
HYMN
HYPE
HYPO
IYNX
JYNX
KYAT
KYLE
KYPE
KYTE
LYAM
LYCH
LYLE
LYLY
LYME
LYNX
LYON
LYRA
LYRE
LYSE
LYTE
MYAL
MYTH
NYAS
NYET
NYOS
OYER
OYEZ
PYAT
PYET
PYOT
PYRE
PYRO
RYAL
RYAN
RYFE
RYND
RYOT
RYVE
SYCE
SYEN
SYKE
SYNC
SYND
SYNE
SYPE
TYKE
TYMP
TYNE
TYPE
TYPO
TYRE
TYRO
TYTE
WYND
WYNN
WYTE
XYST
ZYME
AZAN
AZOV
CZAR
EZRA
IZAR
MZEE
TZAR

4:3

ABAC
ABAS
ACAS
ADAD
ADAM
ADAR
ADAW
AFAR
AGAG
AGAR
AHAB
AJAR
AJAX
ALAI
ALAN
ALAR
ALAS
ALAY
AMAH
ANAK
ANAL
ANAN
ANAS
APAY
ARAB
ARAK
ARAL
ARAM
ARAN
ARAR
ASAP
ASAR
ASAS
ATAP
ATAR
AVAL
AWAY
AYAH
AZAN
BAAL
BAAS
BEAD
BEAK
BEAM
BEAN
BEAR
BEAT
BEAU
BIAS
BLAB
BLAD
BLAE
BLAG
BLAH
BLAT
BLAY
BOAK
BOAR
BOAT
BOAZ
BRAD
BRAE
BRAG
BRAK
BRAM
BRAN
BRAS
BRAT
BRAW
BRAY
BUAT
CFAF
CHAD
CHAI
CHAL
CHAM
CHAN
CHAP
CHAR
CHAT
CHAW
CHAY
CIAO
CLAD
CLAG
CLAM
CLAN
CLAP
CLAT
CLAW
CLAY
COAL
COAT
COAX
CRAB
CRAG
CRAM
CRAN
CRAP
CRAW
CRAX
CRAY
CYAN
CZAR
DEAD
DEAF
DEAL
DEAN
DEAR
DEAW
DHAK
DHAL
DIAL
DIAS
DIAZ
DOAB
DOAT
DRAB
DRAD
DRAG
DRAM
DRAT
DRAW
DRAY
DUAD
DUAL
DUAN
DUAR
DYAD
DYAK
ECAD
EDAL
EDAM
EGAD
EGAL
ELAM
ELAN
ELAT
EOAN
ERAT
ESAU
EVAN
EXAM
EYAS
FEAL
FEAR
FEAT
FIAT
FLAB
FLAG
FLAK
FLAM
FLAN
FLAP
FLAT
FLAW
FLAX
FLAY
FOAL
FOAM
FRAB
FRAE
FRAG
FRAP
FRAU
FRAY
GDAY
GEAL
GEAN
GEAR
GEAT
GHAN
GHAT
GLAD
GLAM
GNAR
GNAT
GNAW
GOAD
GOAF
GOAL
GOAT
GRAB
GRAF
GRAM
GRAN
GRAS
GRAT
GRAY
GUAM
GUAN
GUAR
GYAL
HAAF
HAAL
HAAR
HEAD
HEAL
HEAP
HEAR
HEAT
HOAR
HOAX
IGAD
IKAT
IMAM
IRAN
IRAQ
IRAS
ISAR
IVAN
IZAR
JAAP
JEAT
JIAO
JOAN
JUAN
KEAN
KHAN
KHAT
KNAG
KNAP
KNAR
KOAN
KRAB
KSAR
KWAI
KYAT
LEAD
LEAF
LEAK
LEAL
LEAM
LEAN
LEAP
LEAR
LEAT
LIAM
LIAR
LIAS
LOAD
LOAF
LOAM
LOAN
LUAU
LYAM
MAAM
MAAR
MAAS
MAAT
MEAD
MEAL
MEAN
MEAT
MOAN
MOAT
MYAL
NAAM
NAAN
NEAL
NEAP
NEAR
NEAT
NOAH
NYAS
OBAN
ODAL
OFAY
OGAM
OKAY
OLAF
OMAN
OMAR
OPAH
OPAL
ORAL
ORAN
OVAL
PAAL
PEAG
PEAK
PEAL
PEAN
PEAR
PEAS
PEAT
PIAF
PLAN
PLAP
PLAT
PLAY
PRAD
PRAM
PRAT
PRAU
PRAY
PTAH
PYAT
QUAD
QUAG
QUAT
QUAY
READ
REAK
REAL
REAM
REAN
REAP
REAR
RIAL
ROAD
ROAM
ROAN
ROAR
RYAL
RYAN
SCAB
SCAD
SCAG
SCAM
SCAN
SCAR
SCAT
SCAW
SEAL
SEAM
SEAN
SEAR
SEAS
SEAT
SHAD
SHAG
SHAH
SHAM
SHAN
SHAP
SHAW
SHAY
SIAL
SIAM
SIAN
SKAG
SKAT
SKAW
SLAB
SLAE
SLAG
SLAM
SLAP
SLAT
SLAV
SLAW
SLAY
SNAG
SNAP
SOAK
SOAP
SOAR
SOAY
SPAE
SPAG
SPAM
SPAN
SPAR
SPAT
SPAW
SPAY
STAB
STAG
STAN
STAP
STAR
STAW
STAY
SWAB
SWAD
SWAG
SWAM
SWAN
SWAP
SWAT
SWAY
TAAL
TEAK
TEAL
TEAM
TEAN
TEAR
TEAT
THAE
THAI
THAN
THAR
THAT
THAW
TOAD
TRAD
TRAM
TRAP
TRAY
TSAR
TUAN
TWAE
TWAL
TWAT
TWAY
TZAR
UDAD
UDAL
ULAD
ULAN
UNAU

UPAS
URAL
URAO
USAK
UTAH
UTAS
VAAL
VEAL
VIAL
VOAR
WEAK
WEAL
WEAN
WEAR
WHAM
WHAP
WHAT
WHAU
WOAD
WRAP
XIAN
XMAS
YEAD
YEAH
YEAR
YUAN
ZEAL
ABBA
ABBE
ALBE
ALBI
AMBO
BABA
BABE
BABI
BABU
BABY
BIBB
BOBA
BUBA
BUBO
CABA
COBB
COBH
CUBA
CUBE
CUBS
DABS
DEBT
DIBS
DUBS
EBBW
ELBA
ELBE
GABY
GIBE
GOBI
GOBO
GOBY
GYBE
HABU

HEBE
HOBO
IGBO
INBY
JIBE
JOBE
JUBA
JUBE
KIBE
KOBE
KOBO
LIBS
LOBE
LOBO
LUBA
MOBY
NABK
NEBO
NIBS
OMBU
ORBY
PEBA
PSBR
RABI
RIBS
ROBE
RUBE
RUBY
SABA
SIBB
TABI
TABU
TOBY
TUBA
TUBE
UMBO
UNBE
VIBS
WEBB
ZEBU
ZOBO
ZOBU
ACCT
ANCE
ARCH
ARCO
ASCH
BACA
BACH
BACK
BECK
BICE
BOCK
BUCK
COCA
COCH
COCK
COCO
DACE
DECA
DECK

DECO
DICE
DICH
DICK
DICY
DOCK
DUCE
DUCK
DUCT
EACH
ECCE
ECCO
EECH
ETCH
FACE
FACT
FECK
FICO
FOCH
GECK
HACK
HECH
HECK
HECT
HICK
HOCK
HUCK
INCA
INCH
ITCH
JACK
JOCK
JOCO
KECK
KICK
LACE
LACK
LACY
LECH
LICE
LICH
LICK
LOCH
LOCK
LOCO
LUCE
LUCK
LUCY
LYCH
MACE
MACH
MACK
MICA
MICE
MICK
MICO
MOCH
MOCK
MUCH
MUCK
NECK

NICE
NICK
NOCK
ONCE
ORCA
OUCH
PACA
PACE
PACK
PACO
PACT
PECH
PECK
PICA
PICE
PICK
PICT
POCK
PUCA
PUCE
PUCK
RACA
RACE
RACK
RACY
RECD
RECK
RICA
RICE
RICH
RICK
RICO
ROCA
ROCH
ROCK
RUCK
SACK
SECH
SECT
SICE
SICH
SICK
SOCA
SOCK
SUCH
SUCK
SYCE
TACE
TACH
TACK
TACO
TACT
TECH
TICE
TICH
TICK
TOCO
TUCK
UCCA
UNCE
UNCO

VACH
VICE
VOCE
WACK
WICE
WICK
WOCK
YACK
YOCK
YUCA
YUCK
ZACK
AC/DC
AIDA
AIDE
AIDS
ANDA
AUDE
AUDI
AWDL
BADE
BEDE
BEDS
BEDU
BIDE
BODE
BODY
BUDD
BUDE
BUDO
CADE
CADI
CEDE
CEDI
CODA
CODE
CODY
DADA
DADD
DADO
DIDO
DODO
DUDE
DUDS
EDDA
EDDO
EDDY
ENDS
FADE
FADO
FIDE
FIDO
GADE
GADI
GIDE
GODS
HADE
HADJ
HIDE
HYDE
INDY

JADE
JODO
JUDE
JUDO
JUDY
KADE
KADI
KIDD
KUDU
LADA
LADE
LADY
LEDA
LIDE
LIDO
LODE
LUDD
LUDO
MADE
MEDE
MIDI
MODE
MODO
MODS
NADA
NIDE
NODE
NUDD
NUDE
ODDS
OLDS
OUDS
PODS
PUDU
QADI
RADA
REDD
REDE
REDO
RIDE
RODE
RUDD
RUDE
SADE
SIDA
SIDE
SODA
SUDD
SUDS
TEDY
TIDE
TIDY
TODD
TODO
TODY
UNDE
UNDO
URDÉ
URDU
URDY
VADE

VEDA
VIDE
WADD
WADE
WADI
WADY
WIDE
YEDE
YODH
ABED
ABEL
ABER
ABET
ACER
ACES
ADEN
ADES
AGED
AGEE
AGEN
AGES
AHEM
AJEE
AKEE
ALEC
ALEW
ALEX
AMEN
AMES
ANEW
APEX
AREA
AREG
ARES
ARET
AREW
ATEN
AVER
AVES
AWED
AYER
AYES
BAEL
BEEB
BEEF
BEEN
BEEP
BEER
BEES
BEET
BHEL
BIEN
BIER
BLEB
BLED
BLEE
BLET
BLEW
BLEY
BOER
BRED

BREE
BREN
BRER
BREW
CAEN
CHEF
CHER
CHEW
CIEL
CLEF
CLEG
CLEM
CLEW
COED
CRED
CREE
CREW
DEED
DEEK
DEEM
DEEN
DEEP
DEER
DEEV
DIEB
DIED
DIES
DIET
DIEU
DOEK
DOER
DOES
DREE
DREG
DREW
DREY
DUEL
DUES
DUET
DYER
EDEN
EDER
EGER
EHEU
EMEU
ENEW
EPEE
ETEN
EVEN
EVER
EVET
EWER
EWES
EXES
EYER
EYES
FEED
FEEL
FEER
FEET
FIEF

FLEA
FLED
FLEE
FLEG
FLEW
FLEX
FLEY
FOEN
FREE
FRET
FUEL
GAEA
GAEL
GEED
GEEK
GEEP
GEEZ
GHEE
GIER
GLEE
GLEG
GLEI
GLEN
GLEY
GOEL
GOER
GOES
GOEY
GREE
GREW
GREY
HAEM
HAET
HEED
HEEL
HEEP
HUER
HUEY
IBEX
ICED
ICEL
IDEA
IDEM
IDES
ILEX
INES
ISER
ITEM
IVES
JEEL
JEEP
JEER
JOEL
JOEY
KEEK
KEEL
KEEN
KEEP
KIEL
KIER
KIEV

KLEE
KNEE
KNEW
KOEL
LAER
LEEK
LEEP
LEER
LEES
LEET
LIED
LIEF
LIEN
LIES
LIEU
LNER
LUES
LUEZ
LWEI
MEED
MEEK
MEER
MEET
MIEN
MZEE
NEED
NEEM
NEEP
NIEF
NOEL
NOES
NUER
NYET
OBEY
ODER
OGEE
OGEN
OLEA
OLEO
OMEN
OMER
ONER
ONE'S
OPEC
OPEL
OPEN
OVEL
OVEN
OVER
OWED
OWEN
OXEN
OXER
OYER
OYEZ
PEEK
PEEL
PEEN
PEEP
PEER
PHEW
PIED
PIER
PIES
PIET
PLEA
PLEB
PLED
PLEW
POEM
POET
PREE
PREP
PREY
PUER
PYET
QUEP
QUEY
REED
REEF
REEK
REEL
REEN
RHEA
RIEL
RIEM
RIEN
SEED
SEEK
SEEL
SEEM
SEEN
SEEP
SEER
SHEA
SHED
SHEM
SHET
SIEN
SKED
SKEG
SKEN
SKEO
SKEP
SKER
SKET
SKEW
SLED
SLEE
SLEW
SLEY
SMEE
SMEW
SNEB
SNED
SNEE
SPEC
SPED
SPEE
SPET
SPEW
SPEY
STED
STEM
STEN
STEP
STET
STEW
STEY
SUER
SUET
SUEY
SUEZ
SWEE
SWEY
SYEN
TAEL
TEEM
TEEN
TEER
TEES
THEA
THEE
THEM
THEN
THEW
THEY
TIED
TIER
TOEA
TOEY
TREE
TREK
TRET
TREW
TREY
TREZ
TUES
TWEE
UBER
ULEX
UREA
USED
USER
USES
UVEA
VEEP
VEER
VIED
VIEL
VIES
VIEW
VLEI
WEED
WEEK
WEEL
WEEM
WEEN
WEEP
WEET
WHEE
WHEN
WHET
WHEW
WHEY
WIEL
WIEN
WREN
YBET
YEED
YLEM
YUEN
ZOEA
IDÉE
AFFY
ALFA
ANFO
BAFF
BAFT
BIFF
BOFF
BUFF
BUFO
CAFÉ
COFF
CUFF
DAFF
DAFT
DEFT
DEFY
DOFF
DUFF
FAFF
FIFA
FIFE
FUFF
GAFF
GIFT
GOFF
GUFF
HAFF
HAFT
HEFT
HUFF
IFFY
INFO
JEFF
KOFF
LEFT
LIFE
LIFT
LOFT
LUFF
MIFF
MUFF
NAFF
NIFE
NIFF
OFFA
ORFE
ORFF
PUFF
RAFF
RAFT
REFT
RIFE
RIFF
RIFT
RUFF
RYFE
SAFE
SIFT
SOFA
SOFI
SOFT
SUFI
TAFF
TAFT
TEFF
TIFF
TIFT
TOFF
TOFT
TOFU
TUFA
TUFF
TUFT
UFFA
WAFD
WAFF
WAFT
WEFT
WIFE
YAFF
YUFT
ZIFF
ALGA
ARGO
BAGS
BEGO
BIGA
BIGG
BOGY
BUGS
CAGE
CIGS
DAGO
DIGS
DOGE
DOGS
DOGY
EDGE
EDGY
EGGS
EIGG
ERGO
EUGE
EUGH
FEGS
FIGO
FOGG
FOGY
GAGA
GAGE
GIGA
GIGI
GOGO
GUGA
HAGG
HAGH
HIGH
HOGG
HOGH
HUGE
HUGH
HUGO
IAGO
INGE
INGO
JAGG
JAGS
KAGO
LEGO
LEGS
LOGE
LOGO
LOGS
LOGY
LUGE
LUGH
LUGS
MAGE
MAGG
MAGI
MEGA
NAGA
NIGH
NOGO
ONGO
ORGE
ORGY
PAGE
PEGH
PIGS
POGO
PUGH
RAGA
RAGE
RAGG
RAGI
RAGS
RIGA
RIGG
RIGI
RUGA
SAGA
SAGE
SAGO
SEGO
SIGH
SIGN
TEGG
TIGE
TOGA
TOGE
TOGO
TOGS
UPGO
URGE
VEGA
VIGO
WAGE
WEGG
YAGI
YEGG
YOGA
YOGH
YOGI
YUGA
ACHE
ACHT
AGHA
ASHE
ASHY
BAHT
BUHL
DAHL
DOHA
ECHE
ECHO
ECHT
EPHA
ETHE
FAHD
HAHA
HUHU
JEHU
JOHN
KOHL
LAHN
LEHR
MAHU
MOHR
MOHS
OAHU
OCHE
OTHO
RAHU
RUHR
SOHO
TAHA
TAHR
TEHR
TOHO
TSHI
VEHM
ABIB
ACID
ACIS
ADIT
AGIN
AGIO
AGIS
AKIN
ALIA
ALIF
AMID
AMIE
AMIN
AMIR
AMIS
ANIL
APIA
APIS
ARIA
ARID
ARIL
ARIS
ASIA
AVID
AXIL
AXIS
AYIN
BAIL
BAIT
BEIN
BLIN
BLIP
BOIL
BRIE
BRIG
BRIM
BRIO
BRIS
BRIT
BRIX
BUIK
CAIN
CEIL
CHIC
CHIK
CHIL
CHIN
CHIP
CHIT
CLIO
CLIP
COIF
COIL
COIN
COIR
COIT
CRIB
CRIT
CUIF
CUIT
DAIL
DAIS
DEIL
DOIT
DRIB
DRIP
EDIT
EFIK
EGIS
ELIA
ELIS
EMIR
EMIT
ENID
EPIC
ERIA
ERIC
ERIE
ERIK
ERIN
ERIS
EVIL
EXIT
FAIL
FAIN
FAIR
FAIX
FEIS
FLIC
FLIP
FLIT
FLIX
FOIL
FOIN
FRIG
FRIT
GAIA
GAID
GAIN
GAIR
GAIT
GEIT
GLIA
GLIB
GLID
GLIM
GLIT
GRID
GRIG
GRIM
GRIN
GRIP
GRIS
GRIT
GUID
HAIG
HAIK
HAIL
HAIN
HAIR
HAIT
HEIL
HEIR
HUIA
IBID
IBIS
ILIA
IRID
IRIS
ISIS
IWIS
JAIL
JAIN

JOIN
KAID
KAIE
KAIF
KAIL
KAIM
KAIN
KEIR
KNIT
KRIS
KWIC
LAIC
LAID
LAIK
LAIN
LAIR
LAIS
LEIR
LOID
LOIN
LOIR
LOIS
LUIT
MAIA
MAID
MAIK
MAIL
MAIM
MAIN
MEIN
MEIR
MOIL
MOIT
MUID
MUIL
MUIR
NAIA
NAIK
NAIL
NAIN
NAIR
NEIF
NEIL
NOIL
OBIA
OBIT
ODIN
OHIO
OLID
OLIM
OLIO
OMIT
OPIE
OTIC
OTIS
OVID
PAID
PAIK
PAIL
PAIN
PAIR

PAIS
PEIN
PHIL
PHIZ
PLIÉ
PLIM
PRIG
PRIM
PRIX
QUID
QUIM
QUIN
QUIP
QUIT
QUIZ
RAID
RAIK
RAIL
RAIN
RAIT
REIF
REIK
REIN
REIS
ROIL
ROIN
RUIN
SAIC
SAID
SAIL
SAIM
SAIN
SAIR
SEIF
SEIL
SEIR
SHIE
SHIM
SHIN
SHIP
SHIT
SHIV
SKIA
SKID
SKIM
SKIN
SKIO
SKIP
SKIT
SLID
SLIM
SLIP
SLIT
SMIT
SNIB
SNIG
SNIP
SNIT
SOIL
SPIC
SPIF

SPIK
SPIN
SPIT
SPIV
STIE
STIM
STIR
SUIT
SWIG
SWIM
SWIZ
TAIG
TAIL
TAIN
TAIT
TEIL
THIN
THIR
THIS
TOIL
TRIE
TRIG
TRIM
TRIN
TRIO
TRIP
TWIG
TWIN
TWIT
UNIO
UNIT
URIC
URIM
UTIS
VAIL
VAIN
VAIR
VEIL
VEIN
VOID
VRIL
WAIF
WAIL
WAIN
WAIT
WEID
WEIR
WHID
WHIG
WHIM
WHIN
WHIP
WHIR
WHIT
WHIZ
WRIT
YMIR
YWIS
ZEIN
ZOIC
ZOID

BAJU
DOJO
FIJI
FUJI
GAJO
JUJU
MOJO
NAJA
PUJA
REJA
ROJI
SEJM
SIJO
SOJA
TOJO
ALKY
ANKH
ASKE
ASKR
BAKE
BAKU
BIKE
BOKE
BOKO
BUKE
BYKE
CAKE
COKE
DAKS
DEKE
DIKA
DIKE
DUKE
DYKE
EKKA
ELKS
EOKA
ESKY
FAKE
FIKE
FIKY
FYKE
HAKA
HAKE
HIKE
HOKE
HOKI
HYKE
ICKY
ILKA
INKY
JAKE
JOKE
JUKE
KAKI
KIKE
KOKO
KUKU
LAKE
LAKH
LIKE

LOKE
LOKI
LUKE
MAKE
MAKO
MIKE
MOKE
MOKI
MOKO
NIKE
NUKE
OAKS
OAKY
PEKE
PIKA
PIKE
POKE
POKY
PUKE
RAKE
RAKI
RAKU
RAKY
REKE
ROKE
RUKH
SAKE
SAKI
SEKT
SIKA
SIKE
SIKH
SYKE
TAKA
TAKE
TIKA
TIKE
TIKI
TOKE
TOKO
TYKE
WAKA
WAKE
WAKF
WEKA
WOKE
YIKE
YLKE
YOKE
YUKE
YUKO
AALU
ABLE
ABLY
AGLU
ALLO
ALLY
AMLA
ARLY
ATLI
AULA

AULD
AXLE
BALA
BALD
BALE
BALI
BALK
BALL
BALM
BALT
BALU
BELL
BELT
BILE
BILK
BILL
BOLD
BOLE
BOLL
BOLO
BOLT
BULB
BULK
BULL
CALC
CALF
CALK
CALL
CALM
CALP
CALX
CELL
CELT
CILL
COLA
COLD
COLE
COLL
COLT
CULL
CULM
CULT
DALE
DALI
DBLE
DELE
DELF
DELI
DELL
DILL
DOLE
DOLL
DOLT
DULE
DULL
DULY
EALE
EELS
EILD
ELLA
ELLE

ESLA
FALA
FALL
FALX
FELL
FELT
FILE
FILL
FILM
FILO
FILS
FOLD
FOLK
FULL
GALA
GALE
GALL
GELD
GELT
GILA
GILD
GILL
GILT
GOLD
GOLE
GOLF
GULA
GULE
GULF
GULL
GULP
HALE
HALF
HALL
HALM
HALO
HALS
HALT
HELA
HELD
HELE
HELL
HELM
HELP
HILL
HILO
HILT
HOLD
HOLE
HOLI
HOLM
HOLT
HOLY
HULA
HULE
HULK
HULL
HYLA
HYLE
IDLE
IDLY

ILLE
ILLY
INLY
ISLE
JELL
JILL
JILT
JOLE
JOLL
JOLO
JOLT
JULY
KALE
KALI
KELL
KELP
KELT
KILL
KILN
KILO
KILP
KILT
KOLA
KOLO
KYLE
LALO
LELY
LILL
LILO
LILT
LILY
LOLA
LOLL
LULL
LULU
LYLE
LYLY
MALE
MALI
MALL
MALM
MALO
MALT
MELA
MELD
MELL
MELT
MILD
MILE
MILK
MILL
MILO
MILT
MOLA
MOLD
MOLE
MOLL
MOLT
MOLY
MULE
MULL

NALA
NELL
NILE
NILL
NOLE
NOLL
NOLO
NULL
OGLE
OILS
OILY
OLLA
ONLY
ORLE
ORLY
OSLO
OULK
OWLS
OWLY
PALE
PALI
PALK
PALL
PALM
PALP
PELA
PELE
PELF
PELL
PELT
PILE
PILI
PILL
POLE
POLK
POLL
POLO
POLT
POLY
PULA
PULE
PULI
PULL
PULP
PULU
PULY
RALE
RELY
RILE
RILL
ROLE
ROLF
ROLL
RULE
RULY
SALE
SALK
SALP
SALT
SELE
SELF

SELL
SILD
SILE
SILK
SILL
SILO
SILT
SOLA
SOLD
SOLE
SOLO
SULK
SULU
TALA
TALC
TALE
TALK
TALL
TELA
TELE
TELL
TILE
TILL
TILT
TOLA
TOLD
TOLE
TOLL
TOLT
TOLU
TULE
TULI
TULL
UGLI
UGLY
VALE
VALI
VELA
VELE
VELL
VILE
VILL
VOLA
VOLE
VOLT
VULN
WALD
WALE
WALI
WALK
WALL
WALY
WELD
WELK
WELL
WELT
WILD
WILE
WILI
WILL
WILT

WILY
WOLD
WOLF
WULL
YALE
YALU
YELD
YELL
YELP
YELT
YILL
YOLK
YULE
ZILA
ZOLA
ZULU
ACME
AGMA
ALMA
ALMS
AMMO
ARMS
ARMY
AYMÉ
BEMA
BIMM
BOMA
BOMB
BUMF
BUMP
CAMA
CAME
CAMP
COMA
COMB
COME
COMM
COMO
COMP
CUMA
CYMA
CYME
DAME
DAMN
DAMP
DEME
DEMI
DEMO
DEMY
DIMA
DIME
DOME
DUMA
DUMB
DUMP
EGMA
ELMO
EMMA
EMMY
ESME
FAME

FEME
FUME
GAMB
GAME
GAMP
GAMY
GEMS
GIMP
GUMP
GYMP
HAME
HAMS
HEME
HEMI
HEMP
HOMA
HOME
HOMO
HUMA
HUME
HUMF
HUMP
HYMN
IAMB
ISMY
JAMB
JIMP
JOMO
JUMA
JUMP
KAMA
KAME
KAMI
KEMB
KEMP
LAMA
LAMB
LAME
LAMP
LEME
LIMA
LIMB
LIME
LIMN
LIMO
LIMP
LIMY
LOMA
LOME
LUMP
LYME
MAMA
MAME
MEMO
MIME
MIMI
MOME
MUMP
NAME
NEMO
NOMA

NOME
NUMA
NUMB
OUMA
PIMP
POME
POMP
PUMA
PUMP
PUMY
RAMA
RAMI
RAMP
REME
REMS
RIMA
RIME
RIMU
ROME
ROMP
RUME
RUMI
RUMP
SAMA
SAME
SAMI
SAMP
SEMI
SIMA
SIMI
SIMP
SOMA
SOME
SUMO
SUMP
SUMS
TAME
TAMP
TEME
TEMP
TIME
TOMB
TOME
TUMP
TUMS
TYMP
VAMP
VIMY
WAME
WEMB
WIMP
WOMB
XEMA
YAMA
YOMP
YUMP
ZAMA
ZIMB
ZOMO
ZYME
ACNE

AGNI
AÎNÉ
AINT
AINU
ANNA
ANNE
ANNO
ARNA
ARNE
ARNO
AUNE
AUNT
BANC
BAND
BANE
BANG
BANI
BANK
BANT
BEND
BENE
BENJ
BENN
BENT
BENZ
BIND
BINE
BING
BINK
BINT
BONA
BOND
BONE
BONG
BONK
BONN
BONY
BRNO
BUNA
BUND
BUNG
BUNK
BUNT
BYNG
CANA
CANE
CANN
CANS
CANT
CENS
CENT
CINE
CONE
CONK
CONN
CONS
CONT
CONY
CUNT
DANE
DANG

DANK
DENE
DENT
DENY
DINE
DING
DINK
DINT
DONA
DONE
DONG
DONT
DUNE
DUNG
DUNK
DUNS
DUNT
DYNE
EINE
ENNA
ERNE
ESNE
ETNA
EYNE
FAND
FANE
FANG
FANK
FANS
FEND
FENI
FENT
FIND
FINE
FINK
FINN
FINO
FOND
FONE
FONS
FONT
FUND
FUNG
FUNK
FUNS
GANG
GANT
GENE
GENS
GENT
GENU
GING
GINK
GONE
GONG
GONK
GUNK
GUNN
GUNS
GUNZ
GYNT

HAND
HANG
HANK
HANS
HANT
HEND
HENT
HINC
HIND
HING
HINT
HOND
HONE
HONG
HONI
HONK
HUNG
HUNK
HUNT
INNS
IONA
ISNT
IYNX
JANE
JANN
JENA
JINK
JINX
JUNE
JUNG
JUNK
JUNO
JYNX
KANA
KANE
KANG
KANO
KANS
KANT
KENO
KENT
KINA
KIND
KINE
KING
KINK
KINO
KOND
KONG
KONK
KUNA
LANA
LAND
LANE
LANG
LANK
LANT
LANX
LEND
LENG
LENO

LENS
LENT
LIND
LINE
LING
LINK
LINN
LINO
LINT
LONE
LONG
LUNA
LUNE
LUNG
LUNT
LYNX
MANA
MANE
MANG
MANI
MANN
MANO
MANS
MANU
MANX
MANY
MEND
MENE
MENG
MENT
MENU
MINA
MIND
MINE
MING
MINI
MINK
MINO
MINT
MINX
MONA
MONG
MONK
MONO
MONS
MONY
MUNG
NANA
NAND
NANO
NENE
NINA
NINE
NINO
NONE
NONG
NONO
NUNC
OINK
OINT
OMNI

OONS
OONT
ORNE
OWNS
PAND
PANE
PANG
PANT
PEND
PENE
PENH
PENI
PENK
PENN
PENT
PINA
PINE
PING
PINK
PINS
PINT
POND
PONE
PONG
PONK
PONS
PONT
PONY
PUNA
PUNG
PUNK
PUNT
PUNY
QING
RANA
RAND
RANG
RANI
RANK
RANT
REND
RENE
RENO
RENT
RENY
RIND
RINE
RING
RINK
RINT
RONE
RONG
RONT
RUND
RUNE
RUNG
RUNS
RUNT
RYND
SAND
SANE

SANG	WANK	BROG	FOOD	LYON	SCOT	WHOM	OOPS	AWRY
SANK	WANT	BRON	FOOL	MEOW	SCOW	WHOP	OPPO	AYRE
SANS	WEND	BROO	FOON	MOOD	SHOA	WHOT	OUPA	BARB
SANT	WENT	BROS	FOOT	MOOG	SHOD	WOOD	OUPH	BARD
SENA	WIND	BROW	FROE	MOOI	SHOE	WOOF	PAPA	BARE
SEND	WINE	BUOY	FROG	MOOL	SHOG	WOOL	PEPO	BARF
SENS	WING	CHOC	FROM	MOON	SHOO	WOON	PIPA	BARI
SENT	WINK	CHON	FROW	MOOP	SHOP	WOOT	PIPE	BARK
SIND	WINN	CHOP	GAOL	MOOR	SHOT	YGOE	PIPI	BARM
SINE	WINO	CHOU	GLOB	MOOT	SHOW	YOOF	POPE	BARN
SING	WONG	CHOW	GLOM	MUON	SION	YOOP	PUPA	BARP
SINK	WONT	CHOY	GLOP	NAOS	SKOL	ZION	QOPH	BARS
SINO	WYND	CION	GLOW	NEON	SLOB	ZOOM	RAPE	BART
SONE	WYNN	CLOD	GOOD	NOOK	SLOE	ZOOT	RAPT	BERE
SONG	YANG	CLOG	GOOF	NOON	SLOG	ALPH	REPP	BERG
SUNG	YANK	CLOP	GOOG	NOOP	SLOP	ALPS	REPS	BERK
SUNK	YOND	CLOS	GOOK	NYOS	SLOT	BAPU	RIPE	BERM
SUNN	YONI	CLOT	GOOL	OBOE	SLOW	CAPA	RIPP	BERN
SYNC	YUNX	CLOU	GOON	OBOL	SMOG	CAPE	RIPS	BIRD
SYND	ZANY	CLOW	GOOP	ODOR	SNOB	CAPH	ROPE	BIRK
SYNE	ZENO	CLOY	GOOR	OXON	SNOD	CAPO	ROPY	BIRL
TANA	ZINC	COOF	GROG	PEON	SNOG	CAPT	SEPS	BIRO
TANE	ZING	COOK	GROT	PHOH	SNOT	COPE	SEPT	BIRR
TANG	ZONA	COOL	GROW	PHOT	SNOW	COPS	SIPE	BORA
TANH	ZONE	COOM	GSOH	PION	SOOK	COPY	SOPH	BORD
TANK	ZUNI	COON	HOOD	PLOD	SOOL	CUPS	SYPE	BORE
TEND	ACOL	COOP	HOOF	PLOP	SOOM	DEPT	TAPA	BORN
TENE	AEON	COOT	HOOK	PLOT	SOON	DOPA	TAPE	BORO
TENG	AGOG	CROP	HOON	PLOW	SOOP	DOPE	TAPS	BORS
TENT	AGON	CROW	HOOP	PLOY	SOOT	DUPE	TAPU	BURD
TINA	AHOY	DHOW	HOOT	POOD	SPOT	ESPY	TIPI	BURG
TIND	ALOD	DIOR	HUON	POOF	STOA	EXPO	TIPU	BURK
TINE	ALOE	DOOB	ICON	POOH	STOB	GAPE	TOPE	BURL
TING	ALOW	DOOK	IDOL	POOK	STOL	GAPO	TOPI	BURN
TINK	AMOK	DOOL	IFOR	POOL	STOP	HAPI	TOPS	BURP
TINT	AMOS	DOOM	IGOR	POON	STOT	HEPT	TUPI	BURR
TINY	AMOY	DOON	IKON	POOP	STOW	HIPT	TYPE	BURT
TONE	ANOA	DOOR	IPOH	POOR	SWOB	HOPE	TYPO	BURY
TONG	ANON	DROP	IRON	POOT	SWOP	HOPI	UMPH	BYRD
TONK	ATOC	DROW	IVOR	PROA	SWOT	HOPS	WEPT	BYRE
TONS	ATOK	EBOR	JOOK	PROD	THON	HYPE	WIPE	CARD
TONY	ATOM	EDOM	KAON	PROF	THOR	HYPO	YAPP	CARE
TUNA	ATOP	ELOI	KHOR	PROG	THOS	IMPI	YIPS	CARK
TUND	AVON	ENOL	KNOB	PROM	THOU	JAPE	YMPE	CARL
TUNE	AVOW	ENOS	KNOP	PROO	TOOK	KAPH	ZUPA	CARP
TUNG	AWOL	ENOW	KNOT	PROP	TOOL	KEPI	AARU	CARR
TYNE	AXON	EPOS	KNOW	PROW	TOOM	KEPT	ABRI	CART
ULNA	AZOV	EROS	KNOX	PYOT	TOON	KIPE	ACRE	CARY
VANE	BCOM	ETON	KOOK	QUOD	TOOT	KIPP	ACRI	CERE
VANG	BLOB	EUOI	KROO	QUOP	TROD	KYPE	ACRO	CERO
VENA	BLOC	EVOE	LAON	RIOT	TROG	LAPP	AERO	CERT
VEND	BLOT	EXON	LAOS	ROOD	TRON	LIPS	AFRO	CIRÉ
VENN	BLOW	EXOR	LION	ROOF	TROP	LOPE	AGRA	CIRL
VENT	BOOB	EYOT	LOOF	ROOK	TROT	MAPS	AIRE	CORD
VINA	BOOK	FEOD	LOOK	ROOM	TROU	MOPE	AIRN	CORE
VINE	BOOL	FLOE	LOOM	ROON	TROW	MOPP	AIRS	CORF
VINO	BOOM	FLOG	LOON	ROOP	TROY	NAPE	AIRT	CORK
VINT	BOON	FLOP	LOOP	ROOT	UPON	NIPA	AIRY	CORM
WAND	BOOR	FLOR	LOOR	RYOT	VIOL	NOPE	ARRU	CORN
WANE	BOOT	FLOW	LOOS	SCOG	VTOL	OGPU	ARRY	CORY
WANG	BROD	FLOX	LOOT	SCOP	WHOA	OLPE	AURA	CPRS

CURB
CURD
CURE
CURK
CURL
CURN
CURR
CURT
DARD
DARE
DARG
DARI
DARK
DARN
DART
DERE
DERM
DERN
DERO
DERV
DIRE
DIRK
DIRL
DIRT
DORA
DORÉ
DORM
DORP
DORR
DORT
DORY
DURA
DURE
DURN
DURO
EARD
EARL
EARN
EARP
EARS
EBRO
ECRU
EERY
EIRE
EORL
EURE
EURO
EYRA
EYRE
EYRY
EZRA
FARD
FARE
FARM
FARO
FARR
FART
FERE
FERM
FERN
FIRE
FIRK
FIRM
FIRN
FORB
FORD
FORE
FORK
FORM
FORT
FURL
FURR
FURY
FYRD
GARB
GARE
GART
GARY
GERE
GERM
GIRD
GIRL
GIRN
GIRO
GIRR
GIRT
GORE
GORM
GORP
GORY
GURL
GURN
GURU
GYRE
GYRO
HARD
HARE
HARK
HARL
HARM
HARN
HARO
HARP
HART
HARZ
HERA
HERB
HERD
HERE
HERL
HERM
HERN
HERO
HERR
HERS
HERY
HERZ
HIRE
HORE
HORN
HORS
HURL
HURT
INRI
INRO
IVRY
JARK
JARL
JARP
JERK
JIRD
JURA
JURE
JURY
KARA
KARD
KARL
KART
KERB
KERF
KERN
KIRI
KIRK
KIRN
KORA
KORE
KURD
KURI
KURU
LARD
LARE
LARK
LARN
LERP
LIRA
LIRK
LORD
LORE
LORI
LORN
LORY
LURE
LURK
LYRA
LYRE
MARA
MARC
MARE
MARG
MARI
MARK
MARL
MARM
MARO
MARS
MART
MARY
MERE
MERI
MERK
MERL
MERU
MIRA
MIRE
MIRK
MIRO
MIRV
MORE
MORI
MORN
MORO
MORS
MORT
MURE
MURK
MURL
NARC
NARD
NARE
NARK
NARY
NERD
NERK
NERO
NIRL
NORE
NORI
NORK
NORM
NORN
NURD
NURL
NURR
OARS
OGRE
OKRA
OKRO
OORT
ORRA
OURS
OVRA
OWRE
PARA
PARD
PARE
PARK
PARP
PARR
PART
PÈRE
PERI
PERK
PERM
PERN
PERT
PERU
PIRL
PIRN
PIRO
PORE
PORK
PORN
PORT
PURE
PURI
PURL
PURR
PYRE
PYRO
RARE
RORE
RORO
RORT
RORY
RURP
RURU
SARD
SARI
SARK
SCRY
SERA
SERB
SERE
SERF
SERK
SHRI
SIRE
SIRI
SKRY
SORA
SORB
SORD
SORE
SORN
SORT
SPRY
SURA
SURD
SURE
SURF
TARA
TARE
TARN
TARO
TART
TERA
TERF
TERM
TERN
TERR
THRU
TIRE
TIRL
TIRO
TIRR
TORC
TORE
TORN
TORR
TORT
TORY
TURD
TURF
TURK
TURM
TURN
TYRE
TYRO
VARA
VARE
VARY
VERA
VERB
VERS
VERT
VERY
VIRL
WARB
WARD
WARE
WARK
WARM
WARN
WARP
WART
WARY
WERE
WERT
WIRE
WIRY
WORD
WORE
WORK
WORM
WORN
WORT
WURM
XERO
YARD
YARE
YARN
YARR
YERK
YIRD
YIRK
YIRR
YORE
YORK
ZARF
ZERO
ZORI
ZURF
ABSE
AESC
ALSO
APSE
ARSE
BASE
BASH
BASK
BASS
BAST
BESS
BEST
BISE
BISH
BISK
BISP
BOSH
BOSS
BUSH
BUSK
BUSS
BUST
BUSY
CASA
CASE
CASH
CASK
CAST
CESS
CIST
COSE
COSH
COSS
COST
COSY
CUSH
CUSK
CUSP
CUSS
CYST
DASH
DESK
DISA
DISC
DISH
DISK
DISS
DOSE
DOSH
DOSS
DUSE
DUSH
DUSK
DUST
EASE
EAST
EASY
ELSA
ELSE
ENSI
ERSE
ESSE
FASH
FASO
FAST
FEST
FISC
FISH
FISK
FIST
FOSS
FUSE
FUSS
FUST
GASH
GASP
GAST
GCSE
GEST
GISM
GIST
GOSH
GOSS
GUSH
GUST
HASE
HASH
HASK
HASP
HESP
HESS
HEST
HISH
HISS
HIST
HMSO
HOSE
HOSS
HOST
HUSH
HUSK
HUSO
HUSS
INST
IPSE
JASS
JESS
JEST
JISM
JOSE
JOSH
JOSS
JUST
KESH
KEST
KISH
KISS
KIST
KOSS
LASH
LASS
LAST
LESS
LEST
LISA
LISK
LISP
LIST
LOSE
LOSH
LOSS
LOST
LUSH
LUSK
LUST
LYSE
MASA
MASE
MASH
MASK
MASS
MAST
MASU
MESA
MESE
MESH
MESO
MESS
MISC
MISE
MISO
MISS
MIST
MOSS
MOST
MUSA
MUSE
MUSH
MUSK
MUSO
MUSS
MUST
NASA
NASH
NASO
NESH
NESS
NEST
NISI
NOSE
NOSH
NOSY
OAST
ODSO
OISE
ONST
OOSE
OSSA
OUST
PASE
PASH
PASS
PAST
PESO
PEST
PISE
PISH
PISO
PISS
POSE
POSH
POSS
POST
POSY
PUSH
PUSS
RASC

RASE
RASH
RASP
RAST
RESH
REST
RISE
RISK
RISP
RISS
ROSE
ROSS
ROSY
RUSA
RUSE
RUSH
RUSK
RUST
SASA
SASH
SASS
SESE
SESS
SISS
SIST
SOSS
SUSA
SUSS
SUSU
TASH
TASK
TASS
TESS
TEST
TOSA
TOSE
TOSH
TOSS
TOST
TUSH
TUSK
UIST
UPSY
URSA
USSR
VASE
VAST
VEST
VISA
VISE
WASE
WASH
WASP
WAST
WEST
WISE
WISH
WISP
WIST
WUSS
XOSA
XYST
YESK
YEST
ZEST
ACTA
ACTS
AITU
ALTA
ALTE
ALTO
ANTA
ANTE
ANTI
ANTS
ARTA
ARTS
ARTY
ASTI
ATTO
ATTU
AUTO
BATE
BATH
BATS
BATT
BETA
BETE
BÊTE
BETH
BITE
BITO
BITS
BITT
BOTE
BOTH
BOTS
BOTT
BUTE
BUTT
BYTE
CATE
CATO
CATS
CCTV
CETE
CITE
CITO
CITS
CITY
COTE
COTH
COTT
COTY
CUTE
CYTE
DATA
DATE
DATO
DITA
DITE
DITT
DOTE
DOTH
DOTS
DUTY
EATS
ERTÉ
ESTE
ESTH
ETTA
ETTY
FATE
FATS
FETA
FETE
FETT
FITT
FITZ
GATE
GATH
GATT
GETA
GETT
GITE
GOTA
GOTH
GUTS
GYTE
HATE
HATH
HETE
HETH
HOTE
INTI
INTO
IOTA
JATO
JETÉ
JOTA
JUTE
KATA
KATE
KATI
KETA
KITE
KITH
KOTO
KYTE
LATE
LATH
LATS
LETO
LETS
LETT
LITE
LITH
LOTE
LOTH
LOTI
LOTO
LOTS
LUTE
LUTZ
LYTE
MATE
MATH
MATT
MATY
META
METE
MITE
MITT
MOTE
MOTH
MOTT
MOTU
MUTE
MUTI
MUTT
MYTH
NATO
NETE
NETS
NETT
NITH
NOTE
NOTT
NUTS
OATH
OATS
OCTA
OETA
OKTA
ONTO
ORTS
OTTO
PATE
PATH
PATU
PITA
PITH
PITT
PITY
POTE
POTS
POTT
PUTT
PUTZ
RATA
RATE
RATH
RATS
RATU
RETE
RETT
RITA
RITE
RITT
RITZ
ROTA
ROTE
ROTI
ROTL
RUTA
RUTE
RUTH
SATE
SATI
SATS
SETA
SETT
SITE
SITU
TATA
TATE
TATH
TATI
TATT
TATU
TETE
TETH
TITE
TITI
TITO
TOTE
TOTO
TUTU
TYTE
UNTO
VATU
VETO
VETS
VITA
VITE
VOTE
WATE
WATT
WITE
WITH
WITS
WYTE
YATE
YETI
YETT
YITE
ZATI
ZETA
ZITI
ABUS
ABUT
ADUR
AGUE
ALUM
AMUN
AMUR
ANUS
AQUA
ARUM
ARUN
ASUR
ATUA
ATUM
BAUD
BAUK
BAUR
BLUB
BLUE
BLUR
BLUT
BOUK
BOUN
BOUT
BRUM
BRUT
CAUK
CAUL
CAUM
CAUP
CHUB
CHUG
CHUM
CHUT
CLUB
CLUE
COUE
COUP
COUR
CRUD
CRUE
CRUX
DAUB
DAUD
DAUR
DAUT
DOUC
DOUP
DOUR
DOUT
DRUB
DRUG
DRUM
ELUL
ETUI
EXUL
FAUN
FEUD
FLUB
FLUE
FLUX
FOUD
FOUG
FOUL
FOUR
GAUD
GAUL
GAUM
GAUP
GAUR
GEUM
GLUE
GLUM
GLUT
GOUK
GOUT
GRUB
GRUE
GRUG
GRUM
GRUS
HAUD
HAUL
HAUT
HOUR
HOUT
IRUS
JAUP
JOUK
KHUD
KNUB
KNUR
KNUT
LAUD
LAUF
LOUD
LOUP
LOUR
LOUT
MAUD
MAUL
MAUT
MOUE
MOUL
MOUP
NEUK
NOUN
NOUP
NOUS
NOUT
NUUK
ONUS
OPUS
OTUS
OVUM
OXUS
PAUA
PAUL
PHUT
PIUM
PIUS
PLUE
PLUG
PLUM
PLUS
POUF
POUK
POUR
POUT
PRUH
RAUN
RHUS
ROUD
ROUÉ
ROUL
ROUM
ROUP
ROUT
ROUX
SAUL
SAUT
SCUD
SCUG
SCUL
SCUM
SCUR
SCUT
SEUL
SHUL
SHUN
SHUT
SIUM
SKUA
SKUG
SLUB
SLUE
SLUG
SLUM
SLUR
SLUT
SMUG
SMUR
SMUT
SNUB
SNUG
SOUK
SOUL
SOUM
SOUP
SOUR
SPUD
SPUE
SPUN
SPUR
STUB
STUD
STUM
STUN
STUR
SWUM
TAUT
THUD
THUG
THUN
THUS
TOUK
TOUN
TOUR
TOUT
TRUE
TRUG
URUS
VAUD
VAUT
WAUL
WAUR
YAUD
YAUP
YEUK
YOUD
YOUK
YOUR
ZBUD
ZEUS
ZOUK
ALVA
ARVO
BEVY
CAVE
CAVY
CIVE
COVE
DAVY
DEVA
DEVI
DIVA
DIVE
DOVE
ENVY
FIVE
GAVE
GIVE
GYVE
HAVE
HIVE
HOVA
HOVE
JAVA
JIVE
JOVE
KAVA
KIVA
LAVA
LAVE
LEVA
LEVE
LEVI
LEVY
LIVE
LIVY
LOVE
MEVE
MOVE
MOVY
NAVE
NAVY
NEVA
NEVE
NOVA
NOVO
PAVE
PAVO
RAVE
REVD
RIVA
RIVE
RIVO
ROVE
RSVP
RYVE

SAVE
SEVE
SIVA
SUVA
TOVE
URVA
VIVA
VIVE
VIVO
WAVE
WAVY
WEVE
WIVE
WOVE
YEVE
BAWD
BAWL
BAWN
BAWR
BOWL
BOWR
CAWK
COWL
COWP
COWS
DAWD
DAWK
DAWN
DAWT
DEWY
DOWF
DOWN
DOWT
FAWN
FOWL
GAWD
GAWK
GAWP
GOWF
GOWK
GOWL
GOWN
HAWK
HAWM
HOWE
HOWK
HOWL
IOWA
JAWI
JAWS
JEWS
JOWL
KIWI
LAWN
LEWD
LOWE
MAWK
MAWR
MEWL
MEWS
MOWA
NEWS
NEWT
NOWL
NOWT
NOWY
PAWA
PAWK
PAWL
PAWN
POWN
RAWN
ROWE
ROWT
SAWN
SEWN
SOWM
SOWP
TAWA
TAWS
TAWT
TOWN
TOWT
WAWA
WAWL
WOWF
YAWL
YAWN
YAWP
YAWS
YAWY
YOWE
YOWL
DIXY
DOXY
FOXY
LUXE
MAXI
MOXA
NEXT
NIXY
PIXY
POXY
SAXE
SEXT
SEXY
TAXA
TAXI
TEXT
WAXY
ABYE
AMYL
ARYL
BAYE
BAYS
BAYT
BOYG
BOYO
BOYS
CEYX
CRYO
CUYP
DAYS
EMYS
ERYX
GOYA
GUYS
GWYN
HWYL
ITYS
KAYO
KEYS
LLYR
MAYA
MAYO
MOYA
MOYL
ODYL
ONYX
ORYX
PAYE
PNYX
RAYS
RHYS
SAYE
SCYE
SKYE
SKYR
SNYE
SOYA
STYE
STYX
TOYS
TRYE
VAYU
WAYS
YOYO
ABZU
ADZE
BOZO
BUZZ
COZE
COZY
DAZE
DOZE
DOZY
FAZE
FEZE
FIZZ
FOZY
FUZE
FUZZ
GAZA
GAZE
GIZZ
HAZE
HAZY
JAZZ
JIZZ
LAZE
LAZY
LIZA
MAZE
MEZE
MOZE
MOZZ
NAZE
NAZI
OOZE
OOZY
OUZO
PIZE
RAZE
RAZZ
RIZA
SIZE
TOZE
TUZZ
ZEZE
ZIZZ

4:4

ABBA
ACTA
AGHA
AGMA
AGRA
AIDA
ALFA
ALGA
ALIA
ALMA
ALTA
ALVA
AMLA
ANDA
ANNA
ANOA
ANTA
APIA
AQUA
AREA
ARIA
ARNA
ARTA
ASIA
ATUA
AULA
AURA
BABA
BACA
BALA
BEMA
BETA
BIGA
BOBA
BOMA
BONA
BORA
BUBA
BUNA
CABA
CAMA
CANA
CAPA
CASA
COCA
CODA
COLA
COMA
CUBA
CUMA
CYMA
DADA
DATA
DECA
DEVA
DIKA
DIMA
DISA
DITA
DIVA
DOHA
DONA
DOPA
DORA
DUMA
DURA
EDDA
EGMA
EKKA
ELBA
ELIA
ELLA
ELSA
EMMA
ENNA
EOKA
EPHA
ERIA
ESLA
ETNA
ETTA
EYRA
EZRA
FALA
FETA
FIFA
FLEA
GAEA
GAGA
GAIA
GALA
GAZA
GETA
GIGA
GILA
GLIA
GOTA
GOYA
GUGA
GULA
HAHA
HAKA
HELA
HERA
HOMA
HOVA
HUIA
HULA
HUMA
HYLA
IDEA
ILIA
ILKA
INCA
IONA
IOTA
IOWA
JAVA
JENA
JOTA
JUBA
JUMA
JURA
KAMA
KANA
KARA
KATA
KAVA
KETA
KINA
KIVA
KOLA
KORA
KUNA
LADA
LAMA
LANA
LAVA
LEDA
LEVA
LIMA
LIRA
LISA
LIZA
LOLA
LOMA
LUBA
LUNA
LYRA
MAIA
MAMA
MANA
MARA
MASA
MAYA
MEGA
MELA
MESA
META
MICA
MINA
MIRA
MOLA
MONA
MOWA
MOXA
MOYA
MUSA
NADA
NAGA
NAIA
NAJA
NALA
NANA
NASA
NEVA
NINA
NIPA
NOMA
NOVA
NUMA
OBIA
OCTA
OETA
OFFA
OKRA
OKTA
OLEA
OLLA
ORCA
ORRA
OSSA
OUMA
OUPA
OVRA
PACA
PAPA
PARA
PAUA
PAWA
PEBA
PELA
PICA
PIKA
PINA
PIPA
PITA
PLEA
PROA
PUCA
PUJA
PULA
PUMA
PUNA
PUPA
RACA
RADA
RAGA
RAMA
RANA
RATA
REJA
RHEA
RICA
RIGA
RIMA
RITA
RIVA
RIZA
ROCA
ROTA
RUGA
RUSA
RUTA
SABA
SAGA
SAMA
SASA
SENA
SERA
SETA
SHEA
SHOA
SIDA
SIKA
SIMA
SIVA
SKIA
SKUA
SOCA
SODA
SOFA
SOJA
SOLA
SOMA
SORA
SOYA
STOA
SURA
SUSA
SUVA
TAHA
TAKA
TALA
TANA
TAPA
TARA
TATA
TAWA
TAXA
TELA
TERA
THEA
TIKA
TINA
TOEA
TOGA
TOLA
TOSA
TUBA
TUFA
TUNA
UCCA
UFFA
ULNA
UREA
URSA
URVA
UVEA
VARA
VEDA
VEGA
VELA
VENA
VERA
VINA
VISA
VITA
VIVA
VOLA
WAKA
WAWA
WEKA
WHOA
XEMA
XOSA
YAMA
YOGA
YUCA
YUGA
ZAMA
ZETA
ZILA
ZOEA
ZOLA
ZONA
ZUPA
ABIB
AHAB
ARAB
BARB
BEEB
BIBB
BLAB
BLEB
BLOB
BLUB
BOMB
BOOB
BULB
CHUB
CLUB
COBB
COMB
CRAB
CRIB
CURB
DAUB
DIEB
DOAB
DOOB
DRAB
DRIB
DRUB
DUMB

FLAB
FLUB
FORB
FRAB
GAMB
GARB
GLIB
GLOB
GRAB
GRUB
HERB
IAMB
JAMB
KEMB
KERB
KNOB
KNUB
KRAB
LAMB
LIMB
NUMB
PLEB
SCAB
SERB
SIBB
SLAB
SLOB
SLUB
SNEB
SNIB
SNOB
SNUB
SORB
STAB
STOB
STUB
SWAB
SWOB
TOMB
VERB
WARB
WEBB
WEMB
WOMB
ZIMB
ABAC
AC/DC
AESC
ALEC
ATOC
BANC
BLOC
CALC
CHIC
CHOC
DISC
DOUC
EPIC
ERIC
FISC
FLIC
HINC
KWIC
LAIC
MARC
MISC
NARC
NUNC
OPEC
OTIC
RASC
SAIC
SPEC
SPIC
SYNC
TALC
TORC
URIC
ZINC
ZOIC
ABED
ACID
ADAD
AGED
ALOD
AMID
ARID
AULD
AVID
AWED
BALD
BAND
BARD
BAUD
BAWD
BEAD
BEND
BIND
BIRD
BLAD
BLED
BOLD
BOND
BORD
BRAD
BRED
BROD
BUDD
BUND
BURD
BYRD
CARD
CHAD
CLAD
CLOD
COED
COLD
CORD
CRED
CRUD
CURD
DADD
DARD
DAUD
DAWD
DEAD
DEED
DIED
DRAD
DUAD
DYAD
EARD
ECAD
EGAD
EILD
ENID
FAHD
FAND
FARD
FEED
FEND
FEOD
FEUD
FIND
FLED
FOLD
FOND
FOOD
FORD
FOUD
FUND
FYRD
GAID
GAUD
GAWD
GEED
GELD
GILD
GIRD
GLAD
GLID
GOAD
GOLD
GOOD
GRID
GUID
HAND
HARD
HAUD
HEAD
HEED
HELD
HEND
HERD
HIND
HOLD
HOND
HOOD
IBID
ICED
IGAD
IRID
JIRD
KAID
KARD
KHUD
KIDD
KIND
KOND
KURD
LAID
LAND
LARD
LAUD
LEAD
LEND
LEWD
LIED
LIND
LOAD
LOID
LORD
LOUD
LUDD
MAID
MAUD
MEAD
MEED
MELD
MEND
MILD
MIND
MOLD
MOOD
MUID
NAND
NARD
NEED
NERD
NUDD
NURD
OLID
OVID
OWED
PAID
PAND
PARD
PEND
PIED
PLED
PLOD
POND
POOD
PRAD
PROD
QUAD
QUID
QUOD
RAID
RAND
READ
RECD
REDD
REED
REND
REVD
RIND
ROAD
ROOD
ROUD
RUDD
RUND
RYND
SAID
SAND
SARD
SCAD
SCUD
SEED
SEND
SHAD
SHED
SHOD
SILD
SIND
SKED
SKID
SLED
SLID
SNED
SNOD
SOLD
SORD
SPED
SPUD
STED
STUD
SUDD
SURD
SWAD
SYND
TEND
THUD
TIED
TIND
TOAD
TODD
TOLD
TRAD
TROD
TUND
TURD
UDAD
ULAD
USED
VAUD
VEND
VIED
VOID
WADD
WAFD
WALD
WAND
WARD
WEED
WEID
WELD
WEND
WHID
WILD
WIND
WOAD
WOLD
WOOD
WORD
WYND
YARD
YAUD
YEAD
YEED
YELD
YIRD
YOND
YOUD
ZBUD
ZOID
ABBE
ABLE
ABSE
ABYE
ACHE
ACME
ACNE
ACRE
ADZE
AGEE
AGUE
AIDE
AIRE
AJEE
AKEE
ALBE
ALOE
ALTE
AMIE
ANCE
ANNE
ANTE
APSE
ARNE
ARSE
ASHE
ASKE
AUDE
AUNE
AXLE
AYRE
BABE
BADE
BAKE
BALE
BANE
BARE
BASE
BATE
BAYE
BEDE
BENE
BERE
BETE
BÊTE
BICE
BIDE
BIKE
BILE
BINE
BISE
BITE
BLAE
BLEE
BLUE
BODE
BOKE
BOLE
BONE
BORE
BOTE
BRAE
BREE
BRIE
BUDE
BUKE
BUTE
BYKE
BYRE
BYTE
CADE
CAGE
CAKE
CAME
CANE
CAPE
CARE
CASE
CATE
CAVE
CEDE
CERE
CETE
CINE
CITE
CIVE
CLUE
CODE
COKE
COLE
COME
CONE
COPE
CORE
COSE
COTE
COUE
COVE
COZE
CREE
CRUE
CUBE
CURE
CUTE
CYME
CYTE
DACE
DALE
DAME
DANE
DARE
DATE
DAZE
DBLE
DEKE
DELE
DEME
DENE
DERE
DICE
DIKE
DIME
DINE
DIRE
DITE
DIVE
DOGE
DOLE
DOME
DONE
DOPE
DOSE
DOTE
DOVE
DOZE
DREE
DUCE
DUDE
DUKE
DULE
DUNE
DUPE
DURE
DUSE
DYKE
DYNE
EALE
EASE
ECCE
ECHE
EDGE
EINE
EIRE
ELBE
ELLE
ELSE
EPEE
ERIE
ERNE
ERSE
ESME
ESNE
ESSE
ESTE
ETHE
EUGE
EURE
EVOE
EYNE
EYRE
FACE
FADE
FAKE
FAME
FANE
FARE
FATE
FAZE
FEME
FERE
FETE
FEZE
FIDE
FIFE
FIKE
FILE
FINE
FIRE
FIVE
FLEE
FLOE
FLUE
FONE
FORE
FRAE
FREE
FROE
FUME
FUSE
FUZE
FYKE
GADE
GAGE
GALE
GAME
GAPE
GARE
GATE
GAVE
GAZE
GCSE
GENE
GERE
GHEE
GIBE
GIDE
GITE
GIVE
GLEE
GLUE
GOLE
GONE
GORE

GREE
GRUE
GULE
GYBE
GYRE
GYTE
GYVE
HADE
HAKE
HALE
HAME
HARE
HASE
HATE
HAVE
HAZE
HEBE
HELE
HEME
HERE
HETE
HIDE
HIKE
HIRE
HIVE
HOKE
HOLE
HOME
HONE
HOPE
HORE
HOSE
HOTE
HOVE
HOWE
HUGE
HULE
HUME
HYDE
HYKE
HYLE
HYPE
IDÉE
IDLE
ILLE
INGE
IPSE
ISLE
JADE
JAKE
JANE
JAPE
JIBE
JIVE
JOBE
JOKE
JOLE
JOSE
JOVE
JUBE
JUDE
JUKE
JUNE
JURE
JUTE
KADE
KAIE
KALE
KAME
KANE
KATE
KIBE
KIKE
KINE
KIPE
KITE
KLEE
KNEE
KOBE
KORE
KYLE
KYPE
KYTE
LACE
LADE
LAKE
LAME
LANE
LARE
LATE
LAVE
LAZE
LEME
LEVE
LICE
LIDE
LIFE
LIKE
LIME
LINE
LITE
LIVE
LOBE
LODE
LOGE
LOKE
LOME
LONE
LOPE
LORE
LOSE
LOTE
LOVE
LOWE
LUCE
LUGE
LUKE
LUNE
LURE
LUTE
LUXE
LYLE
LYME
LYRE
LYSE
LYTE
MACE
MADE
MAGE
MAKE
MALE
MAME
MANE
MARE
MASE
MATE
MAZE
MEDE
MENE
MERE
MESE
METE
MEVE
MEZE
MICE
MIKE
MILE
MIME
MINE
MIRE
MISE
MITE
MODE
MOKE
MOLE
MOME
MOPE
MORE
MOTE
MOUE
MOVE
MOZE
MULE
MURE
MUSE
MUTE
MZEE
NAME
NAPE
NARE
NAVE
NAZE
NENE
NETE
NEVE
NICE
NIDE
NIFE
NIKE
NILE
NINE
NODE
NOLE
NOME
NONE
NOPE
NORE
NOSE
NOTE
NUDE
NUKE
OBOE
OCHE
OGEE
OGLE
OGRE
OISE
OLPE
ONCE
OOSE
OOZE
OPIE
ORFE
ORGE
ORLE
ORNE
OWRE
PACE
PAGE
PALE
PANE
PARE
PASE
PATE
PAVE
PAYE
PEKE
PELE
PENE
PÈRE
PICE
PIKE
PILE
PINE
PIPE
PISE
PIZE
PLUE
POKE
POLE
POME
PONE
POPE
PORE
POSE
POTE
PREE
PUCE
PUKE
PULE
PURE
PYRE
RACE
RAGE
RAKE
RALE
RAPE
RARE
RASE
RATE
RAVE
RAZE
REDE
REKE
REME
RENE
RETE
RICE
RIDE
RIFE
RILE
RIME
RINE
RIPE
RISE
RITE
RIVE
ROBE
RODE
ROKE
ROLE
ROME
RONE
ROPE
RORE
ROSE
ROTE
ROVE
ROWE
RUBE
RUDE
RULE
RUME
RUNE
RUSE
RUTE
RYFE
RYVE
SADE
SAFE
SAGE
SAKE
SALE
SAME
SANE
SATE
SAVE
SAXE
SAYE
SCYE
SELE
SERE
SESE
SEVE
SHIE
SHOE
SICE
SIDE
SIKE
SILE
SINE
SIPE
SIRE
SITE
SIZE
SKYE
SLAE
SLEE
SLOE
SLUE
SMEE
SNEE
SNYE
SOLE
SOME
SONE
SORE
SPAE
SPEE
SPUE
STIE
STYE
SURE
SWEE
SYCE
SYKE
SYNE
SYPE
TACE
TAKE
TALE
TAME
TANE
TAPE
TARE
TATE
TELE
TEME
TENE
TETE
THAE
THEE
TICE
TIDE
TIGE
TIKE
TILE
TIME
TINE
TIRE
TITE
TOGE
TOKE
TOLE
TOME
TONE
TOPE
TORE
TOSE
TOTE
TOVE
TOZE
TREE
TRIE
TRUE
TRYE
TUBE
TULE
TUNE
TWAE
TWEE
TYKE
TYNE
TYPE
TYRE
TYTE
UNBE
UNCE
UNDE
URGE
VADE
VALE
VANE
VARE
VASE
VELE
VICE
VIDE
VILE
VINE
VISE
VITE
VIVE
VOCE
VOLE
VOTE
WADE
WAGE
WAKE
WALE
WAME
WANE
WARE
WASE
WATE
WAVE
WERE
WEVE
WHEE
WICE
WIDE
WIFE
WILE
WINE
WIPE
WIRE
WISE
WITE
WIVE
WOKE
WORE
WOVE
WYTE
YALE
YARE
YATE
YEDE
YEVE
YGOE
YIKE
YITE
YLKE
YMPE
YOKE
YORE
YOWE
YUKE
YULE
ZEZE
ZONE
ZYME
AÎNÉ
AYMÉ
CAFÉ
CIRÉ
DORÉ
ERTÉ
JETÉ
PLIÉ
ROUÉ
URDÉ
ALIF
BAFF
BARF
BEEF
BIFF
BOFF
BUFF
BUMF
CALF
CFAF
CHEF
CLEF
COFF
COIF
COOF
CORF
CUFF
CUIF
DAFF
DEAF
DELF
DOFF
DOWF
DUFF
FAFF
FIEF
FUFF
GAFF
GOAF
GOFF
GOLF
GOOF
GOWF
GRAF
GUFF
GULF
HAAF
HAFF
HALF
HOOF
HUFF
HUMF
JEFF
KAIF
KERF
KOFF
LAUF
LEAF
LIEF
LOAF
LOOF
LUFF
MIFF
MUFF
NAFF
NEIF
NIEF
NIFF
OLAF
ORFF
PELF
PIAF
POOF
POUF
PROF
PUFF
RAFF
REEF
REIF
RIFF
ROLF
ROOF
RUFF
SEIF
SELF
SERF
SPIF
SURF
TAFF
TEFF
TERF
TIFF
TOFF
TUFF
TURF
WAFF
WAIF
WAKF

WOLF
WOOF
WOWF
YAFF
YOOF
ZARF
ZIFF
ZURF
AGAG
AGOG
AREG
BANG
BERG
BIGG
BING
BLAG
BONG
BOYG
BRAG
BRIG
BROG
BUNG
BURG
BYNG
CHUG
CLAG
CLEG
CLOG
CRAG
DANG
DARG
DING
DONG
DRAG
DREG
DRUG
DUNG
EIGG
FANG
FLAG
FLEG
FLOG
FOGG
FOUG
FRAG
FRIG
FROG
FUNG
GANG
GING
GLEG
GONG
GOOG
GRIG
GROG
GRUG
HAGG
HAIG
HANG
HING
HOGG
HONG
HUNG
JAGG
JUNG
KANG
KING
KNAG
KONG
LANG
LENG
LING
LONG
LUNG
MAGG
MANG
MARG
MENG
MING
MONG
MOOG
MUNG
NONG
PANG
PEAG
PING
PLUG
PONG
PRIG
PROG
PUNG
QING
QUAG
RAGG
RANG
RIGG
RING
RONG
RUNG
SANG
SCAG
SCOG
SCUG
SHAG
SHOG
SING
SKAG
SKEG
SKUG
SLAG
SLOG
SLUG
SMOG
SMUG
SNAG
SNIG
SNOG
SNUG
SONG
SPAG
STAG
SUNG
SWAG
SWIG
TAIG
TANG
TEGG
TENG
THUG
TING
TONG
TRIG
TROG
TRUG
TUNG
TWIG
VANG
WANG
WEGG
WHIG
WING
WONG
YANG
YEGG
ZING
ALPH
AMAH
ANKH
ARCH
ASCH
AYAH
BACH
BASH
BATH
BETH
BISH
BLAH
BOSH
BOTH
BUSH
CAPH
CASH
COBH
COCH
COSH
COTH
CUSH
DASH
DICH
DISH
DOSH
DOTH
DUSH
EACH
EECH
ESTH
ETCH
EUGH
FASH
FISH
FOCH
GASH
GATH
GOSH
GOTH
GSOH
GUSH
HAGH
HASH
HATH
HECH
HETH
HIGH
HISH
HOGH
HUGH
HUSH
INCH
IPOH
ITCH
JOSH
KAPH
KESH
KISH
KITH
LAKH
LASH
LATH
LECH
LICH
LITH
LOCH
LOSH
LOTH
LUGH
LUSH
LYCH
MACH
MASH
MATH
MESH
MOCH
MOTH
MUCH
MUSH
MYTH
NASH
NESH
NIGH
NITH
NOAH
NOSH
OATH
OPAH
OUCH
OUPH
PASH
PATH
PECH
PEGH
PENH
PHOH
PISH
PITH
POOH
POSH
PRUH
PTAH
PUGH
PUSH
QOPH
RASH
RATH
RESH
RICH
ROCH
RUKH
RUSH
RUTH
SASH
SECH
SHAH
SICH
SIGH
SIKH
SOPH
SUCH
TACH
TANH
TASH
TATH
TECH
TETH
TICH
TOSH
TUSH
UMPH
UTAH
VACH
WASH
WISH
WITH
YEAH
YODH
YOGH
ABRI
ACRI
AGNI
ALAI
ALBI
ANTI
ASTI
ATLI
AUDI
BABI
BALI
BANI
BARI
CADI
CEDI
CHAI
DALI
DARI
DELI
DEMI
DEVI
ELOI
ENSI
ETUI
EUOI
FENI
FIJI
FUJI
GADI
GIGI
GLEI
GOBI
HAPI
HEMI
HOKI
HOLI
HONI
HOPI
IMPI
INRI
INTI
JAWI
KADI
KAKI
KALI
KAMI
KATI
KEPI
KIRI
KIWI
KURI
KWAI
LEVI
LOKI
LORI
LOTI
LWEI
MAGI
MALI
MANI
MARI
MAXI
MERI
MIDI
MIMI
MINI
MOKI
MOOI
MORI
MUTI
NAZI
NISI
NORI
OMNI
PALI
PENI
PERI
PILI
PIPI
PULI
PURI
QADI
RABI
RAGI
RAKI
RAMI
RANI
RIGI
ROJI
ROTI
RUMI
SAKI
SAMI
SARI
SATI
SEMI
SHRI
SIMI
SIRI
SOFI
SUFI
TABI
TATI
TAXI
THAI
TIKI
TIPI
TITI
TOPI
TSHI
TULI
TUPI
UGLI
VALI
VLEI
WADI
WALI
WILI
YAGI
YETI
YOGI
YONI
ZATI
ZITI
ZORI
ZUNI
BENJ
HADJ
AMOK
ANAK
ARAK
ATOK
BACK
BALK
BANK
BARK
BASK
BAUK
BEAK
BECK
BERK
BILK
BINK
BIRK
BISK
BOAK
BOCK
BONK
BOOK
BOUK
BRAK
BUCK
BUIK
BULK
BUNK
BURK
BUSK
CALK
CARK
CASK
CAUK
CAWK
CHIK
COCK
CONK
COOK
CORK
CURK
CUSK
DANK
DARK
DAWK
DECK
DEEK
DESK
DHAK
DICK
DINK
DIRK
DISK
DOCK
DOEK
DOOK
DUCK
DUNK
DUSK
DYAK
EFIK
ERIK
FANK
FECK
FINK
FIRK
FISK
FLAK
FOLK
FORK
FUNK
GAWK
GECK
GEEK
GINK
GONK
GOOK
GOUK
GOWK
GUNK
HACK
HAIK
HANK
HARK
HASK
HAWK
HECK
HICK
HOCK
HONK
HOOK
HOWK
HUCK
HULK
HUNK
HUSK
JACK
JARK
JERK
JINK
JOCK
JOOK
JOUK
JUNK
KECK
KEEK
KICK
KINK
KIRK
KONK
KOOK
LACK
LAIK
LANK
LARK
LEAK
LEEK
LICK
LINK
LIRK
LISK
LOCK
LOOK
LUCK
LURK
LUSK
MACK
MAIK
MARK
MASK
MAWK
MEEK
MERK
MICK
MILK
MINK
MIRK

MOCK
MONK
MUCK
MURK
MUSK
NABK
NAIK
NARK
NECK
NERK
NEUK
NICK
NOCK
NOOK
NORK
NUUK
OINK
OULK
PACK
PAIK
PALK
PARK
PAWK
PEAK
PECK
PEEK
PENK
PERK
PICK
PINK
POCK
POLK
PONK
POOK
PORK
POUK
PUCK
PUNK
RACK
RAIK
RANK
REAK
RECK
REEK
REIK
RICK
RINK
RISK
ROCK
ROOK
RUCK
RUSK
SACK
SALK
SANK
SARK
SEEK
SERK
SICK
SILK
SINK
SOAK
SOCK
SOOK
SOUK
SPIK
SUCK
SULK
SUNK
TACK
TALK
TANK
TASK
TEAK
TICK
TINK
TONK
TOOK
TOUK
TREK
TUCK
TURK
TUSK
USAK
WACK
WALK
WANK
WARK
WEAK
WEEK
WELK
WICK
WINK
WOCK
WORK
YACK
YANK
YERK
YESK
YEUK
YIRK
YOCK
YOLK
YORK
YOUK
YUCK
ZACK
ZOUK
ABEL
ACOL
AMYL
ANAL
ANIL
ARAL
ARIL
ARYL
AVAL
AWDL
AWOL
AXIL
BAAL
BAEL
BAIL
BALL
BAWL
BELL
BHEL
BILL
BIRL
BOIL
BOLL
BOOL
BOWL
BUHL
BULL
BURL
CALL
CARL
CAUL
CEIL
CELL
CHAL
CHIL
CIEL
CILL
CIRL
COAL
COIL
COLL
COOL
COWL
CULL
CURL
DAHL
DAIL
DEAL
DEIL
DELL
DHAL
DIAL
DILL
DIRL
DOLL
DOOL
DUAL
DUEL
DULL
EARL
EDAL
EGAL
ELUL
ENOL
EORL
EVIL
EXUL
FAIL
FALL
FEAL
FEEL
FELL
FILL
FOAL
FOIL
FOOL
FOUL
FOWL
FUEL
FULL
FURL
GAEL
GALL
GAOL
GAUL
GEAL
GILL
GIRL
GOAL
GOEL
GOOL
GOWL
GULL
GURL
GYAL
HAAL
HAIL
HALL
HARL
HAUL
HEAL
HEEL
HEIL
HELL
HERL
HILL
HOWL
HULL
HURL
HWYL
ICEL
IDOL
JAIL
JARL
JEEL
JELL
JILL
JOEL
JOLL
JOWL
KAIL
KARL
KEEL
KELL
KIEL
KILL
KOEL
KOHL
LEAL
LILL
LOLL
LULL
MAIL
MALL
MARL
MAUL
MEAL
MELL
MERL
MEWL
MILL
MOIL
MOLL
MOOL
MOUL
MOYL
MUIL
MULL
MURL
MYAL
NAIL
NEAL
NEIL
NELL
NILL
NIRL
NOEL
NOIL
NOLL
NOWL
NULL
NURL
OBOL
ODAL
ODYL
OPAL
OPEL
ORAL
OVAL
OVEL
PAAL
PAIL
PALL
PAUL
PAWL
PEAL
PEEL
PELL
PHIL
PILL
PIRL
POLL
POOL
PULL
PURL
RAIL
REAL
REEL
RIAL
RIEL
RILL
ROIL
ROLL
ROTL
ROUL
RYAL
SAIL
SAUL
SCUL
SEAL
SEEL
SEIL
SELL
SEUL
SHUL
SIAL
SILL
SKOL
SOIL
SOOL
SOUL
STOL
TAAL
TAEL
TAIL
TALL
TEAL
TEIL
TELL
TILL
TIRL
TOIL
TOLL
TOOL
TULL
TWAL
UDAL
URAL
VAAL
VAIL
VEAL
VEIL
VELL
VIAL
VIEL
VILL
VIOL
VIRL
VRIL
VTOL
WAIL
WALL
WAUL
WAWL
WEAL
WEEL
WELL
WIEL
WILL
WOOL
WULL
YAWL
YELL
YILL
YOWL
ZEAL
ADAM
AHEM
ALUM
ARAM
ARUM
ATOM
ATUM
BALM
BARM
BCOM
BEAM
BERM
BIMM
BOOM
BRAM
BRIM
BRUM
CALM
CAUM
CHAM
CHUM
CLAM
CLEM
COMM
COOM
CORM
CRAM
CULM
DEEM
DERM
DOOM
DORM
DRAM
DRUM
EDAM
EDOM
ELAM
EXAM
FARM
FERM
FILM
FIRM
FLAM
FOAM
FORM
FROM
GAUM
GERM
GEUM
GISM
GLAM
GLIM
GLOM
GLUM
GORM
GRAM
GRIM
GRUM
GUAM
HAEM
HALM
HARM
HAWM
HELM
HERM
HOLM
IDEM
IMAM
ITEM
JISM
KAIM
LEAM
LIAM
LOAM
LOOM
LYAM
MAAM
MAIM
MALM
MARM
NAAM
NEEM
NORM
OGAM
OLIM
OVUM
PALM
PERM
PIUM
PLIM
PLUM
POEM
PRAM
PRIM
PROM
QUIM
REAM
RIEM
ROAM
ROOM
ROUM
SAIM
SCAM
SCUM
SEAM
SEEM
SEJM
SHAM
SHEM
SHIM
SIAM
SIUM
SKIM
SLAM
SLIM
SLUM
SOOM
SOUM
SOWM
SPAM
STEM
STIM
STUM
SWAM
SWIM
SWUM
TEAM
TEEM
TERM
THEM
TOOM
TRAM
TRIM
TURM
URIM
VEHM
WARM
WEEM
WHAM
WHIM
WHOM
WORM
WURM
YLEM
ZOOM
ADEN
AEON
AGEN
AGIN
AGON
AIRN
AKIN
ALAN
AMEN
AMIN
AMUN
ANAN
ANON
ARAN
ARUN
ATEN
AVON
AXON
AYIN
AZAN
BARN
BAWN
BEAN
BEEN
BEIN
BENN
BERN
BIEN
BLIN
BONN
BOON
BORN
BOUN
BRAN
BREN
BRON
BURN
CAEN
CAIN
CANN

CHAN	HYMN	OXON	THIN	BOZO	INGO	NOLO	URAO	GRIP
CHIN	ICON	PAIN	THON	BRIO	INRO	NONO	VETO	GULP
CHON	IKON	PAWN	THUN	BRNO	INTO	NOVO	VIGO	GUMP
CION	IRAN	PEAN	TOON	BROO	JATO	ODSO	VINO	GYMP
CLAN	IRON	PEEN	TORN	BUBO	JIAO	OHIO	VIVO	HARP
COIN	IVAN	PEIN	TOUN	BUDO	JOCO	OKRO	WINO	HASP
CONN	JAIN	PENN	TOWN	BUFO	JODO	OLEO	XERO	HEAP
COON	JANN	PEON	TRIN	CAPO	JOLO	OLIO	YOYO	HEEP
CORN	JOAN	PERN	TRON	CATO	JOMO	ONGO	YUKO	HELP
CRAN	JOHN	PION	TUAN	CERO	JUDO	ONTO	ZENO	HEMP
CURN	JOIN	PIRN	TURN	CIAO	JUNO	OPPO	ZERO	HESP
CYAN	JUAN	PLAN	TWIN	CITO	KAGO	OSLO	ZOBO	HOOP
DAMN	KAIN	POON	ULAN	CLIO	KANO	OTHO	ZOMO	HUMP
DARN	KAON	PORN	UPON	COCO	KAYO	OTTO	ASAP	JAAP
DAWN	KEAN	POWN	VAIN	COMO	KENO	OUZO	ATAP	JARP
DEAN	KEEN	QUIN	VEIN	CRYO	KILO	PACO	ATOP	JAUP
DEEN	KERN	RAIN	VENN	DADO	KINO	PAVO	BARP	JEEP
DERN	KHAN	RAUN	VULN	DAGO	KOBO	PEPO	BEEP	JIMP
DOON	KILN	RAWN	WAIN	DATO	KOKO	PESO	BISP	JUMP
DOWN	KIRN	REAN	WARN	DECO	KOLO	PIRO	BLIP	KEEP
DUAN	KOAN	REEN	WEAN	DEMO	KOTO	PISO	BUMP	KELP
DURN	LAHN	REIN	WEEN	DERO	KROO	POGO	BURP	KEMP
EARN	LAIN	RIEN	WHEN	DIDO	LALO	POLO	CALP	KILP
EDEN	LAON	ROAN	WHIN	DODO	LEGO	PROO	CAMP	KIPP
ELAN	LARN	ROIN	WIEN	DOJO	LENO	PYRO	CARP	KNAP
EOAN	LAWN	ROON	WINN	DURO	LETO	REDO	CAUP	KNOP
ERIN	LEAN	RUIN	WOON	EBRO	LIDO	RENO	CHAP	LAMP
ETEN	LIEN	RYAN	WORN	ECCO	LILO	RICO	CHIP	LAPP
ETON	LIMN	SAIN	WREN	ECHO	LIMO	RIVO	CHOP	LEAP
EVAN	LINN	SAWN	WYNN	EDDO	LINO	RORO	CLAP	LEEP
EVEN	LION	SCAN	XIAN	ELMO	LOBO	SAGO	CLIP	LERP
EXON	LOAN	SEAN	YARN	ERGO	LOCO	SEGO	CLOP	LIMP
FAIN	LOIN	SEEN	YAWN	EURO	LOGO	SHOO	COMP	LISP
FAUN	LOON	SEWN	YUAN	EXPO	LOTO	SIJO	COOP	LOOP
FAWN	LORN	SHAN	YUEN	FADO	LUDO	SILO	COUP	LOUP
FERN	LYON	SHIN	ZEIN	FARO	MAKO	SINO	COWP	LUMP
FINN	MAIN	SHUN	ZION	FASO	MALO	SKEO	CRAP	MOOP
FIRN	MANN	SIAN	ACRO	FICO	MANO	SKIO	CROP	MOPP
FLAN	MEAN	SIEN	AERO	FIDO	MARO	SOHO	CUSP	MOUP
FOEN	MEIN	SIGN	AFRO	FIGO	MAYO	SOLO	CUYP	MUMP
FOIN	MIEN	SION	AGIO	FILO	MEMO	SUMO	DAMP	NEAP
FOON	MOAN	SKEN	ALLO	FINO	MESO	TACO	DEEP	NEEP
GAIN	MOON	SKIN	ALSO	GAJO	MICO	TARO	DORP	NOOP
GEAN	MORN	SOON	ALTO	GAPO	MILO	TIRO	DOUP	NOUP
GHAN	MUON	SORN	AMBO	GIRO	MINO	TITO	DRIP	PALP
GIRN	NAAN	SPAN	AMMO	GOBO	MIRO	TOCO	DROP	PARP
GLEN	NAIN	SPIN	ANFO	GOGO	MISO	TODO	DUMP	PEEP
GOON	NEON	SPUN	ANNO	GYRO	MODO	TOGO	EARP	PIMP
GOWN	NOON	STAN	ARCO	HALO	MOJO	TOHO	FLAP	PLAP
GRAN	NORN	STEN	ARGO	HARO	MOKO	TOJO	FLIP	PLOP
GRIN	NOUN	STUN	ARNO	HERO	MONO	TOKO	FLOP	POMP
GUAN	OBAN	SUNN	ARVO	HILO	MORO	TOTO	FRAP	POOP
GUNN	ODIN	SWAN	ATTO	HMSO	MUSO	TRIO	GAMP	PREP
GURN	OGEN	SYEN	AUTO	HOBO	NANO	TYPO	GASP	PROP
GWYN	OMAN	TAIN	BEGO	HOMO	NASO	TYRO	GAUP	PULP
HAIN	OMEN	TARN	BIRO	HUGO	NATO	UMBO	GAWP	PUMP
HARN	OPEN	TEAN	BITO	HUSO	NEBO	UNCO	GEEP	QUEP
HERN	ORAN	TEEN	BOKO	HYPO	NEMO	UNDO	GIMP	QUIP
HOON	OVEN	TERN	BOLO	IAGO	NERO	UNIO	GLOP	QUOP
HORN	OWEN	THAN	BORO	IGBO	NINO	UNTO	GOOP	RAMP
HUON	OXEN	THEN	BOYO	INFO	NOGO	UPGO	GORP	RASP

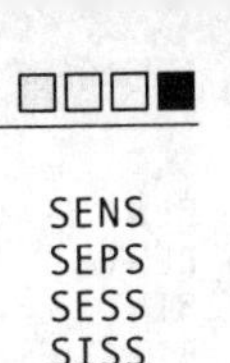

REAP
REPP
RIPP
RISP
ROMP
ROOP
ROUP
RSVP
RUMP
RURP
SALP
SAMP
SCOP
SEEP
SHAP
SHIP
SHOP
SIMP
SKEP
SKIP
SLAP
SLIP
SLOP
SNAP
SNIP
SOAP
SOOP
SOUP
SOWP
STAP
STEP
STOP
SUMP
SWAP
SWOP
TAMP
TEMP
TRAP
TRIP
TROP
TUMP
TYMP
VAMP
VEEP
WARP
WASP
WEEP
WHAP
WHIP
WHOP
WIMP
WISP
WRAP
YAPP
YAUP
YAWP
YELP
YOMP
YOOP
YUMP
IRAQ

ABER
ACER
ADAR
ADUR
AFAR
AGAR
AJAR
ALAR
AMIR
AMUR
ARAR
ASAR
ASKR
ASUR
ATAR
AVER
AYER
BAUR
BAWR
BEAR
BEER
BIER
BIRR
BLUR
BOAR
BOER
BOOR
BOWR
BRER
BURR
CARR
CHAR
CHER
COIR
COUR
CURR
CZAR
DAUR
DEAR
DEER
DIOR
DOER
DOOR
DORR
DOUR
DUAR
DYER
EBOR
EDER
EGER
EMIR
EVER
EWER
EXOR
EYER
FAIR
FARR
FEAR
FEER
FLOR
FOUR

FURR
GAIR
GAUR
GEAR
GIER
GIRR
GNAR
GOER
GOOR
GUAR
HAAR
HAIR
HEAR
HEIR
HERR
HOAR
HOUR
HUER
IFOR
IGOR
ISAR
ISER
IVOR
IZAR
JEER
KEIR
KHOR
KIER
KNAR
KNUR
KSAR
LAER
LAIR
LEAR
LEER
LEHR
LEIR
LIAR
LLYR
LNER
LOIR
LOOR
LOUR
MAAR
MAWR
MEER
MEIR
MOHR
MOOR
MUIR
NAIR
NEAR
NUER
NURR
ODER
ODOR
OMAR
OMER
ONER
OVER
OXER

OYER
PAIR
PARR
PEAR
PEER
PIER
POOR
POUR
PSBR
PUER
PURR
REAR
ROAR
RUHR
SAIR
SCAR
SCUR
SEAR
SEER
SEIR
SKER
SKYR
SLUR
SMUR
SOAR
SOUR
SPAR
SPUR
STAR
STIR
STUR
SUER
TAHR
TEAR
TEER
TEHR
TERR
THAR
THIR
THOR
TIER
TIRR
TORR
TOUR
TSAR
TZAR
UBER
USER
USSR
VAIR
VEER
VOAR
WAUR
WEAR
WEIR
WHIR
YARR
YEAR
YIRR
YMIR
YOUR

ABAS
ABUS
ACAS
ACES
ACIS
ACTS
ADES
AGES
AGIS
AIDS
AIRS
ALAS
ALMS
ALPS
AMES
AMIS
AMOS
ANAS
ANTS
ANUS
APIS
ARES
ARIS
ARMS
ARTS
ASAS
AVES
AXIS
AYES
BAAS
BAGS
BARS
BASS
BATS
BAYS
BEDS
BEES
BESS
BIAS
BITS
BORS
BOSS
BOTS
BOYS
BRAS
BRIS
BROS
BUGS
BUSS
CANS
CATS
CENS
CESS
CIGS
CITS
CLOS
CONS
COPS
COSS
COWS
CPRS

CUBS
CUPS
CUSS
DABS
DAIS
DAKS
DAYS
DIAS
DIBS
DIES
DIGS
DISS
DOES
DOGS
DOSS
DOTS
DUBS
DUDS
DUES
DUNS
EARS
EATS
EELS
EGGS
EGIS
ELIS
ELKS
EMYS
ENDS
ENOS
EPOS
ERIS
EROS
EWES
EXES
EYAS
EYES
FANS
FATS
FEGS
FEIS
FILS
FONS
FOSS
FUNS
FUSS
GEMS
GENS
GODS
GOES
GOSS
GRAS
GRIS
GRUS
GUNS
GUTS
GUYS
HALS
HAMS
HANS
HERS

HESS
HISS
HOPS
HORS
HOSS
HUSS
IBIS
IDES
INES
INNS
IRAS
IRIS
IRUS
ISIS
ITYS
IVES
IWIS
JAGS
JASS
JAWS
JESS
JEWS
JOSS
KANS
KEYS
KISS
KOSS
KRIS
LAIS
LAOS
LASS
LATS
LEES
LEGS
LENS
LESS
LETS
LIAS
LIBS
LIES
LIPS
LOGS
LOIS
LOOS
LOSS
LOTS
LUES
LUGS
MAAS
MANS
MAPS
MARS
MASS
MESS
MEWS
MISS
MODS
MOHS
MONS
MORS
MOSS

MUSS
NAOS
NESS
NETS
NEWS
NIBS
NOES
NOUS
NUTS
NYAS
NYOS
OAKS
OARS
OATS
ODDS
OILS
OLDS
ONE'S
ONUS
OONS
OOPS
OPUS
ORTS
OTIS
OTUS
OUDS
OURS
OWLS
OWNS
OXUS
PAIS
PASS
PEAS
PIES
PIGS
PINS
PISS
PIUS
PLUS
PODS
PONS
POSS
POTS
PUSS
RAGS
RATS
RAYS
REIS
REMS
REPS
RHUS
RHYS
RIBS
RIPS
RISS
ROSS
RUNS
SANS
SASS
SATS
SEAS

SENS
SEPS
SESS
SISS
SOSS
SUDS
SUMS
SUSS
TAPS
TASS
TAWS
TEES
TESS
THIS
THOS
THUS
TOGS
TONS
TOPS
TOSS
TOYS
TUES
TUMS
UPAS
URUS
USES
UTAS
UTIS
VERS
VETS
VIBS
VIES
WAYS
WITS
WUSS
XMAS
YAWS
YIPS
YWIS
ZEUS
ABET
ABUT
ACCT
ACHT
ADIT
AINT
AIRT
ARET
AUNT
BAFT
BAHT
BAIT
BALT
BANT
BART
BAST
BATT
BAYT
BEAT
BEET
BELT

BENT
BEST
BINT
BITT
BLAT
BLET
BLOT
BLUT
BOAT
BOLT
BOOT
BOTT
BOUT
BRAT
BRIT
BRUT
BUAT
BUNT
BURT
BUST
BUTT
CANT
CAPT
CART
CAST
CELT
CENT
CERT
CHAT
CHIT
CHUT
CIST
CLAT
CLOT
COAT
COIT
COLT
CONT
COOT
COST
COTT
CRIT
CUIT
CULT
CUNT
CURT
CYST
DAFT
DART
DAUT
DAWT
DEBT
DEFT
DENT
DEPT
DIET
DINT
DIRT
DITT
DOAT
DOIT
DOLT
DONT
DORT
DOUT
DOWT
DRAT
DUCT
DUET
DUNT
DUST
EAST
ECHT
EDIT
ELAT
EMIT
ERAT
EVET
EXIT
EYOT
FACT
FART
FAST
FEAT
FEET
FELT
FENT
FEST
FETT
FIAT
FIST
FITT
FLAT
FLIT
FONT
FOOT
FORT
FRET
FRIT
FUST
GAIT
GANT
GART
GAST
GATT
GEAT
GEIT
GELT
GENT
GEST
GETT
GHAT
GIFT
GILT
GIRT
GIST
GLIT
GLUT
GNAT
GOAT
GOUT
GRAT
GRIT
GROT
GUST
GYNT
HAET
HAFT
HAIT
HALT
HANT
HART
HAUT
HEAT
HECT
HEFT
HENT
HEPT
HEST
HILT
HINT
HIPT
HIST
HOLT
HOOT
HOST
HOUT
HUNT
HURT
IKAT
INST
ISNT
JEAT
JEST
JILT
JOLT
JUST
KANT
KART
KELT
KENT
KEPT
KEST
KHAT
KILT
KIST
KNIT
KNOT
KNUT
KYAT
LANT
LAST
LEAT
LEET
LEFT
LENT
LEST
LETT
LIFT
LILT
LINT
LIST
LOFT
LOOT
LOST
LOUT
LUIT
LUNT
LUST
MAAT
MALT
MART
MAST
MATT
MAUT
MEAT
MEET
MELT
MENT
MILT
MINT
MIST
MITT
MOAT
MOIT
MOLT
MOOT
MORT
MOST
MOTT
MUST
MUTT
NEAT
NEST
NETT
NEWT
NEXT
NOTT
NOUT
NOWT
NYET
OAST
OBIT
OINT
OMIT
ONST
OONT
OORT
OUST
PACT
PANT
PART
PAST
PEAT
PELT
PENT
PERT
PEST
PHOT
PHUT
PICT
PIET
PINT
PITT
PLAT
PLOT
POET
POLT
PONT
POOT
PORT
POST
POTT
POUT
PRAT
PUNT
PUTT
PYAT
PYET
PYOT
QUAT
QUIT
RAFT
RAIT
RANT
RAPT
RAST
REFT
RENT
REST
RETT
RIFT
RINT
RIOT
RITT
RONT
ROOT
RORT
ROUT
ROWT
RUNT
RUST
RYOT
SALT
SANT
SAUT
SCAT
SCOT
SCUT
SEAT
SECT
SEKT
SENT
SEPT
SETT
SEXT
SHET
SHIT
SHOT
SHUT
SIFT
SILT
SIST
SKAT
SKET
SKIT
SLAT
SLIT
SLOT
SLUT
SMIT
SMUT
SNIT
SNOT
SOFT
SOOT
SORT
SPAT
SPET
SPIT
SPOT
STET
STOT
SUET
SUIT
SWAT
SWOT
TACT
TAFT
TAIT
TART
TATT
TAUT
TAWT
TEAT
TENT
TEST
TEXT
THAT
TIFT
TILT
TINT
TOFT
TOLT
TOOT
TORT
TOST
TOUT
TOWT
TRET
TROT
TUFT
TWAT
TWIT
UIST
UNIT
VAST
VAUT
VENT
VERT
VEST
VINT
VOLT
WAFT
WAIT
WANT
WART
WAST
WATT
WEET
WEFT
WELT
WENT
WEPT
WERT
WEST
WHAT
WHET
WHIT
WHOT
WILT
WIST
WONT
WOOT
WORT
WRIT
XYST
YBET
YELT
YEST
YETT
YUFT
ZEST
ZOOT
AALU
AARU
ABZU
AGLU
AINU
AITU
ARRU
ATTU
BABU
BAJU
BAKU
BALU
BAPU
BEAU
BEDU
CHOU
CLOU
DIEU
ECRU
EHEU
EMEU
ESAU
FRAU
GENU
GURU
HABU
HUHU
JEHU
JUJU
KUDU
KUKU
KURU
LIEU
LUAU
LULU
MAHU
MANU
MASU
MENU
MERU
MOTU
OAHU
OGPU
OMBU
PATU
PERU
PRAU
PUDU
PULU
RAHU
RAKU
RATU
RIMU
RURU
SITU
SULU
SUSU
TABU
TAPU
TATU
THOU
THRU
TIPU
TOFU
TOLU
TROU
TUTU
UNAU
URDU
VATU
VAYU
WHAU
YALU
ZEBU
ZOBU
ZULU
AZOV
CCTV
DEEV
DERV
KIEV
MIRV
SHIV
SLAV
SPIV
ADAW
ALEW
ALOW
ANEW
AREW
AVOW
BLEW
BLOW
BRAW
BREW
BROW
CHAW
CHEW
CHOW
CLAW
CLEW
CLOW
CRAW
CREW
CROW
DEAW
DHOW
DRAW
DREW
DROW
EBBW
ENEW
ENOW
FLAW
FLEW
FLOW
FROW
GLOW
GNAW
GREW
GROW
KNEW
KNOW
MEOW
PHEW
PLEW
PLOW
PROW
SCAW
SCOW
SHAW
SHOW
SKAW
SKEW
SLAW
SLEW
SLOW
SMEW
SNOW
SPAW
SPEW
STAW
STEW
STOW
THAW
THEW
TREW
TROW
VIEW
WHEW
AJAX
ALEX
APEX
BRIX
CALX

CEYX	YUNX	CHAY	EDGY	ICKY	MOLY	PULY	THEY	BUZZ
COAX	ABLY	CHOY	EERY	IDLY	MONY	PUMY	TIDY	DIAZ
CRAX	AFFY	CITY	EMMY	IFFY	MOVY	PUNY	TINY	FITZ
CRUX	AHOY	CLAY	ENVY	ILLY	NARY	QUAY	TOBY	FIZZ
ERYX	AIRY	CLOY	ESKY	INBY	NAVY	QUEY	TODY	FUZZ
FAIX	ALAY	CODY	ESPY	INDY	NIXY	RACY	TOEY	GEEZ
FALX	ALKY	CONY	ETTY	INKY	NOSY	RAKY	TONY	GIZZ
FLAX	ALLY	COPY	EYRY	INLY	NOWY	RELY	TORY	GUNZ
FLEX	AMOY	CORY	FIKY	ISMY	OAKY	RENY	TRAY	HARZ
FLIX	APAY	COSY	FLAY	IVRY	OBEY	ROPY	TREY	HERZ
FLOX	ARLY	COTY	FLEY	JOEY	OFAY	RORY	TROY	JAZZ
FLUX	ARMY	COZY	FOGY	JUDY	OILY	ROSY	TWAY	JIZZ
HOAX	ARRY	CRAY	FOXY	JULY	OKAY	RUBY	UGLY	LUEZ
IBEX	ARTY	DAVY	FOZY	JURY	ONLY	RULY	UPSY	LUTZ
ILEX	ASHY	DEFY	FRAY	LACY	OOZY	SCRY	URDY	MOZZ
IYNX	AWAY	DEMY	FURY	LADY	ORBY	SEXY	VARY	OYEZ
JINX	AWRY	DENY	GABY	LAZY	ORGY	SHAY	VERY	PHIZ
JYNX	BABY	DEWY	GAMY	LELY	ORLY	SKRY	VIMY	PUTZ
KNOX	BEVY	DICY	GARY	LEVY	OWLY	SLAY	WADY	QUIZ
LANX	BLAY	DIXY	GDAY	LILY	PITY	SLEY	WALY	RAZZ
LYNX	BLEY	DOGY	GLEY	LIMY	PIXY	SOAY	WARY	RITZ
MANX	BODY	DORY	GOBY	LIVY	PLAY	SPAY	WAVY	SUEZ
MINX	BOGY	DOXY	GOEY	LOGY	PLOY	SPEY	WAXY	SWIZ
ONYX	BONY	DOZY	GORY	LORY	POKY	SPRY	WHEY	TREZ
ORYX	BRAY	DRAY	GRAY	LUCY	POLY	STAY	WILY	TUZZ
PNYX	BUOY	DREY	GREY	LYLY	PONY	STEY	WIRY	WHIZ
PRIX	BURY	DULY	HAZY	MANY	POSY	SUEY	YAWY	ZIZZ
ROUX	BUSY	DUTY	HERY	MARY	POXY	SWAY	ZANY	
STYX	CARY	EASY	HOLY	MATY	PRAY	SWEY	BENZ	
ULEX	CAVY	EDDY	HUEY	MOBY	PREY	TEDY	BOAZ	

5:1

AARON
ABABA
ABACK
ABACO
ABAFT
ABASE
ABASH
ABATE
ABBAS
ABBEY
ABBOT
ABDAR
ABDUL
ABEAM
ABEAR
ABELE
ABHOR
ABIDE
ABIES
ABLER
ABLOW
ABODE
ABORT
ABOUT
ABOVE
ABRAM
ABRAY
ABRIM
ABSIT
ABUJA
ABUNA
ABUSE
ABYSM
ABYSS
ACCRA
ACERB
ACINI
ACOCK
ACORN
ACRES
ACRID
ACTIN
ACTON
ACTOR
ACUTE
ADAGE
ADAMS
ADAPT
ADDED
ADDER
ADDIO
ADDIS
ADDLE
ADEEM
ADEPT
ADIEU
ADIGE
ADIOS
ADLIB
ADMIN
ADMIT
ADMIX
ADOBE
ADOPT
ADORE
ADORN
ADSUM
ADULT
AEDES
AEGIS
AESOP
AFEAR
AFFIX
AFIRE
AFOOT
AFORE
AFOUL
AFRIT
AFTER
AGAIN
AGAMI
AGAPE
AGATE
AGAVE
AGENT
AGGER
AGGRO
AGILE
AGING
AGIST
AGLEE
AGLET
AGLEY
AGLOW
AGNES
AGONE
AGONY
AGORA
AGREE
AHEAD
AHMED
AIDAN
AIDOS
AIKEN
AINEE
AIOLI
AIRER
AIRES
AISLE
AITCH
AKBAR
AKELA
AKENE
ALACK
ALAMO
ALANS
ALAPA
ALARM
ALATE
ALBAN
ALBEE
ALBUM
ALDAN
ALDER
ALDIS
ALEPH
ALERT
ALEUT
ALFIE
ALGAE
ALGID
ALGOL
ALIAS
ALIBI
ALICE
ALIEN
ALIGN
ALIKE
ALIVE
ALLAH
ALLAN
ALLAY
ALLÉE
ALLEN
ALLEY
ALLOT
ALLOW
ALLOY
ALLYL
ALNUS
ALOES
ALOFT
ALOHA
ALONE
ALONG
ALOOF
ALOUD
ALPHA
ALTAI
ALTAR
ALTER
ALURE
ALVIS
AMAIN
AMANT
AMASS
AMAZE
AMBER
AMBIT
AMBLE
AMEBA
AMEND
AMENE
AMENT
AMICE
AMIEL
AMIGO
AMINE
AMINO
AMISH
AMISS
AMITY
AMMAN
AMONG
AMORT
AMOUR
AMPLE
AMPLY
AMUCK
AMUSE
ANANA
ANDES
ANEAR
ANELE
ANEND
ANENT
ANGEL
ANGER
ANGLE
ANGLO
ANGRY
ANGST
ANGUS
ANIGH
ANIMA
ANION
ANISE
ANITA
ANJOU
ANKER
ANKLE
ANKUS
ANNAL
ANNAM
ANNEX
ANNIE
ANNOY
ANNUL
ANODE
ANOMY
ANSON
ANTAR
ANTIC
ANTON
ANVIL
ANZAC
AORTA
AOSTA
APACE
APAGE
APAID
APART
APEAK
APERT
APHID
APHIS
APODE
APOOP
APPAL
APPAY
APPEL
APPLE
APPLY
APPRO
APPUI
APRIL
APRON
APTLY
AQABA
ARABA
ARBOR
ARCOT
ARCUS
ARDEA
ARDEB
ARDEN
ARDIL
ARDOR
ARECA
AREDE
ARENA
ARENE
ARENT
ARETE
ARGIL
ARGOT
ARGUE
ARGUS
ARIAN
ARICA
ARIEL
ARIES
ARISE
ARISH
ARIST
ARITA
ARKLE
ARLES
ARMED
ARMET
ARMOR
AROID
AROMA
AROSE
ARRAN
ARRAS
ARRAY
ARRÊT
ARRIS
ARROW
ARSON
ARTIE
ARUBA
ARVAL
ARYAN
ASAPH
ASCII
ASCOT
ASCUS
ASDIC
ASHEN
ASHER
ASHES
ASHET
ASIAN
ASIDE
ASKER
ASKEW
ASOKA
ASPEN
ASPER
ASPIC
ASSAI
ASSAM
ASSAY
ASSET
ASTER
ASTIR
ASTON
ASTRA
ASWAN
ATHOS
ATILT
ATLAS
ATLIN
ATMAN
ATOLL
ATOMY
ATONE
ATONY
ATOPY
ATRIP
ATTAR
ATTIC
ATTLE
AUDEN
AUDIO
AUDIT
AUGER
AUGHT
AUGUR
AULIC
AULIS
AUNTY
AURAL
AURIC
AUXIN
AVAIL
AVANT
AVAST
AVENA
AVENS
AVERT
AVIAN
AVION
AVISO
AVOID
AVOUÉ
AWAIT
AWAKE
AWARD
AWARE
AWARN
AWASH
AWEEL
AWFUL
AWOKE
AXIAL
AXIOM
AXOID
AYRIE
AZOIC
AZOTE
AZTEC
AZURE
AZYME
BABAR
BABEL
BABOO
BABUL
BACCY
BACKS
BACON
BADDY
BADEN
BADGE
BADLY
BAFFY
BAGEL
BAGGY
BAHAI
BAHUT
BAIRD
BAIRN
BAIZE
BAJRI
BAKED
BAKER
BAKHA
BALAN
BALER
BALFE
BALLS
BALLY
BALMY
BALOO
BALOR
BALSA
BAMBI
BANAL
BANCO
BANDA
BANDS
BANDY
BANJO
BANKS
BANNS
BANTU
BARGE
BARMY
BARON
BARRA
BARRE
BARRY
BARTS
BASAL
BASAN
BASES
BASHO
BASIC
BASIL
BASIN
BASIS
BASLE
BASRA
BASSO
BASTA
BASTE
BASTO
BATCH
BATED
BATES
BATHE
BATHS
BATIK
BATON
BATTY
BAULK
BAWDY
BAYER
BAYLE
BAYOU
BAZOO
BEACH
BEADS
BEADY
BEALE
BEAMY
BEANO
BEANS
BEARD
BEAST
BEAUT
BEBOP
BECKY
BEDAD
BEDEW
BEECH
BEEFY
BEERY
BEFIT
BEFOG
BEGAD
BEGAN
BEGET
BEGIN
BEGUM
BEGUN
BEHAN
BEIGE
BEING
BEKAA
BELAY
BELCH
BELGA

BELIE
BELLE
BELLS
BELLY
BELOW
BENCH
BENDS
BENDY
BENET
BENIN
BENNE
BEPAT
BERET
BERIA
BEROB
BERRY
BERTH
BERYL
BESET
BESOM
BESOT
BETEL
BETON
BETTE
BETTY
BEVEL
BEVIS
BÉVUE
BEVVY
BEZEL
BHANG
BIBBY
BIBLE
BIDDY
BIDET
BIFID
BIGHT
BIGOT
BIJOU
BIKER
BILGE
BILLY
BIMBO
BINGE
BINGO
BIONT
BIPED
BIPOD
BIRCH
BIRDS
BIRTH
BISON
BITCH
BITER
BITTE
BITTY
BLACK
BLADE
BLAIR
BLAKE
BLAME
BLANC
BLAND
BLANK
BLARE
BLASÉ
BLAST
BLAZE
BLEAK
BLEAR
BLEAT
BLEED
BLEEP
BLEND
BLESS
BLEST
BLIGH
BLIMP
BLIND
BLINI
BLINK
BLISS
BLITZ
BLOAT
BLOCK
BLOKE
BLOND
BLOOD
BLOOM
BLOOP
BLOWN
BLOWY
BLUES
BLUEY
BLUFF
BLUNT
BLURB
BLURT
BLUSH
BOARD
BOAST
BOBBY
BOCHE
BODES
BODGE
BOGEY
BOGGY
BOGIE
BOGLE
BOGUS
BOHEA
BOING
BOLAS
BOLUS
BOMBE
BOMBO
BONAR
BONCE
BONDI
BONDS
BONER
BONES
BONEY
BONGO
BONNY
BONUS
BONZE
BOOBY
BOONE
BOONG
BOOST
BOOTH
BOOTS
BOOTY
BOOZE
BOOZY
BORAX
BORED
BOREE
BORER
BORIC
BORIS
BORNE
BORON
BOSCH
BOSEY
BOSKY
BOSOM
BOSSY
BOSUN
BOTCH
BOTHA
BOTHY
BOTTE
BOUGH
BOULE
BOUND
BOURG
BOWED
BOWEL
BOWER
BOWIE
BOWLS
BOXED
BOXER
BOYAR
BOYAU
BOYCE
BOYLE
BOYNE
BRACE
BRACK
BRACT
BRADY
BRAID
BRAIN
BRAKE
BRAND
BRANK
BRASH
BRASS
BRAVA
BRAVE
BRAVO
BRAWL
BRAWN
BREAD
BREAK
BREAM
BREDA
BREDE
BREED
BREEM
BREME
BRENT
BREST
BREVE
BRIAN
BRIAR
BRIBE
BRICK
BRIDE
BRIEF
BRIER
BRILL
BRINE
BRING
BRINK
BRINY
BRISK
BRIZE
BROAD
BROCK
BROIL
BROKE
BRONX
BROOD
BROOK
BROOL
BROOM
BROSE
BROTH
BROWN
BRUCE
BRUIN
BRUIT
BRULE
BRUME
BRUNO
BRUNT
BRUSH
BRUTE
BUBBY
BUCCA
BUCKO
BUCKS
BUDDY
BUDGE
BUFFO
BUFFS
BUGGY
BUGLE
BUICK
BUILD
BUILT
BULGE
BULKY
BULLA
BULLS
BULLY
BULOW
BUMPH
BUMPY
BUNCE
BUNCH
BUNCO
BUNDY
BUNGY
BUNNY
BURGH
BURIN
BURKE
BURLY
BURMA
BURNS
BURNT
BUROO
BURRO
BURSA
BURST
BUSBY
BUSHY
BUSTY
BUTCH
BUTTE
BUTTY
BUXOM
BUYER
BWANA
BWAZI
BYLAW
BYRON
BYWAY
CABAL
CABAS
CABBY
CABER
CABIN
CABLE
CABOB
CABOT
CACAO
CACHE
CADDY
CADET
CADGE
CADGY
CADRE
CAGEY
CAGOT
CAINE
CAIRN
CAIRO
CAIUS
CAJUN
CALEB
CALIX
CALOR
CALPE
CALVE
CALYX
CAMEL
CAMEO
CAMIS
CAMPO
CAMUS
CANAL
CANDY
CANES
CANNA
CANNY
CANOE
CANON
CANTO
CAPER
CAPET
CAPON
CAPOT
CAPRI
CAPUT
CARAT
CARDS
CARER
CARET
CAREW
CAREY
CARGO
CARIB
CARLE
CAROB
CAROL
CARRY
CARTA
CARTE
CARVE
CARVY
CASCA
CASCO
CASES
CASTE
CATCH
CATER
CATES
CATTY
CAULD
CAULK
CAUSE
CAVAN
CAVIL
CDROM
CEASE
CECIL
CECUM
CEDAR
CELLA
CELLO
CELLS
CENCI
CENSE
CENTO
CEORL
CERES
CERNE
CESAR
CHACO
CHAFE
CHAFF
CHAIN
CHAIR
CHALK
CHAMP
CHANT
CHAOS
CHAPE
CHAPS
CHARD
CHARK
CHARM
CHART
CHARY
CHASE
CHASM
CHEAP
CHEAT
CHECK
CHEEK
CHEEP
CHEER
CHEKA
CHERE
CHERT
CHESS
CHEST
CHEVY
CHEWY
CHIAO
CHICA
CHICK
CHICO
CHIDE
CHIEF
CHILD
CHILE
CHILI
CHILL
CHIME
CHIMP
CHINA
CHINE
CHING
CHINK
CHINO
CHIPS
CHIRK
CHIRL
CHIRP
CHIRR
CHIRT
CHIVE
CHIVY
CHLOE
CHOCK
CHOCO
CHOIR
CHOKE
CHOKO
CHOKY
CHOMP
CHOOK
CHOPS
CHORD
CHORE
CHOSE
CHOTA
CHUBB
CHUCK
CHUFF
CHUMP
CHUNK
CHURL
CHURN
CHURR
CHUTE
CHYLE
CHYME
CHYND
CIBOL
CIDER
CIGAR
CIGGY
CILIA
CILLA
CINCH
CINNA
CIRCA
CIRCE
CISCO
CISSY
CIVET
CIVIC
CIVIL
CIVVY
CLACK
CLAIM
CLAMP
CLANG
CLANK
CLARA
CLARE
CLARK
CLARY
CLASH
CLASP
CLASS
CLAUS
CLAVE
CLEAN
CLEAR

CLEAT
CLECK
CLEEK
CLEEP
CLEFT
CLEPE
CLERK
CLICK
CLIFF
CLIFT
CLIMB
CLIME
CLING
CLINK
CLINT
CLIVE
CLOAK
CLOCK
CLONE
CLOOT
CLOSE
CLOTH
CLOUD
CLOUT
CLOVE
CLOWN
CLOZE
CLUBS
CLUCK
CLUMP
CLUNG
CLUNK
CLYDE
COACH
COADE
COAST
COATI
COBOL
COBRA
COCCI
COCKY
COCOA
COCOS
CODED
CODEX
COHOE
COIGN
COKES
COLET
COLEY
COLIC
COLIN
COLLY
COLON
COLOR
COLTS
COLZA
COMBE
COMBO
COMBS
COMET
COMFY
COMIC
COMMA
COMPO
COMTE
COMUS
CONAN
CONCH
CONDE
CONDO
CONEY
CONGÉ
CONGO
CONIC
CONTE
COOEE
COOKS
COOMB
COOPT
COPER
COPPY
COPRA
COPSE
CORAL
CORAM
CORDS
CORED
CORER
CORFE
CORFU
CORGI
CORIN
CORKY
CORNY
COROT
CORPS
CORSE
CORSO
CORVO
COSEC
COSMO
COSTA
COSTS
COTTA
COUCH
COUDÉ
COUGH
COULD
COUNT
COUPE
COURB
COURT
COUTH
COVEN
COVER
COVET
COVEY
COWAN
COWER
COWRY
COXAL
COXED
COYLY
COYNE
COYPU
COZEN
CRABS
CRACK
CRAFT
CRAIG
CRAKE
CRAMP
CRANE
CRANK
CRAPE
CRAPS
CRARE
CRASH
CRASS
CRATE
CRAVE
CRAWL
CRAZE
CRAZY
CREAK
CREAM
CRECY
CREDO
CREED
CREEK
CREEL
CREEP
CREME
CREON
CREPE
CREPT
CRESS
CREST
CRETE
CREWE
CRICK
CRIED
CRIER
CRIES
CRIME
CRIMP
CRISE
CRISP
CROAK
CROAT
CROCE
CROCK
CROFT
CROME
CRONE
CRONK
CRONY
CROOK
CROPS
CRORE
CROSS
CROUP
CROWD
CROWN
CROZE
CRUCK
CRUDE
CRUEL
CRUET
CRUMB
CRUMP
CRUOR
CRUSE
CRUSH
CRUST
CRWTH
CRYPT
CUBAN
CUBBY
CUBEB
CUBED
CUBIC
CUBIT
CUDDY
CUFFS
CUFFY
CUFIC
CULET
CULEX
CULLY
CUMIN
CUPAR
CUPEL
CUPID
CUPPA
CURDS
CURED
CURER
CURIA
CURIE
CURIO
CURLY
CURRY
CURSE
CURST
CURVE
CURVY
CUSHY
CUTCH
CUTEY
CUTIE
CUTIS
CUTTY
CYCAD
CYCLE
CYMRU
CYMRY
CYNIC
CYRUS
CZECH
DACCA
DACHA
DADDY
DAFFY
DAGON
DAILY
DAIRY
DAISY
DAKAR
DALEK
DALLE
DALLY
DAMAN
DAMME
DAMON
DANAE
DANCE
DANDO
DANDY
DANES
DANTE
DARBY
DARCY
DARTS
DATED
DATER
DATES
DATUK
DATUM
DAUBE
DAUNT
DAVID
DAVIS
DAVIT
DAYAK
DAZED
DEATH
DEBAG
DEBAR
DEBEL
DEBIT
DEBUG
DEBUT
DECAL
DECAY
DECCA
DECKO
DECOR
DECOY
DECRY
DEEDS
DEFER
DEFOE
DEGAS
DEIFY
DEIGN
DEIST
DEITY
DEKKO
DELAY
DELFT
DELHI
DELOS
DELPH
DELTA
DELVE
DEMOB
DEMON
DEMOS
DEMUR
DENIM
DENIS
DENSE
DENYS
DEPOT
DEPTH
DERAY
DERBY
DERMA
DERRY
DESSE
DETER
DEUCE
DEVIL
DEWAN
DEWAR
DEWEY
DHABI
DHOBI
DHOTI
DIALS
DIANA
DIARY
DIAZO
DICEY
DICKY
DIDNT
DIEGO
DIGHT
DIGIT
DIKER
DILDO
DIMLY
DINAR
DINER
DINGE
DINGO
DINGY
DINKA
DINKY
DIODE
DIOTA
DIPPY
DIRGE
DIRTY
DISCO
DISHY
DITAL
DITCH
DITTO
DITTY
DIVAN
DIVER
DIVES
DIVOT
DIVVY
DIWAN
DIXIE
DIZZY
DOBBY
DOBRO
DOCKS
DODDY
DODGE
DODGY
DOGGO
DOGGY
DOGMA
DOILY
DOING
DOLCE
DOLIN
DOLLY
DOMED
DONAR
DONAT
DONEE
DONNA
DONNE
DONOR
DOONE
DOORN
DOORS
DOPEY
DORAS
DOREE
DORIC
DORIS
DORMY
DORTS
DOTTY
DOUAI
DOUAR
DOUAY
DOUBT
DOUCE
DOUGH
DOUMA
DOURA
DOURO
DOUSE
DOVER
DOWDY
DOWEL
DOWER
DOWNS
DOWNY
DOWRY
DOWSE
DOYEN
DOYLE
DOYLY
DOZEN
DRACO
DRAFT
DRAIN
DRAKE
DRAMA
DRANK
DRAPE
DRAWL
DRAWN
DREAD
DREAM
DREAR
DREGS
DRERE
DRESS
DRIED
DRIER
DRIES
DRIFT
DRILL
DRILY
DRINK
DRIVE
DROIT
DROLL
DROME
DRONE
DROOL
DROOP
DROPS
DROSS
DROVE
DROWN
DRUGS
DRUID
DRUNK
DRUPE
DRURY
DRUZE
DRYAD
DRYER
DRYLY
DUBAI
DUCAT
DUCHY
DUCKS
DUCKY
DUDDY
DUKAS
DUKES
DULAC
DUMAS
DUMMY
DUMPS
DUMPY
DUNCE
DUNNO
DUOMO
DUPIN
DURER
DUROY
DURRY
DURST
DURUM

DUSKY
DUSTY
DUTCH
DUVAL
DUVET
DWARF
DWELL
DYFED
DYING
DYKER
DYLAN
DYULA
EAGER
EAGLE
EARLY
EARTH
EASEL
EATER
EAVES
EBOLA
EBONY
ECLAT
EDEMA
EDGAR
EDGED
EDGER
EDICT
EDIFY
EDILE
EDUCE
EDWIN
EERIE
EGDON
EGEST
EGGAR
EGRET
EGYPT
EIDER
EIGER
EIGHT
EIKON
EILAT
EJECT
ELAND
ELATE
ELBOW
ELDER
ELECT
ELEGY
ELENE
ELFIN
ELGAR
ELGIN
ELIAD
ELIAS
ELIDE
ELIHU
ELIOT
ELITE
ELLEN
ELLIS
ELMER
ELOGE
ELOGY
ELOPE
ELSAN
ELTON
ELUDE
ELVAN
ELVER
ELVES
ELVIS
EMAIL
EMBED
EMBER
EMBOW
EMBOX
EMBUS
EMCEE
EMDEN
EMEND
EMERY
EMILE
EMILY
EMLYN
EMMER
EMMET
EMOTE
EMOVE
EMPTY
EMRYS
EMURE
ENACT
ENARM
ENDED
ENDOW
ENDUE
ENEMA
ENEMY
ENJOY
ENMEW
ENNUI
ENOCH
ENORM
ENROL
ENSEW
ENSOR
ENSUE
ENTER
ENTRY
ENUGU
ENURE
ENVOI
ENVOY
EOLIC
EOSIN
EPHOD
EPHOR
EPOCH
EPODE
EPOXY
EPSOM
EQUAL
EQUIP
ERARD
ERASE
ERATO
ERECT
ERGOT
ERICA
ERICK
ERNIE
ERNST
ERODE
ERROR
ERUCA
ERUCT
ERUPT
ESCOT
ESKER
ESROM
ESSAY
ESTER
ESTOC
ESTOP
ETAGE
ETAIN
ETAPE
ETATS
ETHAL
ETHER
ETHIC
ETHOS
ETHYL
ETUDE
ETWEE
EULER
EVADE
EVANS
EVENS
EVENT
EVERT
EVERY
EVIAN
EVICT
EVITA
EVITE
EVOKE
EXACT
EXALT
EXCEL
EXEAT
EXERT
EXILE
EXINE
EXIST
EXODE
EXPEL
EXTOL
EXTRA
EXUDE
EXULT
EXURB
EYRIE
EYTIE
FABER
FABLE
FABRÉ
FACER
FACET
FACIA
FACTO
FACTS
FADDY
FADED
FADGE
FAERY
FAGOT
FAGUS
FAINS
FAINT
FAIRY
FAITH
FAKER
FAKIR
FALDO
FALLA
FALLS
FALSE
FAMED
FANAL
FANCY
FANNY
FANON
FARAD
FARCE
FARCI
FARCY
FARGO
FARNE
FAROE
FARSE
FATAL
FATED
FATTY
FATWA
FAULT
FAUNA
FAURE
FAUST
FAUVE
FAVOR
FAVUS
FEARE
FEAST
FECAL
FECES
FECIT
FEIGN
FEINT
FELIS
FELIX
FELLA
FELON
FEMTO
FEMUR
FENCE
FENNY
FEOFF
FERAL
FERIA
FERMI
FERRY
FESSE
FESTA
FESTE
FETAL
FETCH
FETID
FETOR
FETUS
FEVER
FEWER
FIBER
FIBRE
FIBRO
FICHE
FICHU
FIDEL
FIDES
FIELD
FIEND
FIERE
FIERY
FIFTH
FIFTY
FIGHT
FILCH
FILET
FILLY
FILMS
FILMY
FILTH
FINAL
FINCH
FINER
FINIS
FINKS
FIORD
FIRMA
FIRST
FIRTH
FISHY
FITCH
FIVER
FIVES
FIXED
FIXER
FIZZY
FJORD
FLACK
FLAIL
FLAIR
FLAKE
FLAKY
FLAME
FLANK
FLARE
FLASH
FLASK
FLATS
FLECK
FLEET
FLESH
FLEUR
FLEWS
FLICK
FLIER
FLIES
FLING
FLINT
FLIRT
FLOAT
FLOCK
FLONG
FLOOD
FLOOR
FLOPS
FLORA
FLOSS
FLOTA
FLOUR
FLOUT
FLOWN
FLUFF
FLUID
FLUKE
FLUME
FLUMP
FLUNG
FLUNK
FLUON
FLUSH
FLUTE
FLYER
FLYTE
FOAMY
FOCAL
FOCUS
FOEHN
FOGEY
FOGGY
FOIST
FOLIC
FOLIE
FOLIO
FOLKS
FOLLY
FONDA
FONDS
FOODS
FOOLS
FOOTS
FOOTY
FORAY
FORCE
FOREL
FORGE
FORGO
FORKS
FORME
FORMS
FORTE
FORTH
FORTY
FORUM
FOSSA
FOSSE
FOUET
FOULÉ
FOUND
FOUNT
FOURS
FOVEA
FOYER
FOYLE
FRACK
FRACT
FRAIL
FRAME
FRANC
FRANK
FRANS
FRANZ
FRAUD
FREAK
FREED
FREON
FRESH
FREUD
FRIAR
FRIED
FRIES
FRILL
FRISK
FRIST
FRITH
FRITZ
FROCK
FROND
FRONT
FROST
FROTH
FROWN
FROWY
FROZE
FRUIT
FRUMP
FUBSY
FUCHS
FUDGE
FUERO
FUGAL
FUGGY
FUGUE
FULLY
FUMED
FUMES
FUMET
FUNDI
FUNDS
FUNDY
FUNKY
FUNNY
FUROR
FURRY
FURZE
FUSED
FUSEE
FUSSY
FUSTY
FUTON
FUZEE
FUZZY
FYLDE
GABBY
GABLE
GABON
GADGE
GADUS
GAFFE
GAILY
GAINS
GAIUS
GALAM
GALBA
GALEA
GALEN
GALOP
GAMAY
GAMBA
GAMBO
GAMES
GAMIC
GAMMA
GAMMY
GAMUT
GANJA
GANNY
GAPER
GARBO
GARDA
GARNI
GARTH
GARUM
GASES
GASPÉ
GASSY
GATED
GAUDE
GAUDY
GAUGE
GAULT
GAUNT
GAUSS
GAUZE
GAUZY
GAVEL

GAWKY
GAZON
GÉANT
GEARE
GEBER
GECKO
GEESE
GEIST
GELID
GEMMA
GEMMY
GENET
GENIE
GENOA
GENRE
GENTS
GENTY
GENUS
GEODE
GERBE
GESSE
GESSO
GESTE
GETUP
GHANA
GHATS
GHAZI
GHOST
GHOUL
GHYLL
GIANT
GIBBY
GIBUS
GIDDY
GIFTS
GIGLI
GIGOT
GIGUE
GILES
GILET
GILLS
GILTS
GIMPY
GIPPO
GIPSY
GIRLS
GIRLY
GIRTH
GISMO
GIVEN
GIVER
GIZMO
GLACE
GLADE
GLAIR
GLAND
GLANS
GLASS
GLAZE
GLEAM
GLEAN
GLEBE
GLEEK
GLEET
GLIDE
GLIFF
GLINT
GLISK
GLITZ
GLOAT
GLOBE
GLOGG
GLOOM
GLORY
GLOSS
GLOVE
GLUCK
GLUED
GLUEY
GLUME
GLUON
GLYPH
GNARL
GNASH
GNOME
GOATY
GOBBO
GODET
GODLY
GOFER
GOGOL
GOING
GOLAN
GOLEM
GOLGI
GOLLY
GOMBO
GONAD
GONER
GONNA
GONZO
GOODS
GOODY
GOOEY
GOOFY
GOOLY
GOOSE
GOPAK
GORED
GORGE
GORKY
GORSE
GOSHT
GOSSE
GOTCH
GOTHA
GOTTA
GOUDA
GOUGE
GOURD
GOUTY
GOWAN
GOWER
GRAAL
GRACE
GRADE
GRAFF
GRAFT
GRAIL
GRAIN
GRAND
GRANT
GRAPE
GRAPH
GRASP
GRASS
GRATE
GRAVE
GRAVY
GRAYS
GRAZE
GREAT
GREBE
GREED
GREEK
GREEN
GREER
GREET
GREGG
GRETA
GREYS
GRIEF
GRIEG
GRIFF
GRILL
GRIME
GRIMM
GRIMY
GRIND
GRIOT
GRIPE
GRIST
GRITS
GROAN
GROAT
GROIN
GROOM
GROPE
GROSS
GROSZ
GROUP
GROUT
GROVE
GROWL
GROWN
GRUEL
GRUFE
GRUFF
GRUME
GRUNT
GUACO
GUANA
GUANO
GUARD
GUAVA
GUELF
GUESS
GUEST
GUEUX
GUIDE
GUILD
GUILE
GUILT
GUIMP
GUISE
GULAG
GULCH
GULES
GULLS
GULLY
GULPH
GUMBO
GUMMY
GUNGE
GUNNY
GUPPY
GUSHY
GUSTO
GUSTY
GUTSY
GUTTA
GUYED
GUYON
GUYOT
GWENT
GYGES
GYMNO
GYPPO
GYPSY
GYRUS
HABET
HABIT
HACEK
HADES
HADJI
HADNT
HAFIZ
HAGUE
HAIDA
HAIFA
HAIKU
HAIRS
HAIRY
HAITI
HAKKA
HALER
HALFA
HALLÉ
HALLO
HALMA
HALON
HALSE
HALVE
HAMMY
HANAP
HANCE
HANCH
HANDS
HANDY
HANKY
HANOI
HANSE
HAPPY
HARDY
HAREM
HARPO
HARPY
HARRY
HARSH
HARTY
HASNT
HASTA
HASTE
HASTY
HATCH
HATHI
HATTY
HAUGH
HAULM
HAULT
HAUNT
HAUSA
HAUSE
HAUTE
HAVEL
HAVEN
HAVER
HAVOC
HAWSE
HAYDN
HAYLE
HAZEL
HEADS
HEADY
HEALD
HEAPS
HEARD
HEART
HEATH
HEAVE
HEAVY
HECHT
HECTO
HEDDA
HEDGE
HEELS
HEFTY
HEGEL
HEIGH
HEINE
HEIST
HELEN
HELGA
HELIO
HELIX
HELLO
HELOT
HELVE
HENCE
HENGE
HENNA
HENRY
HERBS
HERMA
HERNE
HEROD
HERON
HERSE
HERTS
HERTZ
HESSE
HETTY
HEUGH
HEVEA
HEWER
HEXAD
HEXAM
HEXYL
HEYER
HIGHT
HIKER
HILAR
HILDA
HILLS
HILLY
HILUM
HINDI
HINDU
HINGE
HINNY
HIPPO
HIPPY
HIRAM
HIRED
HIRER
HITCH
HITHE
HIVER
HIVES
HOARD
HOARE
HOARY
HOAST
HOBBS
HOBBY
HOCUS
HODGE
HOGAN
HOICK
HOIST
HOKEY
HOKUM
HOLED
HOLEY
HOLLA
HOLLY
HOLST
HOMER
HOMME
HONAN
HONDO
HONEY
HONKY
HONOR
HOOCH
HOOEY
HOOKY
HOOSH
HOOVE
HORAH
HORDE
HOREB
HORNE
HORNY
HORSA
HORSE
HORSY
HORUS
HOSEA
HOSEN
HOSTA
HOTCH
HOTEL
HOTLY
HOUGH
HOUND
HOURI
HOURS
HOUSE
HOVEL
HOVER
HOWBE
HOWDY
HOYLE
HUBBY
HUFFY
HULKS
HULLO
HULME
HUMAN
HUMID
HUMOR
HUMPH
HUMUS
HUNCH
HUNKS
HUNKY
HUNTS
HURON
HURRY
HURST
HUSKS
HUSKY
HUSSY
HUTCH
HUZZA
HYDRA
HYDRO
HYENA
HYLUM
HYMEN
HYPER
HYPHA
HYRAX
HYTHE
IBERT
IBIZA
IBSEN
ICENI
ICHOR
ICILY
ICING
ICKER
ICTUS
IDAHO
IDEAL
IDEAS
IDIOM
IDIOT
IDLER
IDRIS
IDYLL
IGAPO
IGLOO
ILEAC
ILEUM
ILEUS
ILIAC
ILIAD
ILIUM
IMAGE
IMAGO
IMARI
IMAUM
IMBED
IMBUE
IMMER
IMMEW
IMPEL
IMPLY
IMPOT
IMSHI
INANE
INAPT
INARI
INARM
INCLE
INCUR
INCUS
INDEW
INDEX
INDIA
INDRA
INDRE
INDRI
INDUE
INDUS
INEPT

INERT
INFER
INFRA
INGLE
INGOT
INIGO
INION
INIUM
INJUN
INLAW
INLAY
INLET
INNER
INNES
INPUT
INSET
INTER
INTRA
INTRO
INUIT
INURE
INWIT
IONIC
IQBAL
IRAQI
IRATE
IRENA
IRENE
IRGUN
IRISH
IROKO
IRONS
IRONY
ISAAC
ISERE
ISLAM
ISLAY
ISLES
ISLET
ISMET
ISOLA
ISSUE
ITALA
ITALY
ITCHY
IVIED
IVORY
IXION
IZARD
IZMIR
IZZAT
JABOT
JACKS
JACOB
JADED
JADIS
JAFFA
JAKES
JALAP
JAMBE
JAMBO
JAMES
JAMMY
JANTY
JANUS
JAPAN
JASEY
JASON
JASPÉ
JAUNT
JAVAN
JAVEL
JAZZY
JEANS
JEBEL
JEHAD
JELAB
JELLO
JELLY
JEMMY
JENNY
JEREZ
JERKS
JERKY
JERRY
JESSE
JESUS
JETTY
JEWEL
JEWRY
JIFFY
JIHAD
JIMMU
JIMMY
JIMPY
JINGO
JINKS
JIRGA
JOCKO
JOINT
JOIST
JOKER
JOLLY
JONAH
JONES
JONTY
JORIS
JORUM
JOUAL
JOULE
JOUNT
JOUST
JOYCE
JUDAS
JUDGE
JUGAL
JUICE
JUICY
JULEP
JUMAR
JUMBO
JUMBY
JUMNA
JUMPS
JUMPY
JUNCO
JUNTA
JUNTO
JUPON
JURAT
JUROR
KAABA
KABOB
KABUL
KAFIR
KAFKA
KALIF
KAMME
KAMPF
KANAK
KANDY
KANJI
KAPOK
KAPPA
KAPUT
KARAT
KARMA
KARNO
KARRI
KARST
KARSY
KASHA
KAURI
KAYAK
KEBAB
KEBEL
KEBLE
KEBOB
KEDAR
KEDGE
KEDGY
KEECH
KEELS
KEEPS
KEFIR
KELIM
KELLS
KELLY
KEMPE
KENDO
KENGA
KENYA
KERAL
KERMA
KERNE
KETCH
KEVIN
KEYED
KEYES
KHAKI
KHAYA
KHAZI
KIANG
KIDDY
KIDGE
KILDA
KILIM
KIMBO
KINGS
KINKY
KIOSK
KIPPS
KIRBY
KIROV
KITTY
KIWIS
KLANG
KLEIN
KLIEG
KLOOF
KNACK
KNARL
KNAVE
KNEAD
KNEEL
KNELL
KNELT
KNIFE
KNOCK
KNOLL
KNOUT
KNOWN
KNURL
KNURR
KOALA
KODAK
KOFTA
KOINE
KOKUM
KONGO
KOOKY
KOORI
KOPJE
KORAN
KOREA
KORMA
KOTOW
KRAAL
KRAFT
KRANG
KRANS
KRANZ
KRAUT
KRIEG
KRILL
KRONA
KRONE
KUALA
KUDOS
KUDZU
KUFIC
KUKRI
KULAK
KURMA
KUTCH
KVASS
KYANG
KYLIE
KYLIN
KYLIX
KYLOE
KYRIE
LABDA
LABEL
LABIS
LABOR
LACET
LACKS
LADEN
LADLE
LAGAN
LAGER
LAGOS
LAIRD
LAIRY
LAITH
LAITY
LAMED
LAMIA
LAMMY
LAMPS
LANCE
LANDE
LANKA
LANKY
LAPEL
LAPIS
LAPSE
LARCH
LARGE
LARGO
LARKS
LARNE
LARRY
LARVA
LASER
LASKI
LASSA
LASSO
LATCH
LATEN
LATER
LATEX
LATHE
LATHI
LATIN
LAUDS
LAUGH
LAURA
LAVER
LAVRA
LAWKS
LAYBY
LAYER
LAZAR
LAZZO
LEACH
LEADS
LEAFY
LEAKY
LEANT
LEAPT
LEARN
LEASE
LEASH
LEAST
LEAVE
LECOQ
LEDGE
LEECH
LEEDS
LEERY
LEESE
LEFTY
LEGAL
LEGER
LEGGE
LEGGY
LEGIT
LEHAR
LEIGH
LEISH
LEITH
LEMAN
LEMMA
LEMON
LEMUR
LENIN
LENTO
LEONE
LEPER
LEPID
LERNA
LERNE
LESHY
LETHE
LEVEE
LEVEL
LEVEN
LEVER
LEVIN
LEVIS
LEWES
LEWIS
LEXIS
LHASA
LIANA
LIANE
LIANG
LIARD
LIBEL
LIBER
LIBRA
LIBYA
LICHT
LICIT
LIEGE
LIFER
LIGGE
LIGHT
LIKED
LIKEN
LIKES
LILAC
LILLE
LILLY
LIMAX
LIMBO
LIMER
LIMES
LIMEY
LIMIT
LINCH
LINED
LINEN
LINER
LINES
LINGO
LININ
LINKS
LINUS
LIONS
LIPID
LIPPI
LISLE
LISTS
LISZT
LITAS
LITER
LITHE
LITRE
LIVED
LIVEN
LIVER
LIVES
LIVID
LIVRE
LLAMA
LLANO
LLOYD
LOAMY
LOATH
LOBAR
LOBBY
LOBED
LOCAL
LOCKE
LOCKS
LOCUM
LOCUS
LODEN
LODGE
LOESS
LOFTY
LOGAN
LOGIC
LOGOS
LOINS
LOIRE
LOLLY
LOMAN
LONER
LONGS
LOOBY
LOOFA
LOONS
LOONY
LOOPY
LOOSE
LORCA
LORDS
LORIS
LORNA
LORNE
LORRY
LOSER
LOTOS
LOTTO
LOTUS
LOUGH
LOUIE
LOUIS
LOUPE
LOUSE
LOUSY
LOUTH
LOVAT
LOVER
LOWAN
LOWER
LOWLY
LOWRY
LOYAL
LOZEN
LUBRA
LUCAN
LUCIA
LUCID
LUCIO
LUCKY
LUCRE
LUDIC
LUFFA
LUGER
LULLY
LUMEN
LUMME
LUMMY
LUMPY
LUNAR
LUNCH
LUNDY
LUNED
LUNGE
LUNGI
LUNGS
LUPIN
LUPUS

LURCH
LURGY
LURID
LUSHY
LUSTY
LUTIN
LUTON
LUZON
LYCÉE
LYCRA
LYDIA
LYING
LYMPH
LYNCH
LYRIC
LYSIN
LYSIS
LYSOL
LYTHE
MACAW
MACER
MACHO
MACLE
MACON
MACRO
MADAM
MADGE
MADLY
MAEVE
MAFIA
MAGIC
MAGMA
MAGNA
MAGOG
MAGUS
MAHDI
MAHOE
MAHUA
MAHWA
MAIKO
MAILE
MAINE
MAINS
MAIRE
MAIZE
MAJOR
MAKAR
MAKER
MALAR
MALAY
MALFI
MALIK
MALMO
MALTA
MAMBA
MAMBO
MAMMA
MAMMY
MANCH
MANED
MANES
MANET
MANGE
MANGO
MANGY
MANIA
MANIC
MANLY
MANNA
MANOR
MANSE
MANTA
MANUL
MANUS
MAORI
MAPLE
MARAT
MARCH
MARCO
MARDI
MARGE
MARIA
MARIE
MARLE
MARLY
MARNE
MAROT
MARRY
MARSH
MASAI
MASER
MASHY
MASON
MASSA
MASSE
MASUS
MATCH
MATER
MATES
MATEY
MATHS
MATIN
MATLO
MAUND
MAUVE
MAVIN
MAVIS
MAXIM
MAYBE
MAYOR
MAZER
MCCOY
MEALS
MEALY
MEANS
MEANT
MEATH
MEATS
MEATY
MEBBE
MECCA
MEDAL
MEDEA
MEDIA
MEDIC
MEDOC
MEETS
MEITH
MELBA
MELEE
MELIA
MELIC
MELON
MELOS
MENAI
MENGE
MENSA
MERAK
MERCY
MERGE
MERIL
MERIT
MERLE
MERRY
MESIC
MESNE
MESON
MESSY
MESTO
METAL
METER
METHS
METIC
METIF
METIS
METOL
METRE
METRO
MEUSE
MEYER
MEZZE
MEZZO
MIAMI
MIAOU
MIAOW
MIAUL
MICAH
MICHE
MICRO
MIDAS
MIDDY
MIDGE
MIDST
MIFFY
MIGHT
MILAN
MILCH
MILER
MILES
MILKY
MILLI
MILLS
MILNE
MIMER
MIMIC
MIMUS
MINCE
MINCH
MINER
MINGY
MINHO
MINIM
MINKE
MINOR
MINOS
MINOT
MINSK
MINUS
MIRTH
MIRZA
MISER
MISSA
MISSY
MISTY
MITES
MITRE
MIXED
MIXER
MIXTE
MIXUP
MOCHA
MODAL
MODEL
MODEM
MODER
MODUS
MOGGY
MOGUL
MOIRA
MOIRE
MOIST
MOLAR
MOLLY
MOLTO
MOMMA
MOMMY
MONAD
MONAL
MONDO
MONET
MONEY
MONKS
MONTE
MONTH
MONZA
MOOCH
MOODY
MOOLI
MOONY
MOORE
MOOSE
MOPED
MOPER
MOPSY
MORAL
MORAN
MORAT
MORAY
MOREL
MORES
MORIA
MORIN
MORNE
MORON
MORPH
MORSE
MORUS
MOSES
MOSEY
MOSSY
MOTEL
MOTET
MOTHS
MOTIF
MOTOR
MOTTE
MOTTO
MOUCH
MOULD
MOULS
MOULT
MOUND
MOUNT
MOURN
MOUSE
MOUSY
MOUTH
MOVED
MOVER
MOVIE
MOWER
MOYLE
MUCID
MUCIN
MUCKY
MUCRO
MUCUS
MUDDY
MUDGE
MUFTI
MUGGY
MULCH
MULCT
MULLA
MULSE
MULTI
MUMMY
MUMPS
MUNCH
MUNDA
MUNGO
MUNRO
MURAL
MUREX
MURKY
MURRE
MURRY
MUSCA
MUSCI
MUSES
MUSHA
MUSHY
MUSIC
MUSIT
MUSKY
MUSSE
MUSSY
MUSTY
MUTED
MUZAK
MUZZY
MVULE
MYNAH
MYOMA
MYRON
MYRRH
NAAFI
NABOB
NACHE
NACHO
NACHT
NACRE
NADER
NADIR
NAGAS
NAGOR
NAHUM
NAIAD
NAILS
NAIRA
NAIVE
NAKED
NAMED
NAMES
NAMIB
NANCE
NANCY
NANDI
NANDU
NANNA
NANNY
NANTZ
NAPPA
NAPPE
NAPPY
NARES
NARKS
NARKY
NASAL
NASHE
NASTY
NATAL
NATCH
NATES
NATTY
NATUS
NAURU
NAVAL
NAVEL
NAVEW
NAVVY
NAWAB
NAXOS
NAZIR
NEAGH
NEALE
NEBEL
NEDDY
NEEDS
NEEDY
NEGEV
NEGRO
NEGUS
NEHRU
NEIGH
NELLY
NEPAL
NERVA
NERVE
NERVI
NERVO
NERVY
NESSA
NESTA
NEVEL
NEVER
NEVIS
NEWEL
NEWLY
NEWSY
NEWTS
NEXUS
NGAIO
NICAD
NICHE
NICOL
NIDOR
NIDUS
NIECE
NIEVE
NIFTY
NIGEL
NIGER
NIGHT
NIHIL
NINJA
NINNY
NINON
NINTH
NIOBE
NIPPY
NISUS
NITID
NITON
NITRE
NIVAL
NIXON
NIZAM
NOBBY
NOBEL
NOBLE
NOBLY
NODAL
NODDY
NODES
NODUS
NOISE
NOISY
NOMAD
NOMEN
NOMIC
NONCE
NONES
NONET
NONNY
NOOKY
NOOSE
NORAH
NORIA
NORMA
NORSE
NORTH
NOSER
NOSEY
NOTAL
NOTCH
NOTED
NOTES
NOTTS
NOTUM
NOVEL
NOVUM
NOXAL
NOYAU
NOYES
NSPCC
NUBIA
NUCHA
NUDGE
NULLA
NUMEN
NUNKY
NURSE
NUTTY
NYALA
NYASA
NYLON
NYMPH
NYSSA
OAKEN
OAKER
OAKUM
OASIS
OATEN
OATES
OBEAH
OBESE
OBIAH

OBIIT
OBOTE
OCCAM
OCCUR
OCEAN
OCHER
OCHRE
OCKER
OCNUS
OCREA
OCTAD
OCTAL
OCTET
ODDER
ODDLY
ODEON
ODETS
ODIUM
ODOUR
OFFAL
OFFAS
OFFER
OFLAG
OFTEN
OGGIN
OGHAM
OGIER
OGIVE
OILED
OILER
OKAPI
OLDEN
OLDER
OLDIE
OLEIC
OLEIN
OLEUM
OLIVE
OLLIE
OMAGH
OMANI
OMBER
OMBRE
OMEGA
ONCER
ONCUS
ONION
ONKUS
ONSET
OOMPH
OPERA
OPHIR
OPINE
OPIUM
OPTIC
ORANG
ORATE
ORBIT
ORCUS
ORDER
ORFEO
ORGAN
ORGUE
ORIEL
ORION
ORLON
ORLOP
ORMER
ORMUZ
ORNIS
ORPEN
ORRIS
ORTHO
ORTON
ORTUS
ORVAL
OSAGE
OSAKA
OSCAR
OSIER
OSMAN
OSSIA
OSTIA
OTARY
OTHER
OTIUM
OTTAR
OTTER
OTWAY
OUGHT
OUIDA
OUIJA
OUNCE
OUSEL
OUTBY
OUTDO
OUTER
OUTGO
OUTRE
OUZEL
OVARY
OVATE
OVERT
OVINE
OVOID
OVULE
OWING
OWLER
OWLET
OWNER
OXBOW
OXEYE
OXIDE
OXIME
OXTER
OZARK
OZONE
PABLO
PACER
PACEY
PACHA
PADDY
PADMA
PADRE
PAEAN
PAGAN
PAGER
PAGES
PAINE
PAINS
PAINT
PAIRE
PAIRS
PAISA
PALEA
PALES
PALET
PALIO
PALLY
PALMY
PALSY
PAMIR
PANDA
PANDY
PANEL
PANGA
PANIC
PANNE
PANSY
PANTO
PANTS
PANTY
PAOLO
PAPAL
PAPAW
PAPER
PARCH
PARDY
PAREO
PAREU
PARIS
PARKA
PARKY
PARMA
PARRY
PARSE
PARSI
PARTI
PARTS
PARTY
PARVO
PASCH
PASEO
PASHA
PASSE
PASTA
PASTE
PASTY
PATCH
PATER
PATIO
PATNA
PATSY
PATTI
PATTY
PAUSE
PAVID
PAWKY
PAYEE
PAYER
PEACE
PEACH
PEAKY
PEARL
PEASE
PEATY
PECAN
PEDAL
PEDRO
PEERS
PEEVE
PEGGY
PEKAN
PEKIN
PEKOE
PELEE
PELLA
PELMA
PENAL
PENCE
PENIS
PENNA
PENNE
PENNY
PEONY
PEPPY
PEPSI
PEPYS
PERAI
PERCE
PERCH
PERCY
PERDU
PERIL
PERKS
PERKY
PERON
PERRY
PERSE
PESKY
PESTO
PETAL
PETER
PETIT
PETRA
PETRE
PETRI
PETTO
PETTY
PHARE
PHASE
PHEBE
PHENO
PHEON
PHIAL
PHILE
PHLOX
PHNOM
PHOBE
PHONE
PHONY
PHOTO
PHYLE
PIANO
PIAVE
PICEA
PICOT
PICUS
PIECE
PIERS
PIERT
PIETA
PIETY
PIEZO
PIGGY
PIGMY
PILAF
PILAU
PILCH
PILED
PILES
PILLS
PILOT
PILUM
PILUS
PINCH
PINES
PINGO
PINKO
PINKY
PINNA
PINNY
PINON
PINOT
PINTA
PINTO
PIOUS
PIPER
PIPIT
PIPPA
PIPUL
PIQUE
PIROG
PISKY
PISTE
PITCH
PITHY
PITON
PITOT
PITTA
PIVOT
PIXEL
PIXIE
PIZZA
PLACE
PLACK
PLAID
PLAIN
PLAIT
PLANE
PLANK
PLANT
PLATE
PLATH
PLATO
PLATY
PLATZ
PLAYA
PLAZA
PLEAD
PLEAT
PLEBS
PLEIN
PLICA
PLIER
PLINY
PLONK
PLOTS
PLUCK
PLUMB
PLUME
PLUMP
PLUNK
PLUSH
PLUTO
POACH
PODEX
PODGE
PODGY
POEMS
POESY
POETS
POILU
POINT
POISE
POKER
POKEY
POLAR
POLIO
POLKA
POLLY
POLYP
POMMY
PONCE
PONDS
PONEY
PONGA
PONGO
PONTY
POOCH
POOLS
POPES
POPOV
POPPA
POPPY
POPSY
POPUP
PORCH
PORGY
PORKY
PORNO
PORTA
PORTE
PORTO
PORTS
POSED
POSER
POSIT
POSSE
POSTE
POTIN
POTOO
POTTO
POTTY
POUCH
POULE
POULT
POUND
POUPE
POWAN
POWER
POWYS
PRADO
PRAHU
PRANA
PRANG
PRANK
PRATE
PRAWL
PRAWN
PREEN
PRESA
PRESS
PREST
PRIAL
PRIAM
PRICE
PRICK
PRIDE
PRILL
PRIMA
PRIME
PRIMO
PRIMP
PRINT
PRION
PRIOR
PRISE
PRISM
PRIVY
PRIZE
PROBE
PROKE
PROLE
PROMO
PRONE
PRONG
PROOF
PROSE
PROSY
PROUD
PROUT
PROVE
PROVO
PROWL
PROXY
PRUDE
PRUNE
PSALM
PSEUD
PSHAW
PSOAS
PSORA
PSYCH
PUBIC
PUBIS
PUDGE
PUDGY
PUDOR
PUFFY
PUGIN
PUKKA
PULEX
PULPY
PULSE
PUNCH
PUNIC
PUNTO
PUPAL
PUPIL
PUPPY
PUREE
PURGE
PURIM
PURSE
PURSY
PUSHY
PUSLE
PUSSY
PUTID
PUTTO
PUTTY
PYGMY
PYLON
PYREX
PYRUS
PYXIS
PZAZZ
QAJAR
QATAR
QUACK
QUADS
QUAFF
QUAIL
QUAKE
QUALM
QUANT
QUARK

QUART
QUASH
QUASI
QUEEN
QUEER
QUELL
QUERN
QUERY
QUEST
QUEUE
QUICK
QUIDS
QUIET
QUIFF
QUILL
QUILP
QUILT
QUINS
QUINT
QUIRE
QUIRK
QUITE
QUITO
QUITS
QUOIF
QUOIN
QUOIT
QUORN
QUOTA
QUOTE
QUOTH
QURAN
RABAT
RABBI
RABID
RACER
RACES
RADAR
RADHA
RADIO
RADIX
RADON
RAGED
RAGGY
RAHAB
RAINE
RAINY
RAISE
RAJAH
RAKED
RAKEE
RAKER
RAKES
RALLY
RALPH
RAMAN
RAMBO
RAMUS
RANCE
RANCH
RANDY
RANEE
RANGE
RANGY
RANKE
RANKS
RAPID
RAREE
RATCH
RATES
RATIO
RATTY
RAVEL
RAVEN
RAVER
RAYED
RAYLE
RAYON
RAZOR
REACH
REACT
READE
READY
REALM
REAMS
REARM
REBEL
REBUS
REBUT
RECAP
RECCE
RECTO
RECUR
REDAN
REDON
REDOX
REECH
REEDE
REEDS
REEDY
REEVE
REFER
REFIT
REGAL
REGAN
REGIA
RÉGIE
REGIS
RÈGLE
REICH
REIGN
REINS
REIST
REITH
REJIG
RELAX
RELAY
RELIC
REMIT
REMUE
REMUS
RENAL
RENAN
RENEW
RENTE
REPAY
REPEL
REPLY
REPOT
REPRO
RERUN
RESET
RESIN
RESIT
RESTS
RETCH
RETRO
REVEL
REVET
REVIE
REVUE
REYES
RHEIN
RHETT
RHEUM
RHINE
RHINO
RHODO
RHOMB
RHONE
RHUMB
RHYME
RIANT
RICAN
RICIN
RIDER
RIDGE
RIFLE
RIGHT
RIGID
RIGOR
RILEY
RILKE
RILLE
RINSE
RIOJA
RIOTS
RIPEN
RIPER
RIPON
RISEN
RISER
RISKY
RISUS
RITES
RITZY
RIVAL
RIVEN
RIVER
RIVET
RIYAL
ROACH
ROAST
ROBES
ROBEY
ROBIN
ROBOT
ROCKS
ROCKY
RODEO
RODIN
ROGER
ROGET
ROGUE
ROHAN
ROIST
ROKER
ROLFE
ROLLO
ROLLS
ROMAN
ROMEO
ROMER
RONDE
RONDO
RONEO
RONNE
ROOKY
ROOMS
ROOMY
ROOPY
ROOST
ROOTS
ROOTY
ROPED
ROPER
ROPES
ROPEY
ROQUE
RORIC
RORKE
RORTY
ROSCO
ROSES
ROSET
ROSIN
ROSIT
ROSSE
ROSSI
ROTOR
ROUEN
ROUGE
ROUGH
ROULE
ROUND
ROUSE
ROUST
ROUTE
ROVER
ROWAN
ROWDY
ROWEL
ROWER
ROYAL
ROZET
RSPCA
RUBIN
RUBLE
RUCHE
RUDDY
RUDGE
RUFUS
RUGBY
RUING
RUINS
RULER
RULES
RUMBA
RUMEN
RUMEX
RUMMY
RUMOR
RUMPY
RUNCH
RUNES
RUNIC
RUNNY
RUNUP
RUPEE
RUPIA
RURAL
RUSHY
RUSSE
RUSSO
RUSTY
RYDAL
SABAL
SABER
SABIN
SABLE
SABOT
SABRA
SABRE
SACHA
SACHS
SACKS
SADHU
SADIE
SADLY
SAGES
SAGGY
SAHEL
SAHIB
SAICE
SAILS
SAINE
SAINT
SAKER
SALAD
SALEM
SALEP
SALES
SALIC
SALIX
SALLE
SALLY
SALMI
SALON
SALSA
SALSE
SALTS
SALTY
SALVE
SALVO
SAMBA
SAMBO
SAMFU
SAMMY
SAMOA
SAMOS
SAMSO
SANDS
SANDY
SANTA
SANTO
SAPID
SAPOR
SAPPY
SARAH
SARAN
SARGE
SARIN
SARKY
SAROS
SARUS
SASHA
SASSE
SASSY
SATAN
SATAY
SATED
SATIE
SATIN
SATIS
SATYR
SAUCE
SAUCH
SAUCY
SAUDI
SAUGH
SAULT
SAUNA
SAUTE
SAVER
SAVOR
SAVOY
SAVVY
SAXON
SAYER
SAYSO
SCADS
SCAFF
SCALA
SCALD
SCALE
SCALP
SCALY
SCAMP
SCANT
SCAPA
SCAPE
SCARE
SCARF
SCARP
SCARY
SCATH
SCAUP
SCAUR
SCENE
SCENT
SCHWA
SCIFI
SCION
SCLIM
SCOFF
SCOLD
SCONE
SCOOP
SCOOT
SCOPE
SCOPS
SCORE
SCORN
SCOTS
SCOTT
SCOUP
SCOUR
SCOUT
SCOWL
SCOWP
SCRAB
SCRAG
SCRAM
SCRAP
SCRAT
SCRAW
SCRAY
SCREE
SCREW
SCRIM
SCRIP
SCROD
SCROG
SCROW
SCRUB
SCRUM
SCUBA
SCUFF
SCULL
SCULP
SCURF
SEALS
SEAMY
SEARE
SECCO
SEDAN
SEDGE
SEDUM
SEEDY
SEGUE
SEINE
SEISM
SEIZE
SELIM
SELLE
SELVA
SEMEN
SEMIS
SENNA
SENOR
SENSE
SENZA
SEOUL
SEPAL
SEPIA
SEPOY
SERAI
SERGE
SERIF
SERIN
SERRA
SERRE
SERUM
SERVE
SERVO
SETUP
SEVEN
SEVER
SEWER
SHACK
SHADE
SHADY
SHAFT
SHAKE
SHAKO
SHAKY
SHALE
SHALL
SHALT
SHAME
SHANG
SHANK
SHANT
SHAPE
SHARD
SHARE
SHARK
SHARP
SHAUN
SHAVE
SHAWL
SHAWM
SHCHI
SHEAF
SHEAR
SHEBA
SHEEL
SHEEN

SHEEP
SHEER
SHEET
SHEIK
SHELF
SHELL
SHERD
SHERE
SHIEL
SHIFT
SHILL
SHINE
SHINY
SHIRE
SHIRK
SHIRR
SHIRT
SHITE
SHIVA
SHIVE
SHLEP
SHOAL
SHOCK
SHOJI
SHOLA
SHONA
SHONE
SHOOK
SHOOT
SHOPS
SHORE
SHORN
SHORT
SHOTS
SHOUT
SHOVE
SHOWN
SHOWY
SHRED
SHREW
SHROW
SHRUB
SHRUG
SHUCK
SHUNT
SHUSH
SHUTE
SHUTS
SHYLY
SIBYL
SIDHA
SIDLE
SIDON
SIEGE
SIEVE
SIGHS
SIGHT
SIGIL
SIGLA
SIGMA
SIGNS
SILAS
SILEX
SILKY
SILLY
SILVA
SIMBA
SIMON
SINAI
SINCE
SINEW
SINGE
SINUS
SIREN
SISAL
SISSY
SITAR
SITIN
SITKA
SITTA
SITUP
SIXER
SIXTH
SIXTY
SIZAR
SKATE
SKEAN
SKEER
SKEET
SKEIN
SKELM
SKELP
SKIER
SKIFF
SKILL
SKIMP
SKINK
SKINS
SKINT
SKIRL
SKIRR
SKIRT
SKIVE
SKOAL
SKRIM
SKULK
SKULL
SKUNK
SLACK
SLADE
SLAIN
SLAKE
SLANG
SLANT
SLASH
SLATE
SLATS
SLATY
SLAVE
SLEEK
SLEEP
SLEET
SLEPT
SLICE
SLICK
SLIDE
SLIGO
SLIME
SLIMY
SLING
SLINK
SLIPE
SLIPS
SLOAN
SLOOP
SLOPE
SLOPS
SLOSH
SLOTH
SLUGS
SLUMP
SLUNG
SLUNK
SLURB
SLURP
SLUSH
SLYLY
SLYPE
SMACK
SMALL
SMARM
SMART
SMASH
SMEAR
SMEEK
SMELL
SMELT
SMILE
SMIRK
SMITE
SMITH
SMOCK
SMOKE
SMOKY
SMOLT
SMOTE
SMUTS
SNACK
SNAFU
SNAGS
SNAIL
SNAKE
SNAKY
SNAPS
SNARE
SNARK
SNARL
SNASH
SNEAD
SNEAK
SNECK
SNEER
SNICK
SNIDE
SNIFF
SNIFT
SNIPE
SNOBS
SNOEK
SNOOD
SNOOK
SNOOP
SNOOT
SNORE
SNORT
SNOUT
SNOWY
SNUFF
SOANE
SOAPY
SOARE
SOBER
SOCKS
SOCLE
SODOM
SODOR
SOFIA
SOFTY
SOGGY
SOKEN
SOKOL
SOLAN
SOLAR
SOLDE
SOLFA
SOLID
SOLON
SOLTI
SOLUM
SOLUS
SOLVE
SOMME
SONAR
SONDE
SONIC
SONNY
SOOTH
SOOTY
SOPHY
SOPPY
SOPRA
SORBO
SORDO
SORES
SOREX
SORRY
SORTS
SOTTO
SOUGH
SOULS
SOUND
SOUSA
SOUSE
SOUTH
SOWER
SOWLE
SOWND
SOWTH
SOYUZ
SPACE
SPADE
SPADO
SPAHI
SPAIN
SPALD
SPALL
SPALT
SPANK
SPARE
SPARK
SPART
SPASM
SPATE
SPATS
SPAWN
SPEAK
SPEAN
SPEAR
SPECK
SPECS
SPEED
SPEER
SPEKE
SPELL
SPELT
SPEND
SPENS
SPENT
SPERM
SPICA
SPICE
SPICK
SPICY
SPIED
SPIEL
SPIES
SPIFF
SPIKE
SPIKY
SPILE
SPILL
SPILT
SPINA
SPINE
SPINY
SPIRE
SPITE
SPITZ
SPLAT
SPLAY
SPLIT
SPODE
SPOHR
SPOIL
SPOKE
SPOOF
SPOOK
SPOOL
SPOON
SPOOR
SPORE
SPORT
SPOTS
SPOUT
SPRAG
SPRAT
SPRAY
SPREE
SPRIG
SPRIT
SPROD
SPROG
SPRUE
SPUME
SPUNK
SPURN
SPURS
SPURT
SQUAB
SQUAD
SQUAT
SQUAW
SQUIB
SQUID
SQUIT
STACK
STADE
STAFF
STAGE
STAGY
STAID
STAIN
STAIR
STAKE
STALE
STALK
STALL
STAMP
STAND
STANK
STAPH
STARE
STARK
STARR
STARS
START
STASH
STASI
STATE
STAVE
STAYS
STEAD
STEAK
STEAL
STEAM
STEED
STEEK
STEEL
STEEN
STEEP
STEER
STEIN
STELA
STELE
STENT
STEPS
STERN
STEVE
STEWS
STEWY
STICK
STIFF
STILE
STILL
STILT
STIME
STIMY
STING
STINK
STINT
STIRP
STOAT
STOCK
STOEP
STOGA
STOGY
STOIC
STOKE
STOLA
STOLE
STOLL
STOMA
STOMP
STONE
STONY
STOOD
STOOK
STOOL
STOOP
STOOR
STOPE
STORE
STORK
STORM
STORY
STOUP
STOUR
STOUT
STOVE
STOWE
STRAD
STRAP
STRAW
STRAY
STREP
STREW
STRIA
STRIP
STROP
STRUM
STRUT
STUCK
STUDY
STUFF
STUKA
STUMP
STUNG
STUNK
STUNT
STUPA
STUPE
STURT
STYLE
STYLO
STYME
SUAVE
SUCKS
SUCRE
SUDAN
SUDOR
SUEDE
SUETY
SUGAN
SUGAR
SUITE
SUITS
SULFA
SULKS
SULKY
SULLA
SULLY
SUMMA
SUNDA
SUNNY
SUOMI
SUPER
SUPPE
SUPRA
SURGE
SURLY
SURYA
SUSAN
SUSHI
SUTCH
SUTOR
SUTRA
SUVLA
SUZIE
SWAIN
SWALE
SWAMI
SWAMP
SWANK
SWANS
SWARD
SWARF
SWARM
SWASH

SWATH
SWATS
SWAZI
SWEAR
SWEAT
SWEDE
SWEEP
SWEET
SWELL
SWELT
SWEPT
SWIFT
SWILL
SWINE
SWING
SWIPE
SWIRE
SWIRL
SWISH
SWISS
SWIZZ
SWOON
SWOOP
SWORD
SWORE
SWORN
SWUNG
SYBIL
SYCEE
SYLPH
SYNGE
SYNOD
SYRAH
SYRIA
SYRUP
TABBY
TABER
TABES
TABLA
TABLE
TABOO
TABOR
TACIT
TACKY
TAFFY
TAGUS
TAIGA
TAILS
TAINE
TAINO
TAINT
TAKEN
TAKER
TALAQ
TALAR
TALEA
TALES
TALKS
TALLY
TALMA
TALON
TALUS
TAMAR
TAMER
TAMIL
TAMIS
TAMMY
TAMPA
TANGA
TANGO
TANGY
TANKA
TANSY
TAPAS
TAPER
TAPET
TAPIR
TAPIS
TARDY
TARGE
TAROT
TARRY
TARTY
TASSE
TASSO
TASTE
TASTY
TATAR
TATER
TATIN
TATRA
TATTY
TAUBE
TAUNT
TAUPE
TAVAH
TAWNY
TAWSE
TAXED
TAXIN
TAXIS
TAXOL
TAXON
TAXUS
TAZZA
TEACH
TEARS
TEASE
TEAZE
TEDDY
TEENS
TEENY
TEETH
TEHEE
TEIGN
TELEX
TELIC
TELLY
TELOS
TEMPE
TEMPO
TEMPT
TENCH
TENDS
TENET
TENON
TENOR
TENSE
TENTH
TENUE
TEPEE
TEPID
TERCE
TEREK
TERES
TERMS
TERNE
TERRA
TERRY
TERSE
TESSA
TESTA
TESTS
TESTY
TETRA
TEXAN
TEXAS
TEXEL
TEXTS
THAIS
THANE
THANK
THECA
THEFT
THEGN
THEIR
THEMA
THEME
THERE
THERM
THESE
THETA
THETE
THEWS
THICK
THIEF
THIGH
THILL
THINE
THING
THINK
THIRD
THIRL
THOFT
THOLE
THONG
THORN
THOSE
THREE
THREW
THRID
THRIP
THROB
THROE
THROW
THRUM
THUGS
THULE
THUMB
THUMP
THUYA
THYME
TIARA
TIBBS
TIBBY
TIBER
TIBET
TIBIA
TIDAL
TIDDY
TIGER
TIGHT
TIGON
TIKKA
TILDE
TILED
TILER
TILES
TILIA
TILTH
TIMER
TIMES
TIMID
TIMON
TIMOR
TINEA
TINGE
TINNY
TIPPY
TIPSY
TIRED
TIREE
TIROS
TITAN
TITCH
TITHE
TITLE
TITRE
TITTY
TITUS
TIZZY
TOADY
TOAST
TOBIT
TODAY
TODDY
TOILE
TOILS
TOISE
TOKAY
TOKEN
TOKYO
TOLAR
TOMMY
TONAL
TONDO
TONER
TONGA
TONGS
TONIC
TONNE
TONUS
TOOLS
TOOTH
TOPAZ
TOPEE
TOPER
TOPIC
TOPSY
TOQUE
TORAH
TORCH
TORII
TORSO
TORTE
TORUS
TOSCA
TOTAL
TOTEM
TOTTY
TOUCH
TOUGH
TOWEL
TOWER
TOWNS
TOWSE
TOWZE
TOXIC
TOXIN
TRACE
TRACK
TRACT
TRADE
TRAIL
TRAIN
TRAIT
TRAMP
TRANS
TRANT
TRAPS
TRASH
TRAWL
TREAD
TREAT
TRECK
TREEN
TREES
TREMA
TREND
TRENT
TRESS
TREVI
TREWS
TRIAD
TRIAL
TRIBE
TRICE
TRICK
TRIED
TRIER
TRIES
TRIKE
TRILL
TRIPE
TRITE
TROIC
TROLL
TROMP
TROON
TROOP
TROPE
TROTH
TROTS
TROUT
TROVE
TRUCE
TRUCK
TRULL
TRULY
TRUMP
TRUNK
TRURO
TRUSS
TRUST
TRUTH
TRYST
TSUBA
TSUGA
TUBBY
TUBER
TUDOR
TUFFE
TULIP
TULLE
TULLY
TUMID
TUMMY
TUMOR
TUNER
TUNIC
TUNIS
TUNKU
TUNNY
TUQUE
TURBO
TURCO
TURIN
TURKI
TURKU
TURPS
TUTOR
TUTSI
TUTTI
TWAIN
TWANG
TWANK
TWEAK
TWEED
TWEET
TWERP
TWICE
TWIGS
TWILL
TWILT
TWINE
TWINS
TWIRL
TWIRP
TWIST
TWIXT
TWOER
TYING
TYLER
TYNED
TYPED
TYPES
TYPHA
TYROL
UDALL
UDDER
UGRIC
UHLAN
UHURU
UKASE
ULCER
ULEMA
ULNAR
ULTRA
UMBEL
UMBER
UMBLE
UMBRA
UMPTY
UNAPT
UNARM
UNBAR
UNBED
UNCAP
UNCLE
UNCUS
UNCUT
UNDAM
UNDER
UNDID
UNDUE
UNFED
UNFIT
UNGET
UNIAT
UNIFY
UNION
UNITA
UNITE
UNITS
UNITY
UNLAW
UNLAY
UNLIT
UNMAN
UNMIX
UNPEN
UNPIN
UNRIG
UNRIP
UNSAY
UNTIE
UNTIL
UNWED
UNZIP
UPEND
UPPER
UPSET
UPSEY
UPTON
URALS
URATE
URBAN
UREDO
URIAH
URINE
URITE
URSON
USAGE
USHER
USING
USTED
USUAL
USURE
USURP
USURY
UTHER
UTTER
UTURN
UVULA
UZBEK
VADUZ
VAGUE
VAGUS
VAILS
VALET
VALID
VALOR
VALSE
VALUE
VALVE
VANCE
VANDA
VANYA
VAPID
VAPOR
VAREC
VARIX
VARUS
VAULT
VAUNT
VEDDA
VEDIC
VEGAN

VEINS
VELAR
VELDT
VELUM
VENAL
VENDA
VENIN
VENOM
VENUE
VENUS
VERDI
VEREY
VERGE
VERNE
VERSA
VERSE
VERSO
VERST
VERTU
VERVE
VESPA
VESTA
VETCH
VEXED
VIAND
VIBES
VICAR
VICHY
VIDEO
VIGIL
VIGOR
VILLA
VILLI
VINYL
VIOLA
VIPER
VIRAL
VIREO
VIRGA
VIRGO
VIRID
VIRTU
VIRUS
VISBY
VISIT
VISON
VISOR
VISTA
VITAE
VITAL
VITIS
VITUS
VIVAT
VIVID
VIXEN
VIZOR
VLACH
VNECK
VOCAL
VODKA
VOGUE
VOICE
VOILA
VOILE
VOLET
VOLGA
VOLTA
VOLTE
VOLVA
VOLVO
VOMER
VOMIT
VOTER
VOTES
VOUCH
VOWEL
VOZHD
VROOM
VULGO
VULVA
WACKY
WADER
WAFER
WAGER
WAGES
WAGGA
WAGON
WAIST
WAITS
WAIVE
WAKEN
WAKES
WALDO
WALER
WALES
WALLY
WALTZ
WANED
WANLY
WARES
WARTY
WASHY
WASNT
WASTE
WATCH
WATER
WATTS
WAUGH
WAVED
WAVER
WAVES
WAXEN
WEALD
WEARY
WEAVE
WEBER
WEDGE
WEEDS
WEEDY
WEEKS
WEENY
WEEPY
WEIGH
WEILL
WEIRD
WELCH
WELLS
WELLY
WELSH
WENCH
WENDY
WESER
WHACK
WHALE
WHANG
WHARF
WHAUP
WHAUR
WHEAL
WHEAT
WHEEL
WHEEN
WHELK
WHELP
WHERE
WHICH
WHIFF
WHIFT
WHILE
WHIMS
WHINE
WHIPS
WHIRL
WHIRR
WHISH
WHISK
WHIST
WHITE
WHIZZ
WHOLE
WHOOP
WHOOT
WHORE
WHORL
WHOSE
WIDEN
WIDOW
WIDTH
WIELD
WIGAN
WIGHT
WILDE
WILDS
WILES
WILGA
WILLY
WILTS
WIMPY
WINCE
WINCH
WINDY
WINEY
WINGS
WIPER
WIRED
WIRES
WISPY
WITAN
WITCH
WITHE
WITHY
WITTY
WIVES
WODEN
WODGE
WOKEN
WOMAN
WOMEN
WONGA
WONKY
WOODS
WOODY
WOOER
WOOFY
WOOLF
WOOZY
WORCS
WORDS
WORDY
WORKS
WORLD
WORMS
WORMY
WORRY
WORSE
WORST
WORTH
WOULD
WOUND
WOVEN
WRACK
WRATH
WREAK
WRECK
WREST
WRING
WRIST
WRITE
WRITS
WRONG
WROTE
WROTH
WRUNG
WRYLY
WURST
WYMAN
XEBEC
XENIA
XENON
XERES
XEROX
XHOSA
XYLEM
XYRIS
YACHT
YAHOO
YAHVE
YAKKA
YAKUT
YALTA
YAMEN
YARFA
YARNS
YARRA
YARTA
YATES
YCLAD
YEARN
YEARS
YEAST
YEATS
YEMEN
YERBA
YEZDI
YIELD
YIKES
YIPPY
YOBBO
YODEL
YOICK
YOKEL
YONKS
YONNE
YOULL
YOUNG
YOURS
YOURT
YOUTH
YOUVE
YPRES
YUCCA
YUCKY
YUKKY
YUKON
YULAN
YUMMY
YUPIK
YUPPY
ZABRA
ZADOK
ZAIRE
ZAKAT
ZAMBO
ZANTE
ZEBRA
ZENOS
ZEPPO
ZERDA
ZIGAN
ZILCH
ZINCO
ZINEB
ZIPPY
ZLOTY
ZOHAR
ZOMBI
ZONAL
ZORBA
ZORRO

5:2

AARON
BABAR
BABEL
BABOO
BABUL
BACCY
BACKS
BACON
BADDY
BADEN
BADGE
BADLY
BAFFY
BAGEL
BAGGY
BAHAI
BAHUT
BAIRD
BAIRN
BAIZE
BAJRI
BAKED
BAKER
BAKHA
BALAN
BALER
BALFE
BALLS
BALLY
BALMY
BALOO
BALOR
BALSA
BAMBI
BANAL
BANCO
BANDA
BANDS
BANDY
BANJO
BANKS
BANNS
BANTU
BARGE
BARMY
BARON
BARRA
BARRE
BARRY
BARTS
BASAL
BASAN
BASES
BASHO
BASIC
BASIL
BASIN
BASIS
BASLE
BASRA
BASSO
BASTA
BASTE
BASTO
BATCH
BATED
BATES
BATHE
BATHS
BATIK
BATON
BATTY
BAULK
BAWDY
BAYER
BAYLE
BAYOU
BAZOO
CABAL
CABAS
CABBY
CABER
CABIN
CABLE
CABOB
CABOT
CACAO
CACHE
CADDY
CADET
CADGE
CADGY
CADRE
CAGEY
CAGOT
CAINE
CAIRN
CAIRO
CAIUS
CAJUN
CALEB
CALIX
CALOR
CALPE
CALVE
CALYX
CAMEL
CAMEO
CAMIS
CAMPO
CAMUS
CANAL
CANDY
CANES
CANNA
CANNY
CANOE
CANON
CANTO
CAPER
CAPET
CAPON
CAPOT
CAPRI
CAPUT
CARAT
CARDS
CARER
CARET
CAREW
CAREY
CARGO
CARIB
CARLE
CAROB
CAROL
CARRY
CARTA
CARTE
CARVE
CARVY
CASCA
CASCO
CASES
CASTE
CATCH
CATER
CATES
CATTY
CAULD
CAULK
CAUSE
CAVAN
CAVIL
DACCA
DACHA
DADDY
DAFFY
DAGON
DAILY
DAIRY
DAISY
DAKAR
DALEK
DALLE
DALLY
DAMAN
DAMME
DAMON
DANAE
DANCE
DANDO
DANDY
DANES
DANTE

DARBY
DARCY
DARTS
DATED
DATER
DATES
DATUK
DATUM
DAUBE
DAUNT
DAVID
DAVIS
DAVIT
DAYAK
DAZED
EAGER
EAGLE
EARLY
EARTH
EASEL
EATER
EAVES
FABER
FABLE
FABRÉ
FACER
FACET
FACIA
FACTO
FACTS
FADDY
FADED
FADGE
FAERY
FAGOT
FAGUS
FAINS
FAINT
FAIRY
FAITH
FAKER
FAKIR
FALDO
FALLA
FALLS
FALSE
FAMED
FANAL
FANCY
FANNY
FANON
FARAD
FARCE
FARCI
FARCY
FARGO
FARNE
FAROE
FARSE
FATAL
FATED
FATTY
FATWA
FAULT
FAUNA
FAURE
FAUST
FAUVE
FAVOR
FAVUS
GABBY
GABLE
GABON
GADGE
GADUS
GAFFE
GAILY
GAINS
GAIUS
GALAM
GALBA
GALEA
GALEN
GALOP
GAMAY
GAMBA
GAMBO
GAMES
GAMIC
GAMMA
GAMMY
GAMUT
GANJA
GANNY
GAPER
GARBO
GARDA
GARNI
GARTH
GARUM
GASES
GASPÉ
GASSY
GATED
GAUDE
GAUDY
GAUGE
GAULT
GAUNT
GAUSS
GAUZE
GAUZY
GAVEL
GAWKY
GAZON
HABET
HABIT
HACEK
HADES
HADJI
HADNT
HAFIZ
HAGUE
HAIDA
HAIFA
HAIKU
HAIRS
HAIRY
HAITI
HAKKA
HALER
HALFA
HALLÉ
HALLO
HALMA
HALON
HALSE
HALVE
HAMMY
HANAP
HANCE
HANCH
HANDS
HANDY
HANKY
HANOI
HANSE
HAPPY
HARDY
HAREM
HARPO
HARPY
HARRY
HARSH
HARTY
HASNT
HASTA
HASTE
HASTY
HATCH
HATHI
HATTY
HAUGH
HAULM
HAULT
HAUNT
HAUSA
HAUSE
HAUTE
HAVEL
HAVEN
HAVER
HAVOC
HAWSE
HAYDN
HAYLE
HAZEL
JABOT
JACKS
JACOB
JADED
JADIS
JAFFA
JAKES
JALAP
JAMBE
JAMBO
JAMES
JAMMY
JANTY
JANUS
JAPAN
JASEY
JASON
JASPÉ
JAUNT
JAVAN
JAVEL
JAZZY
KAABA
KABOB
KABUL
KAFIR
KAFKA
KALIF
KAMME
KAMPF
KANAK
KANDY
KANJI
KAPOK
KAPPA
KAPUT
KARAT
KARMA
KARNO
KARRI
KARST
KARSY
KASHA
KAURI
KAYAK
LABDA
LABEL
LABIS
LABOR
LACET
LACKS
LADEN
LADLE
LAGAN
LAGER
LAGOS
LAIRD
LAIRY
LAITH
LAITY
LAMED
LAMIA
LAMMY
LAMPS
LANCE
LANDE
LANKA
LANKY
LAPEL
LAPIS
LAPSE
LARCH
LARGE
LARGO
LARKS
LARNE
LARRY
LARVA
LASER
LASKI
LASSA
LASSO
LATCH
LATEN
LATER
LATEX
LATHE
LATHI
LATIN
LAUDS
LAUGH
LAURA
LAVER
LAVRA
LAWKS
LAYBY
LAYER
LAZAR
LAZZO
MACAW
MACER
MACHO
MACLE
MACON
MACRO
MADAM
MADGE
MADLY
MAEVE
MAFIA
MAGIC
MAGMA
MAGNA
MAGOG
MAGUS
MAHDI
MAHOE
MAHUA
MAHWA
MAIKO
MAILE
MAINE
MAINS
MAIRE
MAIZE
MAJOR
MAKAR
MAKER
MALAR
MALAY
MALFI
MALIK
MALMO
MALTA
MAMBA
MAMBO
MAMMA
MAMMY
MANCH
MANED
MANES
MANET
MANGE
MANGO
MANGY
MANIA
MANIC
MANLY
MANNA
MANOR
MANSE
MANTA
MANUL
MANUS
MAORI
MAPLE
MARAT
MARCH
MARCO
MARDI
MARGE
MARIA
MARIE
MARLE
MARLY
MARNE
MAROT
MARRY
MARSH
MASAI
MASER
MASHY
MASON
MASSA
MASSE
MASUS
MATCH
MATER
MATES
MATEY
MATHS
MATIN
MATLO
MAUND
MAUVE
MAVIN
MAVIS
MAXIM
MAYBE
MAYOR
MAZER
NAAFI
NABOB
NACHE
NACHO
NACHT
NACRE
NADER
NADIR
NAGAS
NAGOR
NAHUM
NAIAD
NAILS
NAIRA
NAIVE
NAKED
NAMED
NAMES
NAMIB
NANCE
NANCY
NANDI
NANDU
NANNA
NANNY
NANTZ
NAPPA
NAPPE
NAPPY
NARES
NARKS
NARKY
NASAL
NASHE
NASTY
NATAL
NATCH
NATES
NATTY
NATUS
NAURU
NAVAL
NAVEL
NAVEW
NAVVY
NAWAB
NAXOS
NAZIR
OAKEN
OAKER
OAKUM
OASIS
OATEN
OATES
PABLO
PACER
PACEY
PACHA
PADDY
PADMA
PADRE
PAEAN
PAGAN
PAGER
PAGES
PAINE
PAINS
PAINT
PAIRE
PAIRS
PAISA
PALEA
PALES
PALET
PALIO
PALLY
PALMY
PALSY
PAMIR
PANDA
PANDY
PANEL
PANGA
PANIC
PANNE
PANSY
PANTO
PANTS
PANTY
PAOLO
PAPAL
PAPAW
PAPER
PARCH
PARDY
PAREO
PAREU
PARIS
PARKA
PARKY
PARMA
PARRY
PARSE
PARSI
PARTI
PARTS
PARTY
PARVO
PASCH
PASEO
PASHA
PASSE
PASTA
PASTE
PASTY
PATCH
PATER
PATIO
PATNA
PATSY

PATTI
PATTY
PAUSE
PAVID
PAWKY
PAYEE
PAYER
QAJAR
QATAR
RABAT
RABBI
RABID
RACER
RACES
RADAR
RADHA
RADIO
RADIX
RADON
RAGED
RAGGY
RAHAB
RAINE
RAINY
RAISE
RAJAH
RAKED
RAKEE
RAKER
RAKES
RALLY
RALPH
RAMAN
RAMBO
RAMUS
RANCE
RANCH
RANDY
RANEE
RANGE
RANGY
RANKE
RANKS
RAPID
RAREE
RATCH
RATES
RATIO
RATTY
RAVEL
RAVEN
RAVER
RAYED
RAYLE
RAYON
RAZOR
SABAL
SABER
SABIN
SABLE
SABOT
SABRA
SABRE
SACHA
SACHS
SACKS
SADHU
SADIE
SADLY
SAGES
SAGGY
SAHEL
SAHIB
SAICE
SAILS
SAINE
SAINT
SAKER
SALAD
SALEM
SALEP
SALES
SALIC
SALIX
SALLE
SALLY
SALMI
SALON
SALSA
SALSE
SALTS
SALTY
SALVE
SALVO
SAMBA
SAMBO
SAMFU
SAMMY
SAMOA
SAMOS
SAMSO
SANDS
SANDY
SANTA
SANTO
SAPID
SAPOR
SAPPY
SARAH
SARAN
SARGE
SARIN
SARKY
SAROS
SARUS
SASHA
SASSE
SASSY
SATAN
SATAY
SATED
SATIE
SATIN
SATIS
SATYR
SAUCE
SAUCH
SAUCY
SAUDI
SAUGH
SAULT
SAUNA
SAUTE
SAVER
SAVOR
SAVOY
SAVVY
SAXON
SAYER
SAYSO
TABBY
TABER
TABES
TABLA
TABLE
TABOO
TABOR
TACIT
TACKY
TAFFY
TAGUS
TAIGA
TAILS
TAINE
TAINO
TAINT
TAKEN
TAKER
TALAQ
TALAR
TALEA
TALES
TALKS
TALLY
TALMA
TALON
TALUS
TAMAR
TAMER
TAMIL
TAMIS
TAMMY
TAMPA
TANGA
TANGO
TANGY
TANKA
TANSY
TAPAS
TAPER
TAPET
TAPIR
TAPIS
TARDY
TARGE
TAROT
TARRY
TARTY
TASSE
TASSO
TASTE
TASTY
TATAR
TATER
TATIN
TATRA
TATTY
TAUBE
TAUNT
TAUPE
TAVAH
TAWNY
TAWSE
TAXED
TAXIN
TAXIS
TAXOL
TAXON
TAXUS
TAZZA
VADUZ
VAGUE
VAGUS
VAILS
VALET
VALID
VALOR
VALSE
VALUE
VALVE
VANCE
VANDA
VANYA
VAPID
VAPOR
VAREC
VARIX
VARUS
VAULT
VAUNT
WACKY
WADER
WAFER
WAGER
WAGES
WAGGA
WAGON
WAIST
WAITS
WAIVE
WAKEN
WAKES
WALDO
WALER
WALES
WALLY
WALTZ
WANED
WANLY
WARES
WARTY
WASHY
WASNT
WASTE
WATCH
WATER
WATTS
WAUGH
WAVED
WAVER
WAVES
WAXEN
YACHT
YAHOO
YAHVE
YAKKA
YAKUT
YALTA
YAMEN
YARFA
YARNS
YARRA
YARTA
YATES
ZABRA
ZADOK
ZAIRE
ZAKAT
ZAMBO
ZANTE
ABABA
ABACK
ABACO
ABAFT
ABASE
ABASH
ABATE
ABBAS
ABBEY
ABBOT
ABDAR
ABDUL
ABEAM
ABEAR
ABELE
ABHOR
ABIDE
ABIES
ABLER
ABLOW
ABODE
ABORT
ABOUT
ABOVE
ABRAM
ABRAY
ABRIM
ABSIT
ABUJA
ABUNA
ABUSE
ABYSM
ABYSS
EBOLA
EBONY
IBERT
IBIZA
IBSEN
OBEAH
OBESE
OBIAH
OBIIT
OBOTE
ACCRA
ACERB
ACINI
ACOCK
ACORN
ACRES
ACRID
ACTIN
ACTON
ACTOR
ACUTE
ECLAT
ICENI
ICHOR
ICILY
ICING
ICKER
ICTUS
MCCOY
OCCAM
OCCUR
OCEAN
OCHER
OCHRE
OCKER
OCNUS
OCREA
OCTAD
OCTAL
OCTET
SCADS
SCAFF
SCALA
SCALD
SCALE
SCALP
SCALY
SCAMP
SCANT
SCAPA
SCAPE
SCARE
SCARF
SCARP
SCARY
SCATH
SCAUP
SCAUR
SCENE
SCENT
SCHWA
SCIFI
SCION
SCLIM
SCOFF
SCOLD
SCONE
SCOOP
SCOOT
SCOPE
SCOPS
SCORE
SCORN
SCOTS
SCOTT
SCOUP
SCOUR
SCOUT
SCOWL
SCOWP
SCRAB
SCRAG
SCRAM
SCRAP
SCRAT
SCRAW
SCRAY
SCREE
SCREW
SCRIM
SCRIP
SCROD
SCROG
SCROW
SCRUB
SCRUM
SCUBA
SCUFF
SCULL
SCULP
SCURF
YCLAD
ADAGE
ADAMS
ADAPT
ADDED
ADDER
ADDIO
ADDIS
ADDLE
ADEEM
ADEPT
ADIEU
ADIGE
ADIOS
ADLIB
ADMIN
ADMIT
ADMIX
ADOBE
ADOPT
ADORE
ADORN
ADSUM
ADULT
CDROM
EDEMA
EDGAR
EDGED
EDGER
EDICT
EDIFY
EDILE
EDUCE
EDWIN
IDAHO
IDEAL
IDEAS
IDIOM
IDIOT
IDLER
IDRIS
IDYLL
ODDER
ODDLY
ODEON
ODETS
ODIUM
ODOUR
UDALL
UDDER
AEDES
AEGIS
AESOP
BEACH
BEADS
BEADY
BEALE
BEAMY
BEANO
BEANS
BEARD
BEAST
BEAUT
BEBOP
BECKY
BEDAD
BEDEW
BEECH
BEEFY
BEERY
BEFIT
BEFOG
BEGAD
BEGAN

BEGET
BEGIN
BEGUM
BEGUN
BEHAN
BEIGE
BEING
BEKAA
BELAY
BELCH
BELGA
BELIE
BELLE
BELLS
BELLY
BELOW
BENCH
BENDS
BENDY
BENET
BENIN
BENNE
BEPAT
BERET
BERIA
BEROB
BERRY
BERTH
BERYL
BESET
BESOM
BESOT
BETEL
BETON
BETTE
BETTY
BEVEL
BEVIS
BEVVY
BEZEL
CEASE
CECIL
CECUM
CEDAR
CELLA
CELLO
CELLS
CENCI
CENSE
CENTO
CEORL
CERES
CERNE
CESAR
DEATH
DEBAG
DEBAR
DEBEL
DEBIT
DEBUG
DEBUT
DECAL
DECAY
DECCA
DECKO
DECOR
DECOY
DECRY
DEEDS
DEFER
DEFOE
DEGAS
DEIFY
DEIGN
DEIST
DEITY
DEKKO
DELAY
DELFT
DELHI
DELOS
DELPH
DELTA
DELVE
DEMOB
DEMON
DEMOS
DEMUR
DENIM
DENIS
DENSE
DENYS
DEPOT
DEPTH
DERAY
DERBY
DERMA
DERRY
DESSE
DETER
DEUCE
DEVIL
DEWAN
DEWAR
DEWEY
EERIE
FEARE
FEAST
FECAL
FECES
FECIT
FEIGN
FEINT
FELIS
FELIX
FELLA
FELON
FEMTO
FEMUR
FENCE
FENNY
FEOFF
FERAL
FERIA
FERMI
FERRY
FESSE
FESTA
FESTE
FETAL
FETCH
FETID
FETOR
FETUS
FEVER
FEWER
GEARE
GEBER
GECKO
GEESE
GEIST
GELID
GEMMA
GEMMY
GENET
GENIE
GENOA
GENRE
GENTS
GENTY
GENUS
GEODE
GERBE
GESSE
GESSO
GESTE
GETUP
HEADS
HEADY
HEALD
HEAPS
HEARD
HEART
HEATH
HEAVE
HEAVY
HECHT
HECTO
HEDDA
HEDGE
HEELS
HEFTY
HEGEL
HEIGH
HEINE
HEIST
HELEN
HELGA
HELIO
HELIX
HELLO
HELOT
HELVE
HENCE
HENGE
HENNA
HENRY
HERBS
HERMA
HERNE
HEROD
HERON
HERSE
HERTS
HERTZ
HESSE
HETTY
HEUGH
HEVEA
HEWER
HEXAD
HEXAM
HEXYL
HEYER
JEANS
JEBEL
JEHAD
JELAB
JELLO
JELLY
JEMMY
JENNY
JEREZ
JERKS
JERKY
JERRY
JESSE
JESUS
JETTY
JEWEL
JEWRY
KEBAB
KEBEL
KEBLE
KEBOB
KEDAR
KEDGE
KEDGY
KEECH
KEELS
KEEPS
KEFIR
KELIM
KELLS
KELLY
KEMPE
KENDO
KENGA
KENYA
KERAL
KERMA
KERNE
KETCH
KEVIN
KEYED
KEYES
LEACH
LEADS
LEAFY
LEAKY
LEANT
LEAPT
LEARN
LEASE
LEASH
LEAST
LEAVE
LECOQ
LEDGE
LEECH
LEEDS
LEERY
LEESE
LEFTY
LEGAL
LEGER
LEGGE
LEGGY
LEGIT
LEHAR
LEIGH
LEISH
LEITH
LEMAN
LEMMA
LEMON
LEMUR
LENIN
LENTO
LEONE
LEPER
LEPID
LERNA
LERNE
LESHY
LETHE
LEVEE
LEVEL
LEVEN
LEVER
LEVIN
LEVIS
LEWES
LEWIS
LEXIS
MEALS
MEALY
MEANS
MEANT
MEATH
MEATS
MEATY
MEBBE
MECCA
MEDAL
MEDEA
MEDIA
MEDIC
MEDOC
MEETS
MEITH
MELBA
MELEE
MELIA
MELIC
MELON
MELOS
MENAI
MENGE
MENSA
MERAK
MERCY
MERGE
MERIL
MERIT
MERLE
MERRY
MESIC
MESNE
MESON
MESSY
MESTO
METAL
METER
METHS
METIC
METIF
METIS
METOL
METRE
METRO
MEUSE
MEYER
MEZZE
MEZZO
NEAGH
NEALE
NEBEL
NEDDY
NEEDS
NEEDY
NEGEV
NEGRO
NEGUS
NEHRU
NEIGH
NELLY
NEPAL
NERVA
NERVE
NERVI
NERVO
NERVY
NESSA
NESTA
NEVEL
NEVER
NEVIS
NEWEL
NEWLY
NEWSY
NEWTS
NEXUS
PEACE
PEACH
PEAKY
PEARL
PEASE
PEATY
PECAN
PEDAL
PEDRO
PEERS
PEEVE
PEGGY
PEKAN
PEKIN
PEKOE
PELEE
PELLA
PELMA
PENAL
PENCE
PENIS
PENNA
PENNE
PENNY
PEONY
PEPPY
PEPSI
PEPYS
PERAI
PERCE
PERCH
PERCY
PERDU
PERIL
PERKS
PERKY
PERON
PERRY
PERSE
PESKY
PESTO
PETAL
PETER
PETIT
PETRA
PETRE
PETRI
PETTO
PETTY
REACH
REACT
READE
READY
REALM
REAMS
REARM
REBEL
REBUS
REBUT
RECAP
RECCE
RECTO
RECUR
REDAN
REDON
REDOX
REECH
REEDE
REEDS
REEDY
REEVE
REFER
REFIT
REGAL
REGAN
REGIA
REGIS
REICH
REIGN
REINS
REIST
REITH
REJIG
RELAX
RELAY
RELIC
REMIT
REMUE
REMUS
RENAL
RENAN
RENEW
RENTE
REPAY
REPEL
REPLY
REPOT
REPRO
RERUN
RESET
RESIN
RESIT
RESTS
RETCH
RETRO
REVEL
REVET
REVIE
REVUE
REYES
SEALS
SEAMY
SEARE
SECCO
SEDAN

SEDGE
SEDUM
SEEDY
SEGUE
SEINE
SEISM
SEIZE
SELIM
SELLE
SELVA
SEMEN
SEMIS
SENNA
SENOR
SENSE
SENZA
SEOUL
SEPAL
SEPIA
SEPOY
SERAI
SERGE
SERIF
SERIN
SERRA
SERRE
SERUM
SERVE
SERVO
SETUP
SEVEN
SEVER
SEWER
TEACH
TEARS
TEASE
TEAZE
TEDDY
TEENS
TEENY
TEETH
TEHEE
TEIGN
TELEX
TELIC
TELLY
TELOS
TEMPE
TEMPO
TEMPT
TENCH
TENDS
TENET
TENON
TENOR
TENSE
TENTH
TENUE
TEPEE
TEPID
TERCE
TEREK
TERES
TERMS
TERNE
TERRA
TERRY
TERSE
TESSA
TESTA
TESTS
TESTY
TETRA
TEXAN
TEXAS
TEXEL
TEXTS
VEDDA
VEDIC
VEGAN
VEINS
VELAR
VELDT
VELUM
VENAL
VENDA
VENIN
VENOM
VENUE
VENUS
VERDI
VEREY
VERGE
VERNE
VERSA
VERSE
VERSO
VERST
VERTU
VERVE
VESPA
VESTA
VETCH
VEXED
WEALD
WEARY
WEAVE
WEBER
WEDGE
WEEDS
WEEDY
WEEKS
WEENY
WEEPY
WEIGH
WEILL
WEIRD
WELCH
WELLS
WELLY
WELSH
WENCH
WENDY
WESER
XEBEC
XENIA
XENON
XERES
XEROX
YEARN
YEARS
YEAST
YEATS
YEMEN
YERBA
YEZDI
ZEBRA
ZENOS
ZEPPO
ZERDA
BÉVUE
GÉANT
RÉGIE
RÈGLE
AFEAR
AFFIX
AFIRE
AFOOT
AFORE
AFOUL
AFRIT
AFTER
OFFAL
OFFAS
OFFER
OFLAG
OFTEN
AGAIN
AGAMI
AGAPE
AGATE
AGAVE
AGENT
AGGER
AGGRO
AGILE
AGING
AGIST
AGLEE
AGLET
AGLEY
AGLOW
AGNES
AGONE
AGONY
AGORA
AGREE
EGDON
EGEST
EGGAR
EGRET
EGYPT
IGAPO
IGLOO
NGAIO
OGGIN
OGHAM
OGIER
OGIVE
UGRIC
AHEAD
AHMED
BHANG
CHACO
CHAFE
CHAFF
CHAIN
CHAIR
CHALK
CHAMP
CHANT
CHAOS
CHAPE
CHAPS
CHARD
CHARK
CHARM
CHART
CHARY
CHASE
CHASM
CHEAP
CHEAT
CHECK
CHEEK
CHEEP
CHEER
CHEKA
CHERE
CHERT
CHESS
CHEST
CHEVY
CHEWY
CHIAO
CHICA
CHICK
CHICO
CHIDE
CHIEF
CHILD
CHILE
CHILI
CHILL
CHIME
CHIMP
CHINA
CHINE
CHING
CHINK
CHINO
CHIPS
CHIRK
CHIRL
CHIRP
CHIRR
CHIRT
CHIVE
CHIVY
CHLOE
CHOCK
CHOCO
CHOIR
CHOKE
CHOKO
CHOKY
CHOMP
CHOOK
CHOPS
CHORD
CHORE
CHOSE
CHOTA
CHUBB
CHUCK
CHUFF
CHUMP
CHUNK
CHURL
CHURN
CHURR
CHUTE
CHYLE
CHYME
CHYND
DHABI
DHOBI
DHOTI
GHANA
GHATS
GHAZI
GHOST
GHOUL
GHYLL
KHAKI
KHAYA
KHAZI
LHASA
PHARE
PHASE
PHEBE
PHENO
PHEON
PHIAL
PHILE
PHLOX
PHNOM
PHOBE
PHONE
PHONY
PHOTO
PHYLE
RHEIN
RHETT
RHEUM
RHINE
RHINO
RHODO
RHOMB
RHONE
RHUMB
RHYME
SHACK
SHADE
SHADY
SHAFT
SHAKE
SHAKO
SHAKY
SHALE
SHALL
SHALT
SHAME
SHANG
SHANK
SHANT
SHAPE
SHARD
SHARE
SHARK
SHARP
SHAUN
SHAVE
SHAWL
SHAWM
SHCHI
SHEAF
SHEAR
SHEBA
SHEEL
SHEEN
SHEEP
SHEER
SHEET
SHEIK
SHELF
SHELL
SHERD
SHERE
SHIEL
SHIFT
SHILL
SHINE
SHINY
SHIRE
SHIRK
SHIRR
SHIRT
SHITE
SHIVA
SHIVE
SHLEP
SHOAL
SHOCK
SHOJI
SHOLA
SHONA
SHONE
SHOOK
SHOOT
SHOPS
SHORE
SHORN
SHORT
SHOTS
SHOUT
SHOVE
SHOWN
SHOWY
SHRED
SHREW
SHROW
SHRUB
SHRUG
SHUCK
SHUNT
SHUSH
SHUTE
SHUTS
SHYLY
THAIS
THANE
THANK
THECA
THEFT
THEGN
THEIR
THEMA
THEME
THERE
THERM
THESE
THETA
THETE
THEWS
THICK
THIEF
THIGH
THILL
THINE
THING
THINK
THIRD
THIRL
THOFT
THOLE
THONG
THORN
THOSE
THREE
THREW
THRID
THRIP
THROB
THROE
THROW
THRUM
THUGS
THULE
THUMB
THUMP
THUYA
THYME
UHLAN
UHURU
WHACK
WHALE
WHANG
WHARF
WHAUP
WHAUR
WHEAL
WHEAT
WHEEL
WHEEN
WHELK
WHELP
WHERE
WHICH
WHIFF
WHIFT
WHILE
WHIMS
WHINE
WHIPS
WHIRL
WHIRR
WHISH
WHISK
WHIST
WHITE
WHIZZ
WHOLE
WHOOP
WHOOT
WHORE
WHORL
WHOSE
XHOSA
AIDAN
AIDOS
AIKEN
AINEE
AIOLI
AIRER
AIRES
AISLE
AITCH
BIBBY
BIBLE
BIDDY
BIDET
BIFID
BIGHT
BIGOT
BIJOU
BIKER
BILGE

BILLY
BIMBO
BINGE
BINGO
BIONT
BIPED
BIPOD
BIRCH
BIRDS
BIRTH
BISON
BITCH
BITER
BITTE
BITTY
CIBOL
CIDER
CIGAR
CIGGY
CILIA
CILLA
CINCH
CINNA
CIRCA
CIRCE
CISCO
CISSY
CIVET
CIVIC
CIVIL
CIVVY
DIALS
DIANA
DIARY
DIAZO
DICEY
DICKY
DIDNT
DIEGO
DIGHT
DIGIT
DIKER
DILDO
DIMLY
DINAR
DINER
DINGE
DINGO
DINGY
DINKA
DINKY
DIODE
DIOTA
DIPPY
DIRGE
DIRTY
DISCO
DISHY
DITAL
DITCH
DITTO
DITTY
DIVAN
DIVER
DIVES
DIVOT
DIVVY
DIWAN
DIXIE
DIZZY
EIDER
EIGER
EIGHT
EIKON
EILAT
FIBER
FIBRE
FIBRO
FICHE
FICHU
FIDEL
FIDES
FIELD
FIEND
FIERE
FIERY
FIFTH
FIFTY
FIGHT
FILCH
FILET
FILLY
FILMS
FILMY
FILTH
FINAL
FINCH
FINER
FINIS
FINKS
FIORD
FIRMA
FIRST
FIRTH
FISHY
FITCH
FIVER
FIVES
FIXED
FIXER
FIZZY
GIANT
GIBBY
GIBUS
GIDDY
GIFTS
GIGLI
GIGOT
GIGUE
GILES
GILET
GILLS
GILTS
GIMPY
GIPPO
GIPSY
GIRLS
GIRLY
GIRTH
GISMO
GIVEN
GIVER
GIZMO
HIGHT
HIKER
HILAR
HILDA
HILLS
HILLY
HILUM
HINDI
HINDU
HINGE
HINNY
HIPPO
HIPPY
HIRAM
HIRED
HIRER
HITCH
HITHE
HIVER
HIVES
JIFFY
JIHAD
JIMMU
JIMMY
JIMPY
JINGO
JINKS
JIRGA
KIANG
KIDDY
KIDGE
KILDA
KILIM
KIMBO
KINGS
KINKY
KIOSK
KIPPS
KIRBY
KIROV
KITTY
KIWIS
LIANA
LIANE
LIANG
LIARD
LIBEL
LIBER
LIBRA
LIBYA
LICHT
LICIT
LIEGE
LIFER
LIGGE
LIGHT
LIKED
LIKEN
LIKES
LILAC
LILLE
LILLY
LIMAX
LIMBO
LIMER
LIMES
LIMEY
LIMIT
LINCH
LINED
LINEN
LINER
LINES
LINGO
LININ
LINKS
LINUS
LIONS
LIPID
LIPPI
LISLE
LISTS
LISZT
LITAS
LITER
LITHE
LITRE
LIVED
LIVEN
LIVER
LIVES
LIVID
LIVRE
MIAMI
MIAOU
MIAOW
MIAUL
MICAH
MICHE
MICRO
MIDAS
MIDDY
MIDGE
MIDST
MIFFY
MIGHT
MILAN
MILCH
MILER
MILES
MILKY
MILLI
MILLS
MILNE
MIMER
MIMIC
MIMUS
MINCE
MINCH
MINER
MINGY
MINHO
MINIM
MINKE
MINOR
MINOS
MINOT
MINSK
MINUS
MIRTH
MIRZA
MISER
MISSA
MISSY
MISTY
MITES
MITRE
MIXED
MIXER
MIXTE
MIXUP
NICAD
NICHE
NICOL
NIDOR
NIDUS
NIECE
NIEVE
NIFTY
NIGEL
NIGER
NIGHT
NIHIL
NINJA
NINNY
NINON
NINTH
NIOBE
NIPPY
NISUS
NITID
NITON
NITRE
NIVAL
NIXON
NIZAM
OILED
OILER
PIANO
PIAVE
PICEA
PICOT
PICUS
PIECE
PIERS
PIERT
PIETA
PIETY
PIEZO
PIGGY
PIGMY
PILAF
PILAU
PILCH
PILED
PILES
PILLS
PILOT
PILUM
PILUS
PINCH
PINES
PINGO
PINKO
PINKY
PINNA
PINNY
PINON
PINOT
PINTA
PINTO
PIOUS
PIPER
PIPIT
PIPPA
PIPUL
PIQUE
PIROG
PISKY
PISTE
PITCH
PITHY
PITON
PITOT
PITTA
PIVOT
PIXEL
PIXIE
PIZZA
RIANT
RICAN
RICIN
RIDER
RIDGE
RIFLE
RIGHT
RIGID
RIGOR
RILEY
RILKE
RILLE
RINSE
RIOJA
RIOTS
RIPEN
RIPER
RIPON
RISEN
RISER
RISKY
RISUS
RITES
RITZY
RIVAL
RIVEN
RIVER
RIVET
RIYAL
SIBYL
SIDHA
SIDLE
SIDON
SIEGE
SIEVE
SIGHS
SIGHT
SIGIL
SIGLA
SIGMA
SIGNS
SILAS
SILEX
SILKY
SILLY
SILVA
SIMBA
SIMON
SINAI
SINCE
SINEW
SINGE
SINUS
SIREN
SISAL
SISSY
SITAR
SITIN
SITKA
SITTA
SITUP
SIXER
SIXTH
SIXTY
SIZAR
TIARA
TIBBS
TIBBY
TIBER
TIBET
TIBIA
TIDAL
TIDDY
TIGER
TIGHT
TIGON
TIKKA
TILDE
TILED
TILER
TILES
TILIA
TILTH
TIMER
TIMES
TIMID
TIMON
TIMOR
TINEA
TINGE
TINNY
TIPPY
TIPSY
TIRED
TIREE
TIROS
TITAN
TITCH
TITHE
TITLE
TITRE
TITTY
TITUS
TIZZY
VIAND
VIBES
VICAR
VICHY
VIDEO
VIGIL
VIGOR
VILLA
VILLI
VINYL
VIOLA
VIPER
VIRAL
VIREO
VIRGA
VIRGO
VIRID
VIRTU
VIRUS
VISBY
VISIT
VISON
VISOR
VISTA
VITAE
VITAL
VITIS
VITUS
VIVAT
VIVID
VIXEN
VIZOR

WIDEN
WIDOW
WIDTH
WIELD
WIGAN
WIGHT
WILDE
WILDS
WILES
WILGA
WILLY
WILTS
WIMPY
WINCE
WINCH
WINDY
WINEY
WINGS
WIPER
WIRED
WIRES
WISPY
WITAN
WITCH
WITHE
WITHY
WITTY
WIVES
YIELD
YIKES
YIPPY
ZIGAN
ZILCH
ZINCO
ZINEB
ZIPPY
EJECT
FJORD
AKBAR
AKELA
AKENE
OKAPI
SKATE
SKEAN
SKEER
SKEET
SKEIN
SKELM
SKELP
SKIER
SKIFF
SKILL
SKIMP
SKINK
SKINS
SKINT
SKIRL
SKIRR
SKIRT
SKIVE
SKOAL
SKRIM
SKULK
SKULL
SKUNK
UKASE
ALACK
ALAMO
ALANS
ALAPA
ALARM
ALATE
ALBAN
ALBEE
ALBUM
ALDAN
ALDER
ALDIS
ALEPH
ALERT
ALEUT
ALFIE
ALGAE
ALGID
ALGOL
ALIAS
ALIBI
ALICE
ALIEN
ALIGN
ALIKE
ALIVE
ALLAH
ALLAN
ALLAY
ALLÉE
ALLEN
ALLEY
ALLOT
ALLOW
ALLOY
ALLYL
ALNUS
ALOES
ALOFT
ALOHA
ALONE
ALONG
ALOOF
ALOUD
ALPHA
ALTAI
ALTAR
ALTER
ALURE
ALVIS
BLACK
BLADE
BLAIR
BLAKE
BLAME
BLANC
BLAND
BLANK
BLARE
BLASÉ
BLAST
BLAZE
BLEAK
BLEAR
BLEAT
BLEED
BLEEP
BLEND
BLESS
BLEST
BLIGH
BLIMP
BLIND
BLINI
BLINK
BLISS
BLITZ
BLOAT
BLOCK
BLOKE
BLOND
BLOOD
BLOOM
BLOOP
BLOWN
BLOWY
BLUES
BLUEY
BLUFF
BLUNT
BLURB
BLURT
BLUSH
CLACK
CLAIM
CLAMP
CLANG
CLANK
CLARA
CLARE
CLARK
CLARY
CLASH
CLASP
CLASS
CLAUS
CLAVE
CLEAN
CLEAR
CLEAT
CLECK
CLEEK
CLEEP
CLEFT
CLEPE
CLERK
CLICK
CLIFF
CLIFT
CLIMB
CLIME
CLING
CLINK
CLINT
CLIVE
CLOAK
CLOCK
CLONE
CLOOT
CLOSE
CLOTH
CLOUD
CLOUT
CLOVE
CLOWN
CLOZE
CLUBS
CLUCK
CLUMP
CLUNG
CLUNK
CLYDE
ELAND
ELATE
ELBOW
ELDER
ELECT
ELEGY
ELENE
ELFIN
ELGAR
ELGIN
ELIAD
ELIAS
ELIDE
ELIHU
ELIOT
ELITE
ELLEN
ELLIS
ELMER
ELOGE
ELOGY
ELOPE
ELSAN
ELTON
ELUDE
ELVAN
ELVER
ELVES
ELVIS
FLACK
FLAIL
FLAIR
FLAKE
FLAKY
FLAME
FLANK
FLARE
FLASH
FLASK
FLATS
FLECK
FLEET
FLESH
FLEUR
FLEWS
FLICK
FLIER
FLIES
FLING
FLINT
FLIRT
FLOAT
FLOCK
FLONG
FLOOD
FLOOR
FLOPS
FLORA
FLOSS
FLOTA
FLOUR
FLOUT
FLOWN
FLUFF
FLUID
FLUKE
FLUME
FLUMP
FLUNG
FLUNK
FLUON
FLUSH
FLUTE
FLYER
FLYTE
GLACE
GLADE
GLAIR
GLAND
GLANS
GLASS
GLAZE
GLEAM
GLEAN
GLEBE
GLEEK
GLEET
GLIDE
GLIFF
GLINT
GLISK
GLITZ
GLOAT
GLOBE
GLOGG
GLOOM
GLORY
GLOSS
GLOVE
GLUCK
GLUED
GLUEY
GLUME
GLUON
GLYPH
ILEAC
ILEUM
ILEUS
ILIAC
ILIAD
ILIUM
KLANG
KLEIN
KLIEG
KLOOF
LLAMA
LLANO
LLOYD
OLDEN
OLDER
OLDIE
OLEIC
OLEIN
OLEUM
OLIVE
OLLIE
PLACE
PLACK
PLAID
PLAIN
PLAIT
PLANE
PLANK
PLANT
PLATE
PLATH
PLATO
PLATY
PLATZ
PLAYA
PLAZA
PLEAD
PLEAT
PLEBS
PLEIN
PLICA
PLIER
PLINY
PLONK
PLOTS
PLUCK
PLUMB
PLUME
PLUMP
PLUNK
PLUSH
PLUTO
SLACK
SLADE
SLAIN
SLAKE
SLANG
SLANT
SLASH
SLATE
SLATS
SLATY
SLAVE
SLEEK
SLEEP
SLEET
SLEPT
SLICE
SLICK
SLIDE
SLIGO
SLIME
SLIMY
SLING
SLINK
SLIPE
SLIPS
SLOAN
SLOOP
SLOPE
SLOPS
SLOSH
SLOTH
SLUGS
SLUMP
SLUNG
SLUNK
SLURB
SLURP
SLUSH
SLYLY
SLYPE
ULCER
ULEMA
ULNAR
ULTRA
VLACH
ZLOTY
AMAIN
AMANT
AMASS
AMAZE
AMBER
AMBIT
AMBLE
AMEBA
AMEND
AMENE
AMENT
AMICE
AMIEL
AMIGO
AMINE
AMINO
AMISH
AMISS
AMITY
AMMAN
AMONG
AMORT
AMOUR
AMPLE
AMPLY
AMUCK
AMUSE
EMAIL
EMBED
EMBER
EMBOW
EMBOX
EMBUS
EMCEE
EMDEN
EMEND
EMERY
EMILE
EMILY
EMLYN
EMMER
EMMET
EMOTE
EMOVE
EMPTY
EMRYS
EMURE
IMAGE
IMAGO
IMARI
IMAUM
IMBED
IMBUE
IMMER
IMMEW
IMPEL
IMPLY
IMPOT
IMSHI
OMAGH
OMANI
OMBER
OMBRE
OMEGA
SMACK
SMALL
SMARM
SMART
SMASH
SMEAR
SMEEK
SMELL
SMELT
SMILE
SMIRK
SMITE
SMITH

SMOCK
SMOKE
SMOKY
SMOLT
SMOTE
SMUTS
UMBEL
UMBER
UMBLE
UMBRA
UMPTY
ANANA
ANDES
ANEAR
ANELE
ANEND
ANENT
ANGEL
ANGER
ANGLE
ANGLO
ANGRY
ANGST
ANGUS
ANIGH
ANIMA
ANION
ANISE
ANITA
ANJOU
ANKER
ANKLE
ANKUS
ANNAL
ANNAM
ANNEX
ANNIE
ANNOY
ANNUL
ANODE
ANOMY
ANSON
ANTAR
ANTIC
ANTON
ANVIL
ANZAC
ENACT
ENARM
ENDED
ENDOW
ENDUE
ENEMA
ENEMY
ENJOY
ENMEW
ENNUI
ENOCH
ENORM
ENROL
ENSEW
ENSOR
ENSUE
ENTER
ENTRY
ENUGU
ENURE
ENVOI
ENVOY
GNARL
GNASH
GNOME
INANE
INAPT
INARI
INARM
INCLE
INCUR
INCUS
INDEW
INDEX
INDIA
INDRA
INDRE
INDRI
INDUE
INDUS
INEPT
INERT
INFER
INFRA
INGLE
INGOT
INIGO
INION
INIUM
INJUN
INLAW
INLAY
INLET
INNER
INNES
INPUT
INSET
INTER
INTRA
INTRO
INUIT
INURE
INWIT
KNACK
KNARL
KNAVE
KNEAD
KNEEL
KNELL
KNELT
KNIFE
KNOCK
KNOLL
KNOUT
KNOWN
KNURL
KNURR
ONCER
ONCUS
ONION
ONKUS
ONSET
SNACK
SNAFU
SNAGS
SNAIL
SNAKE
SNAKY
SNAPS
SNARE
SNARK
SNARL
SNASH
SNEAD
SNEAK
SNECK
SNEER
SNICK
SNIDE
SNIFF
SNIFT
SNIPE
SNOBS
SNOEK
SNOOD
SNOOK
SNOOP
SNOOT
SNORE
SNORT
SNOUT
SNOWY
SNUFF
UNAPT
UNARM
UNBAR
UNBED
UNCAP
UNCLE
UNCUS
UNCUT
UNDAM
UNDER
UNDID
UNDUE
UNFED
UNFIT
UNGET
UNIAT
UNIFY
UNION
UNITA
UNITE
UNITS
UNITY
UNLAW
UNLAY
UNLIT
UNMAN
UNMIX
UNPEN
UNPIN
UNRIG
UNRIP
UNSAY
UNTIE
UNTIL
UNWED
UNZIP
VNECK
AORTA
AOSTA
BOARD
BOAST
BOBBY
BOCHE
BODES
BODGE
BOGEY
BOGGY
BOGIE
BOGLE
BOGUS
BOHEA
BOING
BOLAS
BOLUS
BOMBE
BOMBO
BONAR
BONCE
BONDI
BONDS
BONER
BONES
BONEY
BONGO
BONNY
BONUS
BONZE
BOOBY
BOONE
BOONG
BOOST
BOOTH
BOOTS
BOOTY
BOOZE
BOOZY
BORAX
BORED
BOREE
BORER
BORIC
BORIS
BORNE
BORON
BOSCH
BOSEY
BOSKY
BOSOM
BOSSY
BOSUN
BOTCH
BOTHA
BOTHY
BOTTE
BOUGH
BOULE
BOUND
BOURG
BOWED
BOWEL
BOWER
BOWIE
BOWLS
BOXED
BOXER
BOYAR
BOYAU
BOYCE
BOYLE
BOYNE
COACH
COADE
COAST
COATI
COBOL
COBRA
COCCI
COCKY
COCOA
COCOS
CODED
CODEX
COHOE
COIGN
COKES
COLET
COLEY
COLIC
COLIN
COLLY
COLON
COLOR
COLTS
COLZA
COMBE
COMBO
COMBS
COMET
COMFY
COMIC
COMMA
COMPO
COMTE
COMUS
CONAN
CONCH
CONDE
CONDO
CONEY
CONGÉ
CONGO
CONIC
CONTE
COOEE
COOKS
COOMB
COOPT
COPER
COPPY
COPRA
COPSE
CORAL
CORAM
CORDS
CORED
CORER
CORFE
CORFU
CORGI
CORIN
CORKY
CORNY
COROT
CORPS
CORSE
CORSO
CORVO
COSEC
COSMO
COSTA
COSTS
COTTA
COUCH
COUDÉ
COUGH
COULD
COUNT
COUPE
COURB
COURT
COUTH
COVEN
COVER
COVET
COVEY
COWAN
COWER
COWRY
COXAL
COXED
COYLY
COYNE
COYPU
COZEN
DOBBY
DOBRO
DOCKS
DODDY
DODGE
DODGY
DOGGO
DOGGY
DOGMA
DOILY
DOING
DOLCE
DOLIN
DOLLY
DOMED
DONAR
DONAT
DONEE
DONNA
DONNE
DONOR
DOONE
DOORN
DOORS
DOPEY
DORAS
DOREE
DORIC
DORIS
DORMY
DORTS
DOTTY
DOUAI
DOUAR
DOUAY
DOUBT
DOUCE
DOUGH
DOUMA
DOURA
DOURO
DOUSE
DOVER
DOWDY
DOWEL
DOWER
DOWNS
DOWNY
DOWRY
DOWSE
DOYEN
DOYLE
DOYLY
DOZEN
EOLIC
EOSIN
FOAMY
FOCAL
FOCUS
FOEHN
FOGEY
FOGGY
FOIST
FOLIC
FOLIE
FOLIO
FOLKS
FOLLY
FONDA
FONDS
FOODS
FOOLS
FOOTS
FOOTY
FORAY
FORCE
FOREL
FORGE
FORGO
FORKS
FORME
FORMS
FORTE
FORTH
FORTY
FORUM
FOSSA
FOSSE
FOUET
FOULÉ
FOUND
FOUNT
FOURS
FOVEA
FOYER
FOYLE
GOATY
GOBBO
GODET
GODLY
GOFER
GOGOL
GOING
GOLAN
GOLEM
GOLGI
GOLLY
GOMBO
GONAD
GONER
GONNA
GONZO
GOODS
GOODY
GOOEY
GOOFY
GOOLY
GOOSE
GOPAK
GORED
GORGE
GORKY
GORSE
GOSHT

GOSSE
GOTCH
GOTHA
GOTTA
GOUDA
GOUGE
GOURD
GOUTY
GOWAN
GOWER
HOARD
HOARE
HOARY
HOAST
HOBBS
HOBBY
HOCUS
HODGE
HOGAN
HOICK
HOIST
HOKEY
HOKUM
HOLED
HOLEY
HOLLA
HOLLY
HOLST
HOMER
HOMME
HONAN
HONDO
HONEY
HONKY
HONOR
HOOCH
HOOEY
HOOKY
HOOSH
HOOVE
HORAH
HORDE
HOREB
HORNE
HORNY
HORSA
HORSE
HORSY
HORUS
HOSEA
HOSEN
HOSTA
HOTCH
HOTEL
HOTLY
HOUGH
HOUND
HOURI
HOURS
HOUSE
HOVEL
HOVER
HOWBE
HOWDY
HOYLE
IONIC
JOCKO
JOINT
JOIST
JOKER
JOLLY
JONAH
JONES
JONTY
JORIS
JORUM
JOUAL
JOULE
JOUNT
JOUST
JOYCE
KOALA
KODAK
KOFTA
KOINE
KOKUM
KONGO
KOOKY
KOORI
KOPJE
KORAN
KOREA
KORMA
KOTOW
LOAMY
LOATH
LOBAR
LOBBY
LOBED
LOCAL
LOCKE
LOCKS
LOCUM
LOCUS
LODEN
LODGE
LOESS
LOFTY
LOGAN
LOGIC
LOGOS
LOINS
LOIRE
LOLLY
LOMAN
LONER
LONGS
LOOBY
LOOFA
LOONS
LOONY
LOOPY
LOOSE
LORCA
LORDS
LORIS
LORNA
LORNE
LORRY
LOSER
LOTOS
LOTTO
LOTUS
LOUGH
LOUIE
LOUIS
LOUPE
LOUSE
LOUSY
LOUTH
LOVAT
LOVER
LOWAN
LOWER
LOWLY
LOWRY
LOYAL
LOZEN
MOCHA
MODAL
MODEL
MODEM
MODER
MODUS
MOGGY
MOGUL
MOIRA
MOIRE
MOIST
MOLAR
MOLLY
MOLTO
MOMMA
MOMMY
MONAD
MONAL
MONDO
MONET
MONEY
MONKS
MONTE
MONTH
MONZA
MOOCH
MOODY
MOOLI
MOONY
MOORE
MOOSE
MOPED
MOPER
MOPSY
MORAL
MORAN
MORAT
MORAY
MOREL
MORES
MORIA
MORIN
MORNE
MORON
MORPH
MORSE
MORUS
MOSES
MOSEY
MOSSY
MOTEL
MOTET
MOTHS
MOTIF
MOTOR
MOTTE
MOTTO
MOUCH
MOULD
MOULS
MOULT
MOUND
MOUNT
MOURN
MOUSE
MOUSY
MOUTH
MOVED
MOVER
MOVIE
MOWER
MOYLE
NOBBY
NOBEL
NOBLE
NOBLY
NODAL
NODDY
NODES
NODUS
NOISE
NOISY
NOMAD
NOMEN
NOMIC
NONCE
NONES
NONET
NONNY
NOOKY
NOOSE
NORAH
NORIA
NORMA
NORSE
NORTH
NOSER
NOSEY
NOTAL
NOTCH
NOTED
NOTES
NOTTS
NOTUM
NOVEL
NOVUM
NOXAL
NOYAU
NOYES
OOMPH
POACH
PODEX
PODGE
PODGY
POEMS
POESY
POETS
POILU
POINT
POISE
POKER
POKEY
POLAR
POLIO
POLKA
POLLY
POLYP
POMMY
PONCE
PONDS
PONEY
PONGA
PONGO
PONTY
POOCH
POOLS
POPES
POPOV
POPPA
POPPY
POPSY
POPUP
PORCH
PORGY
PORKY
PORNO
PORTA
PORTE
PORTO
PORTS
POSED
POSER
POSIT
POSSE
POSTE
POTIN
POTOO
POTTO
POTTY
POUCH
POULE
POULT
POUND
POUPE
POWAN
POWER
POWYS
ROACH
ROAST
ROBES
ROBEY
ROBIN
ROBOT
ROCKS
ROCKY
RODEO
RODIN
ROGER
ROGET
ROGUE
ROHAN
ROIST
ROKER
ROLFE
ROLLO
ROLLS
ROMAN
ROMEO
ROMER
RONDE
RONDO
RONEO
RONNE
ROOKY
ROOMS
ROOMY
ROOPY
ROOST
ROOTS
ROOTY
ROPED
ROPER
ROPES
ROPEY
ROQUE
RORIC
RORKE
RORTY
ROSCO
ROSES
ROSET
ROSIN
ROSIT
ROSSE
ROSSI
ROTOR
ROUEN
ROUGE
ROUGH
ROULE
ROUND
ROUSE
ROUST
ROUTE
ROVER
ROWAN
ROWDY
ROWEL
ROWER
ROYAL
ROZET
SOANE
SOAPY
SOARE
SOBER
SOCKS
SOCLE
SODOM
SODOR
SOFIA
SOFTY
SOGGY
SOKEN
SOKOL
SOLAN
SOLAR
SOLDE
SOLFA
SOLID
SOLON
SOLTI
SOLUM
SOLUS
SOLVE
SOMME
SONAR
SONDE
SONIC
SONNY
SOOTH
SOOTY
SOPHY
SOPPY
SOPRA
SORBO
SORDO
SORES
SOREX
SORRY
SORTS
SOTTO
SOUGH
SOULS
SOUND
SOUSA
SOUSE
SOUTH
SOWER
SOWLE
SOWND
SOWTH
SOYUZ
TOADY
TOAST
TOBIT
TODAY
TODDY
TOILE
TOILS
TOISE
TOKAY
TOKEN
TOKYO
TOLAR
TOMMY
TONAL
TONDO
TONER
TONGA
TONGS
TONIC
TONNE
TONUS
TOOLS
TOOTH
TOPAZ
TOPEE
TOPER
TOPIC
TOPSY
TOQUE
TORAH
TORCH
TORII
TORSO
TORTE
TORUS
TOSCA
TOTAL
TOTEM
TOTTY
TOUCH
TOUGH
TOWEL
TOWER
TOWNS
TOWSE
TOWZE
TOXIC
TOXIN
VOCAL
VODKA
VOGUE
VOICE
VOILA
VOILE
VOLET
VOLGA
VOLTA
VOLTE

VOLVA
VOLVO
VOMER
VOMIT
VOTER
VOTES
VOUCH
VOWEL
VOZHD
WODEN
WODGE
WOKEN
WOMAN
WOMEN
WONGA
WONKY
WOODS
WOODY
WOOER
WOOFY
WOOLF
WOOZY
WORCS
WORDS
WORDY
WORKS
WORLD
WORMS
WORMY
WORRY
WORSE
WORST
WORTH
WOULD
WOUND
WOVEN
YOBBO
YODEL
YOICK
YOKEL
YONKS
YONNE
YOULL
YOUNG
YOURS
YOURT
YOUTH
YOUVE
ZOHAR
ZOMBI
ZONAL
ZORBA
ZORRO
APACE
APAGE
APAID
APART
APEAK
APERT
APHID
APHIS

APODE
APOOP
APPAL
APPAY
APPEL
APPLE
APPLY
APPRO
APPUI
APRIL
APRON
APTLY
EPHOD
EPHOR
EPOCH
EPODE
EPOXY
EPSOM
OPERA
OPHIR
OPINE
OPIUM
OPTIC
SPACE
SPADE
SPADO
SPAHI
SPAIN
SPALD
SPALL
SPALT
SPANK
SPARE
SPARK
SPART
SPASM
SPATE
SPATS
SPAWN
SPEAK
SPEAN
SPEAR
SPECK
SPECS
SPEED
SPEER
SPEKE
SPELL
SPELT
SPEND
SPENS
SPENT
SPERM
SPICA
SPICE
SPICK
SPICY
SPIED
SPIEL
SPIES
SPIFF

SPIKE
SPIKY
SPILE
SPILL
SPILT
SPINA
SPINE
SPINY
SPIRE
SPITE
SPITZ
SPLAT
SPLAY
SPLIT
SPODE
SPOHR
SPOIL
SPOKE
SPOOF
SPOOK
SPOOL
SPOON
SPOOR
SPORE
SPORT
SPOTS
SPOUT
SPRAG
SPRAT
SPRAY
SPREE
SPRIG
SPRIT
SPROD
SPROG
SPRUE
SPUME
SPUNK
SPURN
SPURS
SPURT
UPEND
UPPER
UPSET
UPSEY
UPTON
YPRES
AQABA
EQUAL
EQUIP
IQBAL
SQUAB
SQUAD
SQUAT
SQUAW
SQUIB
SQUID
SQUIT
ARABA
ARBOR
ARCOT

ARCUS
ARDEA
ARDEB
ARDEN
ARDIL
ARDOR
ARECA
AREDE
ARENA
ARENE
ARENT
ARETE
ARGIL
ARGOT
ARGUE
ARGUS
ARIAN
ARICA
ARIEL
ARIES
ARISE
ARISH
ARIST
ARITA
ARKLE
ARLES
ARMED
ARMET
ARMOR
AROID
AROMA
AROSE
ARRAN
ARRAS
ARRAY
ARRÊT
ARRIS
ARROW
ARSON
ARTIE
ARUBA
ARVAL
ARYAN
BRACE
BRACK
BRACT
BRADY
BRAID
BRAIN
BRAKE
BRAND
BRANK
BRASH
BRASS
BRAVA
BRAVE
BRAVO
BRAWL
BRAWN
BREAD
BREAK

BREAM
BREDA
BREDE
BREED
BREEM
BREME
BRENT
BREST
BREVE
BRIAN
BRIAR
BRIBE
BRICK
BRIDE
BRIEF
BRIER
BRILL
BRINE
BRING
BRINK
BRINY
BRISK
BRIZE
BROAD
BROCK
BROIL
BROKE
BRONX
BROOD
BROOK
BROOL
BROOM
BROSE
BROTH
BROWN
BRUCE
BRUIN
BRUIT
BRULE
BRUME
BRUNO
BRUNT
BRUSH
BRUTE
CRABS
CRACK
CRAFT
CRAIG
CRAKE
CRAMP
CRANE
CRANK
CRAPE
CRAPS
CRARE
CRASH
CRASS
CRATE
CRAVE
CRAWL
CRAZE

CRAZY
CREAK
CREAM
CRECY
CREDO
CREED
CREEK
CREEL
CREEP
CREME
CREON
CREPE
CREPT
CRESS
CREST
CRETE
CREWE
CRICK
CRIED
CRIER
CRIES
CRIME
CRIMP
CRISE
CRISP
CROAK
CROAT
CROCE
CROCK
CROFT
CROME
CRONE
CRONK
CRONY
CROOK
CROPS
CRORE
CROSS
CROUP
CROWD
CROWN
CROZE
CRUCK
CRUDE
CRUEL
CRUET
CRUMB
CRUMP
CRUOR
CRUSE
CRUSH
CRUST
CRWTH
CRYPT
DRACO
DRAFT
DRAIN
DRAKE
DRAMA
DRANK
DRAPE

DRAWL
DRAWN
DREAD
DREAM
DREAR
DREGS
DRERE
DRESS
DRIED
DRIER
DRIES
DRIFT
DRILL
DRILY
DRINK
DRIVE
DROIT
DROLL
DROME
DRONE
DROOL
DROOP
DROPS
DROSS
DROVE
DROWN
DRUGS
DRUID
DRUNK
DRUPE
DRURY
DRUZE
DRYAD
DRYER
DRYLY
ERARD
ERASE
ERATO
ERECT
ERGOT
ERICA
ERICK
ERNIE
ERNST
ERODE
ERROR
ERUCA
ERUCT
ERUPT
FRACK
FRACT
FRAIL
FRAME
FRANC
FRANK
FRANS
FRANZ
FRAUD
FREAK
FREED
FREON

FRESH
FREUD
FRIAR
FRIED
FRIES
FRILL
FRISK
FRIST
FRITH
FRITZ
FROCK
FROND
FRONT
FROST
FROTH
FROWN
FROWY
FROZE
FRUIT
FRUMP
GRAAL
GRACE
GRADE
GRAFF
GRAFT
GRAIL
GRAIN
GRAND
GRANT
GRAPE
GRAPH
GRASP
GRASS
GRATE
GRAVE
GRAVY
GRAYS
GRAZE
GREAT
GREBE
GREED
GREEK
GREEN
GREER
GREET
GREGG
GRETA
GREYS
GRIEF
GRIEG
GRIFF
GRILL
GRIME
GRIMM
GRIMY
GRIND
GRIOT
GRIPE
GRIST
GRITS
GROAN

GROAT
GROIN
GROOM
GROPE
GROSS
GROSZ
GROUP
GROUT
GROVE
GROWL
GROWN
GRUEL
GRUFE
GRUFF
GRUME
GRUNT
IRAQI
IRATE
IRENA
IRENE
IRGUN
IRISH
IROKO
IRONS
IRONY
KRAAL
KRAFT
KRANG
KRANS
KRANZ
KRAUT
KRIEG
KRILL
KRONA
KRONE
ORANG
ORATE
ORBIT
ORCUS
ORDER
ORFEO
ORGAN
ORGUE
ORIEL
ORION
ORLON
ORLOP
ORMER
ORMUZ
ORNIS
ORPEN
ORRIS
ORTHO
ORTON
ORTUS
ORVAL
PRADO
PRAHU
PRANA
PRANG
PRANK
PRATE
PRAWL
PRAWN
PREEN
PRESA
PRESS
PREST
PRIAL
PRIAM
PRICE
PRICK
PRIDE
PRILL
PRIMA
PRIME
PRIMO
PRIMP
PRINT
PRION
PRIOR
PRISE
PRISM
PRIVY
PRIZE
PROBE
PROKE
PROLE
PROMO
PRONE
PRONG
PROOF
PROSE
PROSY
PROUD
PROUT
PROVE
PROVO
PROWL
PROXY
PRUDE
PRUNE
TRACE
TRACK
TRACT
TRADE
TRAIL
TRAIN
TRAIT
TRAMP
TRANS
TRANT
TRAPS
TRASH
TRAWL
TREAD
TREAT
TRECK
TREEN
TREES
TREMA
TREND
TRENT
TRESS
TREVI
TREWS
TRIAD
TRIAL
TRIBE
TRICE
TRICK
TRIED
TRIER
TRIES
TRIKE
TRILL
TRIPE
TRITE
TROIC
TROLL
TROMP
TROON
TROOP
TROPE
TROTH
TROTS
TROUT
TROVE
TRUCE
TRUCK
TRULL
TRULY
TRUMP
TRUNK
TRURO
TRUSS
TRUST
TRUTH
TRYST
URALS
URATE
URBAN
UREDO
URIAH
URINE
URITE
URSON
VROOM
WRACK
WRATH
WREAK
WRECK
WREST
WRING
WRIST
WRITE
WRITS
WRONG
WROTE
WROTH
WRUNG
WRYLY
ASAPH
ASCII
ASCOT
ASCUS
ASDIC
ASHEN
ASHER
ASHES
ASHET
ASIAN
ASIDE
ASKER
ASKEW
ASOKA
ASPEN
ASPER
ASPIC
ASSAI
ASSAM
ASSAY
ASSET
ASTER
ASTIR
ASTON
ASTRA
ASWAN
ESCOT
ESKER
ESROM
ESSAY
ESTER
ESTOC
ESTOP
ISAAC
ISERE
ISLAM
ISLAY
ISLES
ISLET
ISMET
ISOLA
ISSUE
NSPCC
OSAGE
OSAKA
OSCAR
OSIER
OSMAN
OSSIA
OSTIA
PSALM
PSEUD
PSHAW
PSOAS
PSORA
PSYCH
RSPCA
TSUBA
TSUGA
USAGE
USHER
USING
USTED
USUAL
USURE
USURP
USURY
ATHOS
ATILT
ATLAS
ATLIN
ATMAN
ATOLL
ATOMY
ATONE
ATONY
ATOPY
ATRIP
ATTAR
ATTIC
ATTLE
ETAGE
ETAIN
ETAPE
ETATS
ETHAL
ETHER
ETHIC
ETHOS
ETHYL
ETUDE
ETWEE
ITALA
ITALY
ITCHY
OTARY
OTHER
OTIUM
OTTAR
OTTER
OTWAY
STACK
STADE
STAFF
STAGE
STAGY
STAID
STAIN
STAIR
STAKE
STALE
STALK
STALL
STAMP
STAND
STANK
STAPH
STARE
STARK
STARR
STARS
START
STASH
STASI
STATE
STAVE
STAYS
STEAD
STEAK
STEAL
STEAM
STEED
STEEK
STEEL
STEEN
STEEP
STEER
STEIN
STELA
STELE
STENT
STEPS
STERN
STEVE
STEWS
STEWY
STICK
STIFF
STILE
STILL
STILT
STIME
STIMY
STING
STINK
STINT
STIRP
STOAT
STOCK
STOEP
STOGA
STOGY
STOIC
STOKE
STOLA
STOLE
STOLL
STOMA
STOMP
STONE
STONY
STOOD
STOOK
STOOL
STOOP
STOOR
STOPE
STORE
STORK
STORM
STORY
STOUP
STOUR
STOUT
STOVE
STOWE
STRAD
STRAP
STRAW
STRAY
STREP
STREW
STRIA
STRIP
STROP
STRUM
STRUT
STUCK
STUDY
STUFF
STUKA
STUMP
STUNG
STUNK
STUNT
STUPA
STUPE
STURT
STYLE
STYLO
STYME
UTHER
UTTER
UTURN
AUDEN
AUDIO
AUDIT
AUGER
AUGHT
AUGUR
AULIC
AULIS
AUNTY
AURAL
AURIC
AUXIN
BUBBY
BUCCA
BUCKO
BUCKS
BUDDY
BUDGE
BUFFO
BUFFS
BUGGY
BUGLE
BUICK
BUILD
BUILT
BULGE
BULKY
BULLA
BULLS
BULLY
BULOW
BUMPH
BUMPY
BUNCE
BUNCH
BUNCO
BUNDY
BUNGY
BUNNY
BURGH
BURIN
BURKE
BURLY
BURMA
BURNS
BURNT
BUROO
BURRO
BURSA
BURST
BUSBY
BUSHY
BUSTY
BUTCH
BUTTE
BUTTY
BUXOM
BUYER
CUBAN
CUBBY
CUBEB
CUBED
CUBIC
CUBIT
CUDDY
CUFFS
CUFFY
CUFIC
CULET
CULEX
CULLY
CUMIN
CUPAR
CUPEL
CUPID
CUPPA
CURDS
CURED
CURER
CURIA
CURIE
CURIO
CURLY
CURRY
CURSE
CURST
CURVE
CURVY
CUSHY
CUTCH
CUTEY
CUTIE

CUTIS
CUTTY
DUBAI
DUCAT
DUCHY
DUCKS
DUCKY
DUDDY
DUKAS
DUKES
DULAC
DUMAS
DUMMY
DUMPS
DUMPY
DUNCE
DUNNO
DUOMO
DUPIN
DURER
DUROY
DURRY
DURST
DURUM
DUSKY
DUSTY
DUTCH
DUVAL
DUVET
EULER
FUBSY
FUCHS
FUDGE
FUERO
FUGAL
FUGGY
FUGUE
FULLY
FUMED
FUMES
FUMET
FUNDI
FUNDS
FUNDY
FUNKY
FUNNY
FUROR
FURRY
FURZE
FUSED
FUSEE
FUSSY
FUSTY
FUTON
FUZEE
FUZZY
GUACO
GUANA
GUANO
GUARD
GUAVA
GUELF
GUESS
GUEST
GUEUX
GUIDE
GUILD
GUILE
GUILT
GUIMP
GUISE
GULAG
GULCH
GULES
GULLS
GULLY
GULPH
GUMBO
GUMMY
GUNGE
GUNNY
GUPPY
GUSHY
GUSTO
GUSTY
GUTSY
GUTTA
GUYED
GUYON
GUYOT
HUBBY
HUFFY
HULKS
HULLO
HULME
HUMAN
HUMID
HUMOR
HUMPH
HUMUS
HUNCH
HUNKS
HUNKY
HUNTS
HURON
HURRY
HURST
HUSKS
HUSKY
HUSSY
HUTCH
HUZZA
JUDAS
JUDGE
JUGAL
JUICE
JUICY
JULEP
JUMAR
JUMBO
JUMBY
JUMNA
JUMPS
JUMPY
JUNCO
JUNTA
JUNTO
JUPON
JURAT
JUROR
KUALA
KUDOS
KUDZU
KUFIC
KUKRI
KULAK
KURMA
KUTCH
LUBRA
LUCAN
LUCIA
LUCID
LUCIO
LUCKY
LUCRE
LUDIC
LUFFA
LUGER
LULLY
LUMEN
LUMME
LUMMY
LUMPY
LUNAR
LUNCH
LUNDY
LUNED
LUNGE
LUNGI
LUNGS
LUPIN
LUPUS
LURCH
LURGY
LURID
LUSHY
LUSTY
LUTIN
LUTON
LUZON
MUCID
MUCIN
MUCKY
MUCRO
MUCUS
MUDDY
MUDGE
MUFTI
MUGGY
MULCH
MULCT
MULLA
MULSE
MULTI
MUMMY
MUMPS
MUNCH
MUNDA
MUNGO
MUNRO
MURAL
MUREX
MURKY
MURRE
MURRY
MUSCA
MUSCI
MUSES
MUSHA
MUSHY
MUSIC
MUSIT
MUSKY
MUSSE
MUSSY
MUSTY
MUTED
MUZAK
MUZZY
NUBIA
NUCHA
NUDGE
NULLA
NUMEN
NUNKY
NURSE
NUTTY
OUGHT
OUIDA
OUIJA
OUNCE
OUSEL
OUTBY
OUTDO
OUTER
OUTGO
OUTRE
OUZEL
PUBIC
PUBIS
PUDGE
PUDGY
PUDOR
PUFFY
PUGIN
PUKKA
PULEX
PULPY
PULSE
PUNCH
PUNIC
PUNTO
PUPAL
PUPIL
PUPPY
PUREE
PURGE
PURIM
PURSE
PURSY
PUSHY
PUSLE
PUSSY
PUTID
PUTTO
PUTTY
QUACK
QUADS
QUAFF
QUAIL
QUAKE
QUALM
QUANT
QUARK
QUART
QUASH
QUASI
QUEEN
QUEER
QUELL
QUERN
QUERY
QUEST
QUEUE
QUICK
QUIDS
QUIET
QUIFF
QUILL
QUILP
QUILT
QUINS
QUINT
QUIRE
QUIRK
QUITE
QUITO
QUITS
QUOIF
QUOIN
QUOIT
QUORN
QUOTA
QUOTE
QUOTH
QURAN
RUBIN
RUBLE
RUCHE
RUDDY
RUDGE
RUFUS
RUGBY
RUING
RUINS
RULER
RULES
RUMBA
RUMEN
RUMEX
RUMMY
RUMOR
RUMPY
RUNCH
RUNES
RUNIC
RUNNY
RUNUP
RUPEE
RUPIA
RURAL
RUSHY
RUSSE
RUSSO
RUSTY
SUAVE
SUCKS
SUCRE
SUDAN
SUDOR
SUEDE
SUETY
SUGAN
SUGAR
SUITE
SUITS
SULFA
SULKS
SULKY
SULLA
SULLY
SUMMA
SUNDA
SUNNY
SUOMI
SUPER
SUPPE
SUPRA
SURGE
SURLY
SURYA
SUSAN
SUSHI
SUTCH
SUTOR
SUTRA
SUVLA
SUZIE
TUBBY
TUBER
TUDOR
TUFFE
TULIP
TULLE
TULLY
TUMID
TUMMY
TUMOR
TUNER
TUNIC
TUNIS
TUNKU
TUNNY
TUQUE
TURBO
TURCO
TURIN
TURKI
TURKU
TURPS
TUTOR
TUTSI
TUTTI
VULGO
VULVA
WURST
YUCCA
YUCKY
YUKKY
YUKON
YULAN
YUMMY
YUPIK
YUPPY
AVAIL
AVANT
AVAST
AVENA
AVENS
AVERT
AVIAN
AVION
AVISO
AVOID
AVOUÉ
EVADE
EVANS
EVENS
EVENT
EVERT
EVERY
EVIAN
EVICT
EVITA
EVITE
EVOKE
IVIED
IVORY
KVASS
MVULE
OVARY
OVATE
OVERT
OVINE
OVOID
OVULE
UVULA
AWAIT
AWAKE
AWARD
AWARE
AWARN
AWASH
AWEEL
AWFUL
AWOKE
BWANA
BWAZI
DWARF
DWELL
GWENT
OWING
OWLER
OWLET
OWNER
SWAIN
SWALE
SWAMI
SWAMP
SWANK
SWANS
SWARD
SWARF
SWARM
SWASH
SWATH
SWATS
SWAZI
SWEAR
SWEAT
SWEDE
SWEEP
SWEET
SWELL
SWELT
SWEPT
SWIFT
SWILL
SWINE
SWING
SWIPE
SWIRE
SWIRL
SWISH
SWISS
SWIZZ
SWOON
SWOOP
SWORD
SWORE
SWORN
SWUNG
TWAIN
TWANG
TWANK
TWEAK
TWEED
TWEET

TWERP
TWICE
TWIGS
TWILL
TWILT
TWINE
TWINS
TWIRL
TWIRP
TWIST
TWIXT
TWOER
AXIAL
AXIOM
AXOID
EXACT
EXALT
EXCEL
EXEAT
EXERT
EXILE
EXINE
EXIST
EXODE
EXPEL
EXTOL
EXTRA
EXUDE
EXULT
EXURB
IXION
OXBOW
OXEYE
OXIDE
OXIME
OXTER
AYRIE
BYLAW
BYRON
BYWAY
CYCAD
CYCLE
CYMRU
CYMRY
CYNIC
CYRUS
DYFED
DYING
DYKER
DYLAN
DYULA
EYRIE
EYTIE
FYLDE
GYGES
GYMNO
GYPPO
GYPSY
GYRUS
HYDRA
HYDRO
HYENA
HYLUM
HYMEN
HYPER
HYPHA
HYRAX
HYTHE
KYANG
KYLIE
KYLIN
KYLIX
KYLOE
KYRIE
LYCÉE
LYCRA
LYDIA
LYING
LYMPH
LYNCH
LYRIC
LYSIN
LYSIS
LYSOL
LYTHE
MYNAH
MYOMA
MYRON
MYRRH
NYALA
NYASA
NYLON
NYMPH
NYSSA
PYGMY
PYLON
PYREX
PYRUS
PYXIS
RYDAL
SYBIL
SYCEE
SYLPH
SYNGE
SYNOD
SYRAH
SYRIA
SYRUP
TYING
TYLER
TYNED
TYPED
TYPES
TYPHA
TYROL
WYMAN
XYLEM
XYRIS
AZOIC
AZOTE
AZTEC
AZURE
AZYME
CZECH
IZARD
IZMIR
IZZAT
OZARK
OZONE
PZAZZ
UZBEK

5:3

ABABA
ABACK
ABACO
ABAFT
ABASE
ABASH
ABATE
ADAGE
ADAMS
ADAPT
AGAIN
AGAMI
AGAPE
AGATE
AGAVE
ALACK
ALAMO
ALANS
ALAPA
ALARM
ALATE
AMAIN
AMANT
AMASS
AMAZE
ANANA
APACE
APAGE
APAID
APART
AQABA
ARABA
ASAPH
AVAIL
AVANT
AVAST
AWAIT
AWAKE
AWARD
AWARE
AWARN
AWASH
BEACH
BEADS
BEADY
BEALE
BEAMY
BEANO
BEANS
BEARD
BEAST
BEAUT
BHANG
BLACK
BLADE
BLAIR
BLAKE
BLAME
BLANC
BLAND
BLANK
BLARE
BLASÉ
BLAST
BLAZE
BOARD
BOAST
BRACE
BRACK
BRACT
BRADY
BRAID
BRAIN
BRAKE
BRAND
BRANK
BRASH
BRASS
BRAVA
BRAVE
BRAVO
BRAWL
BRAWN
BWANA
BWAZI
CEASE
CHACO
CHAFE
CHAFF
CHAIN
CHAIR
CHALK
CHAMP
CHANT
CHAOS
CHAPE
CHAPS
CHARD
CHARK
CHARM
CHART
CHARY
CHASE
CHASM
CLACK
CLAIM
CLAMP
CLANG
CLANK
CLARA
CLARE
CLARK
CLARY
CLASH
CLASP
CLASS
CLAUS
CLAVE
COACH
COADE
COAST
COATI
CRABS
CRACK
CRAFT
CRAIG
CRAKE
CRAMP
CRANE
CRANK
CRAPE
CRAPS
CRARE
CRASH
CRASS
CRATE
CRAVE
CRAWL
CRAZE
CRAZY
DEATH
DHABI
DIALS
DIANA
DIARY
DIAZO
DRACO
DRAFT
DRAIN
DRAKE
DRAMA
DRANK
DRAPE
DRAWL
DRAWN
DWARF
ELAND
ELATE
EMAIL
ENACT
ENARM
ERARD
ERASE
ERATO
ETAGE
ETAIN
ETAPE
ETATS
EVADE
EVANS
EXACT
EXALT
FEARE
FEAST
FLACK
FLAIL
FLAIR
FLAKE
FLAKY
FLAME
FLANK
FLARE
FLASH
FLASK
FLATS
FOAMY
FRACK
FRACT
FRAIL
FRAME
FRANC
FRANK
FRANS
FRANZ
FRAUD
GÉANT
GEARE
GHANA
GHATS
GHAZI
GIANT
GLACE
GLADE
GLAIR
GLAND
GLANS
GLASS
GLAZE
GNARL
GNASH
GOATY
GRAAL
GRACE
GRADE
GRAFF
GRAFT
GRAIL
GRAIN
GRAND
GRANT
GRAPE
GRAPH
GRASP
GRASS
GRATE
GRAVE
GRAVY
GRAYS
GRAZE
GUACO
GUANA
GUANO
GUARD
GUAVA
HEADS
HEADY
HEALD
HEAPS
HEARD
HEART
HEATH
HEAVE
HEAVY
HOARD
HOARE
HOARY
HOAST
IDAHO
IGAPO
IMAGE
IMAGO
IMARI
IMAUM
INANE
INAPT
INARI
INARM
IRAQI
IRATE
ISAAC
ITALA
ITALY
IZARD
JEANS
KAABA
KHAKI
KHAYA
KHAZI
KIANG
KLANG
KNACK
KNARL
KNAVE
KOALA
KRAAL
KRAFT
KRANG
KRANS
KRANZ
KRAUT
KUALA
KVASS
KYANG
LEACH
LEADS
LEAFY
LEAKY
LEANT
LEAPT
LEARN
LEASE
LEASH
LEAST
LEAVE
LHASA
LIANA
LIANE
LIANG
LIARD
LLAMA
LLANO
LOAMY
LOATH
MEALS
MEALY
MEANS
MEANT
MEATH
MEATS
MEATY
MIAMI
MIAOU
MIAOW
MIAUL
NAAFI
NEAGH
NEALE
NGAIO
NYALA
NYASA
OKAPI
OMAGH
OMANI
ORANG
ORATE
OSAGE
OSAKA
OTARY
OVARY
OVATE
OZARK
PEACE
PEACH
PEAKY
PEARL
PEASE
PEATY
PHARE
PHASE
PIANO
PIAVE
PLACE
PLACK
PLAID
PLAIN
PLAIT
PLANE
PLANK
PLANT
PLATE
PLATH
PLATO
PLATY

PLATZ
PLAYA
PLAZA
POACH
PRADO
PRAHU
PRANA
PRANG
PRANK
PRATE
PRAWL
PRAWN
PSALM
PZAZZ
QUACK
QUADS
QUAFF
QUAIL
QUAKE
QUALM
QUANT
QUARK
QUART
QUASH
QUASI
REACH
REACT
READE
READY
REALM
REAMS
REARM
RIANT
ROACH
ROAST
SCADS
SCAFF
SCALA
SCALD
SCALE
SCALP
SCALY
SCAMP
SCANT
SCAPA
SCAPE
SCARE
SCARF
SCARP
SCARY
SCATH
SCAUP
SCAUR
SEALS
SEAMY
SEARE
SHACK
SHADE
SHADY
SHAFT
SHAKE
SHAKO
SHAKY
SHALE
SHALL
SHALT
SHAME
SHANG
SHANK
SHANT
SHAPE
SHARD
SHARE
SHARK
SHARP
SHAUN
SHAVE
SHAWL
SHAWM
SKATE
SLACK
SLADE
SLAIN
SLAKE
SLANG
SLANT
SLASH
SLATE
SLATS
SLATY
SLAVE
SMACK
SMALL
SMARM
SMART
SMASH
SNACK
SNAFU
SNAGS
SNAIL
SNAKE
SNAKY
SNAPS
SNARE
SNARK
SNARL
SNASH
SOANE
SOAPY
SOARE
SPACE
SPADE
SPADO
SPAHI
SPAIN
SPALD
SPALL
SPALT
SPANK
SPARE
SPARK
SPART
SPASM
SPATE
SPATS
SPAWN
STACK
STADE
STAFF
STAGE
STAGY
STAID
STAIN
STAIR
STAKE
STALE
STALK
STALL
STAMP
STAND
STANK
STAPH
STARE
STARK
STARR
STARS
START
STASH
STASI
STATE
STAVE
STAYS
SUAVE
SWAIN
SWALE
SWAMI
SWAMP
SWANK
SWANS
SWARD
SWARF
SWARM
SWASH
SWATH
SWATS
SWAZI
TEACH
TEARS
TEASE
TEAZE
THAIS
THANE
THANK
TIARA
TOADY
TOAST
TRACE
TRACK
TRACT
TRADE
TRAIL
TRAIN
TRAIT
TRAMP
TRANS
TRANT
TRAPS
TRASH
TRAWL
TWAIN
TWANG
TWANK
UDALL
UKASE
UNAPT
UNARM
URALS
URATE
USAGE
VIAND
VLACH
WEALD
WEARY
WEAVE
WHACK
WHALE
WHANG
WHARF
WHAUP
WHAUR
WRACK
WRATH
YEARN
YEARS
YEAST
YEATS
ABBAS
ABBEY
ABBOT
AKBAR
ALBAN
ALBEE
ALBUM
AMBER
AMBIT
AMBLE
ARBOR
BABAR
BABEL
BABOO
BABUL
BEBOP
BIBBY
BIBLE
BOBBY
BUBBY
CABAL
CABAS
CABBY
CABER
CABIN
CABLE
CABOB
CABOT
CIBOL
COBOL
COBRA
CUBAN
CUBBY
CUBEB
CUBED
CUBIC
CUBIT
DEBAG
DEBAR
DEBEL
DEBIT
DEBUG
DEBUT
DOBBY
DOBRO
DUBAI
ELBOW
EMBED
EMBER
EMBOW
EMBOX
EMBUS
FABER
FABLE
FABRÉ
FIBER
FIBRE
FIBRO
FUBSY
GABBY
GABLE
GABON
GEBER
GIBBY
GIBUS
GOBBO
HABET
HABIT
HOBBS
HOBBY
HUBBY
IMBED
IMBUE
IQBAL
JABOT
JEBEL
KABOB
KABUL
KEBAB
KEBEL
KEBLE
KEBOB
LABDA
LABEL
LABIS
LABOR
LIBEL
LIBER
LIBRA
LIBYA
LOBAR
LOBBY
LOBED
LUBRA
MEBBE
NABOB
NEBEL
NOBBY
NOBEL
NOBLE
NOBLY
NUBIA
OMBER
OMBRE
ORBIT
OXBOW
PABLO
PUBIC
PUBIS
RABAT
RABBI
RABID
REBEL
REBUS
REBUT
ROBES
ROBEY
ROBIN
ROBOT
RUBIN
RUBLE
SABAL
SABER
SABIN
SABLE
SABOT
SABRA
SABRE
SIBYL
SOBER
SYBIL
TABBY
TABER
TABES
TABLA
TABLE
TABOO
TABOR
TIBBS
TIBBY
TIBER
TIBET
TIBIA
TOBIT
TUBBY
TUBER
UMBEL
UMBER
UMBLE
UMBRA
UNBAR
UNBED
URBAN
UZBEK
VIBES
WEBER
XEBEC
YOBBO
ZABRA
ZEBRA
ACCRA
ARCOT
ARCUS
ASCII
ASCOT
ASCUS
BACCY
BACKS
BACON
BECKY
BOCHE
BUCCA
BUCKO
BUCKS
CACAO
CACHE
CECIL
CECUM
COCCI
COCKY
COCOA
COCOS
CYCAD
CYCLE
DACCA
DACHA
DECAL
DECAY
DECCA
DECKO
DECOR
DECOY
DECRY
DICEY
DICKY
DOCKS
DUCAT
DUCHY
DUCKS
DUCKY
EMCEE
ESCOT
EXCEL
FACER
FACET
FACIA
FACTO
FACTS
FECAL
FECES
FECIT
FICHE
FICHU
FOCAL
FOCUS
FUCHS
GECKO
HACEK
HECHT
HECTO
HOCUS
INCLE
INCUR
INCUS
ITCHY
JACKS
JACOB
JOCKO
LACET
LACKS
LECOQ
LICHT
LICIT
LOCAL
LOCKE
LOCKS
LOCUM
LOCUS
LUCAN
LUCIA
LUCID
LUCIO
LUCKY
LUCRE
LYCÉE
LYCRA
MACAW
MACER
MACHO
MACLE
MACON
MACRO
MCCOY
MECCA
MICAH
MICHE
MICRO
MOCHA
MUCID
MUCIN
MUCKY
MUCRO
MUCUS
NACHE
NACHO
NACHT
NACRE
NICAD
NICHE
NICOL
NUCHA
OCCAM

OCCUR
ONCER
ONCUS
ORCUS
OSCAR
PACER
PACEY
PACHA
PECAN
PICEA
PICOT
PICUS
RACER
RACES
RECAP
RECCE
RECTO
RECUR
RICAN
RICIN
ROCKS
ROCKY
RUCHE
SACHA
SACHS
SACKS
SECCO
SHCHI
SOCKS
SOCLE
SUCKS
SUCRE
SYCEE
TACIT
TACKY
ULCER
UNCAP
UNCLE
UNCUS
UNCUT
VICAR
VICHY
VOCAL
WACKY
YACHT
YUCCA
YUCKY
ABDAR
ABDUL
ADDED
ADDER
ADDIO
ADDIS
ADDLE
AEDES
AIDAN
AIDOS
ALDAN
ALDER
ALDIS
ANDES
ARDEA
ARDEB
ARDEN
ARDIL
ARDOR
ASDIC
AUDEN
AUDIO
AUDIT
BADDY
BADEN
BADGE
BADLY
BEDAD
BEDEW
BIDDY
BIDET
BODES
BODGE
BUDDY
BUDGE
CADDY
CADET
CADGE
CADGY
CADRE
CEDAR
CIDER
CODED
CODEX
CUDDY
DADDY
DIDNT
DODDY
DODGE
DODGY
DUDDY
EGDON
EIDER
ELDER
EMDEN
ENDED
ENDOW
ENDUE
FADDY
FADED
FADGE
FIDEL
FIDES
FUDGE
GADGE
GADUS
GIDDY
GODET
GODLY
HADES
HADJI
HADNT
HEDDA
HEDGE
HODGE
HYDRA
HYDRO
INDEW
INDEX
INDIA
INDRA
INDRE
INDRI
INDUE
INDUS
JADED
JADIS
JUDAS
JUDGE
KEDAR
KEDGE
KEDGY
KIDDY
KIDGE
KODAK
KUDOS
KUDZU
LADEN
LADLE
LEDGE
LODEN
LODGE
LUDIC
LYDIA
MADAM
MADGE
MADLY
MEDAL
MEDEA
MEDIA
MEDIC
MEDOC
MIDAS
MIDDY
MIDGE
MIDST
MODAL
MODEL
MODEM
MODER
MODUS
MUDDY
MUDGE
NADER
NADIR
NEDDY
NIDOR
NIDUS
NODAL
NODDY
NODES
NODUS
NUDGE
ODDER
ODDLY
OLDEN
OLDER
OLDIE
ORDER
PADDY
PADMA
PADRE
PEDAL
PEDRO
PODEX
PODGE
PODGY
PUDGE
PUDGY
PUDOR
RADAR
RADHA
RADIO
RADIX
RADON
REDAN
REDON
REDOX
RIDER
RIDGE
RODEO
RODIN
RUDDY
RUDGE
RYDAL
SADHU
SADIE
SADLY
SEDAN
SEDGE
SEDUM
SIDHA
SIDLE
SIDON
SODOM
SODOR
SUDAN
SUDOR
TEDDY
TIDAL
TIDDY
TODAY
TODDY
TUDOR
UDDER
UNDAM
UNDER
UNDID
UNDUE
VADUZ
VEDDA
VEDIC
VIDEO
VODKA
WADER
WEDGE
WIDEN
WIDOW
WIDTH
WODEN
WODGE
YODEL
ZADOK
ABEAM
ABEAR
ABELE
ACERB
ADEEM
ADEPT
AFEAR
AGENT
AHEAD
AKELA
AKENE
ALEPH
ALERT
ALEUT
AMEBA
AMEND
AMENE
AMENT
ANEAR
ANELE
ANEND
ANENT
APEAK
APERT
ARECA
AREDE
ARENA
ARENE
ARENT
ARETE
AVENA
AVENS
AVERT
AWEEL
BEECH
BEEFY
BEERY
BLEAK
BLEAR
BLEAT
BLEED
BLEEP
BLEND
BLESS
BLEST
BREAD
BREAK
BREAM
BREDA
BREDE
BREED
BREEM
BREME
BRENT
BREST
BREVE
CHEAP
CHEAT
CHECK
CHEEK
CHEEP
CHEER
CHEKA
CHERE
CHERT
CHESS
CHEST
CHEVY
CHEWY
CLEAN
CLEAR
CLEAT
CLECK
CLEEK
CLEEP
CLEFT
CLEPE
CLERK
CREAK
CREAM
CRECY
CREDO
CREED
CREEK
CREEL
CREEP
CREME
CREON
CREPE
CREPT
CRESS
CREST
CRETE
CREWE
CZECH
DEEDS
DIEGO
DREAD
DREAM
DREAR
DREGS
DRERE
DRESS
DWELL
EDEMA
EGEST
EJECT
ELECT
ELEGY
ELENE
EMEND
EMERY
ENEMA
ENEMY
ERECT
EVENS
EVENT
EVERT
EVERY
EXEAT
EXERT
FAERY
FIELD
FIEND
FIERE
FIERY
FLECK
FLEET
FLESH
FLEUR
FLEWS
FOEHN
FREAK
FREED
FREON
FRESH
FREUD
FUERO
GEESE
GLEAM
GLEAN
GLEBE
GLEEK
GLEET
GREAT
GREBE
GREED
GREEK
GREEN
GREER
GREET
GREGG
GRETA
GREYS
GUELF
GUESS
GUEST
GUEUX
GWENT
HEELS
HYENA
IBERT
ICENI
IDEAL
IDEAS
ILEAC
ILEUM
ILEUS
INEPT
INERT
IRENA
IRENE
ISERE
KEECH
KEELS
KEEPS
KLEIN
KNEAD
KNEEL
KNELL
KNELT
LEECH
LEEDS
LEERY
LEESE
LIEGE
LOESS
MAEVE
MEETS
NEEDS
NEEDY
NIECE
NIEVE
OBEAH
OBESE
OCEAN
ODEON
ODETS
OLEIC
OLEIN
OLEUM
OMEGA
OPERA
OVERT
OXEYE
PAEAN
PEERS
PEEVE
PHEBE
PHENO
PHEON
PIECE
PIERS
PIERT
PIETA
PIETY
PIEZO
PLEAD
PLEAT
PLEBS
PLEIN
POEMS
POESY
POETS
PREEN
PRESA
PRESS
PREST
PSEUD
QUEEN
QUEER
QUELL
QUERN
QUERY
QUEST
QUEUE
REECH
REEDE

REEDS
REEDY
REEVE
RHEIN
RHETT
RHEUM
SCENE
SCENT
SEEDY
SHEAF
SHEAR
SHEBA
SHEEL
SHEEN
SHEEP
SHEER
SHEET
SHEIK
SHELF
SHELL
SHERD
SHERE
SIEGE
SIEVE
SKEAN
SKEER
SKEET
SKEIN
SKELM
SKELP
SLEEK
SLEEP
SLEET
SLEPT
SMEAR
SMEEK
SMELL
SMELT
SNEAD
SNEAK
SNECK
SNEER
SPEAK
SPEAN
SPEAR
SPECK
SPECS
SPEED
SPEER
SPEKE
SPELL
SPELT
SPEND
SPENS
SPENT
SPERM
STEAD
STEAK
STEAL
STEAM
STEED
STEEK
STEEL
STEEN
STEEP
STEER
STEIN
STELA
STELE
STENT
STEPS
STERN
STEVE
STEWS
STEWY
SUEDE
SUETY
SWEAR
SWEAT
SWEDE
SWEEP
SWEET
SWELL
SWELT
SWEPT
TEENS
TEENY
TEETH
THECA
THEFT
THEGN
THEIR
THEMA
THEME
THERE
THERM
THESE
THETA
THETE
THEWS
TREAD
TREAT
TRECK
TREEN
TREES
TREMA
TREND
TRENT
TRESS
TREVI
TREWS
TWEAK
TWEED
TWEET
TWERP
ULEMA
UPEND
UREDO
VNECK
WEEDS
WEEDY
WEEKS
WEENY
WEEPY
WHEAL
WHEAT
WHEEL
WHEEN
WHELK
WHELP
WHERE
WIELD
WREAK
WRECK
WREST
YIELD
AFFIX
ALFIE
AWFUL
BAFFY
BEFIT
BEFOG
BIFID
BUFFO
BUFFS
CUFFS
CUFFY
CUFIC
DAFFY
DEFER
DEFOE
DYFED
ELFIN
FIFTH
FIFTY
GAFFE
GIFTS
GOFER
HAFIZ
HEFTY
HUFFY
INFER
INFRA
JAFFA
JIFFY
KAFIR
KAFKA
KEFIR
KOFTA
KUFIC
LEFTY
LIFER
LOFTY
LUFFA
MAFIA
MIFFY
MUFTI
NIFTY
OFFAL
OFFAS
OFFER
ORFEO
PUFFY
REFER
REFIT
RIFLE
RUFUS
SOFIA
SOFTY
TAFFY
TUFFE
UNFED
UNFIT
WAFER
AEGIS
AGGER
AGGRO
ALGAE
ALGID
ALGOL
ANGEL
ANGER
ANGLE
ANGLO
ANGRY
ANGST
ANGUS
ARGIL
ARGOT
ARGUE
ARGUS
AUGER
AUGHT
AUGUR
BAGEL
BAGGY
BEGAD
BEGAN
BEGET
BEGIN
BEGUM
BEGUN
BIGHT
BIGOT
BOGEY
BOGGY
BOGIE
BOGLE
BOGUS
BUGGY
BUGLE
CAGEY
CAGOT
CIGAR
CIGGY
DAGON
DEGAS
DIGHT
DIGIT
DOGGO
DOGGY
DOGMA
EAGER
EAGLE
EDGAR
EDGED
EDGER
EGGAR
EIGER
EIGHT
ELGAR
ELGIN
ERGOT
FAGOT
FAGUS
FIGHT
FOGEY
FOGGY
FUGAL
FUGGY
FUGUE
GIGLI
GIGOT
GIGUE
GOGOL
GYGES
HAGUE
HEGEL
HIGHT
HOGAN
INGLE
INGOT
IRGUN
JUGAL
LAGAN
LAGER
LAGOS
LEGAL
LEGER
LEGGE
LEGGY
LEGIT
LIGGE
LIGHT
LOGAN
LOGIC
LOGOS
LUGER
MAGIC
MAGMA
MAGNA
MAGOG
MAGUS
MIGHT
MOGGY
MOGUL
MUGGY
NAGAS
NAGOR
NEGEV
NEGRO
NEGUS
NIGEL
NIGER
NIGHT
OGGIN
ORGAN
ORGUE
OUGHT
PAGAN
PAGER
PAGES
PEGGY
PIGGY
PIGMY
PUGIN
PYGMY
RAGED
RAGGY
REGAL
REGAN
REGIA
RÉGIE
REGIS
RÈGLE
RIGHT
RIGID
RIGOR
ROGER
ROGET
ROGUE
RUGBY
SAGES
SAGGY
SEGUE
SIGHS
SIGHT
SIGIL
SIGLA
SIGMA
SIGNS
SOGGY
SUGAN
SUGAR
TAGUS
TIGER
TIGHT
TIGON
UNGET
VAGUE
VAGUS
VEGAN
VIGIL
VIGOR
VOGUE
WAGER
WAGES
WAGGA
WAGON
WIGAN
WIGHT
ZIGAN
ABHOR
APHID
APHIS
ASHEN
ASHER
ASHES
ASHET
ATHOS
BAHAI
BAHUT
BEHAN
BOHEA
COHOE
EPHOD
EPHOR
ETHAL
ETHER
ETHIC
ETHOS
ETHYL
ICHOR
JEHAD
JIHAD
LEHAR
MAHDI
MAHOE
MAHUA
MAHWA
NAHUM
NEHRU
NIHIL
OCHER
OCHRE
OGHAM
OPHIR
OTHER
PSHAW
RAHAB
ROHAN
SAHEL
SAHIB
SCHWA
TEHEE
USHER
UTHER
YAHOO
YAHVE
ZOHAR
ABIDE
ABIES
ACINI
ADIEU
ADIGE
ADIOS
AFIRE
AGILE
AGING
AGIST
ALIAS
ALIBI
ALICE
ALIEN
ALIGN
ALIKE
ALIVE
AMICE
AMIEL
AMIGO
AMINE
AMINO
AMISH
AMISS
AMITY
ANIGH
ANIMA
ANION
ANISE
ANITA
ARIAN
ARICA
ARIEL
ARIES
ARISE
ARISH
ARIST
ARITA
ASIAN
ASIDE
ATILT
AVIAN
AVION
AVISO
AXIAL
AXIOM
BAIRD
BAIRN
BAIZE
BEIGE
BEING
BLIGH
BLIMP
BLIND
BLINI
BLINK
BLISS
BLITZ
BOING
BRIAN
BRIAR
BRIBE
BRICK
BRIDE
BRIEF
BRIER
BRILL
BRINE
BRING
BRINK
BRINY
BRISK
BRIZE
BUICK
BUILD
BUILT
CAINE
CAIRN

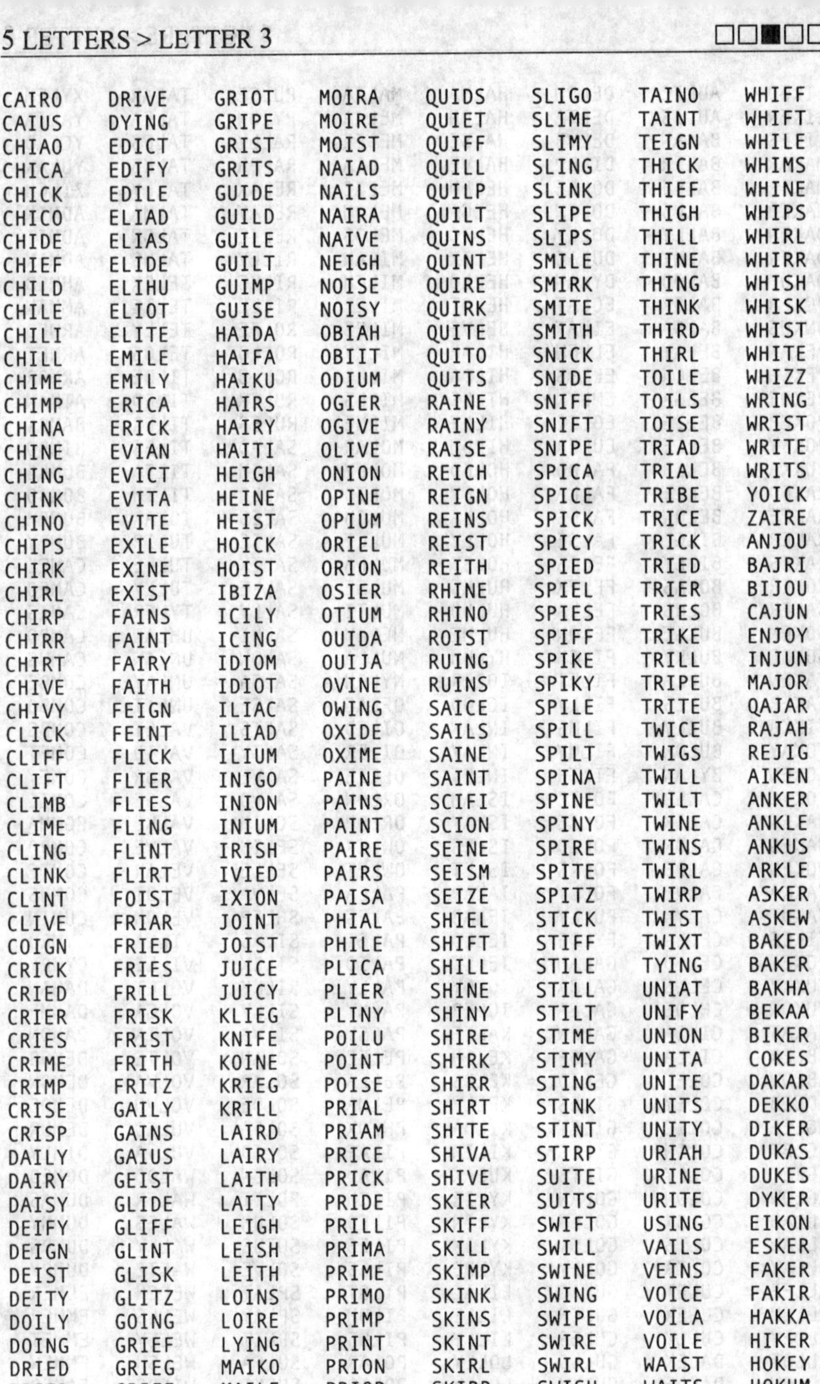

CAIRO
CAIUS
CHIAO
CHICA
CHICK
CHICO
CHIDE
CHIEF
CHILD
CHILE
CHILI
CHILL
CHIME
CHIMP
CHINA
CHINE
CHING
CHINK
CHINO
CHIPS
CHIRK
CHIRL
CHIRP
CHIRR
CHIRT
CHIVE
CHIVY
CLICK
CLIFF
CLIFT
CLIMB
CLIME
CLING
CLINK
CLINT
CLIVE
COIGN
CRICK
CRIED
CRIER
CRIES
CRIME
CRIMP
CRISE
CRISP
DAILY
DAIRY
DAISY
DEIFY
DEIGN
DEIST
DEITY
DOILY
DOING
DRIED
DRIER
DRIES
DRIFT
DRILL
DRILY
DRINK
DRIVE
DYING
EDICT
EDIFY
EDILE
ELIAD
ELIAS
ELIDE
ELIHU
ELIOT
ELITE
EMILE
EMILY
ERICA
ERICK
EVIAN
EVICT
EVITA
EVITE
EXILE
EXINE
EXIST
FAINS
FAINT
FAIRY
FAITH
FEIGN
FEINT
FLICK
FLIER
FLIES
FLING
FLINT
FLIRT
FOIST
FRIAR
FRIED
FRIES
FRILL
FRISK
FRIST
FRITH
FRITZ
GAILY
GAINS
GAIUS
GEIST
GLIDE
GLIFF
GLINT
GLISK
GLITZ
GOING
GRIEF
GRIEG
GRIFF
GRILL
GRIME
GRIMM
GRIMY
GRIND
GRIOT
GRIPE
GRIST
GRITS
GUIDE
GUILD
GUILE
GUILT
GUIMP
GUISE
HAIDA
HAIFA
HAIKU
HAIRS
HAIRY
HAITI
HEIGH
HEINE
HEIST
HOICK
HOIST
IBIZA
ICILY
ICING
IDIOM
IDIOT
ILIAC
ILIAD
ILIUM
INIGO
INION
INIUM
IRISH
IVIED
IXION
JOINT
JOIST
JUICE
JUICY
KLIEG
KNIFE
KOINE
KRIEG
KRILL
LAIRD
LAIRY
LAITH
LAITY
LEIGH
LEISH
LEITH
LOINS
LOIRE
LYING
MAIKO
MAILE
MAINE
MAINS
MAIRE
MAIZE
MEITH
MOIRA
MOIRE
MOIST
NAIAD
NAILS
NAIRA
NAIVE
NEIGH
NOISE
NOISY
OBIAH
OBIIT
ODIUM
OGIER
OGIVE
OLIVE
ONION
OPINE
OPIUM
ORIEL
ORION
OSIER
OTIUM
OUIDA
OUIJA
OVINE
OWING
OXIDE
OXIME
PAINE
PAINS
PAINT
PAIRE
PAIRS
PAISA
PHIAL
PHILE
PLICA
PLIER
PLINY
POILU
POINT
POISE
PRIAL
PRIAM
PRICE
PRICK
PRIDE
PRILL
PRIMA
PRIME
PRIMO
PRIMP
PRINT
PRION
PRIOR
PRISE
PRISM
PRIVY
PRIZE
QUICK
QUIDS
QUIET
QUIFF
QUILL
QUILP
QUILT
QUINS
QUINT
QUIRE
QUIRK
QUITE
QUITO
QUITS
RAINE
RAINY
RAISE
REICH
REIGN
REINS
REIST
REITH
RHINE
RHINO
ROIST
RUING
RUINS
SAICE
SAILS
SAINE
SAINT
SCIFI
SCION
SEINE
SEISM
SEIZE
SHIEL
SHIFT
SHILL
SHINE
SHINY
SHIRE
SHIRK
SHIRR
SHIRT
SHITE
SHIVA
SHIVE
SKIER
SKIFF
SKILL
SKIMP
SKINK
SKINS
SKINT
SKIRL
SKIRR
SKIRT
SKIVE
SLICE
SLICK
SLIDE
SLIGO
SLIME
SLIMY
SLING
SLINK
SLIPE
SLIPS
SMILE
SMIRK
SMITE
SMITH
SNICK
SNIDE
SNIFF
SNIFT
SNIPE
SPICA
SPICE
SPICK
SPICY
SPIED
SPIEL
SPIES
SPIFF
SPIKE
SPIKY
SPILE
SPILL
SPILT
SPINA
SPINE
SPINY
SPIRE
SPITE
SPITZ
STICK
STIFF
STILE
STILL
STILT
STIME
STIMY
STING
STINK
STINT
STIRP
SUITE
SUITS
SWIFT
SWILL
SWINE
SWING
SWIPE
SWIRE
SWIRL
SWISH
SWISS
SWIZZ
TAIGA
TAILS
TAINE
TAINO
TAINT
TEIGN
THICK
THIEF
THIGH
THILL
THINE
THING
THINK
THIRD
THIRL
TOILE
TOILS
TOISE
TRIAD
TRIAL
TRIBE
TRICE
TRICK
TRIED
TRIER
TRIES
TRIKE
TRILL
TRIPE
TRITE
TWICE
TWIGS
TWILL
TWILT
TWINE
TWINS
TWIRL
TWIRP
TWIST
TWIXT
TYING
UNIAT
UNIFY
UNION
UNITA
UNITE
UNITS
UNITY
URIAH
URINE
URITE
USING
VAILS
VEINS
VOICE
VOILA
VOILE
WAIST
WAITS
WAIVE
WEIGH
WEILL
WEIRD
WHICH
WHIFF
WHIFT
WHILE
WHIMS
WHINE
WHIPS
WHIRL
WHIRR
WHISH
WHISK
WHIST
WHITE
WHIZZ
WRING
WRIST
WRITE
WRITS
YOICK
ZAIRE
ANJOU
BAJRI
BIJOU
CAJUN
ENJOY
INJUN
MAJOR
QAJAR
RAJAH
REJIG
AIKEN
ANKER
ANKLE
ANKUS
ARKLE
ASKER
ASKEW
BAKED
BAKER
BAKHA
BEKAA
BIKER
COKES
DAKAR
DEKKO
DIKER
DUKAS
DUKES
DYKER
EIKON
ESKER
FAKER
FAKIR
HAKKA
HIKER
HOKEY
HOKUM
ICKER
JAKES
JOKER
KOKUM
KUKRI

LIKED
LIKEN
LIKES
MAKAR
MAKER
NAKED
OAKEN
OAKER
OAKUM
OCKER
ONKUS
PEKAN
PEKIN
PEKOE
POKER
POKEY
PUKKA
RAKED
RAKEE
RAKER
RAKES
ROKER
SAKER
SOKEN
SOKOL
TAKEN
TAKER
TIKKA
TOKAY
TOKEN
TOKYO
WAKEN
WAKES
WOKEN
YAKKA
YAKUT
YIKES
YOKEL
YUKKY
YUKON
ZAKAT
ABLER
ABLOW
ADLIB
AGLEE
AGLET
AGLEY
AGLOW
ALLAH
ALLAN
ALLAY
ALLÉE
ALLEN
ALLEY
ALLOT
ALLOW
ALLOY
ALLYL
ARLES
ATLAS
ATLIN

AULIC
AULIS
BALAN
BALER
BALFE
BALLS
BALLY
BALMY
BALOO
BALOR
BALSA
BELAY
BELCH
BELGA
BELIE
BELLE
BELLS
BELLY
BELOW
BILGE
BILLY
BOLAS
BOLUS
BULGE
BULKY
BULLA
BULLS
BULLY
BULOW
BYLAW
CALEB
CALIX
CALOR
CALPE
CALVE
CALYX
CELLA
CELLO
CELLS
CHLOE
CILIA
CILLA
COLET
COLEY
COLIC
COLIN
COLLY
COLON
COLOR
COLTS
COLZA
CULET
CULEX
CULLY
DALEK
DALLE
DALLY
DELAY
DELFT
DELHI
DELOS

DELPH
DELTA
DELVE
DILDO
DOLCE
DOLIN
DOLLY
DULAC
DYLAN
ECLAT
EILAT
ELLEN
ELLIS
EMLYN
EOLIC
EULER
FALDO
FALLA
FALLS
FALSE
FELIS
FELIX
FELLA
FELON
FILCH
FILET
FILLY
FILMS
FILMY
FILTH
FOLIC
FOLIE
FOLIO
FOLKS
FOLLY
FULLY
FYLDE
GALAM
GALBA
GALEA
GALEN
GALOP
GELID
GILES
GILET
GILLS
GILTS
GOLAN
GOLEM
GOLGI
GOLLY
GULAG
GULCH
GULES
GULLS
GULLY
GULPH
HALER
HALFA
HALLÉ
HALLO

HALMA
HALON
HALSE
HALVE
HELEN
HELGA
HELIO
HELIX
HELLO
HELOT
HELVE
HILAR
HILDA
HILLS
HILLY
HILUM
HOLED
HOLEY
HOLLA
HOLLY
HOLST
HULKS
HULLO
HULME
HYLUM
IDLER
IGLOO
INLAW
INLAY
INLET
ISLAM
ISLAY
ISLES
ISLET
JALAP
JELAB
JELLO
JELLY
JOLLY
JULEP
KALIF
KELIM
KELLS
KELLY
KILDA
KILIM
KULAK
KYLIE
KYLIN
KYLIX
KYLOE
LILAC
LILLE
LILLY
LOLLY
LULLY
MALAR
MALAY
MALFI
MALIK
MALMO

MALTA
MELBA
MELEE
MELIA
MELIC
MELON
MELOS
MILAN
MILCH
MILER
MILES
MILKY
MILLI
MILLS
MILNE
MOLAR
MOLLY
MOLTO
MULCH
MULCT
MULLA
MULSE
MULTI
NELLY
NULLA
NYLON
OFLAG
OILED
OILER
OLLIE
ORLON
ORLOP
OWLER
OWLET
PALEA
PALES
PALET
PALIO
PALLY
PALMY
PALSY
PELEE
PELLA
PELMA
PHLOX
PILAF
PILAU
PILCH
PILED
PILES
PILLS
PILOT
PILUM
PILUS
POLAR
POLIO
POLKA
POLLY
POLYP
PULEX
PULPY

PULSE
PYLON
RALLY
RALPH
RELAX
RELAY
RELIC
RILEY
RILKE
RILLE
ROLFE
ROLLO
ROLLS
RULER
RULES
SALAD
SALEM
SALEP
SALES
SALIC
SALIX
SALLE
SALLY
SALMI
SALON
SALSA
SALSE
SALTS
SALTY
SALVE
SALVO
SCLIM
SELIM
SELLE
SELVA
SHLEP
SILAS
SILEX
SILKY
SILLY
SILVA
SOLAN
SOLAR
SOLDE
SOLFA
SOLID
SOLON
SOLTI
SOLUM
SOLUS
SOLVE
SPLAT
SPLAY
SPLIT
SULFA
SULKS
SULKY
SULLA
SULLY
SYLPH
TALAQ

TALAR
TALEA
TALES
TALKS
TALLY
TALMA
TALON
TALUS
TELEX
TELIC
TELLY
TELOS
TILDE
TILED
TILER
TILES
TILIA
TILTH
TOLAR
TULIP
TULLE
TULLY
TYLER
UHLAN
UNLAW
UNLAY
UNLIT
VALET
VALID
VALOR
VALSE
VALUE
VALVE
VELAR
VELDT
VELUM
VILLA
VILLI
VOLET
VOLGA
VOLTA
VOLTE
VOLVA
VOLVO
VULGO
VULVA
WALDO
WALER
WALES
WALLY
WALTZ
WELCH
WELLS
WELLY
WELSH
WILDE
WILDS
WILES
WILGA
WILLY
WILTS

XYLEM
YALTA
YCLAD
YULAN
ZILCH
ADMIN
ADMIT
ADMIX
AHMED
AMMAN
ARMED
ARMET
ARMOR
ATMAN
BAMBI
BIMBO
BOMBE
BOMBO
BUMPH
BUMPY
CAMEL
CAMEO
CAMIS
CAMPO
CAMUS
COMBE
COMBO
COMBS
COMET
COMFY
COMIC
COMMA
COMPO
COMTE
COMUS
CUMIN
CYMRU
CYMRY
DAMAN
DAMME
DAMON
DEMOB
DEMON
DEMOS
DEMUR
DIMLY
DOMED
DUMAS
DUMMY
DUMPS
DUMPY
ELMER
EMMER
EMMET
ENMEW
FAMED
FEMTO
FEMUR
FUMED
FUMES
FUMET

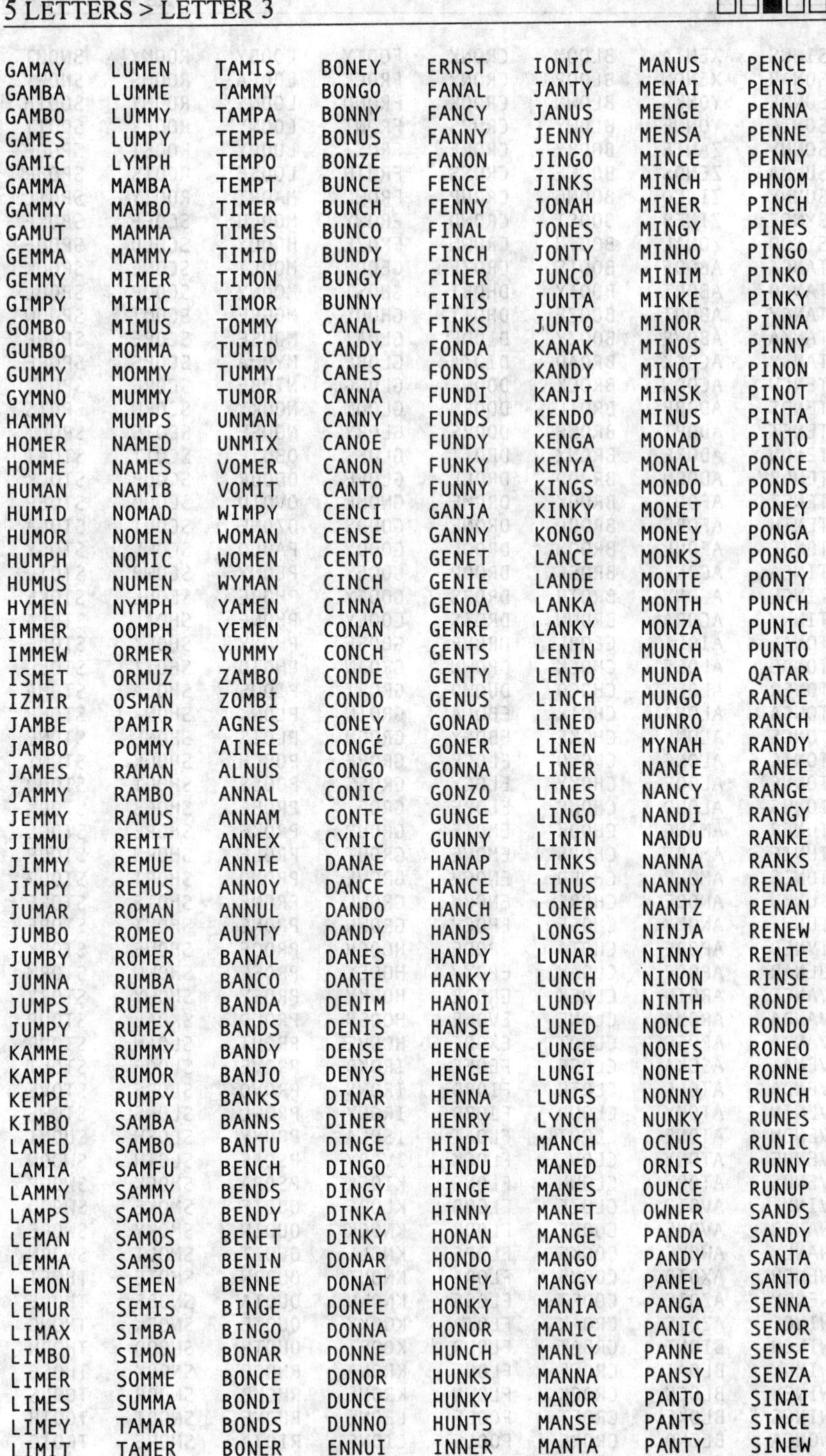

GAMAY
GAMBA
GAMBO
GAMES
GAMIC
GAMMA
GAMMY
GAMUT
GEMMA
GEMMY
GIMPY
GOMBO
GUMBO
GUMMY
GYMNO
HAMMY
HOMER
HOMME
HUMAN
HUMID
HUMOR
HUMPH
HUMUS
HYMEN
IMMER
IMMEW
ISMET
IZMIR
JAMBE
JAMBO
JAMES
JAMMY
JEMMY
JIMMU
JIMMY
JIMPY
JUMAR
JUMBO
JUMBY
JUMNA
JUMPS
JUMPY
KAMME
KAMPF
KEMPE
KIMBO
LAMED
LAMIA
LAMMY
LAMPS
LEMAN
LEMMA
LEMON
LEMUR
LIMAX
LIMBO
LIMER
LIMES
LIMEY
LIMIT
LOMAN

LUMEN
LUMME
LUMMY
LUMPY
LYMPH
MAMBA
MAMBO
MAMMA
MAMMY
MIMER
MIMIC
MIMUS
MOMMA
MOMMY
MUMMY
MUMPS
NAMED
NAMES
NAMIB
NOMAD
NOMEN
NOMIC
NUMEN
NYMPH
OOMPH
ORMER
ORMUZ
OSMAN
PAMIR
POMMY
RAMAN
RAMBO
RAMUS
REMIT
REMUE
REMUS
ROMAN
ROMEO
ROMER
RUMBA
RUMEN
RUMEX
RUMMY
RUMOR
RUMPY
SAMBA
SAMBO
SAMFU
SAMMY
SAMOA
SAMOS
SAMSO
SEMEN
SEMIS
SIMBA
SIMON
SOMME
SUMMA
TAMAR
TAMER
TAMIL

TAMIS
TAMMY
TAMPA
TEMPE
TEMPO
TEMPT
TIMER
TIMES
TIMID
TIMON
TIMOR
TOMMY
TUMID
TUMMY
TUMOR
UNMAN
UNMIX
VOMER
VOMIT
WIMPY
WOMAN
WOMEN
WYMAN
YAMEN
YEMEN
YUMMY
ZAMBO
ZOMBI
AGNES
AINEE
ALNUS
ANNAL
ANNAM
ANNEX
ANNIE
ANNOY
ANNUL
AUNTY
BANAL
BANCO
BANDA
BANDS
BANDY
BANJO
BANKS
BANNS
BANTU
BENCH
BENDS
BENDY
BENET
BENIN
BENNE
BINGE
BINGO
BONAR
BONCE
BONDI
BONDS
BONER
BONES

BONEY
BONGO
BONNY
BONUS
BONZE
BUNCE
BUNCH
BUNCO
BUNDY
BUNGY
BUNNY
CANAL
CANDY
CANES
CANNA
CANNY
CANOE
CANON
CANTO
CENCI
CENSE
CENTO
CINCH
CINNA
CONAN
CONCH
CONDE
CONDO
CONEY
CONGÉ
CONGO
CONIC
CONTE
CYNIC
DANAE
DANCE
DANDO
DANDY
DANES
DANTE
DENIM
DENIS
DENSE
DENYS
DINAR
DINER
DINGE
DINGO
DINGY
DINKA
DINKY
DONAR
DONAT
DONEE
DONNA
DONNE
DONOR
DUNCE
DUNNO
ENNUI
ERNIE

ERNST
FANAL
FANCY
FANNY
FANON
FENCE
FENNY
FINAL
FINCH
FINER
FINIS
FINKS
FONDA
FONDS
FUNDI
FUNDS
FUNDY
FUNKY
FUNNY
GANJA
GANNY
GENET
GENIE
GENOA
GENRE
GENTS
GENTY
GENUS
GONAD
GONER
GONNA
GONZO
GUNGE
GUNNY
HANAP
HANCE
HANCH
HANDS
HANDY
HANKY
HANOI
HANSE
HENCE
HENGE
HENNA
HENRY
HINDI
HINDU
HINGE
HINNY
HONAN
HONDO
HONEY
HONKY
HONOR
HUNCH
HUNKS
HUNKY
HUNTS
INNER
INNES

IONIC
JANTY
JANUS
JENNY
JINGO
JINKS
JONAH
JONES
JONTY
JUNCO
JUNTA
JUNTO
KANAK
KANDY
KANJI
KENDO
KENGA
KENYA
KINGS
KINKY
KONGO
LANCE
LANDE
LANKA
LANKY
LENIN
LENTO
LINCH
LINED
LINEN
LINER
LINES
LINGO
LININ
LINKS
LINUS
LONER
LONGS
LUNAR
LUNCH
LUNDY
LUNED
LUNGE
LUNGI
LUNGS
LYNCH
MANCH
MANED
MANES
MANET
MANGE
MANGO
MANGY
MANIA
MANIC
MANLY
MANNA
MANOR
MANSE
MANTA
MANUL

MANUS
MENAI
MENGE
MENSA
MINCE
MINCH
MINER
MINGY
MINHO
MINIM
MINKE
MINOR
MINOS
MINOT
MINSK
MINUS
MONAD
MONAL
MONDO
MONET
MONEY
MONKS
MONTE
MONTH
MONZA
MUNCH
MUNDA
MUNGO
MUNRO
MYNAH
NANCE
NANCY
NANDI
NANDU
NANNA
NANNY
NANTZ
NINJA
NINNY
NINON
NINTH
NONCE
NONES
NONET
NONNY
NUNKY
OCNUS
ORNIS
OUNCE
OWNER
PANDA
PANDY
PANEL
PANGA
PANIC
PANNE
PANSY
PANTO
PANTS
PANTY
PENAL

PENCE
PENIS
PENNA
PENNE
PENNY
PHNOM
PINCH
PINES
PINGO
PINKO
PINKY
PINNA
PINNY
PINON
PINOT
PINTA
PINTO
PONCE
PONDS
PONEY
PONGA
PONGO
PONTY
PUNCH
PUNIC
PUNTO
QATAR
RANCE
RANCH
RANDY
RANEE
RANGE
RANGY
RANKE
RANKS
RENAL
RENAN
RENEW
RENTE
RINSE
RONDE
RONDO
RONEO
RONNE
RUNCH
RUNES
RUNIC
RUNNY
RUNUP
SANDS
SANDY
SANTA
SANTO
SENNA
SENOR
SENSE
SENZA
SINAI
SINCE
SINEW
SINGE

SINUS
SONAR
SONDE
SONIC
SONNY
SUNDA
SUNNY
SYNGE
SYNOD
TANGA
TANGO
TANGY
TANKA
TANSY
TENCH
TENDS
TENET
TENON
TENOR
TENSE
TENTH
TENUE
TINEA
TINGE
TINNY
TONAL
TONDO
TONER
TONGA
TONGS
TONIC
TONNE
TONUS
TUNER
TUNIC
TUNIS
TUNKU
TUNNY
TYNED
ULNAR
VANCE
VANDA
VANYA
VENAL
VENDA
VENIN
VENOM
VENUE
VENUS
VINYL
WANED
WANLY
WENCH
WENDY
WINCE
WINCH
WINDY
WINEY
WINGS
WONGA
WONKY

XENIA
XENON
YONKS
YONNE
ZANTE
ZENOS
ZINCO
ZINEB
ZONAL
ABODE
ABORT
ABOUT
ABOVE
ACOCK
ACORN
ADOBE
ADOPT
ADORE
ADORN
AFOOT
AFORE
AFOUL
AGONE
AGONY
AGORA
AIOLI
ALOES
ALOFT
ALOHA
ALONE
ALONG
ALOOF
ALOUD
AMONG
AMORT
AMOUR
ANODE
ANOMY
APODE
APOOP
AROID
AROMA
AROSE
ASOKA
ATOLL
ATOMY
ATONE
ATONY
ATOPY
AVOID
AVOUÉ
AWOKE
AXOID
AZOIC
AZOTE
BIONT
BLOAT
BLOCK
BLOKE
BLOND
BLOOD

BLOOM
BLOOP
BLOWN
BLOWY
BOOBY
BOONE
BOONG
BOOST
BOOTH
BOOTS
BOOTY
BOOZE
BOOZY
BROAD
BROCK
BROIL
BROKE
BRONX
BROOD
BROOK
BROOL
BROOM
BROSE
BROTH
BROWN
CEORL
CHOCK
CHOCO
CHOIR
CHOKE
CHOKO
CHOKY
CHOMP
CHOOK
CHOPS
CHORD
CHORE
CHOSE
CHOTA
CLOAK
CLOCK
CLONE
CLOOT
CLOSE
CLOTH
CLOUD
CLOUT
CLOVE
CLOWN
CLOZE
COOEE
COOKS
COOMB
COOPT
CROAK
CROAT
CROCE
CROCK
CROFT
CROME
CRONE

CRONK
CRONY
CROOK
CROPS
CRORE
CROSS
CROUP
CROWD
CROWN
CROZE
DHOBI
DHOTI
DIODE
DIOTA
DOONE
DOORN
DOORS
DROIT
DROLL
DROME
DRONE
DROOL
DROOP
DROPS
DROSS
DROVE
DROWN
DUOMO
EBOLA
EBONY
ELOGE
ELOGY
ELOPE
EMOTE
EMOVE
ENOCH
ENORM
EPOCH
EPODE
EPOXY
ERODE
EVOKE
EXODE
FEOFF
FIORD
FJORD
FLOAT
FLOCK
FLONG
FLOOD
FLOOR
FLOPS
FLORA
FLOSS
FLOTA
FLOUR
FLOUT
FLOWN
FOODS
FOOLS
FOOTS

FOOTY
FROCK
FROND
FRONT
FROST
FROTH
FROWN
FROWY
FROZE
GEODE
GHOST
GHOUL
GLOAT
GLOBE
GLOGG
GLOOM
GLORY
GLOSS
GLOVE
GNOME
GOODS
GOODY
GOOEY
GOOFY
GOOLY
GOOSE
GROAN
GROAT
GROIN
GROOM
GROPE
GROSS
GROSZ
GROUP
GROUT
GROVE
GROWL
GROWN
HOOCH
HOOEY
HOOKY
HOOSH
HOOVE
IROKO
IRONS
IRONY
ISOLA
IVORY
KIOSK
KLOOF
KNOCK
KNOLL
KNOUT
KNOWN
KOOKY
KOORI
KRONA
KRONE
LEONE
LIONS
LLOYD

LOOBY
LOOFA
LOONS
LOONY
LOOPY
LOOSE
MAORI
MOOCH
MOODY
MOOLI
MOONY
MOORE
MOOSE
MYOMA
NIOBE
NOOKY
NOOSE
OBOTE
ODOUR
OVOID
OZONE
PAOLO
PEONY
PHOBE
PHONE
PHONY
PHOTO
PIOUS
PLONK
PLOTS
POOCH
POOLS
PROBE
PROKE
PROLE
PROMO
PRONE
PRONG
PROOF
PROSE
PROSY
PROUD
PROUT
PROVE
PROVO
PROWL
PROXY
PSOAS
PSORA
QUOIF
QUOIN
QUOIT
QUORN
QUOTA
QUOTE
QUOTH
RHODO
RHOMB
RHONE
RIOJA
RIOTS

ROOKY
ROOMS
ROOMY
ROOPY
ROOST
ROOTS
ROOTY
SCOFF
SCOLD
SCONE
SCOOP
SCOOT
SCOPE
SCOPS
SCORE
SCORN
SCOTS
SCOTT
SCOUP
SCOUR
SCOUT
SCOWL
SCOWP
SEOUL
SHOAL
SHOCK
SHOJI
SHOLA
SHONA
SHONE
SHOOK
SHOOT
SHOPS
SHORE
SHORN
SHORT
SHOTS
SHOUT
SHOVE
SHOWN
SHOWY
SKOAL
SLOAN
SLOOP
SLOPE
SLOPS
SLOSH
SLOTH
SMOCK
SMOKE
SMOKY
SMOLT
SMOTE
SNOBS
SNOEK
SNOOD
SNOOK
SNOOP
SNOOT
SNORE
SNORT

SNOUT
SNOWY
SOOTH
SOOTY
SPODE
SPOHR
SPOIL
SPOKE
SPOOF
SPOOK
SPOOL
SPOON
SPOOR
SPORE
SPORT
SPOTS
SPOUT
STOAT
STOCK
STOEP
STOGA
STOGY
STOIC
STOKE
STOLA
STOLE
STOLL
STOMA
STOMP
STONE
STONY
STOOD
STOOK
STOOL
STOOP
STOOR
STOPE
STORE
STORK
STORM
STORY
STOUP
STOUR
STOUT
STOVE
STOWE
SUOMI
SWOON
SWOOP
SWORD
SWORE
SWORN
THOFT
THOLE
THONG
THORN
THOSE
TOOLS
TOOTH
TROIC
TROLL

TROMP
TROON
TROOP
TROPE
TROTH
TROTS
TROUT
TROVE
TWOER
VIOLA
VROOM
WHOLE
WHOOP
WHOOT
WHORE
WHORL
WHOSE
WOODS
WOODY
WOOER
WOOFY
WOOLF
WOOZY
WRONG
WROTE
WROTH
XHOSA
ZLOTY
ALPHA
AMPLE
AMPLY
APPAL
APPAY
APPEL
APPLE
APPLY
APPRO
APPUI
ASPEN
ASPER
ASPIC
BEPAT
BIPED
BIPOD
CAPER
CAPET
CAPON
CAPOT
CAPRI
CAPUT
COPER
COPPY
COPRA
COPSE
CUPAR
CUPEL
CUPID
CUPPA
DEPOT
DEPTH
DIPPY
DOPEY
DUPIN
EMPTY
EXPEL
GAPER
GIPPO
GIPSY
GOPAK
GUPPY
GYPPO
GYPSY
HAPPY
HIPPO
HIPPY
HYPER
HYPHA
IMPEL
IMPLY
IMPOT
INPUT
JAPAN
JUPON
KAPOK
KAPPA
KAPUT
KIPPS
KOPJE
LAPEL
LAPIS
LAPSE
LEPER
LEPID
LIPID
LIPPI
LUPIN
LUPUS
MAPLE
MOPED
MOPER
MOPSY
NAPPA
NAPPE
NAPPY
NEPAL
NIPPY
NSPCC
ORPEN
PAPAL
PAPAW
PAPER
PEPPY
PEPSI
PEPYS
PIPER
PIPIT
PIPPA
PIPUL
POPES
POPOV
POPPA
POPPY
POPSY
POPUP
PUPAL
PUPIL
PUPPY
RAPID
REPAY
REPEL
REPLY
REPOT
REPRO
RIPEN
RIPER
RIPON
ROPED
ROPER
ROPES
ROPEY
RSPCA
RUPEE
RUPIA
SAPID
SAPOR
SAPPY
SEPAL
SEPIA
SEPOY
SOPHY
SOPPY
SOPRA
SUPER
SUPPE
SUPRA
TAPAS
TAPER
TAPET
TAPIR
TAPIS
TEPEE
TEPID
TIPPY
TIPSY
TOPAZ
TOPEE
TOPER
TOPIC
TOPSY
TYPED
TYPES
TYPHA
UMPTY
UNPEN
UNPIN
UPPER
VAPID
VAPOR
VIPER
WIPER
YIPPY
YUPIK
YUPPY
ZEPPO
ZIPPY
PIQUE
ROQUE
TOQUE
TUQUE
AARON
ABRAM
ABRAY
ABRIM
ACRES
ACRID
AFRIT
AGREE
AIRER
AIRES
AORTA
APRIL
APRON
ARRAN
ARRAS
ARRAY
ARRÊT
ARRIS
ARROW
ATRIP
AURAL
AURIC
AYRIE
BARGE
BARMY
BARON
BARRA
BARRE
BARRY
BARTS
BERET
BERIA
BEROB
BERRY
BERTH
BERYL
BIRCH
BIRDS
BIRTH
BORAX
BORED
BOREE
BORER
BORIC
BORIS
BORNE
BORON
BURGH
BURIN
BURKE
BURLY
BURMA
BURNS
BURNT
BUROO
BURRO
BURSA
BURST
BYRON
CARAT
CARDS
CARER
CARET
CAREW
CAREY
CARGO
CARIB
CARLE
CAROB
CAROL
CARRY
CARTA
CARTE
CARVE
CARVY
CDROM
CERES
CERNE
CIRCA
CIRCE
CORAL
CORAM
CORDS
CORED
CORER
CORFE
CORFU
CORGI
CORIN
CORKY
CORNY
COROT
CORPS
CORSE
CORSO
CORVO
CURDS
CURED
CURER
CURIA
CURIE
CURIO
CURLY
CURRY
CURSE
CURST
CURVE
CURVY
CYRUS
DARBY
DARCY
DARTS
DERAY
DERBY
DERMA
DERRY
DIRGE
DIRTY
DORAS
DOREE
DORIC
DORIS
DORMY
DORTS
DURER
DUROY
DURRY
DURST
DURUM
EARLY
EARTH
EERIE
EGRET
EMRYS
ENROL
ERROR
ESROM
EYRIE
FARAD
FARCE
FARCI
FARCY
FARGO
FARNE
FAROE
FARSE
FERAL
FERIA
FERMI
FERRY
FIRMA
FIRST
FIRTH
FORAY
FORCE
FOREL
FORGE
FORGO
FORKS
FORME
FORMS
FORTE
FORTH
FORTY
FORUM
FUROR
FURRY
FURZE
GARBO
GARDA
GARNI
GARTH
GARUM
GERBE
GIRLS
GIRLY
GIRTH
GORED
GORGE
GORKY
GORSE
GYRUS
HARDY
HAREM
HARPO
HARPY
HARRY
HARSH
HARTY
HERBS
HERMA
HERNE
HEROD
HERON
HERSE
HERTS
HERTZ
HIRAM
HIRED
HIRER
HORAH
HORDE
HOREB
HORNE
HORNY
HORSA
HORSE
HORSY
HORUS
HURON
HURRY
HURST
HYRAX
IDRIS
JEREZ
JERKS
JERKY
JERRY
JIRGA
JORIS
JORUM
JURAT
JUROR
KARAT
KARMA
KARNO
KARRI
KARST
KARSY
KERAL
KERMA
KERNE
KIRBY
KIROV
KORAN
KOREA
KORMA
KURMA
KYRIE
LARCH
LARGE
LARGO
LARKS
LARNE
LARRY
LARVA
LERNA
LERNE
LORCA
LORDS
LORIS
LORNA
LORNE
LORRY
LURCH
LURGY
LURID
LYRIC
MARAT
MARCH
MARCO
MARDI
MARGE
MARIA
MARIE
MARLE
MARLY
MARNE
MAROT
MARRY
MARSH
MERAK
MERCY
MERGE
MERIL
MERIT
MERLE
MERRY
MIRTH
MIRZA
MORAL
MORAN
MORAT
MORAY
MOREL
MORES
MORIA
MORIN
MORNE
MORON
MORPH
MORSE
MORUS
MURAL
MUREX
MURKY
MURRE
MURRY
MYRON

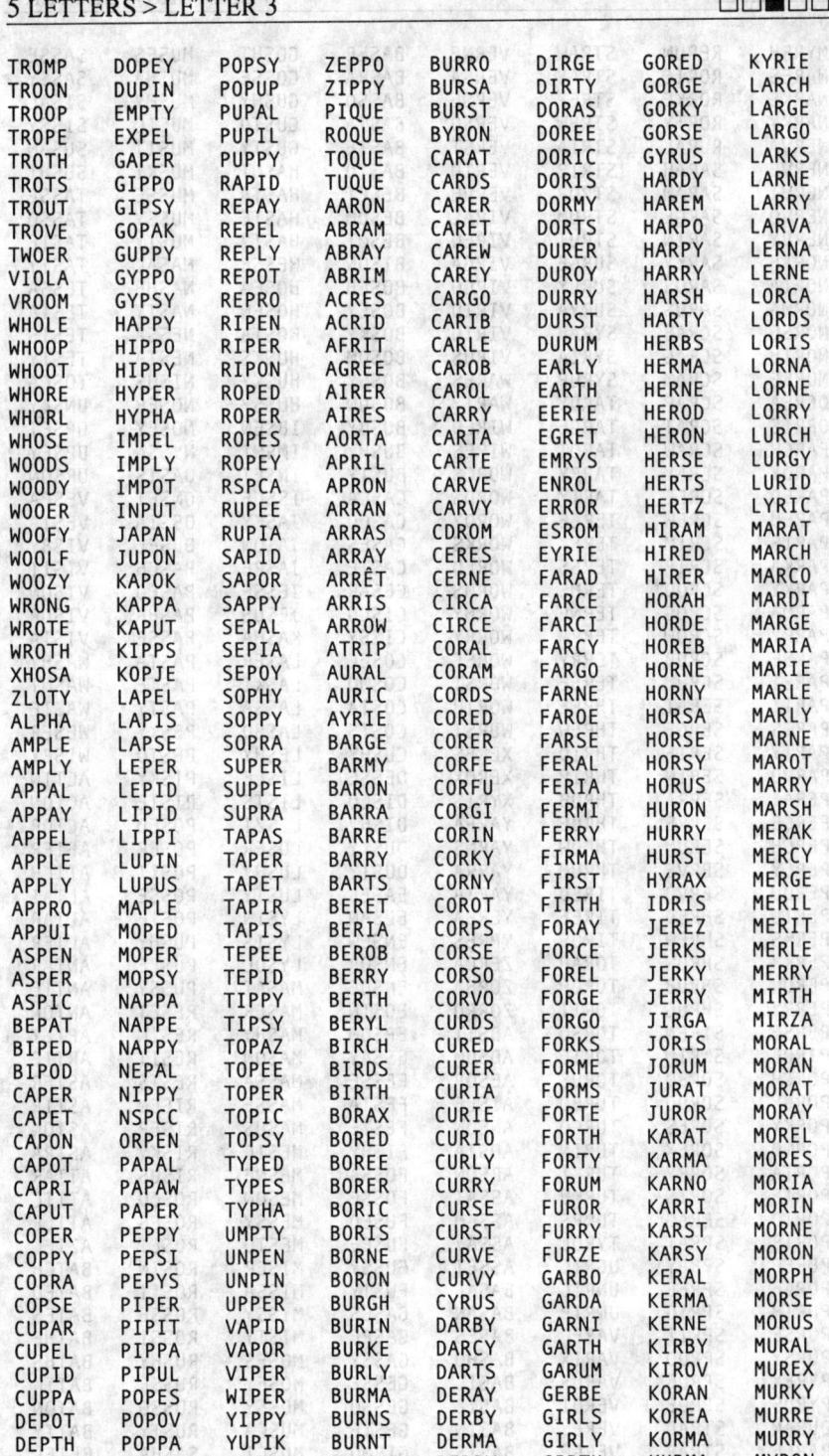

MYRRH
NARES
NARKS
NARKY
NERVA
NERVE
NERVI
NERVO
NERVY
NORAH
NORIA
NORMA
NORSE
NORTH
NURSE
OCREA
ORRIS
PARCH
PARDY
PAREO
PAREU
PARIS
PARKA
PARKY
PARMA
PARRY
PARSE
PARSI
PARTI
PARTS
PARTY
PARVO
PERAI
PERCE
PERCH
PERCY
PERDU
PERIL
PERKS
PERKY
PERON
PERRY
PERSE
PIROG
PORCH
PORGY
PORKY
PORNO
PORTA
PORTE
PORTO
PORTS
PUREE
PURGE
PURIM
PURSE
PURSY
PYREX
PYRUS
QURAN
RAREE
RERUN
RORIC
RORKE
RORTY
RURAL
SARAH
SARAN
SARGE
SARIN
SARKY
SAROS
SARUS
SCRAB
SCRAG
SCRAM
SCRAP
SCRAT
SCRAW
SCRAY
SCREE
SCREW
SCRIM
SCRIP
SCROD
SCROG
SCROW
SCRUB
SCRUM
SERAI
SERGE
SERIF
SERIN
SERRA
SERRE
SERUM
SERVE
SERVO
SHRED
SHREW
SHROW
SHRUB
SHRUG
SIREN
SKRIM
SORBO
SORDO
SORES
SOREX
SORRY
SORTS
SPRAG
SPRAT
SPRAY
SPREE
SPRIG
SPRIT
SPROD
SPROG
SPRUE
STRAD
STRAP
STRAW
STRAY
STREP
STREW
STRIA
STRIP
STROP
STRUM
STRUT
SURGE
SURLY
SURYA
SYRAH
SYRIA
SYRUP
TARDY
TARGE
TAROT
TARRY
TARTY
TERCE
TEREK
TERES
TERMS
TERNE
TERRA
TERRY
TERSE
THREE
THREW
THRID
THRIP
THROB
THROE
THROW
THRUM
TIRED
TIREE
TIROS
TORAH
TORCH
TORII
TORSO
TORTE
TORUS
TURBO
TURCO
TURIN
TURKI
TURKU
TURPS
TYROL
UGRIC
UNRIG
UNRIP
VAREC
VARIX
VARUS
VERDI
VEREY
VERGE
VERNE
VERSA
VERSE
VERSO
VERST
VERTU
VERVE
VIRAL
VIREO
VIRGA
VIRGO
VIRID
VIRTU
VIRUS
WARES
WARTY
WIRED
WIRES
WORCS
WORDS
WORDY
WORKS
WORLD
WORMS
WORMY
WORRY
WORSE
WORST
WORTH
WURST
XERES
XEROX
XYRIS
YARFA
YARNS
YARRA
YARTA
YERBA
YPRES
ZERDA
ZORBA
ZORRO
ABSIT
ADSUM
AESOP
AISLE
ANSON
AOSTA
ARSON
ASSAI
ASSAM
ASSAY
ASSET
BASAL
BASAN
BASES
BASHO
BASIC
BASIL
BASIN
BASIS
BASLE
BASRA
BASSO
BASTA
BASTE
BASTO
BESET
BESOM
BESOT
BISON
BOSCH
BOSEY
BOSKY
BOSOM
BOSSY
BOSUN
BUSBY
BUSHY
BUSTY
CASCA
CASCO
CASES
CASTE
CESAR
CISCO
CISSY
COSEC
COSMO
COSTA
COSTS
CUSHY
DESSE
DISCO
DISHY
DUSKY
DUSTY
EASEL
ELSAN
ENSEW
ENSOR
ENSUE
EOSIN
EPSOM
ESSAY
FESSE
FESTA
FESTE
FISHY
FOSSA
FOSSE
FUSED
FUSEE
FUSSY
FUSTY
GASES
GASPÉ
GASSY
GESSE
GESSO
GESTE
GISMO
GOSHT
GOSSE
GUSHY
GUSTO
GUSTY
HASNT
HASTA
HASTE
HASTY
HESSE
HOSEA
HOSEN
HOSTA
HUSKS
HUSKY
HUSSY
IBSEN
IMSHI
INSET
ISSUE
JASEY
JASON
JASPÉ
JESSE
JESUS
KASHA
LASER
LASKI
LASSA
LASSO
LESHY
LISLE
LISTS
LISZT
LOSER
LUSHY
LUSTY
LYSIN
LYSIS
LYSOL
MASAI
MASER
MASHY
MASON
MASSA
MASSE
MASUS
MESIC
MESNE
MESON
MESSY
MESTO
MISER
MISSA
MISSY
MISTY
MOSES
MOSEY
MOSSY
MUSCA
MUSCI
MUSES
MUSHA
MUSHY
MUSIC
MUSIT
MUSKY
MUSSE
MUSSY
MUSTY
NASAL
NASHE
NASTY
NESSA
NESTA
NISUS
NOSER
NOSEY
NYSSA
OASIS
ONSET
OSSIA
OUSEL
PASCH
PASEO
PASHA
PASSE
PASTA
PASTE
PASTY
PESKY
PESTO
PISKY
PISTE
POSED
POSER
POSIT
POSSE
POSTE
PUSHY
PUSLE
PUSSY
RESET
RESIN
RESIT
RESTS
RISEN
RISER
RISKY
RISUS
ROSCO
ROSES
ROSET
ROSIN
ROSIT
ROSSE
ROSSI
RUSHY
RUSSE
RUSSO
RUSTY
SASHA
SASSE
SASSY
SISAL
SISSY
SUSAN
SUSHI
TASSE
TASSO
TASTE
TASTY
TESSA
TESTA
TESTS
TESTY
TOSCA
UNSAY
UPSET
UPSEY
URSON
VESPA
VESTA
VISBY
VISIT
VISON
VISOR
VISTA
WASHY
WASNT
WASTE
WESER
WISPY
ACTIN
ACTON
ACTOR
AFTER
AITCH
ALTAI
ALTAR
ALTER
ANTAR
ANTIC
ANTON
APTLY
ARTIE
ASTER
ASTIR
ASTON
ASTRA
ATTAR
ATTIC
ATTLE
AZTEC
BATCH
BATED
BATES
BATHE
BATHS
BATIK
BATON
BATTY
BETEL

BETON
BETTE
BETTY
BITCH
BITER
BITTE
BITTY
BOTCH
BOTHA
BOTHY
BOTTE
BUTCH
BUTTE
BUTTY
CATCH
CATER
CATES
CATTY
COTTA
CUTCH
CUTEY
CUTIE
CUTIS
CUTTY
DATED
DATER
DATES
DATUK
DATUM
DETER
DITAL
DITCH
DITTO
DITTY
DOTTY
DUTCH
EATER
ELTON
ENTER
ENTRY
ESTER
ESTOC
ESTOP
EXTOL
EXTRA
EYTIE
FATAL
FATED
FATTY
FATWA
FETAL
FETCH
FETID
FETOR
FETUS
FITCH
FUTON
GATED
GETUP
GOTCH
GOTHA
GOTTA
GUTSY
GUTTA
HATCH
HATHI
HATTY
HETTY
HITCH
HITHE
HOTCH
HOTEL
HOTLY
HUTCH
HYTHE
ICTUS
INTER
INTRA
INTRO
JETTY
KETCH
KITTY
KOTOW
KUTCH
LATCH
LATEN
LATER
LATEX
LATHE
LATHI
LATIN
LETHE
LITAS
LITER
LITHE
LITRE
LOTOS
LOTTO
LOTUS
LUTIN
LUTON
LYTHE
MATCH
MATER
MATES
MATEY
MATHS
MATIN
MATLO
METAL
METER
METHS
METIC
METIF
METIS
METOL
METRE
METRO
MITES
MITRE
MOTEL
MOTET
MOTHS
MOTIF
MOTOR
MOTTE
MOTTO
MUTED
NATAL
NATCH
NATES
NATTY
NATUS
NITID
NITON
NITRE
NOTAL
NOTCH
NOTED
NOTES
NOTTS
NOTUM
NUTTY
OATEN
OATES
OCTAD
OCTAL
OCTET
OFTEN
OPTIC
ORTHO
ORTON
ORTUS
OSTIA
OTTAR
OTTER
OUTBY
OUTDO
OUTER
OUTGO
OUTRE
OXTER
PATCH
PATER
PATIO
PATNA
PATSY
PATTI
PATTY
PETAL
PETER
PETIT
PETRA
PETRE
PETRI
PETTO
PETTY
PITCH
PITHY
PITON
PITOT
PITTA
POTIN
POTOO
POTTO
POTTY
PUTID
PUTTO
PUTTY
RATCH
RATES
RATIO
RATTY
RETCH
RETRO
RITES
RITZY
ROTOR
SATAN
SATAY
SATED
SATIE
SATIN
SATIS
SATYR
SETUP
SITAR
SITIN
SITKA
SITTA
SITUP
SOTTO
SUTCH
SUTOR
SUTRA
TATAR
TATER
TATIN
TATRA
TATTY
TETRA
TITAN
TITCH
TITHE
TITLE
TITRE
TITTY
TITUS
TOTAL
TOTEM
TOTTY
TUTOR
TUTSI
TUTTI
ULTRA
UNTIE
UNTIL
UPTON
USTED
UTTER
VETCH
VITAE
VITAL
VITIS
VITUS
VOTER
VOTES
WATCH
WATER
WATTS
WITAN
WITCH
WITHE
WITHY
WITTY
YATES
ABUJA
ABUNA
ABUSE
ACUTE
ADULT
ALURE
AMUCK
AMUSE
ARUBA
AZURE
BAULK
BLUES
BLUEY
BLUFF
BLUNT
BLURB
BLURT
BLUSH
BOUGH
BOULE
BOUND
BOURG
BRUCE
BRUIN
BRUIT
BRULE
BRUME
BRUNO
BRUNT
BRUSH
BRUTE
CAULD
CAULK
CAUSE
CHUBB
CHUCK
CHUFF
CHUMP
CHUNK
CHURL
CHURN
CHURR
CHUTE
CLUBS
CLUCK
CLUMP
CLUNG
CLUNK
COUCH
COUDÉ
COUGH
COULD
COUNT
COUPE
COURB
COURT
COUTH
CRUCK
CRUDE
CRUEL
CRUET
CRUMB
CRUMP
CRUOR
CRUSE
CRUSH
CRUST
DAUBE
DAUNT
DEUCE
DOUAI
DOUAR
DOUAY
DOUBT
DOUCE
DOUGH
DOUMA
DOURA
DOURO
DOUSE
DRUGS
DRUID
DRUNK
DRUPE
DRURY
DRUZE
DYULA
EDUCE
ELUDE
EMURE
ENUGU
ENURE
EQUAL
EQUIP
ERUCA
ERUCT
ERUPT
ETUDE
EXUDE
EXULT
EXURB
FAULT
FAUNA
FAURE
FAUST
FAUVE
FLUFF
FLUID
FLUKE
FLUME
FLUMP
FLUNG
FLUNK
FLUON
FLUSH
FLUTE
FOUET
FOULÉ
FOUND
FOUNT
FOURS
FRUIT
FRUMP
GAUDE
GAUDY
GAUGE
GAULT
GAUNT
GAUSS
GAUZE
GAUZY
GLUCK
GLUED
GLUEY
GLUME
GLUON
GOUDA
GOUGE
GOURD
GOUTY
GRUEL
GRUFE
GRUFF
GRUME
GRUNT
HAUGH
HAULM
HAULT
HAUNT
HAUSA
HAUSE
HAUTE
HEUGH
HOUGH
HOUND
HOURI
HOURS
HOUSE
INUIT
INURE
JAUNT
JOUAL
JOULE
JOUNT
JOUST
KAURI
KNURL
KNURR
LAUDS
LAUGH
LAURA
LOUGH
LOUIE
LOUIS
LOUPE
LOUSE
LOUSY
LOUTH
MAUND
MAUVE
MEUSE
MOUCH
MOULD
MOULS
MOULT
MOUND
MOUNT
MOURN
MOUSE
MOUSY
MOUTH
MVULE
NAURU
OVULE
PAUSE
PLUCK
PLUMB
PLUME
PLUMP
PLUNK
PLUSH
PLUTO
POUCH
POULE
POULT
POUND
POUPE
PRUDE
PRUNE
RHUMB
ROUEN
ROUGE
ROUGH
ROULE
ROUND
ROUSE
ROUST
ROUTE
SAUCE
SAUCH
SAUCY
SAUDI
SAUGH
SAULT
SAUNA
SAUTE
SCUBA
SCUFF
SCULL
SCULP
SCURF
SHUCK

SHUNT
SHUSH
SHUTE
SHUTS
SKULK
SKULL
SKUNK
SLUGS
SLUMP
SLUNG
SLUNK
SLURB
SLURP
SLUSH
SMUTS
SNUFF
SOUGH
SOULS
SOUND
SOUSA
SOUSE
SOUTH
SPUME
SPUNK
SPURN
SPURS
SPURT
SQUAB
SQUAD
SQUAT
SQUAW
SQUIB
SQUID
SQUIT
STUCK
STUDY
STUFF
STUKA
STUMP
STUNG
STUNK
STUNT
STUPA
STUPE
STURT
SWUNG
TAUBE
TAUNT
TAUPE
THUGS
THULE
THUMB
THUMP
THUYA
TOUCH
TOUGH
TRUCE
TRUCK
TRULL
TRULY
TRUMP
TRUNK
TRURO
TRUSS
TRUST
TRUTH
TSUBA
TSUGA
UHURU
USUAL
USURE
USURP
USURY
UTURN
UVULA
VAULT
VAUNT
VOUCH
WAUGH
WOULD
WOUND
WRUNG
YOULL
YOUNG
YOURS
YOURT
YOUTH
YOUVE
ALVIS
ANVIL
ARVAL
BEVEL
BEVIS
BÉVUE
BEVVY
CAVAN
CAVIL
CIVET
CIVIC
CIVIL
CIVVY
COVEN
COVER
COVET
COVEY
DAVID
DAVIS
DAVIT
DEVIL
DIVAN
DIVER
DIVES
DIVOT
DIVVY
DOVER
DUVAL
DUVET
EAVES
ELVAN
ELVER
ELVES
ELVIS
ENVOI
ENVOY
FAVOR
FAVUS
FEVER
FIVER
FIVES
FOVEA
GAVEL
GIVEN
GIVER
HAVEL
HAVEN
HAVER
HAVOC
HEVEA
HIVER
HIVES
HOVEL
HOVER
JAVAN
JAVEL
KEVIN
LAVER
LAVRA
LEVEE
LEVEL
LEVEN
LEVER
LEVIN
LEVIS
LIVED
LIVEN
LIVER
LIVES
LIVID
LIVRE
LOVAT
LOVER
MAVIN
MAVIS
MOVED
MOVER
MOVIE
NAVAL
NAVEL
NAVEW
NAVVY
NEVEL
NEVER
NEVIS
NIVAL
NOVEL
NOVUM
ORVAL
PAVID
PIVOT
RAVEL
RAVEN
RAVER
REVEL
REVET
REVIE
REVUE
RIVAL
RIVEN
RIVER
RIVET
ROVER
SAVER
SAVOR
SAVOY
SAVVY
SEVEN
SEVER
SUVLA
TAVAH
VIVAT
VIVID
WAVED
WAVER
WAVES
WIVES
WOVEN
ASWAN
BAWDY
BOWED
BOWEL
BOWER
BOWIE
BOWLS
BYWAY
COWAN
COWER
COWRY
CRWTH
DEWAN
DEWAR
DEWEY
DIWAN
DOWDY
DOWEL
DOWER
DOWNS
DOWNY
DOWRY
DOWSE
EDWIN
ETWEE
FEWER
GAWKY
GOWAN
GOWER
HAWSE
HEWER
HOWBE
HOWDY
INWIT
JEWEL
JEWRY
KIWIS
LAWKS
LEWES
LEWIS
LOWAN
LOWER
LOWLY
LOWRY
MOWER
NAWAB
NEWEL
NEWLY
NEWSY
NEWTS
OTWAY
PAWKY
POWAN
POWER
POWYS
ROWAN
ROWDY
ROWEL
ROWER
SEWER
SOWER
SOWLE
SOWND
SOWTH
TAWNY
TAWSE
TOWEL
TOWER
TOWNS
TOWSE
TOWZE
UNWED
VOWEL
AUXIN
BOXED
BOXER
BUXOM
COXAL
COXED
DIXIE
FIXED
FIXER
HEXAD
HEXAM
HEXYL
LEXIS
MAXIM
MIXED
MIXER
MIXTE
MIXUP
NAXOS
NEXUS
NIXON
NOXAL
PIXEL
PIXIE
PYXIS
SAXON
SIXER
SIXTH
SIXTY
TAXED
TAXIN
TAXIS
TAXOL
TAXON
TAXUS
TEXAN
TEXAS
TEXEL
TEXTS
TOXIC
TOXIN
VEXED
VIXEN
WAXEN
ABYSM
ABYSS
ARYAN
AZYME
BAYER
BAYLE
BAYOU
BOYAR
BOYAU
BOYCE
BOYLE
BOYNE
BUYER
CHYLE
CHYME
CHYND
CLYDE
COYLY
COYNE
COYPU
CRYPT
DAYAK
DOYEN
DOYLE
DOYLY
DRYAD
DRYER
DRYLY
EGYPT
FLYER
FLYTE
FOYER
FOYLE
GHYLL
GLYPH
GUYED
GUYON
GUYOT
HAYDN
HAYLE
HEYER
HOYLE
IDYLL
JOYCE
KAYAK
KEYED
KEYES
LAYBY
LAYER
LOYAL
MAYBE
MAYOR
MEYER
MOYLE
NOYAU
NOYES
PAYEE
PAYER
PHYLE
PSYCH
RAYED
RAYLE
RAYON
REYES
RHYME
RIYAL
ROYAL
SAYER
SAYSO
SHYLY
SLYLY
SLYPE
SOYUZ
STYLE
STYLO
STYME
THYME
TRYST
WRYLY
ANZAC
BAZOO
BEZEL
COZEN
DAZED
DIZZY
DOZEN
FIZZY
FUZEE
FUZZY
GAZON
GIZMO
HAZEL
HUZZA
IZZAT
JAZZY
LAZAR
LAZZO
LOZEN
LUZON
MAZER
MEZZE
MEZZO
MUZAK
MUZZY
NAZIR
NIZAM
OUZEL
PIZZA
RAZOR
ROZET
SIZAR
SUZIE
TAZZA
TIZZY
UNZIP
VIZOR
VOZHD
YEZDI

5:4

ABBAS
ABDAR
ABEAM
ABEAR
ABRAM
ABRAY
AFEAR
AHEAD
AIDAN
AKBAR
ALBAN
ALDAN
ALGAE
ALIAS
ALLAH
ALLAN
ALLAY
ALTAI
ALTAR
AMMAN
ANEAR
ANNAL
ANNAM
ANTAR
ANZAC
APEAK
APPAL
APPAY
ARIAN
ARRAN
ARRAS
ARRAY
ARVAL
ARYAN
ASIAN
ASSAI
ASSAM
ASSAY
ASWAN
ATLAS
ATMAN
ATTAR
AURAL

AVIAN
AXIAL
BABAR
BAHAI
BALAN
BANAL
BASAL
BASAN
BEDAD
BEGAD
BEGAN
BEHAN
BEKAA
BELAY
BEPAT
BLEAK
BLEAR
BLEAT
BLOAT
BOLAS
BONAR
BORAX
BOYAR
BOYAU
BREAD
BREAK
BREAM
BRIAN
BRIAR
BROAD
BYLAW
BYWAY
CABAL
CABAS
CACAO
CANAL
CARAT
CAVAN
CEDAR
CESAR
CHEAP
CHEAT
CHIAO
CIGAR
CLEAN
CLEAR
CLEAT
CLOAK
CONAN
CORAL
CORAM
COWAN
COXAL
CREAK
CREAM
CROAK
CROAT
CUBAN
CUPAR
CYCAD
DAKAR

DAMAN
DANAE
DAYAK
DEBAG
DEBAR
DECAL
DECAY
DEGAS
DELAY
DERAY
DEWAN
DEWAR
DINAR
DITAL
DIVAN
DIWAN
DONAR
DONAT
DORAS
DOUAI
DOUAR
DOUAY
DREAD
DREAM
DREAR
DRYAD
DUBAI
DUCAT
DUKAS
DULAC
DUMAS
DUVAL
DYLAN
ECLAT
EDGAR
EGGAR
EILAT
ELGAR
ELIAD
ELIAS
ELSAN
ELVAN
EQUAL
ESSAY
ETHAL
EVIAN
EXEAT
FANAL
FARAD
FATAL
FECAL
FERAL
FETAL
FINAL
FLOAT
FOCAL
FORAY
FREAK
FRIAR
FUGAL
GALAM

GAMAY
GLEAM
GLEAN
GLOAT
GOLAN
GONAD
GOPAK
GOWAN
GRAAL
GREAT
GROAN
GROAT
GULAG
HANAP
HEXAD
HEXAM
HILAR
HIRAM
HOGAN
HONAN
HORAH
HUMAN
HYRAX
IDEAL
IDEAS
ILEAC
ILIAC
ILIAD
INLAW
INLAY
IQBAL
ISAAC
ISLAM
ISLAY
IZZAT
JALAP
JAPAN
JAVAN
JEHAD
JELAB
JIHAD
JONAH
JOUAL
JUDAS
JUGAL
JUMAR
JURAT
KANAK
KARAT
KAYAK
KEBAB
KEDAR
KERAL
KNEAD
KODAK
KORAN
KRAAL
KULAK
LAGAN
LAZAR
LEGAL

LEHAR
LEMAN
LILAC
LIMAX
LITAS
LOBAR
LOCAL
LOGAN
LOMAN
LOVAT
LOWAN
LOYAL
LUCAN
LUNAR
MACAW
MADAM
MAKAR
MALAR
MALAY
MARAT
MASAI
MEDAL
MENAI
MERAK
METAL
MICAH
MIDAS
MILAN
MODAL
MOLAR
MONAD
MONAL
MORAL
MORAN
MORAT
MORAY
MURAL
MUZAK
MYNAH
NAGAS
NAIAD
NASAL
NATAL
NAVAL
NAWAB
NEPAL
NICAD
NIVAL
NIZAM
NODAL
NOMAD
NORAH
NOTAL
NOXAL
NOYAU
OBEAH
OBIAH
OCCAM
OCEAN
OCTAD
OCTAL

OFFAL
OFFAS
OFLAG
OGHAM
ORGAN
ORVAL
OSCAR
OSMAN
OTTAR
OTWAY
PAEAN
PAGAN
PAPAL
PAPAW
PECAN
PEDAL
PEKAN
PENAL
PERAI
PETAL
PHIAL
PILAF
PILAU
PLEAD
PLEAT
POLAR
POWAN
PRIAL
PRIAM
PSHAW
PSOAS
PUPAL
QAJAR
QATAR
QURAN
RABAT
RADAR
RAHAB
RAJAH
RAMAN
RECAP
REDAN
REGAL
REGAN
RELAX
RELAY
RENAL
RENAN
REPAY
RICAN
RIVAL
RIYAL
ROHAN
ROMAN
ROWAN
ROYAL
RURAL
RYDAL
SABAL
SALAD
SARAH

SARAN
SATAN
SATAY
SCRAB
SCRAG
SCRAM
SCRAP
SCRAT
SCRAW
SCRAY
SEDAN
SEPAL
SERAI
SHEAF
SHEAR
SHOAL
SILAS
SINAI
SISAL
SITAR
SIZAR
SKEAN
SKOAL
SLOAN
SMEAR
SNEAD
SNEAK
SOLAN
SOLAR
SONAR
SPEAK
SPEAN
SPEAR
SPLAT
SPLAY
SPRAG
SPRAT
SPRAY
SQUAB
SQUAD
SQUAT
SQUAW
STEAD
STEAK
STEAL
STEAM
STOAT
STRAD
STRAP
STRAW
STRAY
SUDAN
SUGAN
SUGAR
SUSAN
SWEAR
SWEAT
SYRAH
TALAQ
TALAR
TAMAR

TAPAS
TATAR
TAVAH
TEXAN
TEXAS
TIDAL
TITAN
TODAY
TOKAY
TOLAR
TONAL
TOPAZ
TORAH
TOTAL
TREAD
TREAT
TRIAD
TRIAL
TWEAK
UHLAN
ULNAR
UNBAR
UNCAP
UNDAM
UNIAT
UNLAW
UNLAY
UNMAN
UNSAY
URBAN
URIAH
USUAL
VEGAN
VELAR
VENAL
VICAR
VIRAL
VITAE
VITAL
VIVAT
VOCAL
WHEAL
WHEAT
WIGAN
WITAN
WOMAN
WREAK
WYMAN
YCLAD
YULAN
ZAKAT
ZIGAN
ZOHAR
ZONAL
ABABA
ADOBE
ALIBI
AMEBA
AQABA
ARABA
ARUBA

BAMBI
BIBBY
BIMBO
BOBBY
BOMBE
BOMBO
BOOBY
BRIBE
BUBBY
BUSBY
CABBY
CHUBB
CLUBS
COMBE
COMBO
COMBS
CRABS
CUBBY
DARBY
DAUBE
DERBY
DHABI
DHOBI
DOBBY
DOUBT
GABBY
GALBA
GAMBA
GAMBO
GARBO
GERBE
GIBBY
GLEBE
GLOBE
GOBBO
GOMBO
GREBE
GUMBO
HERBS
HOBBS
HOBBY
HOWBE
HUBBY
JAMBE
JAMBO
JUMBO
JUMBY
KAABA
KIMBO
KIRBY
LAYBY
LIMBO
LOBBY
LOOBY
MAMBA
MAMBO
MAYBE
MEBBE
MELBA
NIOBE
NOBBY

OUTBY
PHEBE
PHOBE
PLEBS
PROBE
RABBI
RAMBO
RUGBY
RUMBA
SAMBA
SAMBO
SCUBA
SHEBA
SIMBA
SNOBS
SORBO
TABBY
TAUBE
TIBBS
TIBBY
TRIBE
TSUBA
TUBBY
TURBO
VISBY
YERBA
YOBBO
ZAMBO
ZOMBI
ZORBA
ABACK
ABACO
ACOCK
AITCH
ALACK
ALICE
AMICE
AMUCK
APACE
ARECA
ARICA
BACCY
BANCO
BATCH
BEACH
BEECH
BELCH
BENCH
BIRCH
BITCH
BLACK
BLOCK
BONCE
BOSCH
BOTCH
BOYCE
BRACE
BRACK
BRACT
BRICK
BROCK
BRUCE
BUCCA
BUICK
BUNCE
BUNCH
BUNCO
BUTCH
CASCA
CASCO
CATCH
CENCI
CHACO
CHECK
CHICA
CHICK
CHICO
CHOCK
CHOCO
CHUCK
CINCH
CIRCA
CIRCE
CISCO
CLACK
CLECK
CLICK
CLOCK
CLUCK
COACH
COCCI
CONCH
COUCH
CRACK
CRECY
CRICK
CROCE
CROCK
CRUCK
CUTCH
CZECH
DACCA
DANCE
DARCY
DECCA
DEUCE
DISCO
DITCH
DOLCE
DOUCE
DRACO
DUNCE
DUTCH
EDICT
EDUCE
EJECT
ELECT
ENACT
ENOCH
EPOCH
ERECT
ERICA
ERICK
ERUCA
ERUCT
EVICT
EXACT
FANCY
FARCE
FARCI
FARCY
FENCE
FETCH
FILCH
FINCH
FITCH
FLACK
FLECK
FLICK
FLOCK
FORCE
FRACK
FRACT
FROCK
GLACE
GLUCK
GOTCH
GRACE
GUACO
GULCH
HANCE
HANCH
HATCH
HENCE
HITCH
HOICK
HOOCH
HOTCH
HUNCH
HUTCH
JOYCE
JUICE
JUICY
JUNCO
KEECH
KETCH
KNACK
KNOCK
KUTCH
LANCE
LARCH
LATCH
LEACH
LEECH
LINCH
LORCA
LUNCH
LURCH
LYNCH
MANCH
MARCH
MARCO
MATCH
MECCA
MERCY
MILCH
MINCE
MINCH
MOOCH
MOUCH
MULCH
MULCT
MUNCH
MUSCA
MUSCI
NANCE
NANCY
NATCH
NIECE
NONCE
NOTCH
NSPCC
OUNCE
PARCH
PASCH
PATCH
PEACE
PEACH
PENCE
PERCE
PERCH
PERCY
PIECE
PILCH
PINCH
PITCH
PLACE
PLACK
PLICA
PLUCK
POACH
PONCE
POOCH
PORCH
POUCH
PRICE
PRICK
PSYCH
PUNCH
QUACK
QUICK
RANCE
RANCH
RATCH
REACH
REACT
RECCE
REECH
REICH
RETCH
ROACH
ROSCO
RSPCA
RUNCH
SAICE
SAUCE
SAUCH
SAUCY
SECCO
SHACK
SHOCK
SHUCK
SINCE
SLACK
SLICE
SLICK
SMACK
SMOCK
SNACK
SNECK
SNICK
SPACE
SPECK
SPECS
SPICA
SPICE
SPICK
SPICY
STACK
STICK
STOCK
STUCK
SUTCH
TEACH
TENCH
TERCE
THECA
THICK
TITCH
TORCH
TOSCA
TOUCH
TRACE
TRACK
TRACT
TRECK
TRICE
TRICK
TRUCE
TRUCK
TURCO
TWICE
VANCE
VETCH
VLACH
VNECK
VOICE
VOUCH
WATCH
WELCH
WENCH
WHACK
WHICH
WINCE
WINCH
WITCH
WORCS
WRACK
WRECK
YOICK
YUCCA
ZILCH
ZINCO
ABIDE
ABODE
ANODE
APODE
AREDE
ASIDE
BADDY
BANDA
BANDS
BANDY
BAWDY
BEADS
BEADY
BENDS
BENDY
BIDDY
BIRDS
BLADE
BONDI
BONDS
BRADY
BREDA
BREDE
BRIDE
BUDDY
BUNDY
CADDY
CANDY
CARDS
CHIDE
CLYDE
COADE
CONDE
CONDO
CORDS
COUDÉ
CREDO
CRUDE
CUDDY
CURDS
DADDY
DANDO
DANDY
DEEDS
DILDO
DIODE
DODDY
DOWDY
DUDDY
ELIDE
ELUDE
EPODE
ERODE
ETUDE
EVADE
EXODE
EXUDE
FADDY
FALDO
FONDA
FONDS
FOODS
FUNDI
FUNDS
FUNDY
FYLDE
GARDA
GAUDE
GAUDY
GEODE
GIDDY
GLADE
GLIDE
GOODS
GOODY
GOUDA
GRADE
GUIDE
HAIDA
HANDS
HANDY
HARDY
HAYDN
HEADS
HEADY
HEDDA
HILDA
HINDI
HINDU
HONDO
HORDE
HOWDY
KANDY
KENDO
KIDDY
KILDA
LABDA
LANDE
LAUDS
LEADS
LEEDS
LORDS
LUNDY
MAHDI
MARDI
MIDDY
MONDO
MOODY
MUDDY
MUNDA
NANDI
NANDU
NEDDY
NEEDS
NEEDY
NODDY
OUIDA
OUTDO
OXIDE
PADDY
PANDA
PANDY
PARDY
PERDU
PONDS
PRADO
PRIDE
PRUDE
QUADS
QUIDS
RANDY
READE
READY
REEDE
REEDS
REEDY
RHODO
RONDE
RONDO
ROWDY
RUDDY
SANDS
SANDY
SAUDI
SCADS
SEEDY
SHADE
SHADY
SLADE
SLIDE
SNIDE
SOLDE
SONDE
SORDO
SPADE
SPADO
SPODE
STADE
STUDY
SUEDE
SUNDA
SWEDE
TARDY
TEDDY
TENDS
TIDDY
TILDE
TOADY
TODDY
TONDO
TRADE
UREDO
VANDA
VEDDA
VELDT

VENDA VERDI WALDO WEEDS WEEDY WENDY WILDE WILDS WINDY WOODS WOODY WORDS WORDY YEZDI ZERDA ABBEY ABIES ABLER ACRES ADDED ADDER ADEEM ADIEU AEDES AFTER AGGER AGLEE AGLET AGLEY AGNES AGREE AHMED AIKEN AINEE AIRER AIRES ALBEE ALDER ALIEN ALLEN ALLEY ALOES ALTER AMBER AMIEL ANDES ANGEL ANGER ANKER ANNEX APPEL ARDEA ARDEB ARDEN ARIEL ARIES ARLES ARMED ARMET ASHEN ASHER

ASHES ASHET ASKER ASKEW ASPEN ASPER ASSET ASTER AUDEN AUGER AWEEL AZTEC BABEL BADEN BAGEL BAKED BAKER BALER BASES BATED BATES BAYER BEDEW BEGET BENET BERET BESET BETEL BEVEL BEZEL BIDET BIKER BIPED BITER BLEED BLEEP BLUES BLUEY BODES BOGEY BOHEA BONER BONES BONEY BORED BOREE BORER BOSEY BOWED BOWEL BOWER BOXED BOXER BREED BREEM BRIEF BRIER BUYER CABER CADET CAGEY

CALEB CAMEL CAMEO CANES CAPER CAPET CARER CARET CAREW CAREY CASES CATER CATES CERES CHEEK CHEEP CHEER CHIEF CIDER CIVET CLEEK CLEEP CODED CODEX COKES COLET COLEY COMET CONEY COOEE COPER CORED CORER COSEC COVEN COVER COVET COVEY COWER COXED COZEN CREED CREEK CREEL CREEP CRIED CRIER CRIES CRUEL CRUET CUBEB CUBED CULET CULEX CUPEL CURED CURER CUTEY DALEK DANES DATED

DATER DATES DAZED DEBEL DEFER DETER DEWEY DICEY DIKER DINER DIVER DIVES DOMED DONEE DOPEY DOREE DOVER DOWEL DOWER DOYEN DOZEN DRIED DRIER DRIES DRYER DUKES DURER DUVET DYFED DYKER EAGER EASEL EATER EAVES EDGED EDGER EGRET EIDER EIGER ELDER ELLEN ELMER ELVER ELVES EMBED EMBER EMCEE EMDEN EMMER EMMET ENDED ENMEW ENSEW ENTER ESKER ESTER ETHER ETWEE EULER EXCEL EXPEL

FABER FACER FACET FADED FAKER FAMED FATED FECES FEVER FEWER FIBER FIDEL FIDES FILET FINER FIVER FIVES FIXED FIXER FLEET FLIER FLIES FLYER FOGEY FOREL FOUET FOVEA FOYER FREED FRIED FRIES FUMED FUMES FUMET FUSED FUSEE FUZEE GALEA GALEN GAMES GAPER GASES GATED GAVEL GEBER GENET GILES GILET GIVEN GIVER GLEEK GLEET GLUED GLUEY GODET GOFER GOLEM GONER GOOEY GORED GOWER

GREED GREEK GREEN GREER GREET GRIEF GRIEG GRUEL GULES GUYED GYGES HABET HACEK HADES HALER HAREM HAVEL HAVEN HAVER HAZEL HEGEL HELEN HEVEA HEWER HEYER HIKER HIRED HIRER HIVER HIVES HOKEY HOLED HOLEY HOMER HONEY HOOEY HOREB HOSEA HOSEN HOTEL HOVEL HOVER HYMEN HYPER IBSEN ICKER IDLER IMBED IMMER IMMEW IMPEL INDEW INDEX INFER INLET INNER INNES INSET INTER ISLES ISLET

ISMET IVIED JADED JAKES JAMES JASEY JAVEL JEBEL JEREZ JEWEL JOKER JONES JULEP KEBEL KEYED KEYES KLIEG KNEEL KOREA KRIEG LABEL LACET LADEN LAGER LAMED LAPEL LASER LATEN LATER LATEX LAVER LAYER LEGER LEPER LEVEE LEVEL LEVEN LEVER LEWES LIBEL LIBER LIFER LIKED LIKEN LIKES LIMER LIMES LIMEY LINED LINEN LINER LINES LITER LIVED LIVEN LIVER LIVES LOBED LODEN LONER LOSER

LOVER LOWER LOZEN LUGER LUMEN LUNED MACER MAKER MANED MANES MANET MASER MATER MATES MATEY MAZER MEDEA MELEE METER MEYER MILER MILES MIMER MINER MISER MITES MIXED MIXER MODEL MODEM MODER MONET MONEY MOPED MOPER MOREL MORES MOSES MOSEY MOTEL MOTET MOVED MOVER MOWER MUREX MUSES MUTED NADER NAKED NAMED NAMES NARES NATES NAVEL NAVEW NEBEL NEGEV NEVEL NEVER NEWEL NIGEL

NIGER
NOBEL
NODES
NOMEN
NONES
NONET
NOSER
NOSEY
NOTED
NOTES
NOVEL
NOYES
NUMEN
OAKEN
OAKER
OATEN
OATES
OCHER
OCKER
OCREA
OCTET
ODDER
OFFER
OFTEN
OGIER
OILED
OILER
OLDEN
OLDER
OMBER
ONCER
ONSET
ORDER
ORFEO
ORIEL
ORMER
ORPEN
OSIER
OTHER
OTTER
OUSEL
OUTER
OUZEL
OWLER
OWLET
OWNER
OXTER
PACER
PACEY
PAGER
PAGES
PALEA
PALES
PALET
PANEL
PAPER
PAREO
PAREU
PASEO
PATER
PAYEE
PAYER
PELEE
PETER
PICEA
PILED
PILES
PINES
PIPER
PIXEL
PLIER
PODEX
POKER
POKEY
PONEY
POPES
POSED
POSER
POWER
PREEN
PULEX
PUREE
PYREX
QUEEN
QUEER
QUIET
RACER
RACES
RAGED
RAKED
RAKEE
RAKER
RAKES
RANEE
RAREE
RATES
RAVEL
RAVEN
RAVER
RAYED
REBEL
REFER
RENEW
REPEL
RESET
REVEL
REVET
REYES
RIDER
RILEY
RIPEN
RIPER
RISEN
RISER
RITES
RIVEN
RIVER
RIVET
ROBES
ROBEY
RODEO
ROGER
ROGET
ROKER
ROMEO
ROMER
RONEO
ROPED
ROPER
ROPES
ROPEY
ROSES
ROSET
ROUEN
ROVER
ROWEL
ROWER
ROZET
RULER
RULES
RUMEN
RUMEX
RUNES
RUPEE
SABER
SAGES
SAHEL
SAKER
SALEM
SALEP
SALES
SATED
SAVER
SAYER
SCREE
SCREW
SEMEN
SEVEN
SEVER
SEWER
SHEEL
SHEEN
SHEEP
SHEER
SHEET
SHIEL
SHLEP
SHRED
SHREW
SILEX
SINEW
SIREN
SIXER
SKEER
SKEET
SKIER
SLEEK
SLEEP
SLEET
SMEEK
SNEER
SNOEK
SOBER
SOKEN
SORES
SOREX
SOWER
SPEED
SPEER
SPIED
SPIEL
SPIES
SPREE
STEED
STEEK
STEEL
STEEN
STEEP
STEER
STOEP
STREP
STREW
SUPER
SWEEP
SWEET
SYCEE
TABER
TABES
TAKEN
TAKER
TALEA
TALES
TAMER
TAPER
TAPET
TATER
TAXED
TEHEE
TELEX
TENET
TEPEE
TEREK
TERES
TEXEL
THIEF
THREE
THREW
TIBER
TIBET
TIGER
TILED
TILER
TILES
TIMER
TIMES
TINEA
TIRED
TIREE
TOKEN
TONER
TOPEE
TOPER
TOTEM
TOWEL
TOWER
TREEN
TREES
TRIED
TRIER
TRIES
TUBER
TUNER
TWEED
TWEET
TWOER
TYLER
TYNED
TYPED
TYPES
UDDER
ULCER
UMBEL
UMBER
UNBED
UNDER
UNFED
UNGET
UNPEN
UNWED
UPPER
UPSET
UPSEY
USHER
USTED
UTHER
UTTER
UZBEK
VALET
VAREC
VEREY
VEXED
VIBES
VIDEO
VIPER
VIREO
VIXEN
VOLET
VOMER
VOTER
VOTES
VOWEL
WADER
WAFER
WAGER
WAGES
WAKEN
WAKES
WALER
WALES
WANED
WARES
WATER
WAVED
WAVER
WAVES
WAXEN
WEBER
WESER
WHEEL
WHEEN
WIDEN
WILES
WINEY
WIPER
WIRED
WIRES
WIVES
WODEN
WOKEN
WOMEN
WOOER
WOVEN
XEBEC
XERES
XYLEM
YAMEN
YATES
YEMEN
YIKES
YODEL
YOKEL
YPRES
ZINEB
ALLÉE
LYCÉE
ARRÊT
ABAFT
ALOFT
BAFFY
BALFE
BEEFY
BLUFF
BUFFO
BUFFS
CHAFE
CHAFF
CHUFF
CLEFT
CLIFF
CLIFT
COMFY
CORFE
CORFU
CRAFT
CROFT
CUFFS
CUFFY
DAFFY
DEIFY
DELFT
DRAFT
DRIFT
EDIFY
FEOFF
FLUFF
GAFFE
GLIFF
GOOFY
GRAFF
GRAFT
GRIFF
GRUFE
GRUFF
HAIFA
HALFA
HUFFY
JAFFA
JIFFY
KNIFE
KRAFT
LEAFY
LOOFA
LUFFA
MALFI
MIFFY
NAAFI
PUFFY
QUAFF
QUIFF
ROLFE
SAMFU
SCAFF
SCIFI
SCOFF
SCUFF
SHAFT
SHIFT
SKIFF
SNAFU
SNIFF
SNIFT
SNUFF
SOLFA
SPIFF
STAFF
STIFF
STUFF
SULFA
SWIFT
TAFFY
THEFT
THOFT
TUFFE
UNIFY
WHIFF
WHIFT
WOOFY
YARFA
ADAGE
ADIGE
ALIGN
AMIGO
ANIGH
APAGE
BADGE
BAGGY
BARGE
BEIGE
BELGA
BILGE
BINGE
BINGO
BLIGH
BODGE
BOGGY
BONGO
BOUGH
BUDGE
BUGGY
BULGE
BUNGY
BURGH
CADGE
CADGY
CARGO
CIGGY
COIGN
CONGÉ
CONGO
CORGI
COUGH
DEIGN
DIEGO
DINGE
DINGO
DINGY
DIRGE
DODGE
DODGY
DOGGO
DOGGY
DOUGH
DREGS
DRUGS
ELEGY
ELOGE
ELOGY
ENUGU
ETAGE
FADGE
FARGO
FEIGN
FOGGY
FORGE
FORGO
FUDGE
FUGGY
GADGE
GAUGE
GLOGG
GOLGI
GORGE
GOUGE
GREGG
GUNGE
HAUGH
HEDGE
HEIGH

HELGA	PONGA	ALOHA	NACHO	ANVIL	CILIA	FLAIR	LUCID
HENGE	PONGO	ALPHA	NACHT	APAID	CIVIC	FLUID	LUCIO
HEUGH	PORGY	AUGHT	NASHE	APHID	CIVIL	FOLIC	LUDIC
HINGE	PUDGE	BAKHA	NICHE	APHIS	CLAIM	FOLIE	LUPIN
HODGE	PUDGY	BASHO	NIGHT	APRIL	COLIC	FOLIO	LURID
HOUGH	PURGE	BATHE	NUCHA	ARDIL	COLIN	FRAIL	LUTIN
IMAGE	RAGGY	BATHS	ORTHO	ARGIL	COMIC	FRUIT	LYDIA
IMAGO	RANGE	BIGHT	OUGHT	AROID	CONIC	GAMIC	LYRIC
INIGO	RANGY	BOCHE	PACHA	ARRIS	CORIN	GELID	LYSIN
JINGO	REIGN	BOTHA	PASHA	ARTIE	CRAIG	GENIE	LYSIS
JIRGA	RIDGE	BOTHY	PITHY	ASCII	CUBIC	GLAIR	MAFIA
JUDGE	ROUGE	BUSHY	PRAHU	ASDIC	CUBIT	GRAIL	MAGIC
KEDGE	ROUGH	CACHE	PUSHY	ASPIC	CUFIC	GRAIN	MALIK
KEDGY	RUDGE	CUSHY	RADHA	ASTIR	CUMIN	GROIN	MANIA
KENGA	SAGGY	DACHA	RIGHT	ATLIN	CUPID	HABIT	MANIC
KIDGE	SARGE	DELHI	RUCHE	ATRIP	CURIA	HAFIZ	MARIA
KINGS	SAUGH	DIGHT	RUSHY	ATTIC	CURIE	HELIO	MARIE
KONGO	SEDGE	DISHY	SACHA	AUDIO	CURIO	HELIX	MATIN
LARGE	SERGE	DUCHY	SACHS	AUDIT	CUTIE	HUMID	MAVIN
LARGO	SIEGE	EIGHT	SADHU	AULIC	CUTIS	IDRIS	MAVIS
LAUGH	SINGE	ELIHU	SASHA	AULIS	CYNIC	INDIA	MAXIM
LEDGE	SLIGO	FICHE	SHCHI	AURIC	DAVID	INUIT	MEDIA
LEGGE	SLUGS	FICHU	SIDHA	AUXIN	DAVIS	INWIT	MEDIC
LEGGY	SNAGS	FIGHT	SIGHS	AVAIL	DAVIT	IONIC	MELIA
LEIGH	SOGGY	FISHY	SIGHT	AVOID	DEBIT	IZMIR	MELIC
LIEGE	SOUGH	FOEHN	SOPHY	AWAIT	DENIM	JADIS	MERIL
LIGGE	STAGE	FUCHS	SPAHI	AXOID	DENIS	JORIS	MERIT
LINGO	STAGY	GOSHT	SPOHR	AYRIE	DEVIL	KAFIR	MESIC
LODGE	STOGA	GOTHA	SUSHI	AZOIC	DIGIT	KALIF	METIC
LONGS	STOGY	GUSHY	TIGHT	BASIC	DIXIE	KEFIR	METIF
LOUGH	SURGE	HATHI	TITHE	BASIL	DOLIN	KELIM	METIS
LUNGE	SYNGE	HECHT	TYPHA	BASIN	DORIC	KEVIN	MIMIC
LUNGI	TAIGA	HIGHT	VICHY	BASIS	DORIS	KILIM	MINIM
LUNGS	TANGA	HITHE	VOZHD	BATIK	DRAIN	KIWIS	MORIA
LURGY	TANGO	HYPHA	WASHY	BEFIT	DROIT	KLEIN	MORIN
MADGE	TANGY	HYTHE	WIGHT	BEGIN	DRUID	KUFIC	MOTIF
MANGE	TARGE	IDAHO	WITHE	BELIE	DUPIN	KYLIE	MOVIE
MANGO	TEIGN	IMSHI	WITHY	BENIN	EDWIN	KYLIN	MUCID
MANGY	THEGN	ITCHY	YACHT	BERIA	EERIE	KYLIX	MUCIN
MARGE	THIGH	KASHA	ABRIM	BEVIS	ELFIN	KYRIE	MUSIC
MENGE	THUGS	LATHE	ABSIT	BIFID	ELGIN	LABIS	MUSIT
MERGE	TINGE	LATHI	ACRID	BLAIR	ELLIS	LAMIA	NADIR
MIDGE	TONGA	LESHY	ACTIN	BOGIE	ELVIS	LAPIS	NAMIB
MINGY	TONGS	LETHE	ADDIO	BORIC	EMAIL	LATIN	NAZIR
MOGGY	TOUGH	LICHT	ADDIS	BORIS	EOLIC	LEGIT	NEVIS
MUDGE	TSUGA	LIGHT	ADLIB	BOWIE	EOSIN	LENIN	NGAIO
MUGGY	TWIGS	LITHE	ADMIN	BRAID	EQUIP	LEPID	NIHIL
MUNGO	USAGE	LUSHY	ADMIT	BRAIN	ERNIE	LEVIN	NITID
NEAGH	VERGE	LYTHE	ADMIX	BROIL	ETAIN	LEVIS	NOMIC
NEIGH	VIRGA	MACHO	AEGIS	BRUIN	ETHIC	LEWIS	NORIA
NUDGE	VIRGO	MASHY	AFFIX	BRUIT	EYRIE	LEXIS	NUBIA
OMAGH	VOLGA	MATHS	AFRIT	BURIN	EYTIE	LICIT	OASIS
OMEGA	VULGO	METHS	AGAIN	CABIN	FACIA	LIMIT	OBIIT
OSAGE	WAGGA	MICHE	ALDIS	CALIX	FAKIR	LININ	OGGIN
OUTGO	WAUGH	MIGHT	ALFIE	CAMIS	FECIT	LIPID	OLDIE
PANGA	WEDGE	MINHO	ALGID	CARIB	FELIS	LIVID	OLEIC
PEGGY	WEIGH	MOCHA	ALVIS	CAVIL	FELIX	LOGIC	OLEIN
PIGGY	WILGA	MOTHS	AMAIN	CECIL	FERIA	LORIS	OLLIE
PINGO	WINGS	MUSHA	AMBIT	CHAIN	FETID	LOUIE	OPHIR
PODGE	WODGE	MUSHY	ANNIE	CHAIR	FINIS	LOUIS	OPTIC
PODGY	WONGA	NACHE	ANTIC	CHOIR	FLAIL	LUCIA	ORBIT

ORNIS
ORRIS
OSSIA
OSTIA
OVOID
PALIO
PAMIR
PANIC
PARIS
PATIO
PAVID
PEKIN
PENIS
PERIL
PETIT
PIPIT
PIXIE
PLAID
PLAIN
PLAIT
PLEIN
POLIO
POSIT
POTIN
PUBIC
PUBIS
PUGIN
PUNIC
PUPIL
PURIM
PUTID
PYXIS
QUAIL
QUOIF
QUOIN
QUOIT
RABID
RADIO
RADIX
RAPID
RATIO
REFIT
REGIA
RÉGIE
REGIS
REJIG
RELIC
REMIT
RESIN
RESIT
REVIE
RHEIN
RICIN
RIGID
ROBIN
RODIN
RORIC
ROSIN
ROSIT
RUBIN
RUNIC

RUPIA
SABIN
SADIE
SAHIB
SALIC
SALIX
SAPID
SARIN
SATIE
SATIN
SATIS
SCLIM
SCRIM
SCRIP
SELIM
SEMIS
SEPIA
SERIF
SERIN
SHEIK
SIGIL
SITIN
SKEIN
SKRIM
SLAIN
SNAIL
SOFIA
SOLID
SONIC
SPAIN
SPLIT
SPOIL
SPRIG
SPRIT
SQUIB
SQUID
SQUIT
STAID
STAIN
STAIR
STEIN
STOIC
STRIA
STRIP
SUZIE
SWAIN
SYBIL
SYRIA
TACIT
TAMIL
TAMIS
TAPIR
TAPIS
TATIN
TAXIN
TAXIS
TELIC
TEPID
THAIS
THEIR
THRID

THRIP
TIBIA
TILIA
TIMID
TOBIT
TONIC
TOPIC
TORII
TOXIC
TOXIN
TRAIL
TRAIN
TRAIT
TROIC
TULIP
TUMID
TUNIC
TUNIS
TURIN
TWAIN
UGRIC
UNDID
UNFIT
UNLIT
UNMIX
UNPIN
UNRIG
UNRIP
UNTIE
UNTIL
UNZIP
VALID
VAPID
VARIX
VEDIC
VENIN
VIGIL
VIRID
VISIT
VITIS
VIVID
VOMIT
XENIA
XYRIS
YUPIK
ABUJA
BANJO
GANJA
HADJI
KANJI
KOPJE
NINJA
OUIJA
RIOJA
SHOJI
ALIKE
ASOKA
AWAKE
AWOKE
BACKS
BANKS

BECKY
BLAKE
BLOKE
BOSKY
BRAKE
BROKE
BUCKO
BUCKS
BULKY
BURKE
CHEKA
CHOKE
CHOKO
CHOKY
COCKY
COOKS
CORKY
CRAKE
DECKO
DEKKO
DICKY
DINKA
DINKY
DOCKS
DRAKE
DUCKS
DUCKY
DUSKY
EVOKE
FINKS
FLAKE
FLAKY
FLUKE
FOLKS
FORKS
FUNKY
GAWKY
GECKO
GORKY
HAIKU
HAKKA
HANKY
HONKY
HOOKY
HULKS
HUNKS
HUNKY
HUSKS
HUSKY
IROKO
JACKS
JERKS
JERKY
JINKS
JOCKO
KAFKA
KHAKI
KINKY
KOOKY
LACKS
LANKA

LANKY
LARKS
LASKI
LAWKS
LEAKY
LINKS
LOCKE
LOCKS
LUCKY
MAIKO
MILKY
MINKE
MONKS
MUCKY
MURKY
MUSKY
NARKS
NARKY
NOOKY
NUNKY
OSAKA
PARKA
PARKY
PAWKY
PEAKY
PERKS
PERKY
PESKY
PINKO
PINKY
PISKY
POLKA
PORKY
PROKE
PUKKA
QUAKE
RANKE
RANKS
RILKE
RISKY
ROCKS
ROCKY
ROOKY
RORKE
SACKS
SARKY
SHAKE
SHAKO
SHAKY
SILKY
SITKA
SLAKE
SMOKE
SMOKY
SNAKE
SNAKY
SOCKS
SPEKE
SPIKE
SPIKY
SPOKE

STAKE
STOKE
STUKA
SUCKS
SULKS
SULKY
TACKY
TALKS
TANKA
TIKKA
TRIKE
TUNKU
TURKI
TURKU
VODKA
WACKY
WEEKS
WONKY
WORKS
YAKKA
YONKS
YUCKY
YUKKY
ABELE
ADDLE
ADULT
AGILE
AIOLI
AISLE
AKELA
AMBLE
AMPLE
AMPLY
ANELE
ANGLE
ANGLO
ANKLE
APPLE
APPLY
APTLY
ARKLE
ATILT
ATOLL
ATTLE
BADLY
BALLS
BALLY
BASLE
BAULK
BAYLE
BEALE
BELLE
BELLS
BELLY
BIBLE
BILLY
BOGLE
BOULE
BOWLS
BOYLE
BRILL

BRULE
BUGLE
BUILD
BUILT
BULLA
BULLS
BULLY
BURLY
CABLE
CARLE
CAULD
CAULK
CELLA
CELLO
CELLS
CHALK
CHILD
CHILE
CHILI
CHILL
CHYLE
CILLA
COLLY
COULD
COYLY
CULLY
CURLY
CYCLE
DAILY
DALLE
DALLY
DIALS
DIMLY
DOILY
DOLLY
DOYLE
DOYLY
DRILL
DRILY
DROLL
DRYLY
DWELL
DYULA
EAGLE
EARLY
EBOLA
EDILE
EMILE
EMILY
EXALT
EXILE
EXULT
FABLE
FALLA
FALLS
FAULT
FELLA
FIELD
FILLY
FOLLY
FOOLS

FOULÉ
FOYLE
FRILL
FULLY
GABLE
GAILY
GAULT
GHYLL
GIGLI
GILLS
GIRLS
GIRLY
GODLY
GOLLY
GOOLY
GRILL
GUELF
GUILD
GUILE
GUILT
GULLS
GULLY
HALLÉ
HALLO
HAULM
HAULT
HAYLE
HEALD
HEELS
HELLO
HILLS
HILLY
HOLLA
HOLLY
HOTLY
HOYLE
HULLO
ICILY
IDYLL
IMPLY
INCLE
INGLE
ISOLA
ITALA
ITALY
JELLO
JELLY
JOLLY
JOULE
KEBLE
KEELS
KELLS
KELLY
KNELL
KNELT
KNOLL
KOALA
KRILL
KUALA
LADLE
LILLE

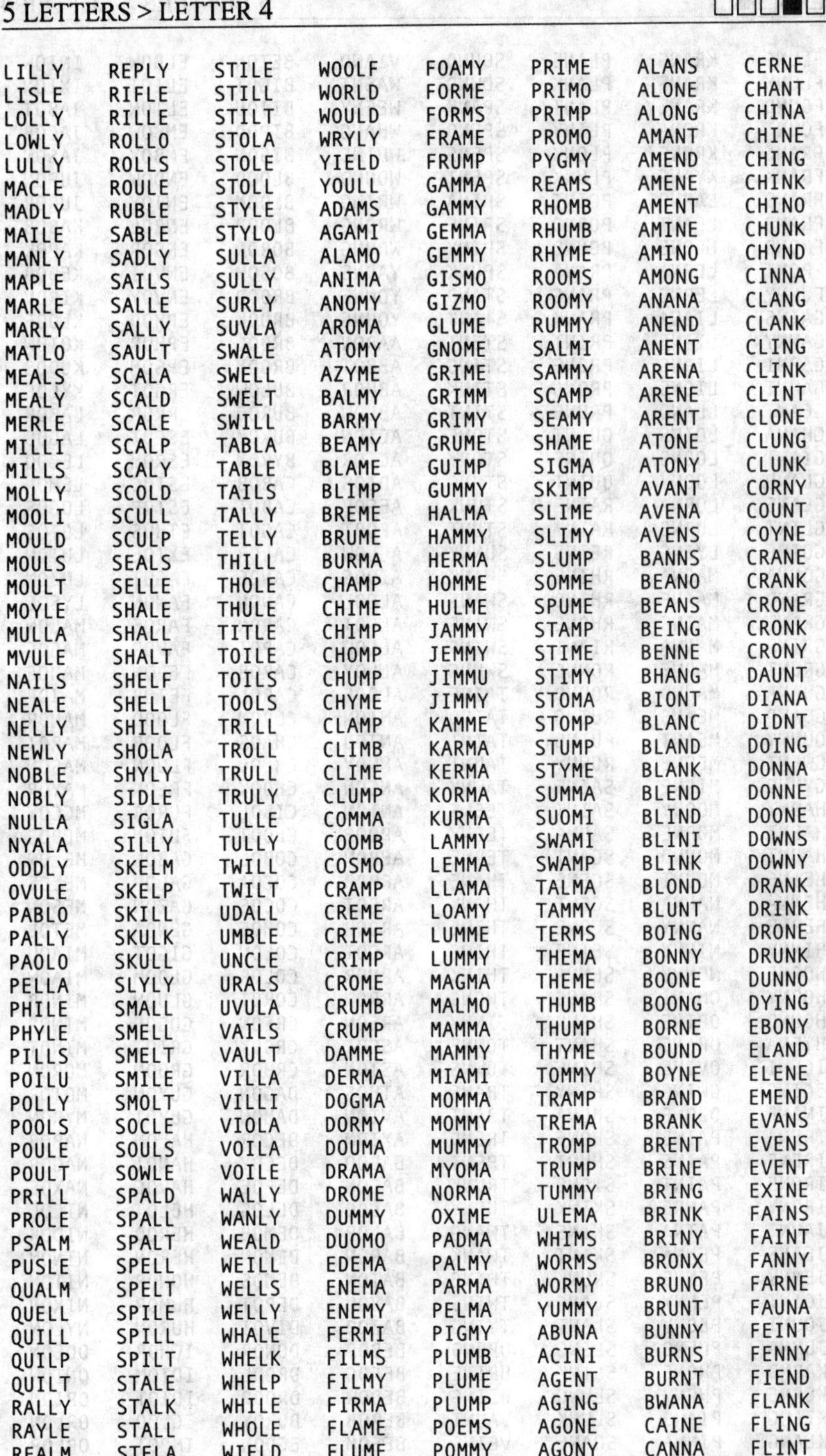

LILLY
LISLE
LOLLY
LOWLY
LULLY
MACLE
MADLY
MAILE
MANLY
MAPLE
MARLE
MARLY
MATLO
MEALS
MEALY
MERLE
MILLI
MILLS
MOLLY
MOOLI
MOULD
MOULS
MOULT
MOYLE
MULLA
MVULE
NAILS
NEALE
NELLY
NEWLY
NOBLE
NOBLY
NULLA
NYALA
ODDLY
OVULE
PABLO
PALLY
PAOLO
PELLA
PHILE
PHYLE
PILLS
POILU
POLLY
POOLS
POULE
POULT
PRILL
PROLE
PSALM
PUSLE
QUALM
QUELL
QUILL
QUILP
QUILT
RALLY
RAYLE
REALM
RÈGLE

REPLY
RIFLE
RILLE
ROLLO
ROLLS
ROULE
RUBLE
SABLE
SADLY
SAILS
SALLE
SALLY
SAULT
SCALA
SCALD
SCALE
SCALP
SCALY
SCOLD
SCULL
SCULP
SEALS
SELLE
SHALE
SHALL
SHALT
SHELF
SHELL
SHILL
SHOLA
SHYLY
SIDLE
SIGLA
SILLY
SKELM
SKELP
SKILL
SKULK
SKULL
SLYLY
SMALL
SMELL
SMELT
SMILE
SMOLT
SOCLE
SOULS
SOWLE
SPALD
SPALL
SPALT
SPELL
SPELT
SPILE
SPILL
SPILT
STALE
STALK
STALL
STELA
STELE

STILE
STILL
STILT
STOLA
STOLE
STOLL
STYLE
STYLO
SULLA
SULLY
SURLY
SUVLA
SWALE
SWELL
SWELT
SWILL
TABLA
TABLE
TAILS
TALLY
TELLY
THILL
THOLE
THULE
TITLE
TOILE
TOILS
TOOLS
TRILL
TROLL
TRULL
TRULY
TULLE
TULLY
TWILL
TWILT
UDALL
UMBLE
UNCLE
URALS
UVULA
VAILS
VAULT
VILLA
VILLI
VIOLA
VOILA
VOILE
WALLY
WANLY
WEALD
WEILL
WELLS
WELLY
WHALE
WHELK
WHELP
WHILE
WHOLE
WIELD
WILLY

WOOLF
WORLD
WOULD
WRYLY
YIELD
YOULL
ADAMS
AGAMI
ALAMO
ANIMA
ANOMY
AROMA
ATOMY
AZYME
BALMY
BARMY
BEAMY
BLAME
BLIMP
BREME
BRUME
BURMA
CHAMP
CHIME
CHIMP
CHOMP
CHUMP
CHYME
CLAMP
CLIMB
CLIME
CLUMP
COMMA
COOMB
COSMO
CRAMP
CREME
CRIME
CRIMP
CROME
CRUMB
CRUMP
DAMME
DERMA
DOGMA
DORMY
DOUMA
DRAMA
DROME
DUMMY
DUOMO
EDEMA
ENEMA
ENEMY
FERMI
FILMS
FILMY
FIRMA
FLAME
FLUME
FLUMP

FOAMY
FORME
FORMS
FRAME
FRUMP
GAMMA
GAMMY
GEMMA
GEMMY
GISMO
GIZMO
GLUME
GNOME
GRIME
GRIMM
GRIMY
GRUME
GUIMP
GUMMY
HALMA
HAMMY
HERMA
HOMME
HULME
JAMMY
JEMMY
JIMMU
JIMMY
KAMME
KARMA
KERMA
KORMA
KURMA
LAMMY
LEMMA
LLAMA
LOAMY
LUMME
LUMMY
MAGMA
MALMO
MAMMA
MAMMY
MIAMI
MOMMA
MOMMY
MUMMY
MYOMA
NORMA
OXIME
PADMA
PALMY
PARMA
PELMA
PIGMY
PLUMB
PLUME
PLUMP
POEMS
POMMY
PRIMA

PRIME
PRIMO
PRIMP
PROMO
PYGMY
REAMS
RHOMB
RHUMB
RHYME
ROOMS
ROOMY
RUMMY
SALMI
SAMMY
SCAMP
SEAMY
SHAME
SIGMA
SKIMP
SLIME
SLIMY
SLUMP
SOMME
SPUME
STAMP
STIME
STIMY
STOMA
STOMP
STUMP
STYME
SUMMA
SUOMI
SWAMI
SWAMP
TALMA
TAMMY
TERMS
THEMA
THEME
THUMB
THUMP
THYME
TOMMY
TRAMP
TREMA
TROMP
TRUMP
TUMMY
ULEMA
WHIMS
WORMS
WORMY
YUMMY
ABUNA
ACINI
AGENT
AGING
AGONE
AGONY
AKENE

ALANS
ALONE
ALONG
AMANT
AMEND
AMENE
AMENT
AMINE
AMINO
AMONG
ANANA
ANEND
ANENT
ARENA
ARENE
ARENT
ATONE
ATONY
AVANT
AVENA
AVENS
BANNS
BEANO
BEANS
BEING
BENNE
BHANG
BIONT
BLANC
BLAND
BLANK
BLEND
BLIND
BLINI
BLINK
BLOND
BLUNT
BOING
BONNY
BOONE
BOONG
BORNE
BOUND
BOYNE
BRAND
BRANK
BRENT
BRINE
BRING
BRINK
BRINY
BRONX
BRUNO
BRUNT
BUNNY
BURNS
BURNT
BWANA
CAINE
CANNA
CANNY

CERNE
CHANT
CHINA
CHINE
CHING
CHINK
CHINO
CHUNK
CHYND
CINNA
CLANG
CLANK
CLING
CLINK
CLINT
CLONE
CLUNG
CLUNK
CORNY
COUNT
COYNE
CRANE
CRANK
CRONE
CRONK
CRONY
DAUNT
DIANA
DIDNT
DOING
DONNA
DONNE
DOONE
DOWNS
DOWNY
DRANK
DRINK
DRONE
DRUNK
DUNNO
DYING
EBONY
ELAND
ELENE
EMEND
EVANS
EVENS
EVENT
EXINE
FAINS
FAINT
FANNY
FARNE
FAUNA
FEINT
FENNY
FIEND
FLANK
FLING
FLINT
FLONG

FLUNG
FLUNK
FOUND
FOUNT
FRANC
FRANK
FRANS
FRANZ
FROND
FRONT
FUNNY
GAINS
GANNY
GARNI
GAUNT
GÉANT
GHANA
GIANT
GLAND
GLANS
GLINT
GOING
GONNA
GRAND
GRANT
GRIND
GRUNT
GUANA
GUANO
GUNNY
GWENT
GYMNO
HADNT
HASNT
HAUNT
HEINE
HENNA
HERNE
HINNY
HORNE
HORNY
HOUND
HYENA
ICENI
ICING
INANE
IRENA
IRENE
IRONS
IRONY
JAUNT
JEANS
JENNY
JOINT
JOUNT
JUMNA
KARNO
KERNE
KIANG
KLANG
KOINE
KRANG
KRANS
KRANZ
KRONA
KRONE
KYANG
LARNE
LEANT
LEONE
LERNA
LERNE
LIANA
LIANE
LIANG
LIONS
LLANO
LOINS
LOONS
LOONY
LORNA
LORNE
LYING
MAGNA
MAINE
MAINS
MANNA
MARNE
MAUND
MEANS
MEANT
MESNE
MILNE
MOONY
MORNE
MOUND
MOUNT
NANNA
NANNY
NINNY
NONNY
OMANI
OPINE
ORANG
OVINE
OWING
OZONE
PAINE
PAINS
PAINT
PANNE
PATNA
PENNA
PENNE
PENNY
PEONY
PHENO
PHONE
PHONY
PIANO
PINNA
PINNY
PLANE
PLANK
PLANT
PLINY
PLONK
PLUNK
POINT
PORNO
POUND
PRANA
PRANG
PRANK
PRINT
PRONE
PRONG
PRUNE
QUANT
QUINS
QUINT
RAINE
RAINY
REINS
RHINE
RHINO
RHONE
RIANT
RONNE
ROUND
RUING
RUINS
RUNNY
SAINE
SAINT
SAUNA
SCANT
SCENE
SCENT
SCONE
SEINE
SENNA
SHANG
SHANK
SHANT
SHINE
SHINY
SHONA
SHONE
SHUNT
SIGNS
SKINK
SKINS
SKINT
SKUNK
SLANG
SLANT
SLING
SLINK
SLUNG
SLUNK
SOANE
SONNY
SOUND
SOWND
SPANK
SPEND
SPENS
SPENT
SPINA
SPINE
SPINY
SPUNK
STAND
STANK
STENT
STING
STINK
STINT
STONE
STONY
STUNG
STUNK
STUNT
SUNNY
SWANK
SWANS
SWINE
SWING
SWUNG
TAINE
TAINO
TAINT
TAUNT
TAWNY
TEENS
TEENY
TERNE
THANE
THANK
THINE
THING
THINK
THONG
TINNY
TONNE
TOWNS
TRANS
TRANT
TREND
TRENT
TRUNK
TUNNY
TWANG
TWANK
TWINE
TWINS
TYING
UPEND
URINE
USING
VAUNT
VEINS
VERNE
VIAND
WASNT
WEENY
WHANG
WHINE
WOUND
WRING
WRONG
WRUNG
YARNS
YONNE
YOUNG
AARON
ABBOT
ABHOR
ABLOW
ACTON
ACTOR
ADIOS
AESOP
AFOOT
AGLOW
AIDOS
ALGOL
ALLOT
ALLOW
ALLOY
ALOOF
ANION
ANJOU
ANNOY
ANSON
ANTON
APOOP
APRON
ARBOR
ARCOT
ARDOR
ARGOT
ARMOR
ARROW
ARSON
ASCOT
ASTON
ATHOS
AVION
AXIOM
BABOO
BACON
BALOO
BALOR
BARON
BATON
BAYOU
BAZOO
BEBOP
BEFOG
BELOW
BEROB
BESOM
BESOT
BETON
BIGOT
BIJOU
BIPOD
BISON
BLOOD
BLOOM
BLOOP
BORON
BOSOM
BROOD
BROOK
BROOL
BROOM
BULOW
BUROO
BUXOM
BYRON
CABOB
CABOT
CAGOT
CALOR
CANOE
CANON
CAPON
CAPOT
CAROB
CAROL
CDROM
CHAOS
CHLOE
CHOOK
CIBOL
CLOOT
COBOL
COCOA
COCOS
COHOE
COLON
COLOR
COROT
CREON
CROOK
CRUOR
DAGON
DAMON
DECOR
DECOY
DEFOE
DELOS
DEMOB
DEMON
DEMOS
DEPOT
DIVOT
DONOR
DROOL
DROOP
DUROY
EGDON
EIKON
ELBOW
ELIOT
ELTON
EMBOW
EMBOX
ENDOW
ENJOY
ENROL
ENSOR
ENVOI
ENVOY
EPHOD
EPHOR
EPSOM
ERGOT
ERROR
ESCOT
ESROM
ESTOC
ESTOP
ETHOS
EXTOL
FAGOT
FANON
FAROE
FAVOR
FELON
FETOR
FLOOD
FLOOR
FLUON
FREON
FUROR
FUTON
GABON
GALOP
GAZON
GENOA
GIGOT
GLOOM
GLUON
GOGOL
GRIOT
GROOM
GUYON
GUYOT
HALON
HANOI
HAVOC
HELOT
HEROD
HERON
HONOR
HUMOR
HURON
ICHOR
IDIOM
IDIOT
IGLOO
IMPOT
INGOT
INION
IXION
JABOT
JACOB
JASON
JUPON
JUROR
KABOB
KAPOK
KEBOB
KIROV
KLOOF
KOTOW
KUDOS
KYLOE
LABOR
LAGOS
LECOQ
LEMON
LOGOS
LOTOS
LUTON
LUZON
LYSOL
MACON
MAGOG
MAHOE
MAJOR
MANOR
MAROT
MASON
MAYOR
MCCOY
MEDOC
MELON
MELOS
MESON
METOL
MIAOU
MIAOW
MINOR
MINOS
MINOT
MORON
MOTOR
MYRON
NABOB
NAGOR
NAXOS
NICOL
NIDOR
NINON
NITON
NIXON
NYLON
ODEON
ONION
ORION
ORLON
ORLOP
ORTON

OXBOW
PEKOE
PERON
PHEON
PHLOX
PHNOM
PICOT
PILOT
PINON
PINOT
PIROG
PITON
PITOT
PIVOT
POPOV
POTOO
PRION
PRIOR
PROOF
PUDOR
PYLON
RADON
RAYON
RAZOR
REDON
REDOX
REPOT
RIGOR
RIPON
ROBOT
ROTOR
RUMOR
SABOT
SALON
SAMOA
SAMOS
SAPOR
SAROS
SAVOR
SAVOY
SAXON
SCION
SCOOP
SCOOT
SCROD
SCROG
SCROW
SENOR
SEPOY
SHOOK
SHOOT
SHROW
SIDON
SIMON
SLOOP
SNOOD
SNOOK
SNOOP
SNOOT
SODOM
SODOR
SOKOL
SOLON
SPOOF
SPOOK
SPOOL
SPOON
SPOOR
SPROD
SPROG
STOOD
STOOK
STOOL
STOOP
STOOR
STROP
SUDOR
SUTOR
SWOON
SWOOP
SYNOD
TABOO
TABOR
TALON
TAROT
TAXOL
TAXON
TELOS
TENON
TENOR
THROB
THROE
THROW
TIGON
TIMON
TIMOR
TIROS
TROON
TROOP
TUDOR
TUMOR
TUTOR
TYROL
UNION
UPTON
URSON
VALOR
VAPOR
VENOM
VIGOR
VISON
VISOR
VIZOR
VROOM
WAGON
WHOOP
WHOOT
WIDOW
XENON
XEROX
YAHOO
YUKON
ZADOK
ZENOS
ADAPT
ADEPT
ADOPT
AGAPE
ALAPA
ALEPH
ASAPH
ATOPY
BUMPH
BUMPY
CALPE
CAMPO
CHAPE
CHAPS
CHIPS
CHOPS
CLEPE
COMPO
COOPT
COPPY
CORPS
COUPE
COYPU
CRAPE
CRAPS
CREPE
CREPT
CROPS
CRYPT
CUPPA
DELPH
DIPPY
DRAPE
DROPS
DRUPE
DUMPS
DUMPY
EGYPT
ELOPE
ERUPT
ETAPE
FLOPS
GASPÉ
GIMPY
GIPPO
GLYPH
GRAPE
GRAPH
GRIPE
GROPE
GULPH
GUPPY
GYPPO
HAPPY
HARPO
HARPY
HEAPS
HIPPO
HIPPY
HUMPH
IGAPO
INAPT
INEPT
JASPÉ
JIMPY
JUMPS
JUMPY
KAMPF
KAPPA
KEEPS
KEMPE
KIPPS
LAMPS
LEAPT
LIPPI
LOOPY
LOUPE
LUMPY
LYMPH
MORPH
MUMPS
NAPPA
NAPPE
NAPPY
NIPPY
NYMPH
OKAPI
OOMPH
PEPPY
PIPPA
POPPA
POPPY
POUPE
PULPY
PUPPY
RALPH
ROOPY
RUMPY
SAPPY
SCAPA
SCAPE
SCOPE
SCOPS
SHAPE
SHOPS
SLEPT
SLIPE
SLIPS
SLOPE
SLOPS
SLYPE
SNAPS
SNIPE
SOAPY
SOPPY
STAPH
STEPS
STOPE
STUPA
STUPE
SUPPE
SWEPT
SWIPE
SYLPH
TAMPA
TAUPE
TEMPE
TEMPO
TEMPT
TIPPY
TRAPS
TRIPE
TROPE
TURPS
UNAPT
VESPA
WEEPY
WHIPS
WIMPY
WISPY
YIPPY
YUPPY
ZEPPO
ZIPPY
IRAQI
ABORT
ACCRA
ACERB
ACORN
ADORE
ADORN
AFIRE
AFORE
AGGRO
AGORA
ALARM
ALERT
ALURE
AMORT
ANGRY
APART
APERT
APPRO
ASTRA
AVERT
AWARD
AWARE
AWARN
AZURE
BAIRD
BAIRN
BAJRI
BARRA
BARRE
BARRY
BASRA
BEARD
BEERY
BERRY
BLARE
BLURB
BLURT
BOARD
BOURG
BURRO
CADRE
CAIRN
CAIRO
CAPRI
CARRY
CEORL
CHARD
CHARK
CHARM
CHART
CHARY
CHERE
CHERT
CHIRK
CHIRL
CHIRP
CHIRR
CHIRT
CHORD
CHORE
CHURL
CHURN
CHURR
CLARA
CLARE
CLARK
CLARY
CLERK
COBRA
COPRA
COURB
COURT
COWRY
CRARE
CRORE
CURRY
CYMRU
CYMRY
DAIRY
DECRY
DERRY
DIARY
DOBRO
DOORN
DOORS
DOURA
DOURO
DOWRY
DRERE
DRURY
DURRY
DWARF
EMERY
EMURE
ENARM
ENORM
ENTRY
ENURE
ERARD
EVERT
EVERY
EXERT
EXTRA
EXURB
FABRÉ
FAERY
FAIRY
FAURE
FEARE
FERRY
FIBRE
FIBRO
FIERE
FIERY
FIORD
FJORD
FLARE
FLIRT
FLORA
FOURS
FUERO
FURRY
GEARE
GENRE
GLORY
GNARL
GOURD
GUARD
HAIRS
HAIRY
HARRY
HEARD
HEART
HENRY
HOARD
HOARE
HOARY
HOURI
HOURS
HURRY
HYDRA
HYDRO
IBERT
IMARI
INARI
INARM
INDRA
INDRE
INDRI
INERT
INFRA
INTRA
INTRO
INURE
ISERE
IVORY
IZARD
JERRY
JEWRY
KARRI
KAURI
KNARL
KNURL
KNURR
KOORI
KUKRI
LAIRD
LAIRY
LARRY
LAURA
LAVRA
LEARN
LEERY
LIARD
LIBRA
LITRE
LIVRE
LOIRE
LORRY
LOWRY
LUBRA
LUCRE
LYCRA
MACRO
MAIRE
MAORI
MARRY
MERRY
METRE
METRO
MICRO
MITRE
MOIRA
MOIRE
MOORE
MOURN
MUCRO
MUNRO
MURRE
MURRY
MYRRH
NACRE
NAIRA
NAURU
NEGRO
NEHRU
NITRE
OCHRE
OMBRE
OPERA
OTARY
OUTRE
OVARY
OVERT
OZARK
PADRE
PAIRE
PAIRS
PARRY

PEARL
PEDRO
PEERS
PERRY
PETRA
PETRE
PETRI
PHARE
PIERS
PIERT
PSORA
QUARK
QUART
QUERN
QUERY
QUIRE
QUIRK
QUORN
REARM
REPRO
RETRO
SABRA
SABRE
SCARE
SCARF
SCARP
SCARY
SCORE
SCORN
SCURF
SEARE
SERRA
SERRE
SHARD
SHARE
SHARK
SHARP
SHERD
SHERE
SHIRE
SHIRK
SHIRR
SHIRT
SHORE
SHORN
SHORT
SKIRL
SKIRR
SKIRT
SLURB
SLURP
SMARM
SMART
SMIRK
SNARE
SNARK
SNARL
SNORE
SNORT
SOARE
SOPRA
SORRY
SPARE
SPARK
SPART
SPERM
SPIRE
SPORE
SPORT
SPURN
SPURS
SPURT
STARE
STARK
STARR
STARS
START
STERN
STIRP
STORE
STORK
STORM
STORY
STURT
SUCRE
SUPRA
SUTRA
SWARD
SWARF
SWARM
SWIRE
SWIRL
SWORD
SWORE
SWORN
TARRY
TATRA
TEARS
TERRA
TERRY
TETRA
THERE
THERM
THIRD
THIRL
THORN
TIARA
TITRE
TRURO
TWERP
TWIRL
TWIRP
UHURU
ULTRA
UMBRA
UNARM
USURE
USURP
USURY
UTURN
WEARY
WEIRD
WHARF
WHERE
WHIRL
WHIRR
WHORE
WHORL
WORRY
YARRA
YEARN
YEARS
YOURS
YOURT
ZABRA
ZAIRE
ZEBRA
ZORRO
ABASE
ABASH
ABUSE
ABYSM
ABYSS
AGIST
AMASS
AMISH
AMISS
AMUSE
ANGST
ANISE
ARISE
ARISH
ARIST
AROSE
AVAST
AVISO
AWASH
BALSA
BASSO
BEAST
BLASÉ
BLAST
BLESS
BLEST
BLISS
BLUSH
BOAST
BOOST
BOSSY
BRASH
BRASS
BREST
BRISK
BROSE
BRUSH
BURSA
BURST
CAUSE
CEASE
CENSE
CHASE
CHASM
CHESS
CHEST
CHOSE
CISSY
CLASH
CLASP
CLASS
CLOSE
COAST
COPSE
CORSE
CORSO
CRASH
CRASS
CRESS
CREST
CRISE
CRISP
CROSS
CRUSE
CRUSH
CRUST
CURSE
CURST
DAISY
DEIST
DENSE
DESSE
DOUSE
DOWSE
DRESS
DROSS
DURST
EGEST
ERASE
ERNST
EXIST
FALSE
FARSE
FAUST
FEAST
FESSE
FIRST
FLASH
FLASK
FLESH
FLOSS
FLUSH
FOIST
FOSSA
FOSSE
FRESH
FRISK
FRIST
FROST
FUBSY
FUSSY
GASSY
GAUSS
GEESE
GEIST
GESSE
GESSO
GHOST
GIPSY
GLASS
GLISK
GLOSS
GNASH
GOOSE
GORSE
GOSSE
GRASP
GRASS
GRIST
GROSS
GROSZ
GUESS
GUEST
GUISE
GUTSY
GYPSY
HALSE
HANSE
HARSH
HAUSA
HAUSE
HAWSE
HEIST
HERSE
HESSE
HOAST
HOIST
HOLST
HOOSH
HORSA
HORSE
HORSY
HOUSE
HURST
HUSSY
IRISH
JESSE
JOIST
JOUST
KARST
KARSY
KIOSK
KVASS
LAPSE
LASSA
LASSO
LEASE
LEASH
LEAST
LEESE
LEISH
LHASA
LOESS
LOOSE
LOUSE
LOUSY
MANSE
MARSH
MASSA
MASSE
MENSA
MESSY
MEUSE
MIDST
MINSK
MISSA
MISSY
MOIST
MOOSE
MOPSY
MORSE
MOSSY
MOUSE
MOUSY
MULSE
MUSSE
MUSSY
NESSA
NEWSY
NOISE
NOISY
NOOSE
NORSE
NURSE
NYASA
NYSSA
OBESE
PAISA
PALSY
PANSY
PARSE
PARSI
PASSE
PATSY
PAUSE
PEASE
PEPSI
PERSE
PHASE
PLUSH
POESY
POISE
POPSY
POSSE
PRESA
PRESS
PREST
PRISE
PRISM
PROSE
PROSY
PULSE
PURSE
PURSY
PUSSY
QUASH
QUASI
QUEST
RAISE
REIST
RINSE
ROAST
ROIST
ROOST
ROSSE
ROSSI
ROUSE
ROUST
RUSSE
RUSSO
SALSA
SALSE
SAMSO
SASSE
SASSY
SAYSO
SEISM
SENSE
SHUSH
SISSY
SLASH
SLOSH
SLUSH
SMASH
SNASH
SOUSA
SOUSE
SPASM
STASH
STASI
SWASH
SWISH
SWISS
TANSY
TASSE
TASSO
TAWSE
TEASE
TENSE
TERSE
TESSA
THESE
THOSE
TIPSY
TOAST
TOISE
TOPSY
TORSO
TOWSE
TRASH
TRESS
TRUSS
TRUST
TRYST
TUTSI
TWIST
UKASE
VALSE
VERSA
VERSE
VERSO
VERST
WAIST
WELSH
WHISH
WHISK
WHIST
WHOSE
WORSE
WORST
WREST
WRIST
WURST
XHOSA
YEAST
ABATE
ACUTE
AGATE
ALATE
AMITY
ANITA
AORTA
AOSTA
ARETE
ARITA
AUNTY
AZOTE
BANTU
BARTS
BASTA
BASTE
BASTO
BATTY
BERTH
BETTE
BETTY
BIRTH
BITTE
BITTY
BLITZ
BOOTH
BOOTS
BOOTY
BOTTE
BROTH
BRUTE
BUSTY
BUTTE
BUTTY
CANTO
CARTA
CARTE
CASTE
CATTY
CENTO
CHOTA
CHUTE
CLOTH
COATI
COLTS

COMTE
CONTE
COSTA
COSTS
COTTA
COUTH
CRATE
CRETE
CRWTH
CUTTY
DANTE
DARTS
DEATH
DEITY
DELTA
DEPTH
DHOTI
DIOTA
DIRTY
DITTO
DITTY
DORTS
DOTTY
DUSTY
EARTH
ELATE
ELITE
EMOTE
EMPTY
ERATO
ETATS
EVITA
EVITE
FACTO
FACTS
FAITH
FATTY
FEMTO
FESTA
FESTE
FIFTH
FIFTY
FILTH
FIRTH
FLATS
FLOTA
FLUTE
FLYTE
FOOTS
FOOTY
FORTE
FORTH
FORTY
FRITH
FRITZ
FROTH
FUSTY
GARTH
GENTS
GENTY
GESTE

GHATS
GIFTS
GILTS
GIRTH
GLITZ
GOATY
GOTTA
GOUTY
GRATE
GRETA
GRITS
GUSTO
GUSTY
GUTTA
HAITI
HARTY
HASTA
HASTE
HASTY
HATTY
HAUTE
HEATH
HECTO
HEFTY
HERTS
HERTZ
HETTY
HOSTA
HUNTS
IRATE
JANTY
JETTY
JONTY
JUNTA
JUNTO
KITTY
KOFTA
LAITH
LAITY
LEFTY
LEITH
LENTO
LISTS
LOATH
LOFTY
LOTTO
LOUTH
LUSTY
MALTA
MANTA
MEATH
MEATS
MEATY
MEETS
MEITH
MESTO
MIRTH
MISTY
MIXTE
MOLTO
MONTE

MONTH
MOTTE
MOTTO
MOUTH
MUFTI
MULTI
MUSTY
NANTZ
NASTY
NATTY
NESTA
NEWTS
NIFTY
NINTH
NORTH
NOTTS
NUTTY
OBOTE
ODETS
ORATE
OVATE
PANTO
PANTS
PANTY
PARTI
PARTS
PARTY
PASTA
PASTE
PASTY
PATTI
PATTY
PEATY
PESTO
PETTO
PETTY
PHOTO
PIETA
PIETY
PINTA
PINTO
PISTE
PITTA
PLATE
PLATH
PLATO
PLATY
PLATZ
PLOTS
PLUTO
POETS
PONTY
PORTA
PORTE
PORTO
PORTS
POSTE
POTTO
POTTY
PRATE
PUNTO

PUTTO
PUTTY
QUITE
QUITO
QUITS
QUOTA
QUOTE
QUOTH
RATTY
RECTO
REITH
RENTE
RESTS
RHETT
RIOTS
ROOTS
ROOTY
RORTY
ROUTE
RUSTY
SALTS
SALTY
SANTA
SANTO
SAUTE
SCATH
SCOTS
SCOTT
SHITE
SHOTS
SHUTE
SHUTS
SITTA
SIXTH
SIXTY
SKATE
SLATE
SLATS
SLATY
SLOTH
SMITE
SMITH
SMOTE
SMUTS
SOFTY
SOLTI
SOOTH
SOOTY
SORTS
SOTTO
SOUTH
SOWTH
SPATE
SPATS
SPITE
SPITZ
SPOTS
STATE
SUETY
SUITE
SUITS

SWATH
SWATS
TARTY
TASTE
TASTY
TATTY
TEETH
TENTH
TESTA
TESTS
TESTY
TEXTS
THETA
THETE
TILTH
TITTY
TOOTH
TORTE
TOTTY
TRITE
TROTH
TROTS
TRUTH
TUTTI
UMPTY
UNITA
UNITE
UNITS
UNITY
URATE
URITE
VERTU
VESTA
VIRTU
VISTA
VOLTA
VOLTE
WAITS
WALTZ
WARTY
WASTE
WATTS
WHITE
WIDTH
WILTS
WITTY
WORTH
WRATH
WRITE
WRITS
WROTE
WROTH
YALTA
YARTA
YEATS
YOUTH
ZANTE
ZLOTY
ABDUL
ABOUT
ADSUM

AFOUL
ALBUM
ALEUT
ALNUS
ALOUD
AMOUR
ANGUS
ANKUS
ANNUL
APPUI
ARCUS
ARGUE
ARGUS
ASCUS
AUGUR
AVOUÉ
AWFUL
BABUL
BAHUT
BEAUT
BEGUM
BEGUN
BÉVUE
BOGUS
BOLUS
BONUS
BOSUN
CAIUS
CAJUN
CAMUS
CAPUT
CECUM
CLAUS
CLOUD
CLOUT
COMUS
CROUP
CYRUS
DATUK
DATUM
DEBUG
DEBUT
DEMUR
DURUM
EMBUS
ENDUE
ENNUI
ENSUE
FAGUS
FAVUS
FEMUR
FETUS
FLEUR
FLOUR
FLOUT
FOCUS
FORUM
FRAUD
FREUD
FUGUE
GADUS

GAIUS
GAMUT
GARUM
GENUS
GETUP
GHOUL
GIBUS
GIGUE
GROUP
GROUT
GUEUX
GYRUS
HAGUE
HILUM
HOCUS
HOKUM
HORUS
HUMUS
HYLUM
ICTUS
ILEUM
ILEUS
ILIUM
IMAUM
IMBUE
INCUR
INCUS
INDUE
INDUS
INIUM
INJUN
INPUT
IRGUN
ISSUE
JANUS
JESUS
JORUM
KABUL
KAPUT
KNOUT
KOKUM
KRAUT
LEMUR
LINUS
LOCUM
LOCUS
LOTUS
LUPUS
MAGUS
MAHUA
MANUL
MANUS
MASUS
MIAUL
MIMUS
MINUS
MIXUP
MODUS
MOGUL
MORUS
MUCUS

NAHUM
NATUS
NEGUS
NEXUS
NIDUS
NISUS
NODUS
NOTUM
NOVUM
OAKUM
OCCUR
OCNUS
ODIUM
ODOUR
OLEUM
ONCUS
ONKUS
OPIUM
ORCUS
ORGUE
ORMUZ
ORTUS
OTIUM
PICUS
PILUM
PILUS
PIOUS
PIPUL
PIQUE
POPUP
PROUD
PROUT
PSEUD
PYRUS
QUEUE
RAMUS
REBUS
REBUT
RECUR
REMUE
REMUS
RERUN
REVUE
RHEUM
RISUS
ROGUE
ROQUE
RUFUS
RUNUP
SARUS
SCAUP
SCAUR
SCOUP
SCOUR
SCOUT
SCRUB
SCRUM
SEDUM
SEGUE
SEOUL
SERUM

SETUP
SHAUN
SHOUT
SHRUB
SHRUG
SINUS
SITUP
SNOUT
SOLUM
SOLUS
SOYUZ
SPOUT
SPRUE
STOUP
STOUR
STOUT
STRUM
STRUT
SYRUP
TAGUS
TALUS
TAXUS
TENUE
THRUM
TITUS
TONUS
TOQUE
TORUS
TROUT
TUQUE
UNCUS
UNCUT
UNDUE
VADUZ
VAGUE
VAGUS
VALUE
VARUS
VELUM
VENUE
VENUS
VIRUS
VITUS
VOGUE
WHAUP
WHAUR
YAKUT
ABOVE
AGAVE
ALIVE
BEVVY
BRAVA
BRAVE
BRAVO
BREVE
CALVE
CARVE
CARVY
CHEVY
CHIVE
CHIVY
CIVVY
CLAVE
CLIVE
CLOVE
CORVO
CRAVE
CURVE
CURVY
DELVE
DIVVY
DRIVE
DROVE
EMOVE
FAUVE
GLOVE
GRAVE
GRAVY
GROVE
GUAVA
HALVE
HEAVE
HEAVY
HELVE
HOOVE
KNAVE
LARVA
LEAVE
MAEVE
MAUVE
NAIVE
NAVVY
NERVA
NERVE
NERVI
NERVO
NERVY
NIEVE
OGIVE
OLIVE
PARVO
PEEVE
PIAVE
PRIVY
PROVE
PROVO
REEVE
SALVE
SALVO
SAVVY
SELVA
SERVE
SERVO
SHAVE
SHIVA
SHIVE
SHOVE
SIEVE
SILVA
SKIVE
SLAVE
SOLVE
STAVE
STEVE
STOVE
SUAVE
TREVI
TROVE
VALVE
VERVE
VOLVA
VOLVO
VULVA
WAIVE
WEAVE
YAHVE
YOUVE
BLOWN
BLOWY
BRAWL
BRAWN
BROWN
CHEWY
CLOWN
CRAWL
CREWE
CROWD
CROWN
DRAWL
DRAWN
DROWN
FATWA
FLEWS
FLOWN
FROWN
FROWY
GROWL
GROWN
KNOWN
MAHWA
PRAWL
PRAWN
PROWL
SCHWA
SCOWL
SCOWP
SHAWL
SHAWM
SHOWN
SHOWY
SNOWY
SPAWN
STEWS
STEWY
STOWE
THEWS
TRAWL
TREWS
EPOXY
PROXY
TWIXT
ALLYL
BERYL
CALYX
DENYS
EMLYN
EMRYS
ETHYL
GRAYS
GREYS
HEXYL
KENYA
KHAYA
LIBYA
LLOYD
OXEYE
PEPYS
PLAYA
POLYP
POWYS
SATYR
SIBYL
STAYS
SURYA
THUYA
TOKYO
VANYA
VINYL
AMAZE
BAIZE
BLAZE
BONZE
BOOZE
BOOZY
BRIZE
BWAZI
CLOZE
COLZA
CRAZE
CRAZY
CROZE
DIAZO
DIZZY
DRUZE
FIZZY
FROZE
FURZE
FUZZY
GAUZE
GAUZY
GHAZI
GLAZE
GONZO
GRAZE
HUZZA
IBIZA
JAZZY
KHAZI
KUDZU
LAZZO
LISZT
MAIZE
MEZZE
MEZZO
MIRZA
MONZA
MUZZY
PIEZO
PIZZA
PLAZA
PRIZE
PZAZZ
RITZY
SEIZE
SENZA
SWAZI
SWIZZ
TAZZA
TEAZE
TIZZY
TOWZE
WHIZZ
WOOZY

5:5

ABABA
ABUJA
ABUNA
ACCRA
AGORA
AKELA
ALAPA
ALOHA
ALPHA
AMEBA
ANANA
ANIMA
ANITA
AORTA
AOSTA
AQABA
ARABA
ARDEA
ARECA
ARENA
ARICA
ARITA
AROMA
ARUBA
ASOKA
ASTRA
AVENA
BAKHA
BALSA
BANDA
BARRA
BASRA
BASTA
BEKAA
BELGA
BERIA
BOHEA
BOTHA
BRAVA
BREDA
BUCCA
BULLA
BURMA
BURSA
BWANA
CANNA
CARTA
CASCA
CELLA
CHEKA
CHICA
CHINA
CHOTA
CILIA
CILLA
CINNA
CIRCA
CLARA
COBRA
COCOA
COLZA
COMMA
COPRA
COSTA
COTTA
CUPPA
CURIA
DACCA
DACHA
DECCA
DELTA
DERMA
DIANA
DINKA
DIOTA
DOGMA
DONNA
DOUMA
DOURA
DRAMA
DYULA
EBOLA
EDEMA
ENEMA
ERICA
ERUCA
EVITA
EXTRA
FACIA
FALLA
FATWA
FAUNA
FELLA
FERIA
FESTA
FIRMA
FLORA
FLOTA
FONDA
FOSSA
FOVEA
GALBA
GALEA
GAMBA
GAMMA
GANJA
GARDA
GEMMA
GENOA
GHANA
GONNA
GOTHA
GOTTA
GOUDA
GRETA
GUANA
GUAVA
GUTTA
HAIDA
HAIFA
HAKKA
HALFA
HALMA
HASTA
HAUSA
HEDDA
HELGA
HENNA
HERMA
HEVEA
HILDA
HOLLA
HORSA
HOSEA
HOSTA
HUZZA
HYDRA
HYENA
HYPHA
IBIZA
INDIA
INDRA
INFRA
INTRA
IRENA
ISOLA
ITALA
JAFFA
JIRGA
JUMNA
JUNTA
KAABA
KAFKA
KAPPA
KARMA
KASHA
KENGA
KENYA
KERMA
KHAYA
KILDA
KOALA
KOFTA
KOREA
KORMA
KRONA
KUALA
KURMA
LABDA
LAMIA
LANKA
LARVA
LASSA
LAURA
LAVRA
LEMMA
LERNA
LHASA
LIANA
LIBRA
LIBYA
LLAMA
LOOFA
LORCA
LORNA
LUBRA
LUCIA
LUFFA
LYCRA
LYDIA
MAFIA
MAGMA
MAGNA
MAHUA
MAHWA
MALTA
MAMBA
MAMMA
MANIA
MANNA
MANTA
MARIA
MASSA
MECCA
MEDEA
MEDIA
MELBA
MELIA
MENSA
MIRZA
MISSA
MOCHA
MOIRA
MOMMA
MONZA
MORIA
MULLA
MUNDA
MUSCA
MUSHA
MYOMA

NAIRA
NANNA
NAPPA
NERVA
NESSA
NESTA
NINJA
NORIA
NORMA
NUBIA
NUCHA
NULLA
NYALA
NYASA
NYSSA
OCREA
OMEGA
OPERA
OSAKA
OSSIA
OSTIA
OUIDA
OUIJA
PACHA
PADMA
PAISA
PALEA
PANDA
PANGA
PARKA
PARMA
PASHA
PASTA
PATNA
PELLA
PELMA
PENNA
PETRA
PICEA
PIETA
PINNA
PINTA
PIPPA
PITTA
PIZZA
PLAYA
PLAZA
PLICA
POLKA
PONGA
POPPA
PORTA
PRANA
PRESA
PRIMA
PSORA
PUKKA
QUOTA
RADHA
REGIA
RIOJA
RSPCA
RUMBA
RUPIA
SABRA
SACHA
SALSA
SAMBA
SAMOA
SANTA
SASHA
SAUNA
SCALA
SCAPA
SCHWA
SCUBA
SELVA
SENNA
SENZA
SEPIA
SERRA
SHEBA
SHIVA
SHOLA
SHONA
SIDHA
SIGLA
SIGMA
SILVA
SIMBA
SITKA
SITTA
SOFIA
SOLFA
SOPRA
SOUSA
SPICA
SPINA
STELA
STOGA
STOLA
STOMA
STRIA
STUKA
STUPA
SULFA
SULLA
SUMMA
SUNDA
SUPRA
SURYA
SUTRA
SUVLA
SYRIA
TABLA
TAIGA
TALEA
TALMA
TAMPA
TANGA
TANKA
TATRA
TAZZA
TERRA
TESSA
TESTA
TETRA
THECA
THEMA
THETA
THUYA
TIARA
TIBIA
TIKKA
TILIA
TINEA
TONGA
TOSCA
TREMA
TSUBA
TSUGA
TYPHA
ULEMA
ULTRA
UMBRA
UNITA
UVULA
VANDA
VANYA
VEDDA
VENDA
VERSA
VESPA
VESTA
VILLA
VIOLA
VIRGA
VISTA
VODKA
VOILA
VOLGA
VOLTA
VOLVA
VULVA
WAGGA
WILGA
WONGA
XENIA
XHOSA
YAKKA
YALTA
YARFA
YARRA
YARTA
YERBA
YUCCA
ZABRA
ZEBRA
ZERDA
ZORBA
ACERB
ADLIB
ARDEB
BEROB
BLURB
CABOB
CALEB
CARIB
CAROB
CHUBB
CLIMB
COOMB
COURB
CRUMB
CUBEB
DEMOB
EXURB
HOREB
JACOB
JELAB
KABOB
KEBAB
KEBOB
NABOB
NAMIB
NAWAB
PLUMB
RAHAB
RHOMB
RHUMB
SAHIB
SCRAB
SCRUB
SHRUB
SLURB
SQUAB
SQUIB
THROB
THUMB
ZINEB
ANTIC
ANZAC
ASDIC
ASPIC
ATTIC
AULIC
AURIC
AZOIC
AZTEC
BASIC
BLANC
BORIC
CIVIC
COLIC
COMIC
CONIC
COSEC
CUBIC
CUFIC
CYNIC
DORIC
DULAC
EOLIC
ESTOC
ETHIC
FOLIC
FRANC
GAMIC
HAVOC
ILEAC
ILIAC
IONIC
ISAAC
KUFIC
LILAC
LOGIC
LUDIC
LYRIC
MAGIC
MANIC
MEDIC
MEDOC
MELIC
MESIC
METIC
MIMIC
MUSIC
NOMIC
NSPCC
OLEIC
OPTIC
PANIC
PUBIC
PUNIC
RELIC
RORIC
RUNIC
SALIC
SONIC
STOIC
TELIC
TONIC
TOPIC
TOXIC
TROIC
TUNIC
UGRIC
VAREC
VEDIC
XEBEC
ACRID
ADDED
AHEAD
AHMED
ALGID
ALOUD
AMEND
ANEND
APAID
APHID
ARMED
AROID
AVOID
AWARD
AXOID
BAIRD
BAKED
BATED
BEARD
BEDAD
BEGAD
BIFID
BIPED
BIPOD
BLAND
BLEED
BLEND
BLIND
BLOND
BLOOD
BOARD
BORED
BOUND
BOWED
BOXED
BRAID
BRAND
BREAD
BREED
BROAD
BROOD
BUILD
CAULD
CHARD
CHILD
CHORD
CHYND
CLOUD
CODED
CORED
COULD
COXED
CREED
CRIED
CROWD
CUBED
CUPID
CURED
CYCAD
DATED
DAVID
DAZED
DOMED
DREAD
DRIED
DRUID
DRYAD
DYFED
EDGED
ELAND
ELIAD
EMBED
EMEND
ENDED
EPHOD
ERARD
FADED
FAMED
FARAD
FATED
FETID
FIELD
FIEND
FIORD
FIXED
FJORD
FLOOD
FLUID
FOUND
FRAUD
FREED
FREUD
FRIED
FROND
FUMED
FUSED
GATED
GELID
GLAND
GLUED
GONAD
GORED
GOURD
GRAND
GREED
GRIND
GUARD
GUILD
GUYED
HEALD
HEARD
HEROD
HEXAD
HIRED
HOARD
HOLED
HOUND
HUMID
ILIAD
IMBED
IVIED
IZARD
JADED
JEHAD
JIHAD
KEYED
KNEAD
LAIRD
LAMED
LEPID
LIARD
LIKED
LINED
LIPID
LIVED
LIVID
LLOYD
LOBED
LUCID
LUNED
LURID
MANED
MAUND
MIXED
MONAD
MOPED
MOULD
MOUND
MOVED
MUCID
MUTED
NAIAD
NAKED
NAMED
NICAD
NITID
NOMAD
NOTED
OCTAD
OILED
OVOID
PAVID
PILED
PLAID
PLEAD
POSED
POUND
PROUD
PSEUD
PUTID
RABID
RAGED
RAKED
RAPID
RAYED
RIGID
ROPED
ROUND
SALAD
SAPID
SATED
SCALD
SCOLD
SCROD
SHARD
SHERD
SHRED
SNEAD
SNOOD
SOLID
SOUND
SOWND
SPALD
SPEED
SPEND
SPIED
SPROD
SQUAD

SQUID
STAID
STAND
STEAD
STEED
STOOD
STRAD
SWARD
SWORD
SYNOD
TAXED
TEPID
THIRD
THRID
TILED
TIMID
TIRED
TREAD
TREND
TRIAD
TRIED
TUMID
TWEED
TYNED
TYPED
UNBED
UNDID
UNFED
UNWED
UPEND
USTED
VALID
VAPID
VEXED
VIAND
VIRID
VIVID
VOZHD
WANED
WAVED
WEALD
WEIRD
WIELD
WIRED
WORLD
WOULD
WOUND
YCLAD
YIELD
ABASE
ABATE
ABELE
ABIDE
ABODE
ABOVE
ABUSE
ACUTE
ADAGE
ADDLE
ADIGE
ADOBE
ADORE
AFIRE
AFORE
AGAPE
AGATE
AGAVE
AGILE
AGLEE
AGONE
AGREE
AINEE
AISLE
AKENE
ALATE
ALBEE
ALFIE
ALGAE
ALICE
ALIKE
ALIVE
ALLÉE
ALONE
ALURE
AMAZE
AMBLE
AMENE
AMICE
AMINE
AMPLE
AMUSE
ANELE
ANGLE
ANISE
ANKLE
ANNIE
ANODE
APACE
APAGE
APODE
APPLE
AREDE
ARENE
ARETE
ARGUE
ARISE
ARKLE
AROSE
ARTIE
ASIDE
ATONE
ATTLE
AWAKE
AWARE
AWOKE
AYRIE
AZOTE
AZURE
AZYME
BADGE
BAIZE
BALFE
BARGE
BARRE
BASLE
BASTE
BATHE
BAYLE
BEALE
BEIGE
BELIE
BELLE
BENNE
BETTE
BÉVUE
BIBLE
BILGE
BINGE
BITTE
BLADE
BLAKE
BLAME
BLARE
BLAZE
BLOKE
BOCHE
BODGE
BOGIE
BOGLE
BOMBE
BONCE
BONZE
BOONE
BOOZE
BOREE
BORNE
BOTTE
BOULE
BOWIE
BOYCE
BOYLE
BOYNE
BRACE
BRAKE
BRAVE
BREDE
BREME
BREVE
BRIBE
BRIDE
BRINE
BRIZE
BROKE
BROSE
BRUCE
BRULE
BRUME
BRUTE
BUDGE
BUGLE
BULGE
BUNCE
BURKE
BUTTE
CABLE
CACHE
CADGE
CADRE
CAINE
CALPE
CALVE
CANOE
CARLE
CARTE
CARVE
CASTE
CAUSE
CEASE
CENSE
CERNE
CHAFE
CHAPE
CHASE
CHERE
CHIDE
CHILE
CHIME
CHINE
CHIVE
CHLOE
CHOKE
CHORE
CHOSE
CHUTE
CHYLE
CHYME
CIRCE
CLARE
CLAVE
CLEPE
CLIME
CLIVE
CLONE
CLOSE
CLOVE
CLOZE
CLYDE
COADE
COHOE
COMBE
COMTE
CONDE
CONTE
COOEE
COPSE
CORFE
CORSE
COUPE
COYNE
CRAKE
CRANE
CRAPE
CRARE
CRATE
CRAVE
CRAZE
CREME
CREPE
CRETE
CREWE
CRIME
CRISE
CROCE
CROME
CRONE
CRORE
CROZE
CRUDE
CRUSE
CURIE
CURSE
CURVE
CUTIE
CYCLE
DALLE
DAMME
DANAE
DANCE
DANTE
DAUBE
DEFOE
DELVE
DENSE
DESSE
DEUCE
DINGE
DIODE
DIRGE
DIXIE
DODGE
DOLCE
DONEE
DONNE
DOONE
DOREE
DOUCE
DOUSE
DOWSE
DOYLE
DRAKE
DRAPE
DRERE
DRIVE
DROME
DRONE
DROVE
DRUPE
DRUZE
DUNCE
EAGLE
EDILE
EDUCE
EERIE
ELATE
ELENE
ELIDE
ELITE
ELOGE
ELOPE
ELUDE
EMCEE
EMILE
EMOTE
EMOVE
EMURE
ENDUE
ENSUE
ENURE
EPODE
ERASE
ERNIE
ERODE
ETAGE
ETAPE
ETUDE
ETWEE
EVADE
EVITE
EVOKE
EXILE
EXINE
EXODE
EXUDE
EYRIE
EYTIE
FABLE
FADGE
FALSE
FARCE
FARNE
FAROE
FARSE
FAURE
FAUVE
FEARE
FENCE
FESSE
FESTE
FIBRE
FICHE
FIERE
FLAKE
FLAME
FLARE
FLUKE
FLUME
FLUTE
FLYTE
FOLIE
FORCE
FORGE
FORME
FORTE
FOSSE
FOYLE
FRAME
FROZE
FUDGE
FUGUE
FURZE
FUSEE
FUZEE
FYLDE
GABLE
GADGE
GAFFE
GAUDE
GAUGE
GAUZE
GEARE
GEESE
GENIE
GENRE
GEODE
GERBE
GESSE
GESTE
GIGUE
GLACE
GLADE
GLAZE
GLEBE
GLIDE
GLOBE
GLOVE
GLUME
GNOME
GOOSE
GORGE
GORSE
GOSSE
GOUGE
GRACE
GRADE
GRAPE
GRATE
GRAVE
GRAZE
GREBE
GRIME
GRIPE
GROPE
GROVE
GRUFE
GRUME
GUIDE
GUILE
GUISE
GUNGE
HAGUE
HALSE
HALVE
HANCE
HANSE
HASTE
HAUSE
HAUTE
HAWSE
HAYLE
HEAVE
HEDGE
HEINE
HELVE
HENCE
HENGE
HERNE
HERSE
HESSE
HINGE
HITHE
HOARE
HODGE
HOMME
HOOVE
HORDE
HORNE
HORSE
HOUSE
HOWBE
HOYLE
HULME
HYTHE
IMAGE
IMBUE
INANE
INCLE
INDRE
INDUE
INGLE
INURE
IRATE
IRENE
ISERE
ISSUE
JAMBE
JESSE
JOULE
JOYCE
JUDGE
JUICE
KAMME
KEBLE
KEDGE
KEMPE
KERNE
KIDGE
KNAVE
KNIFE
KOINE
KOPJE
KRONE
KYLIE
KYLOE
KYRIE
LADLE
LANCE
LANDE
LAPSE

LARGE
LARNE
LATHE
LEASE
LEAVE
LEDGE
LEESE
LEGGE
LEONE
LERNE
LETHE
LEVEE
LIANE
LIEGE
LIGGE
LILLE
LISLE
LITHE
LITRE
LIVRE
LOCKE
LODGE
LOIRE
LOOSE
LORNE
LOUIE
LOUPE
LOUSE
LUCRE
LUMME
LUNGE
LYCÉE
LYTHE
MACLE
MADGE
MAEVE
MAHOE
MAILE
MAINE
MAIRE
MAIZE
MANGE
MANSE
MAPLE
MARGE
MARIE
MARLE
MARNE
MASSE
MAUVE
MAYBE
MEBBE
MELEE
MENGE
MERGE
MERLE
MESNE
METRE
MEUSE
MEZZE
MICHE
MIDGE
MILNE
MINCE
MINKE
MITRE
MIXTE
MOIRE
MONTE
MOORE
MOOSE
MORNE
MORSE
MOTTE
MOUSE
MOVIE
MOYLE
MUDGE
MULSE
MURRE
MUSSE
MVULE
NACHE
NACRE
NAIVE
NANCE
NAPPE
NASHE
NEALE
NERVE
NICHE
NIECE
NIEVE
NIOBE
NITRE
NOBLE
NOISE
NONCE
NOOSE
NORSE
NUDGE
NURSE
OBESE
OBOTE
OCHRE
OGIVE
OLDIE
OLIVE
OLLIE
OMBRE
OPINE
ORATE
ORGUE
OSAGE
OUNCE
OUTRE
OVATE
OVINE
OVULE
OXEYE
OXIDE
OXIME
OZONE
PADRE
PAINE
PAIRE
PANNE
PARSE
PASSE
PASTE
PAUSE
PAYEE
PEACE
PEASE
PEEVE
PEKOE
PELEE
PENCE
PENNE
PERCE
PERSE
PETRE
PHARE
PHASE
PHEBE
PHILE
PHOBE
PHONE
PHYLE
PIAVE
PIECE
PIQUE
PISTE
PIXIE
PLACE
PLANE
PLATE
PLUME
PODGE
POISE
PONCE
PORTE
POSSE
POSTE
POULE
POUPE
PRATE
PRICE
PRIDE
PRIME
PRISE
PRIZE
PROBE
PROKE
PROLE
PRONE
PROSE
PROVE
PRUDE
PRUNE
PUDGE
PULSE
PUREE
PURGE
PURSE
PUSLE
QUAKE
QUEUE
QUIRE
QUITE
QUOTE
RAINE
RAISE
RAKEE
RANCE
RANEE
RANGE
RANKE
RAREE
RAYLE
READE
RECCE
REEDE
REEVE
RÉGIE
RÈGLE
REMUE
RENTE
REVIE
REVUE
RHINE
RHONE
RHYME
RIDGE
RIFLE
RILKE
RILLE
RINSE
ROGUE
ROLFE
RONDE
RONNE
ROQUE
RORKE
ROSSE
ROUGE
ROULE
ROUSE
ROUTE
RUBLE
RUCHE
RUDGE
RUPEE
RUSSE
SABLE
SABRE
SADIE
SAICE
SAINE
SALLE
SALSE
SALVE
SARGE
SASSE
SATIE
SAUCE
SAUTE
SCALE
SCAPE
SCARE
SCENE
SCONE
SCOPE
SCORE
SCREE
SEARE
SEDGE
SEGUE
SEINE
SEIZE
SELLE
SENSE
SERGE
SERRE
SERVE
SHADE
SHAKE
SHALE
SHAME
SHAPE
SHARE
SHAVE
SHERE
SHINE
SHIRE
SHITE
SHIVE
SHONE
SHORE
SHOVE
SHUTE
SIDLE
SIEGE
SIEVE
SINCE
SINGE
SKATE
SKIVE
SLADE
SLAKE
SLATE
SLAVE
SLICE
SLIDE
SLIME
SLIPE
SLOPE
SLYPE
SMILE
SMITE
SMOKE
SMOTE
SNAKE
SNARE
SNIDE
SNIPE
SNORE
SOANE
SOARE
SOCLE
SOLDE
SOLVE
SOMME
SONDE
SOUSE
SOWLE
SPACE
SPADE
SPARE
SPATE
SPEKE
SPICE
SPIKE
SPILE
SPINE
SPIRE
SPITE
SPODE
SPOKE
SPORE
SPREE
SPRUE
SPUME
STADE
STAGE
STAKE
STALE
STARE
STATE
STAVE
STELE
STEVE
STILE
STIME
STOKE
STOLE
STONE
STOPE
STORE
STOVE
STOWE
STUPE
STYLE
STYME
SUAVE
SUCRE
SUEDE
SUITE
SUPPE
SURGE
SUZIE
SWALE
SWEDE
SWINE
SWIPE
SWIRE
SWORE
SYCEE
SYNGE
TABLE
TAINE
TARGE
TASSE
TASTE
TAUBE
TAUPE
TAWSE
TEASE
TEAZE
TEHEE
TEMPE
TENSE
TENUE
TEPEE
TERCE
TERNE
TERSE
THANE
THEME
THERE
THESE
THETE
THINE
THOLE
THOSE
THREE
THROE
THULE
THYME
TILDE
TINGE
TIREE
TITHE
TITLE
TITRE
TOILE
TOISE
TONNE
TOPEE
TOQUE
TORTE
TOWSE
TOWZE
TRACE
TRADE
TRIBE
TRICE
TRIKE
TRIPE
TRITE
TROPE
TROVE
TRUCE
TUFFE
TULLE
TUQUE
TWICE
TWINE
UKASE
UMBLE
UNCLE
UNDUE
UNITE
UNTIE
URATE
URINE
URITE
USAGE
USURE
VAGUE
VALSE
VALUE
VALVE
VANCE
VENUE
VERGE
VERNE
VERSE
VERVE
VITAE
VOGUE
VOICE
VOILE
VOLTE
VOLVO
WAIVE
WASTE
WEAVE
WEDGE
WHALE
WHERE
WHILE
WHINE
WHITE
WHOLE
WHORE
WHOSE
WILDE
WINCE
WITHE
WODGE
WORSE
WRITE
WROTE
YAHVE
YONNE
YOUVE
ZAIRE
ZANTE
AVOUÉ
BLASÉ
CONGÉ
COUDÉ
FABRÉ
FOULÉ
GASPÉ
HALLÉ
JASPÉ

ALOOF	CRAIG	ANIGH	FRESH	MOOCH	SMITH	BLINI	NERVI
BLUFF	DEBAG	ARISH	FRITH	MORPH	SNASH	BONDI	OKAPI
BRIEF	DEBUG	ASAPH	FROTH	MOUCH	SOOTH	BWAZI	OMANI
CHAFF	DOING	AWASH	GARTH	MOUTH	SOUGH	CAPRI	PARSI
CHIEF	DYING	BATCH	GIRTH	MULCH	SOUTH	CENCI	PARTI
CHUFF	FLING	BEACH	GLYPH	MUNCH	SOWTH	CHILI	PATTI
CLIFF	FLONG	BEECH	GNASH	MYNAH	STAPH	COATI	PEPSI
DWARF	FLUNG	BELCH	GOTCH	MYRRH	STASH	COCCI	PERAI
FEOFF	GLOGG	BENCH	GRAPH	NATCH	SUTCH	CORGI	PETRI
FLUFF	GOING	BERTH	GULCH	NEAGH	SWASH	DELHI	QUASI
GLIFF	GREGG	BIRCH	GULPH	NEIGH	SWATH	DHABI	RABBI
GRAFF	GRIEG	BIRTH	HANCH	NINTH	SWISH	DHOBI	ROSSI
GRIEF	GULAG	BITCH	HARSH	NORAH	SYLPH	DHOTI	SALMI
GRIFF	ICING	BLIGH	HATCH	NORTH	SYRAH	DOUAI	SAUDI
GRUFF	KIANG	BLUSH	HAUGH	NOTCH	TAVAH	DUBAI	SCIFI
GUELF	KLANG	BOOTH	HEATH	NYMPH	TEACH	ENNUI	SERAI
KALIF	KLIEG	BOSCH	HEIGH	OBEAH	TEETH	ENVOI	SHCHI
KAMPF	KRANG	BOTCH	HEUGH	OBIAH	TENCH	FARCI	SHOJI
KLOOF	KRIEG	BOUGH	HITCH	OMAGH	TENTH	FERMI	SINAI
METIF	KYANG	BRASH	HOOCH	OOMPH	THIGH	FUNDI	SOLTI
MOTIF	LIANG	BROTH	HOOSH	PARCH	TILTH	GARNI	SPAHI
PILAF	LYING	BRUSH	HORAH	PASCH	TITCH	GHAZI	STASI
PROOF	MAGOG	BUMPH	HOTCH	PATCH	TOOTH	GIGLI	SUOMI
QUAFF	OFLAG	BUNCH	HOUGH	PEACH	TORAH	GOLGI	SUSHI
QUIFF	ORANG	BURGH	HUMPH	PERCH	TORCH	HADJI	SWAMI
QUOIF	OWING	BUTCH	HUNCH	PILCH	TOUCH	HAITI	SWAZI
SCAFF	PIROG	CATCH	HUTCH	PINCH	TOUGH	HANOI	TORII
SCARF	PRANG	CINCH	IRISH	PITCH	TRASH	HATHI	TREVI
SCOFF	PRONG	CLASH	JONAH	PLATH	TROTH	HINDI	TURKI
SCUFF	REJIG	CLOTH	KEECH	PLUSH	TRUTH	HOURI	TUTSI
SCURF	RUING	COACH	KETCH	POACH	URIAH	ICENI	TUTTI
SERIF	SCRAG	CONCH	KUTCH	POOCH	VETCH	IMARI	VERDI
SHEAF	SCROG	COUCH	LAITH	PORCH	VLACH	IMSHI	VILLI
SHELF	SHANG	COUGH	LARCH	POUCH	VOUCH	INARI	YEZDI
SKIFF	SHRUG	COUTH	LATCH	PSYCH	WATCH	INDRI	ZOMBI
SNIFF	SLANG	CRASH	LAUGH	PUNCH	WAUGH	IRAQI	ABACK
SNUFF	SLING	CRUSH	LEACH	QUASH	WEIGH	KANJI	ACOCK
SPIFF	SLUNG	CRWTH	LEASH	QUOTH	WELCH	KARRI	ALACK
SPOOF	SPRAG	CUTCH	LEECH	RAJAH	WELSH	KAURI	AMUCK
STAFF	SPRIG	CZECH	LEIGH	RALPH	WENCH	KHAKI	APEAK
STIFF	SPROG	DEATH	LEISH	RANCH	WHICH	KHAZI	BATIK
STUFF	STING	DELPH	LEITH	RATCH	WHISH	KOORI	BAULK
SWARF	STUNG	DEPTH	LINCH	REACH	WIDTH	KUKRI	BLACK
THIEF	SWING	DITCH	LOATH	REECH	WINCH	LASKI	BLANK
WHARF	SWUNG	DOUGH	LOUGH	REICH	WITCH	LATHI	BLEAK
WHIFF	THING	DUTCH	LOUTH	REITH	WORTH	LIPPI	BLINK
WOOLF	THONG	EARTH	LUNCH	RETCH	WRATH	LUNGI	BLOCK
AGING	TWANG	ENOCH	LURCH	ROACH	WROTH	MAHDI	BRACK
ALONG	TYING	EPOCH	LYMPH	ROUGH	YOUTH	MALFI	BRANK
AMONG	UNRIG	FAITH	LYNCH	RUNCH	ZILCH	MAORI	BREAK
BEFOG	USING	FETCH	MANCH	SARAH	ACINI	MARDI	BRICK
BEING	WHANG	FIFTH	MARCH	SAUCH	AGAMI	MASAI	BRINK
BHANG	WRING	FILCH	MARSH	SAUGH	AIOLI	MENAI	BRISK
BOING	WRONG	FILTH	MATCH	SCATH	ALIBI	MIAMI	BROCK
BOONG	WRUNG	FINCH	MEATH	SHUSH	ALTAI	MILLI	BROOK
BOURG	YOUNG	FIRTH	MEITH	SIXTH	APPUI	MOOLI	BUICK
BRING	ABASH	FITCH	MICAH	SLASH	ASCII	MUFTI	CAULK
CHING	AITCH	FLASH	MILCH	SLOSH	ASSAI	MULTI	CHALK
CLANG	ALEPH	FLESH	MINCH	SLOTH	BAHAI	MUSCI	CHARK
CLING	ALLAH	FLUSH	MIRTH	SLUSH	BAJRI	NAAFI	CHECK
CLUNG	AMISH	FORTH	MONTH	SMASH	BAMBI	NANDI	CHEEK

CHICK
CHINK
CHIRK
CHOCK
CHOOK
CHUCK
CHUNK
CLACK
CLANK
CLARK
CLECK
CLEEK
CLERK
CLICK
CLINK
CLOAK
CLOCK
CLUCK
CLUNK
CRACK
CRANK
CREAK
CREEK
CRICK
CROAK
CROCK
CRONK
CROOK
CRUCK
DALEK
DATUK
DAYAK
DRANK
DRINK
DRUNK
ERICK
FLACK
FLANK
FLASK
FLECK
FLICK
FLOCK
FLUNK
FRACK
FRANK
FREAK
FRISK
FROCK
GLEEK
GLISK
GLUCK
GOPAK
GREEK
HACEK
HOICK
KANAK
KAPOK
KAYAK
KIOSK
KNACK
KNOCK
KODAK
KULAK
MALIK
MERAK
MINSK
MUZAK
OZARK
PLACK
PLANK
PLONK
PLUCK
PLUNK
PRANK
PRICK
QUACK
QUARK
QUICK
QUIRK
SHACK
SHANK
SHARK
SHEIK
SHIRK
SHOCK
SHOOK
SHUCK
SKINK
SKULK
SKUNK
SLACK
SLEEK
SLICK
SLINK
SLUNK
SMACK
SMEEK
SMIRK
SMOCK
SNACK
SNARK
SNEAK
SNECK
SNICK
SNOEK
SNOOK
SPANK
SPARK
SPEAK
SPECK
SPICK
SPOOK
SPUNK
STACK
STALK
STANK
STARK
STEAK
STEEK
STICK
STINK
STOCK
STOOK
STORK
STUCK
STUNK
SWANK
TEREK
THANK
THICK
THINK
TRACK
TRECK
TRICK
TRUCK
TRUNK
TWANK
TWEAK
UZBEK
VNECK
WHACK
WHELK
WHISK
WRACK
WREAK
WRECK
YOICK
YUPIK
ZADOK
ABDUL
AFOUL
ALGOL
ALLYL
AMIEL
ANGEL
ANNAL
ANNUL
ANVIL
APPAL
APPEL
APRIL
ARDIL
ARGIL
ARIEL
ARVAL
ATOLL
AURAL
AVAIL
AWEEL
AWFUL
AXIAL
BABEL
BABUL
BAGEL
BANAL
BASAL
BASIL
BERYL
BETEL
BEVEL
BEZEL
BOWEL
BRAWL
BRILL
BROIL
BROOL
CABAL
CAMEL
CANAL
CAROL
CAVIL
CECIL
CEORL
CHILL
CHIRL
CHURL
CIBOL
CIVIL
COBOL
CORAL
COXAL
CRAWL
CREEL
CRUEL
CUPEL
DEBEL
DECAL
DEVIL
DITAL
DOWEL
DRAWL
DRILL
DROLL
DROOL
DUVAL
DWELL
EASEL
EMAIL
ENROL
EQUAL
ETHAL
ETHYL
EXCEL
EXPEL
EXTOL
FANAL
FATAL
FECAL
FERAL
FETAL
FIDEL
FINAL
FLAIL
FOCAL
FOREL
FRAIL
FRILL
FUGAL
GAVEL
GHOUL
GHYLL
GNARL
GOGOL
GRAAL
GRAIL
GRILL
GROWL
GRUEL
HAVEL
HAZEL
HEGEL
HEXYL
HOTEL
HOVEL
IDEAL
IDYLL
IMPEL
IQBAL
JAVEL
JEBEL
JEWEL
JOUAL
JUGAL
KABUL
KEBEL
KERAL
KNARL
KNEEL
KNELL
KNOLL
KNURL
KRAAL
KRILL
LABEL
LAPEL
LEGAL
LEVEL
LIBEL
LOCAL
LOYAL
LYSOL
MANUL
MEDAL
MERIL
METAL
METOL
MIAUL
MODAL
MODEL
MOGUL
MONAL
MORAL
MOREL
MOTEL
MURAL
NASAL
NATAL
NAVAL
NAVEL
NEBEL
NEPAL
NEVEL
NEWEL
NICOL
NIGEL
NIHIL
NIVAL
NOBEL
NODAL
NOTAL
NOVEL
NOXAL
OCTAL
OFFAL
ORIEL
ORVAL
OUSEL
OUZEL
PANEL
PAPAL
PEARL
PEDAL
PENAL
PERIL
PETAL
PHIAL
PIPUL
PIXEL
PRAWL
PRIAL
PRILL
PROWL
PUPAL
PUPIL
QUAIL
QUELL
QUILL
RAVEL
REBEL
REGAL
RENAL
REPEL
REVEL
RIVAL
RIYAL
ROWEL
ROYAL
RURAL
RYDAL
SABAL
SAHEL
SCOWL
SCULL
SEOUL
SEPAL
SHALL
SHAWL
SHEEL
SHELL
SHIEL
SHILL
SHOAL
SIBYL
SIGIL
SISAL
SKILL
SKIRL
SKOAL
SKULL
SMALL
SMELL
SNAIL
SNARL
SOKOL
SPALL
SPELL
SPIEL
SPILL
SPOIL
SPOOL
STALL
STEAL
STEEL
STILL
STOLL
STOOL
SWELL
SWILL
SWIRL
SYBIL
TAMIL
TAXOL
TEXEL
THILL
THIRL
TIDAL
TONAL
TOTAL
TOWEL
TRAIL
TRAWL
TRIAL
TRILL
TROLL
TRULL
TWILL
TWIRL
TYROL
UDALL
UMBEL
UNTIL
USUAL
VENAL
VIGIL
VINYL
VIRAL
VITAL
VOCAL
VOWEL
WEILL
WHEAL
WHEEL
WHIRL
WHORL
YODEL
YOKEL
YOULL
ZONAL
ABEAM
ABRAM
ABRIM
ABYSM
ADEEM
ADSUM
ALARM
ALBUM
ANNAM
ASSAM
AXIOM
BEGUM
BESOM
BLOOM
BOSOM
BREAM
BREEM
BROOM
BUXOM
CDROM
CECUM
CHARM
CHASM
CLAIM
CORAM
CREAM
DATUM
DENIM
DREAM
DURUM
ENARM
ENORM
EPSOM
ESROM
FORUM
GALAM
GARUM
GLEAM
GLOOM
GOLEM
GRIMM
GROOM
HAREM
HAULM
HEXAM
HILUM
HIRAM
HOKUM
HYLUM
IDIOM
ILEUM
ILIUM
IMAUM
INARM
INIUM
ISLAM
JORUM
KELIM
KILIM
KOKUM

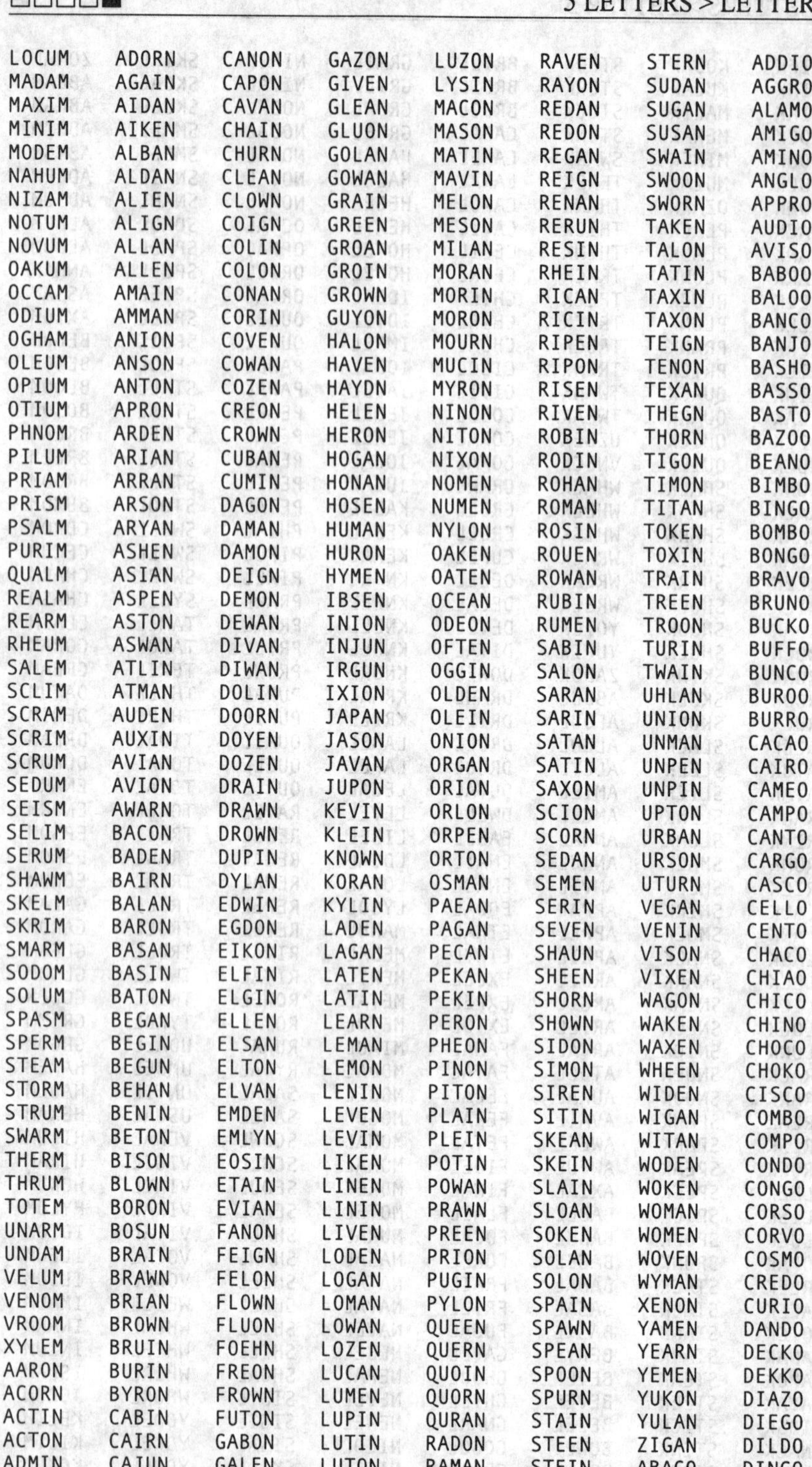

LOCUM
MADAM
MAXIM
MINIM
MODEM
NAHUM
NIZAM
NOTUM
NOVUM
OAKUM
OCCAM
ODIUM
OGHAM
OLEUM
OPIUM
OTIUM
PHNOM
PILUM
PRIAM
PRISM
PSALM
PURIM
QUALM
REALM
REARM
RHEUM
SALEM
SCLIM
SCRAM
SCRIM
SCRUM
SEDUM
SEISM
SELIM
SERUM
SHAWM
SKELM
SKRIM
SMARM
SODOM
SOLUM
SPASM
SPERM
STEAM
STORM
STRUM
SWARM
THERM
THRUM
TOTEM
UNARM
UNDAM
VELUM
VENOM
VROOM
XYLEM
AARON
ACORN
ACTIN
ACTON
ADMIN
ADORN
AGAIN
AIDAN
AIKEN
ALBAN
ALDAN
ALIEN
ALIGN
ALLAN
ALLEN
AMAIN
AMMAN
ANION
ANSON
ANTON
APRON
ARDEN
ARIAN
ARRAN
ARSON
ARYAN
ASHEN
ASIAN
ASPEN
ASTON
ASWAN
ATLIN
ATMAN
AUDEN
AUXIN
AVIAN
AVION
AWARN
BACON
BADEN
BAIRN
BALAN
BARON
BASAN
BASIN
BATON
BEGAN
BEGIN
BEGUN
BEHAN
BENIN
BETON
BISON
BLOWN
BORON
BOSUN
BRAIN
BRAWN
BRIAN
BROWN
BRUIN
BURIN
BYRON
CABIN
CAIRN
CAJUN
CANON
CAPON
CAVAN
CHAIN
CHURN
CLEAN
CLOWN
COIGN
COLIN
COLON
CONAN
CORIN
COVEN
COWAN
COZEN
CREON
CROWN
CUBAN
CUMIN
DAGON
DAMAN
DAMON
DEIGN
DEMON
DEWAN
DIVAN
DIWAN
DOLIN
DOORN
DOYEN
DOZEN
DRAIN
DRAWN
DROWN
DUPIN
DYLAN
EDWIN
EGDON
EIKON
ELFIN
ELGIN
ELLEN
ELSAN
ELTON
ELVAN
EMDEN
EMLYN
EOSIN
ETAIN
EVIAN
FANON
FEIGN
FELON
FLOWN
FLUON
FOEHN
FREON
FROWN
FUTON
GABON
GALEN
GAZON
GIVEN
GLEAN
GLUON
GOLAN
GOWAN
GRAIN
GREEN
GROAN
GROIN
GROWN
GUYON
HALON
HAVEN
HAYDN
HELEN
HERON
HOGAN
HONAN
HOSEN
HUMAN
HURON
HYMEN
IBSEN
INION
INJUN
IRGUN
IXION
JAPAN
JASON
JAVAN
JUPON
KEVIN
KLEIN
KNOWN
KORAN
KYLIN
LADEN
LAGAN
LATEN
LATIN
LEARN
LEMAN
LEMON
LENIN
LEVEN
LEVIN
LIKEN
LINEN
LININ
LIVEN
LODEN
LOGAN
LOMAN
LOWAN
LOZEN
LUCAN
LUMEN
LUPIN
LUTIN
LUTON
LUZON
LYSIN
MACON
MASON
MATIN
MAVIN
MELON
MESON
MILAN
MORAN
MORIN
MORON
MOURN
MUCIN
MYRON
NINON
NITON
NIXON
NOMEN
NUMEN
NYLON
OAKEN
OATEN
OCEAN
ODEON
OFTEN
OGGIN
OLDEN
OLEIN
ONION
ORGAN
ORION
ORLON
ORPEN
ORTON
OSMAN
PAEAN
PAGAN
PECAN
PEKAN
PEKIN
PERON
PHEON
PINON
PITON
PLAIN
PLEIN
POTIN
POWAN
PRAWN
PREEN
PRION
PUGIN
PYLON
QUEEN
QUERN
QUOIN
QUORN
QURAN
RADON
RAMAN
RAVEN
RAYON
REDAN
REDON
REGAN
REIGN
RENAN
RERUN
RESIN
RHEIN
RICAN
RICIN
RIPEN
RIPON
RISEN
RIVEN
ROBIN
RODIN
ROHAN
ROMAN
ROSIN
ROUEN
ROWAN
RUBIN
RUMEN
SABIN
SALON
SARAN
SARIN
SATAN
SATIN
SAXON
SCION
SCORN
SEDAN
SEMEN
SERIN
SEVEN
SHAUN
SHEEN
SHORN
SHOWN
SIDON
SIMON
SIREN
SITIN
SKEAN
SKEIN
SLAIN
SLOAN
SOKEN
SOLAN
SOLON
SPAIN
SPAWN
SPEAN
SPOON
SPURN
STAIN
STEEN
STEIN
STERN
SUDAN
SUGAN
SUSAN
SWAIN
SWOON
SWORN
TAKEN
TALON
TATIN
TAXIN
TAXON
TEIGN
TENON
TEXAN
THEGN
THORN
TIGON
TIMON
TITAN
TOKEN
TOXIN
TRAIN
TREEN
TROON
TURIN
TWAIN
UHLAN
UNION
UNMAN
UNPEN
UNPIN
UPTON
URBAN
URSON
UTURN
VEGAN
VENIN
VISON
VIXEN
WAGON
WAKEN
WAXEN
WHEEN
WIDEN
WIGAN
WITAN
WODEN
WOKEN
WOMAN
WOMEN
WOVEN
WYMAN
XENON
YAMEN
YEARN
YEMEN
YUKON
YULAN
ZIGAN
ABACO
ADDIO
AGGRO
ALAMO
AMIGO
AMINO
ANGLO
APPRO
AUDIO
AVISO
BABOO
BALOO
BANCO
BANJO
BASHO
BASSO
BASTO
BAZOO
BEANO
BIMBO
BINGO
BOMBO
BONGO
BRAVO
BRUNO
BUCKO
BUFFO
BUNCO
BUROO
BURRO
CACAO
CAIRO
CAMEO
CAMPO
CANTO
CARGO
CASCO
CELLO
CENTO
CHACO
CHIAO
CHICO
CHINO
CHOCO
CHOKO
CISCO
COMBO
COMPO
CONDO
CONGO
CORSO
CORVO
COSMO
CREDO
CURIO
DANDO
DECKO
DEKKO
DIAZO
DIEGO
DILDO
DINGO

DISCO
DITTO
DOBRO
DOGGO
DOURO
DRACO
DUNNO
DUOMO
ERATO
FACTO
FALDO
FARGO
FEMTO
FIBRO
FOLIO
FORGO
FUERO
GAMBO
GARBO
GECKO
GESSO
GIPPO
GISMO
GIZMO
GOBBO
GOMBO
GONZO
GUACO
GUANO
GUMBO
GUSTO
GYMNO
GYPPO
HALLO
HARPO
HECTO
HELIO
HELLO
HIPPO
HONDO
HULLO
HYDRO
IDAHO
IGAPO
IGLOO
IMAGO
INIGO
INTRO
IROKO
JAMBO
JELLO
JINGO
JOCKO
JUMBO
JUNCO
JUNTO
KARNO
KENDO
KIMBO
KONGO
LARGO
LASSO
LAZZO
LENTO
LIMBO
LINGO
LLANO
LOTTO
LUCIO
MACHO
MACRO
MAIKO
MALMO
MAMBO
MANGO
MARCO
MATLO
MESTO
METRO
MEZZO
MICRO
MINHO
MOLTO
MONDO
MOTTO
MUCRO
MUNGO
MUNRO
NACHO
NEGRO
NERVO
NGAIO
ORFEO
ORTHO
OUTDO
OUTGO
PABLO
PALIO
PANTO
PAOLO
PAREO
PARVO
PASEO
PATIO
PEDRO
PESTO
PETTO
PHENO
PHOTO
PIANO
PIEZO
PINGO
PINKO
PINTO
PLATO
PLUTO
POLIO
PONGO
PORNO
PORTO
POTOO
POTTO
PRADO
PRIMO
PROMO
PROVO
PUNTO
PUTTO
QUITO
RADIO
RAMBO
RATIO
RECTO
REPRO
RETRO
RHINO
RHODO
RODEO
ROLLO
ROMEO
RONDO
RONEO
ROSCO
RUSSO
SALVO
SAMBO
SAMSO
SANTO
SAYSO
SECCO
SERVO
SHAKO
SLIGO
SORBO
SORDO
SOTTO
SPADO
STYLO
TABOO
TAINO
TANGO
TASSO
TEMPO
TOKYO
TONDO
TORSO
TRURO
TURBO
TURCO
UREDO
VERSO
VIDEO
VIREO
VIRGO
VULGO
WALDO
YAHOO
YOBBO
ZAMBO
ZEPPO
ZINCO
ZORRO
AESOP
APOOP
ATRIP
BEBOP
BLEEP
BLIMP
BLOOP
CHAMP
CHEAP
CHEEP
CHIMP
CHIRP
CHOMP
CHUMP
CLAMP
CLASP
CLEEP
CLUMP
CRAMP
CREEP
CRIMP
CRISP
CROUP
CRUMP
DROOP
EQUIP
ESTOP
FLUMP
FRUMP
GALOP
GETUP
GRASP
GROUP
GUIMP
HANAP
JALAP
JULEP
MIXUP
ORLOP
PLUMP
POLYP
POPUP
PRIMP
QUILP
RECAP
RUNUP
SALEP
SCALP
SCAMP
SCARP
SCAUP
SCOOP
SCOUP
SCOWP
SCRAP
SCRIP
SCULP
SETUP
SHARP
SHEEP
SHLEP
SITUP
SKELP
SKIMP
SLEEP
SLOOP
SLUMP
SLURP
SNOOP
STAMP
STEEP
STIRP
STOEP
STOMP
STOOP
STOUP
STRAP
STREP
STRIP
STROP
STUMP
SWAMP
SWEEP
SWOOP
SYRUP
THRIP
THUMP
TRAMP
TROMP
TROOP
TRUMP
TULIP
TWERP
TWIRP
UNCAP
UNRIP
UNZIP
USURP
WHAUP
WHELP
WHOOP
LECOQ
TALAQ
ABDAR
ABEAR
ABHOR
ABLER
ACTOR
ADDER
AFEAR
AFTER
AGGER
AIRER
AKBAR
ALDER
ALTAR
ALTER
AMBER
AMOUR
ANEAR
ANGER
ANKER
ANTAR
ARBOR
ARDOR
ARMOR
ASHER
ASKER
ASPER
ASTER
ASTIR
ATTAR
AUGER
AUGUR
BABAR
BAKER
BALER
BALOR
BAYER
BIKER
BITER
BLAIR
BLEAR
BONAR
BONER
BORER
BOWER
BOXER
BOYAR
BRIAR
BRIER
BUYER
CABER
CALOR
CAPER
CARER
CATER
CEDAR
CESAR
CHAIR
CHEER
CHIRR
CHOIR
CHURR
CIDER
CIGAR
CLEAR
COLOR
COPER
CORER
COVER
COWER
CRIER
CRUOR
CUPAR
CURER
DAKAR
DATER
DEBAR
DECOR
DEFER
DEMUR
DETER
DEWAR
DIKER
DINAR
DINER
DIVER
DONAR
DONOR
DOUAR
DOVER
DOWER
DREAR
DRIER
DRYER
DURER
DYKER
EAGER
EATER
EDGAR
EDGER
EGGAR
EIDER
EIGER
ELDER
ELGAR
ELMER
ELVER
EMBER
EMMER
ENSOR
ENTER
EPHOR
ERROR
ESKER
ESTER
ETHER
EULER
FABER
FACER
FAKER
FAKIR
FAVOR
FEMUR
FETOR
FEVER
FEWER
FIBER
FINER
FIVER
FIXER
FLAIR
FLEUR
FLIER
FLOOR
FLOUR
FLYER
FOYER
FRIAR
FUROR
GAPER
GEBER
GIVER
GLAIR
GOFER
GONER
GOWER
GREER
HALER
HAVER
HEWER
HEYER
HIKER
HILAR
HIRER
HIVER
HOMER
HONOR
HOVER
HUMOR
HYPER
ICHOR
ICKER
IDLER
IMMER
INCUR
INFER
INNER
INTER
IZMIR
JOKER
JUMAR
JUROR
KAFIR
KEDAR
KEFIR
KNURR
LABOR
LAGER
LASER
LATER
LAVER
LAYER
LAZAR
LEGER
LEHAR
LEMUR
LEPER
LEVER
LIBER
LIFER
LIMER
LINER
LITER
LIVER
LOBAR
LONER
LOSER
LOVER
LOWER
LUGER
LUNAR
MACER
MAJOR
MAKAR

MAKER
MALAR
MANOR
MASER
MATER
MAYOR
MAZER
METER
MEYER
MILER
MIMER
MINER
MINOR
MISER
MIXER
MODER
MOLAR
MOPER
MOTOR
MOVER
MOWER
NADER
NADIR
NAGOR
NAZIR
NEVER
NIDOR
NIGER
NOSER
OAKER
OCCUR
OCHER
OCKER
ODDER
ODOUR
OFFER
OGIER
OILER
OLDER
OMBER
ONCER
OPHIR
ORDER
ORMER
OSCAR
OSIER
OTHER
OTTAR
OTTER
OUTER
OWLER
OWNER
OXTER
PACER
PAGER
PAMIR
PAPER
PATER
PAYER
PETER
PIPER
PLIER
POKER
POLAR
POSER
POWER
PRIOR
PUDOR
QAJAR
QUEER
RACER
RADAR
RAKER
RAVER
RAZOR
RECUR
REFER
RIDER
RIGOR
RIPER
RISER
RIVER
ROGER
ROKER
ROMER
ROPER
ROTOR
ROVER
ROWER
RULER
RUMOR
SABER
SAKER
SAPOR
SATYR
SAVER
SAVOR
SAYER
SCAUR
SCOUR
SENOR
SEVER
SEWER
SHEAR
SHEER
SHIRR
SITAR
SIXER
SIZAR
SKEER
SKIER
SKIRR
SMEAR
SNEER
SOBER
SODOR
SOLAR
SONAR
SOWER
SPEAR
SPEER
SPOHR
SPOOR
STAIR
STARR
STEER
STOOR
STOUR
SUDOR
SUGAR
SUPER
SUTOR
SWEAR
TABER
TABOR
TAKER
TALAR
TAMAR
TAMER
TAPER
TAPIR
TATAR
TATER
TENOR
THEIR
TIBER
TIGER
TILER
TIMER
TIMOR
TOLAR
TONER
TOPER
TOWER
TRIER
TUBER
TUDOR
TUMOR
TUNER
TUTOR
TWOER
TYLER
UDDER
ULCER
ULNAR
UMBER
UNBAR
UNDER
UPPER
USHER
UTHER
UTTER
VALOR
VAPOR
VELAR
VICAR
VIGOR
VIPER
VISOR
VIZOR
VOMER
VOTER
WADER
WAFER
WAGER
WALER
WATER
WAVER
WEBER
WESER
WHAUR
WHIRR
WIPER
WOOER
ZOHAR
ABBAS
ABIES
ABYSS
ACRES
ADAMS
ADDIS
ADIOS
AEDES
AEGIS
AGNES
AIDOS
AIRES
ALANS
ALDIS
ALIAS
ALNUS
ALOES
ALVIS
AMASS
AMISS
ANDES
ANGUS
ANKUS
APHIS
ARCUS
ARGUS
ARIES
ARLES
ARRAS
ARRIS
ASCUS
ASHES
ATHOS
ATLAS
AULIS
AVENS
BACKS
BALLS
BANDS
BANKS
BANNS
BARTS
BASES
BASIS
BATES
BATHS
BEADS
BEANS
BELLS
BENDS
BEVIS
BIRDS
BLESS
BLISS
BLUES
BODES
BOGUS
BOLAS
BOLUS
BONDS
BONES
BONUS
BOOTS
BORIS
BOWLS
BRASS
BUCKS
BUFFS
BULLS
BURNS
CABAS
CAIUS
CAMIS
CAMUS
CANES
CARDS
CASES
CATES
CELLS
CERES
CHAOS
CHAPS
CHESS
CHIPS
CHOPS
CLASS
CLAUS
CLUBS
COCOS
COKES
COLTS
COMBS
COMUS
COOKS
CORDS
CORPS
COSTS
CRABS
CRAPS
CRASS
CRESS
CRIES
CROPS
CROSS
CUFFS
CURDS
CUTIS
CYRUS
DANES
DARTS
DATES
DAVIS
DEEDS
DEGAS
DELOS
DEMOS
DENIS
DENYS
DIALS
DIVES
DOCKS
DOORS
DORAS
DORIS
DORTS
DOWNS
DREGS
DRESS
DRIES
DROPS
DROSS
DRUGS
DUCKS
DUKAS
DUKES
DUMAS
DUMPS
EAVES
ELIAS
ELLIS
ELVES
ELVIS
EMBUS
EMRYS
ETATS
ETHOS
EVANS
EVENS
FACTS
FAGUS
FAINS
FALLS
FAVUS
FECES
FELIS
FETUS
FIDES
FILMS
FINIS
FINKS
FIVES
FLATS
FLEWS
FLIES
FLOPS
FLOSS
FOCUS
FOLKS
FONDS
FOODS
FOOLS
FOOTS
FORKS
FORMS
FOURS
FRANS
FRIES
FUCHS
FUMES
FUNDS
GADUS
GAINS
GAIUS
GAMES
GASES
GAUSS
GENTS
GENUS
GHATS
GIBUS
GIFTS
GILES
GILLS
GILTS
GIRLS
GLANS
GLASS
GLOSS
GOODS
GRASS
GRAYS
GREYS
GRITS
GROSS
GUESS
GULES
GULLS
GYGES
GYRUS
HADES
HAIRS
HANDS
HEADS
HEAPS
HEELS
HERBS
HERTS
HILLS
HIVES
HOBBS
HOCUS
HORUS
HOURS
HULKS
HUMUS
HUNKS
HUNTS
HUSKS
ICTUS
IDEAS
IDRIS
ILEUS
INCUS
INDUS
INNES
IRONS
ISLES
JACKS
JADIS
JAKES
JAMES
JANUS
JEANS
JERKS
JESUS
JINKS
JONES
JORIS
JUDAS
JUMPS
KEELS
KEEPS
KELLS
KEYES
KINGS
KIPPS
KIWIS
KRANS
KUDOS
KVASS
LABIS
LACKS
LAGOS
LAMPS
LAPIS
LARKS
LAUDS
LAWKS
LEADS
LEEDS
LEVIS
LEWES
LEWIS
LEXIS
LIKES
LIMES
LINES
LINKS
LINUS
LIONS
LISTS
LITAS
LIVES
LOCKS
LOCUS
LOESS
LOGOS
LOINS
LONGS
LOONS
LORDS
LORIS
LOTOS

LOTUS
LOUIS
LUNGS
LUPUS
LYSIS
MAGUS
MAINS
MANES
MANUS
MASUS
MATES
MATHS
MAVIS
MEALS
MEANS
MEATS
MEETS
MELOS
METHS
METIS
MIDAS
MILES
MILLS
MIMUS
MINOS
MINUS
MITES
MODUS
MONKS
MORES
MORUS
MOSES
MOTHS
MOULS
MUCUS
MUMPS
MUSES
NAGAS
NAILS
NAMES
NARES
NARKS
NATES
NATUS
NAXOS
NEEDS
NEGUS
NEVIS
NEWTS
NEXUS
NIDUS
NISUS
NODES
NODUS
NONES
NOTES
NOTTS
NOYES
OASIS
OATES
OCNUS
ODETS
OFFAS
ONCUS
ONKUS
ORCUS
ORNIS
ORRIS
ORTUS
PAGES
PAINS
PAIRS
PALES
PANTS
PARIS
PARTS
PEERS
PENIS
PEPYS
PERKS
PICUS
PIERS
PILES
PILLS
PILUS
PINES
PIOUS
PLEBS
PLOTS
POEMS
POETS
PONDS
POOLS
POPES
PORTS
POWYS
PRESS
PSOAS
PUBIS
PYRUS
PYXIS
QUADS
QUIDS
QUINS
QUITS
RACES
RAKES
RAMUS
RANKS
RATES
REAMS
REBUS
REEDS
REGIS
REINS
REMUS
RESTS
REYES
RIOTS
RISUS
RITES
ROBES
ROCKS
ROLLS
ROOMS
ROOTS
ROPES
ROSES
RUFUS
RUINS
RULES
RUNES
SACHS
SACKS
SAGES
SAILS
SALES
SALTS
SAMOS
SANDS
SAROS
SARUS
SATIS
SCADS
SCOPS
SCOTS
SEALS
SEMIS
SHOPS
SHOTS
SHUTS
SIGHS
SIGNS
SILAS
SINUS
SKINS
SLATS
SLIPS
SLOPS
SLUGS
SMUTS
SNAGS
SNAPS
SNOBS
SOCKS
SOLUS
SORES
SORTS
SOULS
SPATS
SPECS
SPENS
SPIES
SPOTS
SPURS
STARS
STAYS
STEPS
STEWS
SUCKS
SUITS
SULKS
SWANS
SWATS
SWISS
TABES
TAGUS
TAILS
TALES
TALKS
TALUS
TAMIS
TAPAS
TAPIS
TAXIS
TAXUS
TEARS
TEENS
TELOS
TENDS
TERES
TERMS
TESTS
TEXAS
TEXTS
THAIS
THEWS
THUGS
TIBBS
TILES
TIMES
TIROS
TITUS
TOILS
TONGS
TONUS
TOOLS
TORUS
TOWNS
TRANS
TRAPS
TREES
TRESS
TREWS
TRIES
TROTS
TRUSS
TUNIS
TURPS
TWIGS
TWINS
TYPES
UNCUS
UNITS
URALS
VAGUS
VAILS
VARUS
VEINS
VENUS
VIBES
VIRUS
VITIS
VITUS
VOTES
WAGES
WAITS
WAKES
WALES
WARES
WATTS
WAVES
WEEDS
WEEKS
WELLS
WHIMS
WHIPS
WILDS
WILES
WILTS
WINGS
WIRES
WIVES
WOODS
WORCS
WORDS
WORKS
WORMS
WRITS
XERES
XYRIS
YARNS
YATES
YEARS
YEATS
YIKES
YONKS
YOURS
YPRES
ZENOS
ABAFT
ABBOT
ABORT
ABOUT
ABSIT
ADAPT
ADEPT
ADMIT
ADOPT
ADULT
AFOOT
AFRIT
AGENT
AGIST
AGLET
ALERT
ALEUT
ALLOT
ALOFT
AMANT
AMBIT
AMENT
AMORT
ANENT
ANGST
APART
APERT
ARCOT
ARENT
ARGOT
ARIST
ARMET
ARRÊT
ASCOT
ASHET
ASSET
ATILT
AUDIT
AUGHT
AVANT
AVAST
AVERT
AWAIT
BAHUT
BEAST
BEAUT
BEFIT
BEGET
BENET
BEPAT
BERET
BESET
BESOT
BIDET
BIGHT
BIGOT
BIONT
BLAST
BLEAT
BLEST
BLOAT
BLUNT
BLURT
BOAST
BOOST
BRACT
BRENT
BREST
BRUIT
BRUNT
BUILT
BURNT
BURST
CABOT
CADET
CAGOT
CAPET
CAPOT
CAPUT
CARAT
CARET
CHANT
CHART
CHEAT
CHERT
CHEST
CHIRT
CIVET
CLEAT
CLEFT
CLIFT
CLINT
CLOOT
CLOUT
COAST
COLET
COMET
COOPT
COROT
COUNT
COURT
COVET
CRAFT
CREPT
CREST
CROAT
CROFT
CRUET
CRUST
CRYPT
CUBIT
CULET
CURST
DAUNT
DAVIT
DEBIT
DEBUT
DEIST
DELFT
DEPOT
DIDNT
DIGHT
DIGIT
DIVOT
DONAT
DOUBT
DRAFT
DRIFT
DROIT
DUCAT
DURST
DUVET
ECLAT
EDICT
EGEST
EGRET
EGYPT
EIGHT
EILAT
EJECT
ELECT
ELIOT
EMMET
ENACT
ERECT
ERGOT
ERNST
ERUCT
ERUPT
ESCOT
EVENT
EVERT
EVICT
EXACT
EXALT
EXEAT
EXERT
EXIST
EXULT
FACET
FAGOT
FAINT
FAULT
FAUST
FEAST
FECIT
FEINT
FIGHT
FILET
FIRST
FLEET
FLINT
FLIRT
FLOAT
FLOUT
FOIST
FOUET
FOUNT
FRACT
FRIST
FRONT
FROST
FRUIT
FUMET
GAMUT
GAULT
GAUNT
GÉANT
GEIST
GENET
GHOST
GIANT
GIGOT
GILET
GLEET
GLINT
GLOAT
GODET
GOSHT
GRAFT
GRANT
GREAT
GREET
GRIOT
GRIST
GROAT
GROUT
GRUNT

GUEST
GUILT
GUYOT
GWENT
HABET
HABIT
HADNT
HASNT
HAULT
HAUNT
HEART
HECHT
HEIST
HELOT
HIGHT
HOAST
HOIST
HOLST
HURST
IBERT
IDIOT
IMPOT
INAPT
INEPT
INERT
INGOT
INLET
INPUT
INSET
INUIT
INWIT
ISLET
ISMET
IZZAT
JABOT
JAUNT
JOINT
JOIST
JOUNT
JOUST
JURAT
KAPUT
KARAT
KARST
KNELT
KNOUT
KRAFT
KRAUT
LACET
LEANT
LEAPT
LEAST
LEGIT
LICHT
LICIT
LIGHT
LIMIT
LISZT
LOVAT
MANET
MARAT
MAROT
MEANT
MERIT
MIDST
MIGHT
MINOT
MOIST
MONET
MORAT
MOTET
MOULT
MOUNT
MULCT
MUSIT
NACHT
NIGHT
NONET
OBIIT
OCTET
ONSET
ORBIT
OUGHT
OVERT
OWLET
PAINT
PALET
PETIT
PICOT
PIERT
PILOT
PINOT
PIPIT
PITOT
PIVOT
PLAIT
PLANT
PLEAT
POINT
POSIT
POULT
PREST
PRINT
PROUT
QATAR
QUANT
QUART
QUEST
QUIET
QUILT
QUINT
QUOIT
RABAT
REACT
REBUT
REFIT
REIST
REMIT
REPOT
RESET
RESIT
REVET
RHETT
RIANT
RIGHT
RIVET
ROAST
ROBOT
ROGET
ROIST
ROOST
ROSET
ROSIT
ROUST
ROZET
SABOT
SAINT
SAULT
SCANT
SCENT
SCOOT
SCOTT
SCOUT
SCRAT
SHAFT
SHALT
SHANT
SHEET
SHIFT
SHIRT
SHOOT
SHORT
SHOUT
SHUNT
SIGHT
SKEET
SKINT
SKIRT
SLANT
SLEET
SLEPT
SMART
SMELT
SMOLT
SNIFT
SNOOT
SNORT
SNOUT
SPALT
SPART
SPELT
SPENT
SPILT
SPLAT
SPLIT
SPORT
SPOUT
SPRAT
SPRIT
SPURT
SQUAT
SQUIT
START
STENT
STILT
STINT
STOAT
STOUT
STRUT
STUNT
STURT
SWEAT
SWEET
SWELT
SWEPT
SWIFT
TACIT
TAINT
TAPET
TAROT
TAUNT
TEMPT
TENET
THEFT
THOFT
TIBET
TIGHT
TOAST
TOBIT
TRACT
TRAIT
TRANT
TREAT
TRENT
TROUT
TRUST
TRYST
TWEET
TWILT
TWIST
TWIXT
UNAPT
UNCUT
UNFIT
UNGET
UNIAT
UNLIT
UPSET
VALET
VAULT
VAUNT
VELDT
VERST
VISIT
VIVAT
VOLET
VOMIT
WAIST
WASNT
WHEAT
WHIFT
WHIST
WHOOT
WIGHT
WORST
WREST
WRIST
WURST
YACHT
YAKUT
YEAST
YOURT
ZAKAT
ADIEU
ANJOU
BANTU
BAYOU
BIJOU
BOYAU
CORFU
COYPU
CYMRU
ELIHU
ENUGU
FICHU
HAIKU
HINDU
JIMMU
KUDZU
MIAOU
NANDU
NAURU
NEHRU
NOYAU
PAREU
PERDU
PILAU
POILU
PRAHU
SADHU
SAMFU
SNAFU
TUNKU
TURKU
UHURU
VERTU
VIRTU
KIROV
NEGEV
POPOV
ABLOW
AGLOW
ALLOW
ARROW
ASKEW
BEDEW
BELOW
BULOW
BYLAW
CAREW
ELBOW
EMBOW
ENDOW
ENMEW
ENSEW
IMMEW
INDEW
INLAW
KOTOW
MACAW
MIAOW
NAVEW
OXBOW
PAPAW
PSHAW
RENEW
SCRAW
SCREW
SCROW
SHREW
SHROW
SINEW
SQUAW
STRAW
STREW
THREW
THROW
UNLAW
WIDOW
ADMIX
AFFIX
ANNEX
BORAX
BRONX
CALIX
CALYX
CODEX
CULEX
EMBOX
FELIX
GUEUX
HELIX
HYRAX
INDEX
KYLIX
LATEX
LIMAX
MUREX
PHLOX
PODEX
PULEX
PYREX
RADIX
REDOX
RELAX
RUMEX
SALIX
SILEX
SOREX
TELEX
UNMIX
VARIX
XEROX
ABBEY
ABRAY
AGLEY
AGONY
ALLAY
ALLEY
ALLOY
AMITY
AMPLY
ANGRY
ANNOY
ANOMY
APPAY
APPLY
APTLY
ARRAY
ASSAY
ATOMY
ATONY
ATOPY
AUNTY
BACCY
BADDY
BADLY
BAFFY
BAGGY
BALLY
BALMY
BANDY
BARMY
BARRY
BATTY
BAWDY
BEADY
BEAMY
BECKY
BEEFY
BEERY
BELAY
BELLY
BENDY
BERRY
BETTY
BEVVY
BIBBY
BIDDY
BILLY
BITTY
BLOWY
BLUEY
BOBBY
BOGEY
BOGGY
BONEY
BONNY
BOOBY
BOOTY
BOOZY
BOSEY
BOSKY
BOSSY
BOTHY
BRADY
BRINY
BUBBY
BUDDY
BUGGY
BULKY
BULLY
BUMPY
BUNDY
BUNGY
BUNNY
BURLY
BUSBY
BUSHY
BUSTY
BUTTY
BYWAY
CABBY
CADDY
CADGY
CAGEY
CANDY
CANNY
CAREY
CARRY
CARVY
CATTY
CHARY
CHEVY
CHEWY
CHIVY
CHOKY
CIGGY
CISSY
CIVVY
CLARY
COCKY
COLEY
COLLY
COMFY
CONEY
COPPY
CORKY
CORNY
COVEY
COWRY
COYLY
CRAZY
CRECY
CRONY
CUBBY
CUDDY
CUFFY
CULLY
CURLY
CURRY
CURVY
CUSHY
CUTEY
CUTTY
CYMRY
DADDY
DAFFY

DAILY
DAIRY
DAISY
DALLY
DANDY
DARBY
DARCY
DECAY
DECOY
DECRY
DEIFY
DEITY
DELAY
DERAY
DERBY
DERRY
DEWEY
DIARY
DICEY
DICKY
DIMLY
DINGY
DINKY
DIPPY
DIRTY
DISHY
DITTY
DIVVY
DIZZY
DOBBY
DODDY
DODGY
DOGGY
DOILY
DOLLY
DOPEY
DORMY
DOTTY
DOUAY
DOWDY
DOWNY
DOWRY
DOYLY
DRILY
DRURY
DRYLY
DUCHY
DUCKY
DUDDY
DUMMY
DUMPY
DUROY
DURRY
DUSKY
DUSTY
EARLY
EBONY
EDIFY
ELEGY
ELOGY
EMERY
EMILY
EMPTY
ENEMY
ENJOY
ENTRY
ENVOY
EPOXY
ESSAY
EVERY
FADDY
FAERY
FAIRY
FANCY
FANNY
FARCY
FATTY
FENNY
FERRY
FIERY
FIFTY
FILLY
FILMY
FISHY
FIZZY
FLAKY
FOAMY
FOGEY
FOGGY
FOLLY
FOOTY
FORAY
FORTY
FROWY
FUBSY
FUGGY
FULLY
FUNDY
FUNKY
FUNNY
FURRY
FUSSY
FUSTY
FUZZY
GABBY
GAILY
GAMAY
GAMMY
GANNY
GASSY
GAUDY
GAUZY
GAWKY
GEMMY
GENTY
GIBBY
GIDDY
GIMPY
GIPSY
GIRLY
GLORY
GLUEY
GOATY
GODLY
GOLLY
GOODY
GOOEY
GOOFY
GOOLY
GORKY
GOUTY
GRAVY
GRIMY
GULLY
GUMMY
GUNNY
GUPPY
GUSHY
GUSTY
GUTSY
GYPSY
HAIRY
HAMMY
HANDY
HANKY
HAPPY
HARDY
HARPY
HARRY
HARTY
HASTY
HATTY
HEADY
HEAVY
HEFTY
HENRY
HETTY
HILLY
HINNY
HIPPY
HOARY
HOBBY
HOKEY
HOLEY
HOLLY
HONEY
HONKY
HOOEY
HOOKY
HORNY
HORSY
HOTLY
HOWDY
HUBBY
HUFFY
HUNKY
HURRY
HUSKY
HUSSY
ICILY
IMPLY
INLAY
IRONY
ISLAY
ITALY
ITCHY
IVORY
JAMMY
JANTY
JASEY
JAZZY
JELLY
JEMMY
JENNY
JERKY
JERRY
JETTY
JEWRY
JIFFY
JIMMY
JIMPY
JOLLY
JONTY
JUICY
JUMBY
JUMPY
KANDY
KARSY
KEDGY
KELLY
KIDDY
KINKY
KIRBY
KITTY
KOOKY
LAIRY
LAITY
LAMMY
LANKY
LARRY
LAYBY
LEAFY
LEAKY
LEERY
LEFTY
LEGGY
LESHY
LILLY
LIMEY
LOAMY
LOBBY
LOFTY
LOLLY
LOOBY
LOONY
LOOPY
LORRY
LOUSY
LOWLY
LOWRY
LUCKY
LULLY
LUMMY
LUMPY
LUNDY
LURGY
LUSHY
LUSTY
MADLY
MALAY
MAMMY
MANGY
MANLY
MARLY
MARRY
MASHY
MATEY
MCCOY
MEALY
MEATY
MERCY
MERRY
MESSY
MIDDY
MIFFY
MILKY
MINGY
MISSY
MISTY
MOGGY
MOLLY
MOMMY
MONEY
MOODY
MOONY
MOPSY
MORAY
MOSEY
MOSSY
MOUSY
MUCKY
MUDDY
MUGGY
MUMMY
MURKY
MURRY
MUSHY
MUSKY
MUSSY
MUSTY
MUZZY
NANCY
NANNY
NAPPY
NARKY
NASTY
NATTY
NAVVY
NEDDY
NEEDY
NELLY
NERVY
NEWLY
NEWSY
NIFTY
NINNY
NIPPY
NOBBY
NOBLY
NODDY
NOISY
NONNY
NOOKY
NOSEY
NUNKY
NUTTY
ODDLY
OTARY
OTWAY
OUTBY
OVARY
PACEY
PADDY
PALLY
PALMY
PALSY
PANDY
PANSY
PANTY
PARDY
PARKY
PARRY
PARTY
PASTY
PATSY
PATTY
PAWKY
PEAKY
PEATY
PEGGY
PENNY
PEONY
PEPPY
PERCY
PERKY
PERRY
PESKY
PETTY
PHONY
PIETY
PIGGY
PIGMY
PINKY
PINNY
PISKY
PITHY
PLATY
PLINY
PODGY
POESY
POKEY
POLLY
POMMY
PONEY
PONTY
POPPY
POPSY
PORGY
PORKY
POTTY
PRIVY
PROSY
PROXY
PUDGY
PUFFY
PULPY
PUPPY
PURSY
PUSHY
PUSSY
PUTTY
PYGMY
QUERY
RAGGY
RAINY
RALLY
RANDY
RANGY
RATTY
READY
REEDY
RELAY
REPAY
REPLY
RILEY
RISKY
RITZY
ROBEY
ROCKY
ROOKY
ROOMY
ROOPY
ROOTY
ROPEY
RORTY
ROWDY
RUDDY
RUGBY
RUMMY
RUMPY
RUNNY
RUSHY
RUSTY
SADLY
SAGGY
SALLY
SALTY
SAMMY
SANDY
SAPPY
SARKY
SASSY
SATAY
SAUCY
SAVOY
SAVVY
SCALY
SCARY
SCRAY
SEAMY
SEEDY
SEPOY
SHADY
SHAKY
SHINY
SHOWY
SHYLY
SILKY
SILLY
SISSY
SIXTY
SLATY
SLIMY
SLYLY
SMOKY
SNAKY
SNOWY
SOAPY
SOFTY
SOGGY
SONNY
SOOTY
SOPHY
SOPPY
SORRY
SPICY
SPIKY
SPINY
SPLAY
SPRAY
STAGY
STEWY
STIMY
STOGY
STONY
STORY
STRAY
STUDY
SUETY
SULKY
SULLY
SUNNY
SURLY
TABBY
TACKY
TAFFY
TALLY
TAMMY
TANGY
TANSY
TARDY
TARRY
TARTY
TASTY
TATTY
TAWNY
TEDDY
TEENY

TELLY
TERRY
TESTY
TIBBY
TIDDY
TINNY
TIPPY
TIPSY
TITTY
TIZZY
TOADY
TODAY
TODDY
TOKAY
TOMMY
TOPSY
TOTTY
TRULY
TUBBY
TULLY
TUMMY
TUNNY
UMPTY
UNIFY
UNITY
UNLAY
UNSAY
UPSEY
USURY
VEREY
VICHY
VISBY
WACKY
WALLY
WANLY
WARTY
WASHY
WEARY
WEEDY
WEENY
WEEPY
WELLY
WENDY
WILLY
WIMPY
WINDY
WINEY
WISPY
WITHY
WITTY
WONKY
WOODY
WOOFY
WOOZY
WORDY
WORMY
WORRY
WRYLY
YIPPY
YUCKY
YUKKY
YUMMY
YUPPY
ZIPPY
ZLOTY
BLITZ
FRANZ
FRITZ
GLITZ
GROSZ
HAFIZ
HERTZ
JEREZ
KRANZ
NANTZ
ORMUZ
PLATZ
PZAZZ
SOYUZ
SPITZ
SWIZZ
TOPAZ
VADUZ
WALTZ
WHIZZ

6:1

AARONS
ABACUS
ABADAN
ABATOR
ABATTU
ABBACY
ABBESS
ABDABS
ABDIEL
ABDUCT
ABELIA
ABJECT
ABJURE
ABLATE
ABLAUT
ABLAZE
ABLOOM
ABLUSH
ABOARD
ABONDE
ABOUND
ABRADE
ABREGE
ABROAD
ABROMA
ABRUPT
ABSEIL
ABSENT
ABSORB
ABSURD
ABULIA
ABYDOS
ACACIA
ACADIA
ACAJOU
ACARID
ACARUS
ACATES
ACCEDE
ACCEND
ACCENT
ACCEPT
ACCESS
ACCORD
ACCOST
ACCRUE
ACCUSE
ACEDIA
ACETIC
ACHENE
ACHING
ACIDIC
ACINUS
ACKERS
ACORNS
ACQUIT
ACRAWL
ACROSS
ACTING
ACTION
ACTIUM
ACTIVE
ACTORS
ACTUAL
ACUITY
ACUMEN
ADAGIO
ADDEEM
ADDEND
ADDICT
ADDLED
ADDUCE
ADDUCT
ADHERE
ADJOIN
ADJURE
ADJUST
ADMIRE
ADNATE
ADONAI
ADONIS
ADORER
ADRIAN
ADRIFT
ADROIT
ADSORB
ADSUKI
ADVENE
ADVENT
ADVERB
ADVERT
ADVICE
ADVISE
AEDILE
AEGEAN
AEGEUS
AEGINA
AENEID
AEOLIC
AEOLIS
AEOLUS
AERATE
AERIAL
AEROBE
AFEARS
AFFAIR
AFFECT
AFFIRM
AFFORD
AFFRAY
AFFRET
AFGHAN
AFIELD
AFLAME
AFLOAT
AFRAID
AFREET
AFRESH
AFRICA
AFTERS
AGADIR
AGARIC
AGATHA
AGEING
AGENCY
AGENDA
AGHAST
AGLAIA
AGNAIL
AGNATE
AGONIC
AGOUTI
AGREED
AGRÉGÉ
AGUISE
AGUISH
AGUIZE
AIDANT
AIGLET
AIKIDO
AILING
AIRBED
AIRBUS
AIRGUN
AIRILY
AIRING
AIRMAN
AIRWAY
AKIMBO
ALACUS
ALALIA
ALARIC
ALARUM
ALASKA
ALBANY
ALBEDO
ALBEIT
ALBERT
ALBINO
ALBION
ALBITE
ALBUGO
ALCINA
ALCOCK
ALCOVE
ALDINE
ALDOSE
ALDRIN
ALECTO
ALEGAR
ALERCE
ALEXIA
ALEXIN
ALEXIS
ALFRED
ALIGHT
ALIPED
ALIYAH
ALKALI
ALKANE
ALKENE
ALLEGE
ALLELE
ALLEYN
ALLIED
ALLIER
ALLIUM
ALLUDE
ALLURE
ALMAIN
ALMERY
ALMOND
ALMOST
ALOGIA
ALONSO
ALPACA
ALPINE
ALPINO
ALTAIR
ALTHEA
ALUDEL
ALUMNI
ALWAYS
AMADOU
AMAZED
AMAZON
AMBAGE
AMBLER
AMBUSH
AMELIA
AMENDE
AMENDS
AMERCE
AMHARA
AMIDOL
AMIDST
AMNION
AMOEBA
AMORAL
AMORCE
AMORET
AMOUNT
AMPERE
AMTRAK
AMULET
AMUSED
AMYCUS
AMYTAL
ANABAS
ANADEM
ANADYR
ANALOG
ANANAS
ANCHOR
ANCILE
ANCOME
ANCONA
ANCORA
ANDEAN
ANDREW
ANEMIA
ANEMIC
ANGARY
ANGELA
ANGELS
ANGERS
ANGICO
ANGINA
ANGLED
ANGLER
ANGLIA
ANGOLA
ANGORA
ANIMAL
ANIMUS
ANKARA
ANKLET
ANKOLE
ANNALS
ANNEAL
ANNEXE
ANNUAL
ANOINT
ANONYM
ANORAK
ANOXIA
ANOXIC
ANSELM
ANSWER
ANTHEM
ANTHER
ANTICS
ANTLER
ANTLIA
ANTONY
ANTRIM
ANTRUM
ANUBIS
ANYHOW
ANYONE
ANYWAY
AORIST
AORTAL
APACHE
APATHY
APEPSY
APERÇU
APHONY
APHTHA
APIARY
APICAL
APIECE
APLITE
APLOMB
APNOEA
APOGEE
APOLLO
APORIA
APPALL
APPEAL
APPEAR
APPEND
APPIAN
APPLES
APPORT
APPOSE
AQUILA
ARABIA
ARABIC
ARABIS
ARABLE
ARAFAT
ARAGON
ARALIA
ARAMIS
ARANDA
ARARAT
ARBOUR
ARCADE
ARCADY
ARCANA
ARCANE
ARCHED
ARCHER
ARCHES
ARCHIE
ARCHIL
ARCHON
ARCTIC
ARDENT
ARDOUR
AREOLA
AREOLE
ARGENT
ARGHAN
ARGIVE
ARGOSY
ARGUED
ARGUTE
ARGYLE
ARGYLL
ARIOCH
ARIOSO
ARISTA
ARKOSE
ARMADA
ARMAGH
ARMFUL
ARMLET
ARMORY
ARMOUR
ARMPIT
ARMURE
ARNAUT
ARNHEM
ARNICA
ARNOLD
AROINT
AROLLA
AROUET
AROUND
AROUSE
ARPENT
ARRACK
ARRANT
ARREAR
ARREST
ARRIAN
ARRIVE
ARROBA
ARROYO
ARSÈNE
ARSINE
ARTAUD
ARTERY
ARTFUL
ARTHUR
ARTIST
ARTURO
ASARUM
ASCEND
ASCENT
ASCHAM
ASCIAN
ASCIUS
ASGARD
ASHCAN
ASHDOD
ASHINE
ASHLAR
ASHLEY
ASHORE
ASHPAN
ASHTAR
ASHTON
ASIMOV
ASKARI
ASKING
ASLANT
ASLEEP
ASLOPE
ASMARA
ASPECT
ASPIRE
ASSAIL
ASSART
ASSENT
ASSERT
ASSESS
ASSETS
ASSIGN
ASSIST
ASSIZE
ASSOIL
ASSORT
ASSUME
ASSURE
ASTART
ASTERN
ASTHMA
ASTONE
ASTRAL
ASTRAY
ASTUTE

ASWARM
ASYLUM
ATABAL
ATABEG
ATAMAN
ATAXIA
ATAXIC
ATHENE
ATHENS
ATHROB
ATKINS
ATOCIA
ATOMIC
ATONAL
ATONIC
ATRIAL
ATRIDE
ATRIUM
ATTACH
ATTACK
ATTAIN
ATTEND
ATTEST
ATTILA
ATTIRE
ATTLEE
ATTONE
ATTORN
ATTRAP
ATTUNE
AUBADE
AUBREY
AUBURN
AUCUBA
AUDILE
AUDLEY
AUDREY
AUGEAN
AUGITE
AUGURY
AUGUST
AUMBRY
AUNTIE
AUREUS
AURIGA
AURORA
AUSPEX
AUSSIE
AUSTEN
AUSTER
AUSTIN
AUTHOR
AUTISM
AUTUMN
AVALON
AVATAR
AVAUNT
AVENGE
AVENUE
AVERNO
AVERSE

AVIARY
AVIATE
AVIDLY
AVOCET
AVOUCH
AVOWAL
AVOWED
AVULSE
AWAKEN
AWHILE
AWNING
AWOKEN
AXEMAN
AXILLA
AYESHA
AYMARA
AZALEA
AZOLLA
AZORES
AZOTIC
AZRAEL
BABBIT
BABBLE
BABOON
BACCHI
BACKER
BACKET
BACKRA
BACKUP
BADGER
BADMAN
BAFFIN
BAFFLE
BAGFUL
BAGMAN
BAGNIO
BAGUIO
BAHADA
BAHRAM
BAIKAL
BAILEE
BAILER
BAILEY
BAILIE
BAILLY
BAKERS
BAKERY
BAKING
BALAAM
BALBOA
BALDER
BALDLY
BALEEN
BALKAN
BALKIS
BALLAD
BALLET
BALLOT
BALSAM
BALTIC
BALZAC

BAMAKO
BAMBOO
BANANA
BANDAR
BANDIT
BANDOG
BANGER
BANGLE
BANGUI
BANIAN
BANISH
BANJAX
BANJUL
BANKER
BANNED
BANNER
BANNET
BANTAM
BANTER
BANTRY
BANYAN
BANZAI
BAOBAB
BARBED
BARBEL
BARBER
BARBET
BARÈGE
BARELY
BARGEE
BARHAM
BARING
BARIUM
BARKER
BARKIS
BARLEY
BARMAN
BARNES
BARNET
BARNEY
BARNUM
BARODA
BARQUE
BARRED
BARREL
BARREN
BARRIE
BARRIO
BARROW
BARSAC
BARTER
BARTOK
BARTON
BARYTA
BASALT
BASHER
BASICS
BASKET
BASQUE
BASSET
BASUTO

BATEAU
BATHER
BATHOS
BATMAN
BATTEN
BATTER
BATTLE
BATTUE
BAUBLE
BAUCIS
BAWBEE
BAXTER
BAYARD
BAYEUX
BAZAAR
BEACHY
BEACON
BEADED
BEADLE
BEAGLE
BEAKER
BEANIE
BEARER
BEATEN
BEATER
BEATTY
BEAUNE
BEAUTY
BEAVER
BECALM
BECAME
BECKET
BECKON
BECOME
BEDASH
BEDAUB
BEDDER
BEDECK
BEDLAM
BEDPAN
BEDSIT
BEEGHA
BEENAH
BEEPER
BEETLE
BEETON
BEFALL
BEFOOL
BEFORE
BEGGAR
BEGONE
BEHALF
BEHAVE
BEHEAD
BEHELD
BEHEST
BEHIND
BEHOLD
BEHOOF
BEHOVE
BEHRAM

BEIRUT
BEJADE
BELAMY
BELFRY
BELIAL
BELIEF
BELIKE
BELIZE
BELLOC
BELLOW
BELONG
BELSEN
BELTED
BELUGA
BEMEAN
BEMOAN
BEMOIL
BEMUSE
BENAME
BENBOW
BENDED
BENDER
BENGAL
BENIGN
BENITO
BENNET
BENSON
BENUMB
BERATE
BERBER
BEREFT
BERGEN
BERING
BERLIN
BERTHA
BERTHE
BERTIE
BESANT
BESEEM
BESIDE
BESORT
BESSEL
BESSIE
BESSUS
BESTED
BESTIR
BESTOW
BETAKE
BETHEL
BETIDE
BETIME
BETISE
BETONY
BETRAY
BETTER
BETTOR
BEULAH
BEURRÉ
BEWAIL
BEWARE
BEYOND

BEZANT
BEZOAR
BEZZLE
BHAJAN
BHAJEE
BHARAT
BIASED
BICARB
BICEPS
BICKER
BIDDER
BIDENT
BIFFIN
BIFOLD
BIGAMY
BIGGER
BIGGIN
BIGWIG
BIKINI
BILLET
BILLIE
BILLOW
BILLYO
BINARY
BINATE
BINDER
BIOGEN
BIONIC
BIOPIC
BIOPSY
BIOTIC
BIOTIN
BIRDIE
BIREME
BIRNAM
BISCAY
BISECT
BISHOP
BISQUE
BISTER
BISTRE
BISTRO
BITCHY
BITING
BITTEN
BITTER
BLACKS
BLAISE
BLAMED
BLANCH
BLANCO
BLAZER
BLAZON
BLEACH
BLEARY
BLENCH
BLENDE
BLENNY
BLIGHT
BLIMEY
BLINKS

BLITHE
BLOCKS
BLONDE
BLOODY
BLOTCH
BLOTTO
BLOUSE
BLOWER
BLOWZY
BLUDGE
BLUISH
BOARDS
BOATER
BOBBIN
BOBBLE
BOBCAT
BOBWIG
BOCAGE
BODACH
BODEGA
BODGER
BODGIE
BODICE
BODIES
BODILY
BODKIN
BODONI
BOEING
BOFFIN
BOFORS
BOGART
BOGGLE
BOGOTA
BOHUNK
BOILED
BOILER
BOLDLY
BOLERO
BOLEYN
BOLIDE
BOLLEN
BOLSHY
BOLTER
BOMBAY
BOMBER
BOMBYX
BONBON
BONDED
BONDER
BONITO
BONNET
BONNIE
BONSAI
BONXIE
BONZER
BOOBOO
BOODLE
BOOGIE
BOOHOO
BOOJUM
BOOKED

BOOKER
BOOKIE
BOOMER
BOOTEE
BOOTLE
BOOZER
BORAGE
BORATE
BORDAR
BORDER
BOREAS
BORGIA
BORING
BORNEO
BORROW
BORSCH
BORZOI
BOSKET
BOSSED
BOSTON
BOSUNS
BOTANY
BOTHAM
BOTHER
BOTHIE
BOTLEY
BOTTLE
BOTTOM
BOUCHE
BOUCLÉ
BOUFFE
BOUGHT
BOULLE
BOUNCE
BOUNCY
BOUNDS
BOUNTY
BOURÉE
BOURNE
BOURSE
BOUSER
BOUTON
BOVATE
BOVINE
BOVRIL
BOWELS
BOWERY
BOWLED
BOWLER
BOWMAN
BOWSER
BOWWOW
BOXCAR
BOXING
BOYISH
BRACER
BRACES
BRAHMA
BRAHMS
BRAINS
BRAINY

BRAISE
BRAMAH
BRANCH
BRANDY
BRAQUE
BRASSY
BRAWNY
BRAZEN
BRAZIL
BREACH
BREAST
BREATH
BRECHT
BREECH
BREEZE
BREEZY
BREGMA
BREMEN
BRETON
BREVET
BREWER
BREWIS
BRIAND
BRIARD
BRICKS
BRIDAL
BRIDGE
BRIDIE
BRIDLE
BRIEFS
BRIGHT
BRIONY
BRITON
BROACH
BROADS
BROGAN
BROGUE
BROKEN
BROKER
BROLLY
BRONCO
BRONTE
BRONZE
BROOCH
BROODY
BROOKE
BROOKS
BROWNE
BROWSE
BRUISE
BRUMAL
BRUMBY
BRUNCH
BRUNEI
BRUNEL
BRUTAL
BRUTUS
BRYANT
BRYONY
BUBBLE
BUBBLY

BUCCAL
BUCHAN
BUCKED
BUCKER
BUCKET
BUCKLE
BUDDHA
BUDGET
BUDGIE
BUENOS
BUFFER
BUFFET
BUFFON
BUGGER
BUGLER
BUKSHI
BULBIL
BULBUL
BULGAR
BULGER
BULIMY
BULLER
BULLET
BUMALO
BUMBLE
BUMPER
BUNCHY
BUNDLE
BUNGAY
BUNGEE
BUNGLE
BUNION
BUNJEE
BUNKER
BUNKUM
BUNSEN
BUNTER
BUNYAN
BURBLE
BURBOT
BURDEN
BUREAU
BURGEE
BURGER
BURGLE
BURIAL
BURIED
BURKHA
BURLAP
BURLEY
BURNER
BURNET
BURROW
BURSAR
BURTON
BUSBOY
BUSHED
BUSHEL
BUSILY
BUSKER
BUSKET

BUSKIN
BUSMAN
BUSONI
BUSTED
BUSTER
BUSTLE
BUTANE
BUTENE
BUTLER
BUTTER
BUTTON
BUYERS
BUYING
BUYOUT
BUZFUZ
BUZZER
BYEBYE
BYELAW
BYGONE
BYLINE
BYPASS
BYRNIE
BYSSUS
BYWORD
CABALE
CABBIE
CACCIA
CACHET
CACHOU
CACKLE
CACOON
CACTUS
CADDIE
CADDIS
CADETS
CADGER
CADMUS
CAECUM
CAESAR
CAFARD
CAFTAN
CAGILY
CAHIER
CAHOOT
CAIMAN
CAIQUE
CAJOLE
CALAIS
CALCED
CALICO
CALIMA
CALIPH
CALKER
CALKIN
CALLAS
CALLED
CALLER
CALLET
CALLID
CALLOP
CALLOW

CALLUP
CALLUS
CALMLY
CALQUE
CALVER
CALVIN
CAMAIL
CAMBER
CAMDEN
CAMERA
CAMION
CAMISE
CAMOTE
CAMPED
CAMPER
CAMPUS
CANAAN
CANADA
CANAPÉ
CANARD
CANARY
CANCEL
CANCER
CANDID
CANDLE
CANDOR
CANGUE
CANINE
CANING
CANKER
CANNAE
CANNED
CANNEL
CANNON
CANNOT
CANOPY
CANTAB
CANTAL
CANTAR
CANTER
CANTLE
CANTON
CANTOR
CANUCK
CANUTE
CANVAS
CANVEY
CANYON
CAPIAS
CAPLET
CAPONE
CAPOTE
CAPPED
CAPSID
CAPTAN
CAPTOR
CARAFE
CARBON
CARBOY
CARDAN
CAREEN

CAREER
CAREME
CARESS
CARFAX
CARIES
CARINA
CARING
CARLIN
CARMEL
CARMEN
CARNAL
CARNET
CARNOT
CARPAL
CARPEL
CARPER
CARPET
CARPUS
CARREL
CARROT
CARSON
CARTEL
CARTER
CARTON
CARUSO
CARVED
CARVEL
CARVER
CASBAH
CASEIN
CASHEW
CASING
CASINO
CASKET
CASLON
CASPAR
CASQUE
CASSIA
CASSIO
CASSIS
CASTER
CASTLE
CASTOR
CASTRO
CASUAL
CATCHY
CATGUT
CATHAR
CATHAY
CATKIN
CATNAP
CATNIP
CATSUP
CATTLE
CAUCUS
CAUDEX
CAUDLE
CAUGHT
CAUSAL
CAUSED
CAUSEY

CAVEAT
CAVEIN
CAVELL
CAVERN
CAVITY
CAVORT
CAVOUR
CAYMAN
CECILS
CECITY
CEDRIC
CEDULA
CEEFAX
CELERY
CELIAC
CELLAR
CELTIC
CEMENT
CENSER
CENSOR
CENSUS
CENTER
CENTRE
CENTUM
CERATE
CERCAL
CERCUS
CEREAL
CEREUS
CERISE
CERIUM
CEROON
CERTES
CERUSE
CERVIX
CESARE
CESIUM
CESTUI
CESTUS
CESURA
CETERA
CEYLON
CHADOR
CHAFER
CHAINS
CHAIRS
CHAISE
CHAKRA
CHALET
CHALKY
CHAMPS
CHANCE
CHANCY
CHANEY
CHANGE
CHAPEL
CHAPKA
CHARGE
CHARON
CHARTA
CHASER

CHASSE
CHASTE
CHATON
CHATTY
CHAZAN
CHEDER
CHEEKY
CHEERS
CHEERY
CHEESE
CHEESY
CHEMIC
CHEMMY
CHENET
CHEOPS
CHEQUE
CHERIE
CHERRY
CHERUB
CHERUP
CHESIL
CHESTY
CHEVAL
CHEVET
CHIBOL
CHICHI
CHICLE
CHICON
CHILDE
CHILLI
CHILLY
CHIMER
CHIMES
CHINAR
CHINCH
CHINTZ
CHIPPY
CHIRON
CHIRPY
CHISEL
CHITAL
CHITIN
CHITON
CHITTY
CHIVES
CHIVVY
CHOANA
CHOICE
CHOKED
CHOKER
CHOKEY
CHOLER
CHOOSE
CHOOSY
CHOPIN
CHOPPY
CHORAL
CHOREA
CHOREE
CHORUS
CHOSEN
CHOUAN
CHOUGH
CHOWRY
CHRISM
CHRIST
CHROMA
CHROME
CHROMO
CHUBBY
CHUFFY
CHUKKA
CHUMMY
CHUNKY
CHURCH
CHYPRE
CICADA
CICALA
CICELY
CICERO
CIERGE
CILICE
CILIUM
CINDER
CINEMA
CINQUE
CIPHER
CIRCLE
CIRCUS
CIRQUE
CIRRUS
CITRIC
CITRIN
CITRON
CITRUS
CIVICS
CIVISM
CLAGGY
CLAIMS
CLAMMY
CLAMOR
CLAQUE
CLARET
CLARTY
CLASSY
CLAUDE
CLAUSE
CLAVIS
CLAYEY
CLEAVE
CLENCH
CLERGY
CLERIC
CLERKS
CLEVER
CLICHÉ
CLIENT
CLIFFS
CLIMAX
CLIMES
CLINCH
CLINIC
CLIPPY
CLIQUE
CLOACA
CLOAKS
CLOCHE
CLONIC
CLONUS
CLOSED
CLOSER
CLOSET
CLOTHE
CLOUDY
CLOUGH
CLOVEN
CLOVER
CLOVIS
CLUMPS
CLUMSY
CLUNCH
CLUTCH
COALER
COARSE
COATED
COATES
COBALT
COBBER
COBBLE
COBDEN
COBURG
COBWEB
COCCID
COCCUS
COCCYX
COCHIN
COCKER
COCKLE
COCOON
CODDLE
CODGER
CODIFY
CODING
COERCE
COEVAL
COFFEE
COFFER
COFFIN
COGENT
COGGER
COGNAC
COHERE
COHORT
COILED
COINER
COITUS
COLDLY
COLLAR
COLLET
COLLIE
COLLOP
COLMAR
COLONY
COLOUR
COLTER
COLUMN
COMART
COMATE
COMBAT
COMBED
COMBER
COMBLE
COMEDO
COMEDY
COMELY
COMFIT
COMICE
COMING
COMITY
COMMIS
COMMIT
COMMON
COMPEL
COMPLY
COMSAT
CONCHA
CONCHY
CONCUR
CONDOM
CONDOR
CONFAB
CONFER
CONGEE
CONGER
CONICS
CONKER
CONMAN
CONNER
CONRAD
CONSUL
CONTRA
CONVEX
CONVEY
CONVOY
COOING
COOKED
COOKER
COOKIE
COOLER
COOLIE
COOLLY
COOLTH
COOPER
COOTIE
COPECK
COPIED
COPIER
COPING
COPPER
COPPIN
COPTIC
COQUET
CORALS
CORBEL
CORBIE
CORDON
CORIUM
CORKED
CORKER
CORMUS
CORNEA
CORNED
CORNEL
CORNER
CORNET
CORNUA
CORNUS
CORONA
CORPSE
CORPUS
CORRAL
CORRIE
CORSET
CORTES
CORTEX
CORTEZ
CORVÉE
CORVUS
CORYZA
COSHER
COSIER
COSILY
COSINE
COSMEA
COSMIC
COSMOS
COSSET
COSSIE
COSTAR
COSTER
COSTLY
COTTAR
COTTON
COTYLE
COUGAR
COULEE
COULIS
COUNTY
COUPLE
COUPON
COURSE
COUSIN
COVENT
COVERT
COVING
COWAGE
COWARD
COWBOY
COWMAN
COWPAT
COWPER
COWRIE
COYOTE
COZIER
CRABBE
CRABBY
CRADLE
CRAFTY
CRAGGY
CRAMBO
CRANCH
CRANKY
CRANNY
CRANTS
CRAPLE
CRASIS
CRATCH
CRATER
CRATON
CRATUR
CRAVAT
CRAVEN
CRAYER
CRAYON
CRAZED
CREACH
CREAGH
CREAKY
CREAMY
CREANT
CREASE
CREATE
CRÈCHE
CREDIT
CREEPS
CREEPY
CREESE
CREESH
CREMOR
CRENAL
CRENEL
CREOLE
CRESOL
CRESTA
CRETAN
CRETIC
CRETIN
CREWEL
CRIANT
CRIBLE
CRIKEY
CRIMEA
CRINAL
CRINGE
CRINUM
CRIPES
CRISIS
CRISPY
CRISTA
CRITIC
CROAKY
CROCHE
CROCKS
CROCUS
CRONET
CRONOS
CROPPY
CROSBY
CROSSE
CROTAL
CROTCH
CROTON
CROUCH
CROUPE
CROUPY
CROUSE
CROUTE
CROUTH
CRUELS
CRUFTS
CRUISE
CRUIVE
CRUMBS
CRUMEN
CRUMMY
CRUNCH
CRURAL
CRUSET
CRUSOE
CRUSTA
CRUSTY
CRUTCH
CRYING
CRYPTO
CUBAGE
CUBICA
CUBISM
CUBIST
CUCKOO
CUDDLE
CUDDLY
CUDGEL
CUEIST
CUERPO
CUESTA
CUFFEE
CUFFIN
CUISSE
CUITER
CULDEE
CULLET
CULLIS
CULMEN
CULTCH
CULTER
CULTUS
CULVER
CUMBER
CUMMER
CUMMIN
CUNEAL
CUNNER
CUPFUL
CUPMAN
CUPOLA
CUPPED
CUPPER

CUPULE
CURACY
CURARE
CURARI
CURATE
CURDLE
CURFEW
CURIET
CURIUM
CURLER
CURLEW
CURPEL
CURRIE
CURSAL
CURSED
CURSOR
CURSUS
CURTAL
CURTAX
CURTLY
CURTSY
CURULE
CURVED
CURVET
CUSCUS
CUSHAT
CUSSED
CUSSER
CUSTER
CUSTOM
CUSTOS
CUTCHA
CUTLER
CUTLET
CUTOFF
CUTTER
CUTTLE
CUTTOE
CYANIN
CYBELE
CYBORG
CYBRID
CYCLIC
CYCLUS
CYDNUS
CYESIS
CYGNET
CYGNUS
CYMBAL
CYMRIC
CYNIPS
CYPHER
CYPRID
CYPRIS
CYPRUS
CYRANO
CYRENE
CYSTIC
CYTASE
CYTODE
CYTOID
CZAPKA
DABBLE
DACOIT
DACTYL
DADDLE
DAEDAL
DAEMON
DAFTIE
DAGGER
DAGGLE
DAHLIA
DAIMIO
DAINTY
DAISHO
DAKOTA
DALASI
DALTON
DAMAGE
DAMASK
DAMMIT
DAMNED
DAMPEN
DAMPER
DAMSEL
DAMSON
DANCER
DANDER
DANDLE
DANGER
DANGLE
DANIEL
DANISH
DANTON
DANUBE
DANZIG
DAPHNE
DAPPER
DAPPLE
DARGLE
DARIEN
DARING
DARIUS
DARKEN
DARKEY
DARKIE
DARKLY
DARTER
DARTLE
DARWIN
DASHED
DATING
DATIVE
DATURA
DAUDET
DAWDLE
DAWNEY
DAWSON
DAYBED
DAZZLE
DEACON
DEADEN
DEADLY
DEAFEN
DEALER
DEARER
DEARIE
DEARLY
DEARTH
DEBASE
DEBATE
DEBILE
DEBRIS
DEBTOR
DEBUNK
DECADE
DECAFF
DECAMP
DECANE
DECANI
DECANT
DECCAN
DECEIT
DECENT
DECIDE
DÉCIME
DECKED
DECKER
DECKLE
DECODE
DECOKE
DECREE
DECREW
DEDANS
DEDUCE
DEDUCT
DEEPEN
DEEPER
DEEPLY
DEFACE
DEFAME
DEFEAT
DEFECT
DEFEND
DEFILE
DEFINE
DEFORM
DEFRAY
DEFTLY
DEFUSE
DÉGAGÉ
DEGREE
DEHORN
DEIDRE
DEJECT
DEKKER
DELATE
DELETE
DELIAN
DELICE
DELICT
DELIUS
DELPHI
DELUDE
DELUGE
DELUXE
DELVED
DEMAIN
DEMAND
DEMEAN
DEMENT
DEMISE
DEMIST
DEMOTE
DEMURE
DENGUE
DENIAL
DENIED
DENIER
DENIMS
DENNIS
DENOTE
DENTAL
DENUDE
DENVER
DEODAR
DEPART
DEPEND
DEPICT
DEPLOY
DEPONE
DEPORT
DEPOSE
DEPTHS
DEPUTE
DEPUTY
DERAIL
DERAIN
DERGUE
DERHAM
DERIDE
DERIVE
DERMAL
DERMIS
DERRIS
DESCRY
DESERT
DESIGN
DESIRE
DESIST
DESORB
DESPOT
DETACH
DETAIL
DETAIN
DETECT
DETENT
DETENU
DETEST
DETOUR
DEVEST
DEVICE
DEVILS
DEVISE
DEVOID
DEVOTE
DEVOUR
DEVOUT
DEWALI
DEWITT
DEWLAP
DEXTER
DHARMA
DHOOTI
DIADEM
DIALOG
DIANAS
DIAPER
DIATOM
DIAXON
DIBBER
DIBBLE
DICAST
DICKER
DICKEY
DICTUM
DIDDLE
DIEPPE
DIESEL
DIESIS
DIETER
DIFFER
DIGEST
DIGGER
DIGLOT
DIKDIK
DIKKOP
DIKTAT
DILATE
DILUTE
DIMITY
DIMMER
DIMPLE
DIMWIT
DINERO
DINGHY
DINGLE
DINGLY
DINING
DINKUM
DINNER
DIODON
DIOXIN
DIPLOE
DIPNOI
DIPOLE
DIPPER
DIQUAT
DIRECT
DIRHAM
DIRNDL
DISARM
DISBAR
DISBUD
DISCUS

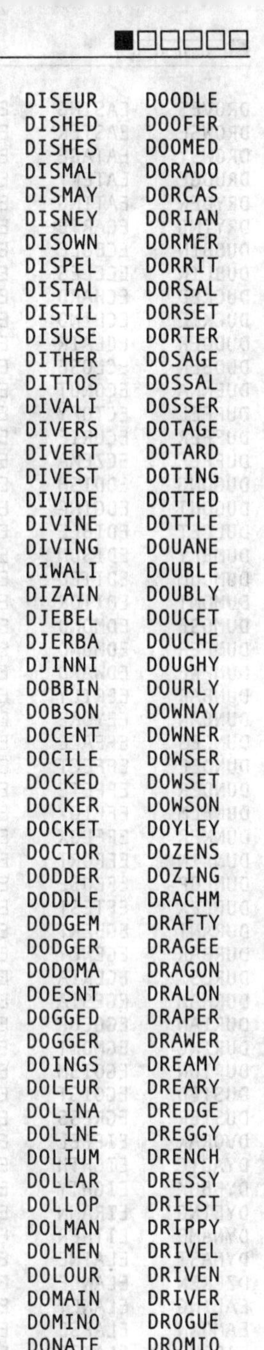

DISEUR
DISHED
DISHES
DISMAL
DISMAY
DISNEY
DISOWN
DISPEL
DISTAL
DISTIL
DISUSE
DITHER
DITTOS
DIVALI
DIVERS
DIVERT
DIVEST
DIVIDE
DIVINE
DIVING
DIWALI
DIZAIN
DJEBEL
DJERBA
DJINNI
DOBBIN
DOBSON
DOCENT
DOCILE
DOCKED
DOCKER
DOCKET
DOCTOR
DODDER
DODDLE
DODGEM
DODGER
DODOMA
DOESNT
DOGGED
DOGGER
DOINGS
DOLEUR
DOLINA
DOLINE
DOLIUM
DOLLAR
DOLLOP
DOLMAN
DOLMEN
DOLOUR
DOMAIN
DOMINO
DONATE
DONGLE
DONJON
DONKEY
DONNÉE
DONZEL
DOODAD
DOODAH
DOODLE
DOOFER
DOOMED
DORADO
DORCAS
DORIAN
DORMER
DORRIT
DORSAL
DORSET
DORTER
DOSAGE
DOSSAL
DOSSER
DOTAGE
DOTARD
DOTING
DOTTED
DOTTLE
DOUANE
DOUBLE
DOUBLY
DOUCET
DOUCHE
DOUGHY
DOURLY
DOWNAY
DOWNER
DOWSER
DOWSET
DOWSON
DOYLEY
DOZENS
DOZING
DRACHM
DRAFTY
DRAGEE
DRAGON
DRALON
DRAPER
DRAWER
DREAMY
DREARY
DREDGE
DREGGY
DRENCH
DRESSY
DRIEST
DRIPPY
DRIVEL
DRIVEN
DRIVER
DROGUE
DROMIO
DROMOS
DRONES
DRONGO
DROOPY
DROPSY
DROSKY
DROVER

DROVES
DROWSE
DROWSY
DRUDGE
DRYDEN
DRYING
DUBBIN
DUBLIN
DUCKED
DUCKIE
DUDDER
DUDEEN
DUENNA
DUFFEL
DUFFER
DUFFLE
DUGONG
DUGOUT
DULCET
DUMBLY
DUMDUM
DUMONT
DUMOSE
DUMPER
DUMPLE
DUNBAR
DUNCAN
DUNCES
DUNDEE
DUNDER
DUNELM
DUNKER
DUNLIN
DUNLOP
DUPLEX
DURANT
DURBAR
DURESS
DURHAM
DURIAN
DURING
DURION
DUSTED
DUSTER
DVORAK
DYADIC
DYBBUK
DYEING
DYNAMO
DYNAST
DZEREN
EALING
EAMONN
EARFUL
EARING
EARNED
EARNER
EARTHY
EARWIG
EASIER
EASILY
EASING
EASTER
EATAGE
EATERY
EATING
ECARTÉ
ECBOLE
ECCLES
ECHARD
ECHINO
ECLAIR
ECLOSE
ECONUT
ECTOPY
ECURIE
ECZEMA
EDDISH
EDGING
EDIBLE
EDISON
EDITED
EDITOR
EDMOND
EDMUND
EDWARD
EERILY
EEYORE
EFFACE
EFFECT
EFFETE
EFFIGY
EFFLUX
EFFORT
EFFUSE
EFTEST
EGBERT
EGENCY
EGERIA
EGESTA
EGGCUP
EGMONT
EGOISM
EGOIST
EGRESS
EIFFEL
EIGHTH
EIGHTY
EIRANN
EITHER
ELAINE
ELANCE
ELANET
ELAPSE
ELATED
ELBRUS
ELDERS
ELDEST
ELEVEN
ELFISH
ELICIT
ELIJAH
ELISHA
ELIXIR
ELLERY
ELLICE
ELODEA
ELOHIM
ELOIGN
ELOISE
ELOPER
ELTCHI
ELUANT
ELUATE
ELUTOR
ELYSEE
EMBAIL
EMBALE
EMBALM
EMBARK
EMBERS
EMBLEM
EMBODY
EMBOSS
EMBRUE
EMBRYO
EMBUSY
EMERGE
EMETIC
EMEUTE
EMIGRÉ
EMPIRE
EMPLOY
EMULGE
EMUNGE
ENABLE
ENAMEL
ENAMOR
ENARCH
ENCALM
ENCAMP
ENCASE
ENCASH
ENCODE
ENCORE
ENDEAR
ENDING
ENDIVE
ENDURE
ENERGY
ENFIRE
ENFOLD
ENFREE
ENGAGE
ENGELS
ENGINE
ENGLUT
ENGULF
ENIGMA
ENJOIN
ENLACE
ENLIST
ENMESH
ENMITY
ENNIUS
ENODAL
ENOSIS
ENOUGH
ENRAGE
ENRAPT
ENRICH
ENROBE
ENROLL
ENSATE
ENSEAL
ENSIGN
ENSILE
ENSURE
ENTAIL
ENTICE
ENTIRE
ENTITY
ENTOMB
ENTRAP
ENTREE
ENWRAP
ENZIAN
ENZYME
EOCENE
EOLITH
EOTHEN
EOZOON
EPARCH
EPAULE
EPERDU
EPHEBE
EPICAL
EPIGON
EPILOG
EPIRUS
EPONYM
EPOPEE
EPPING
EPRISE
EPULIS
EQUALS
EQUANT
EQUATE
EQUINE
EQUIPE
EQUITY
ERASED
ERASER
ERBIUM
EREBUS
EREMIC
ERINYS
ERMINE
ERMITE
ERNANI
ERODED
EROICA
EROTIC
ERRAND
ERRANT
ERSATZ
ESCAPE
ESCARP
ESCHAR
ESCHEW
ESCORT
ESCROC
ESCROW
ESCUDO
ESKIMO
ESPADA
ESPRIT
ESSENE
ESTATE
ESTEEM
ESTHER
ESTRAY
ETALON
ETCHER
ETHANE
ETHENE
ETHICS
ETHIOP
ETHNIC
ETRIER
ETYMON
EUBOEA
EUCHRE
EUCLID
EUGENE
EULOGY
EUNUCH
EUREKA
EUROPA
EUROPE
EUSTON
EUTAXY
EUXINE
EVELYN
EVENLY
EVINCE
EVOLUÉ
EVOLVE
EVULSE
EVZONE
EXARCH
EXCEED
EXCEPT
EXCESS
EXCISE
EXCITE
EXCUSE
EXEDRA
EXEMPT
EXETER
EXHALE
EXHORT
EXHUME
EXISTS
EXMOOR
EXOCET
EXODUS
EXOGEN
EXOTIC
EXPAND
EXPECT
EXPEDE
EXPEND
EXPERT
EXPIRE
EXPIRY
EXPORT
EXPOSE
EXPUGN
EXSERT
EXTANT
EXTEND
EXTENT
EXTERN
EXTIRP
EXTOLL
EXTORT
EYEFUL
EYELET
EYELID
FABIAN
FABIUS
FABLED
FABLES
FABRIC
FACADE
FACIAL
FACIES
FACILE
FACING
FACTOR
FACTUM
FADING
FAECAL
FAECES
FAGGED
FAGGOT
FAIBLE
FAINTS
FAIRLY
FAKING
FALCON
FALLEN
FALLOW
FALTER
FAMILY
FAMINE
FAMISH
FAMOUS
FANGLE
FANION
FANTAN
FARAND
FARCIN
FARDEL
FARDLE
FARINA
FARMER
FAROFF
FAROUK
FARROW
FASCES
FASCIA
FASTEN
FATHER
FATHOM
FATIMA
FATTEN
FAUCES
FAUCET
FAULTY
FAUNUS
FAVELA
FAVISM
FAVOSE
FAVOUR
FAWKES
FEALTY
FECULA
FECUND
FEDORA
FEEBLE
FEEBLY
FEEDER
FEELER
FEERIE
FEINTS
FEISTY
FELINE
FELLER
FELLOE
FELLOW
FELONY
FEMALE
FENCER
FENDER
FENIAN
FENNEL
FERIAL
FERMAT
FERRET
FERRIS
FERULA
FERULE
FERVID
FERVOR
FESCUE
FESTAL
FESTER
FETISH
FETTER
FETTES
FETTLE
FEUDAL
FEWEST
FIACRE
FIANCÉ

FIASCO
FIBBED
FIBBER
FIBULA
FICKLE
FIDDLE
FIDDLY
FIDGET
FIELDS
FIERCE
FIESTA
FIGARO
FIGURE
FILFOT
FILIAL
FILING
FILLED
FILLER
FILLET
FILLIP
FILOSE
FILTER
FILTHY
FILTRÉ
FIMBRA
FINALE
FINDER
FINELY
FINERY
FINEST
FINGAL
FINGER
FINIAL
FINISH
FINITE
FINLAY
FINNAN
FIPPLE
FIRING
FIRKIN
FIRLOT
FIRMAN
FIRMER
FIRMLY
FISCAL
FISHER
FITFUL
FITOUT
FITTED
FITTER
FIXITY
FIZGIG
FIZZED
FIZZER
FIZZLE
FLABBY
FLACON
FLAGGY
FLAGON
FLAMBÉ
FLAMEN
FLANCH
FLANGE
FLANKS
FLARES
FLASHY
FLATLY
FLATUS
FLAUNT
FLAVOR
FLAWED
FLAXEN
FLECHE
FLEDGE
FLEECE
FLEECY
FLENSE
FLESHY
FLETCH
FLEURY
FLICKS
FLIGHT
FLIMSY
FLINCH
FLINTY
FLITCH
FLOOZY
FLOPPY
FLORAL
FLORET
FLORID
FLORIN
FLOSSY
FLOURY
FLOUSH
FLOWER
FLUENT
FLUFFY
FLUNKY
FLURRY
FLUSHY
FLUTED
FLUTER
FLUTES
FLYING
FOCSLE
FODDER
FOETAL
FOETID
FOETUS
FOIBLE
FOILED
FOKINE
FOKKER
FOLDED
FOLDER
FOLIAR
FOLIOS
FOLIOT
FOLIUM
FOLKSY
FOLLOW
FOMENT
FONDLE
FONDLY
FONDUE
FOOTER
FOOTLE
FOOZLE
FORAGE
FORBID
FORÇAT
FORCED
FORCES
FOREDO
FOREGO
FOREST
FORGED
FORGER
FORGET
FORGOT
FORINT
FORKED
FORMAL
FORMAT
FORMER
FORMIC
FORNAX
FORNIX
FORPIT
FORRAD
FORRAY
FORSAY
FORTHY
FOSSIL
FOSTER
FOUGHT
FOULLY
FOURTH
FOUTRE
FOWLER
FRACAS
FRAGOR
FRAISE
FRAMED
FRANCE
FRANCK
FRANCO
FRANZY
FRAPPÉ
FRATER
FRAYED
FREELY
FREEZE
FRENCH
FRENUM
FRENZY
FRESCO
FRIAND
FRIARY
FRIDAY
FRIDGE
FRIEND
FRIEZE
FRIGGA
FRIGHT
FRIGID
FRILLS
FRILLY
FRINGE
FRIPON
FRISKY
FRIVOL
FRIZZY
FROLIC
FRONDE
FROSTY
FROTHY
FROUDE
FROWST
FROWZY
FROZEN
FRUGAL
FRUICT
FRUITS
FRUITY
FRUMPY
FRUTEX
FRYING
FUDDLE
FUGATO
FUHRER
FULFIL
FULGID
FULHAM
FULLER
FULMAR
FUMADO
FUMBLE
FUNDED
FUNDUS
FUNGAL
FUNGUS
FUNNEL
FUREUR
FURFUR
FURIES
FURORE
FURPHY
FURROW
FUSAIN
FUSELI
FUSION
FUSTIC
FUSTOC
FUTILE
FUTURE
FUZZLE
FYLFOT
GABBLE
GABBRO
GABION
GABLED
GADFLY
GADGET
GADOID
GAELIC
GAFFER
GAGGLE
GAIETY
GAIJIN
GAINER
GAINLY
GAITER
GALANT
GALAXY
GALENA
GALERE
GALIOT
GALLEN
GALLET
GALLEY
GALLIC
GALLIO
GALLON
GALLOP
GALLOW
GALLUP
GALLUS
GALOOT
GALORE
GALOSH
GAMBET
GAMBIA
GAMBIT
GAMBLE
GAMBOL
GAMELY
GAMETE
GAMINE
GAMING
GAMMER
GAMMON
GANDER
GANDHI
GANGER
GANGES
GANGLY
GANGUE
GANION
GANNET
GANTRY
GAOLER
GAPING
GARAGE
GARBED
GARBLE
GARÇON
GARDEN
GARETH
GARGET
GARGLE
GARISH
GARLIC
GARNER
GARNET
GARRET
GARROT
GARRYA
GARTER
GARUDA
GASBAG
GASCON
GASKET
GASMAN
GASPAR
GASPER
GASSER
GASTER
GASTON
GATEAU
GATHER
GAUCHE
GAUCHO
GAUFRE
GAUGER
GAVAGE
GAVIAL
GAWAIN
GAZEBO
GAZUMP
GEASON
GEEZER
GEIGER
GEISHA
GELADA
GELATO
GELLER
GEMINI
GEMMAN
GENDER
GENERA
GENEVA
GENIAL
GENIUS
GENOME
GENTES
GENTLE
GENTLY
GENTRY
GEORGE
GERBIL
GERENT
GERMAN
GERUND
GETTER
GEWGAW
GEYSER
GHARRY
GHAZAL
GHEBER
GHERAO
GHETTO
GHOSTS
GIAOUR
GIBBER
GIBBET
GIBBON
GIBSON
GIDDUP
GIDEON
GIFTED
GIGGLE
GIGLET
GIGLOT
GIGOLO
GILDAS
GILDED
GILDER
GILEAD
GILGAI
GILLET
GILLIE
GILPIN
GIMLET
GIMMER
GINGER
GINGKO
GINKGO
GIORGI
GIOTTO
GIRDER
GIRDLE
GIRKIN
GIRLIE
GIRTON
GITANO
GIUSTO
GIVING
GIZZEN
GLACIS
GLADLY
GLAGOL
GLAIRE
GLAIVE
GLAMIS
GLAMOR
GLANCE
GLASSY
GLAZED
GLIBLY
GLIDER
GLIÈRE
GLINKA
GLIOMA
GLITCH
GLITZY
GLOBAL
GLOIRE
GLOOMY
GLORIA
GLOSSA
GLOSSY
GLOVED
GLOWER
GLUMPS
GLUTEN

GLYCOL
GNAWER
GNEISS
GNOMIC
GNOMON
GOALIE
GOANNA
GOATEE
GOBBET
GOBBLE
GOBLET
GOBLIN
GOCART
GODIVA
GODOWN
GODSON
GODWIN
GODWIT
GOETHE
GOFFER
GOGGLE
GOITER
GOITRE
GOKART
GOLDEN
GOLFER
GOLLOP
GOLOSH
GONION
GONIUM
GOOBER
GOODLY
GOOGIE
GOOGLE
GOOGLY
GOOGOL
GOOLEY
GOOLIE
GOPHER
GORDON
GORGED
GORGES
GORGET
GORGIA
GORGIO
GORGON
GORING
GOSPEL
GOSSIP
GOTHAM
GOTHIC
GOTTEN
GOUNOD
GOURDE
GOURDS
GOUTTE
GOVERN
GRABEN
GRACES
GRADED
GRADES
GRADUS
GRAFIN
GRAHAM
GRAINS
GRAINY
GRAMME
GRAMMY
GRAMPS
GRANBY
GRANGE
GRANNY
GRANTA
GRAPES
GRAPPA
GRASSY
GRATED
GRATER
GRATIN
GRATIS
GRAVEL
GRAVEN
GRAVER
GRAVES
GRAVID
GREASE
GREASY
GREATS
GREAVE
GREECE
GREEDY
GREEKS
GREENE
GREENS
GRETNA
GREUZE
GRIEVE
GRIGRI
GRILLE
GRILSE
GRIMES
GRIMLY
GRIMMS
GRINGO
GRIPES
GRIPPE
GRISLY
GRISON
GRITTY
GROATS
GROCER
GROGGY
GROOVE
GROOVY
GROPER
GROSSO
GROTTO
GROTTY
GROUCH
GROUND
GROUPS
GROUSE
GROUTS
GROUTY
GROVEL
GROWER
GROWTH
GROYNE
GRUBBY
GRUDGE
GRUMPH
GRUMPS
GRUMPY
GRUNDY
GRUNGE
GRUTCH
GRYFON
GUARDI
GUARDS
GUBBAH
GUELPH
GUENON
GUESTS
GUFFAW
GUGGLE
GUIANA
GUIDES
GUIDON
GUILDS
GUILTY
GUINEA
GUITAR
GULLAH
GULLET
GULLEY
GULPER
GUMMED
GUNDOG
GUNGHO
GUNMAN
GUNNEL
GUNNER
GUNTER
GURGLE
GURKHA
GURLET
GURNET
GURNEY
GUSHER
GUSLAR
GUSSET
GUTTER
GUTTLE
GUYANA
GUZZLE
GYPSUM
GYRATE
HABILE
HACHIS
HACKEE
HACKER
HACKLE
HAEMAL
HAEMON
HAGDEN
HAGGAI
HAGGIS
HAGGLE
HAILER
HAIRDO
HALIDE
HALITE
HALLAL
HALLEY
HALLOO
HALLOW
HALLUX
HALOID
HALTER
HALVED
HALVES
HAMATE
HAMBLE
HAMITE
HAMLET
HAMMAM
HAMMER
HAMOSE
HAMPER
HANDEL
HANDLE
HANGAR
HANGER
HANGUP
HANKER
HANKIE
HANNAH
HANSOM
HAPPEN
HAPTEN
HAPTIC
HARARE
HARASS
HARBOR
HARDEN
HARDLY
HARKEN
HARLOT
HARMED
HAROLD
HARPIC
HARRIS
HARROW
HARVEY
HASHED
HASLET
HASSAR
HASSLE
HASTEN
HATING
HATRED
HATTER
HAUNCH
HAVANA
HAVENT
HAVERS
HAVING
HAWAII
HAWKED
HAWKER
HAWSER
HAYBOX
HAYDON
HAYLEY
HAYMOW
HAZARD
HAZILY
HEADED
HEADER
HEALER
HEALTH
HEAPED
HEARER
HEARSE
HEARTH
HEARTS
HEARTY
HEATED
HEATER
HEAUME
HEAVED
HEAVEN
HEAVES
HEBREW
HECATE
HECKLE
HECTIC
HECTOR
HECUBA
HEDERA
HEEDED
HEEHAW
HEELED
HEGIRA
HEIFER
HEIGHT
HEJIRA
HELENA
HELIOS
HELIUM
HELLER
HELMET
HELPER
HEMPEN
HENBIT
HENLEY
HENNIN
HENSON
HEPTAD
HERALD
HERBAL
HERDEN
HERDER
HEREBY
HEREIN
HERERO
HERESY
HERETO
HERIOT
HERMES
HERMIT
HERMON
HERNIA
HEROIC
HEROIN
HERONS
HERPES
HERREN
HESIOD
HETERO
HETMAN
HEXANE
HEXOSE
HEYDAY
HIATUS
HICCUP
HICKEY
HIDAGE
HIDDEN
HIDING
HIGHER
HIGHLY
HIGHUP
HIJACK
HIKING
HILARY
HILTON
HIMMEL
HINDER
HINGED
HINGES
HIPPED
HIPPUS
HIRING
HIRSEL
HISPID
HITECH
HITHER
HITLER
HITMAN
HITTER
HOARSE
HOAXER
HOBART
HOBBES
HOBBLE
HOBDAY
HOBNOB
HOCKEY
HODDER
HOGGAR
HOGGET
HOGTIE
HOIDEN
HOLDER
HOLDUP
HOLISM
HOLIST
HOLLER
HOLLOW
HOLMES
HOMAGE
HOMBRE
HOMELY
HOMILY
HOMING
HOMINY
HONCHO
HONEST
HONIED
HONOUR
HONSHU
HOODED
HOOFED
HOOFER
HOOHAH
HOOKAH
HOOKED
HOOKER
HOOKEY
HOOKUP
HOOPER
HOOPLA
HOOPOE
HOORAH
HOORAY
HOOTCH
HOOTER
HOOVER
HOPPER
HORACE
HORMUZ
HORNED
HORNER
HORNET
HORRID
HORROR
HORSED
HOSIER
HOSING
HOSTEL
HOTAIR
HOTBED
HOTPOT
HOTTER
HOUDAH
HOUNDS
HOURLY
HOUSES
HOWARD
HOWDAH
HOWDIE
HOWLER
HOYDEN
HUBBLE
HUBBUB
HUBRIS

HUCKLE
HUDDLE
HUDSON
HUGELY
HUGHES
HUGHIE
HULLED
HUMANE
HUMBER
HUMBLE
HUMBUG
HUMECT
HUMITE
HUMMEL
HUMMER
HUMMUS
HUMOUR
HUMPED
HUMPTY
HUNGER
HUNGRY
HUNKER
HUNTER
HURDLE
HURLEY
HURRAH
HURRAY
HURTLE
HUSHED
HUSSAR
HUSSIF
HUSTLE
HUXLEY
HUZZAH
HYADES
HYAENA
HYBRID
HYBRIS
HYDRAX
HYDRIA
HYMNAL
HYPATE
HYPHAL
HYPHEN
HYPNIC
HYPNOS
HYPNUM
HYSSOP
IAMBIC
IAMBUS
IBADAN
IBERIA
IBIDEM
ICARUS
ICEBOX
ICEMAN
ICICLE
ICONIC
IDIOCY
IFFISH
IGNITE
IGNORE
IGUANA
ILKLEY
ILLITE
ILLUDE
IMBARN
IMBASE
IMBIBE
IMBOSS
IMBRUE
IMMUNE
IMMURE
IMOGEN
IMPACT
IMPAIR
IMPALA
IMPALE
IMPART
IMPAWN
IMPEDE
IMPEND
IMPISH
IMPORT
IMPOSE
IMPOST
IMPUGN
IMPURE
IMPUTE
INBORN
INBRED
INCASE
INCEDE
INCEPT
INCEST
INCHES
INCHON
INCISE
INCITE
INCOME
INDABA
INDEED
INDENT
INDIAN
INDICT
INDIES
INDIGN
INDIGO
INDITE
INDIUM
INDOOR
INDUCE
INDUCT
INFAME
INFAMY
INFANT
INFARE
INFECT
INFEST
INFIRM
INFLOW
INFLUX
INFOLD
INFORM
INFUSE
INGATE
INGEST
INGOTS
INGRAM
INGRES
INGROW
INGULF
INHALE
INHERE
INHUME
INJECT
INJURE
INJURY
INKJET
INKPOT
INLAID
INLAND
INLAWS
INLINE
INMATE
INMESH
INMOST
INNATE
INNING
INROAD
INRUSH
INSANE
INSECT
INSERT
INSIDE
INSIST
INSOLE
INSTAL
INSTAR
INSTEP
INSTIL
INSULA
INSULT
INSURE
INTACT
INTAKE
INTEND
INTENT
INTERN
INTIME
INTONE
INTOWN
INTRAY
INTRON
INVADE
INVENT
INVERT
INVEST
INVITE
INVOKE
INWARD
IODINE
IODIZE
IOLITE
IONIAN
IONIZE
IPECAC
IRAQIS
IREFUL
IRETON
IRONED
IRONIC
IRRUPT
IRVING
IRWELL
ISABEL
ISAIAH
ISCHIA
ISEULT
ISHTAR
ISLAND
ISLETS
ISOBAR
ISOLDE
ISOMER
ISOPOD
ISRAEL
ISSUES
ISTRIA
ITALIC
ITCHEN
ITERUM
ITHACA
ITSELF
IZZARD
JABBER
JABBLE
JABIRU
JACANA
JACENT
JACKAL
JACKET
JACOBS
JAEGER
JAGGED
JAGGER
JAGUAR
JAILER
JAILOR
JALOPY
JAMBOK
JAMBON
JAMMED
JAMPOT
JANGLE
JARGON
JARVEY
JASPER
JAUNTY
JAWBOX
JAZZER
JEEVES
JEJUNE
JEKYLL
JEMIMA
JENNER
JENNET
JERBOA
JEREMY
JERKER
JERKIN
JEROME
JERSEY
JESTER
JESUIT
JETHRO
JETLAG
JETSAM
JETTON
JEWELS
JEWESS
JEWISH
JIBBAH
JIGGER
JIGGLE
JIGSAW
JILLET
JIMJAM
JINGAL
JINGLE
JINXED
JISSOM
JITNEY
JITTER
JOANNA
JOBBER
JOCKEY
JOCOSE
JOCUND
JOGGER
JOGGLE
JOHNNY
JOINER
JOJOBA
JONSON
JOPLIN
JORDAN
JOSEPH
JOSHUA
JOSIAH
JOSKIN
JOSSER
JOSTLE
JOTTER
JOVIAL
JOYFUL
JOYOUS
JUBATE
JUBBAH
JUDDER
JUDGES
JUDICA
JUGGER
JUGGLE
JUJUBE
JULIAN
JULIET
JULIUS
JUMBAL
JUMBLE
JUMPER
JUNCUS
JUNGLE
JUNIOR
JUNKER
JUNKET
JUNKIE
JURANT
JURIST
JUSTIN
JUSTLY
KABAKA
KABELE
KABUKI
KABYLE
KAFFER
KAFFIR
KAFTAN
KAISER
KAKAPO
KALMIA
KALPAK
KANAKA
KANOON
KANSAS
KANTEN
KANTHA
KANUCK
KAOLIN
KAPUTT
KARATE
KARIBA
KARITE
KASBAH
KATANA
KAZAKH
KEATON
KEBELE
KECKSY
KEDDAH
KEELER
KEENER
KEENLY
KEEPER
KELLYS
KELOID
KELPER
KELPIE
KELTER
KELTIC
KELTIE
KELVIN
KENDAL
KENNEL
KENNET
KENSAL
KENYAN
KEPHIR
KEPLER
KERALA
KERMES
KERMIS
KERNEL
KETMIR
KETONE
KETOSE
KETTLE
KEVLAR
KEWPIE
KEYNES
KEYPAD
KEYWAY
KHALAT
KHALIF
KHALSA
KHARIF
KHILAT
KHILIM
KHYBER
KIAORA
KIBBLE
KIBOSH
KICKER
KIDDIE
KIDDLE
KIDNAP
KIDNEY
KIGALI
KIKUYU
KILLER
KILNER
KILTED
KILTER
KILTIE
KIMMER
KIMONO
KINASE
KINDER
KINDLE
KINDLY
KINGLY
KIPPER
KIRBEH
KIRMAN
KIRSCH
KIRTLE
KISMET
KISSEL
KISSER
KITBAG
KITCAT
KITSCH
KITTEN
KITTLE
KLAXON
KLUDGE
KNAGGY

KNIGHT
KNIVES
KNOBBY
KNOTTY
KODIAK
KOMODO
KOODOO
KOOKIE
KOOLAH
KOREAN
KORUNA
KOSHER
KOSMOS
KOTWAL
KOUROS
KOWTOW
KRAKEN
KRANTZ
KRATER
KRATON
KRONER
KRONOS
KRUGER
KRUMAN
KUFIAH
KUMARA
KUMERA
KUMISS
KUMMEL
KVETCH
KWACHA
KWANZA
KYBOSH
KYUSHU
LAAGER
LABIAL
LABILE
LABIUM
LABLAB
LABOUR
LABRUM
LABRYS
LACHES
LACING
LACKEY
LACTIC
LACUNA
LADAKH
LADDER
LADDIE
LADIES
LADING
LADOGA
LAFFER
LAGOON
LAGUNA
LAGUNE
LAICAL
LAISSE
LALLAN
LAMBDA
LAMELY
LAMENT
LAMINA
LAMMAS
LAMMER
LANATE
LANCER
LANCET
LANCIA
LANDAU
LANDED
LANDER
LANDOR
LANUGO
LAPDOG
LAPITH
LAPPER
LAPPET
LAPSED
LAPSUS
LAPTOP
LAPUTA
LARDER
LARDON
LARIAT
LARKIN
LARRUP
LARVAE
LARVAL
LARYNX
LASCAR
LASHED
LASHER
LASKET
LASSIE
LASSUS
LASTLY
LATEEN
LATELY
LATENT
LATEST
LATHER
LATRON
LATTEN
LATTER
LATVIA
LAUDER
LAUNCE
LAUNCH
LAUREL
LAURIC
LAURIE
LAVABO
LAVAGE
LAVISH
LAWFUL
LAWMAN
LAWYER
LAXIST
LAXITY
LAYARD
LAYERS
LAYING
LAYMAN
LAYOFF
LAYOUT
LAZILY
LEADEN
LEADER
LEAGUE
LEALTY
LEANTO
LEAVEN
LEAVER
LEAVES
LECHER
LECTOR
LEDGER
LEEWAY
LEGACY
LEGATE
LEGATO
LEGEND
LEGGED
LEGION
LEGIST
LEGLET
LEGMAN
LEGUME
LEMNOS
LEMONY
LEMUEL
LEMURE
LENDER
LENGTH
LENTEL
LENTEN
LENTIC
LENTIL
LENTOR
LEONID
LEPTON
LESBOS
LESION
LESLIE
LESSEE
LESSEN
LESSER
LESSON
LESSOR
LESTER
LETHAL
LETOUT
LETTER
LEVANT
LEVITE
LEVITY
LEWDLY
LEXEME
LEYDEN
LHOTSE
LIABLE
LIAISE
LIBBER
LIBIDO
LIBYAN
LICHEN
LICTOR
LIEBIG
LIEDER
LIERNE
LIFTED
LIFTER
LIGASE
LIGATE
LIGETI
LIGGER
LIGHTS
LIGNUM
LIGULA
LIGURE
LIKELY
LIKING
LILIAN
LILITH
LIMBED
LIMBER
LIMBIC
LIMITS
LIMNER
LIMPET
LIMPID
LIMPLY
LINDEN
LINEAL
LINEAR
LINEUP
LINGER
LINGOT
LINING
LINKER
LINKUP
LINNET
LINTEL
LIONEL
LIPARI
LIPASE
LIPIDE
LIPOMA
LIPPED
LIQUID
LIQUOR
LISBON
LISPER
LISSOM
LISTEL
LISTEN
LISTER
LITANY
LITCHI
LITHIA
LITMUS
LITTER
LITTLE
LIVELY
LIVERY
LIVING
LIZARD
LIZZIE
LLOYDS
LOADED
LOADER
LOAFER
LOATHE
LOAVES
LOCALE
LOCATE
LOCHIA
LOCKED
LOCKER
LOCKET
LOCKUP
LOCULE
LOCUST
LODGED
LODGER
LOGGER
LOGGIA
LOGJAM
LOITER
LOLITA
LOLIUM
LOLLOP
LOMOND
LONDON
LONELY
LONGER
LOOFAH
LOONIE
LOOPED
LOOPER
LOOSEN
LOOTER
LOQUAT
LORCHA
LORDLY
LORETO
LORICA
LORIOT
LOSING
LOTION
LOUCHE
LOUDEN
LOUDLY
LOUNGE
LOURIE
LOUVER
LOUVRE
LOVAGE
LOVELL
LOVELY
LOVING
LOWBOY
LOWELL
LOWEST
LOWKEY
LOYOLA
LUANDA
LUBBER
LUBRIC
LUCENT
LUCIAN
LUCINA
LUDWIG
LUGANO
LUGGER
LUMBAR
LUMBER
LUMINA
LUMMOX
LUMPUR
LUNACY
LUNARY
LUNATE
LUNULE
LUPINE
LURING
LURIST
LUSAKA
LUSTER
LUSTRE
LUTEAL
LUTEIN
LUTHER
LUTINE
LUTIST
LUXATE
LUXURY
LUZERN
LYCEUM
LYCHEE
LYCOSA
LYDIAN
LYMPNE
LYRICS
LYRIST
LYTTON
MACRON
MACULA
MACULE
MADAME
MADCAP
MADDEN
MADDER
MADEUP
MADMAN
MADRAS
MADRID
MADURA
MADURO
MAENAD
MAFFIA
MAGGIE
MAGGOT
MAGLEV
MAGNES
MAGNET
MAGNON
MAGNUM
MAGNUS
MAGPIE
MAGYAR
MAHLER
MAHOUT
MAIDAN
MAIDEN
MAILER
MAINLY
MAINOR
MAÎTRE
MAJLIS
MAKEUP
MAKING
MALAGA
MALATE
MALAWI
MALDON
MALGRE
MALIAN
MALIBU
MALICE
MALIGN
MALLAM
MALLEE
MALLET
MALLOW
MALONE
MALONY
MALORY
MALTED
MAMMAL
MAMMON
MAMZER
MANAGE
MANANA
MANATI
MANCHE
MANCHU
MANEGE
MANFUL
MANGER
MANGLE
MANIAC
MANILA
MANIOC
MANITO
MANNER
MANNIN
MANQUÉ
MANTIS
MANTLE
MANTRA
MANTUA
MANUAL
MANURE
MAOIST

MAOTAI
MAPUTO
MAQUIS
MARACA
MARAUD
MARBLE
MARCEL
MARGIN
MARIAN
MARINA
MARINE
MARISH
MARIST
MARKED
MARKER
MARKET
MARKKA
MARKUP
MARLIN
MARMOT
MARNER
MAROON
MARQUE
MARRAM
MARRON
MARROW
MARSHY
MARTEL
MARTEN
MARTHA
MARTIN
MARTYR
MARVEL
MASADA
MASCOT
MASHAM
MASHED
MASHER
MASHIE
MASKED
MASLIN
MASQUE
MASSED
MASSES
MASSIF
MASTER
MASTIC
MATHIS
MATING
MATINS
MATLOW
MATRIX
MATRON
MATTED
MATTER
MATURE
MAUGRE
MAUNDY
MAUSER
MAWKIN
MAXIMS
MAYBUG
MAYDAY
MAYFLY
MAYHEM
MAZOUT
MAZUMA
MEADOW
MEAGER
MEAGRE
MEALIE
MEANIE
MEANLY
MEASLY
MEATUS
MEDDLE
MEDIAL
MEDIAN
MEDICI
MEDICO
MEDINA
MEDISM
MEDIUM
MEDIUS
MEDLAR
MEDLEY
MEDUSA
MEDWAY
MEEKLY
MEGRIM
MEJLIS
MEKONG
MELIUS
MELLOW
MELODY
MELTED
MELTON
MEMBER
MEMNON
MEMOIR
MEMORY
MENACE
MENAGE
MENDEL
MENDER
MENDES
MENDIP
MENHIR
MENIAL
MENINX
MENSAL
MENTAL
MENTOR
MENTUM
MERCAT
MERCER
MERCIA
MERELY
MERGER
MERINO
MERKIN
MERLIN
MERLOT
MERMAN
MEROPE
MERRIE
MERROW
MERSEY
MERTON
MESAIL
MESCAL
MESIAL
MESMER
MESSRS
METAGE
METATE
METEOR
METHOD
METHYL
METIER
METOPE
METRIC
METTLE
MEXICO
MIASMA
MICKEY
MICKLE
MICMAC
MICRON
MIDDAY
MIDDEN
MIDDLE
MIDGET
MIDWAY
MIGHTY
MIGNON
MIKADO
MILADY
MILDEW
MILDLY
MILIEU
MILLER
MILLET
MILORD
MILTON
MIMOSA
MINCER
MINDED
MINDEL
MINDER
MINGLE
MINING
MINION
MINNIE
MINNOW
MINOAN
MINTON
MINUET
MINUTE
MIRAGE
MIRROR
MISÈRE
MISERY
MISFIT
MISHAP
MISHIT
MISLAY
MISLED
MISSAL
MISSED
MISSEL
MISSIS
MISSUS
MISTER
MISUSE
MITRAL
MITRED
MITTEN
MIZZEN
MIZZLE
MOANER
MOATED
MOBCAP
MOBILE
MOBIUS
MOCKER
MOCKUP
MODELS
MODENA
MODERN
MODEST
MODIFY
MODISH
MODIST
MODIUS
MODULE
MOGGIE
MOHAIR
MOHAWK
MOHOCK
MOIDER
MOIETY
MOJAVE
MOLECH
MOLEST
MOLINE
MOLLAH
MOLLIE
MOLOCH
MOLTEN
MOMENT
MONACO
MONDAY
MONGER
MONGOL
MONIAL
MONICA
MONISM
MONIST
MONKEY
MONODY
MONROE
MONTEM
MONTHS
MOOCOW
MOOLAH
MOOMBA
MOPING
MOPISH
MOPPET
MOPSUS
MORALE
MORALS
MORASS
MORBID
MORBUS
MOREEN
MORGAN
MORGEN
MORGUE
MORION
MORMON
MORNAY
MORNED
MOROSE
MORRIS
MORROW
MORSEL
MORTAL
MORTAR
MORTEM
MOSAIC
MOSCOW
MOSLEM
MOSQUE
MOSSAD
MOSTLY
MOTHER
MOTILE
MOTION
MOTIVE
MOTLEY
MOTOWN
MOTTLE
MOUJIK
MOULDY
MOULIN
MOUSER
MOUSEY
MOUSSE
MOUTAN
MOUTER
MOUTON
MOVIES
MOVING
MOWING
MOZART
MOZZLE
MUCATE
MUCKER
MUCKLE
MUCOID
MUCOUS
MUDDER
MUDDLE
MUESLI
MUFFET
MUFFIN
MUFFLE
MUFLON
MUGGER
MULISH
MULLAH
MULLER
MULLET
MULTUM
MUMBLE
MUMMER
MUNICH
MUNIFY
MUNITE
MUNSHI
MUPPET
MURAGE
MURALS
MURDER
MURIEL
MURINE
MURLIN
MURMUR
MURPHY
MURRAM
MURRAY
MURRHA
MURRIN
MUSANG
MUSCAT
MUSCLE
MUSEUM
MUSING
MUSIVE
MUSKEG
MUSKET
MUSLIM
MUSLIN
MUSSEL
MUSTER
MUTANT
MUTATE
MUTELY
MUTINY
MUTTER
MUTTON
MUTUAL
MUZHIK
MUZZLE
MYELIN
MYELON
MYGALE
MYOGEN
MYOPIA
MYOPIC
MYOSIN
MYOSIS
MYRIAD
MYRTLE
MYSELF
MYSORE
MYSTIC
MYTHOS
NAEVUS
NAGANA
NAGARI
NAILED
NAILER
NALLAH
NAMELY
NANDOO
NANISM
NANKIN
NANSEN
NANTES
NAPALM
NAPERY
NAPIER
NAPKIN
NAPLES
NAPPER
NARROW
NASEBY
NASION
NASSAU
NASSER
NASTIC
NATANT
NATION
NATIVE
NATRON
NATTER
NATURE
NAUGHT
NAUSEA
NAUTCH
NAVAHO
NAVAJO
NEAPED
NEARBY
NEARER
NEARLY
NEATEN
NEATLY
NEBBUK
NEBECK
NEBISH
NEBULA
NEBULE
NECKAR
NECKED
NECTAR
NEEDED
NEEDLE
NEEDNT
NEFAST
NEGATE
NELLIE
NELSON
NEPALI

NEPETA
NEPHEW
NEREID
NEREUS
NERINE
NERIUM
NEROLI
NERVAL
NERVES
NERVII
NESSIE
NESSUS
NESTLE
NESTOR
NETHER
NETTLE
NEURAL
NEURON
NEUTER
NEVADA
NEWELL
NEWEST
NEWMAN
NEWTON
NIACIN
NIAMEY
NIBBLE
NICELY
NICENE
NICETY
NICKED
NICKEL
NICKER
NIDGET
NIDIFY
NIELLO
NIGGER
NIGGLE
NIGGLY
NIGHTS
NIGHTY
NIGNOG
NIKKEI
NILGAI
NILGAU
NILOTE
NIMBLE
NIMBLY
NIMBUS
NIMROD
NINETY
NINIAN
NIPPER
NIPPLE
NIPPON
NISSEN
NITERY
NITRIC
NITRYL
NITWIT
NIVOSE

NOBBLE
NOBBUT
NOBODY
NOCENT
NOCTUA
NODDED
NODDLE
NODOSE
NODULE
NOGGIN
NOMADE
NOMISM
NONAGE
NONARY
NONCOM
NOODLE
NOOKIE
NORDIC
NORMAL
NORMAN
NORROY
NORVIC
NORWAY
NOSILY
NOTARY
NOTATE
NOTICE
NOTIFY
NOTION
NOUGAT
NOUGHT
NOUNCE
NOVENA
NOVIAL
NOVICE
NOWISE
NOYADE
NOYOUS
NOZZLE
NUANCE
NUBBIN
NUBBLE
NUBILE
NUCULE
NUDISM
NUDIST
NUDITY
NUDNIK
NUGGAR
NUGGET
NULLAH
NUMBER
NUMBLY
NUMPTY
NUNCIO
NUTANT
NUTATE
NUTMEG
NUTTER
NUZZER
NUZZLE

NYANZA
NYLONS
OAFISH
OAKLEY
OAKNUT
OARLAP
OBECHE
OBELUS
OBERON
OBIISM
OBITAL
OBITER
OBJECT
OBLAST
OBLATE
OBLIGE
OBLONG
OBOIST
OBOLUS
OBSESS
OBTAIN
OBTECT
OBTEND
OBTUND
OBTUSE
OBVERT
OCCULT
OCCUPY
OCEANS
OCELOT
OCHONE
OCHREA
OCKERS
OCTANE
OCTANS
OCTANT
OCTAVE
OCTAVO
OCTROI
OCULAR
ODDITY
ODDSON
ODENSE
ODESSA
ODIOUS
OEDEMA
OENONE
OERLAY
OEUVRE
OFFCUT
OFFEND
OFFICE
OFFING
OFFISH
OFFSET
OGADEN
OGAMIC
OGRESS
OILCAN
OILERS
OILMAN

OILRIG
OLDISH
OLEATE
OLEFIN
OLENUS
OLIVER
OLIVET
OLIVIA
OMASUM
OMELET
OMENTA
OMERTA
OMNIUM
ONAGER
ONAGRA
ONCOME
ONCOST
ONDINE
ONEDIN
ONEGIN
ONEIDA
ONEMAN
ONEWAY
ONIONS
ONLINE
ONRUSH
ONSIDE
ONWARD
OOCYTE
OODLES
OOKPIK
OOLITE
OOLONG
OOMPAH
OPAQUE
OPENER
OPENLY
OPHISM
OPHITE
OPIATE
OPPOSE
OPPUGN
OPTICS
OPTIMA
OPTIME
OPTION
OPTOUT
ORACHE
ORACLE
ORALLY
ORANGE
ORATOR
ORBITA
ORCHID
ORCHIS
ORCINE
ORDAIN
ORDEAL
ORDERS
ORDURE
OREGON

OREXIS
ORGANS
ORGASM
ORGEAT
ORGONE
ORIANO
ORIENT
ORIGEN
ORIGIN
ORIOLE
ORISON
ORKNEY
ORMOLU
ORNATE
ORNERY
ORPHAN
ORPHIC
ORRERY
ORSINO
ORTEGA
ORWELL
OSBERT
OSIERY
OSIRIS
OSMIUM
OSMOSE
OSPREY
OSSIAN
OSSIFY
OSTEND
OSTIUM
OSTLER
OSTREA
OSWALD
OTALGY
OTELLO
OTHERS
OTIOSE
OTITIS
OTTAVA
OTTAWA
OULONG
OUNCES
OUNDLE
OURALI
OUTAGE
OUTBAR
OUTBID
OUTCRY
OUTFIT
OUTGAS
OUTING
OUTLAW
OUTLAY
OUTLET
OUTLIE
OUTPUT
OUTRUN
OUTSET
OUTTOP
OUTVIE

OUTWIT
OVERDO
OVERLY
OVIBOS
OWLCAR
OWLISH
OXALIC
OXALIS
OXFORD
OXGATE
OXHEAD
OXHIDE
OXTAIL
OXYGEN
OYSTER
PACIFY
PACKED
PACKER
PACKET
PADANG
PADDED
PADDLE
PADUAN
PAELLA
PAEONY
PAGODA
PAHARI
PAIDUP
PAINED
PAINTS
PAINTY
PAIRER
PAKHTI
PAKHTO
PAKHTU
PALACE
PALAIS
PALATE
PALING
PALLAH
PALLAS
PALLET
PALLID
PALLOR
PALMER
PALTRY
PAMELA
PAMIRS
PAMPAS
PAMPER
PAMYAT
PANADA
PANAMA
PANDER
PANDIT
PANFRY
PANOPE
PANTER
PANTON
PANTRY
PANZER

PAPACY
PAPAYA
PAPERS
PAPERY
PAPHOS
PAPIST
PAPULE
PARADE
PARAMO
PARANA
PARAPH
PARCEL
PARDIE
PARDON
PARENT
PARETO
PARGET
PARIAH
PARISH
PARITY
PARKED
PARKER
PARKIN
PARLEY
PARLOR
PARODY
PAROLE
PARROT
PARSEC
PARSEE
PARSON
PARTLY
PARTON
PARURE
PARVIS
PASCAL
PASHTO
PASHTU
PASQUE
PASSED
PASSES
PASSIM
PASTEL
PASTIL
PASTIS
PASTON
PASTOR
PASTRY
PATACA
PATCHY
PATENT
PATHAN
PATHIC
PATHOS
PATINA
PATMOS
PATOIS
PATROL
PATRON
PATTEN
PATTER

PATTON
PAUNCE
PAUNCH
PAUPER
PAVANE
PAVING
PAVLOV
PAWNEE
PAWPAW
PAYDAY
PAYING
PAYNIM
PAYOFF
PAYOLA
PEAHEN
PEAKED
PEANUT
PEARLS
PEARLY
PEBBLE
PEBBLY
PECKER
PECTEN
PECTIN
PEDALO
PEDANT
PEDDER
PEDDLE
PEDLAR
PEELED
PEELER
PEEPER
PEEVED
PEEWEE
PEEWIT
PEGLEG
PEKING
PELHAM
PELION
PELLET
PELMET
PELOID
PELOTA
PELVIC
PELVIS
PENANG
PENCEL
PENCIL
PENMAN
PENNAE
PENNAL
PENNON
PENSÉE
PENSUM
PENTAD
PENTEL
PENTUP
PENURY
PEOPLE
PEPLOS
PEPLUM
PEPPER
PEPTIC
PEQUOD
PERDUE
PERHAP
PERILS
PERIOD
PERISH
PERKIN
PERMIT
PERNOD
PERRON
PERSON
PERUKE
PERUSE
PESADE
PESETA
PESHWA
PESTER
PESTLE
PÉTAIN
PETARD
PETARY
PETERS
PETIPA
PETITE
PETREL
PETROL
PEWTER
PEYOTE
PHAROS
PHASIS
PHASMA
PHENOL
PHENYL
PHILIP
PHIZOG
PHLEGM
PHLEUM
PHLOEM
PHOBIA
PHOBIC
PHOEBE
PHONAL
PHONEY
PHONIC
PHOOEY
PHOTON
PHRASE
PHYLLO
PHYLUM
PHYSIC
PHYSIO
PIAFFE
PIAZZA
PICARD
PICKAX
PICKED
PICKER
PICKET
PICKLE
PICKUP
PICNIC
PIDDLE
PIDGIN
PIECES
PIEDOG
PIEMAN
PIERCE
PIERIS
PIFFLE
PIGEON
PIGLET
PIGOTT
PIGPEN
PIGSTY
PILAFF
PILAGE
PILATE
PILEUM
PILEUP
PILEUS
PILFER
PILING
PILLAR
PILLOW
PILOSE
PIMENT
PIMPLE
PIMPLY
PINCER
PINDAR
PINEAL
PINERO
PINGER
PINING
PINION
PINITE
PINKIE
PINTER
PINTLE
PINXIT
PINYIN
PIPING
PIPKIN
PIPPIN
PIQUET
PIRACY
PIRATE
PIRENE
PISANO
PISCES
PISGAH
PISSED
PISTIL
PISTOL
PISTON
PITMAN
PITTED
PITTER
PLACED
PLACER
PLACID
PLAGUE
PLAICE
PLAINS
PLAINT
PLANCH
PLANET
PLANKS
PLAQUE
PLASMA
PLATED
PLATEN
PLATER
PLATES
PLAYER
PLEACH
PLEASE
PLEDGE
PLENTY
PLENUM
PLEURA
PLEXOR
PLEXUS
PLIANT
PLIERS
PLIGHT
PLINTH
PLISSÉ
PLONGE
PLOUGH
PLOVER
PLUCKY
PLUMED
PLUMMY
PLUNGE
PLURAL
PLUTUS
PLYING
PNEUMA
POBBLE
POCKET
PODIUM
PODSOL
PODZOL
POETIC
POETRY
POGROM
POINTE
POINTS
POIROT
POISED
POISON
POLACK
POLAND
POLDER
POLICE
POLICY
POLISH
POLITE
POLITY
POLLAN
POLLED
POLLEN
POLLEX
POLLUX
POLONY
POLYPS
POMACE
POMADE
POMELO
POMMEL
POMMIE
POMONA
POMPEY
POMPOM
PONCHO
PONDER
PONENT
PONGEE
PONGID
PONTIC
POODLE
POORLY
POOTER
POPEYE
POPLAR
POPLIN
POPPER
POPPET
POPPIT
PORGIE
PORKER
POROUS
PORTAL
PORTER
PORTIA
PORTLY
POSADA
POSEUR
POSSER
POSSET
POSSUM
POSTAL
POSTER
POSTIL
POTASH
POTATO
POTEEN
POTENT
POTHER
POTION
POTTED
POTTER
POTTLE
POUDRE
POUFFE
POUNCE
POUNDS
POURER
POUTER
POWDER
POWERS
POWNIE
POWTER
POWWOW
PRAGUE
PRAISE
PRANCE
PRANKS
PRATER
PRAVDA
PRAXIS
PRAYER
PREACE
PREACH
PRECIS
PREFAB
PREFER
PREFIX
PRELIM
PREPAY
PREPPY
PRESTO
PRETAX
PRETTY
PREVIN
PREWAR
PRICED
PRICEY
PRIEST
PRIMAL
PRIMED
PRIMER
PRIMLY
PRIMUS
PRINCE
PRIORY
PRISMS
PRISON
PRISSY
PRIVET
PRIZES
PROBIT
PROFIT
PROLEG
PROLIX
PROLOG
PROMPT
PRONTO
PROPEL
PROPER
PROPYL
PROSIT
PROTEA
PROTON
PROUST
PROVEN
PRUNER
PRYING
PSEUDO
PSYCHE
PSYCHO
PTERIN
PTERIS
PTOSIS
PUBLIC
PUCKER
PUDDLE
PUDSEY
PUEBLO
PUERTO
PUFFED
PUFFER
PUFFIN
PUISNE
PULLET
PULLEY
PULPIT
PULSAR
PULVER
PUMICE
PUMMEL
PUNCHY
PUNCTO
PUNDIT
PUNISH
PUNJAB
PUNKAH
PUNNET
PUNTER
PUPATE
PUPPET
PURDAH
PURELY
PURIFY
PURINE
PURIST
PURITY
PURLER
PURLIN
PURPLE
PURSED
PURSER
PURSUE
PURVEY
PUSHER
PUSHTU
PUSHUP
PUSSER
PUTEAL
PUTOIS
PUTRID
PUTSCH
PUTTEE
PUTTER
PUZZLE
PYEDOG
PYRENE
PYRONE
PYROPE
PYRRHO
PYTHIA
PYTHON
QUAGGA

QUAHOG
QUAICH
QUAIGH
QUAINT
QUAKER
QUALMS
QUANGO
QUARRY
QUARTO
QUARTZ
QUASAR
QUAVER
QUEASY
QUEBEC
QUEENS
QUELCH
QUENCH
QUETCH
QUICHE
QUIDAM
QUINCE
QUINSY
QUINTA
QUIRKY
QUITCH
QUIVER
QUOITS
QUORUM
QUOTED
QWERTY
RABATO
RABBET
RABBIT
RABBLE
RABIES
RACEME
RACHEL
RACHIS
RACIAL
RACINE
RACING
RACISM
RACIST
RACKET
RADDLE
RADIAL
RADIAN
RADISH
RADIUM
RADIUS
RADULA
RAFALE
RAFFIA
RAFFLE
RAFTER
RAGBAG
RAGGED
RAGGLE
RAGING
RAGLAN
RAGMAN
RAGOUT
RAGTOP
RAGUSA
RAIDER
RAISED
RAISER
RAISIN
RAKING
RAKISH
RAMBLE
RAMEAU
RAMIFY
RAMJET
RAMOSE
RAMOUS
RAMROD
RANCEL
RANCHO
RANCID
RANCOR
RANDOM
RANGER
RANKED
RANKER
RANKLE
RANSOM
RANTER
RANULA
RAPHIA
RAPIDS
RAPIER
RAPINE
RAPIST
RAPPED
RAPPEL
RAPPER
RAPTLY
RAPTOR
RAREFY
RARELY
RARING
RARITY
RASCAL
RASHER
RASHLY
RASPER
RASTER
RATBAG
RATHER
RATIFY
RATINE
RATING
RATION
RATOON
RATTAN
RATTER
RATTLE
RATTON
RAUNCH
RAVAGE
RAVINE
RAVING
RAVISH
RAZURE
RAZZIA
RAZZLE
READER
REALIA
REALLY
REALTY
REAMER
REAPER
REASON
REBATE
REBECK
REBITE
REBORE
REBORN
REBUFF
REBUKE
RECALL
RECANT
RECAST
RECEDE
RECENT
RECESS
RECIFE
RECIPE
RECITE
RECKON
RECOIL
RECORD
RECOUP
RECTAL
RECTOR
RECTUM
RECTUS
REDACT
REDCAP
REDCAR
REDDEN
REDEEM
REDEYE
REDLEG
REDRAW
REDTOP
REDUCE
REEBOK
REEFER
REEKIE
REELER
REFACE
REFECT
REFILL
REFINE
REFLET
REFLEX
REFLUX
REFORM
REFUEL
REFUGE
REFUND
REFUSE
REFUTE
REGAIN
REGALE
REGARD
REGENT
REGEST
REGGAE
REGIME
REGINA
REGION
REGIUS
REGLET
REGRET
REGULO
REHASH
REHEAT
REHEEL
REJECT
REJOIN
RELATE
RELENT
RELICS
RELICT
RELIEF
RELISH
RELIVE
REMAIN
REMAKE
REMAND
REMARK
REMEDY
REMIND
REMISS
REMOTE
REMOVE
RENAME
RENDER
RENEGE
RENNET
RENNIN
RENOIR
RENOWN
RENTAL
RENTER
RENVOI
RENVOY
REOPEN
REPAID
REPAIR
REPAST
REPEAL
REPEAT
REPENT
REPINE
REPLAY
REPORT
REPOSE
REPTON
REPUGN
REPUTE
REREAD
RESALE
RESCUE
RESEAU
RESECT
RESEDA
RESENT
RESIDE
RESIGN
RESIST
RESORT
RESULT
RESUME
RETAIL
RETAIN
RETAKE
RETARD
RETINA
RETIRE
RETOOL
RETORT
RETOUR
RETURN
REUBEN
REUTER
REVAMP
REVEAL
REVERE
REVERS
REVERT
REVERY
RÊVEUR
REVIEW
REVILE
REVISE
REVIVE
REVOKE
REVOLT
REWARD
REWIND
REWIRE
REWORD
REWORK
RHAPHE
RHEIMS
RHESUS
RHETOR
RHEUMY
RHEXIS
RHODES
RHYMER
RHYTHM
RIALTO
RIBALD
RIBAND
RIBBED
RIBBLE
RIBBON
RIBOSE
RICHES
RICHLY
RICKER
RICKEY
RICRAC
RICTAL
RICTUS
RIDDLE
RIDENT
RIDGED
RIDING
RIENZI
RIFFLE
RIGGED
RIGGER
RIGHTO
RIGHTS
RIGOUR
RIMINI
RIMMED
RINGED
RINGER
RIOTER
RIPOFF
RIPPER
RIPPLE
RIPPON
RIPSAW
RISING
RISQUÉ
RITUAL
RIVAGE
RIVERA
RIVLIN
RIYADH
ROADIE
ROAMER
ROARER
ROBBED
ROBBER
ROBERT
ROBING
ROBSON
ROBUST
ROCKER
ROCKET
ROCOCO
RODENT
RODHAM
RODNEY
ROEMER
ROGNON
ROGUES
ROKEBY
ROLAND
ROLLER
ROMANO
ROMANS
ROMANY
ROMISH
ROMMEL
ROMNEY
RONDEL
ROOFER
ROOKIE
ROOMER
ROOTED
ROOTER
ROOTLE
ROPERY
ROQUET
ROSACE
ROSARY
ROSCID
ROSCOE
ROSERY
ROSINA
ROSSER
ROSTER
ROSTOV
ROSYTH
ROTARY
ROTATE
ROTGUT
ROTHER
ROTHKO
ROTTEN
ROTTER
ROTULA
ROTUND
ROUBLE
ROUGED
ROUGHY
ROUNCE
ROUNDS
ROUTER
ROVING
ROWING
ROXANE
ROYALS
ROZZER
RUBBED
RUBBER
RUBBLE
RUBBRA
RUBENS
RUBIES
RUBIKS
RUBRIC
RUCHED
RUCKLE
RUCKUS
RUDDER
RUDDLE
RUDELY
RUEFUL
RUELLE
RUFFLE
RUGGED
RUGGER
RUGOSE
RUGOUS
RUINED
RULING

RUMBLE
RUMKIN
RUMMER
RUMORS
RUMOUR
RUMPLE
RUMPUS
RUNDLE
RUNNEL
RUNNER
RUNOFF
RUNWAY
RUNYON
RUPEES
RUPERT
RUPIAH
RUPIAS
RUSHED
RUSKIN
RUSSET
RUSSIA
RUSTAM
RUSTEM
RUSTIC
RUSTLE
RUSTUM
RUTTED
RUTTER
RWANDA
RYOKAN
SAANEN
SABELE
SABINE
SABRES
SACHET
SACRED
SACRUM
SADDEN
SADDHU
SADDLE
SADISM
SADIST
SAFARI
SAFELY
SAFETY
SAGELY
SAGGAR
SAHARA
SAILOR
SAINTS
SAITHE
SALAAM
SALADE
SALAMI
SALARY
SALINA
SALINE
SALIVA
SALLEE
SALLET
SALLOW
SALMIS
SALMON
SALOME
SALOON
SALOOP
SALUKI
SALUTE
SALVER
SALVIA
SAMARA
SAMBAL
SAMBAR
SAMBUR
SAMFOO
SAMIAN
SAMIEL
SAMIOT
SAMITE
SAMLET
SAMOSA
SAMPAN
SAMPLE
SAMSON
SAMUEL
SANCHO
SANDAL
SANDER
SANELY
SANITY
SANSEI
SANTAL
SANTON
SAPELE
SAPHAR
SAPIUM
SAPOTA
SAPPER
SAPPHO
SARGUS
SARNIE
SARONG
SARSEN
SARTOR
SARTRE
SASHAY
SATEEN
SATINY
SATIRE
SATIVE
SATORI
SATRAP
SATURN
SATYRA
SAUCER
SAUGER
SAURIA
SAVAGE
SAVANT
SAVATE
SAVING
SAVIOR
SAVOIE
SAVORY
SAVOUR
SAVVEY
SAWDER
SAWNEY
SAWYER
SAXONY
SAYERS
SAYING
SBIRRO
SCABBY
SCAITH
SCALAR
SCALER
SCALES
SCAMPI
SCAMPO
SCANTY
SCAPUS
SCARAB
SCARCE
SCARED
SCARER
SCATCH
SCATHE
SCATTY
SCENIC
SCHEMA
SCHEME
SCHISM
SCHIST
SCHIZO
SCHLEP
SCHMOE
SCHOOL
SCHUSS
SCHUYT
SCILLA
SCILLY
SCIPIO
SCIROC
SCIRON
SCLERA
SCLERE
SCOLEX
SCONCE
SCOOBS
SCOOSH
SCOPUS
SCORCH
SCORER
SCORIA
SCORSE
SCOTCH
SCOTER
SCOTIA
SCOUSE
SCRAMB
SCRAPE
SCRAPS
SCRAWL
SCRAWM
SCREAM
SCREED
SCREEN
SCREWY
SCRIBE
SCRIMP
SCRIPT
SCROLL
SCROOP
SCRUBS
SCRUFF
SCRUNT
SCULPT
SCUMMY
SCUNGE
SCURRY
SCURVY
SCUTCH
SCUTUM
SCUZZY
SCYLLA
SCYTHE
SDEATH
SEABEE
SEALED
SEAMAN
SEAMEN
SEAMER
SEAMUS
SEANCE
SEARCH
SEASON
SEATED
SEAWAY
SEBATE
SECANT
SECEDE
SECOND
SECRET
SECTOR
SECURE
SEDATE
SEDUCE
SEEDED
SEEDER
SEEING
SEEKER
SEEMLY
SEESAW
SEETHE
SEICHE
SEISIN
SELDOM
SELECT
SELENE
SELFED
SELJUK
SELLBY
SELLER
SELWYN
SEMELE
SEMITE
SEMPRE
SEMTEX
SENATE
SENDAL
SENDER
SENECA
SENILE
SENIOR
SENLAC
SENNET
SENORA
SENSED
SENSES
SENSOR
SENTRY
SEPIUM
SEPSIS
SEPTAL
SEPTET
SEPTIC
SEQUEL
SEQUIN
SERAIL
SERANG
SERAPE
SERAPH
SERBIA
SERDAB
SERENE
SERIAL
SERIES
SERINE
SERMON
SEROSA
SERVAL
SERVER
SESAME
SETOSE
SETTEE
SETTER
SETTLE
SEUMAS
SEURAT
SEVENS
SEVERE
SEVERN
SEVERY
SÈVRES
SEWAGE
SEWELL
SEWING
SEXISM
SEXIST
SEXTAN
SEXTET
SEXTON
SEXUAL
SHABBY
SHADED
SHADES
SHADOW
SHADUF
SHAGGY
SHAKEN
SHAKER
SHAKES
SHALOM
SHAMAN
SHAMBA
SHAMMY
SHAMUS
SHANDY
SHANKS
SHANTY
SHAPED
SHARED
SHARER
SHARES
SHARIA
SHARIF
SHARON
SHARPS
SHASTA
SHAVEN
SHAVER
SHEARS
SHEATH
SHEAVE
SHEENY
SHEERS
SHEETS
SHEIKH
SHEILA
SHEKEL
SHELVE
SHERIF
SHERPA
SHERRY
SHIELD
SHIFTY
SHIITE
SHILOH
SHIMMY
SHINDY
SHINER
SHINNY
SHINTO
SHINTY
SHIPKA
SHIRAZ
SHIRRA
SHIRTY
SHIVER
SHODDY
SHOFAR
SHOGUN
SHORTS
SHOULD
SHOVEL
SHOWER
SHRANK
SHREWD
SHRIEK
SHRIFT
SHRIKE
SHRILL
SHRIMP
SHRINE
SHRINK
SHRIVE
SHROFF
SHROUD
SHROVE
SHRUNK
SHTCHI
SHTETL
SHUFTI
SHUFTY
SICILY
SICKEN
SICKER
SICKLE
SICKLY
SIDDHA
SIDING
SIDNEY
SIENNA
SIERRA
SIESTA
SIFFLE
SIFTER
SIGHTS
SIGNAL
SIGNET
SIGNOR
SIKKIM
SILAGE
SILENE
SILENT
SILICA
SILKEN
SILVAN
SILVER
SIMEON
SIMIAN
SIMILE
SIMKIN
SIMMER
SIMNEL
SIMONY
SIMOON
SIMPER
SIMPLE
SIMPLY
SINBAD
SINDER
SINEWY
SINFUL
SINGER
SINGLE

SINGLY SINKER SINNER SIPHON SIPPET SIPPLE SIRDAR SIRIUS SIRKAR SIRRAH SIRREE SISKIN SISTER SITCOM SITREP SITTER SIZZLE SKATER SKATES SKELLY SKERRY SKETCH SKEWED SKEWER SKIDOO SKIING SKIMPY SKINNY SKIVER SKIVVY SKURRY SKYLAB SKYMAN SLACKS SLALOM SLANGY SLATCH SLATER SLAVER SLAVES SLAYER SLEAVE SLEAZE SLEAZY SLEDGE SLEEKY SLEEPY SLEEVE SLEEZY SLEIGH SLEUTH SLEWED SLICER SLIDER SLIGHT SLINKY SLIPPY SLIPUP SLITHY SLIVER SLOANE

SLOGAN SLOPES SLOPPY SLOSHY SLOUCH SLOUGH SLOVAK SLOVEN SLOWLY SLUDGE SLUICE SLUMMY SLURRY SLUSHY SMACKS SMALLS SMARMY SMARTY SMEARY SMEATH SMEGMA SMELLY SMIGHT SMILER SMILES SMILEY SMIRCH SMITHS SMITHY SMOKER SMOKEY SMOOCH SMOOTH SMUDGE SMUDGY SMUGLY SMUTTY SMYRNA SNAGGY SNAILY SNAKED SNAPPY SNATCH SNAZZY SNEAKY SNEATH SNEEZE SNEEZY SNIFFY SNIFTY SNIPER SNITCH SNIVEL SNOOTY SNOOZE SNORER SNOTTY SNOUTY SNOWED SNUDGE SNUGLY

SOAKED SOBEIT SOCAGE SOCCER SOCIAL SOCKET SODDEN SODIUM SODOMY SOFFIT SOFTEN SOFTIE SOFTLY SOHRAB SOIGNÉ SOILED SOIREE SOLACE SOLANO SOLDER SOLEIL SOLELY SOLEMN SOLENT SOLERA SOLEUS SOLIVE SOLUTE SOLVAY SOLVED SOLVER SOMALI SOMBER SOMBRE SONANT SONATA SONICS SONNET SONTAG SOONER SOOTHE SOPHIA SORAGE SORBET SORDES SORDID SORELL SORELY SORGHO SORREL SORROW SORTER SORTES SORTIE SOUGHT SOUPER SOUPLE SOURCE SOURLY SOUSED SOUTER

SOVIET SOWBUG SOWING SOWSED SOWTER SOZZLE SPACED SPACER SPADES SPADIX SPARKS SPARKY SPARSE SPARTA SPARTH SPATHE SPAULD SPAVIN SPECIE SPEECH SPEEDO SPEEDY SPEISS SPENCE SPHENE SPHERE SPHINX SPICED SPICER SPIDER SPIGOT SPIKED SPILTH SPINAL SPINAR SPINET SPIRAL SPIRIT SPITAL SPLAKE SPLASH SPLEEN SPLENT SPLICE SPLIFF SPLINT SPLITS SPLOSH SPOILS SPOILT SPOKEN SPOKES SPONGE SPONGY SPOOKY SPOONY SPORTS SPORTY SPOTTY SPOUSE SPRAIN

SPRANG SPRAWL SPREAD SPRING SPRINT SPRITE SPRITZ SPROUT SPRUCE SPRUNG SPRYLY SPUNGE SPURGE SPUTUM SPYING SQUAIL SQUALL SQUAMA SQUARE SQUASH SQUAWK SQUEAK SQUEAL SQUILL SQUINT SQUIRE SQUIRM SQUIRT SQUISH STABLE STABLY STACKS STAFFA STAGER STAGEY STAIRS STAKES STALAG STALIN STALKS STALKY STALLS STAMEN STAMPS STANCE STANCH STANZA STAPES STAPLE STARCH STARES STARRY STARVE STASIS STATAL STATED STATEN STATER STATES STATIC STATOR

STATUE STATUS STAYER STEADY STEAMY STEELE STEELY STEERS STEMMA STENCH STEPPE STEREO STERIC STERNE STEROL STEVEN STEWED STICKS STICKY STIFLE STIGMA STILTS STILTY STINGO STINGY STINKO STINKS STIPES STITCH STOCKS STOCKY STODGE STODGY STOGIE STOKER STOKES STOLEN STOLID STOLON STONED STONER STONES STOOGE STOOKS STOOLS STORER STOREY STORMY STOVER STOWER STRABO STRAFE STRAIN STRAIT STRAKE STRAND STRASS STRATA STRAWS STRAWY STREAK

STREAM STREET STREGA STRENE STRESS STRICK STRICT STRIDE STRIFE STRIKE STRINE STRING STRIPE STRIPY STRIVE STROBE STRODE STROKE STROLL STRONG STROUD STROUP STROVE STRUCK STRUNG STRUNT STUART STUBBS STUBBY STUCCO STUDIO STUFFY STUMER STUMPS STUMPY STUPID STUPOR STURDY STYLET STYLUS STYMIE STYRAX SUBDUE SUBLET SUBMIT SUBORN SUBSET SUBTLE SUBTLY SUBURB SUBWAY SUCCOR SUCCUS SUCKEN SUCKER SUCKET SUCKLE SUDARY SUDATE SUDDEN SUFFER

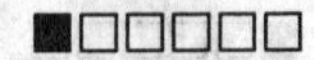

SUFFIX
SUGARY
SUITED
SUITOR
SUIVEZ
SULCUS
SULFUR
SULLEN
SULPHA
SULTAN
SULTRY
SUMACH
SUMMER
SUMMIT
SUMMON
SUNDAE
SUNDAY
SUNDER
SUNDEW
SUNDRY
SUNHAT
SUNKEN
SUNLIT
SUNRAY
SUNSET
SUNTAN
SUPERB
SUPINE
SUPLEX
SUPPER
SUPPLE
SUPPLY
SURELY
SURETÉ
SURETY
SURFER
SURREY
SURTAX
SURVEY
SUSSEX
SUTLER
SUTTEE
SUTURE
SVELTE
SWABIA
SWAMPY
SWANEE
SWANKY
SWARTY
SWATCH
SWATHE
SWEATY
SWEDEN
SWEENY
SWEETS
SWERVE
SWINGE
SWIPES
SWITCH
SWIVEL
SWIVET
SWOOSH
SYDNEY
SYLVAN
SYLVIA
SYMBOL
SYNCOM
SYNDIC
SYNTAX
SYPHER
SYPHON
SYRIAN
SYRINX
SYRISM
SYRUPY
SYSTEM
SYZYGY
TABARD
TABLET
TABULA
TACKET
TACKLE
TACOMA
TACTIC
TAENIA
TAGORE
TAHINA
TAHINI
TAHITI
TAIGLE
TAILLE
TAILOR
TAIPAN
TAIPEI
TAIWAN
TAKING
TALBOT
TALCUM
TALENT
TALION
TALKER
TALKIE
TALLIS
TALLOT
TALLOW
TALMUD
TAMALE
TAMANU
TAMARA
TAMARI
TAMELY
TAMINE
TAMISE
TAMMUZ
TAMPER
TAMPON
TANDEM
TANGLE
TANKER
TANKIA
TANNAH
TANNED
TANNER
TANNIC
TANNIN
TANNOY
TANTRA
TAOISM
TAOIST
TAPPER
TAPPET
TAPPIT
TARCEL
TARDIS
TARGET
TARGUM
TARIFF
TARMAC
TARROW
TARSAL
TARSEL
TARSIA
TARSUS
TARTAN
TARTAR
TARTLY
TASMAN
TASSEL
TASSET
TASSIE
TASTER
TATAMI
TATERS
TATLER
TATTER
TATTLE
TATTOO
TAUGHT
TAURUS
TAUTEN
TAUTLY
TAVERN
TAWDRY
TAWPIE
TAXEME
TAXING
TAXMAN
TEABAG
TEACUP
TEAGUE
TEAPOT
TEAPOY
TEASEL
TEASER
TECHNO
TECKEL
TECTUM
TEDIUM
TEENSY
TEEPEE
TEETER
TEETHE
TEFLON
TEGMEN
TEGULA
TEHRAN
TELEGA
TELEGU
TELLAR
TELLER
TELLUS
TELUGU
TEMPER
TEMPLE
TENACE
TENANT
TENDER
TENDON
TENDRE
TENGKU
TENNER
TENNIS
TENPIN
TENSON
TENSOR
TENURE
TEOPAN
TEPHRA
TERCET
TERCIO
TEREDO
TERESA
TERETE
TERGUM
TERMES
TERMLY
TERNAL
TERRAE
TERROR
TERTIA
TESTER
TESTES
TESTIS
TETANY
TETCHY
TETHER
TETHYS
TETRAD
TETRYL
TETTIX
TEUTON
TEVIOT
THALER
THALES
THALIA
THAMES
THANAH
THANET
THANKS
THATCH
THEAVE
THEBAN
THEBES
THECAL
THEIRS
THEISM
THEIST
THEMIS
THENAR
THENCE
THEORY
THERMO
THESIS
THETIC
THETIS
THEYRE
THICKY
THIERS
THIEVE
THINGS
THINGY
THINLY
THIRST
THIRTY
THISBE
THOLOS
THOLUS
THOMAS
THORAH
THORAX
THORNE
THORNY
THORPE
THOUGH
THRALL
THRASH
THRAWN
THREAD
THREAP
THREAT
THRENE
THRESH
THRICE
THRIFT
THRILL
THRIPS
THRIST
THRIVE
THROAT
THROES
THRONE
THRONG
THROVE
THROWN
THRUSH
THRUST
THWACK
THWART
THYMOL
THYMUS
TICINO
TICKER
TICKET
TICKEY
TICKLE
TICKLY
TIDBIT
TIDDLE
TIDDLY
TIDILY
TIEPIN
TIERCE
TIERED
TIFFIN
TIGHTS
TIGRIS
TILLER
TILSIT
TIMBER
TIMBRE
TIMELY
TIMING
TINDER
TINGED
TINGLE
TINKER
TINKLE
TINNED
TINNIE
TINPAN
TINPOT
TINSEL
TINTED
TINTIN
TIPCAT
TIPOFF
TIPPED
TIPPER
TIPPET
TIPPLE
TIPPOO
TIPTOE
TIPTOP
TIPULA
TIRADE
TIRANA
TIRING
TISANE
TISSOT
TISSUE
TITBIT
TITCHY
TITFER
TITIAN
TITLED
TITTER
TITTLE
TITTUP
TITULE
TIVOLI
TIZWAZ
TMESIS
TOBAGO
TOBIAS
TOCSIN
TODDLE
TOECAP
TOERAG
TOFFEE
TOGGED
TOGGLE
TOILET
TOLEDO
TOLLED
TOLLER
TOLOSA
TOLTEC
TOLUIC
TOLUOL
TOLZEY
TOMATO
TOMBOY
TOMCAT
TOMIAL
TOMIUM
TOMTOM
TONANT
TONGAN
TONGUE
TONITE
TONSIL
TONSOR
TOOTER
TOOTHY
TOOTLE
TOOTSY
TOPHUS
TOPPER
TOPPLE
TORERO
TORPID
TORPOR
TORQUE
TORRES
TORRID
TOSHER
TOSSUP
TOTTER
TOTTIE
TOUCAN
TOUCHE
TOUCHY
TOUPEE
TOUPET
TOURER
TOUSER
TOUSLE
TOWAGE
TOWARD
TOWBAR
TOWHEE
TOWNEE
TOWNLY
TOWSER
TOYISH
TRACER
TRADER

TRADES
TRAGIC
TRAGUS
TRAJAN
TRALEE
TRANCE
TRANNY
TRAPES
TRASHY
TRAUMA
TRAVEL
TRAVIS
TREATY
TREBLE
TREBLY
TREMOR
TRENCH
TRENDY
TREPAN
TRESCO
TRIAGE
TRIBAL
TRIBES
TRICAR
TRICKS
TRICKY
TRICOT
TRIFLE
TRIGON
TRILBY
TRIMLY
TRIODE
TRIPLE
TRIPOD
TRIPOS
TRISTE
TRITON
TRIVET
TRIVIA
TROCAR
TROCHE
TROIKA
TROJAN
TROMPE
TROOPS
TROPHE
TROPHY
TROPIC
TROPPO
TROUGH
TROUPE
TROUVÉ
TROVER
TROWEL
TROYES
TRUANT
TRUDGE
TRUISM
TRUMAN
TRUMPS
TRUNKS
TRUSTY
TRUTHS
TRYING
TSETSE
TSHIRT
TSWANA
TUAREG
TUBERS
TUBING
TUBULE
TUCKER
TUCKET
TUFFET
TUFTED
TUGRIK
TUILLE
TULBAN
TULIPA
TUMBLE
TUMEFY
TUMOUR
TUMULT
TUNDRA
TUNING
TUNNEL
TUPELO
TURBAN
TURBID
TURBOT
TUREEN
TURGID
TURKEY
TURNED
TURNER
TURNIP
TURNUP
TURPIN
TURRET
TURTLE
TURVES
TUSCAN
TUSKER
TUSSAH
TUSSIS
TUSSLE
TUVALU
TUXEDO
TWAITE
TWEEDS
TWEEDY
TWEENY
TWEEZE
TWELVE
TWENTY
TWICER
TWIGGY
TWIGHT
TWINED
TWINGE
TWIRLY
TWISTY
TWITCH
TWOBIT
TYBALT
TYBURN
TYCOON
TYMBAL
TYMPAN
TYPHUS
TYPIFY
TYPING
TYPIST
TYRANT
TYRONE
UBIETY
UCKERS
UFFIZI
UGANDA
UGARIT
UGRIAN
ULCERS
ULITIS
ULLAGE
ULLING
ULSTER
ULTIMA
ULTIMO
UMBLES
UMBREL
UMBRIA
UMBRIL
UMLAUT
UMPIRE
UNABLE
UNBEND
UNBENT
UNBIND
UNBOLT
UNBORN
UNBRED
UNBUSY
UNCAGE
UNCIAL
UNCLAD
UNCOIL
UNCOOL
UNCORK
UNDATE
UNDECK
UNDIES
UNDINE
UNDONE
UNDULY
UNDYED
UNEASE
UNEASY
UNEVEN
UNFAIR
UNFOLD
UNFURL
UNGAIN
UNGULA
UNHAND
UNHOLY
UNHOOK
UNHURT
UNIATE
UNIQUE
UNISEX
UNISON
UNITED
UNJUST
UNKIND
UNLACE
UNLESS
UNLIKE
UNLOAD
UNLOCK
UNMADE
UNMASK
UNMEET
UNPACK
UNPAID
UNPICK
UNPLUG
UNREAD
UNREAL
UNREEL
UNREST
UNRIPE
UNROLL
UNRULY
UNSAFE
UNSAID
UNSEAM
UNSEAT
UNSEEN
UNSENT
UNSEXY
UNSHOD
UNSOLD
UNSUNG
UNSURE
UNTIDY
UNTOLD
UNTRUE
UNUSED
UNVEIL
UNWARY
UNWELL
UNWIND
UNWISE
UNWRAP
UNYOKE
UPBEAT
UPDATE
UPFLOW
UPHELD
UPHILL
UPHOLD
UPKEEP
UPLAND
UPLIFT
UPLINK
UPPISH
UPPITY
UPRATE
UPROAR
UPROOT
UPSHOT
UPSIDE
UPTAKE
UPTOWN
UPTURN
UPWARD
URANIA
URANIC
URANUS
URBANE
URCHIN
URETER
URGENT
URINAL
URSINE
URSULA
URTICA
USABLE
USANCE
USEFUL
USHANT
USURER
UTERUS
UTMOST
UTOPIA
VACANT
VACATE
VACUUM
VADOSE
VAGARY
VAGINA
VAHINE
VAINLY
VALENS
VALETA
VALGUS
VALINE
VALISE
VALIUM
VALLEY
VALLUM
VALOUR
VALUER
VALUTA
VANDAL
VANISH
VANITY
VAPOUR
VARECH
VARESE
VARIED
VARLET
VASSAL
VASTLY
VATHEK
VATMAN
VAUNCE
VECTIS
VECTOR
VEDDAH
VEDUTA
VEILED
VEINED
VELCRO
VELETA
VELLUM
VELOCE
VELOUR
VELURE
VELVET
VENDEE
VENDER
VENDOR
VENDUE
VENEER
VENERY
VENIAL
VENICE
VENITE
VENOSE
VENOUS
VENTIL
VENTRE
VERBAL
VERDIN
VERDUN
VEREIN
VERGER
VERGES
VERIFY
VERILY
VERISM
VERITY
VERMIN
VERMIS
VERNAL
VERNON
VERSAL
VERSED
VERSES
VERSET
VERSUS
VERVET
VESICA
VESPER
VESSEL
VESTAL
VESTED
VESTRY
VIABLE
VIANDS
VIATOR
VIBRIO
VICTIM
VICTOR
VICUNA
VIENNA
VIENNE
VIEWER
VIGOUR
VIKING
VILELY
VILIFY
VILLUS
VINERY
VINOUS
VIOLET
VIOLIN
VIRAGO
VIRGIL
VIRGIN
VIRILE
VIROUS
VIRTUE
VISAGE
VISCID
VISHNU
VISIER
VISION
VISUAL
VITALS
VIVACE
VIVIAN
VIVIEN
VIZARD
VIZIER
VOICED
VOIDED
VOIDEE
VOIDER
VOLAGE
VOLANS
VOLANT
VOLENS
VOLLEY
VOLUME
VOLUTE
VOMICA
VOODOO
VORTEX
VOSGES
VOTARY
VOTING
VOTIVE
VOWELS
VOYAGE
VOYEUR
VULCAN
VULGAR
VULGUS
WABASH
WACKER
WADDLE
WADERS
WADHAM
WAFFLE
WAFTED

WAGGLE
WAGGON
WAGNER
WAGRAM
WAILER
WAITER
WAIVER
WAKING
WALKER
WALLAH
WALLED
WALLER
WALLET
WALLOP
WALLOW
WALNUT
WALRUS
WALTER
WALTON
WAMBLE
WAMPUM
WAMPUS
WANDER
WANDLE
WANGLE
WANKEL
WANTED
WANTON
WAPITI
WARBLE
WARCRY
WARDEN
WARDER
WARHOL
WARILY
WARMER
WARMLY
WARMTH
WARNER
WARPED
WARREN
WARSAW
WASHED
WASHER
WASTED
WASTEL
WASTER
WATERS
WATERY
WATSON
WATTLE
WAVELL
WAVING
WAXING
WAYLAY
WAYOUT
WEAKEN
WEAKER
WEAKLY
WEALTH
WEAPON
WEARER
WEASEL
WEAVER
WEBBED
WEDDED
WEDGED
WEEKLY
WEEPIE
WEEVIL
WEEWEE
WEIGHT
WEIMAR
WEIRDO
WELDER
WELKIN
WELLER
WELLES
WELLIE
WELTER
WELWYN
WENSUM
WERENT
WESKER
WESLEY
WESSEX
WETBOB
WETHER
WHACKO
WHACKY
WHALER
WHALES
WHAMMY
WHARFE
WHEELS
WHEELY
WHEEZE
WHEEZY
WHENCE
WHERRY
WHILOM
WHILST
WHIMSY
WHINGE
WHINNY
WHISHT
WHISKY
WHITBY
WHITED
WHITEN
WHITES
WHOLLY
WHOOPS
WHOOSH
WICKED
WICKER
WICKET
WIDELY
WIDGET
WIDOWS
WIENER
WIFELY
WIGEON
WIGGLE
WIGGLY
WIGWAM
WILDER
WILDLY
WILFUL
WILLED
WILLET
WILLIE
WILLOW
WILSON
WIMBLE
WIMPLE
WIMSEY
WINDER
WINDOW
WINDUP
WINGED
WINGER
WINKER
WINKLE
WINNER
WINNIE
WINNOW
WINTER
WINTRY
WIPERS
WIPING
WIRING
WIRRAL
WISDEN
WISDOM
WISELY
WISHES
WITHAL
WITHER
WITHIN
WITTED
WIVERN
WIZARD
WIZIER
WOBBLE
WOBBLY
WOBURN
WOEFUL
WOMBAT
WOMENS
WONDER
WONTED
WONTON
WOODED
WOODEN
WOODIE
WOOFER
WOOKEY
WOOLEN
WOOLLY
WORKED
WORKER
WORSEN
WORTHY
WORTLE
WOWSER
WRAITH
WRASSE
WREATH
WREKIN
WRENCH
WRETCH
WRIGHT
WRITER
WRITHE
WYVERN
XANADU
XAVIER
XENIAL
XENIUM
XEROMA
XERXES
XYLOID
YABBER
YAFFLE
YAHWEH
YAKKER
YAKUZA
YAMMER
YANKEE
YANKER
YAOURT
YARDIE
YARROW
YATTER
YEARLY
YEASTY
YELLOW
YEMENI
YEOMAN
YEOMEN
YESMAN
YESTER
YEZIDI
YIPPEE
YOGURT
YOICKS
YOKING
YONDER
YORICK
YORKER
YORUBA
YUCKER
YUKATA
YUMYUM
YUPPIE
ZAFTIG
ZAGREB
ZAMBIA
ZANDER
ZAPATA
ZEALOT
ZEBECK
ZENANA
ZENDIK
ZENITH
ZEPHYR
ZEUGMA
ZIGZAG
ZIMMER
ZINGER
ZINNIA
ZIPPER
ZIRCON
ZITHER
ZODIAC
ZOMBIE
ZONING
ZONKED
ZOPHAR
ZOSTER
ZOUAVE
ZOUNDS
ZURICH
ZYGOMA
ZYGOTE
ZYRIAN

6:2

AARONS
BABBIT
BABBLE
BABOON
BACCHI
BACKER
BACKET
BACKRA
BACKUP
BADGER
BADMAN
BAFFIN
BAFFLE
BAGFUL
BAGMAN
BAGNIO
BAGUIO
BAHADA
BAHRAM
BAIKAL
BAILEE
BAILER
BAILEY
BAILIE
BAILLY
BAKERS
BAKERY
BAKING
BALAAM
BALBOA
BALDER
BALDLY
BALEEN
BALKAN
BALKIS
BALLAD
BALLET
BALLOT
BALSAM
BALTIC
BALZAC
BAMAKO
BAMBOO
BANANA
BANDAR
BANDIT
BANDOG
BANGER
BANGLE
BANGUI
BANIAN
BANISH
BANJAX
BANJUL
BANKER
BANNED
BANNER
BANNET
BANTAM
BANTER
BANTRY
BANYAN
BANZAI
BAOBAB
BARBED
BARBEL
BARBER
BARBET
BARÈGE
BARELY
BARGEE
BARHAM
BARING
BARIUM
BARKER
BARKIS
BARLEY
BARMAN
BARNES
BARNET
BARNEY
BARNUM
BARODA
BARQUE
BARRED
BARREL
BARREN
BARRIE
BARRIO
BARROW
BARSAC
BARTER
BARTOK
BARTON
BARYTA
BASALT
BASHER
BASICS
BASKET
BASQUE
BASSET
BASUTO
BATEAU
BATHER
BATHOS
BATMAN
BATTEN
BATTER
BATTLE
BATTUE
BAUBLE
BAUCIS
BAWBEE
BAXTER
BAYARD
BAYEUX
BAZAAR
CABALE
CABBIE
CACCIA
CACHET
CACHOU
CACKLE
CACOON
CACTUS
CADDIE
CADDIS
CADETS
CADGER
CADMUS
CAECUM
CAESAR
CAFARD
CAFTAN
CAGILY
CAHIER
CAHOOT
CAIMAN
CAIQUE
CAJOLE
CALAIS
CALCED
CALICO
CALIMA
CALIPH
CALKER
CALKIN
CALLAS
CALLED
CALLER
CALLET
CALLID
CALLOP
CALLOW
CALLUP
CALLUS

CALMLY
CALQUE
CALVER
CALVIN
CAMAIL
CAMBER
CAMDEN
CAMERA
CAMION
CAMISE
CAMOTE
CAMPED
CAMPER
CAMPUS
CANAAN
CANADA
CANAPÉ
CANARD
CANARY
CANCEL
CANCER
CANDID
CANDLE
CANDOR
CANGUE
CANINE
CANING
CANKER
CANNAE
CANNED
CANNEL
CANNON
CANNOT
CANOPY
CANTAB
CANTAL
CANTAR
CANTER
CANTLE
CANTON
CANTOR
CANUCK
CANUTE
CANVAS
CANVEY
CANYON
CAPIAS
CAPLET
CAPONE
CAPOTE
CAPPED
CAPSID
CAPTAN
CAPTOR
CARAFE
CARBON
CARBOY
CARDAN
CAREEN
CAREER
CAREME
CARESS
CARFAX
CARIES
CARINA
CARING
CARLIN
CARMEL
CARMEN
CARNAL
CARNET
CARNOT
CARPAL
CARPEL
CARPER
CARPET
CARPUS
CARREL
CARROT
CARSON
CARTEL
CARTER
CARTON
CARUSO
CARVED
CARVEL
CARVER
CASBAH
CASEIN
CASHEW
CASING
CASINO
CASKET
CASLON
CASPAR
CASQUE
CASSIA
CASSIO
CASSIS
CASTER
CASTLE
CASTOR
CASTRO
CASUAL
CATCHY
CATGUT
CATHAR
CATHAY
CATKIN
CATNAP
CATNIP
CATSUP
CATTLE
CAUCUS
CAUDEX
CAUDLE
CAUGHT
CAUSAL
CAUSED
CAUSEY
CAVEAT
CAVEIN
CAVELL
CAVERN
CAVITY
CAVORT
CAVOUR
CAYMAN
DABBLE
DACOIT
DACTYL
DADDLE
DAEDAL
DAEMON
DAFTIE
DAGGER
DAGGLE
DAHLIA
DAIMIO
DAINTY
DAISHO
DAKOTA
DALASI
DALTON
DAMAGE
DAMASK
DAMMIT
DAMNED
DAMPEN
DAMPER
DAMSEL
DAMSON
DANCER
DANDER
DANDLE
DANGER
DANGLE
DANIEL
DANISH
DANTON
DANUBE
DANZIG
DAPHNE
DAPPER
DAPPLE
DARGLE
DARIEN
DARING
DARIUS
DARKEN
DARKEY
DARKIE
DARKLY
DARTER
DARTLE
DARWIN
DASHED
DATING
DATIVE
DATURA
DAUDET
DAWDLE
DAWNEY
DAWSON
DAYBED
DAZZLE
EALING
EAMONN
EARFUL
EARING
EARNED
EARNER
EARTHY
EARWIG
EASIER
EASILY
EASING
EASTER
EATAGE
EATERY
EATING
FABIAN
FABIUS
FABLED
FABLES
FABRIC
FACADE
FACIAL
FACIES
FACILE
FACING
FACTOR
FACTUM
FADING
FAECAL
FAECES
FAGGED
FAGGOT
FAIBLE
FAINTS
FAIRLY
FAKING
FALCON
FALLEN
FALLOW
FALTER
FAMILY
FAMINE
FAMISH
FAMOUS
FANGLE
FANION
FANTAN
FARAND
FARCIN
FARDEL
FARDLE
FARINA
FARMER
FAROFF
FAROUK
FARROW
FASCES
FASCIA
FASTEN
FATHER
FATHOM
FATIMA
FATTEN
FAUCES
FAUCET
FAULTY
FAUNUS
FAVELA
FAVISM
FAVOSE
FAVOUR
FAWKES
GABBLE
GABBRO
GABION
GABLED
GADFLY
GADGET
GADOID
GAELIC
GAFFER
GAGGLE
GAIETY
GAIJIN
GAINER
GAINLY
GAITER
GALANT
GALAXY
GALENA
GALERE
GALIOT
GALLEN
GALLET
GALLEY
GALLIC
GALLIO
GALLON
GALLOP
GALLOW
GALLUP
GALLUS
GALOOT
GALORE
GALOSH
GAMBET
GAMBIA
GAMBIT
GAMBLE
GAMBOL
GAMELY
GAMETE
GAMINE
GAMING
GAMMER
GAMMON
GANDER
GANDHI
GANGER
GANGES
GANGLY
GANGUE
GANION
GANNET
GANTRY
GAOLER
GAPING
GARAGE
GARBED
GARBLE
GARÇON
GARDEN
GARETH
GARGET
GARGLE
GARISH
GARLIC
GARNER
GARNET
GARRET
GARROT
GARRYA
GARTER
GARUDA
GASBAG
GASCON
GASKET
GASMAN
GASPAR
GASPER
GASSER
GASTER
GASTON
GATEAU
GATHER
GAUCHE
GAUCHO
GAUFRE
GAUGER
GAVAGE
GAVIAL
GAWAIN
GAZEBO
GAZUMP
HABILE
HACHIS
HACKEE
HACKER
HACKLE
HAEMAL
HAEMON
HAGDEN
HAGGAI
HAGGIS
HAGGLE
HAILER
HAIRDO
HALIDE
HALITE
HALLAL
HALLEY
HALLOO
HALLOW
HALLUX
HALOID
HALTER
HALVED
HALVES
HAMATE
HAMBLE
HAMITE
HAMLET
HAMMAM
HAMMER
HAMOSE
HAMPER
HANDEL
HANDLE
HANGAR
HANGER
HANGUP
HANKER
HANKIE
HANNAH
HANSOM
HAPPEN
HAPTEN
HAPTIC
HARARE
HARASS
HARBOR
HARDEN
HARDLY
HARKEN
HARLOT
HARMED
HAROLD
HARPIC
HARRIS
HARROW
HARVEY
HASHED
HASLET
HASSAR
HASSLE
HASTEN
HATING
HATRED
HATTER
HAUNCH
HAVANA
HAVENT
HAVERS
HAVING
HAWAII
HAWKED
HAWKER
HAWSER
HAYBOX
HAYDON
HAYLEY

HAYMOW
HAZARD
HAZILY
IAMBIC
IAMBUS
JABBER
JABBLE
JABIRU
JACANA
JACENT
JACKAL
JACKET
JACOBS
JAEGER
JAGGED
JAGGER
JAGUAR
JAILER
JAILOR
JALOPY
JAMBOK
JAMBON
JAMMED
JAMPOT
JANGLE
JARGON
JARVEY
JASPER
JAUNTY
JAWBOX
JAZZER
KABAKA
KABELE
KABUKI
KABYLE
KAFFER
KAFFIR
KAFTAN
KAISER
KAKAPO
KALMIA
KALPAK
KANAKA
KANOON
KANSAS
KANTEN
KANTHA
KANUCK
KAOLIN
KAPUTT
KARATE
KARIBA
KARITE
KASBAH
KATANA
KAZAKH
LAAGER
LABIAL
LABILE
LABIUM
LABLAB
LABOUR
LABRUM
LABRYS
LACHES
LACING
LACKEY
LACTIC
LACUNA
LADAKH
LADDER
LADDIE
LADIES
LADING
LADOGA
LAFFER
LAGOON
LAGUNA
LAGUNE
LAICAL
LAISSE
LALLAN
LAMBDA
LAMELY
LAMENT
LAMINA
LAMMAS
LAMMER
LANATE
LANCER
LANCET
LANCIA
LANDAU
LANDED
LANDER
LANDOR
LANUGO
LAPDOG
LAPITH
LAPPER
LAPPET
LAPSED
LAPSUS
LAPTOP
LAPUTA
LARDER
LARDON
LARIAT
LARKIN
LARRUP
LARVAE
LARVAL
LARYNX
LASCAR
LASHED
LASHER
LASKET
LASSIE
LASSUS
LASTLY
LATEEN
LATELY
LATENT
LATEST
LATHER
LATRON
LATTEN
LATTER
LATVIA
LAUDER
LAUNCE
LAUNCH
LAUREL
LAURIC
LAURIE
LAVABO
LAVAGE
LAVISH
LAWFUL
LAWMAN
LAWYER
LAXIST
LAXITY
LAYARD
LAYERS
LAYING
LAYMAN
LAYOFF
LAYOUT
LAZILY
MACRON
MACULA
MACULE
MADAME
MADCAP
MADDEN
MADDER
MADEUP
MADMAN
MADRAS
MADRID
MADURA
MADURO
MAENAD
MAFFIA
MAGGIE
MAGGOT
MAGLEV
MAGNES
MAGNET
MAGNON
MAGNUM
MAGNUS
MAGPIE
MAGYAR
MAHLER
MAHOUT
MAIDAN
MAIDEN
MAILER
MAINLY
MAINOR
MAÎTRE
MAJLIS
MAKEUP
MAKING
MALAGA
MALATE
MALAWI
MALDON
MALGRE
MALIAN
MALIBU
MALICE
MALIGN
MALLAM
MALLEE
MALLET
MALLOW
MALONE
MALONY
MALORY
MALTED
MAMMAL
MAMMON
MAMZER
MANAGE
MANANA
MANATI
MANCHE
MANCHU
MANEGE
MANFUL
MANGER
MANGLE
MANIAC
MANILA
MANIOC
MANITO
MANNER
MANNIN
MANQUÉ
MANTIS
MANTLE
MANTRA
MANTUA
MANUAL
MANURE
MAOIST
MAOTAI
MAPUTO
MAQUIS
MARACA
MARAUD
MARBLE
MARCEL
MARGIN
MARIAN
MARINA
MARINE
MARISH
MARIST
MARKED
MARKER
MARKET
MARKKA
MARKUP
MARLIN
MARMOT
MARNER
MAROON
MARQUE
MARRAM
MARRON
MARROW
MARSHY
MARTEL
MARTEN
MARTHA
MARTIN
MARTYR
MARVEL
MASADA
MASCOT
MASHAM
MASHED
MASHER
MASHIE
MASKED
MASLIN
MASQUE
MASSED
MASSES
MASSIF
MASTER
MASTIC
MATHIS
MATING
MATINS
MATLOW
MATRIX
MATRON
MATTED
MATTER
MATURE
MAUGRE
MAUNDY
MAUSER
MAWKIN
MAXIMS
MAYBUG
MAYDAY
MAYFLY
MAYHEM
MAZOUT
MAZUMA
NAEVUS
NAGANA
NAGARI
NAILED
NAILER
NALLAH
NAMELY
NANDOO
NANISM
NANKIN
NANSEN
NANTES
NAPALM
NAPERY
NAPIER
NAPKIN
NAPLES
NAPPER
NARROW
NASEBY
NASION
NASSAU
NASSER
NASTIC
NATANT
NATION
NATIVE
NATRON
NATTER
NATURE
NAUGHT
NAUSEA
NAUTCH
NAVAHO
NAVAJO
OAFISH
OAKLEY
OAKNUT
OARLAP
PACIFY
PACKED
PACKER
PACKET
PADANG
PADDED
PADDLE
PADUAN
PAELLA
PAEONY
PAGODA
PAHARI
PAIDUP
PAINED
PAINTS
PAINTY
PAIRER
PAKHTI
PAKHTO
PAKHTU
PALACE
PALAIS
PALATE
PALING
PALLAH
PALLAS
PALLET
PALLID
PALLOR
PALMER
PALTRY
PAMELA
PAMIRS
PAMPAS
PAMPER
PAMYAT
PANADA
PANAMA
PANDER
PANDIT
PANFRY
PANOPE
PANTER
PANTON
PANTRY
PANZER
PAPACY
PAPAYA
PAPERS
PAPERY
PAPHOS
PAPIST
PAPULE
PARADE
PARAMO
PARANA
PARAPH
PARCEL
PARDIE
PARDON
PARENT
PARETO
PARGET
PARIAH
PARISH
PARITY
PARKED
PARKER
PARKIN
PARLEY
PARLOR
PARODY
PAROLE
PARROT
PARSEC
PARSEE
PARSON
PARTLY
PARTON
PARURE
PARVIS
PASCAL
PASHTO
PASHTU
PASQUE
PASSED
PASSES
PASSIM
PASTEL
PASTIL
PASTIS
PASTON

PASTOR
PASTRY
PATACA
PATCHY
PATENT
PATHAN
PATHIC
PATHOS
PATINA
PATMOS
PATOIS
PATROL
PATRON
PATTEN
PATTER
PATTON
PAUNCE
PAUNCH
PAUPER
PAVANE
PAVING
PAVLOV
PAWNEE
PAWPAW
PAYDAY
PAYING
PAYNIM
PAYOFF
PAYOLA
RABATO
RABBET
RABBIT
RABBLE
RABIES
RACEME
RACHEL
RACHIS
RACIAL
RACINE
RACING
RACISM
RACIST
RACKET
RADDLE
RADIAL
RADIAN
RADISH
RADIUM
RADIUS
RADULA
RAFALE
RAFFIA
RAFFLE
RAFTER
RAGBAG
RAGGED
RAGGLE
RAGING
RAGLAN
RAGMAN
RAGOUT
RAGTOP
RAGUSA
RAIDER
RAISED
RAISER
RAISIN
RAKING
RAKISH
RAMBLE
RAMEAU
RAMIFY
RAMJET
RAMOSE
RAMOUS
RAMROD
RANCEL
RANCHO
RANCID
RANCOR
RANDOM
RANGER
RANKED
RANKER
RANKLE
RANSOM
RANTER
RANULA
RAPHIA
RAPIDS
RAPIER
RAPINE
RAPIST
RAPPED
RAPPEL
RAPPER
RAPTLY
RAPTOR
RAREFY
RARELY
RARING
RARITY
RASCAL
RASHER
RASHLY
RASPER
RASTER
RATBAG
RATHER
RATIFY
RATINE
RATING
RATION
RATOON
RATTAN
RATTER
RATTLE
RATTON
RAUNCH
RAVAGE
RAVINE
RAVING
RAVISH
RAZURE
RAZZIA
RAZZLE
SAANEN
SABELE
SABINE
SABRES
SACHET
SACRED
SACRUM
SADDEN
SADDHU
SADDLE
SADISM
SADIST
SAFARI
SAFELY
SAFETY
SAGELY
SAGGAR
SAHARA
SAILOR
SAINTS
SAITHE
SALAAM
SALADE
SALAMI
SALARY
SALINA
SALINE
SALIVA
SALLEE
SALLET
SALLOW
SALMIS
SALMON
SALOME
SALOON
SALOOP
SALUKI
SALUTE
SALVER
SALVIA
SAMARA
SAMBAL
SAMBAR
SAMBUR
SAMFOO
SAMIAN
SAMIEL
SAMIOT
SAMITE
SAMLET
SAMOSA
SAMPAN
SAMPLE
SAMSON
SAMUEL
SANCHO
SANDAL
SANDER
SANELY
SANITY
SANSEI
SANTAL
SANTON
SAPELE
SAPHAR
SAPIUM
SAPOTA
SAPPER
SAPPHO
SARGUS
SARNIE
SARONG
SARSEN
SARTOR
SARTRE
SASHAY
SATEEN
SATINY
SATIRE
SATIVE
SATORI
SATRAP
SATURN
SATYRA
SAUCER
SAUGER
SAURIA
SAVAGE
SAVANT
SAVATE
SAVING
SAVIOR
SAVOIE
SAVORY
SAVOUR
SAVVEY
SAWDER
SAWNEY
SAWYER
SAXONY
SAYERS
SAYING
TABARD
TABLET
TABULA
TACKET
TACKLE
TACOMA
TACTIC
TAENIA
TAGORE
TAHINA
TAHINI
TAHITI
TAIGLE
TAILLE
TAILOR
TAIPAN
TAIPEI
TAIWAN
TAKING
TALBOT
TALCUM
TALENT
TALION
TALKER
TALKIE
TALLIS
TALLOT
TALLOW
TALMUD
TAMALE
TAMANU
TAMARA
TAMARI
TAMELY
TAMINE
TAMISE
TAMMUZ
TAMPER
TAMPON
TANDEM
TANGLE
TANKER
TANKIA
TANNAH
TANNED
TANNER
TANNIC
TANNIN
TANNOY
TANTRA
TAOISM
TAOIST
TAPPER
TAPPET
TAPPIT
TARCEL
TARDIS
TARGET
TARGUM
TARIFF
TARMAC
TARROW
TARSAL
TARSEL
TARSIA
TARSUS
TARTAN
TARTAR
TARTLY
TASMAN
TASSEL
TASSET
TASSIE
TASTER
TATAMI
TATERS
TATLER
TATTER
TATTLE
TATTOO
TAUGHT
TAURUS
TAUTEN
TAUTLY
TAVERN
TAWDRY
TAWPIE
TAXEME
TAXING
TAXMAN
VACANT
VACATE
VACUUM
VADOSE
VAGARY
VAGINA
VAHINE
VAINLY
VALENS
VALETA
VALGUS
VALINE
VALISE
VALIUM
VALLEY
VALLUM
VALOUR
VALUER
VALUTA
VANDAL
VANISH
VANITY
VAPOUR
VARECH
VARESE
VARIED
VARLET
VASSAL
VASTLY
VATHEK
VATMAN
VAUNCE
WABASH
WACKER
WADDLE
WADERS
WADHAM
WAFFLE
WAFTED
WAGGLE
WAGGON
WAGNER
WAGRAM
WAILER
WAITER
WAIVER
WAKING
WALKER
WALLAH
WALLED
WALLER
WALLET
WALLOP
WALLOW
WALNUT
WALRUS
WALTER
WALTON
WAMBLE
WAMPUM
WAMPUS
WANDER
WANDLE
WANGLE
WANKEL
WANTED
WANTON
WAPITI
WARBLE
WARCRY
WARDEN
WARDER
WARHOL
WARILY
WARMER
WARMLY
WARMTH
WARNER
WARPED
WARREN
WARSAW
WASHED
WASHER
WASTED
WASTEL
WASTER
WATERS
WATERY
WATSON
WATTLE
WAVELL
WAVING
WAXING
WAYLAY
WAYOUT
XANADU
XAVIER
YABBER
YAFFLE
YAHWEH
YAKKER
YAKUZA
YAMMER
YANKEE
YANKER
YAOURT
YARDIE
YARROW
YATTER

ZAFTIG
ZAGREB
ZAMBIA
ZANDER
ZAPATA
ABACUS
ABADAN
ABATOR
ABATTU
ABBACY
ABBESS
ABDABS
ABDIEL
ABDUCT
ABELIA
ABJECT
ABJURE
ABLATE
ABLAUT
ABLAZE
ABLOOM
ABLUSH
ABOARD
ABONDE
ABOUND
ABRADE
ABREGE
ABROAD
ABROMA
ABRUPT
ABSEIL
ABSENT
ABSORB
ABSURD
ABULIA
ABYDOS
IBADAN
IBERIA
IBIDEM
OBECHE
OBELUS
OBERON
OBIISM
OBITAL
OBITER
OBJECT
OBLAST
OBLATE
OBLIGE
OBLONG
OBOIST
OBOLUS
OBSESS
OBTAIN
OBTECT
OBTEND
OBTUND
OBTUSE
OBVERT
SBIRRO
UBIETY
ACACIA
ACADIA
ACAJOU
ACARID
ACARUS
ACATES
ACCEDE
ACCEND
ACCENT
ACCEPT
ACCESS
ACCORD
ACCOST
ACCRUE
ACCUSE
ACEDIA
ACETIC
ACHENE
ACHING
ACIDIC
ACINUS
ACKERS
ACORNS
ACQUIT
ACRAWL
ACROSS
ACTING
ACTION
ACTIUM
ACTIVE
ACTORS
ACTUAL
ACUITY
ACUMEN
ECARTÉ
ECBOLE
ECCLES
ECHARD
ECHINO
ECLAIR
ECLOSE
ECONUT
ECTOPY
ECURIE
ECZEMA
ICARUS
ICEBOX
ICEMAN
ICICLE
ICONIC
OCCULT
OCCUPY
OCEANS
OCELOT
OCHONE
OCHREA
OCKERS
OCTANE
OCTANS
OCTANT
OCTAVE
OCTAVO
OCTROI
OCULAR
SCABBY
SCAITH
SCALAR
SCALER
SCALES
SCAMPI
SCAMPO
SCANTY
SCAPUS
SCARAB
SCARCE
SCARED
SCARER
SCATCH
SCATHE
SCATTY
SCENIC
SCHEMA
SCHEME
SCHISM
SCHIST
SCHIZO
SCHLEP
SCHMOE
SCHOOL
SCHUSS
SCHUYT
SCILLA
SCILLY
SCIPIO
SCIROC
SCIRON
SCLERA
SCLERE
SCOLEX
SCONCE
SCOOBS
SCOOSH
SCOPUS
SCORCH
SCORER
SCORIA
SCORSE
SCOTCH
SCOTER
SCOTIA
SCOUSE
SCRAMB
SCRAPE
SCRAPS
SCRAWL
SCRAWM
SCREAM
SCREED
SCREEN
SCREWY
SCRIBE
SCRIMP
SCRIPT
SCROLL
SCROOP
SCRUBS
SCRUFF
SCRUNT
SCULPT
SCUMMY
SCUNGE
SCURRY
SCURVY
SCUTCH
SCUTUM
SCUZZY
SCYLLA
SCYTHE
UCKERS
ADAGIO
ADDEEM
ADDEND
ADDICT
ADDLED
ADDUCE
ADDUCT
ADHERE
ADJOIN
ADJURE
ADJUST
ADMIRE
ADNATE
ADONAI
ADONIS
ADORER
ADRIAN
ADRIFT
ADROIT
ADSORB
ADSUKI
ADVENE
ADVENT
ADVERB
ADVERT
ADVICE
ADVISE
EDDISH
EDGING
EDIBLE
EDISON
EDITED
EDITOR
EDMOND
EDMUND
EDWARD
IDIOCY
ODDITY
ODDSON
ODENSE
ODESSA
ODIOUS
SDEATH
AEDILE
AEGEAN
AEGEUS
AEGINA
AENEID
AEOLIC
AEOLIS
AEOLUS
AERATE
AERIAL
AEROBE
BEACHY
BEACON
BEADED
BEADLE
BEAGLE
BEAKER
BEANIE
BEARER
BEATEN
BEATER
BEATTY
BEAUNE
BEAUTY
BEAVER
BECALM
BECAME
BECKET
BECKON
BECOME
BEDASH
BEDAUB
BEDDER
BEDECK
BEDLAM
BEDPAN
BEDSIT
BEEGHA
BEENAH
BEEPER
BEETLE
BEETON
BEFALL
BEFOOL
BEFORE
BEGGAR
BEGONE
BEHALF
BEHAVE
BEHEAD
BEHELD
BEHEST
BEHIND
BEHOLD
BEHOOF
BEHOVE
BEHRAM
BEIRUT
BEJADE
BELAMY
BELFRY
BELIAL
BELIEF
BELIKE
BELIZE
BELLOC
BELLOW
BELONG
BELSEN
BELTED
BELUGA
BEMEAN
BEMOAN
BEMOIL
BEMUSE
BENAME
BENBOW
BENDED
BENDER
BENGAL
BENIGN
BENITO
BENNET
BENSON
BENUMB
BERATE
BERBER
BEREFT
BERGEN
BERING
BERLIN
BERTHA
BERTHE
BERTIE
BESANT
BESEEM
BESIDE
BESORT
BESSEL
BESSIE
BESSUS
BESTED
BESTIR
BESTOW
BETAKE
BETHEL
BETIDE
BETIME
BETISE
BETONY
BETRAY
BETTER
BETTOR
BEULAH
BEURRÉ
BEWAIL
BEWARE
BEYOND
BEZANT
BEZOAR
BEZZLE
CECILS
CECITY
CEDRIC
CEDULA
CEEFAX
CELERY
CELIAC
CELLAR
CELTIC
CEMENT
CENSER
CENSOR
CENSUS
CENTER
CENTRE
CENTUM
CERATE
CERCAL
CERCUS
CEREAL
CEREUS
CERISE
CERIUM
CEROON
CERTES
CERUSE
CERVIX
CESARE
CESIUM
CESTUI
CESTUS
CESURA
CETERA
CEYLON
DEACON
DEADEN
DEADLY
DEAFEN
DEALER
DEARER
DEARIE
DEARLY
DEARTH
DEBASE
DEBATE
DEBILE
DEBRIS
DEBTOR
DEBUNK
DECADE
DECAFF
DECAMP
DECANE
DECANI
DECANT
DECCAN
DECEIT
DECENT
DECIDE
DECKED
DECKER
DECKLE
DECODE

DECOKE
DECREE
DECREW
DEDANS
DEDUCE
DEDUCT
DEEPEN
DEEPER
DEEPLY
DEFACE
DEFAME
DEFEAT
DEFECT
DEFEND
DEFILE
DEFINE
DEFORM
DEFRAY
DEFTLY
DEFUSE
DEGREE
DEHORN
DEIDRE
DEJECT
DEKKER
DELATE
DELETE
DELIAN
DELICE
DELICT
DELIUS
DELPHI
DELUDE
DELUGE
DELUXE
DELVED
DEMAIN
DEMAND
DEMEAN
DEMENT
DEMISE
DEMIST
DEMOTE
DEMURE
DENGUE
DENIAL
DENIED
DENIER
DENIMS
DENNIS
DENOTE
DENTAL
DENUDE
DENVER
DEODAR
DEPART
DEPEND
DEPICT
DEPLOY
DEPONE
DEPORT
DEPOSE
DEPTHS
DEPUTE
DEPUTY
DERAIL
DERAIN
DERGUE
DERHAM
DERIDE
DERIVE
DERMAL
DERMIS
DERRIS
DESCRY
DESERT
DESIGN
DESIRE
DESIST
DESORB
DESPOT
DETACH
DETAIL
DETAIN
DETECT
DETENT
DETENU
DETEST
DETOUR
DEVEST
DEVICE
DEVILS
DEVISE
DEVOID
DEVOTE
DEVOUR
DEVOUT
DEWALI
DEWITT
DEWLAP
DEXTER
EERILY
EEYORE
FEALTY
FECULA
FECUND
FEDORA
FEEBLE
FEEBLY
FEEDER
FEELER
FEERIE
FEINTS
FEISTY
FELINE
FELLER
FELLOE
FELLOW
FELONY
FEMALE
FENCER
FENDER
FENIAN
FENNEL
FERIAL
FERMAT
FERRET
FERRIS
FERULA
FERULE
FERVID
FERVOR
FESCUE
FESTAL
FESTER
FETISH
FETTER
FETTES
FETTLE
FEUDAL
FEWEST
GEASON
GEEZER
GEIGER
GEISHA
GELADA
GELATO
GELLER
GEMINI
GEMMAN
GENDER
GENERA
GENEVA
GENIAL
GENIUS
GENOME
GENTES
GENTLE
GENTLY
GENTRY
GEORGE
GERBIL
GERENT
GERMAN
GERUND
GETTER
GEWGAW
GEYSER
HEADED
HEADER
HEALER
HEALTH
HEAPED
HEARER
HEARSE
HEARTH
HEARTS
HEARTY
HEATED
HEATER
HEAUME
HEAVED
HEAVEN
HEAVES
HEBREW
HECATE
HECKLE
HECTIC
HECTOR
HECUBA
HEDERA
HEEDED
HEEHAW
HEELED
HEGIRA
HEIFER
HEIGHT
HEJIRA
HELENA
HELIOS
HELIUM
HELLER
HELMET
HELPER
HEMPEN
HENBIT
HENLEY
HENNIN
HENSON
HEPTAD
HERALD
HERBAL
HERDEN
HERDER
HEREBY
HEREIN
HERERO
HERESY
HERETO
HERIOT
HERMES
HERMIT
HERMON
HERNIA
HEROIC
HEROIN
HERONS
HERPES
HERREN
HESIOD
HETERO
HETMAN
HEXANE
HEXOSE
HEYDAY
JEEVES
JEJUNE
JEKYLL
JEMIMA
JENNER
JENNET
JERBOA
JEREMY
JERKER
JERKIN
JEROME
JERSEY
JESTER
JESUIT
JETHRO
JETLAG
JETSAM
JETTON
JEWELS
JEWESS
JEWISH
KEATON
KEBELE
KECKSY
KEDDAH
KEELER
KEENER
KEENLY
KEEPER
KELLYS
KELOID
KELPER
KELPIE
KELTER
KELTIC
KELTIE
KELVIN
KENDAL
KENNEL
KENNET
KENSAL
KENYAN
KEPHIR
KEPLER
KERALA
KERMES
KERMIS
KERNEL
KETMIR
KETONE
KETOSE
KETTLE
KEVLAR
KEWPIE
KEYNES
KEYPAD
KEYWAY
LEADEN
LEADER
LEAGUE
LEALTY
LEANTO
LEAVEN
LEAVER
LEAVES
LECHER
LECTOR
LEDGER
LEEWAY
LEGACY
LEGATE
LEGATO
LEGEND
LEGGED
LEGION
LEGIST
LEGLET
LEGMAN
LEGUME
LEMNOS
LEMONY
LEMUEL
LEMURE
LENDER
LENGTH
LENTEL
LENTEN
LENTIC
LENTIL
LENTOR
LEONID
LEPTON
LESBOS
LESION
LESLIE
LESSEE
LESSEN
LESSER
LESSON
LESSOR
LESTER
LETHAL
LETOUT
LETTER
LEVANT
LEVITE
LEVITY
LEWDLY
LEXEME
LEYDEN
MEADOW
MEAGER
MEAGRE
MEALIE
MEANIE
MEANLY
MEASLY
MEATUS
MEDDLE
MEDIAL
MEDIAN
MEDICI
MEDICO
MEDINA
MEDISM
MEDIUM
MEDIUS
MEDLAR
MEDLEY
MEDUSA
MEDWAY
MEEKLY
MEGRIM
MEJLIS
MEKONG
MELIUS
MELLOW
MELODY
MELTED
MELTON
MEMBER
MEMNON
MEMOIR
MEMORY
MENACE
MENAGE
MENDEL
MENDER
MENDES
MENDIP
MENHIR
MENIAL
MENINX
MENSAL
MENTAL
MENTOR
MENTUM
MERCAT
MERCER
MERCIA
MERELY
MERGER
MERINO
MERKIN
MERLIN
MERLOT
MERMAN
MEROPE
MERRIE
MERROW
MERSEY
MERTON
MESAIL
MESCAL
MESIAL
MESMER
MESSRS
METAGE
METATE
METEOR
METHOD
METHYL
METIER
METOPE
METRIC
METTLE
MEXICO
NEAPED
NEARBY
NEARER
NEARLY
NEATEN

NEATLY
NEBBUK
NEBECK
NEBISH
NEBULA
NEBULE
NECKAR
NECKED
NECTAR
NEEDED
NEEDLE
NEEDNT
NEFAST
NEGATE
NELLIE
NELSON
NEPALI
NEPETA
NEPHEW
NEREID
NEREUS
NERINE
NERIUM
NEROLI
NERVAL
NERVES
NERVII
NESSIE
NESSUS
NESTLE
NESTOR
NETHER
NETTLE
NEURAL
NEURON
NEUTER
NEVADA
NEWELL
NEWEST
NEWMAN
NEWTON
OEDEMA
OENONE
OERLAY
OEUVRE
PEAHEN
PEAKED
PEANUT
PEARLS
PEARLY
PEBBLE
PEBBLY
PECKER
PECTEN
PECTIN
PEDALO
PEDANT
PEDDER
PEDDLE
PEDLAR
PEELED
PEELER
PEEPER
PEEVED
PEEWEE
PEEWIT
PEGLEG
PEKING
PELHAM
PELION
PELLET
PELMET
PELOID
PELOTA
PELVIC
PELVIS
PENANG
PENCEL
PENCIL
PENMAN
PENNAE
PENNAL
PENNON
PENSÉE
PENSUM
PENTAD
PENTEL
PENTUP
PENURY
PEOPLE
PEPLOS
PEPLUM
PEPPER
PEPTIC
PEQUOD
PERDUE
PERHAP
PERILS
PERIOD
PERISH
PERKIN
PERMIT
PERNOD
PERRON
PERSON
PERUKE
PERUSE
PESADE
PESETA
PESHWA
PESTER
PESTLE
PETARD
PETARY
PETERS
PETIPA
PETITE
PETREL
PETROL
PEWTER
PEYOTE
READER
REALIA
REALLY
REALTY
REAMER
REAPER
REASON
REBATE
REBECK
REBITE
REBORE
REBORN
REBUFF
REBUKE
RECALL
RECANT
RECAST
RECEDE
RECENT
RECESS
RECIFE
RECIPE
RECITE
RECKON
RECOIL
RECORD
RECOUP
RECTAL
RECTOR
RECTUM
RECTUS
REDACT
REDCAP
REDCAR
REDDEN
REDEEM
REDEYE
REDLEG
REDRAW
REDTOP
REDUCE
REEBOK
REEFER
REEKIE
REELER
REFACE
REFECT
REFILL
REFINE
REFLET
REFLEX
REFLUX
REFORM
REFUEL
REFUGE
REFUND
REFUSE
REFUTE
REGAIN
REGALE
REGARD
REGENT
REGEST
REGGAE
REGIME
REGINA
REGION
REGIUS
REGLET
REGRET
REGULO
REHASH
REHEAT
REHEEL
REJECT
REJOIN
RELATE
RELENT
RELICS
RELICT
RELIEF
RELISH
RELIVE
REMAIN
REMAKE
REMAND
REMARK
REMEDY
REMIND
REMISS
REMOTE
REMOVE
RENAME
RENDER
RENEGE
RENNET
RENNIN
RENOIR
RENOWN
RENTAL
RENTER
RENVOI
RENVOY
REOPEN
REPAID
REPAIR
REPAST
REPEAL
REPEAT
REPENT
REPINE
REPLAY
REPORT
REPOSE
REPTON
REPUGN
REPUTE
REREAD
RESALE
RESCUE
RESEAU
RESECT
RESEDA
RESENT
RESIDE
RESIGN
RESIST
RESORT
RESULT
RESUME
RETAIL
RETAIN
RETAKE
RETARD
RETINA
RETIRE
RETOOL
RETORT
RETOUR
RETURN
REUBEN
REUTER
REVAMP
REVEAL
REVERE
REVERS
REVERT
REVERY
REVIEW
REVILE
REVISE
REVIVE
REVOKE
REVOLT
REWARD
REWIND
REWIRE
REWORD
REWORK
SEABEE
SEALED
SEAMAN
SEAMEN
SEAMER
SEAMUS
SEANCE
SEARCH
SEASON
SEATED
SEAWAY
SEBATE
SECANT
SECEDE
SECOND
SECRET
SECTOR
SECURE
SEDATE
SEDUCE
SEEDED
SEEDER
SEEING
SEEKER
SEEMLY
SEESAW
SEETHE
SEICHE
SEISIN
SELDOM
SELECT
SELENE
SELFED
SELJUK
SELLBY
SELLER
SELWYN
SEMELE
SEMITE
SEMPRE
SEMTEX
SENATE
SENDAL
SENDER
SENECA
SENILE
SENIOR
SENLAC
SENNET
SENORA
SENSED
SENSES
SENSOR
SENTRY
SEPIUM
SEPSIS
SEPTAL
SEPTET
SEPTIC
SEQUEL
SEQUIN
SERAIL
SERANG
SERAPE
SERAPH
SERBIA
SERDAB
SERENE
SERIAL
SERIES
SERINE
SERMON
SEROSA
SERVAL
SERVER
SESAME
SETOSE
SETTEE
SETTER
SETTLE
SEUMAS
SEURAT
SEVENS
SEVERE
SEVERN
SEVERY
SEWAGE
SEWELL
SEWING
SEXISM
SEXIST
SEXTAN
SEXTET
SEXTON
SEXUAL
TEABAG
TEACUP
TEAGUE
TEAPOT
TEAPOY
TEASEL
TEASER
TECHNO
TECKEL
TECTUM
TEDIUM
TEENSY
TEEPEE
TEETER
TEETHE
TEFLON
TEGMEN
TEGULA
TEHRAN
TELEGA
TELEGU
TELLAR
TELLER
TELLUS
TELUGU
TEMPER
TEMPLE
TENACE
TENANT
TENDER
TENDON
TENDRE
TENGKU
TENNER
TENNIS
TENPIN
TENSON
TENSOR
TENURE
TEOPAN
TEPHRA
TERCET
TERCIO
TEREDO
TERESA
TERETE
TERGUM
TERMES
TERMLY
TERNAL
TERRAE
TERROR

TERTIA
TESTER
TESTES
TESTIS
TETANY
TETCHY
TETHER
TETHYS
TETRAD
TETRYL
TETTIX
TEUTON
TEVIOT
VECTIS
VECTOR
VEDDAH
VEDUTA
VEILED
VEINED
VELCRO
VELETA
VELLUM
VELOCE
VELOUR
VELURE
VELVET
VENDEE
VENDER
VENDOR
VENDUE
VENEER
VENERY
VENIAL
VENICE
VENITE
VENOSE
VENOUS
VENTIL
VENTRE
VERBAL
VERDIN
VERDUN
VEREIN
VERGER
VERGES
VERIFY
VERILY
VERISM
VERITY
VERMIN
VERMIS
VERNAL
VERNON
VERSAL
VERSED
VERSES
VERSET
VERSUS
VERVET
VESICA
VESPER
VESSEL
VESTAL
VESTED
VESTRY
WEAKEN
WEAKER
WEAKLY
WEALTH
WEAPON
WEARER
WEASEL
WEAVER
WEBBED
WEDDED
WEDGED
WEEKLY
WEEPIE
WEEVIL
WEEWEE
WEIGHT
WEIMAR
WEIRDO
WELDER
WELKIN
WELLER
WELLES
WELLIE
WELTER
WELWYN
WENSUM
WERENT
WESKER
WESLEY
WESSEX
WETBOB
WETHER
XENIAL
XENIUM
XEROMA
XERXES
YEARLY
YEASTY
YELLOW
YEMENI
YEOMAN
YEOMEN
YESMAN
YESTER
YEZIDI
ZEALOT
ZEBECK
ZENANA
ZENDIK
ZENITH
ZEPHYR
ZEUGMA
DÉCIME
DÉGAGÉ
PÉTAIN
SÈVRES
RÊVEUR
AFEARS
AFFAIR
AFFECT
AFFIRM
AFFORD
AFFRAY
AFFRET
AFGHAN
AFIELD
AFLAME
AFLOAT
AFRAID
AFREET
AFRESH
AFRICA
AFTERS
EFFACE
EFFECT
EFFETE
EFFIGY
EFFLUX
EFFORT
EFFUSE
EFTEST
IFFISH
OFFCUT
OFFEND
OFFICE
OFFING
OFFISH
OFFSET
UFFIZI
AGADIR
AGARIC
AGATHA
AGEING
AGENCY
AGENDA
AGHAST
AGLAIA
AGNAIL
AGNATE
AGONIC
AGOUTI
AGREED
AGRÉGÉ
AGUISE
AGUISH
AGUIZE
EGBERT
EGENCY
EGERIA
EGESTA
EGGCUP
EGMONT
EGOISM
EGOIST
EGRESS
IGNITE
IGNORE
IGUANA
OGADEN
OGAMIC
OGRESS
UGANDA
UGARIT
UGRIAN
BHAJAN
BHAJEE
BHARAT
CHADOR
CHAFER
CHAINS
CHAIRS
CHAISE
CHAKRA
CHALET
CHALKY
CHAMPS
CHANCE
CHANCY
CHANEY
CHANGE
CHAPEL
CHAPKA
CHARGE
CHARON
CHARTA
CHASER
CHASSE
CHASTE
CHATON
CHATTY
CHAZAN
CHEDER
CHEEKY
CHEERS
CHEERY
CHEESE
CHEESY
CHEMIC
CHEMMY
CHENET
CHEOPS
CHEQUE
CHERIE
CHERRY
CHERUB
CHERUP
CHESIL
CHESTY
CHEVAL
CHEVET
CHIBOL
CHICHI
CHICLE
CHICON
CHILDE
CHILLI
CHILLY
CHIMER
CHIMES
CHINAR
CHINCH
CHINTZ
CHIPPY
CHIRON
CHIRPY
CHISEL
CHITAL
CHITIN
CHITON
CHITTY
CHIVES
CHIVVY
CHOANA
CHOICE
CHOKED
CHOKER
CHOKEY
CHOLER
CHOOSE
CHOOSY
CHOPIN
CHOPPY
CHORAL
CHOREA
CHOREE
CHORUS
CHOSEN
CHOUAN
CHOUGH
CHOWRY
CHRISM
CHRIST
CHROMA
CHROME
CHROMO
CHUBBY
CHUFFY
CHUKKA
CHUMMY
CHUNKY
CHURCH
CHYPRE
DHARMA
DHOOTI
GHARRY
GHAZAL
GHEBER
GHERAO
GHETTO
GHOSTS
KHALAT
KHALIF
KHALSA
KHARIF
KHILAT
KHILIM
KHYBER
LHOTSE
PHAROS
PHASIS
PHASMA
PHENOL
PHENYL
PHILIP
PHIZOG
PHLEGM
PHLEUM
PHLOEM
PHOBIA
PHOBIC
PHOEBE
PHONAL
PHONEY
PHONIC
PHOOEY
PHOTON
PHRASE
PHYLLO
PHYLUM
PHYSIC
PHYSIO
RHAPHE
RHEIMS
RHESUS
RHETOR
RHEUMY
RHEXIS
RHODES
RHYMER
RHYTHM
SHABBY
SHADED
SHADES
SHADOW
SHADUF
SHAGGY
SHAKEN
SHAKER
SHAKES
SHALOM
SHAMAN
SHAMBA
SHAMMY
SHAMUS
SHANDY
SHANKS
SHANTY
SHAPED
SHARED
SHARER
SHARES
SHARIA
SHARIF
SHARON
SHARPS
SHASTA
SHAVEN
SHAVER
SHEARS
SHEATH
SHEAVE
SHEENY
SHEERS
SHEETS
SHEIKH
SHEILA
SHEKEL
SHELVE
SHERIF
SHERPA
SHERRY
SHIELD
SHIFTY
SHIITE
SHILOH
SHIMMY
SHINDY
SHINER
SHINNY
SHINTO
SHINTY
SHIPKA
SHIRAZ
SHIRRA
SHIRTY
SHIVER
SHODDY
SHOFAR
SHOGUN
SHORTS
SHOULD
SHOVEL
SHOWER
SHRANK
SHREWD
SHRIEK
SHRIFT
SHRIKE
SHRILL
SHRIMP
SHRINE
SHRINK
SHRIVE
SHROFF
SHROUD
SHROVE
SHRUNK
SHTCHI
SHTETL
SHUFTI
SHUFTY
THALER
THALES
THALIA
THAMES
THANAH
THANET
THANKS
THATCH
THEAVE
THEBAN
THEBES

THECAL
THEIRS
THEISM
THEIST
THEMIS
THENAR
THENCE
THEORY
THERMO
THESIS
THETIC
THETIS
THEYRE
THICKY
THIERS
THIEVE
THINGS
THINGY
THINLY
THIRST
THIRTY
THISBE
THOLOS
THOLUS
THOMAS
THORAH
THORAX
THORNE
THORNY
THORPE
THOUGH
THRALL
THRASH
THRAWN
THREAD
THREAP
THREAT
THRENE
THRESH
THRICE
THRIFT
THRILL
THRIPS
THRIST
THRIVE
THROAT
THROES
THRONE
THRONG
THROVE
THROWN
THRUSH
THRUST
THWACK
THWART
THYMOL
THYMUS
WHACKO
WHACKY
WHALER
WHALES
WHAMMY
WHARFE
WHEELS
WHEELY
WHEEZE
WHEEZY
WHENCE
WHERRY
WHILOM
WHILST
WHIMSY
WHINGE
WHINNY
WHISHT
WHISKY
WHITBY
WHITED
WHITEN
WHITES
WHOLLY
WHOOPS
WHOOSH
AIDANT
AIGLET
AIKIDO
AILING
AIRBED
AIRBUS
AIRGUN
AIRILY
AIRING
AIRMAN
AIRWAY
BIASED
BICARB
BICEPS
BICKER
BIDDER
BIDENT
BIFFIN
BIFOLD
BIGAMY
BIGGER
BIGGIN
BIGWIG
BIKINI
BILLET
BILLIE
BILLOW
BILLYO
BINARY
BINATE
BINDER
BIOGEN
BIONIC
BIOPIC
BIOPSY
BIOTIC
BIOTIN
BIRDIE
BIREME
BIRNAM
BISCAY
BISECT
BISHOP
BISQUE
BISTER
BISTRE
BISTRO
BITCHY
BITING
BITTEN
BITTER
CICADA
CICALA
CICELY
CICERO
CIERGE
CILICE
CILIUM
CINDER
CINEMA
CINQUE
CIPHER
CIRCLE
CIRCUS
CIRQUE
CIRRUS
CITRIC
CITRIN
CITRON
CITRUS
CIVICS
CIVISM
DIADEM
DIALOG
DIANAS
DIAPER
DIATOM
DIAXON
DIBBER
DIBBLE
DICAST
DICKER
DICKEY
DICTUM
DIDDLE
DIEPPE
DIESEL
DIESIS
DIETER
DIFFER
DIGEST
DIGGER
DIGLOT
DIKDIK
DIKKOP
DIKTAT
DILATE
DILUTE
DIMITY
DIMMER
DIMPLE
DIMWIT
DINERO
DINGHY
DINGLE
DINGLY
DINING
DINKUM
DINNER
DIODON
DIOXIN
DIPLOE
DIPNOI
DIPOLE
DIPPER
DIQUAT
DIRECT
DIRHAM
DIRNDL
DISARM
DISBAR
DISBUD
DISCUS
DISEUR
DISHED
DISHES
DISMAL
DISMAY
DISNEY
DISOWN
DISPEL
DISTAL
DISTIL
DISUSE
DITHER
DITTOS
DIVALI
DIVERS
DIVERT
DIVEST
DIVIDE
DIVINE
DIVING
DIWALI
DIZAIN
EIFFEL
EIGHTH
EIGHTY
EIRANN
EITHER
FIACRE
FIANCÉ
FIASCO
FIBBED
FIBBER
FIBULA
FICKLE
FIDDLE
FIDDLY
FIDGET
FIELDS
FIERCE
FIESTA
FIGARO
FIGURE
FILFOT
FILIAL
FILING
FILLED
FILLER
FILLET
FILLIP
FILOSE
FILTER
FILTHY
FILTRÉ
FIMBRA
FINALE
FINDER
FINELY
FINERY
FINEST
FINGAL
FINGER
FINIAL
FINISH
FINITE
FINLAY
FINNAN
FIPPLE
FIRING
FIRKIN
FIRLOT
FIRMAN
FIRMER
FIRMLY
FISCAL
FISHER
FITFUL
FITOUT
FITTED
FITTER
FIXITY
FIZGIG
FIZZED
FIZZER
FIZZLE
GIAOUR
GIBBER
GIBBET
GIBBON
GIBSON
GIDDUP
GIDEON
GIFTED
GIGGLE
GIGLET
GIGLOT
GIGOLO
GILDAS
GILDED
GILDER
GILEAD
GILGAI
GILLET
GILLIE
GILPIN
GIMLET
GIMMER
GINGER
GINGKO
GINKGO
GIORGI
GIOTTO
GIRDER
GIRDLE
GIRKIN
GIRLIE
GIRTON
GITANO
GIUSTO
GIVING
GIZZEN
HIATUS
HICCUP
HICKEY
HIDAGE
HIDDEN
HIDING
HIGHER
HIGHLY
HIGHUP
HIJACK
HIKING
HILARY
HILTON
HIMMEL
HINDER
HINGED
HINGES
HIPPED
HIPPUS
HIRING
HIRSEL
HISPID
HITECH
HITHER
HITLER
HITMAN
HITTER
JIBBAH
JIGGER
JIGGLE
JIGSAW
JILLET
JIMJAM
JINGAL
JINGLE
JINXED
JISSOM
JITNEY
JITTER
KIAORA
KIBBLE
KIBOSH
KICKER
KIDDIE
KIDDLE
KIDNAP
KIDNEY
KIGALI
KIKUYU
KILLER
KILNER
KILTED
KILTER
KILTIE
KIMMER
KIMONO
KINASE
KINDER
KINDLE
KINDLY
KINGLY
KIPPER
KIRBEH
KIRMAN
KIRSCH
KIRTLE
KISMET
KISSEL
KISSER
KITBAG
KITCAT
KITSCH
KITTEN
KITTLE
LIABLE
LIAISE
LIBBER
LIBIDO
LIBYAN
LICHEN
LICTOR
LIEBIG
LIEDER
LIERNE
LIFTED
LIFTER
LIGASE
LIGATE
LIGETI
LIGGER
LIGHTS
LIGNUM
LIGULA
LIGURE
LIKELY
LIKING
LILIAN
LILITH
LIMBED
LIMBER
LIMBIC

LIMITS
LIMNER
LIMPET
LIMPID
LIMPLY
LINDEN
LINEAL
LINEAR
LINEUP
LINGER
LINGOT
LINING
LINKER
LINKUP
LINNET
LINTEL
LIONEL
LIPARI
LIPASE
LIPIDE
LIPOMA
LIPPED
LIQUID
LIQUOR
LISBON
LISPER
LISSOM
LISTEL
LISTEN
LISTER
LITANY
LITCHI
LITHIA
LITMUS
LITTER
LITTLE
LIVELY
LIVERY
LIVING
LIZARD
LIZZIE
MIASMA
MICKEY
MICKLE
MICMAC
MICRON
MIDDAY
MIDDEN
MIDDLE
MIDGET
MIDWAY
MIGHTY
MIGNON
MIKADO
MILADY
MILDEW
MILDLY
MILIEU
MILLER
MILLET
MILORD
MILTON
MIMOSA
MINCER
MINDED
MINDEL
MINDER
MINGLE
MINING
MINION
MINNIE
MINNOW
MINOAN
MINTON
MINUET
MINUTE
MIRAGE
MIRROR
MISÈRE
MISERY
MISFIT
MISHAP
MISHIT
MISLAY
MISLED
MISSAL
MISSED
MISSEL
MISSIS
MISSUS
MISTER
MISUSE
MITRAL
MITRED
MITTEN
MIZZEN
MIZZLE
NIACIN
NIAMEY
NIBBLE
NICELY
NICENE
NICETY
NICKED
NICKEL
NICKER
NIDGET
NIDIFY
NIELLO
NIGGER
NIGGLE
NIGGLY
NIGHTS
NIGHTY
NIGNOG
NIKKEI
NILGAI
NILGAU
NILOTE
NIMBLE
NIMBLY
NIMBUS
NIMROD
NINETY
NINIAN
NIPPER
NIPPLE
NIPPON
NISSEN
NITERY
NITRIC
NITRYL
NITWIT
NIVOSE
OILCAN
OILERS
OILMAN
OILRIG
PIAFFE
PIAZZA
PICARD
PICKAX
PICKED
PICKER
PICKET
PICKLE
PICKUP
PICNIC
PIDDLE
PIDGIN
PIECES
PIEDOG
PIEMAN
PIERCE
PIERIS
PIFFLE
PIGEON
PIGLET
PIGOTT
PIGPEN
PIGSTY
PILAFF
PILAGE
PILATE
PILEUM
PILEUP
PILEUS
PILFER
PILING
PILLAR
PILLOW
PILOSE
PIMENT
PIMPLE
PIMPLY
PINCER
PINDAR
PINEAL
PINERO
PINGER
PINING
PINION
PINITE
PINKIE
PINTER
PINTLE
PINXIT
PINYIN
PIPING
PIPKIN
PIPPIN
PIQUET
PIRACY
PIRATE
PIRENE
PISANO
PISCES
PISGAH
PISSED
PISTIL
PISTOL
PISTON
PITMAN
PITTED
PITTER
RIALTO
RIBALD
RIBAND
RIBBED
RIBBLE
RIBBON
RIBOSE
RICHES
RICHLY
RICKER
RICKEY
RICRAC
RICTAL
RICTUS
RIDDLE
RIDENT
RIDGED
RIDING
RIENZI
RIFFLE
RIGGED
RIGGER
RIGHTO
RIGHTS
RIGOUR
RIMINI
RIMMED
RINGED
RINGER
RIOTER
RIPOFF
RIPPER
RIPPLE
RIPPON
RIPSAW
RISING
RISQUÉ
RITUAL
RIVAGE
RIVERA
RIVLIN
RIYADH
SICILY
SICKEN
SICKER
SICKLE
SICKLY
SIDDHA
SIDING
SIDNEY
SIENNA
SIERRA
SIESTA
SIFFLE
SIFTER
SIGHTS
SIGNAL
SIGNET
SIGNOR
SIKKIM
SILAGE
SILENE
SILENT
SILICA
SILKEN
SILVAN
SILVER
SIMEON
SIMIAN
SIMILE
SIMKIN
SIMMER
SIMNEL
SIMONY
SIMOON
SIMPER
SIMPLE
SIMPLY
SINBAD
SINDER
SINEWY
SINFUL
SINGER
SINGLE
SINGLY
SINKER
SINNER
SIPHON
SIPPET
SIPPLE
SIRDAR
SIRIUS
SIRKAR
SIRRAH
SIRREE
SISKIN
SISTER
SITCOM
SITREP
SITTER
SIZZLE
TICINO
TICKER
TICKET
TICKEY
TICKLE
TICKLY
TIDBIT
TIDDLE
TIDDLY
TIDILY
TIEPIN
TIERCE
TIERED
TIFFIN
TIGHTS
TIGRIS
TILLER
TILSIT
TIMBER
TIMBRE
TIMELY
TIMING
TINDER
TINGED
TINGLE
TINKER
TINKLE
TINNED
TINNIE
TINPAN
TINPOT
TINSEL
TINTED
TINTIN
TIPCAT
TIPOFF
TIPPED
TIPPER
TIPPET
TIPPLE
TIPPOO
TIPTOE
TIPTOP
TIPULA
TIRADE
TIRANA
TIRING
TISANE
TISSOT
TISSUE
TITBIT
TITCHY
TITFER
TITIAN
TITLED
TITTER
TITTLE
TITTUP
TITULE
TIVOLI
TIZWAZ
VIABLE
VIANDS
VIATOR
VIBRIO
VICTIM
VICTOR
VICUNA
VIENNA
VIENNE
VIEWER
VIGOUR
VIKING
VILELY
VILIFY
VILLUS
VINERY
VINOUS
VIOLET
VIOLIN
VIRAGO
VIRGIL
VIRGIN
VIRILE
VIROUS
VIRTUE
VISAGE
VISCID
VISHNU
VISIER
VISION
VISUAL
VITALS
VIVACE
VIVIAN
VIVIEN
VIZARD
VIZIER
WICKED
WICKER
WICKET
WIDELY
WIDGET
WIDOWS
WIENER
WIFELY
WIGEON
WIGGLE
WIGGLY
WIGWAM
WILDER
WILDLY
WILFUL
WILLED
WILLET
WILLIE
WILLOW
WILSON
WIMBLE
WIMPLE
WIMSEY

WINDER
WINDOW
WINDUP
WINGED
WINGER
WINKER
WINKLE
WINNER
WINNIE
WINNOW
WINTER
WINTRY
WIPERS
WIPING
WIRING
WIRRAL
WISDEN
WISDOM
WISELY
WISHES
WITHAL
WITHER
WITHIN
WITTED
WIVERN
WIZARD
WIZIER
YIPPEE
ZIGZAG
ZIMMER
ZINGER
ZINNIA
ZIPPER
ZIRCON
ZITHER
DJEBEL
DJERBA
DJINNI
AKIMBO
SKATER
SKATES
SKELLY
SKERRY
SKETCH
SKEWED
SKEWER
SKIDOO
SKIING
SKIMPY
SKINNY
SKIVER
SKIVVY
SKURRY
SKYLAB
SKYMAN
ALACUS
ALALIA
ALARIC
ALARUM
ALASKA
ALBANY
ALBEDO
ALBEIT
ALBERT
ALBINO
ALBION
ALBITE
ALBUGO
ALCINA
ALCOCK
ALCOVE
ALDINE
ALDOSE
ALDRIN
ALECTO
ALEGAR
ALERCE
ALEXIA
ALEXIN
ALEXIS
ALFRED
ALIGHT
ALIPED
ALIYAH
ALKALI
ALKANE
ALKENE
ALLEGE
ALLELE
ALLEYN
ALLIED
ALLIER
ALLIUM
ALLUDE
ALLURE
ALMAIN
ALMERY
ALMOND
ALMOST
ALOGIA
ALONSO
ALPACA
ALPINE
ALPINO
ALTAIR
ALTHEA
ALUDEL
ALUMNI
ALWAYS
BLACKS
BLAISE
BLAMED
BLANCH
BLANCO
BLAZER
BLAZON
BLEACH
BLEARY
BLENCH
BLENDE
BLENNY
BLIGHT
BLIMEY
BLINKS
BLITHE
BLOCKS
BLONDE
BLOODY
BLOTCH
BLOTTO
BLOUSE
BLOWER
BLOWZY
BLUDGE
BLUISH
CLAGGY
CLAIMS
CLAMMY
CLAMOR
CLAQUE
CLARET
CLARTY
CLASSY
CLAUDE
CLAUSE
CLAVIS
CLAYEY
CLEAVE
CLENCH
CLERGY
CLERIC
CLERKS
CLEVER
CLICHÉ
CLIENT
CLIFFS
CLIMAX
CLIMES
CLINCH
CLINIC
CLIPPY
CLIQUE
CLOACA
CLOAKS
CLOCHE
CLONIC
CLONUS
CLOSED
CLOSER
CLOSET
CLOTHE
CLOUDY
CLOUGH
CLOVEN
CLOVER
CLOVIS
CLUMPS
CLUMSY
CLUNCH
CLUTCH
ELAINE
ELANCE
ELANET
ELAPSE
ELATED
ELBRUS
ELDERS
ELDEST
ELEVEN
ELFISH
ELICIT
ELIJAH
ELISHA
ELIXIR
ELLERY
ELLICE
ELODEA
ELOHIM
ELOIGN
ELOISE
ELOPER
ELTCHI
ELUANT
ELUATE
ELUTOR
ELYSEE
FLABBY
FLACON
FLAGGY
FLAGON
FLAMBÉ
FLAMEN
FLANCH
FLANGE
FLANKS
FLARES
FLASHY
FLATLY
FLATUS
FLAUNT
FLAVOR
FLAWED
FLAXEN
FLECHE
FLEDGE
FLEECE
FLEECY
FLENSE
FLESHY
FLETCH
FLEURY
FLICKS
FLIGHT
FLIMSY
FLINCH
FLINTY
FLITCH
FLOOZY
FLOPPY
FLORAL
FLORET
FLORID
FLORIN
FLOSSY
FLOURY
FLOUSH
FLOWER
FLUENT
FLUFFY
FLUNKY
FLURRY
FLUSHY
FLUTED
FLUTER
FLUTES
FLYING
GLACIS
GLADLY
GLAGOL
GLAIRE
GLAIVE
GLAMIS
GLAMOR
GLANCE
GLASSY
GLAZED
GLIBLY
GLIDER
GLIÈRE
GLINKA
GLIOMA
GLITCH
GLITZY
GLOBAL
GLOIRE
GLOOMY
GLORIA
GLOSSA
GLOSSY
GLOVED
GLOWER
GLUMPS
GLUTEN
GLYCOL
ILKLEY
ILLITE
ILLUDE
KLAXON
KLUDGE
LLOYDS
OLDISH
OLEATE
OLEFIN
OLENUS
OLIVER
OLIVET
OLIVIA
PLACED
PLACER
PLACID
PLAGUE
PLAICE
PLAINS
PLAINT
PLANCH
PLANET
PLANKS
PLAQUE
PLASMA
PLATED
PLATEN
PLATER
PLATES
PLAYER
PLEACH
PLEASE
PLEDGE
PLENTY
PLENUM
PLEURA
PLEXOR
PLEXUS
PLIANT
PLIERS
PLIGHT
PLINTH
PLISSÉ
PLONGE
PLOUGH
PLOVER
PLUCKY
PLUMED
PLUMMY
PLUNGE
PLURAL
PLUTUS
PLYING
SLACKS
SLALOM
SLANGY
SLATCH
SLATER
SLAVER
SLAVES
SLAYER
SLEAVE
SLEAZE
SLEAZY
SLEDGE
SLEEKY
SLEEPY
SLEEVE
SLEEZY
SLEIGH
SLEUTH
SLEWED
SLICER
SLIDER
SLIGHT
SLINKY
SLIPPY
SLIPUP
SLITHY
SLIVER
SLOANE
SLOGAN
SLOPES
SLOPPY
SLOSHY
SLOUCH
SLOUGH
SLOVAK
SLOVEN
SLOWLY
SLUDGE
SLUICE
SLUMMY
SLURRY
SLUSHY
ULCERS
ULITIS
ULLAGE
ULLING
ULSTER
ULTIMA
ULTIMO
AMADOU
AMAZED
AMAZON
AMBAGE
AMBLER
AMBUSH
AMELIA
AMENDE
AMENDS
AMERCE
AMHARA
AMIDOL
AMIDST
AMNION
AMOEBA
AMORAL
AMORCE
AMORET
AMOUNT
AMPERE
AMTRAK
AMULET
AMUSED
AMYCUS
AMYTAL
EMBAIL
EMBALE
EMBALM
EMBARK
EMBERS
EMBLEM
EMBODY
EMBOSS
EMBRUE
EMBRYO
EMBUSY
EMERGE
EMETIC
EMEUTE
EMIGRÉ
EMPIRE

EMPLOY
EMULGE
EMUNGE
IMBARN
IMBASE
IMBIBE
IMBOSS
IMBRUE
IMMUNE
IMMURE
IMOGEN
IMPACT
IMPAIR
IMPALA
IMPALE
IMPART
IMPAWN
IMPEDE
IMPEND
IMPISH
IMPORT
IMPOSE
IMPOST
IMPUGN
IMPURE
IMPUTE
OMASUM
OMELET
OMENTA
OMERTA
OMNIUM
SMACKS
SMALLS
SMARMY
SMARTY
SMEARY
SMEATH
SMEGMA
SMELLY
SMIGHT
SMILER
SMILES
SMILEY
SMIRCH
SMITHS
SMITHY
SMOKER
SMOKEY
SMOOCH
SMOOTH
SMUDGE
SMUDGY
SMUGLY
SMUTTY
SMYRNA
TMESIS
UMBLES
UMBREL
UMBRIA
UMBRIL
UMLAUT
UMPIRE
ANABAS
ANADEM
ANADYR
ANALOG
ANANAS
ANCHOR
ANCILE
ANCOME
ANCONA
ANCORA
ANDEAN
ANDREW
ANEMIA
ANEMIC
ANGARY
ANGELA
ANGELS
ANGERS
ANGICO
ANGINA
ANGLED
ANGLER
ANGLIA
ANGOLA
ANGORA
ANIMAL
ANIMUS
ANKARA
ANKLET
ANKOLE
ANNALS
ANNEAL
ANNEXE
ANNUAL
ANOINT
ANONYM
ANORAK
ANOXIA
ANOXIC
ANSELM
ANSWER
ANTHEM
ANTHER
ANTICS
ANTLER
ANTLIA
ANTONY
ANTRIM
ANTRUM
ANUBIS
ANYHOW
ANYONE
ANYWAY
ENABLE
ENAMEL
ENAMOR
ENARCH
ENCALM
ENCAMP
ENCASE
ENCASH
ENCODE
ENCORE
ENDEAR
ENDING
ENDIVE
ENDURE
ENERGY
ENFIRE
ENFOLD
ENFREE
ENGAGE
ENGELS
ENGINE
ENGLUT
ENGULF
ENIGMA
ENJOIN
ENLACE
ENLIST
ENMESH
ENMITY
ENNIUS
ENODAL
ENOSIS
ENOUGH
ENRAGE
ENRAPT
ENRICH
ENROBE
ENROLL
ENSATE
ENSEAL
ENSIGN
ENSILE
ENSURE
ENTAIL
ENTICE
ENTIRE
ENTITY
ENTOMB
ENTRAP
ENTREE
ENWRAP
ENZIAN
ENZYME
GNAWER
GNEISS
GNOMIC
GNOMON
INBORN
INBRED
INCASE
INCEDE
INCEPT
INCEST
INCHES
INCHON
INCISE
INCITE
INCOME
INDABA
INDEED
INDENT
INDIAN
INDICT
INDIES
INDIGN
INDIGO
INDITE
INDIUM
INDOOR
INDUCE
INDUCT
INFAME
INFAMY
INFANT
INFARE
INFECT
INFEST
INFIRM
INFLOW
INFLUX
INFOLD
INFORM
INFUSE
INGATE
INGEST
INGOTS
INGRAM
INGRES
INGROW
INGULF
INHALE
INHERE
INHUME
INJECT
INJURE
INJURY
INKJET
INKPOT
INLAID
INLAND
INLAWS
INLINE
INMATE
INMESH
INMOST
INNATE
INNING
INROAD
INRUSH
INSANE
INSECT
INSERT
INSIDE
INSIST
INSOLE
INSTAL
INSTAR
INSTEP
INSTIL
INSULA
INSULT
INSURE
INTACT
INTAKE
INTEND
INTENT
INTERN
INTIME
INTONE
INTOWN
INTRAY
INTRON
INVADE
INVENT
INVERT
INVEST
INVITE
INVOKE
INWARD
KNAGGY
KNIGHT
KNIVES
KNOBBY
KNOTTY
ONAGER
ONAGRA
ONCOME
ONCOST
ONDINE
ONEDIN
ONEGIN
ONEIDA
ONEMAN
ONEWAY
ONIONS
ONLINE
ONRUSH
ONSIDE
ONWARD
PNEUMA
SNAGGY
SNAILY
SNAKED
SNAPPY
SNATCH
SNAZZY
SNEAKY
SNEATH
SNEEZE
SNEEZY
SNIFFY
SNIFTY
SNIPER
SNITCH
SNIVEL
SNOOTY
SNOOZE
SNORER
SNOTTY
SNOUTY
SNOWED
SNUDGE
SNUGLY
UNABLE
UNBEND
UNBENT
UNBIND
UNBOLT
UNBORN
UNBRED
UNBUSY
UNCAGE
UNCIAL
UNCLAD
UNCOIL
UNCOOL
UNCORK
UNDATE
UNDECK
UNDIES
UNDINE
UNDONE
UNDULY
UNDYED
UNEASE
UNEASY
UNEVEN
UNFAIR
UNFOLD
UNFURL
UNGAIN
UNGULA
UNHAND
UNHOLY
UNHOOK
UNHURT
UNIATE
UNIQUE
UNISEX
UNISON
UNITED
UNJUST
UNKIND
UNLACE
UNLESS
UNLIKE
UNLOAD
UNLOCK
UNMADE
UNMASK
UNMEET
UNPACK
UNPAID
UNPICK
UNPLUG
UNREAD
UNREAL
UNREEL
UNREST
UNRIPE
UNROLL
UNRULY
UNSAFE
UNSAID
UNSEAM
UNSEAT
UNSEEN
UNSENT
UNSEXY
UNSHOD
UNSOLD
UNSUNG
UNSURE
UNTIDY
UNTOLD
UNTRUE
UNUSED
UNVEIL
UNWARY
UNWELL
UNWIND
UNWISE
UNWRAP
UNYOKE
AORIST
AORTAL
BOARDS
BOATER
BOBBIN
BOBBLE
BOBCAT
BOBWIG
BOCAGE
BODACH
BODEGA
BODGER
BODGIE
BODICE
BODIES
BODILY
BODKIN
BODONI
BOEING
BOFFIN
BOFORS
BOGART
BOGGLE
BOGOTA
BOHUNK
BOILED
BOILER
BOLDLY
BOLERO
BOLEYN
BOLIDE
BOLLEN
BOLSHY
BOLTER
BOMBAY
BOMBER
BOMBYX
BONBON

BONDED
BONDER
BONITO
BONNET
BONNIE
BONSAI
BONXIE
BONZER
BOOBOO
BOODLE
BOOGIE
BOOHOO
BOOJUM
BOOKED
BOOKER
BOOKIE
BOOMER
BOOTEE
BOOTLE
BOOZER
BORAGE
BORATE
BORDAR
BORDER
BOREAS
BORGIA
BORING
BORNEO
BORROW
BORSCH
BORZOI
BOSKET
BOSSED
BOSTON
BOSUNS
BOTANY
BOTHAM
BOTHER
BOTHIE
BOTLEY
BOTTLE
BOTTOM
BOUCHE
BOUCLÉ
BOUFFE
BOUGHT
BOULLE
BOUNCE
BOUNCY
BOUNDS
BOUNTY
BOURÉE
BOURNE
BOURSE
BOUSER
BOUTON
BOVATE
BOVINE
BOVRIL
BOWELS
BOWERY
BOWLED
BOWLER
BOWMAN
BOWSER
BOWWOW
BOXCAR
BOXING
BOYISH
COALER
COARSE
COATED
COATES
COBALT
COBBER
COBBLE
COBDEN
COBURG
COBWEB
COCCID
COCCUS
COCCYX
COCHIN
COCKER
COCKLE
COCOON
CODDLE
CODGER
CODIFY
CODING
COERCE
COEVAL
COFFEE
COFFER
COFFIN
COGENT
COGGER
COGNAC
COHERE
COHORT
COILED
COINER
COITUS
COLDLY
COLLAR
COLLET
COLLIE
COLLOP
COLMAR
COLONY
COLOUR
COLTER
COLUMN
COMART
COMATE
COMBAT
COMBED
COMBER
COMBLE
COMEDO
COMEDY
COMELY
COMFIT
COMICE
COMING
COMITY
COMMIS
COMMIT
COMMON
COMPEL
COMPLY
COMSAT
CONCHA
CONCHY
CONCUR
CONDOM
CONDOR
CONFAB
CONFER
CONGEE
CONGER
CONICS
CONKER
CONMAN
CONNER
CONRAD
CONSUL
CONTRA
CONVEX
CONVEY
CONVOY
COOING
COOKED
COOKER
COOKIE
COOLER
COOLIE
COOLLY
COOLTH
COOPER
COOTIE
COPECK
COPIED
COPIER
COPING
COPPER
COPPIN
COPTIC
COQUET
CORALS
CORBEL
CORBIE
CORDON
CORIUM
CORKED
CORKER
CORMUS
CORNEA
CORNED
CORNEL
CORNER
CORNET
CORNUA
CORNUS
CORONA
CORPSE
CORPUS
CORRAL
CORRIE
CORSET
CORTES
CORTEX
CORTEZ
CORVÉE
CORVUS
CORYZA
COSHER
COSIER
COSILY
COSINE
COSMEA
COSMIC
COSMOS
COSSET
COSSIE
COSTAR
COSTER
COSTLY
COTTAR
COTTON
COTYLE
COUGAR
COULEE
COULIS
COUNTY
COUPLE
COUPON
COURSE
COUSIN
COVENT
COVERT
COVING
COWAGE
COWARD
COWBOY
COWMAN
COWPAT
COWPER
COWRIE
COYOTE
COZIER
DOBBIN
DOBSON
DOCENT
DOCILE
DOCKED
DOCKER
DOCKET
DOCTOR
DODDER
DODDLE
DODGEM
DODGER
DODOMA
DOESNT
DOGGED
DOGGER
DOINGS
DOLEUR
DOLINA
DOLINE
DOLIUM
DOLLAR
DOLLOP
DOLMAN
DOLMEN
DOLOUR
DOMAIN
DOMINO
DONATE
DONGLE
DONJON
DONKEY
DONNÉE
DONZEL
DOODAD
DOODAH
DOODLE
DOOFER
DOOMED
DORADO
DORCAS
DORIAN
DORMER
DORRIT
DORSAL
DORSET
DORTER
DOSAGE
DOSSAL
DOSSER
DOTAGE
DOTARD
DOTING
DOTTED
DOTTLE
DOUANE
DOUBLE
DOUBLY
DOUCET
DOUCHE
DOUGHY
DOURLY
DOWNAY
DOWNER
DOWSER
DOWSET
DOWSON
DOYLEY
DOZENS
DOZING
EOCENE
EOLITH
EOTHEN
EOZOON
FOCSLE
FODDER
FOETAL
FOETID
FOETUS
FOIBLE
FOILED
FOKINE
FOKKER
FOLDED
FOLDER
FOLIAR
FOLIOS
FOLIOT
FOLIUM
FOLKSY
FOLLOW
FOMENT
FONDLE
FONDLY
FONDUE
FOOTER
FOOTLE
FOOZLE
FORAGE
FORBID
FORÇAT
FORCED
FORCES
FOREDO
FOREGO
FOREST
FORGED
FORGER
FORGET
FORGOT
FORINT
FORKED
FORMAL
FORMAT
FORMER
FORMIC
FORNAX
FORNIX
FORPIT
FORRAD
FORRAY
FORSAY
FORTHY
FOSSIL
FOSTER
FOUGHT
FOULLY
FOURTH
FOUTRE
FOWLER
GOALIE
GOANNA
GOATEE
GOBBET
GOBBLE
GOBLET
GOBLIN
GOCART
GODIVA
GODOWN
GODSON
GODWIN
GODWIT
GOETHE
GOFFER
GOGGLE
GOITER
GOITRE
GOKART
GOLDEN
GOLFER
GOLLOP
GOLOSH
GONION
GONIUM
GOOBER
GOODLY
GOOGIE
GOOGLE
GOOGLY
GOOGOL
GOOLEY
GOOLIE
GOPHER
GORDON
GORGED
GORGES
GORGET
GORGIA
GORGIO
GORGON
GORING
GOSPEL
GOSSIP
GOTHAM
GOTHIC
GOTTEN
GOUNOD
GOURDE
GOURDS
GOUTTE
GOVERN
HOARSE
HOAXER
HOBART
HOBBES
HOBBLE
HOBDAY
HOBNOB
HOCKEY
HODDER
HOGGAR
HOGGET
HOGTIE
HOIDEN
HOLDER

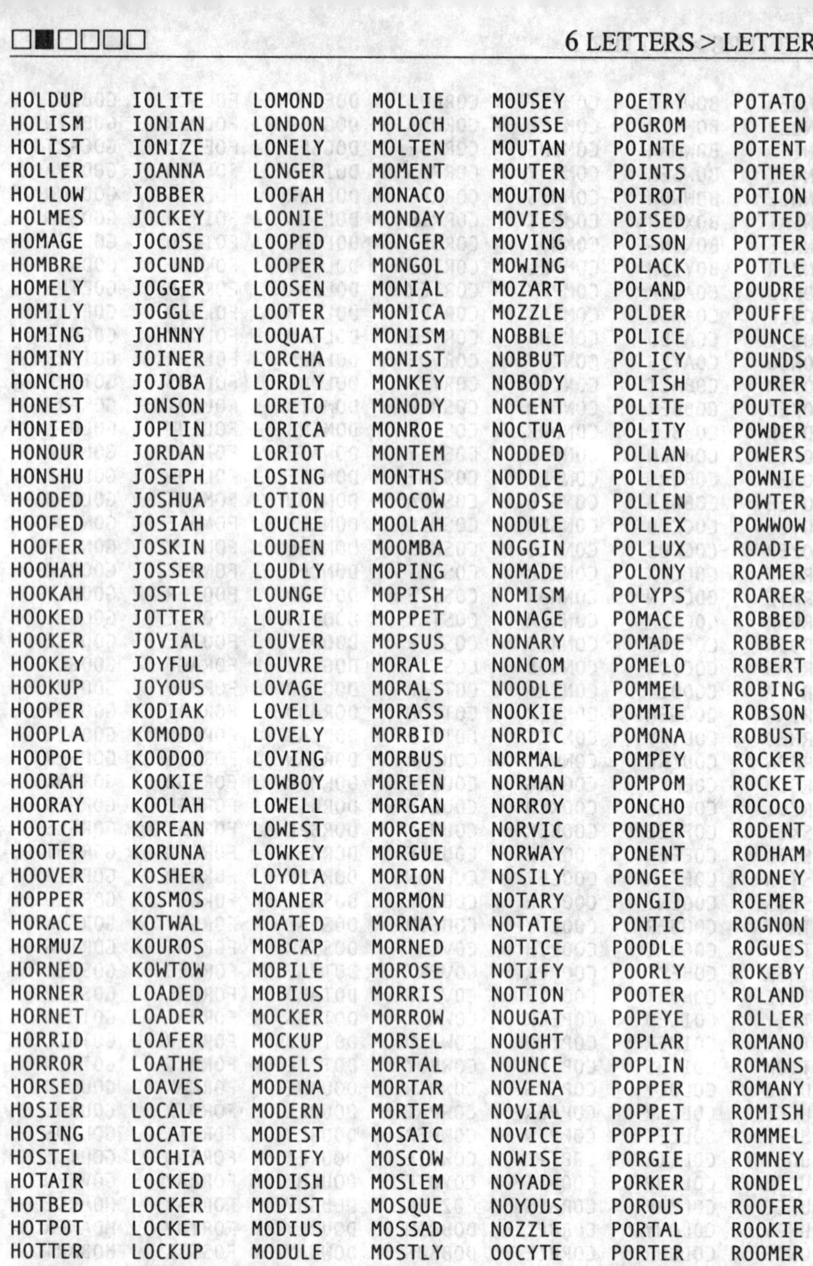

HOLDUP
HOLISM
HOLIST
HOLLER
HOLLOW
HOLMES
HOMAGE
HOMBRE
HOMELY
HOMILY
HOMING
HOMINY
HONCHO
HONEST
HONIED
HONOUR
HONSHU
HOODED
HOOFED
HOOFER
HOOHAH
HOOKAH
HOOKED
HOOKER
HOOKEY
HOOKUP
HOOPER
HOOPLA
HOOPOE
HOORAH
HOORAY
HOOTCH
HOOTER
HOOVER
HOPPER
HORACE
HORMUZ
HORNED
HORNER
HORNET
HORRID
HORROR
HORSED
HOSIER
HOSING
HOSTEL
HOTAIR
HOTBED
HOTPOT
HOTTER
HOUDAH
HOUNDS
HOURLY
HOUSES
HOWARD
HOWDAH
HOWDIE
HOWLER
HOYDEN
IODINE
IODIZE
IOLITE
IONIAN
IONIZE
JOANNA
JOBBER
JOCKEY
JOCOSE
JOCUND
JOGGER
JOGGLE
JOHNNY
JOINER
JOJOBA
JONSON
JOPLIN
JORDAN
JOSEPH
JOSHUA
JOSIAH
JOSKIN
JOSSER
JOSTLE
JOTTER
JOVIAL
JOYFUL
JOYOUS
KODIAK
KOMODO
KOODOO
KOOKIE
KOOLAH
KOREAN
KORUNA
KOSHER
KOSMOS
KOTWAL
KOUROS
KOWTOW
LOADED
LOADER
LOAFER
LOATHE
LOAVES
LOCALE
LOCATE
LOCHIA
LOCKED
LOCKER
LOCKET
LOCKUP
LOCULE
LOCUST
LODGED
LODGER
LOGGER
LOGGIA
LOGJAM
LOITER
LOLITA
LOLIUM
LOLLOP
LOMOND
LONDON
LONELY
LONGER
LOOFAH
LOONIE
LOOPED
LOOPER
LOOSEN
LOOTER
LOQUAT
LORCHA
LORDLY
LORETO
LORICA
LORIOT
LOSING
LOTION
LOUCHE
LOUDEN
LOUDLY
LOUNGE
LOURIE
LOUVER
LOUVRE
LOVAGE
LOVELL
LOVELY
LOVING
LOWBOY
LOWELL
LOWEST
LOWKEY
LOYOLA
MOANER
MOATED
MOBCAP
MOBILE
MOBIUS
MOCKER
MOCKUP
MODELS
MODENA
MODERN
MODEST
MODIFY
MODISH
MODIST
MODIUS
MODULE
MOGGIE
MOHAIR
MOHAWK
MOHOCK
MOIDER
MOIETY
MOJAVE
MOLECH
MOLEST
MOLINE
MOLLAH
MOLLIE
MOLOCH
MOLTEN
MOMENT
MONACO
MONDAY
MONGER
MONGOL
MONIAL
MONICA
MONISM
MONIST
MONKEY
MONODY
MONROE
MONTEM
MONTHS
MOOCOW
MOOLAH
MOOMBA
MOPING
MOPISH
MOPPET
MOPSUS
MORALE
MORALS
MORASS
MORBID
MORBUS
MOREEN
MORGAN
MORGEN
MORGUE
MORION
MORMON
MORNAY
MORNED
MOROSE
MORRIS
MORROW
MORSEL
MORTAL
MORTAR
MORTEM
MOSAIC
MOSCOW
MOSLEM
MOSQUE
MOSSAD
MOSTLY
MOTHER
MOTILE
MOTION
MOTIVE
MOTLEY
MOTOWN
MOTTLE
MOUJIK
MOULDY
MOULIN
MOUSER
MOUSEY
MOUSSE
MOUTAN
MOUTER
MOUTON
MOVIES
MOVING
MOWING
MOZART
MOZZLE
NOBBLE
NOBBUT
NOBODY
NOCENT
NOCTUA
NODDED
NODDLE
NODOSE
NODULE
NOGGIN
NOMADE
NOMISM
NONAGE
NONARY
NONCOM
NOODLE
NOOKIE
NORDIC
NORMAL
NORMAN
NORROY
NORVIC
NORWAY
NOSILY
NOTARY
NOTATE
NOTICE
NOTIFY
NOTION
NOUGAT
NOUGHT
NOUNCE
NOVENA
NOVIAL
NOVICE
NOWISE
NOYADE
NOYOUS
NOZZLE
OOCYTE
OODLES
OOKPIK
OOLITE
OOLONG
OOMPAH
POBBLE
POCKET
PODIUM
PODSOL
PODZOL
POETIC
POETRY
POGROM
POINTE
POINTS
POIROT
POISED
POISON
POLACK
POLAND
POLDER
POLICE
POLICY
POLISH
POLITE
POLITY
POLLAN
POLLED
POLLEN
POLLEX
POLLUX
POLONY
POLYPS
POMACE
POMADE
POMELO
POMMEL
POMMIE
POMONA
POMPEY
POMPOM
PONCHO
PONDER
PONENT
PONGEE
PONGID
PONTIC
POODLE
POORLY
POOTER
POPEYE
POPLAR
POPLIN
POPPER
POPPET
POPPIT
PORGIE
PORKER
POROUS
PORTAL
PORTER
PORTIA
PORTLY
POSADA
POSEUR
POSSER
POSSET
POSSUM
POSTAL
POSTER
POSTIL
POTASH
POTATO
POTEEN
POTENT
POTHER
POTION
POTTED
POTTER
POTTLE
POUDRE
POUFFE
POUNCE
POUNDS
POURER
POUTER
POWDER
POWERS
POWNIE
POWTER
POWWOW
ROADIE
ROAMER
ROARER
ROBBED
ROBBER
ROBERT
ROBING
ROBSON
ROBUST
ROCKER
ROCKET
ROCOCO
RODENT
RODHAM
RODNEY
ROEMER
ROGNON
ROGUES
ROKEBY
ROLAND
ROLLER
ROMANO
ROMANS
ROMANY
ROMISH
ROMMEL
ROMNEY
RONDEL
ROOFER
ROOKIE
ROOMER
ROOTED
ROOTER
ROOTLE
ROPERY
ROQUET
ROSACE
ROSARY
ROSCID
ROSCOE
ROSERY
ROSINA

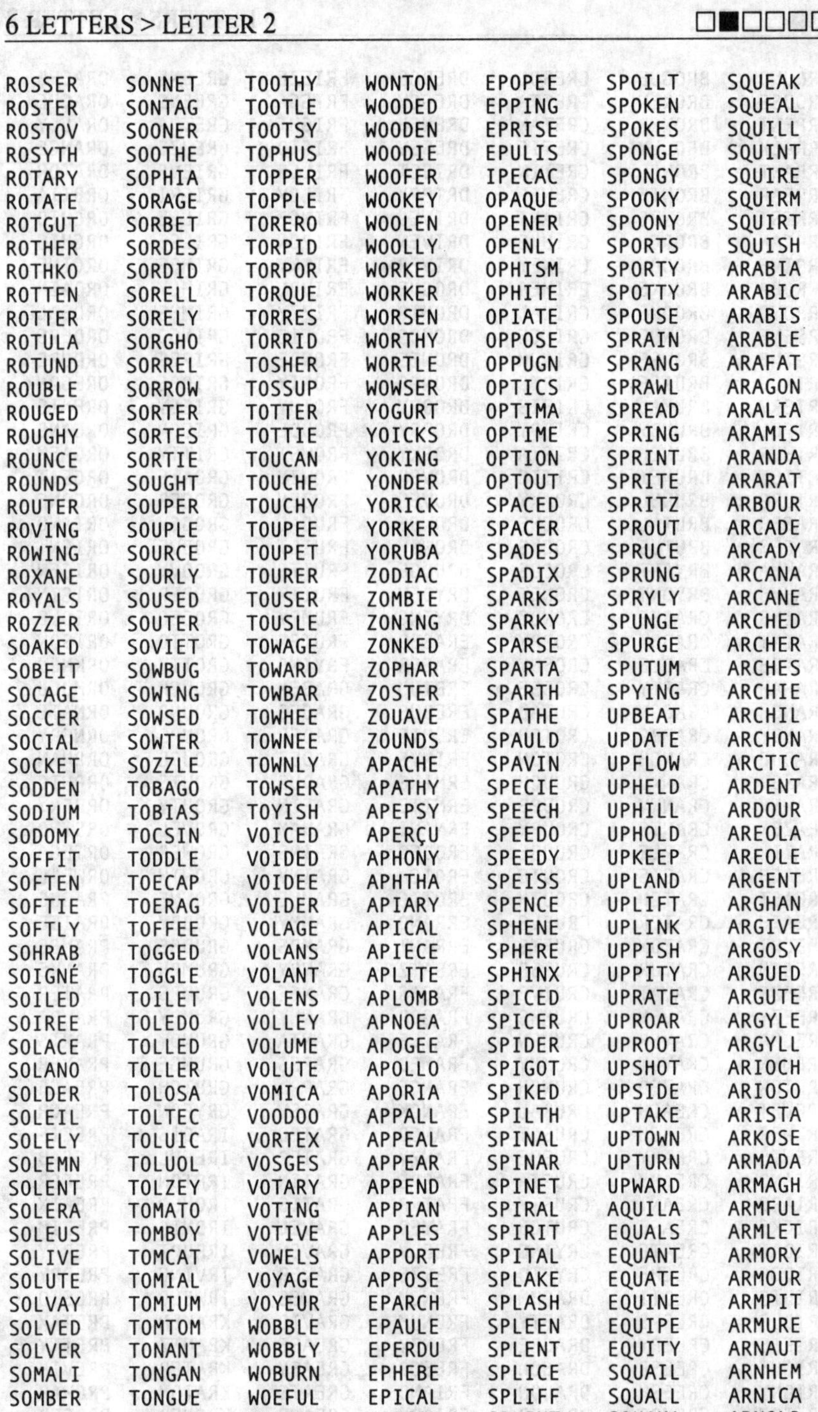

ROSSER
ROSTER
ROSTOV
ROSYTH
ROTARY
ROTATE
ROTGUT
ROTHER
ROTHKO
ROTTEN
ROTTER
ROTULA
ROTUND
ROUBLE
ROUGED
ROUGHY
ROUNCE
ROUNDS
ROUTER
ROVING
ROWING
ROXANE
ROYALS
ROZZER
SOAKED
SOBEIT
SOCAGE
SOCCER
SOCIAL
SOCKET
SODDEN
SODIUM
SODOMY
SOFFIT
SOFTEN
SOFTIE
SOFTLY
SOHRAB
SOIGNÉ
SOILED
SOIREE
SOLACE
SOLANO
SOLDER
SOLEIL
SOLELY
SOLEMN
SOLENT
SOLERA
SOLEUS
SOLIVE
SOLUTE
SOLVAY
SOLVED
SOLVER
SOMALI
SOMBER
SOMBRE
SONANT
SONATA
SONICS
SONNET
SONTAG
SOONER
SOOTHE
SOPHIA
SORAGE
SORBET
SORDES
SORDID
SORELL
SORELY
SORGHO
SORREL
SORROW
SORTER
SORTES
SORTIE
SOUGHT
SOUPER
SOUPLE
SOURCE
SOURLY
SOUSED
SOUTER
SOVIET
SOWBUG
SOWING
SOWSED
SOWTER
SOZZLE
TOBAGO
TOBIAS
TOCSIN
TODDLE
TOECAP
TOERAG
TOFFEE
TOGGED
TOGGLE
TOILET
TOLEDO
TOLLED
TOLLER
TOLOSA
TOLTEC
TOLUIC
TOLUOL
TOLZEY
TOMATO
TOMBOY
TOMCAT
TOMIAL
TOMIUM
TOMTOM
TONANT
TONGAN
TONGUE
TONITE
TONSIL
TONSOR
TOOTER
TOOTHY
TOOTLE
TOOTSY
TOPHUS
TOPPER
TOPPLE
TORERO
TORPID
TORPOR
TORQUE
TORRES
TORRID
TOSHER
TOSSUP
TOTTER
TOTTIE
TOUCAN
TOUCHE
TOUCHY
TOUPEE
TOUPET
TOURER
TOUSER
TOUSLE
TOWAGE
TOWARD
TOWBAR
TOWHEE
TOWNEE
TOWNLY
TOWSER
TOYISH
VOICED
VOIDED
VOIDEE
VOIDER
VOLAGE
VOLANS
VOLANT
VOLENS
VOLLEY
VOLUME
VOLUTE
VOMICA
VOODOO
VORTEX
VOSGES
VOTARY
VOTING
VOTIVE
VOWELS
VOYAGE
VOYEUR
WOBBLE
WOBBLY
WOBURN
WOEFUL
WOMBAT
WOMENS
WONDER
WONTED
WONTON
WOODED
WOODEN
WOODIE
WOOFER
WOOKEY
WOOLEN
WOOLLY
WORKED
WORKER
WORSEN
WORTHY
WORTLE
WOWSER
YOGURT
YOICKS
YOKING
YONDER
YORICK
YORKER
YORUBA
ZODIAC
ZOMBIE
ZONING
ZONKED
ZOPHAR
ZOSTER
ZOUAVE
ZOUNDS
APACHE
APATHY
APEPSY
APERÇU
APHONY
APHTHA
APIARY
APICAL
APIECE
APLITE
APLOMB
APNOEA
APOGEE
APOLLO
APORIA
APPALL
APPEAL
APPEAR
APPEND
APPIAN
APPLES
APPORT
APPOSE
EPARCH
EPAULE
EPERDU
EPHEBE
EPICAL
EPIGON
EPILOG
EPIRUS
EPONYM
EPOPEE
EPPING
EPRISE
EPULIS
IPECAC
OPAQUE
OPENER
OPENLY
OPHISM
OPHITE
OPIATE
OPPOSE
OPPUGN
OPTICS
OPTIMA
OPTIME
OPTION
OPTOUT
SPACED
SPACER
SPADES
SPADIX
SPARKS
SPARKY
SPARSE
SPARTA
SPARTH
SPATHE
SPAULD
SPAVIN
SPECIE
SPEECH
SPEEDO
SPEEDY
SPEISS
SPENCE
SPHENE
SPHERE
SPHINX
SPICED
SPICER
SPIDER
SPIGOT
SPIKED
SPILTH
SPINAL
SPINAR
SPINET
SPIRAL
SPIRIT
SPITAL
SPLAKE
SPLASH
SPLEEN
SPLENT
SPLICE
SPLIFF
SPLINT
SPLITS
SPLOSH
SPOILS
SPOILT
SPOKEN
SPOKES
SPONGE
SPONGY
SPOOKY
SPOONY
SPORTS
SPORTY
SPOTTY
SPOUSE
SPRAIN
SPRANG
SPRAWL
SPREAD
SPRING
SPRINT
SPRITE
SPRITZ
SPROUT
SPRUCE
SPRUNG
SPRYLY
SPUNGE
SPURGE
SPUTUM
SPYING
UPBEAT
UPDATE
UPFLOW
UPHELD
UPHILL
UPHOLD
UPKEEP
UPLAND
UPLIFT
UPLINK
UPPISH
UPPITY
UPRATE
UPROAR
UPROOT
UPSHOT
UPSIDE
UPTAKE
UPTOWN
UPTURN
UPWARD
AQUILA
EQUALS
EQUANT
EQUATE
EQUINE
EQUIPE
EQUITY
SQUAIL
SQUALL
SQUAMA
SQUARE
SQUASH
SQUAWK
SQUEAK
SQUEAL
SQUILL
SQUINT
SQUIRE
SQUIRM
SQUIRT
SQUISH
ARABIA
ARABIC
ARABIS
ARABLE
ARAFAT
ARAGON
ARALIA
ARAMIS
ARANDA
ARARAT
ARBOUR
ARCADE
ARCADY
ARCANA
ARCANE
ARCHED
ARCHER
ARCHES
ARCHIE
ARCHIL
ARCHON
ARCTIC
ARDENT
ARDOUR
AREOLA
AREOLE
ARGENT
ARGHAN
ARGIVE
ARGOSY
ARGUED
ARGUTE
ARGYLE
ARGYLL
ARIOCH
ARIOSO
ARISTA
ARKOSE
ARMADA
ARMAGH
ARMFUL
ARMLET
ARMORY
ARMOUR
ARMPIT
ARMURE
ARNAUT
ARNHEM
ARNICA
ARNOLD
AROINT
AROLLA
AROUET

AROUND
AROUSE
ARPENT
ARRACK
ARRANT
ARREAR
ARREST
ARRIAN
ARRIVE
ARROBA
ARROYO
ARSÈNE
ARSINE
ARTAUD
ARTERY
ARTFUL
ARTHUR
ARTIST
ARTURO
BRACER
BRACES
BRAHMA
BRAHMS
BRAINS
BRAINY
BRAISE
BRAMAH
BRANCH
BRANDY
BRAQUE
BRASSY
BRAWNY
BRAZEN
BRAZIL
BREACH
BREAST
BREATH
BRECHT
BREECH
BREEZE
BREEZY
BREGMA
BREMEN
BRETON
BREVET
BREWER
BREWIS
BRIAND
BRIARD
BRICKS
BRIDAL
BRIDGE
BRIDIE
BRIDLE
BRIEFS
BRIGHT
BRIONY
BRITON
BROACH
BROADS
BROGAN
BROGUE
BROKEN
BROKER
BROLLY
BRONCO
BRONTE
BRONZE
BROOCH
BROODY
BROOKE
BROOKS
BROWNE
BROWSE
BRUISE
BRUMAL
BRUMBY
BRUNCH
BRUNEI
BRUNEL
BRUTAL
BRUTUS
BRYANT
BRYONY
CRABBE
CRABBY
CRADLE
CRAFTY
CRAGGY
CRAMBO
CRANCH
CRANKY
CRANNY
CRANTS
CRAPLE
CRASIS
CRATCH
CRATER
CRATON
CRATUR
CRAVAT
CRAVEN
CRAYER
CRAYON
CRAZED
CREACH
CREAGH
CREAKY
CREAMY
CREANT
CREASE
CREATE
CRÈCHE
CREDIT
CREEPS
CREEPY
CREESE
CREESH
CREMOR
CRENAL
CRENEL
CREOLE
CRESOL
CRESTA
CRETAN
CRETIC
CRETIN
CREWEL
CRIANT
CRIBLE
CRIKEY
CRIMEA
CRINAL
CRINGE
CRINUM
CRIPES
CRISIS
CRISPY
CRISTA
CRITIC
CROAKY
CROCHE
CROCKS
CROCUS
CRONET
CRONOS
CROPPY
CROSBY
CROSSE
CROTAL
CROTCH
CROTON
CROUCH
CROUPE
CROUPY
CROUSE
CROUTE
CROUTH
CRUELS
CRUFTS
CRUISE
CRUIVE
CRUMBS
CRUMEN
CRUMMY
CRUNCH
CRURAL
CRUSET
CRUSOE
CRUSTA
CRUSTY
CRUTCH
CRYING
CRYPTO
DRACHM
DRAFTY
DRAGEE
DRAGON
DRALON
DRAPER
DRAWER
DREAMY
DREARY
DREDGE
DREGGY
DRENCH
DRESSY
DRIEST
DRIPPY
DRIVEL
DRIVEN
DRIVER
DROGUE
DROMIO
DROMOS
DRONES
DRONGO
DROOPY
DROPSY
DROSKY
DROVER
DROVES
DROWSE
DROWSY
DRUDGE
DRYDEN
DRYING
ERASED
ERASER
ERBIUM
EREBUS
EREMIC
ERINYS
ERMINE
ERMITE
ERNANI
ERODED
EROICA
EROTIC
ERRAND
ERRANT
ERSATZ
FRACAS
FRAGOR
FRAISE
FRAMED
FRANCE
FRANCK
FRANCO
FRANZY
FRAPPÉ
FRATER
FRAYED
FREELY
FREEZE
FRENCH
FRENUM
FRENZY
FRESCO
FRIAND
FRIARY
FRIDAY
FRIDGE
FRIEND
FRIEZE
FRIGGA
FRIGHT
FRIGID
FRILLS
FRILLY
FRINGE
FRIPON
FRISKY
FRIVOL
FRIZZY
FROLIC
FRONDE
FROSTY
FROTHY
FROUDE
FROWST
FROWZY
FROZEN
FRUGAL
FRUICT
FRUITS
FRUITY
FRUMPY
FRUTEX
FRYING
GRABEN
GRACES
GRADED
GRADES
GRADUS
GRAFIN
GRAHAM
GRAINS
GRAINY
GRAMME
GRAMMY
GRAMPS
GRANBY
GRANGE
GRANNY
GRANTA
GRAPES
GRAPPA
GRASSY
GRATED
GRATER
GRATIN
GRATIS
GRAVEL
GRAVEN
GRAVER
GRAVES
GRAVID
GREASE
GREASY
GREATS
GREAVE
GREECE
GREEDY
GREEKS
GREENE
GREENS
GRETNA
GREUZE
GRIEVE
GRIGRI
GRILLE
GRILSE
GRIMES
GRIMLY
GRIMMS
GRINGO
GRIPES
GRIPPE
GRISLY
GRISON
GRITTY
GROATS
GROCER
GROGGY
GROOVE
GROOVY
GROPER
GROSSO
GROTTO
GROTTY
GROUCH
GROUND
GROUPS
GROUSE
GROUTS
GROUTY
GROVEL
GROWER
GROWTH
GROYNE
GRUBBY
GRUDGE
GRUMPH
GRUMPS
GRUMPY
GRUNDY
GRUNGE
GRUTCH
GRYFON
IRAQIS
IREFUL
IRETON
IRONED
IRONIC
IRRUPT
IRVING
IRWELL
KRAKEN
KRANTZ
KRATER
KRATON
KRONER
KRONOS
KRUGER
KRUMAN
ORACHE
ORACLE
ORALLY
ORANGE
ORATOR
ORBITA
ORCHID
ORCHIS
ORCINE
ORDAIN
ORDEAL
ORDERS
ORDURE
OREGON
OREXIS
ORGANS
ORGASM
ORGEAT
ORGONE
ORIANO
ORIENT
ORIGEN
ORIGIN
ORIOLE
ORISON
ORKNEY
ORMOLU
ORNATE
ORNERY
ORPHAN
ORPHIC
ORRERY
ORSINO
ORTEGA
ORWELL
PRAGUE
PRAISE
PRANCE
PRANKS
PRATER
PRAVDA
PRAXIS
PRAYER
PREACE
PREACH
PRECIS
PREFAB
PREFER
PREFIX
PRELIM
PREPAY
PREPPY
PRESTO
PRETAX
PRETTY
PREVIN
PREWAR
PRICED
PRICEY
PRIEST
PRIMAL

PRIMED
PRIMER
PRIMLY
PRIMUS
PRINCE
PRIORY
PRISMS
PRISON
PRISSY
PRIVET
PRIZES
PROBIT
PROFIT
PROLEG
PROLIX
PROLOG
PROMPT
PRONTO
PROPEL
PROPER
PROPYL
PROSIT
PROTEA
PROTON
PROUST
PROVEN
PRUNER
PRYING
TRACER
TRADER
TRADES
TRAGIC
TRAGUS
TRAJAN
TRALEE
TRANCE
TRANNY
TRAPES
TRASHY
TRAUMA
TRAVEL
TRAVIS
TREATY
TREBLE
TREBLY
TREMOR
TRENCH
TRENDY
TREPAN
TRESCO
TRIAGE
TRIBAL
TRIBES
TRICAR
TRICKS
TRICKY
TRICOT
TRIFLE
TRIGON
TRILBY
TRIMLY
TRIODE
TRIPLE
TRIPOD
TRIPOS
TRISTE
TRITON
TRIVET
TRIVIA
TROCAR
TROCHE
TROIKA
TROJAN
TROMPE
TROOPS
TROPHE
TROPHY
TROPIC
TROPPO
TROUGH
TROUPE
TROUVÉ
TROVER
TROWEL
TROYES
TRUANT
TRUDGE
TRUISM
TRUMAN
TRUMPS
TRUNKS
TRUSTY
TRUTHS
TRYING
URANIA
URANIC
URANUS
URBANE
URCHIN
URETER
URGENT
URINAL
URSINE
URSULA
URTICA
WRAITH
WRASSE
WREATH
WREKIN
WRENCH
WRETCH
WRIGHT
WRITER
WRITHE
ASARUM
ASCEND
ASCENT
ASCHAM
ASCIAN
ASCIUS
ASGARD
ASHCAN
ASHDOD
ASHINE
ASHLAR
ASHLEY
ASHORE
ASHPAN
ASHTAR
ASHTON
ASIMOV
ASKARI
ASKING
ASLANT
ASLEEP
ASLOPE
ASMARA
ASPECT
ASPIRE
ASSAIL
ASSART
ASSENT
ASSERT
ASSESS
ASSETS
ASSIGN
ASSIST
ASSIZE
ASSOIL
ASSORT
ASSUME
ASSURE
ASTART
ASTERN
ASTHMA
ASTONE
ASTRAL
ASTRAY
ASTUTE
ASWARM
ASYLUM
ESCAPE
ESCARP
ESCHAR
ESCHEW
ESCORT
ESCROC
ESCROW
ESCUDO
ESKIMO
ESPADA
ESPRIT
ESSENE
ESTATE
ESTEEM
ESTHER
ESTRAY
ISABEL
ISAIAH
ISCHIA
ISEULT
ISHTAR
ISLAND
ISLETS
ISOBAR
ISOLDE
ISOMER
ISOPOD
ISRAEL
ISSUES
ISTRIA
OSBERT
OSIERY
OSIRIS
OSMIUM
OSMOSE
OSPREY
OSSIAN
OSSIFY
OSTEND
OSTIUM
OSTLER
OSTREA
OSWALD
PSEUDO
PSYCHE
PSYCHO
TSETSE
TSHIRT
TSWANA
USABLE
USANCE
USEFUL
USHANT
USURER
ATABAL
ATABEG
ATAMAN
ATAXIA
ATAXIC
ATHENE
ATHENS
ATHROB
ATKINS
ATOCIA
ATOMIC
ATONAL
ATONIC
ATRIAL
ATRIDE
ATRIUM
ATTACH
ATTACK
ATTAIN
ATTEND
ATTEST
ATTILA
ATTIRE
ATTLEE
ATTONE
ATTORN
ATTRAP
ATTUNE
ETALON
ETCHER
ETHANE
ETHENE
ETHICS
ETHIOP
ETHNIC
ETRIER
ETYMON
ITALIC
ITCHEN
ITERUM
ITHACA
ITSELF
OTALGY
OTELLO
OTHERS
OTIOSE
OTITIS
OTTAVA
OTTAWA
PTERIN
PTERIS
PTOSIS
STABLE
STABLY
STACKS
STAFFA
STAGER
STAGEY
STAIRS
STAKES
STALAG
STALIN
STALKS
STALKY
STALLS
STAMEN
STAMPS
STANCE
STANCH
STANZA
STAPES
STAPLE
STARCH
STARES
STARRY
STARVE
STASIS
STATAL
STATED
STATEN
STATER
STATES
STATIC
STATOR
STATUE
STATUS
STAYER
STEADY
STEAMY
STEELE
STEELY
STEERS
STEMMA
STENCH
STEPPE
STEREO
STERIC
STERNE
STEROL
STEVEN
STEWED
STICKS
STICKY
STIFLE
STIGMA
STILTS
STILTY
STINGO
STINGY
STINKO
STINKS
STIPES
STITCH
STOCKS
STOCKY
STODGE
STODGY
STOGIE
STOKER
STOKES
STOLEN
STOLID
STOLON
STONED
STONER
STONES
STOOGE
STOOKS
STOOLS
STORER
STOREY
STORMY
STOVER
STOWER
STRABO
STRAFE
STRAIN
STRAIT
STRAKE
STRAND
STRASS
STRATA
STRAWS
STRAWY
STREAK
STREAM
STREET
STREGA
STRENE
STRESS
STRICK
STRICT
STRIDE
STRIFE
STRIKE
STRINE
STRING
STRIPE
STRIPY
STRIVE
STROBE
STRODE
STROKE
STROLL
STRONG
STROUD
STROUP
STROVE
STRUCK
STRUNG
STRUNT
STUART
STUBBS
STUBBY
STUCCO
STUDIO
STUFFY
STUMER
STUMPS
STUMPY
STUPID
STUPOR
STURDY
STYLET
STYLUS
STYMIE
STYRAX
UTERUS
UTMOST
UTOPIA
AUBADE
AUBREY
AUBURN
AUCUBA
AUDILE
AUDLEY
AUDREY
AUGEAN
AUGITE
AUGURY
AUGUST
AUMBRY
AUNTIE
AUREUS
AURIGA
AURORA
AUSPEX
AUSSIE
AUSTEN
AUSTER
AUSTIN
AUTHOR

AUTISM
AUTUMN
BUBBLE
BUBBLY
BUCCAL
BUCHAN
BUCKED
BUCKER
BUCKET
BUCKLE
BUDDHA
BUDGET
BUDGIE
BUENOS
BUFFER
BUFFET
BUFFON
BUGGER
BUGLER
BUKSHI
BULBIL
BULBUL
BULGAR
BULGER
BULIMY
BULLER
BULLET
BUMALO
BUMBLE
BUMPER
BUNCHY
BUNDLE
BUNGAY
BUNGEE
BUNGLE
BUNION
BUNJEE
BUNKER
BUNKUM
BUNSEN
BUNTER
BUNYAN
BURBLE
BURBOT
BURDEN
BUREAU
BURGEE
BURGER
BURGLE
BURIAL
BURIED
BURKHA
BURLAP
BURLEY
BURNER
BURNET
BURROW
BURSAR
BURTON
BUSBOY
BUSHED
BUSHEL
BUSILY
BUSKER
BUSKET
BUSKIN
BUSMAN
BUSONI
BUSTED
BUSTER
BUSTLE
BUTANE
BUTENE
BUTLER
BUTTER
BUTTON
BUYERS
BUYING
BUYOUT
BUZFUZ
BUZZER
CUBAGE
CUBICA
CUBISM
CUBIST
CUCKOO
CUDDLE
CUDDLY
CUDGEL
CUEIST
CUERPO
CUESTA
CUFFEE
CUFFIN
CUISSE
CUITER
CULDEE
CULLET
CULLIS
CULMEN
CULTCH
CULTER
CULTUS
CULVER
CUMBER
CUMMER
CUMMIN
CUNEAL
CUNNER
CUPFUL
CUPMAN
CUPOLA
CUPPED
CUPPER
CUPULE
CURACY
CURARE
CURARI
CURATE
CURDLE
CURFEW
CURIET
CURIUM
CURLER
CURLEW
CURPEL
CURRIE
CURSAL
CURSED
CURSOR
CURSUS
CURTAL
CURTAX
CURTLY
CURTSY
CURULE
CURVED
CURVET
CUSCUS
CUSHAT
CUSSED
CUSSER
CUSTER
CUSTOM
CUSTOS
CUTCHA
CUTLER
CUTLET
CUTOFF
CUTTER
CUTTLE
CUTTOE
DUBBIN
DUBLIN
DUCKED
DUCKIE
DUDDER
DUDEEN
DUENNA
DUFFEL
DUFFER
DUFFLE
DUGONG
DUGOUT
DULCET
DUMBLY
DUMDUM
DUMONT
DUMOSE
DUMPER
DUMPLE
DUNBAR
DUNCAN
DUNCES
DUNDEE
DUNDER
DUNELM
DUNKER
DUNLIN
DUNLOP
DUPLEX
DURANT
DURBAR
DURESS
DURHAM
DURIAN
DURING
DURION
DUSTED
DUSTER
EUBOEA
EUCHRE
EUCLID
EUGENE
EULOGY
EUNUCH
EUREKA
EUROPA
EUROPE
EUSTON
EUTAXY
EUXINE
FUDDLE
FUGATO
FUHRER
FULFIL
FULGID
FULHAM
FULLER
FULMAR
FUMADO
FUMBLE
FUNDED
FUNDUS
FUNGAL
FUNGUS
FUNNEL
FUREUR
FURFUR
FURIES
FURORE
FURPHY
FURROW
FUSAIN
FUSELI
FUSION
FUSTIC
FUSTOC
FUTILE
FUTURE
FUZZLE
GUARDI
GUARDS
GUBBAH
GUELPH
GUENON
GUESTS
GUFFAW
GUGGLE
GUIANA
GUIDES
GUIDON
GUILDS
GUILTY
GUINEA
GUITAR
GULLAH
GULLET
GULLEY
GULPER
GUMMED
GUNDOG
GUNGHO
GUNMAN
GUNNEL
GUNNER
GUNTER
GURGLE
GURKHA
GURLET
GURNET
GURNEY
GUSHER
GUSLAR
GUSSET
GUTTER
GUTTLE
GUYANA
GUZZLE
HUBBLE
HUBBUB
HUBRIS
HUCKLE
HUDDLE
HUDSON
HUGELY
HUGHES
HUGHIE
HULLED
HUMANE
HUMBER
HUMBLE
HUMBUG
HUMECT
HUMITE
HUMMEL
HUMMER
HUMMUS
HUMOUR
HUMPED
HUMPTY
HUNGER
HUNGRY
HUNKER
HUNTER
HURDLE
HURLEY
HURRAH
HURRAY
HURTLE
HUSHED
HUSSAR
HUSSIF
HUSTLE
HUXLEY
HUZZAH
JUBATE
JUBBAH
JUDDER
JUDGES
JUDICA
JUGGER
JUGGLE
JUJUBE
JULIAN
JULIET
JULIUS
JUMBAL
JUMBLE
JUMPER
JUNCUS
JUNGLE
JUNIOR
JUNKER
JUNKET
JUNKIE
JURANT
JURIST
JUSTIN
JUSTLY
KUFIAH
KUMARA
KUMERA
KUMISS
KUMMEL
LUANDA
LUBBER
LUBRIC
LUCENT
LUCIAN
LUCINA
LUDWIG
LUGANO
LUGGER
LUMBAR
LUMBER
LUMINA
LUMMOX
LUMPUR
LUNACY
LUNARY
LUNATE
LUNULE
LUPINE
LURING
LURIST
LUSAKA
LUSTER
LUSTRE
LUTEAL
LUTEIN
LUTHER
LUTINE
LUTIST
LUXATE
LUXURY
LUZERN
MUCATE
MUCKER
MUCKLE
MUCOID
MUCOUS
MUDDER
MUDDLE
MUESLI
MUFFET
MUFFIN
MUFFLE
MUFLON
MUGGER
MULISH
MULLAH
MULLER
MULLET
MULTUM
MUMBLE
MUMMER
MUNICH
MUNIFY
MUNITE
MUNSHI
MUPPET
MURAGE
MURALS
MURDER
MURIEL
MURINE
MURLIN
MURMUR
MURPHY
MURRAM
MURRAY
MURRHA
MURRIN
MUSANG
MUSCAT
MUSCLE
MUSEUM
MUSING
MUSIVE
MUSKEG
MUSKET
MUSLIM
MUSLIN
MUSSEL
MUSTER
MUTANT
MUTATE
MUTELY
MUTINY
MUTTER
MUTTON
MUTUAL
MUZHIK
MUZZLE
NUANCE
NUBBIN

NUBBLE
NUBILE
NUCULE
NUDISM
NUDIST
NUDITY
NUDNIK
NUGGAR
NUGGET
NULLAH
NUMBER
NUMBLY
NUMPTY
NUNCIO
NUTANT
NUTATE
NUTMEG
NUTTER
NUZZER
NUZZLE
OULONG
OUNCES
OUNDLE
OURALI
OUTAGE
OUTBAR
OUTBID
OUTCRY
OUTFIT
OUTGAS
OUTING
OUTLAW
OUTLAY
OUTLET
OUTLIE
OUTPUT
OUTRUN
OUTSET
OUTTOP
OUTVIE
OUTWIT
PUBLIC
PUCKER
PUDDLE
PUDSEY
PUEBLO
PUERTO
PUFFED
PUFFER
PUFFIN
PUISNE
PULLET
PULLEY
PULPIT
PULSAR
PULVER
PUMICE
PUMMEL
PUNCHY
PUNCTO
PUNDIT
PUNISH
PUNJAB
PUNKAH
PUNNET
PUNTER
PUPATE
PUPPET
PURDAH
PURELY
PURIFY
PURINE
PURIST
PURITY
PURLER
PURLIN
PURPLE
PURSED
PURSER
PURSUE
PURVEY
PUSHER
PUSHTU
PUSHUP
PUSSER
PUTEAL
PUTOIS
PUTRID
PUTSCH
PUTTEE
PUTTER
PUZZLE
QUAGGA
QUAHOG
QUAICH
QUAIGH
QUAINT
QUAKER
QUALMS
QUANGO
QUARRY
QUARTO
QUARTZ
QUASAR
QUAVER
QUEASY
QUEBEC
QUEENS
QUELCH
QUENCH
QUETCH
QUICHE
QUIDAM
QUINCE
QUINSY
QUINTA
QUIRKY
QUITCH
QUIVER
QUOITS
QUORUM
QUOTED
RUBBED
RUBBER
RUBBLE
RUBBRA
RUBENS
RUBIES
RUBIKS
RUBRIC
RUCHED
RUCKLE
RUCKUS
RUDDER
RUDDLE
RUDELY
RUEFUL
RUELLE
RUFFLE
RUGGED
RUGGER
RUGOSE
RUGOUS
RUINED
RULING
RUMBLE
RUMKIN
RUMMER
RUMORS
RUMOUR
RUMPLE
RUMPUS
RUNDLE
RUNNEL
RUNNER
RUNOFF
RUNWAY
RUNYON
RUPEES
RUPERT
RUPIAH
RUPIAS
RUSHED
RUSKIN
RUSSET
RUSSIA
RUSTAM
RUSTEM
RUSTIC
RUSTLE
RUSTUM
RUTTED
RUTTER
SUBDUE
SUBLET
SUBMIT
SUBORN
SUBSET
SUBTLE
SUBTLY
SUBURB
SUBWAY
SUCCOR
SUCCUS
SUCKEN
SUCKER
SUCKET
SUCKLE
SUDARY
SUDATE
SUDDEN
SUFFER
SUFFIX
SUGARY
SUITED
SUITOR
SUIVEZ
SULCUS
SULFUR
SULLEN
SULPHA
SULTAN
SULTRY
SUMACH
SUMMER
SUMMIT
SUMMON
SUNDAE
SUNDAY
SUNDER
SUNDEW
SUNDRY
SUNHAT
SUNKEN
SUNLIT
SUNRAY
SUNSET
SUNTAN
SUPERB
SUPINE
SUPLEX
SUPPER
SUPPLE
SUPPLY
SURELY
SURETÉ
SURETY
SURFER
SURREY
SURTAX
SURVEY
SUSSEX
SUTLER
SUTTEE
SUTURE
TUAREG
TUBERS
TUBING
TUBULE
TUCKER
TUCKET
TUFFET
TUFTED
TUGRIK
TUILLE
TULBAN
TULIPA
TUMBLE
TUMEFY
TUMOUR
TUMULT
TUNDRA
TUNING
TUNNEL
TUPELO
TURBAN
TURBID
TURBOT
TUREEN
TURGID
TURKEY
TURNED
TURNER
TURNIP
TURNUP
TURPIN
TURRET
TURTLE
TURVES
TUSCAN
TUSKER
TUSSAH
TUSSIS
TUSSLE
TUVALU
TUXEDO
VULCAN
VULGAR
VULGUS
YUCKER
YUKATA
YUMYUM
YUPPIE
ZURICH
AVALON
AVATAR
AVAUNT
AVENGE
AVENUE
AVERNO
AVERSE
AVIARY
AVIATE
AVIDLY
AVOCET
AVOUCH
AVOWAL
AVOWED
AVULSE
DVORAK
EVELYN
EVENLY
EVINCE
EVOLUÉ
EVOLVE
EVULSE
EVZONE
KVETCH
OVERDO
OVERLY
OVIBOS
SVELTE
AWAKEN
AWHILE
AWNING
AWOKEN
KWACHA
KWANZA
OWLCAR
OWLISH
QWERTY
RWANDA
SWABIA
SWAMPY
SWANEE
SWANKY
SWARTY
SWATCH
SWATHE
SWEATY
SWEDEN
SWEENY
SWEETS
SWERVE
SWINGE
SWIPES
SWITCH
SWIVEL
SWIVET
SWOOSH
TWAITE
TWEEDS
TWEEDY
TWEENY
TWEEZE
TWELVE
TWENTY
TWICER
TWIGGY
TWIGHT
TWINED
TWINGE
TWIRLY
TWISTY
TWITCH
TWOBIT
AXEMAN
AXILLA
EXARCH
EXCEED
EXCEPT
EXCESS
EXCISE
EXCITE
EXCUSE
EXEDRA
EXEMPT
EXETER
EXHALE
EXHORT
EXHUME
EXISTS
EXMOOR
EXOCET
EXODUS
EXOGEN
EXOTIC
EXPAND
EXPECT
EXPEDE
EXPEND
EXPERT
EXPIRE
EXPIRY
EXPORT
EXPOSE
EXPUGN
EXSERT
EXTANT
EXTEND
EXTENT
EXTERN
EXTIRP
EXTOLL
EXTORT
OXALIC
OXALIS
OXFORD
OXGATE
OXHEAD
OXHIDE
OXTAIL
OXYGEN
AYESHA
AYMARA
BYEBYE
BYELAW
BYGONE
BYLINE
BYPASS
BYRNIE
BYSSUS
BYWORD
CYANIN
CYBELE
CYBORG
CYBRID
CYCLIC
CYCLUS
CYDNUS
CYESIS
CYGNET
CYGNUS
CYMBAL
CYMRIC
CYNIPS
CYPHER

CYPRID
CYPRIS
CYPRUS
CYRANO
CYRENE
CYSTIC
CYTASE
CYTODE
CYTOID
DYADIC
DYBBUK
DYEING
DYNAMO
DYNAST
EYEFUL
EYELET
EYELID
FYLFOT
GYPSUM
GYRATE
HYADES
HYAENA
HYBRID
HYBRIS
HYDRAX
HYDRIA
HYMNAL
HYPATE
HYPHAL
HYPHEN
HYPNIC
HYPNOS
HYPNUM
HYSSOP
KYBOSH
KYUSHU
LYCEUM
LYCHEE
LYCOSA
LYDIAN
LYMPNE
LYRICS
LYRIST
LYTTON
MYELIN
MYELON
MYGALE
MYOGEN
MYOPIA
MYOPIC
MYOSIN
MYOSIS
MYRIAD
MYRTLE
MYSELF
MYSORE
MYSTIC
MYTHOS
NYANZA
NYLONS
OYSTER
PYEDOG
PYRENE
PYRONE
PYROPE
PYRRHO
PYTHIA
PYTHON
RYOKAN
SYDNEY
SYLVAN
SYLVIA
SYMBOL
SYNCOM
SYNDIC
SYNTAX
SYPHER
SYPHON
SYRIAN
SYRINX
SYRISM
SYRUPY
SYSTEM
SYZYGY
TYBALT
TYBURN
TYCOON
TYMBAL
TYMPAN
TYPHUS
TYPIFY
TYPING
TYPIST
TYRANT
TYRONE
WYVERN
XYLOID
ZYGOMA
ZYGOTE
ZYRIAN
AZALEA
AZOLLA
AZORES
AZOTIC
AZRAEL
CZAPKA
DZEREN
IZZARD

6:3

ABACUS
ABADAN
ABATOR
ABATTU
ACACIA
ACADIA
ACAJOU
ACARID
ACARUS
ACATES
ADAGIO
AGADIR
AGARIC
AGATHA
ALACUS
ALALIA
ALARIC
ALARUM
ALASKA
AMADOU
AMAZED
AMAZON
ANABAS
ANADEM
ANADYR
ANALOG
ANANAS
APACHE
APATHY
ARABIA
ARABIC
ARABIS
ARABLE
ARAFAT
ARAGON
ARALIA
ARAMIS
ARANDA
ARARAT
ASARUM
ATABAL
ATABEG
ATAMAN
ATAXIA
ATAXIC
AVALON
AVATAR
AVAUNT
AWAKEN
AZALEA
BEACHY
BEACON
BEADED
BEADLE
BEAGLE
BEAKER
BEANIE
BEARER
BEATEN
BEATER
BEATTY
BEAUNE
BEAUTY
BEAVER
BHAJAN
BHAJEE
BHARAT
BIASED
BLACKS
BLAISE
BLAMED
BLANCH
BLANCO
BLAZER
BLAZON
BOARDS
BOATER
BRACER
BRACES
BRAHMA
BRAHMS
BRAINS
BRAINY
BRAISE
BRAMAH
BRANCH
BRANDY
BRAQUE
BRASSY
BRAWNY
BRAZEN
BRAZIL
CHADOR
CHAFER
CHAINS
CHAIRS
CHAISE
CHAKRA
CHALET
CHALKY
CHAMPS
CHANCE
CHANCY
CHANEY
CHANGE
CHAPEL
CHAPKA
CHARGE
CHARON
CHARTA
CHASER
CHASSE
CHASTE
CHATON
CHATTY
CHAZAN
CLAGGY
CLAIMS
CLAMMY
CLAMOR
CLAQUE
CLARET
CLARTY
CLASSY
CLAUDE
CLAUSE
CLAVIS
CLAYEY
COALER
COARSE
COATED
COATES
CRABBE
CRABBY
CRADLE
CRAFTY
CRAGGY
CRAMBO
CRANCH
CRANKY
CRANNY
CRANTS
CRAPLE
CRASIS
CRATCH
CRATER
CRATON
CRATUR
CRAVAT
CRAVEN
CRAYER
CRAYON
CRAZED
CYANIN
CZAPKA
DEACON
DEADEN
DEADLY
DEAFEN
DEALER
DEARER
DEARIE
DEARLY
DEARTH
DHARMA
DIADEM
DIALOG
DIANAS
DIAPER
DIATOM
DIAXON
DRACHM
DRAFTY
DRAGEE
DRAGON
DRALON
DRAPER
DRAWER
DYADIC
ECARTÉ
ELAINE
ELANCE
ELANET
ELAPSE
ELATED
ENABLE
ENAMEL
ENAMOR
ENARCH
EPARCH
EPAULE
ERASED
ERASER
ETALON
EXARCH
FEALTY
FIACRE
FIANCÉ
FIASCO
FLABBY
FLACON
FLAGGY
FLAGON
FLAMBÉ
FLAMEN
FLANCH
FLANGE
FLANKS
FLARES
FLASHY
FLATLY
FLATUS
FLAUNT
FLAVOR
FLAWED
FLAXEN
FRACAS
FRAGOR
FRAISE
FRAMED
FRANCE
FRANCK
FRANCO
FRANZY
FRAPPÉ
FRATER
FRAYED
GEASON
GHARRY
GHAZAL
GIAOUR
GLACIS
GLADLY
GLAGOL
GLAIRE
GLAIVE
GLAMIS
GLAMOR
GLANCE
GLASSY
GLAZED
GNAWER
GOALIE
GOANNA
GOATEE
GRABEN
GRACES
GRADED
GRADES
GRADUS
GRAFIN
GRAHAM
GRAINS
GRAINY
GRAMME
GRAMMY
GRAMPS
GRANBY
GRANGE
GRANNY
GRANTA
GRAPES
GRAPPA
GRASSY
GRATED
GRATER
GRATIN
GRATIS
GRAVEL
GRAVEN
GRAVER
GRAVES
GRAVID
GUARDI
GUARDS
HEADED
HEADER
HEALER
HEALTH
HEAPED
HEARER
HEARSE
HEARTH
HEARTS
HEARTY
HEATED
HEATER
HEAUME
HEAVED
HEAVEN
HEAVES
HIATUS
HOARSE
HOAXER
HYADES
HYAENA
IBADAN
ICARUS
IRAQIS
ISABEL
ISAIAH
ITALIC
JOANNA
KEATON
KHALAT
KHALIF
KHALSA
KHARIF
KIAORA
KLAXON
KNAGGY
KRAKEN
KRANTZ
KRATER
KRATON

KWACHA
KWANZA
LAAGER
LEADEN
LEADER
LEAGUE
LEALTY
LEANTO
LEAVEN
LEAVER
LEAVES
LIABLE
LIAISE
LOADED
LOADER
LOAFER
LOATHE
LOAVES
LUANDA
MEADOW
MEAGER
MEAGRE
MEALIE
MEANIE
MEANLY
MEASLY
MEATUS
MIASMA
MOANER
MOATED
NEAPED
NEARBY
NEARER
NEARLY
NEATEN
NEATLY
NIACIN
NIAMEY
NUANCE
NYANZA
OGADEN
OGAMIC
OMASUM
ONAGER
ONAGRA
OPAQUE
ORACHE
ORACLE
ORALLY
ORANGE
ORATOR
OTALGY
OXALIC
OXALIS
PEAHEN
PEAKED
PEANUT
PEARLS
PEARLY
PHAROS
PHASIS
PHASMA
PIAFFE
PIAZZA
PLACED
PLACER
PLACID
PLAGUE
PLAICE
PLAINS
PLAINT
PLANCH
PLANET
PLANKS
PLAQUE
PLASMA
PLATED
PLATEN
PLATER
PLATES
PLAYER
PRAGUE
PRAISE
PRANCE
PRANKS
PRATER
PRAVDA
PRAXIS
PRAYER
QUAGGA
QUAHOG
QUAICH
QUAIGH
QUAINT
QUAKER
QUALMS
QUANGO
QUARRY
QUARTO
QUARTZ
QUASAR
QUAVER
READER
REALIA
REALLY
REALTY
REAMER
REAPER
REASON
RHAPHE
RIALTO
ROADIE
ROAMER
ROARER
RWANDA
SAANEN
SCABBY
SCAITH
SCALAR
SCALER
SCALES
SCAMPI
SCAMPO
SCANTY
SCAPUS
SCARAB
SCARCE
SCARED
SCARER
SCATCH
SCATHE
SCATTY
SEABEE
SEALED
SEAMAN
SEAMEN
SEAMER
SEAMUS
SEANCE
SEARCH
SEASON
SEATED
SEAWAY
SHABBY
SHADED
SHADES
SHADOW
SHADUF
SHAGGY
SHAKEN
SHAKER
SHAKES
SHALOM
SHAMAN
SHAMBA
SHAMMY
SHAMUS
SHANDY
SHANKS
SHANTY
SHAPED
SHARED
SHARER
SHARES
SHARIA
SHARIF
SHARON
SHARPS
SHASTA
SHAVEN
SHAVER
SKATER
SKATES
SLACKS
SLALOM
SLANGY
SLATCH
SLATER
SLAVER
SLAVES
SLAYER
SMACKS
SMALLS
SMARMY
SMARTY
SNAGGY
SNAILY
SNAKED
SNAPPY
SNATCH
SNAZZY
SOAKED
SPACED
SPACER
SPADES
SPADIX
SPARKS
SPARKY
SPARSE
SPARTA
SPARTH
SPATHE
SPAULD
SPAVIN
STABLE
STABLY
STACKS
STAFFA
STAGER
STAGEY
STAIRS
STAKES
STALAG
STALIN
STALKS
STALKY
STALLS
STAMEN
STAMPS
STANCE
STANCH
STANZA
STAPES
STAPLE
STARCH
STARES
STARRY
STARVE
STASIS
STATAL
STATED
STATEN
STATER
STATES
STATIC
STATOR
STATUE
STATUS
STAYER
SWABIA
SWAMPY
SWANEE
SWANKY
SWARTY
SWATCH
SWATHE
TEABAG
TEACUP
TEAGUE
TEAPOT
TEAPOY
TEASEL
TEASER
THALER
THALES
THALIA
THAMES
THANAH
THANET
THANKS
THATCH
TRACER
TRADER
TRADES
TRAGIC
TRAGUS
TRAJAN
TRALEE
TRANCE
TRANNY
TRAPES
TRASHY
TRAUMA
TRAVEL
TRAVIS
TUAREG
TWAITE
UGANDA
UGARIT
UNABLE
URANIA
URANIC
URANUS
USABLE
USANCE
VIABLE
VIANDS
VIATOR
WEAKEN
WEAKER
WEAKLY
WEALTH
WEAPON
WEARER
WEASEL
WEAVER
WHACKO
WHACKY
WHALER
WHALES
WHAMMY
WHARFE
WRAITH
WRASSE
YEARLY
YEASTY
ZEALOT
ABBACY
ABBESS
ALBANY
ALBEDO
ALBEIT
ALBERT
ALBINO
ALBION
ALBITE
ALBUGO
AMBAGE
AMBLER
AMBUSH
ARBOUR
AUBADE
AUBREY
AUBURN
BABBIT
BABBLE
BABOON
BOBBIN
BOBBLE
BOBCAT
BOBWIG
BUBBLE
BUBBLY
CABALE
CABBIE
COBALT
COBBER
COBBLE
COBDEN
COBURG
COBWEB
CUBAGE
CUBICA
CUBISM
CUBIST
CYBELE
CYBORG
CYBRID
DABBLE
DEBASE
DEBATE
DEBILE
DEBRIS
DEBTOR
DEBUNK
DIBBER
DIBBLE
DOBBIN
DOBSON
DUBBIN
DUBLIN
DYBBUK
ECBOLE
EGBERT
ELBRUS
EMBAIL
EMBALE
EMBALM
EMBARK
EMBERS
EMBLEM
EMBODY
EMBOSS
EMBRUE
EMBRYO
EMBUSY
ERBIUM
EUBOEA
FABIAN
FABIUS
FABLED
FABLES
FABRIC
FIBBED
FIBBER
FIBULA
GABBLE
GABBRO
GABION
GABLED
GIBBER
GIBBET
GIBBON
GIBSON
GOBBET
GOBBLE
GOBLET
GOBLIN
GUBBAH
HABILE
HEBREW
HOBART
HOBBES
HOBBLE
HOBDAY
HOBNOB
HUBBLE
HUBBUB
HUBRIS
HYBRID
HYBRIS
IMBARN
IMBASE
IMBIBE
IMBOSS
IMBRUE
INBORN
INBRED
JABBER
JABBLE
JABIRU
JIBBAH
JOBBER
JUBATE
JUBBAH
KABAKA
KABELE

KABUKI
KABYLE
KEBELE
KIBBLE
KIBOSH
KYBOSH
LABIAL
LABILE
LABIUM
LABLAB
LABOUR
LABRUM
LABRYS
LIBBER
LIBIDO
LIBYAN
LUBBER
LUBRIC
MOBCAP
MOBILE
MOBIUS
NEBBUK
NEBECK
NEBISH
NEBULA
NEBULE
NIBBLE
NOBBLE
NOBBUT
NOBODY
NUBBIN
NUBBLE
NUBILE
ORBITA
OSBERT
PEBBLE
PEBBLY
POBBLE
PUBLIC
RABATO
RABBET
RABBIT
RABBLE
RABIES
REBATE
REBECK
REBITE
REBORE
REBORN
REBUFF
REBUKE
RIBALD
RIBAND
RIBBED
RIBBLE
RIBBON
RIBOSE
ROBBED
ROBBER
ROBERT
ROBING
ROBSON
ROBUST
RUBBED
RUBBER
RUBBLE
RUBBRA
RUBENS
RUBIES
RUBIKS
RUBRIC
SABELE
SABINE
SABRES
SEBATE
SOBEIT
SUBDUE
SUBLET
SUBMIT
SUBORN
SUBSET
SUBTLE
SUBTLY
SUBURB
SUBWAY
TABARD
TABLET
TABULA
TOBAGO
TOBIAS
TUBERS
TUBING
TUBULE
TYBALT
TYBURN
UMBLES
UMBREL
UMBRIA
UMBRIL
UNBEND
UNBENT
UNBIND
UNBOLT
UNBORN
UNBRED
UNBUSY
UPBEAT
URBANE
VIBRIO
WABASH
WEBBED
WOBBLE
WOBBLY
WOBURN
YABBER
ZEBECK
ACCEDE
ACCEND
ACCENT
ACCEPT
ACCESS
ACCORD
ACCOST
ACCRUE
ACCUSE
ALCINA
ALCOCK
ALCOVE
ANCHOR
ANCILE
ANCOME
ANCONA
ANCORA
ARCADE
ARCADY
ARCANA
ARCANE
ARCHED
ARCHER
ARCHES
ARCHIE
ARCHIL
ARCHON
ARCTIC
ASCEND
ASCENT
ASCHAM
ASCIAN
ASCIUS
AUCUBA
BACCHI
BACKER
BACKET
BACKRA
BACKUP
BECALM
BECAME
BECKET
BECKON
BECOME
BICARB
BICEPS
BICKER
BOCAGE
BUCCAL
BUCHAN
BUCKED
BUCKER
BUCKET
BUCKLE
CACCIA
CACHET
CACHOU
CACKLE
CACOON
CACTUS
CECILS
CECITY
CICADA
CICALA
CICELY
CICERO
COCCID
COCCUS
COCCYX
COCHIN
COCKER
COCKLE
COCOON
CUCKOO
CYCLIC
CYCLUS
DACOIT
DACTYL
DECADE
DECAFF
DECAMP
DECANE
DECANI
DECANT
DECCAN
DECEIT
DECENT
DECIDE
DÉCIME
DECKED
DECKER
DECKLE
DECODE
DECOKE
DECREE
DECREW
DICAST
DICKER
DICKEY
DICTUM
DOCENT
DOCILE
DOCKED
DOCKER
DOCKET
DOCTOR
DUCKED
DUCKIE
ECCLES
ENCALM
ENCAMP
ENCASE
ENCASH
ENCODE
ENCORE
EOCENE
ESCAPE
ESCARP
ESCHAR
ESCHEW
ESCORT
ESCROC
ESCROW
ESCUDO
ETCHER
EUCHRE
EUCLID
EXCEED
EXCEPT
EXCESS
EXCISE
EXCITE
EXCUSE
FACADE
FACIAL
FACIES
FACILE
FACING
FACTOR
FACTUM
FECULA
FECUND
FICKLE
FOCSLE
GOCART
HACHIS
HACKEE
HACKER
HACKLE
HECATE
HECKLE
HECTIC
HECTOR
HECUBA
HICCUP
HICKEY
HOCKEY
HUCKLE
INCASE
INCEDE
INCEPT
INCEST
INCHES
INCHON
INCISE
INCITE
INCOME
ISCHIA
ITCHEN
JACANA
JACENT
JACKAL
JACKET
JACOBS
JOCKEY
JOCOSE
JOCUND
KECKSY
KICKER
LACHES
LACING
LACKEY
LACTIC
LACUNA
LECHER
LECTOR
LICHEN
LICTOR
LOCALE
LOCATE
LOCHIA
LOCKED
LOCKER
LOCKET
LOCKUP
LOCULE
LOCUST
LUCENT
LUCIAN
LUCINA
LYCEUM
LYCHEE
LYCOSA
MACRON
MACULA
MACULE
MICKEY
MICKLE
MICMAC
MICRON
MOCKER
MOCKUP
MUCATE
MUCKER
MUCKLE
MUCOID
MUCOUS
NECKAR
NECKED
NECTAR
NICELY
NICENE
NICETY
NICKED
NICKEL
NICKER
NOCENT
NOCTUA
NUCULE
OCCULT
OCCUPY
ONCOME
ONCOST
OOCYTE
ORCHID
ORCHIS
ORCINE
PACIFY
PACKED
PACKER
PACKET
PECKER
PECTEN
PECTIN
PICARD
PICKAX
PICKED
PICKER
PICKET
PICKLE
PICKUP
PICNIC
POCKET
PUCKER
RACEME
RACHEL
RACHIS
RACIAL
RACINE
RACING
RACISM
RACIST
RACKET
RECALL
RECANT
RECAST
RECEDE
RECENT
RECESS
RECIFE
RECIPE
RECITE
RECKON
RECOIL
RECORD
RECOUP
RECTAL
RECTOR
RECTUM
RECTUS
RICHES
RICHLY
RICKER
RICKEY
RICRAC
RICTAL
RICTUS
ROCKER
ROCKET
ROCOCO
RUCHED
RUCKLE
RUCKUS
SACHET
SACRED
SACRUM
SECANT
SECEDE
SECOND
SECRET
SECTOR
SECURE
SICILY
SICKEN
SICKER
SICKLE
SICKLY
SOCAGE
SOCCER
SOCIAL
SOCKET

SUCCOR
SUCCUS
SUCKEN
SUCKER
SUCKET
SUCKLE
TACKET
TACKLE
TACOMA
TACTIC
TECHNO
TECKEL
TECTUM
TICINO
TICKER
TICKET
TICKEY
TICKLE
TICKLY
TOCSIN
TUCKER
TUCKET
TYCOON
ULCERS
UNCAGE
UNCIAL
UNCLAD
UNCOIL
UNCOOL
UNCORK
URCHIN
VACANT
VACATE
VACUUM
VECTIS
VECTOR
VICTIM
VICTOR
VICUNA
WACKER
WICKED
WICKER
WICKET
YUCKER
ABDABS
ABDIEL
ABDUCT
ADDEEM
ADDEND
ADDICT
ADDLED
ADDUCE
ADDUCT
AEDILE
AIDANT
ALDINE
ALDOSE
ALDRIN
ANDEAN
ANDREW
ARDENT

ARDOUR
AUDILE
AUDLEY
AUDREY
BADGER
BADMAN
BEDASH
BEDAUB
BEDDER
BEDECK
BEDLAM
BEDPAN
BEDSIT
BIDDER
BIDENT
BODACH
BODEGA
BODGER
BODGIE
BODICE
BODIES
BODILY
BODKIN
BODONI
BUDDHA
BUDGET
BUDGIE
CADDIE
CADDIS
CADETS
CADGER
CADMUS
CEDRIC
CEDULA
CODDLE
CODGER
CODIFY
CODING
CUDDLE
CUDDLY
CUDGEL
CYDNUS
DADDLE
DEDANS
DEDUCE
DEDUCT
DIDDLE
DODDER
DODDLE
DODGEM
DODGER
DODOMA
DUDDER
DUDEEN
EDDISH
ELDERS
ELDEST
ENDEAR
ENDING
ENDIVE
ENDURE

FADING
FEDORA
FIDDLE
FIDDLY
FIDGET
FODDER
FUDDLE
GADFLY
GADGET
GADOID
GIDDUP
GIDEON
GODIVA
GODOWN
GODSON
GODWIN
GODWIT
HEDERA
HIDAGE
HIDDEN
HIDING
HODDER
HUDDLE
HUDSON
HYDRAX
HYDRIA
INDABA
INDEED
INDENT
INDIAN
INDICT
INDIES
INDIGN
INDIGO
INDITE
INDIUM
INDOOR
INDUCE
INDUCT
IODINE
IODIZE
JUDDER
JUDGES
JUDICA
KEDDAH
KIDDIE
KIDDLE
KIDNAP
KIDNEY
KODIAK
LADAKH
LADDER
LADDIE
LADIES
LADING
LADOGA
LEDGER
LODGED
LODGER
LUDWIG
LYDIAN

MADAME
MADCAP
MADDEN
MADDER
MADEUP
MADMAN
MADRAS
MADRID
MADURA
MADURO
MEDDLE
MEDIAL
MEDIAN
MEDICI
MEDICO
MEDINA
MEDISM
MEDIUM
MEDIUS
MEDLAR
MEDLEY
MEDUSA
MEDWAY
MIDDAY
MIDDEN
MIDDLE
MIDGET
MIDWAY
MODELS
MODENA
MODERN
MODEST
MODIFY
MODISH
MODIST
MODIUS
MODULE
MUDDER
MUDDLE
NIDGET
NIDIFY
NODDED
NODDLE
NODOSE
NODULE
NUDISM
NUDIST
NUDITY
NUDNIK
ODDITY
ODDSON
OEDEMA
OLDISH
ONDINE
OODLES
ORDAIN
ORDEAL
ORDERS
ORDURE
PADANG
PADDED

PADDLE
PADUAN
PEDALO
PEDANT
PEDDER
PEDDLE
PEDLAR
PIDDLE
PIDGIN
PODIUM
PODSOL
PODZOL
PUDDLE
PUDSEY
RADDLE
RADIAL
RADIAN
RADISH
RADIUM
RADIUS
RADULA
REDACT
REDCAP
REDCAR
REDDEN
REDEEM
REDEYE
REDLEG
REDRAW
REDTOP
REDUCE
RIDDLE
RIDENT
RIDGED
RIDING
RODENT
RODHAM
RODNEY
RUDDER
RUDDLE
RUDELY
SADDEN
SADDHU
SADDLE
SADISM
SADIST
SEDATE
SEDUCE
SIDDHA
SIDING
SIDNEY
SODDEN
SODIUM
SODOMY
SUDARY
SUDATE
SUDDEN
SYDNEY
TEDIUM
TIDBIT
TIDDLE

TIDDLY
TIDILY
TODDLE
UNDATE
UNDECK
UNDIES
UNDINE
UNDONE
UNDULY
UNDYED
UPDATE
VADOSE
VEDDAH
VEDUTA
WADDLE
WADERS
WADHAM
WEDDED
WEDGED
WIDELY
WIDGET
WIDOWS
ZODIAC
ABELIA
ACEDIA
ACETIC
AFEARS
AGEING
AGENCY
AGENDA
ALECTO
ALEGAR
ALERCE
ALEXIA
ALEXIN
ALEXIS
AMELIA
AMENDE
AMENDS
AMERCE
ANEMIA
ANEMIC
APEPSY
APERÇU
AREOLA
AREOLE
AVENGE
AVENUE
AVERNO
AVERSE
AXEMAN
AYESHA
BEEGHA
BEENAH
BEEPER
BEETLE
BEETON
BLEACH
BLEARY
BLENCH
BLENDE

BLENNY
BOEING
BREACH
BREAST
BREATH
BRECHT
BREECH
BREEZE
BREEZY
BREGMA
BREMEN
BRETON
BREVET
BREWER
BREWIS
BUENOS
BYEBYE
BYELAW
CAECUM
CAESAR
CEEFAX
CHEDER
CHEEKY
CHEERS
CHEERY
CHEESE
CHEESY
CHEMIC
CHEMMY
CHENET
CHEOPS
CHEQUE
CHERIE
CHERRY
CHERUB
CHERUP
CHESIL
CHESTY
CHEVAL
CHEVET
CIERGE
CLEAVE
CLENCH
CLERGY
CLERIC
CLERKS
CLEVER
COERCE
COEVAL
CREACH
CREAGH
CREAKY
CREAMY
CREANT
CREASE
CREATE
CREDIT
CREEPS
CREEPY
CREESE
CREESH

CREMOR
CRENAL
CRENEL
CREOLE
CRESOL
CRESTA
CRETAN
CRETIC
CRETIN
CREWEL
CUEIST
CUERPO
CUESTA
CYESIS
DAEDAL
DAEMON
DEEPEN
DEEPER
DEEPLY
DIEPPE
DIESEL
DIESIS
DIETER
DJEBEL
DJERBA
DOESNT
DREAMY
DREARY
DREDGE
DREGGY
DRENCH
DRESSY
DUENNA
DYEING
DZEREN
EGENCY
EGERIA
EGESTA
ELEVEN
EMERGE
EMETIC
EMEUTE
ENERGY
EPERDU
EREBUS
EREMIC
EVELYN
EVENLY
EXEDRA
EXEMPT
EXETER
EYEFUL
EYELET
EYELID
FAECAL
FAECES
FEEBLE
FEEBLY
FEEDER
FEELER
FEERIE
FIELDS
FIERCE
FIESTA
FLECHE
FLEDGE
FLEECE
FLEECY
FLENSE
FLESHY
FLETCH
FLEURY
FOETAL
FOETID
FOETUS
FREELY
FREEZE
FRENCH
FRENUM
FRENZY
FRESCO
GAELIC
GEEZER
GHEBER
GHERAO
GHETTO
GNEISS
GOETHE
GREASE
GREASY
GREATS
GREAVE
GREECE
GREEDY
GREEKS
GREENE
GREENS
GRETNA
GREUZE
GUELPH
GUENON
GUESTS
HAEMAL
HAEMON
HEEDED
HEEHAW
HEELED
IBERIA
ICEBOX
ICEMAN
IPECAC
IREFUL
IRETON
ISEULT
ITERUM
JAEGER
JEEVES
KEELER
KEENER
KEENLY
KEEPER
KVETCH
LEEWAY
LIEBIG
LIEDER
LIERNE
MAENAD
MEEKLY
MUESLI
MYELIN
MYELON
NAEVUS
NEEDED
NEEDLE
NEEDNT
NIELLO
OBECHE
OBELUS
OBERON
OCEANS
OCELOT
ODENSE
ODESSA
OLEATE
OLEFIN
OLENUS
OMELET
OMENTA
OMERTA
ONEDIN
ONEGIN
ONEIDA
ONEMAN
ONEWAY
OPENER
OPENLY
OREGON
OREXIS
OTELLO
OVERDO
OVERLY
PAELLA
PAEONY
PEELED
PEELER
PEEPER
PEEVED
PEEWEE
PEEWIT
PHENOL
PHENYL
PIECES
PIEDOG
PIEMAN
PIERCE
PIERIS
PLEACH
PLEASE
PLEDGE
PLENTY
PLENUM
PLEURA
PLEXOR
PLEXUS
PNEUMA
POETIC
POETRY
PREACE
PREACH
PRECIS
PREFAB
PREFER
PREFIX
PRELIM
PREPAY
PREPPY
PRESTO
PRETAX
PRETTY
PREVIN
PREWAR
PSEUDO
PTERIN
PTERIS
PUEBLO
PUERTO
PYEDOG
QUEASY
QUEBEC
QUEENS
QUELCH
QUENCH
QUETCH
QWERTY
REEBOK
REEFER
REEKIE
REELER
RHEIMS
RHESUS
RHETOR
RHEUMY
RHEXIS
RIENZI
ROEMER
RUEFUL
RUELLE
SCENIC
SDEATH
SEEDED
SEEDER
SEEING
SEEKER
SEEMLY
SEESAW
SEETHE
SHEARS
SHEATH
SHEAVE
SHEENY
SHEERS
SHEETS
SHEIKH
SHEILA
SHEKEL
SHELVE
SHERIF
SHERPA
SHERRY
SIENNA
SIERRA
SIESTA
SKELLY
SKERRY
SKETCH
SKEWED
SKEWER
SLEAVE
SLEAZE
SLEAZY
SLEDGE
SLEEKY
SLEEPY
SLEEVE
SLEEZY
SLEIGH
SLEUTH
SLEWED
SMEARY
SMEATH
SMEGMA
SMELLY
SNEAKY
SNEATH
SNEEZE
SNEEZY
SPECIE
SPEECH
SPEEDO
SPEEDY
SPEISS
SPENCE
STEADY
STEAMY
STEELE
STEELY
STEERS
STEMMA
STENCH
STEPPE
STEREO
STERIC
STERNE
STEROL
STEVEN
STEWED
SVELTE
SWEATY
SWEDEN
SWEENY
SWEETS
SWERVE
TAENIA
TEENSY
TEEPEE
TEETER
TEETHE
THEAVE
THEBAN
THEBES
THECAL
THEIRS
THEISM
THEIST
THEMIS
THENAR
THENCE
THEORY
THERMO
THESIS
THETIC
THETIS
THEYRE
TIEPIN
TIERCE
TIERED
TMESIS
TOECAP
TOERAG
TREATY
TREBLE
TREBLY
TREMOR
TRENCH
TRENDY
TREPAN
TRESCO
TSETSE
TWEEDS
TWEEDY
TWEENY
TWEEZE
TWELVE
TWENTY
UNEASE
UNEASY
UNEVEN
URETER
USEFUL
UTERUS
VIENNA
VIENNE
VIEWER
WEEKLY
WEEPIE
WEEVIL
WEEWEE
WHEELS
WHEELY
WHEEZE
WHEEZY
WHENCE
WHERRY
WIENER
WOEFUL
WREATH
WREKIN
WRENCH
WRETCH
CRÈCHE
AFFAIR
AFFECT
AFFIRM
AFFORD
AFFRAY
AFFRET
ALFRED
BAFFIN
BAFFLE
BEFALL
BEFOOL
BEFORE
BIFFIN
BIFOLD
BOFFIN
BOFORS
BUFFER
BUFFET
BUFFON
CAFARD
CAFTAN
COFFEE
COFFER
COFFIN
CUFFEE
CUFFIN
DAFTIE
DEFACE
DEFAME
DEFEAT
DEFECT
DEFEND
DEFILE
DEFINE
DEFORM
DEFRAY
DEFTLY
DEFUSE
DIFFER
DUFFEL
DUFFER
DUFFLE
EFFACE
EFFECT
EFFETE
EFFIGY
EFFLUX
EFFORT
EFFUSE
EIFFEL
ELFISH
ENFIRE
ENFOLD
ENFREE
GAFFER
GIFTED
GOFFER

GUFFAW
IFFISH
INFAME
INFAMY
INFANT
INFARE
INFECT
INFEST
INFIRM
INFLOW
INFLUX
INFOLD
INFORM
INFUSE
KAFFER
KAFFIR
KAFTAN
KUFIAH
LAFFER
LIFTED
LIFTER
MAFFIA
MUFFET
MUFFIN
MUFFLE
MUFLON
NEFAST
OAFISH
OFFCUT
OFFEND
OFFICE
OFFING
OFFISH
OFFSET
OXFORD
PIFFLE
PUFFED
PUFFER
PUFFIN
RAFALE
RAFFIA
RAFFLE
RAFTER
REFACE
REFECT
REFILL
REFINE
REFLET
REFLEX
REFLUX
REFORM
REFUEL
REFUGE
REFUND
REFUSE
REFUTE
RIFFLE
RUFFLE
SAFARI
SAFELY
SAFETY
SIFFLE
SIFTER
SOFFIT
SOFTEN
SOFTIE
SOFTLY
SUFFER
SUFFIX
TEFLON
TIFFIN
TOFFEE
TUFFET
TUFTED
UFFIZI
UNFAIR
UNFOLD
UNFURL
UPFLOW
WAFFLE
WAFTED
WIFELY
YAFFLE
ZAFTIG
AEGEAN
AEGEUS
AEGINA
AFGHAN
AIGLET
ANGARY
ANGELA
ANGELS
ANGERS
ANGICO
ANGINA
ANGLED
ANGLER
ANGLIA
ANGOLA
ANGORA
ARGENT
ARGHAN
ARGIVE
ARGOSY
ARGUED
ARGUTE
ARGYLE
ARGYLL
ASGARD
AUGEAN
AUGITE
AUGURY
AUGUST
BAGFUL
BAGMAN
BAGNIO
BAGUIO
BEGGAR
BEGONE
BIGAMY
BIGGER
BIGGIN
BIGWIG
BOGART
BOGGLE
BOGOTA
BUGGER
BUGLER
BYGONE
CAGILY
COGENT
COGGER
COGNAC
CYGNET
CYGNUS
DAGGER
DAGGLE
DÉGAGÉ
DEGREE
DIGEST
DIGGER
DIGLOT
DOGGED
DOGGER
DUGONG
DUGOUT
EDGING
EGGCUP
EIGHTH
EIGHTY
ENGAGE
ENGELS
ENGINE
ENGLUT
ENGULF
EUGENE
FAGGED
FAGGOT
FIGARO
FIGURE
FUGATO
GAGGLE
GIGGLE
GIGLET
GIGLOT
GIGOLO
GOGGLE
GUGGLE
HAGDEN
HAGGAI
HAGGIS
HAGGLE
HEGIRA
HIGHER
HIGHLY
HIGHUP
HOGGAR
HOGGET
HOGTIE
HUGELY
HUGHES
HUGHIE
INGATE
INGEST
INGOTS
INGRAM
INGRES
INGROW
INGULF
JAGGED
JAGGER
JAGUAR
JIGGER
JIGGLE
JIGSAW
JOGGER
JOGGLE
JUGGER
JUGGLE
KIGALI
LAGOON
LAGUNA
LAGUNE
LEGACY
LEGATE
LEGATO
LEGEND
LEGGED
LEGION
LEGIST
LEGLET
LEGMAN
LEGUME
LIGASE
LIGATE
LIGETI
LIGGER
LIGHTS
LIGNUM
LIGULA
LIGURE
LOGGER
LOGGIA
LOGJAM
LUGANO
LUGGER
MAGGIE
MAGGOT
MAGLEV
MAGNES
MAGNET
MAGNON
MAGNUM
MAGNUS
MAGPIE
MAGYAR
MEGRIM
MIGHTY
MIGNON
MOGGIE
MUGGER
MYGALE
NAGANA
NAGARI
NEGATE
NIGGER
NIGGLE
NIGGLY
NIGHTS
NIGHTY
NIGNOG
NOGGIN
NUGGAR
NUGGET
ORGANS
ORGASM
ORGEAT
ORGONE
OXGATE
PAGODA
PEGLEG
PIGEON
PIGLET
PIGOTT
PIGPEN
PIGSTY
POGROM
RAGBAG
RAGGED
RAGGLE
RAGING
RAGLAN
RAGMAN
RAGOUT
RAGTOP
RAGUSA
REGAIN
REGALE
REGARD
REGENT
REGEST
REGGAE
REGIME
REGINA
REGION
REGIUS
REGLET
REGRET
REGULO
RIGGED
RIGGER
RIGHTO
RIGHTS
RIGOUR
ROGNON
ROGUES
RUGGED
RUGGER
RUGOSE
RUGOUS
SAGELY
SAGGAR
SIGHTS
SIGNAL
SIGNET
SIGNOR
SUGARY
TAGORE
TEGMEN
TEGULA
TIGHTS
TIGRIS
TOGGED
TOGGLE
TUGRIK
UNGAIN
UNGULA
URGENT
VAGARY
VAGINA
VIGOUR
WAGGLE
WAGGON
WAGNER
WAGRAM
WIGEON
WIGGLE
WIGGLY
WIGWAM
YOGURT
ZAGREB
ZIGZAG
ZYGOMA
ZYGOTE
ACHENE
ACHING
ADHERE
AGHAST
AMHARA
APHONY
APHTHA
ASHCAN
ASHDOD
ASHINE
ASHLAR
ASHLEY
ASHORE
ASHPAN
ASHTAR
ASHTON
ATHENE
ATHENS
ATHROB
AWHILE
BAHADA
BAHRAM
BEHALF
BEHAVE
BEHEAD
BEHELD
BEHEST
BEHIND
BEHOLD
BEHOOF
BEHOVE
BEHRAM
BOHUNK
CAHIER
CAHOOT
COHERE
COHORT
DAHLIA
DEHORN
ECHARD
ECHINO
EPHEBE
ETHANE
ETHENE
ETHICS
ETHIOP
ETHNIC
EXHALE
EXHORT
EXHUME
FUHRER
INHALE
INHERE
INHUME
ISHTAR
ITHACA
JOHNNY
MAHLER
MAHOUT
MOHAIR
MOHAWK
MOHOCK
OCHONE
OCHREA
OPHISM
OPHITE
OTHERS
OXHEAD
OXHIDE
PAHARI
REHASH
REHEAT
REHEEL
SAHARA
SCHEMA
SCHEME
SCHISM
SCHIST
SCHIZO
SCHLEP
SCHMOE
SCHOOL
SCHUSS
SCHUYT
SOHRAB
SPHENE
SPHERE
SPHINX
TAHINA
TAHINI
TAHITI
TEHRAN
TSHIRT

UNHAND
UNHOLY
UNHOOK
UNHURT
UPHELD
UPHILL
UPHOLD
USHANT
VAHINE
YAHWEH
ACIDIC
ACINUS
AFIELD
AKIMBO
ALIGHT
ALIPED
ALIYAH
AMIDOL
AMIDST
ANIMAL
ANIMUS
APIARY
APICAL
APIECE
ARIOCH
ARIOSO
ARISTA
ASIMOV
AVIARY
AVIATE
AVIDLY
AXILLA
BAIKAL
BAILEE
BAILER
BAILEY
BAILIE
BAILLY
BEIRUT
BLIGHT
BLIMEY
BLINKS
BLITHE
BOILED
BOILER
BRIAND
BRIARD
BRICKS
BRIDAL
BRIDGE
BRIDIE
BRIDLE
BRIEFS
BRIGHT
BRIONY
BRITON
CAIMAN
CAIQUE
CHIBOL
CHICHI
CHICLE

CHICON
CHILDE
CHILLI
CHILLY
CHIMER
CHIMES
CHINAR
CHINCH
CHINTZ
CHIPPY
CHIRON
CHIRPY
CHISEL
CHITAL
CHITIN
CHITON
CHITTY
CHIVES
CHIVVY
CLICHÉ
CLIENT
CLIFFS
CLIMAX
CLIMES
CLINCH
CLINIC
CLIPPY
CLIQUE
COILED
COINER
COITUS
CRIANT
CRIBLE
CRIKEY
CRIMEA
CRINAL
CRINGE
CRINUM
CRIPES
CRISIS
CRISPY
CRISTA
CRITIC
CUISSE
CUITER
DAIMIO
DAINTY
DAISHO
DEIDRE
DJINNI
DOINGS
DRIEST
DRIPPY
DRIVEL
DRIVEN
DRIVER
EDIBLE
EDISON
EDITED
EDITOR
ELICIT

ELIJAH
ELISHA
ELIXIR
EMIGRÉ
ENIGMA
EPICAL
EPIGON
EPILOG
EPIRUS
ERINYS
EVINCE
EXISTS
FAIBLE
FAINTS
FAIRLY
FEINTS
FEISTY
FLICKS
FLIGHT
FLIMSY
FLINCH
FLINTY
FLITCH
FOIBLE
FOILED
FRIAND
FRIARY
FRIDAY
FRIDGE
FRIEND
FRIEZE
FRIGGA
FRIGHT
FRIGID
FRILLS
FRILLY
FRINGE
FRIPON
FRISKY
FRIVOL
FRIZZY
GAIETY
GAIJIN
GAINER
GAINLY
GAITER
GEIGER
GEISHA
GLIBLY
GLIDER
GLIÈRE
GLINKA
GLIOMA
GLITCH
GLITZY
GOITER
GOITRE
GRIEVE
GRIGRI
GRILLE
GRILSE

GRIMES
GRIMLY
GRIMMS
GRINGO
GRIPES
GRIPPE
GRISLY
GRISON
GRITTY
GUIANA
GUIDES
GUIDON
GUILDS
GUILTY
GUINEA
GUITAR
HAILER
HAIRDO
HEIFER
HEIGHT
HOIDEN
IBIDEM
ICICLE
IDIOCY
JAILER
JAILOR
JOINER
KAISER
KHILAT
KHILIM
KNIGHT
KNIVES
LAICAL
LAISSE
LOITER
MAIDAN
MAIDEN
MAILER
MAINLY
MAINOR
MOIDER
MOIETY
NAILED
NAILER
OBIISM
OBITAL
OBITER
ODIOUS
OLIVER
OLIVET
OLIVIA
ONIONS
OPIATE
ORIANO
ORIENT
ORIGEN
ORIGIN
ORIOLE
ORISON
OSIERY
OSIRIS

OTIOSE
OTITIS
OVIBOS
PAIDUP
PAINED
PAINTS
PAINTY
PAIRER
PHILIP
PHIZOG
PLIANT
PLIERS
PLIGHT
PLINTH
PLISSÉ
POINTE
POINTS
POIROT
POISED
POISON
PRICED
PRICEY
PRIEST
PRIMAL
PRIMED
PRIMER
PRIMLY
PRIMUS
PRINCE
PRIORY
PRISMS
PRISON
PRISSY
PRIVET
PRIZES
PUISNE
QUICHE
QUIDAM
QUINCE
QUINSY
QUINTA
QUIRKY
QUITCH
QUIVER
RAIDER
RAISED
RAISER
RAISIN
RUINED
SAILOR
SAINTS
SAITHE
SBIRRO
SCILLA
SCILLY
SCIPIO
SCIROC
SCIRON
SEICHE
SEISIN
SHIELD

SHIFTY
SHIITE
SHILOH
SHIMMY
SHINDY
SHINER
SHINNY
SHINTO
SHINTY
SHIPKA
SHIRAZ
SHIRRA
SHIRTY
SHIVER
SKIDOO
SKIING
SKIMPY
SKINNY
SKIVER
SKIVVY
SLICER
SLIDER
SLIGHT
SLINKY
SLIPPY
SLIPUP
SLITHY
SLIVER
SMIGHT
SMILER
SMILES
SMILEY
SMIRCH
SMITHS
SMITHY
SNIFFY
SNIFTY
SNIPER
SNITCH
SNIVEL
SOIGNÉ
SOILED
SOIREE
SPICED
SPICER
SPIDER
SPIGOT
SPIKED
SPILTH
SPINAL
SPINAR
SPINET
SPIRAL
SPIRIT
SPITAL
STICKS
STICKY
STIFLE
STIGMA
STILTS
STILTY

STINGO
STINGY
STINKO
STINKS
STIPES
STITCH
SUITED
SUITOR
SUIVEZ
SWINGE
SWIPES
SWITCH
SWIVEL
SWIVET
TAIGLE
TAILLE
TAILOR
TAIPAN
TAIPEI
TAIWAN
THICKY
THIERS
THIEVE
THINGS
THINGY
THINLY
THIRST
THIRTY
THISBE
TOILET
TRIAGE
TRIBAL
TRIBES
TRICAR
TRICKS
TRICKY
TRICOT
TRIFLE
TRIGON
TRILBY
TRIMLY
TRIODE
TRIPLE
TRIPOD
TRIPOS
TRISTE
TRITON
TRIVET
TRIVIA
TUILLE
TWICER
TWIGGY
TWIGHT
TWINED
TWINGE
TWIRLY
TWISTY
TWITCH
UBIETY
ULITIS
UNIATE

UNIQUE
UNISEX
UNISON
UNITED
URINAL
VAINLY
VEILED
VEINED
VOICED
VOIDED
VOIDEE
VOIDER
WAILER
WAITER
WAIVER
WEIGHT
WEIMAR
WEIRDO
WHILOM
WHILST
WHIMSY
WHINGE
WHINNY
WHISHT
WHISKY
WHITBY
WHITED
WHITEN
WHITES
WRIGHT
WRITER
WRITHE
YOICKS
MAÎTRE
ABJECT
ABJURE
ADJOIN
ADJURE
ADJUST
BEJADE
CAJOLE
DEJECT
ENJOIN
HEJIRA
HIJACK
INJECT
INJURE
INJURY
JEJUNE
JOJOBA
JUJUBE
MAJLIS
MEJLIS
MOJAVE
OBJECT
REJECT
REJOIN
UNJUST
ACKERS
AIKIDO
ALKALI
ALKANE
ALKENE
ANKARA
ANKLET
ANKOLE
ARKOSE
ASKARI
ASKING
ATKINS
BAKERS
BAKERY
BAKING
BIKINI
BUKSHI
DAKOTA
DEKKER
DIKDIK
DIKKOP
DIKTAT
ESKIMO
FAKING
FOKINE
FOKKER
GOKART
HIKING
ILKLEY
INKJET
INKPOT
JEKYLL
KAKAPO
KIKUYU
LIKELY
LIKING
MAKEUP
MAKING
MEKONG
MIKADO
NIKKEI
OAKLEY
OAKNUT
OCKERS
OOKPIK
ORKNEY
PAKHTI
PAKHTO
PAKHTU
PEKING
RAKING
RAKISH
ROKEBY
SIKKIM
TAKING
UCKERS
UNKIND
UPKEEP
VIKING
WAKING
YAKKER
YAKUZA
YOKING
YUKATA
ABLATE
ABLAUT
ABLAZE
ABLOOM
ABLUSH
AFLAME
AFLOAT
AGLAIA
AILING
ALLEGE
ALLELE
ALLEYN
ALLIED
ALLIER
ALLIUM
ALLUDE
ALLURE
APLITE
APLOMB
ASLANT
ASLEEP
ASLOPE
BALAAM
BALBOA
BALDER
BALDLY
BALEEN
BALKAN
BALKIS
BALLAD
BALLET
BALLOT
BALSAM
BALTIC
BALZAC
BELAMY
BELFRY
BELIAL
BELIEF
BELIKE
BELIZE
BELLOC
BELLOW
BELONG
BELSEN
BELTED
BELUGA
BILLET
BILLIE
BILLOW
BILLYO
BOLDLY
BOLERO
BOLEYN
BOLIDE
BOLLEN
BOLSHY
BOLTER
BULBIL
BULBUL
BULGAR
BULGER
BULIMY
BULLER
BULLET
BYLINE
CALAIS
CALCED
CALICO
CALIMA
CALIPH
CALKER
CALKIN
CALLAS
CALLED
CALLER
CALLET
CALLID
CALLOP
CALLOW
CALLUP
CALLUS
CALMLY
CALQUE
CALVER
CALVIN
CELERY
CELIAC
CELLAR
CELTIC
CILICE
CILIUM
COLDLY
COLLAR
COLLET
COLLIE
COLLOP
COLMAR
COLONY
COLOUR
COLTER
COLUMN
CULDEE
CULLET
CULLIS
CULMEN
CULTCH
CULTER
CULTUS
CULVER
DALASI
DALTON
DELATE
DELETE
DELIAN
DELICE
DELICT
DELIUS
DELPHI
DELUDE
DELUGE
DELUXE
DELVED
DILATE
DILUTE
DOLEUR
DOLINA
DOLINE
DOLIUM
DOLLAR
DOLLOP
DOLMAN
DOLMEN
DOLOUR
DULCET
EALING
ECLAIR
ECLOSE
ELLERY
ELLICE
ENLACE
ENLIST
EOLITH
EULOGY
FALCON
FALLEN
FALLOW
FALTER
FELINE
FELLER
FELLOE
FELLOW
FELONY
FILFOT
FILIAL
FILING
FILLED
FILLER
FILLET
FILLIP
FILOSE
FILTER
FILTHY
FILTRÉ
FOLDED
FOLDER
FOLIAR
FOLIOS
FOLIOT
FOLIUM
FOLKSY
FOLLOW
FULFIL
FULGID
FULHAM
FULLER
FULMAR
FYLFOT
GALANT
GALAXY
GALENA
GALERE
GALIOT
GALLEN
GALLET
GALLEY
GALLIC
GALLIO
GALLON
GALLOP
GALLOW
GALLUP
GALLUS
GALOOT
GALORE
GALOSH
GELADA
GELATO
GELLER
GILDAS
GILDED
GILDER
GILEAD
GILGAI
GILLET
GILLIE
GILPIN
GOLDEN
GOLFER
GOLLOP
GOLOSH
GULLAH
GULLET
GULLEY
GULPER
HALIDE
HALITE
HALLAL
HALLEY
HALLOO
HALLOW
HALLUX
HALOID
HALTER
HALVED
HALVES
HELENA
HELIOS
HELIUM
HELLER
HELMET
HELPER
HILARY
HILTON
HOLDER
HOLDUP
HOLISM
HOLIST
HOLLER
HOLLOW
HOLMES
HULLED
ILLITE
ILLUDE
INLAID
INLAND
INLAWS
INLINE
IOLITE
ISLAND
ISLETS
JALOPY
JILLET
JULIAN
JULIET
JULIUS
KALMIA
KALPAK
KELLYS
KELOID
KELPER
KELPIE
KELTER
KELTIC
KELTIE
KELVIN
KILLER
KILNER
KILTED
KILTER
KILTIE
LALLAN
LILIAN
LILITH
LOLITA
LOLIUM
LOLLOP
MALAGA
MALATE
MALAWI
MALDON
MALGRE
MALIAN
MALIBU
MALICE
MALIGN
MALLAM
MALLEE
MALLET
MALLOW
MALONE
MALONY
MALORY
MALTED
MELIUS
MELLOW
MELODY
MELTED
MELTON
MILADY
MILDEW
MILDLY
MILIEU
MILLER
MILLET

MILORD
MILTON
MOLECH
MOLEST
MOLINE
MOLLAH
MOLLIE
MOLOCH
MOLTEN
MULISH
MULLAH
MULLER
MULLET
MULTUM
NALLAH
NELLIE
NELSON
NILGAI
NILGAU
NILOTE
NULLAH
NYLONS
OBLAST
OBLATE
OBLIGE
OBLONG
OILCAN
OILERS
OILMAN
OILRIG
ONLINE
OOLITE
OOLONG
OULONG
OWLCAR
OWLISH
PALACE
PALAIS
PALATE
PALING
PALLAH
PALLAS
PALLET
PALLID
PALLOR
PALMER
PALTRY
PELHAM
PELION
PELLET
PELMET
PELOID
PELOTA
PELVIC
PELVIS
PHLEGM
PHLEUM
PHLOEM
PILAFF
PILAGE
PILATE
PILEUM
PILEUP
PILEUS
PILFER
PILING
PILLAR
PILLOW
PILOSE
POLACK
POLAND
POLDER
POLICE
POLICY
POLISH
POLITE
POLITY
POLLAN
POLLED
POLLEN
POLLEX
POLLUX
POLONY
POLYPS
PULLET
PULLEY
PULPIT
PULSAR
PULVER
RELATE
RELENT
RELICS
RELICT
RELIEF
RELISH
RELIVE
ROLAND
ROLLER
RULING
SALAAM
SALADE
SALAMI
SALARY
SALINA
SALINE
SALIVA
SALLEE
SALLET
SALLOW
SALMIS
SALMON
SALOME
SALOON
SALOOP
SALUKI
SALUTE
SALVER
SALVIA
SCLERA
SCLERE
SELDOM
SELECT
SELENE
SELFED
SELJUK
SELLBY
SELLER
SELWYN
SILAGE
SILENE
SILENT
SILICA
SILKEN
SILVAN
SILVER
SOLACE
SOLANO
SOLDER
SOLEIL
SOLELY
SOLEMN
SOLENT
SOLERA
SOLEUS
SOLIVE
SOLUTE
SOLVAY
SOLVED
SOLVER
SPLAKE
SPLASH
SPLEEN
SPLENT
SPLICE
SPLIFF
SPLINT
SPLITS
SPLOSH
SULCUS
SULFUR
SULLEN
SULPHA
SULTAN
SULTRY
SYLVAN
SYLVIA
TALBOT
TALCUM
TALENT
TALION
TALKER
TALKIE
TALLIS
TALLOT
TALLOW
TALMUD
TELEGA
TELEGU
TELLAR
TELLER
TELLUS
TELUGU
TILLER
TILSIT
TOLEDO
TOLLED
TOLLER
TOLOSA
TOLTEC
TOLUIC
TOLUOL
TOLZEY
TULBAN
TULIPA
ULLAGE
ULLING
UMLAUT
UNLACE
UNLESS
UNLIKE
UNLOAD
UNLOCK
UPLAND
UPLIFT
UPLINK
VALENS
VALETA
VALGUS
VALINE
VALISE
VALIUM
VALLEY
VALLUM
VALOUR
VALUER
VALUTA
VELCRO
VELETA
VELLUM
VELOCE
VELOUR
VELURE
VELVET
VILELY
VILIFY
VILLUS
VOLAGE
VOLANS
VOLANT
VOLENS
VOLLEY
VOLUME
VOLUTE
VULCAN
VULGAR
VULGUS
WALKER
WALLAH
WALLED
WALLER
WALLET
WALLOP
WALLOW
WALNUT
WALRUS
WALTER
WALTON
WELDER
WELKIN
WELLER
WELLES
WELLIE
WELTER
WELWYN
WILDER
WILDLY
WILFUL
WILLED
WILLET
WILLIE
WILLOW
WILSON
XYLOID
YELLOW
ADMIRE
ALMAIN
ALMERY
ALMOND
ALMOST
ARMADA
ARMAGH
ARMFUL
ARMLET
ARMORY
ARMOUR
ARMPIT
ARMURE
ASMARA
AUMBRY
AYMARA
BAMAKO
BAMBOO
BEMEAN
BEMOAN
BEMOIL
BEMUSE
BOMBAY
BOMBER
BOMBYX
BUMALO
BUMBLE
BUMPER
CAMAIL
CAMBER
CAMDEN
CAMERA
CAMION
CAMISE
CAMOTE
CAMPED
CAMPER
CAMPUS
CEMENT
COMART
COMATE
COMBAT
COMBED
COMBER
COMBLE
COMEDO
COMEDY
COMELY
COMFIT
COMICE
COMING
COMITY
COMMIS
COMMIT
COMMON
COMPEL
COMPLY
COMSAT
CUMBER
CUMMER
CUMMIN
CYMBAL
CYMRIC
DAMAGE
DAMASK
DAMMIT
DAMNED
DAMPEN
DAMPER
DAMSEL
DAMSON
DEMAIN
DEMAND
DEMEAN
DEMENT
DEMISE
DEMIST
DEMOTE
DEMURE
DIMITY
DIMMER
DIMPLE
DIMWIT
DOMAIN
DOMINO
DUMBLY
DUMDUM
DUMONT
DUMOSE
DUMPER
DUMPLE
EAMONN
EDMOND
EDMUND
EGMONT
ENMESH
ENMITY
ERMINE
ERMITE
EXMOOR
FAMILY
FAMINE
FAMISH
FAMOUS
FEMALE
FIMBRA
FOMENT
FUMADO
FUMBLE
GAMBET
GAMBIA
GAMBIT
GAMBLE
GAMBOL
GAMELY
GAMETE
GAMINE
GAMING
GAMMER
GAMMON
GEMINI
GEMMAN
GIMLET
GIMMER
GUMMED
HAMATE
HAMBLE
HAMITE
HAMLET
HAMMAM
HAMMER
HAMOSE
HAMPER
HEMPEN
HIMMEL
HOMAGE
HOMBRE
HOMELY
HOMILY
HOMING
HOMINY
HUMANE
HUMBER
HUMBLE
HUMBUG
HUMECT
HUMITE
HUMMEL
HUMMER
HUMMUS
HUMOUR
HUMPED
HUMPTY
HYMNAL
IAMBIC
IAMBUS
IMMUNE
IMMURE
INMATE
INMESH
INMOST
JAMBOK
JAMBON

JAMMED
JAMPOT
JEMIMA
JIMJAM
JUMBAL
JUMBLE
JUMPER
KIMMER
KIMONO
KOMODO
KUMARA
KUMERA
KUMISS
KUMMEL
LAMBDA
LAMELY
LAMENT
LAMINA
LAMMAS
LAMMER
LEMNOS
LEMONY
LEMUEL
LEMURE
LIMBED
LIMBER
LIMBIC
LIMITS
LIMNER
LIMPET
LIMPID
LIMPLY
LOMOND
LUMBAR
LUMBER
LUMINA
LUMMOX
LUMPUR
LYMPNE
MAMMAL
MAMMON
MAMZER
MEMBER
MEMNON
MEMOIR
MEMORY
MIMOSA
MOMENT
MUMBLE
MUMMER
NAMELY
NIMBLE
NIMBLY
NIMBUS
NIMROD
NOMADE
NOMISM
NUMBER
NUMBLY
NUMPTY
OOMPAH
ORMOLU
OSMIUM
OSMOSE
PAMELA
PAMIRS
PAMPAS
PAMPER
PAMYAT
PIMENT
PIMPLE
PIMPLY
POMACE
POMADE
POMELO
POMMEL
POMMIE
POMONA
POMPEY
POMPOM
PUMICE
PUMMEL
RAMBLE
RAMEAU
RAMIFY
RAMJET
RAMOSE
RAMOUS
RAMROD
REMAIN
REMAKE
REMAND
REMARK
REMEDY
REMIND
REMISS
REMOTE
REMOVE
RIMINI
RIMMED
ROMANO
ROMANS
ROMANY
ROMISH
ROMMEL
ROMNEY
RUMBLE
RUMKIN
RUMMER
RUMORS
RUMOUR
RUMPLE
RUMPUS
SAMARA
SAMBAL
SAMBAR
SAMBUR
SAMFOO
SAMIAN
SAMIEL
SAMIOT
SAMITE
SAMLET
SAMOSA
SAMPAN
SAMPLE
SAMSON
SAMUEL
SEMELE
SEMITE
SEMPRE
SEMTEX
SIMEON
SIMIAN
SIMILE
SIMKIN
SIMMER
SIMNEL
SIMONY
SIMOON
SIMPER
SIMPLE
SIMPLY
SOMALI
SOMBER
SOMBRE
SUMACH
SUMMER
SUMMIT
SUMMON
SYMBOL
TAMALE
TAMANU
TAMARA
TAMARI
TAMELY
TAMINE
TAMISE
TAMMUZ
TAMPER
TAMPON
TEMPER
TEMPLE
TIMBER
TIMBRE
TIMELY
TIMING
TOMATO
TOMBOY
TOMCAT
TOMIAL
TOMIUM
TOMTOM
TUMBLE
TUMEFY
TUMOUR
TUMULT
TYMBAL
TYMPAN
UNMADE
UNMASK
UNMEET
UTMOST
VOMICA
WAMBLE
WAMPUM
WAMPUS
WIMBLE
WIMPLE
WIMSEY
WOMBAT
WOMENS
YAMMER
YEMENI
YUMYUM
ZAMBIA
ZIMMER
ZOMBIE
ADNATE
AENEID
AGNAIL
AGNATE
AMNION
ANNALS
ANNEAL
ANNEXE
ANNUAL
APNOEA
ARNAUT
ARNHEM
ARNICA
ARNOLD
AUNTIE
AWNING
BANANA
BANDAR
BANDIT
BANDOG
BANGER
BANGLE
BANGUI
BANIAN
BANISH
BANJAX
BANJUL
BANKER
BANNED
BANNER
BANNET
BANTAM
BANTER
BANTRY
BANYAN
BANZAI
BENAME
BENBOW
BENDED
BENDER
BENGAL
BENIGN
BENITO
BENNET
BENSON
BENUMB
BINARY
BINATE
BINDER
BONBON
BONDED
BONDER
BONITO
BONNET
BONNIE
BONSAI
BONXIE
BONZER
BUNCHY
BUNDLE
BUNGAY
BUNGEE
BUNGLE
BUNION
BUNJEE
BUNKER
BUNKUM
BUNSEN
BUNTER
BUNYAN
CANAAN
CANADA
CANAPÉ
CANARD
CANARY
CANCEL
CANCER
CANDID
CANDLE
CANDOR
CANGUE
CANINE
CANING
CANKER
CANNAE
CANNED
CANNEL
CANNON
CANNOT
CANOPY
CANTAB
CANTAL
CANTAR
CANTER
CANTLE
CANTON
CANTOR
CANUCK
CANUTE
CANVAS
CANVEY
CANYON
CENSER
CENSOR
CENSUS
CENTER
CENTRE
CENTUM
CINDER
CINEMA
CINQUE
CONCHA
CONCHY
CONCUR
CONDOM
CONDOR
CONFAB
CONFER
CONGEE
CONGER
CONICS
CONKER
CONMAN
CONNER
CONRAD
CONSUL
CONTRA
CONVEX
CONVEY
CONVOY
CUNEAL
CUNNER
CYNIPS
DANCER
DANDER
DANDLE
DANGER
DANGLE
DANIEL
DANISH
DANTON
DANUBE
DANZIG
DENGUE
DENIAL
DENIED
DENIER
DENIMS
DENNIS
DENOTE
DENTAL
DENUDE
DENVER
DINERO
DINGHY
DINGLE
DINGLY
DINING
DINKUM
DINNER
DONATE
DONGLE
DONJON
DONKEY
DONNÉE
DONZEL
DUNBAR
DUNCAN
DUNCES
DUNDEE
DUNDER
DUNELM
DUNKER
DUNLIN
DUNLOP
DYNAMO
DYNAST
ENNIUS
ERNANI
EUNUCH
FANGLE
FANION
FANTAN
FENCER
FENDER
FENIAN
FENNEL
FINALE
FINDER
FINELY
FINERY
FINEST
FINGAL
FINGER
FINIAL
FINISH
FINITE
FINLAY
FINNAN
FONDLE
FONDLY
FONDUE
FUNDED
FUNDUS
FUNGAL
FUNGUS
FUNNEL
GANDER
GANDHI
GANGER
GANGES
GANGLY
GANGUE
GANION
GANNET
GANTRY
GENDER
GENERA
GENEVA
GENIAL
GENIUS
GENOME
GENTES
GENTLE
GENTLY
GENTRY
GINGER
GINGKO
GINKGO

GONION
GONIUM
GUNDOG
GUNGHO
GUNMAN
GUNNEL
GUNNER
GUNTER
HANDEL
HANDLE
HANGAR
HANGER
HANGUP
HANKER
HANKIE
HANNAH
HANSOM
HENBIT
HENLEY
HENNIN
HENSON
HINDER
HINGED
HINGES
HONCHO
HONEST
HONIED
HONOUR
HONSHU
HUNGER
HUNGRY
HUNKER
HUNTER
IGNITE
IGNORE
INNATE
INNING
IONIAN
IONIZE
JANGLE
JENNER
JENNET
JINGAL
JINGLE
JINXED
JONSON
JUNCUS
JUNGLE
JUNIOR
JUNKER
JUNKET
JUNKIE
KANAKA
KANOON
KANSAS
KANTEN
KANTHA
KANUCK
KENDAL
KENNEL
KENNET

KENSAL
KENYAN
KINASE
KINDER
KINDLE
KINDLY
KINGLY
LANATE
LANCER
LANCET
LANCIA
LANDAU
LANDED
LANDER
LANDOR
LANUGO
LENDER
LENGTH
LENTEL
LENTEN
LENTIC
LENTIL
LENTOR
LINDEN
LINEAL
LINEAR
LINEUP
LINGER
LINGOT
LINING
LINKER
LINKUP
LINNET
LINTEL
LONDON
LONELY
LONGER
LUNACY
LUNARY
LUNATE
LUNULE
MANAGE
MANANA
MANATI
MANCHE
MANCHU
MANEGE
MANFUL
MANGER
MANGLE
MANIAC
MANILA
MANIOC
MANITO
MANNER
MANNIN
MANQUÉ
MANTIS
MANTLE
MANTRA
MANTUA

MANUAL
MANURE
MENACE
MENAGE
MENDEL
MENDER
MENDES
MENDIP
MENHIR
MENIAL
MENINX
MENSAL
MENTAL
MENTOR
MENTUM
MINCER
MINDED
MINDEL
MINDER
MINGLE
MINING
MINION
MINNIE
MINNOW
MINOAN
MINTON
MINUET
MINUTE
MONACO
MONDAY
MONGER
MONGOL
MONIAL
MONICA
MONISM
MONIST
MONKEY
MONODY
MONROE
MONTEM
MONTHS
MUNICH
MUNIFY
MUNITE
MUNSHI
NANDOO
NANISM
NANKIN
NANSEN
NANTES
NINETY
NINIAN
NONAGE
NONARY
NONCOM
NUNCIO
OENONE
OMNIUM
ORNATE
ORNERY
OUNCES

OUNDLE
PANADA
PANAMA
PANDER
PANDIT
PANFRY
PANOPE
PANTER
PANTON
PANTRY
PANZER
PENANG
PENCEL
PENCIL
PENMAN
PENNAE
PENNAL
PENNON
PENSÉE
PENSUM
PENTAD
PENTEL
PENTUP
PENURY
PINCER
PINDAR
PINEAL
PINERO
PINGER
PINING
PINION
PINITE
PINKIE
PINTER
PINTLE
PINXIT
PINYIN
PONCHO
PONDER
PONENT
PONGEE
PONGID
PONTIC
PUNCHY
PUNCTO
PUNDIT
PUNISH
PUNJAB
PUNKAH
PUNNET
PUNTER
RANCEL
RANCHO
RANCID
RANCOR
RANDOM
RANGER
RANKED
RANKER
RANKLE
RANSOM

RANTER
RANULA
RENAME
RENDER
RENEGE
RENNET
RENNIN
RENOIR
RENOWN
RENTAL
RENTER
RENVOI
RENVOY
RINGED
RINGER
RONDEL
RUNDLE
RUNNEL
RUNNER
RUNOFF
RUNWAY
RUNYON
SANCHO
SANDAL
SANDER
SANELY
SANITY
SANSEI
SANTAL
SANTON
SENATE
SENDAL
SENDER
SENECA
SENILE
SENIOR
SENLAC
SENNET
SENORA
SENSED
SENSES
SENSOR
SENTRY
SINBAD
SINDER
SINEWY
SINFUL
SINGER
SINGLE
SINGLY
SINKER
SINNER
SONANT
SONATA
SONICS
SONNET
SONTAG
SUNDAE
SUNDAY
SUNDER
SUNDEW

SUNDRY
SUNHAT
SUNKEN
SUNLIT
SUNRAY
SUNSET
SUNTAN
SYNCOM
SYNDIC
SYNTAX
TANDEM
TANGLE
TANKER
TANKIA
TANNAH
TANNED
TANNER
TANNIC
TANNIN
TANNOY
TANTRA
TENACE
TENANT
TENDER
TENDON
TENDRE
TENGKU
TENNER
TENNIS
TENPIN
TENSON
TENSOR
TENURE
TINDER
TINGED
TINGLE
TINKER
TINKLE
TINNED
TINNIE
TINPAN
TINPOT
TINSEL
TINTED
TINTIN
TONANT
TONGAN
TONGUE
TONITE
TONSIL
TONSOR
TUNDRA
TUNING
TUNNEL
VANDAL
VANISH
VANITY
VENDEE
VENDER
VENDOR
VENDUE

VENEER
VENERY
VENIAL
VENICE
VENITE
VENOSE
VENOUS
VENTIL
VENTRE
VINERY
VINOUS
WANDER
WANDLE
WANGLE
WANKEL
WANTED
WANTON
WENSUM
WINDER
WINDOW
WINDUP
WINGED
WINGER
WINKER
WINKLE
WINNER
WINNIE
WINNOW
WINTER
WINTRY
WONDER
WONTED
WONTON
XANADU
XENIAL
XENIUM
YANKEE
YANKER
YONDER
ZANDER
ZENANA
ZENDIK
ZENITH
ZINGER
ZINNIA
ZONING
ZONKED
ABOARD
ABONDE
ABOUND
ACORNS
ADONAI
ADONIS
ADORER
AEOLIC
AEOLIS
AEOLUS
AGONIC
AGOUTI
ALOGIA
ALONSO

AMOEBA
AMORAL
AMORCE
AMORET
AMOUNT
ANOINT
ANONYM
ANORAK
ANOXIA
ANOXIC
APOGEE
APOLLO
APORIA
AROINT
AROLLA
AROUET
AROUND
AROUSE
ATOCIA
ATOMIC
ATONAL
ATONIC
AVOCET
AVOUCH
AVOWAL
AVOWED
AWOKEN
AZOLLA
AZORES
AZOTIC
BAOBAB
BIOGEN
BIONIC
BIOPIC
BIOPSY
BIOTIC
BIOTIN
BLOCKS
BLONDE
BLOODY
BLOTCH
BLOTTO
BLOUSE
BLOWER
BLOWZY
BOOBOO
BOODLE
BOOGIE
BOOHOO
BOOJUM
BOOKED
BOOKER
BOOKIE
BOOMER
BOOTEE
BOOTLE
BOOZER
BROACH
BROADS
BROGAN
BROGUE
BROKEN
BROKER
BROLLY
BRONCO
BRONTE
BRONZE
BROOCH
BROODY
BROOKE
BROOKS
BROWNE
BROWSE
CHOANA
CHOICE
CHOKED
CHOKER
CHOKEY
CHOLER
CHOOSE
CHOOSY
CHOPIN
CHOPPY
CHORAL
CHOREA
CHOREE
CHORUS
CHOSEN
CHOUAN
CHOUGH
CHOWRY
CLOACA
CLOAKS
CLOCHE
CLONIC
CLONUS
CLOSED
CLOSER
CLOSET
CLOTHE
CLOUDY
CLOUGH
CLOVEN
CLOVER
CLOVIS
COOING
COOKED
COOKER
COOKIE
COOLER
COOLIE
COOLLY
COOLTH
COOPER
COOTIE
CROAKY
CROCHE
CROCKS
CROCUS
CRONET
CRONOS
CROPPY
CROSBY
CROSSE
CROTAL
CROTCH
CROTON
CROUCH
CROUPE
CROUPY
CROUSE
CROUTE
CROUTH
DEODAR
DHOOTI
DIODON
DIOXIN
DOODAD
DOODAH
DOODLE
DOOFER
DOOMED
DROGUE
DROMIO
DROMOS
DRONES
DRONGO
DROOPY
DROPSY
DROSKY
DROVER
DROVES
DROWSE
DROWSY
DVORAK
ECONUT
EGOISM
EGOIST
ELODEA
ELOHIM
ELOIGN
ELOISE
ELOPER
ENODAL
ENOSIS
ENOUGH
EPONYM
EPOPEE
ERODED
EROICA
EROTIC
EVOLUÉ
EVOLVE
EXOCET
EXODUS
EXOGEN
EXOTIC
FLOOZY
FLOPPY
FLORAL
FLORET
FLORID
FLORIN
FLOSSY
FLOURY
FLOUSH
FLOWER
FOOTER
FOOTLE
FOOZLE
FROLIC
FRONDE
FROSTY
FROTHY
FROUDE
FROWST
FROWZY
FROZEN
GAOLER
GEORGE
GHOSTS
GIORGI
GIOTTO
GLOBAL
GLOIRE
GLOOMY
GLORIA
GLOSSA
GLOSSY
GLOVED
GLOWER
GNOMIC
GNOMON
GOOBER
GOODLY
GOOGIE
GOOGLE
GOOGLY
GOOGOL
GOOLEY
GOOLIE
GROATS
GROCER
GROGGY
GROOVE
GROOVY
GROPER
GROSSO
GROTTO
GROTTY
GROUCH
GROUND
GROUPS
GROUSE
GROUTS
GROUTY
GROVEL
GROWER
GROWTH
GROYNE
HOODED
HOOFED
HOOFER
HOOHAH
HOOKAH
HOOKED
HOOKER
HOOKEY
HOOKUP
HOOPER
HOOPLA
HOOPOE
HOORAH
HOORAY
HOOTCH
HOOTER
HOOVER
ICONIC
IMOGEN
IRONED
IRONIC
ISOBAR
ISOLDE
ISOMER
ISOPOD
KAOLIN
KNOBBY
KNOTTY
KOODOO
KOOKIE
KOOLAH
KRONER
KRONOS
LEONID
LHOTSE
LIONEL
LLOYDS
LOOFAH
LOONIE
LOOPED
LOOPER
LOOSEN
LOOTER
MAOIST
MAOTAI
MOOCOW
MOOLAH
MOOMBA
MYOGEN
MYOPIA
MYOPIC
MYOSIN
MYOSIS
NOODLE
NOOKIE
OBOIST
OBOLUS
PEOPLE
PHOBIA
PHOBIC
PHOEBE
PHONAL
PHONEY
PHONIC
PHOOEY
PHOTON
PLONGE
PLOUGH
PLOVER
POODLE
POORLY
POOTER
PROBIT
PROFIT
PROLEG
PROLIX
PROLOG
PROMPT
PRONTO
PROPEL
PROPER
PROPYL
PROSIT
PROTEA
PROTON
PROUST
PROVEN
PTOSIS
QUOITS
QUORUM
QUOTED
REOPEN
RHODES
RIOTER
ROOFER
ROOKIE
ROOMER
ROOTED
ROOTER
ROOTLE
RYOKAN
SCOLEX
SCONCE
SCOOBS
SCOOSH
SCOPUS
SCORCH
SCORER
SCORIA
SCORSE
SCOTCH
SCOTER
SCOTIA
SCOUSE
SHODDY
SHOFAR
SHOGUN
SHORTS
SHOULD
SHOVEL
SHOWER
SLOANE
SLOGAN
SLOPES
SLOPPY
SLOSHY
SLOUCH
SLOUGH
SLOVAK
SLOVEN
SLOWLY
SMOKER
SMOKEY
SMOOCH
SMOOTH
SNOOTY
SNOOZE
SNORER
SNOTTY
SNOUTY
SNOWED
SOONER
SOOTHE
SPOILS
SPOILT
SPOKEN
SPOKES
SPONGE
SPONGY
SPOOKY
SPOONY
SPORTS
SPORTY
SPOTTY
SPOUSE
STOCKS
STOCKY
STODGE
STODGY
STOGIE
STOKER
STOKES
STOLEN
STOLID
STOLON
STONED
STONER
STONES
STOOGE
STOOKS
STOOLS
STORER
STOREY
STORMY
STOVER
STOWER
SWOOSH
TAOISM
TAOIST
TEOPAN
THOLOS
THOLUS
THOMAS
THORAH
THORAX
THORNE
THORNY

THORPE
THOUGH
TOOTER
TOOTHY
TOOTLE
TOOTSY
TROCAR
TROCHE
TROIKA
TROJAN
TROMPE
TROOPS
TROPHE
TROPHY
TROPIC
TROPPO
TROUGH
TROUPE
TROUVÉ
TROVER
TROWEL
TROYES
TWOBIT
UTOPIA
VIOLET
VIOLIN
VOODOO
WHOLLY
WHOOPS
WHOOSH
WOODED
WOODEN
WOODIE
WOOFER
WOOKEY
WOOLEN
WOOLLY
YAOURT
YEOMAN
YEOMEN
ALPACA
ALPINE
ALPINO
AMPERE
APPALL
APPEAL
APPEAR
APPEND
APPIAN
APPLES
APPORT
APPOSE
ARPENT
ASPECT
ASPIRE
BYPASS
CAPIAS
CAPLET
CAPONE
CAPOTE
CAPPED
CAPSID
CAPTAN
CAPTOR
CIPHER
COPECK
COPIED
COPIER
COPING
COPPER
COPPIN
COPTIC
CUPFUL
CUPMAN
CUPOLA
CUPPED
CUPPER
CUPULE
CYPHER
CYPRID
CYPRIS
CYPRUS
DAPHNE
DAPPER
DAPPLE
DEPART
DEPEND
DEPICT
DEPLOY
DEPONE
DEPORT
DEPOSE
DEPTHS
DEPUTE
DEPUTY
DIPLOE
DIPNOI
DIPOLE
DIPPER
DUPLEX
EMPIRE
EMPLOY
EPPING
ESPADA
ESPRIT
EXPAND
EXPECT
EXPEDE
EXPEND
EXPERT
EXPIRE
EXPIRY
EXPORT
EXPOSE
EXPUGN
FIPPLE
GAPING
GOPHER
GYPSUM
HAPPEN
HAPTEN
HAPTIC
HEPTAD
HIPPED
HIPPUS
HOPPER
HYPATE
HYPHAL
HYPHEN
HYPNIC
HYPNOS
HYPNUM
IMPACT
IMPAIR
IMPALA
IMPALE
IMPART
IMPAWN
IMPEDE
IMPEND
IMPISH
IMPORT
IMPOSE
IMPOST
IMPUGN
IMPURE
IMPUTE
JOPLIN
KAPUTT
KEPHIR
KEPLER
KIPPER
LAPDOG
LAPITH
LAPPER
LAPPET
LAPSED
LAPSUS
LAPTOP
LAPUTA
LEPTON
LIPARI
LIPASE
LIPIDE
LIPOMA
LIPPED
LUPINE
MAPUTO
MOPING
MOPISH
MOPPET
MOPSUS
MUPPET
NAPALM
NAPERY
NAPIER
NAPKIN
NAPLES
NAPPER
NEPALI
NEPETA
NEPHEW
NIPPER
NIPPLE
NIPPON
OPPOSE
OPPUGN
ORPHAN
ORPHIC
OSPREY
PAPACY
PAPAYA
PAPERS
PAPERY
PAPHOS
PAPIST
PAPULE
PEPLOS
PEPLUM
PEPPER
PEPTIC
PIPING
PIPKIN
PIPPIN
POPEYE
POPLAR
POPLIN
POPPER
POPPET
POPPIT
PUPATE
PUPPET
RAPHIA
RAPIDS
RAPIER
RAPINE
RAPIST
RAPPED
RAPPEL
RAPPER
RAPTLY
RAPTOR
REPAID
REPAIR
REPAST
REPEAL
REPEAT
REPENT
REPINE
REPLAY
REPORT
REPOSE
REPTON
REPUGN
REPUTE
RIPOFF
RIPPER
RIPPLE
RIPPON
RIPSAW
ROPERY
RUPEES
RUPERT
RUPIAH
RUPIAS
SAPELE
SAPHAR
SAPIUM
SAPOTA
SAPPER
SAPPHO
SEPIUM
SEPSIS
SEPTAL
SEPTET
SEPTIC
SIPHON
SIPPET
SIPPLE
SOPHIA
SUPERB
SUPINE
SUPLEX
SUPPER
SUPPLE
SUPPLY
SYPHER
SYPHON
TAPPER
TAPPET
TAPPIT
TEPHRA
TIPCAT
TIPOFF
TIPPED
TIPPER
TIPPET
TIPPLE
TIPPOO
TIPTOE
TIPTOP
TIPULA
TOPHUS
TOPPER
TOPPLE
TUPELO
TYPHUS
TYPIFY
TYPING
TYPIST
UMPIRE
UNPACK
UNPAID
UNPICK
UNPLUG
UPPISH
UPPITY
VAPOUR
WAPITI
WIPERS
WIPING
YIPPEE
YUPPIE
ZAPATA
ZEPHYR
ZIPPER
ZOPHAR
ACQUIT
COQUET
DIQUAT
LIQUID
LIQUOR
LOQUAT
MAQUIS
PEQUOD
PIQUET
ROQUET
SEQUEL
SEQUIN
AARONS
ABRADE
ABREGE
ABROAD
ABROMA
ABRUPT
ACRAWL
ACROSS
ADRIAN
ADRIFT
ADROIT
AERATE
AERIAL
AEROBE
AFRAID
AFREET
AFRESH
AFRICA
AGREED
AGRÉGÉ
AIRBED
AIRBUS
AIRGUN
AIRILY
AIRING
AIRMAN
AIRWAY
AORIST
AORTAL
ARRACK
ARRANT
ARREAR
ARREST
ARRIAN
ARRIVE
ARROBA
ARROYO
ATRIAL
ATRIDE
ATRIUM
AUREUS
AURIGA
AURORA
AZRAEL
BARBED
BARBEL
BARBER
BARBET
BARÈGE
BARELY
BARGEE
BARHAM
BARING
BARIUM
BARKER
BARKIS
BARLEY
BARMAN
BARNES
BARNET
BARNEY
BARNUM
BARODA
BARQUE
BARRED
BARREL
BARREN
BARRIE
BARRIO
BARROW
BARSAC
BARTER
BARTOK
BARTON
BARYTA
BERATE
BERBER
BEREFT
BERGEN
BERING
BERLIN
BERTHA
BERTHE
BERTIE
BIRDIE
BIREME
BIRNAM
BORAGE
BORATE
BORDAR
BORDER
BOREAS
BORGIA
BORING
BORNEO
BORROW
BORSCH
BORZOI
BURBLE
BURBOT
BURDEN
BUREAU
BURGEE
BURGER
BURGLE
BURIAL
BURIED
BURKHA

BURLAP
BURLEY
BURNER
BURNET
BURROW
BURSAR
BURTON
BYRNIE
CARAFE
CARBON
CARBOY
CARDAN
CAREEN
CAREER
CAREME
CARESS
CARFAX
CARIES
CARINA
CARING
CARLIN
CARMEL
CARMEN
CARNAL
CARNET
CARNOT
CARPAL
CARPEL
CARPER
CARPET
CARPUS
CARREL
CARROT
CARSON
CARTEL
CARTER
CARTON
CARUSO
CARVED
CARVEL
CARVER
CERATE
CERCAL
CERCUS
CEREAL
CEREUS
CERISE
CERIUM
CEROON
CERTES
CERUSE
CERVIX
CHRISM
CHRIST
CHROMA
CHROME
CHROMO
CIRCLE
CIRCUS
CIRQUE
CIRRUS
CORALS
CORBEL
CORBIE
CORDON
CORIUM
CORKED
CORKER
CORMUS
CORNEA
CORNED
CORNEL
CORNER
CORNET
CORNUA
CORNUS
CORONA
CORPSE
CORPUS
CORRAL
CORRIE
CORSET
CORTES
CORTEX
CORTEZ
CORVÉE
CORVUS
CORYZA
CURACY
CURARE
CURARI
CURATE
CURDLE
CURFEW
CURIET
CURIUM
CURLER
CURLEW
CURPEL
CURRIE
CURSAL
CURSED
CURSOR
CURSUS
CURTAL
CURTAX
CURTLY
CURTSY
CURULE
CURVED
CURVET
CYRANO
CYRENE
DARGLE
DARIEN
DARING
DARIUS
DARKEN
DARKEY
DARKIE
DARKLY
DARTER
DARTLE
DARWIN
DERAIL
DERAIN
DERGUE
DERHAM
DERIDE
DERIVE
DERMAL
DERMIS
DERRIS
DIRECT
DIRHAM
DIRNDL
DORADO
DORCAS
DORIAN
DORMER
DORRIT
DORSAL
DORSET
DORTER
DURANT
DURBAR
DURESS
DURHAM
DURIAN
DURING
DURION
EARFUL
EARING
EARNED
EARNER
EARTHY
EARWIG
EERILY
EGRESS
EIRANN
ENRAGE
ENRAPT
ENRICH
ENROBE
ENROLL
EPRISE
ERRAND
ERRANT
ETRIER
EUREKA
EUROPA
EUROPE
FARAND
FARCIN
FARDEL
FARDLE
FARINA
FARMER
FAROFF
FAROUK
FARROW
FERIAL
FERMAT
FERRET
FERRIS
FERULA
FERULE
FERVID
FERVOR
FIRING
FIRKIN
FIRLOT
FIRMAN
FIRMER
FIRMLY
FORAGE
FORBID
FORÇAT
FORCED
FORCES
FOREDO
FOREGO
FOREST
FORGED
FORGER
FORGET
FORGOT
FORINT
FORKED
FORMAL
FORMAT
FORMER
FORMIC
FORNAX
FORNIX
FORPIT
FORRAD
FORRAY
FORSAY
FORTHY
FUREUR
FURFUR
FURIES
FURORE
FURPHY
FURROW
GARAGE
GARBED
GARBLE
GARÇON
GARDEN
GARETH
GARGET
GARGLE
GARISH
GARLIC
GARNER
GARNET
GARRET
GARROT
GARRYA
GARTER
GARUDA
GERBIL
GERENT
GERMAN
GERUND
GIRDER
GIRDLE
GIRKIN
GIRLIE
GIRTON
GORDON
GORGED
GORGES
GORGET
GORGIA
GORGIO
GORGON
GORING
GURGLE
GURKHA
GURLET
GURNET
GURNEY
GYRATE
HARARE
HARASS
HARBOR
HARDEN
HARDLY
HARKEN
HARLOT
HARMED
HAROLD
HARPIC
HARRIS
HARROW
HARVEY
HERALD
HERBAL
HERDEN
HERDER
HEREBY
HEREIN
HERERO
HERESY
HERETO
HERIOT
HERMES
HERMIT
HERMON
HERNIA
HEROIC
HEROIN
HERONS
HERPES
HERREN
HIRING
HIRSEL
HORACE
HORMUZ
HORNED
HORNER
HORNET
HORRID
HORROR
HORSED
HURDLE
HURLEY
HURRAH
HURRAY
HURTLE
INROAD
INRUSH
IRRUPT
ISRAEL
JARGON
JARVEY
JERBOA
JEREMY
JERKER
JERKIN
JEROME
JERSEY
JORDAN
JURANT
JURIST
KARATE
KARIBA
KARITE
KERALA
KERMES
KERMIS
KERNEL
KIRBEH
KIRMAN
KIRSCH
KIRTLE
KOREAN
KORUNA
LARDER
LARDON
LARIAT
LARKIN
LARRUP
LARVAE
LARVAL
LARYNX
LORCHA
LORDLY
LORETO
LORICA
LORIOT
LURING
LURIST
LYRICS
LYRIST
MARACA
MARAUD
MARBLE
MARCEL
MARGIN
MARIAN
MARINA
MARINE
MARISH
MARIST
MARKED
MARKER
MARKET
MARKKA
MARKUP
MARLIN
MARMOT
MARNER
MAROON
MARQUE
MARRAM
MARRON
MARROW
MARSHY
MARTEL
MARTEN
MARTHA
MARTIN
MARTYR
MARVEL
MERCAT
MERCER
MERCIA
MERELY
MERGER
MERINO
MERKIN
MERLIN
MERLOT
MERMAN
MEROPE
MERRIE
MERROW
MERSEY
MERTON
MIRAGE
MIRROR
MORALE
MORALS
MORASS
MORBID
MORBUS
MOREEN
MORGAN
MORGEN
MORGUE
MORION
MORMON
MORNAY
MORNED
MOROSE
MORRIS
MORROW
MORSEL
MORTAL
MORTAR
MORTEM
MURAGE
MURALS

MURDER
MURIEL
MURINE
MURLIN
MURMUR
MURPHY
MURRAM
MURRAY
MURRHA
MURRIN
MYRIAD
MYRTLE
NARROW
NEREID
NEREUS
NERINE
NERIUM
NEROLI
NERVAL
NERVES
NERVII
NORDIC
NORMAL
NORMAN
NORROY
NORVIC
NORWAY
OARLAP
OERLAY
OGRESS
ONRUSH
ORRERY
OURALI
PARADE
PARAMO
PARANA
PARAPH
PARCEL
PARDIE
PARDON
PARENT
PARETO
PARGET
PARIAH
PARISH
PARITY
PARKED
PARKER
PARKIN
PARLEY
PARLOR
PARODY
PAROLE
PARROT
PARSEC
PARSEE
PARSON
PARTLY
PARTON
PARURE
PARVIS
PERDUE
PERHAP
PERILS
PERIOD
PERISH
PERKIN
PERMIT
PERNOD
PERRON
PERSON
PERUKE
PERUSE
PHRASE
PIRACY
PIRATE
PIRENE
PORGIE
PORKER
POROUS
PORTAL
PORTER
PORTIA
PORTLY
PURDAH
PURELY
PURIFY
PURINE
PURIST
PURITY
PURLER
PURLIN
PURPLE
PURSED
PURSER
PURSUE
PURVEY
PYRENE
PYRONE
PYROPE
PYRRHO
RAREFY
RARELY
RARING
RARITY
REREAD
SARGUS
SARNIE
SARONG
SARSEN
SARTOR
SARTRE
SCRAMB
SCRAPE
SCRAPS
SCRAWL
SCRAWM
SCREAM
SCREED
SCREEN
SCREWY
SCRIBE
SCRIMP
SCRIPT
SCROLL
SCROOP
SCRUBS
SCRUFF
SCRUNT
SERAIL
SERANG
SERAPE
SERAPH
SERBIA
SERDAB
SERENE
SERIAL
SERIES
SERINE
SERMON
SEROSA
SERVAL
SERVER
SHRANK
SHREWD
SHRIEK
SHRIFT
SHRIKE
SHRILL
SHRIMP
SHRINE
SHRINK
SHRIVE
SHROFF
SHROUD
SHROVE
SHRUNK
SIRDAR
SIRIUS
SIRKAR
SIRRAH
SIRREE
SORAGE
SORBET
SORDES
SORDID
SORELL
SORELY
SORGHO
SORREL
SORROW
SORTER
SORTES
SORTIE
SPRAIN
SPRANG
SPRAWL
SPREAD
SPRING
SPRINT
SPRITE
SPRITZ
SPROUT
SPRUCE
SPRUNG
SPRYLY
STRABO
STRAFE
STRAIN
STRAIT
STRAKE
STRAND
STRASS
STRATA
STRAWS
STRAWY
STREAK
STREAM
STREET
STREGA
STRENE
STRESS
STRICK
STRICT
STRIDE
STRIFE
STRIKE
STRINE
STRING
STRIPE
STRIPY
STRIVE
STROBE
STRODE
STROKE
STROLL
STRONG
STROUD
STROUP
STROVE
STRUCK
STRUNG
STRUNT
SURELY
SURETÉ
SURETY
SURFER
SURREY
SURTAX
SURVEY
SYRIAN
SYRINX
SYRISM
SYRUPY
TARCEL
TARDIS
TARGET
TARGUM
TARIFF
TARMAC
TARROW
TARSAL
TARSEL
TARSIA
TARSUS
TARTAN
TARTAR
TARTLY
TERCET
TERCIO
TEREDO
TERESA
TERETE
TERGUM
TERMES
TERMLY
TERNAL
TERRAE
TERROR
TERTIA
THRALL
THRASH
THRAWN
THREAD
THREAP
THREAT
THRENE
THRESH
THRICE
THRIFT
THRILL
THRIPS
THRIST
THRIVE
THROAT
THROES
THRONE
THRONG
THROVE
THROWN
THRUSH
THRUST
TIRADE
TIRANA
TIRING
TORERO
TORPID
TORPOR
TORQUE
TORRES
TORRID
TURBAN
TURBID
TURBOT
TUREEN
TURGID
TURKEY
TURNED
TURNER
TURNIP
TURNUP
TURPIN
TURRET
TURTLE
TURVES
TYRANT
TYRONE
UGRIAN
UNREAD
UNREAL
UNREEL
UNREST
UNRIPE
UNROLL
UNRULY
UPRATE
UPROAR
UPROOT
VARECH
VARESE
VARIED
VARLET
VERBAL
VERDIN
VERDUN
VEREIN
VERGER
VERGES
VERIFY
VERILY
VERISM
VERITY
VERMIN
VERMIS
VERNAL
VERNON
VERSAL
VERSED
VERSES
VERSET
VERSUS
VERVET
VIRAGO
VIRGIL
VIRGIN
VIRILE
VIROUS
VIRTUE
VORTEX
WARBLE
WARCRY
WARDEN
WARDER
WARHOL
WARILY
WARMER
WARMLY
WARMTH
WARNER
WARPED
WARREN
WARSAW
WERENT
WIRING
WIRRAL
WORKED
WORKER
WORSEN
WORTHY
WORTLE
XEROMA
XERXES
YARDIE
YARROW
YORICK
YORKER
YORUBA
ZIRCON
ZURICH
ZYRIAN
ABSEIL
ABSENT
ABSORB
ABSURD
ADSORB
ADSUKI
ANSELM
ANSWER
ARSÈNE
ARSINE
ASSAIL
ASSART
ASSENT
ASSERT
ASSESS
ASSETS
ASSIGN
ASSIST
ASSIZE
ASSOIL
ASSORT
ASSUME
ASSURE
AUSPEX
AUSSIE
AUSTEN
AUSTER
AUSTIN
BASALT
BASHER
BASICS
BASKET
BASQUE
BASSET
BASUTO
BESANT
BESEEM
BESIDE
BESORT
BESSEL
BESSIE
BESSUS
BESTED
BESTIR
BESTOW
BISCAY
BISECT

BISHOP
BISQUE
BISTER
BISTRE
BISTRO
BOSKET
BOSSED
BOSTON
BOSUNS
BUSBOY
BUSHED
BUSHEL
BUSILY
BUSKER
BUSKET
BUSKIN
BUSMAN
BUSONI
BUSTED
BUSTER
BUSTLE
BYSSUS
CASBAH
CASEIN
CASHEW
CASING
CASINO
CASKET
CASLON
CASPAR
CASQUE
CASSIA
CASSIO
CASSIS
CASTER
CASTLE
CASTOR
CASTRO
CASUAL
CESARE
CESIUM
CESTUI
CESTUS
CESURA
COSHER
COSIER
COSILY
COSINE
COSMEA
COSMIC
COSMOS
COSSET
COSSIE
COSTAR
COSTER
COSTLY
CUSCUS
CUSHAT
CUSSED
CUSSER
CUSTER
CUSTOM
CUSTOS
CYSTIC
DASHED
DESCRY
DESERT
DESIGN
DESIRE
DESIST
DESORB
DESPOT
DISARM
DISBAR
DISBUD
DISCUS
DISEUR
DISHED
DISHES
DISMAL
DISMAY
DISNEY
DISOWN
DISPEL
DISTAL
DISTIL
DISUSE
DOSAGE
DOSSAL
DOSSER
DUSTED
DUSTER
EASIER
EASILY
EASING
EASTER
ENSATE
ENSEAL
ENSIGN
ENSILE
ENSURE
ERSATZ
ESSENE
EUSTON
EXSERT
FASCES
FASCIA
FASTEN
FESCUE
FESTAL
FESTER
FISCAL
FISHER
FOSSIL
FOSTER
FUSAIN
FUSELI
FUSION
FUSTIC
FUSTOC
GASBAG
GASCON
GASKET
GASMAN
GASPAR
GASPER
GASSER
GASTER
GASTON
GOSPEL
GOSSIP
GUSHER
GUSLAR
GUSSET
HASHED
HASLET
HASSAR
HASSLE
HASTEN
HESIOD
HISPID
HOSIER
HOSING
HOSTEL
HUSHED
HUSSAR
HUSSIF
HUSTLE
HYSSOP
INSANE
INSECT
INSERT
INSIDE
INSIST
INSOLE
INSTAL
INSTAR
INSTEP
INSTIL
INSULA
INSULT
INSURE
ISSUES
ITSELF
JASPER
JESTER
JESUIT
JISSOM
JOSEPH
JOSHUA
JOSIAH
JOSKIN
JOSSER
JOSTLE
JUSTIN
JUSTLY
KASBAH
KISMET
KISSEL
KISSER
KOSHER
KOSMOS
LASCAR
LASHED
LASHER
LASKET
LASSIE
LASSUS
LASTLY
LESBOS
LESION
LESLIE
LESSEE
LESSEN
LESSER
LESSON
LESSOR
LESTER
LISBON
LISPER
LISSOM
LISTEL
LISTEN
LISTER
LOSING
LUSAKA
LUSTER
LUSTRE
MASADA
MASCOT
MASHAM
MASHED
MASHER
MASHIE
MASKED
MASLIN
MASQUE
MASSED
MASSES
MASSIF
MASTER
MASTIC
MESAIL
MESCAL
MESIAL
MESMER
MESSRS
MISÈRE
MISERY
MISFIT
MISHAP
MISHIT
MISLAY
MISLED
MISSAL
MISSED
MISSEL
MISSIS
MISSUS
MISTER
MISUSE
MOSAIC
MOSCOW
MOSLEM
MOSQUE
MOSSAD
MOSTLY
MUSANG
MUSCAT
MUSCLE
MUSEUM
MUSING
MUSIVE
MUSKEG
MUSKET
MUSLIM
MUSLIN
MUSSEL
MUSTER
MYSELF
MYSORE
MYSTIC
NASEBY
NASION
NASSAU
NASSER
NASTIC
NESSIE
NESSUS
NESTLE
NESTOR
NISSEN
NOSILY
OBSESS
ONSIDE
ORSINO
OSSIAN
OSSIFY
OYSTER
PASCAL
PASHTO
PASHTU
PASQUE
PASSED
PASSES
PASSIM
PASTEL
PASTIL
PASTIS
PASTON
PASTOR
PASTRY
PESADE
PESETA
PESHWA
PESTER
PESTLE
PISANO
PISCES
PISGAH
PISSED
PISTIL
PISTOL
PISTON
POSADA
POSEUR
POSSER
POSSET
POSSUM
POSTAL
POSTER
POSTIL
PUSHER
PUSHTU
PUSHUP
PUSSER
RASCAL
RASHER
RASHLY
RASPER
RASTER
RESALE
RESCUE
RESEAU
RESECT
RESEDA
RESENT
RESIDE
RESIGN
RESIST
RESORT
RESULT
RESUME
RISING
RISQUÉ
ROSACE
ROSARY
ROSCID
ROSCOE
ROSERY
ROSINA
ROSSER
ROSTER
ROSTOV
ROSYTH
RUSHED
RUSKIN
RUSSET
RUSSIA
RUSTAM
RUSTEM
RUSTIC
RUSTLE
RUSTUM
SASHAY
SESAME
SISKIN
SISTER
SUSSEX
SYSTEM
TASMAN
TASSEL
TASSET
TASSIE
TASTER
TESTER
TESTES
TESTIS
TISANE
TISSOT
TISSUE
TOSHER
TOSSUP
TUSCAN
TUSKER
TUSSAH
TUSSIS
TUSSLE
ULSTER
UNSAFE
UNSAID
UNSEAM
UNSEAT
UNSEEN
UNSENT
UNSEXY
UNSHOD
UNSOLD
UNSUNG
UNSURE
UPSHOT
UPSIDE
URSINE
URSULA
VASSAL
VASTLY
VESICA
VESPER
VESSEL
VESTAL
VESTED
VESTRY
VISAGE
VISCID
VISHNU
VISIER
VISION
VISUAL
VOSGES
WASHED
WASHER
WASTED
WASTEL
WASTER
WESKER
WESLEY
WESSEX
WISDEN
WISDOM
WISELY
WISHES
YESMAN
YESTER
ZOSTER
ACTING
ACTION
ACTIUM

ACTIVE
ACTORS
ACTUAL
AFTERS
ALTAIR
ALTHEA
AMTRAK
ANTHEM
ANTHER
ANTICS
ANTLER
ANTLIA
ANTONY
ANTRIM
ANTRUM
ARTAUD
ARTERY
ARTFUL
ARTHUR
ARTIST
ARTURO
ASTART
ASTERN
ASTHMA
ASTONE
ASTRAL
ASTRAY
ASTUTE
ATTACH
ATTACK
ATTAIN
ATTEND
ATTEST
ATTILA
ATTIRE
ATTLEE
ATTONE
ATTORN
ATTRAP
ATTUNE
AUTHOR
AUTISM
AUTUMN
BATEAU
BATHER
BATHOS
BATMAN
BATTEN
BATTER
BATTLE
BATTUE
BETAKE
BETHEL
BETIDE
BETIME
BETISE
BETONY
BETRAY
BETTER
BETTOR
BITCHY
BITING
BITTEN
BITTER
BOTANY
BOTHAM
BOTHER
BOTHIE
BOTLEY
BOTTLE
BOTTOM
BUTANE
BUTENE
BUTLER
BUTTER
BUTTON
CATCHY
CATGUT
CATHAR
CATHAY
CATKIN
CATNAP
CATNIP
CATSUP
CATTLE
CETERA
CITRIC
CITRIN
CITRON
CITRUS
COTTAR
COTTON
COTYLE
CUTCHA
CUTLER
CUTLET
CUTOFF
CUTTER
CUTTLE
CUTTOE
CYTASE
CYTODE
CYTOID
DATING
DATIVE
DATURA
DETACH
DETAIL
DETAIN
DETECT
DETENT
DETENU
DETEST
DETOUR
DITHER
DITTOS
DOTAGE
DOTARD
DOTING
DOTTED
DOTTLE
EATAGE
EATERY
EATING
ECTOPY
EFTEST
EITHER
ELTCHI
ENTAIL
ENTICE
ENTIRE
ENTITY
ENTOMB
ENTRAP
ENTREE
EOTHEN
ESTATE
ESTEEM
ESTHER
ESTRAY
EUTAXY
EXTANT
EXTEND
EXTENT
EXTERN
EXTIRP
EXTOLL
EXTORT
FATHER
FATHOM
FATIMA
FATTEN
FETISH
FETTER
FETTES
FETTLE
FITFUL
FITOUT
FITTED
FITTER
FUTILE
FUTURE
GATEAU
GATHER
GETTER
GITANO
GOTHAM
GOTHIC
GOTTEN
GUTTER
GUTTLE
HATING
HATRED
HATTER
HETERO
HETMAN
HITECH
HITHER
HITLER
HITMAN
HITTER
HOTAIR
HOTBED
HOTPOT
HOTTER
INTACT
INTAKE
INTEND
INTENT
INTERN
INTIME
INTONE
INTOWN
INTRAY
INTRON
ISTRIA
JETHRO
JETLAG
JETSAM
JETTON
JITNEY
JITTER
JOTTER
KATANA
KETMIR
KETONE
KETOSE
KETTLE
KITBAG
KITCAT
KITSCH
KITTEN
KITTLE
KOTWAL
LATEEN
LATELY
LATENT
LATEST
LATHER
LATRON
LATTEN
LATTER
LATVIA
LETHAL
LETOUT
LETTER
LITANY
LITCHI
LITHIA
LITMUS
LITTER
LITTLE
LOTION
LUTEAL
LUTEIN
LUTHER
LUTINE
LUTIST
LYTTON
MATHIS
MATING
MATINS
MATLOW
MATRIX
MATRON
MATTED
MATTER
MATURE
METAGE
METATE
METEOR
METHOD
METHYL
METIER
METOPE
METRIC
METTLE
MITRAL
MITRED
MITTEN
MOTHER
MOTILE
MOTION
MOTIVE
MOTLEY
MOTOWN
MOTTLE
MUTANT
MUTATE
MUTELY
MUTINY
MUTTER
MUTTON
MUTUAL
MYTHOS
NATANT
NATION
NATIVE
NATRON
NATTER
NATURE
NETHER
NETTLE
NITERY
NITRIC
NITRYL
NITWIT
NOTARY
NOTATE
NOTICE
NOTIFY
NOTION
NUTANT
NUTATE
NUTMEG
NUTTER
OBTAIN
OBTECT
OBTEND
OBTUND
OBTUSE
OCTANE
OCTANS
OCTANT
OCTAVE
OCTAVO
OCTROI
OPTICS
OPTIMA
OPTIME
OPTION
OPTOUT
ORTEGA
OSTEND
OSTIUM
OSTLER
OSTREA
OTTAVA
OTTAWA
OUTAGE
OUTBAR
OUTBID
OUTCRY
OUTFIT
OUTGAS
OUTING
OUTLAW
OUTLAY
OUTLET
OUTLIE
OUTPUT
OUTRUN
OUTSET
OUTTOP
OUTVIE
OUTWIT
OXTAIL
PATACA
PATCHY
PATENT
PATHAN
PATHIC
PATHOS
PATINA
PATMOS
PATOIS
PATROL
PATRON
PATTEN
PATTER
PATTON
PÉTAIN
PETARD
PETARY
PETERS
PETIPA
PETITE
PETREL
PETROL
PITMAN
PITTED
PITTER
POTASH
POTATO
POTEEN
POTENT
POTHER
POTION
POTTED
POTTER
POTTLE
PUTEAL
PUTOIS
PUTRID
PUTSCH
PUTTEE
PUTTER
PYTHIA
PYTHON
RATBAG
RATHER
RATIFY
RATINE
RATING
RATION
RATOON
RATTAN
RATTER
RATTLE
RATTON
RETAIL
RETAIN
RETAKE
RETARD
RETINA
RETIRE
RETOOL
RETORT
RETOUR
RETURN
RITUAL
ROTARY
ROTATE
ROTGUT
ROTHER
ROTHKO
ROTTEN
ROTTER
ROTULA
ROTUND
RUTTED
RUTTER
SATEEN
SATINY
SATIRE
SATIVE
SATORI
SATRAP
SATURN
SATYRA
SETOSE
SETTEE
SETTER
SETTLE
SHTCHI
SHTETL
SITCOM

SITREP
SITTER
SUTLER
SUTTEE
SUTURE
TATAMI
TATERS
TATLER
TATTER
TATTLE
TATTOO
TETANY
TETCHY
TETHER
TETHYS
TETRAD
TETRYL
TETTIX
TITBIT
TITCHY
TITFER
TITIAN
TITLED
TITTER
TITTLE
TITTUP
TITULE
TOTTER
TOTTIE
ULTIMA
ULTIMO
UNTIDY
UNTOLD
UNTRUE
UPTAKE
UPTOWN
UPTURN
URTICA
VATHEK
VATMAN
VITALS
VOTARY
VOTING
VOTIVE
WATERS
WATERY
WATSON
WATTLE
WETBOB
WETHER
WITHAL
WITHER
WITHIN
WITTED
YATTER
ZITHER
ABULIA
ACUITY
ACUMEN
AGUISE
AGUISH
AGUIZE
ALUDEL
ALUMNI
AMULET
AMUSED
ANUBIS
AQUILA
AVULSE
BAUBLE
BAUCIS
BEULAH
BEURRÉ
BLUDGE
BLUISH
BOUCHE
BOUCLÉ
BOUFFE
BOUGHT
BOULLE
BOUNCE
BOUNCY
BOUNDS
BOUNTY
BOURÉE
BOURNE
BOURSE
BOUSER
BOUTON
BRUISE
BRUMAL
BRUMBY
BRUNCH
BRUNEI
BRUNEL
BRUTAL
BRUTUS
CAUCUS
CAUDEX
CAUDLE
CAUGHT
CAUSAL
CAUSED
CAUSEY
CHUBBY
CHUFFY
CHUKKA
CHUMMY
CHUNKY
CHURCH
CLUMPS
CLUMSY
CLUNCH
CLUTCH
COUGAR
COULEE
COULIS
COUNTY
COUPLE
COUPON
COURSE
COUSIN
CRUELS
CRUFTS
CRUISE
CRUIVE
CRUMBS
CRUMEN
CRUMMY
CRUNCH
CRURAL
CRUSET
CRUSOE
CRUSTA
CRUSTY
CRUTCH
DAUDET
DOUANE
DOUBLE
DOUBLY
DOUCET
DOUCHE
DOUGHY
DOURLY
DRUDGE
ECURIE
ELUANT
ELUATE
ELUTOR
EMULGE
EMUNGE
EPULIS
EQUALS
EQUANT
EQUATE
EQUINE
EQUIPE
EQUITY
EVULSE
FAUCES
FAUCET
FAULTY
FAUNUS
FEUDAL
FLUENT
FLUFFY
FLUNKY
FLURRY
FLUSHY
FLUTED
FLUTER
FLUTES
FOUGHT
FOULLY
FOURTH
FOUTRE
FRUGAL
FRUICT
FRUITS
FRUITY
FRUMPY
FRUTEX
GAUCHE
GAUCHO
GAUFRE
GAUGER
GIUSTO
GLUMPS
GLUTEN
GOUNOD
GOURDE
GOURDS
GOUTTE
GRUBBY
GRUDGE
GRUMPH
GRUMPS
GRUMPY
GRUNDY
GRUNGE
GRUTCH
HAUNCH
HOUDAH
HOUNDS
HOURLY
HOUSES
IGUANA
JAUNTY
KLUDGE
KOUROS
KRUGER
KRUMAN
KYUSHU
LAUDER
LAUNCE
LAUNCH
LAUREL
LAURIC
LAURIE
LOUCHE
LOUDEN
LOUDLY
LOUNGE
LOURIE
LOUVER
LOUVRE
MAUGRE
MAUNDY
MAUSER
MOUJIK
MOULDY
MOULIN
MOUSER
MOUSEY
MOUSSE
MOUTAN
MOUTER
MOUTON
NAUGHT
NAUSEA
NAUTCH
NEURAL
NEURON
NEUTER
NOUGAT
NOUGHT
NOUNCE
OCULAR
OEUVRE
PAUNCE
PAUNCH
PAUPER
PLUCKY
PLUMED
PLUMMY
PLUNGE
PLURAL
PLUTUS
POUDRE
POUFFE
POUNCE
POUNDS
POURER
POUTER
PRUNER
RAUNCH
REUBEN
REUTER
ROUBLE
ROUGED
ROUGHY
ROUNCE
ROUNDS
ROUTER
SAUCER
SAUGER
SAURIA
SCULPT
SCUMMY
SCUNGE
SCURRY
SCURVY
SCUTCH
SCUTUM
SCUZZY
SEUMAS
SEURAT
SHUFTI
SHUFTY
SKURRY
SLUDGE
SLUICE
SLUMMY
SLURRY
SLUSHY
SMUDGE
SMUDGY
SMUGLY
SMUTTY
SNUDGE
SNUGLY
SOUGHT
SOUPER
SOUPLE
SOURCE
SOURLY
SOUSED
SOUTER
SPUNGE
SPURGE
SPUTUM
SQUAIL
SQUALL
SQUAMA
SQUARE
SQUASH
SQUAWK
SQUEAK
SQUEAL
SQUILL
SQUINT
SQUIRE
SQUIRM
SQUIRT
SQUISH
STUART
STUBBS
STUBBY
STUCCO
STUDIO
STUFFY
STUMER
STUMPS
STUMPY
STUPID
STUPOR
STURDY
TAUGHT
TAURUS
TAUTEN
TAUTLY
TEUTON
TOUCAN
TOUCHE
TOUCHY
TOUPEE
TOUPET
TOURER
TOUSER
TOUSLE
TRUANT
TRUDGE
TRUISM
TRUMAN
TRUMPS
TRUNKS
TRUSTY
TRUTHS
UNUSED
USURER
VAUNCE
ZEUGMA
ZOUAVE
ZOUNDS
ADVENE
ADVENT
ADVERB
ADVERT
ADVICE
ADVISE
BOVATE
BOVINE
BOVRIL
CAVEAT
CAVEIN
CAVELL
CAVERN
CAVITY
CAVORT
CAVOUR
CIVICS
CIVISM
COVENT
COVERT
COVING
DEVEST
DEVICE
DEVILS
DEVISE
DEVOID
DEVOTE
DEVOUR
DEVOUT
DIVALI
DIVERS
DIVERT
DIVEST
DIVIDE
DIVINE
DIVING
FAVELA
FAVISM
FAVOSE
FAVOUR
GAVAGE
GAVIAL
GIVING
GOVERN
HAVANA
HAVENT
HAVERS
HAVING
INVADE
INVENT
INVERT
INVEST
INVITE
INVOKE
IRVING
JOVIAL
KEVLAR
LAVABO
LAVAGE
LAVISH
LEVANT
LEVITE
LEVITY

LIVELY
LIVERY
LIVING
LOVAGE
LOVELL
LOVELY
LOVING
MOVIES
MOVING
NAVAHO
NAVAJO
NEVADA
NIVOSE
NOVENA
NOVIAL
NOVICE
OBVERT
PAVANE
PAVING
PAVLOV
RAVAGE
RAVINE
RAVING
RAVISH
REVAMP
REVEAL
REVERE
REVERS
REVERT
REVERY
RÊVEUR
REVIEW
REVILE
REVISE
REVIVE
REVOKE
REVOLT
RIVAGE
RIVERA
RIVLIN
ROVING
SAVAGE
SAVANT
SAVATE
SAVING
SAVIOR
SAVOIE
SAVORY
SAVOUR
SAVVEY
SEVENS
SEVERE
SEVERN
SEVERY
SÈVRES
SOVIET
TAVERN
TEVIOT
TIVOLI
TUVALU
UNVEIL
VIVACE
VIVIAN
VIVIEN
WAVELL
WAVING
WIVERN
WYVERN
XAVIER
ALWAYS
ASWARM
BAWBEE
BEWAIL
BEWARE
BOWELS
BOWERY
BOWLED
BOWLER
BOWMAN
BOWSER
BOWWOW
BYWORD
COWAGE
COWARD
COWBOY
COWMAN
COWPAT
COWPER
COWRIE
DAWDLE
DAWNEY
DAWSON
DEWALI
DEWITT
DEWLAP
DIWALI
DOWNAY
DOWNER
DOWSER
DOWSET
DOWSON
EDWARD
ENWRAP
FAWKES
FEWEST
FOWLER
GAWAIN
GEWGAW
HAWAII
HAWKED
HAWKER
HAWSER
HOWARD
HOWDAH
HOWDIE
HOWLER
INWARD
IRWELL
JAWBOX
JEWELS
JEWESS
JEWISH
KEWPIE
KOWTOW
LAWFUL
LAWMAN
LAWYER
LEWDLY
LOWBOY
LOWELL
LOWEST
LOWKEY
MAWKIN
MOWING
NEWELL
NEWEST
NEWMAN
NEWTON
NOWISE
ONWARD
ORWELL
OSWALD
PAWNEE
PAWPAW
PEWTER
POWDER
POWERS
POWNIE
POWTER
POWWOW
REWARD
REWIND
REWIRE
REWORD
REWORK
ROWING
SAWDER
SAWNEY
SAWYER
SEWAGE
SEWELL
SEWING
SOWBUG
SOWING
SOWSED
SOWTER
TAWDRY
TAWPIE
THWACK
THWART
TOWAGE
TOWARD
TOWBAR
TOWHEE
TOWNEE
TOWNLY
TOWSER
TSWANA
UNWARY
UNWELL
UNWIND
UNWISE
UNWRAP
UPWARD
VOWELS
WOWSER
BAXTER
BOXCAR
BOXING
DEXTER
EUXINE
FIXITY
HEXANE
HEXOSE
HUXLEY
LAXIST
LAXITY
LEXEME
LUXATE
LUXURY
MAXIMS
MEXICO
ROXANE
SAXONY
SEXISM
SEXIST
SEXTAN
SEXTET
SEXTON
SEXUAL
TAXEME
TAXING
TAXMAN
TUXEDO
WAXING
ABYDOS
AMYCUS
AMYTAL
ANYHOW
ANYONE
ANYWAY
ASYLUM
BAYARD
BAYEUX
BEYOND
BOYISH
BRYANT
BRYONY
BUYERS
BUYING
BUYOUT
CAYMAN
CEYLON
CHYPRE
COYOTE
CRYING
CRYPTO
DAYBED
DOYLEY
DRYDEN
DRYING
EEYORE
ELYSEE
ETYMON
FLYING
FRYING
GEYSER
GLYCOL
GRYFON
GUYANA
HAYBOX
HAYDON
HAYLEY
HAYMOW
HEYDAY
HOYDEN
JOYFUL
JOYOUS
KEYNES
KEYPAD
KEYWAY
KHYBER
LAYARD
LAYERS
LAYING
LAYMAN
LAYOFF
LAYOUT
LEYDEN
LOYOLA
MAYBUG
MAYDAY
MAYFLY
MAYHEM
NOYADE
NOYOUS
OXYGEN
PAYDAY
PAYING
PAYNIM
PAYOFF
PAYOLA
PEYOTE
PHYLLO
PHYLUM
PHYSIC
PHYSIO
PLYING
PRYING
PSYCHE
PSYCHO
RHYMER
RHYTHM
RIYADH
ROYALS
SAYERS
SAYING
SCYLLA
SCYTHE
SKYLAB
SKYMAN
SMYRNA
SPYING
STYLET
STYLUS
STYMIE
STYRAX
THYMOL
THYMUS
TOYISH
TRYING
UNYOKE
VOYAGE
VOYEUR
WAYLAY
WAYOUT
BAZAAR
BEZANT
BEZOAR
BEZZLE
BUZFUZ
BUZZER
COZIER
DAZZLE
DIZAIN
DOZENS
DOZING
ECZEMA
ENZIAN
ENZYME
EOZOON
EVZONE
FIZGIG
FIZZED
FIZZER
FIZZLE
FUZZLE
GAZEBO
GAZUMP
GIZZEN
GUZZLE
HAZARD
HAZILY
HUZZAH
IZZARD
JAZZER
KAZAKH
LAZILY
LIZARD
LIZZIE
LUZERN
MAZOUT
MAZUMA
MIZZEN
MIZZLE
MOZART
MOZZLE
MUZHIK
MUZZLE
NOZZLE
NUZZER
NUZZLE
PUZZLE
RAZURE
RAZZIA
RAZZLE
ROZZER
SIZZLE
SOZZLE
SYZYGY
TIZWAZ
VIZARD
VIZIER
WIZARD
WIZIER
YEZIDI

6:4

ABBACY
ABDABS
ABLATE
ABLAUT
ABLAZE
ABOARD
ABRADE
ACRAWL
ADNATE
AERATE
AFEARS
AFFAIR
AFLAME
AFRAID
AGHAST
AGLAIA
AGNAIL
AGNATE
AIDANT
ALBANY
ALKALI
ALKANE
ALMAIN
ALPACA
ALTAIR
ALWAYS
AMBAGE
AMHARA
ANGARY
ANKARA
ANNALS
APIARY
APPALL
ARCADE
ARCADY
ARCANA
ARCANE
ARMADA
ARMAGH
ARNAUT
ARRACK
ARRANT
ARTAUD
ASGARD
ASKARI
ASLANT
ASMARA

ASSAIL
ASSART
ASTART
ASWARM
ATTACH
ATTACK
ATTAIN
AUBADE
AVIARY
AVIATE
AYMARA
AZRAEL
BAHADA
BALAAM
BAMAKO
BANANA
BASALT
BAYARD
BAZAAR
BECALM
BECAME
BEDASH
BEDAUB
BEFALL
BEHALF
BEHAVE
BEJADE
BELAMY
BENAME
BERATE
BESANT
BETAKE
BEWAIL
BEWARE
BEZANT
BICARB
BIGAMY
BINARY
BINATE
BLEACH
BLEARY
BOCAGE
BODACH
BOGART
BORAGE
BORATE
BOTANY
BOVATE
BREACH
BREAST
BREATH
BRIAND
BRIARD
BROACH
BROADS
BRYANT
BUMALO
BUTANE
BYPASS
CABALE
CAFARD
CALAIS
CAMAIL
CANAAN
CANADA
CANAPÉ
CANARD
CANARY
CARAFE
CERATE
CESARE
CHOANA
CICADA
CICALA
CLEAVE
CLOACA
CLOAKS
COBALT
COMART
COMATE
CORALS
COWAGE
COWARD
CREACH
CREAGH
CREAKY
CREAMY
CREANT
CREASE
CREATE
CRIANT
CROAKY
CUBAGE
CURACY
CURARE
CURARI
CURATE
CYRANO
CYTASE
DALASI
DAMAGE
DAMASK
DEBASE
DEBATE
DECADE
DECAFF
DECAMP
DECANE
DECANI
DECANT
DEDANS
DEFACE
DEFAME
DÉGAGÉ
DELATE
DEMAIN
DEMAND
DEPART
DERAIL
DERAIN
DETACH
DETAIL
DETAIN
DEWALI
DICAST
DILATE
DISARM
DIVALI
DIWALI
DIZAIN
DOMAIN
DONATE
DORADO
DOSAGE
DOTAGE
DOTARD
DOUANE
DREAMY
DREARY
DURANT
DYNAMO
DYNAST
EATAGE
ECHARD
ECLAIR
EDWARD
EFFACE
EIRANN
ELUANT
ELUATE
EMBAIL
EMBALE
EMBALM
EMBARK
ENCALM
ENCAMP
ENCASE
ENCASH
ENGAGE
ENLACE
ENRAGE
ENRAPT
ENSATE
ENTAIL
EQUALS
EQUANT
EQUATE
ERNANI
ERRAND
ERRANT
ERSATZ
ESCAPE
ESCARP
ESPADA
ESTATE
ETHANE
EUTAXY
EXHALE
EXPAND
EXTANT
FACADE
FARAND
FEMALE
FIGARO
FINALE
FORAGE
FRIAND
FRIARY
FUGATO
FUMADO
FUSAIN
GALANT
GALAXY
GARAGE
GAVAGE
GAWAIN
GELADA
GELATO
GITANO
GOCART
GOKART
GREASE
GREASY
GREATS
GREAVE
GROATS
GUIANA
GUYANA
GYRATE
HAMATE
HARARE
HARASS
HAVANA
HAWAII
HAZARD
HECATE
HERALD
HEXANE
HIDAGE
HIJACK
HILARY
HOBART
HOMAGE
HORACE
HOTAIR
HOWARD
HUMANE
HYPATE
IGUANA
IMBARN
IMBASE
IMPACT
IMPAIR
IMPALA
IMPALE
IMPART
IMPAWN
INCASE
INDABA
INFAME
INFAMY
INFANT
INFARE
INGATE
INHALE
INLAID
INLAND
INLAWS
INMATE
INNATE
INSANE
INTACT
INTAKE
INVADE
INWARD
ISLAND
ISRAEL
ITHACA
IZZARD
JACANA
JUBATE
JURANT
KABAKA
KAKAPO
KANAKA
KARATE
KATANA
KAZAKH
KERALA
KIGALI
KINASE
KUMARA
LADAKH
LANATE
LAVABO
LAVAGE
LAYARD
LEGACY
LEGATE
LEGATO
LEVANT
LIGASE
LIGATE
LIPARI
LIPASE
LITANY
LIZARD
LOCALE
LOCATE
LOVAGE
LUGANO
LUNACY
LUNARY
LUNATE
LUSAKA
LUXATE
MADAME
MALAGA
MALATE
MALAWI
MANAGE
MANANA
MANATI
MARACA
MARAUD
MASADA
MENACE
MENAGE
MESAIL
METAGE
METATE
MIKADO
MILADY
MIRAGE
MOHAIR
MOHAWK
MOJAVE
MONACO
MORALE
MORALS
MORASS
MOSAIC
MOZART
MUCATE
MURAGE
MURALS
MUSANG
MUTANT
MUTATE
MYGALE
NAGANA
NAGARI
NAPALM
NATANT
NAVAHO
NAVAJO
NEFAST
NEGATE
NEPALI
NEVADA
NOMADE
NONAGE
NONARY
NOTARY
NOTATE
NOYADE
NUTANT
NUTATE
OBLAST
OBLATE
OBTAIN
OCEANS
OCTANE
OCTANS
OCTANT
OCTAVE
OCTAVO
OLEATE
ONWARD
OPIATE
ORDAIN
ORGANS
ORGASM
ORIANO
ORNATE
OSWALD
OTTAVA
OTTAWA
OURALI
OUTAGE
OXGATE
OXTAIL
PADANG
PAHARI
PALACE
PALAIS
PALATE
PANADA
PANAMA
PAPACY
PAPAYA
PARADE
PARAMO
PARANA
PARAPH
PATACA
PAVANE
PEDALO
PEDANT
PENANG
PESADE
PÉTAIN
PETARD
PETARY
PHRASE
PICARD
PILAFF
PILAGE
PILATE
PIRACY
PIRATE
PISANO
PLEACH
PLEASE
PLIANT
POLACK
POLAND
POMACE
POMADE
POSADA
POTASH
POTATO
PREACE
PREACH
PUPATE
QUEASY
RABATO
RAFALE
RAVAGE
REBATE
RECALL
RECANT
RECAST
REDACT
REFACE
REGAIN
REGALE

REGARD
REHASH
RELATE
REMAIN
REMAKE
REMAND
REMARK
RENAME
REPAID
REPAIR
REPAST
RESALE
RETAIL
RETAIN
RETAKE
RETARD
REVAMP
REWARD
RIBALD
RIBAND
RIVAGE
RIYADH
ROLAND
ROMANO
ROMANS
ROMANY
ROSACE
ROSARY
ROTARY
ROTATE
ROXANE
ROYALS
SAFARI
SAHARA
SALAAM
SALADE
SALAMI
SALARY
SAMARA
SAVAGE
SAVANT
SAVATE
SCRAMB
SCRAPE
SCRAPS
SCRAWL
SCRAWM
SDEATH
SEBATE
SECANT
SEDATE
SENATE
SERAIL
SERANG
SERAPE
SERAPH
SESAME
SEWAGE
SHEARS
SHEATH
SHEAVE

SHRANK
SILAGE
SLEAVE
SLEAZE
SLEAZY
SLOANE
SMEARY
SMEATH
SNEAKY
SNEATH
SOCAGE
SOLACE
SOLANO
SOMALI
SONANT
SONATA
SORAGE
SPLAKE
SPLASH
SPRAIN
SPRANG
SPRAWL
SQUAIL
SQUALL
SQUAMA
SQUARE
SQUASH
SQUAWK
STEADY
STEAMY
STRABO
STRAFE
STRAIN
STRAIT
STRAKE
STRAND
STRASS
STRATA
STRAWS
STRAWY
STUART
SUDARY
SUDATE
SUGARY
SUMACH
SWEATY
TABARD
TAMALE
TAMANU
TAMARA
TAMARI
TATAMI
TENACE
TENANT
TETANY
THEAVE
THRALL
THRASH
THRAWN
THWACK
THWART

TIRADE
TIRANA
TISANE
TOBAGO
TOMATO
TONANT
TOWAGE
TOWARD
TREATY
TRIAGE
TRUANT
TSWANA
TUVALU
TYBALT
TYRANT
ULLAGE
UMLAUT
UNCAGE
UNDATE
UNEASE
UNEASY
UNFAIR
UNGAIN
UNHAND
UNIATE
UNLACE
UNMADE
UNMASK
UNPACK
UNPAID
UNSAFE
UNSAID
UNWARY
UPDATE
UPLAND
UPRATE
UPTAKE
UPWARD
URBANE
USHANT
VACANT
VACATE
VAGARY
VIRAGO
VISAGE
VITALS
VIVACE
VIZARD
VOLAGE
VOLANS
VOLANT
VOTARY
VOYAGE
WABASH
WIZARD
WREATH
XANADU
YUKATA
ZAPATA
ZENANA
ZOUAVE

AIRBED
AIRBUS
ANABAS
ANUBIS
ARABIA
ARABIC
ARABIS
ARABLE
ATABAL
ATABEG
AUMBRY
BABBIT
BABBLE
BALBOA
BAMBOO
BAOBAB
BARBED
BARBEL
BARBER
BARBET
BAUBLE
BAWBEE
BENBOW
BERBER
BOBBIN
BOBBLE
BOMBAY
BOMBER
BOMBYX
BONBON
BOOBOO
BUBBLE
BUBBLY
BULBIL
BULBUL
BUMBLE
BURBLE
BURBOT
BUSBOY
BYEBYE
CABBIE
CAMBER
CARBON
CARBOY
CASBAH
CHIBOL
CHUBBY
COBBER
COBBLE
COMBAT
COMBED
COMBER
COMBLE
CORBEL
CORBIE
COWBOY
CRABBE
CRABBY
CRIBLE
CUMBER
CYMBAL

DABBLE
DAYBED
DIBBER
DIBBLE
DISBAR
DISBUD
DJEBEL
DOBBIN
DOUBLE
DOUBLY
DUBBIN
DUMBLY
DUNBAR
DURBAR
DYBBUK
EDIBLE
ENABLE
EREBUS
FAIBLE
FEEBLE
FEEBLY
FIBBED
FIBBER
FIMBRA
FLABBY
FOIBLE
FORBID
FUMBLE
GABBLE
GABBRO
GAMBET
GAMBIA
GAMBIT
GAMBLE
GAMBOL
GARBED
GARBLE
GASBAG
GERBIL
GHEBER
GIBBER
GIBBET
GIBBON
GLIBLY
GLOBAL
GOBBET
GOBBLE
GOOBER
GRABEN
GRUBBY
GUBBAH
HAMBLE
HARBOR
HAYBOX
HENBIT
HERBAL
HOBBES
HOBBLE
HOMBRE
HOTBED
HUBBLE

HUBBUB
HUMBER
HUMBLE
HUMBUG
IAMBIC
IAMBUS
ICEBOX
ISABEL
ISOBAR
JABBER
JABBLE
JAMBOK
JAMBON
JAWBOX
JERBOA
JIBBAH
JOBBER
JUBBAH
JUMBAL
JUMBLE
KASBAH
KHYBER
KIBBLE
KIRBEH
KITBAG
KNOBBY
LAMBDA
LESBOS
LIABLE
LIBBER
LIEBIG
LIMBED
LIMBER
LIMBIC
LISBON
LOWBOY
LUBBER
LUMBAR
LUMBER
MARBLE
MAYBUG
MEMBER
MORBID
MORBUS
MUMBLE
NEBBUK
NIBBLE
NIMBLE
NIMBLY
NIMBUS
NOBBLE
NOBBUT
NUBBIN
NUBBLE
NUMBER
NUMBLY
OUTBAR
OUTBID
OVIBOS
PEBBLE
PEBBLY

PHOBIA
PHOBIC
POBBLE
PROBIT
PUEBLO
QUEBEC
RABBET
RABBIT
RABBLE
RAGBAG
RAMBLE
RATBAG
REEBOK
REUBEN
RIBBED
RIBBLE
RIBBON
ROBBED
ROBBER
ROUBLE
RUBBED
RUBBER
RUBBLE
RUBBRA
RUMBLE
SAMBAL
SAMBAR
SAMBUR
SCABBY
SEABEE
SERBIA
SHABBY
SINBAD
SOMBER
SOMBRE
SORBET
SOWBUG
STABLE
STABLY
STUBBS
STUBBY
SWABIA
SYMBOL
TALBOT
TEABAG
THEBAN
THEBES
TIDBIT
TIMBER
TIMBRE
TITBIT
TOMBOY
TOWBAR
TREBLE
TREBLY
TRIBAL
TRIBES
TULBAN
TUMBLE
TURBAN
TURBID

TURBOT
TWOBIT
TYMBAL
UNABLE
USABLE
VERBAL
VIABLE
WAMBLE
WARBLE
WEBBED
WETBOB
WIMBLE
WOBBLE
WOBBLY
WOMBAT
YABBER
ZAMBIA
ZOMBIE
ABACUS
ACACIA
ALACUS
ALECTO
AMYCUS
APACHE
APICAL
ASHCAN
ATOCIA
AVOCET
BACCHI
BAUCIS
BEACHY
BEACON
BISCAY
BITCHY
BLACKS
BLOCKS
BOBCAT
BOUCHE
BOUCLÉ
BOXCAR
BRACER
BRACES
BRECHT
BRICKS
BUCCAL
BUNCHY
CACCIA
CAECUM
CALCED
CANCEL
CANCER
CATCHY
CAUCUS
CERCAL
CERCUS
CHICHI
CHICLE
CHICON
CIRCLE
CIRCUS
CLICHÉ
CLOCHE
COCCID
COCCUS
COCCYX
CONCHA
CONCHY
CONCUR
CRÈCHE
CROCHE
CROCKS
CROCUS
CUSCUS
CUTCHA
DANCER
DEACON
DECCAN
DESCRY
DISCUS
DORCAS
DOUCET
DOUCHE
DRACHM
DULCET
DUNCAN
DUNCES
EGGCUP
ELICIT
ELTCHI
EPICAL
EXOCET
FAECAL
FAECES
FALCON
FARCIN
FASCES
FASCIA
FAUCES
FAUCET
FENCER
FESCUE
FIACRE
FISCAL
FLACON
FLECHE
FLICKS
FORCED
FORCES
FRACAS
GASCON
GAUCHE
GAUCHO
GLACIS
GLYCOL
GRACES
GROCER
HICCUP
HONCHO
ICICLE
IPECAC
JUNCUS
KITCAT
KWACHA
LAICAL
LANCER
LANCET
LANCIA
LASCAR
LITCHI
LORCHA
LOUCHE
MADCAP
MANCHE
MANCHU
MARCEL
MASCOT
MERCAT
MERCER
MERCIA
MESCAL
MINCER
MOBCAP
MOOCOW
MOSCOW
MUSCAT
MUSCLE
NIACIN
NONCOM
NUNCIO
OBECHE
OFFCUT
OILCAN
ORACHE
ORACLE
OUNCES
OUTCRY
OWLCAR
PARCEL
PASCAL
PATCHY
PENCEL
PENCIL
PIECES
PINCER
PISCES
PLACED
PLACER
PLACID
PLUCKY
PONCHO
PRECIS
PRICED
PRICEY
PSYCHE
PSYCHO
PUNCHY
PUNCTO
QUICHE
RANCEL
RANCHO
RANCID
RANCOR
RASCAL
REDCAP
REDCAR
RESCUE
ROSCID
ROSCOE
SANCHO
SAUCER
SEICHE
SHTCHI
SITCOM
SLACKS
SLICER
SMACKS
SOCCER
SPACED
SPACER
SPECIE
SPICED
SPICER
STACKS
STICKS
STICKY
STOCKS
STOCKY
STUCCO
SUCCOR
SUCCUS
SULCUS
SYNCOM
TALCUM
TARCEL
TEACUP
TERCET
TERCIO
TETCHY
THECAL
THICKY
TIPCAT
TITCHY
TOECAP
TOMCAT
TOUCAN
TOUCHE
TOUCHY
TRACER
TRICAR
TRICKS
TRICKY
TRICOT
TROCAR
TROCHE
TUSCAN
TWICER
VELCRO
VISCID
VOICED
VULCAN
WARCRY
WHACKO
WHACKY
YOICKS
ZIRCON
FORÇAT
GARÇON
ABADAN
ABYDOS
ACADIA
ACEDIA
ACIDIC
AGADIR
ALUDEL
AMADOU
AMIDOL
AMIDST
ANADEM
ANADYR
ASHDOD
AVIDLY
BALDER
BALDLY
BANDAR
BANDIT
BANDOG
BEADED
BEADLE
BEDDER
BENDED
BENDER
BIDDER
BINDER
BIRDIE
BLUDGE
BOLDLY
BONDED
BONDER
BOODLE
BORDAR
BORDER
BRIDAL
BRIDGE
BRIDIE
BRIDLE
BUDDHA
BUNDLE
BURDEN
CADDIE
CADDIS
CAMDEN
CANDID
CANDLE
CANDOR
CARDAN
CAUDEX
CAUDLE
CHADOR
CHEDER
CINDER
COBDEN
CODDLE
COLDLY
CONDOM
CONDOR
CORDON
CRADLE
CREDIT
CUDDLE
CUDDLY
CULDEE
CURDLE
DADDLE
DAEDAL
DANDER
DANDLE
DAUDET
DAWDLE
DEADEN
DEADLY
DEIDRE
DEODAR
DIADEM
DIDDLE
DIKDIK
DIODON
DODDER
DODDLE
DOODAD
DOODAH
DOODLE
DREDGE
DRUDGE
DRYDEN
DUDDER
DUMDUM
DUNDEE
DUNDER
DYADIC
ELODEA
ENODAL
ERODED
EXEDRA
EXODUS
FARDEL
FARDLE
FEEDER
FENDER
FEUDAL
FIDDLE
FIDDLY
FINDER
FLEDGE
FODDER
FOLDED
FOLDER
FONDLE
FONDLY
FONDUE
FRIDAY
FRIDGE
FUDDLE
FUNDED
FUNDUS
GANDER
GANDHI
GARDEN
GENDER
GIDDUP
GILDAS
GILDED
GILDER
GIRDER
GIRDLE
GLADLY
GLIDER
GOLDEN
GOODLY
GORDON
GRADED
GRADES
GRADUS
GRUDGE
GUIDES
GUIDON
GUNDOG
HAGDEN
HANDEL
HANDLE
HARDEN
HARDLY
HAYDON
HEADED
HEADER
HEEDED
HERDEN
HERDER
HEYDAY
HIDDEN
HINDER
HOBDAY
HODDER
HOIDEN
HOLDER
HOLDUP
HOODED
HOUDAH
HOWDAH
HOWDIE
HOYDEN
HUDDLE
HURDLE
HYADES
IBADAN
IBIDEM
JORDAN
JUDDER
KEDDAH
KENDAL
KIDDIE
KIDDLE
KINDER
KINDLE
KINDLY
KLUDGE
KOODOO
LADDER

LADDIE
LANDAU
LANDED
LANDER
LANDOR
LAPDOG
LARDER
LARDON
LAUDER
LEADEN
LEADER
LENDER
LEWDLY
LEYDEN
LIEDER
LINDEN
LOADED
LOADER
LONDON
LORDLY
LOUDEN
LOUDLY
MADDEN
MADDER
MAIDAN
MAIDEN
MALDON
MAYDAY
MEADOW
MEDDLE
MENDEL
MENDER
MENDES
MENDIP
MIDDAY
MIDDEN
MIDDLE
MILDEW
MILDLY
MINDED
MINDEL
MINDER
MOIDER
MONDAY
MUDDER
MUDDLE
MURDER
NANDOO
NEEDED
NEEDLE
NEEDNT
NODDED
NODDLE
NOODLE
NORDIC
OGADEN
ONEDIN
OUNDLE
PADDED
PADDLE
PAIDUP

PANDER
PANDIT
PARDIE
PARDON
PAYDAY
PEDDER
PEDDLE
PERDUE
PIDDLE
PIEDOG
PINDAR
PLEDGE
POLDER
PONDER
POODLE
POUDRE
POWDER
PUDDLE
PUNDIT
PURDAH
PYEDOG
QUIDAM
RADDLE
RAIDER
RANDOM
READER
REDDEN
RENDER
RHODES
RIDDLE
ROADIE
RONDEL
RUDDER
RUDDLE
RUNDLE
SADDEN
SADDHU
SADDLE
SANDAL
SANDER
SAWDER
SEEDED
SEEDER
SELDOM
SENDAL
SENDER
SERDAB
SHADED
SHADES
SHADOW
SHADUF
SHODDY
SIDDHA
SINDER
SIRDAR
SKIDOO
SLEDGE
SLIDER
SLUDGE
SMUDGE
SMUDGY

SNUDGE
SODDEN
SOLDER
SORDES
SORDID
SPADES
SPADIX
SPIDER
STODGE
STODGY
STUDIO
SUBDUE
SUDDEN
SUNDAE
SUNDAY
SUNDER
SUNDEW
SUNDRY
SWEDEN
SYNDIC
TANDEM
TARDIS
TAWDRY
TENDER
TENDON
TENDRE
TIDDLE
TIDDLY
TINDER
TODDLE
TRADER
TRADES
TRUDGE
TUNDRA
VANDAL
VEDDAH
VENDEE
VENDER
VENDOR
VENDUE
VERDIN
VERDUN
VOIDED
VOIDEE
VOIDER
VOODOO
WADDLE
WANDER
WANDLE
WARDEN
WARDER
WEDDED
WELDER
WILDER
WILDLY
WINDER
WINDOW
WINDUP
WISDEN
WISDOM
WONDER

WOODED
WOODEN
WOODIE
YARDIE
YONDER
ZANDER
ZENDIK
ABBESS
ABJECT
ABREGE
ABSEIL
ABSENT
ACCEDE
ACCEND
ACCENT
ACCEPT
ACCESS
ACHENE
ACKERS
ADDEEM
ADDEND
ADHERE
ADVENE
ADVENT
ADVERB
ADVERT
AEGEAN
AEGEUS
AENEID
AFFECT
AFIELD
AFREET
AFRESH
AFTERS
AGREED
ALBEDO
ALBEIT
ALBERT
ALKENE
ALLEGE
ALLELE
ALLEYN
ALMERY
AMOEBA
AMPERE
ANDEAN
ANGELA
ANGELS
ANGERS
ANNEAL
ANNEXE
ANSELM
APIECE
APPEAL
APPEAR
APPEND
ARDENT
ARGENT
ARPENT
ARREAR
ARREST

ARTERY
ASCEND
ASCENT
ASLEEP
ASPECT
ASSENT
ASSERT
ASSESS
ASSETS
ASTERN
ATHENE
ATHENS
ATTEND
ATTEST
AUGEAN
AUREUS
BAKERS
BAKERY
BALEEN
BARELY
BATEAU
BAYEUX
BEDECK
BEHEAD
BEHELD
BEHEST
BEMEAN
BEREFT
BESEEM
BICEPS
BIDENT
BIREME
BISECT
BODEGA
BOLERO
BOLEYN
BOREAS
BOWELS
BOWERY
BREECH
BREEZE
BREEZY
BRIEFS
BUREAU
BUTENE
BUYERS
CADETS
CAMERA
CAREEN
CAREER
CAREME
CARESS
CASEIN
CAVEAT
CAVEIN
CAVELL
CAVERN
CELERY
CEMENT
CEREAL
CEREUS

CETERA
CHEEKY
CHEERS
CHEERY
CHEESE
CHEESY
CICELY
CICERO
CINEMA
CLIENT
COGENT
COHERE
COMEDO
COMEDY
COMELY
COPECK
COVENT
COVERT
CREEPS
CREEPY
CREESE
CREESH
CRUELS
CUNEAL
CYBELE
CYRENE
DECEIT
DECENT
DEFEAT
DEFECT
DEFEND
DEJECT
DELETE
DEMEAN
DEMENT
DEPEND
DESERT
DETECT
DETENT
DETENU
DETEST
DEVEST
DIGEST
DINERO
DIRECT
DISEUR
DIVERS
DIVERT
DIVEST
DOCENT
DOLEUR
DOZENS
DRIEST
DUDEEN
DUNELM
DURESS
EATERY
ECZEMA
EFFECT
EFFETE
EFTEST

EGBERT
EGRESS
ELDERS
ELDEST
ELLERY
EMBERS
ENDEAR
ENGELS
ENMESH
ENSEAL
EOCENE
EPHEBE
ESSENE
ESTEEM
ETHENE
EUGENE
EUREKA
EXCEED
EXCEPT
EXCESS
EXPECT
EXPEDE
EXPEND
EXPERT
EXSERT
EXTEND
EXTENT
EXTERN
FAVELA
FEWEST
FINELY
FINERY
FINEST
FLEECE
FLEECY
FLUENT
FOMENT
FOREDO
FOREGO
FOREST
FREELY
FREEZE
FRIEND
FRIEZE
FUREUR
FUSELI
GAIETY
GALENA
GALERE
GAMELY
GAMETE
GARETH
GATEAU
GAZEBO
GENERA
GENEVA
GERENT
GIDEON
GILEAD
GOVERN
GREECE

GREEDY
GREEKS
GREENE
GREENS
GRIEVE
HAVENT
HAVERS
HEDERA
HELENA
HEREBY
HEREIN
HERERO
HERESY
HERETO
HETERO
HITECH
HOMELY
HONEST
HUGELY
HUMECT
HYAENA
IMPEDE
IMPEND
INCEDE
INCEPT
INCEST
INDEED
INDENT
INFECT
INFEST
INGEST
INHERE
INJECT
INMESH
INSECT
INSERT
INTEND
INTENT
INTERN
INVENT
INVERT
INVEST
IRWELL
ISLETS
ITSELF
JACENT
JEREMY
JEWELS
JEWESS
JOSEPH
KABELE
KEBELE
KOREAN
KUMERA
LAMELY
LAMENT
LATEEN
LATELY
LATENT
LATEST
LAYERS
LEGEND
LEXEME
LIGETI
LIKELY
LINEAL
LINEAR
LINEUP
LIVELY
LIVERY
LONELY
LORETO
LOVELL
LOVELY
LOWELL
LOWEST
LUCENT
LUTEAL
LUTEIN
LUZERN
LYCEUM
MADEUP
MAKEUP
MANEGE
MERELY
METEOR
MISERY
MODELS
MODENA
MODERN
MODEST
MOIETY
MOLECH
MOLEST
MOMENT
MOREEN
MUSEUM
MUTELY
MYSELF
NAMELY
NAPERY
NASEBY
NEBECK
NEPETA
NEREID
NEREUS
NEWELL
NEWEST
NICELY
NICENE
NICETY
NINETY
NITERY
NOCENT
NOVENA
OBJECT
OBSESS
OBTECT
OBTEND
OBVERT
OCKERS
OEDEMA
OFFEND
OGRESS
OILERS
ORDEAL
ORDERS
ORGEAT
ORIENT
ORNERY
ORRERY
ORTEGA
ORWELL
OSBERT
OSIERY
OSTEND
OTHERS
OXHEAD
PAMELA
PAPERS
PAPERY
PARENT
PARETO
PATENT
PESETA
PETERS
PHLEGM
PHLEUM
PHOEBE
PIGEON
PILEUM
PILEUP
PILEUS
PIMENT
PINEAL
PINERO
PIRENE
PLIERS
POMELO
PONENT
POPEYE
POSEUR
POTEEN
POTENT
POWERS
PRIEST
PURELY
PUTEAL
PYRENE
QUEENS
RACEME
RAMEAU
RAREFY
RARELY
REBECK
RECEDE
RECENT
RECESS
REDEEM
REDEYE
REFECT
REGENT
REGEST
REHEAT
REHEEL
REJECT
RELENT
REMEDY
RENEGE
REPEAL
REPEAT
REPENT
REREAD
RESEAU
RESECT
RESEDA
RESENT
REVEAL
REVERE
REVERS
REVERT
REVERY
RÊVEUR
RIDENT
RIVERA
ROBERT
RODENT
ROKEBY
ROPERY
ROSERY
RUBENS
RUDELY
RUPEES
RUPERT
SABELE
SAFELY
SAFETY
SAGELY
SANELY
SAPELE
SATEEN
SAYERS
SCHEMA
SCHEME
SCLERA
SCLERE
SCREAM
SCREED
SCREEN
SCREWY
SECEDE
SELECT
SELENE
SEMELE
SENECA
SERENE
SEVENS
SEVERE
SEVERN
SEVERY
SEWELL
SHEENY
SHEERS
SHEETS
SHIELD
SHREWD
SHTETL
SILENE
SILENT
SIMEON
SINEWY
SLEEKY
SLEEPY
SLEEVE
SLEEZY
SNEEZE
SNEEZY
SOBEIT
SOLEIL
SOLELY
SOLEMN
SOLENT
SOLERA
SOLEUS
SORELL
SORELY
SPEECH
SPEEDO
SPEEDY
SPHENE
SPHERE
SPLEEN
SPLENT
SPREAD
SQUEAK
SQUEAL
STEELE
STEELY
STEERS
STREAK
STREAM
STREET
STREGA
STRENE
STRESS
SUPERB
SURELY
SURETÉ
SURETY
SWEENY
SWEETS
TALENT
TAMELY
TATERS
TAVERN
TAXEME
TELEGA
TELEGU
TEREDO
TERESA
TERETE
THIERS
THIEVE
THREAD
THREAP
THREAT
THRENE
THRESH
TIMELY
TOLEDO
TORERO
TUBERS
TUMEFY
TUPELO
TUREEN
TUXEDO
TWEEDS
TWEEDY
TWEENY
TWEEZE
UBIETY
UCKERS
ULCERS
UNBEND
UNBENT
UNDECK
UNLESS
UNMEET
UNREAD
UNREAL
UNREEL
UNREST
UNSEAM
UNSEAT
UNSEEN
UNSENT
UNSEXY
UNVEIL
UNWELL
UPBEAT
UPHELD
UPKEEP
URGENT
VALENS
VALETA
VARECH
VARESE
VELETA
VENEER
VENERY
VEREIN
VILELY
VINERY
VOLENS
VOWELS
VOYEUR
WADERS
WATERS
WATERY
WAVELL
WERENT
WHEELS
WHEELY
WHEEZE
WHEEZY
WIDELY
WIFELY
WIGEON
WIPERS
WISELY
WIVERN
WOMENS
WYVERN
YEMENI
ZEBECK
AGRÉGÉ
ARSÈNE
BARÈGE
GLIÈRE
MISÈRE
ARAFAT
ARMFUL
ARTFUL
BAFFIN
BAFFLE
BAGFUL
BELFRY
BIFFIN
BOFFIN
BOUFFE
BUFFER
BUFFET
BUFFON
BUZFUZ
CARFAX
CEEFAX
CHAFER
CHUFFY
CLIFFS
COFFEE
COFFER
COFFIN
COMFIT
CONFAB
CONFER
CRAFTY
CRUFTS
CUFFEE
CUFFIN
CUPFUL
CURFEW
DEAFEN
DIFFER
DOOFER
DRAFTY
DUFFEL
DUFFER
DUFFLE
EARFUL
EIFFEL
EYEFUL
FILFOT
FITFUL
FLUFFY
FULFIL
FURFUR
FYLFOT

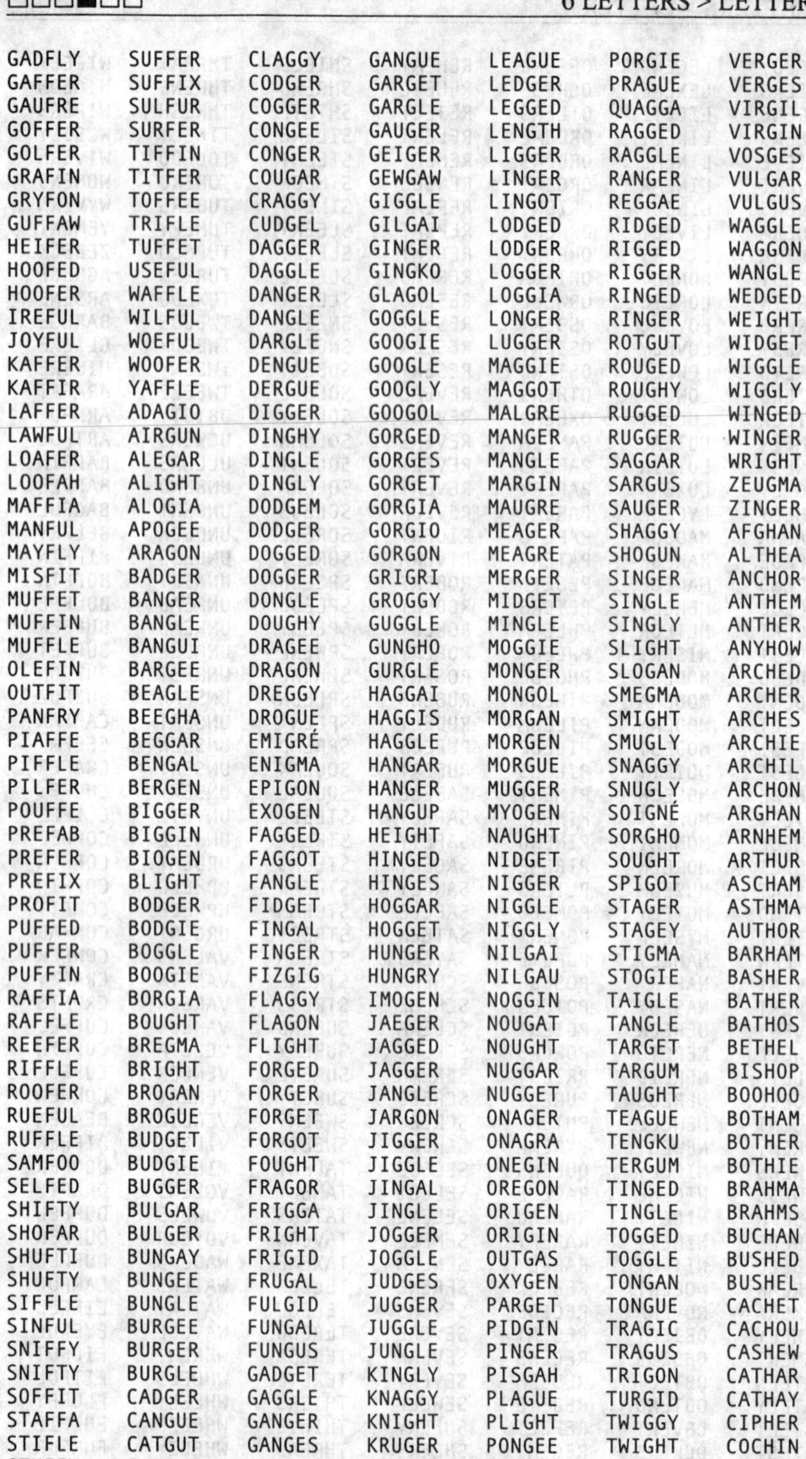

GADFLY
GAFFER
GAUFRE
GOFFER
GOLFER
GRAFIN
GRYFON
GUFFAW
HEIFER
HOOFED
HOOFER
IREFUL
JOYFUL
KAFFER
KAFFIR
LAFFER
LAWFUL
LOAFER
LOOFAH
MAFFIA
MANFUL
MAYFLY
MISFIT
MUFFET
MUFFIN
MUFFLE
OLEFIN
OUTFIT
PANFRY
PIAFFE
PIFFLE
PILFER
POUFFE
PREFAB
PREFER
PREFIX
PROFIT
PUFFED
PUFFER
PUFFIN
RAFFIA
RAFFLE
REEFER
RIFFLE
ROOFER
RUEFUL
RUFFLE
SAMFOO
SELFED
SHIFTY
SHOFAR
SHUFTI
SHUFTY
SIFFLE
SINFUL
SNIFFY
SNIFTY
SOFFIT
STAFFA
STIFLE
STUFFY
SUFFER
SUFFIX
SULFUR
SURFER
TIFFIN
TITFER
TOFFEE
TRIFLE
TUFFET
USEFUL
WAFFLE
WILFUL
WOEFUL
WOOFER
YAFFLE
ADAGIO
AIRGUN
ALEGAR
ALIGHT
ALOGIA
APOGEE
ARAGON
BADGER
BANGER
BANGLE
BANGUI
BARGEE
BEAGLE
BEEGHA
BEGGAR
BENGAL
BERGEN
BIGGER
BIGGIN
BIOGEN
BLIGHT
BODGER
BODGIE
BOGGLE
BOOGIE
BORGIA
BOUGHT
BREGMA
BRIGHT
BROGAN
BROGUE
BUDGET
BUDGIE
BUGGER
BULGAR
BULGER
BUNGAY
BUNGEE
BUNGLE
BURGEE
BURGER
BURGLE
CADGER
CANGUE
CATGUT
CAUGHT
CLAGGY
CODGER
COGGER
CONGEE
CONGER
COUGAR
CRAGGY
CUDGEL
DAGGER
DAGGLE
DANGER
DANGLE
DARGLE
DENGUE
DERGUE
DIGGER
DINGHY
DINGLE
DINGLY
DODGEM
DODGER
DOGGED
DOGGER
DONGLE
DOUGHY
DRAGEE
DRAGON
DREGGY
DROGUE
EMIGRÉ
ENIGMA
EPIGON
EXOGEN
FAGGED
FAGGOT
FANGLE
FIDGET
FINGAL
FINGER
FIZGIG
FLAGGY
FLAGON
FLIGHT
FORGED
FORGER
FORGET
FORGOT
FOUGHT
FRAGOR
FRIGGA
FRIGHT
FRIGID
FRUGAL
FULGID
FUNGAL
FUNGUS
GADGET
GAGGLE
GANGER
GANGES
GANGLY
GANGUE
GARGET
GARGLE
GAUGER
GEIGER
GEWGAW
GIGGLE
GILGAI
GINGER
GINGKO
GLAGOL
GOGGLE
GOOGIE
GOOGLE
GOOGLY
GOOGOL
GORGED
GORGES
GORGET
GORGIA
GORGIO
GORGON
GRIGRI
GROGGY
GUGGLE
GUNGHO
GURGLE
HAGGAI
HAGGIS
HAGGLE
HANGAR
HANGER
HANGUP
HEIGHT
HINGED
HINGES
HOGGAR
HOGGET
HUNGER
HUNGRY
IMOGEN
JAEGER
JAGGED
JAGGER
JANGLE
JARGON
JIGGER
JIGGLE
JINGAL
JINGLE
JOGGER
JOGGLE
JUDGES
JUGGER
JUGGLE
JUNGLE
KINGLY
KNAGGY
KNIGHT
KRUGER
LAAGER
LEAGUE
LEDGER
LEGGED
LENGTH
LIGGER
LINGER
LINGOT
LODGED
LODGER
LOGGER
LOGGIA
LONGER
LUGGER
MAGGIE
MAGGOT
MALGRE
MANGER
MANGLE
MARGIN
MAUGRE
MEAGER
MEAGRE
MERGER
MIDGET
MINGLE
MOGGIE
MONGER
MONGOL
MORGAN
MORGEN
MORGUE
MUGGER
MYOGEN
NAUGHT
NIDGET
NIGGER
NIGGLE
NIGGLY
NILGAI
NILGAU
NOGGIN
NOUGAT
NOUGHT
NUGGAR
NUGGET
ONAGER
ONAGRA
ONEGIN
OREGON
ORIGEN
ORIGIN
OUTGAS
OXYGEN
PARGET
PIDGIN
PINGER
PISGAH
PLAGUE
PLIGHT
PONGEE
PONGID
PORGIE
PRAGUE
QUAGGA
RAGGED
RAGGLE
RANGER
REGGAE
RIDGED
RIGGED
RIGGER
RINGED
RINGER
ROTGUT
ROUGED
ROUGHY
RUGGED
RUGGER
SAGGAR
SARGUS
SAUGER
SHAGGY
SHOGUN
SINGER
SINGLE
SINGLY
SLIGHT
SLOGAN
SMEGMA
SMIGHT
SMUGLY
SNAGGY
SNUGLY
SOIGNÉ
SORGHO
SOUGHT
SPIGOT
STAGER
STAGEY
STIGMA
STOGIE
TAIGLE
TANGLE
TARGET
TARGUM
TAUGHT
TEAGUE
TENGKU
TERGUM
TINGED
TINGLE
TOGGED
TOGGLE
TONGAN
TONGUE
TRAGIC
TRAGUS
TRIGON
TURGID
TWIGGY
TWIGHT
VALGUS
VERGER
VERGES
VIRGIL
VIRGIN
VOSGES
VULGAR
VULGUS
WAGGLE
WAGGON
WANGLE
WEDGED
WEIGHT
WIDGET
WIGGLE
WIGGLY
WINGED
WINGER
WRIGHT
ZEUGMA
ZINGER
AFGHAN
ALTHEA
ANCHOR
ANTHEM
ANTHER
ANYHOW
ARCHED
ARCHER
ARCHES
ARCHIE
ARCHIL
ARCHON
ARGHAN
ARNHEM
ARTHUR
ASCHAM
ASTHMA
AUTHOR
BARHAM
BASHER
BATHER
BATHOS
BETHEL
BISHOP
BOOHOO
BOTHAM
BOTHER
BOTHIE
BRAHMA
BRAHMS
BUCHAN
BUSHED
BUSHEL
CACHET
CACHOU
CASHEW
CATHAR
CATHAY
CIPHER
COCHIN
COSHER

CUSHAT
CYPHER
DAPHNE
DASHED
DERHAM
DIRHAM
DISHED
DISHES
DITHER
DURHAM
EIGHTH
EIGHTY
EITHER
ELOHIM
EOTHEN
ESCHAR
ESCHEW
ESTHER
ETCHER
EUCHRE
FATHER
FATHOM
FISHER
FULHAM
GATHER
GOPHER
GOTHAM
GOTHIC
GRAHAM
GUSHER
HACHIS
HASHED
HEEHAW
HIGHER
HIGHLY
HIGHUP
HITHER
HOOHAH
HUGHES
HUGHIE
HUSHED
HYPHAL
HYPHEN
INCHES
INCHON
ISCHIA
ITCHEN
JETHRO
JOSHUA
KEPHIR
KOSHER
LACHES
LASHED
LASHER
LATHER
LECHER
LETHAL
LICHEN
LIGHTS
LITHIA
LOCHIA
LUTHER
LYCHEE
MASHAM
MASHED
MASHER
MASHIE
MATHIS
MAYHEM
MENHIR
METHOD
METHYL
MIGHTY
MISHAP
MISHIT
MOTHER
MUZHIK
MYTHOS
NEPHEW
NETHER
NIGHTS
NIGHTY
ORCHID
ORCHIS
ORPHAN
ORPHIC
PAKHTI
PAKHTO
PAKHTU
PAPHOS
PASHTO
PASHTU
PATHAN
PATHIC
PATHOS
PEAHEN
PELHAM
PERHAP
PESHWA
POTHER
PUSHER
PUSHTU
PUSHUP
PYTHIA
PYTHON
QUAHOG
RACHEL
RACHIS
RAPHIA
RASHER
RASHLY
RATHER
RICHES
RICHLY
RIGHTO
RIGHTS
RODHAM
ROTHER
ROTHKO
RUCHED
RUSHED
SACHET
SAPHAR
SASHAY
SIGHTS
SIPHON
SOPHIA
SUNHAT
SYPHER
SYPHON
TECHNO
TEPHRA
TETHER
TETHYS
TIGHTS
TOPHUS
TOSHER
TOWHEE
TYPHUS
UNSHOD
UPSHOT
URCHIN
VATHEK
VISHNU
WADHAM
WARHOL
WASHED
WASHER
WETHER
WISHES
WITHAL
WITHER
WITHIN
ZEPHYR
ZITHER
ZOPHAR
ABDIEL
ACHING
ACTING
ACTION
ACTIUM
ACTIVE
ACUITY
ADDICT
ADMIRE
ADRIAN
ADRIFT
ADVICE
ADVISE
AEDILE
AEGINA
AERIAL
AFFIRM
AFRICA
AGEING
AGUISE
AGUISH
AGUIZE
AIKIDO
AILING
AIRILY
AIRING
ALBINO
ALBION
ALBITE
ALCINA
ALDINE
ALLIED
ALLIER
ALLIUM
ALPINE
ALPINO
AMNION
ANCILE
ANGICO
ANGINA
ANOINT
ANTICS
AORIST
APLITE
APPIAN
AQUILA
ARGIVE
ARNICA
AROINT
ARRIAN
ARRIVE
ARSINE
ARTIST
ASCIAN
ASCIUS
ASHINE
ASKING
ASPIRE
ASSIGN
ASSIST
ASSIZE
ATKINS
ATRIAL
ATRIDE
ATRIUM
ATTILA
ATTIRE
AUDILE
AUGITE
AURIGA
AUTISM
AWHILE
AWNING
BAKING
BANIAN
BANISH
BARING
BARIUM
BASICS
BEHIND
BELIAL
BELIEF
BELIKE
BELIZE
BENIGN
BENITO
BERING
BESIDE
BETIDE
BETIME
BETISE
BIKINI
BITING
BLAISE
BLUISH
BODICE
BODIES
BODILY
BOEING
BOLIDE
BONITO
BORING
BOVINE
BOXING
BOYISH
BRAINS
BRAINY
BRAISE
BRUISE
BULIMY
BUNION
BURIAL
BURIED
BUSILY
BUYING
BYLINE
CAGILY
CAHIER
CALICO
CALIMA
CALIPH
CAMION
CAMISE
CANINE
CANING
CAPIAS
CARIES
CARINA
CARING
CASING
CASINO
CAVITY
CECILS
CECITY
CELIAC
CERISE
CERIUM
CESIUM
CHAINS
CHAIRS
CHAISE
CHOICE
CHRISM
CHRIST
CILICE
CILIUM
CIVICS
CIVISM
CLAIMS
CODIFY
CODING
COMICE
COMING
COMITY
CONICS
COOING
COPIED
COPIER
COPING
CORIUM
COSIER
COSILY
COSINE
COVING
COZIER
CRUISE
CRUIVE
CRYING
CUBICA
CUBISM
CUBIST
CUEIST
CURIET
CURIUM
CYNIPS
DANIEL
DANISH
DARIEN
DARING
DARIUS
DATING
DATIVE
DEBILE
DECIDE
DÉCIME
DEFILE
DEFINE
DELIAN
DELICE
DELICT
DELIUS
DEMISE
DEMIST
DENIAL
DENIED
DENIER
DENIMS
DEPICT
DERIDE
DERIVE
DESIGN
DESIRE
DESIST
DEVICE
DEVILS
DEVISE
DEWITT
DIMITY
DINING
DIVIDE
DIVINE
DIVING
DOCILE
DOLINA
DOLINE
DOLIUM
DOMINO
DORIAN
DOTING
DOZING
DRYING
DURIAN
DURING
DURION
DYEING
EALING
EARING
EASIER
EASILY
EASING
EATING
ECHINO
EDDISH
EDGING
EERILY
EFFIGY
EGOISM
EGOIST
ELAINE
ELFISH
ELLICE
ELOIGN
ELOISE
EMPIRE
ENDING
ENDIVE
ENFIRE
ENGINE
ENLIST
ENMITY
ENNIUS
ENRICH
ENSIGN
ENSILE
ENTICE
ENTIRE
ENTITY
ENZIAN
EOLITH
EPPING
EPRISE
EQUINE
EQUIPE
EQUITY
ERBIUM
ERMINE
ERMITE
EROICA
ESKIMO
ETHICS
ETHIOP

ETRIER
EUXINE
EXCISE
EXCITE
EXPIRE
EXPIRY
EXTIRP
FABIAN
FABIUS
FACIAL
FACIES
FACILE
FACING
FADING
FAKING
FAMILY
FAMINE
FAMISH
FANION
FARINA
FATIMA
FAVISM
FELINE
FENIAN
FERIAL
FETISH
FILIAL
FILING
FINIAL
FINISH
FINITE
FIRING
FIXITY
FLYING
FOKINE
FOLIAR
FOLIOS
FOLIOT
FOLIUM
FORINT
FRAISE
FRUICT
FRUITS
FRUITY
FRYING
FURIES
FUSION
FUTILE
GABION
GALIOT
GAMINE
GAMING
GANION
GAPING
GARISH
GAVIAL
GEMINI
GENIAL
GENIUS
GIVING
GLAIRE
GLAIVE
GLOIRE
GNEISS
GODIVA
GONION
GONIUM
GORING
GRAINS
GRAINY
HABILE
HALIDE
HALITE
HAMITE
HATING
HAVING
HAZILY
HEGIRA
HEJIRA
HELIOS
HELIUM
HERIOT
HESIOD
HIDING
HIKING
HIRING
HOLISM
HOLIST
HOMILY
HOMING
HOMINY
HONIED
HOSIER
HOSING
HUMITE
IFFISH
IGNITE
ILLITE
IMBIBE
IMPISH
INCISE
INCITE
INDIAN
INDICT
INDIES
INDIGN
INDIGO
INDITE
INDIUM
INFIRM
INLINE
INNING
INSIDE
INSIST
INTIME
INVITE
IODINE
IODIZE
IOLITE
IONIAN
IONIZE
IRVING
ISAIAH
JABIRU
JEMIMA
JEWISH
JOSIAH
JOVIAL
JUDICA
JULIAN
JULIET
JULIUS
JUNIOR
JURIST
KARIBA
KARITE
KODIAK
KUFIAH
KUMISS
LABIAL
LABILE
LABIUM
LACING
LADIES
LADING
LAMINA
LAPITH
LARIAT
LAVISH
LAXIST
LAXITY
LAYING
LAZILY
LEGION
LEGIST
LESION
LEVITE
LEVITY
LIAISE
LIBIDO
LIKING
LILIAN
LILITH
LIMITS
LINING
LIPIDE
LIVING
LOLITA
LOLIUM
LORICA
LORIOT
LOSING
LOTION
LOVING
LUCIAN
LUCINA
LUMINA
LUPINE
LURING
LURIST
LUTINE
LUTIST
LYDIAN
LYRICS
LYRIST
MAKING
MALIAN
MALIBU
MALICE
MALIGN
MANIAC
MANILA
MANIOC
MANITO
MAOIST
MARIAN
MARINA
MARINE
MARISH
MARIST
MATING
MATINS
MAXIMS
MEDIAL
MEDIAN
MEDICI
MEDICO
MEDINA
MEDISM
MEDIUM
MEDIUS
MELIUS
MENIAL
MENINX
MERINO
MESIAL
METIER
MEXICO
MILIEU
MINING
MINION
MOBILE
MOBIUS
MODIFY
MODISH
MODIST
MODIUS
MOLINE
MONIAL
MONICA
MONISM
MONIST
MOPING
MOPISH
MORION
MOTILE
MOTION
MOTIVE
MOVIES
MOVING
MOWING
MULISH
MUNICH
MUNIFY
MUNITE
MURIEL
MURINE
MUSING
MUSIVE
MUTINY
MYRIAD
NANISM
NAPIER
NASION
NATION
NATIVE
NEBISH
NERINE
NERIUM
NIDIFY
NINIAN
NOMISM
NOSILY
NOTICE
NOTIFY
NOTION
NOVIAL
NOVICE
NOWISE
NUBILE
NUDISM
NUDIST
NUDITY
OAFISH
OBIISM
OBLIGE
OBOIST
ODDITY
OFFICE
OFFING
OFFISH
OLDISH
OMNIUM
ONDINE
ONEIDA
ONLINE
ONSIDE
OOLITE
OPHISM
OPHITE
OPTICS
OPTIMA
OPTIME
OPTION
ORBITA
ORCINE
ORSINO
OSMIUM
OSSIAN
OSSIFY
OSTIUM
OUTING
OWLISH
OXHIDE
PACIFY
PALING
PAMIRS
PAPIST
PARIAH
PARISH
PARITY
PATINA
PAVING
PAYING
PEKING
PELION
PERILS
PERIOD
PERISH
PETIPA
PETITE
PILING
PINING
PINION
PINITE
PIPING
PLAICE
PLAINS
PLAINT
PLYING
PODIUM
POLICE
POLICY
POLISH
POLITE
POLITY
POTION
PRAISE
PRYING
PUMICE
PUNISH
PURIFY
PURINE
PURIST
PURITY
QUAICH
QUAIGH
QUAINT
QUOITS
RABIES
RACIAL
RACINE
RACING
RACISM
RACIST
RADIAL
RADIAN
RADISH
RADIUM
RADIUS
RAGING
RAKING
RAKISH
RAMIFY
RAPIDS
RAPIER
RAPINE
RAPIST
RARING
RARITY
RATIFY
RATINE
RATING
RATION
RAVINE
RAVING
RAVISH
REBITE
RECIFE
RECIPE
RECITE
REFILL
REFINE
REGIME
REGINA
REGION
REGIUS
RELICS
RELICT
RELIEF
RELISH
RELIVE
REMIND
REMISS
REPINE
RESIDE
RESIGN
RESIST
RETINA
RETIRE
REVIEW
REVILE
REVISE
REVIVE
REWIND
REWIRE
RHEIMS
RIDING
RIMINI
RISING
ROBING
ROMISH
ROSINA
ROVING
ROWING
RUBIES
RUBIKS
RULING
RUPIAH
RUPIAS
SABINE
SADISM
SADIST
SALINA
SALINE
SALIVA
SAMIAN

SAMIEL
SAMIOT
SAMITE
SANITY
SAPIUM
SATINY
SATIRE
SATIVE
SAVING
SAVIOR
SAYING
SCAITH
SCHISM
SCHIST
SCHIZO
SCRIBE
SCRIMP
SCRIPT
SEEING
SEMITE
SENILE
SENIOR
SEPIUM
SERIAL
SERIES
SERINE
SEWING
SEXISM
SEXIST
SHEIKH
SHEILA
SHIITE
SHRIEK
SHRIFT
SHRIKE
SHRILL
SHRIMP
SHRINE
SHRINK
SHRIVE
SICILY
SIDING
SILICA
SIMIAN
SIMILE
SIRIUS
SKIING
SLEIGH
SLUICE
SNAILY
SOCIAL
SODIUM
SOLIVE
SONICS
SOVIET
SOWING
SPEISS
SPHINX
SPLICE
SPLIFF
SPLINT
SPLITS
SPOILS
SPOILT
SPRING
SPRINT
SPRITE
SPRITZ
SPYING
SQUILL
SQUINT
SQUIRE
SQUIRM
SQUIRT
SQUISH
STAIRS
STRICK
STRICT
STRIDE
STRIFE
STRIKE
STRINE
STRING
STRIPE
STRIPY
STRIVE
SUPINE
SYRIAN
SYRINX
SYRISM
TAHINA
TAHINI
TAHITI
TAKING
TALION
TAMINE
TAMISE
TAOISM
TAOIST
TARIFF
TAXING
TEDIUM
TEVIOT
THEIRS
THEISM
THEIST
THRICE
THRIFT
THRILL
THRIPS
THRIST
THRIVE
TICINO
TIDILY
TIMING
TIRING
TITIAN
TOBIAS
TOMIAL
TOMIUM
TONITE
TOYISH
TROIKA
TRUISM
TRYING
TSHIRT
TUBING
TULIPA
TUNING
TWAITE
TYPIFY
TYPING
TYPIST
UFFIZI
UGRIAN
ULLING
ULTIMA
ULTIMO
UMPIRE
UNBIND
UNCIAL
UNDIES
UNDINE
UNKIND
UNLIKE
UNPICK
UNRIPE
UNTIDY
UNWIND
UNWISE
UPHILL
UPLIFT
UPLINK
UPPISH
UPPITY
UPSIDE
URSINE
URTICA
VAGINA
VAHINE
VALINE
VALISE
VALIUM
VANISH
VANITY
VARIED
VENIAL
VENICE
VENITE
VERIFY
VERILY
VERISM
VERITY
VESICA
VIKING
VILIFY
VIRILE
VISIER
VISION
VIVIAN
VIVIEN
VIZIER
VOMICA
VOTING
VOTIVE
WAKING
WAPITI
WARILY
WAVING
WAXING
WIPING
WIRING
WIZIER
WRAITH
XAVIER
XENIAL
XENIUM
YEZIDI
YOKING
YORICK
ZENITH
ZODIAC
ZONING
ZURICH
ZYRIAN
ACAJOU
BANJAX
BANJUL
BHAJAN
BHAJEE
BOOJUM
BUNJEE
DONJON
ELIJAH
GAIJIN
INKJET
JIMJAM
LOGJAM
MOUJIK
PUNJAB
RAMJET
SELJUK
TRAJAN
TROJAN
AWAKEN
AWOKEN
BACKER
BACKET
BACKRA
BACKUP
BAIKAL
BALKAN
BALKIS
BANKER
BARKER
BARKIS
BASKET
BEAKER
BECKET
BECKON
BICKER
BODKIN
BOOKED
BOOKER
BOOKIE
BOSKET
BROKEN
BROKER
BUCKED
BUCKER
BUCKET
BUCKLE
BUNKER
BUNKUM
BURKHA
BUSKER
BUSKET
BUSKIN
CACKLE
CALKER
CALKIN
CANKER
CASKET
CATKIN
CHAKRA
CHOKED
CHOKER
CHOKEY
CHUKKA
COCKER
COCKLE
CONKER
COOKED
COOKER
COOKIE
CORKED
CORKER
CRIKEY
CUCKOO
DARKEN
DARKEY
DARKIE
DARKLY
DECKED
DECKER
DECKLE
DEKKER
DICKER
DICKEY
DIKKOP
DINKUM
DOCKED
DOCKER
DOCKET
DONKEY
DUCKED
DUCKIE
DUNKER
FAWKES
FICKLE
FIRKIN
FOKKER
FOLKSY
FORKED
GASKET
GINKGO
GIRKIN
GURKHA
HACKEE
HACKER
HACKLE
HANKER
HANKIE
HARKEN
HAWKED
HAWKER
HECKLE
HICKEY
HOCKEY
HOOKAH
HOOKED
HOOKER
HOOKEY
HOOKUP
HUCKLE
HUNKER
JACKAL
JACKET
JERKER
JERKIN
JOCKEY
JOSKIN
JUNKER
JUNKET
JUNKIE
KECKSY
KICKER
KOOKIE
KRAKEN
LACKEY
LARKIN
LASKET
LINKER
LINKUP
LOCKED
LOCKER
LOCKET
LOCKUP
LOWKEY
MARKED
MARKER
MARKET
MARKKA
MARKUP
MASKED
MAWKIN
MEEKLY
MERKIN
MICKEY
MICKLE
MOCKER
MOCKUP
MONKEY
MUCKER
MUCKLE
MUSKEG
MUSKET
NANKIN
NAPKIN
NECKAR
NECKED
NICKED
NICKEL
NICKER
NIKKEI
NOOKIE
PACKED
PACKER
PACKET
PARKED
PARKER
PARKIN
PEAKED
PECKER
PERKIN
PICKAX
PICKED
PICKER
PICKET
PICKLE
PICKUP
PINKIE
PIPKIN
POCKET
PORKER
PUCKER
PUNKAH
QUAKER
RACKET
RANKED
RANKER
RANKLE
RECKON
REEKIE
RICKER
RICKEY
ROCKER
ROCKET
ROOKIE
RUCKLE
RUCKUS
RUMKIN
RUSKIN
RYOKAN
SEEKER
SHAKEN
SHAKER
SHAKES
SHEKEL
SICKEN
SICKER
SICKLE
SICKLY
SIKKIM
SILKEN
SIMKIN
SINKER

SIRKAR
SISKIN
SMOKER
SMOKEY
SNAKED
SOAKED
SOCKET
SPIKED
SPOKEN
SPOKES
STAKES
STOKER
STOKES
SUCKEN
SUCKER
SUCKET
SUCKLE
SUNKEN
TACKET
TACKLE
TALKER
TALKIE
TANKER
TANKIA
TECKEL
TICKER
TICKET
TICKEY
TICKLE
TICKLY
TINKER
TINKLE
TUCKER
TUCKET
TURKEY
TUSKER
WACKER
WALKER
WANKEL
WEAKEN
WEAKER
WEAKLY
WEEKLY
WELKIN
WESKER
WICKED
WICKER
WICKET
WINKER
WINKLE
WOOKEY
WORKED
WORKER
WREKIN
YAKKER
YANKEE
YANKER
YORKER
YUCKER
ZONKED
ABELIA
ABULIA
ADDLED
AEOLIC
AEOLIS
AEOLUS
AIGLET
ALALIA
AMBLER
AMELIA
AMULET
ANALOG
ANGLED
ANGLER
ANGLIA
ANKLET
ANTLER
ANTLIA
APOLLO
APPLES
ARALIA
ARMLET
AROLLA
ASHLAR
ASHLEY
ASYLUM
ATTLEE
AUDLEY
AVALON
AVULSE
AXILLA
AZALEA
AZOLLA
BAILEE
BAILER
BAILEY
BAILIE
BAILLY
BALLAD
BALLET
BALLOT
BARLEY
BEDLAM
BELLOC
BELLOW
BERLIN
BEULAH
BILLET
BILLIE
BILLOW
BILLYO
BOILED
BOILER
BOLLEN
BOTLEY
BOULLE
BOWLED
BOWLER
BROLLY
BUGLER
BULLER
BULLET
BURLAP
BURLEY
BUTLER
BYELAW
CALLAS
CALLED
CALLER
CALLET
CALLID
CALLOP
CALLOW
CALLUP
CALLUS
CAPLET
CARLIN
CASLON
CELLAR
CEYLON
CHALET
CHALKY
CHILDE
CHILLI
CHILLY
CHOLER
COALER
COILED
COLLAR
COLLET
COLLIE
COLLOP
COOLER
COOLIE
COOLLY
COOLTH
COULEE
COULIS
CULLET
CULLIS
CURLER
CURLEW
CUTLER
CUTLET
CYCLIC
CYCLUS
DAHLIA
DEALER
DEPLOY
DEWLAP
DIALOG
DIGLOT
DIPLOE
DOLLAR
DOLLOP
DOYLEY
DRALON
DUBLIN
DUNLIN
DUNLOP
DUPLEX
ECCLES
EFFLUX
EMBLEM
EMPLOY
EMULGE
ENGLUT
EPILOG
EPULIS
ETALON
EUCLID
EVELYN
EVOLUÉ
EVOLVE
EVULSE
EYELET
EYELID
FABLED
FABLES
FALLEN
FALLOW
FAULTY
FEALTY
FEELER
FELLER
FELLOE
FELLOW
FIELDS
FILLED
FILLER
FILLET
FILLIP
FINLAY
FIRLOT
FOILED
FOLLOW
FOULLY
FOWLER
FRILLS
FRILLY
FROLIC
FULLER
GABLED
GAELIC
GALLEN
GALLET
GALLEY
GALLIC
GALLIO
GALLON
GALLOP
GALLOW
GALLUP
GALLUS
GAOLER
GARLIC
GELLER
GIGLET
GIGLOT
GILLET
GILLIE
GIMLET
GIRLIE
GOALIE
GOBLET
GOBLIN
GOLLOP
GOOLEY
GOOLIE
GRILLE
GRILSE
GUELPH
GUILDS
GUILTY
GULLAH
GULLET
GULLEY
GURLET
GUSLAR
HAILER
HALLAL
HALLEY
HALLOO
HALLOW
HALLUX
HAMLET
HARLOT
HASLET
HAYLEY
HEALER
HEALTH
HEELED
HELLER
HENLEY
HITLER
HOLLER
HOLLOW
HOWLER
HULLED
HURLEY
HUXLEY
ILKLEY
INFLOW
INFLUX
ISOLDE
ITALIC
JAILER
JAILOR
JETLAG
JILLET
JOPLIN
KAOLIN
KEELER
KELLYS
KEPLER
KEVLAR
KHALAT
KHALIF
KHALSA
KHILAT
KHILIM
KILLER
KOOLAH
LABLAB
LALLAN
LEALTY
LEGLET
LESLIE
LOLLOP
MAGLEV
MAHLER
MAILER
MAJLIS
MALLAM
MALLEE
MALLET
MALLOW
MARLIN
MASLIN
MATLOW
MEALIE
MEDLAR
MEDLEY
MEJLIS
MELLOW
MERLIN
MERLOT
MILLER
MILLET
MISLAY
MISLED
MOLLAH
MOLLIE
MOOLAH
MOSLEM
MOTLEY
MOULDY
MOULIN
MUFLON
MULLAH
MULLER
MULLET
MURLIN
MUSLIM
MUSLIN
MYELIN
MYELON
NAILED
NAILER
NALLAH
NAPLES
NELLIE
NIELLO
NULLAH
OAKLEY
OARLAP
OBELUS
OBOLUS
OCELOT
OCULAR
OERLAY
OMELET
OODLES
ORALLY
OSTLER
OTALGY
OTELLO
OUTLAW
OUTLAY
OUTLET
OUTLIE
OXALIC
OXALIS
PAELLA
PALLAH
PALLAS
PALLET
PALLID
PALLOR
PARLEY
PARLOR
PAVLOV
PEDLAR
PEELED
PEELER
PEGLEG
PELLET
PEPLOS
PEPLUM
PHILIP
PHYLLO
PHYLUM
PIGLET
PILLAR
PILLOW
POLLAN
POLLED
POLLEN
POLLEX
POLLUX
POPLAR
POPLIN
PRELIM
PROLEG
PROLIX
PROLOG
PUBLIC
PULLET
PULLEY
PURLER
PURLIN
QUALMS
QUELCH
RAGLAN
REALIA
REALLY
REALTY
REDLEG
REELER
REFLET
REFLEX
REFLUX
REGLET
REPLAY
RIALTO
RIVLIN
ROLLER

RUELLE
SAILOR
SALLEE
SALLET
SALLOW
SAMLET
SCALAR
SCALER
SCALES
SCHLEP
SCILLA
SCILLY
SCOLEX
SCULPT
SCYLLA
SEALED
SELLBY
SELLER
SENLAC
SHALOM
SHELVE
SHILOH
SKELLY
SKYLAB
SLALOM
SMALLS
SMELLY
SMILER
SMILES
SMILEY
SOILED
SPILTH
STALAG
STALIN
STALKS
STALKY
STALLS
STILTS
STILTY
STOLEN
STOLID
STOLON
STYLET
STYLUS
SUBLET
SULLEN
SUNLIT
SUPLEX
SUTLER
SVELTE
TABLET
TAILLE
TAILOR
TALLIS
TALLOT
TALLOW
TATLER
TEFLON
TELLAR
TELLER
TELLUS
THALER
THALES
THALIA
THOLOS
THOLUS
TILLER
TITLED
TOILET
TOLLED
TOLLER
TRALEE
TRILBY
TUILLE
TWELVE
UMBLES
UNCLAD
UNPLUG
UPFLOW
VALLEY
VALLUM
VARLET
VEILED
VELLUM
VILLUS
VIOLET
VIOLIN
VOLLEY
WAILER
WALLAH
WALLED
WALLER
WALLET
WALLOP
WALLOW
WAYLAY
WEALTH
WELLER
WELLES
WELLIE
WESLEY
WHALER
WHALES
WHILOM
WHILST
WHOLLY
WILLED
WILLET
WILLIE
WILLOW
WOOLEN
WOOLLY
YELLOW
ZEALOT
ACUMEN
AIRMAN
AKIMBO
ALUMNI
ANEMIA
ANEMIC
ANIMAL
ANIMUS
ARAMIS
ASIMOV
ATAMAN
ATOMIC
AXEMAN
BADMAN
BAGMAN
BARMAN
BATMAN
BLAMED
BLIMEY
BOOMER
BOWMAN
BRAMAH
BREMEN
BRUMAL
BRUMBY
BUSMAN
CADMUS
CAIMAN
CALMLY
CARMEL
CARMEN
CAYMAN
CHAMPS
CHEMIC
CHEMMY
CHIMER
CHIMES
CHUMMY
CLAMMY
CLAMOR
CLIMAX
CLIMES
CLUMPS
CLUMSY
COLMAR
COMMIS
COMMIT
COMMON
CONMAN
CORMUS
COSMEA
COSMIC
COSMOS
COWMAN
CRAMBO
CREMOR
CRIMEA
CRUMBS
CRUMEN
CRUMMY
CULMEN
CUMMER
CUMMIN
CUPMAN
DAEMON
DAIMIO
DAMMIT
DERMAL
DERMIS
DIMMER
DISMAL
DISMAY
DOLMAN
DOLMEN
DOOMED
DORMER
DROMIO
DROMOS
ENAMEL
ENAMOR
EREMIC
ETYMON
EXEMPT
FARMER
FERMAT
FIRMAN
FIRMER
FIRMLY
FLAMBÉ
FLAMEN
FLIMSY
FORMAL
FORMAT
FORMER
FORMIC
FRAMED
FRUMPY
FULMAR
GAMMER
GAMMON
GASMAN
GEMMAN
GERMAN
GIMMER
GLAMIS
GLAMOR
GLUMPS
GNOMIC
GNOMON
GRAMME
GRAMMY
GRAMPS
GRIMES
GRIMLY
GRIMMS
GRUMPH
GRUMPS
GRUMPY
GUMMED
GUNMAN
HAEMAL
HAEMON
HAMMAM
HAMMER
HARMED
HAYMOW
HELMET
HERMES
HERMIT
HERMON
HETMAN
HIMMEL
HITMAN
HOLMES
HORMUZ
HUMMEL
HUMMER
HUMMUS
ICEMAN
ISOMER
JAMMED
KALMIA
KERMES
KERMIS
KETMIR
KIMMER
KIRMAN
KISMET
KOSMOS
KRUMAN
KUMMEL
LAMMAS
LAMMER
LAWMAN
LAYMAN
LEGMAN
LITMUS
LUMMOX
MADMAN
MAMMAL
MAMMON
MARMOT
MERMAN
MESMER
MICMAC
MOOMBA
MORMON
MUMMER
MURMUR
NEWMAN
NIAMEY
NORMAL
NORMAN
NUTMEG
OGAMIC
OILMAN
ONEMAN
PALMER
PATMOS
PELMET
PENMAN
PERMIT
PIEMAN
PITMAN
PLUMED
PLUMMY
POMMEL
POMMIE
PRIMAL
PRIMED
PRIMER
PRIMLY
PRIMUS
PROMPT
PUMMEL
RAGMAN
REAMER
RHYMER
RIMMED
ROAMER
ROEMER
ROMMEL
ROOMER
RUMMER
SALMIS
SALMON
SCAMPI
SCAMPO
SCHMOE
SCUMMY
SEAMAN
SEAMEN
SEAMER
SEAMUS
SEEMLY
SERMON
SEUMAS
SHAMAN
SHAMBA
SHAMMY
SHAMUS
SHIMMY
SIMMER
SKIMPY
SKYMAN
SLUMMY
STAMEN
STAMPS
STEMMA
STUMER
STUMPS
STUMPY
STYMIE
SUBMIT
SUMMER
SUMMIT
SUMMON
SWAMPY
TALMUD
TAMMUZ
TARMAC
TASMAN
TAXMAN
TEGMEN
TERMES
TERMLY
THAMES
THEMIS
THOMAS
THYMOL
THYMUS
TREMOR
TRIMLY
TROMPE
TRUMAN
TRUMPS
VATMAN
VERMIN
VERMIS
WARMER
WARMLY
WARMTH
WEIMAR
WHAMMY
WHIMSY
YAMMER
YEOMAN
YEOMEN
YESMAN
ZIMMER
ABONDE
ACINUS
ADONAI
ADONIS
AGENCY
AGENDA
AGONIC
ALONSO
AMENDE
AMENDS
ANANAS
ANONYM
ARANDA
ATONAL
ATONIC
AVENGE
AVENUE
BAGNIO
BANNED
BANNER
BANNET
BARNES
BARNET
BARNEY
BARNUM
BEANIE
BEENAH
BENNET
BIONIC
BIRNAM
BLANCH
BLANCO
BLENCH
BLENDE
BLENNY
BLINKS
BLONDE
BONNET
BONNIE
BORNEO
BOUNCE
BOUNCY
BOUNDS

BOUNTY
BRANCH
BRANDY
BRONCO
BRONTE
BRONZE
BRUNCH
BRUNEI
BRUNEL
BUENOS
BURNER
BURNET
BYRNIE
CANNAE
CANNED
CANNEL
CANNON
CANNOT
CARNAL
CARNET
CARNOT
CATNAP
CATNIP
CHANCE
CHANCY
CHANEY
CHANGE
CHENET
CHINAR
CHINCH
CHINTZ
CHUNKY
CLENCH
CLINCH
CLINIC
CLONIC
CLONUS
CLUNCH
COGNAC
COINER
CONNER
CORNEA
CORNED
CORNEL
CORNER
CORNET
CORNUA
CORNUS
COUNTY
CRANCH
CRANKY
CRANNY
CRANTS
CRENAL
CRENEL
CRINAL
CRINGE
CRINUM
CRONET
CRONOS
CRUNCH
CUNNER
CYANIN
CYDNUS
CYGNET
CYGNUS
DAINTY
DAMNED
DAWNEY
DENNIS
DIANAS
DINNER
DIPNOI
DIRNDL
DISNEY
DJINNI
DOINGS
DONNÉE
DOWNAY
DOWNER
DRENCH
DRONES
DRONGO
DUENNA
EARNED
EARNER
ECONUT
EGENCY
ELANCE
ELANET
EMUNGE
EPONYM
ERINYS
ETHNIC
EVENLY
EVINCE
FAINTS
FAUNUS
FEINTS
FENNEL
FIANCÉ
FINNAN
FLANCH
FLANGE
FLANKS
FLENSE
FLINCH
FLINTY
FLUNKY
FORNAX
FORNIX
FRANCE
FRANCK
FRANCO
FRANZY
FRENCH
FRENUM
FRENZY
FRINGE
FRONDE
FUNNEL
GAINER
GAINLY
GANNET
GARNER
GARNET
GLANCE
GLINKA
GOANNA
GOUNOD
GRANBY
GRANGE
GRANNY
GRANTA
GRINGO
GRUNDY
GRUNGE
GUENON
GUINEA
GUNNEL
GUNNER
GURNET
GURNEY
HANNAH
HAUNCH
HENNIN
HERNIA
HOBNOB
HORNED
HORNER
HORNET
HOUNDS
HYMNAL
HYPNIC
HYPNOS
HYPNUM
ICONIC
IRONED
IRONIC
JAUNTY
JENNER
JENNET
JITNEY
JOANNA
JOHNNY
JOINER
KEENER
KEENLY
KENNEL
KENNET
KERNEL
KEYNES
KIDNAP
KIDNEY
KILNER
KRANTZ
KRONER
KRONOS
KWANZA
LAUNCE
LAUNCH
LEANTO
LEMNOS
LEONID
LIGNUM
LIMNER
LINNET
LIONEL
LOONIE
LOUNGE
LUANDA
MAENAD
MAGNES
MAGNET
MAGNON
MAGNUM
MAGNUS
MAINLY
MAINOR
MANNER
MANNIN
MARNER
MAUNDY
MEANIE
MEANLY
MEMNON
MIGNON
MINNIE
MINNOW
MOANER
MORNAY
MORNED
NIGNOG
NOUNCE
NUANCE
NUDNIK
NYANZA
OAKNUT
ODENSE
OLENUS
OMENTA
OPENER
OPENLY
ORANGE
ORKNEY
PAINED
PAINTS
PAINTY
PAUNCE
PAUNCH
PAWNEE
PAYNIM
PEANUT
PENNAE
PENNAL
PENNON
PERNOD
PHENOL
PHENYL
PHONAL
PHONEY
PHONIC
PICNIC
PLANCH
PLANET
PLANKS
PLENTY
PLENUM
PLINTH
PLONGE
PLUNGE
POINTE
POINTS
POUNCE
POUNDS
POWNIE
PRANCE
PRANKS
PRINCE
PRONTO
PRUNER
PUNNET
QUANGO
QUENCH
QUINCE
QUINSY
QUINTA
RAUNCH
RENNET
RENNIN
RIENZI
RODNEY
ROGNON
ROMNEY
ROUNCE
ROUNDS
RUINED
RUNNEL
RUNNER
RWANDA
SAANEN
SAINTS
SARNIE
SAWNEY
SCANTY
SCENIC
SCONCE
SCUNGE
SEANCE
SENNET
SHANDY
SHANKS
SHANTY
SHINDY
SHINER
SHINNY
SHINTO
SHINTY
SIDNEY
SIENNA
SIGNAL
SIGNET
SIGNOR
SIMNEL
SINNER
SKINNY
SLANGY
SLINKY
SONNET
SOONER
SPENCE
SPINAL
SPINAR
SPINET
SPONGE
SPONGY
SPUNGE
STANCE
STANCH
STANZA
STENCH
STINGO
STINGY
STINKO
STINKS
STONED
STONER
STONES
SWANEE
SWANKY
SWINGE
SYDNEY
TAENIA
TANNAH
TANNED
TANNER
TANNIC
TANNIN
TANNOY
TEENSY
TENNER
TENNIS
TERNAL
THANAH
THANET
THANKS
THENAR
THENCE
THINGS
THINGY
THINLY
TINNED
TINNIE
TOWNEE
TOWNLY
TRANCE
TRANNY
TRENCH
TRENDY
TRUNKS
TUNNEL
TURNED
TURNER
TURNIP
TURNUP
TWENTY
TWINED
TWINGE
UGANDA
URANIA
URANIC
URANUS
URINAL
USANCE
VAINLY
VAUNCE
VEINED
VERNAL
VERNON
VIANDS
VIENNA
VIENNE
WAGNER
WALNUT
WARNER
WHENCE
WHINGE
WHINNY
WIENER
WINNER
WINNIE
WINNOW
WRENCH
ZINNIA
ZOUNDS
AARONS
ABLOOM
ABROAD
ABROMA
ABSORB
ACCORD
ACCOST
ACROSS
ACTORS
ADJOIN
ADROIT
ADSORB
AEROBE
AFFORD
AFLOAT
ALCOCK
ALCOVE
ALDOSE
ALMOND
ALMOST
ANCOME
ANCONA
ANCORA
ANGOLA
ANGORA
ANKOLE
ANTONY
ANYONE
APHONY
APLOMB
APNOEA
APPORT

APPOSE
ARBOUR
ARDOUR
AREOLA
AREOLE
ARGOSY
ARIOCH
ARIOSO
ARKOSE
ARMORY
ARMOUR
ARNOLD
ARROBA
ARROYO
ASHORE
ASLOPE
ASSOIL
ASSORT
ASTONE
ATTONE
ATTORN
AURORA
BABOON
BARODA
BECOME
BEFOOL
BEFORE
BEGONE
BEHOLD
BEHOOF
BEHOVE
BELONG
BEMOAN
BEMOIL
BESORT
BETONY
BEYOND
BEZOAR
BIFOLD
BLOODY
BODONI
BOFORS
BOGOTA
BRIONY
BROOCH
BROODY
BROOKE
BROOKS
BRYONY
BUSONI
BUYOUT
BYGONE
BYWORD
CACOON
CAHOOT
CAJOLE
CAMOTE
CANOPY
CAPONE
CAPOTE
CAVORT
CAVOUR
CEROON
CHEOPS
CHOOSE
CHOOSY
CHROMA
CHROME
CHROMO
COCOON
COHORT
COLONY
COLOUR
CORONA
COYOTE
CREOLE
CUPOLA
CUTOFF
CYBORG
CYTODE
CYTOID
DACOIT
DAKOTA
DECODE
DECOKE
DEFORM
DEHORN
DEMOTE
DENOTE
DEPONE
DEPORT
DEPOSE
DESORB
DETOUR
DEVOID
DEVOTE
DEVOUR
DEVOUT
DHOOTI
DIPOLE
DISOWN
DODOMA
DOLOUR
DROOPY
DUGONG
DUGOUT
DUMONT
DUMOSE
EAMONN
ECBOLE
ECLOSE
ECTOPY
EDMOND
EEYORE
EFFORT
EGMONT
EMBODY
EMBOSS
ENCODE
ENCORE
ENFOLD
ENJOIN
ENROBE
ENROLL
ENTOMB
EOZOON
ESCORT
EUBOEA
EULOGY
EUROPA
EUROPE
EVZONE
EXHORT
EXMOOR
EXPORT
EXPOSE
EXTOLL
EXTORT
FAMOUS
FAROFF
FAROUK
FAVOSE
FAVOUR
FEDORA
FELONY
FILOSE
FITOUT
FLOOZY
FURORE
GADOID
GALOOT
GALORE
GALOSH
GENOME
GIAOUR
GIGOLO
GLIOMA
GLOOMY
GODOWN
GOLOSH
GROOVE
GROOVY
HALOID
HAMOSE
HAROLD
HEROIC
HEROIN
HERONS
HEXOSE
HONOUR
HUMOUR
IDIOCY
IGNORE
IMBOSS
IMPORT
IMPOSE
IMPOST
INBORN
INCOME
INDOOR
INFOLD
INFORM
INGOTS
INMOST
INROAD
INSOLE
INTONE
INTOWN
INVOKE
JACOBS
JALOPY
JEROME
JOCOSE
JOJOBA
JOYOUS
KANOON
KELOID
KETONE
KETOSE
KIAORA
KIBOSH
KIMONO
KOMODO
KYBOSH
LABOUR
LADOGA
LAGOON
LAYOFF
LAYOUT
LEMONY
LETOUT
LIPOMA
LOMOND
LOYOLA
LYCOSA
MAHOUT
MALONE
MALONY
MALORY
MAROON
MAZOUT
MEKONG
MELODY
MEMOIR
MEMORY
MEROPE
METOPE
MILORD
MIMOSA
MINOAN
MOHOCK
MOLOCH
MONODY
MOROSE
MOTOWN
MUCOID
MUCOUS
MYSORE
NEROLI
NILOTE
NIVOSE
NOBODY
NODOSE
NOYOUS
NYLONS
OBLONG
OCHONE
ODIOUS
OENONE
ONCOME
ONCOST
ONIONS
OOLONG
OPPOSE
OPTOUT
ORGONE
ORIOLE
ORMOLU
OSMOSE
OTIOSE
OULONG
OXFORD
PAEONY
PAGODA
PANOPE
PARODY
PAROLE
PATOIS
PAYOFF
PAYOLA
PELOID
PELOTA
PEYOTE
PHLOEM
PHOOEY
PIGOTT
PILOSE
POLONY
POMONA
POROUS
PRIORY
PUTOIS
PYRONE
PYROPE
RAGOUT
RAMOSE
RAMOUS
RATOON
REBORE
REBORN
RECOIL
RECORD
RECOUP
REFORM
REJOIN
REMOTE
REMOVE
RENOIR
RENOWN
REPORT
REPOSE
RESORT
RETOOL
RETORT
RETOUR
REVOKE
REVOLT
REWORD
REWORK
RIBOSE
RIGOUR
RIPOFF
ROCOCO
RUGOSE
RUGOUS
RUMORS
RUMOUR
RUNOFF
SALOME
SALOON
SALOOP
SAMOSA
SAPOTA
SARONG
SATORI
SAVOIE
SAVORY
SAVOUR
SAXONY
SCHOOL
SCOOBS
SCOOSH
SCROLL
SCROOP
SECOND
SENORA
SEROSA
SETOSE
SHROFF
SHROUD
SHROVE
SIMONY
SIMOON
SMOOCH
SMOOTH
SNOOTY
SNOOZE
SODOMY
SPLOSH
SPOOKY
SPOONY
SPROUT
STOOGE
STOOKS
STOOLS
STROBE
STRODE
STROKE
STROLL
STRONG
STROUD
STROUP
STROVE
SUBORN
SWOOSH
TACOMA
TAGORE
THEORY
THROAT
THROES
THRONE
THRONG
THROVE
THROWN
TIPOFF
TIVOLI
TOLOSA
TRIODE
TROOPS
TUMOUR
TYCOON
TYRONE
UNBOLT
UNBORN
UNCOIL
UNCOOL
UNCORK
UNDONE
UNFOLD
UNHOLY
UNHOOK
UNLOAD
UNLOCK
UNROLL
UNSOLD
UNTOLD
UNYOKE
UPHOLD
UPROAR
UPROOT
UPTOWN
UTMOST
VADOSE
VALOUR
VAPOUR
VELOCE
VELOUR
VENOSE
VENOUS
VIGOUR
VINOUS
VIROUS
WAYOUT
WHOOPS
WHOOSH
WIDOWS
XEROMA
XYLOID
ZYGOMA
ZYGOTE
ALIPED
APEPSY
ARMPIT
ASHPAN
AUSPEX
BEDPAN
BEEPER

BIOPIC
BIOPSY
BUMPER
CAMPED
CAMPER
CAMPUS
CAPPED
CARPAL
CARPEL
CARPER
CARPET
CARPUS
CASPAR
CHAPEL
CHAPKA
CHIPPY
CHOPIN
CHOPPY
CHYPRE
CLIPPY
COMPEL
COMPLY
COOPER
COPPER
COPPIN
CORPSE
CORPUS
COUPLE
COUPON
COWPAT
COWPER
CRAPLE
CRIPES
CROPPY
CRYPTO
CUPPED
CUPPER
CURPEL
CZAPKA
DAMPEN
DAMPER
DAPPER
DAPPLE
DEEPEN
DEEPER
DEEPLY
DELPHI
DESPOT
DIAPER
DIEPPE
DIMPLE
DIPPER
DISPEL
DRAPER
DRIPPY
DROPSY
DUMPER
DUMPLE
ELAPSE
ELOPER
EPOPEE
FIPPLE
FLOPPY
FORPIT
FRAPPÉ
FRIPON
FURPHY
GASPAR
GASPER
GILPIN
GOSPEL
GRAPES
GRAPPA
GRIPES
GRIPPE
GROPER
GULPER
HAMPER
HAPPEN
HARPIC
HEAPED
HELPER
HEMPEN
HERPES
HIPPED
HIPPUS
HISPID
HOOPER
HOOPLA
HOOPOE
HOPPER
HOTPOT
HUMPED
HUMPTY
INKPOT
ISOPOD
JAMPOT
JASPER
JUMPER
KALPAK
KEEPER
KELPER
KELPIE
KEWPIE
KEYPAD
KIPPER
LAPPER
LAPPET
LIMPET
LIMPID
LIMPLY
LIPPED
LISPER
LOOPED
LOOPER
LUMPUR
LYMPNE
MAGPIE
MOPPET
MUPPET
MURPHY
MYOPIA
MYOPIC
NAPPER
NEAPED
NIPPER
NIPPLE
NIPPON
NUMPTY
OOKPIK
OOMPAH
OUTPUT
PAMPAS
PAMPER
PAUPER
PAWPAW
PEEPER
PEOPLE
PEPPER
PIGPEN
PIMPLE
PIMPLY
PIPPIN
POMPEY
POMPOM
POPPER
POPPET
POPPIT
PREPAY
PREPPY
PROPEL
PROPER
PROPYL
PULPIT
PUPPET
PURPLE
RAPPED
RAPPEL
RAPPER
RASPER
REAPER
REOPEN
RHAPHE
RIPPER
RIPPLE
RIPPON
RUMPLE
RUMPUS
SAMPAN
SAMPLE
SAPPER
SAPPHO
SCAPUS
SCIPIO
SCOPUS
SEMPRE
SHAPED
SHIPKA
SIMPER
SIMPLE
SIMPLY
SIPPET
SIPPLE
SLIPPY
SLIPUP
SLOPES
SLOPPY
SNAPPY
SNIPER
SOUPER
SOUPLE
STAPES
STAPLE
STEPPE
STIPES
STUPID
STUPOR
SULPHA
SUPPER
SUPPLE
SUPPLY
SWIPES
TAIPAN
TAIPEI
TAMPER
TAMPON
TAPPER
TAPPET
TAPPIT
TAWPIE
TEAPOT
TEAPOY
TEEPEE
TEMPER
TEMPLE
TENPIN
TEOPAN
TIEPIN
TINPAN
TINPOT
TIPPED
TIPPER
TIPPET
TIPPLE
TIPPOO
TOPPER
TOPPLE
TORPID
TORPOR
TOUPEE
TOUPET
TRAPES
TREPAN
TRIPLE
TRIPOD
TRIPOS
TROPHE
TROPHY
TROPIC
TROPPO
TURPIN
TYMPAN
UTOPIA
VESPER
WAMPUM
WAMPUS
WARPED
WEAPON
WEEPIE
WIMPLE
YIPPEE
YUPPIE
ZIPPER
BARQUE
BASQUE
BISQUE
BRAQUE
CAIQUE
CALQUE
CASQUE
CHEQUE
CINQUE
CIRQUE
CLAQUE
CLIQUE
IRAQIS
MANQUÉ
MARQUE
MASQUE
MOSQUE
OPAQUE
PASQUE
PLAQUE
RISQUÉ
TORQUE
UNIQUE
ACARID
ACARUS
ACCRUE
ACORNS
ADORER
AFFRAY
AFFRET
AGARIC
ALARIC
ALARUM
ALDRIN
ALERCE
ALFRED
AMERCE
AMORAL
AMORCE
AMORET
AMTRAK
ANDREW
ANORAK
ANTRIM
ANTRUM
APERÇU
APORIA
ARARAT
ASARUM
ASTRAL
ASTRAY
ATHROB
ATTRAP
AUBREY
AUDREY
AVERNO
AVERSE
AZORES
BAHRAM
BARRED
BARREL
BARREN
BARRIE
BARRIO
BARROW
BEARER
BEHRAM
BEIRUT
BETRAY
BEURRÉ
BHARAT
BOARDS
BORROW
BOURÉE
BOURNE
BOURSE
BOVRIL
BURROW
CARREL
CARROT
CEDRIC
CHARGE
CHARON
CHARTA
CHERIE
CHERRY
CHERUB
CHERUP
CHIRON
CHIRPY
CHORAL
CHOREA
CHOREE
CHORUS
CHURCH
CIERGE
CIRRUS
CITRIC
CITRIN
CITRON
CITRUS
CLARET
CLARTY
CLERGY
CLERIC
CLERKS
COARSE
COERCE
CONRAD
CORRAL
CORRIE
COURSE
COWRIE
CRURAL
CUERPO
CURRIE
CYBRID
CYMRIC
CYPRID
CYPRIS
CYPRUS
DEARER
DEARIE
DEARLY
DEARTH
DEBRIS
DECREE
DECREW
DEFRAY
DEGREE
DERRIS
DHARMA
DJERBA
DORRIT
DOURLY
DVORAK
DZEREN
ECARTÉ
ECURIE
EGERIA
ELBRUS
EMBRUE
EMBRYO
EMERGE
ENARCH
ENERGY
ENFREE
ENTRAP
ENTREE
ENWRAP
EPARCH
EPERDU
EPIRUS
ESCROC
ESCROW
ESPRIT
ESTRAY
EXARCH
FABRIC
FAIRLY
FARROW
FEERIE
FERRET
FERRIS
FIERCE
FLARES
FLORAL
FLORET
FLORID
FLORIN
FLURRY
FORRAD
FORRAY
FOURTH

FUHRER
FURROW
GARRET
GARROT
GARRYA
GEORGE
GHARRY
GHERAO
GIORGI
GLORIA
GOURDE
GOURDS
GUARDI
GUARDS
HAIRDO
HARRIS
HARROW
HATRED
HEARER
HEARSE
HEARTH
HEARTS
HEARTY
HEBREW
HERREN
HOARSE
HOORAH
HOORAY
HORRID
HORROR
HOURLY
HUBRIS
HURRAH
HURRAY
HYBRID
HYBRIS
HYDRAX
HYDRIA
IBERIA
ICARUS
IMBRUE
INBRED
INGRAM
INGRES
INGROW
INTRAY
INTRON
ISTRIA
ITERUM
KHARIF
KOUROS
LABRUM
LABRYS
LARRUP
LATRON
LAUREL
LAURIC
LAURIE
LIERNE
LOURIE
LUBRIC

MACRON
MADRAS
MADRID
MARRAM
MARRON
MARROW
MATRIX
MATRON
MEGRIM
MERRIE
MERROW
METRIC
MICRON
MIRROR
MITRAL
MITRED
MONROE
MORRIS
MORROW
MURRAM
MURRAY
MURRHA
MURRIN
NARROW
NATRON
NEARBY
NEARER
NEARLY
NEURAL
NEURON
NIMROD
NITRIC
NITRYL
NORROY
OBERON
OCHREA
OCTROI
OILRIG
OMERTA
OSIRIS
OSPREY
OSTREA
OUTRUN
OVERDO
OVERLY
PAIRER
PARROT
PATROL
PATRON
PEARLS
PEARLY
PERRON
PETREL
PETROL
PHAROS
PIERCE
PIERIS
PLURAL
POGROM
POIROT
POORLY

POURER
PTERIN
PTERIS
PUERTO
PUTRID
PYRRHO
QUARRY
QUARTO
QUARTZ
QUIRKY
QUORUM
QWERTY
RAMROD
REDRAW
REGRET
RICRAC
ROARER
RUBRIC
SABRES
SACRED
SACRUM
SATRAP
SAURIA
SBIRRO
SCARAB
SCARCE
SCARED
SCARER
SCIROC
SCIRON
SCORCH
SCORER
SCORIA
SCORSE
SCURRY
SCURVY
SEARCH
SECRET
SEURAT
SÈVRES
SHARED
SHARER
SHARES
SHARIA
SHARIF
SHARON
SHARPS
SHERIF
SHERPA
SHERRY
SHIRAZ
SHIRRA
SHIRTY
SHORTS
SIERRA
SIRRAH
SIRREE
SITREP
SKERRY
SKURRY
SLURRY

SMARMY
SMARTY
SMIRCH
SMYRNA
SNORER
SOHRAB
SOIREE
SORREL
SORROW
SOURCE
SOURLY
SPARKS
SPARKY
SPARSE
SPARTA
SPARTH
SPIRAL
SPIRIT
SPORTS
SPORTY
SPURGE
STARCH
STARES
STARRY
STARVE
STEREO
STERIC
STERNE
STEROL
STORER
STOREY
STORMY
STURDY
STYRAX
SUNRAY
SURREY
SWARTY
SWERVE
TARROW
TAURUS
TEHRAN
TERRAE
TERROR
TETRAD
TETRYL
THERMO
THIRST
THIRTY
THORAH
THORAX
THORNE
THORNY
THORPE
TIERCE
TIERED
TIGRIS
TOERAG
TORRES
TORRID
TOURER
TUAREG

TUGRIK
TURRET
TWIRLY
UGARIT
UMBREL
UMBRIA
UMBRIL
UNBRED
UNTRUE
UNWRAP
USURER
UTERUS
VIBRIO
WAGRAM
WALRUS
WARREN
WEARER
WEIRDO
WHARFE
WHERRY
WIRRAL
YARROW
YEARLY
ZAGREB
ALASKA
AMUSED
ARISTA
AUSSIE
AYESHA
BALSAM
BARSAC
BASSET
BEDSIT
BELSEN
BENSON
BESSEL
BESSIE
BESSUS
BIASED
BOLSHY
BONSAI
BORSCH
BOSSED
BOUSER
BOWSER
BRASSY
BUKSHI
BUNSEN
BURSAR
BYSSUS
CAESAR
CAPSID
CARSON
CASSIA
CASSIO
CASSIS
CATSUP
CAUSAL
CAUSED
CAUSEY
CENSER

CENSOR
CENSUS
CHASER
CHASSE
CHASTE
CHESIL
CHESTY
CHISEL
CHOSEN
CLASSY
CLOSED
CLOSER
CLOSET
COMSAT
CONSUL
CORSET
COSSET
COSSIE
COUSIN
CRASIS
CRESOL
CRESTA
CRISIS
CRISPY
CRISTA
CROSBY
CROSSE
CRUSET
CRUSOE
CRUSTA
CRUSTY
CUESTA
CUISSE
CURSAL
CURSED
CURSOR
CURSUS
CUSSED
CUSSER
CYESIS
DAISHO
DAMSEL
DAMSON
DAWSON
DIESEL
DIESIS
DOBSON
DOESNT
DORSAL
DORSET
DOSSAL
DOSSER
DOWSER
DOWSET
DOWSON
DRESSY
DROSKY
EDISON
EGESTA
ELISHA
ELYSEE

ENOSIS
ERASED
ERASER
EXISTS
FEISTY
FIASCO
FIESTA
FLASHY
FLESHY
FLOSSY
FLUSHY
FOCSLE
FORSAY
FOSSIL
FRESCO
FRISKY
FROSTY
GASSER
GEASON
GEISHA
GEYSER
GHOSTS
GIBSON
GIUSTO
GLASSY
GLOSSA
GLOSSY
GODSON
GOSSIP
GRASSY
GRISLY
GRISON
GROSSO
GUESTS
GUSSET
GYPSUM
HANSOM
HASSAR
HASSLE
HAWSER
HENSON
HIRSEL
HONSHU
HORSED
HOUSES
HUDSON
HUSSAR
HUSSIF
HYSSOP
JERSEY
JETSAM
JIGSAW
JISSOM
JONSON
JOSSER
KAISER
KANSAS
KENSAL
KIRSCH
KISSEL
KISSER

KITSCH
KYUSHU
LAISSE
LAPSED
LAPSUS
LASSIE
LASSUS
LESSEE
LESSEN
LESSER
LESSON
LESSOR
LISSOM
LOOSEN
MARSHY
MASSED
MASSES
MASSIF
MAUSER
MEASLY
MENSAL
MERSEY
MESSRS
MIASMA
MISSAL
MISSED
MISSEL
MISSIS
MISSUS
MOPSUS
MORSEL
MOSSAD
MOUSER
MOUSEY
MOUSSE
MUESLI
MUNSHI
MUSSEL
MYOSIN
MYOSIS
NANSEN
NASSAU
NASSER
NAUSEA
NELSON
NESSIE
NESSUS
NISSEN
ODDSON
ODESSA
OFFSET
OMASUM
ORISON
OUTSET
PARSEC
PARSEE
PARSON
PASSED
PASSES
PASSIM
PENSÉE
PENSUM
PERSON
PHASIS
PHASMA
PHYSIC
PHYSIO
PIGSTY
PISSED
PLASMA
PLISSÉ
PODSOL
POISED
POISON
POSSER
POSSET
POSSUM
PRESTO
PRISMS
PRISON
PRISSY
PROSIT
PTOSIS
PUDSEY
PUISNE
PULSAR
PURSED
PURSER
PURSUE
PUSSER
PUTSCH
QUASAR
RAISED
RAISER
RAISIN
RANSOM
REASON
RHESUS
RIPSAW
ROBSON
ROSSER
RUSSET
RUSSIA
SAMSON
SANSEI
SARSEN
SEASON
SEESAW
SEISIN
SENSED
SENSES
SENSOR
SEPSIS
SHASTA
SIESTA
SLOSHY
SLUSHY
SOUSED
SOWSED
STASIS
SUBSET
SUNSET
SUSSEX
TARSAL
TARSEL
TARSIA
TARSUS
TASSEL
TASSET
TASSIE
TEASEL
TEASER
TENSON
TENSOR
THESIS
THISBE
TILSIT
TINSEL
TISSOT
TISSUE
TMESIS
TOCSIN
TONSIL
TONSOR
TOSSUP
TOUSER
TOUSLE
TOWSER
TRASHY
TRESCO
TRISTE
TRUSTY
TUSSAH
TUSSIS
TUSSLE
TWISTY
UNISEX
UNISON
UNUSED
VASSAL
VERSAL
VERSED
VERSES
VERSET
VERSUS
VESSEL
WARSAW
WATSON
WEASEL
WENSUM
WESSEX
WHISHT
WHISKY
WILSON
WIMSEY
WORSEN
WOWSER
WRASSE
YEASTY
ABATOR
ABATTU
ACATES
ACETIC
AGATHA
AMYTAL
AORTAL
APATHY
APHTHA
ARCTIC
ASHTAR
ASHTON
AUNTIE
AUSTEN
AUSTER
AUSTIN
AVATAR
AZOTIC
BALTIC
BANTAM
BANTER
BANTRY
BARTER
BARTOK
BARTON
BATTEN
BATTER
BATTLE
BATTUE
BAXTER
BEATEN
BEATER
BEATTY
BEETLE
BEETON
BELTED
BERTHA
BERTHE
BERTIE
BESTED
BESTIR
BESTOW
BETTER
BETTOR
BIOTIC
BIOTIN
BISTER
BISTRE
BISTRO
BITTEN
BITTER
BLITHE
BLOTCH
BLOTTO
BOATER
BOLTER
BOOTEE
BOOTLE
BOSTON
BOTTLE
BOTTOM
BOUTON
BRETON
BRITON
BRUTAL
BRUTUS
BUNTER
BURTON
BUSTED
BUSTER
BUSTLE
BUTTER
BUTTON
CACTUS
CAFTAN
CANTAB
CANTAL
CANTAR
CANTER
CANTLE
CANTON
CANTOR
CAPTAN
CAPTOR
CARTEL
CARTER
CARTON
CASTER
CASTLE
CASTOR
CASTRO
CATTLE
CELTIC
CENTER
CENTRE
CENTUM
CERTES
CESTUI
CESTUS
CHATON
CHATTY
CHITAL
CHITIN
CHITON
CHITTY
CLOTHE
CLUTCH
COATED
COATES
COITUS
COLTER
CONTRA
COOTIE
COPTIC
CORTES
CORTEX
CORTEZ
COSTAR
COSTER
COSTLY
COTTAR
COTTON
CRATCH
CRATER
CRATON
CRATUR
CRETAN
CRETIC
CRETIN
CRITIC
CROTAL
CROTCH
CROTON
CRUTCH
CUITER
CULTCH
CULTER
CULTUS
CURTAL
CURTAX
CURTLY
CURTSY
CUSTER
CUSTOM
CUSTOS
CUTTER
CUTTLE
CUTTOE
CYSTIC
DACTYL
DAFTIE
DALTON
DANTON
DARTER
DARTLE
DEBTOR
DEFTLY
DENTAL
DEPTHS
DEXTER
DIATOM
DICTUM
DIETER
DIKTAT
DISTAL
DISTIL
DITTOS
DOCTOR
DORTER
DOTTED
DOTTLE
DUSTED
DUSTER
EARTHY
EASTER
EDITED
EDITOR
ELATED
ELUTOR
EMETIC
EROTIC
EUSTON
EXETER
EXOTIC
FACTOR
FACTUM
FALTER
FANTAN
FASTEN
FATTEN
FESTAL
FESTER
FETTER
FETTES
FETTLE
FILTER
FILTHY
FILTRÉ
FITTED
FITTER
FLATLY
FLATUS
FLETCH
FLITCH
FLUTED
FLUTER
FLUTES
FOETAL
FOETID
FOETUS
FOOTER
FOOTLE
FORTHY
FOSTER
FOUTRE
FRATER
FROTHY
FRUTEX
FUSTIC
FUSTOC
GAITER
GANTRY
GARTER
GASTER
GASTON
GENTES
GENTLE
GENTLY
GENTRY
GETTER
GHETTO
GIFTED
GIOTTO
GIRTON
GLITCH
GLITZY
GLUTEN
GOATEE
GOETHE
GOITER
GOITRE
GOTTEN
GOUTTE
GRATED
GRATER
GRATIN
GRATIS
GRETNA

GRITTY
GROTTO
GROTTY
GRUTCH
GUITAR
GUNTER
GUTTER
GUTTLE
HALTER
HAPTEN
HAPTIC
HASTEN
HATTER
HEATED
HEATER
HECTIC
HECTOR
HEPTAD
HIATUS
HILTON
HITTER
HOGTIE
HOOTCH
HOOTER
HOSTEL
HOTTER
HUNTER
HURTLE
HUSTLE
INSTAL
INSTAR
INSTEP
INSTIL
IRETON
ISHTAR
JESTER
JETTON
JITTER
JOSTLE
JOTTER
JUSTIN
JUSTLY
KAFTAN
KANTEN
KANTHA
KEATON
KELTER
KELTIC
KELTIE
KETTLE
KILTED
KILTER
KILTIE
KIRTLE
KITTEN
KITTLE
KNOTTY
KOWTOW
KRATER
KRATON
KVETCH

LACTIC
LAPTOP
LASTLY
LATTEN
LATTER
LECTOR
LENTEL
LENTEN
LENTIC
LENTIL
LENTOR
LEPTON
LESTER
LETTER
LHOTSE
LICTOR
LIFTED
LIFTER
LINTEL
LISTEL
LISTEN
LISTER
LITTER
LITTLE
LOATHE
LOITER
LOOTER
LUSTER
LUSTRE
LYTTON
MAÎTRE
MALTED
MANTIS
MANTLE
MANTRA
MANTUA
MAOTAI
MARTEL
MARTEN
MARTHA
MARTIN
MARTYR
MASTER
MASTIC
MATTED
MATTER
MEATUS
MELTED
MELTON
MENTAL
MENTOR
MENTUM
MERTON
METTLE
MILTON
MINTON
MISTER
MITTEN
MOATED
MOLTEN
MONTEM

MONTHS
MORTAL
MORTAR
MORTEM
MOSTLY
MOTTLE
MOUTAN
MOUTER
MOUTON
MULTUM
MUSTER
MUTTER
MUTTON
MYRTLE
MYSTIC
NANTES
NASTIC
NATTER
NAUTCH
NEATEN
NEATLY
NECTAR
NESTLE
NESTOR
NETTLE
NEUTER
NEWTON
NOCTUA
NUTTER
OBITAL
OBITER
ORATOR
OTITIS
OUTTOP
OYSTER
PALTRY
PANTER
PANTON
PANTRY
PARTLY
PARTON
PASTEL
PASTIL
PASTIS
PASTON
PASTOR
PASTRY
PATTEN
PATTER
PATTON
PECTEN
PECTIN
PENTAD
PENTEL
PENTUP
PEPTIC
PESTER
PESTLE
PEWTER
PHOTON
PINTER

PINTLE
PISTIL
PISTOL
PISTON
PITTED
PITTER
PLATED
PLATEN
PLATER
PLATES
PLUTUS
POETIC
POETRY
PONTIC
POOTER
PORTAL
PORTER
PORTIA
PORTLY
POSTAL
POSTER
POSTIL
POTTED
POTTER
POTTLE
POUTER
POWTER
PRATER
PRETAX
PRETTY
PROTEA
PROTON
PUNTER
PUTTEE
PUTTER
QUETCH
QUITCH
QUOTED
RAFTER
RAGTOP
RANTER
RAPTLY
RAPTOR
RASTER
RATTAN
RATTER
RATTLE
RATTON
RECTAL
RECTOR
RECTUM
RECTUS
REDTOP
RENTAL
RENTER
REPTON
REUTER
RHETOR
RHYTHM
RICTAL
RICTUS

RIOTER
ROOTED
ROOTER
ROOTLE
ROSTER
ROSTOV
ROTTEN
ROTTER
ROUTER
RUSTAM
RUSTEM
RUSTIC
RUSTLE
RUSTUM
RUTTED
RUTTER
SAITHE
SANTAL
SANTON
SARTOR
SARTRE
SCATCH
SCATHE
SCATTY
SCOTCH
SCOTER
SCOTIA
SCUTCH
SCUTUM
SCYTHE
SEATED
SECTOR
SEETHE
SEMTEX
SENTRY
SEPTAL
SEPTET
SEPTIC
SETTEE
SETTER
SETTLE
SEXTAN
SEXTET
SEXTON
SIFTER
SISTER
SITTER
SKATER
SKATES
SKETCH
SLATCH
SLATER
SLITHY
SMITHS
SMITHY
SMUTTY
SNATCH
SNITCH
SNOTTY
SOFTEN
SOFTIE

SOFTLY
SONTAG
SOOTHE
SORTER
SORTES
SORTIE
SOUTER
SOWTER
SPATHE
SPITAL
SPOTTY
SPUTUM
STATAL
STATED
STATEN
STATER
STATES
STATIC
STATOR
STATUE
STATUS
STITCH
SUBTLE
SUBTLY
SUITED
SUITOR
SULTAN
SULTRY
SUNTAN
SURTAX
SUTTEE
SWATCH
SWATHE
SWITCH
SYNTAX
SYSTEM
TACTIC
TANTRA
TARTAN
TARTAR
TARTLY
TASTER
TATTER
TATTLE
TATTOO
TAUTEN
TAUTLY
TECTUM
TEETER
TEETHE
TERTIA
TESTER
TESTES
TESTIS
TETTIX
TEUTON
THATCH
THETIC
THETIS
TINTED
TINTIN

TIPTOE
TIPTOP
TITTER
TITTLE
TITTUP
TOLTEC
TOMTOM
TOOTER
TOOTHY
TOOTLE
TOOTSY
TOTTER
TOTTIE
TRITON
TRUTHS
TSETSE
TUFTED
TURTLE
TWITCH
ULITIS
ULSTER
UNITED
URETER
VASTLY
VECTIS
VECTOR
VENTIL
VENTRE
VESTAL
VESTED
VESTRY
VIATOR
VICTIM
VICTOR
VIRTUE
VORTEX
WAFTED
WAITER
WALTER
WALTON
WANTED
WANTON
WASTED
WASTEL
WASTER
WATTLE
WELTER
WHITBY
WHITED
WHITEN
WHITES
WINTER
WINTRY
WITTED
WONTED
WONTON
WORTHY
WORTLE
WRETCH
WRITER
WRITHE

YATTER
YESTER
ZAFTIG
ZOSTER
ABDUCT
ABJURE
ABLUSH
ABOUND
ABRUPT
ABSURD
ACCUSE
ACQUIT
ACTUAL
ADDUCE
ADDUCT
ADJURE
ADJUST
ADSUKI
AGOUTI
ALBUGO
ALLUDE
ALLURE
AMBUSH
AMOUNT
ANNUAL
ARGUED
ARGUTE
ARMURE
AROUET
AROUND
AROUSE
ARTURO
ASSUME
ASSURE
ASTUTE
ATTUNE
AUBURN
AUCUBA
AUGURY
AUGUST
AUTUMN
AVAUNT
AVOUCH
BAGUIO
BASUTO
BEAUNE
BEAUTY
BELUGA
BEMUSE
BENUMB
BLOUSE
BOHUNK
BOSUNS
CANUCK
CANUTE
CARUSO
CASUAL
CEDULA
CERUSE
CESURA
CHOUAN

CHOUGH
CLAUDE
CLAUSE
CLOUDY
CLOUGH
COBURG
COLUMN
COQUET
CROUCH
CROUPE
CROUPY
CROUSE
CROUTE
CROUTH
CUPULE
CURULE
DANUBE
DATURA
DEBUNK
DEDUCE
DEDUCT
DEFUSE
DELUDE
DELUGE
DELUXE
DEMURE
DENUDE
DEPUTE
DEPUTY
DILUTE
DIQUAT
DISUSE
EDMUND
EFFUSE
EMBUSY
EMEUTE
ENDURE
ENGULF
ENOUGH
ENSURE
EPAULE
ESCUDO
EUNUCH
EXCUSE
EXHUME
EXPUGN
FECULA
FECUND
FERULA
FERULE
FIBULA
FIGURE
FLAUNT
FLEURY
FLOURY
FLOUSH
FROUDE
FUTURE
GARUDA
GAZUMP
GERUND

GREUZE
GROUCH
GROUND
GROUPS
GROUSE
GROUTS
GROUTY
HEAUME
HECUBA
ILLUDE
IMMUNE
IMMURE
IMPUGN
IMPURE
IMPUTE
INDUCE
INDUCT
INFUSE
INGULF
INHUME
INJURE
INJURY
INRUSH
INSULA
INSULT
INSURE
IRRUPT
ISEULT
ISSUES
JAGUAR
JEJUNE
JESUIT
JOCUND
JUJUBE
KABUKI
KANUCK
KAPUTT
KIKUYU
KORUNA
LACUNA
LAGUNA
LAGUNE
LANUGO
LAPUTA
LEGUME
LEMUEL
LEMURE
LIGULA
LIGURE
LIQUID
LIQUOR
LOCULE
LOCUST
LOQUAT
LUNULE
LUXURY
MACULA
MACULE
MADURA
MADURO
MANUAL

MANURE
MAPUTO
MAQUIS
MATURE
MAZUMA
MEDUSA
MINUET
MINUTE
MISUSE
MODULE
MUTUAL
NATURE
NEBULA
NEBULE
NODULE
NUCULE
OBTUND
OBTUSE
OCCULT
OCCUPY
ONRUSH
OPPUGN
ORDURE
PADUAN
PAPULE
PARURE
PENURY
PEQUOD
PERUKE
PERUSE
PIQUET
PLEURA
PLOUGH
PNEUMA
PROUST
PSEUDO
RADULA
RAGUSA
RANULA
RAZURE
REBUFF
REBUKE
REDUCE
REFUEL
REFUGE
REFUND
REFUSE
REFUTE
REGULO
REPUGN
REPUTE
RESULT
RESUME
RETURN
RHEUMY
RITUAL
ROBUST
ROGUES
ROQUET
ROTULA
ROTUND

SALUKI
SALUTE
SAMUEL
SATURN
SCHUSS
SCHUYT
SCOUSE
SCRUBS
SCRUFF
SCRUNT
SECURE
SEDUCE
SEQUEL
SEQUIN
SEXUAL
SHOULD
SHRUNK
SLEUTH
SLOUCH
SLOUGH
SNOUTY
SOLUTE
SPAULD
SPOUSE
SPRUCE
SPRUNG
STRUCK
STRUNG
STRUNT
SUBURB
SUTURE
SYRUPY
TABULA
TEGULA
TELUGU
TENURE
THOUGH
THRUSH
THRUST
TIPULA
TITULE
TOLUIC
TOLUOL
TRAUMA
TROUGH
TROUPE
TROUVÉ
TUBULE
TUMULT
TYBURN
UNBUSY
UNDULY
UNFURL
UNGULA
UNHURT
UNJUST
UNRULY
UNSUNG
UNSURE
UPTURN
URSULA

VACUUM
VALUER
VALUTA
VEDUTA
VELURE
VICUNA
VISUAL
VOLUME
VOLUTE
WOBURN
YAKUZA
YAOURT
YOGURT
YORUBA
BEAVER
BREVET
CALVER
CALVIN
CANVAS
CANVEY
CARVED
CARVEL
CARVER
CERVIX
CHEVAL
CHEVET
CHIVES
CHIVVY
CLAVIS
CLEVER
CLOVEN
CLOVER
CLOVIS
COEVAL
CONVEX
CONVEY
CONVOY
CORVÉE
CORVUS
CRAVAT
CRAVEN
CULVER
CURVED
CURVET
DELVED
DENVER
DRIVEL
DRIVEN
DRIVER
DROVER
DROVES
ELEVEN
FERVID
FERVOR
FLAVOR
FRIVOL
GLOVED
GRAVEL
GRAVEN
GRAVER
GRAVES

GRAVID
GROVEL
HALVED
HALVES
HARVEY
HEAVED
HEAVEN
HEAVES
HOOVER
JARVEY
JEEVES
KELVIN
KNIVES
LARVAE
LARVAL
LATVIA
LEAVEN
LEAVER
LEAVES
LOAVES
LOUVER
LOUVRE
MARVEL
NAEVUS
NERVAL
NERVES
NERVII
NORVIC
OEUVRE
OLIVER
OLIVET
OLIVIA
OUTVIE
PARVIS
PEEVED
PELVIC
PELVIS
PLOVER
PRAVDA
PREVIN
PRIVET
PROVEN
PULVER
PURVEY
QUAVER
QUIVER
RENVOI
RENVOY
SALVER
SALVIA
SAVVEY
SERVAL
SERVER
SHAVEN
SHAVER
SHIVER
SHOVEL
SILVAN
SILVER
SKIVER
SKIVVY

SLAVER
SLAVES
SLIVER
SLOVAK
SLOVEN
SNIVEL
SOLVAY
SOLVED
SOLVER
SPAVIN
STEVEN
STOVER
SUIVEZ
SURVEY
SWIVEL
SWIVET
SYLVAN
SYLVIA
TRAVEL
TRAVIS
TRIVET
TRIVIA
TROVER
TURVES
UNEVEN
VELVET
VERVET
WAIVER
WEAVER
WEEVIL
AIRWAY
ANSWER
ANYWAY
AVOWAL
AVOWED
BIGWIG
BLOWER
BLOWZY
BOBWIG
BOWWOW
BRAWNY
BREWER
BREWIS
BROWNE
BROWSE
CHOWRY
COBWEB
CREWEL
DARWIN
DIMWIT
DRAWER
DROWSE
DROWSY
EARWIG
FLAWED
FLOWER
FROWST
FROWZY
GLOWER
GNAWER
GODWIN
GODWIT
GROWER
GROWTH
KEYWAY
KOTWAL
LEEWAY
LUDWIG
MEDWAY
MIDWAY
NITWIT
NORWAY
ONEWAY
OUTWIT
PEEWEE
PEEWIT
POWWOW
PREWAR
RUNWAY
SEAWAY
SELWYN
SHOWER
SKEWED
SKEWER
SLEWED
SLOWLY
SNOWED
STEWED
STOWER
SUBWAY
TAIWAN
TIZWAZ
TROWEL
VIEWER
WEEWEE
WELWYN
WIGWAM
YAHWEH
ALEXIA
ALEXIN
ALEXIS
ANOXIA
ANOXIC
ATAXIA
ATAXIC
BONXIE
DIAXON
DIOXIN
ELIXIR
FLAXEN
HOAXER
JINXED
KLAXON
OREXIS
PINXIT
PLEXOR
PLEXUS
PRAXIS
RHEXIS
XERXES
ALIYAH
ARGYLE
ARGYLL
BANYAN
BARYTA
BUNYAN
CANYON
CLAYEY
CORYZA
COTYLE
CRAYER
CRAYON
ENZYME
FRAYED
GROYNE
JEKYLL
KABYLE
KENYAN
LARYNX
LAWYER
LIBYAN
LLOYDS
MAGYAR
OOCYTE
PAMYAT
PINYIN
PLAYER
POLYPS
PRAYER
ROSYTH
RUNYON
SATYRA
SAWYER
SLAYER
SPRYLY
STAYER
SYZYGY
THEYRE
TROYES
UNDYED
YUMYUM
AMAZED
AMAZON
BALZAC
BANZAI
BEZZLE
BLAZER
BLAZON
BONZER
BOOZER
BORZOI
BRAZEN
BRAZIL
BUZZER
CHAZAN
CRAZED
DANZIG
DAZZLE
DONZEL
FIZZED
FIZZER
FIZZLE
FOOZLE
FRIZZY
FROZEN
FUZZLE
GEEZER
GHAZAL
GIZZEN
GLAZED
GUZZLE
HUZZAH
JAZZER
LIZZIE
MAMZER
MIZZEN
MIZZLE
MOZZLE
MUZZLE
NOZZLE
NUZZER
NUZZLE
PANZER
PHIZOG
PIAZZA
PODZOL
PRIZES
PUZZLE
RAZZIA
RAZZLE
ROZZER
SCUZZY
SIZZLE
SNAZZY
SOZZLE
TOLZEY
ZIGZAG

6:5

ABADAN
ABROAD
ACTUAL
ADONAI
ADRIAN
AEGEAN
AERIAL
AFFRAY
AFGHAN
AFLOAT
AIRMAN
AIRWAY
ALEGAR
ALIYAH
AMORAL
AMTRAK
AMYTAL
ANABAS
ANANAS
ANDEAN
ANIMAL
ANNEAL
ANNUAL
ANORAK
ANYWAY
AORTAL
APICAL
APPEAL
APPEAR
APPIAN
ARAFAT
ARARAT
ARGHAN
ARREAR
ARRIAN
ASCHAM
ASCIAN
ASHCAN
ASHLAR
ASHPAN
ASHTAR
ASTRAL
ASTRAY
ATABAL
ATAMAN
ATONAL
ATRIAL
ATTRAP
AUGEAN
AVATAR
AVOWAL
AXEMAN
BADMAN
BAGMAN
BAHRAM
BAIKAL
BALAAM
BALKAN
BALLAD
BALSAM
BALZAC
BANDAR
BANIAN
BANJAX
BANTAM
BANYAN
BANZAI
BAOBAB
BARHAM
BARMAN
BARSAC
BATEAU
BATMAN
BAZAAR
BEDLAM
BEDPAN
BEENAH
BEGGAR
BEHEAD
BEHRAM
BELIAL
BEMEAN
BEMOAN
BENGAL
BETRAY
BEULAH
BEZOAR
BHAJAN
BHARAT
BIRNAM
BISCAY
BOBCAT
BOMBAY
BONSAI
BORDAR
BOREAS
BOTHAM
BOWMAN
BOXCAR
BRAMAH
BRIDAL
BROGAN
BRUMAL
BRUTAL
BUCCAL
BUCHAN
BULGAR
BUNGAY
BUNYAN
BUREAU
BURIAL
BURLAP
BURSAR
BUSMAN
BYELAW
CAESAR
CAFTAN
CAIMAN
CALLAS
CANAAN
CANNAE
CANTAB
CANTAL
CANTAR
CANVAS
CAPIAS
CAPTAN
CARDAN
CARFAX
CARNAL
CARPAL
CASBAH
CASPAR
CASUAL
CATHAR
CATHAY
CATNAP
CAUSAL
CAVEAT
CAYMAN
CEEFAX
CELIAC
CELLAR
CERCAL
CEREAL
CHAZAN
CHEVAL
CHINAR
CHITAL
CHORAL
CHOUAN
CLIMAX
COEVAL
COGNAC
COLLAR
COLMAR
COMBAT
COMSAT
CONFAB
CONMAN
CONRAD
CORRAL
COSTAR
COTTAR
COUGAR
COWMAN
COWPAT
CRAVAT
CRENAL
CRETAN
CRINAL
CROTAL
CRURAL
CUNEAL
CUPMAN
CURSAL
CURTAL
CURTAX
CUSHAT
CYMBAL
DAEDAL
DECCAN
DEFEAT
DEFRAY
DELIAN
DEMEAN
DENIAL
DENTAL
DEODAR
DERHAM
DERMAL
DEWLAP
DIANAS
DIKTAT
DIQUAT
DIRHAM
DISBAR
DISMAL
DISMAY
DISTAL
DOLLAR
DOLMAN
DOODAD
DOODAH
DORCAS
DORIAN

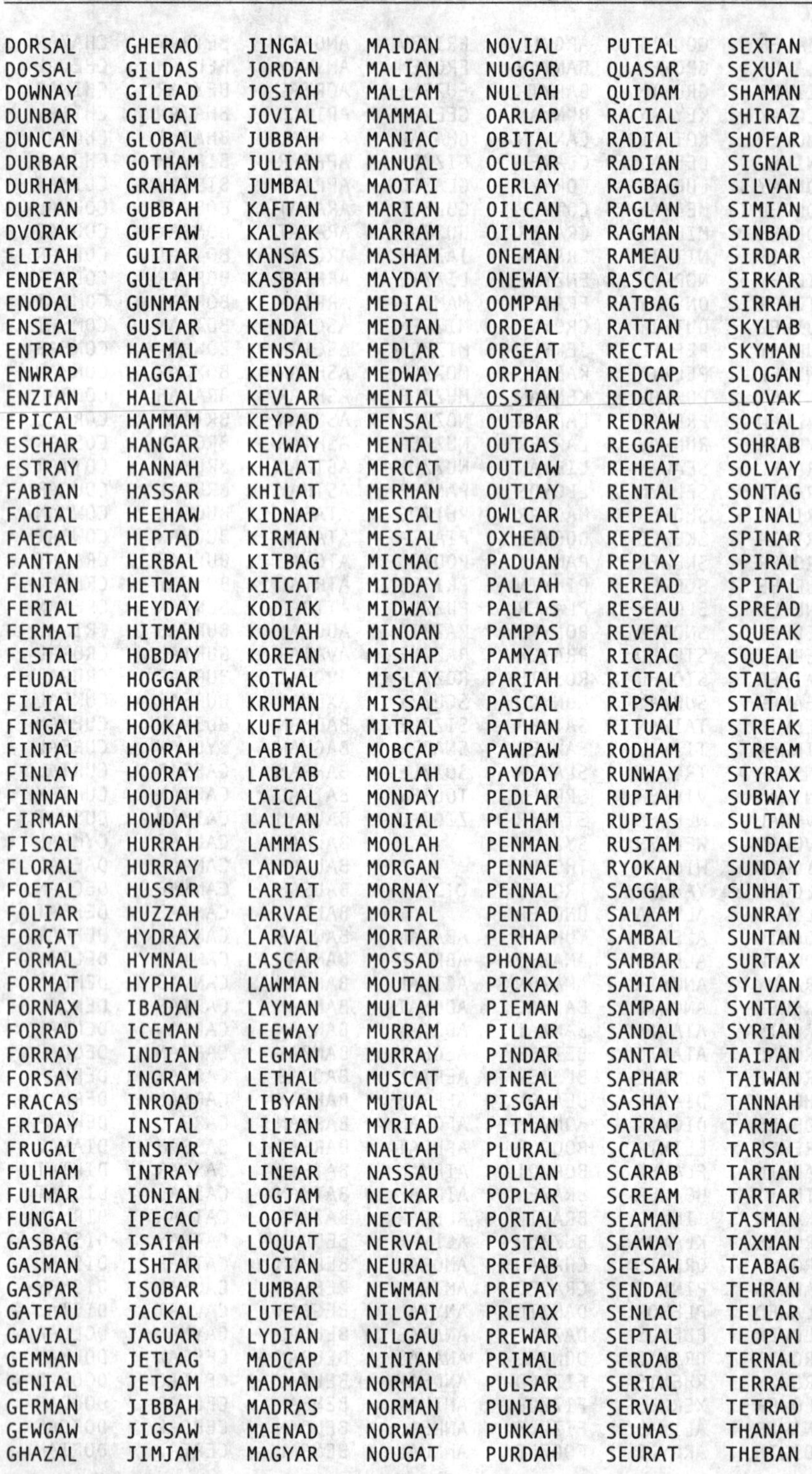

DORSAL
DOSSAL
DOWNAY
DUNBAR
DUNCAN
DURBAR
DURHAM
DURIAN
DVORAK
ELIJAH
ENDEAR
ENODAL
ENSEAL
ENTRAP
ENWRAP
ENZIAN
EPICAL
ESCHAR
ESTRAY
FABIAN
FACIAL
FAECAL
FANTAN
FENIAN
FERIAL
FERMAT
FESTAL
FEUDAL
FILIAL
FINGAL
FINIAL
FINLAY
FINNAN
FIRMAN
FISCAL
FLORAL
FOETAL
FOLIAR
FORÇAT
FORMAL
FORMAT
FORNAX
FORRAD
FORRAY
FORSAY
FRACAS
FRIDAY
FRUGAL
FULHAM
FULMAR
FUNGAL
GASBAG
GASMAN
GASPAR
GATEAU
GAVIAL
GEMMAN
GENIAL
GERMAN
GEWGAW
GHAZAL
GHERAO
GILDAS
GILEAD
GILGAI
GLOBAL
GOTHAM
GRAHAM
GUBBAH
GUFFAW
GUITAR
GULLAH
GUNMAN
GUSLAR
HAEMAL
HAGGAI
HALLAL
HAMMAM
HANGAR
HANNAH
HASSAR
HEEHAW
HEPTAD
HERBAL
HETMAN
HEYDAY
HITMAN
HOBDAY
HOGGAR
HOOHAH
HOOKAH
HOORAH
HOORAY
HOUDAH
HOWDAH
HURRAH
HURRAY
HUSSAR
HUZZAH
HYDRAX
HYMNAL
HYPHAL
IBADAN
ICEMAN
INDIAN
INGRAM
INROAD
INSTAL
INSTAR
INTRAY
IONIAN
IPECAC
ISAIAH
ISHTAR
ISOBAR
JACKAL
JAGUAR
JETLAG
JETSAM
JIBBAH
JIGSAW
JIMJAM
JINGAL
JORDAN
JOSIAH
JOVIAL
JUBBAH
JULIAN
JUMBAL
KAFTAN
KALPAK
KANSAS
KASBAH
KEDDAH
KENDAL
KENSAL
KENYAN
KEVLAR
KEYPAD
KEYWAY
KHALAT
KHILAT
KIDNAP
KIRMAN
KITBAG
KITCAT
KODIAK
KOOLAH
KOREAN
KOTWAL
KRUMAN
KUFIAH
LABIAL
LABLAB
LAICAL
LALLAN
LAMMAS
LANDAU
LARIAT
LARVAE
LARVAL
LASCAR
LAWMAN
LAYMAN
LEEWAY
LEGMAN
LETHAL
LIBYAN
LILIAN
LINEAL
LINEAR
LOGJAM
LOOFAH
LOQUAT
LUCIAN
LUMBAR
LUTEAL
LYDIAN
MADCAP
MADMAN
MADRAS
MAENAD
MAGYAR
MAIDAN
MALIAN
MALLAM
MAMMAL
MANIAC
MANUAL
MAOTAI
MARIAN
MARRAM
MASHAM
MAYDAY
MEDIAL
MEDIAN
MEDLAR
MEDWAY
MENIAL
MENSAL
MENTAL
MERCAT
MERMAN
MESCAL
MESIAL
MICMAC
MIDDAY
MIDWAY
MINOAN
MISHAP
MISLAY
MISSAL
MITRAL
MOBCAP
MOLLAH
MONDAY
MONIAL
MOOLAH
MORGAN
MORNAY
MORTAL
MORTAR
MOSSAD
MOUTAN
MULLAH
MURRAM
MURRAY
MUSCAT
MUTUAL
MYRIAD
NALLAH
NASSAU
NECKAR
NECTAR
NERVAL
NEURAL
NEWMAN
NILGAI
NILGAU
NINIAN
NORMAL
NORMAN
NORWAY
NOUGAT
NOVIAL
NUGGAR
NULLAH
OARLAP
OBITAL
OCULAR
OERLAY
OILCAN
OILMAN
ONEMAN
ONEWAY
OOMPAH
ORDEAL
ORGEAT
ORPHAN
OSSIAN
OUTBAR
OUTGAS
OUTLAW
OUTLAY
OWLCAR
OXHEAD
PADUAN
PALLAH
PALLAS
PAMPAS
PAMYAT
PARIAH
PASCAL
PATHAN
PAWPAW
PAYDAY
PEDLAR
PELHAM
PENMAN
PENNAE
PENNAL
PENTAD
PERHAP
PHONAL
PICKAX
PIEMAN
PILLAR
PINDAR
PINEAL
PISGAH
PITMAN
PLURAL
POLLAN
POPLAR
PORTAL
POSTAL
PREFAB
PREPAY
PRETAX
PREWAR
PRIMAL
PULSAR
PUNJAB
PUNKAH
PURDAH
PUTEAL
QUASAR
QUIDAM
RACIAL
RADIAL
RADIAN
RAGBAG
RAGLAN
RAGMAN
RAMEAU
RASCAL
RATBAG
RATTAN
RECTAL
REDCAP
REDCAR
REDRAW
REGGAE
REHEAT
RENTAL
REPEAL
REPEAT
REPLAY
REREAD
RESEAU
REVEAL
RICRAC
RICTAL
RIPSAW
RITUAL
RODHAM
RUNWAY
RUPIAH
RUPIAS
RUSTAM
RYOKAN
SAGGAR
SALAAM
SAMBAL
SAMBAR
SAMIAN
SAMPAN
SANDAL
SANTAL
SAPHAR
SASHAY
SATRAP
SCALAR
SCARAB
SCREAM
SEAMAN
SEAWAY
SEESAW
SENDAL
SENLAC
SEPTAL
SERDAB
SERIAL
SERVAL
SEUMAS
SEURAT
SEXTAN
SEXUAL
SHAMAN
SHIRAZ
SHOFAR
SIGNAL
SILVAN
SIMIAN
SINBAD
SIRDAR
SIRKAR
SIRRAH
SKYLAB
SKYMAN
SLOGAN
SLOVAK
SOCIAL
SOHRAB
SOLVAY
SONTAG
SPINAL
SPINAR
SPIRAL
SPITAL
SPREAD
SQUEAK
SQUEAL
STALAG
STATAL
STREAK
STREAM
STYRAX
SUBWAY
SULTAN
SUNDAE
SUNDAY
SUNHAT
SUNRAY
SUNTAN
SURTAX
SYLVAN
SYNTAX
SYRIAN
TAIPAN
TAIWAN
TANNAH
TARMAC
TARSAL
TARTAN
TARTAR
TASMAN
TAXMAN
TEABAG
TEHRAN
TELLAR
TEOPAN
TERNAL
TERRAE
TETRAD
THANAH
THEBAN

THECAL
THENAR
THOMAS
THORAH
THORAX
THREAD
THREAP
THREAT
THROAT
TINPAN
TIPCAT
TITIAN
TIZWAZ
TOBIAS
TOECAP
TOERAG
TOMCAT
TOMIAL
TONGAN
TOUCAN
TOWBAR
TRAJAN
TREPAN
TRIBAL
TRICAR
TROCAR
TROJAN
TRUMAN
TULBAN
TURBAN
TUSCAN
TUSSAH
TYMBAL
TYMPAN
UGRIAN
UNCIAL
UNCLAD
UNLOAD
UNREAD
UNREAL
UNSEAM
UNSEAT
UNWRAP
UPBEAT
UPROAR
URINAL
VANDAL
VASSAL
VATMAN
VEDDAH
VENIAL
VERBAL
VERNAL
VERSAL
VESTAL
VISUAL
VIVIAN
VULCAN
VULGAR
WADHAM
WAGRAM
WALLAH
WARSAW
WAYLAY
WEIMAR
WIGWAM
WIRRAL
WITHAL
WOMBAT
XENIAL
YEOMAN
YESMAN
ZIGZAG
ZODIAC
ZOPHAR
ZYRIAN
ABDABS
AEROBE
AKIMBO
AMOEBA
ARROBA
AUCUBA
BRUMBY
CHUBBY
CRABBE
CRABBY
CRAMBO
CROSBY
CRUMBS
DANUBE
DJERBA
ENROBE
EPHEBE
FLABBY
FLAMBÉ
GAZEBO
GRANBY
GRUBBY
HECUBA
HEREBY
IMBIBE
INDABA
JACOBS
JOJOBA
JUJUBE
KARIBA
KNOBBY
LAVABO
MALIBU
MOOMBA
NASEBY
NEARBY
PHOEBE
ROKEBY
SCABBY
SCOOBS
SCRIBE
SCRUBS
SELLBY
SHABBY
SHAMBA
STRABO
STROBE
STUBBS
STUBBY
THISBE
TRILBY
WHITBY
YORUBA
ABBACY
ABDUCT
ABJECT
ADDICT
ADDUCE
ADDUCT
ADVICE
AFFECT
AFRICA
AGENCY
ALCOCK
ALERCE
ALPACA
AMERCE
AMORCE
ANGICO
ANTICS
APIECE
ARIOCH
ARNICA
ARRACK
ASPECT
ATTACH
ATTACK
AVOUCH
BASICS
BEDECK
BISECT
BLANCH
BLANCO
BLEACH
BLENCH
BLOTCH
BODACH
BODICE
BORSCH
BOUNCE
BOUNCY
BRANCH
BREACH
BREECH
BROACH
BRONCO
BROOCH
BRUNCH
CALICO
CANUCK
CHANCE
CHANCY
CHINCH
CHOICE
CHURCH
CILICE
CIVICS
CLENCH
CLINCH
CLOACA
CLUNCH
CLUTCH
COERCE
COMICE
CONICS
COPECK
CRANCH
CRATCH
CREACH
CROTCH
CROUCH
CRUNCH
CRUTCH
CUBICA
CULTCH
CURACY
DEDUCE
DEDUCT
DEFACE
DEFECT
DEJECT
DELICE
DELICT
DEPICT
DETACH
DETECT
DEVICE
DIRECT
DRENCH
EFFACE
EFFECT
EGENCY
ELANCE
ELLICE
ENARCH
ENLACE
ENRICH
ENTICE
EPARCH
EROICA
ETHICS
EUNUCH
EVINCE
EXARCH
EXPECT
FIANCÉ
FIASCO
FIERCE
FLANCH
FLEECE
FLEECY
FLETCH
FLINCH
FLITCH
FRANCE
FRANCK
FRANCO
FRENCH
FRESCO
FRUICT
GLANCE
GLITCH
GREECE
GROUCH
GRUTCH
HAUNCH
HIJACK
HITECH
HOOTCH
HORACE
HUMECT
IDIOCY
IMPACT
INDICT
INDUCE
INDUCT
INFECT
INJECT
INSECT
INTACT
ITHACA
JUDICA
KANUCK
KIRSCH
KITSCH
KVETCH
LAUNCE
LAUNCH
LEGACY
LORICA
LUNACY
LYRICS
MALICE
MARACA
MEDICI
MEDICO
MENACE
MEXICO
MOHOCK
MOLECH
MOLOCH
MONACO
MONICA
MUNICH
NAUTCH
NEBECK
NOTICE
NOUNCE
NOVICE
NUANCE
OBJECT
OBTECT
OFFICE
OPTICS
PALACE
PAPACY
PATACA
PAUNCE
PAUNCH
PIERCE
PIRACY
PLAICE
PLANCH
PLEACH
POLACK
POLICE
POLICY
POMACE
POUNCE
PRANCE
PREACE
PREACH
PRINCE
PUMICE
PUTSCH
QUAICH
QUELCH
QUENCH
QUETCH
QUINCE
QUITCH
RAUNCH
REBECK
REDACT
REDUCE
REFACE
REFECT
REJECT
RELICS
RELICT
RESECT
ROCOCO
ROSACE
ROUNCE
SCARCE
SCATCH
SCONCE
SCORCH
SCOTCH
SCUTCH
SEANCE
SEARCH
SEDUCE
SELECT
SENECA
SILICA
SKETCH
SLATCH
SLOUCH
SLUICE
SMIRCH
SMOOCH
SNATCH
SNITCH
SOLACE
SONICS
SOURCE
SPEECH
SPENCE
SPLICE
SPRUCE
STANCE
STANCH
STARCH
STENCH
STITCH
STRICK
STRICT
STRUCK
STUCCO
SUMACH
SWATCH
SWITCH
TENACE
THATCH
THENCE
THRICE
THWACK
TIERCE
TRANCE
TRENCH
TRESCO
TWITCH
UNDECK
UNLACE
UNLOCK
UNPACK
UNPICK
URTICA
USANCE
VARECH
VAUNCE
VELOCE
VENICE
VESICA
VIVACE
VOMICA
WHENCE
WRENCH
WRETCH
YORICK
ZEBECK
ZURICH
APERÇU
ABONDE
ABRADE
ACCEDE
AGENDA
AIKIDO
ALBEDO
ALLUDE
AMENDE
AMENDS
ARANDA
ARCADE
ARCADY
ARMADA
ATRIDE
AUBADE
BAHADA
BARODA

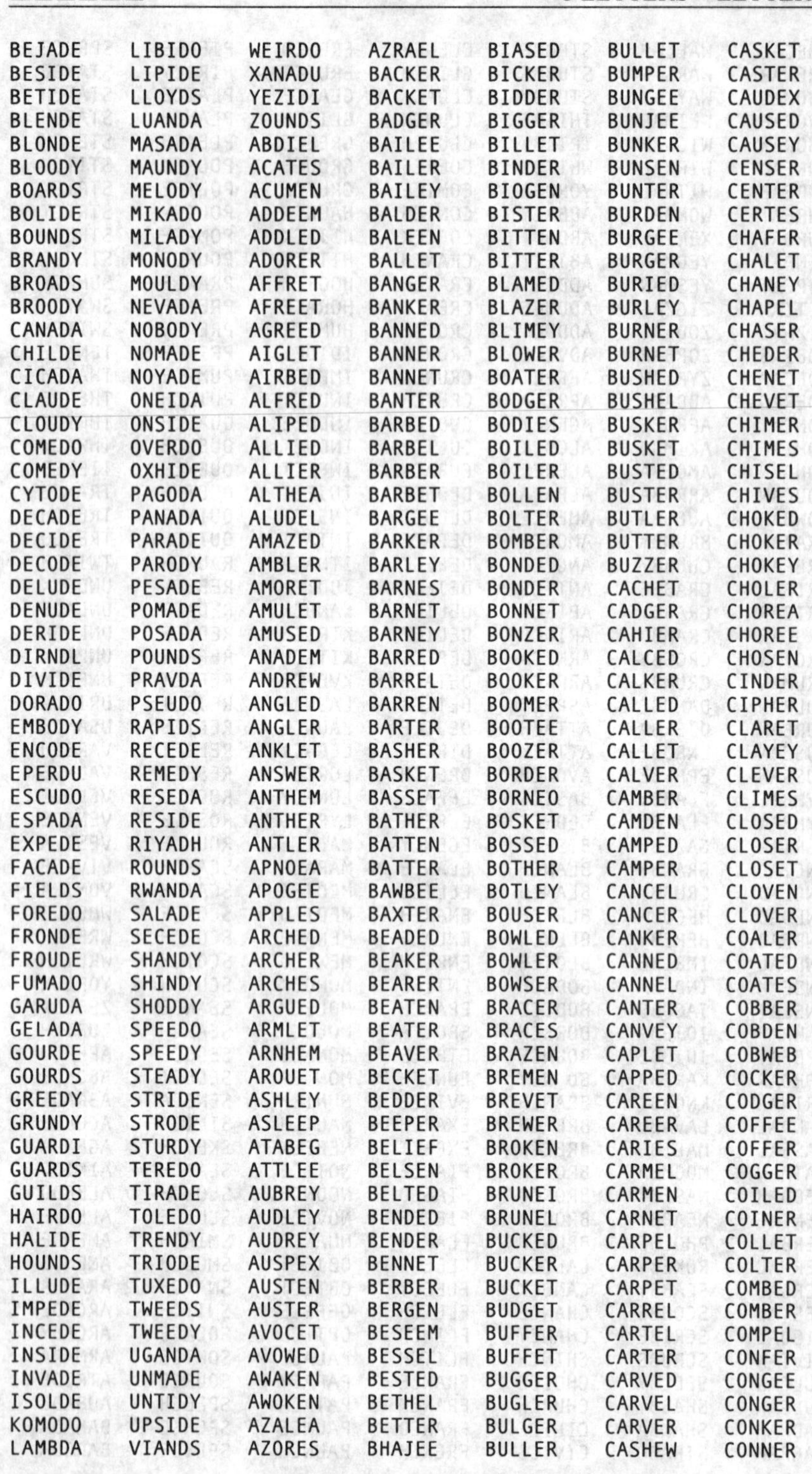

BEJADE
BESIDE
BETIDE
BLENDE
BLONDE
BLOODY
BOARDS
BOLIDE
BOUNDS
BRANDY
BROADS
BROODY
CANADA
CHILDE
CICADA
CLAUDE
CLOUDY
COMEDO
COMEDY
CYTODE
DECADE
DECIDE
DECODE
DELUDE
DENUDE
DERIDE
DIRNDL
DIVIDE
DORADO
EMBODY
ENCODE
EPERDU
ESCUDO
ESPADA
EXPEDE
FACADE
FIELDS
FOREDO
FRONDE
FROUDE
FUMADO
GARUDA
GELADA
GOURDE
GOURDS
GREEDY
GRUNDY
GUARDI
GUARDS
GUILDS
HAIRDO
HALIDE
HOUNDS
ILLUDE
IMPEDE
INCEDE
INSIDE
INVADE
ISOLDE
KOMODO
LAMBDA
LIBIDO
LIPIDE
LLOYDS
LUANDA
MASADA
MAUNDY
MELODY
MIKADO
MILADY
MONODY
MOULDY
NEVADA
NOBODY
NOMADE
NOYADE
ONEIDA
ONSIDE
OVERDO
OXHIDE
PAGODA
PANADA
PARADE
PARODY
PESADE
POMADE
POSADA
POUNDS
PRAVDA
PSEUDO
RAPIDS
RECEDE
REMEDY
RESEDA
RESIDE
RIYADH
ROUNDS
RWANDA
SALADE
SECEDE
SHANDY
SHINDY
SHODDY
SPEEDO
SPEEDY
STEADY
STRIDE
STRODE
STURDY
TEREDO
TIRADE
TOLEDO
TRENDY
TRIODE
TUXEDO
TWEEDS
TWEEDY
UGANDA
UNMADE
UNTIDY
UPSIDE
VIANDS
WEIRDO
XANADU
YEZIDI
ZOUNDS
ABDIEL
ACATES
ACUMEN
ADDEEM
ADDLED
ADORER
AFFRET
AFREET
AGREED
AIGLET
AIRBED
ALFRED
ALIPED
ALLIED
ALLIER
ALTHEA
ALUDEL
AMAZED
AMBLER
AMORET
AMULET
AMUSED
ANADEM
ANDREW
ANGLED
ANGLER
ANKLET
ANSWER
ANTHEM
ANTHER
ANTLER
APNOEA
APOGEE
APPLES
ARCHED
ARCHER
ARCHES
ARGUED
ARMLET
ARNHEM
AROUET
ASHLEY
ASLEEP
ATABEG
ATTLEE
AUBREY
AUDLEY
AUDREY
AUSPEX
AUSTEN
AUSTER
AVOCET
AVOWED
AWAKEN
AWOKEN
AZALEA
AZORES
AZRAEL
BACKER
BACKET
BADGER
BAILEE
BAILER
BAILEY
BALDER
BALEEN
BALLET
BANGER
BANKER
BANNED
BANNER
BANNET
BANTER
BARBED
BARBEL
BARBER
BARBET
BARGEE
BARKER
BARLEY
BARNES
BARNET
BARNEY
BARRED
BARREL
BARREN
BARTER
BASHER
BASKET
BASSET
BATHER
BATTEN
BATTER
BAWBEE
BAXTER
BEADED
BEAKER
BEARER
BEATEN
BEATER
BEAVER
BECKET
BEDDER
BEEPER
BELIEF
BELSEN
BELTED
BENDED
BENDER
BENNET
BERBER
BERGEN
BESEEM
BESSEL
BESTED
BETHEL
BETTER
BHAJEE
BIASED
BICKER
BIDDER
BIGGER
BILLET
BINDER
BIOGEN
BISTER
BITTEN
BITTER
BLAMED
BLAZER
BLIMEY
BLOWER
BOATER
BODGER
BODIES
BOILED
BOILER
BOLLEN
BOLTER
BOMBER
BONDED
BONDER
BONNET
BONZER
BOOKED
BOOKER
BOOMER
BOOTEE
BOOZER
BORDER
BORNEO
BOSKET
BOSSED
BOTHER
BOTLEY
BOUSER
BOWLED
BOWLER
BOWSER
BRACER
BRACES
BRAZEN
BREMEN
BREVET
BREWER
BROKEN
BROKER
BRUNEI
BRUNEL
BUCKED
BUCKER
BUCKET
BUDGET
BUFFER
BUFFET
BUGGER
BUGLER
BULGER
BULLER
BULLET
BUMPER
BUNGEE
BUNJEE
BUNKER
BUNSEN
BUNTER
BURDEN
BURGEE
BURGER
BURIED
BURLEY
BURNER
BURNET
BUSHED
BUSHEL
BUSKER
BUSKET
BUSTED
BUSTER
BUTLER
BUTTER
BUZZER
CACHET
CADGER
CAHIER
CALCED
CALKER
CALLED
CALLER
CALLET
CALVER
CAMBER
CAMDEN
CAMPED
CAMPER
CANCEL
CANCER
CANKER
CANNED
CANNEL
CANTER
CANVEY
CAPLET
CAPPED
CAREEN
CAREER
CARIES
CARMEL
CARMEN
CARNET
CARPEL
CARPER
CARPET
CARREL
CARTEL
CARTER
CARVED
CARVEL
CARVER
CASHEW
CASKET
CASTER
CAUDEX
CAUSED
CAUSEY
CENSER
CENTER
CERTES
CHAFER
CHALET
CHANEY
CHAPEL
CHASER
CHEDER
CHENET
CHEVET
CHIMER
CHIMES
CHISEL
CHIVES
CHOKED
CHOKER
CHOKEY
CHOLER
CHOREA
CHOREE
CHOSEN
CINDER
CIPHER
CLARET
CLAYEY
CLEVER
CLIMES
CLOSED
CLOSER
CLOSET
CLOVEN
CLOVER
COALER
COATED
COATES
COBBER
COBDEN
COBWEB
COCKER
CODGER
COFFEE
COFFER
COGGER
COILED
COINER
COLLET
COLTER
COMBED
COMBER
COMPEL
CONFER
CONGEE
CONGER
CONKER
CONNER

CONVEX
CONVEY
COOKED
COOKER
COOLER
COOPER
COPIED
COPIER
COPPER
COQUET
CORBEL
CORKED
CORKER
CORNEA
CORNED
CORNEL
CORNER
CORNET
CORSET
CORTES
CORTEX
CORTEZ
COSHER
COSIER
COSMEA
COSSET
COSTER
COULEE
COWPER
COZIER
CRATER
CRAVEN
CRAYER
CRAZED
CRENEL
CREWEL
CRIKEY
CRIMEA
CRIPES
CRONET
CRUMEN
CRUSET
CUDGEL
CUFFEE
CUITER
CULDEE
CULLET
CULMEN
CULTER
CULVER
CUMBER
CUMMER
CUNNER
CUPPED
CUPPER
CURFEW
CURIET
CURLER
CURLEW
CURPEL
CURSED
CURVED
CURVET
CUSSED
CUSSER
CUSTER
CUTLER
CUTLET
CUTTER
CYGNET
CYPHER
DAGGER
DAMNED
DAMPEN
DAMPER
DAMSEL
DANCER
DANDER
DANGER
DANIEL
DAPPER
DARIEN
DARKEN
DARKEY
DARTER
DASHED
DAUDET
DAWNEY
DAYBED
DEADEN
DEAFEN
DEALER
DEARER
DECKED
DECKER
DECREE
DECREW
DEEPEN
DEEPER
DEGREE
DEKKER
DELVED
DENIED
DENIER
DENVER
DEXTER
DIADEM
DIAPER
DIBBER
DICKER
DICKEY
DIESEL
DIETER
DIFFER
DIGGER
DIMMER
DINNER
DIPPER
DISHED
DISHES
DISNEY
DISPEL
DITHER
DJEBEL
DOCKED
DOCKER
DOCKET
DODDER
DODGEM
DODGER
DOGGED
DOGGER
DOLMEN
DONKEY
DONZEL
DOOFER
DOOMED
DORMER
DORSET
DORTER
DOSSER
DOTTED
DOUCET
DOWNER
DOWSER
DOWSET
DOYLEY
DRAGEE
DRAPER
DRAWER
DRIVEL
DRIVEN
DRIVER
DRONES
DROVER
DROVES
DRYDEN
DUCKED
DUDDER
DUDEEN
DUFFEL
DUFFER
DULCET
DUMPER
DUNCES
DUNDEE
DUNDER
DUNKER
DUPLEX
DUSTED
DUSTER
DZEREN
EARNED
EARNER
EASIER
EASTER
ECCLES
EDITED
EIFFEL
EITHER
ELANET
ELATED
ELEVEN
ELODEA
ELOPER
ELYSEE
EMBLEM
ENAMEL
ENFREE
ENTREE
EOTHEN
EPOPEE
ERASED
ERASER
ERODED
ESCHEW
ESTEEM
ESTHER
ETCHER
ETRIER
EUBOEA
EXCEED
EXETER
EXOCET
EXOGEN
EYELET
FABLED
FABLES
FACIES
FAECES
FAGGED
FALLEN
FALTER
FARDEL
FARMER
FASCES
FASTEN
FATHER
FATTEN
FAUCES
FAUCET
FAWKES
FEEDER
FEELER
FELLER
FENCER
FENDER
FENNEL
FERRET
FESTER
FETTER
FETTES
FIBBED
FIBBER
FIDGET
FILLED
FILLER
FILLET
FILTER
FINDER
FINGER
FIRMER
FISHER
FITTED
FITTER
FIZZED
FIZZER
FLAMEN
FLARES
FLAWED
FLAXEN
FLORET
FLOWER
FLUTED
FLUTER
FLUTES
FODDER
FOILED
FOKKER
FOLDED
FOLDER
FOOTER
FORCED
FORCES
FORGED
FORGER
FORGET
FORKED
FORMER
FOSTER
FOWLER
FRAMED
FRATER
FRAYED
FROZEN
FRUTEX
FUHRER
FULLER
FUNDED
FUNNEL
FURIES
GABLED
GADGET
GAFFER
GAINER
GAITER
GALLEN
GALLET
GALLEY
GAMBET
GAMMER
GANDER
GANGER
GANGES
GANNET
GAOLER
GARBED
GARDEN
GARGET
GARNER
GARNET
GARRET
GARTER
GASKET
GASPER
GASSER
GASTER
GATHER
GAUGER
GEEZER
GEIGER
GELLER
GENDER
GENTES
GETTER
GEYSER
GHEBER
GIBBER
GIBBET
GIFTED
GIGLET
GILDED
GILDER
GILLET
GIMLET
GIMMER
GINGER
GIRDER
GIZZEN
GLAZED
GLIDER
GLOVED
GLOWER
GLUTEN
GNAWER
GOATEE
GOBBET
GOBLET
GOFFER
GOITER
GOLDEN
GOLFER
GOOBER
GOOLEY
GOPHER
GORGED
GORGES
GORGET
GOSPEL
GOTTEN
GRABEN
GRACES
GRADED
GRADES
GRAPES
GRATED
GRATER
GRAVEL
GRAVEN
GRAVER
GRAVES
GRIMES
GRIPES
GROCER
GROPER
GROVEL
GROWER
GUIDES
GUINEA
GULLET
GULLEY
GULPER
GUMMED
GUNNEL
GUNNER
GUNTER
GURLET
GURNET
GURNEY
GUSHER
GUSSET
GUTTER
HACKEE
HACKER
HAGDEN
HAILER
HALLEY
HALTER
HALVED
HALVES
HAMLET
HAMMER
HAMPER
HANDEL
HANGER
HANKER
HAPPEN
HAPTEN
HARDEN
HARKEN
HARMED
HARVEY
HASHED
HASLET
HASTEN
HATRED
HATTER
HAWKED
HAWKER
HAWSER
HAYLEY
HEADED
HEADER
HEALER
HEAPED
HEARER
HEATED
HEATER
HEAVED
HEAVEN
HEAVES
HEBREW
HEEDED
HEELED
HEIFER
HELLER
HELMET

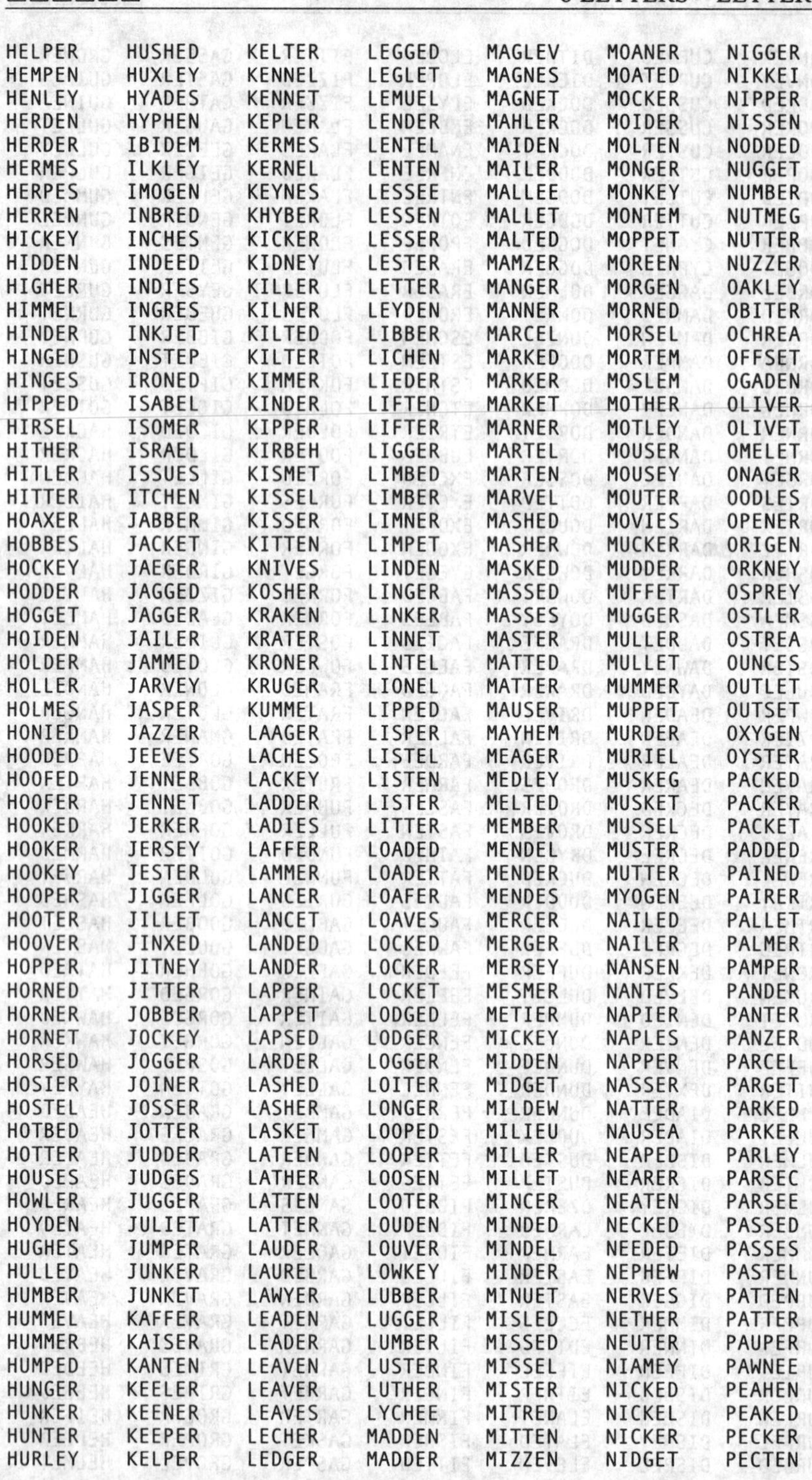

HELPER
HEMPEN
HENLEY
HERDEN
HERDER
HERMES
HERPES
HERREN
HICKEY
HIDDEN
HIGHER
HIMMEL
HINDER
HINGED
HINGES
HIPPED
HIRSEL
HITHER
HITLER
HITTER
HOAXER
HOBBES
HOCKEY
HODDER
HOGGET
HOIDEN
HOLDER
HOLLER
HOLMES
HONIED
HOODED
HOOFED
HOOFER
HOOKED
HOOKER
HOOKEY
HOOPER
HOOTER
HOOVER
HOPPER
HORNED
HORNER
HORNET
HORSED
HOSIER
HOSTEL
HOTBED
HOTTER
HOUSES
HOWLER
HOYDEN
HUGHES
HULLED
HUMBER
HUMMEL
HUMMER
HUMPED
HUNGER
HUNKER
HUNTER
HURLEY
HUSHED
HUXLEY
HYADES
HYPHEN
IBIDEM
ILKLEY
IMOGEN
INBRED
INCHES
INDEED
INDIES
INGRES
INKJET
INSTEP
IRONED
ISABEL
ISOMER
ISRAEL
ISSUES
ITCHEN
JABBER
JACKET
JAEGER
JAGGED
JAGGER
JAILER
JAMMED
JARVEY
JASPER
JAZZER
JEEVES
JENNER
JENNET
JERKER
JERSEY
JESTER
JIGGER
JILLET
JINXED
JITNEY
JITTER
JOBBER
JOCKEY
JOGGER
JOINER
JOSSER
JOTTER
JUDDER
JUDGES
JUGGER
JULIET
JUMPER
JUNKER
JUNKET
KAFFER
KAISER
KANTEN
KEELER
KEENER
KEEPER
KELPER
KELTER
KENNEL
KENNET
KEPLER
KERMES
KERNEL
KEYNES
KHYBER
KICKER
KIDNEY
KILLER
KILNER
KILTED
KILTER
KIMMER
KINDER
KIPPER
KIRBEH
KISMET
KISSEL
KISSER
KITTEN
KNIVES
KOSHER
KRAKEN
KRATER
KRONER
KRUGER
KUMMEL
LAAGER
LACHES
LACKEY
LADDER
LADIES
LAFFER
LAMMER
LANCER
LANCET
LANDED
LANDER
LAPPER
LAPPET
LAPSED
LARDER
LASHED
LASHER
LASKET
LATEEN
LATHER
LATTEN
LATTER
LAUDER
LAUREL
LAWYER
LEADEN
LEADER
LEAVEN
LEAVER
LEAVES
LECHER
LEDGER
LEGGED
LEGLET
LEMUEL
LENDER
LENTEL
LENTEN
LESSEE
LESSEN
LESSER
LESTER
LETTER
LEYDEN
LIBBER
LICHEN
LIEDER
LIFTED
LIFTER
LIGGER
LIMBED
LIMBER
LIMNER
LIMPET
LINDEN
LINGER
LINKER
LINNET
LINTEL
LIONEL
LIPPED
LISPER
LISTEL
LISTEN
LISTER
LITTER
LOADED
LOADER
LOAFER
LOAVES
LOCKED
LOCKER
LOCKET
LODGED
LODGER
LOGGER
LOITER
LONGER
LOOPED
LOOPER
LOOSEN
LOOTER
LOUDEN
LOUVER
LOWKEY
LUBBER
LUGGER
LUMBER
LUSTER
LUTHER
LYCHEE
MADDEN
MADDER
MAGLEV
MAGNES
MAGNET
MAHLER
MAIDEN
MAILER
MALLEE
MALLET
MALTED
MAMZER
MANGER
MANNER
MARCEL
MARKED
MARKER
MARKET
MARNER
MARTEL
MARTEN
MARVEL
MASHED
MASHER
MASKED
MASSED
MASSES
MASTER
MATTED
MATTER
MAUSER
MAYHEM
MEAGER
MEDLEY
MELTED
MEMBER
MENDEL
MENDER
MENDES
MERCER
MERGER
MERSEY
MESMER
METIER
MICKEY
MIDDEN
MIDGET
MILDEW
MILIEU
MILLER
MILLET
MINCER
MINDED
MINDEL
MINDER
MINUET
MISLED
MISSED
MISSEL
MISTER
MITRED
MITTEN
MIZZEN
MOANER
MOATED
MOCKER
MOIDER
MOLTEN
MONGER
MONKEY
MONTEM
MOPPET
MOREEN
MORGEN
MORNED
MORSEL
MORTEM
MOSLEM
MOTHER
MOTLEY
MOUSER
MOUSEY
MOUTER
MOVIES
MUCKER
MUDDER
MUFFET
MUGGER
MULLER
MULLET
MUMMER
MUPPET
MURDER
MURIEL
MUSKEG
MUSKET
MUSSEL
MUSTER
MUTTER
MYOGEN
NAILED
NAILER
NANSEN
NANTES
NAPIER
NAPLES
NAPPER
NASSER
NATTER
NAUSEA
NEAPED
NEARER
NEATEN
NECKED
NEEDED
NEPHEW
NERVES
NETHER
NEUTER
NIAMEY
NICKED
NICKEL
NICKER
NIDGET
NIGGER
NIKKEI
NIPPER
NISSEN
NODDED
NUGGET
NUMBER
NUTMEG
NUTTER
NUZZER
OAKLEY
OBITER
OCHREA
OFFSET
OGADEN
OLIVER
OLIVET
OMELET
ONAGER
OODLES
OPENER
ORIGEN
ORKNEY
OSPREY
OSTLER
OSTREA
OUNCES
OUTLET
OUTSET
OXYGEN
OYSTER
PACKED
PACKER
PACKET
PADDED
PAINED
PAIRER
PALLET
PALMER
PAMPER
PANDER
PANTER
PANZER
PARCEL
PARGET
PARKED
PARKER
PARLEY
PARSEC
PARSEE
PASSED
PASSES
PASTEL
PATTEN
PATTER
PAUPER
PAWNEE
PEAHEN
PEAKED
PECKER
PECTEN

PEDDER
PEELED
PEELER
PEEPER
PEEVED
PEEWEE
PEGLEG
PELLET
PELMET
PENCEL
PENTEL
PEPPER
PESTER
PETREL
PEWTER
PHLOEM
PHONEY
PHOOEY
PICKED
PICKER
PICKET
PIECES
PIGLET
PIGPEN
PILFER
PINCER
PINGER
PINTER
PIQUET
PISCES
PISSED
PITTED
PITTER
PLACED
PLACER
PLANET
PLATED
PLATEN
PLATER
PLATES
PLAYER
PLOVER
PLUMED
POCKET
POISED
POLDER
POLLED
POLLEN
POLLEX
POMMEL
POMPEY
PONDER
PONGEE
POOTER
POPPER
POPPET
PORKER
PORTER
POSSER
POSSET
POSTER
POTEEN
POTHER
POTTED
POTTER
POURER
POUTER
POWDER
POWTER
PRATER
PRAYER
PREFER
PRICED
PRICEY
PRIMED
PRIMER
PRIVET
PRIZES
PROLEG
PROPEL
PROPER
PROTEA
PROVEN
PRUNER
PUCKER
PUDSEY
PUFFED
PUFFER
PULLET
PULLEY
PULVER
PUMMEL
PUNNET
PUNTER
PUPPET
PURLER
PURSED
PURSER
PURVEY
PUSHER
PUSSER
PUTTEE
PUTTER
QUAKER
QUAVER
QUEBEC
QUIVER
QUOTED
RABBET
RABIES
RACHEL
RACKET
RAFTER
RAGGED
RAIDER
RAISED
RAISER
RAMJET
RANCEL
RANGER
RANKED
RANKER
RANTER
RAPIER
RAPPED
RAPPEL
RAPPER
RASHER
RASPER
RASTER
RATHER
RATTER
READER
REAMER
REAPER
REDDEN
REDEEM
REDLEG
REEFER
REELER
REFLET
REFLEX
REFUEL
REGLET
REGRET
REHEEL
RELIEF
RENDER
RENNET
RENTER
REOPEN
REUBEN
REUTER
REVIEW
RHODES
RHYMER
RIBBED
RICHES
RICKER
RICKEY
RIDGED
RIGGED
RIGGER
RIMMED
RINGED
RINGER
RIOTER
RIPPER
ROAMER
ROARER
ROBBED
ROBBER
ROCKER
ROCKET
RODNEY
ROEMER
ROGUES
ROLLER
ROMMEL
ROMNEY
RONDEL
ROOFER
ROOMER
ROOTED
ROOTER
ROQUET
ROSSER
ROSTER
ROTHER
ROTTEN
ROTTER
ROUGED
ROUTER
ROZZER
RUBBED
RUBBER
RUBIES
RUCHED
RUDDER
RUGGED
RUGGER
RUINED
RUMMER
RUNNEL
RUNNER
RUPEES
RUSHED
RUSSET
RUSTEM
RUTTED
RUTTER
SAANEN
SABRES
SACHET
SACRED
SADDEN
SALLEE
SALLET
SALVER
SAMIEL
SAMLET
SAMUEL
SANDER
SANSEI
SAPPER
SARSEN
SATEEN
SAUCER
SAUGER
SAVVEY
SAWDER
SAWNEY
SAWYER
SCALER
SCALES
SCARED
SCARER
SCHLEP
SCOLEX
SCORER
SCOTER
SCREED
SCREEN
SEABEE
SEALED
SEAMEN
SEAMER
SEATED
SECRET
SEEDED
SEEDER
SEEKER
SELFED
SELLER
SEMTEX
SENDER
SENNET
SENSED
SENSES
SEPTET
SEQUEL
SERIES
SERVER
SETTEE
SETTER
SÈVRES
SEXTET
SHADED
SHADES
SHAKEN
SHAKER
SHAKES
SHAPED
SHARED
SHARER
SHARES
SHAVEN
SHAVER
SHEKEL
SHINER
SHIVER
SHOVEL
SHOWER
SHRIEK
SICKEN
SICKER
SIDNEY
SIFTER
SIGNET
SILKEN
SILVER
SIMMER
SIMNEL
SIMPER
SINDER
SINGER
SINKER
SINNER
SIPPET
SIRREE
SISTER
SITREP
SITTER
SKATER
SKATES
SKEWED
SKEWER
SKIVER
SLATER
SLAVER
SLAVES
SLAYER
SLEWED
SLICER
SLIDER
SLIVER
SLOPES
SLOVEN
SMILER
SMILES
SMILEY
SMOKER
SMOKEY
SNAKED
SNIPER
SNIVEL
SNORER
SNOWED
SOAKED
SOCCER
SOCKET
SODDEN
SOFTEN
SOILED
SOIREE
SOLDER
SOLVED
SOLVER
SOMBER
SONNET
SOONER
SORBET
SORDES
SORREL
SORTER
SORTES
SOUPER
SOUSED
SOUTER
SOVIET
SOWSED
SOWTER
SPACED
SPACER
SPADES
SPICED
SPICER
SPIDER
SPIKED
SPINET
SPLEEN
SPOKEN
SPOKES
STAGER
STAGEY
STAKES
STAMEN
STAPES
STARES
STATED
STATEN
STATER
STATES
STAYER
STEREO
STEVEN
STEWED
STIPES
STOKER
STOKES
STOLEN
STONED
STONER
STONES
STORER
STOREY
STOVER
STOWER
STREET
STUMER
STYLET
SUBLET
SUBSET
SUCKEN
SUCKER
SUCKET
SUDDEN
SUFFER
SUITED
SUIVEZ
SULLEN
SUMMER
SUNDER
SUNDEW
SUNKEN
SUNSET
SUPLEX
SUPPER
SURFER
SURREY
SURVEY
SUSSEX
SUTLER
SUTTEE
SWANEE
SWEDEN
SWIPES
SWIVEL
SWIVET
SYDNEY
SYPHER
SYSTEM
TABLET
TACKET
TAIPEI
TALKER
TAMPER

TANDEM
TANKER
TANNED
TANNER
TAPPER
TAPPET
TARCEL
TARGET
TARSEL
TASSEL
TASSET
TASTER
TATLER
TATTER
TAUTEN
TEASEL
TEASER
TECKEL
TEEPEE
TEETER
TEGMEN
TELLER
TEMPER
TENDER
TENNER
TERCET
TERMES
TESTER
TESTES
TETHER
THALER
THALES
THAMES
THANET
THEBES
THROES
TICKER
TICKET
TICKEY
TIERED
TILLER
TIMBER
TINDER
TINGED
TINKER
TINNED
TINSEL
TINTED
TIPPED
TIPPER
TIPPET
TITFER
TITLED
TITTER
TOFFEE
TOGGED
TOILET
TOLLED
TOLLER
TOLTEC
TOLZEY
TOOTER
TOPPER
TORRES
TOSHER
TOTTER
TOUPEE
TOUPET
TOURER
TOUSER
TOWHEE
TOWNEE
TOWSER
TRACER
TRADER
TRADES
TRALEE
TRAPES
TRAVEL
TRIBES
TRIVET
TROVER
TROWEL
TROYES
TUAREG
TUCKER
TUCKET
TUFFET
TUFTED
TUNNEL
TUREEN
TURKEY
TURNED
TURNER
TURRET
TURVES
TUSKER
TWICER
TWINED
ULSTER
UMBLES
UMBREL
UNBRED
UNDIES
UNDYED
UNEVEN
UNISEX
UNITED
UNMEET
UNREEL
UNSEEN
UNUSED
UPKEEP
URETER
USURER
VALLEY
VALUER
VARIED
VARLET
VATHEK
VEILED
VEINED
VELVET
VENDEE
VENDER
VENEER
VERGER
VERGES
VERSED
VERSES
VERSET
VERVET
VESPER
VESSEL
VESTED
VIEWER
VIOLET
VISIER
VIVIEN
VIZIER
VOICED
VOIDED
VOIDEE
VOIDER
VOLLEY
VORTEX
VOSGES
WACKER
WAFTED
WAGNER
WAILER
WAITER
WAIVER
WALKER
WALLED
WALLER
WALLET
WALTER
WANDER
WANKEL
WANTED
WARDEN
WARDER
WARMER
WARNER
WARPED
WARREN
WASHED
WASHER
WASTED
WASTEL
WASTER
WEAKEN
WEAKER
WEARER
WEASEL
WEAVER
WEBBED
WEDDED
WEDGED
WEEWEE
WELDER
WELLER
WELLES
WELTER
WESKER
WESLEY
WESSEX
WETHER
WHALER
WHALES
WHITED
WHITEN
WHITES
WICKED
WICKER
WICKET
WIDGET
WIENER
WILDER
WILLED
WILLET
WIMSEY
WINDER
WINGED
WINGER
WINKER
WINNER
WINTER
WISDEN
WISHES
WITHER
WITTED
WIZIER
WONDER
WONTED
WOODED
WOODEN
WOOFER
WOOKEY
WOOLEN
WORKED
WORKER
WORSEN
WOWSER
WRITER
XAVIER
XERXES
YABBER
YAHWEH
YAKKER
YAMMER
YANKEE
YANKER
YATTER
YEOMEN
YESTER
YIPPEE
YONDER
YORKER
YUCKER
ZAGREB
ZANDER
ZIMMER
ZINGER
ZIPPER
ZITHER
ZONKED
ZOSTER
BOURÉE
CORVÉE
DONNÉE
PENSÉE
ADRIFT
BEREFT
BOUFFE
BRIEFS
CARAFE
CHUFFY
CLIFFS
CODIFY
CUTOFF
DECAFF
FAROFF
FLUFFY
LAYOFF
MODIFY
MUNIFY
NIDIFY
NOTIFY
OSSIFY
PACIFY
PAYOFF
PIAFFE
PILAFF
POUFFE
PURIFY
RAMIFY
RAREFY
RATIFY
REBUFF
RECIFE
RIPOFF
RUNOFF
SCRUFF
SHRIFT
SHROFF
SNIFFY
SPLIFF
STAFFA
STRAFE
STRIFE
STUFFY
TARIFF
THRIFT
TIPOFF
TUMEFY
TYPIFY
UNSAFE
UPLIFT
VERIFY
VILIFY
WHARFE
ABREGE
AGRÉGÉ
ALBUGO
ALLEGE
AMBAGE
ARMAGH
ASSIGN
AURIGA
AVENGE
BARÈGE
BELUGA
BENIGN
BLUDGE
BOCAGE
BODEGA
BORAGE
BRIDGE
CHANGE
CHARGE
CHOUGH
CIERGE
CLAGGY
CLERGY
CLOUGH
COWAGE
CRAGGY
CREAGH
CRINGE
CUBAGE
DAMAGE
DÉGAGÉ
DELUGE
DESIGN
DOINGS
DOSAGE
DOTAGE
DREDGE
DREGGY
DRONGO
DRUDGE
EATAGE
EFFIGY
ELOIGN
EMERGE
EMULGE
EMUNGE
ENERGY
ENGAGE
ENOUGH
ENRAGE
ENSIGN
EULOGY
EXPUGN
FLAGGY
FLANGE
FLEDGE
FORAGE
FOREGO
FRIDGE
FRIGGA
FRINGE
GARAGE
GAVAGE
GEORGE
GINKGO
GIORGI
GRANGE
GRINGO
GROGGY
GRUDGE
GRUNGE
HIDAGE
HOMAGE
IMPUGN
INDIGN
INDIGO
KLUDGE
KNAGGY
LADOGA
LANUGO
LAVAGE
LOUNGE
LOVAGE
MALAGA
MALIGN
MANAGE
MANEGE
MENAGE
METAGE
MIRAGE
MURAGE
NONAGE
OBLIGE
OPPUGN
ORANGE
ORTEGA
OTALGY
OUTAGE
PHLEGM
PILAGE
PLEDGE
PLONGE
PLOUGH
PLUNGE
QUAGGA
QUAIGH
QUANGO
RAVAGE
REFUGE
RENEGE
REPUGN
RESIGN
RIVAGE
SAVAGE
SCUNGE
SEWAGE
SHAGGY
SILAGE
SLANGY
SLEDGE
SLEIGH
SLOUGH
SLUDGE
SMUDGE

SMUDGY
SNAGGY
SNUDGE
SOCAGE
SORAGE
SPONGE
SPONGY
SPUNGE
SPURGE
STINGO
STINGY
STODGE
STODGY
STOOGE
STREGA
SWINGE
SYZYGY
TELEGA
TELEGU
TELUGU
THINGS
THINGY
THOUGH
TOBAGO
TOWAGE
TRIAGE
TROUGH
TRUDGE
TWIGGY
TWINGE
ULLAGE
UNCAGE
VIRAGO
VISAGE
VOLAGE
VOYAGE
WHINGE
AGATHA
ALIGHT
APACHE
APATHY
APHTHA
AYESHA
BACCHI
BEACHY
BEEGHA
BERTHA
BERTHE
BITCHY
BLIGHT
BLITHE
BOLSHY
BOUCHE
BOUGHT
BRECHT
BRIGHT
BUDDHA
BUKSHI
BUNCHY
BURKHA
CATCHY
CAUGHT
CHICHI
CLICHÉ
CLOCHE
CLOTHE
CONCHA
CONCHY
CRÈCHE
CROCHE
CUTCHA
DAISHO
DELPHI
DEPTHS
DINGHY
DOUCHE
DOUGHY
DRACHM
EARTHY
ELISHA
ELTCHI
FILTHY
FLASHY
FLECHE
FLESHY
FLIGHT
FLUSHY
FORTHY
FOUGHT
FRIGHT
FROTHY
FURPHY
GANDHI
GAUCHE
GAUCHO
GEISHA
GOETHE
GUNGHO
GURKHA
HEIGHT
HONCHO
HONSHU
KANTHA
KNIGHT
KWACHA
KYUSHU
LITCHI
LOATHE
LORCHA
LOUCHE
MANCHE
MANCHU
MARSHY
MARTHA
MONTHS
MUNSHI
MURPHY
MURRHA
NAUGHT
NAVAHO
NOUGHT
OBECHE
ORACHE
PATCHY
PLIGHT
PONCHO
PSYCHE
PSYCHO
PUNCHY
PYRRHO
QUICHE
RANCHO
RHAPHE
RHYTHM
ROUGHY
SADDHU
SAITHE
SANCHO
SAPPHO
SCATHE
SCYTHE
SEETHE
SEICHE
SHTCHI
SIDDHA
SLIGHT
SLITHY
SLOSHY
SLUSHY
SMIGHT
SMITHS
SMITHY
SOOTHE
SORGHO
SOUGHT
SPATHE
SULPHA
SWATHE
TAUGHT
TEETHE
TETCHY
TITCHY
TOOTHY
TOUCHE
TOUCHY
TRASHY
TROCHE
TROPHE
TROPHY
TRUTHS
TWIGHT
WEIGHT
WHISHT
WORTHY
WRIGHT
WRITHE
ABELIA
ABSEIL
ABULIA
ACACIA
ACADIA
ACARID
ACEDIA
ACETIC
ACIDIC
ACQUIT
ADAGIO
ADJOIN
ADONIS
ADROIT
AENEID
AEOLIC
AEOLIS
AFFAIR
AFRAID
AGADIR
AGARIC
AGLAIA
AGNAIL
AGONIC
ALALIA
ALARIC
ALBEIT
ALDRIN
ALEXIA
ALEXIN
ALEXIS
ALMAIN
ALOGIA
ALTAIR
AMELIA
ANEMIA
ANEMIC
ANGLIA
ANOXIA
ANOXIC
ANTLIA
ANTRIM
ANUBIS
APORIA
ARABIA
ARABIC
ARABIS
ARALIA
ARAMIS
ARCHIE
ARCHIL
ARCTIC
ARMPIT
ASSAIL
ASSOIL
ATAXIA
ATAXIC
ATOCIA
ATOMIC
ATONIC
ATTAIN
AUNTIE
AUSSIE
AUSTIN
AZOTIC
BABBIT
BAFFIN
BAGNIO
BAGUIO
BAILIE
BALKIS
BALTIC
BANDIT
BARKIS
BARRIE
BARRIO
BAUCIS
BEANIE
BEDSIT
BEMOIL
BERLIN
BERTIE
BESSIE
BESTIR
BEWAIL
BIFFIN
BIGGIN
BIGWIG
BILLIE
BIONIC
BIOPIC
BIOTIC
BIOTIN
BIRDIE
BOBBIN
BOBWIG
BODGIE
BODKIN
BOFFIN
BONNIE
BONXIE
BOOGIE
BOOKIE
BORGIA
BOTHIE
BOVRIL
BRAZIL
BREWIS
BRIDIE
BUDGIE
BULBIL
BUSKIN
BYRNIE
CABBIE
CACCIA
CADDIE
CADDIS
CALAIS
CALKIN
CALLID
CALVIN
CAMAIL
CANDID
CAPSID
CARLIN
CASEIN
CASSIA
CASSIO
CASSIS
CATKIN
CATNIP
CAVEIN
CEDRIC
CELTIC
CERVIX
CHEMIC
CHERIE
CHESIL
CHITIN
CHOPIN
CITRIC
CITRIN
CLAVIS
CLERIC
CLINIC
CLONIC
CLOVIS
COCCID
COCHIN
COFFIN
COLLIE
COMFIT
COMMIS
COMMIT
COOKIE
COOLIE
COOTIE
COPPIN
COPTIC
CORBIE
CORRIE
COSMIC
COSSIE
COULIS
COUSIN
COWRIE
CRASIS
CREDIT
CRETIC
CRETIN
CRISIS
CRITIC
CUFFIN
CULLIS
CUMMIN
CURRIE
CYANIN
CYBRID
CYCLIC
CYESIS
CYMRIC
CYPRID
CYPRIS
CYSTIC
CYTOID
DACOIT
DAFTIE
DAHLIA
DAIMIO
DAMMIT
DANZIG
DARKIE
DARWIN
DEARIE
DEBRIS
DECEIT
DEMAIN
DENNIS
DERAIL
DERAIN
DERMIS
DERRIS
DETAIL
DETAIN
DEVOID
DIESIS
DIKDIK
DIMWIT
DIOXIN
DISTIL
DIZAIN
DOBBIN
DOMAIN
DORRIT
DROMIO
DUBBIN
DUBLIN
DUCKIE
DUNLIN
DYADIC
EARWIG
ECLAIR
ECURIE
EGERIA
ELICIT
ELIXIR
ELOHIM
EMBAIL
EMETIC
ENJOIN
ENOSIS
ENTAIL
EPULIS
EREMIC
EROTIC
ESPRIT
ETHNIC
EUCLID
EXOTIC
EYELID
FABRIC
FARCIN
FASCIA
FEERIE
FERRIS
FERVID
FILLIP
FIRKIN
FIZGIG
FLORID
FLORIN

FOETID
FORBID
FORMIC
FORNIX
FORPIT
FOSSIL
FRIGID
FROLIC
FULFIL
FULGID
FUSAIN
FUSTIC
GADOID
GAELIC
GAIJIN
GALLIC
GALLIO
GAMBIA
GAMBIT
GARLIC
GAWAIN
GERBIL
GILLIE
GILPIN
GIRKIN
GIRLIE
GLACIS
GLAMIS
GLORIA
GNOMIC
GOALIE
GOBLIN
GODWIN
GODWIT
GOOGIE
GOOLIE
GORGIA
GORGIO
GOSSIP
GOTHIC
GRAFIN
GRATIN
GRATIS
GRAVID
HACHIS
HAGGIS
HALOID
HANKIE
HAPTIC
HARPIC
HARRIS
HAWAII
HECTIC
HENBIT
HENNIN
HEREIN
HERMIT
HERNIA
HEROIC
HEROIN
HISPID
HOGTIE
HORRID
HOTAIR
HOWDIE
HUBRIS
HUGHIE
HUSSIF
HYBRID
HYBRIS
HYDRIA
HYPNIC
IAMBIC
IBERIA
ICONIC
IMPAIR
INLAID
INSTIL
IRAQIS
IRONIC
ISCHIA
ISTRIA
ITALIC
JERKIN
JESUIT
JOPLIN
JOSKIN
JUNKIE
JUSTIN
KAFFIR
KALMIA
KAOLIN
KELOID
KELPIE
KELTIC
KELTIE
KELVIN
KEPHIR
KERMIS
KETMIR
KEWPIE
KHALIF
KHARIF
KHILIM
KIDDIE
KILTIE
KOOKIE
LACTIC
LADDIE
LANCIA
LARKIN
LASSIE
LATVIA
LAURIC
LAURIE
LENTIC
LENTIL
LEONID
LESLIE
LIEBIG
LIMBIC
LIMPID
LIQUID
LITHIA
LIZZIE
LOCHIA
LOGGIA
LOONIE
LOURIE
LUBRIC
LUDWIG
LUTEIN
MADRID
MAFFIA
MAGGIE
MAGPIE
MAJLIS
MANNIN
MANTIS
MAQUIS
MARGIN
MARLIN
MARTIN
MASHIE
MASLIN
MASSIF
MASTIC
MATHIS
MATRIX
MAWKIN
MEALIE
MEANIE
MEGRIM
MEJLIS
MEMOIR
MENDIP
MENHIR
MERCIA
MERKIN
MERLIN
MERRIE
MESAIL
METRIC
MINNIE
MISFIT
MISHIT
MISSIS
MOGGIE
MOHAIR
MOLLIE
MORBID
MORRIS
MOSAIC
MOUJIK
MOULIN
MUCOID
MUFFIN
MURLIN
MURRIN
MUSLIM
MUSLIN
MUZHIK
MYELIN
MYOPIA
MYOPIC
MYOSIN
MYOSIS
MYSTIC
NANKIN
NAPKIN
NASTIC
NELLIE
NEREID
NERVII
NESSIE
NIACIN
NITRIC
NITWIT
NOGGIN
NOOKIE
NORDIC
NORVIC
NUBBIN
NUDNIK
NUNCIO
OBTAIN
OGAMIC
OILRIG
OLEFIN
OLIVIA
ONEDIN
ONEGIN
OOKPIK
ORCHID
ORCHIS
ORDAIN
OREXIS
ORIGIN
ORPHIC
OSIRIS
OTITIS
OUTBID
OUTFIT
OUTLIE
OUTVIE
OUTWIT
OXALIC
OXALIS
OXTAIL
PALAIS
PALLID
PANDIT
PARDIE
PARKIN
PARVIS
PASSIM
PASTIL
PASTIS
PATHIC
PATOIS
PAYNIM
PECTIN
PEEWIT
PELOID
PELVIC
PELVIS
PENCIL
PEPTIC
PERKIN
PERMIT
PÉTAIN
PHASIS
PHILIP
PHOBIA
PHOBIC
PHONIC
PHYSIC
PHYSIO
PICNIC
PIDGIN
PIERIS
PINKIE
PINXIT
PINYIN
PIPKIN
PIPPIN
PISTIL
PLACID
POETIC
POMMIE
PONGID
PONTIC
POPLIN
POPPIT
PORGIE
PORTIA
POSTIL
POWNIE
PRAXIS
PRECIS
PREFIX
PRELIM
PREVIN
PROBIT
PROFIT
PROLIX
PROSIT
PTERIN
PTERIS
PTOSIS
PUBLIC
PUFFIN
PULPIT
PUNDIT
PURLIN
PUTOIS
PUTRID
PYTHIA
RABBIT
RACHIS
RAFFIA
RAISIN
RANCID
RAPHIA
RAZZIA
REALIA
RECOIL
REEKIE
REGAIN
REJOIN
REMAIN
RENNIN
RENOIR
REPAID
REPAIR
RETAIL
RETAIN
RHEXIS
RIVLIN
ROADIE
ROOKIE
ROSCID
RUBRIC
RUMKIN
RUSKIN
RUSSIA
RUSTIC
SALMIS
SALVIA
SARNIE
SAURIA
SAVOIE
SCENIC
SCIPIO
SCORIA
SCOTIA
SEISIN
SEPSIS
SEPTIC
SEQUIN
SERAIL
SERBIA
SHARIA
SHARIF
SHERIF
SIKKIM
SIMKIN
SISKIN
SOBEIT
SOFFIT
SOFTIE
SOLEIL
SOPHIA
SORDID
SORTIE
SPADIX
SPAVIN
SPECIE
SPIRIT
SPRAIN
SQUAIL
STALIN
STASIS
STATIC
STERIC
STOGIE
STOLID
STRAIN
STRAIT
STUDIO
STUPID
STYMIE
SUBMIT
SUFFIX
SUMMIT
SUNLIT
SWABIA
SYLVIA
SYNDIC
TACTIC
TAENIA
TALKIE
TALLIS
TANKIA
TANNIC
TANNIN
TAPPIT
TARDIS
TARSIA
TASSIE
TAWPIE
TENNIS
TENPIN
TERCIO
TERTIA
TESTIS
TETTIX
THALIA
THEMIS
THESIS
THETIC
THETIS
TIDBIT
TIEPIN
TIFFIN
TIGRIS
TILSIT
TINNIE
TINTIN
TITBIT
TMESIS
TOCSIN
TOLUIC
TONSIL
TORPID
TORRID
TOTTIE
TRAGIC
TRAVIS
TRIVIA
TROPIC
TUGRIK
TURBID
TURGID
TURNIP
TURPIN
TUSSIS

TWCBIT
UGARIT
ULITIS
UMBRIA
UMBRIL
UNCOIL
UNFAIR
UNGAIN
UNPAID
UNSAID
UNVEIL
URANIA
URANIC
URCHIN
UTOPIA
VECTIS
VENTIL
VERDIN
VEREIN
VERMIN
VERMIS
VIBRIO
VICTIM
VIOLIN
VIRGIL
VIRGIN
VISCID
WEEPIE
WEEVIL
WELKIN
WELLIE
WILLIE
WINNIE
WITHIN
WOODIE
WREKIN
XYLOID
YARDIE
YUPPIE
ZAFTIG
ZAMBIA
ZENDIK
ZINNIA
ZOMBIE
NAVAJO
ADSUKI
ALASKA
BAMAKO
BELIKE
BETAKE
BLACKS
BLINKS
BLOCKS
BRICKS
BROOKE
BROOKS
CHALKY
CHAPKA
CHEEKY
CHUKKA
CHUNKY
CLERKS
CLOAKS
CRANKY
CREAKY
CROAKY
CROCKS
CZAPKA
DECOKE
DROSKY
EUREKA
FLANKS
FLICKS
FLUNKY
FRISKY
GINGKO
GLINKA
GREEKS
INTAKE
INVOKE
KABAKA
KABUKI
KANAKA
KAZAKH
LADAKH
LUSAKA
MARKKA
PERUKE
PLANKS
PLUCKY
PRANKS
QUIRKY
REBUKE
REMAKE
RETAKE
REVOKE
ROTHKO
RUBIKS
SALUKI
SHANKS
SHEIKH
SHIPKA
SHRIKE
SLACKS
SLEEKY
SLINKY
SMACKS
SNEAKY
SPARKS
SPARKY
SPLAKE
SPOOKY
STACKS
STALKS
STALKY
STICKS
STICKY
STINKO
STINKS
STOCKS
STOCKY
STOOKS
STRAKE
STRIKE
STROKE
SWANKY
TENGKU
THANKS
THICKY
TRICKS
TRICKY
TROIKA
TRUNKS
UNLIKE
UNYOKE
UPTAKE
WHACKO
WHACKY
WHISKY
YOICKS
AEDILE
AFIELD
AIRILY
ALKALI
ALLELE
ANCILE
ANGELA
ANGELS
ANGOLA
ANKOLE
ANNALS
ANSELM
APOLLO
APPALL
AQUILA
ARABLE
AREOLA
AREOLE
ARGYLE
ARGYLL
ARNOLD
AROLLA
ATTILA
AUDILE
AVIDLY
AWHILE
AXILLA
AZOLLA
BABBLE
BAFFLE
BAILLY
BALDLY
BANGLE
BARELY
BASALT
BATTLE
BAUBLE
BEADLE
BEAGLE
BECALM
BEETLE
BEFALL
BEHALF
BEHELD
BEHOLD
BEZZLE
BIFOLD
BOBBLE
BODILY
BOGGLE
BOLDLY
BOODLE
BOOTLE
BOTTLE
BOUCLÉ
BOULLE
BOWELS
BRIDLE
BROLLY
BUBBLE
BUBBLY
BUCKLE
BUMALO
BUMBLE
BUNDLE
BUNGLE
BURBLE
BURGLE
BUSILY
BUSTLE
CABALE
CACKLE
CAGILY
CAJOLE
CALMLY
CANDLE
CANTLE
CASTLE
CATTLE
CAUDLE
CAVELL
CECILS
CEDULA
CHICLE
CHILLI
CHILLY
CICALA
CICELY
CIRCLE
COBALT
COBBLE
COCKLE
CODDLE
COLDLY
COMBLE
COMELY
COMPLY
COOLLY
CORALS
COSILY
COSTLY
COTYLE
COUPLE
CRADLE
CRAPLE
CREOLE
CRIBLE
CRUELS
CUDDLE
CUDDLY
CUPOLA
CUPULE
CURDLE
CURTLY
CURULE
CUTTLE
CYBELE
DABBLE
DADDLE
DAGGLE
DANDLE
DANGLE
DAPPLE
DARGLE
DARKLY
DARTLE
DAWDLE
DAZZLE
DEADLY
DEARLY
DEBILE
DECKLE
DEEPLY
DEFILE
DEFTLY
DEVILS
DEWALI
DIBBLE
DIDDLE
DIMPLE
DINGLE
DINGLY
DIPOLE
DIVALI
DIWALI
DOCILE
DODDLE
DONGLE
DOODLE
DOTTLE
DOUBLE
DOUBLY
DOURLY
DUFFLE
DUMBLY
DUMPLE
DUNELM
EASILY
ECBOLE
EDIBLE
EERILY
EMBALE
EMBALM
ENABLE
ENCALM
ENFOLD
ENGELS
ENGULF
ENROLL
ENSILE
EPAULE
EQUALS
EVENLY
EXHALE
EXTOLL
FACILE
FAIBLE
FAIRLY
FAMILY
FANGLE
FARDLE
FAVELA
FECULA
FEEBLE
FEEBLY
FEMALE
FERULA
FERULE
FETTLE
FIBULA
FICKLE
FIDDLE
FIDDLY
FINALE
FINELY
FIPPLE
FIRMLY
FIZZLE
FLATLY
FOCSLE
FOIBLE
FONDLE
FONDLY
FOOTLE
FOOZLE
FOULLY
FREELY
FRILLS
FRILLY
FUDDLE
FUMBLE
FUSELI
FUTILE
FUZZLE
GABBLE
GADFLY
GAGGLE
GAINLY
GAMBLE
GAMELY
GANGLY
GARBLE
GARGLE
GENTLE
GENTLY
GIGGLE
GIGOLO
GIRDLE
GLADLY
GLIBLY
GOBBLE
GOGGLE
GOODLY
GOOGLE
GOOGLY
GRILLE
GRIMLY
GRISLY
GUGGLE
GURGLE
GUTTLE
GUZZLE
HABILE
HACKLE
HAGGLE
HAMBLE
HANDLE
HARDLY
HAROLD
HASSLE
HAZILY
HECKLE
HERALD
HIGHLY
HOBBLE
HOMELY
HOMILY
HOOPLA
HOURLY
HUBBLE
HUCKLE
HUDDLE
HUGELY
HUMBLE
HURDLE
HURTLE
HUSTLE
ICICLE
IMPALA
IMPALE
INFOLD
INGULF
INHALE
INSOLE
INSULA
INSULT
IRWELL
ISEULT
ITSELF
JABBLE
JANGLE
JEKYLL
JEWELS
JIGGLE
JINGLE
JOGGLE
JOSTLE

JUGGLE
JUMBLE
JUNGLE
JUSTLY
KABELE
KABYLE
KEBELE
KEENLY
KERALA
KETTLE
KIBBLE
KIDDLE
KIGALI
KINDLE
KINDLY
KINGLY
KIRTLE
KITTLE
LABILE
LAMELY
LASTLY
LATELY
LAZILY
LEWDLY
LIABLE
LIGULA
LIKELY
LIMPLY
LITTLE
LIVELY
LOCALE
LOCULE
LONELY
LORDLY
LOUDLY
LOVELL
LOVELY
LOWELL
LOYOLA
LUNULE
MACULA
MACULE
MAINLY
MANGLE
MANILA
MANTLE
MARBLE
MAYFLY
MEANLY
MEASLY
MEDDLE
MEEKLY
MERELY
METTLE
MICKLE
MIDDLE
MILDLY
MINGLE
MIZZLE
MOBILE
MODELS

MODULE
MORALE
MORALS
MOSTLY
MOTILE
MOTTLE
MOZZLE
MUCKLE
MUDDLE
MUESLI
MUFFLE
MUMBLE
MURALS
MUSCLE
MUTELY
MUZZLE
MYGALE
MYRTLE
MYSELF
NAMELY
NAPALM
NEARLY
NEATLY
NEBULA
NEBULE
NEEDLE
NEPALI
NEROLI
NESTLE
NETTLE
NEWELL
NIBBLE
NICELY
NIELLO
NIGGLE
NIGGLY
NIMBLE
NIMBLY
NIPPLE
NOBBLE
NODDLE
NODULE
NOODLE
NOSILY
NOZZLE
NUBBLE
NUBILE
NUCULE
NUMBLY
NUZZLE
OCCULT
OPENLY
ORACLE
ORALLY
ORIOLE
ORMOLU
ORWELL
OSWALD
OTELLO
OUNDLE
OURALI

OVERLY
PADDLE
PAELLA
PAMELA
PAPULE
PAROLE
PARTLY
PAYOLA
PEARLS
PEARLY
PEBBLE
PEBBLY
PEDALO
PEDDLE
PEOPLE
PERILS
PESTLE
PHYLLO
PICKLE
PIDDLE
PIFFLE
PIMPLE
PIMPLY
PINTLE
POBBLE
POMELO
POODLE
POORLY
PORTLY
POTTLE
PRIMLY
PUDDLE
PUEBLO
PURELY
PURPLE
PUZZLE
RABBLE
RADDLE
RADULA
RAFALE
RAFFLE
RAGGLE
RAMBLE
RANKLE
RANULA
RAPTLY
RARELY
RASHLY
RATTLE
RAZZLE
REALLY
RECALL
REFILL
REGALE
REGULO
RESALE
RESULT
REVILE
REVOLT
RIBALD
RIBBLE

RICHLY
RIDDLE
RIFFLE
RIPPLE
ROOTLE
ROTULA
ROUBLE
ROYALS
RUBBLE
RUCKLE
RUDDLE
RUDELY
RUELLE
RUFFLE
RUMBLE
RUMPLE
RUNDLE
RUSTLE
SABELE
SADDLE
SAFELY
SAGELY
SAMPLE
SANELY
SAPELE
SCILLA
SCILLY
SCROLL
SCYLLA
SEEMLY
SEMELE
SENILE
SETTLE
SEWELL
SHEILA
SHIELD
SHOULD
SHRILL
SICILY
SICKLE
SICKLY
SIFFLE
SIMILE
SIMPLE
SIMPLY
SINGLE
SINGLY
SIPPLE
SIZZLE
SKELLY
SLOWLY
SMALLS
SMELLY
SMUGLY
SNAILY
SNUGLY
SOFTLY
SOLELY
SOMALI
SORELL
SORELY

SOUPLE
SOURLY
SOZZLE
SPAULD
SPOILS
SPOILT
SPRYLY
SQUALL
SQUILL
STABLE
STABLY
STALLS
STAPLE
STEELE
STEELY
STIFLE
STOOLS
STROLL
SUBTLE
SUBTLY
SUCKLE
SUPPLE
SUPPLY
SURELY
TABULA
TACKLE
TAIGLE
TAILLE
TAMALE
TAMELY
TANGLE
TARTLY
TATTLE
TAUTLY
TEGULA
TEMPLE
TERMLY
THINLY
THRALL
THRILL
TICKLE
TICKLY
TIDDLE
TIDDLY
TIDILY
TIMELY
TINGLE
TINKLE
TIPPLE
TIPULA
TITTLE
TITULE
TIVOLI
TODDLE
TOGGLE
TOOTLE
TOPPLE
TOUSLE
TOWNLY
TREBLE
TREBLY

TRIFLE
TRIMLY
TRIPLE
TUBULE
TUILLE
TUMBLE
TUMULT
TUPELO
TURTLE
TUSSLE
TUVALU
TWIRLY
TYBALT
UNABLE
UNBOLT
UNDULY
UNFOLD
UNGULA
UNHOLY
UNROLL
UNRULY
UNSOLD
UNTOLD
UNWELL
UPHELD
UPHILL
UPHOLD
URSULA
USABLE
VAINLY
VASTLY
VERILY
VIABLE
VILELY
VIRILE
VITALS
VOWELS
WADDLE
WAFFLE
WAGGLE
WAMBLE
WANDLE
WANGLE
WARBLE
WARILY
WARMLY
WATTLE
WAVELL
WEAKLY
WEEKLY
WHEELS
WHEELY
WHOLLY
WIDELY
WIFELY
WIGGLE
WIGGLY
WILDLY
WIMBLE
WIMPLE
WINKLE

WISELY
WOBBLE
WOBBLY
WOOLLY
WORTLE
YAFFLE
YEARLY
ABROMA
AFLAME
ANCOME
APLOMB
ASSUME
ASTHMA
AUTUMN
BECAME
BECOME
BELAMY
BENAME
BENUMB
BETIME
BIGAMY
BIREME
BRAHMA
BRAHMS
BREGMA
BULIMY
CALIMA
CAREME
CHEMMY
CHROMA
CHROME
CHROMO
CHUMMY
CINEMA
CLAIMS
CLAMMY
COLUMN
CREAMY
CRUMMY
DECAMP
DÉCIME
DEFAME
DENIMS
DHARMA
DODOMA
DREAMY
DYNAMO
ECZEMA
ENCAMP
ENIGMA
ENTOMB
ENZYME
ESKIMO
EXHUME
FATIMA
GAZUMP
GENOME
GLIOMA
GLOOMY
GRAMME
GRAMMY

GRIMMS
HEAUME
INCOME
INFAME
INFAMY
INHUME
INTIME
JEMIMA
JEREMY
JEROME
LEGUME
LEXEME
LIPOMA
MADAME
MAXIMS
MAZUMA
MIASMA
OEDEMA
ONCOME
OPTIMA
OPTIME
PANAMA
PARAMO
PHASMA
PLASMA
PLUMMY
PNEUMA
PRISMS
QUALMS
RACEME
REGIME
RENAME
RESUME
REVAMP
RHEIMS
RHEUMY
SALAMI
SALOME
SCHEMA
SCHEME
SCRAMB
SCRIMP
SCUMMY
SESAME
SHAMMY
SHIMMY
SHRIMP
SLUMMY
SMARMY
SMEGMA
SODOMY
SOLEMN
SQUAMA
STEAMY
STEMMA
STIGMA
STORMY
TACOMA
TATAMI
TAXEME
THERMO
TRAUMA
ULTIMA
ULTIMO
VOLUME
WHAMMY
XEROMA
ZEUGMA
ZYGOMA
AARONS
ABOUND
ABSENT
ACCEND
ACCENT
ACHENE
ACHING
ACORNS
ACTING
ADDEND
ADVENE
ADVENT
AEGINA
AGEING
AIDANT
AILING
AIRING
ALBANY
ALBINO
ALCINA
ALDINE
ALKANE
ALKENE
ALMOND
ALPINE
ALPINO
ALUMNI
AMOUNT
ANCONA
ANGINA
ANOINT
ANTONY
ANYONE
APHONY
APPEND
ARCANA
ARCANE
ARDENT
ARGENT
AROINT
AROUND
ARPENT
ARRANT
ARSÈNE
ARSINE
ASCEND
ASCENT
ASHINE
ASKING
ASLANT
ASSENT
ASTONE
ATHENE
ATHENS
ATKINS
ATTEND
ATTONE
ATTUNE
AVAUNT
AVERNO
AWNING
BAKING
BANANA
BARING
BEAUNE
BEGONE
BEHIND
BELONG
BERING
BESANT
BETONY
BEYOND
BEZANT
BIDENT
BIKINI
BITING
BLENNY
BODONI
BOEING
BOHUNK
BORING
BOSUNS
BOTANY
BOURNE
BOVINE
BOXING
BRAINS
BRAINY
BRAWNY
BRIAND
BRIONY
BROWNE
BRYANT
BRYONY
BUSONI
BUTANE
BUTENE
BUYING
BYGONE
BYLINE
CANINE
CANING
CAPONE
CARINA
CARING
CASING
CASINO
CEMENT
CHAINS
CHOANA
CLIENT
CODING
COGENT
COLONY
COMING
COOING
COPING
CORONA
COSINE
COVENT
COVING
CRANNY
CREANT
CRIANT
CRYING
CYRANO
CYRENE
DAPHNE
DARING
DATING
DEBUNK
DECANE
DECANI
DECANT
DECENT
DEDANS
DEFEND
DEFINE
DEMAND
DEMENT
DEPEND
DEPONE
DETENT
DETENU
DINING
DIVINE
DIVING
DJINNI
DOCENT
DOESNT
DOLINA
DOLINE
DOMINO
DOTING
DOUANE
DOZENS
DOZING
DRYING
DUENNA
DUGONG
DUMONT
DURANT
DURING
DYEING
EALING
EAMONN
EARING
EASING
EATING
ECHINO
EDGING
EDMOND
EDMUND
EGMONT
EIRANN
ELAINE
ELUANT
ENDING
ENGINE
EOCENE
EPPING
EQUANT
EQUINE
ERMINE
ERNANI
ERRAND
ERRANT
ESSENE
ETHANE
ETHENE
EUGENE
EUXINE
EVZONE
EXPAND
EXPEND
EXTANT
EXTEND
EXTENT
FACING
FADING
FAKING
FAMINE
FARAND
FARINA
FECUND
FELINE
FELONY
FILING
FIRING
FLAUNT
FLUENT
FLYING
FOKINE
FOMENT
FORINT
FRIAND
FRIEND
FRYING
GALANT
GALENA
GAMINE
GAMING
GAPING
GEMINI
GERENT
GERUND
GITANO
GIVING
GOANNA
GORING
GRAINS
GRAINY
GRANNY
GREENE
GREENS
GRETNA
GROUND
GROYNE
GUIANA
GUYANA
HATING
HAVANA
HAVENT
HAVING
HELENA
HERONS
HEXANE
HIDING
HIKING
HIRING
HOMING
HOMINY
HOSING
HUMANE
HYAENA
IGUANA
IMMUNE
IMPEND
INDENT
INFANT
INLAND
INLINE
INNING
INSANE
INTEND
INTENT
INTONE
INVENT
IODINE
IRVING
ISLAND
JACANA
JACENT
JEJUNE
JOANNA
JOCUND
JOHNNY
JURANT
KATANA
KETONE
KIMONO
KORUNA
LACING
LACUNA
LADING
LAGUNA
LAGUNE
LAMENT
LAMINA
LARYNX
LATENT
LAYING
LEGEND
LEMONY
LEVANT
LIERNE
LIKING
LINING
LITANY
LIVING
LOMOND
LOSING
LOVING
LUCENT
LUCINA
LUGANO
LUMINA
LUPINE
LURING
LUTINE
LYMPNE
MAKING
MALONE
MALONY
MANANA
MARINA
MARINE
MATING
MATINS
MEDINA
MEKONG
MENINX
MERINO
MINING
MODENA
MOLINE
MOMENT
MOPING
MOVING
MOWING
MURINE
MUSANG
MUSING
MUTANT
MUTINY
NAGANA
NATANT
NEEDNT
NERINE
NICENE
NOCENT
NOVENA
NUTANT
NYLONS
OBLONG
OBTEND
OBTUND
OCEANS
OCHONE
OCTANE
OCTANS
OCTANT
OENONE
OFFEND
OFFING
ONDINE
ONIONS
ONLINE

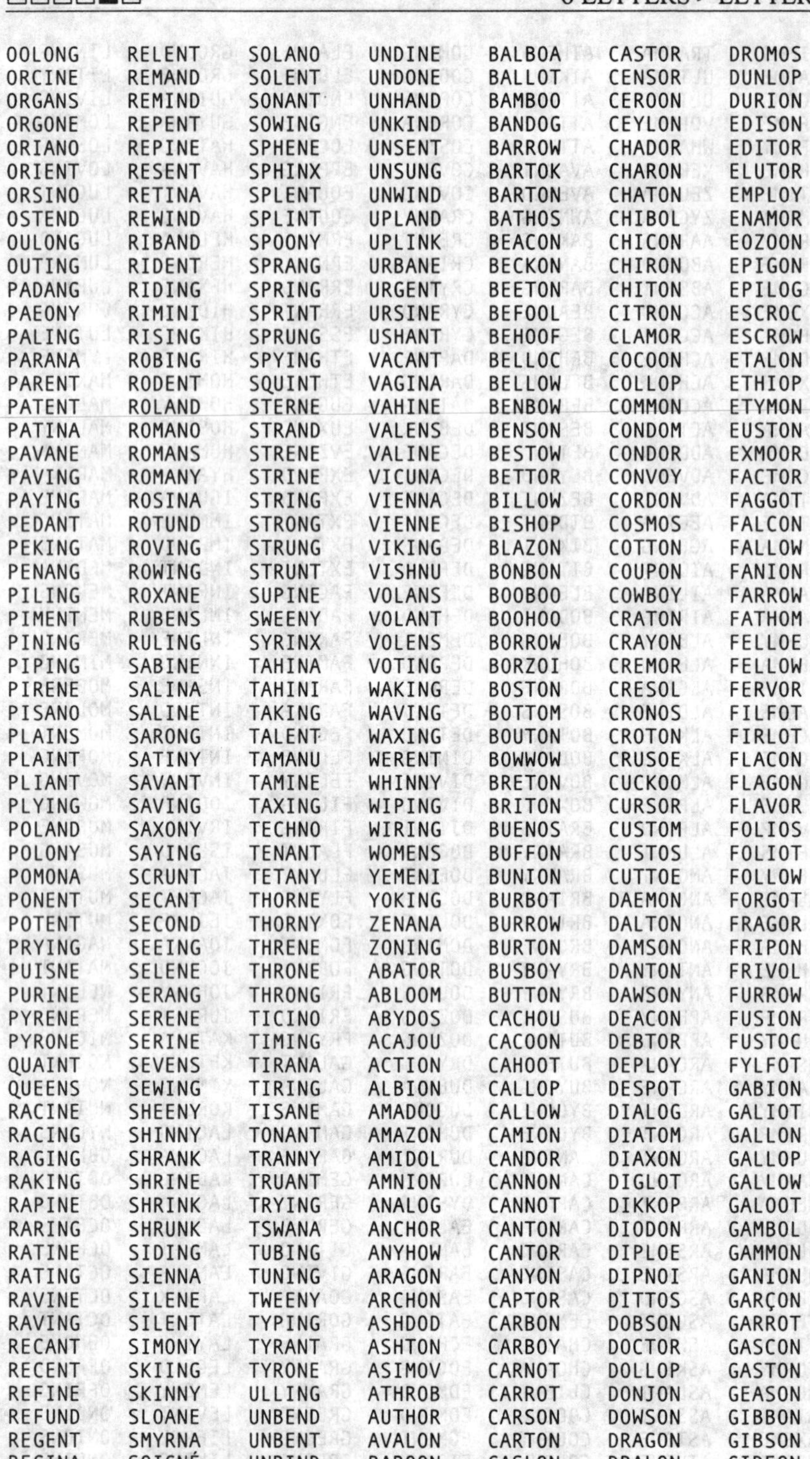

OOLONG
ORCINE
ORGANS
ORGONE
ORIANO
ORIENT
ORSINO
OSTEND
OULONG
OUTING
PADANG
PAEONY
PALING
PARANA
PARENT
PATENT
PATINA
PAVANE
PAVING
PAYING
PEDANT
PEKING
PENANG
PILING
PIMENT
PINING
PIPING
PIRENE
PISANO
PLAINS
PLAINT
PLIANT
PLYING
POLAND
POLONY
POMONA
PONENT
POTENT
PRYING
PUISNE
PURINE
PYRENE
PYRONE
QUAINT
QUEENS
RACINE
RACING
RAGING
RAKING
RAPINE
RARING
RATINE
RATING
RAVINE
RAVING
RECANT
RECENT
REFINE
REFUND
REGENT
REGINA
RELENT
REMAND
REMIND
REPENT
REPINE
RESENT
RETINA
REWIND
RIBAND
RIDENT
RIDING
RIMINI
RISING
ROBING
RODENT
ROLAND
ROMANO
ROMANS
ROMANY
ROSINA
ROTUND
ROVING
ROWING
ROXANE
RUBENS
RULING
SABINE
SALINA
SALINE
SARONG
SATINY
SAVANT
SAVING
SAXONY
SAYING
SCRUNT
SECANT
SECOND
SEEING
SELENE
SERANG
SERENE
SERINE
SEVENS
SEWING
SHEENY
SHINNY
SHRANK
SHRINE
SHRINK
SHRUNK
SIDING
SIENNA
SILENE
SILENT
SIMONY
SKIING
SKINNY
SLOANE
SMYRNA
SOIGNÉ
SOLANO
SOLENT
SONANT
SOWING
SPHENE
SPHINX
SPLENT
SPLINT
SPOONY
SPRANG
SPRING
SPRINT
SPRUNG
SPYING
SQUINT
STERNE
STRAND
STRENE
STRINE
STRING
STRONG
STRUNG
STRUNT
SUPINE
SWEENY
SYRINX
TAHINA
TAHINI
TAKING
TALENT
TAMANU
TAMINE
TAXING
TECHNO
TENANT
TETANY
THORNE
THORNY
THRENE
THRONE
THRONG
TICINO
TIMING
TIRANA
TIRING
TISANE
TONANT
TRANNY
TRUANT
TRYING
TSWANA
TUBING
TUNING
TWEENY
TYPING
TYRANT
TYRONE
ULLING
UNBEND
UNBENT
UNBIND
UNDINE
UNDONE
UNHAND
UNKIND
UNSENT
UNSUNG
UNWIND
UPLAND
UPLINK
URBANE
URGENT
URSINE
USHANT
VACANT
VAGINA
VAHINE
VALENS
VALINE
VICUNA
VIENNA
VIENNE
VIKING
VISHNU
VOLANS
VOLANT
VOLENS
VOTING
WAKING
WAVING
WAXING
WERENT
WHINNY
WIPING
WIRING
WOMENS
YEMENI
YOKING
ZENANA
ZONING
ABATOR
ABLOOM
ABYDOS
ACAJOU
ACTION
ALBION
AMADOU
AMAZON
AMIDOL
AMNION
ANALOG
ANCHOR
ANYHOW
ARAGON
ARCHON
ASHDOD
ASHTON
ASIMOV
ATHROB
AUTHOR
AVALON
BABOON
BALBOA
BALLOT
BAMBOO
BANDOG
BARROW
BARTOK
BARTON
BATHOS
BEACON
BECKON
BEETON
BEFOOL
BEHOOF
BELLOC
BELLOW
BENBOW
BENSON
BESTOW
BETTOR
BILLOW
BISHOP
BLAZON
BONBON
BOOBOO
BOOHOO
BORROW
BORZOI
BOSTON
BOTTOM
BOUTON
BOWWOW
BRETON
BRITON
BUENOS
BUFFON
BUNION
BURBOT
BURROW
BURTON
BUSBOY
BUTTON
CACHOU
CACOON
CAHOOT
CALLOP
CALLOW
CAMION
CANDOR
CANNON
CANNOT
CANTON
CANTOR
CANYON
CAPTOR
CARBON
CARBOY
CARNOT
CARROT
CARSON
CARTON
CASLON
CASTOR
CENSOR
CEROON
CEYLON
CHADOR
CHARON
CHATON
CHIBOL
CHICON
CHIRON
CHITON
CITRON
CLAMOR
COCOON
COLLOP
COMMON
CONDOM
CONDOR
CONVOY
CORDON
COSMOS
COTTON
COUPON
COWBOY
CRATON
CRAYON
CREMOR
CRESOL
CRONOS
CROTON
CRUSOE
CUCKOO
CURSOR
CUSTOM
CUSTOS
CUTTOE
DAEMON
DALTON
DAMSON
DANTON
DAWSON
DEACON
DEBTOR
DEPLOY
DESPOT
DIALOG
DIATOM
DIAXON
DIGLOT
DIKKOP
DIODON
DIPLOE
DIPNOI
DITTOS
DOBSON
DOCTOR
DOLLOP
DONJON
DOWSON
DRAGON
DRALON
DROMOS
DUNLOP
DURION
EDISON
EDITOR
ELUTOR
EMPLOY
ENAMOR
EOZOON
EPIGON
EPILOG
ESCROC
ESCROW
ETALON
ETHIOP
ETYMON
EUSTON
EXMOOR
FACTOR
FAGGOT
FALCON
FALLOW
FANION
FARROW
FATHOM
FELLOE
FELLOW
FERVOR
FILFOT
FIRLOT
FLACON
FLAGON
FLAVOR
FOLIOS
FOLIOT
FOLLOW
FORGOT
FRAGOR
FRIPON
FRIVOL
FURROW
FUSION
FUSTOC
FYLFOT
GABION
GALIOT
GALLON
GALLOP
GALLOW
GALOOT
GAMBOL
GAMMON
GANION
GARÇON
GARROT
GASCON
GASTON
GEASON
GIBBON
GIBSON
GIDEON

GIGLOT
GIRTON
GLAGOL
GLAMOR
GLYCOL
GNOMON
GODSON
GOLLOP
GONION
GOOGOL
GORDON
GORGON
GOUNOD
GRISON
GRYFON
GUENON
GUIDON
GUNDOG
HAEMON
HALLOO
HALLOW
HANSOM
HARBOR
HARLOT
HARROW
HAYBOX
HAYDON
HAYMOW
HECTOR
HELIOS
HENSON
HERIOT
HERMON
HESIOD
HILTON
HOBNOB
HOLLOW
HOOPOE
HORROR
HOTPOT
HUDSON
HYPNOS
HYSSOP
ICEBOX
INCHON
INDOOR
INFLOW
INGROW
INKPOT
INTRON
IRETON
ISOPOD
JAILOR
JAMBOK
JAMBON
JAMPOT
JARGON
JAWBOX
JERBOA
JETTON
JISSOM
JONSON
JUNIOR
KANOON
KEATON
KLAXON
KOODOO
KOSMOS
KOUROS
KOWTOW
KRATON
KRONOS
LAGOON
LANDOR
LAPDOG
LAPTOP
LARDON
LATRON
LECTOR
LEGION
LEMNOS
LENTOR
LEPTON
LESBOS
LESION
LESSON
LESSOR
LICTOR
LINGOT
LIQUOR
LISBON
LISSOM
LOLLOP
LONDON
LORIOT
LOTION
LOWBOY
LUMMOX
LYTTON
MACRON
MAGGOT
MAGNON
MAINOR
MALDON
MALLOW
MAMMON
MANIOC
MARMOT
MAROON
MARRON
MARROW
MASCOT
MATLOW
MATRON
MEADOW
MELLOW
MELTON
MEMNON
MENTOR
MERLOT
MERROW
MERTON
METEOR
METHOD
MICRON
MIGNON
MILTON
MINION
MINNOW
MINTON
MIRROR
MONGOL
MONROE
MOOCOW
MORION
MORMON
MORROW
MOSCOW
MOTION
MOUTON
MUFLON
MUTTON
MYELON
MYTHOS
NANDOO
NARROW
NASION
NATION
NATRON
NELSON
NESTOR
NEURON
NEWTON
NIGNOG
NIMROD
NIPPON
NONCOM
NORROY
NOTION
OBERON
OCELOT
OCTROI
ODDSON
OPTION
ORATOR
OREGON
ORISON
OUTTOP
OVIBOS
PALLOR
PANTON
PAPHOS
PARDON
PARLOR
PARROT
PARSON
PARTON
PASTON
PASTOR
PATHOS
PATMOS
PATROL
PATRON
PATTON
PAVLOV
PELION
PENNON
PEPLOS
PEQUOD
PERIOD
PERNOD
PERRON
PERSON
PETROL
PHAROS
PHENOL
PHIZOG
PHOTON
PIEDOG
PIGEON
PILLOW
PINION
PISTOL
PISTON
PLEXOR
PODSOL
PODZOL
POGROM
POIROT
POISON
POMPOM
POTION
POWWOW
PRISON
PROLOG
PROTON
PYEDOG
PYTHON
QUAHOG
RAGTOP
RAMROD
RANCOR
RANDOM
RANSOM
RAPTOR
RATION
RATOON
RATTON
REASON
RECKON
RECTOR
REDTOP
REEBOK
REGION
RENVOI
RENVOY
REPTON
RETOOL
RHETOR
RIBBON
RIPPON
ROBSON
ROGNON
ROSCOE
ROSTOV
RUNYON
SAILOR
SALLOW
SALMON
SALOON
SALOOP
SAMFOO
SAMIOT
SAMSON
SANTON
SARTOR
SAVIOR
SCHMOE
SCHOOL
SCIROC
SCIRON
SCROOP
SEASON
SECTOR
SELDOM
SENIOR
SENSOR
SERMON
SEXTON
SHADOW
SHALOM
SHARON
SHILOH
SIGNOR
SIMEON
SIMOON
SIPHON
SITCOM
SKIDOO
SLALOM
SORROW
SPIGOT
STATOR
STEROL
STOLON
STUPOR
SUCCOR
SUITOR
SUMMON
SYMBOL
SYNCOM
SYPHON
TAILOR
TALBOT
TALION
TALLOT
TALLOW
TAMPON
TANNOY
TARROW
TATTOO
TEAPOT
TEAPOY
TEFLON
TENDON
TENSON
TENSOR
TERROR
TEUTON
TEVIOT
THOLOS
THYMOL
TINPOT
TIPPOO
TIPTOE
TIPTOP
TISSOT
TOLUOL
TOMBOY
TOMTOM
TONSOR
TORPOR
TREMOR
TRICOT
TRIGON
TRIPOD
TRIPOS
TRITON
TURBOT
TYCOON
UNCOOL
UNHOOK
UNISON
UNSHOD
UPFLOW
UPROOT
UPSHOT
VECTOR
VENDOR
VERNON
VIATOR
VICTOR
VISION
VOODOO
WAGGON
WALLOP
WALLOW
WALTON
WANTON
WARHOL
WATSON
WEAPON
WETBOB
WHILOM
WIGEON
WILLOW
WILSON
WINDOW
WINNOW
WISDOM
WONTON
YARROW
YELLOW
ZEALOT
ZIRCON
ABRUPT
ACCEPT
ASLOPE
BICEPS
CALIPH
CANAPÉ
CANOPY
CHAMPS
CHEOPS
CHIPPY
CHIRPY
CHOPPY
CLIPPY
CLUMPS
CREEPS
CREEPY
CRISPY
CROPPY
CROUPE
CROUPY
CUERPO
CYNIPS
DIEPPE
DRIPPY
DROOPY
ECTOPY
ENRAPT
EQUIPE
ESCAPE
EUROPA
EUROPE
EXCEPT
EXEMPT
FLOPPY
FRAPPÉ
FRUMPY
GLUMPS
GRAMPS
GRAPPA
GRIPPE
GROUPS
GRUMPH
GRUMPS
GRUMPY
GUELPH
INCEPT
IRRUPT
JALOPY
JOSEPH
KAKAPO
MEROPE
METOPE
OCCUPY
PANOPE
PARAPH
PETIPA
POLYPS
PREPPY
PROMPT
PYROPE
RECIPE
SCAMPI

SCAMPO
SCRAPE
SCRAPS
SCRIPT
SCULPT
SERAPE
SERAPH
SHARPS
SHERPA
SKIMPY
SLEEPY
SLIPPY
SLOPPY
SNAPPY
STAMPS
STEPPE
STRIPE
STRIPY
STUMPS
STUMPY
SWAMPY
SYRUPY
THORPE
THRIPS
TROMPE
TROOPS
TROPPO
TROUPE
TRUMPS
TULIPA
UNRIPE
WHOOPS
ABJURE
ABOARD
ABSORB
ABSURD
ACCORD
ACKERS
ACTORS
ADHERE
ADJURE
ADMIRE
ADSORB
ADVERB
ADVERT
AFEARS
AFFIRM
AFFORD
AFTERS
ALBERT
ALLURE
ALMERY
AMHARA
AMPERE
ANCORA
ANGARY
ANGERS
ANGORA
ANKARA
APIARY
APPORT
ARMORY
ARMURE
ARTERY
ARTURO
ASGARD
ASHORE
ASKARI
ASMARA
ASPIRE
ASSART
ASSERT
ASSORT
ASSURE
ASTART
ASTERN
ASWARM
ATTIRE
ATTORN
AUBURN
AUGURY
AUMBRY
AURORA
AVIARY
AYMARA
BACKRA
BAKERS
BAKERY
BANTRY
BAYARD
BEFORE
BELFRY
BESORT
BEURRÉ
BEWARE
BICARB
BINARY
BISTRE
BISTRO
BLEARY
BOFORS
BOGART
BOLERO
BOWERY
BRIARD
BUYERS
BYWORD
CAFARD
CAMERA
CANARD
CANARY
CASTRO
CAVERN
CAVORT
CELERY
CENTRE
CESARE
CESURA
CETERA
CHAIRS
CHAKRA
CHEERS
CHEERY
CHERRY
CHOWRY
CHYPRE
CICERO
COBURG
COHERE
COHORT
COMART
CONTRA
COVERT
COWARD
CURARE
CURARI
CYBORG
DATURA
DEFORM
DEHORN
DEIDRE
DEMURE
DEPART
DEPORT
DESCRY
DESERT
DESIRE
DESORB
DINERO
DISARM
DIVERS
DIVERT
DOTARD
DREARY
EATERY
ECHARD
EDWARD
EEYORE
EFFORT
EGBERT
ELDERS
ELLERY
EMBARK
EMBERS
EMIGRÉ
EMPIRE
ENCORE
ENDURE
ENFIRE
ENSURE
ENTIRE
ESCARP
ESCORT
EUCHRE
EXEDRA
EXHORT
EXPERT
EXPIRE
EXPIRY
EXPORT
EXSERT
EXTERN
EXTIRP
EXTORT
FEDORA
FIACRE
FIGARO
FIGURE
FILTRÉ
FIMBRA
FINERY
FLEURY
FLOURY
FLURRY
FOUTRE
FRIARY
FURORE
FUTURE
GABBRO
GALERE
GALORE
GANTRY
GAUFRE
GENERA
GENTRY
GHARRY
GLAIRE
GLIÈRE
GLOIRE
GOCART
GOITRE
GOKART
GOVERN
GRIGRI
HARARE
HAVERS
HAZARD
HEDERA
HEGIRA
HEJIRA
HERERO
HETERO
HILARY
HOBART
HOMBRE
HOWARD
HUNGRY
IGNORE
IMBARN
IMMURE
IMPART
IMPORT
IMPURE
INBORN
INFARE
INFIRM
INFORM
INHERE
INJURE
INJURY
INSERT
INSURE
INTERN
INVERT
INWARD
IZZARD
JABIRU
JETHRO
KIAORA
KUMARA
KUMERA
LAYARD
LAYERS
LEMURE
LIGURE
LIPARI
LIVERY
LIZARD
LOUVRE
LUNARY
LUSTRE
LUXURY
LUZERN
MADURA
MADURO
MAÎTRE
MALGRE
MALORY
MANTRA
MANURE
MATURE
MAUGRE
MEAGRE
MEMORY
MESSRS
MILORD
MISÈRE
MISERY
MODERN
MOZART
MYSORE
NAGARI
NAPERY
NATURE
NITERY
NONARY
NOTARY
OBVERT
OCKERS
OEUVRE
OILERS
ONAGRA
ONWARD
ORDERS
ORDURE
ORNERY
ORRERY
OSBERT
OSIERY
OTHERS
OUTCRY
OXFORD
PAHARI
PALTRY
PAMIRS
PANFRY
PANTRY
PAPERS
PAPERY
PARURE
PASTRY
PENURY
PETARD
PETARY
PETERS
PICARD
PINERO
PLEURA
PLIERS
POETRY
POUDRE
POWERS
PRIORY
QUARRY
RAZURE
REBORE
REBORN
RECORD
REFORM
REGARD
REMARK
REPORT
RESORT
RETARD
RETIRE
RETORT
RETURN
REVERE
REVERS
REVERT
REVERY
REWARD
REWIRE
REWORD
REWORK
RIVERA
ROBERT
ROPERY
ROSARY
ROSERY
ROTARY
RUBBRA
RUMORS
RUPERT
SAFARI
SAHARA
SALARY
SAMARA
SARTRE
SATIRE
SATORI
SATURN
SATYRA
SAVORY
SAYERS
SBIRRO
SCLERA
SCLERE
SCURRY
SECURE
SEMPRE
SENORA
SENTRY
SEVERE
SEVERN
SEVERY
SHEARS
SHEERS
SHERRY
SHIRRA
SIERRA
SKERRY
SKURRY
SLURRY
SMEARY
SOLERA
SOMBRE
SPHERE
SQUARE
SQUIRE
SQUIRM
SQUIRT
STAIRS
STARRY
STEERS
STUART
SUBORN
SUBURB
SUDARY
SUGARY
SULTRY
SUNDRY
SUPERB
SUTURE
TABARD
TAGORE
TAMARA
TAMARI
TANTRA
TATERS
TAVERN
TAWDRY
TENDRE
TENURE
TEPHRA
THEIRS
THEORY
THEYRE
THIERS
THWART
TIMBRE
TORERO
TOWARD
TSHIRT
TUBERS
TUNDRA
TYBURN

UCKERS
ULCERS
UMPIRE
UNBORN
UNCORK
UNFURL
UNHURT
UNSURE
UNWARY
UPTURN
UPWARD
VAGARY
VELCRO
VELURE
VENERY
VENTRE
VESTRY
VINERY
VIZARD
VOTARY
WADERS
WARCRY
WATERS
WATERY
WHERRY
WINTRY
WIPERS
WIVERN
WIZARD
WOBURN
WYVERN
YAOURT
YOGURT
ABBESS
ABLUSH
ACCESS
ACCOST
ACCUSE
ACROSS
ADJUST
ADVISE
AFRESH
AGHAST
AGUISE
AGUISH
ALDOSE
ALMOST
ALONSO
AMBUSH
AMIDST
AORIST
APEPSY
APPOSE
ARGOSY
ARIOSO
ARKOSE
AROUSE
ARREST
ARTIST
ASSESS
ASSIST
ATTEST
AUGUST
AUTISM
AVERSE
AVULSE
BANISH
BEDASH
BEHEST
BEMUSE
BETISE
BIOPSY
BLAISE
BLOUSE
BLUISH
BOURSE
BOYISH
BRAISE
BRASSY
BREAST
BROWSE
BRUISE
BYPASS
CAMISE
CARESS
CARUSO
CERISE
CERUSE
CHAISE
CHASSE
CHEESE
CHEESY
CHOOSE
CHOOSY
CHRISM
CHRIST
CIVISM
CLASSY
CLAUSE
CLUMSY
COARSE
CORPSE
COURSE
CREASE
CREESE
CREESH
CROSSE
CROUSE
CRUISE
CUBISM
CUBIST
CUEIST
CUISSE
CURTSY
CYTASE
DALASI
DAMASK
DANISH
DEBASE
DEFUSE
DEMISE
DEMIST
DEPOSE
DESIST
DETEST
DEVEST
DEVISE
DICAST
DIGEST
DISUSE
DIVEST
DRESSY
DRIEST
DROPSY
DROWSE
DROWSY
DUMOSE
DURESS
DYNAST
ECLOSE
EDDISH
EFFUSE
EFTEST
EGOISM
EGOIST
EGRESS
ELAPSE
ELDEST
ELFISH
ELOISE
EMBOSS
EMBUSY
ENCASE
ENCASH
ENLIST
ENMESH
EPRISE
EVULSE
EXCESS
EXCISE
EXCUSE
EXPOSE
FAMISH
FAVISM
FAVOSE
FETISH
FEWEST
FILOSE
FINEST
FINISH
FLENSE
FLIMSY
FLOSSY
FLOUSH
FOLKSY
FOREST
FRAISE
FROWST
GALOSH
GARISH
GLASSY
GLOSSA
GLOSSY
GNEISS
GOLOSH
GRASSY
GREASE
GREASY
GRILSE
GROSSO
GROUSE
HAMOSE
HARASS
HEARSE
HERESY
HEXOSE
HOARSE
HOLISM
HOLIST
HONEST
IFFISH
IMBASE
IMBOSS
IMPISH
IMPOSE
IMPOST
INCASE
INCEST
INCISE
INFEST
INFUSE
INGEST
INMESH
INMOST
INRUSH
INSIST
INVEST
JEWESS
JEWISH
JOCOSE
JURIST
KECKSY
KETOSE
KHALSA
KIBOSH
KINASE
KUMISS
KYBOSH
LAISSE
LATEST
LAVISH
LAXIST
LEGIST
LHOTSE
LIAISE
LIGASE
LIPASE
LOCUST
LOWEST
LURIST
LUTIST
LYCOSA
LYRIST
MAOIST
MARISH
MARIST
MEDISM
MEDUSA
MIMOSA
MISUSE
MODEST
MODISH
MODIST
MOLEST
MONISM
MONIST
MOPISH
MORASS
MOROSE
MOUSSE
MULISH
NANISM
NEBISH
NEFAST
NEWEST
NIVOSE
NODOSE
NOMISM
NOWISE
NUDISM
NUDIST
OAFISH
OBIISM
OBLAST
OBOIST
OBSESS
OBTUSE
ODENSE
ODESSA
OFFISH
OGRESS
OLDISH
ONCOST
ONRUSH
OPHISM
OPPOSE
ORGASM
OSMOSE
OTIOSE
OWLISH
PAPIST
PARISH
PERISH
PERUSE
PHRASE
PILOSE
PLEASE
PLISSÉ
POLISH
POTASH
PRAISE
PRIEST
PRISSY
PROUST
PUNISH
PURIST
QUEASY
QUINSY
RACISM
RACIST
RADISH
RAGUSA
RAKISH
RAMOSE
RAPIST
RAVISH
RECAST
RECESS
REFUSE
REGEST
REHASH
RELISH
REMISS
REPAST
REPOSE
RESIST
REVISE
RIBOSE
ROBUST
ROMISH
RUGOSE
SADISM
SADIST
SAMOSA
SCHISM
SCHIST
SCHUSS
SCOOSH
SCORSE
SCOUSE
SEROSA
SETOSE
SEXISM
SEXIST
SPARSE
SPEISS
SPLASH
SPLOSH
SPOUSE
SQUASH
SQUISH
STRASS
STRESS
SWOOSH
SYRISM
TAMISE
TAOISM
TAOIST
TEENSY
TERESA
THEISM
THEIST
THIRST
THRASH
THRESH
THRIST
THRUSH
THRUST
TOLOSA
TOOTSY
TOYISH
TRUISM
TSETSE
TYPIST
UNBUSY
UNEASE
UNEASY
UNJUST
UNLESS
UNMASK
UNREST
UNWISE
UPPISH
UTMOST
VADOSE
VALISE
VANISH
VARESE
VENOSE
VERISM
WABASH
WHILST
WHIMSY
WHOOSH
WRASSE
ABATTU
ABLATE
ACUITY
ADNATE
AERATE
AGNATE
AGOUTI
ALBITE
ALECTO
APLITE
ARGUTE
ARISTA
ASSETS
ASTUTE
AUGITE
AVIATE
BARYTA
BASUTO
BEATTY
BEAUTY
BENITO
BERATE
BINATE
BLOTTO
BOGOTA
BONITO
BORATE
BOUNTY
BOVATE
BREATH
BRONTE
CADETS

CAMOTE
CANUTE
CAPOTE
CAVITY
CECITY
CERATE
CHARTA
CHASTE
CHATTY
CHESTY
CHINTZ
CHITTY
CLARTY
COMATE
COMITY
COOLTH
COUNTY
COYOTE
CRAFTY
CRANTS
CREATE
CRESTA
CRISTA
CROUTE
CROUTH
CRUFTS
CRUSTA
CRUSTY
CRYPTO
CUESTA
CURATE
DAINTY
DAKOTA
DEARTH
DEBATE
DELATE
DELETE
DEMOTE
DENOTE
DEPUTE
DEPUTY
DEVOTE
DEWITT
DHOOTI
DILATE
DILUTE
DIMITY
DONATE
DRAFTY
ECARTÉ
EFFETE
EGESTA
EIGHTH
EIGHTY
ELUATE
EMEUTE
ENMITY
ENSATE
ENTITY
EOLITH
EQUATE
EQUITY
ERMITE
ERSATZ
ESTATE
EXCITE
EXISTS
FAINTS
FAULTY
FEALTY
FEINTS
FEISTY
FIESTA
FINITE
FIXITY
FLINTY
FOURTH
FROSTY
FRUITS
FRUITY
FUGATO
GAIETY
GAMETE
GARETH
GELATO
GHETTO
GHOSTS
GIOTTO
GIUSTO
GOUTTE
GRANTA
GREATS
GRITTY
GROATS
GROTTO
GROTTY
GROUTS
GROUTY
GROWTH
GUESTS
GUILTY
GYRATE
HALITE
HAMATE
HAMITE
HEALTH
HEARTH
HEARTS
HEARTY
HECATE
HERETO
HUMITE
HUMPTY
HYPATE
IGNITE
ILLITE
IMPUTE
INCITE
INDITE
INGATE
INGOTS
INMATE
INNATE
INVITE
IOLITE
ISLETS
JAUNTY
JUBATE
KAPUTT
KARATE
KARITE
KNOTTY
KRANTZ
LANATE
LAPITH
LAPUTA
LAXITY
LEALTY
LEANTO
LEGATE
LEGATO
LENGTH
LEVITE
LEVITY
LIGATE
LIGETI
LIGHTS
LILITH
LIMITS
LOCATE
LOLITA
LORETO
LUNATE
LUXATE
MALATE
MANATI
MANITO
MAPUTO
METATE
MIGHTY
MINUTE
MOIETY
MUCATE
MUNITE
MUTATE
NEGATE
NEPETA
NICETY
NIGHTS
NIGHTY
NILOTE
NINETY
NOTATE
NUDITY
NUMPTY
NUTATE
OBLATE
ODDITY
OLEATE
OMENTA
OMERTA
OOCYTE
OOLITE
OPHITE
OPIATE
ORBITA
ORNATE
OXGATE
PAINTS
PAINTY
PAKHTI
PAKHTO
PAKHTU
PALATE
PARETO
PARITY
PASHTO
PASHTU
PELOTA
PESETA
PETITE
PEYOTE
PIGOTT
PIGSTY
PILATE
PINITE
PIRATE
PLENTY
PLINTH
POINTE
POINTS
POLITE
POLITY
POTATO
PRESTO
PRETTY
PRONTO
PUERTO
PUNCTO
PUPATE
PURITY
PUSHTU
QUARTO
QUARTZ
QUINTA
QUOITS
QWERTY
RABATO
RARITY
REALTY
REBATE
REBITE
RECITE
REFUTE
RELATE
REMOTE
REPUTE
RIALTO
RIGHTO
RIGHTS
ROSYTH
ROTATE
SAFETY
SAINTS
SALUTE
SAMITE
SANITY
SAPOTA
SAVATE
SCAITH
SCANTY
SCATTY
SDEATH
SEBATE
SEDATE
SEMITE
SENATE
SHANTY
SHASTA
SHEATH
SHEETS
SHIFTY
SHIITE
SHINTO
SHINTY
SHIRTY
SHORTS
SHTETL
SHUFTI
SHUFTY
SIESTA
SIGHTS
SLEUTH
SMARTY
SMEATH
SMOOTH
SMUTTY
SNEATH
SNIFTY
SNOOTY
SNOTTY
SNOUTY
SOLUTE
SONATA
SPARTA
SPARTH
SPILTH
SPLITS
SPORTS
SPORTY
SPOTTY
SPRITE
SPRITZ
STILTS
STILTY
STRATA
SUDATE
SURETÉ
SURETY
SVELTE
SWARTY
SWEATY
SWEETS
TAHITI
TERETE
THIRTY
TIGHTS
TOMATO
TONITE
TREATY
TRISTE
TRUSTY
TWAITE
TWENTY
TWISTY
UBIETY
UNDATE
UNIATE
UPDATE
UPPITY
UPRATE
VACATE
VALETA
VALUTA
VANITY
VEDUTA
VELETA
VENITE
VERITY
VOLUTE
WAPITI
WARMTH
WEALTH
WRAITH
WREATH
YEASTY
YUKATA
ZAPATA
ZENITH
ZYGOTE
ABACUS
ABLAUT
ACARUS
ACCRUE
ACINUS
ACTIUM
AEGEUS
AEOLUS
AIRBUS
AIRGUN
ALACUS
ALARUM
ALLIUM
AMYCUS
ANIMUS
ANTRUM
ARBOUR
ARDOUR
ARMFUL
ARMOUR
ARNAUT
ARTAUD
ARTFUL
ARTHUR
ASARUM
ASCIUS
ASYLUM
ATRIUM
AUREUS
AVENUE
BACKUP
BAGFUL
BANGUI
BANJUL
BARIUM
BARNUM
BARQUE
BASQUE
BATTUE
BAYEUX
BEDAUB
BEIRUT
BESSUS
BISQUE
BOOJUM
BRAQUE
BROGUE
BRUTUS
BULBUL
BUNKUM
BUYOUT
BUZFUZ
BYSSUS
CACTUS
CADMUS
CAECUM
CAIQUE
CALLUP
CALLUS
CALQUE
CAMPUS
CANGUE
CARPUS
CASQUE
CATGUT
CATSUP
CAUCUS
CAVOUR
CENSUS
CENTUM
CERCUS
CEREUS
CERIUM
CESIUM
CESTUI
CESTUS
CHEQUE
CHERUB
CHERUP
CHORUS
CILIUM
CINQUE
CIRCUS
CIRQUE
CIRRUS
CITRUS
CLAQUE

CLIQUE
CLONUS
COCCUS
COITUS
COLOUR
CONCUR
CONSUL
CORIUM
CORMUS
CORNUA
CORNUS
CORPUS
CORVUS
CRATUR
CRINUM
CROCUS
CULTUS
CUPFUL
CURIUM
CURSUS
CUSCUS
CYCLUS
CYDNUS
CYGNUS
CYPRUS
DARIUS
DELIUS
DENGUE
DERGUE
DETOUR
DEVOUR
DEVOUT
DICTUM
DINKUM
DISBUD
DISCUS
DISEUR
DOLEUR
DOLIUM
DOLOUR
DROGUE
DUGOUT
DUMDUM
DYBBUK
EARFUL
ECONUT
EFFLUX
EGGCUP
ELBRUS
EMBRUE
ENGLUT
ENNIUS
EPIRUS
ERBIUM
EREBUS
EVOLUÉ
EXODUS
EYEFUL
FABIUS
FACTUM
FAMOUS
FAROUK
FAUNUS
FAVOUR
FESCUE
FITFUL
FITOUT
FLATUS
FOETUS
FOLIUM
FONDUE
FRENUM
FUNDUS
FUNGUS
FUREUR
FURFUR
GALLUP
GALLUS
GANGUE
GENIUS
GIAOUR
GIDDUP
GONIUM
GRADUS
GYPSUM
HALLUX
HANGUP
HELIUM
HIATUS
HICCUP
HIGHUP
HIPPUS
HOLDUP
HONOUR
HOOKUP
HORMUZ
HUBBUB
HUMBUG
HUMMUS
HUMOUR
HYPNUM
IAMBUS
ICARUS
IMBRUE
INDIUM
INFLUX
IREFUL
ITERUM
JOSHUA
JOYFUL
JOYOUS
JULIUS
JUNCUS
LABIUM
LABOUR
LABRUM
LAPSUS
LARRUP
LASSUS
LAWFUL
LAYOUT
LEAGUE
LETOUT
LIGNUM
LINEUP
LINKUP
LITMUS
LOCKUP
LOLIUM
LUMPUR
LYCEUM
MADEUP
MAGNUM
MAGNUS
MAHOUT
MAKEUP
MANFUL
MANQUÉ
MANTUA
MARAUD
MARKUP
MARQUE
MASQUE
MAYBUG
MAZOUT
MEATUS
MEDIUM
MEDIUS
MELIUS
MENTUM
MISSUS
MOBIUS
MOCKUP
MODIUS
MOPSUS
MORBUS
MORGUE
MOSQUE
MUCOUS
MULTUM
MURMUR
MUSEUM
NAEVUS
NEBBUK
NEREUS
NERIUM
NESSUS
NIMBUS
NOBBUT
NOCTUA
NOYOUS
OAKNUT
OBELUS
OBOLUS
ODIOUS
OFFCUT
OLENUS
OMASUM
OMNIUM
OPAQUE
OPTOUT
OSMIUM
OSTIUM
OUTPUT
OUTRUN
PAIDUP
PASQUE
PEANUT
PENSUM
PENTUP
PEPLUM
PERDUE
PHLEUM
PHYLUM
PICKUP
PILEUM
PILEUP
PILEUS
PLAGUE
PLAQUE
PLENUM
PLEXUS
PLUTUS
PODIUM
POLLUX
POROUS
POSEUR
POSSUM
PRAGUE
PRIMUS
PURSUE
PUSHUP
QUORUM
RADIUM
RADIUS
RAGOUT
RAMOUS
RECOUP
RECTUM
RECTUS
REFLUX
REGIUS
RESCUE
RETOUR
RÊVEUR
RHESUS
RICTUS
RIGOUR
RISQUÉ
ROTGUT
RUCKUS
RUEFUL
RUGOUS
RUMOUR
RUMPUS
RUSTUM
SACRUM
SAMBUR
SAPIUM
SARGUS
SAVOUR
SCAPUS
SCOPUS
SCUTUM
SEAMUS
SELJUK
SEPIUM
SHADUF
SHAMUS
SHOGUN
SHROUD
SINFUL
SIRIUS
SLIPUP
SODIUM
SOLEUS
SOWBUG
SPROUT
SPUTUM
STATUE
STATUS
STROUD
STROUP
STYLUS
SUBDUE
SUCCUS
SULCUS
SULFUR
TALCUM
TALMUD
TAMMUZ
TARGUM
TARSUS
TAURUS
TEACUP
TEAGUE
TECTUM
TEDIUM
TELLUS
TERGUM
THOLUS
THYMUS
TISSUE
TITTUP
TOMIUM
TONGUE
TOPHUS
TORQUE
TOSSUP
TRAGUS
TUMOUR
TURNUP
TYPHUS
UMLAUT
UNIQUE
UNPLUG
UNTRUE
URANUS
USEFUL
UTERUS
VACUUM
VALGUS
VALIUM
VALLUM
VALOUR
VAPOUR
VELLUM
VELOUR
VENDUE
VENOUS
VERDUN
VERSUS
VIGOUR
VILLUS
VINOUS
VIROUS
VIRTUE
VOYEUR
VULGUS
WALNUT
WALRUS
WAMPUM
WAMPUS
WAYOUT
WENSUM
WILFUL
WINDUP
WOEFUL
XENIUM
YUMYUM
ACTIVE
ALCOVE
ARGIVE
ARRIVE
BEHAVE
BEHOVE
CHIVVY
CLEAVE
CRUIVE
DATIVE
DERIVE
ENDIVE
EVOLVE
GENEVA
GLAIVE
GODIVA
GREAVE
GRIEVE
GROOVE
GROOVY
MOJAVE
MOTIVE
MUSIVE
NATIVE
OCTAVE
OCTAVO
OTTAVA
RELIVE
REMOVE
REVIVE
SALIVA
SATIVE
SCURVY
SHEAVE
SHELVE
SHRIVE
SHROVE
SKIVVY
SLEAVE
SLEEVE
SOLIVE
STARVE
STRIVE
STROVE
SWERVE
THEAVE
THIEVE
THRIVE
THROVE
TROUVÉ
TWELVE
VOTIVE
ZOUAVE
ACRAWL
DISOWN
GODOWN
IMPAWN
INLAWS
INTOWN
MALAWI
MOHAWK
MOTOWN
OTTAWA
PESHWA
RENOWN
SCRAWL
SCRAWM
SCREWY
SHREWD
SINEWY
SPRAWL
SQUAWK
STRAWS
STRAWY
THRAWN
THROWN
UPTOWN
WIDOWS
ANNEXE
DELUXE
EUTAXY
GALAXY
UNSEXY
ALLEYN
ALWAYS
ANADYR
ANONYM
ARROYO
BILLYO
BOLEYN
BOMBYX
BYEBYE
COCCYX
DACTYL
EMBRYO
EPONYM
ERINYS

EVELYN
GARRYA
KELLYS
KIKUYU
LABRYS
MARTYR
METHYL
NITRYL
PAPAYA
PHENYL
POPEYE
PROPYL
REDEYE
SCHUYT
SELWYN
TETHYS
TETRYL
WELWYN
ZEPHYR
ABLAZE
AGUIZE
ASSIZE
BELIZE
BLOWZY
BREEZE
BREEZY
BRONZE
CORYZA
FLOOZY
FRANZY
FREEZE
FRENZY
FRIEZE
FRIZZY
FROWZY
GLITZY
GREUZE
IODIZE
IONIZE
KWANZA
NYANZA
PIAZZA
RIENZI
SCHIZO
SCUZZY
SLEAZE
SLEAZY
SLEEZY
SNAZZY
SNEEZE
SNEEZY
SNOOZE
STANZA
TWEEZE
UFFIZI
WHEEZE
WHEEZY
YAKUZA

6:6

ABELIA
ABROMA
ABULIA
ACACIA
ACADIA
ACEDIA
AEGINA
AFRICA
AGATHA
AGENDA
AGLAIA
ALALIA
ALASKA
ALCINA
ALEXIA
ALOGIA
ALPACA
ALTHEA
AMELIA
AMHARA
AMOEBA
ANCONA
ANCORA
ANEMIA
ANGELA
ANGINA
ANGLIA
ANGOLA
ANGORA
ANKARA
ANOXIA
ANTLIA
APHTHA
APNOEA
APORIA
AQUILA
ARABIA
ARALIA
ARANDA
ARCANA
AREOLA
ARISTA
ARMADA
ARNICA
AROLLA
ARROBA
ASMARA
ASTHMA
ATAXIA
ATOCIA
ATTILA
AUCUBA
AURIGA
AURORA
AXILLA
AYESHA
AYMARA
AZALEA
AZOLLA
BACKRA
BAHADA
BALBOA
BANANA
BARODA
BARYTA
BEEGHA
BELUGA
BERTHA
BODEGA
BOGOTA
BORGIA
BRAHMA
BREGMA
BUDDHA
BURKHA
CACCIA
CALIMA
CAMERA
CANADA
CARINA
CASSIA
CEDULA
CESURA
CETERA
CHAKRA
CHAPKA
CHARTA
CHOANA
CHOREA
CHROMA
CHUKKA
CICADA
CICALA
CINEMA
CLOACA
CONCHA
CONTRA
CORNEA
CORNUA
CORONA
CORYZA
COSMEA
CRESTA
CRIMEA
CRISTA
CRUSTA
CUBICA
CUESTA
CUPOLA
CUTCHA
CZAPKA
DAHLIA
DAKOTA
DATURA
DHARMA
DJERBA
DODOMA
DOLINA
DUENNA
ECZEMA
EGERIA
EGESTA
ELISHA
ELODEA
ENIGMA
EROICA
ESPADA
EUBOEA
EUREKA
EUROPA
EXEDRA
FARINA
FASCIA
FATIMA
FAVELA
FECULA
FEDORA
FERULA
FIBULA
FIESTA
FIMBRA
FRIGGA
GALENA
GAMBIA
GARRYA
GARUDA
GEISHA
GELADA
GENERA
GENEVA
GLINKA
GLIOMA
GLORIA
GLOSSA
GOANNA
GODIVA
GORGIA
GRANTA
GRAPPA
GRETNA
GUIANA
GUINEA
GURKHA
GUYANA
HAVANA
HECUBA
HEDERA
HEGIRA
HEJIRA
HELENA
HERNIA
HOOPLA
HYAENA
HYDRIA
IBERIA
IGUANA
IMPALA
INDABA
INSULA
ISCHIA
ISTRIA
ITHACA
JACANA
JEMIMA
JERBOA
JOANNA
JOJOBA
JOSHUA
JUDICA
KABAKA
KALMIA
KANAKA
KANTHA
KARIBA
KATANA
KERALA
KHALSA
KIAORA
KORUNA
KUMARA
KUMERA
KWACHA
KWANZA
LACUNA
LADOGA
LAGUNA
LAMBDA
LAMINA
LANCIA
LAPUTA
LATVIA
LIGULA
LIPOMA
LITHIA
LOCHIA
LOGGIA
LOLITA
LORCHA
LORICA
LOYOLA
LUANDA
LUCINA
LUMINA
LUSAKA
LYCOSA
MACULA
MADURA
MAFFIA
MALAGA
MANANA
MANILA
MANTRA
MANTUA
MARACA
MARINA
MARKKA
MARTHA
MASADA
MAZUMA
MEDINA
MEDUSA
MERCIA
MIASMA
MIMOSA
MODENA
MONICA
MOOMBA
MURRHA
MYOPIA
NAGANA
NAUSEA
NEBULA
NEPETA
NEVADA
NOCTUA
NOVENA
NYANZA
OCHREA
ODESSA
OEDEMA
OLIVIA
OMENTA
OMERTA
ONAGRA
ONEIDA
OPTIMA
ORBITA
ORTEGA
OSTREA
OTTAVA
OTTAWA
PAELLA
PAGODA
PAMELA
PANADA
PANAMA
PAPAYA
PARANA
PATACA
PATINA
PAYOLA
PELOTA
PESETA
PESHWA
PETIPA
PHASMA
PHOBIA
PIAZZA
PLASMA
PLEURA
PNEUMA
POMONA
PORTIA
POSADA
PRAVDA
PROTEA
PYTHIA
QUAGGA
QUINTA
RADULA
RAFFIA
RAGUSA
RANULA
RAPHIA
RAZZIA
REALIA
REGINA
RESEDA
RETINA
RIVERA
ROSINA
ROTULA
RUBBRA
RUSSIA
RWANDA
SAHARA
SALINA
SALIVA
SALVIA
SAMARA
SAMOSA
SAPOTA
SATYRA
SAURIA
SCHEMA
SCILLA
SCLERA
SCORIA
SCOTIA
SCYLLA
SENECA
SENORA
SERBIA
SEROSA
SHAMBA
SHARIA
SHASTA
SHEILA
SHERPA
SHIPKA
SHIRRA
SIDDHA
SIENNA
SIERRA
SIESTA
SILICA
SMEGMA
SMYRNA
SOLERA
SONATA
SOPHIA
SPARTA
SQUAMA
STAFFA
STANZA
STEMMA
STIGMA
STRATA
STREGA
SULPHA
SWABIA
SYLVIA
TABULA

TACOMA
TAENIA
TAHINA
TAMARA
TANKIA
TANTRA
TARSIA
TEGULA
TELEGA
TEPHRA
TERESA
TERTIA
THALIA
TIPULA
TIRANA
TOLOSA
TRAUMA
TRIVIA
TROIKA
TSWANA
TULIPA
TUNDRA
UGANDA
ULTIMA
UMBRIA
UNGULA
URANIA
URSULA
URTICA
UTOPIA
VAGINA
VALETA
VALUTA
VEDUTA
VELETA
VESICA
VICUNA
VIENNA
VOMICA
XEROMA
YAKUZA
YORUBA
YUKATA
ZAMBIA
ZAPATA
ZENANA
ZEUGMA
ZINNIA
ZYGOMA
ABSORB
ADSORB
ADVERB
APLOMB
ATHROB
BAOBAB
BEDAUB
BENUMB
BICARB
CANTAB
CHERUB
COBWEB
CONFAB
DESORB
ENTOMB
HOBNOB
HUBBUB
LABLAB
PREFAB
PUNJAB
SCARAB
SCRAMB
SERDAB
SKYLAB
SOHRAB
SUBURB
SUPERB
WETBOB
ZAGREB
ACETIC
ACIDIC
AEOLIC
AGARIC
AGONIC
ALARIC
ANEMIC
ANOXIC
ARABIC
ARCTIC
ATAXIC
ATOMIC
ATONIC
AZOTIC
BALTIC
BALZAC
BARSAC
BELLOC
BIONIC
BIOPIC
BIOTIC
CEDRIC
CELIAC
CELTIC
CHEMIC
CITRIC
CLERIC
CLINIC
CLONIC
COGNAC
COPTIC
COSMIC
CRETIC
CRITIC
CYCLIC
CYMRIC
CYSTIC
DYADIC
EMETIC
EREMIC
EROTIC
ESCROC
ETHNIC
EXOTIC
FABRIC
FORMIC
FROLIC
FUSTIC
FUSTOC
GAELIC
GALLIC
GARLIC
GNOMIC
GOTHIC
HAPTIC
HARPIC
HECTIC
HEROIC
HYPNIC
IAMBIC
ICONIC
IPECAC
IRONIC
ITALIC
KELTIC
LACTIC
LAURIC
LENTIC
LIMBIC
LUBRIC
MANIAC
MANIOC
MASTIC
METRIC
MICMAC
MOSAIC
MYOPIC
MYSTIC
NASTIC
NITRIC
NORDIC
NORVIC
OGAMIC
ORPHIC
OXALIC
PARSEC
PATHIC
PELVIC
PEPTIC
PHOBIC
PHONIC
PHYSIC
PICNIC
POETIC
PONTIC
PUBLIC
QUEBEC
RICRAC
RUBRIC
RUSTIC
SCENIC
SCIROC
SENLAC
SEPTIC
STATIC
STERIC
SYNDIC
TACTIC
TANNIC
TARMAC
THETIC
TOLTEC
TOLUIC
TRAGIC
TROPIC
URANIC
ZODIAC
ABOARD
ABOUND
ABROAD
ABSURD
ACARID
ACCEND
ACCORD
ADDEND
ADDLED
AENEID
AFFORD
AFIELD
AFRAID
AGREED
AIRBED
ALFRED
ALIPED
ALLIED
ALMOND
AMAZED
AMUSED
ANGLED
APPEND
ARCHED
ARGUED
ARNOLD
AROUND
ARTAUD
ASCEND
ASGARD
ASHDOD
ATTEND
AVOWED
BALLAD
BANNED
BARBED
BARRED
BAYARD
BEADED
BEHEAD
BEHELD
BEHIND
BEHOLD
BELTED
BENDED
BESTED
BEYOND
BIASED
BIFOLD
BLAMED
BOILED
BONDED
BOOKED
BOSSED
BOWLED
BRIAND
BRIARD
BUCKED
BURIED
BUSHED
BUSTED
BYWORD
CAFARD
CALCED
CALLED
CALLID
CAMPED
CANARD
CANDID
CANNED
CAPPED
CAPSID
CARVED
CAUSED
CHOKED
CLOSED
COATED
COCCID
COILED
COMBED
CONRAD
COOKED
COPIED
CORKED
CORNED
COWARD
CRAZED
CUPPED
CURSED
CURVED
CUSSED
CYBRID
CYPRID
CYTOID
DAMNED
DASHED
DAYBED
DECKED
DEFEND
DELVED
DEMAND
DENIED
DEPEND
DEVOID
DISBUD
DISHED
DOCKED
DOGGED
DOODAD
DOOMED
DOTARD
DOTTED
DUCKED
DUSTED
EARNED
ECHARD
EDITED
EDMOND
EDMUND
EDWARD
ELATED
ENFOLD
ERASED
ERODED
ERRAND
EUCLID
EXCEED
EXPAND
EXPEND
EXTEND
EYELID
FABLED
FAGGED
FARAND
FECUND
FERVID
FIBBED
FILLED
FITTED
FIZZED
FLAWED
FLORID
FLUTED
FOETID
FOILED
FOLDED
FORBID
FORCED
FORGED
FORKED
FORRAD
FRAMED
FRAYED
FRIAND
FRIEND
FRIGID
FULGID
FUNDED
GABLED
GADOID
GARBED
GERUND
GIFTED
GILDED
GILEAD
GLAZED
GLOVED
GORGED
GOUNOD
GRADED
GRATED
GRAVID
GROUND
GUMMED
HALOID
HALVED
HARMED
HAROLD
HASHED
HATRED
HAWKED
HAZARD
HEADED
HEAPED
HEATED
HEAVED
HEEDED
HEELED
HEPTAD
HERALD
HESIOD
HINGED
HIPPED
HISPID
HONIED
HOODED
HOOFED
HOOKED
HORNED
HORRID
HORSED
HOTBED
HOWARD
HULLED
HUMPED
HUSHED
HYBRID
IMPEND
INBRED
INDEED
INFOLD
INLAID
INLAND
INROAD
INTEND
INWARD
IRONED
ISLAND
ISOPOD
IZZARD
JAGGED
JAMMED
JINXED
JOCUND
KELOID
KEYPAD
KILTED
LANDED
LAPSED
LASHED
LAYARD
LEGEND

LEGGED
LEONID
LIFTED
LIMBED
LIMPID
LIPPED
LIQUID
LIZARD
LOADED
LOCKED
LODGED
LOMOND
LOOPED
MADRID
MAENAD
MALTED
MARAUD
MARKED
MASHED
MASKED
MASSED
MATTED
MELTED
METHOD
MI·LORD
MINDED
MISLED
MISSED
MITRED
MOATED
MORBID
MORNED
MOSSAD
MUCOID
MYRIAD
NAILED
NEAPED
NECKED
NEEDED
NEREID
NICKED
NIMROD
NODDED
OBTEND
OBTUND
OFFEND
ONWARD
ORCHID
OSTEND
OSWALD
OUTBID
OXFORD
OXHEAD
PACKED
PADDED
PAINED
PALLID
PARKED
PASSED
PEAKED
PEELED

PEEVED
PELOID
PENTAD
PEQUOD
PERIOD
PERNOD
PETARD
PICARD
PICKED
PISSED
PITTED
PLACED
PLACID
PLATED
PLUMED
POISED
POLAND
POLLED
PONGID
POTTED
PRICED
PRIMED
PUFFED
PURSED
PUTRID
QUOTED
RAGGED
RAISED
RAMROD
RANCID
RANKED
RAPPED
RECORD
REFUND
REGARD
REMAND
REMIND
REPAID
REREAD
RETARD
REWARD
REWIND
REWORD
RIBALD
RIBAND
RIBBED
RIDGED
RIGGED
RIMMED
RINGED
ROBBED
ROLAND
ROOTED
ROSCID
ROTUND
ROUGED
RUBBED
RUCHED
RUGGED
RUINED
RUSHED

RUTTED
SACRED
SCARED
SCREED
SEALED
SEATED
SECOND
SEEDED
SELFED
SENSED
SHADED
SHAPED
SHARED
SHIELD
SHOULD
SHREWD
SHROUD
SINBAD
SKEWED
SLEWED
SNAKED
SNOWED
SOAKED
SOILED
SOLVED
SORDID
SOUSED
SOWSED
SPACED
SPAULD
SPICED
SPIKED
SPREAD
STATED
STEWED
STOLID
STONED
STRAND
STROUD
STUPID
SUITED
TABARD
TALMUD
TANNED
TETRAD
THREAD
TIERED
TINGED
TINNED
TINTED
TIPPED
TITLED
TOGGED
TOLLED
TORPID
TORRID
TOWARD
TRIPOD
TUFTED
TURBID
TURGID

TURNED
TWINED
UNBEND
UNBIND
UNBRED
UNCLAD
UNDYED
UNFOLD
UNHAND
UNITED
UNKIND
UNLOAD
UNPAID
UNREAD
UNSAID
UNSHOD
UNSOLD
UNTOLD
UNUSED
UNWIND
UPHELD
UPHOLD
UPLAND
UPWARD
VARIED
VEILED
VEINED
VERSED
VESTED
VISCID
VIZARD
VOICED
VOIDED
WAFTED
WALLED
WANTED
WARPED
WASHED
WASTED
WEBBED
WEDDED
WEDGED
WHITED
WICKED
WILLED
WINGED
WITTED
WIZARD
WONTED
WOODED
WORKED
XYLOID
ZONKED
ABJURE
ABLATE
ABLAZE
ABONDE
ABRADE
ABREGE
ACCEDE
ACCRUE

ACCUSE
ACHENE
ACTIVE
ADDUCE
ADHERE
ADJURE
ADMIRE
ADNATE
ADVENE
ADVICE
ADVISE
AEDILE
AERATE
AEROBE
AFLAME
AGNATE
AGUISE
AGUIZE
ALBITE
ALCOVE
ALDINE
ALDOSE
ALERCE
ALKANE
ALKENE
ALLEGE
ALLELE
ALLUDE
ALLURE
ALPINE
AMBAGE
AMENDE
AMERCE
AMORCE
AMPERE
ANCILE
ANCOME
ANKOLE
ANNEXE
ANYONE
APACHE
APIECE
APLITE
APOGEE
APPOSE
ARABLE
ARCADE
ARCANE
ARCHIE
AREOLE
ARGIVE
ARGUTE
ARGYLE
ARKOSE
ARMURE
AROUSE
ARRIVE
ARSÈNE
ARSINE
ASHINE
ASHORE

ASLOPE
ASPIRE
ASSIZE
ASSUME
ASSURE
ASTONE
ASTUTE
ATHENE
ATRIDE
ATTIRE
ATTLEE
ATTONE
ATTUNE
AUBADE
AUDILE
AUGITE
AUNTIE
AUSSIE
AVENGE
AVENUE
AVERSE
AVIATE
AVULSE
AWHILE
BABBLE
BAFFLE
BAILEE
BAILIE
BANGLE
BARÈGE
BARGEE
BARQUE
BARRIE
BASQUE
BATTLE
BATTUE
BAUBLE
BAWBEE
BEADLE
BEAGLE
BEANIE
BEAUNE
BECAME
BECOME
BEETLE
BEFORE
BEGONE
BEHAVE
BEHOVE
BEJADE
BELIKE
BELIZE
BEMUSE
BENAME
BERATE
BERTHE
BERTIE
BESIDE
BESSIE
BETAKE
BETIDE

BETIME
BETISE
BEWARE
BEZZLE
BHAJEE
BILLIE
BINATE
BIRDIE
BIREME
BISQUE
BISTRE
BLAISE
BLENDE
BLITHE
BLONDE
BLOUSE
BLUDGE
BOBBLE
BOCAGE
BODGIE
BODICE
BOGGLE
BOLIDE
BONNIE
BONXIE
BOODLE
BOOGIE
BOOKIE
BOOTEE
BOOTLE
BORAGE
BORATE
BOTHIE
BOTTLE
BOUCHE
BOUFFE
BOULLE
BOUNCE
BOURÉE
BOURNE
BOURSE
BOVATE
BOVINE
BRAISE
BRAQUE
BREEZE
BRIDGE
BRIDIE
BRIDLE
BROGUE
BRONTE
BRONZE
BROOKE
BROWNE
BROWSE
BRUISE
BUBBLE
BUCKLE
BUDGIE
BUMBLE
BUNDLE

BUNGEE
BUNGLE
BUNJEE
BURBLE
BURGEE
BURGLE
BUSTLE
BUTANE
BUTENE
BYEBYE
BYGONE
BYLINE
BYRNIE
CABALE
CABBIE
CACKLE
CADDIE
CAIQUE
CAJOLE
CALQUE
CAMISE
CAMOTE
CANDLE
CANGUE
CANINE
CANNAE
CANTLE
CANUTE
CAPONE
CAPOTE
CARAFE
CAREME
CASQUE
CASTLE
CATTLE
CAUDLE
CENTRE
CERATE
CERISE
CERUSE
CESARE
CHAISE
CHANCE
CHANGE
CHARGE
CHASSE
CHASTE
CHEESE
CHEQUE
CHERIE
CHICLE
CHILDE
CHOICE
CHOOSE
CHOREE
CHROME
CHYPRE
CIERGE
CILICE
CINQUE
CIRCLE
CIRQUE
CLAQUE
CLAUDE
CLAUSE
CLEAVE
CLIQUE
CLOCHE
CLOTHE
COARSE
COBBLE
COCKLE
CODDLE
COERCE
COFFEE
COHERE
COLLIE
COMATE
COMBLE
COMICE
CONGEE
COOKIE
COOLIE
COOTIE
CORBIE
CORPSE
CORRIE
CORVÉE
COSINE
COSSIE
COTYLE
COULEE
COUPLE
COURSE
COWAGE
COWRIE
COYOTE
CRABBE
CRADLE
CRAPLE
CREASE
CREATE
CRÈCHE
CREESE
CREOLE
CRIBLE
CRINGE
CROCHE
CROSSE
CROUPE
CROUSE
CROUTE
CRUISE
CRUIVE
CRUSOE
CUBAGE
CUDDLE
CUFFEE
CUISSE
CULDEE
CUPULE
CURARE
CURATE
CURDLE
CURRIE
CURULE
CUTTLE
CUTTOE
CYBELE
CYRENE
CYTASE
CYTODE
DABBLE
DADDLE
DAFTIE
DAGGLE
DAMAGE
DANDLE
DANGLE
DANUBE
DAPHNE
DAPPLE
DARGLE
DARKIE
DARTLE
DATIVE
DAWDLE
DAZZLE
DEARIE
DEBASE
DEBATE
DEBILE
DECADE
DECANE
DECIDE
DÉCIME
DECKLE
DECODE
DECOKE
DECREE
DEDUCE
DEFACE
DEFAME
DEFILE
DEFINE
DEFUSE
DEGREE
DEIDRE
DELATE
DELETE
DELICE
DELUDE
DELUGE
DELUXE
DEMISE
DEMOTE
DEMURE
DENGUE
DENOTE
DENUDE
DEPONE
DEPOSE
DEPUTE
DERGUE
DERIDE
DERIVE
DESIRE
DEVICE
DEVISE
DEVOTE
DIBBLE
DIDDLE
DIEPPE
DILATE
DILUTE
DIMPLE
DINGLE
DIPLOE
DIPOLE
DISUSE
DIVIDE
DIVINE
DOCILE
DODDLE
DOLINE
DONATE
DONGLE
DONNÉE
DOODLE
DOSAGE
DOTAGE
DOTTLE
DOUANE
DOUBLE
DOUCHE
DRAGEE
DREDGE
DROGUE
DROWSE
DRUDGE
DUCKIE
DUFFLE
DUMOSE
DUMPLE
DUNDEE
EATAGE
ECBOLE
ECLOSE
ECURIE
EDIBLE
EEYORE
EFFACE
EFFETE
EFFUSE
ELAINE
ELANCE
ELAPSE
ELLICE
ELOISE
ELUATE
ELYSEE
EMBALE
EMBRUE
EMERGE
EMEUTE
EMPIRE
EMULGE
EMUNGE
ENABLE
ENCASE
ENCODE
ENCORE
ENDIVE
ENDURE
ENFIRE
ENFREE
ENGAGE
ENGINE
ENLACE
ENRAGE
ENROBE
ENSATE
ENSILE
ENSURE
ENTICE
ENTIRE
ENTREE
ENZYME
EOCENE
EPAULE
EPHEBE
EPOPEE
EPRISE
EQUATE
EQUINE
EQUIPE
ERMINE
ERMITE
ESCAPE
ESSENE
ESTATE
ETHANE
ETHENE
EUCHRE
EUGENE
EUROPE
EUXINE
EVINCE
EVOLVE
EVULSE
EVZONE
EXCISE
EXCITE
EXCUSE
EXHALE
EXHUME
EXPEDE
EXPIRE
EXPOSE
FACADE
FACILE
FAIBLE
FAMINE
FANGLE
FARDLE
FAVOSE
FEEBLE
FEERIE
FELINE
FELLOE
FEMALE
FERULE
FESCUE
FETTLE
FIACRE
FICKLE
FIDDLE
FIERCE
FIGURE
FILOSE
FINALE
FINITE
FIPPLE
FIZZLE
FLANGE
FLECHE
FLEDGE
FLEECE
FLENSE
FOCSLE
FOIBLE
FOKINE
FONDLE
FONDUE
FOOTLE
FOOZLE
FORAGE
FOUTRE
FRAISE
FRANCE
FREEZE
FRIDGE
FRIEZE
FRINGE
FRONDE
FROUDE
FUDDLE
FUMBLE
FURORE
FUTILE
FUTURE
FUZZLE
GABBLE
GAGGLE
GALERE
GALORE
GAMBLE
GAMETE
GAMINE
GANGUE
GARAGE
GARBLE
GARGLE
GAUCHE
GAUFRE
GAVAGE
GENOME
GENTLE
GEORGE
GIGGLE
GILLIE
GIRDLE
GIRLIE
GLAIRE
GLAIVE
GLANCE
GLIÈRE
GLOIRE
GOALIE
GOATEE
GOBBLE
GOETHE
GOGGLE
GOITRE
GOOGIE
GOOGLE
GOOLIE
GOURDE
GOUTTE
GRAMME
GRANGE
GREASE
GREAVE
GREECE
GREENE
GREUZE
GRIEVE
GRILLE
GRILSE
GRIPPE
GROOVE
GROUSE
GROYNE
GRUDGE
GRUNGE
GUGGLE
GURGLE
GUTTLE
GUZZLE
GYRATE
HABILE
HACKEE
HACKLE
HAGGLE
HALIDE
HALITE
HAMATE
HAMBLE
HAMITE
HAMOSE
HANDLE
HANKIE
HARARE
HASSLE
HEARSE
HEAUME
HECATE

HECKLE
HEXANE
HEXOSE
HIDAGE
HOARSE
HOBBLE
HOGTIE
HOMAGE
HOMBRE
HOOPOE
HORACE
HOWDIE
HUBBLE
HUCKLE
HUDDLE
HUGHIE
HUMANE
HUMBLE
HUMITE
HURDLE
HURTLE
HUSTLE
HYPATE
ICICLE
IGNITE
IGNORE
ILLITE
ILLUDE
IMBASE
IMBIBE
IMBRUE
IMMUNE
IMMURE
IMPALE
IMPEDE
IMPOSE
IMPURE
IMPUTE
INCASE
INCEDE
INCISE
INCITE
INCOME
INDITE
INDUCE
INFAME
INFARE
INFUSE
INGATE
INHALE
INHERE
INHUME
INJURE
INLINE
INMATE
INNATE
INSANE
INSIDE
INSOLE
INSURE
INTAKE
INTIME
INTONE
INVADE
INVITE
INVOKE
IODINE
IODIZE
IOLITE
IONIZE
ISOLDE
JABBLE
JANGLE
JEJUNE
JEROME
JIGGLE
JINGLE
JOCOSE
JOGGLE
JOSTLE
JUBATE
JUGGLE
JUJUBE
JUMBLE
JUNGLE
JUNKIE
KABELE
KABYLE
KARATE
KARITE
KEBELE
KELPIE
KELTIE
KETONE
KETOSE
KETTLE
KEWPIE
KIBBLE
KIDDIE
KIDDLE
KILTIE
KINASE
KINDLE
KIRTLE
KITTLE
KLUDGE
KOOKIE
LABILE
LADDIE
LAGUNE
LAISSE
LANATE
LARVAE
LASSIE
LAUNCE
LAURIE
LAVAGE
LEAGUE
LEGATE
LEGUME
LEMURE
LESLIE
LESSEE
LEVITE
LEXEME
LHOTSE
LIABLE
LIAISE
LIERNE
LIGASE
LIGATE
LIGURE
LIPASE
LIPIDE
LITTLE
LIZZIE
LOATHE
LOCALE
LOCATE
LOCULE
LOONIE
LOUCHE
LOUNGE
LOURIE
LOUVRE
LOVAGE
LUNATE
LUNULE
LUPINE
LUSTRE
LUTINE
LUXATE
LYCHEE
LYMPNE
MACULE
MADAME
MAGGIE
MAGPIE
MAÎTRE
MALATE
MALGRE
MALICE
MALLEE
MALONE
MANAGE
MANCHE
MANEGE
MANGLE
MANTLE
MANURE
MARBLE
MARINE
MARQUE
MASHIE
MASQUE
MATURE
MAUGRE
MEAGRE
MEALIE
MEANIE
MEDDLE
MENACE
MENAGE
MEROPE
MERRIE
METAGE
METATE
METOPE
METTLE
MICKLE
MIDDLE
MINGLE
MINNIE
MINUTE
MIRAGE
MISÈRE
MISUSE
MIZZLE
MOBILE
MODULE
MOGGIE
MOJAVE
MOLINE
MOLLIE
MONROE
MORALE
MORGUE
MOROSE
MOSQUE
MOTILE
MOTIVE
MOTTLE
MOUSSE
MOZZLE
MUCATE
MUCKLE
MUDDLE
MUFFLE
MUMBLE
MUNITE
MURAGE
MURINE
MUSCLE
MUSIVE
MUTATE
MUZZLE
MYGALE
MYRTLE
MYSORE
NATIVE
NATURE
NEBULE
NEEDLE
NEGATE
NELLIE
NERINE
NESSIE
NESTLE
NETTLE
NIBBLE
NICENE
NIGGLE
NILOTE
NIMBLE
NIPPLE
NIVOSE
NOBBLE
NODDLE
NODOSE
NODULE
NOMADE
NONAGE
NOODLE
NOOKIE
NOTATE
NOTICE
NOUNCE
NOVICE
NOWISE
NOYADE
NOZZLE
NUANCE
NUBBLE
NUBILE
NUCULE
NUTATE
NUZZLE
OBECHE
OBLATE
OBLIGE
OBTUSE
OCHONE
OCTANE
OCTAVE
ODENSE
OENONE
OEUVRE
OFFICE
OLEATE
ONCOME
ONDINE
ONLINE
ONSIDE
OOCYTE
OOLITE
OPAQUE
OPHITE
OPIATE
OPPOSE
OPTIME
ORACHE
ORACLE
ORANGE
ORCINE
ORDURE
ORGONE
ORIOLE
ORNATE
OSMOSE
OTIOSE
OUNDLE
OUTAGE
OUTLIE
OUTVIE
OXGATE
OXHIDE
PADDLE
PALACE
PALATE
PANOPE
PAPULE
PARADE
PARDIE
PAROLE
PARSEE
PARURE
PASQUE
PAUNCE
PAVANE
PAWNEE
PEBBLE
PEDDLE
PEEWEE
PENNAE
PENSÉE
PEOPLE
PERDUE
PERUKE
PERUSE
PESADE
PESTLE
PETITE
PEYOTE
PHOEBE
PHRASE
PIAFFE
PICKLE
PIDDLE
PIERCE
PIFFLE
PILAGE
PILATE
PILOSE
PIMPLE
PINITE
PINKIE
PINTLE
PIRATE
PIRENE
PLAGUE
PLAICE
PLAQUE
PLEASE
PLEDGE
PLONGE
PLUNGE
POBBLE
POINTE
POLICE
POLITE
POMACE
POMADE
POMMIE
PONGEE
POODLE
POPEYE
PORGIE
POTTLE
POUDRE
POUFFE
POUNCE
POWNIE
PRAGUE
PRAISE
PRANCE
PREACE
PRINCE
PSYCHE
PUDDLE
PUISNE
PUMICE
PUPATE
PURINE
PURPLE
PURSUE
PUTTEE
PUZZLE
PYRENE
PYRONE
PYROPE
QUICHE
QUINCE
RABBLE
RACEME
RACINE
RADDLE
RAFALE
RAFFLE
RAGGLE
RAMBLE
RAMOSE
RANKLE
RAPINE
RATINE
RATTLE
RAVAGE
RAVINE
RAZURE
RAZZLE
REBATE
REBITE
REBORE
REBUKE
RECEDE
RECIFE
RECIPE
RECITE
REDEYE
REDUCE
REEKIE
REFACE
REFINE
REFUGE
REFUSE
REFUTE
REGALE
REGGAE

REGIME
RELATE
RELIVE
REMAKE
REMOTE
REMOVE
RENAME
RENEGE
REPINE
REPOSE
REPUTE
RESALE
RESCUE
RESIDE
RESUME
RETAKE
RETIRE
REVERE
REVILE
REVISE
REVIVE
REVOKE
REWIRE
RHAPHE
RIBBLE
RIBOSE
RIDDLE
RIFFLE
RIPPLE
RIVAGE
ROADIE
ROOKIE
ROOTLE
ROSACE
ROSCOE
ROTATE
ROUBLE
ROUNCE
ROXANE
RUBBLE
RUCKLE
RUDDLE
RUELLE
RUFFLE
RUGOSE
RUMBLE
RUMPLE
RUNDLE
RUSTLE
SABELE
SABINE
SADDLE
SAITHE
SALADE
SALINE
SALLEE
SALOME
SALUTE
SAMITE
SAMPLE
SAPELE

SARNIE
SARTRE
SATIRE
SATIVE
SAVAGE
SAVATE
SAVOIE
SCARCE
SCATHE
SCHEME
SCHMOE
SCLERE
SCONCE
SCORSE
SCOUSE
SCRAPE
SCRIBE
SCUNGE
SCYTHE
SEABEE
SEANCE
SEBATE
SECEDE
SECURE
SEDATE
SEDUCE
SEETHE
SEICHE
SELENE
SEMELE
SEMITE
SEMPRE
SENATE
SENILE
SERAPE
SERENE
SERINE
SESAME
SETOSE
SETTEE
SETTLE
SEVERE
SEWAGE
SHEAVE
SHELVE
SHIITE
SHRIKE
SHRINE
SHRIVE
SHROVE
SICKLE
SIFFLE
SILAGE
SILENE
SIMILE
SIMPLE
SINGLE
SIPPLE
SIRREE
SIZZLE
SLEAVE

SLEAZE
SLEDGE
SLEEVE
SLOANE
SLUDGE
SLUICE
SMUDGE
SNEEZE
SNOOZE
SNUDGE
SOCAGE
SOFTIE
SOIREE
SOLACE
SOLIVE
SOLUTE
SOMBRE
SOOTHE
SORAGE
SORTIE
SOUPLE
SOURCE
SOZZLE
SPARSE
SPATHE
SPECIE
SPENCE
SPHENE
SPHERE
SPLAKE
SPLICE
SPONGE
SPOUSE
SPRITE
SPRUCE
SPUNGE
SPURGE
SQUARE
SQUIRE
STABLE
STANCE
STAPLE
STARVE
STATUE
STEELE
STEPPE
STERNE
STIFLE
STODGE
STOGIE
STOOGE
STRAFE
STRAKE
STRENE
STRIDE
STRIFE
STRIKE
STRINE
STRIPE
STRIVE
STROBE

STRODE
STROKE
STROVE
STYMIE
SUBDUE
SUBTLE
SUCKLE
SUDATE
SUNDAE
SUPINE
SUPPLE
SUTTEE
SUTURE
SVELTE
SWANEE
SWATHE
SWERVE
SWINGE
TACKLE
TAGORE
TAIGLE
TAILLE
TALKIE
TAMALE
TAMINE
TAMISE
TANGLE
TASSIE
TATTLE
TAWPIE
TAXEME
TEAGUE
TEEPEE
TEETHE
TEMPLE
TENACE
TENDRE
TENURE
TERETE
TERRAE
THEAVE
THENCE
THEYRE
THIEVE
THISBE
THORNE
THORPE
THRENE
THRICE
THRIVE
THRONE
THROVE
TICKLE
TIDDLE
TIERCE
TIMBRE
TINGLE
TINKLE
TINNIE
TIPPLE
TIPTOE

TIRADE
TISANE
TISSUE
TITTLE
TITULE
TODDLE
TOFFEE
TOGGLE
TONGUE
TONITE
TOOTLE
TOPPLE
TORQUE
TOTTIE
TOUCHE
TOUPEE
TOUSLE
TOWAGE
TOWHEE
TOWNEE
TRALEE
TRANCE
TREBLE
TRIAGE
TRIFLE
TRIODE
TRIPLE
TRISTE
TROCHE
TROMPE
TROPHE
TROUPE
TRUDGE
TSETSE
TUBULE
TUILLE
TUMBLE
TURTLE
TUSSLE
TWAITE
TWEEZE
TWELVE
TWINGE
TYRONE
ULLAGE
UMPIRE
UNABLE
UNCAGE
UNDATE
UNDINE
UNDONE
UNEASE
UNIATE
UNIQUE
UNLACE
UNLIKE
UNMADE
UNRIPE
UNSAFE
UNSURE
UNTRUE

UNWISE
UNYOKE
UPDATE
UPRATE
UPSIDE
UPTAKE
URBANE
URSINE
USABLE
USANCE
VACATE
VADOSE
VAHINE
VALINE
VALISE
VARESE
VAUNCE
VELOCE
VELURE
VENDEE
VENDUE
VENICE
VENITE
VENOSE
VENTRE
VIABLE
VIENNE
VIRILE
VIRTUE
VISAGE
VIVACE
VOIDEE
VOLAGE
VOLUME
VOLUTE
VOTIVE
VOYAGE
WADDLE
WAFFLE
WAGGLE
WAMBLE
WANDLE
WANGLE
WARBLE
WATTLE
WEEPIE
WEEWEE
WELLIE
WHARFE
WHEEZE
WHENCE
WHINGE
WIGGLE
WILLIE
WIMBLE
WIMPLE
WINKLE
WINNIE
WOBBLE
WOODIE
WORTLE

WRASSE
WRITHE
YAFFLE
YANKEE
YARDIE
YIPPEE
YUPPIE
ZOMBIE
ZOUAVE
ZYGOTE
AGRÉGÉ
BEURRÉ
BOUCLÉ
CANAPÉ
CLICHÉ
DÉGAGÉ
ECARTÉ
EMIGRÉ
EVOLUÉ
FIANCÉ
FILTRÉ
FLAMBÉ
FRAPPÉ
MANQUÉ
PLISSÉ
RISQUÉ
SOIGNÉ
SURETÉ
TROUVÉ
BEHALF
BEHOOF
BELIEF
CUTOFF
DECAFF
ENGULF
FAROFF
HUSSIF
INGULF
ITSELF
KHALIF
KHARIF
LAYOFF
MASSIF
MYSELF
PAYOFF
PILAFF
REBUFF
RELIEF
RIPOFF
RUNOFF
SCRUFF
SHADUF
SHARIF
SHERIF
SHROFF
SPLIFF
TARIFF
TIPOFF
ACHING
ACTING
AGEING

AILING	GIVING	PRYING	ZIGZAG	ELIJAH	KITSCH	RELISH
AIRING	GORING	PYEDOG	ZONING	ENARCH	KOOLAH	RIYADH
ANALOG	GUNDOG	QUAHOG	ABLUSH	ENCASH	KUFIAH	ROMISH
ASKING	HATING	RACING	AFRESH	ENMESH	KVETCH	ROSYTH
ATABEG	HAVING	RAGBAG	AGUISH	ENOUGH	KYBOSH	RUPIAH
AWNING	HIDING	RAGING	ALIYAH	ENRICH	LADAKH	SCAITH
BAKING	HIKING	RAKING	AMBUSH	EOLITH	LAPITH	SCATCH
BANDOG	HIRING	RARING	ARIOCH	EPARCH	LAUNCH	SCOOSH
BARING	HOMING	RATBAG	ARMAGH	EUNUCH	LAVISH	SCORCH
BELONG	HOSING	RATING	ATTACH	EXARCH	LENGTH	SCOTCH
BERING	HUMBUG	RAVING	AVOUCH	FAMISH	LILITH	SCUTCH
BIGWIG	INNING	REDLEG	BANISH	FETISH	LOOFAH	SDEATH
BITING	IRVING	RIDING	BEDASH	FINISH	MARISH	SEARCH
BOBWIG	JETLAG	RISING	BEENAH	FLANCH	MODISH	SERAPH
BOEING	KITBAG	ROBING	BEULAH	FLETCH	MOLECH	SHEATH
BORING	LACING	ROVING	BLANCH	FLINCH	MOLLAH	SHEIKH
BOXING	LADING	ROWING	BLEACH	FLITCH	MOLOCH	SHILOH
BUYING	LAPDOG	RULING	BLENCH	FLOUSH	MOOLAH	SIRRAH
CANING	LAYING	SARONG	BLOTCH	FOURTH	MOPISH	SKETCH
CARING	LIEBIG	SAVING	BLUISH	FRENCH	MULISH	SLATCH
CASING	LIKING	SAYING	BODACH	GALOSH	MULLAH	SLEIGH
COBURG	LINING	SEEING	BORSCH	GARETH	MUNICH	SLEUTH
CODING	LIVING	SERANG	BOYISH	GARISH	NALLAH	SLOUCH
COMING	LOSING	SEWING	BRAMAH	GLITCH	NAUTCH	SLOUGH
COOING	LOVING	SIDING	BRANCH	GOLOSH	NEBISH	SMEATH
COPING	LUDWIG	SKIING	BREACH	GROUCH	NULLAH	SMIRCH
COVING	LURING	SONTAG	BREATH	GROWTH	OAFISH	SMOOCH
CRYING	MAKING	SOWBUG	BREECH	GRUMPH	OFFISH	SMOOTH
CYBORG	MATING	SOWING	BROACH	GRUTCH	OLDISH	SNATCH
DANZIG	MAYBUG	SPRANG	BROOCH	GUBBAH	ONRUSH	SNEATH
DARING	MEKONG	SPRING	BRUNCH	GUELPH	OOMPAH	SNITCH
DATING	MINING	SPRUNG	CALIPH	GULLAH	OWLISH	SPARTH
DIALOG	MOPING	SPYING	CASBAH	HANNAH	PALLAH	SPEECH
DINING	MOVING	STALAG	CHINCH	HAUNCH	PARAPH	SPILTH
DIVING	MOWING	STRING	CHOUGH	HEALTH	PARIAH	SPLASH
DOTING	MUSANG	STRONG	CHURCH	HEARTH	PARISH	SPLOSH
DOZING	MUSING	STRUNG	CLENCH	HITECH	PAUNCH	SQUASH
DRYING	MUSKEG	TAKING	CLINCH	HOOHAH	PERISH	SQUISH
DUGONG	NIGNOG	TAXING	CLOUGH	HOOKAH	PISGAH	STANCH
DURING	NUTMEG	TEABAG	CLUNCH	HOORAH	PLANCH	STARCH
DYEING	OBLONG	THRONG	CLUTCH	HOOTCH	PLEACH	STENCH
EALING	OFFING	TIMING	COOLTH	HOUDAH	PLINTH	STITCH
EARING	OILRIG	TIRING	CRANCH	HOWDAH	PLOUGH	SUMACH
EARWIG	OOLONG	TOERAG	CRATCH	HURRAH	POLISH	SWATCH
EASING	OULONG	TRYING	CREACH	HUZZAH	POTASH	SWITCH
EATING	OUTING	TUAREG	CREAGH	IFFISH	PREACH	SWOOSH
EDGING	PADANG	TUBING	CREESH	IMPISH	PUNISH	TANNAH
ENDING	PALING	TUNING	CROTCH	INMESH	PUNKAH	THANAH
EPILOG	PAVING	TYPING	CROUCH	INRUSH	PURDAH	THATCH
EPPING	PAYING	ULLING	CROUTH	ISAIAH	PUTSCH	THORAH
FACING	PEGLEG	UNPLUG	CRUNCH	JEWISH	QUAICH	THOUGH
FADING	PEKING	UNSUNG	CRUTCH	JIBBAH	QUAIGH	THRASH
FAKING	PENANG	VIKING	CULTCH	JOSEPH	QUELCH	THRESH
FILING	PHIZOG	VOTING	DANISH	JOSIAH	QUENCH	THRUSH
FIRING	PIEDOG	WAKING	DEARTH	JUBBAH	QUETCH	TOYISH
FIZGIG	PILING	WAVING	DETACH	KASBAH	QUITCH	TRENCH
FLYING	PINING	WAXING	DOODAH	KAZAKH	RADISH	TROUGH
FRYING	PIPING	WIPING	DRENCH	KEDDAH	RAKISH	TUSSAH
GAMING	PLYING	WIRING	EDDISH	KIBOSH	RAUNCH	TWITCH
GAPING	PROLEG	YOKING	EIGHTH	KIRBEH	RAVISH	UPPISH
GASBAG	PROLOG	ZAFTIG	ELFISH	KIRSCH	REHASH	VANISH

VARECH
VEDDAH
WABASH
WALLAH
WARMTH
WEALTH
WHOOSH
WRAITH
WREATH
WRENCH
WRETCH
YAHWEH
ZENITH
ZURICH
ADONAI
ADSUKI
AGOUTI
ALKALI
ALUMNI
ASKARI
BACCHI
BANGUI
BANZAI
BIKINI
BODONI
BONSAI
BORZOI
BRUNEI
BUKSHI
BUSONI
CESTUI
CHICHI
CHILLI
CURARI
DALASI
DECANI
DELPHI
DEWALI
DHOOTI
DIPNOI
DIVALI
DIWALI
DJINNI
ELTCHI
ERNANI
FUSELI
GANDHI
GEMINI
GILGAI
GIORGI
GRIGRI
GUARDI
HAGGAI
HAWAII
KABUKI
KIGALI
LIGETI
LIPARI
LITCHI
MALAWI
MANATI
MAOTAI
MEDICI
MILADY
MUESLI
MUNSHI
NAGARI
NEPALI
NEROLI
NERVII
NIKKEI
NILGAI
OCTROI
OURALI
PAHARI
PAKHTI
RENVOI
RIENZI
RIMINI
SAFARI
SALAMI
SALUKI
SANSEI
SATORI
SCAMPI
SHTCHI
SHUFTI
SOMALI
TAHINI
TAHITI
TAIPEI
TAMARI
TATAMI
TIVOLI
UFFIZI
WAPITI
YEMENI
YEZIDI
ALCOCK
AMTRAK
ANORAK
ARRACK
ATTACK
BARTOK
BEDECK
BOHUNK
CANUCK
COPECK
DAMASK
DEBUNK
DIKDIK
DVORAK
DYBBUK
EMBARK
FAROUK
FRANCK
HIJACK
JAMBOK
KALPAK
KANUCK
KODIAK
MOHAWK
MOHOCK
MOUJIK
MUZHIK
NEBBUK
NEBECK
NUDNIK
OOKPIK
POLACK
REBECK
REEBOK
REMARK
REWORK
SELJUK
SHRANK
SHRIEK
SHRINK
SHRUNK
SLOVAK
SQUAWK
SQUEAK
STREAK
STRICK
STRUCK
THWACK
TUGRIK
UNCORK
UNDECK
UNHOOK
UNLOCK
UNMASK
UNPACK
UNPICK
UPLINK
VATHEK
YORICK
ZEBECK
ZENDIK
ABDIEL
ABSEIL
ACRAWL
ACTUAL
AERIAL
AGNAIL
ALUDEL
AMIDOL
AMORAL
AMYTAL
ANIMAL
ANNEAL
ANNUAL
AORTAL
APICAL
APPALL
APPEAL
ARCHIL
ARGYLL
ARMFUL
ARTFUL
ASSAIL
ASSOIL
ASTRAL
ATABAL
ATONAL
ATRIAL
AVOWAL
AZRAEL
BAGFUL
BAIKAL
BANJUL
BARBEL
BARREL
BEFALL
BEFOOL
BELIAL
BEMOIL
BENGAL
BESSEL
BETHEL
BEWAIL
BOVRIL
BRAZIL
BRIDAL
BRUMAL
BRUNEL
BRUTAL
BUCCAL
BULBIL
BULBUL
BURIAL
BUSHEL
CAMAIL
CANCEL
CANNEL
CANTAL
CARMEL
CARNAL
CARPAL
CARPEL
CARREL
CARTEL
CARVEL
CASUAL
CAUSAL
CAVELL
CERCAL
CEREAL
CHAPEL
CHESIL
CHEVAL
CHIBOL
CHISEL
CHITAL
CHORAL
COEVAL
COMPEL
CONSUL
CORBEL
CORNEL
CORRAL
CRENAL
CRENEL
CRESOL
CREWEL
CRINAL
CROTAL
CRURAL
CUDGEL
CUNEAL
CUPFUL
CURPEL
CURSAL
CURTAL
CYMBAL
DACTYL
DAEDAL
DAMSEL
DANIEL
DENIAL
DENTAL
DERAIL
DERMAL
DETAIL
DIESEL
DIRNDL
DISMAL
DISPEL
DISTAL
DISTIL
DJEBEL
DONZEL
DORSAL
DOSSAL
DRIVEL
DUFFEL
EARFUL
EIFFEL
EMBAIL
ENAMEL
ENODAL
ENROLL
ENSEAL
ENTAIL
EPICAL
EXTOLL
EYEFUL
FACIAL
FAECAL
FARDEL
FENNEL
FERIAL
FESTAL
FEUDAL
FILIAL
FINGAL
FINIAL
FISCAL
FITFUL
FLORAL
FOETAL
FORMAL
FOSSIL
FRIVOL
FRUGAL
FULFIL
FUNGAL
FUNNEL
GAMBOL
GAVIAL
GENIAL
GERBIL
GHAZAL
GLAGOL
GLOBAL
GLYCOL
GOOGOL
GOSPEL
GRAVEL
GROVEL
GUNNEL
HAEMAL
HALLAL
HANDEL
HERBAL
HIMMEL
HIRSEL
HOSTEL
HUMMEL
HYMNAL
HYPHAL
INSTAL
INSTIL
IREFUL
IRWELL
ISABEL
ISRAEL
JACKAL
JEKYLL
JINGAL
JOVIAL
JOYFUL
JUMBAL
KENDAL
KENNEL
KENSAL
KERNEL
KISSEL
KOTWAL
KUMMEL
LABIAL
LAICAL
LARVAL
LAUREL
LAWFUL
LEMUEL
LENTEL
LENTIL
LETHAL
LINEAL
LINTEL
LIONEL
LISTEL
LOVELL
LOWELL
LUTEAL
MAMMAL
MANFUL
MANUAL
MARCEL
MARTEL
MARVEL
MEDIAL
MENDEL
MENIAL
MENSAL
MENTAL
MESAIL
MESCAL
MESIAL
METHYL
MINDEL
MISSAL
MISSEL
MITRAL
MONGOL
MONIAL
MORSEL
MORTAL
MURIEL
MUSSEL
MUTUAL
NERVAL
NEURAL
NEWELL
NICKEL
NITRYL
NORMAL
NOVIAL
OBITAL
ORDEAL
ORWELL
OXTAIL
PARCEL
PASCAL
PASTEL
PASTIL
PATROL
PENCEL
PENCIL
PENNAL
PENTEL
PETREL
PETROL
PHENOL
PHENYL
PHONAL
PINEAL
PISTIL
PISTOL
PLURAL
PODSOL
PODZOL
POMMEL
PORTAL
POSTAL
POSTIL

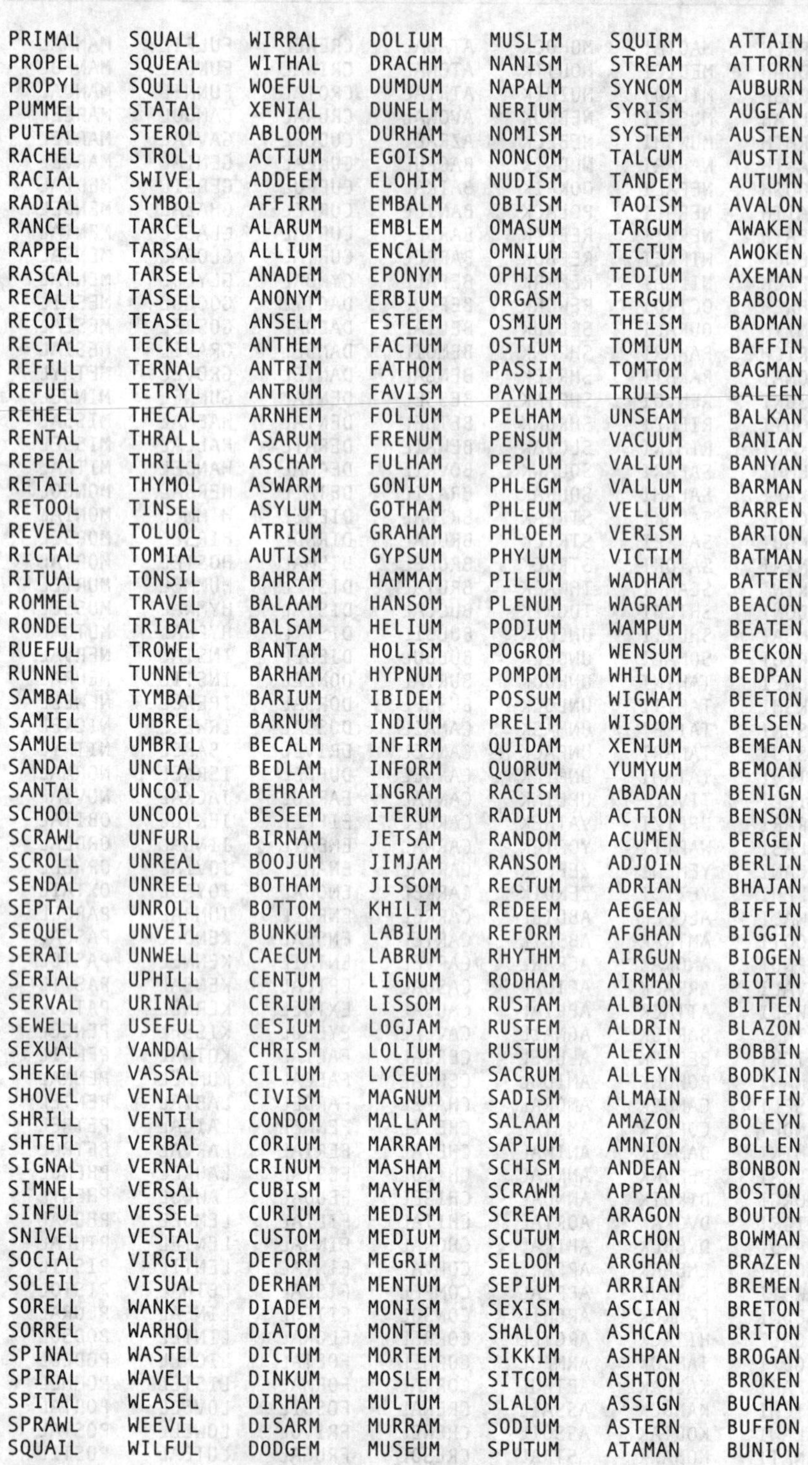

PRIMAL
PROPEL
PROPYL
PUMMEL
PUTEAL
RACHEL
RACIAL
RADIAL
RANCEL
RAPPEL
RASCAL
RECALL
RECOIL
RECTAL
REFILL
REFUEL
REHEEL
RENTAL
REPEAL
RETAIL
RETOOL
REVEAL
RICTAL
RITUAL
ROMMEL
RONDEL
RUEFUL
RUNNEL
SAMBAL
SAMIEL
SAMUEL
SANDAL
SANTAL
SCHOOL
SCRAWL
SCROLL
SENDAL
SEPTAL
SEQUEL
SERAIL
SERIAL
SERVAL
SEWELL
SEXUAL
SHEKEL
SHOVEL
SHRILL
SHTETL
SIGNAL
SIMNEL
SINFUL
SNIVEL
SOCIAL
SOLEIL
SORELL
SORREL
SPINAL
SPIRAL
SPITAL
SPRAWL
SQUAIL
SQUALL
SQUEAL
SQUILL
STATAL
STEROL
STROLL
SWIVEL
SYMBOL
TARCEL
TARSAL
TARSEL
TASSEL
TEASEL
TECKEL
TERNAL
TETRYL
THECAL
THRALL
THRILL
THYMOL
TINSEL
TOLUOL
TOMIAL
TONSIL
TRAVEL
TRIBAL
TROWEL
TUNNEL
TYMBAL
UMBREL
UMBRIL
UNCIAL
UNCOIL
UNCOOL
UNFURL
UNREAL
UNREEL
UNROLL
UNVEIL
UNWELL
UPHILL
URINAL
USEFUL
VANDAL
VASSAL
VENIAL
VENTIL
VERBAL
VERNAL
VERSAL
VESSEL
VESTAL
VIRGIL
VISUAL
WANKEL
WARHOL
WASTEL
WAVELL
WEASEL
WEEVIL
WILFUL
WIRRAL
WITHAL
WOEFUL
XENIAL
ABLOOM
ACTIUM
ADDEEM
AFFIRM
ALARUM
ALLIUM
ANADEM
ANONYM
ANSELM
ANTHEM
ANTRIM
ANTRUM
ARNHEM
ASARUM
ASCHAM
ASWARM
ASYLUM
ATRIUM
AUTISM
BAHRAM
BALAAM
BALSAM
BANTAM
BARHAM
BARIUM
BARNUM
BECALM
BEDLAM
BEHRAM
BESEEM
BIRNAM
BOOJUM
BOTHAM
BOTTOM
BUNKUM
CAECUM
CENTUM
CERIUM
CESIUM
CHRISM
CILIUM
CIVISM
CONDOM
CORIUM
CRINUM
CUBISM
CURIUM
CUSTOM
DEFORM
DERHAM
DIADEM
DIATOM
DICTUM
DINKUM
DIRHAM
DISARM
DODGEM
DOLIUM
DRACHM
DUMDUM
DUNELM
DURHAM
EGOISM
ELOHIM
EMBALM
EMBLEM
ENCALM
EPONYM
ERBIUM
ESTEEM
FACTUM
FATHOM
FAVISM
FOLIUM
FRENUM
FULHAM
GONIUM
GOTHAM
GRAHAM
GYPSUM
HAMMAM
HANSOM
HELIUM
HOLISM
HYPNUM
IBIDEM
INDIUM
INFIRM
INFORM
INGRAM
ITERUM
JETSAM
JIMJAM
JISSOM
KHILIM
LABIUM
LABRUM
LIGNUM
LISSOM
LOGJAM
LOLIUM
LYCEUM
MAGNUM
MALLAM
MARRAM
MASHAM
MAYHEM
MEDISM
MEDIUM
MEGRIM
MENTUM
MONISM
MONTEM
MORTEM
MOSLEM
MULTUM
MURRAM
MUSEUM
MUSLIM
NANISM
NAPALM
NERIUM
NOMISM
NONCOM
NUDISM
OBIISM
OMASUM
OMNIUM
OPHISM
ORGASM
OSMIUM
OSTIUM
PASSIM
PAYNIM
PELHAM
PENSUM
PEPLUM
PHLEGM
PHLEUM
PHLOEM
PHYLUM
PILEUM
PLENUM
PODIUM
POGROM
POMPOM
POSSUM
PRELIM
QUIDAM
QUORUM
RACISM
RADIUM
RANDOM
RANSOM
RECTUM
REDEEM
REFORM
RHYTHM
RODHAM
RUSTAM
RUSTEM
RUSTUM
SACRUM
SADISM
SALAAM
SAPIUM
SCHISM
SCRAWM
SCREAM
SCUTUM
SELDOM
SEPIUM
SEXISM
SHALOM
SIKKIM
SITCOM
SLALOM
SODIUM
SPUTUM
SQUIRM
STREAM
SYNCOM
SYRISM
SYSTEM
TALCUM
TANDEM
TAOISM
TARGUM
TECTUM
TEDIUM
TERGUM
THEISM
TOMIUM
TOMTOM
TRUISM
UNSEAM
VACUUM
VALIUM
VALLUM
VELLUM
VERISM
VICTIM
WADHAM
WAGRAM
WAMPUM
WENSUM
WHILOM
WIGWAM
WISDOM
XENIUM
YUMYUM
ABADAN
ACTION
ACUMEN
ADJOIN
ADRIAN
AEGEAN
AFGHAN
AIRGUN
AIRMAN
ALBION
ALDRIN
ALEXIN
ALLEYN
ALMAIN
AMAZON
AMNION
ANDEAN
APPIAN
ARAGON
ARCHON
ARGHAN
ARRIAN
ASCIAN
ASHCAN
ASHPAN
ASHTON
ASSIGN
ASTERN
ATAMAN
ATTAIN
ATTORN
AUBURN
AUGEAN
AUSTEN
AUSTIN
AUTUMN
AVALON
AWAKEN
AWOKEN
AXEMAN
BABOON
BADMAN
BAFFIN
BAGMAN
BALEEN
BALKAN
BANIAN
BANYAN
BARMAN
BARREN
BARTON
BATMAN
BATTEN
BEACON
BEATEN
BECKON
BEDPAN
BEETON
BELSEN
BEMEAN
BEMOAN
BENIGN
BENSON
BERGEN
BERLIN
BHAJAN
BIFFIN
BIGGIN
BIOGEN
BIOTIN
BITTEN
BLAZON
BOBBIN
BODKIN
BOFFIN
BOLEYN
BOLLEN
BONBON
BOSTON
BOUTON
BOWMAN
BRAZEN
BREMEN
BRETON
BRITON
BROGAN
BROKEN
BUCHAN
BUFFON
BUNION

BUNSEN
BUNYAN
BURDEN
BURTON
BUSKIN
BUSMAN
BUTTON
CACOON
CAFTAN
CAIMAN
CALKIN
CALVIN
CAMDEN
CAMION
CANAAN
CANNON
CANTON
CANYON
CAPTAN
CARBON
CARDAN
CAREEN
CARLIN
CARMEN
CARSON
CARTON
CASEIN
CASLON
CATKIN
CAVEIN
CAVERN
CAYMAN
CEROON
CEYLON
CHARON
CHATON
CHAZAN
CHICON
CHIRON
CHITIN
CHITON
CHOPIN
CHOSEN
CHOUAN
CITRIN
CITRON
CLOVEN
COBDEN
COCHIN
COCOON
COFFIN
COLUMN
COMMON
CONMAN
COPPIN
CORDON
COTTON
COUPON
COUSIN
COWMAN
CRATON
CRAVEN
CRAYON
CRETAN
CRETIN
CROTON
CRUMEN
CUFFIN
CULMEN
CUMMIN
CUPMAN
CYANIN
DAEMON
DALTON
DAMPEN
DAMSON
DANTON
DARIEN
DARKEN
DARWIN
DAWSON
DEACON
DEADEN
DEAFEN
DECCAN
DEEPEN
DEHORN
DELIAN
DEMAIN
DEMEAN
DERAIN
DESIGN
DETAIN
DIAXON
DIODON
DIOXIN
DISOWN
DIZAIN
DOBBIN
DOBSON
DOLMAN
DOLMEN
DOMAIN
DONJON
DORIAN
DOWSON
DRAGON
DRALON
DRIVEN
DRYDEN
DUBBIN
DUBLIN
DUDEEN
DUNCAN
DUNLIN
DURIAN
DURION
DZEREN
EAMONN
EDISON
EIRANN
ELEVEN
ELOIGN
ENJOIN
ENSIGN
ENZIAN
EOTHEN
EOZOON
EPIGON
ETALON
ETYMON
EUSTON
EVELYN
EXOGEN
EXPUGN
EXTERN
FABIAN
FALCON
FALLEN
FANION
FANTAN
FARCIN
FASTEN
FATTEN
FENIAN
FINNAN
FIRKIN
FIRMAN
FLACON
FLAGON
FLAMEN
FLAXEN
FLORIN
FRIPON
FROZEN
FUSAIN
FUSION
GABION
GAIJIN
GALLEN
GALLON
GAMMON
GANION
GARÇON
GARDEN
GASCON
GASMAN
GASTON
GAWAIN
GEASON
GEMMAN
GERMAN
GIBBON
GIBSON
GIDEON
GILPIN
GIRKIN
GIRTON
GIZZEN
GLUTEN
GNOMON
GOBLIN
GODOWN
GODSON
GODWIN
GOLDEN
GONION
GORDON
GORGON
GOTTEN
GOVERN
GRABEN
GRAFIN
GRATIN
GRAVEN
GRISON
GRYFON
GUENON
GUIDON
GUNMAN
HAEMON
HAGDEN
HAPPEN
HAPTEN
HARDEN
HARKEN
HASTEN
HAYDON
HEAVEN
HEMPEN
HENNIN
HENSON
HERDEN
HEREIN
HERMON
HEROIN
HERREN
HETMAN
HIDDEN
HILTON
HITMAN
HOIDEN
HOYDEN
HUDSON
HYPHEN
IBADAN
ICEMAN
IMBARN
IMOGEN
IMPAWN
IMPUGN
INBORN
INCHON
INDIAN
INDIGN
INTERN
INTOWN
INTRON
IONIAN
IRETON
ITCHEN
JAMBON
JARGON
JERKIN
JETTON
JONSON
JOPLIN
JORDAN
JOSKIN
JULIAN
JUSTIN
KAFTAN
KANOON
KANTEN
KAOLIN
KEATON
KELVIN
KENYAN
KIRMAN
KITTEN
KLAXON
KOREAN
KRAKEN
KRATON
KRUMAN
LAGOON
LALLAN
LARDON
LARKIN
LATEEN
LATRON
LATTEN
LAWMAN
LAYMAN
LEADEN
LEAVEN
LEGION
LEGMAN
LENTEN
LEPTON
LESION
LESSEN
LESSON
LEYDEN
LIBYAN
LICHEN
LILIAN
LINDEN
LISBON
LISTEN
LONDON
LOOSEN
LOTION
LOUDEN
LUCIAN
LUTEIN
LUZERN
LYDIAN
LYTTON
MACRON
MADDEN
MADMAN
MAGNON
MAIDAN
MAIDEN
MALDON
MALIAN
MALIGN
MAMMON
MANNIN
MARGIN
MARIAN
MARLIN
MAROON
MARRON
MARTEN
MARTIN
MASLIN
MATRON
MAWKIN
MEDIAN
MELTON
MEMNON
MERKIN
MERLIN
MERMAN
MERTON
MICRON
MIDDEN
MIGNON
MILTON
MINION
MINOAN
MINTON
MITTEN
MIZZEN
MODERN
MOLTEN
MOREEN
MORGAN
MORGEN
MORION
MORMON
MOTION
MOTOWN
MOULIN
MOUTAN
MOUTON
MUFFIN
MUFLON
MURLIN
MURRIN
MUSLIN
MUTTON
MYELIN
MYELON
MYOGEN
MYOSIN
NANKIN
NANSEN
NAPKIN
NASION
NATION
NATRON
NEATEN
NELSON
NEURON
NEWMAN
NEWTON
NIACIN
NINIAN
NIPPON
NISSEN
NOGGIN
NORMAN
NOTION
NUBBIN
OBERON
OBTAIN
ODDSON
OGADEN
OILCAN
OILMAN
OLEFIN
ONEDIN
ONEGIN
ONEMAN
OPPUGN
OPTION
ORDAIN
OREGON
ORIGEN
ORIGIN
ORISON
ORPHAN
OSSIAN
OUTRUN
OXYGEN
PADUAN
PANTON
PARDON
PARKIN
PARSON
PARTON
PASTON
PATHAN
PATRON
PATTEN
PATTON
PEAHEN
PECTEN
PECTIN
PELION
PENMAN
PENNON
PERKIN
PERRON
PERSON
PÉTAIN
PHOTON
PIDGIN
PIEMAN
PIGEON
PIGPEN
PINION
PINYIN
PIPKIN

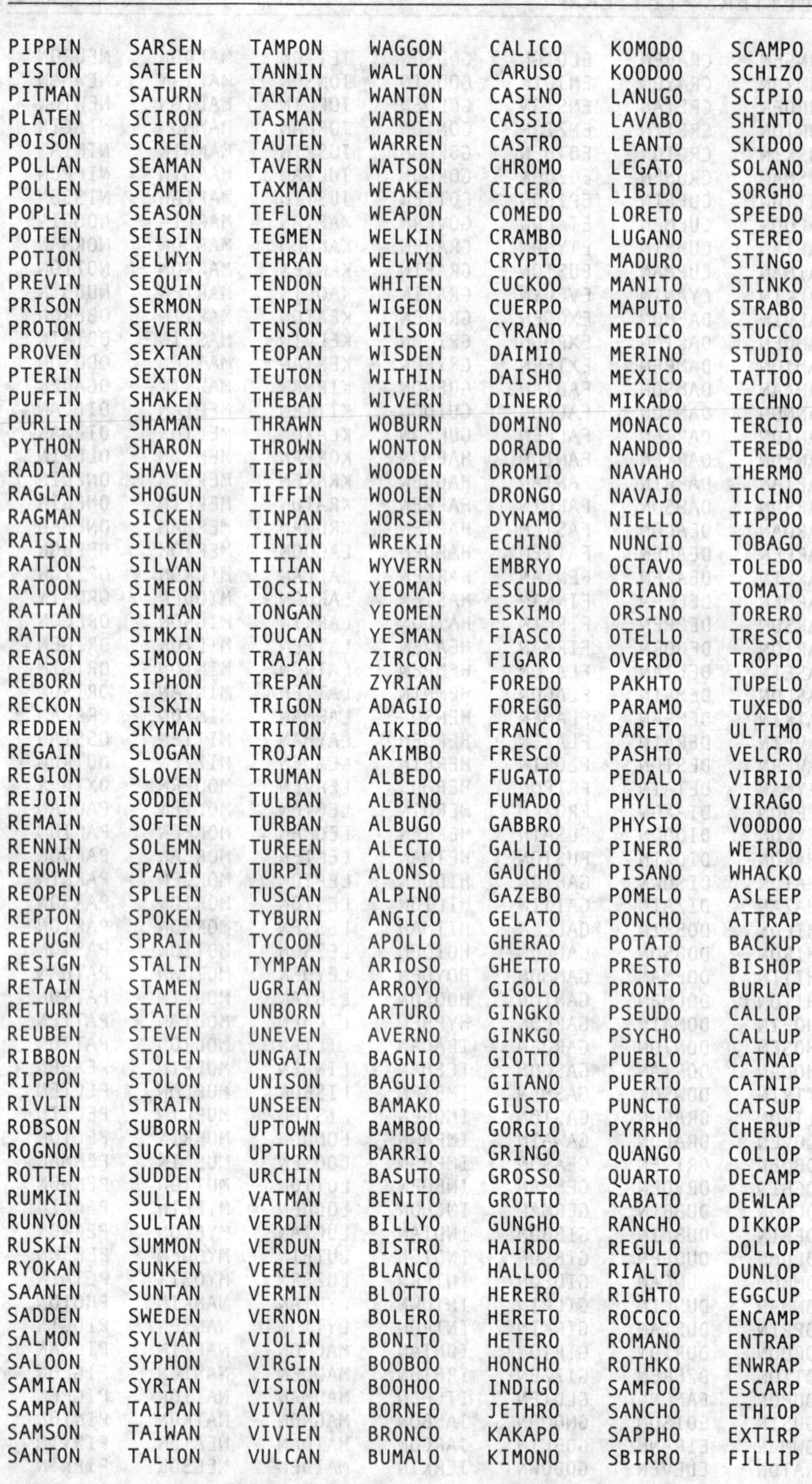

PIPPIN
PISTON
PITMAN
PLATEN
POISON
POLLAN
POLLEN
POPLIN
POTEEN
POTION
PREVIN
PRISON
PROTON
PROVEN
PTERIN
PUFFIN
PURLIN
PYTHON
RADIAN
RAGLAN
RAGMAN
RAISIN
RATION
RATOON
RATTAN
RATTON
REASON
REBORN
RECKON
REDDEN
REGAIN
REGION
REJOIN
REMAIN
RENNIN
RENOWN
REOPEN
REPTON
REPUGN
RESIGN
RETAIN
RETURN
REUBEN
RIBBON
RIPPON
RIVLIN
ROBSON
ROGNON
ROTTEN
RUMKIN
RUNYON
RUSKIN
RYOKAN
SAANEN
SADDEN
SALMON
SALOON
SAMIAN
SAMPAN
SAMSON
SANTON
SARSEN
SATEEN
SATURN
SCIRON
SCREEN
SEAMAN
SEAMEN
SEASON
SEISIN
SELWYN
SEQUIN
SERMON
SEVERN
SEXTAN
SEXTON
SHAKEN
SHAMAN
SHARON
SHAVEN
SHOGUN
SICKEN
SILKEN
SILVAN
SIMEON
SIMIAN
SIMKIN
SIMOON
SIPHON
SISKIN
SKYMAN
SLOGAN
SLOVEN
SODDEN
SOFTEN
SOLEMN
SPAVIN
SPLEEN
SPOKEN
SPRAIN
STALIN
STAMEN
STATEN
STEVEN
STOLEN
STOLON
STRAIN
SUBORN
SUCKEN
SUDDEN
SULLEN
SULTAN
SUMMON
SUNKEN
SUNTAN
SWEDEN
SYLVAN
SYPHON
SYRIAN
TAIPAN
TAIWAN
TALION
TAMPON
TANNIN
TARTAN
TASMAN
TAUTEN
TAVERN
TAXMAN
TEFLON
TEGMEN
TEHRAN
TENDON
TENPIN
TENSON
TEOPAN
TEUTON
THEBAN
THRAWN
THROWN
TIEPIN
TIFFIN
TINPAN
TINTIN
TITIAN
TOCSIN
TONGAN
TOUCAN
TRAJAN
TREPAN
TRIGON
TRITON
TROJAN
TRUMAN
TULBAN
TURBAN
TUREEN
TURPIN
TUSCAN
TYBURN
TYCOON
TYMPAN
UGRIAN
UNBORN
UNEVEN
UNGAIN
UNISON
UNSEEN
UPTOWN
UPTURN
URCHIN
VATMAN
VERDIN
VERDUN
VEREIN
VERMIN
VERNON
VIOLIN
VIRGIN
VISION
VIVIAN
VIVIEN
VULCAN
WAGGON
WALTON
WANTON
WARDEN
WARREN
WATSON
WEAKEN
WEAPON
WELKIN
WELWYN
WHITEN
WIGEON
WILSON
WISDEN
WITHIN
WIVERN
WOBURN
WONTON
WOODEN
WOOLEN
WORSEN
WREKIN
WYVERN
YEOMAN
YEOMEN
YESMAN
ZIRCON
ZYRIAN
ADAGIO
AIKIDO
AKIMBO
ALBEDO
ALBINO
ALBUGO
ALECTO
ALONSO
ALPINO
ANGICO
APOLLO
ARIOSO
ARROYO
ARTURO
AVERNO
BAGNIO
BAGUIO
BAMAKO
BAMBOO
BARRIO
BASUTO
BENITO
BILLYO
BISTRO
BLANCO
BLOTTO
BOLERO
BONITO
BOOBOO
BOOHOO
BORNEO
BRONCO
BUMALO
CALICO
CARUSO
CASINO
CASSIO
CASTRO
CHROMO
CICERO
COMEDO
CRAMBO
CRYPTO
CUCKOO
CUERPO
CYRANO
DAIMIO
DAISHO
DINERO
DOMINO
DORADO
DROMIO
DRONGO
DYNAMO
ECHINO
EMBRYO
ESCUDO
ESKIMO
FIASCO
FIGARO
FOREDO
FOREGO
FRANCO
FRESCO
FUGATO
FUMADO
GABBRO
GALLIO
GAUCHO
GAZEBO
GELATO
GHERAO
GHETTO
GIGOLO
GINGKO
GINKGO
GIOTTO
GITANO
GIUSTO
GORGIO
GRINGO
GROSSO
GROTTO
GUNGHO
HAIRDO
HALLOO
HERERO
HERETO
HETERO
HONCHO
INDIGO
JETHRO
KAKAPO
KIMONO
KOMODO
KOODOO
LANUGO
LAVABO
LEANTO
LEGATO
LIBIDO
LORETO
LUGANO
MADURO
MANITO
MAPUTO
MEDICO
MERINO
MEXICO
MIKADO
MONACO
NANDOO
NAVAHO
NAVAJO
NIELLO
NUNCIO
OCTAVO
ORIANO
ORSINO
OTELLO
OVERDO
PAKHTO
PARAMO
PARETO
PASHTO
PEDALO
PHYLLO
PHYSIO
PINERO
PISANO
POMELO
PONCHO
POTATO
PRESTO
PRONTO
PSEUDO
PSYCHO
PUEBLO
PUERTO
PUNCTO
PYRRHO
QUANGO
QUARTO
RABATO
RANCHO
REGULO
RIALTO
RIGHTO
ROCOCO
ROMANO
ROTHKO
SAMFOO
SANCHO
SAPPHO
SBIRRO
SCAMPO
SCHIZO
SCIPIO
SHINTO
SKIDOO
SOLANO
SORGHO
SPEEDO
STEREO
STINGO
STINKO
STRABO
STUCCO
STUDIO
TATTOO
TECHNO
TERCIO
TEREDO
THERMO
TICINO
TIPPOO
TOBAGO
TOLEDO
TOMATO
TORERO
TRESCO
TROPPO
TUPELO
TUXEDO
ULTIMO
VELCRO
VIBRIO
VIRAGO
VOODOO
WEIRDO
WHACKO
ASLEEP
ATTRAP
BACKUP
BISHOP
BURLAP
CALLOP
CALLUP
CATNAP
CATNIP
CATSUP
CHERUP
COLLOP
DECAMP
DEWLAP
DIKKOP
DOLLOP
DUNLOP
EGGCUP
ENCAMP
ENTRAP
ENWRAP
ESCARP
ETHIOP
EXTIRP
FILLIP

GALLOP
GALLUP
GAZUMP
GIDDUP
GOLLOP
GOSSIP
HANGUP
HICCUP
HIGHUP
HOLDUP
HOOKUP
HYSSOP
INSTEP
KIDNAP
LAPTOP
LARRUP
LINEUP
LINKUP
LOCKUP
LOLLOP
MADCAP
MADEUP
MAKEUP
MARKUP
MENDIP
MISHAP
MOBCAP
MOCKUP
OARLAP
OUTTOP
PAIDUP
PENTUP
PERHAP
PHILIP
PICKUP
PILEUP
PUSHUP
RAGTOP
RECOUP
REDCAP
REDTOP
REVAMP
SALOOP
SATRAP
SCHLEP
SCRIMP
SCROOP
SHRIMP
SITREP
SLIPUP
STROUP
TEACUP
THREAP
TIPTOP
TITTUP
TOECAP
TOSSUP
TURNIP
TURNUP
UNWRAP
UPKEEP
WALLOP
WINDUP
ABATOR
ADORER
AFFAIR
AGADIR
ALEGAR
ALLIER
ALTAIR
AMBLER
ANADYR
ANCHOR
ANGLER
ANSWER
ANTHER
ANTLER
APPEAR
ARBOUR
ARCHER
ARDOUR
ARMOUR
ARREAR
ARTHUR
ASHLAR
ASHTAR
AUSTER
AUTHOR
AVATAR
BACKER
BADGER
BAILER
BALDER
BANDAR
BANGER
BANKER
BANNER
BANTER
BARBER
BARKER
BARTER
BASHER
BATHER
BATTER
BAXTER
BAZAAR
BEAKER
BEARER
BEATER
BEAVER
BEDDER
BEEPER
BEGGAR
BENDER
BERBER
BESTIR
BETTER
BETTOR
BEZOAR
BICKER
BIDDER
BIGGER
BINDER
BISTER
BITTER
BLAZER
BLOWER
BOATER
BODGER
BOILER
BOLTER
BOMBER
BONDER
BONZER
BOOKER
BOOMER
BOOZER
BORDAR
BORDER
BOTHER
BOUSER
BOWLER
BOWSER
BOXCAR
BRACER
BREWER
BROKER
BUCKER
BUFFER
BUGGER
BUGLER
BULGAR
BULGER
BULLER
BUMPER
BUNKER
BUNTER
BURGER
BURNER
BURSAR
BUSKER
BUSTER
BUTLER
BUTTER
BUZZER
CADGER
CAESAR
CAHIER
CALKER
CALLER
CALVER
CAMBER
CAMPER
CANCER
CANDOR
CANKER
CANTAR
CANTER
CANTOR
CAPTOR
CAREER
CARPER
CARTER
CARVER
CASPAR
CASTER
CASTOR
CATHAR
CAVOUR
CELLAR
CENSER
CENSOR
CENTER
CHADOR
CHAFER
CHASER
CHEDER
CHIMER
CHINAR
CHOKER
CHOLER
CINDER
CIPHER
CLAMOR
CLEVER
CLOSER
CLOVER
COALER
COBBER
COCKER
CODGER
COFFER
COGGER
COINER
COLLAR
COLMAR
COLOUR
COLTER
COMBER
CONCUR
CONDOR
CONFER
CONGER
CONKER
CONNER
COOKER
COOLER
COOPER
COPIER
COPPER
CORKER
CORNER
COSHER
COSIER
COSTAR
COSTER
COTTAR
COUGAR
COWPER
COZIER
CRATER
CRATUR
CRAYER
CREMOR
CUITER
CULTER
CULVER
CUMBER
CUMMER
CUNNER
CUPPER
CURLER
CURSOR
CUSSER
CUSTER
CUTLER
CUTTER
CYPHER
DAGGER
DAMPER
DANCER
DANDER
DANGER
DAPPER
DARTER
DEALER
DEARER
DEBTOR
DECKER
DEEPER
DEKKER
DENIER
DENVER
DEODAR
DETOUR
DEVOUR
DEXTER
DIAPER
DIBBER
DICKER
DIETER
DIFFER
DIGGER
DIMMER
DINNER
DIPPER
DISBAR
DISEUR
DITHER
DOCKER
DOCTOR
DODDER
DODGER
DOGGER
DOLEUR
DOLLAR
DOLOUR
DOOFER
DORMER
DORTER
DOSSER
DOWNER
DOWSER
DRAPER
DRAWER
DRIVER
DROVER
DUDDER
DUFFER
DUMPER
DUNBAR
DUNDER
DUNKER
DURBAR
DUSTER
EARNER
EASIER
EASTER
ECLAIR
EDITOR
EITHER
ELIXIR
ELOPER
ELUTOR
ENAMOR
ENDEAR
ERASER
ESCHAR
ESTHER
ETCHER
ETRIER
EXETER
EXMOOR
FACTOR
FALTER
FARMER
FATHER
FAVOUR
FEEDER
FEELER
FELLER
FENCER
FENDER
FERVOR
FESTER
FETTER
FIBBER
FILLER
FILTER
FINDER
FINGER
FIRMER
FISHER
FITTER
FIZZER
FLAVOR
FLOWER
FLUTER
FODDER
FOKKER
FOLDER
FOLIAR
FOOTER
FORGER
FORMER
FOSTER
FOWLER
FRAGOR
FRATER
FUHRER
FULLER
FULMAR
FUREUR
FURFUR
GAFFER
GAINER
GAITER
GAMMER
GANDER
GANGER
GAOLER
GARNER
GARTER
GASPAR
GASPER
GASSER
GASTER
GATHER
GAUGER
GEEZER
GEIGER
GELLER
GENDER
GETTER
GEYSER
GHEBER
GIAOUR
GIBBER
GILDER
GIMMER
GINGER
GIRDER
GLAMOR
GLIDER
GLOWER
GNAWER
GOFFER
GOITER
GOLFER
GOOBER
GOPHER
GRATER
GRAVER
GROCER
GROPER
GROWER
GUITAR
GULPER
GUNNER
GUNTER
GUSHER
GUSLAR
GUTTER
HACKER
HAILER
HALTER
HAMMER

HAMPER
HANGAR
HANGER
HANKER
HARBOR
HASSAR
HATTER
HAWKER
HAWSER
HEADER
HEALER
HEARER
HEATER
HECTOR
HEIFER
HELLER
HELPER
HERDER
HIGHER
HINDER
HITHER
HITLER
HITTER
HOAXER
HODDER
HOGGAR
HOLDER
HOLLER
HONOUR
HOOFER
HOOKER
HOOPER
HOOTER
HOOVER
HOPPER
HORNER
HORROR
HOSIER
HOTAIR
HOTTER
HOWLER
HUMBER
HUMMER
HUMOUR
HUNGER
HUNKER
HUNTER
HUSSAR
IMPAIR
INDOOR
INSTAR
ISHTAR
ISOBAR
ISOMER
JABBER
JAEGER
JAGGER
JAGUAR
JAILER
JAILOR
JASPER
JAZZER
JENNER
JERKER
JESTER
JIGGER
JITTER
JOBBER
JOGGER
JOINER
JOSSER
JOTTER
JUDDER
JUGGER
JUMPER
JUNIOR
JUNKER
KAFFER
KAFFIR
KAISER
KEELER
KEENER
KEEPER
KELPER
KELTER
KEPHIR
KEPLER
KETMIR
KEVLAR
KHYBER
KICKER
KILLER
KILNER
KILTER
KIMMER
KINDER
KIPPER
KISSER
KOSHER
KRATER
KRONER
KRUGER
LAAGER
LABOUR
LADDER
LAFFER
LAMMER
LANCER
LANDER
LANDOR
LAPPER
LARDER
LASCAR
LASHER
LATHER
LATTER
LAUDER
LAWYER
LEADER
LEAVER
LECHER
LECTOR
LEDGER
LENDER
LENTOR
LESSER
LESSOR
LESTER
LETTER
LIBBER
LICTOR
LIEDER
LIFTER
LIGGER
LIMBER
LIMNER
LINEAR
LINGER
LINKER
LIQUOR
LISPER
LISTER
LITTER
LOADER
LOAFER
LOCKER
LODGER
LOGGER
LOITER
LONGER
LOOPER
LOOTER
LOUVER
LUBBER
LUGGER
LUMBAR
LUMBER
LUMPUR
LUSTER
LUTHER
MADDER
MAGYAR
MAHLER
MAILER
MAINOR
MAMZER
MANGER
MANNER
MARKER
MARNER
MARTYR
MASHER
MASTER
MATTER
MAUSER
MEAGER
MEDLAR
MEMBER
MEMOIR
MENDER
MENHIR
MENTOR
MERCER
MERGER
MESMER
METEOR
METIER
MILLER
MINCER
MINDER
MIRROR
MISTER
MOANER
MOCKER
MOHAIR
MOIDER
MONGER
MORTAR
MOTHER
MOUSER
MOUTER
MUCKER
MUDDER
MUGGER
MULLER
MUMMER
MURDER
MURMUR
MUSTER
MUTTER
NAILER
NAPIER
NAPPER
NASSER
NATTER
NEARER
NECKAR
NECTAR
NESTOR
NETHER
NEUTER
NICKER
NIGGER
NIPPER
NUGGAR
NUMBER
NUTTER
NUZZER
OBITER
OCULAR
OLIVER
ONAGER
OPENER
ORATOR
OSTLER
OUTBAR
OWLCAR
OYSTER
PACKER
PAIRER
PALLOR
PALMER
PAMPER
PANDER
PANTER
PANZER
PARKER
PARLOR
PASTOR
PATTER
PAUPER
PECKER
PEDDER
PEDLAR
PEELER
PEEPER
PEPPER
PESTER
PEWTER
PICKER
PILFER
PILLAR
PINCER
PINDAR
PINGER
PINTER
PITTER
PLACER
PLATER
PLAYER
PLEXOR
PLOVER
POLDER
PONDER
POOTER
POPLAR
POPPER
PORKER
PORTER
POSEUR
POSSER
POSTER
POTHER
POTTER
POURER
POUTER
POWDER
POWTER
PRATER
PRAYER
PREFER
PREWAR
PRIMER
PROPER
PRUNER
PUCKER
PUFFER
PULSAR
PULVER
PUNTER
PURLER
PURSER
PUSHER
PUSSER
PUTTER
QUAKER
QUASAR
QUAVER
QUIVER
RAFTER
RAIDER
RAISER
RANCOR
RANGER
RANKER
RANTER
RAPIER
RAPPER
RAPTOR
RASHER
RASPER
RASTER
RATHER
RATTER
READER
REAMER
REAPER
RECTOR
REDCAR
REEFER
REELER
RENDER
RENOIR
RENTER
REPAIR
RETOUR
REUTER
RÊVEUR
RHETOR
RHYMER
RICKER
RIGGER
RIGOUR
RINGER
RIOTER
RIPPER
ROAMER
ROARER
ROBBER
ROCKER
ROEMER
ROLLER
ROOFER
ROOMER
ROOTER
ROSSER
ROSTER
ROTHER
ROTTER
ROUTER
ROZZER
RUBBER
RUDDER
RUGGER
RUMMER
RUMOUR
RUNNER
RUTTER
SAGGAR
SAILOR
SALVER
SAMBAR
SAMBUR
SANDER
SAPHAR
SAPPER
SARTOR
SAUCER
SAUGER
SAVIOR
SAVOUR
SAWDER
SAWYER
SCALAR
SCALER
SCARER
SCORER
SCOTER
SEAMER
SECTOR
SEEDER
SEEKER
SELLER
SENDER
SENIOR
SENSOR
SERVER
SETTER
SHAKER
SHARER
SHAVER
SHINER
SHIVER
SHOFAR
SHOWER
SICKER
SIFTER
SIGNOR
SILVER
SIMMER
SIMPER
SINDER
SINGER
SINKER
SINNER
SIRDAR
SIRKAR
SISTER
SITTER
SKATER
SKEWER
SKIVER
SLATER
SLAVER
SLAYER
SLICER
SLIDER

SLIVER
SMILER
SMOKER
SNIPER
SNORER
SOCCER
SOLDER
SOLVER
SOMBER
SOONER
SORTER
SOUPER
SOUTER
SOWTER
SPACER
SPICER
SPIDER
SPINAR
STAGER
STATER
STATOR
STAYER
STOKER
STONER
STORER
STOVER
STOWER
STUMER
STUPOR
SUCCOR
SUCKER
SUFFER
SUITOR
SULFUR
SUMMER
SUNDER
SUPPER
SURFER
SUTLER
SYPHER
TAILOR
TALKER
TAMPER
TANKER
TANNER
TAPPER
TARTAR
TASTER
TATLER
TATTER
TEASER
TEETER
TELLAR
TELLER
TEMPER
TENDER
TENNER
TENSOR
TERROR
TESTER
TETHER
THALER
THENAR
TICKER
TILLER
TIMBER
TINDER
TINKER
TIPPER
TITFER
TITTER
TOLLER
TONSOR
TOOTER
TOPPER
TORPOR
TOSHER
TOTTER
TOURER
TOUSER
TOWBAR
TOWSER
TRACER
TRADER
TREMOR
TRICAR
TROCAR
TROVER
TUCKER
TUMOUR
TURNER
TUSKER
TWICER
ULSTER
UNFAIR
UPROAR
URETER
USURER
VALOUR
VALUER
VAPOUR
VECTOR
VELOUR
VENDER
VENDOR
VENEER
VERGER
VESPER
VIATOR
VICTOR
VIEWER
VIGOUR
VISIER
VIZIER
VOIDER
VOYEUR
VULGAR
WACKER
WAGNER
WAILER
WAITER
WAIVER
WALKER
WALLER
WALTER
WANDER
WARDER
WARMER
WARNER
WASHER
WASTER
WEAKER
WEARER
WEAVER
WEIMAR
WELDER
WELLER
WELTER
WESKER
WETHER
WHALER
WICKER
WIENER
WILDER
WINDER
WINGER
WINKER
WINNER
WINTER
WITHER
WIZIER
WONDER
WOOFER
WORKER
WOWSER
WRITER
XAVIER
YABBER
YAKKER
YAMMER
YANKER
YATTER
YESTER
YONDER
YORKER
YUCKER
ZANDER
ZEPHYR
ZIMMER
ZINGER
ZIPPER
ZITHER
ZOPHAR
ZOSTER
AARONS
ABACUS
ABBESS
ABDABS
ABYDOS
ACARUS
ACATES
ACCESS
ACINUS
ACKERS
ACORNS
ACROSS
ACTORS
ADONIS
AEGEUS
AEOLIS
AEOLUS
AFEARS
AFTERS
AIRBUS
ALACUS
ALEXIS
ALWAYS
AMENDS
AMYCUS
ANABAS
ANANAS
ANGELS
ANGERS
ANIMUS
ANNALS
ANTICS
ANUBIS
APPLES
ARABIS
ARAMIS
ARCHES
ASCIUS
ASSESS
ASSETS
ATHENS
ATKINS
AUREUS
AZORES
BAKERS
BALKIS
BARKIS
BARNES
BASICS
BATHOS
BAUCIS
BESSUS
BICEPS
BLACKS
BLINKS
BLOCKS
BOARDS
BODIES
BOFORS
BOREAS
BOSUNS
BOUNDS
BOWELS
BRACES
BRAHMS
BRAINS
BREWIS
BRICKS
BRIEFS
BROADS
BROOKS
BRUTUS
BUENOS
BUYERS
BYPASS
BYSSUS
CACTUS
CADDIS
CADETS
CADMUS
CALAIS
CALLAS
CALLUS
CAMPUS
CANVAS
CAPIAS
CARESS
CARIES
CARPUS
CASSIS
CAUCUS
CECILS
CENSUS
CERCUS
CEREUS
CERTES
CESTUS
CHAINS
CHAIRS
CHAMPS
CHEERS
CHEOPS
CHIMES
CHIVES
CHORUS
CIRCUS
CIRRUS
CITRUS
CIVICS
CLAIMS
CLAVIS
CLERKS
CLIFFS
CLIMES
CLOAKS
CLONUS
CLOVIS
CLUMPS
COATES
COCCUS
COITUS
COMMIS
CONICS
CORALS
CORMUS
CORNUS
CORPUS
CORTES
CORVUS
COSMOS
COULIS
CRANTS
CRASIS
CREEPS
CRIPES
CRISIS
CROCKS
CROCUS
CRONOS
CRUELS
CRUFTS
CRUMBS
CULLIS
CULTUS
CURSUS
CUSCUS
CUSTOS
CYCLUS
CYDNUS
CYESIS
CYGNUS
CYNIPS
CYPRIS
CYPRUS
DARIUS
DEBRIS
DEDANS
DELIUS
DENIMS
DENNIS
DEPTHS
DERMIS
DERRIS
DEVILS
DIANAS
DIESIS
DISCUS
DISHES
DITTOS
DIVERS
DOINGS
DORCAS
DOZENS
DROMOS
DRONES
DROVES
DUNCES
DURESS
ECCLES
EGRESS
ELBRUS
ELDERS
EMBERS
EMBOSS
ENGELS
ENNIUS
ENOSIS
EPIRUS
EPULIS
EQUALS
EREBUS
ERINYS
ETHICS
EXCESS
EXISTS
EXODUS
FABIUS
FABLES
FACIES
FAECES
FAINTS
FAMOUS
FASCES
FAUCES
FAUNUS
FAWKES
FEINTS
FERRIS
FETTES
FIELDS
FLANKS
FLARES
FLATUS
FLICKS
FLUTES
FOETUS
FOLIOS
FORCES
FRACAS
FRILLS
FRUITS
FUNDUS
FUNGUS
FURIES
GALLUS
GANGES
GENIUS
GENTES
GHOSTS
GILDAS
GLACIS
GLAMIS
GLUMPS
GNEISS
GORGES
GOURDS
GRACES
GRADES
GRADUS
GRAINS
GRAMPS
GRAPES
GRATIS
GRAVES
GREATS
GREEKS
GREENS
GRIMES
GRIMMS
GRIPES
GROATS
GROUPS
GROUTS

GRUMPS
GUARDS
GUESTS
GUIDES
GUILDS
HACHIS
HAGGIS
HALVES
HARASS
HARRIS
HAVERS
HEARTS
HEAVES
HELIOS
HERMES
HERONS
HERPES
HIATUS
HINGES
HIPPUS
HOBBES
HOLMES
HOUNDS
HOUSES
HUBRIS
HUGHES
HUMMUS
HYADES
HYBRIS
HYPNOS
IAMBUS
ICARUS
IMBOSS
INCHES
INDIES
INGOTS
INGRES
INLAWS
IRAQIS
ISLETS
ISSUES
JACOBS
JEEVES
JEWELS
JEWESS
JOYOUS
JUDGES
JULIUS
JUNCUS
KANSAS
KELLYS
KERMES
KERMIS
KEYNES
KNIVES
KOSMOS
KOUROS
KRONOS
KUMISS
LABRYS
LACHES
LADIES
LAMMAS
LAPSUS
LASSUS
LAYERS
LEAVES
LEMNOS
LESBOS
LIGHTS
LIMITS
LITMUS
LLOYDS
LOAVES
LYRICS
MADRAS
MAGNES
MAGNUS
MAJLIS
MANTIS
MAQUIS
MASSES
MATHIS
MATINS
MAXIMS
MEATUS
MEDIUS
MEJLIS
MELIUS
MENDES
MESSRS
MISSIS
MISSUS
MOBIUS
MODELS
MODIUS
MONTHS
MOPSUS
MORALS
MORASS
MORBUS
MORRIS
MOVIES
MUCOUS
MURALS
MYOSIS
MYTHOS
NAEVUS
NANTES
NAPLES
NEREUS
NERVES
NESSUS
NIGHTS
NIMBUS
NOYOUS
NYLONS
OBELUS
OBOLUS
OBSESS
OCEANS
OCKERS
OCTANS
ODIOUS
OGRESS
OILERS
OLENUS
ONIONS
OODLES
OPTICS
ORCHIS
ORDERS
OREXIS
ORGANS
OSIRIS
OTHERS
OTITIS
OUNCES
OUTGAS
OVIBOS
OXALIS
PAINTS
PALAIS
PALLAS
PAMIRS
PAMPAS
PAPERS
PAPHOS
PARVIS
PASSES
PASTIS
PATHOS
PATMOS
PATOIS
PEARLS
PELVIS
PEPLOS
PERILS
PETERS
PHAROS
PHASIS
PIECES
PIERIS
PILEUS
PISCES
PLAINS
PLANKS
PLATES
PLEXUS
PLIERS
PLUTUS
POINTS
POLYPS
POROUS
POUNDS
POWERS
PRANKS
PRAXIS
PRECIS
PRIMUS
PRISMS
PRIZES
PTERIS
PTOSIS
PUTOIS
QUALMS
QUEENS
QUOITS
RABIES
RACHIS
RADIUS
RAMOUS
RAPIDS
RECESS
RECTUS
REGIUS
RELICS
REMISS
REVERS
RHEIMS
RHESUS
RHEXIS
RHODES
RICHES
RICTUS
RIGHTS
ROGUES
ROMANS
ROUNDS
ROYALS
RUBENS
RUBIES
RUBIKS
RUCKUS
RUGOUS
RUMORS
RUMPUS
RUPEES
RUPIAS
SABRES
SAINTS
SALMIS
SARGUS
SAYERS
SCALES
SCAPUS
SCHUSS
SCOOBS
SCOPUS
SCRAPS
SCRUBS
SEAMUS
SENSES
SEPSIS
SERIES
SEUMAS
SEVENS
SÈVRES
SHADES
SHAKES
SHAMUS
SHANKS
SHARES
SHARPS
SHEARS
SHEERS
SHEETS
SHORTS
SIGHTS
SIRIUS
SKATES
SLACKS
SLAVES
SLOPES
SMACKS
SMALLS
SMILES
SMITHS
SOLEUS
SONICS
SORDES
SORTES
SPADES
SPARKS
SPEISS
SPLITS
SPOILS
SPOKES
SPORTS
STACKS
STAIRS
STAKES
STALKS
STALLS
STAMPS
STAPES
STARES
STASIS
STATES
STATUS
STEERS
STICKS
STILTS
STINKS
STIPES
STOCKS
STOKES
STONES
STOOKS
STOOLS
STRASS
STRAWS
STRESS
STUBBS
STUMPS
STYLUS
SUCCUS
SULCUS
SWEETS
SWIPES
TALLIS
TARDIS
TARSUS
TATERS
TAURUS
TELLUS
TENNIS
TERMES
TESTES
TESTIS
TETHYS
THALES
THAMES
THANKS
THEBES
THEIRS
THEMIS
THESIS
THETIS
THIERS
THINGS
THOLOS
THOLUS
THOMAS
THRIPS
THROES
THYMUS
TIGHTS
TIGRIS
TMESIS
TOBIAS
TOPHUS
TORRES
TRADES
TRAGUS
TRAPES
TRAVIS
TRIBES
TRICKS
TRIPOS
TROOPS
TROYES
TRUMPS
TRUNKS
TRUTHS
TUBERS
TURVES
TUSSIS
TWEEDS
TYPHUS
UCKERS
ULCERS
ULITIS
UMBLES
UNDIES
UNLESS
URANUS
UTERUS
VALENS
VALGUS
VECTIS
VENOUS
VERGES
VERMIS
VERSES
VERSUS
VIANDS
VILLUS
VINOUS
VIROUS
VITALS
VOLANS
VOLENS
VOSGES
VOWELS
VULGUS
WADERS
WALRUS
WAMPUS
WATERS
WELLES
WHALES
WHEELS
WHITES
WHOOPS
WIDOWS
WIPERS
WISHES
WOMENS
XERXES
YOICKS
ZOUNDS
ABDUCT
ABJECT
ABLAUT
ABRUPT
ABSENT
ACCENT
ACCEPT
ACCOST
ACQUIT
ADDICT
ADDUCT
ADJUST
ADRIFT
ADROIT
ADVENT
ADVERT
AFFECT
AFFRET
AFLOAT
AFREET
AGHAST
AIDANT
AIGLET
ALBEIT
ALBERT
ALIGHT
ALMOST
AMIDST
AMORET
AMOUNT
AMULET
ANKLET
ANOINT
AORIST
APPORT

ARAFAT
ARARAT
ARDENT
ARGENT
ARMLET
ARMPIT
ARNAUT
AROINT
AROUET
ARPENT
ARRANT
ARREST
ARTIST
ASCENT
ASLANT
ASPECT
ASSART
ASSENT
ASSERT
ASSIST
ASSORT
ASTART
ATTEST
AUGUST
AVAUNT
AVOCET
BABBIT
BACKET
BALLET
BALLOT
BANDIT
BANNET
BARBET
BARNET
BASALT
BASKET
BASSET
BECKET
BEDSIT
BEHEST
BEIRUT
BENNET
BEREFT
BESANT
BESORT
BEZANT
BHARAT
BIDENT
BILLET
BISECT
BLIGHT
BOBCAT
BOGART
BONNET
BOSKET
BOUGHT
BREAST
BRECHT
BREVET
BRIGHT
BRYANT

BUCKET
BUDGET
BUFFET
BULLET
BURBOT
BURNET
BUSKET
BUYOUT
CACHET
CAHOOT
CALLET
CANNOT
CAPLET
CARNET
CARNOT
CARPET
CARROT
CASKET
CATGUT
CAUGHT
CAVEAT
CAVORT
CEMENT
CHALET
CHENET
CHEVET
CHRIST
CLARET
CLIENT
CLOSET
COBALT
COGENT
COHORT
COLLET
COMART
COMBAT
COMFIT
COMMIT
COMSAT
COQUET
CORNET
CORSET
COSSET
COVENT
COVERT
COWPAT
CRAVAT
CREANT
CREDIT
CRIANT
CRONET
CRUSET
CUBIST
CUEIST
CULLET
CURIET
CURVET
CUSHAT
CUTLET
CYGNET
DACOIT

DAMMIT
DAUDET
DECANT
DECEIT
DECENT
DEDUCT
DEFEAT
DEFECT
DEJECT
DELICT
DEMENT
DEMIST
DEPART
DEPICT
DEPORT
DESERT
DESIST
DESPOT
DETECT
DETENT
DETEST
DEVEST
DEVOUT
DEWITT
DICAST
DIGEST
DIGLOT
DIKTAT
DIMWIT
DIQUAT
DIRECT
DIVERT
DIVEST
DOCENT
DOCKET
DOESNT
DORRIT
DORSET
DOUCET
DOWSET
DRIEST
DUGOUT
DULCET
DUMONT
DURANT
DYNAST
ECONUT
EFFECT
EFFORT
EFTEST
EGBERT
EGMONT
EGOIST
ELANET
ELDEST
ELICIT
ELUANT
ENGLUT
ENLIST
ENRAPT
EQUANT

ERRANT
ESCORT
ESPRIT
EXCEPT
EXEMPT
EXHORT
EXOCET
EXPECT
EXPERT
EXPORT
EXSERT
EXTANT
EXTENT
EXTORT
EYELET
FAGGOT
FAUCET
FERMAT
FERRET
FEWEST
FIDGET
FILFOT
FILLET
FINEST
FIRLOT
FITOUT
FLAUNT
FLIGHT
FLORET
FLUENT
FOLIOT
FOMENT
FORÇAT
FOREST
FORGET
FORGOT
FORINT
FORMAT
FORPIT
FOUGHT
FRIGHT
FROWST
FRUICT
FYLFOT
GADGET
GALANT
GALIOT
GALLET
GALOOT
GAMBET
GAMBIT
GANNET
GARGET
GARNET
GARRET
GARROT
GASKET
GERENT
GIBBET
GIGLET
GIGLOT

GILLET
GIMLET
GOBBET
GOBLET
GOCART
GODWIT
GOKART
GORGET
GULLET
GURLET
GURNET
GUSSET
HAMLET
HARLOT
HASLET
HAVENT
HEIGHT
HELMET
HENBIT
HERIOT
HERMIT
HOBART
HOGGET
HOLIST
HONEST
HORNET
HOTPOT
HUMECT
IMPACT
IMPART
IMPORT
IMPOST
INCEPT
INCEST
INDENT
INDICT
INDUCT
INFANT
INFECT
INFEST
INGEST
INJECT
INKJET
INKPOT
INMOST
INSECT
INSERT
INSIST
INSULT
INTACT
INTENT
INVENT
INVERT
INVEST
IRRUPT
ISEULT
JACENT
JACKET
JAMPOT
JENNET
JESUIT

JILLET
JULIET
JUNKET
JURANT
JURIST
KAPUTT
KENNET
KHALAT
KHILAT
KISMET
KITCAT
KNIGHT
LAMENT
LANCET
LAPPET
LARIAT
LASKET
LATENT
LATEST
LAXIST
LAYOUT
LEGIST
LEGLET
LETOUT
LEVANT
LIMPET
LINGOT
LINNET
LOCKET
LOCUST
LOQUAT
LORIOT
LOWEST
LUCENT
LURIST
LUTIST
LYRIST
MAGGOT
MAGNET
MAHOUT
MALLET
MAOIST
MARIST
MARKET
MARMOT
MASCOT
MAZOUT
MERCAT
MERLOT
MIDGET
MILLET
MINUET
MISFIT
MISHIT
MODEST
MODIST
MOLEST
MOMENT
MONIST
MOPPET
MOZART

MUFFET
MULLET
MUPPET
MUSCAT
MUSKET
MUTANT
NATANT
NAUGHT
NEEDNT
NEFAST
NEWEST
NIDGET
NITWIT
NOBBUT
NOCENT
NOUGAT
NOUGHT
NUDIST
NUGGET
NUTANT
OAKNUT
OBJECT
OBLAST
OBOIST
OBTECT
OBVERT
OCCULT
OCELOT
OCTANT
OFFCUT
OFFSET
OLIVET
OMELET
ONCOST
OPTOUT
ORGEAT
ORIENT
OSBERT
OUTFIT
OUTLET
OUTPUT
OUTSET
OUTWIT
PACKET
PALLET
PAMYAT
PANDIT
PAPIST
PARENT
PARGET
PARROT
PATENT
PEANUT
PEDANT
PEEWIT
PELLET
PELMET
PERMIT
PICKET
PIGLET
PIGOTT

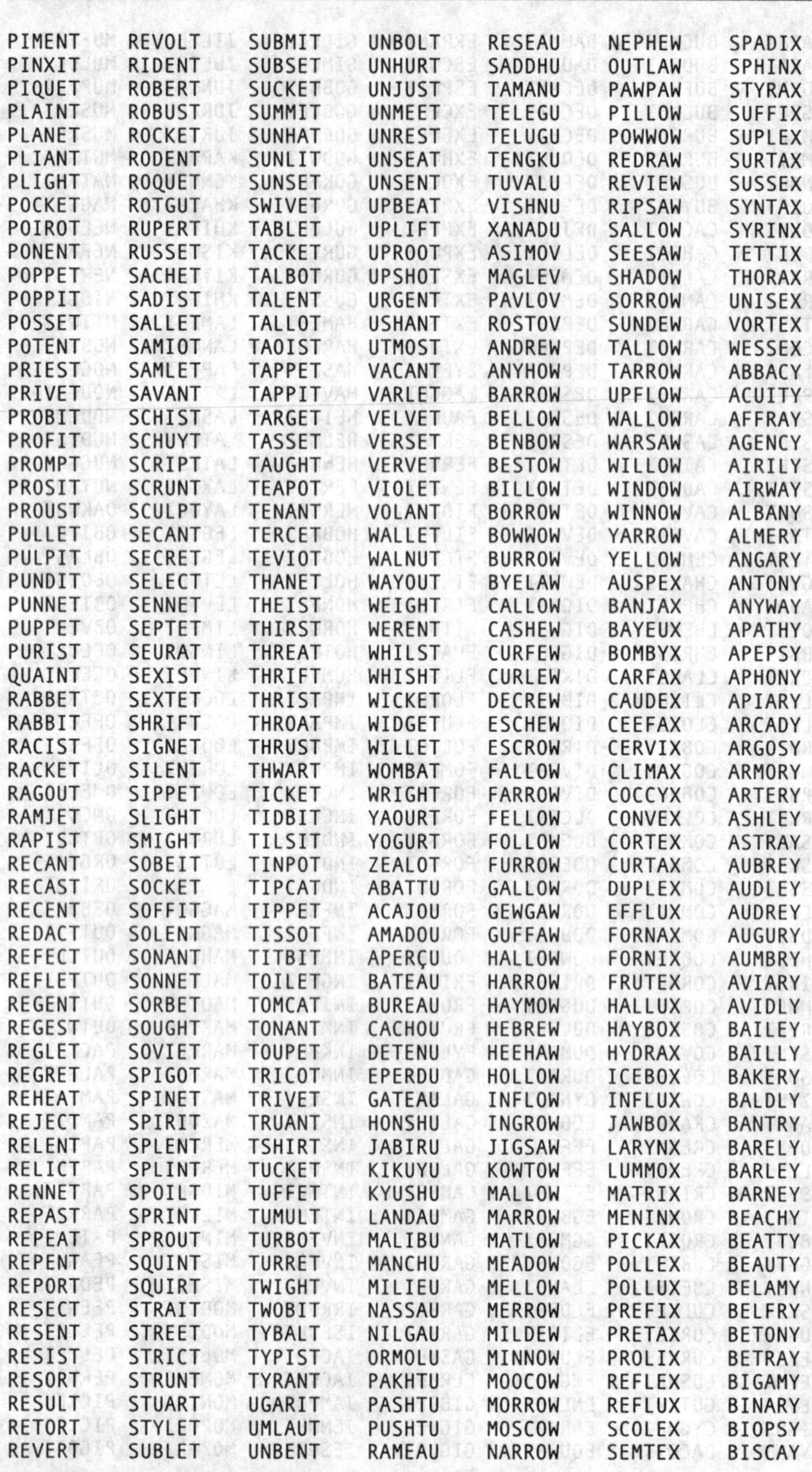

PIMENT
PINXIT
PIQUET
PLAINT
PLANET
PLIANT
PLIGHT
POCKET
POIROT
PONENT
POPPET
POPPIT
POSSET
POTENT
PRIEST
PRIVET
PROBIT
PROFIT
PROMPT
PROSIT
PROUST
PULLET
PULPIT
PUNDIT
PUNNET
PUPPET
PURIST
QUAINT
RABBET
RABBIT
RACIST
RACKET
RAGOUT
RAMJET
RAPIST
RECANT
RECAST
RECENT
REDACT
REFECT
REFLET
REGENT
REGEST
REGLET
REGRET
REHEAT
REJECT
RELENT
RELICT
RENNET
REPAST
REPEAT
REPENT
REPORT
RESECT
RESENT
RESIST
RESORT
RESULT
RETORT
REVERT
REVOLT
RIDENT
ROBERT
ROBUST
ROCKET
RODENT
ROQUET
ROTGUT
RUPERT
RUSSET
SACHET
SADIST
SALLET
SAMIOT
SAMLET
SAVANT
SCHIST
SCHUYT
SCRIPT
SCRUNT
SCULPT
SECANT
SECRET
SELECT
SENNET
SEPTET
SEURAT
SEXIST
SEXTET
SHRIFT
SIGNET
SILENT
SIPPET
SLIGHT
SMIGHT
SOBEIT
SOCKET
SOFFIT
SOLENT
SONANT
SONNET
SORBET
SOUGHT
SOVIET
SPIGOT
SPINET
SPIRIT
SPLENT
SPLINT
SPOILT
SPRINT
SPROUT
SQUINT
SQUIRT
STRAIT
STREET
STRICT
STRUNT
STUART
STYLET
SUBLET
SUBMIT
SUBSET
SUCKET
SUMMIT
SUNHAT
SUNLIT
SUNSET
SWIVET
TABLET
TACKET
TALBOT
TALENT
TALLOT
TAOIST
TAPPET
TAPPIT
TARGET
TASSET
TAUGHT
TEAPOT
TENANT
TERCET
TEVIOT
THANET
THEIST
THIRST
THREAT
THRIFT
THRIST
THROAT
THRUST
THWART
TICKET
TIDBIT
TILSIT
TINPOT
TIPCAT
TIPPET
TISSOT
TITBIT
TOILET
TOMCAT
TONANT
TOUPET
TRICOT
TRIVET
TRUANT
TSHIRT
TUCKET
TUFFET
TUMULT
TURBOT
TURRET
TWIGHT
TWOBIT
TYBALT
TYPIST
TYRANT
UGARIT
UMLAUT
UNBENT
UNBOLT
UNHURT
UNJUST
UNMEET
UNREST
UNSEAT
UNSENT
UPBEAT
UPLIFT
UPROOT
UPSHOT
URGENT
USHANT
UTMOST
VACANT
VARLET
VELVET
VERSET
VERVET
VIOLET
VOLANT
WALLET
WALNUT
WAYOUT
WEIGHT
WERENT
WHILST
WHISHT
WICKET
WIDGET
WILLET
WOMBAT
WRIGHT
YAOURT
YOGURT
ZEALOT
ABATTU
ACAJOU
AMADOU
APERÇU
BATEAU
BUREAU
CACHOU
DETENU
EPERDU
GATEAU
HONSHU
JABIRU
KIKUYU
KYUSHU
LANDAU
MALIBU
MANCHU
MILIEU
NASSAU
NILGAU
ORMOLU
PAKHTU
PASHTU
PUSHTU
RAMEAU
RESEAU
SADDHU
TAMANU
TELEGU
TELUGU
TENGKU
TUVALU
VISHNU
XANADU
ASIMOV
MAGLEV
PAVLOV
ROSTOV
ANDREW
ANYHOW
BARROW
BELLOW
BENBOW
BESTOW
BILLOW
BORROW
BOWWOW
BURROW
BYELAW
CALLOW
CASHEW
CURFEW
CURLEW
DECREW
ESCHEW
ESCROW
FALLOW
FARROW
FELLOW
FOLLOW
FURROW
GALLOW
GEWGAW
GUFFAW
HALLOW
HARROW
HAYMOW
HEBREW
HEEHAW
HOLLOW
INFLOW
INGROW
JIGSAW
KOWTOW
MALLOW
MARROW
MATLOW
MEADOW
MELLOW
MERROW
MILDEW
MINNOW
MOOCOW
MORROW
MOSCOW
NARROW
NEPHEW
OUTLAW
PAWPAW
PILLOW
POWWOW
REDRAW
REVIEW
RIPSAW
SALLOW
SEESAW
SHADOW
SORROW
SUNDEW
TALLOW
TARROW
UPFLOW
WALLOW
WARSAW
WILLOW
WINDOW
WINNOW
YARROW
YELLOW
AUSPEX
BANJAX
BAYEUX
BOMBYX
CARFAX
CAUDEX
CEEFAX
CERVIX
CLIMAX
COCCYX
CONVEX
CORTEX
CURTAX
DUPLEX
EFFLUX
FORNAX
FORNIX
FRUTEX
HALLUX
HAYBOX
HYDRAX
ICEBOX
INFLUX
JAWBOX
LARYNX
LUMMOX
MATRIX
MENINX
PICKAX
POLLEX
POLLUX
PREFIX
PRETAX
PROLIX
REFLEX
REFLUX
SCOLEX
SEMTEX
SPADIX
SPHINX
STYRAX
SUFFIX
SUPLEX
SURTAX
SUSSEX
SYNTAX
SYRINX
TETTIX
THORAX
UNISEX
VORTEX
WESSEX
ABBACY
ACUITY
AFFRAY
AGENCY
AIRILY
AIRWAY
ALBANY
ALMERY
ANGARY
ANTONY
ANYWAY
APATHY
APEPSY
APHONY
APIARY
ARCADY
ARGOSY
ARMORY
ARTERY
ASHLEY
ASTRAY
AUBREY
AUDLEY
AUDREY
AUGURY
AUMBRY
AVIARY
AVIDLY
BAILEY
BAILLY
BAKERY
BALDLY
BANTRY
BARELY
BARLEY
BARNEY
BEACHY
BEATTY
BEAUTY
BELAMY
BELFRY
BETONY
BETRAY
BIGAMY
BINARY
BIOPSY
BISCAY

BITCHY
BLEARY
BLENNY
BLIMEY
BLOODY
BLOWZY
BODILY
BOLDLY
BOLSHY
BOMBAY
BOTANY
BOTLEY
BOUNCY
BOUNTY
BOWERY
BRAINY
BRANDY
BRASSY
BRAWNY
BREEZY
BRIONY
BROLLY
BROODY
BRUMBY
BRYONY
BUBBLY
BULIMY
BUNCHY
BUNGAY
BURLEY
BUSBOY
BUSILY
CAGILY
CALMLY
CANARY
CANOPY
CANVEY
CARBOY
CATCHY
CATHAY
CAUSEY
CAVITY
CECITY
CELERY
CHALKY
CHANCY
CHANEY
CHATTY
CHEEKY
CHEERY
CHEESY
CHEMMY
CHERRY
CHESTY
CHILLY
CHIPPY
CHIRPY
CHITTY
CHIVVY
CHOKEY
CHOOSY
CHOPPY
CHOWRY
CHUBBY
CHUFFY
CHUMMY
CHUNKY
CICELY
CLAGGY
CLAMMY
CLARTY
CLASSY
CLAYEY
CLERGY
CLIPPY
CLOUDY
CLUMSY
CODIFY
COLDLY
COLONY
COMEDY
COMELY
COMITY
COMPLY
CONCHY
CONVEY
CONVOY
COOLLY
COSILY
COSTLY
COUNTY
COWBOY
CRABBY
CRAFTY
CRAGGY
CRANKY
CRANNY
CREAKY
CREAMY
CREEPY
CRIKEY
CRISPY
CROAKY
CROPPY
CROSBY
CROUPY
CRUMMY
CRUSTY
CUDDLY
CURACY
CURTLY
CURTSY
DAINTY
DARKEY
DARKLY
DAWNEY
DEADLY
DEARLY
DEEPLY
DEFRAY
DEFTLY
DEPLOY
DEPUTY
DESCRY
DICKEY
DIMITY
DINGHY
DINGLY
DISMAY
DISNEY
DONKEY
DOUBLY
DOUGHY
DOURLY
DOWNAY
DOYLEY
DRAFTY
DREAMY
DREARY
DREGGY
DRESSY
DRIPPY
DROOPY
DROPSY
DROSKY
DROWSY
DUMBLY
EARTHY
EASILY
EATERY
ECTOPY
EERILY
EFFIGY
EGENCY
EIGHTY
ELLERY
EMBODY
EMBUSY
EMPLOY
ENERGY
ENMITY
ENTITY
EQUITY
ESTRAY
EULOGY
EUTAXY
EVENLY
EXPIRY
FAIRLY
FAMILY
FAULTY
FEALTY
FEEBLY
FEISTY
FELONY
FIDDLY
FILTHY
FINELY
FINERY
FINLAY
FIRMLY
FIXITY
FLABBY
FLAGGY
FLASHY
FLATLY
FLEECY
FLESHY
FLEURY
FLIMSY
FLINTY
FLOOZY
FLOPPY
FLOSSY
FLOURY
FLUFFY
FLUNKY
FLURRY
FLUSHY
FOLKSY
FONDLY
FORRAY
FORSAY
FORTHY
FOULLY
FRANZY
FREELY
FRENZY
FRIARY
FRIDAY
FRILLY
FRISKY
FRIZZY
FROSTY
FROTHY
FROWZY
FRUITY
FRUMPY
FURPHY
GADFLY
GAIETY
GAINLY
GALAXY
GALLEY
GAMELY
GANGLY
GANTRY
GENTLY
GENTRY
GHARRY
GLADLY
GLASSY
GLIBLY
GLITZY
GLOOMY
GLOSSY
GOODLY
GOOGLY
GOOLEY
GRAINY
GRAMMY
GRANBY
GRANNY
GRASSY
GREASY
GREEDY
GRIMLY
GRISLY
GRITTY
GROGGY
GROOVY
GROTTY
GROUTY
GRUBBY
GRUMPY
GRUNDY
GUILTY
GULLEY
GURNEY
HALLEY
HARDLY
HARVEY
HAYLEY
HAZILY
HEARTY
HENLEY
HEREBY
HERESY
HEYDAY
HICKEY
HIGHLY
HILARY
HOBDAY
HOCKEY
HOMELY
HOMILY
HOMINY
HOOKEY
HOORAY
HOURLY
HUGELY
HUMPTY
HUNGRY
HURLEY
HURRAY
HUXLEY
IDIOCY
ILKLEY
INFAMY
INJURY
INTRAY
JALOPY
JARVEY
JAUNTY
JEREMY
JERSEY
JITNEY
JOCKEY
JOHNNY
JUSTLY
KECKSY
KEENLY
KEYWAY
KIDNEY
KINDLY
KINGLY
KNAGGY
KNOBBY
KNOTTY
LACKEY
LAMELY
LASTLY
LATELY
LAXITY
LAZILY
LEALTY
LEEWAY
LEGACY
LEMONY
LEVITY
LEWDLY
LIKELY
LIMPLY
LITANY
LIVELY
LIVERY
LONELY
LORDLY
LOUDLY
LOVELY
LOWBOY
LOWKEY
LUNACY
LUNARY
LUXURY
MAINLY
MALONY
MALORY
MARSHY
MAUNDY
MAYDAY
MAYFLY
MEANLY
MEASLY
MEDLEY
MEDWAY
MEEKLY
MELODY
MEMORY
MERELY
MERSEY
MICKEY
MIDDAY
MIDWAY
MIGHTY
MILDLY
MISERY
MISLAY
MODIFY
MOIETY
MONDAY
MONKEY
MONODY
MORNAY
MOSTLY
MOTLEY
MOULDY
MOUSEY
MUNIFY
MURPHY
MURRAY
MUTELY
MUTINY
NAMELY
NAPERY
NASEBY
NEARBY
NEARLY
NEATLY
NIAMEY
NICELY
NICETY
NIDIFY
NIGGLY
NIGHTY
NIMBLY
NINETY
NITERY
NOBODY
NONARY
NORROY
NORWAY
NOSILY
NOTARY
NOTIFY
NUDITY
NUMBLY
NUMPTY
OAKLEY
OCCUPY
ODDITY
OERLAY
ONEWAY
OPENLY
ORALLY
ORKNEY
ORNERY
ORRERY
OSIERY
OSPREY
OSSIFY
OTALGY
OUTCRY
OUTLAY
OVERLY
PACIFY
PAEONY
PAINTY
PALTRY
PANFRY
PANTRY
PAPACY
PAPERY
PARITY
PARLEY
PARODY
PARTLY

PASTRY
PATCHY
PAYDAY
PEARLY
PEBBLY
PENURY
PETARY
PHONEY
PHOOEY
PIGSTY
PIMPLY
PIRACY
PLENTY
PLUCKY
PLUMMY
POETRY
POLICY
POLITY
POLONY
POMPEY
POORLY
PORTLY
PREPAY
PREPPY
PRETTY
PRICEY
PRIMLY
PRIORY
PRISSY
PUDSEY
PULLEY
PUNCHY
PURELY
PURIFY
PURITY
PURVEY
QUARRY
QUEASY
QUINSY
QUIRKY
QWERTY
RAMIFY
RAPTLY
RAREFY
RARELY
RARITY
RASHLY
RATIFY

REALLY
REALTY
REMEDY
RENVOY
REPLAY
REVERY
RHEUMY
RICHLY
RICKEY
RODNEY
ROKEBY
ROMANY
ROMNEY
ROPERY
ROSARY
ROSERY
ROTARY
ROUGHY
RUDELY
RUNWAY
SAFELY
SAFETY
SAGELY
SALARY
SANELY
SANITY
SASHAY
SATINY
SAVORY
SAVVEY
SAWNEY
SAXONY
SCABBY
SCANTY
SCATTY
SCILLY
SCREWY
SCUMMY
SCURRY
SCURVY
SCUZZY
SEAWAY
SEEMLY
SELLBY
SENTRY
SEVERY
SHABBY
SHAGGY

SHAMMY
SHANDY
SHANTY
SHEENY
SHERRY
SHIFTY
SHIMMY
SHINDY
SHINNY
SHINTY
SHIRTY
SHODDY
SHUFTY
SICILY
SICKLY
SIDNEY
SIMONY
SIMPLY
SINEWY
SINGLY
SKELLY
SKERRY
SKIMPY
SKINNY
SKIVVY
SKURRY
SLANGY
SLEAZY
SLEEKY
SLEEPY
SLEEZY
SLINKY
SLIPPY
SLITHY
SLOPPY
SLOSHY
SLOWLY
SLUMMY
SLURRY
SLUSHY
SMARMY
SMARTY
SMEARY
SMELLY
SMILEY
SMITHY
SMOKEY
SMUDGY

SMUGLY
SMUTTY
SNAGGY
SNAILY
SNAPPY
SNAZZY
SNEAKY
SNEEZY
SNIFFY
SNIFTY
SNOOTY
SNOTTY
SNOUTY
SNUGLY
SODOMY
SOFTLY
SOLELY
SOLVAY
SORELY
SOURLY
SPARKY
SPEEDY
SPONGY
SPOOKY
SPOONY
SPORTY
SPOTTY
SPRYLY
STABLY
STAGEY
STALKY
STARRY
STEADY
STEAMY
STEELY
STICKY
STILTY
STINGY
STOCKY
STODGY
STOREY
STORMY
STRAWY
STRIPY
STUBBY
STUFFY
STUMPY
STURDY

SUBTLY
SUBWAY
SUDARY
SUGARY
SULTRY
SUNDAY
SUNDRY
SUNRAY
SUPPLY
SURELY
SURETY
SURREY
SURVEY
SWAMPY
SWANKY
SWARTY
SWEATY
SWEENY
SYDNEY
SYRUPY
SYZYGY
TAMELY
TANNOY
TARTLY
TAUTLY
TAWDRY
TEAPOY
TEENSY
TERMLY
TETANY
TETCHY
THEORY
THICKY
THINGY
THINLY
THIRTY
THORNY
TICKEY
TICKLY
TIDDLY
TIDILY
TIMELY
TITCHY
TOLZEY
TOMBOY
TOOTHY
TOOTSY
TOUCHY

TOWNLY
TRANNY
TRASHY
TREATY
TREBLY
TRENDY
TRICKY
TRILBY
TRIMLY
TROPHY
TRUSTY
TUMEFY
TURKEY
TWEEDY
TWEENY
TWENTY
TWIGGY
TWIRLY
TWISTY
TYPIFY
UBIETY
UNBUSY
UNDULY
UNEASY
UNHOLY
UNRULY
UNSEXY
UNTIDY
UNWARY
UPPITY
VAGARY
VAINLY
VALLEY
VANITY
VASTLY
VENERY
VERIFY
VERILY
VERITY
VESTRY
VILELY
VILIFY
VINERY
VOLLEY
VOTARY
WARCRY
WARILY
WARMLY

WATERY
WAYLAY
WEAKLY
WEEKLY
WESLEY
WHACKY
WHAMMY
WHEELY
WHEEZY
WHERRY
WHIMSY
WHINNY
WHISKY
WHITBY
WHOLLY
WIDELY
WIFELY
WIGGLY
WILDLY
WIMSEY
WINTRY
WISELY
WOBBLY
WOOKEY
WOOLLY
WORTHY
YEARLY
YEASTY
BUZFUZ
CHINTZ
CORTEZ
ERSATZ
HORMUZ
KRANTZ
QUARTZ
SHIRAZ
SPRITZ
SUIVEZ
TAMMUZ
TIZWAZ

7:1

AARONIC
ABALONE
ABANDON
ABASHED
ABATTIS
ABBASID
ABDOMEN
ABELARD
ABETTOR
ABIDING
ABIDJAN
ABIGAIL
ABILITY
ABIOSIS
ABJOINT
ABLATOR
ABOLISH
ABOUKIR
ABOULIA
ABRAHAM
ABRAXIS
ABREAST
ABRIDGE
ABSCESS
ABSCOND
ABSENCE
ABSINTH
ABSOLVE
ABSTAIN
ABUSIVE
ABYSMAL
ABYSSAL
ACADEME
ACADEMY
ACADIAN
ACARIDA
ACAUDAL
ACCLAIM
ACCOUNT
ACCRETE
ACCRUAL
ACCURSE
ACCUSED
ACCUSER
ACERBIC
ACESTES
ACETATE
ACETONE
ACHAEAN
ACHATES
ACHERON
ACHESON
ACHIEVE
ACHTUNG
ACIDIFY
ACIDITY
ACIFORM
ACOLYTE
ACONITE
ACQUIRE
ACREAGE
ACROBAT
ACRONYM
ACRYLIC
ACTAEON
ACTINAL
ACTINIA
ACTINIC
ACTRESS
ACTUARY
ACTUATE
ACUTELY
ADAMANT
ADAMITE
ADAPTER
ADAPTOR
ADDISON
ADDRESS
ADELINE
ADELPHI
ADENOID
ADENOMA
ADIPOSE
ADJOINT
ADJOURN
ADJUNCT
ADMIRAL
ADMIRED
ADMIRER
ADONAIS
ADOPTED
ADORING
ADORNED
ADRENAL
ADULATE
ADVANCE
ADVERSE
ADVISER
ADVISOR
AEOLIAN
AERATED
AEROBIC
AEROSOL
AFFABLE
AFFABLY
AFFAIRS
AFFIXED
AFFLICT
AFFRONT
AFGHANI
AFRICAN
AGAINST
AGELESS
AGELONG
AGGRESS
AGILITY
AGISTOR
AGITATE
AGITATO
AGONIST
AGONIZE
AGRAPHA
AGRIPPA
AGROUND
AIDANCE
AILERON
AILMENT
AIMLESS
AINTREE
AIRBASE
AIRCREW
AIRFLOW
AIRLESS
AIRLIFT
AIRLINE
AIRLOCK
AIRMAIL
AIRPORT
AIRSHIP
AIRSICK
AIRSTOP
ALABAMA
ALADDIN
ALAMEIN
ALAMODE
ALANINE
ALARMED
ALASKAN
ALBANIA
ALBENIZ
ALBERGO
ALBERTA
ALBERTI
ALBUMEN
ALBUMIN
ALCALDE
ALCHEMY
ALCOHOL
ALCORAN
ALDABRA
ALDRICH
ALECOST
ALEMBIC
ALENÇON
ALEPINE
ALEWIFE
ALFALFA
ALFONSO
ALGEBRA
ALGERIA
ALGIERS
ALICANT
ALIDADE
ALIGNED
ALIMENT
ALIMONY
ALIQUID
ALIQUOT
ALKANET
ALKORAN
ALLEGED
ALLEGRI
ALLEGRO
ALLENBY
ALLERGY
ALLONGE
ALLOWED
ALLSTAR
ALMACKS
ALMANAC
ALMONER
ALPHEUS
ALREADY
ALRIGHT
ALSATIA
ALTERED
ALTHAEA
ALTHING
ALUMINA
ALUMNAE
ALUMNUS
ALVEOLE
ALYSSUM
AMALGAM
AMANITA
AMATEUR
AMATORY
AMAZING
AMBAGES
AMBIENT
AMBOYNA
AMBROSE
AMENITY
AMERICA
AMERIGO
AMERIND
AMHARIC
AMIABLE
AMIABLY
AMMETER
AMMONAL
AMMONIA
AMNESIA
AMNESTY
AMOEBIC
AMONGST
AMORIST
AMORITE
AMOROSO
AMOROUS
AMPHORA
AMPLIFY
AMPOULE
AMPULLA
AMTRACK
AMUSING
AMYGDAL
AMYLASE
AMYLOID
ANAEMIA
ANAEMIC
ANAGRAM
ANALOGY
ANALYST
ANALYZE
ANANIAS
ANARCHY
ANATOLE
ANATOMY
ANCHOVY
ANCIENT
ANDAMAN
ANDANTE
ANDIRON
ANDORRA
ANDROID
ANEMONE
ANEROID
ANGELIC
ANGELUS
ANGEVIN
ANGIOMA
ANGLING
ANGOLAN
ANGRILY
ANGUISH
ANGULAR
ANILINE
ANIMALS
ANIMATE
ANIMIST
ANISEED
ANNELID
ANNOYED
ANNUITY
ANNULAR
ANNULET
ANNULUS
ANODIZE
ANODYNE
ANOMALY
ANOSMIA
ANOTHER
ANTACID
ANTARES
ANTENNA
ANTHILL
ANTHONY
ANTHRAX
ANTIBES
ANTIGEN
ANTIGUA
ANTIOCH
ANTIQUE
ANTLERS
ANTONIO
ANTONYM
ANTWERP
ANXIETY
ANXIOUS
ANYBODY
ANYMORE
APELIKE
APEPSIA
APHAGIA
APHASIA
APHELIA
APHESIS
APHONIA
APHONIC
APHOTIC
APHTHAE
APICIUS
APLASIA
APOCOPE
APOGEAN
APOLOGY
APOSTLE
APPARAT
APPAREL
APPEASE
APPLAUD
APPLIED
APPOINT
APPOSED
APPRIZE
APPROVE
APRICOT
APROPOS
APSIDAL
APTERAL
APTERYX
APTNESS
AQUATIC
AQUAVIT
AQUEOUS
AQUIFER
AQUILON
AQUINAS
AQUINUS
ARABIAN
ARABICA
ARACHNE
ARAMAIC
ARBITER
ARBUTUS
ARCADIA
ARCHAIC
ARCHERY
ARCHIVE
ARCHWAY
ARCUATE
ARDUOUS
ARETINO
ARIADNE
ARIDITY
ARIETTA
ARIOSTO
ARIZONA
ARMBAND
ARMHOLE
ARMORED
ARMORIC
ARMOURY
ARMREST
AROUSAL
ARRAIGN
ARRANGE
ARRAYED
ARREARS
ARRIVAL
ARRIVED
ARSENAL
ARSENIC
ARTEMIS
ARTEMUS
ARTICLE
ARTISAN
ARTISTE
ARTLESS
ARTWORK
ARUNDEL
ASCARID
ASCETIC
ASCITES
ASCRIBE
ASEPTIC
ASEXUAL
ASHAMED
ASHANTI
ASHDOWN
ASHTRAY
ASIATIC
ASININE
ASKANCE
ASOCIAL
ASPASIA
ASPERGE
ASPHALT
ASPIRIN
ASQUITH
ASSAULT
ASSEGAI
ASSIEGE
ASSISTS
ASSIZES
ASSUAGE
ASSUMED
ASSURED
ASSYRIA
ASTARTE
ASTILBE
ASTOUND
ASTRIDE
ASUNDER
ATACTIC
ATAGHAN
ATARAXY
ATAVISM
ATELIER
ATHEISM
ATHEIST
ATHIRST
ATHLETE

ATHWART
ATINGLE
ATISHOO
ATOMIST
ATOMIZE
ATROPHY
ATTABOY
ATTACHE
ATTAINT
ATTEMPT
ATTICUS
ATTIRED
ATTRACT
AUBERGE
AUCTION
AUDIBLE
AUDIBLY
AUDITOR
AUDUBON
AUGMENT
AUGUSTA
AUGUSTE
AURALLY
AUREATE
AURELIA
AUREOLA
AUREOLE
AURICLE
AUROCHS
AUSLESE
AUSTERE
AUSTRAL
AUSTRIA
AUTARKY
AUTOCUE
AUTOMAT
AUTOPSY
AVARICE
AVEBURY
AVENGER
AVERAGE
AVIATOR
AVIDITY
AVIGNON
AVOCADO
AVOIDER
AWESOME
AWFULLY
AWKWARD
AXOLOTL
AZIMUTH
AZYGOUS
BABBITT
BABBLER
BABOOSH
BABYISH
BABYLON
BABYSIT
BACARDI
BACCHIC
BACCHUS
BACILLI
BACKING
BACKLOG
BACKSET
BADNESS
BAFFLED
BAGASSE
BAGEHOT
BAGGAGE
BAGHDAD
BAGPIPE
BAHADUR
BAHAMAS
BAHRAIN
BAHREIN
BAILIFF
BAJAZET
BAKLAVA
BALANCE
BALATON
BALCONY
BALDING
BALDRIC
BALDWIN
BALEFUL
BALFOUR
BALLADE
BALLAST
BALLBOY
BALLIOL
BALLOON
BALONEY
BAMBINO
BANANAS
BANBURY
BANDAGE
BANDAID
BANDBOX
BANDEAU
BANGING
BANGKOK
BANKING
BANKSIA
BANNOCK
BANQUET
BANSHEE
BAPTISM
BAPTIST
BAPTIZE
BARBARA
BARBARY
BARENTS
BARGAIN
BARKERS
BARKING
BARMAID
BARNABY
BARONET
BAROQUE
BARRACK
BARRAGE
BARRIER
BARRING
BARYTES
BASCULE
BASHFUL
BASINET
BASKING
BASMATI
BASSOON
BASTARD
BASTIDE
BASTION
BATAVIA
BATHERS
BATHING
BATHMAT
BATHTUB
BATSMAN
BATTELS
BATTERY
BATTING
BAUHAUS
BAUXITE
BAYONET
BAZOOKA
BEACHED
BEACHES
BEADING
BEAMING
BEARDED
BEARHUG
BEARING
BEARISH
BEASTLY
BEATIFY
BEATING
BEATLES
BEATNIK
BECAUSE
BECKETT
BEDDING
BEDEVIL
BEDFORD
BEDOUIN
BEDPOST
BEDROCK
BEDROOM
BEDSIDE
BEDSORE
BEDTIME
BEEHIVE
BEELINE
BEERMAT
BEESWAX
BEGGARY
BEGGING
BEGONIA
BEGORRA
BEGUILE
BEHAVED
BEHOOVE
BEIJING
BEJEWEL
BELABOR
BELARUS
BELATED
BELGIAN
BELGIUM
BELIEVE
BELINDA
BELISHA
BELLBOY
BELLEEK
BELLHOP
BELLINI
BELLMAN
BELLOWS
BELOVED
BEMUSED
BENARES
BENCHER
BENDING
BENEATH
BENEFIT
BENGALI
BENISON
BENNETT
BENTHAM
BENTHOS
BENZENE
BENZINE
BENZOIN
BEOWULF
BEQUEST
BERCEAU
BEREAVE
BERGSON
BERLINE
BERMUDA
BERNARD
BERNINI
BERSEEM
BERSERK
BERTRAM
BESEECH
BESHREW
BESIDES
BESIEGE
BESMEAR
BESPEAK
BESPOKE
BESTIAL
BESTREW
BETHINK
BETHUMB
BETIMES
BETOKEN
BETROTH
BETTING
BETWEEN
BETWIXT
BEVERLY
BEWITCH
BEZIQUE
BIAFRAN
BIASSED
BIBELOT
BICYCLE
BIDDING
BIFOCAL
BIGFOOT
BIGHEAD
BIGHORN
BIGOTED
BIGOTRY
BIGSHOT
BILIOUS
BILLION
BILLMAN
BILLOWS
BILTONG
BINDERY
BINDING
BIOLOGY
BIOMASS
BIPLANE
BIRDMAN
BIRETTA
BISCUIT
BISMUTH
BISTORT
BITTERN
BITTERS
BITUMEN
BIVALVE
BIVOUAC
BIZARRE
BLABBER
BLACKEN
BLADDER
BLANDLY
BLANKET
BLANKLY
BLASTED
BLASTER
BLATANT
BLATHER
BLATTER
BLAZERS
BLAZING
BLEAKLY
BLEEPER
BLEMISH
BLENDER
BLESSED
BLESSES
BLETHER
BLIGHTY
BLINDER
BLINDLY
BLINKER
BLISTER
BLITZED
BLOATED
BLOATER
BLOCKED
BLOCKER
BLOOMER
BLOOPER
BLOSSOM
BLOTCHY
BLOTTER
BLOUSON
BLOWFLY
BLOWOUT
BLUBBER
BLUFFLY
BLUNDER
BLUNTED
BLUNTLY
BLURRED
BLUSHER
BLUSTER
BOARDER
BOASTER
BOATING
BOATMAN
BOBSLED
BOHEMIA
BOILEAU
BOILING
BOLETUS
BOLIVAR
BOLIVIA
BOLLARD
BOLOGNA
BOLONEY
BOLSHIE
BOLSHOI
BOLSTER
BOMBARD
BOMBAST
BOMBING
BONANZA
BONDAGE
BONDMAN
BONFIRE
BONKERS
BONNARD
BOOKIES
BOOKING
BOOKISH
BOOKLET
BOOKMAN
BOOLEAN
BOOMING
BOORISH
BOOSTER
BOOTLEG
BORACIC
BORDERS
BOREDOM
BORODIN
BOROUGH
BORSTAL
BOSWELL
BOTANIC
BOTARGO
BOTTEGA
BOTTLED
BOTTLES
BOUCLÉE
BOUDOIR
BOUILLI
BOULDER
BOUNCER
BOUNDED
BOUNDEN
BOUNDER
BOUQUET
BOURBON
BOURDON
BOURSIN
BOUTADE
BOWDLER
BOWHEAD
BOWLING
BOWSHOT
BOXROOM
BOYCOTT
BOYHOOD
BRACING
BRACKEN
BRACKET
BRADAWL
BRADMAN
BRAEMAR
BRAHMIN
BRAILLE
BRAKING
BRAMBLE
BRANDED
BRANDER
BRANTUB
BRASERO
BRAVADO
BRAVELY
BRAVERY
BRAVURA
BRAWLER
BRAZIER
BREADED
BREADTH
BREAKER
BREATHE
BREEDER
BRENDAN
BRENNER
BREVITY
BREWERY
BREWING
BRIBERY
BRICKIE
BRIDGES
BRIDGET

BRIDLER
BRIDLES
BRIEFLY
BRIGADE
BRIGAND
BRIGHAM
BRIMFUL
BRINDLE
BRINJAL
BRIOCHE
BRISKET
BRISKLY
BRISTLE
BRISTLY
BRISTOL
BRITAIN
BRITISH
BRITONS
BRITTLE
BRITZKA
BRIXTON
BROADEN
BROADLY
BROCADE
BROILER
BROKERS
BROMIDE
BROMINE
BRONCHI
BRONZED
BROTHEL
BROTHER
BROUGHT
BROWNED
BROWNIE
BROWSER
BRUISED
BRUISER
BRUSHER
BRUSQUE
BRUTISH
BUBBLES
BUBONIC
BUCKETS
BUCKEYE
BUCKLER
BUCKRAM
BUCOLIC
BUDDING
BUFFALO
BUFFOON
BUGABOO
BUGBEAR
BUGGING
BUGGINS
BUGLOSS
BUILDER
BULBOUS
BULGHUR
BULGING
BULIMIA
BULLACE
BULLDOG
BULLETS
BULLION
BULLISH
BULLOCK
BULLPEN
BULRUSH
BULWARK
BUMBOAT
BUMMALO
BUMPKIN
BUNDOOK
BUNGLER
BUNTING
BUOYANT
BURBAGE
BURDOCK
BURETTE
BURGEON
BURGESS
BURGHER
BURGLAR
BURKINA
BURMESE
BURNELL
BURNHAM
BURNING
BURNISH
BURNOUS
BURNOUT
BURSARY
BURSTER
BURUNDI
BUSHIDO
BUSHMAN
BUSHMEN
BUSKINS
BUSSING
BUSTARD
BUSTLER
BUSTLES
BUTCHER
BUTTERY
BUTTONS
BUZZARD
BYRONIC
CABARET
CABBAGE
CABINET
CABLING
CABOOSE
CACHEXY
CACIQUE
CADAVER
CADDISH
CADENCE
CADENZA
CADMIUM
CADOGAN
CAEDMON
CAESIUM
CAESURA
CAGOULE
CAHOOTS
CAINITE
CAIRENE
CAISSON
CAITIFF
CALABAR
CALAMUS
CALCIFY
CALCINE
CALCITE
CALCIUM
CALCULI
CALDERA
CALDRON
CALECHE
CALENDS
CALEPIN
CALIBAN
CALIBER
CALIBRE
CALLBOX
CALLBOY
CALLING
CALLOUS
CALMUCK
CALOMEL
CALORIC
CALORIE
CALTROP
CALUMET
CALUMNY
CALVARY
CALYPSO
CAMBIUM
CAMBRAI
CAMBRIC
CAMELOT
CAMERON
CAMILLA
CAMORRA
CAMPANA
CAMPARI
CAMPHOR
CAMPING
CAMPION
CANASTA
CANDACE
CANDELA
CANDIDA
CANDIDE
CANDIED
CANDOUR
CANELLA
CANIDAE
CANNERY
CANNILY
CANNING
CANNOCK
CANNULA
CANONRY
CANTATA
CANTEEN
CANTHUS
CANTRIP
CANTUAR
CANVASS
CAPABLE
CAPABLY
CAPELLA
CAPITAL
CAPITOL
CAPORAL
CAPRICE
CAPSIZE
CAPSTAN
CAPSULE
CAPTAIN
CAPTION
CAPTIVE
CAPTURE
CARACAS
CARACUL
CARADOC
CARAMBA
CARAMEL
CARAVAN
CARAVEL
CARAWAY
CARBIDE
CARBINE
CARCASE
CARCASS
CARDIAC
CARDOON
CARDUUS
CAREERS
CAREFUL
CARGOES
CARIBOU
CARIOCA
CARIOLE
CARITAS
CARLYLE
CARMINE
CARNABY
CARNAGE
CAROLUS
CAROTID
CAROTIN
CAROUSE
CARPORT
CARRELL
CARRIED
CARRIER
CARRIES
CARRION
CARROLL
CARROTS
CARROTY
CARSICK
CARTIER
CARTOON
CARVING
CASCADE
CASCARA
CASEASE
CASHBOX
CASHIER
CASPIAN
CASSATA
CASSAVA
CASSOCK
CASTILE
CASTING
CASTLED
CASTOFF
CASUALS
CASUISM
CASUIST
CATALAN
CATALOG
CATALPA
CATARRH
CATCALL
CATCHER
CATCHUP
CATELOG
CATERER
CATESBY
CATFISH
CATHEAD
CATHODE
CATKINS
CATLIKE
CATLING
CATMINT
CATSEYE
CATSPAW
CATTISH
CATWALK
CAUSTIC
CAUTERY
CAUTION
CAVALRY
CAVEMAN
CAVIARE
CAYENNE
CECILIA
CEDILLA
CEILIDH
CEILING
CELADON
CELEBES
CELESTA
CELESTE
CELLINI
CELLIST
CELLULE
CELSIUS
CEMBALO
CENACLE
CENSURE
CENTAUR
CENTAVO
CENTRAL
CENTRED
CENTRUM
CENTURY
CERAMIC
CERTAIN
CERTIFY
CESSION
CESSPIT
CESTODE
CESTOID
CEVICHE
CÉZANNE
CHABLIS
CHAFING
CHAGALL
CHAGRIN
CHAINED
CHALDEE
CHALICE
CHALKER
CHALONE
CHAMBER
CHAMBRÉ
CHAMFER
CHAMOIS
CHANCEL
CHANCRE
CHANGED
CHANGES
CHANNEL
CHANSON
CHANTER
CHAOTIC
CHAPATI
CHAPEAU
CHAPLET
CHAPMAN
CHAPPED
CHAPTER
CHARADE
CHARDIN
CHARGED
CHARGER
CHARGES
CHARIOT
CHARITY
CHARLES
CHARLEY
CHARMED
CHARMER
CHARNEL
CHARPOY
CHARRED
CHARTER
CHASING
CHASSIS
CHASTEN
CHATEAU
CHATHAM
CHATTEL
CHATTER
CHAUCER
CHAYOTE
CHEAPEN
CHEAPLY
CHEATER
CHECKED
CHECKIN
CHECKUP
CHEDDAR
CHEERIO
CHEESED
CHEETAH
CHEKHOV
CHELSEA
CHEMISE
CHEMIST
CHEQUER
CHERISH
CHEROOT
CHERVIL
CHESTER
CHEVIOT
CHEVRON
CHEWING
CHIANTI
CHIASMA
CHICAGO
CHICANE
CHICANO
CHICKEN
CHICORY
CHIEFLY
CHIFFON
CHIGGER
CHIGNON
CHILEAN
CHILLER
CHILLON
CHIMERA
CHIMNEY
CHINDIT
CHINESE
CHINOOK
CHINTZY
CHINWAG
CHIPPED
CHIPPER
CHIPPIE
CHIRRUP
CHLAMYS
CHLORAL
CHOCTAW
CHOKING
CHOLERA
CHOOKIE
CHOPINE

CHOPPER
CHORALE
CHORDAE
CHORION
CHORIZO
CHOROID
CHORTLE
CHOWDER
CHRISOM
CHRISTY
CHRONIC
CHUCKLE
CHUFFED
CHUKKER
CHUNDER
CHUPATI
CHUTNEY
CIMABUE
CINDERS
CINEMAS
CINEREA
CIRCLET
CIRCLIP
CIRCUIT
CIRROSE
CISSOID
CISTERN
CITADEL
CITHARA
CITIZEN
CITRINE
CITROEN
CIVILLY
CIVVIES
CLACHAN
CLAMBER
CLAMOUR
CLAMPER
CLANGER
CLAPPER
CLARIFY
CLARION
CLARITY
CLASSIC
CLASTIC
CLATTER
CLEANER
CLEANLY
CLEANSE
CLEANUP
CLEARLY
CLEARUP
CLEAVER
CLEMENT
CLICKER
CLIMATE
CLIMBER
CLINGER
CLINKER
CLIPPED
CLIPPER
CLIPPIE
CLIQUEY
CLOBBER
CLOISON
CLOSELY
CLOSEUP
CLOSING
CLOSURE
CLOTHED
CLOTHES
CLOTURE
CLOUDED
CLOYING
CLUBMAN
CLUMBER
CLUNIAC
CLUSTER
CLUTTER
COARSEN
COASTAL
COASTER
COATING
COAXIAL
COBBLED
COBBLER
COCAINE
COCHLEA
COCKADE
COCKLES
COCKNEY
COCKPIT
COCONUT
COCOTTE
CODEINE
CODICIL
CODLING
COELIAC
COEXIST
COFFERS
COGENCY
COGNATE
COHABIT
COINAGE
COITION
COLCHIS
COLDITZ
COLIBRI
COLITIS
COLLAGE
COLLARD
COLLATE
COLLECT
COLLEEN
COLLEGE
COLLIDE
COLLIER
COLLOID
COLLUDE
COLOGNE
COLOMBO
COLONEL
COLORED
COLOURS
COLUMNS
COMBINE
COMBING
COMFORT
COMFREY
COMICAL
COMMAND
COMMEND
COMMENT
COMMODE
COMMODO
COMMONS
COMMUNE
COMMUTE
COMPACT
COMPANY
COMPARE
COMPASS
COMPERE
COMPETE
COMPILE
COMPLEX
COMPORT
COMPOSE
COMPOST
COMPOTE
COMPUTE
COMRADE
CONAKRY
CONCAVE
CONCEAL
CONCEDE
CONCEIT
CONCEPT
CONCERN
CONCERT
CONCISE
CONCOCT
CONCORD
CONCUSS
CONDEMN
CONDOLE
CONDONE
CONDUCT
CONDUIT
CONFESS
CONFIDE
CONFINE
CONFIRM
CONFORM
CONFUSE
CONGEAL
CONICAL
CONIFER
CONJOIN
CONJURE
CONNATE
CONNECT
CONNIVE
CONNOTE
CONQUER
CONSENT
CONSIGN
CONSIST
CONSOLE
CONSOLS
CONSORT
CONSULT
CONSUME
CONTACT
CONTAIN
CONTEMN
CONTEND
CONTENT
CONTEST
CONTEXT
CONTORT
CONTOUR
CONTROL
CONVENE
CONVENT
CONVERT
CONVICT
CONVOKE
COOKERY
COOKING
COOLANT
COOLING
COPILOT
COPIOUS
COPLAND
COPPERS
COPPICE
COPYCAT
COPYING
COPYIST
CORACLE
CORANTO
CORBEAU
CORBETT
CORDATE
CORDIAL
CORDITE
CORDOBA
CORELLI
CORINTH
CORKAGE
CORKING
CORNCOB
CORNEAL
CORNELL
CORNICE
CORNISH
COROLLA
CORONER
CORONET
CORRECT
CORRIDA
CORRODE
CORRUPT
CORSAGE
CORSAIR
CORTEGE
CORTINA
CORUNNA
CORYDON
COSSACK
COSTARD
COSTING
COSTIVE
COSTUME
COTERIE
COTTAGE
COTTONY
COUCHÉE
COULDNT
COULOMB
COULTER
COUNCIL
COUNSEL
COUNTED
COUNTER
COUNTRY
COUPLER
COUPLET
COUPONS
COURAGE
COURBET
COURIER
COURSER
COURSES
COURTLY
COUSINS
COUTURE
COVERED
COVERUP
COVETED
COWGIRL
COWHAND
COWHERD
COWLICK
COWLING
COWPOKE
COWSHED
COWSLIP
COXCOMB
COXLESS
COYNESS
CRACKED
CRACKER
CRACKLE
CRACKLY
CRAMMED
CRAMMER
CRAMPED
CRAMPON
CRANACH
CRANIAL
CRANIUM
CRANMER
CRASHES
CRASSUS
CRAVING
CRAWLER
CRAZILY
CREATED
CREATOR
CREEPER
CREMATE
CRENATE
CRESTED
CREVICE
CREWCUT
CREWMAN
CRICKET
CRICKEY
CRICOID
CRIMEAN
CRIMSON
CRINKLE
CRINKLY
CRINOID
CRIPPLE
CRISPIN
CRITTER
CROAKER
CROATIA
CROCHET
CROCKET
CROESUS
CROFTER
CROOKED
CROONER
CROPPED
CROPPER
CROQUET
CROQUIS
CROSIER
CROSSED
CROSSLY
CROUTON
CROWBAR
CROWDED
CROWING
CROZIER
CRUCIAL
CRUCIFY
CRUDELY
CRUDITY
CRUELLS
CRUELLY
CRUELTY
CRUISER
CRUMBLE
CRUMBLY
CRUMPET
CRUMPLE
CRUNCHY
CRUPPER
CRUSADE
CRUSHED
CRUSHER
CRYPTIC
CRYPTON
CRYSTAL
CSARDAS
CUBICLE
CUCKING
CUCKOLD
CUIRASS
CUISINE
CULPRIT
CULTURE
CULVERT
CUMBRIA
CUMSHAW
CUMULUS
CUNNING
CURABLE
CURACAO
CURATOR
CURCUMA
CURDLED
CURETTE
CURIOUS
CURLING
CURRAGH
CURRANT
CURRENT
CURRIED
CURSIVE
CURSORY
CURTAIL
CURTAIN
CURTSEY
CUSHION
CUSTARD
CUSTODY
CUSTOMS
CUTAWAY
CUTBACK
CUTICLE
CUTLASS
CUTLERY
CUTTERS
CUTTING
CUTWORM
CUVETTE
CYANIDE
CYCLING
CYCLIST
CYCLONE
CYCLOPS
CYMBALS
CYNICAL
CYNTHIA
CYPRESS
CYPRIOT
CYSTOID
CYTISUS
DABBLER
DADAISM
DADAIST

DAGGERS
DAGWOOD
DAIMLER
DALILAH
DAMAGED
DAMAGES
DAMNING
DAMOSEL
DAMPIER
DAMPING
DANCING
DANTEAN
DAPHNID
DAPHNIS
DAPPLED
DARLING
DARNING
DASHING
DASHPOT
DASTARD
DATABLE
DAUPHIN
DAWDLER
DAYBOOK
DAYMARK
DAYSTAR
DAYTIME
DAZZLED
DEADEYE
DEADPAN
DEADSET
DEALING
DEANERY
DEAREST
DEATHLY
DEBACLE
DEBASED
DEBATER
DEBAUCH
DEBORAH
DEBOUCH
DEBRETT
DEBRIEF
DEBUSSY
DECANAL
DECAYED
DECEASE
DECEIVE
DECENCY
DECIBEL
DECIDED
DECIDER
DECIMAL
DECLAIM
DECLARE
DECLINE
DECODER
DECORUM
DECREED
DECRYPT
DEEPFRY
DEFACED
DEFAULT
DEFENCE
DEFENSE
DEFIANT
DEFICIT
DEFILED
DEFINED
DEFLATE
DEFLECT
DEFRAUD
DEFROCK
DEFROST
DEFUNCT
DEGAUSS
DEGRADE
DEGREES
DEHISCE
DEIRDRE
DEJECTA
DELAYED
DELIBES
DELIGHT
DELILAH
DELIMIT
DELIVER
DELOUSE
DELPHIC
DELTOID
DELUDED
DEMERGE
DEMERIT
DEMESNE
DEMETER
DEMIGOD
DEMONIC
DEMOTIC
DENDRON
DENIZEN
DENMARK
DENSELY
DENSITY
DENTINE
DENTIST
DENTURE
DEPLETE
DEPLORE
DEPOSIT
DEPRAVE
DEPRESS
DEPRIVE
DERANGE
DERONDA
DERRICK
DERVISH
DERWENT
DESCANT
DESCEND
DESCENT
DESERTS
DESERVE
DESMOND
DESPAIR
DESPISE
DESPITE
DESPOIL
DESPOND
DESSERT
DESTINE
DESTINY
DESTROY
DETAILS
DETENTE
DETRACT
DETRAIN
DEVALUE
DEVELOP
DEVIANT
DEVIATE
DEVILRY
DEVIOUS
DEVISED
DEVISEE
DEVOLVE
DEVOTED
DEVOTEE
DEWDROP
DEXTRIN
DIABOLO
DIAGRAM
DIALECT
DIALING
DIALYSE
DIAMINE
DIAMOND
DIAPSID
DIARCHY
DIARIST
DIBBLER
DICKENS
DICTATE
DICTION
DIDEROT
DIDICOY
DIDYMUS
DIECAST
DIEDRAL
DIEHARD
DIETARY
DIETINE
DIFFUSE
DIGGING
DIGITAL
DIGLYPH
DIGNIFY
DIGNITY
DIGONAL
DIGRAPH
DIGRESS
DILATED
DILATOR
DILEMMA
DILUENT
DILUTED
DIMNESS
DIMPLED
DINETTE
DINGBAT
DINMONT
DIOCESE
DIOPTER
DIOPTRE
DIORAMA
DIORITE
DIOXIDE
DIPLOCK
DIPLOMA
DIPOLAR
DIPTERA
DIPTYCH
DISABLE
DISAVOW
DISBAND
DISBARK
DISCARD
DISCERN
DISCORD
DISCUSS
DISDAIN
DISEASE
DISGUST
DISJOIN
DISLIKE
DISMAST
DISMISS
DISOBEY
DISPLAY
DISPORT
DISPOSE
DISPRIN
DISPUTE
DISROBE
DISRUPT
DISSECT
DISSENT
DISTAFF
DISTANT
DISTEND
DISTENT
DISTILL
DISTORT
DISTURB
DISUSED
DITHERY
DITTANY
DITTIES
DIURNAL
DIVERGE
DIVERSE
DIVIDED
DIVINER
DIVISOR
DIVORCE
DIVULGE
DIZZILY
DNIEPER
DOCKING
DOCTORS
DODDERY
DODGEMS
DOESKIN
DOGCART
DOGFISH
DOGFOOD
DOGGONE
DOGROSE
DOGWOOD
DOLEFUL
DOLLARS
DOLORES
DOLPHIN
DOMAINE
DOMINGO
DOMINIC
DONEGAL
DONNISH
DOODLER
DOORKEY
DOORMAN
DOORMAT
DOORWAY
DOPPLER
DORKING
DORMANT
DOROTHY
DOSSIER
DOUBLES
DOUBLET
DOUBTER
DOUGHTY
DOUGLAS
DOWAGER
DOWDILY
DOWLAND
DOWSING
DRABBLE
DRACHMA
DRACULA
DRAFTED
DRAFTEE
DRAGGLE
DRAGNET
DRAGOON
DRAINED
DRAPERY
DRASTIC
DRAUGHT
DRAWBAR
DRAWERS
DRAWING
DREADED
DREAMER
DREDGER
DRESDEN
DRESSED
DRESSER
DREYFUS
DRIBBLE
DRIBLET
DRIFTER
DRINKER
DRIVERS
DRIVING
DRIZZLE
DRIZZLY
DROPLET
DROPOUT
DROPPER
DROSHKY
DROUGHT
DRUGGED
DRUGGET
DRUMLIN
DRUMMER
DRUNKEN
DRYNESS
DUALITY
DUBBING
DUBIETY
DUBIOUS
DUCHESS
DUCKING
DUCTILE
DUDGEON
DUKEDOM
DULLARD
DUMPISH
DUNCIAD
DUNEDIN
DUNGEON
DUNKIRK
DUNNAGE
DUNNOCK
DUNSTAN
DUOPOLY
DURABLE
DURABLY
DURAMEN
DURRELL
DUSTBIN
DUSTING
DUSTMAN
DUSTPAN
DUTIFUL
DVORNIK
DWELLER
DWINDLE
DYARCHY
DYNAMIC
DYNASTY
EAGERLY
EARACHE
EARDRUM
EARLDOM
EARLIER
EARLOBE
EARMARK
EARNEST
EARRING
EARSHOT
EARTHEN
EARTHLY
EASIEST
EASTERN
EATABLE
EBBTIDE
EBONITE
ECBOLIC
ECCRINE
ECDYSIS
ECHELON
ECHIDNA
ECHINUS
ECLIPSE
ECLOGUE
ECOLOGY
ECONOMY
ECSTASY
ECTASIS
ECTOPIA
ECUADOR
EDAPHIC
EDIFICE
EDITION
EDUCATE
EFFECTS
EFFENDI
EFFORCE
EGALITY
EGGHEAD
EGLOGUE
EGOTISM
EGOTIST
EJECTOR
ELASTIC
ELASTIN
ELATION
ELDERLY
ELEANOR
ELECTED
ELECTOR
ELECTRA
ELECTRO
ELEGANT
ELEGIAC
ELEGIST
ELEMENT
ELEVATE
ELISION
ELITISM
ELITIST
ELLIPSE
ELOGIUM
ELUSIVE
ELUSORY
ELYSIAN

ELYSIUM
ELZEVIR
EMANATE
EMBARGO
EMBASSY
EMBLAZE
EMBOLUS
EMBOWER
EMBRACE
EMBROIL
EMERALD
EMERSON
EMINENT
EMIRATE
EMOTION
EMOTIVE
EMPANEL
EMPATHY
EMPEROR
EMPIRIC
EMPLOYS
EMPOWER
EMPRESS
EMPYEMA
EMULATE
EMULSIN
ENACTOR
ENAMOUR
ENCHANT
ENCLASP
ENCLAVE
ENCLOSE
ENCRUST
ENDEMIC
ENDGAME
ENDLESS
ENDOGEN
ENDORSE
ENDURED
ENDWAYS
ENERGIC
ENFEOFF
ENFIELD
ENFORCE
ENGAGED
ENGINED
ENGLAND
ENGLISH
ENGORGE
ENGRAFT
ENGRAIN
ENGRAVE
ENGROSS
ENHANCE
ENLARGE
ENLIVEN
ENNOBLE
ENPRINT
ENQUIRE
ENQUIRY
ENRAGED
ENSLAVE
ENSNARE
ENSNARL
ENSUING
ENSUITE
ENTEBBE
ENTENTE
ENTERIC
ENTERON
ENTHRAL
ENTHUSE
ENTITLE
ENTRAIN
ENTRANT
ENTREAT
ENTRUST
ENTWINE
ENVELOP
ENVENOM
ENVIOUS
EPAULET
EPERGNE
EPHEBUS
EPHEDRA
EPHESUS
EPHRAIM
EPICARP
EPICENE
EPICURE
EPIDOTE
EPIGONE
EPIGRAM
EPISODE
EPISTLE
EPITAPH
EPITAXY
EPITHET
EPITOME
EPIZOON
EPSILON
EPSTEIN
EQUABLE
EQUABLY
EQUALLY
EQUATOR
EQUERRY
EQUINOX
ERASMUS
ERASURE
ERECTOR
EREMITE
ERINYES
ERISKAY
ERITREA
ERODIUM
EROSION
EROTICA
ERRATIC
ERRATUM
ERUDITE
ESCALOP
ESCAPEE
ESCHEAT
ESPARTO
ESPOUSE
ESQUIRE
ESSENCE
ESSENES
ESTIVAL
ESTOVER
ESTREAT
ESTUARY
ETAGÈRE
ETAPLES
ETCHING
ETERNAL
ETESIAN
ETHANOL
ETHICAL
ETHMOID
ETONIAN
ETRURIA
ETTRICK
EUGENIA
EUGENIC
EUGENIE
EULALIE
EUPEPSY
EUPHONY
EUSTACE
EUTERPE
EVACUEE
EVANDER
EVASION
EVASIVE
EVENING
EVENTER
EVEREST
EVIDENT
EXACTLY
EXALTED
EXAMINE
EXAMPLE
EXCERPT
EXCITED
EXCLAIM
EXCLUDE
EXCRETA
EXCRETE
EXECUTE
EXEGETE
EXEMPLA
EXHAUST
EXHEDRA
EXHIBIT
EXIGENT
EXISTED
EXITING
EXOGAMY
EXPANSE
EXPENSE
EXPIATE
EXPIRED
EXPLAIN
EXPLODE
EXPLOIT
EXPLORE
EXPOSED
EXPOUND
EXPRESS
EXPUNGE
EXTINCT
EXTRACT
EXTREME
EXTRUDE
EYEBALL
EYEBATH
EYEBROW
EYELASH
EYELESS
EYELIDS
EYESHOT
EYESORE
EYEWASH
EZEKIEL
FACETED
FACTION
FACTORS
FACTORY
FACTUAL
FACULTY
FADDISH
FADDIST
FAGGOTS
FAIENCE
FAILING
FAILURE
FAINTED
FAINTLY
FAIRING
FAIRISH
FAIRWAY
FAJITAS
FALAFEL
FALLACY
FALLING
FALLOUT
FALSELY
FALSIES
FALSIFY
FANATIC
FANCIED
FANCIER
FANFARE
FANGLED
FANTAIL
FANTASY
FANZINE
FARADAY
FARAWAY
FARCEUR
FARMERS
FARMING
FARNESE
FARRAGO
FARRIER
FARTHER
FASCISM
FASCIST
FASHION
FASTING
FASTNET
FATALLY
FATEFUL
FATHEAD
FATIGUE
FATNESS
FATUITY
FATUOUS
FAUSTUS
FAUVISM
FAUVIST
FAVELLA
FAVORED
FAWNING
FEARFUL
FEATHER
FEATURE
FEBRILE
FEDERAL
FEEDING
FEELING
FEIGNED
FELLOWS
FELSPAR
FELUCCA
FEMORAL
FENCING
FENELON
FENLAND
FERMENT
FERMIUM
FERROUS
FERRULE
FERTILE
FERVENT
FERVOUR
FESTIVE
FESTOON
FETICHE
FETLOCK
FETTERS
FEVERED
FEYDEAU
FIANCÉE
FIBROID
FIBROMA
FIBROUS
FICTION
FIDDLER
FIDELIO
FIDGETS
FIDGETY
FIELDER
FIFTEEN
FIGHTER
FIGLEAF
FIGMENT
FIGURES
FILARIA
FILASSE
FILBERT
FILCHER
FILINGS
FILLETS
FILLING
FILMING
FIMBRIA
FINAGLE
FINALLY
FINANCE
FINDING
FINESSE
FINGERS
FINICAL
FINICKY
FINLAND
FINNISH
FIRCONE
FIREARM
FIREBUG
FIREDOG
FIREFLY
FIREMAN
FIRSTLY
FISHERY
FISHEYE
FISHING
FISHNET
FISSILE
FISSION
FISSURE
FISTFUL
FISTULA
FISTULE
FITMENT
FITNESS
FITTEST
FITTING
FIXATED
FIXEDLY
FIXINGS
FIXTURE
FLACCID
FLAGDAY
FLAMING
FLANKER
FLANNEL
FLAPPED
FLAPPER
FLAREUP
FLASHER
FLATCAR
FLATLET
FLATTEN
FLATTER
FLAUNCH
FLAVOUR
FLEAPIT
FLECKED
FLECKER
FLEDGED
FLEEING
FLEMING
FLEMISH
FLEURET
FLEURON
FLICKER
FLIGHTY
FLIPPER
FLITTER
FLIVVER
FLOATER
FLODDEN
FLOGGER
FLOODED
FLOOZIE
FLORIDA
FLORIST
FLOTSAM
FLOUNCE
FLOWERS
FLOWERY
FLOWING
FLUENCY
FLUMMOX
FLUNKEY
FLUSHED
FLUSTER
FLUTIST
FLUTTER
FLUVIAL
FLYHALF
FLYLEAF
FLYOVER
FLYPAST
FOGHORN
FOGLAMP
FOLDING
FOLIAGE
FOLLIES
FONDANT
FOOLISH
FOOTAGE
FOOTING
FOOTMAN
FOOTPAD
FOOTSIE
FOPPISH
FORAMEN
FORBADE
FORBEAR
FORCEPS
FOREARM
FOREIGN
FORELEG

FOREMAN
FOREPAW
FORESEE
FOREVER
FORFEIT
FORFEND
FORGAVE
FORGERY
FORGIVE
FORGONE
FORLORN
FORMICA
FORMING
FORMOSA
FORMULA
FORSAKE
FORSTER
FORTIES
FORTIFY
FORTRAN
FORTUNE
FORWARD
FOSSICK
FOSSULA
FOULARD
FOUNDER
FOUNDRY
FOXHOLE
FOXTROT
FRAGILE
FRAILTY
FRANCIS
FRANKLY
FRANTIC
FRAUGHT
FRAZZLE
FRECKLE
FREEBIE
FREEDOM
FREEMAN
FREESIA
FREEWAY
FREEZER
FREIGHT
FRESHEN
FRESHER
FRESHET
FRESHLY
FRETFUL
FRETSAW
FRETTED
FRIABLE
FRIENDS
FRIGATE
FRILLED
FRINGED
FRISBEE
FRISIAN
FRISSON
FRITTER
FRIZZLE
FRIZZLY
FROEBEL
FROGMAN
FRONTAL
FROSTED
FROWSTY
FRUMPLE
FUCHSIA
FUDDLED
FULCRUM
FULFILL
FULGENT
FULLERS
FULSOME
FUMETTE
FUNCHAL
FUNDING
FUNERAL
FUNFAIR
FUNGOID
FUNGOUS
FUNNILY
FURBISH
FURIOUS
FURLONG
FURNACE
FURNISH
FURRIER
FURTHER
FURTIVE
FUSEBOX
FUSIBLE
FUSILLI
FUSSILY
FUSTIAN
FUTTOCK
FUTURES
GABBLER
GABELLE
GABFEST
GABRIEL
GADROON
GADWALL
GAEKWAR
GAINFUL
GAINSAY
GAITERS
GALAHAD
GALATEA
GALETTE
GALILEE
GALILEO
GALIPOT
GALLANT
GALLEON
GALLERY
GALLING
GALLIUM
GALLONS
GALLOWS
GALOCHE
GALOPIN
GALUMPH
GAMBIAN
GAMBLER
GAMBOGE
GAMELAN
GANELON
GANGWAY
GARBAGE
GARBLED
GARBOIL
GARBURE
GARDENS
GARLAND
GARMENT
GARNISH
GARONNE
GAROTTE
GARRICK
GASCONY
GASEOUS
GASFIRE
GASMASK
GASOHOL
GASPING
GASTHOF
GASTRIC
GASTRIN
GATEWAY
GATLING
GAUDILY
GAUGUIN
GAUTAMA
GAVOTTE
GAWKISH
GAYNESS
GAZELLE
GAZETTE
GEARBOX
GEARING
GEELONG
GEFILTE
GEHENNA
GELATIN
GELDING
GEMMATE
GENERAL
GENERIC
GENESIS
GENETIC
GENISTA
GENITAL
GENOESE
GENTEEL
GENTIAN
GENTILE
GENUINE
GEODESY
GEOLOGY
GEORDIE
GEORGIA
GEORGIC
GERAINT
GERBERA
GERMANE
GERMANY
GESTALT
GESTAPO
GESTATE
GESTURE
GETAWAY
GETTING
GHASTLY
GHERKIN
GHOSTLY
GIBBONS
GIBBOUS
GIBLETS
GIDDILY
GIELGUD
GILBERT
GILDING
GILLRAY
GIMBALS
GIMBLET
GIMMICK
GINGHAM
GINSENG
GIRAFFE
GIRLISH
GIRONDE
GISELLE
GIZZARD
GLACIAL
GLACIER
GLADDEN
GLAMOUR
GLARING
GLASGOW
GLASSES
GLAZIER
GLAZING
GLEANER
GLEEFUL
GLENCOE
GLENOID
GLIDING
GLIMMER
GLIMPSE
GLISTEN
GLITTER
GLOBULE
GLORIFY
GLOTTAL
GLOTTIS
GLOWING
GLUCOSE
GLUTTON
GLYPTAL
GLYPTIC
GNARLED
GNAWING
GNOCCHI
GNOSTIC
GOAHEAD
GOBBLER
GOBELIN
GODDESS
GODETIA
GODLESS
GODLIKE
GODSEND
GODUNOV
GOGGLES
GOLDING
GOLDONI
GOLFING
GOLIARD
GOLIATH
GOMBEEN
GOMORRA
GONDOLA
GOODBYE
GOODIES
GOODISH
GOODMAN
GOODWIN
GOOLIES
GORDIAN
GORDIUS
GORILLA
GORSEDD
GOSHAWK
GOSLING
GOSSIPY
GOUACHE
GOULASH
GOURMET
GRACCHI
GRACILE
GRACKLE
GRADATE
GRADELY
GRADUAL
GRAFTER
GRAINED
GRAINER
GRAMMAR
GRAMPUS
GRANARY
GRANDAD
GRANDEE
GRANDLY
GRANDMA
GRANDPA
GRANITA
GRANITE
GRANNIE
GRANOLA
GRANTED
GRANTEE
GRANULE
GRAPHIC
GRAPHIS
GRAPNEL
GRAPPLE
GRATIFY
GRATING
GRAVITY
GRAVURE
GRAYISH
GRAZING
GREASER
GREATEN
GREATLY
GREAVES
GRECIAN
GREENER
GREGORY
GREMLIN
GRENADA
GRENADE
GRENDEL
GREYISH
GREYLAG
GRIDDLE
GRIFFON
GRIFTER
GRILLED
GRIMACE
GRIMOND
GRIMSBY
GRINDER
GRISTLE
GRISTLY
GRIZZLE
GRIZZLY
GROCERS
GROCERY
GROCKLE
GROGRAM
GROINED
GROLIER
GROMMET
GROOVED
GROPIUS
GROSSLY
GROTIUS
GROUCHO
GROUCHY
GROUNDS
GROUPER
GROUPIE
GROUSER
GROWING
GROWLER
GROWNUP
GRUFFLY
GRUMBLE
GRUMMET
GRUYÈRE
GRYPHON
GUANACO
GUARANA
GUARANI
GUARDED
GUBBINS
GUDGEON
GUIDING
GUIGNOL
GUILDER
GUINEAN
GUINEAS
GUMBOIL
GUMBOOT
GUMDROP
GUMSHOE
GUNBOAT
GUNFIRE
GUNNERA
GUNNERY
GUNPLAY
GUNROOM
GUNSHOT
GUNWALE
GUSHING
GUTLESS
GUTTATE
GUYROPE
GUZZLER
GWYNETH
GYMNAST
GYMSLIP
HABITAT
HACHURE
HACKERY
HACKING
HACKLES
HACKNEY
HACKSAW
HADDOCK
HADRIAN
HAFNIUM
HAGBOLT
HAGGADA
HAGGARD
HAGGERY
HAHNIUM
HAIRCUT
HAIRNET
HAIRPIN
HAITIAN
HALBERD
HALBERT
HALCYON
HALFWAY
HALFWIT
HALIBUT
HALIFAX
HALITUS
HALLALI
HALLWAY
HALOGEN
HALTING
HALYARD

HAMMOCK
HAMSTER
HANDBAG
HANDFUL
HANDGUN
HANDILY
HANDLED
HANDLER
HANDOUT
HANDSAW
HANDSEL
HANDSET
HANGDOG
HANGING
HANGMAN
HANGMEN
HANGOUT
HANOVER
HANSARD
HAPLESS
HAPORTH
HAPPILY
HARBOUR
HARDPAN
HARDTOP
HARELIP
HARICOT
HARLECH
HARMFUL
HARMONY
HARNESS
HARPIST
HARPOON
HARRIER
HARRIET
HARSHLY
HARVARD
HARVEST
HARWICH
HARWOOD
HASHISH
HASSOCK
HASTATE
HASTILY
HATBAND
HATCHET
HATEFUL
HATLESS
HATTOCK
HAUGHTY
HAULAGE
HAULIER
HAUNTED
HAUTBOY
HAWKEYE
HAYSEED
HAYWARD
HAYWIRE
HAZLETT
HEADING
HEADMAN
HEADSET
HEADWAY
HEALING
HEALTHY
HEARING
HEARKEN
HEARSAY
HEARTEN
HEATHEN
HEATHER
HEATING
HEAVENS
HEAVIER
HEAVILY
HECKLER
HECTARE
HEDGING
HEEDFUL
HEIGHTS
HEINOUS
HEIRESS
HELICAL
HELICON
HELIPAD
HELLCAT
HELLENE
HELLION
HELLISH
HELLUVA
HELPFUL
HELPING
HEMLINE
HEMLOCK
HENBANE
HENGIST
HENNAED
HENPECK
HEPARIN
HEPATIC
HEPTANE
HERBAGE
HERBERT
HERBERY
HERBIST
HEREDIA
HERETIC
HEROINE
HEROISM
HERRICK
HERRIES
HERRING
HERSELF
HESSIAN
HETAERA
HEURISM
HEXAGON
HEXAPOD
HEXARCH
HIBACHI
HICKORY
HIDALGO
HIDEOUS
HIDEOUT
HIGGINS
HIGHEST
HIGHMAN
HIGHWAY
HILDING
HILLMAN
HILLMEN
HILLOCK
HILLTOP
HIMSELF
HINDLEG
HIPSTER
HIRSUTE
HISPANO
HISSING
HISTOID
HISTORY
HITTITE
HOARDER
HOBNAIL
HOBSONS
HOEDOWN
HOGARTH
HOGBACK
HOGGING
HOGWASH
HOLBEIN
HOLDALL
HOLDING
HOLIDAY
HOLLAND
HOLSTER
HOMBURG
HOMERIC
HOMINID
HOMONYM
HONESTY
HONEYED
HONITON
HONOURS
HOODLUM
HOPEFUL
HOPKINS
HOPLITE
HOPPING
HOPSACK
HORATIO
HORDEUM
HORIZON
HORMONE
HORRIFY
HORRORS
HORSING
HOSANNA
HOSIERY
HOSPICE
HOSTAGE
HOSTESS
HOSTILE
HOTFOOT
HOTHEAD
HOTLINE
HOTSHOT
HOTSPUR
HOUDINI
HOUSING
HOWEVER
HOWLING
HUBBARD
HULKING
HUMANLY
HUMBLES
HUMDRUM
HUMERUS
HUMIDOR
HUMMING
HUMMOCK
HUNCHED
HUNDRED
HUNGARY
HUNKERS
HUNTING
HURDLER
HURLING
HURRIED
HURTFUL
HUSBAND
HUSKILY
HUSSARS
HUSSITE
HUSTLER
HYALINE
HYALOID
HYDATID
HYDRANT
HYDRATE
HYGIENE
HYPOGEA
IAMBIST
IBERIAN
ICEBERG
ICEFLOE
ICELAND
ICHABOD
ICHNITE
ICINESS
ICTERIC
ICTERUS
IDEALLY
IDIOTIC
IDOLIZE
IDYLLIC
IGNEOUS
IGNOBLE
IGNORED
IKEBANA
ILIACUS
ILLBRED
ILLEGAL
ILLICIT
ILLNESS
IMAGERY
IMAGINE
IMAGING
IMAGISM
IMAGIST
IMHOTEP
IMITATE
IMMENSE
IMMERGE
IMMERSE
IMMORAL
IMPASSE
IMPASTO
IMPAVID
IMPEACH
IMPERIL
IMPETUS
IMPIETY
IMPINGE
IMPIOUS
IMPLANT
IMPLIED
IMPLODE
IMPLORE
IMPOUND
IMPRESS
IMPREST
IMPRINT
IMPROVE
IMPULSE
INANITY
INBOARD
INBUILT
INBURST
INCENSE
INCISOR
INCLINE
INCLUDE
INCOMER
INCONNU
INCRUST
INCUBUS
INDEPTH
INDEXER
INDIANA
INDOORS
INDULGE
INERTIA
INEXACT
INFANCY
INFARCT
INFERNO
INFIDEL
INFIELD
INFLAME
INFLATE
INFLECT
INFLICT
INGENUE
INGRAIN
INGRATE
INGRESS
INHABIT
INHALER
INHERIT
INHIBIT
INHOUSE
INHUMAN
INITIAL
INJURED
INKLING
INKWELL
INNARDS
INNERVE
INNINGS
INQUEST
INQUIRE
INQUIRY
INROADS
INSCAPE
INSECTS
INSHORE
INSIDER
INSIDES
INSIGHT
INSIPID
INSPECT
INSPIRE
INSTALL
INSTANT
INSTATE
INSTEAD
INSTILL
INSULAR
INSULIN
INSURER
INTEGER
INTENSE
INTERIM
INTERNE
INTROIT
INTRUDE
INVADER
INVALID
INVEIGH
INVERSE
INVIOUS
INVOICE
INVOLVE
INWARDS
IONESCO
IPOMOEA
IRANIAN
IRELAND
IRIDISE
IRIDIUM
IRKSOME
IRONING
ISADORA
ISCHIUM
ISLAMIC
ISLANDS
ISMAILI
ISOBASE
ISODORE
ISOGRAM
ISOHYET
ISOLATE
ISOMERE
ISOTONE
ISOTOPE
ISRAELI
ISSUANT
ISTHMUS
ITALIAN
ITCHING
ITEMIZE
ITERATE
IVANHOE
IVORIAN
IVORIEN
IVRESSE
JACKASS
JACKDAW
JACKETS
JACKPOT
JACKSON
JACOBIN
JACOBUS
JACQUES
JACUZZI
JAGGERY
JAKARTA
JAMAICA
JAMESON
JAMMING
JAMPANI
JANITOR
JANKERS
JANUARY
JAPLISH
JASMINE
JAVELIN
JAVELLE
JAWBONE
JAZZMAN
JEALOUS
JEEPERS
JEEPNEY
JEERING
JEHOVAH
JEJUNUM
JELLABA
JELLIED
JENKINS
JERICHO
JERKILY
JERSEYS
JESTING
JEWELER
JEWELRY
JEZEBEL

JIMJAMS
JITTERS
JITTERY
JOBBERY
JOBBING
JOBLESS
JOCASTA
JOCULAR
JOGGING
JOGTROT
JOHNNIE
JOHNSON
JOINERY
JOINING
JOINTED
JOINTLY
JOLLITY
JONQUIL
JOURNAL
JOURNEY
JOYLESS
JOYRIDE
JUBILEE
JUDAISM
JUGGINS
JUGGLER
JUGLANS
JUGULAR
JUJITSU
JUKEBOX
JUMBLED
JUMBLES
JUMPING
JUNIPER
JUPITER
JURYBOX
JURYMAN
JUSSIVE
JUSTICE
JUSTIFY
JUTLAND
JUVENAL
KADDISH
KAINITE
KALENDS
KALMUCK
KAMERAD
KAMPALA
KAMPONG
KARACHI
KARAJAN
KARAKUL
KARAOKE
KASHMIR
KATORGA
KATRINE
KEARTON
KEELING
KEEPING
KENNEDY
KENNELS
KENNING
KENOSIS
KENOTIC
KENTISH
KERATIN
KERMESS
KERNITE
KEROGEN
KESTREL
KETCHUP
KEYHOLE
KEYNOTE
KEYWORD
KHALIFA
KHAMSIN
KHANATE
KHEDIVE
KIBBUTZ
KICKING
KICKOFF
KIDNEYS
KIELDER
KILDARE
KILLICK
KILLING
KILLJOY
KILVERT
KINDRED
KINESIS
KINETIC
KINGCUP
KINGDOM
KINGLET
KINGPIN
KINSHIP
KINSMAN
KINTYRE
KIPLING
KIPPERS
KISSING
KITCHEN
KITHARA
KIWANIS
KLAVIER
KLEENEX
KLINKER
KNACKER
KNAPPER
KNAVERY
KNEECAP
KNEELER
KNELLER
KNESSET
KNICKER
KNITTED
KNITTER
KNOBBLE
KNOBBLY
KNOCKER
KNOTTED
KNOWALL
KNOWHOW
KNOWING
KNUCKLE
KOLKHOZ
KONTIKI
KOUMISS
KOWLOON
KREMLIN
KRISHNA
KRYPTON
KUBELIK
KUFIYAH
KUMQUAT
KURHAUS
KURSAAL
KYANITE
LABIATE
LABORED
LABORER
LACERTA
LACEUPS
LACKING
LACONIC
LACQUER
LACTASE
LACTATE
LACTEAL
LACTOSE
LACUNAE
LADYBUG
LAETARE
LAGGARD
LAGGING
LAGONDA
LAKSHMI
LALIQUE
LALLANS
LAMAISM
LAMAIST
LAMBADA
LAMBAST
LAMBENT
LAMBERT
LAMBETH
LAMBING
LAMELLA
LAMPOON
LAMPREY
LANCERS
LANCING
LANDING
LANGLEY
LANGTON
LANGUID
LANGUOR
LANOLIN
LANTANA
LANTERN
LANYARD
LAOCOON
LAOTIAN
LAPPING
LAPSANG
LAPUTAN
LAPWING
LARCENY
LARDOON
LARGELY
LARGESS
LARGEST
LASAGNA
LASAGNE
LASHING
LASTING
LATCHET
LATERAL
LATERAN
LATIMER
LATRINE
LATTICE
LATVIAN
LAUNDER
LAUNDRY
LAURELS
LAVATER
LAVOLTA
LAWLESS
LAWSUIT
LAWYERS
LAXNESS
LAYERED
LAYETTE
LAYINGS
LEACOCK
LEADERS
LEADING
LEAFLET
LEAGUER
LEAKAGE
LEANDER
LEANING
LEAPING
LEARNED
LEARNER
LEASING
LEASOWE
LEATHER
LEAVING
LEBANON
LECHERY
LECTERN
LECTURE
LEEWARD
LEFTIST
LEGALLY
LEGATEE
LEGGING
LEGIBLE
LEGIBLY
LEGIONS
LEGLESS
LEGPULL
LEGROOM
LEGWORK
LEISURE
LEMMATA
LEMMING
LEMPIRA
LENDING
LENGTHY
LENIENT
LENTIGO
LENTILS
LEONARD
LEONINE
LEOPARD
LEOPOLD
LEOTARD
LEPANTO
LEPROSY
LEPROUS
LESBIAN
LESOTHO
LESSING
LETDOWN
LETTERS
LETTING
LETTUCE
LEUCINE
LEUCOMA
LEVERET
LEXICON
LIAISON
LIBERAL
LIBERIA
LIBERTY
LIBRARY
LIBRIUM
LICENCE
LICENSE
LICKING
LIEDOWN
LIFTOFF
LIGHTEN
LIGHTER
LIGHTLY
LIGNITE
LIKENED
LILTING
LIMINAL
LIMITED
LIMITER
LIMPOPO
LINACRE
LINCOLN
LINCTUS
LINDANE
LINEAGE
LINEMAN
LINGUAL
LININGS
LINKAGE
LINKING
LINKMAN
LINNEAN
LINOCUT
LINSANG
LINSEED
LIONESS
LIONIZE
LIPREAD
LIQUEFY
LIQUEUR
LIQUIDS
LISSOME
LISTING
LITCHEE
LITERAL
LITHELY
LITHIUM
LITOTES
LITURGY
LOBELIA
LOBSTER
LOCALLY
LOCKJAW
LOCKNUT
LOCKOUT
LOCUSTS
LODGING
LOFTILY
LOGBOOK
LOGGING
LOGICAL
LOGWOOD
LOLLARD
LONGBOW
LONGING
LOOKING
LOOKOUT
LOOMING
LOOSELY
LOOTING
LORDING
LORELEI
LOTHAIR
LOTHIAN
LOTTERY
LOUNGER
LOURDES
LOURING
LOUTISH
LOUVRED
LOVABLE
LOWBROW
LOWDOWN
LOWLAND
LOWPAID
LOYALLY
LOYALTY
LOZENGE
LUCARNE
LUCERNE
LUCIDLY
LUCIFER
LUCKILY
LUDDITE
LUDGATE
LUGGAGE
LUGHOLE
LUGWORM
LULLABY
LUMBAGO
LUMPISH
LUMPKIN
LUNATIC
LURCHER
LURIDLY
LURKING
LUSTFUL
LUSTILY
LUSTRUM
LUTYENS
LYCHNIS
LYMNAEA
LYNCHET
LYRICAL
MACABRE
MACADAM
MACAQUE
MACBETH
MACEDON
MACHETE
MACHINE
MACRAMÉ
MADEIRA
MADISON
MADNESS
MADONNA
MAENADS
MAESTRO
MAFIOSO
MAGENTA
MAGGOTY
MAGHREB
MAGICAL
MAGINOT
MAGNATE
MAGNETO
MAGNIFY
MAGUIRE
MAHATMA
MAHJONG
MAHONIA
MAIGRET
MAILBAG
MAILBOX
MAILCAR
MAILING
MAILMAN
MAJESTY
MAJORCA
MAKINGS
MALACCA
MALAISE

MALARIA
MALAYAN
MALEFIC
MALLARD
MALLEUS
MALLING
MALMSEY
MALTASE
MALTESE
MALTHUS
MAMILLA
MAMMARY
MAMMOTH
MANACLE
MANAGER
MANAGUA
MANATEE
MANDALA
MANDATE
MANDIOC
MANGOLD
MANHOLE
MANHOOD
MANHUNT
MANIHOC
MANIKIN
MANILLA
MANITOU
MANKIND
MANMADE
MANNERS
MANNING
MANNISH
MANSARD
MANSION
MANSIZE
MANTUAN
MANUMIT
MANXMAN
MAPPING
MARABOU
MARACAS
MARANTA
MARATHA
MARBLED
MARBLES
MARBURG
MARCHER
MARCONI
MARCUSE
MAREMMA
MARENGO
MARGERY
MARIBOU
MARINER
MARITAL
MARKING
MARLENE
MARLINE
MARLOWE
MARMARA
MARMION
MARMITE
MARQUEE
MARQUIS
MARRIED
MARRYAT
MARSALA
MARSHAL
MARSYAS
MARTENS
MARTIAL
MARTIAN
MARTINI
MARTLET
MARTYRS
MARVELL
MARXISM
MARXIST
MASCARA
MASONIC
MASONRY
MASSAGE
MASSEUR
MASSINE
MASSIVE
MASTERS
MASTERY
MASTIFF
MASTOID
MASURKA
MATADOR
MATCHED
MATCHET
MATELOT
MATILDA
MATINEE
MATISSE
MATTERS
MATTHEW
MATTING
MATTINS
MATTOCK
MAUDLIN
MAUGHAM
MAUNDER
MAWKISH
MAXILLA
MAXIMUM
MAXWELL
MAYFAIR
MAYPOLE
MAZARIN
MAZEPPA
MAZURKA
MEACOCK
MEANDER
MEANING
MEASLES
MEASURE
MECONIC
MEDDLER
MEDIATE
MEDICAL
MEDULLA
MEERKAT
MEETING
MEGARON
MEGATON
MEIOSIS
MEISSEN
MELANIN
MELLITE
MELODIC
MELROSE
MELTING
MEMBERS
MEMENTO
MEMOIRS
MENDING
MENFOLK
MENORAH
MENTHOL
MENTION
MENUHIN
MERCERY
MERCIES
MERCURY
MERITED
MERMAID
MERRIER
MERRILY
MESCLUN
MESEEMS
MESSAGE
MESSIAH
MESSIER
MESSILY
MESSINA
METALLY
METAYER
METHANE
METHINK
METICAL
MÉTISSE
METONIC
METONYM
METTLED
MEXICAN
MIASMIC
MICHAEL
MICROBE
MIDLAND
MIDRIFF
MIDSHIP
MIDTERM
MIDWEEK
MIDWEST
MIDWIFE
MIGRANT
MIGRATE
MILEAGE
MILFOIL
MILITIA
MILKING
MILKMAN
MILKSOP
MILLAIS
MILLING
MILLION
MIMICRY
MIMULUS
MINARET
MINCING
MINDFUL
MINDSET
MINERAL
MINERVA
MINIBUS
MINICAB
MINIMAL
MINIMAX
MINIMUM
MINORCA
MINSTER
MINUEND
MINUTED
MINUTES
MINUTIA
MIOCENE
MIRACLE
MIRADOR
MIRANDA
MIRIFIC
MISCAST
MISDEED
MISERLY
MISFIRE
MISLEAD
MISPLAY
MISREAD
MISRULE
MISSILE
MISSING
MISSION
MISSIVE
MISSTEP
MISTAKE
MISTIME
MISTOOK
MISTRAL
MITHRAS
MITOSIS
MITTENS
MITZVAH
MIXTURE
MOABITE
MOANING
MOBSTER
MOCKERS
MOCKERY
MOCKING
MODESTY
MODICUM
MODISTE
MODULAR
MODULUS
MOELLON
MOFETTE
MOHICAN
MOIDORE
MOISTEN
MOITHER
MOLDING
MOLIÈRE
MOLLIFY
MOLLUSC
MOLOTOV
MOLUCCA
MOMBASA
MOMENTS
MONARCH
MONEYED
MONGREL
MONILIA
MONITOR
MONKISH
MONOCLE
MONOLOG
MONOPLY
MONSOON
MONSTER
MONTAGE
MONTAGU
MONTANA
MONTANT
MONTERO
MONTHLY
MOODILY
MOONING
MOONLIT
MOORHEN
MOORING
MOORISH
MOPPING
MORAINE
MORALLY
MORAVIA
MORDANT
MOREISH
MORELLO
MORESBY
MORESCO
MORLAND
MORNING
MOROCCO
MORONIC
MORPHIA
MORRELL
MORTALS
MORTICE
MORTIFY
MORTISE
MOSELLE
MOTHERS
MOTTLED
MOUFLON
MOUILLÉ
MOULAGE
MOULDED
MOULDER
MOUNTED
MOUNTIE
MOURNER
MOVABLE
MUDDLED
MUDEJAR
MUDFLAP
MUDLARK
MUDPACK
MUEZZIN
MUFFLED
MUFFLER
MUGGING
MUGWORT
MUGWUMP
MULATTO
MULLEIN
MULLION
MUMMERS
MUMMERY
MUMMIFY
MUNDANE
MUNSTER
MUNTJAC
MURAENA
MURIATE
MURILLO
MURRAIN
MUSCOID
MUSCOVY
MUSETTE
MUSICAL
MUSSELS
MUSTANG
MUSTARD
MUTABLE
MUTAGEN
MYALGIA
MYANMAR
MYCELLA
MYCENAE
MYCETES
MYELINE
MYELOID
MYELOMA
MYIASIS
MYRINGA
MYSTERY
MYSTIFY
NABOKOV
NACELLE
NACROUS
NAGGING
NAILBED
NAIPAUL
NAIROBI
NAIVELY
NAIVETÉ
NAIVETY
NAKEDLY
NAMIBIA
NANKEEN
NAPHTHA
NAPPING
NARRATE
NARROWS
NARTHEX
NARWHAL
NASALLY
NASCENT
NASTILY
NATCHEZ
NATIONS
NATIVES
NATRIUM
NATURAL
NAUGHTY
NAVARIN
NAVARRE
NAVETTE
NEAREST
NEARING
NEBBISH
NEBULAR
NECKING
NECKLET
NECKTIE
NECROSE
NECTARY
NEEDFUL
NEEDLES
NEGLECT
NÉGLIGÉ
NEGRESS
NEGROID
NEITHER
NEMESIA
NEMESIS
NEMORAL
NEOLITH
NEPTUNE
NERITIC
NERVOSA
NERVOUS
NERVURE
NETBALL
NETSUKE
NETTING
NETWORK
NEURINE
NEURONE
NEUTRAL
NEUTRON
NEVILLE
NEWBOLT
NEWBORN

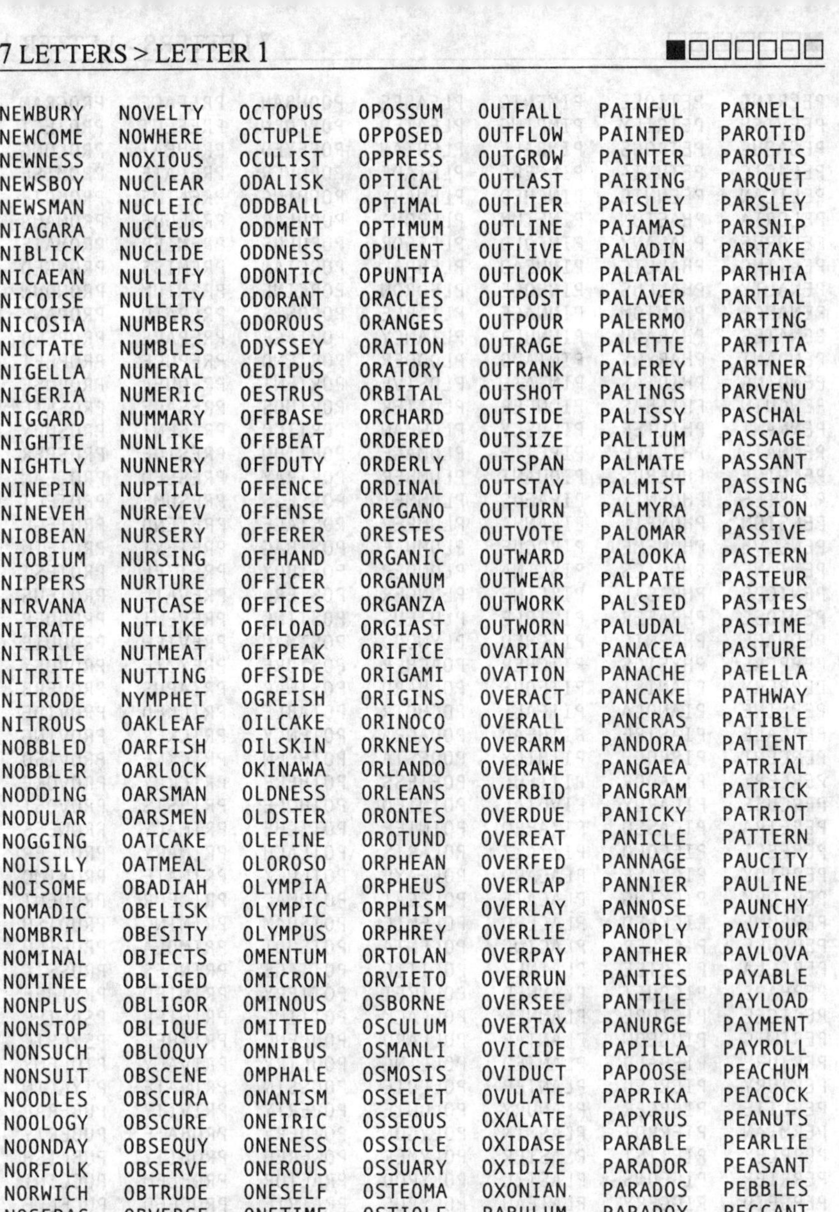

NEWBURY
NEWCOME
NEWNESS
NEWSBOY
NEWSMAN
NIAGARA
NIBLICK
NICAEAN
NICOISE
NICOSIA
NICTATE
NIGELLA
NIGERIA
NIGGARD
NIGHTIE
NIGHTLY
NINEPIN
NINEVEH
NIOBEAN
NIOBIUM
NIPPERS
NIRVANA
NITRATE
NITRILE
NITRITE
NITRODE
NITROUS
NOBBLED
NOBBLER
NODDING
NODULAR
NOGGING
NOISILY
NOISOME
NOMADIC
NOMBRIL
NOMINAL
NOMINEE
NONPLUS
NONSTOP
NONSUCH
NONSUIT
NOODLES
NOOLOGY
NOONDAY
NORFOLK
NORWICH
NOSEBAG
NOSEGAY
NOSTRIL
NOSTRUM
NOTABLE
NOTABLY
NOTCHED
NOTEPAD
NOTHING
NOTIONS
NOURISH
NOUVEAU
NOVELLA
NOVELLO
NOVELTY
NOWHERE
NOXIOUS
NUCLEAR
NUCLEIC
NUCLEUS
NUCLIDE
NULLIFY
NULLITY
NUMBERS
NUMBLES
NUMERAL
NUMERIC
NUMMARY
NUNLIKE
NUNNERY
NUPTIAL
NUREYEV
NURSERY
NURSING
NURTURE
NUTCASE
NUTLIKE
NUTMEAT
NUTTING
NYMPHET
OAKLEAF
OARFISH
OARLOCK
OARSMAN
OARSMEN
OATCAKE
OATMEAL
OBADIAH
OBELISK
OBESITY
OBJECTS
OBLIGED
OBLIGOR
OBLIQUE
OBLOQUY
OBSCENE
OBSCURA
OBSCURE
OBSEQUY
OBSERVE
OBTRUDE
OBVERSE
OBVIATE
OBVIOUS
OCARINA
OCCIPUT
OCCLUDE
OCEANIA
OCEANIC
OCEANID
OCELLAR
OCELLUS
OCTAGON
OCTOBER
OCTOPOD
OCTOPUS
OCTUPLE
OCULIST
ODALISK
ODDBALL
ODDMENT
ODDNESS
ODONTIC
ODORANT
ODOROUS
ODYSSEY
OEDIPUS
OESTRUS
OFFBASE
OFFBEAT
OFFDUTY
OFFENCE
OFFENSE
OFFERER
OFFHAND
OFFICER
OFFICES
OFFLOAD
OFFPEAK
OFFSIDE
OGREISH
OILCAKE
OILSKIN
OKINAWA
OLDNESS
OLDSTER
OLEFINE
OLOROSO
OLYMPIA
OLYMPIC
OLYMPUS
OMENTUM
OMICRON
OMINOUS
OMITTED
OMNIBUS
OMPHALE
ONANISM
ONEIRIC
ONENESS
ONEROUS
ONESELF
ONETIME
ONGOING
ONMIBUS
ONSHORE
ONSTAGE
ONTARIO
ONWARDS
OPACITY
OPALINE
OPENING
OPERAND
OPERANT
OPERATE
OPINION
OPOSSUM
OPPOSED
OPPRESS
OPTICAL
OPTIMAL
OPTIMUM
OPULENT
OPUNTIA
ORACLES
ORANGES
ORATION
ORATORY
ORBITAL
ORCHARD
ORDERED
ORDERLY
ORDINAL
OREGANO
ORESTES
ORGANIC
ORGANUM
ORGANZA
ORGIAST
ORIFICE
ORIGAMI
ORIGINS
ORINOCO
ORKNEYS
ORLANDO
ORLEANS
ORONTES
OROTUND
ORPHEAN
ORPHEUS
ORPHISM
ORPHREY
ORTOLAN
ORVIETO
OSBORNE
OSCULUM
OSMANLI
OSMOSIS
OSSELET
OSSEOUS
OSSICLE
OSSUARY
OSTEOMA
OSTIOLE
OSTRICH
OTALGIA
OTHELLO
OTRANTO
OTTOMAN
OUSTITI
OUTBACK
OUTCAST
OUTCOME
OUTCROP
OUTDARE
OUTDOOR
OUTFACE
OUTFALL
OUTFLOW
OUTGROW
OUTLAST
OUTLIER
OUTLINE
OUTLIVE
OUTLOOK
OUTPOST
OUTPOUR
OUTRAGE
OUTRANK
OUTSHOT
OUTSIDE
OUTSIZE
OUTSPAN
OUTSTAY
OUTTURN
OUTVOTE
OUTWARD
OUTWEAR
OUTWORK
OUTWORN
OVARIAN
OVATION
OVERACT
OVERALL
OVERARM
OVERAWE
OVERBID
OVERDUE
OVEREAT
OVERFED
OVERLAP
OVERLAY
OVERLIE
OVERPAY
OVERRUN
OVERSEE
OVERTAX
OVICIDE
OVIDUCT
OVULATE
OXALATE
OXIDASE
OXIDIZE
OXONIAN
PABULUM
PACIFIC
PACKAGE
PACKING
PACKMAN
PADDING
PADDLER
PADDOCK
PADLOCK
PADRONE
PAESTUM
PAGEANT
PAGEBOY
PAHLAVI
PAINFUL
PAINTED
PAINTER
PAIRING
PAISLEY
PAJAMAS
PALADIN
PALATAL
PALAVER
PALERMO
PALETTE
PALFREY
PALINGS
PALISSY
PALLIUM
PALMATE
PALMIST
PALMYRA
PALOMAR
PALOOKA
PALPATE
PALSIED
PALUDAL
PANACEA
PANACHE
PANCAKE
PANCRAS
PANDORA
PANGAEA
PANGRAM
PANICKY
PANICLE
PANNAGE
PANNIER
PANNOSE
PANOPLY
PANTHER
PANTIES
PANTILE
PANURGE
PAPILLA
PAPOOSE
PAPRIKA
PAPYRUS
PARABLE
PARADOR
PARADOS
PARADOX
PARAGON
PARAPET
PARASOL
PARBOIL
PARCHED
PARENTS
PARESIS
PARFAIT
PARINGS
PARKING
PARKWAY
PARLOUR
PARLOUS
PARNELL
PAROTID
PAROTIS
PARQUET
PARSLEY
PARSNIP
PARTAKE
PARTHIA
PARTIAL
PARTING
PARTITA
PARTNER
PARVENU
PASCHAL
PASSAGE
PASSANT
PASSING
PASSION
PASSIVE
PASTERN
PASTEUR
PASTIES
PASTIME
PASTURE
PATELLA
PATHWAY
PATIBLE
PATIENT
PATRIAL
PATRICK
PATRIOT
PATTERN
PAUCITY
PAULINE
PAUNCHY
PAVIOUR
PAVLOVA
PAYABLE
PAYLOAD
PAYMENT
PAYROLL
PEACHUM
PEACOCK
PEANUTS
PEARLIE
PEASANT
PEBBLES
PECCANT
PECCARY
PECCAVI
PECKING
PECKISH
PECTASE
PEDDLER
PEDICAB
PEDICEL
PEDICLE
PEELING
PEEPING
PEERAGE
PEERESS

PEERING
PEEVISH
PEGASUS
PELAGIC
PELICAN
PELORIA
PELORUS
PELTING
PENALTY
PENANCE
PENATES
PENDANT
PENDING
PENGUIN
PENNANT
PENNATE
PENNINE
PENSILE
PENSION
PENSIVE
PENTANE
PENTODE
PENTOSE
PEONAGE
PEPPERS
PEPPERY
PEPSINE
PERCALE
PERCENT
PERCEPT
PERCUSS
PEREIRA
PERFECT
PERFIDY
PERFORM
PERFUME
PERFUSE
PERGOLA
PERHAPS
PERIGEE
PERIWIG
PERJURE
PERJURY
PERLITE
PERMIAN
PERPLEX
PERRIER
PERSEID
PERSEUS
PERSIAN
PERSIST
PERSONA
PERSONS
PERSPEX
PERTAIN
PERTURB
PERTUSE
PERUSAL
PERVADE
PERVERT
PESSARY
PETIOLE
PETRIFY
PETROUS
PETUNIA
PFENNIG
PHAETON
PHALANX
PHALLIC
PHALLUS
PHANTOM
PHARAOH
PHARYNX
PHIDIAS
PHILEAS
PHILTER
PHILTRE
PHOEBUS
PHOENIX
PHONEIN
PHONEME
PHONICS
PHRASAL
PHRASER
PHRENIC
PHYSICS
PIANIST
PIANOLA
PIASTRE
PIBROCH
PICADOR
PICARDY
PICASSO
PICCOLO
PICKAXE
PICKING
PICKLED
PICKLER
PICOTEE
PICQUET
PICTURE
PIDGEON
PIEBALD
PIERCED
PIERCER
PIERROT
PIETIST
PIGEONS
PIGGERY
PIGLING
PIGMEAT
PIGMENT
PIGSKIN
PIGTAIL
PIKELET
PILATUS
PILCHER
PILGRIM
PILLAGE
PILLBOX
PILLION
PILLORY
PIMENTO
PIMPING
PINBALL
PINCERS
PINCHED
PINETUM
PINFOLD
PINHEAD
PINHOLE
PINNACE
PINNULA
PINTADO
PINTAIL
PIONEER
PIOUSLY
PIPETTE
PIQUANT
PIRAEUS
PIRANHA
PIROGUE
PISCINA
PISCINE
PISTOLE
PITCHED
PITCHER
PITEOUS
PITFALL
PITHEAD
PITHILY
PITIFUL
PIVOTAL
PIZARRO
PIZZAZZ
PLACARD
PLACATE
PLACEBO
PLACING
PLAINLY
PLANNED
PLANNER
PLANTAR
PLANTED
PLANTER
PLANURY
PLASMIN
PLASTER
PLASTIC
PLATEAU
PLATOON
PLATTER
PLAUDIT
PLAUTUS
PLAYBOY
PLAYERS
PLAYFUL
PLAYING
PLAYLET
PLAYOFF
PLAYPEN
PLEADER
PLEASED
PLEASES
PLEATED
PLEBIAN
PLEIADE
PLENARY
PLEROMA
PLESSOR
PLEURAL
PLEURON
PLIABLE
PLIANCY
PLODDER
PLOSIVE
PLOTTER
PLOWMAN
PLUMAGE
PLUMBER
PLUMMET
PLUMPER
PLUMULE
PLUNDER
PLUNGER
PLUTEUS
PLYWOOD
POACHER
POCHARD
POCHOIR
PODAGRA
PODESTA
POETESS
POINTED
POINTER
POLARIS
POLEAXE
POLECAT
POLEMIC
POLENTA
POLITIC
POLIZEI
POLLACK
POLLARD
POLLING
POLLUTE
POLONIE
POLYGON
POLYMER
POLYPOD
POLYPUS
POMEROL
POMEROY
POMFRET
POMMARD
POMPEII
POMPOON
POMPOUS
PONIARD
PONTIAC
PONTIFF
PONTINE
PONTOON
POOFTER
POOHBAH
POPCORN
POPEYED
POPOVER
POPPING
POPULAR
POPULUS
PORCIAN
PORCINE
POROSIS
PORTAGE
PORTEND
PORTENT
PORTHOS
PORTICO
PORTION
PORTRAY
POSSESS
POSTAGE
POSTBAG
POSTBOX
POSTERN
POSTING
POSTMAN
POSTURE
POSTWAR
POTABLE
POTENCY
POTHEEN
POTHERB
POTHOLE
POTICHE
POTLACH
POTLUCK
POTOMAC
POTSDAM
POTSHOT
POTTAGE
POTTERY
POTTING
POULENC
POULTRY
POUSSIN
POVERTY
POWDERY
POWERED
PRAETOR
PRAIRIE
PRALINE
PRATTLE
PRAYING
PREBEND
PRECAST
PRECEDE
PRECEPT
PRECISE
PREDATE
PREDIAL
PREDICT
PREDOOM
PREEMPT
PREFACE
PREFECT
PREHEAT
PRELATE
PRELIMS
PRELUDE
PREMIER
PREMISS
PREMIUM
PREPAID
PREPARE
PREPUCE
PREQUEL
PRESAGE
PRESENT
PRESIDE
PRESSED
PRESUME
PRETEND
PRETEXT
PRETZEL
PREVAIL
PREVENT
PREVIEW
PREZZIE
PRIAPUS
PRICKED
PRICKER
PRICKLE
PRICKLY
PRIESTS
PRIMACY
PRIMARY
PRIMATE
PRIMEUR
PRIMING
PRIMULA
PRINCES
PRINTED
PRINTER
PRITHEE
PRIVACY
PRIVATE
PRIVITY
PROBATE
PROBITY
PROBLEM
PROCEED
PROCESS
PROCTOR
PROCURE
PRODIGY
PRODUCE
PRODUCT
PROFANE
PROFESS
PROFFER
PROFILE
PROFITS
PROFUSE
PROGENY
PROGRAM
PROJECT
PROLONG
PROMISE
PROMOTE
PRONAOS
PRONATE
PRONGED
PRONOUN
PROPANE
PROPEND
PROPHET
PROPOSE
PROSAIC
PROSODY
PROSPER
PROTEAN
PROTECT
PROTEGE
PROTEIN
PROTEST
PROTEUS
PROUDER
PROUDIE
PROUDLY
PROVERB
PROVIDE
PROVING
PROVISO
PROVOKE
PROVOST
PROWESS
PROWLER
PROXIMO
PRUDENT
PRUDISH
PRURIGO
PRUSSIC
PRYTHEE
PSALTER
PSYCHIC
PTOLEMY
PTYALIN
PUBERAL
PUBERTY
PUBLISH
PUCCINI
PUCELLE
PUCKISH
PUDDING
PUERILE
PUGWASH
PULLMAN
PULSATE
PULSING
PUMPKIN
PUNCHED
PUNCHER
PUNGENT
PUNJABI
PUNSTER

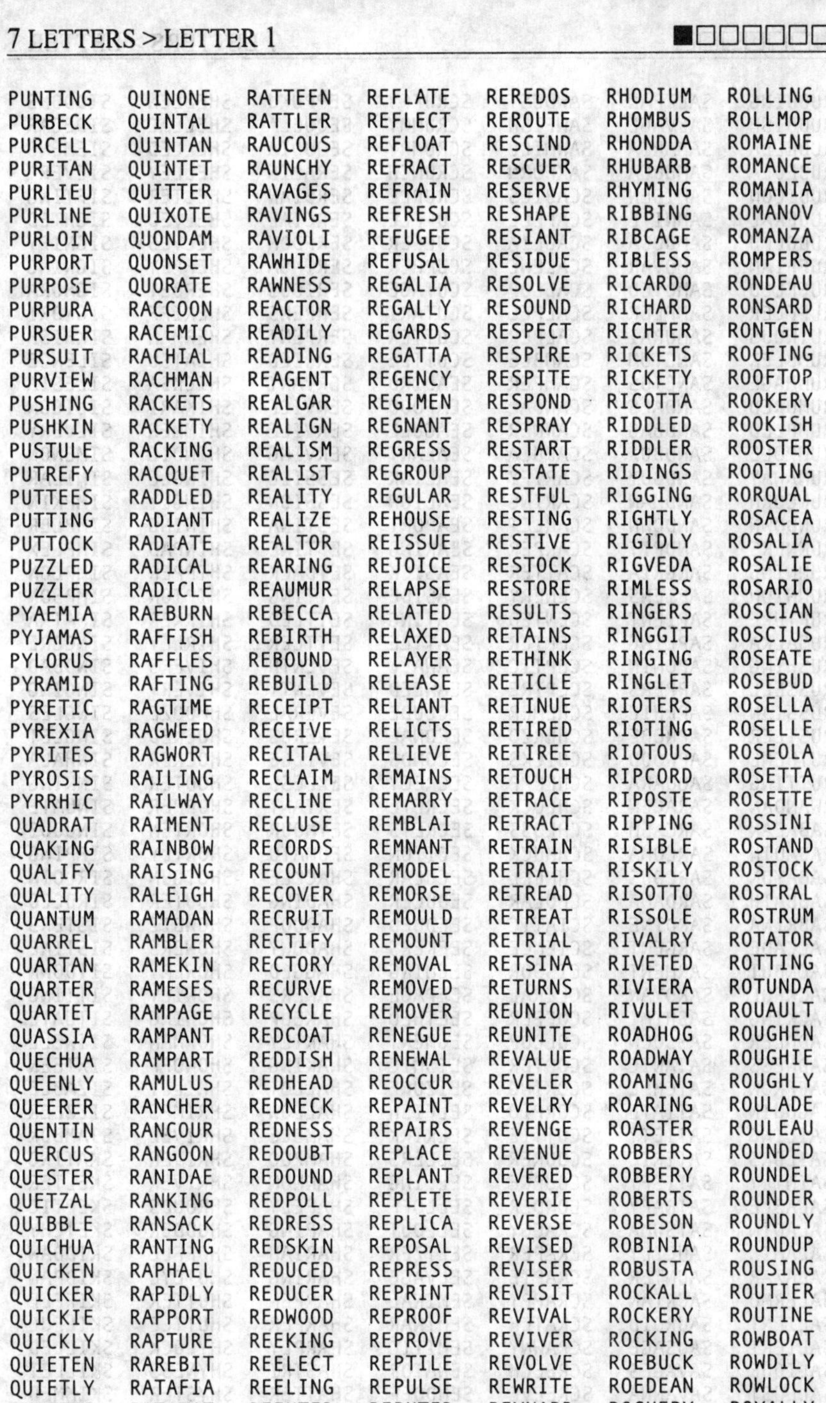

PUNTING
PURBECK
PURCELL
PURITAN
PURLIEU
PURLINE
PURLOIN
PURPORT
PURPOSE
PURPURA
PURSUER
PURSUIT
PURVIEW
PUSHING
PUSHKIN
PUSTULE
PUTREFY
PUTTEES
PUTTING
PUTTOCK
PUZZLED
PUZZLER
PYAEMIA
PYJAMAS
PYLORUS
PYRAMID
PYRETIC
PYREXIA
PYRITES
PYROSIS
PYRRHIC
QUADRAT
QUAKING
QUALIFY
QUALITY
QUANTUM
QUARREL
QUARTAN
QUARTER
QUARTET
QUASSIA
QUECHUA
QUEENLY
QUEERER
QUENTIN
QUERCUS
QUESTER
QUETZAL
QUIBBLE
QUICHUA
QUICKEN
QUICKER
QUICKIE
QUICKLY
QUIETEN
QUIETLY
QUIETUS
QUILTED
QUILTER
QUINCHE
QUININE
QUINONE
QUINTAL
QUINTAN
QUINTET
QUITTER
QUIXOTE
QUONDAM
QUONSET
QUORATE
RACCOON
RACEMIC
RACHIAL
RACHMAN
RACKETS
RACKETY
RACKING
RACQUET
RADDLED
RADIANT
RADIATE
RADICAL
RADICLE
RAEBURN
RAFFISH
RAFFLES
RAFTING
RAGTIME
RAGWEED
RAGWORT
RAILING
RAILWAY
RAIMENT
RAINBOW
RAISING
RALEIGH
RAMADAN
RAMBLER
RAMEKIN
RAMESES
RAMPAGE
RAMPANT
RAMPART
RAMULUS
RANCHER
RANCOUR
RANGOON
RANIDAE
RANKING
RANSACK
RANTING
RAPHAEL
RAPIDLY
RAPPORT
RAPTURE
RAREBIT
RATAFIA
RATATAT
RATCHET
RATIONS
RATLINE
RATPACK
RATTEEN
RATTLER
RAUCOUS
RAUNCHY
RAVAGES
RAVINGS
RAVIOLI
RAWHIDE
RAWNESS
REACTOR
READILY
READING
REAGENT
REALGAR
REALIGN
REALISM
REALIST
REALITY
REALIZE
REALTOR
REARING
REAUMUR
REBECCA
REBIRTH
REBOUND
REBUILD
RECEIPT
RECEIVE
RECITAL
RECLAIM
RECLINE
RECLUSE
RECORDS
RECOUNT
RECOVER
RECRUIT
RECTIFY
RECTORY
RECURVE
RECYCLE
REDCOAT
REDDISH
REDHEAD
REDNECK
REDNESS
REDOUBT
REDOUND
REDPOLL
REDRESS
REDSKIN
REDUCED
REDUCER
REDWOOD
REEKING
REELECT
REELING
REENTER
REENTRY
REFEREE
REFINED
REFINER
REFLATE
REFLECT
REFLOAT
REFRACT
REFRAIN
REFRESH
REFUGEE
REFUSAL
REGALIA
REGALLY
REGARDS
REGATTA
REGENCY
REGIMEN
REGNANT
REGRESS
REGROUP
REGULAR
REHOUSE
REISSUE
REJOICE
RELAPSE
RELATED
RELAXED
RELAYER
RELEASE
RELIANT
RELICTS
RELIEVE
REMAINS
REMARRY
REMBLAI
REMNANT
REMODEL
REMORSE
REMOULD
REMOUNT
REMOVAL
REMOVED
REMOVER
RENEGUE
RENEWAL
REOCCUR
REPAINT
REPAIRS
REPLACE
REPLANT
REPLETE
REPLICA
REPOSAL
REPRESS
REPRINT
REPROOF
REPROVE
REPTILE
REPULSE
REPUTED
REQUEST
REQUIEM
REQUIRE
REQUITE
REREDOS
REROUTE
RESCIND
RESCUER
RESERVE
RESHAPE
RESIANT
RESIDUE
RESOLVE
RESOUND
RESPECT
RESPIRE
RESPITE
RESPOND
RESPRAY
RESTART
RESTATE
RESTFUL
RESTING
RESTIVE
RESTOCK
RESTORE
RESULTS
RETAINS
RETHINK
RETICLE
RETINUE
RETIRED
RETIREE
RETOUCH
RETRACE
RETRACT
RETRAIN
RETRAIT
RETREAD
RETREAT
RETRIAL
RETSINA
RETURNS
REUNION
REUNITE
REVALUE
REVELER
REVELRY
REVENGE
REVENUE
REVERED
REVERIE
REVERSE
REVISED
REVISER
REVISIT
REVIVAL
REVIVER
REVOLVE
REWRITE
REYNARD
RHENISH
RHIZOID
RHIZOME
RHODIAN
RHODIUM
RHOMBUS
RHONDDA
RHUBARB
RHYMING
RIBBING
RIBCAGE
RIBLESS
RICARDO
RICHARD
RICHTER
RICKETS
RICKETY
RICOTTA
RIDDLED
RIDDLER
RIDINGS
RIGGING
RIGHTLY
RIGIDLY
RIGVEDA
RIMLESS
RINGERS
RINGGIT
RINGING
RINGLET
RIOTERS
RIOTING
RIOTOUS
RIPCORD
RIPOSTE
RIPPING
RISIBLE
RISKILY
RISOTTO
RISSOLE
RIVALRY
RIVETED
RIVIERA
RIVULET
ROADHOG
ROADWAY
ROAMING
ROARING
ROASTER
ROBBERS
ROBBERY
ROBERTS
ROBESON
ROBINIA
ROBUSTA
ROCKALL
ROCKERY
ROCKING
ROEBUCK
ROEDEAN
ROGUERY
ROGUISH
ROISTER
ROLLERS
ROLLICK
ROLLING
ROLLMOP
ROMAINE
ROMANCE
ROMANIA
ROMANOV
ROMANZA
ROMPERS
RONDEAU
RONSARD
RONTGEN
ROOFING
ROOFTOP
ROOKERY
ROOKISH
ROOSTER
ROOTING
RORQUAL
ROSACEA
ROSALIA
ROSALIE
ROSARIO
ROSCIAN
ROSCIUS
ROSEATE
ROSEBUD
ROSELLA
ROSELLE
ROSEOLA
ROSETTA
ROSETTE
ROSSINI
ROSTAND
ROSTOCK
ROSTRAL
ROSTRUM
ROTATOR
ROTTING
ROTUNDA
ROUAULT
ROUGHEN
ROUGHIE
ROUGHLY
ROULADE
ROULEAU
ROUNDED
ROUNDEL
ROUNDER
ROUNDLY
ROUNDUP
ROUSING
ROUTIER
ROUTINE
ROWBOAT
ROWDILY
ROWLOCK
ROYALLY
ROYALTY
ROZZERS
RUBBERS
RUBBERY

RUBBING
RUBBISH
RUBELLA
RUBEOLA
RUBICON
RUDERAL
RUDOLPH
RUFFIAN
RUFFLED
RUFFLER
RUINOUS
RUMBLER
RUMMAGE
RUMORED
RUMPLED
RUMPOLE
RUNAWAY
RUNCORN
RUNDOWN
RUNNERS
RUNNING
RUNNION
RUPTURE
RUSALKA
RUSHING
RUSSELL
RUSSIAN
RUSTLER
RUTHENE
RUTTING
RWANDAN
SABAEAN
SABAOTH
SABAYON
SABBATH
SABRINA
SACCADE
SACKBUT
SACKFUL
SACKING
SADDLER
SADNESS
SAFFRON
SAGOUIN
SAILING
SAILORS
SAINTLY
SALABLE
SALADIN
SALAMIS
SALAZAR
SALERMO
SALIENT
SALIERI
SALIQUE
SALLUST
SALPINX
SALSIFY
SALTATE
SALTING
SALTIRE
SALTPAN
SALVAGE
SAMARIA
SAMBUCA
SAMISEN
SAMNITE
SAMOOSA
SAMOVAR
SAMOYED
SAMPLER
SAMURAI
SANCTUM
SANCTUS
SANDALS
SANDBAG
SANDBOX
SANDBOY
SANDMAN
SANDOWN
SANDPIT
SANGRIA
SAPIENS
SAPIENT
SAPLING
SAPONIN
SAPPERS
SAPPHIC
SAPROBE
SAPWOOD
SAQQARA
SARACEN
SARCASM
SARCOMA
SARCOUS
SARDANA
SARDINE
SARGENT
SARMENT
SAROYAN
SASHIMI
SASSOON
SATANIC
SATCHEL
SATIATE
SATIETY
SATIRIC
SATISFY
SATRAPY
SATSUMA
SAUCILY
SAUNTER
SAURIAN
SAUROID
SAUSAGE
SAVAGES
SAVANNA
SAVELOY
SAVINGS
SAVIOUR
SAVOURY
SAWBILL
SAWDUST
SAWFISH
SAWMILL
SAXHORN
SCABIES
SCAFELL
SCAGLIA
SCALENE
SCALLOP
SCALPEL
SCALPER
SCAMBLE
SCAMPER
SCANDAL
SCANNER
SCAPULA
SCARIFY
SCARING
SCARLET
SCARPER
SCATTER
SCENERY
SCENTED
SCEPTER
SCEPTIC
SCEPTRE
SCHEMER
SCHERZO
SCHICKS
SCHLEPP
SCHLOCK
SCHLOSS
SCHMUCK
SCHNELL
SCHOLAR
SCIATIC
SCIENCE
SCISSOR
SCLERAL
SCOFFER
SCOLLOP
SCOOTER
SCORING
SCORPIO
SCOTTIE
SCOURER
SCOURGE
SCOWDER
SCRAGGY
SCRAPER
SCRAPIE
SCRAPPY
SCRATCH
SCRAWNY
SCREECH
SCREEVE
SCREWED
SCROOGE
SCROTAL
SCROTUM
SCRUBBY
SCRUFFY
SCRUMMY
SCRUMPY
SCRUNCH
SCRUPLE
SCUFFLE
SCULLER
SCUPPER
SCUTAGE
SCUTARI
SCUTTER
SCUTTLE
SEABIRD
SEAFOOD
SEAGULL
SEALANT
SEALINK
SEALION
SEAPORT
SEARING
SEASICK
SEASIDE
SEATING
SEATTLE
SEAWALL
SEAWEED
SECLUDE
SECONAL
SECONDS
SECRECY
SECRETE
SECRETS
SECTION
SECULAR
SEDUCER
SEEDBED
SEEKERS
SEEMING
SEEPAGE
SEETHED
SEGMENT
SEISMIC
SEIZURE
SELFISH
SELKIRK
SELLERS
SELLING
SELLOFF
SELLOUT
SELTZER
SELVAGE
SEMINAL
SEMINAR
SEMITIC
SENATOR
SENDOFF
SENECIO
SENEGAL
SENSATE
SENSORY
SENSUAL
SEPPUKU
SEQUELA
SEQUOIA
SERAPIS
SERBIAN
SERCIAL
SERFDOM
SERINGA
SERIOUS
SERPENS
SERPENT
SERRIED
SERVANT
SERVICE
SERVILE
SERVING
SESSILE
SESSION
SESTINA
SESTINE
SETBACK
SETTING
SETTLED
SETTLER
SEVENTH
SEVENTY
SEVERAL
SEVERUS
SEVILLE
SEXLESS
SEXTANT
SEYMOUR
SFUMATO
SHACKLE
SHADING
SHADOOF
SHADOWY
SHAGGED
SHAKERS
SHAKEUP
SHAKILY
SHAKING
SHALLOT
SHALLOW
SHAMBLE
SHAMPOO
SHANNON
SHAPELY
SHAPING
SHARIAH
SHARING
SHARPEN
SHARPER
SHARPLY
SHASTRI
SHATTER
SHAVING
SHEARER
SHEATHE
SHEAVES
SHEBANG
SHEBEEN
SHELLAC
SHELLED
SHELLEY
SHELTER
SHELVED
SHELVES
SHEPPEY
SHERBET
SHERIFF
SHERMAN
SHIATSU
SHICKSA
SHIKARI
SHIMMER
SHINDIG
SHINGLE
SHINGLY
SHINING
SHINPAD
SHIPPER
SHIPTON
SHIRKER
SHIRLEY
SHIVERS
SHIVERY
SHMOOZE
SHOCKED
SHOCKER
SHOOTER
SHOPPER
SHORTEN
SHORTLY
SHOTGUN
SHOUTER
SHOWBIZ
SHOWERS
SHOWERY
SHOWILY
SHOWING
SHOWMAN
SHOWOFF
SHRILLY
SHRIMPS
SHRIVEL
SHRIVEN
SHRIVER
SHROUDS
SHUDDER
SHUFFLE
SHUTEYE
SHUTTER
SHUTTLE
SHYLOCK
SHYNESS
SHYSTER
SIAMESE
SIBLING
SICKBAY
SICKBED
SICKERT
SIDDONS
SIDECAR
SIEMENS
SIEVERT
SIFTING
SIGHTED
SIGNIFY
SIGNING
SIGNORA
SIGNORI
SIKHISM
SILENCE
SILESIA
SILICON
SILVERY
SIMENON
SIMILAR
SIMPKIN
SIMPLER
SIMPLEX
SIMPLON
SIMPSON
SINATRA
SINCERE
SINDBAD
SINGING
SINGLES
SINGLET
SINHALA
SINKING
SINUATE
SINUOUS
SIPPING
SIRLOIN
SIROCCO
SISTERS
SISTINE
SITDOWN
SITTING
SITUATE
SITWELL
SIXTEEN
SIZABLE
SIZZLER
SJAMBOK
SKATING
SKELTER
SKEPTIC
SKETCHY
SKIDDAW
SKIDPAN
SKIFFLE
SKILFUL
SKILLED
SKILLET
SKIMMED
SKIMMER
SKIMMIA
SKINFUL
SKINNED
SKINNER

SKIPPED
SKIPPER
SKITTER
SKITTLE
SKYBLUE
SKYHIGH
SKYLARK
SKYLINE
SKYWARD
SLACKEN
SLACKER
SLACKLY
SLAMMER
SLANDER
SLAPPER
SLASHED
SLATTED
SLAVERY
SLAVISH
SLAYING
SLEEKLY
SLEEPER
SLEEVED
SLEIGHT
SLENDER
SLICKER
SLIDING
SLIMMER
SLIPPED
SLIPPER
SLIPWAY
SLITHER
SLOBBER
SLOGGER
SLOPING
SLOSHED
SLOTTED
SLOVENE
SLOWING
SLUMBER
SLYNESS
SMACKER
SMALLER
SMARTEN
SMARTIE
SMARTLY
SMASHED
SMASHER
SMATTER
SMELTER
SMETANA
SMICKLY
SMIDGIN
SMILING
SMITHER
SMITTEN
SMOKING
SMOLDER
SMOOTHE
SMOTHER
SMUDGED
SMUGGLE
SNAFFLE
SNAPPER
SNARLER
SNARLUP
SNEAKER
SNICKER
SNIFFER
SNIFFLE
SNIFTER
SNIGGER
SNIPPET
SNOOKER
SNOOPER
SNORING
SNORKEL
SNORTER
SNORTLE
SNOWDON
SNOWMAN
SNUFFLE
SNUGGLE
SOAKING
SOAPBOX
SOARING
SOBERLY
SOCAGER
SOCIETY
SOCKEYE
SOCKING
SOCOTRA
SOFABED
SOJOURN
SOLANUM
SOLDIER
SOLICIT
SOLIDLY
SOLIDUS
SOLOIST
SOLOMON
SOLUBLE
SOLVENT
SOMALIA
SOMEHOW
SOMEONE
SONDAGE
SOPHISM
SOPHIST
SOPPING
SOPRANO
SOPWITH
SORCERY
SORGHUM
SOROSIS
SORROWS
SORTING
SOUBISE
SOUFFLE
SOULFUL
SOUNDED
SOUNDER
SOUNDLY
SOURSOP
SOUTANE
SOUTHEY
SOVKHOZ
SOZZLED
SPACING
SPADGER
SPANDAU
SPANDEX
SPANGLE
SPANIEL
SPANISH
SPANKER
SPANNER
SPARING
SPARKLE
SPARROW
SPARTAN
SPASTIC
SPATIAL
SPATTER
SPATULA
SPAVINE
SPEAKER
SPECIAL
SPECIES
SPECIFY
SPECKLE
SPECTER
SPECTRE
SPELLER
SPENCER
SPENDER
SPENSER
SPHENIC
SPICATE
SPICULA
SPIDERS
SPIDERY
SPINACH
SPINATE
SPINDLE
SPINDLY
SPINNER
SPINNEY
SPINOFF
SPINOZA
SPIRITS
SPITTLE
SPLASHY
SPLAYED
SPLICED
SPLICER
SPLODGE
SPLOTCH
SPLURGE
SPOILED
SPOILER
SPONDEE
SPONDYL
SPONGER
SPONSON
SPONSOR
SPOONER
SPORRAN
SPOTTED
SPOTTER
SPOUSAL
SPRAINT
SPRAYER
SPRINGE
SPRINGS
SPRINGY
SPROUTS
SPURREY
SPURWAY
SPUTNIK
SPUTTER
SPYHOLE
SQUADDY
SQUALID
SQUALLY
SQUALOR
SQUARED
SQUARES
SQUASHY
SQUEAKY
SQUEERS
SQUEEZE
SQUELCH
SQUIFFY
SQUINCH
SQUISHY
STABLES
STACHYS
STADDLE
STADIUM
STAFFER
STAGGER
STAGING
STAINED
STAINER
STALKED
STALKER
STAMINA
STAMMER
STAMPED
STAMPER
STANDBY
STANDIN
STANDUP
STANLEY
STANNIC
STAPLER
STARCHY
STARDOM
STARETS
STARING
STARKLY
STARLET
STARLIT
STARTED
STARTER
STARTLE
STARVED
STATELY
STATICS
STATION
STATIST
STATURE
STATUTE
STAUNCH
STAYING
STEALTH
STEAMED
STEAMER
STEARIC
STEEPEN
STEEPLE
STEEPLY
STEERER
STELLAR
STEMMED
STENCIL
STENGAH
STENGUN
STENTOR
STEPHEN
STEPNEY
STEPSON
STERILE
STERNAL
STERNLY
STERNUM
STEROID
STETSON
STEVENS
STEWARD
STEWING
STICKER
STICKLE
STIFFEN
STIFFLY
STILTED
STILTON
STINGER
STINKER
STIPEND
STIPPLE
STIRFRY
STIRPES
STIRRED
STIRRUP
STOICAL
STOLLEN
STOMACH
STONILY
STONKER
STOPGAP
STOPPED
STOPPER
STORAGE
STORIED
STORIES
STOUTLY
STRAITS
STRANGE
STRATUM
STRATUS
STRAUSS
STREAKY
STRETCH
STREWTH
STRIATE
STRIDES
STRIDOR
STRIGIL
STRIKER
STRINGS
STRINGY
STRIPED
STRIPER
STRIPES
STROBIC
STROPHE
STROPPY
STRUDEL
STUBBLE
STUBBLY
STUDDED
STUDENT
STUDIED
STUFFED
STUMBLE
STUMPED
STUNNER
STUNTED
STUPEFY
STURMER
STUTTER
STYGIAN
STYLING
STYLISH
STYLIST
STYLITE
STYLIZE
STYPTIC
SUAVELY
SUAVITY
SUBAQUA
SUBATOM
SUBDUCT
SUBDUED
SUBEDAR
SUBEDIT
SUBFUSC
SUBJECT
SUBJOIN
SUBLIME
SUBSIDE
SUBSIDY
SUBSIST
SUBSOIL
SUBSUME
SUBTEEN
SUBTEND
SUBVERT
SUBZERO
SUCCEED
SUCCESS
SUCCOUR
SUCCUMB
SUCROSE
SUCTION
SUDETEN
SUFFETE
SUFFICE
SUFFOLK
SUFFUSE
SUGARED
SUGGEST
SUICIDE
SULFATE
SULKILY
SULLAGE
SULPHUR
SULTANA
SUMATRA
SUMMARY
SUMMERY
SUMMING
SUMMONS
SUNBEAM
SUNBURN
SUNDECK
SUNDIAL
SUNDOWN
SUNLAMP
SUNLESS
SUNNILY
SUNNITE
SUNRISE
SUNROOF
SUNSPOT
SUNTRAP
SUPPORT
SUPPOSE
SUPREME
SUPREMO
SURCOAT
SURDITY
SURFACE
SURFEIT
SURFING
SURGEON
SURGERY
SURINAM
SURMISE
SURNAME
SURPASS
SURPLUS
SURREAL
SURVIVE
SUSANNA

SUSPECT
SUSPEND
SUSTAIN
SUZETTE
SWADDLE
SWAGGER
SWAGMAN
SWAHILI
SWALLOW
SWANSEA
SWAPPED
SWARTHY
SWAYING
SWEATED
SWEATER
SWEDISH
SWEEPER
SWEETEN
SWEETIE
SWEETLY
SWELTER
SWIDDEN
SWIFTER
SWIFTLY
SWIMMER
SWINDLE
SWINGER
SWINGLE
SWITHIN
SWIZZLE
SWOLLEN
SYCORAX
SYCOSIS
SYMPTOM
SYNAPSE
SYNAXIS
SYNCOPE
SYNERGY
SYNONYM
SYNOVIA
SYRINGA
SYRINGE
SYSTOLE
TABANID
TABARET
TABASCO
TABITHA
TABLEAU
TABLOID
TABULAR
TACHISM
TACITLY
TACITUS
TACKLER
TACTFUL
TACTICS
TACTILE
TADPOLE
TAFFETA
TAGALOG
TAGETES
TAILORS
TAINTED
TAKEOFF
TAKEOUT
TAKINGS
TALIPES
TALIPOT
TALKING
TALLBOY
TALOOKA
TAMARIN
TAMBOUR
TAMESIS
TAMMANY
TAMPICO
TAMPION
TANAGER
TANAGRA
TANCRED
TANGENT
TANGIER
TANGLED
TANKARD
TANNATE
TANNERY
TANNING
TANTARA
TANTIVY
TANTRUM
TAPIOCA
TAPLASH
TAPPICE
TAPPING
TAPROOT
TAPSTER
TARANTO
TARDILY
TARDIVE
TARNISH
TARPEIA
TARQUIN
TARSIER
TARTARE
TARTARY
TARTINE
TASSILI
TATARIC
TATIANA
TATTERS
TATTING
TATTLER
TAURINE
TAVERNA
TAXABLE
TAXFREE
TAXICAB
TBILISI
TEACAKE
TEACHER
TEALEAF
TEARFUL
TEARING
TEAROOM
TEASHOP
TEASING
TEATIME
TEDIOUS
TEEMING
TEENAGE
TEHERAN
TEKTITE
TELFORD
TELLING
TELSTAR
TEMPERA
TEMPEST
TEMPLAR
TEMPLET
TEMPTER
TEMPURA
TENABLE
TENANCY
TENANTS
TENDRIL
TENFOLD
TENNIEL
TENSELY
TENSILE
TENSING
TENSION
TENUOUS
TEQUILA
TERBIUM
TERENCE
TERMITE
TERRACE
TERRAIN
TERRENE
TERRIER
TERRIFY
TERRINE
TERSELY
TERSION
TERTIAL
TERTIAN
TESSERA
TESTATE
TESTIFY
TESTILY
TESTING
TESTUDO
TETANUS
TEXTILE
TEXTUAL
TEXTURE
THALLUS
THEATER
THEATRE
THEORBO
THEOREM
THERAPY
THEREBY
THEREIN
THERESA
THERETO
THERMAL
THERMIC
THERMOS
THESEUS
THICKEN
THICKET
THICKLY
THIEVES
THIMBLE
THINKER
THINNER
THIRDLY
THIRSTY
THISTLE
THITHER
THOMISM
THOMIST
THOMSON
THOREAU
THORIUM
THOUGHT
THREADS
THRENOS
THRIFTY
THRISTY
THROATY
THROUGH
THROWER
THROWIN
THRUWAY
THUGGEE
THULIUM
THUMPER
THUNDER
THYROID
THYRSIS
THYSELF
THYSSEN
TIBETAN
TICKING
TICKLER
TIDDLER
TIDEWAY
TIDINGS
TIEPOLO
TIERCEL
TIERCET
TIFFANY
TIGHTEN
TIGHTLY
TIGRESS
TIGRISH
TILAPIA
TILBURY
TILLAGE
TIMBALE
TIMBERS
TIMBREL
TIMELAG
TIMIDLY
TIMOTHY
TIMPANI
TINFOIL
TINGLER
TINTACK
TINTERN
TIPCART
TIPPING
TIPPLER
TIPSILY
TIPSTER
TITANIA
TITANIC
TITOISM
TITOIST
TITRATE
TITULAR
TOASTED
TOASTER
TOBACCO
TOCCATA
TODDLER
TOEHOLD
TOENAIL
TOLKIEN
TOLLMAN
TOLSTOY
TOLUENE
TOMBOLA
TOMFOOL
TOMPION
TONGUES
TONIGHT
TONNAGE
TONNEAU
TONNISH
TONSURE
TONTINE
TOOLBOX
TOOLING
TOOTHED
TOOTSIE
TOPCOAT
TOPIARY
TOPICAL
TOPKAPI
TOPKNOT
TOPLESS
TOPMAST
TOPMOST
TOPPING
TOPSIDE
TOPSOIL
TORCHON
TORMENT
TORNADE
TORNADO
TORONTO
TORPEDO
TORPIDS
TORREFY
TORRENT
TORSADE
TORSION
TORTILE
TORTRIX
TORTURE
TOSSPOT
TOTALLY
TOTEMIC
TOTIENT
TOTTERY
TOUCHED
TOUGHEN
TOURING
TOURISM
TOURIST
TOWARDS
TOWHEAD
TOWLINE
TOWPATH
TOXEMIA
TOYNBEE
TOYSHOP
TRACERY
TRACHEA
TRACING
TRACKER
TRACTOR
TRADEIN
TRADING
TRADUCE
TRAFFIC
TRAGEDY
TRAILER
TRAINED
TRAINEE
TRAINER
TRAIPSE
TRAITOR
TRAMCAR
TRAMMEL
TRAMPLE
TRAMWAY
TRANCHE
TRANSIT
TRANSOM
TRANTER
TRAPEZE
TRAPPED
TRAPPER
TRAVAIL
TRAWLER
TREACLE
TREACLY
TREADLE
TREASON
TREATED
TREETOP
TREFOIL
TREKKER
TRELLIS
TREMBLE
TREMBLY
TREMOLO
TREPANG
TRESSES
TRESTLE
TRIANON
TRIATIC
TRIBUNE
TRIBUTE
TRICEPS
TRICKLE
TRIDENT
TRIESTE
TRIFFID
TRIFLER
TRIFLES
TRIGGER
TRILLED
TRILLER
TRILOGY
TRIMMER
TRINGLE
TRINITY
TRINKET
TRIPLET
TRIPLEX
TRIPODY
TRIPOLI
TRIPPER
TRIPSIS
TRIREME
TRISECT
TRISHAW
TRISTAN
TRITELY
TRITIUM
TRITOMA
TRIUMPH
TRIVIAL
TRIVIUM
TROCHEE
TROCHUS
TRODDEN
TROILUS
TROLLEY
TROLLOP
TROOPER
TROPHIC
TROPICS
TROPISM
TROTSKY
TROTTER
TROUBLE
TROUNCE
TROUPER
TROUSER
TRUANCY
TRUCIAL

TRUCKER
TRUCKLE
TRUDGEN
TRUFFLE
TRUMEAU
TRUMPET
TRUNDLE
TRUSTEE
TRYPSIN
TSARINA
TSARIST
TSIGANE
TSIGANY
TSUNAMI
TUBULAR
TUBULIN
TUESDAY
TUGBOAT
TUITION
TUMBLER
TUMBREL
TUMBRIL
TUMULUS
TUNABLE
TUNEFUL
TUNISIA
TURBARY
TURBINE
TURENNE
TURGENT
TURKISH
TURMOIL
TURNERY
TURNING
TURNKEY
TURNOUT
TUSCANY
TUSSOCK
TUSSORE
TUTELAR
TWADDLE
TWEEDLE
TWEETER
TWELFTH
TWIDDLE
TWIDDLY
TWIGGER
TWINKLE
TWINSET
TWISTED
TWISTER
TWITCHY
TWITTER
TWOFOLD
TWOSOME
TWOSTEP
TWOTIME
TYLOSIS
TYMPANO
TYMPANY
TYNWALD
TYPHOID
TYPHOON
TYPICAL
TYRANNY
TZARINA
UCCELLO
UGANDAN
UGOLINO
UKRAINE
UKULELE
ULEXITE
ULULANT
ULULATE
ULYSSES
UMBRAGE
UMBRIAN
UMPTEEN
UNAIDED
UNAIRED
UNALIKE
UNALIVE
UNARMED
UNASKED
UNAWARE
UNBLOCK
UNBOSOM
UNBOUND
UNBOWED
UNCANNY
UNCARED
UNCINUS
UNCIVIL
UNCLASP
UNCLEAN
UNCLEAR
UNCOUTH
UNCOVER
UNCTION
UNCURED
UNDATED
UNDERGO
UNDOING
UNDRESS
UNDYING
UNEARTH
UNEQUAL
UNFADED
UNFIXED
UNFROCK
UNGODLY
UNGUENT
UNHAPPY
UNHEARD
UNHINGE
UNHITCH
UNHORSE
UNICORN
UNIFORM
UNITARY
UNITIES
UNKEMPT
UNKNOWN
UNLADEN
UNLATCH
UNLEASH
UNLINED
UNLOOSE
UNLOVED
UNLUCKY
UNMIXED
UNMOVED
UNNAMED
UNNERVE
UNOWNED
UNQUIET
UNQUOTE
UNRAVEL
UNREADY
UNSCREW
UNSNARL
UNSOUND
UNSTICK
UNSTOCK
UNSTUCK
UNTAMED
UNTRIED
UNTRUTH
UNTWINE
UNUSUAL
UNWOUND
UPBRAID
UPGRADE
UPRAISE
UPRIGHT
UPSHOOT
UPSIDES
UPSILON
UPSTAGE
UPSTART
UPSTATE
UPSURGE
UPSWING
UPTIGHT
UPWARDS
URAEMIA
URALITE
URANIAN
URANISM
URANITE
URANIUM
URETHRA
URGENCY
URINARY
URINATE
UROLITH
URUGUAY
USELESS
USUALLY
USURPER
UTENSIL
UTERINE
UTILITY
UTILIZE
UTOPIAN
UTRECHT
UTRICLE
UTRILLO
UTTERLY
UXORIAL
VACANCY
VACCINE
VACUITY
VACUOLE
VACUOUS
VAGINAL
VAGRANT
VAGUELY
VALENCE
VALENCY
VALIANT
VAMOOSE
VAMPIRE
VANDALS
VANDYKE
VANESSA
VANILLA
VANITAS
VANTAGE
VANUATU
VAPOURS
VARIANT
VARIETY
VARIOLA
VARIOUS
VARMINT
VARNISH
VARSITY
VARYING
VASSAIL
VATICAN
VAUDOIS
VAUGHAN
VAULTED
VEDANTA
VEDETTE
VEHICLE
VELOURS
VELVETY
VENDING
VENDOME
VENERER
VENISON
VENTOSE
VENTRAL
VENTURE
VERBENA
VERBOSE
VERDANT
VERDICT
VERDURE
VERMEER
VERMONT
VERONAL
VERRUCA
VERSANT
VERSIFY
VERSION
VERTIGO
VERULAM
VERVAIN
VESICLE
VESPERS
VESTIGE
VETERAN
VETIVER
VETTING
VIADUCT
VIBRANT
VIBRATE
VIBRATO
VICEROY
VICINAL
VICIOUS
VICTORY
VICTUAL
VIDIMUS
VIETNAM
VIKINGS
VILLAGE
VILLAIN
VILLEIN
VILNIUS
VINASSE
VINCENT
VINEGAR
VINTAGE
VINTNER
VIOLATE
VIOLENT
VIRELAY
VIRGATE
VIRGULE
VIRTUAL
VISCERA
VISCOSE
VISCOUS
VISIBLE
VISIBLY
VISITOR
VISTULA
VITALLY
VITAMIN
VITIATE
VITRAIL
VITRIFY
VITRIOL
VIVALDI
VIVIDLY
VOCALIC
VOCALLY
VOIVODE
VOLANTE
VOLAPUK
VOLCANO
VOLTAGE
VOLTAIC
VOLUBLE
VOLUBLY
VOUCHER
VOYAGER
VULGATE
VULPINE
VULTURE
WADDING
WAFTING
WAGGISH
WAGGLER
WAGONER
WAGTAIL
WAILING
WAITING
WAKEFUL
WALKING
WALKMAN
WALKOUT
WALKWAY
WALLABY
WALLACE
WALLIES
WALLOON
WALPOLE
WALTZER
WANGLER
WANTING
WAPPING
WARBECK
WARBLER
WARBURG
WARDOUR
WARFARE
WARHEAD
WARLIKE
WARLING
WARLOCK
WARLORD
WARMING
WARNING
WARPATH
WARRANT
WARRING
WARRIOR
WARSHIP
WARTHOG
WARTIME
WARWICK
WASHDAY
WASHERS
WASHING
WASHOUT
WASHTUB
WASPISH
WASSAIL
WASTAGE
WASTING
WASTREL
WATCHER
WATERED
WATTAGE
WATTEAU
WATTLES
WATUTSI
WAVERER
WAXBILL
WAXWING
WAXWORK
WAYBILL
WAYLAND
WAYMARK
WAYSIDE
WAYWARD
WEAKEST
WEALDEN
WEALTHY
WEAPONS
WEARILY
WEARING
WEATHER
WEAVING
WEBBING
WEBSTER
WEDDING
WEDLOCK
WEEKDAY
WEEKEND
WEEPING
WEIGELA
WEIGHIN
WEIGHTS
WEIGHTY
WEIRDLY
WELCOME
WELDING
WELFARE
WELLIES
WELLOFF
WENDELL
WENLOCK
WESTERN
WETBACK
WETLAND
WETNESS
WETSUIT
WETTING
WHACKED
WHACKER
WHALING
WHARTON
WHATNOT
WHATSIT
WHEATEN
WHEEDLE
WHEELED
WHEELER
WHEELIE
WHEREAS
WHEREBY

WHEREIN
WHETHER
WHIMPER
WHIMSEY
WHINGER
WHIPCAT
WHIPPED
WHIPPET
WHISKER
WHISKEY
WHISPER
WHISTLE
WHITHER
WHITING
WHITISH
WHITLOW
WHITSUN
WHITTLE
WHOEVER
WHOOPEE
WHOOPER
WHOPPER
WICKIUP
WICKLOW
WIDGEON
WIDOWED
WIDOWER
WIGGING
WILDCAT
WILFRED
WILLIAM
WILLIES
WILLING
WILLOWY
WIMPISH
WINDBAG
WINDING
WINDOWS
WINDROW
WINDSOR
WINNING
WINNOCK
WINSOME
WINSTON
WIPEOUT
WIRETAP
WISHFUL
WISHING
WISTFUL
WITCHES
WITHERS
WITHOUT
WITLESS
WITLOOF
WITNESS
WIZENED
WOLFISH
WOLFRAM
WOMANLY
WONDERS
WOODCUT
WOODMAN
WOOLLEN
WOOMERA
WOOSTER
WORDILY
WORDING
WORKERS
WORKING
WORKMAN
WORKMEN
WORKOUT
WORKSHY
WORKTOP
WORLDLY
WORRIED
WORRIER
WORSHIP
WORSTED
WOTCHER
WOULDBE
WOULDNT
WOUNDED
WRANGLE
WRAPPED
WRAPPER
WRAUGHT
WREATHE
WRECKED
WRECKER
WRESTLE
WRIGGLE
WRINGER
WRINKLE
WRINKLY
WRITEUP
WRITING
WRITTEN
WRONGLY
WROUGHT
WRYBILL
WRYNECK
WRYNOSE
WYOMING
WYSIWYG
XANTHOS
XENOPUS
XERAFIN
XEROSIS
XIMENES
YANGTSE
YAOUNDE
YARDAGE
YARDARM
YASHMAK
YAWNING
YELLOWS
YEREVAN
YEZIDEE
YIDDISH
YOGHURT
YONKERS
YORKIST
YOUNGER
YPSILON
YTTRIUM
YUCATAN
ZAIREAN
ZAKUSKA
ZAMBESI
ZAMBIAN
ZAMORIN
ZAPOTEC
ZEALAND
ZEALOUS
ZEDOARY
ZEMSTVO
ZEOLITE
ZEPHIEL
ZESTFUL
ZETLAND
ZILLION
ZINGARO
ZIONIST
ZIZANIA
ZOFFANY
ZOOLITE
ZOOLOGY
ZOOTOMY
ZYGOSIS
ZYMOSIS
ZYMURGY

7:2

AARONIC
BABBITT
BABBLER
BABOOSH
BABYISH
BABYLON
BABYSIT
BACARDI
BACCHIC
BACCHUS
BACILLI
BACKING
BACKLOG
BACKSET
BADNESS
BAFFLED
BAGASSE
BAGEHOT
BAGGAGE
BAGHDAD
BAGPIPE
BAHADUR
BAHAMAS
BAHRAIN
BAHREIN
BAILIFF
BAJAZET
BAKLAVA
BALANCE
BALATON
BALCONY
BALDING
BALDRIC
BALDWIN
BALEFUL
BALFOUR
BALLADE
BALLAST
BALLBOY
BALLIOL
BALLOON
BALONEY
BAMBINO
BANANAS
BANBURY
BANDAGE
BANDAID
BANDBOX
BANDEAU
BANGING
BANGKOK
BANKING
BANKSIA
BANNOCK
BANQUET
BANSHEE
BAPTISM
BAPTIST
BAPTIZE
BARBARA
BARBARY
BARENTS
BARGAIN
BARKERS
BARKING
BARMAID
BARNABY
BARONET
BAROQUE
BARRACK
BARRAGE
BARRIER
BARRING
BARYTES
BASCULE
BASHFUL
BASINET
BASKING
BASMATI
BASSOON
BASTARD
BASTIDE
BASTION
BATAVIA
BATHERS
BATHING
BATHMAT
BATHTUB
BATSMAN
BATTELS
BATTERY
BATTING
BAUHAUS
BAUXITE
BAYONET
BAZOOKA
CABARET
CABBAGE
CABINET
CABLING
CABOOSE
CACHEXY
CACIQUE
CADAVER
CADDISH
CADENCE
CADENZA
CADMIUM
CADOGAN
CAEDMON
CAESIUM
CAESURA
CAGOULE
CAHOOTS
CAINITE
CAIRENE
CAISSON
CAITIFF
CALABAR
CALAMUS
CALCIFY
CALCINE
CALCITE
CALCIUM
CALCULI
CALDERA
CALDRON
CALECHE
CALENDS
CALEPIN
CALIBAN
CALIBER
CALIBRE
CALLBOX
CALLBOY
CALLING
CALLOUS
CALMUCK
CALOMEL
CALORIC
CALORIE
CALTROP
CALUMET
CALUMNY
CALVARY
CALYPSO
CAMBIUM
CAMBRAI
CAMBRIC
CAMELOT
CAMERON
CAMILLA
CAMORRA
CAMPANA
CAMPARI
CAMPHOR
CAMPING
CAMPION
CANASTA
CANDACE
CANDELA
CANDIDA
CANDIDE
CANDIED
CANDOUR
CANELLA
CANIDAE
CANNERY
CANNILY
CANNING
CANNOCK
CANNULA
CANONRY
CANTATA
CANTEEN
CANTHUS
CANTRIP
CANTUAR
CANVASS
CAPABLE
CAPABLY
CAPELLA
CAPITAL
CAPITOL
CAPORAL
CAPRICE
CAPSIZE
CAPSTAN
CAPSULE
CAPTAIN
CAPTION
CAPTIVE
CAPTURE
CARACAS
CARACUL
CARADOC
CARAMBA
CARAMEL
CARAVAN
CARAVEL
CARAWAY
CARBIDE
CARBINE
CARCASE
CARCASS
CARDIAC
CARDOON
CARDUUS
CAREERS
CAREFUL
CARGOES
CARIBOU
CARIOCA
CARIOLE
CARITAS
CARLYLE
CARMINE
CARNABY
CARNAGE
CAROLUS
CAROTID
CAROTIN
CAROUSE
CARPORT
CARRELL
CARRIED
CARRIER
CARRIES
CARRION
CARROLL
CARROTS
CARROTY
CARSICK
CARTIER
CARTOON
CARVING
CASCADE
CASCARA
CASEASE
CASHBOX
CASHIER
CASPIAN
CASSATA
CASSAVA
CASSOCK
CASTILE
CASTING
CASTLED
CASTOFF
CASUALS
CASUISM
CASUIST
CATALAN
CATALOG
CATALPA
CATARRH
CATCALL
CATCHER
CATCHUP
CATELOG
CATERER
CATESBY
CATFISH
CATHEAD
CATHODE
CATKINS
CATLIKE
CATLING
CATMINT
CATSEYE
CATSPAW

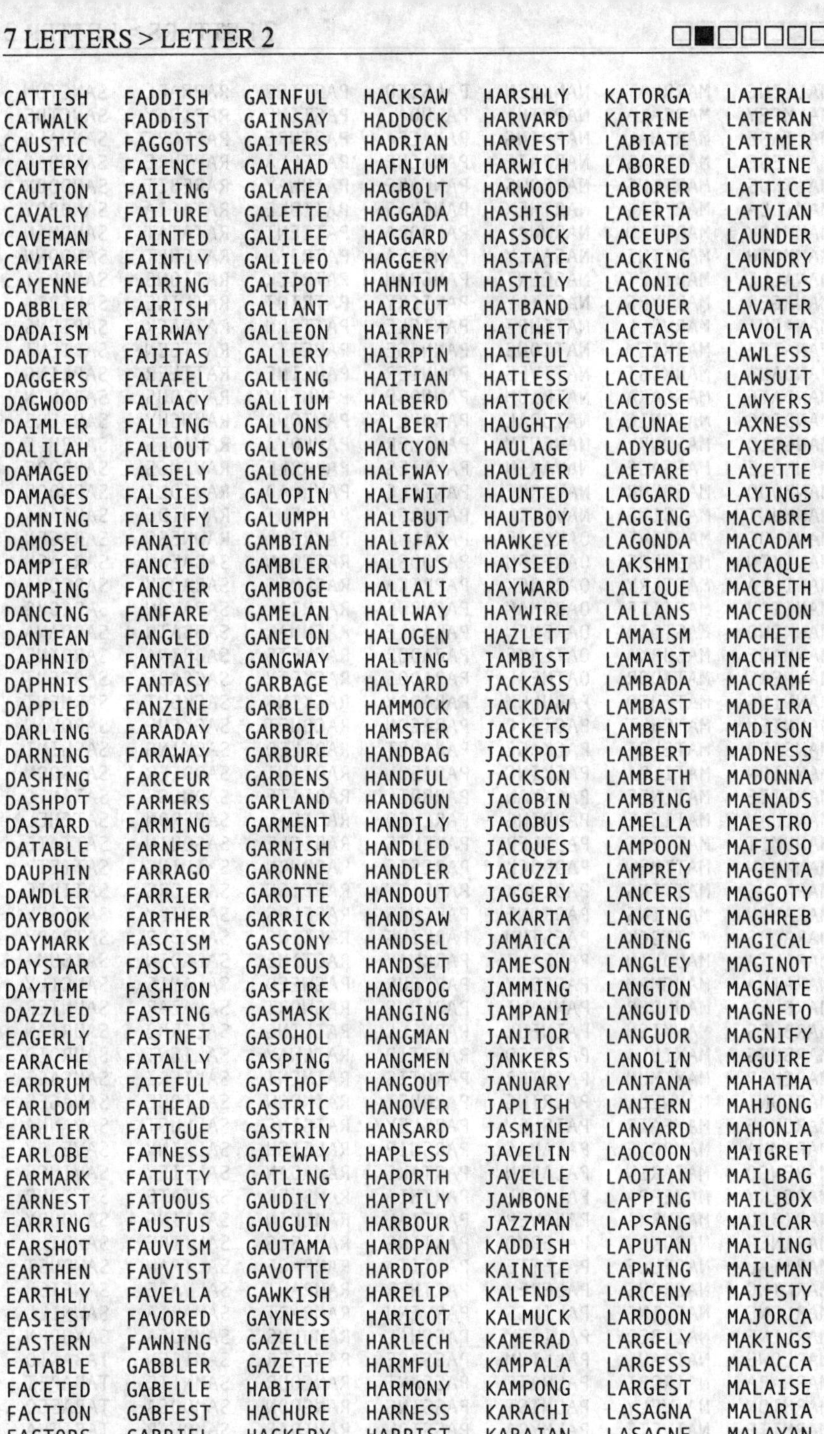

CATTISH
CATWALK
CAUSTIC
CAUTERY
CAUTION
CAVALRY
CAVEMAN
CAVIARE
CAYENNE
DABBLER
DADAISM
DADAIST
DAGGERS
DAGWOOD
DAIMLER
DALILAH
DAMAGED
DAMAGES
DAMNING
DAMOSEL
DAMPIER
DAMPING
DANCING
DANTEAN
DAPHNID
DAPHNIS
DAPPLED
DARLING
DARNING
DASHING
DASHPOT
DASTARD
DATABLE
DAUPHIN
DAWDLER
DAYBOOK
DAYMARK
DAYSTAR
DAYTIME
DAZZLED
EAGERLY
EARACHE
EARDRUM
EARLDOM
EARLIER
EARLOBE
EARMARK
EARNEST
EARRING
EARSHOT
EARTHEN
EARTHLY
EASIEST
EASTERN
EATABLE
FACETED
FACTION
FACTORS
FACTORY
FACTUAL
FACULTY
FADDISH
FADDIST
FAGGOTS
FAIENCE
FAILING
FAILURE
FAINTED
FAINTLY
FAIRING
FAIRISH
FAIRWAY
FAJITAS
FALAFEL
FALLACY
FALLING
FALLOUT
FALSELY
FALSIES
FALSIFY
FANATIC
FANCIED
FANCIER
FANFARE
FANGLED
FANTAIL
FANTASY
FANZINE
FARADAY
FARAWAY
FARCEUR
FARMERS
FARMING
FARNESE
FARRAGO
FARRIER
FARTHER
FASCISM
FASCIST
FASHION
FASTING
FASTNET
FATALLY
FATEFUL
FATHEAD
FATIGUE
FATNESS
FATUITY
FATUOUS
FAUSTUS
FAUVISM
FAUVIST
FAVELLA
FAVORED
FAWNING
GABBLER
GABELLE
GABFEST
GABRIEL
GADROON
GADWALL
GAEKWAR
GAINFUL
GAINSAY
GAITERS
GALAHAD
GALATEA
GALETTE
GALILEE
GALILEO
GALIPOT
GALLANT
GALLEON
GALLERY
GALLING
GALLIUM
GALLONS
GALLOWS
GALOCHE
GALOPIN
GALUMPH
GAMBIAN
GAMBLER
GAMBOGE
GAMELAN
GANELON
GANGWAY
GARBAGE
GARBLED
GARBOIL
GARBURE
GARDENS
GARLAND
GARMENT
GARNISH
GARONNE
GAROTTE
GARRICK
GASCONY
GASEOUS
GASFIRE
GASMASK
GASOHOL
GASPING
GASTHOF
GASTRIC
GASTRIN
GATEWAY
GATLING
GAUDILY
GAUGUIN
GAUTAMA
GAVOTTE
GAWKISH
GAYNESS
GAZELLE
GAZETTE
HABITAT
HACHURE
HACKERY
HACKING
HACKLES
HACKNEY
HACKSAW
HADDOCK
HADRIAN
HAFNIUM
HAGBOLT
HAGGADA
HAGGARD
HAGGERY
HAHNIUM
HAIRCUT
HAIRNET
HAIRPIN
HAITIAN
HALBERD
HALBERT
HALCYON
HALFWAY
HALFWIT
HALIBUT
HALIFAX
HALITUS
HALLALI
HALLWAY
HALOGEN
HALTING
HALYARD
HAMMOCK
HAMSTER
HANDBAG
HANDFUL
HANDGUN
HANDILY
HANDLED
HANDLER
HANDOUT
HANDSAW
HANDSEL
HANDSET
HANGDOG
HANGING
HANGMAN
HANGMEN
HANGOUT
HANOVER
HANSARD
HAPLESS
HAPORTH
HAPPILY
HARBOUR
HARDPAN
HARDTOP
HARELIP
HARICOT
HARLECH
HARMFUL
HARMONY
HARNESS
HARPIST
HARPOON
HARRIER
HARRIET
HARSHLY
HARVARD
HARVEST
HARWICH
HARWOOD
HASHISH
HASSOCK
HASTATE
HASTILY
HATBAND
HATCHET
HATEFUL
HATLESS
HATTOCK
HAUGHTY
HAULAGE
HAULIER
HAUNTED
HAUTBOY
HAWKEYE
HAYSEED
HAYWARD
HAYWIRE
HAZLETT
IAMBIST
JACKASS
JACKDAW
JACKETS
JACKPOT
JACKSON
JACOBIN
JACOBUS
JACQUES
JACUZZI
JAGGERY
JAKARTA
JAMAICA
JAMESON
JAMMING
JAMPANI
JANITOR
JANKERS
JANUARY
JAPLISH
JASMINE
JAVELIN
JAVELLE
JAWBONE
JAZZMAN
KADDISH
KAINITE
KALENDS
KALMUCK
KAMERAD
KAMPALA
KAMPONG
KARACHI
KARAJAN
KARAKUL
KARAOKE
KASHMIR
KATORGA
KATRINE
LABIATE
LABORED
LABORER
LACERTA
LACEUPS
LACKING
LACONIC
LACQUER
LACTASE
LACTATE
LACTEAL
LACTOSE
LACUNAE
LADYBUG
LAETARE
LAGGARD
LAGGING
LAGONDA
LAKSHMI
LALIQUE
LALLANS
LAMAISM
LAMAIST
LAMBADA
LAMBAST
LAMBENT
LAMBERT
LAMBETH
LAMBING
LAMELLA
LAMPOON
LAMPREY
LANCERS
LANCING
LANDING
LANGLEY
LANGTON
LANGUID
LANGUOR
LANOLIN
LANTANA
LANTERN
LANYARD
LAOCOON
LAOTIAN
LAPPING
LAPSANG
LAPUTAN
LAPWING
LARCENY
LARDOON
LARGELY
LARGESS
LARGEST
LASAGNA
LASAGNE
LASHING
LASTING
LATCHET
LATERAL
LATERAN
LATIMER
LATRINE
LATTICE
LATVIAN
LAUNDER
LAUNDRY
LAURELS
LAVATER
LAVOLTA
LAWLESS
LAWSUIT
LAWYERS
LAXNESS
LAYERED
LAYETTE
LAYINGS
MACABRE
MACADAM
MACAQUE
MACBETH
MACEDON
MACHETE
MACHINE
MACRAMÉ
MADEIRA
MADISON
MADNESS
MADONNA
MAENADS
MAESTRO
MAFIOSO
MAGENTA
MAGGOTY
MAGHREB
MAGICAL
MAGINOT
MAGNATE
MAGNETO
MAGNIFY
MAGUIRE
MAHATMA
MAHJONG
MAHONIA
MAIGRET
MAILBAG
MAILBOX
MAILCAR
MAILING
MAILMAN
MAJESTY
MAJORCA
MAKINGS
MALACCA
MALAISE
MALARIA
MALAYAN
MALEFIC
MALLARD
MALLEUS

MALLING
MALMSEY
MALTASE
MALTESE
MALTHUS
MAMILLA
MAMMARY
MAMMOTH
MANACLE
MANAGER
MANAGUA
MANATEE
MANDALA
MANDATE
MANDIOC
MANGOLD
MANHOLE
MANHOOD
MANHUNT
MANIHOC
MANIKIN
MANILLA
MANITOU
MANKIND
MANMADE
MANNERS
MANNING
MANNISH
MANSARD
MANSION
MANSIZE
MANTUAN
MANUMIT
MANXMAN
MAPPING
MARABOU
MARACAS
MARANTA
MARATHA
MARBLED
MARBLES
MARBURG
MARCHER
MARCONI
MARCUSE
MAREMMA
MARENGO
MARGERY
MARIBOU
MARINER
MARITAL
MARKING
MARLENE
MARLINE
MARLOWE
MARMARA
MARMION
MARMITE
MARQUEE
MARQUIS
MARRIED
MARRYAT
MARSALA
MARSHAL
MARSYAS
MARTENS
MARTIAL
MARTIAN
MARTINI
MARTLET
MARTYRS
MARVELL
MARXISM
MARXIST
MASCARA
MASONIC
MASONRY
MASSAGE
MASSEUR
MASSINE
MASSIVE
MASTERS
MASTERY
MASTIFF
MASTOID
MASURKA
MATADOR
MATCHED
MATCHET
MATELOT
MATILDA
MATINEE
MATISSE
MATTERS
MATTHEW
MATTING
MATTINS
MATTOCK
MAUDLIN
MAUGHAM
MAUNDER
MAWKISH
MAXILLA
MAXIMUM
MAXWELL
MAYFAIR
MAYPOLE
MAZARIN
MAZEPPA
MAZURKA
NABOKOV
NACELLE
NACROUS
NAGGING
NAILBED
NAIPAUL
NAIROBI
NAIVELY
NAIVETÉ
NAIVETY
NAKEDLY
NAMIBIA
NANKEEN
NAPHTHA
NAPPING
NARRATE
NARROWS
NARTHEX
NARWHAL
NASALLY
NASCENT
NASTILY
NATCHEZ
NATIONS
NATIVES
NATRIUM
NATURAL
NAUGHTY
NAVARIN
NAVARRE
NAVETTE
OAKLEAF
OARFISH
OARLOCK
OARSMAN
OARSMEN
OATCAKE
OATMEAL
PABULUM
PACIFIC
PACKAGE
PACKING
PACKMAN
PADDING
PADDLER
PADDOCK
PADLOCK
PADRONE
PAESTUM
PAGEANT
PAGEBOY
PAHLAVI
PAINFUL
PAINTED
PAINTER
PAIRING
PAISLEY
PAJAMAS
PALADIN
PALATAL
PALAVER
PALERMO
PALETTE
PALFREY
PALINGS
PALISSY
PALLIUM
PALMATE
PALMIST
PALMYRA
PALOMAR
PALOOKA
PALPATE
PALSIED
PALUDAL
PANACEA
PANACHE
PANCAKE
PANCRAS
PANDORA
PANGAEA
PANGRAM
PANICKY
PANICLE
PANNAGE
PANNIER
PANNOSE
PANOPLY
PANTHER
PANTIES
PANTILE
PANURGE
PAPILLA
PAPOOSE
PAPRIKA
PAPYRUS
PARABLE
PARADOR
PARADOS
PARADOX
PARAGON
PARAPET
PARASOL
PARBOIL
PARCHED
PARENTS
PARESIS
PARFAIT
PARINGS
PARKING
PARKWAY
PARLOUR
PARLOUS
PARNELL
PAROTID
PAROTIS
PARQUET
PARSLEY
PARSNIP
PARTAKE
PARTHIA
PARTIAL
PARTING
PARTITA
PARTNER
PARVENU
PASCHAL
PASSAGE
PASSANT
PASSING
PASSION
PASSIVE
PASTERN
PASTEUR
PASTIES
PASTIME
PASTURE
PATELLA
PATHWAY
PATIBLE
PATIENT
PATRIAL
PATRICK
PATRIOT
PATTERN
PAUCITY
PAULINE
PAUNCHY
PAVIOUR
PAVLOVA
PAYABLE
PAYLOAD
PAYMENT
PAYROLL
RACCOON
RACEMIC
RACHIAL
RACHMAN
RACKETS
RACKETY
RACKING
RACQUET
RADDLED
RADIANT
RADIATE
RADICAL
RADICLE
RAEBURN
RAFFISH
RAFFLES
RAFTING
RAGTIME
RAGWEED
RAGWORT
RAILING
RAILWAY
RAIMENT
RAINBOW
RAISING
RALEIGH
RAMADAN
RAMBLER
RAMEKIN
RAMESES
RAMPAGE
RAMPANT
RAMPART
RAMULUS
RANCHER
RANCOUR
RANGOON
RANIDAE
RANKING
RANSACK
RANTING
RAPHAEL
RAPIDLY
RAPPORT
RAPTURE
RAREBIT
RATAFIA
RATATAT
RATCHET
RATIONS
RATLINE
RATPACK
RATTEEN
RATTLER
RAUCOUS
RAUNCHY
RAVAGES
RAVINGS
RAVIOLI
RAWHIDE
RAWNESS
SABAEAN
SABAOTH
SABAYON
SABBATH
SABRINA
SACCADE
SACKBUT
SACKFUL
SACKING
SADDLER
SADNESS
SAFFRON
SAGOUIN
SAILING
SAILORS
SAINTLY
SALABLE
SALADIN
SALAMIS
SALAZAR
SALERMO
SALIENT
SALIERI
SALIQUE
SALLUST
SALPINX
SALSIFY
SALTATE
SALTING
SALTIRE
SALTPAN
SALVAGE
SAMARIA
SAMBUCA
SAMISEN
SAMNITE
SAMOOSA
SAMOVAR
SAMOYED
SAMPLER
SAMURAI
SANCTUM
SANCTUS
SANDALS
SANDBAG
SANDBOX
SANDBOY
SANDMAN
SANDOWN
SANDPIT
SANGRIA
SAPIENS
SAPIENT
SAPLING
SAPONIN
SAPPERS
SAPPHIC
SAPROBE
SAPWOOD
SAQQARA
SARACEN
SARCASM
SARCOMA
SARCOUS
SARDANA
SARDINE
SARGENT
SARMENT
SAROYAN
SASHIMI
SASSOON
SATANIC
SATCHEL
SATIATE
SATIETY
SATIRIC
SATISFY
SATRAPY
SATSUMA
SAUCILY
SAUNTER
SAURIAN
SAUROID
SAUSAGE
SAVAGES
SAVANNA
SAVELOY
SAVINGS
SAVIOUR
SAVOURY
SAWBILL
SAWDUST
SAWFISH
SAWMILL
SAXHORN
TABANID
TABARET
TABASCO
TABITHA
TABLEAU
TABLOID
TABULAR

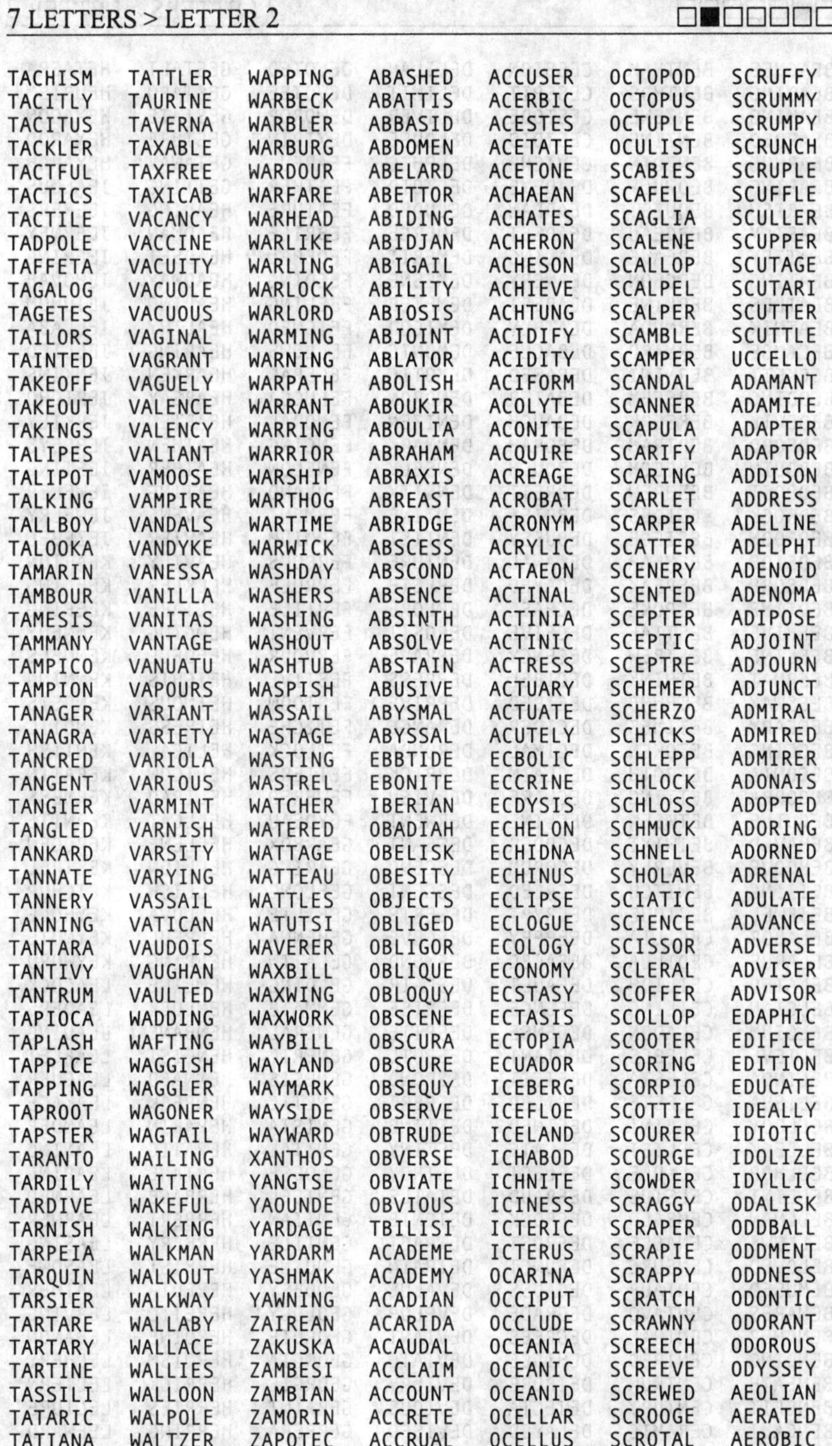

TACHISM
TACITLY
TACITUS
TACKLER
TACTFUL
TACTICS
TACTILE
TADPOLE
TAFFETA
TAGALOG
TAGETES
TAILORS
TAINTED
TAKEOFF
TAKEOUT
TAKINGS
TALIPES
TALIPOT
TALKING
TALLBOY
TALOOKA
TAMARIN
TAMBOUR
TAMESIS
TAMMANY
TAMPICO
TAMPION
TANAGER
TANAGRA
TANCRED
TANGENT
TANGIER
TANGLED
TANKARD
TANNATE
TANNERY
TANNING
TANTARA
TANTIVY
TANTRUM
TAPIOCA
TAPLASH
TAPPICE
TAPPING
TAPROOT
TAPSTER
TARANTO
TARDILY
TARDIVE
TARNISH
TARPEIA
TARQUIN
TARSIER
TARTARE
TARTARY
TARTINE
TASSILI
TATARIC
TATIANA
TATTERS
TATTING
TATTLER
TAURINE
TAVERNA
TAXABLE
TAXFREE
TAXICAB
VACANCY
VACCINE
VACUITY
VACUOLE
VACUOUS
VAGINAL
VAGRANT
VAGUELY
VALENCE
VALENCY
VALIANT
VAMOOSE
VAMPIRE
VANDALS
VANDYKE
VANESSA
VANILLA
VANITAS
VANTAGE
VANUATU
VAPOURS
VARIANT
VARIETY
VARIOLA
VARIOUS
VARMINT
VARNISH
VARSITY
VARYING
VASSAIL
VATICAN
VAUDOIS
VAUGHAN
VAULTED
WADDING
WAFTING
WAGGISH
WAGGLER
WAGONER
WAGTAIL
WAILING
WAITING
WAKEFUL
WALKING
WALKMAN
WALKOUT
WALKWAY
WALLABY
WALLACE
WALLIES
WALLOON
WALPOLE
WALTZER
WANGLER
WANTING
WAPPING
WARBECK
WARBLER
WARBURG
WARDOUR
WARFARE
WARHEAD
WARLIKE
WARLING
WARLOCK
WARLORD
WARMING
WARNING
WARPATH
WARRANT
WARRING
WARRIOR
WARSHIP
WARTHOG
WARTIME
WARWICK
WASHDAY
WASHERS
WASHING
WASHOUT
WASHTUB
WASPISH
WASSAIL
WASTAGE
WASTING
WASTREL
WATCHER
WATERED
WATTAGE
WATTEAU
WATTLES
WATUTSI
WAVERER
WAXBILL
WAXWING
WAXWORK
WAYBILL
WAYLAND
WAYMARK
WAYSIDE
WAYWARD
XANTHOS
YANGTSE
YAOUNDE
YARDAGE
YARDARM
YASHMAK
YAWNING
ZAIREAN
ZAKUSKA
ZAMBESI
ZAMBIAN
ZAMORIN
ZAPOTEC
ABALONE
ABANDON
ABASHED
ABATTIS
ABBASID
ABDOMEN
ABELARD
ABETTOR
ABIDING
ABIDJAN
ABIGAIL
ABILITY
ABIOSIS
ABJOINT
ABLATOR
ABOLISH
ABOUKIR
ABOULIA
ABRAHAM
ABRAXIS
ABREAST
ABRIDGE
ABSCESS
ABSCOND
ABSENCE
ABSINTH
ABSOLVE
ABSTAIN
ABUSIVE
ABYSMAL
ABYSSAL
EBBTIDE
EBONITE
IBERIAN
OBADIAH
OBELISK
OBESITY
OBJECTS
OBLIGED
OBLIGOR
OBLIQUE
OBLOQUY
OBSCENE
OBSCURA
OBSCURE
OBSEQUY
OBSERVE
OBTRUDE
OBVERSE
OBVIATE
OBVIOUS
TBILISI
ACADEME
ACADEMY
ACADIAN
ACARIDA
ACAUDAL
ACCLAIM
ACCOUNT
ACCRETE
ACCRUAL
ACCURSE
ACCUSED
ACCUSER
ACERBIC
ACESTES
ACETATE
ACETONE
ACHAEAN
ACHATES
ACHERON
ACHESON
ACHIEVE
ACHTUNG
ACIDIFY
ACIDITY
ACIFORM
ACOLYTE
ACONITE
ACQUIRE
ACREAGE
ACROBAT
ACRONYM
ACRYLIC
ACTAEON
ACTINAL
ACTINIA
ACTINIC
ACTRESS
ACTUARY
ACTUATE
ACUTELY
ECBOLIC
ECCRINE
ECDYSIS
ECHELON
ECHIDNA
ECHINUS
ECLIPSE
ECLOGUE
ECOLOGY
ECONOMY
ECSTASY
ECTASIS
ECTOPIA
ECUADOR
ICEBERG
ICEFLOE
ICELAND
ICHABOD
ICHNITE
ICINESS
ICTERIC
ICTERUS
OCARINA
OCCIPUT
OCCLUDE
OCEANIA
OCEANIC
OCEANID
OCELLAR
OCELLUS
OCTAGON
OCTOBER
OCTOPOD
OCTOPUS
OCTUPLE
OCULIST
SCABIES
SCAFELL
SCAGLIA
SCALENE
SCALLOP
SCALPEL
SCALPER
SCAMBLE
SCAMPER
SCANDAL
SCANNER
SCAPULA
SCARIFY
SCARING
SCARLET
SCARPER
SCATTER
SCENERY
SCENTED
SCEPTER
SCEPTIC
SCEPTRE
SCHEMER
SCHERZO
SCHICKS
SCHLEPP
SCHLOCK
SCHLOSS
SCHMUCK
SCHNELL
SCHOLAR
SCIATIC
SCIENCE
SCISSOR
SCLERAL
SCOFFER
SCOLLOP
SCOOTER
SCORING
SCORPIO
SCOTTIE
SCOURER
SCOURGE
SCOWDER
SCRAGGY
SCRAPER
SCRAPIE
SCRAPPY
SCRATCH
SCRAWNY
SCREECH
SCREEVE
SCREWED
SCROOGE
SCROTAL
SCROTUM
SCRUBBY
SCRUFFY
SCRUMMY
SCRUMPY
SCRUNCH
SCRUPLE
SCUFFLE
SCULLER
SCUPPER
SCUTAGE
SCUTARI
SCUTTER
SCUTTLE
UCCELLO
ADAMANT
ADAMITE
ADAPTER
ADAPTOR
ADDISON
ADDRESS
ADELINE
ADELPHI
ADENOID
ADENOMA
ADIPOSE
ADJOINT
ADJOURN
ADJUNCT
ADMIRAL
ADMIRED
ADMIRER
ADONAIS
ADOPTED
ADORING
ADORNED
ADRENAL
ADULATE
ADVANCE
ADVERSE
ADVISER
ADVISOR
EDAPHIC
EDIFICE
EDITION
EDUCATE
IDEALLY
IDIOTIC
IDOLIZE
IDYLLIC
ODALISK
ODDBALL
ODDMENT
ODDNESS
ODONTIC
ODORANT
ODOROUS
ODYSSEY
AEOLIAN
AERATED
AEROBIC
AEROSOL
BEACHED

BEACHES
BEADING
BEAMING
BEARDED
BEARHUG
BEARING
BEARISH
BEASTLY
BEATIFY
BEATING
BEATLES
BEATNIK
BECAUSE
BECKETT
BEDDING
BEDEVIL
BEDFORD
BEDOUIN
BEDPOST
BEDROCK
BEDROOM
BEDSIDE
BEDSORE
BEDTIME
BEEHIVE
BEELINE
BEERMAT
BEESWAX
BEGGARY
BEGGING
BEGONIA
BEGORRA
BEGUILE
BEHAVED
BEHOOVE
BEIJING
BEJEWEL
BELABOR
BELARUS
BELATED
BELGIAN
BELGIUM
BELIEVE
BELINDA
BELISHA
BELLBOY
BELLEEK
BELLHOP
BELLINI
BELLMAN
BELLOWS
BELOVED
BEMUSED
BENARES
BENCHER
BENDING
BENEATH
BENEFIT
BENGALI
BENISON
BENNETT
BENTHAM
BENTHOS
BENZENE
BENZINE
BENZOIN
BEOWULF
BEQUEST
BERCEAU
BEREAVE
BERGSON
BERLINE
BERMUDA
BERNARD
BERNINI
BERSEEM
BERSERK
BERTRAM
BESEECH
BESHREW
BESIDES
BESIEGE
BESMEAR
BESPEAK
BESPOKE
BESTIAL
BESTREW
BETHINK
BETHUMB
BETIMES
BETOKEN
BETROTH
BETTING
BETWEEN
BETWIXT
BEVERLY
BEWITCH
BEZIQUE
CECILIA
CEDILLA
CEILIDH
CEILING
CELADON
CELEBES
CELESTA
CELESTE
CELLINI
CELLIST
CELLULE
CELSIUS
CEMBALO
CENACLE
CENSURE
CENTAUR
CENTAVO
CENTRAL
CENTRED
CENTRUM
CENTURY
CERAMIC
CERTAIN
CERTIFY
CESSION
CESSPIT
CESTODE
CESTOID
CEVICHE
DEADEYE
DEADPAN
DEADSET
DEALING
DEANERY
DEAREST
DEATHLY
DEBACLE
DEBASED
DEBATER
DEBAUCH
DEBORAH
DEBOUCH
DEBRETT
DEBRIEF
DEBUSSY
DECANAL
DECAYED
DECEASE
DECEIVE
DECENCY
DECIBEL
DECIDED
DECIDER
DECIMAL
DECLAIM
DECLARE
DECLINE
DECODER
DECORUM
DECREED
DECRYPT
DEEPFRY
DEFACED
DEFAULT
DEFENCE
DEFENSE
DEFIANT
DEFICIT
DEFILED
DEFINED
DEFLATE
DEFLECT
DEFRAUD
DEFROCK
DEFROST
DEFUNCT
DEGAUSS
DEGRADE
DEGREES
DEHISCE
DEIRDRE
DEJECTA
DELAYED
DELIBES
DELIGHT
DELILAH
DELIMIT
DELIVER
DELOUSE
DELPHIC
DELTOID
DELUDED
DEMERGE
DEMERIT
DEMESNE
DEMETER
DEMIGOD
DEMONIC
DEMOTIC
DENDRON
DENIZEN
DENMARK
DENSELY
DENSITY
DENTINE
DENTIST
DENTURE
DEPLETE
DEPLORE
DEPOSIT
DEPRAVE
DEPRESS
DEPRIVE
DERANGE
DERONDA
DERRICK
DERVISH
DERWENT
DESCANT
DESCEND
DESCENT
DESERTS
DESERVE
DESMOND
DESPAIR
DESPISE
DESPITE
DESPOIL
DESPOND
DESSERT
DESTINE
DESTINY
DESTROY
DETAILS
DETENTE
DETRACT
DETRAIN
DEVALUE
DEVELOP
DEVIANT
DEVIATE
DEVILRY
DEVIOUS
DEVISED
DEVISEE
DEVOLVE
DEVOTED
DEVOTEE
DEWDROP
DEXTRIN
FEARFUL
FEATHER
FEATURE
FEBRILE
FEDERAL
FEEDING
FEELING
FEIGNED
FELLOWS
FELSPAR
FELUCCA
FEMORAL
FENCING
FENELON
FENLAND
FERMENT
FERMIUM
FERROUS
FERRULE
FERTILE
FERVENT
FERVOUR
FESTIVE
FESTOON
FETICHE
FETLOCK
FETTERS
FEVERED
FEYDEAU
GEARBOX
GEARING
GEELONG
GEFILTE
GEHENNA
GELATIN
GELDING
GEMMATE
GENERAL
GENERIC
GENESIS
GENETIC
GENISTA
GENITAL
GENOESE
GENTEEL
GENTIAN
GENTILE
GENUINE
GEODESY
GEOLOGY
GEORDIE
GEORGIA
GEORGIC
GERAINT
GERBERA
GERMANE
GERMANY
GESTALT
GESTAPO
GESTATE
GESTURE
GETAWAY
GETTING
HEADING
HEADMAN
HEADSET
HEADWAY
HEALING
HEALTHY
HEARING
HEARKEN
HEARSAY
HEARTEN
HEATHEN
HEATHER
HEATING
HEAVENS
HEAVIER
HEAVILY
HECKLER
HECTARE
HEDGING
HEEDFUL
HEIGHTS
HEINOUS
HEIRESS
HELICAL
HELICON
HELIPAD
HELLCAT
HELLENE
HELLION
HELLISH
HELLUVA
HELPFUL
HELPING
HEMLINE
HEMLOCK
HENBANE
HENGIST
HENNAED
HENPECK
HEPARIN
HEPATIC
HEPTANE
HERBAGE
HERBERT
HERBERY
HERBIST
HEREDIA
HERETIC
HEROINE
HEROISM
HERRICK
HERRIES
HERRING
HERSELF
HESSIAN
HETAERA
HEURISM
HEXAGON
HEXAPOD
HEXARCH
JEALOUS
JEEPERS
JEEPNEY
JEERING
JEHOVAH
JEJUNUM
JELLABA
JELLIED
JENKINS
JERICHO
JERKILY
JERSEYS
JESTING
JEWELER
JEWELRY
JEZEBEL
KEARTON
KEELING
KEEPING
KENNEDY
KENNELS
KENNING
KENOSIS
KENOTIC
KENTISH
KERATIN
KERMESS
KERNITE
KEROGEN
KESTREL
KETCHUP
KEYHOLE
KEYNOTE
KEYWORD
LEACOCK
LEADERS
LEADING
LEAFLET
LEAGUER
LEAKAGE
LEANDER
LEANING
LEAPING
LEARNED
LEARNER
LEASING
LEASOWE
LEATHER
LEAVING
LEBANON
LECHERY
LECTERN
LECTURE
LEEWARD
LEFTIST
LEGALLY

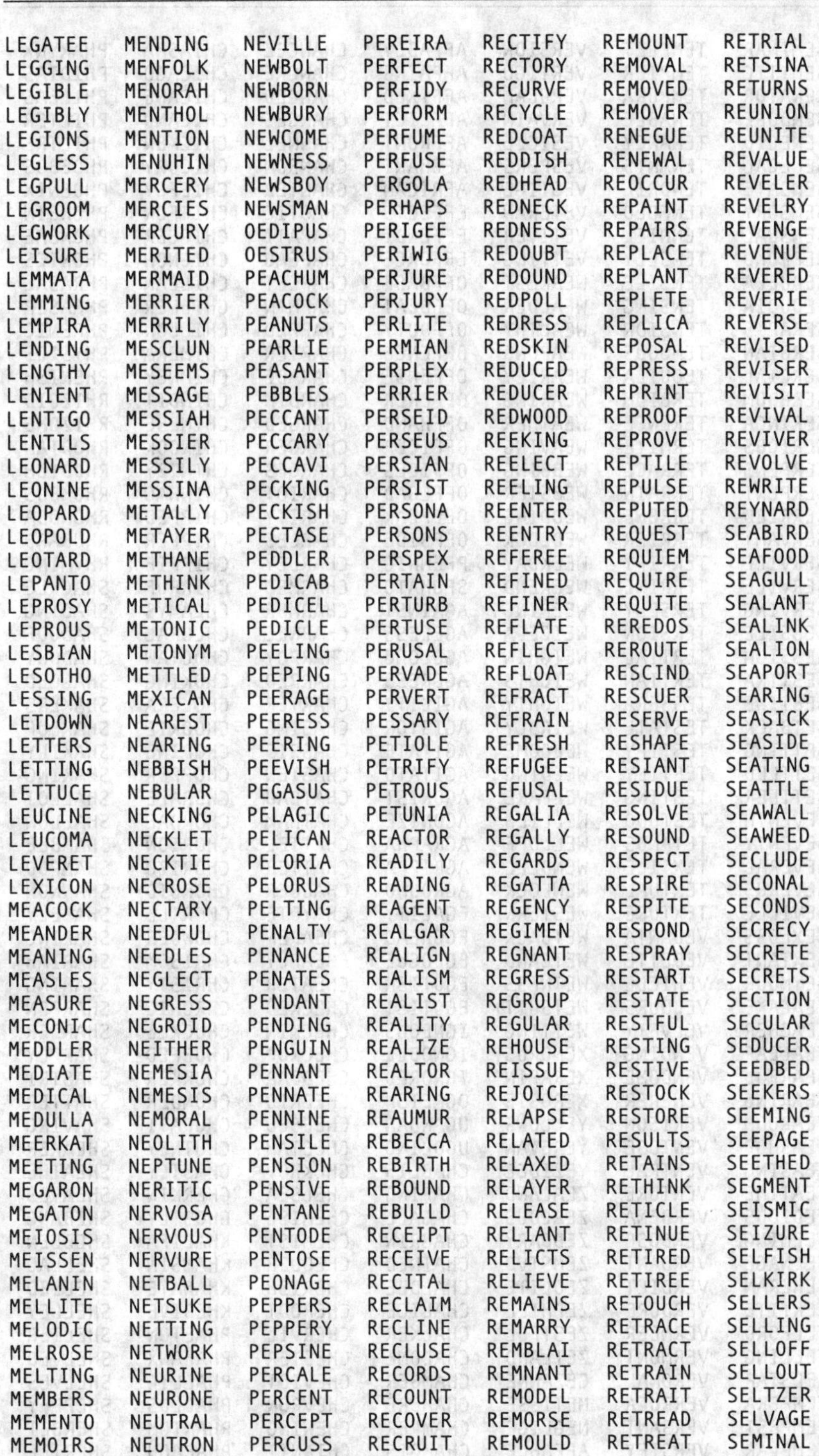

LEGATEE
LEGGING
LEGIBLE
LEGIBLY
LEGIONS
LEGLESS
LEGPULL
LEGROOM
LEGWORK
LEISURE
LEMMATA
LEMMING
LEMPIRA
LENDING
LENGTHY
LENIENT
LENTIGO
LENTILS
LEONARD
LEONINE
LEOPARD
LEOPOLD
LEOTARD
LEPANTO
LEPROSY
LEPROUS
LESBIAN
LESOTHO
LESSING
LETDOWN
LETTERS
LETTING
LETTUCE
LEUCINE
LEUCOMA
LEVERET
LEXICON
MEACOCK
MEANDER
MEANING
MEASLES
MEASURE
MECONIC
MEDDLER
MEDIATE
MEDICAL
MEDULLA
MEERKAT
MEETING
MEGARON
MEGATON
MEIOSIS
MEISSEN
MELANIN
MELLITE
MELODIC
MELROSE
MELTING
MEMBERS
MEMENTO
MEMOIRS
MENDING
MENFOLK
MENORAH
MENTHOL
MENTION
MENUHIN
MERCERY
MERCIES
MERCURY
MERITED
MERMAID
MERRIER
MERRILY
MESCLUN
MESEEMS
MESSAGE
MESSIAH
MESSIER
MESSILY
MESSINA
METALLY
METAYER
METHANE
METHINK
METICAL
METONIC
METONYM
METTLED
MEXICAN
NEAREST
NEARING
NEBBISH
NEBULAR
NECKING
NECKLET
NECKTIE
NECROSE
NECTARY
NEEDFUL
NEEDLES
NEGLECT
NEGRESS
NEGROID
NEITHER
NEMESIA
NEMESIS
NEMORAL
NEOLITH
NEPTUNE
NERITIC
NERVOSA
NERVOUS
NERVURE
NETBALL
NETSUKE
NETTING
NETWORK
NEURINE
NEURONE
NEUTRAL
NEUTRON
NEVILLE
NEWBOLT
NEWBORN
NEWBURY
NEWCOME
NEWNESS
NEWSBOY
NEWSMAN
OEDIPUS
OESTRUS
PEACHUM
PEACOCK
PEANUTS
PEARLIE
PEASANT
PEBBLES
PECCANT
PECCARY
PECCAVI
PECKING
PECKISH
PECTASE
PEDDLER
PEDICAB
PEDICEL
PEDICLE
PEELING
PEEPING
PEERAGE
PEERESS
PEERING
PEEVISH
PEGASUS
PELAGIC
PELICAN
PELORIA
PELORUS
PELTING
PENALTY
PENANCE
PENATES
PENDANT
PENDING
PENGUIN
PENNANT
PENNATE
PENNINE
PENSILE
PENSION
PENSIVE
PENTANE
PENTODE
PENTOSE
PEONAGE
PEPPERS
PEPPERY
PEPSINE
PERCALE
PERCENT
PERCEPT
PERCUSS
PEREIRA
PERFECT
PERFIDY
PERFORM
PERFUME
PERFUSE
PERGOLA
PERHAPS
PERIGEE
PERIWIG
PERJURE
PERJURY
PERLITE
PERMIAN
PERPLEX
PERRIER
PERSEID
PERSEUS
PERSIAN
PERSIST
PERSONA
PERSONS
PERSPEX
PERTAIN
PERTURB
PERTUSE
PERUSAL
PERVADE
PERVERT
PESSARY
PETIOLE
PETRIFY
PETROUS
PETUNIA
REACTOR
READILY
READING
REAGENT
REALGAR
REALIGN
REALISM
REALIST
REALITY
REALIZE
REALTOR
REARING
REAUMUR
REBECCA
REBIRTH
REBOUND
REBUILD
RECEIPT
RECEIVE
RECITAL
RECLAIM
RECLINE
RECLUSE
RECORDS
RECOUNT
RECOVER
RECRUIT
RECTIFY
RECTORY
RECURVE
RECYCLE
REDCOAT
REDDISH
REDHEAD
REDNECK
REDNESS
REDOUBT
REDOUND
REDPOLL
REDRESS
REDSKIN
REDUCED
REDUCER
REDWOOD
REEKING
REELECT
REELING
REENTER
REENTRY
REFEREE
REFINED
REFINER
REFLATE
REFLECT
REFLOAT
REFRACT
REFRAIN
REFRESH
REFUGEE
REFUSAL
REGALIA
REGALLY
REGARDS
REGATTA
REGENCY
REGIMEN
REGNANT
REGRESS
REGROUP
REGULAR
REHOUSE
REISSUE
REJOICE
RELAPSE
RELATED
RELAXED
RELAYER
RELEASE
RELIANT
RELICTS
RELIEVE
REMAINS
REMARRY
REMBLAI
REMNANT
REMODEL
REMORSE
REMOULD
REMOUNT
REMOVAL
REMOVED
REMOVER
RENEGUE
RENEWAL
REOCCUR
REPAINT
REPAIRS
REPLACE
REPLANT
REPLETE
REPLICA
REPOSAL
REPRESS
REPRINT
REPROOF
REPROVE
REPTILE
REPULSE
REPUTED
REQUEST
REQUIEM
REQUIRE
REQUITE
REREDOS
REROUTE
RESCIND
RESCUER
RESERVE
RESHAPE
RESIANT
RESIDUE
RESOLVE
RESOUND
RESPECT
RESPIRE
RESPITE
RESPOND
RESPRAY
RESTART
RESTATE
RESTFUL
RESTING
RESTIVE
RESTOCK
RESTORE
RESULTS
RETAINS
RETHINK
RETICLE
RETINUE
RETIRED
RETIREE
RETOUCH
RETRACE
RETRACT
RETRAIN
RETRAIT
RETREAD
RETREAT
RETRIAL
RETSINA
RETURNS
REUNION
REUNITE
REVALUE
REVELER
REVELRY
REVENGE
REVENUE
REVERED
REVERIE
REVERSE
REVISED
REVISER
REVISIT
REVIVAL
REVIVER
REVOLVE
REWRITE
REYNARD
SEABIRD
SEAFOOD
SEAGULL
SEALANT
SEALINK
SEALION
SEAPORT
SEARING
SEASICK
SEASIDE
SEATING
SEATTLE
SEAWALL
SEAWEED
SECLUDE
SECONAL
SECONDS
SECRECY
SECRETE
SECRETS
SECTION
SECULAR
SEDUCER
SEEDBED
SEEKERS
SEEMING
SEEPAGE
SEETHED
SEGMENT
SEISMIC
SEIZURE
SELFISH
SELKIRK
SELLERS
SELLING
SELLOFF
SELLOUT
SELTZER
SELVAGE
SEMINAL

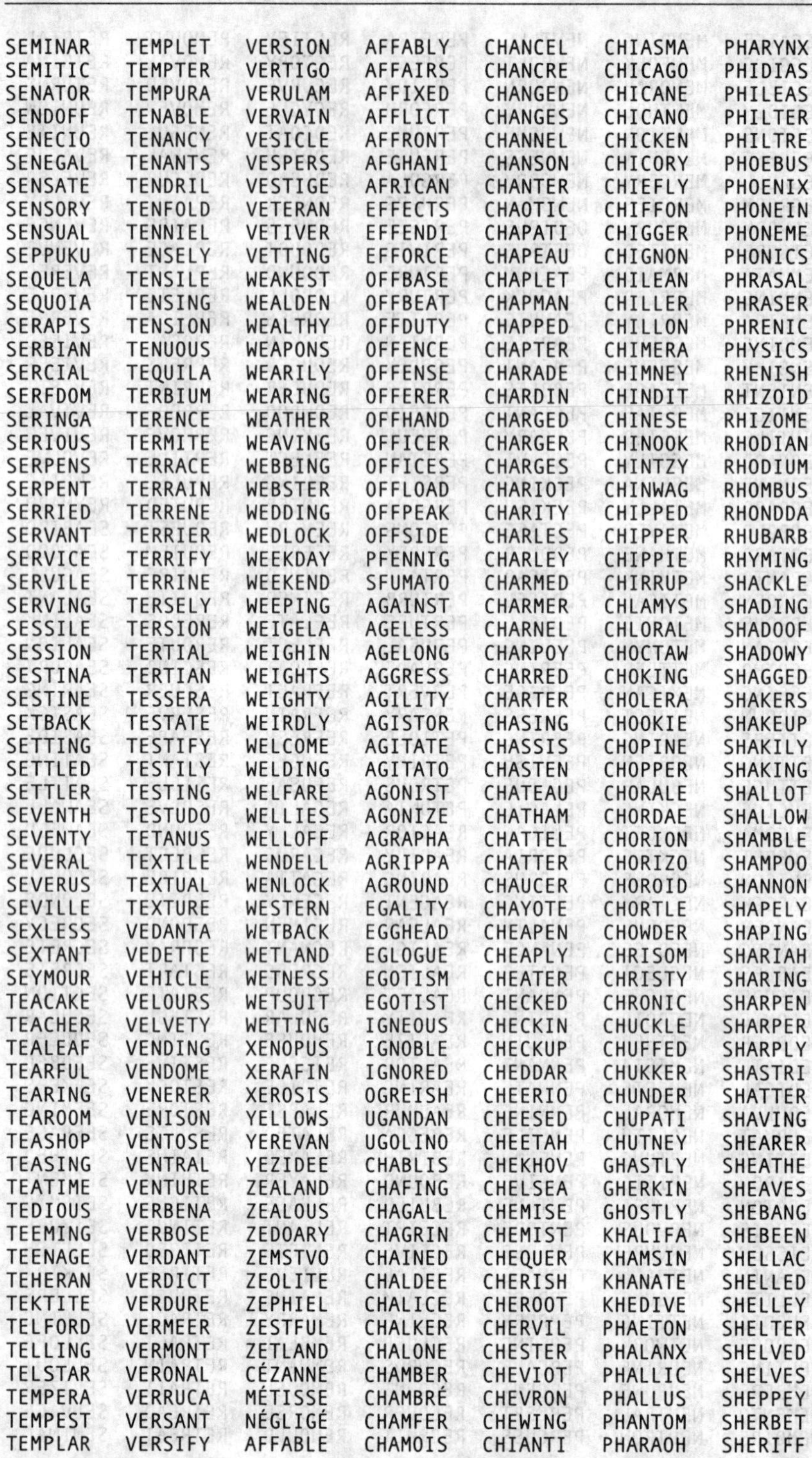

SEMINAR
SEMITIC
SENATOR
SENDOFF
SENECIO
SENEGAL
SENSATE
SENSORY
SENSUAL
SEPPUKU
SEQUELA
SEQUOIA
SERAPIS
SERBIAN
SERCIAL
SERFDOM
SERINGA
SERIOUS
SERPENS
SERPENT
SERRIED
SERVANT
SERVICE
SERVILE
SERVING
SESSILE
SESSION
SESTINA
SESTINE
SETBACK
SETTING
SETTLED
SETTLER
SEVENTH
SEVENTY
SEVERAL
SEVERUS
SEVILLE
SEXLESS
SEXTANT
SEYMOUR
TEACAKE
TEACHER
TEALEAF
TEARFUL
TEARING
TEAROOM
TEASHOP
TEASING
TEATIME
TEDIOUS
TEEMING
TEENAGE
TEHERAN
TEKTITE
TELFORD
TELLING
TELSTAR
TEMPERA
TEMPEST
TEMPLAR
TEMPLET
TEMPTER
TEMPURA
TENABLE
TENANCY
TENANTS
TENDRIL
TENFOLD
TENNIEL
TENSELY
TENSILE
TENSING
TENSION
TENUOUS
TEQUILA
TERBIUM
TERENCE
TERMITE
TERRACE
TERRAIN
TERRENE
TERRIER
TERRIFY
TERRINE
TERSELY
TERSION
TERTIAL
TERTIAN
TESSERA
TESTATE
TESTIFY
TESTILY
TESTING
TESTUDO
TETANUS
TEXTILE
TEXTUAL
TEXTURE
VEDANTA
VEDETTE
VEHICLE
VELOURS
VELVETY
VENDING
VENDOME
VENERER
VENISON
VENTOSE
VENTRAL
VENTURE
VERBENA
VERBOSE
VERDANT
VERDICT
VERDURE
VERMEER
VERMONT
VERONAL
VERRUCA
VERSANT
VERSIFY
VERSION
VERTIGO
VERULAM
VERVAIN
VESICLE
VESPERS
VESTIGE
VETERAN
VETIVER
VETTING
WEAKEST
WEALDEN
WEALTHY
WEAPONS
WEARILY
WEARING
WEATHER
WEAVING
WEBBING
WEBSTER
WEDDING
WEDLOCK
WEEKDAY
WEEKEND
WEEPING
WEIGELA
WEIGHIN
WEIGHTS
WEIGHTY
WEIRDLY
WELCOME
WELDING
WELFARE
WELLIES
WELLOFF
WENDELL
WENLOCK
WESTERN
WETBACK
WETLAND
WETNESS
WETSUIT
WETTING
XENOPUS
XERAFIN
XEROSIS
YELLOWS
YEREVAN
YEZIDEE
ZEALAND
ZEALOUS
ZEDOARY
ZEMSTVO
ZEOLITE
ZEPHIEL
ZESTFUL
ZETLAND
CÉZANNE
MÉTISSE
NÉGLIGÉ
AFFABLE
AFFABLY
AFFAIRS
AFFIXED
AFFLICT
AFFRONT
AFGHANI
AFRICAN
EFFECTS
EFFENDI
EFFORCE
OFFBASE
OFFBEAT
OFFDUTY
OFFENCE
OFFENSE
OFFERER
OFFHAND
OFFICER
OFFICES
OFFLOAD
OFFPEAK
OFFSIDE
PFENNIG
SFUMATO
AGAINST
AGELESS
AGELONG
AGGRESS
AGILITY
AGISTOR
AGITATE
AGITATO
AGONIST
AGONIZE
AGRAPHA
AGRIPPA
AGROUND
EGALITY
EGGHEAD
EGLOGUE
EGOTISM
EGOTIST
IGNEOUS
IGNOBLE
IGNORED
OGREISH
UGANDAN
UGOLINO
CHABLIS
CHAFING
CHAGALL
CHAGRIN
CHAINED
CHALDEE
CHALICE
CHALKER
CHALONE
CHAMBER
CHAMBRÉ
CHAMFER
CHAMOIS
CHANCEL
CHANCRE
CHANGED
CHANGES
CHANNEL
CHANSON
CHANTER
CHAOTIC
CHAPATI
CHAPEAU
CHAPLET
CHAPMAN
CHAPPED
CHAPTER
CHARADE
CHARDIN
CHARGED
CHARGER
CHARGES
CHARIOT
CHARITY
CHARLES
CHARLEY
CHARMED
CHARMER
CHARNEL
CHARPOY
CHARRED
CHARTER
CHASING
CHASSIS
CHASTEN
CHATEAU
CHATHAM
CHATTEL
CHATTER
CHAUCER
CHAYOTE
CHEAPEN
CHEAPLY
CHEATER
CHECKED
CHECKIN
CHECKUP
CHEDDAR
CHEERIO
CHEESED
CHEETAH
CHEKHOV
CHELSEA
CHEMISE
CHEMIST
CHEQUER
CHERISH
CHEROOT
CHERVIL
CHESTER
CHEVIOT
CHEVRON
CHEWING
CHIANTI
CHIASMA
CHICAGO
CHICANE
CHICANO
CHICKEN
CHICORY
CHIEFLY
CHIFFON
CHIGGER
CHIGNON
CHILEAN
CHILLER
CHILLON
CHIMERA
CHIMNEY
CHINDIT
CHINESE
CHINOOK
CHINTZY
CHINWAG
CHIPPED
CHIPPER
CHIPPIE
CHIRRUP
CHLAMYS
CHLORAL
CHOCTAW
CHOKING
CHOLERA
CHOOKIE
CHOPINE
CHOPPER
CHORALE
CHORDAE
CHORION
CHORIZO
CHOROID
CHORTLE
CHOWDER
CHRISOM
CHRISTY
CHRONIC
CHUCKLE
CHUFFED
CHUKKER
CHUNDER
CHUPATI
CHUTNEY
GHASTLY
GHERKIN
GHOSTLY
KHALIFA
KHAMSIN
KHANATE
KHEDIVE
PHAETON
PHALANX
PHALLIC
PHALLUS
PHANTOM
PHARAOH
PHARYNX
PHIDIAS
PHILEAS
PHILTER
PHILTRE
PHOEBUS
PHOENIX
PHONEIN
PHONEME
PHONICS
PHRASAL
PHRASER
PHRENIC
PHYSICS
RHENISH
RHIZOID
RHIZOME
RHODIAN
RHODIUM
RHOMBUS
RHONDDA
RHUBARB
RHYMING
SHACKLE
SHADING
SHADOOF
SHADOWY
SHAGGED
SHAKERS
SHAKEUP
SHAKILY
SHAKING
SHALLOT
SHALLOW
SHAMBLE
SHAMPOO
SHANNON
SHAPELY
SHAPING
SHARIAH
SHARING
SHARPEN
SHARPER
SHARPLY
SHASTRI
SHATTER
SHAVING
SHEARER
SHEATHE
SHEAVES
SHEBANG
SHEBEEN
SHELLAC
SHELLED
SHELLEY
SHELTER
SHELVED
SHELVES
SHEPPEY
SHERBET
SHERIFF

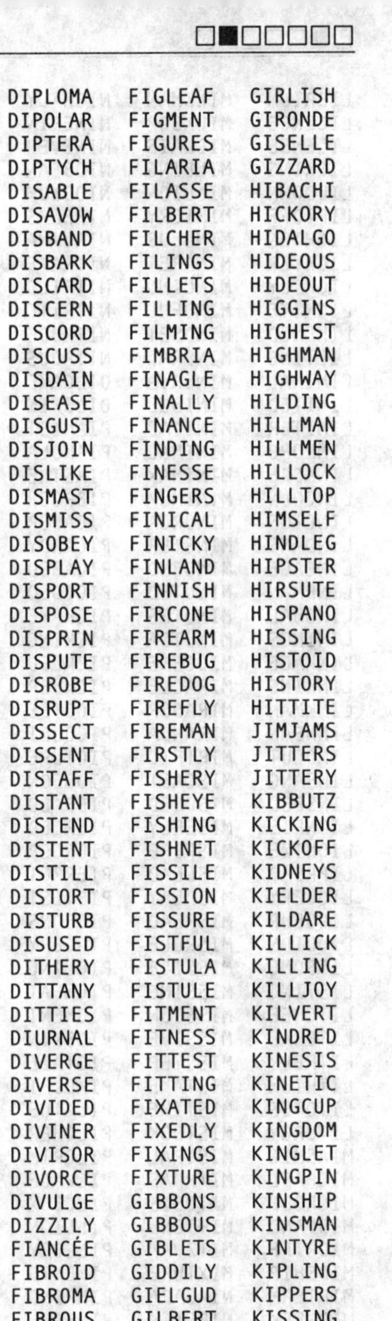

SHERMAN
SHIATSU
SHICKSA
SHIKARI
SHIMMER
SHINDIG
SHINGLE
SHINGLY
SHINING
SHINPAD
SHIPPER
SHIPTON
SHIRKER
SHIRLEY
SHIVERS
SHIVERY
SHMOOZE
SHOCKED
SHOCKER
SHOOTER
SHOPPER
SHORTEN
SHORTLY
SHOTGUN
SHOUTER
SHOWBIZ
SHOWERS
SHOWERY
SHOWILY
SHOWING
SHOWMAN
SHOWOFF
SHRILLY
SHRIMPS
SHRIVEL
SHRIVEN
SHRIVER
SHROUDS
SHUDDER
SHUFFLE
SHUTEYE
SHUTTER
SHUTTLE
SHYLOCK
SHYNESS
SHYSTER
THALLUS
THEATER
THEATRE
THEORBO
THEOREM
THERAPY
THEREBY
THEREIN
THERESA
THERETO
THERMAL
THERMIC
THERMOS
THESEUS
THICKEN
THICKET
THICKLY
THIEVES
THIMBLE
THINKER
THINNER
THIRDLY
THIRSTY
THISTLE
THITHER
THOMISM
THOMIST
THOMSON
THOREAU
THORIUM
THOUGHT
THREADS
THRENOS
THRIFTY
THRISTY
THROATY
THROUGH
THROWER
THROWIN
THRUWAY
THUGGEE
THULIUM
THUMPER
THUNDER
THYROID
THYRSIS
THYSELF
THYSSEN
WHACKED
WHACKER
WHALING
WHARTON
WHATNOT
WHATSIT
WHEATEN
WHEEDLE
WHEELED
WHEELER
WHEELIE
WHEREAS
WHEREBY
WHEREIN
WHETHER
WHIMPER
WHIMSEY
WHINGER
WHIPCAT
WHIPPED
WHIPPET
WHISKER
WHISKEY
WHISPER
WHISTLE
WHITHER
WHITING
WHITISH
WHITLOW
WHITSUN
WHITTLE
WHOEVER
WHOOPEE
WHOOPER
WHOPPER
AIDANCE
AILERON
AILMENT
AIMLESS
AINTREE
AIRBASE
AIRCREW
AIRFLOW
AIRLESS
AIRLIFT
AIRLINE
AIRLOCK
AIRMAIL
AIRPORT
AIRSHIP
AIRSICK
AIRSTOP
BIAFRAN
BIASSED
BIBELOT
BICYCLE
BIDDING
BIFOCAL
BIGFOOT
BIGHEAD
BIGHORN
BIGOTED
BIGOTRY
BIGSHOT
BILIOUS
BILLION
BILLMAN
BILLOWS
BILTONG
BINDERY
BINDING
BIOLOGY
BIOMASS
BIPLANE
BIRDMAN
BIRETTA
BISCUIT
BISMUTH
BISTORT
BITTERN
BITTERS
BITUMEN
BIVALVE
BIVOUAC
BIZARRE
CIMABUE
CINDERS
CINEMAS
CINEREA
CIRCLET
CIRCLIP
CIRCUIT
CIRROSE
CISSOID
CISTERN
CITADEL
CITHARA
CITIZEN
CITRINE
CITROEN
CIVILLY
CIVVIES
DIABOLO
DIAGRAM
DIALECT
DIALING
DIALYSE
DIAMINE
DIAMOND
DIAPSID
DIARCHY
DIARIST
DIBBLER
DICKENS
DICTATE
DICTION
DIDEROT
DIDICOY
DIDYMUS
DIECAST
DIEDRAL
DIEHARD
DIETARY
DIETINE
DIFFUSE
DIGGING
DIGITAL
DIGLYPH
DIGNIFY
DIGNITY
DIGONAL
DIGRAPH
DIGRESS
DILATED
DILATOR
DILEMMA
DILUENT
DILUTED
DIMNESS
DIMPLED
DINETTE
DINGBAT
DINMONT
DIOCESE
DIOPTER
DIOPTRE
DIORAMA
DIORITE
DIOXIDE
DIPLOCK
DIPLOMA
DIPOLAR
DIPTERA
DIPTYCH
DISABLE
DISAVOW
DISBAND
DISBARK
DISCARD
DISCERN
DISCORD
DISCUSS
DISDAIN
DISEASE
DISGUST
DISJOIN
DISLIKE
DISMAST
DISMISS
DISOBEY
DISPLAY
DISPORT
DISPOSE
DISPRIN
DISPUTE
DISROBE
DISRUPT
DISSECT
DISSENT
DISTAFF
DISTANT
DISTEND
DISTENT
DISTILL
DISTORT
DISTURB
DISUSED
DITHERY
DITTANY
DITTIES
DIURNAL
DIVERGE
DIVERSE
DIVIDED
DIVINER
DIVISOR
DIVORCE
DIVULGE
DIZZILY
FIANCÉE
FIBROID
FIBROMA
FIBROUS
FICTION
FIDDLER
FIDELIO
FIDGETS
FIDGETY
FIELDER
FIFTEEN
FIGHTER
FIGLEAF
FIGMENT
FIGURES
FILARIA
FILASSE
FILBERT
FILCHER
FILINGS
FILLETS
FILLING
FILMING
FIMBRIA
FINAGLE
FINALLY
FINANCE
FINDING
FINESSE
FINGERS
FINICAL
FINICKY
FINLAND
FINNISH
FIRCONE
FIREARM
FIREBUG
FIREDOG
FIREFLY
FIREMAN
FIRSTLY
FISHERY
FISHEYE
FISHING
FISHNET
FISSILE
FISSION
FISSURE
FISTFUL
FISTULA
FISTULE
FITMENT
FITNESS
FITTEST
FITTING
FIXATED
FIXEDLY
FIXINGS
FIXTURE
GIBBONS
GIBBOUS
GIBLETS
GIDDILY
GIELGUD
GILBERT
GILDING
GILLRAY
GIMBALS
GIMBLET
GIMMICK
GINGHAM
GINSENG
GIRAFFE
GIRLISH
GIRONDE
GISELLE
GIZZARD
HIBACHI
HICKORY
HIDALGO
HIDEOUS
HIDEOUT
HIGGINS
HIGHEST
HIGHMAN
HIGHWAY
HILDING
HILLMAN
HILLMEN
HILLOCK
HILLTOP
HIMSELF
HINDLEG
HIPSTER
HIRSUTE
HISPANO
HISSING
HISTOID
HISTORY
HITTITE
JIMJAMS
JITTERS
JITTERY
KIBBUTZ
KICKING
KICKOFF
KIDNEYS
KIELDER
KILDARE
KILLICK
KILLING
KILLJOY
KILVERT
KINDRED
KINESIS
KINETIC
KINGCUP
KINGDOM
KINGLET
KINGPIN
KINSHIP
KINSMAN
KINTYRE
KIPLING
KIPPERS
KISSING
KITCHEN
KITHARA
KIWANIS
LIAISON
LIBERAL
LIBERIA
LIBERTY
LIBRARY

LIBRIUM
LICENCE
LICENSE
LICKING
LIEDOWN
LIFTOFF
LIGHTEN
LIGHTER
LIGHTLY
LIGNITE
LIKENED
LILTING
LIMINAL
LIMITED
LIMITER
LIMPOPO
LINACRE
LINCOLN
LINCTUS
LINDANE
LINEAGE
LINEMAN
LINGUAL
LININGS
LINKAGE
LINKING
LINKMAN
LINNEAN
LINOCUT
LINSANG
LINSEED
LIONESS
LIONIZE
LIPREAD
LIQUEFY
LIQUEUR
LIQUIDS
LISSOME
LISTING
LITCHEE
LITERAL
LITHELY
LITHIUM
LITOTES
LITURGY
MIASMIC
MICHAEL
MICROBE
MIDLAND
MIDRIFF
MIDSHIP
MIDTERM
MIDWEEK
MIDWEST
MIDWIFE
MIGRANT
MIGRATE
MILEAGE
MILFOIL
MILITIA
MILKING
MILKMAN
MILKSOP
MILLAIS
MILLING
MILLION
MIMICRY
MIMULUS
MINARET
MINCING
MINDFUL
MINDSET
MINERAL
MINERVA
MINIBUS
MINICAB
MINIMAL
MINIMAX
MINIMUM
MINORCA
MINSTER
MINUEND
MINUTED
MINUTES
MINUTIA
MIOCENE
MIRACLE
MIRADOR
MIRANDA
MIRIFIC
MISCAST
MISDEED
MISERLY
MISFIRE
MISLEAD
MISPLAY
MISREAD
MISRULE
MISSILE
MISSING
MISSION
MISSIVE
MISSTEP
MISTAKE
MISTIME
MISTOOK
MISTRAL
MITHRAS
MITOSIS
MITTENS
MITZVAH
MIXTURE
NIAGARA
NIBLICK
NICAEAN
NICOISE
NICOSIA
NICTATE
NIGELLA
NIGERIA
NIGGARD
NIGHTIE
NIGHTLY
NINEPIN
NINEVEH
NIOBEAN
NIOBIUM
NIPPERS
NIRVANA
NITRATE
NITRILE
NITRITE
NITRODE
NITROUS
OILCAKE
OILSKIN
PIANIST
PIANOLA
PIASTRE
PIBROCH
PICADOR
PICARDY
PICASSO
PICCOLO
PICKAXE
PICKING
PICKLED
PICKLER
PICOTEE
PICQUET
PICTURE
PIDGEON
PIEBALD
PIERCED
PIERCER
PIERROT
PIETIST
PIGEONS
PIGGERY
PIGLING
PIGMEAT
PIGMENT
PIGSKIN
PIGTAIL
PIKELET
PILATUS
PILCHER
PILGRIM
PILLAGE
PILLBOX
PILLION
PILLORY
PIMENTO
PIMPING
PINBALL
PINCERS
PINCHED
PINETUM
PINFOLD
PINHEAD
PINHOLE
PINNACE
PINNULA
PINTADO
PINTAIL
PIONEER
PIOUSLY
PIPETTE
PIQUANT
PIRAEUS
PIRANHA
PIROGUE
PISCINA
PISCINE
PISTOLE
PITCHED
PITCHER
PITEOUS
PITFALL
PITHEAD
PITHILY
PITIFUL
PIVOTAL
PIZARRO
PIZZAZZ
RIBBING
RIBCAGE
RIBLESS
RICARDO
RICHARD
RICHTER
RICKETS
RICKETY
RICOTTA
RIDDLED
RIDDLER
RIDINGS
RIGGING
RIGHTLY
RIGIDLY
RIGVEDA
RIMLESS
RINGERS
RINGGIT
RINGING
RINGLET
RIOTERS
RIOTING
RIOTOUS
RIPCORD
RIPOSTE
RIPPING
RISIBLE
RISKILY
RISOTTO
RISSOLE
RIVALRY
RIVETED
RIVIERA
RIVULET
SIAMESE
SIBLING
SICKBAY
SICKBED
SICKERT
SIDDONS
SIDECAR
SIEMENS
SIEVERT
SIFTING
SIGHTED
SIGNIFY
SIGNING
SIGNORA
SIGNORI
SIKHISM
SILENCE
SILESIA
SILICON
SILVERY
SIMENON
SIMILAR
SIMPKIN
SIMPLER
SIMPLEX
SIMPLON
SIMPSON
SINATRA
SINCERE
SINDBAD
SINGING
SINGLES
SINGLET
SINHALA
SINKING
SINUATE
SINUOUS
SIPPING
SIRLOIN
SIROCCO
SISTERS
SISTINE
SITDOWN
SITTING
SITUATE
SITWELL
SIXTEEN
SIZABLE
SIZZLER
TIBETAN
TICKING
TICKLER
TIDDLER
TIDEWAY
TIDINGS
TIEPOLO
TIERCEL
TIERCET
TIFFANY
TIGHTEN
TIGHTLY
TIGRESS
TIGRISH
TILAPIA
TILBURY
TILLAGE
TIMBALE
TIMBERS
TIMBREL
TIMELAG
TIMIDLY
TIMOTHY
TIMPANI
TINFOIL
TINGLER
TINTACK
TINTERN
TIPCART
TIPPING
TIPPLER
TIPSILY
TIPSTER
TITANIA
TITANIC
TITOISM
TITOIST
TITRATE
TITULAR
VIADUCT
VIBRANT
VIBRATE
VIBRATO
VICEROY
VICINAL
VICIOUS
VICTORY
VICTUAL
VIDIMUS
VIETNAM
VIKINGS
VILLAGE
VILLAIN
VILLEIN
VILNIUS
VINASSE
VINCENT
VINEGAR
VINTAGE
VINTNER
VIOLATE
VIOLENT
VIRELAY
VIRGATE
VIRGULE
VIRTUAL
VISCERA
VISCOSE
VISCOUS
VISIBLE
VISIBLY
VISITOR
VISTULA
VITALLY
VITAMIN
VITIATE
VITRAIL
VITRIFY
VITRIOL
VIVALDI
VIVIDLY
WICKIUP
WICKLOW
WIDGEON
WIDOWED
WIDOWER
WIGGING
WILDCAT
WILFRED
WILLIAM
WILLIES
WILLING
WILLOWY
WIMPISH
WINDBAG
WINDING
WINDOWS
WINDROW
WINDSOR
WINNING
WINNOCK
WINSOME
WINSTON
WIPEOUT
WIRETAP
WISHFUL
WISHING
WISTFUL
WITCHES
WITHERS
WITHOUT
WITLESS
WITLOOF
WITNESS
WIZENED
XIMENES
YIDDISH
ZILLION
ZINGARO
ZIONIST
ZIZANIA
EJECTOR
SJAMBOK
IKEBANA
OKINAWA
SKATING
SKELTER
SKEPTIC
SKETCHY
SKIDDAW
SKIDPAN
SKIFFLE
SKILFUL
SKILLED
SKILLET
SKIMMED
SKIMMER
SKIMMIA

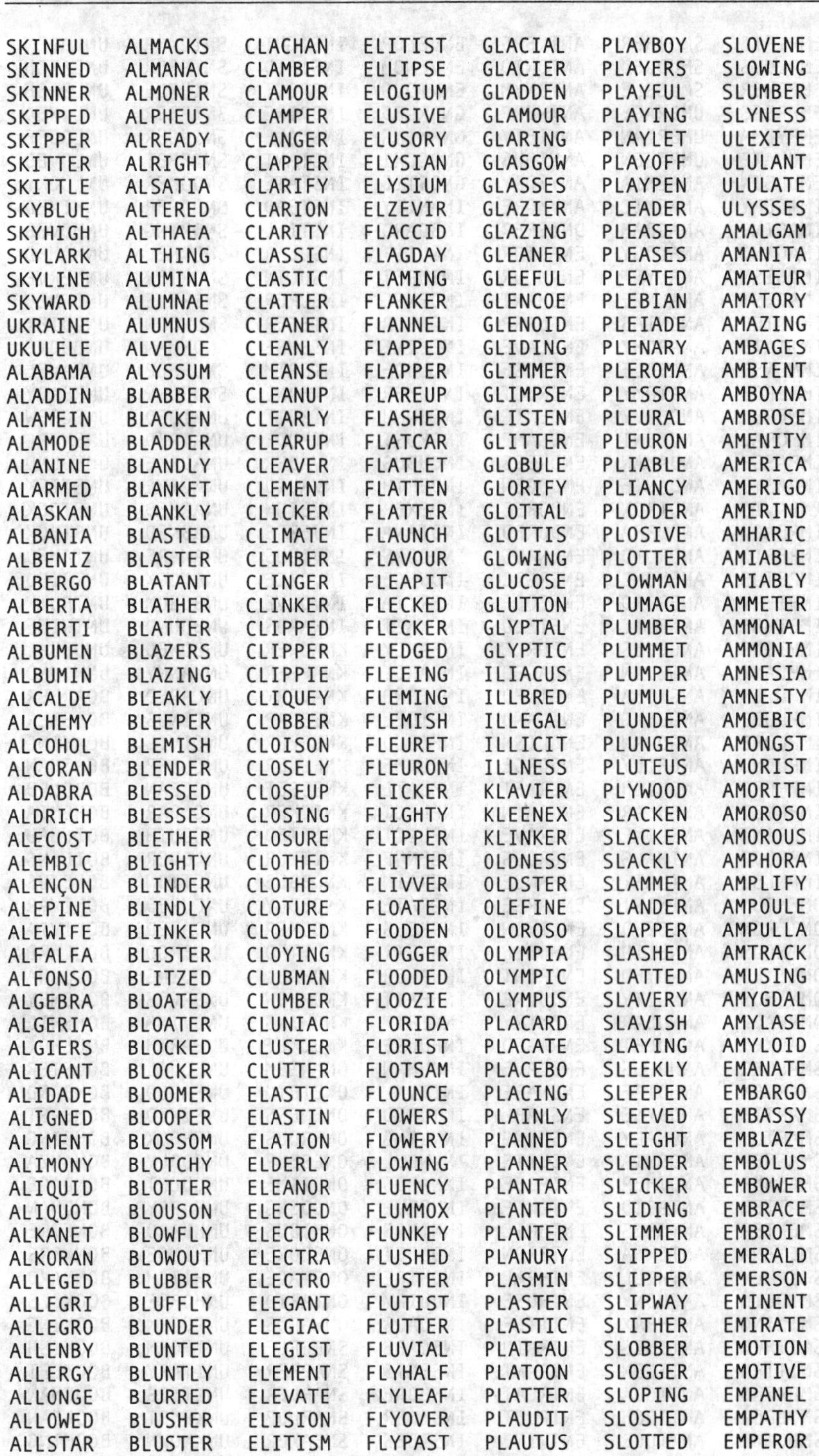

SKINFUL
SKINNED
SKINNER
SKIPPED
SKIPPER
SKITTER
SKITTLE
SKYBLUE
SKYHIGH
SKYLARK
SKYLINE
SKYWARD
UKRAINE
UKULELE
ALABAMA
ALADDIN
ALAMEIN
ALAMODE
ALANINE
ALARMED
ALASKAN
ALBANIA
ALBENIZ
ALBERGO
ALBERTA
ALBERTI
ALBUMEN
ALBUMIN
ALCALDE
ALCHEMY
ALCOHOL
ALCORAN
ALDABRA
ALDRICH
ALECOST
ALEMBIC
ALENÇON
ALEPINE
ALEWIFE
ALFALFA
ALFONSO
ALGEBRA
ALGERIA
ALGIERS
ALICANT
ALIDADE
ALIGNED
ALIMENT
ALIMONY
ALIQUID
ALIQUOT
ALKANET
ALKORAN
ALLEGED
ALLEGRI
ALLEGRO
ALLENBY
ALLERGY
ALLONGE
ALLOWED
ALLSTAR

ALMACKS
ALMANAC
ALMONER
ALPHEUS
ALREADY
ALRIGHT
ALSATIA
ALTERED
ALTHAEA
ALTHING
ALUMINA
ALUMNAE
ALUMNUS
ALVEOLE
ALYSSUM
BLABBER
BLACKEN
BLADDER
BLANDLY
BLANKET
BLANKLY
BLASTED
BLASTER
BLATANT
BLATHER
BLATTER
BLAZERS
BLAZING
BLEAKLY
BLEEPER
BLEMISH
BLENDER
BLESSED
BLESSES
BLETHER
BLIGHTY
BLINDER
BLINDLY
BLINKER
BLISTER
BLITZED
BLOATED
BLOATER
BLOCKED
BLOCKER
BLOOMER
BLOOPER
BLOSSOM
BLOTCHY
BLOTTER
BLOUSON
BLOWFLY
BLOWOUT
BLUBBER
BLUFFLY
BLUNDER
BLUNTED
BLUNTLY
BLURRED
BLUSHER
BLUSTER

CLACHAN
CLAMBER
CLAMOUR
CLAMPER
CLANGER
CLAPPER
CLARIFY
CLARION
CLARITY
CLASSIC
CLASTIC
CLATTER
CLEANER
CLEANLY
CLEANSE
CLEANUP
CLEARLY
CLEARUP
CLEAVER
CLEMENT
CLICKER
CLIMATE
CLIMBER
CLINGER
CLINKER
CLIPPED
CLIPPER
CLIPPIE
CLIQUEY
CLOBBER
CLOISON
CLOSELY
CLOSEUP
CLOSING
CLOSURE
CLOTHED
CLOTHES
CLOTURE
CLOUDED
CLOYING
CLUBMAN
CLUMBER
CLUNIAC
CLUSTER
CLUTTER
ELASTIC
ELASTIN
ELATION
ELDERLY
ELEANOR
ELECTED
ELECTOR
ELECTRA
ELECTRO
ELEGANT
ELEGIAC
ELEGIST
ELEMENT
ELEVATE
ELISION
ELITISM

ELITIST
ELLIPSE
ELOGIUM
ELUSIVE
ELUSORY
ELYSIAN
ELYSIUM
ELZEVIR
FLACCID
FLAGDAY
FLAMING
FLANKER
FLANNEL
FLAPPED
FLAPPER
FLAREUP
FLASHER
FLATCAR
FLATLET
FLATTEN
FLATTER
FLAUNCH
FLAVOUR
FLEAPIT
FLECKED
FLECKER
FLEDGED
FLEEING
FLEMING
FLEMISH
FLEURET
FLEURON
FLICKER
FLIGHTY
FLIPPER
FLITTER
FLIVVER
FLOATER
FLODDEN
FLOGGER
FLOODED
FLOOZIE
FLORIDA
FLORIST
FLOTSAM
FLOUNCE
FLOWERS
FLOWERY
FLOWING
FLUENCY
FLUMMOX
FLUNKEY
FLUSHED
FLUSTER
FLUTIST
FLUTTER
FLUVIAL
FLYHALF
FLYLEAF
FLYOVER
FLYPAST

GLACIAL
GLACIER
GLADDEN
GLAMOUR
GLARING
GLASGOW
GLASSES
GLAZIER
GLAZING
GLEANER
GLEEFUL
GLENCOE
GLENOID
GLIDING
GLIMMER
GLIMPSE
GLISTEN
GLITTER
GLOBULE
GLORIFY
GLOTTAL
GLOTTIS
GLOWING
GLUCOSE
GLUTTON
GLYPTAL
GLYPTIC
ILIACUS
ILLBRED
ILLEGAL
ILLICIT
ILLNESS
KLAVIER
KLEENEX
KLINKER
OLDNESS
OLDSTER
OLEFINE
OLOROSO
OLYMPIA
OLYMPIC
OLYMPUS
PLACARD
PLACATE
PLACEBO
PLACING
PLAINLY
PLANNED
PLANNER
PLANTAR
PLANTED
PLANTER
PLANURY
PLASMIN
PLASTER
PLASTIC
PLATEAU
PLATOON
PLATTER
PLAUDIT
PLAUTUS

PLAYBOY
PLAYERS
PLAYFUL
PLAYING
PLAYLET
PLAYOFF
PLAYPEN
PLEADER
PLEASED
PLEASES
PLEATED
PLEBIAN
PLEIADE
PLENARY
PLEROMA
PLESSOR
PLEURAL
PLEURON
PLIABLE
PLIANCY
PLODDER
PLOSIVE
PLOTTER
PLOWMAN
PLUMAGE
PLUMBER
PLUMMET
PLUMPER
PLUMULE
PLUNDER
PLUNGER
PLUTEUS
PLYWOOD
SLACKEN
SLACKER
SLACKLY
SLAMMER
SLANDER
SLAPPER
SLASHED
SLATTED
SLAVERY
SLAVISH
SLAYING
SLEEKLY
SLEEPER
SLEEVED
SLEIGHT
SLENDER
SLICKER
SLIDING
SLIMMER
SLIPPED
SLIPPER
SLIPWAY
SLITHER
SLOBBER
SLOGGER
SLOPING
SLOSHED
SLOTTED

SLOVENE
SLOWING
SLUMBER
SLYNESS
ULEXITE
ULULANT
ULULATE
ULYSSES
AMALGAM
AMANITA
AMATEUR
AMATORY
AMAZING
AMBAGES
AMBIENT
AMBOYNA
AMBROSE
AMENITY
AMERICA
AMERIGO
AMERIND
AMHARIC
AMIABLE
AMIABLY
AMMETER
AMMONAL
AMMONIA
AMNESIA
AMNESTY
AMOEBIC
AMONGST
AMORIST
AMORITE
AMOROSO
AMOROUS
AMPHORA
AMPLIFY
AMPOULE
AMPULLA
AMTRACK
AMUSING
AMYGDAL
AMYLASE
AMYLOID
EMANATE
EMBARGO
EMBASSY
EMBLAZE
EMBOLUS
EMBOWER
EMBRACE
EMBROIL
EMERALD
EMERSON
EMINENT
EMIRATE
EMOTION
EMOTIVE
EMPANEL
EMPATHY
EMPEROR

EMPIRIC
EMPLOYS
EMPOWER
EMPRESS
EMPYEMA
EMULATE
EMULSIN
IMAGERY
IMAGINE
IMAGING
IMAGISM
IMAGIST
IMHOTEP
IMITATE
IMMENSE
IMMERGE
IMMERSE
IMMORAL
IMPASSE
IMPASTO
IMPAVID
IMPEACH
IMPERIL
IMPETUS
IMPIETY
IMPINGE
IMPIOUS
IMPLANT
IMPLIED
IMPLODE
IMPLORE
IMPOUND
IMPRESS
IMPREST
IMPRINT
IMPROVE
IMPULSE
OMENTUM
OMICRON
OMINOUS
OMITTED
OMNIBUS
OMPHALE
SMACKER
SMALLER
SMARTEN
SMARTIE
SMARTLY
SMASHED
SMASHER
SMATTER
SMELTER
SMETANA
SMICKLY
SMIDGIN
SMILING
SMITHER
SMITTEN
SMOKING
SMOLDER
SMOOTHE
SMOTHER
SMUDGED
SMUGGLE
UMBRAGE
UMBRIAN
UMPTEEN
ANAEMIA
ANAEMIC
ANAGRAM
ANALOGY
ANALYST
ANALYZE
ANANIAS
ANARCHY
ANATOLE
ANATOMY
ANCHOVY
ANCIENT
ANDAMAN
ANDANTE
ANDIRON
ANDORRA
ANDROID
ANEMONE
ANEROID
ANGELIC
ANGELUS
ANGEVIN
ANGIOMA
ANGLING
ANGOLAN
ANGRILY
ANGUISH
ANGULAR
ANILINE
ANIMALS
ANIMATE
ANIMIST
ANISEED
ANNELID
ANNOYED
ANNUITY
ANNULAR
ANNULET
ANNULUS
ANODIZE
ANODYNE
ANOMALY
ANOSMIA
ANOTHER
ANTACID
ANTARES
ANTENNA
ANTHILL
ANTHONY
ANTHRAX
ANTIBES
ANTIGEN
ANTIGUA
ANTIOCH
ANTIQUE
ANTLERS
ANTONIO
ANTONYM
ANTWERP
ANXIETY
ANXIOUS
ANYBODY
ANYMORE
DNIEPER
ENACTOR
ENAMOUR
ENCHANT
ENCLASP
ENCLAVE
ENCLOSE
ENCRUST
ENDEMIC
ENDGAME
ENDLESS
ENDOGEN
ENDORSE
ENDURED
ENDWAYS
ENERGIC
ENFEOFF
ENFIELD
ENFORCE
ENGAGED
ENGINED
ENGLAND
ENGLISH
ENGORGE
ENGRAFT
ENGRAIN
ENGRAVE
ENGROSS
ENHANCE
ENLARGE
ENLIVEN
ENNOBLE
ENPRINT
ENQUIRE
ENQUIRY
ENRAGED
ENSLAVE
ENSNARE
ENSNARL
ENSUING
ENSUITE
ENTEBBE
ENTENTE
ENTERIC
ENTERON
ENTHRAL
ENTHUSE
ENTITLE
ENTRAIN
ENTRANT
ENTREAT
ENTRUST
ENTWINE
ENVELOP
ENVENOM
ENVIOUS
GNARLED
GNAWING
GNOCCHI
GNOSTIC
INANITY
INBOARD
INBUILT
INBURST
INCENSE
INCISOR
INCLINE
INCLUDE
INCOMER
INCONNU
INCRUST
INCUBUS
INDEPTH
INDEXER
INDIANA
INDOORS
INDULGE
INERTIA
INEXACT
INFANCY
INFARCT
INFERNO
INFIDEL
INFIELD
INFLAME
INFLATE
INFLECT
INFLICT
INGENUE
INGRAIN
INGRATE
INGRESS
INHABIT
INHALER
INHERIT
INHIBIT
INHOUSE
INHUMAN
INITIAL
INJURED
INKLING
INKWELL
INNARDS
INNERVE
INNINGS
INQUEST
INQUIRE
INQUIRY
INROADS
INSCAPE
INSECTS
INSHORE
INSIDER
INSIDES
INSIGHT
INSIPID
INSPECT
INSPIRE
INSTALL
INSTANT
INSTATE
INSTEAD
INSTILL
INSULAR
INSULIN
INSURER
INTEGER
INTENSE
INTERIM
INTERNE
INTROIT
INTRUDE
INVADER
INVALID
INVEIGH
INVERSE
INVIOUS
INVOICE
INVOLVE
INWARDS
KNACKER
KNAPPER
KNAVERY
KNEECAP
KNEELER
KNELLER
KNESSET
KNICKER
KNITTED
KNITTER
KNOBBLE
KNOBBLY
KNOCKER
KNOTTED
KNOWALL
KNOWHOW
KNOWING
KNUCKLE
ONANISM
ONEIRIC
ONENESS
ONEROUS
ONESELF
ONETIME
ONGOING
ONMIBUS
ONSHORE
ONSTAGE
ONTARIO
ONWARDS
SNAFFLE
SNAPPER
SNARLER
SNARLUP
SNEAKER
SNICKER
SNIFFER
SNIFFLE
SNIFTER
SNIGGER
SNIPPET
SNOOKER
SNOOPER
SNORING
SNORKEL
SNORTER
SNORTLE
SNOWDON
SNOWMAN
SNUFFLE
SNUGGLE
UNAIDED
UNAIRED
UNALIKE
UNALIVE
UNARMED
UNASKED
UNAWARE
UNBLOCK
UNBOSOM
UNBOUND
UNBOWED
UNCANNY
UNCARED
UNCINUS
UNCIVIL
UNCLASP
UNCLEAN
UNCLEAR
UNCOUTH
UNCOVER
UNCTION
UNCURED
UNDATED
UNDERGO
UNDOING
UNDRESS
UNDYING
UNEARTH
UNEQUAL
UNFADED
UNFIXED
UNFROCK
UNGODLY
UNGUENT
UNHAPPY
UNHEARD
UNHINGE
UNHITCH
UNHORSE
UNICORN
UNIFORM
UNITARY
UNITIES
UNKEMPT
UNKNOWN
UNLADEN
UNLATCH
UNLEASH
UNLINED
UNLOOSE
UNLOVED
UNLUCKY
UNMIXED
UNMOVED
UNNAMED
UNNERVE
UNOWNED
UNQUIET
UNQUOTE
UNRAVEL
UNREADY
UNSCREW
UNSNARL
UNSOUND
UNSTICK
UNSTOCK
UNSTUCK
UNTAMED
UNTRIED
UNTRUTH
UNTWINE
UNUSUAL
UNWOUND
BOARDER
BOASTER
BOATING
BOATMAN
BOBSLED
BOHEMIA
BOILEAU
BOILING
BOLETUS
BOLIVAR
BOLIVIA
BOLLARD
BOLOGNA
BOLONEY
BOLSHIE
BOLSHOI
BOLSTER
BOMBARD
BOMBAST
BOMBING
BONANZA
BONDAGE
BONDMAN
BONFIRE
BONKERS
BONNARD
BOOKIES
BOOKING
BOOKISH
BOOKLET
BOOKMAN
BOOLEAN
BOOMING

BOORISH
BOOSTER
BOOTLEG
BORACIC
BORDERS
BOREDOM
BORODIN
BOROUGH
BORSTAL
BOSWELL
BOTANIC
BOTARGO
BOTTEGA
BOTTLED
BOTTLES
BOUCLÉE
BOUDOIR
BOUILLI
BOULDER
BOUNCER
BOUNDED
BOUNDEN
BOUNDER
BOUQUET
BOURBON
BOURDON
BOURSIN
BOUTADE
BOWDLER
BOWHEAD
BOWLING
BOWSHOT
BOXROOM
BOYCOTT
BOYHOOD
COARSEN
COASTAL
COASTER
COATING
COAXIAL
COBBLED
COBBLER
COCAINE
COCHLEA
COCKADE
COCKLES
COCKNEY
COCKPIT
COCONUT
COCOTTE
CODEINE
CODICIL
CODLING
COELIAC
COEXIST
COFFERS
COGENCY
COGNATE
COHABIT
COINAGE
COITION
COLCHIS
COLDITZ
COLIBRI
COLITIS
COLLAGE
COLLARD
COLLATE
COLLECT
COLLEEN
COLLEGE
COLLIDE
COLLIER
COLLOID
COLLUDE
COLOGNE
COLOMBO
COLONEL
COLORED
COLOURS
COLUMNS
COMBINE
COMBING
COMFORT
COMFREY
COMICAL
COMMAND
COMMEND
COMMENT
COMMODE
COMMODO
COMMONS
COMMUNE
COMMUTE
COMPACT
COMPANY
COMPARE
COMPASS
COMPERE
COMPETE
COMPILE
COMPLEX
COMPORT
COMPOSE
COMPOST
COMPOTE
COMPUTE
COMRADE
CONAKRY
CONCAVE
CONCEAL
CONCEDE
CONCEIT
CONCEPT
CONCERN
CONCERT
CONCISE
CONCOCT
CONCORD
CONCUSS
CONDEMN
CONDOLE
CONDONE
CONDUCT
CONDUIT
CONFESS
CONFIDE
CONFINE
CONFIRM
CONFORM
CONFUSE
CONGEAL
CONICAL
CONIFER
CONJOIN
CONJURE
CONNATE
CONNECT
CONNIVE
CONNOTE
CONQUER
CONSENT
CONSIGN
CONSIST
CONSOLE
CONSOLS
CONSORT
CONSULT
CONSUME
CONTACT
CONTAIN
CONTEMN
CONTEND
CONTENT
CONTEST
CONTEXT
CONTORT
CONTOUR
CONTROL
CONVENE
CONVENT
CONVERT
CONVICT
CONVOKE
COOKERY
COOKING
COOLANT
COOLING
COPILOT
COPIOUS
COPLAND
COPPERS
COPPICE
COPYCAT
COPYING
COPYIST
CORACLE
CORANTO
CORBEAU
CORBETT
CORDATE
CORDIAL
CORDITE
CORDOBA
CORELLI
CORINTH
CORKAGE
CORKING
CORNCOB
CORNEAL
CORNELL
CORNICE
CORNISH
COROLLA
CORONER
CORONET
CORRECT
CORRIDA
CORRODE
CORRUPT
CORSAGE
CORSAIR
CORTEGE
CORTINA
CORUNNA
CORYDON
COSSACK
COSTARD
COSTING
COSTIVE
COSTUME
COTERIE
COTTAGE
COTTONY
COUCHÉE
COULDNT
COULOMB
COULTER
COUNCIL
COUNSEL
COUNTED
COUNTER
COUNTRY
COUPLER
COUPLET
COUPONS
COURAGE
COURBET
COURIER
COURSER
COURSES
COURTLY
COUSINS
COUTURE
COVERED
COVERUP
COVETED
COWGIRL
COWHAND
COWHERD
COWLICK
COWLING
COWPOKE
COWSHED
COWSLIP
COXCOMB
COXLESS
COYNESS
DOCKING
DOCTORS
DODDERY
DODGEMS
DOESKIN
DOGCART
DOGFISH
DOGFOOD
DOGGONE
DOGROSE
DOGWOOD
DOLEFUL
DOLLARS
DOLORES
DOLPHIN
DOMAINE
DOMINGO
DOMINIC
DONEGAL
DONNISH
DOODLER
DOORKEY
DOORMAN
DOORMAT
DOORWAY
DOPPLER
DORKING
DORMANT
DOROTHY
DOSSIER
DOUBLES
DOUBLET
DOUBTER
DOUGHTY
DOUGLAS
DOWAGER
DOWDILY
DOWLAND
DOWSING
FOGHORN
FOGLAMP
FOLDING
FOLIAGE
FOLLIES
FONDANT
FOOLISH
FOOTAGE
FOOTING
FOOTMAN
FOOTPAD
FOOTSIE
FOPPISH
FORAMEN
FORBADE
FORBEAR
FORCEPS
FOREARM
FOREIGN
FORELEG
FOREMAN
FOREPAW
FORESEE
FOREVER
FORFEIT
FORFEND
FORGAVE
FORGERY
FORGIVE
FORGONE
FORLORN
FORMICA
FORMING
FORMOSA
FORMULA
FORSAKE
FORSTER
FORTIES
FORTIFY
FORTRAN
FORTUNE
FORWARD
FOSSICK
FOSSULA
FOULARD
FOUNDER
FOUNDRY
FOXHOLE
FOXTROT
GOAHEAD
GOBBLER
GOBELIN
GODDESS
GODETIA
GODLESS
GODLIKE
GODSEND
GODUNOV
GOGGLES
GOLDING
GOLDONI
GOLFING
GOLIARD
GOLIATH
GOMBEEN
GOMORRA
GONDOLA
GOODBYE
GOODIES
GOODISH
GOODMAN
GOODWIN
GOOLIES
GORDIAN
GORDIUS
GORILLA
GORSEDD
GOSHAWK
GOSLING
GOSSIPY
GOUACHE
GOULASH
GOURMET
HOARDER
HOBNAIL
HOBSONS
HOEDOWN
HOGARTH
HOGBACK
HOGGING
HOGWASH
HOLBEIN
HOLDALL
HOLDING
HOLIDAY
HOLLAND
HOLSTER
HOMBURG
HOMERIC
HOMINID
HOMONYM
HONESTY
HONEYED
HONITON
HONOURS
HOODLUM
HOPEFUL
HOPKINS
HOPLITE
HOPPING
HOPSACK
HORATIO
HORDEUM
HORIZON
HORMONE
HORRIFY
HORRORS
HORSING
HOSANNA
HOSIERY
HOSPICE
HOSTAGE
HOSTESS
HOSTILE
HOTFOOT
HOTHEAD
HOTLINE
HOTSHOT
HOTSPUR
HOUDINI
HOUSING
HOWEVER
HOWLING
IONESCO
JOBBERY
JOBBING
JOBLESS
JOCASTA
JOCULAR
JOGGING

JOGTROT
JOHNNIE
JOHNSON
JOINERY
JOINING
JOINTED
JOINTLY
JOLLITY
JONQUIL
JOURNAL
JOURNEY
JOYLESS
JOYRIDE
KOLKHOZ
KONTIKI
KOUMISS
KOWLOON
LOBELIA
LOBSTER
LOCALLY
LOCKJAW
LOCKNUT
LOCKOUT
LOCUSTS
LODGING
LOFTILY
LOGBOOK
LOGGING
LOGICAL
LOGWOOD
LOLLARD
LONGBOW
LONGING
LOOKING
LOOKOUT
LOOMING
LOOSELY
LOOTING
LORDING
LORELEI
LOTHAIR
LOTHIAN
LOTTERY
LOUNGER
LOURDES
LOURING
LOUTISH
LOUVRED
LOVABLE
LOWBROW
LOWDOWN
LOWLAND
LOWPAID
LOYALLY
LOYALTY
LOZENGE
MOABITE
MOANING
MOBSTER
MOCKERS
MOCKERY
MOCKING
MODESTY
MODICUM
MODISTE
MODULAR
MODULUS
MOELLON
MOFETTE
MOHICAN
MOIDORE
MOISTEN
MOITHER
MOLDING
MOLIÈRE
MOLLIFY
MOLLUSC
MOLOTOV
MOLUCCA
MOMBASA
MOMENTS
MONARCH
MONEYED
MONGREL
MONILIA
MONITOR
MONKISH
MONOCLE
MONOLOG
MONOPLY
MONSOON
MONSTER
MONTAGE
MONTAGU
MONTANA
MONTANT
MONTERO
MONTHLY
MOODILY
MOONING
MOONLIT
MOORHEN
MOORING
MOORISH
MOPPING
MORAINE
MORALLY
MORAVIA
MORDANT
MOREISH
MORELLO
MORESBY
MORESCO
MORLAND
MORNING
MOROCCO
MORONIC
MORPHIA
MORRELL
MORTALS
MORTICE
MORTIFY
MORTISE
MOSELLE
MOTHERS
MOTTLED
MOUFLON
MOUILLÉ
MOULAGE
MOULDED
MOULDER
MOUNTED
MOUNTIE
MOURNER
MOVABLE
NOBBLED
NOBBLER
NODDING
NODULAR
NOGGING
NOISILY
NOISOME
NOMADIC
NOMBRIL
NOMINAL
NOMINEE
NONPLUS
NONSTOP
NONSUCH
NONSUIT
NOODLES
NOOLOGY
NOONDAY
NORFOLK
NORWICH
NOSEBAG
NOSEGAY
NOSTRIL
NOSTRUM
NOTABLE
NOTABLY
NOTCHED
NOTEPAD
NOTHING
NOTIONS
NOURISH
NOUVEAU
NOVELLA
NOVELLO
NOVELTY
NOWHERE
NOXIOUS
POACHER
POCHARD
POCHOIR
PODAGRA
PODESTA
POETESS
POINTED
POINTER
POLARIS
POLEAXE
POLECAT
POLEMIC
POLENTA
POLITIC
POLIZEI
POLLACK
POLLARD
POLLING
POLLUTE
POLONIE
POLYGON
POLYMER
POLYPOD
POLYPUS
POMEROL
POMEROY
POMFRET
POMMARD
POMPEII
POMPOON
POMPOUS
PONIARD
PONTIAC
PONTIFF
PONTINE
PONTOON
POOFTER
POOHBAH
POPCORN
POPEYED
POPOVER
POPPING
POPULAR
POPULUS
PORCIAN
PORCINE
POROSIS
PORTAGE
PORTEND
PORTENT
PORTHOS
PORTICO
PORTION
PORTRAY
POSSESS
POSTAGE
POSTBAG
POSTBOX
POSTERN
POSTING
POSTMAN
POSTURE
POSTWAR
POTABLE
POTENCY
POTHEEN
POTHERB
POTHOLE
POTICHE
POTLACH
POTLUCK
POTOMAC
POTSDAM
POTSHOT
POTTAGE
POTTERY
POTTING
POULENC
POULTRY
POUSSIN
POVERTY
POWDERY
POWERED
ROADHOG
ROADWAY
ROAMING
ROARING
ROASTER
ROBBERS
ROBBERY
ROBERTS
ROBESON
ROBINIA
ROBUSTA
ROCKALL
ROCKERY
ROCKING
ROEBUCK
ROEDEAN
ROGUERY
ROGUISH
ROISTER
ROLLERS
ROLLICK
ROLLING
ROLLMOP
ROMAINE
ROMANCE
ROMANIA
ROMANOV
ROMANZA
ROMPERS
RONDEAU
RONSARD
RONTGEN
ROOFING
ROOFTOP
ROOKERY
ROOKISH
ROOSTER
ROOTING
RORQUAL
ROSACEA
ROSALIA
ROSALIE
ROSARIO
ROSCIAN
ROSCIUS
ROSEATE
ROSEBUD
ROSELLA
ROSELLE
ROSEOLA
ROSETTA
ROSETTE
ROSSINI
ROSTAND
ROSTOCK
ROSTRAL
ROSTRUM
ROTATOR
ROTTING
ROTUNDA
ROUAULT
ROUGHEN
ROUGHIE
ROUGHLY
ROULADE
ROULEAU
ROUNDED
ROUNDEL
ROUNDER
ROUNDLY
ROUNDUP
ROUSING
ROUTIER
ROUTINE
ROWBOAT
ROWDILY
ROWLOCK
ROYALLY
ROYALTY
ROZZERS
SOAKING
SOAPBOX
SOARING
SOBERLY
SOCAGER
SOCIETY
SOCKEYE
SOCKING
SOCOTRA
SOFABED
SOJOURN
SOLANUM
SOLDIER
SOLICIT
SOLIDLY
SOLIDUS
SOLOIST
SOLOMON
SOLUBLE
SOLVENT
SOMALIA
SOMEHOW
SOMEONE
SONDAGE
SOPHISM
SOPHIST
SOPPING
SOPRANO
SOPWITH
SORCERY
SORGHUM
SOROSIS
SORROWS
SORTING
SOUBISE
SOUFFLE
SOULFUL
SOUNDED
SOUNDER
SOUNDLY
SOURSOP
SOUTANE
SOUTHEY
SOVKHOZ
SOZZLED
TOASTED
TOASTER
TOBACCO
TOCCATA
TODDLER
TOEHOLD
TOENAIL
TOLKIEN
TOLLMAN
TOLSTOY
TOLUENE
TOMBOLA
TOMFOOL
TOMPION
TONGUES
TONIGHT
TONNAGE
TONNEAU
TONNISH
TONSURE
TONTINE
TOOLBOX
TOOLING
TOOTHED
TOOTSIE
TOPCOAT
TOPIARY
TOPICAL
TOPKAPI
TOPKNOT
TOPLESS
TOPMAST
TOPMOST
TOPPING
TOPSIDE
TOPSOIL
TORCHON
TORMENT
TORNADE
TORNADO
TORONTO
TORPEDO
TORPIDS
TORREFY
TORRENT
TORSADE
TORSION

TORTILE
TORTRIX
TORTURE
TOSSPOT
TOTALLY
TOTEMIC
TOTIENT
TOTTERY
TOUCHED
TOUGHEN
TOURING
TOURISM
TOURIST
TOWARDS
TOWHEAD
TOWLINE
TOWPATH
TOXEMIA
TOYNBEE
TOYSHOP
VOCALIC
VOCALLY
VOIVODE
VOLANTE
VOLAPUK
VOLCANO
VOLTAGE
VOLTAIC
VOLUBLE
VOLUBLY
VOUCHER
VOYAGER
WOLFISH
WOLFRAM
WOMANLY
WONDERS
WOODCUT
WOODMAN
WOOLLEN
WOOMERA
WOOSTER
WORDILY
WORDING
WORKERS
WORKING
WORKMAN
WORKMEN
WORKOUT
WORKSHY
WORKTOP
WORLDLY
WORRIED
WORRIER
WORSHIP
WORSTED
WOTCHER
WOULDBE
WOULDNT
WOUNDED
YOGHURT
YONKERS
YORKIST
YOUNGER
ZOFFANY
ZOOLITE
ZOOLOGY
ZOOTOMY
APELIKE
APEPSIA
APHAGIA
APHASIA
APHELIA
APHESIS
APHONIA
APHONIC
APHOTIC
APHTHAE
APICIUS
APLASIA
APOCOPE
APOGEAN
APOLOGY
APOSTLE
APPARAT
APPAREL
APPEASE
APPLAUD
APPLIED
APPOINT
APPOSED
APPRIZE
APPROVE
APRICOT
APROPOS
APSIDAL
APTERAL
APTERYX
APTNESS
EPAULET
EPERGNE
EPHEBUS
EPHEDRA
EPHESUS
EPHRAIM
EPICARP
EPICENE
EPICURE
EPIDOTE
EPIGONE
EPIGRAM
EPISODE
EPISTLE
EPITAPH
EPITAXY
EPITHET
EPITOME
EPIZOON
EPSILON
EPSTEIN
IPOMOEA
OPACITY
OPALINE
OPENING
OPERAND
OPERANT
OPERATE
OPINION
OPOSSUM
OPPOSED
OPPRESS
OPTICAL
OPTIMAL
OPTIMUM
OPULENT
OPUNTIA
SPACING
SPADGER
SPANDAU
SPANDEX
SPANGLE
SPANIEL
SPANISH
SPANKER
SPANNER
SPARING
SPARKLE
SPARROW
SPARTAN
SPASTIC
SPATIAL
SPATTER
SPATULA
SPAVINE
SPEAKER
SPECIAL
SPECIES
SPECIFY
SPECKLE
SPECTER
SPECTRE
SPELLER
SPENCER
SPENDER
SPENSER
SPHENIC
SPICATE
SPICULA
SPIDERS
SPIDERY
SPINACH
SPINATE
SPINDLE
SPINDLY
SPINNER
SPINNEY
SPINOFF
SPINOZA
SPIRITS
SPITTLE
SPLASHY
SPLAYED
SPLICED
SPLICER
SPLODGE
SPLOTCH
SPLURGE
SPOILED
SPOILER
SPONDEE
SPONDYL
SPONGER
SPONSON
SPONSOR
SPOONER
SPORRAN
SPOTTED
SPOTTER
SPOUSAL
SPRAINT
SPRAYER
SPRINGE
SPRINGS
SPRINGY
SPROUTS
SPURREY
SPURWAY
SPUTNIK
SPUTTER
SPYHOLE
UPBRAID
UPGRADE
UPRAISE
UPRIGHT
UPSHOOT
UPSIDES
UPSILON
UPSTAGE
UPSTART
UPSTATE
UPSURGE
UPSWING
UPTIGHT
UPWARDS
YPSILON
AQUATIC
AQUAVIT
AQUEOUS
AQUIFER
AQUILON
AQUINAS
AQUINUS
EQUABLE
EQUABLY
EQUALLY
EQUATOR
EQUERRY
EQUINOX
SQUADDY
SQUALID
SQUALLY
SQUALOR
SQUARED
SQUARES
SQUASHY
SQUEAKY
SQUEERS
SQUEEZE
SQUELCH
SQUIFFY
SQUINCH
SQUISHY
ARABIAN
ARABICA
ARACHNE
ARAMAIC
ARBITER
ARBUTUS
ARCADIA
ARCHAIC
ARCHERY
ARCHIVE
ARCHWAY
ARCUATE
ARDUOUS
ARETINO
ARIADNE
ARIDITY
ARIETTA
ARIOSTO
ARIZONA
ARMBAND
ARMHOLE
ARMORED
ARMORIC
ARMOURY
ARMREST
AROUSAL
ARRAIGN
ARRANGE
ARRAYED
ARREARS
ARRIVAL
ARRIVED
ARSENAL
ARSENIC
ARTEMIS
ARTEMUS
ARTICLE
ARTISAN
ARTISTE
ARTLESS
ARTWORK
ARUNDEL
BRACING
BRACKEN
BRACKET
BRADAWL
BRADMAN
BRAEMAR
BRAHMIN
BRAILLE
BRAKING
BRAMBLE
BRANDED
BRANDER
BRANTUB
BRASERO
BRAVADO
BRAVELY
BRAVERY
BRAVURA
BRAWLER
BRAZIER
BREADED
BREADTH
BREAKER
BREATHE
BREEDER
BRENDAN
BRENNER
BREVITY
BREWERY
BREWING
BRIBERY
BRICKIE
BRIDGES
BRIDGET
BRIDLER
BRIDLES
BRIEFLY
BRIGADE
BRIGAND
BRIGHAM
BRIMFUL
BRINDLE
BRINJAL
BRIOCHE
BRISKET
BRISKLY
BRISTLE
BRISTLY
BRISTOL
BRITAIN
BRITISH
BRITONS
BRITTLE
BRITZKA
BRIXTON
BROADEN
BROADLY
BROCADE
BROILER
BROKERS
BROMIDE
BROMINE
BRONCHI
BRONZED
BROTHEL
BROTHER
BROUGHT
BROWNED
BROWNIE
BROWSER
BRUISED
BRUISER
BRUSHER
BRUSQUE
BRUTISH
CRACKED
CRACKER
CRACKLE
CRACKLY
CRAMMED
CRAMMER
CRAMPED
CRAMPON
CRANACH
CRANIAL
CRANIUM
CRANMER
CRASHES
CRASSUS
CRAVING
CRAWLER
CRAZILY
CREATED
CREATOR
CREEPER
CREMATE
CRENATE
CRESTED
CREVICE
CREWCUT
CREWMAN
CRICKET
CRICKEY
CRICOID
CRIMEAN
CRIMSON
CRINKLE
CRINKLY
CRINOID
CRIPPLE
CRISPIN
CRITTER
CROAKER
CROATIA
CROCHET
CROCKET
CROESUS
CROFTER
CROOKED
CROONER
CROPPED
CROPPER
CROQUET
CROQUIS
CROSIER
CROSSED
CROSSLY
CROUTON
CROWBAR
CROWDED
CROWING
CROZIER
CRUCIAL
CRUCIFY

CRUDELY
CRUDITY
CRUELLS
CRUELLY
CRUELTY
CRUISER
CRUMBLE
CRUMBLY
CRUMPET
CRUMPLE
CRUNCHY
CRUPPER
CRUSADE
CRUSHED
CRUSHER
CRYPTIC
CRYPTON
CRYSTAL
DRABBLE
DRACHMA
DRACULA
DRAFTED
DRAFTEE
DRAGGLE
DRAGNET
DRAGOON
DRAINED
DRAPERY
DRASTIC
DRAUGHT
DRAWBAR
DRAWERS
DRAWING
DREADED
DREAMER
DREDGER
DRESDEN
DRESSED
DRESSER
DREYFUS
DRIBBLE
DRIBLET
DRIFTER
DRINKER
DRIVERS
DRIVING
DRIZZLE
DRIZZLY
DROPLET
DROPOUT
DROPPER
DROSHKY
DROUGHT
DRUGGED
DRUGGET
DRUMLIN
DRUMMER
DRUNKEN
DRYNESS
ERASMUS
ERASURE
ERECTOR
EREMITE
ERINYES
ERISKAY
ERITREA
ERODIUM
EROSION
EROTICA
ERRATIC
ERRATUM
ERUDITE
FRAGILE
FRAILTY
FRANCIS
FRANKLY
FRANTIC
FRAUGHT
FRAZZLE
FRECKLE
FREEBIE
FREEDOM
FREEMAN
FREESIA
FREEWAY
FREEZER
FREIGHT
FRESHEN
FRESHER
FRESHET
FRESHLY
FRETFUL
FRETSAW
FRETTED
FRIABLE
FRIENDS
FRIGATE
FRILLED
FRINGED
FRISBEE
FRISIAN
FRISSON
FRITTER
FRIZZLE
FRIZZLY
FROEBEL
FROGMAN
FRONTAL
FROSTED
FROWSTY
FRUMPLE
GRACCHI
GRACILE
GRACKLE
GRADATE
GRADELY
GRADUAL
GRAFTER
GRAINED
GRAINER
GRAMMAR
GRAMPUS
GRANARY
GRANDAD
GRANDEE
GRANDLY
GRANDMA
GRANDPA
GRANITA
GRANITE
GRANNIE
GRANOLA
GRANTED
GRANTEE
GRANULE
GRAPHIC
GRAPHIS
GRAPNEL
GRAPPLE
GRATIFY
GRATING
GRAVITY
GRAVURE
GRAYISH
GRAZING
GREASER
GREATEN
GREATLY
GREAVES
GRECIAN
GREENER
GREGORY
GREMLIN
GRENADA
GRENADE
GRENDEL
GREYISH
GREYLAG
GRIDDLE
GRIFFON
GRIFTER
GRILLED
GRIMACE
GRIMOND
GRIMSBY
GRINDER
GRISTLE
GRISTLY
GRIZZLE
GRIZZLY
GROCERS
GROCERY
GROCKLE
GROGRAM
GROINED
GROLIER
GROMMET
GROOVED
GROPIUS
GROSSLY
GROTIUS
GROUCHO
GROUCHY
GROUNDS
GROUPER
GROUPIE
GROUSER
GROWING
GROWLER
GROWNUP
GRUFFLY
GRUMBLE
GRUMMET
GRUYÈRE
GRYPHON
IRANIAN
IRELAND
IRIDISE
IRIDIUM
IRKSOME
IRONING
KREMLIN
KRISHNA
KRYPTON
ORACLES
ORANGES
ORATION
ORATORY
ORBITAL
ORCHARD
ORDERED
ORDERLY
ORDINAL
OREGANO
ORESTES
ORGANIC
ORGANUM
ORGANZA
ORGIAST
ORIFICE
ORIGAMI
ORIGINS
ORINOCO
ORKNEYS
ORLANDO
ORLEANS
ORONTES
OROTUND
ORPHEAN
ORPHEUS
ORPHISM
ORPHREY
ORTOLAN
ORVIETO
PRAETOR
PRAIRIE
PRALINE
PRATTLE
PRAYING
PREBEND
PRECAST
PRECEDE
PRECEPT
PRECISE
PREDATE
PREDIAL
PREDICT
PREDOOM
PREEMPT
PREFACE
PREFECT
PREHEAT
PRELATE
PRELIMS
PRELUDE
PREMIER
PREMISS
PREMIUM
PREPAID
PREPARE
PREPUCE
PREQUEL
PRESAGE
PRESENT
PRESIDE
PRESSED
PRESUME
PRETEND
PRETEXT
PRETZEL
PREVAIL
PREVENT
PREVIEW
PREZZIE
PRIAPUS
PRICKED
PRICKER
PRICKLE
PRICKLY
PRIESTS
PRIMACY
PRIMARY
PRIMATE
PRIMEUR
PRIMING
PRIMULA
PRINCES
PRINTED
PRINTER
PRITHEE
PRIVACY
PRIVATE
PRIVITY
PROBATE
PROBITY
PROBLEM
PROCEED
PROCESS
PROCTOR
PROCURE
PRODIGY
PRODUCE
PRODUCT
PROFANE
PROFESS
PROFFER
PROFILE
PROFITS
PROFUSE
PROGENY
PROGRAM
PROJECT
PROLONG
PROMISE
PROMOTE
PRONAOS
PRONATE
PRONGED
PRONOUN
PROPANE
PROPEND
PROPHET
PROPOSE
PROSAIC
PROSODY
PROSPER
PROTEAN
PROTECT
PROTEGE
PROTEIN
PROTEST
PROTEUS
PROUDER
PROUDIE
PROUDLY
PROVERB
PROVIDE
PROVING
PROVISO
PROVOKE
PROVOST
PROWESS
PROWLER
PROXIMO
PRUDENT
PRUDISH
PRURIGO
PRUSSIC
PRYTHEE
TRACERY
TRACHEA
TRACING
TRACKER
TRACTOR
TRADEIN
TRADING
TRADUCE
TRAFFIC
TRAGEDY
TRAILER
TRAINED
TRAINEE
TRAINER
TRAIPSE
TRAITOR
TRAMCAR
TRAMMEL
TRAMPLE
TRAMWAY
TRANCHE
TRANSIT
TRANSOM
TRANTER
TRAPEZE
TRAPPED
TRAPPER
TRAVAIL
TRAWLER
TREACLE
TREACLY
TREADLE
TREASON
TREATED
TREETOP
TREFOIL
TREKKER
TRELLIS
TREMBLE
TREMBLY
TREMOLO
TREPANG
TRESSES
TRESTLE
TRIANON
TRIATIC
TRIBUNE
TRIBUTE
TRICEPS
TRICKLE
TRIDENT
TRIESTE
TRIFFID
TRIFLER
TRIFLES
TRIGGER
TRILLED
TRILLER
TRILOGY
TRIMMER
TRINGLE
TRINITY
TRINKET
TRIPLET
TRIPLEX
TRIPODY
TRIPOLI
TRIPPER
TRIPSIS
TRIREME
TRISECT
TRISHAW
TRISTAN
TRITELY
TRITIUM
TRITOMA
TRIUMPH
TRIVIAL

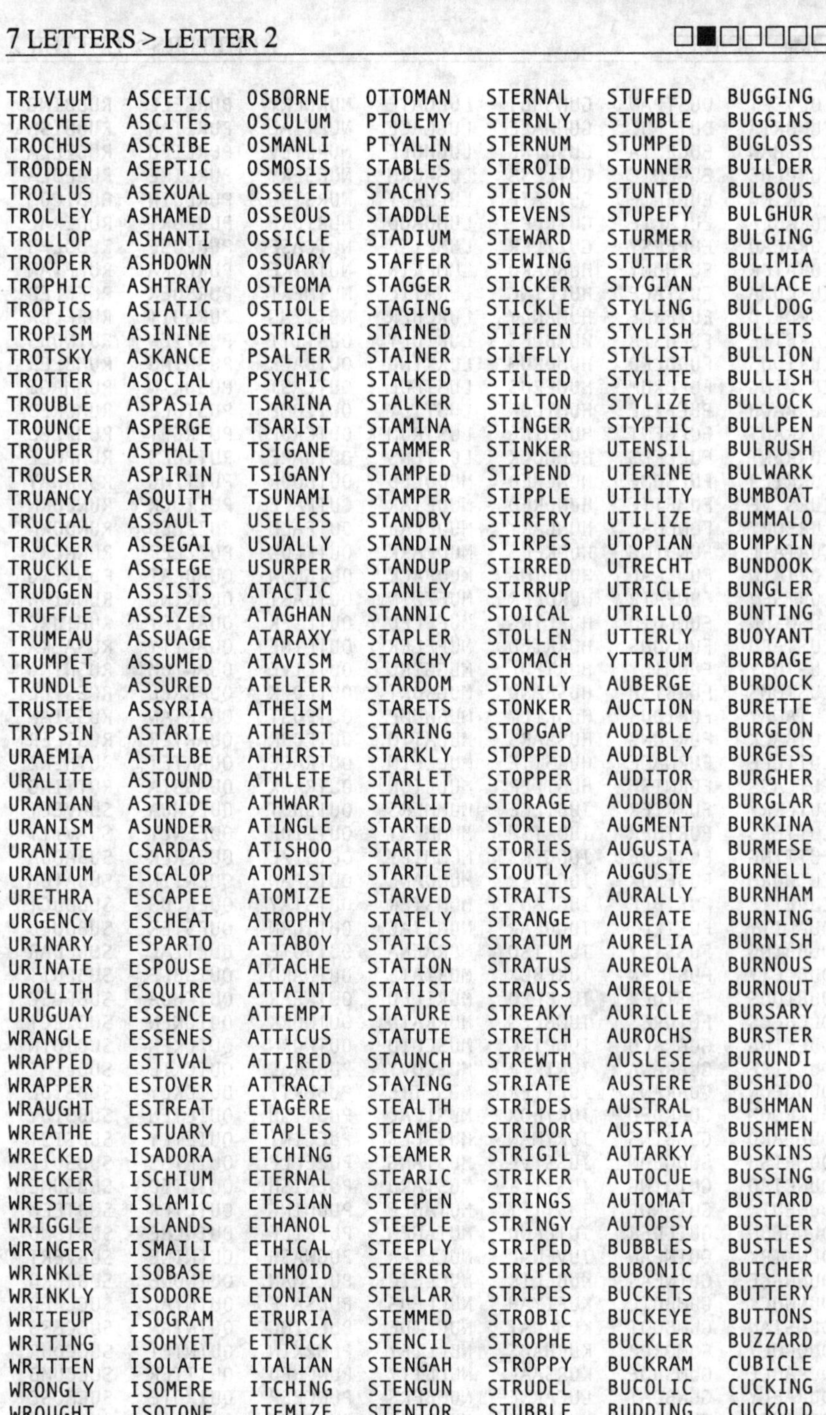

TRIVIUM
TROCHEE
TROCHUS
TRODDEN
TROILUS
TROLLEY
TROLLOP
TROOPER
TROPHIC
TROPICS
TROPISM
TROTSKY
TROTTER
TROUBLE
TROUNCE
TROUPER
TROUSER
TRUANCY
TRUCIAL
TRUCKER
TRUCKLE
TRUDGEN
TRUFFLE
TRUMEAU
TRUMPET
TRUNDLE
TRUSTEE
TRYPSIN
URAEMIA
URALITE
URANIAN
URANISM
URANITE
URANIUM
URETHRA
URGENCY
URINARY
URINATE
UROLITH
URUGUAY
WRANGLE
WRAPPED
WRAPPER
WRAUGHT
WREATHE
WRECKED
WRECKER
WRESTLE
WRIGGLE
WRINGER
WRINKLE
WRINKLY
WRITEUP
WRITING
WRITTEN
WRONGLY
WROUGHT
WRYBILL
WRYNECK
WRYNOSE
ASCARID
ASCETIC
ASCITES
ASCRIBE
ASEPTIC
ASEXUAL
ASHAMED
ASHANTI
ASHDOWN
ASHTRAY
ASIATIC
ASININE
ASKANCE
ASOCIAL
ASPASIA
ASPERGE
ASPHALT
ASPIRIN
ASQUITH
ASSAULT
ASSEGAI
ASSIEGE
ASSISTS
ASSIZES
ASSUAGE
ASSUMED
ASSURED
ASSYRIA
ASTARTE
ASTILBE
ASTOUND
ASTRIDE
ASUNDER
CSARDAS
ESCALOP
ESCAPEE
ESCHEAT
ESPARTO
ESPOUSE
ESQUIRE
ESSENCE
ESSENES
ESTIVAL
ESTOVER
ESTREAT
ESTUARY
ISADORA
ISCHIUM
ISLAMIC
ISLANDS
ISMAILI
ISOBASE
ISODORE
ISOGRAM
ISOHYET
ISOLATE
ISOMERE
ISOTONE
ISOTOPE
ISRAELI
ISSUANT
ISTHMUS
OSBORNE
OSCULUM
OSMANLI
OSMOSIS
OSSELET
OSSEOUS
OSSICLE
OSSUARY
OSTEOMA
OSTIOLE
OSTRICH
PSALTER
PSYCHIC
TSARINA
TSARIST
TSIGANE
TSIGANY
TSUNAMI
USELESS
USUALLY
USURPER
ATACTIC
ATAGHAN
ATARAXY
ATAVISM
ATELIER
ATHEISM
ATHEIST
ATHIRST
ATHLETE
ATHWART
ATINGLE
ATISHOO
ATOMIST
ATOMIZE
ATROPHY
ATTABOY
ATTACHE
ATTAINT
ATTEMPT
ATTICUS
ATTIRED
ATTRACT
ETAGÈRE
ETAPLES
ETCHING
ETERNAL
ETESIAN
ETHANOL
ETHICAL
ETHMOID
ETONIAN
ETRURIA
ETTRICK
ITALIAN
ITCHING
ITEMIZE
ITERATE
OTALGIA
OTHELLO
OTRANTO
OTTOMAN
PTOLEMY
PTYALIN
STABLES
STACHYS
STADDLE
STADIUM
STAFFER
STAGGER
STAGING
STAINED
STAINER
STALKED
STALKER
STAMINA
STAMMER
STAMPED
STAMPER
STANDBY
STANDIN
STANDUP
STANLEY
STANNIC
STAPLER
STARCHY
STARDOM
STARETS
STARING
STARKLY
STARLET
STARLIT
STARTED
STARTER
STARTLE
STARVED
STATELY
STATICS
STATION
STATIST
STATURE
STATUTE
STAUNCH
STAYING
STEALTH
STEAMED
STEAMER
STEARIC
STEEPEN
STEEPLE
STEEPLY
STEERER
STELLAR
STEMMED
STENCIL
STENGAH
STENGUN
STENTOR
STEPHEN
STEPNEY
STEPSON
STERILE
STERNAL
STERNLY
STERNUM
STEROID
STETSON
STEVENS
STEWARD
STEWING
STICKER
STICKLE
STIFFEN
STIFFLY
STILTED
STILTON
STINGER
STINKER
STIPEND
STIPPLE
STIRFRY
STIRPES
STIRRED
STIRRUP
STOICAL
STOLLEN
STOMACH
STONILY
STONKER
STOPGAP
STOPPED
STOPPER
STORAGE
STORIED
STORIES
STOUTLY
STRAITS
STRANGE
STRATUM
STRATUS
STRAUSS
STREAKY
STRETCH
STREWTH
STRIATE
STRIDES
STRIDOR
STRIGIL
STRIKER
STRINGS
STRINGY
STRIPED
STRIPER
STRIPES
STROBIC
STROPHE
STROPPY
STRUDEL
STUBBLE
STUBBLY
STUDDED
STUDENT
STUDIED
STUFFED
STUMBLE
STUMPED
STUNNER
STUNTED
STUPEFY
STURMER
STUTTER
STYGIAN
STYLING
STYLISH
STYLIST
STYLITE
STYLIZE
STYPTIC
UTENSIL
UTERINE
UTILITY
UTILIZE
UTOPIAN
UTRECHT
UTRICLE
UTRILLO
UTTERLY
YTTRIUM
AUBERGE
AUCTION
AUDIBLE
AUDIBLY
AUDITOR
AUDUBON
AUGMENT
AUGUSTA
AUGUSTE
AURALLY
AUREATE
AURELIA
AUREOLA
AUREOLE
AURICLE
AUROCHS
AUSLESE
AUSTERE
AUSTRAL
AUSTRIA
AUTARKY
AUTOCUE
AUTOMAT
AUTOPSY
BUBBLES
BUBONIC
BUCKETS
BUCKEYE
BUCKLER
BUCKRAM
BUCOLIC
BUDDING
BUFFALO
BUFFOON
BUGABOO
BUGBEAR
BUGGING
BUGGINS
BUGLOSS
BUILDER
BULBOUS
BULGHUR
BULGING
BULIMIA
BULLACE
BULLDOG
BULLETS
BULLION
BULLISH
BULLOCK
BULLPEN
BULRUSH
BULWARK
BUMBOAT
BUMMALO
BUMPKIN
BUNDOOK
BUNGLER
BUNTING
BUOYANT
BURBAGE
BURDOCK
BURETTE
BURGEON
BURGESS
BURGHER
BURGLAR
BURKINA
BURMESE
BURNELL
BURNHAM
BURNING
BURNISH
BURNOUS
BURNOUT
BURSARY
BURSTER
BURUNDI
BUSHIDO
BUSHMAN
BUSHMEN
BUSKINS
BUSSING
BUSTARD
BUSTLER
BUSTLES
BUTCHER
BUTTERY
BUTTONS
BUZZARD
CUBICLE
CUCKING
CUCKOLD
CUIRASS
CUISINE
CULPRIT
CULTURE

CULVERT
CUMBRIA
CUMSHAW
CUMULUS
CUNNING
CURABLE
CURACAO
CURATOR
CURCUMA
CURDLED
CURETTE
CURIOUS
CURLING
CURRAGH
CURRANT
CURRENT
CURRIED
CURSIVE
CURSORY
CURTAIL
CURTAIN
CURTSEY
CUSHION
CUSTARD
CUSTODY
CUSTOMS
CUTAWAY
CUTBACK
CUTICLE
CUTLASS
CUTLERY
CUTTERS
CUTTING
CUTWORM
CUVETTE
DUALITY
DUBBING
DUBIETY
DUBIOUS
DUCHESS
DUCKING
DUCTILE
DUDGEON
DUKEDOM
DULLARD
DUMPISH
DUNCIAD
DUNEDIN
DUNGEON
DUNKIRK
DUNNAGE
DUNNOCK
DUNSTAN
DUOPOLY
DURABLE
DURABLY
DURAMEN
DURRELL
DUSTBIN
DUSTING
DUSTMAN
DUSTPAN
DUTIFUL
EUGENIA
EUGENIC
EUGENIE
EULALIE
EUPEPSY
EUPHONY
EUSTACE
EUTERPE
FUCHSIA
FUDDLED
FULCRUM
FULFILL
FULGENT
FULLERS
FULSOME
FUMETTE
FUNCHAL
FUNDING
FUNERAL
FUNFAIR
FUNGOID
FUNGOUS
FUNNILY
FURBISH
FURIOUS
FURLONG
FURNACE
FURNISH
FURRIER
FURTHER
FURTIVE
FUSEBOX
FUSIBLE
FUSILLI
FUSSILY
FUSTIAN
FUTTOCK
FUTURES
GUANACO
GUARANA
GUARANI
GUARDED
GUBBINS
GUDGEON
GUIDING
GUIGNOL
GUILDER
GUINEAN
GUINEAS
GUMBOIL
GUMBOOT
GUMDROP
GUMSHOE
GUNBOAT
GUNFIRE
GUNNERA
GUNNERY
GUNPLAY
GUNROOM
GUNSHOT
GUNWALE
GUSHING
GUTLESS
GUTTATE
GUYROPE
GUZZLER
HUBBARD
HULKING
HUMANLY
HUMBLES
HUMDRUM
HUMERUS
HUMIDOR
HUMMING
HUMMOCK
HUNCHED
HUNDRED
HUNGARY
HUNKERS
HUNTING
HURDLER
HURLING
HURRIED
HURTFUL
HUSBAND
HUSKILY
HUSSARS
HUSSITE
HUSTLER
JUBILEE
JUDAISM
JUGGINS
JUGGLER
JUGLANS
JUGULAR
JUJITSU
JUKEBOX
JUMBLED
JUMBLES
JUMPING
JUNIPER
JUPITER
JURYBOX
JURYMAN
JUSSIVE
JUSTICE
JUSTIFY
JUTLAND
JUVENAL
KUBELIK
KUFIYAH
KUMQUAT
KURHAUS
KURSAAL
LUCARNE
LUCERNE
LUCIDLY
LUCIFER
LUCKILY
LUDDITE
LUDGATE
LUGGAGE
LUGHOLE
LUGWORM
LULLABY
LUMBAGO
LUMPISH
LUMPKIN
LUNATIC
LURCHER
LURIDLY
LURKING
LUSTFUL
LUSTILY
LUSTRUM
LUTYENS
MUDDLED
MUDEJAR
MUDFLAP
MUDLARK
MUDPACK
MUEZZIN
MUFFLED
MUFFLER
MUGGING
MUGWORT
MUGWUMP
MULATTO
MULLEIN
MULLION
MUMMERS
MUMMERY
MUMMIFY
MUNDANE
MUNSTER
MUNTJAC
MURAENA
MURIATE
MURILLO
MURRAIN
MUSCOID
MUSCOVY
MUSETTE
MUSICAL
MUSSELS
MUSTANG
MUSTARD
MUTABLE
MUTAGEN
NUCLEAR
NUCLEIC
NUCLEUS
NUCLIDE
NULLIFY
NULLITY
NUMBERS
NUMBLES
NUMERAL
NUMERIC
NUMMARY
NUNLIKE
NUNNERY
NUPTIAL
NUREYEV
NURSERY
NURSING
NURTURE
NUTCASE
NUTLIKE
NUTMEAT
NUTTING
OUSTITI
OUTBACK
OUTCAST
OUTCOME
OUTCROP
OUTDARE
OUTDOOR
OUTFACE
OUTFALL
OUTFLOW
OUTGROW
OUTLAST
OUTLIER
OUTLINE
OUTLIVE
OUTLOOK
OUTPOST
OUTPOUR
OUTRAGE
OUTRANK
OUTSHOT
OUTSIDE
OUTSIZE
OUTSPAN
OUTSTAY
OUTTURN
OUTVOTE
OUTWARD
OUTWEAR
OUTWORK
OUTWORN
PUBERAL
PUBERTY
PUBLISH
PUCCINI
PUCELLE
PUCKISH
PUDDING
PUERILE
PUGWASH
PULLMAN
PULSATE
PULSING
PUMPKIN
PUNCHED
PUNCHER
PUNGENT
PUNJABI
PUNSTER
PUNTING
PURBECK
PURCELL
PURITAN
PURLIEU
PURLINE
PURLOIN
PURPORT
PURPOSE
PURPURA
PURSUER
PURSUIT
PURVIEW
PUSHING
PUSHKIN
PUSTULE
PUTREFY
PUTTEES
PUTTING
PUTTOCK
PUZZLED
PUZZLER
QUADRAT
QUAKING
QUALIFY
QUALITY
QUANTUM
QUARREL
QUARTAN
QUARTER
QUARTET
QUASSIA
QUECHUA
QUEENLY
QUEERER
QUENTIN
QUERCUS
QUESTER
QUETZAL
QUIBBLE
QUICHUA
QUICKEN
QUICKER
QUICKIE
QUICKLY
QUIETEN
QUIETLY
QUIETUS
QUILTED
QUILTER
QUINCHE
QUININE
QUINONE
QUINTAL
QUINTAN
QUINTET
QUITTER
QUIXOTE
QUONDAM
QUONSET
QUORATE
RUBBERS
RUBBERY
RUBBING
RUBBISH
RUBELLA
RUBEOLA
RUBICON
RUDERAL
RUDOLPH
RUFFIAN
RUFFLED
RUFFLER
RUINOUS
RUMBLER
RUMMAGE
RUMORED
RUMPLED
RUMPOLE
RUNAWAY
RUNCORN
RUNDOWN
RUNNERS
RUNNING
RUNNION
RUPTURE
RUSALKA
RUSHING
RUSSELL
RUSSIAN
RUSTLER
RUTHENE
RUTTING
SUAVELY
SUAVITY
SUBAQUA
SUBATOM
SUBDUCT
SUBDUED
SUBEDAR
SUBEDIT
SUBFUSC
SUBJECT
SUBJOIN
SUBLIME
SUBSIDE
SUBSIDY
SUBSIST
SUBSOIL
SUBSUME
SUBTEEN
SUBTEND
SUBVERT
SUBZERO
SUCCEED
SUCCESS
SUCCOUR
SUCCUMB
SUCROSE
SUCTION
SUDETEN
SUFFETE
SUFFICE
SUFFOLK

SUFFUSE
SUGARED
SUGGEST
SUICIDE
SULFATE
SULKILY
SULLAGE
SULPHUR
SULTANA
SUMATRA
SUMMARY
SUMMERY
SUMMING
SUMMONS
SUNBEAM
SUNBURN
SUNDECK
SUNDIAL
SUNDOWN
SUNLAMP
SUNLESS
SUNNILY
SUNNITE
SUNRISE
SUNROOF
SUNSPOT
SUNTRAP
SUPPORT
SUPPOSE
SUPREME
SUPREMO
SURCOAT
SURDITY
SURFACE
SURFEIT
SURFING
SURGEON
SURGERY
SURINAM
SURMISE
SURNAME
SURPASS
SURPLUS
SURREAL
SURVIVE
SUSANNA
SUSPECT
SUSPEND
SUSTAIN
SUZETTE
TUBULAR
TUBULIN
TUESDAY
TUGBOAT
TUITION
TUMBLER
TUMBREL
TUMBRIL
TUMULUS
TUNABLE
TUNEFUL
TUNISIA
TURBARY
TURBINE
TURENNE
TURGENT
TURKISH
TURMOIL
TURNERY
TURNING
TURNKEY
TURNOUT
TUSCANY
TUSSOCK
TUSSORE
TUTELAR
VULGATE
VULPINE
VULTURE
YUCATAN
AVARICE
AVEBURY
AVENGER
AVERAGE
AVIATOR
AVIDITY
AVIGNON
AVOCADO
AVOIDER
DVORNIK
EVACUEE
EVANDER
EVASION
EVASIVE
EVENING
EVENTER
EVEREST
EVIDENT
IVANHOE
IVORIAN
IVORIEN
IVRESSE
OVARIAN
OVATION
OVERACT
OVERALL
OVERARM
OVERAWE
OVERBID
OVERDUE
OVEREAT
OVERFED
OVERLAP
OVERLAY
OVERLIE
OVERPAY
OVERRUN
OVERSEE
OVERTAX
OVICIDE
OVIDUCT
OVULATE
AWESOME
AWFULLY
AWKWARD
DWELLER
DWINDLE
GWYNETH
RWANDAN
SWADDLE
SWAGGER
SWAGMAN
SWAHILI
SWALLOW
SWANSEA
SWAPPED
SWARTHY
SWAYING
SWEATED
SWEATER
SWEDISH
SWEEPER
SWEETEN
SWEETIE
SWEETLY
SWELTER
SWIDDEN
SWIFTER
SWIFTLY
SWIMMER
SWINDLE
SWINGER
SWINGLE
SWITHIN
SWIZZLE
SWOLLEN
TWADDLE
TWEEDLE
TWEETER
TWELFTH
TWIDDLE
TWIDDLY
TWIGGER
TWINKLE
TWINSET
TWISTED
TWISTER
TWITCHY
TWITTER
TWOFOLD
TWOSOME
TWOSTEP
TWOTIME
AXOLOTL
EXACTLY
EXALTED
EXAMINE
EXAMPLE
EXCERPT
EXCITED
EXCLAIM
EXCLUDE
EXCRETA
EXCRETE
EXECUTE
EXEGETE
EXEMPLA
EXHAUST
EXHEDRA
EXHIBIT
EXIGENT
EXISTED
EXITING
EXOGAMY
EXPANSE
EXPENSE
EXPIATE
EXPIRED
EXPLAIN
EXPLODE
EXPLOIT
EXPLORE
EXPOSED
EXPOUND
EXPRESS
EXPUNGE
EXTINCT
EXTRACT
EXTREME
EXTRUDE
OXALATE
OXIDASE
OXIDIZE
OXONIAN
UXORIAL
BYRONIC
CYANIDE
CYCLING
CYCLIST
CYCLONE
CYCLOPS
CYMBALS
CYNICAL
CYNTHIA
CYPRESS
CYPRIOT
CYSTOID
CYTISUS
DYARCHY
DYNAMIC
DYNASTY
EYEBALL
EYEBATH
EYEBROW
EYELASH
EYELESS
EYELIDS
EYESHOT
EYESORE
EYEWASH
GYMNAST
GYMSLIP
HYALINE
HYALOID
HYDATID
HYDRANT
HYDRATE
HYGIENE
HYPOGEA
KYANITE
LYCHNIS
LYMNAEA
LYNCHET
LYRICAL
MYALGIA
MYANMAR
MYCELLA
MYCENAE
MYCETES
MYELINE
MYELOID
MYELOMA
MYIASIS
MYRINGA
MYSTERY
MYSTIFY
NYMPHET
PYAEMIA
PYJAMAS
PYLORUS
PYRAMID
PYRETIC
PYREXIA
PYRITES
PYROSIS
PYRRHIC
SYCORAX
SYCOSIS
SYMPTOM
SYNAPSE
SYNAXIS
SYNCOPE
SYNERGY
SYNONYM
SYNOVIA
SYRINGA
SYRINGE
SYSTOLE
TYLOSIS
TYMPANO
TYMPANY
TYNWALD
TYPHOID
TYPHOON
TYPICAL
TYRANNY
WYOMING
WYSIWYG
ZYGOSIS
ZYMOSIS
ZYMURGY
AZIMUTH
AZYGOUS
EZEKIEL
TZARINA

7:3

ABALONE
ABANDON
ABASHED
ABATTIS
ACADEME
ACADEMY
ACADIAN
ACARIDA
ACAUDAL
ADAMANT
ADAMITE
ADAPTER
ADAPTOR
AGAINST
ALABAMA
ALADDIN
ALAMEIN
ALAMODE
ALANINE
ALARMED
ALASKAN
AMALGAM
AMANITA
AMATEUR
AMATORY
AMAZING
ANAEMIA
ANAEMIC
ANAGRAM
ANALOGY
ANALYST
ANALYZE
ANANIAS
ANARCHY
ANATOLE
ANATOMY
ARABIAN
ARABICA
ARACHNE
ARAMAIC
ATACTIC
ATAGHAN
ATARAXY
ATAVISM
AVARICE
BEACHED
BEACHES
BEADING
BEAMING
BEARDED
BEARHUG
BEARING
BEARISH
BEASTLY
BEATIFY
BEATING
BEATLES
BEATNIK
BIAFRAN
BIASSED
BLABBER
BLACKEN
BLADDER
BLANDLY
BLANKET
BLANKLY
BLASTED
BLASTER
BLATANT
BLATHER
BLATTER
BLAZERS
BLAZING
BOARDER
BOASTER
BOATING
BOATMAN
BRACING
BRACKEN
BRACKET
BRADAWL
BRADMAN
BRAEMAR
BRAHMIN
BRAILLE
BRAKING
BRAMBLE
BRANDED
BRANDER
BRANTUB
BRASERO
BRAVADO
BRAVELY
BRAVERY
BRAVURA
BRAWLER
BRAZIER
CHABLIS
CHAFING
CHAGALL
CHAGRIN
CHAINED
CHALDEE
CHALICE
CHALKER
CHALONE
CHAMBER
CHAMBRÉ
CHAMFER
CHAMOIS
CHANCEL
CHANCRE
CHANGED
CHANGES
CHANNEL
CHANSON
CHANTER
CHAOTIC
CHAPATI

CHAPEAU
CHAPLET
CHAPMAN
CHAPPED
CHAPTER
CHARADE
CHARDIN
CHARGED
CHARGER
CHARGES
CHARIOT
CHARITY
CHARLES
CHARLEY
CHARMED
CHARMER
CHARNEL
CHARPOY
CHARRED
CHARTER
CHASING
CHASSIS
CHASTEN
CHATEAU
CHATHAM
CHATTEL
CHATTER
CHAUCER
CHAYOTE
CLACHAN
CLAMBER
CLAMOUR
CLAMPER
CLANGER
CLAPPER
CLARIFY
CLARION
CLARITY
CLASSIC
CLASTIC
CLATTER
COARSEN
COASTAL
COASTER
COATING
COAXIAL
CRACKED
CRACKER
CRACKLE
CRACKLY
CRAMMED
CRAMMER
CRAMPED
CRAMPON
CRANACH
CRANIAL
CRANIUM
CRANMER
CRASHES
CRASSUS
CRAVING
CRAWLER
CRAZILY
CSARDAS
CYANIDE
DEADEYE
DEADPAN
DEADSET
DEALING
DEANERY
DEAREST
DEATHLY
DIABOLO
DIAGRAM
DIALECT
DIALING
DIALYSE
DIAMINE
DIAMOND
DIAPSID
DIARCHY
DIARIST
DRABBLE
DRACHMA
DRACULA
DRAFTED
DRAFTEE
DRAGGLE
DRAGNET
DRAGOON
DRAINED
DRAPERY
DRASTIC
DRAUGHT
DRAWBAR
DRAWERS
DRAWING
DUALITY
DYARCHY
EDAPHIC
EGALITY
ELASTIC
ELASTIN
ELATION
EMANATE
ENACTOR
ENAMOUR
EPAULET
ERASMUS
ERASURE
ETAGÈRE
ETAPLES
EVACUEE
EVANDER
EVASION
EVASIVE
EXACTLY
EXALTED
EXAMINE
EXAMPLE
FEARFUL
FEATHER
FEATURE
FIANCÉE
FLACCID
FLAGDAY
FLAMING
FLANKER
FLANNEL
FLAPPED
FLAPPER
FLAREUP
FLASHER
FLATCAR
FLATLET
FLATTEN
FLATTER
FLAUNCH
FLAVOUR
FRAGILE
FRAILTY
FRANCIS
FRANKLY
FRANTIC
FRAUGHT
FRAZZLE
GEARBOX
GEARING
GHASTLY
GLACIAL
GLACIER
GLADDEN
GLAMOUR
GLARING
GLASGOW
GLASSES
GLAZIER
GLAZING
GNARLED
GNAWING
GOAHEAD
GRACCHI
GRACILE
GRACKLE
GRADATE
GRADELY
GRADUAL
GRAFTER
GRAINED
GRAINER
GRAMMAR
GRAMPUS
GRANARY
GRANDAD
GRANDEE
GRANDLY
GRANDMA
GRANDPA
GRANITA
GRANITE
GRANNIE
GRANOLA
GRANTED
GRANTEE
GRANULE
GRAPHIC
GRAPHIS
GRAPNEL
GRAPPLE
GRATIFY
GRATING
GRAVITY
GRAVURE
GRAYISH
GRAZING
GUANACO
GUARANA
GUARANI
GUARDED
HEADING
HEADMAN
HEADSET
HEADWAY
HEALING
HEALTHY
HEARING
HEARKEN
HEARSAY
HEARTEN
HEATHEN
HEATHER
HEATING
HEAVENS
HEAVIER
HEAVILY
HOARDER
HYALINE
HYALOID
IMAGERY
IMAGINE
IMAGING
IMAGISM
IMAGIST
INANITY
IRANIAN
ISADORA
ITALIAN
IVANHOE
JEALOUS
KEARTON
KHALIFA
KHAMSIN
KHANATE
KLAVIER
KNACKER
KNAPPER
KNAVERY
KYANITE
LEACOCK
LEADERS
LEADING
LEAFLET
LEAGUER
LEAKAGE
LEANDER
LEANING
LEAPING
LEARNED
LEARNER
LEASING
LEASOWE
LEATHER
LEAVING
LIAISON
MEACOCK
MEANDER
MEANING
MEASLES
MEASURE
MIASMIC
MOABITE
MOANING
MYALGIA
MYANMAR
NEAREST
NEARING
NIAGARA
OBADIAH
OCARINA
ODALISK
ONANISM
OPACITY
OPALINE
ORACLES
ORANGES
ORATION
ORATORY
OTALGIA
OVARIAN
OVATION
OXALATE
PEACHUM
PEACOCK
PEANUTS
PEARLIE
PEASANT
PHAETON
PHALANX
PHALLIC
PHALLUS
PHANTOM
PHARAOH
PHARYNX
PIANIST
PIANOLA
PIASTRE
PLACARD
PLACATE
PLACEBO
PLACING
PLAINLY
PLANNED
PLANNER
PLANTAR
PLANTED
PLANTER
PLANURY
PLASMIN
PLASTER
PLASTIC
PLATEAU
PLATOON
PLATTER
PLAUDIT
PLAUTUS
PLAYBOY
PLAYERS
PLAYFUL
PLAYING
PLAYLET
PLAYOFF
PLAYPEN
POACHER
PRAETOR
PRAIRIE
PRALINE
PRATTLE
PRAYING
PSALTER
PYAEMIA
QUADRAT
QUAKING
QUALIFY
QUALITY
QUANTUM
QUARREL
QUARTAN
QUARTER
QUARTET
QUASSIA
REACTOR
READILY
READING
REAGENT
REALGAR
REALIGN
REALISM
REALIST
REALITY
REALIZE
REALTOR
REARING
REAUMUR
ROADHOG
ROADWAY
ROAMING
ROARING
ROASTER
RWANDAN
SCABIES
SCAFELL
SCAGLIA
SCALENE
SCALLOP
SCALPEL
SCALPER
SCAMBLE
SCAMPER
SCANDAL
SCANNER
SCAPULA
SCARIFY
SCARING
SCARLET
SCARPER
SCATTER
SEABIRD
SEAFOOD
SEAGULL
SEALANT
SEALINK
SEALION
SEAPORT
SEARING
SEASICK
SEASIDE
SEATING
SEATTLE
SEAWALL
SEAWEED
SHACKLE
SHADING
SHADOOF
SHADOWY
SHAGGED
SHAKERS
SHAKEUP
SHAKILY
SHAKING
SHALLOT
SHALLOW
SHAMBLE
SHAMPOO
SHANNON
SHAPELY
SHAPING
SHARIAH
SHARING
SHARPEN
SHARPER
SHARPLY
SHASTRI
SHATTER
SHAVING
SIAMESE
SJAMBOK
SKATING
SLACKEN
SLACKER
SLACKLY
SLAMMER
SLANDER
SLAPPER
SLASHED
SLATTED
SLAVERY
SLAVISH

SLAYING
SMACKER
SMALLER
SMARTEN
SMARTIE
SMARTLY
SMASHED
SMASHER
SMATTER
SNAFFLE
SNAPPER
SNARLER
SNARLUP
SOAKING
SOAPBOX
SOARING
SPACING
SPADGER
SPANDAU
SPANDEX
SPANGLE
SPANIEL
SPANISH
SPANKER
SPANNER
SPARING
SPARKLE
SPARROW
SPARTAN
SPASTIC
SPATIAL
SPATTER
SPATULA
SPAVINE
STABLES
STACHYS
STADDLE
STADIUM
STAFFER
STAGGER
STAGING
STAINED
STAINER
STALKED
STALKER
STAMINA
STAMMER
STAMPED
STAMPER
STANDBY
STANDIN
STANDUP
STANLEY
STANNIC
STAPLER
STARCHY
STARDOM
STARETS
STARING
STARKLY
STARLET
STARLIT
STARTED
STARTER
STARTLE
STARVED
STATELY
STATICS
STATION
STATIST
STATURE
STATUTE
STAUNCH
STAYING
SUAVELY
SUAVITY
SWADDLE
SWAGGER
SWAGMAN
SWAHILI
SWALLOW
SWANSEA
SWAPPED
SWARTHY
SWAYING
TEACAKE
TEACHER
TEALEAF
TEARFUL
TEARING
TEAROOM
TEASHOP
TEASING
TEATIME
THALLUS
TOASTED
TOASTER
TRACERY
TRACHEA
TRACING
TRACKER
TRACTOR
TRADEIN
TRADING
TRADUCE
TRAFFIC
TRAGEDY
TRAILER
TRAINED
TRAINEE
TRAINER
TRAIPSE
TRAITOR
TRAMCAR
TRAMMEL
TRAMPLE
TRAMWAY
TRANCHE
TRANSIT
TRANSOM
TRANTER
TRAPEZE
TRAPPED
TRAPPER
TRAVAIL
TRAWLER
TSARINA
TSARIST
TWADDLE
TZARINA
UGANDAN
UNAIDED
UNAIRED
UNALIKE
UNALIVE
UNARMED
UNASKED
UNAWARE
URAEMIA
URALITE
URANIAN
URANISM
URANITE
URANIUM
VIADUCT
WEAKEST
WEALDEN
WEALTHY
WEAPONS
WEARILY
WEARING
WEATHER
WEAVING
WHACKED
WHACKER
WHALING
WHARTON
WHATNOT
WHATSIT
WRANGLE
WRAPPED
WRAPPER
WRAUGHT
ZEALAND
ZEALOUS
ABBASID
ALBANIA
ALBENIZ
ALBERGO
ALBERTA
ALBERTI
ALBUMEN
ALBUMIN
AMBAGES
AMBIENT
AMBOYNA
AMBROSE
ARBITER
ARBUTUS
AUBERGE
BABBITT
BABBLER
BABOOSH
BABYISH
BABYLON
BABYSIT
BIBELOT
BOBSLED
BUBBLES
BUBONIC
CABARET
CABBAGE
CABINET
CABLING
CABOOSE
COBBLED
COBBLER
CUBICLE
DABBLER
DEBACLE
DEBASED
DEBATER
DEBAUCH
DEBORAH
DEBOUCH
DEBRETT
DEBRIEF
DEBUSSY
DIBBLER
DUBBING
DUBIETY
DUBIOUS
EBBTIDE
ECBOLIC
EMBARGO
EMBASSY
EMBLAZE
EMBOLUS
EMBOWER
EMBRACE
EMBROIL
FEBRILE
FIBROID
FIBROMA
FIBROUS
GABBLER
GABELLE
GABFEST
GABRIEL
GIBBONS
GIBBOUS
GIBLETS
GOBBLER
GOBELIN
GUBBINS
HABITAT
HIBACHI
HOBNAIL
HOBSONS
HUBBARD
INBOARD
INBUILT
INBURST
JOBBERY
JOBBING
JOBLESS
JUBILEE
KIBBUTZ
KUBELIK
LABIATE
LABORED
LABORER
LEBANON
LIBERAL
LIBERIA
LIBERTY
LIBRARY
LIBRIUM
LOBELIA
LOBSTER
MOBSTER
NABOKOV
NEBBISH
NEBULAR
NIBLICK
NOBBLED
NOBBLER
ORBITAL
OSBORNE
PABULUM
PEBBLES
PIBROCH
PUBERAL
PUBERTY
PUBLISH
REBECCA
REBIRTH
REBOUND
REBUILD
RIBBING
RIBCAGE
RIBLESS
ROBBERS
ROBBERY
ROBERTS
ROBESON
ROBINIA
ROBUSTA
RUBBERS
RUBBERY
RUBBING
RUBBISH
RUBELLA
RUBEOLA
RUBICON
SABAEAN
SABAOTH
SABAYON
SABBATH
SABRINA
SIBLING
SOBERLY
SUBAQUA
SUBATOM
SUBDUCT
SUBDUED
SUBEDAR
SUBEDIT
SUBFUSC
SUBJECT
SUBJOIN
SUBLIME
SUBSIDE
SUBSIDY
SUBSIST
SUBSOIL
SUBSUME
SUBTEEN
SUBTEND
SUBVERT
SUBZERO
TABANID
TABARET
TABASCO
TABITHA
TABLEAU
TABLOID
TABULAR
TIBETAN
TOBACCO
TUBULAR
TUBULIN
UMBRAGE
UMBRIAN
UNBLOCK
UNBOSOM
UNBOUND
UNBOWED
UPBRAID
VIBRANT
VIBRATE
VIBRATO
WEBBING
WEBSTER
ACCLAIM
ACCOUNT
ACCRETE
ACCRUAL
ACCURSE
ACCUSED
ACCUSER
ALCALDE
ALCHEMY
ALCOHOL
ALCORAN
ANCHOVY
ANCIENT
ARCADIA
ARCHAIC
ARCHERY
ARCHIVE
ARCHWAY
ARCUATE
ASCARID
ASCETIC
ASCITES
ASCRIBE
AUCTION
BACARDI
BACCHIC
BACCHUS
BACILLI
BACKING
BACKLOG
BACKSET
BECAUSE
BECKETT
BICYCLE
BUCKETS
BUCKEYE
BUCKLER
BUCKRAM
BUCOLIC
CACHEXY
CACIQUE
CECILIA
COCAINE
COCHLEA
COCKADE
COCKLES
COCKNEY
COCKPIT
COCONUT
COCOTTE
CUCKING
CUCKOLD
CYCLING
CYCLIST
CYCLONE
CYCLOPS
DECANAL
DECAYED
DECEASE
DECEIVE
DECENCY
DECIBEL
DECIDED
DECIDER
DECIMAL
DECLAIM
DECLARE
DECLINE
DECODER
DECORUM
DECREED
DECRYPT
DICKENS
DICTATE
DICTION
DOCKING
DOCTORS
DUCHESS
DUCKING
DUCTILE
ECCRINE
ENCHANT
ENCLASP

ENCLAVE
ENCLOSE
ENCRUST
ESCALOP
ESCAPEE
ESCHEAT
ETCHING
EXCERPT
EXCITED
EXCLAIM
EXCLUDE
EXCRETA
EXCRETE
FACETED
FACTION
FACTORS
FACTORY
FACTUAL
FACULTY
FICTION
FUCHSIA
HACHURE
HACKERY
HACKING
HACKLES
HACKNEY
HACKSAW
HECKLER
HECTARE
HICKORY
INCENSE
INCISOR
INCLINE
INCLUDE
INCOMER
INCONNU
INCRUST
INCUBUS
ISCHIUM
ITCHING
JACKASS
JACKDAW
JACKETS
JACKPOT
JACKSON
JACOBIN
JACOBUS
JACQUES
JACUZZI
JOCASTA
JOCULAR
KICKING
KICKOFF
LACERTA
LACEUPS
LACKING
LACONIC
LACQUER
LACTASE
LACTATE
LACTEAL
LACTOSE
LACUNAE
LECHERY
LECTERN
LECTURE
LICENCE
LICENSE
LICKING
LOCALLY
LOCKJAW
LOCKNUT
LOCKOUT
LOCUSTS
LUCARNE
LUCERNE
LUCIDLY
LUCIFER
LUCKILY
LYCHNIS
MACABRE
MACADAM
MACAQUE
MACBETH
MACEDON
MACHETE
MACHINE
MACRAMÉ
MECONIC
MICHAEL
MICROBE
MOCKERS
MOCKERY
MOCKING
MYCELLA
MYCENAE
MYCETES
NACELLE
NACROUS
NECKING
NECKLET
NECKTIE
NECROSE
NECTARY
NICAEAN
NICOISE
NICOSIA
NICTATE
NUCLEAR
NUCLEIC
NUCLEUS
NUCLIDE
OCCIPUT
OCCLUDE
ORCHARD
OSCULUM
PACIFIC
PACKAGE
PACKING
PACKMAN
PECCANT
PECCARY
PECCAVI
PECKING
PECKISH
PECTASE
PICADOR
PICARDY
PICASSO
PICCOLO
PICKAXE
PICKING
PICKLED
PICKLER
PICOTEE
PICQUET
PICTURE
POCHARD
POCHOIR
PUCCINI
PUCELLE
PUCKISH
RACCOON
RACEMIC
RACHIAL
RACHMAN
RACKETS
RACKETY
RACKING
RACQUET
RECEIPT
RECEIVE
RECITAL
RECLAIM
RECLINE
RECLUSE
RECORDS
RECOUNT
RECOVER
RECRUIT
RECTIFY
RECTORY
RECURVE
RECYCLE
RICARDO
RICHARD
RICHTER
RICKETS
RICKETY
RICOTTA
ROCKALL
ROCKERY
ROCKING
SACCADE
SACKBUT
SACKFUL
SACKING
SECLUDE
SECONAL
SECONDS
SECRECY
SECRETE
SECRETS
SECTION
SECULAR
SICKBAY
SICKBED
SICKERT
SOCAGER
SOCIETY
SOCKEYE
SOCKING
SOCOTRA
SUCCEED
SUCCESS
SUCCOUR
SUCCUMB
SUCROSE
SUCTION
SYCORAX
SYCOSIS
TACHISM
TACITLY
TACITUS
TACKLER
TACTFUL
TACTICS
TACTILE
TICKING
TICKLER
TOCCATA
UCCELLO
UNCANNY
UNCARED
UNCINUS
UNCIVIL
UNCLASP
UNCLEAN
UNCLEAR
UNCOUTH
UNCOVER
UNCTION
UNCURED
VACANCY
VACCINE
VACUITY
VACUOLE
VACUOUS
VICEROY
VICINAL
VICIOUS
VICTORY
VICTUAL
VOCALIC
VOCALLY
WICKIUP
WICKLOW
YUCATAN
ABDOMEN
ADDISON
ADDRESS
AIDANCE
ALDABRA
ALDRICH
ANDAMAN
ANDANTE
ANDIRON
ANDORRA
ANDROID
ARDUOUS
AUDIBLE
AUDIBLY
AUDITOR
AUDUBON
BADNESS
BEDDING
BEDEVIL
BEDFORD
BEDOUIN
BEDPOST
BEDROCK
BEDROOM
BEDSIDE
BEDSORE
BEDTIME
BIDDING
BUDDING
CADAVER
CADDISH
CADENCE
CADENZA
CADMIUM
CADOGAN
CEDILLA
CODEINE
CODICIL
CODLING
DADAISM
DADAIST
DIDEROT
DIDICOY
DIDYMUS
DODDERY
DODGEMS
DUDGEON
ECDYSIS
ELDERLY
ENDEMIC
ENDGAME
ENDLESS
ENDOGEN
ENDORSE
ENDURED
ENDWAYS
FADDISH
FADDIST
FEDERAL
FIDDLER
FIDELIO
FIDGETS
FIDGETY
FUDDLED
GADROON
GADWALL
GIDDILY
GODDESS
GODETIA
GODLESS
GODLIKE
GODSEND
GODUNOV
GUDGEON
HADDOCK
HADRIAN
HEDGING
HIDALGO
HIDEOUS
HIDEOUT
HYDATID
HYDRANT
HYDRATE
INDEPTH
INDEXER
INDIANA
INDOORS
INDULGE
JUDAISM
KADDISH
KIDNEYS
LADYBUG
LODGING
LUDDITE
LUDGATE
MADEIRA
MADISON
MADNESS
MADONNA
MEDDLER
MEDIATE
MEDICAL
MEDULLA
MIDLAND
MIDRIFF
MIDSHIP
MIDTERM
MIDWEEK
MIDWEST
MIDWIFE
MODESTY
MODICUM
MODISTE
MODULAR
MODULUS
MUDDLED
MUDEJAR
MUDFLAP
MUDLARK
MUDPACK
NODDING
NODULAR
ODDBALL
ODDMENT
ODDNESS
OEDIPUS
OLDNESS
OLDSTER
ORDERED
ORDERLY
ORDINAL
PADDING
PADDLER
PADDOCK
PADLOCK
PADRONE
PEDDLER
PEDICAB
PEDICEL
PEDICLE
PIDGEON
PODAGRA
PODESTA
PUDDING
RADDLED
RADIANT
RADIATE
RADICAL
RADICLE
REDCOAT
REDDISH
REDHEAD
REDNECK
REDNESS
REDOUBT
REDOUND
REDPOLL
REDRESS
REDSKIN
REDUCED
REDUCER
REDWOOD
RIDDLED
RIDDLER
RIDINGS
RUDERAL
RUDOLPH
SADDLER
SADNESS
SEDUCER
SIDDONS
SIDECAR
SUDETEN
TADPOLE
TEDIOUS
TIDDLER
TIDEWAY
TIDINGS
TODDLER
UNDATED
UNDERGO
UNDOING
UNDRESS
UNDYING
VEDANTA
VEDETTE
VIDIMUS
WADDING
WEDDING

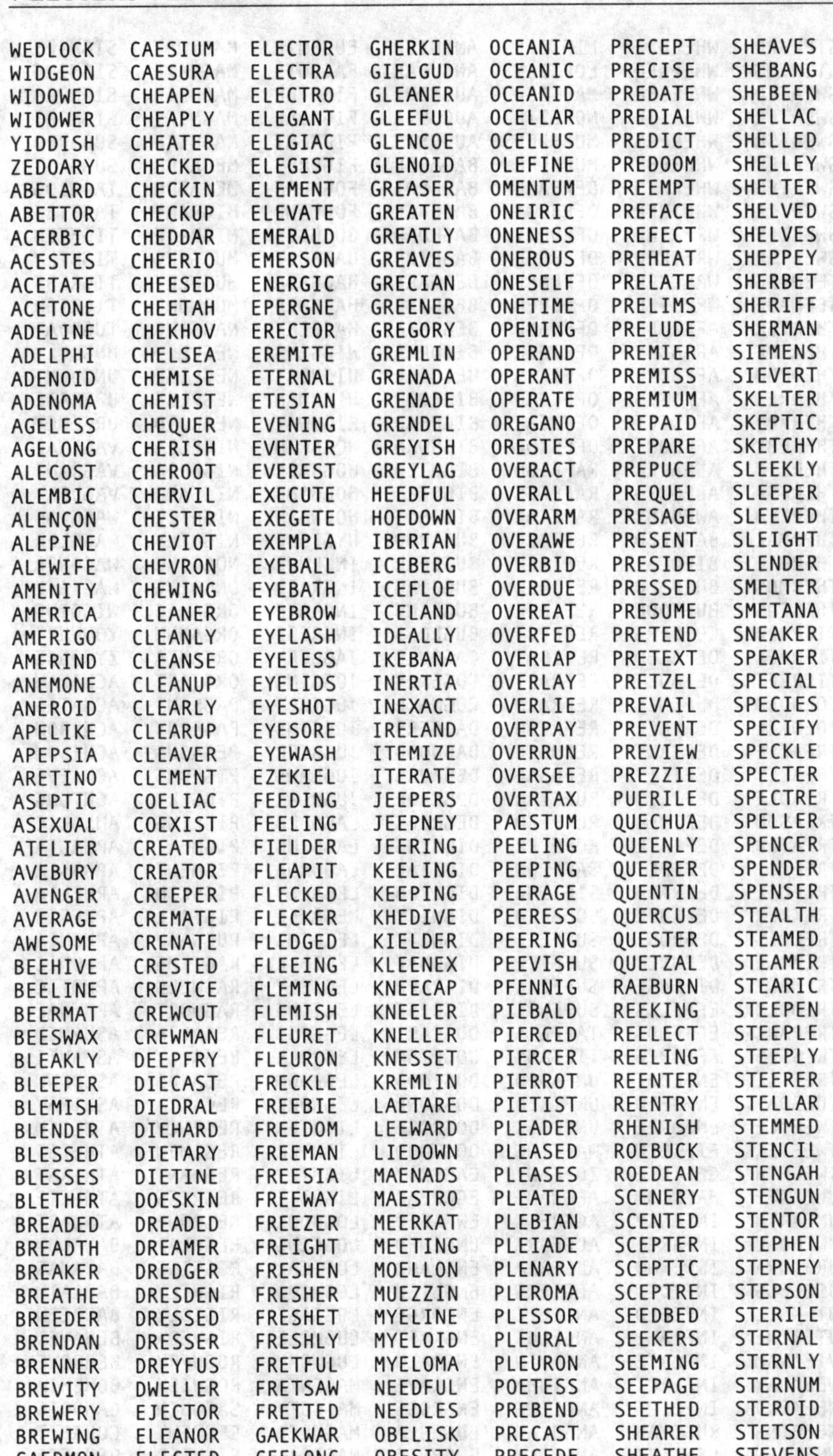

WEDLOCK
WIDGEON
WIDOWED
WIDOWER
YIDDISH
ZEDOARY
ABELARD
ABETTOR
ACERBIC
ACESTES
ACETATE
ACETONE
ADELINE
ADELPHI
ADENOID
ADENOMA
AGELESS
AGELONG
ALECOST
ALEMBIC
ALENÇON
ALEPINE
ALEWIFE
AMENITY
AMERICA
AMERIGO
AMERIND
ANEMONE
ANEROID
APELIKE
APEPSIA
ARETINO
ASEPTIC
ASEXUAL
ATELIER
AVEBURY
AVENGER
AVERAGE
AWESOME
BEEHIVE
BEELINE
BEERMAT
BEESWAX
BLEAKLY
BLEEPER
BLEMISH
BLENDER
BLESSED
BLESSES
BLETHER
BREADED
BREADTH
BREAKER
BREATHE
BREEDER
BRENDAN
BRENNER
BREVITY
BREWERY
BREWING
CAEDMON
CAESIUM
CAESURA
CHEAPEN
CHEAPLY
CHEATER
CHECKED
CHECKIN
CHECKUP
CHEDDAR
CHEERIO
CHEESED
CHEETAH
CHEKHOV
CHELSEA
CHEMISE
CHEMIST
CHEQUER
CHERISH
CHEROOT
CHERVIL
CHESTER
CHEVIOT
CHEVRON
CHEWING
CLEANER
CLEANLY
CLEANSE
CLEANUP
CLEARLY
CLEARUP
CLEAVER
CLEMENT
COELIAC
COEXIST
CREATED
CREATOR
CREEPER
CREMATE
CRENATE
CRESTED
CREVICE
CREWCUT
CREWMAN
DEEPFRY
DIECAST
DIEDRAL
DIEHARD
DIETARY
DIETINE
DOESKIN
DREADED
DREAMER
DREDGER
DRESDEN
DRESSED
DRESSER
DREYFUS
DWELLER
EJECTOR
ELEANOR
ELECTED
ELECTOR
ELECTRA
ELECTRO
ELEGANT
ELEGIAC
ELEGIST
ELEMENT
ELEVATE
EMERALD
EMERSON
ENERGIC
EPERGNE
ERECTOR
EREMITE
ETERNAL
ETESIAN
EVENING
EVENTER
EVEREST
EXECUTE
EXEGETE
EXEMPLA
EYEBALL
EYEBATH
EYEBROW
EYELASH
EYELESS
EYELIDS
EYESHOT
EYESORE
EYEWASH
EZEKIEL
FEEDING
FEELING
FIELDER
FLEAPIT
FLECKED
FLECKER
FLEDGED
FLEEING
FLEMING
FLEMISH
FLEURET
FLEURON
FRECKLE
FREEBIE
FREEDOM
FREEMAN
FREESIA
FREEWAY
FREEZER
FREIGHT
FRESHEN
FRESHER
FRESHET
FRESHLY
FRETFUL
FRETSAW
FRETTED
GAEKWAR
GEELONG
GHERKIN
GIELGUD
GLEANER
GLEEFUL
GLENCOE
GLENOID
GREASER
GREATEN
GREATLY
GREAVES
GRECIAN
GREENER
GREGORY
GREMLIN
GRENADA
GRENADE
GRENDEL
GREYISH
GREYLAG
HEEDFUL
HOEDOWN
IBERIAN
ICEBERG
ICEFLOE
ICELAND
IDEALLY
IKEBANA
INERTIA
INEXACT
IRELAND
ITEMIZE
ITERATE
JEEPERS
JEEPNEY
JEERING
KEELING
KEEPING
KHEDIVE
KIELDER
KLEENEX
KNEECAP
KNEELER
KNELLER
KNESSET
KREMLIN
LAETARE
LEEWARD
LIEDOWN
MAENADS
MAESTRO
MEERKAT
MEETING
MOELLON
MUEZZIN
MYELINE
MYELOID
MYELOMA
NEEDFUL
NEEDLES
OBELISK
OBESITY
OCEANIA
OCEANIC
OCEANID
OCELLAR
OCELLUS
OLEFINE
OMENTUM
ONEIRIC
ONENESS
ONEROUS
ONESELF
ONETIME
OPENING
OPERAND
OPERANT
OPERATE
OREGANO
ORESTES
OVERACT
OVERALL
OVERARM
OVERAWE
OVERBID
OVERDUE
OVEREAT
OVERFED
OVERLAP
OVERLAY
OVERLIE
OVERPAY
OVERRUN
OVERSEE
OVERTAX
PAESTUM
PEELING
PEEPING
PEERAGE
PEERESS
PEERING
PEEVISH
PFENNIG
PIEBALD
PIERCED
PIERCER
PIERROT
PIETIST
PLEADER
PLEASED
PLEASES
PLEATED
PLEBIAN
PLEIADE
PLENARY
PLEROMA
PLESSOR
PLEURAL
PLEURON
POETESS
PREBEND
PRECAST
PRECEDE
PRECEPT
PRECISE
PREDATE
PREDIAL
PREDICT
PREDOOM
PREEMPT
PREFACE
PREFECT
PREHEAT
PRELATE
PRELIMS
PRELUDE
PREMIER
PREMISS
PREMIUM
PREPAID
PREPARE
PREPUCE
PREQUEL
PRESAGE
PRESENT
PRESIDE
PRESSED
PRESUME
PRETEND
PRETEXT
PRETZEL
PREVAIL
PREVENT
PREVIEW
PREZZIE
PUERILE
QUECHUA
QUEENLY
QUEERER
QUENTIN
QUERCUS
QUESTER
QUETZAL
RAEBURN
REEKING
REELECT
REELING
REENTER
REENTRY
RHENISH
ROEBUCK
ROEDEAN
SCENERY
SCENTED
SCEPTER
SCEPTIC
SCEPTRE
SEEDBED
SEEKERS
SEEMING
SEEPAGE
SEETHED
SHEARER
SHEATHE
SHEAVES
SHEBANG
SHEBEEN
SHELLAC
SHELLED
SHELLEY
SHELTER
SHELVED
SHELVES
SHEPPEY
SHERBET
SHERIFF
SHERMAN
SIEMENS
SIEVERT
SKELTER
SKEPTIC
SKETCHY
SLEEKLY
SLEEPER
SLEEVED
SLEIGHT
SLENDER
SMELTER
SMETANA
SNEAKER
SPEAKER
SPECIAL
SPECIES
SPECIFY
SPECKLE
SPECTER
SPECTRE
SPELLER
SPENCER
SPENDER
SPENSER
STEALTH
STEAMED
STEAMER
STEARIC
STEEPEN
STEEPLE
STEEPLY
STEERER
STELLAR
STEMMED
STENCIL
STENGAH
STENGUN
STENTOR
STEPHEN
STEPNEY
STEPSON
STERILE
STERNAL
STERNLY
STERNUM
STEROID
STETSON
STEVENS

STEWARD
STEWING
SWEATED
SWEATER
SWEDISH
SWEEPER
SWEETEN
SWEETIE
SWEETLY
SWELTER
TEEMING
TEENAGE
THEATER
THEATRE
THEORBO
THEOREM
THERAPY
THEREBY
THEREIN
THERESA
THERETO
THERMAL
THERMIC
THERMOS
THESEUS
TIEPOLO
TIERCEL
TIERCET
TOEHOLD
TOENAIL
TREACLE
TREACLY
TREADLE
TREASON
TREATED
TREETOP
TREFOIL
TREKKER
TRELLIS
TREMBLE
TREMBLY
TREMOLO
TREPANG
TRESSES
TRESTLE
TUESDAY
TWEEDLE
TWEETER
TWELFTH
ULEXITE
UNEARTH
UNEQUAL
URETHRA
USELESS
UTENSIL
UTERINE
VIETNAM
WEEKDAY
WEEKEND
WEEPING
WHEATEN
WHEEDLE
WHEELED
WHEELER
WHEELIE
WHEREAS
WHEREBY
WHEREIN
WHETHER
WREATHE
WRECKED
WRECKER
WRESTLE
AFFABLE
AFFABLY
AFFAIRS
AFFIXED
AFFLICT
AFFRONT
ALFALFA
ALFONSO
AWFULLY
BAFFLED
BIFOCAL
BUFFALO
BUFFOON
COFFERS
DEFACED
DEFAULT
DEFENCE
DEFENSE
DEFIANT
DEFICIT
DEFILED
DEFINED
DEFLATE
DEFLECT
DEFRAUD
DEFROCK
DEFROST
DEFUNCT
DIFFUSE
EFFECTS
EFFENDI
EFFORCE
ENFEOFF
ENFIELD
ENFORCE
FIFTEEN
GEFILTE
HAFNIUM
INFANCY
INFARCT
INFERNO
INFIDEL
INFIELD
INFLAME
INFLATE
INFLECT
INFLICT
KUFIYAH
LEFTIST
LIFTOFF
LOFTILY
MAFIOSO
MOFETTE
MUFFLED
MUFFLER
OFFBASE
OFFBEAT
OFFDUTY
OFFENCE
OFFENSE
OFFERER
OFFHAND
OFFICER
OFFICES
OFFLOAD
OFFPEAK
OFFSIDE
RAFFISH
RAFFLES
RAFTING
REFEREE
REFINED
REFINER
REFLATE
REFLECT
REFLOAT
REFRACT
REFRAIN
REFRESH
REFUGEE
REFUSAL
RUFFIAN
RUFFLED
RUFFLER
SAFFRON
SIFTING
SOFABED
SUFFETE
SUFFICE
SUFFOLK
SUFFUSE
TAFFETA
TIFFANY
UNFADED
UNFIXED
UNFROCK
WAFTING
ZOFFANY
AFGHANI
AGGRESS
ALGEBRA
ALGERIA
ALGIERS
ANGELIC
ANGELUS
ANGEVIN
ANGIOMA
ANGLING
ANGOLAN
ANGRILY
ANGUISH
ANGULAR
AUGMENT
AUGUSTA
AUGUSTE
BAGASSE
BAGEHOT
BAGGAGE
BAGHDAD
BAGPIPE
BEGGARY
BEGGING
BEGONIA
BEGORRA
BEGUILE
BIGFOOT
BIGHEAD
BIGHORN
BIGOTED
BIGOTRY
BIGSHOT
BUGABOO
BUGBEAR
BUGGING
BUGGINS
BUGLOSS
CAGOULE
COGENCY
COGNATE
DAGGERS
DAGWOOD
DEGAUSS
DEGRADE
DEGREES
DIGGING
DIGITAL
DIGLYPH
DIGNIFY
DIGNITY
DIGONAL
DIGRAPH
DIGRESS
DOGCART
DOGFISH
DOGFOOD
DOGGONE
DOGROSE
DOGWOOD
EAGERLY
EGGHEAD
ENGAGED
ENGINED
ENGLAND
ENGLISH
ENGORGE
ENGRAFT
ENGRAIN
ENGRAVE
ENGROSS
EUGENIA
EUGENIC
EUGENIE
FAGGOTS
FIGHTER
FIGLEAF
FIGMENT
FIGURES
FOGHORN
FOGLAMP
GOGGLES
HAGBOLT
HAGGADA
HAGGARD
HAGGERY
HIGGINS
HIGHEST
HIGHMAN
HIGHWAY
HOGARTH
HOGBACK
HOGGING
HOGWASH
HYGIENE
INGENUE
INGRAIN
INGRATE
INGRESS
JAGGERY
JOGGING
JOGTROT
JUGGINS
JUGGLER
JUGLANS
JUGULAR
LAGGARD
LAGGING
LAGONDA
LEGALLY
LEGATEE
LEGGING
LEGIBLE
LEGIBLY
LEGIONS
LEGLESS
LEGPULL
LEGROOM
LEGWORK
LIGHTEN
LIGHTER
LIGHTLY
LIGNITE
LOGBOOK
LOGGING
LOGICAL
LOGWOOD
LUGGAGE
LUGHOLE
LUGWORM
MAGENTA
MAGGOTY
MAGHREB
MAGICAL
MAGINOT
MAGNATE
MAGNETO
MAGNIFY
MAGUIRE
MEGARON
MEGATON
MIGRANT
MIGRATE
MUGGING
MUGWORT
MUGWUMP
NAGGING
NEGLECT
NÉGLIGÉ
NEGRESS
NEGROID
NIGELLA
NIGERIA
NIGGARD
NIGHTIE
NIGHTLY
NOGGING
ONGOING
ORGANIC
ORGANUM
ORGANZA
ORGIAST
PAGEANT
PAGEBOY
PEGASUS
PIGEONS
PIGGERY
PIGLING
PIGMEAT
PIGMENT
PIGSKIN
PIGTAIL
PUGWASH
RAGTIME
RAGWEED
RAGWORT
REGALIA
REGALLY
REGARDS
REGATTA
REGENCY
REGIMEN
REGNANT
REGRESS
REGROUP
REGULAR
RIGGING
RIGHTLY
RIGIDLY
RIGVEDA
ROGUERY
ROGUISH
SAGOUIN
SEGMENT
SIGHTED
SIGNIFY
SIGNING
SIGNORA
SIGNORI
SUGARED
SUGGEST
TAGALOG
TAGETES
TIGHTEN
TIGHTLY
TIGRESS
TIGRISH
TUGBOAT
UNGODLY
UNGUENT
UPGRADE
URGENCY
VAGINAL
VAGRANT
VAGUELY
WAGGISH
WAGGLER
WAGONER
WAGTAIL
WIGGING
YOGHURT
ZYGOSIS
ACHAEAN
ACHATES
ACHERON
ACHESON
ACHIEVE
ACHTUNG
AMHARIC
APHAGIA
APHASIA
APHELIA
APHESIS
APHONIA
APHONIC
APHOTIC
APHTHAE
ASHAMED
ASHANTI
ASHDOWN
ASHTRAY
ATHEISM
ATHEIST
ATHIRST
ATHLETE
ATHWART
BAHADUR
BAHAMAS
BAHRAIN
BAHREIN
BEHAVED
BEHOOVE
BOHEMIA
CAHOOTS
COHABIT
DEHISCE

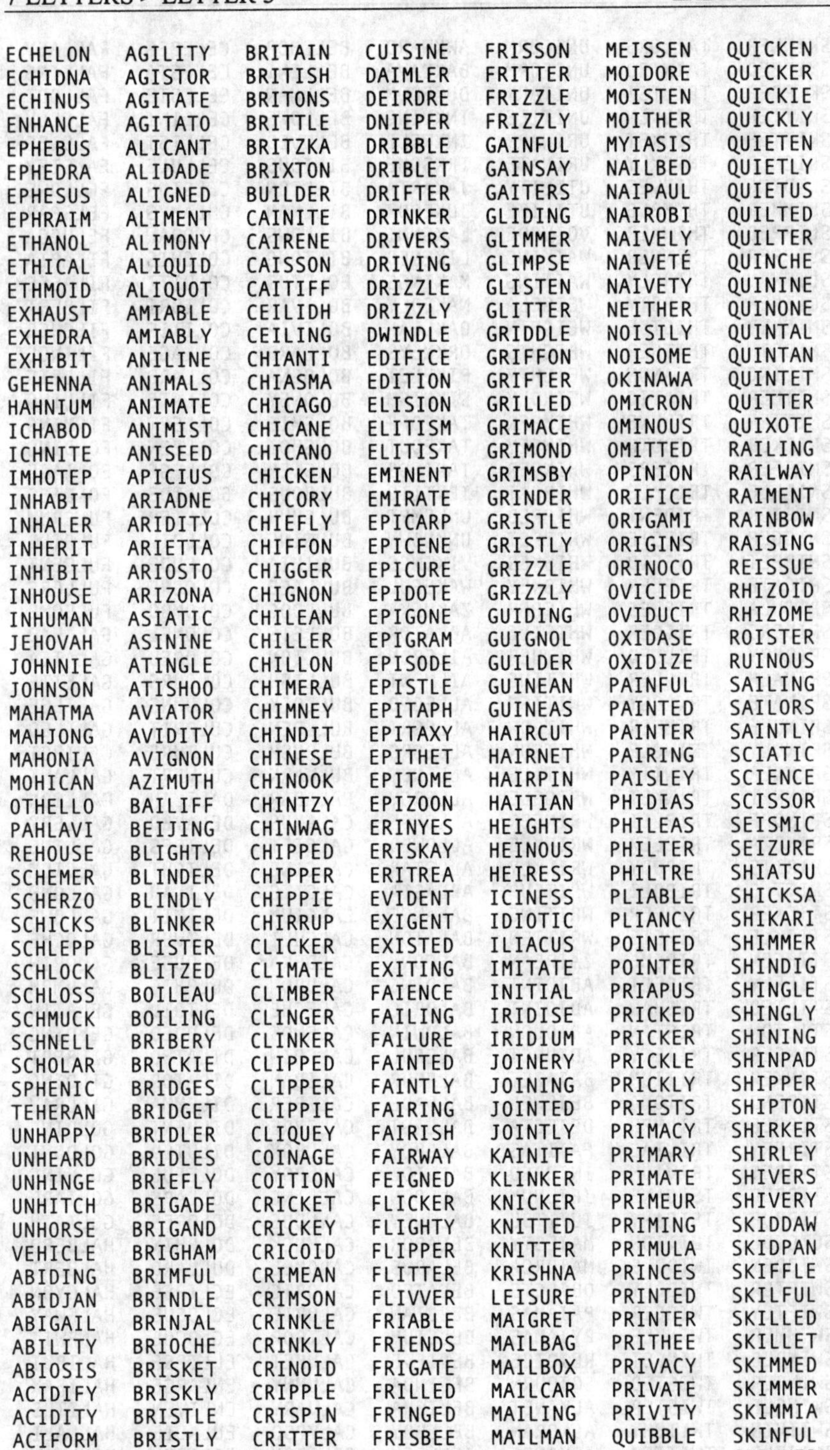

ECHELON
ECHIDNA
ECHINUS
ENHANCE
EPHEBUS
EPHEDRA
EPHESUS
EPHRAIM
ETHANOL
ETHICAL
ETHMOID
EXHAUST
EXHEDRA
EXHIBIT
GEHENNA
HAHNIUM
ICHABOD
ICHNITE
IMHOTEP
INHABIT
INHALER
INHERIT
INHIBIT
INHOUSE
INHUMAN
JEHOVAH
JOHNNIE
JOHNSON
MAHATMA
MAHJONG
MAHONIA
MOHICAN
OTHELLO
PAHLAVI
REHOUSE
SCHEMER
SCHERZO
SCHICKS
SCHLEPP
SCHLOCK
SCHLOSS
SCHMUCK
SCHNELL
SCHOLAR
SPHENIC
TEHERAN
UNHAPPY
UNHEARD
UNHINGE
UNHITCH
UNHORSE
VEHICLE
ABIDING
ABIDJAN
ABIGAIL
ABILITY
ABIOSIS
ACIDIFY
ACIDITY
ACIFORM
ADIPOSE

AGILITY
AGISTOR
AGITATE
AGITATO
ALICANT
ALIDADE
ALIGNED
ALIMENT
ALIMONY
ALIQUID
ALIQUOT
AMIABLE
AMIABLY
ANILINE
ANIMALS
ANIMATE
ANIMIST
ANISEED
APICIUS
ARIADNE
ARIDITY
ARIETTA
ARIOSTO
ARIZONA
ASIATIC
ASININE
ATINGLE
ATISHOO
AVIATOR
AVIDITY
AVIGNON
AZIMUTH
BAILIFF
BEIJING
BLIGHTY
BLINDER
BLINDLY
BLINKER
BLISTER
BLITZED
BOILEAU
BOILING
BRIBERY
BRICKIE
BRIDGES
BRIDGET
BRIDLER
BRIDLES
BRIEFLY
BRIGADE
BRIGAND
BRIGHAM
BRIMFUL
BRINDLE
BRINJAL
BRIOCHE
BRISKET
BRISKLY
BRISTLE
BRISTLY
BRISTOL

BRITAIN
BRITISH
BRITONS
BRITTLE
BRITZKA
BRIXTON
BUILDER
CAINITE
CAIRENE
CAISSON
CAITIFF
CEILIDH
CEILING
CHIANTI
CHIASMA
CHICAGO
CHICANE
CHICANO
CHICKEN
CHICORY
CHIEFLY
CHIFFON
CHIGGER
CHIGNON
CHILEAN
CHILLER
CHILLON
CHIMERA
CHIMNEY
CHINDIT
CHINESE
CHINOOK
CHINTZY
CHINWAG
CHIPPED
CHIPPER
CHIPPIE
CHIRRUP
CLICKER
CLIMATE
CLIMBER
CLINGER
CLINKER
CLIPPED
CLIPPER
CLIPPIE
CLIQUEY
COINAGE
COITION
CRICKET
CRICKEY
CRICOID
CRIMEAN
CRIMSON
CRINKLE
CRINKLY
CRINOID
CRIPPLE
CRISPIN
CRITTER
CUIRASS

CUISINE
DAIMLER
DEIRDRE
DNIEPER
DRIBBLE
DRIBLET
DRIFTER
DRINKER
DRIVERS
DRIVING
DRIZZLE
DRIZZLY
DWINDLE
EDIFICE
EDITION
ELISION
ELITISM
ELITIST
EMINENT
EMIRATE
EPICARP
EPICENE
EPICURE
EPIDOTE
EPIGONE
EPIGRAM
EPISODE
EPISTLE
EPITAPH
EPITAXY
EPITHET
EPITOME
EPIZOON
ERINYES
ERISKAY
ERITREA
EVIDENT
EXIGENT
EXISTED
EXITING
FAIENCE
FAILING
FAILURE
FAINTED
FAINTLY
FAIRING
FAIRISH
FAIRWAY
FEIGNED
FLICKER
FLIGHTY
FLIPPER
FLITTER
FLIVVER
FRIABLE
FRIENDS
FRIGATE
FRILLED
FRINGED
FRISBEE
FRISIAN

FRISSON
FRITTER
FRIZZLE
FRIZZLY
GAINFUL
GAINSAY
GAITERS
GLIDING
GLIMMER
GLIMPSE
GLISTEN
GLITTER
GRIDDLE
GRIFFON
GRIFTER
GRILLED
GRIMACE
GRIMOND
GRIMSBY
GRINDER
GRISTLE
GRISTLY
GRIZZLE
GRIZZLY
GUIDING
GUIGNOL
GUILDER
GUINEAN
GUINEAS
HAIRCUT
HAIRNET
HAIRPIN
HAITIAN
HEIGHTS
HEINOUS
HEIRESS
ICINESS
IDIOTIC
ILIACUS
IMITATE
INITIAL
IRIDISE
IRIDIUM
JOINERY
JOINING
JOINTED
JOINTLY
KAINITE
KLINKER
KNICKER
KNITTED
KNITTER
KRISHNA
LEISURE
MAIGRET
MAILBAG
MAILBOX
MAILCAR
MAILING
MAILMAN
MEIOSIS

MEISSEN
MOIDORE
MOISTEN
MOITHER
MYIASIS
NAILBED
NAIPAUL
NAIROBI
NAIVELY
NAIVETÉ
NAIVETY
NEITHER
NOISILY
NOISOME
OKINAWA
OMICRON
OMINOUS
OMITTED
OPINION
ORIFICE
ORIGAMI
ORIGINS
ORINOCO
OVICIDE
OVIDUCT
OXIDASE
OXIDIZE
PAINFUL
PAINTED
PAINTER
PAIRING
PAISLEY
PHIDIAS
PHILEAS
PHILTER
PHILTRE
PLIABLE
PLIANCY
POINTED
POINTER
PRIAPUS
PRICKED
PRICKER
PRICKLE
PRICKLY
PRIESTS
PRIMACY
PRIMARY
PRIMATE
PRIMEUR
PRIMING
PRIMULA
PRINCES
PRINTED
PRINTER
PRITHEE
PRIVACY
PRIVATE
PRIVITY
QUIBBLE
QUICHUA

QUICKEN
QUICKER
QUICKIE
QUICKLY
QUIETEN
QUIETLY
QUIETUS
QUILTED
QUILTER
QUINCHE
QUININE
QUINONE
QUINTAL
QUINTAN
QUINTET
QUITTER
QUIXOTE
RAILING
RAILWAY
RAIMENT
RAINBOW
RAISING
REISSUE
RHIZOID
RHIZOME
ROISTER
RUINOUS
SAILING
SAILORS
SAINTLY
SCIATIC
SCIENCE
SCISSOR
SEISMIC
SEIZURE
SHIATSU
SHICKSA
SHIKARI
SHIMMER
SHINDIG
SHINGLE
SHINGLY
SHINING
SHINPAD
SHIPPER
SHIPTON
SHIRKER
SHIRLEY
SHIVERS
SHIVERY
SKIDDAW
SKIDPAN
SKIFFLE
SKILFUL
SKILLED
SKILLET
SKIMMED
SKIMMER
SKIMMIA
SKINFUL
SKINNED

SKINNER
SKIPPED
SKIPPER
SKITTER
SKITTLE
SLICKER
SLIDING
SLIMMER
SLIPPED
SLIPPER
SLIPWAY
SLITHER
SMICKLY
SMIDGIN
SMILING
SMITHER
SMITTEN
SNICKER
SNIFFER
SNIFFLE
SNIFTER
SNIGGER
SNIPPET
SPICATE
SPICULA
SPIDERS
SPIDERY
SPINACH
SPINATE
SPINDLE
SPINDLY
SPINNER
SPINNEY
SPINOFF
SPINOZA
SPIRITS
SPITTLE
STICKER
STICKLE
STIFFEN
STIFFLY
STILTED
STILTON
STINGER
STINKER
STIPEND
STIPPLE
STIRFRY
STIRPES
STIRRED
STIRRUP
SUICIDE
SWIDDEN
SWIFTER
SWIFTLY
SWIMMER
SWINDLE
SWINGER
SWINGLE
SWITHIN
SWIZZLE
TAILORS
TAINTED
TBILISI
THICKEN
THICKET
THICKLY
THIEVES
THIMBLE
THINKER
THINNER
THIRDLY
THIRSTY
THISTLE
THITHER
TRIANON
TRIATIC
TRIBUNE
TRIBUTE
TRICEPS
TRICKLE
TRIDENT
TRIESTE
TRIFFID
TRIFLER
TRIFLES
TRIGGER
TRILLED
TRILLER
TRILOGY
TRIMMER
TRINGLE
TRINITY
TRINKET
TRIPLET
TRIPLEX
TRIPODY
TRIPOLI
TRIPPER
TRIPSIS
TRIREME
TRISECT
TRISHAW
TRISTAN
TRITELY
TRITIUM
TRITOMA
TRIUMPH
TRIVIAL
TRIVIUM
TSIGANE
TSIGANY
TUITION
TWIDDLE
TWIDDLY
TWIGGER
TWINKLE
TWINSET
TWISTED
TWISTER
TWITCHY
TWITTER
UNICORN
UNIFORM
UNITARY
UNITIES
URINARY
URINATE
UTILITY
UTILIZE
VOIVODE
WAILING
WAITING
WEIGELA
WEIGHIN
WEIGHTS
WEIGHTY
WEIRDLY
WHIMPER
WHIMSEY
WHINGER
WHIPCAT
WHIPPED
WHIPPET
WHISKER
WHISKEY
WHISPER
WHISTLE
WHITHER
WHITING
WHITISH
WHITLOW
WHITSUN
WHITTLE
WRIGGLE
WRINGER
WRINKLE
WRINKLY
WRITEUP
WRITING
WRITTEN
ZAIREAN
ABJOINT
ADJOINT
ADJOURN
ADJUNCT
BAJAZET
BEJEWEL
DEJECTA
FAJITAS
INJURED
JEJUNUM
JUJITSU
MAJESTY
MAJORCA
OBJECTS
PAJAMAS
PYJAMAS
REJOICE
SOJOURN
ALKANET
ALKORAN
ASKANCE
AWKWARD
BAKLAVA
DUKEDOM
INKLING
INKWELL
IRKSOME
JAKARTA
JUKEBOX
LAKSHMI
LIKENED
MAKINGS
NAKEDLY
OAKLEAF
ORKNEYS
PIKELET
SIKHISM
TAKEOFF
TAKEOUT
TAKINGS
TEKTITE
UNKEMPT
UNKNOWN
VIKINGS
WAKEFUL
ZAKUSKA
ABLATOR
AILERON
AILMENT
ALLEGED
ALLEGRI
ALLEGRO
ALLENBY
ALLERGY
ALLONGE
ALLOWED
ALLSTAR
APLASIA
BALANCE
BALATON
BALCONY
BALDING
BALDRIC
BALDWIN
BALEFUL
BALFOUR
BALLADE
BALLAST
BALLBOY
BALLIOL
BALLOON
BALONEY
BELABOR
BELARUS
BELATED
BELGIAN
BELGIUM
BELIEVE
BELINDA
BELISHA
BELLBOY
BELLEEK
BELLHOP
BELLINI
BELLMAN
BELLOWS
BELOVED
BILIOUS
BILLION
BILLMAN
BILLOWS
BILTONG
BOLETUS
BOLIVAR
BOLIVIA
BOLLARD
BOLOGNA
BOLONEY
BOLSHIE
BOLSHOI
BOLSTER
BULBOUS
BULGHUR
BULGING
BULIMIA
BULLACE
BULLDOG
BULLETS
BULLION
BULLISH
BULLOCK
BULLPEN
BULRUSH
BULWARK
CALABAR
CALAMUS
CALCIFY
CALCINE
CALCITE
CALCIUM
CALCULI
CALDERA
CALDRON
CALECHE
CALENDS
CALEPIN
CALIBAN
CALIBER
CALIBRE
CALLBOX
CALLBOY
CALLING
CALLOUS
CALMUCK
CALOMEL
CALORIC
CALORIE
CALTROP
CALUMET
CALUMNY
CALVARY
CALYPSO
CELADON
CELEBES
CELESTA
CELESTE
CELLINI
CELLIST
CELLULE
CELSIUS
CHLAMYS
CHLORAL
COLCHIS
COLDITZ
COLIBRI
COLITIS
COLLAGE
COLLARD
COLLATE
COLLECT
COLLEEN
COLLEGE
COLLIDE
COLLIER
COLLOID
COLLUDE
COLOGNE
COLOMBO
COLONEL
COLORED
COLOURS
COLUMNS
CULPRIT
CULTURE
CULVERT
DALILAH
DELAYED
DELIBES
DELIGHT
DELILAH
DELIMIT
DELIVER
DELOUSE
DELPHIC
DELTOID
DELUDED
DILATED
DILATOR
DILEMMA
DILUENT
DILUTED
DOLEFUL
DOLLARS
DOLORES
DOLPHIN
DULLARD
ECLIPSE
ECLOGUE
EGLOGUE
ELLIPSE
ENLARGE
ENLIVEN
EULALIE
FALAFEL
FALLACY
FALLING
FALLOUT
FALSELY
FALSIES
FALSIFY
FELLOWS
FELSPAR
FELUCCA
FILARIA
FILASSE
FILBERT
FILCHER
FILINGS
FILLETS
FILLING
FILMING
FOLDING
FOLIAGE
FOLLIES
FULCRUM
FULFILL
FULGENT
FULLERS
FULSOME
GALAHAD
GALATEA
GALETTE
GALILEE
GALILEO
GALIPOT
GALLANT
GALLEON
GALLERY
GALLING
GALLIUM
GALLONS
GALLOWS
GALOCHE
GALOPIN
GALUMPH
GELATIN
GELDING
GILBERT
GILDING
GILLRAY
GOLDING
GOLDONI
GOLFING
GOLIARD
GOLIATH
HALBERD
HALBERT
HALCYON
HALFWAY
HALFWIT
HALIBUT
HALIFAX
HALITUS
HALLALI
HALLWAY

HALOGEN
HALTING
HALYARD
HELICAL
HELICON
HELIPAD
HELLCAT
HELLENE
HELLION
HELLISH
HELLUVA
HELPFUL
HELPING
HILDING
HILLMAN
HILLMEN
HILLOCK
HILLTOP
HOLBEIN
HOLDALL
HOLDING
HOLIDAY
HOLLAND
HOLSTER
HULKING
ILLBRED
ILLEGAL
ILLICIT
ILLNESS
ISLAMIC
ISLANDS
JELLABA
JELLIED
JOLLITY
KALENDS
KALMUCK
KILDARE
KILLICK
KILLING
KILLJOY
KILVERT
KOLKHOZ
LALIQUE
LALLANS
LILTING
LOLLARD
LULLABY
MALACCA
MALAISE
MALARIA
MALAYAN
MALEFIC
MALLARD
MALLEUS
MALLING
MALMSEY
MALTASE
MALTESE
MALTHUS
MELANIN
MELLITE
MELODIC
MELROSE
MELTING
MILEAGE
MILFOIL
MILITIA
MILKING
MILKMAN
MILKSOP
MILLAIS
MILLING
MILLION
MOLDING
MOLIÈRE
MOLLIFY
MOLLUSC
MOLOTOV
MOLUCCA
MULATTO
MULLEIN
MULLION
NULLIFY
NULLITY
OBLIGED
OBLIGOR
OBLIQUE
OBLOQUY
OILCAKE
OILSKIN
ORLANDO
ORLEANS
PALADIN
PALATAL
PALAVER
PALERMO
PALETTE
PALFREY
PALINGS
PALISSY
PALLIUM
PALMATE
PALMIST
PALMYRA
PALOMAR
PALOOKA
PALPATE
PALSIED
PALUDAL
PELAGIC
PELICAN
PELORIA
PELORUS
PELTING
PILATUS
PILCHER
PILGRIM
PILLAGE
PILLBOX
PILLION
PILLORY
POLARIS
POLEAXE
POLECAT
POLEMIC
POLENTA
POLITIC
POLIZEI
POLLACK
POLLARD
POLLING
POLLUTE
POLONIE
POLYGON
POLYMER
POLYPOD
POLYPUS
PULLMAN
PULSATE
PULSING
PYLORUS
RALEIGH
RELAPSE
RELATED
RELAXED
RELAYER
RELEASE
RELIANT
RELICTS
RELIEVE
ROLLERS
ROLLICK
ROLLING
ROLLMOP
SALABLE
SALADIN
SALAMIS
SALAZAR
SALERMO
SALIENT
SALIERI
SALIQUE
SALLUST
SALPINX
SALSIFY
SALTATE
SALTING
SALTIRE
SALTPAN
SALVAGE
SCLERAL
SELFISH
SELKIRK
SELLERS
SELLING
SELLOFF
SELLOUT
SELTZER
SELVAGE
SILENCE
SILESIA
SILICON
SILVERY
SOLANUM
SOLDIER
SOLICIT
SOLIDLY
SOLIDUS
SOLOIST
SOLOMON
SOLUBLE
SOLVENT
SPLASHY
SPLAYED
SPLICED
SPLICER
SPLODGE
SPLOTCH
SPLURGE
SULFATE
SULKILY
SULLAGE
SULPHUR
SULTANA
TALIPES
TALIPOT
TALKING
TALLBOY
TALOOKA
TELFORD
TELLING
TELSTAR
TILAPIA
TILBURY
TILLAGE
TOLKIEN
TOLLMAN
TOLSTOY
TOLUENE
TYLOSIS
UNLADEN
UNLATCH
UNLEASH
UNLINED
UNLOOSE
UNLOVED
UNLUCKY
VALENCE
VALENCY
VALIANT
VELOURS
VELVETY
VILLAGE
VILLAIN
VILLEIN
VILNIUS
VOLANTE
VOLAPUK
VOLCANO
VOLTAGE
VOLTAIC
VOLUBLE
VOLUBLY
VULGATE
VULPINE
VULTURE
WALKING
WALKMAN
WALKOUT
WALKWAY
WALLABY
WALLACE
WALLIES
WALLOON
WALPOLE
WALTZER
WELCOME
WELDING
WELFARE
WELLIES
WELLOFF
WILDCAT
WILFRED
WILLIAM
WILLIES
WILLING
WILLOWY
WOLFISH
WOLFRAM
YELLOWS
ZILLION
ADMIRAL
ADMIRED
ADMIRER
AIMLESS
ALMACKS
ALMANAC
ALMONER
AMMETER
AMMONAL
AMMONIA
ARMBAND
ARMHOLE
ARMORED
ARMORIC
ARMOURY
ARMREST
BAMBINO
BEMUSED
BOMBARD
BOMBAST
BOMBING
BUMBOAT
BUMMALO
BUMPKIN
CAMBIUM
CAMBRAI
CAMBRIC
CAMELOT
CAMERON
CAMILLA
CAMORRA
CAMPANA
CAMPARI
CAMPHOR
CAMPING
CAMPION
CEMBALO
CIMABUE
COMBINE
COMBING
COMFORT
COMFREY
COMICAL
COMMAND
COMMEND
COMMENT
COMMODE
COMMODO
COMMONS
COMMUNE
COMMUTE
COMPACT
COMPANY
COMPARE
COMPASS
COMPERE
COMPETE
COMPILE
COMPLEX
COMPORT
COMPOSE
COMPOST
COMPOTE
COMPUTE
COMRADE
CUMBRIA
CUMSHAW
CUMULUS
CYMBALS
DAMAGED
DAMAGES
DAMNING
DAMOSEL
DAMPIER
DAMPING
DEMERGE
DEMERIT
DEMESNE
DEMETER
DEMIGOD
DEMONIC
DEMOTIC
DIMNESS
DIMPLED
DOMAINE
DOMINGO
DOMINIC
DUMPISH
FEMORAL
FIMBRIA
FUMETTE
GAMBIAN
GAMBLER
GAMBOGE
GAMELAN
GEMMATE
GIMBALS
GIMBLET
GIMMICK
GOMBEEN
GOMORRA
GUMBOIL
GUMBOOT
GUMDROP
GUMSHOE
GYMNAST
GYMSLIP
HAMMOCK
HAMSTER
HEMLINE
HEMLOCK
HIMSELF
HOMBURG
HOMERIC
HOMINID
HOMONYM
HUMANLY
HUMBLES
HUMDRUM
HUMERUS
HUMIDOR
HUMMING
HUMMOCK
IAMBIST
IMMENSE
IMMERGE
IMMERSE
IMMORAL
ISMAILI
JAMAICA
JAMESON
JAMMING
JAMPANI
JIMJAMS
JUMBLED
JUMBLES
JUMPING
KAMERAD
KAMPALA
KAMPONG
KUMQUAT
LAMAISM
LAMAIST
LAMBADA
LAMBAST
LAMBENT
LAMBERT
LAMBETH
LAMBING
LAMELLA
LAMPOON
LAMPREY
LEMMATA
LEMMING
LEMPIRA
LIMINAL

LIMITED
LIMITER
LIMPOPO
LUMBAGO
LUMPISH
LUMPKIN
LYMNAEA
MAMILLA
MAMMARY
MAMMOTH
MEMBERS
MEMENTO
MEMOIRS
MIMICRY
MIMULUS
MOMBASA
MOMENTS
MUMMERS
MUMMERY
MUMMIFY
NAMIBIA
NEMESIA
NEMESIS
NEMORAL
NOMADIC
NOMBRIL
NOMINAL
NOMINEE
NUMBERS
NUMBLES
NUMERAL
NUMERIC
NUMMARY
NYMPHET
ONMIBUS
OSMANLI
OSMOSIS
PIMENTO
PIMPING
POMEROL
POMEROY
POMFRET
POMMARD
POMPEII
POMPOON
POMPOUS
PUMPKIN
RAMADAN
RAMBLER
RAMEKIN
RAMESES
RAMPAGE
RAMPANT
RAMPART
RAMULUS
REMAINS
REMARRY
REMBLAI
REMNANT
REMODEL
REMORSE
REMOULD
REMOUNT
REMOVAL
REMOVED
REMOVER
RIMLESS
ROMAINE
ROMANCE
ROMANIA
ROMANOV
ROMANZA
ROMPERS
RUMBLER
RUMMAGE
RUMORED
RUMPLED
RUMPOLE
SAMARIA
SAMBUCA
SAMISEN
SAMNITE
SAMOOSA
SAMOVAR
SAMOYED
SAMPLER
SAMURAI
SEMINAL
SEMINAR
SEMITIC
SHMOOZE
SIMENON
SIMILAR
SIMPKIN
SIMPLER
SIMPLEX
SIMPLON
SIMPSON
SOMALIA
SOMEHOW
SOMEONE
SUMATRA
SUMMARY
SUMMERY
SUMMING
SUMMONS
SYMPTOM
TAMARIN
TAMBOUR
TAMESIS
TAMMANY
TAMPICO
TAMPION
TEMPERA
TEMPEST
TEMPLAR
TEMPLET
TEMPTER
TEMPURA
TIMBALE
TIMBERS
TIMBREL
TIMELAG
TIMIDLY
TIMOTHY
TIMPANI
TOMBOLA
TOMFOOL
TOMPION
TUMBLER
TUMBREL
TUMBRIL
TUMULUS
TYMPANO
TYMPANY
UNMIXED
UNMOVED
VAMOOSE
VAMPIRE
WIMPISH
WOMANLY
XIMENES
ZAMBESI
ZAMBIAN
ZAMORIN
ZEMSTVO
ZYMOSIS
ZYMURGY
AINTREE
AMNESIA
AMNESTY
ANNELID
ANNOYED
ANNUITY
ANNULAR
ANNULET
ANNULUS
BANANAS
BANBURY
BANDAGE
BANDAID
BANDBOX
BANDEAU
BANGING
BANGKOK
BANKING
BANKSIA
BANNOCK
BANQUET
BANSHEE
BENARES
BENCHER
BENDING
BENEATH
BENEFIT
BENGALI
BENISON
BENNETT
BENTHAM
BENTHOS
BENZENE
BENZINE
BENZOIN
BINDERY
BINDING
BONANZA
BONDAGE
BONDMAN
BONFIRE
BONKERS
BONNARD
BUNDOOK
BUNGLER
BUNTING
CANASTA
CANDACE
CANDELA
CANDIDA
CANDIDE
CANDIED
CANDOUR
CANELLA
CANIDAE
CANNERY
CANNILY
CANNING
CANNOCK
CANNULA
CANONRY
CANTATA
CANTEEN
CANTHUS
CANTRIP
CANTUAR
CANVASS
CENACLE
CENSURE
CENTAUR
CENTAVO
CENTRAL
CENTRED
CENTRUM
CENTURY
CINDERS
CINEMAS
CINEREA
CONAKRY
CONCAVE
CONCEAL
CONCEDE
CONCEIT
CONCEPT
CONCERN
CONCERT
CONCISE
CONCOCT
CONCORD
CONCUSS
CONDEMN
CONDOLE
CONDONE
CONDUCT
CONDUIT
CONFESS
CONFIDE
CONFINE
CONFIRM
CONFORM
CONFUSE
CONGEAL
CONICAL
CONIFER
CONJOIN
CONJURE
CONNATE
CONNECT
CONNIVE
CONNOTE
CONQUER
CONSENT
CONSIGN
CONSIST
CONSOLE
CONSOLS
CONSORT
CONSULT
CONSUME
CONTACT
CONTAIN
CONTEMN
CONTEND
CONTENT
CONTEST
CONTEXT
CONTORT
CONTOUR
CONTROL
CONVENE
CONVENT
CONVERT
CONVICT
CONVOKE
CUNNING
CYNICAL
CYNTHIA
DANCING
DANTEAN
DENDRON
DENIZEN
DENMARK
DENSELY
DENSITY
DENTINE
DENTIST
DENTURE
DINETTE
DINGBAT
DINMONT
DONEGAL
DONNISH
DUNCIAD
DUNEDIN
DUNGEON
DUNKIRK
DUNNAGE
DUNNOCK
DUNSTAN
DYNAMIC
DYNASTY
ENNOBLE
FANATIC
FANCIED
FANCIER
FANFARE
FANGLED
FANTAIL
FANTASY
FANZINE
FENCING
FENELON
FENLAND
FINAGLE
FINALLY
FINANCE
FINDING
FINESSE
FINGERS
FINICAL
FINICKY
FINLAND
FINNISH
FONDANT
FUNCHAL
FUNDING
FUNERAL
FUNFAIR
FUNGOID
FUNGOUS
FUNNILY
GANELON
GANGWAY
GENERAL
GENERIC
GENESIS
GENETIC
GENISTA
GENITAL
GENOESE
GENTEEL
GENTIAN
GENTILE
GENUINE
GINGHAM
GINSENG
GONDOLA
GUNBOAT
GUNFIRE
GUNNERA
GUNNERY
GUNPLAY
GUNROOM
GUNSHOT
GUNWALE
HANDBAG
HANDFUL
HANDGUN
HANDILY
HANDLED
HANDLER
HANDOUT
HANDSAW
HANDSEL
HANDSET
HANGDOG
HANGING
HANGMAN
HANGMEN
HANGOUT
HANOVER
HANSARD
HENBANE
HENGIST
HENNAED
HENPECK
HINDLEG
HONESTY
HONEYED
HONITON
HONOURS
HUNCHED
HUNDRED
HUNGARY
HUNKERS
HUNTING
IGNEOUS
IGNOBLE
IGNORED
INNARDS
INNERVE
INNINGS
IONESCO
JANITOR
JANKERS
JANUARY
JENKINS
JONQUIL
JUNIPER
KENNEDY
KENNELS
KENNING
KENOSIS
KENOTIC
KENTISH
KINDRED
KINESIS
KINETIC
KINGCUP
KINGDOM
KINGLET
KINGPIN
KINSHIP
KINSMAN
KINTYRE
KONTIKI
LANCERS
LANCING
LANDING

LANGLEY
LANGTON
LANGUID
LANGUOR
LANOLIN
LANTANA
LANTERN
LANYARD
LENDING
LENGTHY
LENIENT
LENTIGO
LENTILS
LINACRE
LINCOLN
LINCTUS
LINDANE
LINEAGE
LINEMAN
LINGUAL
LININGS
LINKAGE
LINKING
LINKMAN
LINNEAN
LINOCUT
LINSANG
LINSEED
LONGBOW
LONGING
LUNATIC
LYNCHET
MANACLE
MANAGER
MANAGUA
MANATEE
MANDALA
MANDATE
MANDIOC
MANGOLD
MANHOLE
MANHOOD
MANHUNT
MANIHOC
MANIKIN
MANILLA
MANITOU
MANKIND
MANMADE
MANNERS
MANNING
MANNISH
MANSARD
MANSION
MANSIZE
MANTUAN
MANUMIT
MANXMAN
MENDING
MENFOLK
MENORAH
MENTHOL
MENTION
MENUHIN
MINARET
MINCING
MINDFUL
MINDSET
MINERAL
MINERVA
MINIBUS
MINICAB
MINIMAL
MINIMAX
MINIMUM
MINORCA
MINSTER
MINUEND
MINUTED
MINUTES
MINUTIA
MONARCH
MONEYED
MONGREL
MONILIA
MONITOR
MONKISH
MONOCLE
MONOLOG
MONOPLY
MONSOON
MONSTER
MONTAGE
MONTAGU
MONTANA
MONTANT
MONTERO
MONTHLY
MUNDANE
MUNSTER
MUNTJAC
NANKEEN
NINEPIN
NINEVEH
NONPLUS
NONSTOP
NONSUCH
NONSUIT
NUNLIKE
NUNNERY
OMNIBUS
PANACEA
PANACHE
PANCAKE
PANCRAS
PANDORA
PANGAEA
PANGRAM
PANICKY
PANICLE
PANNAGE
PANNIER
PANNOSE
PANOPLY
PANTHER
PANTIES
PANTILE
PANURGE
PENALTY
PENANCE
PENATES
PENDANT
PENDING
PENGUIN
PENNANT
PENNATE
PENNINE
PENSILE
PENSION
PENSIVE
PENTANE
PENTODE
PENTOSE
PINBALL
PINCERS
PINCHED
PINETUM
PINFOLD
PINHEAD
PINHOLE
PINNACE
PINNULA
PINTADO
PINTAIL
PONIARD
PONTIAC
PONTIFF
PONTINE
PONTOON
PUNCHED
PUNCHER
PUNGENT
PUNJABI
PUNSTER
PUNTING
RANCHER
RANCOUR
RANGOON
RANIDAE
RANKING
RANSACK
RANTING
RENEGUE
RENEWAL
RINGERS
RINGGIT
RINGING
RINGLET
RONDEAU
RONSARD
RONTGEN
RUNAWAY
RUNCORN
RUNDOWN
RUNNERS
RUNNING
RUNNION
SANCTUM
SANCTUS
SANDALS
SANDBAG
SANDBOX
SANDBOY
SANDMAN
SANDOWN
SANDPIT
SANGRIA
SENATOR
SENDOFF
SENECIO
SENEGAL
SENSATE
SENSORY
SENSUAL
SINATRA
SINCERE
SINDBAD
SINGING
SINGLES
SINGLET
SINHALA
SINKING
SINUATE
SINUOUS
SONDAGE
SUNBEAM
SUNBURN
SUNDECK
SUNDIAL
SUNDOWN
SUNLAMP
SUNLESS
SUNNILY
SUNNITE
SUNRISE
SUNROOF
SUNSPOT
SUNTRAP
SYNAPSE
SYNAXIS
SYNCOPE
SYNERGY
SYNONYM
SYNOVIA
TANAGER
TANAGRA
TANCRED
TANGENT
TANGIER
TANGLED
TANKARD
TANNATE
TANNERY
TANNING
TANTARA
TANTIVY
TANTRUM
TENABLE
TENANCY
TENANTS
TENDRIL
TENFOLD
TENNIEL
TENSELY
TENSILE
TENSING
TENSION
TENUOUS
TINFOIL
TINGLER
TINTACK
TINTERN
TONGUES
TONIGHT
TONNAGE
TONNEAU
TONNISH
TONSURE
TONTINE
TUNABLE
TUNEFUL
TUNISIA
TYNWALD
UNNAMED
UNNERVE
VANDALS
VANDYKE
VANESSA
VANILLA
VANITAS
VANTAGE
VANUATU
VENDING
VENDOME
VENERER
VENISON
VENTOSE
VENTRAL
VENTURE
VINASSE
VINCENT
VINEGAR
VINTAGE
VINTNER
WANGLER
WANTING
WENDELL
WENLOCK
WINDBAG
WINDING
WINDOWS
WINDROW
WINDSOR
WINNING
WINNOCK
WINSOME
WINSTON
WONDERS
XANTHOS
XENOPUS
YANGTSE
YONKERS
ZINGARO
ABOLISH
ABOUKIR
ABOULIA
ACOLYTE
ACONITE
ADONAIS
ADOPTED
ADORING
ADORNED
AEOLIAN
AGONIST
AGONIZE
AMOEBIC
AMONGST
AMORIST
AMORITE
AMOROSO
AMOROUS
ANODIZE
ANODYNE
ANOMALY
ANOSMIA
ANOTHER
APOCOPE
APOGEAN
APOLOGY
APOSTLE
AROUSAL
ASOCIAL
ATOMIST
ATOMIZE
AVOCADO
AVOIDER
AXOLOTL
BEOWULF
BIOLOGY
BIOMASS
BLOATED
BLOATER
BLOCKED
BLOCKER
BLOOMER
BLOOPER
BLOSSOM
BLOTCHY
BLOTTER
BLOUSON
BLOWFLY
BLOWOUT
BOOKIES
BOOKING
BOOKISH
BOOKLET
BOOKMAN
BOOLEAN
BOOMING
BOORISH
BOOSTER
BOOTLEG
BROADEN
BROADLY
BROCADE
BROILER
BROKERS
BROMIDE
BROMINE
BRONCHI
BRONZED
BROTHEL
BROTHER
BROUGHT
BROWNED
BROWNIE
BROWSER
BUOYANT
CHOCTAW
CHOKING
CHOLERA
CHOOKIE
CHOPINE
CHOPPER
CHORALE
CHORDAE
CHORION
CHORIZO
CHOROID
CHORTLE
CHOWDER
CLOBBER
CLOISON
CLOSELY
CLOSEUP
CLOSING
CLOSURE
CLOTHED
CLOTHES
CLOTURE
CLOUDED
CLOYING
COOKERY
COOKING
COOLANT
COOLING
CROAKER
CROATIA
CROCHET
CROCKET
CROESUS
CROFTER
CROOKED
CROONER
CROPPED
CROPPER
CROQUET

CROQUIS
CROSIER
CROSSED
CROSSLY
CROUTON
CROWBAR
CROWDED
CROWING
CROZIER
DIOCESE
DIOPTER
DIOPTRE
DIORAMA
DIORITE
DIOXIDE
DOODLER
DOORKEY
DOORMAN
DOORMAT
DOORWAY
DROPLET
DROPOUT
DROPPER
DROSHKY
DROUGHT
DUOPOLY
DVORNIK
EBONITE
ECOLOGY
ECONOMY
EGOTISM
EGOTIST
ELOGIUM
EMOTION
EMOTIVE
ERODIUM
EROSION
EROTICA
ETONIAN
EXOGAMY
FLOATER
FLODDEN
FLOGGER
FLOODED
FLOOZIE
FLORIDA
FLORIST
FLOTSAM
FLOUNCE
FLOWERS
FLOWERY
FLOWING
FOOLISH
FOOTAGE
FOOTING
FOOTMAN
FOOTPAD
FOOTSIE
FROEBEL
FROGMAN
FRONTAL

FROSTED
FROWSTY
GEODESY
GEOLOGY
GEORDIE
GEORGIA
GEORGIC
GHOSTLY
GLOBULE
GLORIFY
GLOTTAL
GLOTTIS
GLOWING
GNOCCHI
GNOSTIC
GOODBYE
GOODIES
GOODISH
GOODMAN
GOODWIN
GOOLIES
GROCERS
GROCERY
GROCKLE
GROGRAM
GROINED
GROLIER
GROMMET
GROOVED
GROPIUS
GROSSLY
GROTIUS
GROUCHO
GROUCHY
GROUNDS
GROUPER
GROUPIE
GROUSER
GROWING
GROWLER
GROWNUP
HOODLUM
IDOLIZE
IPOMOEA
IRONING
ISOBASE
ISODORE
ISOGRAM
ISOHYET
ISOLATE
ISOMERE
ISOTONE
ISOTOPE
IVORIAN
IVORIEN
KNOBBLE
KNOBBLY
KNOCKER
KNOTTED
KNOWALL
KNOWHOW

KNOWING
LAOCOON
LAOTIAN
LEONARD
LEONINE
LEOPARD
LEOPOLD
LEOTARD
LIONESS
LIONIZE
LOOKING
LOOKOUT
LOOMING
LOOSELY
LOOTING
MIOCENE
MOODILY
MOONING
MOONLIT
MOORHEN
MOORING
MOORISH
NEOLITH
NIOBEAN
NIOBIUM
NOODLES
NOOLOGY
NOONDAY
ODONTIC
ODORANT
ODOROUS
OLOROSO
OPOSSUM
ORONTES
OROTUND
OXONIAN
PEONAGE
PHOEBUS
PHOENIX
PHONEIN
PHONEME
PHONICS
PIONEER
PIOUSLY
PLODDER
PLOSIVE
PLOTTER
PLOWMAN
POOFTER
POOHBAH
PROBATE
PROBITY
PROBLEM
PROCEED
PROCESS
PROCTOR
PROCURE
PRODIGY
PRODUCE
PRODUCT
PROFANE

PROFESS
PROFFER
PROFILE
PROFITS
PROFUSE
PROGENY
PROGRAM
PROJECT
PROLONG
PROMISE
PROMOTE
PRONAOS
PRONATE
PRONGED
PRONOUN
PROPANE
PROPEND
PROPHET
PROPOSE
PROSAIC
PROSODY
PROSPER
PROTEAN
PROTECT
PROTEGE
PROTEIN
PROTEST
PROTEUS
PROUDER
PROUDIE
PROUDLY
PROVERB
PROVIDE
PROVING
PROVISO
PROVOKE
PROVOST
PROWESS
PROWLER
PROXIMO
PTOLEMY
QUONDAM
QUONSET
QUORATE
REOCCUR
RHODIAN
RHODIUM
RHOMBUS
RHONDDA
RIOTERS
RIOTING
RIOTOUS
ROOFING
ROOFTOP
ROOKERY
ROOKISH
ROOSTER
ROOTING
SCOFFER
SCOLLOP
SCOOTER

SCORING
SCORPIO
SCOTTIE
SCOURER
SCOURGE
SCOWDER
SHOCKED
SHOCKER
SHOOTER
SHOPPER
SHORTEN
SHORTLY
SHOTGUN
SHOUTER
SHOWBIZ
SHOWERS
SHOWERY
SHOWILY
SHOWING
SHOWMAN
SHOWOFF
SLOBBER
SLOGGER
SLOPING
SLOSHED
SLOTTED
SLOVENE
SLOWING
SMOKING
SMOLDER
SMOOTHE
SMOTHER
SNOOKER
SNOOPER
SNORING
SNORKEL
SNORTER
SNORTLE
SNOWDON
SNOWMAN
SPOILED
SPOILER
SPONDEE
SPONDYL
SPONGER
SPONSON
SPONSOR
SPOONER
SPORRAN
SPOTTED
SPOTTER
SPOUSAL
STOICAL
STOLLEN
STOMACH
STONILY
STONKER
STOPGAP
STOPPED
STOPPER
STORAGE

STORIED
STORIES
STOUTLY
SWOLLEN
THOMISM
THOMIST
THOMSON
THOREAU
THORIUM
THOUGHT
TOOLBOX
TOOLING
TOOTHED
TOOTSIE
TROCHEE
TROCHUS
TRODDEN
TROILUS
TROLLEY
TROLLOP
TROOPER
TROPHIC
TROPICS
TROPISM
TROTSKY
TROTTER
TROUBLE
TROUNCE
TROUPER
TROUSER
TWOFOLD
TWOSOME
TWOSTEP
TWOTIME
UGOLINO
UNOWNED
UROLITH
UTOPIAN
UXORIAL
VIOLATE
VIOLENT
WHOEVER
WHOOPEE
WHOOPER
WHOPPER
WOODCUT
WOODMAN
WOOLLEN
WOOMERA
WOOSTER
WRONGLY
WROUGHT
WYOMING
YAOUNDE
ZEOLITE
ZIONIST
ZOOLITE
ZOOLOGY
ZOOTOMY
ALPHEUS
AMPHORA

AMPLIFY
AMPOULE
AMPULLA
APPARAT
APPAREL
APPEASE
APPLAUD
APPLIED
APPOINT
APPOSED
APPRIZE
APPROVE
ASPASIA
ASPERGE
ASPHALT
ASPIRIN
BAPTISM
BAPTIST
BAPTIZE
BIPLANE
CAPABLE
CAPABLY
CAPELLA
CAPITAL
CAPITOL
CAPORAL
CAPRICE
CAPSIZE
CAPSTAN
CAPSULE
CAPTAIN
CAPTION
CAPTIVE
CAPTURE
COPILOT
COPIOUS
COPLAND
COPPERS
COPPICE
COPYCAT
COPYING
COPYIST
CYPRESS
CYPRIOT
DAPHNID
DAPHNIS
DAPPLED
DEPLETE
DEPLORE
DEPOSIT
DEPRAVE
DEPRESS
DEPRIVE
DIPLOCK
DIPLOMA
DIPOLAR
DIPTERA
DIPTYCH
DOPPLER
EMPANEL
EMPATHY

EMPEROR
EMPIRIC
EMPLOYS
EMPOWER
EMPRESS
EMPYEMA
ENPRINT
ESPARTO
ESPOUSE
EUPEPSY
EUPHONY
EXPANSE
EXPENSE
EXPIATE
EXPIRED
EXPLAIN
EXPLODE
EXPLOIT
EXPLORE
EXPOSED
EXPOUND
EXPRESS
EXPUNGE
FOPPISH
HAPLESS
HAPORTH
HAPPILY
HEPARIN
HEPATIC
HEPTANE
HIPSTER
HOPEFUL
HOPKINS
HOPLITE
HOPPING
HOPSACK
HYPOGEA
IMPASSE
IMPASTO
IMPAVID
IMPEACH
IMPERIL
IMPETUS
IMPIETY
IMPINGE
IMPIOUS
IMPLANT
IMPLIED
IMPLODE
IMPLORE
IMPOUND
IMPRESS
IMPREST
IMPRINT
IMPROVE
IMPULSE
JAPLISH
JUPITER
KIPLING
KIPPERS
LAPPING
LAPSANG
LAPUTAN
LAPWING
LEPANTO
LEPROSY
LEPROUS
LIPREAD
MAPPING
MOPPING
NAPHTHA
NAPPING
NEPTUNE
NIPPERS
NUPTIAL
OMPHALE
OPPOSED
OPPRESS
ORPHEAN
ORPHEUS
ORPHISM
ORPHREY
PAPILLA
PAPOOSE
PAPRIKA
PAPYRUS
PEPPERS
PEPPERY
PEPSINE
PIPETTE
POPCORN
POPEYED
POPOVER
POPPING
POPULAR
POPULUS
RAPHAEL
RAPIDLY
RAPPORT
RAPTURE
REPAINT
REPAIRS
REPLACE
REPLANT
REPLETE
REPLICA
REPOSAL
REPRESS
REPRINT
REPROOF
REPROVE
REPTILE
REPULSE
REPUTED
RIPCORD
RIPOSTE
RIPPING
RUPTURE
SAPIENS
SAPIENT
SAPLING
SAPONIN
SAPPERS
SAPPHIC
SAPROBE
SAPWOOD
SEPPUKU
SIPPING
SOPHISM
SOPHIST
SOPPING
SOPRANO
SOPWITH
SUPPORT
SUPPOSE
SUPREME
SUPREMO
TAPIOCA
TAPLASH
TAPPICE
TAPPING
TAPROOT
TAPSTER
TIPCART
TIPPING
TIPPLER
TIPSILY
TIPSTER
TOPCOAT
TOPIARY
TOPICAL
TOPKAPI
TOPKNOT
TOPLESS
TOPMAST
TOPMOST
TOPPING
TOPSIDE
TOPSOIL
TYPHOID
TYPHOON
TYPICAL
UMPTEEN
VAPOURS
WAPPING
WIPEOUT
ZAPOTEC
ZEPHIEL
ACQUIRE
ASQUITH
BEQUEST
ENQUIRE
ENQUIRY
ESQUIRE
INQUEST
INQUIRE
INQUIRY
LIQUEFY
LIQUEUR
LIQUIDS
PIQUANT
REQUEST
REQUIEM
REQUIRE
REQUITE
SAQQARA
SEQUELA
SEQUOIA
TEQUILA
UNQUIET
UNQUOTE
AARONIC
ABRAHAM
ABRAXIS
ABREAST
ABRIDGE
ACREAGE
ACROBAT
ACRONYM
ACRYLIC
ADRENAL
AERATED
AEROBIC
AEROSOL
AFRICAN
AGRAPHA
AGRIPPA
AGROUND
AIRBASE
AIRCREW
AIRFLOW
AIRLESS
AIRLIFT
AIRLINE
AIRLOCK
AIRMAIL
AIRPORT
AIRSHIP
AIRSICK
AIRSTOP
ALREADY
ALRIGHT
APRICOT
APROPOS
ARRAIGN
ARRANGE
ARRAYED
ARREARS
ARRIVAL
ARRIVED
ATROPHY
AURALLY
AUREATE
AURELIA
AUREOLA
AUREOLE
AURICLE
AUROCHS
BARBARA
BARBARY
BARENTS
BARGAIN
BARKERS
BARKING
BARMAID
BARNABY
BARONET
BAROQUE
BARRACK
BARRAGE
BARRIER
BARRING
BARYTES
BERCEAU
BEREAVE
BERGSON
BERLINE
BERMUDA
BERNARD
BERNINI
BERSEEM
BERSERK
BERTRAM
BIRDMAN
BIRETTA
BORACIC
BORDERS
BOREDOM
BORODIN
BOROUGH
BORSTAL
BURBAGE
BURDOCK
BURETTE
BURGEON
BURGESS
BURGHER
BURGLAR
BURKINA
BURMESE
BURNELL
BURNHAM
BURNING
BURNISH
BURNOUS
BURNOUT
BURSARY
BURSTER
BURUNDI
BYRONIC
CARACAS
CARACUL
CARADOC
CARAMBA
CARAMEL
CARAVAN
CARAVEL
CARAWAY
CARBIDE
CARBINE
CARCASE
CARCASS
CARDIAC
CARDOON
CARDUUS
CAREERS
CAREFUL
CARGOES
CARIBOU
CARIOCA
CARIOLE
CARITAS
CARLYLE
CARMINE
CARNABY
CARNAGE
CAROLUS
CAROTID
CAROTIN
CAROUSE
CARPORT
CARRELL
CARRIED
CARRIER
CARRIES
CARRION
CARROLL
CARROTS
CARROTY
CARSICK
CARTIER
CARTOON
CARVING
CERAMIC
CERTAIN
CERTIFY
CHRISOM
CHRISTY
CHRONIC
CIRCLET
CIRCLIP
CIRCUIT
CIRROSE
CORACLE
CORANTO
CORBEAU
CORBETT
CORDATE
CORDIAL
CORDITE
CORDOBA
CORELLI
CORINTH
CORKAGE
CORKING
CORNCOB
CORNEAL
CORNELL
CORNICE
CORNISH
COROLLA
CORONER
CORONET
CORRECT
CORRIDA
CORRODE
CORRUPT
CORSAGE
CORSAIR
CORTEGE
CORTINA
CORUNNA
CORYDON
CURABLE
CURACAO
CURATOR
CURCUMA
CURDLED
CURETTE
CURIOUS
CURLING
CURRAGH
CURRANT
CURRENT
CURRIED
CURSIVE
CURSORY
CURTAIL
CURTAIN
CURTSEY
DARLING
DARNING
DERANGE
DERONDA
DERRICK
DERVISH
DERWENT
DORKING
DORMANT
DOROTHY
DURABLE
DURABLY
DURAMEN
DURRELL
EARACHE
EARDRUM
EARLDOM
EARLIER
EARLOBE
EARMARK
EARNEST
EARRING
EARSHOT
EARTHEN
EARTHLY
ENRAGED
ERRATIC
ERRATUM
ETRURIA
FARADAY
FARAWAY
FARCEUR
FARMERS
FARMING
FARNESE
FARRAGO
FARRIER

FARTHER
FERMENT
FERMIUM
FERROUS
FERRULE
FERTILE
FERVENT
FERVOUR
FIRCONE
FIREARM
FIREBUG
FIREDOG
FIREFLY
FIREMAN
FIRSTLY
FORAMEN
FORBADE
FORBEAR
FORCEPS
FOREARM
FOREIGN
FORELEG
FOREMAN
FOREPAW
FORESEE
FOREVER
FORFEIT
FORFEND
FORGAVE
FORGERY
FORGIVE
FORGONE
FORLORN
FORMICA
FORMING
FORMOSA
FORMULA
FORSAKE
FORSTER
FORTIES
FORTIFY
FORTRAN
FORTUNE
FORWARD
FURBISH
FURIOUS
FURLONG
FURNACE
FURNISH
FURRIER
FURTHER
FURTIVE
GARBAGE
GARBLED
GARBOIL
GARBURE
GARDENS
GARLAND
GARMENT
GARNISH
GARONNE
GAROTTE
GARRICK
GERAINT
GERBERA
GERMANE
GERMANY
GIRAFFE
GIRLISH
GIRONDE
GORDIAN
GORDIUS
GORILLA
GORSEDD
HARBOUR
HARDPAN
HARDTOP
HARELIP
HARICOT
HARLECH
HARMFUL
HARMONY
HARNESS
HARPIST
HARPOON
HARRIER
HARRIET
HARSHLY
HARVARD
HARVEST
HARWICH
HARWOOD
HERBAGE
HERBERT
HERBERY
HERBIST
HEREDIA
HERETIC
HEROINE
HEROISM
HERRICK
HERRIES
HERRING
HERSELF
HIRSUTE
HORATIO
HORDEUM
HORIZON
HORMONE
HORRIFY
HORRORS
HORSING
HURDLER
HURLING
HURRIED
HURTFUL
INROADS
ISRAELI
IVRESSE
JERICHO
JERKILY
JERSEYS
JURYBOX
JURYMAN
KARACHI
KARAJAN
KARAKUL
KARAOKE
KERATIN
KERMESS
KERNITE
KEROGEN
KURHAUS
KURSAAL
LARCENY
LARDOON
LARGELY
LARGESS
LARGEST
LORDING
LORELEI
LURCHER
LURIDLY
LURKING
LYRICAL
MARABOU
MARACAS
MARANTA
MARATHA
MARBLED
MARBLES
MARBURG
MARCHER
MARCONI
MARCUSE
MAREMMA
MARENGO
MARGERY
MARIBOU
MARINER
MARITAL
MARKING
MARLENE
MARLINE
MARLOWE
MARMARA
MARMION
MARMITE
MARQUEE
MARQUIS
MARRIED
MARRYAT
MARSALA
MARSHAL
MARSYAS
MARTENS
MARTIAL
MARTIAN
MARTINI
MARTLET
MARTYRS
MARVELL
MARXISM
MARXIST
MERCERY
MERCIES
MERCURY
MERITED
MERMAID
MERRIER
MERRILY
MIRACLE
MIRADOR
MIRANDA
MIRIFIC
MORAINE
MORALLY
MORAVIA
MORDANT
MOREISH
MORELLO
MORESBY
MORESCO
MORLAND
MORNING
MOROCCO
MORONIC
MORPHIA
MORRELL
MORTALS
MORTICE
MORTIFY
MORTISE
MURAENA
MURIATE
MURILLO
MURRAIN
MYRINGA
NARRATE
NARROWS
NARTHEX
NARWHAL
NERITIC
NERVOSA
NERVOUS
NERVURE
NIRVANA
NORFOLK
NORWICH
NUREYEV
NURSERY
NURSING
NURTURE
OARFISH
OARLOCK
OARSMAN
OARSMEN
OGREISH
OTRANTO
PARABLE
PARADOR
PARADOS
PARADOX
PARAGON
PARAPET
PARASOL
PARBOIL
PARCHED
PARENTS
PARESIS
PARFAIT
PARINGS
PARKING
PARKWAY
PARLOUR
PARLOUS
PARNELL
PAROTID
PAROTIS
PARQUET
PARSLEY
PARSNIP
PARTAKE
PARTHIA
PARTIAL
PARTING
PARTITA
PARTNER
PARVENU
PERCALE
PERCENT
PERCEPT
PERCUSS
PEREIRA
PERFECT
PERFIDY
PERFORM
PERFUME
PERFUSE
PERGOLA
PERHAPS
PERIGEE
PERIWIG
PERJURE
PERJURY
PERLITE
PERMIAN
PERPLEX
PERRIER
PERSEID
PERSEUS
PERSIAN
PERSIST
PERSONA
PERSONS
PERSPEX
PERTAIN
PERTURB
PERTUSE
PERUSAL
PERVADE
PERVERT
PHRASAL
PHRASER
PHRENIC
PIRAEUS
PIRANHA
PIROGUE
PORCIAN
PORCINE
POROSIS
PORTAGE
PORTEND
PORTENT
PORTHOS
PORTICO
PORTION
PORTRAY
PURBECK
PURCELL
PURITAN
PURLIEU
PURLINE
PURLOIN
PURPORT
PURPOSE
PURPURA
PURSUER
PURSUIT
PURVIEW
PYRAMID
PYRETIC
PYREXIA
PYRITES
PYROSIS
PYRRHIC
RAREBIT
REREDOS
REROUTE
RORQUAL
SARACEN
SARCASM
SARCOMA
SARCOUS
SARDANA
SARDINE
SARGENT
SARMENT
SAROYAN
SCRAGGY
SCRAPER
SCRAPIE
SCRAPPY
SCRATCH
SCRAWNY
SCREECH
SCREEVE
SCREWED
SCROOGE
SCROTAL
SCROTUM
SCRUBBY
SCRUFFY
SCRUMMY
SCRUMPY
SCRUNCH
SCRUPLE
SERAPIS
SERBIAN
SERCIAL
SERFDOM
SERINGA
SERIOUS
SERPENS
SERPENT
SERRIED
SERVANT
SERVICE
SERVILE
SERVING
SHRILLY
SHRIMPS
SHRIVEL
SHRIVEN
SHRIVER
SHROUDS
SIRLOIN
SIROCCO
SORCERY
SORGHUM
SOROSIS
SORROWS
SORTING
SPRAINT
SPRAYER
SPRINGE
SPRINGS
SPRINGY
SPROUTS
STRAITS
STRANGE
STRATUM
STRATUS
STRAUSS
STREAKY
STRETCH
STREWTH
STRIATE
STRIDES
STRIDOR
STRIGIL
STRIKER
STRINGS
STRINGY
STRIPED
STRIPER
STRIPES
STROBIC
STROPHE
STROPPY
STRUDEL
SURCOAT
SURDITY
SURFACE
SURFEIT
SURFING
SURGEON

SURGERY
SURINAM
SURMISE
SURNAME
SURPASS
SURPLUS
SURREAL
SURVIVE
SYRINGA
SYRINGE
TARANTO
TARDILY
TARDIVE
TARNISH
TARPEIA
TARQUIN
TARSIER
TARTARE
TARTARY
TARTINE
TERBIUM
TERENCE
TERMITE
TERRACE
TERRAIN
TERRENE
TERRIER
TERRIFY
TERRINE
TERSELY
TERSION
TERTIAL
TERTIAN
THREADS
THRENOS
THRIFTY
THRISTY
THROATY
THROUGH
THROWER
THROWIN
THRUWAY
TORCHON
TORMENT
TORNADE
TORNADO
TORONTO
TORPEDO
TORPIDS
TORREFY
TORRENT
TORSADE
TORSION
TORTILE
TORTRIX
TORTURE
TURBARY
TURBINE
TURENNE
TURGENT
TURKISH
TURMOIL
TURNERY
TURNING
TURNKEY
TURNOUT
TYRANNY
UKRAINE
UNRAVEL
UNREADY
UPRAISE
UPRIGHT
UTRECHT
UTRICLE
UTRILLO
VARIANT
VARIETY
VARIOLA
VARIOUS
VARMINT
VARNISH
VARSITY
VARYING
VERBENA
VERBOSE
VERDANT
VERDICT
VERDURE
VERMEER
VERMONT
VERONAL
VERRUCA
VERSANT
VERSIFY
VERSION
VERTIGO
VERULAM
VERVAIN
VIRELAY
VIRGATE
VIRGULE
VIRTUAL
WARBECK
WARBLER
WARBURG
WARDOUR
WARFARE
WARHEAD
WARLIKE
WARLING
WARLOCK
WARLORD
WARMING
WARNING
WARPATH
WARRANT
WARRING
WARRIOR
WARSHIP
WARTHOG
WARTIME
WARWICK
WIRETAP
WORDILY
WORDING
WORKERS
WORKING
WORKMAN
WORKMEN
WORKOUT
WORKSHY
WORKTOP
WORLDLY
WORRIED
WORRIER
WORSHIP
WORSTED
XERAFIN
XEROSIS
YARDAGE
YARDARM
YEREVAN
YORKIST
ABSCESS
ABSCOND
ABSENCE
ABSINTH
ABSOLVE
ABSTAIN
ALSATIA
APSIDAL
ARSENAL
ARSENIC
ASSAULT
ASSEGAI
ASSIEGE
ASSISTS
ASSIZES
ASSUAGE
ASSUMED
ASSURED
ASSYRIA
AUSLESE
AUSTERE
AUSTRAL
AUSTRIA
BASCULE
BASHFUL
BASINET
BASKING
BASMATI
BASSOON
BASTARD
BASTIDE
BASTION
BESEECH
BESHREW
BESIDES
BESIEGE
BESMEAR
BESPEAK
BESPOKE
BESTIAL
BESTREW
BISCUIT
BISMUTH
BISTORT
BOSWELL
BUSHIDO
BUSHMAN
BUSHMEN
BUSKINS
BUSSING
BUSTARD
BUSTLER
BUSTLES
CASCADE
CASCARA
CASEASE
CASHBOX
CASHIER
CASPIAN
CASSATA
CASSAVA
CASSOCK
CASTILE
CASTING
CASTLED
CASTOFF
CASUALS
CASUISM
CASUIST
CESSION
CESSPIT
CESTODE
CESTOID
CISSOID
CISTERN
COSSACK
COSTARD
COSTING
COSTIVE
COSTUME
CUSHION
CUSTARD
CUSTODY
CUSTOMS
CYSTOID
DASHING
DASHPOT
DASTARD
DESCANT
DESCEND
DESCENT
DESERTS
DESERVE
DESMOND
DESPAIR
DESPISE
DESPITE
DESPOIL
DESPOND
DESSERT
DESTINE
DESTINY
DESTROY
DISABLE
DISAVOW
DISBAND
DISBARK
DISCARD
DISCERN
DISCORD
DISCUSS
DISDAIN
DISEASE
DISGUST
DISJOIN
DISLIKE
DISMAST
DISMISS
DISOBEY
DISPLAY
DISPORT
DISPOSE
DISPRIN
DISPUTE
DISROBE
DISRUPT
DISSECT
DISSENT
DISTAFF
DISTANT
DISTEND
DISTENT
DISTILL
DISTORT
DISTURB
DISUSED
DOSSIER
DUSTBIN
DUSTING
DUSTMAN
DUSTPAN
EASIEST
EASTERN
ECSTASY
ENSLAVE
ENSNARE
ENSNARL
ENSUING
ENSUITE
EPSILON
EPSTEIN
ESSENCE
ESSENES
EUSTACE
FASCISM
FASCIST
FASHION
FASTING
FASTNET
FESTIVE
FESTOON
FISHERY
FISHEYE
FISHING
FISHNET
FISSILE
FISSION
FISSURE
FISTFUL
FISTULA
FISTULE
FOSSICK
FOSSULA
FUSEBOX
FUSIBLE
FUSILLI
FUSSILY
FUSTIAN
GASCONY
GASEOUS
GASFIRE
GASMASK
GASOHOL
GASPING
GASTHOF
GASTRIC
GASTRIN
GESTALT
GESTAPO
GESTATE
GESTURE
GISELLE
GOSHAWK
GOSLING
GOSSIPY
GUSHING
HASHISH
HASSOCK
HASTATE
HASTILY
HESSIAN
HISPANO
HISSING
HISTOID
HISTORY
HOSANNA
HOSIERY
HOSPICE
HOSTAGE
HOSTESS
HOSTILE
HUSBAND
HUSKILY
HUSSARS
HUSSITE
HUSTLER
INSCAPE
INSECTS
INSHORE
INSIDER
INSIDES
INSIGHT
INSIPID
INSPECT
INSPIRE
INSTALL
INSTANT
INSTATE
INSTEAD
INSTILL
INSULAR
INSULIN
INSURER
ISSUANT
JASMINE
JESTING
JUSSIVE
JUSTICE
JUSTIFY
KASHMIR
KESTREL
KISSING
LASAGNA
LASAGNE
LASHING
LASTING
LESBIAN
LESOTHO
LESSING
LISSOME
LISTING
LUSTFUL
LUSTILY
LUSTRUM
MASCARA
MASONIC
MASONRY
MASSAGE
MASSEUR
MASSINE
MASSIVE
MASTERS
MASTERY
MASTIFF
MASTOID
MASURKA
MESCLUN
MESEEMS
MESSAGE
MESSIAH
MESSIER
MESSILY
MESSINA
MISCAST
MISDEED
MISERLY
MISFIRE
MISLEAD
MISPLAY
MISREAD
MISRULE
MISSILE
MISSING
MISSION

MISSIVE
MISSTEP
MISTAKE
MISTIME
MISTOOK
MISTRAL
MOSELLE
MUSCOID
MUSCOVY
MUSETTE
MUSICAL
MUSSELS
MUSTANG
MUSTARD
MYSTERY
MYSTIFY
NASALLY
NASCENT
NASTILY
NOSEBAG
NOSEGAY
NOSTRIL
NOSTRUM
OBSCENE
OBSCURA
OBSCURE
OBSEQUY
OBSERVE
OESTRUS
ONSHORE
ONSTAGE
OSSELET
OSSEOUS
OSSICLE
OSSUARY
OUSTITI
PASCHAL
PASSAGE
PASSANT
PASSING
PASSION
PASSIVE
PASTERN
PASTEUR
PASTIES
PASTIME
PASTURE
PESSARY
PISCINA
PISCINE
PISTOLE
POSSESS
POSTAGE
POSTBAG
POSTBOX
POSTERN
POSTING
POSTMAN
POSTURE
POSTWAR
PUSHING
PUSHKIN
PUSTULE
RESCIND
RESCUER
RESERVE
RESHAPE
RESIANT
RESIDUE
RESOLVE
RESOUND
RESPECT
RESPIRE
RESPITE
RESPOND
RESPRAY
RESTART
RESTATE
RESTFUL
RESTING
RESTIVE
RESTOCK
RESTORE
RESULTS
RISIBLE
RISKILY
RISOTTO
RISSOLE
ROSACEA
ROSALIA
ROSALIE
ROSARIO
ROSCIAN
ROSCIUS
ROSEATE
ROSEBUD
ROSELLA
ROSELLE
ROSEOLA
ROSETTA
ROSETTE
ROSSINI
ROSTAND
ROSTOCK
ROSTRAL
ROSTRUM
RUSALKA
RUSHING
RUSSELL
RUSSIAN
RUSTLER
SASHIMI
SASSOON
SESSILE
SESSION
SESTINA
SESTINE
SISTERS
SISTINE
SUSANNA
SUSPECT
SUSPEND
SUSTAIN
SYSTOLE
TASSILI
TESSERA
TESTATE
TESTIFY
TESTILY
TESTING
TESTUDO
TOSSPOT
TUSCANY
TUSSOCK
TUSSORE
UNSCREW
UNSNARL
UNSOUND
UNSTICK
UNSTOCK
UNSTUCK
UPSHOOT
UPSIDES
UPSILON
UPSTAGE
UPSTART
UPSTATE
UPSURGE
UPSWING
VASSAIL
VESICLE
VESPERS
VESTIGE
VISCERA
VISCOSE
VISCOUS
VISIBLE
VISIBLY
VISITOR
VISTULA
WASHDAY
WASHERS
WASHING
WASHOUT
WASHTUB
WASPISH
WASSAIL
WASTAGE
WASTING
WASTREL
WESTERN
WISHFUL
WISHING
WISTFUL
WYSIWYG
YASHMAK
YPSILON
ZESTFUL
ACTAEON
ACTINAL
ACTINIA
ACTINIC
ACTRESS
ACTUARY
ACTUATE
ALTERED
ALTHAEA
ALTHING
AMTRACK
ANTACID
ANTARES
ANTENNA
ANTHILL
ANTHONY
ANTHRAX
ANTIBES
ANTIGEN
ANTIGUA
ANTIOCH
ANTIQUE
ANTLERS
ANTONIO
ANTONYM
ANTWERP
APTERAL
APTERYX
APTNESS
ARTEMIS
ARTEMUS
ARTICLE
ARTISAN
ARTISTE
ARTLESS
ARTWORK
ASTARTE
ASTILBE
ASTOUND
ASTRIDE
ATTABOY
ATTACHE
ATTAINT
ATTEMPT
ATTICUS
ATTIRED
ATTRACT
AUTARKY
AUTOCUE
AUTOMAT
AUTOPSY
BATAVIA
BATHERS
BATHING
BATHMAT
BATHTUB
BATSMAN
BATTELS
BATTERY
BATTING
BETHINK
BETHUMB
BETIMES
BETOKEN
BETROTH
BETTING
BETWEEN
BETWIXT
BITTERN
BITTERS
BITUMEN
BOTANIC
BOTARGO
BOTTEGA
BOTTLED
BOTTLES
BUTCHER
BUTTERY
BUTTONS
CATALAN
CATALOG
CATALPA
CATARRH
CATCALL
CATCHER
CATCHUP
CATELOG
CATERER
CATESBY
CATFISH
CATHEAD
CATHODE
CATKINS
CATLIKE
CATLING
CATMINT
CATSEYE
CATSPAW
CATTISH
CATWALK
CITADEL
CITHARA
CITIZEN
CITRINE
CITROEN
COTERIE
COTTAGE
COTTONY
CUTAWAY
CUTBACK
CUTICLE
CUTLASS
CUTLERY
CUTTERS
CUTTING
CUTWORM
CYTISUS
DATABLE
DETAILS
DETENTE
DETRACT
DETRAIN
DITHERY
DITTANY
DITTIES
DUTIFUL
EATABLE
ECTASIS
ECTOPIA
ENTEBBE
ENTENTE
ENTERIC
ENTERON
ENTHRAL
ENTHUSE
ENTITLE
ENTRAIN
ENTRANT
ENTREAT
ENTRUST
ENTWINE
ESTIVAL
ESTOVER
ESTREAT
ESTUARY
ETTRICK
EUTERPE
EXTINCT
EXTRACT
EXTREME
EXTRUDE
FATALLY
FATEFUL
FATHEAD
FATIGUE
FATNESS
FATUITY
FATUOUS
FETICHE
FETLOCK
FETTERS
FITMENT
FITNESS
FITTEST
FITTING
FUTTOCK
FUTURES
GATEWAY
GATLING
GETAWAY
GETTING
GUTLESS
GUTTATE
HATBAND
HATCHET
HATEFUL
HATLESS
HATTOCK
HETAERA
HITTITE
HOTFOOT
HOTHEAD
HOTLINE
HOTSHOT
HOTSPUR
ICTERIC
ICTERUS
INTEGER
INTENSE
INTERIM
INTERNE
INTROIT
INTRUDE
ISTHMUS
JITTERS
JITTERY
JUTLAND
KATORGA
KATRINE
KETCHUP
KITCHEN
KITHARA
LATCHET
LATERAL
LATERAN
LATIMER
LATRINE
LATTICE
LATVIAN
LETDOWN
LETTERS
LETTING
LETTUCE
LITCHEE
LITERAL
LITHELY
LITHIUM
LITOTES
LITURGY
LOTHAIR
LOTHIAN
LOTTERY
LUTYENS
MATADOR
MATCHED
MATCHET
MATELOT
MATILDA
MATINEE
MATISSE
MATTERS
MATTHEW
MATTING
MATTINS
MATTOCK
METALLY
METAYER
METHANE
METHINK
METICAL
MÉTISSE
METONIC
METONYM
METTLED
MITHRAS
MITOSIS
MITTENS
MITZVAH
MOTHERS

MOTTLED
MUTABLE
MUTAGEN
NATCHEZ
NATIONS
NATIVES
NATRIUM
NATURAL
NETBALL
NETSUKE
NETTING
NETWORK
NITRATE
NITRILE
NITRITE
NITRODE
NITROUS
NOTABLE
NOTABLY
NOTCHED
NOTEPAD
NOTHING
NOTIONS
NUTCASE
NUTLIKE
NUTMEAT
NUTTING
OATCAKE
OATMEAL
OBTRUDE
OCTAGON
OCTOBER
OCTOPOD
OCTOPUS
OCTUPLE
ONTARIO
OPTICAL
OPTIMAL
OPTIMUM
ORTOLAN
OSTEOMA
OSTIOLE
OSTRICH
OTTOMAN
OUTBACK
OUTCAST
OUTCOME
OUTCROP
OUTDARE
OUTDOOR
OUTFACE
OUTFALL
OUTFLOW
OUTGROW
OUTLAST
OUTLIER
OUTLINE
OUTLIVE
OUTLOOK
OUTPOST
OUTPOUR
OUTRAGE
OUTRANK
OUTSHOT
OUTSIDE
OUTSIZE
OUTSPAN
OUTSTAY
OUTTURN
OUTVOTE
OUTWARD
OUTWEAR
OUTWORK
OUTWORN
PATELLA
PATHWAY
PATIBLE
PATIENT
PATRIAL
PATRICK
PATRIOT
PATTERN
PETIOLE
PETRIFY
PETROUS
PETUNIA
PITCHED
PITCHER
PITEOUS
PITFALL
PITHEAD
PITHILY
PITIFUL
POTABLE
POTENCY
POTHEEN
POTHERB
POTHOLE
POTICHE
POTLACH
POTLUCK
POTOMAC
POTSDAM
POTSHOT
POTTAGE
POTTERY
POTTING
PUTREFY
PUTTEES
PUTTING
PUTTOCK
RATAFIA
RATATAT
RATCHET
RATIONS
RATLINE
RATPACK
RATTEEN
RATTLER
RETAINS
RETHINK
RETICLE
RETINUE
RETIRED
RETIREE
RETOUCH
RETRACE
RETRACT
RETRAIN
RETRAIT
RETREAD
RETREAT
RETRIAL
RETSINA
RETURNS
ROTATOR
ROTTING
ROTUNDA
RUTHENE
RUTTING
SATANIC
SATCHEL
SATIATE
SATIETY
SATIRIC
SATISFY
SATRAPY
SATSUMA
SETBACK
SETTING
SETTLED
SETTLER
SITDOWN
SITTING
SITUATE
SITWELL
TATARIC
TATIANA
TATTERS
TATTING
TATTLER
TETANUS
TITANIA
TITANIC
TITOISM
TITOIST
TITRATE
TITULAR
TOTALLY
TOTEMIC
TOTIENT
TOTTERY
TUTELAR
UNTAMED
UNTRIED
UNTRUTH
UNTWINE
UPTIGHT
UTTERLY
VATICAN
VETERAN
VETIVER
VETTING
VITALLY
VITAMIN
VITIATE
VITRAIL
VITRIFY
VITRIOL
WATCHER
WATERED
WATTAGE
WATTEAU
WATTLES
WATUTSI
WETBACK
WETLAND
WETNESS
WETSUIT
WETTING
WITCHES
WITHERS
WITHOUT
WITLESS
WITLOOF
WITNESS
WOTCHER
YTTRIUM
ZETLAND
ABUSIVE
ACUTELY
ADULATE
ALUMINA
ALUMNAE
ALUMNUS
AMUSING
AQUATIC
AQUAVIT
AQUEOUS
AQUIFER
AQUILON
AQUINAS
AQUINUS
ARUNDEL
ASUNDER
BAUHAUS
BAUXITE
BLUBBER
BLUFFLY
BLUNDER
BLUNTED
BLUNTLY
BLURRED
BLUSHER
BLUSTER
BOUCLÉE
BOUDOIR
BOUILLI
BOULDER
BOUNCER
BOUNDED
BOUNDEN
BOUNDER
BOUQUET
BOURBON
BOURDON
BOURSIN
BOUTADE
BRUISED
BRUISER
BRUSHER
BRUSQUE
BRUTISH
CAUSTIC
CAUTERY
CAUTION
CHUCKLE
CHUFFED
CHUKKER
CHUNDER
CHUPATI
CHUTNEY
CLUBMAN
CLUMBER
CLUNIAC
CLUSTER
CLUTTER
COUCHÉE
COULDNT
COULOMB
COULTER
COUNCIL
COUNSEL
COUNTED
COUNTER
COUNTRY
COUPLER
COUPLET
COUPONS
COURAGE
COURBET
COURIER
COURSER
COURSES
COURTLY
COUSINS
COUTURE
CRUCIAL
CRUCIFY
CRUDELY
CRUDITY
CRUELLS
CRUELLY
CRUELTY
CRUISER
CRUMBLE
CRUMBLY
CRUMPET
CRUMPLE
CRUNCHY
CRUPPER
CRUSADE
CRUSHED
CRUSHER
DAUPHIN
DIURNAL
DOUBLES
DOUBLET
DOUBTER
DOUGHTY
DOUGLAS
DRUGGED
DRUGGET
DRUMLIN
DRUMMER
DRUNKEN
ECUADOR
EDUCATE
ELUSIVE
ELUSORY
EMULATE
EMULSIN
EQUABLE
EQUABLY
EQUALLY
EQUATOR
EQUERRY
EQUINOX
ERUDITE
FAUSTUS
FAUVISM
FAUVIST
FLUENCY
FLUMMOX
FLUNKEY
FLUSHED
FLUSTER
FLUTIST
FLUTTER
FLUVIAL
FOULARD
FOUNDER
FOUNDRY
FRUMPLE
GAUDILY
GAUGUIN
GAUTAMA
GLUCOSE
GLUTTON
GOUACHE
GOULASH
GOURMET
GRUFFLY
GRUMBLE
GRUMMET
GRUYÈRE
HAUGHTY
HAULAGE
HAULIER
HAUNTED
HAUTBOY
HEURISM
HOUDINI
HOUSING
JOURNAL
JOURNEY
KNUCKLE
KOUMISS
LAUNDER
LAUNDRY
LAURELS
LEUCINE
LEUCOMA
LOUNGER
LOURDES
LOURING
LOUTISH
LOUVRED
MAUDLIN
MAUGHAM
MAUNDER
MOUFLON
MOUILLÉ
MOULAGE
MOULDED
MOULDER
MOUNTED
MOUNTIE
MOURNER
NAUGHTY
NEURINE
NEURONE
NEUTRAL
NEUTRON
NOURISH
NOUVEAU
OCULIST
OPULENT
OPUNTIA
OVULATE
PAUCITY
PAULINE
PAUNCHY
PLUMAGE
PLUMBER
PLUMMET
PLUMPER
PLUMULE
PLUNDER
PLUNGER
PLUTEUS
POULENC
POULTRY
POUSSIN
PRUDENT
PRUDISH
PRURIGO
PRUSSIC
RAUCOUS
RAUNCHY
REUNION
REUNITE
RHUBARB
ROUAULT
ROUGHEN
ROUGHIE
ROUGHLY

ROULADE
ROULEAU
ROUNDED
ROUNDEL
ROUNDER
ROUNDLY
ROUNDUP
ROUSING
ROUTIER
ROUTINE
SAUCILY
SAUNTER
SAURIAN
SAUROID
SAUSAGE
SCUFFLE
SCULLER
SCUPPER
SCUTAGE
SCUTARI
SCUTTER
SCUTTLE
SFUMATO
SHUDDER
SHUFFLE
SHUTEYE
SHUTTER
SHUTTLE
SLUMBER
SMUDGED
SMUGGLE
SNUFFLE
SNUGGLE
SOUBISE
SOUFFLE
SOULFUL
SOUNDED
SOUNDER
SOUNDLY
SOURSOP
SOUTANE
SOUTHEY
SPURREY
SPURWAY
SPUTNIK
SPUTTER
SQUADDY
SQUALID
SQUALLY
SQUALOR
SQUARED
SQUARES
SQUASHY
SQUEAKY
SQUEERS
SQUEEZE
SQUELCH
SQUIFFY
SQUINCH
SQUISHY
STUBBLE

STUBBLY
STUDDED
STUDENT
STUDIED
STUFFED
STUMBLE
STUMPED
STUNNER
STUNTED
STUPEFY
STURMER
STUTTER
TAURINE
THUGGEE
THULIUM
THUMPER
THUNDER
TOUCHED
TOUGHEN
TOURING
TOURISM
TOURIST
TRUANCY
TRUCIAL
TRUCKER
TRUCKLE
TRUDGEN
TRUFFLE
TRUMEAU
TRUMPET
TRUNDLE
TRUSTEE
TSUNAMI
UKULELE
ULULANT
ULULATE
UNUSUAL
URUGUAY
USUALLY
USURPER
VAUDOIS
VAUGHAN
VAULTED
VOUCHER
WOULDBE
WOULDNT
WOUNDED
YOUNGER
ADVANCE
ADVERSE
ADVISER
ADVISOR
ALVEOLE
BEVERLY
BIVALVE
BIVOUAC
CAVALRY
CAVEMAN
CAVIARE
CEVICHE
CIVILLY

CIVVIES
COVERED
COVERUP
COVETED
CUVETTE
DEVALUE
DEVELOP
DEVIANT
DEVIATE
DEVILRY
DEVIOUS
DEVISED
DEVISEE
DEVOLVE
DEVOTED
DEVOTEE
DIVERGE
DIVERSE
DIVIDED
DIVINER
DIVISOR
DIVORCE
DIVULGE
ENVELOP
ENVENOM
ENVIOUS
FAVELLA
FAVORED
FEVERED
GAVOTTE
INVADER
INVALID
INVEIGH
INVERSE
INVIOUS
INVOICE
INVOLVE
JAVELIN
JAVELLE
JUVENAL
LAVATER
LAVOLTA
LEVERET
LOVABLE
MOVABLE
NAVARIN
NAVARRE
NAVETTE
NEVILLE
NOVELLA
NOVELLO
NOVELTY
OBVERSE
OBVIATE
OBVIOUS
ORVIETO
PAVIOUR
PAVLOVA
PIVOTAL
POVERTY
RAVAGES

RAVINGS
RAVIOLI
REVALUE
REVELER
REVELRY
REVENGE
REVENUE
REVERED
REVERIE
REVERSE
REVISED
REVISER
REVISIT
REVIVAL
REVIVER
REVOLVE
RIVALRY
RIVETED
RIVIERA
RIVULET
SAVAGES
SAVANNA
SAVELOY
SAVINGS
SAVIOUR
SAVOURY
SEVENTH
SEVENTY
SEVERAL
SEVERUS
SEVILLE
SOVKHOZ
TAVERNA
VIVALDI
VIVIDLY
WAVERER
BEWITCH
BOWDLER
BOWHEAD
BOWLING
BOWSHOT
COWGIRL
COWHAND
COWHERD
COWLICK
COWLING
COWPOKE
COWSHED
COWSLIP
DAWDLER
DEWDROP
DOWAGER
DOWDILY
DOWLAND
DOWSING
FAWNING
GAWKISH
HAWKEYE
HOWEVER
HOWLING
INWARDS

JAWBONE
JEWELER
JEWELRY
KIWANIS
KOWLOON
LAWLESS
LAWSUIT
LAWYERS
LOWBROW
LOWDOWN
LOWLAND
LOWPAID
MAWKISH
NEWBOLT
NEWBORN
NEWBURY
NEWCOME
NEWNESS
NEWSBOY
NEWSMAN
NOWHERE
ONWARDS
POWDERY
POWERED
RAWHIDE
RAWNESS
REWRITE
ROWBOAT
ROWDILY
ROWLOCK
SAWBILL
SAWDUST
SAWFISH
SAWMILL
TOWARDS
TOWHEAD
TOWLINE
TOWPATH
UNWOUND
UPWARDS
YAWNING
ANXIETY
ANXIOUS
BOXROOM
COXCOMB
COXLESS
DEXTRIN
FIXATED
FIXEDLY
FIXINGS
FIXTURE
FOXHOLE
FOXTROT
HEXAGON
HEXAPOD
HEXARCH
LAXNESS
LEXICON
MAXILLA
MAXIMUM
MAXWELL

MEXICAN
MIXTURE
NOXIOUS
SAXHORN
SEXLESS
SEXTANT
SIXTEEN
TAXABLE
TAXFREE
TAXICAB
TEXTILE
TEXTUAL
TEXTURE
TOXEMIA
WAXBILL
WAXWING
WAXWORK
ABYSMAL
ABYSSAL
ALYSSUM
AMYGDAL
AMYLASE
AMYLOID
ANYBODY
ANYMORE
AZYGOUS
BAYONET
BOYCOTT
BOYHOOD
CAYENNE
COYNESS
CRYPTIC
CRYPTON
CRYSTAL
DAYBOOK
DAYMARK
DAYSTAR
DAYTIME
DRYNESS
ELYSIAN
ELYSIUM
FEYDEAU
FLYHALF
FLYLEAF
FLYOVER
FLYPAST
GAYNESS
GLYPTAL
GLYPTIC
GRYPHON
GUYROPE
GWYNETH
HAYSEED
HAYWARD
HAYWIRE
IDYLLIC
JOYLESS
JOYRIDE
KEYHOLE
KEYNOTE
KEYWORD

KRYPTON
LAYERED
LAYETTE
LAYINGS
LOYALLY
LOYALTY
MAYFAIR
MAYPOLE
ODYSSEY
OLYMPIA
OLYMPIC
OLYMPUS
PAYABLE
PAYLOAD
PAYMENT
PAYROLL
PHYSICS
PLYWOOD
PRYTHEE
PSYCHIC
PTYALIN
REYNARD
RHYMING
ROYALLY
ROYALTY
SEYMOUR
SHYLOCK
SHYNESS
SHYSTER
SKYBLUE
SKYHIGH
SKYLARK
SKYLINE
SKYWARD
SLYNESS
SPYHOLE
STYGIAN
STYLING
STYLISH
STYLIST
STYLITE
STYLIZE
STYPTIC
THYROID
THYRSIS
THYSELF
THYSSEN
TOYNBEE
TOYSHOP
TRYPSIN
ULYSSES
VOYAGER
WAYBILL
WAYLAND
WAYMARK
WAYSIDE
WAYWARD
WRYBILL
WRYNECK
WRYNOSE
BAZOOKA

BEZIQUE
BIZARRE
BUZZARD
CÉZANNE
DAZZLED
DIZZILY
ELZEVIR
GAZELLE
GAZETTE
GIZZARD
GUZZLER
HAZLETT
JAZZMAN
JEZEBEL
LOZENGE
MAZARIN
MAZEPPA
MAZURKA
PIZARRO
PIZZAZZ
PUZZLED
PUZZLER
ROZZERS
SIZABLE
SIZZLER
SOZZLED
SUZETTE
WIZENED
YEZIDEE
ZIZANIA

7:4

ABBASID
ABLATOR
ABRAHAM
ABRAXIS
ACHAEAN
ACHATES
ACTAEON
ADVANCE
AERATED
AFFABLE
AFFABLY
AFFAIRS
AGRAPHA
AIDANCE
ALBANIA
ALCALDE
ALDABRA
ALFALFA
ALKANET
ALMACKS
ALMANAC
ALSATIA
AMBAGES
AMHARIC
AMIABLE
AMIABLY
ANDAMAN
ANDANTE
ANTACID
ANTARES
APHAGIA
APHASIA
APLASIA
APPARAT
APPAREL
AQUATIC
AQUAVIT
ARCADIA
ARIADNE
ARRAIGN
ARRANGE
ARRAYED
ASCARID
ASHAMED
ASHANTI
ASIATIC
ASKANCE
ASPASIA
ASSAULT
ASTARTE
ATTABOY
ATTACHE
ATTAINT
AURALLY
AUTARKY
AVIATOR
BACARDI
BAGASSE
BAHADUR
BAHAMAS
BAJAZET
BALANCE
BALATON
BANANAS
BATAVIA
BECAUSE
BEHAVED
BELABOR
BELARUS
BELATED
BENARES
BIVALVE
BIZARRE
BLEAKLY
BLOATED
BLOATER
BONANZA
BORACIC
BOTANIC
BOTARGO
BREADED
BREADTH
BREAKER
BREATHE
BROADEN
BROADLY
BUGABOO
CABARET
CADAVER
CALABAR
CALAMUS
CANASTA
CAPABLE
CAPABLY
CARACAS
CARACUL
CARADOC
CARAMBA
CARAMEL
CARAVAN
CARAVEL
CARAWAY
CATALAN
CATALOG
CATALPA
CATARRH
CAVALRY
CELADON
CENACLE
CERAMIC
CÉZANNE
CHEAPEN
CHEAPLY
CHEATER
CHIANTI
CHIASMA
CHLAMYS
CIMABUE
CITADEL
CLEANER
CLEANLY
CLEANSE
CLEANUP
CLEARLY
CLEARUP
CLEAVER
COCAINE
COHABIT
CONAKRY
CORACLE
CORANTO
CREATED
CREATOR
CROAKER
CROATIA
CURABLE
CURACAO
CURATOR
CUTAWAY
DADAISM
DADAIST
DAMAGED
DAMAGES
DATABLE
DEBACLE
DEBASED
DEBATER
DEBAUCH
DECANAL
DECAYED
DEFACED
DEFAULT
DEGAUSS
DELAYED
DERANGE
DETAILS
DEVALUE
DILATED
DILATOR
DISABLE
DISAVOW
DOMAINE
DOWAGER
DREADED
DREAMER
DURABLE
DURABLY
DURAMEN
DYNAMIC
DYNASTY
EARACHE
EATABLE
ECTASIS
ECUADOR
ELEANOR
EMBARGO
EMBASSY
EMPANEL
EMPATHY
ENGAGED
ENHANCE
ENLARGE
ENRAGED
EQUABLE
EQUABLY
EQUALLY
EQUATOR
ERRATIC
ERRATUM
ESCALOP
ESCAPEE
ESPARTO
ETHANOL
EULALIE
EXHAUST
EXPANSE
FALAFEL
FANATIC
FARADAY
FARAWAY
FATALLY
FILARIA
FILASSE
FINAGLE
FINALLY
FINANCE
FIXATED
FLEAPIT
FLOATER
FORAMEN
FRIABLE
GALAHAD
GALATEA
GELATIN
GERAINT
GETAWAY
GIRAFFE
GLEANER
GOUACHE
GREASER
GREATEN
GREATLY
GREAVES
HEPARIN
HEPATIC
HETAERA
HEXAGON
HEXAPOD
HEXARCH
HIBACHI
HIDALGO
HOGARTH
HORATIO
HOSANNA
HUMANLY
HYDATID
ICHABOD
IDEALLY
ILIACUS
IMPASSE
IMPASTO
IMPAVID
INFANCY
INFARCT
INHABIT
INHALER
INNARDS
INVADER
INVALID
INWARDS
ISLAMIC
ISLANDS
ISMAILI
ISRAELI
JAKARTA
JAMAICA
JOCASTA
JUDAISM
KARACHI
KARAJAN
KARAKUL
KARAOKE
KERATIN
KIWANIS
LAMAISM
LAMAIST
LASAGNA
LASAGNE
LAVATER
LEBANON
LEGALLY
LEGATEE
LEPANTO
LINACRE
LOCALLY
LOVABLE
LOYALLY
LOYALTY
LUCARNE
LUNATIC
MACABRE
MACADAM
MACAQUE
MAHATMA
MALACCA
MALAISE
MALARIA
MALAYAN
MANACLE
MANAGER
MANAGUA
MANATEE
MARABOU
MARACAS
MARANTA
MARATHA
MATADOR
MAZARIN
MEGARON
MEGATON
MELANIN
METALLY
METAYER
MINARET
MIRACLE
MIRADOR
MIRANDA
MONARCH
MORAINE
MORALLY
MORAVIA
MOVABLE
MULATTO
MURAENA
MUTABLE
MUTAGEN
MYIASIS
NASALLY
NAVARIN
NAVARRE
NICAEAN
NOMADIC
NOTABLE
NOTABLY
OCEANIA
OCEANIC
OCEANID
OCTAGON
ONTARIO
ONWARDS
ORGANIC
ORGANUM
ORGANZA
ORLANDO
OSMANLI
OTRANTO
PAJAMAS
PALADIN
PALATAL
PALAVER
PANACEA
PANACHE
PARABLE
PARADOR
PARADOS
PARADOX
PARAGON
PARAPET
PARASOL
PAYABLE
PEGASUS
PELAGIC
PENALTY
PENANCE
PENATES
PHRASAL
PHRASER
PICADOR
PICARDY
PICASSO
PILATUS
PIRAEUS
PIRANHA
PIZARRO
PLEADER
PLEASED
PLEASES
PLEATED
PLIABLE
PLIANCY
PODAGRA
POLARIS
POTABLE
PRIAPUS
PTYALIN
PYJAMAS
PYRAMID
RAMADAN
RATAFIA
RATATAT
RAVAGES
REGALIA
REGALLY
REGARDS
REGATTA
RELAPSE
RELATED
RELAXED
RELAYER
REMAINS
REMARRY
REPAINT
REPAIRS

RETAINS
REVALUE
RICARDO
RIVALRY
ROMAINE
ROMANCE
ROMANIA
ROMANOV
ROMANZA
ROSACEA
ROSALIA
ROSALIE
ROSARIO
ROTATOR
ROUAULT
ROYALLY
ROYALTY
RUNAWAY
RUSALKA
SABAEAN
SABAOTH
SABAYON
SALABLE
SALADIN
SALAMIS
SALAZAR
SAMARIA
SARACEN
SATANIC
SAVAGES
SAVANNA
SCIATIC
SCRAGGY
SCRAPER
SCRAPIE
SCRAPPY
SCRATCH
SCRAWNY
SENATOR
SERAPIS
SHEARER
SHEATHE
SHEAVES
SHIATSU
SINATRA
SIZABLE
SNEAKER
SOCAGER
SOFABED
SOLANUM
SOMALIA
SPEAKER
SPLASHY
SPLAYED
SPRAINT
SPRAYER
SQUADDY
SQUALID
SQUALLY
SQUALOR
SQUARED
SQUARES
SQUASHY
STEALTH
STEAMED
STEAMER
STEARIC
STRAITS
STRANGE
STRATUM
STRATUS
STRAUSS
SUBAQUA
SUBATOM
SUGARED
SUMATRA
SUSANNA
SWEATED
SWEATER
SYNAPSE
SYNAXIS
TABANID
TABARET
TABASCO
TAGALOG
TAMARIN
TANAGER
TANAGRA
TARANTO
TATARIC
TAXABLE
TENABLE
TENANCY
TENANTS
TETANUS
THEATER
THEATRE
TILAPIA
TITANIA
TITANIC
TOBACCO
TOTALLY
TOWARDS
TREACLE
TREACLY
TREADLE
TREASON
TREATED
TRIANON
TRIATIC
TRUANCY
TUNABLE
TYRANNY
UKRAINE
UNCANNY
UNCARED
UNDATED
UNEARTH
UNFADED
UNHAPPY
UNLADEN
UNLATCH
UNNAMED
UNRAVEL
UNTAMED
UPRAISE
UPWARDS
USUALLY
VACANCY
VEDANTA
VINASSE
VITALLY
VITAMIN
VIVALDI
VOCALIC
VOCALLY
VOLANTE
VOLAPUK
VOYAGER
WHEATEN
WOMANLY
WREATHE
XERAFIN
YUCATAN
ZIZANIA
AIRBASE
ALABAMA
ANYBODY
ARABIAN
ARABICA
ARMBAND
AVEBURY
BABBITT
BABBLER
BAMBINO
BANBURY
BARBARA
BARBARY
BLABBER
BLUBBER
BOMBARD
BOMBAST
BOMBING
BRIBERY
BUBBLES
BUGBEAR
BULBOUS
BUMBOAT
BURBAGE
CABBAGE
CAMBIUM
CAMBRAI
CAMBRIC
CARBIDE
CARBINE
CEMBALO
CHABLIS
CLOBBER
CLUBMAN
COBBLED
COBBLER
COMBINE
COMBING
CORBEAU
CORBETT
CUMBRIA
CUTBACK
CYMBALS
DABBLER
DAYBOOK
DIABOLO
DIBBLER
DISBAND
DISBARK
DOUBLES
DOUBLET
DOUBTER
DRABBLE
DRIBBLE
DRIBLET
DUBBING
EYEBALL
EYEBATH
EYEBROW
FILBERT
FIMBRIA
FORBADE
FORBEAR
FURBISH
GABBLER
GAMBIAN
GAMBLER
GAMBOGE
GARBAGE
GARBLED
GARBOIL
GARBURE
GERBERA
GIBBONS
GIBBOUS
GILBERT
GIMBALS
GIMBLET
GLOBULE
GOBBLER
GOMBEEN
GUBBINS
GUMBOIL
GUMBOOT
GUNBOAT
HAGBOLT
HALBERD
HALBERT
HARBOUR
HATBAND
HENBANE
HERBAGE
HERBERT
HERBERY
HERBIST
HOGBACK
HOLBEIN
HOMBURG
HUBBARD
HUMBLES
HUSBAND
IAMBIST
ICEBERG
IKEBANA
ILLBRED
ISOBASE
JAWBONE
JOBBERY
JOBBING
JUMBLED
JUMBLES
KIBBUTZ
KNOBBLE
KNOBBLY
LAMBADA
LAMBAST
LAMBENT
LAMBERT
LAMBETH
LAMBING
LESBIAN
LOGBOOK
LOWBROW
LUMBAGO
MACBETH
MARBLED
MARBLES
MARBURG
MEMBERS
MOABITE
MOMBASA
NEBBISH
NETBALL
NEWBOLT
NEWBORN
NEWBURY
NIOBEAN
NIOBIUM
NOBBLED
NOBBLER
NOMBRIL
NUMBERS
NUMBLES
ODDBALL
OFFBASE
OFFBEAT
OUTBACK
PARBOIL
PEBBLES
PIEBALD
PINBALL
PLEBIAN
PREBEND
PROBATE
PROBITY
PROBLEM
PURBECK
QUIBBLE
RAEBURN
RAMBLER
REMBLAI
RHUBARB
RIBBING
ROBBERS
ROBBERY
ROEBUCK
ROWBOAT
RUBBERS
RUBBERY
RUBBING
RUBBISH
RUMBLER
SABBATH
SAMBUCA
SAWBILL
SCABIES
SEABIRD
SERBIAN
SETBACK
SHEBANG
SHEBEEN
SKYBLUE
SLOBBER
SOUBISE
STABLES
STUBBLE
STUBBLY
SUNBEAM
SUNBURN
TAMBOUR
TERBIUM
TILBURY
TIMBALE
TIMBERS
TIMBREL
TOMBOLA
TRIBUNE
TRIBUTE
TUGBOAT
TUMBLER
TUMBREL
TUMBRIL
TURBARY
TURBINE
VERBENA
VERBOSE
WARBECK
WARBLER
WARBURG
WAXBILL
WAYBILL
WEBBING
WETBACK
WRYBILL
ZAMBESI
ZAMBIAN
ABSCESS
ABSCOND
AIRCREW
ALECOST
ALICANT
APICIUS
APOCOPE
ARACHNE
ASOCIAL
ATACTIC
AVOCADO
BACCHIC
BACCHUS
BALCONY
BASCULE
BEACHED
BEACHES
BENCHER
BERCEAU
BISCUIT
BLACKEN
BLOCKED
BLOCKER
BOUCLÉE
BOYCOTT
BRACING
BRACKEN
BRACKET
BRICKIE
BROCADE
BUTCHER
CALCIFY
CALCINE
CALCITE
CALCIUM
CALCULI
CARCASE
CARCASS
CASCADE
CASCARA
CATCALL
CATCHER
CATCHUP
CHECKED
CHECKIN
CHECKUP
CHICAGO
CHICANE
CHICANO
CHICKEN
CHICORY
CHOCTAW
CHUCKLE
CIRCLET
CIRCLIP
CIRCUIT
CLACHAN
CLICKER
COLCHIS
CONCAVE
CONCEAL
CONCEDE
CONCEIT
CONCEPT
CONCERN
CONCERT

CONCISE
CONCOCT
CONCORD
CONCUSS
COUCHÉE
COXCOMB
CRACKED
CRACKER
CRACKLE
CRACKLY
CRICKET
CRICKEY
CRICOID
CROCHET
CROCKET
CRUCIAL
CRUCIFY
CURCUMA
DANCING
DESCANT
DESCEND
DESCENT
DIECAST
DIOCESE
DISCARD
DISCERN
DISCORD
DISCUSS
DOGCART
DRACHMA
DRACULA
DUNCIAD
EDUCATE
EJECTOR
ELECTED
ELECTOR
ELECTRA
ELECTRO
ENACTOR
EPICARP
EPICENE
EPICURE
ERECTOR
EVACUEE
EXACTLY
EXECUTE
FANCIED
FANCIER
FARCEUR
FASCISM
FASCIST
FENCING
FILCHER
FIRCONE
FLACCID
FLECKED
FLECKER
FLICKER
FORCEPS
FRECKLE
FULCRUM
FUNCHAL
GASCONY
GLACIAL
GLACIER
GLUCOSE
GNOCCHI
GRACCHI
GRACILE
GRACKLE
GRECIAN
GROCERS
GROCERY
GROCKLE
HALCYON
HATCHET
HUNCHED
INSCAPE
KETCHUP
KITCHEN
KNACKER
KNICKER
KNOCKER
KNUCKLE
LANCERS
LANCING
LAOCOON
LARCENY
LATCHET
LEACOCK
LEUCINE
LEUCOMA
LINCOLN
LINCTUS
LITCHEE
LURCHER
LYNCHET
MARCHER
MARCONI
MARCUSE
MASCARA
MATCHED
MATCHET
MEACOCK
MERCERY
MERCIES
MERCURY
MESCLUN
MINCING
MIOCENE
MISCAST
MUSCOID
MUSCOVY
NASCENT
NATCHEZ
NEWCOME
NOTCHED
NUTCASE
OATCAKE
OBSCENE
OBSCURA
OBSCURE
OILCAKE
OMICRON
OPACITY
ORACLES
OUTCAST
OUTCOME
OUTCROP
OVICIDE
PANCAKE
PANCRAS
PARCHED
PASCHAL
PAUCITY
PEACHUM
PEACOCK
PECCANT
PECCARY
PECCAVI
PERCALE
PERCENT
PERCEPT
PERCUSS
PICCOLO
PILCHER
PINCERS
PINCHED
PISCINA
PISCINE
PITCHED
PITCHER
PLACARD
PLACATE
PLACEBO
PLACING
POACHER
POPCORN
PORCIAN
PORCINE
PRECAST
PRECEDE
PRECEPT
PRECISE
PRICKED
PRICKER
PRICKLE
PRICKLY
PROCEED
PROCESS
PROCTOR
PROCURE
PSYCHIC
PUCCINI
PUNCHED
PUNCHER
PURCELL
QUECHUA
QUICHUA
QUICKEN
QUICKER
QUICKIE
QUICKLY
RACCOON
RANCHER
RANCOUR
RATCHET
RAUCOUS
REACTOR
REDCOAT
REOCCUR
RESCIND
RESCUER
RIBCAGE
RIPCORD
ROSCIAN
ROSCIUS
RUNCORN
SACCADE
SANCTUM
SANCTUS
SARCASM
SARCOMA
SARCOUS
SATCHEL
SAUCILY
SERCIAL
SHACKLE
SHICKSA
SHOCKED
SHOCKER
SINCERE
SLACKEN
SLACKER
SLACKLY
SLICKER
SMACKER
SMICKLY
SNICKER
SORCERY
SPACING
SPECIAL
SPECIES
SPECIFY
SPECKLE
SPECTER
SPECTRE
SPICATE
SPICULA
STACHYS
STICKER
STICKLE
SUCCEED
SUCCESS
SUCCOUR
SUCCUMB
SUICIDE
SURCOAT
SYNCOPE
TANCRED
TEACAKE
TEACHER
THICKEN
THICKET
THICKLY
TIPCART
TOCCATA
TOPCOAT
TORCHON
TOUCHED
TRACERY
TRACHEA
TRACING
TRACKER
TRACTOR
TRICEPS
TRICKLE
TROCHEE
TROCHUS
TRUCIAL
TRUCKER
TRUCKLE
TUSCANY
UNICORN
UNSCREW
VACCINE
VINCENT
VISCERA
VISCOSE
VISCOUS
VOLCANO
VOUCHER
WATCHER
WELCOME
WHACKED
WHACKER
WITCHES
WOTCHER
WRECKED
WRECKER
ABIDING
ABIDJAN
ACADEME
ACADEMY
ACADIAN
ACIDIFY
ACIDITY
ALADDIN
ALIDADE
ANODIZE
ANODYNE
ARIDITY
ASHDOWN
AVIDITY
BALDING
BALDRIC
BALDWIN
BANDAGE
BANDAID
BANDBOX
BANDEAU
BEADING
BEDDING
BENDING
BIDDING
BINDERY
BINDING
BIRDMAN
BLADDER
BONDAGE
BONDMAN
BORDERS
BOUDOIR
BOWDLER
BRADAWL
BRADMAN
BRIDGES
BRIDGET
BRIDLER
BRIDLES
BUDDING
BUNDOOK
BURDOCK
CADDISH
CAEDMON
CALDERA
CALDRON
CANDACE
CANDELA
CANDIDA
CANDIDE
CANDIED
CANDOUR
CARDIAC
CARDOON
CARDUUS
CHEDDAR
CINDERS
COLDITZ
CONDEMN
CONDOLE
CONDONE
CONDUCT
CONDUIT
CORDATE
CORDIAL
CORDITE
CORDOBA
CRUDELY
CRUDITY
CURDLED
DAWDLER
DEADEYE
DEADPAN
DEADSET
DENDRON
DEWDROP
DIEDRAL
DISDAIN
DODDERY
DOODLER
DOWDILY
DREDGER
EARDRUM
EPIDOTE
ERODIUM
ERUDITE
EVIDENT
FADDISH
FADDIST
FEEDING
FEYDEAU
FIDDLER
FINDING
FLEDGED
FLODDEN
FOLDING
FONDANT
FUDDLED
FUNDING
GARDENS
GAUDILY
GELDING
GEODESY
GIDDILY
GILDING
GLADDEN
GLIDING
GODDESS
GOLDING
GOLDONI
GONDOLA
GOODBYE
GOODIES
GOODISH
GOODMAN
GOODWIN
GORDIAN
GORDIUS
GRADATE
GRADELY
GRADUAL
GRIDDLE
GUIDING
GUMDROP
HADDOCK
HANDBAG
HANDFUL
HANDGUN
HANDILY
HANDLED
HANDLER
HANDOUT
HANDSAW
HANDSEL
HANDSET
HARDPAN
HARDTOP
HEADING
HEADMAN
HEADSET
HEADWAY
HEEDFUL
HILDING
HINDLEG
HOEDOWN
HOLDALL

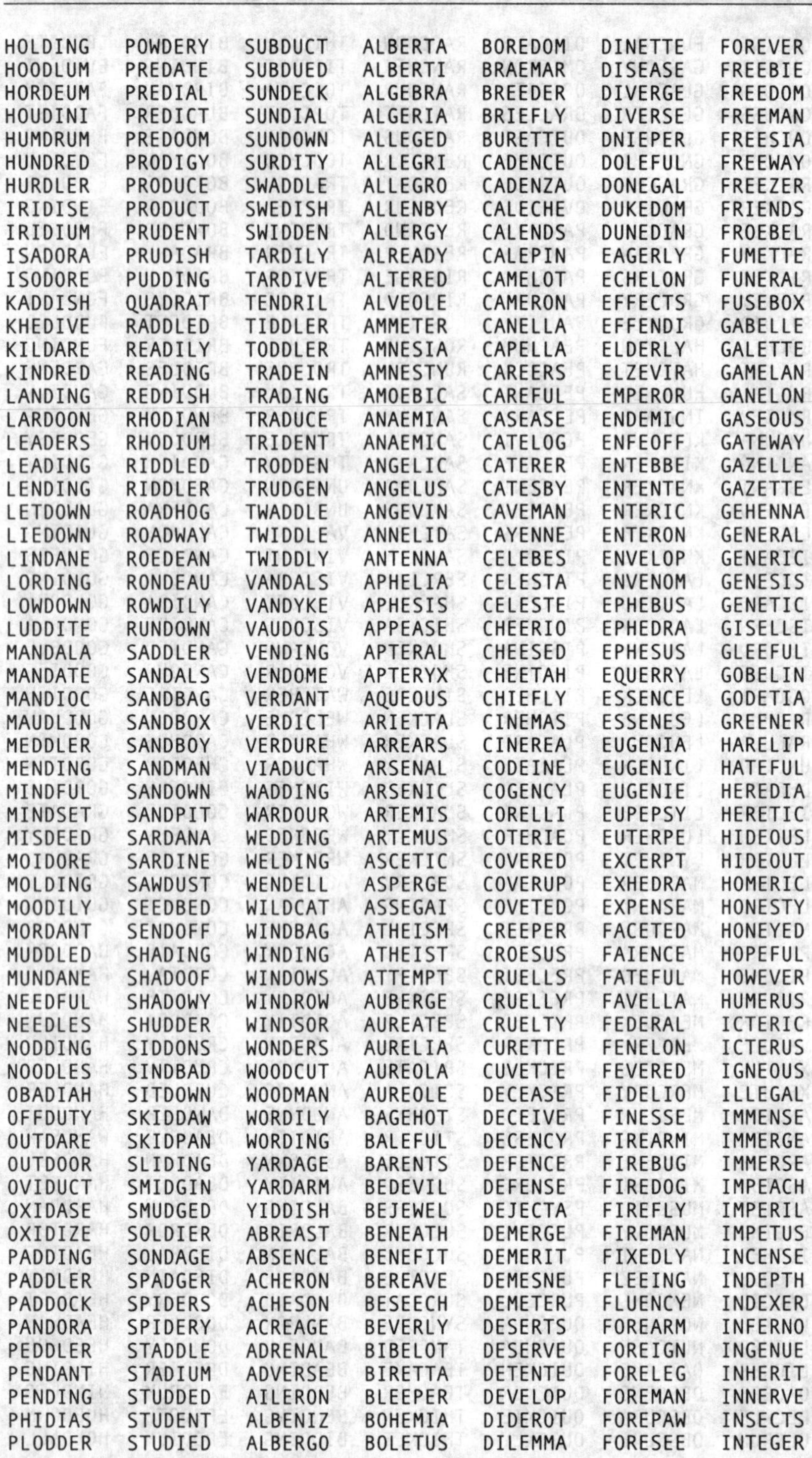

HOLDING
HOODLUM
HORDEUM
HOUDINI
HUMDRUM
HUNDRED
HURDLER
IRIDISE
IRIDIUM
ISADORA
ISODORE
KADDISH
KHEDIVE
KILDARE
KINDRED
LANDING
LARDOON
LEADERS
LEADING
LENDING
LETDOWN
LIEDOWN
LINDANE
LORDING
LOWDOWN
LUDDITE
MANDALA
MANDATE
MANDIOC
MAUDLIN
MEDDLER
MENDING
MINDFUL
MINDSET
MISDEED
MOIDORE
MOLDING
MOODILY
MORDANT
MUDDLED
MUNDANE
NEEDFUL
NEEDLES
NODDING
NOODLES
OBADIAH
OFFDUTY
OUTDARE
OUTDOOR
OVIDUCT
OXIDASE
OXIDIZE
PADDING
PADDLER
PADDOCK
PANDORA
PEDDLER
PENDANT
PENDING
PHIDIAS
PLODDER
POWDERY
PREDATE
PREDIAL
PREDICT
PREDOOM
PRODIGY
PRODUCE
PRODUCT
PRUDENT
PRUDISH
PUDDING
QUADRAT
RADDLED
READILY
READING
REDDISH
RHODIAN
RHODIUM
RIDDLED
RIDDLER
ROADHOG
ROADWAY
ROEDEAN
RONDEAU
ROWDILY
RUNDOWN
SADDLER
SANDALS
SANDBAG
SANDBOX
SANDBOY
SANDMAN
SANDOWN
SANDPIT
SARDANA
SARDINE
SAWDUST
SEEDBED
SENDOFF
SHADING
SHADOOF
SHADOWY
SHUDDER
SIDDONS
SINDBAD
SITDOWN
SKIDDAW
SKIDPAN
SLIDING
SMIDGIN
SMUDGED
SOLDIER
SONDAGE
SPADGER
SPIDERS
SPIDERY
STADDLE
STADIUM
STUDDED
STUDENT
STUDIED
SUBDUCT
SUBDUED
SUNDECK
SUNDIAL
SUNDOWN
SURDITY
SWADDLE
SWEDISH
SWIDDEN
TARDILY
TARDIVE
TENDRIL
TIDDLER
TODDLER
TRADEIN
TRADING
TRADUCE
TRIDENT
TRODDEN
TRUDGEN
TWADDLE
TWIDDLE
TWIDDLY
VANDALS
VANDYKE
VAUDOIS
VENDING
VENDOME
VERDANT
VERDICT
VERDURE
VIADUCT
WADDING
WARDOUR
WEDDING
WELDING
WENDELL
WILDCAT
WINDBAG
WINDING
WINDOWS
WINDROW
WINDSOR
WONDERS
WOODCUT
WOODMAN
WORDILY
WORDING
YARDAGE
YARDARM
YIDDISH
ABREAST
ABSENCE
ACHERON
ACHESON
ACREAGE
ADRENAL
ADVERSE
AILERON
ALBENIZ
ALBERGO
ALBERTA
ALBERTI
ALGEBRA
ALGERIA
ALLEGED
ALLEGRI
ALLEGRO
ALLENBY
ALLERGY
ALREADY
ALTERED
ALVEOLE
AMMETER
AMNESIA
AMNESTY
AMOEBIC
ANAEMIA
ANAEMIC
ANGELIC
ANGELUS
ANGEVIN
ANNELID
ANTENNA
APHELIA
APHESIS
APPEASE
APTERAL
APTERYX
AQUEOUS
ARIETTA
ARREARS
ARSENAL
ARSENIC
ARTEMIS
ARTEMUS
ASCETIC
ASPERGE
ASSEGAI
ATHEISM
ATHEIST
ATTEMPT
AUBERGE
AUREATE
AURELIA
AUREOLA
AUREOLE
BAGEHOT
BALEFUL
BARENTS
BEDEVIL
BEJEWEL
BENEATH
BENEFIT
BEREAVE
BESEECH
BEVERLY
BIBELOT
BIRETTA
BLEEPER
BOHEMIA
BOLETUS
BOREDOM
BRAEMAR
BREEDER
BRIEFLY
BURETTE
CADENCE
CADENZA
CALECHE
CALENDS
CALEPIN
CAMELOT
CAMERON
CANELLA
CAPELLA
CAREERS
CAREFUL
CASEASE
CATELOG
CATERER
CATESBY
CAVEMAN
CAYENNE
CELEBES
CELESTA
CELESTE
CHEERIO
CHEESED
CHEETAH
CHIEFLY
CINEMAS
CINEREA
CODEINE
COGENCY
CORELLI
COTERIE
COVERED
COVERUP
COVETED
CREEPER
CROESUS
CRUELLS
CRUELLY
CRUELTY
CURETTE
CUVETTE
DECEASE
DECEIVE
DECENCY
DEFENCE
DEFENSE
DEJECTA
DEMERGE
DEMERIT
DEMESNE
DEMETER
DESERTS
DESERVE
DETENTE
DEVELOP
DIDEROT
DILEMMA
DINETTE
DISEASE
DIVERGE
DIVERSE
DNIEPER
DOLEFUL
DONEGAL
DUKEDOM
DUNEDIN
EAGERLY
ECHELON
EFFECTS
EFFENDI
ELDERLY
ELZEVIR
EMPEROR
ENDEMIC
ENFEOFF
ENTEBBE
ENTENTE
ENTERIC
ENTERON
ENVELOP
ENVENOM
EPHEBUS
EPHEDRA
EPHESUS
EQUERRY
ESSENCE
ESSENES
EUGENIA
EUGENIC
EUGENIE
EUPEPSY
EUTERPE
EXCERPT
EXHEDRA
EXPENSE
FACETED
FAIENCE
FATEFUL
FAVELLA
FEDERAL
FENELON
FEVERED
FIDELIO
FINESSE
FIREARM
FIREBUG
FIREDOG
FIREFLY
FIREMAN
FIXEDLY
FLEEING
FLUENCY
FOREARM
FOREIGN
FORELEG
FOREMAN
FOREPAW
FORESEE
FOREVER
FREEBIE
FREEDOM
FREEMAN
FREESIA
FREEWAY
FREEZER
FRIENDS
FROEBEL
FUMETTE
FUNERAL
FUSEBOX
GABELLE
GALETTE
GAMELAN
GANELON
GASEOUS
GATEWAY
GAZELLE
GAZETTE
GEHENNA
GENERAL
GENERIC
GENESIS
GENETIC
GISELLE
GLEEFUL
GOBELIN
GODETIA
GREENER
HARELIP
HATEFUL
HEREDIA
HERETIC
HIDEOUS
HIDEOUT
HOMERIC
HONESTY
HONEYED
HOPEFUL
HOWEVER
HUMERUS
ICTERIC
ICTERUS
IGNEOUS
ILLEGAL
IMMENSE
IMMERGE
IMMERSE
IMPEACH
IMPERIL
IMPETUS
INCENSE
INDEPTH
INDEXER
INFERNO
INGENUE
INHERIT
INNERVE
INSECTS
INTEGER

INTENSE
INTERIM
INTERNE
INVEIGH
INVERSE
IONESCO
IVRESSE
JAMESON
JAVELIN
JAVELLE
JEWELER
JEWELRY
JEZEBEL
JUKEBOX
JUVENAL
KALENDS
KAMERAD
KINESIS
KINETIC
KLEENEX
KNEECAP
KNEELER
KUBELIK
LACERTA
LACEUPS
LAMELLA
LATERAL
LATERAN
LAYERED
LAYETTE
LEVERET
LIBERAL
LIBERIA
LIBERTY
LICENCE
LICENSE
LIKENED
LINEAGE
LINEMAN
LITERAL
LOBELIA
LORELEI
LOZENGE
LUCERNE
MACEDON
MADEIRA
MAGENTA
MAJESTY
MALEFIC
MAREMMA
MARENGO
MATELOT
MAZEPPA
MEMENTO
MESEEMS
MILEAGE
MINERAL
MINERVA
MISERLY
MODESTY
MOFETTE
MOMENTS
MONEYED
MOREISH
MORELLO
MORESBY
MORESCO
MOSELLE
MUDEJAR
MUSETTE
MYCELLA
MYCENAE
MYCETES
NACELLE
NAKEDLY
NAVETTE
NEMESIA
NEMESIS
NIGELLA
NIGERIA
NINEPIN
NINEVEH
NOSEBAG
NOSEGAY
NOTEPAD
NOVELLA
NOVELLO
NOVELTY
NUMERAL
NUMERIC
NUREYEV
OBJECTS
OBSEQUY
OBSERVE
OBVERSE
OFFENCE
OFFENSE
OFFERER
OGREISH
ORDERED
ORDERLY
ORLEANS
OSSELET
OSSEOUS
OSTEOMA
OTHELLO
PAGEANT
PAGEBOY
PALERMO
PALETTE
PARENTS
PARESIS
PATELLA
PEREIRA
PHAETON
PHOEBUS
PHOENIX
PHRENIC
PIGEONS
PIKELET
PIMENTO
PINETUM
PIPETTE
PITEOUS
PODESTA
POLEAXE
POLECAT
POLEMIC
POLENTA
POMEROL
POMEROY
POPEYED
POTENCY
POVERTY
POWERED
PRAETOR
PREEMPT
PRIESTS
PUBERAL
PUBERTY
PUCELLE
PYAEMIA
PYRETIC
PYREXIA
QUEENLY
QUEERER
QUIETEN
QUIETLY
QUIETUS
RACEMIC
RALEIGH
RAMEKIN
RAMESES
RAREBIT
REBECCA
RECEIPT
RECEIVE
REFEREE
REGENCY
RELEASE
RENEGUE
RENEWAL
REREDOS
RESERVE
REVELER
REVELRY
REVENGE
REVENUE
REVERED
REVERIE
REVERSE
RIVETED
ROBERTS
ROBESON
ROSEATE
ROSEBUD
ROSELLA
ROSELLE
ROSEOLA
ROSETTA
ROSETTE
RUBELLA
RUBEOLA
RUDERAL
SALERMO
SAVELOY
SCHEMER
SCHERZO
SCIENCE
SCLERAL
SCREECH
SCREEVE
SCREWED
SENECIO
SENEGAL
SEVENTH
SEVENTY
SEVERAL
SEVERUS
SIDECAR
SILENCE
SILESIA
SIMENON
SLEEKLY
SLEEPER
SLEEVED
SOBERLY
SOMEHOW
SOMEONE
SPHENIC
SQUEAKY
SQUEERS
SQUEEZE
SQUELCH
STEEPEN
STEEPLE
STEEPLY
STEERER
STREAKY
STRETCH
STREWTH
SUBEDAR
SUBEDIT
SUDETEN
SUZETTE
SWEEPER
SWEETEN
SWEETIE
SWEETLY
SYNERGY
TAGETES
TAKEOFF
TAKEOUT
TAMESIS
TAVERNA
TEHERAN
TERENCE
THIEVES
THREADS
THRENOS
TIBETAN
TIDEWAY
TIMELAG
TOTEMIC
TOXEMIA
TREETOP
TRIESTE
TUNEFUL
TURENNE
TUTELAR
TWEEDLE
TWEETER
UCCELLO
UNDERGO
UNHEARD
UNKEMPT
UNLEASH
UNNERVE
UNREADY
URAEMIA
URGENCY
UTRECHT
UTTERLY
VALENCE
VALENCY
VANESSA
VEDETTE
VENERER
VETERAN
VICEROY
VINEGAR
VIRELAY
WAKEFUL
WATERED
WAVERER
WHEEDLE
WHEELED
WHEELER
WHEELIE
WHOEVER
WIPEOUT
WIRETAP
WIZENED
XIMENES
YEREVAN
ACIFORM
AIRFLOW
BAFFLED
BALFOUR
BEDFORD
BIAFRAN
BIGFOOT
BLUFFLY
BONFIRE
BUFFALO
BUFFOON
CATFISH
CHAFING
CHIFFON
CHUFFED
COFFERS
COMFORT
COMFREY
CONFESS
CONFIDE
CONFINE
CONFIRM
CONFORM
CONFUSE
CROFTER
DIFFUSE
DOGFISH
DOGFOOD
DRAFTED
DRAFTEE
DRIFTER
EDIFICE
FANFARE
FORFEIT
FORFEND
FULFILL
FUNFAIR
GABFEST
GASFIRE
GOLFING
GRAFTER
GRIFFON
GRIFTER
GRUFFLY
GUNFIRE
HALFWAY
HALFWIT
HOTFOOT
ICEFLOE
LEAFLET
MAYFAIR
MENFOLK
MILFOIL
MISFIRE
MOUFLON
MUDFLAP
MUFFLED
MUFFLER
NORFOLK
OARFISH
OLEFINE
ORIFICE
OUTFACE
OUTFALL
OUTFLOW
PALFREY
PARFAIT
PERFECT
PERFIDY
PERFORM
PERFUME
PERFUSE
PINFOLD
PITFALL
POMFRET
POOFTER
PREFACE
PREFECT
PROFANE
PROFESS
PROFFER
PROFILE
PROFITS
PROFUSE
RAFFISH
RAFFLES
ROOFING
ROOFTOP
RUFFIAN
RUFFLED
RUFFLER
SAFFRON
SAWFISH
SCAFELL
SCOFFER
SCUFFLE
SEAFOOD
SELFISH
SERFDOM
SHUFFLE
SKIFFLE
SNAFFLE
SNIFFER
SNIFFLE
SNIFTER
SNUFFLE
SOUFFLE
STAFFER
STIFFEN
STIFFLY
STUFFED
SUBFUSC
SUFFETE
SUFFICE
SUFFOLK
SUFFUSE
SULFATE
SURFACE
SURFEIT
SURFING
SWIFTER
SWIFTLY
TAFFETA
TAXFREE
TELFORD
TENFOLD
TIFFANY
TINFOIL
TOMFOOL
TRAFFIC
TREFOIL
TRIFFID
TRIFLER
TRIFLES
TRUFFLE
TWOFOLD
UNIFORM
WARFARE
WELFARE
WILFRED
WOLFISH
WOLFRAM

ZOFFANY
ABIGAIL
ALIGNED
AMYGDAL
ANAGRAM
APOGEAN
ATAGHAN
AVIGNON
AZYGOUS
BAGGAGE
BANGING
BANGKOK
BARGAIN
BEGGARY
BEGGING
BELGIAN
BELGIUM
BENGALI
BERGSON
BLIGHTY
BRIGADE
BRIGAND
BRIGHAM
BUGGING
BUGGINS
BULGHUR
BULGING
BUNGLER
BURGEON
BURGESS
BURGHER
BURGLAR
CARGOES
CHAGALL
CHAGRIN
CHIGGER
CHIGNON
CONGEAL
COWGIRL
DAGGERS
DIAGRAM
DIGGING
DINGBAT
DISGUST
DODGEMS
DOGGONE
DOUGHTY
DOUGLAS
DRAGGLE
DRAGNET
DRAGOON
DRUGGED
DRUGGET
DUDGEON
DUNGEON
ELEGANT
ELEGIAC
ELEGIST
ELOGIUM
ENDGAME
EPIGONE

EPIGRAM
ETAGÈRE
EXEGETE
EXIGENT
EXOGAMY
FAGGOTS
FANGLED
FEIGNED
FIDGETS
FIDGETY
FINGERS
FLAGDAY
FLIGHTY
FLOGGER
FORGAVE
FORGERY
FORGIVE
FORGONE
FRAGILE
FRIGATE
FROGMAN
FULGENT
FUNGOID
FUNGOUS
GANGWAY
GAUGUIN
GINGHAM
GOGGLES
GREGORY
GROGRAM
GUDGEON
GUIGNOL
HAGGADA
HAGGARD
HAGGERY
HANGDOG
HANGING
HANGMAN
HANGMEN
HANGOUT
HAUGHTY
HEDGING
HEIGHTS
HENGIST
HIGGINS
HOGGING
HUNGARY
IMAGERY
IMAGINE
IMAGING
IMAGISM
IMAGIST
ISOGRAM
JAGGERY
JOGGING
JUGGINS
JUGGLER
KINGCUP
KINGDOM
KINGLET
KINGPIN

LAGGARD
LAGGING
LANGLEY
LANGTON
LANGUID
LANGUOR
LARGELY
LARGESS
LARGEST
LEAGUER
LEGGING
LENGTHY
LINGUAL
LODGING
LOGGING
LONGBOW
LONGING
LUDGATE
LUGGAGE
MAGGOTY
MAIGRET
MANGOLD
MARGERY
MAUGHAM
MONGREL
MUGGING
NAGGING
NAUGHTY
NIAGARA
NIGGARD
NOGGING
OREGANO
ORIGAMI
ORIGINS
OUTGROW
PANGAEA
PANGRAM
PENGUIN
PERGOLA
PIDGEON
PIGGERY
PILGRIM
PROGENY
PROGRAM
PUNGENT
RANGOON
REAGENT
RIGGING
RINGERS
RINGGIT
RINGING
RINGLET
ROUGHEN
ROUGHIE
ROUGHLY
SANGRIA
SARGENT
SCAGLIA
SEAGULL
SHAGGED
SINGING

SINGLES
SINGLET
SLOGGER
SMUGGLE
SNIGGER
SNUGGLE
SORGHUM
STAGGER
STAGING
STYGIAN
SUGGEST
SURGEON
SURGERY
SWAGGER
SWAGMAN
TANGENT
TANGIER
TANGLED
THUGGEE
TINGLER
TONGUES
TOUGHEN
TRAGEDY
TRIGGER
TSIGANE
TSIGANY
TURGENT
TWIGGER
URUGUAY
VAUGHAN
VIRGATE
VIRGULE
VULGATE
WAGGISH
WAGGLER
WANGLER
WEIGELA
WEIGHIN
WEIGHTS
WEIGHTY
WIDGEON
WIGGING
WRIGGLE
YANGTSE
ZINGARO
AFGHANI
ALCHEMY
ALPHEUS
ALTHAEA
ALTHING
AMPHORA
ANCHOVY
ANTHILL
ANTHONY
ANTHRAX
ARCHAIC
ARCHERY
ARCHIVE
ARCHWAY
ARMHOLE
ASPHALT

BAGHDAD
BASHFUL
BATHERS
BATHING
BATHMAT
BATHTUB
BAUHAUS
BEEHIVE
BESHREW
BETHINK
BETHUMB
BIGHEAD
BIGHORN
BOWHEAD
BOYHOOD
BRAHMIN
BUSHIDO
BUSHMAN
BUSHMEN
CACHEXY
CASHBOX
CASHIER
CATHEAD
CATHODE
CITHARA
COCHLEA
COWHAND
COWHERD
CUSHION
DAPHNID
DAPHNIS
DASHING
DASHPOT
DIEHARD
DITHERY
DUCHESS
EGGHEAD
ENCHANT
ENTHRAL
ENTHUSE
ESCHEAT
ETCHING
EUPHONY
FASHION
FATHEAD
FIGHTER
FISHERY
FISHEYE
FISHING
FISHNET
FLYHALF
FOGHORN
FOXHOLE
FUCHSIA
GOAHEAD
GOSHAWK
GUSHING
HACHURE
HASHISH
HIGHEST
HIGHMAN

HIGHWAY
HOTHEAD
INSHORE
ISCHIUM
ISOHYET
ISTHMUS
ITCHING
KASHMIR
KEYHOLE
KITHARA
KURHAUS
LASHING
LECHERY
LIGHTEN
LIGHTER
LIGHTLY
LITHELY
LITHIUM
LOTHAIR
LOTHIAN
LUGHOLE
LYCHNIS
MACHETE
MACHINE
MAGHREB
MANHOLE
MANHOOD
MANHUNT
METHANE
METHINK
MICHAEL
MITHRAS
MOTHERS
NAPHTHA
NIGHTIE
NIGHTLY
NOTHING
NOWHERE
OFFHAND
OMPHALE
ONSHORE
ORCHARD
ORPHEAN
ORPHEUS
ORPHISM
ORPHREY
PATHWAY
PERHAPS
PINHEAD
PINHOLE
PITHEAD
PITHILY
POCHARD
POCHOIR
POOHBAH
POTHEEN
POTHERB
POTHOLE
PREHEAT
PUSHING
PUSHKIN

RACHIAL
RACHMAN
RAPHAEL
RAWHIDE
REDHEAD
RESHAPE
RETHINK
RICHARD
RICHTER
RIGHTLY
RUSHING
RUTHENE
SASHIMI
SAXHORN
SIGHTED
SIKHISM
SINHALA
SKYHIGH
SOPHISM
SOPHIST
SPYHOLE
SWAHILI
TACHISM
TIGHTEN
TIGHTLY
TOEHOLD
TOWHEAD
TYPHOID
TYPHOON
UPSHOOT
WARHEAD
WASHDAY
WASHERS
WASHING
WASHOUT
WASHTUB
WISHFUL
WISHING
WITHERS
WITHOUT
YASHMAK
YOGHURT
ZEPHIEL
ABRIDGE
ABSINTH
ACHIEVE
ACTINAL
ACTINIA
ACTINIC
ADDISON
ADMIRAL
ADMIRED
ADMIRER
ADVISER
ADVISOR
AFFIXED
AFRICAN
AGAINST
AGRIPPA
ALGIERS
ALRIGHT

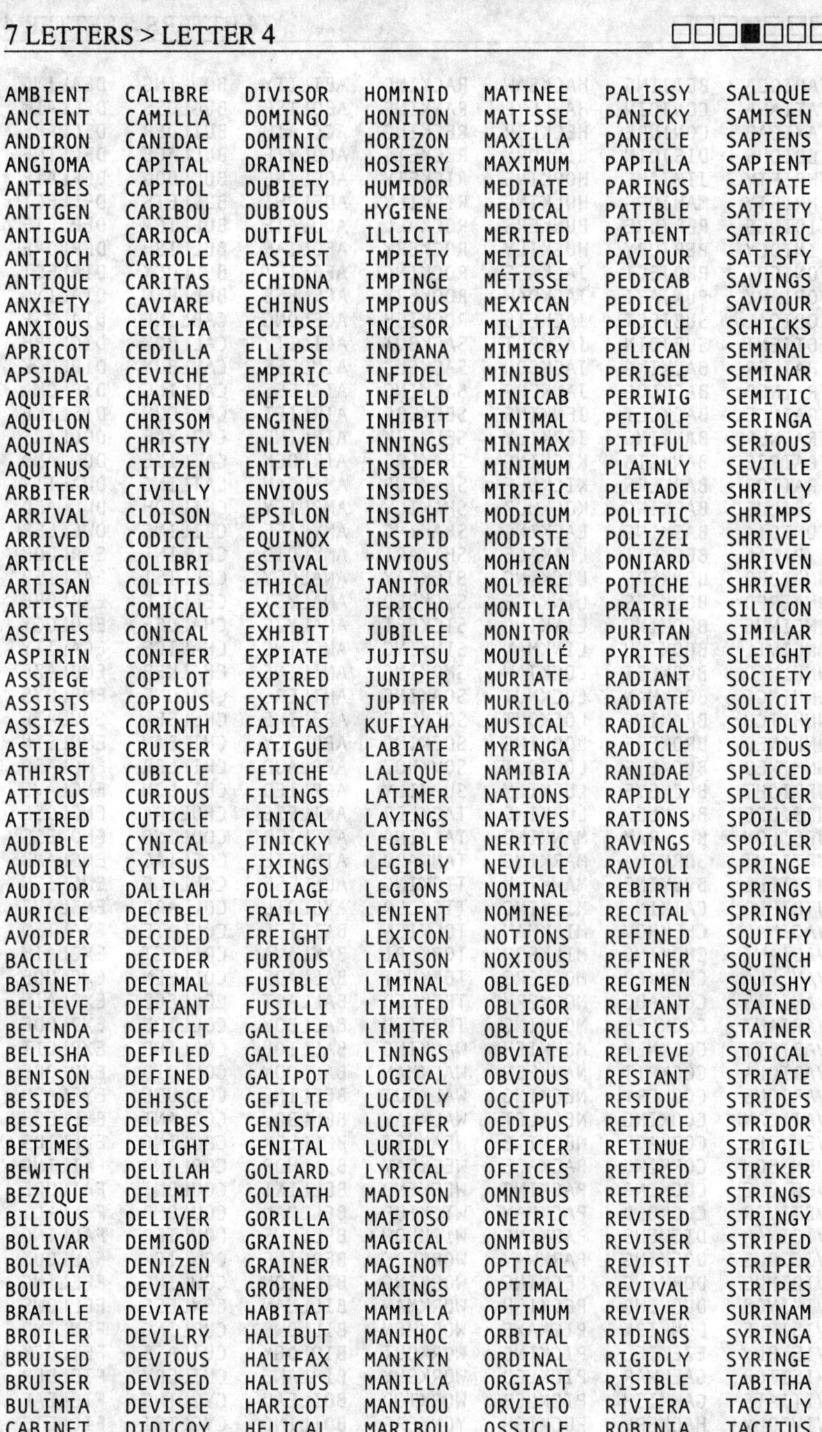

AMBIENT
ANCIENT
ANDIRON
ANGIOMA
ANTIBES
ANTIGEN
ANTIGUA
ANTIOCH
ANTIQUE
ANXIETY
ANXIOUS
APRICOT
APSIDAL
AQUIFER
AQUILON
AQUINAS
AQUINUS
ARBITER
ARRIVAL
ARRIVED
ARTICLE
ARTISAN
ARTISTE
ASCITES
ASPIRIN
ASSIEGE
ASSISTS
ASSIZES
ASTILBE
ATHIRST
ATTICUS
ATTIRED
AUDIBLE
AUDIBLY
AUDITOR
AURICLE
AVOIDER
BACILLI
BASINET
BELIEVE
BELINDA
BELISHA
BENISON
BESIDES
BESIEGE
BETIMES
BEWITCH
BEZIQUE
BILIOUS
BOLIVAR
BOLIVIA
BOUILLI
BRAILLE
BROILER
BRUISED
BRUISER
BULIMIA
CABINET
CACIQUE
CALIBAN
CALIBER
CALIBRE
CAMILLA
CANIDAE
CAPITAL
CAPITOL
CARIBOU
CARIOCA
CARIOLE
CARITAS
CAVIARE
CECILIA
CEDILLA
CEVICHE
CHAINED
CHRISOM
CHRISTY
CITIZEN
CIVILLY
CLOISON
CODICIL
COLIBRI
COLITIS
COMICAL
CONICAL
CONIFER
COPILOT
COPIOUS
CORINTH
CRUISER
CUBICLE
CURIOUS
CUTICLE
CYNICAL
CYTISUS
DALILAH
DECIBEL
DECIDED
DECIDER
DECIMAL
DEFIANT
DEFICIT
DEFILED
DEFINED
DEHISCE
DELIBES
DELIGHT
DELILAH
DELIMIT
DELIVER
DEMIGOD
DENIZEN
DEVIANT
DEVIATE
DEVILRY
DEVIOUS
DEVISED
DEVISEE
DIDICOY
DIGITAL
DIVIDED
DIVINER
DIVISOR
DOMINGO
DOMINIC
DRAINED
DUBIETY
DUBIOUS
DUTIFUL
EASIEST
ECHIDNA
ECHINUS
ECLIPSE
ELLIPSE
EMPIRIC
ENFIELD
ENGINED
ENLIVEN
ENTITLE
ENVIOUS
EPSILON
EQUINOX
ESTIVAL
ETHICAL
EXCITED
EXHIBIT
EXPIATE
EXPIRED
EXTINCT
FAJITAS
FATIGUE
FETICHE
FILINGS
FINICAL
FINICKY
FIXINGS
FOLIAGE
FRAILTY
FREIGHT
FURIOUS
FUSIBLE
FUSILLI
GALILEE
GALILEO
GALIPOT
GEFILTE
GENISTA
GENITAL
GOLIARD
GOLIATH
GORILLA
GRAINED
GRAINER
GROINED
HABITAT
HALIBUT
HALIFAX
HALITUS
HARICOT
HELICAL
HELICON
HELIPAD
HOLIDAY
HOMINID
HONITON
HORIZON
HOSIERY
HUMIDOR
HYGIENE
ILLICIT
IMPIETY
IMPINGE
IMPIOUS
INCISOR
INDIANA
INFIDEL
INFIELD
INHIBIT
INNINGS
INSIDER
INSIDES
INSIGHT
INSIPID
INVIOUS
JANITOR
JERICHO
JUBILEE
JUJITSU
JUNIPER
JUPITER
KUFIYAH
LABIATE
LALIQUE
LATIMER
LAYINGS
LEGIBLE
LEGIBLY
LEGIONS
LENIENT
LEXICON
LIAISON
LIMINAL
LIMITED
LIMITER
LININGS
LOGICAL
LUCIDLY
LUCIFER
LURIDLY
LYRICAL
MADISON
MAFIOSO
MAGICAL
MAGINOT
MAKINGS
MAMILLA
MANIHOC
MANIKIN
MANILLA
MANITOU
MARIBOU
MARINER
MARITAL
MATILDA
MATINEE
MATISSE
MAXILLA
MAXIMUM
MEDIATE
MEDICAL
MERITED
METICAL
MÉTISSE
MEXICAN
MILITIA
MIMICRY
MINIBUS
MINICAB
MINIMAL
MINIMAX
MINIMUM
MIRIFIC
MODICUM
MODISTE
MOHICAN
MOLIÈRE
MONILIA
MONITOR
MOUILLÉ
MURIATE
MURILLO
MUSICAL
MYRINGA
NAMIBIA
NATIONS
NATIVES
NERITIC
NEVILLE
NOMINAL
NOMINEE
NOTIONS
NOXIOUS
OBLIGED
OBLIGOR
OBLIQUE
OBVIATE
OBVIOUS
OCCIPUT
OEDIPUS
OFFICER
OFFICES
OMNIBUS
ONEIRIC
ONMIBUS
OPTICAL
OPTIMAL
OPTIMUM
ORBITAL
ORDINAL
ORGIAST
ORVIETO
OSSICLE
OSTIOLE
PACIFIC
PALINGS
PALISSY
PANICKY
PANICLE
PAPILLA
PARINGS
PATIBLE
PATIENT
PAVIOUR
PEDICAB
PEDICEL
PEDICLE
PELICAN
PERIGEE
PERIWIG
PETIOLE
PITIFUL
PLAINLY
PLEIADE
POLITIC
POLIZEI
PONIARD
POTICHE
PRAIRIE
PURITAN
PYRITES
RADIANT
RADIATE
RADICAL
RADICLE
RANIDAE
RAPIDLY
RATIONS
RAVINGS
RAVIOLI
REBIRTH
RECITAL
REFINED
REFINER
REGIMEN
RELIANT
RELICTS
RELIEVE
RESIANT
RESIDUE
RETICLE
RETINUE
RETIRED
RETIREE
REVISED
REVISER
REVISIT
REVIVAL
REVIVER
RIDINGS
RIGIDLY
RISIBLE
RIVIERA
ROBINIA
RUBICON
SALIENT
SALIERI
SALIQUE
SAMISEN
SAPIENS
SAPIENT
SATIATE
SATIETY
SATIRIC
SATISFY
SAVINGS
SAVIOUR
SCHICKS
SEMINAL
SEMINAR
SEMITIC
SERINGA
SERIOUS
SEVILLE
SHRILLY
SHRIMPS
SHRIVEL
SHRIVEN
SHRIVER
SILICON
SIMILAR
SLEIGHT
SOCIETY
SOLICIT
SOLIDLY
SOLIDUS
SPLICED
SPLICER
SPOILED
SPOILER
SPRINGE
SPRINGS
SPRINGY
SQUIFFY
SQUINCH
SQUISHY
STAINED
STAINER
STOICAL
STRIATE
STRIDES
STRIDOR
STRIGIL
STRIKER
STRINGS
STRINGY
STRIPED
STRIPER
STRIPES
SURINAM
SYRINGA
SYRINGE
TABITHA
TACITLY
TACITUS
TAKINGS
TALIPES
TALIPOT

TAPIOCA
TATIANA
TAXICAB
TEDIOUS
THRIFTY
THRISTY
TIDINGS
TIMIDLY
TONIGHT
TOPIARY
TOPICAL
TOTIENT
TRAILER
TRAINED
TRAINEE
TRAINER
TRAIPSE
TRAITOR
TROILUS
TUNISIA
TYPICAL
UNAIDED
UNAIRED
UNCINUS
UNCIVIL
UNFIXED
UNHINGE
UNHITCH
UNLINED
UNMIXED
UPRIGHT
UPSIDES
UPSILON
UPTIGHT
UTRICLE
UTRILLO
VAGINAL
VALIANT
VANILLA
VANITAS
VARIANT
VARIETY
VARIOLA
VARIOUS
VATICAN
VEHICLE
VENISON
VESICLE
VETIVER
VICINAL
VICIOUS
VIDIMUS
VIKINGS
VISIBLE
VISIBLY
VISITOR
VITIATE
VIVIDLY
WYSIWYG
YEZIDEE
YPSILON
BEIJING
CONJOIN
CONJURE
DISJOIN
JIMJAMS
MAHJONG
PERJURE
PERJURY
PROJECT
PUNJABI
SUBJECT
SUBJOIN
BACKING
BACKLOG
BACKSET
BANKING
BANKSIA
BARKERS
BARKING
BASKING
BECKETT
BONKERS
BOOKIES
BOOKING
BOOKISH
BOOKLET
BOOKMAN
BRAKING
BROKERS
BUCKETS
BUCKEYE
BUCKLER
BUCKRAM
BURKINA
BUSKINS
CATKINS
CHEKHOV
CHOKING
CHUKKER
COCKADE
COCKLES
COCKNEY
COCKPIT
COOKERY
COOKING
CORKAGE
CORKING
CUCKING
CUCKOLD
DICKENS
DOCKING
DORKING
DUCKING
DUNKIRK
EZEKIEL
GAEKWAR
GAWKISH
HACKERY
HACKING
HACKLES
HACKNEY
HACKSAW
HAWKEYE
HECKLER
HICKORY
HOPKINS
HULKING
HUNKERS
HUSKILY
JACKASS
JACKDAW
JACKETS
JACKPOT
JACKSON
JANKERS
JENKINS
JERKILY
KICKING
KICKOFF
KOLKHOZ
LACKING
LEAKAGE
LICKING
LINKAGE
LINKING
LINKMAN
LOCKJAW
LOCKNUT
LOCKOUT
LOOKING
LOOKOUT
LUCKILY
LURKING
MANKIND
MARKING
MAWKISH
MILKING
MILKMAN
MILKSOP
MOCKERS
MOCKERY
MOCKING
MONKISH
NANKEEN
NECKING
NECKLET
NECKTIE
PACKAGE
PACKING
PACKMAN
PARKING
PARKWAY
PECKING
PECKISH
PICKAXE
PICKING
PICKLED
PICKLER
PUCKISH
QUAKING
RACKETS
RACKETY
RACKING
RANKING
REEKING
RICKETS
RICKETY
RISKILY
ROCKALL
ROCKERY
ROCKING
ROOKERY
ROOKISH
SACKBUT
SACKFUL
SACKING
SEEKERS
SELKIRK
SHAKERS
SHAKEUP
SHAKILY
SHAKING
SHIKARI
SICKBAY
SICKBED
SICKERT
SINKING
SMOKING
SOAKING
SOCKEYE
SOCKING
SOVKHOZ
SULKILY
TACKLER
TALKING
TANKARD
TICKING
TICKLER
TOLKIEN
TOPKAPI
TOPKNOT
TREKKER
TURKISH
WALKING
WALKMAN
WALKOUT
WALKWAY
WEAKEST
WEEKDAY
WEEKEND
WICKIUP
WICKLOW
WORKERS
WORKING
WORKMAN
WORKMEN
WORKOUT
WORKSHY
WORKTOP
YONKERS
YORKIST
ABALONE
ABELARD
ABILITY
ABOLISH
ACCLAIM
ACOLYTE
ADELINE
ADELPHI
ADULATE
AEOLIAN
AFFLICT
AGELESS
AGELONG
AGILITY
AIMLESS
AIRLESS
AIRLIFT
AIRLINE
AIRLOCK
AMALGAM
AMPLIFY
AMYLASE
AMYLOID
ANALOGY
ANALYST
ANALYZE
ANGLING
ANILINE
ANTLERS
APELIKE
APOLOGY
APPLAUD
APPLIED
ARTLESS
ATELIER
ATHLETE
AUSLESE
AXOLOTL
BAILIFF
BAKLAVA
BALLADE
BALLAST
BALLBOY
BALLIOL
BALLOON
BEELINE
BELLBOY
BELLEEK
BELLHOP
BELLINI
BELLMAN
BELLOWS
BERLINE
BILLION
BILLMAN
BILLOWS
BIOLOGY
BIPLANE
BOILEAU
BOILING
BOLLARD
BOOLEAN
BOULDER
BOWLING
BUGLOSS
BUILDER
BULLACE
BULLDOG
BULLETS
BULLION
BULLISH
BULLOCK
BULLPEN
CABLING
CALLBOX
CALLBOY
CALLING
CALLOUS
CARLYLE
CATLIKE
CATLING
CEILIDH
CEILING
CELLINI
CELLIST
CELLULE
CHALDEE
CHALICE
CHALKER
CHALONE
CHELSEA
CHILEAN
CHILLER
CHILLON
CHOLERA
CODLING
COELIAC
COLLAGE
COLLARD
COLLATE
COLLECT
COLLEEN
COLLEGE
COLLIDE
COLLIER
COLLOID
COLLUDE
COOLANT
COOLING
COPLAND
COULDNT
COULOMB
COULTER
COWLICK
COWLING
COXLESS
CURLING
CUTLASS
CUTLERY
CYCLING
CYCLIST
CYCLONE
CYCLOPS
DARLING
DEALING
DECLAIM
DECLARE
DECLINE
DEFLATE
DEFLECT
DEPLETE
DEPLORE
DIALECT
DIALING
DIALYSE
DIGLYPH
DIPLOCK
DIPLOMA
DISLIKE
DOLLARS
DOWLAND
DUALITY
DULLARD
DWELLER
EARLDOM
EARLIER
EARLOBE
ECOLOGY
EGALITY
EMBLAZE
EMPLOYS
EMULATE
EMULSIN
ENCLASP
ENCLAVE
ENCLOSE
ENDLESS
ENGLAND
ENGLISH
ENSLAVE
EXALTED
EXCLAIM
EXCLUDE
EXPLAIN
EXPLODE
EXPLOIT
EXPLORE
EYELASH
EYELESS
EYELIDS
FAILING
FAILURE
FALLACY
FALLING
FALLOUT
FEELING
FELLOWS
FENLAND
FETLOCK
FIELDER
FIGLEAF
FILLETS
FILLING
FINLAND
FLYLEAF

FOGLAMP
FOLLIES
FOOLISH
FORLORN
FOULARD
FRILLED
FULLERS
FURLONG
GALLANT
GALLEON
GALLERY
GALLING
GALLIUM
GALLONS
GALLOWS
GARLAND
GATLING
GEELONG
GEOLOGY
GIBLETS
GIELGUD
GILLRAY
GIRLISH
GODLESS
GODLIKE
GOOLIES
GOSLING
GOULASH
GRILLED
GROLIER
GUILDER
GUTLESS
HALLALI
HALLWAY
HAPLESS
HARLECH
HATLESS
HAULAGE
HAULIER
HAZLETT
HEALING
HEALTHY
HELLCAT
HELLENE
HELLION
HELLISH
HELLUVA
HEMLINE
HEMLOCK
HILLMAN
HILLMEN
HILLOCK
HILLTOP
HOLLAND
HOPLITE
HOTLINE
HOWLING
HURLING
HYALINE
HYALOID
ICELAND
IDOLIZE
IDYLLIC
IMPLANT
IMPLIED
IMPLODE
IMPLORE
INCLINE
INCLUDE
INFLAME
INFLATE
INFLECT
INFLICT
INKLING
IRELAND
ISOLATE
ITALIAN
JAPLISH
JEALOUS
JELLABA
JELLIED
JOBLESS
JOLLITY
JOYLESS
JUGLANS
JUTLAND
KEELING
KHALIFA
KIELDER
KILLICK
KILLING
KILLJOY
KIPLING
KNELLER
KOWLOON
LALLANS
LAWLESS
LEGLESS
LOLLARD
LOWLAND
LULLABY
MAILBAG
MAILBOX
MAILCAR
MAILING
MAILMAN
MALLARD
MALLEUS
MALLING
MARLENE
MARLINE
MARLOWE
MELLITE
MIDLAND
MILLAIS
MILLING
MILLION
MISLEAD
MOELLON
MOLLIFY
MOLLUSC
MORLAND
MOULAGE
MOULDED
MOULDER
MUDLARK
MULLEIN
MULLION
MYALGIA
MYELINE
MYELOID
MYELOMA
NAILBED
NEGLECT
NÉGLIGÉ
NEOLITH
NIBLICK
NOOLOGY
NUCLEAR
NUCLEIC
NUCLEUS
NUCLIDE
NULLIFY
NULLITY
NUNLIKE
NUTLIKE
OAKLEAF
OARLOCK
OBELISK
OCCLUDE
OCELLAR
OCELLUS
OCULIST
ODALISK
OFFLOAD
OPALINE
OPULENT
OTALGIA
OUTLAST
OUTLIER
OUTLINE
OUTLIVE
OUTLOOK
OVULATE
OXALATE
PADLOCK
PAHLAVI
PALLIUM
PARLOUR
PARLOUS
PAULINE
PAVLOVA
PAYLOAD
PEELING
PERLITE
PHALANX
PHALLIC
PHALLUS
PHILEAS
PHILTER
PHILTRE
PIGLING
PILLAGE
PILLBOX
PILLION
PILLORY
POLLACK
POLLARD
POLLING
POLLUTE
POTLACH
POTLUCK
POULENC
POULTRY
PRALINE
PRELATE
PRELIMS
PRELUDE
PROLONG
PSALTER
PTOLEMY
PUBLISH
PULLMAN
PURLIEU
PURLINE
PURLOIN
QUALIFY
QUALITY
QUILTED
QUILTER
RAILING
RAILWAY
RATLINE
REALGAR
REALIGN
REALISM
REALIST
REALITY
REALIZE
REALTOR
RECLAIM
RECLINE
RECLUSE
REELECT
REELING
REFLATE
REFLECT
REFLOAT
REPLACE
REPLANT
REPLETE
REPLICA
RIBLESS
RIMLESS
ROLLERS
ROLLICK
ROLLING
ROLLMOP
ROULADE
ROULEAU
ROWLOCK
SAILING
SAILORS
SALLUST
SAPLING
SCALENE
SCALLOP
SCALPEL
SCALPER
SCHLEPP
SCHLOCK
SCHLOSS
SCOLLOP
SCULLER
SEALANT
SEALINK
SEALION
SECLUDE
SELLERS
SELLING
SELLOFF
SELLOUT
SEXLESS
SHALLOT
SHALLOW
SHELLAC
SHELLED
SHELLEY
SHELTER
SHELVED
SHELVES
SHYLOCK
SIBLING
SIRLOIN
SKELTER
SKILFUL
SKILLED
SKILLET
SKYLARK
SKYLINE
SMALLER
SMELTER
SMILING
SMOLDER
SOULFUL
SPELLER
STALKED
STALKER
STELLAR
STILTED
STILTON
STOLLEN
STYLING
STYLISH
STYLIST
STYLITE
STYLIZE
SUBLIME
SULLAGE
SUNLAMP
SUNLESS
SWALLOW
SWELTER
SWOLLEN
TABLEAU
TABLOID
TAILORS
TALLBOY
TAPLASH
TBILISI
TEALEAF
TELLING
THALLUS
THULIUM
TILLAGE
TOLLMAN
TOOLBOX
TOOLING
TOPLESS
TOWLINE
TRELLIS
TRILLED
TRILLER
TRILOGY
TROLLEY
TROLLOP
TWELFTH
UGOLINO
UKULELE
ULULANT
ULULATE
UNALIKE
UNALIVE
UNBLOCK
UNCLASP
UNCLEAN
UNCLEAR
URALITE
UROLITH
USELESS
UTILITY
UTILIZE
VAULTED
VILLAGE
VILLAIN
VILLEIN
VIOLATE
VIOLENT
WAILING
WALLABY
WALLACE
WALLIES
WALLOON
WARLIKE
WARLING
WARLOCK
WARLORD
WAYLAND
WEALDEN
WEALTHY
WEDLOCK
WELLIES
WELLOFF
WENLOCK
WETLAND
WHALING
WILLIAM
WILLIES
WILLING
WILLOWY
WITLESS
WITLOOF
WOOLLEN
WORLDLY
WOULDBE
WOULDNT
YELLOWS
ZEALAND
ZEALOUS
ZEOLITE
ZETLAND
ZILLION
ZOOLITE
ZOOLOGY
ADAMANT
ADAMITE
AILMENT
AIRMAIL
ALAMEIN
ALAMODE
ALEMBIC
ALIMENT
ALIMONY
ALUMINA
ALUMNAE
ALUMNUS
ANEMONE
ANIMALS
ANIMATE
ANIMIST
ANOMALY
ANYMORE
ARAMAIC
ATOMIST
ATOMIZE
AUGMENT
AZIMUTH
BARMAID
BASMATI
BEAMING
BERMUDA
BESMEAR
BIOMASS
BISMUTH
BLEMISH
BOOMING
BRAMBLE
BRIMFUL
BROMIDE
BROMINE
BUMMALO
BURMESE
CADMIUM
CALMUCK
CARMINE
CATMINT
CHAMBER

CHAMBRÉ
CHAMFER
CHAMOIS
CHEMISE
CHEMIST
CHIMERA
CHIMNEY
CLAMBER
CLAMOUR
CLAMPER
CLEMENT
CLIMATE
CLIMBER
CLUMBER
COMMAND
COMMEND
COMMENT
COMMODE
COMMODO
COMMONS
COMMUNE
COMMUTE
CRAMMED
CRAMMER
CRAMPED
CRAMPON
CREMATE
CRIMEAN
CRIMSON
CRUMBLE
CRUMBLY
CRUMPET
CRUMPLE
DAIMLER
DAYMARK
DENMARK
DESMOND
DIAMINE
DIAMOND
DINMONT
DISMAST
DISMISS
DORMANT
DRUMLIN
DRUMMER
EARMARK
ELEMENT
ENAMOUR
EREMITE
ETHMOID
EXAMINE
EXAMPLE
EXEMPLA
FARMERS
FARMING
FERMENT
FERMIUM
FIGMENT
FILMING
FITMENT
FLAMING
FLEMING
FLEMISH
FLUMMOX
FORMICA
FORMING
FORMOSA
FORMULA
FRUMPLE
GARMENT
GASMASK
GEMMATE
GERMANE
GERMANY
GIMMICK
GLAMOUR
GLIMMER
GLIMPSE
GRAMMAR
GRAMPUS
GREMLIN
GRIMACE
GRIMOND
GRIMSBY
GROMMET
GRUMBLE
GRUMMET
HAMMOCK
HARMFUL
HARMONY
HORMONE
HUMMING
HUMMOCK
IPOMOEA
ISOMERE
ITEMIZE
JAMMING
JASMINE
KALMUCK
KERMESS
KHAMSIN
KOUMISS
KREMLIN
LEMMATA
LEMMING
LOOMING
MALMSEY
MAMMARY
MAMMOTH
MANMADE
MARMARA
MARMION
MARMITE
MERMAID
MUMMERS
MUMMERY
MUMMIFY
NUMMARY
NUTMEAT
OATMEAL
ODDMENT
OLYMPIA
OLYMPIC
OLYMPUS
PALMATE
PALMIST
PALMYRA
PAYMENT
PERMIAN
PIGMEAT
PIGMENT
PLUMAGE
PLUMBER
PLUMMET
PLUMPER
PLUMULE
POMMARD
PREMIER
PREMISS
PREMIUM
PRIMACY
PRIMARY
PRIMATE
PRIMEUR
PRIMING
PRIMULA
PROMISE
PROMOTE
RAIMENT
RHOMBUS
RHYMING
ROAMING
RUMMAGE
SARMENT
SAWMILL
SCAMBLE
SCAMPER
SCHMUCK
SEEMING
SEGMENT
SEYMOUR
SFUMATO
SHAMBLE
SHAMPOO
SHIMMER
SIAMESE
SIEMENS
SJAMBOK
SKIMMED
SKIMMER
SKIMMIA
SLAMMER
SLIMMER
SLUMBER
STAMINA
STAMMER
STAMPED
STAMPER
STEMMED
STOMACH
STUMBLE
STUMPED
SUMMARY
SUMMERY
SUMMING
SUMMONS
SURMISE
SWIMMER
TAMMANY
TEEMING
TERMITE
THIMBLE
THOMISM
THOMIST
THOMSON
THUMPER
TOPMAST
TOPMOST
TORMENT
TRAMCAR
TRAMMEL
TRAMPLE
TRAMWAY
TREMBLE
TREMBLY
TREMOLO
TRIMMER
TRUMEAU
TRUMPET
TURMOIL
VARMINT
VERMEER
VERMONT
WARMING
WAYMARK
WHIMPER
WHIMSEY
WOOMERA
WYOMING
ABANDON
ACONITE
ADENOID
ADENOMA
ADONAIS
AGONIST
AGONIZE
ALANINE
ALENÇON
AMANITA
AMENITY
AMONGST
ANANIAS
APTNESS
ARUNDEL
ASININE
ASUNDER
ATINGLE
AVENGER
BADNESS
BANNOCK
BARNABY
BENNETT
BERNARD
BERNINI
BLANDLY
BLANKET
BLANKLY
BLENDER
BLINDER
BLINDLY
BLINKER
BLUNDER
BLUNTED
BLUNTLY
BONNARD
BOUNCER
BOUNDED
BOUNDEN
BOUNDER
BRANDED
BRANDER
BRANTUB
BRENDAN
BRENNER
BRINDLE
BRINJAL
BRONCHI
BRONZED
BURNELL
BURNHAM
BURNING
BURNISH
BURNOUS
BURNOUT
CAINITE
CANNERY
CANNILY
CANNING
CANNOCK
CANNULA
CARNABY
CARNAGE
CHANCEL
CHANCRE
CHANGED
CHANGES
CHANNEL
CHANSON
CHANTER
CHINDIT
CHINESE
CHINOOK
CHINTZY
CHINWAG
CHUNDER
CLANGER
CLINGER
CLINKER
CLUNIAC
COGNATE
COINAGE
CONNATE
CONNECT
CONNIVE
CONNOTE
CORNCOB
CORNEAL
CORNELL
CORNICE
CORNISH
COUNCIL
COUNSEL
COUNTED
COUNTER
COUNTRY
COYNESS
CRANACH
CRANIAL
CRANIUM
CRANMER
CRENATE
CRINKLE
CRINKLY
CRINOID
CRUNCHY
CUNNING
CYANIDE
DAMNING
DARNING
DEANERY
DIGNIFY
DIGNITY
DIMNESS
DONNISH
DRINKER
DRUNKEN
DRYNESS
DUNNAGE
DUNNOCK
DWINDLE
EARNEST
EBONITE
ECONOMY
EMANATE
EMINENT
ENSNARE
ENSNARL
ERINYES
ETONIAN
EVANDER
EVENING
EVENTER
FAINTED
FAINTLY
FARNESE
FATNESS
FAWNING
FIANCÉE
FINNISH
FITNESS
FLANKER
FLANNEL
FLUNKEY
FOUNDER
FOUNDRY
FRANCIS
FRANKLY
FRANTIC
FRINGED
FRONTAL
FUNNILY
FURNACE
FURNISH
GAINFUL
GAINSAY
GARNISH
GAYNESS
GLENCOE
GLENOID
GRANARY
GRANDAD
GRANDEE
GRANDLY
GRANDMA
GRANDPA
GRANITA
GRANITE
GRANNIE
GRANOLA
GRANTED
GRANTEE
GRANULE
GRENADA
GRENADE
GRENDEL
GRINDER
GUANACO
GUINEAN
GUINEAS
GUNNERA
GUNNERY
GWYNETH
GYMNAST
HAFNIUM
HAHNIUM
HARNESS
HAUNTED
HEINOUS
HENNAED
HOBNAIL
ICHNITE
ICINESS
ILLNESS
INANITY
IRANIAN
IRONING
IVANHOE
JOHNNIE
JOHNSON
JOINERY
JOINING
JOINTED
JOINTLY
KAINITE
KENNEDY
KENNELS
KENNING

KERNITE
KEYNOTE
KHANATE
KIDNEYS
KLINKER
KYANITE
LAUNDER
LAUNDRY
LAXNESS
LEANDER
LEANING
LEONARD
LEONINE
LIGNITE
LINNEAN
LIONESS
LIONIZE
LOUNGER
LYMNAEA
MADNESS
MAENADS
MAGNATE
MAGNETO
MAGNIFY
MANNERS
MANNING
MANNISH
MAUNDER
MEANDER
MEANING
MOANING
MOONING
MOONLIT
MORNING
MOUNTED
MOUNTIE
MYANMAR
NEWNESS
NOONDAY
NUNNERY
ODDNESS
ODONTIC
OKINAWA
OLDNESS
OMENTUM
OMINOUS
ONANISM
ONENESS
OPENING
OPINION
OPUNTIA
ORANGES
ORINOCO
ORKNEYS
ORONTES
OXONIAN
PAINFUL
PAINTED
PAINTER
PANNAGE
PANNIER
PANNOSE
PARNELL
PAUNCHY
PEANUTS
PENNANT
PENNATE
PENNINE
PEONAGE
PFENNIG
PHANTOM
PHONEIN
PHONEME
PHONICS
PIANIST
PIANOLA
PINNACE
PINNULA
PIONEER
PLANNED
PLANNER
PLANTAR
PLANTED
PLANTER
PLANURY
PLENARY
PLUNDER
PLUNGER
POINTED
POINTER
PRINCES
PRINTED
PRINTER
PRONAOS
PRONATE
PRONGED
PRONOUN
QUANTUM
QUENTIN
QUINCHE
QUININE
QUINONE
QUINTAL
QUINTAN
QUINTET
QUONDAM
QUONSET
RAINBOW
RAUNCHY
RAWNESS
REDNECK
REDNESS
REENTER
REENTRY
REGNANT
REMNANT
REUNION
REUNITE
REYNARD
RHENISH
RHONDDA
ROUNDED
ROUNDEL
ROUNDER
ROUNDLY
ROUNDUP
RUINOUS
RUNNERS
RUNNING
RUNNION
RWANDAN
SADNESS
SAINTLY
SAMNITE
SAUNTER
SCANDAL
SCANNER
SCENERY
SCENTED
SCHNELL
SHANNON
SHINDIG
SHINGLE
SHINGLY
SHINING
SHINPAD
SHYNESS
SIGNIFY
SIGNING
SIGNORA
SIGNORI
SKINFUL
SKINNED
SKINNER
SLANDER
SLENDER
SLYNESS
SOUNDED
SOUNDER
SOUNDLY
SPANDAU
SPANDEX
SPANGLE
SPANIEL
SPANISH
SPANKER
SPANNER
SPENCER
SPENDER
SPENSER
SPINACH
SPINATE
SPINDLE
SPINDLY
SPINNER
SPINNEY
SPINOFF
SPINOZA
SPONDEE
SPONDYL
SPONGER
SPONSON
SPONSOR
STANDBY
STANDIN
STANDUP
STANLEY
STANNIC
STENCIL
STENGAH
STENGUN
STENTOR
STINGER
STINKER
STONILY
STONKER
STUNNER
STUNTED
SUNNILY
SUNNITE
SURNAME
SWANSEA
SWINDLE
SWINGER
SWINGLE
TAINTED
TANNATE
TANNERY
TANNING
TARNISH
TEENAGE
TENNIEL
THINKER
THINNER
THUNDER
TOENAIL
TONNAGE
TONNEAU
TONNISH
TORNADE
TORNADO
TOYNBEE
TRANCHE
TRANSIT
TRANSOM
TRANTER
TRINGLE
TRINITY
TRINKET
TRUNDLE
TSUNAMI
TURNERY
TURNING
TURNKEY
TURNOUT
TWINKLE
TWINSET
UGANDAN
UNKNOWN
UNSNARL
URANIAN
URANISM
URANITE
URANIUM
URINARY
URINATE
UTENSIL
VARNISH
VILNIUS
WARNING
WETNESS
WHINGER
WINNING
WINNOCK
WITNESS
WOUNDED
WRANGLE
WRINGER
WRINKLE
WRINKLY
WRONGLY
WRYNECK
WRYNOSE
YAWNING
YOUNGER
ZIONIST
AARONIC
ABDOMEN
ABIOSIS
ABJOINT
ABSOLVE
ACCOUNT
ACROBAT
ACRONYM
ADJOINT
ADJOURN
AEROBIC
AEROSOL
AGROUND
ALCOHOL
ALCORAN
ALFONSO
ALKORAN
ALLONGE
ALLOWED
ALMONER
AMBOYNA
AMMONAL
AMMONIA
AMPOULE
ANDORRA
ANGOLAN
ANNOYED
ANTONIO
ANTONYM
APHONIA
APHONIC
APHOTIC
APPOINT
APPOSED
APROPOS
ARIOSTO
ARMORED
ARMORIC
ARMOURY
ASTOUND
ATROPHY
AUROCHS
AUTOCUE
AUTOMAT
AUTOPSY
BABOOSH
BALONEY
BARONET
BAROQUE
BAYONET
BAZOOKA
BEDOUIN
BEGONIA
BEGORRA
BEHOOVE
BELOVED
BETOKEN
BIFOCAL
BIGOTED
BIGOTRY
BIVOUAC
BLOOMER
BLOOPER
BOLOGNA
BOLONEY
BORODIN
BOROUGH
BRIOCHE
BUBONIC
BUCOLIC
BYRONIC
CABOOSE
CADOGAN
CAGOULE
CAHOOTS
CALOMEL
CALORIC
CALORIE
CAMORRA
CANONRY
CAPORAL
CAROLUS
CAROTID
CAROTIN
CAROUSE
CHAOTIC
CHLORAL
CHOOKIE
CHRONIC
COCONUT
COCOTTE
COLOGNE
COLOMBO
COLONEL
COLORED
COLOURS
COROLLA
CORONER
CORONET
CROOKED
CROONER
DAMOSEL
DEBORAH
DEBOUCH
DECODER
DECORUM
DELOUSE
DEMONIC
DEMOTIC
DEPOSIT
DERONDA
DEVOLVE
DEVOTED
DEVOTEE
DIGONAL
DIPOLAR
DISOBEY
DIVORCE
DOLORES
DOROTHY
ECBOLIC
ECLOGUE
ECTOPIA
EFFORCE
EGLOGUE
EMBOLUS
EMBOWER
EMPOWER
ENDOGEN
ENDORSE
ENFORCE
ENGORGE
ENNOBLE
ESPOUSE
ESTOVER
EXPOSED
EXPOUND
FAVORED
FEMORAL
FLOODED
FLOOZIE
FLYOVER
GALOCHE
GALOPIN
GARONNE
GAROTTE
GASOHOL
GAVOTTE
GENOESE
GIRONDE
GOMORRA
GROOVED
HALOGEN
HANOVER
HAPORTH
HEROINE
HEROISM
HOMONYM
HONOURS
HYPOGEA
IDIOTIC

IGNOBLE
IGNORED
IMHOTEP
IMMORAL
IMPOUND
INBOARD
INCOMER
INCONNU
INDOORS
INHOUSE
INROADS
INVOICE
INVOLVE
JACOBIN
JACOBUS
JEHOVAH
KATORGA
KENOSIS
KENOTIC
KEROGEN
LABORED
LABORER
LACONIC
LAGONDA
LANOLIN
LAVOLTA
LESOTHO
LINOCUT
LITOTES
MADONNA
MAHONIA
MAJORCA
MASONIC
MASONRY
MECONIC
MEIOSIS
MELODIC
MEMOIRS
MENORAH
METONIC
METONYM
MINORCA
MITOSIS
MOLOTOV
MONOCLE
MONOLOG
MONOPLY
MOROCCO
MORONIC
NABOKOV
NEMORAL
NICOISE
NICOSIA
OBLOQUY
OCTOBER
OCTOPOD
OCTOPUS
ONGOING
OPPOSED
ORTOLAN
OSBORNE
OSMOSIS
OTTOMAN
PALOMAR
PALOOKA
PANOPLY
PAPOOSE
PAROTID
PAROTIS
PELORIA
PELORUS
PICOTEE
PIROGUE
PIVOTAL
POLONIE
POPOVER
POROSIS
POTOMAC
PYLORUS
PYROSIS
REBOUND
RECORDS
RECOUNT
RECOVER
REDOUBT
REDOUND
REHOUSE
REJOICE
REMODEL
REMORSE
REMOULD
REMOUNT
REMOVAL
REMOVED
REMOVER
REPOSAL
REROUTE
RESOLVE
RESOUND
RETOUCH
REVOLVE
RICOTTA
RIPOSTE
RISOTTO
RUDOLPH
RUMORED
SAGOUIN
SAMOOSA
SAMOVAR
SAMOYED
SAPONIN
SAROYAN
SAVOURY
SCHOLAR
SCOOTER
SCROOGE
SCROTAL
SCROTUM
SECONAL
SECONDS
SHMOOZE
SHOOTER
SHROUDS
SIROCCO
SMOOTHE
SNOOKER
SNOOPER
SOCOTRA
SOJOURN
SOLOIST
SOLOMON
SOROSIS
SPLODGE
SPLOTCH
SPOONER
SPROUTS
STROBIC
STROPHE
STROPPY
SYCORAX
SYCOSIS
SYNONYM
SYNOVIA
TALOOKA
THEORBO
THEOREM
THROATY
THROUGH
THROWER
THROWIN
TIMOTHY
TITOISM
TITOIST
TORONTO
TROOPER
TYLOSIS
UNBOSOM
UNBOUND
UNBOWED
UNCOUTH
UNCOVER
UNDOING
UNGODLY
UNHORSE
UNLOOSE
UNLOVED
UNMOVED
UNSOUND
UNWOUND
VAMOOSE
VAPOURS
VELOURS
VERONAL
WAGONER
WHOOPEE
WHOOPER
WIDOWED
WIDOWER
XENOPUS
XEROSIS
ZAMORIN
ZAPOTEC
ZEDOARY
ZYGOSIS
ZYMOSIS
ADAPTER
ADAPTOR
ADIPOSE
ADOPTED
AIRPORT
ALEPINE
APEPSIA
ASEPTIC
BAGPIPE
BEDPOST
BESPEAK
BESPOKE
BUMPKIN
CAMPANA
CAMPARI
CAMPHOR
CAMPING
CAMPION
CARPORT
CASPIAN
CHAPATI
CHAPEAU
CHAPLET
CHAPMAN
CHAPPED
CHAPTER
CHIPPED
CHIPPER
CHIPPIE
CHOPINE
CHOPPER
CHUPATI
CLAPPER
CLIPPED
CLIPPER
CLIPPIE
COMPACT
COMPANY
COMPARE
COMPASS
COMPERE
COMPETE
COMPILE
COMPLEX
COMPORT
COMPOSE
COMPOST
COMPOTE
COMPUTE
COPPERS
COPPICE
COUPLER
COUPLET
COUPONS
COWPOKE
CRIPPLE
CROPPED
CROPPER
CRUPPER
CRYPTIC
CRYPTON
CULPRIT
DAMPIER
DAMPING
DAPPLED
DAUPHIN
DEEPFRY
DELPHIC
DESPAIR
DESPISE
DESPITE
DESPOIL
DESPOND
DIAPSID
DIMPLED
DIOPTER
DIOPTRE
DISPLAY
DISPORT
DISPOSE
DISPRIN
DISPUTE
DOLPHIN
DOPPLER
DRAPERY
DROPLET
DROPOUT
DROPPER
DUMPISH
DUOPOLY
EDAPHIC
ETAPLES
FLAPPED
FLAPPER
FLIPPER
FLYPAST
FOPPISH
GASPING
GLYPTAL
GLYPTIC
GRAPHIC
GRAPHIS
GRAPNEL
GRAPPLE
GROPIUS
GRYPHON
GUNPLAY
HAPPILY
HARPIST
HARPOON
HELPFUL
HELPING
HENPECK
HISPANO
HOPPING
HOSPICE
INSPECT
INSPIRE
JAMPANI
JEEPERS
JEEPNEY
JUMPING
KAMPALA
KAMPONG
KEEPING
KIPPERS
KNAPPER
KRYPTON
LAMPOON
LAMPREY
LAPPING
LEAPING
LEGPULL
LEMPIRA
LEOPARD
LEOPOLD
LIMPOPO
LOWPAID
LUMPISH
LUMPKIN
MAPPING
MAYPOLE
MISPLAY
MOPPING
MORPHIA
MUDPACK
NAIPAUL
NAPPING
NIPPERS
NONPLUS
NYMPHET
OFFPEAK
OUTPOST
OUTPOUR
PALPATE
PEEPING
PEPPERS
PEPPERY
PERPLEX
PIMPING
POMPEII
POMPOON
POMPOUS
POPPING
PREPAID
PREPARE
PREPUCE
PROPANE
PROPEND
PROPHET
PROPOSE
PUMPKIN
PURPORT
PURPOSE
PURPURA
RAMPAGE
RAMPANT
RAMPART
RAPPORT
RATPACK
REDPOLL
RESPECT
RESPIRE
RESPITE
RESPOND
RESPRAY
RIPPING
ROMPERS
RUMPLED
RUMPOLE
SALPINX
SAMPLER
SAPPERS
SAPPHIC
SCAPULA
SCEPTER
SCEPTIC
SCEPTRE
SCUPPER
SEAPORT
SEEPAGE
SEPPUKU
SERPENS
SERPENT
SHAPELY
SHAPING
SHEPPEY
SHIPPER
SHIPTON
SHOPPER
SIMPKIN
SIMPLER
SIMPLEX
SIMPLON
SIMPSON
SIPPING
SKEPTIC
SKIPPED
SKIPPER
SLAPPER
SLIPPED
SLIPPER
SLIPWAY
SLOPING
SNAPPER
SNIPPET
SOAPBOX
SOPPING
STAPLER
STEPHEN
STEPNEY
STEPSON
STIPEND
STIPPLE
STOPGAP
STOPPED
STOPPER
STUPEFY
STYPTIC
SULPHUR
SUPPORT
SUPPOSE

SURPASS
SURPLUS
SUSPECT
SUSPEND
SWAPPED
SYMPTOM
TADPOLE
TAMPICO
TAMPION
TAPPICE
TAPPING
TARPEIA
TEMPERA
TEMPEST
TEMPLAR
TEMPLET
TEMPTER
TEMPURA
TIEPOLO
TIMPANI
TIPPING
TIPPLER
TOMPION
TOPPING
TORPEDO
TORPIDS
TOWPATH
TRAPEZE
TRAPPED
TRAPPER
TREPANG
TRIPLET
TRIPLEX
TRIPODY
TRIPOLI
TRIPPER
TRIPSIS
TROPHIC
TROPICS
TROPISM
TRYPSIN
TYMPANO
TYMPANY
UTOPIAN
VAMPIRE
VESPERS
VULPINE
WALPOLE
WAPPING
WARPATH
WASPISH
WEAPONS
WEEPING
WHIPCAT
WHIPPED
WHIPPET
WHOPPER
WIMPISH
WRAPPED
WRAPPER
ALIQUID
ALIQUOT
BANQUET
BOUQUET
CHEQUER
CLIQUEY
CONQUER
CROQUET
CROQUIS
JACQUES
JONQUIL
KUMQUAT
LACQUER
MARQUEE
MARQUIS
PARQUET
PICQUET
PREQUEL
RACQUET
RORQUAL
SAQQARA
TARQUIN
UNEQUAL
ACARIDA
ACCRETE
ACCRUAL
ACERBIC
ACTRESS
ADDRESS
ADORING
ADORNED
AFFRONT
AGGRESS
ALARMED
ALDRICH
AMBROSE
AMERICA
AMERIGO
AMERIND
AMORIST
AMORITE
AMOROSO
AMOROUS
AMTRACK
ANARCHY
ANDROID
ANEROID
ANGRILY
APPRIZE
APPROVE
ARMREST
ASCRIBE
ASTRIDE
ATARAXY
ATTRACT
AVARICE
AVERAGE
BAHRAIN
BAHREIN
BARRACK
BARRAGE
BARRIER
BARRING
BEARDED
BEARHUG
BEARING
BEARISH
BEDROCK
BEDROOM
BEERMAT
BETROTH
BLURRED
BOARDER
BOORISH
BOURBON
BOURDON
BOURSIN
BOXROOM
BULRUSH
CAIRENE
CAPRICE
CARRELL
CARRIED
CARRIER
CARRIES
CARRION
CARROLL
CARROTS
CARROTY
CHARADE
CHARDIN
CHARGED
CHARGER
CHARGES
CHARIOT
CHARITY
CHARLES
CHARLEY
CHARMED
CHARMER
CHARNEL
CHARPOY
CHARRED
CHARTER
CHERISH
CHEROOT
CHERVIL
CHIRRUP
CHORALE
CHORDAE
CHORION
CHORIZO
CHOROID
CHORTLE
CIRROSE
CITRINE
CITROEN
CLARIFY
CLARION
CLARITY
COARSEN
COMRADE
CORRECT
CORRIDA
CORRODE
CORRUPT
COURAGE
COURBET
COURIER
COURSER
COURSES
COURTLY
CSARDAS
CUIRASS
CURRAGH
CURRANT
CURRENT
CURRIED
CYPRESS
CYPRIOT
DEAREST
DEBRETT
DEBRIEF
DECREED
DECRYPT
DEFRAUD
DEFROCK
DEFROST
DEGRADE
DEGREES
DEIRDRE
DEPRAVE
DEPRESS
DEPRIVE
DERRICK
DETRACT
DETRAIN
DIARCHY
DIARIST
DIGRAPH
DIGRESS
DIORAMA
DIORITE
DISROBE
DISRUPT
DIURNAL
DOGROSE
DOORKEY
DOORMAN
DOORMAT
DOORWAY
DURRELL
DVORNIK
DYARCHY
EARRING
ECCRINE
EMBRACE
EMBROIL
EMERALD
EMERSON
EMIRATE
EMPRESS
ENCRUST
ENERGIC
ENGRAFT
ENGRAIN
ENGRAVE
ENGROSS
ENPRINT
ENTRAIN
ENTRANT
ENTREAT
ENTRUST
EPERGNE
EPHRAIM
ESTREAT
ETERNAL
ETTRICK
EVEREST
EXCRETA
EXCRETE
EXPRESS
EXTRACT
EXTREME
EXTRUDE
FAIRING
FAIRISH
FAIRWAY
FARRAGO
FARRIER
FEARFUL
FEBRILE
FERROUS
FERRULE
FIBROID
FIBROMA
FIBROUS
FLAREUP
FLORIDA
FLORIST
FURRIER
GABRIEL
GADROON
GARRICK
GEARBOX
GEARING
GEORDIE
GEORGIA
GEORGIC
GHERKIN
GLARING
GLORIFY
GNARLED
GOURMET
GUARANA
GUARANI
GUARDED
GUNROOM
GUYROPE
HADRIAN
HAIRCUT
HAIRNET
HAIRPIN
HARRIER
HARRIET
HEARING
HEARKEN
HEARSAY
HEARTEN
HEIRESS
HERRICK
HERRIES
HERRING
HEURISM
HOARDER
HORRIFY
HORRORS
HURRIED
HYDRANT
HYDRATE
IBERIAN
IMPRESS
IMPREST
IMPRINT
IMPROVE
INCRUST
INERTIA
INGRAIN
INGRATE
INGRESS
INTROIT
INTRUDE
ITERATE
IVORIAN
IVORIEN
JEERING
JOURNAL
JOURNEY
JOYRIDE
KATRINE
KEARTON
LATRINE
LAURELS
LEARNED
LEARNER
LEGROOM
LEPROSY
LEPROUS
LIBRARY
LIBRIUM
LIPREAD
LOURDES
LOURING
MACRAMÉ
MARRIED
MARRYAT
MEERKAT
MELROSE
MERRIER
MERRILY
MICROBE
MIDRIFF
MIGRANT
MIGRATE
MISREAD
MISRULE
MOORHEN
MOORING
MOORISH
MORRELL
MOURNER
MURRAIN
NACROUS
NAIROBI
NARRATE
NARROWS
NATRIUM
NEAREST
NEARING
NECROSE
NEGRESS
NEGROID
NEURINE
NEURONE
NITRATE
NITRILE
NITRITE
NITRODE
NITROUS
NOURISH
OBTRUDE
OCARINA
ODORANT
ODOROUS
OLOROSO
ONEROUS
OPERAND
OPERANT
OPERATE
OPPRESS
OSTRICH
OUTRAGE
OUTRANK
OVARIAN
OVERACT
OVERALL
OVERARM
OVERAWE
OVERBID
OVERDUE
OVEREAT
OVERFED
OVERLAP
OVERLAY
OVERLIE
OVERPAY
OVERRUN
OVERSEE
OVERTAX
PADRONE
PAIRING
PAPRIKA
PATRIAL
PATRICK
PATRIOT
PAYROLL
PEARLIE

PEERAGE
PEERESS
PEERING
PERRIER
PETRIFY
PETROUS
PHARAOH
PHARYNX
PIBROCH
PIERCED
PIERCER
PIERROT
PLEROMA
PRURIGO
PUERILE
PUTREFY
PYRRHIC
QUARREL
QUARTAN
QUARTER
QUARTET
QUERCUS
QUORATE
REARING
RECRUIT
REDRESS
REFRACT
REFRAIN
REFRESH
REGRESS
REGROUP
REPRESS
REPRINT
REPROOF
REPROVE
RETRACE
RETRACT
RETRAIN
RETRAIT
RETREAD
RETREAT
RETRIAL
REWRITE
ROARING
SABRINA
SAPROBE
SATRAPY
SAURIAN
SAUROID
SCARIFY
SCARING
SCARLET
SCARPER
SCORING
SCORPIO
SEARING
SECRECY
SECRETE
SECRETS
SERRIED
SHARIAH

SHARING
SHARPEN
SHARPER
SHARPLY
SHERBET
SHERIFF
SHERMAN
SHIRKER
SHIRLEY
SHORTEN
SHORTLY
SMARTEN
SMARTIE
SMARTLY
SNARLER
SNARLUP
SNORING
SNORKEL
SNORTER
SNORTLE
SOARING
SOPRANO
SORROWS
SOURSOP
SPARING
SPARKLE
SPARROW
SPARTAN
SPIRITS
SPORRAN
SPURREY
SPURWAY
STARCHY
STARDOM
STARETS
STARING
STARKLY
STARLET
STARLIT
STARTED
STARTER
STARTLE
STARVED
STERILE
STERNAL
STERNLY
STERNUM
STEROID
STIRFRY
STIRPES
STIRRED
STIRRUP
STORAGE
STORIED
STORIES
STURMER
SUCROSE
SUNRISE
SUNROOF
SUPREME
SUPREMO

SURREAL
SWARTHY
TAPROOT
TAURINE
TEARFUL
TEARING
TEAROOM
TERRACE
TERRAIN
TERRENE
TERRIER
TERRIFY
TERRINE
THERAPY
THEREBY
THEREIN
THERESA
THERETO
THERMAL
THERMIC
THERMOS
THIRDLY
THIRSTY
THOREAU
THORIUM
THYROID
THYRSIS
TIERCEL
TIERCET
TIGRESS
TIGRISH
TITRATE
TORREFY
TORRENT
TOURING
TOURISM
TOURIST
TRIREME
TSARINA
TSARIST
TZARINA
UMBRAGE
UMBRIAN
UNARMED
UNDRESS
UNFROCK
UNTRIED
UNTRUTH
UPBRAID
UPGRADE
USURPER
UTERINE
UXORIAL
VAGRANT
VERRUCA
VIBRANT
VIBRATE
VIBRATO
VITRAIL
VITRIFY
VITRIOL

WARRANT
WARRING
WARRIOR
WEARILY
WEARING
WEIRDLY
WHARTON
WHEREAS
WHEREBY
WHEREIN
WORRIED
WORRIER
YTTRIUM
ZAIREAN
ABASHED
ABUSIVE
ABYSMAL
ABYSSAL
ACESTES
AGISTOR
AIRSHIP
AIRSICK
AIRSTOP
ALASKAN
ALLSTAR
ALYSSUM
AMUSING
ANISEED
ANOSMIA
APOSTLE
ATISHOO
AWESOME
BANSHEE
BASSOON
BATSMAN
BEASTLY
BEDSIDE
BEDSORE
BEESWAX
BERSEEM
BERSERK
BIASSED
BIGSHOT
BLASTED
BLASTER
BLESSED
BLESSES
BLISTER
BLOSSOM
BLUSHER
BLUSTER
BOASTER
BOBSLED
BOLSHIE
BOLSHOI
BOLSTER
BOOSTER
BORSTAL
BOWSHOT
BRASERO
BRISKET

BRISKLY
BRISTLE
BRISTLY
BRISTOL
BRUSHER
BRUSQUE
BURSARY
BURSTER
BUSSING
CAESIUM
CAESURA
CAISSON
CAPSIZE
CAPSTAN
CAPSULE
CARSICK
CASSATA
CASSAVA
CASSOCK
CATSEYE
CATSPAW
CAUSTIC
CELSIUS
CENSURE
CESSION
CESSPIT
CHASING
CHASSIS
CHASTEN
CHESTER
CISSOID
CLASSIC
CLASTIC
CLOSELY
CLOSEUP
CLOSING
CLOSURE
CLUSTER
COASTAL
COASTER
CONSENT
CONSIGN
CONSIST
CONSOLE
CONSOLS
CONSORT
CONSULT
CONSUME
CORSAGE
CORSAIR
COSSACK
COUSINS
COWSHED
COWSLIP
CRASHES
CRASSUS
CRESTED
CRISPIN
CROSIER
CROSSED
CROSSLY

CRUSADE
CRUSHED
CRUSHER
CRYSTAL
CUISINE
CUMSHAW
CURSIVE
CURSORY
DAYSTAR
DENSELY
DENSITY
DESSERT
DISSECT
DISSENT
DOESKIN
DOSSIER
DOWSING
DRASTIC
DRESDEN
DRESSED
DRESSER
DROSHKY
DUNSTAN
EARSHOT
ELASTIC
ELASTIN
ELISION
ELUSIVE
ELUSORY
ELYSIAN
ELYSIUM
EPISODE
EPISTLE
ERASMUS
ERASURE
ERISKAY
EROSION
ETESIAN
EVASION
EVASIVE
EXISTED
EYESHOT
EYESORE
FALSELY
FALSIES
FALSIFY
FAUSTUS
FELSPAR
FIRSTLY
FISSILE
FISSION
FISSURE
FLASHER
FLUSHED
FLUSTER
FORSAKE
FORSTER
FOSSICK
FOSSULA
FRESHEN
FRESHER

FRESHET
FRESHLY
FRISBEE
FRISIAN
FRISSON
FROSTED
FULSOME
FUSSILY
GHASTLY
GHOSTLY
GINSENG
GLASGOW
GLASSES
GLISTEN
GNOSTIC
GODSEND
GORSEDD
GOSSIPY
GRISTLE
GRISTLY
GROSSLY
GUMSHOE
GUNSHOT
GYMSLIP
HAMSTER
HANSARD
HARSHLY
HASSOCK
HAYSEED
HERSELF
HESSIAN
HIMSELF
HIPSTER
HIRSUTE
HISSING
HOBSONS
HOLSTER
HOPSACK
HORSING
HOTSHOT
HOTSPUR
HOUSING
HUSSARS
HUSSITE
IRKSOME
JERSEYS
JUSSIVE
KINSHIP
KINSMAN
KISSING
KNESSET
KRISHNA
KURSAAL
LAKSHMI
LAPSANG
LAWSUIT
LEASING
LEASOWE
LEISURE
LESSING
LINSANG

LINSEED
LISSOME
LOBSTER
LOOSELY
MAESTRO
MANSARD
MANSION
MANSIZE
MARSALA
MARSHAL
MARSYAS
MASSAGE
MASSEUR
MASSINE
MASSIVE
MEASLES
MEASURE
MEISSEN
MESSAGE
MESSIAH
MESSIER
MESSILY
MESSINA
MIASMIC
MIDSHIP
MINSTER
MISSILE
MISSING
MISSION
MISSIVE
MISSTEP
MOBSTER
MOISTEN
MONSOON
MONSTER
MUNSTER
MUSSELS
NETSUKE
NEWSBOY
NEWSMAN
NOISILY
NOISOME
NONSTOP
NONSUCH
NONSUIT
NURSERY
NURSING
OARSMAN
OARSMEN
OBESITY
ODYSSEY
OFFSIDE
OILSKIN
OLDSTER
ONESELF
OPOSSUM
ORESTES
OUTSHOT
OUTSIDE
OUTSIZE
OUTSPAN
OUTSTAY
PAESTUM
PAISLEY
PALSIED
PARSLEY
PARSNIP
PASSAGE
PASSANT
PASSING
PASSION
PASSIVE
PEASANT
PENSILE
PENSION
PENSIVE
PEPSINE
PERSEID
PERSEUS
PERSIAN
PERSIST
PERSONA
PERSONS
PERSPEX
PESSARY
PHYSICS
PIASTRE
PIGSKIN
PLASMIN
PLASTER
PLASTIC
PLESSOR
PLOSIVE
POSSESS
POTSDAM
POTSHOT
POUSSIN
PRESAGE
PRESENT
PRESIDE
PRESSED
PRESUME
PROSAIC
PROSODY
PROSPER
PRUSSIC
PULSATE
PULSING
PUNSTER
PURSUER
PURSUIT
QUASSIA
QUESTER
RAISING
RANSACK
REDSKIN
REISSUE
RETSINA
RISSOLE
ROASTER
ROISTER
RONSARD
ROOSTER
ROSSINI
ROUSING
RUSSELL
RUSSIAN
SALSIFY
SASSOON
SATSUMA
SAUSAGE
SCISSOR
SEASICK
SEASIDE
SEISMIC
SENSATE
SENSORY
SENSUAL
SESSILE
SESSION
SHASTRI
SHYSTER
SLASHED
SLOSHED
SMASHED
SMASHER
SPASTIC
SUBSIDE
SUBSIDY
SUBSIST
SUBSOIL
SUBSUME
SUNSPOT
TAPSTER
TARSIER
TASSILI
TEASHOP
TEASING
TELSTAR
TENSELY
TENSILE
TENSING
TENSION
TERSELY
TERSION
TESSERA
THESEUS
THISTLE
THYSELF
THYSSEN
TIPSILY
TIPSTER
TOASTED
TOASTER
TOLSTOY
TONSURE
TOPSIDE
TOPSOIL
TORSADE
TORSION
TOSSPOT
TOYSHOP
TRESSES
TRESTLE
TRISECT
TRISHAW
TRISTAN
TRUSTEE
TUESDAY
TUSSOCK
TUSSORE
TWISTED
TWISTER
TWOSOME
TWOSTEP
ULYSSES
UNASKED
UNUSUAL
VARSITY
VASSAIL
VERSANT
VERSIFY
VERSION
WARSHIP
WASSAIL
WAYSIDE
WEBSTER
WETSUIT
WHISKER
WHISKEY
WHISPER
WHISTLE
WINSOME
WINSTON
WOOSTER
WORSHIP
WORSTED
WRESTLE
ZEMSTVO
ABATTIS
ABETTOR
ABSTAIN
ACETATE
ACETONE
ACHTUNG
ACUTELY
AGITATE
AGITATO
AINTREE
AMATEUR
AMATORY
ANATOLE
ANATOMY
ANOTHER
APHTHAE
ARETINO
ASHTRAY
AUCTION
AUSTERE
AUSTRAL
AUSTRIA
BAPTISM
BAPTIST
BAPTIZE
BASTARD
BASTIDE
BASTION
BATTELS
BATTERY
BATTING
BEATIFY
BEATING
BEATLES
BEATNIK
BEDTIME
BENTHAM
BENTHOS
BERTRAM
BESTIAL
BESTREW
BETTING
BILTONG
BISTORT
BITTERN
BITTERS
BLATANT
BLATHER
BLATTER
BLETHER
BLITZED
BLOTCHY
BLOTTER
BOATING
BOATMAN
BOOTLEG
BOTTEGA
BOTTLED
BOTTLES
BOUTADE
BRITAIN
BRITISH
BRITONS
BRITTLE
BRITZKA
BROTHEL
BROTHER
BRUTISH
BUNTING
BUSTARD
BUSTLER
BUSTLES
BUTTERY
BUTTONS
CAITIFF
CALTROP
CANTATA
CANTEEN
CANTHUS
CANTRIP
CANTUAR
CAPTAIN
CAPTION
CAPTIVE
CAPTURE
CARTIER
CARTOON
CASTILE
CASTING
CASTLED
CASTOFF
CATTISH
CAUTERY
CAUTION
CENTAUR
CENTAVO
CENTRAL
CENTRED
CENTRUM
CENTURY
CERTAIN
CERTIFY
CESTODE
CESTOID
CHATEAU
CHATHAM
CHATTEL
CHATTER
CHUTNEY
CISTERN
CLATTER
CLOTHED
CLOTHES
CLOTURE
CLUTTER
COATING
COITION
CONTACT
CONTAIN
CONTEMN
CONTEND
CONTENT
CONTEST
CONTEXT
CONTORT
CONTOUR
CONTROL
CORTEGE
CORTINA
COSTARD
COSTING
COSTIVE
COSTUME
COTTAGE
COTTONY
COUTURE
CRITTER
CULTURE
CURTAIL
CURTAIN
CURTSEY
CUSTARD
CUSTODY
CUSTOMS
CUTTERS
CUTTING
CYNTHIA
CYSTOID
DANTEAN
DASTARD
DAYTIME
DEATHLY
DELTOID
DENTINE
DENTIST
DENTURE
DESTINE
DESTINY
DESTROY
DEXTRIN
DICTATE
DICTION
DIETARY
DIETINE
DIPTERA
DIPTYCH
DISTAFF
DISTANT
DISTEND
DISTENT
DISTILL
DISTORT
DISTURB
DITTANY
DITTIES
DOCTORS
DUCTILE
DUSTBIN
DUSTING
DUSTMAN
DUSTPAN
EARTHEN
EARTHLY
EASTERN
EBBTIDE
ECSTASY
EDITION
EGOTISM
EGOTIST
ELATION
ELITISM
ELITIST
EMOTION
EMOTIVE
EPITAPH
EPITAXY
EPITHET
EPITOME
EPSTEIN
ERITREA
EROTICA
EUSTACE
EXITING
FACTION
FACTORS
FACTORY
FACTUAL
FANTAIL

FANTASY
FARTHER
FASTING
FASTNET
FEATHER
FEATURE
FERTILE
FESTIVE
FESTOON
FETTERS
FICTION
FIFTEEN
FISTFUL
FISTULA
FISTULE
FITTEST
FITTING
FIXTURE
FLATCAR
FLATLET
FLATTEN
FLATTER
FLITTER
FLOTSAM
FLUTIST
FLUTTER
FOOTAGE
FOOTING
FOOTMAN
FOOTPAD
FOOTSIE
FORTIES
FORTIFY
FORTRAN
FORTUNE
FOXTROT
FRETFUL
FRETSAW
FRETTED
FRITTER
FURTHER
FURTIVE
FUSTIAN
FUTTOCK
GAITERS
GASTHOF
GASTRIC
GASTRIN
GAUTAMA
GENTEEL
GENTIAN
GENTILE
GESTALT
GESTAPO
GESTATE
GESTURE
GETTING
GLITTER
GLOTTAL
GLOTTIS
GLUTTON
GRATIFY
GRATING
GROTIUS
GUTTATE
HAITIAN
HALTING
HASTATE
HASTILY
HATTOCK
HAUTBOY
HEATHEN
HEATHER
HEATING
HECTARE
HEPTANE
HISTOID
HISTORY
HITTITE
HOSTAGE
HOSTESS
HOSTILE
HUNTING
HURTFUL
HUSTLER
IMITATE
INITIAL
INSTALL
INSTANT
INSTATE
INSTEAD
INSTILL
ISOTONE
ISOTOPE
JESTING
JITTERS
JITTERY
JOGTROT
JUSTICE
JUSTIFY
KENTISH
KESTREL
KINTYRE
KNITTED
KNITTER
KNOTTED
KONTIKI
LACTASE
LACTATE
LACTEAL
LACTOSE
LAETARE
LANTANA
LANTERN
LAOTIAN
LASTING
LATTICE
LEATHER
LECTERN
LECTURE
LEFTIST
LENTIGO
LENTILS
LEOTARD
LETTERS
LETTING
LETTUCE
LIFTOFF
LILTING
LISTING
LOFTILY
LOOTING
LOTTERY
LOUTISH
LUSTFUL
LUSTILY
LUSTRUM
MALTASE
MALTESE
MALTHUS
MANTUAN
MARTENS
MARTIAL
MARTIAN
MARTINI
MARTLET
MARTYRS
MASTERS
MASTERY
MASTIFF
MASTOID
MATTERS
MATTHEW
MATTING
MATTINS
MATTOCK
MEETING
MELTING
MENTHOL
MENTION
METTLED
MIDTERM
MISTAKE
MISTIME
MISTOOK
MISTRAL
MITTENS
MIXTURE
MOITHER
MONTAGE
MONTAGU
MONTANA
MONTANT
MONTERO
MONTHLY
MORTALS
MORTICE
MORTIFY
MORTISE
MOTTLED
MUNTJAC
MUSTANG
MUSTARD
MYSTERY
MYSTIFY
NARTHEX
NASTILY
NECTARY
NEITHER
NEPTUNE
NETTING
NEUTRAL
NEUTRON
NICTATE
NOSTRIL
NOSTRUM
NUPTIAL
NURTURE
NUTTING
OESTRUS
OMITTED
ONETIME
ONSTAGE
ORATION
ORATORY
OROTUND
OUSTITI
OUTTURN
OVATION
PANTHER
PANTIES
PANTILE
PARTAKE
PARTHIA
PARTIAL
PARTING
PARTITA
PARTNER
PASTERN
PASTEUR
PASTIES
PASTIME
PASTURE
PATTERN
PECTASE
PELTING
PENTANE
PENTODE
PENTOSE
PERTAIN
PERTURB
PERTUSE
PICTURE
PIETIST
PIGTAIL
PINTADO
PINTAIL
PISTOLE
PLATEAU
PLATOON
PLATTER
PLOTTER
PLUTEUS
POETESS
PONTIAC
PONTIFF
PONTINE
PONTOON
PORTAGE
PORTEND
PORTENT
PORTHOS
PORTICO
PORTION
PORTRAY
POSTAGE
POSTBAG
POSTBOX
POSTERN
POSTING
POSTMAN
POSTURE
POSTWAR
POTTAGE
POTTERY
POTTING
PRATTLE
PRETEND
PRETEXT
PRETZEL
PRITHEE
PROTEAN
PROTECT
PROTEGE
PROTEIN
PROTEST
PROTEUS
PRYTHEE
PUNTING
PUSTULE
PUTTEES
PUTTING
PUTTOCK
QUETZAL
QUITTER
RAFTING
RAGTIME
RANTING
RAPTURE
RATTEEN
RATTLER
RECTIFY
RECTORY
REPTILE
RESTART
RESTATE
RESTFUL
RESTING
RESTIVE
RESTOCK
RESTORE
RIOTERS
RIOTING
RIOTOUS
RONTGEN
ROOTING
ROSTAND
ROSTOCK
ROSTRAL
ROSTRUM
ROTTING
ROUTIER
ROUTINE
RUPTURE
RUSTLER
RUTTING
SALTATE
SALTING
SALTIRE
SALTPAN
SCATTER
SCOTTIE
SCUTAGE
SCUTARI
SCUTTER
SCUTTLE
SEATING
SEATTLE
SECTION
SEETHED
SELTZER
SESTINA
SESTINE
SETTING
SETTLED
SETTLER
SEXTANT
SHATTER
SHOTGUN
SHUTEYE
SHUTTER
SHUTTLE
SIFTING
SISTERS
SISTINE
SITTING
SIXTEEN
SKATING
SKETCHY
SKITTER
SKITTLE
SLATTED
SLITHER
SLOTTED
SMATTER
SMETANA
SMITHER
SMITTEN
SMOTHER
SORTING
SOUTANE
SOUTHEY
SPATIAL
SPATTER
SPATULA
SPITTLE
SPOTTED
SPOTTER
SPUTNIK
SPUTTER
STATELY
STATICS
STATION
STATIST
STATURE
STATUTE
STETSON
STUTTER
SUBTEEN
SUBTEND
SUCTION
SULTANA
SUNTRAP
SUSTAIN
SWITHIN
SYSTOLE
TACTFUL
TACTICS
TACTILE
TANTARA
TANTIVY
TANTRUM
TARTARE
TARTARY
TARTINE
TATTERS
TATTING
TATTLER
TEATIME
TEKTITE
TERTIAL
TERTIAN
TESTATE
TESTIFY
TESTILY
TESTING
TESTUDO
TEXTILE
TEXTUAL
TEXTURE
THITHER
TINTACK
TINTERN
TONTINE
TOOTHED
TOOTSIE
TORTILE
TORTRIX
TORTURE
TOTTERY
TRITELY
TRITIUM
TRITOMA
TROTSKY
TROTTER
TUITION
TWITCHY

TWITTER
TWOTIME
UMPTEEN
UNCTION
UNITARY
UNITIES
UNSTICK
UNSTOCK
UNSTUCK
UPSTAGE
UPSTART
UPSTATE
URETHRA
VANTAGE
VENTOSE
VENTRAL
VENTURE
VERTIGO
VESTIGE
VETTING
VICTORY
VICTUAL
VIETNAM
VINTAGE
VINTNER
VIRTUAL
VISTULA
VOLTAGE
VOLTAIC
VULTURE
WAFTING
WAGTAIL
WAITING
WALTZER
WANTING
WARTHOG
WARTIME
WASTAGE
WASTING
WASTREL
WATTAGE
WATTEAU
WATTLES
WEATHER
WESTERN
WETTING
WHATNOT
WHATSIT
WHETHER
WHITHER
WHITING
WHITISH
WHITLOW
WHITSUN
WHITTLE
WISTFUL
WRITEUP
WRITING
WRITTEN
XANTHOS
ZESTFUL
ZOOTOMY
ABOUKIR
ABOULIA
ACAUDAL
ACCURSE
ACCUSED
ACCUSER
ACQUIRE
ACTUARY
ACTUATE
ADJUNCT
ALBUMEN
ALBUMIN
AMPULLA
ANGUISH
ANGULAR
ANNUITY
ANNULAR
ANNULET
ANNULUS
ARBUTUS
ARCUATE
ARDUOUS
AROUSAL
ASQUITH
ASSUAGE
ASSUMED
ASSURED
AUDUBON
AUGUSTA
AUGUSTE
AWFULLY
BEGUILE
BEMUSED
BEQUEST
BITUMEN
BLOUSON
BROUGHT
BURUNDI
CALUMET
CALUMNY
CASUALS
CASUISM
CASUIST
CHAUCER
CLOUDED
COLUMNS
CORUNNA
CROUTON
CUMULUS
DEBUSSY
DEFUNCT
DELUDED
DILUENT
DILUTED
DISUSED
DIVULGE
DRAUGHT
DROUGHT
ENDURED
ENQUIRE
ENQUIRY
ENSUING
ENSUITE
EPAULET
ESQUIRE
ESTUARY
ETRURIA
EXPUNGE
FACULTY
FATUITY
FATUOUS
FELUCCA
FIGURES
FLAUNCH
FLEURET
FLEURON
FLOUNCE
FRAUGHT
FUTURES
GALUMPH
GENUINE
GODUNOV
GROUCHO
GROUCHY
GROUNDS
GROUPER
GROUPIE
GROUSER
IMPULSE
INBUILT
INBURST
INCUBUS
INDULGE
INHUMAN
INJURED
INQUEST
INQUIRE
INQUIRY
INSULAR
INSULIN
INSURER
ISSUANT
JACUZZI
JANUARY
JEJUNUM
JOCULAR
JUGULAR
LACUNAE
LAPUTAN
LIQUEFY
LIQUEUR
LIQUIDS
LITURGY
LOCUSTS
MAGUIRE
MANUMIT
MASURKA
MAZURKA
MEDULLA
MENUHIN
MIMULUS
MINUEND
MINUTED
MINUTES
MINUTIA
MODULAR
MODULUS
MOLUCCA
NATURAL
NEBULAR
NODULAR
OCTUPLE
OSCULUM
OSSUARY
PABULUM
PALUDAL
PANURGE
PERUSAL
PETUNIA
PIOUSLY
PIQUANT
PLAUDIT
PLAUTUS
PLEURAL
PLEURON
POPULAR
POPULUS
PROUDER
PROUDIE
PROUDLY
RAMULUS
REAUMUR
REBUILD
RECURVE
REDUCED
REDUCER
REFUGEE
REFUSAL
REGULAR
REPULSE
REPUTED
REQUEST
REQUIEM
REQUIRE
REQUITE
RESULTS
RETURNS
RIVULET
ROBUSTA
ROGUERY
ROGUISH
ROTUNDA
SAMURAI
SCOURER
SCOURGE
SCRUBBY
SCRUFFY
SCRUMMY
SCRUMPY
SCRUNCH
SCRUPLE
SECULAR
SEDUCER
SEQUELA
SEQUOIA
SHOUTER
SINUATE
SINUOUS
SITUATE
SOLUBLE
SPLURGE
SPOUSAL
STAUNCH
STOUTLY
STRUDEL
TABULAR
TENUOUS
TEQUILA
THOUGHT
THRUWAY
TITULAR
TOLUENE
TRIUMPH
TROUBLE
TROUNCE
TROUPER
TROUSER
TUBULAR
TUBULIN
TUMULUS
UNCURED
UNGUENT
UNLUCKY
UNQUIET
UNQUOTE
UPSURGE
VACUITY
VACUOLE
VACUOUS
VAGUELY
VANUATU
VERULAM
VOLUBLE
VOLUBLY
WATUTSI
WRAUGHT
WROUGHT
YAOUNDE
ZAKUSKA
ZYMURGY
ATAVISM
BRAVADO
BRAVELY
BRAVERY
BRAVURA
BREVITY
CALVARY
CANVASS
CARVING
CHEVIOT
CHEVRON
CIVVIES
CONVENE
CONVENT
CONVERT
CONVICT
CONVOKE
CRAVING
CREVICE
CULVERT
DERVISH
DRIVERS
DRIVING
ELEVATE
FAUVISM
FAUVIST
FERVENT
FERVOUR
FLAVOUR
FLIVVER
FLUVIAL
GRAVITY
GRAVURE
HARVARD
HARVEST
HEAVENS
HEAVIER
HEAVILY
KILVERT
KLAVIER
KNAVERY
LATVIAN
LEAVING
LOUVRED
MARVELL
NAIVELY
NAIVETÉ
NAIVETY
NERVOSA
NERVOUS
NERVURE
NIRVANA
NOUVEAU
OUTVOTE
PARVENU
PEEVISH
PERVADE
PERVERT
PREVAIL
PREVENT
PREVIEW
PRIVACY
PRIVATE
PRIVITY
PROVERB
PROVIDE
PROVING
PROVISO
PROVOKE
PROVOST
PURVIEW
RIGVEDA
SALVAGE
SELVAGE
SERVANT
SERVICE
SERVILE
SERVING
SHAVING
SHIVERS
SHIVERY
SIEVERT
SILVERY
SLAVERY
SLAVISH
SLOVENE
SOLVENT
SPAVINE
STEVENS
SUAVELY
SUAVITY
SUBVERT
SURVIVE
TRAVAIL
TRIVIAL
TRIVIUM
VELVETY
VERVAIN
VOIVODE
WEAVING
ALEWIFE
ANTWERP
ARTWORK
ATHWART
AWKWARD
BEOWULF
BETWEEN
BETWIXT
BLOWFLY
BLOWOUT
BOSWELL
BRAWLER
BREWERY
BREWING
BROWNED
BROWNIE
BROWSER
BULWARK
CATWALK
CHEWING
CHOWDER
CRAWLER
CREWCUT
CREWMAN
CROWBAR
CROWDED
CROWING
CUTWORM
DAGWOOD
DERWENT
DOGWOOD
DRAWBAR
DRAWERS
DRAWING
ENDWAYS

ENTWINE
EYEWASH
FLOWERS
FLOWERY
FLOWING
FORWARD
FROWSTY
GADWALL
GLOWING
GNAWING
GROWING
GROWLER
GROWNUP
GUNWALE
HARWICH
HARWOOD
HAYWARD
HAYWIRE
HOGWASH
INKWELL
KEYWORD
KNOWALL
KNOWHOW
KNOWING
LAPWING
LEEWARD
LEGWORK
LOGWOOD
LUGWORM
MAXWELL
MIDWEEK
MIDWEST
MIDWIFE
MUGWORT
MUGWUMP
NARWHAL
NETWORK
NORWICH
OUTWARD
OUTWEAR
OUTWORK
OUTWORN
PLOWMAN
PLYWOOD
PROWESS
PROWLER
PUGWASH
RAGWEED
RAGWORT
REDWOOD
SAPWOOD
SCOWDER
SEAWALL
SEAWEED
SHOWBIZ
SHOWERS
SHOWERY
SHOWILY
SHOWING
SHOWMAN
SHOWOFF
SITWELL
SKYWARD
SLOWING
SNOWDON
SNOWMAN
SOPWITH
STEWARD
STEWING
TRAWLER
TYNWALD
UNAWARE
UNOWNED
UNTWINE
UPSWING
WARWICK
WAXWING
WAXWORK
WAYWARD
ASEXUAL
BAUXITE
BRIXTON
COAXIAL
COEXIST
DIOXIDE
INEXACT
MANXMAN
MARXISM
MARXIST
PROXIMO
QUIXOTE
ULEXITE
ACRYLIC
ASSYRIA
BABYISH
BABYLON
BABYSIT
BARYTES
BICYCLE
BUOYANT
CALYPSO
CHAYOTE
CLOYING
COPYCAT
COPYING
COPYIST
CORYDON
DIDYMUS
DREYFUS
ECDYSIS
EMPYEMA
GRAYISH
GREYISH
GREYLAG
GRUYÈRE
HALYARD
JURYBOX
JURYMAN
LADYBUG
LANYARD
LAWYERS
LUTYENS
PAPYRUS
PLAYBOY
PLAYERS
PLAYFUL
PLAYING
PLAYLET
PLAYOFF
PLAYPEN
POLYGON
POLYMER
POLYPOD
POLYPUS
PRAYING
RECYCLE
SLAYING
STAYING
SWAYING
UNDYING
VARYING
AMAZING
ARIZONA
BENZENE
BENZINE
BENZOIN
BLAZERS
BLAZING
BRAZIER
BUZZARD
CRAZILY
CROZIER
DAZZLED
DIZZILY
DRIZZLE
DRIZZLY
EPIZOON
FANZINE
FRAZZLE
FRIZZLE
FRIZZLY
GIZZARD
GLAZIER
GLAZING
GRAZING
GRIZZLE
GRIZZLY
GUZZLER
JAZZMAN
MITZVAH
MUEZZIN
PIZZAZZ
PREZZIE
PUZZLED
PUZZLER
RHIZOID
RHIZOME
ROZZERS
SEIZURE
SIZZLER
SOZZLED
SUBZERO
SWIZZLE

7:5

ABELARD
ABIGAIL
ABREAST
ABSTAIN
ACCLAIM
ACETATE
ACREAGE
ACTUARY
ACTUATE
ADAMANT
ADONAIS
ADULATE
AFGHANI
AGITATE
AGITATO
AIRBASE
AIRMAIL
ALABAMA
ALICANT
ALIDADE
ALREADY
ALTHAEA
AMTRACK
AMYLASE
ANIMALS
ANIMATE
ANOMALY
APPEASE
APPLAUD
ARAMAIC
ARCHAIC
ARCUATE
ARMBAND
ARREARS
ASPHALT
ASSUAGE
ATARAXY
ATHWART
ATTRACT
AUREATE
AVERAGE
AVOCADO
AWKWARD
BAGGAGE
BAHRAIN
BAKLAVA
BALLADE
BALLAST
BANDAGE
BANDAID
BARBARA
BARBARY
BARGAIN
BARMAID
BARNABY
BARRACK
BARRAGE
BASMATI
BASTARD
BAUHAUS
BEGGARY
BENEATH
BENGALI
BEREAVE
BERNARD
BIOMASS
BIPLANE
BLATANT
BOLLARD
BOMBARD
BOMBAST
BONDAGE
BONNARD
BOUTADE
BRADAWL
BRAVADO
BRIGADE
BRIGAND
BRITAIN
BROCADE
BUFFALO
BULLACE
BULWARK
BUMMALO
BUOYANT
BURBAGE
BURSARY
BUSTARD
BUZZARD
CABBAGE
CALVARY
CAMPANA
CAMPARI
CANDACE
CANTATA
CANVASS
CAPTAIN
CARCASE
CARCASS
CARNABY
CARNAGE
CASCADE
CASCARA
CASEASE
CASSATA
CASSAVA
CASUALS
CATCALL
CATWALK
CAVIARE
CEMBALO
CENTAUR
CENTAVO
CERTAIN
CHAGALL
CHAPATI
CHARADE
CHICAGO
CHICANE
CHICANO
CHORALE
CHUPATI
CITHARA
CLIMATE
COCKADE
COGNATE
COINAGE
COLLAGE
COLLARD
COLLATE
COMMAND
COMPACT
COMPANY
COMPARE
COMPASS
COMRADE
CONCAVE
CONNATE
CONTACT
CONTAIN
COOLANT
COPLAND
CORDATE
CORKAGE
CORSAGE
CORSAIR
COSSACK
COSTARD
COTTAGE
COURAGE
COWHAND
CRANACH
CREMATE
CRENATE
CRUSADE
CUIRASS
CURRAGH
CURRANT
CURTAIL
CURTAIN
CUSTARD
CUTBACK
CUTLASS
CYMBALS
DASTARD
DAYMARK
DECEASE
DECLAIM
DECLARE
DEFIANT
DEFLATE
DEFRAUD
DEGRADE
DENMARK
DEPRAVE
DESCANT
DESPAIR
DETRACT
DETRAIN
DEVIANT
DEVIATE
DICTATE
DIECAST
DIEHARD
DIETARY
DIGRAPH
DIORAMA
DISBAND
DISBARK
DISCARD
DISDAIN
DISEASE
DISMAST
DISTAFF
DISTANT
DITTANY
DOGCART
DOLLARS
DORMANT
DOWLAND
DULLARD
DUNNAGE
EARMARK
ECSTASY
EDUCATE
ELEGANT
ELEVATE
EMANATE
EMBLAZE
EMBRACE
EMERALD
EMIRATE
EMULATE
ENCHANT
ENCLASP
ENCLAVE
ENDGAME
ENDWAYS
ENGLAND
ENGRAFT
ENGRAIN
ENGRAVE
ENSLAVE
ENSNARE
ENSNARL
ENTRAIN
ENTRANT
EPHRAIM
EPICARP
EPITAPH
EPITAXY
ESTUARY
EUSTACE
EXCLAIM
EXOGAMY
EXPIATE
EXPLAIN
EXTRACT
EYEBALL
EYEBATH
EYELASH

EYEWASH
FALLACY
FANFARE
FANTAIL
FANTASY
FARRAGO
FENLAND
FINLAND
FIREARM
FLYHALF
FLYPAST
FOGLAMP
FOLIAGE
FONDANT
FOOTAGE
FORBADE
FOREARM
FORGAVE
FORSAKE
FORWARD
FOULARD
FRIGATE
FUNFAIR
FURNACE
GADWALL
GALLANT
GARBAGE
GARLAND
GASMASK
GAUTAMA
GEMMATE
GERMANE
GERMANY
GESTALT
GESTAPO
GESTATE
GIMBALS
GIZZARD
GOLIARD
GOLIATH
GOSHAWK
GOULASH
GRADATE
GRANARY
GRENADA
GRENADE
GRIMACE
GUANACO
GUARANA
GUARANI
GUNWALE
GUTTATE
GYMNAST
HAGGADA
HAGGARD
HALLALI
HALYARD
HANSARD
HARVARD
HASTATE
HATBAND
HAULAGE
HAYWARD
HECTARE
HENBANE
HENNAED
HEPTANE
HERBAGE
HISPANO
HOBNAIL
HOGBACK
HOGWASH
HOLDALL
HOLLAND
HOPSACK
HOSTAGE
HUBBARD
HUNGARY
HUSBAND
HUSSARS
HYDRANT
HYDRATE
ICELAND
IKEBANA
IMITATE
IMPEACH
IMPLANT
INBOARD
INDIANA
INEXACT
INFLAME
INFLATE
INGRAIN
INGRATE
INROADS
INSCAPE
INSTALL
INSTANT
INSTATE
IRELAND
ISOBASE
ISOLATE
ISSUANT
ITERATE
JACKASS
JAMPANI
JANUARY
JELLABA
JIMJAMS
JUGLANS
JUTLAND
KAMPALA
KHANATE
KILDARE
KITHARA
KNOWALL
KURHAUS
KURSAAL
LABIATE
LACTASE
LACTATE
LAETARE
LAGGARD
LALLANS
LAMBADA
LAMBAST
LANTANA
LANYARD
LAPSANG
LEAKAGE
LEEWARD
LEMMATA
LEONARD
LEOPARD
LEOTARD
LIBRARY
LINDANE
LINEAGE
LINKAGE
LINSANG
LOLLARD
LOTHAIR
LOWLAND
LOWPAID
LUDGATE
LUGGAGE
LULLABY
LUMBAGO
LYMNAEA
MACRAMÉ
MAENADS
MAGNATE
MALLARD
MALTASE
MAMMARY
MANDALA
MANDATE
MANMADE
MANSARD
MARMARA
MARSALA
MASCARA
MASSAGE
MAYFAIR
MEDIATE
MERMAID
MESSAGE
METHANE
MICHAEL
MIDLAND
MIGRANT
MIGRATE
MILEAGE
MILLAIS
MISCAST
MISTAKE
MOMBASA
MONTAGE
MONTAGU
MONTANA
MONTANT
MORDANT
MORLAND
MORTALS
MOULAGE
MUDLARK
MUDPACK
MUNDANE
MURIATE
MURRAIN
MUSTANG
MUSTARD
NAIPAUL
NARRATE
NECTARY
NETBALL
NIAGARA
NICTATE
NIGGARD
NIRVANA
NITRATE
NUMMARY
NUTCASE
OATCAKE
OBVIATE
ODDBALL
ODORANT
OFFBASE
OFFHAND
OILCAKE
OKINAWA
OMPHALE
ONSTAGE
OPERAND
OPERANT
OPERATE
ORCHARD
OREGANO
ORGIAST
ORIGAMI
ORLEANS
OSSUARY
OUTBACK
OUTCAST
OUTDARE
OUTFACE
OUTFALL
OUTLAST
OUTRAGE
OUTRANK
OUTWARD
OVERACT
OVERALL
OVERARM
OVERAWE
OVULATE
OXALATE
OXIDASE
PACKAGE
PAGEANT
PAHLAVI
PALMATE
PALPATE
PANCAKE
PANGAEA
PANNAGE
PARFAIT
PARTAKE
PASSAGE
PASSANT
PEASANT
PECCANT
PECCARY
PECCAVI
PECTASE
PEERAGE
PENDANT
PENNANT
PENNATE
PENTANE
PEONAGE
PERCALE
PERHAPS
PERTAIN
PERVADE
PESSARY
PHALANX
PHARAOH
PICKAXE
PIEBALD
PIGTAIL
PILLAGE
PINBALL
PINNACE
PINTADO
PINTAIL
PIQUANT
PITFALL
PIZZAZZ
PLACARD
PLACATE
PLEIADE
PLENARY
PLUMAGE
POCHARD
POLEAXE
POLLACK
POLLARD
POMMARD
PONIARD
PORTAGE
POSTAGE
POTLACH
POTTAGE
PRECAST
PREDATE
PREFACE
PRELATE
PREPAID
PREPARE
PRESAGE
PREVAIL
PRIMACY
PRIMARY
PRIMATE
PRIVACY
PRIVATE
PROBATE
PROFANE
PRONAOS
PRONATE
PROPANE
PROSAIC
PUGWASH
PULSATE
PUNJABI
QUORATE
RADIANT
RADIATE
RAMPAGE
RAMPANT
RAMPART
RANSACK
RAPHAEL
RATPACK
RECLAIM
REFLATE
REFRACT
REFRAIN
REGNANT
RELEASE
RELIANT
REMNANT
REPLACE
REPLANT
RESHAPE
RESIANT
RESTART
RESTATE
RETRACE
RETRACT
RETRAIN
RETRAIT
REYNARD
RHUBARB
RIBCAGE
RICHARD
ROCKALL
RONSARD
ROSEATE
ROSTAND
ROULADE
RUMMAGE
SABBATH
SACCADE
SALTATE
SALVAGE
SANDALS
SAQQARA
SARCASM
SARDANA
SATIATE
SATRAPY
SAUSAGE
SCUTAGE
SCUTARI
SEALANT
SEAWALL
SEEPAGE
SELVAGE
SENSATE
SERVANT
SETBACK
SEXTANT
SFUMATO
SHEBANG
SHIKARI
SINHALA
SINUATE
SITUATE
SKYLARK
SKYWARD
SMETANA
SONDAGE
SOPRANO
SOUTANE
SPICATE
SPINACH
SPINATE
SQUEAKY
STEWARD
STOMACH
STORAGE
STREAKY
STRIATE
SULFATE
SULLAGE
SULTANA
SUMMARY
SUNLAMP
SURFACE
SURNAME
SURPASS
SUSTAIN
TAMMANY
TANKARD
TANNATE
TANTARA
TAPLASH
TARTARE
TARTARY
TATIANA
TEACAKE
TEENAGE
TERRACE
TERRAIN
TESTATE
THERAPY
THREADS
THROATY
TIFFANY
TILLAGE
TIMBALE
TIMPANI
TINTACK
TIPCART
TITRATE

TOCCATA
TOENAIL
TONNAGE
TOPIARY
TOPKAPI
TOPMAST
TORNADE
TORNADO
TORSADE
TOWPATH
TRAVAIL
TREPANG
TSIGANE
TSIGANY
TSUNAMI
TURBARY
TUSCANY
TYMPANO
TYMPANY
TYNWALD
ULULANT
ULULATE
UMBRAGE
UNAWARE
UNCLASP
UNHEARD
UNITARY
UNLEASH
UNREADY
UNSNARL
UPBRAID
UPGRADE
UPSTAGE
UPSTART
UPSTATE
URINARY
URINATE
VAGRANT
VALIANT
VANDALS
VANTAGE
VANUATU
VARIANT
VASSAIL
VERDANT
VERSANT
VERVAIN
VIBRANT
VIBRATE
VIBRATO
VILLAGE
VILLAIN
VINTAGE
VIOLATE
VIRGATE
VITIATE
VITRAIL
VOLCANO
VOLTAGE
VOLTAIC
VULGATE
WAGTAIL
WALLABY
WALLACE
WARFARE
WARPATH
WARRANT
WASSAIL
WASTAGE
WATTAGE
WAYLAND
WAYMARK
WAYWARD
WELFARE
WETBACK
WETLAND
YARDAGE
YARDARM
ZEALAND
ZEDOARY
ZETLAND
ZINGARO
ZOFFANY
ACERBIC
ACROBAT
AEROBIC
AFFABLE
AFFABLY
ALDABRA
ALEMBIC
ALGEBRA
AMIABLE
AMIABLY
AMOEBIC
ANTIBES
ATTABOY
AUDIBLE
AUDIBLY
AUDUBON
BALLBOY
BANDBOX
BELABOR
BELLBOY
BLABBER
BLUBBER
BOURBON
BRAMBLE
BUGABOO
CALABAR
CALIBAN
CALIBER
CALIBRE
CALLBOX
CALLBOY
CAPABLE
CAPABLY
CARIBOU
CASHBOX
CELEBES
CHAMBER
CHAMBRÉ
CIMABUE
CLAMBER
CLIMBER
CLOBBER
CLUMBER
COHABIT
COLIBRI
COURBET
CROWBAR
CRUMBLE
CRUMBLY
CURABLE
DATABLE
DECIBEL
DELIBES
DINGBAT
DISABLE
DISOBEY
DRABBLE
DRAWBAR
DRIBBLE
DURABLE
DURABLY
DUSTBIN
EATABLE
ENNOBLE
ENTEBBE
EPHEBUS
EQUABLE
EQUABLY
EXHIBIT
FIREBUG
FREEBIE
FRIABLE
FRISBEE
FROEBEL
FUSEBOX
FUSIBLE
GEARBOX
GOODBYE
GRUMBLE
HALIBUT
HANDBAG
HAUTBOY
ICHABOD
IGNOBLE
INCUBUS
INHABIT
INHIBIT
JACOBIN
JACOBUS
JEZEBEL
JUKEBOX
JURYBOX
KNOBBLE
KNOBBLY
LADYBUG
LEGIBLE
LEGIBLY
LONGBOW
LOVABLE
MACABRE
MAILBAG
MAILBOX
MARABOU
MARIBOU
MINIBUS
MOVABLE
MUTABLE
NAILBED
NAMIBIA
NEWSBOY
NOSEBAG
NOTABLE
NOTABLY
OCTOBER
OMNIBUS
ONMIBUS
OVERBID
PAGEBOY
PARABLE
PATIBLE
PAYABLE
PHOEBUS
PILLBOX
PLAYBOY
PLIABLE
PLUMBER
POOHBAH
POSTBAG
POSTBOX
POTABLE
QUIBBLE
RAINBOW
RAREBIT
RHOMBUS
RISIBLE
ROSEBUD
SACKBUT
SALABLE
SANDBAG
SANDBOX
SANDBOY
SCAMBLE
SCRUBBY
SEEDBED
SHAMBLE
SHERBET
SHOWBIZ
SICKBAY
SICKBED
SINDBAD
SIZABLE
SJAMBOK
SLOBBER
SLUMBER
SOAPBOX
SOFABED
SOLUBLE
STROBIC
STUBBLE
STUBBLY
STUMBLE
TALLBOY
TAXABLE
TENABLE
THIMBLE
TOOLBOX
TOYNBEE
TREMBLE
TREMBLY
TROUBLE
TUNABLE
VISIBLE
VISIBLY
VOLUBLE
VOLUBLY
WINDBAG
AFRICAN
ALMACKS
ANARCHY
ANTACID
APRICOT
ARTICLE
ATTACHE
ATTICUS
AURICLE
AUROCHS
AUTOCUE
BICYCLE
BIFOCAL
BLOTCHY
BORACIC
BOUNCER
BRIOCHE
BRONCHI
CALECHE
CARACAS
CARACUL
CENACLE
CEVICHE
CHANCEL
CHANCRE
CHAUCER
CODICIL
COMICAL
CONICAL
COPYCAT
CORACLE
CORNCOB
COUNCIL
CREWCUT
CRUNCHY
CUBICLE
CURACAO
CUTICLE
CYNICAL
DEBACLE
DEFACED
DEFICIT
DEJECTA
DIARCHY
DIDICOY
DYARCHY
EARACHE
EFFECTS
ETHICAL
FELUCCA
FETICHE
FIANCÉE
FINICAL
FINICKY
FLACCID
FLATCAR
FRANCIS
GALOCHE
GLENCOE
GNOCCHI
GOUACHE
GRACCHI
GROUCHO
GROUCHY
HAIRCUT
HARICOT
HELICAL
HELICON
HELLCAT
HIBACHI
ILIACUS
ILLICIT
INSECTS
JERICHO
KARACHI
KINGCUP
KNEECAP
LEXICON
LINACRE
LINOCUT
LOGICAL
LYRICAL
MAGICAL
MAILCAR
MALACCA
MANACLE
MARACAS
MEDICAL
METICAL
MEXICAN
MIMICRY
MINICAB
MIRACLE
MODICUM
MOHICAN
MOLUCCA
MONOCLE
MOROCCO
MUSICAL
OBJECTS
OFFICER
OFFICES
OPTICAL
OSSICLE
PANACEA
PANACHE
PANICKY
PANICLE
PAUNCHY
PEDICAB
PEDICEL
PEDICLE
PELICAN
PIERCED
PIERCER
POLECAT
POTICHE
PRINCES
QUERCUS
QUINCHE
RADICAL
RADICLE
RAUNCHY
REBECCA
RECYCLE
REDUCED
REDUCER
RELICTS
REOCCUR
RETICLE
ROSACEA
RUBICON
SARACEN
SCHICKS
SEDUCER
SENECIO
SIDECAR
SILICON
SIROCCO
SKETCHY
SOLICIT
SPENCER
SPLICED
SPLICER
STARCHY
STENCIL
STOICAL
TAXICAB
TIERCEL
TIERCET
TOBACCO
TOPICAL
TRAMCAR
TRANCHE
TREACLE
TREACLY
TWITCHY
TYPICAL
UNLUCKY
UTRECHT
UTRICLE
VATICAN
VEHICLE
VESICLE
WHIPCAT
WILDCAT
WOODCUT
ALENÇON

ABANDON
ABRIDGE
ACAUDAL
ALADDIN
AMYGDAL
APSIDAL
ARCADIA
ARIADNE
ARUNDEL
ASUNDER
AVOIDER
BAGHDAD
BAHADUR
BEARDED
BESIDES
BLADDER
BLANDLY
BLENDER
BLINDER
BLINDLY
BLUNDER
BOARDER
BOREDOM
BORODIN
BOULDER
BOUNDED
BOUNDEN
BOUNDER
BOURDON
BRANDED
BRANDER
BREADED
BREADTH
BREEDER
BRENDAN
BRINDLE
BROADEN
BROADLY
BUILDER
BULLDOG
CANIDAE
CARADOC
CELADON
CHALDEE
CHARDIN
CHEDDAR
CHINDIT
CHORDAE
CHOWDER
CHUNDER
CITADEL
CLOUDED
CORYDON
COULDNT
CROWDED
CSARDAS
DECIDED
DECIDER
DECODER
DEIRDRE
DELUDED

DIVIDED
DREADED
DRESDEN
DUKEDOM
DUNEDIN
DWINDLE
EARLDOM
ECHIDNA
ECUADOR
EPHEDRA
EVANDER
EXHEDRA
FARADAY
FIELDER
FIREDOG
FIXEDLY
FLAGDAY
FLODDEN
FLOODED
FOUNDER
FOUNDRY
FREEDOM
GEORDIE
GLADDEN
GRANDAD
GRANDEE
GRANDLY
GRANDMA
GRANDPA
GRENDEL
GRIDDLE
GRINDER
GUARDED
GUILDER
HANGDOG
HEREDIA
HOARDER
HOLIDAY
HUMIDOR
INFIDEL
INSIDER
INSIDES
INVADER
JACKDAW
KIELDER
KINGDOM
LAUNDER
LAUNDRY
LEANDER
LOURDES
LUCIDLY
LURIDLY
MACADAM
MACEDON
MATADOR
MAUNDER
MEANDER
MELODIC
MIRADOR
MOULDED
MOULDER

NAKEDLY
NOMADIC
NOONDAY
OVERDUE
PALADIN
PALUDAL
PARADOR
PARADOS
PARADOX
PICADOR
PLAUDIT
PLEADER
PLODDER
PLUNDER
POTSDAM
PROUDER
PROUDIE
PROUDLY
QUONDAM
RAMADAN
RANIDAE
RAPIDLY
REMODEL
REREDOS
RESIDUE
RHONDDA
RIGIDLY
ROUNDED
ROUNDEL
ROUNDER
ROUNDLY
ROUNDUP
RWANDAN
SALADIN
SCANDAL
SCOWDER
SERFDOM
SHINDIG
SHUDDER
SKIDDAW
SLANDER
SLENDER
SMOLDER
SNOWDON
SOLIDLY
SOLIDUS
SOUNDED
SOUNDER
SOUNDLY
SPANDAU
SPANDEX
SPENDER
SPINDLE
SPINDLY
SPLODGE
SPONDEE
SPONDYL
SQUADDY
STADDLE
STANDBY
STANDIN

STANDUP
STARDOM
STRIDES
STRIDOR
STRUDEL
STUDDED
SUBEDAR
SUBEDIT
SWADDLE
SWIDDEN
SWINDLE
THIRDLY
THUNDER
TIMIDLY
TREADLE
TRODDEN
TRUNDLE
TUESDAY
TWADDLE
TWEEDLE
TWIDDLE
TWIDDLY
UGANDAN
UNAIDED
UNFADED
UNGODLY
UNLADEN
UPSIDES
VIVIDLY
WASHDAY
WEALDEN
WEEKDAY
WEIRDLY
WHEEDLE
WORLDLY
WOULDBE
WOULDNT
WOUNDED
YEZIDEE
ABSCESS
ACADEME
ACADEMY
ACCRETE
ACHAEAN
ACHIEVE
ACTAEON
ACTRESS
ACUTELY
ADDRESS
AGELESS
AGGRESS
AILMENT
AIMLESS
AIRLESS
ALAMEIN
ALCHEMY
ALGIERS
ALIMENT
ALPHEUS
AMATEUR
AMBIENT

ANCIENT
ANISEED
ANTLERS
ANTWERP
ANXIETY
APOGEAN
APTNESS
ARCHERY
ARMREST
ARTLESS
ASSIEGE
ATHLETE
AUGMENT
AUSLESE
AUSTERE
BADNESS
BAHREIN
BANDEAU
BARKERS
BATHERS
BATTELS
BATTERY
BECKETT
BELIEVE
BELLEEK
BENNETT
BENZENE
BEQUEST
BERCEAU
BERSEEM
BERSERK
BESEECH
BESIEGE
BESMEAR
BESPEAK
BETWEEN
BIGHEAD
BINDERY
BITTERN
BITTERS
BLAZERS
BOILEAU
BONKERS
BOOLEAN
BORDERS
BOSWELL
BOTTEGA
BOWHEAD
BRASERO
BRAVELY
BRAVERY
BREWERY
BRIBERY
BROKERS
BUCKETS
BUCKEYE
BUGBEAR
BULLETS
BURGEON
BURGESS
BURMESE

BURNELL
BUTTERY
CACHEXY
CAIRENE
CALDERA
CANDELA
CANNERY
CANTEEN
CAREERS
CARRELL
CATHEAD
CATSEYE
CAUTERY
CHAPEAU
CHATEAU
CHILEAN
CHIMERA
CHINESE
CHOLERA
CINDERS
CISTERN
CLEMENT
CLOSELY
CLOSEUP
COFFERS
COLLECT
COLLEEN
COLLEGE
COMMEND
COMMENT
COMPERE
COMPETE
CONCEAL
CONCEDE
CONCEIT
CONCEPT
CONCERN
CONCERT
CONDEMN
CONFESS
CONGEAL
CONNECT
CONSENT
CONTEMN
CONTEND
CONTENT
CONTEST
CONTEXT
CONVENE
CONVENT
CONVERT
COOKERY
COPPERS
CORBEAU
CORBETT
CORNEAL
CORNELL
CORRECT
CORTEGE
COWHERD
COXLESS

COYNESS
CRIMEAN
CRUDELY
CULVERT
CURRENT
CUTLERY
CUTTERS
CYPRESS
DAGGERS
DANTEAN
DEADEYE
DEANERY
DEAREST
DEBRETT
DECREED
DEFLECT
DEGREES
DENSELY
DEPLETE
DEPRESS
DERWENT
DESCEND
DESCENT
DESSERT
DIALECT
DICKENS
DIGRESS
DILUENT
DIMNESS
DIOCESE
DIPTERA
DISCERN
DISSECT
DISSENT
DISTEND
DISTENT
DITHERY
DODDERY
DODGEMS
DRAPERY
DRAWERS
DRIVERS
DRYNESS
DUBIETY
DUCHESS
DUDGEON
DUNGEON
DURRELL
EARNEST
EASIEST
EASTERN
EGGHEAD
ELEMENT
EMINENT
EMPRESS
EMPYEMA
ENDLESS
ENFIELD
ENTREAT
EPICENE
EPSTEIN

ESCHEAT
ESTREAT
EVEREST
EVIDENT
EXCRETA
EXCRETE
EXEGETE
EXIGENT
EXPRESS
EXTREME
EYELESS
FALSELY
FARCEUR
FARMERS
FARNESE
FATHEAD
FATNESS
FERMENT
FERVENT
FETTERS
FEYDEAU
FIDGETS
FIDGETY
FIFTEEN
FIGLEAF
FIGMENT
FILBERT
FILLETS
FINGERS
FISHERY
FISHEYE
FITMENT
FITNESS
FITTEST
FLAREUP
FLOWERS
FLOWERY
FLYLEAF
FORBEAR
FORCEPS
FORFEIT
FORFEND
FORGERY
FULGENT
FULLERS
GABFEST
GAITERS
GALLEON
GALLERY
GARDENS
GARMENT
GAYNESS
GENOESE
GENTEEL
GEODESY
GERBERA
GIBLETS
GILBERT
GINSENG
GOAHEAD
GODDESS
GODLESS
GODSEND
GOMBEEN
GORSEDD
GRADELY
GROCERS
GROCERY
GUDGEON
GUINEAN
GUINEAS
GUNNERA
GUNNERY
GUTLESS
GWYNETH
HACKERY
HAGGERY
HALBERD
HALBERT
HAPLESS
HARLECH
HARNESS
HARVEST
HATLESS
HAWKEYE
HAYSEED
HAZLETT
HEAVENS
HEIRESS
HELLENE
HENPECK
HERBERT
HERBERY
HERSELF
HETAERA
HIGHEST
HIMSELF
HOLBEIN
HORDEUM
HOSIERY
HOSTESS
HOTHEAD
HUNKERS
HYGIENE
ICEBERG
ICINESS
ILLNESS
IMAGERY
IMPIETY
IMPRESS
IMPREST
INFIELD
INFLECT
INGRESS
INKWELL
INQUEST
INSPECT
INSTEAD
ISOMERE
ISRAELI
JACKETS
JAGGERY
JANKERS
JEEPERS
JERSEYS
JITTERS
JITTERY
JOBBERY
JOBLESS
JOINERY
JOYLESS
KENNEDY
KENNELS
KERMESS
KIDNEYS
KILVERT
KIPPERS
KNAVERY
LACTEAL
LAMBENT
LAMBERT
LAMBETH
LANCERS
LANTERN
LARCENY
LARGELY
LARGESS
LARGEST
LAURELS
LAWLESS
LAWYERS
LAXNESS
LEADERS
LECHERY
LECTERN
LEGLESS
LENIENT
LETTERS
LINNEAN
LINSEED
LIONESS
LIPREAD
LIQUEFY
LIQUEUR
LITHELY
LOOSELY
LOTTERY
LUTYENS
MACBETH
MACHETE
MADNESS
MAGNETO
MALLEUS
MALTESE
MANNERS
MARGERY
MARLENE
MARTENS
MARVELL
MASSEUR
MASTERS
MASTERY
MATTERS
MAXWELL
MEMBERS
MERCERY
MESEEMS
MIDTERM
MIDWEEK
MIDWEST
MINUEND
MIOCENE
MISDEED
MISLEAD
MISREAD
MITTENS
MOCKERS
MOCKERY
MONTERO
MORRELL
MOTHERS
MULLEIN
MUMMERS
MUMMERY
MURAENA
MUSSELS
MYSTERY
NAIVELY
NAIVETÉ
NAIVETY
NANKEEN
NASCENT
NEAREST
NEGLECT
NEGRESS
NEWNESS
NICAEAN
NIOBEAN
NIPPERS
NOUVEAU
NOWHERE
NUCLEAR
NUCLEIC
NUCLEUS
NUMBERS
NUNNERY
NURSERY
NUTMEAT
OAKLEAF
OATMEAL
OBSCENE
ODDMENT
ODDNESS
OFFBEAT
OFFPEAK
OLDNESS
ONENESS
ONESELF
OPPRESS
OPULENT
ORKNEYS
ORPHEAN
ORPHEUS
ORVIETO
OUTWEAR
OVEREAT
PARNELL
PARVENU
PASTERN
PASTEUR
PATIENT
PATTERN
PAYMENT
PEERESS
PEPPERS
PEPPERY
PERCENT
PERCEPT
PERFECT
PERSEID
PERSEUS
PERVERT
PHILEAS
PHONEIN
PHONEME
PIDGEON
PIGGERY
PIGMEAT
PIGMENT
PINCERS
PINHEAD
PIONEER
PIRAEUS
PITHEAD
PLACEBO
PLATEAU
PLAYERS
PLUTEUS
POETESS
POMPEII
PORTEND
PORTENT
POSSESS
POSTERN
POTHEEN
POTHERB
POTTERY
POULENC
POWDERY
PREBEND
PRECEDE
PRECEPT
PREFECT
PREHEAT
PRESENT
PRETEND
PRETEXT
PREVENT
PRIMEUR
PROCEED
PROCESS
PROFESS
PROGENY
PROJECT
PROPEND
PROTEAN
PROTECT
PROTEGE
PROTEIN
PROTEST
PROTEUS
PROVERB
PROWESS
PRUDENT
PTOLEMY
PUNGENT
PURBECK
PURCELL
PUTREFY
PUTTEES
RACKETS
RACKETY
RAGWEED
RAIMENT
RATTEEN
RAWNESS
REAGENT
REDHEAD
REDNECK
REDNESS
REDRESS
REELECT
REFLECT
REFRESH
REGRESS
RELIEVE
REPLETE
REPRESS
REQUEST
RESPECT
RETREAD
RETREAT
RIBLESS
RICKETS
RICKETY
RIGVEDA
RIMLESS
RINGERS
RIOTERS
RIVIERA
ROBBERS
ROBBERY
ROCKERY
ROEDEAN
ROGUERY
ROLLERS
ROMPERS
RONDEAU
ROOKERY
ROULEAU
ROZZERS
RUBBERS
RUBBERY
RUNNERS
RUSSELL
RUTHENE
SABAEAN
SADNESS
SALIENT
SALIERI
SAPIENS
SAPIENT
SAPPERS
SARGENT
SARMENT
SATIETY
SCAFELL
SCALENE
SCENERY
SCHLEPP
SCHNELL
SCREECH
SCREEVE
SEAWEED
SECRECY
SECRETE
SECRETS
SEEKERS
SEGMENT
SELLERS
SEQUELA
SERPENS
SERPENT
SEXLESS
SHAKERS
SHAKEUP
SHAPELY
SHEBEEN
SHIVERS
SHIVERY
SHOWERS
SHOWERY
SHUTEYE
SHYNESS
SIAMESE
SICKERT
SIEMENS
SIEVERT
SILVERY
SINCERE
SISTERS
SITWELL
SIXTEEN
SLAVERY
SLOVENE
SLYNESS
SOCIETY
SOCKEYE
SOLVENT
SORCERY
SPIDERS
SPIDERY
SQUEERS
SQUEEZE
STARETS
STATELY
STEVENS

STIPEND
STUDENT
STUPEFY
SUAVELY
SUBJECT
SUBTEEN
SUBTEND
SUBVERT
SUBZERO
SUCCEED
SUCCESS
SUFFETE
SUGGEST
SUMMERY
SUNBEAM
SUNDECK
SUNLESS
SUPREME
SUPREMO
SURFEIT
SURGEON
SURGERY
SURREAL
SUSPECT
SUSPEND
TABLEAU
TAFFETA
TANGENT
TANNERY
TARPEIA
TATTERS
TEALEAF
TEMPERA
TEMPEST
TENSELY
TERRENE
TERSELY
TESSERA
THEREBY
THEREIN
THERESA
THERETO
THESEUS
THOREAU
THYSELF
TIGRESS
TIMBERS
TINTERN
TOLUENE
TONNEAU
TOPLESS
TORMENT
TORPEDO
TORREFY
TORRENT
TOTIENT
TOTTERY
TOWHEAD
TRACERY
TRADEIN
TRAGEDY

TRAPEZE
TRICEPS
TRIDENT
TRIREME
TRISECT
TRITELY
TRUMEAU
TURGENT
TURNERY
UKULELE
UMPTEEN
UNCLEAN
UNCLEAR
UNDRESS
UNGUENT
USELESS
VAGUELY
VARIETY
VELVETY
VERBENA
VERMEER
VESPERS
VILLEIN
VINCENT
VIOLENT
VISCERA
WARBECK
WARHEAD
WASHERS
WATTEAU
WEAKEST
WEEKEND
WEIGELA
WENDELL
WESTERN
WETNESS
WHEREAS
WHEREBY
WHEREIN
WIDGEON
WITHERS
WITLESS
WITNESS
WONDERS
WOOMERA
WORKERS
WRITEUP
WRYNECK
YONKERS
ZAIREAN
ZAMBESI
ETAGÈRE
GRUYÈRE
MOLIÈRE
AQUIFER
BALEFUL
BASHFUL
BENEFIT
BLOWFLY
BLUFFLY
BRIEFLY

BRIMFUL
CAREFUL
CHAMFER
CHIEFLY
CHIFFON
CHUFFED
CONIFER
DEEPFRY
DOLEFUL
DREYFUS
DUTIFUL
FALAFEL
FATEFUL
FEARFUL
FIREFLY
FISTFUL
FRETFUL
GAINFUL
GIRAFFE
GLEEFUL
GRIFFON
GRUFFLY
HALIFAX
HANDFUL
HARMFUL
HATEFUL
HEEDFUL
HELPFUL
HOPEFUL
HURTFUL
LUCIFER
LUSTFUL
MALEFIC
MINDFUL
MIRIFIC
NEEDFUL
OVERFED
PACIFIC
PAINFUL
PITIFUL
PLAYFUL
PROFFER
RATAFIA
RESTFUL
SACKFUL
SCOFFER
SCRUFFY
SCUFFLE
SHUFFLE
SKIFFLE
SKILFUL
SKINFUL
SNAFFLE
SNIFFER
SNIFFLE
SNUFFLE
SOUFFLE
SOULFUL
SQUIFFY
STAFFER
STIFFEN

STIFFLY
STIRFRY
STUFFED
TACTFUL
TEARFUL
THRIFTY
TRAFFIC
TRIFFID
TRUFFLE
TUNEFUL
TWELFTH
WAKEFUL
WISHFUL
WISTFUL
XERAFIN
ZESTFUL
ALLEGED
ALLEGRI
ALLEGRO
ALRIGHT
AMALGAM
AMBAGES
AMONGST
ANTIGEN
ANTIGUA
APHAGIA
ASSEGAI
ATINGLE
AVENGER
BOLOGNA
BRIDGES
BRIDGET
BROUGHT
CADOGAN
CHANGED
CHANGES
CHARGED
CHARGER
CHARGES
CHIGGER
CLANGER
CLINGER
COLOGNE
DAMAGED
DAMAGES
DELIGHT
DEMIGOD
DONEGAL
DOWAGER
DRAGGLE
DRAUGHT
DREDGER
DROUGHT
DRUGGED
DRUGGET
ECLOGUE
EGLOGUE
ENDOGEN
ENERGIC
ENGAGED
ENRAGED

EPERGNE
FATIGUE
FINAGLE
FLEDGED
FLOGGER
FRAUGHT
FREIGHT
FRINGED
GEORGIA
GEORGIC
GIELGUD
GLASGOW
HALOGEN
HANDGUN
HEXAGON
HYPOGEA
ILLEGAL
INSIGHT
INTEGER
KEROGEN
LASAGNA
LASAGNE
LOUNGER
MANAGER
MANAGUA
MUTAGEN
MYALGIA
NOSEGAY
OBLIGED
OBLIGOR
OCTAGON
ORANGES
OTALGIA
PARAGON
PELAGIC
PERIGEE
PIROGUE
PLUNGER
PODAGRA
POLYGON
PRONGED
RAVAGES
REALGAR
REFUGEE
RENEGUE
RINGGIT
RONTGEN
SAVAGES
SCRAGGY
SENEGAL
SHAGGED
SHINGLE
SHINGLY
SHOTGUN
SLEIGHT
SLOGGER
SMIDGIN
SMUDGED
SMUGGLE
SNIGGER
SNUGGLE

SOCAGER
SPADGER
SPANGLE
SPONGER
STAGGER
STENGAH
STENGUN
STINGER
STOPGAP
STRIGIL
SWAGGER
SWINGER
SWINGLE
TANAGER
TANAGRA
THOUGHT
THUGGEE
TONIGHT
TRIGGER
TRINGLE
TRUDGEN
TWIGGER
UPRIGHT
UPTIGHT
VINEGAR
VOYAGER
WHINGER
WRANGLE
WRAUGHT
WRIGGLE
WRINGER
WRONGLY
WROUGHT
YOUNGER
ABASHED
ABRAHAM
AIRSHIP
ALCOHOL
ANOTHER
APHTHAE
ARACHNE
ATAGHAN
ATISHOO
BACCHIC
BACCHUS
BAGEHOT
BANSHEE
BEACHED
BEACHES
BEARHUG
BELLHOP
BENCHER
BENTHAM
BENTHOS
BIGSHOT
BLATHER
BLETHER
BLIGHTY
BLUSHER
BOLSHIE
BOLSHOI

BOWSHOT
BRIGHAM
BROTHEL
BROTHER
BRUSHER
BULGHUR
BURGHER
BURNHAM
BUTCHER
CAMPHOR
CANTHUS
CATCHER
CATCHUP
CHATHAM
CHEKHOV
CLACHAN
CLOTHED
CLOTHES
COLCHIS
COUCHÉE
COWSHED
CRASHES
CROCHET
CRUSHED
CRUSHER
CUMSHAW
CYNTHIA
DAUPHIN
DEATHLY
DELPHIC
DOLPHIN
DOUGHTY
DRACHMA
DROSHKY
EARSHOT
EARTHEN
EARTHLY
EDAPHIC
EPITHET
EYESHOT
FARTHER
FEATHER
FILCHER
FLASHER
FLIGHTY
FLUSHED
FRESHEN
FRESHER
FRESHET
FRESHLY
FUNCHAL
FURTHER
GALAHAD
GASOHOL
GASTHOF
GINGHAM
GRAPHIC
GRAPHIS
GRYPHON
GUMSHOE
GUNSHOT

HARSHLY
HATCHET
HAUGHTY
HEATHEN
HEATHER
HEIGHTS
HOTSHOT
HUNCHED
IVANHOE
KETCHUP
KINSHIP
KITCHEN
KNOWHOW
KOLKHOZ
KRISHNA
LAKSHMI
LATCHET
LEATHER
LITCHEE
LURCHER
LYNCHET
MALTHUS
MANIHOC
MARCHER
MARSHAL
MATCHED
MATCHET
MATTHEW
MAUGHAM
MENTHOL
MENUHIN
MIDSHIP
MOITHER
MONTHLY
MOORHEN
MORPHIA
NARTHEX
NARWHAL
NATCHEZ
NAUGHTY
NEITHER
NOTCHED
NYMPHET
OUTSHOT
PANTHER
PARCHED
PARTHIA
PASCHAL
PEACHUM
PILCHER
PINCHED
PITCHED
PITCHER
POACHER
PORTHOS
POTSHOT
PRITHEE
PROPHET
PRYTHEE
PSYCHIC
PUNCHED
PUNCHER
PYRRHIC
QUECHUA
QUICHUA
RANCHER
RATCHET
ROADHOG
ROUGHEN
ROUGHIE
ROUGHLY
SAPPHIC
SATCHEL
SEETHED
SLASHED
SLITHER
SLOSHED
SMASHED
SMASHER
SMITHER
SMOTHER
SOMEHOW
SORGHUM
SOUTHEY
SOVKHOZ
STACHYS
STEPHEN
SULPHUR
SWITHIN
TEACHER
TEASHOP
THITHER
TOOTHED
TORCHON
TOUCHED
TOUGHEN
TOYSHOP
TRACHEA
TRISHAW
TROCHEE
TROCHUS
TROPHIC
URETHRA
VAUGHAN
VOUCHER
WARSHIP
WARTHOG
WATCHER
WEATHER
WEIGHIN
WEIGHTS
WEIGHTY
WHETHER
WHITHER
WITCHES
WORSHIP
WOTCHER
XANTHOS
ABIDING
ABILITY
ABJOINT
ABOLISH
ABUSIVE
ACADIAN
ACARIDA
ACIDIFY
ACIDITY
ACONITE
ACQUIRE
ADAMITE
ADELINE
ADJOINT
ADORING
AEOLIAN
AFFAIRS
AFFLICT
AGILITY
AGONIST
AGONIZE
AIRLIFT
AIRLINE
AIRSICK
ALANINE
ALDRICH
ALEPINE
ALEWIFE
ALTHING
ALUMINA
AMANITA
AMAZING
AMENITY
AMERICA
AMERIGO
AMERIND
AMORIST
AMORITE
AMPLIFY
AMUSING
ANANIAS
ANGLING
ANGRILY
ANGUISH
ANILINE
ANIMIST
ANNUITY
ANODIZE
ANTHILL
APELIKE
APICIUS
APPLIED
APPOINT
APPRIZE
ARABIAN
ARABICA
ARCHIVE
ARETINO
ARIDITY
ARRAIGN
ASCRIBE
ASININE
ASOCIAL
ASQUITH
ASTRIDE
ATAVISM
ATELIER
ATHEISM
ATHEIST
ATOMIST
ATOMIZE
ATTAINT
AUCTION
AVARICE
AVIDITY
BABBITT
BABYISH
BACKING
BAGPIPE
BAILIFF
BALDING
BALLIOL
BAMBINO
BANGING
BANKING
BAPTISM
BAPTIST
BAPTIZE
BARKING
BARRIER
BARRING
BASKING
BASTIDE
BASTION
BATHING
BATTING
BAUXITE
BEADING
BEAMING
BEARING
BEARISH
BEATIFY
BEATING
BEDDING
BEDSIDE
BEDTIME
BEEHIVE
BEELINE
BEGGING
BEGUILE
BEIJING
BELGIAN
BELGIUM
BELLINI
BENDING
BENZINE
BERLINE
BERNINI
BESTIAL
BETHINK
BETTING
BETWIXT
BIDDING
BILLION
BINDING
BLAZING
BLEMISH
BOATING
BOILING
BOMBING
BONFIRE
BOOKIES
BOOKING
BOOKISH
BOOMING
BOORISH
BOWLING
BRACING
BRAKING
BRAZIER
BREVITY
BREWING
BRITISH
BROMIDE
BROMINE
BRUTISH
BUDDING
BUGGING
BUGGINS
BULGING
BULLION
BULLISH
BUNTING
BURKINA
BURNING
BURNISH
BUSHIDO
BUSKINS
BUSSING
CABLING
CADDISH
CADMIUM
CAESIUM
CAINITE
CAITIFF
CALCIFY
CALCINE
CALCITE
CALCIUM
CALLING
CAMBIUM
CAMPING
CAMPION
CANDIDA
CANDIDE
CANDIED
CANNILY
CANNING
CAPRICE
CAPSIZE
CAPTION
CAPTIVE
CARBIDE
CARBINE
CARDIAC
CARMINE
CARRIED
CARRIER
CARRIES
CARRION
CARSICK
CARTIER
CARVING
CASHIER
CASPIAN
CASTILE
CASTING
CASUISM
CASUIST
CATFISH
CATKINS
CATLIKE
CATLING
CATMINT
CATTISH
CAUTION
CEILIDH
CEILING
CELLINI
CELLIST
CELSIUS
CERTIFY
CESSION
CHAFING
CHALICE
CHARIOT
CHARITY
CHASING
CHEMISE
CHEMIST
CHERISH
CHEVIOT
CHEWING
CHOKING
CHOPINE
CHORION
CHORIZO
CITRINE
CIVVIES
CLARIFY
CLARION
CLARITY
CLOSING
CLOYING
CLUNIAC
COATING
COAXIAL
COCAINE
CODEINE
CODLING
COELIAC
COEXIST
COITION
COLDITZ
COLLIDE
COLLIER
COMBINE
COMBING
COMPILE
CONCISE
CONFIDE
CONFINE
CONFIRM
CONNIVE
CONSIGN
CONSIST
CONVICT
COOKING
COOLING
COPPICE
COPYING
COPYIST
CORDIAL
CORDITE
CORKING
CORNICE
CORNISH
CORRIDA
CORTINA
COSTING
COSTIVE
COURIER
COUSINS
COWGIRL
COWLICK
COWLING
CRANIAL
CRANIUM
CRAVING
CRAZILY
CREVICE
CROSIER
CROWING
CROZIER
CRUCIAL
CRUCIFY
CRUDITY
CUCKING
CUISINE
CUNNING
CURLING
CURRIED
CURSIVE
CUSHION
CUTTING
CYANIDE
CYCLING
CYCLIST
CYPRIOT
DADAISM
DADAIST
DAMNING
DAMPIER
DAMPING
DANCING
DARLING
DARNING
DASHING
DAYTIME

DEALING
DEBRIEF
DECEIVE
DECLINE
DENSITY
DENTINE
DENTIST
DEPRIVE
DERRICK
DERVISH
DESPISE
DESPITE
DESTINE
DESTINY
DETAILS
DIALING
DIAMINE
DIARIST
DICTION
DIETINE
DIGGING
DIGNIFY
DIGNITY
DIORITE
DIOXIDE
DISLIKE
DISMISS
DISTILL
DITTIES
DIZZILY
DOCKING
DOGFISH
DOMAINE
DONNISH
DORKING
DOSSIER
DOWDILY
DOWSING
DRAWING
DRIVING
DUALITY
DUBBING
DUCKING
DUCTILE
DUMPISH
DUNCIAD
DUNKIRK
DUSTING
EARLIER
EARRING
EBBTIDE
EBONITE
ECCRINE
EDIFICE
EDITION
EGALITY
EGOTISM
EGOTIST
ELATION
ELEGIAC
ELEGIST
ELISION
ELITISM
ELITIST
ELOGIUM
ELUSIVE
ELYSIAN
ELYSIUM
EMOTION
EMOTIVE
ENGLISH
ENPRINT
ENQUIRE
ENQUIRY
ENSUING
ENSUITE
ENTWINE
EREMITE
ERODIUM
EROSION
EROTICA
ERUDITE
ESQUIRE
ETCHING
ETESIAN
ETONIAN
ETTRICK
EVASION
EVASIVE
EVENING
EXAMINE
EXITING
EYELIDS
EZEKIEL
FACTION
FADDISH
FADDIST
FAILING
FAIRING
FAIRISH
FALLING
FALSIES
FALSIFY
FANCIED
FANCIER
FANZINE
FARMING
FARRIER
FASCISM
FASCIST
FASHION
FASTING
FATUITY
FAUVISM
FAUVIST
FAWNING
FEBRILE
FEEDING
FEELING
FENCING
FERMIUM
FERTILE
FESTIVE
FICTION
FILLING
FILMING
FINDING
FINNISH
FISHING
FISSILE
FISSION
FITTING
FLAMING
FLEEING
FLEMING
FLEMISH
FLORIDA
FLORIST
FLOWING
FLUTIST
FLUVIAL
FOLDING
FOLLIES
FOOLISH
FOOTING
FOPPISH
FOREIGN
FORGIVE
FORMICA
FORMING
FORTIES
FORTIFY
FOSSICK
FRAGILE
FRISIAN
FULFILL
FUNDING
FUNNILY
FURBISH
FURNISH
FURRIER
FURTIVE
FUSSILY
FUSTIAN
GABRIEL
GALLING
GALLIUM
GAMBIAN
GARNISH
GARRICK
GASFIRE
GASPING
GATLING
GAUDILY
GAWKISH
GEARING
GELDING
GENTIAN
GENTILE
GENUINE
GERAINT
GETTING
GIDDILY
GILDING
GIMMICK
GIRLISH
GLACIAL
GLACIER
GLARING
GLAZIER
GLAZING
GLIDING
GLORIFY
GLOWING
GNAWING
GODLIKE
GOLDING
GOLFING
GOODIES
GOODISH
GOOLIES
GORDIAN
GORDIUS
GOSLING
GOSSIPY
GRACILE
GRANITA
GRANITE
GRATIFY
GRATING
GRAVITY
GRAYISH
GRAZING
GRECIAN
GREYISH
GROLIER
GROPIUS
GROTIUS
GROWING
GUBBINS
GUIDING
GUNFIRE
GUSHING
HACKING
HADRIAN
HAFNIUM
HAHNIUM
HAITIAN
HALTING
HANDILY
HANGING
HAPPILY
HARPIST
HARRIER
HARRIET
HARWICH
HASHISH
HASTILY
HAULIER
HAYWIRE
HEADING
HEALING
HEARING
HEATING
HEAVIER
HEAVILY
HEDGING
HELLION
HELLISH
HELPING
HEMLINE
HENGIST
HERBIST
HEROINE
HEROISM
HERRICK
HERRIES
HERRING
HESSIAN
HEURISM
HIGGINS
HILDING
HISSING
HITTITE
HOGGING
HOLDING
HOPKINS
HOPLITE
HOPPING
HORRIFY
HORSING
HOSPICE
HOSTILE
HOTLINE
HOUDINI
HOUSING
HOWLING
HULKING
HUMMING
HUNTING
HURLING
HURRIED
HUSKILY
HUSSITE
HYALINE
IAMBIST
IBERIAN
ICHNITE
IDOLIZE
IMAGINE
IMAGING
IMAGISM
IMAGIST
IMPLIED
IMPRINT
INANITY
INBUILT
INCLINE
INFLICT
INITIAL
INKLING
INQUIRE
INQUIRY
INSPIRE
INSTILL
INVEIGH
INVOICE
IRANIAN
IRIDISE
IRIDIUM
IRONING
ISCHIUM
ISMAILI
ITALIAN
ITCHING
ITEMIZE
IVORIAN
IVORIEN
JAMAICA
JAMMING
JAPLISH
JASMINE
JEERING
JELLIED
JENKINS
JERKILY
JESTING
JOBBING
JOGGING
JOINING
JOLLITY
JOYRIDE
JUDAISM
JUGGINS
JUMPING
JUSSIVE
JUSTICE
JUSTIFY
KADDISH
KAINITE
KATRINE
KEELING
KEEPING
KENNING
KENTISH
KERNITE
KHALIFA
KHEDIVE
KICKING
KILLICK
KILLING
KIPLING
KISSING
KLAVIER
KNOWING
KONTIKI
KOUMISS
KYANITE
LACKING
LAGGING
LAMAISM
LAMAIST
LAMBING
LANCING
LANDING
LAOTIAN
LAPPING
LAPWING
LASHING
LASTING
LATRINE
LATTICE
LATVIAN
LEADING
LEANING
LEAPING
LEASING
LEAVING
LEFTIST
LEGGING
LEMMING
LEMPIRA
LENDING
LENTIGO
LENTILS
LEONINE
LESBIAN
LESSING
LETTING
LEUCINE
LIBRIUM
LICKING
LIGNITE
LILTING
LINKING
LIONIZE
LIQUIDS
LISTING
LITHIUM
LODGING
LOFTILY
LOGGING
LONGING
LOOKING
LOOMING
LOOTING
LORDING
LOTHIAN
LOURING
LOUTISH
LUCKILY
LUDDITE
LUMPISH
LURKING
LUSTILY
MACHINE
MADEIRA
MAGNIFY
MAGUIRE
MAILING
MALAISE
MALLING
MANDIOC
MANKIND
MANNING
MANNISH
MANSION

MANSIZE
MAPPING
MARKING
MARLINE
MARMION
MARMITE
MARRIED
MARTIAL
MARTIAN
MARTINI
MARXISM
MARXIST
MASSINE
MASSIVE
MASTIFF
MATTING
MATTINS
MAWKISH
MEANING
MEETING
MELLITE
MELTING
MEMOIRS
MENDING
MENTION
MERCIES
MERRIER
MERRILY
MESSIAH
MESSIER
MESSILY
MESSINA
METHINK
MIDRIFF
MIDWIFE
MILKING
MILLING
MILLION
MINCING
MISFIRE
MISSILE
MISSING
MISSION
MISSIVE
MISTIME
MOABITE
MOANING
MOCKING
MOLDING
MOLLIFY
MONKISH
MOODILY
MOONING
MOORING
MOORISH
MOPPING
MORAINE
MOREISH
MORNING
MORTICE
MORTIFY
MORTISE
MUGGING
MULLION
MUMMIFY
MYELINE
MYSTIFY
NAGGING
NAPPING
NASTILY
NATRIUM
NEARING
NEBBISH
NECKING
NÉGLIGÉ
NEOLITH
NETTING
NEURINE
NIBLICK
NICOISE
NIOBIUM
NITRILE
NITRITE
NODDING
NOGGING
NOISILY
NORWICH
NOTHING
NOURISH
NUCLIDE
NULLIFY
NULLITY
NUNLIKE
NUPTIAL
NURSING
NUTLIKE
NUTTING
OARFISH
OBADIAH
OBELISK
OBESITY
OCARINA
OCULIST
ODALISK
OFFSIDE
OGREISH
OLEFINE
ONANISM
ONETIME
ONGOING
OPACITY
OPALINE
OPENING
OPINION
ORATION
ORIFICE
ORIGINS
ORPHISM
OSTRICH
OUSTITI
OUTLIER
OUTLINE
OUTLIVE
OUTSIDE
OUTSIZE
OVARIAN
OVATION
OVICIDE
OXIDIZE
OXONIAN
PACKING
PADDING
PAIRING
PALLIUM
PALMIST
PALSIED
PANNIER
PANTIES
PANTILE
PAPRIKA
PARKING
PARTIAL
PARTING
PARTITA
PASSING
PASSION
PASSIVE
PASTIES
PASTIME
PATRIAL
PATRICK
PATRIOT
PAUCITY
PAULINE
PECKING
PECKISH
PEELING
PEEPING
PEERING
PEEVISH
PELTING
PENDING
PENNINE
PENSILE
PENSION
PENSIVE
PEPSINE
PEREIRA
PERFIDY
PERLITE
PERMIAN
PERRIER
PERSIAN
PERSIST
PETRIFY
PHIDIAS
PHONICS
PHYSICS
PIANIST
PICKING
PIETIST
PIGLING
PILLION
PIMPING
PISCINA
PISCINE
PITHILY
PLACING
PLAYING
PLEBIAN
PLOSIVE
POLLING
PONTIAC
PONTIFF
PONTINE
POPPING
PORCIAN
PORCINE
PORTICO
PORTION
POSTING
POTTING
PRALINE
PRAYING
PRECISE
PREDIAL
PREDICT
PRELIMS
PREMIER
PREMISS
PREMIUM
PRESIDE
PREVIEW
PRIMING
PRIVITY
PROBITY
PRODIGY
PROFILE
PROFITS
PROMISE
PROVIDE
PROVING
PROVISO
PROXIMO
PRUDISH
PRURIGO
PUBLISH
PUCCINI
PUCKISH
PUDDING
PUERILE
PULSING
PUNTING
PURLIEU
PURLINE
PURVIEW
PUSHING
PUTTING
QUAKING
QUALIFY
QUALITY
QUININE
RACHIAL
RACKING
RAFFISH
RAFTING
RAGTIME
RAILING
RAISING
RALEIGH
RANKING
RANTING
RATLINE
RAWHIDE
READILY
READING
REALIGN
REALISM
REALIST
REALITY
REALIZE
REARING
REBUILD
RECEIPT
RECEIVE
RECLINE
RECTIFY
REDDISH
REEKING
REELING
REJOICE
REMAINS
REPAINT
REPAIRS
REPLICA
REPRINT
REPTILE
REQUIEM
REQUIRE
REQUITE
RESCIND
RESPIRE
RESPITE
RESTING
RESTIVE
RETAINS
RETHINK
RETRIAL
RETSINA
REUNION
REUNITE
REWRITE
RHENISH
RHODIAN
RHODIUM
RHYMING
RIBBING
RIGGING
RINGING
RIOTING
RIPPING
RISKILY
ROAMING
ROARING
ROCKING
ROGUISH
ROLLICK
ROLLING
ROMAINE
ROOFING
ROOKISH
ROOTING
ROSCIAN
ROSCIUS
ROSSINI
ROTTING
ROUSING
ROUTIER
ROUTINE
ROWDILY
RUBBING
RUBBISH
RUFFIAN
RUNNING
RUNNION
RUSHING
RUSSIAN
RUTTING
SABRINA
SACKING
SAILING
SALPINX
SALSIFY
SALTING
SALTIRE
SAMNITE
SAPLING
SARDINE
SASHIMI
SAUCILY
SAURIAN
SAWBILL
SAWFISH
SAWMILL
SCABIES
SCARIFY
SCARING
SCORING
SEABIRD
SEALINK
SEALION
SEARING
SEASICK
SEASIDE
SEATING
SECTION
SEEMING
SELFISH
SELKIRK
SELLING
SERBIAN
SERCIAL
SERRIED
SERVICE
SERVILE
SERVING
SESSILE
SESSION
SESTINA
SESTINE
SETTING
SHADING
SHAKILY
SHAKING
SHAPING
SHARIAH
SHARING
SHAVING
SHERIFF
SHINING
SHOWILY
SHOWING
SIBLING
SIFTING
SIGNIFY
SIGNING
SIKHISM
SINGING
SINKING
SIPPING
SISTINE
SITTING
SKATING
SKYHIGH
SKYLINE
SLAVISH
SLAYING
SLIDING
SLOPING
SLOWING
SMILING
SMOKING
SNORING
SOAKING
SOARING
SOCKING
SOLDIER
SOLOIST
SOPHISM
SOPHIST
SOPPING
SOPWITH
SORTING
SOUBISE
SPACING
SPANIEL
SPANISH
SPARING
SPATIAL
SPAVINE
SPECIAL
SPECIES
SPECIFY
SPIRITS
SPRAINT
STADIUM
STAGING

STAMINA
STARING
STATICS
STATION
STATIST
STAYING
STERILE
STEWING
STONILY
STORIED
STORIES
STRAITS
STUDIED
STYGIAN
STYLING
STYLISH
STYLIST
STYLITE
STYLIZE
SUAVITY
SUBLIME
SUBSIDE
SUBSIDY
SUBSIST
SUCTION
SUFFICE
SUICIDE
SULKILY
SUMMING
SUNDIAL
SUNNILY
SUNNITE
SUNRISE
SURDITY
SURFING
SURMISE
SURVIVE
SWAHILI
SWAYING
SWEDISH
TACHISM
TACTICS
TACTILE
TALKING
TAMPICO
TAMPION
TANGIER
TANNING
TANTIVY
TAPPICE
TAPPING
TARDILY
TARDIVE
TARNISH
TARSIER
TARTINE
TASSILI
TATTING
TAURINE
TBILISI
TEARING

TEASING
TEATIME
TEEMING
TEKTITE
TELLING
TENNIEL
TENSILE
TENSING
TENSION
TEQUILA
TERBIUM
TERMITE
TERRIER
TERRIFY
TERRINE
TERSION
TERTIAL
TERTIAN
TESTIFY
TESTILY
TESTING
TEXTILE
THOMISM
THOMIST
THORIUM
THULIUM
TICKING
TIGRISH
TIPPING
TIPSILY
TITOISM
TITOIST
TOLKIEN
TOMPION
TONNISH
TONTINE
TOOLING
TOPPING
TOPSIDE
TORPIDS
TORSION
TORTILE
TOURING
TOURISM
TOURIST
TOWLINE
TRACING
TRADING
TRINITY
TRITIUM
TRIVIAL
TRIVIUM
TROPICS
TROPISM
TRUCIAL
TSARINA
TSARIST
TUITION
TURBINE
TURKISH
TURNING

TWOTIME
TZARINA
UGOLINO
UKRAINE
ULEXITE
UMBRIAN
UNALIKE
UNALIVE
UNCTION
UNDOING
UNDYING
UNITIES
UNQUIET
UNSTICK
UNTRIED
UNTWINE
UPRAISE
UPSWING
URALITE
URANIAN
URANISM
URANITE
URANIUM
UROLITH
UTERINE
UTILITY
UTILIZE
UTOPIAN
UXORIAL
VACCINE
VACUITY
VAMPIRE
VARMINT
VARNISH
VARSITY
VARYING
VENDING
VERDICT
VERSIFY
VERSION
VERTIGO
VESTIGE
VETTING
VILNIUS
VITRIFY
VITRIOL
VULPINE
WADDING
WAFTING
WAGGISH
WAILING
WAITING
WALKING
WALLIES
WANTING
WAPPING
WARLIKE
WARLING
WARMING
WARNING
WARRING

WARRIOR
WARTIME
WARWICK
WASHING
WASPISH
WASTING
WAXBILL
WAXWING
WAYBILL
WAYSIDE
WEARILY
WEARING
WEAVING
WEBBING
WEDDING
WEEPING
WELDING
WELLIES
WETTING
WHALING
WHITING
WHITISH
WICKIUP
WIGGING
WILLIAM
WILLIES
WILLING
WIMPISH
WINDING
WINNING
WISHING
WOLFISH
WORDILY
WORDING
WORKING
WORRIED
WORRIER
WRITING
WRYBILL
WYOMING
YAWNING
YIDDISH
YORKIST
YTTRIUM
ZAMBIAN
ZEOLITE
ZEPHIEL
ZILLION
ZIONIST
ZOOLITE
ABIDJAN
BRINJAL
KARAJAN
KILLJOY
LOCKJAW
MUDEJAR
MUNTJAC
ABOUKIR
ALASKAN
BANGKOK
BETOKEN

BLACKEN
BLANKET
BLANKLY
BLEAKLY
BLINKER
BLOCKED
BLOCKER
BRACKEN
BRACKET
BREAKER
BRICKIE
BRISKET
BRISKLY
BUMPKIN
CHALKER
CHECKED
CHECKIN
CHECKUP
CHICKEN
CHOOKIE
CHUCKLE
CHUKKER
CLICKER
CLINKER
CONAKRY
CRACKED
CRACKER
CRACKLE
CRACKLY
CRICKET
CRICKEY
CRINKLE
CRINKLY
CROAKER
CROCKET
CROOKED
DOESKIN
DOORKEY
DRINKER
DRUNKEN
ERISKAY
FLANKER
FLECKED
FLECKER
FLICKER
FLUNKEY
FRANKLY
FRECKLE
GHERKIN
GRACKLE
GROCKLE
HEARKEN
KARAKUL
KLINKER
KNACKER
KNICKER
KNOCKER
KNUCKLE
LUMPKIN
MANIKIN
MEERKAT

NABOKOV
OILSKIN
PIGSKIN
PRICKED
PRICKER
PRICKLE
PRICKLY
PUMPKIN
PUSHKIN
QUICKEN
QUICKER
QUICKIE
QUICKLY
RAMEKIN
REDSKIN
SHACKLE
SHICKSA
SHIRKER
SHOCKED
SHOCKER
SIMPKIN
SLACKEN
SLACKER
SLACKLY
SLEEKLY
SLICKER
SMACKER
SMICKLY
SNEAKER
SNICKER
SNOOKER
SNORKEL
SPANKER
SPARKLE
SPEAKER
SPECKLE
STALKED
STALKER
STARKLY
STICKER
STICKLE
STINKER
STONKER
STRIKER
THICKEN
THICKET
THICKLY
THINKER
TRACKER
TREKKER
TRICKLE
TRINKET
TRUCKER
TRUCKLE
TURNKEY
TWINKLE
UNASKED
WHACKED
WHACKER
WHISKER
WHISKEY

WRECKED
WRECKER
WRINKLE
WRINKLY
ABOULIA
ABSOLVE
ACRYLIC
AIRFLOW
ALCALDE
ALFALFA
AMPULLA
ANGELIC
ANGELUS
ANGOLAN
ANGULAR
ANNELID
ANNULAR
ANNULET
ANNULUS
APHELIA
AQUILON
ASTILBE
AURALLY
AURELIA
AWFULLY
BABBLER
BABYLON
BACILLI
BACKLOG
BAFFLED
BEATLES
BIBELOT
BIVALVE
BOBSLED
BOOKLET
BOOTLEG
BOTTLED
BOTTLES
BOUCLÉE
BOUILLI
BOWDLER
BRAILLE
BRAWLER
BRIDLER
BRIDLES
BROILER
BUBBLES
BUCKLER
BUCOLIC
BUNGLER
BURGLAR
BUSTLER
BUSTLES
CAMELOT
CAMILLA
CANELLA
CAPELLA
CAROLUS
CASTLED
CATALAN
CATALOG

CATALPA
CATELOG
CAVALRY
CECILIA
CEDILLA
CHABLIS
CHAPLET
CHARLES
CHARLEY
CHILLER
CHILLON
CIRCLET
CIRCLIP
CIVILLY
COBBLED
COBBLER
COCHLEA
COCKLES
COMPLEX
COPILOT
CORELLI
COROLLA
COUPLER
COUPLET
COWSLIP
CRAWLER
CRUELLS
CRUELLY
CRUELTY
CUMULUS
CURDLED
DABBLER
DAIMLER
DALILAH
DAPPLED
DAWDLER
DAZZLED
DEFILED
DELILAH
DEVALUE
DEVELOP
DEVILRY
DEVOLVE
DIBBLER
DIMPLED
DIPOLAR
DISPLAY
DIVULGE
DOODLER
DOPPLER
DOUBLES
DOUBLET
DOUGLAS
DRIBLET
DROPLET
DRUMLIN
DWELLER
ECBOLIC
ECHELON
EMBOLUS
ENVELOP
EPAULET
EPSILON
EQUALLY
ESCALOP
ETAPLES
EULALIE
FACULTY
FANGLED
FATALLY
FAVELLA
FENELON
FIDDLER
FIDELIO
FINALLY
FLATLET
FORELEG
FRAILTY
FRILLED
FUDDLED
FUSILLI
GABBLER
GABELLE
GALILEE
GALILEO
GAMBLER
GAMELAN
GANELON
GARBLED
GAZELLE
GEFILTE
GIMBLET
GISELLE
GNARLED
GOBBLER
GOBELIN
GOGGLES
GORILLA
GREMLIN
GREYLAG
GRILLED
GROWLER
GUNPLAY
GUZZLER
GYMSLIP
HACKLES
HANDLED
HANDLER
HARELIP
HECKLER
HIDALGO
HINDLEG
HOODLUM
HUMBLES
HURDLER
HUSTLER
ICEFLOE
IDEALLY
IDYLLIC
IMPULSE
INDULGE
INHALER
INSULAR
INSULIN
INVALID
INVOLVE
JAVELIN
JAVELLE
JEWELER
JEWELRY
JOCULAR
JUBILEE
JUGGLER
JUGULAR
JUMBLED
JUMBLES
KINGLET
KNEELER
KNELLER
KREMLIN
KUBELIK
LAMELLA
LANGLEY
LANOLIN
LAVOLTA
LEAFLET
LEGALLY
LOBELIA
LOCALLY
LORELEI
LOYALLY
LOYALTY
MAMILLA
MANILLA
MARBLED
MARBLES
MARTLET
MATELOT
MATILDA
MAUDLIN
MAXILLA
MEASLES
MEDDLER
MEDULLA
MESCLUN
METALLY
METTLED
MIMULUS
MISPLAY
MODULAR
MODULUS
MOELLON
MONILIA
MONOLOG
MOONLIT
MORALLY
MORELLO
MOSELLE
MOTTLED
MOUFLON
MOUILLÉ
MUDDLED
MUDFLAP
MUFFLED
MUFFLER
MURILLO
MYCELLA
NACELLE
NASALLY
NEBULAR
NECKLET
NEEDLES
NEVILLE
NIGELLA
NOBBLED
NOBBLER
NODULAR
NONPLUS
NOODLES
NOVELLA
NOVELLO
NOVELTY
NUMBLES
OCELLAR
OCELLUS
ORACLES
ORTOLAN
OSCULUM
OSSELET
OTHELLO
OUTFLOW
OVERLAP
OVERLAY
OVERLIE
PABULUM
PADDLER
PAISLEY
PAPILLA
PARSLEY
PATELLA
PEARLIE
PEBBLES
PEDDLER
PENALTY
PERPLEX
PHALLIC
PHALLUS
PICKLED
PICKLER
PIKELET
PLAYLET
POPULAR
POPULUS
PROBLEM
PROWLER
PTYALIN
PUCELLE
PUZZLED
PUZZLER
RADDLED
RAFFLES
RAMBLER
RAMULUS
RATTLER
REGALIA
REGALLY
REGULAR
REMBLAI
REPULSE
RESOLVE
RESULTS
REVALUE
REVELER
REVELRY
REVOLVE
RIDDLED
RIDDLER
RINGLET
RIVALRY
RIVULET
ROSALIA
ROSALIE
ROSELLA
ROSELLE
ROYALLY
ROYALTY
RUBELLA
RUDOLPH
RUFFLED
RUFFLER
RUMBLER
RUMPLED
RUSALKA
RUSTLER
SADDLER
SAMPLER
SAVELOY
SCAGLIA
SCALLOP
SCARLET
SCHOLAR
SCOLLOP
SCULLER
SECULAR
SETTLED
SETTLER
SEVILLE
SHALLOT
SHALLOW
SHELLAC
SHELLED
SHELLEY
SHIRLEY
SHRILLY
SIMILAR
SIMPLER
SIMPLEX
SIMPLON
SINGLES
SINGLET
SIZZLER
SKILLED
SKILLET
SKYBLUE
SMALLER
SNARLER
SNARLUP
SOMALIA
SOZZLED
SPELLER
SPOILED
SPOILER
SQUALID
SQUALLY
SQUALOR
SQUELCH
STABLES
STANLEY
STAPLER
STARLET
STARLIT
STEALTH
STELLAR
STOLLEN
SURPLUS
SWALLOW
SWOLLEN
TABULAR
TACKLER
TAGALOG
TANGLED
TATTLER
TEMPLAR
TEMPLET
THALLUS
TICKLER
TIDDLER
TIMELAG
TINGLER
TIPPLER
TITULAR
TODDLER
TOTALLY
TRAILER
TRAWLER
TRELLIS
TRIFLER
TRIFLES
TRILLED
TRILLER
TRIPLET
TRIPLEX
TROILUS
TROLLEY
TROLLOP
TUBULAR
TUBULIN
TUMBLER
TUMULUS
TUTELAR
UCCELLO
UPSILON
USUALLY
UTRILLO
VANILLA
VERULAM
VIRELAY
VITALLY
VIVALDI
VOCALIC
VOCALLY
WAGGLER
WANGLER
WARBLER
WATTLES
WHEELED
WHEELER
WHEELIE
WHITLOW
WICKLOW
WOOLLEN
YPSILON
ABDOMEN
ABYSMAL
ALARMED
ALBUMEN
ALBUMIN
ANAEMIA
ANAEMIC
ANDAMAN
ANOSMIA
ARTEMIS
ARTEMUS
ASHAMED
ASSUMED
ATTEMPT
AUTOMAT
BAHAMAS
BATHMAT
BATSMAN
BEERMAT
BELLMAN
BETIMES
BILLMAN
BIRDMAN
BITUMEN
BLOOMER
BOATMAN
BOHEMIA
BONDMAN
BOOKMAN
BRADMAN
BRAEMAR
BRAHMIN
BULIMIA
BUSHMAN
BUSHMEN
CAEDMON
CALAMUS
CALOMEL
CALUMET
CALUMNY
CARAMBA
CARAMEL
CAVEMAN
CERAMIC
CHAPMAN

CHARMED
CHARMER
CHLAMYS
CINEMAS
CLUBMAN
COLOMBO
COLUMNS
CRAMMED
CRAMMER
CRANMER
CREWMAN
DECIMAL
DELIMIT
DIDYMUS
DILEMMA
DOORMAN
DOORMAT
DREAMER
DRUMMER
DURAMEN
DUSTMAN
DYNAMIC
ENDEMIC
ERASMUS
FIREMAN
FLUMMOX
FOOTMAN
FORAMEN
FOREMAN
FREEMAN
FROGMAN
GALUMPH
GLIMMER
GOODMAN
GOURMET
GRAMMAR
GROMMET
GRUMMET
HANGMAN
HANGMEN
HEADMAN
HIGHMAN
HILLMAN
HILLMEN
INCOMER
INHUMAN
ISLAMIC
ISTHMUS
JAZZMAN
JURYMAN
KASHMIR
KINSMAN
LATIMER
LINEMAN
LINKMAN
MAILMAN
MANUMIT
MANXMAN
MAREMMA
MAXIMUM
MIASMIC
MILKMAN
MINIMAL
MINIMAX
MINIMUM
MYANMAR
NEWSMAN
OARSMAN
OARSMEN
OPTIMAL
OPTIMUM
OTTOMAN
PACKMAN
PAJAMAS
PALOMAR
PLASMIN
PLOWMAN
PLUMMET
POLEMIC
POLYMER
POSTMAN
POTOMAC
PREEMPT
PULLMAN
PYAEMIA
PYJAMAS
PYRAMID
RACEMIC
RACHMAN
REAUMUR
REGIMEN
ROLLMOP
SALAMIS
SANDMAN
SCHEMER
SCRUMMY
SCRUMPY
SEISMIC
SHERMAN
SHIMMER
SHOWMAN
SHRIMPS
SKIMMED
SKIMMER
SKIMMIA
SLAMMER
SLIMMER
SNOWMAN
SOLOMON
STAMMER
STEAMED
STEAMER
STEMMED
STURMER
SWAGMAN
SWIMMER
THERMAL
THERMIC
THERMOS
TOLLMAN
TOTEMIC
TOXEMIA
TRAMMEL
TRIMMER
TRIUMPH
UNARMED
UNKEMPT
UNNAMED
UNTAMED
URAEMIA
VIDIMUS
VITAMIN
WALKMAN
WOODMAN
WORKMAN
WORKMEN
YASHMAK
AARONIC
ABSENCE
ABSINTH
ACRONYM
ACTINAL
ACTINIA
ACTINIC
ADJUNCT
ADORNED
ADRENAL
ADVANCE
AGAINST
AIDANCE
ALBANIA
ALBENIZ
ALFONSO
ALIGNED
ALKANET
ALLENBY
ALLONGE
ALMANAC
ALMONER
ALUMNAE
ALUMNUS
AMMONAL
AMMONIA
ANDANTE
ANTENNA
ANTONIO
ANTONYM
APHONIA
APHONIC
AQUINAS
AQUINUS
ARRANGE
ARSENAL
ARSENIC
ASHANTI
ASKANCE
AVIGNON
BALANCE
BALONEY
BANANAS
BARENTS
BARONET
BASINET
BAYONET
BEATNIK
BEGONIA
BELINDA
BOLONEY
BONANZA
BOTANIC
BRENNER
BROWNED
BROWNIE
BUBONIC
BURUNDI
BYRONIC
CABINET
CADENCE
CADENZA
CALENDS
CANONRY
CAYENNE
CÉZANNE
CHAINED
CHANNEL
CHARNEL
CHIANTI
CHIGNON
CHIMNEY
CHRONIC
CHUTNEY
CLEANER
CLEANLY
CLEANSE
CLEANUP
COCKNEY
COCONUT
COGENCY
COLONEL
CORANTO
CORINTH
CORONER
CORONET
CORUNNA
CROONER
DAPHNID
DAPHNIS
DECANAL
DECENCY
DEFENCE
DEFENSE
DEFINED
DEFUNCT
DEMONIC
DERANGE
DERONDA
DETENTE
DIGONAL
DIURNAL
DIVINER
DOMINGO
DOMINIC
DRAGNET
DRAINED
DVORNIK
ECHINUS
EFFENDI
ELEANOR
EMPANEL
ENGINED
ENHANCE
ENTENTE
ENVENOM
EQUINOX
ESSENCE
ESSENES
ETERNAL
ETHANOL
EUGENIA
EUGENIC
EUGENIE
EXPANSE
EXPENSE
EXPUNGE
EXTINCT
FAIENCE
FASTNET
FEIGNED
FILINGS
FINANCE
FISHNET
FIXINGS
FLANNEL
FLAUNCH
FLOUNCE
FLUENCY
FRIENDS
GARONNE
GEHENNA
GIRONDE
GLEANER
GODUNOV
GRAINED
GRAINER
GRANNIE
GRAPNEL
GREENER
GROINED
GROUNDS
GROWNUP
GUIGNOL
HACKNEY
HAIRNET
HOMINID
HOMONYM
HOSANNA
HUMANLY
IMMENSE
IMPINGE
INCENSE
INCONNU
INFANCY
INGENUE
INNINGS
INTENSE
ISLANDS
JEEPNEY
JEJUNUM
JOHNNIE
JOURNAL
JOURNEY
JUVENAL
KALENDS
KIWANIS
KLEENEX
LACONIC
LACUNAE
LAGONDA
LAYINGS
LEARNED
LEARNER
LEBANON
LEPANTO
LICENCE
LICENSE
LIKENED
LIMINAL
LININGS
LOCKNUT
LOZENGE
LYCHNIS
MADONNA
MAGENTA
MAGINOT
MAHONIA
MAKINGS
MARANTA
MARENGO
MARINER
MASONIC
MASONRY
MATINEE
MECONIC
MELANIN
MEMENTO
METONIC
METONYM
MIRANDA
MOMENTS
MORONIC
MOURNER
MYCENAE
MYRINGA
NOMINAL
NOMINEE
OCEANIA
OCEANIC
OCEANID
OFFENCE
OFFENSE
ORDINAL
ORGANIC
ORGANUM
ORGANZA
ORLANDO
OSMANLI
OTRANTO
PALINGS
PARENTS
PARINGS
PARSNIP
PARTNER
PENANCE
PETUNIA
PFENNIG
PHOENIX
PHRENIC
PIMENTO
PIRANHA
PLAINLY
PLANNED
PLANNER
PLIANCY
POLENTA
POLONIE
POTENCY
QUEENLY
RAVINGS
REFINED
REFINER
REGENCY
RETINUE
REVENGE
REVENUE
RIDINGS
ROBINIA
ROMANCE
ROMANIA
ROMANOV
ROMANZA
ROTUNDA
SAPONIN
SATANIC
SAVANNA
SAVINGS
SCANNER
SCIENCE
SCRUNCH
SECONAL
SECONDS
SEMINAL
SEMINAR
SERINGA
SEVENTH
SEVENTY
SHANNON
SILENCE
SIMENON
SKINNED
SKINNER
SOLANUM
SPANNER
SPHENIC
SPINNER
SPINNEY
SPOONER
SPRINGE

SPRINGS
SPRINGY
SPUTNIK
SQUINCH
STAINED
STAINER
STANNIC
STAUNCH
STEPNEY
STERNAL
STERNLY
STERNUM
STRANGE
STRINGS
STRINGY
STUNNER
SURINAM
SUSANNA
SYNONYM
SYRINGA
SYRINGE
TABANID
TAKINGS
TARANTO
TENANCY
TENANTS
TERENCE
TETANUS
THINNER
THRENOS
TIDINGS
TITANIA
TITANIC
TOPKNOT
TORONTO
TRAINED
TRAINEE
TRAINER
TRIANON
TROUNCE
TRUANCY
TURENNE
TYRANNY
UNCANNY
UNCINUS
UNHINGE
UNLINED
UNOWNED
URGENCY
VACANCY
VAGINAL
VALENCE
VALENCY
VEDANTA
VERONAL
VICINAL
VIETNAM
VIKINGS
VINTNER
VOLANTE
WAGONER
WHATNOT
WIZENED
WOMANLY
XIMENES
YAOUNDE
ZIZANIA
ABALONE
ABSCOND
ACETONE
ACIFORM
ADENOID
ADENOMA
ADIPOSE
AFFRONT
AGELONG
AIRLOCK
AIRPORT
ALAMODE
ALECOST
ALIMONY
ALVEOLE
AMATORY
AMBROSE
AMOROSO
AMOROUS
AMPHORA
AMYLOID
ANALOGY
ANATOLE
ANATOMY
ANCHOVY
ANDROID
ANEMONE
ANEROID
ANGIOMA
ANTHONY
ANTIOCH
ANXIOUS
ANYBODY
ANYMORE
APOCOPE
APOLOGY
APPROVE
AQUEOUS
ARDUOUS
ARIZONA
ARMHOLE
ARTWORK
ASHDOWN
AUREOLA
AUREOLE
AWESOME
AXOLOTL
AZYGOUS
BABOOSH
BALCONY
BALFOUR
BALLOON
BANNOCK
BASSOON
BAZOOKA
BEDFORD
BEDPOST
BEDROCK
BEDROOM
BEDSORE
BEHOOVE
BELLOWS
BENZOIN
BESPOKE
BETROTH
BIGFOOT
BIGHORN
BILIOUS
BILLOWS
BILTONG
BIOLOGY
BISTORT
BLOWOUT
BOUDOIR
BOXROOM
BOYCOTT
BOYHOOD
BRITONS
BUFFOON
BUGLOSS
BULBOUS
BULLOCK
BUMBOAT
BUNDOOK
BURDOCK
BURNOUS
BURNOUT
BUTTONS
CABOOSE
CAHOOTS
CALLOUS
CANDOUR
CANNOCK
CARDOON
CARGOES
CARIOCA
CARIOLE
CARPORT
CARROLL
CARROTS
CARROTY
CARTOON
CASSOCK
CASTOFF
CATHODE
CESTODE
CESTOID
CHALONE
CHAMOIS
CHAYOTE
CHEROOT
CHICORY
CHINOOK
CHOROID
CIRROSE
CISSOID
CITROEN
CLAMOUR
COLLOID
COMFORT
COMMODE
COMMODO
COMMONS
COMPORT
COMPOSE
COMPOST
COMPOTE
CONCOCT
CONCORD
CONDOLE
CONDONE
CONFORM
CONJOIN
CONNOTE
CONSOLE
CONSOLS
CONSORT
CONTORT
CONTOUR
CONVOKE
COPIOUS
CORDOBA
CORRODE
COTTONY
COULOMB
COUPONS
COWPOKE
COXCOMB
CRICOID
CRINOID
CUCKOLD
CURIOUS
CURSORY
CUSTODY
CUSTOMS
CUTWORM
CYCLONE
CYCLOPS
CYSTOID
DAGWOOD
DAYBOOK
DEFROCK
DEFROST
DELTOID
DEPLORE
DESMOND
DESPOIL
DESPOND
DEVIOUS
DIABOLO
DIAMOND
DINMONT
DIPLOCK
DIPLOMA
DISCORD
DISJOIN
DISPORT
DISPOSE
DISROBE
DISTORT
DOCTORS
DOGFOOD
DOGGONE
DOGROSE
DOGWOOD
DRAGOON
DROPOUT
DUBIOUS
DUNNOCK
DUOPOLY
EARLOBE
ECOLOGY
ECONOMY
ELUSORY
EMBROIL
EMPLOYS
ENAMOUR
ENCLOSE
ENFEOFF
ENGROSS
ENVIOUS
EPIDOTE
EPIGONE
EPISODE
EPITOME
EPIZOON
ETHMOID
EUPHONY
EXPLODE
EXPLOIT
EXPLORE
EYESORE
FACTORS
FACTORY
FAGGOTS
FALLOUT
FATUOUS
FELLOWS
FERROUS
FERVOUR
FESTOON
FETLOCK
FIBROID
FIBROMA
FIBROUS
FIRCONE
FLAVOUR
FOGHORN
FORGONE
FORLORN
FORMOSA
FOXHOLE
FULSOME
FUNGOID
FUNGOUS
FURIOUS
FURLONG
FUTTOCK
GADROON
GALLONS
GALLOWS
GAMBOGE
GARBOIL
GASCONY
GASEOUS
GEELONG
GEOLOGY
GIBBONS
GIBBOUS
GLAMOUR
GLENOID
GLUCOSE
GOLDONI
GONDOLA
GRANOLA
GREGORY
GRIMOND
GUMBOIL
GUMBOOT
GUNBOAT
GUNROOM
GUYROPE
HADDOCK
HAGBOLT
HAMMOCK
HANDOUT
HANGOUT
HARBOUR
HARMONY
HARPOON
HARWOOD
HASSOCK
HATTOCK
HEINOUS
HEMLOCK
HICKORY
HIDEOUS
HIDEOUT
HILLOCK
HISTOID
HISTORY
HOBSONS
HOEDOWN
HORMONE
HORRORS
HOTFOOT
HUMMOCK
HYALOID
IGNEOUS
IMPIOUS
IMPLODE
IMPLORE
IMPROVE
INDOORS
INSHORE
INTROIT
INVIOUS
IPOMOEA
IRKSOME
ISADORA
ISODORE
ISOTONE
ISOTOPE
JAWBONE
JEALOUS
KAMPONG
KARAOKE
KEYHOLE
KEYNOTE
KEYWORD
KICKOFF
KOWLOON
LACTOSE
LAMPOON
LAOCOON
LARDOON
LEACOCK
LEASOWE
LEGIONS
LEGROOM
LEGWORK
LEOPOLD
LEPROSY
LEPROUS
LETDOWN
LEUCOMA
LIEDOWN
LIFTOFF
LIMPOPO
LINCOLN
LISSOME
LOCKOUT
LOGBOOK
LOGWOOD
LOOKOUT
LOWDOWN
LUGHOLE
LUGWORM
MAFIOSO
MAGGOTY
MAHJONG
MAMMOTH
MANGOLD
MANHOLE
MANHOOD
MARCONI
MARLOWE
MASTOID
MATTOCK
MAYPOLE
MEACOCK
MELROSE
MENFOLK
MICROBE
MILFOIL
MISTOOK
MOIDORE
MONSOON
MUGWORT
MUSCOID

MUSCOVY
MYELOID
MYELOMA
NACROUS
NAIROBI
NARROWS
NATIONS
NECROSE
NEGROID
NERVOSA
NERVOUS
NETWORK
NEURONE
NEWBOLT
NEWBORN
NEWCOME
NITRODE
NITROUS
NOISOME
NOOLOGY
NORFOLK
NOTIONS
NOXIOUS
OARLOCK
OBVIOUS
ODOROUS
OFFLOAD
OLOROSO
OMINOUS
ONEROUS
ONSHORE
ORATORY
ORINOCO
OSSEOUS
OSTEOMA
OSTIOLE
OUTCOME
OUTDOOR
OUTLOOK
OUTPOST
OUTPOUR
OUTVOTE
OUTWORK
OUTWORN
PADDOCK
PADLOCK
PADRONE
PALOOKA
PANDORA
PANNOSE
PAPOOSE
PARBOIL
PARLOUR
PARLOUS
PAVIOUR
PAVLOVA
PAYLOAD
PAYROLL
PEACOCK
PENTODE
PENTOSE
PERFORM
PERGOLA
PERSONA
PERSONS
PETIOLE
PETROUS
PIANOLA
PIBROCH
PICCOLO
PIGEONS
PILLORY
PINFOLD
PINHOLE
PISTOLE
PITEOUS
PLATOON
PLAYOFF
PLEROMA
PLYWOOD
POCHOIR
POMPOON
POMPOUS
PONTOON
POPCORN
POTHOLE
PREDOOM
PROLONG
PROMOTE
PRONOUN
PROPOSE
PROSODY
PROVOKE
PROVOST
PURLOIN
PURPORT
PURPOSE
PUTTOCK
QUINONE
QUIXOTE
RACCOON
RAGWORT
RANCOUR
RANGOON
RAPPORT
RATIONS
RAUCOUS
RAVIOLI
RECTORY
REDCOAT
REDPOLL
REDWOOD
REFLOAT
REGROUP
REPROOF
REPROVE
RESPOND
RESTOCK
RESTORE
RHIZOID
RHIZOME
RIOTOUS
RIPCORD
RISSOLE
ROSEOLA
ROSTOCK
ROWBOAT
ROWLOCK
RUBEOLA
RUINOUS
RUMPOLE
RUNCORN
RUNDOWN
SABAOTH
SAILORS
SAMOOSA
SANDOWN
SAPROBE
SAPWOOD
SARCOMA
SARCOUS
SASSOON
SAUROID
SAVIOUR
SAXHORN
SCHLOCK
SCHLOSS
SCROOGE
SEAFOOD
SEAPORT
SELLOFF
SELLOUT
SENDOFF
SENSORY
SEQUOIA
SERIOUS
SEYMOUR
SHADOOF
SHADOWY
SHMOOZE
SHOWOFF
SHYLOCK
SIDDONS
SIGNORA
SIGNORI
SINUOUS
SIRLOIN
SITDOWN
SOMEONE
SORROWS
SPINOFF
SPINOZA
SPYHOLE
STEROID
SUBJOIN
SUBSOIL
SUCCOUR
SUCROSE
SUFFOLK
SUMMONS
SUNDOWN
SUNROOF
SUPPORT
SUPPOSE
SURCOAT
SYNCOPE
SYSTOLE
TABLOID
TADPOLE
TAILORS
TAKEOFF
TAKEOUT
TALOOKA
TAMBOUR
TAPIOCA
TAPROOT
TEAROOM
TEDIOUS
TELFORD
TENFOLD
TENUOUS
THYROID
TIEPOLO
TINFOIL
TOEHOLD
TOMBOLA
TOMFOOL
TOPCOAT
TOPMOST
TOPSOIL
TREFOIL
TREMOLO
TRILOGY
TRIPODY
TRIPOLI
TRITOMA
TUGBOAT
TURMOIL
TURNOUT
TUSSOCK
TUSSORE
TWOFOLD
TWOSOME
TYPHOID
TYPHOON
UNBLOCK
UNFROCK
UNICORN
UNIFORM
UNKNOWN
UNLOOSE
UNQUOTE
UNSTOCK
UPSHOOT
VACUOLE
VACUOUS
VAMOOSE
VARIOLA
VARIOUS
VAUDOIS
VENDOME
VENTOSE
VERBOSE
VERMONT
VICIOUS
VICTORY
VISCOSE
VISCOUS
VOIVODE
WALKOUT
WALLOON
WALPOLE
WARDOUR
WARLOCK
WARLORD
WASHOUT
WAXWORK
WEAPONS
WEDLOCK
WELCOME
WELLOFF
WENLOCK
WILLOWY
WINDOWS
WINNOCK
WINSOME
WIPEOUT
WITHOUT
WITLOOF
WORKOUT
WRYNOSE
YELLOWS
ZEALOUS
ZOOLOGY
ZOOTOMY
ADELPHI
AGRAPHA
AGRIPPA
APROPOS
ATROPHY
AUTOPSY
BLEEPER
BLOOPER
BULLPEN
CALEPIN
CALYPSO
CATSPAW
CESSPIT
CHAPPED
CHARPOY
CHEAPEN
CHEAPLY
CHIPPED
CHIPPER
CHIPPIE
CHOPPER
CLAMPER
CLAPPER
CLIPPED
CLIPPER
CLIPPIE
COCKPIT
CRAMPED
CRAMPON
CREEPER
CRIPPLE
CRISPIN
CROPPED
CROPPER
CRUMPET
CRUMPLE
CRUPPER
DASHPOT
DEADPAN
DNIEPER
DROPPER
DUSTPAN
ECLIPSE
ECTOPIA
ELLIPSE
ESCAPEE
EUPEPSY
EXAMPLE
EXEMPLA
FELSPAR
FLAPPED
FLAPPER
FLEAPIT
FLIPPER
FOOTPAD
FOREPAW
FRUMPLE
GALIPOT
GALOPIN
GLIMPSE
GRAMPUS
GRAPPLE
GROUPER
GROUPIE
HAIRPIN
HARDPAN
HELIPAD
HEXAPOD
HOTSPUR
INDEPTH
INSIPID
JACKPOT
JUNIPER
KINGPIN
KNAPPER
MAZEPPA
MONOPLY
NINEPIN
NOTEPAD
OCCIPUT
OCTOPOD
OCTOPUS
OCTUPLE
OEDIPUS
OLYMPIA
OLYMPIC
OLYMPUS
OUTSPAN
OVERPAY
PANOPLY
PARAPET
PERSPEX
PLAYPEN
PLUMPER
POLYPOD
POLYPUS
PRIAPUS
PROSPER
RELAPSE
SALTPAN
SANDPIT
SCALPEL
SCALPER
SCAMPER
SCARPER
SCORPIO
SCRAPER
SCRAPIE
SCRAPPY
SCRUPLE
SCUPPER
SERAPIS
SHAMPOO
SHARPEN
SHARPER
SHARPLY
SHEPPEY
SHINPAD
SHIPPER
SHOPPER
SKIDPAN
SKIPPED
SKIPPER
SLAPPER
SLEEPER
SLIPPED
SLIPPER
SNAPPER
SNIPPET
SNOOPER
STAMPED
STAMPER
STEEPEN
STEEPLE
STEEPLY
STIPPLE
STIRPES
STOPPED
STOPPER
STRIPED
STRIPER
STRIPES
STROPHE
STROPPY
STUMPED
SUNSPOT
SWAPPED
SWEEPER
SYNAPSE
TALIPES
TALIPOT
THUMPER

TILAPIA
TOSSPOT
TRAIPSE
TRAMPLE
TRAPPED
TRAPPER
TRIPPER
TROOPER
TROUPER
TRUMPET
UNHAPPY
USURPER
VOLAPUK
WHIMPER
WHIPPED
WHIPPET
WHISPER
WHOOPEE
WHOOPER
WHOPPER
WRAPPED
WRAPPER
XENOPUS
ANTIQUE
BAROQUE
BEZIQUE
BRUSQUE
CACIQUE
LALIQUE
MACAQUE
OBLIQUE
OBLOQUY
OBSEQUY
SALIQUE
SUBAQUA
ACCURSE
ACHERON
ADMIRAL
ADMIRED
ADMIRER
ADVERSE
AILERON
AINTREE
AIRCREW
ALBERGO
ALBERTA
ALBERTI
ALCORAN
ALGERIA
ALKORAN
ALLERGY
ALTERED
AMHARIC
ANAGRAM
ANDIRON
ANDORRA
ANTARES
ANTHRAX
APPARAT
APPAREL
APTERAL
APTERYX
ARMORED
ARMORIC
ASCARID
ASHTRAY
ASPERGE
ASPIRIN
ASSURED
ASSYRIA
ASTARTE
ATHIRST
ATTIRED
AUBERGE
AUSTRAL
AUSTRIA
AUTARKY
BACARDI
BALDRIC
BEGORRA
BELARUS
BENARES
BERTRAM
BESHREW
BESTREW
BEVERLY
BIAFRAN
BIZARRE
BLURRED
BOTARGO
BUCKRAM
CABARET
CALDRON
CALORIC
CALORIE
CALTROP
CAMBRAI
CAMBRIC
CAMERON
CAMORRA
CANTRIP
CAPORAL
CATARRH
CATERER
CENTRAL
CENTRED
CENTRUM
CHAGRIN
CHARRED
CHEERIO
CHEVRON
CHIRRUP
CHLORAL
CINEREA
CLEARLY
CLEARUP
COLORED
COMFREY
CONTROL
COTERIE
COVERED
COVERUP
CULPRIT
CUMBRIA
DEBORAH
DECORUM
DEMERGE
DEMERIT
DENDRON
DESERTS
DESERVE
DESTROY
DEWDROP
DEXTRIN
DIAGRAM
DIDEROT
DIEDRAL
DISPRIN
DIVERGE
DIVERSE
DIVORCE
DOLORES
EAGERLY
EARDRUM
EFFORCE
ELDERLY
EMBARGO
EMPEROR
EMPIRIC
ENDORSE
ENDURED
ENFORCE
ENGORGE
ENLARGE
ENTERIC
ENTERON
ENTHRAL
EPIGRAM
EQUERRY
ERITREA
ESPARTO
ETRURIA
EUTERPE
EXCERPT
EXPIRED
EYEBROW
FAVORED
FEDERAL
FEMORAL
FEVERED
FIGURES
FILARIA
FIMBRIA
FLEURET
FLEURON
FORTRAN
FOXTROT
FULCRUM
FUNERAL
FUTURES
GASTRIC
GASTRIN
GENERAL
GENERIC
GILLRAY
GOMORRA
GROGRAM
GUMDROP
HAPORTH
HEPARIN
HEXARCH
HOGARTH
HOMERIC
HUMDRUM
HUMERUS
HUNDRED
ICTERIC
ICTERUS
IGNORED
ILLBRED
IMMERGE
IMMERSE
IMMORAL
IMPERIL
INBURST
INFARCT
INFERNO
INHERIT
INJURED
INNARDS
INNERVE
INSURER
INTERIM
INTERNE
INVERSE
INWARDS
ISOGRAM
JAKARTA
JOGTROT
KAMERAD
KATORGA
KESTREL
KINDRED
LABORED
LABORER
LACERTA
LAMPREY
LATERAL
LATERAN
LAYERED
LEVERET
LIBERAL
LIBERIA
LIBERTY
LITERAL
LITURGY
LOUVRED
LOWBROW
LUCARNE
LUCERNE
LUSTRUM
MAGHREB
MAIGRET
MAJORCA
MALARIA
MASURKA
MAZARIN
MAZURKA
MEGARON
MENORAH
MINARET
MINERAL
MINERVA
MINORCA
MISERLY
MISTRAL
MITHRAS
MONARCH
MONGREL
NATURAL
NAVARIN
NAVARRE
NEMORAL
NEUTRAL
NEUTRON
NIGERIA
NOMBRIL
NOSTRIL
NOSTRUM
NUMERAL
NUMERIC
OBSERVE
OBVERSE
OESTRUS
OFFERER
OMICRON
ONEIRIC
ONTARIO
ONWARDS
ORDERED
ORDERLY
ORPHREY
OSBORNE
OUTCROP
OUTGROW
OVERRUN
PALERMO
PALFREY
PANCRAS
PANGRAM
PANURGE
PAPYRUS
PELORIA
PELORUS
PICARDY
PIERROT
PILGRIM
PIZARRO
PLEURAL
PLEURON
POLARIS
POMEROL
POMEROY
POMFRET
PORTRAY
POVERTY
POWERED
PRAIRIE
PROGRAM
PUBERAL
PUBERTY
PYLORUS
QUADRAT
QUARREL
QUEERER
REBIRTH
RECORDS
RECURVE
REFEREE
REGARDS
REMARRY
REMORSE
RESERVE
RESPRAY
RETIRED
RETIREE
RETURNS
REVERED
REVERIE
REVERSE
RICARDO
ROBERTS
ROSARIO
ROSTRAL
ROSTRUM
RUDERAL
RUMORED
SAFFRON
SALERMO
SAMARIA
SAMURAI
SANGRIA
SATIRIC
SCHERZO
SCLERAL
SCOURER
SCOURGE
SEVERAL
SEVERUS
SHEARER
SOBERLY
SPARROW
SPLURGE
SPORRAN
SPURREY
SQUARED
SQUARES
STEARIC
STEERER
STIRRED
STIRRUP
SUGARED
SUNTRAP
SYCORAX
SYNERGY
TABARET
TAMARIN
TANCRED
TANTRUM
TATARIC
TAVERNA
TAXFREE
TEHERAN
TENDRIL
THEORBO
THEOREM
TIMBREL
TORTRIX
TOWARDS
TUMBREL
TUMBRIL
UNAIRED
UNCARED
UNCURED
UNDERGO
UNEARTH
UNHORSE
UNNERVE
UNSCREW
UPSURGE
UPWARDS
UTTERLY
VENERER
VENTRAL
VETERAN
VICEROY
WASTREL
WATERED
WAVERER
WILFRED
WINDROW
WOLFRAM
ZAMORIN
ZYMURGY
ABBASID
ABIOSIS
ABYSSAL
ACCUSED
ACCUSER
ACHESON
ADDISON
ADVISER
ADVISOR
AEROSOL
ALYSSUM
AMNESIA
AMNESTY
APEPSIA
APHASIA
APHESIS
APLASIA
APPOSED
ARIOSTO
AROUSAL
ARTISAN
ARTISTE
ASPASIA

ASSISTS
AUGUSTA
AUGUSTE
BABYSIT
BACKSET
BAGASSE
BANKSIA
BELISHA
BEMUSED
BENISON
BERGSON
BIASSED
BLESSED
BLESSES
BLOSSOM
BLOUSON
BOURSIN
BROWSER
BRUISED
BRUISER
CAISSON
CANASTA
CATESBY
CELESTA
CELESTE
CHANSON
CHASSIS
CHEESED
CHELSEA
CHIASMA
CHRISOM
CHRISTY
CLASSIC
CLOISON
COARSEN
COUNSEL
COURSER
COURSES
CRASSUS
CRIMSON
CROESUS
CROSSED
CROSSLY
CRUISER
CURTSEY
CYTISUS
DAMOSEL
DEADSET
DEBASED
DEBUSSY
DEHISCE
DEMESNE
DEPOSIT
DEVISED
DEVISEE
DIAPSID
DISUSED
DIVISOR
DRESSED
DRESSER
DYNASTY
ECDYSIS
ECTASIS
EMBASSY
EMERSON
EMULSIN
EPHESUS
EXPOSED
FILASSE
FINESSE
FLOTSAM
FOOTSIE
FORESEE
FREESIA
FRETSAW
FRISSON
FROWSTY
FUCHSIA
GAINSAY
GENESIS
GENISTA
GLASSES
GREASER
GRIMSBY
GROSSLY
GROUSER
HACKSAW
HANDSAW
HANDSEL
HANDSET
HEADSET
HEARSAY
HONESTY
IMPASSE
IMPASTO
INCISOR
IONESCO
IVRESSE
JACKSON
JAMESON
JOCASTA
JOHNSON
KENOSIS
KHAMSIN
KINESIS
KNESSET
LIAISON
LOCUSTS
MADISON
MAJESTY
MALMSEY
MATISSE
MEIOSIS
MEISSEN
MÉTISSE
MILKSOP
MINDSET
MITOSIS
MODESTY
MODISTE
MORESBY
MORESCO
MYIASIS
NEMESIA
NEMESIS
NICOSIA
ODYSSEY
OPOSSUM
OPPOSED
OSMOSIS
OVERSEE
PALISSY
PARASOL
PARESIS
PEGASUS
PERUSAL
PHRASAL
PHRASER
PICASSO
PIOUSLY
PLEASED
PLEASES
PLESSOR
PODESTA
POROSIS
POUSSIN
PRESSED
PRIESTS
PRUSSIC
PYROSIS
QUASSIA
QUONSET
RAMESES
REFUSAL
REISSUE
REPOSAL
REVISED
REVISER
REVISIT
RIPOSTE
ROBESON
ROBUSTA
SAMISEN
SATISFY
SCISSOR
SILESIA
SIMPSON
SOROSIS
SOURSOP
SPENSER
SPLASHY
SPONSON
SPONSOR
SPOUSAL
SQUASHY
SQUISHY
STEPSON
STETSON
SWANSEA
SYCOSIS
TABASCO
TAMESIS
THIRSTY
THOMSON
THRISTY
THYRSIS
THYSSEN
TOOTSIE
TRANSIT
TRANSOM
TREASON
TRESSES
TRIESTE
TRIPSIS
TROTSKY
TROUSER
TRYPSIN
TUNISIA
TWINSET
TYLOSIS
ULYSSES
UNBOSOM
UTENSIL
VANESSA
VENISON
VINASSE
WHATSIT
WHIMSEY
WHITSUN
WINDSOR
WORKSHY
XEROSIS
ZAKUSKA
ZYGOSIS
ZYMOSIS
ABATTIS
ABETTOR
ABLATOR
ACESTES
ACHATES
ADAPTER
ADAPTOR
ADOPTED
AERATED
AGISTOR
AIRSTOP
ALLSTAR
ALSATIA
AMMETER
APHOTIC
APOSTLE
AQUATIC
ARBITER
ARBUTUS
ARIETTA
ASCETIC
ASCITES
ASEPTIC
ASIATIC
ATACTIC
AUDITOR
AVIATOR
BALATON
BARYTES
BATHTUB
BEASTLY
BELATED
BEWITCH
BIGOTED
BIGOTRY
BIRETTA
BLASTED
BLASTER
BLATTER
BLISTER
BLOATED
BLOATER
BLOTTER
BLUNTED
BLUNTLY
BLUSTER
BOASTER
BOLETUS
BOLSTER
BOOSTER
BORSTAL
BRANTUB
BREATHE
BRISTLE
BRISTLY
BRISTOL
BRITTLE
BRIXTON
BURETTE
BURSTER
CAPITAL
CAPITOL
CAPSTAN
CARITAS
CAROTID
CAROTIN
CAUSTIC
CHANTER
CHAOTIC
CHAPTER
CHARTER
CHASTEN
CHATTEL
CHATTER
CHEATER
CHEETAH
CHESTER
CHINTZY
CHOCTAW
CHORTLE
CLASTIC
CLATTER
CLUSTER
CLUTTER
COASTAL
COASTER
COCOTTE
COLITIS
COULTER
COUNTED
COUNTER
COUNTRY
COURTLY
COVETED
CREATED
CREATOR
CRESTED
CRITTER
CROATIA
CROFTER
CROUTON
CRYPTIC
CRYPTON
CRYSTAL
CURATOR
CURETTE
CUVETTE
DAYSTAR
DEBATER
DEMETER
DEMOTIC
DEVOTED
DEVOTEE
DIGITAL
DILATED
DILATOR
DILUTED
DINETTE
DIOPTER
DIOPTRE
DOROTHY
DOUBTER
DRAFTED
DRAFTEE
DRASTIC
DRIFTER
DUNSTAN
EJECTOR
ELASTIC
ELASTIN
ELECTED
ELECTOR
ELECTRA
ELECTRO
EMPATHY
ENACTOR
ENTITLE
EPISTLE
EQUATOR
ERECTOR
ERRATIC
ERRATUM
EVENTER
EXACTLY
EXALTED
EXCITED
EXISTED
FACETED
FAINTED
FAINTLY
FAJITAS
FANATIC
FAUSTUS
FIGHTER
FIRSTLY
FIXATED
FLATTEN
FLATTER
FLITTER
FLOATER
FLUSTER
FLUTTER
FORSTER
FRANTIC
FRETTED
FRITTER
FRONTAL
FROSTED
FUMETTE
GALATEA
GALETTE
GAROTTE
GAVOTTE
GAZETTE
GELATIN
GENETIC
GENITAL
GHASTLY
GHOSTLY
GLISTEN
GLITTER
GLOTTAL
GLOTTIS
GLUTTON
GLYPTAL
GLYPTIC
GNOSTIC
GODETIA
GRAFTER
GRANTED
GRANTEE
GREATEN
GREATLY
GRIFTER
GRISTLE
GRISTLY
HABITAT
HALITUS
HAMSTER
HARDTOP
HAUNTED
HEALTHY
HEARTEN
HEPATIC
HERETIC
HILLTOP
HIPSTER
HOLSTER
HONITON
HORATIO
HYDATID
IDIOTIC

IMHOTEP
IMPETUS
INERTIA
JANITOR
JOINTED
JOINTLY
JUJITSU
JUPITER
KEARTON
KENOTIC
KERATIN
KINETIC
KNITTED
KNITTER
KNOTTED
KRYPTON
LANGTON
LAPUTAN
LAVATER
LAYETTE
LEGATEE
LENGTHY
LESOTHO
LIGHTEN
LIGHTER
LIGHTLY
LIMITED
LIMITER
LINCTUS
LITOTES
LOBSTER
LUNATIC
MAESTRO
MAHATMA
MANATEE
MANITOU
MARATHA
MARITAL
MEGATON
MERITED
MILITIA
MINSTER
MINUTED
MINUTES
MINUTIA
MISSTEP
MOBSTER
MOFETTE
MOISTEN
MOLOTOV
MONITOR
MONSTER
MOUNTED
MOUNTIE
MULATTO
MUNSTER
MUSETTE
MYCETES
NAPHTHA
NAVETTE
NECKTIE
NERITIC
NIGHTIE
NIGHTLY
NONSTOP
ODONTIC
OLDSTER
OMENTUM
OMITTED
OPUNTIA
ORBITAL
ORESTES
ORONTES
OUTSTAY
OVERTAX
PAESTUM
PAINTED
PAINTER
PALATAL
PALETTE
PAROTID
PAROTIS
PENATES
PHAETON
PHANTOM
PHILTER
PHILTRE
PIASTRE
PICOTEE
PILATUS
PINETUM
PIPETTE
PIVOTAL
PLANTAR
PLANTED
PLANTER
PLASTER
PLASTIC
PLATTER
PLAUTUS
PLEATED
PLOTTER
POINTED
POINTER
POLITIC
POOFTER
POULTRY
PRAETOR
PRATTLE
PRINTED
PRINTER
PROCTOR
PSALTER
PUNSTER
PURITAN
PYRETIC
PYRITES
QUANTUM
QUARTAN
QUARTER
QUARTET
QUENTIN
QUESTER
QUIETEN
QUIETLY
QUIETUS
QUILTED
QUILTER
QUINTAL
QUINTAN
QUINTET
QUITTER
RATATAT
REACTOR
REALTOR
RECITAL
REENTER
REENTRY
REGATTA
RELATED
REPUTED
RICHTER
RICOTTA
RIGHTLY
RISOTTO
RIVETED
ROASTER
ROISTER
ROOFTOP
ROOSTER
ROSETTA
ROSETTE
ROTATOR
SAINTLY
SANCTUM
SANCTUS
SAUNTER
SCATTER
SCENTED
SCEPTER
SCEPTIC
SCEPTRE
SCIATIC
SCOOTER
SCOTTIE
SCRATCH
SCROTAL
SCROTUM
SCUTTER
SCUTTLE
SEATTLE
SEMITIC
SENATOR
SHASTRI
SHATTER
SHEATHE
SHELTER
SHIATSU
SHIPTON
SHOOTER
SHORTEN
SHORTLY
SHOUTER
SHUTTER
SHUTTLE
SHYSTER
SIGHTED
SINATRA
SKELTER
SKEPTIC
SKITTER
SKITTLE
SLATTED
SLOTTED
SMARTEN
SMARTIE
SMARTLY
SMATTER
SMELTER
SMITTEN
SMOOTHE
SNIFTER
SNORTER
SNORTLE
SOCOTRA
SPARTAN
SPASTIC
SPATTER
SPECTER
SPECTRE
SPITTLE
SPLOTCH
SPOTTED
SPOTTER
SPUTTER
STARTED
STARTER
STARTLE
STENTOR
STILTED
STILTON
STOUTLY
STRATUM
STRATUS
STRETCH
STUNTED
STUTTER
STYPTIC
SUBATOM
SUDETEN
SUMATRA
SUZETTE
SWARTHY
SWEATED
SWEATER
SWEETEN
SWEETIE
SWEETLY
SWELTER
SWIFTER
SWIFTLY
SYMPTOM
TABITHA
TACITLY
TACITUS
TAGETES
TAINTED
TAPSTER
TELSTAR
TEMPTER
THEATER
THEATRE
THISTLE
TIBETAN
TIGHTEN
TIGHTLY
TIMOTHY
TIPSTER
TOASTED
TOASTER
TOLSTOY
TRACTOR
TRAITOR
TRANTER
TREATED
TREETOP
TRESTLE
TRIATIC
TRISTAN
TROTTER
TRUSTEE
TWEETER
TWISTED
TWISTER
TWITTER
TWOSTEP
UNDATED
UNHITCH
UNLATCH
VANITAS
VAULTED
VEDETTE
VISITOR
WASHTUB
WATUTSI
WEALTHY
WEBSTER
WHARTON
WHEATEN
WHISTLE
WHITTLE
WINSTON
WIRETAP
WOOSTER
WORKTOP
WORSTED
WREATHE
WRESTLE
WRITTEN
YANGTSE
YUCATAN
ZAPOTEC
ZEMSTVO
ACCOUNT
ACCRUAL
ACHTUNG
ADJOURN
AGROUND
ALIQUID
ALIQUOT
AMPOULE
ARMOURY
ASEXUAL
ASSAULT
ASTOUND
AVEBURY
AZIMUTH
BANBURY
BANQUET
BASCULE
BECAUSE
BEDOUIN
BEOWULF
BERMUDA
BETHUMB
BISCUIT
BISMUTH
BIVOUAC
BOROUGH
BOUQUET
BRAVURA
BULRUSH
CAESURA
CAGOULE
CALCULI
CALMUCK
CANNULA
CANTUAR
CAPSULE
CAPTURE
CARDUUS
CAROUSE
CELLULE
CENSURE
CENTURY
CHEQUER
CIRCUIT
CLIQUEY
CLOSURE
CLOTURE
COLLUDE
COLOURS
COMMUNE
COMMUTE
COMPUTE
CONCUSS
CONDUCT
CONDUIT
CONFUSE
CONJURE
CONQUER
CONSULT
CONSUME
CORRUPT
COSTUME
COUTURE
CROQUET
CROQUIS
CULTURE
CURCUMA
DEBAUCH
DEBOUCH
DEFAULT
DEGAUSS
DELOUSE
DENTURE
DIFFUSE
DISCUSS
DISGUST
DISPUTE
DISRUPT
DISTURB
DRACULA
ENCRUST
ENTHUSE
ENTRUST
EPICURE
ERASURE
ESPOUSE
EVACUEE
EXCLUDE
EXECUTE
EXHAUST
EXPOUND
EXTRUDE
FACTUAL
FAILURE
FEATURE
FERRULE
FISSURE
FISTULA
FISTULE
FIXTURE
FORMULA
FORTUNE
FOSSULA
GARBURE
GAUGUIN
GESTURE
GLOBULE
GRADUAL
GRANULE
GRAVURE
HACHURE
HELLUVA
HIRSUTE
HOMBURG
HONOURS
IMPOUND
INCLUDE
INCRUST
INHOUSE
INTRUDE
JACQUES
JONQUIL
KALMUCK
KIBBUTZ

KUMQUAT
LACEUPS
LACQUER
LANGUID
LANGUOR
LAWSUIT
LEAGUER
LECTURE
LEGPULL
LEISURE
LETTUCE
LINGUAL
MANHUNT
MANTUAN
MARBURG
MARCUSE
MARQUEE
MARQUIS
MEASURE
MERCURY
MISRULE
MIXTURE
MOLLUSC
MUGWUMP
NEPTUNE
NERVURE
NETSUKE
NEWBURY
NONSUCH
NONSUIT
NURTURE
OBSCURA
OBSCURE
OBTRUDE
OCCLUDE
OFFDUTY
OROTUND
OUTTURN
OVIDUCT
PARQUET
PASTURE
PEANUTS
PENGUIN
PERCUSS
PERFUME
PERFUSE
PERJURE
PERJURY
PERTURB
PERTUSE
PICQUET
PICTURE
PINNULA
PLANURY
PLUMULE
POLLUTE
POSTURE
POTLUCK
PRELUDE
PREPUCE
PREQUEL
PRESUME
PRIMULA
PROCURE
PRODUCE
PRODUCT
PROFUSE
PURPURA
PURSUER
PURSUIT
PUSTULE
RACQUET
RAEBURN
RAPTURE
REBOUND
RECLUSE
RECOUNT
RECRUIT
REDOUBT
REDOUND
REHOUSE
REMOULD
REMOUNT
REROUTE
RESCUER
RESOUND
RETOUCH
ROEBUCK
RORQUAL
ROUAULT
RUPTURE
SAGOUIN
SALLUST
SAMBUCA
SATSUMA
SAVOURY
SAWDUST
SCAPULA
SCHMUCK
SEAGULL
SECLUDE
SEIZURE
SENSUAL
SEPPUKU
SHROUDS
SOJOURN
SPATULA
SPICULA
SPROUTS
STATURE
STATUTE
STRAUSS
SUBDUCT
SUBDUED
SUBFUSC
SUBSUME
SUCCUMB
SUFFUSE
SUNBURN
TARQUIN
TEMPURA
TESTUDO
TEXTUAL
TEXTURE
THROUGH
TILBURY
TONGUES
TONSURE
TORTURE
TRADUCE
TRIBUNE
TRIBUTE
UNBOUND
UNCOUTH
UNEQUAL
UNSOUND
UNSTUCK
UNTRUTH
UNUSUAL
UNWOUND
URUGUAY
VAPOURS
VELOURS
VENTURE
VERDURE
VERRUCA
VIADUCT
VICTUAL
VIRGULE
VIRTUAL
VISTULA
VULTURE
WARBURG
WETSUIT
YOGHURT
ANGEVIN
AQUAVIT
ARRIVAL
ARRIVED
BATAVIA
BEDEVIL
BEHAVED
BELOVED
BOLIVAR
BOLIVIA
CADAVER
CARAVAN
CARAVEL
CHERVIL
CLEAVER
DELIVER
DISAVOW
ELZEVIR
ENLIVEN
ESTIVAL
ESTOVER
FLIVVER
FLYOVER
FOREVER
GREAVES
GROOVED
HANOVER
HOWEVER
IMPAVID
JEHOVAH
MITZVAH
MORAVIA
NATIVES
NINEVEH
PALAVER
POPOVER
RECOVER
REMOVAL
REMOVED
REMOVER
REVIVAL
REVIVER
SAMOVAR
SHEAVES
SHELVED
SHELVES
SHRIVEL
SHRIVEN
SHRIVER
SLEEVED
STARVED
SYNOVIA
THIEVES
UNCIVIL
UNCOVER
UNLOVED
UNMOVED
UNRAVEL
VETIVER
WHOEVER
YEREVAN
ALLOWED
ARCHWAY
BALDWIN
BEESWAX
BEJEWEL
CARAWAY
CHINWAG
CUTAWAY
DOORWAY
EMBOWER
EMPOWER
FAIRWAY
FARAWAY
FREEWAY
GAEKWAR
GANGWAY
GATEWAY
GETAWAY
GOODWIN
HALFWAY
HALFWIT
HALLWAY
HEADWAY
HIGHWAY
PARKWAY
PATHWAY
PERIWIG
POSTWAR
RAILWAY
RENEWAL
ROADWAY
RUNAWAY
SCRAWNY
SCREWED
SLIPWAY
SPURWAY
STREWTH
THROWER
THROWIN
THRUWAY
TIDEWAY
TRAMWAY
UNBOWED
WALKWAY
WIDOWED
WIDOWER
WYSIWYG
ABRAXIS
AFFIXED
INDEXER
PYREXIA
RELAXED
SYNAXIS
UNFIXED
UNMIXED
ACOLYTE
AMBOYNA
ANALYST
ANALYZE
ANNOYED
ANODYNE
ARRAYED
CARLYLE
DECAYED
DECRYPT
DELAYED
DIALYSE
DIGLYPH
DIPTYCH
ERINYES
HALCYON
HONEYED
ISOHYET
KINTYRE
KUFIYAH
MALAYAN
MARRYAT
MARSYAS
MARTYRS
METAYER
MONEYED
NUREYEV
PALMYRA
PHARYNX
POPEYED
RELAYER
SABAYON
SAMOYED
SAROYAN
SPLAYED
SPRAYER
VANDYKE
ASSIZES
BAJAZET
BLITZED
BRITZKA
BRONZED
CITIZEN
DENIZEN
DRIZZLE
DRIZZLY
FLOOZIE
FRAZZLE
FREEZER
FRIZZLE
FRIZZLY
GRIZZLE
GRIZZLY
HORIZON
JACUZZI
MUEZZIN
POLIZEI
PRETZEL
PREZZIE
QUETZAL
SALAZAR
SELTZER
SWIZZLE
WALTZER

7:6

ABIDJAN
ABRAHAM
ABYSMAL
ABYSSAL
ACADIAN
ACAUDAL
ACCRUAL
ACHAEAN
ACROBAT
ACTINAL
ADMIRAL
ADRENAL
AEOLIAN
AFRICAN
ALASKAN
ALCORAN
ALKORAN
ALLSTAR
ALMANAC
ALUMNAE
AMALGAM
AMMONAL
AMYGDAL
ANAGRAM
ANANIAS
ANDAMAN
ANGOLAN
ANGULAR
ANNULAR
ANTHRAX
APHTHAE
APOGEAN
APPARAT
APSIDAL
APTERAL
AQUINAS
ARABIAN
ARCHWAY
AROUSAL
ARRIVAL
ARSENAL
ARTISAN
ASEXUAL
ASHTRAY
ASOCIAL
ASSEGAI
ATAGHAN
AUSTRAL
AUTOMAT
BAGHDAD
BAHAMAS
BANANAS
BANDEAU
BATHMAT
BATSMAN
BEERMAT
BEESWAX
BELGIAN
BELLMAN
BENTHAM
BERCEAU
BERTRAM
BESMEAR
BESPEAK
BESTIAL
BIAFRAN
BIFOCAL
BIGHEAD
BILLMAN
BIRDMAN
BIVOUAC
BOATMAN
BOILEAU
BOLIVAR
BONDMAN
BOOKMAN
BOOLEAN
BORSTAL
BOWHEAD
BRADMAN
BRAEMAR
BRENDAN
BRIGHAM
BRINJAL
BUCKRAM
BUGBEAR
BUMBOAT
BURGLAR

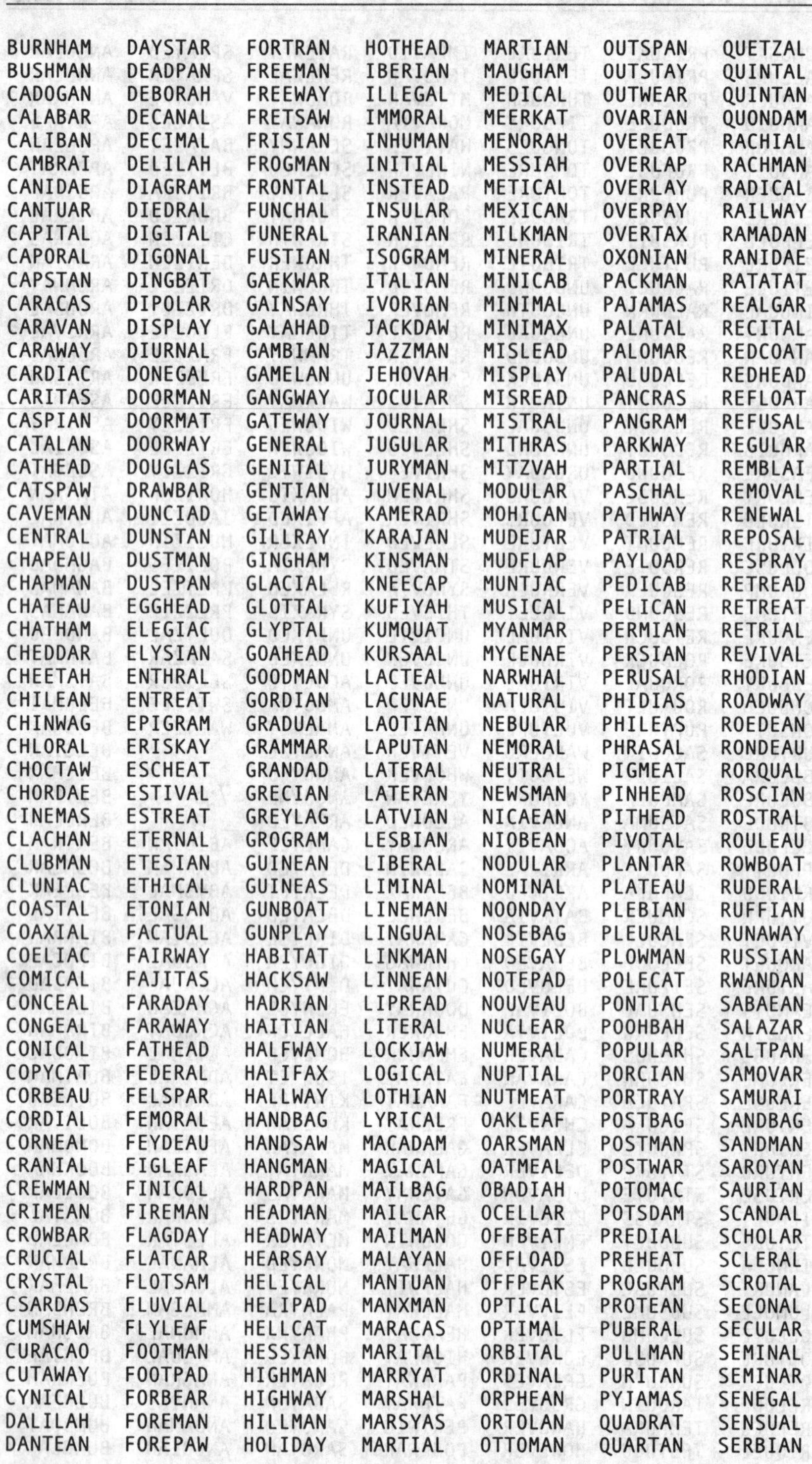

BURNHAM
BUSHMAN
CADOGAN
CALABAR
CALIBAN
CAMBRAI
CANIDAE
CANTUAR
CAPITAL
CAPORAL
CAPSTAN
CARACAS
CARAVAN
CARAWAY
CARDIAC
CARITAS
CASPIAN
CATALAN
CATHEAD
CATSPAW
CAVEMAN
CENTRAL
CHAPEAU
CHAPMAN
CHATEAU
CHATHAM
CHEDDAR
CHEETAH
CHILEAN
CHINWAG
CHLORAL
CHOCTAW
CHORDAE
CINEMAS
CLACHAN
CLUBMAN
CLUNIAC
COASTAL
COAXIAL
COELIAC
COMICAL
CONCEAL
CONGEAL
CONICAL
COPYCAT
CORBEAU
CORDIAL
CORNEAL
CRANIAL
CREWMAN
CRIMEAN
CROWBAR
CRUCIAL
CRYSTAL
CSARDAS
CUMSHAW
CURACAO
CUTAWAY
CYNICAL
DALILAH
DANTEAN
DAYSTAR
DEADPAN
DEBORAH
DECANAL
DECIMAL
DELILAH
DIAGRAM
DIEDRAL
DIGITAL
DIGONAL
DINGBAT
DIPOLAR
DISPLAY
DIURNAL
DONEGAL
DOORMAN
DOORMAT
DOORWAY
DOUGLAS
DRAWBAR
DUNCIAD
DUNSTAN
DUSTMAN
DUSTPAN
EGGHEAD
ELEGIAC
ELYSIAN
ENTHRAL
ENTREAT
EPIGRAM
ERISKAY
ESCHEAT
ESTIVAL
ESTREAT
ETERNAL
ETESIAN
ETHICAL
ETONIAN
FACTUAL
FAIRWAY
FAJITAS
FARADAY
FARAWAY
FATHEAD
FEDERAL
FELSPAR
FEMORAL
FEYDEAU
FIGLEAF
FINICAL
FIREMAN
FLAGDAY
FLATCAR
FLOTSAM
FLUVIAL
FLYLEAF
FOOTMAN
FOOTPAD
FORBEAR
FOREMAN
FOREPAW
FORTRAN
FREEMAN
FREEWAY
FRETSAW
FRISIAN
FROGMAN
FRONTAL
FUNCHAL
FUNERAL
FUSTIAN
GAEKWAR
GAINSAY
GALAHAD
GAMBIAN
GAMELAN
GANGWAY
GATEWAY
GENERAL
GENITAL
GENTIAN
GETAWAY
GILLRAY
GINGHAM
GLACIAL
GLOTTAL
GLYPTAL
GOAHEAD
GOODMAN
GORDIAN
GRADUAL
GRAMMAR
GRANDAD
GRECIAN
GREYLAG
GROGRAM
GUINEAN
GUINEAS
GUNBOAT
GUNPLAY
HABITAT
HACKSAW
HADRIAN
HAITIAN
HALFWAY
HALIFAX
HALLWAY
HANDBAG
HANDSAW
HANGMAN
HARDPAN
HEADMAN
HEADWAY
HEARSAY
HELICAL
HELIPAD
HELLCAT
HESSIAN
HIGHMAN
HIGHWAY
HILLMAN
HOLIDAY
HOTHEAD
IBERIAN
ILLEGAL
IMMORAL
INHUMAN
INITIAL
INSTEAD
INSULAR
IRANIAN
ISOGRAM
ITALIAN
IVORIAN
JACKDAW
JAZZMAN
JEHOVAH
JOCULAR
JOURNAL
JUGULAR
JURYMAN
JUVENAL
KAMERAD
KARAJAN
KINSMAN
KNEECAP
KUFIYAH
KUMQUAT
KURSAAL
LACTEAL
LACUNAE
LAOTIAN
LAPUTAN
LATERAL
LATERAN
LATVIAN
LESBIAN
LIBERAL
LIMINAL
LINEMAN
LINGUAL
LINKMAN
LINNEAN
LIPREAD
LITERAL
LOCKJAW
LOGICAL
LOTHIAN
LYRICAL
MACADAM
MAGICAL
MAILBAG
MAILCAR
MAILMAN
MALAYAN
MANTUAN
MANXMAN
MARACAS
MARITAL
MARRYAT
MARSHAL
MARSYAS
MARTIAL
MARTIAN
MAUGHAM
MEDICAL
MEERKAT
MENORAH
MESSIAH
METICAL
MEXICAN
MILKMAN
MINERAL
MINICAB
MINIMAL
MINIMAX
MISLEAD
MISPLAY
MISREAD
MISTRAL
MITHRAS
MITZVAH
MODULAR
MOHICAN
MUDEJAR
MUDFLAP
MUNTJAC
MUSICAL
MYANMAR
MYCENAE
NARWHAL
NATURAL
NEBULAR
NEMORAL
NEUTRAL
NEWSMAN
NICAEAN
NIOBEAN
NODULAR
NOMINAL
NOONDAY
NOSEBAG
NOSEGAY
NOTEPAD
NOUVEAU
NUCLEAR
NUMERAL
NUPTIAL
NUTMEAT
OAKLEAF
OARSMAN
OATMEAL
OBADIAH
OCELLAR
OFFBEAT
OFFLOAD
OFFPEAK
OPTICAL
OPTIMAL
ORBITAL
ORDINAL
ORPHEAN
ORTOLAN
OTTOMAN
OUTSPAN
OUTSTAY
OUTWEAR
OVARIAN
OVEREAT
OVERLAP
OVERLAY
OVERPAY
OVERTAX
OXONIAN
PACKMAN
PAJAMAS
PALATAL
PALOMAR
PALUDAL
PANCRAS
PANGRAM
PARKWAY
PARTIAL
PASCHAL
PATHWAY
PATRIAL
PAYLOAD
PEDICAB
PELICAN
PERMIAN
PERSIAN
PERUSAL
PHIDIAS
PHILEAS
PHRASAL
PIGMEAT
PINHEAD
PITHEAD
PIVOTAL
PLANTAR
PLATEAU
PLEBIAN
PLEURAL
PLOWMAN
POLECAT
PONTIAC
POOHBAH
POPULAR
PORCIAN
PORTRAY
POSTBAG
POSTMAN
POSTWAR
POTOMAC
POTSDAM
PREDIAL
PREHEAT
PROGRAM
PROTEAN
PUBERAL
PULLMAN
PURITAN
PYJAMAS
QUADRAT
QUARTAN
QUETZAL
QUINTAL
QUINTAN
QUONDAM
RACHIAL
RACHMAN
RADICAL
RAILWAY
RAMADAN
RANIDAE
RATATAT
REALGAR
RECITAL
REDCOAT
REDHEAD
REFLOAT
REFUSAL
REGULAR
REMBLAI
REMOVAL
RENEWAL
REPOSAL
RESPRAY
RETREAD
RETREAT
RETRIAL
REVIVAL
RHODIAN
ROADWAY
ROEDEAN
RONDEAU
RORQUAL
ROSCIAN
ROSTRAL
ROULEAU
ROWBOAT
RUDERAL
RUFFIAN
RUNAWAY
RUSSIAN
RWANDAN
SABAEAN
SALAZAR
SALTPAN
SAMOVAR
SAMURAI
SANDBAG
SANDMAN
SAROYAN
SAURIAN
SCANDAL
SCHOLAR
SCLERAL
SCROTAL
SECONAL
SECULAR
SEMINAL
SEMINAR
SENEGAL
SENSUAL
SERBIAN

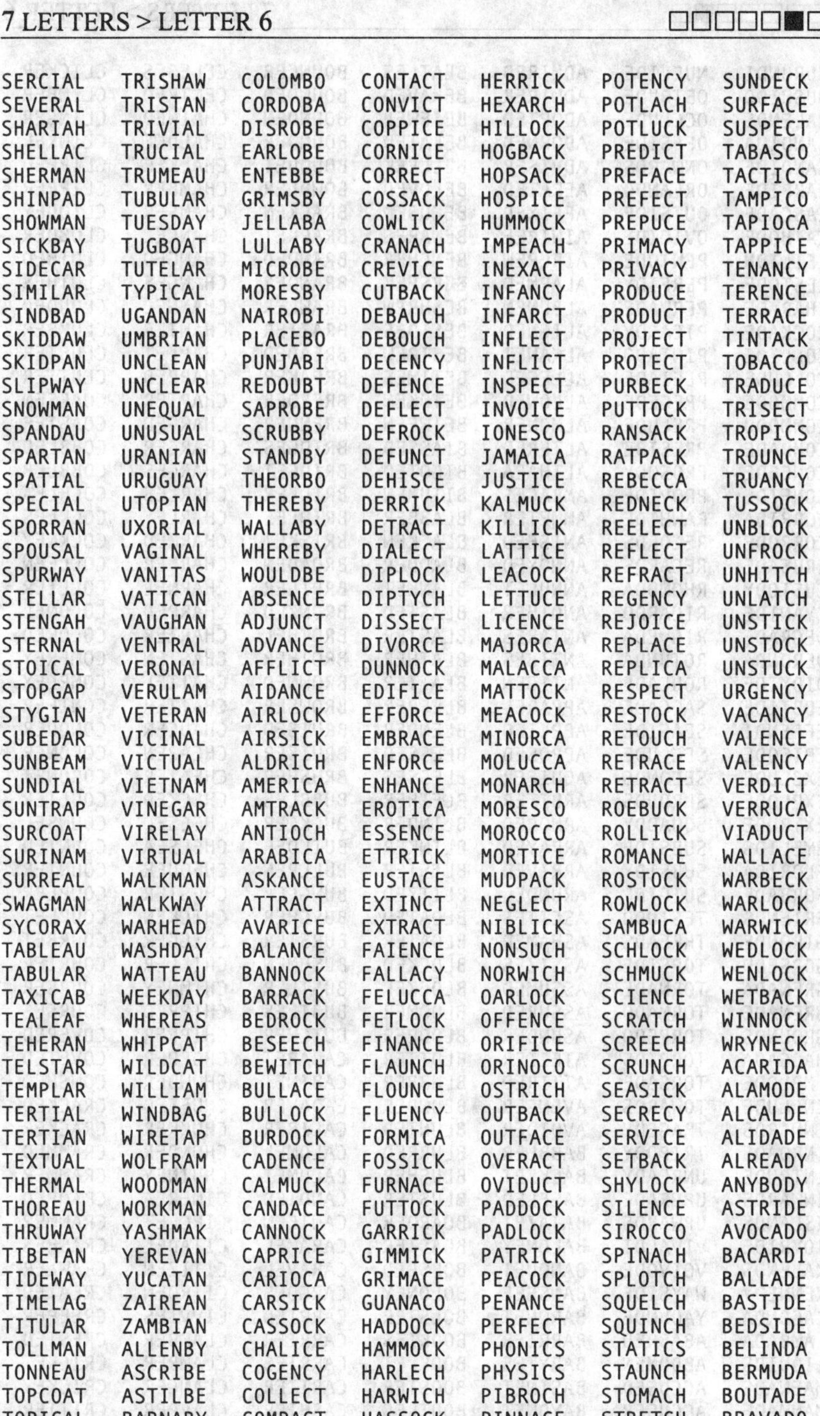

SERCIAL
SEVERAL
SHARIAH
SHELLAC
SHERMAN
SHINPAD
SHOWMAN
SICKBAY
SIDECAR
SIMILAR
SINDBAD
SKIDDAW
SKIDPAN
SLIPWAY
SNOWMAN
SPANDAU
SPARTAN
SPATIAL
SPECIAL
SPORRAN
SPOUSAL
SPURWAY
STELLAR
STENGAH
STERNAL
STOICAL
STOPGAP
STYGIAN
SUBEDAR
SUNBEAM
SUNDIAL
SUNTRAP
SURCOAT
SURINAM
SURREAL
SWAGMAN
SYCORAX
TABLEAU
TABULAR
TAXICAB
TEALEAF
TEHERAN
TELSTAR
TEMPLAR
TERTIAL
TERTIAN
TEXTUAL
THERMAL
THOREAU
THRUWAY
TIBETAN
TIDEWAY
TIMELAG
TITULAR
TOLLMAN
TONNEAU
TOPCOAT
TOPICAL
TOWHEAD
TRAMCAR
TRAMWAY
TRISHAW
TRISTAN
TRIVIAL
TRUCIAL
TRUMEAU
TUBULAR
TUESDAY
TUGBOAT
TUTELAR
TYPICAL
UGANDAN
UMBRIAN
UNCLEAN
UNCLEAR
UNEQUAL
UNUSUAL
URANIAN
URUGUAY
UTOPIAN
UXORIAL
VAGINAL
VANITAS
VATICAN
VAUGHAN
VENTRAL
VERONAL
VERULAM
VETERAN
VICINAL
VICTUAL
VIETNAM
VINEGAR
VIRELAY
VIRTUAL
WALKMAN
WALKWAY
WARHEAD
WASHDAY
WATTEAU
WEEKDAY
WHEREAS
WHIPCAT
WILDCAT
WILLIAM
WINDBAG
WIRETAP
WOLFRAM
WOODMAN
WORKMAN
YASHMAK
YEREVAN
YUCATAN
ZAIREAN
ZAMBIAN
ALLENBY
ASCRIBE
ASTILBE
BARNABY
CARAMBA
CARNABY
CATESBY
COLOMBO
CORDOBA
DISROBE
EARLOBE
ENTEBBE
GRIMSBY
JELLABA
LULLABY
MICROBE
MORESBY
NAIROBI
PLACEBO
PUNJABI
REDOUBT
SAPROBE
SCRUBBY
STANDBY
THEORBO
THEREBY
WALLABY
WHEREBY
WOULDBE
ABSENCE
ADJUNCT
ADVANCE
AFFLICT
AIDANCE
AIRLOCK
AIRSICK
ALDRICH
AMERICA
AMTRACK
ANTIOCH
ARABICA
ASKANCE
ATTRACT
AVARICE
BALANCE
BANNOCK
BARRACK
BEDROCK
BESEECH
BEWITCH
BULLACE
BULLOCK
BURDOCK
CADENCE
CALMUCK
CANDACE
CANNOCK
CAPRICE
CARIOCA
CARSICK
CASSOCK
CHALICE
COGENCY
COLLECT
COMPACT
CONCOCT
CONDUCT
CONNECT
CONTACT
CONVICT
COPPICE
CORNICE
CORRECT
COSSACK
COWLICK
CRANACH
CREVICE
CUTBACK
DEBAUCH
DEBOUCH
DECENCY
DEFENCE
DEFLECT
DEFROCK
DEFUNCT
DEHISCE
DERRICK
DETRACT
DIALECT
DIPLOCK
DIPTYCH
DISSECT
DIVORCE
DUNNOCK
EDIFICE
EFFORCE
EMBRACE
ENFORCE
ENHANCE
EROTICA
ESSENCE
ETTRICK
EUSTACE
EXTINCT
EXTRACT
FAIENCE
FALLACY
FELUCCA
FETLOCK
FINANCE
FLAUNCH
FLOUNCE
FLUENCY
FORMICA
FOSSICK
FURNACE
FUTTOCK
GARRICK
GIMMICK
GRIMACE
GUANACO
HADDOCK
HAMMOCK
HARLECH
HARWICH
HASSOCK
HATTOCK
HEMLOCK
HENPECK
HERRICK
HEXARCH
HILLOCK
HOGBACK
HOPSACK
HOSPICE
HUMMOCK
IMPEACH
INEXACT
INFANCY
INFARCT
INFLECT
INFLICT
INSPECT
INVOICE
IONESCO
JAMAICA
JUSTICE
KALMUCK
KILLICK
LATTICE
LEACOCK
LETTUCE
LICENCE
MAJORCA
MALACCA
MATTOCK
MEACOCK
MINORCA
MOLUCCA
MONARCH
MORESCO
MOROCCO
MORTICE
MUDPACK
NEGLECT
NIBLICK
NONSUCH
NORWICH
OARLOCK
OFFENCE
ORIFICE
ORINOCO
OSTRICH
OUTBACK
OUTFACE
OVERACT
OVIDUCT
PADDOCK
PADLOCK
PATRICK
PEACOCK
PENANCE
PERFECT
PHONICS
PHYSICS
PIBROCH
PINNACE
PLIANCY
POLLACK
PORTICO
POTENCY
POTLACH
POTLUCK
PREDICT
PREFACE
PREFECT
PREPUCE
PRIMACY
PRIVACY
PRODUCE
PRODUCT
PROJECT
PROTECT
PURBECK
PUTTOCK
RANSACK
RATPACK
REBECCA
REDNECK
REELECT
REFLECT
REFRACT
REGENCY
REJOICE
REPLACE
REPLICA
RESPECT
RESTOCK
RETOUCH
RETRACE
RETRACT
ROEBUCK
ROLLICK
ROMANCE
ROSTOCK
ROWLOCK
SAMBUCA
SCHLOCK
SCHMUCK
SCIENCE
SCRATCH
SCREECH
SCRUNCH
SEASICK
SECRECY
SERVICE
SETBACK
SHYLOCK
SILENCE
SIROCCO
SPINACH
SPLOTCH
SQUELCH
SQUINCH
STATICS
STAUNCH
STOMACH
STRETCH
SUBDUCT
SUBJECT
SUFFICE
SUNDECK
SURFACE
SUSPECT
TABASCO
TACTICS
TAMPICO
TAPIOCA
TAPPICE
TENANCY
TERENCE
TERRACE
TINTACK
TOBACCO
TRADUCE
TRISECT
TROPICS
TROUNCE
TRUANCY
TUSSOCK
UNBLOCK
UNFROCK
UNHITCH
UNLATCH
UNSTICK
UNSTOCK
UNSTUCK
URGENCY
VACANCY
VALENCE
VALENCY
VERDICT
VERRUCA
VIADUCT
WALLACE
WARBECK
WARLOCK
WARWICK
WEDLOCK
WENLOCK
WETBACK
WINNOCK
WRYNECK
ACARIDA
ALAMODE
ALCALDE
ALIDADE
ALREADY
ANYBODY
ASTRIDE
AVOCADO
BACARDI
BALLADE
BASTIDE
BEDSIDE
BELINDA
BERMUDA
BOUTADE
BRAVADO
BRIGADE
BROCADE
BROMIDE

BURUNDI
BUSHIDO
CALENDS
CANDIDA
CANDIDE
CARBIDE
CASCADE
CATHODE
CEILIDH
CESTODE
CHARADE
COCKADE
COLLIDE
COLLUDE
COMMODE
COMMODO
COMRADE
CONCEDE
CONFIDE
CORRIDA
CORRODE
CRUSADE
CUSTODY
CYANIDE
DEGRADE
DERONDA
DIOXIDE
EBBTIDE
EFFENDI
EPISODE
EXCLUDE
EXPLODE
EXTRUDE
EYELIDS
FLORIDA
FORBADE
FRIENDS
GIRONDE
GORSEDD
GRENADA
GRENADE
GROUNDS
HAGGADA
IMPLODE
INCLUDE
INNARDS
INROADS
INTRUDE
INWARDS
ISLANDS
JOYRIDE
KALENDS
KENNEDY
LAGONDA
LAMBADA
LIQUIDS
MAENADS
MANMADE
MATILDA
MIRANDA
NITRODE
NUCLIDE
OBTRUDE
OCCLUDE
OFFSIDE
ONWARDS
ORLANDO
OUTSIDE
OVICIDE
PENTODE
PERFIDY
PERVADE
PICARDY
PINTADO
PLEIADE
PRECEDE
PRELUDE
PRESIDE
PROSODY
PROVIDE
RAWHIDE
RECORDS
REGARDS
RHONDDA
RICARDO
RIGVEDA
ROTUNDA
ROULADE
SACCADE
SEASIDE
SECLUDE
SECONDS
SHROUDS
SQUADDY
SUBSIDE
SUBSIDY
SUICIDE
TESTUDO
THREADS
TOPSIDE
TORNADE
TORNADO
TORPEDO
TORPIDS
TORSADE
TOWARDS
TRAGEDY
TRIPODY
UNREADY
UPGRADE
UPWARDS
VIVALDI
VOIVODE
WAYSIDE
YAOUNDE
ABASHED
ABDOMEN
ACCUSED
ACCUSER
ACESTES
ACHATES
ADAPTER
ADMIRED
ADMIRER
ADOPTED
ADORNED
ADVISER
AERATED
AFFIXED
AINTREE
AIRCREW
ALARMED
ALBUMEN
ALIGNED
ALKANET
ALLEGED
ALLOWED
ALMONER
ALTERED
ALTHAEA
AMBAGES
AMMETER
ANISEED
ANNOYED
ANNULET
ANOTHER
ANTARES
ANTIBES
ANTIGEN
APPAREL
APPLIED
APPOSED
AQUIFER
ARBITER
ARMORED
ARRAYED
ARRIVED
ARUNDEL
ASCITES
ASHAMED
ASSIZES
ASSUMED
ASSURED
ASUNDER
ATELIER
ATTIRED
AVENGER
AVOIDER
BABBLER
BACKSET
BAFFLED
BAJAZET
BALONEY
BANQUET
BANSHEE
BARONET
BARRIER
BARYTES
BASINET
BAYONET
BEACHED
BEACHES
BEARDED
BEATLES
BEHAVED
BEJEWEL
BELATED
BELLEEK
BELOVED
BEMUSED
BENARES
BENCHER
BERSEEM
BESHREW
BESIDES
BESTREW
BETIMES
BETOKEN
BETWEEN
BIASSED
BIGOTED
BITUMEN
BLABBER
BLACKEN
BLADDER
BLANKET
BLASTED
BLASTER
BLATHER
BLATTER
BLEEPER
BLENDER
BLESSED
BLESSES
BLETHER
BLINDER
BLINKER
BLISTER
BLITZED
BLOATED
BLOATER
BLOCKED
BLOCKER
BLOOMER
BLOOPER
BLOTTER
BLUBBER
BLUNDER
BLUNTED
BLURRED
BLUSHER
BLUSTER
BOARDER
BOASTER
BOBSLED
BOLONEY
BOLSTER
BOOKIES
BOOKLET
BOOSTER
BOOTLEG
BOTTLED
BOTTLES
BOULDER
BOUNCER
BOUNDED
BOUNDEN
BOUNDER
BOUQUET
BOWDLER
BRACKEN
BRACKET
BRANDED
BRANDER
BRAWLER
BRAZIER
BREADED
BREAKER
BREEDER
BRENNER
BRIDGES
BRIDGET
BRIDLER
BRIDLES
BRISKET
BROADEN
BROILER
BRONZED
BROTHEL
BROTHER
BROWNED
BROWSER
BRUISED
BRUISER
BRUSHER
BUBBLES
BUCKLER
BUILDER
BULLPEN
BUNGLER
BURGHER
BURSTER
BUSHMEN
BUSTLER
BUSTLES
BUTCHER
CABARET
CABINET
CADAVER
CALIBER
CALOMEL
CALUMET
CANDIED
CANTEEN
CARAMEL
CARAVEL
CARGOES
CARRIED
CARRIER
CARRIES
CARTIER
CASHIER
CASTLED
CATCHER
CATERER
CELEBES
CENTRED
CHAINED
CHALDEE
CHALKER
CHAMBER
CHAMFER
CHANCEL
CHANGED
CHANGES
CHANNEL
CHANTER
CHAPLET
CHAPPED
CHAPTER
CHARGED
CHARGER
CHARGES
CHARLES
CHARLEY
CHARMED
CHARMER
CHARNEL
CHARRED
CHARTER
CHASTEN
CHATTEL
CHATTER
CHAUCER
CHEAPEN
CHEATER
CHECKED
CHEESED
CHELSEA
CHEQUER
CHESTER
CHICKEN
CHIGGER
CHILLER
CHIMNEY
CHIPPED
CHIPPER
CHOPPER
CHOWDER
CHUFFED
CHUKKER
CHUNDER
CHUTNEY
CINEREA
CIRCLET
CITADEL
CITIZEN
CITROEN
CIVVIES
CLAMBER
CLAMPER
CLANGER
CLAPPER
CLATTER
CLEANER
CLEAVER
CLICKER
CLIMBER
CLINGER
CLINKER
CLIPPED
CLIPPER
CLIQUEY
CLOBBER
CLOTHED
CLOTHES
CLOUDED
CLUMBER
CLUSTER
CLUTTER
COARSEN
COASTER
COBBLED
COBBLER
COCHLEA
COCKLES
COCKNEY
COLLEEN
COLLIER
COLONEL
COLORED
COMFREY
COMPLEX
CONIFER
CONQUER
CORONER
CORONET
COULTER
COUNSEL
COUNTED
COUNTER
COUPLER
COUPLET
COURBET
COURIER
COURSER
COURSES
COVERED
COVETED
COWSHED
CRACKED
CRACKER
CRAMMED
CRAMMER
CRAMPED
CRANMER
CRASHES
CRAWLER
CREATED
CREEPER
CRESTED
CRICKET
CRICKEY
CRITTER
CROAKER
CROCHET
CROCKET

CROFTER
CROOKED
CROONER
CROPPED
CROPPER
CROQUET
CROSIER
CROSSED
CROWDED
CROZIER
CRUISER
CRUMPET
CRUPPER
CRUSHED
CRUSHER
CURDLED
CURRIED
CURTSEY
DABBLER
DAIMLER
DAMAGED
DAMAGES
DAMOSEL
DAMPIER
DAPPLED
DAWDLER
DAZZLED
DEADSET
DEBASED
DEBATER
DEBRIEF
DECAYED
DECIBEL
DECIDED
DECIDER
DECODER
DECREED
DEFACED
DEFILED
DEFINED
DEGREES
DELAYED
DELIBES
DELIVER
DELUDED
DEMETER
DENIZEN
DEVISED
DEVISEE
DEVOTED
DEVOTEE
DIBBLER
DILATED
DILUTED
DIMPLED
DIOPTER
DISOBEY
DISUSED
DITTIES
DIVIDED
DIVINER

DNIEPER
DOLORES
DOODLER
DOORKEY
DOPPLER
DOSSIER
DOUBLES
DOUBLET
DOUBTER
DOWAGER
DRAFTED
DRAFTEE
DRAGNET
DRAINED
DREADED
DREAMER
DREDGER
DRESDEN
DRESSED
DRESSER
DRIBLET
DRIFTER
DRINKER
DROPLET
DROPPER
DRUGGED
DRUGGET
DRUMMER
DRUNKEN
DURAMEN
DWELLER
EARLIER
EARTHEN
ELECTED
EMBOWER
EMPANEL
EMPOWER
ENDOGEN
ENDURED
ENGAGED
ENGINED
ENLIVEN
ENRAGED
EPAULET
EPITHET
ERINYES
ERITREA
ESCAPEE
ESSENES
ESTOVER
ETAPLES
EVACUEE
EVANDER
EVENTER
EXALTED
EXCITED
EXISTED
EXPIRED
EXPOSED
EZEKIEL
FACETED

FAINTED
FALAFEL
FALSIES
FANCIED
FANCIER
FANGLED
FARRIER
FARTHER
FASTNET
FAVORED
FEATHER
FEIGNED
FEVERED
FIDDLER
FIELDER
FIFTEEN
FIGHTER
FIGURES
FILCHER
FISHNET
FIXATED
FLANKER
FLANNEL
FLAPPED
FLAPPER
FLASHER
FLATLET
FLATTEN
FLATTER
FLECKED
FLECKER
FLEDGED
FLEURET
FLICKER
FLIPPER
FLITTER
FLIVVER
FLOATER
FLODDEN
FLOGGER
FLOODED
FLUNKEY
FLUSHED
FLUSTER
FLUTTER
FLYOVER
FOLLIES
FORAMEN
FORELEG
FORESEE
FOREVER
FORSTER
FORTIES
FOUNDER
FREEZER
FRESHEN
FRESHER
FRESHET
FRETTED
FRILLED
FRINGED

FRISBEE
FRITTER
FROEBEL
FROSTED
FUDDLED
FURRIER
FURTHER
FUTURES
GABBLER
GABRIEL
GALATEA
GALILEE
GALILEO
GAMBLER
GARBLED
GENTEEL
GIMBLET
GLACIER
GLADDEN
GLASSES
GLAZIER
GLEANER
GLIMMER
GLISTEN
GLITTER
GNARLED
GOBBLER
GOGGLES
GOMBEEN
GOODIES
GOOLIES
GOURMET
GRAFTER
GRAINED
GRAINER
GRANDEE
GRANTED
GRANTEE
GRAPNEL
GREASER
GREATEN
GREAVES
GREENER
GRENDEL
GRIFTER
GRILLED
GRINDER
GROINED
GROLIER
GROMMET
GROOVED
GROUPER
GROUSER
GROWLER
GRUMMET
GUARDED
GUILDER
GUZZLER
HACKLES
HACKNEY
HAIRNET

HALOGEN
HAMSTER
HANDLED
HANDLER
HANDSEL
HANDSET
HANGMEN
HANOVER
HARRIER
HARRIET
HATCHET
HAULIER
HAUNTED
HAYSEED
HEADSET
HEARKEN
HEARTEN
HEATHEN
HEATHER
HEAVIER
HECKLER
HENNAED
HERRIES
HILLMEN
HINDLEG
HIPSTER
HOARDER
HOLSTER
HONEYED
HOWEVER
HUMBLES
HUNCHED
HUNDRED
HURDLER
HURRIED
HUSTLER
HYPOGEA
IGNORED
ILLBRED
IMHOTEP
IMPLIED
INCOMER
INDEXER
INFIDEL
INHALER
INJURED
INSIDER
INSIDES
INSURER
INTEGER
INVADER
IPOMOEA
ISOHYET
IVORIEN
JACQUES
JEEPNEY
JELLIED
JEWELER
JEZEBEL
JOINTED
JOURNEY

JUBILEE
JUGGLER
JUMBLED
JUMBLES
JUNIPER
JUPITER
KEROGEN
KESTREL
KIELDER
KINDRED
KINGLET
KITCHEN
KLAVIER
KLEENEX
KLINKER
KNACKER
KNAPPER
KNEELER
KNELLER
KNESSET
KNICKER
KNITTED
KNITTER
KNOCKER
KNOTTED
LABORED
LABORER
LACQUER
LAMPREY
LANGLEY
LATCHET
LATIMER
LAUNDER
LAVATER
LAYERED
LEAFLET
LEAGUER
LEANDER
LEARNED
LEARNER
LEATHER
LEGATEE
LEVERET
LIGHTEN
LIGHTER
LIKENED
LIMITED
LIMITER
LINSEED
LITCHEE
LITOTES
LOBSTER
LORELEI
LOUNGER
LOURDES
LOUVRED
LUCIFER
LURCHER
LYMNAEA
LYNCHET
MAGHREB

MAIGRET
MALMSEY
MANAGER
MANATEE
MARBLED
MARBLES
MARCHER
MARINER
MARQUEE
MARRIED
MARTLET
MATCHED
MATCHET
MATINEE
MATTHEW
MAUNDER
MEANDER
MEASLES
MEDDLER
MEISSEN
MERCIES
MERITED
MERRIER
MESSIER
METAYER
METTLED
MICHAEL
MIDWEEK
MINARET
MINDSET
MINSTER
MINUTED
MINUTES
MISDEED
MISSTEP
MOBSTER
MOISTEN
MOITHER
MONEYED
MONGREL
MONSTER
MOORHEN
MOTTLED
MOULDED
MOULDER
MOUNTED
MOURNER
MUDDLED
MUFFLED
MUFFLER
MUNSTER
MUTAGEN
MYCETES
NAILBED
NANKEEN
NARTHEX
NATCHEZ
NATIVES
NECKLET
NEEDLES
NEITHER

NINEVEH
NOBBLED
NOBBLER
NOMINEE
NOODLES
NOTCHED
NUMBLES
NUREYEV
NYMPHET
OARSMEN
OBLIGED
OCTOBER
ODYSSEY
OFFERER
OFFICER
OFFICES
OLDSTER
OMITTED
OPPOSED
ORACLES
ORANGES
ORDERED
ORESTES
ORONTES
ORPHREY
OSSELET
OUTLIER
OVERFED
OVERSEE
PADDLER
PAINTED
PAINTER
PAISLEY
PALAVER
PALFREY
PALSIED
PANACEA
PANGAEA
PANNIER
PANTHER
PANTIES
PARAPET
PARCHED
PARQUET
PARSLEY
PARTNER
PASTIES
PEBBLES
PEDDLER
PEDICEL
PENATES
PERIGEE
PERPLEX
PERRIER
PERSPEX
PHILTER
PHRASER
PICKLED
PICKLER
PICOTEE
PICQUET
PIERCED
PIERCER
PIKELET
PILCHER
PINCHED
PIONEER
PITCHED
PITCHER
PLANNED
PLANNER
PLANTED
PLANTER
PLASTER
PLATTER
PLAYLET
PLAYPEN
PLEADER
PLEASED
PLEASES
PLEATED
PLODDER
PLOTTER
PLUMBER
PLUMMET
PLUMPER
PLUNDER
PLUNGER
POACHER
POINTED
POINTER
POLIZEI
POLYMER
POMFRET
POOFTER
POPEYED
POPOVER
POTHEEN
POWERED
PREMIER
PREQUEL
PRESSED
PRETZEL
PREVIEW
PRICKED
PRICKER
PRINCES
PRINTED
PRINTER
PRITHEE
PROBLEM
PROCEED
PROFFER
PRONGED
PROPHET
PROSPER
PROUDER
PROWLER
PRYTHEE
PSALTER
PUNCHED
PUNCHER
PUNSTER
PURLIEU
PURSUER
PURVIEW
PUTTEES
PUZZLED
PUZZLER
PYRITES
QUARREL
QUARTER
QUARTET
QUEERER
QUESTER
QUICKEN
QUICKER
QUIETEN
QUILTED
QUILTER
QUINTET
QUITTER
QUONSET
RACQUET
RADDLED
RAFFLES
RAGWEED
RAMBLER
RAMESES
RANCHER
RAPHAEL
RATCHET
RATTEEN
RATTLER
RAVAGES
RECOVER
REDUCED
REDUCER
REENTER
REFEREE
REFINED
REFINER
REFUGEE
REGIMEN
RELATED
RELAXED
RELAYER
REMODEL
REMOVED
REMOVER
REPUTED
REQUIEM
RESCUER
RETIRED
RETIREE
REVELER
REVERED
REVISED
REVISER
REVIVER
RICHTER
RIDDLED
RIDDLER
RINGLET
RIVETED
RIVULET
ROASTER
ROISTER
RONTGEN
ROOSTER
ROSACEA
ROUGHEN
ROUNDED
ROUNDEL
ROUNDER
ROUTIER
RUFFLED
RUFFLER
RUMBLER
RUMORED
RUMPLED
RUSTLER
SADDLER
SAMISEN
SAMOYED
SAMPLER
SARACEN
SATCHEL
SAUNTER
SAVAGES
SCABIES
SCALPEL
SCALPER
SCAMPER
SCANNER
SCARLET
SCARPER
SCATTER
SCENTED
SCEPTER
SCHEMER
SCOFFER
SCOOTER
SCOURER
SCOWDER
SCRAPER
SCREWED
SCULLER
SCUPPER
SCUTTER
SEAWEED
SEDUCER
SEEDBED
SEETHED
SELTZER
SERRIED
SETTLED
SETTLER
SHAGGED
SHARPEN
SHARPER
SHATTER
SHEARER
SHEAVES
SHEBEEN
SHELLED
SHELLEY
SHELTER
SHELVED
SHELVES
SHEPPEY
SHERBET
SHIMMER
SHIPPER
SHIRKER
SHIRLEY
SHOCKED
SHOCKER
SHOOTER
SHOPPER
SHORTEN
SHOUTER
SHRIVEL
SHRIVEN
SHRIVER
SHUDDER
SHUTTER
SHYSTER
SICKBED
SIGHTED
SIMPLER
SIMPLEX
SINGLES
SINGLET
SIXTEEN
SIZZLER
SKELTER
SKILLED
SKILLET
SKIMMED
SKIMMER
SKINNED
SKINNER
SKIPPED
SKIPPER
SKITTER
SLACKEN
SLACKER
SLAMMER
SLANDER
SLAPPER
SLASHED
SLATTED
SLEEPER
SLEEVED
SLENDER
SLICKER
SLIMMER
SLIPPED
SLIPPER
SLITHER
SLOBBER
SLOGGER
SLOSHED
SLOTTED
SLUMBER
SMACKER
SMALLER
SMARTEN
SMASHED
SMASHER
SMATTER
SMELTER
SMITHER
SMITTEN
SMOLDER
SMOTHER
SMUDGED
SNAPPER
SNARLER
SNEAKER
SNICKER
SNIFFER
SNIFTER
SNIGGER
SNIPPET
SNOOKER
SNOOPER
SNORKEL
SNORTER
SOCAGER
SOFABED
SOLDIER
SOUNDED
SOUNDER
SOUTHEY
SOZZLED
SPADGER
SPANDEX
SPANIEL
SPANKER
SPANNER
SPATTER
SPEAKER
SPECIES
SPECTER
SPELLER
SPENCER
SPENDER
SPENSER
SPINNER
SPINNEY
SPLAYED
SPLICED
SPLICER
SPOILED
SPOILER
SPONDEE
SPONGER
SPOONER
SPOTTED
SPOTTER
SPRAYER
SPURREY
SPUTTER
SQUARED
SQUARES
STABLES
STAFFER
STAGGER
STAINED
STAINER
STALKED
STALKER
STAMMER
STAMPED
STAMPER
STANLEY
STAPLER
STARLET
STARTED
STARTER
STARVED
STEAMED
STEAMER
STEEPEN
STEERER
STEMMED
STEPHEN
STEPNEY
STICKER
STIFFEN
STILTED
STINGER
STINKER
STIRPES
STIRRED
STOLLEN
STONKER
STOPPED
STOPPER
STORIED
STORIES
STRIDES
STRIKER
STRIPED
STRIPER
STRIPES
STRUDEL
STUDDED
STUDIED
STUFFED
STUMPED
STUNNER
STUNTED
STURMER
STUTTER
SUBDUED
SUBTEEN
SUCCEED
SUDETEN
SUGARED
SWAGGER
SWANSEA
SWAPPED
SWEATED
SWEATER

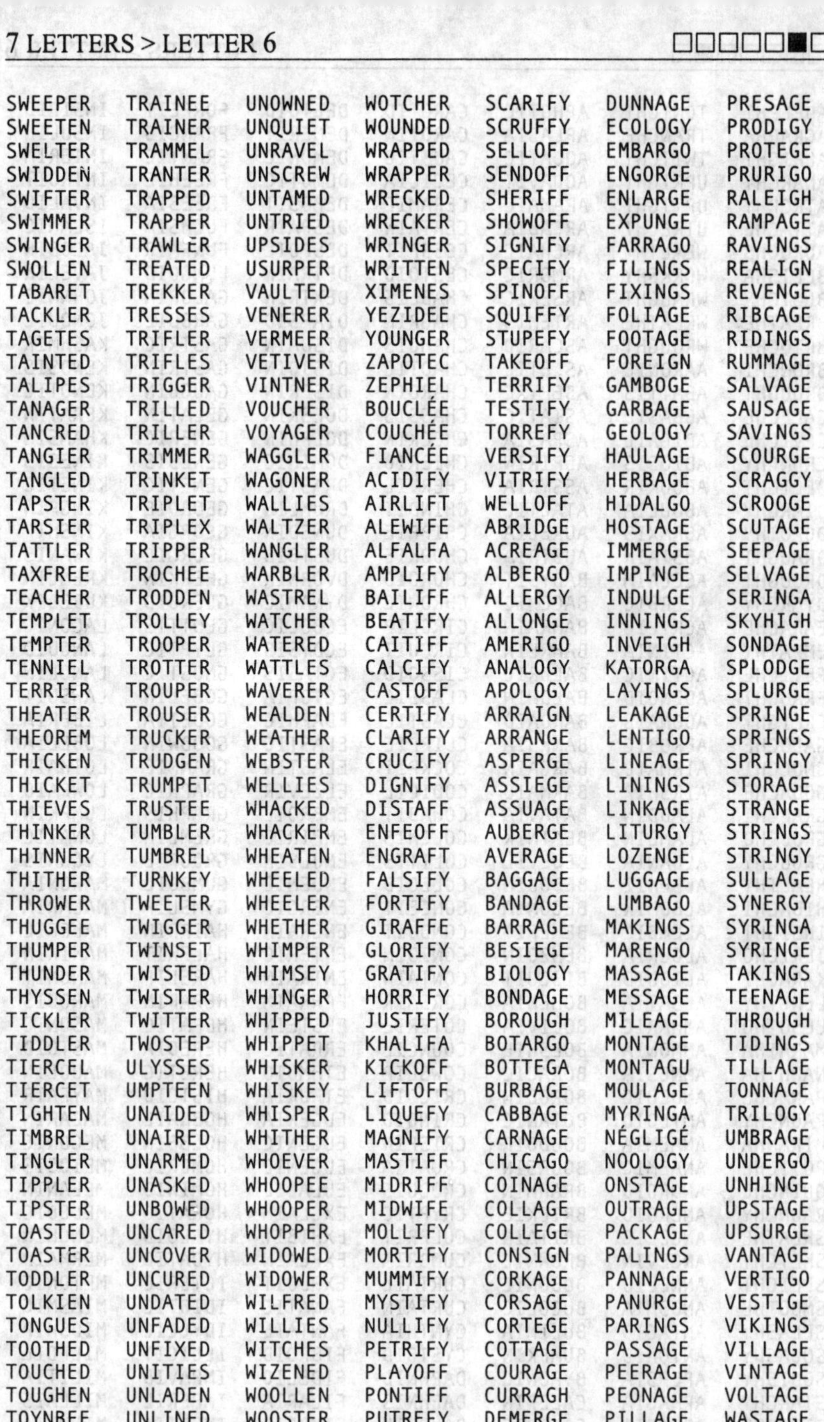

SWEEPER
SWEETEN
SWELTER
SWIDDEN
SWIFTER
SWIMMER
SWINGER
SWOLLEN
TABARET
TACKLER
TAGETES
TAINTED
TALIPES
TANAGER
TANCRED
TANGIER
TANGLED
TAPSTER
TARSIER
TATTLER
TAXFREE
TEACHER
TEMPLET
TEMPTER
TENNIEL
TERRIER
THEATER
THEOREM
THICKEN
THICKET
THIEVES
THINKER
THINNER
THITHER
THROWER
THUGGEE
THUMPER
THUNDER
THYSSEN
TICKLER
TIDDLER
TIERCEL
TIERCET
TIGHTEN
TIMBREL
TINGLER
TIPPLER
TIPSTER
TOASTED
TOASTER
TODDLER
TOLKIEN
TONGUES
TOOTHED
TOUCHED
TOUGHEN
TOYNBEE
TRACHEA
TRACKER
TRAILER
TRAINED
TRAINEE
TRAINER
TRAMMEL
TRANTER
TRAPPED
TRAPPER
TRAWLER
TREATED
TREKKER
TRESSES
TRIFLER
TRIFLES
TRIGGER
TRILLED
TRILLER
TRIMMER
TRINKET
TRIPLET
TRIPLEX
TRIPPER
TROCHEE
TRODDEN
TROLLEY
TROOPER
TROTTER
TROUPER
TROUSER
TRUCKER
TRUDGEN
TRUMPET
TRUSTEE
TUMBLER
TUMBREL
TURNKEY
TWEETER
TWIGGER
TWINSET
TWISTED
TWISTER
TWITTER
TWOSTEP
ULYSSES
UMPTEEN
UNAIDED
UNAIRED
UNARMED
UNASKED
UNBOWED
UNCARED
UNCOVER
UNCURED
UNDATED
UNFADED
UNFIXED
UNITIES
UNLADEN
UNLINED
UNLOVED
UNMIXED
UNMOVED
UNNAMED
UNOWNED
UNQUIET
UNRAVEL
UNSCREW
UNTAMED
UNTRIED
UPSIDES
USURPER
VAULTED
VENERER
VERMEER
VETIVER
VINTNER
VOUCHER
VOYAGER
WAGGLER
WAGONER
WALLIES
WALTZER
WANGLER
WARBLER
WASTREL
WATCHER
WATERED
WATTLES
WAVERER
WEALDEN
WEATHER
WEBSTER
WELLIES
WHACKED
WHACKER
WHEATEN
WHEELED
WHEELER
WHETHER
WHIMPER
WHIMSEY
WHINGER
WHIPPED
WHIPPET
WHISKER
WHISKEY
WHISPER
WHITHER
WHOEVER
WHOOPEE
WHOOPER
WHOPPER
WIDOWED
WIDOWER
WILFRED
WILLIES
WITCHES
WIZENED
WOOLLEN
WOOSTER
WORKMEN
WORRIED
WORRIER
WORSTED
WOTCHER
WOUNDED
WRAPPED
WRAPPER
WRECKED
WRECKER
WRINGER
WRITTEN
XIMENES
YEZIDEE
YOUNGER
ZAPOTEC
ZEPHIEL
BOUCLÉE
COUCHÉE
FIANCÉE
ACIDIFY
AIRLIFT
ALEWIFE
ALFALFA
AMPLIFY
BAILIFF
BEATIFY
CAITIFF
CALCIFY
CASTOFF
CERTIFY
CLARIFY
CRUCIFY
DIGNIFY
DISTAFF
ENFEOFF
ENGRAFT
FALSIFY
FORTIFY
GIRAFFE
GLORIFY
GRATIFY
HORRIFY
JUSTIFY
KHALIFA
KICKOFF
LIFTOFF
LIQUEFY
MAGNIFY
MASTIFF
MIDRIFF
MIDWIFE
MOLLIFY
MORTIFY
MUMMIFY
MYSTIFY
NULLIFY
PETRIFY
PLAYOFF
PONTIFF
PUTREFY
QUALIFY
RECTIFY
SALSIFY
SATISFY
SCARIFY
SCRUFFY
SELLOFF
SENDOFF
SHERIFF
SHOWOFF
SIGNIFY
SPECIFY
SPINOFF
SQUIFFY
STUPEFY
TAKEOFF
TERRIFY
TESTIFY
TORREFY
VERSIFY
VITRIFY
WELLOFF
ABRIDGE
ACREAGE
ALBERGO
ALLERGY
ALLONGE
AMERIGO
ANALOGY
APOLOGY
ARRAIGN
ARRANGE
ASPERGE
ASSIEGE
ASSUAGE
AUBERGE
AVERAGE
BAGGAGE
BANDAGE
BARRAGE
BESIEGE
BIOLOGY
BONDAGE
BOROUGH
BOTARGO
BOTTEGA
BURBAGE
CABBAGE
CARNAGE
CHICAGO
COINAGE
COLLAGE
COLLEGE
CONSIGN
CORKAGE
CORSAGE
CORTEGE
COTTAGE
COURAGE
CURRAGH
DEMERGE
DERANGE
DIVERGE
DIVULGE
DOMINGO
DUNNAGE
ECOLOGY
EMBARGO
ENGORGE
ENLARGE
EXPUNGE
FARRAGO
FILINGS
FIXINGS
FOLIAGE
FOOTAGE
FOREIGN
GAMBOGE
GARBAGE
GEOLOGY
HAULAGE
HERBAGE
HIDALGO
HOSTAGE
IMMERGE
IMPINGE
INDULGE
INNINGS
INVEIGH
KATORGA
LAYINGS
LEAKAGE
LENTIGO
LINEAGE
LININGS
LINKAGE
LITURGY
LOZENGE
LUGGAGE
LUMBAGO
MAKINGS
MARENGO
MASSAGE
MESSAGE
MILEAGE
MONTAGE
MONTAGU
MOULAGE
MYRINGA
NÉGLIGÉ
NOOLOGY
ONSTAGE
OUTRAGE
PACKAGE
PALINGS
PANNAGE
PANURGE
PARINGS
PASSAGE
PEERAGE
PEONAGE
PILLAGE
PLUMAGE
PORTAGE
POSTAGE
POTTAGE
PRESAGE
PRODIGY
PROTEGE
PRURIGO
RALEIGH
RAMPAGE
RAVINGS
REALIGN
REVENGE
RIBCAGE
RIDINGS
RUMMAGE
SALVAGE
SAUSAGE
SAVINGS
SCOURGE
SCRAGGY
SCROOGE
SCUTAGE
SEEPAGE
SELVAGE
SERINGA
SKYHIGH
SONDAGE
SPLODGE
SPLURGE
SPRINGE
SPRINGS
SPRINGY
STORAGE
STRANGE
STRINGS
STRINGY
SULLAGE
SYNERGY
SYRINGA
SYRINGE
TAKINGS
TEENAGE
THROUGH
TIDINGS
TILLAGE
TONNAGE
TRILOGY
UMBRAGE
UNDERGO
UNHINGE
UPSTAGE
UPSURGE
VANTAGE
VERTIGO
VESTIGE
VIKINGS
VILLAGE
VINTAGE
VOLTAGE
WASTAGE
WATTAGE
YARDAGE
ZOOLOGY
ZYMURGY

ADELPHI
AGRAPHA
ALRIGHT
ANARCHY
ATROPHY
ATTACHE
AUROCHS
BELISHA
BLOTCHY
BREATHE
BRIOCHE
BRONCHI
BROUGHT
CALECHE
CEVICHE
CRUNCHY
DELIGHT
DIARCHY
DOROTHY
DRAUGHT
DROUGHT
DYARCHY
EARACHE
EMPATHY
FETICHE
FRAUGHT
FREIGHT
GALOCHE
GNOCCHI
GOUACHE
GRACCHI
GROUCHO
GROUCHY
HEALTHY
HIBACHI
INSIGHT
JERICHO
KARACHI
LENGTHY
LESOTHO
MARATHA
NAPHTHA
PANACHE
PAUNCHY
PIRANHA
POTICHE
QUINCHE
RAUNCHY
SHEATHE
SKETCHY
SLEIGHT
SMOOTHE
SPLASHY
SQUASHY
SQUISHY
STARCHY
STROPHE
SWARTHY
TABITHA
THOUGHT
TIMOTHY
TONIGHT
TRANCHE
TWITCHY
UPRIGHT
UPTIGHT
UTRECHT
WEALTHY
WORKSHY
WRAUGHT
WREATHE
WROUGHT
AARONIC
ABATTIS
ABBASID
ABIGAIL
ABIOSIS
ABOUKIR
ABOULIA
ABRAXIS
ABSTAIN
ACCLAIM
ACERBIC
ACRYLIC
ACTINIA
ACTINIC
ADENOID
ADONAIS
AEROBIC
AIRMAIL
AIRSHIP
ALADDIN
ALAMEIN
ALBANIA
ALBENIZ
ALBUMIN
ALEMBIC
ALGERIA
ALIQUID
ALSATIA
AMHARIC
AMMONIA
AMNESIA
AMOEBIC
AMYLOID
ANAEMIA
ANAEMIC
ANDROID
ANEROID
ANGELIC
ANGEVIN
ANNELID
ANOSMIA
ANTACID
ANTONIO
APEPSIA
APHAGIA
APHASIA
APHELIA
APHESIS
APHONIA
APHONIC
APHOTIC
APLASIA
AQUATIC
AQUAVIT
ARAMAIC
ARCADIA
ARCHAIC
ARMORIC
ARSENIC
ARTEMIS
ASCARID
ASCETIC
ASEPTIC
ASIATIC
ASPASIA
ASPIRIN
ASSYRIA
ATACTIC
AURELIA
AUSTRIA
BABYSIT
BACCHIC
BAHRAIN
BAHREIN
BALDRIC
BALDWIN
BANDAID
BANKSIA
BARGAIN
BARMAID
BATAVIA
BEATNIK
BEDEVIL
BEDOUIN
BEGONIA
BENEFIT
BENZOIN
BISCUIT
BOHEMIA
BOLIVIA
BOLSHIE
BORACIC
BORODIN
BOTANIC
BOUDOIR
BOURSIN
BRAHMIN
BRICKIE
BRITAIN
BROWNIE
BUBONIC
BUCOLIC
BULIMIA
BUMPKIN
BYRONIC
CALEPIN
CALORIC
CALORIE
CAMBRIC
CANTRIP
CAPTAIN
CAROTID
CAROTIN
CAUSTIC
CECILIA
CERAMIC
CERTAIN
CESSPIT
CESTOID
CHABLIS
CHAGRIN
CHAMOIS
CHAOTIC
CHARDIN
CHASSIS
CHECKIN
CHEERIO
CHERVIL
CHINDIT
CHIPPIE
CHOOKIE
CHOROID
CHRONIC
CIRCLIP
CIRCUIT
CISSOID
CLASSIC
CLASTIC
CLIPPIE
COCKPIT
CODICIL
COHABIT
COLCHIS
COLITIS
COLLOID
CONCEIT
CONDUIT
CONJOIN
CONTAIN
CORSAIR
COTERIE
COUNCIL
COWSLIP
CRICOID
CRINOID
CRISPIN
CROATIA
CROQUIS
CRYPTIC
CULPRIT
CUMBRIA
CURTAIL
CURTAIN
CYNTHIA
CYSTOID
DAPHNID
DAPHNIS
DAUPHIN
DECLAIM
DEFICIT
DELIMIT
DELPHIC
DELTOID
DEMERIT
DEMONIC
DEMOTIC
DEPOSIT
DESPAIR
DESPOIL
DETRAIN
DEXTRIN
DIAPSID
DISDAIN
DISJOIN
DISPRIN
DOESKIN
DOLPHIN
DOMINIC
DRASTIC
DRUMLIN
DUNEDIN
DUSTBIN
DVORNIK
DYNAMIC
ECBOLIC
ECDYSIS
ECTASIS
ECTOPIA
EDAPHIC
ELASTIC
ELASTIN
ELZEVIR
EMBROIL
EMPIRIC
EMULSIN
ENDEMIC
ENERGIC
ENGRAIN
ENTERIC
ENTRAIN
EPHRAIM
EPSTEIN
ERRATIC
ETHMOID
ETRURIA
EUGENIA
EUGENIC
EUGENIE
EULALIE
EXCLAIM
EXHIBIT
EXPLAIN
EXPLOIT
FANATIC
FANTAIL
FIBROID
FIDELIO
FILARIA
FIMBRIA
FLACCID
FLEAPIT
FLOOZIE
FOOTSIE
FORFEIT
FRANCIS
FRANTIC
FREEBIE
FREESIA
FUCHSIA
FUNFAIR
FUNGOID
GALOPIN
GARBOIL
GASTRIC
GASTRIN
GAUGUIN
GELATIN
GENERIC
GENESIS
GENETIC
GEORDIE
GEORGIA
GEORGIC
GHERKIN
GLENOID
GLOTTIS
GLYPTIC
GNOSTIC
GOBELIN
GODETIA
GOODWIN
GRANNIE
GRAPHIC
GRAPHIS
GREMLIN
GROUPIE
GUMBOIL
GYMSLIP
HAIRPIN
HALFWIT
HARELIP
HEPARIN
HEPATIC
HEREDIA
HERETIC
HISTOID
HOBNAIL
HOLBEIN
HOMERIC
HOMINID
HORATIO
HYALOID
HYDATID
ICTERIC
IDIOTIC
IDYLLIC
ILLICIT
IMPAVID
IMPERIL
INERTIA
INGRAIN
INHABIT
INHERIT
INHIBIT
INSIPID
INSULIN
INTERIM
INTROIT
INVALID
ISLAMIC
JACOBIN
JAVELIN
JOHNNIE
JONQUIL
KASHMIR
KENOSIS
KENOTIC
KERATIN
KHAMSIN
KINESIS
KINETIC
KINGPIN
KINSHIP
KIWANIS
KREMLIN
KUBELIK
LACONIC
LANGUID
LANOLIN
LAWSUIT
LIBERIA
LOBELIA
LOTHAIR
LOWPAID
LUMPKIN
LUNATIC
LYCHNIS
MAHONIA
MALARIA
MALEFIC
MANIKIN
MANUMIT
MARQUIS
MASONIC
MASTOID
MAUDLIN
MAYFAIR
MAZARIN
MECONIC
MEIOSIS
MELANIN
MELODIC
MENUHIN
MERMAID
METONIC
MIASMIC
MIDSHIP
MILFOIL
MILITIA
MILLAIS
MINUTIA
MIRIFIC
MITOSIS
MONILIA
MOONLIT

MORAVIA
MORONIC
MORPHIA
MOUNTIE
MUEZZIN
MULLEIN
MURRAIN
MUSCOID
MYALGIA
MYELOID
MYIASIS
NAMIBIA
NAVARIN
NECKTIE
NEGROID
NEMESIA
NEMESIS
NERITIC
NICOSIA
NIGERIA
NIGHTIE
NINEPIN
NOMADIC
NOMBRIL
NONSUIT
NOSTRIL
NUCLEIC
NUMERIC
OCEANIA
OCEANIC
OCEANID
ODONTIC
OILSKIN
OLYMPIA
OLYMPIC
ONEIRIC
ONTARIO
OPUNTIA
ORGANIC
OSMOSIS
OTALGIA
OVERBID
OVERLIE
PACIFIC
PALADIN
PARBOIL
PARESIS
PARFAIT
PAROTID
PAROTIS
PARSNIP
PARTHIA
PEARLIE
PELAGIC
PELORIA
PENGUIN
PERIWIG
PERSEID
PERTAIN
PETUNIA
PFENNIG
PHALLIC
PHOENIX
PHONEIN
PHRENIC
PIGSKIN
PIGTAIL
PILGRIM
PINTAIL
PLASMIN
PLASTIC
PLAUDIT
POCHOIR
POLARIS
POLEMIC
POLITIC
POLONIE
POMPEII
POROSIS
POUSSIN
PRAIRIE
PREPAID
PREVAIL
PREZZIE
PROSAIC
PROTEIN
PROUDIE
PRUSSIC
PSYCHIC
PTYALIN
PUMPKIN
PURLOIN
PURSUIT
PUSHKIN
PYAEMIA
PYRAMID
PYRETIC
PYREXIA
PYROSIS
PYRRHIC
QUASSIA
QUENTIN
QUICKIE
RACEMIC
RAMEKIN
RAREBIT
RATAFIA
RECLAIM
RECRUIT
REDSKIN
REFRAIN
REGALIA
RETRAIN
RETRAIT
REVERIE
REVISIT
RHIZOID
RINGGIT
ROBINIA
ROMANIA
ROSALIA
ROSALIE
ROSARIO
ROUGHIE
SAGOUIN
SALADIN
SALAMIS
SAMARIA
SANDPIT
SANGRIA
SAPONIN
SAPPHIC
SATANIC
SATIRIC
SAUROID
SCAGLIA
SCEPTIC
SCIATIC
SCORPIO
SCOTTIE
SCRAPIE
SEISMIC
SEMITIC
SENECIO
SEQUOIA
SERAPIS
SHINDIG
SHOWBIZ
SILESIA
SIMPKIN
SIRLOIN
SKEPTIC
SKIMMIA
SMARTIE
SMIDGIN
SOLICIT
SOMALIA
SOROSIS
SPASTIC
SPHENIC
SPUTNIK
SQUALID
STANDIN
STANNIC
STARLIT
STEARIC
STENCIL
STEROID
STRIGIL
STROBIC
STYPTIC
SUBEDIT
SUBJOIN
SUBSOIL
SURFEIT
SUSTAIN
SWEETIE
SWITHIN
SYCOSIS
SYNAXIS
SYNOVIA
TABANID
TABLOID
TAMARIN
TAMESIS
TARPEIA
TARQUIN
TATARIC
TENDRIL
TERRAIN
THEREIN
THERMIC
THROWIN
THYROID
THYRSIS
TILAPIA
TINFOIL
TITANIA
TITANIC
TOENAIL
TOOTSIE
TOPSOIL
TORTRIX
TOTEMIC
TOXEMIA
TRADEIN
TRAFFIC
TRANSIT
TRAVAIL
TREFOIL
TRELLIS
TRIATIC
TRIFFID
TRIPSIS
TROPHIC
TRYPSIN
TUBULIN
TUMBRIL
TUNISIA
TURMOIL
TYLOSIS
TYPHOID
UNCIVIL
UPBRAID
URAEMIA
UTENSIL
VASSAIL
VAUDOIS
VERVAIN
VILLAIN
VILLEIN
VITAMIN
VITRAIL
VOCALIC
VOLTAIC
WAGTAIL
WARSHIP
WASSAIL
WEIGHIN
WETSUIT
WHATSIT
WHEELIE
WHEREIN
WORSHIP
XERAFIN
XEROSIS
ZAMORIN
ZIZANIA
ZYGOSIS
ZYMOSIS
ALMACKS
APELIKE
AUTARKY
BAZOOKA
BESPOKE
BRITZKA
CATLIKE
CONVOKE
COWPOKE
DISLIKE
DROSHKY
FINICKY
FORSAKE
GODLIKE
KARAOKE
KONTIKI
MASURKA
MAZURKA
MISTAKE
NETSUKE
NUNLIKE
NUTLIKE
OATCAKE
OILCAKE
PALOOKA
PANCAKE
PANICKY
PAPRIKA
PARTAKE
PROVOKE
RUSALKA
SCHICKS
SEPPUKU
SQUEAKY
STREAKY
TALOOKA
TEACAKE
TROTSKY
UNALIKE
UNLUCKY
VANDYKE
WARLIKE
ZAKUSKA
ACUTELY
AFFABLE
AFFABLY
ALVEOLE
AMIABLE
AMIABLY
AMPOULE
AMPULLA
ANATOLE
ANGRILY
ANIMALS
ANOMALY
ANTHILL
APOSTLE
ARMHOLE
ARTICLE
ASPHALT
ASSAULT
ATINGLE
AUDIBLE
AUDIBLY
AURALLY
AUREOLA
AUREOLE
AURICLE
AWFULLY
BACILLI
BASCULE
BATTELS
BEASTLY
BEGUILE
BENGALI
BEOWULF
BEVERLY
BICYCLE
BLANDLY
BLANKLY
BLEAKLY
BLINDLY
BLOWFLY
BLUFFLY
BLUNTLY
BOSWELL
BOUILLI
BRAILLE
BRAMBLE
BRAVELY
BRIEFLY
BRINDLE
BRISKLY
BRISTLE
BRISTLY
BRITTLE
BROADLY
BUFFALO
BUMMALO
BURNELL
CAGOULE
CALCULI
CAMILLA
CANDELA
CANELLA
CANNILY
CANNULA
CAPABLE
CAPABLY
CAPELLA
CAPSULE
CARIOLE
CARLYLE
CARRELL
CARROLL
CASTILE
CASUALS
CATCALL
CATWALK
CEDILLA
CELLULE
CEMBALO
CENACLE
CHAGALL
CHEAPLY
CHIEFLY
CHORALE
CHORTLE
CHUCKLE
CIVILLY
CLEANLY
CLEARLY
CLOSELY
COMPILE
CONDOLE
CONSOLE
CONSOLS
CONSULT
CORACLE
CORELLI
CORNELL
COROLLA
COURTLY
CRACKLE
CRACKLY
CRAZILY
CRINKLE
CRINKLY
CRIPPLE
CROSSLY
CRUDELY
CRUELLS
CRUELLY
CRUMBLE
CRUMBLY
CRUMPLE
CUBICLE
CUCKOLD
CURABLE
CUTICLE
CYMBALS
DATABLE
DEATHLY
DEBACLE
DEFAULT
DENSELY
DETAILS
DIABOLO
DISABLE
DISTILL
DIZZILY
DOWDILY
DRABBLE
DRACULA
DRAGGLE
DRIBBLE
DRIZZLE

DRIZZLY
DUCTILE
DUOPOLY
DURABLE
DURABLY
DURRELL
DWINDLE
EAGERLY
EARTHLY
EATABLE
ELDERLY
EMERALD
ENFIELD
ENNOBLE
ENTITLE
EPISTLE
EQUABLE
EQUABLY
EQUALLY
EXACTLY
EXAMPLE
EXEMPLA
EYEBALL
FAINTLY
FALSELY
FATALLY
FAVELLA
FEBRILE
FERRULE
FERTILE
FINAGLE
FINALLY
FIREFLY
FIRSTLY
FISSILE
FISTULA
FISTULE
FIXEDLY
FLYHALF
FORMULA
FOSSULA
FOXHOLE
FRAGILE
FRANKLY
FRAZZLE
FRECKLE
FRESHLY
FRIABLE
FRIZZLE
FRIZZLY
FRUMPLE
FULFILL
FUNNILY
FUSIBLE
FUSILLI
FUSSILY
GABELLE
GADWALL
GAUDILY
GAZELLE
GENTILE
GESTALT
GHASTLY
GHOSTLY
GIDDILY
GIMBALS
GISELLE
GLOBULE
GONDOLA
GORILLA
GRACILE
GRACKLE
GRADELY
GRANDLY
GRANOLA
GRANULE
GRAPPLE
GREATLY
GRIDDLE
GRISTLE
GRISTLY
GRIZZLE
GRIZZLY
GROCKLE
GROSSLY
GRUFFLY
GRUMBLE
GUNWALE
HAGBOLT
HALLALI
HANDILY
HAPPILY
HARSHLY
HASTILY
HEAVILY
HERSELF
HIMSELF
HOLDALL
HOSTILE
HUMANLY
HUSKILY
IDEALLY
IGNOBLE
INBUILT
INFIELD
INKWELL
INSTALL
INSTILL
ISMAILI
ISRAELI
JAVELLE
JERKILY
JOINTLY
KAMPALA
KENNELS
KEYHOLE
KNOBBLE
KNOBBLY
KNOWALL
KNUCKLE
LAMELLA
LARGELY
LAURELS
LEGALLY
LEGIBLE
LEGIBLY
LEGPULL
LENTILS
LEOPOLD
LIGHTLY
LINCOLN
LITHELY
LOCALLY
LOFTILY
LOOSELY
LOVABLE
LOYALLY
LUCIDLY
LUCKILY
LUGHOLE
LURIDLY
LUSTILY
MAMILLA
MANACLE
MANDALA
MANGOLD
MANHOLE
MANILLA
MARSALA
MARVELL
MAXILLA
MAXWELL
MAYPOLE
MEDULLA
MENFOLK
MERRILY
MESSILY
METALLY
MIRACLE
MISERLY
MISRULE
MISSILE
MONOCLE
MONOPLY
MONTHLY
MOODILY
MORALLY
MORELLO
MORRELL
MORTALS
MOSELLE
MOUILLÉ
MOVABLE
MURILLO
MUSSELS
MUTABLE
MYCELLA
NACELLE
NAIVELY
NAKEDLY
NASALLY
NASTILY
NETBALL
NEVILLE
NEWBOLT
NIGELLA
NIGHTLY
NITRILE
NOISILY
NORFOLK
NOTABLE
NOTABLY
NOVELLA
NOVELLO
OCTUPLE
ODDBALL
OMPHALE
ONESELF
ORDERLY
OSMANLI
OSSICLE
OSTIOLE
OTHELLO
OUTFALL
OVERALL
PANICLE
PANOPLY
PANTILE
PAPILLA
PARABLE
PARNELL
PATELLA
PATIBLE
PAYABLE
PAYROLL
PEDICLE
PENSILE
PERCALE
PERGOLA
PETIOLE
PIANOLA
PICCOLO
PIEBALD
PINBALL
PINFOLD
PINHOLE
PINNULA
PIOUSLY
PISTOLE
PITFALL
PITHILY
PLAINLY
PLIABLE
PLUMULE
POTABLE
POTHOLE
PRATTLE
PRICKLE
PRICKLY
PRIMULA
PROFILE
PROUDLY
PUCELLE
PUERILE
PURCELL
PUSTULE
QUEENLY
QUIBBLE
QUICKLY
QUIETLY
RADICLE
RAPIDLY
RAVIOLI
READILY
REBUILD
RECYCLE
REDPOLL
REGALLY
REMOULD
REPTILE
RETICLE
RIGHTLY
RIGIDLY
RISIBLE
RISKILY
RISSOLE
ROCKALL
ROSELLA
ROSELLE
ROSEOLA
ROUAULT
ROUGHLY
ROUNDLY
ROWDILY
ROYALLY
RUBELLA
RUBEOLA
RUMPOLE
RUSSELL
SAINTLY
SALABLE
SANDALS
SAUCILY
SAWBILL
SAWMILL
SCAFELL
SCAMBLE
SCAPULA
SCHNELL
SCRUPLE
SCUFFLE
SCUTTLE
SEAGULL
SEATTLE
SEAWALL
SEQUELA
SERVILE
SESSILE
SEVILLE
SHACKLE
SHAKILY
SHAMBLE
SHAPELY
SHARPLY
SHINGLE
SHINGLY
SHORTLY
SHOWILY
SHRILLY
SHUFFLE
SHUTTLE
SINHALA
SITWELL
SIZABLE
SKIFFLE
SKITTLE
SLACKLY
SLEEKLY
SMARTLY
SMICKLY
SMUGGLE
SNAFFLE
SNIFFLE
SNORTLE
SNUFFLE
SNUGGLE
SOBERLY
SOLIDLY
SOLUBLE
SOUFFLE
SOUNDLY
SPANGLE
SPARKLE
SPATULA
SPECKLE
SPICULA
SPINDLE
SPINDLY
SPITTLE
SPYHOLE
SQUALLY
STADDLE
STARKLY
STARTLE
STATELY
STEEPLE
STEEPLY
STERILE
STERNLY
STICKLE
STIFFLY
STIPPLE
STONILY
STOUTLY
STUBBLE
STUBBLY
STUMBLE
SUAVELY
SUFFOLK
SULKILY
SUNNILY
SWADDLE
SWAHILI
SWEETLY
SWIFTLY
SWINDLE
SWINGLE
SWIZZLE
SYSTOLE
TACITLY
TACTILE
TADPOLE
TARDILY
TASSILI
TAXABLE
TENABLE
TENFOLD
TENSELY
TENSILE
TEQUILA
TERSELY
TESTILY
TEXTILE
THICKLY
THIMBLE
THIRDLY
THISTLE
THYSELF
TIEPOLO
TIGHTLY
TIMBALE
TIMIDLY
TIPSILY
TOEHOLD
TOMBOLA
TORTILE
TOTALLY
TRAMPLE
TREACLE
TREACLY
TREADLE
TREMBLE
TREMBLY
TREMOLO
TRESTLE
TRICKLE
TRINGLE
TRIPOLI
TRITELY
TROUBLE
TRUCKLE
TRUFFLE
TRUNDLE
TUNABLE
TWADDLE
TWEEDLE
TWIDDLE
TWIDDLY
TWINKLE
TWOFOLD
TYNWALD
UCCELLO
UKULELE
UNGODLY
USUALLY
UTRICLE
UTRILLO

UTTERLY
VACUOLE
VAGUELY
VANDALS
VANILLA
VARIOLA
VEHICLE
VESICLE
VIRGULE
VISIBLE
VISIBLY
VISTULA
VITALLY
VIVIDLY
VOCALLY
VOLUBLE
VOLUBLY
WALPOLE
WAXBILL
WAYBILL
WEARILY
WEIGELA
WEIRDLY
WENDELL
WHEEDLE
WHISTLE
WHITTLE
WOMANLY
WORDILY
WORLDLY
WRANGLE
WRESTLE
WRIGGLE
WRINKLE
WRINKLY
WRONGLY
WRYBILL
ACADEME
ACADEMY
ADENOMA
ALABAMA
ALCHEMY
ANATOMY
ANGIOMA
AWESOME
BEDTIME
BETHUMB
CHIASMA
CONDEMN
CONSUME
CONTEMN
COSTUME
COULOMB
COXCOMB
CURCUMA
CUSTOMS
DAYTIME
DILEMMA
DIORAMA
DIPLOMA
DODGEMS
DRACHMA
ECONOMY
EMPYEMA
ENDGAME
EPITOME
EXOGAMY
EXTREME
FIBROMA
FOGLAMP
FULSOME
GAUTAMA
GRANDMA
INFLAME
IRKSOME
JIMJAMS
LAKSHMI
LEUCOMA
LISSOME
MACRAMÉ
MAHATMA
MAREMMA
MESEEMS
MISTIME
MUGWUMP
MYELOMA
NEWCOME
NOISOME
ONETIME
ORIGAMI
OSTEOMA
OUTCOME
PALERMO
PASTIME
PERFUME
PHONEME
PLEROMA
PRELIMS
PRESUME
PROXIMO
PTOLEMY
RAGTIME
RHIZOME
SALERMO
SARCOMA
SASHIMI
SATSUMA
SCRUMMY
SUBLIME
SUBSUME
SUCCUMB
SUNLAMP
SUPREME
SUPREMO
SURNAME
TEATIME
TRIREME
TRITOMA
TSUNAMI
TWOSOME
TWOTIME
VENDOME
WARTIME
WELCOME
WINSOME
ZOOTOMY
ABALONE
ABIDING
ABJOINT
ABSCOND
ACCOUNT
ACETONE
ACHTUNG
ADAMANT
ADELINE
ADJOINT
ADORING
AFFRONT
AFGHANI
AGELONG
AGROUND
AILMENT
AIRLINE
ALANINE
ALEPINE
ALICANT
ALIMENT
ALIMONY
ALTHING
ALUMINA
AMAZING
AMBIENT
AMBOYNA
AMERIND
AMUSING
ANCIENT
ANEMONE
ANGLING
ANILINE
ANODYNE
ANTENNA
ANTHONY
APPOINT
ARACHNE
ARETINO
ARIADNE
ARIZONA
ARMBAND
ASININE
ASTOUND
ATTAINT
AUGMENT
BACKING
BALCONY
BALDING
BAMBINO
BANGING
BANKING
BARKING
BARRING
BASKING
BATHING
BATTING
BEADING
BEAMING
BEARING
BEATING
BEDDING
BEELINE
BEGGING
BEIJING
BELLINI
BENDING
BENZENE
BENZINE
BERLINE
BERNINI
BETHINK
BETTING
BIDDING
BILTONG
BINDING
BIPLANE
BLATANT
BLAZING
BOATING
BOILING
BOLOGNA
BOMBING
BOOKING
BOOMING
BOWLING
BRACING
BRAKING
BREWING
BRIGAND
BRITONS
BROMINE
BUDDING
BUGGING
BUGGINS
BULGING
BUNTING
BUOYANT
BURKINA
BURNING
BUSKINS
BUSSING
BUTTONS
CABLING
CAIRENE
CALCINE
CALLING
CALUMNY
CAMPANA
CAMPING
CANNING
CARBINE
CARMINE
CARVING
CASTING
CATKINS
CATLING
CATMINT
CAYENNE
CEILING
CELLINI
CÉZANNE
CHAFING
CHALONE
CHASING
CHEWING
CHICANE
CHICANO
CHOKING
CHOPINE
CITRINE
CLEMENT
CLOSING
CLOYING
COATING
COCAINE
CODEINE
CODLING
COLOGNE
COLUMNS
COMBINE
COMBING
COMMAND
COMMEND
COMMENT
COMMONS
COMMUNE
COMPANY
CONDONE
CONFINE
CONSENT
CONTEND
CONTENT
CONVENE
CONVENT
COOKING
COOLANT
COOLING
COPLAND
COPYING
CORKING
CORTINA
CORUNNA
COSTING
COTTONY
COULDNT
COUPONS
COUSINS
COWHAND
COWLING
CRAVING
CROWING
CUCKING
CUISINE
CUNNING
CURLING
CURRANT
CURRENT
CUTTING
CYCLING
CYCLONE
DAMNING
DAMPING
DANCING
DARLING
DARNING
DASHING
DEALING
DECLINE
DEFIANT
DEMESNE
DENTINE
DERWENT
DESCANT
DESCEND
DESCENT
DESMOND
DESPOND
DESTINE
DESTINY
DEVIANT
DIALING
DIAMINE
DIAMOND
DICKENS
DIETINE
DIGGING
DILUENT
DINMONT
DISBAND
DISSENT
DISTANT
DISTEND
DISTENT
DITTANY
DOCKING
DOGGONE
DOMAINE
DORKING
DORMANT
DOWLAND
DOWSING
DRAWING
DRIVING
DUBBING
DUCKING
DUSTING
EARRING
ECCRINE
ECHIDNA
ELEGANT
ELEMENT
EMINENT
ENCHANT
ENGLAND
ENPRINT
ENSUING
ENTRANT
ENTWINE
EPERGNE
EPICENE
EPIGONE
ETCHING
EUPHONY
EVENING
EVIDENT
EXAMINE
EXIGENT
EXITING
EXPOUND
FAILING
FAIRING
FALLING
FANZINE
FARMING
FASTING
FAWNING
FEEDING
FEELING
FENCING
FENLAND
FERMENT
FERVENT
FIGMENT
FILLING
FILMING
FINDING
FINLAND
FIRCONE
FISHING
FITMENT
FITTING
FLAMING
FLEEING
FLEMING
FLOWING
FOLDING
FONDANT
FOOTING
FORFEND
FORGONE
FORMING
FORTUNE
FULGENT
FUNDING
FURLONG
GALLANT
GALLING
GALLONS
GARDENS
GARLAND
GARMENT
GARONNE
GASCONY
GASPING
GATLING
GEARING
GEELONG
GEHENNA
GELDING
GENUINE

GERAINT
GERMANE
GERMANY
GETTING
GIBBONS
GILDING
GINSENG
GLARING
GLAZING
GLIDING
GLOWING
GNAWING
GODSEND
GOLDING
GOLDONI
GOLFING
GOSLING
GRATING
GRAZING
GRIMOND
GROWING
GUARANA
GUARANI
GUBBINS
GUIDING
GUSHING
HACKING
HALTING
HANGING
HARMONY
HATBAND
HEADING
HEALING
HEARING
HEATING
HEAVENS
HEDGING
HELLENE
HELPING
HEMLINE
HENBANE
HEPTANE
HEROINE
HERRING
HIGGINS
HILDING
HISPANO
HISSING
HOBSONS
HOGGING
HOLDING
HOLLAND
HOPKINS
HOPPING
HORMONE
HORSING
HOSANNA
HOTLINE
HOUDINI
HOUSING
HOWLING
HULKING
HUMMING
HUNTING
HURLING
HUSBAND
HYALINE
HYDRANT
HYGIENE
ICELAND
IKEBANA
IMAGINE
IMAGING
IMPLANT
IMPOUND
IMPRINT
INCLINE
INCONNU
INDIANA
INFERNO
INKLING
INSTANT
INTERNE
IRELAND
IRONING
ISOTONE
ISSUANT
ITCHING
JAMMING
JAMPANI
JASMINE
JAWBONE
JEERING
JENKINS
JESTING
JOBBING
JOGGING
JOINING
JUGGINS
JUGLANS
JUMPING
JUTLAND
KAMPONG
KATRINE
KEELING
KEEPING
KENNING
KICKING
KILLING
KIPLING
KISSING
KNOWING
KRISHNA
LACKING
LAGGING
LALLANS
LAMBENT
LAMBING
LANCING
LANDING
LANTANA
LAPPING
LAPSANG
LAPWING
LARCENY
LASAGNA
LASAGNE
LASHING
LASTING
LATRINE
LEADING
LEANING
LEAPING
LEASING
LEAVING
LEGGING
LEGIONS
LEMMING
LENDING
LENIENT
LEONINE
LESSING
LETTING
LEUCINE
LICKING
LILTING
LINDANE
LINKING
LINSANG
LISTING
LODGING
LOGGING
LONGING
LOOKING
LOOMING
LOOTING
LORDING
LOURING
LOWLAND
LUCARNE
LUCERNE
LURKING
LUTYENS
MACHINE
MADONNA
MAHJONG
MAILING
MALLING
MANHUNT
MANKIND
MANNING
MAPPING
MARCONI
MARKING
MARLENE
MARLINE
MARTENS
MARTINI
MASSINE
MATTING
MATTINS
MEANING
MEETING
MELTING
MENDING
MESSINA
METHANE
METHINK
MIDLAND
MIGRANT
MILKING
MILLING
MINCING
MINUEND
MIOCENE
MISSING
MITTENS
MOANING
MOCKING
MOLDING
MONTANA
MONTANT
MOONING
MOORING
MOPPING
MORAINE
MORDANT
MORLAND
MORNING
MUGGING
MUNDANE
MURAENA
MUSTANG
MYELINE
NAGGING
NAPPING
NASCENT
NATIONS
NEARING
NECKING
NEPTUNE
NETTING
NEURINE
NEURONE
NIRVANA
NODDING
NOGGING
NOTHING
NOTIONS
NURSING
NUTTING
OBSCENE
OCARINA
ODDMENT
ODORANT
OFFHAND
OLEFINE
ONGOING
OPALINE
OPENING
OPERAND
OPERANT
OPULENT
OREGANO
ORIGINS
ORLEANS
OROTUND
OSBORNE
OUTLINE
OUTRANK
PACKING
PADDING
PADRONE
PAGEANT
PAIRING
PARKING
PARTING
PARVENU
PASSANT
PASSING
PATIENT
PAULINE
PAYMENT
PEASANT
PECCANT
PECKING
PEELING
PEEPING
PEERING
PELTING
PENDANT
PENDING
PENNANT
PENNINE
PENTANE
PEPSINE
PERCENT
PERSONA
PERSONS
PHALANX
PHARYNX
PICKING
PIGEONS
PIGLING
PIGMENT
PIMPING
PIQUANT
PISCINA
PISCINE
PLACING
PLAYING
POLLING
PONTINE
POPPING
PORCINE
PORTEND
PORTENT
POSTING
POTTING
POULENC
PRALINE
PRAYING
PREBEND
PRESENT
PRETEND
PREVENT
PRIMING
PROFANE
PROGENY
PROLONG
PROPANE
PROPEND
PROVING
PRUDENT
PUCCINI
PUDDING
PULSING
PUNGENT
PUNTING
PURLINE
PUSHING
PUTTING
QUAKING
QUININE
QUINONE
RACKING
RADIANT
RAFTING
RAILING
RAIMENT
RAISING
RAMPANT
RANKING
RANTING
RATIONS
RATLINE
READING
REAGENT
REARING
REBOUND
RECLINE
RECOUNT
REDOUND
REEKING
REELING
REGNANT
RELIANT
REMAINS
REMNANT
REMOUNT
REPAINT
REPLANT
REPRINT
RESCIND
RESIANT
RESOUND
RESPOND
RESTING
RETAINS
RETHINK
RETSINA
RETURNS
RHYMING
RIBBING
RIGGING
RINGING
RIOTING
RIPPING
ROAMING
ROARING
ROCKING
ROLLING
ROMAINE
ROOFING
ROOTING
ROSSINI
ROSTAND
ROTTING
ROUSING
ROUTINE
RUBBING
RUNNING
RUSHING
RUTHENE
RUTTING
SABRINA
SACKING
SAILING
SALIENT
SALPINX
SALTING
SAPIENS
SAPIENT
SAPLING
SARDANA
SARDINE
SARGENT
SARMENT
SAVANNA
SCALENE
SCARING
SCORING
SCRAWNY
SEALANT
SEALINK
SEARING
SEATING
SEEMING
SEGMENT
SELLING
SERPENS
SERPENT
SERVANT
SERVING
SESTINA
SESTINE
SETTING
SEXTANT
SHADING
SHAKING
SHAPING
SHARING
SHAVING
SHEBANG
SHINING
SHOWING
SIBLING

SIDDONS
SIEMENS
SIFTING
SIGNING
SINGING
SINKING
SIPPING
SISTINE
SITTING
SKATING
SKYLINE
SLAYING
SLIDING
SLOPING
SLOVENE
SLOWING
SMETANA
SMILING
SMOKING
SNORING
SOAKING
SOARING
SOCKING
SOLVENT
SOMEONE
SOPPING
SOPRANO
SORTING
SOUTANE
SPACING
SPARING
SPAVINE
SPRAINT
STAGING
STAMINA
STARING
STAYING
STEVENS
STEWING
STIPEND
STUDENT
STYLING
SUBTEND
SULTANA
SUMMING
SUMMONS
SURFING
SUSANNA
SUSPEND
SWAYING
TALKING
TAMMANY
TANGENT
TANNING
TAPPING
TARTINE
TATIANA
TATTING
TAURINE
TAVERNA
TEARING
TEASING
TEEMING
TELLING
TENSING
TERRENE
TERRINE
TESTING
TICKING
TIFFANY
TIMPANI
TIPPING
TOLUENE
TONTINE
TOOLING
TOPPING
TORMENT
TORRENT
TOTIENT
TOURING
TOWLINE
TRACING
TRADING
TREPANG
TRIBUNE
TRIDENT
TSARINA
TSIGANE
TSIGANY
TURBINE
TURENNE
TURGENT
TURNING
TUSCANY
TYMPANO
TYMPANY
TYRANNY
TZARINA
UGOLINO
UKRAINE
ULULANT
UNBOUND
UNCANNY
UNDOING
UNDYING
UNGUENT
UNSOUND
UNTWINE
UNWOUND
UPSWING
UTERINE
VACCINE
VAGRANT
VALIANT
VARIANT
VARMINT
VARYING
VENDING
VERBENA
VERDANT
VERMONT
VERSANT
VETTING
VIBRANT
VINCENT
VIOLENT
VOLCANO
VULPINE
WADDING
WAFTING
WAILING
WAITING
WALKING
WANTING
WAPPING
WARLING
WARMING
WARNING
WARRANT
WARRING
WASHING
WASTING
WAXWING
WAYLAND
WEAPONS
WEARING
WEAVING
WEBBING
WEDDING
WEEKEND
WEEPING
WELDING
WETLAND
WETTING
WHALING
WHITING
WIGGING
WILLING
WINDING
WINNING
WISHING
WORDING
WORKING
WOULDNT
WRITING
WYOMING
YAWNING
ZEALAND
ZETLAND
ZOFFANY
ABANDON
ABETTOR
ABLATOR
ACHERON
ACHESON
ACTAEON
ADAPTOR
ADDISON
ADVISOR
AEROSOL
AGISTOR
AILERON
AIRFLOW
AIRSTOP
ALCOHOL
ALENÇON
ALIQUOT
ANDIRON
APRICOT
APROPOS
AQUILON
ATISHOO
ATTABOY
AUCTION
AUDITOR
AUDUBON
AVIATOR
AVIGNON
BABYLON
BACKLOG
BAGEHOT
BALATON
BALLBOY
BALLIOL
BALLOON
BANDBOX
BANGKOK
BASSOON
BASTION
BEDROOM
BELABOR
BELLBOY
BELLHOP
BENISON
BENTHOS
BERGSON
BIBELOT
BIGFOOT
BIGSHOT
BILLION
BLOSSOM
BLOUSON
BOLSHOI
BOREDOM
BOURBON
BOURDON
BOWSHOT
BOXROOM
BOYHOOD
BRISTOL
BRIXTON
BUFFOON
BUGABOO
BULLDOG
BULLION
BUNDOOK
BURGEON
CAEDMON
CAISSON
CALDRON
CALLBOX
CALLBOY
CALTROP
CAMELOT
CAMERON
CAMPHOR
CAMPION
CAPITOL
CAPTION
CARADOC
CARDOON
CARIBOU
CARRION
CARTOON
CASHBOX
CATALOG
CATELOG
CAUTION
CELADON
CESSION
CHANSON
CHARIOT
CHARPOY
CHEKHOV
CHEROOT
CHEVIOT
CHEVRON
CHIFFON
CHIGNON
CHILLON
CHINOOK
CHORION
CHRISOM
CLARION
CLOISON
COITION
CONTROL
COPILOT
CORNCOB
CORYDON
CRAMPON
CREATOR
CRIMSON
CROUTON
CRYPTON
CURATOR
CUSHION
CYPRIOT
DAGWOOD
DASHPOT
DAYBOOK
DEMIGOD
DENDRON
DESTROY
DEVELOP
DEWDROP
DICTION
DIDEROT
DIDICOY
DILATOR
DISAVOW
DIVISOR
DOGFOOD
DOGWOOD
DRAGOON
DUDGEON
DUKEDOM
DUNGEON
EARLDOM
EARSHOT
ECHELON
ECUADOR
EDITION
EJECTOR
ELATION
ELEANOR
ELECTOR
ELISION
EMERSON
EMOTION
EMPEROR
ENACTOR
ENTERON
ENVELOP
ENVENOM
EPIZOON
EPSILON
EQUATOR
EQUINOX
ERECTOR
EROSION
ESCALOP
ETHANOL
EVASION
EYEBROW
EYESHOT
FACTION
FASHION
FENELON
FESTOON
FICTION
FIREDOG
FISSION
FLEURON
FLUMMOX
FOXTROT
FREEDOM
FRISSON
FUSEBOX
GADROON
GALIPOT
GALLEON
GANELON
GASOHOL
GASTHOF
GEARBOX
GLASGOW
GLENCOE
GLUTTON
GODUNOV
GRIFFON
GRYPHON
GUDGEON
GUIGNOL
GUMBOOT
GUMDROP
GUMSHOE
GUNROOM
GUNSHOT
HALCYON
HANGDOG
HARDTOP
HARICOT
HARPOON
HARWOOD
HAUTBOY
HELICON
HELLION
HEXAGON
HEXAPOD
HILLTOP
HONITON
HORIZON
HOTFOOT
HOTSHOT
HUMIDOR
ICEFLOE
ICHABOD
INCISOR
IVANHOE
JACKPOT
JACKSON
JAMESON
JANITOR
JOGTROT
JOHNSON
JUKEBOX
JURYBOX
KEARTON
KILLJOY
KINGDOM
KNOWHOW
KOLKHOZ
KOWLOON
KRYPTON
LAMPOON
LANGTON
LANGUOR
LAOCOON
LARDOON
LEBANON
LEGROOM
LEXICON
LIAISON
LOGBOOK
LOGWOOD
LONGBOW
LOWBROW
MACEDON
MADISON
MAGINOT
MAILBOX
MANDIOC
MANHOOD
MANIHOC
MANITOU
MANSION

MARABOU
MARIBOU
MARMION
MATADOR
MATELOT
MEGARON
MEGATON
MENTHOL
MENTION
MILKSOP
MILLION
MIRADOR
MISSION
MISTOOK
MOELLON
MOLOTOV
MONITOR
MONOLOG
MONSOON
MOUFLON
MULLION
NABOKOV
NEUTRON
NEWSBOY
NONSTOP
OBLIGOR
OCTAGON
OCTOPOD
OMICRON
OPINION
ORATION
OUTCROP
OUTDOOR
OUTFLOW
OUTGROW
OUTLOOK
OUTSHOT
OVATION
PAGEBOY
PARADOR
PARADOS
PARADOX
PARAGON
PARASOL
PASSION
PATRIOT
PENSION
PHAETON
PHANTOM
PHARAOH
PICADOR
PIDGEON
PIERROT
PILLBOX
PILLION
PLATOON
PLAYBOY
PLESSOR
PLEURON
PLYWOOD
POLYGON
POLYPOD
POMEROL
POMEROY
POMPOON
PONTOON
PORTHOS
PORTION
POSTBOX
POTSHOT
PRAETOR
PREDOOM
PROCTOR
PRONAOS
RACCOON
RAINBOW
RANGOON
REACTOR
REALTOR
REDWOOD
REPROOF
REREDOS
REUNION
ROADHOG
ROBESON
ROLLMOP
ROMANOV
ROOFTOP
ROTATOR
RUBICON
RUNNION
SABAYON
SAFFRON
SANDBOX
SANDBOY
SAPWOOD
SASSOON
SAVELOY
SCALLOP
SCISSOR
SCOLLOP
SEAFOOD
SEALION
SECTION
SENATOR
SERFDOM
SESSION
SHADOOF
SHALLOT
SHALLOW
SHAMPOO
SHANNON
SHIPTON
SILICON
SIMENON
SIMPLON
SIMPSON
SJAMBOK
SNOWDON
SOAPBOX
SOLOMON
SOMEHOW
SOURSOP
SOVKHOZ
SPARROW
SPONSON
SPONSOR
SQUALOR
STARDOM
STATION
STENTOR
STEPSON
STETSON
STILTON
STRIDOR
SUBATOM
SUCTION
SUNROOF
SUNSPOT
SURGEON
SWALLOW
SYMPTOM
TAGALOG
TALIPOT
TALLBOY
TAMPION
TAPROOT
TEAROOM
TEASHOP
TENSION
TERSION
THERMOS
THOMSON
THRENOS
TOLSTOY
TOMFOOL
TOMPION
TOOLBOX
TOPKNOT
TORCHON
TORSION
TOSSPOT
TOYSHOP
TRACTOR
TRAITOR
TRANSOM
TREASON
TREETOP
TRIANON
TROLLOP
TUITION
TYPHOON
UNBOSOM
UNCTION
UPSHOOT
UPSILON
VENISON
VERSION
VICEROY
VISITOR
VITRIOL
WALLOON
WARRIOR
WARTHOG
WHARTON
WHATNOT
WHITLOW
WICKLOW
WIDGEON
WINDROW
WINDSOR
WINSTON
WITLOOF
WORKTOP
XANTHOS
YPSILON
ZILLION
AGRIPPA
APOCOPE
ATTEMPT
BAGPIPE
CATALPA
CONCEPT
CORRUPT
CYCLOPS
DECRYPT
DIGLYPH
DIGRAPH
DISRUPT
EPITAPH
EUTERPE
EXCERPT
FORCEPS
GALUMPH
GESTAPO
GOSSIPY
GRANDPA
GUYROPE
INSCAPE
ISOTOPE
LACEUPS
LIMPOPO
MAZEPPA
PERCEPT
PERHAPS
PRECEPT
PREEMPT
RECEIPT
RESHAPE
RUDOLPH
SATRAPY
SCHLEPP
SCRAPPY
SCRUMPY
SHRIMPS
STROPPY
SYNCOPE
THERAPY
TOPKAPI
TRICEPS
TRIUMPH
UNHAPPY
UNKEMPT
ABELARD
ACIFORM
ACQUIRE
ACTUARY
ADJOURN
AFFAIRS
AIRPORT
ALDABRA
ALGEBRA
ALGIERS
ALLEGRI
ALLEGRO
AMATORY
AMPHORA
ANDORRA
ANTLERS
ANTWERP
ANYMORE
ARCHERY
ARMOURY
ARREARS
ARTWORK
ATHWART
AUSTERE
AVEBURY
AWKWARD
BANBURY
BARBARA
BARBARY
BARKERS
BASTARD
BATHERS
BATTERY
BEDFORD
BEDSORE
BEGGARY
BEGORRA
BERNARD
BERSERK
BIGHORN
BIGOTRY
BINDERY
BISTORT
BITTERN
BITTERS
BIZARRE
BLAZERS
BOLLARD
BOMBARD
BONFIRE
BONKERS
BONNARD
BORDERS
BRASERO
BRAVERY
BRAVURA
BREWERY
BRIBERY
BROKERS
BULWARK
BURSARY
BUSTARD
BUTTERY
BUZZARD
CAESURA
CALDERA
CALIBRE
CALVARY
CAMORRA
CAMPARI
CANNERY
CANONRY
CAPTURE
CAREERS
CARPORT
CASCARA
CATARRH
CAUTERY
CAVALRY
CAVIARE
CENSURE
CENTURY
CHAMBRÉ
CHANCRE
CHICORY
CHIMERA
CHOLERA
CINDERS
CISTERN
CITHARA
CLOSURE
CLOTURE
COFFERS
COLIBRI
COLLARD
COLOURS
COMFORT
COMPARE
COMPERE
COMPORT
CONAKRY
CONCERN
CONCERT
CONCORD
CONFIRM
CONFORM
CONJURE
CONSORT
CONTORT
CONVERT
COOKERY
COPPERS
COSTARD
COUNTRY
COUTURE
COWGIRL
COWHERD
CULTURE
CULVERT
CURSORY
CUSTARD
CUTLERY
CUTTERS
CUTWORM
DAGGERS
DASTARD
DAYMARK
DEANERY
DECLARE
DEEPFRY
DEIRDRE
DENMARK
DENTURE
DEPLORE
DESSERT
DEVILRY
DIEHARD
DIETARY
DIOPTRE
DIPTERA
DISBARK
DISCARD
DISCERN
DISCORD
DISPORT
DISTORT
DISTURB
DITHERY
DOCTORS
DODDERY
DOGCART
DOLLARS
DRAPERY
DRAWERS
DRIVERS
DULLARD
DUNKIRK
EARMARK
EASTERN
ELECTRA
ELECTRO
ELUSORY
ENQUIRE
ENQUIRY
ENSNARE
ENSNARL
EPHEDRA
EPICARP
EPICURE
EQUERRY
ERASURE
ESQUIRE
ESTUARY
ETAGÈRE
EXHEDRA
EXPLORE
EYESORE
FACTORS
FACTORY
FAILURE
FANFARE
FARMERS
FEATURE
FETTERS

FILBERT
FINGERS
FIREARM
FISHERY
FISSURE
FIXTURE
FLOWERS
FLOWERY
FOGHORN
FOREARM
FORGERY
FORLORN
FORWARD
FOULARD
FOUNDRY
FULLERS
GAITERS
GALLERY
GARBURE
GASFIRE
GERBERA
GESTURE
GILBERT
GIZZARD
GOLIARD
GOMORRA
GRANARY
GRAVURE
GREGORY
GROCERS
GROCERY
GRUYÈRE
GUNFIRE
GUNNERA
GUNNERY
HACHURE
HACKERY
HAGGARD
HAGGERY
HALBERD
HALBERT
HALYARD
HANSARD
HARVARD
HAYWARD
HAYWIRE
HECTARE
HERBERT
HERBERY
HETAERA
HICKORY
HISTORY
HOMBURG
HONOURS
HORRORS
HOSIERY
HUBBARD
HUNGARY
HUNKERS
HUSSARS
ICEBERG
IMAGERY
IMPLORE
INBOARD
INDOORS
INQUIRE
INQUIRY
INSHORE
INSPIRE
ISADORA
ISODORE
ISOMERE
JAGGERY
JANKERS
JANUARY
JEEPERS
JEWELRY
JITTERS
JITTERY
JOBBERY
JOINERY
KEYWORD
KILDARE
KILVERT
KINTYRE
KIPPERS
KITHARA
KNAVERY
LAETARE
LAGGARD
LAMBERT
LANCERS
LANTERN
LANYARD
LAUNDRY
LAWYERS
LEADERS
LECHERY
LECTERN
LECTURE
LEEWARD
LEGWORK
LEISURE
LEMPIRA
LEONARD
LEOPARD
LEOTARD
LETTERS
LIBRARY
LINACRE
LOLLARD
LOTTERY
LUGWORM
MACABRE
MADEIRA
MAESTRO
MAGUIRE
MALLARD
MAMMARY
MANNERS
MANSARD
MARBURG
MARGERY
MARMARA
MARTYRS
MASCARA
MASONRY
MASTERS
MASTERY
MATTERS
MEASURE
MEMBERS
MEMOIRS
MERCERY
MERCURY
MIDTERM
MIMICRY
MISFIRE
MIXTURE
MOCKERS
MOCKERY
MOIDORE
MOLIÈRE
MONTERO
MOTHERS
MUDLARK
MUGWORT
MUMMERS
MUMMERY
MUSTARD
MYSTERY
NAVARRE
NECTARY
NERVURE
NETWORK
NEWBORN
NEWBURY
NIAGARA
NIGGARD
NIPPERS
NOWHERE
NUMBERS
NUMMARY
NUNNERY
NURSERY
NURTURE
OBSCURA
OBSCURE
ONSHORE
ORATORY
ORCHARD
OSSUARY
OUTDARE
OUTTURN
OUTWARD
OUTWORK
OUTWORN
OVERARM
PALMYRA
PANDORA
PASTERN
PASTURE
PATTERN
PECCARY
PEPPERS
PEPPERY
PEREIRA
PERFORM
PERJURE
PERJURY
PERTURB
PERVERT
PESSARY
PHILTRE
PIASTRE
PICTURE
PIGGERY
PILLORY
PINCERS
PIZARRO
PLACARD
PLANURY
PLAYERS
PLENARY
POCHARD
PODAGRA
POLLARD
POMMARD
PONIARD
POPCORN
POSTERN
POSTURE
POTHERB
POTTERY
POULTRY
POWDERY
PREPARE
PRIMARY
PROCURE
PROVERB
PURPORT
PURPURA
RAEBURN
RAGWORT
RAMPART
RAPPORT
RAPTURE
RECTORY
REENTRY
REMARRY
REPAIRS
REQUIRE
RESPIRE
RESTART
RESTORE
REVELRY
REYNARD
RHUBARB
RICHARD
RINGERS
RIOTERS
RIPCORD
RIVALRY
RIVIERA
ROBBERS
ROBBERY
ROCKERY
ROGUERY
ROLLERS
ROMPERS
RONSARD
ROOKERY
ROZZERS
RUBBERS
RUBBERY
RUNCORN
RUNNERS
RUPTURE
SAILORS
SALIERI
SALTIRE
SAPPERS
SAQQARA
SAVOURY
SAXHORN
SCENERY
SCEPTRE
SCUTARI
SEABIRD
SEAPORT
SEEKERS
SEIZURE
SELKIRK
SELLERS
SENSORY
SHAKERS
SHASTRI
SHIKARI
SHIVERS
SHIVERY
SHOWERS
SHOWERY
SICKERT
SIEVERT
SIGNORA
SIGNORI
SILVERY
SINATRA
SINCERE
SISTERS
SKYLARK
SKYWARD
SLAVERY
SOCOTRA
SOJOURN
SORCERY
SPECTRE
SPIDERS
SPIDERY
SQUEERS
STATURE
STEWARD
STIRFRY
SUBVERT
SUBZERO
SUMATRA
SUMMARY
SUMMERY
SUNBURN
SUPPORT
SURGERY
TAILORS
TANAGRA
TANKARD
TANNERY
TANTARA
TARTARE
TARTARY
TATTERS
TELFORD
TEMPERA
TEMPURA
TESSERA
TEXTURE
THEATRE
TILBURY
TIMBERS
TINTERN
TIPCART
TONSURE
TOPIARY
TORTURE
TOTTERY
TRACERY
TURBARY
TURNERY
TUSSORE
UNAWARE
UNHEARD
UNICORN
UNIFORM
UNITARY
UNSNARL
UPSTART
URETHRA
URINARY
VAMPIRE
VAPOURS
VELOURS
VENTURE
VERDURE
VESPERS
VICTORY
VISCERA
VULTURE
WARBURG
WARFARE
WARLORD
WASHERS
WAXWORK
WAYMARK
WAYWARD
WELFARE
WESTERN
WITHERS
WONDERS
WOOMERA
WORKERS
YARDARM
YOGHURT
YONKERS
ZEDOARY
ZINGARO
ABOLISH
ABREAST
ABSCESS
ACCURSE
ACTRESS
ADDRESS
ADIPOSE
ADVERSE
AGAINST
AGELESS
AGGRESS
AGONIST
AIMLESS
AIRBASE
AIRLESS
ALECOST
ALFONSO
AMBROSE
AMONGST
AMORIST
AMOROSO
AMYLASE
ANALYST
ANGUISH
ANIMIST
APPEASE
APTNESS
ARMREST
ARTLESS
ATAVISM
ATHEISM
ATHEIST
ATHIRST
ATOMIST
AUSLESE
AUTOPSY
BABOOSH
BABYISH
BADNESS
BAGASSE
BALLAST
BAPTISM
BAPTIST
BEARISH
BECAUSE
BEDPOST
BEQUEST
BIOMASS
BLEMISH
BOMBAST
BOOKISH
BOORISH
BRITISH
BRUTISH

BUGLOSS
BULLISH
BULRUSH
BURGESS
BURMESE
BURNISH
CABOOSE
CADDISH
CALYPSO
CANVASS
CARCASE
CARCASS
CAROUSE
CASEASE
CASUISM
CASUIST
CATFISH
CATTISH
CELLIST
CHEMISE
CHEMIST
CHERISH
CHINESE
CIRROSE
CLEANSE
COEXIST
COMPASS
COMPOSE
COMPOST
CONCISE
CONCUSS
CONFESS
CONFUSE
CONSIST
CONTEST
COPYIST
CORNISH
COXLESS
COYNESS
CUIRASS
CUTLASS
CYCLIST
CYPRESS
DADAISM
DADAIST
DEAREST
DEBUSSY
DECEASE
DEFENSE
DEFROST
DEGAUSS
DELOUSE
DENTIST
DEPRESS
DERVISH
DESPISE
DIALYSE
DIARIST
DIECAST
DIFFUSE
DIGRESS
DIMNESS
DIOCESE
DISCUSS
DISEASE
DISGUST
DISMAST
DISMISS
DISPOSE
DIVERSE
DOGFISH
DOGROSE
DONNISH
DRYNESS
DUCHESS
DUMPISH
EARNEST
EASIEST
ECLIPSE
ECSTASY
EGOTISM
EGOTIST
ELEGIST
ELITISM
ELITIST
ELLIPSE
EMBASSY
EMPRESS
ENCLASP
ENCLOSE
ENCRUST
ENDLESS
ENDORSE
ENGLISH
ENGROSS
ENTHUSE
ENTRUST
ESPOUSE
EUPEPSY
EVEREST
EXHAUST
EXPANSE
EXPENSE
EXPRESS
EYELASH
EYELESS
EYEWASH
FADDISH
FADDIST
FAIRISH
FANTASY
FARNESE
FASCISM
FASCIST
FATNESS
FAUVISM
FAUVIST
FILASSE
FINESSE
FINNISH
FITNESS
FITTEST
FLEMISH
FLORIST
FLUTIST
FLYPAST
FOOLISH
FOPPISH
FORMOSA
FURBISH
FURNISH
GABFEST
GARNISH
GASMASK
GAWKISH
GAYNESS
GENOESE
GEODESY
GIRLISH
GLIMPSE
GLUCOSE
GODDESS
GODLESS
GOODISH
GOULASH
GRAYISH
GREYISH
GUTLESS
GYMNAST
HAPLESS
HARNESS
HARPIST
HARVEST
HASHISH
HATLESS
HEIRESS
HELLISH
HENGIST
HERBIST
HEROISM
HEURISM
HIGHEST
HOGWASH
HOSTESS
IAMBIST
ICINESS
ILLNESS
IMAGISM
IMAGIST
IMMENSE
IMMERSE
IMPASSE
IMPRESS
IMPREST
IMPULSE
INBURST
INCENSE
INCRUST
INGRESS
INHOUSE
INQUEST
INTENSE
INVERSE
IRIDISE
ISOBASE
IVRESSE
JACKASS
JAPLISH
JOBLESS
JOYLESS
JUDAISM
JUJITSU
KADDISH
KENTISH
KERMESS
KOUMISS
LACTASE
LACTOSE
LAMAISM
LAMAIST
LAMBAST
LARGESS
LARGEST
LAWLESS
LAXNESS
LEFTIST
LEGLESS
LEPROSY
LICENSE
LIONESS
LOUTISH
LUMPISH
MADNESS
MAFIOSO
MALAISE
MALTASE
MALTESE
MANNISH
MARCUSE
MARXISM
MARXIST
MATISSE
MAWKISH
MELROSE
MÉTISSE
MIDWEST
MISCAST
MOLLUSC
MOMBASA
MONKISH
MOORISH
MOREISH
MORTISE
NEAREST
NEBBISH
NECROSE
NEGRESS
NERVOSA
NEWNESS
NICOISE
NOURISH
NUTCASE
OARFISH
OBELISK
OBVERSE
OCULIST
ODALISK
ODDNESS
OFFBASE
OFFENSE
OGREISH
OLDNESS
OLOROSO
ONANISM
ONENESS
OPPRESS
ORGIAST
ORPHISM
OUTCAST
OUTLAST
OUTPOST
OXIDASE
PALISSY
PALMIST
PANNOSE
PAPOOSE
PECKISH
PECTASE
PEERESS
PEEVISH
PENTOSE
PERCUSS
PERFUSE
PERSIST
PERTUSE
PIANIST
PICASSO
PIETIST
POETESS
POSSESS
PRECAST
PRECISE
PREMISS
PROCESS
PROFESS
PROFUSE
PROMISE
PROPOSE
PROTEST
PROVISO
PROVOST
PROWESS
PRUDISH
PUBLISH
PUCKISH
PUGWASH
PURPOSE
RAFFISH
RAWNESS
REALISM
REALIST
RECLUSE
REDDISH
REDNESS
REDRESS
REFRESH
REGRESS
REHOUSE
RELAPSE
RELEASE
REMORSE
REPRESS
REPULSE
REQUEST
REVERSE
RHENISH
RIBLESS
RIMLESS
ROGUISH
ROOKISH
RUBBISH
SADNESS
SALLUST
SAMOOSA
SARCASM
SAWDUST
SAWFISH
SCHLOSS
SELFISH
SEXLESS
SHIATSU
SHICKSA
SHYNESS
SIAMESE
SIKHISM
SLAVISH
SLYNESS
SOLOIST
SOPHISM
SOPHIST
SOUBISE
SPANISH
STATIST
STRAUSS
STYLISH
STYLIST
SUBFUSC
SUBSIST
SUCCESS
SUCROSE
SUFFUSE
SUGGEST
SUNLESS
SUNRISE
SUPPOSE
SURMISE
SURPASS
SWEDISH
SYNAPSE
TACHISM
TAPLASH
TARNISH
TBILISI
TEMPEST
THERESA
THOMISM
THOMIST
TIGRESS
TIGRISH
TITOISM
TITOIST
TONNISH
TOPLESS
TOPMAST
TOPMOST
TOURISM
TOURIST
TRAIPSE
TROPISM
TSARIST
TURKISH
UNCLASP
UNDRESS
UNHORSE
UNLEASH
UNLOOSE
UPRAISE
URANISM
USELESS
VAMOOSE
VANESSA
VARNISH
VENTOSE
VERBOSE
VINASSE
VISCOSE
WAGGISH
WASPISH
WATUTSI
WEAKEST
WETNESS
WHITISH
WIMPISH
WITLESS
WITNESS
WOLFISH
WRYNOSE
YANGTSE
YIDDISH
YORKIST
ZAMBESI
ZIONIST
ABILITY
ABSINTH
ACCRETE
ACETATE
ACIDITY
ACOLYTE
ACONITE
ACTUATE
ADAMITE
ADULATE
AGILITY
AGITATE
AGITATO
ALBERTA
ALBERTI

AMANITA
AMENITY
AMNESTY
AMORITE
ANDANTE
ANIMATE
ANNUITY
ANXIETY
ARCUATE
ARIDITY
ARIETTA
ARIOSTO
ARTISTE
ASHANTI
ASQUITH
ASSISTS
ASTARTE
ATHLETE
AUGUSTA
AUGUSTE
AUREATE
AVIDITY
AXOLOTL
AZIMUTH
BABBITT
BARENTS
BASMATI
BAUXITE
BECKETT
BENEATH
BENNETT
BETROTH
BIRETTA
BISMUTH
BLIGHTY
BOYCOTT
BREADTH
BREVITY
BUCKETS
BULLETS
BURETTE
CAHOOTS
CAINITE
CALCITE
CANASTA
CANTATA
CARROTS
CARROTY
CASSATA
CELESTA
CELESTE
CHAPATI
CHARITY
CHAYOTE
CHIANTI
CHRISTY
CHUPATI
CLARITY
CLIMATE
COCOTTE
COGNATE
COLDITZ
COLLATE
COMMUTE
COMPETE
COMPOTE
COMPUTE
CONNATE
CONNOTE
CORANTO
CORBETT
CORDATE
CORDITE
CORINTH
CREMATE
CRENATE
CRUDITY
CRUELTY
CURETTE
CUVETTE
DEBRETT
DEFLATE
DEJECTA
DENSITY
DEPLETE
DESERTS
DESPITE
DETENTE
DEVIATE
DICTATE
DIGNITY
DINETTE
DIORITE
DISPUTE
DOUGHTY
DUALITY
DUBIETY
DYNASTY
EBONITE
EDUCATE
EFFECTS
EGALITY
ELEVATE
EMANATE
EMIRATE
EMULATE
ENSUITE
ENTENTE
EPIDOTE
EREMITE
ERUDITE
ESPARTO
EXCRETA
EXCRETE
EXECUTE
EXEGETE
EXPIATE
EYEBATH
FACULTY
FAGGOTS
FATUITY
FIDGETS
FIDGETY
FILLETS
FLIGHTY
FRAILTY
FRIGATE
FROWSTY
FUMETTE
GALETTE
GAROTTE
GAVOTTE
GAZETTE
GEFILTE
GEMMATE
GENISTA
GESTATE
GIBLETS
GOLIATH
GRADATE
GRANITA
GRANITE
GRAVITY
GUTTATE
GWYNETH
HAPORTH
HASTATE
HAUGHTY
HAZLETT
HEIGHTS
HIRSUTE
HITTITE
HOGARTH
HONESTY
HOPLITE
HUSSITE
HYDRATE
ICHNITE
IMITATE
IMPASTO
IMPIETY
INANITY
INDEPTH
INFLATE
INGRATE
INSECTS
INSTATE
ISOLATE
ITERATE
JACKETS
JAKARTA
JOCASTA
JOLLITY
KAINITE
KERNITE
KEYNOTE
KHANATE
KIBBUTZ
KYANITE
LABIATE
LACERTA
LACTATE
LAMBETH
LAVOLTA
LAYETTE
LEMMATA
LEPANTO
LIBERTY
LIGNITE
LOCUSTS
LOYALTY
LUDDITE
LUDGATE
MACBETH
MACHETE
MAGENTA
MAGGOTY
MAGNATE
MAGNETO
MAJESTY
MAMMOTH
MANDATE
MARANTA
MARMITE
MEDIATE
MELLITE
MEMENTO
MIGRATE
MOABITE
MODESTY
MODISTE
MOFETTE
MOMENTS
MULATTO
MURIATE
MUSETTE
NAIVETÉ
NAIVETY
NARRATE
NAUGHTY
NAVETTE
NEOLITH
NICTATE
NITRATE
NITRITE
NOVELTY
NULLITY
OBESITY
OBJECTS
OBVIATE
OFFDUTY
OPACITY
OPERATE
ORVIETO
OTRANTO
OUSTITI
OUTVOTE
OVULATE
OXALATE
PALETTE
PALMATE
PALPATE
PARENTS
PARTITA
PAUCITY
PEANUTS
PENALTY
PENNATE
PERLITE
PIMENTO
PIPETTE
PLACATE
PODESTA
POLENTA
POLLUTE
POVERTY
PREDATE
PRELATE
PRIESTS
PRIMATE
PRIVATE
PRIVITY
PROBATE
PROBITY
PROFITS
PROMOTE
PRONATE
PUBERTY
PULSATE
QUALITY
QUIXOTE
QUORATE
RACKETS
RACKETY
RADIATE
REALITY
REBIRTH
REFLATE
REGATTA
RELICTS
REPLETE
REQUITE
REROUTE
RESPITE
RESTATE
RESULTS
REUNITE
REWRITE
RICKETS
RICKETY
RICOTTA
RIPOSTE
RISOTTO
ROBERTS
ROBUSTA
ROSEATE
ROSETTA
ROSETTE
ROYALTY
SABAOTH
SABBATH
SALTATE
SAMNITE
SATIATE
SATIETY
SECRETE
SECRETS
SENSATE
SEVENTH
SEVENTY
SFUMATO
SINUATE
SITUATE
SOCIETY
SOPWITH
SPICATE
SPINATE
SPIRITS
SPROUTS
STARETS
STATUTE
STEALTH
STRAITS
STREWTH
STRIATE
STYLITE
SUAVITY
SUFFETE
SULFATE
SUNNITE
SURDITY
SUZETTE
TAFFETA
TANNATE
TARANTO
TEKTITE
TENANTS
TERMITE
TESTATE
THERETO
THIRSTY
THRIFTY
THRISTY
THROATY
TITRATE
TOCCATA
TORONTO
TOWPATH
TRIBUTE
TRIESTE
TRINITY
TWELFTH
ULEXITE
ULULATE
UNCOUTH
UNEARTH
UNQUOTE
UNTRUTH
UPSTATE
URALITE
URANITE
URINATE
UROLITH
UTILITY
VACUITY
VANUATU
VARIETY
VARSITY
VEDANTA
VEDETTE
VELVETY
VIBRATE
VIBRATO
VIOLATE
VIRGATE
VITIATE
VOLANTE
VULGATE
WARPATH
WEIGHTS
WEIGHTY
ZEOLITE
ZOOLITE
ALPHEUS
ALUMNUS
ALYSSUM
AMATEUR
AMOROUS
ANGELUS
ANNULUS
ANTIGUA
ANTIQUE
ANXIOUS
APICIUS
APPLAUD
AQUEOUS
AQUINUS
ARBUTUS
ARDUOUS
ARTEMUS
ATTICUS
AUTOCUE
AZYGOUS
BACCHUS
BAHADUR
BALEFUL
BALFOUR
BAROQUE
BASHFUL
BATHTUB
BAUHAUS
BEARHUG
BELARUS
BELGIUM
BEZIQUE
BILIOUS
BLOWOUT
BOLETUS
BRANTUB
BRIMFUL
BRUSQUE
BULBOUS
BULGHUR
BURNOUS
BURNOUT
CACIQUE
CADMIUM

CAESIUM
CALAMUS
CALCIUM
CALLOUS
CAMBIUM
CANDOUR
CANTHUS
CARACUL
CARDUUS
CAREFUL
CAROLUS
CATCHUP
CELSIUS
CENTAUR
CENTRUM
CHECKUP
CHIRRUP
CIMABUE
CLAMOUR
CLEANUP
CLEARUP
CLOSEUP
COCONUT
CONTOUR
COPIOUS
COVERUP
CRANIUM
CRASSUS
CREWCUT
CROESUS
CUMULUS
CURIOUS
CYTISUS
DECORUM
DEFRAUD
DEVALUE
DEVIOUS
DIDYMUS
DOLEFUL
DREYFUS
DROPOUT
DUBIOUS
DUTIFUL
EARDRUM
ECHINUS
ECLOGUE
EGLOGUE
ELOGIUM
ELYSIUM
EMBOLUS
ENAMOUR
ENVIOUS
EPHEBUS
EPHESUS
ERASMUS
ERODIUM
ERRATUM
FALLOUT
FARCEUR
FATEFUL
FATIGUE
FATUOUS
FAUSTUS
FEARFUL
FERMIUM
FERROUS
FERVOUR
FIBROUS
FIREBUG
FISTFUL
FLAREUP
FLAVOUR
FRETFUL
FULCRUM
FUNGOUS
FURIOUS
GAINFUL
GALLIUM
GASEOUS
GIBBOUS
GIELGUD
GLAMOUR
GLEEFUL
GORDIUS
GRAMPUS
GROPIUS
GROTIUS
GROWNUP
HAFNIUM
HAHNIUM
HAIRCUT
HALIBUT
HALITUS
HANDFUL
HANDGUN
HANDOUT
HANGOUT
HARBOUR
HARMFUL
HATEFUL
HEEDFUL
HEINOUS
HELPFUL
HIDEOUS
HIDEOUT
HOODLUM
HOPEFUL
HORDEUM
HOTSPUR
HUMDRUM
HUMERUS
HURTFUL
ICTERUS
IGNEOUS
ILIACUS
IMPETUS
IMPIOUS
INCUBUS
INGENUE
INVIOUS
IRIDIUM
ISCHIUM
ISTHMUS
JACOBUS
JEALOUS
JEJUNUM
KARAKUL
KETCHUP
KINGCUP
KURHAUS
LADYBUG
LALIQUE
LEPROUS
LIBRIUM
LINCTUS
LINOCUT
LIQUEUR
LITHIUM
LOCKNUT
LOCKOUT
LOOKOUT
LUSTFUL
LUSTRUM
MACAQUE
MALLEUS
MALTHUS
MANAGUA
MASSEUR
MAXIMUM
MESCLUN
MIMULUS
MINDFUL
MINIBUS
MINIMUM
MODICUM
MODULUS
NACROUS
NAIPAUL
NATRIUM
NEEDFUL
NERVOUS
NIOBIUM
NITROUS
NONPLUS
NOSTRUM
NOXIOUS
NUCLEUS
OBLIQUE
OBLOQUY
OBSEQUY
OBVIOUS
OCCIPUT
OCELLUS
OCTOPUS
ODOROUS
OEDIPUS
OESTRUS
OLYMPUS
OMENTUM
OMINOUS
OMNIBUS
ONEROUS
ONMIBUS
OPOSSUM
OPTIMUM
ORGANUM
ORPHEUS
OSCULUM
OSSEOUS
OUTPOUR
OVERDUE
OVERRUN
PABULUM
PAESTUM
PAINFUL
PALLIUM
PAPYRUS
PARLOUR
PARLOUS
PASTEUR
PAVIOUR
PEACHUM
PEGASUS
PELORUS
PERSEUS
PETROUS
PHALLUS
PHOEBUS
PILATUS
PINETUM
PIRAEUS
PIROGUE
PITEOUS
PITIFUL
PLAUTUS
PLAYFUL
PLUTEUS
POLYPUS
POMPOUS
POPULUS
PREMIUM
PRIAPUS
PRIMEUR
PRONOUN
PROTEUS
PYLORUS
QUANTUM
QUECHUA
QUERCUS
QUICHUA
QUIETUS
RAMULUS
RANCOUR
RAUCOUS
REAUMUR
REGROUP
REISSUE
RENEGUE
REOCCUR
RESIDUE
RESTFUL
RETINUE
REVALUE
REVENUE
RHODIUM
RHOMBUS
RIOTOUS
ROSCIUS
ROSEBUD
ROSTRUM
ROUNDUP
RUINOUS
SACKBUT
SACKFUL
SALIQUE
SANCTUM
SANCTUS
SARCOUS
SAVIOUR
SCROTUM
SELLOUT
SERIOUS
SEVERUS
SEYMOUR
SHAKEUP
SHOTGUN
SINUOUS
SKILFUL
SKINFUL
SKYBLUE
SNARLUP
SOLANUM
SOLIDUS
SORGHUM
SOULFUL
STADIUM
STANDUP
STENGUN
STERNUM
STIRRUP
STRATUM
STRATUS
SUBAQUA
SUCCOUR
SULPHUR
SURPLUS
TACITUS
TACTFUL
TAKEOUT
TAMBOUR
TANTRUM
TEARFUL
TEDIOUS
TENUOUS
TERBIUM
TETANUS
THALLUS
THESEUS
THORIUM
THULIUM
TRITIUM
TRIVIUM
TROCHUS
TROILUS
TUMULUS
TUNEFUL
TURNOUT
UNCINUS
URANIUM
VACUOUS
VARIOUS
VICIOUS
VIDIMUS
VILNIUS
VISCOUS
VOLAPUK
WAKEFUL
WALKOUT
WARDOUR
WASHOUT
WASHTUB
WHITSUN
WICKIUP
WIPEOUT
WISHFUL
WISTFUL
WITHOUT
WOODCUT
WORKOUT
WRITEUP
XENOPUS
YTTRIUM
ZEALOUS
ZESTFUL
ABSOLVE
ABUSIVE
ACHIEVE
ANCHOVY
APPROVE
ARCHIVE
BAKLAVA
BEEHIVE
BEHOOVE
BELIEVE
BEREAVE
BIVALVE
CAPTIVE
CASSAVA
CENTAVO
CONCAVE
CONNIVE
COSTIVE
CURSIVE
DECEIVE
DEPRAVE
DEPRIVE
DESERVE
DEVOLVE
ELUSIVE
EMOTIVE
ENCLAVE
ENGRAVE
ENSLAVE
EVASIVE
FESTIVE
FORGAVE
FORGIVE
FURTIVE
HELLUVA
IMPROVE
INNERVE
INVOLVE
JUSSIVE
KHEDIVE
MASSIVE
MINERVA
MISSIVE
MUSCOVY
OBSERVE
OUTLIVE
PAHLAVI
PASSIVE
PAVLOVA
PECCAVI
PENSIVE
PLOSIVE
RECEIVE
RECURVE
RELIEVE
REPROVE
RESERVE
RESOLVE
RESTIVE
REVOLVE
SCREEVE
SURVIVE
TANTIVY
TARDIVE
UNALIVE
UNNERVE
ZEMSTVO
ASHDOWN
BELLOWS
BILLOWS
BRADAWL
FELLOWS
GALLOWS
GOSHAWK
HOEDOWN
LEASOWE
LETDOWN
LIEDOWN
LOWDOWN
MARLOWE
NARROWS
OKINAWA
OVERAWE
RUNDOWN
SANDOWN
SHADOWY
SITDOWN
SORROWS
SUNDOWN
UNKNOWN
WILLOWY
WINDOWS
YELLOWS

ATARAXY
BETWIXT
CACHEXY
CONTEXT
EPITAXY
PICKAXE
POLEAXE
PRETEXT
ACRONYM
ANTONYM
APTERYX
BUCKEYE
CATSEYE
CHLAMYS
DEADEYE
EMPLOYS
ENDWAYS
FISHEYE
GOODBYE
HAWKEYE
HOMONYM
JERSEYS
KIDNEYS
METONYM
ORKNEYS
SHUTEYE
SOCKEYE
SPONDYL
STACHYS
SYNONYM
WYSIWYG
AGONIZE
ANALYZE
ANODIZE
APPRIZE
ATOMIZE
BAPTIZE
BONANZA
CADENZA
CAPSIZE
CHINTZY
CHORIZO
EMBLAZE
IDOLIZE
ITEMIZE
JACUZZI
LIONIZE
MANSIZE
ORGANZA
OUTSIZE
OXIDIZE
PIZZAZZ
REALIZE
ROMANZA
SCHERZO
SHMOOZE
SPINOZA
SQUEEZE
STYLIZE
TRAPEZE
UTILIZE

7:7

ABOULIA
ACARIDA
ACTINIA
ADENOMA
AGRAPHA
AGRIPPA
ALABAMA
ALBANIA
ALBERTA
ALDABRA
ALFALFA
ALGEBRA
ALGERIA
ALSATIA
ALTHAEA
ALUMINA
AMANITA
AMBOYNA
AMERICA
AMMONIA
AMNESIA
AMPHORA
AMPULLA
ANAEMIA
ANDORRA
ANGIOMA
ANOSMIA
ANTENNA
ANTIGUA
APEPSIA
APHAGIA
APHASIA
APHELIA
APHONIA
APLASIA
ARABICA
ARCADIA
ARIETTA
ARIZONA
ASPASIA
ASSYRIA
AUGUSTA
AURELIA
AUREOLA
AUSTRIA
BAKLAVA
BANKSIA
BARBARA
BATAVIA
BAZOOKA
BEGONIA
BEGORRA
BELINDA
BELISHA
BERMUDA
BIRETTA
BOHEMIA
BOLIVIA
BOLOGNA
BONANZA
BOTTEGA
BRAVURA
BRITZKA
BULIMIA
BURKINA
CADENZA
CAESURA
CALDERA
CAMILLA
CAMORRA
CAMPANA
CANASTA
CANDELA
CANDIDA
CANELLA
CANNULA
CANTATA
CAPELLA
CARAMBA
CARIOCA
CASCARA
CASSATA
CASSAVA
CATALPA
CECILIA
CEDILLA
CELESTA
CHELSEA
CHIASMA
CHIMERA
CHOLERA
CINEREA
CITHARA
COCHLEA
CORDOBA
COROLLA
CORRIDA
CORTINA
CORUNNA
CROATIA
CUMBRIA
CURCUMA
CYNTHIA
DEJECTA
DERONDA
DILEMMA
DIORAMA
DIPLOMA
DIPTERA
DRACHMA
DRACULA
ECHIDNA
ECTOPIA
ELECTRA
EMPYEMA
EPHEDRA
ERITREA
EROTICA
ETRURIA
EUGENIA
EXCRETA
EXEMPLA
EXHEDRA
FAVELLA
FELUCCA
FIBROMA
FILARIA
FIMBRIA
FISTULA
FLORIDA
FORMICA
FORMOSA
FORMULA
FOSSULA
FREESIA
FUCHSIA
GALATEA
GAUTAMA
GEHENNA
GENISTA
GEORGIA
GERBERA
GODETIA
GOMORRA
GONDOLA
GORILLA
GRANDMA
GRANDPA
GRANITA
GRANOLA
GRENADA
GUARANA
GUNNERA
HAGGADA
HELLUVA
HEREDIA
HETAERA
HOSANNA
HYPOGEA
IKEBANA
INDIANA
INERTIA
IPOMOEA
ISADORA
JAKARTA
JAMAICA
JELLABA
JOCASTA
KAMPALA
KATORGA
KHALIFA
KITHARA
KRISHNA
LACERTA
LAGONDA
LAMBADA
LAMELLA
LANTANA
LASAGNA
LAVOLTA
LEMMATA
LEMPIRA
LEUCOMA
LIBERIA
LOBELIA
LYMNAEA
MADEIRA
MADONNA
MAGENTA
MAHATMA
MAHONIA
MAJORCA
MALACCA
MALARIA
MAMILLA
MANAGUA
MANDALA
MANILLA
MARANTA
MARATHA
MAREMMA
MARMARA
MARSALA
MASCARA
MASURKA
MATILDA
MAXILLA
MAZEPPA
MAZURKA
MEDULLA
MESSINA
MILITIA
MINERVA
MINORCA
MINUTIA
MIRANDA
MOLUCCA
MOMBASA
MONILIA
MONTANA
MORAVIA
MORPHIA
MURAENA
MYALGIA
MYCELLA
MYELOMA
MYRINGA
NAMIBIA
NAPHTHA
NEMESIA
NERVOSA
NIAGARA
NICOSIA
NIGELLA
NIGERIA
NIRVANA
NOVELLA
OBSCURA
OCARINA
OCEANIA
OKINAWA
OLYMPIA
OPUNTIA
ORGANZA
OSTEOMA
OTALGIA
PALMYRA
PALOOKA
PANACEA
PANDORA
PANGAEA
PAPILLA
PAPRIKA
PARTHIA
PARTITA
PATELLA
PAVLOVA
PELORIA
PEREIRA
PERGOLA
PERSONA
PETUNIA
PIANOLA
PINNULA
PIRANHA
PISCINA
PLEROMA
PODAGRA
PODESTA
POLENTA
PRIMULA
PURPURA
PYAEMIA
PYREXIA
QUASSIA
QUECHUA
QUICHUA
RATAFIA
REBECCA
REGALIA
REGATTA
REPLICA
RETSINA
RHONDDA
RICOTTA
RIGVEDA
RIVIERA
ROBINIA
ROBUSTA
ROMANIA
ROMANZA
ROSACEA
ROSALIA
ROSELLA
ROSEOLA
ROSETTA
ROTUNDA
RUBELLA
RUBEOLA
RUSALKA
SABRINA
SAMARIA
SAMBUCA
SAMOOSA
SANGRIA
SAQQARA
SARCOMA
SARDANA
SATSUMA
SAVANNA
SCAGLIA
SCAPULA
SEQUELA
SEQUOIA
SERINGA
SESTINA
SHICKSA
SIGNORA
SILESIA
SINATRA
SINHALA
SKIMMIA
SMETANA
SOCOTRA
SOMALIA
SPATULA
SPICULA
SPINOZA
STAMINA
SUBAQUA
SULTANA
SUMATRA
SUSANNA
SWANSEA
SYNOVIA
SYRINGA
TABITHA
TAFFETA
TALOOKA
TANAGRA
TANTARA
TAPIOCA
TARPEIA
TATIANA
TAVERNA
TEMPERA
TEMPURA
TEQUILA
TESSERA
THERESA
TILAPIA
TITANIA
TOCCATA
TOMBOLA
TOXEMIA
TRACHEA
TRITOMA
TSARINA
TUNISIA
TZARINA
URAEMIA
URETHRA
VANESSA

VANILLA
VARIOLA
VEDANTA
VERBENA
VERRUCA
VISCERA
VISTULA
WEIGELA
WOOMERA
ZAKUSKA
ZIZANIA
BATHTUB
BETHUMB
BRANTUB
CORNCOB
COULOMB
COXCOMB
DISTURB
MAGHREB
MINICAB
PEDICAB
PERTURB
POTHERB
PROVERB
RHUBARB
SUCCUMB
TAXICAB
WASHTUB
AARONIC
ACERBIC
ACRYLIC
ACTINIC
AEROBIC
ALEMBIC
ALMANAC
AMHARIC
AMOEBIC
ANAEMIC
ANGELIC
APHONIC
APHOTIC
AQUATIC
ARAMAIC
ARCHAIC
ARMORIC
ARSENIC
ASCETIC
ASEPTIC
ASIATIC
ATACTIC
BACCHIC
BALDRIC
BIVOUAC
BORACIC
BOTANIC
BUBONIC
BUCOLIC
BYRONIC
CALORIC
CAMBRIC
CARADOC
CARDIAC
CAUSTIC
CERAMIC
CHAOTIC
CHRONIC
CLASSIC
CLASTIC
CLUNIAC
COELIAC
CRYPTIC
DELPHIC
DEMONIC
DEMOTIC
DOMINIC
DRASTIC
DYNAMIC
ECBOLIC
EDAPHIC
ELASTIC
ELEGIAC
EMPIRIC
ENDEMIC
ENERGIC
ENTERIC
ERRATIC
EUGENIC
FANATIC
FRANTIC
GASTRIC
GENERIC
GENETIC
GEORGIC
GLYPTIC
GNOSTIC
GRAPHIC
HEPATIC
HERETIC
HOMERIC
ICTERIC
IDIOTIC
IDYLLIC
ISLAMIC
KENOTIC
KINETIC
LACONIC
LUNATIC
MALEFIC
MANDIOC
MANIHOC
MASONIC
MECONIC
MELODIC
METONIC
MIASMIC
MIRIFIC
MOLLUSC
MORONIC
MUNTJAC
NERITIC
NOMADIC
NUCLEIC
NUMERIC
OCEANIC
ODONTIC
OLYMPIC
ONEIRIC
ORGANIC
PACIFIC
PELAGIC
PHALLIC
PHRENIC
PLASTIC
POLEMIC
POLITIC
PONTIAC
POTOMAC
POULENC
PROSAIC
PRUSSIC
PSYCHIC
PYRETIC
PYRRHIC
RACEMIC
SAPPHIC
SATANIC
SATIRIC
SCEPTIC
SCIATIC
SEISMIC
SEMITIC
SHELLAC
SKEPTIC
SPASTIC
SPHENIC
STANNIC
STEARIC
STROBIC
STYPTIC
SUBFUSC
TATARIC
THERMIC
TITANIC
TOTEMIC
TRAFFIC
TRIATIC
TROPHIC
VOCALIC
VOLTAIC
ZAPOTEC
ABASHED
ABBASID
ABELARD
ABSCOND
ACCUSED
ADENOID
ADMIRED
ADOPTED
ADORNED
AERATED
AFFIXED
AGROUND
ALARMED
ALIGNED
ALIQUID
ALLEGED
ALLOWED
ALTERED
AMERIND
AMYLOID
ANDROID
ANEROID
ANISEED
ANNELID
ANNOYED
ANTACID
APPLAUD
APPLIED
APPOSED
ARMBAND
ARMORED
ARRAYED
ARRIVED
ASCARID
ASHAMED
ASSUMED
ASSURED
ASTOUND
ATTIRED
AWKWARD
BAFFLED
BAGHDAD
BANDAID
BARMAID
BASTARD
BEACHED
BEARDED
BEDFORD
BEHAVED
BELATED
BELOVED
BEMUSED
BERNARD
BIASSED
BIGHEAD
BIGOTED
BLASTED
BLESSED
BLITZED
BLOATED
BLOCKED
BLUNTED
BLURRED
BOBSLED
BOLLARD
BOMBARD
BONNARD
BOTTLED
BOUNDED
BOWHEAD
BOYHOOD
BRANDED
BREADED
BRIGAND
BRONZED
BROWNED
BRUISED
BUSTARD
BUZZARD
CANDIED
CAROTID
CARRIED
CASTLED
CATHEAD
CENTRED
CESTOID
CHAINED
CHANGED
CHAPPED
CHARGED
CHARMED
CHARRED
CHECKED
CHEESED
CHIPPED
CHOROID
CHUFFED
CISSOID
CLIPPED
CLOTHED
CLOUDED
COBBLED
COLLARD
COLLOID
COLORED
COMMAND
COMMEND
CONCORD
CONTEND
COPLAND
COSTARD
COUNTED
COVERED
COVETED
COWHAND
COWHERD
COWSHED
CRACKED
CRAMMED
CRAMPED
CREATED
CRESTED
CRICOID
CRINOID
CROOKED
CROPPED
CROSSED
CROWDED
CRUSHED
CUCKOLD
CURDLED
CURRIED
CUSTARD
CYSTOID
DAGWOOD
DAMAGED
DAPHNID
DAPPLED
DASTARD
DAZZLED
DEBASED
DECAYED
DECIDED
DECREED
DEFACED
DEFILED
DEFINED
DEFRAUD
DELAYED
DELTOID
DELUDED
DEMIGOD
DESCEND
DESMOND
DESPOND
DEVISED
DEVOTED
DIAMOND
DIAPSID
DIEHARD
DILATED
DILUTED
DIMPLED
DISBAND
DISCARD
DISCORD
DISTEND
DISUSED
DIVIDED
DOGFOOD
DOGWOOD
DOWLAND
DRAFTED
DRAINED
DREADED
DRESSED
DRUGGED
DULLARD
DUNCIAD
EGGHEAD
ELECTED
EMERALD
ENDURED
ENFIELD
ENGAGED
ENGINED
ENGLAND
ENRAGED
ETHMOID
EXALTED
EXCITED
EXISTED
EXPIRED
EXPOSED
EXPOUND
FACETED
FAINTED
FANCIED
FANGLED
FATHEAD
FAVORED
FEIGNED
FENLAND
FEVERED
FIBROID
FINLAND
FIXATED
FLACCID
FLAPPED
FLECKED
FLEDGED
FLOODED
FLUSHED
FOOTPAD
FORFEND
FORWARD
FOULARD
FRETTED
FRILLED
FRINGED
FROSTED
FUDDLED
FUNGOID
GALAHAD
GARBLED
GARLAND
GIELGUD
GIZZARD
GLENOID
GNARLED
GOAHEAD
GODSEND
GOLIARD
GORSEDD
GRAINED
GRANDAD
GRANTED
GRILLED
GRIMOND
GROINED
GROOVED
GUARDED
HAGGARD
HALBERD
HALYARD
HANDLED
HANSARD
HARVARD
HARWOOD
HATBAND
HAUNTED
HAYSEED
HAYWARD
HELIPAD
HENNAED
HEXAPOD
HISTOID

HOLLAND
HOMINID
HONEYED
HOTHEAD
HUBBARD
HUNCHED
HUNDRED
HURRIED
HUSBAND
HYALOID
HYDATID
ICELAND
ICHABOD
IGNORED
ILLBRED
IMPAVID
IMPLIED
IMPOUND
INBOARD
INFIELD
INJURED
INSIPID
INSTEAD
INVALID
IRELAND
JELLIED
JOINTED
JUMBLED
JUTLAND
KAMERAD
KEYWORD
KINDRED
KNITTED
KNOTTED
LABORED
LAGGARD
LANGUID
LANYARD
LAYERED
LEARNED
LEEWARD
LEONARD
LEOPARD
LEOPOLD
LEOTARD
LIKENED
LIMITED
LINSEED
LIPREAD
LOGWOOD
LOLLARD
LOUVRED
LOWLAND
LOWPAID
MALLARD
MANGOLD
MANHOOD
MANKIND
MANSARD
MARBLED
MARRIED
MASTOID
MATCHED
MERITED
MERMAID
METTLED
MIDLAND
MINUEND
MINUTED
MISDEED
MISLEAD
MISREAD
MONEYED
MORLAND
MOTTLED
MOULDED
MOUNTED
MUDDLED
MUFFLED
MUSCOID
MUSTARD
MYELOID
NAILBED
NEGROID
NIGGARD
NOBBLED
NOTCHED
NOTEPAD
OBLIGED
OCEANID
OCTOPOD
OFFHAND
OFFLOAD
OMITTED
OPERAND
OPPOSED
ORCHARD
ORDERED
OROTUND
OUTWARD
OVERBID
OVERFED
PAINTED
PALSIED
PARCHED
PAROTID
PAYLOAD
PERSEID
PICKLED
PIEBALD
PIERCED
PINCHED
PINFOLD
PINHEAD
PITCHED
PITHEAD
PLACARD
PLANNED
PLANTED
PLEASED
PLEATED
PLYWOOD
POCHARD
POINTED
POLLARD
POLYPOD
POMMARD
PONIARD
POPEYED
PORTEND
POWERED
PREBEND
PREPAID
PRESSED
PRETEND
PRICKED
PRINTED
PROCEED
PRONGED
PROPEND
PUNCHED
PUZZLED
PYRAMID
QUILTED
RADDLED
RAGWEED
REBOUND
REBUILD
REDHEAD
REDOUND
REDUCED
REDWOOD
REFINED
RELATED
RELAXED
REMOULD
REMOVED
REPUTED
RESCIND
RESOUND
RESPOND
RETIRED
RETREAD
REVERED
REVISED
REYNARD
RHIZOID
RICHARD
RIDDLED
RIPCORD
RIVETED
RONSARD
ROSEBUD
ROSTAND
ROUNDED
RUFFLED
RUMORED
RUMPLED
SAMOYED
SAPWOOD
SAUROID
SCENTED
SCREWED
SEABIRD
SEAFOOD
SEAWEED
SEEDBED
SEETHED
SERRIED
SETTLED
SHAGGED
SHELLED
SHELVED
SHINPAD
SHOCKED
SICKBED
SIGHTED
SINDBAD
SKILLED
SKIMMED
SKINNED
SKIPPED
SKYWARD
SLASHED
SLATTED
SLEEVED
SLIPPED
SLOSHED
SLOTTED
SMASHED
SMUDGED
SOFABED
SOUNDED
SOZZLED
SPLAYED
SPLICED
SPOILED
SPOTTED
SQUALID
SQUARED
STAINED
STALKED
STAMPED
STARTED
STARVED
STEAMED
STEMMED
STEROID
STEWARD
STILTED
STIPEND
STIRRED
STOPPED
STORIED
STRIPED
STUDDED
STUDIED
STUFFED
STUMPED
STUNTED
SUBDUED
SUBTEND
SUCCEED
SUGARED
SUSPEND
SWAPPED
SWEATED
TABANID
TABLOID
TAINTED
TANCRED
TANGLED
TANKARD
TELFORD
TENFOLD
THYROID
TOASTED
TOEHOLD
TOOTHED
TOUCHED
TOWHEAD
TRAINED
TRAPPED
TREATED
TRIFFID
TRILLED
TWISTED
TWOFOLD
TYNWALD
TYPHOID
UNAIDED
UNAIRED
UNARMED
UNASKED
UNBOUND
UNBOWED
UNCARED
UNCURED
UNDATED
UNFADED
UNFIXED
UNHEARD
UNLINED
UNLOVED
UNMIXED
UNMOVED
UNNAMED
UNOWNED
UNSOUND
UNTAMED
UNTRIED
UNWOUND
UPBRAID
VAULTED
WARHEAD
WARLORD
WATERED
WAYLAND
WAYWARD
WEEKEND
WETLAND
WHACKED
WHEELED
WHIPPED
WIDOWED
WILFRED
WIZENED
WORRIED
WORSTED
WOUNDED
WRAPPED
WRECKED
ZEALAND
ZETLAND
ABALONE
ABRIDGE
ABSENCE
ABSOLVE
ABUSIVE
ACADEME
ACCRETE
ACCURSE
ACETATE
ACETONE
ACHIEVE
ACOLYTE
ACONITE
ACQUIRE
ACREAGE
ACTUATE
ADAMITE
ADELINE
ADIPOSE
ADULATE
ADVANCE
ADVERSE
AFFABLE
AGITATE
AGONIZE
AIDANCE
AINTREE
AIRBASE
AIRLINE
ALAMODE
ALANINE
ALCALDE
ALEPINE
ALEWIFE
ALIDADE
ALLONGE
ALUMNAE
ALVEOLE
AMBROSE
AMIABLE
AMORITE
AMPOULE
AMYLASE
ANALYZE
ANATOLE
ANDANTE
ANEMONE
ANILINE
ANIMATE
ANODIZE
ANODYNE
ANTIQUE
ANYMORE
APELIKE
APHTHAE
APOCOPE
APOSTLE
APPEASE
APPRIZE
APPROVE
ARACHNE
ARCHIVE
ARCUATE
ARIADNE
ARMHOLE
ARRANGE
ARTICLE
ARTISTE
ASCRIBE
ASININE
ASKANCE
ASPERGE
ASSIEGE
ASSUAGE
ASTARTE
ASTILBE
ASTRIDE
ATHLETE
ATINGLE
ATOMIZE
ATTACHE
AUBERGE
AUDIBLE
AUGUSTE
AUREATE
AUREOLE
AURICLE
AUSLESE
AUSTERE
AUTOCUE
AVARICE
AVERAGE
AWESOME
BAGASSE
BAGGAGE
BAGPIPE
BALANCE
BALLADE
BANDAGE
BANSHEE
BAPTIZE
BAROQUE
BARRAGE
BASCULE
BASTIDE
BAUXITE
BECAUSE
BEDSIDE
BEDSORE
BEDTIME
BEEHIVE
BEELINE
BEGUILE

BEHOOVE
BELIEVE
BENZENE
BENZINE
BEREAVE
BERLINE
BESIEGE
BESPOKE
BEZIQUE
BICYCLE
BIPLANE
BIVALVE
BIZARRE
BOLSHIE
BONDAGE
BONFIRE
BOUCLÉE
BOUTADE
BRAILLE
BRAMBLE
BREATHE
BRICKIE
BRIGADE
BRINDLE
BRIOCHE
BRISTLE
BRITTLE
BROCADE
BROMIDE
BROMINE
BROWNIE
BRUSQUE
BUCKEYE
BULLACE
BURBAGE
BURETTE
BURMESE
CABBAGE
CABOOSE
CACIQUE
CADENCE
CAGOULE
CAINITE
CAIRENE
CALCINE
CALCITE
CALECHE
CALIBRE
CALORIE
CANDACE
CANDIDE
CANIDAE
CAPABLE
CAPRICE
CAPSIZE
CAPSULE
CAPTIVE
CAPTURE
CARBIDE
CARBINE
CARCASE
CARIOLE
CARLYLE
CARMINE
CARNAGE
CAROUSE
CASCADE
CASEASE
CASTILE
CATHODE
CATLIKE
CATSEYE
CAVIARE
CAYENNE
CELESTE
CELLULE
CENACLE
CENSURE
CESTODE
CEVICHE
CÉZANNE
CHALDEE
CHALICE
CHALONE
CHANCRE
CHARADE
CHAYOTE
CHEMISE
CHICANE
CHINESE
CHIPPIE
CHOOKIE
CHOPINE
CHORALE
CHORDAE
CHORTLE
CHUCKLE
CIMABUE
CIRROSE
CITRINE
CLEANSE
CLIMATE
CLIPPIE
CLOSURE
CLOTURE
COCAINE
COCKADE
COCOTTE
CODEINE
COGNATE
COINAGE
COLLAGE
COLLATE
COLLEGE
COLLIDE
COLLUDE
COLOGNE
COMBINE
COMMODE
COMMUNE
COMMUTE
COMPARE
COMPERE
COMPETE
COMPILE
COMPOSE
COMPOTE
COMPUTE
COMRADE
CONCAVE
CONCEDE
CONCISE
CONDOLE
CONDONE
CONFIDE
CONFINE
CONFUSE
CONJURE
CONNATE
CONNIVE
CONNOTE
CONSOLE
CONSUME
CONVENE
CONVOKE
COPPICE
CORACLE
CORDATE
CORDITE
CORKAGE
CORNICE
CORRODE
CORSAGE
CORTEGE
COSTIVE
COSTUME
COTERIE
COTTAGE
COUCHÉE
COURAGE
COUTURE
COWPOKE
CRACKLE
CREMATE
CRENATE
CREVICE
CRINKLE
CRIPPLE
CRUMBLE
CRUMPLE
CRUSADE
CUBICLE
CUISINE
CULTURE
CURABLE
CURETTE
CURSIVE
CUTICLE
CUVETTE
CYANIDE
CYCLONE
DATABLE
DAYTIME
DEADEYE
DEBACLE
DECEASE
DECEIVE
DECLARE
DECLINE
DEFENCE
DEFENSE
DEFLATE
DEGRADE
DEHISCE
DEIRDRE
DELOUSE
DEMERGE
DEMESNE
DENTINE
DENTURE
DEPLETE
DEPLORE
DEPRAVE
DEPRIVE
DERANGE
DESERVE
DESPISE
DESPITE
DESTINE
DETENTE
DEVALUE
DEVIATE
DEVISEE
DEVOLVE
DEVOTEE
DIALYSE
DIAMINE
DICTATE
DIETINE
DIFFUSE
DINETTE
DIOCESE
DIOPTRE
DIORITE
DIOXIDE
DISABLE
DISEASE
DISLIKE
DISPOSE
DISPUTE
DISROBE
DIVERGE
DIVERSE
DIVORCE
DIVULGE
DOGGONE
DOGROSE
DOMAINE
DRABBLE
DRAFTEE
DRAGGLE
DRIBBLE
DRIZZLE
DUCTILE
DUNNAGE
DURABLE
DWINDLE
EARACHE
EARLOBE
EATABLE
EBBTIDE
EBONITE
ECCRINE
ECLIPSE
ECLOGUE
EDIFICE
EDUCATE
EFFORCE
EGLOGUE
ELEVATE
ELLIPSE
ELUSIVE
EMANATE
EMBLAZE
EMBRACE
EMIRATE
EMOTIVE
EMULATE
ENCLAVE
ENCLOSE
ENDGAME
ENDORSE
ENFORCE
ENGORGE
ENGRAVE
ENHANCE
ENLARGE
ENNOBLE
ENQUIRE
ENSLAVE
ENSNARE
ENSUITE
ENTEBBE
ENTENTE
ENTHUSE
ENTITLE
ENTWINE
EPERGNE
EPICENE
EPICURE
EPIDOTE
EPIGONE
EPISODE
EPISTLE
EPITOME
EQUABLE
ERASURE
EREMITE
ERUDITE
ESCAPEE
ESPOUSE
ESQUIRE
ESSENCE
ETAGÈRE
EUGENIE
EULALIE
EUSTACE
EUTERPE
EVACUEE
EVASIVE
EXAMINE
EXAMPLE
EXCLUDE
EXCRETE
EXECUTE
EXEGETE
EXPANSE
EXPENSE
EXPIATE
EXPLODE
EXPLORE
EXPUNGE
EXTREME
EXTRUDE
EYESORE
FAIENCE
FAILURE
FANFARE
FANZINE
FARNESE
FATIGUE
FEATURE
FEBRILE
FERRULE
FERTILE
FESTIVE
FETICHE
FIANCÉE
FILASSE
FINAGLE
FINANCE
FINESSE
FIRCONE
FISHEYE
FISSILE
FISSURE
FISTULE
FIXTURE
FLOOZIE
FLOUNCE
FOLIAGE
FOOTAGE
FOOTSIE
FORBADE
FORESEE
FORGAVE
FORGIVE
FORGONE
FORSAKE
FORTUNE
FOXHOLE
FRAGILE
FRAZZLE
FRECKLE
FREEBIE
FRIABLE
FRIGATE
FRISBEE
FRIZZLE
FRUMPLE
FULSOME
FUMETTE
FURNACE
FURTIVE
FUSIBLE
GABELLE
GALETTE
GALILEE
GALOCHE
GAMBOGE
GARBAGE
GARBURE
GARONNE
GAROTTE
GASFIRE
GAVOTTE
GAZELLE
GAZETTE
GEFILTE
GEMMATE
GENOESE
GENTILE
GENUINE
GEORDIE
GERMANE
GESTATE
GESTURE
GIRAFFE
GIRONDE
GISELLE
GLENCOE
GLIMPSE
GLOBULE
GLUCOSE
GODLIKE
GOODBYE
GOUACHE
GRACILE
GRACKLE
GRADATE
GRANDEE
GRANITE
GRANNIE
GRANTEE
GRANULE
GRAPPLE
GRAVURE
GRENADE
GRIDDLE
GRIMACE
GRISTLE
GRIZZLE
GROCKLE
GROUPIE
GRUMBLE
GRUYÈRE
GUMSHOE

GUNFIRE
GUNWALE
GUTTATE
GUYROPE
HACHURE
HASTATE
HAULAGE
HAWKEYE
HAYWIRE
HECTARE
HELLENE
HEMLINE
HENBANE
HEPTANE
HERBAGE
HEROINE
HIRSUTE
HITTITE
HOPLITE
HORMONE
HOSPICE
HOSTAGE
HOSTILE
HOTLINE
HUSSITE
HYALINE
HYDRATE
HYGIENE
ICEFLOE
ICHNITE
IDOLIZE
IGNOBLE
IMAGINE
IMITATE
IMMENSE
IMMERGE
IMMERSE
IMPASSE
IMPINGE
IMPLODE
IMPLORE
IMPROVE
IMPULSE
INCENSE
INCLINE
INCLUDE
INDULGE
INFLAME
INFLATE
INGENUE
INGRATE
INHOUSE
INNERVE
INQUIRE
INSCAPE
INSHORE
INSPIRE
INSTATE
INTENSE
INTERNE
INTRUDE
INVERSE
INVOICE
INVOLVE
IRIDISE
IRKSOME
ISOBASE
ISODORE
ISOLATE
ISOMERE
ISOTONE
ISOTOPE
ITEMIZE
ITERATE
IVANHOE
IVRESSE
JASMINE
JAVELLE
JAWBONE
JOHNNIE
JOYRIDE
JUBILEE
JUSSIVE
JUSTICE
KAINITE
KARAOKE
KATRINE
KERNITE
KEYHOLE
KEYNOTE
KHANATE
KHEDIVE
KILDARE
KINTYRE
KNOBBLE
KNUCKLE
KYANITE
LABIATE
LACTASE
LACTATE
LACTOSE
LACUNAE
LAETARE
LALIQUE
LASAGNE
LATRINE
LATTICE
LAYETTE
LEAKAGE
LEASOWE
LECTURE
LEGATEE
LEGIBLE
LEISURE
LEONINE
LETTUCE
LEUCINE
LICENCE
LICENSE
LIGNITE
LINACRE
LINDANE
LINEAGE
LINKAGE
LIONIZE
LISSOME
LITCHEE
LOVABLE
LOZENGE
LUCARNE
LUCERNE
LUDDITE
LUDGATE
LUGGAGE
LUGHOLE
MACABRE
MACAQUE
MACHETE
MACHINE
MAGNATE
MAGUIRE
MALAISE
MALTASE
MALTESE
MANACLE
MANATEE
MANDATE
MANHOLE
MANMADE
MANSIZE
MARCUSE
MARLENE
MARLINE
MARLOWE
MARMITE
MARQUEE
MASSAGE
MASSINE
MASSIVE
MATINEE
MATISSE
MAYPOLE
MEASURE
MEDIATE
MELLITE
MELROSE
MESSAGE
METHANE
MÉTISSE
MICROBE
MIDWIFE
MIGRATE
MILEAGE
MIOCENE
MIRACLE
MISFIRE
MISRULE
MISSILE
MISSIVE
MISTAKE
MISTIME
MIXTURE
MOABITE
MODISTE
MOFETTE
MOIDORE
MOLIÈRE
MONOCLE
MONTAGE
MORAINE
MORTICE
MORTISE
MOSELLE
MOULAGE
MOUNTIE
MOVABLE
MUNDANE
MURIATE
MUSETTE
MUTABLE
MYCENAE
MYELINE
NACELLE
NARRATE
NAVARRE
NAVETTE
NECKTIE
NECROSE
NEPTUNE
NERVURE
NETSUKE
NEURINE
NEURONE
NEVILLE
NEWCOME
NICOISE
NICTATE
NIGHTIE
NITRATE
NITRILE
NITRITE
NITRODE
NOISOME
NOMINEE
NOTABLE
NOWHERE
NUCLIDE
NUNLIKE
NURTURE
NUTCASE
NUTLIKE
OATCAKE
OBLIQUE
OBSCENE
OBSCURE
OBSERVE
OBTRUDE
OBVERSE
OBVIATE
OCCLUDE
OCTUPLE
OFFBASE
OFFENCE
OFFENSE
OFFSIDE
OILCAKE
OLEFINE
OMPHALE
ONETIME
ONSHORE
ONSTAGE
OPALINE
OPERATE
ORIFICE
OSBORNE
OSSICLE
OSTIOLE
OUTCOME
OUTDARE
OUTFACE
OUTLINE
OUTLIVE
OUTRAGE
OUTSIDE
OUTSIZE
OUTVOTE
OVERAWE
OVERDUE
OVERLIE
OVERSEE
OVICIDE
OVULATE
OXALATE
OXIDASE
OXIDIZE
PACKAGE
PADRONE
PALETTE
PALMATE
PALPATE
PANACHE
PANCAKE
PANICLE
PANNAGE
PANNOSE
PANTILE
PANURGE
PAPOOSE
PARABLE
PARTAKE
PASSAGE
PASSIVE
PASTIME
PASTURE
PATIBLE
PAULINE
PAYABLE
PEARLIE
PECTASE
PEDICLE
PEERAGE
PENANCE
PENNATE
PENNINE
PENSILE
PENSIVE
PENTANE
PENTODE
PENTOSE
PEONAGE
PEPSINE
PERCALE
PERFUME
PERFUSE
PERIGEE
PERJURE
PERLITE
PERTUSE
PERVADE
PETIOLE
PHILTRE
PHONEME
PIASTRE
PICKAXE
PICOTEE
PICTURE
PILLAGE
PINHOLE
PINNACE
PIPETTE
PIROGUE
PISCINE
PISTOLE
PLACATE
PLEIADE
PLIABLE
PLOSIVE
PLUMAGE
PLUMULE
POLEAXE
POLLUTE
POLONIE
PONTINE
PORCINE
PORTAGE
POSTAGE
POSTURE
POTABLE
POTHOLE
POTICHE
POTTAGE
PRAIRIE
PRALINE
PRATTLE
PRECEDE
PRECISE
PREDATE
PREFACE
PRELATE
PRELUDE
PREPARE
PREPUCE
PRESAGE
PRESIDE
PRESUME
PREZZIE
PRICKLE
PRIMATE
PRITHEE
PRIVATE
PROBATE
PROCURE
PRODUCE
PROFANE
PROFILE
PROFUSE
PROMISE
PROMOTE
PRONATE
PROPANE
PROPOSE
PROTEGE
PROUDIE
PROVIDE
PROVOKE
PRYTHEE
PUCELLE
PUERILE
PULSATE
PURLINE
PURPOSE
PUSTULE
QUIBBLE
QUICKIE
QUINCHE
QUININE
QUINONE
QUIXOTE
QUORATE
RADIATE
RADICLE
RAGTIME
RAMPAGE
RANIDAE
RAPTURE
RATLINE
RAWHIDE
REALIZE
RECEIVE
RECLINE
RECLUSE
RECURVE
RECYCLE
REFEREE
REFLATE
REFUGEE
REHOUSE
REISSUE
REJOICE
RELAPSE
RELEASE
RELIEVE
REMORSE
RENEGUE
REPLACE
REPLETE
REPROVE

REPTILE
REPULSE
REQUIRE
REQUITE
REROUTE
RESERVE
RESHAPE
RESIDUE
RESOLVE
RESPIRE
RESPITE
RESTATE
RESTIVE
RESTORE
RETICLE
RETINUE
RETIREE
RETRACE
REUNITE
REVALUE
REVENGE
REVENUE
REVERIE
REVERSE
REVOLVE
REWRITE
RHIZOME
RIBCAGE
RIPOSTE
RISIBLE
RISSOLE
ROMAINE
ROMANCE
ROSALIE
ROSEATE
ROSELLE
ROSETTE
ROUGHIE
ROULADE
ROUTINE
RUMMAGE
RUMPOLE
RUPTURE
RUTHENE
SACCADE
SALABLE
SALIQUE
SALTATE
SALTIRE
SALVAGE
SAMNITE
SAPROBE
SARDINE
SATIATE
SAUSAGE
SCALENE
SCAMBLE
SCEPTRE
SCIENCE
SCOTTIE
SCOURGE
SCRAPIE
SCREEVE
SCROOGE
SCRUPLE
SCUFFLE
SCUTAGE
SCUTTLE
SEASIDE
SEATTLE
SECLUDE
SECRETE
SEEPAGE
SEIZURE
SELVAGE
SENSATE
SERVICE
SERVILE
SESSILE
SESTINE
SEVILLE
SHACKLE
SHAMBLE
SHEATHE
SHINGLE
SHMOOZE
SHUFFLE
SHUTEYE
SHUTTLE
SIAMESE
SILENCE
SINCERE
SINUATE
SISTINE
SITUATE
SIZABLE
SKIFFLE
SKITTLE
SKYBLUE
SKYLINE
SLOVENE
SMARTIE
SMOOTHE
SMUGGLE
SNAFFLE
SNIFFLE
SNORTLE
SNUFFLE
SNUGGLE
SOCKEYE
SOLUBLE
SOMEONE
SONDAGE
SOUBISE
SOUFFLE
SOUTANE
SPANGLE
SPARKLE
SPAVINE
SPECKLE
SPECTRE
SPICATE
SPINATE
SPINDLE
SPITTLE
SPLODGE
SPLURGE
SPONDEE
SPRINGE
SPYHOLE
SQUEEZE
STADDLE
STARTLE
STATURE
STATUTE
STEEPLE
STERILE
STICKLE
STIPPLE
STORAGE
STRANGE
STRIATE
STROPHE
STUBBLE
STUMBLE
STYLITE
STYLIZE
SUBLIME
SUBSIDE
SUBSUME
SUCROSE
SUFFETE
SUFFICE
SUFFUSE
SUICIDE
SULFATE
SULLAGE
SUNNITE
SUNRISE
SUPPOSE
SUPREME
SURFACE
SURMISE
SURNAME
SURVIVE
SUZETTE
SWADDLE
SWEETIE
SWINDLE
SWINGLE
SWIZZLE
SYNAPSE
SYNCOPE
SYRINGE
SYSTOLE
TACTILE
TADPOLE
TANNATE
TAPPICE
TARDIVE
TARTARE
TARTINE
TAURINE
TAXABLE
TAXFREE
TEACAKE
TEATIME
TEENAGE
TEKTITE
TENABLE
TENSILE
TERENCE
TERMITE
TERRACE
TERRENE
TERRINE
TESTATE
TEXTILE
TEXTURE
THEATRE
THIMBLE
THISTLE
THUGGEE
TILLAGE
TIMBALE
TITRATE
TOLUENE
TONNAGE
TONSURE
TONTINE
TOOTSIE
TOPSIDE
TORNADE
TORSADE
TORTILE
TORTURE
TOWLINE
TOYNBEE
TRADUCE
TRAINEE
TRAIPSE
TRAMPLE
TRANCHE
TRAPEZE
TREACLE
TREADLE
TREMBLE
TRESTLE
TRIBUNE
TRIBUTE
TRICKLE
TRIESTE
TRINGLE
TRIREME
TROCHEE
TROUBLE
TROUNCE
TRUCKLE
TRUFFLE
TRUNDLE
TRUSTEE
TSIGANE
TUNABLE
TURBINE
TURENNE
TUSSORE
TWADDLE
TWEEDLE
TWIDDLE
TWINKLE
TWOSOME
TWOTIME
UKRAINE
UKULELE
ULEXITE
ULULATE
UMBRAGE
UNALIKE
UNALIVE
UNAWARE
UNHINGE
UNHORSE
UNLOOSE
UNNERVE
UNQUOTE
UNTWINE
UPGRADE
UPRAISE
UPSTAGE
UPSTATE
UPSURGE
URALITE
URANITE
URINATE
UTERINE
UTILIZE
UTRICLE
VACCINE
VACUOLE
VALENCE
VAMOOSE
VAMPIRE
VANDYKE
VANTAGE
VEDETTE
VEHICLE
VENDOME
VENTOSE
VENTURE
VERBOSE
VERDURE
VESICLE
VESTIGE
VIBRATE
VILLAGE
VINASSE
VINTAGE
VIOLATE
VIRGATE
VIRGULE
VISCOSE
VISIBLE
VITIATE
VOIVODE
VOLANTE
VOLTAGE
VOLUBLE
VULGATE
VULPINE
VULTURE
WALLACE
WALPOLE
WARFARE
WARLIKE
WARTIME
WASTAGE
WATTAGE
WAYSIDE
WELCOME
WELFARE
WHEEDLE
WHEELIE
WHISTLE
WHITTLE
WHOOPEE
WINSOME
WOULDBE
WRANGLE
WREATHE
WRESTLE
WRIGGLE
WRINKLE
WRYNOSE
YANGTSE
YAOUNDE
YARDAGE
YEZIDEE
ZEOLITE
ZOOLITE
CHAMBRÉ
MACRAMÉ
MOUILLÉ
NAIVETÉ
NÉGLIGÉ
BAILIFF
BEOWULF
CAITIFF
CASTOFF
DEBRIEF
DISTAFF
ENFEOFF
FIGLEAF
FLYHALF
FLYLEAF
GASTHOF
HERSELF
HIMSELF
KICKOFF
LIFTOFF
MASTIFF
MIDRIFF
OAKLEAF
ONESELF
PLAYOFF
PONTIFF
REPROOF
SELLOFF
SENDOFF
SHADOOF
SHERIFF
SHOWOFF
SPINOFF
SUNROOF
TAKEOFF
TEALEAF
THYSELF
WELLOFF
WITLOOF
ABIDING
ACHTUNG
ADORING
AGELONG
ALTHING
AMAZING
AMUSING
ANGLING
BACKING
BACKLOG
BALDING
BANGING
BANKING
BARKING
BARRING
BASKING
BATHING
BATTING
BEADING
BEAMING
BEARHUG
BEARING
BEATING
BEDDING
BEGGING
BEIJING
BENDING
BETTING
BIDDING
BILTONG
BINDING
BLAZING
BOATING
BOILING
BOMBING
BOOKING
BOOMING
BOOTLEG
BOWLING
BRACING
BRAKING
BREWING
BUDDING
BUGGING
BULGING
BULLDOG
BUNTING
BURNING
BUSSING

CABLING
CALLING
CAMPING
CANNING
CARVING
CASTING
CATALOG
CATELOG
CATLING
CEILING
CHAFING
CHASING
CHEWING
CHINWAG
CHOKING
CLOSING
CLOYING
COATING
CODLING
COMBING
COOKING
COOLING
COPYING
CORKING
COSTING
COWLING
CRAVING
CROWING
CUCKING
CUNNING
CURLING
CUTTING
CYCLING
DAMNING
DAMPING
DANCING
DARLING
DARNING
DASHING
DEALING
DIALING
DIGGING
DOCKING
DORKING
DOWSING
DRAWING
DRIVING
DUBBING
DUCKING
DUSTING
EARRING
ENSUING
ETCHING
EVENING
EXITING
FAILING
FAIRING
FALLING
FARMING
FASTING
FAWNING
FEEDING
FEELING
FENCING
FILLING
FILMING
FINDING
FIREBUG
FIREDOG
FISHING
FITTING
FLAMING
FLEEING
FLEMING
FLOWING
FOLDING
FOOTING
FORELEG
FORMING
FUNDING
FURLONG
GALLING
GASPING
GATLING
GEARING
GEELONG
GELDING
GETTING
GILDING
GINSENG
GLARING
GLAZING
GLIDING
GLOWING
GNAWING
GOLDING
GOLFING
GOSLING
GRATING
GRAZING
GREYLAG
GROWING
GUIDING
GUSHING
HACKING
HALTING
HANDBAG
HANGDOG
HANGING
HEADING
HEALING
HEARING
HEATING
HEDGING
HELPING
HERRING
HILDING
HINDLEG
HISSING
HOGGING
HOLDING
HOMBURG
HOPPING
HORSING
HOUSING
HOWLING
HULKING
HUMMING
HUNTING
HURLING
ICEBERG
IMAGING
INKLING
IRONING
ITCHING
JAMMING
JEERING
JESTING
JOBBING
JOGGING
JOINING
JUMPING
KAMPONG
KEELING
KEEPING
KENNING
KICKING
KILLING
KIPLING
KISSING
KNOWING
LACKING
LADYBUG
LAGGING
LAMBING
LANCING
LANDING
LAPPING
LAPSANG
LAPWING
LASHING
LASTING
LEADING
LEANING
LEAPING
LEASING
LEAVING
LEGGING
LEMMING
LENDING
LESSING
LETTING
LICKING
LILTING
LINKING
LINSANG
LISTING
LODGING
LOGGING
LONGING
LOOKING
LOOMING
LOOTING
LORDING
LOURING
LURKING
MAHJONG
MAILBAG
MAILING
MALLING
MANNING
MAPPING
MARBURG
MARKING
MATTING
MEANING
MEETING
MELTING
MENDING
MILKING
MILLING
MINCING
MISSING
MOANING
MOCKING
MOLDING
MONOLOG
MOONING
MOORING
MOPPING
MORNING
MUGGING
MUSTANG
NAGGING
NAPPING
NEARING
NECKING
NETTING
NODDING
NOGGING
NOSEBAG
NOTHING
NURSING
NUTTING
ONGOING
OPENING
PACKING
PADDING
PAIRING
PARKING
PARTING
PASSING
PECKING
PEELING
PEEPING
PEERING
PELTING
PENDING
PERIWIG
PFENNIG
PICKING
PIGLING
PIMPING
PLACING
PLAYING
POLLING
POPPING
POSTBAG
POSTING
POTTING
PRAYING
PRIMING
PROLONG
PROVING
PUDDING
PULSING
PUNTING
PUSHING
PUTTING
QUAKING
RACKING
RAFTING
RAILING
RAISING
RANKING
RANTING
READING
REARING
REEKING
REELING
RESTING
RHYMING
RIBBING
RIGGING
RINGING
RIOTING
RIPPING
ROADHOG
ROAMING
ROARING
ROCKING
ROLLING
ROOFING
ROOTING
ROTTING
ROUSING
RUBBING
RUNNING
RUSHING
RUTTING
SACKING
SAILING
SALTING
SANDBAG
SAPLING
SCARING
SCORING
SEARING
SEATING
SEEMING
SELLING
SERVING
SETTING
SHADING
SHAKING
SHAPING
SHARING
SHAVING
SHEBANG
SHINDIG
SHINING
SHOWING
SIBLING
SIFTING
SIGNING
SINGING
SINKING
SIPPING
SITTING
SKATING
SLAYING
SLIDING
SLOPING
SLOWING
SMILING
SMOKING
SNORING
SOAKING
SOARING
SOCKING
SOPPING
SORTING
SPACING
SPARING
STAGING
STARING
STAYING
STEWING
STYLING
SUMMING
SURFING
SWAYING
TAGALOG
TALKING
TANNING
TAPPING
TATTING
TEARING
TEASING
TEEMING
TELLING
TENSING
TESTING
TICKING
TIMELAG
TIPPING
TOOLING
TOPPING
TOURING
TRACING
TRADING
TREPANG
TURNING
UNDOING
UNDYING
UPSWING
VARYING
VENDING
VETTING
WADDING
WAFTING
WAILING
WAITING
WALKING
WANTING
WAPPING
WARBURG
WARLING
WARMING
WARNING
WARRING
WARTHOG
WASHING
WASTING
WAXWING
WEARING
WEAVING
WEBBING
WEDDING
WEEPING
WELDING
WETTING
WHALING
WHITING
WIGGING
WILLING
WINDBAG
WINDING
WINNING
WISHING
WORDING
WORKING
WRITING
WYOMING
WYSIWYG
YAWNING
ABOLISH
ABSINTH
ALDRICH
ANGUISH
ANTIOCH
ASQUITH
AZIMUTH
BABOOSH
BABYISH
BEARISH
BENEATH
BESEECH
BETROTH
BEWITCH
BISMUTH
BLEMISH
BOOKISH
BOORISH
BOROUGH
BREADTH
BRITISH

BRUTISH
BULLISH
BULRUSH
BURNISH
CADDISH
CATARRH
CATFISH
CATTISH
CEILIDH
CHEETAH
CHERISH
CORINTH
CORNISH
CRANACH
CURRAGH
DALILAH
DEBAUCH
DEBORAH
DEBOUCH
DELILAH
DERVISH
DIGLYPH
DIGRAPH
DIPTYCH
DOGFISH
DONNISH
DUMPISH
ENGLISH
EPITAPH
EYEBATH
EYELASH
EYEWASH
FADDISH
FAIRISH
FINNISH
FLAUNCH
FLEMISH
FOOLISH
FOPPISH
FURBISH
FURNISH
GALUMPH
GARNISH
GAWKISH
GIRLISH
GOLIATH
GOODISH
GOULASH
GRAYISH
GREYISH
GWYNETH
HAPORTH
HARLECH
HARWICH
HASHISH
HELLISH
HEXARCH
HOGARTH
HOGWASH
IMPEACH
INDEPTH
INVEIGH
JAPLISH
JEHOVAH
KADDISH
KENTISH
KUFIYAH
LAMBETH
LOUTISH
LUMPISH
MACBETH
MAMMOTH
MANNISH
MAWKISH
MENORAH
MESSIAH
MITZVAH
MONARCH
MONKISH
MOORISH
MOREISH
NEBBISH
NEOLITH
NINEVEH
NONSUCH
NORWICH
NOURISH
OARFISH
OBADIAH
OGREISH
OSTRICH
PECKISH
PEEVISH
PHARAOH
PIBROCH
POOHBAH
POTLACH
PRUDISH
PUBLISH
PUCKISH
PUGWASH
RAFFISH
RALEIGH
REBIRTH
REDDISH
REFRESH
RETOUCH
RHENISH
ROGUISH
ROOKISH
RUBBISH
RUDOLPH
SABAOTH
SABBATH
SAWFISH
SCRATCH
SCREECH
SCRUNCH
SELFISH
SEVENTH
SHARIAH
SKYHIGH
SLAVISH
SOPWITH
SPANISH
SPINACH
SPLOTCH
SQUELCH
SQUINCH
STAUNCH
STEALTH
STENGAH
STOMACH
STRETCH
STREWTH
STYLISH
SWEDISH
TAPLASH
TARNISH
THROUGH
TIGRISH
TONNISH
TOWPATH
TRIUMPH
TURKISH
TWELFTH
UNCOUTH
UNEARTH
UNHITCH
UNLATCH
UNLEASH
UNTRUTH
UROLITH
VARNISH
WAGGISH
WARPATH
WASPISH
WHITISH
WIMPISH
WOLFISH
YIDDISH
ADELPHI
AFGHANI
ALBERTI
ALLEGRI
ASHANTI
ASSEGAI
BACARDI
BACILLI
BASMATI
BELLINI
BENGALI
BERNINI
BOLSHOI
BOUILLI
BRONCHI
BURUNDI
CALCULI
CAMBRAI
CAMPARI
CELLINI
CHAPATI
CHIANTI
CHUPATI
COLIBRI
CORELLI
EFFENDI
FUSILLI
GNOCCHI
GOLDONI
GRACCHI
GUARANI
HALLALI
HIBACHI
HOUDINI
ISMAILI
ISRAELI
JACUZZI
JAMPANI
KARACHI
KONTIKI
LAKSHMI
LORELEI
MARCONI
MARTINI
NAIROBI
ORIGAMI
OSMANLI
OUSTITI
PAHLAVI
PECCAVI
POLIZEI
POMPEII
PUCCINI
PUNJABI
RAVIOLI
REMBLAI
ROSSINI
SALIERI
SAMURAI
SASHIMI
SCUTARI
SHASTRI
SHIKARI
SIGNORI
SWAHILI
TASSILI
TBILISI
TIMPANI
TOPKAPI
TRIPOLI
TSUNAMI
VIVALDI
WATUTSI
ZAMBESI
AIRLOCK
AIRSICK
AMTRACK
ARTWORK
BANGKOK
BANNOCK
BARRACK
BEATNIK
BEDROCK
BELLEEK
BERSERK
BESPEAK
BETHINK
BULLOCK
BULWARK
BUNDOOK
BURDOCK
CALMUCK
CANNOCK
CARSICK
CASSOCK
CATWALK
CHINOOK
COSSACK
COWLICK
CUTBACK
DAYBOOK
DAYMARK
DEFROCK
DENMARK
DERRICK
DIPLOCK
DISBARK
DUNKIRK
DUNNOCK
DVORNIK
EARMARK
ETTRICK
FETLOCK
FOSSICK
FUTTOCK
GARRICK
GASMASK
GIMMICK
GOSHAWK
HADDOCK
HAMMOCK
HASSOCK
HATTOCK
HEMLOCK
HENPECK
HERRICK
HILLOCK
HOGBACK
HOPSACK
HUMMOCK
KALMUCK
KILLICK
KUBELIK
LEACOCK
LEGWORK
LOGBOOK
MATTOCK
MEACOCK
MENFOLK
METHINK
MIDWEEK
MISTOOK
MUDLARK
MUDPACK
NETWORK
NIBLICK
NORFOLK
OARLOCK
OBELISK
ODALISK
OFFPEAK
OUTBACK
OUTLOOK
OUTRANK
OUTWORK
PADDOCK
PADLOCK
PATRICK
PEACOCK
POLLACK
POTLUCK
PURBECK
PUTTOCK
RANSACK
RATPACK
REDNECK
RESTOCK
RETHINK
ROEBUCK
ROLLICK
ROSTOCK
ROWLOCK
SCHLOCK
SCHMUCK
SEALINK
SEASICK
SELKIRK
SETBACK
SHYLOCK
SJAMBOK
SKYLARK
SPUTNIK
SUFFOLK
SUNDECK
TINTACK
TUSSOCK
UNBLOCK
UNFROCK
UNSTICK
UNSTOCK
UNSTUCK
VOLAPUK
WARBECK
WARLOCK
WARWICK
WAXWORK
WAYMARK
WEDLOCK
WENLOCK
WETBACK
WINNOCK
WRYNECK
YASHMAK
ABIGAIL
ABYSMAL
ABYSSAL
ACAUDAL
ACCRUAL
ACTINAL
ADMIRAL
ADRENAL
AEROSOL
AIRMAIL
ALCOHOL
AMMONAL
AMYGDAL
ANTHILL
APPAREL
APSIDAL
APTERAL
AROUSAL
ARRIVAL
ARSENAL
ARUNDEL
ASEXUAL
ASOCIAL
AUSTRAL
AXOLOTL
BALEFUL
BALLIOL
BASHFUL
BEDEVIL
BEJEWEL
BESTIAL
BIFOCAL
BORSTAL
BOSWELL
BRADAWL
BRIMFUL
BRINJAL
BRISTOL
BROTHEL
BURNELL
CALOMEL
CAPITAL
CAPITOL
CAPORAL
CARACUL
CARAMEL
CARAVEL
CAREFUL
CARRELL
CARROLL
CATCALL
CENTRAL
CHAGALL
CHANCEL
CHANNEL
CHARNEL
CHATTEL
CHERVIL
CHLORAL
CITADEL
COASTAL
COAXIAL
CODICIL

COLONEL
COMICAL
CONCEAL
CONGEAL
CONICAL
CONTROL
CORDIAL
CORNEAL
CORNELL
COUNCIL
COUNSEL
COWGIRL
CRANIAL
CRUCIAL
CRYSTAL
CURTAIL
CYNICAL
DAMOSEL
DECANAL
DECIBEL
DECIMAL
DESPOIL
DIEDRAL
DIGITAL
DIGONAL
DISTILL
DIURNAL
DOLEFUL
DONEGAL
DURRELL
DUTIFUL
EMBROIL
EMPANEL
ENSNARL
ENTHRAL
ESTIVAL
ETERNAL
ETHANOL
ETHICAL
EYEBALL
EZEKIEL
FACTUAL
FALAFEL
FANTAIL
FATEFUL
FEARFUL
FEDERAL
FEMORAL
FINICAL
FISTFUL
FLANNEL
FLUVIAL
FRETFUL
FROEBEL
FRONTAL
FULFILL
FUNCHAL
FUNERAL
GABRIEL
GADWALL
GAINFUL
GARBOIL
GASOHOL
GENERAL
GENITAL
GENTEEL
GLACIAL
GLEEFUL
GLOTTAL
GLYPTAL
GRADUAL
GRAPNEL
GRENDEL
GUIGNOL
GUMBOIL
HANDFUL
HANDSEL
HARMFUL
HATEFUL
HEEDFUL
HELICAL
HELPFUL
HOBNAIL
HOLDALL
HOPEFUL
HURTFUL
ILLEGAL
IMMORAL
IMPERIL
INFIDEL
INITIAL
INKWELL
INSTALL
INSTILL
JEZEBEL
JONQUIL
JOURNAL
JUVENAL
KARAKUL
KESTREL
KNOWALL
KURSAAL
LACTEAL
LATERAL
LEGPULL
LIBERAL
LIMINAL
LINGUAL
LITERAL
LOGICAL
LUSTFUL
LYRICAL
MAGICAL
MARITAL
MARSHAL
MARTIAL
MARVELL
MAXWELL
MEDICAL
MENTHOL
METICAL
MICHAEL
MILFOIL
MINDFUL
MINERAL
MINIMAL
MISTRAL
MONGREL
MORRELL
MUSICAL
NAIPAUL
NARWHAL
NATURAL
NEEDFUL
NEMORAL
NETBALL
NEUTRAL
NOMBRIL
NOMINAL
NOSTRIL
NUMERAL
NUPTIAL
OATMEAL
ODDBALL
OPTICAL
OPTIMAL
ORBITAL
ORDINAL
OUTFALL
OVERALL
PAINFUL
PALATAL
PALUDAL
PARASOL
PARBOIL
PARNELL
PARTIAL
PASCHAL
PATRIAL
PAYROLL
PEDICEL
PERUSAL
PHRASAL
PIGTAIL
PINBALL
PINTAIL
PITFALL
PITIFUL
PIVOTAL
PLAYFUL
PLEURAL
POMEROL
PREDIAL
PREQUEL
PRETZEL
PREVAIL
PUBERAL
PURCELL
QUARREL
QUETZAL
QUINTAL
RACHIAL
RADICAL
RAPHAEL
RECITAL
REDPOLL
REFUSAL
REMODEL
REMOVAL
RENEWAL
REPOSAL
RESTFUL
RETRIAL
REVIVAL
ROCKALL
RORQUAL
ROSTRAL
ROUNDEL
RUDERAL
RUSSELL
SACKFUL
SATCHEL
SAWBILL
SAWMILL
SCAFELL
SCALPEL
SCANDAL
SCHNELL
SCLERAL
SCROTAL
SEAGULL
SEAWALL
SECONAL
SEMINAL
SENEGAL
SENSUAL
SERCIAL
SEVERAL
SHRIVEL
SITWELL
SKILFUL
SKINFUL
SNORKEL
SOULFUL
SPANIEL
SPATIAL
SPECIAL
SPONDYL
SPOUSAL
STENCIL
STERNAL
STOICAL
STRIGIL
STRUDEL
SUBSOIL
SUNDIAL
SURREAL
TACTFUL
TEARFUL
TENDRIL
TENNIEL
TERTIAL
TEXTUAL
THERMAL
TIERCEL
TIMBREL
TINFOIL
TOENAIL
TOMFOOL
TOPICAL
TOPSOIL
TRAMMEL
TRAVAIL
TREFOIL
TRIVIAL
TRUCIAL
TUMBREL
TUMBRIL
TUNEFUL
TURMOIL
TYPICAL
UNCIVIL
UNEQUAL
UNRAVEL
UNSNARL
UNUSUAL
UTENSIL
UXORIAL
VAGINAL
VASSAIL
VENTRAL
VERONAL
VICINAL
VICTUAL
VIRTUAL
VITRAIL
VITRIOL
WAGTAIL
WAKEFUL
WASSAIL
WASTREL
WAXBILL
WAYBILL
WENDELL
WISHFUL
WISTFUL
WRYBILL
ZEPHIEL
ZESTFUL
ABRAHAM
ACCLAIM
ACIFORM
ACRONYM
ALYSSUM
AMALGAM
ANAGRAM
ANTONYM
ATAVISM
ATHEISM
BAPTISM
BEDROOM
BELGIUM
BENTHAM
BERSEEM
BERTRAM
BLOSSOM
BOREDOM
BOXROOM
BRIGHAM
BUCKRAM
BURNHAM
CADMIUM
CAESIUM
CALCIUM
CAMBIUM
CASUISM
CENTRUM
CHATHAM
CHRISOM
CONFIRM
CONFORM
CRANIUM
CUTWORM
DADAISM
DECLAIM
DECORUM
DIAGRAM
DUKEDOM
EARDRUM
EARLDOM
EGOTISM
ELITISM
ELOGIUM
ELYSIUM
ENVENOM
EPHRAIM
EPIGRAM
ERODIUM
ERRATUM
EXCLAIM
FASCISM
FAUVISM
FERMIUM
FIREARM
FLOTSAM
FOREARM
FREEDOM
FULCRUM
GALLIUM
GINGHAM
GROGRAM
GUNROOM
HAFNIUM
HAHNIUM
HEROISM
HEURISM
HOMONYM
HOODLUM
HORDEUM
HUMDRUM
IMAGISM
INTERIM
IRIDIUM
ISCHIUM
ISOGRAM
JEJUNUM
JUDAISM
KINGDOM
LAMAISM
LEGROOM
LIBRIUM
LITHIUM
LUGWORM
LUSTRUM
MACADAM
MARXISM
MAUGHAM
MAXIMUM
METONYM
MIDTERM
MINIMUM
MODICUM
NATRIUM
NIOBIUM
NOSTRUM
OMENTUM
ONANISM
OPOSSUM
OPTIMUM
ORGANUM
ORPHISM
OSCULUM
OVERARM
PABULUM
PAESTUM
PALLIUM
PANGRAM
PEACHUM
PERFORM
PHANTOM
PILGRIM
PINETUM
POTSDAM
PREDOOM
PREMIUM
PROBLEM
PROGRAM
QUANTUM
QUONDAM
REALISM
RECLAIM
REQUIEM
RHODIUM
ROSTRUM
SANCTUM
SARCASM
SCROTUM
SERFDOM
SIKHISM
SOLANUM
SOPHISM
SORGHUM
STADIUM
STARDOM
STERNUM
STRATUM
SUBATOM

SUNBEAM
SURINAM
SYMPTOM
SYNONYM
TACHISM
TANTRUM
TEAROOM
TERBIUM
THEOREM
THOMISM
THORIUM
THULIUM
TITOISM
TOURISM
TRANSOM
TRITIUM
TRIVIUM
TROPISM
UNBOSOM
UNIFORM
URANISM
URANIUM
VERULAM
VIETNAM
WILLIAM
WOLFRAM
YARDARM
YTTRIUM
ABANDON
ABDOMEN
ABIDJAN
ABSTAIN
ACADIAN
ACHAEAN
ACHERON
ACHESON
ACTAEON
ADDISON
ADJOURN
AEOLIAN
AFRICAN
AILERON
ALADDIN
ALAMEIN
ALASKAN
ALBUMEN
ALBUMIN
ALCORAN
ALENÇON
ALKORAN
ANDAMAN
ANDIRON
ANGEVIN
ANGOLAN
ANTIGEN
APOGEAN
AQUILON
ARABIAN
ARRAIGN
ARTISAN
ASHDOWN
ASPIRIN
ATAGHAN
AUCTION
AUDUBON
AVIGNON
BABYLON
BAHRAIN
BAHREIN
BALATON
BALDWIN
BALLOON
BARGAIN
BASSOON
BASTION
BATSMAN
BEDOUIN
BELGIAN
BELLMAN
BENISON
BENZOIN
BERGSON
BETOKEN
BETWEEN
BIAFRAN
BIGHORN
BILLION
BILLMAN
BIRDMAN
BITTERN
BITUMEN
BLACKEN
BLOUSON
BOATMAN
BONDMAN
BOOKMAN
BOOLEAN
BORODIN
BOUNDEN
BOURBON
BOURDON
BOURSIN
BRACKEN
BRADMAN
BRAHMIN
BRENDAN
BRITAIN
BRIXTON
BROADEN
BUFFOON
BULLION
BULLPEN
BUMPKIN
BURGEON
BUSHMAN
BUSHMEN
CADOGAN
CAEDMON
CAISSON
CALDRON
CALEPIN
CALIBAN
CAMERON
CAMPION
CANTEEN
CAPSTAN
CAPTAIN
CAPTION
CARAVAN
CARDOON
CAROTIN
CARRION
CARTOON
CASPIAN
CATALAN
CAUTION
CAVEMAN
CELADON
CERTAIN
CESSION
CHAGRIN
CHANSON
CHAPMAN
CHARDIN
CHASTEN
CHEAPEN
CHECKIN
CHEVRON
CHICKEN
CHIFFON
CHIGNON
CHILEAN
CHILLON
CHORION
CISTERN
CITIZEN
CITROEN
CLACHAN
CLARION
CLOISON
CLUBMAN
COARSEN
COITION
COLLEEN
CONCERN
CONDEMN
CONJOIN
CONSIGN
CONTAIN
CONTEMN
CORYDON
CRAMPON
CREWMAN
CRIMEAN
CRIMSON
CRISPIN
CROUTON
CRYPTON
CURTAIN
CUSHION
DANTEAN
DAUPHIN
DEADPAN
DENDRON
DENIZEN
DETRAIN
DEXTRIN
DICTION
DISCERN
DISDAIN
DISJOIN
DISPRIN
DOESKIN
DOLPHIN
DOORMAN
DRAGOON
DRESDEN
DRUMLIN
DRUNKEN
DUDGEON
DUNEDIN
DUNGEON
DUNSTAN
DURAMEN
DUSTBIN
DUSTMAN
DUSTPAN
EARTHEN
EASTERN
ECHELON
EDITION
ELASTIN
ELATION
ELISION
ELYSIAN
EMERSON
EMOTION
EMULSIN
ENDOGEN
ENGRAIN
ENLIVEN
ENTERON
ENTRAIN
EPIZOON
EPSILON
EPSTEIN
EROSION
ETESIAN
ETONIAN
EVASION
EXPLAIN
FACTION
FASHION
FENELON
FESTOON
FICTION
FIFTEEN
FIREMAN
FISSION
FLATTEN
FLEURON
FLODDEN
FOGHORN
FOOTMAN
FORAMEN
FOREIGN
FOREMAN
FORLORN
FORTRAN
FREEMAN
FRESHEN
FRISIAN
FRISSON
FROGMAN
FUSTIAN
GADROON
GALLEON
GALOPIN
GAMBIAN
GAMELAN
GANELON
GASTRIN
GAUGUIN
GELATIN
GENTIAN
GHERKIN
GLADDEN
GLISTEN
GLUTTON
GOBELIN
GOMBEEN
GOODMAN
GOODWIN
GORDIAN
GREATEN
GRECIAN
GREMLIN
GRIFFON
GRYPHON
GUDGEON
GUINEAN
HADRIAN
HAIRPIN
HAITIAN
HALCYON
HALOGEN
HANDGUN
HANGMAN
HANGMEN
HARDPAN
HARPOON
HEADMAN
HEARKEN
HEARTEN
HEATHEN
HELICON
HELLION
HEPARIN
HESSIAN
HEXAGON
HIGHMAN
HILLMAN
HILLMEN
HOEDOWN
HOLBEIN
HONITON
HORIZON
IBERIAN
INGRAIN
INHUMAN
INSULIN
IRANIAN
ITALIAN
IVORIAN
IVORIEN
JACKSON
JACOBIN
JAMESON
JAVELIN
JAZZMAN
JOHNSON
JURYMAN
KARAJAN
KEARTON
KERATIN
KEROGEN
KHAMSIN
KINGPIN
KINSMAN
KITCHEN
KOWLOON
KREMLIN
KRYPTON
LAMPOON
LANGTON
LANOLIN
LANTERN
LAOCOON
LAOTIAN
LAPUTAN
LARDOON
LATERAN
LATVIAN
LEBANON
LECTERN
LESBIAN
LETDOWN
LEXICON
LIAISON
LIEDOWN
LIGHTEN
LINCOLN
LINEMAN
LINKMAN
LINNEAN
LOTHIAN
LOWDOWN
LUMPKIN
MACEDON
MADISON
MAILMAN
MALAYAN
MANIKIN
MANSION
MANTUAN
MANXMAN
MARMION
MARTIAN
MAUDLIN
MAZARIN
MEGARON
MEGATON
MEISSEN
MELANIN
MENTION
MENUHIN
MESCLUN
MEXICAN
MILKMAN
MILLION
MISSION
MOELLON
MOHICAN
MOISTEN
MONSOON
MOORHEN
MOUFLON
MUEZZIN
MULLEIN
MULLION
MURRAIN
MUTAGEN
NANKEEN
NAVARIN
NEUTRON
NEWBORN
NEWSMAN
NICAEAN
NINEPIN
NIOBEAN
OARSMAN
OARSMEN
OCTAGON
OILSKIN
OMICRON
OPINION
ORATION
ORPHEAN
ORTOLAN
OTTOMAN
OUTSPAN
OUTTURN
OUTWORN
OVARIAN
OVATION
OVERRUN
OXONIAN
PACKMAN
PALADIN
PARAGON
PASSION
PASTERN
PATTERN
PELICAN
PENGUIN
PENSION
PERMIAN

PERSIAN
PERTAIN
PHAETON
PHONEIN
PIDGEON
PIGSKIN
PILLION
PLASMIN
PLATOON
PLAYPEN
PLEBIAN
PLEURON
PLOWMAN
POLYGON
POMPOON
PONTOON
POPCORN
PORCIAN
PORTION
POSTERN
POSTMAN
POTHEEN
POUSSIN
PRONOUN
PROTEAN
PROTEIN
PTYALIN
PULLMAN
PUMPKIN
PURITAN
PURLOIN
PUSHKIN
QUARTAN
QUENTIN
QUICKEN
QUIETEN
QUINTAN
RACCOON
RACHMAN
RAEBURN
RAMADAN
RAMEKIN
RANGOON
RATTEEN
REALIGN
REDSKIN
REFRAIN
REGIMEN
RETRAIN
REUNION
RHODIAN
ROBESON
ROEDEAN
RONTGEN
ROSCIAN
ROUGHEN
RUBICON
RUFFIAN
RUNCORN
RUNDOWN
RUNNION
RUSSIAN
RWANDAN
SABAEAN
SABAYON
SAFFRON
SAGOUIN
SALADIN
SALTPAN
SAMISEN
SANDMAN
SANDOWN
SAPONIN
SARACEN
SAROYAN
SASSOON
SAURIAN
SAXHORN
SEALION
SECTION
SERBIAN
SESSION
SHANNON
SHARPEN
SHEBEEN
SHERMAN
SHIPTON
SHORTEN
SHOTGUN
SHOWMAN
SHRIVEN
SILICON
SIMENON
SIMPKIN
SIMPLON
SIMPSON
SIRLOIN
SITDOWN
SIXTEEN
SKIDPAN
SLACKEN
SMARTEN
SMIDGIN
SMITTEN
SNOWDON
SNOWMAN
SOJOURN
SOLOMON
SPARTAN
SPONSON
SPORRAN
STANDIN
STATION
STEEPEN
STENGUN
STEPHEN
STEPSON
STETSON
STIFFEN
STILTON
STOLLEN
STYGIAN
SUBJOIN
SUBTEEN
SUCTION
SUDETEN
SUNBURN
SUNDOWN
SURGEON
SUSTAIN
SWAGMAN
SWEETEN
SWIDDEN
SWITHIN
SWOLLEN
TAMARIN
TAMPION
TARQUIN
TEHERAN
TENSION
TERRAIN
TERSION
TERTIAN
THEREIN
THICKEN
THOMSON
THROWIN
THYSSEN
TIBETAN
TIGHTEN
TINTERN
TOLKIEN
TOLLMAN
TOMPION
TORCHON
TORSION
TOUGHEN
TRADEIN
TREASON
TRIANON
TRISTAN
TRODDEN
TRUDGEN
TRYPSIN
TUBULIN
TUITION
TYPHOON
UGANDAN
UMBRIAN
UMPTEEN
UNCLEAN
UNCTION
UNICORN
UNKNOWN
UNLADEN
UPSILON
URANIAN
UTOPIAN
VATICAN
VAUGHAN
VENISON
VERSION
VERVAIN
VETERAN
VILLAIN
VILLEIN
VITAMIN
WALKMAN
WALLOON
WEALDEN
WEIGHIN
WESTERN
WHARTON
WHEATEN
WHEREIN
WHITSUN
WIDGEON
WINSTON
WOODMAN
WOOLLEN
WORKMAN
WORKMEN
WRITTEN
XERAFIN
YEREVAN
YPSILON
YUCATAN
ZAIREAN
ZAMBIAN
ZAMORIN
ZILLION
AGITATO
ALBERGO
ALFONSO
ALLEGRO
AMERIGO
AMOROSO
ANTONIO
ARETINO
ARIOSTO
ATISHOO
AVOCADO
BAMBINO
BOTARGO
BRASERO
BRAVADO
BUFFALO
BUGABOO
BUMMALO
BUSHIDO
CALYPSO
CEMBALO
CENTAVO
CHEERIO
CHICAGO
CHICANO
CHORIZO
COLOMBO
COMMODO
CORANTO
CURACAO
DIABOLO
DOMINGO
ELECTRO
EMBARGO
ESPARTO
FARRAGO
FIDELIO
GALILEO
GESTAPO
GROUCHO
GUANACO
HIDALGO
HISPANO
HORATIO
IMPASTO
INFERNO
IONESCO
JERICHO
LENTIGO
LEPANTO
LESOTHO
LIMPOPO
LUMBAGO
MAESTRO
MAFIOSO
MAGNETO
MARENGO
MEMENTO
MONTERO
MORELLO
MORESCO
MOROCCO
MULATTO
MURILLO
NOVELLO
OLOROSO
ONTARIO
OREGANO
ORINOCO
ORLANDO
ORVIETO
OTHELLO
OTRANTO
PALERMO
PICASSO
PICCOLO
PIMENTO
PINTADO
PIZARRO
PLACEBO
PORTICO
PROVISO
PROXIMO
PRURIGO
RICARDO
RISOTTO
ROSARIO
SALERMO
SCHERZO
SCORPIO
SENECIO
SFUMATO
SHAMPOO
SIROCCO
SOPRANO
SUBZERO
SUPREMO
TABASCO
TAMPICO
TARANTO
TESTUDO
THEORBO
THERETO
TIEPOLO
TOBACCO
TORNADO
TORONTO
TORPEDO
TREMOLO
TYMPANO
UCCELLO
UGOLINO
UNDERGO
UTRILLO
VERTIGO
VIBRATO
VOLCANO
ZEMSTVO
ZINGARO
AIRSHIP
AIRSTOP
ANTWERP
BELLHOP
CALTROP
CANTRIP
CATCHUP
CHECKUP
CHIRRUP
CIRCLIP
CLEANUP
CLEARUP
CLOSEUP
COVERUP
COWSLIP
DEVELOP
DEWDROP
ENCLASP
ENVELOP
EPICARP
ESCALOP
FLAREUP
FOGLAMP
GROWNUP
GUMDROP
GYMSLIP
HARDTOP
HARELIP
HILLTOP
IMHOTEP
KETCHUP
KINGCUP
KINSHIP
KNEECAP
MIDSHIP
MILKSOP
MISSTEP
MUDFLAP
MUGWUMP
NONSTOP
OUTCROP
OVERLAP
PARSNIP
REGROUP
ROLLMOP
ROOFTOP
ROUNDUP
SCALLOP
SCHLEPP
SCOLLOP
SHAKEUP
SNARLUP
SOURSOP
STANDUP
STIRRUP
STOPGAP
SUNLAMP
SUNTRAP
TEASHOP
TOYSHOP
TREETOP
TROLLOP
TWOSTEP
UNCLASP
WARSHIP
WICKIUP
WIRETAP
WORKTOP
WORSHIP
WRITEUP
ABETTOR
ABLATOR
ABOUKIR
ACCUSER
ADAPTER
ADAPTOR
ADMIRER
ADVISER
ADVISOR
AGISTOR
ALLSTAR
ALMONER
AMATEUR
AMMETER
ANGULAR
ANNULAR
ANOTHER
AQUIFER
ARBITER
ASUNDER
ATELIER
AUDITOR
AVENGER
AVIATOR
AVOIDER
BABBLER
BAHADUR

BALFOUR
BARRIER
BELABOR
BENCHER
BESMEAR
BLABBER
BLADDER
BLASTER
BLATHER
BLATTER
BLEEPER
BLENDER
BLETHER
BLINDER
BLINKER
BLISTER
BLOATER
BLOCKER
BLOOMER
BLOOPER
BLOTTER
BLUBBER
BLUNDER
BLUSHER
BLUSTER
BOARDER
BOASTER
BOLIVAR
BOLSTER
BOOSTER
BOUDOIR
BOULDER
BOUNCER
BOUNDER
BOWDLER
BRAEMAR
BRANDER
BRAWLER
BRAZIER
BREAKER
BREEDER
BRENNER
BRIDLER
BROILER
BROTHER
BROWSER
BRUISER
BRUSHER
BUCKLER
BUGBEAR
BUILDER
BULGHUR
BUNGLER
BURGHER
BURGLAR
BURSTER
BUSTLER
BUTCHER
CADAVER
CALABAR
CALIBER
CAMPHOR
CANDOUR
CANTUAR
CARRIER
CARTIER
CASHIER
CATCHER
CATERER
CENTAUR
CHALKER
CHAMBER
CHAMFER
CHANTER
CHAPTER
CHARGER
CHARMER
CHARTER
CHATTER
CHAUCER
CHEATER
CHEDDAR
CHEQUER
CHESTER
CHIGGER
CHILLER
CHIPPER
CHOPPER
CHOWDER
CHUKKER
CHUNDER
CLAMBER
CLAMOUR
CLAMPER
CLANGER
CLAPPER
CLATTER
CLEANER
CLEAVER
CLICKER
CLIMBER
CLINGER
CLINKER
CLIPPER
CLOBBER
CLUMBER
CLUSTER
CLUTTER
COASTER
COBBLER
COLLIER
CONIFER
CONQUER
CONTOUR
CORONER
CORSAIR
COULTER
COUNTER
COUPLER
COURIER
COURSER
CRACKER
CRAMMER
CRANMER
CRAWLER
CREATOR
CREEPER
CRITTER
CROAKER
CROFTER
CROONER
CROPPER
CROSIER
CROWBAR
CROZIER
CRUISER
CRUPPER
CRUSHER
CURATOR
DABBLER
DAIMLER
DAMPIER
DAWDLER
DAYSTAR
DEBATER
DECIDER
DECODER
DELIVER
DEMETER
DESPAIR
DIBBLER
DILATOR
DIOPTER
DIPOLAR
DIVINER
DIVISOR
DNIEPER
DOODLER
DOPPLER
DOSSIER
DOUBTER
DOWAGER
DRAWBAR
DREAMER
DREDGER
DRESSER
DRIFTER
DRINKER
DROPPER
DRUMMER
DWELLER
EARLIER
ECUADOR
EJECTOR
ELEANOR
ELECTOR
ELZEVIR
EMBOWER
EMPEROR
EMPOWER
ENACTOR
ENAMOUR
EQUATOR
ERECTOR
ESTOVER
EVANDER
EVENTER
FANCIER
FARCEUR
FARRIER
FARTHER
FEATHER
FELSPAR
FERVOUR
FIDDLER
FIELDER
FIGHTER
FILCHER
FLANKER
FLAPPER
FLASHER
FLATCAR
FLATTER
FLAVOUR
FLECKER
FLICKER
FLIPPER
FLITTER
FLIVVER
FLOATER
FLOGGER
FLUSTER
FLUTTER
FLYOVER
FORBEAR
FOREVER
FORSTER
FOUNDER
FREEZER
FRESHER
FRITTER
FUNFAIR
FURRIER
FURTHER
GABBLER
GAEKWAR
GAMBLER
GLACIER
GLAMOUR
GLAZIER
GLEANER
GLIMMER
GLITTER
GOBBLER
GRAFTER
GRAINER
GRAMMAR
GREASER
GREENER
GRIFTER
GRINDER
GROLIER
GROUPER
GROUSER
GROWLER
GUILDER
GUZZLER
HAMSTER
HANDLER
HANOVER
HARBOUR
HARRIER
HAULIER
HEATHER
HEAVIER
HECKLER
HIPSTER
HOARDER
HOLSTER
HOTSPUR
HOWEVER
HUMIDOR
HURDLER
HUSTLER
INCISOR
INCOMER
INDEXER
INHALER
INSIDER
INSULAR
INSURER
INTEGER
INVADER
JANITOR
JEWELER
JOCULAR
JUGGLER
JUGULAR
JUNIPER
JUPITER
KASHMIR
KIELDER
KLAVIER
KLINKER
KNACKER
KNAPPER
KNEELER
KNELLER
KNICKER
KNITTER
KNOCKER
LABORER
LACQUER
LANGUOR
LATIMER
LAUNDER
LAVATER
LEAGUER
LEANDER
LEARNER
LEATHER
LIGHTER
LIMITER
LIQUEUR
LOBSTER
LOTHAIR
LOUNGER
LUCIFER
LURCHER
MAILCAR
MANAGER
MARCHER
MARINER
MASSEUR
MATADOR
MAUNDER
MAYFAIR
MEANDER
MEDDLER
MERRIER
MESSIER
METAYER
MINSTER
MIRADOR
MOBSTER
MODULAR
MOITHER
MONITOR
MONSTER
MOULDER
MOURNER
MUDEJAR
MUFFLER
MUNSTER
MYANMAR
NEBULAR
NEITHER
NOBBLER
NODULAR
NUCLEAR
OBLIGOR
OCELLAR
OCTOBER
OFFERER
OFFICER
OLDSTER
OUTDOOR
OUTLIER
OUTPOUR
OUTWEAR
PADDLER
PAINTER
PALAVER
PALOMAR
PANNIER
PANTHER
PARADOR
PARLOUR
PARTNER
PASTEUR
PAVIOUR
PEDDLER
PERRIER
PHILTER
PHRASER
PICADOR
PICKLER
PIERCER
PILCHER
PIONEER
PITCHER
PLANNER
PLANTAR
PLANTER
PLASTER
PLATTER
PLEADER
PLESSOR
PLODDER
PLOTTER
PLUMBER
PLUMPER
PLUNDER
PLUNGER
POACHER
POCHOIR
POINTER
POLYMER
POOFTER
POPOVER
POPULAR
POSTWAR
PRAETOR
PREMIER
PRICKER
PRIMEUR
PRINTER
PROCTOR
PROFFER
PROSPER
PROUDER
PROWLER
PSALTER
PUNCHER
PUNSTER
PURSUER
PUZZLER
QUARTER
QUEERER
QUESTER
QUICKER
QUILTER
QUITTER
RAMBLER
RANCHER
RANCOUR
RATTLER
REACTOR
REALGAR
REALTOR
REAUMUR
RECOVER
REDUCER
REENTER
REFINER
REGULAR
RELAYER

REMOVER
REOCCUR
RESCUER
REVELER
REVISER
REVIVER
RICHTER
RIDDLER
ROASTER
ROISTER
ROOSTER
ROTATOR
ROUNDER
ROUTIER
RUFFLER
RUMBLER
RUSTLER
SADDLER
SALAZAR
SAMOVAR
SAMPLER
SAUNTER
SAVIOUR
SCALPER
SCAMPER
SCANNER
SCARPER
SCATTER
SCEPTER
SCHEMER
SCHOLAR
SCISSOR
SCOFFER
SCOOTER
SCOURER
SCOWDER
SCRAPER
SCULLER
SCUPPER
SCUTTER
SECULAR
SEDUCER
SELTZER
SEMINAR
SENATOR
SETTLER
SEYMOUR
SHARPER
SHATTER
SHEARER
SHELTER
SHIMMER
SHIPPER
SHIRKER
SHOCKER
SHOOTER
SHOPPER
SHOUTER
SHRIVER
SHUDDER
SHUTTER
SHYSTER
SIDECAR
SIMILAR
SIMPLER
SIZZLER
SKELTER
SKIMMER
SKINNER
SKIPPER
SKITTER
SLACKER
SLAMMER
SLANDER
SLAPPER
SLEEPER
SLENDER
SLICKER
SLIMMER
SLIPPER
SLITHER
SLOBBER
SLOGGER
SLUMBER
SMACKER
SMALLER
SMASHER
SMATTER
SMELTER
SMITHER
SMOLDER
SMOTHER
SNAPPER
SNARLER
SNEAKER
SNICKER
SNIFFER
SNIFTER
SNIGGER
SNOOKER
SNOOPER
SNORTER
SOCAGER
SOLDIER
SOUNDER
SPADGER
SPANKER
SPANNER
SPATTER
SPEAKER
SPECTER
SPELLER
SPENCER
SPENDER
SPENSER
SPINNER
SPLICER
SPOILER
SPONGER
SPONSOR
SPOONER
SPOTTER
SPRAYER
SPUTTER
SQUALOR
STAFFER
STAGGER
STAINER
STALKER
STAMMER
STAMPER
STAPLER
STARTER
STEAMER
STEERER
STELLAR
STENTOR
STICKER
STINGER
STINKER
STONKER
STOPPER
STRIDOR
STRIKER
STRIPER
STUNNER
STURMER
STUTTER
SUBEDAR
SUCCOUR
SULPHUR
SWAGGER
SWEATER
SWEEPER
SWELTER
SWIFTER
SWIMMER
SWINGER
TABULAR
TACKLER
TAMBOUR
TANAGER
TANGIER
TAPSTER
TARSIER
TATTLER
TEACHER
TELSTAR
TEMPLAR
TEMPTER
TERRIER
THEATER
THINKER
THINNER
THITHER
THROWER
THUMPER
THUNDER
TICKLER
TIDDLER
TINGLER
TIPPLER
TIPSTER
TITULAR
TOASTER
TODDLER
TRACKER
TRACTOR
TRAILER
TRAINER
TRAITOR
TRAMCAR
TRANTER
TRAPPER
TRAWLER
TREKKER
TRIFLER
TRIGGER
TRILLER
TRIMMER
TRIPPER
TROOPER
TROTTER
TROUPER
TROUSER
TRUCKER
TUBULAR
TUMBLER
TUTELAR
TWEETER
TWIGGER
TWISTER
TWITTER
UNCLEAR
UNCOVER
USURPER
VENERER
VERMEER
VETIVER
VINEGAR
VINTNER
VISITOR
VOUCHER
VOYAGER
WAGGLER
WAGONER
WALTZER
WANGLER
WARBLER
WARDOUR
WARRIOR
WATCHER
WAVERER
WEATHER
WEBSTER
WHACKER
WHEELER
WHETHER
WHIMPER
WHINGER
WHISKER
WHISPER
WHITHER
WHOEVER
WHOOPER
WHOPPER
WIDOWER
WINDSOR
WOOSTER
WORRIER
WOTCHER
WRAPPER
WRECKER
WRINGER
YOUNGER
ABATTIS
ABIOSIS
ABRAXIS
ABSCESS
ACESTES
ACHATES
ACTRESS
ADDRESS
ADONAIS
AFFAIRS
AGELESS
AGGRESS
AIMLESS
AIRLESS
ALGIERS
ALMACKS
ALPHEUS
ALUMNUS
AMBAGES
AMOROUS
ANANIAS
ANGELUS
ANIMALS
ANNULUS
ANTARES
ANTIBES
ANTLERS
ANXIOUS
APHESIS
APICIUS
APROPOS
APTNESS
AQUEOUS
AQUINAS
AQUINUS
ARBUTUS
ARDUOUS
ARREARS
ARTEMIS
ARTEMUS
ARTLESS
ASCITES
ASSISTS
ASSIZES
ATTICUS
AUROCHS
AZYGOUS
BACCHUS
BADNESS
BAHAMAS
BANANAS
BARENTS
BARKERS
BARYTES
BATHERS
BATTELS
BAUHAUS
BEACHES
BEATLES
BELARUS
BELLOWS
BENARES
BENTHOS
BESIDES
BETIMES
BILIOUS
BILLOWS
BIOMASS
BITTERS
BLAZERS
BLESSES
BOLETUS
BONKERS
BOOKIES
BORDERS
BOTTLES
BRIDGES
BRIDLES
BRITONS
BROKERS
BUBBLES
BUCKETS
BUGGINS
BUGLOSS
BULBOUS
BULLETS
BURGESS
BURNOUS
BUSKINS
BUSTLES
BUTTONS
CAHOOTS
CALAMUS
CALENDS
CALLOUS
CANTHUS
CANVASS
CARACAS
CARCASS
CARDUUS
CAREERS
CARGOES
CARITAS
CAROLUS
CARRIES
CARROTS
CASUALS
CATKINS
CELEBES
CELSIUS
CHABLIS
CHAMOIS
CHANGES
CHARGES
CHARLES
CHASSIS
CHLAMYS
CINDERS
CINEMAS
CIVVIES
CLOTHES
COCKLES
COFFERS
COLCHIS
COLITIS
COLOURS
COLUMNS
COMMONS
COMPASS
CONCUSS
CONFESS
CONSOLS
COPIOUS
COPPERS
COUPONS
COURSES
COUSINS
COXLESS
COYNESS
CRASHES
CRASSUS
CROESUS
CROQUIS
CRUELLS
CSARDAS
CUIRASS
CUMULUS
CURIOUS
CUSTOMS
CUTLASS
CUTTERS
CYCLOPS
CYMBALS
CYPRESS
CYTISUS
DAGGERS
DAMAGES
DAPHNIS
DEGAUSS
DEGREES
DELIBES
DEPRESS
DESERTS
DETAILS
DEVIOUS
DICKENS
DIDYMUS
DIGRESS
DIMNESS
DISCUSS
DISMISS
DITTIES

DOCTORS
DODGEMS
DOLLARS
DOLORES
DOUBLES
DOUGLAS
DRAWERS
DREYFUS
DRIVERS
DRYNESS
DUBIOUS
DUCHESS
ECDYSIS
ECHINUS
ECTASIS
EFFECTS
EMBOLUS
EMPLOYS
EMPRESS
ENDLESS
ENDWAYS
ENGROSS
ENVIOUS
EPHEBUS
EPHESUS
ERASMUS
ERINYES
ESSENES
ETAPLES
EXPRESS
EYELESS
EYELIDS
FACTORS
FAGGOTS
FAJITAS
FALSIES
FARMERS
FATNESS
FATUOUS
FAUSTUS
FELLOWS
FERROUS
FETTERS
FIBROUS
FIDGETS
FIGURES
FILINGS
FILLETS
FINGERS
FITNESS
FIXINGS
FLOWERS
FOLLIES
FORCEPS
FORTIES
FRANCIS
FRIENDS
FULLERS
FUNGOUS
FURIOUS
FUTURES
GAITERS
GALLONS
GALLOWS
GARDENS
GASEOUS
GAYNESS
GENESIS
GIBBONS
GIBBOUS
GIBLETS
GIMBALS
GLASSES
GLOTTIS
GODDESS
GODLESS
GOGGLES
GOODIES
GOOLIES
GORDIUS
GRAMPUS
GRAPHIS
GREAVES
GROCERS
GROPIUS
GROTIUS
GROUNDS
GUBBINS
GUINEAS
GUTLESS
HACKLES
HALITUS
HAPLESS
HARNESS
HATLESS
HEAVENS
HEIGHTS
HEINOUS
HEIRESS
HERRIES
HIDEOUS
HIGGINS
HOBSONS
HONOURS
HOPKINS
HORRORS
HOSTESS
HUMBLES
HUMERUS
HUNKERS
HUSSARS
ICINESS
ICTERUS
IGNEOUS
ILIACUS
ILLNESS
IMPETUS
IMPIOUS
IMPRESS
INCUBUS
INDOORS
INGRESS
INNARDS
INNINGS
INROADS
INSECTS
INSIDES
INVIOUS
INWARDS
ISLANDS
ISTHMUS
JACKASS
JACKETS
JACOBUS
JACQUES
JANKERS
JEALOUS
JEEPERS
JENKINS
JERSEYS
JIMJAMS
JITTERS
JOBLESS
JOYLESS
JUGGINS
JUGLANS
JUMBLES
KALENDS
KENNELS
KENOSIS
KERMESS
KIDNEYS
KINESIS
KIPPERS
KIWANIS
KOUMISS
KURHAUS
LACEUPS
LALLANS
LANCERS
LARGESS
LAURELS
LAWLESS
LAWYERS
LAXNESS
LAYINGS
LEADERS
LEGIONS
LEGLESS
LENTILS
LEPROUS
LETTERS
LINCTUS
LININGS
LIONESS
LIQUIDS
LITOTES
LOCUSTS
LOURDES
LUTYENS
LYCHNIS
MADNESS
MAENADS
MAKINGS
MALLEUS
MALTHUS
MANNERS
MARACAS
MARBLES
MARQUIS
MARSYAS
MARTENS
MARTYRS
MASTERS
MATTERS
MATTINS
MEASLES
MEIOSIS
MEMBERS
MEMOIRS
MERCIES
MESEEMS
MILLAIS
MIMULUS
MINIBUS
MINUTES
MITHRAS
MITOSIS
MITTENS
MOCKERS
MODULUS
MOMENTS
MORTALS
MOTHERS
MUMMERS
MUSSELS
MYCETES
MYIASIS
NACROUS
NARROWS
NATIONS
NATIVES
NEEDLES
NEGRESS
NEMESIS
NERVOUS
NEWNESS
NIPPERS
NITROUS
NONPLUS
NOODLES
NOTIONS
NOXIOUS
NUCLEUS
NUMBERS
NUMBLES
OBJECTS
OBVIOUS
OCELLUS
OCTOPUS
ODDNESS
ODOROUS
OEDIPUS
OESTRUS
OFFICES
OLDNESS
OLYMPUS
OMINOUS
OMNIBUS
ONENESS
ONEROUS
ONMIBUS
ONWARDS
OPPRESS
ORACLES
ORANGES
ORESTES
ORIGINS
ORKNEYS
ORLEANS
ORONTES
ORPHEUS
OSMOSIS
OSSEOUS
PAJAMAS
PALINGS
PANCRAS
PANTIES
PAPYRUS
PARADOS
PARENTS
PARESIS
PARINGS
PARLOUS
PAROTIS
PASTIES
PEANUTS
PEBBLES
PEERESS
PEGASUS
PELORUS
PENATES
PEPPERS
PERCUSS
PERHAPS
PERSEUS
PERSONS
PETROUS
PHALLUS
PHIDIAS
PHILEAS
PHOEBUS
PHONICS
PHYSICS
PIGEONS
PILATUS
PINCERS
PIRAEUS
PITEOUS
PLAUTUS
PLAYERS
PLEASES
PLUTEUS
POETESS
POLARIS
POLYPUS
POMPOUS
POPULUS
POROSIS
PORTHOS
POSSESS
PRELIMS
PREMISS
PRIAPUS
PRIESTS
PRINCES
PROCESS
PROFESS
PROFITS
PRONAOS
PROTEUS
PROWESS
PUTTEES
PYJAMAS
PYLORUS
PYRITES
PYROSIS
QUERCUS
QUIETUS
RACKETS
RAFFLES
RAMESES
RAMULUS
RATIONS
RAUCOUS
RAVAGES
RAVINGS
RAWNESS
RECORDS
REDNESS
REDRESS
REGARDS
REGRESS
RELICTS
REMAINS
REPAIRS
REPRESS
REREDOS
RESULTS
RETAINS
RETURNS
RHOMBUS
RIBLESS
RICKETS
RIDINGS
RIMLESS
RINGERS
RIOTERS
RIOTOUS
ROBBERS
ROBERTS
ROLLERS
ROMPERS
ROSCIUS
ROZZERS
RUBBERS
RUINOUS
RUNNERS
SADNESS
SAILORS
SALAMIS
SANCTUS
SANDALS
SAPIENS
SAPPERS
SARCOUS
SAVAGES
SAVINGS
SCABIES
SCHICKS
SCHLOSS
SECONDS
SECRETS
SEEKERS
SELLERS
SERAPIS
SERIOUS
SERPENS
SEVERUS
SEXLESS
SHAKERS
SHEAVES
SHELVES
SHIVERS
SHOWERS
SHRIMPS
SHROUDS
SHYNESS
SIDDONS
SIEMENS
SINGLES
SINUOUS
SISTERS
SLYNESS
SOLIDUS
SOROSIS
SORROWS
SPECIES
SPIDERS
SPIRITS
SPRINGS
SPROUTS
SQUARES
SQUEERS
STABLES
STACHYS
STARETS
STATICS
STEVENS
STIRPES
STORIES
STRAITS
STRATUS
STRAUSS
STRIDES
STRINGS
STRIPES

SUCCESS
SUMMONS
SUNLESS
SURPASS
SURPLUS
SYCOSIS
SYNAXIS
TACITUS
TACTICS
TAGETES
TAILORS
TAKINGS
TALIPES
TAMESIS
TATTERS
TEDIOUS
TENANTS
TENUOUS
TETANUS
THALLUS
THERMOS
THESEUS
THIEVES
THREADS
THRENOS
THYRSIS
TIDINGS
TIGRESS
TIMBERS
TONGUES
TOPLESS
TORPIDS
TOWARDS
TRELLIS
TRESSES
TRICEPS
TRIFLES
TRIPSIS
TROCHUS
TROILUS
TROPICS
TUMULUS
TYLOSIS
ULYSSES
UNCINUS
UNDRESS
UNITIES
UPSIDES
UPWARDS
USELESS
VACUOUS
VANDALS
VANITAS
VAPOURS
VARIOUS
VAUDOIS
VELOURS
VESPERS
VICIOUS
VIDIMUS
VIKINGS
VILNIUS
VISCOUS
WALLIES
WASHERS
WATTLES
WEAPONS
WEIGHTS
WELLIES
WETNESS
WHEREAS
WILLIES
WINDOWS
WITCHES
WITHERS
WITLESS
WITNESS
WONDERS
WORKERS
XANTHOS
XENOPUS
XEROSIS
XIMENES
YELLOWS
YONKERS
ZEALOUS
ZYGOSIS
ZYMOSIS
ABJOINT
ABREAST
ACCOUNT
ACROBAT
ADAMANT
ADJOINT
ADJUNCT
AFFLICT
AFFRONT
AGAINST
AGONIST
AILMENT
AIRLIFT
AIRPORT
ALECOST
ALICANT
ALIMENT
ALIQUOT
ALKANET
ALRIGHT
AMBIENT
AMONGST
AMORIST
ANALYST
ANCIENT
ANIMIST
ANNULET
APPARAT
APPOINT
APRICOT
AQUAVIT
ARMREST
ASPHALT
ASSAULT
ATHEIST
ATHIRST
ATHWART
ATOMIST
ATTAINT
ATTEMPT
ATTRACT
AUGMENT
AUTOMAT
BABBITT
BABYSIT
BACKSET
BAGEHOT
BAJAZET
BALLAST
BANQUET
BAPTIST
BARONET
BASINET
BATHMAT
BAYONET
BECKETT
BEDPOST
BEERMAT
BENEFIT
BENNETT
BEQUEST
BETWIXT
BIBELOT
BIGFOOT
BIGSHOT
BISCUIT
BISTORT
BLANKET
BLATANT
BLOWOUT
BOMBAST
BOOKLET
BOUQUET
BOWSHOT
BOYCOTT
BRACKET
BRIDGET
BRISKET
BROUGHT
BUMBOAT
BUOYANT
BURNOUT
CABARET
CABINET
CALUMET
CAMELOT
CARPORT
CASUIST
CATMINT
CELLIST
CESSPIT
CHAPLET
CHARIOT
CHEMIST
CHEROOT
CHEVIOT
CHINDIT
CIRCLET
CIRCUIT
CLEMENT
COCKPIT
COCONUT
COEXIST
COHABIT
COLLECT
COMFORT
COMMENT
COMPACT
COMPORT
COMPOST
CONCEIT
CONCEPT
CONCERT
CONCOCT
CONDUCT
CONDUIT
CONNECT
CONSENT
CONSIST
CONSORT
CONSULT
CONTACT
CONTENT
CONTEST
CONTEXT
CONTORT
CONVENT
CONVERT
CONVICT
COOLANT
COPILOT
COPYCAT
COPYIST
CORBETT
CORONET
CORRECT
CORRUPT
COULDNT
COUPLET
COURBET
CREWCUT
CRICKET
CROCHET
CROCKET
CROQUET
CRUMPET
CULPRIT
CULVERT
CURRANT
CURRENT
CYCLIST
CYPRIOT
DADAIST
DASHPOT
DEADSET
DEAREST
DEBRETT
DECRYPT
DEFAULT
DEFIANT
DEFICIT
DEFLECT
DEFROST
DEFUNCT
DELIGHT
DELIMIT
DEMERIT
DENTIST
DEPOSIT
DERWENT
DESCANT
DESCENT
DESSERT
DETRACT
DEVIANT
DIALECT
DIARIST
DIDEROT
DIECAST
DILUENT
DINGBAT
DINMONT
DISGUST
DISMAST
DISPORT
DISRUPT
DISSECT
DISSENT
DISTANT
DISTENT
DISTORT
DOGCART
DOORMAT
DORMANT
DOUBLET
DRAGNET
DRAUGHT
DRIBLET
DROPLET
DROPOUT
DROUGHT
DRUGGET
EARNEST
EARSHOT
EASIEST
EGOTIST
ELEGANT
ELEGIST
ELEMENT
ELITIST
EMINENT
ENCHANT
ENCRUST
ENGRAFT
ENPRINT
ENTRANT
ENTREAT
ENTRUST
EPAULET
EPITHET
ESCHEAT
ESTREAT
EVEREST
EVIDENT
EXCERPT
EXHAUST
EXHIBIT
EXIGENT
EXPLOIT
EXTINCT
EXTRACT
EYESHOT
FADDIST
FALLOUT
FASCIST
FASTNET
FAUVIST
FERMENT
FERVENT
FIGMENT
FILBERT
FISHNET
FITMENT
FITTEST
FLATLET
FLEAPIT
FLEURET
FLORIST
FLUTIST
FLYPAST
FONDANT
FORFEIT
FOXTROT
FRAUGHT
FREIGHT
FRESHET
FULGENT
GABFEST
GALIPOT
GALLANT
GARMENT
GERAINT
GESTALT
GILBERT
GIMBLET
GOURMET
GROMMET
GRUMMET
GUMBOOT
GUNBOAT
GUNSHOT
GYMNAST
HABITAT
HAGBOLT
HAIRCUT
HAIRNET
HALBERT
HALFWIT
HALIBUT
HANDOUT
HANDSET
HANGOUT
HARICOT
HARPIST
HARRIET
HARVEST
HATCHET
HAZLETT
HEADSET
HELLCAT
HENGIST
HERBERT
HERBIST
HIDEOUT
HIGHEST
HOTFOOT
HOTSHOT
HYDRANT
IAMBIST
ILLICIT
IMAGIST
IMPLANT
IMPREST
IMPRINT
INBUILT
INBURST
INCRUST
INEXACT
INFARCT
INFLECT
INFLICT
INHABIT
INHERIT
INHIBIT
INQUEST
INSIGHT
INSPECT
INSTANT
INTROIT
ISOHYET
ISSUANT
JACKPOT
JOGTROT
KILVERT
KINGLET
KNESSET
KUMQUAT
LAMAIST
LAMBAST
LAMBENT
LAMBERT
LARGEST
LATCHET
LAWSUIT
LEAFLET
LEFTIST
LENIENT
LEVERET
LINOCUT

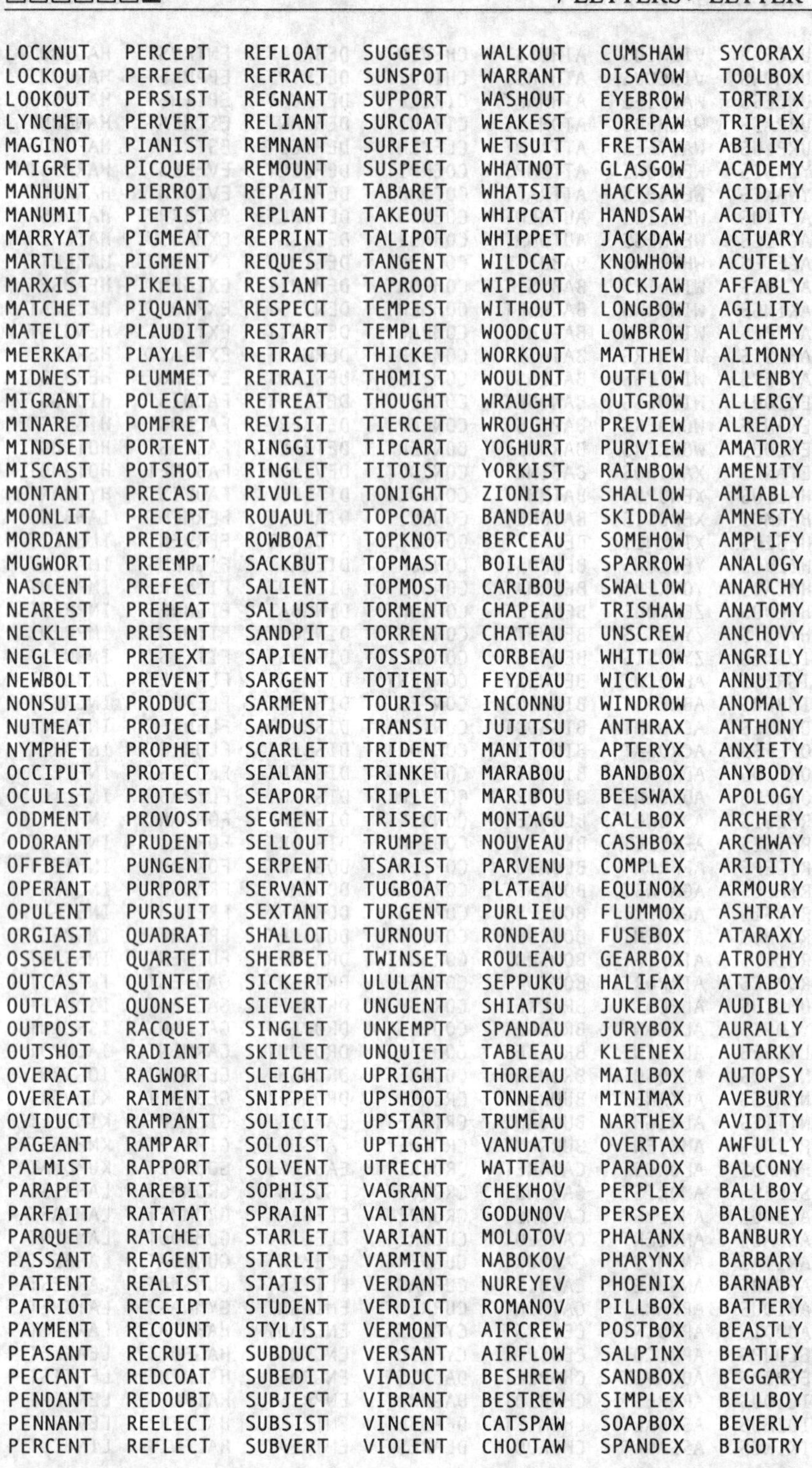

LOCKNUT
LOCKOUT
LOOKOUT
LYNCHET
MAGINOT
MAIGRET
MANHUNT
MANUMIT
MARRYAT
MARTLET
MARXIST
MATCHET
MATELOT
MEERKAT
MIDWEST
MIGRANT
MINARET
MINDSET
MISCAST
MONTANT
MOONLIT
MORDANT
MUGWORT
NASCENT
NEAREST
NECKLET
NEGLECT
NEWBOLT
NONSUIT
NUTMEAT
NYMPHET
OCCIPUT
OCULIST
ODDMENT
ODORANT
OFFBEAT
OPERANT
OPULENT
ORGIAST
OSSELET
OUTCAST
OUTLAST
OUTPOST
OUTSHOT
OVERACT
OVEREAT
OVIDUCT
PAGEANT
PALMIST
PARAPET
PARFAIT
PARQUET
PASSANT
PATIENT
PATRIOT
PAYMENT
PEASANT
PECCANT
PENDANT
PENNANT
PERCENT

PERCEPT
PERFECT
PERSIST
PERVERT
PIANIST
PICQUET
PIERROT
PIETIST
PIGMEAT
PIGMENT
PIKELET
PIQUANT
PLAUDIT
PLAYLET
PLUMMET
POLECAT
POMFRET
PORTENT
POTSHOT
PRECAST
PRECEPT
PREDICT
PREEMPT
PREFECT
PREHEAT
PRESENT
PRETEXT
PREVENT
PRODUCT
PROJECT
PROPHET
PROTECT
PROTEST
PROVOST
PRUDENT
PUNGENT
PURPORT
PURSUIT
QUADRAT
QUARTET
QUINTET
QUONSET
RACQUET
RADIANT
RAGWORT
RAIMENT
RAMPANT
RAMPART
RAPPORT
RAREBIT
RATATAT
RATCHET
REAGENT
REALIST
RECEIPT
RECOUNT
RECRUIT
REDCOAT
REDOUBT
REELECT
REFLECT

REFLOAT
REFRACT
REGNANT
RELIANT
REMNANT
REMOUNT
REPAINT
REPLANT
REPRINT
REQUEST
RESIANT
RESPECT
RESTART
RETRACT
RETRAIT
RETREAT
REVISIT
RINGGIT
RINGLET
RIVULET
ROUAULT
ROWBOAT
SACKBUT
SALIENT
SALLUST
SANDPIT
SAPIENT
SARGENT
SARMENT
SAWDUST
SCARLET
SEALANT
SEAPORT
SEGMENT
SELLOUT
SERPENT
SERVANT
SEXTANT
SHALLOT
SHERBET
SICKERT
SIEVERT
SINGLET
SKILLET
SLEIGHT
SNIPPET
SOLICIT
SOLOIST
SOLVENT
SOPHIST
SPRAINT
STARLET
STARLIT
STATIST
STUDENT
STYLIST
SUBDUCT
SUBEDIT
SUBJECT
SUBSIST
SUBVERT

SUGGEST
SUNSPOT
SUPPORT
SURCOAT
SURFEIT
SUSPECT
TABARET
TAKEOUT
TALIPOT
TANGENT
TAPROOT
TEMPEST
TEMPLET
THICKET
THOMIST
THOUGHT
TIERCET
TIPCART
TITOIST
TONIGHT
TOPCOAT
TOPKNOT
TOPMAST
TOPMOST
TORMENT
TORRENT
TOSSPOT
TOTIENT
TOURIST
TRANSIT
TRIDENT
TRINKET
TRIPLET
TRISECT
TRUMPET
TSARIST
TUGBOAT
TURGENT
TURNOUT
TWINSET
ULULANT
UNGUENT
UNKEMPT
UNQUIET
UPRIGHT
UPSHOOT
UPSTART
UPTIGHT
UTRECHT
VAGRANT
VALIANT
VARIANT
VARMINT
VERDANT
VERDICT
VERMONT
VERSANT
VIADUCT
VIBRANT
VINCENT
VIOLENT

WALKOUT
WARRANT
WASHOUT
WEAKEST
WETSUIT
WHATNOT
WHATSIT
WHIPCAT
WHIPPET
WILDCAT
WIPEOUT
WITHOUT
WOODCUT
WORKOUT
WOULDNT
WRAUGHT
WROUGHT
YOGHURT
YORKIST
ZIONIST
BANDEAU
BERCEAU
BOILEAU
CARIBOU
CHAPEAU
CHATEAU
CORBEAU
FEYDEAU
INCONNU
JUJITSU
MANITOU
MARABOU
MARIBOU
MONTAGU
NOUVEAU
PARVENU
PLATEAU
PURLIEU
RONDEAU
ROULEAU
SEPPUKU
SHIATSU
SPANDAU
TABLEAU
THOREAU
TONNEAU
TRUMEAU
VANUATU
WATTEAU
CHEKHOV
GODUNOV
MOLOTOV
NABOKOV
NUREYEV
ROMANOV
AIRCREW
AIRFLOW
BESHREW
BESTREW
CATSPAW
CHOCTAW

CUMSHAW
DISAVOW
EYEBROW
FOREPAW
FRETSAW
GLASGOW
HACKSAW
HANDSAW
JACKDAW
KNOWHOW
LOCKJAW
LONGBOW
LOWBROW
MATTHEW
OUTFLOW
OUTGROW
PREVIEW
PURVIEW
RAINBOW
SHALLOW
SKIDDAW
SOMEHOW
SPARROW
SWALLOW
TRISHAW
UNSCREW
WHITLOW
WICKLOW
WINDROW
ANTHRAX
APTERYX
BANDBOX
BEESWAX
CALLBOX
CASHBOX
COMPLEX
EQUINOX
FLUMMOX
FUSEBOX
GEARBOX
HALIFAX
JUKEBOX
JURYBOX
KLEENEX
MAILBOX
MINIMAX
NARTHEX
OVERTAX
PARADOX
PERPLEX
PERSPEX
PHALANX
PHARYNX
PHOENIX
PILLBOX
POSTBOX
SALPINX
SANDBOX
SIMPLEX
SOAPBOX
SPANDEX

SYCORAX
TOOLBOX
TORTRIX
TRIPLEX
ABILITY
ACADEMY
ACIDIFY
ACIDITY
ACTUARY
ACUTELY
AFFABLY
AGILITY
ALCHEMY
ALIMONY
ALLENBY
ALLERGY
ALREADY
AMATORY
AMENITY
AMIABLY
AMNESTY
AMPLIFY
ANALOGY
ANARCHY
ANATOMY
ANCHOVY
ANGRILY
ANNUITY
ANOMALY
ANTHONY
ANXIETY
ANYBODY
APOLOGY
ARCHERY
ARCHWAY
ARIDITY
ARMOURY
ASHTRAY
ATARAXY
ATROPHY
ATTABOY
AUDIBLY
AURALLY
AUTARKY
AUTOPSY
AVEBURY
AVIDITY
AWFULLY
BALCONY
BALLBOY
BALONEY
BANBURY
BARBARY
BARNABY
BATTERY
BEASTLY
BEATIFY
BEGGARY
BELLBOY
BEVERLY
BIGOTRY

BINDERY
BIOLOGY
BLANDLY
BLANKLY
BLEAKLY
BLIGHTY
BLINDLY
BLOTCHY
BLOWFLY
BLUFFLY
BLUNTLY
BOLONEY
BRAVELY
BRAVERY
BREVITY
BREWERY
BRIBERY
BRIEFLY
BRISKLY
BRISTLY
BROADLY
BURSARY
BUTTERY
CACHEXY
CALCIFY
CALLBOY
CALUMNY
CALVARY
CANNERY
CANNILY
CANONRY
CAPABLY
CARAWAY
CARNABY
CARROTY
CATESBY
CAUTERY
CAVALRY
CENTURY
CERTIFY
CHARITY
CHARLEY
CHARPOY
CHEAPLY
CHICORY
CHIEFLY
CHIMNEY
CHINTZY
CHRISTY
CHUTNEY
CIVILLY
CLARIFY
CLARITY
CLEANLY
CLEARLY
CLIQUEY
CLOSELY
COCKNEY
COGENCY
COMFREY
COMPANY
CONAKRY
COOKERY
COTTONY
COUNTRY
COURTLY
CRACKLY
CRAZILY
CRICKEY
CRINKLY
CROSSLY
CRUCIFY
CRUDELY
CRUDITY
CRUELLY
CRUELTY
CRUMBLY
CRUNCHY
CURSORY
CURTSEY
CUSTODY
CUTAWAY
CUTLERY
DEANERY
DEATHLY
DEBUSSY
DECENCY
DEEPFRY
DENSELY
DENSITY
DESTINY
DESTROY
DEVILRY
DIARCHY
DIDICOY
DIETARY
DIGNIFY
DIGNITY
DISOBEY
DISPLAY
DITHERY
DITTANY
DIZZILY
DODDERY
DOORKEY
DOORWAY
DOROTHY
DOUGHTY
DOWDILY
DRAPERY
DRIZZLY
DROSHKY
DUALITY
DUBIETY
DUOPOLY
DURABLY
DYARCHY
DYNASTY
EAGERLY
EARTHLY
ECOLOGY
ECONOMY
ECSTASY
EGALITY
ELDERLY
ELUSORY
EMBASSY
EMPATHY
ENQUIRY
EPITAXY
EQUABLY
EQUALLY
EQUERRY
ERISKAY
ESTUARY
EUPEPSY
EUPHONY
EXACTLY
EXOGAMY
FACTORY
FACULTY
FAINTLY
FAIRWAY
FALLACY
FALSELY
FALSIFY
FANTASY
FARADAY
FARAWAY
FATALLY
FATUITY
FIDGETY
FINALLY
FINICKY
FIREFLY
FIRSTLY
FISHERY
FIXEDLY
FLAGDAY
FLIGHTY
FLOWERY
FLUENCY
FLUNKEY
FORGERY
FORTIFY
FOUNDRY
FRAILTY
FRANKLY
FREEWAY
FRESHLY
FRIZZLY
FROWSTY
FUNNILY
FUSSILY
GAINSAY
GALLERY
GANGWAY
GASCONY
GATEWAY
GAUDILY
GEODESY
GEOLOGY
GERMANY
GETAWAY
GHASTLY
GHOSTLY
GIDDILY
GILLRAY
GLORIFY
GOSSIPY
GRADELY
GRANARY
GRANDLY
GRATIFY
GRAVITY
GREATLY
GREGORY
GRIMSBY
GRISTLY
GRIZZLY
GROCERY
GROSSLY
GROUCHY
GRUFFLY
GUNNERY
GUNPLAY
HACKERY
HACKNEY
HAGGERY
HALFWAY
HALLWAY
HANDILY
HAPPILY
HARMONY
HARSHLY
HASTILY
HAUGHTY
HAUTBOY
HEADWAY
HEALTHY
HEARSAY
HEAVILY
HERBERY
HICKORY
HIGHWAY
HISTORY
HOLIDAY
HONESTY
HORRIFY
HOSIERY
HUMANLY
HUNGARY
HUSKILY
IDEALLY
IMAGERY
IMPIETY
INANITY
INFANCY
INQUIRY
JAGGERY
JANUARY
JEEPNEY
JERKILY
JEWELRY
JITTERY
JOBBERY
JOINERY
JOINTLY
JOLLITY
JOURNEY
JUSTIFY
KENNEDY
KILLJOY
KNAVERY
KNOBBLY
LAMPREY
LANGLEY
LARCENY
LARGELY
LAUNDRY
LECHERY
LEGALLY
LEGIBLY
LENGTHY
LEPROSY
LIBERTY
LIBRARY
LIGHTLY
LIQUEFY
LITHELY
LITURGY
LOCALLY
LOFTILY
LOOSELY
LOTTERY
LOYALLY
LOYALTY
LUCIDLY
LUCKILY
LULLABY
LURIDLY
LUSTILY
MAGGOTY
MAGNIFY
MAJESTY
MALMSEY
MAMMARY
MARGERY
MASONRY
MASTERY
MERCERY
MERCURY
MERRILY
MESSILY
METALLY
MIMICRY
MISERLY
MISPLAY
MOCKERY
MODESTY
MOLLIFY
MONOPLY
MONTHLY
MOODILY
MORALLY
MORESBY
MORTIFY
MUMMERY
MUMMIFY
MUSCOVY
MYSTERY
MYSTIFY
NAIVELY
NAIVETY
NAKEDLY
NASALLY
NASTILY
NAUGHTY
NECTARY
NEWBURY
NEWSBOY
NIGHTLY
NOISILY
NOOLOGY
NOONDAY
NOSEGAY
NOTABLY
NOVELTY
NULLIFY
NULLITY
NUMMARY
NUNNERY
NURSERY
OBESITY
OBLOQUY
OBSEQUY
ODYSSEY
OFFDUTY
OPACITY
ORATORY
ORDERLY
ORPHREY
OSSUARY
OUTSTAY
OVERLAY
OVERPAY
PAGEBOY
PAISLEY
PALFREY
PALISSY
PANICKY
PANOPLY
PARKWAY
PARSLEY
PATHWAY
PAUCITY
PAUNCHY
PECCARY
PENALTY
PEPPERY
PERFIDY
PERJURY
PESSARY
PETRIFY
PICARDY
PIGGERY
PILLORY
PIOUSLY
PITHILY
PLAINLY
PLANURY
PLAYBOY
PLENARY
PLIANCY
POMEROY
PORTRAY
POTENCY
POTTERY
POULTRY
POVERTY
POWDERY
PRICKLY
PRIMACY
PRIMARY
PRIVACY
PRIVITY
PROBITY
PRODIGY
PROGENY
PROSODY
PROUDLY
PTOLEMY
PUBERTY
PUTREFY
QUALIFY
QUALITY
QUEENLY
QUICKLY
QUIETLY
RACKETY
RAILWAY
RAPIDLY
RAUNCHY
READILY
REALITY
RECTIFY
RECTORY
REENTRY
REGALLY
REGENCY
REMARRY
RESPRAY
REVELRY
RICKETY
RIGHTLY
RIGIDLY
RISKILY
RIVALRY
ROADWAY
ROBBERY
ROCKERY
ROGUERY
ROOKERY
ROUGHLY
ROUNDLY
ROWDILY
ROYALLY

ROYALTY
RUBBERY
RUNAWAY
SAINTLY
SALSIFY
SANDBOY
SATIETY
SATISFY
SATRAPY
SAUCILY
SAVELOY
SAVOURY
SCARIFY
SCENERY
SCRAGGY
SCRAPPY
SCRAWNY
SCRUBBY
SCRUFFY
SCRUMMY
SCRUMPY
SECRECY
SENSORY
SEVENTY
SHADOWY
SHAKILY
SHAPELY
SHARPLY
SHELLEY
SHEPPEY
SHINGLY
SHIRLEY
SHIVERY
SHORTLY
SHOWERY
SHOWILY
SHRILLY
SICKBAY
SIGNIFY
SILVERY
SKETCHY
SLACKLY
SLAVERY
SLEEKLY
SLIPWAY
SMARTLY
SMICKLY
SOBERLY
SOCIETY
SOLIDLY
SORCERY
SOUNDLY
SOUTHEY
SPECIFY
SPIDERY
SPINDLY
SPINNEY
SPLASHY
SPRINGY
SPURREY
SPURWAY
SQUADDY
SQUALLY
SQUASHY
SQUEAKY
SQUIFFY
SQUISHY
STANDBY
STANLEY
STARCHY
STARKLY
STATELY
STEEPLY
STEPNEY
STERNLY
STIFFLY
STIRFRY
STONILY
STOUTLY
STREAKY
STRINGY
STROPPY
STUBBLY
STUPEFY
SUAVELY
SUAVITY
SUBSIDY
SULKILY
SUMMARY
SUMMERY
SUNNILY
SURDITY
SURGERY
SWARTHY
SWEETLY
SWIFTLY
SYNERGY
TACITLY
TALLBOY
TAMMANY
TANNERY
TANTIVY
TARDILY
TARTARY
TENANCY
TENSELY
TERRIFY
TERSELY
TESTIFY
TESTILY
THERAPY
THEREBY
THICKLY
THIRDLY
THIRSTY
THRIFTY
THRISTY
THROATY
THRUWAY
TIDEWAY
TIFFANY
TIGHTLY
TILBURY
TIMIDLY
TIMOTHY
TIPSILY
TOLSTOY
TOPIARY
TORREFY
TOTALLY
TOTTERY
TRACERY
TRAGEDY
TRAMWAY
TREACLY
TREMBLY
TRILOGY
TRINITY
TRIPODY
TRITELY
TROLLEY
TROTSKY
TRUANCY
TSIGANY
TUESDAY
TURBARY
TURNERY
TURNKEY
TUSCANY
TWIDDLY
TWITCHY
TYMPANY
TYRANNY
UNCANNY
UNGODLY
UNHAPPY
UNITARY
UNLUCKY
UNREADY
URGENCY
URINARY
URUGUAY
USUALLY
UTILITY
UTTERLY
VACANCY
VACUITY
VAGUELY
VALENCY
VARIETY
VARSITY
VELVETY
VERSIFY
VICEROY
VICTORY
VIRELAY
VISIBLY
VITALLY
VITRIFY
VIVIDLY
VOCALLY
VOLUBLY
WALKWAY
WALLABY
WASHDAY
WEALTHY
WEARILY
WEEKDAY
WEIGHTY
WEIRDLY
WHEREBY
WHIMSEY
WHISKEY
WILLOWY
WOMANLY
WORDILY
WORKSHY
WORLDLY
WRINKLY
WRONGLY
ZEDOARY
ZOFFANY
ZOOLOGY
ZOOTOMY
ZYMURGY
ALBENIZ
COLDITZ
KIBBUTZ
KOLKHOZ
NATCHEZ
PIZZAZZ
SHOWBIZ
SOVKHOZ

8:1

AARDVARK
AASVOGEL
ABATTOIR
ABBASIDE
ABDICATE
ABDUCENS
ABDUCTED
ABDUCTOR
ABERDEEN
ABERRANT
ABESSIVE
ABEYANCE
ABINGDON
ABJECTLY
ABLATION
ABLATIVE
ABLUTION
ABNEGATE
ABNORMAL
ABOMASUM
ABORTION
ABORTIVE
ABRASION
ABRASIVE
ABRIDGED
ABROGATE
ABRUPTLY
ABSCISSA
ABSENTEE
ABSINTHE
ABSOLUTE
ABSOLVED
ABSORBED
ABSORBER
ABSTRACT
ABSTRUSE
ABSURDLY
ABUNDANT
ABUTILON
ABUTMENT
ACADEMIC
ACANTHUS
ACAPULCO
ACCENTED
ACCENTOR
ACCEPTED
ACCIDENT
ACCOLADE
ACCOUNTS
ACCREDIT
ACCURACY
ACCURATE
ACCURSED
ACCUSING
ACCUSTOM
ACERBATE
ACERBITY
ACHIEVED
ACHIEVER
ACHILLES
ACIDHEAD
ACOUSTIC
ACQUAINT
ACQUIRED
ACQUIRER
ACRIMONY
ACROMION
ACROSTIC
ACTINIDE
ACTINIUM
ACTIVATE
ACTIVELY
ACTIVISM
ACTIVIST
ACTIVITY
ACTUALLY
ADDENDUM
ADDICTED
ADDITION
ADDITIVE
ADELAIDE
ADENITIS
ADENOIDS
ADEQUACY
ADEQUATE
ADESSIVE
ADHERENT
ADHESION
ADHESIVE
ADJACENT
ADJUSTER
ADJUSTOR
ADJUTAGE
ADJUTANT
ADJUVANT
ADMIRING
ADMONISH
ADOPTION
ADOPTIVE
ADORABLE
ADRIATIC
ADROITLY
ADULATOR
ADULTERY
ADVANCED
ADVANCER
ADVISORY
ADVOCACY
ADVOCATE
AEGROTAT
AEROBICS
AERODYNE
AEROFLOT
AEROFOIL
AEROGRAM
AEROLITH
AERONAUT
AEROSTAT
AESTHETE
AFFECTED
AFFINITY
AFFLATUS
AFFLUENT
AFFUSION
AGACERIE
AGGRIEVE
AGITATED
AGITATOR
AGITPROP
AGNATION
AGNOSTIC
AGONIZED
AGRARIAN
AGREEING
AGRICOLA
AGRIMONY
AGRONOMY
AIGRETTE
AIGUILLE
AIRBORNE
AIRBRAKE
AIRCRAFT
AIREDALE
AIRFIELD
AIRINESS
AIRLINER
AIRPLANE
AIRSCREW
AIRSPEED
AIRSTRIP
AIRTIGHT
AIRWAVES
AKKADIAN
ALACRITY
ALARMING
ALARMIST
ALBACORE
ALBANIAN
ALBERICH
ALBINONI
ALBURNUM
ALCATRAZ
ALCESTIS
ALCHEMIC
ALDEHYDE
ALDERMAN
ALDERNEY
ALEATORY
ALEHOUSE
ALEMAINE
ALEUTIAN
ALFRESCO
ALGERIAN
ALGERINE
ALGORISM
ALHAMBRA
ALICANTE
ALIENATE
ALIENISM
ALIENIST
ALKALIFY
ALKALINE
ALKALOID
ALLEGORY
ALLELUIA
ALLERGEN
ALLERGIC
ALLEYWAY
ALLIANCE
ALLOCATE
ALLOGAMY
ALLOPATH
ALLOWING
ALLSPICE
ALLURING
ALLUSION
ALLUSIVE
ALLUVIAL
ALLUVIUM
ALMIGHTY
ALOPECIA
ALPHABET
ALPINIST
ALSATIAN
ALTHOUGH
ALTITUDE
ALTRUISM
ALTRUIST
ALUMINUM
ALVEOLUS
AMANDINE
AMARANTH
AMARETTO
AMATEURS
AMBIANCE
AMBIENCE
AMBITION
AMBROSIA
AMBULANT
AMBULATE
AMBUSHED
AMENABLE
AMERICAN
AMERICAS
AMETHYST
AMICABLE
AMICABLY
AMMONIAC
AMMONITE
AMORETTI
AMORETTO
AMORTIZE
AMPERAGE
AMPUTATE
AMRITSAR
AMUNDSEN
AMUSETTE
AMYGDALA
ANABASIS
ANABATIC
ANACONDA
ANACREON
ANAGLYPH
ANALECTA
ANALEMMA
ANALOGUE
ANALYSER
ANALYSIS
ANAPAEST
ANARCHIC
ANATHEMA
ANATOLIA
ANATOMIC
ANCESTOR
ANCESTRY
ANCHISES
ANCHORET
ANDERSON
ANDORRAN
ANDREWES
ANECDOTE
ANEURYSM
ANGELICA
ANGLESEY
ANGLICAN
ANGSTROM
ANGUILLA
ANIMATED
ANISETTE
ANNALIST
ANNAMITE
ANNEALER
ANNELIDA
ANNOTATE
ANNOUNCE
ANNOYING
ANNUALLY
ANOREXIA
ANOREXIC
ANSERINE
ANTECEDE
ANTEDATE
ANTELOPE
ANTENNAE
ANTEPOST
ANTERIOR
ANTEROOM
ANTIBODY
ANTIDOTE
ANTILLES
ANTILOPE
ANTIMONY
ANTIPHON
ANTIPOPE
ANYPLACE
ANYTHING
ANYWHERE
AOTEAROA
APERIENT
APERITIF
APERTURE
APHELION
APHORISM
APIARIST
APOLLYON
APOLOGIA
APOLOGUE
APOPLEXY
APOSTASY
APOSTATE
APOSTLES
APOTHEGM
APPALLED
APPANAGE
APPARENT
APPELANT
APPENDIX
APPETITE
APPLAUSE
APPLETON
APPLIQUÉ
APPOSITE
APPRAISE
APPRISED
APPROACH
APPROVAL
APPROVED
APTITUDE
AQUALUNG
AQUARIUM
AQUARIUS
AQUATINT
AQUEDUCT
AQUILINE
ARACHNID
ARALDITE
ARAMAEAN
ARAMANTH
ARBALEST

ARBOREAL
ARCADIAN
ARCHAISM
ARCHDUKE
ARCHIVES
ARCTURUS
ARDENNES
ARDENTLY
ARETHUSA
ARGESTES
ARGININE
ARGONAUT
ARGUABLE
ARGUABLY
ARGUMENT
ARKANSAS
ARMAGNAC
ARMALITE
ARMAMENT
ARMATURE
ARMCHAIR
ARMENIAN
ARMORIAL
ARMORICA
ARMOURED
AROMATIC
ARPEGGIO
ARQUEBUS
ARRANGER
ARRESTED
ARRESTER
ARROGANT
ARROGATE
ARSONIST
ARTEFACT
ARTERIAL
ARTESIAN
ARTFULLY
ARTICLED
ARTICLES
ARTIFACT
ARTIFICE
ARTISTIC
ARTISTRY
ASBESTOS
ASCIDIAN
ASCIDIUM
ASCORBIC
ASMODEUS
ASPERGES
ASPERITY
ASPHODEL
ASPHYXIA
ASPIRANT
ASPIRATE
ASPIRING
ASSASSIN
ASSEMBLE
ASSEMBLY
ASSESSOR
ASSIGNEE
ASSORTED
ASSUMING
ASSYRIAN
ASTATINE
ASTERISK
ASTEROID
ASTHENIA
ASTONISH
ASTUTELY
ASUNCION
ATALANTA
ATARAXIA
ATARAXIC
ATHANASY
ATHELING
ATHENIAN
ATHEROMA
ATHETISE
ATHETOID
ATHLETIC
ATLANTIC
ATLANTIS
ATOMIZER
ATROCITY
ATTACHED
ATTACKER
ATTENDER
ATTESTOR
ATTITUDE
ATTORNEY
ATYPICAL
AUBUSSON
AUCASSIN
AUDACITY
AUDIENCE
AUDITION
AUDITORY
AUGUSTUS
AURELIAN
AUSPICES
AUSTRIAN
AUTARCHY
AUTISTIC
AUTOBAHN
AUTOCRAT
AUTOGAMY
AUTOGYRO
AUTOMATE
AUTONOMY
AUTOTYPE
AUTUMNAL
AVAILING
AVENTINE
AVERSION
AVIATION
AVICENNA
AVIFAUNA
AVOGADRO
AVULSION
AYRSHIRE
BAATHIST
BABBLING
BABUSHKA
BABYHOOD
BACCARAT
BACCHANT
BACHELOR
BACILLUS
BACKACHE
BACKBITE
BACKBONE
BACKCHAT
BACKCOMB
BACKDATE
BACKDROP
BACKFIRE
BACKHAND
BACKLASH
BACKLESS
BACKPACK
BACKROOM
BACKSIDE
BACKWARD
BACKYARD
BACTERIA
BACTRIAN
BADINAGE
BADLANDS
BAEDEKER
BAFFLING
BAGHEERA
BAGPIPES
BAGUETTE
BAHAMIAN
BAHRAINI
BAILMENT
BAKELITE
BALANCED
BALDNESS
BALDRICK
BALEARIC
BALINESE
BALLCOCK
BALLGIRL
BALLISTA
BALLOCKS
BALLPARK
BALLROOM
BALLYHOO
BALMORAL
BALUSTER
BANALITY
BANDANNA
BANDEROL
BANDITTI
BANDSMAN
BANISTER
BANKBOOK
BANKNOTE
BANKROLL
BANKRUPT
BANLIEUE
BANTLING
BAPTISED
BARABBAS
BARATHEA
BARBADOS
BARBARIC
BARBECUE
BARBICAN
BARBIZON
BARDOLPH
BAREBACK
BAREFOOT
BARENESS
BARGELLO
BARGEMAN
BARITONE
BARNABAS
BARNACLE
BARNARDS
BARNYARD
BARONESS
BARONETS
BARONIAL
BARRACKS
BARRATRY
BARRETTE
BARTERED
BASEBALL
BASEBORN
BASELESS
BASELINE
BASEMENT
BASENESS
BASIDIUM
BASILICA
BASILISK
BASINFUL
BASKETRY
BASSINET
BASTILLE
BATAVIAN
BATHETIC
BATHROBE
BATHROOM
BATTERED
BAUDRICK
BAVARIAN
BAYREUTH
BEAKLESS
BEANPOLE
BEARABLE
BEARINGS
BEARSKIN
BEATIFIC
BEAUFORT
BEAUMONT
BEAUTIFY
BECALMED
BECHAMEL
BECOMING
BEDABBLE
BEDCOVER
BEDMAKER
BEDSTEAD
BEDSTRAW
BEERBOHM
BEESWING
BEETLING
BEETROOT
BEFRIEND
BEFUDDLE
BEGETTER
BEGGARLY
BEGINNER
BEGORRAH
BEGRUDGE
BEHAVIOR
BEHEMOTH
BEHOLDEN
BEHOLDER
BELABOUR
BELGRADE
BELIEVER
BELITTLE
BELLPUSH
BELLYFUL
BELPAESE
BENEDICK
BENEDICT
BENEFICE
BENEFITS
BENENDEN
BENGHAZI
BENJAMIN
BEQUEATH
BERBERIS
BERCEUSE
BEREAVED
BERGAMOT
BERGERAC
BERIBERI
BERKELEY
BERTRAND
BESIEGED
BESMIRCH
BESOTTED
BESOUGHT
BESPOKEN
BESSEMER
BESTIARY
BESTOWER
BESTRIDE
BETATRON
BETHESDA
BETJEMAN
BETRAYAL
BETRAYER
BEVERAGE
BEWILDER
BIANNUAL
BIATHLON
BIBLICAL
BIBULOUS
BICONVEX
BICUSPID
BIENNIAL
BIFOCALS
BIGAMIST
BIGAMOUS
BIGARADE
BILBERRY
BILLFOLD
BILLHOOK
BILLYBOY
BILLYCAN
BINDWEED
BINNACLE
BINOMIAL
BIOGRAPH
BIOSCOPE
BIRDCAGE
BIRDSEED
BIRTHDAY
BISCAYAN
BISEXUAL
BISMARCK
BITTERLY
BLACKBOY
BLACKCAP
BLACKFLY
BLACKING
BLACKISH
BLACKLEG
BLACKOUT
BLANDISH
BLASTOFF
BLASTULA
BLEACHER
BLEEDING

BLENDING
BLENHEIM
BLESSING
BLIGHTER
BLINDING
BLINKERS
BLINKING
BLISSFUL
BLITHELY
BLIZZARD
BLOCKADE
BLOCKAGE
BLOOMERS
BLOOMING
BLOTCHED
BLOWFISH
BLOWHOLE
BLOWLAMP
BLOWPIPE
BLUDGEON
BLUEBACK
BLUEBELL
BLUECOAT
BLUENOSE
BLURRING
BLUSHING
BLUSTERY
BOADICEA
BOARDING
BOASTFUL
BOASTING
BOATLOAD
BOBBYPIN
BOBOLINK
BODLEIAN
BODYLINE
BODYWORK
BOEOTIAN
BOGEYMAN
BOHEMIAN
BOLDNESS
BOLIVIAN
BOLLOCKS
BOLTHOLE
BONDSMAN
BONEHEAD
BONELESS
BONEYARD
BONHOMIE
BONIFACE
BONSPIEL
BOOKABLE
BOOKCASE
BOOKMARK
BOOKROOM
BOOKSHOP
BOOKWORK
BOOKWORM
BOOTLESS
BOOTNECK
BORACITE
BORDEAUX
BORDELLO
BORDERER
BORECOLE
BOREHOLE
BORODINO
BORROWED
BORROWER
BORSTALL
BOSWORTH
BOTANIST
BOTHERED
BOTHWELL
BOTSWANA
BOTTLING
BOTTOMRY
BOTULISM
BOUFFANT
BOUNCING
BOUNDARY
BOUTIQUE
BOUZOUKI
BOWSPRIT
BRABAZON
BRACELET
BRACHIAL
BRACKETS
BRACKISH
BRADBURY
BRADSHAW
BRAGANZA
BRAGGART
BRAGGING
BRAMANTE
BRANCHED
BRANDADE
BRANDISH
BRANDNEW
BRASILIA
BRASSARD
BRASSICA
BRATPACK
BREACHES
BREAKING
BREAKOUT
BREATHER
BREECHES
BREEDING
BREEZILY
BRETHREN
BREVIARY
BRIBABLE
BRICKBAT
BRIDGING
BRIEFING
BRIGHTEN
BRIGHTLY
BRIGHTON
BRIMMING
BRINDISI
BRINDLED
BRINGING
BRISLING
BRISTLED
BRISTLES
BROADWAY
BROCCOLI
BROCHURE
BROILING
BROMELIA
BROMPTON
BRONCHUS
BROODING
BROUGHAM
BROUHAHA
BROWBEAT
BROWNING
BROWNISH
BROWSING
BRUCKNER
BRUISING
BRUMAIRE
BRUNETTE
BRUSSELS
BRUTALLY
BUBBLING
BUCKFAST
BUCKLING
BUCKSHEE
BUCKSHOT
BUCKSKIN
BUDAPEST
BUDDHISM
BUDDHIST
BUDDLEIA
BUGGERED
BUILDING
BULGARIA
BULKHEAD
BULLDOZE
BULLETIN
BULLFROG
BULLHORN
BULLRING
BULLYRAG
BUMBLING
BUMMAREE
BUNFIGHT
BUNGALOW
BUNGLING
BUOYANCY
BURBERRY
BURDENED
BURGLARY
BURGRAVE
BURGUNDY
BURNTOUT
BURROWER
BURSITIS
BURSTING
BUSINESS
BUSTLING
BUSYBODY
BUTCHERS
BUTCHERY
BUTTERED
BUTTOCKS
BUTTRESS
BUZZWORD
CABERNET
CABLECAR
CABLEWAY
CABOCHON
CABOODLE
CABOTAGE
CABRIOLE
CACHALOT
CACHEPOT
CACHEXIA
CADASTRE
CADILLAC
CADUCEUS
CAERLEON
CAFFEINE
CAGINESS
CAJOLERY
CAKEHOLE
CAKEWALK
CALABASH
CALAMINE
CALAMITY
CALCEATE
CALCULUS
CALCUTTA
CALDERON
CALENDAR
CALENDER
CALIGULA
CALIPERS
CALLGIRL
CALLIOPE
CALLIPER
CALLISTO
CALMNESS
CALOTYPE
CALTHROP
CALVADOS
CAMARGUE
CAMBERED
CAMBODIA
CAMBRIAN
CAMELLIA
CAMEROON
CAMISOLE
CAMOMILE
CAMPAIGN
CAMPBELL
CAMPSITE
CAMPTOWN
CAMSHAFT
CAMSTONE
CANADIAN
CANAILLE
CANALISE
CANARIES
CANBERRA
CANDIDLY
CANISTER
CANNABIS
CANNIBAL
CANOEING
CANOEIST
CANONIZE
CANOODLE
CANTICLE
CAPACITY
CAPERING
CAPITALS
CAPRIOLE
CAPSICUM
CAPSIZED
CAPSTONE
CAPTIOUS
CAPUCHIN
CAPYBARA
CARABINE
CARACOLE
CARAPACE
CARBOLIC
CARBONIC
CARCAJOU
CARCANET
CARDAMOM
CARDIGAN
CARDINAL
CAREFREE
CARELESS
CAREWORN
CARILLON
CARJACOU
CARNEGIE
CARNIVAL
CAROLINA
CAROLINE
CAROTENE
CAROUSAL
CAROUSEL
CARRAWAY
CARRIAGE
CARRIOLE
CARRYALL
CARRYCOT
CARRYING
CARTHAGE
CARTLOAD
CARUCATE
CARYATID
CASANOVA
CASEMATE
CASEMENT
CASHMERE
CASSETTE
CASTANET
CASTAWAY
CASTOFFS
CASTRATE
CASTRATO
CASUALLY
CASUALTY
CATACOMB
CATALYST
CATAMITE
CATAPULT
CATARACT
CATATONY
CATCHING
CATEGORY
CATERING
CATHEDRA
CATHETER
CATHOLIC
CATHOUSE
CATILINE
CATSMEAT
CATTLEYA
CATULLUS
CAUDILLO
CAULDRON
CAUSEWAY
CAUTIOUS
CAVALIER
CAVATINA
CELANESE
CELERIAC
CELERITY
CELIBACY
CELIBATE
CELLARER
CELLULAR
CEMETERY
CENOBITE

CENOTAPH
CENTAURY
CENTERED
CENTRIST
CENTRODE
CERAMICS
CERATOID
CERBERUS
CEREBRAL
CEREBRUM
CEREMENT
CEREMONY
CERULEAN
CERVELAT
CERVICAL
CESSPOOL
CETACEAN
CHACONNE
CHADBAND
CHAINSAW
CHAIRMAN
CHALDEAN
CHALDRON
CHAMBERS
CHAMPERS
CHAMPION
CHANCERY
CHANDLER
CHANGING
CHANTAGE
CHANTREY
CHAPATTI
CHAPERON
CHAPLAIN
CHARCOAL
CHARGING
CHARISMA
CHARLADY
CHARLOCK
CHARMING
CHARTISM
CHARTIST
CHARTRES
CHASSEUR
CHASTISE
CHASTITY
CHASUBLE
CHATTELS
CHEATERS
CHEATING
CHECKERS
CHECKING
CHECKOUT
CHEEKILY
CHEERFUL
CHEERILY
CHEERING
CHEMICAL
CHENILLE
CHEQUERS
CHEROKEE
CHERUBIC
CHERUBIM
CHERWELL
CHESHIRE
CHESSMAN
CHESSMEN
CHESTNUT
CHEVIOTS
CHEYENNE
CHIASMUS
CHICKENS
CHICKPEA
CHILDERS
CHILDISH
CHILDREN
CHILIAST
CHILLADA
CHILLING
CHILTERN
CHIMAERA
CHINAMAN
CHINDITS
CHIPMUNK
CHITCHAT
CHIVALRY
CHLORATE
CHLORIDE
CHLORINE
CHOIRBOY
CHOLERIC
CHOOSING
CHOPPING
CHORDATA
CHORDATE
CHORIAMB
CHRISTEN
CHRISTIE
CHRISTOM
CHROMITE
CHROMIUM
CHUMMAGE
CHURLISH
CHUTZPAH
CIBORIUM
CICATRIX
CICERONE
CICISBEO
CILIATED
CINCHONA
CINERAMA
CINEREAL
CINGULUM
CINNABAR
CINNAMON
CIRCULAR
CITATION
CIVILIAN
CIVILITY
CIVILIZE
CLADDING
CLAIMANT
CLAMBAKE
CLANGING
CLANGOUR
CLANNISH
CLANSMAN
CLAPPERS
CLAPPING
CLAPTRAP
CLARENCE
CLARINET
CLASHING
CLASPING
CLASSICS
CLASSIFY
CLAUDIUS
CLAVECIN
CLAVICLE
CLAWBACK
CLAYMORE
CLEANERS
CLEANING
CLEANSED
CLEANSER
CLEARCUT
CLEARING
CLEARWAY
CLEAVAGE
CLEAVERS
CLEMATIS
CLEMENCY
CLERICAL
CLERIHEW
CLEVERLY
CLIFFORD
CLIMATIC
CLIMBING
CLINCHER
CLINGING
CLINICAL
CLINKERS
CLIPPERS
CLIPPING
CLIQUISH
CLITORIS
CLIVEDEN
CLODPOLL
CLOISTER
CLOTHIER
CLOTHING
CLOWNISH
CLUBFOOT
CLUELESS
CLUMSILY
COACHING
COACHMAN
COALESCE
COALHOLE
COALMINE
COALPORT
COARSELY
COATRACK
COATTAIL
COAUTHOR
COBBLERS
COBWEBBY
COCACOLA
COCCIDAE
COCHLEAR
COCKATOO
COCKAYNE
COCKCROW
COCKEREL
COCKEYED
COCKTAIL
CODPIECE
COERCION
COERCIVE
COGITATE
COGNOMEN
COGWHEEL
COHERENT
COHESION
COHESIVE
COIFFEUR
COIFFURE
COINCIDE
COLANDER
COLDNESS
COLESLAW
COLISEUM
COLLAGEN
COLLAPSE
COLLARED
COLLATOR
COLLECTS
COLLEGES
COLLIERS
COLLIERY
COLLOQUY
COLOMBIA
COLONIAL
COLONIST
COLONIZE
COLOPHON
COLORADO
COLORANT
COLORFUL
COLORING
COLOSSAL
COLOSSUS
COLOURED
COLUMBAN
COLUMBUS
COMATOSE
COMBINED
COMEBACK
COMEDIAN
COMEDOWN
COMMANDO
COMMENCE
COMMERCE
COMMONER
COMMONLY
COMMUNAL
COMMUTER
COMPARED
COMPILER
COMPLAIN
COMPLETE
COMPLINE
COMPOSED
COMPOSER
COMPOUND
COMPRESS
COMPRISE
COMPUTER
CONCEIVE
CONCERTO
CONCHOID
CONCLAVE
CONCLUDE
CONCORDE
CONCRETE
CONDENSE
CONFETTI
CONFINED
CONFINES
CONFLATE
CONFLICT
CONFOUND
CONFRONT
CONFUSED
CONGRESS
CONJUGAL
CONJURER
CONJUROR
CONQUEST
CONSERVE
CONSIDER
CONSOMMÉ
CONSPIRE
CONSTANT
CONSTRUE
CONSULAR
CONSUMED
CONSUMER
CONTANGO
CONTEMPT
CONTENTS
CONTINUE
CONTINUO
CONTRACT
CONTRARY
CONTRAST
CONTRITE
CONTRIVE
CONTROLS
CONVENER
CONVERGE
CONVERSE
CONVEYOR
CONVINCE
CONVULSE
COOKBOOK
COOKWARE
COOLNESS
COPULATE
COPYBOOK
COPYHOLD
COQUETRY
COQUETTE
CORDOVAN
CORDUROY
CORDWAIN
CORIOLIS
CORMORAN
CORNETTO
CORNHILL
CORNICHE
CORNWALL
CORONARY
CORONOID
CORPORAL
CORRAGIO
CORRIDOR
CORRODED
CORSELET
CORSICAN
CORVETTE
COSINESS
COSMETIC
COSTMARY
COTOPAXI
COTSWOLD
COTTAGER
COUCHANT
COUCHING
COUGHING
COUNTESS
COUNTIES

COUNTING
COUPERIN
COUPLING
COURTESY
COUSCOUS
COVALENT
COVENANT
COVENTRY
COVERAGE
COVERING
COVERLET
COVETOUS
COWARDLY
COXSWAIN
COYSTRIL
COZINESS
CRACKERS
CRACKING
CRACKPOT
CRAFTILY
CRAMOISY
CRANEFLY
CRATCHIT
CRAVATES
CRAWFISH
CRAWLING
CRAYFISH
CREAMERY
CREATION
CREATIVE
CREATURE
CREDIBLE
CREDIBLY
CREDITOR
CREOSOTE
CREPITUS
CRESCENT
CRETONNE
CREVASSE
CRIBBAGE
CRICHTON
CRIMINAL
CRINGING
CRIPPLED
CRISPIAN
CRITICAL
CRITIQUE
CROATIAN
CROCKERY
CROCKETT
CROMLECH
CROMWELL
CRONYISM
CROONING
CROSSBAR
CROSSING
CROSSLET
CROTCHET
CROUPIER
CROWFOOT
CROWNING
CRUCIATE
CRUCIBLE
CRUCIFER
CRUCIFIX
CRUMHORN
CRUMMOCK
CRUNCHIE
CRUSADER
CRUSHING
CRUTCHED
CRUZEIRO
CRYSTALS
CUCUMBER
CUCURBIT
CULINARY
CULLINAN
CULLODEN
CULPABLE
CULTURAL
CULTURED
CULVERIN
CUPBOARD
CUPIDITY
CURATIVE
CURLICUE
CURRENCY
CURRICLE
CURSITOR
CURTAINS
CURTNESS
CUSPIDOR
CUSTOMER
CUTENESS
CUTHBERT
CUTPRICE
CUTPURSE
CUTWATER
CYANOGEN
CYANOSIS
CYCLADES
CYCLAMEN
CYCLICAL
CYLINDER
CYNICISM
CYNOSURE
CYRENIAC
CYRILLIC
CYSTITIS
CYTOLOGY
CZAREVNA
DABCHICK
DAEDALUS
DAFFODIL
DAINTIES
DAINTILY
DAIQUIRI
DAIRYMAN
DALMATIC
DAMASCUS
DAMNABLE
DAMOCLES
DAMPNESS
DANDRUFF
DANEGELD
DANKNESS
DARKENED
DARKNESS
DARKROOM
DARTMOOR
DASHWOOD
DATABASE
DATELESS
DATELINE
DAUGHTER
DAUNTING
DAVIDSON
DAYBREAK
DAYDREAM
DAYLIGHT
DAZZLING
DEADBEAT
DEADENED
DEADENER
DEADHEAD
DEADLINE
DEADLOCK
DEADWOOD
DEAFNESS
DEALINGS
DEATHBED
DEBILITY
DEBONAIR
DECADENT
DECANTER
DECAYING
DECEASED
DECEIVER
DECEMBER
DECEMVIR
DECENTLY
DECIMATE
DECIPHER
DECISION
DECISIVE
DECKHAND
DECLUTCH
DECORATE
DECOROUS
DECOUPLE
DECREASE
DECREPIT
DECRETAL
DEDICATE
DEEPNESS
DEERSKIN
DEFEATED
DEFECATE
DEFECTOR
DEFENDER
DEFIANCE
DEFINITE
DEFLOWER
DEFORMED
DEFREEZE
DEFTNESS
DEGRADED
DEJECTED
DELAWARE
DELEGATE
DELETION
DELICACY
DELICATE
DELIRIUM
DELIVERY
DELUSION
DEMEANOR
DEMENTED
DEMENTIA
DEMERARA
DEMERSAL
DEMIJOHN
DEMISTER
DEMIURGE
DEMOCRAT
DEMOLISH
DEMONIAC
DEMOTION
DEMURELY
DEMURRAL
DENARIUS
DENATURE
DENDRITE
DENDROID
DENOUNCE
DENTURES
DEPARTED
DEPILATE
DEPORTEE
DEPRAVED
DEPRIVED
DEPUTIZE
DERANGED
DERELICT
DERISION
DERISIVE
DERISORY
DEROGATE
DESCRIBE
DESELECT
DESERTED
DESERTER
DESERVED
DESIGNER
DESIROUS
DESOLATE
DESPATCH
DESPOTIC
DESTINED
DESTRUCT
DETACHED
DETAILED
DETAINEE
DETAINER
DETECTOR
DETHRONE
DETONATE
DETRITUS
DEVIANCE
DEVILISH
DEVILLED
DEVOTION
DEWBERRY
DEWYEYED
DEXTROSE
DEXTROUS
DIABETES
DIABETIC
DIABOLIC
DIAGNOSE
DIAGONAL
DIALLING
DIALOGUE
DIALYSIS
DIAMANTE
DIAMETER
DIAMONDS
DIANTHUS
DIAPASON
DIAPHONE
DIARESIS
DIARRHEA
DIASPORA
DIASTASE
DIASTOLE
DIATONIC
DIATRIBE
DIAZEPAM
DICTATES
DICTATOR
DICYCLIC
DIDACTIC
DIDDICOY
DIEHARDS
DIELDRIN
DIERESIS
DIFFRACT
DIGGINGS
DIGITIZE
DILATION
DILATORY
DILIGENT
DILUTION
DIMINISH
DINGBATS
DINOSAUR
DIOCESAN
DIOGENES
DIONYSUS
DIOPTRIC
DIPHENYL
DIPLOMAT
DIPSTICK
DIPTERAL
DIRECTLY
DIRECTOR
DISABLED
DISABUSE
DISAGREE
DISALLOW
DISARRAY
DISASTER
DISBURSE
DISCIPLE
DISCLAIM
DISCLOSE
DISCOLOR
DISCOUNT
DISCOVER
DISCREET
DISCRETE
DISEASED
DISFAVOR
DISGORGE
DISGRACE
DISGUISE
DISHEVEL
DISHONOR
DISINTER
DISKETTE
DISLIKED
DISLODGE
DISLOYAL
DISMALLY
DISMAYED
DISMOUNT
DISORDER
DISPATCH
DISPENSE
DISPERSE
DISPIRIT
DISPLACE

DISPOSAL
DISPOSED
DISPROVE
DISPUTED
DISQUIET
DISRAELI
DISSOLVE
DISSUADE
DISTANCE
DISTASTE
DISTINCT
DISTRACT
DISTRAIN
DISTRAIT
DISTRESS
DISTRICT
DISTRUST
DISUNION
DISUNITE
DISUNITY
DIURETIC
DIVIDEND
DIVIDERS
DIVINITY
DIVISION
DIVISIVE
DIVORCED
DIVORCEE
DJIBOUTI
DOCILITY
DOCKLAND
DOCKSIDE
DOCKYARD
DOCTORAL
DOCTORED
DOCTRINE
DOCUMENT
DOGBERRY
DOGGEDLY
DOGGEREL
DOGHOUSE
DOGMATIC
DOGSBODY
DOGSTAIL
DOGWATCH
DOLDRUMS
DOLOMITE
DOLOROUS
DOMESDAY
DOMESTIC
DOMICILE
DOMINANT
DOMINATE
DOMINEER
DOMINION
DOMINOES
DONATION
DONATIST
DOOLALLY
DOOMSDAY
DOORBELL
DOORKNOB
DOORPOST
DOORSTEP
DOPAMINE
DORMOUSE
DOTTEREL
DOUBLOON
DOUBTFUL
DOUBTING
DOUGHBOY
DOUGHNUT
DOVECOTE
DOVETAIL
DOWNBEAT
DOWNCAST
DOWNFALL
DOWNHILL
DOWNLOAD
DOWNPLAY
DOWNPOUR
DOWNSIDE
DOWNSIZE
DOWNTOWN
DOWNTURN
DOWNWARD
DOXOLOGY
DRACAENA
DRACONIC
DRAGOONS
DRAGSTER
DRAINAGE
DRAINING
DRAMATIC
DRAUGHTS
DRAUGHTY
DRAWBACK
DREADFUL
DREAMILY
DREARILY
DRESSAGE
DRESSING
DRIBLETS
DRIFTING
DRINKING
DRIPPING
DRIVEWAY
DROOPING
DROPHEAD
DROPPING
DROPSHOT
DROWNING
DROWSILY
DRUBBING
DRUDGERY
DRUGGIST
DRUMBEAT
DRUMHEAD
DRUMLINE
DRUMMING
DRUNKARD
DRYCLEAN
DRYGOODS
DRYSTONE
DUBONNET
DUCHESSE
DUCKBILL
DUCKLING
DUCKWEED
DUELLIST
DULCIMER
DULCINEA
DULLNESS
DUMBBELL
DUMBNESS
DUMFOUND
DUMPLING
DUNGHILL
DUODENAL
DUODENUM
DURABLES
DURATION
DUTCHMAN
DUTIABLE
DUTYFREE
DWARFISH
DWARFISM
DWELLING
DYNAMICS
DYNAMISM
DYNAMITE
DYNASTIC
DYNATRON
DYSLEXIA
DYSLEXIC
EARLIEST
EARNINGS
EARPHONE
EARPIECE
EASEMENT
EASINESS
EASTERLY
EASTLAKE
EASTWARD
EATABLES
ECHINATE
ECHINOPS
ECLECTIC
ECLOSION
ECOFREAK
ECONOMIC
ECSTASIS
ECSTATIC
ECTODERM
EDENTATE
EDGEHILL
EDGEWAYS
EDGEWISE
EDUCATED
EDUCATOR
EERINESS
EFFICACY
EFFLUENT
EFFLUVIA
EFFUSION
EFFUSIVE
EGGPLANT
EGGSHELL
EGGTIMER
EGOISTIC
EGOMANIA
EGYPTIAN
EIDECTIC
EIGHTEEN
EINSTEIN
EJECTION
ELDORADO
ELDRITCH
ELECTION
ELECTIVE
ELECTORS
ELECTRIC
ELECTRON
ELECTRUM
ELEGANCE
ELEMENTS
ELEPHANT
ELEVATED
ELEVATOR
ELEVENTH
ELIGIBLE
ELKHOUND
ELLIPSIS
ELLIPTIC
ELONGATE
ELOQUENT
ELSINORE
EMACIATE
EMBATTLE
EMBEDDED
EMBEZZLE
EMBITTER
EMBLAZON
EMBODIED
EMBOLDEN
EMBOLISM
EMBOSSED
EMBRACED
EMBRACES
EMERGENT
EMERGING
EMERITUS
EMERSION
EMIGRANT
EMIGRATE
EMINENCE
EMIRATES
EMISSARY
EMISSION
EMMANUEL
EMPHASIS
EMPHATIC
EMPLOYED
EMPLOYEE
EMPLOYER
EMPORIUM
EMPYREAN
EMULGENT
EMULSIFY
EMULSION
ENCAENIA
ENCAMPED
ENCIRCLE
ENCLOSED
ENCLOTHE
ENCOMIUM
ENCROACH
ENCUMBER
ENDANGER
ENDEAVOR
ENDOCARP
ENDODERM
ENDOGAMY
ENDURING
ENDYMION
ENERGIZE
ENERVATE
ENFEEBLE
ENFILADE
ENGAGING
ENGENDER
ENGINEER
ENGRAVER
ENIWETOK
ENKINDLE
ENLARGED
ENLARGER
ENMESHED
ENORMITY
ENORMOUS
ENRICHED
ENSCONCE
ENSEMBLE
ENSHRINE
ENSHROUD
ENSIFORM
ENSILAGE
ENTANGLE
ENTHRALL
ENTHRONE
ENTICING
ENTIRELY
ENTIRETY
ENTITLED
ENTRAILS
ENTRANCE
ENTREATY
ENTRENCH
ENTREPOT
ENTRYISM
ENVELOPE
ENVIABLE
ENVIRONS
ENVISAGE
ENVISION
EOHIPPUS
EPHEMERA
EPHESIAN
EPICURUS
EPIDEMIC
EPIDURAL
EPIGAMIC
EPIGRAPH
EPILEPSY
EPILOGUE
EPIPHANY
EPIPHYTE
EPIPLOON
EPISODIC
EPISTYLE
EPITASIS
EPITHEMA
EQUALITY
EQUALIZE
EQUATION
EQUIPAGE
EQUITANT
ERADIATE
ERECTILE
ERECTING
ERECTION
ERGOTISE
ERGOTISM
ERIKSSON
ERUCTATE
ERUPTION
ERUPTURE
ERYTHEMA
ESCALADE
ESCALATE
ESCALOPE
ESCAPADE

ESCAPISM
ESCAPIST
ESCARGOT
ESCORIAL
ESCULENT
ESOTERIC
ESPALIER
ESPECIAL
ESPOUSAL
ESPRESSO
ESSAYIST
ESTANCIA
ESTEEMED
ESTHETIC
ESTIMATE
ESTIVATE
ESTONIAN
ESTOPPEL
ESTOVERS
ESTRAGON
ESTROGEN
ETCETERA
ETERNITY
ETHEREAL
ETHERISE
ETHIOPIA
ETHNARCH
ETHYLENE
ETIOLATE
ETRURIAN
ETRUSCAN
EUCYCLIC
EUDOXIAN
EUGENICS
EULOGIST
EULOGIUM
EULOGIZE
EUPEPSIA
EUPHONIA
EUPHONIC
EUPHORIA
EUPHORIC
EUPHUISM
EURASIAN
EUROLAND
EUROPEAN
EUROSTAR
EURYDICE
EUSTATIC
EUTROPHY
EUTROPIC
EVACUANT
EVACUATE
EVALUATE
EVANESCE
EVENNESS
EVENSONG
EVENTFUL
EVENTIDE
EVENTUAL
EVERMORE
EVERYDAY
EVERYMAN
EVERYONE
EVICTION
EVIDENCE
EVILDOER
EWIGKEIT
EXACTING
EXACTION
EXAMINEE
EXAMINER
EXCAVATE
EXCHANGE
EXCISION
EXCITING
EXECRATE
EXECUTED
EXECUTOR
EXEGESIS
EXEGETIC
EXEMPLAR
EXERCISE
EXERTION
EXHUMATE
EXIGENCY
EXIGUITY
EXIGUOUS
EXISTENT
EXISTING
EXOCRINE
EXORCISM
EXORCIST
EXORCIZE
EXORDIUM
EXPECTED
EXPEDITE
EXPENDED
EXPENSES
EXPLICIT
EXPLODED
EXPLORER
EXPONENT
EXPORTER
EXPOSURE
EXPRESSO
EXTENDED
EXTENSOR
EXTERIOR
EXTERNAL
EXTERNAT
EXTRADOS
EXULTANT
EXULTING
EYEGLASS
EYELINER
EYEPIECE
EYESHADE
EYESIGHT
EYETOOTH
FABULOUS
FACEACHE
FACELESS
FACELIFT
FACILITY
FACTIOUS
FACTOTUM
FAINITES
FAINTING
FAIRNESS
FAITHFUL
FALCONRY
FALKLAND
FALLIBLE
FALSETTO
FAMILIAR
FAMISHED
FAMOUSLY
FANCIFUL
FANCYMAN
FANDANGO
FANLIGHT
FANTASIA
FARCICAL
FAREWELL
FARMHAND
FARMLAND
FARMYARD
FAROUCHE
FARRIERY
FARTHEST
FARTHING
FASCICLE
FASTBACK
FASTENER
FASTNESS
FATALISM
FATALIST
FATALITY
FATHERLY
FATIGUED
FATIGUES
FATSTOCK
FAULKNER
FAVORITE
FAVOURED
FEARLESS
FEARSOME
FEASIBLE
FEASIBLY
FEATHERS
FEATHERY
FEATURED
FEATURES
FEBRUARY
FECKLESS
FECULENT
FEDAYEEN
FEDERACY
FEDERATE
FEEDBACK
FEELGOOD
FEELINGS
FELDSPAR
FELICITY
FELLAHIN
FEMININE
FEMINISM
FEMINIST
FEMINITY
FENCIBLE
FENESTRA
FEROCITY
FERRYMAN
FESTIVAL
FETCHING
FEVERFEW
FEVERISH
FIBROSIS
FIDDLING
FIDELITY
FIELDING
FIENDISH
FIERCELY
FIFTIETH
FIGHTING
FIGURINE
FILAGREE
FILAMENT
FILARIUM
FILENAME
FILIGREE
FILIPINO
FILTHILY
FILTRATE
FINALIST
FINALITY
FINALIZE
FINDINGS
FINESPUN
FINISHED
FINISHER
FIREARMS
FIREBACK
FIREBALL
FIREBIRD
FIREBOLT
FIREDAMP
FIRESIDE
FIRESTEP
FIRETRAP
FIREWEED
FIREWOOD
FIREWORK
FIRMNESS
FISHBONE
FISHCAKE
FISHMEAL
FISHPOND
FISHWIFE
FITFULLY
FIXATION
FIXATIVE
FLAGGING
FLAGPOLE
FLAGRANT
FLAGSHIP
FLAMENCO
FLAMINGO
FLANDERS
FLANNELS
FLAPJACK
FLAPPING
FLASHGUN
FLASHILY
FLASHING
FLATFISH
FLATFOOT
FLATMATE
FLATTERY
FLATWARE
FLATWORM
FLAUBERT
FLAUTIST
FLAVORED
FLAWLESS
FLEABITE
FLEETING
FLEXIBLE
FLEXIBLY
FLIMSILY
FLINDERS
FLIPPANT
FLIPPERS
FLIPPING
FLIRTING
FLOATING
FLOGGING
FLOODING
FLOODLIT
FLOORING
FLORENCE
FLOTILLA
FLOUNCED
FLOUNDER
FLOURISH
FLUENTLY
FLUIDITY
FLUMMERY
FLUORIDE
FLUORINE
FLUORITE
FLUSHING
FLYBLOWN
FLYDRIVE
FLYSHEET
FLYWHEEL
FOGBOUND
FOGLIGHT
FOLDEROL
FOLKLORE
FOLKSONG
FOLLICLE
FOLLOWED
FOLLOWER
FOLLOWUP
FONDLING
FONDNESS
FOOLSCAP
FOOTBALL
FOOTFALL
FOOTHOLD
FOOTLING
FOOTNOTE
FOOTPATH
FOOTREST
FOOTSORE
FOOTSTEP
FOOTWEAR
FOOTWORK
FORCEFUL
FORCIBLE
FORCIBLY
FOREBEAR
FOREBODE
FORECAST
FOREDECK
FOREDOOM
FOREFOOT
FOREGONE
FOREHAND
FOREHEAD
FORELAND
FORELOCK
FOREMOST
FORENAME
FORENOON
FORENSIC
FORESAIL
FORESHIP
FORESKIN
FORESTAY

FORESTER
FORESTRY
FORETELL
FOREWARN
FOREWORD
FORFEITS
FORKLIFT
FORKTAIL
FORMALIN
FORMALLY
FORMERLY
FORMLESS
FORMOSAN
FORSAKEN
FORSLACK
FORSOOTH
FORSWEAR
FORTIETH
FORTRESS
FORTUITY
FORWARDS
FOULNESS
FOUNDING
FOUNTAIN
FOURFOLD
FOURPART
FOURSOME
FOURTEEN
FOXGLOVE
FOXHOUND
FRABJOUS
FRACTION
FRACTURE
FRAGMENT
FRAGRANT
FRANCIUM
FRANKISH
FRANKLIN
FRAULEIN
FRAXINUS
FRAZZLED
FREAKISH
FRECKLED
FRECKLES
FREEHAND
FREEHOLD
FREEPOST
FREETOWN
FREEZING
FREMITUS
FRENETIC
FRENULUM
FRENZIED
FREQUENT
FRESHEST
FRESHMAN
FRETWORK
FREUDIAN
FRICTION
FRIENDLY
FRIGHTEN
FRIGIDLY
FRIPPERY
FRISKILY
FRONDEUR
FRONTAGE
FRONTIER
FRONTMAN
FROSTILY
FROSTING
FRUCTIFY
FRUCTOSE
FRUGALLY
FRUITFUL
FRUITING
FRUITION
FRUMENTY
FRUMPISH
FUCHSITE
FUGITIVE
FUGLEMAN
FULLBACK
FULLNESS
FULLPAGE
FULLSIZE
FULLTIME
FUMAROLE
FUMBLING
FUMIGATE
FUMITORY
FUNCTION
FUNERARY
FUNEREAL
FURBELOW
FURLOUGH
FURROWED
FURTHEST
FURUNCLE
FUSAROLE
FUSELAGE
FUSEWIRE
FUSIFORM
FUSILIER
FUTILITY
FUTURISM
FUTURIST
GABONESE
GABORONE
GADABOUT
GADARENE
GADGETRY
GADOGADO
GADZOOKS
GAILLARD
GALACTIC
GALBANUM
GALILEAN
GALLERIA
GALLIARD
GALLIPOT
GALLOPER
GALLOWAY
GALLUMPH
GALOSHES
GALVANIC
GAMBLING
GAMEBIRD
GAMENESS
GANGLAND
GANGLING
GANGLION
GANGRENE
GANGSTER
GANYMEDE
GAOLBIRD
GARAMOND
GARDENER
GARDENIA
GARDYLOO
GARGANEY
GARGOYLE
GARISHLY
GARLICKY
GARMENTS
GARRIGUE
GARRISON
GARROTTE
GASOLIER
GASOLINE
GASTRULA
GASWORKS
GATEPOST
GATHERED
GAUNTLET
GAZPACHO
GAZUNDER
GELASTIC
GELATINE
GEMINATE
GEMOLOGY
GENDARME
GENERATE
GENEROUS
GENETICS
GENETRIX
GENIALLY
GENITALS
GENITIVE
GENOCIDE
GENTRIFY
GEODESIC
GEOMANCY
GEOMETER
GEOMETRY
GEOPHONE
GEORGIAN
GEOTAXIS
GERANIUM
GERMAINE
GERMANIC
GERMINAL
GERONIMO
GERTRUDE
GESTURES
GHANAIAN
GHOULISH
GIACONDA
GIANTESS
GIGANTIC
GIGLAMPS
GIMCRACK
GINGERLY
GINGIVAL
GIOCONDA
GIOVANNI
GIRASOLE
GIRLHOOD
GIRONDIN
GIVEAWAY
GLABELLA
GLABROUS
GLADNESS
GLADSOME
GLANCING
GLANDERS
GLASNOST
GLASSFUL
GLAUCOMA
GLAUCOUS
GLEAMING
GLEESOME
GLISSADE
GLOAMING
GLOATING
GLOBALLY
GLOBULAR
GLOBULIN
GLOOMILY
GLORIANA
GLORIOLE
GLORIOUS
GLOSSARY
GLOSSEME
GLOXINIA
GLUMPISH
GLUTAEUS
GLUTTONY
GLYCERIN
GLYCOGEN
GNASHING
GOALPOST
GOATSKIN
GOBSMACK
GODCHILD
GOLDFISH
GOLDMINE
GOLFBALL
GOLFCLUB
GOLGOTHA
GOLLIWOG
GONDWANA
GONFALON
GOODNESS
GOODSIRE
GOODWIFE
GOODWILL
GOODWOOD
GOODYEAR
GOOFBALL
GOOSEGOG
GORGEOUS
GORMLESS
GOSSAMER
GOURMAND
GOVERNOR
GRACEFUL
GRACIOUS
GRADIENT
GRADUATE
GRAFFITI
GRAINING
GRAMERCY
GRANDEUR
GRANDSON
GRANULAR
GRANULES
GRAPHEME
GRAPHICS
GRAPHITE
GRASPING
GRATEFUL
GRATUITY
GRAVAMEN
GRAVELLY
GRAVITAS
GRAYLING
GREATEST
GREEDILY
GREENBAG
GREENERY
GREENFLY
GREENING
GREENISH
GREENOCK
GREETING
GRIDIRON
GRIDLOCK
GRIEVOUS
GRILLING
GRIMALDI
GRIMNESS
GRINDING
GRIPPING
GRISELDA
GRISETTE
GRIZZLED
GROGGILY
GROOMING
GROSBEAK
GROSCHEN
GROUNDED
GROUPING
GROUTING
GROWLING
GRUDGING
GRUESOME
GRUMBLER
GRUMPILY
GUARDIAN
GUERIDON
GUERILLA
GUERNSEY
GUIANIAN
GUIDANCE
GUILTILY
GUJARATI
GULLIBLE
GULLIVER
GUMMOSIS
GUMPTION
GUNMETAL
GUNPOINT
GUNSMITH
GURDWARA
GUSSETED
GUTTURAL
GUYANESE
GYMKHANA
GYRATION
GYRATORY
GYROSTAT
HABAKKUK
HABANERA
HABITUAL
HABSBURG
HACIENDA
HAGGADAH
HAIRLESS
HAIRLIKE
HAIRLINE
HALFFULL
HALFHOUR

HALFMAST
HALFTERM
HALFTIME
HALFYEAR
HALLIARD
HALLMARK
HALLOWED
HAMILTON
HAMMERED
HANDBALL
HANDBILL
HANDBOOK
HANDCART
HANDCLAP
HANDCUFF
HANDHELD
HANDICAP
HANDMADE
HANDMAID
HANDOVER
HANDRAIL
HANDSOME
HANDYMAN
HANGINGS
HANGNAIL
HANGOVER
HANNIBAL
HANUKKAH
HAPSBURG
HARANGUE
HARASSED
HARDBACK
HARDCORE
HARDENED
HARDLINE
HARDNESS
HARDSHIP
HARDTACK
HARDWARE
HARDWOOD
HAREBELL
HARFLEUR
HARMLESS
HARMONIC
HARRIDAN
HARRISON
HARTFORD
HARUSPEX
HASTINGS
HATCHERY
HATCHING
HATCHWAY
HATHAWAY
HATTERAS
HAUNCHES
HAUNTING
HAVILDAR
HAWAIIAN
HAWFINCH
HAWTHORN
HAYFEVER
HAYFIELD
HAYMAKER
HAYSTACK
HAZELNUT
HAZINESS
HEADACHE
HEADBAND
HEADGEAR
HEADHUNT
HEADLAMP
HEADLAND
HEADLESS
HEADLINE
HEADLONG
HEADMARK
HEADMOST
HEADREST
HEADROOM
HEADSHIP
HEADWIND
HEADWORD
HEARTIES
HEARTILY
HEATEDLY
HEATSPOT
HEATWAVE
HEAVENLY
HEBETUDE
HEBRIDES
HECATOMB
HECKLING
HEDGEHOG
HEDGEROW
HEDONISM
HEDONIST
HEEDLESS
HEELBALL
HEELTAPS
HEGEMONY
HEIGHTEN
HEIRLESS
HEIRLOOM
HELIPORT
HELLADIC
HELLBENT
HELLENIC
HELLFIRE
HELMETED
HELMSMAN
HELPLESS
HELPLINE
HELPMATE
HELSINKI
HELVETIA
HENCHMAN
HENHOUSE
HEPATICA
HEPTAGON
HEPTARCH
HERACLES
HERACLID
HERALDIC
HERALDRY
HERCULES
HERDSMAN
HEREDITY
HEREFORD
HEREWARD
HEREWITH
HERITAGE
HERMETIC
HERMIONE
HERPETIC
HERSCHEL
HESITANT
HESITATE
HETAIRIA
HEXAGRAM
HEYTHROP
HIAWATHA
HIBERNIA
HIBISCUS
HICCOUGH
HIDEAWAY
HIDROSIS
HIERARCH
HIERATIC
HIGHBALL
HIGHBORN
HIGHBROW
HIGHGATE
HIGHLAND
HIGHNESS
HIGHRISE
HIGHROAD
HIJACKER
HILARITY
HILLSIDE
HINDMOST
HINDUISM
HINDWARD
HIPSTERS
HIRAGANA
HIRELING
HISPANIC
HISTORIC
HITHERTO
HOARDING
HOARSELY
HOBBLING
HOGMANAY
HOGSHEAD
HOKKAIDO
HOLDINGS
HOLIDAYS
HOLINESS
HOLISTIC
HOLLOWAY
HOLOGRAM
HOLYHEAD
HOLYROOD
HOMELAND
HOMELESS
HOMEMADE
HOMESICK
HOMESPUN
HOMEWARD
HOMEWORK
HOMICIDE
HONDURAN
HONDURAS
HONESTLY
HONEYDEW
HONEYPOT
HONGKONG
HONOLULU
HONORARY
HOODWINK
HOOKWORM
HOOLIGAN
HOPELESS
HOPFIELD
HORATIAN
HORATIUS
HORLICKS
HORMONAL
HORNBEAM
HORNBILL
HORNBOOK
HORNPIPE
HOROLOGY
HORRIBLE
HORRIBLY
HORRIFIC
HORSEBOX
HORSEFLY
HORSEMAN
HORSEMEN
HOSEPIPE
HOSPITAL
HOSTELRY
HOTELIER
HOTHOUSE
HOTPLATE
HOUSEMAN
HOVERFLY
HOWDYEDO
HOWITZER
HUCKSTER
HUMANELY
HUMANISM
HUMANIST
HUMANITY
HUMANIZE
HUMIDIFY
HUMIDITY
HUMILITY
HUMORIST
HUMOROUS
HUMPBACK
HUMPHREY
HUNDREDS
HUNGRILY
HUNTRESS
HUNTSMAN
HURDLING
HUSHHUSH
HUSTINGS
HYACINTH
HYDATOID
HYDROGEN
HYGIENIC
HYPERION
HYPNOSIS
HYPNOTIC
HYSTERIA
HYSTERIC
ICEFIELD
ICEHOUSE
IDEALISM
IDEALIST
IDEALIZE
IDENTIFY
IDENTITY
IDEOGRAM
IDEOLOGY
IDLENESS
IDOLATER
IDOLATRY
IGNITION
IGNOMINY
IGNORANT
ILLFATED
ILLINOIS
ILLUMINE
ILLUSION
ILLUSIVE
ILLUSORY
IMAGINED
IMBECILE
IMITATOR
IMMANENT
IMMANUEL
IMMATURE
IMMERSED
IMMINENT
IMMOBILE
IMMODEST
IMMOLATE
IMMORTAL
IMMUNITY
IMMUNIZE
IMPACTED
IMPAIRED
IMPELLED
IMPERIAL
IMPETIGO
IMPLICIT
IMPOLITE
IMPORTER
IMPOSING
IMPOSTER
IMPOSTOR
IMPOTENT
IMPRISON
IMPROPER
IMPROVED
IMPROVER
IMPUDENT
IMPUNITY
IMPURIFY
IMPURITY
INACTION
INACTIVE
INASMUCH
INCENSED
INCHOATE
INCIDENT
INCISION
INCISIVE
INCLINED
INCLUDED
INCOMING
INCREASE
INCUBATE
INDEBTED
INDECENT
INDENTED
INDEXING
INDIAMAN
INDICANT
INDICATE
INDIGENT
INDIRECT
INDOLENT
INDUCIVE
INDUSTRY
INEDIBLE
INEQUITY
INEXPERT
INFAMOUS

INFANTRY
INFECTED
INFERIOR
INFERNAL
INFESTED
INFINITE
INFINITY
INFLAMED
INFLATED
INFLIGHT
INFORMAL
INFORMED
INFORMER
INFRARED
INFRINGE
INFUSION
INGROWTH
INGUINAL
INHALANT
INHERENT
INHUMANE
INIMICAL
INIQUITY
INITIATE
INJECTOR
INKSTAIN
INNOCENT
INNOVATE
INNUENDO
INQUIRER
INSANELY
INSANITY
INSCRIBE
INSECURE
INSIGNIA
INSOLENT
INSOMNIA
INSPIRED
INSPIRIT
INSTANCE
INSTINCT
INSTRUCT
INSULATE
INTAGLIO
INTEGRAL
INTELSAT
INTENDED
INTENTLY
INTERACT
INTERCOM
INTEREST
INTERIOR
INTERMIT
INTERNAL
INTERNEE
INTERNET
INTERPOL
INTERVAL
INTIFADA
INTIMACY
INTIMATE
INTRADOS
INTRENCH
INTREPID
INTRIGUE
INTRUDER
INUNDATE
INVASION
INVASIVE
INVEIGLE
INVENTED
INVENTOR
INVERTED
INVESTOR
INVITING
INVOLUTE
INVOLVED
INWARDLY
IOLANTHE
IRISCOPE
IRISHISM
IRISHMAN
IRISHMEN
IRONCLAD
IRONICAL
IRONSIDE
IRONWARE
IRONWOOD
IRONWORK
IROQUOIS
IRRIGATE
IRRITANT
IRRITATE
ISABELLA
ISABELLE
ISLANDER
ISOGLOSS
ISOGONAL
ISOLATED
ISOSTASY
ISOTHERE
ISOTHERM
ISTANBUL
ISTHMIAN
IVOIRIEN
JACKAROO
JACKBOOT
JACKETED
JACOBEAN
JACOBITE
JACQUARD
JAILBIRD
JALOUSIE
JAMAICAN
JAMBOREE
JANGLING
JAPANESE
JAPONICA
JAUNDICE
JAUNTILY
JEALOUSY
JEANETTE
JEBUSITE
JEFFREYS
JEHOVAHS
JELLICOE
JEOPARDY
JEPHTHAH
JEREBOAM
JEREMIAD
JEREMIAH
JEROBOAM
JERRYCAN
JETTISON
JEWELLED
JEWELLER
JIGGERED
JIMCRACK
JINGOISM
JINGOIST
JODHPURS
JOHANNES
JOHNSONS
JOINTURE
JOKINGLY
JONATHAN
JONCANOE
JONGLEUR
JORROCKS
JOTTINGS
JOVIALLY
JOYFULLY
JOYSTICK
JUBILANT
JUBILATE
JUDGMENT
JUDICIAL
JUGGLING
JULIENNE
JUMPSUIT
JUNCTION
JUNCTURE
JURASSIC
JURATORY
JUSTNESS
JUVENILE
KACHAHRI
KALAHARI
KAMIKAZE
KANGAROO
KATAKANA
KATMANDU
KATTEGAT
KEDGEREE
KEELHAUL
KEENNESS
KEEPSAKE
KENTUCKY
KERCHIEF
KERMESSE
KEROSENE
KESTEVEN
KEYBOARD
KEYSTONE
KHARTOUM
KIBITZER
KICKBACK
KICKSHAW
KIDGLOVE
KILKENNY
KILLDEER
KILOBYTE
KILOGRAM
KILOVOLT
KILOWATT
KINDLING
KINDNESS
KINETICS
KINGPOST
KINGSHIP
KINGSIZE
KINGSLEY
KINGSTON
KINKAJOU
KINSFOLK
KINSHASA
KIPPERED
KITEMARK
KLONDIKE
KNACKERS
KNAPSACK
KNAPWEED
KNEEDEEP
KNEEHIGH
KNICKERS
KNIGHTLY
KNITTING
KNITWEAR
KNOBLESS
KNOCKERS
KNOCKING
KNOCKOUT
KNOTWEED
KNOTWORK
KOHLRABI
KOMSOMOL
KORRIGAN
KOURMISS
KOUSKOUS
KRAKATOA
KREPLACH
KROMESKY
KUFFIYEH
KYPHOSIS
LABOURED
LABOURER
LABRADOR
LABURNUM
LACERATE
LACEWING
LACINATE
LACKADAY
LACKLAND
LACONIAN
LACROSSE
LADRONES
LADYBIRD
LADYLIKE
LADYSHIP
LAIDBACK
LAKELAND
LAMASERY
LAMBSKIN
LAMENESS
LAMENTED
LAMINATE
LAMPPOST
LANCELOT
LANDFALL
LANDFILL
LANDLADY
LANDLOCK
LANDLORD
LANDMARK
LANDMASS
LANDMINE
LANDRACE
LANDSEER
LANDSLIP
LANDWARD
LANGLAND
LANGLAUF
LANGUAGE
LANGUISH
LANOLINE
LANSBURY
LAPIDARY
LAPIDATE
LARGESSE
LARKSPUR
LAROUSSE
LASHINGS
LATCHKEY
LATENESS
LATERITE
LATINIST
LATITUDE
LATTERLY
LAUDABLE
LAUDABLY
LAUDANUM
LAUGHING
LAUGHTER
LAUREATE
LAURENCE
LAVATORY
LAVENDER
LAVENGRO
LAVISHLY
LAWCOURT
LAWFULLY
LAWMAKER
LAWRENCE
LAXATIVE
LAYABOUT
LAZINESS
LEACHING
LEADSMAN
LEAFLESS
LEAPFROG
LEARNING
LEATHERY
LEAVENED
LEAVINGS
LEBANESE
LECITHIN
LECTURER
LECTURES
LEFTHAND
LEFTOVER
LEFTWARD
LEFTWING
LEGALISM
LEGALITY
LEGALIZE
LEGATION
LEGGINGS
LEINSTER
LEISURED
LEMONADE
LENGTHEN
LENIENCY
LEONARDO
LEONIDAS
LETHARGY
LETTERED
LEUKEMIA
LEVELLER
LEVERAGE
LEVITATE
LEWDNESS
LEWISITE

LIBATION
LIBELOUS
LIBERATE
LIBERIAN
LIBRETTO
LICENSED
LICENSEE
LICORICE
LIEGEMAN
LIENTERY
LIFEBELT
LIFEBOAT
LIFEBUOY
LIFELESS
LIFELIKE
LIFELINE
LIFELONG
LIFESPAN
LIFETIME
LIGAMENT
LIGATURE
LIGHTING
LIGNEOUS
LIKEABLE
LIKENESS
LIKEWISE
LILONGWE
LIMBLESS
LIMERICK
LIMITING
LIMONITE
LIMPNESS
LINCHPIN
LINCOLNS
LINESMAN
LINGERIE
LINGUIST
LINIMENT
LINNAEAN
LINNAEUS
LINOLEUM
LINOTYPE
LIPSTICK
LISTENER
LISTERIA
LISTLESS
LITERACY
LITERARY
LITERATE
LITERATI
LITIGANT
LITIGATE
LITTORAL
LIVELONG
LIVERIED
LIVERISH
LIVEWARE
LIVIDITY
LOADSTAR
LOATHING
LOBBYIST
LOBELINE
LOBOTOMY
LOCALITY
LOCALIZE
LOCATION
LOCATIVE
LOCKABLE
LODESTAR
LODGINGS
LOGISTIC
LOITERER
LOLLIPOP
LOMBARDY
LONDONER
LONESOME
LONGBOAT
LONGHAND
LONGHAUL
LONGHORN
LONGLAND
LONGSTAY
LONGSTOP
LONGTERM
LONGTIME
LONICERA
LONSDALE
LOOPHOLE
LOOSEBOX
LOPSIDED
LORDOSIS
LORDSHIP
LORRAINE
LOTHARIO
LOUDNESS
LOUVERED
LOVEBIRD
LOVELACE
LOVELESS
LOVELORN
LOVESICK
LOVINGLY
LOWCLASS
LOWERING
LOWLANDS
LOWLYING
LOYALIST
LUCIDITY
LUCKLESS
LUKEWARM
LULWORTH
LUMINARY
LUMINOUS
LUMPFISH
LUNCHEON
LUNGFISH
LUPERCAL
LUSCIOUS
LUSHNESS
LUSTRINE
LUSTROUS
LUTHERAN
LYNCHING
LYREBIRD
LYRICISM
LYRICIST
LYSANDER
LYSERGIC
MACARONI
MACAROON
MACASSAR
MACAULAY
MACERATE
MACHEATH
MACHINES
MACHISMO
MACKEREL
MACMAHON
MACREADY
MACULATE
MADHOUSE
MADRIGAL
MADWOMAN
MAECENAS
MAESTOSO
MAGAZINE
MAGELLAN
MAGICIAN
MAGISTER
MAGNESIA
MAGNETIC
MAGNOLIA
MAHARAJA
MAHARANI
MAHJONGG
MAHOGANY
MAIDENLY
MAILBOAT
MAILSHOT
MAINLAND
MAINLINE
MAINMAST
MAINSAIL
MAINSTAY
MAINTAIN
MAINYARD
MAJESTIC
MAJOLICA
MAJORITY
MALAGASY
MALAKOFF
MALARIAL
MALARKEY
MALAWIAN
MALAYSIA
MALDIVES
MALGRADO
MALINGER
MALLARMÉ
MALLEATE
MALLORCA
MALODOUR
MALTREAT
MALVASIA
MALVOLIO
MAMELUKE
MANAGING
MANCIPLE
MANDAMUS
MANDARIN
MANDATED
MANDIBLE
MANDIOCA
MANDOLIN
MANDRAKE
MANDRILL
MANEUVER
MANFULLY
MANGONEL
MANGROVE
MANIACAL
MANICURE
MANIFEST
MANIFOLD
MANITOBA
MANNERED
MANNERLY
MANNIKIN
MANORIAL
MANPOWER
MANTILLA
MANTISSA
MANUALLY
MAQUETTE
MARABOUT
MARASMUS
MARATHON
MARAUDER
MARCELLA
MARCELLO
MARGARET
MARGINAL
MARGRAVE
MARIACHI
MARIANAS
MARIGOLD
MARINADE
MARINATE
MARITIME
MARJORAM
MARKDOWN
MARKEDLY
MARKSMAN
MARMOSET
MARONITE
MARQUESA
MARQUESS
MARQUISE
MARRIAGE
MARSHALL
MARTELLO
MARTINET
MARTYRED
MARYLAND
MARZIPAN
MASCARON
MASSACRE
MASSENET
MASSEUSE
MASSICOT
MASTERLY
MASTHEAD
MASTODON
MATABELE
MATAMORE
MATCHBOX
MATCHING
MATERIAL
MATERNAL
MATHURIN
MATRONLY
MATTRESS
MATURATE
MATURITY
MAVERICK
MAXIMIZE
MAYORESS
MAZARINE
MCKINLEY
MEALTIME
MEALYBUG
MEANNESS
MEANTIME
MEASURED
MEATLESS
MECHANIC
MEDALIST
MEDDLING
MEDIATOR
MEDICATE
MEDICINE
MEDIEVAL
MEDIOCRE
MEDITATE
MEEKNESS
MEGABYTE
MEGALITH
MEGAWATT
MELAMINE
MELANITE
MELANOMA
MELCHIOR
MELEAGER
MELTDOWN
MEMBRANE
MEMORIAL
MEMORIAM
MEMORIZE
MEMSAHIB
MENACING
MENANDER
MENELAUS
MENISCUS
MENSWEAR
MENTALLY
MERCALLI
MERCATOR
MERCEDES
MERCHANT
MERCIFUL
MEREDITH
MERIDIAN
MERINGUE
MERISTEM
MESCALIN
MESMERIC
MESOLITE
MESSAGER
MESSIDOR
MESSMATE
MESSUAGE
METABOLA
MÉTAIRIE
METALLED
METALLIC
METAPHOR
METEORIC
METHANOL
METHODIC
METONYMY
METRICAL
METRITIS
MEUNIÈRE
MICHIGAN
MICRODOT
MIDDLING
MIDFIELD
MIDLANDS
MIDNIGHT
MIDPOINT
MIGHTILY
MIGNONNE

MIGRAINE
MILANESE
MILDEWED
MILDNESS
MILITANT
MILITARY
MILITATE
MILKLESS
MILKMAID
MILKWEED
MILKWORT
MILLIBAR
MILLINER
MILLIONS
MILLPOND
MILLRACE
MINAMATA
MINATORY
MINCEPIE
MINDANAO
MINDLESS
MINEHEAD
MINIMIZE
MINISTER
MINISTRY
MINORESS
MINORITE
MINORITY
MINOTAUR
MINSTREL
MINUTELY
MINUTIAE
MIREPOIX
MIRLITON
MIRRORED
MIRTHFUL
MISAPPLY
MISCARRY
MISCHIEF
MISCOUNT
MISERERE
MISGUIDE
MISHMASH
MISJUDGE
MISMATCH
MISNOMER
MISOGYNY
MISPLACE
MISPRINT
MISQUOTE
MISSOURI
MISSPELL
MISSPENT
MISTAKEN
MISTREAT
MISTRESS
MISTRUST

MITIGATE
MNEMONIC
MOBILITY
MOBILIZE
MOCASSIN
MOCCASIN
MODELING
MODELLER
MODERATE
MODERATO
MODESTLY
MODIFIER
MODULATE
MOHAMMED
MOISTURE
MOLASSES
MOLECULE
MOLEHILL
MOLESKIN
MOLESTER
MOLLUSCS
MOLUCCAS
MOMENTUM
MONADISM
MONARCHY
MONASTIC
MONAURAL
MONDRIAN
MONETARY
MONETISE
MONEYBOX
MONGOLIA
MONGOOSE
MONICKER
MONMOUTH
MONOGAMY
MONOGRAM
MONOHULL
MONOLITH
MONOPOLY
MONORAIL
MONOTONY
MONOTYPE
MONOXIDE
MONROVIA
MONSTERA
MONTCALM
MONTEITH
MONUMENT
MOONBEAM
MOORCOCK
MOORINGS
MOORLAND
MOQUETTE
MORALIST
MORALITY
MORALIZE

MORAVIAN
MORBIDLY
MORBILLI
MOREOVER
MORIBUND
MOROCCAN
MOROSELY
MORPHEME
MORPHEUS
MORPHINE
MORRISON
MORTALLY
MORTGAGE
MORTIMER
MORTUARY
MOSQUITO
MOTHBALL
MOTHERLY
MOTIVATE
MOTORCAR
MOTORING
MOTORIST
MOTORIZE
MOTORMAN
MOTORWAY
MOUFFLON
MOULDING
MOUNTAIN
MOUNTING
MOURNFUL
MOURNING
MOUSSAKA
MOUTHFUL
MOVEABLE
MOVEMENT
MUCHNESS
MUCILAGE
MUDFLATS
MUDGUARD
MUDSTONE
MUHAMMAD
MULBERRY
MULETEER
MULEWORT
MULLIGAN
MULTIPLE
MULTIPLY
MUMBLING
MUNCHKIN
MUNIMENT
MURDERER
MUSCADET
MUSCATEL
MUSCULAR
MUSHROOM
MUSICIAN
MUSQUASH

MUSTACHE
MUTATION
MUTCHKIN
MUTILATE
MUTINEER
MUTINOUS
MUTUALLY
MYCELIUM
MYCOLOGY
MYELITIS
MYOBLAST
MYOSOTIS
MYRIAPOD
MYRMIDON
MYSTICAL
MYSTIQUE
MYTHICAL
NAGASAKI
NAMELESS
NAMESAKE
NAMIBIAN
NAPOLEON
NARCOSES
NARCOSIS
NARCOTIC
NARGILEH
NARRATOR
NARROWLY
NATALITY
NATIONAL
NATIVITY
NATTERED
NATURISM
NATURIST
NAUPLIUS
NAUSEATE
NAUSEOUS
NAUTICAL
NAUTILUS
NAVARINO
NAVIGATE
NAZARENE
NDJAMENA
NEARNESS
NEATHERD
NEATNESS
NEBRASKA
NEBULOUS
NECKBAND
NECKLACE
NECKLINE
NECKWEAR
NECROSIS
NEEDLESS
NEGATION
NEGATIVE
NEGLIGEE

NEIGHBOR
NEMATODE
NEMATOID
NEMBUTAL
NENUPHAR
NEOMYCIN
NEOPHYTE
NEPALESE
NEPENTHE
NEPHRITE
NEPIONIC
NEPOTISM
NESCIENT
NESTLING
NEURITIS
NEUROSIS
NEUROTIC
NEUTRINO
NEWCOMER
NEWFOUND
NEWHAVEN
NEWSCAST
NEWSHAWK
NEWSPEAK
NEWSREEL
NEWSROOM
NIBELUNG
NICENESS
NICHOLAS
NICKNACK
NICKNAME
NICOTINE
NIDATION
NIGERIAN
NIGERIEN
NIGGLING
NIGHTCAP
NIGHTJAR
NIHILISM
NIHILIST
NIJINSKY
NINEPINS
NINETEEN
NITROGEN
NOBELIUM
NOBILITY
NOBLEMAN
NOCTURNE
NOISETTE
NOMINATE
NOMOGRAM
NONESUCH
NONSENSE
NONSTICK
NOONTIME
NORMALLY
NORMANDY

NORSEMAN
NORSEMEN
NORTHERN
NOSEBAND
NOSEDIVE
NOSOLOGY
NOSTRILS
NOSTROMO
NOTARIAL
NOTATION
NOTEBOOK
NOTECASE
NOTIONAL
NOVELIST
NOVEMBER
NOWADAYS
NUCLEOLE
NUFFIELD
NUGATORY
NUISANCE
NUMBNESS
NUMERACY
NUMERALS
NUMERATE
NUMEROUS
NUMINOUS
NUPTIALS
NURSLING
NUTHATCH
NUTHOUSE
NUTRIENT
NUTSHELL
OBDURACY
OBDURATE
OBEDIENT
OBITUARY
OBJECTOR
OBLATION
OBLIGATE
OBLIGING
OBLIVION
OBSCURED
OBSERVED
OBSERVER
OBSESSED
OBSIDIAN
OBSOLETE
OBSTACLE
OBSTRUCT
OBTAINED
OBTUSELY
OCCAMIST
OCCASION
OCCIDENT
OCCUPANT
OCCUPIED
OCCUPIER

OCTAROON
ODDMENTS
ODIOUSLY
ODOMETER
ODYSSEUS
OEDIPEAN
OEILLADE
OENOLOGY
OENOPHIL
OFFBREAK
OFFCOLOR
OFFENDED
OFFENDER
OFFERING
OFFICERS
OFFICIAL
OFFSHOOT
OFFSHORE
OFFSIDER
OFFSTAGE
OILCLOTH
OILFIELD
OILINESS
OILSKINS
OILSLICK
OINTMENT
OKLAHOMA
OLDSTYLE
OLDWORLD
OLEACEAE
OLEANDER
OLIGARCH
OLIPHANT
OLYMPIAD
OLYMPIAN
OLYMPICS
OMDURMAN
OMELETTE
OMISSION
OMNIFORM
OMPHALOS
ONCOLOGY
ONCOMING
ONESIDED
ONETRACK
ONLOOKER
ONSCREEN
ONTOLOGY
OOPHORON
OPENCAST
OPENDOOR
OPENNESS
OPENPLAN
OPENWORK
OPERABLE
OPERATIC
OPERATOR
OPERETTA
OPHIDIAN
OPOPANAX
OPPONENT
OPPOSING
OPPOSITE
OPTICIAN
OPTIMATE
OPTIMISM
OPTIMIST
OPTIONAL
OPULENCE
OPUSCULE
ORANGERY
ORATORIO
ORCADIAN
ORCHITIS
ORDERING
ORDINAND
ORDINARY
ORDINATE
ORDNANCE
ORESTEIA
ORGANDIE
ORGANISM
ORGANIST
ORGANIZE
ORIENTAL
ORIGINAL
ORNAMENT
ORPHANED
ORPIMENT
ORTHODOX
OSCULATE
OSTERLEY
OTOSCOPE
OTTAVINO
OUISTITI
OUTBOARD
OUTBREAK
OUTBURST
OUTCLASS
OUTDATED
OUTDOORS
OUTFIELD
OUTFLANK
OUTGOING
OUTHOUSE
OUTLYING
OUTMATCH
OUTMODED
OUTREACH
OUTREMER
OUTRIDER
OUTRIGHT
OUTSHINE
OUTSIDER
OUTSMART
OUTSTRIP
OUTWARDS
OUTWEIGH
OVENWARE
OVERALLS
OVERBOOK
OVERCAST
OVERCOAT
OVERCOME
OVERDONE
OVERDOSE
OVERDRAW
OVERFEED
OVERFILL
OVERFLOW
OVERFULL
OVERHANG
OVERHAUL
OVERHEAD
OVERHEAR
OVERHEAT
OVERKILL
OVERLAID
OVERLAND
OVERLEAF
OVERLOAD
OVERLOOK
OVERLORD
OVERMUCH
OVERPASS
OVERPLAY
OVERRATE
OVERRIDE
OVERRIPE
OVERRULE
OVERSEAS
OVERSEER
OVERSHOE
OVERSHOT
OVERSIZE
OVERSTAY
OVERSTEP
OVERTAKE
OVERTIME
OVERTONE
OVERTURE
OVERTURN
OVERVIEW
OVERWORK
OXBRIDGE
OXPECKER
OXYMORON
OXYTOCIN
PABULOUS
PACHINKO
PACIFIER
PACIFISM
PACIFIST
PACKAGED
PADDLING
PAGANINI
PAGINATE
PAINLESS
PAINTING
PAKISTAN
PALATIAL
PALATINE
PALEFACE
PALENESS
PALGRAVE
PALIMONY
PALINODE
PALISADE
PALLADIO
PALLIATE
PALMATED
PALMETTO
PALPABLE
PALPABLY
PALUDISM
PAMPERED
PAMPHLET
PANATELA
PANCREAS
PANDARUS
PANDEMIC
PANDOWDY
PANEGYRY
PANELING
PANELLED
PANGLOSS
PANGOLIN
PANNICLE
PANNIKIN
PANORAMA
PANTALON
PANTHEON
PAPILLON
PARABOLA
PARADIGM
PARADISE
PARAFFIN
PARAGUAY
PARAKEET
PARALLAX
PARALLEL
PARALYZE
PARAMOUR
PARANOIA
PARANOID
PARAQUAT
PARASITE
PARDONER
PARENTAL
PARIETAL
PARISIAN
PARKLAND
PARLANCE
PARMESAN
PARODIST
PAROLLES
PAROXYSM
PARSIFAL
PARTERRE
PARTHIAN
PARTICLE
PARTISAN
PARTTIME
PASHMINA
PASSABLE
PASSABLY
PASSBOOK
PASSERBY
PASSIBLE
PASSOVER
PASSPORT
PASSWORD
PASTICHE
PASTILLE
PASTORAL
PASTRAMI
PASTURES
PATCHILY
PATELLAR
PATENTED
PATENTEE
PATENTLY
PATERNAL
PATHETIC
PATHOGEN
PATIENCE
PATULOUS
PAULINUS
PAVEMENT
PAVILION
PAWNSHOP
PAYCHECK
PEACEFUL
PEARLING
PEARMAIN
PECORINO
PECTORAL
PECULATE
PECULIAR
PEDAGOGY
PEDANTIC
PEDANTRY
PEDDLING
PEDERAST
PEDESTAL
PEDICURE
PEDIGREE
PEDIMENT
PEDUNCLE
PEEKABOO
PEELINGS
PEEPHOLE
PEERLESS
PEIGNOIR
PEKINESE
PELAGIUS
PELLAGRA
PELLETED
PELLICLE
PELLMELL
PELLUCID
PEMBROKE
PEMMICAN
PENALIZE
PENCHANT
PENDULUM
PENELOPE
PENITENT
PENKNIFE
PENNINES
PENOLOGY
PENTACLE
PENTAGON
PENTARCH
PENUMBRA
PENZANCE
PEPERONI
PERACUTE
PERCEIVE
PERCEVAL
PERCIVAL
PERFECTA
PERFECTO
PERFORCE
PERFUMED
PERIANTH
PERICARP
PERICLES
PERIDERM
PERILOUS
PERIODIC
PERIPETY
PERISHED
PERISHER
PERJURED
PERJURER
PERMEATE
PEROXIDE
PERSHING
PERSONAL
PERSPIRE
PERSUADE

PERSUANT
PERTNESS
PERUVIAN
PERVERSE
PERVIOUS
PETANQUE
PETERLOO
PETITION
PETRARCH
PETULANT
PEVENSEY
PHALANGE
PHANTASM
PHARISEE
PHARMACY
PHEASANT
PHILEMON
PHILIPPI
PHILLIPS
PHILOMEL
PHLEGMON
PHONETIC
PHORMIUM
PHOSGENE
PHOTOFIT
PHOTOPSY
PHREATIC
PHRYGIAN
PHTHISIS
PHYLLOME
PHYSALIA
PHYSICAL
PHYSIQUE
PICAROON
PICKINGS
PICKLOCK
PICKMEUP
PICKWICK
PICTURES
PIDDLING
PIECHART
PIECRUST
PIERCING
PIERETTE
PIERIDES
PIGSWILL
PILASTER
PILCHARD
PILFERER
PILGRIMS
PILLAGER
PILLARED
PILOTAGE
PILSENER
PILTDOWN
PIMIENTO
PINAFORE
PINDARIC
PINEWOOD
PINNACLE
PINNIPED
PINOCHLE
PINPOINT
PINPRICK
PINTABLE
PINWHEEL
PIPELINE
PIPERINE
PIQUANCY
PIRANESI
PIROZHKI
PISCATOR
PISSHEAD
PITCAIRN
PITHLESS
PITIABLE
PITILESS
PITTANCE
PIZZERIA
PLACABLE
PLACEMAT
PLACEMEN
PLACENTA
PLACIDLY
PLANCHET
PLANGENT
PLANKING
PLANKTON
PLANNING
PLANTAIN
PLASTRON
PLATANUS
PLATEFUL
PLATELET
PLATFORM
PLATINUM
PLATONIC
PLATYPUS
PLAUDITS
PLAYBACK
PLAYBILL
PLAYFAIR
PLAYGIRL
PLAYMATE
PLAYROOM
PLAYSUIT
PLAYTIME
PLEADING
PLEASANT
PLEASING
PLEASURE
PLEBEIAN
PLECTRUM
PLEIADES
PLEONASM
PLETHORA
PLEURISY
PLIMSOLL
PLIOCENE
PLOTINUS
PLOUGHED
PLUCKILY
PLUCKING
PLUGHOLE
PLUMBAGO
PLUMBING
PLUNGING
PLUTARCH
PLYMOUTH
POCHETTE
PODARGUS
POETICAL
POIGNANT
POISONER
POITIERS
POLARIZE
POLISHED
POLISHER
POLITELY
POLITICO
POLITICS
POLLSTER
POLLUTED
POLLUTER
POLONIUM
POLTROON
POLYANNA
POLYARCH
POLYCARP
POLYGAMY
POLYGLOT
POLYMATH
POLYSEME
POLYSEMY
POMANDER
PONSONBY
PONYTAIL
POOLROOM
POORNESS
POPINJAY
POPPADOM
POPSICLE
POPULACE
POPULATE
POPULIST
POPULOUS
POROSITY
PORPHYRA
PORPHYRY
PORPOISE
PORRIDGE
PORTABLE
PORTHOLE
PORTIÈRE
PORTLAND
PORTRAIT
PORTUGAL
POSEIDON
POSITION
POSITIVE
POSITRON
POSOLOGY
POSSIBLE
POSSIBLY
POSTCARD
POSTCODE
POSTDATE
POSTMARK
POSTPAID
POSTPONE
POTATOES
POTBELLY
POTBOUND
POTEMKIN
POTHOLER
POTLATCH
POTSHERD
POULAINE
POULTICE
POUNDAGE
POWDERED
POWERFUL
PRACTICE
PRACTISE
PRAIRIAL
PRANDIAL
PRATFALL
PRATTLER
PREACHER
PREAMBLE
PRECINCT
PRECIOUS
PRECLUDE
PRECURSE
PREDATOR
PREDELLA
PREGNANT
PREJUDGE
PREMIERE
PREMISES
PREMOLAR
PRENATAL
PREPARED
PRESENCE
PRESERVE
PRESSING
PRESSMAN
PRESSURE
PRESTIGE
PRETENCE
PRETENSE
PRETORIA
PRETTILY
PREVIOUS
PRIAPISM
PRIESTLY
PRIGGISH
PRIMEVAL
PRIMNESS
PRIMROSE
PRINCELY
PRINCESS
PRINTING
PRINTOUT
PRIORESS
PRIORITY
PRISONER
PRISTINE
PRIVATES
PROBABLE
PROBABLY
PROCEEDS
PROCLAIM
PROCURER
PRODIGAL
PRODUCER
PRODUCES
PRODUCTS
PROFORMA
PROFOUND
PROFUSER
PROGERIA
PROGRESS
PROHIBIT
PROLAPSE
PROLIFIC
PROLOGUE
PROMISED
PROMOTER
PROMPTER
PROMPTLY
PROPERLY
PROPERTY
PROPHECY
PROPHESY
PROPOSAL
PROPOSED
PROPOSER
PROPOUND
PROROGUE
PROSPECT
PROSPERO
PROSTATE
PROTEASE
PROTÉGÉE
PROTOCOL
PROTOZOA
PROTRUDE
PROVABLE
PROVERBS
PROVIDED
PROVIDER
PROVINCE
PRUDENCE
PRUNELLA
PRURIENT
PRUSSIAN
PSALMIST
PSALMODY
PSALTERY
PSEUDERY
PTOMAINE
PUBLICAN
PUBLICLY
PUCKERED
PUDENDUM
PUFFBALL
PUGILISM
PUGILIST
PUGNOSED
PUISSANT
PULITZER
PULLDOWN
PULLOVER
PUNCTUAL
PUNCTURE
PUNGENCY
PUNISHED
PUNITIVE
PURBLIND
PURCHASE
PURIFIED
PURIFIER
PURLIEUS
PURPLISH
PURSLANE
PURULENT
PURVEYOR
PUSHBIKE
PUSHCART
PUSHOVER
PUSSYCAT
PUSTULAR
PUTATIVE
PUZZLING
PYELITIS
PYORRHEA
PYRAMIDS
PYRENEES
PYRIFORM
QUADRANT
QUADRATE

QUADRIGA
QUADROON
QUAESTOR
QUAGMIRE
QUAINTLY
QUANDARY
QUANTIFY
QUANTITY
QUARTERS
QUARTIER
QUARTILE
QUATORZE
QUATRAIN
QUAYSIDE
QUENELLE
QUESTION
QUIBBLER
QUICKSET
QUIETUDE
QUILTING
QUINCUNX
QUINTAIN
QUIRINAL
QUISLING
QUIXOTIC
QUOTABLE
QUOTIENT
RABELAIS
RACHITIS
RACIALLY
RACINESS
RACKRENT
RACLETTE
RADIANCE
RADIATOR
RAGSTONE
RAILHEAD
RAILINGS
RAILLERY
RAILROAD
RAINBIRD
RAINCOAT
RAINDROP
RAINFALL
RAINWEAR
RAISONNÉ
RAMBLING
RAMBUTAN
RAMEQUIN
RAMPARTS
RANDOMLY
RANELAGH
RANKNESS
RAPACITY
RAPECAKE
RAPIDITY
RAREFIED

RASCALLY
RASHNESS
RASPUTIN
RASSELAS
RATEABLE
RATIONAL
RATTIGAN
RATTLING
RAVENOUS
REACTION
REACTIVE
READABLE
READIEST
READJUST
REAFFIRM
REALTIME
REAPPEAR
REARMOST
REARWARD
REASONED
REASSERT
REASSESS
REASSIGN
REASSUME
REASSURE
REAWAKEN
REBUTTAL
RECEDING
RECEIPTS
RECEIVED
RECEIVER
RECENTLY
RECEPTOR
RECESSED
RECHARGE
RECKLESS
RECKONER
RECORDER
RECOURSE
RECOVERY
RECREATE
RECRUITS
RECUSANT
REDACTOR
REDBRICK
REDEEMER
REDEFINE
REDEPLOY
REDESIGN
REDIRECT
REDLIGHT
REDOLENT
REDOUBLE
REDSHANK
REDSTART
REEDLING
REEDSMAN

REEMPLOY
REFERRAL
REFINERY
REFORMED
REFORMER
REFRINGE
REFUGIUM
REGAINED
REGICIDE
REGIMENT
REGIONAL
REGISTER
REGISTRY
REGULATE
REHEARSE
REIGNING
REINDEER
REINSURE
REINVEST
REJOINED
REKINDLE
RELATING
RELATION
RELATIVE
RELAXING
RELAYING
RELEASED
RELEGATE
RELEVANT
RELIABLE
RELIABLY
RELIANCE
RELIEVED
RELIGION
RELOCATE
REMEDIAL
REMEMBER
REMINDER
REMITTAL
REMNANTS
REMOTELY
REMOUNTS
RENEGADE
RENMINBI
RENOUNCE
RENOVATE
RENOWNED
REORIENT
REPAIRER
REPARTEE
REPAYING
REPEATED
REPEATER
REPHRASE
REPLEVIN
REPORTED
REPORTER

REPOUSSÉ
REPRIEVE
REPRISAL
REPROACH
REPUBLIC
REQUIRED
RESEARCH
RESEMBLE
RESERVED
RESETTLE
RESIDENT
RESIDUAL
RESIDUUM
RESIGNED
RESINOUS
RESISTOR
RESOLUTE
RESOLVED
RESONANT
RESONATE
RESOURCE
RESPECTS
RESPIGHI
RESPONSE
RESTLESS
RESTORER
RESTRAIN
RESTRICT
RESTROOM
RETAILER
RETAINER
RETARDED
RETICENT
RETICULE
RETIRING
RETRENCH
RETRIEVE
REUSABLE
REVANCHE
REVEALED
REVEILLE
REVELLER
REVEREND
REVERENT
REVERSAL
REVERSED
REVIEWER
REVISION
REVIVIFY
REVIVING
REVOLVER
REYNOLDS
RHAPSODY
RHEOSTAT
RHETORIC
RHOMBOID
RHONCHUS

RHYTHMIC
RIBALDRY
RIBSTONE
RICHNESS
RICKSHAW
RICOCHET
RIDDANCE
RIDGEWAY
RIDICULE
RIESLING
RIFFRAFF
RIFLEMAN
RIGATONI
RIGHTFUL
RIGHTIST
RIGIDITY
RIGOROUS
RINGDOVE
RINGSIDE
RINGTAIL
RINGWALL
RINGWORM
RIPARIAN
RIPENESS
RIPPLING
RISSOLES
RITUALLY
RIVALISE
RIVERAIN
RIVERINE
RIVETING
ROADSHOW
ROADSIDE
ROADSTER
ROASTING
ROBINSON
ROBOTICS
ROBUSTLY
ROCHDALE
ROCKETRY
RODERICK
ROENTGEN
ROGATION
ROLLCALL
ROLYPOLY
ROMANCER
ROMANIAN
ROMANSCH
ROMANTIC
ROOFLESS
ROOFTOPS
ROOMMATE
ROOTLESS
ROSALIND
ROSALINE
ROSAMOND
ROSEMARY

ROSEWOOD
ROSINESS
ROSSETTI
ROTATION
ROTATORY
ROTENONE
ROUGHAGE
ROULETTE
ROUNDERS
ROUSSEAU
ROYALIST
RUBAIYAT
RUBBISHY
RUBICUND
RUCKSACK
RUCTIONS
RUDENESS
RUDIMENT
RUEFULLY
RUGGEDLY
RULEBOOK
RUMBLING
RUMINANT
RUMINATE
RUMOURED
RUNABOUT
RUNCIBLE
RUNNERUP
RUSHMORE
RUSTLESS
RUSTLING
RUTABAGA
RUTHLESS
RYEGRASS
SABOTAGE
SABOTEUR
SACRISTY
SADDLERY
SADDLING
SADDUCEE
SADISTIC
SAGACITY
SAGENESS
SAILBOAT
SAINFOIN
SALACITY
SALARIED
SALEABLE
SALEROOM
SALESMAN
SALINGER
SALINITY
SALIVARY
SALIVATE
SALTLICK
SALTNESS
SALUTARY

SALUTORY
SALVADOR
SAMENESS
SAMIZDAT
SAMPHIRE
SANCTIFY
SANCTION
SANCTITY
SANDBANK
SANDWICH
SANGLIER
SANGUINE
SANITARY
SANITIZE
SANSERIF
SANSKRIT
SANTIAGO
SAPONITE
SAPPHIRE
SAPPHIST
SARABAND
SARATOGA
SARDINIA
SARDONIC
SARDONYX
SARGASSO
SASSANID
SATIATED
SATIRIST
SATIRIZE
SATURATE
SATURDAY
SATURNIA
SAUCEPAN
SAUROPOD
SAUSAGES
SAVAGELY
SAVAGERY
SAVANNAH
SAVOURED
SAVOYARD
SAWBONES
SAXATILE
SAYONARA
SCABBARD
SCABIOUS
SCABROUS
SCAFFOLD
SCALDING
SCALENUS
SCALLION
SCANDIUM
SCANNING
SCANSION
SCANTIES
SCANTILY
SCAPHOID
SCAPULAR
SCARCELY
SCARCITY
SCARFACE
SCATHING
SCAVENGE
SCENARIO
SCHAPSKA
SCHEDULE
SCHEMING
SCHILLER
SCHIZOID
SCHMALTZ
SCHMOOZE
SCHNAPPS
SCHOONER
SCHUBERT
SCHUMANN
SCIATICA
SCIENCES
SCILICET
SCIMITAR
SCIROCCO
SCISSION
SCISSORS
SCOFFING
SCOLDING
SCORCHED
SCORCHER
SCORNFUL
SCORPION
SCOTLAND
SCOTSMAN
SCOTTISH
SCOURING
SCOWLING
SCRABBLE
SCRAMBLE
SCRAPPLE
SCRATCHY
SCRAWLED
SCREAMER
SCREENED
SCREWTOP
SCRIABIN
SCRIBBLE
SCRIBBLY
SCRIPTUM
SCROFULA
SCROUNGE
SCRUBBER
SCRUPLES
SCRUTINY
SCULLERY
SCULLION
SCULPTOR
SCYBALUM
SEABOARD
SEABORNE
SEAFARER
SEAFORTH
SEAFRONT
SEAGOING
SEALSKIN
SEALYHAM
SEAMLESS
SEAMSTER
SEAPLANE
SEARCHER
SEASCAPE
SEASHELL
SEASHORE
SEASONAL
SEASONED
SEAWARDS
SECLUDED
SECONDER
SECONDLY
SECRETLY
SECURELY
SECURITY
SEDATELY
SEDATION
SEDATIVE
SEDIMENT
SEDITION
SEDULOUS
SEEDLESS
SEEDLING
SEEDSMAN
SEETHING
SELASSIE
SELBORNE
SELECTED
SELECTOR
SELENITE
SELENIUM
SELEUCID
SELFHELP
SELFLESS
SELFMADE
SELFPITY
SELFSAME
SELVEDGE
SEMESTER
SEMINARY
SEMIOTIC
SEMITONE
SEMOLINA
SENGREEN
SENILITY
SENORITA
SENSIBLE
SENSIBLY
SENSUOUS
SENTENCE
SENTIENT
SENTINEL
SEPARATE
SEQUENCE
SERAFILE
SERAGLIO
SERAPHIC
SERAPHIM
SERENADE
SERENATA
SERENELY
SERENITY
SERGEANT
SERIATIM
SERJEANT
SEROLOGY
SEROTYPE
SERRATED
SERVICES
SERVIENT
SERVITOR
SEVERELY
SEVEREST
SEVERITY
SEWERAGE
SEXOLOGY
SEXUALLY
SHABBILY
SHACKLES
SHADRACH
SHAGREEN
SHAKEOUT
SHALLOWS
SHAMBLES
SHAMEFUL
SHAMROCK
SHANGHAI
SHANTUNG
SHAREOUT
SHEARMAN
SHEEPDOG
SHEEPISH
SHEIKDOM
SHELDUCK
SHELVING
SHEPHERD
SHERATON
SHERIDAN
SHERLOCK
SHERWOOD
SHETLAND
SHIELING
SHIFTING
SHIGELLA
SHIITAKE
SHILLING
SHINGLES
SHIPMATE
SHIPMENT
SHIPPING
SHIPYARD
SHIVERED
SHOCKING
SHODDILY
SHOEHORN
SHOELACE
SHOELESS
SHOETREE
SHOOTING
SHOOTOUT
SHOPPING
SHOPTALK
SHORTAGE
SHOULDER
SHOUTING
SHOWBOAT
SHOWCASE
SHOWDOWN
SHOWGIRL
SHOWROOM
SHRAPNEL
SHREDDER
SHREWDLY
SHREWISH
SHROUDED
SHRUNKEN
SHUTDOWN
SHUTTERS
SIBERIAN
SIBILANT
SICILIAN
SICKLIST
SICKNESS
SICKROOM
SIDEKICK
SIDELINE
SIDELONG
SIDEREAL
SIDERITE
SIDESHOW
SIDESLIP
SIDESMAN
SIDESTEP
SIDEWALK
SIDEWAYS
SIGHTING
SIGNALER
SIGNALLY
SIGNORIA
SIGNPOST
SILENCER
SILENTLY
SILESIAN
SILICATE
SILICONE
SILKTAIL
SILKWORM
SILURIAN
SIMPLIFY
SIMULATE
SINAPISM
SINCLAIR
SINECURE
SINFONIA
SINGSONG
SINGULAR
SINISTER
SIRENIAN
SISTERLY
SISYPHUS
SITUATED
SIXPENCE
SIXTIETH
SIZEABLE
SIZZLING
SKELETAL
SKELETON
SKEWBALD
SKIBOOTS
SKIDDING
SKILLFUL
SKILLING
SKILLION
SKINDEEP
SKINHEAD
SKINWORK
SKIPJACK
SKIPPING
SKIRMISH
SKIRTING
SKITTISH
SKITTLES
SKULKING
SKULLCAP
SKYLIGHT
SKYPILOT
SLANGING
SLANTING
SLAPBANG
SLAPDASH
SLAPJACK
SLATTERN
SLEEPERS
SLEEPILY
SLEEPING
SLIGHTED
SLIGHTLY
SLIMNESS
SLIPOVER

SLIPPERS
SLIPPERY
SLIPPING
SLIPSHOD
SLIPSLOP
SLOBBERY
SLOPPILY
SLOTHFUL
SLOVAKIA
SLOVENIA
SLOVENLY
SLOWDOWN
SLOWNESS
SLOWPOKE
SLUGABED
SLUGFEST
SLUGGARD
SLUGGISH
SLUMMING
SLURRING
SLUTTISH
SLYBOOTS
SMALLEST
SMALLPOX
SMARTEST
SMASHING
SMELTING
SMIDGEON
SMOCKING
SMOLLETT
SMOOTHER
SMOOTHLY
SMOULDER
SMUGGLED
SMUGGLER
SMUGNESS
SNACKBAR
SNAPPILY
SNAPSHOT
SNATCHER
SNEAKERS
SNEAKING
SNEERING
SNEEZING
SNIFFLER
SNOBBERY
SNOBBISH
SNOOTILY
SNORTING
SNOWBALL
SNOWDROP
SNOWFALL
SNOWLINE
SNUFFBOX
SOAKAWAY
SOAPSUDS
SOBERING
SOBRIETY
SOCALLED
SOCIABLE
SOCIALLY
SOCRATES
SOCRATIC
SODALITE
SODALITY
SOFTBALL
SOFTENER
SOFTNESS
SOFTWARE
SOFTWOOD
SOLARIUM
SOLDIERS
SOLDIERY
SOLECISM
SOLEMNLY
SOLENOID
SOLIDIFY
SOLIDITY
SOLITARY
SOLITUDE
SOLSTICE
SOLUTION
SOLVABLE
SOLVENCY
SOMBRELY
SOMBRERO
SOMEBODY
SOMERSET
SOMETIME
SOMEWHAT
SONATINA
SONGBIRD
SONGSTER
SONOROUS
SOOTHING
SOOTHSAY
SORBONNE
SORCERER
SORDIDLY
SORENESS
SORORITY
SOUCHONG
SOULLESS
SOUNDING
SOURCING
SOURNESS
SOURPUSS
SOUTHEND
SOUTHERN
SOUTHPAW
SOUVENIR
SPACEMAN
SPACIOUS
SPADEFUL
SPANDREL
SPANGLED
SPANIARD
SPANKING
SPANNING
SPARAXIS
SPARKING
SPARKLER
SPARRING
SPARSELY
SPARSITY
SPARTANS
SPAVINED
SPAWNING
SPEAKERS
SPEAKING
SPECIFIC
SPECIMEN
SPECIOUS
SPECKLED
SPECTRAL
SPECTRUM
SPECULUM
SPEEDILY
SPEEDWAY
SPELLING
SPELLMAN
SPENDING
SPHAGNUM
SPICCATO
SPIFFING
SPILLAGE
SPILLWAY
SPINNING
SPINSTER
SPINTEXT
SPIRACLE
SPIRALLY
SPIRITED
SPIRITUS
SPITEFUL
SPITFIRE
SPITHEAD
SPITTING
SPITTOON
SPLASHER
SPLATTER
SPLENDID
SPLENDOR
SPLINTER
SPLITTER
SPLUTTER
SPOILAGE
SPOILING
SPOLIATE
SPOONFUL
SPORADIC
SPORTING
SPORTIVE
SPOTLESS
SPOTTING
SPRAINED
SPRAWLED
SPREADER
SPRINGER
SPRINKLE
SPRINTER
SPRITELY
SPRITZER
SPROCKET
SPRUCELY
SPRYNESS
SPURIOUS
SPURNING
SPYGLASS
SQUABBLE
SQUADDIE
SQUADRON
SQUAMATA
SQUANDER
SQUARELY
SQUATTER
SQUEAKER
SQUEALER
SQUEEGEE
SQUEEZER
SQUIGGLE
SQUIRREL
STABBING
STABLING
STACCATO
STAFFING
STAFFORD
STAGGERS
STAGHORN
STAGNANT
STAGNATE
STAIRWAY
STAKEOUT
STALKING
STALLION
STALWART
STAMENED
STAMPEDE
STANDARD
STANDING
STANDISH
STANDOFF
STANHOPE
STANNARY
STANNITE
STAPHYLE
STARCHED
STARDUST
STARFISH
STARGAZE
STARKERS
STARLESS
STARLING
STAROSTA
STARTERS
STARTING
STARVING
STATUARY
STAYSAIL
STEADILY
STEALING
STEALTHY
STEATITE
STEATOMA
STEERAGE
STEERING
STEINWAY
STELLATE
STENDHAL
STENOSED
STENOSIS
STEPHENS
STERLING
STICCATO
STICKILY
STICKING
STICKLER
STIFLING
STIGMATA
STILETTO
STILWELL
STIMULUS
STINGING
STINGRAY
STINKING
STIRLING
STIRRING
STOCCATA
STOCKADE
STOCKCAR
STOCKING
STOCKIST
STOCKMAN
STOCKPOT
STOICISM
STOKESAY
STOLIDLY
STOPCOCK
STOPOVER
STOPPAGE
STOPPING
STOREMAN
STOREYED
STORMING
STORMONT
STOWAWAY
STRABISM
STRACHEY
STRADDLE
STRAGGLE
STRAGGLY
STRAIGHT
STRAINED
STRAINER
STRAITEN
STRANDED
STRANGER
STRANGLE
STRAPPED
STRAPPER
STRATEGY
STRATIFY
STREAKED
STREAKER
STREAMER
STRENGTH
STRESSED
STRETCHY
STRIATED
STRIATUM
STRICKEN
STRICTLY
STRIDENT
STRIKING
STRINGED
STRINGER
STRIPPED
STRIPPER
STRIVING
STROLLER
STRONGLY
STRUGGLE
STRUMPET
STUBBORN
STUCCOED
STUDENTS
STUDIOUS
STUFFILY
STUFFING
STULTIFY
STUNNING
STUPIDLY
STURDILY
STURGEON
STYLIZED
SUBHUMAN
SUBJECTS
SUBLEASE
SUBMERGE
SUBPOENA
SUBSONIC
SUBTENSE

SUBTITLE
SUBTLETY
SUBTOPIA
SUBTOTAL
SUBTRACT
SUBURBAN
SUBURBIA
SUCCEEDS
SUCCINCT
SUCCUBUS
SUCHLIKE
SUCKLING
SUDAMENT
SUDAMINA
SUDANESE
SUDARIUM
SUDDENLY
SUFFERER
SUFFRAGE
SUICIDAL
SUITABLE
SUITABLY
SUITCASE
SUKIYAKI
SULFURIC
SULLENLY
SULLIVAN
SULPHATE
SULPHIDE
SUMERIAN
SUMMITRY
SUNBATHE
SUNBURNT
SUNBURST
SUNCREAM
SUNDANCE
SUNDRIED
SUNDRIES
SUNLIGHT
SUNSHADE
SUNSHINE
SUPERBLY
SUPERIOR
SUPERMAN
SUPERNAL
SUPERTAX
SUPPLANT
SUPPLIER
SUPPLIES
SUPPOSED
SUPPRESS
SURENESS
SURFBOAT
SURGICAL
SURMOUNT
SURPLICE
SURPRISE
SURROUND
SURVEYOR
SURVIVAL
SURVIVOR
SUSPENSE
SUZERAIN
SVENGALI
SWADDLER
SWANSKIN
SWANSONG
SWARMING
SWASTIKA
SWEARING
SWEATING
SWEEPING
SWELLING
SWERVING
SWILLING
SWIMMING
SWIMSUIT
SWINDLER
SWINGING
SWIRLING
SYBARITE
SYCAMORE
SYLLABIC
SYLLABLE
SYLLABUB
SYLLABUS
SYLVANER
SYMBIONT
SYMBOLIC
SYMMETRY
SYMPATHY
SYMPHONY
SYMPTOMS
SYNCLINE
SYNDROME
SYNOPSIS
SYNOPTIC
SYNTEXIS
SYPHILIS
SYRACUSE
SYRINGES
SYSTEMIC
TABBYCAT
TABLEMAT
TABULATE
TACITURN
TACTICAL
TACTLESS
TAFFRAIL
TAHITIAN
TAILBACK
TAILGATE
TAILLESS
TAILPIPE
TAILSKID
TAILSPIN
TAKEAWAY
TAKEHOME
TAKEOVER
TALENTED
TALISMAN
TAMARIND
TAMARISK
TAMENESS
TAMWORTH
TANDOORI
TANGIBLE
TANGIBLY
TANTALUM
TANTALUS
TANZANIA
TAPENADE
TAPERING
TAPESTRY
TAPEWORM
TAPHOUSE
TARBOOSH
TARRAGON
TARTARIC
TARTARUS
TARTNESS
TARTRATE
TARTUFFE
TASHKENT
TASMANIA
TASTEFUL
TATTERED
TAUTNESS
TAVERNER
TAXATION
TAXONOMY
TAXPAYER
TAYBERRY
TEACHERS
TEACHING
TEACLOTH
TEAMMATE
TEAMSTER
TEAMWORK
TEARABLE
TEARAWAY
TEARDROP
TEASPOON
TECTONIC
TEENAGER
TEESHIRT
TEETHING
TEETOTAL
TEGUMENT
TELECAST
TELEFILM
TELEGONY
TELEGRAM
TELEMARK
TELETHON
TELEVISE
TELLTALE
TELLURIC
TEMERITY
TEMPERED
TEMPLATE
TEMPORAL
TEMPTING
TENACITY
TENDENCY
TENDERLY
TENEBRAE
TENEBRIO
TENEMENT
TENESMUS
TENNYSON
TENTACLE
TEQUILLA
TERATOMA
TERIYAKI
TERMINAL
TERMINUS
TERRACED
TERRAPIN
TERRIBLE
TERRIBLY
TERRIFIC
TERTIARY
TERYLENE
TESTATOR
TESTATUM
TESTICLE
TETCHILY
TETRAGON
TETRAPOD
TETRARCH
TEUTONIC
TEXTBOOK
TEXTURED
THAILAND
THALAMUS
THALLIUM
THANATOS
THANKFUL
THATAWAY
THATCHED
THATCHER
THEATRIC
THEMATIC
THEOCRAT
THEOLOGY
THEORIST
THEORIZE
THESPIAN
THIAMINE
THICKSET
THIEVERY
THIEVING
THIEVISH
THINGAMY
THINKING
THINNESS
THINNING
THIRTEEN
THOMPSON
THORACIC
THOROUGH
THOUGHTS
THOUSAND
THRACIAN
THRALDOM
THRASHER
THREATEN
THRENODY
THRESHER
THRILLER
THROMBIN
THROMBUS
THROTTLE
THRUSTER
THUMPING
THUNDERY
THURIBLE
THURIFER
THURSDAY
TIBERIAS
TIBERIUS
TICKLING
TICKLISH
TICKTACK
TICKTOCK
TIDEMARK
TIDINESS
TIEBREAK
TIGHTWAD
TIMBERED
TIMELESS
TIMIDITY
TIMOROUS
TINCTURE
TINGLING
TINNITUS
TINSELLY
TINTAGEL
TIPSTAFF
TIRAMISU
TIRELESS
TIRESIAS
TIRESOME
TITANESS
TITANISM
TITANITE
TITANIUM
TITICACA
TITIVATE
TITMOUSE
TOBOGGAN
TOGETHER
TOILSOME
TOISEACH
TOLBOOTH
TOLERANT
TOLERATE
TOLLGATE
TOMAHAWK
TOMATOES
TOMENTUM
TOMORROW
TONALITY
TONELESS
TONSURED
TOPCLASS
TOPHEAVY
TOPLEVEL
TOPNOTCH
TOPOLOGY
TOREADOR
TORTILLA
TORTOISE
TORTUOUS
TORTURED
TORTURER
TOTALITY
TOTALIZE
TOUCHING
TOULOUSE
TOVARICH
TOWELING
TOWERING
TOWNSHIP
TOWNSMAN
TOXAEMIA
TOXICITY
TOXOCARA
TRACHOMA
TRACKING
TRACTION
TRADEOFF
TRAILING
TRAINING
TRAITORS
TRAMLINE
TRANQUIL
TRANSACT
TRANSECT
TRANSEPT
TRANSFER

TRANSFIX TRUENESS UNAWARES UNLEADED URGENTLY VERLAINE
TRANSHIP TRUMPERY UNBEATEN UNLIKELY URSULINE VERMOUTH
TRANSKEI TRUNCATE UNBIASED UNLISTED USEFULLY VERONESE
TRANSMIT TRUNNION UNBIDDEN UNLOADED USUFRUCT VERONICA
TRAPDOOR TRUSTFUL UNBROKEN UNLOCKED USURIOUS VERSICLE
TRAPPIST TRUSTING UNBURDEN UNLOVELY UTENSILS VERTEBRA
TRASHCAN TRUTHFUL UNBUTTON UNMANNED UXORIOUS VERTICAL
TRAVELER TSAREVNA UNCARING UNMARKED VACANTLY VESPERAL
TRAVERSE TUBELESS UNCHASTE UNNERVED VACATION VESPUCCI
TRAVESTY TUBERCLE UNCLOVEN UNPERSON VAGABOND VESTIARY
TREASURE TUBEROSE UNCOMBED UNPLACED VAGARIES VESTMENT
TREASURY TUBEROUS UNCOMMON UNREASON VAGRANCY VESUVIUS
TREATISE TUNGSTEN UNCOOKED UNSALTED VALENCIA VEXATION
TREELESS TUNISIAN UNCOUPLE UNSAVORY VALERIAN VEXILLUM
TREELINE TUPAMARO UNCTUOUS UNSEALED VALETING VIATICUM
TREETOPS TUPPENNY UNCURBED UNSEEDED VALHALLA VIBRANCY
TREMBLER TURANDOT UNDERAGE UNSEEMLY VALIDATE VIBRATOR
TRENCHER TURBANED UNDERARM UNSETTLE VALIDITY VIBURNUM
TRESPASS TURBOJET UNDERCUT UNSHAKEN VALKYRIE VICARAGE
TRIANGLE TURGENEV UNDERDOG UNSIGNED VALLETTA VICARIAL
TRIASSIC TURGIDLY UNDERFED UNSOCIAL VALUABLE VICINITY
TRIBUNAL TURKOMAN UNDERLAY UNSOLVED VALVULAR VICTORIA
TRICHOID TURMERIC UNDERLIE UNSPOILT VANADIUM VICTUALS
TRICKERY TURNBACK UNDERPIN UNSPOKEN VANBRUGH VIGILANT
TRICYCLE TURNCOAT UNDERSEA UNSTABLE VANGUARD VIGNETTE
TRIFLING TURNCOCK UNDERTOW UNSTATED VANISHED VIGOROUS
TRIGLYPH TURNOVER UNDULANT UNSTEADY VANQUISH VILENESS
TRILEMMA TURNPIKE UNDULATE UNSUITED VAPORIZE VILLAGER
TRILLING TURNSPIT UNEARNED UNTANGLE VARIABLE VILLAINY
TRILLION TURRETED UNEASILY UNTAPPED VARIANCE VINCIBLE
TRILLIUM TUSITALA UNENDING UNTHREAD VARICOSE VINCULUM
TRIMARAN TUTELAGE UNERRING UNTIDILY VARIETAL VINDALOO
TRIMMING TUTELARY UNEVENLY UNTILLED VARIFORM VINEGARY
TRIMNESS TUTORIAL UNFADING UNTIMELY VARIORUM VINEYARD
TRINCULO TWEEZERS UNFASTEN UNTOWARD VASCULAR VIOLATOR
TRINIDAD TWELVEMO UNFETTER UNUSABLE VASTNESS VIOLENCE
TRIPLING TWILIGHT UNFILLED UNVARIED VAULTING VIPEROUS
TRIPTANE TWIRLING UNFORCED UNVERSED VAUXHALL VIREMENT
TRIPTYCH TWISTING UNFREEZE UNVOICED VEGETATE VIRGINAL
TRISTICH TWITCHER UNGAINLY UNWANTED VEHEMENT VIRGINIA
TRISTRAM TWOPENNY UNGULATE UNWEANED VELLEITY VIRILITY
TRITICAL TWOPIECE UNHARMED UNWIELDY VELOCITY VIROLOGY
TRITICUM TYMPANUM UNHEATED UNWONTED VENALITY VIRTUOSI
TROCHAIC TYPECAST UNHEROIC UNWORTHY VENDETTA VIRTUOSO
TROCHLEA TYPEFACE UNHINGED UPCOMING VENERATE VIRTUOUS
TROLLOPE TYROLEAN UNIFYING UPHEAVAL VENEREAL VIRULENT
TROMBONE TYROSINE UNIONISM UPHOLDER VENETIAN VISCERAL
TROOPING TZATZIKI UNIONIST UPMARKET VENGEFUL VISCOUNT
TROPICAL UBIQUITY UNIONIZE UPPERCUT VENOMOUS VISELIKE
TROTTERS UDOMETER UNIPOLAR UPRIGHTS VENTURED VISIGOTH
TROTTOIR UGLINESS UNIQUELY UPRISING VERACITY VISITANT
TROUBLED ULCERATE UNITEDLY UPSTAIRS VERANDAH VISITING
TROUBLES ULCEROUS UNIVALVE UPSTREAM VERBALLY VISUALLY
TROUNCER ULTERIOR UNIVERSE UPTURNED VERBATIM VITALITY
TROUSERS ULTIMATE UNJUSTLY URBANITY VERBIAGE VITALIZE
TRUCKING UMBRELLA UNKINDLY URBANIZE VERDERER VITAMINS
TRUCKLED UNABATED UNLAWFUL URETHANE VERJUICE VITELLUS

VITILIGO
VITREOUS
VIVACITY
VIVARIUM
VOCALIST
VOCALIZE
VOCATION
VOCATIVE
VOIDANCE
VOLATILE
VOLCANIC
VOLITION
VOLPLANE
VOLSCIAN
VOLTAIRE
VOMITING
VOMITORY
VORACITY
VOYAGEUR
VULGARLY
WAGGONER
WAINSCOT
WAITRESS
WALKOVER
WALKYRIE
WALLSEND
WALLWORT
WALTZING
WAMBLING
WANDERER
WARDRESS
WARDROBE
WARDROOM
WARDSHIP
WARFARIN
WARHORSE
WARINESS
WARPAINT
WARPLANE
WARRANTY
WASHABLE
WASHBOWL
WASHDOWN
WASHROOM
WASTEFUL
WATCHDOG
WATCHFUL
WATCHING
WATCHMAN
WATERBUG
WATERING
WATERLOO
WATERMAN
WATERWAY
WAVEBAND
WAVERING
WAVERLEY
WAXWORKS
WAYFARER
WEAKLING
WEAKNESS
WEAPONRY
WEARABLE
WEDGWOOD
WEIGHING
WELLBRED
WELLNIGH
WELLPAID
WELSHMAN
WEREWOLF
WESLEYAN
WESTERLY
WESTWARD
WETLANDS
WHACKING
WHARFAGE
WHATEVER
WHEATEAR
WHEEZILY
WHEEZING
WHENEVER
WHEREVER
WHIMBREL
WHINCHAT
WHIPCORD
WHIPHAND
WHIPJACK
WHIPLASH
WHIPPING
WHIRLING
WHISKERS
WHISKERY
WHISTLER
WHITECAP
WHITEHOT
WHITENER
WHITLING
WHODUNIT
WHOOPING
WHOPPING
WICKEDLY
WIDENING
WILDFELL
WILDFIRE
WILDFOWL
WILDLIFE
WILDNESS
WILFULLY
WILINESS
WILLIAMS
WINDBURN
WINDFALL
WINDHOEK
WINDINGS
WINDLASS
WINDLESS
WINDMILL
WINDPIPE
WINDSOCK
WINDWARD
WINGLESS
WINGSPAN
WINIFRED
WINNINGS
WINNIPEG
WIRELESS
WIREWORM
WISEACRE
WISHBONE
WISTERIA
WITCHERY
WITCHING
WITHDRAW
WITHERED
WITHHOLD
WIZARDRY
WOBBLING
WOEFULLY
WOLFBANE
WOLSELEY
WOMANISH
WOMANIZE
WONDROUS
WOODBINE
WOODCOCK
WOODENLY
WOODLAND
WOODSHED
WOODSMAN
WOODWARD
WOODWIND
WOODWORK
WOODWORM
WOOLLENS
WOOLPACK
WOOLSACK
WORDBOOK
WORDLESS
WORKABLE
WORKADAY
WORKBOOK
WORKINGS
WORKLOAD
WORKMATE
WORKROOM
WORKSHOP
WORMCAST
WORMWOOD
WORRYING
WORTHIES
WORTHILY
WRANGLER
WRAPPING
WRATHFUL
WREATHED
WRECKAGE
WRESTLER
WRETCHED
WRINGING
WRINKLED
WRISTLET
WRITEOFF
WRITHING
WRITINGS
WRONGFUL
WYCLIFFE
XANTHOMA
XANTIPPE
XENOGAMY
XENOLITH
XENOPHON
XERAPHIM
YACHTING
YAKITORI
YARMULKA
YATAGHAN
YEARBOOK
YEARLING
YEARLONG
YEARNING
YEOMANRY
YERSINIA
YIELDING
YODELLER
YOGHOURT
YOKOHAMA
YOSEMITE
YOUNGEST
YOURSELF
YOUTHFUL
YUGOSLAV
YULETIDE
ZAKOUSKI
ZAMINDAR
ZARZUELA
ZASTRUGA
ZEDEKIAH
ZEPHYRUS
ZEPPELIN
ZIBELINE
ZIGGURAT
ZIMBABWE
ZIRCONIA
ZODIACAL
ZOETROPE
ZOONOSIS
ZOOPHYTE
ZOOSPERM
ZOOSPORE
ZUCCHINI
ZWIEBACK

8:2

AARDVARK
AASVOGEL
BAATHIST
BABBLING
BABUSHKA
BABYHOOD
BACCARAT
BACCHANT
BACHELOR
BACILLUS
BACKACHE
BACKBITE
BACKBONE
BACKCHAT
BACKCOMB
BACKDATE
BACKDROP
BACKFIRE
BACKHAND
BACKLASH
BACKLESS
BACKPACK
BACKROOM
BACKSIDE
BACKWARD
BACKYARD
BACTERIA
BACTRIAN
BADINAGE
BADLANDS
BAEDEKER
BAFFLING
BAGHEERA
BAGPIPES
BAGUETTE
BAHAMIAN
BAHRAINI
BAILMENT
BAKELITE
BALANCED
BALDNESS
BALDRICK
BALEARIC
BALINESE
BALLCOCK
BALLGIRL
BALLISTA
BALLOCKS
BALLPARK
BALLROOM
BALLYHOO
BALMORAL
BALUSTER
BANALITY
BANDANNA
BANDEROL
BANDITTI
BANDSMAN
BANISTER
BANKBOOK
BANKNOTE
BANKROLL
BANKRUPT
BANLIEUE
BANTLING
BAPTISED
BARABBAS
BARATHEA
BARBADOS
BARBARIC
BARBECUE
BARBICAN
BARBIZON
BARDOLPH
BAREBACK
BAREFOOT
BARENESS
BARGELLO
BARGEMAN
BARITONE
BARNABAS
BARNACLE
BARNARDS
BARNYARD
BARONESS
BARONETS
BARONIAL
BARRACKS
BARRATRY
BARRETTE
BARTERED
BASEBALL
BASEBORN
BASELESS
BASELINE
BASEMENT
BASENESS
BASIDIUM
BASILICA
BASILISK
BASINFUL
BASKETRY
BASSINET
BASTILLE
BATAVIAN
BATHETIC
BATHROBE

BATHROOM
BATTERED
BAUDRICK
BAVARIAN
BAYREUTH
CABERNET
CABLECAR
CABLEWAY
CABOCHON
CABOODLE
CABOTAGE
CABRIOLE
CACHALOT
CACHEPOT
CACHEXIA
CADASTRE
CADILLAC
CADUCEUS
CAERLEON
CAFFEINE
CAGINESS
CAJOLERY
CAKEHOLE
CAKEWALK
CALABASH
CALAMINE
CALAMITY
CALCEATE
CALCULUS
CALCUTTA
CALDERON
CALENDAR
CALENDER
CALIGULA
CALIPERS
CALLGIRL
CALLIOPE
CALLIPER
CALLISTO
CALMNESS
CALOTYPE
CALTHROP
CALVADOS
CAMARGUE
CAMBERED
CAMBODIA
CAMBRIAN
CAMELLIA
CAMEROON
CAMISOLE
CAMOMILE
CAMPAIGN
CAMPBELL
CAMPSITE
CAMPTOWN
CAMSHAFT
CAMSTONE
CANADIAN
CANAILLE
CANALISE
CANARIES
CANBERRA
CANDIDLY
CANISTER
CANNABIS
CANNIBAL
CANOEING
CANOEIST
CANONIZE
CANOODLE
CANTICLE
CAPACITY
CAPERING
CAPITALS
CAPRIOLE
CAPSICUM
CAPSIZED
CAPSTONE
CAPTIOUS
CAPUCHIN
CAPYBARA
CARABINE
CARACOLE
CARAPACE
CARBOLIC
CARBONIC
CARCAJOU
CARCANET
CARDAMOM
CARDIGAN
CARDINAL
CAREFREE
CARELESS
CAREWORN
CARILLON
CARJACOU
CARNEGIE
CARNIVAL
CAROLINA
CAROLINE
CAROTENE
CAROUSAL
CAROUSEL
CARRAWAY
CARRIAGE
CARRIOLE
CARRYALL
CARRYCOT
CARRYING
CARTHAGE
CARTLOAD
CARUCATE
CARYATID
CASANOVA
CASEMATE
CASEMENT
CASHMERE
CASSETTE
CASTANET
CASTAWAY
CASTOFFS
CASTRATE
CASTRATO
CASUALLY
CASUALTY
CATACOMB
CATALYST
CATAMITE
CATAPULT
CATARACT
CATATONY
CATCHING
CATEGORY
CATERING
CATHEDRA
CATHETER
CATHOLIC
CATHOUSE
CATILINE
CATSMEAT
CATTLEYA
CATULLUS
CAUDILLO
CAULDRON
CAUSEWAY
CAUTIOUS
CAVALIER
CAVATINA
DABCHICK
DAEDALUS
DAFFODIL
DAINTIES
DAINTILY
DAIQUIRI
DAIRYMAN
DALMATIC
DAMASCUS
DAMNABLE
DAMOCLES
DAMPNESS
DANDRUFF
DANEGELD
DANKNESS
DARKENED
DARKNESS
DARKROOM
DARTMOOR
DASHWOOD
DATABASE
DATELESS
DATELINE
DAUGHTER
DAUNTING
DAVIDSON
DAYBREAK
DAYDREAM
DAYLIGHT
DAZZLING
EARLIEST
EARNINGS
EARPHONE
EARPIECE
EASEMENT
EASINESS
EASTERLY
EASTLAKE
EASTWARD
EATABLES
FABULOUS
FACEACHE
FACELESS
FACELIFT
FACILITY
FACTIOUS
FACTOTUM
FAINITES
FAINTING
FAIRNESS
FAITHFUL
FALCONRY
FALKLAND
FALLIBLE
FALSETTO
FAMILIAR
FAMISHED
FAMOUSLY
FANCIFUL
FANCYMAN
FANDANGO
FANLIGHT
FANTASIA
FARCICAL
FAREWELL
FARMHAND
FARMLAND
FARMYARD
FAROUCHE
FARRIERY
FARTHEST
FARTHING
FASCICLE
FASTBACK
FASTENER
FASTNESS
FATALISM
FATALIST
FATALITY
FATHERLY
FATIGUED
FATIGUES
FATSTOCK
FAULKNER
FAVORITE
FAVOURED
GABONESE
GABORONE
GADABOUT
GADARENE
GADGETRY
GADOGADO
GADZOOKS
GAILLARD
GALACTIC
GALBANUM
GALILEAN
GALLERIA
GALLIARD
GALLIPOT
GALLOPER
GALLOWAY
GALLUMPH
GALOSHES
GALVANIC
GAMBLING
GAMEBIRD
GAMENESS
GANGLAND
GANGLING
GANGLION
GANGRENE
GANGSTER
GANYMEDE
GAOLBIRD
GARAMOND
GARDENER
GARDENIA
GARDYLOO
GARGANEY
GARGOYLE
GARISHLY
GARLICKY
GARMENTS
GARRIGUE
GARRISON
GARROTTE
GASOLIER
GASOLINE
GASTRULA
GASWORKS
GATEPOST
GATHERED
GAUNTLET
GAZPACHO
GAZUNDER
HABAKKUK
HABANERA
HABITUAL
HABSBURG
HACIENDA
HAGGADAH
HAIRLESS
HAIRLIKE
HAIRLINE
HALFFULL
HALFHOUR
HALFMAST
HALFTERM
HALFTIME
HALFYEAR
HALLIARD
HALLMARK
HALLOWED
HAMILTON
HAMMERED
HANDBALL
HANDBILL
HANDBOOK
HANDCART
HANDCLAP
HANDCUFF
HANDHELD
HANDICAP
HANDMADE
HANDMAID
HANDOVER
HANDRAIL
HANDSOME
HANDYMAN
HANGINGS
HANGNAIL
HANGOVER
HANNIBAL
HANUKKAH
HAPSBURG
HARANGUE
HARASSED
HARDBACK
HARDCORE
HARDENED
HARDLINE
HARDNESS
HARDSHIP
HARDTACK
HARDWARE
HARDWOOD
HAREBELL
HARFLEUR
HARMLESS
HARMONIC
HARRIDAN
HARRISON
HARTFORD

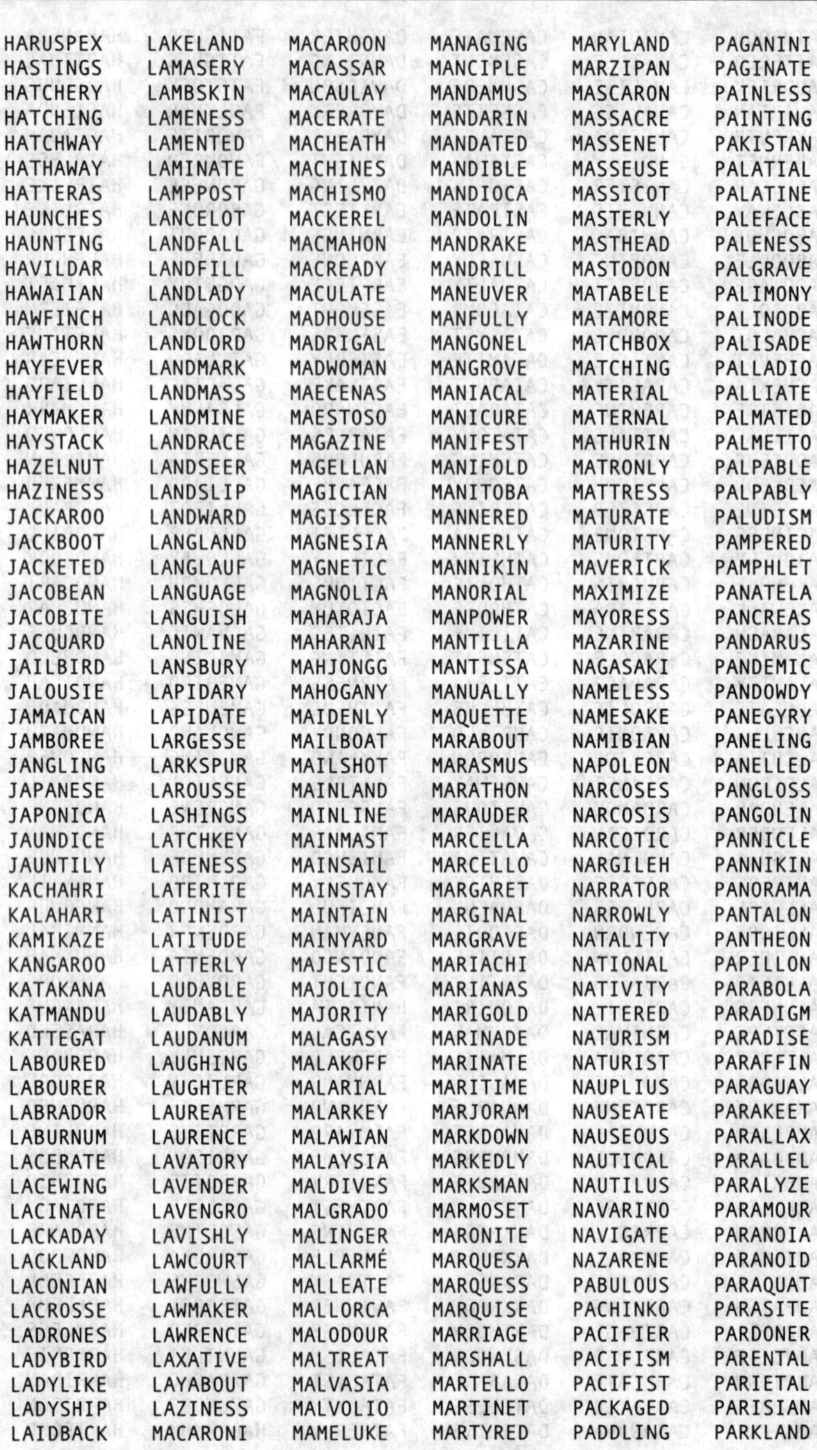

HARUSPEX
HASTINGS
HATCHERY
HATCHING
HATCHWAY
HATHAWAY
HATTERAS
HAUNCHES
HAUNTING
HAVILDAR
HAWAIIAN
HAWFINCH
HAWTHORN
HAYFEVER
HAYFIELD
HAYMAKER
HAYSTACK
HAZELNUT
HAZINESS
JACKAROO
JACKBOOT
JACKETED
JACOBEAN
JACOBITE
JACQUARD
JAILBIRD
JALOUSIE
JAMAICAN
JAMBOREE
JANGLING
JAPANESE
JAPONICA
JAUNDICE
JAUNTILY
KACHAHRI
KALAHARI
KAMIKAZE
KANGAROO
KATAKANA
KATMANDU
KATTEGAT
LABOURED
LABOURER
LABRADOR
LABURNUM
LACERATE
LACEWING
LACINATE
LACKADAY
LACKLAND
LACONIAN
LACROSSE
LADRONES
LADYBIRD
LADYLIKE
LADYSHIP
LAIDBACK
LAKELAND
LAMASERY
LAMBSKIN
LAMENESS
LAMENTED
LAMINATE
LAMPPOST
LANCELOT
LANDFALL
LANDFILL
LANDLADY
LANDLOCK
LANDLORD
LANDMARK
LANDMASS
LANDMINE
LANDRACE
LANDSEER
LANDSLIP
LANDWARD
LANGLAND
LANGLAUF
LANGUAGE
LANGUISH
LANOLINE
LANSBURY
LAPIDARY
LAPIDATE
LARGESSE
LARKSPUR
LAROUSSE
LASHINGS
LATCHKEY
LATENESS
LATERITE
LATINIST
LATITUDE
LATTERLY
LAUDABLE
LAUDABLY
LAUDANUM
LAUGHING
LAUGHTER
LAUREATE
LAURENCE
LAVATORY
LAVENDER
LAVENGRO
LAVISHLY
LAWCOURT
LAWFULLY
LAWMAKER
LAWRENCE
LAXATIVE
LAYABOUT
LAZINESS
MACARONI
MACAROON
MACASSAR
MACAULAY
MACERATE
MACHEATH
MACHINES
MACHISMO
MACKEREL
MACMAHON
MACREADY
MACULATE
MADHOUSE
MADRIGAL
MADWOMAN
MAECENAS
MAESTOSO
MAGAZINE
MAGELLAN
MAGICIAN
MAGISTER
MAGNESIA
MAGNETIC
MAGNOLIA
MAHARAJA
MAHARANI
MAHJONGG
MAHOGANY
MAIDENLY
MAILBOAT
MAILSHOT
MAINLAND
MAINLINE
MAINMAST
MAINSAIL
MAINSTAY
MAINTAIN
MAINYARD
MAJESTIC
MAJOLICA
MAJORITY
MALAGASY
MALAKOFF
MALARIAL
MALARKEY
MALAWIAN
MALAYSIA
MALDIVES
MALGRADO
MALINGER
MALLARMÉ
MALLEATE
MALLORCA
MALODOUR
MALTREAT
MALVASIA
MALVOLIO
MAMELUKE
MANAGING
MANCIPLE
MANDAMUS
MANDARIN
MANDATED
MANDIBLE
MANDIOCA
MANDOLIN
MANDRAKE
MANDRILL
MANEUVER
MANFULLY
MANGONEL
MANGROVE
MANIACAL
MANICURE
MANIFEST
MANIFOLD
MANITOBA
MANNERED
MANNERLY
MANNIKIN
MANORIAL
MANPOWER
MANTILLA
MANTISSA
MANUALLY
MAQUETTE
MARABOUT
MARASMUS
MARATHON
MARAUDER
MARCELLA
MARCELLO
MARGARET
MARGINAL
MARGRAVE
MARIACHI
MARIANAS
MARIGOLD
MARINADE
MARINATE
MARITIME
MARJORAM
MARKDOWN
MARKEDLY
MARKSMAN
MARMOSET
MARONITE
MARQUESA
MARQUESS
MARQUISE
MARRIAGE
MARSHALL
MARTELLO
MARTINET
MARTYRED
MARYLAND
MARZIPAN
MASCARON
MASSACRE
MASSENET
MASSEUSE
MASSICOT
MASTERLY
MASTHEAD
MASTODON
MATABELE
MATAMORE
MATCHBOX
MATCHING
MATERIAL
MATERNAL
MATHURIN
MATRONLY
MATTRESS
MATURATE
MATURITY
MAVERICK
MAXIMIZE
MAYORESS
MAZARINE
NAGASAKI
NAMELESS
NAMESAKE
NAMIBIAN
NAPOLEON
NARCOSES
NARCOSIS
NARCOTIC
NARGILEH
NARRATOR
NARROWLY
NATALITY
NATIONAL
NATIVITY
NATTERED
NATURISM
NATURIST
NAUPLIUS
NAUSEATE
NAUSEOUS
NAUTICAL
NAUTILUS
NAVARINO
NAVIGATE
NAZARENE
PABULOUS
PACHINKO
PACIFIER
PACIFISM
PACIFIST
PACKAGED
PADDLING
PAGANINI
PAGINATE
PAINLESS
PAINTING
PAKISTAN
PALATIAL
PALATINE
PALEFACE
PALENESS
PALGRAVE
PALIMONY
PALINODE
PALISADE
PALLADIO
PALLIATE
PALMATED
PALMETTO
PALPABLE
PALPABLY
PALUDISM
PAMPERED
PAMPHLET
PANATELA
PANCREAS
PANDARUS
PANDEMIC
PANDOWDY
PANEGYRY
PANELING
PANELLED
PANGLOSS
PANGOLIN
PANNICLE
PANNIKIN
PANORAMA
PANTALON
PANTHEON
PAPILLON
PARABOLA
PARADIGM
PARADISE
PARAFFIN
PARAGUAY
PARAKEET
PARALLAX
PARALLEL
PARALYZE
PARAMOUR
PARANOIA
PARANOID
PARAQUAT
PARASITE
PARDONER
PARENTAL
PARIETAL
PARISIAN
PARKLAND

PARLANCE
PARMESAN
PARODIST
PAROLLES
PAROXYSM
PARSIFAL
PARTERRE
PARTHIAN
PARTICLE
PARTISAN
PARTTIME
PASHMINA
PASSABLE
PASSABLY
PASSBOOK
PASSERBY
PASSIBLE
PASSOVER
PASSPORT
PASSWORD
PASTICHE
PASTILLE
PASTORAL
PASTRAMI
PASTURES
PATCHILY
PATELLAR
PATENTED
PATENTEE
PATENTLY
PATERNAL
PATHETIC
PATHOGEN
PATIENCE
PATULOUS
PAULINUS
PAVEMENT
PAVILION
PAWNSHOP
PAYCHECK
RABELAIS
RACHITIS
RACIALLY
RACINESS
RACKRENT
RACLETTE
RADIANCE
RADIATOR
RAGSTONE
RAILHEAD
RAILINGS
RAILLERY
RAILROAD
RAINBIRD
RAINCOAT
RAINDROP
RAINFALL
RAINWEAR
RAISONNÉ
RAMBLING
RAMBUTAN
RAMEQUIN
RAMPARTS
RANDOMLY
RANELAGH
RANKNESS
RAPACITY
RAPECAKE
RAPIDITY
RAREFIED
RASCALLY
RASHNESS
RASPUTIN
RASSELAS
RATEABLE
RATIONAL
RATTIGAN
RATTLING
RAVENOUS
SABOTAGE
SABOTEUR
SACRISTY
SADDLERY
SADDLING
SADDUCEE
SADISTIC
SAGACITY
SAGENESS
SAILBOAT
SAINFOIN
SALACITY
SALARIED
SALEABLE
SALEROOM
SALESMAN
SALINGER
SALINITY
SALIVARY
SALIVATE
SALTLICK
SALTNESS
SALUTARY
SALUTORY
SALVADOR
SAMENESS
SAMIZDAT
SAMPHIRE
SANCTIFY
SANCTION
SANCTITY
SANDBANK
SANDWICH
SANGLIER
SANGUINE
SANITARY
SANITIZE
SANSERIF
SANSKRIT
SANTIAGO
SAPONITE
SAPPHIRE
SAPPHIST
SARABAND
SARATOGA
SARDINIA
SARDONIC
SARDONYX
SARGASSO
SASSANID
SATIATED
SATIRIST
SATIRIZE
SATURATE
SATURDAY
SATURNIA
SAUCEPAN
SAUROPOD
SAUSAGES
SAVAGELY
SAVAGERY
SAVANNAH
SAVOURED
SAVOYARD
SAWBONES
SAXATILE
SAYONARA
TABBYCAT
TABLEMAT
TABULATE
TACITURN
TACTICAL
TACTLESS
TAFFRAIL
TAHITIAN
TAILBACK
TAILGATE
TAILLESS
TAILPIPE
TAILSKID
TAILSPIN
TAKEAWAY
TAKEHOME
TAKEOVER
TALENTED
TALISMAN
TAMARIND
TAMARISK
TAMENESS
TAMWORTH
TANDOORI
TANGIBLE
TANGIBLY
TANTALUM
TANTALUS
TANZANIA
TAPENADE
TAPERING
TAPESTRY
TAPEWORM
TAPHOUSE
TARBOOSH
TARRAGON
TARTARIC
TARTARUS
TARTNESS
TARTRATE
TARTUFFE
TASHKENT
TASMANIA
TASTEFUL
TATTERED
TAUTNESS
TAVERNER
TAXATION
TAXONOMY
TAXPAYER
TAYBERRY
VACANTLY
VACATION
VAGABOND
VAGARIES
VAGRANCY
VALENCIA
VALERIAN
VALETING
VALHALLA
VALIDATE
VALIDITY
VALKYRIE
VALLETTA
VALUABLE
VALVULAR
VANADIUM
VANBRUGH
VANGUARD
VANISHED
VANQUISH
VAPORIZE
VARIABLE
VARIANCE
VARICOSE
VARIETAL
VARIFORM
VARIORUM
VASCULAR
VASTNESS
VAULTING
VAUXHALL
WAGGONER
WAINSCOT
WAITRESS
WALKOVER
WALKYRIE
WALLSEND
WALLWORT
WALTZING
WAMBLING
WANDERER
WARDRESS
WARDROBE
WARDROOM
WARDSHIP
WARFARIN
WARHORSE
WARINESS
WARPAINT
WARPLANE
WARRANTY
WASHABLE
WASHBOWL
WASHDOWN
WASHROOM
WASTEFUL
WATCHDOG
WATCHFUL
WATCHING
WATCHMAN
WATERBUG
WATERING
WATERLOO
WATERMAN
WATERWAY
WAVEBAND
WAVERING
WAVERLEY
WAXWORKS
WAYFARER
XANTHOMA
XANTIPPE
YACHTING
YAKITORI
YARMULKA
YATAGHAN
ZAKOUSKI
ZAMINDAR
ZARZUELA
ZASTRUGA
ABATTOIR
ABBASIDE
ABDICATE
ABDUCENS
ABDUCTED
ABDUCTOR
ABERDEEN
ABERRANT
ABESSIVE
ABEYANCE
ABINGDON
ABJECTLY
ABLATION
ABLATIVE
ABLUTION
ABNEGATE
ABNORMAL
ABOMASUM
ABORTION
ABORTIVE
ABRASION
ABRASIVE
ABRIDGED
ABROGATE
ABRUPTLY
ABSCISSA
ABSENTEE
ABSINTHE
ABSOLUTE
ABSOLVED
ABSORBED
ABSORBER
ABSTRACT
ABSTRUSE
ABSURDLY
ABUNDANT
ABUTILON
ABUTMENT
OBDURACY
OBDURATE
OBEDIENT
OBITUARY
OBJECTOR
OBLATION
OBLIGATE
OBLIGING
OBLIVION
OBSCURED
OBSERVED
OBSERVER
OBSESSED
OBSIDIAN
OBSOLETE
OBSTACLE
OBSTRUCT
OBTAINED
OBTUSELY
UBIQUITY
ACADEMIC
ACANTHUS
ACAPULCO
ACCENTED
ACCENTOR
ACCEPTED
ACCIDENT

ACCOLADE
ACCOUNTS
ACCREDIT
ACCURACY
ACCURATE
ACCURSED
ACCUSING
ACCUSTOM
ACERBATE
ACERBITY
ACHIEVED
ACHIEVER
ACHILLES
ACIDHEAD
ACOUSTIC
ACQUAINT
ACQUIRED
ACQUIRER
ACRIMONY
ACROMION
ACROSTIC
ACTINIDE
ACTINIUM
ACTIVATE
ACTIVELY
ACTIVISM
ACTIVIST
ACTIVITY
ACTUALLY
ECHINATE
ECHINOPS
ECLECTIC
ECLOSION
ECOFREAK
ECONOMIC
ECSTASIS
ECSTATIC
ECTODERM
ICEFIELD
ICEHOUSE
MCKINLEY
OCCAMIST
OCCASION
OCCIDENT
OCCUPANT
OCCUPIED
OCCUPIER
OCTAROON
SCABBARD
SCABIOUS
SCABROUS
SCAFFOLD
SCALDING
SCALENUS
SCALLION
SCANDIUM
SCANNING
SCANSION
SCANTIES
SCANTILY
SCAPHOID
SCAPULAR
SCARCELY
SCARCITY
SCARFACE
SCATHING
SCAVENGE
SCENARIO
SCHAPSKA
SCHEDULE
SCHEMING
SCHILLER
SCHIZOID
SCHMALTZ
SCHMOOZE
SCHNAPPS
SCHOONER
SCHUBERT
SCHUMANN
SCIATICA
SCIENCES
SCILICET
SCIMITAR
SCIROCCO
SCISSION
SCISSORS
SCOFFING
SCOLDING
SCORCHED
SCORCHER
SCORNFUL
SCORPION
SCOTLAND
SCOTSMAN
SCOTTISH
SCOURING
SCOWLING
SCRABBLE
SCRAMBLE
SCRAPPLE
SCRATCHY
SCRAWLED
SCREAMER
SCREENED
SCREWTOP
SCRIABIN
SCRIBBLE
SCRIBBLY
SCRIPTUM
SCROFULA
SCROUNGE
SCRUBBER
SCRUPLES
SCRUTINY
SCULLERY
SCULLION
SCULPTOR
SCYBALUM
ADDENDUM
ADDICTED
ADDITION
ADDITIVE
ADELAIDE
ADENITIS
ADENOIDS
ADEQUACY
ADEQUATE
ADESSIVE
ADHERENT
ADHESION
ADHESIVE
ADJACENT
ADJUSTER
ADJUSTOR
ADJUTAGE
ADJUTANT
ADJUVANT
ADMIRING
ADMONISH
ADOPTION
ADOPTIVE
ADORABLE
ADRIATIC
ADROITLY
ADULATOR
ADULTERY
ADVANCED
ADVANCER
ADVISORY
ADVOCACY
ADVOCATE
EDENTATE
EDGEHILL
EDGEWAYS
EDGEWISE
EDUCATED
EDUCATOR
IDEALISM
IDEALIST
IDEALIZE
IDENTIFY
IDENTITY
IDEOGRAM
IDEOLOGY
IDLENESS
IDOLATER
IDOLATRY
NDJAMENA
ODDMENTS
ODIOUSLY
ODOMETER
ODYSSEUS
UDOMETER
AEGROTAT
AEROBICS
AERODYNE
AEROFLOT
AEROFOIL
AEROGRAM
AEROLITH
AERONAUT
AEROSTAT
AESTHETE
BEAKLESS
BEANPOLE
BEARABLE
BEARINGS
BEARSKIN
BEATIFIC
BEAUFORT
BEAUMONT
BEAUTIFY
BECALMED
BECHAMEL
BECOMING
BEDABBLE
BEDCOVER
BEDMAKER
BEDSTEAD
BEDSTRAW
BEERBOHM
BEESWING
BEETLING
BEETROOT
BEFRIEND
BEFUDDLE
BEGETTER
BEGGARLY
BEGINNER
BEGORRAH
BEGRUDGE
BEHAVIOR
BEHEMOTH
BEHOLDEN
BEHOLDER
BELABOUR
BELGRADE
BELIEVER
BELITTLE
BELLPUSH
BELLYFUL
BELPAESE
BENEDICK
BENEDICT
BENEFICE
BENEFITS
BENENDEN
BENGHAZI
BENJAMIN
BEQUEATH
BERBERIS
BERCEUSE
BEREAVED
BERGAMOT
BERGERAC
BERIBERI
BERKELEY
BERTRAND
BESIEGED
BESMIRCH
BESOTTED
BESOUGHT
BESPOKEN
BESSEMER
BESTIARY
BESTOWER
BESTRIDE
BETATRON
BETHESDA
BETJEMAN
BETRAYAL
BETRAYER
BEVERAGE
BEWILDER
CELANESE
CELERIAC
CELERITY
CELIBACY
CELIBATE
CELLARER
CELLULAR
CEMETERY
CENOBITE
CENOTAPH
CENTAURY
CENTERED
CENTRIST
CENTRODE
CERAMICS
CERATOID
CERBERUS
CEREBRAL
CEREBRUM
CEREMENT
CEREMONY
CERULEAN
CERVELAT
CERVICAL
CESSPOOL
CETACEAN
DEADBEAT
DEADENED
DEADENER
DEADHEAD
DEADLINE
DEADLOCK
DEADWOOD
DEAFNESS
DEALINGS
DEATHBED
DEBILITY
DEBONAIR
DECADENT
DECANTER
DECAYING
DECEASED
DECEIVER
DECEMBER
DECEMVIR
DECENTLY
DECIMATE
DECIPHER
DECISION
DECISIVE
DECKHAND
DECLUTCH
DECORATE
DECOROUS
DECOUPLE
DECREASE
DECREPIT
DECRETAL
DEDICATE
DEEPNESS
DEERSKIN
DEFEATED
DEFECATE
DEFECTOR
DEFENDER
DEFIANCE
DEFINITE
DEFLOWER
DEFORMED
DEFREEZE
DEFTNESS
DEGRADED
DEJECTED
DELAWARE
DELEGATE
DELETION
DELICACY
DELICATE
DELIRIUM
DELIVERY
DELUSION
DEMEANOR
DEMENTED
DEMENTIA
DEMERARA
DEMERSAL
DEMIJOHN
DEMISTER

DEMIURGE
DEMOCRAT
DEMOLISH
DEMONIAC
DEMOTION
DEMURELY
DEMURRAL
DENARIUS
DENATURE
DENDRITE
DENDROID
DENOUNCE
DENTURES
DEPARTED
DEPILATE
DEPORTEE
DEPRAVED
DEPRIVED
DEPUTIZE
DERANGED
DERELICT
DERISION
DERISIVE
DERISORY
DEROGATE
DESCRIBE
DESELECT
DESERTED
DESERTER
DESERVED
DESIGNER
DESIROUS
DESOLATE
DESPATCH
DESPOTIC
DESTINED
DESTRUCT
DETACHED
DETAILED
DETAINEE
DETAINER
DETECTOR
DETHRONE
DETONATE
DETRITUS
DEVIANCE
DEVILISH
DEVILLED
DEVOTION
DEWBERRY
DEWYEYED
DEXTROSE
DEXTROUS
EERINESS
FEARLESS
FEARSOME
FEASIBLE
FEASIBLY
FEATHERS
FEATHERY
FEATURED
FEATURES
FEBRUARY
FECKLESS
FECULENT
FEDAYEEN
FEDERACY
FEDERATE
FEEDBACK
FEELGOOD
FEELINGS
FELDSPAR
FELICITY
FELLAHIN
FEMININE
FEMINISM
FEMINIST
FEMINITY
FENCIBLE
FENESTRA
FEROCITY
FERRYMAN
FESTIVAL
FETCHING
FEVERFEW
FEVERISH
GELASTIC
GELATINE
GEMINATE
GEMOLOGY
GENDARME
GENERATE
GENEROUS
GENETICS
GENETRIX
GENIALLY
GENITALS
GENITIVE
GENOCIDE
GENTRIFY
GEODESIC
GEOMANCY
GEOMETER
GEOMETRY
GEOPHONE
GEORGIAN
GEOTAXIS
GERANIUM
GERMAINE
GERMANIC
GERMINAL
GERONIMO
GERTRUDE
GESTURES
HEADACHE
HEADBAND
HEADGEAR
HEADHUNT
HEADLAMP
HEADLAND
HEADLESS
HEADLINE
HEADLONG
HEADMARK
HEADMOST
HEADREST
HEADROOM
HEADSHIP
HEADWIND
HEADWORD
HEARTIES
HEARTILY
HEATEDLY
HEATSPOT
HEATWAVE
HEAVENLY
HEBETUDE
HEBRIDES
HECATOMB
HECKLING
HEDGEHOG
HEDGEROW
HEDONISM
HEDONIST
HEEDLESS
HEELBALL
HEELTAPS
HEGEMONY
HEIGHTEN
HEIRLESS
HEIRLOOM
HELIPORT
HELLADIC
HELLBENT
HELLENIC
HELLFIRE
HELMETED
HELMSMAN
HELPLESS
HELPLINE
HELPMATE
HELSINKI
HELVETIA
HENCHMAN
HENHOUSE
HEPATICA
HEPTAGON
HEPTARCH
HERACLES
HERACLID
HERALDIC
HERALDRY
HERCULES
HERDSMAN
HEREDITY
HEREFORD
HEREWARD
HEREWITH
HERITAGE
HERMETIC
HERMIONE
HERPETIC
HERSCHEL
HESITANT
HESITATE
HETAIRIA
HEXAGRAM
HEYTHROP
JEALOUSY
JEANETTE
JEBUSITE
JEFFREYS
JEHOVAHS
JELLICOE
JEOPARDY
JEPHTHAH
JEREBOAM
JEREMIAD
JEREMIAH
JEROBOAM
JERRYCAN
JETTISON
JEWELLED
JEWELLER
KEDGEREE
KEELHAUL
KEENNESS
KEEPSAKE
KENTUCKY
KERCHIEF
KERMESSE
KEROSENE
KESTEVEN
KEYBOARD
KEYSTONE
LEACHING
LEADSMAN
LEAFLESS
LEAPFROG
LEARNING
LEATHERY
LEAVENED
LEAVINGS
LEBANESE
LECITHIN
LECTURER
LECTURES
LEFTHAND
LEFTOVER
LEFTWARD
LEFTWING
LEGALISM
LEGALITY
LEGALIZE
LEGATION
LEGGINGS
LEINSTER
LEISURED
LEMONADE
LENGTHEN
LENIENCY
LEONARDO
LEONIDAS
LETHARGY
LETTERED
LEUKEMIA
LEVELLER
LEVERAGE
LEVITATE
LEWDNESS
LEWISITE
MEALTIME
MEALYBUG
MEANNESS
MEANTIME
MEASURED
MEATLESS
MECHANIC
MEDALIST
MEDDLING
MEDIATOR
MEDICATE
MEDICINE
MEDIEVAL
MEDIOCRE
MEDITATE
MEEKNESS
MEGABYTE
MEGALITH
MEGAWATT
MELAMINE
MELANITE
MELANOMA
MELCHIOR
MELEAGER
MELTDOWN
MEMBRANE
MEMORIAL
MEMORIAM
MEMORIZE
MEMSAHIB
MENACING
MENANDER
MENELAUS
MENISCUS
MENSWEAR
MENTALLY
MERCALLI
MERCATOR
MERCEDES
MERCHANT
MERCIFUL
MEREDITH
MERIDIAN
MERINGUE
MERISTEM
MESCALIN
MESMERIC
MESOLITE
MESSAGER
MESSIDOR
MESSMATE
MESSUAGE
METABOLA
METALLED
METALLIC
METAPHOR
METEORIC
METHANOL
METHODIC
METONYMY
METRICAL
METRITIS
MEUNIÈRE
NEARNESS
NEATHERD
NEATNESS
NEBRASKA
NEBULOUS
NECKBAND
NECKLACE
NECKLINE
NECKWEAR
NECROSIS
NEEDLESS
NEGATION
NEGATIVE
NEGLIGEE
NEIGHBOR
NEMATODE
NEMATOID
NEMBUTAL
NENUPHAR
NEOMYCIN
NEOPHYTE
NEPALESE
NEPENTHE
NEPHRITE
NEPIONIC
NEPOTISM
NESCIENT
NESTLING

NEURITIS
NEUROSIS
NEUROTIC
NEUTRINO
NEWCOMER
NEWFOUND
NEWHAVEN
NEWSCAST
NEWSHAWK
NEWSPEAK
NEWSREEL
NEWSROOM
OEDIPEAN
OEILLADE
OENOLOGY
OENOPHIL
PEACEFUL
PEARLING
PEARMAIN
PECORINO
PECTORAL
PECULATE
PECULIAR
PEDAGOGY
PEDANTIC
PEDANTRY
PEDDLING
PEDERAST
PEDESTAL
PEDICURE
PEDIGREE
PEDIMENT
PEDUNCLE
PEEKABOO
PEELINGS
PEEPHOLE
PEERLESS
PEIGNOIR
PEKINESE
PELAGIUS
PELLAGRA
PELLETED
PELLICLE
PELLMELL
PELLUCID
PEMBROKE
PEMMICAN
PENALIZE
PENCHANT
PENDULUM
PENELOPE
PENITENT
PENKNIFE
PENNINES
PENOLOGY
PENTACLE
PENTAGON
PENTARCH
PENUMBRA
PENZANCE
PEPERONI
PERACUTE
PERCEIVE
PERCEVAL
PERCIVAL
PERFECTA
PERFECTO
PERFORCE
PERFUMED
PERIANTH
PERICARP
PERICLES
PERIDERM
PERILOUS
PERIODIC
PERIPETY
PERISHED
PERISHER
PERJURED
PERJURER
PERMEATE
PEROXIDE
PERSHING
PERSONAL
PERSPIRE
PERSUADE
PERSUANT
PERTNESS
PERUVIAN
PERVERSE
PERVIOUS
PETANQUE
PETERLOO
PETITION
PETRARCH
PETULANT
PEVENSEY
REACTION
REACTIVE
READABLE
READIEST
READJUST
REAFFIRM
REALTIME
REAPPEAR
REARMOST
REARWARD
REASONED
REASSERT
REASSESS
REASSIGN
REASSUME
REASSURE
REAWAKEN
REBUTTAL
RECEDING
RECEIPTS
RECEIVED
RECEIVER
RECENTLY
RECEPTOR
RECESSED
RECHARGE
RECKLESS
RECKONER
RECORDER
RECOURSE
RECOVERY
RECREATE
RECRUITS
RECUSANT
REDACTOR
REDBRICK
REDEEMER
REDEFINE
REDEPLOY
REDESIGN
REDIRECT
REDLIGHT
REDOLENT
REDOUBLE
REDSHANK
REDSTART
REEDLING
REEDSMAN
REEMPLOY
REFERRAL
REFINERY
REFORMED
REFORMER
REFRINGE
REFUGIUM
REGAINED
REGICIDE
REGIMENT
REGIONAL
REGISTER
REGISTRY
REGULATE
REHEARSE
REIGNING
REINDEER
REINSURE
REINVEST
REJOINED
REKINDLE
RELATING
RELATION
RELATIVE
RELAXING
RELAYING
RELEASED
RELEGATE
RELEVANT
RELIABLE
RELIABLY
RELIANCE
RELIEVED
RELIGION
RELOCATE
REMEDIAL
REMEMBER
REMINDER
REMITTAL
REMNANTS
REMOTELY
REMOUNTS
RENEGADE
RENMINBI
RENOUNCE
RENOVATE
RENOWNED
REORIENT
REPAIRER
REPARTEE
REPAYING
REPEATED
REPEATER
REPHRASE
REPLEVIN
REPORTED
REPORTER
REPOUSSÉ
REPRIEVE
REPRISAL
REPROACH
REPUBLIC
REQUIRED
RESEARCH
RESEMBLE
RESERVED
RESETTLE
RESIDENT
RESIDUAL
RESIDUUM
RESIGNED
RESINOUS
RESISTOR
RESOLUTE
RESOLVED
RESONANT
RESONATE
RESOURCE
RESPECTS
RESPIGHI
RESPONSE
RESTLESS
RESTORER
RESTRAIN
RESTRICT
RESTROOM
RETAILER
RETAINER
RETARDED
RETICENT
RETICULE
RETIRING
RETRENCH
RETRIEVE
REUSABLE
REVANCHE
REVEALED
REVEILLE
REVELLER
REVEREND
REVERENT
REVERSAL
REVERSED
REVIEWER
REVISION
REVIVIFY
REVIVING
REVOLVER
REYNOLDS
SEABOARD
SEABORNE
SEAFARER
SEAFORTH
SEAFRONT
SEAGOING
SEALSKIN
SEALYHAM
SEAMLESS
SEAMSTER
SEAPLANE
SEARCHER
SEASCAPE
SEASHELL
SEASHORE
SEASONAL
SEASONED
SEAWARDS
SECLUDED
SECONDER
SECONDLY
SECRETLY
SECURELY
SECURITY
SEDATELY
SEDATION
SEDATIVE
SEDIMENT
SEDITION
SEDULOUS
SEEDLESS
SEEDLING
SEEDSMAN
SEETHING
SELASSIE
SELBORNE
SELECTED
SELECTOR
SELENITE
SELENIUM
SELEUCID
SELFHELP
SELFLESS
SELFMADE
SELFPITY
SELFSAME
SELVEDGE
SEMESTER
SEMINARY
SEMIOTIC
SEMITONE
SEMOLINA
SENGREEN
SENILITY
SENORITA
SENSIBLE
SENSIBLY
SENSUOUS
SENTENCE
SENTIENT
SENTINEL
SEPARATE
SEQUENCE
SERAFILE
SERAGLIO
SERAPHIC
SERAPHIM
SERENADE
SERENATA
SERENELY
SERENITY
SERGEANT
SERIATIM
SERJEANT
SEROLOGY
SEROTYPE
SERRATED
SERVICES
SERVIENT
SERVITOR
SEVERELY
SEVEREST
SEVERITY
SEWERAGE
SEXOLOGY
SEXUALLY
TEACHERS
TEACHING

TEACLOTH
TEAMMATE
TEAMSTER
TEAMWORK
TEARABLE
TEARAWAY
TEARDROP
TEASPOON
TECTONIC
TEENAGER
TEESHIRT
TEETHING
TEETOTAL
TEGUMENT
TELECAST
TELEFILM
TELEGONY
TELEGRAM
TELEMARK
TELETHON
TELEVISE
TELLTALE
TELLURIC
TEMERITY
TEMPERED
TEMPLATE
TEMPORAL
TEMPTING
TENACITY
TENDENCY
TENDERLY
TENEBRAE
TENEBRIO
TENEMENT
TENESMUS
TENNYSON
TENTACLE
TEQUILLA
TERATOMA
TERIYAKI
TERMINAL
TERMINUS
TERRACED
TERRAPIN
TERRIBLE
TERRIBLY
TERRIFIC
TERTIARY
TERYLENE
TESTATOR
TESTATUM
TESTICLE
TETCHILY
TETRAGON
TETRAPOD
TETRARCH
TEUTONIC
TEXTBOOK
TEXTURED
VEGETATE
VEHEMENT
VELLEITY
VELOCITY
VENALITY
VENDETTA
VENERATE
VENEREAL
VENETIAN
VENGEFUL
VENOMOUS
VENTURED
VERACITY
VERANDAH
VERBALLY
VERBATIM
VERBIAGE
VERDERER
VERJUICE
VERLAINE
VERMOUTH
VERONESE
VERONICA
VERSICLE
VERTEBRA
VERTICAL
VESPERAL
VESPUCCI
VESTIARY
VESTMENT
VESUVIUS
VEXATION
VEXILLUM
WEAKLING
WEAKNESS
WEAPONRY
WEARABLE
WEDGWOOD
WEIGHING
WELLBRED
WELLNIGH
WELLPAID
WELSHMAN
WEREWOLF
WESLEYAN
WESTERLY
WESTWARD
WETLANDS
XENOGAMY
XENOLITH
XENOPHON
XERAPHIM
YEARBOOK
YEARLING
YEARLONG
YEARNING
YEOMANRY
YERSINIA
ZEDEKIAH
ZEPHYRUS
ZEPPELIN
MÉTAIRIE
AFFECTED
AFFINITY
AFFLATUS
AFFLUENT
AFFUSION
EFFICACY
EFFLUENT
EFFLUVIA
EFFUSION
EFFUSIVE
OFFBREAK
OFFCOLOR
OFFENDED
OFFENDER
OFFERING
OFFICERS
OFFICIAL
OFFSHOOT
OFFSHORE
OFFSIDER
OFFSTAGE
AGACERIE
AGGRIEVE
AGITATED
AGITATOR
AGITPROP
AGNATION
AGNOSTIC
AGONIZED
AGRARIAN
AGREEING
AGRICOLA
AGRIMONY
AGRONOMY
EGGPLANT
EGGSHELL
EGGTIMER
EGOISTIC
EGOMANIA
EGYPTIAN
IGNITION
IGNOMINY
IGNORANT
UGLINESS
CHACONNE
CHADBAND
CHAINSAW
CHAIRMAN
CHALDEAN
CHALDRON
CHAMBERS
CHAMPERS
CHAMPION
CHANCERY
CHANDLER
CHANGING
CHANTAGE
CHANTREY
CHAPATTI
CHAPERON
CHAPLAIN
CHARCOAL
CHARGING
CHARISMA
CHARLADY
CHARLOCK
CHARMING
CHARTISM
CHARTIST
CHARTRES
CHASSEUR
CHASTISE
CHASTITY
CHASUBLE
CHATTELS
CHEATERS
CHEATING
CHECKERS
CHECKING
CHECKOUT
CHEEKILY
CHEERFUL
CHEERILY
CHEERING
CHEMICAL
CHENILLE
CHEQUERS
CHEROKEE
CHERUBIC
CHERUBIM
CHERWELL
CHESHIRE
CHESSMAN
CHESSMEN
CHESTNUT
CHEVIOTS
CHEYENNE
CHIASMUS
CHICKENS
CHICKPEA
CHILDERS
CHILDISH
CHILDREN
CHILIAST
CHILLADA
CHILLING
CHILTERN
CHIMAERA
CHINAMAN
CHINDITS
CHIPMUNK
CHITCHAT
CHIVALRY
CHLORATE
CHLORIDE
CHLORINE
CHOIRBOY
CHOLERIC
CHOOSING
CHOPPING
CHORDATA
CHORDATE
CHORIAMB
CHRISTEN
CHRISTIE
CHRISTOM
CHROMITE
CHROMIUM
CHUMMAGE
CHURLISH
CHUTZPAH
GHANAIAN
GHOULISH
KHARTOUM
PHALANGE
PHANTASM
PHARISEE
PHARMACY
PHEASANT
PHILEMON
PHILIPPI
PHILLIPS
PHILOMEL
PHLEGMON
PHONETIC
PHORMIUM
PHOSGENE
PHOTOFIT
PHOTOPSY
PHREATIC
PHRYGIAN
PHTHISIS
PHYLLOME
PHYSALIA
PHYSICAL
PHYSIQUE
RHAPSODY
RHEOSTAT
RHETORIC
RHOMBOID
RHONCHUS
RHYTHMIC
SHABBILY
SHACKLES
SHADRACH
SHAGREEN
SHAKEOUT
SHALLOWS
SHAMBLES
SHAMEFUL
SHAMROCK
SHANGHAI
SHANTUNG
SHAREOUT
SHEARMAN
SHEEPDOG
SHEEPISH
SHEIKDOM
SHELDUCK
SHELVING
SHEPHERD
SHERATON
SHERIDAN
SHERLOCK
SHERWOOD
SHETLAND
SHIELING
SHIFTING
SHIGELLA
SHIITAKE
SHILLING
SHINGLES
SHIPMATE
SHIPMENT
SHIPPING
SHIPYARD
SHIVERED
SHOCKING
SHODDILY
SHOEHORN
SHOELACE
SHOELESS
SHOETREE
SHOOTING
SHOOTOUT
SHOPPING
SHOPTALK
SHORTAGE
SHOULDER
SHOUTING
SHOWBOAT
SHOWCASE
SHOWDOWN
SHOWGIRL
SHOWROOM
SHRAPNEL
SHREDDER
SHREWDLY
SHREWISH
SHROUDED
SHRUNKEN

SHUTDOWN
SHUTTERS
THAILAND
THALAMUS
THALLIUM
THANATOS
THANKFUL
THATAWAY
THATCHED
THATCHER
THEATRIC
THEMATIC
THEOCRAT
THEOLOGY
THEORIST
THEORIZE
THESPIAN
THIAMINE
THICKSET
THIEVERY
THIEVING
THIEVISH
THINGAMY
THINKING
THINNESS
THINNING
THIRTEEN
THOMPSON
THORACIC
THOROUGH
THOUGHTS
THOUSAND
THRACIAN
THRALDOM
THRASHER
THREATEN
THRENODY
THRESHER
THRILLER
THROMBIN
THROMBUS
THROTTLE
THRUSTER
THUMPING
THUNDERY
THURIBLE
THURIFER
THURSDAY
WHACKING
WHARFAGE
WHATEVER
WHEATEAR
WHEEZILY
WHEEZING
WHENEVER
WHEREVER
WHIMBREL
WHINCHAT
WHIPCORD
WHIPHAND
WHIPJACK
WHIPLASH
WHIPPING
WHIRLING
WHISKERS
WHISKERY
WHISTLER
WHITECAP
WHITEHOT
WHITENER
WHITLING
WHODUNIT
WHOOPING
WHOPPING
AIGRETTE
AIGUILLE
AIRBORNE
AIRBRAKE
AIRCRAFT
AIREDALE
AIRFIELD
AIRINESS
AIRLINER
AIRPLANE
AIRSCREW
AIRSPEED
AIRSTRIP
AIRTIGHT
AIRWAVES
BIANNUAL
BIATHLON
BIBLICAL
BIBULOUS
BICONVEX
BICUSPID
BIENNIAL
BIFOCALS
BIGAMIST
BIGAMOUS
BIGARADE
BILBERRY
BILLFOLD
BILLHOOK
BILLYBOY
BILLYCAN
BINDWEED
BINNACLE
BINOMIAL
BIOGRAPH
BIOSCOPE
BIRDCAGE
BIRDSEED
BIRTHDAY
BISCAYAN
BISEXUAL
BISMARCK
BITTERLY
CIBORIUM
CICATRIX
CICERONE
CICISBEO
CILIATED
CINCHONA
CINERAMA
CINEREAL
CINGULUM
CINNABAR
CINNAMON
CIRCULAR
CITATION
CIVILIAN
CIVILITY
CIVILIZE
DIABETES
DIABETIC
DIABOLIC
DIAGNOSE
DIAGONAL
DIALLING
DIALOGUE
DIALYSIS
DIAMANTE
DIAMETER
DIAMONDS
DIANTHUS
DIAPASON
DIAPHONE
DIARESIS
DIARRHEA
DIASPORA
DIASTASE
DIASTOLE
DIATONIC
DIATRIBE
DIAZEPAM
DICTATES
DICTATOR
DICYCLIC
DIDACTIC
DIDDICOY
DIEHARDS
DIELDRIN
DIERESIS
DIFFRACT
DIGGINGS
DIGITIZE
DILATION
DILATORY
DILIGENT
DILUTION
DIMINISH
DINGBATS
DINOSAUR
DIOCESAN
DIOGENES
DIONYSUS
DIOPTRIC
DIPHENYL
DIPLOMAT
DIPSTICK
DIPTERAL
DIRECTLY
DIRECTOR
DISABLED
DISABUSE
DISAGREE
DISALLOW
DISARRAY
DISASTER
DISBURSE
DISCIPLE
DISCLAIM
DISCLOSE
DISCOLOR
DISCOUNT
DISCOVER
DISCREET
DISCRETE
DISEASED
DISFAVOR
DISGORGE
DISGRACE
DISGUISE
DISHEVEL
DISHONOR
DISINTER
DISKETTE
DISLIKED
DISLODGE
DISLOYAL
DISMALLY
DISMAYED
DISMOUNT
DISORDER
DISPATCH
DISPENSE
DISPERSE
DISPIRIT
DISPLACE
DISPOSAL
DISPOSED
DISPROVE
DISPUTED
DISQUIET
DISRAELI
DISSOLVE
DISSUADE
DISTANCE
DISTASTE
DISTINCT
DISTRACT
DISTRAIN
DISTRAIT
DISTRESS
DISTRICT
DISTRUST
DISUNION
DISUNITE
DISUNITY
DIURETIC
DIVIDEND
DIVIDERS
DIVINITY
DIVISION
DIVISIVE
DIVORCED
DIVORCEE
EIDECTIC
EIGHTEEN
EINSTEIN
FIBROSIS
FIDDLING
FIDELITY
FIELDING
FIENDISH
FIERCELY
FIFTIETH
FIGHTING
FIGURINE
FILAGREE
FILAMENT
FILARIUM
FILENAME
FILIGREE
FILIPINO
FILTHILY
FILTRATE
FINALIST
FINALITY
FINALIZE
FINDINGS
FINESPUN
FINISHED
FINISHER
FIREARMS
FIREBACK
FIREBALL
FIREBIRD
FIREBOLT
FIREDAMP
FIRESIDE
FIRESTEP
FIRETRAP
FIREWEED
FIREWOOD
FIREWORK
FIRMNESS
FISHBONE
FISHCAKE
FISHMEAL
FISHPOND
FISHWIFE
FITFULLY
FIXATION
FIXATIVE
GIACONDA
GIANTESS
GIGANTIC
GIGLAMPS
GIMCRACK
GINGERLY
GINGIVAL
GIOCONDA
GIOVANNI
GIRASOLE
GIRLHOOD
GIRONDIN
GIVEAWAY
HIAWATHA
HIBERNIA
HIBISCUS
HICCOUGH
HIDEAWAY
HIDROSIS
HIERARCH
HIERATIC
HIGHBALL
HIGHBORN
HIGHBROW
HIGHGATE
HIGHLAND
HIGHNESS
HIGHRISE
HIGHROAD
HIJACKER
HILARITY
HILLSIDE
HINDMOST
HINDUISM
HINDWARD
HIPSTERS
HIRAGANA
HIRELING
HISPANIC
HISTORIC
HITHERTO
JIGGERED
JIMCRACK
JINGOISM
JINGOIST
KIBITZER
KICKBACK

KICKSHAW
KIDGLOVE
KILKENNY
KILLDEER
KILOBYTE
KILOGRAM
KILOVOLT
KILOWATT
KINDLING
KINDNESS
KINETICS
KINGPOST
KINGSHIP
KINGSIZE
KINGSLEY
KINGSTON
KINKAJOU
KINSFOLK
KINSHASA
KIPPERED
KITEMARK
LIBATION
LIBELOUS
LIBERATE
LIBERIAN
LIBRETTO
LICENSED
LICENSEE
LICORICE
LIEGEMAN
LIENTERY
LIFEBELT
LIFEBOAT
LIFEBUOY
LIFELESS
LIFELIKE
LIFELINE
LIFELONG
LIFESPAN
LIFETIME
LIGAMENT
LIGATURE
LIGHTING
LIGNEOUS
LIKEABLE
LIKENESS
LIKEWISE
LILONGWE
LIMBLESS
LIMERICK
LIMITING
LIMONITE
LIMPNESS
LINCHPIN
LINCOLNS
LINESMAN
LINGERIE
LINGUIST
LINIMENT
LINNAEAN
LINNAEUS
LINOLEUM
LINOTYPE
LIPSTICK
LISTENER
LISTERIA
LISTLESS
LITERACY
LITERARY
LITERATE
LITERATI
LITIGANT
LITIGATE
LITTORAL
LIVELONG
LIVERIED
LIVERISH
LIVEWARE
LIVIDITY
MICHIGAN
MICRODOT
MIDDLING
MIDFIELD
MIDLANDS
MIDNIGHT
MIDPOINT
MIGHTILY
MIGNONNE
MIGRAINE
MILANESE
MILDEWED
MILDNESS
MILITANT
MILITARY
MILITATE
MILKLESS
MILKMAID
MILKWEED
MILKWORT
MILLIBAR
MILLINER
MILLIONS
MILLPOND
MILLRACE
MINAMATA
MINATORY
MINCEPIE
MINDANAO
MINDLESS
MINEHEAD
MINIMIZE
MINISTER
MINISTRY
MINORESS
MINORITE
MINORITY
MINOTAUR
MINSTREL
MINUTELY
MINUTIAE
MIREPOIX
MIRLITON
MIRRORED
MIRTHFUL
MISAPPLY
MISCARRY
MISCHIEF
MISCOUNT
MISERERE
MISGUIDE
MISHMASH
MISJUDGE
MISMATCH
MISNOMER
MISOGYNY
MISPLACE
MISPRINT
MISQUOTE
MISSOURI
MISSPELL
MISSPENT
MISTAKEN
MISTREAT
MISTRESS
MISTRUST
MITIGATE
NIBELUNG
NICENESS
NICHOLAS
NICKNACK
NICKNAME
NICOTINE
NIDATION
NIGERIAN
NIGERIEN
NIGGLING
NIGHTCAP
NIGHTJAR
NIHILISM
NIHILIST
NIJINSKY
NINEPINS
NINETEEN
NITROGEN
OILCLOTH
OILFIELD
OILINESS
OILSKINS
OILSLICK
OINTMENT
PICAROON
PICKINGS
PICKLOCK
PICKMEUP
PICKWICK
PICTURES
PIDDLING
PIECHART
PIECRUST
PIERCING
PIERETTE
PIERIDES
PIGSWILL
PILASTER
PILCHARD
PILFERER
PILGRIMS
PILLAGER
PILLARED
PILOTAGE
PILSENER
PILTDOWN
PIMIENTO
PINAFORE
PINDARIC
PINEWOOD
PINNACLE
PINNIPED
PINOCHLE
PINPOINT
PINPRICK
PINTABLE
PINWHEEL
PIPELINE
PIPERINE
PIQUANCY
PIRANESI
PIROZHKI
PISCATOR
PISSHEAD
PITCAIRN
PITHLESS
PITIABLE
PITILESS
PITTANCE
PIZZERIA
RIBALDRY
RIBSTONE
RICHNESS
RICKSHAW
RICOCHET
RIDDANCE
RIDGEWAY
RIDICULE
RIESLING
RIFFRAFF
RIFLEMAN
RIGATONI
RIGHTFUL
RIGHTIST
RIGIDITY
RIGOROUS
RINGDOVE
RINGSIDE
RINGTAIL
RINGWALL
RINGWORM
RIPARIAN
RIPENESS
RIPPLING
RISSOLES
RITUALLY
RIVALISE
RIVERAIN
RIVERINE
RIVETING
SIBERIAN
SIBILANT
SICILIAN
SICKLIST
SICKNESS
SICKROOM
SIDEKICK
SIDELINE
SIDELONG
SIDEREAL
SIDERITE
SIDESHOW
SIDESLIP
SIDESMAN
SIDESTEP
SIDEWALK
SIDEWAYS
SIGHTING
SIGNALER
SIGNALLY
SIGNORIA
SIGNPOST
SILENCER
SILENTLY
SILESIAN
SILICATE
SILICONE
SILKTAIL
SILKWORM
SILURIAN
SIMPLIFY
SIMULATE
SINAPISM
SINCLAIR
SINECURE
SINFONIA
SINGSONG
SINGULAR
SINISTER
SIRENIAN
SISTERLY
SISYPHUS
SITUATED
SIXPENCE
SIXTIETH
SIZEABLE
SIZZLING
TIBERIAS
TIBERIUS
TICKLING
TICKLISH
TICKTACK
TICKTOCK
TIDEMARK
TIDINESS
TIEBREAK
TIGHTWAD
TIMBERED
TIMELESS
TIMIDITY
TIMOROUS
TINCTURE
TINGLING
TINNITUS
TINSELLY
TINTAGEL
TIPSTAFF
TIRAMISU
TIRELESS
TIRESIAS
TIRESOME
TITANESS
TITANISM
TITANITE
TITANIUM
TITICACA
TITIVATE
TITMOUSE
VIATICUM
VIBRANCY
VIBRATOR
VIBURNUM
VICARAGE
VICARIAL
VICINITY
VICTORIA
VICTUALS
VIGILANT
VIGNETTE
VIGOROUS
VILENESS
VILLAGER
VILLAINY
VINCIBLE
VINCULUM
VINDALOO

VINEGARY
VINEYARD
VIOLATOR
VIOLENCE
VIPEROUS
VIREMENT
VIRGINAL
VIRGINIA
VIRILITY
VIROLOGY
VIRTUOSI
VIRTUOSO
VIRTUOUS
VIRULENT
VISCERAL
VISCOUNT
VISELIKE
VISIGOTH
VISITANT
VISITING
VISUALLY
VITALITY
VITALIZE
VITAMINS
VITELLUS
VITILIGO
VITREOUS
VIVACITY
VIVARIUM
WICKEDLY
WIDENING
WILDFELL
WILDFIRE
WILDFOWL
WILDLIFE
WILDNESS
WILFULLY
WILINESS
WILLIAMS
WINDBURN
WINDFALL
WINDHOEK
WINDINGS
WINDLASS
WINDLESS
WINDMILL
WINDPIPE
WINDSOCK
WINDWARD
WINGLESS
WINGSPAN
WINIFRED
WINNINGS
WINNIPEG
WIRELESS
WIREWORM
WISEACRE
WISHBONE
WISTERIA
WITCHERY
WITCHING
WITHDRAW
WITHERED
WITHHOLD
WIZARDRY
YIELDING
ZIBELINE
ZIGGURAT
ZIMBABWE
ZIRCONIA
DJIBOUTI
EJECTION
AKKADIAN
OKLAHOMA
SKELETAL
SKELETON
SKEWBALD
SKIBOOTS
SKIDDING
SKILLFUL
SKILLING
SKILLION
SKINDEEP
SKINHEAD
SKINWORK
SKIPJACK
SKIPPING
SKIRMISH
SKIRTING
SKITTISH
SKITTLES
SKULKING
SKULLCAP
SKYLIGHT
SKYPILOT
ALACRITY
ALARMING
ALARMIST
ALBACORE
ALBANIAN
ALBERICH
ALBINONI
ALBURNUM
ALCATRAZ
ALCESTIS
ALCHEMIC
ALDEHYDE
ALDERMAN
ALDERNEY
ALEATORY
ALEHOUSE
ALEMAINE
ALEUTIAN
ALFRESCO
ALGERIAN
ALGERINE
ALGORISM
ALHAMBRA
ALICANTE
ALIENATE
ALIENISM
ALIENIST
ALKALIFY
ALKALINE
ALKALOID
ALLEGORY
ALLELUIA
ALLERGEN
ALLERGIC
ALLEYWAY
ALLIANCE
ALLOCATE
ALLOGAMY
ALLOPATH
ALLOWING
ALLSPICE
ALLURING
ALLUSION
ALLUSIVE
ALLUVIAL
ALLUVIUM
ALMIGHTY
ALOPECIA
ALPHABET
ALPINIST
ALSATIAN
ALTHOUGH
ALTITUDE
ALTRUISM
ALTRUIST
ALUMINUM
ALVEOLUS
BLACKBOY
BLACKCAP
BLACKFLY
BLACKING
BLACKISH
BLACKLEG
BLACKOUT
BLANDISH
BLASTOFF
BLASTULA
BLEACHER
BLEEDING
BLENDING
BLENHEIM
BLESSING
BLIGHTER
BLINDING
BLINKERS
BLINKING
BLISSFUL
BLITHELY
BLIZZARD
BLOCKADE
BLOCKAGE
BLOOMERS
BLOOMING
BLOTCHED
BLOWFISH
BLOWHOLE
BLOWLAMP
BLOWPIPE
BLUDGEON
BLUEBACK
BLUEBELL
BLUECOAT
BLUENOSE
BLURRING
BLUSHING
BLUSTERY
CLADDING
CLAIMANT
CLAMBAKE
CLANGING
CLANGOUR
CLANNISH
CLANSMAN
CLAPPERS
CLAPPING
CLAPTRAP
CLARENCE
CLARINET
CLASHING
CLASPING
CLASSICS
CLASSIFY
CLAUDIUS
CLAVECIN
CLAVICLE
CLAWBACK
CLAYMORE
CLEANERS
CLEANING
CLEANSED
CLEANSER
CLEARCUT
CLEARING
CLEARWAY
CLEAVAGE
CLEAVERS
CLEMATIS
CLEMENCY
CLERICAL
CLERIHEW
CLEVERLY
CLIFFORD
CLIMATIC
CLIMBING
CLINCHER
CLINGING
CLINICAL
CLINKERS
CLIPPERS
CLIPPING
CLIQUISH
CLITORIS
CLIVEDEN
CLODPOLL
CLOISTER
CLOTHIER
CLOTHING
CLOWNISH
CLUBFOOT
CLUELESS
CLUMSILY
ELDORADO
ELDRITCH
ELECTION
ELECTIVE
ELECTORS
ELECTRIC
ELECTRON
ELECTRUM
ELEGANCE
ELEMENTS
ELEPHANT
ELEVATED
ELEVATOR
ELEVENTH
ELIGIBLE
ELKHOUND
ELLIPSIS
ELLIPTIC
ELONGATE
ELOQUENT
ELSINORE
FLAGGING
FLAGPOLE
FLAGRANT
FLAGSHIP
FLAMENCO
FLAMINGO
FLANDERS
FLANNELS
FLAPJACK
FLAPPING
FLASHGUN
FLASHILY
FLASHING
FLATFISH
FLATFOOT
FLATMATE
FLATTERY
FLATWARE
FLATWORM
FLAUBERT
FLAUTIST
FLAVORED
FLAWLESS
FLEABITE
FLEETING
FLEXIBLE
FLEXIBLY
FLIMSILY
FLINDERS
FLIPPANT
FLIPPERS
FLIPPING
FLIRTING
FLOATING
FLOGGING
FLOODING
FLOODLIT
FLOORING
FLORENCE
FLOTILLA
FLOUNCED
FLOUNDER
FLOURISH
FLUENTLY
FLUIDITY
FLUMMERY
FLUORIDE
FLUORINE
FLUORITE
FLUSHING
FLYBLOWN
FLYDRIVE
FLYSHEET
FLYWHEEL
GLABELLA
GLABROUS
GLADNESS
GLADSOME
GLANCING
GLANDERS
GLASNOST
GLASSFUL
GLAUCOMA
GLAUCOUS
GLEAMING
GLEESOME
GLISSADE
GLOAMING
GLOATING
GLOBALLY
GLOBULAR
GLOBULIN
GLOOMILY
GLORIANA
GLORIOLE

GLORIOUS
GLOSSARY
GLOSSEME
GLOXINIA
GLUMPISH
GLUTAEUS
GLUTTONY
GLYCERIN
GLYCOGEN
ILLFATED
ILLINOIS
ILLUMINE
ILLUSION
ILLUSIVE
ILLUSORY
KLONDIKE
OLDSTYLE
OLDWORLD
OLEACEAE
OLEANDER
OLIGARCH
OLIPHANT
OLYMPIAD
OLYMPIAN
OLYMPICS
PLACABLE
PLACEMAT
PLACEMEN
PLACENTA
PLACIDLY
PLANCHET
PLANGENT
PLANKING
PLANKTON
PLANNING
PLANTAIN
PLASTRON
PLATANUS
PLATEFUL
PLATELET
PLATFORM
PLATINUM
PLATONIC
PLATYPUS
PLAUDITS
PLAYBACK
PLAYBILL
PLAYFAIR
PLAYGIRL
PLAYMATE
PLAYROOM
PLAYSUIT
PLAYTIME
PLEADING
PLEASANT
PLEASING
PLEASURE
PLEBEIAN
PLECTRUM
PLEIADES
PLEONASM
PLETHORA
PLEURISY
PLIMSOLL
PLIOCENE
PLOTINUS
PLOUGHED
PLUCKILY
PLUCKING
PLUGHOLE
PLUMBAGO
PLUMBING
PLUNGING
PLUTARCH
PLYMOUTH
SLANGING
SLANTING
SLAPBANG
SLAPDASH
SLAPJACK
SLATTERN
SLEEPERS
SLEEPILY
SLEEPING
SLIGHTED
SLIGHTLY
SLIMNESS
SLIPOVER
SLIPPERS
SLIPPERY
SLIPPING
SLIPSHOD
SLIPSLOP
SLOBBERY
SLOPPILY
SLOTHFUL
SLOVAKIA
SLOVENIA
SLOVENLY
SLOWDOWN
SLOWNESS
SLOWPOKE
SLUGABED
SLUGFEST
SLUGGARD
SLUGGISH
SLUMMING
SLURRING
SLUTTISH
SLYBOOTS
ULCERATE
ULCEROUS
ULTERIOR
ULTIMATE
AMANDINE
AMARANTH
AMARETTO
AMATEURS
AMBIANCE
AMBIENCE
AMBITION
AMBROSIA
AMBULANT
AMBULATE
AMBUSHED
AMENABLE
AMERICAN
AMERICAS
AMETHYST
AMICABLE
AMICABLY
AMMONIAC
AMMONITE
AMORETTI
AMORETTO
AMORTIZE
AMPERAGE
AMPUTATE
AMRITSAR
AMUNDSEN
AMUSETTE
AMYGDALA
EMACIATE
EMBATTLE
EMBEDDED
EMBEZZLE
EMBITTER
EMBLAZON
EMBODIED
EMBOLDEN
EMBOLISM
EMBOSSED
EMBRACED
EMBRACES
EMERGENT
EMERGING
EMERITUS
EMERSION
EMIGRANT
EMIGRATE
EMINENCE
EMIRATES
EMISSARY
EMISSION
EMMANUEL
EMPHASIS
EMPHATIC
EMPLOYED
EMPLOYEE
EMPLOYER
EMPORIUM
EMPYREAN
EMULGENT
EMULSIFY
EMULSION
IMAGINED
IMBECILE
IMITATOR
IMMANENT
IMMANUEL
IMMATURE
IMMERSED
IMMINENT
IMMOBILE
IMMODEST
IMMOLATE
IMMORTAL
IMMUNITY
IMMUNIZE
IMPACTED
IMPAIRED
IMPELLED
IMPERIAL
IMPETIGO
IMPLICIT
IMPOLITE
IMPORTER
IMPOSING
IMPOSTER
IMPOSTOR
IMPOTENT
IMPRISON
IMPROPER
IMPROVED
IMPROVER
IMPUDENT
IMPUNITY
IMPURIFY
IMPURITY
OMDURMAN
OMELETTE
OMISSION
OMNIFORM
OMPHALOS
SMALLEST
SMALLPOX
SMARTEST
SMASHING
SMELTING
SMIDGEON
SMOCKING
SMOLLETT
SMOOTHER
SMOOTHLY
SMOULDER
SMUGGLED
SMUGGLER
SMUGNESS
UMBRELLA
ANABASIS
ANABATIC
ANACONDA
ANACREON
ANAGLYPH
ANALECTA
ANALEMMA
ANALOGUE
ANALYSER
ANALYSIS
ANAPAEST
ANARCHIC
ANATHEMA
ANATOLIA
ANATOMIC
ANCESTOR
ANCESTRY
ANCHISES
ANCHORET
ANDERSON
ANDORRAN
ANDREWES
ANECDOTE
ANEURYSM
ANGELICA
ANGLESEY
ANGLICAN
ANGSTROM
ANGUILLA
ANIMATED
ANISETTE
ANNALIST
ANNAMITE
ANNEALER
ANNELIDA
ANNOTATE
ANNOUNCE
ANNOYING
ANNUALLY
ANOREXIA
ANOREXIC
ANSERINE
ANTECEDE
ANTEDATE
ANTELOPE
ANTENNAE
ANTEPOST
ANTERIOR
ANTEROOM
ANTIBODY
ANTIDOTE
ANTILLES
ANTILOPE
ANTIMONY
ANTIPHON
ANTIPOPE
ANYPLACE
ANYTHING
ANYWHERE
ENCAENIA
ENCAMPED
ENCIRCLE
ENCLOSED
ENCLOTHE
ENCOMIUM
ENCROACH
ENCUMBER
ENDANGER
ENDEAVOR
ENDOCARP
ENDODERM
ENDOGAMY
ENDURING
ENDYMION
ENERGIZE
ENERVATE
ENFEEBLE
ENFILADE
ENGAGING
ENGENDER
ENGINEER
ENGRAVER
ENIWETOK
ENKINDLE
ENLARGED
ENLARGER
ENMESHED
ENORMITY
ENORMOUS
ENRICHED
ENSCONCE
ENSEMBLE
ENSHRINE
ENSHROUD
ENSIFORM
ENSILAGE
ENTANGLE
ENTHRALL
ENTHRONE
ENTICING
ENTIRELY
ENTIRETY
ENTITLED
ENTRAILS
ENTRANCE
ENTREATY
ENTRENCH
ENTREPOT
ENTRYISM
ENVELOPE
ENVIABLE
ENVIRONS
ENVISAGE

ENVISION
GNASHING
INACTION
INACTIVE
INASMUCH
INCENSED
INCHOATE
INCIDENT
INCISION
INCISIVE
INCLINED
INCLUDED
INCOMING
INCREASE
INCUBATE
INDEBTED
INDECENT
INDENTED
INDEXING
INDIAMAN
INDICANT
INDICATE
INDIGENT
INDIRECT
INDOLENT
INDUCIVE
INDUSTRY
INEDIBLE
INEQUITY
INEXPERT
INFAMOUS
INFANTRY
INFECTED
INFERIOR
INFERNAL
INFESTED
INFINITE
INFINITY
INFLAMED
INFLATED
INFLIGHT
INFORMAL
INFORMED
INFORMER
INFRARED
INFRINGE
INFUSION
INGROWTH
INGUINAL
INHALANT
INHERENT
INHUMANE
INIMICAL
INIQUITY
INITIATE
INJECTOR
INKSTAIN
INNOCENT
INNOVATE
INNUENDO
INQUIRER
INSANELY
INSANITY
INSCRIBE
INSECURE
INSIGNIA
INSOLENT
INSOMNIA
INSPIRED
INSPIRIT
INSTANCE
INSTINCT
INSTRUCT
INSULATE
INTAGLIO
INTEGRAL
INTELSAT
INTENDED
INTENTLY
INTERACT
INTERCOM
INTEREST
INTERIOR
INTERMIT
INTERNAL
INTERNEE
INTERNET
INTERPOL
INTERVAL
INTIFADA
INTIMACY
INTIMATE
INTRADOS
INTRENCH
INTREPID
INTRIGUE
INTRUDER
INUNDATE
INVASION
INVASIVE
INVEIGLE
INVENTED
INVENTOR
INVERTED
INVESTOR
INVITING
INVOLUTE
INVOLVED
INWARDLY
KNACKERS
KNAPSACK
KNAPWEED
KNEEDEEP
KNEEHIGH
KNICKERS
KNIGHTLY
KNITTING
KNITWEAR
KNOBLESS
KNOCKERS
KNOCKING
KNOCKOUT
KNOTWEED
KNOTWORK
MNEMONIC
ONCOLOGY
ONCOMING
ONESIDED
ONETRACK
ONLOOKER
ONSCREEN
ONTOLOGY
SNACKBAR
SNAPPILY
SNAPSHOT
SNATCHER
SNEAKERS
SNEAKING
SNEERING
SNEEZING
SNIFFLER
SNOBBERY
SNOBBISH
SNOOTILY
SNORTING
SNOWBALL
SNOWDROP
SNOWFALL
SNOWLINE
SNUFFBOX
UNABATED
UNAWARES
UNBEATEN
UNBIASED
UNBIDDEN
UNBROKEN
UNBURDEN
UNBUTTON
UNCARING
UNCHASTE
UNCLOVEN
UNCOMBED
UNCOMMON
UNCOOKED
UNCOUPLE
UNCTUOUS
UNCURBED
UNDERAGE
UNDERARM
UNDERCUT
UNDERDOG
UNDERFED
UNDERLAY
UNDERLIE
UNDERPIN
UNDERSEA
UNDERTOW
UNDULANT
UNDULATE
UNEARNED
UNEASILY
UNENDING
UNERRING
UNEVENLY
UNFADING
UNFASTEN
UNFETTER
UNFILLED
UNFORCED
UNFREEZE
UNGAINLY
UNGULATE
UNHARMED
UNHEATED
UNHEROIC
UNHINGED
UNIFYING
UNIONISM
UNIONIST
UNIONIZE
UNIPOLAR
UNIQUELY
UNITEDLY
UNIVALVE
UNIVERSE
UNJUSTLY
UNKINDLY
UNLAWFUL
UNLEADED
UNLIKELY
UNLISTED
UNLOADED
UNLOCKED
UNLOVELY
UNMANNED
UNMARKED
UNNERVED
UNPERSON
UNPLACED
UNREASON
UNSALTED
UNSAVORY
UNSEALED
UNSEEDED
UNSEEMLY
UNSETTLE
UNSHAKEN
UNSIGNED
UNSOCIAL
UNSOLVED
UNSPOILT
UNSPOKEN
UNSTABLE
UNSTATED
UNSTEADY
UNSUITED
UNTANGLE
UNTAPPED
UNTHREAD
UNTIDILY
UNTILLED
UNTIMELY
UNTOWARD
UNUSABLE
UNVARIED
UNVERSED
UNVOICED
UNWANTED
UNWEANED
UNWIELDY
UNWONTED
UNWORTHY
AOTEAROA
BOADICEA
BOARDING
BOASTFUL
BOASTING
BOATLOAD
BOBBYPIN
BOBOLINK
BODLEIAN
BODYLINE
BODYWORK
BOEOTIAN
BOGEYMAN
BOHEMIAN
BOLDNESS
BOLIVIAN
BOLLOCKS
BOLTHOLE
BONDSMAN
BONEHEAD
BONELESS
BONEYARD
BONHOMIE
BONIFACE
BONSPIEL
BOOKABLE
BOOKCASE
BOOKMARK
BOOKROOM
BOOKSHOP
BOOKWORK
BOOKWORM
BOOTLESS
BOOTNECK
BORACITE
BORDEAUX
BORDELLO
BORDERER
BORECOLE
BOREHOLE
BORODINO
BORROWED
BORROWER
BORSTALL
BOSWORTH
BOTANIST
BOTHERED
BOTHWELL
BOTSWANA
BOTTLING
BOTTOMRY
BOTULISM
BOUFFANT
BOUNCING
BOUNDARY
BOUTIQUE
BOUZOUKI
BOWSPRIT
COACHING
COACHMAN
COALESCE
COALHOLE
COALMINE
COALPORT
COARSELY
COATRACK
COATTAIL
COAUTHOR
COBBLERS
COBWEBBY
COCACOLA
COCCIDAE
COCHLEAR
COCKATOO
COCKAYNE
COCKCROW
COCKEREL
COCKEYED
COCKTAIL
CODPIECE
COERCION
COERCIVE
COGITATE
COGNOMEN
COGWHEEL
COHERENT
COHESION
COHESIVE
COIFFEUR
COIFFURE

COINCIDE
COLANDER
COLDNESS
COLESLAW
COLISEUM
COLLAGEN
COLLAPSE
COLLARED
COLLATOR
COLLECTS
COLLEGES
COLLIERS
COLLIERY
COLLOQUY
COLOMBIA
COLONIAL
COLONIST
COLONIZE
COLOPHON
COLORADO
COLORANT
COLORFUL
COLORING
COLOSSAL
COLOSSUS
COLOURED
COLUMBAN
COLUMBUS
COMATOSE
COMBINED
COMEBACK
COMEDIAN
COMEDOWN
COMMANDO
COMMENCE
COMMERCE
COMMONER
COMMONLY
COMMUNAL
COMMUTER
COMPARED
COMPILER
COMPLAIN
COMPLETE
COMPLINE
COMPOSED
COMPOSER
COMPOUND
COMPRESS
COMPRISE
COMPUTER
CONCEIVE
CONCERTO
CONCHOID
CONCLAVE
CONCLUDE
CONCORDE
CONCRETE
CONDENSE
CONFETTI
CONFINED
CONFINES
CONFLATE
CONFLICT
CONFOUND
CONFRONT
CONFUSED
CONGRESS
CONJUGAL
CONJURER
CONJUROR
CONQUEST
CONSERVE
CONSIDER
CONSOMMÉ
CONSPIRE
CONSTANT
CONSTRUE
CONSULAR
CONSUMED
CONSUMER
CONTANGO
CONTEMPT
CONTENTS
CONTINUE
CONTINUO
CONTRACT
CONTRARY
CONTRAST
CONTRITE
CONTRIVE
CONTROLS
CONVENER
CONVERGE
CONVERSE
CONVEYOR
CONVINCE
CONVULSE
COOKBOOK
COOKWARE
COOLNESS
COPULATE
COPYBOOK
COPYHOLD
COQUETRY
COQUETTE
CORDOVAN
CORDUROY
CORDWAIN
CORIOLIS
CORMORAN
CORNETTO
CORNHILL
CORNICHE
CORNWALL
CORONARY
CORONOID
CORPORAL
CORRAGIO
CORRIDOR
CORRODED
CORSELET
CORSICAN
CORVETTE
COSINESS
COSMETIC
COSTMARY
COTOPAXI
COTSWOLD
COTTAGER
COUCHANT
COUCHING
COUGHING
COUNTESS
COUNTIES
COUNTING
COUPERIN
COUPLING
COURTESY
COUSCOUS
COVALENT
COVENANT
COVENTRY
COVERAGE
COVERING
COVERLET
COVETOUS
COWARDLY
COXSWAIN
COYSTRIL
COZINESS
DOCILITY
DOCKLAND
DOCKSIDE
DOCKYARD
DOCTORAL
DOCTORED
DOCTRINE
DOCUMENT
DOGBERRY
DOGGEDLY
DOGGEREL
DOGHOUSE
DOGMATIC
DOGSBODY
DOGSTAIL
DOGWATCH
DOLDRUMS
DOLOMITE
DOLOROUS
DOMESDAY
DOMESTIC
DOMICILE
DOMINANT
DOMINATE
DOMINEER
DOMINION
DOMINOES
DONATION
DONATIST
DOOLALLY
DOOMSDAY
DOORBELL
DOORKNOB
DOORPOST
DOORSTEP
DOPAMINE
DORMOUSE
DOTTEREL
DOUBLOON
DOUBTFUL
DOUBTING
DOUGHBOY
DOUGHNUT
DOVECOTE
DOVETAIL
DOWNBEAT
DOWNCAST
DOWNFALL
DOWNHILL
DOWNLOAD
DOWNPLAY
DOWNPOUR
DOWNSIDE
DOWNSIZE
DOWNTOWN
DOWNTURN
DOWNWARD
DOXOLOGY
EOHIPPUS
FOGBOUND
FOGLIGHT
FOLDEROL
FOLKLORE
FOLKSONG
FOLLICLE
FOLLOWED
FOLLOWER
FOLLOWUP
FONDLING
FONDNESS
FOOLSCAP
FOOTBALL
FOOTFALL
FOOTHOLD
FOOTLING
FOOTNOTE
FOOTPATH
FOOTREST
FOOTSORE
FOOTSTEP
FOOTWEAR
FOOTWORK
FORCEFUL
FORCIBLE
FORCIBLY
FOREBEAR
FOREBODE
FORECAST
FOREDECK
FOREDOOM
FOREFOOT
FOREGONE
FOREHAND
FOREHEAD
FORELAND
FORELOCK
FOREMOST
FORENAME
FORENOON
FORENSIC
FORESAIL
FORESHIP
FORESKIN
FORESTAY
FORESTER
FORESTRY
FORETELL
FOREWARN
FOREWORD
FORFEITS
FORKLIFT
FORKTAIL
FORMALIN
FORMALLY
FORMERLY
FORMLESS
FORMOSAN
FORSAKEN
FORSLACK
FORSOOTH
FORSWEAR
FORTIETH
FORTRESS
FORTUITY
FORWARDS
FOULNESS
FOUNDING
FOUNTAIN
FOURFOLD
FOURPART
FOURSOME
FOURTEEN
FOXGLOVE
FOXHOUND
GOALPOST
GOATSKIN
GOBSMACK
GODCHILD
GOLDFISH
GOLDMINE
GOLFBALL
GOLFCLUB
GOLGOTHA
GOLLIWOG
GONDWANA
GONFALON
GOODNESS
GOODSIRE
GOODWIFE
GOODWILL
GOODWOOD
GOODYEAR
GOOFBALL
GOOSEGOG
GORGEOUS
GORMLESS
GOSSAMER
GOURMAND
GOVERNOR
HOARDING
HOARSELY
HOBBLING
HOGMANAY
HOGSHEAD
HOKKAIDO
HOLDINGS
HOLIDAYS
HOLINESS
HOLISTIC
HOLLOWAY
HOLOGRAM
HOLYHEAD
HOLYROOD
HOMELAND
HOMELESS
HOMEMADE
HOMESICK
HOMESPUN
HOMEWARD
HOMEWORK
HOMICIDE
HONDURAN
HONDURAS
HONESTLY
HONEYDEW
HONEYPOT
HONGKONG
HONOLULU
HONORARY
HOODWINK
HOOKWORM

HOOLIGAN
HOPELESS
HOPFIELD
HORATIAN
HORATIUS
HORLICKS
HORMONAL
HORNBEAM
HORNBILL
HORNBOOK
HORNPIPE
HOROLOGY
HORRIBLE
HORRIBLY
HORRIFIC
HORSEBOX
HORSEFLY
HORSEMAN
HORSEMEN
HOSEPIPE
HOSPITAL
HOSTELRY
HOTELIER
HOTHOUSE
HOTPLATE
HOUSEMAN
HOVERFLY
HOWDYEDO
HOWITZER
IOLANTHE
JODHPURS
JOHANNES
JOHNSONS
JOINTURE
JOKINGLY
JONATHAN
JONCANOE
JONGLEUR
JORROCKS
JOTTINGS
JOVIALLY
JOYFULLY
JOYSTICK
KOHLRABI
KOMSOMOL
KORRIGAN
KOURMISS
KOUSKOUS
LOADSTAR
LOATHING
LOBBYIST
LOBELINE
LOBOTOMY
LOCALITY
LOCALIZE
LOCATION
LOCATIVE

LOCKABLE
LODESTAR
LODGINGS
LOGISTIC
LOITERER
LOLLIPOP
LOMBARDY
LONDONER
LONESOME
LONGBOAT
LONGHAND
LONGHAUL
LONGHORN
LONGLAND
LONGSTAY
LONGSTOP
LONGTERM
LONGTIME
LONICERA
LONSDALE
LOOPHOLE
LOOSEBOX
LOPSIDED
LORDOSIS
LORDSHIP
LORRAINE
LOTHARIO
LOUDNESS
LOUVERED
LOVEBIRD
LOVELACE
LOVELESS
LOVELORN
LOVESICK
LOVINGLY
LOWCLASS
LOWERING
LOWLANDS
LOWLYING
LOYALIST
MOBILITY
MOBILIZE
MOCASSIN
MOCCASIN
MODELING
MODELLER
MODERATE
MODERATO
MODESTLY
MODIFIER
MODULATE
MOHAMMED
MOISTURE
MOLASSES
MOLECULE
MOLEHILL
MOLESKIN

MOLESTER
MOLLUSCS
MOLUCCAS
MOMENTUM
MONADISM
MONARCHY
MONASTIC
MONAURAL
MONDRIAN
MONETARY
MONETISE
MONEYBOX
MONGOLIA
MONGOOSE
MONICKER
MONMOUTH
MONOGAMY
MONOGRAM
MONOHULL
MONOLITH
MONOPOLY
MONORAIL
MONOTONY
MONOTYPE
MONOXIDE
MONROVIA
MONSTERA
MONTCALM
MONTEITH
MONUMENT
MOONBEAM
MOORCOCK
MOORINGS
MOORLAND
MOQUETTE
MORALIST
MORALITY
MORALIZE
MORAVIAN
MORBIDLY
MORBILLI
MOREOVER
MORIBUND
MOROCCAN
MOROSELY
MORPHEME
MORPHEUS
MORPHINE
MORRISON
MORTALLY
MORTGAGE
MORTIMER
MORTUARY
MOSQUITO
MOTHBALL
MOTHERLY
MOTIVATE

MOTORCAR
MOTORING
MOTORIST
MOTORIZE
MOTORMAN
MOTORWAY
MOUFFLON
MOULDING
MOUNTAIN
MOUNTING
MOURNFUL
MOURNING
MOUSSAKA
MOUTHFUL
MOVEABLE
MOVEMENT
NOBELIUM
NOBILITY
NOBLEMAN
NOCTURNE
NOISETTE
NOMINATE
NOMOGRAM
NONESUCH
NONSENSE
NONSTICK
NOONTIME
NORMALLY
NORMANDY
NORSEMAN
NORSEMEN
NORTHERN
NOSEBAND
NOSEDIVE
NOSOLOGY
NOSTRILS
NOSTROMO
NOTARIAL
NOTATION
NOTEBOOK
NOTECASE
NOTIONAL
NOVELIST
NOVEMBER
NOWADAYS
OOPHORON
POCHETTE
PODARGUS
POETICAL
POIGNANT
POISONER
POITIERS
POLARIZE
POLISHED
POLISHER
POLITELY
POLITICO

POLITICS
POLLSTER
POLLUTED
POLLUTER
POLONIUM
POLTROON
POLYANNA
POLYARCH
POLYCARP
POLYGAMY
POLYGLOT
POLYMATH
POLYSEME
POLYSEMY
POMANDER
PONSONBY
PONYTAIL
POOLROOM
POORNESS
POPINJAY
POPPADOM
POPSICLE
POPULACE
POPULATE
POPULIST
POPULOUS
POROSITY
PORPHYRA
PORPHYRY
PORPOISE
PORRIDGE
PORTABLE
PORTHOLE
PORTIÈRE
PORTLAND
PORTRAIT
PORTUGAL
POSEIDON
POSITION
POSITIVE
POSITRON
POSOLOGY
POSSIBLE
POSSIBLY
POSTCARD
POSTCODE
POSTDATE
POSTMARK
POSTPAID
POSTPONE
POTATOES
POTBELLY
POTBOUND
POTEMKIN
POTHOLER
POTLATCH
POTSHERD

POULAINE
POULTICE
POUNDAGE
POWDERED
POWERFUL
ROADSHOW
ROADSIDE
ROADSTER
ROASTING
ROBINSON
ROBOTICS
ROBUSTLY
ROCHDALE
ROCKETRY
RODERICK
ROENTGEN
ROGATION
ROLLCALL
ROLYPOLY
ROMANCER
ROMANIAN
ROMANSCH
ROMANTIC
ROOFLESS
ROOFTOPS
ROOMMATE
ROOTLESS
ROSALIND
ROSALINE
ROSAMOND
ROSEMARY
ROSEWOOD
ROSINESS
ROSSETTI
ROTATION
ROTATORY
ROTENONE
ROUGHAGE
ROULETTE
ROUNDERS
ROUSSEAU
ROYALIST
SOAKAWAY
SOAPSUDS
SOBERING
SOBRIETY
SOCALLED
SOCIABLE
SOCIALLY
SOCRATES
SOCRATIC
SODALITE
SODALITY
SOFTBALL
SOFTENER
SOFTNESS
SOFTWARE

SOFTWOOD
SOLARIUM
SOLDIERS
SOLDIERY
SOLECISM
SOLEMNLY
SOLENOID
SOLIDIFY
SOLIDITY
SOLITARY
SOLITUDE
SOLSTICE
SOLUTION
SOLVABLE
SOLVENCY
SOMBRELY
SOMBRERO
SOMEBODY
SOMERSET
SOMETIME
SOMEWHAT
SONATINA
SONGBIRD
SONGSTER
SONOROUS
SOOTHING
SOOTHSAY
SORBONNE
SORCERER
SORDIDLY
SORENESS
SORORITY
SOUCHONG
SOULLESS
SOUNDING
SOURCING
SOURNESS
SOURPUSS
SOUTHEND
SOUTHERN
SOUTHPAW
SOUVENIR
TOBOGGAN
TOGETHER
TOILSOME
TOISEACH
TOLBOOTH
TOLERANT
TOLERATE
TOLLGATE
TOMAHAWK
TOMATOES
TOMENTUM
TOMORROW
TONALITY
TONELESS
TONSURED
TOPCLASS
TOPHEAVY
TOPLEVEL
TOPNOTCH
TOPOLOGY
TOREADOR
TORTILLA
TORTOISE
TORTUOUS
TORTURED
TORTURER
TOTALITY
TOTALIZE
TOUCHING
TOULOUSE
TOVARICH
TOWELING
TOWERING
TOWNSHIP
TOWNSMAN
TOXAEMIA
TOXICITY
TOXOCARA
VOCALIST
VOCALIZE
VOCATION
VOCATIVE
VOIDANCE
VOLATILE
VOLCANIC
VOLITION
VOLPLANE
VOLSCIAN
VOLTAIRE
VOMITING
VOMITORY
VORACITY
VOYAGEUR
WOBBLING
WOEFULLY
WOLFBANE
WOLSELEY
WOMANISH
WOMANIZE
WONDROUS
WOODBINE
WOODCOCK
WOODENLY
WOODLAND
WOODSHED
WOODSMAN
WOODWARD
WOODWIND
WOODWORK
WOODWORM
WOOLLENS
WOOLPACK
WOOLSACK
WORDBOOK
WORDLESS
WORKABLE
WORKADAY
WORKBOOK
WORKINGS
WORKLOAD
WORKMATE
WORKROOM
WORKSHOP
WORMCAST
WORMWOOD
WORRYING
WORTHIES
WORTHILY
YODELLER
YOGHOURT
YOKOHAMA
YOSEMITE
YOUNGEST
YOURSELF
YOUTHFUL
ZODIACAL
ZOETROPE
ZOONOSIS
ZOOPHYTE
ZOOSPERM
ZOOSPORE
APERIENT
APERITIF
APERTURE
APHELION
APHORISM
APIARIST
APOLLYON
APOLOGIA
APOLOGUE
APOPLEXY
APOSTASY
APOSTATE
APOSTLES
APOTHEGM
APPALLED
APPANAGE
APPARENT
APPELANT
APPENDIX
APPETITE
APPLAUSE
APPLETON
APPLIQUÉ
APPOSITE
APPRAISE
APPRISED
APPROACH
APPROVAL
APPROVED
APTITUDE
EPHEMERA
EPHESIAN
EPICURUS
EPIDEMIC
EPIDURAL
EPIGAMIC
EPIGRAPH
EPILEPSY
EPILOGUE
EPIPHANY
EPIPHYTE
EPIPLOON
EPISODIC
EPISTYLE
EPITASIS
EPITHEMA
OPENCAST
OPENDOOR
OPENNESS
OPENPLAN
OPENWORK
OPERABLE
OPERATIC
OPERATOR
OPERETTA
OPHIDIAN
OPOPANAX
OPPONENT
OPPOSING
OPPOSITE
OPTICIAN
OPTIMATE
OPTIMISM
OPTIMIST
OPTIONAL
OPULENCE
OPUSCULE
SPACEMAN
SPACIOUS
SPADEFUL
SPANDREL
SPANGLED
SPANIARD
SPANKING
SPANNING
SPARAXIS
SPARKING
SPARKLER
SPARRING
SPARSELY
SPARSITY
SPARTANS
SPAVINED
SPAWNING
SPEAKERS
SPEAKING
SPECIFIC
SPECIMEN
SPECIOUS
SPECKLED
SPECTRAL
SPECTRUM
SPECULUM
SPEEDILY
SPEEDWAY
SPELLING
SPELLMAN
SPENDING
SPHAGNUM
SPICCATO
SPIFFING
SPILLAGE
SPILLWAY
SPINNING
SPINSTER
SPINTEXT
SPIRACLE
SPIRALLY
SPIRITED
SPIRITUS
SPITEFUL
SPITFIRE
SPITHEAD
SPITTING
SPITTOON
SPLASHER
SPLATTER
SPLENDID
SPLENDOR
SPLINTER
SPLITTER
SPLUTTER
SPOILAGE
SPOILING
SPOLIATE
SPOONFUL
SPORADIC
SPORTING
SPORTIVE
SPOTLESS
SPOTTING
SPRAINED
SPRAWLED
SPREADER
SPRINGER
SPRINKLE
SPRINTER
SPRITELY
SPRITZER
SPROCKET
SPRUCELY
SPRYNESS
SPURIOUS
SPURNING
SPYGLASS
UPCOMING
UPHEAVAL
UPHOLDER
UPMARKET
UPPERCUT
UPRIGHTS
UPRISING
UPSTAIRS
UPSTREAM
UPTURNED
AQUALUNG
AQUARIUM
AQUARIUS
AQUATINT
AQUEDUCT
AQUILINE
EQUALITY
EQUALIZE
EQUATION
EQUIPAGE
EQUITANT
SQUABBLE
SQUADDIE
SQUADRON
SQUAMATA
SQUANDER
SQUARELY
SQUATTER
SQUEAKER
SQUEALER
SQUEEGEE
SQUEEZER
SQUIGGLE
SQUIRREL
ARACHNID
ARALDITE
ARAMAEAN
ARAMANTH
ARBALEST
ARBOREAL
ARCADIAN
ARCHAISM
ARCHDUKE
ARCHIVES
ARCTURUS
ARDENNES
ARDENTLY
ARETHUSA
ARGESTES
ARGININE
ARGONAUT
ARGUABLE
ARGUABLY
ARGUMENT

ARKANSAS
ARMAGNAC
ARMALITE
ARMAMENT
ARMATURE
ARMCHAIR
ARMENIAN
ARMORIAL
ARMORICA
ARMOURED
AROMATIC
ARPEGGIO
ARQUEBUS
ARRANGER
ARRESTED
ARRESTER
ARROGANT
ARROGATE
ARSONIST
ARTEFACT
ARTERIAL
ARTESIAN
ARTFULLY
ARTICLED
ARTICLES
ARTIFACT
ARTIFICE
ARTISTIC
ARTISTRY
BRABAZON
BRACELET
BRACHIAL
BRACKETS
BRACKISH
BRADBURY
BRADSHAW
BRAGANZA
BRAGGART
BRAGGING
BRAMANTE
BRANCHED
BRANDADE
BRANDISH
BRANDNEW
BRASILIA
BRASSARD
BRASSICA
BRATPACK
BREACHES
BREAKING
BREAKOUT
BREATHER
BREECHES
BREEDING
BREEZILY
BRETHREN
BREVIARY
BRIBABLE
BRICKBAT
BRIDGING
BRIEFING
BRIGHTEN
BRIGHTLY
BRIGHTON
BRIMMING
BRINDISI
BRINDLED
BRINGING
BRISLING
BRISTLED
BRISTLES
BROADWAY
BROCCOLI
BROCHURE
BROILING
BROMELIA
BROMPTON
BRONCHUS
BROODING
BROUGHAM
BROUHAHA
BROWBEAT
BROWNING
BROWNISH
BROWSING
BRUCKNER
BRUISING
BRUMAIRE
BRUNETTE
BRUSSELS
BRUTALLY
CRACKERS
CRACKING
CRACKPOT
CRAFTILY
CRAMOISY
CRANEFLY
CRATCHIT
CRAVATES
CRAWFISH
CRAWLING
CRAYFISH
CREAMERY
CREATION
CREATIVE
CREATURE
CREDIBLE
CREDIBLY
CREDITOR
CREOSOTE
CREPITUS
CRESCENT
CRETONNE
CREVASSE
CRIBBAGE
CRICHTON
CRIMINAL
CRINGING
CRIPPLED
CRISPIAN
CRITICAL
CRITIQUE
CROATIAN
CROCKERY
CROCKETT
CROMLECH
CROMWELL
CRONYISM
CROONING
CROSSBAR
CROSSING
CROSSLET
CROTCHET
CROUPIER
CROWFOOT
CROWNING
CRUCIATE
CRUCIBLE
CRUCIFER
CRUCIFIX
CRUMHORN
CRUMMOCK
CRUNCHIE
CRUSADER
CRUSHING
CRUTCHED
CRUZEIRO
CRYSTALS
DRACAENA
DRACONIC
DRAGOONS
DRAGSTER
DRAINAGE
DRAINING
DRAMATIC
DRAUGHTS
DRAUGHTY
DRAWBACK
DREADFUL
DREAMILY
DREARILY
DRESSAGE
DRESSING
DRIBLETS
DRIFTING
DRINKING
DRIPPING
DRIVEWAY
DROOPING
DROPHEAD
DROPPING
DROPSHOT
DROWNING
DROWSILY
DRUBBING
DRUDGERY
DRUGGIST
DRUMBEAT
DRUMHEAD
DRUMLINE
DRUMMING
DRUNKARD
DRYCLEAN
DRYGOODS
DRYSTONE
ERADIATE
ERECTILE
ERECTING
ERECTION
ERGOTISE
ERGOTISM
ERIKSSON
ERUCTATE
ERUPTION
ERUPTURE
ERYTHEMA
FRABJOUS
FRACTION
FRACTURE
FRAGMENT
FRAGRANT
FRANCIUM
FRANKISH
FRANKLIN
FRAULEIN
FRAXINUS
FRAZZLED
FREAKISH
FRECKLED
FRECKLES
FREEHAND
FREEHOLD
FREEPOST
FREETOWN
FREEZING
FREMITUS
FRENETIC
FRENULUM
FRENZIED
FREQUENT
FRESHEST
FRESHMAN
FRETWORK
FREUDIAN
FRICTION
FRIENDLY
FRIGHTEN
FRIGIDLY
FRIPPERY
FRISKILY
FRONDEUR
FRONTAGE
FRONTIER
FRONTMAN
FROSTILY
FROSTING
FRUCTIFY
FRUCTOSE
FRUGALLY
FRUITFUL
FRUITING
FRUITION
FRUMENTY
FRUMPISH
GRACEFUL
GRACIOUS
GRADIENT
GRADUATE
GRAFFITI
GRAINING
GRAMERCY
GRANDEUR
GRANDSON
GRANULAR
GRANULES
GRAPHEME
GRAPHICS
GRAPHITE
GRASPING
GRATEFUL
GRATUITY
GRAVAMEN
GRAVELLY
GRAVITAS
GRAYLING
GREATEST
GREEDILY
GREENBAG
GREENERY
GREENFLY
GREENING
GREENISH
GREENOCK
GREETING
GRIDIRON
GRIDLOCK
GRIEVOUS
GRILLING
GRIMALDI
GRIMNESS
GRINDING
GRIPPING
GRISELDA
GRISETTE
GRIZZLED
GROGGILY
GROOMING
GROSBEAK
GROSCHEN
GROUNDED
GROUPING
GROUTING
GROWLING
GRUDGING
GRUESOME
GRUMBLER
GRUMPILY
IRISCOPE
IRISHISM
IRISHMAN
IRISHMEN
IRONCLAD
IRONICAL
IRONSIDE
IRONWARE
IRONWOOD
IRONWORK
IROQUOIS
IRRIGATE
IRRITANT
IRRITATE
KRAKATOA
KREPLACH
KROMESKY
ORANGERY
ORATORIO
ORCADIAN
ORCHITIS
ORDERING
ORDINAND
ORDINARY
ORDINATE
ORDNANCE
ORESTEIA
ORGANDIE
ORGANISM
ORGANIST
ORGANIZE
ORIENTAL
ORIGINAL
ORNAMENT
ORPHANED
ORPIMENT
ORTHODOX
PRACTICE
PRACTISE
PRAIRIAL
PRANDIAL
PRATFALL
PRATTLER
PREACHER
PREAMBLE

PRECINCT
PRECIOUS
PRECLUDE
PRECURSE
PREDATOR
PREDELLA
PREGNANT
PREJUDGE
PREMIERE
PREMISES
PREMOLAR
PRENATAL
PREPARED
PRESENCE
PRESERVE
PRESSING
PRESSMAN
PRESSURE
PRESTIGE
PRETENCE
PRETENSE
PRETORIA
PRETTILY
PREVIOUS
PRIAPISM
PRIESTLY
PRIGGISH
PRIMEVAL
PRIMNESS
PRIMROSE
PRINCELY
PRINCESS
PRINTING
PRINTOUT
PRIORESS
PRIORITY
PRISONER
PRISTINE
PRIVATES
PROBABLE
PROBABLY
PROCEEDS
PROCLAIM
PROCURER
PRODIGAL
PRODUCER
PRODUCES
PRODUCTS
PROFORMA
PROFOUND
PROFUSER
PROGERIA
PROGRESS
PROHIBIT
PROLAPSE
PROLIFIC
PROLOGUE
PROMISED
PROMOTER
PROMPTER
PROMPTLY
PROPERLY
PROPERTY
PROPHECY
PROPHESY
PROPOSAL
PROPOSED
PROPOSER
PROPOUND
PROROGUE
PROSPECT
PROSPERO
PROSTATE
PROTEASE
PROTÉGÉE
PROTOCOL
PROTOZOA
PROTRUDE
PROVABLE
PROVERBS
PROVIDED
PROVIDER
PROVINCE
PRUDENCE
PRUNELLA
PRURIENT
PRUSSIAN
TRACHOMA
TRACKING
TRACTION
TRADEOFF
TRAILING
TRAINING
TRAITORS
TRAMLINE
TRANQUIL
TRANSACT
TRANSECT
TRANSEPT
TRANSFER
TRANSFIX
TRANSHIP
TRANSKEI
TRANSMIT
TRAPDOOR
TRAPPIST
TRASHCAN
TRAVELER
TRAVERSE
TRAVESTY
TREASURE
TREASURY
TREATISE
TREELESS
TREELINE
TREETOPS
TREMBLER
TRENCHER
TRESPASS
TRIANGLE
TRIASSIC
TRIBUNAL
TRICHOID
TRICKERY
TRICYCLE
TRIFLING
TRIGLYPH
TRILEMMA
TRILLING
TRILLION
TRILLIUM
TRIMARAN
TRIMMING
TRIMNESS
TRINCULO
TRINIDAD
TRIPLING
TRIPTANE
TRIPTYCH
TRISTICH
TRISTRAM
TRITICAL
TRITICUM
TROCHAIC
TROCHLEA
TROLLOPE
TROMBONE
TROOPING
TROPICAL
TROTTERS
TROTTOIR
TROUBLED
TROUBLES
TROUNCER
TROUSERS
TRUCKING
TRUCKLED
TRUENESS
TRUMPERY
TRUNCATE
TRUNNION
TRUSTFUL
TRUSTING
TRUTHFUL
URBANITY
URBANIZE
URETHANE
URGENTLY
URSULINE
WRANGLER
WRAPPING
WRATHFUL
WREATHED
WRECKAGE
WRESTLER
WRETCHED
WRINGING
WRINKLED
WRISTLET
WRITEOFF
WRITHING
WRITINGS
WRONGFUL
ASBESTOS
ASCIDIAN
ASCIDIUM
ASCORBIC
ASMODEUS
ASPERGES
ASPERITY
ASPHODEL
ASPHYXIA
ASPIRANT
ASPIRATE
ASPIRING
ASSASSIN
ASSEMBLE
ASSEMBLY
ASSESSOR
ASSIGNEE
ASSORTED
ASSUMING
ASSYRIAN
ASTATINE
ASTERISK
ASTEROID
ASTHENIA
ASTONISH
ASTUTELY
ASUNCION
ESCALADE
ESCALATE
ESCALOPE
ESCAPADE
ESCAPISM
ESCAPIST
ESCARGOT
ESCORIAL
ESCULENT
ESOTERIC
ESPALIER
ESPECIAL
ESPOUSAL
ESPRESSO
ESSAYIST
ESTANCIA
ESTEEMED
ESTHETIC
ESTIMATE
ESTIVATE
ESTONIAN
ESTOPPEL
ESTOVERS
ESTRAGON
ESTROGEN
ISABELLA
ISABELLE
ISLANDER
ISOGLOSS
ISOGONAL
ISOLATED
ISOSTASY
ISOTHERE
ISOTHERM
ISTANBUL
ISTHMIAN
OSCULATE
OSTERLEY
PSALMIST
PSALMODY
PSALTERY
PSEUDERY
TSAREVNA
USEFULLY
USUFRUCT
USURIOUS
ATALANTA
ATARAXIA
ATARAXIC
ATHANASY
ATHELING
ATHENIAN
ATHEROMA
ATHETISE
ATHETOID
ATHLETIC
ATLANTIC
ATLANTIS
ATOMIZER
ATROCITY
ATTACHED
ATTACKER
ATTENDER
ATTESTOR
ATTITUDE
ATTORNEY
ATYPICAL
ETCETERA
ETERNITY
ETHEREAL
ETHERISE
ETHIOPIA
ETHNARCH
ETHYLENE
ETIOLATE
ETRURIAN
ETRUSCAN
OTOSCOPE
OTTAVINO
PTOMAINE
STABBING
STABLING
STACCATO
STAFFING
STAFFORD
STAGGERS
STAGHORN
STAGNANT
STAGNATE
STAIRWAY
STAKEOUT
STALKING
STALLION
STALWART
STAMENED
STAMPEDE
STANDARD
STANDING
STANDISH
STANDOFF
STANHOPE
STANNARY
STANNITE
STAPHYLE
STARCHED
STARDUST
STARFISH
STARGAZE
STARKERS
STARLESS
STARLING
STAROSTA
STARTERS
STARTING
STARVING
STATUARY
STAYSAIL
STEADILY
STEALING
STEALTHY
STEATITE
STEATOMA
STEERAGE
STEERING
STEINWAY
STELLATE
STENDHAL
STENOSED
STENOSIS
STEPHENS
STERLING
STICCATO

STICKILY
STICKING
STICKLER
STIFLING
STIGMATA
STILETTO
STILWELL
STIMULUS
STINGING
STINGRAY
STINKING
STIRLING
STIRRING
STOCCATA
STOCKADE
STOCKCAR
STOCKING
STOCKIST
STOCKMAN
STOCKPOT
STOICISM
STOKESAY
STOLIDLY
STOPCOCK
STOPOVER
STOPPAGE
STOPPING
STOREMAN
STOREYED
STORMING
STORMONT
STOWAWAY
STRABISM
STRACHEY
STRADDLE
STRAGGLE
STRAGGLY
STRAIGHT
STRAINED
STRAINER
STRAITEN
STRANDED
STRANGER
STRANGLE
STRAPPED
STRAPPER
STRATEGY
STRATIFY
STREAKED
STREAKER
STREAMER
STRENGTH
STRESSED
STRETCHY
STRIATED
STRIATUM
STRICKEN
STRICTLY
STRIDENT
STRIKING
STRINGED
STRINGER
STRIPPED
STRIPPER
STRIVING
STROLLER
STRONGLY
STRUGGLE
STRUMPET
STUBBORN
STUCCOED
STUDENTS
STUDIOUS
STUFFILY
STUFFING
STULTIFY
STUNNING
STUPIDLY
STURDILY
STURGEON
STYLIZED
UTENSILS
AUBUSSON
AUCASSIN
AUDACITY
AUDIENCE
AUDITION
AUDITORY
AUGUSTUS
AURELIAN
AUSPICES
AUSTRIAN
AUTARCHY
AUTISTIC
AUTOBAHN
AUTOCRAT
AUTOGAMY
AUTOGYRO
AUTOMATE
AUTONOMY
AUTOTYPE
AUTUMNAL
BUBBLING
BUCKFAST
BUCKLING
BUCKSHEE
BUCKSHOT
BUCKSKIN
BUDAPEST
BUDDHISM
BUDDHIST
BUDDLEIA
BUGGERED
BUILDING
BULGARIA
BULKHEAD
BULLDOZE
BULLETIN
BULLFROG
BULLHORN
BULLRING
BULLYRAG
BUMBLING
BUMMAREE
BUNFIGHT
BUNGALOW
BUNGLING
BUOYANCY
BURBERRY
BURDENED
BURGLARY
BURGRAVE
BURGUNDY
BURNTOUT
BURROWER
BURSITIS
BURSTING
BUSINESS
BUSTLING
BUSYBODY
BUTCHERS
BUTCHERY
BUTTERED
BUTTOCKS
BUTTRESS
BUZZWORD
CUCUMBER
CUCURBIT
CULINARY
CULLINAN
CULLODEN
CULPABLE
CULTURAL
CULTURED
CULVERIN
CUPBOARD
CUPIDITY
CURATIVE
CURLICUE
CURRENCY
CURRICLE
CURSITOR
CURTAINS
CURTNESS
CUSPIDOR
CUSTOMER
CUTENESS
CUTHBERT
CUTPRICE
CUTPURSE
CUTWATER
DUBONNET
DUCHESSE
DUCKBILL
DUCKLING
DUCKWEED
DUELLIST
DULCIMER
DULCINEA
DULLNESS
DUMBBELL
DUMBNESS
DUMFOUND
DUMPLING
DUNGHILL
DUODENAL
DUODENUM
DURABLES
DURATION
DUTCHMAN
DUTIABLE
DUTYFREE
EUCYCLIC
EUDOXIAN
EUGENICS
EULOGIST
EULOGIUM
EULOGIZE
EUPEPSIA
EUPHONIA
EUPHONIC
EUPHORIA
EUPHORIC
EUPHUISM
EURASIAN
EUROLAND
EUROPEAN
EUROSTAR
EURYDICE
EUSTATIC
EUTROPHY
EUTROPIC
FUCHSITE
FUGITIVE
FUGLEMAN
FULLBACK
FULLNESS
FULLPAGE
FULLSIZE
FULLTIME
FUMAROLE
FUMBLING
FUMIGATE
FUMITORY
FUNCTION
FUNERARY
FUNEREAL
FURBELOW
FURLOUGH
FURROWED
FURTHEST
FURUNCLE
FUSAROLE
FUSELAGE
FUSEWIRE
FUSIFORM
FUSILIER
FUTILITY
FUTURISM
FUTURIST
GUARDIAN
GUERIDON
GUERILLA
GUERNSEY
GUIANIAN
GUIDANCE
GUILTILY
GUJARATI
GULLIBLE
GULLIVER
GUMMOSIS
GUMPTION
GUNMETAL
GUNPOINT
GUNSMITH
GURDWARA
GUSSETED
GUTTURAL
GUYANESE
HUCKSTER
HUMANELY
HUMANISM
HUMANIST
HUMANITY
HUMANIZE
HUMIDIFY
HUMIDITY
HUMILITY
HUMORIST
HUMOROUS
HUMPBACK
HUMPHREY
HUNDREDS
HUNGRILY
HUNTRESS
HUNTSMAN
HURDLING
HUSHHUSH
HUSTINGS
JUBILANT
JUBILATE
JUDGMENT
JUDICIAL
JUGGLING
JULIENNE
JUMPSUIT
JUNCTION
JUNCTURE
JURASSIC
JURATORY
JUSTNESS
JUVENILE
KUFFIYEH
LUCIDITY
LUCKLESS
LUKEWARM
LULWORTH
LUMINARY
LUMINOUS
LUMPFISH
LUNCHEON
LUNGFISH
LUPERCAL
LUSCIOUS
LUSHNESS
LUSTRINE
LUSTROUS
LUTHERAN
MUCHNESS
MUCILAGE
MUDFLATS
MUDGUARD
MUDSTONE
MUHAMMAD
MULBERRY
MULETEER
MULEWORT
MULLIGAN
MULTIPLE
MULTIPLY
MUMBLING
MUNCHKIN
MUNIMENT
MURDERER
MUSCADET
MUSCATEL
MUSCULAR
MUSHROOM
MUSICIAN
MUSQUASH
MUSTACHE
MUTATION
MUTCHKIN
MUTILATE
MUTINEER
MUTINOUS
MUTUALLY
NUCLEOLE
NUFFIELD
NUGATORY
NUISANCE
NUMBNESS

NUMERACY
NUMERALS
NUMERATE
NUMEROUS
NUMINOUS
NUPTIALS
NURSLING
NUTHATCH
NUTHOUSE
NUTRIENT
NUTSHELL
OUISTITI
OUTBOARD
OUTBREAK
OUTBURST
OUTCLASS
OUTDATED
OUTDOORS
OUTFIELD
OUTFLANK
OUTGOING
OUTHOUSE
OUTLYING
OUTMATCH
OUTMODED
OUTREACH
OUTREMER
OUTRIDER
OUTRIGHT
OUTSHINE
OUTSIDER
OUTSMART
OUTSTRIP
OUTWARDS
OUTWEIGH
PUBLICAN
PUBLICLY
PUCKERED
PUDENDUM
PUFFBALL
PUGILISM
PUGILIST
PUGNOSED
PUISSANT
PULITZER
PULLDOWN
PULLOVER
PUNCTUAL
PUNCTURE
PUNGENCY
PUNISHED
PUNITIVE
PURBLIND
PURCHASE
PURIFIED
PURIFIER
PURLIEUS
PURPLISH
PURSLANE
PURULENT
PURVEYOR
PUSHBIKE
PUSHCART
PUSHOVER
PUSSYCAT
PUSTULAR
PUTATIVE
PUZZLING
QUADRANT
QUADRATE
QUADRIGA
QUADROON
QUAESTOR
QUAGMIRE
QUAINTLY
QUANDARY
QUANTIFY
QUANTITY
QUARTERS
QUARTIER
QUARTILE
QUATORZE
QUATRAIN
QUAYSIDE
QUENELLE
QUESTION
QUIBBLER
QUICKSET
QUIETUDE
QUILTING
QUINCUNX
QUINTAIN
QUIRINAL
QUISLING
QUIXOTIC
QUOTABLE
QUOTIENT
RUBAIYAT
RUBBISHY
RUBICUND
RUCKSACK
RUCTIONS
RUDENESS
RUDIMENT
RUEFULLY
RUGGEDLY
RULEBOOK
RUMBLING
RUMINANT
RUMINATE
RUMOURED
RUNABOUT
RUNCIBLE
RUNNERUP
RUSHMORE
RUSTLESS
RUSTLING
RUTABAGA
RUTHLESS
SUBHUMAN
SUBJECTS
SUBLEASE
SUBMERGE
SUBPOENA
SUBSONIC
SUBTENSE
SUBTITLE
SUBTLETY
SUBTOPIA
SUBTOTAL
SUBTRACT
SUBURBAN
SUBURBIA
SUCCEEDS
SUCCINCT
SUCCUBUS
SUCHLIKE
SUCKLING
SUDAMENT
SUDAMINA
SUDANESE
SUDARIUM
SUDDENLY
SUFFERER
SUFFRAGE
SUICIDAL
SUITABLE
SUITABLY
SUITCASE
SUKIYAKI
SULFURIC
SULLENLY
SULLIVAN
SULPHATE
SULPHIDE
SUMERIAN
SUMMITRY
SUNBATHE
SUNBURNT
SUNBURST
SUNCREAM
SUNDANCE
SUNDRIED
SUNDRIES
SUNLIGHT
SUNSHADE
SUNSHINE
SUPERBLY
SUPERIOR
SUPERMAN
SUPERNAL
SUPERTAX
SUPPLANT
SUPPLIER
SUPPLIES
SUPPOSED
SUPPRESS
SURENESS
SURFBOAT
SURGICAL
SURMOUNT
SURPLICE
SURPRISE
SURROUND
SURVEYOR
SURVIVAL
SURVIVOR
SUSPENSE
SUZERAIN
TUBELESS
TUBERCLE
TUBEROSE
TUBEROUS
TUNGSTEN
TUNISIAN
TUPAMARO
TUPPENNY
TURANDOT
TURBANED
TURBOJET
TURGENEV
TURGIDLY
TURKOMAN
TURMERIC
TURNBACK
TURNCOAT
TURNCOCK
TURNOVER
TURNPIKE
TURNSPIT
TURRETED
TUSITALA
TUTELAGE
TUTELARY
TUTORIAL
VULGARLY
YUGOSLAV
YULETIDE
ZUCCHINI
AVAILING
AVENTINE
AVERSION
AVIATION
AVICENNA
AVIFAUNA
AVOGADRO
AVULSION
EVACUANT
EVACUATE
EVALUATE
EVANESCE
EVENNESS
EVENSONG
EVENTFUL
EVENTIDE
EVENTUAL
EVERMORE
EVERYDAY
EVERYMAN
EVERYONE
EVICTION
EVIDENCE
EVILDOER
IVOIRIEN
OVENWARE
OVERALLS
OVERBOOK
OVERCAST
OVERCOAT
OVERCOME
OVERDONE
OVERDOSE
OVERDRAW
OVERFEED
OVERFILL
OVERFLOW
OVERFULL
OVERHANG
OVERHAUL
OVERHEAD
OVERHEAR
OVERHEAT
OVERKILL
OVERLAID
OVERLAND
OVERLEAF
OVERLOAD
OVERLOOK
OVERLORD
OVERMUCH
OVERPASS
OVERPLAY
OVERRATE
OVERRIDE
OVERRIPE
OVERRULE
OVERSEAS
OVERSEER
OVERSHOE
OVERSHOT
OVERSIZE
OVERSTAY
OVERSTEP
OVERTAKE
OVERTIME
OVERTONE
OVERTURE
OVERTURN
OVERVIEW
OVERWORK
SVENGALI
DWARFISH
DWARFISM
DWELLING
EWIGKEIT
SWADDLER
SWANSKIN
SWANSONG
SWARMING
SWASTIKA
SWEARING
SWEATING
SWEEPING
SWELLING
SWERVING
SWILLING
SWIMMING
SWIMSUIT
SWINDLER
SWINGING
SWIRLING
TWEEZERS
TWELVEMO
TWILIGHT
TWIRLING
TWISTING
TWITCHER
TWOPENNY
TWOPIECE
ZWIEBACK
EXACTING
EXACTION
EXAMINEE
EXAMINER
EXCAVATE
EXCHANGE
EXCISION
EXCITING
EXECRATE
EXECUTED
EXECUTOR
EXEGESIS
EXEGETIC
EXEMPLAR
EXERCISE
EXERTION
EXHUMATE
EXIGENCY
EXIGUITY
EXIGUOUS
EXISTENT
EXISTING

EXOCRINE
EXORCISM
EXORCIST
EXORCIZE
EXORDIUM
EXPECTED
EXPEDITE
EXPENDED
EXPENSES
EXPLICIT
EXPLODED
EXPLORER
EXPONENT
EXPORTER
EXPOSURE
EXPRESSO
EXTENDED
EXTENSOR
EXTERIOR
EXTERNAL
EXTERNAT
EXTRADOS
EXULTANT
EXULTING
OXBRIDGE
OXPECKER
OXYMORON
OXYTOCIN
UXORIOUS
AYRSHIRE
CYANOGEN
CYANOSIS
CYCLADES
CYCLAMEN
CYCLICAL
CYLINDER
CYNICISM
CYNOSURE
CYRENIAC
CYRILLIC
CYSTITIS
CYTOLOGY
DYNAMICS
DYNAMISM
DYNAMITE
DYNASTIC
DYNATRON
DYSLEXIA
DYSLEXIC
EYEGLASS
EYELINER
EYEPIECE
EYESHADE
EYESIGHT
EYETOOTH
GYMKHANA
GYRATION
GYRATORY
GYROSTAT
HYACINTH
HYDATOID
HYDROGEN
HYGIENIC
HYPERION
HYPNOSIS
HYPNOTIC
HYSTERIA
HYSTERIC
KYPHOSIS
LYNCHING
LYREBIRD
LYRICISM
LYRICIST
LYSANDER
LYSERGIC
MYCELIUM
MYCOLOGY
MYELITIS
MYOBLAST
MYOSOTIS
MYRIAPOD
MYRMIDON
MYSTICAL
MYSTIQUE
MYTHICAL
PYELITIS
PYORRHEA
PYRAMIDS
PYRENEES
PYRIFORM
RYEGRASS
SYBARITE
SYCAMORE
SYLLABIC
SYLLABLE
SYLLABUB
SYLLABUS
SYLVANER
SYMBIONT
SYMBOLIC
SYMMETRY
SYMPATHY
SYMPHONY
SYMPTOMS
SYNCLINE
SYNDROME
SYNOPSIS
SYNOPTIC
SYNTEXIS
SYPHILIS
SYRACUSE
SYRINGES
SYSTEMIC
TYMPANUM
TYPECAST
TYPEFACE
TYROLEAN
TYROSINE
WYCLIFFE
CZAREVNA
TZATZIKI

8:3

ABATTOIR
ACADEMIC
ACANTHUS
ACAPULCO
AGACERIE
ALACRITY
ALARMING
ALARMIST
AMANDINE
AMARANTH
AMARETTO
AMATEURS
ANABASIS
ANABATIC
ANACONDA
ANACREON
ANAGLYPH
ANALECTA
ANALEMMA
ANALOGUE
ANALYSER
ANALYSIS
ANAPAEST
ANARCHIC
ANATHEMA
ANATOLIA
ANATOMIC
ARACHNID
ARALDITE
ARAMAEAN
ARAMANTH
ATALANTA
ATARAXIA
ATARAXIC
AVAILING
BAATHIST
BEAKLESS
BEANPOLE
BEARABLE
BEARINGS
BEARSKIN
BEATIFIC
BEAUFORT
BEAUMONT
BEAUTIFY
BIANNUAL
BIATHLON
BLACKBOY
BLACKCAP
BLACKFLY
BLACKING
BLACKISH
BLACKLEG
BLACKOUT
BLANDISH
BLASTOFF
BLASTULA
BOADICEA
BOARDING
BOASTFUL
BOASTING
BOATLOAD
BRABAZON
BRACELET
BRACHIAL
BRACKETS
BRACKISH
BRADBURY
BRADSHAW
BRAGANZA
BRAGGART
BRAGGING
BRAMANTE
BRANCHED
BRANDADE
BRANDISH
BRANDNEW
BRASILIA
BRASSARD
BRASSICA
BRATPACK
CHACONNE
CHADBAND
CHAINSAW
CHAIRMAN
CHALDEAN
CHALDRON
CHAMBERS
CHAMPERS
CHAMPION
CHANCERY
CHANDLER
CHANGING
CHANTAGE
CHANTREY
CHAPATTI
CHAPERON
CHAPLAIN
CHARCOAL
CHARGING
CHARISMA
CHARLADY
CHARLOCK
CHARMING
CHARTISM
CHARTIST
CHARTRES
CHASSEUR
CHASTISE
CHASTITY
CHASUBLE
CHATTELS
CLADDING
CLAIMANT
CLAMBAKE
CLANGING
CLANGOUR
CLANNISH
CLANSMAN
CLAPPERS
CLAPPING
CLAPTRAP
CLARENCE
CLARINET
CLASHING
CLASPING
CLASSICS
CLASSIFY
CLAUDIUS
CLAVECIN
CLAVICLE
CLAWBACK
CLAYMORE
COACHING
COACHMAN
COALESCE
COALHOLE
COALMINE
COALPORT
COARSELY
COATRACK
COATTAIL
COAUTHOR
CRACKERS
CRACKING
CRACKPOT
CRAFTILY
CRAMOISY
CRANEFLY
CRATCHIT
CRAVATES
CRAWFISH
CRAWLING
CRAYFISH
CYANOGEN
CYANOSIS
CZAREVNA
DEADBEAT
DEADENED
DEADENER
DEADHEAD
DEADLINE
DEADLOCK
DEADWOOD
DEAFNESS
DEALINGS
DEATHBED
DIABETES
DIABETIC
DIABOLIC
DIAGNOSE
DIAGONAL
DIALLING
DIALOGUE
DIALYSIS
DIAMANTE
DIAMETER
DIAMONDS
DIANTHUS
DIAPASON
DIAPHONE
DIARESIS
DIARRHEA
DIASPORA
DIASTASE
DIASTOLE
DIATONIC
DIATRIBE
DIAZEPAM
DRACAENA
DRACONIC
DRAGOONS
DRAGSTER
DRAINAGE
DRAINING
DRAMATIC
DRAUGHTS
DRAUGHTY
DRAWBACK
DWARFISH
DWARFISM
EMACIATE
ERADIATE
EVACUANT
EVACUATE
EVALUATE
EVANESCE
EXACTING
EXACTION
EXAMINEE
EXAMINER
FEARLESS
FEARSOME
FEASIBLE
FEASIBLY
FEATHERS
FEATHERY

FEATURED
FEATURES
FLAGGING
FLAGPOLE
FLAGRANT
FLAGSHIP
FLAMENCO
FLAMINGO
FLANDERS
FLANNELS
FLAPJACK
FLAPPING
FLASHGUN
FLASHILY
FLASHING
FLATFISH
FLATFOOT
FLATMATE
FLATTERY
FLATWARE
FLATWORM
FLAUBERT
FLAUTIST
FLAVORED
FLAWLESS
FRABJOUS
FRACTION
FRACTURE
FRAGMENT
FRAGRANT
FRANCIUM
FRANKISH
FRANKLIN
FRAULEIN
FRAXINUS
FRAZZLED
GHANAIAN
GIACONDA
GIANTESS
GLABELLA
GLABROUS
GLADNESS
GLADSOME
GLANCING
GLANDERS
GLASNOST
GLASSFUL
GLAUCOMA
GLAUCOUS
GNASHING
GOALPOST
GOATSKIN
GRACEFUL
GRACIOUS
GRADIENT
GRADUATE
GRAFFITI
GRAINING
GRAMERCY
GRANDEUR
GRANDSON
GRANULAR
GRANULES
GRAPHEME
GRAPHICS
GRAPHITE
GRASPING
GRATEFUL
GRATUITY
GRAVAMEN
GRAVELLY
GRAVITAS
GRAYLING
GUARDIAN
HEADACHE
HEADBAND
HEADGEAR
HEADHUNT
HEADLAMP
HEADLAND
HEADLESS
HEADLINE
HEADLONG
HEADMARK
HEADMOST
HEADREST
HEADROOM
HEADSHIP
HEADWIND
HEADWORD
HEARTIES
HEARTILY
HEATEDLY
HEATSPOT
HEATWAVE
HEAVENLY
HIAWATHA
HOARDING
HOARSELY
HYACINTH
IMAGINED
INACTION
INACTIVE
INASMUCH
ISABELLA
ISABELLE
JEALOUSY
JEANETTE
KHARTOUM
KNACKERS
KNAPSACK
KNAPWEED
KRAKATOA
LEACHING
LEADSMAN
LEAFLESS
LEAPFROG
LEARNING
LEATHERY
LEAVENED
LEAVINGS
LOADSTAR
LOATHING
MEALTIME
MEALYBUG
MEANNESS
MEANTIME
MEASURED
MEATLESS
NEARNESS
NEATHERD
NEATNESS
ORANGERY
ORATORIO
PEACEFUL
PEARLING
PEARMAIN
PHALANGE
PHANTASM
PHARISEE
PHARMACY
PLACABLE
PLACEMAT
PLACEMEN
PLACENTA
PLACIDLY
PLANCHET
PLANGENT
PLANKING
PLANKTON
PLANNING
PLANTAIN
PLASTRON
PLATANUS
PLATEFUL
PLATELET
PLATFORM
PLATINUM
PLATONIC
PLATYPUS
PLAUDITS
PLAYBACK
PLAYBILL
PLAYFAIR
PLAYGIRL
PLAYMATE
PLAYROOM
PLAYSUIT
PLAYTIME
PRACTICE
PRACTISE
PRAIRIAL
PRANDIAL
PRATFALL
PRATTLER
PSALMIST
PSALMODY
PSALTERY
QUADRANT
QUADRATE
QUADRIGA
QUADROON
QUAESTOR
QUAGMIRE
QUAINTLY
QUANDARY
QUANTIFY
QUANTITY
QUARTERS
QUARTIER
QUARTILE
QUATORZE
QUATRAIN
QUAYSIDE
REACTION
REACTIVE
READABLE
READIEST
READJUST
REAFFIRM
REALTIME
REAPPEAR
REARMOST
REARWARD
REASONED
REASSERT
REASSESS
REASSIGN
REASSUME
REASSURE
REAWAKEN
RHAPSODY
ROADSHOW
ROADSIDE
ROADSTER
ROASTING
SCABBARD
SCABIOUS
SCABROUS
SCAFFOLD
SCALDING
SCALENUS
SCALLION
SCANDIUM
SCANNING
SCANSION
SCANTIES
SCANTILY
SCAPHOID
SCAPULAR
SCARCELY
SCARCITY
SCARFACE
SCATHING
SCAVENGE
SEABOARD
SEABORNE
SEAFARER
SEAFORTH
SEAFRONT
SEAGOING
SEALSKIN
SEALYHAM
SEAMLESS
SEAMSTER
SEAPLANE
SEARCHER
SEASCAPE
SEASHELL
SEASHORE
SEASONAL
SEASONED
SEAWARDS
SHABBILY
SHACKLES
SHADRACH
SHAGREEN
SHAKEOUT
SHALLOWS
SHAMBLES
SHAMEFUL
SHAMROCK
SHANGHAI
SHANTUNG
SHAREOUT
SLANGING
SLANTING
SLAPBANG
SLAPDASH
SLAPJACK
SLATTERN
SMALLEST
SMALLPOX
SMARTEST
SMASHING
SNACKBAR
SNAPPILY
SNAPSHOT
SNATCHER
SOAKAWAY
SOAPSUDS
SPACEMAN
SPACIOUS
SPADEFUL
SPANDREL
SPANGLED
SPANIARD
SPANKING
SPANNING
SPARAXIS
SPARKING
SPARKLER
SPARRING
SPARSELY
SPARSITY
SPARTANS
SPAVINED
SPAWNING
STABBING
STABLING
STACCATO
STAFFING
STAFFORD
STAGGERS
STAGHORN
STAGNANT
STAGNATE
STAIRWAY
STAKEOUT
STALKING
STALLION
STALWART
STAMENED
STAMPEDE
STANDARD
STANDING
STANDISH
STANDOFF
STANHOPE
STANNARY
STANNITE
STAPHYLE
STARCHED
STARDUST
STARFISH
STARGAZE
STARKERS
STARLESS
STARLING
STAROSTA
STARTERS
STARTING
STARVING
STATUARY
STAYSAIL
SWADDLER
SWANSKIN
SWANSONG
SWARMING
SWASTIKA
TEACHERS
TEACHING

TEACLOTH
TEAMMATE
TEAMSTER
TEAMWORK
TEARABLE
TEARAWAY
TEARDROP
TEASPOON
THAILAND
THALAMUS
THALLIUM
THANATOS
THANKFUL
THATAWAY
THATCHED
THATCHER
TRACHOMA
TRACKING
TRACTION
TRADEOFF
TRAILING
TRAINING
TRAITORS
TRAMLINE
TRANQUIL
TRANSACT
TRANSECT
TRANSEPT
TRANSFER
TRANSFIX
TRANSHIP
TRANSKEI
TRANSMIT
TRAPDOOR
TRAPPIST
TRASHCAN
TRAVELER
TRAVERSE
TRAVESTY
TSAREVNA
TZATZIKI
UNABATED
UNAWARES
VIATICUM
WEAKLING
WEAKNESS
WEAPONRY
WEARABLE
WHACKING
WHARFAGE
WHATEVER
WRANGLER
WRAPPING
WRATHFUL
YEARBOOK
YEARLING
YEARLONG
YEARNING
ABBASIDE
ALBACORE
ALBANIAN
ALBERICH
ALBINONI
ALBURNUM
AMBIANCE
AMBIENCE
AMBITION
AMBROSIA
AMBULANT
AMBULATE
AMBUSHED
ARBALEST
ARBOREAL
ASBESTOS
AUBUSSON
BABBLING
BABUSHKA
BABYHOOD
BIBLICAL
BIBULOUS
BOBBYPIN
BOBOLINK
BUBBLING
CABERNET
CABLECAR
CABLEWAY
CABOCHON
CABOODLE
CABOTAGE
CABRIOLE
CIBORIUM
COBBLERS
COBWEBBY
DABCHICK
DEBILITY
DEBONAIR
DUBONNET
EMBATTLE
EMBEDDED
EMBEZZLE
EMBITTER
EMBLAZON
EMBODIED
EMBOLDEN
EMBOLISM
EMBOSSED
EMBRACED
EMBRACES
FABULOUS
FEBRUARY
FIBROSIS
GABONESE
GABORONE
GOBSMACK
HABAKKUK
HABANERA
HABITUAL
HABSBURG
HEBETUDE
HEBRIDES
HIBERNIA
HIBISCUS
HOBBLING
IMBECILE
JEBUSITE
JUBILANT
JUBILATE
KIBITZER
LABOURED
LABOURER
LABRADOR
LABURNUM
LEBANESE
LIBATION
LIBELOUS
LIBERATE
LIBERIAN
LIBRETTO
LOBBYIST
LOBELINE
LOBOTOMY
MOBILITY
MOBILIZE
NEBRASKA
NEBULOUS
NIBELUNG
NOBELIUM
NOBILITY
NOBLEMAN
OXBRIDGE
PABULOUS
PUBLICAN
PUBLICLY
RABELAIS
REBUTTAL
RIBALDRY
RIBSTONE
ROBINSON
ROBOTICS
ROBUSTLY
RUBAIYAT
RUBBISHY
RUBICUND
SABOTAGE
SABOTEUR
SIBERIAN
SIBILANT
SOBERING
SOBRIETY
SUBHUMAN
SUBJECTS
SUBLEASE
SUBMERGE
SUBPOENA
SUBSONIC
SUBTENSE
SUBTITLE
SUBTLETY
SUBTOPIA
SUBTOTAL
SUBTRACT
SUBURBAN
SUBURBIA
SYBARITE
TABBYCAT
TABLEMAT
TABULATE
TIBERIAS
TIBERIUS
TOBOGGAN
TUBELESS
TUBERCLE
TUBEROSE
TUBEROUS
UMBRELLA
UNBEATEN
UNBIASED
UNBIDDEN
UNBROKEN
UNBURDEN
UNBUTTON
URBANITY
URBANIZE
VIBRANCY
VIBRATOR
VIBURNUM
WOBBLING
ZIBELINE
ACCENTED
ACCENTOR
ACCEPTED
ACCIDENT
ACCOLADE
ACCOUNTS
ACCREDIT
ACCURACY
ACCURATE
ACCURSED
ACCUSING
ACCUSTOM
ALCATRAZ
ALCESTIS
ALCHEMIC
ANCESTOR
ANCESTRY
ANCHISES
ANCHORET
ARCADIAN
ARCHAISM
ARCHDUKE
ARCHIVES
ARCTURUS
ASCIDIAN
ASCIDIUM
ASCORBIC
AUCASSIN
BACCARAT
BACCHANT
BACHELOR
BACILLUS
BACKACHE
BACKBITE
BACKBONE
BACKCHAT
BACKCOMB
BACKDATE
BACKDROP
BACKFIRE
BACKHAND
BACKLASH
BACKLESS
BACKPACK
BACKROOM
BACKSIDE
BACKWARD
BACKYARD
BACTERIA
BACTRIAN
BECALMED
BECHAMEL
BECOMING
BICONVEX
BICUSPID
BUCKFAST
BUCKLING
BUCKSHEE
BUCKSHOT
BUCKSKIN
CACHALOT
CACHEPOT
CACHEXIA
CICATRIX
CICERONE
CICISBEO
COCACOLA
COCCIDAE
COCHLEAR
COCKATOO
COCKAYNE
COCKCROW
COCKEREL
COCKEYED
COCKTAIL
CUCUMBER
CUCURBIT
CYCLADES
CYCLAMEN
CYCLICAL
DECADENT
DECANTER
DECAYING
DECEASED
DECEIVER
DECEMBER
DECEMVIR
DECENTLY
DECIMATE
DECIPHER
DECISION
DECISIVE
DECKHAND
DECLUTCH
DECORATE
DECOROUS
DECOUPLE
DECREASE
DECREPIT
DECRETAL
DICTATES
DICTATOR
DICYCLIC
DOCILITY
DOCKLAND
DOCKSIDE
DOCKYARD
DOCTORAL
DOCTORED
DOCTRINE
DOCUMENT
DUCHESSE
DUCKBILL
DUCKLING
DUCKWEED
ENCAENIA
ENCAMPED
ENCIRCLE
ENCLOSED
ENCLOTHE
ENCOMIUM
ENCROACH
ENCUMBER
ESCALADE
ESCALATE
ESCALOPE
ESCAPADE
ESCAPISM
ESCAPIST
ESCARGOT
ESCORIAL
ESCULENT
ETCETERA
EUCYCLIC

EXCAVATE
EXCHANGE
EXCISION
EXCITING
FACEACHE
FACELESS
FACELIFT
FACILITY
FACTIOUS
FACTOTUM
FECKLESS
FECULENT
FUCHSITE
HACIENDA
HECATOMB
HECKLING
HICCOUGH
HUCKSTER
INCENSED
INCHOATE
INCIDENT
INCISION
INCISIVE
INCLINED
INCLUDED
INCOMING
INCREASE
INCUBATE
JACKAROO
JACKBOOT
JACKETED
JACOBEAN
JACOBITE
JACQUARD
KACHAHRI
KICKBACK
KICKSHAW
LACERATE
LACEWING
LACINATE
LACKADAY
LACKLAND
LACONIAN
LACROSSE
LECITHIN
LECTURER
LECTURES
LICENSED
LICENSEE
LICORICE
LOCALITY
LOCALIZE
LOCATION
LOCATIVE
LOCKABLE
LUCIDITY
LUCKLESS
MACARONI
MACAROON
MACASSAR
MACAULAY
MACERATE
MACHEATH
MACHINES
MACHISMO
MACKEREL
MACMAHON
MACREADY
MACULATE
MECHANIC
MICHIGAN
MICRODOT
MOCASSIN
MOCCASIN
MUCHNESS
MUCILAGE
MYCELIUM
MYCOLOGY
NECKBAND
NECKLACE
NECKLINE
NECKWEAR
NECROSIS
NICENESS
NICHOLAS
NICKNACK
NICKNAME
NICOTINE
NOCTURNE
NUCLEOLE
OCCAMIST
OCCASION
OCCIDENT
OCCUPANT
OCCUPIED
OCCUPIER
ONCOLOGY
ONCOMING
ORCADIAN
ORCHITIS
OSCULATE
PACHINKO
PACIFIER
PACIFISM
PACIFIST
PACKAGED
PECORINO
PECTORAL
PECULATE
PECULIAR
PICAROON
PICKINGS
PICKLOCK
PICKMEUP
PICKWICK
PICTURES
POCHETTE
PUCKERED
RACHITIS
RACIALLY
RACINESS
RACKRENT
RACLETTE
RECEDING
RECEIPTS
RECEIVED
RECEIVER
RECENTLY
RECEPTOR
RECESSED
RECHARGE
RECKLESS
RECKONER
RECORDER
RECOURSE
RECOVERY
RECREATE
RECRUITS
RECUSANT
RICHNESS
RICKSHAW
RICOCHET
ROCHDALE
ROCKETRY
RUCKSACK
RUCTIONS
SACRISTY
SECLUDED
SECONDER
SECONDLY
SECRETLY
SECURELY
SECURITY
SICILIAN
SICKLIST
SICKNESS
SICKROOM
SOCALLED
SOCIABLE
SOCIALLY
SOCRATES
SOCRATIC
SUCCEEDS
SUCCINCT
SUCCUBUS
SUCHLIKE
SUCKLING
SYCAMORE
TACITURN
TACTICAL
TACTLESS
TECTONIC
TICKLING
TICKLISH
TICKTACK
TICKTOCK
ULCERATE
ULCEROUS
UNCARING
UNCHASTE
UNCLOVEN
UNCOMBED
UNCOMMON
UNCOOKED
UNCOUPLE
UNCTUOUS
UNCURBED
UPCOMING
VACANTLY
VACATION
VICARAGE
VICARIAL
VICINITY
VICTORIA
VICTUALS
VOCALIST
VOCALIZE
VOCATION
VOCATIVE
WICKEDLY
WYCLIFFE
YACHTING
ZUCCHINI
ABDICATE
ABDUCENS
ABDUCTED
ABDUCTOR
ADDENDUM
ADDICTED
ADDITION
ADDITIVE
ALDEHYDE
ALDERMAN
ALDERNEY
ANDERSON
ANDORRAN
ANDREWES
ARDENNES
ARDENTLY
AUDACITY
AUDIENCE
AUDITION
AUDITORY
BADINAGE
BADLANDS
BEDABBLE
BEDCOVER
BEDMAKER
BEDSTEAD
BEDSTRAW
BODLEIAN
BODYLINE
BODYWORK
BUDAPEST
BUDDHISM
BUDDHIST
BUDDLEIA
CADASTRE
CADILLAC
CADUCEUS
CODPIECE
DEDICATE
DIDACTIC
DIDDICOY
EIDECTIC
ELDORADO
ELDRITCH
ENDANGER
ENDEAVOR
ENDOCARP
ENDODERM
ENDOGAMY
ENDURING
ENDYMION
EUDOXIAN
FEDAYEEN
FEDERACY
FEDERATE
FIDDLING
FIDELITY
GADABOUT
GADARENE
GADGETRY
GADOGADO
GADZOOKS
GODCHILD
HEDGEHOG
HEDGEROW
HEDONISM
HEDONIST
HIDEAWAY
HIDROSIS
HYDATOID
HYDROGEN
INDEBTED
INDECENT
INDENTED
INDEXING
INDIAMAN
INDICANT
INDICATE
INDIGENT
INDIRECT
INDOLENT
INDUCIVE
INDUSTRY
JODHPURS
JUDGMENT
JUDICIAL
KEDGEREE
KIDGLOVE
LADRONES
LADYBIRD
LADYLIKE
LADYSHIP
LODESTAR
LODGINGS
MADHOUSE
MADRIGAL
MADWOMAN
MEDALIST
MEDDLING
MEDIATOR
MEDICATE
MEDICINE
MEDIEVAL
MEDIOCRE
MEDITATE
MIDDLING
MIDFIELD
MIDLANDS
MIDNIGHT
MIDPOINT
MODELING
MODELLER
MODERATE
MODERATO
MODESTLY
MODIFIER
MODULATE
MUDFLATS
MUDGUARD
MUDSTONE
NIDATION
OBDURACY
OBDURATE
ODDMENTS
OEDIPEAN
OLDSTYLE
OLDWORLD
OMDURMAN
ORDERING
ORDINAND
ORDINARY
ORDINATE
ORDNANCE
PADDLING
PEDAGOGY
PEDANTIC
PEDANTRY
PEDDLING
PEDERAST

PEDESTAL
PEDICURE
PEDIGREE
PEDIMENT
PEDUNCLE
PIDDLING
PODARGUS
PUDENDUM
RADIANCE
RADIATOR
REDACTOR
REDBRICK
REDEEMER
REDEFINE
REDEPLOY
REDESIGN
REDIRECT
REDLIGHT
REDOLENT
REDOUBLE
REDSHANK
REDSTART
RIDDANCE
RIDGEWAY
RIDICULE
RODERICK
RUDENESS
RUDIMENT
SADDLERY
SADDLING
SADDUCEE
SADISTIC
SEDATELY
SEDATION
SEDATIVE
SEDIMENT
SEDITION
SEDULOUS
SIDEKICK
SIDELINE
SIDELONG
SIDEREAL
SIDERITE
SIDESHOW
SIDESLIP
SIDESMAN
SIDESTEP
SIDEWALK
SIDEWAYS
SODALITE
SODALITY
SUDAMENT
SUDAMINA
SUDANESE
SUDARIUM
SUDDENLY
TIDEMARK
TIDINESS
UNDERAGE
UNDERARM
UNDERCUT
UNDERDOG
UNDERFED
UNDERLAY
UNDERLIE
UNDERPIN
UNDERSEA
UNDERTOW
UNDULANT
UNDULATE
WEDGWOOD
WIDENING
YODELLER
ZEDEKIAH
ZODIACAL
ABERDEEN
ABERRANT
ABESSIVE
ABEYANCE
ACERBATE
ACERBITY
ADELAIDE
ADENITIS
ADENOIDS
ADEQUACY
ADEQUATE
ADESSIVE
ALEATORY
ALEHOUSE
ALEMAINE
ALEUTIAN
AMENABLE
AMERICAN
AMERICAS
AMETHYST
ANECDOTE
ANEURYSM
APERIENT
APERITIF
APERTURE
ARETHUSA
AVENTINE
AVERSION
BAEDEKER
BEERBOHM
BEESWING
BEETLING
BEETROOT
BIENNIAL
BLEACHER
BLEEDING
BLENDING
BLENHEIM
BLESSING
BOEOTIAN
BREACHES
BREAKING
BREAKOUT
BREATHER
BREECHES
BREEDING
BREEZILY
BRETHREN
BREVIARY
CAERLEON
CHEATERS
CHEATING
CHECKERS
CHECKING
CHECKOUT
CHEEKILY
CHEERFUL
CHEERILY
CHEERING
CHEMICAL
CHENILLE
CHEQUERS
CHEROKEE
CHERUBIC
CHERUBIM
CHERWELL
CHESHIRE
CHESSMAN
CHESSMEN
CHESTNUT
CHEVIOTS
CHEYENNE
CLEANERS
CLEANING
CLEANSED
CLEANSER
CLEARCUT
CLEARING
CLEARWAY
CLEAVAGE
CLEAVERS
CLEMATIS
CLEMENCY
CLERICAL
CLERIHEW
CLEVERLY
COERCION
COERCIVE
CREAMERY
CREATION
CREATIVE
CREATURE
CREDIBLE
CREDIBLY
CREDITOR
CREOSOTE
CREPITUS
CRESCENT
CRETONNE
CREVASSE
DAEDALUS
DEEPNESS
DEERSKIN
DIEHARDS
DIELDRIN
DIERESIS
DREADFUL
DREAMILY
DREARILY
DRESSAGE
DRESSING
DUELLIST
DWELLING
EDENTATE
EJECTION
ELECTION
ELECTIVE
ELECTORS
ELECTRIC
ELECTRON
ELECTRUM
ELEGANCE
ELEMENTS
ELEPHANT
ELEVATED
ELEVATOR
ELEVENTH
EMERGENT
EMERGING
EMERITUS
EMERSION
ENERGIZE
ENERVATE
ERECTILE
ERECTING
ERECTION
ETERNITY
EVENNESS
EVENSONG
EVENTFUL
EVENTIDE
EVENTUAL
EVERMORE
EVERYDAY
EVERYMAN
EVERYONE
EXECRATE
EXECUTED
EXECUTOR
EXEGESIS
EXEGETIC
EXEMPLAR
EXERCISE
EXERTION
EYEGLASS
EYELINER
EYEPIECE
EYESHADE
EYESIGHT
EYETOOTH
FEEDBACK
FEELGOOD
FEELINGS
FIELDING
FIENDISH
FIERCELY
FLEABITE
FLEETING
FLEXIBLE
FLEXIBLY
FREAKISH
FRECKLED
FRECKLES
FREEHAND
FREEHOLD
FREEPOST
FREETOWN
FREEZING
FREMITUS
FRENETIC
FRENULUM
FRENZIED
FREQUENT
FRESHEST
FRESHMAN
FRETWORK
FREUDIAN
GLEAMING
GLEESOME
GREATEST
GREEDILY
GREENBAG
GREENERY
GREENFLY
GREENING
GREENISH
GREENOCK
GREETING
GUERIDON
GUERILLA
GUERNSEY
HEEDLESS
HEELBALL
HEELTAPS
HIERARCH
HIERATIC
ICEFIELD
ICEHOUSE
IDEALISM
IDEALIST
IDEALIZE
IDENTIFY
IDENTITY
IDEOGRAM
IDEOLOGY
INEDIBLE
INEQUITY
INEXPERT
KEELHAUL
KEENNESS
KEEPSAKE
KNEEDEEP
KNEEHIGH
KREPLACH
LIEGEMAN
LIENTERY
MAECENAS
MAESTOSO
MEEKNESS
MNEMONIC
MYELITIS
NEEDLESS
OBEDIENT
OLEACEAE
OLEANDER
OMELETTE
ONESIDED
ONETRACK
OPENCAST
OPENDOOR
OPENNESS
OPENPLAN
OPENWORK
OPERABLE
OPERATIC
OPERATOR
OPERETTA
ORESTEIA
OVENWARE
OVERALLS
OVERBOOK
OVERCAST
OVERCOAT
OVERCOME
OVERDONE
OVERDOSE
OVERDRAW
OVERFEED
OVERFILL
OVERFLOW
OVERFULL
OVERHANG
OVERHAUL
OVERHEAD
OVERHEAR
OVERHEAT
OVERKILL

OVERLAID
OVERLAND
OVERLEAF
OVERLOAD
OVERLOOK
OVERLORD
OVERMUCH
OVERPASS
OVERPLAY
OVERRATE
OVERRIDE
OVERRIPE
OVERRULE
OVERSEAS
OVERSEER
OVERSHOE
OVERSHOT
OVERSIZE
OVERSTAY
OVERSTEP
OVERTAKE
OVERTIME
OVERTONE
OVERTURE
OVERTURN
OVERVIEW
OVERWORK
PEEKABOO
PEELINGS
PEEPHOLE
PEERLESS
PHEASANT
PIECHART
PIECRUST
PIERCING
PIERETTE
PIERIDES
PLEADING
PLEASANT
PLEASING
PLEASURE
PLEBEIAN
PLECTRUM
PLEIADES
PLEONASM
PLETHORA
PLEURISY
POETICAL
PREACHER
PREAMBLE
PRECINCT
PRECIOUS
PRECLUDE
PRECURSE
PREDATOR
PREDELLA
PREGNANT
PREJUDGE
PREMIERE
PREMISES
PREMOLAR
PRENATAL
PREPARED
PRESENCE
PRESERVE
PRESSING
PRESSMAN
PRESSURE
PRESTIGE
PRETENCE
PRETENSE
PRETORIA
PRETTILY
PREVIOUS
PSEUDERY
PYELITIS
QUENELLE
QUESTION
REEDLING
REEDSMAN
REEMPLOY
RHEOSTAT
RHETORIC
RIESLING
ROENTGEN
RUEFULLY
RYEGRASS
SCENARIO
SEEDLESS
SEEDLING
SEEDSMAN
SEETHING
SHEARMAN
SHEEPDOG
SHEEPISH
SHEIKDOM
SHELDUCK
SHELVING
SHEPHERD
SHERATON
SHERIDAN
SHERLOCK
SHERWOOD
SHETLAND
SKELETAL
SKELETON
SKEWBALD
SLEEPERS
SLEEPILY
SLEEPING
SMELTING
SNEAKERS
SNEAKING
SNEERING
SNEEZING
SPEAKERS
SPEAKING
SPECIFIC
SPECIMEN
SPECIOUS
SPECKLED
SPECTRAL
SPECTRUM
SPECULUM
SPEEDILY
SPEEDWAY
SPELLING
SPELLMAN
SPENDING
STEADILY
STEALING
STEALTHY
STEATITE
STEATOMA
STEERAGE
STEERING
STEINWAY
STELLATE
STENDHAL
STENOSED
STENOSIS
STEPHENS
STERLING
SVENGALI
SWEARING
SWEATING
SWEEPING
SWELLING
SWERVING
TEENAGER
TEESHIRT
TEETHING
TEETOTAL
THEATRIC
THEMATIC
THEOCRAT
THEOLOGY
THEORIST
THEORIZE
THESPIAN
TIEBREAK
TREASURE
TREASURY
TREATISE
TREELESS
TREELINE
TREETOPS
TREMBLER
TRENCHER
TRESPASS
TWEEZERS
TWELVEMO
UNEARNED
UNEASILY
UNENDING
UNERRING
UNEVENLY
URETHANE
USEFULLY
UTENSILS
WHEATEAR
WHEEZILY
WHEEZING
WHENEVER
WHEREVER
WOEFULLY
WREATHED
WRECKAGE
WRESTLER
WRETCHED
YIELDING
ZOETROPE
AFFECTED
AFFINITY
AFFLATUS
AFFLUENT
AFFUSION
ALFRESCO
BAFFLING
BEFRIEND
BEFUDDLE
BIFOCALS
CAFFEINE
DAFFODIL
DEFEATED
DEFECATE
DEFECTOR
DEFENDER
DEFIANCE
DEFINITE
DEFLOWER
DEFORMED
DEFREEZE
DEFTNESS
DIFFRACT
EFFICACY
EFFLUENT
EFFLUVIA
EFFUSION
EFFUSIVE
ENFEEBLE
ENFILADE
FIFTIETH
INFAMOUS
INFANTRY
INFECTED
INFERIOR
INFERNAL
INFESTED
INFINITE
INFINITY
INFLAMED
INFLATED
INFLIGHT
INFORMAL
INFORMED
INFORMER
INFRARED
INFRINGE
INFUSION
JEFFREYS
KUFFIYEH
LEFTHAND
LEFTOVER
LEFTWARD
LEFTWING
LIFEBELT
LIFEBOAT
LIFEBUOY
LIFELESS
LIFELIKE
LIFELINE
LIFELONG
LIFESPAN
LIFETIME
NUFFIELD
OFFBREAK
OFFCOLOR
OFFENDED
OFFENDER
OFFERING
OFFICERS
OFFICIAL
OFFSHOOT
OFFSHORE
OFFSIDER
OFFSTAGE
PUFFBALL
REFERRAL
REFINERY
REFORMED
REFORMER
REFRINGE
REFUGIUM
RIFFRAFF
RIFLEMAN
SOFTBALL
SOFTENER
SOFTNESS
SOFTWARE
SOFTWOOD
SUFFERER
SUFFRAGE
TAFFRAIL
UNFADING
UNFASTEN
UNFETTER
UNFILLED
UNFORCED
UNFREEZE
AEGROTAT
AGGRIEVE
AIGRETTE
AIGUILLE
ALGERIAN
ALGERINE
ALGORISM
ANGELICA
ANGLESEY
ANGLICAN
ANGSTROM
ANGUILLA
ARGESTES
ARGININE
ARGONAUT
ARGUABLE
ARGUABLY
ARGUMENT
AUGUSTUS
BAGHEERA
BAGPIPES
BAGUETTE
BEGETTER
BEGGARLY
BEGINNER
BEGORRAH
BEGRUDGE
BIGAMIST
BIGAMOUS
BIGARADE
BOGEYMAN
BUGGERED
CAGINESS
COGITATE
COGNOMEN
COGWHEEL
DEGRADED
DIGGINGS
DIGITIZE
DOGBERRY
DOGGEDLY
DOGGEREL
DOGHOUSE
DOGMATIC
DOGSBODY
DOGSTAIL
DOGWATCH
EDGEHILL
EDGEWAYS
EDGEWISE
EGGPLANT
EGGSHELL

EGGTIMER
EIGHTEEN
ENGAGING
ENGENDER
ENGINEER
ENGRAVER
ERGOTISE
ERGOTISM
EUGENICS
FIGHTING
FIGURINE
FOGBOUND
FOGLIGHT
FUGITIVE
FUGLEMAN
GIGANTIC
GIGLAMPS
HAGGADAH
HEGEMONY
HIGHBALL
HIGHBORN
HIGHBROW
HIGHGATE
HIGHLAND
HIGHNESS
HIGHRISE
HIGHROAD
HOGMANAY
HOGSHEAD
HYGIENIC
INGROWTH
INGUINAL
JIGGERED
JUGGLING
LEGALISM
LEGALITY
LEGALIZE
LEGATION
LEGGINGS
LIGAMENT
LIGATURE
LIGHTING
LIGNEOUS
LOGISTIC
MAGAZINE
MAGELLAN
MAGICIAN
MAGISTER
MAGNESIA
MAGNETIC
MAGNOLIA
MEGABYTE
MEGALITH
MEGAWATT
MIGHTILY
MIGNONNE
MIGRAINE
NAGASAKI
NEGATION
NEGATIVE
NEGLIGEE
NIGERIAN
NIGERIEN
NIGGLING
NIGHTCAP
NIGHTJAR
NUGATORY
ORGANDIE
ORGANISM
ORGANIST
ORGANIZE
PAGANINI
PAGINATE
PIGSWILL
PUGILISM
PUGILIST
PUGNOSED
RAGSTONE
REGAINED
REGICIDE
REGIMENT
REGIONAL
REGISTER
REGISTRY
REGULATE
RIGATONI
RIGHTFUL
RIGHTIST
RIGIDITY
RIGOROUS
ROGATION
RUGGEDLY
SAGACITY
SAGENESS
SIGHTING
SIGNALER
SIGNALLY
SIGNORIA
SIGNPOST
TEGUMENT
TIGHTWAD
TOGETHER
UNGAINLY
UNGULATE
URGENTLY
VAGABOND
VAGARIES
VAGRANCY
VEGETATE
VIGILANT
VIGNETTE
VIGOROUS
WAGGONER
YOGHOURT
YUGOSLAV
ZIGGURAT
ACHIEVED
ACHIEVER
ACHILLES
ADHERENT
ADHESION
ADHESIVE
ALHAMBRA
APHELION
APHORISM
ATHANASY
ATHELING
ATHENIAN
ATHEROMA
ATHETISE
ATHETOID
ATHLETIC
BAHAMIAN
BAHRAINI
BEHAVIOR
BEHEMOTH
BEHOLDEN
BEHOLDER
BOHEMIAN
COHERENT
COHESION
COHESIVE
ECHINATE
ECHINOPS
EOHIPPUS
EPHEMERA
EPHESIAN
ETHEREAL
ETHERISE
ETHIOPIA
ETHNARCH
ETHYLENE
EXHUMATE
INHALANT
INHERENT
INHUMANE
JEHOVAHS
JOHANNES
JOHNSONS
KOHLRABI
MAHARAJA
MAHARANI
MAHJONGG
MAHOGANY
MOHAMMED
MUHAMMAD
NIHILISM
NIHILIST
OPHIDIAN
REHEARSE
SCHAPSKA
SCHEDULE
SCHEMING
SCHILLER
SCHIZOID
SCHMALTZ
SCHMOOZE
SCHNAPPS
SCHOONER
SCHUBERT
SCHUMANN
SPHAGNUM
TAHITIAN
UNHARMED
UNHEATED
UNHEROIC
UNHINGED
UPHEAVAL
UPHOLDER
VEHEMENT
ABINGDON
ACIDHEAD
AGITATED
AGITATOR
AGITPROP
ALICANTE
ALIENATE
ALIENISM
ALIENIST
AMICABLE
AMICABLY
ANIMATED
ANISETTE
APIARIST
AVIATION
AVICENNA
AVIFAUNA
BAILMENT
BLIGHTER
BLINDING
BLINKERS
BLINKING
BLISSFUL
BLITHELY
BLIZZARD
BRIBABLE
BRICKBAT
BRIDGING
BRIEFING
BRIGHTEN
BRIGHTLY
BRIGHTON
BRIMMING
BRINDISI
BRINDLED
BRINGING
BRISLING
BRISTLED
BRISTLES
BUILDING
CHIASMUS
CHICKENS
CHICKPEA
CHILDERS
CHILDISH
CHILDREN
CHILIAST
CHILLADA
CHILLING
CHILTERN
CHIMAERA
CHINAMAN
CHINDITS
CHIPMUNK
CHITCHAT
CHIVALRY
CLIFFORD
CLIMATIC
CLIMBING
CLINCHER
CLINGING
CLINICAL
CLINKERS
CLIPPERS
CLIPPING
CLIQUISH
CLITORIS
CLIVEDEN
COIFFEUR
COIFFURE
COINCIDE
CRIBBAGE
CRICHTON
CRIMINAL
CRINGING
CRIPPLED
CRISPIAN
CRITICAL
CRITIQUE
DAINTIES
DAINTILY
DAIQUIRI
DAIRYMAN
DJIBOUTI
DRIBLETS
DRIFTING
DRINKING
DRIPPING
DRIVEWAY
ELIGIBLE
EMIGRANT
EMIGRATE
EMINENCE
EMIRATES
EMISSARY
EMISSION
ENIWETOK
EPICURUS
EPIDEMIC
EPIDURAL
EPIGAMIC
EPIGRAPH
EPILEPSY
EPILOGUE
EPIPHANY
EPIPHYTE
EPIPLOON
EPISODIC
EPISTYLE
EPITASIS
EPITHEMA
ERIKSSON
ETIOLATE
EVICTION
EVIDENCE
EVILDOER
EWIGKEIT
EXIGENCY
EXIGUITY
EXIGUOUS
EXISTENT
EXISTING
FAINITES
FAINTING
FAIRNESS
FAITHFUL
FLIMSILY
FLINDERS
FLIPPANT
FLIPPERS
FLIPPING
FLIRTING
FRICTION
FRIENDLY
FRIGHTEN
FRIGIDLY
FRIPPERY
FRISKILY
GAILLARD
GLISSADE
GRIDIRON
GRIDLOCK
GRIEVOUS
GRILLING
GRIMALDI
GRIMNESS
GRINDING
GRIPPING
GRISELDA
GRISETTE
GRIZZLED
GUIANIAN

GUIDANCE
GUILTILY
HAIRLESS
HAIRLIKE
HAIRLINE
HEIGHTEN
HEIRLESS
HEIRLOOM
IMITATOR
INIMICAL
INIQUITY
INITIATE
IRISCOPE
IRISHISM
IRISHMAN
IRISHMEN
JAILBIRD
JOINTURE
KNICKERS
KNIGHTLY
KNITTING
KNITWEAR
LAIDBACK
LEINSTER
LEISURED
LOITERER
MAIDENLY
MAILBOAT
MAILSHOT
MAINLAND
MAINLINE
MAINMAST
MAINSAIL
MAINSTAY
MAINTAIN
MAINYARD
MOISTURE
NEIGHBOR
NOISETTE
NUISANCE
OBITUARY
ODIOUSLY
OEILLADE
OLIGARCH
OLIPHANT
OMISSION
ORIENTAL
ORIGINAL
OUISTITI
PAINLESS
PAINTING
PEIGNOIR
PHILEMON
PHILIPPI
PHILLIPS
PHILOMEL
PLIMSOLL
PLIOCENE
POIGNANT
POISONER
POITIERS
PRIAPISM
PRIESTLY
PRIGGISH
PRIMEVAL
PRIMNESS
PRIMROSE
PRINCELY
PRINCESS
PRINTING
PRINTOUT
PRIORESS
PRIORITY
PRISONER
PRISTINE
PRIVATES
PUISSANT
QUIBBLER
QUICKSET
QUIETUDE
QUILTING
QUINCUNX
QUINTAIN
QUIRINAL
QUISLING
QUIXOTIC
RAILHEAD
RAILINGS
RAILLERY
RAILROAD
RAINBIRD
RAINCOAT
RAINDROP
RAINFALL
RAINWEAR
RAISONNÉ
REIGNING
REINDEER
REINSURE
REINVEST
SAILBOAT
SAINFOIN
SCIATICA
SCIENCES
SCILICET
SCIMITAR
SCIROCCO
SCISSION
SCISSORS
SHIELING
SHIFTING
SHIGELLA
SHIITAKE
SHILLING
SHINGLES
SHIPMATE
SHIPMENT
SHIPPING
SHIPYARD
SHIVERED
SKIBOOTS
SKIDDING
SKILLFUL
SKILLING
SKILLION
SKINDEEP
SKINHEAD
SKINWORK
SKIPJACK
SKIPPING
SKIRMISH
SKIRTING
SKITTISH
SKITTLES
SLIGHTED
SLIGHTLY
SLIMNESS
SLIPOVER
SLIPPERS
SLIPPERY
SLIPPING
SLIPSHOD
SLIPSLOP
SMIDGEON
SNIFFLER
SPICCATO
SPIFFING
SPILLAGE
SPILLWAY
SPINNING
SPINSTER
SPINTEXT
SPIRACLE
SPIRALLY
SPIRITED
SPIRITUS
SPITEFUL
SPITFIRE
SPITHEAD
SPITTING
SPITTOON
STICCATO
STICKILY
STICKING
STICKLER
STIFLING
STIGMATA
STILETTO
STILWELL
STIMULUS
STINGING
STINGRAY
STINKING
STIRLING
STIRRING
SUICIDAL
SUITABLE
SUITABLY
SUITCASE
SWILLING
SWIMMING
SWIMSUIT
SWINDLER
SWINGING
SWIRLING
TAILBACK
TAILGATE
TAILLESS
TAILPIPE
TAILSKID
TAILSPIN
THIAMINE
THICKSET
THIEVERY
THIEVING
THIEVISH
THINGAMY
THINKING
THINNESS
THINNING
THIRTEEN
TOILSOME
TOISEACH
TRIANGLE
TRIASSIC
TRIBUNAL
TRICHOID
TRICKERY
TRICYCLE
TRIFLING
TRIGLYPH
TRILEMMA
TRILLING
TRILLION
TRILLIUM
TRIMARAN
TRIMMING
TRIMNESS
TRINCULO
TRINIDAD
TRIPLING
TRIPTANE
TRIPTYCH
TRISTICH
TRISTRAM
TRITICAL
TRITICUM
TWILIGHT
TWIRLING
TWISTING
TWITCHER
UBIQUITY
UNIFYING
UNIONISM
UNIONIST
UNIONIZE
UNIPOLAR
UNIQUELY
UNITEDLY
UNIVALVE
UNIVERSE
VOIDANCE
WAINSCOT
WAITRESS
WEIGHING
WHIMBREL
WHINCHAT
WHIPCORD
WHIPHAND
WHIPJACK
WHIPLASH
WHIPPING
WHIRLING
WHISKERS
WHISKERY
WHISTLER
WHITECAP
WHITEHOT
WHITENER
WHITLING
WRINGING
WRINKLED
WRISTLET
WRITEOFF
WRITHING
WRITINGS
ZWIEBACK
ABJECTLY
ADJACENT
ADJUSTER
ADJUSTOR
ADJUTAGE
ADJUTANT
ADJUVANT
CAJOLERY
DEJECTED
GUJARATI
HIJACKER
INJECTOR
MAJESTIC
MAJOLICA
MAJORITY
NDJAMENA
NIJINSKY
OBJECTOR
REJOINED
UNJUSTLY
AKKADIAN
ALKALIFY
ALKALINE
ALKALOID
ARKANSAS
BAKELITE
CAKEHOLE
CAKEWALK
ELKHOUND
ENKINDLE
HOKKAIDO
INKSTAIN
JOKINGLY
LAKELAND
LIKEABLE
LIKENESS
LIKEWISE
LUKEWARM
MCKINLEY
PAKISTAN
PEKINESE
REKINDLE
SUKIYAKI
TAKEAWAY
TAKEHOME
TAKEOVER
UNKINDLY
YAKITORI
YOKOHAMA
ZAKOUSKI
ABLATION
ABLATIVE
ABLUTION
ALLEGORY
ALLELUIA
ALLERGEN
ALLERGIC
ALLEYWAY
ALLIANCE
ALLOCATE
ALLOGAMY
ALLOPATH
ALLOWING
ALLSPICE
ALLURING
ALLUSION
ALLUSIVE
ALLUVIAL
ALLUVIUM
ATLANTIC
ATLANTIS
BALANCED
BALDNESS
BALDRICK
BALEARIC

BALINESE
BALLCOCK
BALLGIRL
BALLISTA
BALLOCKS
BALLPARK
BALLROOM
BALLYHOO
BALMORAL
BALUSTER
BELABOUR
BELGRADE
BELIEVER
BELITTLE
BELLPUSH
BELLYFUL
BELPAESE
BILBERRY
BILLFOLD
BILLHOOK
BILLYBOY
BILLYCAN
BOLDNESS
BOLIVIAN
BOLLOCKS
BOLTHOLE
BULGARIA
BULKHEAD
BULLDOZE
BULLETIN
BULLFROG
BULLHORN
BULLRING
BULLYRAG
CALABASH
CALAMINE
CALAMITY
CALCEATE
CALCULUS
CALCUTTA
CALDERON
CALENDAR
CALENDER
CALIGULA
CALIPERS
CALLGIRL
CALLIOPE
CALLIPER
CALLISTO
CALMNESS
CALOTYPE
CALTHROP
CALVADOS
CELANESE
CELERIAC
CELERITY
CELIBACY
CELIBATE
CELLARER
CELLULAR
CHLORATE
CHLORIDE
CHLORINE
CILIATED
COLANDER
COLDNESS
COLESLAW
COLISEUM
COLLAGEN
COLLAPSE
COLLARED
COLLATOR
COLLECTS
COLLEGES
COLLIERS
COLLIERY
COLLOQUY
COLOMBIA
COLONIAL
COLONIST
COLONIZE
COLOPHON
COLORADO
COLORANT
COLORFUL
COLORING
COLOSSAL
COLOSSUS
COLOURED
COLUMBAN
COLUMBUS
CULINARY
CULLINAN
CULLODEN
CULPABLE
CULTURAL
CULTURED
CULVERIN
CYLINDER
DALMATIC
DELAWARE
DELEGATE
DELETION
DELICACY
DELICATE
DELIRIUM
DELIVERY
DELUSION
DILATION
DILATORY
DILIGENT
DILUTION
DOLDRUMS
DOLOMITE
DOLOROUS
DULCIMER
DULCINEA
DULLNESS
ECLECTIC
ECLOSION
ELLIPSIS
ELLIPTIC
ENLARGED
ENLARGER
EULOGIST
EULOGIUM
EULOGIZE
FALCONRY
FALKLAND
FALLIBLE
FALSETTO
FELDSPAR
FELICITY
FELLAHIN
FILAGREE
FILAMENT
FILARIUM
FILENAME
FILIGREE
FILIPINO
FILTHILY
FILTRATE
FOLDEROL
FOLKLORE
FOLKSONG
FOLLICLE
FOLLOWED
FOLLOWER
FOLLOWUP
FULLBACK
FULLNESS
FULLPAGE
FULLSIZE
FULLTIME
GALACTIC
GALBANUM
GALILEAN
GALLERIA
GALLIARD
GALLIPOT
GALLOPER
GALLOWAY
GALLUMPH
GALOSHES
GALVANIC
GELASTIC
GELATINE
GOLDFISH
GOLDMINE
GOLFBALL
GOLFCLUB
GOLGOTHA
GOLLIWOG
GULLIBLE
GULLIVER
HALFFULL
HALFHOUR
HALFMAST
HALFTERM
HALFTIME
HALFYEAR
HALLIARD
HALLMARK
HALLOWED
HELIPORT
HELLADIC
HELLBENT
HELLENIC
HELLFIRE
HELMETED
HELMSMAN
HELPLESS
HELPLINE
HELPMATE
HELSINKI
HELVETIA
HILARITY
HILLSIDE
HOLDINGS
HOLIDAYS
HOLINESS
HOLISTIC
HOLLOWAY
HOLOGRAM
HOLYHEAD
HOLYROOD
IDLENESS
ILLFATED
ILLINOIS
ILLUMINE
ILLUSION
ILLUSIVE
ILLUSORY
IOLANTHE
ISLANDER
JALOUSIE
JELLICOE
JULIENNE
KALAHARI
KILKENNY
KILLDEER
KILOBYTE
KILOGRAM
KILOVOLT
KILOWATT
LILONGWE
LOLLIPOP
LULWORTH
MALAGASY
MALAKOFF
MALARIAL
MALARKEY
MALAWIAN
MALAYSIA
MALDIVES
MALGRADO
MALINGER
MALLARMÉ
MALLEATE
MALLORCA
MALODOUR
MALTREAT
MALVASIA
MALVOLIO
MELAMINE
MELANITE
MELANOMA
MELCHIOR
MELEAGER
MELTDOWN
MILANESE
MILDEWED
MILDNESS
MILITANT
MILITARY
MILITATE
MILKLESS
MILKMAID
MILKWEED
MILKWORT
MILLIBAR
MILLINER
MILLIONS
MILLPOND
MILLRACE
MOLASSES
MOLECULE
MOLEHILL
MOLESKIN
MOLESTER
MOLLUSCS
MOLUCCAS
MULBERRY
MULETEER
MULEWORT
MULLIGAN
MULTIPLE
MULTIPLY
OBLATION
OBLIGATE
OBLIGING
OBLIVION
OILCLOTH
OILFIELD
OILINESS
OILSKINS
OILSLICK
OKLAHOMA
ONLOOKER
PALATIAL
PALATINE
PALEFACE
PALENESS
PALGRAVE
PALIMONY
PALINODE
PALISADE
PALLADIO
PALLIATE
PALMATED
PALMETTO
PALPABLE
PALPABLY
PALUDISM
PELAGIUS
PELLAGRA
PELLETED
PELLICLE
PELLMELL
PELLUCID
PHLEGMON
PILASTER
PILCHARD
PILFERER
PILGRIMS
PILLAGER
PILLARED
PILOTAGE
PILSENER
PILTDOWN
POLARIZE
POLISHED
POLISHER
POLITELY
POLITICO
POLITICS
POLLSTER
POLLUTED
POLLUTER
POLONIUM
POLTROON
POLYANNA
POLYARCH
POLYCARP
POLYGAMY
POLYGLOT
POLYMATH
POLYSEME
POLYSEMY
PULITZER
PULLDOWN
PULLOVER

RELATING
RELATION
RELATIVE
RELAXING
RELAYING
RELEASED
RELEGATE
RELEVANT
RELIABLE
RELIABLY
RELIANCE
RELIEVED
RELIGION
RELOCATE
ROLLCALL
ROLYPOLY
RULEBOOK
SALACITY
SALARIED
SALEABLE
SALEROOM
SALESMAN
SALINGER
SALINITY
SALIVARY
SALIVATE
SALTLICK
SALTNESS
SALUTARY
SALUTORY
SALVADOR
SELASSIE
SELBORNE
SELECTED
SELECTOR
SELENITE
SELENIUM
SELEUCID
SELFHELP
SELFLESS
SELFMADE
SELFPITY
SELFSAME
SELVEDGE
SILENCER
SILENTLY
SILESIAN
SILICATE
SILICONE
SILKTAIL
SILKWORM
SILURIAN
SOLARIUM
SOLDIERS
SOLDIERY
SOLECISM
SOLEMNLY
SOLENOID
SOLIDIFY
SOLIDITY
SOLITARY
SOLITUDE
SOLSTICE
SOLUTION
SOLVABLE
SOLVENCY
SPLASHER
SPLATTER
SPLENDID
SPLENDOR
SPLINTER
SPLITTER
SPLUTTER
SULFURIC
SULLENLY
SULLIVAN
SULPHATE
SULPHIDE
SYLLABIC
SYLLABLE
SYLLABUB
SYLLABUS
SYLVANER
TALENTED
TALISMAN
TELECAST
TELEFILM
TELEGONY
TELEGRAM
TELEMARK
TELETHON
TELEVISE
TELLTALE
TELLURIC
TOLBOOTH
TOLERANT
TOLERATE
TOLLGATE
UGLINESS
UNLAWFUL
UNLEADED
UNLIKELY
UNLISTED
UNLOADED
UNLOCKED
UNLOVELY
VALENCIA
VALERIAN
VALETING
VALHALLA
VALIDATE
VALIDITY
VALKYRIE
VALLETTA
VALUABLE
VALVULAR
VELLEITY
VELOCITY
VILENESS
VILLAGER
VILLAINY
VOLATILE
VOLCANIC
VOLITION
VOLPLANE
VOLSCIAN
VOLTAIRE
VULGARLY
WALKOVER
WALKYRIE
WALLSEND
WALLWORT
WALTZING
WELLBRED
WELLNIGH
WELLPAID
WELSHMAN
WILDFELL
WILDFIRE
WILDFOWL
WILDLIFE
WILDNESS
WILFULLY
WILINESS
WILLIAMS
WOLFBANE
WOLSELEY
YULETIDE
ADMIRING
ADMONISH
ALMIGHTY
AMMONIAC
AMMONITE
ARMAGNAC
ARMALITE
ARMAMENT
ARMATURE
ARMCHAIR
ARMENIAN
ARMORIAL
ARMORICA
ARMOURED
ASMODEUS
BUMBLING
BUMMAREE
CAMARGUE
CAMBERED
CAMBODIA
CAMBRIAN
CAMELLIA
CAMEROON
CAMISOLE
CAMOMILE
CAMPAIGN
CAMPBELL
CAMPSITE
CAMPTOWN
CAMSHAFT
CAMSTONE
CEMETERY
COMATOSE
COMBINED
COMEBACK
COMEDIAN
COMEDOWN
COMMANDO
COMMENCE
COMMERCE
COMMONER
COMMONLY
COMMUNAL
COMMUTER
COMPARED
COMPILER
COMPLAIN
COMPLETE
COMPLINE
COMPOSED
COMPOSER
COMPOUND
COMPRESS
COMPRISE
COMPUTER
DAMASCUS
DAMNABLE
DAMOCLES
DAMPNESS
DEMEANOR
DEMENTED
DEMENTIA
DEMERARA
DEMERSAL
DEMIJOHN
DEMISTER
DEMIURGE
DEMOCRAT
DEMOLISH
DEMONIAC
DEMOTION
DEMURELY
DEMURRAL
DIMINISH
DOMESDAY
DOMESTIC
DOMICILE
DOMINANT
DOMINATE
DOMINEER
DOMINION
DOMINOES
DUMBBELL
DUMBNESS
DUMFOUND
DUMPLING
EMMANUEL
ENMESHED
FAMILIAR
FAMISHED
FAMOUSLY
FEMININE
FEMINISM
FEMINIST
FEMINITY
FUMAROLE
FUMBLING
FUMIGATE
FUMITORY
GAMBLING
GAMEBIRD
GAMENESS
GEMINATE
GEMOLOGY
GIMCRACK
GUMMOSIS
GUMPTION
GYMKHANA
HAMILTON
HAMMERED
HOMELAND
HOMELESS
HOMEMADE
HOMESICK
HOMESPUN
HOMEWARD
HOMEWORK
HOMICIDE
HUMANELY
HUMANISM
HUMANIST
HUMANITY
HUMANIZE
HUMIDIFY
HUMIDITY
HUMILITY
HUMORIST
HUMOROUS
HUMPBACK
HUMPHREY
IMMANENT
IMMANUEL
IMMATURE
IMMERSED
IMMINENT
IMMOBILE
IMMODEST
IMMOLATE
IMMORTAL
IMMUNITY
IMMUNIZE
JAMAICAN
JAMBOREE
JIMCRACK
JUMPSUIT
KAMIKAZE
KOMSOMOL
LAMASERY
LAMBSKIN
LAMENESS
LAMENTED
LAMINATE
LAMPPOST
LEMONADE
LIMBLESS
LIMERICK
LIMITING
LIMONITE
LIMPNESS
LOMBARDY
LUMINARY
LUMINOUS
LUMPFISH
MAMELUKE
MEMBRANE
MEMORIAL
MEMORIAM
MEMORIZE
MEMSAHIB
MOMENTUM
MUMBLING
NAMELESS
NAMESAKE
NAMIBIAN
NEMATODE
NEMATOID
NEMBUTAL
NOMINATE
NOMOGRAM
NUMBNESS
NUMERACY
NUMERALS
NUMERATE
NUMEROUS
NUMINOUS
PAMPERED
PAMPHLET
PEMBROKE
PEMMICAN
PIMIENTO
POMANDER
RAMBLING
RAMBUTAN
RAMEQUIN

RAMPARTS
REMEDIAL
REMEMBER
REMINDER
REMITTAL
REMNANTS
REMOTELY
REMOUNTS
ROMANCER
ROMANIAN
ROMANSCH
ROMANTIC
RUMBLING
RUMINANT
RUMINATE
RUMOURED
SAMENESS
SAMIZDAT
SAMPHIRE
SEMESTER
SEMINARY
SEMIOTIC
SEMITONE
SEMOLINA
SIMPLIFY
SIMULATE
SOMBRELY
SOMBRERO
SOMEBODY
SOMERSET
SOMETIME
SOMEWHAT
SUMERIAN
SUMMITRY
SYMBIONT
SYMBOLIC
SYMMETRY
SYMPATHY
SYMPHONY
SYMPTOMS
TAMARIND
TAMARISK
TAMENESS
TAMWORTH
TEMERITY
TEMPERED
TEMPLATE
TEMPORAL
TEMPTING
TIMBERED
TIMELESS
TIMIDITY
TIMOROUS
TOMAHAWK
TOMATOES
TOMENTUM
TOMORROW
TYMPANUM
UNMANNED
UNMARKED
UPMARKET
VOMITING
VOMITORY
WAMBLING
WOMANISH
WOMANIZE
ZAMINDAR
ZIMBABWE
ABNEGATE
ABNORMAL
AGNATION
AGNOSTIC
ANNALIST
ANNAMITE
ANNEALER
ANNELIDA
ANNOTATE
ANNOUNCE
ANNOYING
ANNUALLY
BANALITY
BANDANNA
BANDEROL
BANDITTI
BANDSMAN
BANISTER
BANKBOOK
BANKNOTE
BANKROLL
BANKRUPT
BANLIEUE
BANTLING
BENEDICK
BENEDICT
BENEFICE
BENEFITS
BENENDEN
BENGHAZI
BENJAMIN
BINDWEED
BINNACLE
BINOMIAL
BONDSMAN
BONEHEAD
BONELESS
BONEYARD
BONHOMIE
BONIFACE
BONSPIEL
BUNFIGHT
BUNGALOW
BUNGLING
CANADIAN
CANAILLE
CANALISE
CANARIES
CANBERRA
CANDIDLY
CANISTER
CANNABIS
CANNIBAL
CANOEING
CANOEIST
CANONIZE
CANOODLE
CANTICLE
CENOBITE
CENOTAPH
CENTAURY
CENTERED
CENTRIST
CENTRODE
CINCHONA
CINERAMA
CINEREAL
CINGULUM
CINNABAR
CINNAMON
CONCEIVE
CONCERTO
CONCHOID
CONCLAVE
CONCLUDE
CONCORDE
CONCRETE
CONDENSE
CONFETTI
CONFINED
CONFINES
CONFLATE
CONFLICT
CONFOUND
CONFRONT
CONFUSED
CONGRESS
CONJUGAL
CONJURER
CONJUROR
CONQUEST
CONSERVE
CONSIDER
CONSOMMÉ
CONSPIRE
CONSTANT
CONSTRUE
CONSULAR
CONSUMED
CONSUMER
CONTANGO
CONTEMPT
CONTENTS
CONTINUE
CONTINUO
CONTRACT
CONTRARY
CONTRAST
CONTRITE
CONTRIVE
CONTROLS
CONVENER
CONVERGE
CONVERSE
CONVEYOR
CONVINCE
CONVULSE
CYNICISM
CYNOSURE
DANDRUFF
DANEGELD
DANKNESS
DENARIUS
DENATURE
DENDRITE
DENDROID
DENOUNCE
DENTURES
DINGBATS
DINOSAUR
DONATION
DONATIST
DUNGHILL
DYNAMICS
DYNAMISM
DYNAMITE
DYNASTIC
DYNATRON
EINSTEIN
FANCIFUL
FANCYMAN
FANDANGO
FANLIGHT
FANTASIA
FENCIBLE
FENESTRA
FINALIST
FINALITY
FINALIZE
FINDINGS
FINESPUN
FINISHED
FINISHER
FONDLING
FONDNESS
FUNCTION
FUNERARY
FUNEREAL
GANGLAND
GANGLING
GANGLION
GANGRENE
GANGSTER
GANYMEDE
GENDARME
GENERATE
GENEROUS
GENETICS
GENETRIX
GENIALLY
GENITALS
GENITIVE
GENOCIDE
GENTRIFY
GINGERLY
GINGIVAL
GONDWANA
GONFALON
GUNMETAL
GUNPOINT
GUNSMITH
HANDBALL
HANDBILL
HANDBOOK
HANDCART
HANDCLAP
HANDCUFF
HANDHELD
HANDICAP
HANDMADE
HANDMAID
HANDOVER
HANDRAIL
HANDSOME
HANDYMAN
HANGINGS
HANGNAIL
HANGOVER
HANNIBAL
HANUKKAH
HENCHMAN
HENHOUSE
HINDMOST
HINDUISM
HINDWARD
HONDURAN
HONDURAS
HONESTLY
HONEYDEW
HONEYPOT
HONGKONG
HONOLULU
HONORARY
HUNDREDS
HUNGRILY
HUNTRESS
HUNTSMAN
IGNITION
IGNOMINY
IGNORANT
INNOCENT
INNOVATE
INNUENDO
JANGLING
JINGOISM
JINGOIST
JONATHAN
JONCANOE
JONGLEUR
JUNCTION
JUNCTURE
KANGAROO
KENTUCKY
KINDLING
KINDNESS
KINETICS
KINGPOST
KINGSHIP
KINGSIZE
KINGSLEY
KINGSTON
KINKAJOU
KINSFOLK
KINSHASA
LANCELOT
LANDFALL
LANDFILL
LANDLADY
LANDLOCK
LANDLORD
LANDMARK
LANDMASS
LANDMINE
LANDRACE
LANDSEER
LANDSLIP
LANDWARD
LANGLAND
LANGLAUF
LANGUAGE
LANGUISH
LANOLINE
LANSBURY
LENGTHEN
LENIENCY
LINCHPIN
LINCOLNS
LINESMAN
LINGERIE
LINGUIST
LINIMENT
LINNAEAN
LINNAEUS
LINOLEUM

LINOTYPE
LONDONER
LONESOME
LONGBOAT
LONGHAND
LONGHAUL
LONGHORN
LONGLAND
LONGSTAY
LONGSTOP
LONGTERM
LONGTIME
LONICERA
LONSDALE
LUNCHEON
LUNGFISH
LYNCHING
MANAGING
MANCIPLE
MANDAMUS
MANDARIN
MANDATED
MANDIBLE
MANDIOCA
MANDOLIN
MANDRAKE
MANDRILL
MANEUVER
MANFULLY
MANGONEL
MANGROVE
MANIACAL
MANICURE
MANIFEST
MANIFOLD
MANITOBA
MANNERED
MANNERLY
MANNIKIN
MANORIAL
MANPOWER
MANTILLA
MANTISSA
MANUALLY
MENACING
MENANDER
MENELAUS
MENISCUS
MENSWEAR
MENTALLY
MINAMATA
MINATORY
MINCEPIE
MINDANAO
MINDLESS
MINEHEAD
MINIMIZE
MINISTER
MINISTRY
MINORESS
MINORITE
MINORITY
MINOTAUR
MINSTREL
MINUTELY
MINUTIAE
MONADISM
MONARCHY
MONASTIC
MONAURAL
MONDRIAN
MONETARY
MONETISE
MONEYBOX
MONGOLIA
MONGOOSE
MONICKER
MONMOUTH
MONOGAMY
MONOGRAM
MONOHULL
MONOLITH
MONOPOLY
MONORAIL
MONOTONY
MONOTYPE
MONOXIDE
MONROVIA
MONSTERA
MONTCALM
MONTEITH
MONUMENT
MUNCHKIN
MUNIMENT
NENUPHAR
NINEPINS
NINETEEN
NONESUCH
NONSENSE
NONSTICK
OENOLOGY
OENOPHIL
OINTMENT
OMNIFORM
ORNAMENT
PANATELA
PANCREAS
PANDARUS
PANDEMIC
PANDOWDY
PANEGYRY
PANELING
PANELLED
PANGLOSS
PANGOLIN
PANNICLE
PANNIKIN
PANORAMA
PANTALON
PANTHEON
PENALIZE
PENCHANT
PENDULUM
PENELOPE
PENITENT
PENKNIFE
PENNINES
PENOLOGY
PENTACLE
PENTAGON
PENTARCH
PENUMBRA
PENZANCE
PINAFORE
PINDARIC
PINEWOOD
PINNACLE
PINNIPED
PINOCHLE
PINPOINT
PINPRICK
PINTABLE
PINWHEEL
PONSONBY
PONYTAIL
PUNCTUAL
PUNCTURE
PUNGENCY
PUNISHED
PUNITIVE
RANDOMLY
RANELAGH
RANKNESS
RENEGADE
RENMINBI
RENOUNCE
RENOVATE
RENOWNED
RINGDOVE
RINGSIDE
RINGTAIL
RINGWALL
RINGWORM
RUNABOUT
RUNCIBLE
RUNNERUP
SANCTIFY
SANCTION
SANCTITY
SANDBANK
SANDWICH
SANGLIER
SANGUINE
SANITARY
SANITIZE
SANSERIF
SANSKRIT
SANTIAGO
SENGREEN
SENILITY
SENORITA
SENSIBLE
SENSIBLY
SENSUOUS
SENTENCE
SENTIENT
SENTINEL
SINAPISM
SINCLAIR
SINECURE
SINFONIA
SINGSONG
SINGULAR
SINISTER
SONATINA
SONGBIRD
SONGSTER
SONOROUS
SUNBATHE
SUNBURNT
SUNBURST
SUNCREAM
SUNDANCE
SUNDRIED
SUNDRIES
SUNLIGHT
SUNSHADE
SUNSHINE
SYNCLINE
SYNDROME
SYNOPSIS
SYNOPTIC
SYNTEXIS
TANDOORI
TANGIBLE
TANGIBLY
TANTALUM
TANTALUS
TANZANIA
TENACITY
TENDENCY
TENDERLY
TENEBRAE
TENEBRIO
TENEMENT
TENESMUS
TENNYSON
TENTACLE
TINCTURE
TINGLING
TINNITUS
TINSELLY
TINTAGEL
TONALITY
TONELESS
TONSURED
TUNGSTEN
TUNISIAN
UNNERVED
VANADIUM
VANBRUGH
VANGUARD
VANISHED
VANQUISH
VENALITY
VENDETTA
VENERATE
VENEREAL
VENETIAN
VENGEFUL
VENOMOUS
VENTURED
VINCIBLE
VINCULUM
VINDALOO
VINEGARY
VINEYARD
WANDERER
WINDBURN
WINDFALL
WINDHOEK
WINDINGS
WINDLASS
WINDLESS
WINDMILL
WINDPIPE
WINDSOCK
WINDWARD
WINGLESS
WINGSPAN
WINIFRED
WINNINGS
WINNIPEG
WONDROUS
XANTHOMA
XANTIPPE
XENOGAMY
XENOLITH
XENOPHON
ABOMASUM
ABORTION
ABORTIVE
ACOUSTIC
ADOPTION
ADOPTIVE
ADORABLE
AGONIZED
ALOPECIA
AMORETTI
AMORETTO
AMORTIZE
ANOREXIA
ANOREXIC
APOLLYON
APOLOGIA
APOLOGUE
APOPLEXY
APOSTASY
APOSTATE
APOSTLES
APOTHEGM
AROMATIC
ATOMIZER
AVOGADRO
BIOGRAPH
BIOSCOPE
BLOCKADE
BLOCKAGE
BLOOMERS
BLOOMING
BLOTCHED
BLOWFISH
BLOWHOLE
BLOWLAMP
BLOWPIPE
BOOKABLE
BOOKCASE
BOOKMARK
BOOKROOM
BOOKSHOP
BOOKWORK
BOOKWORM
BOOTLESS
BOOTNECK
BROADWAY
BROCCOLI
BROCHURE
BROILING
BROMELIA
BROMPTON
BRONCHUS
BROODING
BROUGHAM
BROUHAHA
BROWBEAT
BROWNING
BROWNISH
BROWSING
BUOYANCY
CHOIRBOY
CHOLERIC
CHOOSING

CHOPPING
CHORDATA
CHORDATE
CHORIAMB
CLODPOLL
CLOISTER
CLOTHIER
CLOTHING
CLOWNISH
COOKBOOK
COOKWARE
COOLNESS
CROATIAN
CROCKERY
CROCKETT
CROMLECH
CROMWELL
CRONYISM
CROONING
CROSSBAR
CROSSING
CROSSLET
CROTCHET
CROUPIER
CROWFOOT
CROWNING
DIOCESAN
DIOGENES
DIONYSUS
DIOPTRIC
DOOLALLY
DOOMSDAY
DOORBELL
DOORKNOB
DOORPOST
DOORSTEP
DROOPING
DROPHEAD
DROPPING
DROPSHOT
DROWNING
DROWSILY
DUODENAL
DUODENUM
ECOFREAK
ECONOMIC
EGOISTIC
EGOMANIA
ELONGATE
ELOQUENT
ENORMITY
ENORMOUS
ESOTERIC
EXOCRINE
EXORCISM
EXORCIST
EXORCIZE
EXORDIUM
FLOATING
FLOGGING
FLOODING
FLOODLIT
FLOORING
FLORENCE
FLOTILLA
FLOUNCED
FLOUNDER
FLOURISH
FOOLSCAP
FOOTBALL
FOOTFALL
FOOTHOLD
FOOTLING
FOOTNOTE
FOOTPATH
FOOTREST
FOOTSORE
FOOTSTEP
FOOTWEAR
FOOTWORK
FRONDEUR
FRONTAGE
FRONTIER
FRONTMAN
FROSTILY
FROSTING
GAOLBIRD
GEODESIC
GEOMANCY
GEOMETER
GEOMETRY
GEOPHONE
GEORGIAN
GEOTAXIS
GHOULISH
GIOCONDA
GIOVANNI
GLOAMING
GLOATING
GLOBALLY
GLOBULAR
GLOBULIN
GLOOMILY
GLORIANA
GLORIOLE
GLORIOUS
GLOSSARY
GLOSSEME
GLOXINIA
GOODNESS
GOODSIRE
GOODWIFE
GOODWILL
GOODWOOD
GOODYEAR
GOOFBALL
GOOSEGOG
GROGGILY
GROOMING
GROSBEAK
GROSCHEN
GROUNDED
GROUPING
GROUTING
GROWLING
HOODWINK
HOOKWORM
HOOLIGAN
IDOLATER
IDOLATRY
IRONCLAD
IRONICAL
IRONSIDE
IRONWARE
IRONWOOD
IRONWORK
IROQUOIS
ISOGLOSS
ISOGONAL
ISOLATED
ISOSTASY
ISOTHERE
ISOTHERM
IVOIRIEN
JEOPARDY
KLONDIKE
KNOBLESS
KNOCKERS
KNOCKING
KNOCKOUT
KNOTWEED
KNOTWORK
KROMESKY
LEONARDO
LEONIDAS
LOOPHOLE
LOOSEBOX
MOONBEAM
MOORCOCK
MOORINGS
MOORLAND
MYOBLAST
MYOSOTIS
NEOMYCIN
NEOPHYTE
NOONTIME
ODOMETER
OPOPANAX
OTOSCOPE
PHONETIC
PHORMIUM
PHOSGENE
PHOTOFIT
PHOTOPSY
PLOTINUS
PLOUGHED
POOLROOM
POORNESS
PROBABLE
PROBABLY
PROCEEDS
PROCLAIM
PROCURER
PRODIGAL
PRODUCER
PRODUCES
PRODUCTS
PROFORMA
PROFOUND
PROFUSER
PROGERIA
PROGRESS
PROHIBIT
PROLAPSE
PROLIFIC
PROLOGUE
PROMISED
PROMOTER
PROMPTER
PROMPTLY
PROPERLY
PROPERTY
PROPHECY
PROPHESY
PROPOSAL
PROPOSED
PROPOSER
PROPOUND
PROROGUE
PROSPECT
PROSPERO
PROSTATE
PROTEASE
PROTÉGÉE
PROTOCOL
PROTOZOA
PROTRUDE
PROVABLE
PROVERBS
PROVIDED
PROVIDER
PROVINCE
PTOMAINE
PYORRHEA
QUOTABLE
QUOTIENT
REORIENT
RHOMBOID
RHONCHUS
ROOFLESS
ROOFTOPS
ROOMMATE
ROOTLESS
SCOFFING
SCOLDING
SCORCHED
SCORCHER
SCORNFUL
SCORPION
SCOTLAND
SCOTSMAN
SCOTTISH
SCOURING
SCOWLING
SHOCKING
SHODDILY
SHOEHORN
SHOELACE
SHOELESS
SHOETREE
SHOOTING
SHOOTOUT
SHOPPING
SHOPTALK
SHORTAGE
SHOULDER
SHOUTING
SHOWBOAT
SHOWCASE
SHOWDOWN
SHOWGIRL
SHOWROOM
SLOBBERY
SLOPPILY
SLOTHFUL
SLOVAKIA
SLOVENIA
SLOVENLY
SLOWDOWN
SLOWNESS
SLOWPOKE
SMOCKING
SMOLLETT
SMOOTHER
SMOOTHLY
SMOULDER
SNOBBERY
SNOBBISH
SNOOTILY
SNORTING
SNOWBALL
SNOWDROP
SNOWFALL
SNOWLINE
SOOTHING
SOOTHSAY
SPOILAGE
SPOILING
SPOLIATE
SPOONFUL
SPORADIC
SPORTING
SPORTIVE
SPOTLESS
SPOTTING
STOCCATA
STOCKADE
STOCKCAR
STOCKING
STOCKIST
STOCKMAN
STOCKPOT
STOICISM
STOKESAY
STOLIDLY
STOPCOCK
STOPOVER
STOPPAGE
STOPPING
STOREMAN
STOREYED
STORMING
STORMONT
STOWAWAY
THOMPSON
THORACIC
THOROUGH
THOUGHTS
THOUSAND
TROCHAIC
TROCHLEA
TROLLOPE
TROMBONE
TROOPING
TROPICAL
TROTTERS
TROTTOIR
TROUBLED
TROUBLES
TROUNCER
TROUSERS
TWOPENNY
TWOPIECE
UDOMETER
UXORIOUS
VIOLATOR
VIOLENCE
WHODUNIT
WHOOPING
WHOPPING
WOODBINE
WOODCOCK

WOODENLY
WOODLAND
WOODSHED
WOODSMAN
WOODWARD
WOODWIND
WOODWORK
WOODWORM
WOOLLENS
WOOLPACK
WOOLSACK
WRONGFUL
YEOMANRY
ZOONOSIS
ZOOPHYTE
ZOOSPERM
ZOOSPORE
ALPHABET
ALPINIST
AMPERAGE
AMPUTATE
APPALLED
APPANAGE
APPARENT
APPELANT
APPENDIX
APPETITE
APPLAUSE
APPLETON
APPLIQUÉ
APPOSITE
APPRAISE
APPRISED
APPROACH
APPROVAL
APPROVED
ARPEGGIO
ASPERGES
ASPERITY
ASPHODEL
ASPHYXIA
ASPIRANT
ASPIRATE
ASPIRING
BAPTISED
CAPACITY
CAPERING
CAPITALS
CAPRIOLE
CAPSICUM
CAPSIZED
CAPSTONE
CAPTIOUS
CAPUCHIN
CAPYBARA
COPULATE
COPYBOOK
COPYHOLD
CUPBOARD
CUPIDITY
DEPARTED
DEPILATE
DEPORTEE
DEPRAVED
DEPRIVED
DEPUTIZE
DIPHENYL
DIPLOMAT
DIPSTICK
DIPTERAL
DOPAMINE
EMPHASIS
EMPHATIC
EMPLOYED
EMPLOYEE
EMPLOYER
EMPORIUM
EMPYREAN
ESPALIER
ESPECIAL
ESPOUSAL
ESPRESSO
EUPEPSIA
EUPHONIA
EUPHONIC
EUPHORIA
EUPHORIC
EUPHUISM
EXPECTED
EXPEDITE
EXPENDED
EXPENSES
EXPLICIT
EXPLODED
EXPLORER
EXPONENT
EXPORTER
EXPOSURE
EXPRESSO
HAPSBURG
HEPATICA
HEPTAGON
HEPTARCH
HIPSTERS
HOPELESS
HOPFIELD
HYPERION
HYPNOSIS
HYPNOTIC
IMPACTED
IMPAIRED
IMPELLED
IMPERIAL
IMPETIGO
IMPLICIT
IMPOLITE
IMPORTER
IMPOSING
IMPOSTER
IMPOSTOR
IMPOTENT
IMPRISON
IMPROPER
IMPROVED
IMPROVER
IMPUDENT
IMPUNITY
IMPURIFY
IMPURITY
JAPANESE
JAPONICA
JEPHTHAH
KIPPERED
KYPHOSIS
LAPIDARY
LAPIDATE
LIPSTICK
LOPSIDED
LUPERCAL
NAPOLEON
NEPALESE
NEPENTHE
NEPHRITE
NEPIONIC
NEPOTISM
NUPTIALS
OMPHALOS
OOPHORON
OPPONENT
OPPOSING
OPPOSITE
ORPHANED
ORPIMENT
OXPECKER
PAPILLON
PEPERONI
PIPELINE
PIPERINE
POPINJAY
POPPADOM
POPSICLE
POPULACE
POPULATE
POPULIST
POPULOUS
RAPACITY
RAPECAKE
RAPIDITY
REPAIRER
REPARTEE
REPAYING
REPEATED
REPEATER
REPHRASE
REPLEVIN
REPORTED
REPORTER
REPOUSSÉ
REPRIEVE
REPRISAL
REPROACH
REPUBLIC
RIPARIAN
RIPENESS
RIPPLING
SAPONITE
SAPPHIRE
SAPPHIST
SEPARATE
SUPERBLY
SUPERIOR
SUPERMAN
SUPERNAL
SUPERTAX
SUPPLANT
SUPPLIER
SUPPLIES
SUPPOSED
SUPPRESS
SYPHILIS
TAPENADE
TAPERING
TAPESTRY
TAPEWORM
TAPHOUSE
TIPSTAFF
TOPCLASS
TOPHEAVY
TOPLEVEL
TOPNOTCH
TOPOLOGY
TUPAMARO
TUPPENNY
TYPECAST
TYPEFACE
UNPERSON
UNPLACED
UPPERCUT
VAPORIZE
VIPEROUS
ZEPHYRUS
ZEPPELIN
ACQUAINT
ACQUIRED
ACQUIRER
ARQUEBUS
BEQUEATH
COQUETRY
COQUETTE
INQUIRER
MAQUETTE
MOQUETTE
PIQUANCY
REQUIRED
SEQUENCE
TEQUILLA
AARDVARK
ABRASION
ABRASIVE
ABRIDGED
ABROGATE
ABRUPTLY
ACRIMONY
ACROMION
ACROSTIC
ADRIATIC
ADROITLY
AEROBICS
AERODYNE
AEROFLOT
AEROFOIL
AEROGRAM
AEROLITH
AERONAUT
AEROSTAT
AGRARIAN
AGREEING
AGRICOLA
AGRIMONY
AGRONOMY
AIRBORNE
AIRBRAKE
AIRCRAFT
AIREDALE
AIRFIELD
AIRINESS
AIRLINER
AIRPLANE
AIRSCREW
AIRSPEED
AIRSTRIP
AIRTIGHT
AIRWAVES
AMRITSAR
ARRANGER
ARRESTED
ARRESTER
ARROGANT
ARROGATE
ATROCITY
AURELIAN
AYRSHIRE
BARABBAS
BARATHEA
BARBADOS
BARBARIC
BARBECUE
BARBICAN
BARBIZON
BARDOLPH
BAREBACK
BAREFOOT
BARENESS
BARGELLO
BARGEMAN
BARITONE
BARNABAS
BARNACLE
BARNARDS
BARNYARD
BARONESS
BARONETS
BARONIAL
BARRACKS
BARRATRY
BARRETTE
BARTERED
BERBERIS
BERCEUSE
BEREAVED
BERGAMOT
BERGERAC
BERIBERI
BERKELEY
BERTRAND
BIRDCAGE
BIRDSEED
BIRTHDAY
BORACITE
BORDEAUX
BORDELLO
BORDERER
BORECOLE
BOREHOLE
BORODINO
BORROWED
BORROWER
BORSTALL
BURBERRY
BURDENED
BURGLARY
BURGRAVE
BURGUNDY
BURNTOUT
BURROWER
BURSITIS
BURSTING
CARABINE
CARACOLE
CARAPACE
CARBOLIC
CARBONIC

CARCAJOU
CARCANET
CARDAMOM
CARDIGAN
CARDINAL
CAREFREE
CARELESS
CAREWORN
CARILLON
CARJACOU
CARNEGIE
CARNIVAL
CAROLINA
CAROLINE
CAROTENE
CAROUSAL
CAROUSEL
CARRAWAY
CARRIAGE
CARRIOLE
CARRYALL
CARRYCOT
CARRYING
CARTHAGE
CARTLOAD
CARUCATE
CARYATID
CERAMICS
CERATOID
CERBERUS
CEREBRAL
CEREBRUM
CEREMENT
CEREMONY
CERULEAN
CERVELAT
CERVICAL
CHRISTEN
CHRISTIE
CHRISTOM
CHROMITE
CHROMIUM
CIRCULAR
CORDOVAN
CORDUROY
CORDWAIN
CORIOLIS
CORMORAN
CORNETTO
CORNHILL
CORNICHE
CORNWALL
CORONARY
CORONOID
CORPORAL
CORRAGIO
CORRIDOR
CORRODED
CORSELET
CORSICAN
CORVETTE
CURATIVE
CURLICUE
CURRENCY
CURRICLE
CURSITOR
CURTAINS
CURTNESS
CYRENIAC
CYRILLIC
DARKENED
DARKNESS
DARKROOM
DARTMOOR
DERANGED
DERELICT
DERISION
DERISIVE
DERISORY
DEROGATE
DIRECTLY
DIRECTOR
DORMOUSE
DURABLES
DURATION
EARLIEST
EARNINGS
EARPHONE
EARPIECE
EERINESS
ENRICHED
ETRURIAN
ETRUSCAN
EURASIAN
EUROLAND
EUROPEAN
EUROSTAR
EURYDICE
FARCICAL
FAREWELL
FARMHAND
FARMLAND
FARMYARD
FAROUCHE
FARRIERY
FARTHEST
FARTHING
FEROCITY
FERRYMAN
FIREARMS
FIREBACK
FIREBALL
FIREBIRD
FIREBOLT
FIREDAMP
FIRESIDE
FIRESTEP
FIRETRAP
FIREWEED
FIREWOOD
FIREWORK
FIRMNESS
FORCEFUL
FORCIBLE
FORCIBLY
FOREBEAR
FOREBODE
FORECAST
FOREDECK
FOREDOOM
FOREFOOT
FOREGONE
FOREHAND
FOREHEAD
FORELAND
FORELOCK
FOREMOST
FORENAME
FORENOON
FORENSIC
FORESAIL
FORESHIP
FORESKIN
FORESTAY
FORESTER
FORESTRY
FORETELL
FOREWARN
FOREWORD
FORFEITS
FORKLIFT
FORKTAIL
FORMALIN
FORMALLY
FORMERLY
FORMLESS
FORMOSAN
FORSAKEN
FORSLACK
FORSOOTH
FORSWEAR
FORTIETH
FORTRESS
FORTUITY
FORWARDS
FURBELOW
FURLOUGH
FURROWED
FURTHEST
FURUNCLE
GARAMOND
GARDENER
GARDENIA
GARDYLOO
GARGANEY
GARGOYLE
GARISHLY
GARLICKY
GARMENTS
GARRIGUE
GARRISON
GARROTTE
GERANIUM
GERMAINE
GERMANIC
GERMINAL
GERONIMO
GERTRUDE
GIRASOLE
GIRLHOOD
GIRONDIN
GORGEOUS
GORMLESS
GURDWARA
GYRATION
GYRATORY
GYROSTAT
HARANGUE
HARASSED
HARDBACK
HARDCORE
HARDENED
HARDLINE
HARDNESS
HARDSHIP
HARDTACK
HARDWARE
HARDWOOD
HAREBELL
HARFLEUR
HARMLESS
HARMONIC
HARRIDAN
HARRISON
HARTFORD
HARUSPEX
HERACLES
HERACLID
HERALDIC
HERALDRY
HERCULES
HERDSMAN
HEREDITY
HEREFORD
HEREWARD
HEREWITH
HERITAGE
HERMETIC
HERMIONE
HERPETIC
HERSCHEL
HIRAGANA
HIRELING
HORATIAN
HORATIUS
HORLICKS
HORMONAL
HORNBEAM
HORNBILL
HORNBOOK
HORNPIPE
HOROLOGY
HORRIBLE
HORRIBLY
HORRIFIC
HORSEBOX
HORSEFLY
HORSEMAN
HORSEMEN
HURDLING
IRRIGATE
IRRITANT
IRRITATE
JEREBOAM
JEREMIAD
JEREMIAH
JEROBOAM
JERRYCAN
JORROCKS
JURASSIC
JURATORY
KERCHIEF
KERMESSE
KEROSENE
KORRIGAN
LARGESSE
LARKSPUR
LAROUSSE
LORDOSIS
LORDSHIP
LORRAINE
LYREBIRD
LYRICISM
LYRICIST
MARABOUT
MARASMUS
MARATHON
MARAUDER
MARCELLA
MARCELLO
MARGARET
MARGINAL
MARGRAVE
MARIACHI
MARIANAS
MARIGOLD
MARINADE
MARINATE
MARITIME
MARJORAM
MARKDOWN
MARKEDLY
MARKSMAN
MARMOSET
MARONITE
MARQUESA
MARQUESS
MARQUISE
MARRIAGE
MARSHALL
MARTELLO
MARTINET
MARTYRED
MARYLAND
MARZIPAN
MERCALLI
MERCATOR
MERCEDES
MERCHANT
MERCIFUL
MEREDITH
MERIDIAN
MERINGUE
MERISTEM
MIREPOIX
MIRLITON
MIRRORED
MIRTHFUL
MORALIST
MORALITY
MORALIZE
MORAVIAN
MORBIDLY
MORBILLI
MOREOVER
MORIBUND
MOROCCAN
MOROSELY
MORPHEME
MORPHEUS
MORPHINE
MORRISON
MORTALLY
MORTGAGE
MORTIMER
MORTUARY
MURDERER
MYRIAPOD
MYRMIDON
NARCOSES
NARCOSIS
NARCOTIC

NARGILEH
NARRATOR
NARROWLY
NORMALLY
NORMANDY
NORSEMAN
NORSEMEN
NORTHERN
NURSLING
PARABOLA
PARADIGM
PARADISE
PARAFFIN
PARAGUAY
PARAKEET
PARALLAX
PARALLEL
PARALYZE
PARAMOUR
PARANOIA
PARANOID
PARAQUAT
PARASITE
PARDONER
PARENTAL
PARIETAL
PARISIAN
PARKLAND
PARLANCE
PARMESAN
PARODIST
PAROLLES
PAROXYSM
PARSIFAL
PARTERRE
PARTHIAN
PARTICLE
PARTISAN
PARTTIME
PERACUTE
PERCEIVE
PERCEVAL
PERCIVAL
PERFECTA
PERFECTO
PERFORCE
PERFUMED
PERIANTH
PERICARP
PERICLES
PERIDERM
PERILOUS
PERIODIC
PERIPETY
PERISHED
PERISHER
PERJURED
PERJURER
PERMEATE
PEROXIDE
PERSHING
PERSONAL
PERSPIRE
PERSUADE
PERSUANT
PERTNESS
PERUVIAN
PERVERSE
PERVIOUS
PHREATIC
PHRYGIAN
PIRANESI
PIROZHKI
POROSITY
PORPHYRA
PORPHYRY
PORPOISE
PORRIDGE
PORTABLE
PORTHOLE
PORTIÈRE
PORTLAND
PORTRAIT
PORTUGAL
PURBLIND
PURCHASE
PURIFIED
PURIFIER
PURLIEUS
PURPLISH
PURSLANE
PURULENT
PURVEYOR
PYRAMIDS
PYRENEES
PYRIFORM
RAREFIED
SARABAND
SARATOGA
SARDINIA
SARDONIC
SARDONYX
SARGASSO
SCRABBLE
SCRAMBLE
SCRAPPLE
SCRATCHY
SCRAWLED
SCREAMER
SCREENED
SCREWTOP
SCRIABIN
SCRIBBLE
SCRIBBLY
SCRIPTUM
SCROFULA
SCROUNGE
SCRUBBER
SCRUPLES
SCRUTINY
SERAFILE
SERAGLIO
SERAPHIC
SERAPHIM
SERENADE
SERENATA
SERENELY
SERENITY
SERGEANT
SERIATIM
SERJEANT
SEROLOGY
SEROTYPE
SERRATED
SERVICES
SERVIENT
SERVITOR
SHRAPNEL
SHREDDER
SHREWDLY
SHREWISH
SHROUDED
SHRUNKEN
SIRENIAN
SORBONNE
SORCERER
SORDIDLY
SORENESS
SORORITY
SPRAINED
SPRAWLED
SPREADER
SPRINGER
SPRINKLE
SPRINTER
SPRITELY
SPRITZER
SPROCKET
SPRUCELY
SPRYNESS
STRABISM
STRACHEY
STRADDLE
STRAGGLE
STRAGGLY
STRAIGHT
STRAINED
STRAINER
STRAITEN
STRANDED
STRANGER
STRANGLE
STRAPPED
STRAPPER
STRATEGY
STRATIFY
STREAKED
STREAKER
STREAMER
STRENGTH
STRESSED
STRETCHY
STRIATED
STRIATUM
STRICKEN
STRICTLY
STRIDENT
STRIKING
STRINGED
STRINGER
STRIPPED
STRIPPER
STRIVING
STROLLER
STRONGLY
STRUGGLE
STRUMPET
SURENESS
SURFBOAT
SURGICAL
SURMOUNT
SURPLICE
SURPRISE
SURROUND
SURVEYOR
SURVIVAL
SURVIVOR
SYRACUSE
SYRINGES
TARBOOSH
TARRAGON
TARTARIC
TARTARUS
TARTNESS
TARTRATE
TARTUFFE
TERATOMA
TERIYAKI
TERMINAL
TERMINUS
TERRACED
TERRAPIN
TERRIBLE
TERRIBLY
TERRIFIC
TERTIARY
TERYLENE
THRACIAN
THRALDOM
THRASHER
THREATEN
THRENODY
THRESHER
THRILLER
THROMBIN
THROMBUS
THROTTLE
THRUSTER
TIRAMISU
TIRELESS
TIRESIAS
TIRESOME
TOREADOR
TORTILLA
TORTOISE
TORTUOUS
TORTURED
TORTURER
TURANDOT
TURBANED
TURBOJET
TURGENEV
TURGIDLY
TURKOMAN
TURMERIC
TURNBACK
TURNCOAT
TURNCOCK
TURNOVER
TURNPIKE
TURNSPIT
TURRETED
TYROLEAN
TYROSINE
UNREASON
UPRIGHTS
UPRISING
VARIABLE
VARIANCE
VARICOSE
VARIETAL
VARIFORM
VARIORUM
VERACITY
VERANDAH
VERBALLY
VERBATIM
VERBIAGE
VERDERER
VERJUICE
VERLAINE
VERMOUTH
VERONESE
VERONICA
VERSICLE
VERTEBRA
VERTICAL
VIREMENT
VIRGINAL
VIRGINIA
VIRILITY
VIROLOGY
VIRTUOSI
VIRTUOSO
VIRTUOUS
VIRULENT
VORACITY
WARDRESS
WARDROBE
WARDROOM
WARDSHIP
WARFARIN
WARHORSE
WARINESS
WARPAINT
WARPLANE
WARRANTY
WEREWOLF
WIRELESS
WIREWORM
WORDBOOK
WORDLESS
WORKABLE
WORKADAY
WORKBOOK
WORKINGS
WORKLOAD
WORKMATE
WORKROOM
WORKSHOP
WORMCAST
WORMWOOD
WORRYING
WORTHIES
WORTHILY
XERAPHIM
YARMULKA
YERSINIA
ZARZUELA
ZIRCONIA
AASVOGEL
ABSCISSA
ABSENTEE
ABSINTHE
ABSOLUTE
ABSOLVED
ABSORBED
ABSORBER
ABSTRACT
ABSTRUSE
ABSURDLY
AESTHETE

ALSATIAN
ANSERINE
ARSONIST
ASSASSIN
ASSEMBLE
ASSEMBLY
ASSESSOR
ASSIGNEE
ASSORTED
ASSUMING
ASSYRIAN
AUSPICES
AUSTRIAN
BASEBALL
BASEBORN
BASELESS
BASELINE
BASEMENT
BASENESS
BASIDIUM
BASILICA
BASILISK
BASINFUL
BASKETRY
BASSINET
BASTILLE
BESIEGED
BESMIRCH
BESOTTED
BESOUGHT
BESPOKEN
BESSEMER
BESTIARY
BESTOWER
BESTRIDE
BISCAYAN
BISEXUAL
BISMARCK
BOSWORTH
BUSINESS
BUSTLING
BUSYBODY
CASANOVA
CASEMATE
CASEMENT
CASHMERE
CASSETTE
CASTANET
CASTAWAY
CASTOFFS
CASTRATE
CASTRATO
CASUALLY
CASUALTY
CESSPOOL
COSINESS
COSMETIC
COSTMARY
CUSPIDOR
CUSTOMER
CYSTITIS
DASHWOOD
DESCRIBE
DESELECT
DESERTED
DESERTER
DESERVED
DESIGNER
DESIROUS
DESOLATE
DESPATCH
DESPOTIC
DESTINED
DESTRUCT
DISABLED
DISABUSE
DISAGREE
DISALLOW
DISARRAY
DISASTER
DISBURSE
DISCIPLE
DISCLAIM
DISCLOSE
DISCOLOR
DISCOUNT
DISCOVER
DISCREET
DISCRETE
DISEASED
DISFAVOR
DISGORGE
DISGRACE
DISGUISE
DISHEVEL
DISHONOR
DISINTER
DISKETTE
DISLIKED
DISLODGE
DISLOYAL
DISMALLY
DISMAYED
DISMOUNT
DISORDER
DISPATCH
DISPENSE
DISPERSE
DISPIRIT
DISPLACE
DISPOSAL
DISPOSED
DISPROVE
DISPUTED
DISQUIET
DISRAELI
DISSOLVE
DISSUADE
DISTANCE
DISTASTE
DISTINCT
DISTRACT
DISTRAIN
DISTRAIT
DISTRESS
DISTRICT
DISTRUST
DISUNION
DISUNITE
DISUNITY
DYSLEXIA
DYSLEXIC
EASEMENT
EASINESS
EASTERLY
EASTLAKE
EASTWARD
ECSTASIS
ECSTATIC
ELSINORE
ENSCONCE
ENSEMBLE
ENSHRINE
ENSHROUD
ENSIFORM
ENSILAGE
ESSAYIST
EUSTATIC
FASCICLE
FASTBACK
FASTENER
FASTNESS
FESTIVAL
FISHBONE
FISHCAKE
FISHMEAL
FISHPOND
FISHWIFE
FUSAROLE
FUSELAGE
FUSEWIRE
FUSIFORM
FUSILIER
GASOLIER
GASOLINE
GASTRULA
GASWORKS
GESTURES
GOSSAMER
GUSSETED
HASTINGS
HESITANT
HESITATE
HISPANIC
HISTORIC
HOSEPIPE
HOSPITAL
HOSTELRY
HUSHHUSH
HUSTINGS
HYSTERIA
HYSTERIC
INSANELY
INSANITY
INSCRIBE
INSECURE
INSIGNIA
INSOLENT
INSOMNIA
INSPIRED
INSPIRIT
INSTANCE
INSTINCT
INSTRUCT
INSULATE
JUSTNESS
KESTEVEN
LASHINGS
LISTENER
LISTERIA
LISTLESS
LUSCIOUS
LUSHNESS
LUSTRINE
LUSTROUS
LYSANDER
LYSERGIC
MASCARON
MASSACRE
MASSENET
MASSEUSE
MASSICOT
MASTERLY
MASTHEAD
MASTODON
MESCALIN
MESMERIC
MESOLITE
MESSAGER
MESSIDOR
MESSMATE
MESSUAGE
MISAPPLY
MISCARRY
MISCHIEF
MISCOUNT
MISERERE
MISGUIDE
MISHMASH
MISJUDGE
MISMATCH
MISNOMER
MISOGYNY
MISPLACE
MISPRINT
MISQUOTE
MISSOURI
MISSPELL
MISSPENT
MISTAKEN
MISTREAT
MISTRESS
MISTRUST
MOSQUITO
MUSCADET
MUSCATEL
MUSCULAR
MUSHROOM
MUSICIAN
MUSQUASH
MUSTACHE
MYSTICAL
MYSTIQUE
NESCIENT
NESTLING
NOSEBAND
NOSEDIVE
NOSOLOGY
NOSTRILS
NOSTROMO
OBSCURED
OBSERVED
OBSERVER
OBSESSED
OBSIDIAN
OBSOLETE
OBSTACLE
OBSTRUCT
ONSCREEN
PASHMINA
PASSABLE
PASSABLY
PASSBOOK
PASSERBY
PASSIBLE
PASSOVER
PASSPORT
PASSWORD
PASTICHE
PASTILLE
PASTORAL
PASTRAMI
PASTURES
PISCATOR
PISSHEAD
POSEIDON
POSITION
POSITIVE
POSITRON
POSOLOGY
POSSIBLE
POSSIBLY
POSTCARD
POSTCODE
POSTDATE
POSTMARK
POSTPAID
POSTPONE
PUSHBIKE
PUSHCART
PUSHOVER
PUSSYCAT
PUSTULAR
RASCALLY
RASHNESS
RASPUTIN
RASSELAS
RESEARCH
RESEMBLE
RESERVED
RESETTLE
RESIDENT
RESIDUAL
RESIDUUM
RESIGNED
RESINOUS
RESISTOR
RESOLUTE
RESOLVED
RESONANT
RESONATE
RESOURCE
RESPECTS
RESPIGHI
RESPONSE
RESTLESS
RESTORER
RESTRAIN
RESTRICT
RESTROOM
RISSOLES
ROSALIND
ROSALINE
ROSAMOND
ROSEMARY
ROSEWOOD
ROSINESS
ROSSETTI
RUSHMORE
RUSTLESS
RUSTLING
SASSANID

SISTERLY
SISYPHUS
SUSPENSE
SYSTEMIC
TASHKENT
TASMANIA
TASTEFUL
TESTATOR
TESTATUM
TESTICLE
TUSITALA
UNSALTED
UNSAVORY
UNSEALED
UNSEEDED
UNSEEMLY
UNSETTLE
UNSHAKEN
UNSIGNED
UNSOCIAL
UNSOLVED
UNSPOILT
UNSPOKEN
UNSTABLE
UNSTATED
UNSTEADY
UNSUITED
UPSTAIRS
UPSTREAM
URSULINE
VASCULAR
VASTNESS
VESPERAL
VESPUCCI
VESTIARY
VESTMENT
VESUVIUS
VISCERAL
VISCOUNT
VISELIKE
VISIGOTH
VISITANT
VISITING
VISUALLY
WASHABLE
WASHBOWL
WASHDOWN
WASHROOM
WASTEFUL
WESLEYAN
WESTERLY
WESTWARD
WISEACRE
WISHBONE
WISTERIA
YOSEMITE
ZASTRUGA
ACTINIDE
ACTINIUM
ACTIVATE
ACTIVELY
ACTIVISM
ACTIVIST
ACTIVITY
ACTUALLY
ALTHOUGH
ALTITUDE
ALTRUISM
ALTRUIST
ANTECEDE
ANTEDATE
ANTELOPE
ANTENNAE
ANTEPOST
ANTERIOR
ANTEROOM
ANTIBODY
ANTIDOTE
ANTILLES
ANTILOPE
ANTIMONY
ANTIPHON
ANTIPOPE
AOTEAROA
APTITUDE
ARTEFACT
ARTERIAL
ARTESIAN
ARTFULLY
ARTICLED
ARTICLES
ARTIFACT
ARTIFICE
ARTISTIC
ARTISTRY
ASTATINE
ASTERISK
ASTEROID
ASTHENIA
ASTONISH
ASTUTELY
ATTACHED
ATTACKER
ATTENDER
ATTESTOR
ATTITUDE
ATTORNEY
AUTARCHY
AUTISTIC
AUTOBAHN
AUTOCRAT
AUTOGAMY
AUTOGYRO
AUTOMATE
AUTONOMY
AUTOTYPE
AUTUMNAL
BATAVIAN
BATHETIC
BATHROBE
BATHROOM
BATTERED
BETATRON
BETHESDA
BETJEMAN
BETRAYAL
BETRAYER
BITTERLY
BOTANIST
BOTHERED
BOTHWELL
BOTSWANA
BOTTLING
BOTTOMRY
BOTULISM
BUTCHERS
BUTCHERY
BUTTERED
BUTTOCKS
BUTTRESS
CATACOMB
CATALYST
CATAMITE
CATAPULT
CATARACT
CATATONY
CATCHING
CATEGORY
CATERING
CATHEDRA
CATHETER
CATHOLIC
CATHOUSE
CATILINE
CATSMEAT
CATTLEYA
CATULLUS
CETACEAN
CITATION
COTOPAXI
COTSWOLD
COTTAGER
CUTENESS
CUTHBERT
CUTPRICE
CUTPURSE
CUTWATER
CYTOLOGY
DATABASE
DATELESS
DATELINE
DETACHED
DETAILED
DETAINEE
DETAINER
DETECTOR
DETHRONE
DETONATE
DETRITUS
DOTTEREL
DUTCHMAN
DUTIABLE
DUTYFREE
EATABLES
ECTODERM
ENTANGLE
ENTHRALL
ENTHRONE
ENTICING
ENTIRELY
ENTIRETY
ENTITLED
ENTRAILS
ENTRANCE
ENTREATY
ENTRENCH
ENTREPOT
ENTRYISM
ESTANCIA
ESTEEMED
ESTHETIC
ESTIMATE
ESTIVATE
ESTONIAN
ESTOPPEL
ESTOVERS
ESTRAGON
ESTROGEN
EUTROPHY
EUTROPIC
EXTENDED
EXTENSOR
EXTERIOR
EXTERNAL
EXTERNAT
EXTRADOS
FATALISM
FATALIST
FATALITY
FATHERLY
FATIGUED
FATIGUES
FATSTOCK
FETCHING
FITFULLY
FUTILITY
FUTURISM
FUTURIST
GATEPOST
GATHERED
GUTTURAL
HATCHERY
HATCHING
HATCHWAY
HATHAWAY
HATTERAS
HETAIRIA
HITHERTO
HOTELIER
HOTHOUSE
HOTPLATE
INTAGLIO
INTEGRAL
INTELSAT
INTENDED
INTENTLY
INTERACT
INTERCOM
INTEREST
INTERIOR
INTERMIT
INTERNAL
INTERNEE
INTERNET
INTERPOL
INTERVAL
INTIFADA
INTIMACY
INTIMATE
INTRADOS
INTRENCH
INTREPID
INTRIGUE
INTRUDER
ISTANBUL
ISTHMIAN
JETTISON
JOTTINGS
KATAKANA
KATMANDU
KATTEGAT
KITEMARK
LATCHKEY
LATENESS
LATERITE
LATINIST
LATITUDE
LATTERLY
LETHARGY
LETTERED
LITERACY
LITERARY
LITERATE
LITERATI
LITIGANT
LITIGATE
LITTORAL
LOTHARIO
LUTHERAN
MATABELE
MATAMORE
MATCHBOX
MATCHING
MATERIAL
MATERNAL
MATHURIN
MATRONLY
MATTRESS
MATURATE
MATURITY
METABOLA
MÉTAIRIE
METALLED
METALLIC
METAPHOR
METEORIC
METHANOL
METHODIC
METONYMY
METRICAL
METRITIS
MITIGATE
MOTHBALL
MOTHERLY
MOTIVATE
MOTORCAR
MOTORING
MOTORIST
MOTORIZE
MOTORMAN
MOTORWAY
MUTATION
MUTCHKIN
MUTILATE
MUTINEER
MUTINOUS
MUTUALLY
MYTHICAL
NATALITY
NATIONAL
NATIVITY
NATTERED
NATURISM
NATURIST
NITROGEN
NOTARIAL
NOTATION
NOTEBOOK
NOTECASE
NOTIONAL
NUTHATCH
NUTHOUSE

NUTRIENT
NUTSHELL
OBTAINED
OBTUSELY
OCTAROON
ONTOLOGY
OPTICIAN
OPTIMATE
OPTIMISM
OPTIMIST
OPTIONAL
ORTHODOX
OSTERLEY
OTTAVINO
OUTBOARD
OUTBREAK
OUTBURST
OUTCLASS
OUTDATED
OUTDOORS
OUTFIELD
OUTFLANK
OUTGOING
OUTHOUSE
OUTLYING
OUTMATCH
OUTMODED
OUTREACH
OUTREMER
OUTRIDER
OUTRIGHT
OUTSHINE
OUTSIDER
OUTSMART
OUTSTRIP
OUTWARDS
OUTWEIGH
PATCHILY
PATELLAR
PATENTED
PATENTEE
PATENTLY
PATERNAL
PATHETIC
PATHOGEN
PATIENCE
PATULOUS
PETANQUE
PETERLOO
PETITION
PETRARCH
PETULANT
PHTHISIS
PITCAIRN
PITHLESS
PITIABLE
PITILESS
PITTANCE
POTATOES
POTBELLY
POTBOUND
POTEMKIN
POTHOLER
POTLATCH
POTSHERD
PUTATIVE
RATEABLE
RATIONAL
RATTIGAN
RATTLING
RETAILER
RETAINER
RETARDED
RETICENT
RETICULE
RETIRING
RETRENCH
RETRIEVE
RITUALLY
ROTATION
ROTATORY
ROTENONE
RUTABAGA
RUTHLESS
SATIATED
SATIRIST
SATIRIZE
SATURATE
SATURDAY
SATURNIA
SITUATED
TATTERED
TETCHILY
TETRAGON
TETRAPOD
TETRARCH
TITANESS
TITANISM
TITANITE
TITANIUM
TITICACA
TITIVATE
TITMOUSE
TOTALITY
TOTALIZE
TUTELAGE
TUTELARY
TUTORIAL
ULTERIOR
ULTIMATE
UNTANGLE
UNTAPPED
UNTHREAD
UNTIDILY
UNTILLED
UNTIMELY
UNTOWARD
UPTURNED
VITALITY
VITALIZE
VITAMINS
VITELLUS
VITILIGO
VITREOUS
WATCHDOG
WATCHFUL
WATCHING
WATCHMAN
WATERBUG
WATERING
WATERLOO
WATERMAN
WATERWAY
WETLANDS
WITCHERY
WITCHING
WITHDRAW
WITHERED
WITHHOLD
YATAGHAN
ABUNDANT
ABUTILON
ABUTMENT
ADULATOR
ADULTERY
ALUMINUM
AMUNDSEN
AMUSETTE
AQUALUNG
AQUARIUM
AQUARIUS
AQUATINT
AQUEDUCT
AQUILINE
ASUNCION
AVULSION
BAUDRICK
BLUDGEON
BLUEBACK
BLUEBELL
BLUECOAT
BLUENOSE
BLURRING
BLUSHING
BLUSTERY
BOUFFANT
BOUNCING
BOUNDARY
BOUTIQUE
BOUZOUKI
BRUCKNER
BRUISING
BRUMAIRE
BRUNETTE
BRUSSELS
BRUTALLY
CAUDILLO
CAULDRON
CAUSEWAY
CAUTIOUS
CHUMMAGE
CHURLISH
CHUTZPAH
CLUBFOOT
CLUELESS
CLUMSILY
COUCHANT
COUCHING
COUGHING
COUNTESS
COUNTIES
COUNTING
COUPERIN
COUPLING
COURTESY
COUSCOUS
CRUCIATE
CRUCIBLE
CRUCIFER
CRUCIFIX
CRUMHORN
CRUMMOCK
CRUNCHIE
CRUSADER
CRUSHING
CRUTCHED
CRUZEIRO
DAUGHTER
DAUNTING
DIURETIC
DOUBLOON
DOUBTFUL
DOUBTING
DOUGHBOY
DOUGHNUT
DRUBBING
DRUDGERY
DRUGGIST
DRUMBEAT
DRUMHEAD
DRUMLINE
DRUMMING
DRUNKARD
EDUCATED
EDUCATOR
EMULGENT
EMULSIFY
EMULSION
EQUALITY
EQUALIZE
EQUATION
EQUIPAGE
EQUITANT
ERUCTATE
ERUPTION
ERUPTURE
EXULTANT
EXULTING
FAULKNER
FLUENTLY
FLUIDITY
FLUMMERY
FLUORIDE
FLUORINE
FLUORITE
FLUSHING
FOULNESS
FOUNDING
FOUNTAIN
FOURFOLD
FOURPART
FOURSOME
FOURTEEN
FRUCTIFY
FRUCTOSE
FRUGALLY
FRUITFUL
FRUITING
FRUITION
FRUMENTY
FRUMPISH
GAUNTLET
GLUMPISH
GLUTAEUS
GLUTTONY
GOURMAND
GRUDGING
GRUESOME
GRUMBLER
GRUMPILY
HAUNCHES
HAUNTING
HOUSEMAN
INUNDATE
JAUNDICE
JAUNTILY
KOURMISS
KOUSKOUS
LAUDABLE
LAUDABLY
LAUDANUM
LAUGHING
LAUGHTER
LAUREATE
LAURENCE
LEUKEMIA
LOUDNESS
LOUVERED
MEUNIÈRE
MOUFFLON
MOULDING
MOUNTAIN
MOUNTING
MOURNFUL
MOURNING
MOUSSAKA
MOUTHFUL
NAUPLIUS
NAUSEATE
NAUSEOUS
NAUTICAL
NAUTILUS
NEURITIS
NEUROSIS
NEUROTIC
NEUTRINO
OPULENCE
OPUSCULE
PAULINUS
PLUCKILY
PLUCKING
PLUGHOLE
PLUMBAGO
PLUMBING
PLUNGING
PLUTARCH
POULAINE
POULTICE
POUNDAGE
PRUDENCE
PRUNELLA
PRURIENT
PRUSSIAN
REUSABLE
ROUGHAGE
ROULETTE
ROUNDERS
ROUSSEAU
SAUCEPAN
SAUROPOD
SAUSAGES
SCULLERY
SCULLION
SCULPTOR
SHUTDOWN
SHUTTERS
SKULKING
SKULLCAP
SLUGABED
SLUGFEST
SLUGGARD
SLUGGISH

SLUMMING
SLURRING
SLUTTISH
SMUGGLED
SMUGGLER
SMUGNESS
SNUFFBOX
SOUCHONG
SOULLESS
SOUNDING
SOURCING
SOURNESS
SOURPUSS
SOUTHEND
SOUTHERN
SOUTHPAW
SOUVENIR
SPURIOUS
SPURNING
SQUABBLE
SQUADDIE
SQUADRON
SQUAMATA
SQUANDER
SQUARELY
SQUATTER
SQUEAKER
SQUEALER
SQUEEGEE
SQUEEZER
SQUIGGLE
SQUIRREL
STUBBORN
STUCCOED
STUDENTS
STUDIOUS
STUFFILY
STUFFING
STULTIFY
STUNNING
STUPIDLY
STURDILY
STURGEON
TAUTNESS
TEUTONIC
THUMPING
THUNDERY
THURIBLE
THURIFER
THURSDAY
TOUCHING
TOULOUSE
TRUCKING
TRUCKLED
TRUENESS
TRUMPERY
TRUNCATE
TRUNNION
TRUSTFUL
TRUSTING
TRUTHFUL
UNUSABLE
USUFRUCT
USURIOUS
VAULTING
VAUXHALL
YOUNGEST
YOURSELF
YOUTHFUL
ADVANCED
ADVANCER
ADVISORY
ADVOCACY
ADVOCATE
ALVEOLUS
BAVARIAN
BEVERAGE
CAVALIER
CAVATINA
CIVILIAN
CIVILITY
CIVILIZE
COVALENT
COVENANT
COVENTRY
COVERAGE
COVERING
COVERLET
COVETOUS
DAVIDSON
DEVIANCE
DEVILISH
DEVILLED
DEVOTION
DIVIDEND
DIVIDERS
DIVINITY
DIVISION
DIVISIVE
DIVORCED
DIVORCEE
DOVECOTE
DOVETAIL
ENVELOPE
ENVIABLE
ENVIRONS
ENVISAGE
ENVISION
FAVORITE
FAVOURED
FEVERFEW
FEVERISH
GIVEAWAY
GOVERNOR
HAVILDAR
HOVERFLY
INVASION
INVASIVE
INVEIGLE
INVENTED
INVENTOR
INVERTED
INVESTOR
INVITING
INVOLUTE
INVOLVED
JOVIALLY
JUVENILE
LAVATORY
LAVENDER
LAVENGRO
LAVISHLY
LEVELLER
LEVERAGE
LEVITATE
LIVELONG
LIVERIED
LIVERISH
LIVEWARE
LIVIDITY
LOVEBIRD
LOVELACE
LOVELESS
LOVELORN
LOVESICK
LOVINGLY
MAVERICK
MOVEABLE
MOVEMENT
NAVARINO
NAVIGATE
NOVELIST
NOVEMBER
PAVEMENT
PAVILION
PEVENSEY
RAVENOUS
REVANCHE
REVEALED
REVEILLE
REVELLER
REVEREND
REVERENT
REVERSAL
REVERSED
REVIEWER
REVISION
REVIVIFY
REVIVING
REVOLVER
RIVALISE
RIVERAIN
RIVERINE
RIVETING
SAVAGELY
SAVAGERY
SAVANNAH
SAVOURED
SAVOYARD
SEVERELY
SEVEREST
SEVERITY
TAVERNER
TOVARICH
UNVARIED
UNVERSED
UNVOICED
VIVACITY
VIVARIUM
WAVEBAND
WAVERING
WAVERLEY
BEWILDER
BOWSPRIT
COWARDLY
DEWBERRY
DEWYEYED
DOWNBEAT
DOWNCAST
DOWNFALL
DOWNHILL
DOWNLOAD
DOWNPLAY
DOWNPOUR
DOWNSIDE
DOWNSIZE
DOWNTOWN
DOWNTURN
DOWNWARD
HAWAIIAN
HAWFINCH
HAWTHORN
HOWDYEDO
HOWITZER
INWARDLY
JEWELLED
JEWELLER
LAWCOURT
LAWFULLY
LAWMAKER
LAWRENCE
LEWDNESS
LEWISITE
LOWCLASS
LOWERING
LOWLANDS
LOWLYING
NEWCOMER
NEWFOUND
NEWHAVEN
NEWSCAST
NEWSHAWK
NEWSPEAK
NEWSREEL
NEWSROOM
NOWADAYS
PAWNSHOP
POWDERED
POWERFUL
SAWBONES
SEWERAGE
TOWELING
TOWERING
TOWNSHIP
TOWNSMAN
UNWANTED
UNWEANED
UNWIELDY
UNWONTED
UNWORTHY
COXSWAIN
DEXTROSE
DEXTROUS
DOXOLOGY
FIXATION
FIXATIVE
FOXGLOVE
FOXHOUND
HEXAGRAM
LAXATIVE
MAXIMIZE
SAXATILE
SEXOLOGY
SEXUALLY
SIXPENCE
SIXTIETH
TAXATION
TAXONOMY
TAXPAYER
TEXTBOOK
TEXTURED
TOXAEMIA
TOXICITY
TOXOCARA
VEXATION
VEXILLUM
WAXWORKS
AMYGDALA
ANYPLACE
ANYTHING
ANYWHERE
ATYPICAL
BAYREUTH
COYSTRIL
CRYSTALS
DAYBREAK
DAYDREAM
DAYLIGHT
DRYCLEAN
DRYGOODS
DRYSTONE
EGYPTIAN
ERYTHEMA
FLYBLOWN
FLYDRIVE
FLYSHEET
FLYWHEEL
GLYCERIN
GLYCOGEN
GUYANESE
HAYFEVER
HAYFIELD
HAYMAKER
HAYSTACK
HEYTHROP
JOYFULLY
JOYSTICK
KEYBOARD
KEYSTONE
LAYABOUT
LOYALIST
MAYORESS
ODYSSEUS
OLYMPIAD
OLYMPIAN
OLYMPICS
OXYMORON
OXYTOCIN
PAYCHECK
PHYLLOME
PHYSALIA
PHYSICAL
PHYSIQUE
PLYMOUTH
REYNOLDS
RHYTHMIC
ROYALIST
SAYONARA
SCYBALUM
SKYLIGHT
SKYPILOT
SLYBOOTS
SPYGLASS
STYLIZED
TAYBERRY
VOYAGEUR
WAYFARER
BUZZWORD
COZINESS
DAZZLING
GAZPACHO
GAZUNDER

HAZELNUT
HAZINESS
LAZINESS
MAZARINE
NAZARENE
PIZZERIA
PUZZLING
SIZEABLE
SIZZLING
SUZERAIN
WIZARDRY

8:4

ABBASIDE
ABLATION
ABLATIVE
ABRASION
ABRASIVE
ADJACENT
ADVANCED
ADVANCER
AGNATION
AGRARIAN
AKKADIAN
ALBACORE
ALBANIAN
ALCATRAZ
ALEATORY
ALHAMBRA
ALKALIFY
ALKALINE
ALKALOID
ALSATIAN
ANNALIST
ANNAMITE
APIARIST
APPALLED
APPANAGE
APPARENT
AQUALUNG
AQUARIUM
AQUARIUS
AQUATINT
ARBALEST
ARCADIAN
ARKANSAS
ARMAGNAC
ARMALITE
ARMAMENT
ARMATURE
ARRANGER
ASSASSIN
ASTATINE
ATHANASY
ATLANTIC
ATLANTIS
ATTACHED
ATTACKER
AUCASSIN
AUDACITY
AUTARCHY
AVIATION
BAHAMIAN
BALANCED
BANALITY
BARABBAS
BARATHEA
BATAVIAN
BAVARIAN
BECALMED
BEDABBLE
BEHAVIOR
BELABOUR
BETATRON
BIGAMIST
BIGAMOUS
BIGARADE
BLEACHER
BORACITE
BOTANIST
BREACHES
BREAKING
BREAKOUT
BREATHER
BROADWAY
BUDAPEST
CADASTRE
CALABASH
CALAMINE
CALAMITY
CAMARGUE
CANADIAN
CANAILLE
CANALISE
CANARIES
CAPACITY
CARABINE
CARACOLE
CARAPACE
CASANOVA
CATACOMB
CATALYST
CATAMITE
CATAPULT
CATARACT
CATATONY
CAVALIER
CAVATINA
CELANESE
CERAMICS
CERATOID
CETACEAN
CHEATERS
CHEATING
CHIASMUS
CICATRIX
CITATION
CLEANERS
CLEANING
CLEANSED
CLEANSER
CLEARCUT
CLEARING
CLEARWAY
CLEAVAGE
CLEAVERS
COCACOLA
COLANDER
COMATOSE
COVALENT
COWARDLY
CREAMERY
CREATION
CREATIVE
CREATURE
CROATIAN
CURATIVE
DAMASCUS
DATABASE
DECADENT
DECANTER
DECAYING
DELAWARE
DENARIUS
DENATURE
DEPARTED
DERANGED
DETACHED
DETAILED
DETAINEE
DETAINER
DIDACTIC
DILATION
DILATORY
DISABLED
DISABUSE
DISAGREE
DISALLOW
DISARRAY
DISASTER
DONATION
DONATIST
DOPAMINE
DREADFUL
DREAMILY
DREARILY
DURABLES
DURATION
DYNAMICS
DYNAMISM
DYNAMITE
DYNASTIC
DYNATRON
EATABLES
EMBATTLE
EMMANUEL
ENCAENIA
ENCAMPED
ENDANGER
ENGAGING
ENLARGED
ENLARGER
ENTANGLE
EQUALITY
EQUALIZE
EQUATION
ESCALADE
ESCALATE
ESCALOPE
ESCAPADE
ESCAPISM
ESCAPIST
ESCARGOT
ESPALIER
ESSAYIST
ESTANCIA
EURASIAN
EXCAVATE
FATALISM
FATALIST
FATALITY
FEDAYEEN
FILAGREE
FILAMENT
FILARIUM
FINALIST
FINALITY
FINALIZE
FIXATION
FIXATIVE
FLEABITE
FLOATING
FREAKISH
FUMAROLE
FUSAROLE
GADABOUT
GADARENE
GALACTIC
GARAMOND
GELASTIC
GELATINE
GERANIUM
GIGANTIC
GIRASOLE
GLEAMING
GLOAMING
GLOATING
GREATEST
GUIANIAN
GUJARATI
GUYANESE
GYRATION
GYRATORY
HABAKKUK
HABANERA
HARANGUE
HARASSED
HAWAIIAN
HECATOMB
HEPATICA
HERACLES
HERACLID
HERALDIC
HERALDRY
HETAIRIA
HEXAGRAM
HIJACKER
HILARITY
HIRAGANA
HORATIAN
HORATIUS
HUMANELY
HUMANISM
HUMANIST
HUMANITY
HUMANIZE
HYDATOID
IDEALISM
IDEALIST
IDEALIZE
IMMANENT
IMMANUEL
IMMATURE
IMPACTED
IMPAIRED
INFAMOUS
INFANTRY
INHALANT
INSANELY
INSANITY
INTAGLIO
INVASION
INVASIVE
INWARDLY
IOLANTHE
ISLANDER
ISTANBUL
JAMAICAN
JAPANESE
JOHANNES
JONATHAN
JURASSIC
JURATORY
KALAHARI
KATAKANA
LAMASERY
LAVATORY
LAXATIVE
LAYABOUT
LEBANESE
LEGALISM
LEGALITY
LEGALIZE
LEGATION
LIBATION
LIGAMENT
LIGATURE
LOCALITY
LOCALIZE
LOCATION
LOCATIVE
LOYALIST
LYSANDER
MACARONI
MACAROON
MACASSAR
MACAULAY
MAGAZINE
MAHARAJA
MAHARANI
MALAGASY
MALAKOFF
MALARIAL
MALARKEY
MALAWIAN
MALAYSIA
MANAGING
MARABOUT
MARASMUS
MARATHON
MARAUDER
MATABELE
MATAMORE
MAZARINE
MEDALIST
MEGABYTE
MEGALITH
MEGAWATT
MELAMINE
MELANITE
MELANOMA
MENACING
MENANDER
METABOLA
MÉTAIRIE
METALLED
METALLIC
METAPHOR
MILANESE
MINAMATA
MINATORY

MISAPPLY
MOCASSIN
MOHAMMED
MOLASSES
MONADISM
MONARCHY
MONASTIC
MONAURAL
MORALIST
MORALITY
MORALIZE
MORAVIAN
MUHAMMAD
MUTATION
NAGASAKI
NATALITY
NAVARINO
NAZARENE
NDJAMENA
NEGATION
NEGATIVE
NEMATODE
NEMATOID
NEPALESE
NIDATION
NOTARIAL
NOTATION
NOWADAYS
NUGATORY
OBLATION
OBTAINED
OCCAMIST
OCCASION
OCTAROON
OKLAHOMA
OLEACEAE
OLEANDER
ORCADIAN
ORGANDIE
ORGANISM
ORGANIST
ORGANIZE
ORNAMENT
OTTAVINO
PAGANINI
PALATIAL
PALATINE
PANATELA
PARABOLA
PARADIGM
PARADISE
PARAFFIN
PARAGUAY
PARAKEET
PARALLAX
PARALLEL
PARALYZE
PARAMOUR
PARANOIA
PARANOID
PARAQUAT
PARASITE
PEDAGOGY
PEDANTIC
PEDANTRY
PELAGIUS
PENALIZE
PERACUTE
PETANQUE
PHEASANT
PICAROON
PILASTER
PINAFORE
PIRANESI
PLEADING
PLEASANT
PLEASING
PLEASURE
PODARGUS
POLARIZE
POMANDER
POTATOES
PREACHER
PREAMBLE
PRIAPISM
PUTATIVE
PYRAMIDS
RAPACITY
REDACTOR
REGAINED
RELATING
RELATION
RELATIVE
RELAXING
RELAYING
REPAIRER
REPARTEE
REPAYING
RETAILER
RETAINER
RETARDED
REVANCHE
RIBALDRY
RIGATONI
RIPARIAN
RIVALISE
ROGATION
ROMANCER
ROMANIAN
ROMANSCH
ROMANTIC
ROSALIND
ROSALINE
ROSAMOND
ROTATION
ROTATORY
ROYALIST
RUBAIYAT
RUNABOUT
RUTABAGA
SAGACITY
SALACITY
SALARIED
SARABAND
SARATOGA
SAVAGELY
SAVAGERY
SAVANNAH
SAXATILE
SCHAPSKA
SCIATICA
SCRABBLE
SCRAMBLE
SCRAPPLE
SCRATCHY
SCRAWLED
SEDATELY
SEDATION
SEDATIVE
SELASSIE
SEPARATE
SERAFILE
SERAGLIO
SERAPHIC
SERAPHIM
SHEARMAN
SHRAPNEL
SINAPISM
SNEAKERS
SNEAKING
SOCALLED
SODALITE
SODALITY
SOLARIUM
SONATINA
SPEAKERS
SPEAKING
SPHAGNUM
SPLASHER
SPLATTER
SPRAINED
SPRAWLED
SQUABBLE
SQUADDIE
SQUADRON
SQUAMATA
SQUANDER
SQUARELY
SQUATTER
STEADILY
STEALING
STEALTHY
STEATITE
STEATOMA
STRABISM
STRACHEY
STRADDLE
STRAGGLE
STRAGGLY
STRAIGHT
STRAINED
STRAINER
STRAITEN
STRANDED
STRANGER
STRANGLE
STRAPPED
STRAPPER
STRATEGY
STRATIFY
SUDAMENT
SUDAMINA
SUDANESE
SUDARIUM
SWEARING
SWEATING
SYBARITE
SYCAMORE
SYRACUSE
TAMARIND
TAMARISK
TAXATION
TENACITY
TERATOMA
THEATRIC
THIAMINE
THRACIAN
THRALDOM
THRASHER
TIRAMISU
TITANESS
TITANISM
TITANITE
TITANIUM
TOMAHAWK
TOMATOES
TONALITY
TOTALITY
TOTALIZE
TOVARICH
TOXAEMIA
TREASURE
TREASURY
TREATISE
TRIANGLE
TRIASSIC
TUPAMARO
TURANDOT
UNCARING
UNEARNED
UNEASILY
UNFADING
UNFASTEN
UNGAINLY
UNHARMED
UNLAWFUL
UNMANNED
UNMARKED
UNSALTED
UNSAVORY
UNTANGLE
UNTAPPED
UNVARIED
UNWANTED
UPMARKET
URBANITY
URBANIZE
VACANTLY
VACATION
VAGABOND
VAGARIES
VANADIUM
VENALITY
VERACITY
VERANDAH
VEXATION
VICARAGE
VICARIAL
VITALITY
VITALIZE
VITAMINS
VIVACITY
VIVARIUM
VOCALIST
VOCALIZE
VOCATION
VOCATIVE
VOLATILE
VORACITY
VOYAGEUR
WHEATEAR
WIZARDRY
WOMANISH
WOMANIZE
WREATHED
XERAPHIM
YATAGHAN
AIRBORNE
AIRBRAKE
ANABASIS
ANABATIC
BABBLING
BARBADOS
BARBARIC
BARBECUE
BARBICAN
BARBIZON
BERBERIS
BILBERRY
BOBBYPIN
BRABAZON
BRIBABLE
BUBBLING
BUMBLING
BURBERRY
CAMBERED
CAMBODIA
CAMBRIAN
CANBERRA
CARBOLIC
CARBONIC
CERBERUS
CLUBFOOT
COBBLERS
COMBINED
CRIBBAGE
CUPBOARD
DAYBREAK
DEWBERRY
DIABETES
DIABETIC
DIABOLIC
DISBURSE
DJIBOUTI
DOGBERRY
DOUBLOON
DOUBTFUL
DOUBTING
DRIBLETS
DRUBBING
DUMBBELL
DUMBNESS
FLYBLOWN
FOGBOUND
FRABJOUS
FUMBLING
FURBELOW
GALBANUM
GAMBLING
GLABELLA
GLABROUS
GLOBALLY
GLOBULAR
GLOBULIN
HOBBLING
ISABELLA
ISABELLE
JAMBOREE
KEYBOARD
KNOBLESS
LAMBSKIN
LIMBLESS

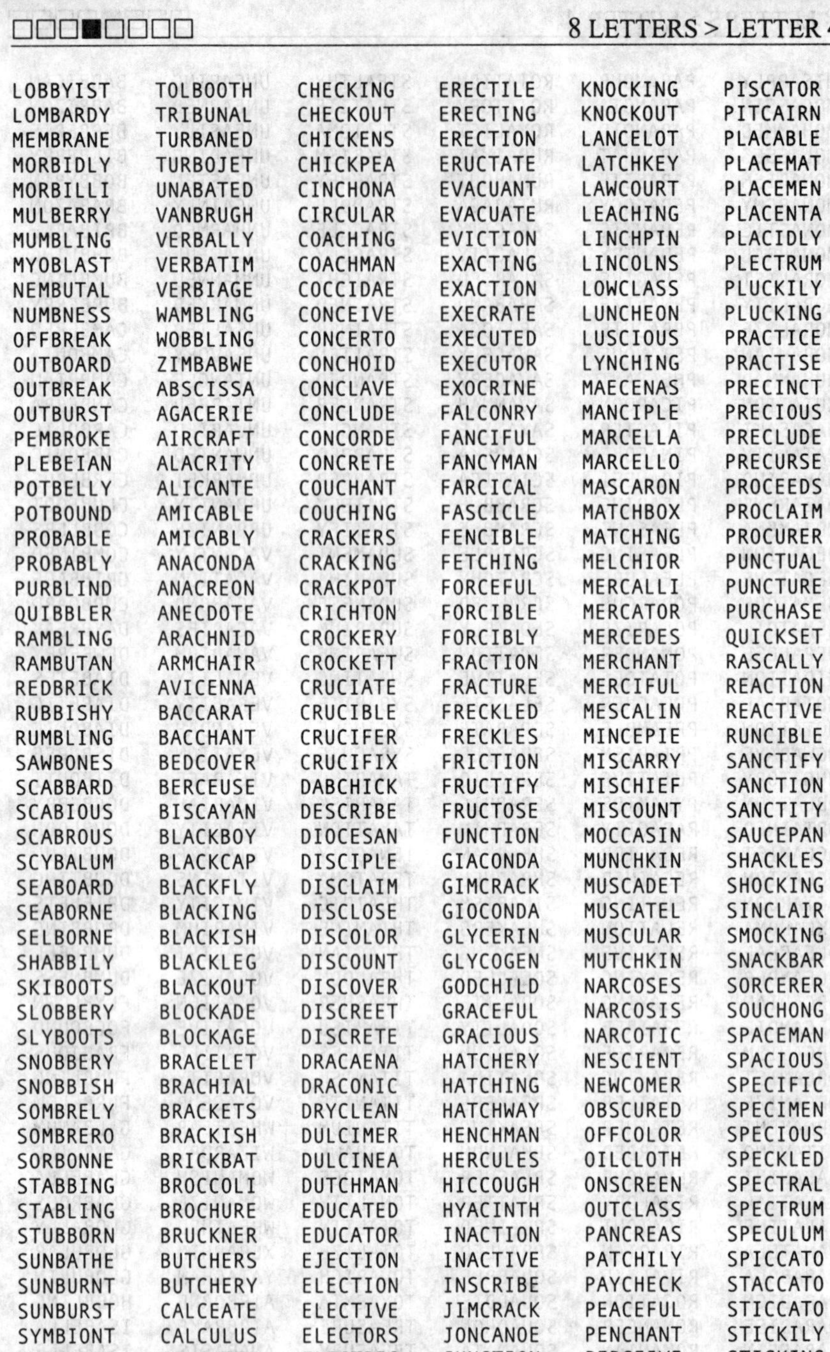

LOBBYIST
LOMBARDY
MEMBRANE
MORBIDLY
MORBILLI
MULBERRY
MUMBLING
MYOBLAST
NEMBUTAL
NUMBNESS
OFFBREAK
OUTBOARD
OUTBREAK
OUTBURST
PEMBROKE
PLEBEIAN
POTBELLY
POTBOUND
PROBABLE
PROBABLY
PURBLIND
QUIBBLER
RAMBLING
RAMBUTAN
REDBRICK
RUBBISHY
RUMBLING
SAWBONES
SCABBARD
SCABIOUS
SCABROUS
SCYBALUM
SEABOARD
SEABORNE
SELBORNE
SHABBILY
SKIBOOTS
SLOBBERY
SLYBOOTS
SNOBBERY
SNOBBISH
SOMBRELY
SOMBRERO
SORBONNE
STABBING
STABLING
STUBBORN
SUNBATHE
SUNBURNT
SUNBURST
SYMBIONT
SYMBOLIC
TABBYCAT
TARBOOSH
TAYBERRY
TIEBREAK
TIMBERED
TOLBOOTH
TRIBUNAL
TURBANED
TURBOJET
UNABATED
VANBRUGH
VERBALLY
VERBATIM
VERBIAGE
WAMBLING
WOBBLING
ZIMBABWE
ABSCISSA
AGACERIE
AIRCRAFT
ALACRITY
ALICANTE
AMICABLE
AMICABLY
ANACONDA
ANACREON
ANECDOTE
ARACHNID
ARMCHAIR
AVICENNA
BACCARAT
BACCHANT
BEDCOVER
BERCEUSE
BISCAYAN
BLACKBOY
BLACKCAP
BLACKFLY
BLACKING
BLACKISH
BLACKLEG
BLACKOUT
BLOCKADE
BLOCKAGE
BRACELET
BRACHIAL
BRACKETS
BRACKISH
BRICKBAT
BROCCOLI
BROCHURE
BRUCKNER
BUTCHERS
BUTCHERY
CALCEATE
CALCULUS
CALCUTTA
CARCAJOU
CARCANET
CATCHING
CHACONNE
CHECKERS
CHECKING
CHECKOUT
CHICKENS
CHICKPEA
CINCHONA
CIRCULAR
COACHING
COACHMAN
COCCIDAE
CONCEIVE
CONCERTO
CONCHOID
CONCLAVE
CONCLUDE
CONCORDE
CONCRETE
COUCHANT
COUCHING
CRACKERS
CRACKING
CRACKPOT
CRICHTON
CROCKERY
CROCKETT
CRUCIATE
CRUCIBLE
CRUCIFER
CRUCIFIX
DABCHICK
DESCRIBE
DIOCESAN
DISCIPLE
DISCLAIM
DISCLOSE
DISCOLOR
DISCOUNT
DISCOVER
DISCREET
DISCRETE
DRACAENA
DRACONIC
DRYCLEAN
DULCIMER
DULCINEA
DUTCHMAN
EDUCATED
EDUCATOR
EJECTION
ELECTION
ELECTIVE
ELECTORS
ELECTRIC
ELECTRON
ELECTRUM
EMACIATE
ENSCONCE
EPICURUS
ERECTILE
ERECTING
ERECTION
ERUCTATE
EVACUANT
EVACUATE
EVICTION
EXACTING
EXACTION
EXECRATE
EXECUTED
EXECUTOR
EXOCRINE
FALCONRY
FANCIFUL
FANCYMAN
FARCICAL
FASCICLE
FENCIBLE
FETCHING
FORCEFUL
FORCIBLE
FORCIBLY
FRACTION
FRACTURE
FRECKLED
FRECKLES
FRICTION
FRUCTIFY
FRUCTOSE
FUNCTION
GIACONDA
GIMCRACK
GIOCONDA
GLYCERIN
GLYCOGEN
GODCHILD
GRACEFUL
GRACIOUS
HATCHERY
HATCHING
HATCHWAY
HENCHMAN
HERCULES
HICCOUGH
HYACINTH
INACTION
INACTIVE
INSCRIBE
JIMCRACK
JONCANOE
JUNCTION
JUNCTURE
KERCHIEF
KNACKERS
KNICKERS
KNOCKERS
KNOCKING
KNOCKOUT
LANCELOT
LATCHKEY
LAWCOURT
LEACHING
LINCHPIN
LINCOLNS
LOWCLASS
LUNCHEON
LUSCIOUS
LYNCHING
MAECENAS
MANCIPLE
MARCELLA
MARCELLO
MASCARON
MATCHBOX
MATCHING
MELCHIOR
MERCALLI
MERCATOR
MERCEDES
MERCHANT
MERCIFUL
MESCALIN
MINCEPIE
MISCARRY
MISCHIEF
MISCOUNT
MOCCASIN
MUNCHKIN
MUSCADET
MUSCATEL
MUSCULAR
MUTCHKIN
NARCOSES
NARCOSIS
NARCOTIC
NESCIENT
NEWCOMER
OBSCURED
OFFCOLOR
OILCLOTH
ONSCREEN
OUTCLASS
PANCREAS
PATCHILY
PAYCHECK
PEACEFUL
PENCHANT
PERCEIVE
PERCEVAL
PERCIVAL
PIECHART
PIECRUST
PILCHARD
PISCATOR
PITCAIRN
PLACABLE
PLACEMAT
PLACEMEN
PLACENTA
PLACIDLY
PLECTRUM
PLUCKILY
PLUCKING
PRACTICE
PRACTISE
PRECINCT
PRECIOUS
PRECLUDE
PRECURSE
PROCEEDS
PROCLAIM
PROCURER
PUNCTUAL
PUNCTURE
PURCHASE
QUICKSET
RASCALLY
REACTION
REACTIVE
RUNCIBLE
SANCTIFY
SANCTION
SANCTITY
SAUCEPAN
SHACKLES
SHOCKING
SINCLAIR
SMOCKING
SNACKBAR
SORCERER
SOUCHONG
SPACEMAN
SPACIOUS
SPECIFIC
SPECIMEN
SPECIOUS
SPECKLED
SPECTRAL
SPECTRUM
SPECULUM
SPICCATO
STACCATO
STICCATO
STICKILY
STICKING
STICKLER
STOCCATA
STOCKADE
STOCKCAR
STOCKING

STOCKIST
STOCKMAN
STOCKPOT
STUCCOED
SUCCEEDS
SUCCINCT
SUCCUBUS
SUICIDAL
SUNCREAM
SYNCLINE
TEACHERS
TEACHING
TEACLOTH
TETCHILY
THICKSET
TINCTURE
TOPCLASS
TOUCHING
TRACHOMA
TRACKING
TRACTION
TRICHOID
TRICKERY
TRICYCLE
TROCHAIC
TROCHLEA
TRUCKING
TRUCKLED
VASCULAR
VINCIBLE
VINCULUM
VISCERAL
VISCOUNT
VOLCANIC
WATCHDOG
WATCHFUL
WATCHING
WATCHMAN
WHACKING
WITCHERY
WITCHING
WRECKAGE
ZIRCONIA
ZUCCHINI
AARDVARK
ACADEMIC
ACIDHEAD
BAEDEKER
BALDNESS
BALDRICK
BANDANNA
BANDEROL
BANDITTI
BANDSMAN
BARDOLPH
BAUDRICK
BINDWEED
BIRDCAGE
BIRDSEED
BLUDGEON
BOADICEA
BOLDNESS
BONDSMAN
BORDEAUX
BORDELLO
BORDERER
BRADBURY
BRADSHAW
BRIDGING
BUDDHISM
BUDDHIST
BUDDLEIA
BURDENED
CALDERON
CANDIDLY
CARDAMOM
CARDIGAN
CARDINAL
CAUDILLO
CHADBAND
CLADDING
CLODPOLL
COLDNESS
CONDENSE
CORDOVAN
CORDUROY
CORDWAIN
CREDIBLE
CREDIBLY
CREDITOR
DAEDALUS
DANDRUFF
DAYDREAM
DEADBEAT
DEADENED
DEADENER
DEADHEAD
DEADLINE
DEADLOCK
DEADWOOD
DENDRITE
DENDROID
DIDDICOY
DOLDRUMS
DRUDGERY
DUODENAL
DUODENUM
EPIDEMIC
EPIDURAL
ERADIATE
EVIDENCE
FANDANGO
FEEDBACK
FELDSPAR
FIDDLING
FINDINGS
FLYDRIVE
FOLDEROL
FONDLING
FONDNESS
GARDENER
GARDENIA
GARDYLOO
GENDARME
GEODESIC
GLADNESS
GLADSOME
GOLDFISH
GOLDMINE
GONDWANA
GOODNESS
GOODSIRE
GOODWIFE
GOODWILL
GOODWOOD
GOODYEAR
GRADIENT
GRADUATE
GRIDIRON
GRIDLOCK
GRUDGING
GUIDANCE
GURDWARA
HANDBALL
HANDBILL
HANDBOOK
HANDCART
HANDCLAP
HANDCUFF
HANDHELD
HANDICAP
HANDMADE
HANDMAID
HANDOVER
HANDRAIL
HANDSOME
HANDYMAN
HARDBACK
HARDCORE
HARDENED
HARDLINE
HARDNESS
HARDSHIP
HARDTACK
HARDWARE
HARDWOOD
HEADACHE
HEADBAND
HEADGEAR
HEADHUNT
HEADLAMP
HEADLAND
HEADLESS
HEADLINE
HEADLONG
HEADMARK
HEADMOST
HEADREST
HEADROOM
HEADSHIP
HEADWIND
HEADWORD
HEEDLESS
HERDSMAN
HINDMOST
HINDUISM
HINDWARD
HOLDINGS
HONDURAN
HONDURAS
HOODWINK
HOWDYEDO
HUNDREDS
HURDLING
INEDIBLE
KINDLING
KINDNESS
LAIDBACK
LANDFALL
LANDFILL
LANDLADY
LANDLOCK
LANDLORD
LANDMARK
LANDMASS
LANDMINE
LANDRACE
LANDSEER
LANDSLIP
LANDWARD
LAUDABLE
LAUDABLY
LAUDANUM
LEADSMAN
LEWDNESS
LOADSTAR
LONDONER
LORDOSIS
LORDSHIP
LOUDNESS
MAIDENLY
MALDIVES
MANDAMUS
MANDARIN
MANDATED
MANDIBLE
MANDIOCA
MANDOLIN
MANDRAKE
MANDRILL
MEDDLING
MIDDLING
MILDEWED
MILDNESS
MINDANAO
MINDLESS
MONDRIAN
MURDERER
NEEDLESS
OBEDIENT
OUTDATED
OUTDOORS
PADDLING
PANDARUS
PANDEMIC
PANDOWDY
PARDONER
PEDDLING
PENDULUM
PIDDLING
PINDARIC
POWDERED
PREDATOR
PREDELLA
PRODIGAL
PRODUCER
PRODUCES
PRODUCTS
PRUDENCE
QUADRANT
QUADRATE
QUADRIGA
QUADROON
RANDOMLY
READABLE
READIEST
READJUST
REEDLING
REEDSMAN
RIDDANCE
ROADSHOW
ROADSIDE
ROADSTER
SADDLERY
SADDLING
SADDUCEE
SANDBANK
SANDWICH
SARDINIA
SARDONIC
SARDONYX
SEEDLESS
SEEDLING
SEEDSMAN
SHADRACH
SHODDILY
SKIDDING
SMIDGEON
SOLDIERS
SOLDIERY
SORDIDLY
SPADEFUL
STUDENTS
STUDIOUS
SUDDENLY
SUNDANCE
SUNDRIED
SUNDRIES
SWADDLER
SYNDROME
TANDOORI
TENDENCY
TENDERLY
TRADEOFF
VENDETTA
VERDERER
VINDALOO
VOIDANCE
WANDERER
WARDRESS
WARDROBE
WARDROOM
WARDSHIP
WHODUNIT
WILDFELL
WILDFIRE
WILDFOWL
WILDLIFE
WILDNESS
WINDBURN
WINDFALL
WINDHOEK
WINDINGS
WINDLASS
WINDLESS
WINDMILL
WINDPIPE
WINDSOCK
WINDWARD
WONDROUS
WOODBINE
WOODCOCK
WOODENLY
WOODLAND
WOODSHED
WOODSMAN
WOODWARD
WOODWIND
WOODWORK
WOODWORM
WORDBOOK
WORDLESS

ABJECTLY
ABNEGATE
ABSENTEE
ACCENTED
ACCENTOR
ACCEPTED
ADDENDUM
ADHERENT
ADHESION
ADHESIVE
AFFECTED
AGREEING
AIREDALE
ALBERICH
ALCESTIS
ALDEHYDE
ALDERMAN
ALDERNEY
ALGERIAN
ALGERINE
ALIENATE
ALIENISM
ALIENIST
ALLEGORY
ALLELUIA
ALLERGEN
ALLERGIC
ALLEYWAY
ALVEOLUS
AMPERAGE
ANCESTOR
ANCESTRY
ANDERSON
ANGELICA
ANNEALER
ANNELIDA
ANSERINE
ANTECEDE
ANTEDATE
ANTELOPE
ANTENNAE
ANTEPOST
ANTERIOR
ANTEROOM
AOTEAROA
APHELION
APPELANT
APPENDIX
APPETITE
AQUEDUCT
ARDENNES
ARDENTLY
ARGESTES
ARMENIAN
ARPEGGIO
ARRESTED
ARRESTER
ARTEFACT
ARTERIAL
ARTESIAN
ASBESTOS
ASPERGES
ASPERITY
ASSEMBLE
ASSEMBLY
ASSESSOR
ASTERISK
ASTEROID
ATHELING
ATHENIAN
ATHEROMA
ATHETISE
ATHETOID
ATTENDER
ATTESTOR
AURELIAN
BAKELITE
BALEARIC
BAREBACK
BAREFOOT
BARENESS
BASEBALL
BASEBORN
BASELESS
BASELINE
BASEMENT
BASENESS
BEGETTER
BEHEMOTH
BENEDICK
BENEDICT
BENEFICE
BENEFITS
BENENDEN
BEREAVED
BEVERAGE
BISEXUAL
BLEEDING
BLUEBACK
BLUEBELL
BLUECOAT
BLUENOSE
BOGEYMAN
BOHEMIAN
BONEHEAD
BONELESS
BONEYARD
BORECOLE
BOREHOLE
BREECHES
BREEDING
BREEZILY
BRIEFING
CABERNET
CAKEHOLE
CAKEWALK
CALENDAR
CALENDER
CAMELLIA
CAMEROON
CAPERING
CAREFREE
CARELESS
CAREWORN
CASEMATE
CASEMENT
CATEGORY
CATERING
CELERIAC
CELERITY
CEMETERY
CEREBRAL
CEREBRUM
CEREMENT
CEREMONY
CHEEKILY
CHEERFUL
CHEERILY
CHEERING
CICERONE
CINERAMA
CINEREAL
CLUELESS
COHERENT
COHESION
COHESIVE
COLESLAW
COMEBACK
COMEDIAN
COMEDOWN
COVENANT
COVENTRY
COVERAGE
COVERING
COVERLET
COVETOUS
CUTENESS
CYRENIAC
DANEGELD
DATELESS
DATELINE
DECEASED
DECEIVER
DECEMBER
DECEMVIR
DECENTLY
DEFEATED
DEFECATE
DEFECTOR
DEFENDER
DEJECTED
DELEGATE
DELETION
DEMEANOR
DEMENTED
DEMENTIA
DEMERARA
DEMERSAL
DERELICT
DESELECT
DESERTED
DESERTER
DESERVED
DETECTOR
DIRECTLY
DIRECTOR
DISEASED
DOMESDAY
DOMESTIC
DOVECOTE
DOVETAIL
EASEMENT
ECLECTIC
EDGEHILL
EDGEWAYS
EDGEWISE
EIDECTIC
EMBEDDED
EMBEZZLE
ENDEAVOR
ENFEEBLE
ENGENDER
ENMESHED
ENSEMBLE
ENVELOPE
EPHEMERA
EPHESIAN
ESPECIAL
ESTEEMED
ETCETERA
ETHEREAL
ETHERISE
EUGENICS
EUPEPSIA
EXPECTED
EXPEDITE
EXPENDED
EXPENSES
EXTENDED
EXTENSOR
EXTERIOR
EXTERNAL
EXTERNAT
FACEACHE
FACELESS
FACELIFT
FAREWELL
FEDERACY
FEDERATE
FENESTRA
FEVERFEW
FEVERISH
FIDELITY
FILENAME
FINESPUN
FIREARMS
FIREBACK
FIREBALL
FIREBIRD
FIREBOLT
FIREDAMP
FIRESIDE
FIRESTEP
FIRETRAP
FIREWEED
FIREWOOD
FIREWORK
FLEETING
FLUENTLY
FOREBEAR
FOREBODE
FORECAST
FOREDECK
FOREDOOM
FOREFOOT
FOREGONE
FOREHAND
FOREHEAD
FORELAND
FORELOCK
FOREMOST
FORENAME
FORENOON
FORENSIC
FORESAIL
FORESHIP
FORESKIN
FORESTAY
FORESTER
FORESTRY
FORETELL
FOREWARN
FOREWORD
FREEHAND
FREEHOLD
FREEPOST
FREETOWN
FREEZING
FRIENDLY
FUNERARY
FUNEREAL
FUSELAGE
FUSEWIRE
GAMEBIRD
GAMENESS
GATEPOST
GENERATE
GENEROUS
GENETICS
GENETRIX
GIVEAWAY
GLEESOME
GOVERNOR
GREEDILY
GREENBAG
GREENERY
GREENFLY
GREENING
GREENISH
GREENOCK
GREETING
GRIEVOUS
GRUESOME
HAREBELL
HAZELNUT
HEBETUDE
HEGEMONY
HEREDITY
HEREFORD
HEREWARD
HEREWITH
HIBERNIA
HIDEAWAY
HIRELING
HOMELAND
HOMELESS
HOMEMADE
HOMESICK
HOMESPUN
HOMEWARD
HOMEWORK
HONESTLY
HONEYDEW
HONEYPOT
HOPELESS
HOSEPIPE
HOTELIER
HOVERFLY
HYPERION
IDLENESS
IMBECILE
IMMERSED
IMPELLED
IMPERIAL
IMPETIGO
INCENSED
INDEBTED
INDECENT
INDENTED
INDEXING
INFECTED
INFERIOR

INFERNAL
INFESTED
INHERENT
INJECTOR
INSECURE
INTEGRAL
INTELSAT
INTENDED
INTENTLY
INTERACT
INTERCOM
INTEREST
INTERIOR
INTERMIT
INTERNAL
INTERNEE
INTERNET
INTERPOL
INTERVAL
INVEIGLE
INVENTED
INVENTOR
INVERTED
INVESTOR
JEREBOAM
JEREMIAD
JEREMIAH
JEWELLED
JEWELLER
JUVENILE
KINETICS
KITEMARK
KNEEDEEP
KNEEHIGH
LACERATE
LACEWING
LAKELAND
LAMENESS
LAMENTED
LATENESS
LATERITE
LAVENDER
LAVENGRO
LEVELLER
LEVERAGE
LIBELOUS
LIBERATE
LIBERIAN
LICENSED
LICENSEE
LIFEBELT
LIFEBOAT
LIFEBUOY
LIFELESS
LIFELIKE
LIFELINE
LIFELONG
LIFESPAN
LIFETIME
LIKEABLE
LIKENESS
LIKEWISE
LIMERICK
LINESMAN
LITERACY
LITERARY
LITERATE
LITERATI
LIVELONG
LIVERIED
LIVERISH
LIVEWARE
LOBELINE
LODESTAR
LONESOME
LOVEBIRD
LOVELACE
LOVELESS
LOVELORN
LOVESICK
LOWERING
LUKEWARM
LUPERCAL
LYREBIRD
LYSERGIC
MACERATE
MAGELLAN
MAJESTIC
MAMELUKE
MANEUVER
MATERIAL
MATERNAL
MAVERICK
MELEAGER
MENELAUS
MEREDITH
METEORIC
MINEHEAD
MIREPOIX
MISERERE
MODELING
MODELLER
MODERATE
MODERATO
MODESTLY
MOLECULE
MOLEHILL
MOLESKIN
MOLESTER
MOMENTUM
MONETARY
MONETISE
MONEYBOX
MOREOVER
MOVEABLE
MOVEMENT
MULETEER
MULEWORT
MYCELIUM
NAMELESS
NAMESAKE
NEPENTHE
NIBELUNG
NICENESS
NIGERIAN
NIGERIEN
NINEPINS
NINETEEN
NOBELIUM
NONESUCH
NOSEBAND
NOSEDIVE
NOTEBOOK
NOTECASE
NOVELIST
NOVEMBER
NUMERACY
NUMERALS
NUMERATE
NUMEROUS
OBJECTOR
OBSERVED
OBSERVER
OBSESSED
OFFENDED
OFFENDER
OFFERING
ORDERING
ORIENTAL
OSTERLEY
OXPECKER
PALEFACE
PALENESS
PANEGYRY
PANELING
PANELLED
PARENTAL
PATELLAR
PATENTED
PATENTEE
PATENTLY
PATERNAL
PAVEMENT
PEDERAST
PEDESTAL
PENELOPE
PEPERONI
PETERLOO
PEVENSEY
PHLEGMON
PHREATIC
PINEWOOD
PIPELINE
PIPERINE
POSEIDON
POTEMKIN
POWERFUL
PRIESTLY
PUDENDUM
PYRENEES
QUAESTOR
QUIETUDE
RABELAIS
RAMEQUIN
RANELAGH
RAPECAKE
RAREFIED
RATEABLE
RAVENOUS
RECEDING
RECEIPTS
RECEIVED
RECEIVER
RECENTLY
RECEPTOR
RECESSED
REDEEMER
REDEFINE
REDEPLOY
REDESIGN
REFERRAL
REHEARSE
RELEASED
RELEGATE
RELEVANT
REMEDIAL
REMEMBER
RENEGADE
REPEATED
REPEATER
RESEARCH
RESEMBLE
RESERVED
RESETTLE
REVEALED
REVEILLE
REVELLER
REVEREND
REVERENT
REVERSAL
REVERSED
RIPENESS
RIVERAIN
RIVERINE
RIVETING
RODERICK
ROSEMARY
ROSEWOOD
ROTENONE
RUDENESS
RULEBOOK
SAGENESS
SALEABLE
SALEROOM
SALESMAN
SAMENESS
SCHEDULE
SCHEMING
SCIENCES
SCREAMER
SCREENED
SCREWTOP
SELECTED
SELECTOR
SELENITE
SELENIUM
SELEUCID
SEMESTER
SERENADE
SERENATA
SERENELY
SERENITY
SEVERELY
SEVEREST
SEVERITY
SEWERAGE
SHEEPDOG
SHEEPISH
SHIELING
SHOEHORN
SHOELACE
SHOELESS
SHOETREE
SHREDDER
SHREWDLY
SHREWISH
SIBERIAN
SIDEKICK
SIDELINE
SIDELONG
SIDEREAL
SIDERITE
SIDESHOW
SIDESLIP
SIDESMAN
SIDESTEP
SIDEWALK
SIDEWAYS
SILENCER
SILENTLY
SILESIAN
SINECURE
SIRENIAN
SIZEABLE
SLEEPERS
SLEEPILY
SLEEPING
SNEERING
SNEEZING
SOBERING
SOLECISM
SOLEMNLY
SOLENOID
SOMEBODY
SOMERSET
SOMETIME
SOMEWHAT
SORENESS
SPEEDILY
SPEEDWAY
SPLENDID
SPLENDOR
SPREADER
SQUEAKER
SQUEALER
SQUEEGEE
SQUEEZER
STEERAGE
STEERING
STREAKED
STREAKER
STREAMER
STRENGTH
STRESSED
STRETCHY
SUMERIAN
SUPERBLY
SUPERIOR
SUPERMAN
SUPERNAL
SUPERTAX
SURENESS
SUZERAIN
SWEEPING
TAKEAWAY
TAKEHOME
TAKEOVER
TALENTED
TAMENESS
TAPENADE
TAPERING
TAPESTRY
TAPEWORM
TAVERNER
TELECAST
TELEFILM
TELEGONY
TELEGRAM
TELEMARK
TELETHON
TELEVISE
TEMERITY

TENEBRAE
TENEBRIO
TENEMENT
TENESMUS
THIEVERY
THIEVING
THIEVISH
THREATEN
THRENODY
THRESHER
TIBERIAS
TIBERIUS
TIDEMARK
TIMELESS
TIRELESS
TIRESIAS
TIRESOME
TOGETHER
TOLERANT
TOLERATE
TOMENTUM
TONELESS
TOREADOR
TOWELING
TOWERING
TREELESS
TREELINE
TREETOPS
TRUENESS
TUBELESS
TUBERCLE
TUBEROSE
TUBEROUS
TUTELAGE
TUTELARY
TWEEZERS
TYPECAST
TYPEFACE
ULCERATE
ULCEROUS
ULTERIOR
UNBEATEN
UNDERAGE
UNDERARM
UNDERCUT
UNDERDOG
UNDERFED
UNDERLAY
UNDERLIE
UNDERPIN
UNDERSEA
UNDERTOW
UNFETTER
UNHEATED
UNHEROIC
UNLEADED
UNNERVED
UNPERSON
UNREASON
UNSEALED
UNSEEDED
UNSEEMLY
UNSETTLE
UNVERSED
UNWEANED
UPHEAVAL
UPPERCUT
URGENTLY
VALENCIA
VALERIAN
VALETING
VEGETATE
VEHEMENT
VENERATE
VENEREAL
VENETIAN
VILENESS
VINEGARY
VINEYARD
VIPEROUS
VIREMENT
VISELIKE
VITELLUS
WATERBUG
WATERING
WATERLOO
WATERMAN
WATERWAY
WAVEBAND
WAVERING
WAVERLEY
WEREWOLF
WHEEZILY
WHEEZING
WIDENING
WIRELESS
WIREWORM
WISEACRE
YODELLER
YOSEMITE
YULETIDE
ZEDEKIAH
ZIBELINE
ZWIEBACK
AIRFIELD
ARTFULLY
AVIFAUNA
BAFFLING
BOUFFANT
BUNFIGHT
CAFFEINE
CLIFFORD
COIFFEUR
COIFFURE
CONFETTI
CONFINED
CONFINES
CONFLATE
CONFLICT
CONFOUND
CONFRONT
CONFUSED
CRAFTILY
DAFFODIL
DEAFNESS
DIFFRACT
DISFAVOR
DRIFTING
DUMFOUND
ECOFREAK
FITFULLY
FORFEITS
GOLFBALL
GOLFCLUB
GONFALON
GOOFBALL
GRAFFITI
HALFFULL
HALFHOUR
HALFMAST
HALFTERM
HALFTIME
HALFYEAR
HARFLEUR
HAWFINCH
HAYFEVER
HAYFIELD
HOPFIELD
ICEFIELD
ILLFATED
JEFFREYS
JOYFULLY
KUFFIYEH
LAWFULLY
LEAFLESS
MANFULLY
MIDFIELD
MOUFFLON
MUDFLATS
NEWFOUND
NUFFIELD
OILFIELD
OUTFIELD
OUTFLANK
PERFECTA
PERFECTO
PERFORCE
PERFUMED
PILFERER
PROFORMA
PROFOUND
PROFUSER
PUFFBALL
REAFFIRM
RIFFRAFF
ROOFLESS
ROOFTOPS
RUEFULLY
SCAFFOLD
SCOFFING
SEAFARER
SEAFORTH
SEAFRONT
SELFHELP
SELFLESS
SELFMADE
SELFPITY
SELFSAME
SHIFTING
SINFONIA
SNIFFLER
SNUFFBOX
SPIFFING
STAFFING
STAFFORD
STIFLING
STUFFILY
STUFFING
SUFFERER
SUFFRAGE
SULFURIC
SURFBOAT
TAFFRAIL
TRIFLING
UNIFYING
USEFULLY
USUFRUCT
WARFARIN
WAYFARER
WILFULLY
WOEFULLY
WOLFBANE
AMYGDALA
ANAGLYPH
AVOGADRO
BARGELLO
BARGEMAN
BEGGARLY
BELGRADE
BENGHAZI
BERGAMOT
BERGERAC
BIOGRAPH
BLIGHTER
BRAGANZA
BRAGGART
BRAGGING
BRIGHTEN
BRIGHTLY
BRIGHTON
BUGGERED
BULGARIA
BUNGALOW
BUNGLING
BURGLARY
BURGRAVE
BURGUNDY
CINGULUM
CONGRESS
COUGHING
DAUGHTER
DIAGNOSE
DIAGONAL
DIGGINGS
DINGBATS
DIOGENES
DISGORGE
DISGRACE
DISGUISE
DOGGEDLY
DOGGEREL
DOUGHBOY
DOUGHNUT
DRAGOONS
DRAGSTER
DRUGGIST
DRYGOODS
DUNGHILL
ELEGANCE
ELIGIBLE
EMIGRANT
EMIGRATE
EPIGAMIC
EPIGRAPH
EWIGKEIT
EXEGESIS
EXEGETIC
EXIGENCY
EXIGUITY
EXIGUOUS
EYEGLASS
FLAGGING
FLAGPOLE
FLAGRANT
FLAGSHIP
FLOGGING
FOXGLOVE
FRAGMENT
FRAGRANT
FRIGHTEN
FRIGIDLY
FRUGALLY
GADGETRY
GANGLAND
GANGLING
GANGLION
GANGRENE
GANGSTER
GARGANEY
GARGOYLE
GINGERLY
GINGIVAL
GOLGOTHA
GORGEOUS
GROGGILY
HAGGADAH
HANGINGS
HANGNAIL
HANGOVER
HEDGEHOG
HEDGEROW
HEIGHTEN
HONGKONG
HUNGRILY
IMAGINED
ISOGLOSS
ISOGONAL
JANGLING
JIGGERED
JINGOISM
JINGOIST
JONGLEUR
JUDGMENT
JUGGLING
KANGAROO
KEDGEREE
KIDGLOVE
KINGPOST
KINGSHIP
KINGSIZE
KINGSLEY
KINGSTON
KNIGHTLY
LANGLAND
LANGLAUF
LANGUAGE
LANGUISH
LARGESSE
LAUGHING
LAUGHTER
LEGGINGS
LENGTHEN
LIEGEMAN
LINGERIE
LINGUIST
LODGINGS
LONGBOAT
LONGHAND
LONGHAUL
LONGHORN
LONGLAND
LONGSTAY

LONGSTOP
LONGTERM
LONGTIME
LUNGFISH
MALGRADO
MANGONEL
MANGROVE
MARGARET
MARGINAL
MARGRAVE
MISGUIDE
MONGOLIA
MONGOOSE
MUDGUARD
NARGILEH
NEIGHBOR
NIGGLING
OLIGARCH
ORIGINAL
OUTGOING
PALGRAVE
PANGLOSS
PANGOLIN
PEIGNOIR
PILGRIMS
PLUGHOLE
POIGNANT
PREGNANT
PRIGGISH
PROGERIA
PROGRESS
PUNGENCY
QUAGMIRE
REIGNING
RIDGEWAY
RINGDOVE
RINGSIDE
RINGTAIL
RINGWALL
RINGWORM
ROUGHAGE
RUGGEDLY
RYEGRASS
SANGLIER
SANGUINE
SARGASSO
SEAGOING
SENGREEN
SERGEANT
SHAGREEN
SHIGELLA
SINGSONG
SINGULAR
SLIGHTED
SLIGHTLY
SLUGABED
SLUGFEST
SLUGGARD
SLUGGISH
SMUGGLED
SMUGGLER
SMUGNESS
SONGBIRD
SONGSTER
SPYGLASS
STAGGERS
STAGHORN
STAGNANT
STAGNATE
STIGMATA
SURGICAL
TANGIBLE
TANGIBLY
TINGLING
TRIGLYPH
TUNGSTEN
TURGENEV
TURGIDLY
VANGUARD
VENGEFUL
VIRGINAL
VIRGINIA
VULGARLY
WAGGONER
WEDGWOOD
WEIGHING
WINGLESS
WINGSPAN
ZIGGURAT
ALCHEMIC
ALEHOUSE
ALPHABET
ALTHOUGH
ANCHISES
ANCHORET
ARCHAISM
ARCHDUKE
ARCHIVES
ASPHODEL
ASPHYXIA
ASTHENIA
BACHELOR
BAGHEERA
BATHETIC
BATHROBE
BATHROOM
BECHAMEL
BETHESDA
BONHOMIE
BOTHERED
BOTHWELL
CACHALOT
CACHEPOT
CACHEXIA
CASHMERE
CATHEDRA
CATHETER
CATHOLIC
CATHOUSE
COCHLEAR
CUTHBERT
DASHWOOD
DETHRONE
DIEHARDS
DIPHENYL
DISHEVEL
DISHONOR
DOGHOUSE
DUCHESSE
EIGHTEEN
ELKHOUND
EMPHASIS
EMPHATIC
ENSHRINE
ENSHROUD
ENTHRALL
ENTHRONE
ESTHETIC
EUPHONIA
EUPHONIC
EUPHORIA
EUPHORIC
EUPHUISM
EXCHANGE
FATHERLY
FIGHTING
FISHBONE
FISHCAKE
FISHMEAL
FISHPOND
FISHWIFE
FOXHOUND
FUCHSITE
GATHERED
HATHAWAY
HENHOUSE
HIGHBALL
HIGHBORN
HIGHBROW
HIGHGATE
HIGHLAND
HIGHNESS
HIGHRISE
HIGHROAD
HITHERTO
HOTHOUSE
HUSHHUSH
ICEHOUSE
INCHOATE
ISTHMIAN
JEPHTHAH
JODHPURS
KACHAHRI
KYPHOSIS
LASHINGS
LETHARGY
LIGHTING
LOTHARIO
LUSHNESS
LUTHERAN
MACHEATH
MACHINES
MACHISMO
MADHOUSE
MATHURIN
MECHANIC
METHANOL
METHODIC
MICHIGAN
MIGHTILY
MISHMASH
MOTHBALL
MOTHERLY
MUCHNESS
MUSHROOM
MYTHICAL
NEPHRITE
NEWHAVEN
NICHOLAS
NIGHTCAP
NIGHTJAR
NUTHATCH
NUTHOUSE
OMPHALOS
OOPHORON
ORCHITIS
ORPHANED
ORTHODOX
OUTHOUSE
PACHINKO
PASHMINA
PATHETIC
PATHOGEN
PHTHISIS
PITHLESS
POCHETTE
POTHOLER
PROHIBIT
PUSHBIKE
PUSHCART
PUSHOVER
RACHITIS
RASHNESS
RECHARGE
REPHRASE
RICHNESS
RIGHTFUL
RIGHTIST
ROCHDALE
RUSHMORE
RUTHLESS
SIGHTING
SUBHUMAN
SUCHLIKE
SYPHILIS
TAPHOUSE
TASHKENT
TIGHTWAD
TOPHEAVY
UNCHASTE
UNSHAKEN
UNTHREAD
VALHALLA
WARHORSE
WASHABLE
WASHBOWL
WASHDOWN
WASHROOM
WISHBONE
WITHDRAW
WITHERED
WITHHOLD
YACHTING
YOGHOURT
ZEPHYRUS
ABDICATE
ABRIDGED
ABSINTHE
ACCIDENT
ACHIEVED
ACHIEVER
ACHILLES
ACRIMONY
ACTINIDE
ACTINIUM
ACTIVATE
ACTIVELY
ACTIVISM
ACTIVIST
ACTIVITY
ADDICTED
ADDITION
ADDITIVE
ADMIRING
ADRIATIC
ADVISORY
AFFINITY
AGRICOLA
AGRIMONY
AIRINESS
ALBINONI
ALLIANCE
ALMIGHTY
ALPINIST
ALTITUDE
AMBIANCE
AMBIENCE
AMBITION
AMRITSAR
ANTIBODY
ANTIDOTE
ANTILLES
ANTILOPE
ANTIMONY
ANTIPHON
ANTIPOPE
APTITUDE
AQUILINE
ARGININE
ARTICLED
ARTICLES
ARTIFACT
ARTIFICE
ARTISTIC
ARTISTRY
ASCIDIAN
ASCIDIUM
ASPIRANT
ASPIRATE
ASPIRING
ASSIGNEE
ATTITUDE
AUDIENCE
AUDITION
AUDITORY
AUTISTIC
AVAILING
BACILLUS
BADINAGE
BALINESE
BANISTER
BARITONE
BASIDIUM
BASILICA
BASILISK
BASINFUL
BEGINNER
BELIEVER
BELITTLE
BERIBERI
BESIEGED
BEWILDER
BOLIVIAN
BONIFACE
BROILING
BRUISING
BUSINESS
CADILLAC
CAGINESS
CALIGULA
CALIPERS
CAMISOLE

CANISTER
CAPITALS
CARILLON
CATILINE
CELIBACY
CELIBATE
CHAINSAW
CHAIRMAN
CHOIRBOY
CHRISTEN
CHRISTIE
CHRISTOM
CICISBEO
CILIATED
CIVILIAN
CIVILITY
CIVILIZE
CLAIMANT
CLOISTER
COGITATE
COLISEUM
CORIOLIS
COSINESS
COZINESS
CULINARY
CUPIDITY
CYLINDER
CYNICISM
CYRILLIC
DAVIDSON
DEBILITY
DECIMATE
DECIPHER
DECISION
DECISIVE
DEDICATE
DEFIANCE
DEFINITE
DELICACY
DELICATE
DELIRIUM
DELIVERY
DEMIJOHN
DEMISTER
DEMIURGE
DEPILATE
DERISION
DERISIVE
DERISORY
DESIGNER
DESIROUS
DEVIANCE
DEVILISH
DEVILLED
DIGITIZE
DILIGENT
DIMINISH
DISINTER
DIVIDEND
DIVIDERS
DIVINITY
DIVISION
DIVISIVE
DOCILITY
DOMICILE
DOMINANT
DOMINATE
DOMINEER
DOMINION
DOMINOES
DRAINAGE
DRAINING
DUTIABLE
EASINESS
ECHINATE
ECHINOPS
EERINESS
EFFICACY
EGOISTIC
ELLIPSIS
ELLIPTIC
ELSINORE
EMBITTER
ENCIRCLE
ENFILADE
ENGINEER
ENKINDLE
ENRICHED
ENSIFORM
ENSILAGE
ENTICING
ENTIRELY
ENTIRETY
ENTITLED
ENVIABLE
ENVIRONS
ENVISAGE
ENVISION
EOHIPPUS
EQUIPAGE
EQUITANT
ESTIMATE
ESTIVATE
ETHIOPIA
EXCISION
EXCITING
FACILITY
FAMILIAR
FAMISHED
FATIGUED
FATIGUES
FELICITY
FEMININE
FEMINISM
FEMINIST
FEMINITY
FILIGREE
FILIPINO
FINISHED
FINISHER
FLUIDITY
FRUITFUL
FRUITING
FRUITION
FUGITIVE
FUMIGATE
FUMITORY
FUSIFORM
FUSILIER
FUTILITY
GALILEAN
GARISHLY
GEMINATE
GENIALLY
GENITALS
GENITIVE
GRAINING
HABITUAL
HACIENDA
HAMILTON
HAVILDAR
HAZINESS
HELIPORT
HERITAGE
HESITANT
HESITATE
HIBISCUS
HOLIDAYS
HOLINESS
HOLISTIC
HOMICIDE
HOWITZER
HUMIDIFY
HUMIDITY
HUMILITY
HYGIENIC
IGNITION
ILLINOIS
IMMINENT
INCIDENT
INCISION
INCISIVE
INDIAMAN
INDICANT
INDICATE
INDIGENT
INDIRECT
INFINITE
INFINITY
INSIGNIA
INTIFADA
INTIMACY
INTIMATE
INVITING
IRRIGATE
IRRITANT
IRRITATE
IVOIRIEN
JOKINGLY
JOVIALLY
JUBILANT
JUBILATE
JUDICIAL
JULIENNE
KAMIKAZE
KIBITZER
LACINATE
LAMINATE
LAPIDARY
LAPIDATE
LATINIST
LATITUDE
LAVISHLY
LAZINESS
LECITHIN
LENIENCY
LEVITATE
LEWISITE
LIMITING
LINIMENT
LITIGANT
LITIGATE
LIVIDITY
LOGISTIC
LONICERA
LOVINGLY
LUCIDITY
LUMINARY
LUMINOUS
LYRICISM
LYRICIST
MAGICIAN
MAGISTER
MALINGER
MANIACAL
MANICURE
MANIFEST
MANIFOLD
MANITOBA
MARIACHI
MARIANAS
MARIGOLD
MARINADE
MARINATE
MARITIME
MAXIMIZE
MCKINLEY
MEDIATOR
MEDICATE
MEDICINE
MEDIEVAL
MEDIOCRE
MEDITATE
MENISCUS
MERIDIAN
MERINGUE
MERISTEM
MILITANT
MILITARY
MILITATE
MINIMIZE
MINISTER
MINISTRY
MITIGATE
MOBILITY
MOBILIZE
MODIFIER
MONICKER
MORIBUND
MOTIVATE
MUCILAGE
MUNIMENT
MUSICIAN
MUTILATE
MUTINEER
MUTINOUS
MYRIAPOD
NAMIBIAN
NATIONAL
NATIVITY
NAVIGATE
NEPIONIC
NIHILISM
NIHILIST
NIJINSKY
NOBILITY
NOMINATE
NOTIONAL
NUMINOUS
OBLIGATE
OBLIGING
OBLIVION
OBSIDIAN
OCCIDENT
OEDIPEAN
OFFICERS
OFFICIAL
OILINESS
OMNIFORM
OPHIDIAN
OPTICIAN
OPTIMATE
OPTIMISM
OPTIMIST
OPTIONAL
ORDINAND
ORDINARY
ORDINATE
ORPIMENT
PACIFIER
PACIFISM
PACIFIST
PAGINATE
PAKISTAN
PALIMONY
PALINODE
PALISADE
PAPILLON
PARIETAL
PARISIAN
PATIENCE
PAVILION
PEDICURE
PEDIGREE
PEDIMENT
PEKINESE
PENITENT
PERIANTH
PERICARP
PERICLES
PERIDERM
PERILOUS
PERIODIC
PERIPETY
PERISHED
PERISHER
PETITION
PIMIENTO
PITIABLE
PITILESS
PLEIADES
POLISHED
POLISHER
POLITELY
POLITICO
POLITICS
POPINJAY
POSITION
POSITIVE
POSITRON
PRAIRIAL
PUGILISM
PUGILIST
PULITZER
PUNISHED
PUNITIVE
PURIFIED
PURIFIER
PYRIFORM
QUAINTLY
RACIALLY
RACINESS

RADIANCE
RADIATOR
RAPIDITY
RATIONAL
REDIRECT
REFINERY
REGICIDE
REGIMENT
REGIONAL
REGISTER
REGISTRY
REKINDLE
RELIABLE
RELIABLY
RELIANCE
RELIEVED
RELIGION
REMINDER
REMITTAL
RESIDENT
RESIDUAL
RESIDUUM
RESIGNED
RESINOUS
RESISTOR
RETICENT
RETICULE
RETIRING
REVIEWER
REVISION
REVIVIFY
REVIVING
RIDICULE
RIGIDITY
ROBINSON
ROSINESS
RUBICUND
RUDIMENT
RUMINANT
RUMINATE
SADISTIC
SALINGER
SALINITY
SALIVARY
SALIVATE
SAMIZDAT
SANITARY
SANITIZE
SATIATED
SATIRIST
SATIRIZE
SCHILLER
SCHIZOID
SCRIABIN
SCRIBBLE
SCRIBBLY
SCRIPTUM
SEDIMENT
SEDITION
SEMINARY
SEMIOTIC
SEMITONE
SENILITY
SERIATIM
SHEIKDOM
SHIITAKE
SIBILANT
SICILIAN
SILICATE
SILICONE
SINISTER
SOCIABLE
SOCIALLY
SOLIDIFY
SOLIDITY
SOLITARY
SOLITUDE
SPLINTER
SPLITTER
SPOILAGE
SPOILING
SPRINGER
SPRINKLE
SPRINTER
SPRITELY
SPRITZER
SQUIGGLE
SQUIRREL
STAIRWAY
STEINWAY
STOICISM
STRIATED
STRIATUM
STRICKEN
STRICTLY
STRIDENT
STRIKING
STRINGED
STRINGER
STRIPPED
STRIPPER
STRIVING
SUKIYAKI
SYRINGES
TACITURN
TAHITIAN
TALISMAN
TERIYAKI
THAILAND
THRILLER
TIDINESS
TIMIDITY
TITICACA
TITIVATE
TOXICITY
TRAILING
TRAINING
TRAITORS
TUNISIAN
TUSITALA
UGLINESS
ULTIMATE
UNBIASED
UNBIDDEN
UNFILLED
UNHINGED
UNKINDLY
UNLIKELY
UNLISTED
UNSIGNED
UNTIDILY
UNTILLED
UNTIMELY
UNWIELDY
UPRIGHTS
UPRISING
VALIDATE
VALIDITY
VANISHED
VARIABLE
VARIANCE
VARICOSE
VARIETAL
VARIFORM
VARIORUM
VEXILLUM
VICINITY
VIGILANT
VIRILITY
VISIGOTH
VISITANT
VISITING
VITILIGO
VOLITION
VOMITING
VOMITORY
WARINESS
WILINESS
WINIFRED
YAKITORI
ZAMINDAR
ZODIACAL
BENJAMIN
BETJEMAN
CARJACOU
CONJUGAL
CONJURER
CONJUROR
MAHJONGG
MARJORAM
MISJUDGE
PERJURED
PERJURER
PREJUDGE
SERJEANT
SUBJECTS
VERJUICE
BACKACHE
BACKBITE
BACKBONE
BACKCHAT
BACKCOMB
BACKDATE
BACKDROP
BACKFIRE
BACKHAND
BACKLASH
BACKLESS
BACKPACK
BACKROOM
BACKSIDE
BACKWARD
BACKYARD
BANKBOOK
BANKNOTE
BANKROLL
BANKRUPT
BASKETRY
BEAKLESS
BERKELEY
BOOKABLE
BOOKCASE
BOOKMARK
BOOKROOM
BOOKSHOP
BOOKWORK
BOOKWORM
BUCKFAST
BUCKLING
BUCKSHEE
BUCKSHOT
BUCKSKIN
BULKHEAD
COCKATOO
COCKAYNE
COCKCROW
COCKEREL
COCKEYED
COCKTAIL
COOKBOOK
COOKWARE
DANKNESS
DARKENED
DARKNESS
DARKROOM
DECKHAND
DISKETTE
DOCKLAND
DOCKSIDE
DOCKYARD
DUCKBILL
DUCKLING
DUCKWEED
ERIKSSON
FALKLAND
FECKLESS
FOLKLORE
FOLKSONG
FORKLIFT
FORKTAIL
GYMKHANA
HECKLING
HOKKAIDO
HOOKWORM
HUCKSTER
JACKAROO
JACKBOOT
JACKETED
KICKBACK
KICKSHAW
KILKENNY
KINKAJOU
KRAKATOA
LACKADAY
LACKLAND
LARKSPUR
LEUKEMIA
LOCKABLE
LUCKLESS
MACKEREL
MARKDOWN
MARKEDLY
MARKSMAN
MEEKNESS
MILKLESS
MILKMAID
MILKWEED
MILKWORT
NECKBAND
NECKLACE
NECKLINE
NECKWEAR
NICKNACK
NICKNAME
PACKAGED
PARKLAND
PEEKABOO
PENKNIFE
PICKINGS
PICKLOCK
PICKMEUP
PICKWICK
PUCKERED
RACKRENT
RANKNESS
RECKLESS
RECKONER
RICKSHAW
ROCKETRY
RUCKSACK
SHAKEOUT
SICKLIST
SICKNESS
SICKROOM
SILKTAIL
SILKWORM
SOAKAWAY
STAKEOUT
STOKESAY
SUCKLING
TICKLING
TICKLISH
TICKTACK
TICKTOCK
TURKOMAN
VALKYRIE
WALKOVER
WALKYRIE
WEAKLING
WEAKNESS
WICKEDLY
WORKABLE
WORKADAY
WORKBOOK
WORKINGS
WORKLOAD
WORKMATE
WORKROOM
WORKSHOP
ADELAIDE
ADULATOR
ADULTERY
AFFLATUS
AFFLUENT
AIRLINER
ANALECTA
ANALEMMA
ANALOGUE
ANALYSER
ANALYSIS
ANGLESEY
ANGLICAN
APOLLYON
APOLOGIA
APOLOGUE
APPLAUSE
APPLETON
APPLIQUÉ
ARALDITE
ATALANTA
ATHLETIC
AVULSION

BADLANDS
BAILMENT
BALLCOCK
BALLGIRL
BALLISTA
BALLOCKS
BALLPARK
BALLROOM
BALLYHOO
BANLIEUE
BELLPUSH
BELLYFUL
BIBLICAL
BILLFOLD
BILLHOOK
BILLYBOY
BILLYCAN
BODLEIAN
BOLLOCKS
BUILDING
BULLDOZE
BULLETIN
BULLFROG
BULLHORN
BULLRING
BULLYRAG
CABLECAR
CABLEWAY
CALLGIRL
CALLIOPE
CALLIPER
CALLISTO
CAULDRON
CELLARER
CELLULAR
CHALDEAN
CHALDRON
CHILDERS
CHILDISH
CHILDREN
CHILIAST
CHILLADA
CHILLING
CHILTERN
CHOLERIC
COALESCE
COALHOLE
COALMINE
COALPORT
COLLAGEN
COLLAPSE
COLLARED
COLLATOR
COLLECTS
COLLEGES
COLLIERS
COLLIERY
COLLOQUY
COOLNESS
CULLINAN
CULLODEN
CURLICUE
CYCLADES
CYCLAMEN
CYCLICAL
DAYLIGHT
DEALINGS
DECLUTCH
DEFLOWER
DIALLING
DIALOGUE
DIALYSIS
DIELDRIN
DIPLOMAT
DISLIKED
DISLODGE
DISLOYAL
DOOLALLY
DUELLIST
DULLNESS
DWELLING
DYSLEXIA
DYSLEXIC
EARLIEST
EFFLUENT
EFFLUVIA
EMBLAZON
EMPLOYED
EMPLOYEE
EMPLOYER
EMULGENT
EMULSIFY
EMULSION
ENCLOSED
ENCLOTHE
EPILEPSY
EPILOGUE
EVALUATE
EVILDOER
EXPLICIT
EXPLODED
EXPLORER
EXULTANT
EXULTING
EYELINER
FALLIBLE
FANLIGHT
FAULKNER
FEELGOOD
FEELINGS
FELLAHIN
FIELDING
FOGLIGHT
FOLLICLE
FOLLOWED
FOLLOWER
FOLLOWUP
FOOLSCAP
FOULNESS
FUGLEMAN
FULLBACK
FULLNESS
FULLPAGE
FULLSIZE
FULLTIME
FURLOUGH
GAILLARD
GALLERIA
GALLIARD
GALLIPOT
GALLOPER
GALLOWAY
GALLUMPH
GAOLBIRD
GARLICKY
GIGLAMPS
GIRLHOOD
GOALPOST
GOLLIWOG
GRILLING
GUILTILY
GULLIBLE
GULLIVER
HALLIARD
HALLMARK
HALLOWED
HEELBALL
HEELTAPS
HELLADIC
HELLBENT
HELLENIC
HELLFIRE
HILLSIDE
HOLLOWAY
HOOLIGAN
HORLICKS
IDOLATER
IDOLATRY
IMPLICIT
INCLINED
INCLUDED
INFLAMED
INFLATED
INFLIGHT
ISOLATED
JAILBIRD
JEALOUSY
JELLICOE
KEELHAUL
KILLDEER
KOHLRABI
LOLLIPOP
LOWLANDS
LOWLYING
MAILBOAT
MAILSHOT
MALLARMÉ
MALLEATE
MALLORCA
MEALTIME
MEALYBUG
MIDLANDS
MILLIBAR
MILLINER
MILLIONS
MILLPOND
MILLRACE
MIRLITON
MOLLUSCS
MOULDING
MULLIGAN
MYELITIS
NEGLIGEE
NOBLEMAN
NUCLEOLE
OEILLADE
OMELETTE
OPULENCE
OUTLYING
PALLADIO
PALLIATE
PARLANCE
PAULINUS
PEELINGS
PELLAGRA
PELLETED
PELLICLE
PELLMELL
PELLUCID
PHALANGE
PHILEMON
PHILIPPI
PHILLIPS
PHILOMEL
PHYLLOME
PILLAGER
PILLARED
POLLSTER
POLLUTED
POLLUTER
POOLROOM
POTLATCH
POULAINE
POULTICE
PROLAPSE
PROLIFIC
PROLOGUE
PSALMIST
PSALMODY
PSALTERY
PUBLICAN
PUBLICLY
PULLDOWN
PULLOVER
PURLIEUS
PYELITIS
QUILTING
RACLETTE
RAILHEAD
RAILINGS
RAILLERY
RAILROAD
REALTIME
REDLIGHT
REPLEVIN
RIFLEMAN
ROLLCALL
ROULETTE
SAILBOAT
SCALDING
SCALENUS
SCALLION
SCILICET
SCOLDING
SCULLERY
SCULLION
SCULPTOR
SEALSKIN
SEALYHAM
SECLUDED
SHALLOWS
SHELDUCK
SHELVING
SHILLING
SKELETAL
SKELETON
SKILLFUL
SKILLING
SKILLION
SKULKING
SKULLCAP
SKYLIGHT
SMALLEST
SMALLPOX
SMELTING
SMOLLETT
SOULLESS
SPELLING
SPELLMAN
SPILLAGE
SPILLWAY
SPOLIATE
STALKING
STALLION
STALWART
STELLATE
STILETTO
STILWELL
STOLIDLY
STULTIFY
STYLIZED
SUBLEASE
SULLENLY
SULLIVAN
SUNLIGHT
SWELLING
SWILLING
SYLLABIC
SYLLABLE
SYLLABUB
SYLLABUS
TABLEMAT
TAILBACK
TAILGATE
TAILLESS
TAILPIPE
TAILSKID
TAILSPIN
TELLTALE
TELLURIC
THALAMUS
THALLIUM
TOILSOME
TOLLGATE
TOPLEVEL
TOULOUSE
TRILEMMA
TRILLING
TRILLION
TRILLIUM
TROLLOPE
TWELVEMO
TWILIGHT
UNCLOVEN
UNPLACED
VALLETTA
VAULTING
VELLEITY
VERLAINE
VILLAGER
VILLAINY
VIOLATOR
VIOLENCE
WALLSEND
WALLWORT
WELLBRED
WELLNIGH
WELLPAID
WESLEYAN
WETLANDS
WILLIAMS
WOOLLENS

WOOLPACK
WOOLSACK
WYCLIFFE
YIELDING
ABOMASUM
ALEMAINE
ALUMINUM
ANIMATED
ARAMAEAN
ARAMANTH
AROMATIC
ATOMIZER
BALMORAL
BEDMAKER
BESMIRCH
BISMARCK
BRAMANTE
BRIMMING
BROMELIA
BROMPTON
BRUMAIRE
BUMMAREE
CALMNESS
CHAMBERS
CHAMPERS
CHAMPION
CHEMICAL
CHIMAERA
CHUMMAGE
CLAMBAKE
CLEMATIS
CLEMENCY
CLIMATIC
CLIMBING
CLUMSILY
COMMANDO
COMMENCE
COMMERCE
COMMONER
COMMONLY
COMMUNAL
COMMUTER
CORMORAN
COSMETIC
CRAMOISY
CRIMINAL
CROMLECH
CROMWELL
CRUMHORN
CRUMMOCK
DALMATIC
DIAMANTE
DIAMETER
DIAMONDS
DISMALLY
DISMAYED
DISMOUNT
DOGMATIC
DOOMSDAY
DORMOUSE
DRAMATIC
DRUMBEAT
DRUMHEAD
DRUMLINE
DRUMMING
EGOMANIA
ELEMENTS
EXAMINEE
EXAMINER
EXEMPLAR
FARMHAND
FARMLAND
FARMYARD
FIRMNESS
FLAMENCO
FLAMINGO
FLIMSILY
FLUMMERY
FORMALIN
FORMALLY
FORMERLY
FORMLESS
FORMOSAN
FREMITUS
FRUMENTY
FRUMPISH
GARMENTS
GEOMANCY
GEOMETER
GEOMETRY
GERMAINE
GERMANIC
GERMINAL
GLUMPISH
GORMLESS
GRAMERCY
GRIMALDI
GRIMNESS
GRUMBLER
GRUMPILY
GUMMOSIS
GUNMETAL
HAMMERED
HARMLESS
HARMONIC
HAYMAKER
HELMETED
HELMSMAN
HERMETIC
HERMIONE
HOGMANAY
HORMONAL
INIMICAL
KATMANDU
KERMESSE
KROMESKY
LAWMAKER
MACMAHON
MARMOSET
MESMERIC
MISMATCH
MNEMONIC
MONMOUTH
MYRMIDON
NEOMYCIN
NORMALLY
NORMANDY
ODDMENTS
ODOMETER
OLYMPIAD
OLYMPIAN
OLYMPICS
OUTMATCH
OUTMODED
OXYMORON
PALMATED
PALMETTO
PARMESAN
PEMMICAN
PERMEATE
PLIMSOLL
PLUMBAGO
PLUMBING
PLYMOUTH
PREMIERE
PREMISES
PREMOLAR
PRIMEVAL
PRIMNESS
PRIMROSE
PROMISED
PROMOTER
PROMPTER
PROMPTLY
PTOMAINE
REEMPLOY
RENMINBI
RHOMBOID
ROOMMATE
SCHMALTZ
SCHMOOZE
SCIMITAR
SEAMLESS
SEAMSTER
SHAMBLES
SHAMEFUL
SHAMROCK
SLIMNESS
SLUMMING
STAMENED
STAMPEDE
STIMULUS
SUBMERGE
SUMMITRY
SURMOUNT
SWIMMING
SWIMSUIT
SYMMETRY
TASMANIA
TEAMMATE
TEAMSTER
TEAMWORK
TERMINAL
TERMINUS
THEMATIC
THOMPSON
THUMPING
TITMOUSE
TRAMLINE
TREMBLER
TRIMARAN
TRIMMING
TRIMNESS
TROMBONE
TRUMPERY
TURMERIC
UDOMETER
VERMOUTH
WHIMBREL
WORMCAST
WORMWOOD
YARMULKA
YEOMANRY
ABINGDON
ABUNDANT
ACANTHUS
ADENITIS
ADENOIDS
AGONIZED
AMANDINE
AMENABLE
AMUNDSEN
ASUNCION
AVENTINE
BARNABAS
BARNACLE
BARNARDS
BARNYARD
BEANPOLE
BIANNUAL
BIENNIAL
BINNACLE
BLANDISH
BLENDING
BLENHEIM
BLINDING
BLINKERS
BLINKING
BOUNCING
BOUNDARY
BRANCHED
BRANDADE
BRANDISH
BRANDNEW
BRINDISI
BRINDLED
BRINGING
BRONCHUS
BRUNETTE
BURNTOUT
CANNABIS
CANNIBAL
CARNEGIE
CARNIVAL
CHANCERY
CHANDLER
CHANGING
CHANTAGE
CHANTREY
CHENILLE
CHINAMAN
CHINDITS
CINNABAR
CINNAMON
CLANGING
CLANGOUR
CLANNISH
CLANSMAN
CLINCHER
CLINGING
CLINICAL
CLINKERS
COGNOMEN
COINCIDE
CORNETTO
CORNHILL
CORNICHE
CORNWALL
COUNTESS
COUNTIES
COUNTING
CRANEFLY
CRINGING
CRONYISM
CRUNCHIE
CYANOGEN
CYANOSIS
DAINTIES
DAINTILY
DAMNABLE
DAUNTING
DIANTHUS
DIONYSUS
DOWNBEAT
DOWNCAST
DOWNFALL
DOWNHILL
DOWNLOAD
DOWNPLAY
DOWNPOUR
DOWNSIDE
DOWNSIZE
DOWNTOWN
DOWNTURN
DOWNWARD
DRINKING
DRUNKARD
EARNINGS
ECONOMIC
EDENTATE
ELONGATE
EMINENCE
ETHNARCH
EVANESCE
EVENNESS
EVENSONG
EVENTFUL
EVENTIDE
EVENTUAL
FAINITES
FAINTING
FIENDISH
FLANDERS
FLANNELS
FLINDERS
FOUNDING
FOUNTAIN
FRANCIUM
FRANKISH
FRANKLIN
FRENETIC
FRENULUM
FRENZIED
FRONDEUR
FRONTAGE
FRONTIER
FRONTMAN
GAUNTLET
GHANAIAN
GIANTESS
GLANCING
GLANDERS
GRANDEUR
GRANDSON
GRANULAR
GRANULES
GRINDING
HANNIBAL
HAUNCHES
HAUNTING
HORNBEAM
HORNBILL

HORNBOOK
HORNPIPE
HYPNOSIS
HYPNOTIC
IDENTIFY
IDENTITY
INUNDATE
IRONCLAD
IRONICAL
IRONSIDE
IRONWARE
IRONWOOD
IRONWORK
JAUNDICE
JAUNTILY
JEANETTE
JOHNSONS
JOINTURE
KEENNESS
KLONDIKE
LEINSTER
LEONARDO
LEONIDAS
LIENTERY
LIGNEOUS
LINNAEAN
LINNAEUS
MAGNESIA
MAGNETIC
MAGNOLIA
MAINLAND
MAINLINE
MAINMAST
MAINSAIL
MAINSTAY
MAINTAIN
MAINYARD
MANNERED
MANNERLY
MANNIKIN
MEANNESS
MEANTIME
MEUNIÈRE
MIDNIGHT
MIGNONNE
MISNOMER
MOONBEAM
MOUNTAIN
MOUNTING
NOONTIME
OPENCAST
OPENDOOR
OPENNESS
OPENPLAN
OPENWORK
ORANGERY
ORDNANCE
OVENWARE
PAINLESS
PAINTING
PANNICLE
PANNIKIN
PAWNSHOP
PENNINES
PHANTASM
PHONETIC
PINNACLE
PINNIPED
PLANCHET
PLANGENT
PLANKING
PLANKTON
PLANNING
PLANTAIN
PLUNGING
POUNDAGE
PRANDIAL
PRENATAL
PRINCELY
PRINCESS
PRINTING
PRINTOUT
PRUNELLA
PUGNOSED
QUANDARY
QUANTIFY
QUANTITY
QUENELLE
QUINCUNX
QUINTAIN
RAINBIRD
RAINCOAT
RAINDROP
RAINFALL
RAINWEAR
REINDEER
REINSURE
REINVEST
REMNANTS
REYNOLDS
RHONCHUS
ROENTGEN
ROUNDERS
RUNNERUP
SAINFOIN
SCANDIUM
SCANNING
SCANSION
SCANTIES
SCANTILY
SCENARIO
SCHNAPPS
SHANGHAI
SHANTUNG
SHINGLES
SIGNALER
SIGNALLY
SIGNORIA
SIGNPOST
SKINDEEP
SKINHEAD
SKINWORK
SLANGING
SLANTING
SOUNDING
SPANDREL
SPANGLED
SPANIARD
SPANKING
SPANNING
SPENDING
SPINNING
SPINSTER
SPINTEXT
STANDARD
STANDING
STANDISH
STANDOFF
STANHOPE
STANNARY
STANNITE
STENDHAL
STENOSED
STENOSIS
STINGING
STINGRAY
STINKING
STUNNING
SVENGALI
SWANSKIN
SWANSONG
SWINDLER
SWINGING
TEENAGER
TENNYSON
THANATOS
THANKFUL
THINGAMY
THINKING
THINNESS
THINNING
THUNDERY
TINNITUS
TOPNOTCH
TOWNSHIP
TOWNSMAN
TRANQUIL
TRANSACT
TRANSECT
TRANSEPT
TRANSFER
TRANSFIX
TRANSHIP
TRANSKEI
TRANSMIT
TRENCHER
TRINCULO
TRINIDAD
TRUNCATE
TRUNNION
TURNBACK
TURNCOAT
TURNCOCK
TURNOVER
TURNPIKE
TURNSPIT
UNENDING
UTENSILS
VIGNETTE
WAINSCOT
WHENEVER
WHINCHAT
WINNINGS
WINNIPEG
WRANGLER
WRINGING
WRINKLED
WRONGFUL
YOUNGEST
ZOONOSIS
ABNORMAL
ABROGATE
ABSOLUTE
ABSOLVED
ABSORBED
ABSORBER
ACCOLADE
ACCOUNTS
ACROMION
ACROSTIC
ADMONISH
ADROITLY
ADVOCACY
ADVOCATE
AEROBICS
AERODYNE
AEROFLOT
AEROFOIL
AEROGRAM
AEROLITH
AERONAUT
AEROSTAT
AGNOSTIC
AGRONOMY
ALGORISM
ALLOCATE
ALLOGAMY
ALLOPATH
ALLOWING
AMMONIAC
AMMONITE
ANDORRAN
ANNOTATE
ANNOUNCE
ANNOYING
APHORISM
APPOSITE
ARBOREAL
ARGONAUT
ARMORIAL
ARMORICA
ARMOURED
ARROGANT
ARROGATE
ARSONIST
ASCORBIC
ASMODEUS
ASSORTED
ASTONISH
ATROCITY
ATTORNEY
AUTOBAHN
AUTOCRAT
AUTOGAMY
AUTOGYRO
AUTOMATE
AUTONOMY
AUTOTYPE
BARONESS
BARONETS
BARONIAL
BECOMING
BEGORRAH
BEHOLDEN
BEHOLDER
BESOTTED
BESOUGHT
BICONVEX
BIFOCALS
BINOMIAL
BLOOMERS
BLOOMING
BOBOLINK
BOEOTIAN
BORODINO
BROODING
CABOCHON
CABOODLE
CABOTAGE
CAJOLERY
CALOTYPE
CAMOMILE
CANOEING
CANOEIST
CANONIZE
CANOODLE
CAROLINA
CAROLINE
CAROTENE
CAROUSAL
CAROUSEL
CENOBITE
CENOTAPH
CHLORATE
CHLORIDE
CHLORINE
CHOOSING
CHROMITE
CHROMIUM
CIBORIUM
COLOMBIA
COLONIAL
COLONIST
COLONIZE
COLOPHON
COLORADO
COLORANT
COLORFUL
COLORING
COLOSSAL
COLOSSUS
COLOURED
CORONARY
CORONOID
COTOPAXI
CREOSOTE
CROONING
CYNOSURE
CYTOLOGY
DAMOCLES
DEBONAIR
DECORATE
DECOROUS
DECOUPLE
DEFORMED
DEMOCRAT
DEMOLISH
DEMONIAC
DEMOTION
DENOUNCE
DEPORTEE
DEROGATE
DESOLATE
DETONATE
DEVOTION
DINOSAUR
DISORDER
DIVORCED
DIVORCEE
DOLOMITE
DOLOROUS
DOXOLOGY

DROOPING
DUBONNET
ECLOSION
ECTODERM
ELDORADO
EMBODIED
EMBOLDEN
EMBOLISM
EMBOSSED
EMPORIUM
ENCOMIUM
ENDOCARP
ENDODERM
ENDOGAMY
ERGOTISE
ERGOTISM
ESCORIAL
ESPOUSAL
ESTONIAN
ESTOPPEL
ESTOVERS
ETIOLATE
EUDOXIAN
EULOGIST
EULOGIUM
EULOGIZE
EUROLAND
EUROPEAN
EUROSTAR
EXPONENT
EXPORTER
EXPOSURE
FAMOUSLY
FAROUCHE
FAVORITE
FAVOURED
FEROCITY
FLOODING
FLOODLIT
FLOORING
FLUORIDE
FLUORINE
FLUORITE
GABONESE
GABORONE
GADOGADO
GALOSHES
GASOLIER
GASOLINE
GEMOLOGY
GENOCIDE
GERONIMO
GIRONDIN
GLOOMILY
GROOMING
GYROSTAT
HEDONISM
HEDONIST
HOLOGRAM
HONOLULU
HONORARY
HOROLOGY
HUMORIST
HUMOROUS
IDEOGRAM
IDEOLOGY
IGNOMINY
IGNORANT
IMMOBILE
IMMODEST
IMMOLATE
IMMORTAL
IMPOLITE
IMPORTER
IMPOSING
IMPOSTER
IMPOSTOR
IMPOTENT
INCOMING
INDOLENT
INFORMAL
INFORMED
INFORMER
INNOCENT
INNOVATE
INSOLENT
INSOMNIA
INVOLUTE
INVOLVED
JACOBEAN
JACOBITE
JALOUSIE
JAPONICA
JEHOVAHS
JEROBOAM
KEROSENE
KILOBYTE
KILOGRAM
KILOVOLT
KILOWATT
LABOURED
LABOURER
LACONIAN
LANOLINE
LAROUSSE
LEMONADE
LICORICE
LILONGWE
LIMONITE
LINOLEUM
LINOTYPE
LOBOTOMY
MAHOGANY
MAJOLICA
MAJORITY
MALODOUR
MANORIAL
MARONITE
MAYORESS
MEMORIAL
MEMORIAM
MEMORIZE
MESOLITE
METONYMY
MINORESS
MINORITE
MINORITY
MINOTAUR
MISOGYNY
MONOGAMY
MONOGRAM
MONOHULL
MONOLITH
MONOPOLY
MONORAIL
MONOTONY
MONOTYPE
MONOXIDE
MOROCCAN
MOROSELY
MOTORCAR
MOTORING
MOTORIST
MOTORIZE
MOTORMAN
MOTORWAY
MYCOLOGY
NAPOLEON
NEPOTISM
NICOTINE
NOMOGRAM
NOSOLOGY
OBSOLETE
ODIOUSLY
OENOLOGY
OENOPHIL
ONCOLOGY
ONCOMING
ONLOOKER
ONTOLOGY
OPPONENT
OPPOSING
OPPOSITE
PANORAMA
PARODIST
PAROLLES
PAROXYSM
PECORINO
PENOLOGY
PEROXIDE
PILOTAGE
PINOCHLE
PIROZHKI
PLEONASM
PLIOCENE
POLONIUM
POROSITY
POSOLOGY
PRIORESS
PRIORITY
RECORDER
RECOURSE
RECOVERY
REDOLENT
REDOUBLE
REFORMED
REFORMER
REJOINED
RELOCATE
REMOTELY
REMOUNTS
RENOUNCE
RENOVATE
RENOWNED
REPORTED
REPORTER
REPOUSSÉ
RESOLUTE
RESOLVED
RESONANT
RESONATE
RESOURCE
REVOLVER
RHEOSTAT
RICOCHET
RIGOROUS
ROBOTICS
RUMOURED
SABOTAGE
SABOTEUR
SAPONITE
SAVOURED
SAVOYARD
SAYONARA
SCHOONER
SCROFULA
SCROUNGE
SECONDER
SECONDLY
SEMOLINA
SENORITA
SEROLOGY
SEROTYPE
SEXOLOGY
SHOOTING
SHOOTOUT
SHROUDED
SMOOTHER
SMOOTHLY
SNOOTILY
SONOROUS
SORORITY
SPOONFUL
SPROCKET
STROLLER
STRONGLY
SYNOPSIS
SYNOPTIC
TAXONOMY
THEOCRAT
THEOLOGY
THEORIST
THEORIZE
THROMBIN
THROMBUS
THROTTLE
TIMOROUS
TOBOGGAN
TOMORROW
TOPOLOGY
TOXOCARA
TROOPING
TUTORIAL
TYROLEAN
TYROSINE
UNCOMBED
UNCOMMON
UNCOOKED
UNCOUPLE
UNFORCED
UNIONISM
UNIONIST
UNIONIZE
UNLOADED
UNLOCKED
UNLOVELY
UNSOCIAL
UNSOLVED
UNTOWARD
UNVOICED
UNWONTED
UNWORTHY
UPCOMING
UPHOLDER
VAPORIZE
VELOCITY
VENOMOUS
VERONESE
VERONICA
VIGOROUS
VIROLOGY
WHOOPING
XENOGAMY
XENOLITH
XENOPHON
YOKOHAMA
YUGOSLAV
ZAKOUSKI
ACAPULCO
ADOPTION
ADOPTIVE
AIRPLANE
ALOPECIA
ANAPAEST
ANYPLACE
APOPLEXY
ATYPICAL
AUSPICES
BAGPIPES
BELPAESE
BESPOKEN
CAMPAIGN
CAMPBELL
CAMPSITE
CAMPTOWN
CHAPATTI
CHAPERON
CHAPLAIN
CHIPMUNK
CHOPPING
CLAPPERS
CLAPPING
CLAPTRAP
CLIPPERS
CLIPPING
CODPIECE
COMPARED
COMPILER
COMPLAIN
COMPLETE
COMPLINE
COMPOSED
COMPOSER
COMPOUND
COMPRESS
COMPRISE
COMPUTER
CORPORAL
COUPERIN
COUPLING
CREPITUS
CRIPPLED
CULPABLE
CUSPIDOR
CUTPRICE
CUTPURSE
DAMPNESS
DEEPNESS
DESPATCH
DESPOTIC
DIAPASON
DIAPHONE

DIOPTRIC
DISPATCH
DISPENSE
DISPERSE
DISPIRIT
DISPLACE
DISPOSAL
DISPOSED
DISPROVE
DISPUTED
DRIPPING
DROPHEAD
DROPPING
DROPSHOT
DUMPLING
EARPHONE
EARPIECE
EGGPLANT
EGYPTIAN
ELEPHANT
EPIPHANY
EPIPHYTE
EPIPLOON
ERUPTION
ERUPTURE
EYEPIECE
FLAPJACK
FLAPPING
FLIPPANT
FLIPPERS
FLIPPING
FRIPPERY
GAZPACHO
GEOPHONE
GRAPHEME
GRAPHICS
GRAPHITE
GRIPPING
GUMPTION
GUNPOINT
HELPLESS
HELPLINE
HELPMATE
HERPETIC
HISPANIC
HOSPITAL
HOTPLATE
HUMPBACK
HUMPHREY
INSPIRED
INSPIRIT
JEOPARDY
JUMPSUIT
KEEPSAKE
KIPPERED
KNAPSACK
KNAPWEED

KREPLACH
LAMPPOST
LEAPFROG
LIMPNESS
LOOPHOLE
LUMPFISH
MANPOWER
MIDPOINT
MISPLACE
MISPRINT
MORPHEME
MORPHEUS
MORPHINE
NAUPLIUS
NEOPHYTE
OLIPHANT
OPOPANAX
PALPABLE
PALPABLY
PAMPERED
PAMPHLET
PEEPHOLE
PINPOINT
PINPRICK
POPPADOM
PORPHYRA
PORPHYRY
PORPOISE
PREPARED
PROPERLY
PROPERTY
PROPHECY
PROPHESY
PROPOSAL
PROPOSED
PROPOSER
PROPOUND
PURPLISH
RAMPARTS
RASPUTIN
REAPPEAR
RESPECTS
RESPIGHI
RESPONSE
RHAPSODY
RIPPLING
SAMPHIRE
SAPPHIRE
SAPPHIST
SCAPHOID
SCAPULAR
SEAPLANE
SHEPHERD
SHIPMATE
SHIPMENT
SHIPPING
SHIPYARD

SHOPPING
SHOPTALK
SIMPLIFY
SIXPENCE
SKIPJACK
SKIPPING
SKYPILOT
SLAPBANG
SLAPDASH
SLAPJACK
SLIPOVER
SLIPPERS
SLIPPERY
SLIPPING
SLIPSHOD
SLIPSLOP
SLOPPILY
SNAPPILY
SNAPSHOT
SOAPSUDS
STAPHYLE
STEPHENS
STOPCOCK
STOPOVER
STOPPAGE
STOPPING
STUPIDLY
SUBPOENA
SULPHATE
SULPHIDE
SUPPLANT
SUPPLIER
SUPPLIES
SUPPOSED
SUPPRESS
SURPLICE
SURPRISE
SUSPENSE
SYMPATHY
SYMPHONY
SYMPTOMS
TAXPAYER
TEMPERED
TEMPLATE
TEMPORAL
TEMPTING
TRAPDOOR
TRAPPIST
TRIPLING
TRIPTANE
TRIPTYCH
TROPICAL
TUPPENNY
TWOPENNY
TWOPIECE
TYMPANUM
UNIPOLAR

UNSPOILT
UNSPOKEN
VESPERAL
VESPUCCI
VOLPLANE
WARPAINT
WARPLANE
WEAPONRY
WHIPCORD
WHIPHAND
WHIPJACK
WHIPLASH
WHIPPING
WHOPPING
WRAPPING
ZEPPELIN
ZOOPHYTE
ADEQUACY
ADEQUATE
CHEQUERS
CLIQUISH
CONQUEST
DAIQUIRI
DISQUIET
ELOQUENT
FREQUENT
INEQUITY
INIQUITY
IROQUOIS
JACQUARD
MARQUESA
MARQUESS
MARQUISE
MISQUOTE
MOSQUITO
MUSQUASH
UBIQUITY
UNIQUELY
VANQUISH
ABERDEEN
ABERRANT
ABORTION
ABORTIVE
ACCREDIT
ACERBATE
ACERBITY
ADORABLE
AEGROTAT
AGGRIEVE
AIGRETTE
ALARMING
ALARMIST
ALFRESCO
ALTRUISM
ALTRUIST
AMARANTH
AMARETTO

AMBROSIA
AMERICAN
AMERICAS
AMORETTI
AMORETTO
AMORTIZE
ANARCHIC
ANDREWES
ANOREXIA
ANOREXIC
APERIENT
APERITIF
APERTURE
APPRAISE
APPRISED
APPROACH
APPROVAL
APPROVED
ATARAXIA
ATARAXIC
AVERSION
BAHRAINI
BARRACKS
BARRATRY
BARRETTE
BAYREUTH
BEARABLE
BEARINGS
BEARSKIN
BEERBOHM
BEFRIEND
BEGRUDGE
BETRAYAL
BETRAYER
BLURRING
BOARDING
BORROWED
BORROWER
BURROWER
CABRIOLE
CAERLEON
CAPRIOLE
CARRAWAY
CARRIAGE
CARRIOLE
CARRYALL
CARRYCOT
CARRYING
CHARCOAL
CHARGING
CHARISMA
CHARLADY
CHARLOCK
CHARMING
CHARTISM
CHARTIST
CHARTRES

CHEROKEE
CHERUBIC
CHERUBIM
CHERWELL
CHORDATA
CHORDATE
CHORIAMB
CHURLISH
CLARENCE
CLARINET
CLERICAL
CLERIHEW
COARSELY
COERCION
COERCIVE
CORRAGIO
CORRIDOR
CORRODED
COURTESY
CURRENCY
CURRICLE
CZAREVNA
DAIRYMAN
DECREASE
DECREPIT
DECRETAL
DEERSKIN
DEFREEZE
DEGRADED
DEPRAVED
DEPRIVED
DETRITUS
DIARESIS
DIARRHEA
DIERESIS
DISRAELI
DIURETIC
DOORBELL
DOORKNOB
DOORPOST
DOORSTEP
DWARFISH
DWARFISM
ELDRITCH
EMBRACED
EMBRACES
EMERGENT
EMERGING
EMERITUS
EMERSION
EMIRATES
ENCROACH
ENERGIZE
ENERVATE
ENGRAVER
ENORMITY
ENORMOUS

ENTRAILS
ENTRANCE
ENTREATY
ENTRENCH
ENTREPOT
ENTRYISM
ESPRESSO
ESTRAGON
ESTROGEN
ETERNITY
EUTROPHY
EUTROPIC
EVERMORE
EVERYDAY
EVERYMAN
EVERYONE
EXERCISE
EXERTION
EXORCISM
EXORCIST
EXORCIZE
EXORDIUM
EXPRESSO
EXTRADOS
FAIRNESS
FARRIERY
FEARLESS
FEARSOME
FEBRUARY
FERRYMAN
FIBROSIS
FIERCELY
FLIRTING
FLORENCE
FOURFOLD
FOURPART
FOURSOME
FOURTEEN
FURROWED
GARRIGUE
GARRISON
GARROTTE
GEORGIAN
GLORIANA
GLORIOLE
GLORIOUS
GOURMAND
GUARDIAN
GUERIDON
GUERILLA
GUERNSEY
HAIRLESS
HAIRLIKE
HAIRLINE
HARRIDAN
HARRISON
HEARTIES
HEARTILY
HEBRIDES
HEIRLESS
HEIRLOOM
HIDROSIS
HIERARCH
HIERATIC
HOARDING
HOARSELY
HORRIBLE
HORRIBLY
HORRIFIC
HYDROGEN
IMPRISON
IMPROPER
IMPROVED
IMPROVER
INCREASE
INFRARED
INFRINGE
INGROWTH
INTRADOS
INTRENCH
INTREPID
INTRIGUE
INTRUDER
JERRYCAN
JORROCKS
KHARTOUM
KORRIGAN
KOURMISS
LABRADOR
LACROSSE
LADRONES
LAUREATE
LAURENCE
LAWRENCE
LEARNING
LIBRETTO
LORRAINE
MACREADY
MADRIGAL
MARRIAGE
MATRONLY
METRICAL
METRITIS
MICRODOT
MIGRAINE
MIRRORED
MONROVIA
MOORCOCK
MOORINGS
MOORLAND
MORRISON
MOURNFUL
MOURNING
NARRATOR
NARROWLY
NEARNESS
NEBRASKA
NECROSIS
NEURITIS
NEUROSIS
NEUROTIC
NITROGEN
NUTRIENT
OPERABLE
OPERATIC
OPERATOR
OPERETTA
OUTREACH
OUTREMER
OUTRIDER
OUTRIGHT
OVERALLS
OVERBOOK
OVERCAST
OVERCOAT
OVERCOME
OVERDONE
OVERDOSE
OVERDRAW
OVERFEED
OVERFILL
OVERFLOW
OVERFULL
OVERHANG
OVERHAUL
OVERHEAD
OVERHEAR
OVERHEAT
OVERKILL
OVERLAID
OVERLAND
OVERLEAF
OVERLOAD
OVERLOOK
OVERLORD
OVERMUCH
OVERPASS
OVERPLAY
OVERRATE
OVERRIDE
OVERRIPE
OVERRULE
OVERSEAS
OVERSEER
OVERSHOE
OVERSHOT
OVERSIZE
OVERSTAY
OVERSTEP
OVERTAKE
OVERTIME
OVERTONE
OVERTURE
OVERTURN
OVERVIEW
OVERWORK
OXBRIDGE
PEARLING
PEARMAIN
PEERLESS
PETRARCH
PHARISEE
PHARMACY
PHORMIUM
PIERCING
PIERETTE
PIERIDES
POORNESS
PORRIDGE
PROROGUE
PRURIENT
PYORRHEA
QUARTERS
QUARTIER
QUARTILE
QUIRINAL
REARMOST
REARWARD
RECREATE
RECRUITS
REFRINGE
REORIENT
REPRIEVE
REPRISAL
REPROACH
RETRENCH
RETRIEVE
SACRISTY
SAUROPOD
SCARCELY
SCARCITY
SCARFACE
SCIROCCO
SCORCHED
SCORCHER
SCORNFUL
SCORPION
SEARCHER
SECRETLY
SERRATED
SHAREOUT
SHERATON
SHERIDAN
SHERLOCK
SHERWOOD
SHORTAGE
SKIRMISH
SKIRTING
SLURRING
SMARTEST
SNORTING
SOBRIETY
SOCRATES
SOCRATIC
SOURCING
SOURNESS
SOURPUSS
SPARAXIS
SPARKING
SPARKLER
SPARRING
SPARSELY
SPARSITY
SPARTANS
SPIRACLE
SPIRALLY
SPIRITED
SPIRITUS
SPORADIC
SPORTING
SPORTIVE
SPURIOUS
SPURNING
STARCHED
STARDUST
STARFISH
STARGAZE
STARKERS
STARLESS
STARLING
STAROSTA
STARTERS
STARTING
STARVING
STERLING
STIRLING
STIRRING
STOREMAN
STOREYED
STORMING
STORMONT
STURDILY
STURGEON
SURROUND
SWARMING
SWERVING
SWIRLING
TARRAGON
TEARABLE
TEARAWAY
TEARDROP
TERRACED
TERRAPIN
TERRIBLE
TERRIBLY
TERRIFIC
TETRAGON
TETRAPOD
TETRARCH
THIRTEEN
THORACIC
THOROUGH
THURIBLE
THURIFER
THURSDAY
TSAREVNA
TURRETED
TWIRLING
UMBRELLA
UNBROKEN
UNERRING
UNFREEZE
USURIOUS
UXORIOUS
VAGRANCY
VIBRANCY
VIBRATOR
VITREOUS
WARRANTY
WEARABLE
WHARFAGE
WHEREVER
WHIRLING
WORRYING
YEARBOOK
YEARLING
YEARLONG
YEARNING
YOURSELF
ABESSIVE
ADESSIVE
AIRSCREW
AIRSPEED
AIRSTRIP
ALLSPICE
AMUSETTE
ANGSTROM
ANISETTE
APOSTASY
APOSTATE
APOSTLES
AYRSHIRE
BASSINET
BEDSTEAD
BEDSTRAW
BEESWING
BESSEMER
BIOSCOPE
BLASTOFF
BLASTULA
BLESSING
BLISSFUL

BLUSHING
BLUSTERY
BOASTFUL
BOASTING
BONSPIEL
BORSTALL
BOTSWANA
BOWSPRIT
BRASILIA
BRASSARD
BRASSICA
BRISLING
BRISTLED
BRISTLES
BRUSSELS
BURSITIS
BURSTING
CAMSHAFT
CAMSTONE
CAPSICUM
CAPSIZED
CAPSTONE
CASSETTE
CATSMEAT
CAUSEWAY
CESSPOOL
CHASSEUR
CHASTISE
CHASTITY
CHASUBLE
CHESHIRE
CHESSMAN
CHESSMEN
CHESTNUT
CLASHING
CLASPING
CLASSICS
CLASSIFY
CONSERVE
CONSIDER
CONSOMMÉ
CONSPIRE
CONSTANT
CONSTRUE
CONSULAR
CONSUMED
CONSUMER
CORSELET
CORSICAN
COTSWOLD
COUSCOUS
COXSWAIN
COYSTRIL
CRESCENT
CRISPIAN
CROSSBAR
CROSSING
CROSSLET
CRUSADER
CRUSHING
CRYSTALS
CURSITOR
DIASPORA
DIASTASE
DIASTOLE
DIPSTICK
DISSOLVE
DISSUADE
DOGSBODY
DOGSTAIL
DRESSAGE
DRESSING
DRYSTONE
EGGSHELL
EINSTEIN
EMISSARY
EMISSION
EPISODIC
EPISTYLE
EXISTENT
EXISTING
EYESHADE
EYESIGHT
FALSETTO
FATSTOCK
FEASIBLE
FEASIBLY
FLASHGUN
FLASHILY
FLASHING
FLUSHING
FLYSHEET
FORSAKEN
FORSLACK
FORSOOTH
FORSWEAR
FRESHEST
FRESHMAN
FRISKILY
FROSTILY
FROSTING
GLASNOST
GLASSFUL
GLISSADE
GLOSSARY
GLOSSEME
GNASHING
GOBSMACK
GOOSEGOG
GOSSAMER
GRASPING
GRISELDA
GRISETTE
GROSBEAK
GROSCHEN
GUNSMITH
GUSSETED
HABSBURG
HAPSBURG
HAYSTACK
HELSINKI
HERSCHEL
HIPSTERS
HOGSHEAD
HORSEBOX
HORSEFLY
HORSEMAN
HORSEMEN
HOUSEMAN
INASMUCH
INKSTAIN
IRISCOPE
IRISHISM
IRISHMAN
IRISHMEN
ISOSTASY
JOYSTICK
KEYSTONE
KINSFOLK
KINSHASA
KOMSOMOL
KOUSKOUS
LANSBURY
LEISURED
LIPSTICK
LONSDALE
LOOSEBOX
LOPSIDED
MAESTOSO
MARSHALL
MASSACRE
MASSENET
MASSEUSE
MASSICOT
MEASURED
MEMSAHIB
MENSWEAR
MESSAGER
MESSIDOR
MESSMATE
MESSUAGE
MINSTREL
MISSOURI
MISSPELL
MISSPENT
MOISTURE
MONSTERA
MOUSSAKA
MUDSTONE
MYOSOTIS
NAUSEATE
NAUSEOUS
NEWSCAST
NEWSHAWK
NEWSPEAK
NEWSREEL
NEWSROOM
NOISETTE
NONSENSE
NONSTICK
NORSEMAN
NORSEMEN
NUISANCE
NURSLING
NUTSHELL
ODYSSEUS
OFFSHOOT
OFFSHORE
OFFSIDER
OFFSTAGE
OILSKINS
OILSLICK
OLDSTYLE
OMISSION
ONESIDED
OPUSCULE
ORESTEIA
OTOSCOPE
OUISTITI
OUTSHINE
OUTSIDER
OUTSMART
OUTSTRIP
PARSIFAL
PASSABLE
PASSABLY
PASSBOOK
PASSERBY
PASSIBLE
PASSOVER
PASSPORT
PASSWORD
PERSHING
PERSONAL
PERSPIRE
PERSUADE
PERSUANT
PHOSGENE
PHYSALIA
PHYSICAL
PHYSIQUE
PIGSWILL
PILSENER
PISSHEAD
PLASTRON
POISONER
PONSONBY
POPSICLE
POSSIBLE
POSSIBLY
POTSHERD
PRESENCE
PRESERVE
PRESSING
PRESSMAN
PRESSURE
PRESTIGE
PRISONER
PRISTINE
PROSPECT
PROSPERO
PROSTATE
PRUSSIAN
PUISSANT
PURSLANE
PUSSYCAT
QUESTION
QUISLING
RAGSTONE
RAISONNÉ
RASSELAS
REASONED
REASSERT
REASSESS
REASSIGN
REASSUME
REASSURE
REDSHANK
REDSTART
REUSABLE
RIBSTONE
RIESLING
RISSOLES
ROASTING
ROSSETTI
ROUSSEAU
SANSERIF
SANSKRIT
SASSANID
SAUSAGES
SCISSION
SCISSORS
SEASCAPE
SEASHELL
SEASHORE
SEASONAL
SEASONED
SENSIBLE
SENSIBLY
SENSUOUS
SMASHING
SOLSTICE
SUBSONIC
SUNSHADE
SUNSHINE
SWASTIKA
TEASPOON
TEESHIRT
THESPIAN
TINSELLY
TIPSTAFF
TOISEACH
TONSURED
TRASHCAN
TRESPASS
TRISTICH
TRISTRAM
TRUSTFUL
TRUSTING
TWISTING
UNUSABLE
VERSICLE
VOLSCIAN
WELSHMAN
WHISKERS
WHISKERY
WHISTLER
WOLSELEY
WRESTLER
WRISTLET
YERSINIA
ZOOSPERM
ZOOSPORE
ABATTOIR
ABSTRACT
ABSTRUSE
ABUTILON
ABUTMENT
AESTHETE
AGITATED
AGITATOR
AGITPROP
AIRTIGHT
AMATEURS
AMETHYST
ANATHEMA
ANATOLIA
ANATOMIC
ANYTHING
APOTHEGM
ARCTURUS
ARETHUSA
AUSTRIAN
BAATHIST
BACTERIA
BACTRIAN
BANTLING
BAPTISED
BARTERED
BASTILLE
BATTERED
BEATIFIC

BEETLING
BEETROOT
BERTRAND
BESTIARY
BESTOWER
BESTRIDE
BIATHLON
BIRTHDAY
BITTERLY
BLITHELY
BLOTCHED
BOATLOAD
BOLTHOLE
BOOTLESS
BOOTNECK
BOTTLING
BOTTOMRY
BOUTIQUE
BRATPACK
BRETHREN
BRUTALLY
BUSTLING
BUTTERED
BUTTOCKS
BUTTRESS
CALTHROP
CANTICLE
CAPTIOUS
CARTHAGE
CARTLOAD
CASTANET
CASTAWAY
CASTOFFS
CASTRATE
CASTRATO
CATTLEYA
CAUTIOUS
CENTAURY
CENTERED
CENTRIST
CENTRODE
CHATTELS
CHITCHAT
CHUTZPAH
CLITORIS
CLOTHIER
CLOTHING
COATRACK
COATTAIL
CONTANGO
CONTEMPT
CONTENTS
CONTINUE
CONTINUO
CONTRACT
CONTRARY
CONTRAST
CONTRITE
CONTRIVE
CONTROLS
COSTMARY
COTTAGER
CRATCHIT
CRETONNE
CRITICAL
CRITIQUE
CROTCHET
CRUTCHED
CULTURAL
CULTURED
CURTAINS
CURTNESS
CUSTOMER
CYSTITIS
DARTMOOR
DEATHBED
DEFTNESS
DENTURES
DESTINED
DESTRUCT
DEXTROSE
DEXTROUS
DIATONIC
DIATRIBE
DICTATES
DICTATOR
DIPTERAL
DISTANCE
DISTASTE
DISTINCT
DISTRACT
DISTRAIN
DISTRAIT
DISTRESS
DISTRICT
DISTRUST
DOCTORAL
DOCTORED
DOCTRINE
DOTTEREL
EASTERLY
EASTLAKE
EASTWARD
ECSTASIS
ECSTATIC
EGGTIMER
EPITASIS
EPITHEMA
ERYTHEMA
ESOTERIC
EUSTATIC
EYETOOTH
FACTIOUS
FACTOTUM
FAITHFUL
FANTASIA
FARTHEST
FARTHING
FASTBACK
FASTENER
FASTNESS
FEATHERS
FEATHERY
FEATURED
FEATURES
FESTIVAL
FIFTIETH
FILTHILY
FILTRATE
FLATFISH
FLATFOOT
FLATMATE
FLATTERY
FLATWARE
FLATWORM
FLOTILLA
FOOTBALL
FOOTFALL
FOOTHOLD
FOOTLING
FOOTNOTE
FOOTPATH
FOOTREST
FOOTSORE
FOOTSTEP
FOOTWEAR
FOOTWORK
FORTIETH
FORTRESS
FORTUITY
FRETWORK
FURTHEST
GASTRULA
GENTRIFY
GEOTAXIS
GERTRUDE
GESTURES
GLUTAEUS
GLUTTONY
GOATSKIN
GRATEFUL
GRATUITY
GUTTURAL
HARTFORD
HASTINGS
HATTERAS
HAWTHORN
HEATEDLY
HEATSPOT
HEATWAVE
HEPTAGON
HEPTARCH
HEYTHROP
HISTORIC
HOSTELRY
HUNTRESS
HUNTSMAN
HUSTINGS
HYSTERIA
HYSTERIC
IMITATOR
INITIATE
INSTANCE
INSTINCT
INSTRUCT
ISOTHERE
ISOTHERM
JETTISON
JOTTINGS
JUSTNESS
KATTEGAT
KENTUCKY
KESTEVEN
KNITTING
KNITWEAR
KNOTWEED
KNOTWORK
LATTERLY
LEATHERY
LECTURER
LECTURES
LEFTHAND
LEFTOVER
LEFTWARD
LEFTWING
LETTERED
LISTENER
LISTERIA
LISTLESS
LITTORAL
LOATHING
LOITERER
LUSTRINE
LUSTROUS
MALTREAT
MANTILLA
MANTISSA
MARTELLO
MARTINET
MARTYRED
MASTERLY
MASTHEAD
MASTODON
MATTRESS
MEATLESS
MELTDOWN
MENTALLY
MIRTHFUL
MISTAKEN
MISTREAT
MISTRESS
MISTRUST
MONTCALM
MONTEITH
MORTALLY
MORTGAGE
MORTIMER
MORTUARY
MOUTHFUL
MULTIPLE
MULTIPLY
MUSTACHE
MYSTICAL
MYSTIQUE
NATTERED
NAUTICAL
NAUTILUS
NEATHERD
NEATNESS
NESTLING
NEUTRINO
NOCTURNE
NORTHERN
NOSTRILS
NOSTROMO
NUPTIALS
OBITUARY
OBSTACLE
OBSTRUCT
OINTMENT
ONETRACK
ORATORIO
OXYTOCIN
PANTALON
PANTHEON
PARTERRE
PARTHIAN
PARTICLE
PARTISAN
PARTTIME
PASTICHE
PASTILLE
PASTORAL
PASTRAMI
PASTURES
PECTORAL
PENTACLE
PENTAGON
PENTARCH
PERTNESS
PHOTOFIT
PHOTOPSY
PICTURES
PILTDOWN
PINTABLE
PITTANCE
PLATANUS
PLATEFUL
PLATELET
PLATFORM
PLATINUM
PLATONIC
PLATYPUS
PLETHORA
PLOTINUS
PLUTARCH
POETICAL
POITIERS
POLTROON
PORTABLE
PORTHOLE
PORTIÈRE
PORTLAND
PORTRAIT
PORTUGAL
POSTCARD
POSTCODE
POSTDATE
POSTMARK
POSTPAID
POSTPONE
PRATFALL
PRATTLER
PRETENCE
PRETENSE
PRETORIA
PRETTILY
PROTEASE
PROTÉGÉE
PROTOCOL
PROTOZOA
PROTRUDE
PUSTULAR
QUATORZE
QUATRAIN
QUOTABLE
QUOTIENT
RATTIGAN
RATTLING
RESTLESS
RESTORER
RESTRAIN
RESTRICT
RESTROOM
RHETORIC
RHYTHMIC
ROOTLESS
RUCTIONS
RUSTLESS
RUSTLING
SALTLICK
SALTNESS

SANTIAGO
SCATHING
SCOTLAND
SCOTSMAN
SCOTTISH
SEETHING
SENTENCE
SENTIENT
SENTINEL
SHETLAND
SHUTDOWN
SHUTTERS
SISTERLY
SIXTIETH
SKITTISH
SKITTLES
SLATTERN
SLOTHFUL
SLUTTISH
SNATCHER
SOFTBALL
SOFTENER
SOFTNESS
SOFTWARE
SOFTWOOD
SOOTHING
SOOTHSAY
SOUTHEND
SOUTHERN
SOUTHPAW
SPITEFUL
SPITFIRE
SPITHEAD
SPITTING
SPITTOON
SPOTLESS
SPOTTING
STATUARY
SUBTENSE
SUBTITLE
SUBTLETY
SUBTOPIA
SUBTOTAL
SUBTRACT
SUITABLE
SUITABLY
SUITCASE
SYNTEXIS
SYSTEMIC
TACTICAL
TACTLESS
TANTALUM
TANTALUS
TARTARIC
TARTARUS
TARTNESS
TARTRATE
TARTUFFE
TASTEFUL
TATTERED
TAUTNESS
TECTONIC
TEETHING
TEETOTAL
TENTACLE
TERTIARY
TESTATOR
TESTATUM
TESTICLE
TEUTONIC
TEXTBOOK
TEXTURED
THATAWAY
THATCHED
THATCHER
TINTAGEL
TORTILLA
TORTOISE
TORTUOUS
TORTURED
TORTURER
TRITICAL
TRITICUM
TROTTERS
TROTTOIR
TRUTHFUL
TWITCHER
TZATZIKI
UNCTUOUS
UNITEDLY
UNSTABLE
UNSTATED
UNSTEADY
UPSTAIRS
UPSTREAM
URETHANE
VASTNESS
VENTURED
VERTEBRA
VERTICAL
VESTIARY
VESTMENT
VIATICUM
VICTORIA
VICTUALS
VIRTUOSI
VIRTUOSO
VIRTUOUS
VOLTAIRE
WAITRESS
WALTZING
WASTEFUL
WESTERLY
WESTWARD
WHATEVER
WHITECAP
WHITEHOT
WHITENER
WHITLING
WISTERIA
WORTHIES
WORTHILY
WRATHFUL
WRETCHED
WRITEOFF
WRITHING
WRITINGS
XANTHOMA
XANTIPPE
YOUTHFUL
ZASTRUGA
ZOETROPE
ABDUCENS
ABDUCTED
ABDUCTOR
ABLUTION
ABRUPTLY
ABSURDLY
ACCURACY
ACCURATE
ACCURSED
ACCUSING
ACCUSTOM
ACOUSTIC
ACQUAINT
ACQUIRED
ACQUIRER
ACTUALLY
ADJUSTER
ADJUSTOR
ADJUTAGE
ADJUTANT
ADJUVANT
AFFUSION
AIGUILLE
ALBURNUM
ALEUTIAN
ALLURING
ALLUSION
ALLUSIVE
ALLUVIAL
ALLUVIUM
AMBULANT
AMBULATE
AMBUSHED
AMPUTATE
ANEURYSM
ANGUILLA
ANNUALLY
ARGUABLE
ARGUABLY
ARGUMENT
ARQUEBUS
ASSUMING
ASTUTELY
AUBUSSON
AUGUSTUS
AUTUMNAL
BABUSHKA
BAGUETTE
BALUSTER
BEAUFORT
BEAUMONT
BEAUTIFY
BEFUDDLE
BEQUEATH
BIBULOUS
BICUSPID
BOTULISM
BROUGHAM
BROUHAHA
CADUCEUS
CAPUCHIN
CARUCATE
CASUALLY
CASUALTY
CATULLUS
CERULEAN
CLAUDIUS
COAUTHOR
COLUMBAN
COLUMBUS
COPULATE
COQUETRY
COQUETTE
CROUPIER
CUCUMBER
CUCURBIT
DELUSION
DEMURELY
DEMURRAL
DEPUTIZE
DILUTION
DISUNION
DISUNITE
DISUNITY
DOCUMENT
DRAUGHTS
DRAUGHTY
EFFUSION
EFFUSIVE
ENCUMBER
ENDURING
ESCULENT
ETRURIAN
ETRUSCAN
EXHUMATE
FABULOUS
FECULENT
FIGURINE
FLAUBERT
FLAUTIST
FLOUNCED
FLOUNDER
FLOURISH
FRAULEIN
FREUDIAN
FURUNCLE
FUTURISM
FUTURIST
GAZUNDER
GHOULISH
GLAUCOMA
GLAUCOUS
GROUNDED
GROUPING
GROUTING
HANUKKAH
HARUSPEX
ILLUMINE
ILLUSION
ILLUSIVE
ILLUSORY
IMMUNITY
IMMUNIZE
IMPUDENT
IMPUNITY
IMPURIFY
IMPURITY
INCUBATE
INDUCIVE
INDUSTRY
INFUSION
INGUINAL
INHUMANE
INNUENDO
INQUIRER
INSULATE
JEBUSITE
LABURNUM
MACULATE
MANUALLY
MAQUETTE
MATURATE
MATURITY
MINUTELY
MINUTIAE
MODULATE
MOLUCCAS
MONUMENT
MOQUETTE
MUTUALLY
NATURISM
NATURIST
NEBULOUS
NENUPHAR
OBDURACY
OBDURATE
OBTUSELY
OCCUPANT
OCCUPIED
OCCUPIER
OMDURMAN
OSCULATE
PABULOUS
PALUDISM
PATULOUS
PECULATE
PECULIAR
PEDUNCLE
PENUMBRA
PERUVIAN
PETULANT
PIQUANCY
PLAUDITS
PLEURISY
PLOUGHED
POPULACE
POPULATE
POPULIST
POPULOUS
PSEUDERY
PURULENT
REBUTTAL
RECUSANT
REFUGIUM
REGULATE
REPUBLIC
REQUIRED
RITUALLY
ROBUSTLY
SALUTARY
SALUTORY
SATURATE
SATURDAY
SATURNIA
SCHUBERT
SCHUMANN
SCOURING
SCRUBBER
SCRUPLES
SCRUTINY
SECURELY
SECURITY
SEDULOUS
SEQUENCE
SEXUALLY
SHOULDER
SHOUTING
SHRUNKEN
SILURIAN
SIMULATE

SITUATED
SMOULDER
SOLUTION
SPLUTTER
SPRUCELY
STRUGGLE
STRUMPET
SUBURBAN
SUBURBIA
TABULATE
TEGUMENT
TEQUILLA
THOUGHTS
THOUSAND
THRUSTER
TROUBLED
TROUBLES
TROUNCER
TROUSERS
UNBURDEN
UNBUTTON
UNCURBED
UNDULANT
UNDULATE
UNGULATE
UNJUSTLY
UNSUITED
UPTURNED
URSULINE
VALUABLE
VESUVIUS
VIBURNUM
VIRULENT
VISUALLY
AASVOGEL
BREVIARY
CALVADOS
CERVELAT
CERVICAL
CHEVIOTS
CHIVALRY
CLAVECIN
CLAVICLE
CLEVERLY
CLIVEDEN
CONVENER
CONVERGE
CONVERSE
CONVEYOR
CONVINCE
CONVULSE
CORVETTE
CRAVATES
CREVASSE
CULVERIN
DRIVEWAY
ELEVATED
ELEVATOR
ELEVENTH
FLAVORED
GALVANIC
GIOVANNI
GRAVAMEN
GRAVELLY
GRAVITAS
HEAVENLY
HELVETIA
LEAVENED
LEAVINGS
LOUVERED
MALVASIA
MALVOLIO
PERVERSE
PERVIOUS
PREVIOUS
PRIVATES
PROVABLE
PROVERBS
PROVIDED
PROVIDER
PROVINCE
PURVEYOR
SALVADOR
SCAVENGE
SELVEDGE
SERVICES
SERVIENT
SERVITOR
SHIVERED
SLOVAKIA
SLOVENIA
SLOVENLY
SOLVABLE
SOLVENCY
SOUVENIR
SPAVINED
SURVEYOR
SURVIVAL
SURVIVOR
SYLVANER
TRAVELER
TRAVERSE
TRAVESTY
UNEVENLY
UNIVALVE
UNIVERSE
VALVULAR
AIRWAVES
ANYWHERE
BLOWFISH
BLOWHOLE
BLOWLAMP
BLOWPIPE
BOSWORTH
BROWBEAT
BROWNING
BROWNISH
BROWSING
CLAWBACK
CLOWNISH
COBWEBBY
COGWHEEL
CRAWFISH
CRAWLING
CROWFOOT
CROWNING
CUTWATER
DOGWATCH
DRAWBACK
DROWNING
DROWSILY
ENIWETOK
FLAWLESS
FLYWHEEL
FORWARDS
GASWORKS
GROWLING
HIAWATHA
LULWORTH
MADWOMAN
OLDWORLD
OUTWARDS
OUTWEIGH
PINWHEEL
REAWAKEN
SCOWLING
SEAWARDS
SHOWBOAT
SHOWCASE
SHOWDOWN
SHOWGIRL
SHOWROOM
SKEWBALD
SLOWDOWN
SLOWNESS
SLOWPOKE
SNOWBALL
SNOWDROP
SNOWFALL
SNOWLINE
SPAWNING
STOWAWAY
TAMWORTH
UNAWARES
WAXWORKS
FLEXIBLE
FLEXIBLY
FRAXINUS
GLOXINIA
INEXPERT
QUIXOTIC
VAUXHALL
ABEYANCE
ASSYRIAN
BABYHOOD
BODYLINE
BODYWORK
BUOYANCY
BUSYBODY
CAPYBARA
CARYATID
CHEYENNE
CLAYMORE
COPYBOOK
COPYHOLD
CRAYFISH
DEWYEYED
DICYCLIC
DUTYFREE
EMPYREAN
ENDYMION
ETHYLENE
EUCYCLIC
EURYDICE
GANYMEDE
GRAYLING
HOLYHEAD
HOLYROOD
LADYBIRD
LADYLIKE
LADYSHIP
MARYLAND
PHRYGIAN
PLAYBACK
PLAYBILL
PLAYFAIR
PLAYGIRL
PLAYMATE
PLAYROOM
PLAYSUIT
PLAYTIME
POLYANNA
POLYARCH
POLYCARP
POLYGAMY
POLYGLOT
POLYMATH
POLYSEME
POLYSEMY
PONYTAIL
QUAYSIDE
ROLYPOLY
SISYPHUS
SPRYNESS
STAYSAIL
TERYLENE
BLIZZARD
BOUZOUKI
BUZZWORD
CRUZEIRO
DAZZLING
DIAZEPAM
FRAZZLED
GADZOOKS
GRIZZLED
MARZIPAN
PENZANCE
PIZZERIA
PUZZLING
SIZZLING
TANZANIA
ZARZUELA

8:5

ABEYANCE
ABOMASUM
ACQUAINT
ACTUALLY
ADELAIDE
ADORABLE
ADRIATIC
ADULATOR
AFFLATUS
AGITATED
AGITATOR
AIRWAVES
ALEMAINE
ALICANTE
ALLIANCE
ALPHABET
AMARANTH
AMBIANCE
AMENABLE
AMICABLE
AMICABLY
ANABASIS
ANABATIC
ANAPAEST
ANIMATED
ANNEALER
ANNUALLY
AOTEAROA
APPLAUSE
APPRAISE
ARAMAEAN
ARAMANTH
ARCHAISM
ARGUABLE
ARGUABLY
AROMATIC
ATALANTA
ATARAXIA
ATARAXIC
AVIFAUNA
AVOGADRO
BACCARAT
BACKACHE
BADLANDS
BAHRAINI
BALEARIC
BANDANNA
BARBADOS
BARBARIC
BARNABAS
BARNACLE
BARNARDS
BARRACKS
BARRATRY
BEARABLE
BECHAMEL
BEDMAKER
BEGGARLY
BELPAESE
BENJAMIN
BEREAVED
BERGAMOT
BETRAYAL
BETRAYER
BINNACLE
BISCAYAN
BISMARCK
BOOKABLE
BRABAZON
BRAGANZA
BRAMANTE
BRIBABLE
BRUMAIRE
BRUTALLY
BULGARIA
BUMMAREE
BUNGALOW
BUOYANCY
CACHALOT
CALVADOS
CAMPAIGN
CANNABIS
CARCAJOU
CARCANET
CARDAMOM
CARJACOU
CARRAWAY
CARYATID
CASTANET
CASTAWAY
CASUALLY
CASUALTY
CELLARER
CENTAURY
CHAPATTI
CHIMAERA

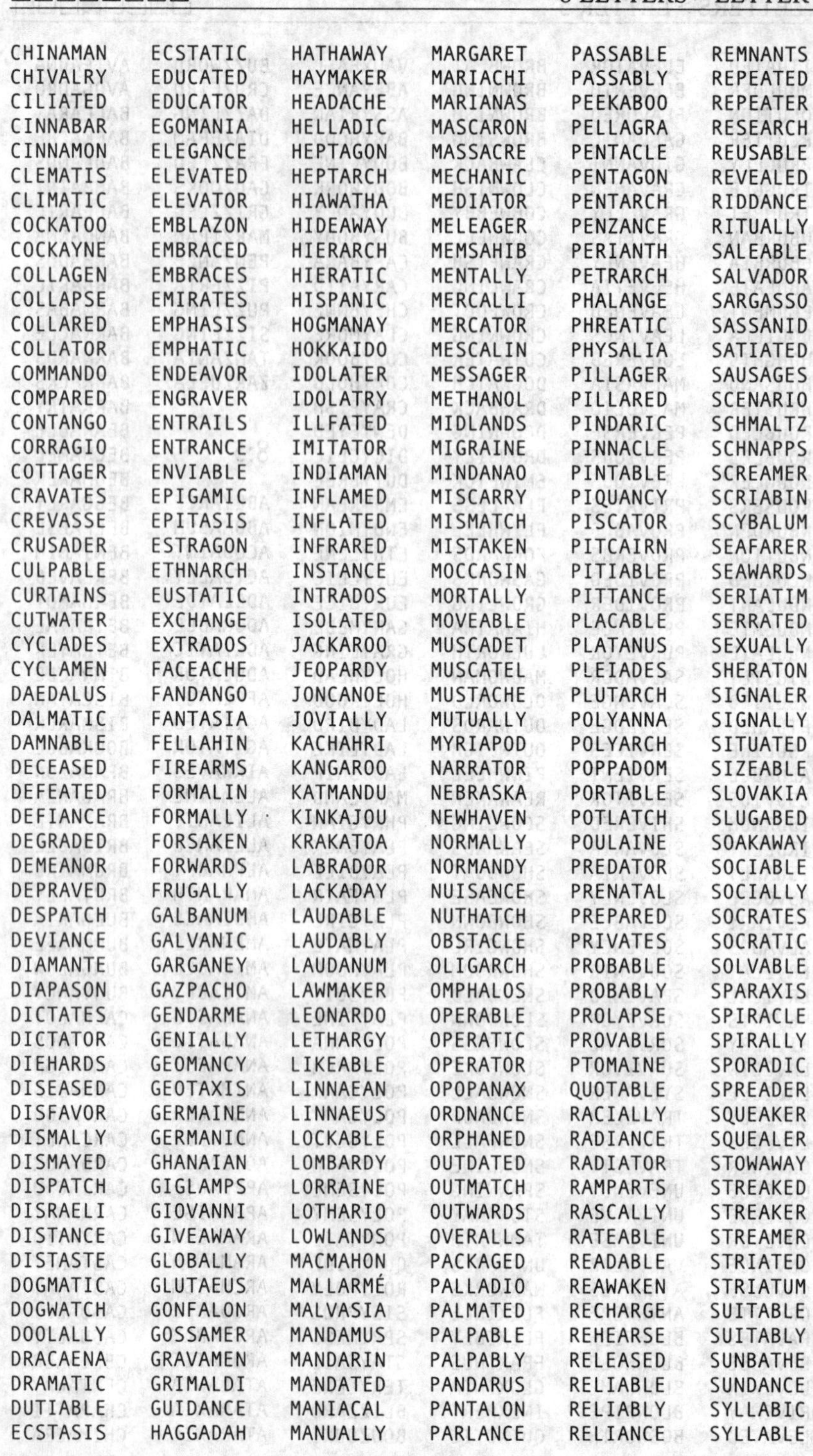

CHINAMAN
CHIVALRY
CILIATED
CINNABAR
CINNAMON
CLEMATIS
CLIMATIC
COCKATOO
COCKAYNE
COLLAGEN
COLLAPSE
COLLARED
COLLATOR
COMMANDO
COMPARED
CONTANGO
CORRAGIO
COTTAGER
CRAVATES
CREVASSE
CRUSADER
CULPABLE
CURTAINS
CUTWATER
CYCLADES
CYCLAMEN
DAEDALUS
DALMATIC
DAMNABLE
DECEASED
DEFEATED
DEFIANCE
DEGRADED
DEMEANOR
DEPRAVED
DESPATCH
DEVIANCE
DIAMANTE
DIAPASON
DICTATES
DICTATOR
DIEHARDS
DISEASED
DISFAVOR
DISMALLY
DISMAYED
DISPATCH
DISRAELI
DISTANCE
DISTASTE
DOGMATIC
DOGWATCH
DOOLALLY
DRACAENA
DRAMATIC
DUTIABLE
ECSTASIS
ECSTATIC
EDUCATED
EDUCATOR
EGOMANIA
ELEGANCE
ELEVATED
ELEVATOR
EMBLAZON
EMBRACED
EMBRACES
EMIRATES
EMPHASIS
EMPHATIC
ENDEAVOR
ENGRAVER
ENTRAILS
ENTRANCE
ENVIABLE
EPIGAMIC
EPITASIS
ESTRAGON
ETHNARCH
EUSTATIC
EXCHANGE
EXTRADOS
FACEACHE
FANDANGO
FANTASIA
FELLAHIN
FIREARMS
FORMALIN
FORMALLY
FORSAKEN
FORWARDS
FRUGALLY
GALBANUM
GALVANIC
GARGANEY
GAZPACHO
GENDARME
GENIALLY
GEOMANCY
GEOTAXIS
GERMAINE
GERMANIC
GHANAIAN
GIGLAMPS
GIOVANNI
GIVEAWAY
GLOBALLY
GLUTAEUS
GONFALON
GOSSAMER
GRAVAMEN
GRIMALDI
GUIDANCE
HAGGADAH
HATHAWAY
HAYMAKER
HEADACHE
HELLADIC
HEPTAGON
HEPTARCH
HIAWATHA
HIDEAWAY
HIERARCH
HIERATIC
HISPANIC
HOGMANAY
HOKKAIDO
IDOLATER
IDOLATRY
ILLFATED
IMITATOR
INDIAMAN
INFLAMED
INFLATED
INFRARED
INSTANCE
INTRADOS
ISOLATED
JACKAROO
JEOPARDY
JONCANOE
JOVIALLY
KACHAHRI
KANGAROO
KATMANDU
KINKAJOU
KRAKATOA
LABRADOR
LACKADAY
LAUDABLE
LAUDABLY
LAUDANUM
LAWMAKER
LEONARDO
LETHARGY
LIKEABLE
LINNAEAN
LINNAEUS
LOCKABLE
LOMBARDY
LORRAINE
LOTHARIO
LOWLANDS
MACMAHON
MALLARMÉ
MALVASIA
MANDAMUS
MANDARIN
MANDATED
MANIACAL
MANUALLY
MARGARET
MARIACHI
MARIANAS
MASCARON
MASSACRE
MECHANIC
MEDIATOR
MELEAGER
MEMSAHIB
MENTALLY
MERCALLI
MERCATOR
MESCALIN
MESSAGER
METHANOL
MIDLANDS
MIGRAINE
MINDANAO
MISCARRY
MISMATCH
MISTAKEN
MOCCASIN
MORTALLY
MOVEABLE
MUSCADET
MUSCATEL
MUSTACHE
MUTUALLY
MYRIAPOD
NARRATOR
NEBRASKA
NEWHAVEN
NORMALLY
NORMANDY
NUISANCE
NUTHATCH
OBSTACLE
OLIGARCH
OMPHALOS
OPERABLE
OPERATIC
OPERATOR
OPOPANAX
ORDNANCE
ORPHANED
OUTDATED
OUTMATCH
OUTWARDS
OVERALLS
PACKAGED
PALLADIO
PALMATED
PALPABLE
PALPABLY
PANDARUS
PANTALON
PARLANCE
PASSABLE
PASSABLY
PEEKABOO
PELLAGRA
PENTACLE
PENTAGON
PENTARCH
PENZANCE
PERIANTH
PETRARCH
PHALANGE
PHREATIC
PHYSALIA
PILLAGER
PILLARED
PINDARIC
PINNACLE
PINTABLE
PIQUANCY
PISCATOR
PITCAIRN
PITIABLE
PITTANCE
PLACABLE
PLATANUS
PLEIADES
PLUTARCH
POLYANNA
POLYARCH
POPPADOM
PORTABLE
POTLATCH
POULAINE
PREDATOR
PRENATAL
PREPARED
PRIVATES
PROBABLE
PROBABLY
PROLAPSE
PROVABLE
PTOMAINE
QUOTABLE
RACIALLY
RADIANCE
RADIATOR
RAMPARTS
RASCALLY
RATEABLE
READABLE
REAWAKEN
RECHARGE
REHEARSE
RELEASED
RELIABLE
RELIABLY
RELIANCE
REMNANTS
REPEATED
REPEATER
RESEARCH
REUSABLE
REVEALED
RIDDANCE
RITUALLY
SALEABLE
SALVADOR
SARGASSO
SASSANID
SATIATED
SAUSAGES
SCENARIO
SCHMALTZ
SCHNAPPS
SCREAMER
SCRIABIN
SCYBALUM
SEAFARER
SEAWARDS
SERIATIM
SERRATED
SEXUALLY
SHERATON
SIGNALER
SIGNALLY
SITUATED
SIZEABLE
SLOVAKIA
SLUGABED
SOAKAWAY
SOCIABLE
SOCIALLY
SOCRATES
SOCRATIC
SOLVABLE
SPARAXIS
SPIRACLE
SPIRALLY
SPORADIC
SPREADER
SQUEAKER
SQUEALER
STOWAWAY
STREAKED
STREAKER
STREAMER
STRIATED
STRIATUM
SUITABLE
SUITABLY
SUNBATHE
SUNDANCE
SYLLABIC
SYLLABLE

SYLLABUB
SYLLABUS
SYLVANER
SYMPATHY
TAKEAWAY
TANTALUM
TANTALUS
TANZANIA
TARRAGON
TARTARIC
TARTARUS
TASMANIA
TAXPAYER
TEARABLE
TEARAWAY
TEENAGER
TENTACLE
TERRACED
TERRAPIN
TESTATOR
TESTATUM
TETRAGON
TETRAPOD
TETRARCH
THALAMUS
THANATOS
THATAWAY
THEMATIC
THORACIC
THREATEN
TINTAGEL
TOREADOR
TRIMARAN
TURBANED
TYMPANUM
UNABATED
UNAWARES
UNBEATEN
UNBIASED
UNCHASTE
UNHEATED
UNIVALVE
UNLEADED
UNLOADED
UNPLACED
UNREASON
UNSEALED
UNSHAKEN
UNSTABLE
UNSTATED
UNUSABLE
UNWEANED
UPHEAVAL
UPSTAIRS
VAGRANCY
VALHALLA
VALUABLE
VARIABLE
VARIANCE
VERBALLY
VERBATIM
VERLAINE
VIBRANCY
VIBRATOR
VILLAGER
VILLAINY
VINDALOO
VIOLATOR
VISUALLY
VOIDANCE
VOLCANIC
VOLTAIRE
VULGARLY
WARFARIN
WARPAINT
WARRANTY
WASHABLE
WAYFARER
WEARABLE
WETLANDS
WISEACRE
WORKABLE
WORKADAY
YEOMANRY
ZIMBABWE
ZODIACAL
ACERBATE
ACERBITY
AEROBICS
ANTIBODY
AUTOBAHN
BACKBITE
BACKBONE
BANKBOOK
BARABBAS
BAREBACK
BASEBALL
BASEBORN
BEDABBLE
BEERBOHM
BELABOUR
BERIBERI
BLUEBACK
BLUEBELL
BRADBURY
BROWBEAT
BUSYBODY
CALABASH
CAMPBELL
CAPYBARA
CARABINE
CELIBACY
CELIBATE
CENOBITE
CEREBRAL
CEREBRUM
CHADBAND
CHAMBERS
CLAMBAKE
CLAWBACK
CLIMBING
COMEBACK
COOKBOOK
COPYBOOK
CRIBBAGE
CUTHBERT
DATABASE
DEADBEAT
DINGBATS
DISABLED
DISABUSE
DOGSBODY
DOORBELL
DOWNBEAT
DRAWBACK
DRUBBING
DRUMBEAT
DUCKBILL
DUMBBELL
DURABLES
EATABLES
FASTBACK
FEEDBACK
FIREBACK
FIREBALL
FIREBIRD
FIREBOLT
FISHBONE
FLAUBERT
FLEABITE
FOOTBALL
FOREBEAR
FOREBODE
FULLBACK
GADABOUT
GAMEBIRD
GAOLBIRD
GOLFBALL
GOOFBALL
GROSBEAK
GRUMBLER
HABSBURG
HANDBALL
HANDBILL
HANDBOOK
HAPSBURG
HARDBACK
HAREBELL
HEADBAND
HEELBALL
HELLBENT
HIGHBALL
HIGHBORN
HIGHBROW
HORNBEAM
HORNBILL
HORNBOOK
HUMPBACK
IMMOBILE
INCUBATE
INDEBTED
JACKBOOT
JACOBEAN
JACOBITE
JAILBIRD
JEREBOAM
JEROBOAM
KICKBACK
KILOBYTE
LADYBIRD
LAIDBACK
LANSBURY
LAYABOUT
LIFEBELT
LIFEBOAT
LIFEBUOY
LONGBOAT
LOVEBIRD
LYREBIRD
MAILBOAT
MARABOUT
MATABELE
MEGABYTE
METABOLA
MOONBEAM
MORIBUND
MOTHBALL
NAMIBIAN
NECKBAND
NOSEBAND
NOTEBOOK
OVERBOOK
PARABOLA
PASSBOOK
PLAYBACK
PLAYBILL
PLUMBAGO
PLUMBING
PUFFBALL
PUSHBIKE
QUIBBLER
RAINBIRD
REPUBLIC
RHOMBOID
RULEBOOK
RUNABOUT
RUTABAGA
SAILBOAT
SANDBANK
SARABAND
SCABBARD
SCHUBERT
SCRABBLE
SCRIBBLE
SCRIBBLY
SCRUBBER
SHABBILY
SHAMBLES
SHOWBOAT
SKEWBALD
SLAPBANG
SLOBBERY
SNOBBERY
SNOBBISH
SNOWBALL
SOFTBALL
SOMEBODY
SONGBIRD
SQUABBLE
STABBING
STRABISM
STUBBORN
SURFBOAT
TAILBACK
TENEBRAE
TENEBRIO
TEXTBOOK
TREMBLER
TROMBONE
TROUBLED
TROUBLES
TURNBACK
VAGABOND
WASHBOWL
WAVEBAND
WELLBRED
WHIMBREL
WINDBURN
WISHBONE
WOLFBANE
WOODBINE
WORDBOOK
WORKBOOK
YEARBOOK
ZWIEBACK
ABDICATE
ABDUCENS
ABDUCTED
ABDUCTOR
ABJECTLY
ADDICTED
ADJACENT
ADVOCACY
ADVOCATE
AFFECTED
AGRICOLA
AIRSCREW
ALBACORE
ALLOCATE
ANARCHIC
ANTECEDE
ARTICLED
ARTICLES
ASUNCION
ATROCITY
ATTACHED
ATTACKER
AUDACITY
AUTOCRAT
BACKCHAT
BACKCOMB
BALLCOCK
BIFOCALS
BIOSCOPE
BIRDCAGE
BLEACHER
BLOTCHED
BLUECOAT
BOOKCASE
BORACITE
BORECOLE
BOUNCING
BRANCHED
BREACHES
BREECHES
BROCCOLI
BRONCHUS
CABOCHON
CADUCEUS
CAPACITY
CAPUCHIN
CARACOLE
CARUCATE
CATACOMB
CETACEAN
CHANCERY
CHARCOAL
CHITCHAT
CLINCHER
COCACOLA
COCKCROW
COERCION
COERCIVE
COINCIDE
COUSCOUS
CRATCHIT
CRESCENT
CROTCHET
CRUNCHIE
CRUTCHED
CYNICISM
DAMOCLES

DEDICATE
DEFECATE
DEFECTOR
DEJECTED
DELICACY
DELICATE
DEMOCRAT
DETACHED
DETECTOR
DICYCLIC
DIDACTIC
DIRECTLY
DIRECTOR
DOMICILE
DOVECOTE
DOWNCAST
ECLECTIC
EFFICACY
EIDECTIC
ENDOCARP
ENRICHED
ENTICING
ESPECIAL
EUCYCLIC
EXERCISE
EXORCISM
EXORCIST
EXORCIZE
EXPECTED
FELICITY
FEROCITY
FIERCELY
FISHCAKE
FORECAST
FRANCIUM
GALACTIC
GENOCIDE
GLANCING
GLAUCOMA
GLAUCOUS
GOLFCLUB
GROSCHEN
HANDCART
HANDCLAP
HANDCUFF
HARDCORE
HAUNCHES
HERACLES
HERACLID
HERSCHEL
HIJACKER
HOMICIDE
IMBECILE
IMPACTED
INDECENT
INDICANT
INDICATE
INDUCIVE
INFECTED
INJECTOR
INNOCENT
INSECURE
IRISCOPE
IRONCLAD
JUDICIAL
LONICERA
LYRICISM
LYRICIST
MAGICIAN
MANICURE
MEDICATE
MEDICINE
MENACING
MOLECULE
MOLUCCAS
MONICKER
MONTCALM
MOORCOCK
MOROCCAN
MUSICIAN
NEWSCAST
NOTECASE
OBJECTOR
OFFICERS
OFFICIAL
OLEACEAE
OPENCAST
OPTICIAN
OPUSCULE
OTOSCOPE
OVERCAST
OVERCOAT
OVERCOME
OXPECKER
PEDICURE
PERACUTE
PERICARP
PERICLES
PIERCING
PINOCHLE
PLANCHET
PLIOCENE
POLYCARP
POSTCARD
POSTCODE
PREACHER
PRINCELY
PRINCESS
PUSHCART
QUINCUNX
RAINCOAT
RAPACITY
RAPECAKE
REDACTOR
REGICIDE
RELOCATE
RETICENT
RETICULE
RHONCHUS
RICOCHET
RIDICULE
ROLLCALL
RUBICUND
SAGACITY
SALACITY
SCARCELY
SCARCITY
SCORCHED
SCORCHER
SEARCHER
SEASCAPE
SELECTED
SELECTOR
SHOWCASE
SILICATE
SILICONE
SINECURE
SNATCHER
SOLECISM
SOURCING
SPICCATO
SPROCKET
SPRUCELY
STACCATO
STARCHED
STICCATO
STOCCATA
STOICISM
STOPCOCK
STRACHEY
STRICKEN
STRICTLY
STUCCOED
SUITCASE
SYRACUSE
TELECAST
TENACITY
THATCHED
THATCHER
THEOCRAT
THRACIAN
TITICACA
TOXICITY
TOXOCARA
TRENCHER
TRINCULO
TRUNCATE
TURNCOAT
TURNCOCK
TWITCHER
TYPECAST
UNLOCKED
UNSOCIAL
VARICOSE
VELOCITY
VERACITY
VIVACITY
VOLSCIAN
VORACITY
WHINCHAT
WHIPCORD
WOODCOCK
WORMCAST
WRETCHED
ABERDEEN
ABRIDGED
ABUNDANT
ACCIDENT
AERODYNE
AIREDALE
AKKADIAN
AMANDINE
AMUNDSEN
AMYGDALA
ANECDOTE
ANTEDATE
ANTIDOTE
AQUEDUCT
ARALDITE
ARCADIAN
ARCHDUKE
ASCIDIAN
ASCIDIUM
ASMODEUS
BACKDATE
BACKDROP
BASIDIUM
BEFUDDLE
BENEDICK
BENEDICT
BLANDISH
BLEEDING
BLENDING
BLINDING
BOARDING
BORODINO
BOUNDARY
BRANDADE
BRANDISH
BRANDNEW
BREEDING
BRINDISI
BRINDLED
BROADWAY
BROODING
BUILDING
BULLDOZE
CANADIAN
CAULDRON
CHALDEAN
CHALDRON
CHANDLER
CHILDERS
CHILDISH
CHILDREN
CHINDITS
CHORDATA
CHORDATE
CLADDING
CLAUDIUS
COMEDIAN
COMEDOWN
CUPIDITY
DAVIDSON
DECADENT
DIELDRIN
DIVIDEND
DIVIDERS
DREADFUL
ECTODERM
EMBEDDED
EMBODIED
ENDODERM
EURYDICE
EVILDOER
EXORDIUM
EXPEDITE
FIELDING
FIENDISH
FIREDAMP
FLANDERS
FLINDERS
FLOODING
FLOODLIT
FLUIDITY
FOREDECK
FOREDOOM
FOUNDING
FREUDIAN
FRONDEUR
GLANDERS
GRANDEUR
GRANDSON
GREEDILY
GRINDING
GUARDIAN
HEREDITY
HOARDING
HOLIDAYS
HUMIDIFY
HUMIDITY
IMMODEST
IMPUDENT
INCIDENT
INUNDATE
JAUNDICE
KILLDEER
KLONDIKE
KNEEDEEP
LAPIDARY
LAPIDATE
LIVIDITY
LONSDALE
LUCIDITY
MALODOUR
MARKDOWN
MELTDOWN
MEREDITH
MERIDIAN
MONADISM
MOULDING
NOSEDIVE
NOWADAYS
OBSIDIAN
OCCIDENT
OPENDOOR
OPHIDIAN
ORCADIAN
OVERDONE
OVERDOSE
OVERDRAW
PALUDISM
PARADIGM
PARADISE
PARODIST
PERIDERM
PILTDOWN
PLAUDITS
PLEADING
POSTDATE
POUNDAGE
PRANDIAL
PSEUDERY
PULLDOWN
QUANDARY
RAINDROP
RAPIDITY
RECEDING
REINDEER
REMEDIAL
RESIDENT
RESIDUAL
RESIDUUM
RIGIDITY
RINGDOVE
ROCHDALE
ROUNDERS
SCALDING
SCANDIUM
SCHEDULE
SCOLDING
SHELDUCK

SHODDILY
SHOWDOWN
SHREDDER
SHUTDOWN
SKIDDING
SKINDEEP
SLAPDASH
SLOWDOWN
SNOWDROP
SOLIDIFY
SOLIDITY
SOUNDING
SPANDREL
SPEEDILY
SPEEDWAY
SPENDING
SQUADDIE
SQUADRON
STANDARD
STANDING
STANDISH
STANDOFF
STARDUST
STEADILY
STENDHAL
STRADDLE
STRIDENT
STURDILY
SWADDLER
SWINDLER
TEARDROP
THUNDERY
TIMIDITY
TRAPDOOR
UNBIDDEN
UNENDING
UNFADING
UNTIDILY
VALIDATE
VALIDITY
VANADIUM
WASHDOWN
WITHDRAW
YIELDING
ACADEMIC
ACCREDIT
ACHIEVED
ACHIEVER
AGACERIE
AGREEING
AIGRETTE
ALCHEMIC
ALFRESCO
ALOPECIA
AMARETTO
AMATEURS
AMBIENCE
AMORETTI
AMORETTO
AMUSETTE
ANALECTA
ANALEMMA
ANDREWES
ANGLESEY
ANISETTE
ANOREXIA
ANOREXIC
APPLETON
ARQUEBUS
ASTHENIA
ATHLETIC
AUDIENCE
AVICENNA
BACHELOR
BACTERIA
BAEDEKER
BAGHEERA
BAGUETTE
BANDEROL
BARBECUE
BARGELLO
BARGEMAN
BARRETTE
BARTERED
BASKETRY
BATHETIC
BATTERED
BAYREUTH
BELIEVER
BEQUEATH
BERBERIS
BERCEUSE
BERGERAC
BERKELEY
BESIEGED
BESSEMER
BETHESDA
BETJEMAN
BILBERRY
BITTERLY
BODLEIAN
BORDEAUX
BORDELLO
BORDERER
BOTHERED
BRACELET
BROMELIA
BRUNETTE
BUGGERED
BULLETIN
BURBERRY
BURDENED
BUTTERED
CABLECAR
CABLEWAY
CACHEPOT
CACHEXIA
CAFFEINE
CALCEATE
CALDERON
CAMBERED
CANBERRA
CANOEING
CANOEIST
CARNEGIE
CASSETTE
CATHEDRA
CATHETER
CAUSEWAY
CENTERED
CERBERUS
CERVELAT
CHAPERON
CHEYENNE
CHOLERIC
CLARENCE
CLAVECIN
CLEMENCY
CLEVERLY
CLIVEDEN
COALESCE
COBWEBBY
COCKEREL
COCKEYED
COLLECTS
COLLEGES
COMMENCE
COMMERCE
CONCEIVE
CONCERTO
CONDENSE
CONFETTI
CONSERVE
CONTEMPT
CONTENTS
CONVENER
CONVERGE
CONVERSE
CONVEYOR
COQUETRY
COQUETTE
CORNETTO
CORSELET
CORVETTE
COSMETIC
COUPERIN
CRANEFLY
CRUZEIRO
CULVERIN
CURRENCY
CZAREVNA
DARKENED
DEADENED
DEADENER
DECREASE
DECREPIT
DECRETAL
DEFREEZE
DEWBERRY
DEWYEYED
DIABETES
DIABETIC
DIAMETER
DIARESIS
DIAZEPAM
DIERESIS
DIOCESAN
DIOGENES
DIPHENYL
DIPTERAL
DISHEVEL
DISKETTE
DISPENSE
DISPERSE
DIURETIC
DOGBERRY
DOGGEDLY
DOGGEREL
DOTTEREL
DRIVEWAY
DUCHESSE
DUODENAL
DUODENUM
DYSLEXIA
DYSLEXIC
EASTERLY
ELEMENTS
ELEVENTH
EMINENCE
ENCAENIA
ENFEEBLE
ENIWETOK
ENTREATY
ENTRENCH
ENTREPOT
EPIDEMIC
EPILEPSY
ESOTERIC
ESPRESSO
ESTEEMED
ESTHETIC
EVANESCE
EVIDENCE
EXEGESIS
EXEGETIC
EXIGENCY
EXPRESSO
FALSETTO
FASTENER
FATHERLY
FLAMENCO
FLORENCE
FOLDEROL
FORCEFUL
FORFEITS
FORMERLY
FRENETIC
FRUMENTY
FUGLEMAN
FURBELOW
GADGETRY
GALLERIA
GARDENER
GARDENIA
GARMENTS
GATHERED
GEODESIC
GEOMETER
GEOMETRY
GINGERLY
GLABELLA
GLYCERIN
GOOSEGOG
GORGEOUS
GRACEFUL
GRAMERCY
GRATEFUL
GRAVELLY
GRISELDA
GRISETTE
GUNMETAL
GUSSETED
HACIENDA
HAMMERED
HARDENED
HATTERAS
HAYFEVER
HEATEDLY
HEAVENLY
HEDGEHOG
HEDGEROW
HELLENIC
HELMETED
HELVETIA
HERMETIC
HERPETIC
HITHERTO
HORSEBOX
HORSEFLY
HORSEMAN
HORSEMEN
HOSTELRY
HOUSEMAN
HYGIENIC
HYSTERIA
HYSTERIC
INCREASE
INNUENDO
INTRENCH
INTREPID
ISABELLA
ISABELLE
JACKETED
JEANETTE
JIGGERED
JULIENNE
KATTEGAT
KEDGEREE
KERMESSE
KESTEVEN
KILKENNY
KIPPERED
KROMESKY
LANCELOT
LARGESSE
LATTERLY
LAUREATE
LAURENCE
LAWRENCE
LEAVENED
LENIENCY
LETTERED
LEUKEMIA
LIBRETTO
LIEGEMAN
LIGNEOUS
LINGERIE
LISTENER
LISTERIA
LOITERER
LOOSEBOX
LOUVERED
LUTHERAN
MACHEATH
MACKEREL
MACREADY
MAECENAS
MAGNESIA
MAGNETIC
MAIDENLY
MALLEATE
MANNERED
MANNERLY
MAQUETTE
MARCELLA
MARCELLO
MARKEDLY
MARTELLO
MASSENET
MASSEUSE
MASTERLY
MEDIEVAL

MERCEDES
MESMERIC
MILDEWED
MINCEPIE
MONTEITH
MOQUETTE
MOTHERLY
MULBERRY
MURDERER
NATTERED
NAUSEATE
NAUSEOUS
NOBLEMAN
NOISETTE
NONSENSE
NORSEMAN
NORSEMEN
NUCLEOLE
ODDMENTS
ODOMETER
OMELETTE
OPERETTA
OPULENCE
OUTREACH
OUTREMER
OUTWEIGH
PALMETTO
PAMPERED
PANDEMIC
PARIETAL
PARMESAN
PARTERRE
PASSERBY
PATHETIC
PATIENCE
PEACEFUL
PELLETED
PERCEIVE
PERCEVAL
PERFECTA
PERFECTO
PERMEATE
PERVERSE
PHILEMON
PHONETIC
PIERETTE
PILFERER
PILSENER
PIMIENTO
PIZZERIA
PLACEMAT
PLACEMEN
PLACENTA
PLATEFUL
PLATELET
PLEBEIAN
POCHETTE
POTBELLY
POWDERED
PREDELLA
PRESENCE
PRESERVE
PRETENCE
PRETENSE
PRIMEVAL
PROCEEDS
PROGERIA
PROPERLY
PROPERTY
PROTEASE
PROVERBS
PRUDENCE
PRUNELLA
PUCKERED
PUNGENCY
PURVEYOR
QUENELLE
RACLETTE
RASSELAS
RECREATE
REDEEMER
RELIEVED
REPLEVIN
RESPECTS
RETRENCH
REVIEWER
RIDGEWAY
RIFLEMAN
ROCKETRY
ROSSETTI
ROULETTE
RUGGEDLY
RUNNERUP
SANSERIF
SAUCEPAN
SCALENUS
SCAVENGE
SCREENED
SECRETLY
SELVEDGE
SENTENCE
SEQUENCE
SERGEANT
SERJEANT
SHAKEOUT
SHAMEFUL
SHAREOUT
SHIGELLA
SHIVERED
SISTERLY
SIXPENCE
SKELETAL
SKELETON
SLOVENIA
SLOVENLY
SOFTENER
SOLVENCY
SORCERER
SOUVENIR
SPACEMAN
SPADEFUL
SPITEFUL
SQUEEGEE
SQUEEZER
STAKEOUT
STAMENED
STILETTO
STOKESAY
STOREMAN
STOREYED
STUDENTS
SUBJECTS
SUBLEASE
SUBMERGE
SUBTENSE
SUCCEEDS
SUDDENLY
SUFFERER
SULLENLY
SURVEYOR
SUSPENSE
SYMMETRY
SYNTEXIS
SYSTEMIC
TABLEMAT
TASTEFUL
TATTERED
TAYBERRY
TEMPERED
TENDENCY
TENDERLY
TIMBERED
TINSELLY
TOISEACH
TOPHEAVY
TOPLEVEL
TOXAEMIA
TRADEOFF
TRAVELER
TRAVERSE
TRAVESTY
TRILEMMA
TSAREVNA
TUPPENNY
TURGENEV
TURMERIC
TURRETED
TWOPENNY
UDOMETER
UMBRELLA
UNEVENLY
UNFREEZE
UNITEDLY
UNIVERSE
UNSEEDED
UNSEEMLY
UNSTEADY
UNWIELDY
VALLETTA
VARIETAL
VELLEITY
VENDETTA
VENGEFUL
VERDERER
VERTEBRA
VESPERAL
VIGNETTE
VIOLENCE
VISCERAL
VITREOUS
WANDERER
WASTEFUL
WESLEYAN
WESTERLY
WHATEVER
WHENEVER
WHEREVER
WHITECAP
WHITEHOT
WHITENER
WICKEDLY
WISTERIA
WITHERED
WOLSELEY
WOODENLY
WRITEOFF
ZEPPELIN
PROTÉGÉE
AEROFLOT
AEROFOIL
ARTEFACT
ARTIFACT
ARTIFICE
BACKFIRE
BAREFOOT
BEAUFORT
BENEFICE
BENEFITS
BILLFOLD
BLOWFISH
BONIFACE
BOUFFANT
BRIEFING
BUCKFAST
BULLFROG
CAREFREE
CLIFFORD
CLUBFOOT
COIFFEUR
COIFFURE
CRAWFISH
CRAYFISH
CROWFOOT
DOWNFALL
DUTYFREE
DWARFISH
DWARFISM
ENSIFORM
FLATFISH
FLATFOOT
FOOTFALL
FOREFOOT
FOURFOLD
FUSIFORM
GOLDFISH
GRAFFITI
HALFFULL
HARTFORD
HELLFIRE
HEREFORD
INTIFADA
KINSFOLK
LANDFALL
LANDFILL
LEAPFROG
LUMPFISH
LUNGFISH
MANIFEST
MANIFOLD
MODIFIER
MOUFFLON
OMNIFORM
OVERFEED
OVERFILL
OVERFLOW
OVERFULL
PACIFIER
PACIFISM
PACIFIST
PALEFACE
PARAFFIN
PINAFORE
PLATFORM
PLAYFAIR
PRATFALL
PURIFIED
PURIFIER
PYRIFORM
RAINFALL
RAREFIED
REAFFIRM
REDEFINE
SAINFOIN
SCAFFOLD
SCARFACE
SCOFFING
SCROFULA
SERAFILE
SLUGFEST
SNIFFLER
SNOWFALL
SNUFFBOX
SPIFFING
SPITFIRE
STAFFING
STAFFORD
STARFISH
STUFFILY
STUFFING
TELEFILM
TYPEFACE
VARIFORM
WHARFAGE
WILDFELL
WILDFIRE
WILDFOWL
WINDFALL
WINIFRED
ABINGDON
ABNEGATE
ABROGATE
AEROGRAM
ALLEGORY
ALLOGAMY
ALMIGHTY
ARMAGNAC
ARPEGGIO
ARROGANT
ARROGATE
ASSIGNEE
AUTOGAMY
AUTOGYRO
BALLGIRL
BLUDGEON
BRAGGART
BRAGGING
BRIDGING
BRINGING
BROUGHAM
CALIGULA
CALLGIRL
CATEGORY
CHANGING
CHARGING
CLANGING
CLANGOUR
CLINGING
CRINGING
DANEGELD
DELEGATE
DEROGATE
DESIGNER

DILIGENT
DISAGREE
DRAUGHTS
DRAUGHTY
DRUDGERY
DRUGGIST
ELONGATE
EMERGENT
EMERGING
EMULGENT
ENDOGAMY
ENERGIZE
ENGAGING
EULOGIST
EULOGIUM
EULOGIZE
FATIGUED
FATIGUES
FEELGOOD
FILAGREE
FILIGREE
FLAGGING
FLOGGING
FOREGONE
FUMIGATE
GADOGADO
GEORGIAN
GROGGILY
GRUDGING
HEADGEAR
HEXAGRAM
HIGHGATE
HIRAGANA
HOLOGRAM
IDEOGRAM
INDIGENT
INSIGNIA
INTAGLIO
INTEGRAL
IRRIGATE
KILOGRAM
LITIGANT
LITIGATE
MAHOGANY
MALAGASY
MANAGING
MARIGOLD
MISOGYNY
MITIGATE
MONOGAMY
MONOGRAM
MORTGAGE
NAVIGATE
NOMOGRAM
OBLIGATE
OBLIGING
ORANGERY

PANEGYRY
PARAGUAY
PEDAGOGY
PEDIGREE
PELAGIUS
PHLEGMON
PHOSGENE
PHRYGIAN
PLANGENT
PLAYGIRL
PLOUGHED
PLUNGING
POLYGAMY
POLYGLOT
PRIGGISH
REFUGIUM
RELEGATE
RELIGION
RENEGADE
RESIGNED
SAVAGELY
SAVAGERY
SERAGLIO
SHANGHAI
SHINGLES
SHOWGIRL
SLANGING
SLUGGARD
SLUGGISH
SMIDGEON
SMUGGLED
SMUGGLER
SPANGLED
SPHAGNUM
SQUIGGLE
STAGGERS
STARGAZE
STINGING
STINGRAY
STRAGGLE
STRAGGLY
STRUGGLE
STURGEON
SVENGALI
SWINGING
TAILGATE
TELEGONY
TELEGRAM
THINGAMY
THOUGHTS
TOBOGGAN
TOLLGATE
UNSIGNED
UPRIGHTS
VINEGARY
VISIGOTH
VOYAGEUR

WRANGLER
WRINGING
WRONGFUL
XENOGAMY
YATAGHAN
YOUNGEST
ACIDHEAD
AESTHETE
ALDEHYDE
AMETHYST
ANATHEMA
ANYTHING
ANYWHERE
APOTHEGM
ARACHNID
ARETHUSA
ARMCHAIR
AYRSHIRE
BAATHIST
BABYHOOD
BACCHANT
BACKHAND
BENGHAZI
BIATHLON
BILLHOOK
BIRTHDAY
BLENHEIM
BLIGHTER
BLITHELY
BLOWHOLE
BLUSHING
BOLTHOLE
BONEHEAD
BOREHOLE
BRACHIAL
BRETHREN
BRIGHTEN
BRIGHTLY
BRIGHTON
BROCHURE
BROUHAHA
BUDDHISM
BUDDHIST
BULKHEAD
BULLHORN
BUTCHERS
BUTCHERY
CAKEHOLE
CALTHROP
CAMSHAFT
CARTHAGE
CATCHING
CHESHIRE
CINCHONA
CLASHING
CLOTHIER
CLOTHING

COACHING
COACHMAN
COALHOLE
COGWHEEL
CONCHOID
COPYHOLD
CORNHILL
COUCHANT
COUCHING
COUGHING
CRICHTON
CRUMHORN
CRUSHING
DABCHICK
DAUGHTER
DEADHEAD
DEATHBED
DECKHAND
DIAPHONE
DOUGHBOY
DOUGHNUT
DOWNHILL
DROPHEAD
DRUMHEAD
DUNGHILL
DUTCHMAN
EARPHONE
EDGEHILL
EGGSHELL
ELEPHANT
EPIPHANY
EPIPHYTE
EPITHEMA
ERYTHEMA
EYESHADE
FAITHFUL
FARMHAND
FARTHEST
FARTHING
FEATHERS
FEATHERY
FETCHING
FILTHILY
FLASHGUN
FLASHILY
FLASHING
FLUSHING
FLYSHEET
FLYWHEEL
FOOTHOLD
FOREHAND
FOREHEAD
FREEHAND
FREEHOLD
FRESHEST
FRESHMAN
FRIGHTEN

FURTHEST
GEOPHONE
GIRLHOOD
GNASHING
GODCHILD
GRAPHEME
GRAPHICS
GRAPHITE
GYMKHANA
HALFHOUR
HANDHELD
HATCHERY
HATCHING
HATCHWAY
HAWTHORN
HEADHUNT
HEIGHTEN
HENCHMAN
HEYTHROP
HOGSHEAD
HOLYHEAD
HUMPHREY
HUSHHUSH
IRISHISM
IRISHMAN
IRISHMEN
ISOTHERE
ISOTHERM
KALAHARI
KEELHAUL
KERCHIEF
KINSHASA
KNEEHIGH
KNIGHTLY
LATCHKEY
LAUGHING
LAUGHTER
LEACHING
LEATHERY
LEFTHAND
LINCHPIN
LOATHING
LONGHAND
LONGHAUL
LONGHORN
LOOPHOLE
LUNCHEON
LYNCHING
MARSHALL
MASTHEAD
MATCHBOX
MATCHING
MELCHIOR
MERCHANT
MINEHEAD
MIRTHFUL
MISCHIEF

MOLEHILL
MONOHULL
MORPHEME
MORPHEUS
MORPHINE
MOUTHFUL
MUNCHKIN
MUTCHKIN
NEATHERD
NEIGHBOR
NEOPHYTE
NEWSHAWK
NORTHERN
NUTSHELL
OFFSHOOT
OFFSHORE
OKLAHOMA
OLIPHANT
OUTSHINE
OVERHANG
OVERHAUL
OVERHEAD
OVERHEAR
OVERHEAT
PAMPHLET
PANTHEON
PARTHIAN
PATCHILY
PAYCHECK
PEEPHOLE
PENCHANT
PERSHING
PIECHART
PILCHARD
PINWHEEL
PISSHEAD
PLETHORA
PLUGHOLE
PORPHYRA
PORPHYRY
PORTHOLE
POTSHERD
PROPHECY
PROPHESY
PURCHASE
RAILHEAD
REDSHANK
RHYTHMIC
ROUGHAGE
SAMPHIRE
SAPPHIRE
SAPPHIST
SCAPHOID
SCATHING
SEASHELL
SEASHORE
SEETHING

SELFHELP
SHEPHERD
SHOEHORN
SKINHEAD
SLIGHTED
SLIGHTLY
SLOTHFUL
SMASHING
SOOTHING
SOOTHSAY
SOUCHONG
SOUTHEND
SOUTHERN
SOUTHPAW
SPITHEAD
STAGHORN
STANHOPE
STAPHYLE
STEPHENS
SULPHATE
SULPHIDE
SUNSHADE
SUNSHINE
SYMPHONY
TAKEHOME
TEACHERS
TEACHING
TEESHIRT
TEETHING
TETCHILY
TOMAHAWK
TOUCHING
TRACHOMA
TRASHCAN
TRICHOID
TROCHAIC
TROCHLEA
TRUTHFUL
URETHANE
VAUXHALL
WATCHDOG
WATCHFUL
WATCHING
WATCHMAN
WEIGHING
WELSHMAN
WHIPHAND
WINDHOEK
WITCHERY
WITCHING
WITHHOLD
WORTHIES
WORTHILY
WRATHFUL
WRITHING
XANTHOMA
YOKOHAMA
YOUTHFUL
ZOOPHYTE
ZUCCHINI
ABSCISSA
ABUTILON
ACQUIRED
ACQUIRER
ADENITIS
ADROITLY
AGGRIEVE
AGONIZED
AIGUILLE
AIRFIELD
AIRLINER
AIRTIGHT
ALUMINUM
AMERICAN
AMERICAS
ANCHISES
ANGLICAN
ANGUILLA
APERIENT
APERITIF
APPLIQUÉ
APPRISED
ARCHIVES
ATOMIZER
ATYPICAL
AUSPICES
BAGPIPES
BALLISTA
BANDITTI
BANLIEUE
BAPTISED
BARBICAN
BARBIZON
BASSINET
BASTILLE
BEARINGS
BEATIFIC
BEFRIEND
BESMIRCH
BESTIARY
BIBLICAL
BOADICEA
BOUTIQUE
BRASILIA
BREVIARY
BUNFIGHT
BURSITIS
CABRIOLE
CALLIOPE
CALLIPER
CALLISTO
CANAILLE
CANDIDLY
CANNIBAL
CANTICLE
CAPRIOLE
CAPSICUM
CAPSIZED
CAPTIOUS
CARDIGAN
CARDINAL
CARNIVAL
CARRIAGE
CARRIOLE
CAUDILLO
CAUTIOUS
CERVICAL
CHARISMA
CHEMICAL
CHENILLE
CHEVIOTS
CHILIAST
CHORIAMB
CLARINET
CLAVICLE
CLERICAL
CLERIHEW
CLINICAL
COCCIDAE
CODPIECE
COLLIERS
COLLIERY
COMBINED
COMPILER
CONFINED
CONFINES
CONSIDER
CONTINUE
CONTINUO
CONVINCE
CORNICHE
CORRIDOR
CORSICAN
CREDIBLE
CREDIBLY
CREDITOR
CREPITUS
CRIMINAL
CRITICAL
CRITIQUE
CRUCIATE
CRUCIBLE
CRUCIFER
CRUCIFIX
CULLINAN
CURLICUE
CURRICLE
CURSITOR
CUSPIDOR
CYCLICAL
CYSTITIS
DAYLIGHT
DEALINGS
DECEIVER
DEPRIVED
DESTINED
DETAILED
DETAINEE
DETAINER
DETRITUS
DIDDICOY
DIGGINGS
DISCIPLE
DISLIKED
DISPIRIT
DISTINCT
DULCIMER
DULCINEA
EARLIEST
EARNINGS
EARPIECE
EGGTIMER
ELDRITCH
ELIGIBLE
EMACIATE
EMERITUS
ERADIATE
EXAMINEE
EXAMINER
EXPLICIT
EYELINER
EYEPIECE
EYESIGHT
FACTIOUS
FAINITES
FALLIBLE
FANCIFUL
FANLIGHT
FARCICAL
FARRIERY
FASCICLE
FEASIBLE
FEASIBLY
FEELINGS
FENCIBLE
FESTIVAL
FIFTIETH
FINDINGS
FLAMINGO
FLEXIBLE
FLEXIBLY
FLOTILLA
FOGLIGHT
FOLLICLE
FORCIBLE
FORCIBLY
FORTIETH
FRAXINUS
FREMITUS
FRIGIDLY
GALLIARD
GALLIPOT
GARLICKY
GARRIGUE
GARRISON
GERMINAL
GINGIVAL
GLORIANA
GLORIOLE
GLORIOUS
GLOXINIA
GOLLIWOG
GRACIOUS
GRADIENT
GRAVITAS
GRIDIRON
GUERIDON
GUERILLA
GULLIBLE
GULLIVER
HALLIARD
HANDICAP
HANGINGS
HANNIBAL
HARRIDAN
HARRISON
HASTINGS
HAWAIIAN
HAWFINCH
HAYFIELD
HEBRIDES
HELSINKI
HERMIONE
HETAIRIA
HOLDINGS
HOOLIGAN
HOPFIELD
HORLICKS
HORRIBLE
HORRIBLY
HORRIFIC
HOSPITAL
HUSTINGS
HYACINTH
ICEFIELD
IMAGINED
IMPAIRED
IMPLICIT
IMPRISON
INCLINED
INEDIBLE
INFLIGHT
INFRINGE
INGUINAL
INIMICAL
INITIATE
INQUIRER
INSPIRED
INSPIRIT
INSTINCT
INTRIGUE
INVEIGLE
IRONICAL
JAMAICAN
JELLICOE
JETTISON
JOTTINGS
KORRIGAN
KUFFIYEH
LASHINGS
LEAVINGS
LEGGINGS
LEONIDAS
LODGINGS
LOLLIPOP
LOPSIDED
LUSCIOUS
MACHINES
MACHISMO
MADRIGAL
MALDIVES
MANCIPLE
MANDIBLE
MANDIOCA
MANNIKIN
MANTILLA
MANTISSA
MARGINAL
MARRIAGE
MARTINET
MARZIPAN
MASSICOT
MERCIFUL
MESSIDOR
MÉTAIRIE
METRICAL
METRITIS
MEUNIÈRE
MICHIGAN
MIDFIELD
MIDNIGHT
MILLIBAR
MILLINER
MILLIONS
MIRLITON
MOORINGS
MORBIDLY
MORBILLI
MORRISON
MORTIMER
MULLIGAN
MULTIPLE

MULTIPLY
MYELITIS
MYRMIDON
MYSTICAL
MYSTIQUE
MYTHICAL
NARGILEH
NAUTICAL
NAUTILUS
NEGLIGEE
NESCIENT
NEURITIS
NUFFIELD
NUPTIALS
NUTRIENT
OBEDIENT
OBTAINED
OFFSIDER
OILFIELD
ONESIDED
ORCHITIS
ORIGINAL
OUTFIELD
OUTRIDER
OUTRIGHT
OUTSIDER
OXBRIDGE
PACHINKO
PALLIATE
PANNICLE
PANNIKIN
PARSIFAL
PARTICLE
PARTISAN
PASSIBLE
PASTICHE
PASTILLE
PAULINUS
PEELINGS
PELLICLE
PEMMICAN
PENNINES
PERCIVAL
PERVIOUS
PHARISEE
PHILIPPI
PHTHISIS
PHYSICAL
PHYSIQUE
PICKINGS
PIERIDES
PINNIPED
PLACIDLY
PLATINUM
PLOTINUS
POETICAL
POITIERS
POPSICLE
PORRIDGE
PORTIÈRE
POSEIDON
POSSIBLE
POSSIBLY
PRECINCT
PRECIOUS
PREMIERE
PREMISES
PREVIOUS
PRODIGAL
PROHIBIT
PROLIFIC
PROMISED
PROVIDED
PROVIDER
PROVINCE
PRURIENT
PUBLICAN
PUBLICLY
PURLIEUS
PYELITIS
QUIRINAL
QUOTIENT
RACHITIS
RAILINGS
RATTIGAN
READIEST
RECEIPTS
RECEIVED
RECEIVER
REDLIGHT
REFRINGE
REGAINED
REJOINED
RENMINBI
REORIENT
REPAIRER
REPRIEVE
REPRISAL
REQUIRED
RESPIGHI
RETAILER
RETAINER
RETRIEVE
REVEILLE
RUBAIYAT
RUBBISHY
RUCTIONS
RUNCIBLE
SACRISTY
SANTIAGO
SARDINIA
SCABIOUS
SCILICET
SCIMITAR
SENSIBLE
SENSIBLY
SENTIENT
SENTINEL
SERVICES
SERVIENT
SERVITOR
SHERIDAN
SIXTIETH
SKYLIGHT
SKYPILOT
SOBRIETY
SOLDIERS
SOLDIERY
SORDIDLY
SPACIOUS
SPANIARD
SPAVINED
SPECIFIC
SPECIMEN
SPECIOUS
SPIRITED
SPIRITUS
SPOLIATE
SPRAINED
SPURIOUS
STOLIDLY
STRAIGHT
STRAINED
STRAINER
STRAITEN
STUDIOUS
STUPIDLY
STYLIZED
SUBTITLE
SUCCINCT
SUICIDAL
SULLIVAN
SUMMITRY
SUNLIGHT
SURGICAL
SURVIVAL
SURVIVOR
SYMBIONT
SYPHILIS
TACTICAL
TANGIBLE
TANGIBLY
TEQUILLA
TERMINAL
TERMINUS
TERRIBLE
TERRIBLY
TERRIFIC
TERTIARY
TESTICLE
THURIBLE
THURIFER
TINNITUS
TORTILLA
TRINIDAD
TRITICAL
TRITICUM
TROPICAL
TURGIDLY
TWILIGHT
TWOPIECE
UNGAINLY
UNSUITED
UNVOICED
USURIOUS
UXORIOUS
VERBIAGE
VERSICLE
VERTICAL
VESTIARY
VIATICUM
VINCIBLE
VIRGINAL
VIRGINIA
WILLIAMS
WINDINGS
WINNINGS
WINNIPEG
WORKINGS
WRITINGS
WYCLIFFE
XANTIPPE
YERSINIA
DEMIJOHN
FLAPJACK
FRABJOUS
READJUST
SKIPJACK
SLAPJACK
WHIPJACK
BLACKBOY
BLACKCAP
BLACKFLY
BLACKING
BLACKISH
BLACKLEG
BLACKOUT
BLINKERS
BLINKING
BLOCKADE
BLOCKAGE
BRACKETS
BRACKISH
BREAKING
BREAKOUT
BRICKBAT
BRUCKNER
CHECKERS
CHECKING
CHECKOUT
CHEEKILY
CHICKENS
CHICKPEA
CLINKERS
CRACKERS
CRACKING
CRACKPOT
CROCKERY
CROCKETT
DOORKNOB
DRINKING
DRUNKARD
EWIGKEIT
FAULKNER
FRANKISH
FRANKLIN
FREAKISH
FRECKLED
FRECKLES
FRISKILY
HABAKKUK
HANUKKAH
HONGKONG
KAMIKAZE
KATAKANA
KNACKERS
KNICKERS
KNOCKERS
KNOCKING
KNOCKOUT
KOUSKOUS
MALAKOFF
OILSKINS
OVERKILL
PARAKEET
PLANKING
PLANKTON
PLUCKILY
PLUCKING
QUICKSET
SANSKRIT
SHACKLES
SHEIKDOM
SHOCKING
SIDEKICK
SKULKING
SMOCKING
SNACKBAR
SNEAKERS
SNEAKING
SPANKING
SPARKING
SPARKLER
SPEAKERS
SPEAKING
SPECKLED
STALKING
STARKERS
STICKILY
STICKING
STICKLER
STINKING
STOCKADE
STOCKCAR
STOCKING
STOCKIST
STOCKMAN
STOCKPOT
STRIKING
TASHKENT
THANKFUL
THICKSET
THINKING
TRACKING
TRICKERY
TRUCKING
TRUCKLED
UNLIKELY
WHACKING
WHISKERS
WHISKERY
WRECKAGE
WRINKLED
ZEDEKIAH
ABSOLUTE
ABSOLVED
ACCOLADE
ACHILLES
AEROLITH
AIRPLANE
ALKALIFY
ALKALINE
ALKALOID
ALLELUIA
AMBULANT
AMBULATE
ANAGLYPH
ANGELICA
ANNALIST
ANNELIDA
ANTELOPE
ANTILLES
ANTILOPE
ANYPLACE
APHELION
APOLLYON
APOPLEXY
APPALLED
APPELANT
AQUALUNG
AQUILINE
ARBALEST

ARMALITE
ATHELING
AURELIAN
AVAILING
BABBLING
BACILLUS
BACKLASH
BACKLESS
BAFFLING
BAKELITE
BANALITY
BANTLING
BASELESS
BASELINE
BASILICA
BASILISK
BEAKLESS
BECALMED
BEETLING
BEHOLDEN
BEHOLDER
BEWILDER
BIBULOUS
BLOWLAMP
BOATLOAD
BOBOLINK
BODYLINE
BONELESS
BOOTLESS
BOTTLING
BOTULISM
BRISLING
BROILING
BUBBLING
BUCKLING
BUDDLEIA
BUMBLING
BUNGLING
BURGLARY
BUSTLING
CADILLAC
CAERLEON
CAJOLERY
CAMELLIA
CANALISE
CARELESS
CARILLON
CAROLINA
CAROLINE
CARTLOAD
CATALYST
CATILINE
CATTLEYA
CATULLUS
CAVALIER
CERULEAN
CHAPLAIN
CHARLADY
CHARLOCK
CHILLADA
CHILLING
CHURLISH
CIVILIAN
CIVILITY
CIVILIZE
CLUELESS
COBBLERS
COCHLEAR
COMPLAIN
COMPLETE
COMPLINE
CONCLAVE
CONCLUDE
CONFLATE
CONFLICT
COPULATE
COUPLING
COVALENT
CRAWLING
CROMLECH
CYRILLIC
CYTOLOGY
DATELESS
DATELINE
DAZZLING
DEADLINE
DEADLOCK
DEBILITY
DEMOLISH
DEPILATE
DERELICT
DESELECT
DESOLATE
DEVILISH
DEVILLED
DIALLING
DISALLOW
DISCLAIM
DISCLOSE
DISPLACE
DOCILITY
DOCKLAND
DOUBLOON
DOWNLOAD
DOXOLOGY
DRIBLETS
DRUMLINE
DRYCLEAN
DUCKLING
DUELLIST
DUMPLING
DWELLING
EASTLAKE
EGGPLANT
EMBOLDEN
EMBOLISM
ENFILADE
ENSILAGE
ENVELOPE
EPIPLOON
EQUALITY
EQUALIZE
ESCALADE
ESCALATE
ESCALOPE
ESCULENT
ESPALIER
ETHYLENE
ETIOLATE
EUROLAND
EYEGLASS
FABULOUS
FACELESS
FACELIFT
FACILITY
FALKLAND
FAMILIAR
FARMLAND
FATALISM
FATALIST
FATALITY
FEARLESS
FECKLESS
FECULENT
FIDDLING
FIDELITY
FINALIST
FINALITY
FINALIZE
FLAWLESS
FLYBLOWN
FOLKLORE
FONDLING
FOOTLING
FORELAND
FORELOCK
FORKLIFT
FORMLESS
FORSLACK
FOXGLOVE
FRAULEIN
FUMBLING
FUSELAGE
FUSILIER
FUTILITY
GAILLARD
GALILEAN
GAMBLING
GANGLAND
GANGLING
GANGLION
GASOLIER
GASOLINE
GEMOLOGY
GHOULISH
GORMLESS
GRAYLING
GRIDLOCK
GRILLING
GROWLING
HAIRLESS
HAIRLIKE
HAIRLINE
HAMILTON
HARDLINE
HARFLEUR
HARMLESS
HAVILDAR
HAZELNUT
HEADLAMP
HEADLAND
HEADLESS
HEADLINE
HEADLONG
HECKLING
HEEDLESS
HEIRLESS
HEIRLOOM
HELPLESS
HELPLINE
HERALDIC
HERALDRY
HIGHLAND
HIRELING
HOBBLING
HOMELAND
HOMELESS
HONOLULU
HOPELESS
HOROLOGY
HOTELIER
HOTPLATE
HUMILITY
HURDLING
IDEALISM
IDEALIST
IDEALIZE
IDEOLOGY
IMMOLATE
IMPELLED
IMPOLITE
INDOLENT
INHALANT
INSOLENT
INSULATE
INTELSAT
INVOLUTE
INVOLVED
ISOGLOSS
JANGLING
JEWELLED
JEWELLER
JONGLEUR
JUBILANT
JUBILATE
JUGGLING
KIDGLOVE
KINDLING
KNOBLESS
KREPLACH
LACKLAND
LADYLIKE
LAKELAND
LANDLADY
LANDLOCK
LANDLORD
LANGLAND
LANGLAUF
LANOLINE
LEAFLESS
LEGALISM
LEGALITY
LEGALIZE
LEVELLER
LIBELOUS
LIFELESS
LIFELIKE
LIFELINE
LIFELONG
LIMBLESS
LINOLEUM
LISTLESS
LIVELONG
LOBELINE
LOCALITY
LOCALIZE
LONGLAND
LOVELACE
LOVELESS
LOVELORN
LOWCLASS
LOYALIST
LUCKLESS
MACULATE
MAGELLAN
MAINLAND
MAINLINE
MAJOLICA
MAMELUKE
MARYLAND
MEATLESS
MEDALIST
MEDDLING
MEGALITH
MENELAUS
MESOLITE
METALLED
METALLIC
MIDDLING
MILKLESS
MINDLESS
MISPLACE
MOBILITY
MOBILIZE
MODELING
MODELLER
MODULATE
MONOLITH
MOORLAND
MORALIST
MORALITY
MORALIZE
MUCILAGE
MUDFLATS
MUMBLING
MUTILATE
MYCELIUM
MYCOLOGY
MYOBLAST
NAMELESS
NAPOLEON
NATALITY
NAUPLIUS
NEBULOUS
NECKLACE
NECKLINE
NEEDLESS
NEPALESE
NESTLING
NIBELUNG
NIGGLING
NIHILISM
NIHILIST
NOBELIUM
NOBILITY
NOSOLOGY
NOVELIST
NURSLING
OBSOLETE
OEILLADE
OENOLOGY
OILCLOTH
OILSLICK
ONCOLOGY
ONTOLOGY
OSCULATE
OUTCLASS
OUTFLANK
OVERLAID
OVERLAND
OVERLEAF
OVERLOAD

OVERLOOK
OVERLORD
PABULOUS
PADDLING
PAINLESS
PANELING
PANELLED
PANGLOSS
PAPILLON
PARALLAX
PARALLEL
PARALYZE
PARKLAND
PAROLLES
PATELLAR
PATULOUS
PAVILION
PEARLING
PECULATE
PECULIAR
PEDDLING
PEERLESS
PENALIZE
PENELOPE
PENOLOGY
PERILOUS
PETULANT
PHILLIPS
PHYLLOME
PICKLOCK
PIDDLING
PIPELINE
PITHLESS
PITILESS
POPULACE
POPULATE
POPULIST
POPULOUS
PORTLAND
POSOLOGY
PRECLUDE
PROCLAIM
PUGILISM
PUGILIST
PURBLIND
PURPLISH
PURSLANE
PURULENT
PUZZLING
QUISLING
RABELAIS
RAILLERY
RAMBLING
RANELAGH
RATTLING
RECKLESS
REDOLENT
REEDLING
REGULATE
RESOLUTE
RESOLVED
RESTLESS
REVELLER
REVOLVER
RIBALDRY
RIESLING
RIPPLING
RIVALISE
ROOFLESS
ROOTLESS
ROSALIND
ROSALINE
ROYALIST
RUMBLING
RUSTLESS
RUSTLING
RUTHLESS
SADDLERY
SADDLING
SALTLICK
SANGLIER
SCALLION
SCHILLER
SCOTLAND
SCOWLING
SCULLERY
SCULLION
SEAMLESS
SEAPLANE
SEDULOUS
SEEDLESS
SEEDLING
SELFLESS
SEMOLINA
SENILITY
SEROLOGY
SEXOLOGY
SHALLOWS
SHERLOCK
SHETLAND
SHIELING
SHILLING
SHOELACE
SHOELESS
SHOULDER
SIBILANT
SICILIAN
SICKLIST
SIDELINE
SIDELONG
SIMPLIFY
SIMULATE
SINCLAIR
SIZZLING
SKILLFUL
SKILLING
SKILLION
SKULLCAP
SMALLEST
SMALLPOX
SMOLLETT
SMOULDER
SNOWLINE
SOCALLED
SODALITE
SODALITY
SOULLESS
SPELLING
SPELLMAN
SPILLAGE
SPILLWAY
SPOILAGE
SPOILING
SPOTLESS
SPYGLASS
STABLING
STALLION
STARLESS
STARLING
STEALING
STEALTHY
STELLATE
STERLING
STIFLING
STIRLING
STROLLER
SUBTLETY
SUCHLIKE
SUCKLING
SUPPLANT
SUPPLIER
SUPPLIES
SURPLICE
SWELLING
SWILLING
SWIRLING
SYNCLINE
TABULATE
TACTLESS
TAILLESS
TEACLOTH
TEMPLATE
TERYLENE
THAILAND
THALLIUM
THEOLOGY
THRALDOM
THRILLER
TICKLING
TICKLISH
TIMELESS
TINGLING
TIRELESS
TONALITY
TONELESS
TOPCLASS
TOPOLOGY
TOTALITY
TOTALIZE
TOWELING
TRAILING
TRAMLINE
TREELESS
TREELINE
TRIFLING
TRIGLYPH
TRILLING
TRILLION
TRILLIUM
TRIPLING
TROLLOPE
TUBELESS
TUTELAGE
TUTELARY
TWIRLING
TYROLEAN
UNDULANT
UNDULATE
UNFILLED
UNGULATE
UNSALTED
UNSOLVED
UNTILLED
UPHOLDER
URSULINE
VENALITY
VEXILLUM
VIGILANT
VIRILITY
VIROLOGY
VIRULENT
VISELIKE
VITALITY
VITALIZE
VITELLUS
VITILIGO
VOCALIST
VOCALIZE
VOLPLANE
WAMBLING
WARPLANE
WEAKLING
WHIPLASH
WHIRLING
WHITLING
WILDLIFE
WINDLASS
WINDLESS
WINGLESS
WIRELESS
WOBBLING
WOODLAND
WOOLLENS
WORDLESS
WORKLOAD
XENOLITH
YEARLING
YEARLONG
YODELLER
ZIBELINE
ABUTMENT
ACRIMONY
ACROMION
AGRIMONY
ALARMING
ALARMIST
ALHAMBRA
ANNAMITE
ANTIMONY
ARGUMENT
ARMAMENT
ASSEMBLE
ASSEMBLY
ASSUMING
AUTOMATE
AUTUMNAL
BAHAMIAN
BAILMENT
BASEMENT
BEAUMONT
BECOMING
BEHEMOTH
BIGAMIST
BIGAMOUS
BINOMIAL
BLOOMERS
BLOOMING
BOHEMIAN
BOOKMARK
BRIMMING
CALAMINE
CALAMITY
CAMOMILE
CASEMATE
CASEMENT
CASHMERE
CATAMITE
CATSMEAT
CERAMICS
CEREMENT
CEREMONY
CHARMING
CHIPMUNK
CHROMITE
CHROMIUM
CHUMMAGE
CLAIMANT
CLAYMORE
COALMINE
COLOMBIA
COLUMBAN
COLUMBUS
COSTMARY
CREAMERY
CRUMMOCK
CUCUMBER
DARTMOOR
DECEMBER
DECEMVIR
DECIMATE
DOCUMENT
DOLOMITE
DOPAMINE
DREAMILY
DRUMMING
DYNAMICS
DYNAMISM
DYNAMITE
EASEMENT
ENCAMPED
ENCOMIUM
ENCUMBER
ENDYMION
ENORMITY
ENORMOUS
ENSEMBLE
EPHEMERA
ESTIMATE
EVERMORE
EXHUMATE
FILAMENT
FISHMEAL
FLATMATE
FLUMMERY
FOREMOST
FRAGMENT
GANYMEDE
GARAMOND
GLEAMING
GLOAMING
GLOOMILY
GOBSMACK
GOLDMINE
GOURMAND
GROOMING
GUNSMITH
HALFMAST
HALLMARK
HANDMADE
HANDMAID
HEADMARK
HEADMOST

HEGEMONY
HELPMATE
HINDMOST
HOMEMADE
IGNOMINY
ILLUMINE
INASMUCH
INCOMING
INFAMOUS
INHUMANE
INSOMNIA
INTIMACY
INTIMATE
ISTHMIAN
JEREMIAD
JEREMIAH
JUDGMENT
KITEMARK
KOURMISS
LANDMARK
LANDMASS
LANDMINE
LIGAMENT
LINIMENT
MAINMAST
MATAMORE
MAXIMIZE
MELAMINE
MESSMATE
MILKMAID
MINAMATA
MINIMIZE
MISHMASH
MOHAMMED
MONUMENT
MOVEMENT
MUHAMMAD
MUNIMENT
NDJAMENA
NOVEMBER
OCCAMIST
OINTMENT
ONCOMING
OPTIMATE
OPTIMISM
OPTIMIST
ORNAMENT
ORPIMENT
OUTSMART
OVERMUCH
PALIMONY
PARAMOUR
PASHMINA
PAVEMENT
PEARMAIN
PEDIMENT
PELLMELL
PENUMBRA
PHARMACY
PHORMIUM
PICKMEUP
PLAYMATE
POLYMATH
POSTMARK
POTEMKIN
PREAMBLE
PSALMIST
PSALMODY
PYRAMIDS
QUAGMIRE
REARMOST
REGIMENT
REMEMBER
RESEMBLE
ROOMMATE
ROSAMOND
ROSEMARY
RUDIMENT
RUSHMORE
SCHEMING
SCHUMANN
SCRAMBLE
SEDIMENT
SELFMADE
SHIPMATE
SHIPMENT
SKIRMISH
SLUMMING
SOLEMNLY
SQUAMATA
STIGMATA
STORMING
STORMONT
STRUMPET
SUDAMENT
SUDAMINA
SWARMING
SWIMMING
SYCAMORE
TEAMMATE
TEGUMENT
TELEMARK
TENEMENT
THIAMINE
THROMBIN
THROMBUS
TIDEMARK
TIRAMISU
TRIMMING
TUPAMARO
ULTIMATE
UNCOMBED
UNCOMMON
UNTIMELY
UPCOMING
VEHEMENT
VENOMOUS
VESTMENT
VIREMENT
VITAMINS
WINDMILL
WORKMATE
YOSEMITE
ABSENTEE
ABSINTHE
ACCENTED
ACCENTOR
ACTINIDE
ACTINIUM
ADDENDUM
ADMONISH
ADVANCED
ADVANCER
AERONAUT
AFFINITY
AGRONOMY
AIRINESS
ALBANIAN
ALBINONI
ALIENATE
ALIENISM
ALIENIST
ALPINIST
AMMONIAC
AMMONITE
ANTENNAE
APPANAGE
APPENDIX
ARDENNES
ARDENTLY
ARGININE
ARGONAUT
ARKANSAS
ARMENIAN
ARRANGER
ARSONIST
ASTONISH
ATHANASY
ATHENIAN
ATLANTIC
ATLANTIS
ATTENDER
AUTONOMY
BADINAGE
BALANCED
BALDNESS
BALINESE
BANKNOTE
BARENESS
BARONESS
BARONETS
BARONIAL
BASENESS
BASINFUL
BEGINNER
BENENDEN
BIANNUAL
BICONVEX
BIENNIAL
BLUENOSE
BOLDNESS
BOOTNECK
BOTANIST
BROWNING
BROWNISH
BUSINESS
CAGINESS
CALENDAR
CALENDER
CALMNESS
CANONIZE
CASANOVA
CELANESE
CHAINSAW
CLANNISH
CLEANERS
CLEANING
CLEANSED
CLEANSER
CLOWNISH
COLANDER
COLDNESS
COLONIAL
COLONIST
COLONIZE
COOLNESS
CORONARY
CORONOID
COSINESS
COVENANT
COVENTRY
COZINESS
CROONING
CROWNING
CULINARY
CURTNESS
CUTENESS
CYLINDER
CYRENIAC
DAMPNESS
DANKNESS
DARKNESS
DEAFNESS
DEBONAIR
DECANTER
DECENTLY
DEEPNESS
DEFENDER
DEFINITE
DEFTNESS
DEMENTED
DEMENTIA
DEMONIAC
DERANGED
DETONATE
DIAGNOSE
DIMINISH
DISINTER
DISUNION
DISUNITE
DISUNITY
DIVINITY
DOMINANT
DOMINATE
DOMINEER
DOMINION
DOMINOES
DRAINAGE
DRAINING
DROWNING
DUBONNET
DULLNESS
DUMBNESS
EASINESS
ECHINATE
ECHINOPS
EERINESS
ELSINORE
EMMANUEL
ENDANGER
ENGENDER
ENGINEER
ENKINDLE
ENTANGLE
ESTANCIA
ESTONIAN
ETERNITY
EUGENICS
EVENNESS
EXPENDED
EXPENSES
EXPONENT
EXTENDED
EXTENSOR
FAIRNESS
FASTNESS
FEMININE
FEMINISM
FEMINIST
FEMINITY
FILENAME
FIRMNESS
FLANNELS
FLOUNCED
FLOUNDER
FLUENTLY
FONDNESS
FOOTNOTE
FORENAME
FORENOON
FORENSIC
FOULNESS
FRIENDLY
FULLNESS
FURUNCLE
GABONESE
GAMENESS
GAZUNDER
GEMINATE
GERANIUM
GERONIMO
GIGANTIC
GIRONDIN
GLADNESS
GLASNOST
GOODNESS
GRAINING
GREENBAG
GREENERY
GREENFLY
GREENING
GREENISH
GREENOCK
GRIMNESS
GROUNDED
GUERNSEY
GUIANIAN
GUYANESE
HABANERA
HANGNAIL
HARANGUE
HARDNESS
HAZINESS
HEDONISM
HEDONIST
HIGHNESS
HOLINESS
HUMANELY
HUMANISM
HUMANIST
HUMANITY
HUMANIZE
IDLENESS
ILLINOIS
IMMANENT
IMMANUEL
IMMINENT
IMMUNITY
IMMUNIZE
IMPUNITY
INCENSED
INDENTED

INFANTRY
INFINITE
INFINITY
INSANELY
INSANITY
INTENDED
INTENTLY
INVENTED
INVENTOR
IOLANTHE
ISLANDER
ISTANBUL
JAPANESE
JAPONICA
JOHANNES
JOKINGLY
JUSTNESS
JUVENILE
KEENNESS
KINDNESS
LACINATE
LACONIAN
LAMENESS
LAMENTED
LAMINATE
LATENESS
LATINIST
LAVENDER
LAVENGRO
LAZINESS
LEARNING
LEBANESE
LEMONADE
LEWDNESS
LICENSED
LICENSEE
LIKENESS
LILONGWE
LIMONITE
LIMPNESS
LOUDNESS
LOVINGLY
LUMINARY
LUMINOUS
LUSHNESS
LYSANDER
MALINGER
MARINADE
MARINATE
MARONITE
MCKINLEY
MEANNESS
MEEKNESS
MELANITE
MELANOMA
MENANDER
MERINGUE
METONYMY
MILANESE
MILDNESS
MOMENTUM
MOURNFUL
MOURNING
MUCHNESS
MUTINEER
MUTINOUS
NEARNESS
NEATNESS
NEPENTHE
NICENESS
NICKNACK
NICKNAME
NIJINSKY
NOMINATE
NUMBNESS
NUMINOUS
OFFENDED
OFFENDER
OILINESS
OLEANDER
OPENNESS
OPPONENT
ORDINAND
ORDINARY
ORDINATE
ORGANDIE
ORGANISM
ORGANIST
ORGANIZE
ORIENTAL
PAGANINI
PAGINATE
PALENESS
PALINODE
PARANOIA
PARANOID
PARENTAL
PATENTED
PATENTEE
PATENTLY
PEDANTIC
PEDANTRY
PEDUNCLE
PEIGNOIR
PEKINESE
PENKNIFE
PERTNESS
PETANQUE
PEVENSEY
PIRANESI
PLANNING
PLEONASM
POIGNANT
POLONIUM
POMANDER
POORNESS
POPINJAY
PREGNANT
PRIMNESS
PUDENDUM
PYRENEES
QUAINTLY
RACINESS
RANKNESS
RASHNESS
RAVENOUS
RECENTLY
REFINERY
REIGNING
REKINDLE
REMINDER
RESINOUS
RESONANT
RESONATE
REVANCHE
RICHNESS
RIPENESS
ROBINSON
ROMANCER
ROMANIAN
ROMANSCH
ROMANTIC
ROSINESS
ROTENONE
RUDENESS
RUMINANT
RUMINATE
SAGENESS
SALINGER
SALINITY
SALTNESS
SAMENESS
SAPONITE
SAVANNAH
SAYONARA
SCANNING
SCIENCES
SCORNFUL
SECONDER
SECONDLY
SELENITE
SELENIUM
SEMINARY
SERENADE
SERENATA
SERENELY
SERENITY
SHRUNKEN
SICKNESS
SILENCER
SILENTLY
SIRENIAN
SLIMNESS
SLOWNESS
SMUGNESS
SOFTNESS
SOLENOID
SORENESS
SOURNESS
SPANNING
SPAWNING
SPINNING
SPLENDID
SPLENDOR
SPLINTER
SPOONFUL
SPRINGER
SPRINKLE
SPRINTER
SPRYNESS
SPURNING
SQUANDER
STAGNANT
STAGNATE
STANNARY
STANNITE
STEINWAY
STRANDED
STRANGER
STRANGLE
STRENGTH
STRINGED
STRINGER
STRONGLY
STUNNING
SUDANESE
SURENESS
SYRINGES
TALENTED
TAMENESS
TAPENADE
TARTNESS
TAUTNESS
TAXONOMY
THINNESS
THINNING
THRENODY
TIDINESS
TITANESS
TITANISM
TITANITE
TITANIUM
TOMENTUM
TRAINING
TRIANGLE
TRIMNESS
TROUNCER
TRUENESS
TRUNNION
TURANDOT
UGLINESS
UNHINGED
UNIONISM
UNIONIST
UNIONIZE
UNKINDLY
UNMANNED
UNTANGLE
UNWANTED
UNWONTED
URBANITY
URBANIZE
URGENTLY
VACANTLY
VALENCIA
VASTNESS
VERANDAH
VERONESE
VERONICA
VICINITY
VILENESS
WARINESS
WEAKNESS
WELLNIGH
WIDENING
WILDNESS
WILINESS
WOMANISH
WOMANIZE
YEARNING
ZAMINDAR
AASVOGEL
ADENOIDS
AEGROTAT
AIRBORNE
ALEHOUSE
ALTHOUGH
ALVEOLUS
AMBROSIA
ANACONDA
ANALOGUE
ANATOLIA
ANATOMIC
ANCHORET
APOLOGIA
APOLOGUE
APPROACH
APPROVAL
APPROVED
ASPHODEL
BALLOCKS
BALMORAL
BARDOLPH
BEDCOVER
BESPOKEN
BESTOWER
BOLLOCKS
BONHOMIE
BORROWED
BORROWER
BOSWORTH
BOTTOMRY
BOUZOUKI
BURROWER
BUTTOCKS
CABOODLE
CAMBODIA
CANOODLE
CARBOLIC
CARBONIC
CASTOFFS
CATHOLIC
CATHOUSE
CHACONNE
CHEROKEE
CLITORIS
COGNOMEN
COLLOQUY
COMMONER
COMMONLY
COMPOSED
COMPOSER
COMPOUND
CONCORDE
CONFOUND
CONSOMMÉ
CORDOVAN
CORIOLIS
CORMORAN
CORPORAL
CORRODED
CRAMOISY
CRETONNE
CULLODEN
CUPBOARD
CUSTOMER
CYANOGEN
CYANOSIS
DAFFODIL
DEFLOWER
DESPOTIC
DIABOLIC
DIAGONAL
DIALOGUE
DIAMONDS
DIATONIC
DIPLOMAT
DISCOLOR
DISCOUNT
DISCOVER
DISGORGE
DISHONOR

DISLODGE
DISLOYAL
DISMOUNT
DISPOSAL
DISPOSED
DISSOLVE
DJIBOUTI
DOCTORAL
DOCTORED
DOGHOUSE
DORMOUSE
DRACONIC
DRAGOONS
DRYGOODS
DUMFOUND
ECONOMIC
ELKHOUND
EMPLOYED
EMPLOYEE
EMPLOYER
ENCLOSED
ENCLOTHE
ENCROACH
ENSCONCE
EPILOGUE
EPISODIC
ESTROGEN
ETHIOPIA
EUPHONIA
EUPHONIC
EUPHORIA
EUPHORIC
EUTROPHY
EUTROPIC
EXPLODED
EXPLORER
EYETOOTH
FACTOTUM
FALCONRY
FIBROSIS
FLAVORED
FOGBOUND
FOLLOWED
FOLLOWER
FOLLOWUP
FORMOSAN
FORSOOTH
FOXHOUND
FURLOUGH
FURROWED
GADZOOKS
GALLOPER
GALLOWAY
GARGOYLE
GARROTTE
GASWORKS
GIACONDA

GIOCONDA
GLYCOGEN
GOLGOTHA
GUMMOSIS
GUNPOINT
HALLOWED
HANDOVER
HANGOVER
HARMONIC
HENHOUSE
HICCOUGH
HIDROSIS
HISTORIC
HOLLOWAY
HORMONAL
HOTHOUSE
HYDROGEN
HYPNOSIS
HYPNOTIC
ICEHOUSE
IMPROPER
IMPROVED
IMPROVER
INCHOATE
INGROWTH
ISOGONAL
JAMBOREE
JEALOUSY
JINGOISM
JINGOIST
JORROCKS
KEYBOARD
KOMSOMOL
KYPHOSIS
LACROSSE
LADRONES
LAWCOURT
LEFTOVER
LINCOLNS
LITTORAL
LONDONER
LORDOSIS
LULWORTH
MADHOUSE
MADWOMAN
MAGNOLIA
MAHJONGG
MALLORCA
MALVOLIO
MANDOLIN
MANGONEL
MANPOWER
MARJORAM
MARMOSET
MASTODON
MATRONLY
MEDIOCRE

METEORIC
METHODIC
MICRODOT
MIDPOINT
MIGNONNE
MIRRORED
MISCOUNT
MISNOMER
MISSOURI
MNEMONIC
MONGOLIA
MONGOOSE
MONMOUTH
MONROVIA
MOREOVER
MYOSOTIS
NARCOSES
NARCOSIS
NARCOTIC
NARROWLY
NATIONAL
NECROSIS
NEPIONIC
NEUROSIS
NEUROTIC
NEWCOMER
NEWFOUND
NICHOLAS
NITROGEN
NOTIONAL
NUTHOUSE
OFFCOLOR
OLDWORLD
ONLOOKER
OOPHORON
OPTIONAL
ORATORIO
ORTHODOX
OUTBOARD
OUTDOORS
OUTGOING
OUTHOUSE
OUTMODED
OXYMORON
OXYTOCIN
PANDOWDY
PANGOLIN
PARDONER
PASSOVER
PASTORAL
PATHOGEN
PECTORAL
PERFORCE
PERIODIC
PERSONAL
PHILOMEL
PHOTOFIT

PHOTOPSY
PINPOINT
PLATONIC
PLYMOUTH
POISONER
PONSONBY
PORPOISE
POTBOUND
POTHOLER
PREMOLAR
PRETORIA
PRISONER
PROFORMA
PROFOUND
PROLOGUE
PROMOTER
PROPOSAL
PROPOSED
PROPOSER
PROPOUND
PROROGUE
PROTOCOL
PROTOZOA
PUGNOSED
PULLOVER
PUSHOVER
QUATORZE
QUIXOTIC
RAISONNÉ
RANDOMLY
RATIONAL
REASONED
RECKONER
REGIONAL
REPROACH
RESPONSE
RESTORER
REYNOLDS
RHETORIC
RISSOLES
SARDONIC
SARDONYX
SAUROPOD
SAWBONES
SCHMOOZE
SCHOONER
SCIROCCO
SEABOARD
SEABORNE
SEAFORTH
SEAGOING
SEASONAL
SEASONED
SELBORNE
SEMIOTIC
SIGNORIA
SINFONIA

SKIBOOTS
SLIPOVER
SLYBOOTS
SORBONNE
STAROSTA
STENOSED
STENOSIS
STOPOVER
SUBPOENA
SUBSONIC
SUBTOPIA
SUBTOTAL
SUPPOSED
SURMOUNT
SURROUND
SYMBOLIC
TAKEOVER
TAMWORTH
TANDOORI
TAPHOUSE
TARBOOSH
TECTONIC
TEETOTAL
TEMPORAL
TEUTONIC
THOROUGH
TITMOUSE
TOLBOOTH
TOPNOTCH
TORTOISE
TOULOUSE
TURBOJET
TURKOMAN
TURNOVER
UNBROKEN
UNCLOVEN
UNCOOKED
UNIPOLAR
UNSPOILT
UNSPOKEN
VARIORUM
VERMOUTH
VICTORIA
VISCOUNT
WAGGONER
WALKOVER
WARHORSE
WAXWORKS
WEAPONRY
YOGHOURT
ZIRCONIA
ZOONOSIS
ABRUPTLY
ACCEPTED
AGITPROP
AIRSPEED
ALLOPATH

ALLSPICE
ANTEPOST
ANTIPHON
ANTIPOPE
BACKPACK
BALLPARK
BEANPOLE
BELLPUSH
BLOWPIPE
BONSPIEL
BOWSPRIT
BRATPACK
BROMPTON
BUDAPEST
CALIPERS
CARAPACE
CATAPULT
CESSPOOL
CHAMPERS
CHAMPION
CHOPPING
CLAPPERS
CLAPPING
CLASPING
CLIPPERS
CLIPPING
CLODPOLL
COALPORT
COLOPHON
CONSPIRE
COTOPAXI
CRIPPLED
CRISPIAN
CROUPIER
DECIPHER
DIASPORA
DOORPOST
DOWNPLAY
DOWNPOUR
DRIPPING
DROOPING
DROPPING
ELLIPSIS
ELLIPTIC
EOHIPPUS
EQUIPAGE
ESCAPADE
ESCAPISM
ESCAPIST
ESTOPPEL
EUPEPSIA
EUROPEAN
EXEMPLAR
FILIPINO
FISHPOND
FLAGPOLE
FLAPPING

FLIPPANT
FLIPPERS
FLIPPING
FOOTPATH
FOURPART
FREEPOST
FRIPPERY
FRUMPISH
FULLPAGE
GATEPOST
GLUMPISH
GOALPOST
GRASPING
GRIPPING
GROUPING
GRUMPILY
HELIPORT
HORNPIPE
HOSEPIPE
INEXPERT
JODHPURS
KINGPOST
LAMPPOST
METAPHOR
MILLPOND
MIREPOIX
MISAPPLY
MISSPELL
MISSPENT
MONOPOLY
NENUPHAR
NEWSPEAK
NINEPINS
OCCUPANT
OCCUPIED
OCCUPIER
OEDIPEAN
OENOPHIL
OLYMPIAD
OLYMPIAN
OLYMPICS
OPENPLAN
OVERPASS
OVERPLAY
PASSPORT
PERIPETY
PERSPIRE
POSTPAID
POSTPONE
PRIAPISM
PROMPTER
PROMPTLY
PROSPECT
PROSPERO
REAPPEAR
RECEPTOR
REDEPLOY
REEMPLOY
ROLYPOLY
SCHAPSKA
SCORPION
SCRAPPLE
SCRIPTUM
SCRUPLES
SCULPTOR
SELFPITY
SERAPHIC
SERAPHIM
SHEEPDOG
SHEEPISH
SHIPPING
SHOPPING
SHRAPNEL
SIGNPOST
SINAPISM
SISYPHUS
SKIPPING
SLEEPERS
SLEEPILY
SLEEPING
SLIPPERS
SLIPPERY
SLIPPING
SLOPPILY
SLOWPOKE
SNAPPILY
SOURPUSS
STAMPEDE
STOPPAGE
STOPPING
STRAPPED
STRAPPER
STRIPPED
STRIPPER
SWEEPING
SYNOPSIS
SYNOPTIC
TAILPIPE
TEASPOON
THESPIAN
THOMPSON
THUMPING
TRAPPIST
TRESPASS
TROOPING
TRUMPERY
TURNPIKE
UNTAPPED
WELLPAID
WHIPPING
WHOOPING
WHOPPING
WINDPIPE
WOOLPACK
WRAPPING
XENOPHON
XERAPHIM
ZOOSPERM
ZOOSPORE
PARAQUAT
RAMEQUIN
TRANQUIL
ABERRANT
ABNORMAL
ABSORBED
ABSORBER
ABSTRACT
ABSTRUSE
ABSURDLY
ACCURACY
ACCURATE
ACCURSED
ADHERENT
ADMIRING
AGRARIAN
AIRBRAKE
AIRCRAFT
ALACRITY
ALBERICH
ALBURNUM
ALDERMAN
ALDERNEY
ALGERIAN
ALGERINE
ALGORISM
ALLERGEN
ALLERGIC
ALLURING
AMPERAGE
ANACREON
ANDERSON
ANDORRAN
ANEURYSM
ANSERINE
ANTERIOR
ANTEROOM
APHORISM
APIARIST
APPARENT
AQUARIUM
AQUARIUS
ARBOREAL
ARMORIAL
ARMORICA
ARTERIAL
ASCORBIC
ASPERGES
ASPERITY
ASPIRANT
ASPIRATE
ASPIRING
ASSORTED
ASSYRIAN
ASTERISK
ASTEROID
ATHEROMA
ATTORNEY
AUSTRIAN
AUTARCHY
BACKROOM
BACTRIAN
BALDRICK
BALLROOM
BANKROLL
BANKRUPT
BATHROBE
BATHROOM
BAUDRICK
BAVARIAN
BEETROOT
BEGORRAH
BELGRADE
BERTRAND
BESTRIDE
BEVERAGE
BIGARADE
BIOGRAPH
BLURRING
BOOKROOM
BULLRING
BURGRAVE
BUTTRESS
CABERNET
CAMARGUE
CAMBRIAN
CAMEROON
CANARIES
CAPERING
CASTRATE
CASTRATO
CATARACT
CATERING
CELERIAC
CELERITY
CENTRIST
CENTRODE
CHAIRMAN
CHEERFUL
CHEERILY
CHEERING
CHLORATE
CHLORIDE
CHLORINE
CHOIRBOY
CIBORIUM
CICERONE
CINERAMA
CINEREAL
CLEARCUT
CLEARING
CLEARWAY
COATRACK
COHERENT
COLORADO
COLORANT
COLORFUL
COLORING
COMPRESS
COMPRISE
CONCRETE
CONFRONT
CONGRESS
CONTRACT
CONTRARY
CONTRAST
CONTRITE
CONTRIVE
CONTROLS
COVERAGE
COVERING
COVERLET
COWARDLY
CUCURBIT
CUTPRICE
DANDRUFF
DARKROOM
DAYBREAK
DAYDREAM
DECORATE
DECOROUS
DEFORMED
DELIRIUM
DEMERARA
DEMERSAL
DEMURELY
DEMURRAL
DENARIUS
DENDRITE
DENDROID
DEPARTED
DEPORTEE
DESCRIBE
DESERTED
DESERTER
DESERVED
DESIROUS
DESTRUCT
DETHRONE
DEXTROSE
DEXTROUS
DIARRHEA
DIATRIBE
DIFFRACT
DISARRAY
DISCREET
DISCRETE
DISGRACE
DISORDER
DISPROVE
DISTRACT
DISTRAIN
DISTRAIT
DISTRESS
DISTRICT
DISTRUST
DIVORCED
DIVORCEE
DOCTRINE
DOLDRUMS
DOLOROUS
DREARILY
ECOFREAK
ELDORADO
EMIGRANT
EMIGRATE
EMPORIUM
EMPYREAN
ENCIRCLE
ENDURING
ENLARGED
ENLARGER
ENSHRINE
ENSHROUD
ENTHRALL
ENTHRONE
ENTIRELY
ENTIRETY
ENVIRONS
EPIGRAPH
ESCARGOT
ESCORIAL
ETHEREAL
ETHERISE
ETRURIAN
EXECRATE
EXOCRINE
EXPORTER
EXTERIOR
EXTERNAL
EXTERNAT
FAVORITE
FEDERACY
FEDERATE
FEVERFEW
FEVERISH
FIGURINE
FILARIUM
FILTRATE
FLAGRANT
FLOORING
FLOURISH
FLUORIDE

FLUORINE INTERCOM MAZARINE OVERRATE REVEREND SUBURBAN
FLUORITE INTEREST MEMBRANE OVERRIDE REVERENT SUBURBIA
FLYDRIVE INTERIOR MEMORIAL OVERRIPE REVERSAL SUDARIUM
FOOTREST INTERMIT MEMORIAM OVERRULE REVERSED SUFFRAGE
FORTRESS INTERNAL MEMORIZE PALGRAVE RIFFRAFF SUMERIAN
FRAGRANT INTERNEE MILLRACE PANCREAS RIGOROUS SUNCREAM
FUMAROLE INTERNET MINORESS PANORAMA RIPARIAN SUNDRIED
FUNERARY INTERPOL MINORITE PASTRAMI RIVERAIN SUNDRIES
FUNEREAL INTERVAL MINORITY PATERNAL RIVERINE SUPERBLY
FUSAROLE INVERTED MISERERE PECORINO RODERICK SUPERIOR
FUTURISM INWARDLY MISPRINT PEDERAST RYEGRASS SUPERMAN
FUTURIST IVOIRIEN MISTREAT PEMBROKE SALARIED SUPERNAL
GABORONE JEFFREYS MISTRESS PEPERONI SALEROOM SUPERTAX
GADARENE JIMCRACK MISTRUST PETERLOO SATIRIST SUPPRESS
GANGRENE KOHLRABI MODERATE PICAROON SATIRIZE SURPRISE
GASTRULA LABURNUM MODERATO PIECRUST SATURATE SUZERAIN
GENERATE LACERATE MONARCHY PILGRIMS SATURDAY SWEARING
GENEROUS LANDRACE MONDRIAN PINPRICK SATURNIA SYBARITE
GENTRIFY LATERITE MONORAIL PIPERINE SCABROUS SYNDROME
GERTRUDE LEVERAGE MOTORCAR PLAYROOM SCOURING TAFFRAIL
GIMCRACK LIBERATE MOTORING PLEURISY SEAFRONT TAMARIND
GLABROUS LIBERIAN MOTORIST PODARGUS SECURELY TAMARISK
GOVERNOR LICORICE MOTORIZE POLARIZE SECURITY TAPERING
GUJARATI LIMERICK MOTORMAN POLTROON SENGREEN TARTRATE
HANDRAIL LITERACY MOTORWAY POOLROOM SENORITA TAVERNER
HEADREST LITERARY MUSHROOM PORTRAIT SEPARATE TEMERITY
HEADROOM LITERATE NATURISM POWERFUL SEVERELY THEORIST
HIBERNIA LITERATI NATURIST PRAIRIAL SEVEREST THEORIZE
HIGHRISE LIVERIED NAVARINO PRIMROSE SEVERITY TIBERIAS
HIGHROAD LIVERISH NAZARENE PRIORESS SEWERAGE TIBERIUS
HILARITY LOWERING NEPHRITE PRIORITY SHADRACH TIEBREAK
HOLYROOD LUPERCAL NEUTRINO PROGRESS SHAGREEN TIMOROUS
HONORARY LUSTRINE NEWSREEL PROTRUDE SHAMROCK TOLERANT
HOVERFLY LUSTROUS NEWSROOM PYORRHEA SHEARMAN TOLERATE
HUMORIST LYSERGIC NIGERIAN QUADRANT SHOWROOM TOMORROW
HUMOROUS MACARONI NIGERIEN QUADRATE SIBERIAN TOVARICH
HUNDREDS MACAROON NOSTRILS QUADRIGA SICKROOM TOWERING
HUNGRILY MACERATE NOSTROMO QUADROON SIDEREAL TUBERCLE
HUNTRESS MAHARAJA NOTARIAL QUATRAIN SIDERITE TUBEROSE
HYPERION MAHARANI NUMERACY RACKRENT SILURIAN TUBEROUS
IGNORANT MAJORITY NUMERALS RAILROAD SLURRING TUTORIAL
IMMERSED MALARIAL NUMERATE RECORDER SNEERING ULCERATE
IMMORTAL MALARKEY NUMEROUS REDBRICK SOBERING ULCEROUS
IMPERIAL MALGRADO OBDURACY REDIRECT SOLARIUM ULTERIOR
IMPORTER MALTREAT OBDURATE REFERRAL SOMBRELY UNBURDEN
IMPURIFY MANDRAKE OBSERVED REFORMED SOMBRERO UNCARING
IMPURITY MANDRILL OBSERVER REFORMER SOMERSET UNCURBED
INDIRECT MANGROVE OBSTRUCT REPARTEE SONOROUS UNDERAGE
INFERIOR MANORIAL OCTAROON REPHRASE SORORITY UNDERARM
INFERNAL MARGRAVE OFFBREAK REPORTED SPARRING UNDERCUT
INFORMAL MATERIAL OFFERING REPORTER SQUARELY UNDERDOG
INFORMED MATERNAL OMDURMAN RESERVED SQUIRREL UNDERFED
INFORMER MATTRESS ONETRACK RESTRAIN STAIRWAY UNDERLAY
INHERENT MATURATE ONSCREEN RESTRICT STEERAGE UNDERLIE
INSCRIBE MATURITY ORDERING RESTROOM STEERING UNDERPIN
INSTRUCT MAVERICK OSTERLEY RETARDED STIRRING UNDERSEA
INTERACT MAYORESS OUTBREAK RETIRING SUBTRACT UNDERTOW

UNEARNED
UNERRING
UNFORCED
UNHARMED
UNHEROIC
UNMARKED
UNNERVED
UNPERSON
UNTHREAD
UNVARIED
UNVERSED
UNWORTHY
UPMARKET
UPPERCUT
UPSTREAM
UPTURNED
USUFRUCT
VAGARIES
VALERIAN
VANBRUGH
VAPORIZE
VENERATE
VENEREAL
VIBURNUM
VICARAGE
VICARIAL
VIGOROUS
VIPEROUS
VIVARIUM
WAITRESS
WARDRESS
WARDROBE
WARDROOM
WASHROOM
WATERBUG
WATERING
WATERLOO
WATERMAN
WATERWAY
WAVERING
WAVERLEY
WIZARDRY
WONDROUS
WORKROOM
ZASTRUGA
ZOETROPE
ABBASIDE
ABESSIVE
ABRASION
ABRASIVE
ACCUSING
ACCUSTOM
ACOUSTIC
ACROSTIC
ADESSIVE
ADHESION
ADHESIVE
ADJUSTER
ADJUSTOR
ADVISORY
AEROSTAT
AFFUSION
AGNOSTIC
ALCESTIS
ALLUSION
ALLUSIVE
AMBUSHED
ANCESTOR
ANCESTRY
APPOSITE
ARGESTES
ARRESTED
ARRESTER
ARTESIAN
ARTISTIC
ARTISTRY
ASBESTOS
ASSASSIN
ASSESSOR
ATTESTOR
AUBUSSON
AUCASSIN
AUGUSTUS
AUTISTIC
AVERSION
AVULSION
BABUSHKA
BACKSIDE
BALUSTER
BANDSMAN
BANISTER
BEARSKIN
BICUSPID
BIRDSEED
BLESSING
BLISSFUL
BONDSMAN
BOOKSHOP
BRADSHAW
BRASSARD
BRASSICA
BROWSING
BRUISING
BRUSSELS
BUCKSHEE
BUCKSHOT
BUCKSKIN
CADASTRE
CAMISOLE
CAMPSITE
CANISTER
CHASSEUR
CHESSMAN
CHESSMEN
CHIASMUS
CHOOSING
CHRISTEN
CHRISTIE
CHRISTOM
CICISBEO
CLANSMAN
CLASSICS
CLASSIFY
CLOISTER
CLUMSILY
COARSELY
COHESION
COHESIVE
COLESLAW
COLISEUM
COLOSSAL
COLOSSUS
CREOSOTE
CROSSBAR
CROSSING
CROSSLET
CYNOSURE
DAMASCUS
DECISION
DECISIVE
DEERSKIN
DELUSION
DEMISTER
DERISION
DERISIVE
DERISORY
DINOSAUR
DISASTER
DIVISION
DIVISIVE
DOCKSIDE
DOMESDAY
DOMESTIC
DOOMSDAY
DOORSTEP
DOWNSIDE
DOWNSIZE
DRAGSTER
DRESSAGE
DRESSING
DROPSHOT
DROWSILY
DYNASTIC
ECLOSION
EFFUSION
EFFUSIVE
EGOISTIC
EMBOSSED
EMERSION
EMISSARY
EMISSION
EMULSIFY
EMULSION
ENMESHED
ENVISAGE
ENVISION
EPHESIAN
ERIKSSON
ETRUSCAN
EURASIAN
EUROSTAR
EVENSONG
EXCISION
EXPOSURE
FAMISHED
FEARSOME
FELDSPAR
FENESTRA
FINESPUN
FINISHED
FINISHER
FIRESIDE
FIRESTEP
FLAGSHIP
FLIMSILY
FOLKSONG
FOOLSCAP
FOOTSORE
FOOTSTEP
FORESAIL
FORESHIP
FORESKIN
FORESTAY
FORESTER
FORESTRY
FOURSOME
FUCHSITE
FULLSIZE
GALOSHES
GANGSTER
GARISHLY
GELASTIC
GIRASOLE
GLADSOME
GLASSFUL
GLEESOME
GLISSADE
GLOSSARY
GLOSSEME
GOATSKIN
GOODSIRE
GRUESOME
GYROSTAT
HANDSOME
HARASSED
HARDSHIP
HARUSPEX
HEADSHIP
HEATSPOT
HELMSMAN
HERDSMAN
HIBISCUS
HILLSIDE
HOARSELY
HOLISTIC
HOMESICK
HOMESPUN
HONESTLY
HUCKSTER
HUNTSMAN
ILLUSION
ILLUSIVE
ILLUSORY
IMPOSING
IMPOSTER
IMPOSTOR
INCISION
INCISIVE
INDUSTRY
INFESTED
INFUSION
INVASION
INVASIVE
INVESTOR
IRONSIDE
JEBUSITE
JOHNSONS
JUMPSUIT
JURASSIC
KEEPSAKE
KEROSENE
KICKSHAW
KINGSHIP
KINGSIZE
KINGSLEY
KINGSTON
KNAPSACK
LADYSHIP
LAMASERY
LAMBSKIN
LANDSEER
LANDSLIP
LARKSPUR
LAVISHLY
LEADSMAN
LEINSTER
LEWISITE
LIFESPAN
LINESMAN
LOADSTAR
LODESTAR
LOGISTIC
LONESOME
LONGSTAY
LONGSTOP
LORDSHIP
LOVESICK
MACASSAR
MAGISTER
MAILSHOT
MAINSAIL
MAINSTAY
MAJESTIC
MARASMUS
MARKSMAN
MENISCUS
MERISTEM
MINISTER
MINISTRY
MOCASSIN
MODESTLY
MOLASSES
MOLESKIN
MOLESTER
MONASTIC
MOROSELY
MOUSSAKA
NAGASAKI
NAMESAKE
NONESUCH
OBSESSED
OBTUSELY
OCCASION
ODYSSEUS
OMISSION
OPPOSING
OPPOSITE
OVERSEAS
OVERSEER
OVERSHOE
OVERSHOT
OVERSIZE
OVERSTAY
OVERSTEP
PAKISTAN
PALISADE
PARASITE
PARISIAN
PAWNSHOP
PEDESTAL
PERISHED
PERISHER
PHEASANT
PILASTER
PLAYSUIT
PLEASANT
PLEASING
PLEASURE
PLIMSOLL
POLISHED
POLISHER
POLLSTER

POLYSEME
POLYSEMY
POROSITY
PRESSING
PRESSMAN
PRESSURE
PRIESTLY
PRUSSIAN
PUISSANT
PUNISHED
QUAESTOR
QUAYSIDE
REASSERT
REASSESS
REASSIGN
REASSUME
REASSURE
RECESSED
RECUSANT
REDESIGN
REEDSMAN
REGISTER
REGISTRY
REINSURE
RESISTOR
REVISION
RHAPSODY
RHEOSTAT
RICKSHAW
RINGSIDE
ROADSHOW
ROADSIDE
ROADSTER
ROBUSTLY
ROUSSEAU
RUCKSACK
SADISTIC
SALESMAN
SCANSION
SCISSION
SCISSORS
SCOTSMAN
SEALSKIN
SEAMSTER
SEEDSMAN
SELASSIE
SELFSAME
SEMESTER
SIDESHOW
SIDESLIP
SIDESMAN
SIDESTEP
SILESIAN
SINGSONG
SINISTER
SLIPSHOD
SLIPSLOP
SNAPSHOT
SOAPSUDS
SONGSTER
SPARSELY
SPARSITY
SPINSTER
SPLASHER
STAYSAIL
STRESSED
SWANSKIN
SWANSONG
SWIMSUIT
TAILSKID
TAILSPIN
TALISMAN
TAPESTRY
TEAMSTER
TENESMUS
THOUSAND
THRASHER
THRESHER
THRUSTER
THURSDAY
TIRESIAS
TIRESOME
TOILSOME
TOWNSHIP
TOWNSMAN
TRANSACT
TRANSECT
TRANSEPT
TRANSFER
TRANSFIX
TRANSHIP
TRANSKEI
TRANSMIT
TREASURE
TREASURY
TRIASSIC
TROUSERS
TUNGSTEN
TUNISIAN
TURNSPIT
TYROSINE
UNEASILY
UNFASTEN
UNJUSTLY
UNLISTED
UPRISING
UTENSILS
VANISHED
WAINSCOT
WALLSEND
WARDSHIP
WINDSOCK
WINGSPAN
WOODSHED
WOODSMAN
WOOLSACK
WORKSHOP
YOURSELF
YUGOSLAV
ABATTOIR
ABLATION
ABLATIVE
ABLUTION
ABORTION
ABORTIVE
ACANTHUS
ADDITION
ADDITIVE
ADJUTAGE
ADJUTANT
ADOPTION
ADOPTIVE
ADULTERY
AGNATION
AIRSTRIP
ALCATRAZ
ALEATORY
ALEUTIAN
ALSATIAN
ALTITUDE
AMBITION
AMORTIZE
AMPUTATE
AMRITSAR
ANGSTROM
ANNOTATE
APERTURE
APOSTASY
APOSTATE
APOSTLES
APPETITE
APTITUDE
AQUATINT
ARMATURE
ASTATINE
ASTUTELY
ATHETISE
ATHETOID
ATTITUDE
AUDITION
AUDITORY
AUTOTYPE
AVENTINE
AVIATION
BARATHEA
BARITONE
BEAUTIFY
BEDSTEAD
BEDSTRAW
BEGETTER
BELITTLE
BESOTTED
BETATRON
BLASTOFF
BLASTULA
BLUSTERY
BOASTFUL
BOASTING
BOEOTIAN
BORSTALL
BREATHER
BRISTLED
BRISTLES
BURNTOUT
BURSTING
CABOTAGE
CALOTYPE
CAMPTOWN
CAMSTONE
CAPITALS
CAPSTONE
CAROTENE
CATATONY
CAVATINA
CEMETERY
CENOTAPH
CERATOID
CHANTAGE
CHANTREY
CHARTISM
CHARTIST
CHARTRES
CHASTISE
CHASTITY
CHATTELS
CHEATERS
CHEATING
CHESTNUT
CHILTERN
CICATRIX
CITATION
CLAPTRAP
COATTAIL
COAUTHOR
COCKTAIL
COGITATE
COMATOSE
CONSTANT
CONSTRUE
COUNTESS
COUNTIES
COUNTING
COURTESY
COVETOUS
COYSTRIL
CRAFTILY
CREATION
CREATIVE
CREATURE
CROATIAN
CRYSTALS
CURATIVE
DAINTIES
DAINTILY
DAUNTING
DELETION
DEMOTION
DENATURE
DEPUTIZE
DEVOTION
DIANTHUS
DIASTASE
DIASTOLE
DIGITIZE
DILATION
DILATORY
DILUTION
DIOPTRIC
DIPSTICK
DOGSTAIL
DONATION
DONATIST
DOUBTFUL
DOUBTING
DOVETAIL
DOWNTOWN
DOWNTURN
DRIFTING
DRYSTONE
DURATION
DYNATRON
EDENTATE
EGYPTIAN
EIGHTEEN
EINSTEIN
EJECTION
ELECTION
ELECTIVE
ELECTORS
ELECTRIC
ELECTRON
ELECTRUM
EMBATTLE
EMBITTER
ENTITLED
EPISTYLE
EQUATION
EQUITANT
ERECTILE
ERECTING
ERECTION
ERGOTISE
ERGOTISM
ERUCTATE
ERUPTION
ERUPTURE
ETCETERA
EVENTFUL
EVENTIDE
EVENTUAL
EVICTION
EXACTING
EXACTION
EXCITING
EXERTION
EXISTENT
EXISTING
EXULTANT
EXULTING
FAINTING
FATSTOCK
FIGHTING
FIRETRAP
FIXATION
FIXATIVE
FLATTERY
FLAUTIST
FLEETING
FLIRTING
FLOATING
FORETELL
FORKTAIL
FOUNTAIN
FOURTEEN
FRACTION
FRACTURE
FREETOWN
FRICTION
FRONTAGE
FRONTIER
FRONTMAN
FROSTILY
FROSTING
FRUCTIFY
FRUCTOSE
FRUITFUL
FRUITING
FRUITION
FUGITIVE
FULLTIME
FUMITORY
FUNCTION
GAUNTLET
GELATINE
GENETICS
GENETRIX
GENITALS
GENITIVE
GIANTESS
GLOATING
GLUTTONY
GREATEST

GREETING
GROUTING
GUILTILY
GUMPTION
GYRATION
GYRATORY
HABITUAL
HALFTERM
HALFTIME
HARDTACK
HAUNTING
HAYSTACK
HEARTIES
HEARTILY
HEBETUDE
HECATOMB
HEELTAPS
HEPATICA
HERITAGE
HESITANT
HESITATE
HIPSTERS
HORATIAN
HORATIUS
HOWITZER
HYDATOID
IDENTIFY
IDENTITY
IGNITION
IMMATURE
IMPETIGO
IMPOTENT
INACTION
INACTIVE
INKSTAIN
INVITING
IRRITANT
IRRITATE
ISOSTASY
JAUNTILY
JEPHTHAH
JOINTURE
JONATHAN
JOYSTICK
JUNCTION
JUNCTURE
JURATORY
KEYSTONE
KHARTOUM
KIBITZER
KINETICS
KNITTING
LATITUDE
LAVATORY
LAXATIVE
LECITHIN
LEGATION
LENGTHEN
LEVITATE
LIBATION
LIENTERY
LIFETIME
LIGATURE
LIGHTING
LIMITING
LINOTYPE
LIPSTICK
LOBOTOMY
LOCATION
LOCATIVE
LONGTERM
LONGTIME
MAESTOSO
MAINTAIN
MANITOBA
MARATHON
MARITIME
MEALTIME
MEANTIME
MEDITATE
MIGHTILY
MILITANT
MILITARY
MILITATE
MINATORY
MINOTAUR
MINSTREL
MINUTELY
MINUTIAE
MOISTURE
MONETARY
MONETISE
MONOTONY
MONOTYPE
MONSTERA
MOUNTAIN
MOUNTING
MUDSTONE
MULETEER
MUTATION
NEGATION
NEGATIVE
NEMATODE
NEMATOID
NEPOTISM
NICOTINE
NIDATION
NIGHTCAP
NIGHTJAR
NINETEEN
NONSTICK
NOONTIME
NOTATION
NUGATORY
OBLATION
OFFSTAGE
OLDSTYLE
ORESTEIA
OUISTITI
OUTSTRIP
OVERTAKE
OVERTIME
OVERTONE
OVERTURE
OVERTURN
PAINTING
PALATIAL
PALATINE
PANATELA
PARTTIME
PENITENT
PETITION
PHANTASM
PILOTAGE
PLANTAIN
PLASTRON
PLAYTIME
PLECTRUM
POLITELY
POLITICO
POLITICS
PONYTAIL
POSITION
POSITIVE
POSITRON
POTATOES
POULTICE
PRACTICE
PRACTISE
PRATTLER
PRESTIGE
PRETTILY
PRINTING
PRINTOUT
PRISTINE
PROSTATE
PSALTERY
PULITZER
PUNCTUAL
PUNCTURE
PUNITIVE
PUTATIVE
QUANTIFY
QUANTITY
QUARTERS
QUARTIER
QUARTILE
QUESTION
QUIETUDE
QUILTING
QUINTAIN
RAGSTONE
REACTION
REACTIVE
REALTIME
REBUTTAL
REDSTART
RELATING
RELATION
RELATIVE
REMITTAL
REMOTELY
RESETTLE
RIBSTONE
RIGATONI
RIGHTFUL
RIGHTIST
RINGTAIL
RIVETING
ROASTING
ROBOTICS
ROENTGEN
ROGATION
ROOFTOPS
ROTATION
ROTATORY
SABOTAGE
SABOTEUR
SALUTARY
SALUTORY
SANCTIFY
SANCTION
SANCTITY
SANITARY
SANITIZE
SARATOGA
SAXATILE
SCANTIES
SCANTILY
SCIATICA
SCOTTISH
SCRATCHY
SCRUTINY
SEDATELY
SEDATION
SEDATIVE
SEDITION
SEMITONE
SEROTYPE
SHANTUNG
SHIFTING
SHIITAKE
SHOETREE
SHOOTING
SHOOTOUT
SHOPTALK
SHORTAGE
SHOUTING
SHUTTERS
SIGHTING
SILKTAIL
SKIRTING
SKITTISH
SKITTLES
SLANTING
SLATTERN
SLUTTISH
SMARTEST
SMELTING
SMOOTHER
SMOOTHLY
SNOOTILY
SNORTING
SOLITARY
SOLITUDE
SOLSTICE
SOLUTION
SOMETIME
SONATINA
SPARTANS
SPECTRAL
SPECTRUM
SPINTEXT
SPITTING
SPITTOON
SPLATTER
SPLITTER
SPLUTTER
SPORTING
SPORTIVE
SPOTTING
SPRITELY
SPRITZER
SQUATTER
STARTERS
STARTING
STEATITE
STEATOMA
STRATEGY
STRATIFY
STRETCHY
STULTIFY
SWASTIKA
SWEATING
SYMPTOMS
TACITURN
TAHITIAN
TAXATION
TELETHON
TELLTALE
TEMPTING
TERATOMA
THEATRIC
THIRTEEN
THROTTLE
TICKTACK
TICKTOCK
TIGHTWAD
TINCTURE
TIPSTAFF
TOGETHER
TOMATOES
TRACTION
TRAITORS
TREATISE
TREETOPS
TRIPTANE
TRIPTYCH
TRISTICH
TRISTRAM
TROTTERS
TROTTOIR
TRUSTFUL
TRUSTING
TUSITALA
TWISTING
UNBUTTON
UNFETTER
UNSETTLE
VACATION
VALETING
VAULTING
VEGETATE
VENETIAN
VEXATION
VISITANT
VISITING
VOCATION
VOCATIVE
VOLATILE
VOLITION
VOMITING
VOMITORY
WHEATEAR
WHISTLER
WREATHED
WRESTLER
WRISTLET
YACHTING
YAKITORI
YULETIDE
ACAPULCO
ACCOUNTS
ADEQUACY
ADEQUATE
AFFLUENT
ALTRUISM
ALTRUIST
ANNOUNCE
ARCTURUS
ARMOURED
ARTFULLY

BEGRUDGE
BESOUGHT
BURGUNDY
CALCULUS
CALCUTTA
CAROUSAL
CAROUSEL
CELLULAR
CHASUBLE
CHEQUERS
CHERUBIC
CHERUBIM
CINGULUM
CIRCULAR
CLIQUISH
COLOURED
COMMUNAL
COMMUTER
COMPUTER
CONFUSED
CONJUGAL
CONJURER
CONJUROR
CONQUEST
CONSULAR
CONSUMED
CONSUMER
CONVULSE
CORDUROY
CULTURAL
CULTURED
CUTPURSE
DAIQUIRI
DECLUTCH
DECOUPLE
DEMIURGE
DENOUNCE
DENTURES
DISBURSE
DISGUISE
DISPUTED
DISQUIET
DISSUADE
EFFLUENT
EFFLUVIA
ELOQUENT
EPICURUS
EPIDURAL
ESPOUSAL
EUPHUISM
EVACUANT
EVACUATE
EVALUATE
EXECUTED
EXECUTOR
EXIGUITY
EXIGUOUS
FAMOUSLY
FAROUCHE
FAVOURED
FEATURED
FEATURES
FEBRUARY
FITFULLY
FORTUITY
FRENULUM
FREQUENT
GALLUMPH
GESTURES
GLOBULAR
GLOBULIN
GRADUATE
GRANULAR
GRANULES
GRATUITY
GUTTURAL
HERCULES
HINDUISM
HONDURAN
HONDURAS
INCLUDED
INEQUITY
INIQUITY
INTRUDER
IROQUOIS
JACQUARD
JALOUSIE
JOYFULLY
KENTUCKY
LABOURED
LABOURER
LANGUAGE
LANGUISH
LAROUSSE
LAWFULLY
LECTURER
LECTURES
LEISURED
LINGUIST
MACAULAY
MANEUVER
MANFULLY
MARAUDER
MARQUESA
MARQUESS
MARQUISE
MATHURIN
MEASURED
MESSUAGE
MISGUIDE
MISJUDGE
MISQUOTE
MOLLUSCS
MONAURAL
MORTUARY
MOSQUITO
MUDGUARD
MUSCULAR
MUSQUASH
NEMBUTAL
NOCTURNE
OBITUARY
OBSCURED
ODIOUSLY
OUTBURST
PASTURES
PELLUCID
PENDULUM
PERFUMED
PERJURED
PERJURER
PERSUADE
PERSUANT
PICTURES
POLLUTED
POLLUTER
PORTUGAL
PRECURSE
PREJUDGE
PROCURER
PRODUCER
PRODUCES
PRODUCTS
PROFUSER
PUSTULAR
RAMBUTAN
RASPUTIN
RECOURSE
RECRUITS
REDOUBLE
REMOUNTS
RENOUNCE
REPOUSSÉ
RESOURCE
RUEFULLY
RUMOURED
SADDUCEE
SANGUINE
SAVOURED
SCAPULAR
SCROUNGE
SECLUDED
SELEUCID
SENSUOUS
SHROUDED
SINGULAR
SPECULUM
STATUARY
STIMULUS
SUBHUMAN
SUCCUBUS
SULFURIC
SUNBURNT
SUNBURST
TARTUFFE
TELLURIC
TEXTURED
TONSURED
TORTUOUS
TORTURED
TORTURER
TRIBUNAL
UBIQUITY
UNCOUPLE
UNCTUOUS
UNIQUELY
USEFULLY
VALVULAR
VANGUARD
VANQUISH
VASCULAR
VENTURED
VERJUICE
VESPUCCI
VICTUALS
VINCULUM
VIRTUOSI
VIRTUOSO
VIRTUOUS
WHODUNIT
WILFULLY
WOEFULLY
YARMULKA
ZAKOUSKI
ZARZUELA
ZIGGURAT
AARDVARK
ACTIVATE
ACTIVELY
ACTIVISM
ACTIVIST
ACTIVITY
ADJUVANT
ALLUVIAL
ALLUVIUM
BATAVIAN
BEHAVIOR
BOLIVIAN
CLEAVAGE
CLEAVERS
DELIVERY
ENERVATE
ESTIVATE
ESTOVERS
EXCAVATE
GRIEVOUS
INNOVATE
JEHOVAHS
KILOVOLT
MORAVIAN
MOTIVATE
NATIVITY
OBLIVION
OTTAVINO
OVERVIEW
PERUVIAN
RECOVERY
REINVEST
RELEVANT
RENOVATE
REVIVIFY
REVIVING
SALIVARY
SALIVATE
SHELVING
STARVING
STRIVING
SWERVING
TELEVISE
THIEVERY
THIEVING
THIEVISH
TITIVATE
TWELVEMO
UNLOVELY
UNSAVORY
VESUVIUS
ALLOWING
BACKWARD
BEESWING
BINDWEED
BODYWORK
BOOKWORK
BOOKWORM
BOTHWELL
BOTSWANA
BUZZWORD
CAKEWALK
CAREWORN
CHERWELL
COOKWARE
CORDWAIN
CORNWALL
COTSWOLD
COXSWAIN
CROMWELL
DASHWOOD
DEADWOOD
DELAWARE
DOWNWARD
DUCKWEED
EASTWARD
EDGEWAYS
EDGEWISE
FAREWELL
FIREWEED
FIREWOOD
FIREWORK
FISHWIFE
FLATWARE
FLATWORM
FOOTWEAR
FOOTWORK
FOREWARN
FOREWORD
FORSWEAR
FRETWORK
FUSEWIRE
GONDWANA
GOODWIFE
GOODWILL
GOODWOOD
GURDWARA
HARDWARE
HARDWOOD
HEADWIND
HEADWORD
HEATWAVE
HEREWARD
HEREWITH
HINDWARD
HOMEWARD
HOMEWORK
HOODWINK
HOOKWORM
IRONWARE
IRONWOOD
IRONWORK
KILOWATT
KNAPWEED
KNITWEAR
KNOTWEED
KNOTWORK
LACEWING
LANDWARD
LEFTWARD
LEFTWING
LIKEWISE
LIVEWARE
LUKEWARM
MALAWIAN
MEGAWATT
MENSWEAR
MILKWEED
MILKWORT
MULEWORT
NECKWEAR
OPENWORK
OVENWARE
OVERWORK
PASSWORD
PICKWICK

PIGSWILL
PINEWOOD
RAINWEAR
REARWARD
RENOWNED
RINGWALL
RINGWORM
ROSEWOOD
SANDWICH
SCRAWLED
SCREWTOP
SHERWOOD
SHREWDLY
SHREWISH
SIDEWALK
SIDEWAYS
SILKWORM
SKINWORK
SOFTWARE
SOFTWOOD
SOMEWHAT
SPRAWLED
STALWART
STILWELL
TAPEWORM
TEAMWORK
UNLAWFUL
UNTOWARD
WALLWORT
WEDGWOOD
WEREWOLF
WESTWARD
WINDWARD
WIREWORM
WOODWARD
WOODWIND
WOODWORK
WOODWORM
WORMWOOD
BISEXUAL
EUDOXIAN
INDEXING
MONOXIDE
PAROXYSM
PEROXIDE
RELAXING
ALLEYWAY
ANALYSER
ANALYSIS
ANNOYING
ASPHYXIA
BACKYARD
BALLYHOO
BARNYARD
BELLYFUL
BILLYBOY
BILLYCAN
BOBBYPIN
BOGEYMAN
BONEYARD
BULLYRAG
CARRYALL
CARRYCOT
CARRYING
CRONYISM
DAIRYMAN
DECAYING
DIALYSIS
DIONYSUS
DOCKYARD
ENTRYISM
ESSAYIST
EVERYDAY
EVERYMAN
EVERYONE
FANCYMAN
FARMYARD
FEDAYEEN
FERRYMAN
GARDYLOO
GOODYEAR
HALFYEAR
HANDYMAN
HONEYDEW
HONEYPOT
HOWDYEDO
JERRYCAN
LOBBYIST
LOWLYING
MAINYARD
MALAYSIA
MARTYRED
MEALYBUG
MONEYBOX
NEOMYCIN
OUTLYING
PLATYPUS
PUSSYCAT
RELAYING
REPAYING
SAVOYARD
SEALYHAM
SHIPYARD
SUKIYAKI
TABBYCAT
TENNYSON
TERIYAKI
TRICYCLE
UNIFYING
VALKYRIE
VINEYARD
WALKYRIE
WORRYING
ZEPHYRUS
BLIZZARD
BREEZILY
CHUTZPAH
EMBEZZLE
FRAZZLED
FREEZING
FRENZIED
GRIZZLED
MAGAZINE
PIROZHKI
SAMIZDAT
SCHIZOID
SNEEZING
TWEEZERS
TZATZIKI
WALTZING
WHEEZILY
WHEEZING

8:6

AARDVARK
ABDICATE
ABERRANT
ABNEGATE
ABROGATE
ABSTRACT
ABUNDANT
ACCOLADE
ACCURACY
ACCURATE
ACERBATE
ACTIVATE
ADEQUACY
ADEQUATE
ADJUTAGE
ADJUTANT
ADJUVANT
ADVOCACY
ADVOCATE
AERONAUT
AIRBRAKE
AIRCRAFT
AIREDALE
AIRPLANE
ALIENATE
ALLOCATE
ALLOGAMY
ALLOPATH
AMBULANT
AMBULATE
AMPERAGE
AMPUTATE
AMYGDALA
ANNOTATE
ANTEDATE
ANYPLACE
APOSTASY
APOSTATE
APPANAGE
APPELANT
APPROACH
ARGONAUT
ARMCHAIR
ARROGANT
ARROGATE
ARTEFACT
ARTIFACT
ASPIRANT
ASPIRATE
ATHANASY
AUTOBAHN
AUTOGAMY
AUTOMATE
BACCHANT
BACKDATE
BACKHAND
BACKLASH
BACKPACK
BACKWARD
BACKYARD
BADINAGE
BALLPARK
BAREBACK
BARNYARD
BASEBALL
BELGRADE
BENGHAZI
BEQUEATH
BERTRAND
BESTIARY
BEVERAGE
BIFOCALS
BIGARADE
BIOGRAPH
BIRDCAGE
BLIZZARD
BLOCKADE
BLOCKAGE
BLOWLAMP
BLUEBACK
BONEYARD
BONIFACE
BOOKCASE
BOOKMARK
BORDEAUX
BORSTALL
BOTSWANA
BOUFFANT
BOUNDARY
BRAGGART
BRANDADE
BRASSARD
BRATPACK
BREVIARY
BROUHAHA
BUCKFAST
BURGLARY
BURGRAVE
CABOTAGE
CAKEWALK
CALABASH
CALCEATE
CAMSHAFT
CAPITALS
CAPYBARA
CARAPACE
CARRIAGE
CARRYALL
CARTHAGE
CARUCATE
CASEMATE
CASTRATE
CASTRATO
CATARACT
CELIBACY
CELIBATE
CENOTAPH
CHADBAND
CHANTAGE
CHAPLAIN
CHARLADY
CHILIAST
CHILLADA
CHLORATE
CHORDATA
CHORDATE
CHORIAMB
CHUMMAGE
CINERAMA
CLAIMANT
CLAMBAKE
CLAWBACK
CLEAVAGE
COATRACK
COATTAIL
COCKTAIL
COGITATE
COLORADO
COLORANT
COMEBACK
COMPLAIN
CONCLAVE
CONFLATE
CONSTANT
CONTRACT
CONTRARY
CONTRAST
COOKWARE
COPULATE
CORDWAIN
CORNWALL
CORONARY
COSTMARY
COTOPAXI
COUCHANT
COVENANT
COVERAGE
COXSWAIN
CRIBBAGE
CRUCIATE
CRYSTALS
CULINARY
CUPBOARD
DATABASE
DEBONAIR
DECIMATE
DECKHAND
DECORATE
DECREASE
DEDICATE
DEFECATE
DELAWARE
DELEGATE
DELICACY
DELICATE
DEMERARA
DEPILATE
DEROGATE
DESOLATE
DETONATE
DIASTASE
DIFFRACT
DINGBATS
DINOSAUR
DISCLAIM
DISGRACE
DISPLACE
DISSUADE
DISTRACT
DISTRAIN
DISTRAIT
DOCKLAND
DOCKYARD
DOGSTAIL
DOMINANT
DOMINATE
DOVETAIL
DOWNCAST
DOWNFALL
DOWNWARD
DRAINAGE
DRAWBACK
DRESSAGE
DRUNKARD
EASTLAKE
EASTWARD

ECHINATE
EDENTATE
EDGEWAYS
EFFICACY
EGGPLANT
ELDORADO
ELEPHANT
ELONGATE
EMACIATE
EMIGRANT
EMIGRATE
EMISSARY
ENCROACH
ENDOCARP
ENDOGAMY
ENERVATE
ENFILADE
ENSILAGE
ENTHRALL
ENTREATY
ENVISAGE
EPIGRAPH
EPIPHANY
EQUIPAGE
EQUITANT
ERADIATE
ERUCTATE
ESCALADE
ESCALATE
ESCAPADE
ESTIMATE
ESTIVATE
ETIOLATE
EUROLAND
EVACUANT
EVACUATE
EVALUATE
EXCAVATE
EXECRATE
EXHUMATE
EXULTANT
EYEGLASS
EYESHADE
FALKLAND
FARMHAND
FARMLAND
FARMYARD
FASTBACK
FEBRUARY
FEDERACY
FEDERATE
FEEDBACK
FILENAME
FILTRATE
FIREBACK
FIREBALL
FIREDAMP
FISHCAKE
FLAGRANT
FLAPJACK
FLATMATE
FLATWARE
FLIPPANT
FOOTBALL
FOOTFALL
FOOTPATH
FORECAST
FOREHAND
FORELAND
FORENAME
FORESAIL
FOREWARN
FORKTAIL
FORSLACK
FOUNTAIN
FOURPART
FRAGRANT
FREEHAND
FRONTAGE
FULLBACK
FULLPAGE
FUMIGATE
FUNERARY
FUSELAGE
GADOGADO
GAILLARD
GALLIARD
GANGLAND
GEMINATE
GENERATE
GENITALS
GIMCRACK
GLISSADE
GLORIANA
GLOSSARY
GOBSMACK
GOLFBALL
GONDWANA
GOOFBALL
GOURMAND
GRADUATE
GUJARATI
GURDWARA
GYMKHANA
HALFMAST
HALLIARD
HALLMARK
HANDBALL
HANDCART
HANDMADE
HANDMAID
HANDRAIL
HANGNAIL
HARDBACK
HARDTACK
HARDWARE
HAYSTACK
HEADBAND
HEADLAMP
HEADLAND
HEADMARK
HEATWAVE
HEELBALL
HEELTAPS
HELPMATE
HEREWARD
HERITAGE
HESITANT
HESITATE
HIGHBALL
HIGHGATE
HIGHLAND
HINDWARD
HIRAGANA
HOLIDAYS
HOMELAND
HOMEMADE
HOMEWARD
HONORARY
HOTPLATE
HUMPBACK
IGNORANT
IMMOLATE
INCHOATE
INCREASE
INCUBATE
INDICANT
INDICATE
INHALANT
INHUMANE
INITIATE
INKSTAIN
INNOVATE
INSULATE
INTERACT
INTIFADA
INTIMACY
INTIMATE
INUNDATE
IRONWARE
IRRIGATE
IRRITANT
IRRITATE
ISOSTASY
JACQUARD
JEHOVAHS
JIMCRACK
JUBILANT
JUBILATE
KALAHARI
KAMIKAZE
KATAKANA
KEELHAUL
KEEPSAKE
KEYBOARD
KICKBACK
KILOWATT
KINSHASA
KITEMARK
KNAPSACK
KOHLRABI
KREPLACH
LACERATE
LACINATE
LACKLAND
LAIDBACK
LAKELAND
LAMINATE
LANDFALL
LANDLADY
LANDMARK
LANDMASS
LANDRACE
LANDWARD
LANGLAND
LANGLAUF
LANGUAGE
LAPIDARY
LAPIDATE
LAUREATE
LEFTHAND
LEFTWARD
LEMONADE
LEVERAGE
LEVITATE
LIBERATE
LITERACY
LITERARY
LITERATE
LITERATI
LITIGANT
LITIGATE
LIVEWARE
LONGHAND
LONGHAUL
LONGLAND
LONSDALE
LOVELACE
LOWCLASS
LUKEWARM
LUMINARY
MACERATE
MACHEATH
MACREADY
MACULATE
MAHARAJA
MAHARANI
MAHOGANY
MAINLAND
MAINMAST
MAINSAIL
MAINTAIN
MAINYARD
MALAGASY
MALGRADO
MALLEATE
MANDRAKE
MARGRAVE
MARINADE
MARINATE
MARRIAGE
MARSHALL
MARYLAND
MATURATE
MEDICATE
MEDITATE
MEGAWATT
MEMBRANE
MENELAUS
MERCHANT
MESSMATE
MESSUAGE
MILITANT
MILITARY
MILITATE
MILKMAID
MILLRACE
MINAMATA
MINOTAUR
MISHMASH
MISPLACE
MITIGATE
MODERATE
MODERATO
MODULATE
MONETARY
MONOGAMY
MONORAIL
MONTCALM
MOORLAND
MORTGAGE
MORTUARY
MOTHBALL
MOTIVATE
MOUNTAIN
MOUSSAKA
MUCILAGE
MUDFLATS
MUDGUARD
MUSQUASH
MUTILATE
MYOBLAST
NAGASAKI
NAMESAKE
NAUSEATE
NAVIGATE
NECKBAND
NECKLACE
NEWSCAST
NEWSHAWK
NICKNACK
NICKNAME
NOMINATE
NOSEBAND
NOTECASE
NOWADAYS
NUMERACY
NUMERALS
NUMERATE
NUPTIALS
OBDURACY
OBDURATE
OBITUARY
OBLIGATE
OCCUPANT
OEILLADE
OFFSTAGE
OLIPHANT
ONETRACK
OPENCAST
OPTIMATE
ORDINAND
ORDINARY
ORDINATE
OSCULATE
OUTBOARD
OUTCLASS
OUTFLANK
OUTREACH
OUTSMART
OVENWARE
OVERCAST
OVERHANG
OVERHAUL
OVERLAID
OVERLAND
OVERPASS
OVERRATE
OVERTAKE
PAGINATE
PALEFACE
PALGRAVE
PALISADE
PALLIATE
PANORAMA
PARKLAND
PASTRAMI
PEARMAIN
PECULATE
PEDERAST
PENCHANT
PERICARP

PERMEATE
PERSUADE
PERSUANT
PETULANT
PHANTASM
PHARMACY
PHEASANT
PIECHART
PILCHARD
PILOTAGE
PLANTAIN
PLAYBACK
PLAYFAIR
PLAYMATE
PLEASANT
PLEONASM
PLUMBAGO
POIGNANT
POLYCARP
POLYGAMY
POLYMATH
PONYTAIL
POPULACE
POPULATE
PORTLAND
PORTRAIT
POSTCARD
POSTDATE
POSTMARK
POSTPAID
POUNDAGE
PRATFALL
PREGNANT
PROCLAIM
PROSTATE
PROTEASE
PUFFBALL
PUISSANT
PURCHASE
PURSLANE
PUSHCART
QUADRANT
QUADRATE
QUANDARY
QUATRAIN
QUINTAIN
RABELAIS
RAINFALL
RANELAGH
RAPECAKE
REARWARD
RECREATE
RECUSANT
REDSHANK
REDSTART
REGULATE
RELEGATE
RELEVANT
RELOCATE
RENEGADE
RENOVATE
REPHRASE
REPROACH
RESONANT
RESONATE
RESTRAIN
RIFFRAFF
RINGTAIL
RINGWALL
RIVERAIN
ROCHDALE
ROLLCALL
ROOMMATE
ROSEMARY
ROUGHAGE
RUCKSACK
RUMINANT
RUMINATE
RUTABAGA
RYEGRASS
SABOTAGE
SALIVARY
SALIVATE
SALUTARY
SANDBANK
SANITARY
SANTIAGO
SARABAND
SATURATE
SAVOYARD
SAYONARA
SCABBARD
SCARFACE
SCHUMANN
SCOTLAND
SEABOARD
SEAPLANE
SEASCAPE
SELFMADE
SELFSAME
SEMINARY
SEPARATE
SERENADE
SERENATA
SERGEANT
SERJEANT
SEWERAGE
SHADRACH
SHETLAND
SHIITAKE
SHIPMATE
SHIPYARD
SHOELACE
SHOPTALK
SHORTAGE
SHOWCASE
SIBILANT
SIDEWALK
SIDEWAYS
SILICATE
SILKTAIL
SIMULATE
SINCLAIR
SKEWBALD
SKIPJACK
SLAPBANG
SLAPDASH
SLAPJACK
SLUGGARD
SNOWBALL
SNOWFALL
SOFTBALL
SOFTWARE
SOLITARY
SPANIARD
SPARTANS
SPICCATO
SPILLAGE
SPOILAGE
SPOLIATE
SPYGLASS
SQUAMATA
STACCATO
STAGNANT
STAGNATE
STALWART
STANDARD
STANNARY
STARGAZE
STATUARY
STAYSAIL
STEERAGE
STELLATE
STICCATO
STIGMATA
STOCCATA
STOCKADE
STOPPAGE
SUBLEASE
SUBTRACT
SUFFRAGE
SUITCASE
SUKIYAKI
SULPHATE
SUNSHADE
SUPPLANT
SUZERAIN
SVENGALI
TABULATE
TAFFRAIL
TAILBACK
TAILGATE
TAPENADE
TARTRATE
TEAMMATE
TELECAST
TELEMARK
TELLTALE
TEMPLATE
TERIYAKI
TERTIARY
THAILAND
THINGAMY
THOUSAND
TICKTACK
TIDEMARK
TIPSTAFF
TITICACA
TITIVATE
TOISEACH
TOLERANT
TOLERATE
TOLLGATE
TOMAHAWK
TOPCLASS
TOPHEAVY
TOXOCARA
TRANSACT
TRESPASS
TRIPTANE
TROCHAIC
TRUNCATE
TUPAMARO
TURNBACK
TUSITALA
TUTELAGE
TUTELARY
TYPECAST
TYPEFACE
ULCERATE
ULTIMATE
UNDERAGE
UNDERARM
UNDULANT
UNDULATE
UNGULATE
UNSTEADY
UNTOWARD
URETHANE
VALIDATE
VANGUARD
VAUXHALL
VEGETATE
VENERATE
VERBIAGE
VESTIARY
VICARAGE
VICTUALS
VIGILANT
VINEGARY
VINEYARD
VISITANT
VOLPLANE
WARPLANE
WAVEBAND
WELLPAID
WESTWARD
WHARFAGE
WHIPHAND
WHIPJACK
WHIPLASH
WILLIAMS
WINDFALL
WINDLASS
WINDWARD
WOLFBANE
WOODLAND
WOODWARD
WOOLPACK
WOOLSACK
WORKMATE
WORMCAST
WRECKAGE
XENOGAMY
YOKOHAMA
ZWIEBACK
ABSORBED
ABSORBER
ADORABLE
ALHAMBRA
ALPHABET
AMENABLE
AMICABLE
AMICABLY
ARGUABLE
ARGUABLY
ARQUEBUS
ASCORBIC
ASSEMBLE
ASSEMBLY
BARABBAS
BARNABAS
BEARABLE
BEDABBLE
BILLYBOY
BLACKBOY
BOOKABLE
BRIBABLE
BRICKBAT
CANNABIS
CANNIBAL
CHASUBLE
CHERUBIC
CHERUBIM
CHOIRBOY
CICISBEO
CINNABAR
COBWEBBY
COLOMBIA
COLUMBAN
COLUMBUS
CREDIBLE
CREDIBLY
CROSSBAR
CRUCIBLE
CUCUMBER
CUCURBIT
CULPABLE
DAMNABLE
DEATHBED
DECEMBER
DOUGHBOY
DUTIABLE
ELIGIBLE
ENCUMBER
ENFEEBLE
ENSEMBLE
ENVIABLE
FALLIBLE
FEASIBLE
FEASIBLY
FENCIBLE
FLEXIBLE
FLEXIBLY
FORCIBLE
FORCIBLY
GREENBAG
GULLIBLE
HANNIBAL
HORRIBLE
HORRIBLY
HORSEBOX
INEDIBLE
ISTANBUL
LAUDABLE
LAUDABLY
LIKEABLE
LOCKABLE
LOOSEBOX
MANDIBLE
MATCHBOX
MEALYBUG
MILLIBAR
MONEYBOX
MOVEABLE
NEIGHBOR
NOVEMBER
OPERABLE
PALPABLE
PALPABLY
PASSABLE
PASSABLY

PASSIBLE
PEEKABOO
PENUMBRA
PINTABLE
PITIABLE
PLACABLE
PORTABLE
POSSIBLE
POSSIBLY
PREAMBLE
PROBABLE
PROBABLY
PROHIBIT
PROVABLE
QUOTABLE
RATEABLE
READABLE
REDOUBLE
RELIABLE
RELIABLY
REMEMBER
RESEMBLE
REUSABLE
RUNCIBLE
SALEABLE
SCRABBLE
SCRAMBLE
SCRIABIN
SCRIBBLE
SCRIBBLY
SCRUBBER
SENSIBLE
SENSIBLY
SIZEABLE
SLUGABED
SNACKBAR
SNUFFBOX
SOCIABLE
SOLVABLE
SQUABBLE
SUBURBAN
SUBURBIA
SUCCUBUS
SUITABLE
SUITABLY
SUPERBLY
SYLLABIC
SYLLABLE
SYLLABUB
SYLLABUS
TANGIBLE
TANGIBLY
TEARABLE
TERRIBLE
TERRIBLY
THROMBIN
THROMBUS
THURIBLE
UNCOMBED
UNCURBED
UNSTABLE
UNUSABLE
VALUABLE
VARIABLE
VERTEBRA
VINCIBLE
WASHABLE
WATERBUG
WEARABLE
WORKABLE
ZIMBABWE
ADVANCED
ADVANCER
ALOPECIA
AMERICAN
AMERICAS
ANALECTA
ANGLICAN
ATYPICAL
AUSPICES
AUTARCHY
BACKACHE
BALANCED
BALLOCKS
BARBECUE
BARBICAN
BARNACLE
BARRACKS
BIBLICAL
BILLYCAN
BINNACLE
BLACKCAP
BOADICEA
BOLLOCKS
BUTTOCKS
CABLECAR
CANTICLE
CAPSICUM
CARJACOU
CARRYCOT
CERVICAL
CHEMICAL
CLAVECIN
CLAVICLE
CLEARCUT
CLERICAL
CLINICAL
COLLECTS
CORNICHE
CORSICAN
CRITICAL
CURLICUE
CURRICLE
CYCLICAL
DAMASCUS
DIDDICOY
DIVORCED
DIVORCEE
EMBRACED
EMBRACES
ENCIRCLE
ESTANCIA
ETRUSCAN
EXPLICIT
FACEACHE
FARCICAL
FAROUCHE
FASCICLE
FLOUNCED
FOLLICLE
FOOLSCAP
FURUNCLE
GARLICKY
GAZPACHO
HANDICAP
HEADACHE
HIBISCUS
HORLICKS
IMPLICIT
INIMICAL
INTERCOM
IRONICAL
JAMAICAN
JELLICOE
JERRYCAN
JORROCKS
KENTUCKY
LUPERCAL
MANIACAL
MARIACHI
MASSACRE
MASSICOT
MEDIOCRE
MENISCUS
METRICAL
MOLUCCAS
MONARCHY
MOROCCAN
MOTORCAR
MUSTACHE
MYSTICAL
MYTHICAL
NAUTICAL
NEOMYCIN
NIGHTCAP
OBSTACLE
OXYTOCIN
PANNICLE
PARTICLE
PASTICHE
PEDUNCLE
PELLICLE
PELLUCID
PEMMICAN
PENTACLE
PERFECTA
PERFECTO
PHYSICAL
PINNACLE
POETICAL
POPSICLE
PRODUCER
PRODUCES
PRODUCTS
PROTOCOL
PUBLICAN
PUBLICLY
PUSSYCAT
RESPECTS
REVANCHE
ROMANCER
SADDUCEE
SCIENCES
SCILICET
SCIROCCO
SCRATCHY
SELEUCID
SERVICES
SILENCER
SKULLCAP
SPIRACLE
STOCKCAR
STRETCHY
SUBJECTS
SURGICAL
TABBYCAT
TACTICAL
TENTACLE
TERRACED
TESTICLE
THORACIC
TRASHCAN
TRICYCLE
TRITICAL
TRITICUM
TROPICAL
TROUNCER
TUBERCLE
UNDERCUT
UNFORCED
UNPLACED
UNVOICED
UPPERCUT
VALENCIA
VERSICLE
VERTICAL
VESPUCCI
VIATICUM
WAINSCOT
WHITECAP
WISEACRE
ZODIACAL
ABINGDON
ABSURDLY
ACCREDIT
ADDENDUM
APPENDIX
ASPHODEL
ATTENDER
AVOGADRO
BARBADOS
BEFUDDLE
BEGRUDGE
BEHOLDEN
BEHOLDER
BENENDEN
BEWILDER
BIRTHDAY
CABOODLE
CALENDAR
CALENDER
CALVADOS
CAMBODIA
CANDIDLY
CANOODLE
CATHEDRA
CLIVEDEN
COCCIDAE
COLANDER
CONSIDER
CORRIDOR
CORRODED
COWARDLY
CRUSADER
CULLODEN
CUSPIDOR
CYCLADES
CYLINDER
DAFFODIL
DEFENDER
DEGRADED
DISLODGE
DISORDER
DOGGEDLY
DOMESDAY
DOOMSDAY
EMBEDDED
EMBOLDEN
ENGENDER
ENKINDLE
EPISODIC
EVERYDAY
EXPENDED
EXPLODED
EXTENDED
EXTRADOS
FLOUNDER
FRIENDLY
FRIGIDLY
GAZUNDER
GIRONDIN
GROUNDED
GUERIDON
HAGGADAH
HARRIDAN
HAVILDAR
HEATEDLY
HEBRIDES
HELLADIC
HERALDIC
HERALDRY
HONEYDEW
INCLUDED
INTENDED
INTRADOS
INTRUDER
INWARDLY
ISLANDER
LABRADOR
LACKADAY
LAVENDER
LEONIDAS
LOPSIDED
LYSANDER
MARAUDER
MARKEDLY
MASTODON
MENANDER
MERCEDES
MESSIDOR
METHODIC
MICRODOT
MISJUDGE
MORBIDLY
MUSCADET
MYRMIDON
OFFENDED
OFFENDER
OFFSIDER
OLEANDER
ONESIDED
ORGANDIE
ORTHODOX
OUTMODED
OUTRIDER
OUTSIDER
OXBRIDGE
PALLADIO
PERIODIC
PIERIDES
PLACIDLY
PLEIADES

POMANDER
POPPADOM
PORRIDGE
POSEIDON
PREJUDGE
PROVIDED
PROVIDER
PUDENDUM
RECORDER
REKINDLE
REMINDER
RETARDED
RIBALDRY
RUGGEDLY
SALVADOR
SAMIZDAT
SATURDAY
SECLUDED
SECONDER
SECONDLY
SELVEDGE
SHEEPDOG
SHEIKDOM
SHERIDAN
SHOULDER
SHREDDER
SHREWDLY
SHROUDED
SMOULDER
SORDIDLY
SPLENDID
SPLENDOR
SPORADIC
SPREADER
SQUADDIE
SQUANDER
STOLIDLY
STRADDLE
STRANDED
STUPIDLY
SUICIDAL
THRALDOM
THURSDAY
TOREADOR
TRINIDAD
TURANDOT
TURGIDLY
UNBIDDEN
UNBURDEN
UNDERDOG
UNITEDLY
UNKINDLY
UNLEADED
UNLOADED
UNSEEDED
UPHOLDER
VERANDAH
WATCHDOG
WICKEDLY
WIZARDRY
WORKADAY
ZAMINDAR
ABDUCENS
ABERDEEN
ABUTMENT
ACCIDENT
ACIDHEAD
ACTIVELY
ADHERENT
ADJACENT
ADULTERY
AESTHETE
AFFLUENT
AGGRIEVE
AIRFIELD
AIRINESS
AIRSPEED
ANACREON
ANAPAEST
ANATHEMA
ANTECEDE
ANYWHERE
APERIENT
APOPLEXY
APOTHEGM
APPARENT
ARAMAEAN
ARBALEST
ARBOREAL
ARGUMENT
ARMAMENT
ASMODEUS
ASTUTELY
BACKLESS
BAGHEERA
BAILMENT
BALDNESS
BALINESE
BANLIEUE
BARENESS
BARONESS
BARONETS
BASELESS
BASEMENT
BASENESS
BEAKLESS
BEDSTEAD
BEFRIEND
BELPAESE
BERIBERI
BINDWEED
BIRDSEED
BLENHEIM
BLINKERS
BLITHELY
BLOOMERS
BLUDGEON
BLUEBELL
BLUSTERY
BOLDNESS
BONEHEAD
BONELESS
BOOTLESS
BOOTNECK
BOTHWELL
BRACKETS
BROWBEAT
BRUSSELS
BUDAPEST
BUDDLEIA
BULKHEAD
BUSINESS
BUTCHERS
BUTCHERY
BUTTRESS
CADUCEUS
CAERLEON
CAGINESS
CAJOLERY
CALIPERS
CALMNESS
CAMPBELL
CARELESS
CAROTENE
CASEMENT
CASHMERE
CATSMEAT
CATTLEYA
CELANESE
CEMETERY
CEREMENT
CERULEAN
CETACEAN
CHALDEAN
CHAMBERS
CHAMPERS
CHANCERY
CHASSEUR
CHATTELS
CHEATERS
CHECKERS
CHEQUERS
CHERWELL
CHICKENS
CHILDERS
CHILTERN
CHIMAERA
CINEREAL
CLAPPERS
CLEANERS
CLEAVERS
CLINKERS
CLIPPERS
CLUELESS
COARSELY
COBBLERS
COCHLEAR
CODPIECE
COGWHEEL
COHERENT
COIFFEUR
COLDNESS
COLISEUM
COLLIERS
COLLIERY
COMPLETE
COMPRESS
CONCRETE
CONGRESS
CONQUEST
COOLNESS
COSINESS
COUNTESS
COURTESY
COVALENT
COZINESS
CRACKERS
CREAMERY
CRESCENT
CROCKERY
CROCKETT
CROMLECH
CROMWELL
CURTNESS
CUTENESS
CUTHBERT
DAMPNESS
DANEGELD
DANKNESS
DARKNESS
DATELESS
DAYBREAK
DAYDREAM
DEADBEAT
DEADHEAD
DEAFNESS
DECADENT
DEEPNESS
DEFREEZE
DEFTNESS
DELIVERY
DEMURELY
DESELECT
DILIGENT
DISCREET
DISCRETE
DISRAELI
DISTRESS
DIVIDEND
DIVIDERS
DOCUMENT
DOMINEER
DOORBELL
DOWNBEAT
DRACAENA
DRIBLETS
DROPHEAD
DRUDGERY
DRUMBEAT
DRUMHEAD
DRYCLEAN
DUCKWEED
DULLNESS
DUMBBELL
DUMBNESS
EARLIEST
EARPIECE
EASEMENT
EASINESS
ECOFREAK
ECTODERM
EERINESS
EFFLUENT
EGGSHELL
EIGHTEEN
EINSTEIN
ELOQUENT
EMERGENT
EMPYREAN
EMULGENT
ENDODERM
ENGINEER
ENTIRELY
ENTIRETY
EPHEMERA
EPITHEMA
ERYTHEMA
ESCULENT
ESTOVERS
ETCETERA
ETHEREAL
ETHYLENE
EUROPEAN
EVENNESS
EWIGKEIT
EXISTENT
EXPONENT
EYEPIECE
FACELESS
FAIRNESS
FAREWELL
FARRIERY
FARTHEST
FASTNESS
FEARLESS
FEATHERS
FEATHERY
FECKLESS
FECULENT
FEDAYEEN
FIERCELY
FIFTIETH
FILAMENT
FIREWEED
FIRMNESS
FISHMEAL
FLANDERS
FLANNELS
FLATTERY
FLAUBERT
FLAWLESS
FLINDERS
FLIPPERS
FLUMMERY
FLYSHEET
FLYWHEEL
FONDNESS
FOOTREST
FOOTWEAR
FOREBEAR
FOREDECK
FOREHEAD
FORETELL
FORMLESS
FORSWEAR
FORTIETH
FORTRESS
FOULNESS
FOURTEEN
FRAGMENT
FRAULEIN
FREQUENT
FRESHEST
FRIPPERY
FRONDEUR
FULLNESS
FUNEREAL
FURTHEST
GABONESE
GADARENE
GALILEAN
GAMENESS
GANGRENE
GANYMEDE
GIANTESS
GLADNESS
GLANDERS
GLOSSEME
GLUTAEUS
GOODNESS
GOODYEAR
GORMLESS

GRADIENT
GRANDEUR
GRAPHEME
GREATEST
GREENERY
GRIMNESS
GROSBEAK
GUYANESE
HABANERA
HAIRLESS
HALFTERM
HALFYEAR
HANDHELD
HARDNESS
HAREBELL
HARFLEUR
HARMLESS
HATCHERY
HAYFIELD
HAZINESS
HEADGEAR
HEADLESS
HEADREST
HEEDLESS
HEIRLESS
HELLBENT
HELPLESS
HIGHNESS
HIPSTERS
HOARSELY
HOGSHEAD
HOLINESS
HOLYHEAD
HOMELESS
HOPELESS
HOPFIELD
HORNBEAM
HOWDYEDO
HUMANELY
HUNDREDS
HUNTRESS
ICEFIELD
IDLENESS
IMMANENT
IMMINENT
IMMODEST
IMPOTENT
IMPUDENT
INCIDENT
INDECENT
INDIGENT
INDIRECT
INDOLENT
INEXPERT
INHERENT
INNOCENT
INSANELY

INSOLENT
INTEREST
ISOTHERE
ISOTHERM
JACOBEAN
JAPANESE
JEFFREYS
JONGLEUR
JUDGMENT
JUSTNESS
KEENNESS
KEROSENE
KILLDEER
KINDNESS
KNACKERS
KNAPWEED
KNEEDEEP
KNICKERS
KNITWEAR
KNOBLESS
KNOCKERS
KNOTWEED
LAMASERY
LAMENESS
LANDSEER
LATENESS
LAZINESS
LEAFLESS
LEATHERY
LEBANESE
LEWDNESS
LIENTERY
LIFEBELT
LIFELESS
LIGAMENT
LIKENESS
LIMBLESS
LIMPNESS
LINIMENT
LINNAEAN
LINNAEUS
LINOLEUM
LISTLESS
LONGTERM
LONICERA
LOUDNESS
LOVELESS
LUCKLESS
LUNCHEON
LUSHNESS
MALTREAT
MANIFEST
MARQUESA
MARQUESS
MASTHEAD
MATABELE
MATTRESS

MAYORESS
MEANNESS
MEATLESS
MEEKNESS
MENSWEAR
MIDFIELD
MILANESE
MILDNESS
MILKLESS
MILKWEED
MINDLESS
MINEHEAD
MINORESS
MINUTELY
MISERERE
MISSPELL
MISSPENT
MISTREAT
MISTRESS
MONSTERA
MONUMENT
MOONBEAM
MOROSELY
MORPHEME
MORPHEUS
MOVEMENT
MUCHNESS
MULETEER
MUNIMENT
MUTINEER
NAMELESS
NAPOLEON
NAZARENE
NDJAMENA
NEARNESS
NEATHERD
NEATNESS
NECKWEAR
NEEDLESS
NEPALESE
NESCIENT
NEWSPEAK
NEWSREEL
NICENESS
NINETEEN
NORTHERN
NUFFIELD
NUMBNESS
NUTRIENT
NUTSHELL
OBEDIENT
OBSOLETE
OBTUSELY
OCCIDENT
ODYSSEUS
OEDIPEAN
OFFBREAK

OFFICERS
OILFIELD
OILINESS
OINTMENT
OLEACEAE
ONSCREEN
OPENNESS
OPPONENT
ORANGERY
ORESTEIA
ORNAMENT
ORPIMENT
OUTBREAK
OUTFIELD
OVERFEED
OVERHEAD
OVERHEAR
OVERHEAT
OVERLEAF
OVERSEAS
OVERSEER
PAINLESS
PALENESS
PANATELA
PANCREAS
PANTHEON
PARAKEET
PAVEMENT
PAYCHECK
PEDIMENT
PEERLESS
PEKINESE
PELLMELL
PENITENT
PERIDERM
PERIPETY
PERTNESS
PHOSGENE
PICKMEUP
PINWHEEL
PIRANESI
PISSHEAD
PITHLESS
PITILESS
PLANGENT
PLIOCENE
POITIERS
POLITELY
POLYSEME
POLYSEMY
POORNESS
POTSHERD
PREMIERE
PRIMNESS
PRINCELY
PRINCESS
PRIORESS

PROCEEDS
PROGRESS
PROPHECY
PROPHESY
PROSPECT
PROSPERO
PRURIENT
PSALTERY
PSEUDERY
PURLIEUS
PURULENT
PYRENEES
QUARTERS
QUOTIENT
RACINESS
RACKRENT
RAILHEAD
RAILLERY
RAINWEAR
RANKNESS
RASHNESS
READIEST
REAPPEAR
REASSERT
REASSESS
RECKLESS
RECOVERY
REDIRECT
REDOLENT
REFINERY
REGIMENT
REINDEER
REINVEST
REMOTELY
REORIENT
REPRIEVE
RESIDENT
RESTLESS
RETICENT
RETRIEVE
REVEREND
REVERENT
RICHNESS
RIPENESS
ROOFLESS
ROOTLESS
ROSINESS
ROUNDERS
ROUSSEAU
RUDENESS
RUDIMENT
RUSTLESS
RUTHLESS
SABOTEUR
SADDLERY
SAGENESS
SALTNESS

SAMENESS
SAVAGELY
SAVAGERY
SCARCELY
SCHUBERT
SCULLERY
SEAMLESS
SEASHELL
SECURELY
SEDATELY
SEDIMENT
SEEDLESS
SELFHELP
SELFLESS
SENGREEN
SENTIENT
SERENELY
SERVIENT
SEVERELY
SEVEREST
SHAGREEN
SHEPHERD
SHIPMENT
SHOELESS
SHUTTERS
SICKNESS
SIDEREAL
SIXTIETH
SKINDEEP
SKINHEAD
SLATTERN
SLEEPERS
SLIMNESS
SLIPPERS
SLIPPERY
SLOBBERY
SLOWNESS
SLUGFEST
SMALLEST
SMARTEST
SMIDGEON
SMOLLETT
SMUGNESS
SNEAKERS
SNOBBERY
SOBRIETY
SOFTNESS
SOLDIERS
SOLDIERY
SOMBRELY
SOMBRERO
SORENESS
SOULLESS
SOURNESS
SOUTHEND
SOUTHERN
SPARSELY

SPEAKERS
SPINTEXT
SPITHEAD
SPOTLESS
SPRITELY
SPRUCELY
SPRYNESS
SQUARELY
STAGGERS
STAMPEDE
STARKERS
STARLESS
STARTERS
STEPHENS
STILWELL
STRATEGY
STRIDENT
STURGEON
SUBPOENA
SUBTLETY
SUCCEEDS
SUDAMENT
SUDANESE
SUNCREAM
SUPPRESS
SURENESS
TACTLESS
TAILLESS
TAMENESS
TARTNESS
TASHKENT
TAUTNESS
TEACHERS
TEGUMENT
TENEMENT
TERYLENE
THIEVERY
THINNESS
THIRTEEN
THUNDERY
TIDINESS
TIEBREAK
TIMELESS
TIRELESS
TITANESS
TONELESS
TRANSECT
TRANSEPT
TREELESS
TRICKERY
TRIMNESS
TROTTERS
TROUSERS
TRUENESS
TRUMPERY
TUBELESS
TWEEZERS
TWELVEMO
TWOPIECE
TYROLEAN
UGLINESS
UNFREEZE
UNIQUELY
UNLIKELY
UNLOVELY
UNTHREAD
UNTIMELY
UPSTREAM
VASTNESS
VEHEMENT
VENEREAL
VERONESE
VESTMENT
VILENESS
VIREMENT
VIRULENT
VOYAGEUR
WAITRESS
WALLSEND
WARDRESS
WARINESS
WEAKNESS
WHEATEAR
WHISKERS
WHISKERY
WILDFELL
WILDNESS
WILINESS
WINDLESS
WINGLESS
WIRELESS
WITCHERY
WOOLLENS
WORDLESS
YOUNGEST
YOURSELF
ZARZUELA
ZOOSPERM
MEUNIÈRE
PORTIÈRE
BASINFUL
BEATIFIC
BELLYFUL
BLACKFLY
BLISSFUL
BOASTFUL
CASTOFFS
CHEERFUL
COLORFUL
CRANEFLY
CRUCIFER
CRUCIFIX
DOUBTFUL
DREADFUL
EVENTFUL
FAITHFUL
FANCIFUL
FEVERFEW
FORCEFUL
FRUITFUL
GLASSFUL
GRACEFUL
GRATEFUL
GREENFLY
HORRIFIC
HORSEFLY
HOVERFLY
MERCIFUL
MIRTHFUL
MOURNFUL
MOUTHFUL
PARAFFIN
PARSIFAL
PEACEFUL
PHOTOFIT
PLATEFUL
POWERFUL
PROLIFIC
RIGHTFUL
SCORNFUL
SHAMEFUL
SKILLFUL
SLOTHFUL
SPADEFUL
SPECIFIC
SPITEFUL
SPOONFUL
TARTUFFE
TASTEFUL
TERRIFIC
THANKFUL
THURIFER
TRANSFER
TRANSFIX
TRUSTFUL
TRUTHFUL
UNDERFED
UNLAWFUL
VENGEFUL
WASTEFUL
WATCHFUL
WRATHFUL
WRONGFUL
WYCLIFFE
YOUTHFUL
AASVOGEL
ABRIDGED
AIRTIGHT
ALLERGEN
ALLERGIC
ANALOGUE
APOLOGIA
APOLOGUE
ARPEGGIO
ARRANGER
ASPERGES
BESIEGED
BESOUGHT
BUNFIGHT
CAMARGUE
CARDIGAN
CARNEGIE
COLLAGEN
COLLEGES
CONJUGAL
CORRAGIO
COTTAGER
CYANOGEN
DAYLIGHT
DERANGED
DIALOGUE
ENDANGER
ENLARGED
ENLARGER
ENTANGLE
EPILOGUE
ESCARGOT
ESTRAGON
ESTROGEN
EYESIGHT
FANLIGHT
FLASHGUN
FOGLIGHT
GARRIGUE
GLYCOGEN
GOOSEGOG
HARANGUE
HEPTAGON
HOOLIGAN
HYDROGEN
INFLIGHT
INTRIGUE
INVEIGLE
JOKINGLY
KATTEGAT
KORRIGAN
LAVENGRO
LILONGWE
LOVINGLY
LYSERGIC
MADRIGAL
MALINGER
MELEAGER
MERINGUE
MESSAGER
MICHIGAN
MIDNIGHT
MULLIGAN
NEGLIGEE
NITROGEN
OUTRIGHT
PACKAGED
PATHOGEN
PELLAGRA
PENTAGON
PILLAGER
PODARGUS
PORTUGAL
PRODIGAL
PROLOGUE
PROROGUE
PROTÉGÉE
RATTIGAN
REDLIGHT
RESPIGHI
ROENTGEN
SALINGER
SAUSAGES
SKYLIGHT
SPRINGER
SQUEEGEE
SQUIGGLE
STRAGGLE
STRAGGLY
STRAIGHT
STRANGER
STRANGLE
STRENGTH
STRINGED
STRINGER
STRONGLY
STRUGGLE
SUNLIGHT
SYRINGES
TARRAGON
TEENAGER
TETRAGON
TINTAGEL
TOBOGGAN
TRIANGLE
TWILIGHT
UNHINGED
UNTANGLE
VILLAGER
ACANTHUS
ALMIGHTY
AMBUSHED
ANARCHIC
ANTIPHON
ATTACHED
BABUSHKA
BACKCHAT
BALLYHOO
BARATHEA
BLEACHER
BLOTCHED
BOOKSHOP
BRADSHAW
BRANCHED
BREACHES
BREATHER
BREECHES
BRONCHUS
BROUGHAM
BUCKSHEE
BUCKSHOT
CABOCHON
CAPUCHIN
CHITCHAT
CLERIHEW
CLINCHER
COAUTHOR
COLOPHON
CRATCHIT
CROTCHET
CRUNCHIE
CRUTCHED
DECIPHER
DETACHED
DIANTHUS
DIARRHEA
DRAUGHTS
DRAUGHTY
DROPSHOT
ENMESHED
ENRICHED
FAMISHED
FELLAHIN
FINISHED
FINISHER
FLAGSHIP
FORESHIP
GALOSHES
GARISHLY
GROSCHEN
HARDSHIP
HAUNCHES
HEADSHIP
HEDGEHOG
HERSCHEL
JEPHTHAH
JONATHAN
KACHAHRI
KICKSHAW
KINGSHIP
LADYSHIP
LAVISHLY
LECITHIN
LENGTHEN
LORDSHIP
MACMAHON
MAILSHOT

MARATHON
MEMSAHIB
METAPHOR
NENUPHAR
OENOPHIL
OVERSHOE
OVERSHOT
PAWNSHOP
PERISHED
PERISHER
PINOCHLE
PIROZHKI
PLANCHET
PLOUGHED
POLISHED
POLISHER
PREACHER
PUNISHED
PYORRHEA
RHONCHUS
RICKSHAW
RICOCHET
ROADSHOW
SCORCHED
SCORCHER
SEALYHAM
SEARCHER
SERAPHIC
SERAPHIM
SHANGHAI
SIDESHOW
SISYPHUS
SLIPSHOD
SMOOTHER
SMOOTHLY
SNAPSHOT
SNATCHER
SOMEWHAT
SPLASHER
STARCHED
STENDHAL
STRACHEY
TELETHON
THATCHED
THATCHER
THOUGHTS
THRASHER
THRESHER
TOGETHER
TOWNSHIP
TRANSHIP
TRENCHER
TWITCHER
UPRIGHTS
VANISHED
WARDSHIP
WHINCHAT
WHITEHOT
WOODSHED
WORKSHOP
WREATHED
WRETCHED
XENOPHON
XERAPHIM
YATAGHAN
ABBASIDE
ABESSIVE
ABLATION
ABLATIVE
ABLUTION
ABORTION
ABORTIVE
ABRASION
ABRASIVE
ACCUSING
ACERBITY
ACQUAINT
ACROMION
ACTINIDE
ACTINIUM
ACTIVISM
ACTIVIST
ACTIVITY
ADDITION
ADDITIVE
ADELAIDE
ADENOIDS
ADESSIVE
ADHESION
ADHESIVE
ADMIRING
ADMONISH
ADOPTION
ADOPTIVE
AEROBICS
AEROLITH
AFFINITY
AFFUSION
AGNATION
AGRARIAN
AGREEING
AKKADIAN
ALACRITY
ALARMING
ALARMIST
ALBANIAN
ALBERICH
ALEMAINE
ALEUTIAN
ALGERIAN
ALGERINE
ALGORISM
ALIENISM
ALIENIST
ALKALIFY
ALKALINE
ALLOWING
ALLSPICE
ALLURING
ALLUSION
ALLUSIVE
ALLUVIAL
ALLUVIUM
ALPINIST
ALSATIAN
ALTRUISM
ALTRUIST
AMANDINE
AMBITION
AMMONIAC
AMMONITE
AMORTIZE
ANGELICA
ANNALIST
ANNAMITE
ANNELIDA
ANNOYING
ANSERINE
ANTERIOR
ANYTHING
APHELION
APHORISM
APIARIST
APPETITE
APPOSITE
APPRAISE
AQUARIUM
AQUARIUS
AQUATINT
AQUILINE
ARALDITE
ARCADIAN
ARCHAISM
ARGININE
ARMALITE
ARMENIAN
ARMORIAL
ARMORICA
ARSONIST
ARTERIAL
ARTESIAN
ARTIFICE
ASCIDIAN
ASCIDIUM
ASPERITY
ASPIRING
ASSUMING
ASSYRIAN
ASTATINE
ASTERISK
ASTONISH
ASUNCION
ATHELING
ATHENIAN
ATHETISE
ATROCITY
AUDACITY
AUDITION
AURELIAN
AUSTRIAN
AVAILING
AVENTINE
AVERSION
AVIATION
AVULSION
AYRSHIRE
BAATHIST
BABBLING
BACKBITE
BACKFIRE
BACKSIDE
BACTRIAN
BAFFLING
BAHAMIAN
BAHRAINI
BAKELITE
BALDRICK
BALLGIRL
BANALITY
BANTLING
BARONIAL
BASELINE
BASIDIUM
BASILICA
BASILISK
BATAVIAN
BAUDRICK
BAVARIAN
BEAUTIFY
BECOMING
BEESWING
BEETLING
BEHAVIOR
BENEDICK
BENEDICT
BENEFICE
BENEFITS
BESTRIDE
BIENNIAL
BIGAMIST
BINOMIAL
BLACKING
BLACKISH
BLANDISH
BLEEDING
BLENDING
BLESSING
BLINDING
BLINKING
BLOOMING
BLOWFISH
BLOWPIPE
BLURRING
BLUSHING
BOARDING
BOASTING
BOBOLINK
BODLEIAN
BODYLINE
BOEOTIAN
BOHEMIAN
BOLIVIAN
BONSPIEL
BORACITE
BORODINO
BOTANIST
BOTTLING
BOTULISM
BOUNCING
BRACHIAL
BRACKISH
BRAGGING
BRANDISH
BRASSICA
BREAKING
BREEDING
BREEZILY
BRIDGING
BRIEFING
BRIMMING
BRINDISI
BRINGING
BRISLING
BROILING
BROODING
BROWNING
BROWNISH
BROWSING
BRUISING
BRUMAIRE
BUBBLING
BUCKLING
BUDDHISM
BUDDHIST
BUILDING
BULLRING
BUMBLING
BUNGLING
BURSTING
BUSTLING
CAFFEINE
CALAMINE
CALAMITY
CALLGIRL
CAMBRIAN
CAMOMILE
CAMPAIGN
CAMPSITE
CANADIAN
CANALISE
CANARIES
CANOEING
CANOEIST
CANONIZE
CAPACITY
CAPERING
CARABINE
CAROLINA
CAROLINE
CARRYING
CATAMITE
CATCHING
CATERING
CATILINE
CAVALIER
CAVATINA
CELERIAC
CELERITY
CENOBITE
CENTRIST
CERAMICS
CHAMPION
CHANGING
CHARGING
CHARMING
CHARTISM
CHARTIST
CHASTISE
CHASTITY
CHEATING
CHECKING
CHEEKILY
CHEERILY
CHEERING
CHESHIRE
CHILDISH
CHILLING
CHINDITS
CHLORIDE
CHLORINE
CHOOSING
CHOPPING
CHROMITE
CHROMIUM
CHURLISH
CIBORIUM
CITATION
CIVILIAN
CIVILITY
CIVILIZE
CLADDING
CLANGING

CLANNISH
CLAPPING
CLASHING
CLASPING
CLASSICS
CLASSIFY
CLAUDIUS
CLEANING
CLEARING
CLIMBING
CLINGING
CLIPPING
CLIQUISH
CLOTHIER
CLOTHING
CLOWNISH
CLUMSILY
COACHING
COALMINE
COERCION
COERCIVE
COHESION
COHESIVE
COINCIDE
COLONIAL
COLONIST
COLONIZE
COLORING
COMEDIAN
COMPLINE
COMPRISE
CONCEIVE
CONFLICT
CONSPIRE
CONTRITE
CONTRIVE
CORNHILL
COUCHING
COUGHING
COUNTIES
COUNTING
COUPLING
COVERING
CRACKING
CRAFTILY
CRAMOISY
CRAWFISH
CRAWLING
CRAYFISH
CREATION
CREATIVE
CRINGING
CRISPIAN
CROATIAN
CRONYISM
CROONING
CROSSING
CROUPIER
CROWNING
CRUSHING
CRUZEIRO
CUPIDITY
CURATIVE
CURTAINS
CUTPRICE
CYNICISM
CYRENIAC
DABCHICK
DAINTIES
DAINTILY
DAIQUIRI
DATELINE
DAUNTING
DAZZLING
DEADLINE
DEBILITY
DECAYING
DECISION
DECISIVE
DEFINITE
DELETION
DELIRIUM
DELUSION
DEMOLISH
DEMONIAC
DEMOTION
DENARIUS
DENDRITE
DEPUTIZE
DERELICT
DERISION
DERISIVE
DESCRIBE
DEVILISH
DEVOTION
DIALLING
DIATRIBE
DIGITIZE
DILATION
DILUTION
DIMINISH
DIPSTICK
DISGUISE
DISQUIET
DISTRICT
DISUNION
DISUNITE
DISUNITY
DIVINITY
DIVISION
DIVISIVE
DOCILITY
DOCKSIDE
DOCTRINE
DOLOMITE
DOMICILE
DOMINION
DONATION
DONATIST
DOPAMINE
DOUBTING
DOWNHILL
DOWNSIDE
DOWNSIZE
DRAINING
DREAMILY
DREARILY
DRESSING
DRIFTING
DRINKING
DRIPPING
DROOPING
DROPPING
DROWNING
DROWSILY
DRUBBING
DRUGGIST
DRUMLINE
DRUMMING
DUCKBILL
DUCKLING
DUELLIST
DUMPLING
DUNGHILL
DURATION
DWARFISH
DWARFISM
DWELLING
DYNAMICS
DYNAMISM
DYNAMITE
ECLOSION
EDGEHILL
EDGEWISE
EFFUSION
EFFUSIVE
EGYPTIAN
EJECTION
ELECTION
ELECTIVE
EMBODIED
EMBOLISM
EMERGING
EMERSION
EMISSION
EMPORIUM
EMULSIFY
EMULSION
ENCOMIUM
ENDURING
ENDYMION
ENERGIZE
ENGAGING
ENORMITY
ENSHRINE
ENTICING
ENTRAILS
ENTRYISM
ENVISION
EPHESIAN
EQUALITY
EQUALIZE
EQUATION
ERECTILE
ERECTING
ERECTION
ERGOTISE
ERGOTISM
ERUPTION
ESCAPISM
ESCAPIST
ESCORIAL
ESPALIER
ESPECIAL
ESSAYIST
ESTONIAN
ETERNITY
ETHERISE
ETRURIAN
EUDOXIAN
EUGENICS
EULOGIST
EULOGIUM
EULOGIZE
EUPHUISM
EURASIAN
EURYDICE
EVENTIDE
EVICTION
EXACTING
EXACTION
EXCISION
EXCITING
EXERCISE
EXERTION
EXIGUITY
EXISTING
EXOCRINE
EXORCISM
EXORCIST
EXORCIZE
EXORDIUM
EXPEDITE
EXTERIOR
EXULTING
FACELIFT
FACILITY
FAINTING
FAMILIAR
FARTHING
FATALISM
FATALIST
FATALITY
FAVORITE
FELICITY
FEMININE
FEMINISM
FEMINIST
FEMINITY
FEROCITY
FETCHING
FEVERISH
FIDDLING
FIDELITY
FIELDING
FIENDISH
FIGHTING
FIGURINE
FILARIUM
FILIPINO
FILTHILY
FINALIST
FINALITY
FINALIZE
FIREBIRD
FIRESIDE
FISHWIFE
FIXATION
FIXATIVE
FLAGGING
FLAPPING
FLASHILY
FLASHING
FLATFISH
FLAUTIST
FLEABITE
FLEETING
FLIMSILY
FLIPPING
FLIRTING
FLOATING
FLOGGING
FLOODING
FLOORING
FLOURISH
FLUIDITY
FLUORIDE
FLUORINE
FLUORITE
FLUSHING
FLYDRIVE
FONDLING
FOOTLING
FORFEITS
FORKLIFT
FORTUITY
FOUNDING
FRACTION
FRANCIUM
FRANKISH
FREAKISH
FREEZING
FRENZIED
FREUDIAN
FRICTION
FRISKILY
FRONTIER
FROSTILY
FROSTING
FRUCTIFY
FRUITING
FRUITION
FRUMPISH
FUCHSITE
FUGITIVE
FULLSIZE
FULLTIME
FUMBLING
FUNCTION
FUSEWIRE
FUSILIER
FUTILITY
FUTURISM
FUTURIST
GAMBLING
GAMEBIRD
GANGLING
GANGLION
GAOLBIRD
GASOLIER
GASOLINE
GELATINE
GENETICS
GENITIVE
GENOCIDE
GENTRIFY
GEORGIAN
GERANIUM
GERMAINE
GERONIMO
GHANAIAN
GHOULISH
GLANCING
GLEAMING
GLOAMING
GLOATING
GLOOMILY
GLUMPISH
GNASHING
GODCHILD
GOLDFISH
GOLDMINE

GOODSIRE
GOODWIFE
GOODWILL
GRAFFITI
GRAINING
GRAPHICS
GRAPHITE
GRASPING
GRATUITY
GRAYLING
GREEDILY
GREENING
GREENISH
GREETING
GRILLING
GRINDING
GRIPPING
GROGGILY
GROOMING
GROUPING
GROUTING
GROWLING
GRUDGING
GRUMPILY
GUARDIAN
GUIANIAN
GUILTILY
GUMPTION
GUNPOINT
GUNSMITH
GYRATION
HAIRLIKE
HAIRLINE
HALFTIME
HANDBILL
HARDLINE
HATCHING
HAUNTING
HAWAIIAN
HEADLINE
HEADWIND
HEARTIES
HEARTILY
HECKLING
HEDONISM
HEDONIST
HELLFIRE
HELPLINE
HEPATICA
HEREDITY
HEREWITH
HIGHRISE
HILARITY
HILLSIDE
HINDUISM
HIRELING
HOARDING
HOBBLING
HOKKAIDO
HOMESICK
HOMICIDE
HOODWINK
HORATIAN
HORATIUS
HORNBILL
HORNPIPE
HOSEPIPE
HOTELIER
HUMANISM
HUMANIST
HUMANITY
HUMANIZE
HUMIDIFY
HUMIDITY
HUMILITY
HUMORIST
HUNGRILY
HURDLING
HYPERION
IDEALISM
IDEALIST
IDEALIZE
IDENTIFY
IDENTITY
IGNITION
IGNOMINY
ILLUMINE
ILLUSION
ILLUSIVE
IMBECILE
IMMOBILE
IMMUNITY
IMMUNIZE
IMPERIAL
IMPETIGO
IMPOLITE
IMPOSING
IMPUNITY
IMPURIFY
IMPURITY
INACTION
INACTIVE
INCISION
INCISIVE
INCOMING
INDEXING
INDUCIVE
INEQUITY
INFERIOR
INFINITE
INFINITY
INFUSION
INIQUITY
INSANITY
INSCRIBE
INTERIOR
INVASION
INVASIVE
INVITING
IRISHISM
IRONSIDE
ISTHMIAN
IVOIRIEN
JACOBITE
JAILBIRD
JANGLING
JAPONICA
JAUNDICE
JAUNTILY
JEBUSITE
JEREMIAD
JEREMIAH
JINGOISM
JINGOIST
JOYSTICK
JUDICIAL
JUGGLING
JUNCTION
JUVENILE
KERCHIEF
KINDLING
KINETICS
KINGSIZE
KLONDIKE
KNEEHIGH
KNITTING
KNOCKING
KOURMISS
LACEWING
LACONIAN
LADYBIRD
LADYLIKE
LANDFILL
LANDMINE
LANGUISH
LANOLINE
LATERITE
LATINIST
LAUGHING
LAXATIVE
LEACHING
LEARNING
LEFTWING
LEGALISM
LEGALITY
LEGALIZE
LEGATION
LEWISITE
LIBATION
LIBERIAN
LICORICE
LIFELIKE
LIFELINE
LIFETIME
LIGHTING
LIKEWISE
LIMERICK
LIMITING
LIMONITE
LINGUIST
LIPSTICK
LIVERIED
LIVERISH
LIVIDITY
LOATHING
LOBBYIST
LOBELINE
LOCALITY
LOCALIZE
LOCATION
LOCATIVE
LONGTIME
LORRAINE
LOVEBIRD
LOVESICK
LOWERING
LOWLYING
LOYALIST
LUCIDITY
LUMPFISH
LUNGFISH
LUSTRINE
LYNCHING
LYREBIRD
LYRICISM
LYRICIST
MAGAZINE
MAGICIAN
MAINLINE
MAJOLICA
MAJORITY
MALARIAL
MALAWIAN
MANAGING
MANDRILL
MANORIAL
MARITIME
MARONITE
MARQUISE
MATCHING
MATERIAL
MATURITY
MAVERICK
MAXIMIZE
MAZARINE
MEALTIME
MEANTIME
MEDALIST
MEDDLING
MEDICINE
MEGALITH
MELAMINE
MELANITE
MELCHIOR
MEMORIAL
MEMORIAM
MEMORIZE
MENACING
MEREDITH
MERIDIAN
MESOLITE
MIDDLING
MIDPOINT
MIGHTILY
MIGRAINE
MINIMIZE
MINORITE
MINORITY
MINUTIAE
MISCHIEF
MISGUIDE
MISPRINT
MOBILITY
MOBILIZE
MODELING
MODIFIER
MOLEHILL
MONADISM
MONDRIAN
MONETISE
MONOLITH
MONOXIDE
MONTEITH
MORALIST
MORALITY
MORALIZE
MORAVIAN
MORPHINE
MOSQUITO
MOTORING
MOTORIST
MOTORIZE
MOULDING
MOUNTING
MOURNING
MUMBLING
MUSICIAN
MUTATION
MYCELIUM
NAMIBIAN
NATALITY
NATIVITY
NATURISM
NATURIST
NAUPLIUS
NAVARINO
NECKLINE
NEGATION
NEGATIVE
NEPHRITE
NEPOTISM
NESTLING
NEUTRINO
NICOTINE
NIDATION
NIGERIAN
NIGERIEN
NIGGLING
NIHILISM
NIHILIST
NINEPINS
NOBELIUM
NOBILITY
NONSTICK
NOONTIME
NOSEDIVE
NOSTRILS
NOTARIAL
NOTATION
NOVELIST
NURSLING
OBLATION
OBLIGING
OBLIVION
OBSIDIAN
OCCAMIST
OCCASION
OCCUPIED
OCCUPIER
OFFERING
OFFICIAL
OILSKINS
OILSLICK
OLYMPIAD
OLYMPIAN
OLYMPICS
OMISSION
ONCOMING
OPHIDIAN
OPPOSING
OPPOSITE
OPTICIAN
OPTIMISM
OPTIMIST
ORCADIAN
ORDERING
ORGANISM
ORGANIST
ORGANIZE
OTTAVINO
OUISTITI
OUTGOING

OUTLYING
OUTSHINE
OUTWEIGH
OVERFILL
OVERKILL
OVERRIDE
OVERRIPE
OVERSIZE
OVERTIME
OVERVIEW
PACIFIER
PACIFISM
PACIFIST
PADDLING
PAGANINI
PAINTING
PALATIAL
PALATINE
PALUDISM
PANELING
PARADIGM
PARADISE
PARASITE
PARISIAN
PARODIST
PARTHIAN
PARTTIME
PASHMINA
PATCHILY
PAVILION
PEARLING
PECORINO
PECULIAR
PEDDLING
PELAGIUS
PENALIZE
PENKNIFE
PERCEIVE
PEROXIDE
PERSHING
PERSPIRE
PERUVIAN
PETITION
PHILLIPS
PHORMIUM
PHRYGIAN
PICKWICK
PIDDLING
PIERCING
PIGSWILL
PILGRIMS
PINPOINT
PINPRICK
PIPELINE
PIPERINE
PITCAIRN
PLANKING
PLANNING
PLAUDITS
PLAYBILL
PLAYGIRL
PLAYTIME
PLEADING
PLEASING
PLEBEIAN
PLEURISY
PLUCKILY
PLUCKING
PLUMBING
PLUNGING
POLARIZE
POLITICO
POLITICS
POLONIUM
POPULIST
POROSITY
PORPOISE
POSITION
POSITIVE
POULAINE
POULTICE
PRACTICE
PRACTISE
PRAIRIAL
PRANDIAL
PRESSING
PRESTIGE
PRETTILY
PRIAPISM
PRIGGISH
PRINTING
PRIORITY
PRISTINE
PRUSSIAN
PSALMIST
PTOMAINE
PUGILISM
PUGILIST
PUNITIVE
PURBLIND
PURIFIED
PURIFIER
PURPLISH
PUSHBIKE
PUTATIVE
PUZZLING
PYRAMIDS
QUADRIGA
QUAGMIRE
QUANTIFY
QUANTITY
QUARTIER
QUARTILE
QUAYSIDE
QUESTION
QUILTING
QUISLING
RAINBIRD
RAMBLING
RAPACITY
RAPIDITY
RAREFIED
RATTLING
REACTION
REACTIVE
REAFFIRM
REALTIME
REASSIGN
RECEDING
RECRUITS
REDBRICK
REDEFINE
REDESIGN
REEDLING
REFUGIUM
REGICIDE
REIGNING
RELATING
RELATION
RELATIVE
RELAXING
RELAYING
RELIGION
REMEDIAL
REPAYING
RESTRICT
RETIRING
REVISION
REVIVIFY
REVIVING
RIESLING
RIGHTIST
RIGIDITY
RINGSIDE
RIPARIAN
RIPPLING
RIVALISE
RIVERINE
RIVETING
ROADSIDE
ROASTING
ROBOTICS
RODERICK
ROGATION
ROMANIAN
ROSALIND
ROSALINE
ROTATION
ROYALIST
RUMBLING
RUSTLING
SADDLING
SAGACITY
SALACITY
SALARIED
SALINITY
SALTLICK
SAMPHIRE
SANCTIFY
SANCTION
SANCTITY
SANDWICH
SANGLIER
SANGUINE
SANITIZE
SAPONITE
SAPPHIRE
SAPPHIST
SATIRIST
SATIRIZE
SAXATILE
SCALDING
SCALLION
SCANDIUM
SCANNING
SCANSION
SCANTIES
SCANTILY
SCARCITY
SCATHING
SCHEMING
SCIATICA
SCISSION
SCOFFING
SCOLDING
SCORPION
SCOTTISH
SCOURING
SCOWLING
SCRUTINY
SCULLION
SEAGOING
SECURITY
SEDATION
SEDATIVE
SEDITION
SEEDLING
SEETHING
SELENITE
SELENIUM
SELFPITY
SEMOLINA
SENILITY
SENORITA
SERAFILE
SERENITY
SEVERITY
SHABBILY
SHEEPISH
SHELVING
SHIELING
SHIFTING
SHILLING
SHIPPING
SHOCKING
SHODDILY
SHOOTING
SHOPPING
SHOUTING
SHOWGIRL
SHREWISH
SIBERIAN
SICILIAN
SICKLIST
SIDEKICK
SIDELINE
SIDERITE
SIGHTING
SILESIAN
SILURIAN
SIMPLIFY
SINAPISM
SIRENIAN
SIZZLING
SKIDDING
SKILLING
SKILLION
SKIPPING
SKIRMISH
SKIRTING
SKITTISH
SKULKING
SLANGING
SLANTING
SLEEPILY
SLEEPING
SLIPPING
SLOPPILY
SLUGGISH
SLUMMING
SLURRING
SLUTTISH
SMASHING
SMELTING
SMOCKING
SNAPPILY
SNEAKING
SNEERING
SNEEZING
SNOBBISH
SNOOTILY
SNORTING
SNOWLINE
SOBERING
SODALITE
SODALITY
SOLARIUM
SOLECISM
SOLIDIFY
SOLIDITY
SOLSTICE
SOLUTION
SOMETIME
SONATINA
SONGBIRD
SOOTHING
SORORITY
SOUNDING
SOURCING
SPANKING
SPANNING
SPARKING
SPARRING
SPARSITY
SPAWNING
SPEAKING
SPEEDILY
SPELLING
SPENDING
SPIFFING
SPINNING
SPITFIRE
SPITTING
SPOILING
SPORTING
SPORTIVE
SPOTTING
SPURNING
STABBING
STABLING
STAFFING
STALKING
STALLION
STANDING
STANDISH
STANNITE
STARFISH
STARLING
STARTING
STARVING
STEADILY
STEALING
STEATITE
STEERING
STERLING
STICKILY
STICKING
STIFLING
STINGING
STINKING
STIRLING
STIRRING

STOCKING
STOCKIST
STOICISM
STOPPING
STORMING
STRABISM
STRATIFY
STRIKING
STRIVING
STUFFILY
STUFFING
STULTIFY
STUNNING
STURDILY
SUCHLIKE
SUCKLING
SUDAMINA
SUDARIUM
SULPHIDE
SUMERIAN
SUNDRIED
SUNDRIES
SUNSHINE
SUPERIOR
SUPPLIER
SUPPLIES
SURPLICE
SURPRISE
SWARMING
SWASTIKA
SWEARING
SWEATING
SWEEPING
SWELLING
SWERVING
SWILLING
SWIMMING
SWINGING
SWIRLING
SYBARITE
SYNCLINE
TAHITIAN
TAILPIPE
TAMARIND
TAMARISK
TAPERING
TAXATION
TEACHING
TEESHIRT
TEETHING
TELEFILM
TELEVISE
TEMERITY
TEMPTING
TENACITY
TETCHILY
THALLIUM
THEORIST
THEORIZE
THESPIAN
THIAMINE
THIEVING
THIEVISH
THINKING
THINNING
THRACIAN
THUMPING
TIBERIAS
TIBERIUS
TICKLING
TICKLISH
TIMIDITY
TINGLING
TIRAMISU
TIRESIAS
TITANISM
TITANITE
TITANIUM
TONALITY
TORTOISE
TOTALITY
TOTALIZE
TOUCHING
TOVARICH
TOWELING
TOWERING
TOXICITY
TRACKING
TRACTION
TRAILING
TRAINING
TRAMLINE
TRAPPIST
TREATISE
TREELINE
TRIFLING
TRILLING
TRILLION
TRILLIUM
TRIMMING
TRIPLING
TRISTICH
TROOPING
TRUCKING
TRUNNION
TRUSTING
TUNISIAN
TURNPIKE
TUTORIAL
TWIRLING
TWISTING
TYROSINE
TZATZIKI
UBIQUITY
ULTERIOR
UNCARING
UNEASILY
UNENDING
UNERRING
UNFADING
UNIFYING
UNIONISM
UNIONIST
UNIONIZE
UNSOCIAL
UNSPOILT
UNTIDILY
UNVARIED
UPCOMING
UPRISING
UPSTAIRS
URBANITY
URBANIZE
URSULINE
UTENSILS
VACATION
VAGARIES
VALERIAN
VALETING
VALIDITY
VANADIUM
VANQUISH
VAPORIZE
VAULTING
VELLEITY
VELOCITY
VENALITY
VENETIAN
VERACITY
VERJUICE
VERLAINE
VERONICA
VESUVIUS
VEXATION
VICARIAL
VICINITY
VILLAINY
VIRILITY
VISELIKE
VISITING
VITALITY
VITALIZE
VITAMINS
VITILIGO
VIVACITY
VIVARIUM
VOCALIST
VOCALIZE
VOCATION
VOCATIVE
VOLATILE
VOLITION
VOLSCIAN
VOLTAIRE
VOMITING
VORACITY
WALTZING
WAMBLING
WARPAINT
WATCHING
WATERING
WAVERING
WEAKLING
WEIGHING
WELLNIGH
WHACKING
WHEEZILY
WHEEZING
WHIPPING
WHIRLING
WHITLING
WHOOPING
WHOPPING
WIDENING
WILDFIRE
WILDLIFE
WINDMILL
WINDPIPE
WITCHING
WOBBLING
WOMANISH
WOMANIZE
WOODBINE
WOODWIND
WORRYING
WORTHIES
WORTHILY
WRAPPING
WRINGING
WRITHING
XENOLITH
YACHTING
YEARLING
YEARNING
YIELDING
YOSEMITE
YULETIDE
ZEDEKIAH
ZIBELINE
ZUCCHINI
CARCAJOU
KINKAJOU
NIGHTJAR
POPINJAY
TURBOJET
ATTACKER
BAEDEKER
BEARSKIN
BEDMAKER
BESPOKEN
BUCKSKIN
CHEROKEE
DEERSKIN
DISLIKED
FORESKIN
FORSAKEN
GOATSKIN
HABAKKUK
HANUKKAH
HAYMAKER
HIJACKER
LAMBSKIN
LATCHKEY
LAWMAKER
MALARKEY
MANNIKIN
MISTAKEN
MOLESKIN
MONICKER
MUNCHKIN
MUTCHKIN
ONLOOKER
OXPECKER
PANNIKIN
POTEMKIN
REAWAKEN
SEALSKIN
SHRUNKEN
SLOVAKIA
SPRINKLE
SPROCKET
SQUEAKER
STREAKED
STREAKER
STRICKEN
SWANSKIN
TAILSKID
TRANSKEI
UNBROKEN
UNCOOKED
UNLOCKED
UNMARKED
UNSHAKEN
UNSPOKEN
UPMARKET
ABUTILON
ACAPULCO
ACHILLES
ACTUALLY
AEROFLOT
AIGUILLE
ALVEOLUS
ANATOLIA
ANGUILLA
ANNEALER
ANNUALLY
ANTILLES
APOSTLES
APPALLED
ARTFULLY
ARTICLED
ARTICLES
BACHELOR
BACILLUS
BARDOLPH
BARGELLO
BASTILLE
BERKELEY
BIATHLON
BLACKLEG
BORDELLO
BRACELET
BRASILIA
BRINDLED
BRISTLED
BRISTLES
BROMELIA
BRUTALLY
BUNGALOW
CACHALOT
CADILLAC
CALCULUS
CAMELLIA
CANAILLE
CARBOLIC
CARILLON
CASUALLY
CASUALTY
CATHOLIC
CATULLUS
CAUDILLO
CELLULAR
CERVELAT
CHANDLER
CHENILLE
CHIVALRY
CINGULUM
CIRCULAR
COLESLAW
COMPILER
CONSULAR
CONVULSE
CORIOLIS
CORSELET
COVERLET
CRIPPLED
CROSSLET
CYRILLIC
DAEDALUS
DAMOCLES
DETAILED
DEVILLED

DIABOLIC
DICYCLIC
DISABLED
DISALLOW
DISCOLOR
DISMALLY
DISSOLVE
DOOLALLY
DOWNPLAY
DURABLES
EATABLES
ENTITLED
EUCYCLIC
EXEMPLAR
FITFULLY
FLOODLIT
FLOTILLA
FORMALIN
FORMALLY
FRANKLIN
FRAZZLED
FRECKLED
FRECKLES
FRENULUM
FRUGALLY
FURBELOW
GARDYLOO
GAUNTLET
GENIALLY
GLABELLA
GLOBALLY
GLOBULAR
GLOBULIN
GOLFCLUB
GONFALON
GRANULAR
GRANULES
GRAVELLY
GRIMALDI
GRISELDA
GRIZZLED
GRUMBLER
GUERILLA
HANDCLAP
HERACLES
HERACLID
HERCULES
HOSTELRY
IMPELLED
INTAGLIO
IRONCLAD
ISABELLA
ISABELLE
JEWELLED
JEWELLER
JOVIALLY
JOYFULLY
KINGSLEY
LANCELOT
LANDSLIP
LAWFULLY
LEVELLER
LINCOLNS
MACAULAY
MAGELLAN
MAGNOLIA
MALVOLIO
MANDOLIN
MANFULLY
MANTILLA
MANUALLY
MARCELLA
MARCELLO
MARTELLO
MCKINLEY
MENTALLY
MERCALLI
MESCALIN
METALLED
METALLIC
MODELLER
MONGOLIA
MORBILLI
MORTALLY
MOUFFLON
MUSCULAR
MUTUALLY
NARGILEH
NAUTILUS
NICHOLAS
NORMALLY
OFFCOLOR
OMPHALOS
OPENPLAN
OSTERLEY
OVERALLS
OVERFLOW
OVERPLAY
PAMPHLET
PANELLED
PANGOLIN
PANTALON
PAPILLON
PARALLAX
PARALLEL
PAROLLES
PASTILLE
PATELLAR
PENDULUM
PERICLES
PETERLOO
PHYSALIA
PLATELET
POLYGLOT
POTBELLY
POTHOLER
PRATTLER
PREDELLA
PREMOLAR
PRUNELLA
PUSTULAR
QUENELLE
QUIBBLER
RACIALLY
RASCALLY
RASSELAS
REDEPLOY
REEMPLOY
REPUBLIC
RETAILER
REVEALED
REVEILLE
REVELLER
REYNOLDS
RISSOLES
RITUALLY
RUEFULLY
SCAPULAR
SCHILLER
SCHMALTZ
SCRAWLED
SCRUPLES
SCYBALUM
SERAGLIO
SEXUALLY
SHACKLES
SHAMBLES
SHIGELLA
SHINGLES
SIDESLIP
SIGNALER
SIGNALLY
SINGULAR
SKITTLES
SKYPILOT
SLIPSLOP
SMUGGLED
SMUGGLER
SNIFFLER
SOCALLED
SOCIALLY
SPANGLED
SPARKLER
SPECKLED
SPECULUM
SPIRALLY
SPRAWLED
SQUEALER
STICKLER
STIMULUS
STROLLER
SWADDLER
SWINDLER
SYMBOLIC
SYPHILIS
TANTALUM
TANTALUS
TEQUILLA
THRILLER
TINSELLY
TORTILLA
TRAVELER
TREMBLER
TROCHLEA
TROUBLED
TROUBLES
TRUCKLED
UMBRELLA
UNDERLAY
UNDERLIE
UNFILLED
UNIPOLAR
UNIVALVE
UNSEALED
UNTILLED
UNWIELDY
USEFULLY
VALHALLA
VALVULAR
VASCULAR
VERBALLY
VEXILLUM
VINCULUM
VINDALOO
VISUALLY
VITELLUS
WATERLOO
WAVERLEY
WHISTLER
WILFULLY
WOEFULLY
WOLSELEY
WRANGLER
WRESTLER
WRINKLED
WRISTLET
YARMULKA
YODELLER
YUGOSLAV
ZEPPELIN
ABNORMAL
ACADEMIC
ALCHEMIC
ALDERMAN
ANALEMMA
ANATOMIC
BANDSMAN
BARGEMAN
BECALMED
BECHAMEL
BENJAMIN
BERGAMOT
BESSEMER
BETJEMAN
BOGEYMAN
BONDSMAN
BONHOMIE
BOTTOMRY
CARDAMOM
CHAIRMAN
CHESSMAN
CHESSMEN
CHIASMUS
CHINAMAN
CINNAMON
CLANSMAN
COACHMAN
COGNOMEN
CONSOMMÉ
CONSUMED
CONSUMER
CONTEMPT
CUSTOMER
CYCLAMEN
DAIRYMAN
DEFORMED
DIPLOMAT
DULCIMER
DUTCHMAN
ECONOMIC
EGGTIMER
EPIDEMIC
EPIGAMIC
ESTEEMED
EVERYMAN
FANCYMAN
FERRYMAN
FRESHMAN
FRONTMAN
FUGLEMAN
GALLUMPH
GIGLAMPS
GOSSAMER
GRAVAMEN
HANDYMAN
HELMSMAN
HENCHMAN
HERDSMAN
HORSEMAN
HORSEMEN
HOUSEMAN
HUNTSMAN
INDIAMAN
INFLAMED
INFORMAL
INFORMED
INFORMER
INTERMIT
IRISHMAN
IRISHMEN
KOMSOMOL
LEADSMAN
LEUKEMIA
LIEGEMAN
LINESMAN
MADWOMAN
MANDAMUS
MARASMUS
MARKSMAN
MISNOMER
MOHAMMED
MORTIMER
MOTORMAN
MUHAMMAD
NEWCOMER
NOBLEMAN
NORSEMAN
NORSEMEN
OMDURMAN
OUTREMER
PANDEMIC
PERFUMED
PHILEMON
PHILOMEL
PHLEGMON
PLACEMAT
PLACEMEN
PRESSMAN
RANDOMLY
REDEEMER
REEDSMAN
REFORMED
REFORMER
RHYTHMIC
RIFLEMAN
SALESMAN
SCOTSMAN
SCREAMER
SEEDSMAN
SHEARMAN
SIDESMAN
SPACEMAN
SPECIMEN
SPELLMAN
STOCKMAN
STOREMAN
STREAMER
SUBHUMAN
SUPERMAN
SYSTEMIC
TABLEMAT
TALISMAN

TENESMUS
THALAMUS
TOWNSMAN
TOXAEMIA
TRANSMIT
TRILEMMA
TURKOMAN
UNCOMMON
UNHARMED
UNSEEMLY
WATCHMAN
WATERMAN
WELSHMAN
WOODSMAN
ABEYANCE
ACCOUNTS
AIRLINER
ALBURNUM
ALDERNEY
ALICANTE
ALLIANCE
ALUMINUM
AMARANTH
AMBIANCE
AMBIENCE
ANACONDA
ANNOUNCE
ANTENNAE
ARACHNID
ARAMANTH
ARDENNES
ARMAGNAC
ASSIGNEE
ASTHENIA
ATALANTA
ATTORNEY
AUDIENCE
AUTUMNAL
AVICENNA
BADLANDS
BANDANNA
BASSINET
BEARINGS
BEGINNER
BRAGANZA
BRAMANTE
BRANDNEW
BRUCKNER
BUOYANCY
BURDENED
BURGUNDY
CABERNET
CARBONIC
CARCANET
CARDINAL
CASTANET
CHACONNE
CHESTNUT
CHEYENNE
CLARENCE
CLARINET
CLEMENCY
COMBINED
COMMANDO
COMMENCE
COMMONER
COMMONLY
COMMUNAL
CONDENSE
CONFINED
CONFINES
CONTANGO
CONTENTS
CONTINUE
CONTINUO
CONVENER
CONVINCE
CRETONNE
CRIMINAL
CULLINAN
CURRENCY
DARKENED
DEADENED
DEADENER
DEALINGS
DEFIANCE
DEMEANOR
DENOUNCE
DESIGNER
DESTINED
DETAINEE
DETAINER
DEVIANCE
DIAGONAL
DIAMANTE
DIAMONDS
DIATONIC
DIGGINGS
DIOGENES
DIPHENYL
DISHONOR
DISPENSE
DISTANCE
DISTINCT
DOORKNOB
DOUGHNUT
DRACONIC
DUBONNET
DULCINEA
DUODENAL
DUODENUM
EARNINGS
EGOMANIA
ELEGANCE
ELEMENTS
ELEVENTH
EMINENCE
ENCAENIA
ENSCONCE
ENTRANCE
ENTRENCH
EUPHONIA
EUPHONIC
EVIDENCE
EXAMINEE
EXAMINER
EXCHANGE
EXIGENCY
EXTERNAL
EXTERNAT
EYELINER
FALCONRY
FANDANGO
FASTENER
FAULKNER
FEELINGS
FINDINGS
FLAMENCO
FLAMINGO
FLORENCE
FRAXINUS
FRUMENTY
GALBANUM
GALVANIC
GARDENER
GARDENIA
GARGANEY
GARMENTS
GEOMANCY
GERMANIC
GERMINAL
GIACONDA
GIOCONDA
GIOVANNI
GLOXINIA
GOVERNOR
GUIDANCE
HACIENDA
HANGINGS
HARDENED
HARMONIC
HASTINGS
HAWFINCH
HAZELNUT
HEAVENLY
HELLENIC
HELSINKI
HIBERNIA
HISPANIC
HOGMANAY
HOLDINGS
HORMONAL
HUSTINGS
HYACINTH
HYGIENIC
IMAGINED
INCLINED
INFERNAL
INFRINGE
INGUINAL
INNUENDO
INSIGNIA
INSOMNIA
INSTANCE
INSTINCT
INTERNAL
INTERNEE
INTERNET
INTRENCH
ISOGONAL
JOHANNES
JONCANOE
JOTTINGS
JULIENNE
KATMANDU
KILKENNY
LABURNUM
LADRONES
LASHINGS
LAUDANUM
LAURENCE
LAWRENCE
LEAVENED
LEAVINGS
LEGGINGS
LENIENCY
LISTENER
LODGINGS
LONDONER
LOWLANDS
MACHINES
MAECENAS
MAHJONGG
MAIDENLY
MANGONEL
MARGINAL
MARIANAS
MARTINET
MASSENET
MATERNAL
MATRONLY
MECHANIC
METHANOL
MIDLANDS
MIGNONNE
MILLINER
MINDANAO
MNEMONIC
MOORINGS
NATIONAL
NEPIONIC
NONSENSE
NORMANDY
NOTIONAL
NUISANCE
OBTAINED
ODDMENTS
OPOPANAX
OPTIONAL
OPULENCE
ORDNANCE
ORIGINAL
ORPHANED
PACHINKO
PARDONER
PARLANCE
PATERNAL
PATIENCE
PAULINUS
PEELINGS
PENNINES
PENZANCE
PERIANTH
PERSONAL
PHALANGE
PICKINGS
PILSENER
PIMIENTO
PIQUANCY
PITTANCE
PLACENTA
PLATANUS
PLATINUM
PLATONIC
PLOTINUS
POISONER
POLYANNA
PONSONBY
PRECINCT
PRESENCE
PRETENCE
PRETENSE
PRISONER
PROVINCE
PRUDENCE
PUNGENCY
QUIRINAL
RADIANCE
RAILINGS
RAISONNÉ
RATIONAL
REASONED
RECKONER
REFRINGE
REGAINED
REGIONAL
REJOINED
RELIANCE
REMNANTS
REMOUNTS
RENMINBI
RENOUNCE
RENOWNED
RESIGNED
RESPONSE
RETAINER
RETRENCH
RIDDANCE
SARDINIA
SARDONIC
SARDONYX
SASSANID
SATURNIA
SAVANNAH
SAWBONES
SCALENUS
SCAVENGE
SCHOONER
SCREENED
SCROUNGE
SEASONAL
SEASONED
SENTENCE
SENTINEL
SEQUENCE
SHRAPNEL
SINFONIA
SIXPENCE
SLOVENIA
SLOVENLY
SOFTENER
SOLEMNLY
SOLVENCY
SORBONNE
SOUVENIR
SPAVINED
SPHAGNUM
SPRAINED
STAMENED
STRAINED
STRAINER
STUDENTS
SUBSONIC
SUBTENSE
SUCCINCT
SUDDENLY
SULLENLY
SUNDANCE
SUPERNAL
SUSPENSE
SYLVANER
TANZANIA

TASMANIA
TAVERNER
TECTONIC
TENDENCY
TERMINAL
TERMINUS
TEUTONIC
TRIBUNAL
TUPPENNY
TURBANED
TURGENEV
TWOPENNY
TYMPANUM
UNEARNED
UNEVENLY
UNGAINLY
UNMANNED
UNSIGNED
UNWEANED
UPTURNED
VAGRANCY
VARIANCE
VIBRANCY
VIBURNUM
VIOLENCE
VIRGINAL
VIRGINIA
VOIDANCE
VOLCANIC
WAGGONER
WARRANTY
WEAPONRY
WETLANDS
WHITENER
WHODUNIT
WINDINGS
WINNINGS
WOODENLY
WORKINGS
WRITINGS
YEOMANRY
YERSINIA
ZIRCONIA
ABATTOIR
ACRIMONY
ADVISORY
AEROFOIL
AGRICOLA
AGRIMONY
AGRONOMY
ALBACORE
ALBINONI
ALEATORY
ALKALOID
ALLEGORY
ANECDOTE
ANTELOPE
ANTEPOST
ANTEROOM
ANTIBODY
ANTIDOTE
ANTILOPE
ANTIMONY
ANTIPOPE
ASTEROID
ATHEROMA
ATHETOID
AUDITORY
AUTONOMY
BABYHOOD
BACKBONE
BACKCOMB
BACKROOM
BALLCOCK
BALLROOM
BANKBOOK
BANKNOTE
BANKROLL
BAREFOOT
BARITONE
BASEBORN
BATHROBE
BATHROOM
BEANPOLE
BEAUFORT
BEAUMONT
BEERBOHM
BEETROOT
BEHEMOTH
BELABOUR
BIBULOUS
BIGAMOUS
BILLFOLD
BILLHOOK
BIOSCOPE
BLACKOUT
BLASTOFF
BLOWHOLE
BLUECOAT
BLUENOSE
BOATLOAD
BODYWORK
BOLTHOLE
BOOKROOM
BOOKWORK
BOOKWORM
BORECOLE
BOREHOLE
BREAKOUT
BROCCOLI
BULLDOZE
BULLHORN
BURNTOUT
BUSYBODY
BUZZWORD
CABRIOLE
CAKEHOLE
CALLIOPE
CAMEROON
CAMISOLE
CAMPTOWN
CAMSTONE
CAPRIOLE
CAPSTONE
CAPTIOUS
CARACOLE
CAREWORN
CARRIOLE
CARTLOAD
CASANOVA
CATACOMB
CATATONY
CATEGORY
CAUTIOUS
CENTRODE
CERATOID
CEREMONY
CESSPOOL
CHARCOAL
CHARLOCK
CHECKOUT
CHEVIOTS
CICERONE
CINCHONA
CLANGOUR
CLAYMORE
CLIFFORD
CLODPOLL
CLUBFOOT
COALHOLE
COALPORT
COCACOLA
COMATOSE
COMEDOWN
CONCHOID
CONFRONT
CONTROLS
COOKBOOK
COPYBOOK
COPYHOLD
CORONOID
COTSWOLD
COUSCOUS
COVETOUS
CREOSOTE
CROWFOOT
CRUMHORN
CRUMMOCK
CYTOLOGY
DARKROOM
DARTMOOR
DASHWOOD
DEADLOCK
DEADWOOD
DECOROUS
DEMIJOHN
DENDROID
DERISORY
DESIROUS
DETHRONE
DEXTROSE
DEXTROUS
DIAGNOSE
DIAPHONE
DIASPORA
DIASTOLE
DILATORY
DISCLOSE
DISPROVE
DOGSBODY
DOLOROUS
DOMINOES
DOORPOST
DOUBLOON
DOVECOTE
DOWNLOAD
DOWNPOUR
DOWNTOWN
DOXOLOGY
DRAGOONS
DRYGOODS
DRYSTONE
EARPHONE
ECHINOPS
ELECTORS
ELSINORE
ENORMOUS
ENSHROUD
ENSIFORM
ENTHRONE
ENVELOPE
ENVIRONS
EPIPLOON
ESCALOPE
EVENSONG
EVERMORE
EVERYONE
EVILDOER
EXIGUOUS
EYETOOTH
FABULOUS
FACTIOUS
FATSTOCK
FEARSOME
FEELGOOD
FIREBOLT
FIREWOOD
FIREWORK
FISHBONE
FISHPOND
FLAGPOLE
FLATFOOT
FLATWORM
FLYBLOWN
FOLKLORE
FOLKSONG
FOOTHOLD
FOOTNOTE
FOOTSORE
FOOTWORK
FOREBODE
FOREDOOM
FOREFOOT
FOREGONE
FORELOCK
FOREMOST
FORENOON
FOREWORD
FORSOOTH
FOURFOLD
FOURSOME
FOXGLOVE
FRABJOUS
FREEHOLD
FREEPOST
FREETOWN
FRETWORK
FRUCTOSE
FUMAROLE
FUMITORY
FUSAROLE
FUSIFORM
GABORONE
GADABOUT
GADZOOKS
GARAMOND
GATEPOST
GEMOLOGY
GENEROUS
GEOPHONE
GIRASOLE
GIRLHOOD
GLABROUS
GLADSOME
GLASNOST
GLAUCOMA
GLAUCOUS
GLEESOME
GLORIOLE
GLORIOUS
GLUTTONY
GOALPOST
GOODWOOD
GORGEOUS
GRACIOUS
GREENOCK
GRIDLOCK
GRIEVOUS
GRUESOME
GYRATORY
HALFHOUR
HANDBOOK
HANDSOME
HARDCORE
HARDWOOD
HARTFORD
HAWTHORN
HEADLONG
HEADMOST
HEADROOM
HEADWORD
HECATOMB
HEGEMONY
HEIRLOOM
HELIPORT
HEREFORD
HERMIONE
HIGHBORN
HIGHROAD
HINDMOST
HOLYROOD
HOMEWORK
HONGKONG
HOOKWORM
HORNBOOK
HOROLOGY
HUMOROUS
HYDATOID
IDEOLOGY
ILLINOIS
ILLUSORY
INFAMOUS
IRISCOPE
IRONWOOD
IRONWORK
IROQUOIS
ISOGLOSS
JACKBOOT
JEREBOAM
JEROBOAM
JOHNSONS
JURATORY
KEYSTONE
KHARTOUM
KIDGLOVE
KILOVOLT
KINGPOST
KINSFOLK
KNOCKOUT
KNOTWORK
KOUSKOUS
LAMPPOST

LANDLOCK
LANDLORD
LAVATORY
LAYABOUT
LIBELOUS
LIFEBOAT
LIFELONG
LIGNEOUS
LIVELONG
LOBOTOMY
LONESOME
LONGBOAT
LONGHORN
LOOPHOLE
LOVELORN
LUMINOUS
LUSCIOUS
LUSTROUS
MACARONI
MACAROON
MAESTOSO
MAILBOAT
MALAKOFF
MALODOUR
MANDIOCA
MANGROVE
MANIFOLD
MANITOBA
MARABOUT
MARIGOLD
MARKDOWN
MATAMORE
MELANOMA
MELTDOWN
METABOLA
MILKWORT
MILLIONS
MILLPOND
MINATORY
MIREPOIX
MISQUOTE
MONGOOSE
MONOPOLY
MONOTONY
MOORCOCK
MUDSTONE
MULEWORT
MUSHROOM
MUTINOUS
MYCOLOGY
NAUSEOUS
NEBULOUS
NEMATODE
NEMATOID
NEWSROOM
NOSOLOGY
NOSTROMO

NOTEBOOK
NUCLEOLE
NUGATORY
NUMEROUS
NUMINOUS
OCTAROON
OENOLOGY
OFFSHOOT
OFFSHORE
OILCLOTH
OKLAHOMA
OMNIFORM
ONCOLOGY
ONTOLOGY
OPENDOOR
OPENWORK
OTOSCOPE
OUTDOORS
OVERBOOK
OVERCOAT
OVERCOME
OVERDONE
OVERDOSE
OVERLOAD
OVERLOOK
OVERLORD
OVERTONE
OVERWORK
PABULOUS
PALIMONY
PALINODE
PANGLOSS
PARABOLA
PARAMOUR
PARANOIA
PARANOID
PASSBOOK
PASSPORT
PASSWORD
PATULOUS
PEDAGOGY
PEEPHOLE
PEIGNOIR
PEMBROKE
PENELOPE
PENOLOGY
PEPERONI
PERILOUS
PERVIOUS
PHYLLOME
PICAROON
PICKLOCK
PILTDOWN
PINAFORE
PINEWOOD
PLATFORM
PLAYROOM

PLETHORA
PLIMSOLL
PLUGHOLE
POLTROON
POOLROOM
POPULOUS
PORTHOLE
POSOLOGY
POSTCODE
POSTPONE
POTATOES
PRECIOUS
PREVIOUS
PRIMROSE
PRINTOUT
PSALMODY
PULLDOWN
PYRIFORM
QUADROON
RAGSTONE
RAILROAD
RAINCOAT
RAVENOUS
REARMOST
RESINOUS
RESTROOM
RHAPSODY
RHOMBOID
RIBSTONE
RIGATONI
RIGOROUS
RINGDOVE
RINGWORM
ROLYPOLY
ROOFTOPS
ROSAMOND
ROSEWOOD
ROTATORY
ROTENONE
RUCTIONS
RULEBOOK
RUNABOUT
RUSHMORE
SAILBOAT
SAINFOIN
SALEROOM
SALUTORY
SARATOGA
SCABIOUS
SCABROUS
SCAFFOLD
SCAPHOID
SCHIZOID
SCHMOOZE
SCISSORS
SEAFRONT
SEASHORE

SEDULOUS
SEMITONE
SENSUOUS
SEROLOGY
SEXOLOGY
SHAKEOUT
SHALLOWS
SHAMROCK
SHAREOUT
SHERLOCK
SHERWOOD
SHOEHORN
SHOOTOUT
SHOWBOAT
SHOWDOWN
SHOWROOM
SHUTDOWN
SICKROOM
SIDELONG
SIGNPOST
SILICONE
SILKWORM
SINGSONG
SKIBOOTS
SKINWORK
SLOWDOWN
SLOWPOKE
SLYBOOTS
SOFTWOOD
SOLENOID
SOMEBODY
SONOROUS
SOUCHONG
SPACIOUS
SPECIOUS
SPITTOON
SPURIOUS
STAFFORD
STAGHORN
STAKEOUT
STANDOFF
STANHOPE
STEATOMA
STOPCOCK
STORMONT
STUBBORN
STUCCOED
STUDIOUS
SURFBOAT
SWANSONG
SYCAMORE
SYMBIONT
SYMPHONY
SYMPTOMS
SYNDROME
TAKEHOME
TANDOORI

TAPEWORM
TARBOOSH
TAXONOMY
TEACLOTH
TEAMWORK
TEASPOON
TELEGONY
TERATOMA
TEXTBOOK
THEOLOGY
THRENODY
TICKTOCK
TIMOROUS
TIRESOME
TOILSOME
TOLBOOTH
TOMATOES
TOPOLOGY
TORTUOUS
TRACHOMA
TRADEOFF
TRAITORS
TRAPDOOR
TREETOPS
TRICHOID
TROLLOPE
TROMBONE
TROTTOIR
TUBEROSE
TUBEROUS
TURNCOAT
TURNCOCK
ULCEROUS
UNCTUOUS
UNHEROIC
UNSAVORY
USURIOUS
UXORIOUS
VAGABOND
VARICOSE
VARIFORM
VENOMOUS
VIGOROUS
VIPEROUS
VIROLOGY
VIRTUOSI
VIRTUOSO
VIRTUOUS
VISIGOTH
VITREOUS
VOMITORY
WALLWORT
WARDROBE
WARDROOM
WASHBOWL
WASHDOWN
WASHROOM

WEDGWOOD
WEREWOLF
WHIPCORD
WILDFOWL
WINDHOEK
WINDSOCK
WIREWORM
WISHBONE
WITHHOLD
WONDROUS
WOODCOCK
WOODWORK
WOODWORM
WORDBOOK
WORKBOOK
WORKLOAD
WORKROOM
WORMWOOD
WRITEOFF
XANTHOMA
YAKITORI
YEARBOOK
YEARLONG
ZOETROPE
ZOOSPORE
BAGPIPES
BICUSPID
BOBBYPIN
CACHEPOT
CALLIPER
CHICKPEA
CHUTZPAH
COLLAPSE
CRACKPOT
DECOUPLE
DECREPIT
DIAZEPAM
DISCIPLE
ENCAMPED
ENTREPOT
EOHIPPUS
EPILEPSY
ESTOPPEL
ETHIOPIA
EUTROPHY
EUTROPIC
FELDSPAR
FINESPUN
GALLIPOT
GALLOPER
HARUSPEX
HEATSPOT
HOMESPUN
HONEYPOT
IMPROPER
INTERPOL
INTREPID

LARKSPUR
LIFESPAN
LINCHPIN
LOLLIPOP
MANCIPLE
MARZIPAN
MINCEPIE
MISAPPLY
MULTIPLE
MULTIPLY
MYRIAPOD
PHILIPPI
PHOTOPSY
PINNIPED
PLATYPUS
PROLAPSE
RECEIPTS
SAUCEPAN
SAUROPOD
SCHNAPPS
SCRAPPLE
SMALLPOX
SOUTHPAW
STOCKPOT
STRAPPED
STRAPPER
STRIPPED
STRIPPER
STRUMPET
SUBTOPIA
TAILSPIN
TERRAPIN
TETRAPOD
TURNSPIT
UNCOUPLE
UNDERPIN
UNTAPPED
WINGSPAN
WINNIPEG
XANTIPPE
APPLIQUÉ
BOUTIQUE
COLLOQUY
CRITIQUE
MYSTIQUE
PETANQUE
PHYSIQUE
ACQUIRED
ACQUIRER
AEROGRAM
AGACERIE
AGITPROP
AIRBORNE
AIRSCREW
AIRSTRIP
ALCATRAZ
ANCHORET
ANDORRAN
ANGSTROM
AOTEAROA
ARCTURUS
ARMOURED
AUTOCRAT
BACCARAT
BACKDROP
BACTERIA
BALEARIC
BALMORAL
BANDEROL
BARBARIC
BARNARDS
BARTERED
BATTERED
BEDSTRAW
BEGGARLY
BEGORRAH
BERBERIS
BERGERAC
BESMIRCH
BETATRON
BILBERRY
BISMARCK
BITTERLY
BORDERER
BOSWORTH
BOTHERED
BOWSPRIT
BRETHREN
BUGGERED
BULGARIA
BULLFROG
BULLYRAG
BUMMAREE
BURBERRY
BUTTERED
CALDERON
CALTHROP
CAMBERED
CANBERRA
CAREFREE
CAULDRON
CELLARER
CENTERED
CERBERUS
CEREBRAL
CEREBRUM
CHALDRON
CHANTREY
CHAPERON
CHARTRES
CHILDREN
CHOLERIC
CICATRIX
CLAPTRAP
CLEVERLY
CLITORIS
COCKCROW
COCKEREL
COLLARED
COLOURED
COMMERCE
COMPARED
CONCERTO
CONCORDE
CONJURER
CONJUROR
CONSERVE
CONSTRUE
CONVERGE
CONVERSE
CORDUROY
CORMORAN
CORPORAL
COUPERIN
COYSTRIL
CULTURAL
CULTURED
CULVERIN
CUTPURSE
DEMIURGE
DEMOCRAT
DEMURRAL
DENTURES
DEWBERRY
DIEHARDS
DIELDRIN
DIOPTRIC
DIPTERAL
DISAGREE
DISARRAY
DISBURSE
DISGORGE
DISPERSE
DISPIRIT
DOCTORAL
DOCTORED
DOGBERRY
DOGGEREL
DOTTEREL
DUTYFREE
DYNATRON
EASTERLY
ELECTRIC
ELECTRON
ELECTRUM
EPICURUS
EPIDURAL
ESOTERIC
ETHNARCH
EUPHORIA
EUPHORIC
EXPLORER
FATHERLY
FAVOURED
FEATURED
FEATURES
FILAGREE
FILIGREE
FIREARMS
FIRETRAP
FLAVORED
FOLDEROL
FORMERLY
FORWARDS
GALLERIA
GASWORKS
GATHERED
GENDARME
GENETRIX
GESTURES
GINGERLY
GLYCERIN
GRAMERCY
GRIDIRON
GUTTURAL
HAMMERED
HATTERAS
HEDGEROW
HEPTARCH
HETAIRIA
HEXAGRAM
HEYTHROP
HIERARCH
HIGHBROW
HISTORIC
HITHERTO
HOLOGRAM
HONDURAN
HONDURAS
HUMPHREY
HYSTERIA
HYSTERIC
IDEOGRAM
IMPAIRED
INFRARED
INQUIRER
INSPIRED
INSPIRIT
INTEGRAL
JACKAROO
JAMBOREE
JEOPARDY
JIGGERED
KANGAROO
KEDGEREE
KILOGRAM
KIPPERED
LABOURED
LABOURER
LATTERLY
LEAPFROG
LECTURER
LECTURES
LEISURED
LEONARDO
LETHARGY
LETTERED
LINGERIE
LISTERIA
LITTORAL
LOITERER
LOMBARDY
LOTHARIO
LOUVERED
LULWORTH
LUTHERAN
MACKEREL
MALLARMÉ
MALLORCA
MANDARIN
MANNERED
MANNERLY
MARGARET
MARJORAM
MARTYRED
MASCARON
MASTERLY
MATHURIN
MEASURED
MESMERIC
MÉTAIRIE
METEORIC
MINSTREL
MIRRORED
MISCARRY
MONAURAL
MONOGRAM
MOTHERLY
MULBERRY
MURDERER
NATTERED
NOCTURNE
NOMOGRAM
OBSCURED
OLDWORLD
OLIGARCH
OOPHORON
ORATORIO
OUTBURST
OUTSTRIP
OUTWARDS
OVERDRAW
OXYMORON
PAMPERED
PANDARUS
PARTERRE
PASSERBY
PASTORAL
PASTURES
PECTORAL
PEDIGREE
PENTARCH
PERFORCE
PERJURED
PERJURER
PERVERSE
PETRARCH
PICTURES
PILFERER
PILLARED
PINDARIC
PIZZERIA
PLASTRON
PLECTRUM
PLUTARCH
POLYARCH
POSITRON
POWDERED
PRECURSE
PREPARED
PRESERVE
PRETORIA
PROCURER
PROFORMA
PROGERIA
PROPERLY
PROPERTY
PROVERBS
PUCKERED
QUATORZE
RAINDROP
RAMPARTS
RECHARGE
RECOURSE
REFERRAL
REHEARSE
REPAIRER
REQUIRED
RESEARCH
RESOURCE
RESTORER
RHETORIC
RUMOURED
RUNNERUP
SANSERIF
SANSKRIT
SAVOURED
SCENARIO
SEABORNE
SEAFARER
SEAFORTH
SEAWARDS

SELBORNE
SHIVERED
SHOETREE
SIGNORIA
SISTERLY
SNOWDROP
SORCERER
SPANDREL
SPECTRAL
SPECTRUM
SQUADRON
SQUIRREL
STINGRAY
SUBMERGE
SUFFERER
SULFURIC
SUNBURNT
SUNBURST
TAMWORTH
TARTARIC
TARTARUS
TATTERED
TAYBERRY
TEARDROP
TELEGRAM
TELLURIC
TEMPERED
TEMPORAL
TENDERLY
TENEBRAE
TENEBRIO
TETRARCH
TEXTURED
THEATRIC
THEOCRAT
TIMBERED
TOMORROW
TONSURED
TORTURED
TORTURER
TRAVERSE
TRIMARAN
TRISTRAM
TURMERIC
UNAWARES
UNIVERSE
VALKYRIE
VARIORUM
VENTURED
VERDERER
VESPERAL
VICTORIA
VISCERAL
VULGARLY
WALKYRIE
WANDERER
WARFARIN
WARHORSE
WAXWORKS
WAYFARER
WELLBRED
WESTERLY
WHIMBREL
WINIFRED
WISTERIA
WITHDRAW
WITHERED
ZEPHYRUS
ZIGGURAT
ABOMASUM
ABSCISSA
ACCURSED
ALFRESCO
AMBROSIA
AMRITSAR
AMUNDSEN
ANABASIS
ANALYSER
ANALYSIS
ANCHISES
ANDERSON
ANGLESEY
APPRISED
ARKANSAS
ASSASSIN
ASSESSOR
AUBUSSON
AUCASSIN
BALLISTA
BAPTISED
BETHESDA
CALLISTO
CAROUSAL
CAROUSEL
CHAINSAW
CHARISMA
CLEANSED
CLEANSER
COALESCE
COLOSSAL
COLOSSUS
COMPOSED
COMPOSER
CONFUSED
CREVASSE
CYANOSIS
DAVIDSON
DECEASED
DEMERSAL
DIALYSIS
DIAPASON
DIARESIS
DIERESIS
DIOCESAN
DIONYSUS
DISEASED
DISPOSAL
DISPOSED
DISTASTE
DUCHESSE
ECSTASIS
ELLIPSIS
EMBOSSED
EMPHASIS
ENCLOSED
EPITASIS
ERIKSSON
ESPOUSAL
ESPRESSO
EUPEPSIA
EVANESCE
EXEGESIS
EXPENSES
EXPRESSO
EXTENSOR
FAMOUSLY
FANTASIA
FIBROSIS
FORENSIC
FORMOSAN
GARRISON
GEODESIC
GRANDSON
GUERNSEY
GUMMOSIS
HARASSED
HARRISON
HIDROSIS
HYPNOSIS
IMMERSED
IMPRISON
INCENSED
INTELSAT
JALOUSIE
JETTISON
JURASSIC
KERMESSE
KROMESKY
KYPHOSIS
LACROSSE
LARGESSE
LAROUSSE
LICENSED
LICENSEE
LORDOSIS
MACASSAR
MACHISMO
MAGNESIA
MALAYSIA
MALVASIA
MANTISSA
MARMOSET
MOCASSIN
MOCCASIN
MOLASSES
MOLLUSCS
MORRISON
NARCOSES
NARCOSIS
NEBRASKA
NECROSIS
NEUROSIS
NIJINSKY
OBSESSED
ODIOUSLY
PARMESAN
PARTISAN
PEVENSEY
PHARISEE
PHTHISIS
PREMISES
PROFUSER
PROMISED
PROPOSAL
PROPOSED
PROPOSER
PUGNOSED
QUICKSET
RECESSED
RELEASED
REPOUSSÉ
REPRISAL
REVERSAL
REVERSED
ROBINSON
ROMANSCH
RUBBISHY
SACRISTY
SARGASSO
SCHAPSKA
SELASSIE
SOMERSET
SOOTHSAY
STAROSTA
STENOSED
STENOSIS
STOKESAY
STRESSED
SUPPOSED
SYNOPSIS
TENNYSON
THICKSET
THOMPSON
TRAVESTY
TRIASSIC
UNBIASED
UNCHASTE
UNDERSEA
UNPERSON
UNREASON
UNVERSED
ZAKOUSKI
ZOONOSIS
ABDUCTED
ABDUCTOR
ABJECTLY
ABRUPTLY
ABSENTEE
ABSINTHE
ACCENTED
ACCENTOR
ACCEPTED
ACCUSTOM
ACOUSTIC
ACROSTIC
ADDICTED
ADENITIS
ADJUSTER
ADJUSTOR
ADRIATIC
ADROITLY
ADULATOR
AEGROTAT
AEROSTAT
AFFECTED
AFFLATUS
AGITATED
AGITATOR
AGNOSTIC
AIGRETTE
ALCESTIS
AMARETTO
AMORETTI
AMORETTO
AMUSETTE
ANABATIC
ANCESTOR
ANCESTRY
ANIMATED
ANISETTE
APERITIF
APPLETON
ARDENTLY
ARGESTES
AROMATIC
ARRESTED
ARRESTER
ARTISTIC
ARTISTRY
ASBESTOS
ASSORTED
ATHLETIC
ATLANTIC
ATLANTIS
ATTESTOR
AUGUSTUS
AUTISTIC
BAGUETTE
BALUSTER
BANDITTI
BANISTER
BARRATRY
BARRETTE
BASKETRY
BATHETIC
BEGETTER
BELITTLE
BESOTTED
BLIGHTER
BRIGHTEN
BRIGHTLY
BRIGHTON
BROMPTON
BRUNETTE
BULLETIN
BURSITIS
CADASTRE
CALCUTTA
CANISTER
CARYATID
CASSETTE
CATHETER
CHAPATTI
CHRISTEN
CHRISTIE
CHRISTOM
CILIATED
CLEMATIS
CLIMATIC
CLOISTER
COCKATOO
COLLATOR
COMMUTER
COMPUTER
CONFETTI
COQUETRY
COQUETTE
CORNETTO
CORVETTE
COSMETIC
COVENTRY
CRAVATES
CREDITOR
CREPITUS
CRICHTON
CURSITOR
CUTWATER
CYSTITIS
DALMATIC
DAUGHTER
DECANTER
DECENTLY

DECLUTCH
DECRETAL
DEFEATED
DEFECTOR
DEJECTED
DEMENTED
DEMENTIA
DEMISTER
DEPARTED
DEPORTEE
DESERTED
DESERTER
DESPATCH
DESPOTIC
DETECTOR
DETRITUS
DIABETES
DIABETIC
DIAMETER
DICTATES
DICTATOR
DIDACTIC
DIRECTLY
DIRECTOR
DISASTER
DISINTER
DISKETTE
DISPATCH
DISPUTED
DIURETIC
DOGMATIC
DOGWATCH
DOMESTIC
DOORSTEP
DRAGSTER
DRAMATIC
DYNASTIC
ECLECTIC
ECSTATIC
EDUCATED
EDUCATOR
EGOISTIC
EIDECTIC
ELDRITCH
ELEVATED
ELEVATOR
ELLIPTIC
EMBATTLE
EMBITTER
EMERITUS
EMIRATES
EMPHATIC
ENCLOTHE
ENIWETOK
ESTHETIC
EUROSTAR
EUSTATIC
EXECUTED
EXECUTOR
EXEGETIC
EXPECTED
EXPORTER
FACTOTUM
FAINITES
FALSETTO
FENESTRA
FIRESTEP
FLUENTLY
FOOTSTEP
FORESTAY
FORESTER
FORESTRY
FREMITUS
FRENETIC
FRIGHTEN
GADGETRY
GALACTIC
GANGSTER
GARROTTE
GELASTIC
GEOMETER
GEOMETRY
GIGANTIC
GOLGOTHA
GRAVITAS
GRISETTE
GUNMETAL
GUSSETED
GYROSTAT
HAMILTON
HEIGHTEN
HELMETED
HELVETIA
HERMETIC
HERPETIC
HIAWATHA
HIERATIC
HOLISTIC
HONESTLY
HOSPITAL
HUCKSTER
HYPNOTIC
IDOLATER
IDOLATRY
ILLFATED
IMITATOR
IMMORTAL
IMPACTED
IMPORTER
IMPOSTER
IMPOSTOR
INDEBTED
INDENTED
INDUSTRY
INFANTRY
INFECTED
INFESTED
INFLATED
INJECTOR
INTENTLY
INVENTED
INVENTOR
INVERTED
INVESTOR
IOLANTHE
ISOLATED
JACKETED
JEANETTE
KINGSTON
KNIGHTLY
KRAKATOA
LAMENTED
LAUGHTER
LEINSTER
LIBRETTO
LOADSTAR
LODESTAR
LOGISTIC
LONGSTAY
LONGSTOP
MAGISTER
MAGNETIC
MAINSTAY
MAJESTIC
MANDATED
MAQUETTE
MEDIATOR
MERCATOR
MERISTEM
METRITIS
MINISTER
MINISTRY
MIRLITON
MISMATCH
MODESTLY
MOLESTER
MOMENTUM
MONASTIC
MOQUETTE
MUSCATEL
MYELITIS
MYOSOTIS
NARCOTIC
NARRATOR
NEMBUTAL
NEPENTHE
NEURITIS
NEUROTIC
NOISETTE
NUTHATCH
OBJECTOR
ODOMETER
OMELETTE
OPERATIC
OPERATOR
OPERETTA
ORCHITIS
ORIENTAL
OUTDATED
OUTMATCH
OVERSTAY
OVERSTEP
PAKISTAN
PALMATED
PALMETTO
PARENTAL
PARIETAL
PATENTED
PATENTEE
PATENTLY
PATHETIC
PEDANTIC
PEDANTRY
PEDESTAL
PELLETED
PHONETIC
PHREATIC
PIERETTE
PILASTER
PISCATOR
PLANKTON
POCHETTE
POLLSTER
POLLUTED
POLLUTER
POTLATCH
PREDATOR
PRENATAL
PRIESTLY
PRIVATES
PROMOTER
PROMPTER
PROMPTLY
PYELITIS
QUAESTOR
QUAINTLY
QUIXOTIC
RACHITIS
RACLETTE
RADIATOR
RAMBUTAN
RASPUTIN
REBUTTAL
RECENTLY
RECEPTOR
REDACTOR
REGISTER
REGISTRY
REMITTAL
REPARTEE
REPEATED
REPEATER
REPORTED
REPORTER
RESETTLE
RESISTOR
RHEOSTAT
ROADSTER
ROBUSTLY
ROCKETRY
ROMANTIC
ROSSETTI
ROULETTE
SADISTIC
SATIATED
SCIMITAR
SCREWTOP
SCRIPTUM
SCULPTOR
SEAMSTER
SECRETLY
SELECTED
SELECTOR
SEMESTER
SEMIOTIC
SERIATIM
SERRATED
SERVITOR
SHERATON
SIDESTEP
SILENTLY
SINISTER
SITUATED
SKELETAL
SKELETON
SLIGHTED
SLIGHTLY
SOCRATES
SOCRATIC
SONGSTER
SPINSTER
SPIRITED
SPIRITUS
SPLATTER
SPLINTER
SPLITTER
SPLUTTER
SPRINTER
SQUATTER
STEALTHY
STILETTO
STRAITEN
STRIATED
STRIATUM
STRICTLY
SUBTITLE
SUBTOTAL
SUMMITRY
SUNBATHE
SUPERTAX
SYMMETRY
SYMPATHY
SYNOPTIC
TALENTED
TAPESTRY
TEAMSTER
TEETOTAL
TESTATOR
TESTATUM
THANATOS
THEMATIC
THREATEN
THROTTLE
THRUSTER
TINNITUS
TOMENTUM
TOPNOTCH
TUNGSTEN
TURRETED
UDOMETER
UNABATED
UNBEATEN
UNBUTTON
UNDERTOW
UNFASTEN
UNFETTER
UNHEATED
UNJUSTLY
UNLISTED
UNSALTED
UNSETTLE
UNSTATED
UNSUITED
UNWANTED
UNWONTED
UNWORTHY
URGENTLY
VACANTLY
VALLETTA
VARIETAL
VENDETTA
VERBATIM
VIBRATOR
VIGNETTE
VIOLATOR
ABSOLUTE
ABSTRUSE
ALEHOUSE
ALLELUIA
ALTHOUGH
ALTITUDE
AMATEURS

APERTURE
APPLAUSE
APTITUDE
AQUALUNG
AQUEDUCT
ARCHDUKE
ARETHUSA
ARMATURE
ATTITUDE
AVIFAUNA
BANKRUPT
BAYREUTH
BELLPUSH
BERCEUSE
BIANNUAL
BISEXUAL
BLASTULA
BOUZOUKI
BRADBURY
BROCHURE
CALIGULA
CATAPULT
CATHOUSE
CENTAURY
CHIPMUNK
COIFFURE
COMPOUND
CONCLUDE
CONFOUND
CREATURE
CYNOSURE
DANDRUFF
DENATURE
DESTRUCT
DISABUSE
DISCOUNT
DISMOUNT
DISTRUST
DJIBOUTI
DOGHOUSE
DOLDRUMS
DORMOUSE
DOWNTURN
DUMFOUND
ELKHOUND
EMMANUEL
ERUPTURE
EVENTUAL
EXPOSURE
FATIGUED
FATIGUES
FOGBOUND
FOXHOUND
FRACTURE
FURLOUGH
GASTRULA
GERTRUDE
HABITUAL
HABSBURG
HALFFULL
HANDCUFF
HAPSBURG
HEADHUNT
HEBETUDE
HENHOUSE
HICCOUGH
HONOLULU
HOTHOUSE
HUSHHUSH
ICEHOUSE
IMMANUEL
IMMATURE
INASMUCH
INSECURE
INSTRUCT
INVOLUTE
JEALOUSY
JODHPURS
JOINTURE
JUMPSUIT
JUNCTURE
LANSBURY
LATITUDE
LAWCOURT
LIFEBUOY
LIGATURE
MADHOUSE
MAMELUKE
MANICURE
MASSEUSE
MISCOUNT
MISSOURI
MISTRUST
MOISTURE
MOLECULE
MONMOUTH
MONOHULL
MORIBUND
NEWFOUND
NIBELUNG
NONESUCH
NUTHOUSE
OBSTRUCT
OPUSCULE
OUTHOUSE
OVERFULL
OVERMUCH
OVERRULE
OVERTURE
OVERTURN
PARAGUAY
PARAQUAT
PEDICURE
PERACUTE
PIECRUST
PLAYSUIT
PLEASURE
PLYMOUTH
POTBOUND
PRECLUDE
PRESSURE
PROFOUND
PROPOUND
PROTRUDE
PUNCTUAL
PUNCTURE
QUIETUDE
QUINCUNX
RAMEQUIN
READJUST
REASSUME
REASSURE
REINSURE
RESIDUAL
RESIDUUM
RESOLUTE
RETICULE
RIDICULE
RUBICUND
SCHEDULE
SCROFULA
SHANTUNG
SHELDUCK
SINECURE
SOAPSUDS
SOLITUDE
SOURPUSS
STARDUST
SURMOUNT
SURROUND
SWIMSUIT
SYRACUSE
TACITURN
TAPHOUSE
THOROUGH
TINCTURE
TITMOUSE
TOULOUSE
TRANQUIL
TREASURE
TREASURY
TRINCULO
USUFRUCT
VANBRUGH
VERMOUTH
VISCOUNT
WINDBURN
YOGHOURT
ZASTRUGA
ABSOLVED
ACHIEVED
ACHIEVER
AIRWAVES
APPROVAL
APPROVED
ARCHIVES
BEDCOVER
BELIEVER
BEREAVED
BICONVEX
CARNIVAL
CORDOVAN
CZAREVNA
DECEIVER
DECEMVIR
DEPRAVED
DEPRIVED
DESERVED
DISCOVER
DISFAVOR
DISHEVEL
EFFLUVIA
ENDEAVOR
ENGRAVER
FESTIVAL
GINGIVAL
GULLIVER
HANDOVER
HANGOVER
HAYFEVER
IMPROVED
IMPROVER
INTERVAL
INVOLVED
KESTEVEN
LEFTOVER
MALDIVES
MANEUVER
MEDIEVAL
MONROVIA
MOREOVER
NEWHAVEN
OBSERVED
OBSERVER
PASSOVER
PERCEVAL
PERCIVAL
PRIMEVAL
PULLOVER
PUSHOVER
RECEIVED
RECEIVER
RELIEVED
REPLEVIN
RESERVED
RESOLVED
REVOLVER
SLIPOVER
STOPOVER
SULLIVAN
SURVIVAL
SURVIVOR
TAKEOVER
TOPLEVEL
TSAREVNA
TURNOVER
UNCLOVEN
UNNERVED
UNSOLVED
UPHEAVAL
WALKOVER
WHATEVER
WHENEVER
WHEREVER
ALLEYWAY
ANDREWES
BESTOWER
BORROWED
BORROWER
BROADWAY
BURROWER
CABLEWAY
CARRAWAY
CASTAWAY
CAUSEWAY
CLEARWAY
DEFLOWER
DRIVEWAY
FOLLOWED
FOLLOWER
FOLLOWUP
FURROWED
GALLOWAY
GIVEAWAY
GOLLIWOG
HALLOWED
HATCHWAY
HATHAWAY
HIDEAWAY
HOLLOWAY
INGROWTH
MANPOWER
MILDEWED
MOTORWAY
NARROWLY
PANDOWDY
REVIEWER
RIDGEWAY
SOAKAWAY
SPEEDWAY
SPILLWAY
STAIRWAY
STEINWAY
STOWAWAY
TAKEAWAY
TEARAWAY
THATAWAY
TIGHTWAD
WATERWAY
ANOREXIA
ANOREXIC
ASPHYXIA
ATARAXIA
ATARAXIC
CACHEXIA
DYSLEXIA
DYSLEXIC
GEOTAXIS
SPARAXIS
SYNTEXIS
AERODYNE
ALDEHYDE
AMETHYST
ANAGLYPH
ANEURYSM
APOLLYON
AUTOGYRO
AUTOTYPE
BETRAYAL
BETRAYER
BISCAYAN
CALOTYPE
CATALYST
COCKAYNE
COCKEYED
CONVEYOR
DEWYEYED
DISLOYAL
DISMAYED
EMPLOYED
EMPLOYEE
EMPLOYER
EPIPHYTE
EPISTYLE
GARGOYLE
KILOBYTE
KUFFIYEH
LINOTYPE
MEGABYTE
METONYMY
MISOGYNY
MONOTYPE
NEOPHYTE
OLDSTYLE
PANEGYRY
PARALYZE
PAROXYSM
PORPHYRA
PORPHYRY
PURVEYOR
RUBAIYAT
SEROTYPE

STAPHYLE
STOREYED
SURVEYOR
TAXPAYER
TRIGLYPH
TRIPTYCH
WESLEYAN
ZOOPHYTE
AGONIZED
ATOMIZER
BARBIZON
BRABAZON
CAPSIZED
EMBEZZLE
EMBLAZON
HOWITZER
KIBITZER
PROTOZOA
PULITZER
SPRITZER
SQUEEZER
STYLIZED

8:7

ABNORMAL
ACIDHEAD
AEGROTAT
AEROGRAM
AEROSTAT
AGRARIAN
AKKADIAN
ALBANIAN
ALCATRAZ
ALDERMAN
ALEUTIAN
ALGERIAN
ALLEYWAY
ALLUVIAL
ALSATIAN
AMERICAN
AMERICAS
AMMONIAC
AMRITSAR
ANDORRAN
ANGLICAN
ANTENNAE
APPROVAL
ARAMAEAN
ARBOREAL
ARCADIAN
ARKANSAS
ARMAGNAC
ARMENIAN
ARMORIAL
ARTERIAL
ARTESIAN
ASCIDIAN
ASSYRIAN
ATHENIAN
ATYPICAL
AURELIAN
AUSTRIAN
AUTOCRAT
AUTUMNAL
BACCARAT
BACKCHAT
BACTRIAN
BAHAMIAN
BALMORAL
BANDSMAN
BARABBAS
BARBICAN
BARGEMAN
BARNABAS
BARONIAL
BATAVIAN
BAVARIAN
BEDSTEAD
BEDSTRAW
BEGORRAH
BERGERAC
BETJEMAN
BETRAYAL
BIANNUAL
BIBLICAL
BIENNIAL
BILLYCAN
BINOMIAL
BIRTHDAY
BISCAYAN
BISEXUAL
BLACKCAP
BLUECOAT
BOATLOAD
BODLEIAN
BOEOTIAN
BOGEYMAN
BOHEMIAN
BOLIVIAN
BONDSMAN
BONEHEAD
BRACHIAL
BRADSHAW
BRICKBAT
BROADWAY
BROUGHAM
BROWBEAT
BULKHEAD
BULLYRAG
CABLECAR
CABLEWAY
CADILLAC
CALENDAR
CAMBRIAN
CANADIAN
CANNIBAL
CARDIGAN
CARDINAL
CARNIVAL
CAROUSAL
CARRAWAY
CARTLOAD
CASTAWAY
CATSMEAT
CAUSEWAY
CELERIAC
CELLULAR
CEREBRAL
CERULEAN
CERVELAT
CERVICAL
CETACEAN
CHAINSAW
CHAIRMAN
CHALDEAN
CHARCOAL
CHEMICAL
CHESSMAN
CHINAMAN
CHITCHAT
CHUTZPAH
CINEREAL
CINNABAR
CIRCULAR
CIVILIAN
CLANSMAN
CLAPTRAP
CLEARWAY
CLERICAL
CLINICAL
COACHMAN
COCCIDAE
COCHLEAR
COLESLAW
COLONIAL
COLOSSAL
COLUMBAN
COMEDIAN
COMMUNAL
CONJUGAL
CONSULAR
CORDOVAN
CORMORAN
CORPORAL
CORSICAN
CRIMINAL
CRISPIAN
CRITICAL
CROATIAN
CROSSBAR
CULLINAN
CULTURAL
CYCLICAL
CYRENIAC
DAIRYMAN
DAYBREAK
DAYDREAM
DEADBEAT
DEADHEAD
DECRETAL
DEMERSAL
DEMOCRAT
DEMONIAC
DEMURRAL
DIAGONAL
DIAZEPAM
DIOCESAN
DIPLOMAT
DIPTERAL
DISARRAY
DISLOYAL
DISPOSAL
DOCTORAL
DOMESDAY
DOOMSDAY
DOWNBEAT
DOWNLOAD
DOWNPLAY
DRIVEWAY
DROPHEAD
DRUMBEAT
DRUMHEAD
DRYCLEAN
DUODENAL
DUTCHMAN
ECOFREAK
EGYPTIAN
EMPYREAN
EPHESIAN
EPIDURAL
ESCORIAL
ESPECIAL
ESPOUSAL
ESTONIAN
ETHEREAL
ETRURIAN
ETRUSCAN
EUDOXIAN
EURASIAN
EUROPEAN
EUROSTAR
EVENTUAL
EVERYDAY
EVERYMAN
EXEMPLAR
EXTERNAL
EXTERNAT
FAMILIAR
FANCYMAN
FARCICAL
FELDSPAR
FERRYMAN
FESTIVAL
FIRETRAP
FISHMEAL
FOOLSCAP
FOOTWEAR
FOREBEAR
FOREHEAD
FORESTAY
FORMOSAN
FORSWEAR
FRESHMAN
FREUDIAN
FRONTMAN
FUGLEMAN
FUNEREAL
GALILEAN
GALLOWAY
GEORGIAN
GERMINAL
GHANAIAN
GINGIVAL
GIVEAWAY
GLOBULAR
GOODYEAR
GRANULAR
GRAVITAS
GREENBAG
GROSBEAK
GUARDIAN
GUIANIAN
GUNMETAL
GUTTURAL
GYROSTAT
HABITUAL
HAGGADAH
HALFYEAR
HANDCLAP
HANDICAP
HANDYMAN
HANNIBAL
HANUKKAH
HARRIDAN
HATCHWAY
HATHAWAY
HATTERAS
HAVILDAR
HAWAIIAN
HEADGEAR
HELMSMAN
HENCHMAN
HERDSMAN
HEXAGRAM
HIDEAWAY
HIGHROAD
HOGMANAY
HOGSHEAD
HOLLOWAY
HOLOGRAM
HOLYHEAD
HONDURAN
HONDURAS
HOOLIGAN
HORATIAN
HORMONAL
HORNBEAM
HORSEMAN
HOSPITAL
HOUSEMAN
HUNTSMAN
IDEOGRAM
IMMORTAL
IMPERIAL
INDIAMAN
INFERNAL
INFORMAL
INGUINAL
INIMICAL
INTEGRAL
INTELSAT
INTERNAL
INTERVAL
IRISHMAN
IRONCLAD
IRONICAL
ISOGONAL
ISTHMIAN
JACOBEAN
JAMAICAN
JEPHTHAH
JEREBOAM
JEREMIAD
JEREMIAH
JEROBOAM
JERRYCAN
JONATHAN
JUDICIAL
KATTEGAT
KICKSHAW
KILOGRAM
KNITWEAR
KORRIGAN
LACKADAY
LACONIAN
LEADSMAN
LEONIDAS
LIBERIAN
LIEGEMAN
LIFEBOAT

LIFESPAN
LINESMAN
LINNAEAN
LITTORAL
LOADSTAR
LODESTAR
LONGBOAT
LONGSTAY
LUPERCAL
LUTHERAN
MACASSAR
MACAULAY
MADRIGAL
MADWOMAN
MAECENAS
MAGELLAN
MAGICIAN
MAILBOAT
MAINSTAY
MALARIAL
MALAWIAN
MALTREAT
MANIACAL
MANORIAL
MARGINAL
MARIANAS
MARJORAM
MARKSMAN
MARZIPAN
MASTHEAD
MATERIAL
MATERNAL
MEDIEVAL
MEMORIAL
MEMORIAM
MENSWEAR
MERIDIAN
METRICAL
MICHIGAN
MILLIBAR
MINDANAO
MINEHEAD
MINUTIAE
MISTREAT
MOLUCCAS
MONAURAL
MONDRIAN
MONOGRAM
MOONBEAM
MORAVIAN
MOROCCAN
MOTORCAR
MOTORMAN
MOTORWAY
MUHAMMAD
MULLIGAN
MUSCULAR
MUSICIAN
MYSTICAL
MYTHICAL
NAMIBIAN
NATIONAL
NAUTICAL
NECKWEAR
NEMBUTAL
NENUPHAR
NEWSPEAK
NICHOLAS
NIGERIAN
NIGHTCAP
NIGHTJAR
NOBLEMAN
NOMOGRAM
NORSEMAN
NOTARIAL
NOTIONAL
OBSIDIAN
OEDIPEAN
OFFBREAK
OFFICIAL
OLEACEAE
OLYMPIAD
OLYMPIAN
OMDURMAN
OPENPLAN
OPHIDIAN
OPOPANAX
OPTICIAN
OPTIONAL
ORCADIAN
ORIENTAL
ORIGINAL
OUTBREAK
OVERCOAT
OVERDRAW
OVERHEAD
OVERHEAR
OVERHEAT
OVERLEAF
OVERLOAD
OVERPLAY
OVERSEAS
OVERSTAY
PAKISTAN
PALATIAL
PANCREAS
PARAGUAY
PARALLAX
PARAQUAT
PARENTAL
PARIETAL
PARISIAN
PARMESAN
PARSIFAL
PARTHIAN
PARTISAN
PASTORAL
PATELLAR
PATERNAL
PECTORAL
PECULIAR
PEDESTAL
PEMMICAN
PERCEVAL
PERCIVAL
PERSONAL
PERUVIAN
PHRYGIAN
PHYSICAL
PISSHEAD
PLACEMAT
PLEBEIAN
POETICAL
POPINJAY
PORTUGAL
PRAIRIAL
PRANDIAL
PREMOLAR
PRENATAL
PRESSMAN
PRIMEVAL
PRODIGAL
PROPOSAL
PRUSSIAN
PUBLICAN
PUNCTUAL
PUSSYCAT
PUSTULAR
QUIRINAL
RAILHEAD
RAILROAD
RAINCOAT
RAINWEAR
RAMBUTAN
RASSELAS
RATIONAL
RATTIGAN
REAPPEAR
REBUTTAL
REEDSMAN
REFERRAL
REGIONAL
REMEDIAL
REMITTAL
REPRISAL
RESIDUAL
REVERSAL
RHEOSTAT
RICKSHAW
RIDGEWAY
RIFLEMAN
RIPARIAN
ROMANIAN
ROUSSEAU
RUBAIYAT
SAILBOAT
SALESMAN
SAMIZDAT
SATURDAY
SAUCEPAN
SAVANNAH
SCAPULAR
SCIMITAR
SCOTSMAN
SEALYHAM
SEASONAL
SEEDSMAN
SHANGHAI
SHEARMAN
SHERIDAN
SHOWBOAT
SIBERIAN
SICILIAN
SIDEREAL
SIDESMAN
SILESIAN
SILURIAN
SINGULAR
SIRENIAN
SKELETAL
SKINHEAD
SKULLCAP
SNACKBAR
SOAKAWAY
SOMEWHAT
SOOTHSAY
SOUTHPAW
SPACEMAN
SPECTRAL
SPEEDWAY
SPELLMAN
SPILLWAY
SPITHEAD
STAIRWAY
STEINWAY
STENDHAL
STINGRAY
STOCKCAR
STOCKMAN
STOKESAY
STOREMAN
STOWAWAY
SUBHUMAN
SUBTOTAL
SUBURBAN
SUICIDAL
SULLIVAN
SUMERIAN
SUNCREAM
SUPERMAN
SUPERNAL
SUPERTAX
SURFBOAT
SURGICAL
SURVIVAL
TABBYCAT
TABLEMAT
TACTICAL
TAHITIAN
TAKEAWAY
TALISMAN
TEARAWAY
TEETOTAL
TELEGRAM
TEMPORAL
TENEBRAE
TERMINAL
THATAWAY
THEOCRAT
THESPIAN
THRACIAN
THURSDAY
TIBERIAS
TIEBREAK
TIGHTWAD
TIRESIAS
TOBOGGAN
TOWNSMAN
TRASHCAN
TRIBUNAL
TRIMARAN
TRINIDAD
TRISTRAM
TRITICAL
TROPICAL
TUNISIAN
TURKOMAN
TURNCOAT
TUTORIAL
TYROLEAN
UNDERLAY
UNIPOLAR
UNSOCIAL
UNTHREAD
UPHEAVAL
UPSTREAM
VALERIAN
VALVULAR
VARIETAL
VASCULAR
VENEREAL
VENETIAN
VERANDAH
VERTICAL
VESPERAL
VICARIAL
VIRGINAL
VISCERAL
VOLSCIAN
WATCHMAN
WATERMAN
WATERWAY
WELSHMAN
WESLEYAN
WHEATEAR
WHINCHAT
WHITECAP
WINGSPAN
WITHDRAW
WOODSMAN
WORKADAY
WORKLOAD
YATAGHAN
YUGOSLAV
ZAMINDAR
ZEDEKIAH
ZIGGURAT
ZODIACAL
BATHROBE
COBWEBBY
DESCRIBE
DIATRIBE
INSCRIBE
KOHLRABI
MANITOBA
PASSERBY
PONSONBY
PROVERBS
RENMINBI
WARDROBE
ABEYANCE
ABSTRACT
ACAPULCO
ACCURACY
ADEQUACY
ADVOCACY
AEROBICS
ALBERICH
ALFRESCO
ALLIANCE
ALLSPICE
AMBIANCE
AMBIENCE
ANGELICA
ANNOUNCE
ANYPLACE
APPROACH
AQUEDUCT
ARMORICA
ARTEFACT
ARTIFACT
ARTIFICE

AUDIENCE
BACKPACK
BALDRICK
BALLCOCK
BAREBACK
BASILICA
BAUDRICK
BENEDICK
BENEDICT
BENEFICE
BESMIRCH
BISMARCK
BLUEBACK
BONIFACE
BOOTNECK
BRASSICA
BRATPACK
BUOYANCY
CARAPACE
CATARACT
CELIBACY
CERAMICS
CHARLOCK
CLARENCE
CLASSICS
CLAWBACK
CLEMENCY
COALESCE
COATRACK
CODPIECE
COMEBACK
COMMENCE
COMMERCE
CONFLICT
CONTRACT
CONVINCE
CROMLECH
CRUMMOCK
CURRENCY
CUTPRICE
DABCHICK
DEADLOCK
DECLUTCH
DEFIANCE
DELICACY
DENOUNCE
DERELICT
DESELECT
DESPATCH
DESTRUCT
DEVIANCE
DIFFRACT
DIPSTICK
DISGRACE
DISPATCH
DISPLACE
DISTANCE
DISTINCT
DISTRACT
DISTRICT
DOGWATCH
DRAWBACK
DYNAMICS
EARPIECE
EFFICACY
ELDRITCH
ELEGANCE
EMINENCE
ENCROACH
ENSCONCE
ENTRANCE
ENTRENCH
ETHNARCH
EUGENICS
EURYDICE
EVANESCE
EVIDENCE
EXIGENCY
EYEPIECE
FASTBACK
FATSTOCK
FEDERACY
FEEDBACK
FIREBACK
FLAMENCO
FLAPJACK
FLORENCE
FOREDECK
FORELOCK
FORSLACK
FULLBACK
GENETICS
GEOMANCY
GIMCRACK
GOBSMACK
GRAMERCY
GRAPHICS
GREENOCK
GRIDLOCK
GUIDANCE
HARDBACK
HARDTACK
HAWFINCH
HAYSTACK
HEPATICA
HEPTARCH
HIERARCH
HOMESICK
HUMPBACK
INASMUCH
INDIRECT
INSTANCE
INSTINCT
INSTRUCT
INTERACT
INTIMACY
INTRENCH
JAPONICA
JAUNDICE
JIMCRACK
JOYSTICK
KICKBACK
KINETICS
KNAPSACK
KREPLACH
LAIDBACK
LANDLOCK
LANDRACE
LAURENCE
LAWRENCE
LENIENCY
LICORICE
LIMERICK
LIPSTICK
LITERACY
LOVELACE
LOVESICK
MAJOLICA
MALLORCA
MANDIOCA
MAVERICK
MILLRACE
MISMATCH
MISPLACE
MOLLUSCS
MOORCOCK
NECKLACE
NICKNACK
NONESUCH
NONSTICK
NUISANCE
NUMERACY
NUTHATCH
OBDURACY
OBSTRUCT
OILSLICK
OLIGARCH
OLYMPICS
ONETRACK
OPULENCE
ORDNANCE
OUTMATCH
OUTREACH
OVERMUCH
PALEFACE
PARLANCE
PATIENCE
PAYCHECK
PENTARCH
PENZANCE
PERFORCE
PETRARCH
PHARMACY
PICKLOCK
PICKWICK
PINPRICK
PIQUANCY
PITTANCE
PLAYBACK
PLUTARCH
POLITICO
POLITICS
POLYARCH
POPULACE
POTLATCH
POULTICE
PRACTICE
PRECINCT
PRESENCE
PRETENCE
PROPHECY
PROSPECT
PROVINCE
PRUDENCE
PUNGENCY
RADIANCE
REDBRICK
REDIRECT
RELIANCE
RENOUNCE
REPROACH
RESEARCH
RESOURCE
RESTRICT
RETRENCH
RIDDANCE
ROBOTICS
RODERICK
ROMANSCH
RUCKSACK
SALTLICK
SANDWICH
SCARFACE
SCIATICA
SCIROCCO
SENTENCE
SEQUENCE
SHADRACH
SHAMROCK
SHELDUCK
SHERLOCK
SHOELACE
SIDEKICK
SIXPENCE
SKIPJACK
SLAPJACK
SOLSTICE
SOLVENCY
STOPCOCK
SUBTRACT
SUCCINCT
SUNDANCE
SURPLICE
TAILBACK
TENDENCY
TETRARCH
TICKTACK
TICKTOCK
TITICACA
TOISEACH
TOPNOTCH
TOVARICH
TRANSACT
TRANSECT
TRIPTYCH
TRISTICH
TURNBACK
TURNCOCK
TWOPIECE
TYPEFACE
USUFRUCT
VAGRANCY
VARIANCE
VERJUICE
VERONICA
VESPUCCI
VIBRANCY
VIOLENCE
VOIDANCE
WHIPJACK
WINDSOCK
WOODCOCK
WOOLPACK
WOOLSACK
ZWIEBACK
ABBASIDE
ACCOLADE
ACTINIDE
ADELAIDE
ADENOIDS
ALDEHYDE
ALTITUDE
ANACONDA
ANNELIDA
ANTECEDE
ANTIBODY
APTITUDE
ATTITUDE
BACKSIDE
BADLANDS
BARNARDS
BELGRADE
BESTRIDE
BETHESDA
BIGARADE
BLOCKADE
BRANDADE
BURGUNDY
BUSYBODY
CENTRODE
CHARLADY
CHILLADA
CHLORIDE
COINCIDE
COLORADO
COMMANDO
CONCLUDE
CONCORDE
DIAMONDS
DIEHARDS
DISSUADE
DOCKSIDE
DOGSBODY
DOWNSIDE
DRYGOODS
ELDORADO
ENFILADE
ESCALADE
ESCAPADE
EVENTIDE
EYESHADE
FIRESIDE
FLUORIDE
FOREBODE
FORWARDS
GADOGADO
GANYMEDE
GENOCIDE
GERTRUDE
GIACONDA
GIOCONDA
GLISSADE
GRIMALDI
GRISELDA
HACIENDA
HANDMADE
HEBETUDE
HILLSIDE
HOKKAIDO
HOMEMADE
HOMICIDE
HOWDYEDO
HUNDREDS
INNUENDO
INTIFADA
IRONSIDE
JEOPARDY
KATMANDU
LANDLADY
LATITUDE
LEMONADE
LEONARDO

LOMBARDY
LOWLANDS
MACREADY
MALGRADO
MARINADE
MIDLANDS
MISGUIDE
MONOXIDE
NEMATODE
NORMANDY
OEILLADE
OUTWARDS
OVERRIDE
PALINODE
PALISADE
PANDOWDY
PEROXIDE
PERSUADE
POSTCODE
PRECLUDE
PROCEEDS
PROTRUDE
PSALMODY
PYRAMIDS
QUAYSIDE
QUIETUDE
REGICIDE
RENEGADE
REYNOLDS
RHAPSODY
RINGSIDE
ROADSIDE
SEAWARDS
SELFMADE
SERENADE
SOAPSUDS
SOLITUDE
SOMEBODY
STAMPEDE
STOCKADE
SUCCEEDS
SULPHIDE
SUNSHADE
TAPENADE
THRENODY
UNSTEADY
UNWIELDY
WETLANDS
YULETIDE
AASVOGEL
ABDUCTED
ABERDEEN
ABRIDGED
ABSENTEE
ABSOLVED
ABSORBED
ABSORBER
ACCENTED
ACCEPTED
ACCURSED
ACHIEVED
ACHIEVER
ACHILLES
ACQUIRED
ACQUIRER
ADDICTED
ADJUSTER
ADVANCED
ADVANCER
AFFECTED
AGITATED
AGONIZED
AIRLINER
AIRSCREW
AIRSPEED
AIRWAVES
ALDERNEY
ALLERGEN
ALPHABET
AMBUSHED
AMUNDSEN
ANALYSER
ANCHISES
ANCHORET
ANDREWES
ANGLESEY
ANIMATED
ANNEALER
ANTILLES
APOSTLES
APPALLED
APPRISED
APPROVED
ARCHIVES
ARDENNES
ARGESTES
ARMOURED
ARRANGER
ARRESTED
ARRESTER
ARTICLED
ARTICLES
ASPERGES
ASPHODEL
ASSIGNEE
ASSORTED
ATOMIZER
ATTACHED
ATTACKER
ATTENDER
ATTORNEY
AUSPICES
BAEDEKER
BAGPIPES
BALANCED
BALUSTER
BANISTER
BAPTISED
BARATHEA
BARTERED
BASSINET
BATTERED
BECALMED
BECHAMEL
BEDCOVER
BEDMAKER
BEGETTER
BEGINNER
BEHOLDEN
BEHOLDER
BELIEVER
BENENDEN
BEREAVED
BERKELEY
BESIEGED
BESOTTED
BESPOKEN
BESSEMER
BESTOWER
BETRAYER
BEWILDER
BICONVEX
BINDWEED
BIRDSEED
BLACKLEG
BLEACHER
BLIGHTER
BLOTCHED
BOADICEA
BONSPIEL
BORDERER
BORROWED
BORROWER
BOTHERED
BRACELET
BRANCHED
BRANDNEW
BREACHES
BREATHER
BREECHES
BRETHREN
BRIGHTEN
BRINDLED
BRISTLED
BRISTLES
BRUCKNER
BUCKSHEE
BUGGERED
BUMMAREE
BURDENED
BURROWER
BUTTERED
CABERNET
CALENDER
CALLIPER
CAMBERED
CANARIES
CANISTER
CAPSIZED
CARCANET
CAREFREE
CAROUSEL
CASTANET
CATHETER
CAVALIER
CELLARER
CENTERED
CHANDLER
CHANTREY
CHARTRES
CHEROKEE
CHESSMEN
CHICKPEA
CHILDREN
CHRISTEN
CICISBEO
CILIATED
CLARINET
CLEANSED
CLEANSER
CLERIHEW
CLINCHER
CLIVEDEN
CLOISTER
CLOTHIER
COCKEREL
COCKEYED
COGNOMEN
COGWHEEL
COLANDER
COLLAGEN
COLLARED
COLLEGES
COLOURED
COMBINED
COMMONER
COMMUTER
COMPARED
COMPILER
COMPOSED
COMPOSER
COMPUTER
CONFINED
CONFINES
CONFUSED
CONJURER
CONSIDER
CONSUMED
CONSUMER
CONVENER
CORRODED
CORSELET
COTTAGER
COUNTIES
COVERLET
CRAVATES
CRIPPLED
CROSSLET
CROTCHET
CROUPIER
CRUCIFER
CRUSADER
CRUTCHED
CUCUMBER
CULLODEN
CULTURED
CUSTOMER
CUTWATER
CYANOGEN
CYCLADES
CYCLAMEN
CYLINDER
DAINTIES
DAMOCLES
DARKENED
DAUGHTER
DEADENED
DEADENER
DEATHBED
DECANTER
DECEASED
DECEIVER
DECEMBER
DECIPHER
DEFEATED
DEFENDER
DEFLOWER
DEFORMED
DEGRADED
DEJECTED
DEMENTED
DEMISTER
DENTURES
DEPARTED
DEPORTEE
DEPRAVED
DEPRIVED
DERANGED
DESERTED
DESERTER
DESERVED
DESIGNER
DESTINED
DETACHED
DETAILED
DETAINEE
DETAINER
DEVILLED
DEWYEYED
DIABETES
DIAMETER
DIARRHEA
DICTATES
DIOGENES
DISABLED
DISAGREE
DISASTER
DISCOVER
DISCREET
DISEASED
DISHEVEL
DISINTER
DISLIKED
DISMAYED
DISORDER
DISPOSED
DISPUTED
DISQUIET
DIVORCED
DIVORCEE
DOCTORED
DOGGEREL
DOMINEER
DOMINOES
DOORSTEP
DOTTEREL
DRAGSTER
DUBONNET
DUCKWEED
DULCIMER
DULCINEA
DURABLES
DUTYFREE
EATABLES
EDUCATED
EGGTIMER
EIGHTEEN
ELEVATED
EMBEDDED
EMBITTER
EMBODIED
EMBOLDEN
EMBOSSED
EMBRACED
EMBRACES
EMIRATES
EMMANUEL
EMPLOYED
EMPLOYEE
EMPLOYER
ENCAMPED
ENCLOSED

ENCUMBER
ENDANGER
ENGENDER
ENGINEER
ENGRAVER
ENLARGED
ENLARGER
ENMESHED
ENRICHED
ENTITLED
ESPALIER
ESTEEMED
ESTOPPEL
ESTROGEN
EVILDOER
EXAMINEE
EXAMINER
EXECUTED
EXPECTED
EXPENDED
EXPENSES
EXPLODED
EXPLORER
EXPORTER
EXTENDED
EYELINER
FAINITES
FAMISHED
FASTENER
FATIGUED
FATIGUES
FAULKNER
FAVOURED
FEATURED
FEATURES
FEDAYEEN
FEVERFEW
FILAGREE
FILIGREE
FINISHED
FINISHER
FIRESTEP
FIREWEED
FLAVORED
FLOUNCED
FLOUNDER
FLYSHEET
FLYWHEEL
FOLLOWED
FOLLOWER
FOOTSTEP
FORESTER
FORSAKEN
FOURTEEN
FRAZZLED
FRECKLED
FRECKLES

FRENZIED
FRIGHTEN
FRONTIER
FURROWED
FUSILIER
GALLOPER
GALOSHES
GANGSTER
GARDENER
GARGANEY
GASOLIER
GATHERED
GAUNTLET
GAZUNDER
GEOMETER
GESTURES
GLYCOGEN
GOSSAMER
GRANULES
GRAVAMEN
GRIZZLED
GROSCHEN
GROUNDED
GRUMBLER
GUERNSEY
GULLIVER
GUSSETED
HALLOWED
HAMMERED
HANDOVER
HANGOVER
HARASSED
HARDENED
HARUSPEX
HAUNCHES
HAYFEVER
HAYMAKER
HEARTIES
HEBRIDES
HEIGHTEN
HELMETED
HERACLES
HERCULES
HERSCHEL
HIJACKER
HONEYDEW
HORSEMEN
HOTELIER
HOWITZER
HUCKSTER
HUMPHREY
HYDROGEN
IDOLATER
ILLFATED
IMAGINED
IMMANUEL
IMMERSED

IMPACTED
IMPAIRED
IMPELLED
IMPORTER
IMPOSTER
IMPROPER
IMPROVED
IMPROVER
INCENSED
INCLINED
INCLUDED
INDEBTED
INDENTED
INFECTED
INFESTED
INFLAMED
INFLATED
INFORMED
INFORMER
INFRARED
INQUIRER
INSPIRED
INTENDED
INTERNEE
INTERNET
INTRUDER
INVENTED
INVERTED
INVOLVED
IRISHMEN
ISLANDER
ISOLATED
IVOIRIEN
JACKETED
JAMBOREE
JEWELLED
JEWELLER
JIGGERED
JOHANNES
KEDGEREE
KERCHIEF
KESTEVEN
KIBITZER
KILLDEER
KINGSLEY
KIPPERED
KNAPWEED
KNEEDEEP
KNOTWEED
KUFFIYEH
LABOURED
LABOURER
LADRONES
LAMENTED
LANDSEER
LATCHKEY
LAUGHTER

LAVENDER
LAWMAKER
LEAVENED
LECTURER
LECTURES
LEFTOVER
LEINSTER
LEISURED
LENGTHEN
LETTERED
LEVELLER
LICENSED
LICENSEE
LISTENER
LIVERIED
LOITERER
LONDONER
LOPSIDED
LOUVERED
LYSANDER
MACHINES
MACKEREL
MAGISTER
MALARKEY
MALDIVES
MALINGER
MANDATED
MANEUVER
MANGONEL
MANNERED
MANPOWER
MARAUDER
MARGARET
MARMOSET
MARTINET
MARTYRED
MASSENET
MCKINLEY
MEASURED
MELEAGER
MENANDER
MERCEDES
MERISTEM
MESSAGER
METALLED
MILDEWED
MILKWEED
MILLINER
MINISTER
MINSTREL
MIRRORED
MISCHIEF
MISNOMER
MISTAKEN
MODELLER
MODIFIER
MOHAMMED

MOLASSES
MOLESTER
MONICKER
MOREOVER
MORTIMER
MULETEER
MURDERER
MUSCADET
MUSCATEL
MUTINEER
NARCOSES
NARGILEH
NATTERED
NEGLIGEE
NEWCOMER
NEWHAVEN
NEWSREEL
NIGERIEN
NINETEEN
NITROGEN
NORSEMEN
NOVEMBER
OBSCURED
OBSERVED
OBSERVER
OBSESSED
OBTAINED
OCCUPIED
OCCUPIER
ODOMETER
OFFENDED
OFFENDER
OFFSIDER
OLEANDER
ONESIDED
ONLOOKER
ONSCREEN
ORPHANED
OSTERLEY
OUTDATED
OUTMODED
OUTREMER
OUTRIDER
OUTSIDER
OVERFEED
OVERSEER
OVERSTEP
OVERVIEW
OXPECKER
PACIFIER
PACKAGED
PALMATED
PAMPERED
PAMPHLET
PANELLED
PARAKEET
PARALLEL

PARDONER
PAROLLES
PASSOVER
PASTURES
PATENTED
PATENTEE
PATHOGEN
PEDIGREE
PELLETED
PENNINES
PERFUMED
PERICLES
PERISHED
PERISHER
PERJURED
PERJURER
PEVENSEY
PHARISEE
PHILOMEL
PICTURES
PIERIDES
PILASTER
PILFERER
PILLAGER
PILLARED
PILSENER
PINNIPED
PINWHEEL
PLACEMEN
PLANCHET
PLATELET
PLEIADES
PLOUGHED
POISONER
POLISHED
POLISHER
POLLSTER
POLLUTED
POLLUTER
POMANDER
POTATOES
POTHOLER
POWDERED
PRATTLER
PREACHER
PREMISES
PREPARED
PRISONER
PRIVATES
PROCURER
PRODUCER
PRODUCES
PROFUSER
PROMISED
PROMOTER
PROMPTER
PROPOSED

PROPOSER
PROVIDED
PROVIDER
PUCKERED
PUGNOSED
PULITZER
PULLOVER
PUNISHED
PURIFIED
PURIFIER
PUSHOVER
PYORRHEA
PYRENEES
QUARTIER
QUIBBLER
QUICKSET
RAREFIED
REASONED
REAWAKEN
RECEIVED
RECEIVER
RECESSED
RECKONER
RECORDER
REDEEMER
REFORMED
REFORMER
REGAINED
REGISTER
REINDEER
REJOINED
RELEASED
RELIEVED
REMEMBER
REMINDER
RENOWNED
REPAIRER
REPARTEE
REPEATED
REPEATER
REPORTED
REPORTER
REQUIRED
RESERVED
RESIGNED
RESOLVED
RESTORER
RETAILER
RETAINER
RETARDED
REVEALED
REVELLER
REVERSED
REVIEWER
REVOLVER
RICOCHET
RISSOLES

ROADSTER
ROENTGEN
ROMANCER
RUMOURED
SADDUCEE
SALARIED
SALINGER
SANGLIER
SATIATED
SAUSAGES
SAVOURED
SAWBONES
SCANTIES
SCHILLER
SCHOONER
SCIENCES
SCILICET
SCORCHED
SCORCHER
SCRAWLED
SCREAMER
SCREENED
SCRUBBER
SCRUPLES
SEAFARER
SEAMSTER
SEARCHER
SEASONED
SECLUDED
SECONDER
SELECTED
SEMESTER
SENGREEN
SENTINEL
SERRATED
SERVICES
SHACKLES
SHAGREEN
SHAMBLES
SHINGLES
SHIVERED
SHOETREE
SHOULDER
SHRAPNEL
SHREDDER
SHROUDED
SHRUNKEN
SIDESTEP
SIGNALER
SILENCER
SINISTER
SITUATED
SKINDEEP
SKITTLES
SLIGHTED
SLIPOVER
SLUGABED

SMOOTHER
SMOULDER
SMUGGLED
SMUGGLER
SNATCHER
SNIFFLER
SOCALLED
SOCRATES
SOFTENER
SOMERSET
SONGSTER
SORCERER
SPANDREL
SPANGLED
SPARKLER
SPAVINED
SPECIMEN
SPECKLED
SPINSTER
SPIRITED
SPLASHER
SPLATTER
SPLINTER
SPLITTER
SPLUTTER
SPRAINED
SPRAWLED
SPREADER
SPRINGER
SPRINTER
SPRITZER
SPROCKET
SQUANDER
SQUATTER
SQUEAKER
SQUEALER
SQUEEGEE
SQUEEZER
SQUIRREL
STAMENED
STARCHED
STENOSED
STICKLER
STOPOVER
STOREYED
STRACHEY
STRAINED
STRAINER
STRAITEN
STRANDED
STRANGER
STRAPPED
STRAPPER
STREAKED
STREAKER
STREAMER
STRESSED

STRIATED
STRICKEN
STRINGED
STRINGER
STRIPPED
STRIPPER
STROLLER
STRUMPET
STUCCOED
STYLIZED
SUFFERER
SUNDRIED
SUNDRIES
SUPPLIER
SUPPLIES
SUPPOSED
SWADDLER
SWINDLER
SYLVANER
SYRINGES
TAKEOVER
TALENTED
TATTERED
TAVERNER
TAXPAYER
TEAMSTER
TEENAGER
TEMPERED
TERRACED
TEXTURED
THATCHED
THATCHER
THICKSET
THIRTEEN
THRASHER
THREATEN
THRESHER
THRILLER
THRUSTER
THURIFER
TIMBERED
TINTAGEL
TOGETHER
TOMATOES
TONSURED
TOPLEVEL
TORTURED
TORTURER
TRANSFER
TRANSKEI
TRAVELER
TREMBLER
TRENCHER
TROCHLEA
TROUBLED
TROUBLES
TROUNCER

TRUCKLED
TUNGSTEN
TURBANED
TURBOJET
TURGENEV
TURNOVER
TURRETED
TWITCHER
UDOMETER
UNABATED
UNAWARES
UNBEATEN
UNBIASED
UNBIDDEN
UNBROKEN
UNBURDEN
UNCLOVEN
UNCOMBED
UNCOOKED
UNCURBED
UNDERFED
UNDERSEA
UNEARNED
UNFASTEN
UNFETTER
UNFILLED
UNFORCED
UNHARMED
UNHEATED
UNHINGED
UNLEADED
UNLISTED
UNLOADED
UNLOCKED
UNMANNED
UNMARKED
UNNERVED
UNPLACED
UNSALTED
UNSEALED
UNSEEDED
UNSHAKEN
UNSIGNED
UNSOLVED
UNSPOKEN
UNSTATED
UNSUITED
UNTAPPED
UNTILLED
UNVARIED
UNVERSED
UNVOICED
UNWANTED
UNWEANED
UNWONTED
UPHOLDER
UPMARKET

UPTURNED
VAGARIES
VANISHED
VENTURED
VERDERER
VILLAGER
WAGGONER
WALKOVER
WANDERER
WAVERLEY
WAYFARER
WELLBRED
WHATEVER
WHENEVER
WHEREVER
WHIMBREL
WHISTLER
WHITENER
WINDHOEK
WINIFRED
WINNIPEG
WITHERED
WOLSELEY
WOODSHED
WORTHIES
WRANGLER
WREATHED
WRESTLER
WRETCHED
WRINKLED
WRISTLET
YODELLER
PROTÉGÉE
AIRCRAFT
ALKALIFY
BEAUTIFY
BLASTOFF
CAMSHAFT
CASTOFFS
CLASSIFY
DANDRUFF
EMULSIFY
FACELIFT
FISHWIFE
FORKLIFT
FRUCTIFY
GENTRIFY
GOODWIFE
HANDCUFF
HUMIDIFY
IDENTIFY
IMPURIFY
MALAKOFF
PENKNIFE
QUANTIFY
REVIVIFY
RIFFRAFF

SANCTIFY
SIMPLIFY
SOLIDIFY
STANDOFF
STRATIFY
STULTIFY
TARTUFFE
TIPSTAFF
TRADEOFF
WILDLIFE
WRITEOFF
WYCLIFFE
ADJUTAGE
ALTHOUGH
AMPERAGE
APOTHEGM
APPANAGE
BADINAGE
BEARINGS
BEGRUDGE
BEVERAGE
BIRDCAGE
BLOCKAGE
CABOTAGE
CAMPAIGN
CARRIAGE
CARTHAGE
CHANTAGE
CHUMMAGE
CLEAVAGE
CONTANGO
CONVERGE
COVERAGE
CRIBBAGE
CYTOLOGY
DEALINGS
DEMIURGE
DIGGINGS
DISGORGE
DISLODGE
DOXOLOGY
DRAINAGE
DRESSAGE
EARNINGS
ENSILAGE
ENVISAGE
EQUIPAGE
EXCHANGE
FANDANGO
FEELINGS
FINDINGS
FLAMINGO
FRONTAGE
FULLPAGE
FURLOUGH
FUSELAGE
GEMOLOGY

HANGINGS
HASTINGS
HERITAGE
HICCOUGH
HOLDINGS
HOROLOGY
HUSTINGS
IDEOLOGY
IMPETIGO
INFRINGE
JOTTINGS
KNEEHIGH
LANGUAGE
LASHINGS
LEAVINGS
LEGGINGS
LETHARGY
LEVERAGE
LODGINGS
MAHJONGG
MARRIAGE
MESSUAGE
MISJUDGE
MOORINGS
MORTGAGE
MUCILAGE
MYCOLOGY
NOSOLOGY
OENOLOGY
OFFSTAGE
ONCOLOGY
ONTOLOGY
OUTWEIGH
OXBRIDGE
PARADIGM
PEDAGOGY
PEELINGS
PENOLOGY
PHALANGE
PICKINGS
PILOTAGE
PLUMBAGO
PORRIDGE
POSOLOGY
POUNDAGE
PREJUDGE
PRESTIGE
QUADRIGA
RAILINGS
RANELAGH
REASSIGN
RECHARGE
REDESIGN
REFRINGE
ROUGHAGE
RUTABAGA
SABOTAGE

SANTIAGO
SARATOGA
SCAVENGE
SCROUNGE
SELVEDGE
SEROLOGY
SEWERAGE
SEXOLOGY
SHORTAGE
SPILLAGE
SPOILAGE
STEERAGE
STOPPAGE
STRATEGY
SUBMERGE
SUFFRAGE
THEOLOGY
THOROUGH
TOPOLOGY
TUTELAGE
UNDERAGE
VANBRUGH
VERBIAGE
VICARAGE
VIROLOGY
VITILIGO
WELLNIGH
WHARFAGE
WINDINGS
WINNINGS
WORKINGS
WRECKAGE
WRITINGS
ZASTRUGA
ABSINTHE
AIRTIGHT
AUTARCHY
AUTOBAHN
BACKACHE
BEERBOHM
BESOUGHT
BROUHAHA
BUNFIGHT
CORNICHE
DAYLIGHT
DEMIJOHN
ENCLOTHE
EUTROPHY
EYESIGHT
FACEACHE
FANLIGHT
FAROUCHE
FOGLIGHT
GAZPACHO
GOLGOTHA
HEADACHE
HIAWATHA

INFLIGHT
IOLANTHE
JEHOVAHS
MARIACHI
MIDNIGHT
MONARCHY
MUSTACHE
NEPENTHE
OUTRIGHT
PASTICHE
REDLIGHT
RESPIGHI
REVANCHE
RUBBISHY
SCRATCHY
SKYLIGHT
STEALTHY
STRAIGHT
STRETCHY
SUNBATHE
SUNLIGHT
SYMPATHY
TWILIGHT
UNWORTHY
ABATTOIR
ACADEMIC
ACCREDIT
ACOUSTIC
ACROSTIC
ADENITIS
ADRIATIC
AEROFOIL
AGACERIE
AGNOSTIC
AIRSTRIP
ALCESTIS
ALCHEMIC
ALKALOID
ALLELUIA
ALLERGIC
ALOPECIA
AMBROSIA
ANABASIS
ANABATIC
ANALYSIS
ANARCHIC
ANATOLIA
ANATOMIC
ANOREXIA
ANOREXIC
APERITIF
APOLOGIA
APPENDIX
ARACHNID
ARMCHAIR
AROMATIC
ARPEGGIO

ARTISTIC
ASCORBIC
ASPHYXIA
ASSASSIN
ASTEROID
ASTHENIA
ATARAXIA
ATARAXIC
ATHETOID
ATHLETIC
ATLANTIC
ATLANTIS
AUCASSIN
AUTISTIC
BACTERIA
BALEARIC
BARBARIC
BATHETIC
BEARSKIN
BEATIFIC
BENJAMIN
BERBERIS
BICUSPID
BLENHEIM
BOBBYPIN
BONHOMIE
BOWSPRIT
BRASILIA
BROMELIA
BUCKSKIN
BUDDLEIA
BULGARIA
BULLETIN
BURSITIS
CACHEXIA
CAMBODIA
CAMELLIA
CANNABIS
CAPUCHIN
CARBOLIC
CARBONIC
CARNEGIE
CARYATID
CATHOLIC
CERATOID
CHAPLAIN
CHERUBIC
CHERUBIM
CHOLERIC
CHRISTIE
CICATRIX
CLAVECIN
CLEMATIS
CLIMATIC
CLITORIS
COATTAIL
COCKTAIL

COLOMBIA
COMPLAIN
CONCHOID
CORDWAIN
CORIOLIS
CORONOID
CORRAGIO
COSMETIC
COUPERIN
COXSWAIN
COYSTRIL
CRATCHIT
CRUCIFIX
CRUNCHIE
CUCURBIT
CULVERIN
CYANOSIS
CYRILLIC
CYSTITIS
DAFFODIL
DALMATIC
DEBONAIR
DECEMVIR
DECREPIT
DEERSKIN
DEMENTIA
DENDROID
DESPOTIC
DIABETIC
DIABOLIC
DIALYSIS
DIARESIS
DIATONIC
DICYCLIC
DIDACTIC
DIELDRIN
DIERESIS
DIOPTRIC
DISCLAIM
DISPIRIT
DISTRAIN
DISTRAIT
DIURETIC
DOGMATIC
DOGSTAIL
DOMESTIC
DOVETAIL
DRACONIC
DRAMATIC
DYNASTIC
DYSLEXIA
DYSLEXIC
ECLECTIC
ECONOMIC
ECSTASIS
ECSTATIC
EFFLUVIA

EGOISTIC
EGOMANIA
EIDECTIC
EINSTEIN
ELECTRIC
ELLIPSIS
ELLIPTIC
EMPHASIS
EMPHATIC
ENCAENIA
EPIDEMIC
EPIGAMIC
EPISODIC
EPITASIS
ESOTERIC
ESTANCIA
ESTHETIC
ETHIOPIA
EUCYCLIC
EUPEPSIA
EUPHONIA
EUPHONIC
EUPHORIA
EUPHORIC
EUSTATIC
EUTROPIC
EWIGKEIT
EXEGESIS
EXEGETIC
EXPLICIT
FANTASIA
FELLAHIN
FIBROSIS
FLAGSHIP
FLOODLIT
FORENSIC
FORESAIL
FORESHIP
FORESKIN
FORKTAIL
FORMALIN
FOUNTAIN
FRANKLIN
FRAULEIN
FRENETIC
GALACTIC
GALLERIA
GALVANIC
GARDENIA
GELASTIC
GENETRIX
GEODESIC
GEOTAXIS
GERMANIC
GIGANTIC
GIRONDIN
GLOBULIN
GLOXINIA
GLYCERIN
GOATSKIN
GUMMOSIS
HANDMAID
HANDRAIL
HANGNAIL
HARDSHIP
HARMONIC
HEADSHIP
HELLADIC
HELLENIC
HELVETIA
HERACLID
HERALDIC
HERMETIC
HERPETIC
HETAIRIA
HIBERNIA
HIDROSIS
HIERATIC
HISPANIC
HISTORIC
HOLISTIC
HORRIFIC
HYDATOID
HYGIENIC
HYPNOSIS
HYPNOTIC
HYSTERIA
HYSTERIC
ILLINOIS
IMPLICIT
INKSTAIN
INSIGNIA
INSOMNIA
INSPIRIT
INTAGLIO
INTERMIT
INTREPID
IROQUOIS
JALOUSIE
JUMPSUIT
JURASSIC
KINGSHIP
KYPHOSIS
LADYSHIP
LAMBSKIN
LANDSLIP
LECITHIN
LEUKEMIA
LINCHPIN
LINGERIE
LISTERIA
LOGISTIC
LORDOSIS
LORDSHIP
LOTHARIO
LYSERGIC
MAGNESIA
MAGNETIC
MAGNOLIA
MAINSAIL
MAINTAIN
MAJESTIC
MALAYSIA
MALVASIA
MALVOLIO
MANDARIN
MANDOLIN
MANNIKIN
MATHURIN
MECHANIC
MEMSAHIB
MESCALIN
MESMERIC
MÉTAIRIE
METALLIC
METEORIC
METHODIC
METRITIS
MILKMAID
MINCEPIE
MIREPOIX
MNEMONIC
MOCASSIN
MOCCASIN
MOLESKIN
MONASTIC
MONGOLIA
MONORAIL
MONROVIA
MOUNTAIN
MUNCHKIN
MUTCHKIN
MYELITIS
MYOSOTIS
NARCOSIS
NARCOTIC
NECROSIS
NEMATOID
NEOMYCIN
NEPIONIC
NEURITIS
NEUROSIS
NEUROTIC
OENOPHIL
OPERATIC
ORATORIO
ORCHITIS
ORESTEIA
ORGANDIE
OUTSTRIP
OVERLAID
OXYTOCIN
PALLADIO
PANDEMIC
PANGOLIN
PANNIKIN
PARAFFIN
PARANOIA
PARANOID
PATHETIC
PEARMAIN
PEDANTIC
PEIGNOIR
PELLUCID
PERIODIC
PHONETIC
PHOTOFIT
PHREATIC
PHTHISIS
PHYSALIA
PINDARIC
PIZZERIA
PLANTAIN
PLATONIC
PLAYFAIR
PLAYSUIT
PONYTAIL
PORTRAIT
POSTPAID
POTEMKIN
PRETORIA
PROCLAIM
PROGERIA
PROHIBIT
PROLIFIC
PYELITIS
QUATRAIN
QUINTAIN
QUIXOTIC
RABELAIS
RACHITIS
RAMEQUIN
RASPUTIN
REPLEVIN
REPUBLIC
RESTRAIN
RHETORIC
RHOMBOID
RHYTHMIC
RINGTAIL
RIVERAIN
ROMANTIC
SADISTIC
SAINFOIN
SANSERIF
SANSKRIT
SARDINIA
SARDONIC
SASSANID
SATURNIA
SCAPHOID
SCENARIO
SCHIZOID
SCRIABIN
SEALSKIN
SELASSIE
SELEUCID
SEMIOTIC
SERAGLIO
SERAPHIC
SERAPHIM
SERIATIM
SIDESLIP
SIGNORIA
SILKTAIL
SINCLAIR
SINFONIA
SLOVAKIA
SLOVENIA
SOCRATIC
SOLENOID
SOUVENIR
SPARAXIS
SPECIFIC
SPLENDID
SPORADIC
SQUADDIE
STAYSAIL
STENOSIS
SUBSONIC
SUBTOPIA
SUBURBIA
SULFURIC
SUZERAIN
SWANSKIN
SWIMSUIT
SYLLABIC
SYMBOLIC
SYNOPSIS
SYNOPTIC
SYNTEXIS
SYPHILIS
SYSTEMIC
TAFFRAIL
TAILSKID
TAILSPIN
TANZANIA
TARTARIC
TASMANIA
TECTONIC
TELLURIC
TENEBRIO
TERRAPIN
TERRIFIC
TEUTONIC
THEATRIC
THEMATIC
THORACIC
THROMBIN
TOWNSHIP
TOXAEMIA
TRANQUIL
TRANSFIX
TRANSHIP
TRANSMIT
TRIASSIC
TRICHOID
TROCHAIC
TROTTOIR
TURMERIC
TURNSPIT
UNDERLIE
UNDERPIN
UNHEROIC
VALENCIA
VALKYRIE
VERBATIM
VICTORIA
VIRGINIA
VOLCANIC
WALKYRIE
WARDSHIP
WARFARIN
WELLPAID
WHODUNIT
WISTERIA
XERAPHIM
YERSINIA
ZEPPELIN
ZIRCONIA
ZOONOSIS
MAHARAJA
AIRBRAKE
ARCHDUKE
BABUSHKA
BALLOCKS
BARRACKS
BOLLOCKS
BOUZOUKI
BUTTOCKS
CLAMBAKE
EASTLAKE
FISHCAKE
GADZOOKS
GARLICKY
GASWORKS
HAIRLIKE
HELSINKI
HORLICKS
JORROCKS
KEEPSAKE
KENTUCKY

KLONDIKE
KROMESKY
LADYLIKE
LIFELIKE
MAMELUKE
MANDRAKE
MOUSSAKA
NAGASAKI
NAMESAKE
NEBRASKA
NIJINSKY
OVERTAKE
PACHINKO
PEMBROKE
PIROZHKI
PUSHBIKE
RAPECAKE
SCHAPSKA
SHIITAKE
SLOWPOKE
SUCHLIKE
SUKIYAKI
SWASTIKA
TERIYAKI
TURNPIKE
TZATZIKI
VISELIKE
WAXWORKS
YARMULKA
ZAKOUSKI
ABJECTLY
ABRUPTLY
ABSURDLY
ACTIVELY
ACTUALLY
ADORABLE
ADROITLY
AGRICOLA
AIGUILLE
AIREDALE
AIRFIELD
AMENABLE
AMICABLE
AMICABLY
AMYGDALA
ANGUILLA
ANNUALLY
ARDENTLY
ARGUABLE
ARGUABLY
ARTFULLY
ASSEMBLE
ASSEMBLY
ASTUTELY
BANKROLL
BARGELLO
BARNACLE
BASEBALL
BASTILLE
BEANPOLE
BEARABLE
BEDABBLE
BEFUDDLE
BEGGARLY
BELITTLE
BIFOCALS
BILLFOLD
BINNACLE
BITTERLY
BLACKFLY
BLASTULA
BLITHELY
BLOWHOLE
BLUEBELL
BOLTHOLE
BOOKABLE
BORDELLO
BORECOLE
BOREHOLE
BORSTALL
BOTHWELL
BREEZILY
BRIBABLE
BRIGHTLY
BROCCOLI
BRUSSELS
BRUTALLY
CABOODLE
CABRIOLE
CAKEHOLE
CAKEWALK
CALIGULA
CAMISOLE
CAMOMILE
CAMPBELL
CANAILLE
CANDIDLY
CANOODLE
CANTICLE
CAPITALS
CAPRIOLE
CARACOLE
CARRIOLE
CARRYALL
CASUALLY
CATAPULT
CAUDILLO
CHASUBLE
CHATTELS
CHEEKILY
CHEERILY
CHENILLE
CHERWELL
CLAVICLE
CLEVERLY
CLODPOLL
CLUMSILY
COALHOLE
COARSELY
COCACOLA
COMMONLY
CONTROLS
COPYHOLD
CORNHILL
CORNWALL
COTSWOLD
COWARDLY
CRAFTILY
CRANEFLY
CREDIBLE
CREDIBLY
CROMWELL
CRUCIBLE
CRYSTALS
CULPABLE
CURRICLE
DAINTILY
DAMNABLE
DANEGELD
DECENTLY
DECOUPLE
DEMURELY
DIASTOLE
DIRECTLY
DISCIPLE
DISMALLY
DISRAELI
DOGGEDLY
DOMICILE
DOOLALLY
DOORBELL
DOWNFALL
DOWNHILL
DREAMILY
DREARILY
DROWSILY
DUCKBILL
DUMBBELL
DUNGHILL
DUTIABLE
EASTERLY
EDGEHILL
EGGSHELL
ELIGIBLE
EMBATTLE
EMBEZZLE
ENCIRCLE
ENFEEBLE
ENKINDLE
ENSEMBLE
ENTANGLE
ENTHRALL
ENTIRELY
ENTRAILS
ENVIABLE
EPISTYLE
ERECTILE
FALLIBLE
FAMOUSLY
FAREWELL
FASCICLE
FATHERLY
FEASIBLE
FEASIBLY
FENCIBLE
FIERCELY
FILTHILY
FIREBALL
FIREBOLT
FITFULLY
FLAGPOLE
FLANNELS
FLASHILY
FLEXIBLE
FLEXIBLY
FLIMSILY
FLOTILLA
FLUENTLY
FOLLICLE
FOOTBALL
FOOTFALL
FOOTHOLD
FORCIBLE
FORCIBLY
FORETELL
FORMALLY
FORMERLY
FOURFOLD
FREEHOLD
FRIENDLY
FRIGIDLY
FRISKILY
FROSTILY
FRUGALLY
FUMAROLE
FURUNCLE
FUSAROLE
GARGOYLE
GARISHLY
GASTRULA
GENIALLY
GENITALS
GINGERLY
GIRASOLE
GLABELLA
GLOBALLY
GLOOMILY
GLORIOLE
GODCHILD
GOLFBALL
GOODWILL
GOOFBALL
GRAVELLY
GREEDILY
GREENFLY
GROGGILY
GRUMPILY
GUERILLA
GUILTILY
GULLIBLE
HALFFULL
HANDBALL
HANDBILL
HANDHELD
HAREBELL
HAYFIELD
HEARTILY
HEATEDLY
HEAVENLY
HEELBALL
HIGHBALL
HOARSELY
HONESTLY
HONOLULU
HOPFIELD
HORNBILL
HORRIBLE
HORRIBLY
HORSEFLY
HOVERFLY
HUMANELY
HUNGRILY
ICEFIELD
IMBECILE
IMMOBILE
INEDIBLE
INSANELY
INTENTLY
INVEIGLE
INWARDLY
ISABELLA
ISABELLE
JAUNTILY
JOKINGLY
JOVIALLY
JOYFULLY
JUVENILE
KILOVOLT
KINSFOLK
KNIGHTLY
LANDFALL
LANDFILL
LATTERLY
LAUDABLE
LAUDABLY
LAVISHLY
LAWFULLY
LIFEBELT
LIKEABLE
LOCKABLE
LONSDALE
LOOPHOLE
LOVINGLY
MAIDENLY
MANCIPLE
MANDIBLE
MANDRILL
MANFULLY
MANIFOLD
MANNERLY
MANTILLA
MANUALLY
MARCELLA
MARCELLO
MARIGOLD
MARKEDLY
MARSHALL
MARTELLO
MASTERLY
MATABELE
MATRONLY
MENTALLY
MERCALLI
METABOLA
MIDFIELD
MIGHTILY
MINUTELY
MISAPPLY
MISSPELL
MODESTLY
MOLECULE
MOLEHILL
MONOHULL
MONOPOLY
MONTCALM
MORBIDLY
MORBILLI
MOROSELY
MORTALLY
MOTHBALL
MOTHERLY
MOVEABLE
MULTIPLE
MULTIPLY
MUTUALLY
NARROWLY
NORMALLY
NOSTRILS
NUCLEOLE
NUFFIELD
NUMERALS
NUPTIALS

NUTSHELL
OBSTACLE
OBTUSELY
ODIOUSLY
OILFIELD
OLDSTYLE
OLDWORLD
OPERABLE
OPUSCULE
OUTFIELD
OVERALLS
OVERFILL
OVERFULL
OVERKILL
OVERRULE
PALPABLE
PALPABLY
PANATELA
PANNICLE
PARABOLA
PARTICLE
PASSABLE
PASSABLY
PASSIBLE
PASTILLE
PATCHILY
PATENTLY
PEDUNCLE
PEEPHOLE
PELLICLE
PELLMELL
PENTACLE
PIGSWILL
PINNACLE
PINOCHLE
PINTABLE
PITIABLE
PLACABLE
PLACIDLY
PLAYBILL
PLIMSOLL
PLUCKILY
PLUGHOLE
POLITELY
POPSICLE
PORTABLE
PORTHOLE
POSSIBLE
POSSIBLY
POTBELLY
PRATFALL
PREAMBLE
PREDELLA
PRETTILY
PRIESTLY
PRINCELY
PROBABLE
PROBABLY
PROMPTLY
PROPERLY
PROVABLE
PRUNELLA
PUBLICLY
PUFFBALL
QUAINTLY
QUARTILE
QUENELLE
QUOTABLE
RACIALLY
RAINFALL
RANDOMLY
RASCALLY
RATEABLE
READABLE
RECENTLY
REDOUBLE
REKINDLE
RELIABLE
RELIABLY
REMOTELY
RESEMBLE
RESETTLE
RETICULE
REUSABLE
REVEILLE
RIDICULE
RINGWALL
RITUALLY
ROBUSTLY
ROCHDALE
ROLLCALL
ROLYPOLY
RUEFULLY
RUGGEDLY
RUNCIBLE
SALEABLE
SAVAGELY
SAXATILE
SCAFFOLD
SCANTILY
SCARCELY
SCHEDULE
SCRABBLE
SCRAMBLE
SCRAPPLE
SCRIBBLE
SCRIBBLY
SCROFULA
SEASHELL
SECONDLY
SECRETLY
SECURELY
SEDATELY
SELFHELP
SENSIBLE
SENSIBLY
SERAFILE
SERENELY
SEVERELY
SEXUALLY
SHABBILY
SHIGELLA
SHODDILY
SHOPTALK
SHREWDLY
SIDEWALK
SIGNALLY
SILENTLY
SISTERLY
SIZEABLE
SKEWBALD
SLEEPILY
SLIGHTLY
SLOPPILY
SLOVENLY
SMOOTHLY
SNAPPILY
SNOOTILY
SNOWBALL
SNOWFALL
SOCIABLE
SOCIALLY
SOFTBALL
SOLEMNLY
SOLVABLE
SOMBRELY
SORDIDLY
SPARSELY
SPEEDILY
SPIRACLE
SPIRALLY
SPRINKLE
SPRITELY
SPRUCELY
SQUABBLE
SQUARELY
SQUIGGLE
STAPHYLE
STEADILY
STICKILY
STILWELL
STOLIDLY
STRADDLE
STRAGGLE
STRAGGLY
STRANGLE
STRICTLY
STRONGLY
STRUGGLE
STUFFILY
STUPIDLY
STURDILY
SUBTITLE
SUDDENLY
SUITABLE
SUITABLY
SULLENLY
SUPERBLY
SVENGALI
SYLLABLE
TANGIBLE
TANGIBLY
TEARABLE
TELEFILM
TELLTALE
TENDERLY
TENTACLE
TEQUILLA
TERRIBLE
TERRIBLY
TESTICLE
TETCHILY
THROTTLE
THURIBLE
TINSELLY
TORTILLA
TRIANGLE
TRICYCLE
TRINCULO
TUBERCLE
TURGIDLY
TUSITALA
UMBRELLA
UNCOUPLE
UNEASILY
UNEVENLY
UNGAINLY
UNIQUELY
UNITEDLY
UNJUSTLY
UNKINDLY
UNLIKELY
UNLOVELY
UNSEEMLY
UNSETTLE
UNSPOILT
UNSTABLE
UNTANGLE
UNTIDILY
UNTIMELY
UNUSABLE
URGENTLY
USEFULLY
UTENSILS
VACANTLY
VALHALLA
VALUABLE
VARIABLE
VAUXHALL
VERBALLY
VERSICLE
VICTUALS
VINCIBLE
VISUALLY
VOLATILE
VULGARLY
WASHABLE
WEARABLE
WEREWOLF
WESTERLY
WHEEZILY
WICKEDLY
WILDFELL
WILFULLY
WINDFALL
WINDMILL
WITHHOLD
WOEFULLY
WOODENLY
WORKABLE
WORTHILY
YOURSELF
ZARZUELA
AGRONOMY
ALLOGAMY
ANALEMMA
ANATHEMA
ATHEROMA
AUTOGAMY
AUTONOMY
BACKCOMB
BLOWLAMP
CATACOMB
CHARISMA
CHORIAMB
CINERAMA
CONSOMMÉ
DOLDRUMS
ENDOGAMY
EPITHEMA
ERYTHEMA
FEARSOME
FILENAME
FIREARMS
FIREDAMP
FORENAME
FOURSOME
FULLTIME
GENDARME
GERONIMO
GLADSOME
GLAUCOMA
GLEESOME
GLOSSEME
GRAPHEME
GRUESOME
HALFTIME
HANDSOME
HEADLAMP
HECATOMB
LIFETIME
LOBOTOMY
LONESOME
LONGTIME
MACHISMO
MALLARMÉ
MARITIME
MEALTIME
MEANTIME
MELANOMA
METONYMY
MONOGAMY
MORPHEME
NICKNAME
NOONTIME
NOSTROMO
OKLAHOMA
OVERCOME
OVERTIME
PANORAMA
PARTTIME
PASTRAMI
PHYLLOME
PILGRIMS
PLAYTIME
POLYGAMY
POLYSEME
POLYSEMY
PROFORMA
REALTIME
REASSUME
SELFSAME
SOMETIME
STEATOMA
SYMPTOMS
SYNDROME
TAKEHOME
TAXONOMY
TERATOMA
THINGAMY
TIRESOME
TOILSOME
TRACHOMA
TRILEMMA
TWELVEMO
WILLIAMS
XANTHOMA
XENOGAMY
YOKOHAMA
ABDUCENS
ABERRANT
ABUNDANT

ABUTMENT
ACCIDENT
ACCUSING
ACQUAINT
ACRIMONY
ADHERENT
ADJACENT
ADJUTANT
ADJUVANT
ADMIRING
AERODYNE
AFFLUENT
AGREEING
AGRIMONY
AIRBORNE
AIRPLANE
ALARMING
ALBINONI
ALEMAINE
ALGERINE
ALKALINE
ALLOWING
ALLURING
AMANDINE
AMBULANT
ANNOYING
ANSERINE
ANTIMONY
ANYTHING
APERIENT
APPARENT
APPELANT
AQUALUNG
AQUATINT
AQUILINE
ARGININE
ARGUMENT
ARMAMENT
ARROGANT
ASPIRANT
ASPIRING
ASSUMING
ASTATINE
ATHELING
AVAILING
AVENTINE
AVICENNA
AVIFAUNA
BABBLING
BACCHANT
BACKBONE
BACKHAND
BAFFLING
BAHRAINI
BAILMENT
BANDANNA
BANTLING
BARITONE
BASELINE
BASEMENT
BEAUMONT
BECOMING
BEESWING
BEETLING
BEFRIEND
BERTRAND
BLACKING
BLEEDING
BLENDING
BLESSING
BLINDING
BLINKING
BLOOMING
BLURRING
BLUSHING
BOARDING
BOASTING
BOBOLINK
BODYLINE
BORODINO
BOTSWANA
BOTTLING
BOUFFANT
BOUNCING
BRAGGING
BREAKING
BREEDING
BRIDGING
BRIEFING
BRIMMING
BRINGING
BRISLING
BROILING
BROODING
BROWNING
BROWSING
BRUISING
BUBBLING
BUCKLING
BUILDING
BULLRING
BUMBLING
BUNGLING
BURSTING
BUSTLING
CAFFEINE
CALAMINE
CAMSTONE
CANOEING
CAPERING
CAPSTONE
CARABINE
CAROLINA
CAROLINE
CAROTENE
CARRYING
CASEMENT
CATATONY
CATCHING
CATERING
CATILINE
CAVATINA
CEREMENT
CEREMONY
CHACONNE
CHADBAND
CHANGING
CHARGING
CHARMING
CHEATING
CHECKING
CHEERING
CHEYENNE
CHICKENS
CHILLING
CHIPMUNK
CHLORINE
CHOOSING
CHOPPING
CICERONE
CINCHONA
CLADDING
CLAIMANT
CLANGING
CLAPPING
CLASHING
CLASPING
CLEANING
CLEARING
CLIMBING
CLINGING
CLIPPING
CLOTHING
COACHING
COALMINE
COCKAYNE
COHERENT
COLORANT
COLORING
COMPLINE
COMPOUND
CONFOUND
CONFRONT
CONSTANT
COUCHANT
COUCHING
COUGHING
COUNTING
COUPLING
COVALENT
COVENANT
COVERING
CRACKING
CRAWLING
CRESCENT
CRETONNE
CRINGING
CROONING
CROSSING
CROWNING
CRUSHING
CURTAINS
CZAREVNA
DATELINE
DAUNTING
DAZZLING
DEADLINE
DECADENT
DECAYING
DECKHAND
DETHRONE
DIALLING
DIAPHONE
DILIGENT
DISCOUNT
DISMOUNT
DIVIDEND
DOCKLAND
DOCTRINE
DOCUMENT
DOMINANT
DOPAMINE
DOUBTING
DRACAENA
DRAGOONS
DRAINING
DRESSING
DRIFTING
DRINKING
DRIPPING
DROOPING
DROPPING
DROWNING
DRUBBING
DRUMLINE
DRUMMING
DRYSTONE
DUCKLING
DUMFOUND
DUMPLING
DWELLING
EARPHONE
EASEMENT
EFFLUENT
EGGPLANT
ELEPHANT
ELKHOUND
ELOQUENT
EMERGENT
EMERGING
EMIGRANT
EMULGENT
ENDURING
ENGAGING
ENSHRINE
ENTHRONE
ENTICING
ENVIRONS
EPIPHANY
EQUITANT
ERECTING
ESCULENT
ETHYLENE
EUROLAND
EVACUANT
EVENSONG
EVERYONE
EXACTING
EXCITING
EXISTENT
EXISTING
EXOCRINE
EXPONENT
EXULTANT
EXULTING
FAINTING
FALKLAND
FARMHAND
FARMLAND
FARTHING
FECULENT
FEMININE
FETCHING
FIDDLING
FIELDING
FIGHTING
FIGURINE
FILAMENT
FILIPINO
FISHBONE
FISHPOND
FLAGGING
FLAGRANT
FLAPPING
FLASHING
FLEETING
FLIPPANT
FLIPPING
FLIRTING
FLOATING
FLOGGING
FLOODING
FLOORING
FLUORINE
FLUSHING
FOGBOUND
FOLKSONG
FONDLING
FOOTLING
FOREGONE
FOREHAND
FORELAND
FOUNDING
FOXHOUND
FRAGMENT
FRAGRANT
FREEHAND
FREEZING
FREQUENT
FROSTING
FRUITING
FUMBLING
GABORONE
GADARENE
GAMBLING
GANGLAND
GANGLING
GANGRENE
GARAMOND
GASOLINE
GELATINE
GEOPHONE
GERMAINE
GIOVANNI
GLANCING
GLEAMING
GLOAMING
GLOATING
GLORIANA
GLUTTONY
GNASHING
GOLDMINE
GONDWANA
GOURMAND
GRADIENT
GRAINING
GRASPING
GRAYLING
GREENING
GREETING
GRILLING
GRINDING
GRIPPING
GROOMING
GROUPING
GROUTING
GROWLING
GRUDGING
GUNPOINT
GYMKHANA
HAIRLINE
HARDLINE

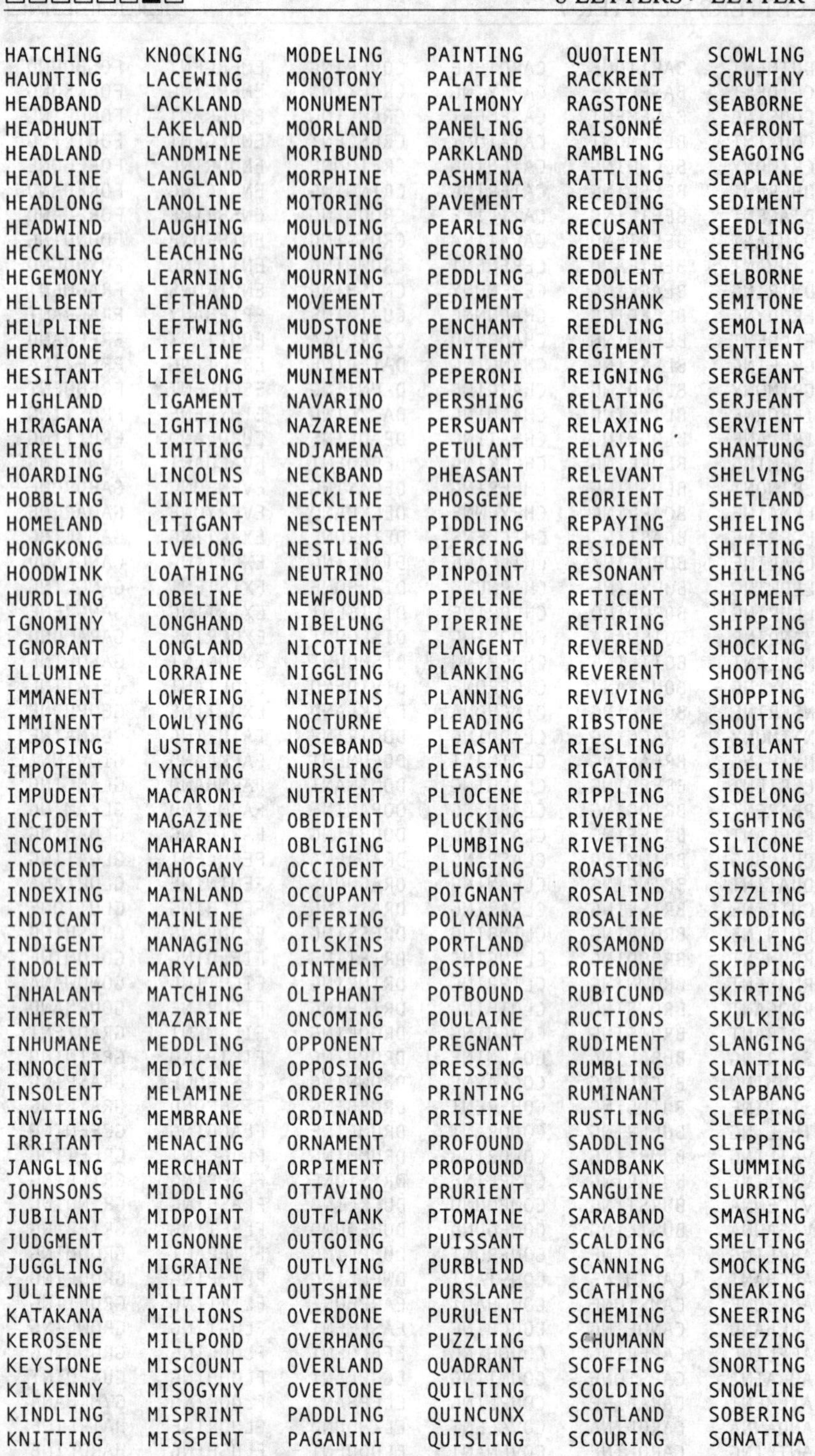

HATCHING
HAUNTING
HEADBAND
HEADHUNT
HEADLAND
HEADLINE
HEADLONG
HEADWIND
HECKLING
HEGEMONY
HELLBENT
HELPLINE
HERMIONE
HESITANT
HIGHLAND
HIRAGANA
HIRELING
HOARDING
HOBBLING
HOMELAND
HONGKONG
HOODWINK
HURDLING
IGNOMINY
IGNORANT
ILLUMINE
IMMANENT
IMMINENT
IMPOSING
IMPOTENT
IMPUDENT
INCIDENT
INCOMING
INDECENT
INDEXING
INDICANT
INDIGENT
INDOLENT
INHALANT
INHERENT
INHUMANE
INNOCENT
INSOLENT
INVITING
IRRITANT
JANGLING
JOHNSONS
JUBILANT
JUDGMENT
JUGGLING
JULIENNE
KATAKANA
KEROSENE
KEYSTONE
KILKENNY
KINDLING
KNITTING
KNOCKING
LACEWING
LACKLAND
LAKELAND
LANDMINE
LANGLAND
LANOLINE
LAUGHING
LEACHING
LEARNING
LEFTHAND
LEFTWING
LIFELINE
LIFELONG
LIGAMENT
LIGHTING
LIMITING
LINCOLNS
LINIMENT
LITIGANT
LIVELONG
LOATHING
LOBELINE
LONGHAND
LONGLAND
LORRAINE
LOWERING
LOWLYING
LUSTRINE
LYNCHING
MACARONI
MAGAZINE
MAHARANI
MAHOGANY
MAINLAND
MAINLINE
MANAGING
MARYLAND
MATCHING
MAZARINE
MEDDLING
MEDICINE
MELAMINE
MEMBRANE
MENACING
MERCHANT
MIDDLING
MIDPOINT
MIGNONNE
MIGRAINE
MILITANT
MILLIONS
MILLPOND
MISCOUNT
MISOGYNY
MISPRINT
MISSPENT
MODELING
MONOTONY
MONUMENT
MOORLAND
MORIBUND
MORPHINE
MOTORING
MOULDING
MOUNTING
MOURNING
MOVEMENT
MUDSTONE
MUMBLING
MUNIMENT
NAVARINO
NAZARENE
NDJAMENA
NECKBAND
NECKLINE
NESCIENT
NESTLING
NEUTRINO
NEWFOUND
NIBELUNG
NICOTINE
NIGGLING
NINEPINS
NOCTURNE
NOSEBAND
NURSLING
NUTRIENT
OBEDIENT
OBLIGING
OCCIDENT
OCCUPANT
OFFERING
OILSKINS
OINTMENT
OLIPHANT
ONCOMING
OPPONENT
OPPOSING
ORDERING
ORDINAND
ORNAMENT
ORPIMENT
OTTAVINO
OUTFLANK
OUTGOING
OUTLYING
OUTSHINE
OVERDONE
OVERHANG
OVERLAND
OVERTONE
PADDLING
PAGANINI
PAINTING
PALATINE
PALIMONY
PANELING
PARKLAND
PASHMINA
PAVEMENT
PEARLING
PECORINO
PEDDLING
PEDIMENT
PENCHANT
PENITENT
PEPERONI
PERSHING
PERSUANT
PETULANT
PHEASANT
PHOSGENE
PIDDLING
PIERCING
PINPOINT
PIPELINE
PIPERINE
PLANGENT
PLANKING
PLANNING
PLEADING
PLEASANT
PLEASING
PLIOCENE
PLUCKING
PLUMBING
PLUNGING
POIGNANT
POLYANNA
PORTLAND
POSTPONE
POTBOUND
POULAINE
PREGNANT
PRESSING
PRINTING
PRISTINE
PROFOUND
PROPOUND
PRURIENT
PTOMAINE
PUISSANT
PURBLIND
PURSLANE
PURULENT
PUZZLING
QUADRANT
QUILTING
QUINCUNX
QUISLING
QUOTIENT
RACKRENT
RAGSTONE
RAISONNÉ
RAMBLING
RATTLING
RECEDING
RECUSANT
REDEFINE
REDOLENT
REDSHANK
REEDLING
REGIMENT
REIGNING
RELATING
RELAXING
RELAYING
RELEVANT
REORIENT
REPAYING
RESIDENT
RESONANT
RETICENT
RETIRING
REVEREND
REVERENT
REVIVING
RIBSTONE
RIESLING
RIGATONI
RIPPLING
RIVERINE
RIVETING
ROASTING
ROSALIND
ROSALINE
ROSAMOND
ROTENONE
RUBICUND
RUCTIONS
RUDIMENT
RUMBLING
RUMINANT
RUSTLING
SADDLING
SANDBANK
SANGUINE
SARABAND
SCALDING
SCANNING
SCATHING
SCHEMING
SCHUMANN
SCOFFING
SCOLDING
SCOTLAND
SCOURING
SCOWLING
SCRUTINY
SEABORNE
SEAFRONT
SEAGOING
SEAPLANE
SEDIMENT
SEEDLING
SEETHING
SELBORNE
SEMITONE
SEMOLINA
SENTIENT
SERGEANT
SERJEANT
SERVIENT
SHANTUNG
SHELVING
SHETLAND
SHIELING
SHIFTING
SHILLING
SHIPMENT
SHIPPING
SHOCKING
SHOOTING
SHOPPING
SHOUTING
SIBILANT
SIDELINE
SIDELONG
SIGHTING
SILICONE
SINGSONG
SIZZLING
SKIDDING
SKILLING
SKIPPING
SKIRTING
SKULKING
SLANGING
SLANTING
SLAPBANG
SLEEPING
SLIPPING
SLUMMING
SLURRING
SMASHING
SMELTING
SMOCKING
SNEAKING
SNEERING
SNEEZING
SNORTING
SNOWLINE
SOBERING
SONATINA

SOOTHING
SORBONNE
SOUCHONG
SOUNDING
SOURCING
SOUTHEND
SPANKING
SPANNING
SPARKING
SPARRING
SPARTANS
SPAWNING
SPEAKING
SPELLING
SPENDING
SPIFFING
SPINNING
SPITTING
SPOILING
SPORTING
SPOTTING
SPURNING
STABBING
STABLING
STAFFING
STAGNANT
STALKING
STANDING
STARLING
STARTING
STARVING
STEALING
STEERING
STEPHENS
STERLING
STICKING
STIFLING
STINGING
STINKING
STIRLING
STIRRING
STOCKING
STOPPING
STORMING
STORMONT
STRIDENT
STRIKING
STRIVING
STUFFING
STUNNING
SUBPOENA
SUCKLING
SUDAMENT
SUDAMINA
SUNBURNT
SUNSHINE
SUPPLANT
SURMOUNT
SURROUND
SWANSONG
SWARMING
SWEARING
SWEATING
SWEEPING
SWELLING
SWERVING
SWILLING
SWIMMING
SWINGING
SWIRLING
SYMBIONT
SYMPHONY
SYNCLINE
TAMARIND
TAPERING
TASHKENT
TEACHING
TEETHING
TEGUMENT
TELEGONY
TEMPTING
TENEMENT
TERYLENE
THAILAND
THIAMINE
THIEVING
THINKING
THINNING
THOUSAND
THUMPING
TICKLING
TINGLING
TOLERANT
TOUCHING
TOWELING
TOWERING
TRACKING
TRAILING
TRAINING
TRAMLINE
TREELINE
TRIFLING
TRILLING
TRIMMING
TRIPLING
TRIPTANE
TROMBONE
TROOPING
TRUCKING
TRUSTING
TSAREVNA
TUPPENNY
TWIRLING
TWISTING
TWOPENNY
TYROSINE
UNCARING
UNDULANT
UNENDING
UNERRING
UNFADING
UNIFYING
UPCOMING
UPRISING
URETHANE
URSULINE
VAGABOND
VALETING
VAULTING
VEHEMENT
VERLAINE
VESTMENT
VIGILANT
VILLAINY
VIREMENT
VIRULENT
VISCOUNT
VISITANT
VISITING
VITAMINS
VOLPLANE
VOMITING
WALLSEND
WALTZING
WAMBLING
WARPAINT
WARPLANE
WATCHING
WATERING
WAVEBAND
WAVERING
WEAKLING
WEIGHING
WHACKING
WHEEZING
WHIPHAND
WHIPPING
WHIRLING
WHITLING
WHOOPING
WHOPPING
WIDENING
WISHBONE
WITCHING
WOBBLING
WOLFBANE
WOODBINE
WOODLAND
WOODWIND
WOOLLENS
WORRYING
WRAPPING
WRINGING
WRITHING
YACHTING
YEARLING
YEARLONG
YEARNING
YIELDING
ZIBELINE
ZUCCHINI
ABDUCTOR
ABINGDON
ABLATION
ABLUTION
ABORTION
ABRASION
ABUTILON
ACCENTOR
ACCUSTOM
ACROMION
ADDITION
ADHESION
ADJUSTOR
ADOPTION
ADULATOR
AEROFLOT
AFFUSION
AGITATOR
AGITPROP
AGNATION
ALLUSION
AMBITION
ANACREON
ANCESTOR
ANDERSON
ANGSTROM
ANTERIOR
ANTEROOM
ANTIPHON
AOTEAROA
APHELION
APOLLYON
APPLETON
ASBESTOS
ASSESSOR
ASUNCION
ATTESTOR
AUBUSSON
AUDITION
AVERSION
AVIATION
AVULSION
BABYHOOD
BACHELOR
BACKDROP
BACKROOM
BALLROOM
BALLYHOO
BANDEROL
BANKBOOK
BARBADOS
BARBIZON
BAREFOOT
BATHROOM
BEETROOT
BEHAVIOR
BERGAMOT
BETATRON
BIATHLON
BILLHOOK
BILLYBOY
BLACKBOY
BLUDGEON
BOOKROOM
BOOKSHOP
BRABAZON
BRIGHTON
BROMPTON
BUCKSHOT
BULLFROG
BUNGALOW
CABOCHON
CACHALOT
CACHEPOT
CAERLEON
CALDERON
CALTHROP
CALVADOS
CAMEROON
CARCAJOU
CARDAMOM
CARILLON
CARJACOU
CARRYCOT
CAULDRON
CESSPOOL
CHALDRON
CHAMPION
CHAPERON
CHOIRBOY
CHRISTOM
CINNAMON
CITATION
CLUBFOOT
COAUTHOR
COCKATOO
COCKCROW
COERCION
COHESION
COLLATOR
COLOPHON
CONJUROR
CONVEYOR
COOKBOOK
COPYBOOK
CORDUROY
CORRIDOR
CRACKPOT
CREATION
CREDITOR
CRICHTON
CROWFOOT
CURSITOR
CUSPIDOR
DARKROOM
DARTMOOR
DASHWOOD
DAVIDSON
DEADWOOD
DECISION
DEFECTOR
DELETION
DELUSION
DEMEANOR
DEMOTION
DERISION
DETECTOR
DEVOTION
DIAPASON
DICTATOR
DIDDICOY
DILATION
DILUTION
DIRECTOR
DISALLOW
DISCOLOR
DISFAVOR
DISHONOR
DISUNION
DIVISION
DOMINION
DONATION
DOORKNOB
DOUBLOON
DOUGHBOY
DROPSHOT
DURATION
DYNATRON
ECLOSION
EDUCATOR
EFFUSION
EJECTION
ELECTION
ELECTRON
ELEVATOR
EMBLAZON
EMERSION
EMISSION
EMULSION
ENDEAVOR
ENDYMION

ENIWETOK
ENTREPOT
ENVISION
EPIPLOON
EQUATION
ERECTION
ERIKSSON
ERUPTION
ESCARGOT
ESTRAGON
EVICTION
EXACTION
EXCISION
EXECUTOR
EXERTION
EXTENSOR
EXTERIOR
EXTRADOS
FEELGOOD
FIREWOOD
FIXATION
FLATFOOT
FOLDEROL
FOREDOOM
FOREFOOT
FORENOON
FRACTION
FRICTION
FRUITION
FUNCTION
FURBELOW
GALLIPOT
GANGLION
GARDYLOO
GARRISON
GIRLHOOD
GOLLIWOG
GONFALON
GOODWOOD
GOOSEGOG
GOVERNOR
GRANDSON
GRIDIRON
GUERIDON
GUMPTION
GYRATION
HAMILTON
HANDBOOK
HARDWOOD
HARRISON
HEADROOM
HEATSPOT
HEDGEHOG
HEDGEROW
HEIRLOOM
HEPTAGON
HEYTHROP
HIGHBROW
HOLYROOD
HONEYPOT
HORNBOOK
HORSEBOX
HYPERION
IGNITION
ILLUSION
IMITATOR
IMPOSTOR
IMPRISON
INACTION
INCISION
INFERIOR
INFUSION
INJECTOR
INTERCOM
INTERIOR
INTERPOL
INTRADOS
INVASION
INVENTOR
INVESTOR
IRONWOOD
JACKAROO
JACKBOOT
JELLICOE
JETTISON
JONCANOE
JUNCTION
KANGAROO
KINGSTON
KINKAJOU
KOMSOMOL
KRAKATOA
LABRADOR
LANCELOT
LEAPFROG
LEGATION
LIBATION
LIFEBUOY
LOCATION
LOLLIPOP
LONGSTOP
LOOSEBOX
LUNCHEON
MACAROON
MACMAHON
MAILSHOT
MARATHON
MASCARON
MASSICOT
MASTODON
MATCHBOX
MEDIATOR
MELCHIOR
MERCATOR
MESSIDOR
METAPHOR
METHANOL
MICRODOT
MIRLITON
MONEYBOX
MORRISON
MOUFFLON
MUSHROOM
MUTATION
MYRIAPOD
MYRMIDON
NAPOLEON
NARRATOR
NEGATION
NEIGHBOR
NEWSROOM
NIDATION
NOTATION
NOTEBOOK
OBJECTOR
OBLATION
OBLIVION
OCCASION
OCTAROON
OFFCOLOR
OFFSHOOT
OMISSION
OMPHALOS
OOPHORON
OPENDOOR
OPERATOR
ORTHODOX
OVERBOOK
OVERFLOW
OVERLOOK
OVERSHOE
OVERSHOT
OXYMORON
PANTALON
PANTHEON
PAPILLON
PASSBOOK
PAVILION
PAWNSHOP
PEEKABOO
PENTAGON
PETERLOO
PETITION
PHILEMON
PHLEGMON
PICAROON
PINEWOOD
PISCATOR
PLANKTON
PLASTRON
PLAYROOM
POLTROON
POLYGLOT
POOLROOM
POPPADOM
POSEIDON
POSITION
POSITRON
PREDATOR
PROTOCOL
PROTOZOA
PURVEYOR
QUADROON
QUAESTOR
QUESTION
RADIATOR
RAINDROP
REACTION
RECEPTOR
REDACTOR
REDEPLOY
REEMPLOY
RELATION
RELIGION
RESISTOR
RESTROOM
REVISION
ROADSHOW
ROBINSON
ROGATION
ROSEWOOD
ROTATION
RULEBOOK
SALEROOM
SALVADOR
SANCTION
SAUROPOD
SCALLION
SCANSION
SCISSION
SCORPION
SCREWTOP
SCULLION
SCULPTOR
SEDATION
SEDITION
SELECTOR
SERVITOR
SHEEPDOG
SHEIKDOM
SHERATON
SHERWOOD
SHOWROOM
SICKROOM
SIDESHOW
SKELETON
SKILLION
SKYPILOT
SLIPSHOD
SLIPSLOP
SMALLPOX
SMIDGEON
SNAPSHOT
SNOWDROP
SNUFFBOX
SOFTWOOD
SOLUTION
SPITTOON
SPLENDOR
SQUADRON
STALLION
STOCKPOT
STURGEON
SUPERIOR
SURVEYOR
SURVIVOR
TARRAGON
TAXATION
TEARDROP
TEASPOON
TELETHON
TENNYSON
TESTATOR
TETRAGON
TETRAPOD
TEXTBOOK
THANATOS
THOMPSON
THRALDOM
TOMORROW
TOREADOR
TRACTION
TRAPDOOR
TRILLION
TRUNNION
TURANDOT
ULTERIOR
UNBUTTON
UNCOMMON
UNDERDOG
UNDERTOW
UNPERSON
UNREASON
VACATION
VEXATION
VIBRATOR
VINDALOO
VIOLATOR
VOCATION
VOLITION
WAINSCOT
WARDROOM
WASHROOM
WATCHDOG
WATERLOO
WEDGWOOD
WHITEHOT
WORDBOOK
WORKBOOK
WORKROOM
WORKSHOP
WORMWOOD
XENOPHON
YEARBOOK
ANAGLYPH
ANTELOPE
ANTILOPE
ANTIPOPE
AUTOTYPE
BANKRUPT
BARDOLPH
BIOGRAPH
BIOSCOPE
BLOWPIPE
CALLIOPE
CALOTYPE
CENOTAPH
CONTEMPT
ECHINOPS
ENVELOPE
EPIGRAPH
ESCALOPE
GALLUMPH
GIGLAMPS
HEELTAPS
HORNPIPE
HOSEPIPE
IRISCOPE
LINOTYPE
MONOTYPE
OTOSCOPE
OVERRIPE
PENELOPE
PHILIPPI
PHILLIPS
ROOFTOPS
SCHNAPPS
SEASCAPE
SEROTYPE
STANHOPE
TAILPIPE
TRANSEPT
TREETOPS
TRIGLYPH
TROLLOPE
WINDPIPE
XANTIPPE
ZOETROPE
AARDVARK
ADULTERY
ADVISORY
ALBACORE

ALEATORY
ALHAMBRA
ALLEGORY
AMATEURS
ANCESTRY
ANYWHERE
APERTURE
ARMATURE
ARTISTRY
AUDITORY
AUTOGYRO
AVOGADRO
AYRSHIRE
BACKFIRE
BACKWARD
BACKYARD
BAGHEERA
BALLGIRL
BALLPARK
BARNYARD
BARRATRY
BASEBORN
BASKETRY
BEAUFORT
BERIBERI
BESTIARY
BILBERRY
BLINKERS
BLIZZARD
BLOOMERS
BLUSTERY
BODYWORK
BONEYARD
BOOKMARK
BOOKWORK
BOOKWORM
BOTTOMRY
BOUNDARY
BRADBURY
BRAGGART
BRASSARD
BREVIARY
BROCHURE
BRUMAIRE
BULLHORN
BURBERRY
BURGLARY
BUTCHERS
BUTCHERY
BUZZWORD
CADASTRE
CAJOLERY
CALIPERS
CALLGIRL
CANBERRA
CAPYBARA
CAREWORN
CASHMERE
CATEGORY
CATHEDRA
CEMETERY
CENTAURY
CHAMBERS
CHAMPERS
CHANCERY
CHEATERS
CHECKERS
CHEQUERS
CHESHIRE
CHILDERS
CHILTERN
CHIMAERA
CHIVALRY
CLAPPERS
CLAYMORE
CLEANERS
CLEAVERS
CLIFFORD
CLINKERS
CLIPPERS
COALPORT
COBBLERS
COIFFURE
COLLIERS
COLLIERY
CONSPIRE
CONTRARY
COOKWARE
COQUETRY
CORONARY
COSTMARY
COVENTRY
CRACKERS
CREAMERY
CREATURE
CROCKERY
CRUMHORN
CRUZEIRO
CULINARY
CUPBOARD
CUTHBERT
CYNOSURE
DAIQUIRI
DELAWARE
DELIVERY
DEMERARA
DENATURE
DERISORY
DEWBERRY
DIASPORA
DILATORY
DIVIDERS
DOCKYARD
DOGBERRY
DOWNTURN
DOWNWARD
DRUDGERY
DRUNKARD
EASTWARD
ECTODERM
ELECTORS
ELSINORE
EMISSARY
ENDOCARP
ENDODERM
ENSIFORM
EPHEMERA
ERUPTURE
ESTOVERS
ETCETERA
EVERMORE
EXPOSURE
FALCONRY
FARMYARD
FARRIERY
FEATHERS
FEATHERY
FEBRUARY
FENESTRA
FIREBIRD
FIREWORK
FLANDERS
FLATTERY
FLATWARE
FLATWORM
FLAUBERT
FLINDERS
FLIPPERS
FLUMMERY
FOLKLORE
FOOTSORE
FOOTWORK
FORESTRY
FOREWARN
FOREWORD
FOURPART
FRACTURE
FRETWORK
FRIPPERY
FUMITORY
FUNERARY
FUSEWIRE
FUSIFORM
GADGETRY
GAILLARD
GALLIARD
GAMEBIRD
GAOLBIRD
GEOMETRY
GLANDERS
GLOSSARY
GOODSIRE
GREENERY
GURDWARA
GYRATORY
HABANERA
HABSBURG
HALFTERM
HALLIARD
HALLMARK
HANDCART
HAPSBURG
HARDCORE
HARDWARE
HARTFORD
HATCHERY
HAWTHORN
HEADMARK
HEADWORD
HELIPORT
HELLFIRE
HERALDRY
HEREFORD
HEREWARD
HIGHBORN
HINDWARD
HIPSTERS
HOMEWARD
HOMEWORK
HONORARY
HOOKWORM
HOSTELRY
IDOLATRY
ILLUSORY
IMMATURE
INDUSTRY
INEXPERT
INFANTRY
INSECURE
IRONWARE
IRONWORK
ISOTHERE
ISOTHERM
JACQUARD
JAILBIRD
JODHPURS
JOINTURE
JUNCTURE
JURATORY
KACHAHRI
KALAHARI
KEYBOARD
KITEMARK
KNACKERS
KNICKERS
KNOCKERS
KNOTWORK
LADYBIRD
LAMASERY
LANDLORD
LANDMARK
LANDWARD
LANSBURY
LAPIDARY
LAVATORY
LAVENGRO
LAWCOURT
LEATHERY
LEFTWARD
LIENTERY
LIGATURE
LITERARY
LIVEWARE
LONGHORN
LONGTERM
LONICERA
LOVEBIRD
LOVELORN
LUKEWARM
LUMINARY
LYREBIRD
MAINYARD
MANICURE
MASSACRE
MATAMORE
MEDIOCRE
MEUNIÈRE
MILITARY
MILKWORT
MINATORY
MINISTRY
MISCARRY
MISERERE
MISSOURI
MOISTURE
MONETARY
MONSTERA
MORTUARY
MUDGUARD
MULBERRY
MULEWORT
NEATHERD
NORTHERN
NUGATORY
OBITUARY
OFFICERS
OFFSHORE
OMNIFORM
OPENWORK
ORANGERY
ORDINARY
OUTBOARD
OUTDOORS
OUTSMART
OVENWARE
OVERLORD
OVERTURE
OVERTURN
OVERWORK
PANEGYRY
PARTERRE
PASSPORT
PASSWORD
PEDANTRY
PEDICURE
PELLAGRA
PENUMBRA
PERICARP
PERIDERM
PERSPIRE
PIECHART
PILCHARD
PINAFORE
PITCAIRN
PLATFORM
PLAYGIRL
PLEASURE
PLETHORA
POITIERS
POLYCARP
PORPHYRA
PORPHYRY
PORTIÈRE
POSTCARD
POSTMARK
POTSHERD
PREMIERE
PRESSURE
PROSPERO
PSALTERY
PSEUDERY
PUNCTURE
PUSHCART
PYRIFORM
QUAGMIRE
QUANDARY
QUARTERS
RAILLERY
RAINBIRD
REAFFIRM
REARWARD
REASSERT
REASSURE
RECOVERY
REDSTART
REFINERY
REGISTRY
REINSURE
RIBALDRY
RINGWORM
ROCKETRY
ROSEMARY

ROTATORY
ROUNDERS
RUSHMORE
SADDLERY
SALIVARY
SALUTARY
SALUTORY
SAMPHIRE
SANITARY
SAPPHIRE
SAVAGERY
SAVOYARD
SAYONARA
SCABBARD
SCHUBERT
SCISSORS
SCULLERY
SEABOARD
SEASHORE
SEMINARY
SHEPHERD
SHIPYARD
SHOEHORN
SHOWGIRL
SHUTTERS
SILKWORM
SINECURE
SKINWORK
SLATTERN
SLEEPERS
SLIPPERS
SLIPPERY
SLOBBERY
SLUGGARD
SNEAKERS
SNOBBERY
SOFTWARE
SOLDIERS
SOLDIERY
SOLITARY
SOMBRERO
SONGBIRD
SOUTHERN
SPANIARD
SPEAKERS
SPITFIRE
STAFFORD
STAGGERS
STAGHORN
STALWART
STANDARD
STANNARY
STARKERS
STARTERS
STATUARY
STUBBORN
SUMMITRY

SYCAMORE
SYMMETRY
TACITURN
TANDOORI
TAPESTRY
TAPEWORM
TAYBERRY
TEACHERS
TEAMWORK
TEESHIRT
TELEMARK
TERTIARY
THIEVERY
THUNDERY
TIDEMARK
TINCTURE
TOXOCARA
TRAITORS
TREASURE
TREASURY
TRICKERY
TROTTERS
TROUSERS
TRUMPERY
TUPAMARO
TUTELARY
TWEEZERS
UNDERARM
UNSAVORY
UNTOWARD
UPSTAIRS
VANGUARD
VARIFORM
VERTEBRA
VESTIARY
VINEGARY
VINEYARD
VOLTAIRE
VOMITORY
WALLWORT
WEAPONRY
WESTWARD
WHIPCORD
WHISKERS
WHISKERY
WILDFIRE
WINDBURN
WINDWARD
WIREWORM
WISEACRE
WITCHERY
WIZARDRY
WOODWARD
WOODWORK
WOODWORM
YAKITORI
YEOMANRY

YOGHOURT
ZOOSPERM
ZOOSPORE
ABSCISSA
ABSTRUSE
ACTIVISM
ACTIVIST
ADMONISH
AIRINESS
ALARMIST
ALEHOUSE
ALGORISM
ALIENISM
ALIENIST
ALPINIST
ALTRUISM
ALTRUIST
AMETHYST
ANAPAEST
ANEURYSM
ANNALIST
ANTEPOST
APHORISM
APIARIST
APOSTASY
APPLAUSE
APPRAISE
ARBALEST
ARCHAISM
ARETHUSA
ARSONIST
ASTERISK
ASTONISH
ATHANASY
ATHETISE
BAATHIST
BACKLASH
BACKLESS
BALDNESS
BALINESE
BARENESS
BARONESS
BASELESS
BASENESS
BASILISK
BEAKLESS
BELLPUSH
BELPAESE
BERCEUSE
BIGAMIST
BLACKISH
BLANDISH
BLOWFISH
BLUENOSE
BOLDNESS
BONELESS
BOOKCASE

BOOTLESS
BOTANIST
BOTULISM
BRACKISH
BRANDISH
BRINDISI
BROWNISH
BUCKFAST
BUDAPEST
BUDDHISM
BUDDHIST
BUSINESS
BUTTRESS
CAGINESS
CALABASH
CALMNESS
CANALISE
CANOEIST
CARELESS
CATALYST
CATHOUSE
CELANESE
CENTRIST
CHARTISM
CHARTIST
CHASTISE
CHILDISH
CHILIAST
CHURLISH
CLANNISH
CLIQUISH
CLOWNISH
CLUELESS
COLDNESS
COLLAPSE
COLONIST
COMATOSE
COMPRESS
COMPRISE
CONDENSE
CONGRESS
CONQUEST
CONTRAST
CONVERSE
CONVULSE
COOLNESS
COSINESS
COUNTESS
COURTESY
COZINESS
CRAMOISY
CRAWFISH
CRAYFISH
CREVASSE
CRONYISM
CURTNESS
CUTENESS

CUTPURSE
CYNICISM
DAMPNESS
DANKNESS
DARKNESS
DATABASE
DATELESS
DEAFNESS
DECREASE
DEEPNESS
DEFTNESS
DEMOLISH
DEVILISH
DEXTROSE
DIAGNOSE
DIASTASE
DIMINISH
DISABUSE
DISBURSE
DISCLOSE
DISGUISE
DISPENSE
DISPERSE
DISTRESS
DISTRUST
DOGHOUSE
DONATIST
DOORPOST
DORMOUSE
DOWNCAST
DRUGGIST
DUCHESSE
DUELLIST
DULLNESS
DUMBNESS
DWARFISH
DWARFISM
DYNAMISM
EARLIEST
EASINESS
EDGEWISE
EERINESS
EMBOLISM
ENTRYISM
EPILEPSY
ERGOTISE
ERGOTISM
ESCAPISM
ESCAPIST
ESPRESSO
ESSAYIST
ETHERISE
EULOGIST
EUPHUISM
EVENNESS
EXERCISE
EXORCISM

EXORCIST
EXPRESSO
EYEGLASS
FACELESS
FAIRNESS
FARTHEST
FASTNESS
FATALISM
FATALIST
FEARLESS
FECKLESS
FEMINISM
FEMINIST
FEVERISH
FIENDISH
FINALIST
FIRMNESS
FLATFISH
FLAUTIST
FLAWLESS
FLOURISH
FONDNESS
FOOTREST
FORECAST
FOREMOST
FORMLESS
FORTRESS
FOULNESS
FRANKISH
FREAKISH
FREEPOST
FRESHEST
FRUCTOSE
FRUMPISH
FULLNESS
FURTHEST
FUTURISM
FUTURIST
GABONESE
GAMENESS
GATEPOST
GHOULISH
GIANTESS
GLADNESS
GLASNOST
GLUMPISH
GOALPOST
GOLDFISH
GOODNESS
GORMLESS
GREATEST
GREENISH
GRIMNESS
GUYANESE
HAIRLESS
HALFMAST
HARDNESS

HARMLESS
HAZINESS
HEADLESS
HEADMOST
HEADREST
HEDONISM
HEDONIST
HEEDLESS
HEIRLESS
HELPLESS
HENHOUSE
HIGHNESS
HIGHRISE
HINDMOST
HINDUISM
HOLINESS
HOMELESS
HOPELESS
HOTHOUSE
HUMANISM
HUMANIST
HUMORIST
HUNTRESS
HUSHHUSH
ICEHOUSE
IDEALISM
IDEALIST
IDLENESS
IMMODEST
INCREASE
INTEREST
IRISHISM
ISOGLOSS
ISOSTASY
JAPANESE
JEALOUSY
JINGOISM
JINGOIST
JUSTNESS
KEENNESS
KERMESSE
KINDNESS
KINGPOST
KINSHASA
KNOBLESS
KOURMISS
LACROSSE
LAMENESS
LAMPPOST
LANDMASS
LANGUISH
LARGESSE
LAROUSSE
LATENESS
LATINIST
LAZINESS
LEAFLESS
LEBANESE
LEGALISM
LEWDNESS
LIFELESS
LIKENESS
LIKEWISE
LIMBLESS
LIMPNESS
LINGUIST
LISTLESS
LIVERISH
LOBBYIST
LOUDNESS
LOVELESS
LOWCLASS
LOYALIST
LUCKLESS
LUMPFISH
LUNGFISH
LUSHNESS
LYRICISM
LYRICIST
MADHOUSE
MAESTOSO
MAINMAST
MALAGASY
MANIFEST
MANTISSA
MARQUESA
MARQUESS
MARQUISE
MASSEUSE
MATTRESS
MAYORESS
MEANNESS
MEATLESS
MEDALIST
MEEKNESS
MILANESE
MILDNESS
MILKLESS
MINDLESS
MINORESS
MISHMASH
MISTRESS
MISTRUST
MONADISM
MONETISE
MONGOOSE
MORALIST
MOTORIST
MUCHNESS
MUSQUASH
MYOBLAST
NAMELESS
NATURISM
NATURIST
NEARNESS
NEATNESS
NEEDLESS
NEPALESE
NEPOTISM
NEWSCAST
NICENESS
NIHILISM
NIHILIST
NONSENSE
NOTECASE
NOVELIST
NUMBNESS
NUTHOUSE
OCCAMIST
OILINESS
OPENCAST
OPENNESS
OPTIMISM
OPTIMIST
ORGANISM
ORGANIST
OUTBURST
OUTCLASS
OUTHOUSE
OVERCAST
OVERDOSE
OVERPASS
PACIFISM
PACIFIST
PAINLESS
PALENESS
PALUDISM
PANGLOSS
PARADISE
PARODIST
PAROXYSM
PEDERAST
PEERLESS
PEKINESE
PERTNESS
PERVERSE
PHANTASM
PHOTOPSY
PIECRUST
PIRANESI
PITHLESS
PITILESS
PLEONASM
PLEURISY
POORNESS
POPULIST
PORPOISE
PRACTISE
PRECURSE
PRETENSE
PRIAPISM
PRIGGISH
PRIMNESS
PRIMROSE
PRINCESS
PRIORESS
PROGRESS
PROLAPSE
PROPHESY
PROTEASE
PSALMIST
PUGILISM
PUGILIST
PURCHASE
PURPLISH
RACINESS
RANKNESS
RASHNESS
READIEST
READJUST
REARMOST
REASSESS
RECKLESS
RECOURSE
REHEARSE
REINVEST
REPHRASE
REPOUSSÉ
RESPONSE
RESTLESS
RICHNESS
RIGHTIST
RIPENESS
RIVALISE
ROOFLESS
ROOTLESS
ROSINESS
ROYALIST
RUDENESS
RUSTLESS
RUTHLESS
RYEGRASS
SAGENESS
SALTNESS
SAMENESS
SAPPHIST
SARGASSO
SATIRIST
SCOTTISH
SEAMLESS
SEEDLESS
SELFLESS
SEVEREST
SHEEPISH
SHOELESS
SHOWCASE
SHREWISH
SICKLIST
SICKNESS
SIGNPOST
SINAPISM
SKIRMISH
SKITTISH
SLAPDASH
SLIMNESS
SLOWNESS
SLUGFEST
SLUGGISH
SLUTTISH
SMALLEST
SMARTEST
SMUGNESS
SNOBBISH
SOFTNESS
SOLECISM
SORENESS
SOULLESS
SOURNESS
SOURPUSS
SPOTLESS
SPRYNESS
SPYGLASS
STANDISH
STARDUST
STARFISH
STARLESS
STOCKIST
STOICISM
STRABISM
SUBLEASE
SUBTENSE
SUDANESE
SUITCASE
SUNBURST
SUPPRESS
SURENESS
SURPRISE
SUSPENSE
SYRACUSE
TACTLESS
TAILLESS
TAMARISK
TAMENESS
TAPHOUSE
TARBOOSH
TARTNESS
TAUTNESS
TELECAST
TELEVISE
THEORIST
THIEVISH
THINNESS
TICKLISH
TIDINESS
TIMELESS
TIRAMISU
TIRELESS
TITANESS
TITANISM
TITMOUSE
TONELESS
TOPCLASS
TORTOISE
TOULOUSE
TRAPPIST
TRAVERSE
TREATISE
TREELESS
TRESPASS
TRIMNESS
TRUENESS
TUBELESS
TUBEROSE
TYPECAST
UGLINESS
UNIONISM
UNIONIST
UNIVERSE
VANQUISH
VARICOSE
VASTNESS
VERONESE
VILENESS
VIRTUOSI
VIRTUOSO
VOCALIST
WAITRESS
WARDRESS
WARHORSE
WARINESS
WEAKNESS
WHIPLASH
WILDNESS
WILINESS
WINDLASS
WINDLESS
WINGLESS
WIRELESS
WOMANISH
WORDLESS
WORMCAST
YOUNGEST
ABDICATE
ABNEGATE
ABROGATE
ABSOLUTE
ACCOUNTS
ACCURATE
ACERBATE
ACERBITY
ACTIVATE
ACTIVITY

ADEQUATE
ADVOCATE
AEROLITH
AESTHETE
AFFINITY
AIGRETTE
ALACRITY
ALICANTE
ALIENATE
ALLOCATE
ALLOPATH
ALMIGHTY
AMARANTH
AMARETTO
AMBULATE
AMMONITE
AMORETTI
AMORETTO
AMPUTATE
AMUSETTE
ANALECTA
ANECDOTE
ANISETTE
ANNAMITE
ANNOTATE
ANTEDATE
ANTIDOTE
APOSTATE
APPETITE
APPOSITE
ARALDITE
ARAMANTH
ARMALITE
ARROGATE
ASPERITY
ASPIRATE
ATALANTA
ATROCITY
AUDACITY
AUTOMATE
BACKBITE
BACKDATE
BAGUETTE
BAKELITE
BALLISTA
BANALITY
BANDITTI
BANKNOTE
BARONETS
BARRETTE
BAYREUTH
BEHEMOTH
BENEFITS
BEQUEATH
BORACITE
BOSWORTH
BRACKETS
BRAMANTE
BRUNETTE
CALAMITY
CALCEATE
CALCUTTA
CALLISTO
CAMPSITE
CAPACITY
CARUCATE
CASEMATE
CASSETTE
CASTRATE
CASTRATO
CASUALTY
CATAMITE
CELERITY
CELIBATE
CENOBITE
CHAPATTI
CHASTITY
CHEVIOTS
CHINDITS
CHLORATE
CHORDATA
CHORDATE
CHROMITE
CIVILITY
COGITATE
COLLECTS
COMPLETE
CONCERTO
CONCRETE
CONFETTI
CONFLATE
CONTENTS
CONTRITE
COPULATE
COQUETTE
CORNETTO
CORVETTE
CREOSOTE
CROCKETT
CRUCIATE
CUPIDITY
DEBILITY
DECIMATE
DECORATE
DEDICATE
DEFECATE
DEFINITE
DELEGATE
DELICATE
DENDRITE
DEPILATE
DEROGATE
DESOLATE
DETONATE
DIAMANTE
DINGBATS
DISCRETE
DISKETTE
DISTASTE
DISUNITE
DISUNITY
DIVINITY
DJIBOUTI
DOCILITY
DOLOMITE
DOMINATE
DOVECOTE
DRAUGHTS
DRAUGHTY
DRIBLETS
DYNAMITE
ECHINATE
EDENTATE
ELEMENTS
ELEVENTH
ELONGATE
EMACIATE
EMIGRATE
ENERVATE
ENORMITY
ENTIRETY
ENTREATY
EPIPHYTE
EQUALITY
ERADIATE
ERUCTATE
ESCALATE
ESTIMATE
ESTIVATE
ETERNITY
ETIOLATE
EVACUATE
EVALUATE
EXCAVATE
EXECRATE
EXHUMATE
EXIGUITY
EXPEDITE
EYETOOTH
FACILITY
FALSETTO
FATALITY
FAVORITE
FEDERATE
FELICITY
FEMINITY
FEROCITY
FIDELITY
FIFTIETH
FILTRATE
FINALITY
FLATMATE
FLEABITE
FLUIDITY
FLUORITE
FOOTNOTE
FOOTPATH
FORFEITS
FORSOOTH
FORTIETH
FORTUITY
FRUMENTY
FUCHSITE
FUMIGATE
FUTILITY
GARMENTS
GARROTTE
GEMINATE
GENERATE
GRADUATE
GRAFFITI
GRAPHITE
GRATUITY
GRISETTE
GUJARATI
GUNSMITH
HELPMATE
HEREDITY
HEREWITH
HESITATE
HIGHGATE
HILARITY
HITHERTO
HOTPLATE
HUMANITY
HUMIDITY
HUMILITY
HYACINTH
IDENTITY
IMMOLATE
IMMUNITY
IMPOLITE
IMPUNITY
IMPURITY
INCHOATE
INCUBATE
INDICATE
INEQUITY
INFINITE
INFINITY
INGROWTH
INIQUITY
INITIATE
INNOVATE
INSANITY
INSULATE
INTIMATE
INUNDATE
INVOLUTE
IRRIGATE
IRRITATE
JACOBITE
JEANETTE
JEBUSITE
JUBILATE
KILOBYTE
KILOWATT
LACERATE
LACINATE
LAMINATE
LAPIDATE
LATERITE
LAUREATE
LEGALITY
LEVITATE
LEWISITE
LIBERATE
LIBRETTO
LIMONITE
LITERATE
LITERATI
LITIGATE
LIVIDITY
LOCALITY
LUCIDITY
LULWORTH
MACERATE
MACHEATH
MACULATE
MAJORITY
MALLEATE
MAQUETTE
MARINATE
MARONITE
MATURATE
MATURITY
MEDICATE
MEDITATE
MEGABYTE
MEGALITH
MEGAWATT
MELANITE
MEREDITH
MESOLITE
MESSMATE
MILITATE
MINAMATA
MINORITE
MINORITY
MISQUOTE
MITIGATE
MOBILITY
MODERATE
MODERATO
MODULATE
MONMOUTH
MONOLITH
MONTEITH
MOQUETTE
MORALITY
MOSQUITO
MOTIVATE
MUDFLATS
MUTILATE
NATALITY
NATIVITY
NAUSEATE
NAVIGATE
NEOPHYTE
NEPHRITE
NOBILITY
NOISETTE
NOMINATE
NUMERATE
OBDURATE
OBLIGATE
OBSOLETE
ODDMENTS
OILCLOTH
OMELETTE
OPERETTA
OPPOSITE
OPTIMATE
ORDINATE
OSCULATE
OUISTITI
OVERRATE
PAGINATE
PALLIATE
PALMETTO
PARASITE
PECULATE
PERACUTE
PERFECTA
PERFECTO
PERIANTH
PERIPETY
PERMEATE
PIERETTE
PIMIENTO
PLACENTA
PLAUDITS
PLAYMATE
PLYMOUTH
POCHETTE
POLYMATH
POPULATE
POROSITY
POSTDATE
PRIORITY
PRODUCTS
PROPERTY

PROSTATE
QUADRATE
QUANTITY
RACLETTE
RAMPARTS
RAPACITY
RAPIDITY
RECEIPTS
RECREATE
RECRUITS
REGULATE
RELEGATE
RELOCATE
REMNANTS
REMOUNTS
RENOVATE
RESOLUTE
RESONATE
RESPECTS
RIGIDITY
ROOMMATE
ROSSETTI
ROULETTE
RUMINATE
SACRISTY
SAGACITY
SALACITY
SALINITY
SALIVATE
SANCTITY
SAPONITE
SATURATE
SCARCITY
SCHMALTZ
SEAFORTH
SECURITY
SELENITE
SELFPITY
SENILITY
SENORITA
SEPARATE
SERENATA
SERENITY
SEVERITY
SHIPMATE
SIDERITE
SILICATE
SIMULATE
SIXTIETH
SKIBOOTS
SLYBOOTS
SMOLLETT
SOBRIETY
SODALITE
SODALITY
SOLIDITY
SORORITY
SPARSITY
SPICCATO
SPOLIATE
SQUAMATA
STACCATO
STAGNATE
STANNITE
STAROSTA
STEATITE
STELLATE
STICCATO
STIGMATA
STILETTO
STOCCATA
STRENGTH
STUDENTS
SUBJECTS
SUBTLETY
SULPHATE
SYBARITE
TABULATE
TAILGATE
TAMWORTH
TARTRATE
TEACLOTH
TEAMMATE
TEMERITY
TEMPLATE
TENACITY
THOUGHTS
TIMIDITY
TITANITE
TITIVATE
TOLBOOTH
TOLERATE
TOLLGATE
TONALITY
TOTALITY
TOXICITY
TRAVESTY
TRUNCATE
UBIQUITY
ULCERATE
ULTIMATE
UNCHASTE
UNDULATE
UNGULATE
UPRIGHTS
URBANITY
VALIDATE
VALIDITY
VALLETTA
VEGETATE
VELLEITY
VELOCITY
VENALITY
VENDETTA
VENERATE
VERACITY
VERMOUTH
VICINITY
VIGNETTE
VIRILITY
VISIGOTH
VITALITY
VIVACITY
VORACITY
WARRANTY
WORKMATE
XENOLITH
YOSEMITE
ZOOPHYTE
ABOMASUM
ACANTHUS
ACTINIUM
ADDENDUM
AERONAUT
AFFLATUS
ALBURNUM
ALLUVIUM
ALUMINUM
ALVEOLUS
ANALOGUE
APOLOGUE
APPLIQUÉ
AQUARIUM
AQUARIUS
ARCTURUS
ARGONAUT
ARQUEBUS
ASCIDIUM
ASMODEUS
AUGUSTUS
BACILLUS
BANLIEUE
BARBECUE
BASIDIUM
BASINFUL
BELABOUR
BELLYFUL
BIBULOUS
BIGAMOUS
BLACKOUT
BLISSFUL
BOASTFUL
BORDEAUX
BOUTIQUE
BREAKOUT
BRONCHUS
BURNTOUT
CADUCEUS
CALCULUS
CAMARGUE
CAPSICUM
CAPTIOUS
CATULLUS
CAUTIOUS
CERBERUS
CEREBRUM
CHASSEUR
CHECKOUT
CHEERFUL
CHESTNUT
CHIASMUS
CHROMIUM
CIBORIUM
CINGULUM
CLANGOUR
CLAUDIUS
CLEARCUT
COIFFEUR
COLISEUM
COLLOQUY
COLORFUL
COLOSSUS
COLUMBUS
CONSTRUE
CONTINUE
CONTINUO
COUSCOUS
COVETOUS
CREPITUS
CRITIQUE
CURLICUE
DAEDALUS
DAMASCUS
DECOROUS
DELIRIUM
DENARIUS
DESIROUS
DETRITUS
DEXTROUS
DIALOGUE
DIANTHUS
DINOSAUR
DIONYSUS
DOLOROUS
DOUBTFUL
DOUGHNUT
DOWNPOUR
DREADFUL
DUODENUM
ELECTRUM
EMERITUS
EMPORIUM
ENCOMIUM
ENORMOUS
ENSHROUD
EOHIPPUS
EPICURUS
EPILOGUE
EULOGIUM
EVENTFUL
EXIGUOUS
EXORDIUM
FABULOUS
FACTIOUS
FACTOTUM
FAITHFUL
FANCIFUL
FILARIUM
FINESPUN
FLASHGUN
FOLLOWUP
FORCEFUL
FRABJOUS
FRANCIUM
FRAXINUS
FREMITUS
FRENULUM
FRONDEUR
FRUITFUL
GADABOUT
GALBANUM
GARRIGUE
GENEROUS
GERANIUM
GLABROUS
GLASSFUL
GLAUCOUS
GLORIOUS
GLUTAEUS
GOLFCLUB
GORGEOUS
GRACEFUL
GRACIOUS
GRANDEUR
GRATEFUL
GRIEVOUS
HABAKKUK
HALFHOUR
HARANGUE
HARFLEUR
HAZELNUT
HIBISCUS
HOMESPUN
HORATIUS
HUMOROUS
INFAMOUS
INTRIGUE
ISTANBUL
JONGLEUR
KEELHAUL
KHARTOUM
KNOCKOUT
KOUSKOUS
LABURNUM
LANGLAUF
LARKSPUR
LAUDANUM
LAYABOUT
LIBELOUS
LIGNEOUS
LINNAEUS
LINOLEUM
LONGHAUL
LUMINOUS
LUSCIOUS
LUSTROUS
MALODOUR
MANDAMUS
MARABOUT
MARASMUS
MEALYBUG
MENELAUS
MENISCUS
MERCIFUL
MERINGUE
MINOTAUR
MIRTHFUL
MOMENTUM
MORPHEUS
MOURNFUL
MOUTHFUL
MUTINOUS
MYCELIUM
MYSTIQUE
NAUPLIUS
NAUSEOUS
NAUTILUS
NEBULOUS
NOBELIUM
NUMEROUS
NUMINOUS
ODYSSEUS
OVERHAUL
PABULOUS
PANDARUS
PARAMOUR
PATULOUS
PAULINUS
PEACEFUL
PELAGIUS
PENDULUM
PERILOUS
PERVIOUS
PETANQUE
PHORMIUM
PHYSIQUE
PICKMEUP
PLATANUS
PLATEFUL
PLATINUM
PLATYPUS
PLECTRUM

PLOTINUS
PODARGUS
POLONIUM
POPULOUS
POWERFUL
PRECIOUS
PREVIOUS
PRINTOUT
PROLOGUE
PROROGUE
PUDENDUM
PURLIEUS
RAVENOUS
REFUGIUM
RESIDUUM
RESINOUS
RHONCHUS
RIGHTFUL
RIGOROUS
RUNABOUT
RUNNERUP
SABOTEUR
SCABIOUS
SCABROUS
SCALENUS
SCANDIUM
SCORNFUL
SCRIPTUM
SCYBALUM
SEDULOUS
SELENIUM
SENSUOUS
SHAKEOUT
SHAMEFUL
SHAREOUT
SHOOTOUT
SISYPHUS
SKILLFUL
SLOTHFUL
SOLARIUM
SONOROUS
SPACIOUS
SPADEFUL
SPECIOUS
SPECTRUM
SPECULUM
SPHAGNUM
SPIRITUS
SPITEFUL
SPOONFUL
SPURIOUS
STAKEOUT
STIMULUS
STRIATUM
STUDIOUS
SUCCUBUS
SUDARIUM
SYLLABUB
SYLLABUS
TANTALUM
TANTALUS
TARTARUS
TASTEFUL
TENESMUS
TERMINUS
TESTATUM
THALAMUS
THALLIUM
THANKFUL
THROMBUS
TIBERIUS
TIMOROUS
TINNITUS
TITANIUM
TOMENTUM
TORTUOUS
TRILLIUM
TRITICUM
TRUSTFUL
TRUTHFUL
TUBEROUS
TYMPANUM
ULCEROUS
UNCTUOUS
UNDERCUT
UNLAWFUL
UPPERCUT
USURIOUS
UXORIOUS
VANADIUM
VARIORUM
VENGEFUL
VENOMOUS
VESUVIUS
VEXILLUM
VIATICUM
VIBURNUM
VIGOROUS
VINCULUM
VIPEROUS
VIRTUOUS
VITELLUS
VITREOUS
VIVARIUM
VOYAGEUR
WASTEFUL
WATCHFUL
WATERBUG
WONDROUS
WRATHFUL
WRONGFUL
YOUTHFUL
ZEPHYRUS
ABESSIVE
ABLATIVE
ABORTIVE
ABRASIVE
ADDITIVE
ADESSIVE
ADHESIVE
ADOPTIVE
AGGRIEVE
ALLUSIVE
BURGRAVE
CASANOVA
COERCIVE
COHESIVE
CONCEIVE
CONCLAVE
CONSERVE
CONTRIVE
CREATIVE
CURATIVE
DECISIVE
DERISIVE
DISPROVE
DISSOLVE
DIVISIVE
EFFUSIVE
ELECTIVE
FIXATIVE
FLYDRIVE
FOXGLOVE
FUGITIVE
GENITIVE
HEATWAVE
ILLUSIVE
INACTIVE
INCISIVE
INDUCIVE
INVASIVE
KIDGLOVE
LAXATIVE
LOCATIVE
MANGROVE
MARGRAVE
NEGATIVE
NOSEDIVE
PALGRAVE
PERCEIVE
POSITIVE
PRESERVE
PUNITIVE
PUTATIVE
REACTIVE
RELATIVE
REPRIEVE
RETRIEVE
RINGDOVE
SEDATIVE
SPORTIVE
TOPHEAVY
UNIVALVE
VOCATIVE
CAMPTOWN
COMEDOWN
DOWNTOWN
FLYBLOWN
FREETOWN
LILONGWE
MARKDOWN
MELTDOWN
NEWSHAWK
PILTDOWN
PULLDOWN
SHALLOWS
SHOWDOWN
SHUTDOWN
SLOWDOWN
TOMAHAWK
WASHBOWL
WASHDOWN
WILDFOWL
ZIMBABWE
APOPLEXY
COTOPAXI
SPINTEXT
CATTLEYA
DIPHENYL
EDGEWAYS
HOLIDAYS
JEFFREYS
NOWADAYS
SARDONYX
SIDEWAYS
AMORTIZE
BENGHAZI
BRAGANZA
BULLDOZE
CANONIZE
CIVILIZE
COLONIZE
DEFREEZE
DEPUTIZE
DIGITIZE
DOWNSIZE
ENERGIZE
EQUALIZE
EULOGIZE
EXORCIZE
FINALIZE
FULLSIZE
HUMANIZE
IDEALIZE
IMMUNIZE
KAMIKAZE
KINGSIZE
LEGALIZE
LOCALIZE
MAXIMIZE
MEMORIZE
MINIMIZE
MOBILIZE
MORALIZE
MOTORIZE
ORGANIZE
OVERSIZE
PARALYZE
PENALIZE
POLARIZE
QUATORZE
SANITIZE
SATIRIZE
SCHMOOZE
STARGAZE
THEORIZE
TOTALIZE
UNFREEZE
UNIONIZE
URBANIZE
VAPORIZE
VITALIZE
VOCALIZE
WOMANIZE

8:8

ABSCISSA
AGRICOLA
ALHAMBRA
ALLELUIA
ALOPECIA
AMBROSIA
AMYGDALA
ANACONDA
ANALECTA
ANALEMMA
ANATHEMA
ANATOLIA
ANGELICA
ANGUILLA
ANNELIDA
ANOREXIA
AOTEAROA
APOLOGIA
ARETHUSA
ARMORICA
ASPHYXIA
ASTHENIA
ATALANTA
ATARAXIA
ATHEROMA
AVICENNA
AVIFAUNA
BABUSHKA
BACTERIA
BAGHEERA
BALLISTA
BANDANNA
BARATHEA
BASILICA
BETHESDA
BLASTULA
BOADICEA
BOTSWANA
BRAGANZA
BRASILIA
BRASSICA
BROMELIA
BROUHAHA
BUDDLEIA
BULGARIA
CACHEXIA
CALCUTTA
CALIGULA
CAMBODIA
CAMELLIA
CANBERRA
CAPYBARA
CAROLINA
CASANOVA
CATHEDRA
CATTLEYA
CAVATINA
CHARISMA
CHICKPEA
CHILLADA
CHIMAERA
CHORDATA
CINCHONA
CINERAMA
COCACOLA
COLOMBIA
CZAREVNA
DEMENTIA
DEMERARA
DIARRHEA
DIASPORA
DRACAENA
DULCINEA
DYSLEXIA
EFFLUVIA
EGOMANIA
ENCAENIA
EPHEMERA
EPITHEMA
ERYTHEMA
ESTANCIA
ETCETERA
ETHIOPIA
EUPEPSIA

EUPHONIA
EUPHORIA
FANTASIA
FENESTRA
FLOTILLA
GALLERIA
GARDENIA
GASTRULA
GIACONDA
GIOCONDA
GLABELLA
GLAUCOMA
GLORIANA
GLOXINIA
GOLGOTHA
GONDWANA
GRISELDA
GUERILLA
GURDWARA
GYMKHANA
HABANERA
HACIENDA
HELVETIA
HEPATICA
HETAIRIA
HIAWATHA
HIBERNIA
HIRAGANA
HYSTERIA
INSIGNIA
INSOMNIA
INTIFADA
ISABELLA
JAPONICA
KATAKANA
KINSHASA
KRAKATOA
LEUKEMIA
LISTERIA
LONICERA
MAGNESIA
MAGNOLIA
MAHARAJA
MAJOLICA
MALAYSIA
MALLORCA
MALVASIA
MANDIOCA
MANITOBA
MANTILLA
MANTISSA
MARCELLA
MARQUESA
MELANOMA
METABOLA
MINAMATA
MONGOLIA
MONROVIA
MONSTERA
MOUSSAKA
NDJAMENA
NEBRASKA
OKLAHOMA
OPERETTA
ORESTEIA
PANATELA
PANORAMA
PARABOLA
PARANOIA
PASHMINA
PELLAGRA
PENUMBRA
PERFECTA
PHYSALIA
PIZZERIA
PLACENTA
PLETHORA
POLYANNA
PORPHYRA
PREDELLA
PRETORIA
PROFORMA
PROGERIA
PROTOZOA
PRUNELLA
PYORRHEA
QUADRIGA
RUTABAGA
SARATOGA
SARDINIA
SATURNIA
SAYONARA
SCHAPSKA
SCIATICA
SCROFULA
SEMOLINA
SENORITA
SERENATA
SHIGELLA
SIGNORIA
SINFONIA
SLOVAKIA
SLOVENIA
SONATINA
SQUAMATA
STAROSTA
STEATOMA
STIGMATA
STOCCATA
SUBPOENA
SUBTOPIA
SUBURBIA
SUDAMINA
SWASTIKA
TANZANIA
TASMANIA
TEQUILLA
TERATOMA
TITICACA
TORTILLA
TOXAEMIA
TOXOCARA
TRACHOMA
TRILEMMA
TROCHLEA
TSAREVNA
TUSITALA
UMBRELLA
UNDERSEA
VALENCIA
VALHALLA
VALLETTA
VENDETTA
VERONICA
VERTEBRA
VICTORIA
VIRGINIA
WISTERIA
XANTHOMA
YARMULKA
YERSINIA
YOKOHAMA
ZARZUELA
ZASTRUGA
ZIRCONIA
BACKCOMB
CATACOMB
CHORIAMB
DOORKNOB
GOLFCLUB
HECATOMB
MEMSAHIB
SYLLABUB
ACADEMIC
ACOUSTIC
ACROSTIC
ADRIATIC
AGNOSTIC
ALCHEMIC
ALLERGIC
AMMONIAC
ANABATIC
ANARCHIC
ANATOMIC
ANOREXIC
ARMAGNAC
AROMATIC
ARTISTIC
ASCORBIC
ATARAXIC
ATHLETIC
ATLANTIC
AUTISTIC
BALEARIC
BARBARIC
BATHETIC
BEATIFIC
BERGERAC
CADILLAC
CARBOLIC
CARBONIC
CATHOLIC
CELERIAC
CHERUBIC
CHOLERIC
CLIMATIC
COSMETIC
CYRENIAC
CYRILLIC
DALMATIC
DEMONIAC
DESPOTIC
DIABETIC
DIABOLIC
DIATONIC
DICYCLIC
DIDACTIC
DIOPTRIC
DIURETIC
DOGMATIC
DOMESTIC
DRACONIC
DRAMATIC
DYNASTIC
DYSLEXIC
ECLECTIC
ECONOMIC
ECSTATIC
EGOISTIC
EIDECTIC
ELECTRIC
ELLIPTIC
EMPHATIC
EPIDEMIC
EPIGAMIC
EPISODIC
ESOTERIC
ESTHETIC
EUCYCLIC
EUPHONIC
EUPHORIC
EUSTATIC
EUTROPIC
EXEGETIC
FORENSIC
FRENETIC
GALACTIC
GALVANIC
GELASTIC
GEODESIC
GERMANIC
GIGANTIC
HARMONIC
HELLADIC
HELLENIC
HERALDIC
HERMETIC
HERPETIC
HIERATIC
HISPANIC
HISTORIC
HOLISTIC
HORRIFIC
HYGIENIC
HYPNOTIC
HYSTERIC
JURASSIC
LOGISTIC
LYSERGIC
MAGNETIC
MAJESTIC
MECHANIC
MESMERIC
METALLIC
METEORIC
METHODIC
MNEMONIC
MONASTIC
NARCOTIC
NEPIONIC
NEUROTIC
OPERATIC
PANDEMIC
PATHETIC
PEDANTIC
PERIODIC
PHONETIC
PHREATIC
PINDARIC
PLATONIC
PROLIFIC
QUIXOTIC
REPUBLIC
RHETORIC
RHYTHMIC
ROMANTIC
SADISTIC
SARDONIC
SEMIOTIC
SERAPHIC
SOCRATIC
SPECIFIC
SPORADIC
SUBSONIC
SULFURIC
SYLLABIC
SYMBOLIC
SYNOPTIC
SYSTEMIC
TARTARIC
TECTONIC
TELLURIC
TERRIFIC
TEUTONIC
THEATRIC
THEMATIC
THORACIC
TRIASSIC
TROCHAIC
TURMERIC
UNHEROIC
VOLCANIC
ABDUCTED
ABRIDGED
ABSOLVED
ABSORBED
ACCENTED
ACCEPTED
ACCURSED
ACHIEVED
ACIDHEAD
ACQUIRED
ADDICTED
ADVANCED
AFFECTED
AGITATED
AGONIZED
AIRFIELD
AIRSPEED
ALKALOID
AMBUSHED
ANIMATED
APPALLED
APPRISED
APPROVED
ARACHNID
ARMOURED
ARRESTED
ARTICLED
ASSORTED
ASTEROID
ATHETOID
ATTACHED
BABYHOOD
BACKHAND
BACKWARD
BACKYARD
BALANCED
BAPTISED
BARNYARD
BARTERED
BATTERED

BECALMED
BEDSTEAD
BEFRIEND
BEREAVED
BERTRAND
BESIEGED
BESOTTED
BICUSPID
BILLFOLD
BINDWEED
BIRDSEED
BLIZZARD
BLOTCHED
BOATLOAD
BONEHEAD
BONEYARD
BORROWED
BOTHERED
BRANCHED
BRASSARD
BRINDLED
BRISTLED
BUGGERED
BULKHEAD
BURDENED
BUTTERED
BUZZWORD
CAMBERED
CAPSIZED
CARTLOAD
CARYATID
CENTERED
CERATOID
CHADBAND
CILIATED
CLEANSED
CLIFFORD
COCKEYED
COLLARED
COLOURED
COMBINED
COMPARED
COMPOSED
COMPOUND
CONCHOID
CONFINED
CONFOUND
CONFUSED
CONSUMED
COPYHOLD
CORONOID
CORRODED
COTSWOLD
CRIPPLED
CRUTCHED
CULTURED
CUPBOARD
DANEGELD
DARKENED
DASHWOOD
DEADENED
DEADHEAD
DEADWOOD
DEATHBED
DECEASED
DECKHAND
DEFEATED
DEFORMED
DEGRADED
DEJECTED
DEMENTED
DENDROID
DEPARTED
DEPRAVED
DEPRIVED
DERANGED
DESERTED
DESERVED
DESTINED
DETACHED
DETAILED
DEVILLED
DEWYEYED
DISABLED
DISEASED
DISLIKED
DISMAYED
DISPOSED
DISPUTED
DIVIDEND
DIVORCED
DOCKLAND
DOCKYARD
DOCTORED
DOWNLOAD
DOWNWARD
DROPHEAD
DRUMHEAD
DRUNKARD
DUCKWEED
DUMFOUND
EASTWARD
EDUCATED
ELEVATED
ELKHOUND
EMBEDDED
EMBODIED
EMBOSSED
EMBRACED
EMPLOYED
ENCAMPED
ENCLOSED
ENLARGED
ENMESHED
ENRICHED
ENSHROUD
ENTITLED
ESTEEMED
EUROLAND
EXECUTED
EXPECTED
EXPENDED
EXPLODED
EXTENDED
FALKLAND
FAMISHED
FARMHAND
FARMLAND
FARMYARD
FATIGUED
FAVOURED
FEATURED
FEELGOOD
FINISHED
FIREBIRD
FIREWEED
FIREWOOD
FISHPOND
FLAVORED
FLOUNCED
FOGBOUND
FOLLOWED
FOOTHOLD
FOREHAND
FOREHEAD
FORELAND
FOREWORD
FOURFOLD
FOXHOUND
FRAZZLED
FRECKLED
FREEHAND
FREEHOLD
FRENZIED
FURROWED
GAILLARD
GALLIARD
GAMEBIRD
GANGLAND
GAOLBIRD
GARAMOND
GATHERED
GIRLHOOD
GODCHILD
GOODWOOD
GOURMAND
GRIZZLED
GROUNDED
GUSSETED
HALLIARD
HALLOWED
HAMMERED
HANDHELD
HANDMAID
HARASSED
HARDENED
HARDWOOD
HARTFORD
HAYFIELD
HEADBAND
HEADLAND
HEADWIND
HEADWORD
HELMETED
HERACLID
HEREFORD
HEREWARD
HIGHLAND
HIGHROAD
HINDWARD
HOGSHEAD
HOLYHEAD
HOLYROOD
HOMELAND
HOMEWARD
HOPFIELD
HYDATOID
ICEFIELD
ILLFATED
IMAGINED
IMMERSED
IMPACTED
IMPAIRED
IMPELLED
IMPROVED
INCENSED
INCLINED
INCLUDED
INDEBTED
INDENTED
INFECTED
INFESTED
INFLAMED
INFLATED
INFORMED
INFRARED
INSPIRED
INTENDED
INTREPID
INVENTED
INVERTED
INVOLVED
IRONCLAD
IRONWOOD
ISOLATED
JACKETED
JACQUARD
JAILBIRD
JEREMIAD
JEWELLED
JIGGERED
KEYBOARD
KIPPERED
KNAPWEED
KNOTWEED
LABOURED
LACKLAND
LADYBIRD
LAKELAND
LAMENTED
LANDLORD
LANDWARD
LANGLAND
LEAVENED
LEFTHAND
LEFTWARD
LEISURED
LETTERED
LICENSED
LIVERIED
LONGHAND
LONGLAND
LOPSIDED
LOUVERED
LOVEBIRD
LYREBIRD
MAINLAND
MAINYARD
MANDATED
MANIFOLD
MANNERED
MARIGOLD
MARTYRED
MARYLAND
MASTHEAD
MEASURED
METALLED
MIDFIELD
MILDEWED
MILKMAID
MILKWEED
MILLPOND
MINEHEAD
MIRRORED
MOHAMMED
MOORLAND
MORIBUND
MUDGUARD
MUHAMMAD
MYRIAPOD
NATTERED
NEATHERD
NECKBAND
NEMATOID
NEWFOUND
NOSEBAND
NUFFIELD
OBSCURED
OBSERVED
OBSESSED
OBTAINED
OCCUPIED
OFFENDED
OILFIELD
OLDWORLD
OLYMPIAD
ONESIDED
ORDINAND
ORPHANED
OUTBOARD
OUTDATED
OUTFIELD
OUTMODED
OVERFEED
OVERHEAD
OVERLAID
OVERLAND
OVERLOAD
OVERLORD
PACKAGED
PALMATED
PAMPERED
PANELLED
PARANOID
PARKLAND
PASSWORD
PATENTED
PELLETED
PELLUCID
PERFUMED
PERISHED
PERJURED
PILCHARD
PILLARED
PINEWOOD
PINNIPED
PISSHEAD
PLOUGHED
POLISHED
POLLUTED
PORTLAND
POSTCARD
POSTPAID
POTBOUND
POTSHERD
POWDERED
PREPARED
PROFOUND
PROMISED
PROPOSED
PROPOUND
PROVIDED

PUCKERED
PUGNOSED
PUNISHED
PURBLIND
PURIFIED
RAILHEAD
RAILROAD
RAINBIRD
RAREFIED
REARWARD
REASONED
RECEIVED
RECESSED
REFORMED
REGAINED
REJOINED
RELEASED
RELIEVED
RENOWNED
REPEATED
REPORTED
REQUIRED
RESERVED
RESIGNED
RESOLVED
RETARDED
REVEALED
REVEREND
REVERSED
RHOMBOID
ROSALIND
ROSAMOND
ROSEWOOD
RUBICUND
RUMOURED
SALARIED
SARABAND
SASSANID
SATIATED
SAUROPOD
SAVOURED
SAVOYARD
SCABBARD
SCAFFOLD
SCAPHOID
SCHIZOID
SCORCHED
SCOTLAND
SCRAWLED
SCREENED
SEABOARD
SEASONED
SECLUDED
SELECTED
SELEUCID
SERRATED
SHEPHERD
SHERWOOD
SHETLAND
SHIPYARD
SHIVERED
SHROUDED
SITUATED
SKEWBALD
SKINHEAD
SLIGHTED
SLIPSHOD
SLUGABED
SLUGGARD
SMUGGLED
SOCALLED
SOFTWOOD
SOLENOID
SONGBIRD
SOUTHEND
SPANGLED
SPANIARD
SPAVINED
SPECKLED
SPIRITED
SPITHEAD
SPLENDID
SPRAINED
SPRAWLED
STAFFORD
STAMENED
STANDARD
STARCHED
STENOSED
STOREYED
STRAINED
STRANDED
STRAPPED
STREAKED
STRESSED
STRIATED
STRINGED
STRIPPED
STUCCOED
STYLIZED
SUNDRIED
SUPPOSED
SURROUND
TAILSKID
TALENTED
TAMARIND
TATTERED
TEMPERED
TERRACED
TETRAPOD
TEXTURED
THAILAND
THATCHED
THOUSAND
TIGHTWAD
TIMBERED
TONSURED
TORTURED
TRICHOID
TRINIDAD
TROUBLED
TRUCKLED
TURBANED
TURRETED
UNABATED
UNBIASED
UNCOMBED
UNCOOKED
UNCURBED
UNDERFED
UNEARNED
UNFILLED
UNFORCED
UNHARMED
UNHEATED
UNHINGED
UNLEADED
UNLISTED
UNLOADED
UNLOCKED
UNMANNED
UNMARKED
UNNERVED
UNPLACED
UNSALTED
UNSEALED
UNSEEDED
UNSIGNED
UNSOLVED
UNSTATED
UNSUITED
UNTAPPED
UNTHREAD
UNTILLED
UNTOWARD
UNVARIED
UNVERSED
UNVOICED
UNWANTED
UNWEANED
UNWONTED
UPTURNED
VAGABOND
VANGUARD
VANISHED
VENTURED
VINEYARD
WALLSEND
WAVEBAND
WEDGWOOD
WELLBRED
WELLPAID
WESTWARD
WHIPCORD
WHIPHAND
WINDWARD
WINIFRED
WITHERED
WITHHOLD
WOODLAND
WOODSHED
WOODWARD
WOODWIND
WORKLOAD
WORMWOOD
WREATHED
WRETCHED
WRINKLED
ABBASIDE
ABDICATE
ABESSIVE
ABEYANCE
ABLATIVE
ABNEGATE
ABORTIVE
ABRASIVE
ABROGATE
ABSENTEE
ABSINTHE
ABSOLUTE
ABSTRUSE
ACCOLADE
ACCURATE
ACERBATE
ACTINIDE
ACTIVATE
ADDITIVE
ADELAIDE
ADEQUATE
ADESSIVE
ADHESIVE
ADJUTAGE
ADOPTIVE
ADORABLE
ADVOCATE
AERODYNE
AESTHETE
AGACERIE
AGGRIEVE
AIGRETTE
AIGUILLE
AIRBORNE
AIRBRAKE
AIREDALE
AIRPLANE
ALBACORE
ALDEHYDE
ALEHOUSE
ALEMAINE
ALGERINE
ALICANTE
ALIENATE
ALKALINE
ALLIANCE
ALLOCATE
ALLSPICE
ALLUSIVE
ALTITUDE
AMANDINE
AMBIANCE
AMBIENCE
AMBULATE
AMENABLE
AMICABLE
AMMONITE
AMORTIZE
AMPERAGE
AMPUTATE
AMUSETTE
ANALOGUE
ANECDOTE
ANISETTE
ANNAMITE
ANNOTATE
ANNOUNCE
ANSERINE
ANTECEDE
ANTEDATE
ANTELOPE
ANTENNAE
ANTIDOTE
ANTILOPE
ANTIPOPE
ANYPLACE
ANYWHERE
APERTURE
APOLOGUE
APOSTATE
APPANAGE
APPETITE
APPLAUSE
APPOSITE
APPRAISE
APTITUDE
AQUILINE
ARALDITE
ARCHDUKE
ARGININE
ARGUABLE
ARMALITE
ARMATURE
ARROGATE
ARTIFICE
ASPIRATE
ASSEMBLE
ASSIGNEE
ASTATINE
ATHETISE
ATTITUDE
AUDIENCE
AUTOMATE
AUTOTYPE
AVENTINE
AYRSHIRE
BACKACHE
BACKBITE
BACKBONE
BACKDATE
BACKFIRE
BACKSIDE
BADINAGE
BAGUETTE
BAKELITE
BALINESE
BANKNOTE
BANLIEUE
BARBECUE
BARITONE
BARNACLE
BARRETTE
BASELINE
BASTILLE
BATHROBE
BEANPOLE
BEARABLE
BEDABBLE
BEFUDDLE
BEGRUDGE
BELGRADE
BELITTLE
BELPAESE
BENEFICE
BERCEUSE
BESTRIDE
BEVERAGE
BIGARADE
BINNACLE
BIOSCOPE
BIRDCAGE
BLOCKADE
BLOCKAGE
BLOWHOLE
BLOWPIPE
BLUENOSE
BODYLINE
BOLTHOLE
BONHOMIE
BONIFACE
BOOKABLE
BOOKCASE
BORACITE
BORECOLE

BOREHOLE
BOUTIQUE
BRAMANTE
BRANDADE
BRIBABLE
BROCHURE
BRUMAIRE
BRUNETTE
BUCKSHEE
BULLDOZE
BUMMAREE
BURGRAVE
CABOODLE
CABOTAGE
CABRIOLE
CADASTRE
CAFFEINE
CAKEHOLE
CALAMINE
CALCEATE
CALLIOPE
CALOTYPE
CAMARGUE
CAMISOLE
CAMOMILE
CAMPSITE
CAMSTONE
CANAILLE
CANALISE
CANONIZE
CANOODLE
CANTICLE
CAPRIOLE
CAPSTONE
CARABINE
CARACOLE
CARAPACE
CAREFREE
CARNEGIE
CAROLINE
CAROTENE
CARRIAGE
CARRIOLE
CARTHAGE
CARUCATE
CASEMATE
CASHMERE
CASSETTE
CASTRATE
CATAMITE
CATHOUSE
CATILINE
CELANESE
CELIBATE
CENOBITE
CENTRODE
CHACONNE
CHANTAGE
CHASTISE
CHASUBLE
CHENILLE
CHEROKEE
CHESHIRE
CHEYENNE
CHLORATE
CHLORIDE
CHLORINE
CHORDATE
CHRISTIE
CHROMITE
CHUMMAGE
CICERONE
CIVILIZE
CLAMBAKE
CLARENCE
CLAVICLE
CLAYMORE
CLEAVAGE
COALESCE
COALHOLE
COALMINE
COCCIDAE
COCKAYNE
CODPIECE
COERCIVE
COGITATE
COHESIVE
COIFFURE
COINCIDE
COLLAPSE
COLONIZE
COMATOSE
COMMENCE
COMMERCE
COMPLETE
COMPLINE
COMPRISE
CONCEIVE
CONCLAVE
CONCLUDE
CONCORDE
CONCRETE
CONDENSE
CONFLATE
CONSERVE
CONSPIRE
CONSTRUE
CONTINUE
CONTRITE
CONTRIVE
CONVERGE
CONVERSE
CONVINCE
CONVULSE
COOKWARE
COPULATE
COQUETTE
CORNICHE
CORVETTE
COVERAGE
CREATIVE
CREATURE
CREDIBLE
CREOSOTE
CRETONNE
CREVASSE
CRIBBAGE
CRITIQUE
CRUCIATE
CRUCIBLE
CRUNCHIE
CULPABLE
CURATIVE
CURLICUE
CURRICLE
CUTPRICE
CUTPURSE
CYNOSURE
DAMNABLE
DATABASE
DATELINE
DEADLINE
DECIMATE
DECISIVE
DECORATE
DECOUPLE
DECREASE
DEDICATE
DEFECATE
DEFIANCE
DEFINITE
DEFREEZE
DELAWARE
DELEGATE
DELICATE
DEMIURGE
DENATURE
DENDRITE
DENOUNCE
DEPILATE
DEPORTEE
DEPUTIZE
DERISIVE
DEROGATE
DESCRIBE
DESOLATE
DETAINEE
DETHRONE
DETONATE
DEVIANCE
DEXTROSE
DIAGNOSE
DIALOGUE
DIAMANTE
DIAPHONE
DIASTASE
DIASTOLE
DIATRIBE
DIGITIZE
DISABUSE
DISAGREE
DISBURSE
DISCIPLE
DISCLOSE
DISCRETE
DISGORGE
DISGRACE
DISGUISE
DISKETTE
DISLODGE
DISPENSE
DISPERSE
DISPLACE
DISPROVE
DISSOLVE
DISSUADE
DISTANCE
DISTASTE
DISUNITE
DIVISIVE
DIVORCEE
DOCKSIDE
DOCTRINE
DOGHOUSE
DOLOMITE
DOMICILE
DOMINATE
DOPAMINE
DORMOUSE
DOVECOTE
DOWNSIDE
DOWNSIZE
DRAINAGE
DRESSAGE
DRUMLINE
DRYSTONE
DUCHESSE
DUTIABLE
DUTYFREE
DYNAMITE
EARPHONE
EARPIECE
EASTLAKE
ECHINATE
EDENTATE
EDGEWISE
EFFUSIVE
ELECTIVE
ELEGANCE
ELIGIBLE
ELONGATE
ELSINORE
EMACIATE
EMBATTLE
EMBEZZLE
EMIGRATE
EMINENCE
EMPLOYEE
ENCIRCLE
ENCLOTHE
ENERGIZE
ENERVATE
ENFEEBLE
ENFILADE
ENKINDLE
ENSCONCE
ENSEMBLE
ENSHRINE
ENSILAGE
ENTANGLE
ENTHRONE
ENTRANCE
ENVELOPE
ENVIABLE
ENVISAGE
EPILOGUE
EPIPHYTE
EPISTYLE
EQUALIZE
EQUIPAGE
ERADIATE
ERECTILE
ERGOTISE
ERUCTATE
ERUPTURE
ESCALADE
ESCALATE
ESCALOPE
ESCAPADE
ESTIMATE
ESTIVATE
ETHERISE
ETHYLENE
ETIOLATE
EULOGIZE
EURYDICE
EVACUATE
EVALUATE
EVANESCE
EVENTIDE
EVERMORE
EVERYONE
EVIDENCE
EXAMINEE
EXCAVATE
EXCHANGE
EXECRATE
EXERCISE
EXHUMATE
EXOCRINE
EXORCIZE
EXPEDITE
EXPOSURE
EYEPIECE
EYESHADE
FACEACHE
FALLIBLE
FAROUCHE
FASCICLE
FAVORITE
FEARSOME
FEASIBLE
FEDERATE
FEMININE
FENCIBLE
FIGURINE
FILAGREE
FILENAME
FILIGREE
FILTRATE
FINALIZE
FIRESIDE
FISHBONE
FISHCAKE
FISHWIFE
FIXATIVE
FLAGPOLE
FLATMATE
FLATWARE
FLEABITE
FLEXIBLE
FLORENCE
FLUORIDE
FLUORINE
FLUORITE
FLYDRIVE
FOLKLORE
FOLLICLE
FOOTNOTE
FOOTSORE
FORCIBLE
FOREBODE
FOREGONE
FORENAME
FOURSOME
FOXGLOVE
FRACTURE
FRONTAGE
FRUCTOSE
FUCHSITE
FUGITIVE
FULLPAGE

FULLSIZE
FULLTIME
FUMAROLE
FUMIGATE
FURUNCLE
FUSAROLE
FUSELAGE
FUSEWIRE
GABONESE
GABORONE
GADARENE
GANGRENE
GANYMEDE
GARGOYLE
GARRIGUE
GARROTTE
GASOLINE
GELATINE
GEMINATE
GENDARME
GENERATE
GENITIVE
GENOCIDE
GEOPHONE
GERMAINE
GERTRUDE
GIRASOLE
GLADSOME
GLEESOME
GLISSADE
GLORIOLE
GLOSSEME
GOLDMINE
GOODSIRE
GOODWIFE
GRADUATE
GRAPHEME
GRAPHITE
GRISETTE
GRUESOME
GUIDANCE
GULLIBLE
GUYANESE
HAIRLIKE
HAIRLINE
HALFTIME
HANDMADE
HANDSOME
HARANGUE
HARDCORE
HARDLINE
HARDWARE
HEADACHE
HEADLINE
HEATWAVE
HEBETUDE
HELLFIRE
HELPLINE
HELPMATE
HENHOUSE
HERITAGE
HERMIONE
HESITATE
HIGHGATE
HIGHRISE
HILLSIDE
HOMEMADE
HOMICIDE
HORNPIPE
HORRIBLE
HOSEPIPE
HOTHOUSE
HOTPLATE
HUMANIZE
ICEHOUSE
IDEALIZE
ILLUMINE
ILLUSIVE
IMBECILE
IMMATURE
IMMOBILE
IMMOLATE
IMMUNIZE
IMPOLITE
INACTIVE
INCHOATE
INCISIVE
INCREASE
INCUBATE
INDICATE
INDUCIVE
INEDIBLE
INFINITE
INFRINGE
INHUMANE
INITIATE
INNOVATE
INSCRIBE
INSECURE
INSTANCE
INSULATE
INTERNEE
INTIMATE
INTRIGUE
INUNDATE
INVASIVE
INVEIGLE
INVOLUTE
IOLANTHE
IRISCOPE
IRONSIDE
IRONWARE
IRRIGATE
IRRITATE
ISABELLE
ISOTHERE
JACOBITE
JALOUSIE
JAMBOREE
JAPANESE
JAUNDICE
JEANETTE
JEBUSITE
JELLICOE
JOINTURE
JONCANOE
JUBILATE
JULIENNE
JUNCTURE
JUVENILE
KAMIKAZE
KEDGEREE
KEEPSAKE
KERMESSE
KEROSENE
KEYSTONE
KIDGLOVE
KILOBYTE
KINGSIZE
KLONDIKE
LACERATE
LACINATE
LACROSSE
LADYLIKE
LAMINATE
LANDMINE
LANDRACE
LANGUAGE
LANOLINE
LAPIDATE
LARGESSE
LAROUSSE
LATERITE
LATITUDE
LAUDABLE
LAUREATE
LAURENCE
LAWRENCE
LAXATIVE
LEBANESE
LEGALIZE
LEMONADE
LEVERAGE
LEVITATE
LEWISITE
LIBERATE
LICENSEE
LICORICE
LIFELIKE
LIFELINE
LIFETIME
LIGATURE
LIKEABLE
LIKEWISE
LILONGWE
LIMONITE
LINGERIE
LINOTYPE
LITERATE
LITIGATE
LIVEWARE
LOBELINE
LOCALIZE
LOCATIVE
LOCKABLE
LONESOME
LONGTIME
LONSDALE
LOOPHOLE
LORRAINE
LOVELACE
LUSTRINE
MACERATE
MACULATE
MADHOUSE
MAGAZINE
MAINLINE
MALLEATE
MAMELUKE
MANCIPLE
MANDIBLE
MANDRAKE
MANGROVE
MANICURE
MAQUETTE
MARGRAVE
MARINADE
MARINATE
MARITIME
MARONITE
MARQUISE
MARRIAGE
MASSACRE
MASSEUSE
MATABELE
MATAMORE
MATURATE
MAXIMIZE
MAZARINE
MEALTIME
MEANTIME
MEDICATE
MEDICINE
MEDIOCRE
MEDITATE
MEGABYTE
MELAMINE
MELANITE
MEMBRANE
MEMORIZE
MERINGUE
MESOLITE
MESSMATE
MESSUAGE
MÉTAIRIE
MEUNIÈRE
MIGNONNE
MIGRAINE
MILANESE
MILITATE
MILLRACE
MINCEPIE
MINIMIZE
MINORITE
MINUTIAE
MISERERE
MISGUIDE
MISJUDGE
MISPLACE
MISQUOTE
MITIGATE
MOBILIZE
MODERATE
MODULATE
MOISTURE
MOLECULE
MONETISE
MONGOOSE
MONOTYPE
MONOXIDE
MOQUETTE
MORALIZE
MORPHEME
MORPHINE
MORTGAGE
MOTIVATE
MOTORIZE
MOVEABLE
MUCILAGE
MUDSTONE
MULTIPLE
MUSTACHE
MUTILATE
MYSTIQUE
NAMESAKE
NAUSEATE
NAVIGATE
NAZARENE
NECKLACE
NECKLINE
NEGATIVE
NEGLIGEE
NEMATODE
NEOPHYTE
NEPALESE
NEPENTHE
NEPHRITE
NICKNAME
NICOTINE
NOCTURNE
NOISETTE
NOMINATE
NONSENSE
NOONTIME
NOSEDIVE
NOTECASE
NUCLEOLE
NUISANCE
NUMERATE
NUTHOUSE
OBDURATE
OBLIGATE
OBSOLETE
OBSTACLE
OEILLADE
OFFSHORE
OFFSTAGE
OLDSTYLE
OLEACEAE
OMELETTE
OPERABLE
OPPOSITE
OPTIMATE
OPULENCE
OPUSCULE
ORDINATE
ORDNANCE
ORGANDIE
ORGANIZE
OSCULATE
OTOSCOPE
OUTHOUSE
OUTSHINE
OVENWARE
OVERCOME
OVERDONE
OVERDOSE
OVERRATE
OVERRIDE
OVERRIPE
OVERRULE
OVERSHOE
OVERSIZE
OVERTAKE
OVERTIME
OVERTONE
OVERTURE
OXBRIDGE
PAGINATE
PALATINE
PALEFACE
PALGRAVE

PALINODE
PALISADE
PALLIATE
PALPABLE
PANNICLE
PARADISE
PARALYZE
PARASITE
PARLANCE
PARTERRE
PARTICLE
PARTTIME
PASSABLE
PASSIBLE
PASTICHE
PASTILLE
PATENTEE
PATIENCE
PECULATE
PEDICURE
PEDIGREE
PEDUNCLE
PEEPHOLE
PEKINESE
PELLICLE
PEMBROKE
PENALIZE
PENELOPE
PENKNIFE
PENTACLE
PENZANCE
PERACUTE
PERCEIVE
PERFORCE
PERMEATE
PEROXIDE
PERSPIRE
PERSUADE
PERVERSE
PETANQUE
PHALANGE
PHARISEE
PHOSGENE
PHYLLOME
PHYSIQUE
PIERETTE
PILOTAGE
PINAFORE
PINNACLE
PINOCHLE
PINTABLE
PIPELINE
PIPERINE
PITIABLE
PITTANCE
PLACABLE
PLAYMATE
PLAYTIME
PLEASURE
PLIOCENE
PLUGHOLE
POCHETTE
POLARIZE
POLYSEME
POPSICLE
POPULACE
POPULATE
PORPOISE
PORRIDGE
PORTABLE
PORTHOLE
PORTIÈRE
POSITIVE
POSSIBLE
POSTCODE
POSTDATE
POSTPONE
POULAINE
POULTICE
POUNDAGE
PRACTICE
PRACTISE
PREAMBLE
PRECLUDE
PRECURSE
PREJUDGE
PREMIERE
PRESENCE
PRESERVE
PRESSURE
PRESTIGE
PRETENCE
PRETENSE
PRIMROSE
PRISTINE
PROBABLE
PROLAPSE
PROLOGUE
PROROGUE
PROSTATE
PROTEASE
PROTÉGÉE
PROTRUDE
PROVABLE
PROVINCE
PRUDENCE
PTOMAINE
PUNCTURE
PUNITIVE
PURCHASE
PURSLANE
PUSHBIKE
PUTATIVE
QUADRATE
QUAGMIRE
QUARTILE
QUATORZE
QUAYSIDE
QUENELLE
QUIETUDE
QUOTABLE
RACLETTE
RADIANCE
RAGSTONE
RAPECAKE
RATEABLE
REACTIVE
READABLE
REALTIME
REASSUME
REASSURE
RECHARGE
RECOURSE
RECREATE
REDEFINE
REDOUBLE
REFRINGE
REGICIDE
REGULATE
REHEARSE
REINSURE
REKINDLE
RELATIVE
RELEGATE
RELIABLE
RELIANCE
RELOCATE
RENEGADE
RENOUNCE
RENOVATE
REPARTEE
REPHRASE
REPRIEVE
RESEMBLE
RESETTLE
RESOLUTE
RESONATE
RESOURCE
RESPONSE
RETICULE
RETRIEVE
REUSABLE
REVANCHE
REVEILLE
RIBSTONE
RIDDANCE
RIDICULE
RINGDOVE
RINGSIDE
RIVALISE
RIVERINE
ROADSIDE
ROCHDALE
ROOMMATE
ROSALINE
ROTENONE
ROUGHAGE
ROULETTE
RUMINATE
RUNCIBLE
RUSHMORE
SABOTAGE
SADDUCEE
SALEABLE
SALIVATE
SAMPHIRE
SANGUINE
SANITIZE
SAPONITE
SAPPHIRE
SATIRIZE
SATURATE
SAXATILE
SCARFACE
SCAVENGE
SCHEDULE
SCHMOOZE
SCRABBLE
SCRAMBLE
SCRAPPLE
SCRIBBLE
SCROUNGE
SEABORNE
SEAPLANE
SEASCAPE
SEASHORE
SEDATIVE
SELASSIE
SELBORNE
SELENITE
SELFMADE
SELFSAME
SELVEDGE
SEMITONE
SENSIBLE
SENTENCE
SEPARATE
SEQUENCE
SERAFILE
SERENADE
SEROTYPE
SEWERAGE
SHIITAKE
SHIPMATE
SHOELACE
SHOETREE
SHORTAGE
SHOWCASE
SIDELINE
SIDERITE
SILICATE
SILICONE
SIMULATE
SINECURE
SIXPENCE
SIZEABLE
SLOWPOKE
SNOWLINE
SOCIABLE
SODALITE
SOFTWARE
SOLITUDE
SOLSTICE
SOLVABLE
SOMETIME
SORBONNE
SPILLAGE
SPIRACLE
SPITFIRE
SPOILAGE
SPOLIATE
SPORTIVE
SPRINKLE
SQUABBLE
SQUADDIE
SQUEEGEE
SQUIGGLE
STAGNATE
STAMPEDE
STANHOPE
STANNITE
STAPHYLE
STARGAZE
STEATITE
STEERAGE
STELLATE
STOCKADE
STOPPAGE
STRADDLE
STRAGGLE
STRANGLE
STRUGGLE
SUBLEASE
SUBMERGE
SUBTENSE
SUBTITLE
SUCHLIKE
SUDANESE
SUFFRAGE
SUITABLE
SUITCASE
SULPHATE
SULPHIDE
SUNBATHE
SUNDANCE
SUNSHADE
SUNSHINE
SURPLICE
SURPRISE
SUSPENSE
SYBARITE
SYCAMORE
SYLLABLE
SYNCLINE
SYNDROME
SYRACUSE
TABULATE
TAILGATE
TAILPIPE
TAKEHOME
TANGIBLE
TAPENADE
TAPHOUSE
TARTRATE
TARTUFFE
TEAMMATE
TEARABLE
TELEVISE
TELLTALE
TEMPLATE
TENEBRAE
TENTACLE
TERRIBLE
TERYLENE
TESTICLE
THEORIZE
THIAMINE
THROTTLE
THURIBLE
TINCTURE
TIRESOME
TITANITE
TITIVATE
TITMOUSE
TOILSOME
TOLERATE
TOLLGATE
TORTOISE
TOTALIZE
TOULOUSE
TRAMLINE
TRAVERSE
TREASURE
TREATISE
TREELINE
TRIANGLE
TRICYCLE
TRIPTANE
TROLLOPE
TROMBONE
TRUNCATE
TUBERCLE

TUBEROSE
TURNPIKE
TUTELAGE
TWOPIECE
TYPEFACE
TYROSINE
ULCERATE
ULTIMATE
UNCHASTE
UNCOUPLE
UNDERAGE
UNDERLIE
UNDULATE
UNFREEZE
UNGULATE
UNIONIZE
UNIVALVE
UNIVERSE
UNSETTLE
UNSTABLE
UNTANGLE
UNUSABLE
URBANIZE
URETHANE
URSULINE
VALIDATE
VALKYRIE
VALUABLE
VAPORIZE
VARIABLE
VARIANCE
VARICOSE
VEGETATE
VENERATE
VERBIAGE
VERJUICE
VERLAINE
VERONESE
VERSICLE
VICARAGE
VIGNETTE
VINCIBLE
VIOLENCE
VISELIKE
VITALIZE
VOCALIZE
VOCATIVE
VOIDANCE
VOLATILE
VOLPLANE
VOLTAIRE
WALKYRIE
WARDROBE
WARHORSE
WARPLANE
WASHABLE
WEARABLE
WHARFAGE
WILDFIRE
WILDLIFE
WINDPIPE
WISEACRE
WISHBONE
WOLFBANE
WOMANIZE
WOODBINE
WORKABLE
WORKMATE
WRECKAGE
WYCLIFFE
XANTIPPE
YOSEMITE
YULETIDE
ZIBELINE
ZIMBABWE
ZOETROPE
ZOOPHYTE
ZOOSPORE
APPLIQUÉ
CONSOMMÉ
MALLARMÉ
RAISONNÉ
REPOUSSÉ
APERITIF
BLASTOFF
DANDRUFF
HANDCUFF
KERCHIEF
LANGLAUF
MALAKOFF
MISCHIEF
OVERLEAF
RIFFRAFF
SANSERIF
STANDOFF
TIPSTAFF
TRADEOFF
WEREWOLF
WRITEOFF
YOURSELF
ACCUSING
ADMIRING
AGREEING
ALARMING
ALLOWING
ALLURING
ANNOYING
ANYTHING
AQUALUNG
ASPIRING
ASSUMING
ATHELING
AVAILING
BABBLING
BAFFLING
BANTLING
BECOMING
BEESWING
BEETLING
BLACKING
BLACKLEG
BLEEDING
BLENDING
BLESSING
BLINDING
BLINKING
BLOOMING
BLURRING
BLUSHING
BOARDING
BOASTING
BOTTLING
BOUNCING
BRAGGING
BREAKING
BREEDING
BRIDGING
BRIEFING
BRIMMING
BRINGING
BRISLING
BROILING
BROODING
BROWNING
BROWSING
BRUISING
BUBBLING
BUCKLING
BUILDING
BULLFROG
BULLRING
BULLYRAG
BUMBLING
BUNGLING
BURSTING
BUSTLING
CANOEING
CAPERING
CARRYING
CATCHING
CATERING
CHANGING
CHARGING
CHARMING
CHEATING
CHECKING
CHEERING
CHILLING
CHOOSING
CHOPPING
CLADDING
CLANGING
CLAPPING
CLASHING
CLASPING
CLEANING
CLEARING
CLIMBING
CLINGING
CLIPPING
CLOTHING
COACHING
COLORING
COUCHING
COUGHING
COUNTING
COUPLING
COVERING
CRACKING
CRAWLING
CRINGING
CROONING
CROSSING
CROWNING
CRUSHING
DAUNTING
DAZZLING
DECAYING
DIALLING
DOUBTING
DRAINING
DRESSING
DRIFTING
DRINKING
DRIPPING
DROOPING
DROPPING
DROWNING
DRUBBING
DRUMMING
DUCKLING
DUMPLING
DWELLING
EMERGING
ENDURING
ENGAGING
ENTICING
ERECTING
EVENSONG
EXACTING
EXCITING
EXISTING
EXULTING
FAINTING
FARTHING
FETCHING
FIDDLING
FIELDING
FIGHTING
FLAGGING
FLAPPING
FLASHING
FLEETING
FLIPPING
FLIRTING
FLOATING
FLOGGING
FLOODING
FLOORING
FLUSHING
FOLKSONG
FONDLING
FOOTLING
FOUNDING
FREEZING
FROSTING
FRUITING
FUMBLING
GAMBLING
GANGLING
GLANCING
GLEAMING
GLOAMING
GLOATING
GNASHING
GOLLIWOG
GOOSEGOG
GRAINING
GRASPING
GRAYLING
GREENBAG
GREENING
GREETING
GRILLING
GRINDING
GRIPPING
GROOMING
GROUPING
GROUTING
GROWLING
GRUDGING
HABSBURG
HAPSBURG
HATCHING
HAUNTING
HEADLONG
HECKLING
HEDGEHOG
HIRELING
HOARDING
HOBBLING
HONGKONG
HURDLING
IMPOSING
INCOMING
INDEXING
INVITING
JANGLING
JUGGLING
KINDLING
KNITTING
KNOCKING
LACEWING
LAUGHING
LEACHING
LEAPFROG
LEARNING
LEFTWING
LIFELONG
LIGHTING
LIMITING
LIVELONG
LOATHING
LOWERING
LOWLYING
LYNCHING
MAHJONGG
MANAGING
MATCHING
MEALYBUG
MEDDLING
MENACING
MIDDLING
MODELING
MOTORING
MOULDING
MOUNTING
MOURNING
MUMBLING
NESTLING
NIBELUNG
NIGGLING
NURSLING
OBLIGING
OFFERING
ONCOMING
OPPOSING
ORDERING
OUTGOING
OUTLYING
OVERHANG
PADDLING
PAINTING
PANELING
PEARLING
PEDDLING
PERSHING
PIDDLING
PIERCING
PLANKING
PLANNING
PLEADING

PLEASING
PLUCKING
PLUMBING
PLUNGING
PRESSING
PRINTING
PUZZLING
QUILTING
QUISLING
RAMBLING
RATTLING
RECEDING
REEDLING
REIGNING
RELATING
RELAXING
RELAYING
REPAYING
RETIRING
REVIVING
RIESLING
RIPPLING
RIVETING
ROASTING
RUMBLING
RUSTLING
SADDLING
SCALDING
SCANNING
SCATHING
SCHEMING
SCOFFING
SCOLDING
SCOURING
SCOWLING
SEAGOING
SEEDLING
SEETHING
SHANTUNG
SHEEPDOG
SHELVING
SHIELING
SHIFTING
SHILLING
SHIPPING
SHOCKING
SHOOTING
SHOPPING
SHOUTING
SIDELONG
SIGHTING
SINGSONG
SIZZLING
SKIDDING
SKILLING
SKIPPING
SKIRTING
SKULKING
SLANGING
SLANTING
SLAPBANG
SLEEPING
SLIPPING
SLUMMING
SLURRING
SMASHING
SMELTING
SMOCKING
SNEAKING
SNEERING
SNEEZING
SNORTING
SOBERING
SOOTHING
SOUCHONG
SOUNDING
SOURCING
SPANKING
SPANNING
SPARKING
SPARRING
SPAWNING
SPEAKING
SPELLING
SPENDING
SPIFFING
SPINNING
SPITTING
SPOILING
SPORTING
SPOTTING
SPURNING
STABBING
STABLING
STAFFING
STALKING
STANDING
STARLING
STARTING
STARVING
STEALING
STEERING
STERLING
STICKING
STIFLING
STINGING
STINKING
STIRLING
STIRRING
STOCKING
STOPPING
STORMING
STRIKING
STRIVING
STUFFING
STUNNING
SUCKLING
SWANSONG
SWARMING
SWEARING
SWEATING
SWEEPING
SWELLING
SWERVING
SWILLING
SWIMMING
SWINGING
SWIRLING
TAPERING
TEACHING
TEETHING
TEMPTING
THIEVING
THINKING
THINNING
THUMPING
TICKLING
TINGLING
TOUCHING
TOWELING
TOWERING
TRACKING
TRAILING
TRAINING
TRIFLING
TRILLING
TRIMMING
TRIPLING
TROOPING
TRUCKING
TRUSTING
TWIRLING
TWISTING
UNCARING
UNDERDOG
UNENDING
UNERRING
UNFADING
UNIFYING
UPCOMING
UPRISING
VALETING
VAULTING
VISITING
VOMITING
WALTZING
WAMBLING
WATCHDOG
WATCHING
WATERBUG
WATERING
WAVERING
WEAKLING
WEIGHING
WHACKING
WHEEZING
WHIPPING
WHIRLING
WHITLING
WHOOPING
WHOPPING
WIDENING
WINNIPEG
WITCHING
WOBBLING
WORRYING
WRAPPING
WRINGING
WRITHING
YACHTING
YEARLING
YEARLONG
YEARNING
YIELDING
ADMONISH
AEROLITH
ALBERICH
ALLOPATH
ALTHOUGH
AMARANTH
ANAGLYPH
APPROACH
ARAMANTH
ASTONISH
BACKLASH
BARDOLPH
BAYREUTH
BEGORRAH
BEHEMOTH
BELLPUSH
BEQUEATH
BESMIRCH
BIOGRAPH
BLACKISH
BLANDISH
BLOWFISH
BOSWORTH
BRACKISH
BRANDISH
BROWNISH
CALABASH
CENOTAPH
CHILDISH
CHURLISH
CHUTZPAH
CLANNISH
CLIQUISH
CLOWNISH
CRAWFISH
CRAYFISH
CROMLECH
DECLUTCH
DEMOLISH
DESPATCH
DEVILISH
DIMINISH
DISPATCH
DOGWATCH
DWARFISH
ELDRITCH
ELEVENTH
ENCROACH
ENTRENCH
EPIGRAPH
ETHNARCH
EYETOOTH
FEVERISH
FIENDISH
FIFTIETH
FLATFISH
FLOURISH
FOOTPATH
FORSOOTH
FORTIETH
FRANKISH
FREAKISH
FRUMPISH
FURLOUGH
GALLUMPH
GHOULISH
GLUMPISH
GOLDFISH
GREENISH
GUNSMITH
HAGGADAH
HANUKKAH
HAWFINCH
HEPTARCH
HEREWITH
HICCOUGH
HIERARCH
HUSHHUSH
HYACINTH
INASMUCH
INGROWTH
INTRENCH
JEPHTHAH
JEREMIAH
KNEEHIGH
KREPLACH
KUFFIYEH
LANGUISH
LIVERISH
LULWORTH
LUMPFISH
LUNGFISH
MACHEATH
MEGALITH
MEREDITH
MISHMASH
MISMATCH
MONMOUTH
MONOLITH
MONTEITH
MUSQUASH
NARGILEH
NONESUCH
NUTHATCH
OILCLOTH
OLIGARCH
OUTMATCH
OUTREACH
OUTWEIGH
OVERMUCH
PENTARCH
PERIANTH
PETRARCH
PLUTARCH
PLYMOUTH
POLYARCH
POLYMATH
POTLATCH
PRIGGISH
PURPLISH
RANELAGH
REPROACH
RESEARCH
RETRENCH
ROMANSCH
SANDWICH
SAVANNAH
SCOTTISH
SEAFORTH
SHADRACH
SHEEPISH
SHREWISH
SIXTIETH
SKIRMISH
SKITTISH
SLAPDASH
SLUGGISH
SLUTTISH
SNOBBISH
STANDISH
STARFISH
STRENGTH
TAMWORTH
TARBOOSH
TEACLOTH
TETRARCH
THIEVISH
THOROUGH

TICKLISH
TOISEACH
TOLBOOTH
TOPNOTCH
TOVARICH
TRIGLYPH
TRIPTYCH
TRISTICH
VANBRUGH
VANQUISH
VERANDAH
VERMOUTH
VISIGOTH
WELLNIGH
WHIPLASH
WOMANISH
XENOLITH
ZEDEKIAH
ALBINONI
AMORETTI
BAHRAINI
BANDITTI
BENGHAZI
BERIBERI
BOUZOUKI
BRINDISI
BROCCOLI
CHAPATTI
CONFETTI
COTOPAXI
DAIQUIRI
DISRAELI
DJIBOUTI
GIOVANNI
GRAFFITI
GRIMALDI
GUJARATI
HELSINKI
KACHAHRI
KALAHARI
KOHLRABI
LITERATI
MACARONI
MAHARANI
MARIACHI
MERCALLI
MISSOURI
MORBILLI
NAGASAKI
OUISTITI
PAGANINI
PASTRAMI
PEPERONI
PHILIPPI
PIRANESI
PIROZHKI
RENMINBI
RESPIGHI
RIGATONI
ROSSETTI
SHANGHAI
SUKIYAKI
SVENGALI
TANDOORI
TERIYAKI
TRANSKEI
TZATZIKI
VESPUCCI
VIRTUOSI
YAKITORI
ZAKOUSKI
ZUCCHINI
AARDVARK
ASTERISK
BACKPACK
BALDRICK
BALLCOCK
BALLPARK
BANKBOOK
BAREBACK
BASILISK
BAUDRICK
BENEDICK
BILLHOOK
BISMARCK
BLUEBACK
BOBOLINK
BODYWORK
BOOKMARK
BOOKWORK
BOOTNECK
BRATPACK
CAKEWALK
CHARLOCK
CHIPMUNK
CLAWBACK
COATRACK
COMEBACK
COOKBOOK
COPYBOOK
CRUMMOCK
DABCHICK
DAYBREAK
DEADLOCK
DIPSTICK
DRAWBACK
ECOFREAK
ENIWETOK
FASTBACK
FATSTOCK
FEEDBACK
FIREBACK
FIREWORK
FLAPJACK
FOOTWORK
FOREDECK
FORELOCK
FORSLACK
FRETWORK
FULLBACK
GIMCRACK
GOBSMACK
GREENOCK
GRIDLOCK
GROSBEAK
HABAKKUK
HALLMARK
HANDBOOK
HARDBACK
HARDTACK
HAYSTACK
HEADMARK
HOMESICK
HOMEWORK
HOODWINK
HORNBOOK
HUMPBACK
IRONWORK
JIMCRACK
JOYSTICK
KICKBACK
KINSFOLK
KITEMARK
KNAPSACK
KNOTWORK
LAIDBACK
LANDLOCK
LANDMARK
LIMERICK
LIPSTICK
LOVESICK
MAVERICK
MOORCOCK
NEWSHAWK
NEWSPEAK
NICKNACK
NONSTICK
NOTEBOOK
OFFBREAK
OILSLICK
ONETRACK
OPENWORK
OUTBREAK
OUTFLANK
OVERBOOK
OVERLOOK
OVERWORK
PASSBOOK
PAYCHECK
PICKLOCK
PICKWICK
PINPRICK
PLAYBACK
POSTMARK
REDBRICK
REDSHANK
RODERICK
RUCKSACK
RULEBOOK
SALTLICK
SANDBANK
SHAMROCK
SHELDUCK
SHERLOCK
SHOPTALK
SIDEKICK
SIDEWALK
SKINWORK
SKIPJACK
SLAPJACK
STOPCOCK
TAILBACK
TAMARISK
TEAMWORK
TELEMARK
TEXTBOOK
TICKTACK
TICKTOCK
TIDEMARK
TIEBREAK
TOMAHAWK
TURNBACK
TURNCOCK
WHIPJACK
WINDHOEK
WINDSOCK
WOODCOCK
WOODWORK
WOOLPACK
WOOLSACK
WORDBOOK
WORKBOOK
YEARBOOK
ZWIEBACK
AASVOGEL
ABNORMAL
AEROFOIL
ALLUVIAL
APPROVAL
ARBOREAL
ARMORIAL
ARTERIAL
ASPHODEL
ATYPICAL
AUTUMNAL
BALLGIRL
BALMORAL
BANDEROL
BANKROLL
BARONIAL
BASEBALL
BASINFUL
BECHAMEL
BELLYFUL
BETRAYAL
BIANNUAL
BIBLICAL
BIENNIAL
BINOMIAL
BISEXUAL
BLISSFUL
BLUEBELL
BOASTFUL
BONSPIEL
BORSTALL
BOTHWELL
BRACHIAL
CALLGIRL
CAMPBELL
CANNIBAL
CARDINAL
CARNIVAL
CAROUSAL
CAROUSEL
CARRYALL
CEREBRAL
CERVICAL
CESSPOOL
CHARCOAL
CHEERFUL
CHEMICAL
CHERWELL
CINEREAL
CLERICAL
CLINICAL
CLODPOLL
COATTAIL
COCKEREL
COCKTAIL
COGWHEEL
COLONIAL
COLORFUL
COLOSSAL
COMMUNAL
CONJUGAL
CORNHILL
CORNWALL
CORPORAL
COYSTRIL
CRIMINAL
CRITICAL
CROMWELL
CULTURAL
CYCLICAL
DAFFODIL
DECRETAL
DEMERSAL
DEMURRAL
DIAGONAL
DIPHENYL
DIPTERAL
DISHEVEL
DISLOYAL
DISPOSAL
DOCTORAL
DOGGEREL
DOGSTAIL
DOORBELL
DOTTEREL
DOUBTFUL
DOVETAIL
DOWNFALL
DOWNHILL
DREADFUL
DUCKBILL
DUMBBELL
DUNGHILL
DUODENAL
EDGEHILL
EGGSHELL
EMMANUEL
ENTHRALL
EPIDURAL
ESCORIAL
ESPECIAL
ESPOUSAL
ESTOPPEL
ETHEREAL
EVENTFUL
EVENTUAL
EXTERNAL
FAITHFUL
FANCIFUL
FARCICAL
FAREWELL
FESTIVAL
FIREBALL
FISHMEAL
FLYWHEEL
FOLDEROL
FOOTBALL
FOOTFALL
FORCEFUL
FORESAIL
FORETELL
FORKTAIL
FRUITFUL
FUNEREAL
GERMINAL
GINGIVAL
GLASSFUL
GOLFBALL

GOODWILL
GOOFBALL
GRACEFUL
GRATEFUL
GUNMETAL
GUTTURAL
HABITUAL
HALFFULL
HANDBALL
HANDBILL
HANDRAIL
HANGNAIL
HANNIBAL
HAREBELL
HEELBALL
HERSCHEL
HIGHBALL
HORMONAL
HORNBILL
HOSPITAL
IMMANUEL
IMMORTAL
IMPERIAL
INFERNAL
INFORMAL
INGUINAL
INIMICAL
INTEGRAL
INTERNAL
INTERPOL
INTERVAL
IRONICAL
ISOGONAL
ISTANBUL
JUDICIAL
KEELHAUL
KOMSOMOL
LANDFALL
LANDFILL
LITTORAL
LONGHAUL
LUPERCAL
MACKEREL
MADRIGAL
MAINSAIL
MALARIAL
MANDRILL
MANGONEL
MANIACAL
MANORIAL
MARGINAL
MARSHALL
MATERIAL
MATERNAL
MEDIEVAL
MEMORIAL
MERCIFUL
METHANOL
METRICAL
MINSTREL
MIRTHFUL
MISSPELL
MOLEHILL
MONAURAL
MONOHULL
MONORAIL
MOTHBALL
MOURNFUL
MOUTHFUL
MUSCATEL
MYSTICAL
MYTHICAL
NATIONAL
NAUTICAL
NEMBUTAL
NEWSREEL
NOTARIAL
NOTIONAL
NUTSHELL
OENOPHIL
OFFICIAL
OPTIONAL
ORIENTAL
ORIGINAL
OVERFILL
OVERFULL
OVERHAUL
OVERKILL
PALATIAL
PARALLEL
PARENTAL
PARIETAL
PARSIFAL
PASTORAL
PATERNAL
PEACEFUL
PECTORAL
PEDESTAL
PELLMELL
PERCEVAL
PERCIVAL
PERSONAL
PHILOMEL
PHYSICAL
PIGSWILL
PINWHEEL
PLATEFUL
PLAYBILL
PLAYGIRL
PLIMSOLL
POETICAL
PONYTAIL
PORTUGAL
POWERFUL
PRAIRIAL
PRANDIAL
PRATFALL
PRENATAL
PRIMEVAL
PRODIGAL
PROPOSAL
PROTOCOL
PUFFBALL
PUNCTUAL
QUIRINAL
RAINFALL
RATIONAL
REBUTTAL
REFERRAL
REGIONAL
REMEDIAL
REMITTAL
REPRISAL
RESIDUAL
REVERSAL
RIGHTFUL
RINGTAIL
RINGWALL
ROLLCALL
SCORNFUL
SEASHELL
SEASONAL
SENTINEL
SHAMEFUL
SHOWGIRL
SHRAPNEL
SIDEREAL
SILKTAIL
SKELETAL
SKILLFUL
SLOTHFUL
SNOWBALL
SNOWFALL
SOFTBALL
SPADEFUL
SPANDREL
SPECTRAL
SPITEFUL
SPOONFUL
SQUIRREL
STAYSAIL
STENDHAL
STILWELL
SUBTOTAL
SUICIDAL
SUPERNAL
SURGICAL
SURVIVAL
TACTICAL
TAFFRAIL
TASTEFUL
TEETOTAL
TEMPORAL
TERMINAL
THANKFUL
TINTAGEL
TOPLEVEL
TRANQUIL
TRIBUNAL
TRITICAL
TROPICAL
TRUSTFUL
TRUTHFUL
TUTORIAL
UNLAWFUL
UNSOCIAL
UPHEAVAL
VARIETAL
VAUXHALL
VENEREAL
VENGEFUL
VERTICAL
VESPERAL
VICARIAL
VIRGINAL
VISCERAL
WASHBOWL
WASTEFUL
WATCHFUL
WHIMBREL
WILDFELL
WILDFOWL
WINDFALL
WINDMILL
WRATHFUL
WRONGFUL
YOUTHFUL
ZODIACAL
ABOMASUM
ACCUSTOM
ACTINIUM
ACTIVISM
ADDENDUM
AEROGRAM
ALBURNUM
ALGORISM
ALIENISM
ALLUVIUM
ALTRUISM
ALUMINUM
ANEURYSM
ANGSTROM
ANTEROOM
APHORISM
APOTHEGM
AQUARIUM
ARCHAISM
ASCIDIUM
BACKROOM
BALLROOM
BASIDIUM
BATHROOM
BEERBOHM
BLENHEIM
BOOKROOM
BOOKWORM
BOTULISM
BROUGHAM
BUDDHISM
CAPSICUM
CARDAMOM
CEREBRUM
CHARTISM
CHERUBIM
CHRISTOM
CHROMIUM
CIBORIUM
CINGULUM
COLISEUM
CRONYISM
CYNICISM
DARKROOM
DAYDREAM
DELIRIUM
DIAZEPAM
DISCLAIM
DUODENUM
DWARFISM
DYNAMISM
ECTODERM
ELECTRUM
EMBOLISM
EMPORIUM
ENCOMIUM
ENDODERM
ENSIFORM
ENTRYISM
ERGOTISM
ESCAPISM
EULOGIUM
EUPHUISM
EXORCISM
EXORDIUM
FACTOTUM
FATALISM
FEMINISM
FILARIUM
FLATWORM
FOREDOOM
FRANCIUM
FRENULUM
FUSIFORM
FUTURISM
GALBANUM
GERANIUM
HALFTERM
HEADROOM
HEDONISM
HEIRLOOM
HEXAGRAM
HINDUISM
HOLOGRAM
HOOKWORM
HORNBEAM
HUMANISM
IDEALISM
IDEOGRAM
INTERCOM
IRISHISM
ISOTHERM
JEREBOAM
JEROBOAM
JINGOISM
KHARTOUM
KILOGRAM
LABURNUM
LAUDANUM
LEGALISM
LINOLEUM
LONGTERM
LUKEWARM
LYRICISM
MARJORAM
MEMORIAM
MERISTEM
MOMENTUM
MONADISM
MONOGRAM
MONTCALM
MOONBEAM
MUSHROOM
MYCELIUM
NATURISM
NEPOTISM
NEWSROOM
NIHILISM
NOBELIUM
NOMOGRAM
OMNIFORM
OPTIMISM
ORGANISM
PACIFISM
PALUDISM
PARADIGM
PAROXYSM
PENDULUM
PERIDERM
PHANTASM
PHORMIUM
PLATFORM
PLATINUM
PLAYROOM

PLECTRUM
PLEONASM
POLONIUM
POOLROOM
POPPADOM
PRIAPISM
PROCLAIM
PUDENDUM
PUGILISM
PYRIFORM
REAFFIRM
REFUGIUM
RESIDUUM
RESTROOM
RINGWORM
SALEROOM
SCANDIUM
SCRIPTUM
SCYBALUM
SEALYHAM
SELENIUM
SERAPHIM
SERIATIM
SHEIKDOM
SHOWROOM
SICKROOM
SILKWORM
SINAPISM
SOLARIUM
SOLECISM
SPECTRUM
SPECULUM
SPHAGNUM
STOICISM
STRABISM
STRIATUM
SUDARIUM
SUNCREAM
TANTALUM
TAPEWORM
TELEFILM
TELEGRAM
TESTATUM
THALLIUM
THRALDOM
TITANISM
TITANIUM
TOMENTUM
TRILLIUM
TRISTRAM
TRITICUM
TYMPANUM
UNDERARM
UNIONISM
UPSTREAM
VANADIUM
VARIFORM
VARIORUM
VERBATIM
VEXILLUM
VIATICUM
VIBURNUM
VINCULUM
VIVARIUM
WARDROOM
WASHROOM
WIREWORM
WOODWORM
WORKROOM
XERAPHIM
ZOOSPERM
ABERDEEN
ABINGDON
ABLATION
ABLUTION
ABORTION
ABRASION
ABUTILON
ACROMION
ADDITION
ADHESION
ADOPTION
AFFUSION
AGNATION
AGRARIAN
AKKADIAN
ALBANIAN
ALDERMAN
ALEUTIAN
ALGERIAN
ALLERGEN
ALLUSION
ALSATIAN
AMBITION
AMERICAN
AMUNDSEN
ANACREON
ANDERSON
ANDORRAN
ANGLICAN
ANTIPHON
APHELION
APOLLYON
APPLETON
ARAMAEAN
ARCADIAN
ARMENIAN
ARTESIAN
ASCIDIAN
ASSASSIN
ASSYRIAN
ASUNCION
ATHENIAN
AUBUSSON
AUCASSIN
AUDITION
AURELIAN
AUSTRIAN
AUTOBAHN
AVERSION
AVIATION
AVULSION
BACTRIAN
BAHAMIAN
BANDSMAN
BARBICAN
BARBIZON
BARGEMAN
BASEBORN
BATAVIAN
BAVARIAN
BEARSKIN
BEHOLDEN
BENENDEN
BENJAMIN
BESPOKEN
BETATRON
BETJEMAN
BIATHLON
BILLYCAN
BISCAYAN
BLUDGEON
BOBBYPIN
BODLEIAN
BOEOTIAN
BOGEYMAN
BOHEMIAN
BOLIVIAN
BONDSMAN
BRABAZON
BRETHREN
BRIGHTEN
BRIGHTON
BROMPTON
BUCKSKIN
BULLETIN
BULLHORN
CABOCHON
CAERLEON
CALDERON
CAMBRIAN
CAMEROON
CAMPAIGN
CAMPTOWN
CANADIAN
CAPUCHIN
CARDIGAN
CAREWORN
CARILLON
CAULDRON
CERULEAN
CETACEAN
CHAIRMAN
CHALDEAN
CHALDRON
CHAMPION
CHAPERON
CHAPLAIN
CHESSMAN
CHESSMEN
CHILDREN
CHILTERN
CHINAMAN
CHRISTEN
CINNAMON
CITATION
CIVILIAN
CLANSMAN
CLAVECIN
CLIVEDEN
COACHMAN
COERCION
COGNOMEN
COHESION
COLLAGEN
COLOPHON
COLUMBAN
COMEDIAN
COMEDOWN
COMPLAIN
CORDOVAN
CORDWAIN
CORMORAN
CORSICAN
COUPERIN
COXSWAIN
CREATION
CRICHTON
CRISPIAN
CROATIAN
CRUMHORN
CULLINAN
CULLODEN
CULVERIN
CYANOGEN
CYCLAMEN
DAIRYMAN
DAVIDSON
DECISION
DEERSKIN
DELETION
DELUSION
DEMIJOHN
DEMOTION
DERISION
DEVOTION
DIAPASON
DIELDRIN
DILATION
DILUTION
DIOCESAN
DISTRAIN
DISUNION
DIVISION
DOMINION
DONATION
DOUBLOON
DOWNTOWN
DOWNTURN
DRYCLEAN
DURATION
DUTCHMAN
DYNATRON
ECLOSION
EFFUSION
EGYPTIAN
EIGHTEEN
EINSTEIN
EJECTION
ELECTION
ELECTRON
EMBLAZON
EMBOLDEN
EMERSION
EMISSION
EMPYREAN
EMULSION
ENDYMION
ENVISION
EPHESIAN
EPIPLOON
EQUATION
ERECTION
ERIKSSON
ERUPTION
ESTONIAN
ESTRAGON
ESTROGEN
ETRURIAN
ETRUSCAN
EUDOXIAN
EURASIAN
EUROPEAN
EVERYMAN
EVICTION
EXACTION
EXCISION
EXERTION
FANCYMAN
FEDAYEEN
FELLAHIN
FERRYMAN
FINESPUN
FIXATION
FLASHGUN
FLYBLOWN
FORENOON
FORESKIN
FOREWARN
FORMALIN
FORMOSAN
FORSAKEN
FOUNTAIN
FOURTEEN
FRACTION
FRANKLIN
FRAULEIN
FREETOWN
FRESHMAN
FREUDIAN
FRICTION
FRIGHTEN
FRONTMAN
FRUITION
FUGLEMAN
FUNCTION
GALILEAN
GANGLION
GARRISON
GEORGIAN
GHANAIAN
GIRONDIN
GLOBULIN
GLYCERIN
GLYCOGEN
GOATSKIN
GONFALON
GRANDSON
GRAVAMEN
GRIDIRON
GROSCHEN
GUARDIAN
GUERIDON
GUIANIAN
GUMPTION
GYRATION
HAMILTON
HANDYMAN
HARRIDAN
HARRISON
HAWAIIAN
HAWTHORN
HEIGHTEN
HELMSMAN
HENCHMAN
HEPTAGON
HERDSMAN
HIGHBORN
HOMESPUN
HONDURAN
HOOLIGAN
HORATIAN

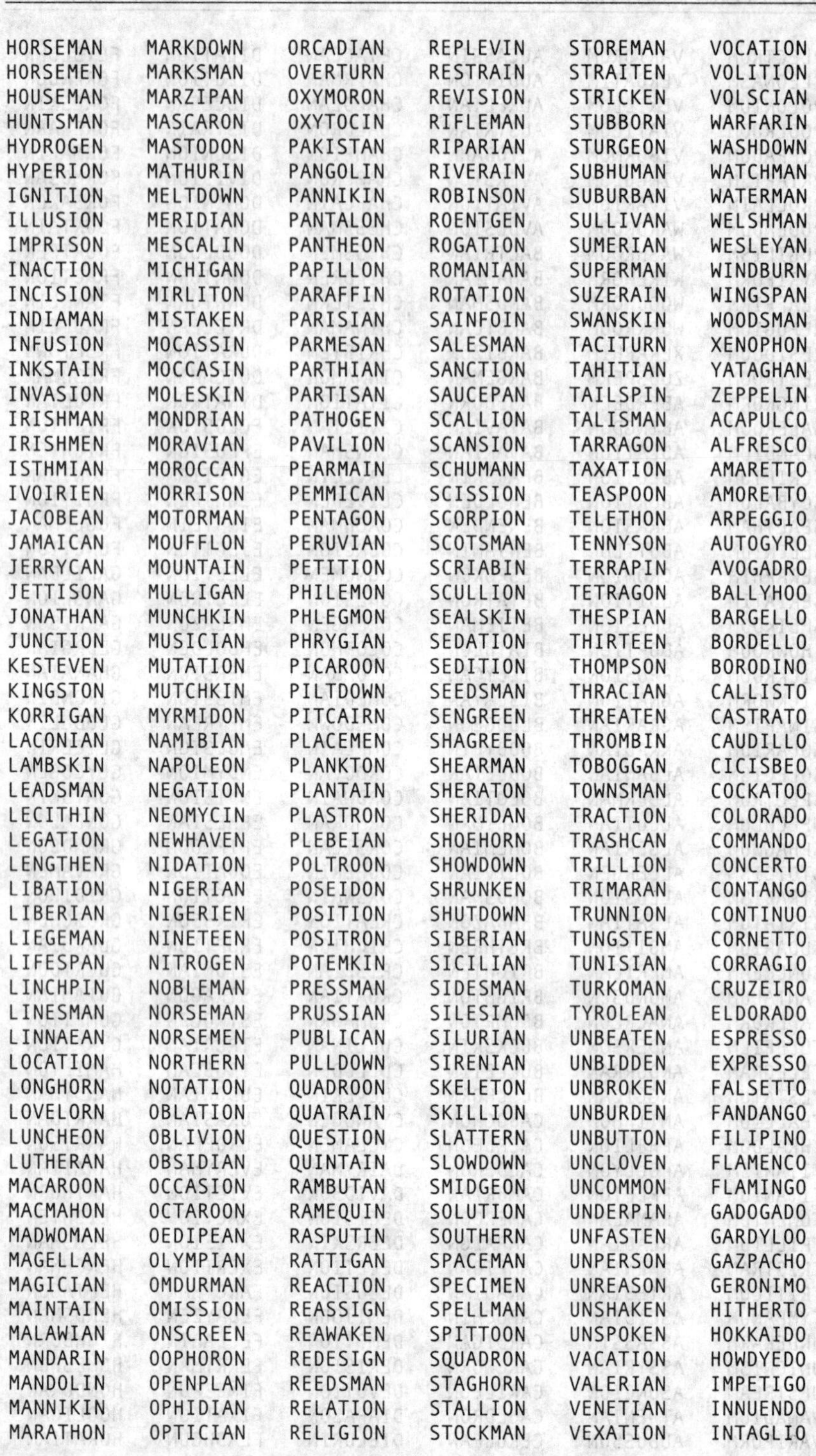

HORSEMAN
HORSEMEN
HOUSEMAN
HUNTSMAN
HYDROGEN
HYPERION
IGNITION
ILLUSION
IMPRISON
INACTION
INCISION
INDIAMAN
INFUSION
INKSTAIN
INVASION
IRISHMAN
IRISHMEN
ISTHMIAN
IVOIRIEN
JACOBEAN
JAMAICAN
JERRYCAN
JETTISON
JONATHAN
JUNCTION
KESTEVEN
KINGSTON
KORRIGAN
LACONIAN
LAMBSKIN
LEADSMAN
LECITHIN
LEGATION
LENGTHEN
LIBATION
LIBERIAN
LIEGEMAN
LIFESPAN
LINCHPIN
LINESMAN
LINNAEAN
LOCATION
LONGHORN
LOVELORN
LUNCHEON
LUTHERAN
MACAROON
MACMAHON
MADWOMAN
MAGELLAN
MAGICIAN
MAINTAIN
MALAWIAN
MANDARIN
MANDOLIN
MANNIKIN
MARATHON
MARKDOWN
MARKSMAN
MARZIPAN
MASCARON
MASTODON
MATHURIN
MELTDOWN
MERIDIAN
MESCALIN
MICHIGAN
MIRLITON
MISTAKEN
MOCASSIN
MOCCASIN
MOLESKIN
MONDRIAN
MORAVIAN
MOROCCAN
MORRISON
MOTORMAN
MOUFFLON
MOUNTAIN
MULLIGAN
MUNCHKIN
MUSICIAN
MUTATION
MUTCHKIN
MYRMIDON
NAMIBIAN
NAPOLEON
NEGATION
NEOMYCIN
NEWHAVEN
NIDATION
NIGERIAN
NIGERIEN
NINETEEN
NITROGEN
NOBLEMAN
NORSEMAN
NORSEMEN
NORTHERN
NOTATION
OBLATION
OBLIVION
OBSIDIAN
OCCASION
OCTAROON
OEDIPEAN
OLYMPIAN
OMDURMAN
OMISSION
ONSCREEN
OOPHORON
OPENPLAN
OPHIDIAN
OPTICIAN
ORCADIAN
OVERTURN
OXYMORON
OXYTOCIN
PAKISTAN
PANGOLIN
PANNIKIN
PANTALON
PANTHEON
PAPILLON
PARAFFIN
PARISIAN
PARMESAN
PARTHIAN
PARTISAN
PATHOGEN
PAVILION
PEARMAIN
PEMMICAN
PENTAGON
PERUVIAN
PETITION
PHILEMON
PHLEGMON
PHRYGIAN
PICAROON
PILTDOWN
PITCAIRN
PLACEMEN
PLANKTON
PLANTAIN
PLASTRON
PLEBEIAN
POLTROON
POSEIDON
POSITION
POSITRON
POTEMKIN
PRESSMAN
PRUSSIAN
PUBLICAN
PULLDOWN
QUADROON
QUATRAIN
QUESTION
QUINTAIN
RAMBUTAN
RAMEQUIN
RASPUTIN
RATTIGAN
REACTION
REASSIGN
REAWAKEN
REDESIGN
REEDSMAN
RELATION
RELIGION
REPLEVIN
RESTRAIN
REVISION
RIFLEMAN
RIPARIAN
RIVERAIN
ROBINSON
ROENTGEN
ROGATION
ROMANIAN
ROTATION
SAINFOIN
SALESMAN
SANCTION
SAUCEPAN
SCALLION
SCANSION
SCHUMANN
SCISSION
SCORPION
SCOTSMAN
SCRIABIN
SCULLION
SEALSKIN
SEDATION
SEDITION
SEEDSMAN
SENGREEN
SHAGREEN
SHEARMAN
SHERATON
SHERIDAN
SHOEHORN
SHOWDOWN
SHRUNKEN
SHUTDOWN
SIBERIAN
SICILIAN
SIDESMAN
SILESIAN
SILURIAN
SIRENIAN
SKELETON
SKILLION
SLATTERN
SLOWDOWN
SMIDGEON
SOLUTION
SOUTHERN
SPACEMAN
SPECIMEN
SPELLMAN
SPITTOON
SQUADRON
STAGHORN
STALLION
STOCKMAN
STOREMAN
STRAITEN
STRICKEN
STUBBORN
STURGEON
SUBHUMAN
SUBURBAN
SULLIVAN
SUMERIAN
SUPERMAN
SUZERAIN
SWANSKIN
TACITURN
TAHITIAN
TAILSPIN
TALISMAN
TARRAGON
TAXATION
TEASPOON
TELETHON
TENNYSON
TERRAPIN
TETRAGON
THESPIAN
THIRTEEN
THOMPSON
THRACIAN
THREATEN
THROMBIN
TOBOGGAN
TOWNSMAN
TRACTION
TRASHCAN
TRILLION
TRIMARAN
TRUNNION
TUNGSTEN
TUNISIAN
TURKOMAN
TYROLEAN
UNBEATEN
UNBIDDEN
UNBROKEN
UNBURDEN
UNBUTTON
UNCLOVEN
UNCOMMON
UNDERPIN
UNFASTEN
UNPERSON
UNREASON
UNSHAKEN
UNSPOKEN
VACATION
VALERIAN
VENETIAN
VEXATION
VOCATION
VOLITION
VOLSCIAN
WARFARIN
WASHDOWN
WATCHMAN
WATERMAN
WELSHMAN
WESLEYAN
WINDBURN
WINGSPAN
WOODSMAN
XENOPHON
YATAGHAN
ZEPPELIN
ACAPULCO
ALFRESCO
AMARETTO
AMORETTO
ARPEGGIO
AUTOGYRO
AVOGADRO
BALLYHOO
BARGELLO
BORDELLO
BORODINO
CALLISTO
CASTRATO
CAUDILLO
CICISBEO
COCKATOO
COLORADO
COMMANDO
CONCERTO
CONTANGO
CONTINUO
CORNETTO
CORRAGIO
CRUZEIRO
ELDORADO
ESPRESSO
EXPRESSO
FALSETTO
FANDANGO
FILIPINO
FLAMENCO
FLAMINGO
GADOGADO
GARDYLOO
GAZPACHO
GERONIMO
HITHERTO
HOKKAIDO
HOWDYEDO
IMPETIGO
INNUENDO
INTAGLIO

JACKAROO
KANGAROO
LAVENGRO
LEONARDO
LIBRETTO
LOTHARIO
MACHISMO
MAESTOSO
MALGRADO
MALVOLIO
MARCELLO
MARTELLO
MINDANAO
MODERATO
MOSQUITO
NAVARINO
NEUTRINO
NOSTROMO
ORATORIO
OTTAVINO
PACHINKO
PALLADIO
PALMETTO
PECORINO
PEEKABOO
PERFECTO
PETERLOO
PIMIENTO
PLUMBAGO
POLITICO
PROSPERO
SANTIAGO
SARGASSO
SCENARIO
SCIROCCO
SERAGLIO
SOMBRERO
SPICCATO
STACCATO
STICCATO
STILETTO
TENEBRIO
TRINCULO
TUPAMARO
TWELVEMO
VINDALOO
VIRTUOSO
VITILIGO
WATERLOO
AGITPROP
AIRSTRIP
BACKDROP
BLACKCAP
BLOWLAMP
BOOKSHOP
CALTHROP
CLAPTRAP
DOORSTEP
ENDOCARP
FIREDAMP
FIRESTEP
FIRETRAP
FLAGSHIP
FOLLOWUP
FOOLSCAP
FOOTSTEP
FORESHIP
HANDCLAP
HANDICAP
HARDSHIP
HEADLAMP
HEADSHIP
HEYTHROP
KINGSHIP
KNEEDEEP
LADYSHIP
LANDSLIP
LOLLIPOP
LONGSTOP
LORDSHIP
NIGHTCAP
OUTSTRIP
OVERSTEP
PAWNSHOP
PERICARP
PICKMEUP
POLYCARP
RAINDROP
RUNNERUP
SCREWTOP
SELFHELP
SIDESLIP
SIDESTEP
SKINDEEP
SKULLCAP
SLIPSLOP
SNOWDROP
TEARDROP
TOWNSHIP
TRANSHIP
WARDSHIP
WHITECAP
WORKSHOP
ABATTOIR
ABDUCTOR
ABSORBER
ACCENTOR
ACHIEVER
ACQUIRER
ADJUSTER
ADJUSTOR
ADULATOR
ADVANCER
AGITATOR
AIRLINER
AMRITSAR
ANALYSER
ANCESTOR
ANNEALER
ANTERIOR
ARMCHAIR
ARRANGER
ARRESTER
ASSESSOR
ATOMIZER
ATTACKER
ATTENDER
ATTESTOR
BACHELOR
BAEDEKER
BALUSTER
BANISTER
BEDCOVER
BEDMAKER
BEGETTER
BEGINNER
BEHAVIOR
BEHOLDER
BELABOUR
BELIEVER
BESSEMER
BESTOWER
BETRAYER
BEWILDER
BLEACHER
BLIGHTER
BORDERER
BORROWER
BREATHER
BRUCKNER
BURROWER
CABLECAR
CALENDAR
CALENDER
CALLIPER
CANISTER
CATHETER
CAVALIER
CELLARER
CELLULAR
CHANDLER
CHASSEUR
CINNABAR
CIRCULAR
CLANGOUR
CLEANSER
CLINCHER
CLOISTER
CLOTHIER
COAUTHOR
COCHLEAR
COIFFEUR
COLANDER
COLLATOR
COMMONER
COMMUTER
COMPILER
COMPOSER
COMPUTER
CONJURER
CONJUROR
CONSIDER
CONSULAR
CONSUMER
CONVENER
CONVEYOR
CORRIDOR
COTTAGER
CREDITOR
CROSSBAR
CROUPIER
CRUCIFER
CRUSADER
CUCUMBER
CURSITOR
CUSPIDOR
CUSTOMER
CUTWATER
CYLINDER
DARTMOOR
DAUGHTER
DEADENER
DEBONAIR
DECANTER
DECEIVER
DECEMBER
DECEMVIR
DECIPHER
DEFECTOR
DEFENDER
DEFLOWER
DEMEANOR
DEMISTER
DESERTER
DESIGNER
DETAINER
DETECTOR
DIAMETER
DICTATOR
DINOSAUR
DIRECTOR
DISASTER
DISCOLOR
DISCOVER
DISFAVOR
DISHONOR
DISINTER
DISORDER
DOMINEER
DOWNPOUR
DRAGSTER
DULCIMER
EDUCATOR
EGGTIMER
ELEVATOR
EMBITTER
EMPLOYER
ENCUMBER
ENDANGER
ENDEAVOR
ENGENDER
ENGINEER
ENGRAVER
ENLARGER
ESPALIER
EUROSTAR
EVILDOER
EXAMINER
EXECUTOR
EXEMPLAR
EXPLORER
EXPORTER
EXTENSOR
EXTERIOR
EYELINER
FAMILIAR
FASTENER
FAULKNER
FELDSPAR
FINISHER
FLOUNDER
FOLLOWER
FOOTWEAR
FOREBEAR
FORESTER
FORSWEAR
FRONDEUR
FRONTIER
FUSILIER
GALLOPER
GANGSTER
GARDENER
GASOLIER
GAZUNDER
GEOMETER
GLOBULAR
GOODYEAR
GOSSAMER
GOVERNOR
GRANDEUR
GRANULAR
GRUMBLER
GULLIVER
HALFHOUR
HALFYEAR
HANDOVER
HANGOVER
HARFLEUR
HAVILDAR
HAYFEVER
HAYMAKER
HEADGEAR
HIJACKER
HOTELIER
HOWITZER
HUCKSTER
IDOLATER
IMITATOR
IMPORTER
IMPOSTER
IMPOSTOR
IMPROPER
IMPROVER
INFERIOR
INFORMER
INJECTOR
INQUIRER
INTERIOR
INTRUDER
INVENTOR
INVESTOR
ISLANDER
JEWELLER
JONGLEUR
KIBITZER
KILLDEER
KNITWEAR
LABOURER
LABRADOR
LANDSEER
LARKSPUR
LAUGHTER
LAVENDER
LAWMAKER
LECTURER
LEFTOVER
LEINSTER
LEVELLER
LISTENER
LOADSTAR
LODESTAR
LOITERER
LONDONER
LYSANDER
MACASSAR
MAGISTER
MALINGER
MALODOUR
MANEUVER
MANPOWER
MARAUDER
MEDIATOR

MELCHIOR
MELEAGER
MENANDER
MENSWEAR
MERCATOR
MESSAGER
MESSIDOR
METAPHOR
MILLIBAR
MILLINER
MINISTER
MINOTAUR
MISNOMER
MODELLER
MODIFIER
MOLESTER
MONICKER
MOREOVER
MORTIMER
MOTORCAR
MULETEER
MURDERER
MUSCULAR
MUTINEER
NARRATOR
NECKWEAR
NEIGHBOR
NENUPHAR
NEWCOMER
NIGHTJAR
NOVEMBER
OBJECTOR
OBSERVER
OCCUPIER
ODOMETER
OFFCOLOR
OFFENDER
OFFSIDER
OLEANDER
ONLOOKER
OPENDOOR
OPERATOR
OUTREMER
OUTRIDER
OUTSIDER
OVERHEAR
OVERSEER
OXPECKER
PACIFIER
PARAMOUR
PARDONER
PASSOVER
PATELLAR
PECULIAR
PEIGNOIR
PERISHER
PERJURER
PILASTER
PILFERER
PILLAGER
PILSENER
PISCATOR
PLAYFAIR
POISONER
POLISHER
POLLSTER
POLLUTER
POMANDER
POTHOLER
PRATTLER
PREACHER
PREDATOR
PREMOLAR
PRISONER
PROCURER
PRODUCER
PROFUSER
PROMOTER
PROMPTER
PROPOSER
PROVIDER
PULITZER
PULLOVER
PURIFIER
PURVEYOR
PUSHOVER
PUSTULAR
QUAESTOR
QUARTIER
QUIBBLER
RADIATOR
RAINWEAR
REAPPEAR
RECEIVER
RECEPTOR
RECKONER
RECORDER
REDACTOR
REDEEMER
REFORMER
REGISTER
REINDEER
REMEMBER
REMINDER
REPAIRER
REPEATER
REPORTER
RESISTOR
RESTORER
RETAILER
RETAINER
REVELLER
REVIEWER
REVOLVER
ROADSTER
ROMANCER
SABOTEUR
SALINGER
SALVADOR
SANGLIER
SCAPULAR
SCHILLER
SCHOONER
SCIMITAR
SCORCHER
SCREAMER
SCRUBBER
SCULPTOR
SEAFARER
SEAMSTER
SEARCHER
SECONDER
SELECTOR
SEMESTER
SERVITOR
SHOULDER
SHREDDER
SIGNALER
SILENCER
SINCLAIR
SINGULAR
SINISTER
SLIPOVER
SMOOTHER
SMOULDER
SMUGGLER
SNACKBAR
SNATCHER
SNIFFLER
SOFTENER
SONGSTER
SORCERER
SOUVENIR
SPARKLER
SPINSTER
SPLASHER
SPLATTER
SPLENDOR
SPLINTER
SPLITTER
SPLUTTER
SPREADER
SPRINGER
SPRINTER
SPRITZER
SQUANDER
SQUATTER
SQUEAKER
SQUEALER
SQUEEZER
STICKLER
STOCKCAR
STOPOVER
STRAINER
STRANGER
STRAPPER
STREAKER
STREAMER
STRINGER
STRIPPER
STROLLER
SUFFERER
SUPERIOR
SUPPLIER
SURVEYOR
SURVIVOR
SWADDLER
SWINDLER
SYLVANER
TAKEOVER
TAVERNER
TAXPAYER
TEAMSTER
TEENAGER
TESTATOR
THATCHER
THRASHER
THRESHER
THRILLER
THRUSTER
THURIFER
TOGETHER
TOREADOR
TORTURER
TRANSFER
TRAPDOOR
TRAVELER
TREMBLER
TRENCHER
TROTTOIR
TROUNCER
TURNOVER
TWITCHER
UDOMETER
ULTERIOR
UNFETTER
UNIPOLAR
UPHOLDER
VALVULAR
VASCULAR
VERDERER
VIBRATOR
VILLAGER
VIOLATOR
VOYAGEUR
WAGGONER
WALKOVER
WANDERER
WAYFARER
WHATEVER
WHEATEAR
WHENEVER
WHEREVER
WHISTLER
WHITENER
WRANGLER
WRESTLER
YODELLER
ZAMINDAR
ABDUCENS
ACANTHUS
ACCOUNTS
ACHILLES
ADENITIS
ADENOIDS
AEROBICS
AFFLATUS
AIRINESS
AIRWAVES
ALCESTIS
ALVEOLUS
AMATEURS
AMERICAS
ANABASIS
ANALYSIS
ANCHISES
ANDREWES
ANTILLES
APOSTLES
AQUARIUS
ARCHIVES
ARCTURUS
ARDENNES
ARGESTES
ARKANSAS
ARQUEBUS
ARTICLES
ASBESTOS
ASMODEUS
ASPERGES
ATLANTIS
AUGUSTUS
AUSPICES
BACILLUS
BACKLESS
BADLANDS
BAGPIPES
BALDNESS
BALLOCKS
BARABBAS
BARBADOS
BARENESS
BARNABAS
BARNARDS
BARONESS
BARONETS
BARRACKS
BASELESS
BASENESS
BEAKLESS
BEARINGS
BENEFITS
BERBERIS
BIBULOUS
BIFOCALS
BIGAMOUS
BLINKERS
BLOOMERS
BOLDNESS
BOLLOCKS
BONELESS
BOOTLESS
BRACKETS
BREACHES
BREECHES
BRISTLES
BRONCHUS
BRUSSELS
BURSITIS
BUSINESS
BUTCHERS
BUTTOCKS
BUTTRESS
CADUCEUS
CAGINESS
CALCULUS
CALIPERS
CALMNESS
CALVADOS
CANARIES
CANNABIS
CAPITALS
CAPTIOUS
CARELESS
CASTOFFS
CATULLUS
CAUTIOUS
CERAMICS
CERBERUS
CHAMBERS
CHAMPERS
CHARTRES
CHATTELS
CHEATERS
CHECKERS
CHEQUERS
CHEVIOTS
CHIASMUS
CHICKENS
CHILDERS
CHINDITS
CLAPPERS

CLASSICS
CLAUDIUS
CLEANERS
CLEAVERS
CLEMATIS
CLINKERS
CLIPPERS
CLITORIS
CLUELESS
COBBLERS
COLDNESS
COLLECTS
COLLEGES
COLLIERS
COLOSSUS
COLUMBUS
COMPRESS
CONFINES
CONGRESS
CONTENTS
CONTROLS
COOLNESS
CORIOLIS
COSINESS
COUNTESS
COUNTIES
COUSCOUS
COVETOUS
COZINESS
CRACKERS
CRAVATES
CREPITUS
CRYSTALS
CURTAINS
CURTNESS
CUTENESS
CYANOSIS
CYCLADES
CYSTITIS
DAEDALUS
DAINTIES
DAMASCUS
DAMOCLES
DAMPNESS
DANKNESS
DARKNESS
DATELESS
DEAFNESS
DEALINGS
DECOROUS
DEEPNESS
DEFTNESS
DENARIUS
DENTURES
DESIROUS
DETRITUS
DEXTROUS
DIABETES
DIALYSIS
DIAMONDS
DIANTHUS
DIARESIS
DICTATES
DIEHARDS
DIERESIS
DIGGINGS
DINGBATS
DIOGENES
DIONYSUS
DISTRESS
DIVIDERS
DOLDRUMS
DOLOROUS
DOMINOES
DRAGOONS
DRAUGHTS
DRIBLETS
DRYGOODS
DULLNESS
DUMBNESS
DURABLES
DYNAMICS
EARNINGS
EASINESS
EATABLES
ECHINOPS
ECSTASIS
EDGEWAYS
EERINESS
ELECTORS
ELEMENTS
ELLIPSIS
EMBRACES
EMERITUS
EMIRATES
EMPHASIS
ENORMOUS
ENTRAILS
ENVIRONS
EOHIPPUS
EPICURUS
EPITASIS
ESTOVERS
EUGENICS
EVENNESS
EXEGESIS
EXIGUOUS
EXPENSES
EXTRADOS
EYEGLASS
FABULOUS
FACELESS
FACTIOUS
FAINITES
FAIRNESS
FASTNESS
FATIGUES
FEARLESS
FEATHERS
FEATURES
FECKLESS
FEELINGS
FIBROSIS
FINDINGS
FIREARMS
FIRMNESS
FLANDERS
FLANNELS
FLAWLESS
FLINDERS
FLIPPERS
FONDNESS
FORFEITS
FORMLESS
FORTRESS
FORWARDS
FOULNESS
FRABJOUS
FRAXINUS
FRECKLES
FREMITUS
FULLNESS
GADZOOKS
GALOSHES
GAMENESS
GARMENTS
GASWORKS
GENEROUS
GENETICS
GENITALS
GEOTAXIS
GESTURES
GIANTESS
GIGLAMPS
GLABROUS
GLADNESS
GLANDERS
GLAUCOUS
GLORIOUS
GLUTAEUS
GOODNESS
GORGEOUS
GORMLESS
GRACIOUS
GRANULES
GRAPHICS
GRAVITAS
GRIEVOUS
GRIMNESS
GUMMOSIS
HAIRLESS
HANGINGS
HARDNESS
HARMLESS
HASTINGS
HATTERAS
HAUNCHES
HAZINESS
HEADLESS
HEARTIES
HEBRIDES
HEEDLESS
HEELTAPS
HEIRLESS
HELPLESS
HERACLES
HERCULES
HIBISCUS
HIDROSIS
HIGHNESS
HIPSTERS
HOLDINGS
HOLIDAYS
HOLINESS
HOMELESS
HONDURAS
HOPELESS
HORATIUS
HORLICKS
HUMOROUS
HUNDREDS
HUNTRESS
HUSTINGS
HYPNOSIS
IDLENESS
ILLINOIS
INFAMOUS
INTRADOS
IROQUOIS
ISOGLOSS
JEFFREYS
JEHOVAHS
JODHPURS
JOHANNES
JOHNSONS
JORROCKS
JOTTINGS
JUSTNESS
KEENNESS
KINDNESS
KINETICS
KNACKERS
KNICKERS
KNOBLESS
KNOCKERS
KOURMISS
KOUSKOUS
KYPHOSIS
LADRONES
LAMENESS
LANDMASS
LASHINGS
LATENESS
LAZINESS
LEAFLESS
LEAVINGS
LECTURES
LEGGINGS
LEONIDAS
LEWDNESS
LIBELOUS
LIFELESS
LIGNEOUS
LIKENESS
LIMBLESS
LIMPNESS
LINCOLNS
LINNAEUS
LISTLESS
LODGINGS
LORDOSIS
LOUDNESS
LOVELESS
LOWCLASS
LOWLANDS
LUCKLESS
LUMINOUS
LUSCIOUS
LUSHNESS
LUSTROUS
MACHINES
MAECENAS
MALDIVES
MANDAMUS
MARASMUS
MARIANAS
MARQUESS
MATTRESS
MAYORESS
MEANNESS
MEATLESS
MEEKNESS
MENELAUS
MENISCUS
MERCEDES
METRITIS
MIDLANDS
MILDNESS
MILKLESS
MILLIONS
MINDLESS
MINORESS
MISTRESS
MOLASSES
MOLLUSCS
MOLUCCAS
MOORINGS
MORPHEUS
MUCHNESS
MUDFLATS
MUTINOUS
MYELITIS
MYOSOTIS
NAMELESS
NARCOSES
NARCOSIS
NAUPLIUS
NAUSEOUS
NAUTILUS
NEARNESS
NEATNESS
NEBULOUS
NECROSIS
NEEDLESS
NEURITIS
NEUROSIS
NICENESS
NICHOLAS
NINEPINS
NOSTRILS
NOWADAYS
NUMBNESS
NUMERALS
NUMEROUS
NUMINOUS
NUPTIALS
ODDMENTS
ODYSSEUS
OFFICERS
OILINESS
OILSKINS
OLYMPICS
OMPHALOS
OPENNESS
ORCHITIS
OUTCLASS
OUTDOORS
OUTWARDS
OVERALLS
OVERPASS
OVERSEAS
PABULOUS
PAINLESS
PALENESS
PANCREAS
PANDARUS
PANGLOSS
PAROLLES
PASTURES
PATULOUS
PAULINUS
PEELINGS

PEERLESS
PELAGIUS
PENNINES
PERICLES
PERILOUS
PERTNESS
PERVIOUS
PHILLIPS
PHTHISIS
PICKINGS
PICTURES
PIERIDES
PILGRIMS
PITHLESS
PITILESS
PLATANUS
PLATYPUS
PLAUDITS
PLEIADES
PLOTINUS
PODARGUS
POITIERS
POLITICS
POORNESS
POPULOUS
POTATOES
PRECIOUS
PREMISES
PREVIOUS
PRIMNESS
PRINCESS
PRIORESS
PRIVATES
PROCEEDS
PRODUCES
PRODUCTS
PROGRESS
PROVERBS
PURLIEUS
PYELITIS
PYRAMIDS
PYRENEES
QUARTERS
RABELAIS
RACHITIS
RACINESS
RAILINGS
RAMPARTS
RANKNESS
RASHNESS
RASSELAS
RAVENOUS
REASSESS
RECEIPTS
RECKLESS
RECRUITS
REMNANTS
REMOUNTS
RESINOUS
RESPECTS
RESTLESS
REYNOLDS
RHONCHUS
RICHNESS
RIGOROUS
RIPENESS
RISSOLES
ROBOTICS
ROOFLESS
ROOFTOPS
ROOTLESS
ROSINESS
ROUNDERS
RUCTIONS
RUDENESS
RUSTLESS
RUTHLESS
RYEGRASS
SAGENESS
SALTNESS
SAMENESS
SAUSAGES
SAWBONES
SCABIOUS
SCABROUS
SCALENUS
SCANTIES
SCHNAPPS
SCIENCES
SCISSORS
SCRUPLES
SEAMLESS
SEAWARDS
SEDULOUS
SEEDLESS
SELFLESS
SENSUOUS
SERVICES
SHACKLES
SHALLOWS
SHAMBLES
SHINGLES
SHOELESS
SHUTTERS
SICKNESS
SIDEWAYS
SISYPHUS
SKIBOOTS
SKITTLES
SLEEPERS
SLIMNESS
SLIPPERS
SLOWNESS
SLYBOOTS
SMUGNESS
SNEAKERS
SOAPSUDS
SOCRATES
SOFTNESS
SOLDIERS
SONOROUS
SORENESS
SOULLESS
SOURNESS
SOURPUSS
SPACIOUS
SPARAXIS
SPARTANS
SPEAKERS
SPECIOUS
SPIRITUS
SPOTLESS
SPRYNESS
SPURIOUS
SPYGLASS
STAGGERS
STARKERS
STARLESS
STARTERS
STENOSIS
STEPHENS
STIMULUS
STUDENTS
STUDIOUS
SUBJECTS
SUCCEEDS
SUCCUBUS
SUNDRIES
SUPPLIES
SUPPRESS
SURENESS
SYLLABUS
SYMPTOMS
SYNOPSIS
SYNTEXIS
SYPHILIS
SYRINGES
TACTLESS
TAILLESS
TAMENESS
TANTALUS
TARTARUS
TARTNESS
TAUTNESS
TEACHERS
TENESMUS
TERMINUS
THALAMUS
THANATOS
THINNESS
THOUGHTS
THROMBUS
TIBERIAS
TIBERIUS
TIDINESS
TIMELESS
TIMOROUS
TINNITUS
TIRELESS
TIRESIAS
TITANESS
TOMATOES
TONELESS
TOPCLASS
TORTUOUS
TRAITORS
TREELESS
TREETOPS
TRESPASS
TRIMNESS
TROTTERS
TROUBLES
TROUSERS
TRUENESS
TUBELESS
TUBEROUS
TWEEZERS
UGLINESS
ULCEROUS
UNAWARES
UNCTUOUS
UPRIGHTS
UPSTAIRS
USURIOUS
UTENSILS
UXORIOUS
VAGARIES
VASTNESS
VENOMOUS
VESUVIUS
VICTUALS
VIGOROUS
VILENESS
VIPEROUS
VIRTUOUS
VITAMINS
VITELLUS
VITREOUS
WAITRESS
WARDRESS
WARINESS
WAXWORKS
WEAKNESS
WETLANDS
WHISKERS
WILDNESS
WILINESS
WILLIAMS
WINDINGS
WINDLASS
WINDLESS
WINGLESS
WINNINGS
WIRELESS
WONDROUS
WOOLLENS
WORDLESS
WORKINGS
WORTHIES
WRITINGS
ZEPHYRUS
ZOONOSIS
ABERRANT
ABSTRACT
ABUNDANT
ABUTMENT
ACCIDENT
ACCREDIT
ACQUAINT
ACTIVIST
ADHERENT
ADJACENT
ADJUTANT
ADJUVANT
AEGROTAT
AEROFLOT
AERONAUT
AEROSTAT
AFFLUENT
AIRCRAFT
AIRTIGHT
ALARMIST
ALIENIST
ALPHABET
ALPINIST
ALTRUIST
AMBULANT
AMETHYST
ANAPAEST
ANCHORET
ANNALIST
ANTEPOST
APERIENT
APIARIST
APPARENT
APPELANT
AQUATINT
AQUEDUCT
ARBALEST
ARGONAUT
ARGUMENT
ARMAMENT
ARROGANT
ARSONIST
ARTEFACT
ARTIFACT
ASPIRANT
AUTOCRAT
BAATHIST
BACCARAT
BACCHANT
BACKCHAT
BAILMENT
BANKRUPT
BAREFOOT
BASEMENT
BASSINET
BEAUFORT
BEAUMONT
BEETROOT
BENEDICT
BERGAMOT
BESOUGHT
BIGAMIST
BLACKOUT
BLUECOAT
BOTANIST
BOUFFANT
BOWSPRIT
BRACELET
BRAGGART
BREAKOUT
BRICKBAT
BROWBEAT
BUCKFAST
BUCKSHOT
BUDAPEST
BUDDHIST
BUNFIGHT
BURNTOUT
CABERNET
CACHALOT
CACHEPOT
CAMSHAFT
CANOEIST
CARCANET
CARRYCOT
CASEMENT
CASTANET
CATALYST
CATAPULT
CATARACT
CATSMEAT
CENTRIST
CEREMENT
CERVELAT
CHARTIST
CHECKOUT
CHESTNUT
CHILIAST
CHITCHAT
CLAIMANT

CLARINET
CLEARCUT
CLUBFOOT
COALPORT
COHERENT
COLONIST
COLORANT
CONFLICT
CONFRONT
CONQUEST
CONSTANT
CONTEMPT
CONTRACT
CONTRAST
CORSELET
COUCHANT
COVALENT
COVENANT
COVERLET
CRACKPOT
CRATCHIT
CRESCENT
CROCKETT
CROSSLET
CROTCHET
CROWFOOT
CUCURBIT
CUTHBERT
DAYLIGHT
DEADBEAT
DECADENT
DECREPIT
DEMOCRAT
DERELICT
DESELECT
DESTRUCT
DIFFRACT
DILIGENT
DIPLOMAT
DISCOUNT
DISCREET
DISMOUNT
DISPIRIT
DISQUIET
DISTINCT
DISTRACT
DISTRAIT
DISTRICT
DISTRUST
DOCUMENT
DOMINANT
DONATIST
DOORPOST
DOUGHNUT
DOWNBEAT
DOWNCAST
DROPSHOT
DRUGGIST
DRUMBEAT
DUBONNET
DUELLIST
EARLIEST
EASEMENT
EFFLUENT
EGGPLANT
ELEPHANT
ELOQUENT
EMERGENT
EMIGRANT
EMULGENT
ENTREPOT
EQUITANT
ESCAPIST
ESCARGOT
ESCULENT
ESSAYIST
EULOGIST
EVACUANT
EWIGKEIT
EXISTENT
EXORCIST
EXPLICIT
EXPONENT
EXTERNAT
EXULTANT
EYESIGHT
FACELIFT
FANLIGHT
FARTHEST
FATALIST
FECULENT
FEMINIST
FILAMENT
FINALIST
FIREBOLT
FLAGRANT
FLATFOOT
FLAUBERT
FLAUTIST
FLIPPANT
FLOODLIT
FLYSHEET
FOGLIGHT
FOOTREST
FORECAST
FOREFOOT
FOREMOST
FORKLIFT
FOURPART
FRAGMENT
FRAGRANT
FREEPOST
FREQUENT
FRESHEST
FURTHEST
FUTURIST
GADABOUT
GALLIPOT
GATEPOST
GAUNTLET
GLASNOST
GOALPOST
GRADIENT
GREATEST
GUNPOINT
GYROSTAT
HALFMAST
HANDCART
HAZELNUT
HEADHUNT
HEADMOST
HEADREST
HEATSPOT
HEDONIST
HELIPORT
HELLBENT
HESITANT
HINDMOST
HONEYPOT
HUMANIST
HUMORIST
IDEALIST
IGNORANT
IMMANENT
IMMINENT
IMMODEST
IMPLICIT
IMPOTENT
IMPUDENT
INCIDENT
INDECENT
INDICANT
INDIGENT
INDIRECT
INDOLENT
INEXPERT
INFLIGHT
INHALANT
INHERENT
INNOCENT
INSOLENT
INSPIRIT
INSTINCT
INSTRUCT
INTELSAT
INTERACT
INTEREST
INTERMIT
INTERNET
IRRITANT
JACKBOOT
JINGOIST
JUBILANT
JUDGMENT
JUMPSUIT
KATTEGAT
KILOVOLT
KILOWATT
KINGPOST
KNOCKOUT
LAMPPOST
LANCELOT
LATINIST
LAWCOURT
LAYABOUT
LIFEBELT
LIFEBOAT
LIGAMENT
LINGUIST
LINIMENT
LITIGANT
LOBBYIST
LONGBOAT
LOYALIST
LYRICIST
MAILBOAT
MAILSHOT
MAINMAST
MALTREAT
MANIFEST
MARABOUT
MARGARET
MARMOSET
MARTINET
MASSENET
MASSICOT
MEDALIST
MEGAWATT
MERCHANT
MICRODOT
MIDNIGHT
MIDPOINT
MILITANT
MILKWORT
MISCOUNT
MISPRINT
MISSPENT
MISTREAT
MISTRUST
MONUMENT
MORALIST
MOTORIST
MOVEMENT
MULEWORT
MUNIMENT
MUSCADET
MYOBLAST
NATURIST
NESCIENT
NEWSCAST
NIHILIST
NOVELIST
NUTRIENT
OBEDIENT
OBSTRUCT
OCCAMIST
OCCIDENT
OCCUPANT
OFFSHOOT
OINTMENT
OLIPHANT
OPENCAST
OPPONENT
OPTIMIST
ORGANIST
ORNAMENT
ORPIMENT
OUTBURST
OUTRIGHT
OUTSMART
OVERCAST
OVERCOAT
OVERHEAT
OVERSHOT
PACIFIST
PAMPHLET
PARAKEET
PARAQUAT
PARODIST
PASSPORT
PAVEMENT
PEDERAST
PEDIMENT
PENCHANT
PENITENT
PERSUANT
PETULANT
PHEASANT
PHOTOFIT
PIECHART
PIECRUST
PINPOINT
PLACEMAT
PLANCHET
PLANGENT
PLATELET
PLAYSUIT
PLEASANT
POIGNANT
POLYGLOT
POPULIST
PORTRAIT
PRECINCT
PREGNANT
PRINTOUT
PROHIBIT
PROSPECT
PRURIENT
PSALMIST
PUGILIST
PUISSANT
PURULENT
PUSHCART
PUSSYCAT
QUADRANT
QUICKSET
QUOTIENT
RACKRENT
RAINCOAT
READIEST
READJUST
REARMOST
REASSERT
RECUSANT
REDIRECT
REDLIGHT
REDOLENT
REDSTART
REGIMENT
REINVEST
RELEVANT
REORIENT
RESIDENT
RESONANT
RESTRICT
RETICENT
REVERENT
RHEOSTAT
RICOCHET
RIGHTIST
ROYALIST
RUBAIYAT
RUDIMENT
RUMINANT
RUNABOUT
SAILBOAT
SAMIZDAT
SANSKRIT
SAPPHIST
SATIRIST
SCHUBERT
SCILICET
SEAFRONT
SEDIMENT
SENTIENT
SERGEANT
SERJEANT
SERVIENT
SEVEREST
SHAKEOUT
SHAREOUT
SHIPMENT

SHOOTOUT
SHOWBOAT
SIBILANT
SICKLIST
SIGNPOST
SKYLIGHT
SKYPILOT
SLUGFEST
SMALLEST
SMARTEST
SMOLLETT
SNAPSHOT
SOMERSET
SOMEWHAT
SPINTEXT
SPROCKET
STAGNANT
STAKEOUT
STALWART
STARDUST
STOCKIST
STOCKPOT
STORMONT
STRAIGHT
STRIDENT
STRUMPET
SUBTRACT
SUCCINCT
SUDAMENT
SUNBURNT
SUNBURST
SUNLIGHT
SUPPLANT
SURFBOAT
SURMOUNT
SWIMSUIT
SYMBIONT
TABBYCAT
TABLEMAT
TASHKENT
TEESHIRT
TEGUMENT
TELECAST
TENEMENT
THEOCRAT
THEORIST
THICKSET
TOLERANT
TRANSACT
TRANSECT
TRANSEPT
TRANSMIT
TRAPPIST
TURANDOT
TURBOJET
TURNCOAT
TURNSPIT
TWILIGHT
TYPECAST
UNDERCUT
UNDULANT
UNIONIST
UNSPOILT
UPMARKET
UPPERCUT
USUFRUCT
VEHEMENT
VESTMENT
VIGILANT
VIREMENT
VIRULENT
VISCOUNT
VISITANT
VOCALIST
WAINSCOT
WALLWORT
WARPAINT
WHINCHAT
WHITEHOT
WHODUNIT
WORMCAST
WRISTLET
YOGHOURT
YOUNGEST
ZIGGURAT
CARCAJOU
CARJACOU
HONOLULU
KATMANDU
KINKAJOU
ROUSSEAU
TIRAMISU
TURGENEV
YUGOSLAV
AIRSCREW
BEDSTRAW
BRADSHAW
BRANDNEW
BUNGALOW
CHAINSAW
CLERIHEW
COCKCROW
COLESLAW
DISALLOW
FEVERFEW
FURBELOW
HEDGEROW
HIGHBROW
HONEYDEW
KICKSHAW
OVERDRAW
OVERFLOW
OVERVIEW
RICKSHAW
ROADSHOW
SIDESHOW
SOUTHPAW
TOMORROW
UNDERTOW
WITHDRAW
APPENDIX
BICONVEX
BORDEAUX
CICATRIX
CRUCIFIX
GENETRIX
HARUSPEX
HORSEBOX
LOOSEBOX
MATCHBOX
MIREPOIX
MONEYBOX
OPOPANAX
ORTHODOX
PARALLAX
QUINCUNX
SARDONYX
SMALLPOX
SNUFFBOX
SUPERTAX
TRANSFIX
ABJECTLY
ABRUPTLY
ABSURDLY
ACCURACY
ACERBITY
ACRIMONY
ACTIVELY
ACTIVITY
ACTUALLY
ADEQUACY
ADROITLY
ADULTERY
ADVISORY
ADVOCACY
AFFINITY
AGRIMONY
AGRONOMY
ALACRITY
ALDERNEY
ALEATORY
ALKALIFY
ALLEGORY
ALLEYWAY
ALLOGAMY
ALMIGHTY
AMICABLY
ANCESTRY
ANGLESEY
ANNUALLY
ANTIBODY
ANTIMONY
APOPLEXY
APOSTASY
ARDENTLY
ARGUABLY
ARTFULLY
ARTISTRY
ASPERITY
ASSEMBLY
ASTUTELY
ATHANASY
ATROCITY
ATTORNEY
AUDACITY
AUDITORY
AUTARCHY
AUTOGAMY
AUTONOMY
BANALITY
BARRATRY
BASKETRY
BEAUTIFY
BEGGARLY
BERKELEY
BESTIARY
BILBERRY
BILLYBOY
BIRTHDAY
BITTERLY
BLACKBOY
BLACKFLY
BLITHELY
BLUSTERY
BOTTOMRY
BOUNDARY
BRADBURY
BREEZILY
BREVIARY
BRIGHTLY
BROADWAY
BRUTALLY
BUOYANCY
BURBERRY
BURGLARY
BURGUNDY
BUSYBODY
BUTCHERY
CABLEWAY
CAJOLERY
CALAMITY
CANDIDLY
CAPACITY
CARRAWAY
CASTAWAY
CASUALLY
CASUALTY
CATATONY
CATEGORY
CAUSEWAY
CELERITY
CELIBACY
CEMETERY
CENTAURY
CEREMONY
CHANCERY
CHANTREY
CHARLADY
CHASTITY
CHEEKILY
CHEERILY
CHIVALRY
CHOIRBOY
CIVILITY
CLASSIFY
CLEARWAY
CLEMENCY
CLEVERLY
CLUMSILY
COARSELY
COBWEBBY
COLLIERY
COLLOQUY
COMMONLY
CONTRARY
COQUETRY
CORDUROY
CORONARY
COSTMARY
COURTESY
COVENTRY
COWARDLY
CRAFTILY
CRAMOISY
CRANEFLY
CREAMERY
CREDIBLY
CROCKERY
CULINARY
CUPIDITY
CURRENCY
CYTOLOGY
DAINTILY
DEBILITY
DECENTLY
DELICACY
DELIVERY
DEMURELY
DERISORY
DEWBERRY
DIDDICOY
DILATORY
DIRECTLY
DISARRAY
DISMALLY
DISUNITY
DIVINITY
DOCILITY
DOGBERRY
DOGGEDLY
DOGSBODY
DOMESDAY
DOOLALLY
DOOMSDAY
DOUGHBOY
DOWNPLAY
DOXOLOGY
DRAUGHTY
DREAMILY
DREARILY
DRIVEWAY
DROWSILY
DRUDGERY
EASTERLY
EFFICACY
EMISSARY
EMULSIFY
ENDOGAMY
ENORMITY
ENTIRELY
ENTIRETY
ENTREATY
EPILEPSY
EPIPHANY
EQUALITY
ETERNITY
EUTROPHY
EVERYDAY
EXIGENCY
EXIGUITY
FACILITY
FALCONRY
FAMOUSLY
FARRIERY
FATALITY
FATHERLY
FEASIBLY
FEATHERY
FEBRUARY
FEDERACY
FELICITY
FEMINITY
FEROCITY
FIDELITY
FIERCELY
FILTHILY
FINALITY
FITFULLY
FLASHILY
FLATTERY
FLEXIBLY
FLIMSILY

FLUENTLY
FLUIDITY
FLUMMERY
FORCIBLY
FORESTAY
FORESTRY
FORMALLY
FORMERLY
FORTUITY
FRIENDLY
FRIGIDLY
FRIPPERY
FRISKILY
FROSTILY
FRUCTIFY
FRUGALLY
FRUMENTY
FUMITORY
FUNERARY
FUTILITY
GADGETRY
GALLOWAY
GARGANEY
GARISHLY
GARLICKY
GEMOLOGY
GENIALLY
GENTRIFY
GEOMANCY
GEOMETRY
GINGERLY
GIVEAWAY
GLOBALLY
GLOOMILY
GLOSSARY
GLUTTONY
GRAMERCY
GRATUITY
GRAVELLY
GREEDILY
GREENERY
GREENFLY
GROGGILY
GRUMPILY
GUERNSEY
GUILTILY
GYRATORY
HATCHERY
HATCHWAY
HATHAWAY
HEARTILY
HEATEDLY
HEAVENLY
HEGEMONY
HERALDRY
HEREDITY
HIDEAWAY
HILARITY
HOARSELY
HOGMANAY
HOLLOWAY
HONESTLY
HONORARY
HOROLOGY
HORRIBLY
HORSEFLY
HOSTELRY
HOVERFLY
HUMANELY
HUMANITY
HUMIDIFY
HUMIDITY
HUMILITY
HUMPHREY
HUNGRILY
IDENTIFY
IDENTITY
IDEOLOGY
IDOLATRY
IGNOMINY
ILLUSORY
IMMUNITY
IMPUNITY
IMPURIFY
IMPURITY
INDUSTRY
INEQUITY
INFANTRY
INFINITY
INIQUITY
INSANELY
INSANITY
INTENTLY
INTIMACY
INWARDLY
ISOSTASY
JAUNTILY
JEALOUSY
JEOPARDY
JOKINGLY
JOVIALLY
JOYFULLY
JURATORY
KENTUCKY
KILKENNY
KINGSLEY
KNIGHTLY
KROMESKY
LACKADAY
LAMASERY
LANDLADY
LANSBURY
LAPIDARY
LATCHKEY
LATTERLY
LAUDABLY
LAVATORY
LAVISHLY
LAWFULLY
LEATHERY
LEGALITY
LENIENCY
LETHARGY
LIENTERY
LIFEBUOY
LITERACY
LITERARY
LIVIDITY
LOBOTOMY
LOCALITY
LOMBARDY
LONGSTAY
LOVINGLY
LUCIDITY
LUMINARY
MACAULAY
MACREADY
MAHOGANY
MAIDENLY
MAINSTAY
MAJORITY
MALAGASY
MALARKEY
MANFULLY
MANNERLY
MANUALLY
MARKEDLY
MASTERLY
MATRONLY
MATURITY
MCKINLEY
MENTALLY
METONYMY
MIGHTILY
MILITARY
MINATORY
MINISTRY
MINORITY
MINUTELY
MISAPPLY
MISCARRY
MISOGYNY
MOBILITY
MODESTLY
MONARCHY
MONETARY
MONOGAMY
MONOPOLY
MONOTONY
MORALITY
MORBIDLY
MOROSELY
MORTALLY
MORTUARY
MOTHERLY
MOTORWAY
MULBERRY
MULTIPLY
MUTUALLY
MYCOLOGY
NARROWLY
NATALITY
NATIVITY
NIJINSKY
NOBILITY
NORMALLY
NORMANDY
NOSOLOGY
NUGATORY
NUMERACY
OBDURACY
OBITUARY
OBTUSELY
ODIOUSLY
OENOLOGY
ONCOLOGY
ONTOLOGY
ORANGERY
ORDINARY
OSTERLEY
OVERPLAY
OVERSTAY
PALIMONY
PALPABLY
PANDOWDY
PANEGYRY
PARAGUAY
PASSABLY
PASSERBY
PATCHILY
PATENTLY
PEDAGOGY
PEDANTRY
PENOLOGY
PERIPETY
PEVENSEY
PHARMACY
PHOTOPSY
PIQUANCY
PLACIDLY
PLEURISY
PLUCKILY
POLITELY
POLYGAMY
POLYSEMY
PONSONBY
POPINJAY
POROSITY
PORPHYRY
POSOLOGY
POSSIBLY
POTBELLY
PRETTILY
PRIESTLY
PRINCELY
PRIORITY
PROBABLY
PROMPTLY
PROPERLY
PROPERTY
PROPHECY
PROPHESY
PSALMODY
PSALTERY
PSEUDERY
PUBLICLY
PUNGENCY
QUAINTLY
QUANDARY
QUANTIFY
QUANTITY
RACIALLY
RAILLERY
RANDOMLY
RAPACITY
RAPIDITY
RASCALLY
RECENTLY
RECOVERY
REDEPLOY
REEMPLOY
REFINERY
REGISTRY
RELIABLY
REMOTELY
REVIVIFY
RHAPSODY
RIBALDRY
RIDGEWAY
RIGIDITY
RITUALLY
ROBUSTLY
ROCKETRY
ROLYPOLY
ROSEMARY
ROTATORY
RUBBISHY
RUEFULLY
RUGGEDLY
SACRISTY
SADDLERY
SAGACITY
SALACITY
SALINITY
SALIVARY
SALUTARY
SALUTORY
SANCTIFY
SANCTITY
SANITARY
SATURDAY
SAVAGELY
SAVAGERY
SCANTILY
SCARCELY
SCARCITY
SCRATCHY
SCRIBBLY
SCRUTINY
SCULLERY
SECONDLY
SECRETLY
SECURELY
SECURITY
SEDATELY
SELFPITY
SEMINARY
SENILITY
SENSIBLY
SERENELY
SERENITY
SEROLOGY
SEVERELY
SEVERITY
SEXOLOGY
SEXUALLY
SHABBILY
SHODDILY
SHREWDLY
SIGNALLY
SILENTLY
SIMPLIFY
SISTERLY
SLEEPILY
SLIGHTLY
SLIPPERY
SLOBBERY
SLOPPILY
SLOVENLY
SMOOTHLY
SNAPPILY
SNOBBERY
SNOOTILY
SOAKAWAY
SOBRIETY
SOCIALLY
SODALITY
SOLDIERY
SOLEMNLY
SOLIDIFY
SOLIDITY
SOLITARY

SOLVENCY
SOMBRELY
SOMEBODY
SOOTHSAY
SORDIDLY
SORORITY
SPARSELY
SPARSITY
SPEEDILY
SPEEDWAY
SPILLWAY
SPIRALLY
SPRITELY
SPRUCELY
SQUARELY
STAIRWAY
STANNARY
STATUARY
STEADILY
STEALTHY
STEINWAY
STICKILY
STINGRAY
STOKESAY
STOLIDLY
STOWAWAY
STRACHEY
STRAGGLY
STRATEGY
STRATIFY
STRETCHY
STRICTLY
STRONGLY
STUFFILY
STULTIFY
STUPIDLY
STURDILY
SUBTLETY
SUDDENLY
SUITABLY
SULLENLY
SUMMITRY
SUPERBLY
SYMMETRY
SYMPATHY
SYMPHONY
TAKEAWAY
TANGIBLY
TAPESTRY
TAXONOMY
TAYBERRY
TEARAWAY
TELEGONY
TEMERITY
TENACITY
TENDENCY
TENDERLY
TERRIBLY
TERTIARY
TETCHILY
THATAWAY
THEOLOGY
THIEVERY
THINGAMY
THRENODY
THUNDERY
THURSDAY
TIMIDITY
TINSELLY
TONALITY
TOPHEAVY
TOPOLOGY
TOTALITY
TOXICITY
TRAVESTY
TREASURY
TRICKERY
TRUMPERY
TUPPENNY
TURGIDLY
TUTELARY
TWOPENNY
UBIQUITY
UNDERLAY
UNEASILY
UNEVENLY
UNGAINLY
UNIQUELY
UNITEDLY
UNJUSTLY
UNKINDLY
UNLIKELY
UNLOVELY
UNSAVORY
UNSEEMLY
UNSTEADY
UNTIDILY
UNTIMELY
UNWIELDY
UNWORTHY
URBANITY
URGENTLY
USEFULLY
VACANTLY
VAGRANCY
VALIDITY
VELLEITY
VELOCITY
VENALITY
VERACITY
VERBALLY
VESTIARY
VIBRANCY
VICINITY
VILLAINY
VINEGARY
VIRILITY
VIROLOGY
VISUALLY
VITALITY
VIVACITY
VOMITORY
VORACITY
VULGARLY
WARRANTY
WATERWAY
WAVERLEY
WEAPONRY
WESTERLY
WHEEZILY
WHISKERY
WICKEDLY
WILFULLY
WITCHERY
WIZARDRY
WOEFULLY
WOLSELEY
WOODENLY
WORKADAY
WORTHILY
XENOGAMY
YEOMANRY
ALCATRAZ
SCHMALTZ

9:1

ABANDONED
ABANDONEE
ABASEMENT
ABATEMENT
ABDOMINAL
ABDUCTION
ABERNETHY
ABERRANCE
ABHORRENT
ABLUTIONS
ABOLITION
ABOMINATE
ABORIGINE
ABOUNDING
ABOUTFACE
ABOUTTURN
ABSCONDER
ABSORBENT
ABSORBING
ABSTAINER
ABSTINENT
ABSURDITY
ABUNDANCE
ABYSMALLY
ACADEMIST
ACARIASIS
ACCESSION
ACCESSORY
ACCIDENTS
ACCLIMATE
ACCLIVITY
ACCOMPANY
ACCORDANT
ACCORDING
ACCORDION
ACCRETION
ACETYLENE
ACIDULATE
ACIDULOUS
ACONCAGUA
ACOUSTICS
ACQUIESCE
ACQUITTAL
ACROBATIC
ACROPHONY
ACROPOLIS
ACTUALITY
ACTUARIAL
ACUMINATE
ACUTENESS
ADAPTABLE
ADDERWORT
ADDICTION
ADDICTIVE
ADDRESSED
ADDRESSEE
ADENOIDAL
ADEPTNESS
ADHERENCE
ADJECTIVE
ADJOINING
ADMIRABLE
ADMIRABLY
ADMIRALTY
ADMISSION
ADMITTING
ADMIXTURE
ADMONITOR
ADORATION
ADORNMENT
ADRENALIN
ADULATION
ADULTERER
ADULTHOOD
ADUMBRATE
ADVANTAGE
ADVECTION
ADVENTIST
ADVENTURE
ADVERBIAL
ADVERSARY
ADVERSELY
ADVERSITY
ADVERTISE
ADVISABLE
ADVISEDLY
ADVOCATED
AEPYORNIS
AERODROME
AEROPLANE
AEROSPACE
AEROTAXIS
AESCHYLUS
AESTHETIC
AFFECTING
AFFECTION
AFFIDAVIT
AFFILIATE
AFFLICTED
AFFLUENCE
AFFRICATE
AFLATOXIN
AFORESAID
AFRIKAANS
AFRIKANER
AFTERCARE
AFTERDAMP
AFTERGLOW
AFTERMATH
AFTERMOST
AFTERNOON
AFTERWORD
AGALACTIC
AGAMEMNON
AGGRAVATE
AGGREGATE
AGGRESSOR
AGGRIEVED
AGINCOURT
AGITATION
AGONIZING
AGREEABLE
AGREEABLY
AGREEMENT
AGUECHEEK
AHASUERUS
AIMLESSLY
AINSWORTH
AIRCOOLED
AIRSTREAM
AITCHBONE
ALABASTER
ALBATROSS
ALBERTINE
ALCHEMIST
ALCOHOLIC
ALDEBARAN
ALERTNESS
ALEURITIS
ALEXANDER
ALEXANDRA
ALGEBRAIC
ALGORITHM
ALIGNMENT
ALLANTOID
ALLANTOIS
ALLEGEDLY
ALLEGIANT
ALLEMANDE
ALLEVIATE
ALLIGATOR
ALLOCARPY
ALLOGRAPH
ALLOPATHY
ALLOTMENT
ALLOWABLE
ALLOWANCE
ALMANDINE
ALONGSIDE
ALOOFNESS
ALPENHORN
ALTERABLE
ALTERCATE
ALTERNATE
ALTIMETER
ALTIPLANO
ALTISSIMO
ALUMINIUM
ALVEOLATE
AMARANTIN
AMARYLLIS
AMAUROSIS
AMAZEMENT
AMBERGRIS
AMBIGUITY
AMBIGUOUS
AMBITIOUS
AMBLYOPIA
AMBROSIAL
AMBROSIAN
AMBROTYPE
AMBULANCE
AMBUSCADE
AMELAKITE
AMENDMENT
AMENHOTEP
AMERICIUM
AMIANTHUS
AMIDSHIPS
AMOROUSLY
AMORPHOUS
AMPERSAND
AMPHIBIAN
AMPLIFIER
AMPLITUDE
AMSTERDAM
AMUSEMENT
AMUSINGLY
AMYGDALUS
ANABOLISM
ANABRANCH
ANAEROBIC
ANAGLYPTA
ANALEPTIC
ANALGESIA
ANALGESIC
ANALOGOUS
ANAPLASTY
ANARCHIST
ANASTASIA
ANATOLIAN
ANATOMIST
ANATOMIZE
ANCESTRAL
ANCHORAGE
ANCHORITE
ANCHORMAN
ANCILLARY
ANCIPITAL
ANDANTINO
ANDROCLES
ANDROMEDA
ANECDOTAL
ANECDOTES
ANGIOGRAM
ANGLICISM
ANGOSTURA
ANGUISHED
ANHYDRIDE
ANHYDRITE
ANHYDROUS
ANIMATION
ANIMISTIC
ANIMOSITY
ANKYLOSIS
ANNAPOLIS
ANNAPURNA
ANNOTATED
ANNOTATOR
ANNOUNCER
ANNOYANCE
ANNULMENT
ANOINTING
ANOMALOUS
ANONYMITY
ANONYMOUS
ANOPHELES
ANSCHLUSS
ANSWERING
ANTARCTIC
ANTENATAL
ANTHOLOGY
ANTICLINE
ANTIGONUS
ANTIHELIX
ANTIPASTO
ANTIPATHY
ANTIPHONY
ANTIPODES
ANTIQUARY
ANTIQUITY
ANTITOXIC
ANTITOXIN
ANTIVENIN
ANTONINUS
ANXIOUSLY
APARTHEID
APARTMENT
APATHETIC
APENNINES
APERIODIC
APERITIVE
APHRODITE
APOCRYPHA
APOLLONUS
APOLOGIST
APOLOGIZE
APOPHATIC
APOPHYSIS
APOSTOLIC
APPALLING
APPARATUS
APPARITOR
APPEALING
APPENDAGE
APPERTAIN
APPETIZER
APPLEJACK
APPLIANCE
APPLICANT
APPOINTED
APPOINTEE
APPORTION
APPRAISAL
APPREHEND
APPROVING
AQUAPLANE
AQUARELLE
AQUILEGIA
ARABESQUE
ARABINOSE
ARACHNOID
ARAGONITE
ARAUCARIA
ARBITRAGE
ARBITRARY
ARBITRATE
ARBORETUM
ARCHANGEL
ARCHETYPE
ARCHIBALD
ARCHITECT
ARCHIVIST
ARCHIVOLT
ARCTOGAEA
ARDUOUSLY
AREOPAGUS
ARGENTINA
ARGENTINE
ARISTOTLE
ARKWRIGHT
ARLINGTON
ARMADILLO
ARMAMENTS
ARMISTICE
ARMSTRONG
ARQUEBUSE
ARRESTING
ARRIVISTE
ARROGANCE
ARROWHEAD
ARROWROOT
ARSENICAL
ARTEMISIA
ARTERIOLE
ARTHRITIC
ARTHRITIS
ARTHROPOD
ARTHROSIS

ARTHURIAN
ARTICHOKE
ARTICULAR
ARTIFICER
ARTILLERY
ASCENDANT
ASCENDING
ASCENSION
ASCERTAIN
ASCLEPIUS
ASHKENAZI
ASHMOLEAN
ASPARAGUS
ASPARTAME
ASPERSION
ASPIRATOR
ASPLENIUM
ASSAILANT
ASSERTING
ASSERTION
ASSERTIVE
ASSIDUITY
ASSIDUOUS
ASSISTANT
ASSOCIATE
ASSONANCE
ASSUETUDE
ASSURANCE
ASSUREDLY
ASTHMATIC
ASTOUNDED
ASTRAGALS
ASTRAKHAN
ASTRODOME
ASTROLABE
ASTROLOGY
ASTRONAUT
ASTRONOMY
ASTROPHEL
ASTROTURF
ASTUCIOUS
ASYMMETRY
ASYNERGIA
ATAHUALPA
ATAVISTIC
ATHEISTIC
ATHELSTAN
ATHENAEUM
ATHLETICS
ATONEMENT
ATROCIOUS
ATTACKING
ATTAINDER
ATTEMPTED
ATTENDANT
ATTENTION
ATTENTIVE
ATTENUATE
ATTITUDES
ATTRIBUTE
ATTRITION
ATTUITION
AUBERGINE
AUBRIETIA
AUCTORIAL
AUDACIOUS
AUGUSTINE
AURICULAR
AUSTERITY
AUSTRALIA
AUTHENTIC
AUTHORESS
AUTHORITY
AUTHORIZE
AUTOCLAVE
AUTOCRACY
AUTOCROSS
AUTOGRAPH
AUTOLATRY
AUTOLYCUS
AUTOLYSIS
AUTOMAKER
AUTOMATED
AUTOMATIC
AUTOMATON
AUTONOMIC
AUTOPILOT
AUTOROUTE
AUTOSCOPY
AUXILIARY
AVAILABLE
AVALANCHE
AVOCATION
AVOIDABLE
AVOIDANCE
AVUNCULAR
AWAKENING
AWARENESS
AWESTRUCK
AWKWARDLY
AXIOMATIC
AXMINSTER
AYATOLLAH
AYCKBOURN
AYLESBURY
BACHARACH
BACKBENCH
BACKBITER
BACKCLOTH
BACKPEDAL
BACKSHISH
BACKSLIDE
BACKSPACE
BACKSTAGE
BACKSWORD
BACKTRACK
BACKWARDS
BACKWATER
BACKWOODS
BACTERIAL
BACTERIUM
BADMINTON
BAGATELLE
BAINMARIE
BAKEHOUSE
BAKSHEESH
BALACLAVA
BALALAIKA
BALDAQUIN
BALEFULLY
BALLADEER
BALLADIST
BALLERINA
BALLISTIC
BALLPOINT
BALTHAZAR
BALTIMORE
BAMBOOZLE
BANDALORE
BANDICOOT
BANDOLEER
BANDOLERO
BANDOLIER
BANDSTAND
BANDWAGON
BANISTERS
BANQUETTE
BANTERING
BAPTISMAL
BARAGOUIN
BARBARIAN
BARBARITY
BARBAROUS
BARBITONE
BARBOTINE
BARCELONA
BAREBONES
BAREFACED
BARMBRACK
BARMECIDE
BARNABITE
BARNACLES
BARNSTORM
BAROMETER
BARRACUDA
BARRICADE
BARRISTER
BARTENDER
BARTHOLDI
BARTHOLIN
BARYSCOPE
BASEBOARD
BASECOURT
BASHFULLY
BASICALLY
BASILICAL
BASILICON
BASKETFUL
BASTINADE
BASTINADO
BATHTOWEL
BATTALION
BATTLEAXE
BEACHHEAD
BEACHWEAR
BEANFEAST
BEARDLESS
BEARDSLEY
BEATITUDE
BEAUTEOUS
BEAUTIFUL
BECHSTEIN
BECQUEREL
BEDFELLOW
BEDJACKET
BEDRAGGLE
BEDRIDDEN
BEDSITTER
BEDSPREAD
BEEFEATER
BEEFSTEAK
BEEKEEPER
BEELZEBUB
BEESTINGS
BEETHOVEN
BEGINNING
BEHAVIOUR
BELATEDLY
BELEAGUER
BELIEVING
BELLICOSE
BELLYACHE
BELLYFLOP
BELONGING
BELVEDERE
BENBECULA
BENCHMARK
BENIGHTED
BERGAMASK
BERGANDER
BERGOMASK
BERKELIUM
BERNSTEIN
BERYLLIUM
BESPANGLE
BETHLEHEM
BETROTHAL
BETROTHED
BETTERTON
BEVERIDGE
BICYCLIST
BIFURCATE
BIGHEADED
BILATERAL
BILINGUAL
BILIRUBIN
BILLABONG
BILLBOARD
BILLIARDS
BILLOWING
BILLYCOCK
BIMONTHLY
BINOCULAR
BIOGRAPHY
BIOLOGIST
BIOSPHERE
BIPARTITE
BIRDBRAIN
BIRDTABLE
BIRTHMARK
BIRTHWORT
BISECTION
BISHOPRIC
BIZARRELY
BLACKBALL
BLACKBIRD
BLACKFACE
BLACKFOOT
BLACKHEAD
BLACKJACK
BLACKLEAD
BLACKLIST
BLACKMAIL
BLACKMORE
BLACKNESS
BLACKWOOD
BLAMELESS
BLANDNESS
BLASPHEME
BLASPHEMY
BLATANTLY
BLEACHERS
BLESSINGS
BLINDFOLD
BLINDNESS
BLINDSPOT
BLINDWORM
BLINKERED
BLISTERED
BLOCKHEAD
BLOODBATH
BLOODLESS
BLOODSHED
BLOODSHOT
BLOWTORCH
BLUEBEARD
BLUEBERRY
BLUEPRINT
BLUESTONE
BLUFFNESS
BLUNDERER
BLUNTNESS
BLUSTERER
BOANERGES
BOARDROOM
BOARDWALK
BOATHOUSE
BOATSWAIN
BOBSLEIGH
BOCCACCIO
BODYGUARD
BOLIVIANO
BOLOGNESE
BOLSHEVIK
BOMBARDON
BOMBASINE
BOMBASTIC
BOMBSHELL
BONAPARTE
BOOBYTRAP
BOOKLOVER
BOOKMAKER
BOOKSHELF
BOOKSTALL
BOOKSTAND
BOOKSTORE
BOOMERANG
BOONDOCKS
BOOTLACES
BORDEREAU
BORDERING
BORNAGAIN
BORROWING
BOSPHORUS
BOSSANOVA
BOSSINESS
BOSTONIAN
BOTANICAL
BOTSWANAN
BOTTLEFUL
BOULEVARD
BOUNDLESS
BOUNTEOUS
BOUNTIFUL
BOURGEOIS
BOXWALLAH
BOYFRIEND
BRACTEOLE
BRADLAUGH
BRAINCASE
BRAINLESS
BRAINWASH

BRAINWAVE
BRAMBLING
BRANCHING
BRANDIRON
BRASENOSE
BRASSERIE
BRASSICAS
BRASSIERE
BRASSWARE
BRATWURST
BRAZILIAN
BREADLINE
BREAKABLE
BREAKAGES
BREAKAWAY
BREAKDOWN
BREAKEVEN
BREAKFAST
BREAKNECK
BREATHING
BREECHING
BRICKWORK
BRICKYARD
BRIDEWELL
BRIDLEWAY
BRIEFCASE
BRIEFNESS
BRIGADIER
BRIGADOON
BRILLIANT
BRIMSTONE
BRIQUETTE
BRISKNESS
BRISTLING
BRITANNIA
BRITANNIC
BRITSCHKA
BROADCAST
BROADLOOM
BROADSIDE
BROKERAGE
BRONCHIAL
BROTHERLY
BROUGHTON
BRUMMAGEM
BRUNHILDE
BRUSHWOOD
BRUSQUELY
BRUTALISM
BRUTALITY
BRUTALIZE
BUCCANEER
BUCENTAUR
BUCHAREST
BUCKETFUL
BUCKTEETH
BUCKTHORN
BUCKWHEAT
BUDGETARY
BULGARIAN
BULKINESS
BULLDOZER
BULLFIGHT
BULLFINCH
BUMBLEBEE
BUMPTIOUS
BUNDESTAG
BURKINABE
BURLESQUE
BURLINESS
BURROUGHS
BURROWING
BURUNDIAN
BUTTERBUR
BUTTERCUP
BUTTERFLY
BUTTERNUT
BYPRODUCT
BYSTANDER
BYZANTINE
CABALLERO
CABLEGRAM
CABRIOLET
CACHAEMIA
CACHECTIC
CACOPHONY
CADASTRAL
CAESAREAN
CAFETERIA
CAFETIERE
CAGOULARD
CAIRNGORM
CAKESTAND
CALABOOSE
CALABRESE
CALCANEUM
CALCANEUS
CALCINATE
CALCULATE
CALDARIUM
CALEDONIA
CALEMBOUR
CALENDULA
CALENTURE
CALIBRATE
CALLIPERS
CALLOSITY
CALLOUSLY
CALORIFIC
CALPURNIA
CALVANISM
CALVINIST
CALVITIES
CAMBODIAN
CAMBRIDGE
CAMBUSCAN
CAMCORDER
CAMEMBERT
CAMERAMAN
CAMPANILE
CAMPANULA
CANALETTO
CANAVERAL
CANCEROUS
CANDIDACY
CANDIDATE
CANDLELIT
CANDLEMAS
CANDYTUFT
CANNELURE
CANNONADE
CANONICAL
CANTABILE
CANTHARIS
CANTHARUS
CANTONESE
CANVASSER
CAPACIOUS
CAPACITOR
CAPARISON
CAPILLARY
CAPITULAR
CAPITULUM
CAPORETTO
CAPRICCIO
CAPRICORN
CAPTAINCY
CAPTIVATE
CAPTIVITY
CARACALLA
CARAMBOLA
CARBAMATE
CARBAMIDE
CARBONADE
CARBONARI
CARBONATE
CARBONIZE
CARBUNCLE
CARCINOMA
CARDBOARD
CAREERIST
CAREFULLY
CARETAKER
CARIBBEAN
CARMELITE
CARNATION
CARNELIAN
CARNIVORE
CARPACCIO
CARPENTER
CARPENTRY
CARPETING
CARTESIAN
CARTHORSE
CARTILAGE
CARTOGRAM
CARTOUCHE
CARTRIDGE
CARTTRACK
CARTULARY
CARTWHEEL
CARYOPSIS
CASHPOINT
CASSANDRA
CASSATION
CASSEROLE
CASSONADE
CASSOULET
CASSOWARY
CASTANETS
CASTIGATE
CASTILIAN
CASTRATED
CASUARINA
CASUISTIC
CASUISTRY
CATACLYSM
CATACOMBS
CATALEPSY
CATALOGUE
CATALYSIS
CATALYTIC
CATAMARAN
CATAPLASM
CATAPLEXY
CATARRHAL
CATATONIA
CATATONIC
CATCHCROP
CATCHMENT
CATCHPOLE
CATCHPOLL
CATCHWORD
CATECHISM
CATECHIZE
CATERWAUL
CATHARSIS
CATHARTIC
CATHEDRAL
CATHEPSIN
CATHERINE
CATSKILLS
CATTLEMAN
CATTLEPEN
CAUCASIAN
CAUSATION
CAUTERIZE
CAVALCADE
CAVENDISH
CAVERNOUS
CAVORTING
CEASEFIRE
CEASELESS
CEDARWOOD
CELANDINE
CELEBRANT
CELEBRATE
CELEBRITY
CELESTIAL
CELLARIST
CELLULITE
CELLULOID
CELLULOSE
CENTAURUS
CENTENARY
CENTERING
CENTIPEDE
CENTRALLY
CENTREING
CENTURION
CERATITIS
CERATODUS
CEREBRATE
CEROMANCY
CERTAINLY
CERTAINTY
CERTIFIED
CERTITUDE
CERVANTES
CESSATION
CEVAPCICI
CEYLONESE
CHABAZITE
CHAFFINCH
CHAIRLIFT
CHALAZION
CHALIAPIN
CHALLENGE
CHALUMEAU
CHAMELEON
CHAMFRAIN
CHAMINADE
CHAMOMILE
CHAMPAGNE
CHAMPAIGN
CHAMPERTY
CHAMPLAIN
CHAMPLEVÉ
CHANTEUSE
CHANTILLY
CHAPARRAL
CHAPERONE
CHARABANC
CHARACTER
CHARGEFUL
CHARIVARI
CHARLATAN
CHARLOTTE
CHAROLAIS
CHARTERED
CHARTREUX
CHARWOMAN
CHARYBDIS
CHASTENED
CHATTERER
CHAUFFEUR
CHAVENDER
CHAWBACON
CHEAPJACK
CHEAPNESS
CHEAPSIDE
CHECKBOOK
CHECKLIST
CHECKMATE
CHECKROOM
CHEEKBONE
CHEERLESS
CHEMISTRY
CHEONGSAM
CHEQUERED
CHERISHED
CHERNOZEM
CHERUBINI
CHEVALIER
CHICANERY
CHICKADEE
CHICKWEED
CHIEFTAIN
CHIHUAHUA
CHILBLAIN
CHILDCARE
CHILDHOOD
CHILDLESS
CHILDLIKE
CHILOPODA
CHINATOWN
CHINOVNIK
CHINSTRAP
CHIPBOARD
CHIPOLATA
CHIPPINGS
CHIROPODY
CHISELLER
CHLAMYDES
CHOCOLATE
CHOLELITH
CHONDRITE
CHONDROID
CHORISTER
CHRISTIAN
CHRISTMAS
CHROMATIC

CHRONICLE
CHRYSALIS
CHURCHILL
CHURCHMAN
CHURIDARS
CIGARETTE
CILIOLATE
CIMMERIAN
CINEMATIC
CINERARIA
CINEREOUS
CIPOLLINO
CIRCADIAN
CIRCINATE
CIRCULATE
CIRRHOSIS
CIVILISED
CIVILIZED
CLAMOROUS
CLAMPDOWN
CLAPBOARD
CLARENDON
CLARIFIER
CLASSICAL
CLASSLESS
CLASSMATE
CLASSROOM
CLEANNESS
CLEANSING
CLEARANCE
CLEARNESS
CLEOPATRA
CLEPSYDRA
CLERGYMAN
CLEVELAND
CLIENTELE
CLIMACTIC
CLINGFILM
CLINICIAN
CLIPBOARD
CLOAKROOM
CLOCKWISE
CLOCKWORK
CLOISONNÉ
CLOSENESS
CLOUDLESS
CLUBHOUSE
CLUSTERED
COACHLOAD
COADJUTOR
COAGULANT
COAGULATE
COALESCED
COALFIELD
COALITION
COALMINER
COARCTATE
COASTLINE
COCHINEAL
COCKAIGNE
COCKATIEL
COCKFIGHT
COCKROACH
COCKSCOMB
COCKSFOOT
COCKSWAIN
COELOSTAT
COEMPTION
COENOBITE
COENOBIUM
COFFERDAM
COFFINITE
COGNITION
COGNITIVE
COGNIZANT
COHERENCE
COINTREAU
COLCHICUM
COLERIDGE
COLLAPSAR
COLLATION
COLLEAGUE
COLLECTED
COLLECTOR
COLLEGIAN
COLLIGATE
COLLIMATE
COLLISION
COLLOCATE
COLLODION
COLLOIDAL
COLLOTYPE
COLLUSION
COLLUSIVE
COLLYRIUM
COLOMBIAN
COLOMBIER
COLONNADE
COLOPHONY
COLORLESS
COLOSSEUM
COLOSTOMY
COLOSTRUM
COLOURFUL
COLOURING
COLOURIST
COLTSFOOT
COLUMBARY
COLUMBATE
COLUMBIAN
COLUMBINE
COLUMBITE
COLUMBIUM
COLUMELLA
COLUMNIST
COMBATANT
COMBATIVE
COMFORTER
COMICALLY
COMINFORM
COMINTERN
COMMANDER
COMMENSAL
COMMISSAR
COMMITTAL
COMMITTED
COMMITTEE
COMMODITY
COMMODORE
COMMOTION
COMMUNION
COMMUNISM
COMMUNIST
COMMUNITY
COMPACTLY
COMPANIES
COMPANION
COMPELLED
COMPETENT
COMPETING
COMPLAINT
COMPLIANT
COMPONENT
COMPOSING
COMPOSITE
COMPOSURE
COMPOTIER
COMPUTING
CONCAVITY
CONCEALED
CONCEITED
CONCERNED
CONCERTED
CONCIERGE
CONCISELY
CONCISION
CONCLUDED
CONCORDAT
CONCOURSE
CONCUBINE
CONCUSSED
CONDEMNED
CONDENSER
CONDIMENT
CONDITION
CONDUCIVE
CONDUCTOR
CONDUCTUS
CONDYLOMA
CONFESSED
CONFESSOR
CONFIDANT
CONFIDENT
CONFIRMED
CONFITEOR
CONFLATED
CONFUCIUS
CONFUSING
CONFUSION
CONGENIAL
CONGERIES
CONGESTED
CONGOLESE
CONGRUENT
CONGRUOUS
CONJUGATE
CONJURING
CONNECTED
CONNECTOR
CONNEXION
CONNOTATE
CONNUBIAL
CONQUEROR
CONSCIOUS
CONSCRIPT
CONSENSUS
CONSIGNEE
CONSIGNOR
CONSONANT
CONSTABLE
CONSTANCE
CONSTANCY
CONSTRICT
CONSTRUCT
CONSULATE
CONSUMING
CONTAGION
CONTAINER
CONTEMPER
CONTENDER
CONTENTED
CONTINENT
CONTINUAL
CONTINUUM
CONTRALTO
CONTRIVED
CONTRIVER
CONTUMACY
CONTUMELY
CONTUSION
CONUNDRUM
CONVECTOR
CONVERTED
CONVERTER
CONVINCED
CONVIVIAL
COOKHOUSE
COOPERATE
COPIOUSLY
COPROLITE
COPYRIGHT
CORALLINE
CORDIALLY
CORDUROYS
CORDYLINE
CORIANDER
CORKSCREW
CORMORANT
CORNBRASH
CORNCRAKE
CORNEILLE
CORNELIAN
CORNERMAN
CORNFIELD
CORNFLOUR
CORNSTALK
COROLLARY
CORPORATE
CORPOREAL
CORPOSANT
CORPULENT
CORPUSCLE
CORRECTED
CORRECTLY
CORRECTOR
CORREGGIO
CORRELATE
CORROSION
CORROSIVE
CORRUGATE
CORRUPTER
CORTISONE
CORUSCATE
COSMETICS
COSMOGONY
COSMOLOGY
COSMONAUT
COSTUMIER
COTANGENT
COTHURNUS
COTYLEDON
COUCHETTE
COUNSELOR
COUNTDOWN
COUNTLESS
COUNTRIES
COURGETTE
COURTELLE
COURTEOUS
COURTESAN
COURTROOM
COURTSHIP
COURTYARD
COUTURIER
COVALENCY
COVELLITE
COVERDALE
COWARDICE
COXSACKIE
CRACKDOWN
CRACKLING
CRACKSMAN
CRACOVIAN
CRAFTSMAN
CRANBERRY
CRANBORNE
CRAPULENT
CRAPULOUS
CRASHLAND
CRAZINESS
CREDULITY
CREDULOUS
CREMATION
CREMATORY
CREPITATE
CREPOLINE
CRESCELLE
CRESCENDO
CRETINOUS
CRIBELLUM
CRICKETER
CRIMINATE
CRINOLINE
CRIPPLING
CRISPNESS
CRITERION
CRITICISM
CRITICIZE
CROCKFORD
CROCODILE
CROISSANT
CROOKBACK
CROOKEDLY
CROQUETTE
CROSSBEAM
CROSSBILL
CROSSBRED
CROSSEYED
CROSSFIRE
CROSSOVER
CROSSWALK
CROSSWIND
CROSSWISE
CROSSWORD
CROTCHETY
CROUSTADE
CROWNLIKE
CROWSBILL
CROWSFOOT
CRUCIALLY
CRUDENESS
CRUMBLING

CRUSTACEA
CRYOGENIC
CRYOMETER
CRYPTOGAM
CTESIPHON
CUBBYHOLE
CUCHULAIN
CUFFLINKS
CULMINATE
CULTIVATE
CUNCTATOR
CUNEIFORM
CUPRESSUS
CURETTAGE
CURFUFFLE
CURIOSITY
CURIOUSLY
CURRENTLY
CURRYCOMB
CURSORILY
CURTILAGE
CURVATURE
CUSPIDORE
CUSTODIAL
CUSTODIAN
CUSTOMARY
CUSTOMIZE
CUTANEOUS
CUTTHROAT
CYCLAMATE
CYCLOLITH
CYCLORAMA
CYCLOTRON
CYMBELINE
CYMBIDIUM
CYNEGETIC
CYNICALLY
DACHSHUND
DAEDALIAN
DAIRYMAID
DALLIANCE
DALMATIAN
DALTONISM
DAMASCENE
DAMBUSTER
DAMNATION
DAMNEDEST
DANDELION
DANDIFIED
DANDYPRAT
DANGEROUS
DAREDEVIL
DARTAGNAN
DARTBOARD
DARTMOUTH
DARWINIAN
DASHBOARD
DASHWHEEL
DASTARDLY
DAUNTLESS
DAVENPORT
DAYSPRING
DEACONESS
DEADLIGHT
DEAFENING
DEATHLESS
DEATHTRAP
DEBATABLE
DEBAUCHED
DEBAUCHEE
DEBENTURE
DEBUTANTE
DECACHORD
DECADENCE
DECALITRE
DECALOGUE
DECAMERON
DECASTYLE
DECATHLON
DECEITFUL
DECEMVIRI
DECEPTION
DECEPTIVE
DECESSION
DECIDEDLY
DECIDUOUS
DECILLION
DECKCHAIR
DECLARING
DECLINING
DECLIVITY
DECOCTION
DECOLLATE
DECOMPOSE
DECONTROL
DECORATED
DECORATOR
DECRETALS
DECUMBENT
DECURSIVE
DECUSSATE
DEDICATED
DEDUCTION
DEDUCTIVE
DEERHOUND
DEFALCATE
DEFAULTER
DEFEATISM
DEFEATIST
DEFECTION
DEFECTIVE
DEFENDANT
DEFENDERS
DEFENSIVE
DEFERENCE
DEFERMENT
DEFICIENT
DEFINABLE
DEFLATION
DEFLECTOR
DEFOLIANT
DEFOLIATE
DEFORMITY
DEGRADING
DEHYDRATE
DEJECTION
DELACROIX
DELICIOUS
DELIGHTED
DELINEATE
DELIRIOUS
DELIVERER
DEMAGOGUE
DEMANDING
DEMARCATE
DEMEANING
DEMEANOUR
DEMETRIUS
DEMITASSE
DEMOCRACY
DEMULCENT
DEMURRAGE
DENIGRATE
DENSENESS
DENTISTRY
DENTITION
DEODORANT
DEODORIZE
DEOXIDISE
DEPARTURE
DEPENDANT
DEPENDENT
DEPENDING
DEPICTION
DEPOSITOR
DEPRAVITY
DEPRECATE
DEPREDATE
DEPRESSED
DERRINGER
DESCARTES
DESECRATE
DESERTION
DESERVING
DESICCATE
DESIGNATE
DESIGNING
DESIPIENT
DESIRABLE
DESPERADO
DESPERATE
DESPOTISM
DESTITUTE
DESTROYED
DESTROYER
DESUETUDE
DESULTORY
DETECTION
DETECTIVE
DETENTION
DETERGENT
DETERMINE
DETERRENT
DETONATOR
DETRACTOR
DETRIMENT
DETRITION
DEUCALION
DEUTERIUM
DEVASTATE
DEVELOPED
DEVELOPER
DEVIATION
DEVILMENT
DEVIOUSLY
DEVONPORT
DEXTERITY
DEXTEROUS
DEXTRORSE
DIABLERIE
DIACRITIC
DIAERESIS
DIAGNOSIS
DIALECTAL
DIALECTIC
DIALOGITE
DIAMETRIC
DIANDROUS
DIANETICS
DIANOETIC
DIAPHRAGM
DIARRHOEA
DIASTASIS
DIATHESIS
DIAZEUXIS
DICHOTOMY
DICTATION
DIDACTICS
DIETETICS
DIETICIAN
DIFFERENT
DIFFICULT
DIFFIDENT
DIFFUSION
DIGASTRIC
DIGESTION
DIGESTIVE
DIGITALIN
DIGITALIS
DIGNIFIED
DIGNITARY
DILIGENCE
DIMENSION
DINGINESS
DINNERSET
DIOCLETES
DIONYSIAN
DIONYSIUS
DIPHTHONG
DIPLOMACY
DIRECTION
DIRECTIVE
DIRECTORS
DIRECTORY
DIRIGIBLE
DIRTINESS
DISABLING
DISAFFIRM
DISAPPEAR
DISARMING
DISBELIEF
DISBURDEN
DISCARDED
DISCHARGE
DISCLOSED
DISCOLOUR
DISCOMFIT
DISCOURSE
DISCOVERT
DISCOVERY
DISCREDIT
DISEMBARK
DISENGAGE
DISENTOMB
DISFAVOUR
DISFIGURE
DISGRACED
DISGUISED
DISGUSTED
DISHCLOTH
DISHONEST
DISHONOUR
DISHWATER
DISINFECT
DISLOCATE
DISMANTLE
DISMEMBER
DISMISSAL
DISOBLIGE
DISORIENT
DISPARAGE
DISPARATE
DISPARITY
DISPENSER
DISPERSAL
DISPERSED
DISPLACED
DISPLAYED
DISPLEASE
DISPUTANT
DISREGARD
DISREPAIR
DISREPUTE
DISSEMBLE
DISSENTER
DISSIDENT
DISSIPATE
DISSOLUTE
DISSOLVED
DISSONANT
DISTANTLY
DISTEMPER
DISTENDED
DISTILLER
DISTORTED
DISTRAINT
DISTURBED
DISUNITED
DITHERING
DITHYRAMB
DIVERGENT
DIVERGING
DIVERSIFY
DIVERSION
DIVERSITY
DIVERTING
DIVIDENDS
DIVISIBLE
DIXIELAND
DIZZINESS
DJELLABAH
DOCTORATE
DOCTRINAL
DOCUMENTS
DODDIPOLL
DOGMATISM
DOGMATIZE
DOLEFULLY
DOLOMITES
DOLOMITIC
DOMICILED
DOMINANCE
DOMINICAL
DOMINICAN
DONATELLO
DONCASTER
DONIZETTI
DOODLEBUG
DORMITION
DORMITORY
DOSSHOUSE
DOTHEBOYS

DOUBTLESS
DOUKHOBOR
DOWELLING
DOWNGRADE
DOWNRIGHT
DOWNSTAGE
DOWNTREND
DOWNWARDS
DRACONIAN
DRAFTSMAN
DRAGONFLY
DRAINPIPE
DRAMATICS
DRAMATIST
DRAMATIZE
DRAVIDIAN
DREAMLESS
DRIFTWOOD
DRINKABLE
DRIPSTONE
DROMEDARY
DROPPINGS
DROPSICAL
DRUGSTORE
DRUMSTICK
DRUNKENLY
DRYASDUST
DUBIOUSLY
DUBROVNIK
DUCKBOARD
DULCINIST
DUMBARTON
DUMBFOUND
DUNDREARY
DUNGAREES
DUNGENESS
DUNGEONER
DUNSINANE
DUNSTABLE
DUODECIMO
DUPLICAND
DUPLICATE
DUPLICITY
DUTIFULLY
DWINDLING
DYNAMITED
DYSENTERY
DYSPEPSIA
DYSPEPTIC
DYSPHAGIA
DYSTROPHY
EAGERNESS
EAGLEWOOD
EALDORMAN
EARNESTLY
EARTHFLAX
EARTHLING
EARTHWORK
EARTHWORM
EASTBOUND
EASTERNER
EASTLINGS
EASTWARDS
EASYGOING
EAVESDROP
EBRILLADE
EBULLIENT
ECARDINES
ECCENTRIC
ECHEVERIA
ECHIDNINE
ECLAMPSIA
ECOLOGIST
ECONOMICS
ECONOMIST
ECONOMIZE
ECOSSAISE
ECOSYSTEM
ECTOMORPH
ECTOPLASM
ECTROPION
EDDINGTON
EDDYSTONE
EDELWEISS
EDGEWORTH
EDINBURGH
EDITORIAL
EDUCATION
EDUCATIVE
EDWARDIAN
EFFECTIVE
EFFECTUAL
EFFICIENT
EFFINGHAM
EFFLUENCE
EFFLUVIUM
EFFULGENT
EGAREMENT
EGLANTINE
EGREGIOUS
EGRESSION
EIDERDOWN
EIDOGRAPH
EIGHTIETH
EIGHTSOME
EJACULATE
ELABORATE
ELAEOLITE
ELASTOMER
ELATERIUM
ELBOWROOM
ELECTORAL
ELECTRESS
ELECTRIFY
ELECTRODE
ELECTUARY
ELEGANTLY
ELEMENTAL
ELEVATION
ELEVENSES
ELIMINATE
ELIZABETH
ELKOSHITE
ELLESMERE
ELLINGTON
ELOCUTION
ELONGATED
ELOPEMENT
ELOQUENCE
ELSEWHERE
ELUCIDATE
ELUTRIATE
EMACIATED
EMANATION
EMBARRASS
EMBASSADE
EMBASSAGE
EMBATTLED
EMBELLISH
EMBEZZLER
EMBRACERY
EMBRACING
EMBRANGLE
EMBRASURE
EMBROCATE
EMBROGLIO
EMBROIDER
EMBROILED
EMBRYONIC
EMERGENCE
EMERGENCY
EMINENTLY
EMMERDALE
EMOLLIATE
EMOLLIENT
EMOLUMENT
EMOTIONAL
EMPAESTIC
EMPANOPLY
EMPENNAGE
EMPHASIZE
EMPHLYSIS
EMPHYSEMA
EMPIRICAL
EMPLECTON
EMPLOYEES
EMPTINESS
EMULATION
ENACTMENT
ENAMELLED
ENAMOURED
ENCANTHIS
ENCAUSTIC
ENCELADUS
ENCHANTED
ENCHANTER
ENCHEASON
ENCHILADA
ENCHORIAL
ENCIRCLED
ENCLOSURE
ENCOLPION
ENCOLPIUM
ENCOMPASS
ENCOUNTER
ENCOURAGE
ENCRATITE
ENCUMBENT
ENDEARING
ENDEAVOUR
ENDECAGON
ENDEICTIC
ENDLESSLY
ENDOCRINE
ENDOMORPH
ENDOSPERM
ENDOWMENT
ENDPAPERS
ENDURABLE
ENDURANCE
ENERGETIC
ENERGUMEN
ENERINITE
ENGARLAND
ENGINEERS
ENGRAINED
ENGRAVING
ENGRENAGE
ENGROSSED
ENGROSSER
ENHYDRITE
ENIGMATIC
ENJOYABLE
ENJOYMENT
ENLIGHTEN
ENLIVENED
ENNERDALE
ENQUIRIES
ENRAPTURE
ENROLMENT
ENSCONCED
ENSHEATHE
ENSORCELL
ENSTATITE
ENTELECHY
ENTERITIS
ENTERTAIN
ENTHYMEME
ENTOPHYTE
ENTOURAGE
ENTRAMMEL
ENTRANCED
ENTRECHAT
ENTRECÔTE
ENTREMETS
ENTROPION
ENTROPIUM
ENUCLEATE
ENUMERATE
ENUNCIATE
ENVERMEIL
EPARCHATE
EPAULETTE
EPEDAPHIC
EPEOLATRY
EPHEDRINE
EPHEMERAL
EPHEMERIS
EPHEMERON
EPHESIANS
EPHIALTES
EPICEDIUM
EPICENTRE
EPICLESIS
EPICUREAN
EPICYCLIC
EPIDERMIS
EPIGAEOUS
EPILEPTIC
EPINASTIC
EPINICION
EPINIKION
EPIPHRAGM
EPIPHYSIS
EPIPHYTIC
EPIPOLISM
EPISCOPAL
EPISTAXIS
EPISTOLER
EPITHESIS
EPITOMIZE
EPONYMOUS
EPULATION
EQUALIZER
EQUIPMENT
EQUIPOISE
EQUISETUM
EQUITABLE
EQUITABLY
EQUIVOCAL
EQUIVOQUE
ERADICATE
ERGATANER
ERIOMETER
ERISTICAL
EROGENOUS
EROSTRATE
EROTICISM
ERPINGHAM
ERRONEOUS
ERSTWHILE
ERUCIFORM
ERUDITION
ESCALATOR
ESCOPETTE
ESCULENTS
ESEMPLASY
ESMERALDA
ESOPHAGUS
ESPAGNOLE
ESPERANCE
ESPERANTO
ESPIONAGE
ESPLANADE
ESQUILINE
ESSENTIAL
ESTABLISH
ESTAFETTE
ESTAMINET
ESTHETICS
ESTIMABLE
ESTRANGED
ESTRAPADE
ESTRELDID
ETCETERAS
ETERNALLY
ETHELBERT
ETHEREOUS
ETHIOPIAN
ETHNOLOGY
ETIOLATED
ETIQUETTE
ETYMOLOGY
EUCHARIST
EUCHLORIC
EUCLIDEAN
EUDAEMONY
EUHEMERUS
EUMENIDES
EUMYCETES
EUPHEMISM
EUPHONIUM
EUPHORBIA
EUPHRATES
EURHYTHMY
EURIPIDES
EUSKARIAN
EUTROPHIC
EVAGATION
EVANGELIC
EVAPORATE
EVASIVELY

EVENTUATE
EVERGLADE
EVERGREEN
EVERYBODY
EVIDENTLY
EVITERNAL
EVOCATION
EVOCATIVE
EVOCATORY
EVOLUTION
EXACTMENT
EXACTNESS
EXANIMATE
EXANTHEMA
EXARATION
EXCALIBUR
EXCAMBION
EXCAVATOR
EXCELLENT
EXCELSIOR
EXCEPTION
EXCESSIVE
EXCHEQUER
EXCIPIENT
EXCISEMAN
EXCITABLE
EXCLAIMED
EXCLUDING
EXCLUSION
EXCLUSIVE
EXCORIATE
EXCREMENT
EXCULPATE
EXCURSION
EXCUSABLE
EXCUSABLY
EXECRABLE
EXECRABLY
EXECUTANT
EXECUTION
EXECUTIVE
EXECUTRIX
EXEMPLARY
EXEMPLIFY
EXEMPTION
EXEQUATUR
EXERCISED
EXERCISES
EXHAUSTED
EXHIBITOR
EXISTENCE
EXODERMIS
EXONERATE
EXORATION
EXOSPHERE
EXOSTOSIS
EXPANSION
EXPANSIVE
EXPATIATE
EXPECTANT
EXPECTING
EXPEDIENT
EXPENSIVE
EXPERTISE
EXPIATION
EXPIATORY
EXPISCATE
EXPLETIVE
EXPLICATE
EXPLOITER
EXPLOSION
EXPLOSIVE
EXPORTING
EXPOSITOR
EXPRESSED
EXPRESSLY
EXPULSION
EXPURGATE
EXQUISITE
EXSICCATE
EXTEMPORE
EXTENSILE
EXTENSION
EXTENSIVE
EXTENUATE
EXTIRPATE
EXTORTION
EXTRACTOR
EXTRADITE
EXTREMELY
EXTREMISM
EXTREMIST
EXTREMITY
EXTRICATE
EXTRINSIC
EXTROVERT
EXTRUSION
EXUBERANT
EXUDATION
EYEBRIGHT
EYELETEER
EYEOPENER
EYESHADOW
EYESPLICE
EYESTRAIN
FABACEOUS
FABRICATE
FABULINUS
FACECLOTH
FACETIOUS
FACSIMILE
FACTIONAL
FACTORISE
FACTUALLY
FACUNDITY
FAINTNESS
FAIRYLAND
FAIRYTALE
FAITHLESS
FALANGIST
FALDSTOOL
FALERNIAN
FALKLANDS
FALLOPIAN
FALSEHOOD
FALSENESS
FAMAGUSTA
FANATICAL
FANDANGLE
FANTASIZE
FANTASTIC
FARANDOLE
FARMHOUSE
FARMSTEAD
FASCINATE
FASHIONED
FASTENING
FASTTRACK
FATIDICAL
FATISCENT
FATTENING
FATUOUSLY
FAULCHION
FAULTLESS
FAVORABLE
FAVORABLY
FAVOURITE
FEARFULLY
FEATHERED
FEBRIFUGE
FECUNDITY
FEDUCIARY
FEEDSTUFF
FENCIBLES
FENUGREEK
FERACIOUS
FERDINAND
FERINGHEE
FERMENTED
FEROCIOUS
FERRYBOAT
FERTILITY
FERTILIZE
FERVENTLY
FESTINATE
FESTIVITY
FEUDALISM
FEUDATORY
FEUILLANT
FIBROLINE
FIBROLITE
FICTIONAL
FIDUCIARY
FIELDFARE
FIELDSMAN
FIELDWORK
FIFTEENTH
FIGURANTE
FILICALES
FILIGRAIN
FILLIPEEN
FILLISTER
FILMMAKER
FILMSTRIP
FILOPLUME
FILOSELLE
FILTERING
FILTERTIP
FINANCIAL
FINANCIER
FINGERING
FINGERTIP
FINICKING
FINICKITY
FINISHING
FINLANDIA
FIREBRAND
FIREBREAK
FIREDRAKE
FIREGUARD
FIRELIGHT
FIREPLACE
FIREPROOF
FIRESTONE
FIREWATER
FIREWORKS
FIRMAMENT
FIRSTEVER
FIRSTHAND
FIRSTRATE
FISHERMAN
FISHGUARD
FISHPLATE
FLABELLUM
FLAGELLIN
FLAGELLUM
FLAGEOLET
FLAGITATE
FLAGRANCE
FLAGSTAFF
FLAGSTONE
FLAMMABLE
FLAMSTEED
FLASHBACK
FLASHBULB
FLASHCUBE
FLATTENED
FLATTENER
FLATTERED
FLATTERER
FLATULENT
FLAVORING
FLAVOURED
FLECHETTE
FLEDGLING
FLEETWOOD
FLESHLESS
FLESHPOTS
FLEXITIME
FLINTLOCK
FLIPPANCY
FLOODGATE
FLOORSHOW
FLOPHOUSE
FLORESTAN
FLORIMELL
FLOTATION
FLOURMILL
FLOWCHART
FLOWERBED
FLOWERING
FLOWERPOT
FLOWSTONE
FLUCTUATE
FLUSTERED
FLYWEIGHT
FOGGINESS
FOGRAMITE
FOLIOLOSE
FOLKETING
FOLKWEAVE
FOLLOWING
FOMALHAUT
FOODSTORE
FOODSTUFF
FOOLHARDY
FOOLISHLY
FOOLPROOF
FOOTBRAKE
FOOTHILLS
FOOTLOOSE
FOOTPLATE
FOOTPRINT
FOOTSTALL
FOOTSTOOL
FORASMUCH
FORBIDDEN
FORCEMEAT
FOREANENT
FOREBEARS
FORECLOSE
FORECOURT
FOREFRONT
FOREGOING
FOREIGNER
FORESHORE
FORESIGHT
FORESPEAK
FORESPEND
FORESTAGE
FORESTALL
FORESTERS
FORETASTE
FORFEITED
FORFICATE
FORGATHER
FORGETFUL
FORGETIVE
FORGIVING
FORGOTTEN
FORJASKIT
FORJESKIT
FORLORNLY
FORMALIST
FORMALITY
FORMALIZE
FORMATION
FORMATIVE
FORMULATE
FORNICATE
FORSYTHIA
FORTALICE
FORTHWINK
FORTHWITH
FORTILAGE
FORTITUDE
FORTNIGHT
FORTUNATE
FORWANDER
FOSSILISE
FOSSORIAL
FOUNDLING
FOURPENCE
FOURWHEEL
FRACTIOUS
FRAGILITY
FRAGMENTS
FRAGONARD
FRAGRANCE
FRAGRANCY
FRAMBOISE
FRAMEWORK
FRANCESCA
FRANCHISE
FRANCOLIN
FRANGLAIS
FRANKNESS
FRATCHETY
FRATERNAL
FREDERICK
FREEBOARD
FREELANCE

FREEMASON
FREEPHONE
FREESTONE
FREESTYLE
FREEWHEEL
FREIGHTER
FRENCHMAN
FRENCHMEN
FREQUENCY
FRESHENER
FRESHNESS
FRETFULLY
FRICASSEE
FRIESLAND
FRIGATOON
FRIGHTFUL
FRIGIDITY
FRITHBORH
FRIVOLITY
FRIVOLOUS
FRIZZANTE
FROBISHER
FROGMARCH
FROGMOUTH
FROGSPAWN
FROISSART
FROSTBITE
FRUCTIDOR
FRUGALITY
FRUITCAKE
FRUITERER
FRUITLESS
FRUSTRATE
FUGACIOUS
FUGGINESS
FULLBLOWN
FULLERENE
FULLGROWN
FULLSCALE
FULMINANT
FULMINATE
FUNDAMENT
FUNGIBLES
FUNGICIDE
FUNICULAR
FURACIOUS
FURIOUSLY
FURNIMENT
FURNITURE
FURTIVELY
FUSILLADE
FUSSINESS
FUSTIGATE
FUSTINESS
FUZZINESS
GABARDINE
GABERDINE
GABIONADE
GAELTACHT
GAINFULLY
GAINSAYER
GALACTOSE
GALANTINE
GALAPAGOS
GALDRAGON
GALENGALE
GALINGALE
GALIONGEE
GALLABEAH
GALLANTLY
GALLANTRY
GALLICISM
GALLINULE
GALLIPOLI
GALLIVANT
GALLOPADE
GALLSTONE
GALLYCROW
GALRAVAGE
GALVANISM
GALVANIZE
GANGPLANK
GARDENING
GARDEROBE
GARGANTUA
GARGARISM
GARIBALDI
GARNISHEE
GARNITURE
GARRULITY
GARRULOUS
GARRYOWEN
GASCONADE
GASHOLDER
GASOMETER
GASPEREAU
GATECRASH
GATESHEAD
GATHERING
GAUDEAMUS
GAUDINESS
GAULEITER
GAUNTNESS
GAVELKIND
GAWKINESS
GAZETTEER
GEARLEVER
GEARSHIFT
GEARSTICK
GEARWHEEL
GELIGNITE
GENEALOGY
GENERALLY
GENERATOR
GENETICAL
GENEVIEVE
GENIALITY
GENITALIA
GENTEELLY
GENTILITY
GENTLEMAN
GENTLEMEN
GENUFLECT
GENUINELY
GEODESIST
GEOGRAPHY
GEOLOGIST
GEOMETRIC
GEOMETRID
GEORGETTE
GERFALCON
GERIATRIC
GERMANCER
GERMANDER
GERMANITE
GERMANIUM
GERMICIDE
GERMINATE
GERUNDIVE
GESSAMINE
GESTATION
GIBBERISH
GIBEONITE
GIBRALTAR
GIDDINESS
GILGAMESH
GINGERADE
GINGLYMUS
GINORMOUS
GIRANDOLE
GIRONDIST
GLABELLAR
GLADIATOR
GLADIOLUS
GLADSTONE
GLAIREOUS
GLAMORIZE
GLAMOROUS
GLANDULAR
GLASSWARE
GLEANINGS
GLEEFULLY
GLENDOWER
GLENGARRY
GLENLIVET
GLISSANDO
GLOMERATE
GLOMERULE
GLORIFIED
GLORYHOLE
GLUCINIUM
GLUCOSIDE
GLUTAMINE
GLUTINOUS
GLYCERIDE
GLYCERINE
GMELINITE
GOALMOUTH
GOBETWEEN
GODDESSES
GODFATHER
GODLINESS
GODMOTHER
GODOLPHIN
GODPARENT
GOLDCREST
GOLDFIELD
GOLDFINCH
GOLDSINNY
GOLDSMITH
GOMPHOSIS
GONDOLIER
GONGORISM
GONIATITE
GOODNIGHT
GOONHILLY
GOOSANDER
GOOSEFOOT
GOOSEHERD
GOOSENECK
GOOSESTEP
GOSLARITE
GOSPELLER
GOSSAMERY
GOSSYPINE
GOSSYPIUM
GOTHAMITE
GOVERNESS
GOVERNING
GRACELESS
GRADATION
GRADGRIND
GRADUALLY
GRADUATED
GRAMPIANS
GRANDIOSE
GRANDNESS
GRANDSIRE
GRANULATE
GRANULITE
GRANULOSE
GRAPESHOT
GRAPETREE
GRAPEVINE
GRAPHICAL
GRAPPLING
GRASSLAND
GRATICULE
GRATITUDE
GRAVADLAX
GRAVESEND
GRAVESIDE
GRAVEYARD
GRAVITATE
GREASEGUN
GREATCOAT
GREATNESS
GREENAWAY
GREENBACK
GREENFEED
GREENGAGE
GREENHEAD
GREENHORN
GREENMAIL
GREENROOM
GREENSAND
GREENWEED
GREENWICH
GREENWOOD
GREENYARD
GREETINGS
GREGARINE
GREGORIAN
GRENADIER
GRENADINE
GRENVILLE
GREYBEARD
GREYHOUND
GREYWACKE
GRIEVANCE
GRIMALKIN
GRIMINESS
GRINGOLET
GRISAILLE
GROCERIES
GROSGRAIN
GROSVENOR
GROTESQUE
GROUNDHOG
GROUNDING
GROUNDNUT
GROUNDSEL
GRUBBINOL
GRUELLING
GRUFFNESS
GRUMBLING
GUACAMOLE
GUARANTEE
GUARANTOR
GUARDROOM
GUARDSMAN
GUATEMALA
GUERRILLA
GUESSWORK
GUIDEBOOK
GUIDELINE
GUILDHALL
GUILELESS
GUILLEMOT
GUILLOCHE
GUILTLESS
GUINEVERE
GUITARIST
GUJARATHI
GUMSHIELD
GUNCOTTON
GUNPOWDER
GUSTATION
GUTENBERG
GUTTERING
GYMNASIUM
GYMNASTIC
GYNOECIUM
GYROMANCY
GYROSCOPE
HABERDINE
HABERGEON
HABITABLE
HABITUATE
HACKAMORE
HACKNEYED
HACQUETON
HADROSAUR
HAECCEITY
HAEMALOMA
HAEMATITE
HAILSTONE
HAILSTORM
HAIRBRUSH
HAIRPIECE
HAIRSTYLE
HALFBAKED
HALFDOZEN
HALFEMPTY
HALFPENNY
HALFSTAFF
HALITOSIS
HALLOWEEN
HALLOWMAS
HALLSTATT
HALOBIONT
HALOPHILE
HALOTHANE
HAMADRYAD
HAMBURGER
HAMFATTER
HAMFISTED
HAMMERING
HAMMURABI
HAMPSTEAD
HAMSTRING
HAMSTRUNG

HANDBRAKE
HANDCUFFS
HANDINESS
HANDIWORK
HANDPIECE
HANDSHAKE
HANDSPIKE
HANDSTAND
HANKERING
HANSEATIC
HAPHAZARD
HAPPENING
HAPPINESS
HARBINGER
HARDANGER
HARDBOARD
HARDCOVER
HARDIHOOD
HARDINESS
HARDLINER
HARDSHELL
HARESTANE
HARIGALDS
HARIOLATE
HARLEQUIN
HARLESTON
HARMALINE
HARMATTAN
HARMONICA
HARMONIST
HARMONIUM
HARMONIZE
HARMOTOME
HARPOONER
HARQUEBUS
HARROGATE
HARROWING
HARSHNESS
HARTSHORN
HARVESTER
HASHEMITE
HASTENING
HASTINESS
HATCHBACK
HATCHMENT
HAUGHTILY
HAUTMONDE
HAVERSACK
HAWCUBITE
HAWKSBILL
HAWTHORNE
HAYMAKING
HAYMARKET
HAYRADDIN
HAZARDOUS
HAZELWORT
HEADBOARD
HEADCLOTH
HEADDRESS
HEADFIRST
HEADINESS
HEADLIGHT
HEADLINED
HEADSCARF
HEADSTALL
HEADSTONE
HEALTHILY
HEARDSMAN
HEARTACHE
HEARTBEAT
HEARTBURN
HEARTFELT
HEARTHRUG
HEARTLAND
HEARTLESS
HEATHLAND
HEAVINESS
HEAVISIDE
HEAVYDUTY
HEBRIDEAN
HECOGENIN
HECTORING
HEDERATED
HEDYPHANE
HELLEBORE
HELPFULLY
HELVELLYN
HEMINGWAY
HEMIPTERA
HEMISTICH
HEMITROPE
HEMSTITCH
HENDIADYS
HENPECKED
HEPATICAL
HEPATITIS
HERBALIST
HERBARIUM
HERBICIDE
HERBIVORE
HERBORIST
HERCULEAN
HEREAFTER
HERETICAL
HERMANDAD
HERMITAGE
HERODOTUS
HERONSHAW
HERPESTES
HESITANCE
HESITANCY
HESPERIAN
HESSONITE
HESTERNAL
HESYCHASM
HESYCHAST
HETERODOX
HETEROSIS
HEURISTIC
HEXAGONAL
HEXAMERON
HEXAMETER
HEXASTICH
HEXATEUCH
HEYPRESTO
HIBERNATE
HIBERNIAN
HIDEBOUND
HIDEOUSLY
HIERARCHY
HIGHCLASS
HIGHFLYER
HIGHLANDS
HIGHLIGHT
HIGHSPEED
HIJACKING
HILARIOUS
HILLBILLY
HIMALAYAN
HIMALAYAS
HIMYARITE
HINDEMITH
HINDRANCE
HINDSIGHT
HINGELESS
HIPPOCRAS
HIPPODAME
HIPPOLYTA
HIPPOLYTE
HIRUNDINE
HISTAMINE
HISTOGRAM
HISTOLOGY
HISTORIAN
HITCHCOCK
HITCHHIKE
HOARFROST
HOARHOUND
HOARSTONE
HOBBINOLL
HOBGOBLIN
HOBNAILED
HOCCAMORE
HODIERNAL
HODMANDOD
HODOGRAPH
HODOMETER
HOLDERBAT
HOLINSHED
HOLLERITH
HOLLYHOCK
HOLLYWOOD
HOLOCAUST
HOLOGRAPH
HOLOPHOTE
HOLYSTONE
HOMEGROWN
HOMEOPATH
HOMEOWNER
HOMESTEAD
HOMEWARDS
HOMICIDAL
HOMOGRAPH
HOMOPHONE
HOMOPTERA
HONEYCOMB
HONEYMOON
HONKYTONK
HONORABLE
HONORIFIC
HOOLACHAN
HOPEFULLY
HOPLOLOGY
HOPSCOTCH
HORDEOLUM
HOREHOUND
HORNSTONE
HOROSCOPE
HORRIFIED
HORSEBACK
HORSEHAIR
HORSELESS
HORSEPLAY
HORSESHOE
HORSETAIL
HORSEWHIP
HORTATIVE
HORTATORY
HOSPITIUM
HOSTILITY
HOTHEADED
HOTTENTOT
HOURGLASS
HOURSTONE
HOUSEBOAT
HOUSECOAT
HOUSEHOLD
HOUSEMAID
HOUSEROOM
HOUSEWIFE
HOUSEWORK
HOUYHNHNM
HOWTOWDIE
HOYDENISH
HUCKABACK
HUMANKIND
HUMDINGER
HUMILIATE
HUMONGOUS
HUMUNGOUS
HUNCHBACK
HUNDREDTH
HUNGARIAN
HUNKYDORY
HURRICANE
HURRICANO
HURRIEDLY
HUSBANDLY
HUSBANDRY
HUSKINESS
HUTTERITE
HYDRANGEA
HYDRAULIC
HYDRAZINE
HYDROFOIL
HYDROPULT
HYDROSTAT
HYGIENIST
HYLOBATES
HYPALLAGE
HYPERBOLA
HYPERBOLE
HYPHENATE
HYPINOSIS
HYPNOTISM
HYPNOTIST
HYPNOTIZE
HYPOCAUST
HYPOCRISY
HYPOCRITE
HYSTERICS
IBUPROFEN
ICELANDER
ICELANDIC
ICHNEUMON
ICHNOLITE
ICTERIDAE
IDEALOGUE
IDENTICAL
IDENTIKIT
IDEOGRAPH
IDEOPATHY
IDIOBLAST
IDIOGRAPH
IDIOMATIC
IDIOPHONE
IDIOPLASM
IDIOTICON
IGNESCENT
IGNORAMUS
IGNORANCE
IGUANODON
ILCHESTER
ILLEGALLY
ILLEGIBLE
ILLEGIBLY
ILLGOTTEN
ILLIBERAL
ILLICITLY
ILLOGICAL
IMAGELESS
IMAGINARY
IMBALANCE
IMBRANGLE
IMBRICATE
IMBROCATE
IMBROGLIO
IMITATION
IMITATIVE
IMMANACLE
IMMANENCE
IMMANENCY
IMMEDIACY
IMMEDIATE
IMMELMANN
IMMENSELY
IMMENSITY
IMMERSION
IMMIGRANT
IMMIGRATE
IMMINENCE
IMMODESTY
IMMORALLY
IMMORTALS
IMMOVABLE
IMMOVABLY
IMMUNISER
IMMUTABLE
IMMUTABLY
IMPACTION
IMPARTIAL
IMPASSION
IMPASSIVE
IMPATIENT
IMPEACHER
IMPEDANCE
IMPELLING
IMPENDING
IMPERATOR
IMPERFECT
IMPERIOUS
IMPETUOUS
IMPLEMENT
IMPLICATE
IMPLUVIUM
IMPOLITIC
IMPORTANT
IMPORTUNE
IMPOSTURE
IMPOTENCE
IMPOUNDER
IMPRECATE

IMPRECISE
IMPRESSED
IMPROBITY
IMPROMPTU
IMPROVING
IMPROVISE
IMPRUDENT
IMPSONITE
IMPUDENCE
IMPULSION
IMPULSIVE
INABILITY
INAMORATA
INAMORATO
INANIMATE
INANITION
INAUDIBLE
INAUDIBLY
INAUGURAL
INCAPABLE
INCARDINE
INCARNATE
INCAUTION
INCENTIVE
INCEPTION
INCESSANT
INCIDENCE
INCIPIENT
INCITATUS
INCLEMENT
INCLUDING
INCLUSION
INCLUSIVE
INCOGNITO
INCOMINGS
INCOMMODE
INCONDITE
INCORRECT
INCREASED
INCREMENT
INCUBATOR
INCULCATE
INCULPATE
INCUMBENT
INCURABLE
INCURABLY
INCURIOUS
INCURSION
INDECENCY
INDECORUM
INDELIBLE
INDELIBLY
INDEMNIFY
INDEMNITY
INDENTURE
INDICATES
INDICATOR
INDICTION
INDIGENCE
INDIGNANT
INDIGNITY
INDOLENCE
INDONESIA
INDRAUGHT
INDUCTION
INDUCTIVE
INDULGENT
INDWELLER
INEBRIATE
INEFFABLE
INELEGANT
INERTNESS
INERUDITE
INFANTILE
INFATUATE
INFECTING
INFECTION
INFERENCE
INFERTILE
INFIELDER
INFIRMARY
INFIRMITY
INFLATION
INFLEXION
INFLUENCE
INFLUENZA
INFORMANT
INFURIATE
INGENIOUS
INGENUITY
INGENUOUS
INGESTION
INGLENOOK
INGRAINED
INGROWING
INHERITED
INHERITOR
INHIBITED
INHUMANLY
INITIALLY
INITIATED
INITIATOR
INJECTION
INJURIOUS
INJUSTICE
INNERMOST
INNISFAIL
INNISFREE
INNKEEPER
INNOCENCE
INNOCUOUS
INNOVATOR
INOCULATE
INOPINATE
INORGANIC
INPATIENT
INQUILINE
INQUINATE
INQUIRING
INQUORATE
INSCRIBED
INSELBERG
INSENSATE
INSERTION
INSHALLAH
INSIDIOUS
INSINCERE
INSINUATE
INSIPIENT
INSISTENT
INSOLENCE
INSOLUBLE
INSOLVENT
INSOMNIAC
INSPECTOR
INSPIRING
INSTANTER
INSTANTLY
INSTIGATE
INSTITUTE
INSULATOR
INSULTING
INSURANCE
INSURGENT
INSWINGER
INTEGRATE
INTEGRITY
INTELLECT
INTENDANT
INTENDING
INTENSELY
INTENSIFY
INTENSITY
INTENSIVE
INTENTION
INTERBRED
INTERCEDE
INTERCEPT
INTERCITY
INTERDICT
INTERFACE
INTERFERE
INTERJECT
INTERLACE
INTERLARD
INTERLOCK
INTERLOPE
INTERLUDE
INTERMENT
INTERNODE
INTERPLAY
INTERPOSE
INTERPRET
INTERRUPT
INTERSECT
INTERVENE
INTERVIEW
INTESTATE
INTESTINE
INTRICACY
INTRICATE
INTRIGUED
INTRIGUER
INTRINSIC
INTRODUCE
INTROITUS
INTROVERT
INTRUSION
INTRUSIVE
INTUITION
INTUITIVE
INTUMESCE
INUMBRATE
INUNCTION
INUSITATE
INVECTIVE
INVENTION
INVENTIVE
INVENTORY
INVERNESS
INVERSION
INVERTASE
INVIDIOUS
INVIOLATE
INVISIBLE
INVOICING
INVOLUCRE
IODOPHILE
IPHIGENIA
IPRINDOLE
IRASCIBLE
IRONSIDES
IRONSTONE
IRONWORKS
IRRADIANT
IRRADIATE
IRRAWADDY
IRREGULAR
IRRITABLE
IRRITABLY
IRRITATED
IRRUPTION
IRVINGISM
ISALLOBAR
ISCHAEMIC
ISINGLASS
ISLAMABAD
ISOCRATES
ISODORIAN
ISOLATION
ISOMERASE
ISOMETRIC
ISOPROPYL
ISOSCELES
ISOTACTIC
ISOTROPIC
ISRAELITE
ITALICIZE
ITINERANT
ITINERARY
ITINERATE
JACARANDA
JACKKNIFE
JACKSNIPE
JACKSTRAW
JACQUERIE
JAGGANATH
JAMBALAYA
JAMPACKED
JANISSARY
JANSENISM
JANSENIST
JARLSBERG
JAUNDICED
JAWBATION
JAYWALKER
JEALOUSLY
JELLYFISH
JENNETING
JEPHTHAHS
JEQUIRITY
JERAHMEEL
JERKINESS
JERKWATER
JERUSALEM
JESSAMINE
JESSERANT
JETSTREAM
JEWELLERY
JIGGUMBOB
JITTERBUG
JOBCENTRE
JOBERNOWL
JOBSEEKER
JOBSWORTH
JOCKSTRAP
JOCKTELEG
JOCULARLY
JOHANNINE
JORDANIAN
JOSEPHINE
JOSEPHSON
JOUISANCE
JOVIALITY
JUBILANCE
JUDGEMENT
JUDICIARY
JUDICIOUS
JUICINESS
JUNEBERRY
JUNKETING
JURIDICAL
JUSTIFIED
JUSTINIAN
JUVENILIA
JUXTAPOSE
KABELJOUW
KALSOMINE
KARABINER
KARAKORAM
KARYOTYPE
KENTIGERN
KENTLEDGE
KEPLARIAN
KERATITIS
KERBSTONE
KERFUFFLE
KERMESITE
KEYHOLDER
KEYSTROKE
KHALIFATE
KHANSAMAH
KICKSHAWS
KIDNAPPED
KIDNAPPER
KIESERITE
KILDERKIN
KILLARNEY
KILOCYCLE
KILOHERTZ
KILOMETER
KILOMETRE
KINGMAKER
KINGSIZED
KINKCOUGH
KINSWOMAN
KINTLEDGE
KISSINGER
KITCHENER
KITTENISH
KITTIWAKE
KLEMPERER
KLENDUSIC
KLINOSTAT
KNACKERED
KNAPSCULL
KNAPSKULL
KNEECORDS
KNIPHOFIA
KNOBSTICK
KNOCKDOWN
KNOWINGLY

KNOWLEDGE
KOMINFORM
KONIMETER
KONISCOPE
KROPOTKIN
KRUMMHORN
LABORIOUS
LABOURITE
LABYRINTH
LACCOLITE
LACERATED
LACHRYMAL
LACINIATE
LACKBEARD
LACONICAL
LACTATION
LADYSMITH
LAEVULOSE
LAFAYETTE
LAGNIAPPE
LAGOMORPH
LAMARTINE
LAMASERAI
LAMBSWOOL
LAMINATED
LAMPADARY
LAMPADION
LAMPBLACK
LAMPLIGHT
LAMPSHADE
LANCASTER
LANCEWOOD
LANCINATE
LANDAULET
LANDDROST
LANDGRAVE
LANDLOPER
LANDOWNER
LANDSCAPE
LANDSLIDE
LANDSMAAL
LANDSTURM
LANDWARDS
LANGOUSTE
LANGRIDGE
LANGSPIEL
LANGUAGES
LANGUEDOC
LANGUETTE
LANGUIDLY
LANKINESS
LANTHANUM
LAODICEAN
LAPLANDER
LAPSTREAK
LARGENESS
LARGHETTO
LARGITION
LASERWORT
LASSITUDE
LASTDITCH
LATECOMER
LATENIGHT
LATERALLY
LATESCENT
LATHYRISM
LATICLAVE
LATRATION
LATTERDAY
LAUDATION
LAUDATORY
LAUGHABLE
LAUNCELOT
LAUNCHING
LAUNDRESS
LAVOISIER
LAWMAKING
LAWMONGER
LAWNMOWER
LAZARETTO
LAZYBONES
LAZZARONE
LEAFMOULD
LEAKPROOF
LEASEHOLD
LEASTWAYS
LEASTWISE
LECANORAM
LECHEROUS
LEFTOVERS
LEGENDARY
LEGIONARY
LEGISLATE
LEHRJAHRE
LEICESTER
LEISURELY
LEITMOTIF
LEITMOTIV
LENGTHILY
LENIENTLY
LENINGRAD
LEPROSERY
LESTRIGON
LETHARGIC
LETTERBOX
LETTERING
LEUCOCYTE
LEUCOTOME
LEUKAEMIA
LEVANTINE
LEVERAGED
LEVIATHAN
LEVITICUS
LIABILITY
LIBELLOUS
LIBERALLY
LIBERATED
LIBERATOR
LIBERTIES
LIBERTINE
LIBRARIAN
LICKERISH
LIENTERIC
LIFEGUARD
LIFESTYLE
LIGHTFOOT
LIGHTLESS
LIGHTNESS
LIGHTNING
LIGHTSHIP
LIGHTSOME
LILYWHITE
LIMBURGER
LIMEHOUSE
LIMELIGHT
LIMESTONE
LIMITLESS
LIMOUSINE
LIMPIDITY
LINDBERGH
LINEAMENT
LINEOLATE
LINGERING
LINGFIELD
LINKLATER
LINTSTOCK
LIONHEART
LIPPITUDE
LIQUEFIED
LIQUIDATE
LIQUIDITY
LIQUIDIZE
LIQUORICE
LIQUORISH
LISTENING
LITERALLY
LITHOCYST
LITHOPONE
LITHUANIA
LITIGIOUS
LIVERPOOL
LIVERWORT
LIVERYMAN
LIVESTOCK
LIVRAISON
LJUBLJANA
LOADSTONE
LOAMSHIRE
LOATHSOME
LOBLOLLYS
LOBSCOUSE
LOCALIZED
LOCELLATE
LOCHINVAR
LOCKSMITH
LODESTONE
LODGEMENT
LOFTINESS
LOGARITHM
LOGICALLY
LOGISTICS
LOGOGRIPH
LOGOTHETE
LOHENGRIN
LOINCLOTH
LOITERING
LOMBARDIC
LONDONESE
LONGCHAMP
LONGEDFOR
LONGEVITY
LONGICORN
LONGINGLY
LONGITUDE
LONGLIVED
LONGRANGE
LONGSHORE
LOOKALIKE
LOOSEHEAD
LOOSELEAF
LOOSENESS
LOQUACITY
LORGNETTE
LOUDMOUTH
LOUISIANA
LOUSEWORT
LOWLANDER
LOWLINESS
LUBAVITCH
LUBRICANT
LUBRICATE
LUCIFERIN
LUCRATIVE
LUCRETIUS
LUCTATION
LUCUBRATE
LUDICROUS
LUMBERING
LUMBRICUS
LUMINAIRE
LUMINANCE
LUNCHTIME
LURIDNESS
LUSTIHOOD
LUSTINESS
LUTESCENT
LUXEMBURG
LUXURIANT
LUXURIATE
LUXURIOUS
LYMESWOLD
LYMPHATIC
LYRICALLY
LYSIMETER
MACADAMIA
MACARONIC
MACARTHUR
MACDONALD
MACEDOINE
MACEDONIA
MACHINATE
MACHINERY
MACHINING
MACHINIST
MACKENZIE
MACQUARIE
MACROCOSM
MACROLOGY
MACTATION
MADARIAGA
MADAROSIS
MADDENING
MADELEINE
MADRASSAH
MADREPORE
MADRESSAH
MADRILENE
MAELSTROM
MAGDALENE
MAGDEBURG
MAGICALLY
MAGNALIUM
MAGNESIUM
MAGNETISM
MAGNETIZE
MAGNETRON
MAGNIFIER
MAGNITUDE
MAHARAJAH
MAHARANEE
MAHARISHI
MAINFRAME
MAINTENON
MAJORDOMO
MAJORETTE
MAJUSCULE
MAKESHIFT
MALACHITE
MALATHION
MALAYSIAN
MALEBOLGE
MALENGINE
MALFORMED
MALICIOUS
MALIGNANT
MALIGNITY
MALLANDER
MALLEABLE
MALLEMUCK
MALLENDER
MALLEOLUS
MAMMALIAN
MANDATORY
MANDICATE
MANDOLINE
MANDUCATE
MANGANATE
MANGANESE
MANGETOUT
MANGOUSTE
MANHANDLE
MANHATTAN
MANIFESTO
MANLINESS
MANNEQUIN
MANNERING
MANNERISM
MANOEUVRE
MANOMETER
MANSFIELD
MANUBRIUM
MAPPEMOND
MARAUDING
MARCASITE
MARCHPANE
MARGARINE
MARIJUANA
MARKETEER
MARKETING
MARMALADE
MARMOREAL
MARQUESAS
MARQUETRY
MARROWFAT
MARSHLAND
MARSUPIAL
MARSUPIUM
MARTINEAU
MARTINMAS
MARTYRDOM
MARVELOUS
MASCULINE
MASEFIELD
MASOCHISM
MASOCHIST
MASSINGER
MASSIVELY
MASSORETE
MASSYMORE
MASTERFUL
MASTERMAN
MASTICATE

MATCHLESS
MATCHLOCK
MATCHWOOD
MATELASSE
MATERNITY
MATHURINE
MATRIARCH
MATRICIDE
MATRIMONY
MATTAMORE
MATUTINAL
MAULSTICK
MAURITIAN
MAURITIUS
MAUSOLEUM
MAVOURNIN
MAXILLARY
MAYFLOWER
MAYORALTY
MEANDRIAN
MEANWHILE
MEASURING
MEATBALLS
MECHANICS
MECHANISM
MECHANIZE
MEDALLION
MEDALLIST
MEDIAEVAL
MEDIATION
MEDICALLY
MEDICATED
MEDICINAL
MEDITATOR
MEDMENHAM
MEDRESSEH
MEGACYCLE
MEGAHERTZ
MEGAPHONE
MEGASCOPE
MEGASPORE
MEHITABEL
MEKOMETER
MELAMPODE
MELANESIA
MELANOTIC
MELBOURNE
MELIORATE
MELODIOUS
MELODRAMA
MELONLIKE
MELPOMENE
MEMORABLE
MEMORITER
MENADIONE
MENAGERIE
MENDACITY
MENDELISM
MENDICANT
MENIPPEAN
MENNONITE
MENOMINEE
MENOPAUSE
MENSHEVIK
MENSTRUAL
MENSTRUUM
MENTALITY
MENTATION
MENTICIDE
MENTIONED
MENUISIER
MEPACRINE
MERCAPTAN
MERCENARY
MERCERIZE
MERCILESS
MERCURIAL
MERESWINE
MERGANSER
MERRIMENT
MESENTERY
MESMERISM
MESMERIZE
MESOBLAST
MESOMORPH
MESSALINA
MESSENGER
MESSIANIC
METABASIS
METABOLIC
METALLOID
METALWORK
METAPELET
METEORITE
METEOROID
METHADONE
METHEGLIN
METHODISM
METHODIST
METRICATE
METROLAND
METRONOME
MEZZANINE
MEZZOTINT
MICKLETON
MICROCHIP
MICROCOSM
MICROCYTE
MICROFILM
MICROLITE
MICROLITH
MICROTOME
MICROTONE
MICROWAVE
MIDDLEMAN
MIDDLESEX
MIDDLETON
MIDDLINGS
MIDIANITE
MIDINETTE
MIDRASHIM
MIDSTREAM
MIDSUMMER
MIDWIFERY
MIDWINTER
MIGRATION
MIGRATORY
MILESTONE
MILITANCY
MILKSHAKE
MILLAMANT
MILLENIAL
MILLENIUM
MILLEPEDE
MILLEPORE
MILLIGRAM
MILLINERY
MILLIONTH
MILLIPEDE
MILLSTONE
MILOMETER
MINACIOUS
MINCEMEAT
MINEFIELD
MINELAYER
MINIATURE
MINISCULE
MINISKIRT
MINKSTONE
MINNESOTA
MINUSCULE
MINUTEMAN
MIRABELLE
MIRTHLESS
MISBEHAVE
MISCHANCE
MISCREANT
MISDIRECT
MISERABLE
MISERABLY
MISFALLEN
MISFIRING
MISGIVING
MISGUIDED
MISHANDLE
MISINFORM
MISLOCATE
MISMANAGE
MISOCLERE
MISONEIST
MISPICKEL
MISPLACED
MISSHAPEN
MISSIONER
MISSTROKE
MISTEMPER
MISTIGRIS
MISTINESS
MISTLETOE
MITHRAISM
MITRAILLE
MNEMOSYNE
MOCCASINS
MOCKERNUT
MODELLING
MODERATOR
MODERNISM
MODERNIST
MODERNITY
MODERNIZE
MODESTINE
MODILLION
MOGADISHU
MOISTNESS
MOLECULAR
MOLESKINS
MOLLITIES
MOLLYMAWK
MOMENTARY
MOMENTOUS
MONACTINE
MONASTERY
MONASTRAL
MONATOMIC
MONERGISM
MONEYWORT
MONGOLIAN
MONGOLISM
MONKSHOOD
MONOCEROS
MONOCHORD
MONOCOQUE
MONOCULAR
MONODRAMA
MONOGRAPH
MONOLOGUE
MONOMACHY
MONOMANIA
MONOMETER
MONOPLANE
MONOSTICH
MONOTROCH
MONOXYLON
MONSIGNOR
MONSTROUS
MONTACUTE
MONTAIGNE
MONTANISM
MONTANIST
MONTESPAN
MONTEZUMA
MONTICULE
MONZONITE
MOODINESS
MOONLIGHT
MOONRAKER
MOONSHINE
MOONSTONE
MORATORIA
MORATORIO
MORBIDITY
MORECAMBE
MORGANITE
MORMONISM
MORTALITY
MORTGAGEE
MORTGAGOR
MORTICIAN
MORTIFIED
MORTSTONE
MOSCHATEL
MOSKONFYT
MOTHBALLS
MOTHEATEN
MOTHERING
MOTOCROSS
MOTORBIKE
MOTORBOAT
MOTORCADE
MOTORISTS
MOURNIVAL
MOUSEHOLE
MOUSELIKE
MOUSETRAP
MOUSTACHE
MOUTHLESS
MOUTHWASH
MOYGASHEL
MRIDAMGAM
MRIDANGAM
MUCHLOVED
MUCKENDER
MUCORALES
MUDDINESS
MUFFETTEE
MUGGLETON
MUGLARITE
MUJAHIDIN
MULTIFORM
MULTIPLEX
MULTITUDE
MUMCHANCE
MUMPSIMUS
MUNDUNGUS
MUNICIPAL
MUNIMENTS
MUNITIONS
MURDERESS
MURDEROUS
MURKINESS
MURMURING
MUSCADINE
MUSCARINE
MUSCOVADO
MUSCOVITE
MUSHINESS
MUSHROOMS
MUSICALLY
MUSICHALL
MUSKETEER
MUSKETOON
MUSKOGEAN
MUSSITATE
MUSSOLINI
MUSSULMAN
MUSTINESS
MUTILATED
MUTOSCOPE
MUTTERING
MUZZINESS
MYRMECOID
MYSTERIES
MYSTICISM
MYTHOLOGY
NABATHEAN
NAKEDNESS
NAMEPLATE
NANTUCKET
NAPIERIAN
NARCISSUS
NARGHILLY
NARRATION
NARRATIVE
NARROWING
NASEBERRY
NASHVILLE
NASTINESS
NATHANIEL
NATHELESS
NATHEMORE
NATROLITE
NATURALLY
NAUGHTILY
NAUMACHIA
NAUSEATED
NAVIGABLE
NAVIGATOR
NEBBISHER
NECESSARY
NECESSITY
NECKVERSE
NECTARINE

NEFANDOUS
NEFARIOUS
NEFERTITI
NEGLECTED
NEGLIGENT
NEGOTIATE
NEGRITUDE
NEIGHBOUR
NEOLITHIC
NEOLOGISM
NEPHALISM
NEPHALIST
NEPHELINE
NEPHRITIC
NEPHRITIS
NEPTUNIUM
NERITIDAE
NERVOUSLY
NESCIENCE
NEUCHATEL
NEURALGIA
NEURALGIC
NEUROGLIA
NEUROLOGY
NEUTRALLY
NEVERMORE
NEWCASTLE
NEWLYWEDS
NEWMARKET
NEWSAGENT
NEWSFLASH
NEWSHOUND
NEWSPAPER
NEWSPRINT
NEWSSHEET
NEWSSTALL
NEWSSTAND
NIAISERIE
NICARAGUA
NICCOLITE
NICKNEVEN
NICODEMUS
NICTITATE
NIDDERING
NIDERLING
NIEBELUNG
NIETZSCHE
NIGGARDLY
NIGHTCLUB
NIGHTFALL
NIGHTFIRE
NIGHTGOWN
NIGHTMARE
NIGHTTIME
NIGHTWORK
NIGRITUDE
NIGROSINE
NINEPENCE
NINETIETH
NIPCHEESE
NIPPERKIN
NITHSDALE
NOBLENESS
NOCTURNAL
NOISELESS
NOISINESS
NOLLEKENS
NOMINALLY
NOMINATOR
NOMOCRACY
NOMOTHETE
NONENTITY
NONILLION
NONPAREIL
NONPROFIT
NONSMOKER
NOOSPHERE
NORMALACY
NORMALITY
NORMALIZE
NORMATIVE
NORTHEAST
NORTHERLY
NORTHWARD
NORTHWEST
NORWEGIAN
NOSEBLEED
NOSTALGIA
NOSTALGIC
NOSTOLOGY
NOTARIKON
NOTCHBACK
NOTEPAPER
NOTOCHORD
NOTONECTA
NOTORIETY
NOTORIOUS
NOVELETTE
NOVICIATE
NOVITIATE
NOVOCAINE
NOVODAMUS
NUCLEOLUS
NUMBSKULL
NUMERAIRE
NUMERATOR
NUMERICAL
NUMMULITE
NUNCUPATE
NUREMBERG
NURSEMAID
NUTJOBBER
NUTRIMENT
NUTRITION
NUTRITIVE
NYSTAGMUS
OARSWOMAN
OASTHOUSE
OBBLIGATO
OBCORDATE
OBEDIENCE
OBEISANCE
OBFUSCATE
OBJECTION
OBJECTIVE
OBJURGATE
OBLIQUELY
OBLIVIOUS
OBNOXIOUS
OBREPTION
OBSCENELY
OBSCENITY
OBSCURELY
OBSCURITY
OBSECRATE
OBSEQUIES
OBSERVANT
OBSESSION
OBSESSIVE
OBSTETRIC
OBSTINACY
OBSTINATE
OBTAINING
OBTRUSION
OBTRUSIVE
OBVENTION
OBVIOUSLY
OCCIPITAL
OCCLUSION
OCCULTIST
OCCUPANCY
OCCUPYING
OCEANIDES
OCHLOCRAT
OCKHAMIST
OCTACHORD
OCTAGONAL
OCTASTICH
OCTILLION
OCTOBRIST
OCULIFORM
ODALISQUE
ODDJOBMAN
ODELSTING
ODOURLESS
OESTROGEN
OFFCHANCE
OFFCOLOUR
OFFENBACH
OFFENDING
OFFENSIVE
OFFERTORY
OFFICIALS
OFFICIANT
OFFICIATE
OFFICIOUS
OFFSEASON
OFFSPRING
OILTANKER
OLECRANON
OLENELLUS
OLEOGRAPH
OLEORESIN
OLFACTORY
OLIGARCHY
OLIGOCENE
OLIVENITE
OMBUDSMAN
OMINOUSLY
OMOPHAGIC
ONCOMETER
ONOMASTIC
ONSLAUGHT
ONTHESPOT
ONTOGENCY
OPENENDED
OPENHEART
OPERATING
OPERATION
OPERATIVE
OPERCULUM
OPHIUCHUS
OPOBALSAM
OPODELDOC
OPPENHEIM
OPPONENTS
OPPORTUNE
OPPRESSED
OPPRESSOR
OPSIMATHY
OPTICALLY
OPTOMETRY
OPTOPHONE
OPULENTLY
ORANGEADE
ORANGEMAN
ORATORIAN
ORBICULAR
ORCHESTRA
ORDINAIRE
ORDINANCE
ORGANELLE
ORGANICAL
ORGANISED
ORGANISER
ORGANIZED
ORGANIZER
ORGANZINE
ORGIASTIC
ORGILLOUS
ORICALCHE
ORIENTATE
ORIFLAMME
ORIGENIST
ORIGINATE
ORMANDINE
OROBANCHE
OROGRAPHY
ORPHANAGE
ORPHARION
ORPINGTON
ORTANIQUE
ORTHODOXY
ORTHOLOGY
ORTHOPTER
ORTHOTONE
OSCILLATE
OSTEODERM
OSTEOPATH
OSTRACISM
OSTRACIZE
OSTROGOTH
OTHERWISE
OTTERBURN
OTTRELITE
OUBLIETTE
OUDENARDE
OUGHTNESS
OUROBOROS
OUROBORUS
OURSELVES
OUTERMOST
OUTFITTER
OUTGOINGS
OUTGROWTH
OUTNUMBER
OUTOFTOWN
OUTRIGGER
OUTROOPER
OUTSIDERS
OUTSKIRTS
OUTSPOKEN
OUTSPREAD
OUTWARDLY
OUTWORKER
OVENPROOF
OVERBLOWN
OVERBOARD
OVERCLOUD
OVERCROWD
OVERDRAFT
OVERDRAWN
OVERDRESS
OVERDRIVE
OVEREXERT
OVERGROWN
OVERHASTY
OVERHEADS
OVERJOYED
OVERLYING
OVERNIGHT
OVERPAINT
OVERPOISE
OVERPOWER
OVERRATED
OVERREACH
OVERREACT
OVERRIDER
OVERSHADE
OVERSHOES
OVERSHOOT
OVERSIGHT
OVERSIZED
OVERSLEEP
OVERSPEND
OVERSPILL
OVERSTATE
OVERSTEER
OVERTHROW
OVERTONES
OVERVALUE
OVERWEIGH
OVERWHELM
OVIPAROUS
OVULATION
OWLEGLASS
OWNERSHIP
OXIDATION
OZOCERITE
OZOKERITE
PACEMAKER
PACHYDERM
PACKAGING
PADEMELON
PAGEANTRY
PAGLIACCI
PAILLASSE
PAILLETTE
PAINFULLY
PAINTWORK
PAKISTANI
PALAESTRA
PALAFITTE
PALAMPORE
PALANKEEN
PALANQUIN
PALATABLE
PALEMPORE
PALEOLITH
PALESTINE
PALINURUS
PALLADIAN

PALLADIUM
PALLIASSE
PALMATION
PALMISTRY
PALMITATE
PALOVERDE
PALPATION
PALPEBRAL
PALPITATE
PALSGRAVE
PALUDRINE
PANATELLA
PANCHAYAT
PANDATION
PANDEMIAN
PANDURATE
PANEGOISM
PANEGYRIC
PANELLING
PANELLIST
PANETTONE
PANHANDLE
PANNIKELL
PANORAMIC
PANTAGAMY
PANTALEON
PANTALOON
PANTHEISM
PANTHENOL
PANTOFFLE
PANTOMIME
PANTOUFLE
PAPARAZZI
PAPARAZZO
PAPERBACK
PAPERCLIP
PAPERWORK
PAPILLOTE
PARABASIS
PARABLAST
PARABOLIC
PARACHUTE
PARACLETE
PARACUSIS
PARAGOGUE
PARAGRAPH
PARALYSIS
PARALYTIC
PARAMEDIC
PARAMETER
PARAMOUNT
PARANOIAC
PARANYMPH
PARASCENE
PARASCEVE
PARASITIC
PARATHION
PARATROOP
PARBUCKLE
PARCHEESI
PARCHMENT
PARDALOTE
PAREGORIC
PARENTAGE
PARENTING
PARFLECHE
PARHELION
PARHYPATE
PARNASITE
PARNASSUS
PAROCHIAL
PAROCHINE
PAROTITIS
PARRICIDE
PARSIMONY
PARSONAGE
PARTAKING
PARTHENON
PARTHOLON
PARTIALLY
PARTICLES
PARTITION
PARTRIDGE
PARTTIMER
PASSAMENT
PASSENGER
PASSEPIED
PASSERINE
PASSIVELY
PASSIVITY
PASTERNAK
PASTICCIO
PASTORALE
PASTURAGE
PATCHOULI
PATCHOULY
PATCHWORK
PATERCOVE
PATERNITY
PATHOGENY
PATHOLOGY
PATHTRAIN
PATIENTLY
PATRIARCH
PATRICIAN
PATRICIDE
PATRIMONY
PATRIOTIC
PATROCLUS
PATROLMAN
PATRONAGE
PATRONESS
PATRONIZE
PATTERNED
PAULOWNIA
PAUSANIAS
PAWKINESS
PAYCHEQUE
PAYMASTER
PEACEABLE
PEACEABLY
PEACETIME
PEARLWORT
PEASANTRY
PEASEWEEP
PECKSNIFF
PECULATOR
PECUNIARY
PEDAGOGUE
PEDERASTY
PEDICULAR
PEDIGREES
PEDOMETER
PEEVISHLY
PEGMATITE
PEIRASTIC
PEKINGESE
PELLAGRIN
PELLITORY
PELMANISM
PEMPHIGUS
PENDENNIS
PENDLETON
PENDRAGON
PENDULATE
PENDULOUS
PENETRATE
PENFRIEND
PENILLION
PENINSULA
PENISTONE
PENITENCE
PENNILESS
PENPUSHER
PENSIONER
PENSIVELY
PENTECOST
PENTHOUSE
PENTOSANE
PENURIOUS
PEPPERONI
PEPPERPOT
PERAEOPOD
PERCALINE
PERCHANCE
PERCHERON
PERCOLATE
PERDITION
PEREGRINE
PERENNIAL
PERFECTLY
PERFERVID
PERFORANS
PERFORATE
PERFORMED
PERFORMER
PERFUMERY
PERGAMENE
PERGUNNAH
PERIAKTOS
PERIANDER
PERIBOLOS
PERICLASE
PERICUTIN
PERIMETER
PERIMORPH
PERIODATE
PERIPATUS
PERIPHERY
PERISCIAN
PERISCOPE
PERISHING
PERISTOME
PERISTYLE
PERMANENT
PERMEABLE
PERMITTED
PERPETUAL
PERPLEXED
PERSECUTE
PERSEVERE
PERSIMMON
PERSONAGE
PERSONATE
PERSONIFY
PERSONNEL
PERSUADED
PERTINENT
PERTURBED
PERTUSATE
PERTUSSIS
PERVASION
PERVASIVE
PERVERTED
PESSIMISM
PESSIMIST
PESTICIDE
PESTILENT
PETAURIST
PETERSHAM
PETHIDINE
PETILLANT
PETRIFIED
PETROLEUM
PETROLOGY
PETTICOAT
PETTINESS
PETTITOES
PETULANCE
PHACOLITE
PHAGOCYTE
PHALANGER
PHALAROPE
PHANARIOT
PHANSIGAR
PHANTASMA
PHARAMOND
PHARISAIC
PHARSALIA
PHELLOGEN
PHENACITE
PHENAKISM
PHEROMONE
PHIGALIAN
PHILANDER
PHILATELY
PHILIPPIC
PHILISTER
PHILLABEG
PHILLIBEG
PHILOLOGY
PHITONIUM
PHLEBITIS
PHONECARD
PHONETICS
PHONOGRAM
PHONOLITE
PHONOLOGY
PHOSPHATE
PHOSPHENE
PHOTOCOPY
PHOTOGENE
PHOTOSTAT
PHRENETIC
PHRENITIS
PHTHALATE
PHYLLOPOD
PHYLOGENY
PHYSICIAN
PHYSICIST
PHYTOLITE
PHYTOTRON
PIACEVOLE
PICKABACK
PICKETING
PICKTHANK
PICNICKER
PICTOGRAM
PICTORIAL
PIECEMEAL
PIECEWORK
PIEPOWDER
PIERGLASS
PIGGYBACK
PIGGYBANK
PIGHEADED
PIGNERATE
PIKESTAFF
PILASTERS
PILFERAGE
PILFERING
PILLICOCK
PIMPERNEL
PINCHBECK
PINCHCOCK
PINEAPPLE
PINHOOKER
PINKERTON
PINOCCHIO
PINSTRIPE
PIPEDREAM
PIPESTONE
PIPSQUEAK
PIQUANTLY
PIRATICAL
PIROUETTE
PISTACHIO
PISTAREEN
PISTOLEER
PITCHFORK
PITCHPINE
PITCHPOLE
PITCHPOLL
PITIFULLY
PITUITARY
PITUITRIN
PIZZICATO
PLACATORY
PLACEMENT
PLACIDITY
PLAINNESS
PLAINSMAN
PLAINSONG
PLAINTIFF
PLAINTIVE
PLANETARY
PLASTERED
PLASTERER
PLATITUDE
PLATONIST
PLAUSIBLE
PLAUSIBLY
PLAUSTRAL
PLAYFULLY
PLAYGROUP
PLAYHOUSE
PLAYTHING
PLEASANCE
PLEIOCENE
PLENITUDE
PLENTEOUS
PLENTIFUL

PLETHORIC
PLIMSOLLS
PLOUGHMAN
PLUMBEOUS
PLUMBLINE
PLUMDAMAS
PLUMPNESS
PLUNDERER
PLURALISM
PLURALITY
PLUTOCRAT
PLUTONIUM
PNEUMATIC
PNEUMONIA
POCKETFUL
POCKMANKY
POETASTER
POIGNANCY
POINTEDLY
POINTLESS
POINTSMAN
POISONING
POISONOUS
POLEMARCH
POLEMICAL
POLIANITE
POLICEMAN
POLITBURO
POLITESSE
POLITICAL
POLITIQUE
POLLINATE
POLLUTANT
POLLUTION
POLONAISE
POLVERINE
POLYANDRY
POLYESTER
POLYGONAL
POLYGRAPH
POLYNESIA
POLYPHONE
POLYPHONY
POLYTHENE
POMOERIUM
POMPADOUR
POMPHOLYX
POMPOSITY
PONDEROSA
PONDEROUS
PONTLEVIS
POORHOUSE
POPLITEAL
POPPERING
POPPYCOCK
POPULARLY
POPULATED
PORBEAGLE
PORCELAIN
PORCUPINE
PORIFERAN
PORPOISES
PORPORATE
PORRINGER
PORTERAGE
PORTFOLIO
PORTRAYAL
PORTREEVE
POSSESSED
POSSESSOR
POSSIBLES
POSTCARDS
POSTERIOR
POSTERITY
POSTHOUSE
POSTNATAL
POSTPONED
POSTULANT
POSTULATE
POSTWOMAN
POTASSIUM
POTBOILER
POTENTATE
POTENTIAL
POTHOLING
POTHUNTER
POTPOURRI
POTTINGAR
POUJADIST
POULTERER
POWELLITE
POWERBOAT
POWERLESS
PRACTICAL
PRACTISED
PRACTOLOL
PRAGMATIC
PRANKSTER
PREBENDAL
PRECATORY
PRECEDENT
PRECEDING
PRECENTOR
PRECEPTOR
PRECIEUSE
PRECINCTS
PRECIPICE
PRECISELY
PRECISIAN
PRECISION
PRECISIVE
PRECOCITY
PRECONISE
PRECURSOR
PREDATORY
PREDICANT
PREDICATE
PREDICTOR
PREDIKANT
PREDILECT
PREFATORY
PREFERRED
PREFIGURE
PREGNANCY
PREHALLUX
PREJUDICE
PRELECTOR
PRELUSORY
PREMATURE
PREMONISH
PREMOTION
PREOCCUPY
PREORDAIN
PREPOLLEX
PRESBYTER
PRESCIENT
PRESCRIBE
PRESCUTUM
PRESENTED
PRESENTER
PRESENTLY
PRESERVED
PRESERVER
PRESERVES
PRESHRUNK
PRESIDENT
PRESIDIAL
PRESIDIUM
PRESSGANG
PRETENDER
PRETERITE
PRETERMIT
PREVALENT
PREVERNAL
PRICELESS
PRIESTESS
PRIESTLEY
PRIMAEVAL
PRIMARILY
PRIMAVERA
PRIMITIAE
PRIMITIVE
PRIMULINE
PRINCETON
PRINCIPAL
PRINCIPLE
PRINTABLE
PRISMATIC
PRIVATEER
PRIVATELY
PRIVATION
PRIVATIZE
PRIVILEGE
PROACTIVE
PROBABLES
PROBATION
PROBOSCIS
PROCACITY
PROCEDURE
PROCERITY
PROCESSOR
PROCLITIC
PROCOELUS
PROCONSUL
PROCREATE
PRODROMAL
PRODROMUS
PROFANELY
PROFANITY
PROFESSED
PROFESSOR
PROFITEER
PROFUSELY
PROFUSION
PROGNOSIS
PROGRAMME
PROJECTED
PROJECTOR
PROKARYON
PROKOFIEV
PROLACTIN
PROLAMINE
PROLEPSIS
PROLIXITY
PROLONGED
PROLUSION
PROMACHOS
PROMENADE
PROMINENT
PROMISING
PROMOTION
PROMPTING
PROMUSCIS
PRONGHORN
PRONOUNCE
PROOFREAD
PROPAGATE
PROPELLED
PROPELLER
PROPELLOR
PROPERDIN
PROPHETIC
PROPIONIC
PROPONENT
PROPRIETY
PROPTOSIS
PROPYLENE
PROROGATE
PROSCRIBE
PROSECUTE
PROSELYTE
PROSTRATE
PROTAMINE
PROTECTOR
PROTESTER
PROTHESIS
PROTHORAX
PROTOSTAR
PROTOTYPE
PROUDHORN
PROUSTITE
PROVEDORE
PROVENDER
PROVIDENT
PROVIDING
PROVISION
PROVOKING
PROVOLONE
PROXIMATE
PROXIMITY
PRUDENTLY
PRURIENCE
PRYTANEUM
PSEUDAXIS
PSEUDONYM
PSORIASIS
PSYCHICAL
PSYCHOSIS
PSYCHOTIC
PTARMIGAN
PTERIDIUM
PTEROSAUR
PUBLICIST
PUBLICITY
PUBLICIZE
PUBLISHED
PUBLISHER
PUCELLAGE
PUERILITY
PUERPERAL
PUFFINESS
PUGNACITY
PUISSANCE
PULLULATE
PULMONARY
PULPITEER
PULSATION
PULVERIZE
PUMMELLED
PUNCHLINE
PUNCTILIO
PUNCTUATE
PUNGENTLY
PUNISHING
PUPILLAGE
PUPPETEER
PURCHASER
PURDONIUM
PURGATIVE
PURGATORY
PURIFYING
PURITANIC
PURPOSELY
PURSUANCE
PURULENCE
PUSHCHAIR
PUSSYFOOT
PYGMALION
PYONGYANG
PYRAMIDAL
PYRETHRUM
PYROMANCY
PYROMANIA
PYRRHONIC
PYTHONESS
QUADRATIC
QUADRATUS
QUADRILLE
QUADRUPED
QUADRUPLE
QUAILPIPE
QUALIFIED
QUALIFIER
QUANTICAL
QUANTOCKS
QUARENDEN
QUARTERLY
QUARTETTE
QUASIMODO
QUAVERING
QUEERNESS
QUENNELLE
QUERCETIN
QUERCETUS
QUERIMONY
QUERULOUS
QUICKLIME
QUICKNESS
QUICKSAND
QUICKSTEP
QUIESCENT
QUIETNESS
QUILLWORT
QUINQUINA
QUINTETTE
QUINTROON
QUINTUPLE
QUITTANCE
QUIVERFUL
QUIVERING
QUIZZICAL
QUODLIBET

QUOTATION
QUOTIDIAN
QUOTITION
RACCABOUT
RACCAHOUT
RACEHORSE
RACETRACK
RACIALISM
RACIALIST
RACKETEER
RACKSTRAW
RACONTEUR
RADCLIFFE
RADDLEMAN
RADIANTLY
RADIATING
RADIATION
RADICALLY
RADICCHIO
RADIOGRAM
RADIOLOGY
RAFFINOSE
RAINCHECK
RAINGAUGE
RAINSTORM
RAINWATER
RAMILLIES
RANCIDITY
RANCOROUS
RANDINESS
RANTIPOLE
RAPACIOUS
RAPTORIAL
RAPTUROUS
RASKOLNIK
RASPATORY
RASPBERRY
RATEPAYER
RATHERIPE
RATHERISH
RATIONALE
RATIONING
RATTLEBAG
RAUCOUSLY
RAVISHING
RAZORBILL
REACHABLE
READDRESS
READINESS
READYEARN
READYMADE
REALISTIC
REALITIES
REANIMATE
REARGUARD
REARHORSE
REARMOUSE
REARRANGE
REARWARDS
REASONING
REBELLION
REBOATION
RECALLING
RECAPTURE
RECEIVING
RECEPTION
RECEPTIVE
RECESSION
RECESSIVE
RECIPIENT
RECKONING
RECLAIMED
RECLAIMER
RECOGNIZE
RECOLLECT
RECOMMEND
RECONCILE
RECONDITE
RECONVENE
RECORDING
RECORDIST
RECOVERED
RECTANGLE
RECTIFIER
RECTITUDE
RECTORIAL
RECUMBENT
RECURRENT
RECURRING
RECUSANCE
REDBREAST
REDDENDUM
REDEEMING
REDHANDED
REDHEADED
REDINGOTE
REDIVIVUS
REDLETTER
REDOLENCE
REDSTREAK
REDUCIBLE
REDUCTION
REDUNDANT
REEDINESS
REEXAMINE
REFECTION
REFECTORY
REFERENCE
REFERRING
REFINANCE
REFLATION
REFLECTOR
REFLEXION
REFLEXIVE
REFORMIST
REFRACTOR
REFRESHER
REFULGENT
REFURBISH
REFUSENIK
REGARDANT
REGARDFUL
REGARDING
REGISSEUR
REGISTRAR
REGRETFUL
REGUERDON
REGULARLY
REGULATOR
REHEARSAL
REICHSRAT
REICHSTAG
REIMBURSE
REINFORCE
REINSTATE
REISTAFEL
REITERATE
REJECTION
REJOICING
REJOINDER
RELATIONS
RELEVANCE
RELIGEUSE
RELIGIOSO
RELIGIOUS
RELIQUARY
RELIQUIAE
RELUCTANT
REMAINDER
REMAINING
REMBRANDT
REMINISCE
REMISSION
REMONTANT
REMOULADE
REMOVABLE
RENASCENT
RENCONTRE
RENDERING
RENDITION
RENEWABLE
RENFIERST
RENOVATOR
RENTALLER
REPAYABLE
REPAYMENT
REPECHAGE
REPELLENT
REPELLING
REPENTANT
REPERCUSS
REPERTORY
REPLACING
REPLENISH
REPLETION
REPLETIVE
REPLICATE
REPORTAGE
REPORTING
REPOSSESS
REPREHEND
REPRESENT
REPRESSED
REPRIMAND
REPROBATE
REPROCESS
REPRODUCE
REPROVING
REPTATION
REPTILIAN
REPUDIATE
REPUGNANT
REPULSION
REPULSIVE
REPUTABLE
REPUTEDLY
REQUISITE
REREMOUSE
RESENTFUL
RESERPINE
RESERVIST
RESERVOIR
RESHUFFLE
RESIDENCE
RESIDENCY
RESIDUARY
RESILIENT
RESISTANT
RESNATRON
RESONANCE
RESONATOR
RESORTING
RESOURCES
RESPECTED
RESPECTER
RESSALDAR
RESTIFORM
RESTITUTE
RESTRAINT
RESULTANT
RESULTING
RESURFACE
RESURGENT
RESURRECT
RETAILING
RETAINING
RETALIATE
RETENTION
RETENTIVE
RETIARIUS
RETICENCE
RETICULUM
RETINITIS
RETORSION
RETORTION
RETRACTOR
RETRIEVAL
RETRIEVER
RETROCEDE
RETROFLEX
RETROVERT
RETURNING
REVEALING
REVELLING
REVERENCE
REVERSING
REVERSION
REVETMENT
REVICTUAL
REVOLTING
REVOLVING
REVULSION
REWARDING
REWORKING
REYKJAVIK
RHAPSODIC
RHEOTAXIS
RHEUMATIC
RHODESIAN
RHODOLITE
RHODOPSIN
RHYMESTER
RIBBONISM
RICERCARE
RICHELIEU
RIDERHOOD
RIDERLESS
RIDGEBACK
RIGHTEOUS
RIGHTHAND
RIGHTNESS
RIGHTWING
RIGMAROLE
RIGOLETTO
RILLETTES
RINGFENCE
RINGSIDER
RIOTOUSLY
RIPIENIST
RISKINESS
RIVERSIDE
ROADBLOCK
ROADHOUSE
ROADSTEAD
ROADWORKS
ROBERTSON
ROCAMBOLE
ROISTERER
ROOSEVELT
ROOTSTOCK
ROQUEFORT
RORSCHACH
ROSCOMMON
ROSEWATER
ROSINANTE
ROSMARINE
ROSMINIAN
ROSTELLUM
ROTAPLANE
ROTTERDAM
ROTUNDATE
ROTUNDITY
ROUGHCAST
ROUGHNECK
ROUGHNESS
ROUGHSHOD
ROUMANIAN
ROUMANSCH
ROUNCEVAL
ROUNCIVAL
ROUNDBACK
ROUNDELAY
ROUNDFISH
ROUNDHAND
ROUNDHEAD
ROUNDSMAN
ROUSSETTE
ROUTINELY
ROWDINESS
ROXBURGHE
ROZINANTE
RUBBERIZE
RUBICELLE
RUDBECKIA
RUDDIGORE
RUDDLEMAN
RUDIMENTS
RUFESCENT
RUFFIANLY
RUGGELACH
RUINATION
RUINOUSLY
RUNAROUND
RUNCINATE
RUNESTAVE
RUNNYMEDE
RUSHLIGHT
RUSTICATE
RUSTINESS
RUTHENIAN
RUTHENIUM
SABBATIAN

SACCHARIN
SACKCLOTH
SACKERSON
SACRAMENT
SACRARIUM
SACRIFICE
SACRILEGE
SACRISTAN
SADDENING
SADDLEBAG
SAFEGUARD
SAFFLOWER
SAGACIOUS
SAGAPENUM
SAGITTARY
SAILCLOTH
SAINTFOIN
SAINTHOOD
SALACIOUS
SALANGANE
SALERATUS
SALESGIRL
SALESLADY
SALICETUM
SALLYPORT
SALLYPOST
SALOPETTE
SALTINESS
SALTPETER
SALTPETRE
SALTWATER
SALUBRITY
SALVARSAN
SALVATION
SAMARITAN
SANCTUARY
SANDALLED
SANDARACH
SANDHURST
SANDPAPER
SANDPIPER
SANDSTONE
SANDSTORM
SANGFROID
SANHEDRIM
SANHEDRIN
SANHEDRON
SANNYASIN
SANTAYANA
SAPSUCKER
SARBACANE
SARCASTIC
SARMENTUM
SARTORIAL
SARTORIUS
SASKATOON
SASQUATCH
SASSAFRAS
SASSENACH
SASSOLITE
SATELLITE
SATIATION
SATINWOOD
SATIRICAL
SATISFIED
SATURATED
SATURNIAN
SATURNINE
SATURNISM
SATYRIDAE
SATYRINAE
SAUCEBOAT
SAUCINESS
SAUCISSON
SAUTERNES
SAUVIGNON
SAVERNAKE
SAXIFRAGE
SAXITOXIN
SAXOPHONE
SCABLANDS
SCAGLIOLA
SCALARIUM
SCALDFISH
SCALEABLE
SCALLAWAG
SCALLIONS
SCALLOPED
SCALLYWAG
SCAMBLING
SCANSORES
SCANTLING
SCAPEGOAT
SCAPOLITE
SCARECROW
SCARIFIER
SCARLATTI
SCATTERED
SCAVENGER
SCELERATE
SCENTLESS
SCEPTICAL
SCHEELITE
SCHEHITAH
SCHELLING
SCHEMATIC
SCHIAVONE
SCHILLING
SCHLEMIEL
SCHLEMIHL
SCHLENTER
SCHLIEREN
SCHMALTZY
SCHMIEDER
SCHMUTTER
SCHNAPPER
SCHNAUZER
SCHNECKEN
SCHNITTKE
SCHNITZEL
SCHNORKEL
SCHNORRER
SCHNOZZLE
SCHOLARCH
SCHOLARLY
SCHOLIAST
SCHOOLBOY
SCHOOLING
SCHOOLMAN
SCIAMACHY
SCIARIDAE
SCIENTISM
SCIENTIST
SCINTILLA
SCIOMANCY
SCISSORER
SCLAUNDER
SCLEROSIS
SCLEROTAL
SCOLECITE
SCOLIOSIS
SCOLIOTIC
SCONCHEON
SCORBUTIC
SCORBUTUS
SCORCHING
SCORODITE
SCOTCHMAN
SCOUNDREL
SCRAMBLER
SCRAPBOOK
SCRAPINGS
SCRAPPING
SCRATCHED
SCRATCHES
SCREENING
SCREWBALL
SCREWEDUP
SCREWPINE
SCREWTAPE
SCRIMMAGE
SCRIMPING
SCRIMSHAW
SCRIPTURE
SCRIVENER
SCRODDLED
SCROUNGER
SCRUBBING
SCRUFFILY
SCRUMMAGE
SCRUMPING
SCRUTATOR
SCUDDALER
SCULPTING
SCULPTURE
SCUNCHEON
SCURRIOUR
SCYTHEMAN
SDEIGNFUL
SEABOTTLE
SEAFARING
SEANNACHY
SEARCHING
SEASONING
SEAWORTHY
SEBACEOUS
SEBASTIAN
SECATEURS
SECESSION
SECLUSION
SECONDARY
SECRETARY
SECRETION
SECRETIVE
SECTARIAN
SECTIONAL
SECTORIAL
SEDENTARY
SEDGEMOOR
SEDITIOUS
SEDUCTION
SEDUCTIVE
SEEMINGLY
SEGMENTED
SEGREGATE
SELACHION
SELECTING
SELECTION
SELECTIVE
SELFISHLY
SELJUKIAN
SELLOTAPE
SEMANTEME
SEMANTICS
SEMANTIDE
SEMANTRON
SEMAPHORE
SEMBLANCE
SEMEIOTIC
SEMIBREVE
SEMICOLON
SEMIFINAL
SEMIOLOGY
SEMIRAMIS
SENESCENT
SENESCHAL
SENIORITY
SENSATION
SENSELESS
SENSILLUM
SENSITIVE
SENSITIZE
SENSORIUM
SENSUALLY
SENTIENCE
SENTIMENT
SEPARABLE
SEPARATED
SEPARATOR
SEPHARDIM
SEPIOLITE
SEPTEMBER
SEPTIMOLE
SEPULCHER
SEPULCHRE
SEPULTURE
SEQUESTER
SEQUINNED
SERAPHINE
SERASKIER
SERBONIAN
SERENADER
SERENGETI
SERIALIST
SERIALIZE
SERIATION
SERIOUSLY
SERMONIZE
SERRATION
SERREFILE
SERVICING
SERVIETTE
SERVILELY
SERVILITY
SERVITUDE
SETACEOUS
SEVENTEEN
SEVERALLY
SEVERANCE
SEXUALITY
SHADINESS
SHAKEDOWN
SHAKINESS
SHAMEFAST
SHAMELESS
SHAMIANAH
SHAPELESS
SHARESMAN
SHARKSKIN
SHARPENER
SHARPNESS
SHASHLICK
SHATTERED
SHAVELING
SHEARLING
SHECHINAH
SHECHITAH
SHEEPFOLD
SHEEPMEAT
SHEEPSKIN
SHEERLEGS
SHEERNESS
SHEFFIELD
SHEIKHDOM
SHELDDUCK
SHELDRAKE
SHELLBACK
SHELLFISH
SHELLSUIT
SHELTERED
SHEMOZZLE
SHENSTONE
SHEPHERDS
SHETLANDS
SHEWBREAD
SHIELDING
SHIFTLESS
SHIFTWORK
SHILLABER
SHINTOISM
SHIPOWNER
SHIPSHAPE
SHIPWRECK
SHIVERING
SHOEMAKER
SHOESHINE
SHOLOKHOV
SHOPFLOOR
SHOPFRONT
SHORTCAKE
SHORTFALL
SHORTHAND
SHORTHAUL
SHORTHOLD
SHORTHORN
SHORTLIST
SHORTNESS
SHORTSTAY
SHORTSTOP
SHORTTERM
SHOVELFUL
SHOVELLER
SHOWINESS
SHOWPIECE
SHRIMPING
SHRINKAGE
SHRINKING
SHRUBBERY
SHUBUNKIN
SHUFFLING
SHUTTERED
SIBILANCE

SIBYLLINE
SICCATIVE
SICILIANO
SICKENING
SIDEBOARD
SIDEBURNS
SIDELIGHT
SIDEROSIS
SIDESWIPE
SIDETRACK
SIDEWARDS
SIEGFRIED
SIGHTLESS
SIGHTSEER
SIGNALLER
SIGNALMAN
SIGNATORY
SIGNATURE
SIGNBOARD
SILICOSIS
SILLINESS
SILTSTONE
SILURIDAE
SIMEONITE
SIMILARLY
SIMPLETON
SIMPLISTE
SIMULATED
SIMULATOR
SIMULCAST
SINCERELY
SINCERITY
SINGALESE
SINGAPORE
SINGLESEX
SINGLETON
SINGSPIEL
SINGULTUS
SINKANSEN
SINUOSITY
SINUSITIS
SIPHUNCLE
SIRBONIAN
SISSERARY
SISYPHEAN
SITUATION
SIXTEENMO
SIXTEENTH
SKEDADDLE
SKEPTICAL
SKETCHILY
SKETCHMAP
SKETCHPAD
SKEWWHIFF
SKIAMACHY
SKILFULLY
SKINDIVER
SKINFLINT
SKINTIGHT
SKYJACKER
SLABSTONE
SLACKNESS
SLAMMAKIN
SLANTWISE
SLAPHAPPY
SLAPSTICK
SLAUGHTER
SLAVISHLY
SLEEKNESS
SLEEPLESS
SLEEPWALK
SLIGHTEST
SLIMINESS
SLINGBACK
SLINGSHOT
SLIVOVICA
SLIVOVITZ
SLOUGHING
SLOVENIAN
SLOWCOACH
SLUGHORNE
SLUMBERER
SMALLNESS
SMALLTIME
SMARTNESS
SMOKEFREE
SMOKELESS
SMUGGLING
SNAKEWEED
SNEERWELL
SNOWBOUND
SNOWDONIA
SNOWDRIFT
SNOWFLAKE
SNOWSHOES
SNOWSTORM
SNOWWHITE
SOAPSTONE
SOBERNESS
SOBRIQUET
SOCIALISM
SOCIALIST
SOCIALITE
SOCIALIZE
SOCIOLECT
SOCIOLOGY
SOFTCOVER
SOFTENING
SOGGINESS
SOLDERING
SOLDIERLY
SOLEMNITY
SOLEMNIZE
SOLFEGGIO
SOLFERINO
SOLFIDIAN
SOLICITOR
SOLILOQUY
SOLIPSISM
SOLITAIRE
SOLLICKER
SOMASCOPE
SOMEPLACE
SOMETHING
SOMETIMES
SOMEWHERE
SOMMELIER
SOMNOLENT
SONGSMITH
SONNETEER
SONOMETER
SOOTERKIN
SOPHISTER
SOPHISTIC
SOPHISTRY
SOPHOCLES
SOPHOMORE
SOPORIFIC
SOPPINESS
SORCERESS
SORROWFUL
SORTILEGE
SOSTENUTO
SOTTISIER
SOUBRETTE
SOUFRIERE
SOULFULLY
SOUNDBITE
SOUNDLESS
SOUNDNESS
SOURDOUGH
SOUTENEUR
SOUTHDOWN
SOUTHEAST
SOUTHERLY
SOUTHWARD
SOUTHWARK
SOUTHWEST
SOUVLAKIA
SOUWESTER
SOVENANCE
SOVEREIGN
SPACELESS
SPACESHIP
SPACESUIT
SPADASSIN
SPAGHETTI
SPARINGLY
SPARKLERS
SPARKLING
SPARTACUS
SPASMODIC
SPATIALLY
SPATTERED
SPEAKEASY
SPEARHEAD
SPEARMINT
SPEARSIDE
SPEARWORT
SPECIALLY
SPECIALTY
SPECIFICS
SPECIFIED
SPECIMENS
SPECTACLE
SPECTATOR
SPECULATE
SPEECHIFY
SPEEDBOAT
SPEEDWELL
SPELDRING
SPELLBIND
SPELUNKER
SPHACELUS
SPHENDONE
SPHERICAL
SPHINCTER
SPICILEGE
SPICINESS
SPIDERWEB
SPIKENARD
SPILLICAN
SPILLIKIN
SPINDRIER
SPINDRIFT
SPINELESS
SPINNAKER
SPINNERET
SPIRITOUS
SPIRITUAL
SPLENDOUR
SPLENETIC
SPLENITIS
SPLINTERS
SPLITTING
SPOFFORTH
SPOILSMAN
SPOKESMAN
SPONGEBAG
SPONSORED
SPOONBILL
SPOONFEED
SPOROCARP
SPORTSMAN
SPORTSMEN
SPOTLIGHT
SPRAICKLE
SPRAUCHLE
SPREADING
SPRECHERY
SPRIGHTLY
SPRINGALD
SPRINGBOK
SPRINGLET
SPRINKLER
SPRITEFUL
SPRITSAIL
SPUNCULID
SQUADRONE
SQUALIDLY
SQUATTERS
SQUEAMISH
SQUINANCY
SQUINTING
SQUIREAGE
SQUIRMING
STABILITY
STABILIZE
STABLEBOY
STABLELAD
STABLEMAN
STAGEHAND
STAGGERED
STAGIRITE
STAGYRITE
STAINLESS
STAIRCASE
STALEMATE
STALENESS
STALWORTH
STAMMERER
STANCHION
STANDARDS
STANDERBY
STANDGALE
STANDPIPE
STANNATOR
STARBOARD
STARGAZER
STARKNESS
STARLIGHT
STARSTONE
STARTLING
STATEHOOD
STATELESS
STATEMENT
STATEROOM
STATESIDE
STATESMAN
STATEWIDE
STATIONED
STATIONER
STATISTIC
STATOLITH
STATUETTE
STATUTORY
STAUNCHLY
STAVANGER
STEADFAST
STEAMBOAT
STEAMSHIP
STEELHEAD
STEELYARD
STEENBRAS
STEENKIRK
STEEPNESS
STEERSMAN
STEGNOSIS
STEGNOTIC
STEGOSAUR
STEINBECK
STEINBOCK
STENOPAIC
STERADIAN
STERCORAL
STERILITY
STERILIZE
STERNFAST
STERNNESS
STEVEDORE
STEVENSON
STIFFENER
STIFFNESS
STILLBORN
STILLNESS
STILLROOM
STILTBIRD
STIMULANT
STIMULATE
STINGAREE
STINKBIRD
STINKHORN
STINKWOOD
STIPULATE
STIRABOUT
STOCKFISH
STOCKHOLM
STOCKINET
STOCKINGS
STOCKPILE
STOCKROOM
STOCKWORK
STOCKYARD
STOICALLY
STOLIDITY
STOMACHIC
STONEBOAT
STONECHAT
STONECROP
STONEHAND
STONELESS
STONEWALL

STONEWARE
STONEWORK
STONEWORT
STONKERED
STOOLBALL
STOREROOM
STORIATED
STORNAWAY
STORYBOOK
STORYLINE
STOUTNESS
STOVEPIPE
STOWNLINS
STRAGGLER
STRAINING
STRANGELY
STRANGLER
STRANGLES
STRANGURY
STRAPHANG
STRAPLESS
STRAPPADO
STRAPPING
STRATAGEM
STRATEGIC
STREAMING
STREETAGE
STREETCAR
STRENUOUS
STRESSFUL
STRETCHED
STRETCHER
STRIATION
STRICTURE
STRIDENCY
STRINGENT
STRINGOPS
STRIPLING
STROBILUS
STROLLING
STROMBOLI
STRONGARM
STRONGYLE
STRONTIUM
STROSSERS
STRUCTURE
STRUMITIS
STRUTTING
STUMBLING
STUMPWORK
STUPEFIED
STUPIDITY
STYLISHLY
STYLISTIC
STYLOBATE
SUBALTERN
SUBCELLAR
SUBCORTEX
SUBDIVIDE
SUBDOLOUS
SUBEDITOR
SUBENTIRE
SUBJACENT
SUBJUGATE
SUBLIMATE
SUBLIMELY
SUBMARINE
SUBMERGED
SUBNORMAL
SUBROGATE
SUBSCRIBE
SUBSCRIPT
SUBSIDIZE
SUBSTANCE
SUBSTRATA
SUBSTRATE
SUBTENANT
SUBTITLED
SUCCEEDED
SUCCENTOR
SUCCESSOR
SUCCINATE
SUCCOTASH
SUCCUBINE
SUCCULENT
SUCCURSAL
SUDORIFIC
SUETONIUS
SUFFERING
SUFFOCATE
SUFFRAGAN
SUFFUSION
SUGARCANE
SULFUROUS
SULKINESS
SULPHONIC
SULPHURIC
SULTANATE
SUMMARILY
SUMMARIZE
SUMMATION
SUMPTUARY
SUMPTUOUS
SUNBATHER
SUNDOWNER
SUNFLOWER
SUNSCREEN
SUNSTROKE
SUNTANNED
SUPERETTE
SUPERFINE
SUPERNOVA
SUPERSEDE
SUPERSTAR
SUPERVENE
SUPERVISE
SUPINATOR
SUPPLIANT
SUPPLICAT
SUPPORTER
SUPPOSING
SUPPURATE
SUPREMACY
SUPREMELY
SUQUAMISH
SURCHARGE
SURCINGLE
SURFBOARD
SURFEITED
SURLINESS
SURMULLET
SURPRISED
SURQUEDRY
SURREJOIN
SURRENDER
SURROGATE
SURVEYING
SURVIVING
SUSCITATE
SUSPECTED
SUSPENDED
SUSPENDER
SUSPENSOR
SUSPICION
SUSTAINED
SWADDLING
SWAGGERER
SWANIMOTE
SWANSDOWN
SWEATBAND
SWEEPINGS
SWEETENER
SWEETMEAT
SWEETNESS
SWEETSHOP
SWIFTNESS
SWINBURNE
SWINEHERD
SWINGEING
SWORDFISH
SWORDPLAY
SWORDSMAN
SWOTHLING
SYBARITIC
SYCOPHANT
SYLLABARY
SYLLABLES
SYLLEPSIS
SYLLOGISM
SYLPHLIKE
SYLVANITE
SYMBIOSIS
SYMBIOTIC
SYMBOLISM
SYMBOLIST
SYMBOLIZE
SYMMETRIC
SYMPHONIC
SYMPHYSIS
SYMPODIUM
SYMPOSIUM
SYNAGOGUE
SYNANGIUM
SYNCHYSIS
SYNCOMIUM
SYNCOPATE
SYNDICATE
SYNEDRION
SYNERGIST
SYNIZESIS
SYNOECETE
SYNOVITIS
SYNTACTIC
SYNTHESIS
SYNTHETIC
SYRIACISM
SYRPHIDAE
TABANIDAE
TABASHEER
TABBOULEH
TABELLION
TABLATURE
TABLELAND
TABLEWARE
TABULATOR
TACAMAHAC
TACHILITE
TACHYLITE
TACHYLYTE
TACKINESS
TACTFULLY
TACTICIAN
TAHSILDAR
TAILBOARD
TAILLEFER
TAILLIGHT
TAILPIECE
TAILPLANE
TALKATIVE
TALMUDIST
TAMERLANE
TAMOXIFEN
TANGERINE
TANTALITE
TANTALIZE
TANTARARA
TANZANIAN
TAOISEACH
TAPDANCER
TARANTASS
TARANTULA
TARAXACUM
TARDINESS
TARGETEER
TARMACKED
TARNATION
TARPAULIN
TARRAGONA
TARTAREAN
TASMANIAN
TASSELLED
TASTELESS
TAUCHNITZ
TAUTOLOGY
TAVERNERS
TAVISTOCK
TAXIDERMY
TAXIMETER
TAYASSUID
TEACHABLE
TEAKETTLE
TEARFULLY
TEARSHEET
TECHNICAL
TECHNIQUE
TECTIFORM
TECTONICS
TECTORIAL
TEDIOSITY
TEDIOUSLY
TEESWATER
TEIRESIAS
TEKNONYMY
TELEGRAPH
TELEOLOGY
TELEPATHY
TELEPHONE
TELEPHONY
TELEPHOTO
TELESALES
TELESCOPE
TELESTICH
TELLINGLY
TELLURIAN
TELLURION
TELLURIUM
TEMPERATE
TEMPORARY
TEMPORIZE
TEMPTRESS
TEMULENCE
TENACIOUS
TENACULUM
TENAILLON
TENDERIZE
TENEBROSE
TENEMENTS
TENNESSEE
TENSENESS
TENTATIVE
TENTORIUM
TENUOUSLY
TEPHILLIN
TEREBINTH
TERMAGANT
TERMAGENT
TERMINATE
TERPINEOL
TERRACING
TERRARIUM
TERRICOLE
TERRIFIED
TERRITORY
TERRORISM
TERRORIST
TERRORIZE
TERSENESS
TESTAMENT
TESTATRIX
TESTDRIVE
TESTICLES
TESTIFIER
TESTIMONY
TETRAGRAM
TETRALOGY
TETRARCHY
TETTEROUS
THACKERAY
THALASSIC
THANATISM
THANKLESS
THATCHING
THAUMATIN
THECODONT
THELEMITE
THELONIUS
THEOBROMA
THEOCRACY
THEOSOPHY
THERALITE
THERAPIST
THEREFORE
THEREUPON
THERMIDOR
THERSITES
THESAURUS
THICKHEAD
THICKNESS
THIGHBONE
THINGUMMY
THINKABLE
THINNINGS

THIRDSMAN
THIRSTILY
THIRSTING
THIRTIETH
THORNBACK
THORNBILL
THORNDYKE
THORNLESS
THOUSANDS
THRALLDOM
THRASHING
THRASONIC
THREADFIN
THREEFOLD
THREESOME
THRENETIC
THREONINE
THRESHOLD
THRIFTILY
THRILLANT
THRILLING
THROATILY
THROBBING
THRONGING
THROWAWAY
THROWBACK
THROWDOWN
THROWSTER
THUMBLING
THUMBNAIL
THUMBTACK
THUNDERER
THYESTEAN
THYLACINE
THYRATRON
THYRISTOR
TICHBORNE
TICTACTOE
TIERCERON
TIGHTENER
TIGHTHEAD
TIGHTNESS
TIGHTROPE
TIMENOGUY
TIMEPIECE
TIMESHARE
TIMETABLE
TIMOCRACY
TIMPANIST
TINGUAITE
TIPPERARY
TIPSINESS
TIPULIDAE
TIREDNESS
TISIPHONE
TITHEBARN
TITILLATE
TITRATION
TITTLEBAT
TOADSTONE
TOADSTOOL
TOASTRACK
TOBERMORY
TOCCATINA
TOLERABLE
TOLERABLY
TOLERANCE
TOLERATED
TOLLHOUSE
TOLPUDDLE
TOMBSTONE
TOMENTOSE
TONBRIDGE
TONOMETER
TONOPLAST
TOOTHACHE
TOOTHCOMB
TOOTHLESS
TOOTHPICK
TOOTHSOME
TOPDRAWER
TOPIARIST
TOPICALLY
TORBANITE
TORMENTER
TORMENTIL
TORMENTOR
TORMENTUM
TORTELIER
TOSCANINI
TOTALIZER
TOTAQUINE
TOTTENHAM
TOUCHDOWN
TOUCHLINE
TOUCHWOOD
TOUGHNESS
TOURNEDOS
TOVARISCH
TOWCESTER
TOWELLING
TOWNSFOLK
TOXOPHILY
TRACEABLE
TRACHINUS
TRACKLESS
TRACKSUIT
TRACTABLE
TRADEMARK
TRADESMAN
TRADEWIND
TRADITION
TRAFALGAR
TRAGEDIAN
TRAGELAPH
TRAINABLE
TRAMLINES
TRANSCEND
TRANSFORM
TRANSFUSE
TRANSHUME
TRANSIENT
TRANSLATE
TRANSMUTE
TRANSPIRE
TRANSPORT
TRANSPOSE
TRANSSHIP
TRANSVAAL
TRAPEZIAL
TRAPEZIST
TRAPEZIUM
TRAPEZIUS
TRAPEZOID
TRAPPINGS
TRASIMENE
TRATTORIA
TRAUMATIC
TRAVELERS
TRAVELING
TRAVELLER
TREACHERY
TREADMILL
TREASURER
TREATMENT
TREBIZOND
TREBUCHET
TREDRILLE
TREETRUNK
TREGEAGLE
TREGETOUR
TREILLAGE
TREMATODE
TREMBLING
TREMOLITE
TREMULATE
TREMULOUS
TRENCHANT
TREVELYAN
TRIANGLED
TRIATHLON
TRIBALISM
TRIBESMAN
TRIBESMEN
TRIBOLOGY
TRIBUNATE
TRIBUTARY
TRICERION
TRICKLESS
TRICKSTER
TRICLINIC
TRICOLOUR
TRIDYMITE
TRIENNIAL
TRIERARCH
TRIETERIC
TRIFORIUM
TRIHEDRON
TRILITHON
TRILOBITE
TRIMESTER
TRIMMINGS
TRINKETER
TRIPITAKA
TRIPMETER
TRISAGION
TRITENESS
TRITICALE
TRITURATE
TRIUMPHAL
TRIVIALLY
TROCHILIC
TROCHILUS
TROMPETTE
TRONDHEIM
TROOPSHIP
TROOSTITE
TROPAELIN
TROPARION
TROSSACHS
TROUBADOR
TROUSSEAU
TRUCKLOAD
TRUCULENT
TRUEPENNY
TRUMPEDUP
TRUMPETER
TRUNCATED
TRUNCHEON
TRUTINATE
TRYPHOEUS
TSAREVICH
TUBBINESS
TUILERIES
TUILLETTE
TUMESCENT
TUMMYACHE
TUNGSTATE
TURBIDITY
TURBINATE
TURBULENT
TURCOPOLE
TURMAGENT
TURNABOUT
TURNBULLS
TURNROUND
TURNSTILE
TURNSTONE
TURNTABLE
TURPITUDE
TURQUOISE
TUTIORISM
TWAYBLADE
TWENTIETH
TWINKLING
TYMPANIST
TYPICALLY
TYRANNIZE
TYRANNOUS
UKRAINIAN
ULIGINOUS
ULLSWATER
ULTIMATUM
ULTRONEUS
UMBILICAL
UMBILICUS
UMBRATILE
UMPTEENTH
UNABASHED
UNADOPTED
UNALLOYED
UNALTERED
UNANIMITY
UNANIMOUS
UNASHAMED
UNBALANCE
UNBEKNOWN
UNBENDING
UNBIASSED
UNBOUNDED
UNBRIDLED
UNCEASING
UNCERTAIN
UNCHANGED
UNCHARGED
UNCHECKED
UNCHRISOM
UNCLAIMED
UNCLOTHED
UNCLOUDED
UNCONCERN
UNCONFINE
UNCORRECT
UNCOUPLED
UNCOURTLY
UNCOVERED
UNCROSSED
UNCROWNED
UNDAMAGED
UNDAUNTED
UNDECIDED
UNDEFILED
UNDEFINED
UNDERBRED
UNDERCAST
UNDERCOAT
UNDERDONE
UNDERFELT
UNDERFOOT
UNDERHAND
UNDERLINE
UNDERLING
UNDERMINE
UNDERMOST
UNDERPAID
UNDERPASS
UNDERRATE
UNDERSEAL
UNDERSELL
UNDERSIDE
UNDERSIGN
UNDERSONG
UNDERTAKE
UNDERTONE
UNDERWALK
UNDERWEAR
UNDERWENT
UNDERWOOD
UNDILUTED
UNDIVIDED
UNDOUBTED
UNDRESSED
UNEARTHLY
UNEATABLE
UNEQUALED
UNETHICAL
UNEXPOSED
UNFAILING
UNFEELING
UNFITTING
UNFLEDGED
UNFOUNDED
UNGUARDED
UNHAPPILY
UNHEALTHY
UNHEEDING
UNHELPFUL
UNHOPEFUL
UNIFORMED
UNIFORMLY
UNINJURED
UNINVITED
UNISEXUAL
UNITARIAN
UNIVALENT
UNIVERSAL
UNKNOWING
UNLEARNED
UNLIMITED
UNLUCKILY
UNMARRIED
UNMATCHED

UNMINDFUL
UNMUSICAL
UNNATURAL
UNNERVING
UNNOTICED
UNOPPOSED
UNPOPULAR
UNPRECISE
UNREFINED
UNRELATED
UNRUFFLED
UNSAVOURY
UNSCATHED
UNSECURED
UNSELFISH
UNSETTLED
UNSHACKLE
UNSHEATHE
UNSIGHTLY
UNSINNING
UNSKILLED
UNSPARING
UNSPOILED
UNSULLIED
UNTENABLE
UNTIMEOUS
UNTOUCHED
UNTRAINED
UNTREATED
UNTRODDEN
UNTUTORED
UNTYPICAL
UNUSUALLY
UNVARYING
UNWATERED
UNWELCOME
UNWILLING
UNWITTING
UNWORRIED
UNWRITTEN
UPAITHRIC
UPANISHAD
UPCOUNTRY
UPHOLSTER
UPLIFTING
UPPERMOST
UPSETTING
URANISCUS
UREDINIAL
URICONIAN
URINATION
UROKINASE
URTICARIA
URUGUAYAN
USHERETTE
UTICENSIS
UTTERANCE
UTTERLESS
UTTERMOST
UVAROVITE
VACCINATE
VACILLATE
VAGUENESS
VAINGLORY
VALDENSES
VALENTINE
VALIANTLY
VALUATION
VALUELESS
VALVASSOR
VANCOUVER
VANDALISM
VANDALIZE
VANISHING
VANTBRASS
VAPORETTO
VAPORIZER
VARANGIAN
VARIATION
VARICELLA
VARIEGATE
VARIOLATE
VARIOUSLY
VARISCITE
VASECTOMY
VEGETABLE
VEGETATOR
VEHEMENCE
VEHICULAR
VEILLEUSE
VELASQUEZ
VELDSKOEN
VELLENAGE
VELLICATE
VELODROME
VELVETEEN
VENERABLE
VENEREOUS
VENEZUELA
VENGEANCE
VENIALITY
VENTIFACT
VENTILATE
VENTRICLE
VENUSBERG
VERACIOUS
VERATRINE
VERBALIZE
VERBASCUM
VERBERATE
VERBOSITY
VERDIGRIS
VERIDICAL
VERITABLE
VERKAMPTE
VERMIFORM
VERMIFUGE
VERMILION
VERMINOUS
VERSATILE
VERSIFIER
VERSIONAL
VERTEBRAE
VERTEBRAL
VERTIPORT
VERTUMNUS
VESICULAR
VESPASIAN
VESTIBULE
VESTIGIAL
VESTITURE
VESTMENTS
VEXATIONS
VEXATIOUS
VEXILLARY
VIABILITY
VIBRATILE
VIBRATION
VIBRATORY
VICARIOUS
VICEREGAL
VICEREINE
VICIOUSLY
VICTIMIZE
VICTORIAN
VICTORINE
VIDELICET
VIDEODISC
VIDEOTAPE
VIENTIANE
VIEWPOINT
VIGESIMAL
VIGILANCE
VIGILANTE
VINDICATE
VIOLATION
VIOLENTLY
VIOLINIST
VIRGINALS
VIRGINIAN
VIRGINITY
VIRGINIUM
VIRGULATE
VIRTUALLY
VIRULENCE
VISAGISTE
VISCOSITY
VISIONARY
VISUALIZE
VITASCOPE
VITELLIUS
VITIATION
VITRIOLIC
VITRUVIAN
VIVACIOUS
VIVIDNESS
VOICELESS
VOLAGEOUS
VOLATIBLE
VOLGOGRAD
VOLKSRAAD
VOLTIGEUR
VOLTINISM
VOLTMETER
VOLTURNUS
VOLUCRINE
VOLUNTARY
VOLUNTEER
VOODOOISM
VORACIOUS
VORTICISM
VORTIGERN
VOUCHSAFE
VULCANIST
VULCANITE
VULCANIZE
VULGARIAN
VULGARISM
VULGARITY
VULPINITE
WAFERTHIN
WAGENBOOM
WAGHALTER
WAGNERIAN
WAGNERITE
WAGONETTE
WAGONLOAD
WAHABIITE
WAISTBAND
WAISTCOAT
WAISTLINE
WAITERAGE
WALDENSES
WALDFLUTE
WALDGRAVE
WALKABOUT
WALLABIES
WALLOPING
WALLOWING
WALLPAPER
WALLYDRAG
WALPURGIS
WAMBENGER
WANCHANCY
WANDERING
WANWORTHY
WAPENTAKE
WAPINSHAW
WAREHOUSE
WARMONGER
WARTCRESS
WASHBASIN
WASHBOARD
WASHCLOTH
WASHERMAN
WASHSTAND
WASPISHLY
WASSERMAN
WASTELAND
WASTWATER
WATCHWORD
WATERBABY
WATERBUTT
WATERFALL
WATERFORD
WATERFOWL
WATERGATE
WATERHOLE
WATERLESS
WATERLILY
WATERLINE
WATERMARK
WATERMILL
WATERSHED
WATERSIDE
WATERWEED
WAVELLITE
WAYZGOOSE
WEAKENING
WEARINESS
WEARISOME
WEBFOOTED
WEDGEWOOD
WEDNESDAY
WEIGHTING
WEIRDNESS
WELCOMING
WELDSTADT
WELLBEING
WELLBUILT
WELLKNOWN
WELSUMMER
WELTGEIST
WENCESLAS
WESTBOUND
WESTERNER
WESTWARDS
WHALEBOAT
WHALEBONE
WHALEMEAT
WHEATGERM
WHEATMEAL
WHEELBASE
WHEREFORE
WHEREUPON
WHERRYMAN
WHETSTONE
WHICHEVER
WHIMSICAL
WHINSTONE
WHIPROUND
WHIPSNADE
WHIRLIGIG
WHIRLPOOL
WHIRLWIND
WHISTLING
WHITAKERS
WHITEBAIT
WHITEDAMP
WHITEFISH
WHITEHALL
WHITEHEAD
WHITENESS
WHITENING
WHITEWALL
WHITEWASH
WHITEWING
WHITEWOOD
WHITTAWER
WHITWORTH
WHIZZBANG
WHODUNNIT
WHOLEFOOD
WHOLEMEAL
WHOLENESS
WHOLESALE
WHOLESOME
WHOSOEVER
WHUNSTANE
WIDOWHOOD
WILDGEESE
WILLEMITE
WILLESDEN
WILLFULLY
WILLINGLY
WILLOWING
WILLPOWER
WIMBLEDON
WINCANTON
WINCOPIPE
WINDBREAK
WINDCHILL
WINDFALLS
WINDHOVER
WINDSCALE
WINDSWEPT
WINEBERRY
WINEGLASS
WINNEBAGO
WISCONSIN
WISECRACK
WISTFULLY

WITCHETTY
WITHDRAWN
WITHERING
WITHERITE
WITHSTAND
WITHYWIND
WITNESSED
WITTICISM
WITTINGLY
WOBBEGONG
WODEHOUSE
WOEBEGONE
WOLFHOUND
WOLLASTON
WOLVERINE
WOMANHOOD
WOMANISER
WOMANIZER
WOMANKIND
WOMENFOLK
WONDERFUL
WOODBORER
WOODCHUCK
WOODCRAFT
WOODENTOP
WOODHOUSE
WOODLANDS
WOODLOUSE
WOODSHOCK
WOOLINESS
WOOMERANG
WORCESTER
WORDINESS
WORDSMITH
WORKFORCE
WORKHORSE
WORKHOUSE
WORKPLACE
WORKSPACE
WORLDWIDE
WORMEATEN
WORRISOME
WORTHLESS
WRANGLERS
WREAKLESS
WRECKFISH
WRESTLING
WRONGDOER
WRONGFOOT
WULFENITE
WURLITZER
WUTHERING
WYANDOTTE
XANTHIPPE
XENOMANIA
XENOPHOBE
XEROPHYTE
XEROSTOMA
XYLOPHONE
YACHTSMAN
YACHTSMEN
YARDSTICK
YELLOWISH
YESTERDAY
YESTEREVE
YGGDRASIL
YOHIMBINE
YORKSHIRE
YOUNGSTER
YTTERBIUM
ZEALANDER
ZEITGEIST
ZENOCRATE
ZIBELLINE
ZINFANDEL
ZINKENITE
ZIRCONIUM
ZOOLOGIST
ZOOMANTIC
ZOOSCOPIC
ZOROASTER
ZUCCHETTO
ZYGOMATIC
ZYGOSPORE

9:2

BACHARACH
BACKBENCH
BACKBITER
BACKCLOTH
BACKPEDAL
BACKSHISH
BACKSLIDE
BACKSPACE
BACKSTAGE
BACKSWORD
BACKTRACK
BACKWARDS
BACKWATER
BACKWOODS
BACTERIAL
BACTERIUM
BADMINTON
BAGATELLE
BAINMARIE
BAKEHOUSE
BAKSHEESH
BALACLAVA
BALALAIKA
BALDAQUIN
BALEFULLY
BALLADEER
BALLADIST
BALLERINA
BALLISTIC
BALLPOINT
BALTHAZAR
BALTIMORE
BAMBOOZLE
BANDALORE
BANDICOOT
BANDOLEER
BANDOLERO
BANDOLIER
BANDOLINE
BANDSTAND
BANDWAGON
BANISTERS
BANQUETTE
BANTERING
BAPTISMAL
BARAGOUIN
BARBARIAN
BARBARITY
BARBAROUS
BARBITONE
BARBOTINE
BARCELONA
BAREBONES
BAREFACED
BARMBRACK
BARMECIDE
BARNABITE
BARNACLES
BARNSTORM
BAROMETER
BARRACUDA
BARRICADE
BARRISTER
BARTENDER
BARTHOLDI
BARTHOLIN
BARYSCOPE
BASEBOARD
BASECOURT
BASHFULLY
BASICALLY
BASILICAL
BASILICON
BASKETFUL
BASTINADE
BASTINADO
BATHTOWEL
BATTALION
BATTLEAXE
CABALLERO
CABLEGRAM
CABRIOLET
CACHAEMIA
CACHECTIC
CACOPHONY
CADASTRAL
CAESAREAN
CAFETERIA
CAFETIERE
CAGOULARD
CAIRNGORM
CAKESTAND
CALABOOSE
CALABRESE
CALCANEUM
CALCANEUS
CALCINATE
CALCULATE
CALDARIUM
CALEDONIA
CALEMBOUR
CALENDULA
CALENTURE
CALIBRATE
CALLIPERS
CALLOSITY
CALLOUSLY
CALORIFIC
CALPURNIA
CALVANISM
CALVINIST
CALVITIES
CAMBODIAN
CAMBRIDGE
CAMBUSCAN
CAMCORDER
CAMEMBERT
CAMERAMAN
CAMPANILE
CAMPANULA
CANALETTO
CANAVERAL
CANCEROUS
CANDIDACY
CANDIDATE
CANDLELIT
CANDLEMAS
CANDYTUFT
CANNELURE
CANNONADE
CANONICAL
CANTABILE
CANTHARIS
CANTHARUS
CANTONESE
CANVASSER
CAPACIOUS
CAPACITOR
CAPARISON
CAPILLARY
CAPITULAR
CAPITULUM
CAPORETTO
CAPRICCIO
CAPRICORN
CAPTAINCY
CAPTIVATE
CAPTIVITY
CARACALLA
CARAMBOLA
CARBAMATE
CARBAMIDE
CARBONADE
CARBONARI
CARBONATE
CARBONIZE
CARBUNCLE
CARCINOMA
CARDBOARD
CAREERIST
CAREFULLY
CARETAKER
CARIBBEAN
CARMELITE
CARNATION
CARNELIAN
CARNIVORE
CARPACCIO
CARPENTER
CARPENTRY
CARPETING
CARTESIAN
CARTHORSE
CARTILAGE
CARTOGRAM
CARTOUCHE
CARTRIDGE
CARTTRACK
CARTULARY
CARTWHEEL
CARYOPSIS
CASHPOINT
CASSANDRA
CASSATION
CASSEROLE
CASSONADE
CASSOULET
CASSOWARY
CASTANETS
CASTIGATE
CASTILIAN
CASTRATED
CASUARINA
CASUISTIC
CASUISTRY
CATACLYSM
CATACOMBS
CATALEPSY
CATALOGUE
CATALYSIS
CATALYTIC
CATAMARAN
CATAPLASM
CATAPLEXY
CATARRHAL
CATATONIA
CATATONIC
CATCHCROP
CATCHMENT
CATCHPOLE
CATCHPOLL
CATCHWORD
CATECHISM
CATECHIZE
CATERWAUL
CATHARSIS
CATHARTIC
CATHEDRAL
CATHEPSIN
CATHERINE
CATSKILLS
CATTLEMAN
CATTLEPEN
CAUCASIAN
CAUSATION
CAUTERIZE
CAVALCADE
CAVENDISH
CAVERNOUS
CAVORTING
DACHSHUND
DAEDALIAN
DAIRYMAID
DALLIANCE
DALMATIAN
DALTONISM
DAMASCENE
DAMBUSTER
DAMNATION
DAMNEDEST
DANDELION
DANDIFIED
DANDYPRAT
DANGEROUS
DAREDEVIL
DARTAGNAN
DARTBOARD
DARTMOUTH
DARWINIAN
DASHBOARD
DASHWHEEL
DASTARDLY
DAUNTLESS
DAVENPORT

DAYSPRING
EAGERNESS
EAGLEWOOD
EALDORMAN
EARNESTLY
EARTHFLAX
EARTHLING
EARTHWORK
EARTHWORM
EASTBOUND
EASTERNER
EASTLINGS
EASTWARDS
EASYGOING
EAVESDROP
FABACEOUS
FABRICATE
FABULINUS
FACECLOTH
FACETIOUS
FACSIMILE
FACTIONAL
FACTORISE
FACTUALLY
FACUNDITY
FAINTNESS
FAIRYLAND
FAIRYTALE
FAITHLESS
FALANGIST
FALDSTOOL
FALERNIAN
FALKLANDS
FALLOPIAN
FALSEHOOD
FALSENESS
FAMAGUSTA
FANATICAL
FANDANGLE
FANTASIZE
FANTASTIC
FARANDOLE
FARMHOUSE
FARMSTEAD
FASCINATE
FASHIONED
FASTENING
FASTTRACK
FATIDICAL
FATISCENT
FATTENING
FATUOUSLY
FAULCHION
FAULTLESS
FAVORABLE
FAVORABLY
FAVOURITE

GABARDINE
GABERDINE
GABIONADE
GAELTACHT
GAINFULLY
GAINSAYER
GALACTOSE
GALANTINE
GALAPAGOS
GALDRAGON
GALENGALE
GALINGALE
GALIONGEE
GALLABEAH
GALLANTLY
GALLANTRY
GALLICISM
GALLINULE
GALLIPOLI
GALLIVANT
GALLOPADE
GALLSTONE
GALLYCROW
GALRAVAGE
GALVANISM
GALVANIZE
GANGPLANK
GARDENING
GARDEROBE
GARGANTUA
GARGARISM
GARIBALDI
GARNISHEE
GARNITURE
GARRULITY
GARRULOUS
GARRYOWEN
GASCONADE
GASHOLDER
GASOMETER
GASPEREAU
GATECRASH
GATESHEAD
GATHERING
GAUDEAMUS
GAUDINESS
GAULEITER
GAUNTNESS
GAVELKIND
GAWKINESS
GAZETTEER
HABERDINE
HABERGEON
HABITABLE
HABITUATE
HACKAMORE
HACKNEYED

HACQUETON
HADROSAUR
HAECCEITY
HAEMALOMA
HAEMATITE
HAILSTONE
HAILSTORM
HAIRBRUSH
HAIRPIECE
HAIRSTYLE
HALFBAKED
HALFDOZEN
HALFEMPTY
HALFPENNY
HALFSTAFF
HALITOSIS
HALLOWEEN
HALLOWMAS
HALLSTATT
HALOBIONT
HALOPHILE
HALOTHANE
HAMADRYAD
HAMBURGER
HAMFATTER
HAMFISTED
HAMMERING
HAMMURABI
HAMPSTEAD
HAMSTRING
HAMSTRUNG
HANDBRAKE
HANDCUFFS
HANDINESS
HANDIWORK
HANDPIECE
HANDSHAKE
HANDSPIKE
HANDSTAND
HANKERING
HANSEATIC
HAPHAZARD
HAPPENING
HAPPINESS
HARBINGER
HARDANGER
HARDBOARD
HARDCOVER
HARDIHOOD
HARDINESS
HARDLINER
HARDSHELL
HARESTANE
HARIGALDS
HARIOLATE
HARLEQUIN
HARLESTON

HARMALINE
HARMATTAN
HARMONICA
HARMONIST
HARMONIUM
HARMONIZE
HARMOTOME
HARPOONER
HARQUEBUS
HARROGATE
HARROWING
HARSHNESS
HARTSHORN
HARVESTER
HASHEMITE
HASTENING
HASTINESS
HATCHBACK
HATCHMENT
HAUGHTILY
HAUTMONDE
HAVERSACK
HAWCUBITE
HAWKSBILL
HAWTHORNE
HAYMAKING
HAYMARKET
HAYRADDIN
HAZARDOUS
HAZELWORT
JACARANDA
JACKKNIFE
JACKSNIPE
JACKSTRAW
JACQUERIE
JAGGANATH
JAMBALAYA
JAMPACKED
JANISSARY
JANSENISM
JANSENIST
JARLSBERG
JAUNDICED
JAWBATION
JAYWALKER
KABELJOUW
KALSOMINE
KARABINER
KARAKORAM
KARYOTYPE
LABORIOUS
LABOURITE
LABYRINTH
LACCOLITE
LACERATED
LACHRYMAL
LACINIATE

LACKBEARD
LACONICAL
LACTATION
LADYSMITH
LAEVULOSE
LAFAYETTE
LAGNIAPPE
LAGOMORPH
LAMARTINE
LAMASERAI
LAMBSWOOL
LAMINATED
LAMPADARY
LAMPADION
LAMPBLACK
LAMPLIGHT
LAMPSHADE
LANCASTER
LANCEWOOD
LANCINATE
LANDAULET
LANDDROST
LANDGRAVE
LANDLOPER
LANDOWNER
LANDSCAPE
LANDSLIDE
LANDSMAAL
LANDSTURM
LANDWARDS
LANGOUSTE
LANGRIDGE
LANGSPIEL
LANGUAGES
LANGUEDOC
LANGUETTE
LANGUIDLY
LANKINESS
LANTHANUM
LAODICEAN
LAPLANDER
LAPSTREAK
LARGENESS
LARGHETTO
LARGITION
LASERWORT
LASSITUDE
LASTDITCH
LATECOMER
LATENIGHT
LATERALLY
LATESCENT
LATHYRISM
LATICLAVE
LATRATION
LATTERDAY
LAUDATION

LAUDATORY
LAUGHABLE
LAUNCELOT
LAUNCHING
LAUNDRESS
LAVOISIER
LAWMAKING
LAWMONGER
LAWNMOWER
LAZARETTO
LAZYBONES
LAZZARONE
MACADAMIA
MACARONIC
MACARTHUR
MACDONALD
MACEDOINE
MACEDONIA
MACHINATE
MACHINERY
MACHINING
MACHINIST
MACKENZIE
MACQUARIE
MACROCOSM
MACROLOGY
MACTATION
MADARIAGA
MADAROSIS
MADDENING
MADELEINE
MADRASSAH
MADREPORE
MADRESSAH
MADRILENE
MAELSTROM
MAGDALENE
MAGDEBURG
MAGICALLY
MAGNALIUM
MAGNESIUM
MAGNETISM
MAGNETIZE
MAGNETRON
MAGNIFIER
MAGNITUDE
MAHARAJAH
MAHARANEE
MAHARISHI
MAINFRAME
MAINTENON
MAJORDOMO
MAJORETTE
MAJUSCULE
MAKESHIFT
MALACHITE
MALATHION

MALAYSIAN
MALEBOLGE
MALENGINE
MALFORMED
MALICIOUS
MALIGNANT
MALIGNITY
MALLANDER
MALLEABLE
MALLEMUCK
MALLENDER
MALLEOLUS
MAMMALIAN
MANDATORY
MANDICATE
MANDOLINE
MANDUCATE
MANGANATE
MANGANESE
MANGETOUT
MANGOUSTE
MANHANDLE
MANHATTAN
MANIFESTO
MANLINESS
MANNEQUIN
MANNERING
MANNERISM
MANOEUVRE
MANOMETER
MANSFIELD
MANUBRIUM
MAPPEMOND
MARAUDING
MARCASITE
MARCHPANE
MARGARINE
MARIJUANA
MARKETEER
MARKETING
MARMALADE
MARMOREAL
MARQUESAS
MARQUETRY
MARROWFAT
MARSHLAND
MARSUPIAL
MARSUPIUM
MARTINEAU
MARTINMAS
MARTYRDOM
MARVELOUS
MASCULINE
MASEFIELD
MASOCHISM
MASOCHIST
MASSINGER

MASSIVELY
MASSORETE
MASSYMORE
MASTERFUL
MASTERMAN
MASTICATE
MATCHLESS
MATCHLOCK
MATCHWOOD
MATELASSE
MATERNITY
MATHURINE
MATRIARCH
MATRICIDE
MATRIMONY
MATTAMORE
MATUTINAL
MAULSTICK
MAURITIAN
MAURITIUS
MAUSOLEUM
MAVOURNIN
MAXILLARY
MAYFLOWER
MAYORALTY
NABATHEAN
NAKEDNESS
NAMEPLATE
NANTUCKET
NAPIERIAN
NARCISSUS
NARGHILLY
NARRATION
NARRATIVE
NARROWING
NASEBERRY
NASHVILLE
NASTINESS
NATHANIEL
NATHELESS
NATHEMORE
NATROLITE
NATURALLY
NAUGHTILY
NAUMACHIA
NAUSEATED
NAVIGABLE
NAVIGATOR
OARSWOMAN
OASTHOUSE
PACEMAKER
PACHYDERM
PACKAGING
PADEMELON
PAGEANTRY
PAGLIACCI
PAILLASSE

PAILLETTE
PAINFULLY
PAINTWORK
PAKISTANI
PALAESTRA
PALAFITTE
PALAMPORE
PALANKEEN
PALANQUIN
PALATABLE
PALEMPORE
PALEOLITH
PALESTINE
PALINURUS
PALLADIAN
PALLADIUM
PALLIASSE
PALMATION
PALMISTRY
PALMITATE
PALOVERDE
PALPATION
PALPEBRAL
PALPITATE
PALSGRAVE
PALUDRINE
PANATELLA
PANCHAYAT
PANDATION
PANDEMIAN
PANDURATE
PANEGOISM
PANEGYRIC
PANELLING
PANELLIST
PANETTONE
PANHANDLE
PANNIKELL
PANORAMIC
PANTAGAMY
PANTALEON
PANTALOON
PANTHEISM
PANTHENOL
PANTOFFLE
PANTOMIME
PANTOUFLE
PAPARAZZI
PAPARAZZO
PAPERBACK
PAPERCLIP
PAPERWORK
PAPILLOTE
PARABASIS
PARABLAST
PARABOLIC
PARACHUTE

PARACLETE
PARACUSIS
PARAGOGUE
PARAGRAPH
PARALYSIS
PARALYTIC
PARAMEDIC
PARAMETER
PARAMOUNT
PARANOIAC
PARANYMPH
PARASCENE
PARASCEVE
PARASITIC
PARATHION
PARATROOP
PARBUCKLE
PARCHEESI
PARCHMENT
PARDALOTE
PAREGORIC
PARENTAGE
PARENTING
PARFLECHE
PARHELION
PARHYPATE
PARNASITE
PARNASSUS
PAROCHIAL
PAROCHINE
PAROTITIS
PARRICIDE
PARSIMONY
PARSONAGE
PARTAKING
PARTHENON
PARTHOLON
PARTIALLY
PARTICLES
PARTITION
PARTRIDGE
PARTTIMER
PASSAMENT
PASSENGER
PASSEPIED
PASSERINE
PASSIVELY
PASSIVITY
PASTERNAK
PASTICCIO
PASTORALE
PASTURAGE
PATCHOULI
PATCHOULY
PATCHWORK
PATERCOVE
PATERNITY

PATHOGENY
PATHOLOGY
PATHTRAIN
PATIENTLY
PATRIARCH
PATRICIAN
PATRICIDE
PATRIMONY
PATRIOTIC
PATROCLUS
PATROLMAN
PATRONAGE
PATRONESS
PATRONIZE
PATTERNED
PAULOWNIA
PAUSANIAS
PAWKINESS
PAYCHEQUE
PAYMASTER
RACCABOUT
RACCAHOUT
RACEHORSE
RACETRACK
RACIALISM
RACIALIST
RACKETEER
RACKSTRAW
RACONTEUR
RADCLIFFE
RADDLEMAN
RADIANTLY
RADIATING
RADIATION
RADICALLY
RADICCHIO
RADIOGRAM
RADIOLOGY
RAFFINOSE
RAINCHECK
RAINGAUGE
RAINSTORM
RAINWATER
RAMILLIES
RANCIDITY
RANCOROUS
RANDINESS
RANTIPOLE
RAPACIOUS
RAPTORIAL
RAPTUROUS
RASKOLNIK
RASPATORY
RASPBERRY
RATEPAYER
RATHERIPE
RATHERISH

RATIONALE
RATIONING
RATTLEBAG
RAUCOUSLY
RAVISHING
RAZORBILL
SABBATIAN
SACCHARIN
SACKCLOTH
SACKERSON
SACRAMENT
SACRARIUM
SACRIFICE
SACRILEGE
SACRISTAN
SADDENING
SADDLEBAG
SAFEGUARD
SAFFLOWER
SAGACIOUS
SAGAPENUM
SAGITTARY
SAILCLOTH
SAINTFOIN
SAINTHOOD
SALACIOUS
SALANGANE
SALERATUS
SALESGIRL
SALESLADY
SALICETUM
SALLYPORT
SALLYPOST
SALOPETTE
SALTINESS
SALTPETER
SALTPETRE
SALTWATER
SALUBRITY
SALVARSAN
SALVATION
SAMARITAN
SANCTUARY
SANDALLED
SANDARACH
SANDHURST
SANDPAPER
SANDPIPER
SANDSTONE
SANDSTORM
SANGFROID
SANHEDRIM
SANHEDRIN
SANHEDRON
SANNYASIN
SANTAYANA
SAPSUCKER

SARBACANE
SARCASTIC
SARMENTUM
SARTORIAL
SARTORIUS
SASKATOON
SASQUATCH
SASSAFRAS
SASSENACH
SASSOLITE
SATELLITE
SATIATION
SATINWOOD
SATIRICAL
SATISFIED
SATURATED
SATURNIAN
SATURNINE
SATURNISM
SATYRIDAE
SATYRINAE
SAUCEBOAT
SAUCINESS
SAUCISSON
SAUTERNES
SAUVIGNON
SAVERNAKE
SAXIFRAGE
SAXITOXIN
SAXOPHONE
TABANIDAE
TABASHEER
TABBOULEH
TABELLION
TABLATURE
TABLELAND
TABLEWARE
TABULATOR
TACAMAHAC
TACHILITE
TACHYLITE
TACHYLYTE
TACKINESS
TACTFULLY
TACTICIAN
TAHSILDAR
TAILBOARD
TAILLEFER
TAILLIGHT
TAILPIECE
TAILPLANE
TALKATIVE
TALMUDIST
TAMERLANE
TAMOXIFEN
TANGERINE
TANTALITE
TANTALIZE
TANTARARA
TANZANIAN
TAOISEACH
TAPDANCER
TARANTASS
TARANTULA
TARAXACUM
TARDINESS
TARGETEER
TARMACKED
TARNATION
TARPAULIN
TARRAGONA
TARTAREAN
TASMANIAN
TASSELLED
TASTELESS
TAUCHNITZ
TAUTOLOGY
TAVERNERS
TAVISTOCK
TAXIDERMY
TAXIMETER
TAYASSUID
VACCINATE
VACILLATE
VAGUENESS
VAINGLORY
VALDENSES
VALENTINE
VALIANTLY
VALUATION
VALUELESS
VALVASSOR
VANCOUVER
VANDALISM
VANDALIZE
VANISHING
VANTBRASS
VAPORETTO
VAPORIZER
VARANGIAN
VARIATION
VARICELLA
VARIEGATE
VARIOLATE
VARIOUSLY
VARISCITE
VASECTOMY
WAFERTHIN
WAGENBOOM
WAGHALTER
WAGNERIAN
WAGNERITE
WAGONETTE
WAGONLOAD
WAHABIITE
WAISTBAND
WAISTCOAT
WAISTLINE
WAITERAGE
WALDENSES
WALDFLUTE
WALDGRAVE
WALKABOUT
WALLABIES
WALLOPING
WALLOWING
WALLPAPER
WALLYDRAG
WALPURGIS
WAMBENGER
WANCHANCY
WANDERING
WANWORTHY
WAPENTAKE
WAPINSHAW
WAREHOUSE
WARMONGER
WARTCRESS
WASHBASIN
WASHBOARD
WASHCLOTH
WASHERMAN
WASHSTAND
WASPISHLY
WASSERMAN
WASTELAND
WASTWATER
WATCHWORD
WATERBABY
WATERBUTT
WATERFALL
WATERFORD
WATERFOWL
WATERGATE
WATERHOLE
WATERLESS
WATERLILY
WATERLINE
WATERMARK
WATERMILL
WATERSHED
WATERSIDE
WATERWEED
WAVELLITE
WAYZGOOSE
XANTHIPPE
YACHTSMAN
YACHTSMEN
YARDSTICK
ABANDONED
ABANDONEE
ABASEMENT
ABATEMENT
ABDOMINAL
ABDUCTION
ABERNETHY
ABERRANCE
ABHORRENT
ABLUTIONS
ABOLITION
ABOMINATE
ABORIGINE
ABOUNDING
ABOUTFACE
ABOUTTURN
ABSCONDER
ABSORBENT
ABSORBING
ABSTAINER
ABSTINENT
ABSURDITY
ABUNDANCE
ABYSMALLY
EBRILLADE
EBULLIENT
IBUPROFEN
OBBLIGATO
OBCORDATE
OBEDIENCE
OBEISANCE
OBFUSCATE
OBJECTION
OBJECTIVE
OBJURGATE
OBLIQUELY
OBLIVIOUS
OBNOXIOUS
OBREPTION
OBSCENELY
OBSCENITY
OBSCURELY
OBSCURITY
OBSECRATE
OBSEQUIES
OBSERVANT
OBSESSION
OBSESSIVE
OBSTETRIC
OBSTINACY
OBSTINATE
OBTAINING
OBTRUSION
OBTRUSIVE
OBVENTION
OBVIOUSLY
ACADEMIST
ACARIASIS
ACCESSION
ACCESSORY
ACCIDENTS
ACCLIMATE
ACCLIVITY
ACCOMPANY
ACCORDANT
ACCORDING
ACCORDION
ACCRETION
ACETYLENE
ACIDULATE
ACIDULOUS
ACONCAGUA
ACOUSTICS
ACQUIESCE
ACQUITTAL
ACROBATIC
ACROPHONY
ACROPOLIS
ACTUALITY
ACTUARIAL
ACUMINATE
ACUTENESS
ECARDINES
ECCENTRIC
ECHEVERIA
ECHIDNINE
ECLAMPSIA
ECOLOGIST
ECONOMICS
ECONOMIST
ECONOMIZE
ECOSSAISE
ECOSYSTEM
ECTOMORPH
ECTOPLASM
ECTROPION
ICELANDER
ICELANDIC
ICHNEUMON
ICHNOLITE
ICTERIDAE
OCCIPITAL
OCCLUSION
OCCULTIST
OCCUPANCY
OCCUPYING
OCEANIDES
OCHLOCRAT
OCKHAMIST
OCTACHORD
OCTAGONAL
OCTASTICH
OCTILLION
OCTOBRIST
OCULIFORM
SCABLANDS
SCAGLIOLA
SCALARIUM
SCALDFISH
SCALEABLE
SCALLAWAG
SCALLIONS
SCALLOPED
SCALLYWAG
SCAMBLING
SCANSORES
SCANTLING
SCAPEGOAT
SCAPOLITE
SCARECROW
SCARIFIER
SCARLATTI
SCATTERED
SCAVENGER
SCELERATE
SCENTLESS
SCEPTICAL
SCHEELITE
SCHEHITAH
SCHELLING
SCHEMATIC
SCHIAVONE
SCHILLING
SCHLEMIEL
SCHLEMIHL
SCHLENTER
SCHLIEREN
SCHMALTZY
SCHMIEDER
SCHMUTTER
SCHNAPPER
SCHNAUZER
SCHNECKEN
SCHNITTKE
SCHNITZEL
SCHNORKEL
SCHNORRER
SCHNOZZLE
SCHOLARCH
SCHOLARLY
SCHOLIAST
SCHOOLBOY
SCHOOLING
SCHOOLMAN
SCIAMACHY
SCIARIDAE
SCIENTISM
SCIENTIST
SCINTILLA
SCIOMANCY
SCISSORER
SCLAUNDER
SCLEROSIS

SCLEROTAL
SCOLECITE
SCOLIOSIS
SCOLIOTIC
SCONCHEON
SCORBUTIC
SCORBUTUS
SCORCHING
SCORODITE
SCOTCHMAN
SCOUNDREL
SCRAMBLER
SCRAPBOOK
SCRAPINGS
SCRAPPING
SCRATCHED
SCRATCHES
SCREENING
SCREWBALL
SCREWEDUP
SCREWPINE
SCREWTAPE
SCRIMMAGE
SCRIMPING
SCRIMSHAW
SCRIPTURE
SCRIVENER
SCRODDLED
SCROUNGER
SCRUBBING
SCRUFFILY
SCRUMMAGE
SCRUMPING
SCRUTATOR
SCUDDALER
SCULPTING
SCULPTURE
SCUNCHEON
SCURRIOUR
SCYTHEMAN
ADAPTABLE
ADDERWORT
ADDICTION
ADDICTIVE
ADDRESSED
ADDRESSEE
ADENOIDAL
ADEPTNESS
ADHERENCE
ADJECTIVE
ADJOINING
ADMIRABLE
ADMIRABLY
ADMIRALTY
ADMISSION
ADMITTING
ADMIXTURE
ADMONITOR
ADORATION
ADORNMENT
ADRENALIN
ADULATION
ADULTERER
ADULTHOOD
ADUMBRATE
ADVANTAGE
ADVECTION
ADVENTIST
ADVENTURE
ADVERBIAL
ADVERSARY
ADVERSELY
ADVERSITY
ADVERTISE
ADVISABLE
ADVISEDLY
ADVOCATED
EDDINGTON
EDDYSTONE
EDELWEISS
EDGEWORTH
EDINBURGH
EDITORIAL
EDUCATION
EDUCATIVE
EDWARDIAN
IDEALOGUE
IDENTICAL
IDENTIKIT
IDEOGRAPH
IDEOPATHY
IDIOBLAST
IDIOGRAPH
IDIOMATIC
IDIOPHONE
IDIOPLASM
IDIOTICON
ODALISQUE
ODDJOBMAN
ODELSTING
ODOURLESS
SDEIGNFUL
AEPYORNIS
AERODROME
AEROPLANE
AEROSPACE
AEROTAXIS
AESCHYLUS
AESTHETIC
BEACHHEAD
BEACHWEAR
BEANFEAST
BEARDLESS
BEARDSLEY
BEATITUDE
BEAUTEOUS
BEAUTIFUL
BECHSTEIN
BECQUEREL
BEDFELLOW
BEDJACKET
BEDRAGGLE
BEDRIDDEN
BEDSITTER
BEDSPREAD
BEEFEATER
BEEFSTEAK
BEEKEEPER
BEELZEBUB
BEESTINGS
BEETHOVEN
BEGINNING
BEHAVIOUR
BELATEDLY
BELEAGUER
BELIEVING
BELLICOSE
BELLYACHE
BELLYFLOP
BELONGING
BELVEDERE
BENBECULA
BENCHMARK
BENIGHTED
BERGAMASK
BERGANDER
BERGOMASK
BERKELIUM
BERNSTEIN
BERYLLIUM
BESPANGLE
BETHLEHEM
BETROTHAL
BETROTHED
BETTERTON
BEVERIDGE
CEASEFIRE
CEASELESS
CEDARWOOD
CELANDINE
CELEBRANT
CELEBRATE
CELEBRITY
CELESTIAL
CELLARIST
CELLULITE
CELLULOID
CELLULOSE
CENTAURUS
CENTENARY
CENTERING
CENTIPEDE
CENTRALLY
CENTREING
CENTURION
CERATITIS
CERATODUS
CEREBRATE
CEROMANCY
CERTAINLY
CERTAINTY
CERTIFIED
CERTITUDE
CERVANTES
CESSATION
CEVAPCICI
CEYLONESE
DEACONESS
DEADLIGHT
DEAFENING
DEATHLESS
DEATHTRAP
DEBATABLE
DEBAUCHED
DEBAUCHEE
DEBENTURE
DEBUTANTE
DECACHORD
DECADENCE
DECALITRE
DECALOGUE
DECAMERON
DECASTYLE
DECATHLON
DECEITFUL
DECEMVIRI
DECEPTION
DECEPTIVE
DECESSION
DECIDEDLY
DECIDUOUS
DECILLION
DECKCHAIR
DECLARING
DECLINING
DECLIVITY
DECOCTION
DECOLLATE
DECOMPOSE
DECONTROL
DECORATED
DECORATOR
DECRETALS
DECUMBENT
DECURSIVE
DECUSSATE
DEDICATED
DEDUCTION
DEDUCTIVE
DEERHOUND
DEFALCATE
DEFAULTER
DEFEATISM
DEFEATIST
DEFECTION
DEFECTIVE
DEFENDANT
DEFENDERS
DEFENSIVE
DEFERENCE
DEFERMENT
DEFICIENT
DEFINABLE
DEFLATION
DEFLECTOR
DEFOLIANT
DEFOLIATE
DEFORMITY
DEGRADING
DEHYDRATE
DEJECTION
DELACROIX
DELICIOUS
DELIGHTED
DELINEATE
DELIRIOUS
DELIVERER
DEMAGOGUE
DEMANDING
DEMARCATE
DEMEANING
DEMEANOUR
DEMETRIUS
DEMITASSE
DEMOCRACY
DEMULCENT
DEMURRAGE
DENIGRATE
DENSENESS
DENTISTRY
DENTITION
DEODORANT
DEODORIZE
DEOXIDISE
DEPARTURE
DEPENDANT
DEPENDENT
DEPENDING
DEPICTION
DEPOSITOR
DEPRAVITY
DEPRECATE
DEPREDATE
DEPRESSED
DERRINGER
DESCARTES
DESECRATE
DESERTION
DESERVING
DESICCATE
DESIGNATE
DESIGNING
DESIPIENT
DESIRABLE
DESPERADO
DESPERATE
DESPOTISM
DESTITUTE
DESTROYED
DESTROYER
DESUETUDE
DESULTORY
DETECTION
DETECTIVE
DETENTION
DETERGENT
DETERMINE
DETERRENT
DETONATOR
DETRACTOR
DETRIMENT
DETRITION
DEUCALION
DEUTERIUM
DEVASTATE
DEVELOPED
DEVELOPER
DEVIATION
DEVILMENT
DEVIOUSLY
DEVONPORT
DEXTERITY
DEXTEROUS
DEXTRORSE
FEARFULLY
FEATHERED
FEBRIFUGE
FECUNDITY
FEDUCIARY
FEEDSTUFF
FENCIBLES
FENUGREEK
FERACIOUS
FERDINAND
FERINGHEE
FERMENTED
FEROCIOUS
FERRYBOAT
FERTILITY
FERTILIZE
FERVENTLY
FESTINATE

FESTIVITY
FEUDALISM
FEUDATORY
FEUILLANT
GEARLEVER
GEARSHIFT
GEARSTICK
GEARWHEEL
GELIGNITE
GENEALOGY
GENERALLY
GENERATOR
GENETICAL
GENEVIEVE
GENIALITY
GENITALIA
GENTEELLY
GENTILITY
GENTLEMAN
GENTLEMEN
GENUFLECT
GENUINELY
GEODESIST
GEOGRAPHY
GEOLOGIST
GEOMETRIC
GEOMETRID
GEORGETTE
GERFALCON
GERIATRIC
GERMANCER
GERMANDER
GERMANITE
GERMANIUM
GERMICIDE
GERMINATE
GERUNDIVE
GESSAMINE
GESTATION
HEADBOARD
HEADCLOTH
HEADDRESS
HEADFIRST
HEADINESS
HEADLIGHT
HEADLINED
HEADSCARF
HEADSTALL
HEADSTONE
HEALTHILY
HEARDSMAN
HEARTACHE
HEARTBEAT
HEARTBURN
HEARTFELT
HEARTHRUG
HEARTLAND
HEARTLESS
HEATHLAND
HEAVINESS
HEAVISIDE
HEAVYDUTY
HEBRIDEAN
HECOGENIN
HECTORING
HEDERATED
HEDYPHANE
HELLEBORE
HELPFULLY
HELVELLYN
HEMINGWAY
HEMIPTERA
HEMISTICH
HEMITROPE
HEMSTITCH
HENDIADYS
HENPECKED
HEPATICAL
HEPATITIS
HERBALIST
HERBARIUM
HERBICIDE
HERBIVORE
HERBORIST
HERCULEAN
HEREAFTER
HERETICAL
HERMANDAD
HERMITAGE
HERODOTUS
HERONSHAW
HERPESTES
HESITANCE
HESITANCY
HESPERIAN
HESSONITE
HESTERNAL
HESYCHASM
HESYCHAST
HETERODOX
HETEROSIS
HEURISTIC
HEXAGONAL
HEXAMERON
HEXAMETER
HEXASTICH
HEXATEUCH
HEYPRESTO
JEALOUSLY
JELLYFISH
JENNETING
JEPHTHAHS
JEQUIRITY
JERAHMEEL
JERKINESS
JERKWATER
JERUSALEM
JESSAMINE
JESSERANT
JETSTREAM
JEWELLERY
KENTIGERN
KENTLEDGE
KEPLARIAN
KERATITIS
KERBSTONE
KERFUFFLE
KERMESITE
KEYHOLDER
KEYSTROKE
LEAFMOULD
LEAKPROOF
LEASEHOLD
LEASTWAYS
LEASTWISE
LECANORAM
LECHEROUS
LEFTOVERS
LEGENDARY
LEGIONARY
LEGISLATE
LEHRJAHRE
LEICESTER
LEISURELY
LEITMOTIF
LEITMOTIV
LENGTHILY
LENIENTLY
LENINGRAD
LEPROSERY
LESTRIGON
LETHARGIC
LETTERBOX
LETTERING
LEUCOCYTE
LEUCOTOME
LEUKAEMIA
LEVANTINE
LEVERAGED
LEVIATHAN
LEVITICUS
MEANDRIAN
MEANWHILE
MEASURING
MEATBALLS
MECHANICS
MECHANISM
MECHANIZE
MEDALLION
MEDALLIST
MEDIAEVAL
MEDIATION
MEDICALLY
MEDICATED
MEDICINAL
MEDITATOR
MEDMENHAM
MEDRESSEH
MEGACYCLE
MEGAHERTZ
MEGAPHONE
MEGASCOPE
MEGASPORE
MEHITABEL
MEKOMETER
MELAMPODE
MELANESIA
MELANOTIC
MELBOURNE
MELIORATE
MELODIOUS
MELODRAMA
MELONLIKE
MELPOMENE
MEMORABLE
MEMORITER
MENADIONE
MENAGERIE
MENDACITY
MENDELISM
MENDICANT
MENIPPEAN
MENNONITE
MENOMINEE
MENOPAUSE
MENSHEVIK
MENSTRUAL
MENSTRUUM
MENTALITY
MENTATION
MENTICIDE
MENTIONED
MENUISIER
MEPACRINE
MERCAPTAN
MERCENARY
MERCERIZE
MERCILESS
MERCURIAL
MERESWINE
MERGANSER
MERRIMENT
MESENTERY
MESMERISM
MESMERIZE
MESOBLAST
MESOMORPH
MESSALINA
MESSENGER
MESSIANIC
METABASIS
METABOLIC
METALLOID
METALWORK
METAPELET
METEORITE
METEOROID
METHADONE
METHEGLIN
METHODISM
METHODIST
METRICATE
METROLAND
METRONOME
MEZZANINE
MEZZOTINT
NEBBISHER
NECESSARY
NECESSITY
NECKVERSE
NECTARINE
NEFANDOUS
NEFARIOUS
NEFERTITI
NEGLECTED
NEGLIGENT
NEGOTIATE
NEGRITUDE
NEIGHBOUR
NEOLITHIC
NEOLOGISM
NEPHALISM
NEPHALIST
NEPHELINE
NEPHRITIC
NEPHRITIS
NEPTUNIUM
NERITIDAE
NERVOUSLY
NESCIENCE
NEUCHATEL
NEURALGIA
NEURALGIC
NEUROGLIA
NEUROLOGY
NEUTRALLY
NEVERMORE
NEWCASTLE
NEWLYWEDS
NEWMARKET
NEWSAGENT
NEWSFLASH
NEWSHOUND
NEWSPAPER
NEWSPRINT
NEWSSHEET
NEWSSTALL
NEWSSTAND
OESTROGEN
PEACEABLE
PEACEABLY
PEACETIME
PEARLWORT
PEASANTRY
PEASEWEEP
PECKSNIFF
PECULATOR
PECUNIARY
PEDAGOGUE
PEDERASTY
PEDICULAR
PEDIGREES
PEDOMETER
PEEVISHLY
PEGMATITE
PEIRASTIC
PEKINGESE
PELLAGRIN
PELLITORY
PELMANISM
PEMPHIGUS
PENDENNIS
PENDLETON
PENDRAGON
PENDULATE
PENDULOUS
PENETRATE
PENFRIEND
PENILLION
PENINSULA
PENISTONE
PENITENCE
PENNILESS
PENPUSHER
PENSIONER
PENSIVELY
PENTECOST
PENTHOUSE
PENTOSANE
PENURIOUS
PEPPERONI
PEPPERPOT
PERAEOPOD
PERCALINE
PERCHANCE
PERCHERON
PERCOLATE
PERDITION
PEREGRINE
PERENNIAL
PERFECTLY
PERFERVID

PERFORANS
PERFORATE
PERFORMED
PERFORMER
PERFUMERY
PERGAMENE
PERGUNNAH
PERIAKTOS
PERIANDER
PERIBOLOS
PERICLASE
PERICUTIN
PERIMETER
PERIMORPH
PERIODATE
PERIPATUS
PERIPHERY
PERISCIAN
PERISCOPE
PERISHING
PERISTOME
PERISTYLE
PERMANENT
PERMEABLE
PERMITTED
PERPETUAL
PERPLEXED
PERSECUTE
PERSEVERE
PERSIMMON
PERSONAGE
PERSONATE
PERSONIFY
PERSONNEL
PERSUADED
PERTINENT
PERTURBED
PERTUSATE
PERTUSSIS
PERVASION
PERVASIVE
PERVERTED
PESSIMISM
PESSIMIST
PESTICIDE
PESTILENT
PETAURIST
PETERSHAM
PETHIDINE
PETILLANT
PETRIFIED
PETROLEUM
PETROLOGY
PETTICOAT
PETTINESS
PETTITOES
PETULANCE

REACHABLE
READDRESS
READINESS
READYEARN
READYMADE
REALISTIC
REALITIES
REANIMATE
REARGUARD
REARHORSE
REARMOUSE
REARRANGE
REARWARDS
REASONING
REBELLION
REBOATION
RECALLING
RECAPTURE
RECEIVING
RECEPTION
RECEPTIVE
RECESSION
RECESSIVE
RECIPIENT
RECKONING
RECLAIMED
RECLAIMER
RECOGNIZE
RECOLLECT
RECOMMEND
RECONCILE
RECONDITE
RECONVENE
RECORDING
RECORDIST
RECOVERED
RECTANGLE
RECTIFIER
RECTITUDE
RECTORIAL
RECUMBENT
RECURRENT
RECURRING
RECUSANCE
REDBREAST
REDDENDUM
REDEEMING
REDHANDED
REDHEADED
REDINGOTE
REDIVIVUS
REDLETTER
REDOLENCE
REDSTREAK
REDUCIBLE
REDUCTION
REDUNDANT

REEDINESS
REEXAMINE
REFECTION
REFECTORY
REFERENCE
REFERRING
REFINANCE
REFLATION
REFLECTOR
REFLEXION
REFLEXIVE
REFORMIST
REFRACTOR
REFRESHER
REFULGENT
REFURBISH
REFUSENIK
REGARDANT
REGARDFUL
REGARDING
REGISSEUR
REGISTRAR
REGRETFUL
REGUERDON
REGULARLY
REGULATOR
REHEARSAL
REICHSRAT
REICHSTAG
REIMBURSE
REINFORCE
REINSTATE
REISTAFEL
REITERATE
REJECTION
REJOICING
REJOINDER
RELATIONS
RELEVANCE
RELIGEUSE
RELIGIOSO
RELIGIOUS
RELIQUARY
RELIQUIAE
RELUCTANT
REMAINDER
REMAINING
REMBRANDT
REMINISCE
REMISSION
REMONTANT
REMOULADE
REMOVABLE
RENASCENT
RENCONTRE
RENDERING
RENDITION

RENEWABLE
RENFIERST
RENOVATOR
RENTALLER
REPAYABLE
REPAYMENT
REPECHAGE
REPELLENT
REPELLING
REPENTANT
REPERCUSS
REPERTORY
REPLACING
REPLENISH
REPLETION
REPLETIVE
REPLICATE
REPORTAGE
REPORTING
REPOSSESS
REPREHEND
REPRESENT
REPRESSED
REPRIMAND
REPROBATE
REPROCESS
REPRODUCE
REPROVING
REPTATION
REPTILIAN
REPUDIATE
REPUGNANT
REPULSION
REPULSIVE
REPUTABLE
REPUTEDLY
REQUISITE
REREMOUSE
RESENTFUL
RESERPINE
RESERVIST
RESERVOIR
RESHUFFLE
RESIDENCE
RESIDENCY
RESIDUARY
RESILIENT
RESISTANT
RESNATRON
RESONANCE
RESONATOR
RESORTING
RESOURCES
RESPECTED
RESPECTER
RESSALDAR
RESTIFORM

RESTITUTE
RESTRAINT
RESULTANT
RESULTING
RESURFACE
RESURGENT
RESURRECT
RETAILING
RETAINING
RETALIATE
RETENTION
RETENTIVE
RETIARIUS
RETICENCE
RETICULUM
RETINITIS
RETORSION
RETORTION
RETRACTOR
RETRIEVAL
RETRIEVER
RETROCEDE
RETROFLEX
RETROVERT
RETURNING
REVEALING
REVELLING
REVERENCE
REVERSING
REVERSION
REVETMENT
REVICTUAL
REVOLTING
REVOLVING
REVULSION
REWARDING
REWORKING
REYKJAVIK
SEABOTTLE
SEAFARING
SEANNACHY
SEARCHING
SEASONING
SEAWORTHY
SEBACEOUS
SEBASTIAN
SECATEURS
SECESSION
SECLUSION
SECONDARY
SECRETARY
SECRETION
SECRETIVE
SECTARIAN
SECTIONAL
SECTORIAL
SEDENTARY

SEDGEMOOR
SEDITIOUS
SEDUCTION
SEDUCTIVE
SEEMINGLY
SEGMENTED
SEGREGATE
SELACHION
SELECTING
SELECTION
SELECTIVE
SELFISHLY
SELJUKIAN
SELLOTAPE
SEMANTEME
SEMANTICS
SEMANTIDE
SEMANTRON
SEMAPHORE
SEMBLANCE
SEMEIOTIC
SEMIBREVE
SEMICOLON
SEMIFINAL
SEMIOLOGY
SEMIRAMIS
SENESCENT
SENESCHAL
SENIORITY
SENSATION
SENSELESS
SENSILLUM
SENSITIVE
SENSITIZE
SENSORIUM
SENSUALLY
SENTIENCE
SENTIMENT
SEPARABLE
SEPARATED
SEPARATOR
SEPHARDIM
SEPIOLITE
SEPTEMBER
SEPTIMOLE
SEPULCHER
SEPULCHRE
SEPULTURE
SEQUESTER
SEQUINNED
SERAPHINE
SERASKIER
SERBONIAN
SERENADER
SERENGETI
SERIALIST
SERIALIZE

SERIATION
SERIOUSLY
SERMONIZE
SERRATION
SERREFILE
SERVICING
SERVIETTE
SERVILELY
SERVILITY
SERVITUDE
SETACEOUS
SEVENTEEN
SEVERALLY
SEVERANCE
SEXUALITY
TEACHABLE
TEAKETTLE
TEARFULLY
TEARSHEET
TECHNICAL
TECHNIQUE
TECTIFORM
TECTONICS
TECTORIAL
TEDIOSITY
TEDIOUSLY
TEESWATER
TEIRESIAS
TEKNONYMY
TELEGRAPH
TELEOLOGY
TELEPATHY
TELEPHONE
TELEPHONY
TELEPHOTO
TELESALES
TELESCOPE
TELESTICH
TELLINGLY
TELLURIAN
TELLURION
TELLURIUM
TEMPERATE
TEMPORARY
TEMPORIZE
TEMPTRESS
TEMULENCE
TENACIOUS
TENACULUM
TENAILLON
TENDERIZE
TENEBROSE
TENEMENTS
TENNESSEE
TENSENESS
TENTATIVE
TENTORIUM
TENUOUSLY
TEPHILLIN
TEREBINTH
TERMAGANT
TERMAGENT
TERMINATE
TERPINEOL
TERRACING
TERRARIUM
TERRICOLE
TERRIFIED
TERRITORY
TERRORISM
TERRORIST
TERRORIZE
TERSENESS
TESTAMENT
TESTATRIX
TESTDRIVE
TESTICLES
TESTIFIER
TESTIMONY
TETRAGRAM
TETRALOGY
TETRARCHY
TETTEROUS
VEGETABLE
VEGETATOR
VEHEMENCE
VEHICULAR
VEILLEUSE
VELASQUEZ
VELDSKOEN
VELLENAGE
VELLICATE
VELODROME
VELVETEEN
VENERABLE
VENEREOUS
VENEZUELA
VENGEANCE
VENIALITY
VENTIFACT
VENTILATE
VENTRICLE
VENUSBERG
VERACIOUS
VERATRINE
VERBALIZE
VERBASCUM
VERBERATE
VERBOSITY
VERDIGRIS
VERIDICAL
VERITABLE
VERKAMPTE
VERMIFORM
VERMIFUGE
VERMILION
VERMINOUS
VERSATILE
VERSIFIER
VERSIONAL
VERTEBRAE
VERTEBRAL
VERTIPORT
VERTUMNUS
VESICULAR
VESPASIAN
VESTIBULE
VESTIGIAL
VESTITURE
VESTMENTS
VEXATIONS
VEXATIOUS
VEXILLARY
WEAKENING
WEARINESS
WEARISOME
WEBFOOTED
WEDGEWOOD
WEDNESDAY
WEIGHTING
WEIRDNESS
WELCOMING
WELDSTADT
WELLBEING
WELLBUILT
WELLKNOWN
WELSUMMER
WELTGEIST
WENCESLAS
WESTBOUND
WESTERNER
WESTWARDS
XENOMANIA
XENOPHOBE
XEROPHYTE
XEROSTOMA
YELLOWISH
YESTERDAY
YESTEREVE
ZEALANDER
ZEITGEIST
ZENOCRATE
AFFECTING
AFFECTION
AFFIDAVIT
AFFILIATE
AFFLICTED
AFFLUENCE
AFFRICATE
AFLATOXIN
AFORESAID
AFRIKAANS
AFRIKANER
AFTERCARE
AFTERDAMP
AFTERGLOW
AFTERMATH
AFTERMOST
AFTERNOON
AFTERWORD
EFFECTIVE
EFFECTUAL
EFFICIENT
EFFINGHAM
EFFLUENCE
EFFLUVIUM
EFFULGENT
OFFCHANCE
OFFCOLOUR
OFFENBACH
OFFENDING
OFFENSIVE
OFFERTORY
OFFICIALS
OFFICIANT
OFFICIATE
OFFICIOUS
OFFSEASON
OFFSPRING
AGALACTIC
AGAMEMNON
AGGRAVATE
AGGREGATE
AGGRESSOR
AGGRIEVED
AGINCOURT
AGITATION
AGONIZING
AGREEABLE
AGREEABLY
AGREEMENT
AGUECHEEK
EGAREMENT
EGLANTINE
EGREGIOUS
EGRESSION
IGNESCENT
IGNORAMUS
IGNORANCE
IGUANODON
YGGDRASIL
AHASUERUS
CHABAZITE
CHAFFINCH
CHAIRLIFT
CHALAZION
CHALIAPIN
CHALLENGE
CHALUMEAU
CHAMELEON
CHAMFRAIN
CHAMINADE
CHAMOMILE
CHAMPAGNE
CHAMPAIGN
CHAMPERTY
CHAMPLAIN
CHAMPLEVÉ
CHANTEUSE
CHANTILLY
CHAPARRAL
CHAPERONE
CHARABANC
CHARACTER
CHARGEFUL
CHARIVARI
CHARLATAN
CHARLOTTE
CHAROLAIS
CHARTERED
CHARTREUX
CHARWOMAN
CHARYBDIS
CHASTENED
CHATTERER
CHAUFFEUR
CHAVENDER
CHAWBACON
CHEAPJACK
CHEAPNESS
CHEAPSIDE
CHECKBOOK
CHECKLIST
CHECKMATE
CHECKROOM
CHEEKBONE
CHEERLESS
CHEMISTRY
CHEONGSAM
CHEQUERED
CHERISHED
CHERNOZEM
CHERUBINI
CHEVALIER
CHICANERY
CHICKADEE
CHICKWEED
CHIEFTAIN
CHIHUAHUA
CHILBLAIN
CHILDCARE
CHILDHOOD
CHILDLESS
CHILDLIKE
CHILOPODA
CHINATOWN
CHINOVNIK
CHINSTRAP
CHIPBOARD
CHIPOLATA
CHIPPINGS
CHIROPODY
CHISELLER
CHLAMYDES
CHOCOLATE
CHOLELITH
CHONDRITE
CHONDROID
CHORISTER
CHRISTIAN
CHRISTMAS
CHROMATIC
CHRONICLE
CHRYSALIS
CHURCHILL
CHURCHMAN
CHURIDARS
KHALIFATE
KHANSAMAH
PHACOLITE
PHAGOCYTE
PHALANGER
PHALAROPE
PHANARIOT
PHANSIGAR
PHANTASMA
PHARAMOND
PHARISAIC
PHARSALIA
PHELLOGEN
PHENACITE
PHENAKISM
PHEROMONE
PHIGALIAN
PHILANDER
PHILATELY
PHILIPPIC
PHILISTER
PHILLABEG
PHILLIBEG
PHILOLOGY
PHITONIUM
PHLEBITIS
PHONECARD
PHONETICS
PHONOGRAM
PHONOLITE
PHONOLOGY
PHOSPHATE
PHOSPHENE
PHOTOCOPY
PHOTOGENE

PHOTOSTAT
PHRENETIC
PHRENITIS
PHTHALATE
PHYLLOPOD
PHYLOGENY
PHYSICIAN
PHYSICIST
PHYTOLITE
PHYTOTRON
RHAPSODIC
RHEOTAXIS
RHEUMATIC
RHODESIAN
RHODOLITE
RHODOPSIN
RHYMESTER
SHADINESS
SHAKEDOWN
SHAKINESS
SHAMEFAST
SHAMELESS
SHAMIANAH
SHAPELESS
SHARESMAN
SHARKSKIN
SHARPENER
SHARPNESS
SHASHLICK
SHATTERED
SHAVELING
SHEARLING
SHECHINAH
SHECHITAH
SHEEPFOLD
SHEEPMEAT
SHEEPSKIN
SHEERLEGS
SHEERNESS
SHEFFIELD
SHEIKHDOM
SHELDDUCK
SHELDRAKE
SHELLBACK
SHELLFISH
SHELLSUIT
SHELTERED
SHEMOZZLE
SHENSTONE
SHEPHERDS
SHETLANDS
SHEWBREAD
SHIELDING
SHIFTLESS
SHIFTWORK
SHILLABER
SHINTOISM
SHIPOWNER
SHIPSHAPE
SHIPWRECK
SHIVERING
SHOEMAKER
SHOESHINE
SHOLOKHOV
SHOPFLOOR
SHOPFRONT
SHORTCAKE
SHORTFALL
SHORTHAND
SHORTHAUL
SHORTHOLD
SHORTHORN
SHORTLIST
SHORTNESS
SHORTSTAY
SHORTSTOP
SHORTTERM
SHOVELFUL
SHOVELLER
SHOWINESS
SHOWPIECE
SHRIMPING
SHRINKAGE
SHRINKING
SHRUBBERY
SHUBUNKIN
SHUFFLING
SHUTTERED
THACKERAY
THALASSIC
THANATISM
THANKLESS
THATCHING
THAUMATIN
THECODONT
THELEMITE
THELONIUS
THEOBROMA
THEOCRACY
THEOSOPHY
THERALITE
THERAPIST
THEREFORE
THEREUPON
THERMIDOR
THERSITES
THESAURUS
THICKHEAD
THICKNESS
THIGHBONE
THINGUMMY
THINKABLE
THINNINGS
THIRDSMAN
THIRSTILY
THIRSTING
THIRTIETH
THORNBACK
THORNBILL
THORNDYKE
THORNLESS
THOUSANDS
THRALLDOM
THRASHING
THRASONIC
THREADFIN
THREEFOLD
THREESOME
THRENETIC
THREONINE
THRESHOLD
THRIFTILY
THRILLANT
THRILLING
THROATILY
THROBBING
THRONGING
THROWAWAY
THROWBACK
THROWDOWN
THROWSTER
THUMBLING
THUMBNAIL
THUMBTACK
THUNDERER
THYESTEAN
THYLACINE
THYRATRON
THYRISTOR
WHALEBOAT
WHALEBONE
WHALEMEAT
WHEATGERM
WHEATMEAL
WHEELBASE
WHEREFORE
WHEREUPON
WHERRYMAN
WHETSTONE
WHICHEVER
WHIMSICAL
WHINSTONE
WHIPROUND
WHIPSNADE
WHIRLIGIG
WHIRLPOOL
WHIRLWIND
WHISTLING
WHITAKERS
WHITEBAIT
WHITEDAMP
WHITEFISH
WHITEHALL
WHITEHEAD
WHITENESS
WHITENING
WHITEWALL
WHITEWASH
WHITEWING
WHITEWOOD
WHITTAWER
WHITWORTH
WHIZZBANG
WHODUNNIT
WHOLEFOOD
WHOLEMEAL
WHOLENESS
WHOLESALE
WHOLESOME
WHOSOEVER
WHUNSTANE
AIMLESSLY
AINSWORTH
AIRCOOLED
AIRSTREAM
AITCHBONE
BICYCLIST
BIFURCATE
BIGHEADED
BILATERAL
BILINGUAL
BILIRUBIN
BILLABONG
BILLBOARD
BILLIARDS
BILLOWING
BILLYCOCK
BIMONTHLY
BINOCULAR
BIOGRAPHY
BIOLOGIST
BIOSPHERE
BIPARTITE
BIRDBRAIN
BIRDTABLE
BIRTHMARK
BIRTHWORT
BISECTION
BISHOPRIC
BIZARRELY
CIGARETTE
CILIOLATE
CIMMERIAN
CINEMATIC
CINERARIA
CINEREOUS
CIPOLLINO
CIRCADIAN
CIRCINATE
CIRCULATE
CIRRHOSIS
CIVILISED
CIVILIZED
DIABLERIE
DIACRITIC
DIAERESIS
DIAGNOSIS
DIALECTAL
DIALECTIC
DIALOGITE
DIAMETRIC
DIANDROUS
DIANETICS
DIANOETIC
DIAPHRAGM
DIARRHOEA
DIASTASIS
DIATHESIS
DIAZEUXIS
DICHOTOMY
DICTATION
DIDACTICS
DIETETICS
DIETICIAN
DIFFERENT
DIFFICULT
DIFFIDENT
DIFFUSION
DIGASTRIC
DIGESTION
DIGESTIVE
DIGITALIN
DIGITALIS
DIGNIFIED
DIGNITARY
DILIGENCE
DIMENSION
DINGINESS
DINNERSET
DIOCLETES
DIONYSIAN
DIONYSIUS
DIPHTHONG
DIPLOMACY
DIRECTION
DIRECTIVE
DIRECTORS
DIRECTORY
DIRIGIBLE
DIRTINESS
DISABLING
DISAFFIRM
DISAPPEAR
DISARMING
DISBELIEF
DISBURDEN
DISCARDED
DISCHARGE
DISCLOSED
DISCOLOUR
DISCOMFIT
DISCOURSE
DISCOVERT
DISCOVERY
DISCREDIT
DISEMBARK
DISENGAGE
DISENTOMB
DISFAVOUR
DISFIGURE
DISGRACED
DISGUISED
DISGUSTED
DISHCLOTH
DISHONEST
DISHONOUR
DISHWATER
DISINFECT
DISLOCATE
DISMANTLE
DISMEMBER
DISMISSAL
DISOBLIGE
DISORIENT
DISPARAGE
DISPARATE
DISPARITY
DISPENSER
DISPERSAL
DISPERSED
DISPLACED
DISPLAYED
DISPLEASE
DISPUTANT
DISREGARD
DISREPAIR
DISREPUTE
DISSEMBLE
DISSENTER
DISSIDENT
DISSIPATE
DISSOLUTE
DISSOLVED
DISSONANT
DISTANTLY
DISTEMPER
DISTENDED
DISTILLER
DISTORTED
DISTRAINT
DISTURBED
DISUNITED

DITHERING
DITHYRAMB
DIVERGENT
DIVERGING
DIVERSIFY
DIVERSION
DIVERSITY
DIVERTING
DIVIDENDS
DIVISIBLE
DIXIELAND
DIZZINESS
EIDERDOWN
EIDOGRAPH
EIGHTIETH
EIGHTSOME
FIBROLINE
FIBROLITE
FICTIONAL
FIDUCIARY
FIELDFARE
FIELDSMAN
FIELDWORK
FIFTEENTH
FIGURANTE
FILICALES
FILIGRAIN
FILLIPEEN
FILLISTER
FILMMAKER
FILMSTRIP
FILOPLUME
FILOSELLE
FILTERING
FILTERTIP
FINANCIAL
FINANCIER
FINGERING
FINGERTIP
FINICKING
FINICKITY
FINISHING
FINLANDIA
FIREBRAND
FIREBREAK
FIREDRAKE
FIREGUARD
FIRELIGHT
FIREPLACE
FIREPROOF
FIRESTONE
FIREWATER
FIREWORKS
FIRMAMENT
FIRSTEVER
FIRSTHAND
FIRSTRATE
FISHERMAN
FISHGUARD
FISHPLATE
GIBBERISH
GIBEONITE
GIBRALTAR
GIDDINESS
GILGAMESH
GINGERADE
GINGLYMUS
GINORMOUS
GIRANDOLE
GIRONDIST
HIBERNATE
HIBERNIAN
HIDEBOUND
HIDEOUSLY
HIERARCHY
HIGHCLASS
HIGHFLYER
HIGHLANDS
HIGHLIGHT
HIGHSPEED
HIJACKING
HILARIOUS
HILLBILLY
HIMALAYAN
HIMALAYAS
HIMYARITE
HINDEMITH
HINDRANCE
HINDSIGHT
HINGELESS
HIPPOCRAS
HIPPODAME
HIPPOLYTA
HIPPOLYTE
HIRUNDINE
HISTAMINE
HISTOGRAM
HISTOLOGY
HISTORIAN
HITCHCOCK
HITCHHIKE
JIGGUMBOB
JITTERBUG
KICKSHAWS
KIDNAPPED
KIDNAPPER
KIESERITE
KILDERKIN
KILLARNEY
KILOCYCLE
KILOHERTZ
KILOMETER
KILOMETRE
KINGMAKER
KINGSIZED
KINKCOUGH
KINSWOMAN
KINTLEDGE
KISSINGER
KITCHENER
KITTENISH
KITTIWAKE
LIABILITY
LIBELLOUS
LIBERALLY
LIBERATED
LIBERATOR
LIBERTIES
LIBERTINE
LIBRARIAN
LICKERISH
LIENTERIC
LIFEGUARD
LIFESTYLE
LIGHTFOOT
LIGHTLESS
LIGHTNESS
LIGHTNING
LIGHTSHIP
LIGHTSOME
LILYWHITE
LIMBURGER
LIMEHOUSE
LIMELIGHT
LIMESTONE
LIMITLESS
LIMOUSINE
LIMPIDITY
LINDBERGH
LINEAMENT
LINEOLATE
LINGERING
LINGFIELD
LINKLATER
LINTSTOCK
LIONHEART
LIPPITUDE
LIQUEFIED
LIQUIDATE
LIQUIDITY
LIQUIDIZE
LIQUORICE
LIQUORISH
LISTENING
LITERALLY
LITHOCYST
LITHOPONE
LITHUANIA
LITIGIOUS
LIVERPOOL
LIVERWORT
LIVERYMAN
LIVESTOCK
LIVRAISON
MICKLETON
MICROCHIP
MICROCOSM
MICROCYTE
MICROFILM
MICROLITE
MICROLITH
MICROTOME
MICROTONE
MICROWAVE
MIDDLEMAN
MIDDLESEX
MIDDLETON
MIDDLINGS
MIDIANITE
MIDINETTE
MIDRASHIM
MIDSTREAM
MIDSUMMER
MIDWIFERY
MIDWINTER
MIGRATION
MIGRATORY
MILESTONE
MILITANCY
MILKSHAKE
MILLAMANT
MILLENIAL
MILLENIUM
MILLEPEDE
MILLEPORE
MILLIGRAM
MILLINERY
MILLIONTH
MILLIPEDE
MILLSTONE
MILOMETER
MINACIOUS
MINCEMEAT
MINEFIELD
MINELAYER
MINIATURE
MINISCULE
MINISKIRT
MINKSTONE
MINNESOTA
MINUSCULE
MINUTEMAN
MIRABELLE
MIRTHLESS
MISBEHAVE
MISCHANCE
MISCREANT
MISDIRECT
MISERABLE
MISERABLY
MISFALLEN
MISFIRING
MISGIVING
MISGUIDED
MISHANDLE
MISINFORM
MISLOCATE
MISMANAGE
MISOCLERE
MISONEIST
MISPICKEL
MISPLACED
MISSHAPEN
MISSIONER
MISSTROKE
MISTEMPER
MISTIGRIS
MISTINESS
MISTLETOE
MITHRAISM
MITRAILLE
NIAISERIE
NICARAGUA
NICCOLITE
NICKNEVEN
NICODEMUS
NICTITATE
NIDDERING
NIDERLING
NIEBELUNG
NIETZSCHE
NIGGARDLY
NIGHTCLUB
NIGHTFALL
NIGHTFIRE
NIGHTGOWN
NIGHTMARE
NIGHTTIME
NIGHTWORK
NIGRITUDE
NIGROSINE
NINEPENCE
NINETIETH
NIPCHEESE
NIPPERKIN
NITHSDALE
OILTANKER
PIACEVOLE
PICKABACK
PICKETING
PICKTHANK
PICNICKER
PICTOGRAM
PICTORIAL
PIECEMEAL
PIECEWORK
PIEPOWDER
PIERGLASS
PIGGYBACK
PIGGYBANK
PIGHEADED
PIGNERATE
PIKESTAFF
PILASTERS
PILFERAGE
PILFERING
PILLICOCK
PIMPERNEL
PINCHBECK
PINCHCOCK
PINEAPPLE
PINHOOKER
PINKERTON
PINOCCHIO
PINSTRIPE
PIPEDREAM
PIPESTONE
PIPSQUEAK
PIQUANTLY
PIRATICAL
PIROUETTE
PISTACHIO
PISTAREEN
PISTOLEER
PITCHFORK
PITCHPINE
PITCHPOLE
PITCHPOLL
PITIFULLY
PITUITARY
PITUITRIN
PIZZICATO
RIBBONISM
RICERCARE
RICHELIEU
RIDERHOOD
RIDERLESS
RIDGEBACK
RIGHTEOUS
RIGHTHAND
RIGHTNESS
RIGHTWING
RIGMAROLE
RIGOLETTO
RILLETTES
RINGFENCE
RINGSIDER
RIOTOUSLY
RIPIENIST
RISKINESS
RIVERSIDE
SIBILANCE

SIBYLLINE
SICCATIVE
SICILIANO
SICKENING
SIDEBOARD
SIDEBURNS
SIDELIGHT
SIDEROSIS
SIDESWIPE
SIDETRACK
SIDEWARDS
SIEGFRIED
SIGHTLESS
SIGHTSEER
SIGNALLER
SIGNALMAN
SIGNATORY
SIGNATURE
SIGNBOARD
SILICOSIS
SILLINESS
SILTSTONE
SILURIDAE
SIMEONITE
SIMILARLY
SIMPLETON
SIMPLISTE
SIMULATED
SIMULATOR
SIMULCAST
SINCERELY
SINCERITY
SINGALESE
SINGAPORE
SINGLESEX
SINGLETON
SINGSPIEL
SINGULTUS
SINKANSEN
SINUOSITY
SINUSITIS
SIPHUNCLE
SIRBONIAN
SISSERARY
SISYPHEAN
SITUATION
SIXTEENMO
SIXTEENTH
TICHBORNE
TICTACTOE
TIERCERON
TIGHTENER
TIGHTHEAD
TIGHTNESS
TIGHTROPE
TIMENOGUY
TIMEPIECE
TIMESHARE
TIMETABLE
TIMOCRACY
TIMPANIST
TINGUAITE
TIPPERARY
TIPSINESS
TIPULIDAE
TIREDNESS
TISIPHONE
TITHEBARN
TITILLATE
TITRATION
TITTLEBAT
VIABILITY
VIBRATILE
VIBRATION
VIBRATORY
VICARIOUS
VICEREGAL
VICEREINE
VICIOUSLY
VICTIMIZE
VICTORIAN
VICTORINE
VIDELICET
VIDEODISC
VIDEOTAPE
VIENTIANE
VIEWPOINT
VIGESIMAL
VIGILANCE
VIGILANTE
VINDICATE
VIOLATION
VIOLENTLY
VIOLINIST
VIRGINALS
VIRGINIAN
VIRGINITY
VIRGINIUM
VIRGULATE
VIRTUALLY
VIRULENCE
VISAGISTE
VISCOSITY
VISIONARY
VISUALIZE
VITASCOPE
VITELLIUS
VITIATION
VITRIOLIC
VITRUVIAN
VIVACIOUS
VIVIDNESS
WIDOWHOOD
WILDGEESE
WILLEMITE
WILLESDEN
WILLFULLY
WILLINGLY
WILLOWING
WILLPOWER
WIMBLEDON
WINCANTON
WINCOPIPE
WINDBREAK
WINDCHILL
WINDFALLS
WINDHOVER
WINDSCALE
WINDSWEPT
WINEBERRY
WINEGLASS
WINNEBAGO
WISCONSIN
WISECRACK
WISTFULLY
WITCHETTY
WITHDRAWN
WITHERING
WITHERITE
WITHSTAND
WITHYWIND
WITNESSED
WITTICISM
WITTINGLY
ZIBELLINE
ZINFANDEL
ZINKENITE
ZIRCONIUM
DJELLABAH
EJACULATE
LJUBLJANA
SKEDADDLE
SKEPTICAL
SKETCHILY
SKETCHMAP
SKETCHPAD
SKEWWHIFF
SKIAMACHY
SKILFULLY
SKINDIVER
SKINFLINT
SKINTIGHT
SKYJACKER
UKRAINIAN
ALABASTER
ALBATROSS
ALBERTINE
ALCHEMIST
ALCOHOLIC
ALDEBARAN
ALERTNESS
ALEURITIS
ALEXANDER
ALEXANDRA
ALGEBRAIC
ALGORITHM
ALIGNMENT
ALLANTOID
ALLANTOIS
ALLEGEDLY
ALLEGIANT
ALLEMANDE
ALLEVIATE
ALLIGATOR
ALLOCARPY
ALLOGRAPH
ALLOPATHY
ALLOTMENT
ALLOWABLE
ALLOWANCE
ALMANDINE
ALONGSIDE
ALOOFNESS
ALPENHORN
ALTERABLE
ALTERCATE
ALTERNATE
ALTIMETER
ALTIPLANO
ALTISSIMO
ALUMINIUM
ALVEOLATE
BLACKBALL
BLACKBIRD
BLACKFACE
BLACKFOOT
BLACKHEAD
BLACKJACK
BLACKLEAD
BLACKLIST
BLACKMAIL
BLACKMORE
BLACKNESS
BLACKWOOD
BLAMELESS
BLANDNESS
BLASPHEME
BLASPHEMY
BLATANTLY
BLEACHERS
BLESSINGS
BLINDFOLD
BLINDNESS
BLINDSPOT
BLINDWORM
BLINKERED
BLISTERED
BLOCKHEAD
BLOODBATH
BLOODLESS
BLOODSHED
BLOODSHOT
BLOWTORCH
BLUEBEARD
BLUEBERRY
BLUEPRINT
BLUESTONE
BLUFFNESS
BLUNDERER
BLUNTNESS
BLUSTERER
CLAMOROUS
CLAMPDOWN
CLAPBOARD
CLARENDON
CLARIFIER
CLASSICAL
CLASSLESS
CLASSMATE
CLASSROOM
CLEANNESS
CLEANSING
CLEARANCE
CLEARNESS
CLEOPATRA
CLEPSYDRA
CLERGYMAN
CLEVELAND
CLIENTELE
CLIMACTIC
CLINGFILM
CLINICIAN
CLIPBOARD
CLOAKROOM
CLOCKWISE
CLOCKWORK
CLOISONNÉ
CLOSENESS
CLOUDLESS
CLUBHOUSE
CLUSTERED
ELABORATE
ELAEOLITE
ELASTOMER
ELATERIUM
ELBOWROOM
ELECTORAL
ELECTRESS
ELECTRIFY
ELECTRODE
ELECTUARY
ELEGANTLY
ELEMENTAL
ELEVATION
ELEVENSES
ELIMINATE
ELIZABETH
ELKOSHITE
ELLESMERE
ELLINGTON
ELOCUTION
ELONGATED
ELOPEMENT
ELOQUENCE
ELSEWHERE
ELUCIDATE
ELUTRIATE
FLABELLUM
FLAGELLIN
FLAGELLUM
FLAGEOLET
FLAGITATE
FLAGRANCE
FLAGSTAFF
FLAGSTONE
FLAMMABLE
FLAMSTEED
FLASHBACK
FLASHBULB
FLASHCUBE
FLATTENED
FLATTENER
FLATTERED
FLATTERER
FLATULENT
FLAVORING
FLAVOURED
FLECHETTE
FLEDGLING
FLEETWOOD
FLESHLESS
FLESHPOTS
FLEXITIME
FLINTLOCK
FLIPPANCY
FLOODGATE
FLOORSHOW
FLOPHOUSE
FLORESTAN
FLORIMELL
FLOTATION
FLOURMILL
FLOWCHART
FLOWERBED
FLOWERING
FLOWERPOT
FLOWSTONE
FLUCTUATE
FLUSTERED
FLYWEIGHT
GLABELLAR
GLADIATOR

GLADIOLUS
GLADSTONE
GLAIREOUS
GLAMORIZE
GLAMOROUS
GLANDULAR
GLASSWARE
GLEANINGS
GLEEFULLY
GLENDOWER
GLENGARRY
GLENLIVET
GLISSANDO
GLOMERATE
GLOMERULE
GLORIFIED
GLORYHOLE
GLUCINIUM
GLUCOSIDE
GLUTAMINE
GLUTINOUS
GLYCERIDE
GLYCERINE
ILCHESTER
ILLEGALLY
ILLEGIBLE
ILLEGIBLY
ILLGOTTEN
ILLIBERAL
ILLICITLY
ILLOGICAL
KLEMPERER
KLENDUSIC
KLINOSTAT
OLECRANON
OLENELLUS
OLEOGRAPH
OLEORESIN
OLFACTORY
OLIGARCHY
OLIGOCENE
OLIVENITE
PLACATORY
PLACEMENT
PLACIDITY
PLAINNESS
PLAINSMAN
PLAINSONG
PLAINTIFF
PLAINTIVE
PLANETARY
PLASTERED
PLASTERER
PLATITUDE
PLATONIST
PLAUSIBLE
PLAUSIBLY
PLAUSTRAL
PLAYFULLY
PLAYGROUP
PLAYHOUSE
PLAYTHING
PLEASANCE
PLEIOCENE
PLENITUDE
PLENTEOUS
PLENTIFUL
PLETHORIC
PLIMSOLLS
PLOUGHMAN
PLUMBEOUS
PLUMBLINE
PLUMDAMAS
PLUMPNESS
PLUNDERER
PLURALISM
PLURALITY
PLUTOCRAT
PLUTONIUM
SLABSTONE
SLACKNESS
SLAMMAKIN
SLANTWISE
SLAPHAPPY
SLAPSTICK
SLAUGHTER
SLAVISHLY
SLEEKNESS
SLEEPLESS
SLEEPWALK
SLIGHTEST
SLIMINESS
SLINGBACK
SLINGSHOT
SLIVOVICA
SLIVOVITZ
SLOUGHING
SLOVENIAN
SLOWCOACH
SLUGHORNE
SLUMBERER
ULIGINOUS
ULLSWATER
ULTIMATUM
ULTRONEUS
AMARANTIN
AMARYLLIS
AMAUROSIS
AMAZEMENT
AMBERGRIS
AMBIGUITY
AMBIGUOUS
AMBITIOUS
AMBLYOPIA
AMBROSIAL
AMBROSIAN
AMBROTYPE
AMBULANCE
AMBUSCADE
AMELAKITE
AMENDMENT
AMENHOTEP
AMERICIUM
AMIANTHUS
AMIDSHIPS
AMOROUSLY
AMORPHOUS
AMPERSAND
AMPHIBIAN
AMPLIFIER
AMPLITUDE
AMSTERDAM
AMUSEMENT
AMUSINGLY
AMYGDALUS
EMACIATED
EMANATION
EMBARRASS
EMBASSADE
EMBASSAGE
EMBATTLED
EMBELLISH
EMBEZZLER
EMBRACERY
EMBRACING
EMBRANGLE
EMBRASURE
EMBROCATE
EMBROGLIO
EMBROIDER
EMBROILED
EMBRYONIC
EMERGENCE
EMERGENCY
EMINENTLY
EMMERDALE
EMOLLIATE
EMOLLIENT
EMOLUMENT
EMOTIONAL
EMPAESTIC
EMPANOPLY
EMPENNAGE
EMPHASIZE
EMPHLYSIS
EMPHYSEMA
EMPIRICAL
EMPLECTON
EMPLOYEES
EMPTINESS
EMULATION
GMELINITE
IMAGELESS
IMAGINARY
IMBALANCE
IMBRANGLE
IMBRICATE
IMBROCATE
IMBROGLIO
IMITATION
IMITATIVE
IMMANACLE
IMMANENCE
IMMANENCY
IMMEDIACY
IMMEDIATE
IMMELMANN
IMMENSELY
IMMENSITY
IMMERSION
IMMIGRANT
IMMIGRATE
IMMINENCE
IMMODESTY
IMMORALLY
IMMORTALS
IMMOVABLE
IMMOVABLY
IMMUNISER
IMMUTABLE
IMMUTABLY
IMPACTION
IMPARTIAL
IMPASSION
IMPASSIVE
IMPATIENT
IMPEACHER
IMPEDANCE
IMPELLING
IMPENDING
IMPERATOR
IMPERFECT
IMPERIOUS
IMPETUOUS
IMPLEMENT
IMPLICATE
IMPLUVIUM
IMPOLITIC
IMPORTANT
IMPORTUNE
IMPOSTURE
IMPOTENCE
IMPOUNDER
IMPRECATE
IMPRECISE
IMPRESSED
IMPROBITY
IMPROMPTU
IMPROVING
IMPROVISE
IMPRUDENT
IMPSONITE
IMPUDENCE
IMPULSION
IMPULSIVE
OMBUDSMAN
OMINOUSLY
OMOPHAGIC
SMALLNESS
SMALLTIME
SMARTNESS
SMOKEFREE
SMOKELESS
SMUGGLING
UMBILICAL
UMBILICUS
UMBRATILE
UMPTEENTH
ANABOLISM
ANABRANCH
ANAEROBIC
ANAGLYPTA
ANALEPTIC
ANALGESIA
ANALGESIC
ANALOGOUS
ANAPLASTY
ANARCHIST
ANASTASIA
ANATOLIAN
ANATOMIST
ANATOMIZE
ANCESTRAL
ANCHORAGE
ANCHORITE
ANCHORMAN
ANCILLARY
ANCIPITAL
ANDANTINO
ANDROCLES
ANDROMEDA
ANECDOTAL
ANECDOTES
ANGIOGRAM
ANGLICISM
ANGOSTURA
ANGUISHED
ANHYDRIDE
ANHYDRITE
ANHYDROUS
ANIMATION
ANIMISTIC
ANIMOSITY
ANKYLOSIS
ANNAPOLIS
ANNAPURNA
ANNOTATED
ANNOTATOR
ANNOUNCER
ANNOYANCE
ANNULMENT
ANOINTING
ANOMALOUS
ANONYMITY
ANONYMOUS
ANOPHELES
ANSCHLUSS
ANSWERING
ANTARCTIC
ANTENATAL
ANTHOLOGY
ANTICLINE
ANTIGONUS
ANTIHELIX
ANTIPASTO
ANTIPATHY
ANTIPHONY
ANTIPODES
ANTIQUARY
ANTIQUITY
ANTITOXIC
ANTITOXIN
ANTIVENIN
ANTONINUS
ANXIOUSLY
ENACTMENT
ENAMELLED
ENAMOURED
ENCANTHIS
ENCAUSTIC
ENCELADUS
ENCHANTED
ENCHANTER
ENCHEASON
ENCHILADA
ENCHORIAL
ENCIRCLED
ENCLOSURE
ENCOLPION
ENCOLPIUM
ENCOMPASS
ENCOUNTER
ENCOURAGE
ENCRATITE
ENCUMBENT
ENDEARING
ENDEAVOUR
ENDECAGON
ENDEICTIC
ENDLESSLY
ENDOCRINE
ENDOMORPH

ENDOSPERM
ENDOWMENT
ENDPAPERS
ENDURABLE
ENDURANCE
ENERGETIC
ENERGUMEN
ENERINITE
ENGARLAND
ENGINEERS
ENGRAINED
ENGRAVING
ENGRENAGE
ENGROSSED
ENGROSSER
ENHYDRITE
ENIGMATIC
ENJOYABLE
ENJOYMENT
ENLIGHTEN
ENLIVENED
ENNERDALE
ENQUIRIES
ENRAPTURE
ENROLMENT
ENSCONCED
ENSHEATHE
ENSORCELL
ENSTATITE
ENTELECHY
ENTERITIS
ENTERTAIN
ENTHYMEME
ENTOPHYTE
ENTOURAGE
ENTRAMMEL
ENTRANCED
ENTRECHAT
ENTRECÔTE
ENTREMETS
ENTROPION
ENTROPIUM
ENUCLEATE
ENUMERATE
ENUNCIATE
ENVERMEIL
INABILITY
INAMORATA
INAMORATO
INANIMATE
INANITION
INAUDIBLE
INAUDIBLY
INAUGURAL
INCAPABLE
INCARDINE
INCARNATE
INCAUTION
INCENTIVE
INCEPTION
INCESSANT
INCIDENCE
INCIPIENT
INCITATUS
INCLEMENT
INCLUDING
INCLUSION
INCLUSIVE
INCOGNITO
INCOMINGS
INCOMMODE
INCONDITE
INCORRECT
INCREASED
INCREMENT
INCUBATOR
INCULCATE
INCULPATE
INCUMBENT
INCURABLE
INCURABLY
INCURIOUS
INCURSION
INDECENCY
INDECORUM
INDELIBLE
INDELIBLY
INDEMNIFY
INDEMNITY
INDENTURE
INDICATES
INDICATOR
INDICTION
INDIGENCE
INDIGNANT
INDIGNITY
INDOLENCE
INDONESIA
INDRAUGHT
INDUCTION
INDUCTIVE
INDULGENT
INDWELLER
INEBRIATE
INEFFABLE
INELEGANT
INERTNESS
INERUDITE
INFANTILE
INFATUATE
INFECTING
INFECTION
INFERENCE
INFERTILE
INFIELDER
INFIRMARY
INFIRMITY
INFLATION
INFLEXION
INFLUENCE
INFLUENZA
INFORMANT
INFURIATE
INGENIOUS
INGENUITY
INGENUOUS
INGESTION
INGLENOOK
INGRAINED
INGROWING
INHERITED
INHERITOR
INHIBITED
INHUMANLY
INITIALLY
INITIATED
INITIATOR
INJECTION
INJURIOUS
INJUSTICE
INNERMOST
INNISFAIL
INNISFREE
INNKEEPER
INNOCENCE
INNOCUOUS
INNOVATOR
INOCULATE
INOPINATE
INORGANIC
INPATIENT
INQUILINE
INQUINATE
INQUIRING
INQUORATE
INSCRIBED
INSELBERG
INSENSATE
INSERTION
INSHALLAH
INSIDIOUS
INSINCERE
INSINUATE
INSIPIENT
INSISTENT
INSOLENCE
INSOLUBLE
INSOLVENT
INSOMNIAC
INSPECTOR
INSPIRING
INSTANTER
INSTANTLY
INSTIGATE
INSTITUTE
INSULATOR
INSULTING
INSURANCE
INSURGENT
INSWINGER
INTEGRATE
INTEGRITY
INTELLECT
INTENDANT
INTENDING
INTENSELY
INTENSIFY
INTENSITY
INTENSIVE
INTENTION
INTERBRED
INTERCEDE
INTERCEPT
INTERCITY
INTERDICT
INTERFACE
INTERFERE
INTERJECT
INTERLACE
INTERLARD
INTERLOCK
INTERLOPE
INTERLUDE
INTERMENT
INTERNODE
INTERPLAY
INTERPOSE
INTERPRET
INTERRUPT
INTERSECT
INTERVENE
INTERVIEW
INTESTATE
INTESTINE
INTRICACY
INTRICATE
INTRIGUED
INTRIGUER
INTRINSIC
INTRODUCE
INTROITUS
INTROVERT
INTRUSION
INTRUSIVE
INTUITION
INTUITIVE
INTUMESCE
INUMBRATE
INUNCTION
INUSITATE
INVECTIVE
INVENTION
INVENTIVE
INVENTORY
INVERNESS
INVERSION
INVERTASE
INVIDIOUS
INVIOLATE
INVISIBLE
INVOICING
INVOLUCRE
KNACKERED
KNAPSCULL
KNAPSKULL
KNEECORDS
KNIPHOFIA
KNOBSTICK
KNOCKDOWN
KNOWINGLY
KNOWLEDGE
MNEMOSYNE
ONCOMETER
ONOMASTIC
ONSLAUGHT
ONTHESPOT
ONTOGENCY
PNEUMATIC
PNEUMONIA
SNAKEWEED
SNEERWELL
SNOWBOUND
SNOWDONIA
SNOWDRIFT
SNOWFLAKE
SNOWSHOES
SNOWSTORM
SNOWWHITE
UNABASHED
UNADOPTED
UNALLOYED
UNALTERED
UNANIMITY
UNANIMOUS
UNASHAMED
UNBALANCE
UNBEKNOWN
UNBENDING
UNBIASSED
UNBOUNDED
UNBRIDLED
UNCEASING
UNCERTAIN
UNCHANGED
UNCHARGED
UNCHECKED
UNCHRISOM
UNCLAIMED
UNCLOTHED
UNCLOUDED
UNCONCERN
UNCONFINE
UNCORRECT
UNCOUPLED
UNCOURTLY
UNCOVERED
UNCROSSED
UNCROWNED
UNDAMAGED
UNDAUNTED
UNDECIDED
UNDEFILED
UNDEFINED
UNDERBRED
UNDERCAST
UNDERCOAT
UNDERDONE
UNDERFELT
UNDERFOOT
UNDERHAND
UNDERLINE
UNDERLING
UNDERMINE
UNDERMOST
UNDERPAID
UNDERPASS
UNDERRATE
UNDERSEAL
UNDERSELL
UNDERSIDE
UNDERSIGN
UNDERSONG
UNDERTAKE
UNDERTONE
UNDERWALK
UNDERWEAR
UNDERWENT
UNDERWOOD
UNDILUTED
UNDIVIDED
UNDOUBTED
UNDRESSED
UNEARTHLY
UNEATABLE
UNEQUALED
UNETHICAL
UNEXPOSED
UNFAILING
UNFEELING
UNFITTING
UNFLEDGED
UNFOUNDED

UNGUARDED
UNHAPPILY
UNHEALTHY
UNHEEDING
UNHELPFUL
UNHOPEFUL
UNIFORMED
UNIFORMLY
UNINJURED
UNINVITED
UNISEXUAL
UNITARIAN
UNIVALENT
UNIVERSAL
UNKNOWING
UNLEARNED
UNLIMITED
UNLUCKILY
UNMARRIED
UNMATCHED
UNMINDFUL
UNMUSICAL
UNNATURAL
UNNERVING
UNNOTICED
UNOPPOSED
UNPOPULAR
UNPRECISE
UNREFINED
UNRELATED
UNRUFFLED
UNSAVOURY
UNSCATHED
UNSECURED
UNSELFISH
UNSETTLED
UNSHACKLE
UNSHEATHE
UNSIGHTLY
UNSINNING
UNSKILLED
UNSPARING
UNSPOILED
UNSULLIED
UNTENABLE
UNTIMEOUS
UNTOUCHED
UNTRAINED
UNTREATED
UNTRODDEN
UNTUTORED
UNTYPICAL
UNUSUALLY
UNVARYING
UNWATERED
UNWELCOME
UNWILLING
UNWITTING
UNWORRIED
UNWRITTEN
BOANERGES
BOARDROOM
BOARDWALK
BOATHOUSE
BOATSWAIN
BOBSLEIGH
BOCCACCIO
BODYGUARD
BOLIVIANO
BOLOGNESE
BOLSHEVIK
BOMBARDON
BOMBASINE
BOMBASTIC
BOMBSHELL
BONAPARTE
BOOBYTRAP
BOOKLOVER
BOOKMAKER
BOOKSHELF
BOOKSTALL
BOOKSTAND
BOOKSTORE
BOOMERANG
BOONDOCKS
BOOTLACES
BORDEREAU
BORDERING
BORNAGAIN
BORROWING
BOSPHORUS
BOSSANOVA
BOSSINESS
BOSTONIAN
BOTANICAL
BOTSWANAN
BOTTLEFUL
BOULEVARD
BOUNDLESS
BOUNTEOUS
BOUNTIFUL
BOURGEOIS
BOXWALLAH
BOYFRIEND
COACHLOAD
COADJUTOR
COAGULANT
COAGULATE
COALESCED
COALFIELD
COALITION
COALMINER
COARCTATE
COASTLINE
COCHINEAL
COCKAIGNE
COCKATIEL
COCKFIGHT
COCKROACH
COCKSCOMB
COCKSFOOT
COCKSWAIN
COELOSTAT
COEMPTION
COENOBITE
COENOBIUM
COFFERDAM
COFFINITE
COGNITION
COGNITIVE
COGNIZANT
COHERENCE
COINTREAU
COLCHICUM
COLERIDGE
COLLAPSAR
COLLATION
COLLEAGUE
COLLECTED
COLLECTOR
COLLEGIAN
COLLIGATE
COLLIMATE
COLLISION
COLLOCATE
COLLODION
COLLOIDAL
COLLOTYPE
COLLUSION
COLLUSIVE
COLLYRIUM
COLOMBIAN
COLOMBIER
COLONNADE
COLOPHONY
COLORLESS
COLOSSEUM
COLOSTOMY
COLOSTRUM
COLOURFUL
COLOURING
COLOURIST
COLTSFOOT
COLUMBARY
COLUMBATE
COLUMBIAN
COLUMBINE
COLUMBITE
COLUMBIUM
COLUMELLA
COLUMNIST
COMBATANT
COMBATIVE
COMFORTER
COMICALLY
COMINFORM
COMINTERN
COMMANDER
COMMENSAL
COMMISSAR
COMMITTAL
COMMITTED
COMMITTEE
COMMODITY
COMMODORE
COMMOTION
COMMUNION
COMMUNISM
COMMUNIST
COMMUNITY
COMPACTLY
COMPANIES
COMPANION
COMPELLED
COMPETENT
COMPETING
COMPLAINT
COMPLIANT
COMPONENT
COMPOSING
COMPOSITE
COMPOSURE
COMPOTIER
COMPUTING
CONCAVITY
CONCEALED
CONCEITED
CONCERNED
CONCERTED
CONCIERGE
CONCISELY
CONCISION
CONCLUDED
CONCORDAT
CONCOURSE
CONCUBINE
CONCUSSED
CONDEMNED
CONDENSER
CONDIMENT
CONDITION
CONDUCIVE
CONDUCTOR
CONDUCTUS
CONDYLOMA
CONFESSED
CONFESSOR
CONFIDANT
CONFIDENT
CONFIRMED
CONFITEOR
CONFLATED
CONFUCIUS
CONFUSING
CONFUSION
CONGENIAL
CONGERIES
CONGESTED
CONGOLESE
CONGRUENT
CONGRUOUS
CONJUGATE
CONJURING
CONNECTED
CONNECTOR
CONNEXION
CONNOTATE
CONNUBIAL
CONQUEROR
CONSCIOUS
CONSCRIPT
CONSENSUS
CONSIGNEE
CONSIGNOR
CONSONANT
CONSTABLE
CONSTANCE
CONSTANCY
CONSTRICT
CONSTRUCT
CONSULATE
CONSUMING
CONTAGION
CONTAINER
CONTEMPER
CONTENDER
CONTENTED
CONTINENT
CONTINUAL
CONTINUUM
CONTRALTO
CONTRIVED
CONTRIVER
CONTUMACY
CONTUMELY
CONTUSION
CONUNDRUM
CONVECTOR
CONVERTED
CONVERTER
CONVINCED
CONVIVIAL
COOKHOUSE
COOPERATE
COPIOUSLY
COPROLITE
COPYRIGHT
CORALLINE
CORDIALLY
CORDUROYS
CORDYLINE
CORIANDER
CORKSCREW
CORMORANT
CORNBRASH
CORNCRAKE
CORNEILLE
CORNELIAN
CORNERMAN
CORNFIELD
CORNFLOUR
CORNSTALK
COROLLARY
CORPORATE
CORPOREAL
CORPOSANT
CORPULENT
CORPUSCLE
CORRECTED
CORRECTLY
CORRECTOR
CORREGGIO
CORRELATE
CORROSION
CORROSIVE
CORRUGATE
CORRUPTER
CORTISONE
CORUSCATE
COSMETICS
COSMOGONY
COSMOLOGY
COSMONAUT
COSTUMIER
COTANGENT
COTHURNUS
COTYLEDON
COUCHETTE
COUNSELOR
COUNTDOWN
COUNTLESS
COUNTRIES
COURGETTE
COURTELLE
COURTEOUS
COURTESAN
COURTROOM
COURTSHIP
COURTYARD
COUTURIER
COVALENCY
COVELLITE

COVERDALE
COWARDICE
COXSACKIE
DOCTORATE
DOCTRINAL
DOCUMENTS
DODDIPOLL
DOGMATISM
DOGMATIZE
DOLEFULLY
DOLOMITES
DOLOMITIC
DOMICILED
DOMINANCE
DOMINICAL
DOMINICAN
DONATELLO
DONCASTER
DONIZETTI
DOODLEBUG
DORMITION
DORMITORY
DOSSHOUSE
DOTHEBOYS
DOUBTLESS
DOUKHOBOR
DOWELLING
DOWNGRADE
DOWNRIGHT
DOWNSTAGE
DOWNTREND
DOWNWARDS
FOGGINESS
FOGRAMITE
FOLIOLOSE
FOLKETING
FOLKWEAVE
FOLLOWING
FOMALHAUT
FOODSTORE
FOODSTUFF
FOOLHARDY
FOOLISHLY
FOOLPROOF
FOOTBRAKE
FOOTHILLS
FOOTLOOSE
FOOTPLATE
FOOTPRINT
FOOTSTALL
FOOTSTOOL
FORASMUCH
FORBIDDEN
FORCEMEAT
FOREANENT
FOREBEARS
FORECLOSE
FORECOURT
FOREFRONT
FOREGOING
FOREIGNER
FORESHORE
FORESIGHT
FORESPEAK
FORESPEND
FORESTAGE
FORESTALL
FORESTERS
FORETASTE
FORFEITED
FORFICATE
FORGATHER
FORGETFUL
FORGETIVE
FORGIVING
FORGOTTEN
FORJASKIT
FORJESKIT
FORLORNLY
FORMALIST
FORMALITY
FORMALIZE
FORMATION
FORMATIVE
FORMULATE
FORNICATE
FORSYTHIA
FORTALICE
FORTHWINK
FORTHWITH
FORTILAGE
FORTITUDE
FORTNIGHT
FORTUNATE
FORWANDER
FOSSILISE
FOSSORIAL
FOUNDLING
FOURPENCE
FOURWHEEL
GOALMOUTH
GOBETWEEN
GODDESSES
GODFATHER
GODLINESS
GODMOTHER
GODOLPHIN
GODPARENT
GOLDCREST
GOLDFIELD
GOLDFINCH
GOLDSINNY
GOLDSMITH
GOMPHOSIS
GONDOLIER
GONGORISM
GONIATITE
GOODNIGHT
GOONHILLY
GOOSANDER
GOOSEFOOT
GOOSEHERD
GOOSENECK
GOOSESTEP
GOSLARITE
GOSPELLER
GOSSAMERY
GOSSYPINE
GOSSYPIUM
GOTHAMITE
GOVERNESS
GOVERNING
HOARFROST
HOARHOUND
HOARSTONE
HOBBINOLL
HOBGOBLIN
HOBNAILED
HOCCAMORE
HODIERNAL
HODMANDOD
HODOGRAPH
HODOMETER
HOLDERBAT
HOLINSHED
HOLLERITH
HOLLYHOCK
HOLLYWOOD
HOLOCAUST
HOLOGRAPH
HOLOPHOTE
HOLYSTONE
HOMEGROWN
HOMEOPATH
HOMEOWNER
HOMESTEAD
HOMEWARDS
HOMICIDAL
HOMOGRAPH
HOMOPHONE
HOMOPTERA
HONEYCOMB
HONEYMOON
HONKYTONK
HONORABLE
HONORIFIC
HOOLACHAN
HOPEFULLY
HOPLOLOGY
HOPSCOTCH
HORDEOLUM
HOREHOUND
HORNSTONE
HOROSCOPE
HORRIFIED
HORSEBACK
HORSEHAIR
HORSELESS
HORSEPLAY
HORSESHOE
HORSETAIL
HORSEWHIP
HORTATIVE
HORTATORY
HOSPITIUM
HOSTILITY
HOTHEADED
HOTTENTOT
HOURGLASS
HOURSTONE
HOUSEBOAT
HOUSECOAT
HOUSEHOLD
HOUSEMAID
HOUSEROOM
HOUSEWIFE
HOUSEWORK
HOUYHNHNM
HOWTOWDIE
HOYDENISH
IODOPHILE
JOBCENTRE
JOBERNOWL
JOBSEEKER
JOBSWORTH
JOCKSTRAP
JOCKTELEG
JOCULARLY
JOHANNINE
JORDANIAN
JOSEPHINE
JOSEPHSON
JOUISANCE
JOVIALITY
KOMINFORM
KONIMETER
KONISCOPE
LOADSTONE
LOAMSHIRE
LOATHSOME
LOBLOLLYS
LOBSCOUSE
LOCALIZED
LOCELLATE
LOCHINVAR
LOCKSMITH
LODESTONE
LODGEMENT
LOFTINESS
LOGARITHM
LOGICALLY
LOGISTICS
LOGOGRIPH
LOGOTHETE
LOHENGRIN
LOINCLOTH
LOITERING
LOMBARDIC
LONDONESE
LONGCHAMP
LONGEDFOR
LONGEVITY
LONGICORN
LONGINGLY
LONGITUDE
LONGLIVED
LONGRANGE
LONGSHORE
LOOKALIKE
LOOSEHEAD
LOOSELEAF
LOOSENESS
LOQUACITY
LORGNETTE
LOUDMOUTH
LOUISIANA
LOUSEWORT
LOWLANDER
LOWLINESS
MOCCASINS
MOCKERNUT
MODELLING
MODERATOR
MODERNISM
MODERNIST
MODERNITY
MODERNIZE
MODESTINE
MODILLION
MOGADISHU
MOISTNESS
MOLECULAR
MOLESKINS
MOLLITIES
MOLLYMAWK
MOMENTARY
MOMENTOUS
MONACTINE
MONASTERY
MONASTRAL
MONATOMIC
MONERGISM
MONEYWORT
MONGOLIAN
MONGOLISM
MONKSHOOD
MONOCEROS
MONOCHORD
MONOCOQUE
MONOCULAR
MONODRAMA
MONOGRAPH
MONOLOGUE
MONOMACHY
MONOMANIA
MONOMETER
MONOPLANE
MONOSTICH
MONOTROCH
MONOXYLON
MONSIGNOR
MONSTROUS
MONTACUTE
MONTAIGNE
MONTANISM
MONTANIST
MONTESPAN
MONTEZUMA
MONTICULE
MONZONITE
MOODINESS
MOONLIGHT
MOONRAKER
MOONSHINE
MOONSTONE
MORATORIA
MORATORIO
MORBIDITY
MORECAMBE
MORGANITE
MORMONISM
MORTALITY
MORTGAGEE
MORTGAGOR
MORTICIAN
MORTIFIED
MORTSTONE
MOSCHATEL
MOSKONFYT
MOTHBALLS
MOTHEATEN
MOTHERING
MOTOCROSS
MOTORBIKE
MOTORBOAT
MOTORCADE
MOTORISTS
MOURNIVAL
MOUSEHOLE
MOUSELIKE
MOUSETRAP
MOUSTACHE

MOUTHLESS
MOUTHWASH
MOYGASHEL
NOBLENESS
NOCTURNAL
NOISELESS
NOISINESS
NOLLEKENS
NOMINALLY
NOMINATOR
NOMOCRACY
NOMOTHETE
NONENTITY
NONILLION
NONPAREIL
NONPROFIT
NONSMOKER
NOOSPHERE
NORMALACY
NORMALITY
NORMALIZE
NORMATIVE
NORTHEAST
NORTHERLY
NORTHWARD
NORTHWEST
NORWEGIAN
NOSEBLEED
NOSTALGIA
NOSTALGIC
NOSTOLOGY
NOTARIKON
NOTCHBACK
NOTEPAPER
NOTOCHORD
NOTONECTA
NOTORIETY
NOTORIOUS
NOVELETTE
NOVICIATE
NOVITIATE
NOVOCAINE
NOVODAMUS
POCKETFUL
POCKMANKY
POETASTER
POIGNANCY
POINTEDLY
POINTLESS
POINTSMAN
POISONING
POISONOUS
POLEMARCH
POLEMICAL
POLIANITE
POLICEMAN
POLITBURO
POLITESSE
POLITICAL
POLITIQUE
POLLINATE
POLLUTANT
POLLUTION
POLONAISE
POLVERINE
POLYANDRY
POLYESTER
POLYGONAL
POLYGRAPH
POLYNESIA
POLYPHONE
POLYPHONY
POLYTHENE
POMOERIUM
POMPADOUR
POMPHOLYX
POMPOSITY
PONDEROSA
PONDEROUS
PONTLEVIS
POORHOUSE
POPLITEAL
POPPERING
POPPYCOCK
POPULARLY
POPULATED
PORBEAGLE
PORCELAIN
PORCUPINE
PORIFERAN
PORPOISES
PORPORATE
PORRINGER
PORTERAGE
PORTFOLIO
PORTRAYAL
PORTREEVE
POSSESSED
POSSESSOR
POSSIBLES
POSTCARDS
POSTERIOR
POSTERITY
POSTHOUSE
POSTNATAL
POSTPONED
POSTULANT
POSTULATE
POSTWOMAN
POTASSIUM
POTBOILER
POTENTATE
POTENTIAL
POTHOLING
POTHUNTER
POTPOURRI
POTTINGAR
POUJADIST
POULTERER
POWELLITE
POWERBOAT
POWERLESS
ROADBLOCK
ROADHOUSE
ROADSTEAD
ROADWORKS
ROBERTSON
ROCAMBOLE
ROISTERER
ROOSEVELT
ROOTSTOCK
ROQUEFORT
RORSCHACH
ROSCOMMON
ROSEWATER
ROSINANTE
ROSMARINE
ROSMINIAN
ROSTELLUM
ROTAPLANE
ROTTERDAM
ROTUNDATE
ROTUNDITY
ROUGHCAST
ROUGHNECK
ROUGHNESS
ROUGHSHOD
ROUMANIAN
ROUMANSCH
ROUNCEVAL
ROUNCIVAL
ROUNDBACK
ROUNDELAY
ROUNDFISH
ROUNDHAND
ROUNDHEAD
ROUNDSMAN
ROUSSETTE
ROUTINELY
ROWDINESS
ROXBURGHE
ROZINANTE
SOAPSTONE
SOBERNESS
SOBRIQUET
SOCIALISM
SOCIALIST
SOCIALITE
SOCIALIZE
SOCIOLECT
SOCIOLOGY
SOFTCOVER
SOFTENING
SOGGINESS
SOLDERING
SOLDIERLY
SOLEMNITY
SOLEMNIZE
SOLFEGGIO
SOLFERINO
SOLFIDIAN
SOLICITOR
SOLILOQUY
SOLIPSISM
SOLITAIRE
SOLLICKER
SOMASCOPE
SOMEPLACE
SOMETHING
SOMETIMES
SOMEWHERE
SOMMELIER
SOMNOLENT
SONGSMITH
SONNETEER
SONOMETER
SOOTERKIN
SOPHISTER
SOPHISTIC
SOPHISTRY
SOPHOCLES
SOPHOMORE
SOPORIFIC
SOPPINESS
SORCERESS
SORROWFUL
SORTILEGE
SOSTENUTO
SOTTISIER
SOUBRETTE
SOUFRIERE
SOULFULLY
SOUNDBITE
SOUNDLESS
SOUNDNESS
SOURDOUGH
SOUTENEUR
SOUTHDOWN
SOUTHEAST
SOUTHERLY
SOUTHWARD
SOUTHWARK
SOUTHWEST
SOUVLAKIA
SOUWESTER
SOVENANCE
SOVEREIGN
TOADSTONE
TOADSTOOL
TOASTRACK
TOBERMORY
TOCCATINA
TOLERABLE
TOLERABLY
TOLERANCE
TOLERATED
TOLLHOUSE
TOLPUDDLE
TOMBSTONE
TOMENTOSE
TONBRIDGE
TONOMETER
TONOPLAST
TOOTHACHE
TOOTHCOMB
TOOTHLESS
TOOTHPICK
TOOTHSOME
TOPDRAWER
TOPIARIST
TOPICALLY
TORBANITE
TORMENTER
TORMENTIL
TORMENTOR
TORMENTUM
TORTELIER
TOSCANINI
TOTALIZER
TOTAQUINE
TOTTENHAM
TOUCHDOWN
TOUCHLINE
TOUCHWOOD
TOUGHNESS
TOURNEDOS
TOVARISCH
TOWCESTER
TOWELLING
TOWNSFOLK
TOXOPHILY
VOICELESS
VOLAGEOUS
VOLATIBLE
VOLGOGRAD
VOLKSRAAD
VOLTIGEUR
VOLTINISM
VOLTMETER
VOLTURNUS
VOLUCRINE
VOLUNTARY
VOLUNTEER
VOODOOISM
VORACIOUS
VORTICISM
VORTIGERN
VOUCHSAFE
WOBBEGONG
WODEHOUSE
WOEBEGONE
WOLFHOUND
WOLLASTON
WOLVERINE
WOMANHOOD
WOMANISER
WOMANIZER
WOMANKIND
WOMENFOLK
WONDERFUL
WOODBORER
WOODCHUCK
WOODCRAFT
WOODENTOP
WOODHOUSE
WOODLANDS
WOODLOUSE
WOODSHOCK
WOOLINESS
WOOMERANG
WORCESTER
WORDINESS
WORDSMITH
WORKFORCE
WORKHORSE
WORKHOUSE
WORKPLACE
WORKSPACE
WORLDWIDE
WORMEATEN
WORRISOME
WORTHLESS
YOHIMBINE
YORKSHIRE
YOUNGSTER
ZOOLOGIST
ZOOMANTIC
ZOOSCOPIC
ZOROASTER
APARTHEID
APARTMENT
APATHETIC
APENNINES
APERIODIC
APERITIVE
APHRODITE
APOCRYPHA
APOLLONUS
APOLOGIST
APOLOGIZE
APOPHATIC
APOPHYSIS

APOSTOLIC
APPALLING
APPARATUS
APPARITOR
APPEALING
APPENDAGE
APPERTAIN
APPETIZER
APPLEJACK
APPLIANCE
APPLICANT
APPOINTED
APPOINTEE
APPORTION
APPRAISAL
APPREHEND
APPROVING
EPARCHATE
EPAULETTE
EPEDAPHIC
EPEOLATRY
EPHEDRINE
EPHEMERAL
EPHEMERIS
EPHEMERON
EPHESIANS
EPHIALTES
EPICEDIUM
EPICENTRE
EPICLESIS
EPICUREAN
EPICYCLIC
EPIDERMIS
EPIGAEOUS
EPILEPTIC
EPINASTIC
EPINICION
EPINIKION
EPIPHRAGM
EPIPHYSIS
EPIPHYTIC
EPIPOLISM
EPISCOPAL
EPISTAXIS
EPISTOLER
EPITHESIS
EPITOMIZE
EPONYMOUS
EPULATION
IPHIGENIA
IPRINDOLE
OPENENDED
OPENHEART
OPERATING
OPERATION
OPERATIVE
OPERCULUM
OPHIUCHUS
OPOBALSAM
OPODELDOC
OPPENHEIM
OPPONENTS
OPPORTUNE
OPPRESSED
OPPRESSOR
OPSIMATHY
OPTICALLY
OPTOMETRY
OPTOPHONE
OPULENTLY
SPACELESS
SPACESHIP
SPACESUIT
SPADASSIN
SPAGHETTI
SPARINGLY
SPARKLERS
SPARKLING
SPARTACUS
SPASMODIC
SPATIALLY
SPATTERED
SPEAKEASY
SPEARHEAD
SPEARMINT
SPEARSIDE
SPEARWORT
SPECIALLY
SPECIALTY
SPECIFICS
SPECIFIED
SPECIMENS
SPECTACLE
SPECTATOR
SPECULATE
SPEECHIFY
SPEEDBOAT
SPEEDWELL
SPELDRING
SPELLBIND
SPELUNKER
SPHACELUS
SPHENDONE
SPHERICAL
SPHINCTER
SPICILEGE
SPICINESS
SPIDERWEB
SPIKENARD
SPILLICAN
SPILLIKIN
SPINDRIER
SPINDRIFT
SPINELESS
SPINNAKER
SPINNERET
SPIRITOUS
SPIRITUAL
SPLENDOUR
SPLENETIC
SPLENITIS
SPLINTERS
SPLITTING
SPOFFORTH
SPOILSMAN
SPOKESMAN
SPONGEBAG
SPONSORED
SPOONBILL
SPOONFEED
SPOROCARP
SPORTSMAN
SPORTSMEN
SPOTLIGHT
SPRAICKLE
SPRAUCHLE
SPREADING
SPRECHERY
SPRIGHTLY
SPRINGALD
SPRINGBOK
SPRINGLET
SPRINKLER
SPRITEFUL
SPRITSAIL
SPUNCULID
UPAITHRIC
UPANISHAD
UPCOUNTRY
UPHOLSTER
UPLIFTING
UPPERMOST
UPSETTING
AQUAPLANE
AQUARELLE
AQUILEGIA
EQUALIZER
EQUIPMENT
EQUIPOISE
EQUISETUM
EQUITABLE
EQUITABLY
EQUIVOCAL
EQUIVOQUE
SQUADRONE
SQUALIDLY
SQUATTERS
SQUEAMISH
SQUINANCY
SQUINTING
SQUIREAGE
SQUIRMING
ARABESQUE
ARABINOSE
ARACHNOID
ARAGONITE
ARAUCARIA
ARBITRAGE
ARBITRARY
ARBITRATE
ARBORETUM
ARCHANGEL
ARCHETYPE
ARCHIBALD
ARCHITECT
ARCHIVIST
ARCHIVOLT
ARCTOGAEA
ARDUOUSLY
AREOPAGUS
ARGENTINA
ARGENTINE
ARISTOTLE
ARKWRIGHT
ARLINGTON
ARMADILLO
ARMAMENTS
ARMISTICE
ARMSTRONG
ARQUEBUSE
ARRESTING
ARRIVISTE
ARROGANCE
ARROWHEAD
ARROWROOT
ARSENICAL
ARTEMISIA
ARTERIOLE
ARTHRITIC
ARTHRITIS
ARTHROPOD
ARTHROSIS
ARTHURIAN
ARTICHOKE
ARTICULAR
ARTIFICER
ARTILLERY
BRACTEOLE
BRADLAUGH
BRAINCASE
BRAINLESS
BRAINWASH
BRAINWAVE
BRAMBLING
BRANCHING
BRANDIRON
BRASENOSE
BRASSERIE
BRASSICAS
BRASSIERE
BRASSWARE
BRATWURST
BRAZILIAN
BREADLINE
BREAKABLE
BREAKAGES
BREAKAWAY
BREAKDOWN
BREAKEVEN
BREAKFAST
BREAKNECK
BREATHING
BREECHING
BRICKWORK
BRICKYARD
BRIDEWELL
BRIDLEWAY
BRIEFCASE
BRIEFNESS
BRIGADIER
BRIGADOON
BRILLIANT
BRIMSTONE
BRIQUETTE
BRISKNESS
BRISTLING
BRITANNIA
BRITANNIC
BRITSCHKA
BROADCAST
BROADLOOM
BROADSIDE
BROKERAGE
BRONCHIAL
BROTHERLY
BROUGHTON
BRUMMAGEM
BRUNHILDE
BRUSHWOOD
BRUSQUELY
BRUTALISM
BRUTALITY
BRUTALIZE
CRACKDOWN
CRACKLING
CRACKSMAN
CRACOVIAN
CRAFTSMAN
CRANBERRY
CRANBORNE
CRAPULENT
CRAPULOUS
CRASHLAND
CRAZINESS
CREDULITY
CREDULOUS
CREMATION
CREMATORY
CREPITATE
CREPOLINE
CRESCELLE
CRESCENDO
CRETINOUS
CRIBELLUM
CRICKETER
CRIMINATE
CRINOLINE
CRIPPLING
CRISPNESS
CRITERION
CRITICISM
CRITICIZE
CROCKFORD
CROCODILE
CROISSANT
CROOKBACK
CROOKEDLY
CROQUETTE
CROSSBEAM
CROSSBILL
CROSSBRED
CROSSEYED
CROSSFIRE
CROSSOVER
CROSSWALK
CROSSWIND
CROSSWISE
CROSSWORD
CROTCHETY
CROUSTADE
CROWNLIKE
CROWSBILL
CROWSFOOT
CRUCIALLY
CRUDENESS
CRUMBLING
CRUSTACEA
CRYOGENIC
CRYOMETER
CRYPTOGAM
DRACONIAN
DRAFTSMAN
DRAGONFLY
DRAINPIPE
DRAMATICS
DRAMATIST
DRAMATIZE
DRAVIDIAN
DREAMLESS
DRIFTWOOD
DRINKABLE
DRIPSTONE

DROMEDARY
DROPPINGS
DROPSICAL
DRUGSTORE
DRUMSTICK
DRUNKENLY
DRYASDUST
ERADICATE
ERGATANER
ERIOMETER
ERISTICAL
EROGENOUS
EROSTRATE
EROTICISM
ERPINGHAM
ERRONEOUS
ERSTWHILE
ERUCIFORM
ERUDITION
FRACTIOUS
FRAGILITY
FRAGMENTS
FRAGONARD
FRAGRANCE
FRAGRANCY
FRAMBOISE
FRAMEWORK
FRANCESCA
FRANCHISE
FRANCOLIN
FRANGLAIS
FRANKNESS
FRATCHETY
FRATERNAL
FREDERICK
FREEBOARD
FREELANCE
FREEMASON
FREEPHONE
FREESTONE
FREESTYLE
FREEWHEEL
FREIGHTER
FRENCHMAN
FRENCHMEN
FREQUENCY
FRESHENER
FRESHNESS
FRETFULLY
FRICASSEE
FRIESLAND
FRIGATOON
FRIGHTFUL
FRIGIDITY
FRITHBORH
FRIVOLITY
FRIVOLOUS
FRIZZANTE
FROBISHER
FROGMARCH
FROGMOUTH
FROGSPAWN
FROISSART
FROSTBITE
FRUCTIDOR
FRUGALITY
FRUITCAKE
FRUITERER
FRUITLESS
FRUSTRATE
GRACELESS
GRADATION
GRADGRIND
GRADUALLY
GRADUATED
GRAMPIANS
GRANDIOSE
GRANDNESS
GRANDSIRE
GRANULATE
GRANULITE
GRANULOSE
GRAPESHOT
GRAPETREE
GRAPEVINE
GRAPHICAL
GRAPPLING
GRASSLAND
GRATICULE
GRATITUDE
GRAVADLAX
GRAVESEND
GRAVESIDE
GRAVEYARD
GRAVITATE
GREASEGUN
GREATCOAT
GREATNESS
GREENAWAY
GREENBACK
GREENFEED
GREENGAGE
GREENHEAD
GREENHORN
GREENMAIL
GREENROOM
GREENSAND
GREENWEED
GREENWICH
GREENWOOD
GREENYARD
GREETINGS
GREGARINE
GREGORIAN
GRENADIER
GRENADINE
GRENVILLE
GREYBEARD
GREYHOUND
GREYWACKE
GRIEVANCE
GRIMALKIN
GRIMINESS
GRINGOLET
GRISAILLE
GROCERIES
GROSGRAIN
GROSVENOR
GROTESQUE
GROUNDHOG
GROUNDING
GROUNDNUT
GROUNDSEL
GRUBBINOL
GRUELLING
GRUFFNESS
GRUMBLING
IRASCIBLE
IRONSIDES
IRONSTONE
IRONWORKS
IRRADIANT
IRRADIATE
IRRAWADDY
IRREGULAR
IRRITABLE
IRRITABLY
IRRITATED
IRRUPTION
IRVINGISM
KROPOTKIN
KRUMMHORN
MRIDAMGAM
MRIDANGAM
ORANGEADE
ORANGEMAN
ORATORIAN
ORBICULAR
ORCHESTRA
ORDINAIRE
ORDINANCE
ORGANELLE
ORGANICAL
ORGANISED
ORGANISER
ORGANIZED
ORGANIZER
ORGANZINE
ORGIASTIC
ORGILLOUS
ORICALCHE
ORIENTATE
ORIFLAMME
ORIGENIST
ORIGINATE
ORMANDINE
OROBANCHE
OROGRAPHY
ORPHANAGE
ORPHARION
ORPINGTON
ORTANIQUE
ORTHODOXY
ORTHOLOGY
ORTHOPTER
ORTHOTONE
PRACTICAL
PRACTISED
PRACTOLOL
PRAGMATIC
PRANKSTER
PREBENDAL
PRECATORY
PRECEDENT
PRECEDING
PRECENTOR
PRECEPTOR
PRECIEUSE
PRECINCTS
PRECIPICE
PRECISELY
PRECISIAN
PRECISION
PRECISIVE
PRECOCITY
PRECONISE
PRECURSOR
PREDATORY
PREDICANT
PREDICATE
PREDICTOR
PREDIKANT
PREDILECT
PREFATORY
PREFERRED
PREFIGURE
PREGNANCY
PREHALLUX
PREJUDICE
PRELECTOR
PRELUSORY
PREMATURE
PREMONISH
PREMOTION
PREOCCUPY
PREORDAIN
PREPOLLEX
PRESBYTER
PRESCIENT
PRESCRIBE
PRESCUTUM
PRESENTED
PRESENTER
PRESENTLY
PRESERVED
PRESERVER
PRESERVES
PRESHRUNK
PRESIDENT
PRESIDIAL
PRESIDIUM
PRESSGANG
PRETENDER
PRETERITE
PRETERMIT
PREVALENT
PREVERNAL
PRICELESS
PRIESTESS
PRIESTLEY
PRIMAEVAL
PRIMARILY
PRIMAVERA
PRIMITIAE
PRIMITIVE
PRIMULINE
PRINCETON
PRINCIPAL
PRINCIPLE
PRINTABLE
PRISMATIC
PRIVATEER
PRIVATELY
PRIVATION
PRIVATIZE
PRIVILEGE
PROACTIVE
PROBABLES
PROBATION
PROBOSCIS
PROCACITY
PROCEDURE
PROCERITY
PROCESSOR
PROCLITIC
PROCOELUS
PROCONSUL
PROCREATE
PRODROMAL
PRODROMUS
PROFANELY
PROFANITY
PROFESSED
PROFESSOR
PROFITEER
PROFUSELY
PROFUSION
PROGNOSIS
PROGRAMME
PROJECTED
PROJECTOR
PROKARYON
PROKOFIEV
PROLACTIN
PROLAMINE
PROLEPSIS
PROLIXITY
PROLONGED
PROLUSION
PROMACHOS
PROMENADE
PROMINENT
PROMISING
PROMOTION
PROMPTING
PROMUSCIS
PRONGHORN
PRONOUNCE
PROOFREAD
PROPAGATE
PROPELLED
PROPELLER
PROPELLOR
PROPERDIN
PROPHETIC
PROPIONIC
PROPONENT
PROPRIETY
PROPTOSIS
PROPYLENE
PROROGATE
PROSCRIBE
PROSECUTE
PROSELYTE
PROSTRATE
PROTAMINE
PROTECTOR
PROTESTER
PROTHESIS
PROTHORAX
PROTOSTAR
PROTOTYPE
PROUDHORN
PROUSTITE
PROVEDORE
PROVENDER
PROVIDENT
PROVIDING
PROVISION
PROVOKING
PROVOLONE
PROXIMATE

PROXIMITY
PRUDENTLY
PRURIENCE
PRYTANEUM
TRACEABLE
TRACHINUS
TRACKLESS
TRACKSUIT
TRACTABLE
TRADEMARK
TRADESMAN
TRADEWIND
TRADITION
TRAFALGAR
TRAGEDIAN
TRAGELAPH
TRAINABLE
TRAMLINES
TRANSCEND
TRANSFORM
TRANSFUSE
TRANSHUME
TRANSIENT
TRANSLATE
TRANSMUTE
TRANSPIRE
TRANSPORT
TRANSPOSE
TRANSSHIP
TRANSVAAL
TRAPEZIAL
TRAPEZIST
TRAPEZIUM
TRAPEZIUS
TRAPEZOID
TRAPPINGS
TRASIMENE
TRATTORIA
TRAUMATIC
TRAVELERS
TRAVELING
TRAVELLER
TREACHERY
TREADMILL
TREASURER
TREATMENT
TREBIZOND
TREBUCHET
TREDRILLE
TREETRUNK
TREGEAGLE
TREGETOUR
TREILLAGE
TREMATODE
TREMBLING
TREMOLITE
TREMULATE
TREMULOUS
TRENCHANT
TREVELYAN
TRIANGLED
TRIATHLON
TRIBALISM
TRIBESMAN
TRIBESMEN
TRIBOLOGY
TRIBUNATE
TRIBUTARY
TRICERION
TRICKLESS
TRICKSTER
TRICLINIC
TRICOLOUR
TRIDYMITE
TRIENNIAL
TRIERARCH
TRIETERIC
TRIFORIUM
TRIHEDRON
TRILITHON
TRILOBITE
TRIMESTER
TRIMMINGS
TRINKETER
TRIPITAKA
TRIPMETER
TRISAGION
TRITENESS
TRITICALE
TRITURATE
TRIUMPHAL
TRIVIALLY
TROCHILIC
TROCHILUS
TROMPETTE
TRONDHEIM
TROOPSHIP
TROOSTITE
TROPAELIN
TROPARION
TROSSACHS
TROUBADOR
TROUSSEAU
TRUCKLOAD
TRUCULENT
TRUEPENNY
TRUMPEDUP
TRUMPETER
TRUNCATED
TRUNCHEON
TRUTINATE
TRYPHOEUS
URANISCUS
UREDINIAL
URICONIAN
URINATION
UROKINASE
URTICARIA
URUGUAYAN
WRANGLERS
WREAKLESS
WRECKFISH
WRESTLING
WRONGDOER
WRONGFOOT
ASCENDANT
ASCENDING
ASCENSION
ASCERTAIN
ASCLEPIUS
ASHKENAZI
ASHMOLEAN
ASPARAGUS
ASPARTAME
ASPERSION
ASPIRATOR
ASPLENIUM
ASSAILANT
ASSERTING
ASSERTION
ASSERTIVE
ASSIDUITY
ASSIDUOUS
ASSISTANT
ASSOCIATE
ASSONANCE
ASSUETUDE
ASSURANCE
ASSUREDLY
ASTHMATIC
ASTOUNDED
ASTRAGALS
ASTRAKHAN
ASTRODOME
ASTROLABE
ASTROLOGY
ASTRONAUT
ASTRONOMY
ASTROPHEL
ASTROTURF
ASTUCIOUS
ASYMMETRY
ASYNERGIA
ESCALATOR
ESCOPETTE
ESCULENTS
ESEMPLASY
ESMERALDA
ESOPHAGUS
ESPAGNOLE
ESPERANCE
ESPERANTO
ESPIONAGE
ESPLANADE
ESQUILINE
ESSENTIAL
ESTABLISH
ESTAFETTE
ESTAMINET
ESTHETICS
ESTIMABLE
ESTRANGED
ESTRAPADE
ESTRELDID
ISALLOBAR
ISCHAEMIC
ISINGLASS
ISLAMABAD
ISOCRATES
ISODORIAN
ISOLATION
ISOMERASE
ISOMETRIC
ISOPROPYL
ISOSCELES
ISOTACTIC
ISOTROPIC
ISRAELITE
OSCILLATE
OSTEODERM
OSTEOPATH
OSTRACISM
OSTRACIZE
OSTROGOTH
PSEUDAXIS
PSEUDONYM
PSORIASIS
PSYCHICAL
PSYCHOSIS
PSYCHOTIC
TSAREVICH
USHERETTE
ATAHUALPA
ATAVISTIC
ATHEISTIC
ATHELSTAN
ATHENAEUM
ATHLETICS
ATONEMENT
ATROCIOUS
ATTACKING
ATTAINDER
ATTEMPTED
ATTENDANT
ATTENTION
ATTENTIVE
ATTENUATE
ATTITUDES
ATTRIBUTE
ATTRITION
ATTUITION
CTESIPHON
ETCETERAS
ETERNALLY
ETHELBERT
ETHEREOUS
ETHIOPIAN
ETHNOLOGY
ETIOLATED
ETIQUETTE
ETYMOLOGY
ITALICIZE
ITINERANT
ITINERARY
ITINERATE
OTHERWISE
OTTERBURN
OTTRELITE
PTARMIGAN
PTERIDIUM
PTEROSAUR
STABILITY
STABILIZE
STABLEBOY
STABLELAD
STABLEMAN
STAGEHAND
STAGGERED
STAGIRITE
STAGYRITE
STAINLESS
STAIRCASE
STALEMATE
STALENESS
STALWORTH
STAMMERER
STANCHION
STANDARDS
STANDERBY
STANDGALE
STANDPIPE
STANNATOR
STARBOARD
STARGAZER
STARKNESS
STARLIGHT
STARSTONE
STARTLING
STATEHOOD
STATELESS
STATEMENT
STATEROOM
STATESIDE
STATESMAN
STATEWIDE
STATIONED
STATIONER
STATISTIC
STATOLITH
STATUETTE
STATUTORY
STAUNCHLY
STAVANGER
STEADFAST
STEAMBOAT
STEAMSHIP
STEELHEAD
STEELYARD
STEENBRAS
STEENKIRK
STEEPNESS
STEERSMAN
STEGNOSIS
STEGNOTIC
STEGOSAUR
STEINBECK
STEINBOCK
STENOPAIC
STERADIAN
STERCORAL
STERILITY
STERILIZE
STERNFAST
STERNNESS
STEVEDORE
STEVENSON
STIFFENER
STIFFNESS
STILLBORN
STILLNESS
STILLROOM
STILTBIRD
STIMULANT
STIMULATE
STINGAREE
STINKBIRD
STINKHORN
STINKWOOD
STIPULATE
STIRABOUT
STOCKFISH
STOCKHOLM
STOCKINET
STOCKINGS
STOCKPILE
STOCKROOM
STOCKWORK
STOCKYARD
STOICALLY
STOLIDITY
STOMACHIC
STONEBOAT

STONECHAT
STONECROP
STONEHAND
STONELESS
STONEWALL
STONEWARE
STONEWORK
STONEWORT
STONKERED
STOOLBALL
STOREROOM
STORIATED
STORNAWAY
STORYBOOK
STORYLINE
STOUTNESS
STOVEPIPE
STOWNLINS
STRAGGLER
STRAINING
STRANGELY
STRANGLER
STRANGLES
STRANGURY
STRAPHANG
STRAPLESS
STRAPPADO
STRAPPING
STRATAGEM
STRATEGIC
STREAMING
STREETAGE
STREETCAR
STRENUOUS
STRESSFUL
STRETCHED
STRETCHER
STRIATION
STRICTURE
STRIDENCY
STRINGENT
STRINGOPS
STRIPLING
STROBILUS
STROLLING
STROMBOLI
STRONGARM
STRONGYLE
STRONTIUM
STROSSERS
STRUCTURE
STRUMITIS
STRUTTING
STUMBLING
STUMPWORK
STUPEFIED
STUPIDITY
STYLISHLY
STYLISTIC
STYLOBATE
UTICENSIS
UTTERANCE
UTTERLESS
UTTERMOST
YTTERBIUM
AUBERGINE
AUBRIETIA
AUCTORIAL
AUDACIOUS
AUGUSTINE
AURICULAR
AUSTERITY
AUSTRALIA
AUTHENTIC
AUTHORESS
AUTHORITY
AUTHORIZE
AUTOCLAVE
AUTOCRACY
AUTOCROSS
AUTOGRAPH
AUTOLATRY
AUTOLYCUS
AUTOLYSIS
AUTOMAKER
AUTOMATED
AUTOMATIC
AUTOMATON
AUTONOMIC
AUTOPILOT
AUTOROUTE
AUTOSCOPY
AUXILIARY
BUCCANEER
BUCENTAUR
BUCHAREST
BUCKETFUL
BUCKTEETH
BUCKTHORN
BUCKWHEAT
BUDGETARY
BULGARIAN
BULKINESS
BULLDOZER
BULLFIGHT
BULLFINCH
BUMBLEBEE
BUMPTIOUS
BUNDESTAG
BURKINABE
BURLESQUE
BURLINESS
BURROUGHS
BURROWING
BURUNDIAN
BUTTERBUR
BUTTERCUP
BUTTERFLY
BUTTERNUT
CUBBYHOLE
CUCHULAIN
CUFFLINKS
CULMINATE
CULTIVATE
CUNCTATOR
CUNEIFORM
CUPRESSUS
CURETTAGE
CURFUFFLE
CURIOSITY
CURIOUSLY
CURRENTLY
CURRYCOMB
CURSORILY
CURTILAGE
CURVATURE
CUSPIDORE
CUSTODIAL
CUSTODIAN
CUSTOMARY
CUSTOMIZE
CUTANEOUS
CUTTHROAT
DUBIOUSLY
DUBROVNIK
DUCKBOARD
DULCINIST
DUMBARTON
DUMBFOUND
DUNDREARY
DUNGAREES
DUNGENESS
DUNGEONER
DUNSINANE
DUNSTABLE
DUODECIMO
DUPLICAND
DUPLICATE
DUPLICITY
DUTIFULLY
EUCHARIST
EUCHLORIC
EUCLIDEAN
EUDAEMONY
EUHEMERUS
EUMENIDES
EUMYCETES
EUPHEMISM
EUPHONIUM
EUPHORBIA
EUPHRATES
EURHYTHMY
EURIPIDES
EUSKARIAN
EUTROPHIC
FUGACIOUS
FUGGINESS
FULLBLOWN
FULLERENE
FULLGROWN
FULLSCALE
FULMINANT
FULMINATE
FUNDAMENT
FUNGIBLES
FUNGICIDE
FUNICULAR
FURACIOUS
FURIOUSLY
FURNIMENT
FURNITURE
FURTIVELY
FUSILLADE
FUSSINESS
FUSTIGATE
FUSTINESS
FUZZINESS
GUACAMOLE
GUARANTEE
GUARANTOR
GUARDROOM
GUARDSMAN
GUATEMALA
GUERRILLA
GUESSWORK
GUIDEBOOK
GUIDELINE
GUILDHALL
GUILELESS
GUILLEMOT
GUILLOCHE
GUILTLESS
GUINEVERE
GUITARIST
GUJARATHI
GUMSHIELD
GUNCOTTON
GUNPOWDER
GUSTATION
GUTENBERG
GUTTERING
HUCKABACK
HUMANKIND
HUMDINGER
HUMILIATE
HUMONGOUS
HUMUNGOUS
HUNCHBACK
HUNDREDTH
HUNGARIAN
HUNKYDORY
HURRICANE
HURRICANO
HURRIEDLY
HUSBANDLY
HUSBANDRY
HUSKINESS
HUTTERITE
JUBILANCE
JUDGEMENT
JUDICIARY
JUDICIOUS
JUICINESS
JUNEBERRY
JUNKETING
JURIDICAL
JUSTIFIED
JUSTINIAN
JUVENILIA
JUXTAPOSE
LUBAVITCH
LUBRICANT
LUBRICATE
LUCIFERIN
LUCRATIVE
LUCRETIUS
LUCTATION
LUCUBRATE
LUDICROUS
LUMBERING
LUMBRICUS
LUMINAIRE
LUMINANCE
LUNCHTIME
LURIDNESS
LUSTIHOOD
LUSTINESS
LUTESCENT
LUXEMBURG
LUXURIANT
LUXURIATE
LUXURIOUS
MUCHLOVED
MUCKENDER
MUCORALES
MUDDINESS
MUFFETTEE
MUGGLETON
MUGLARITE
MUJAHIDIN
MULTIFORM
MULTIPLEX
MULTITUDE
MUMCHANCE
MUMPSIMUS
MUNDUNGUS
MUNICIPAL
MUNIMENTS
MUNITIONS
MURDERESS
MURDEROUS
MURKINESS
MURMURING
MUSCADINE
MUSCARINE
MUSCOVADO
MUSCOVITE
MUSHINESS
MUSHROOMS
MUSICALLY
MUSICHALL
MUSKETEER
MUSKETOON
MUSKOGEAN
MUSSITATE
MUSSOLINI
MUSSULMAN
MUSTINESS
MUTILATED
MUTOSCOPE
MUTTERING
MUZZINESS
NUCLEOLUS
NUMBSKULL
NUMERAIRE
NUMERATOR
NUMERICAL
NUMMULITE
NUNCUPATE
NUREMBERG
NURSEMAID
NUTJOBBER
NUTRIMENT
NUTRITION
NUTRITIVE
OUBLIETTE
OUDENARDE
OUGHTNESS
OUROBOROS
OUROBORUS
OURSELVES
OUTERMOST
OUTFITTER
OUTGOINGS
OUTGROWTH
OUTNUMBER
OUTOFTOWN
OUTRIGGER
OUTROOPER
OUTSIDERS
OUTSKIRTS
OUTSPOKEN

OUTSPREAD
OUTWARDLY
OUTWORKER
PUBLICIST
PUBLICITY
PUBLICIZE
PUBLISHED
PUBLISHER
PUCELLAGE
PUERILITY
PUERPERAL
PUFFINESS
PUGNACITY
PUISSANCE
PULLULATE
PULMONARY
PULPITEER
PULSATION
PULVERIZE
PUMMELLED
PUNCHLINE
PUNCTILIO
PUNCTUATE
PUNGENTLY
PUNISHING
PUPILLAGE
PUPPETEER
PURCHASER
PURDONIUM
PURGATIVE
PURGATORY
PURIFYING
PURITANIC
PURPOSELY
PURSUANCE
PURULENCE
PUSHCHAIR
PUSSYFOOT
QUADRATIC
QUADRATUS
QUADRILLE
QUADRUPED
QUADRUPLE
QUAILPIPE
QUALIFIED
QUALIFIER
QUANTICAL
QUANTOCKS
QUARENDEN
QUARTERLY
QUARTETTE
QUASIMODO
QUAVERING
QUEERNESS
QUENNELLE
QUERCETIN
QUERCETUS
QUERIMONY
QUERULOUS
QUICKLIME
QUICKNESS
QUICKSAND
QUICKSTEP
QUIESCENT
QUIETNESS
QUILLWORT
QUINQUINA
QUINTETTE
QUINTROON
QUINTUPLE
QUITTANCE
QUIVERFUL
QUIVERING
QUIZZICAL
QUODLIBET
QUOTATION
QUOTIDIAN
QUOTITION
RUBBERIZE
RUBICELLE
RUDBECKIA
RUDDIGORE
RUDDLEMAN
RUDIMENTS
RUFESCENT
RUFFIANLY
RUGGELACH
RUINATION
RUINOUSLY
RUNAROUND
RUNCINATE
RUNESTAVE
RUNNYMEDE
RUSHLIGHT
RUSTICATE
RUSTINESS
RUTHENIAN
RUTHENIUM
SUBALTERN
SUBCELLAR
SUBCORTEX
SUBDIVIDE
SUBDOLOUS
SUBEDITOR
SUBENTIRE
SUBJACENT
SUBJUGATE
SUBLIMATE
SUBLIMELY
SUBMARINE
SUBMERGED
SUBNORMAL
SUBROGATE
SUBSCRIBE
SUBSCRIPT
SUBSIDIZE
SUBSTANCE
SUBSTRATA
SUBSTRATE
SUBTENANT
SUBTITLED
SUCCEEDED
SUCCENTOR
SUCCESSOR
SUCCINATE
SUCCOTASH
SUCCUBINE
SUCCULENT
SUCCURSAL
SUDORIFIC
SUETONIUS
SUFFERING
SUFFOCATE
SUFFRAGAN
SUFFUSION
SUGARCANE
SULFUROUS
SULKINESS
SULPHONIC
SULPHURIC
SULTANATE
SUMMARILY
SUMMARIZE
SUMMATION
SUMPTUARY
SUMPTUOUS
SUNBATHER
SUNDOWNER
SUNFLOWER
SUNSCREEN
SUNSTROKE
SUNTANNED
SUPERETTE
SUPERFINE
SUPERNOVA
SUPERSEDE
SUPERSTAR
SUPERVENE
SUPERVISE
SUPINATOR
SUPPLIANT
SUPPLICAT
SUPPORTER
SUPPOSING
SUPPURATE
SUPREMACY
SUPREMELY
SUQUAMISH
SURCHARGE
SURCINGLE
SURFBOARD
SURFEITED
SURLINESS
SURMULLET
SURPRISED
SURQUEDRY
SURREJOIN
SURRENDER
SURROGATE
SURVEYING
SURVIVING
SUSCITATE
SUSPECTED
SUSPENDED
SUSPENDER
SUSPENSOR
SUSPICION
SUSTAINED
TUBBINESS
TUILERIES
TUILLETTE
TUMESCENT
TUMMYACHE
TUNGSTATE
TURBIDITY
TURBINATE
TURBULENT
TURCOPOLE
TURMAGENT
TURNABOUT
TURNBULLS
TURNROUND
TURNSTILE
TURNSTONE
TURNTABLE
TURPITUDE
TURQUOISE
TUTIORISM
VULCANIST
VULCANITE
VULCANIZE
VULGARIAN
VULGARISM
VULGARITY
VULPINITE
WULFENITE
WURLITZER
WUTHERING
ZUCCHETTO
AVAILABLE
AVALANCHE
AVOCATION
AVOIDABLE
AVOIDANCE
AVUNCULAR
EVAGATION
EVANGELIC
EVAPORATE
EVASIVELY
EVENTUATE
EVERGLADE
EVERGREEN
EVERYBODY
EVIDENTLY
EVITERNAL
EVOCATION
EVOCATIVE
EVOCATORY
EVOLUTION
OVENPROOF
OVERBLOWN
OVERBOARD
OVERCLOUD
OVERCROWD
OVERDRAFT
OVERDRAWN
OVERDRESS
OVERDRIVE
OVEREXERT
OVERGROWN
OVERHASTY
OVERHEADS
OVERJOYED
OVERLYING
OVERNIGHT
OVERPAINT
OVERPOISE
OVERPOWER
OVERRATED
OVERREACH
OVERREACT
OVERRIDER
OVERSHADE
OVERSHOES
OVERSHOOT
OVERSIGHT
OVERSIZED
OVERSLEEP
OVERSPEND
OVERSPILL
OVERSTATE
OVERSTEER
OVERTHROW
OVERTONES
OVERVALUE
OVERWEIGH
OVERWHELM
OVIPAROUS
OVULATION
UVAROVITE
AWAKENING
AWARENESS
AWESTRUCK
AWKWARDLY
DWINDLING
OWLEGLASS
OWNERSHIP
SWADDLING
SWAGGERER
SWANIMOTE
SWANSDOWN
SWEATBAND
SWEEPINGS
SWEETENER
SWEETMEAT
SWEETNESS
SWEETSHOP
SWIFTNESS
SWINBURNE
SWINEHERD
SWINGEING
SWORDFISH
SWORDPLAY
SWORDSMAN
SWOTHLING
TWAYBLADE
TWENTIETH
TWINKLING
AXIOMATIC
AXMINSTER
EXACTMENT
EXACTNESS
EXANIMATE
EXANTHEMA
EXARATION
EXCALIBUR
EXCAMBION
EXCAVATOR
EXCELLENT
EXCELSIOR
EXCEPTION
EXCESSIVE
EXCHEQUER
EXCIPIENT
EXCISEMAN
EXCITABLE
EXCLAIMED
EXCLUDING
EXCLUSION
EXCLUSIVE
EXCORIATE
EXCREMENT
EXCULPATE
EXCURSION
EXCUSABLE
EXCUSABLY
EXECRABLE
EXECRABLY
EXECUTANT
EXECUTION
EXECUTIVE
EXECUTRIX

EXEMPLARY
EXEMPLIFY
EXEMPTION
EXEQUATUR
EXERCISED
EXERCISES
EXHAUSTED
EXHIBITOR
EXISTENCE
EXODERMIS
EXONERATE
EXORATION
EXOSPHERE
EXOSTOSIS
EXPANSION
EXPANSIVE
EXPATIATE
EXPECTANT
EXPECTING
EXPEDIENT
EXPENSIVE
EXPERTISE
EXPIATION
EXPIATORY
EXPISCATE
EXPLETIVE
EXPLICATE
EXPLOITER
EXPLOSION
EXPLOSIVE
EXPORTING
EXPOSITOR
EXPRESSED
EXPRESSLY
EXPULSION
EXPURGATE
EXQUISITE
EXSICCATE
EXTEMPORE
EXTENSILE
EXTENSION
EXTENSIVE
EXTENUATE
EXTIRPATE
EXTORTION
EXTRACTOR
EXTRADITE
EXTREMELY
EXTREMISM
EXTREMIST
EXTREMITY
EXTRICATE
EXTRINSIC
EXTROVERT
EXTRUSION
EXUBERANT
EXUDATION
OXIDATION
AYATOLLAH
AYCKBOURN
AYLESBURY
BYPRODUCT
BYSTANDER
BYZANTINE
CYCLAMATE
CYCLOLITH
CYCLORAMA
CYCLOTRON
CYMBELINE
CYMBIDIUM
CYNEGETIC
CYNICALLY
DYNAMITED
DYSENTERY
DYSPEPSIA
DYSPEPTIC
DYSPHAGIA
DYSTROPHY
EYEBRIGHT
EYELETEER
EYEOPENER
EYESHADOW
EYESPLICE
EYESTRAIN
GYMNASIUM
GYMNASTIC
GYNOECIUM
GYROMANCY
GYROSCOPE
HYDRANGEA
HYDRAULIC
HYDRAZINE
HYDROFOIL
HYDROPULT
HYDROSTAT
HYGIENIST
HYLOBATES
HYPALLAGE
HYPERBOLA
HYPERBOLE
HYPHENATE
HYPINOSIS
HYPNOTISM
HYPNOTIST
HYPNOTIZE
HYPOCAUST
HYPOCRISY
HYPOCRITE
HYSTERICS
LYMESWOLD
LYMPHATIC
LYRICALLY
LYSIMETER
MYRMECOID
MYSTERIES
MYSTICISM
MYTHOLOGY
NYSTAGMUS
PYGMALION
PYONGYANG
PYRAMIDAL
PYRETHRUM
PYROMANCY
PYROMANIA
PYRRHONIC
PYTHONESS
SYBARITIC
SYCOPHANT
SYLLABARY
SYLLABLES
SYLLEPSIS
SYLLOGISM
SYLPHLIKE
SYLVANITE
SYMBIOSIS
SYMBIOTIC
SYMBOLISM
SYMBOLIST
SYMBOLIZE
SYMMETRIC
SYMPHONIC
SYMPHYSIS
SYMPODIUM
SYMPOSIUM
SYNAGOGUE
SYNANGIUM
SYNCHYSIS
SYNCOMIUM
SYNCOPATE
SYNDICATE
SYNEDRION
SYNERGIST
SYNIZESIS
SYNOECETE
SYNOVITIS
SYNTACTIC
SYNTHESIS
SYNTHETIC
SYRIACISM
SYRPHIDAE
TYMPANIST
TYPICALLY
TYRANNIZE
TYRANNOUS
WYANDOTTE
XYLOPHONE
ZYGOMATIC
ZYGOSPORE
OZOCERITE
OZOKERITE

9:3

ABANDONED
ABANDONEE
ABASEMENT
ABATEMENT
ACADEMIST
ACARIASIS
ADAPTABLE
AGALACTIC
AGAMEMNON
AHASUERUS
ALABASTER
AMARANTIN
AMARYLLIS
AMAUROSIS
AMAZEMENT
ANABOLISM
ANABRANCH
ANAEROBIC
ANAGLYPTA
ANALEPTIC
ANALGESIA
ANALGESIC
ANALOGOUS
ANAPLASTY
ANARCHIST
ANASTASIA
ANATOLIAN
ANATOMIST
ANATOMIZE
APARTHEID
APARTMENT
APATHETIC
ARABESQUE
ARABINOSE
ARACHNOID
ARAGONITE
ARAUCARIA
ATAHUALPA
ATAVISTIC
AVAILABLE
AVALANCHE
AWAKENING
AWARENESS
AYATOLLAH
BEACHHEAD
BEACHWEAR
BEANFEAST
BEARDLESS
BEARDSLEY
BEATITUDE
BEAUTEOUS
BEAUTIFUL
BLACKBALL
BLACKBIRD
BLACKFACE
BLACKFOOT
BLACKHEAD
BLACKJACK
BLACKLEAD
BLACKLIST
BLACKMAIL
BLACKMORE
BLACKNESS
BLACKWOOD
BLAMELESS
BLANDNESS
BLASPHEME
BLASPHEMY
BLATANTLY
BOANERGES
BOARDROOM
BOARDWALK
BOATHOUSE
BOATSWAIN
BRACTEOLE
BRADLAUGH
BRAINCASE
BRAINLESS
BRAINWASH
BRAINWAVE
BRAMBLING
BRANCHING
BRANDIRON
BRASENOSE
BRASSERIE
BRASSICAS
BRASSIERE
BRASSWARE
BRATWURST
BRAZILIAN
CEASEFIRE
CEASELESS
CHABAZITE
CHAFFINCH
CHAIRLIFT
CHALAZION
CHALIAPIN
CHALLENGE
CHALUMEAU
CHAMELEON
CHAMFRAIN
CHAMINADE
CHAMOMILE
CHAMPAGNE
CHAMPAIGN
CHAMPERTY
CHAMPLAIN
CHAMPLEVÉ
CHANTEUSE
CHANTILLY
CHAPARRAL
CHAPERONE
CHARABANC
CHARACTER
CHARGEFUL
CHARIVARI
CHARLATAN
CHARLOTTE
CHAROLAIS
CHARTERED
CHARTREUX
CHARWOMAN
CHARYBDIS
CHASTENED
CHATTERER
CHAUFFEUR
CHAVENDER
CHAWBACON
CLAMOROUS
CLAMPDOWN
CLAPBOARD
CLARENDON
CLARIFIER
CLASSICAL
CLASSLESS
CLASSMATE
CLASSROOM
COACHLOAD
COADJUTOR
COAGULANT
COAGULATE
COALESCED
COALFIELD
COALITION
COALMINER
COARCTATE
COASTLINE
CRACKDOWN
CRACKLING
CRACKSMAN
CRACOVIAN
CRAFTSMAN
CRANBERRY
CRANBORNE
CRAPULENT
CRAPULOUS
CRASHLAND
CRAZINESS
DEACONESS
DEADLIGHT
DEAFENING
DEATHLESS
DEATHTRAP
DIABLERIE
DIACRITIC
DIAERESIS
DIAGNOSIS
DIALECTAL

DIALECTIC
DIALOGITE
DIAMETRIC
DIANDROUS
DIANETICS
DIANOETIC
DIAPHRAGM
DIARRHOEA
DIASTASIS
DIATHESIS
DIAZEUXIS
DRACONIAN
DRAFTSMAN
DRAGONFLY
DRAINPIPE
DRAMATICS
DRAMATIST
DRAMATIZE
DRAVIDIAN
ECARDINES
EGAREMENT
EJACULATE
ELABORATE
ELAEOLITE
ELASTOMER
ELATERIUM
EMACIATED
EMANATION
ENACTMENT
ENAMELLED
ENAMOURED
EPARCHATE
EPAULETTE
ERADICATE
EVAGATION
EVANGELIC
EVAPORATE
EVASIVELY
EXACTMENT
EXACTNESS
EXANIMATE
EXANTHEMA
EXARATION
FEARFULLY
FEATHERED
FLABELLUM
FLAGELLIN
FLAGELLUM
FLAGEOLET
FLAGITATE
FLAGRANCE
FLAGSTAFF
FLAGSTONE
FLAMMABLE
FLAMSTEED
FLASHBACK
FLASHBULB
FLASHCUBE
FLATTENED
FLATTENER
FLATTERED
FLATTERER
FLATULENT
FLAVORING
FLAVOURED
FRACTIOUS
FRAGILITY
FRAGMENTS
FRAGONARD
FRAGRANCE
FRAGRANCY
FRAMBOISE
FRAMEWORK
FRANCESCA
FRANCHISE
FRANCOLIN
FRANGLAIS
FRANKNESS
FRATCHETY
FRATERNAL
GEARLEVER
GEARSHIFT
GEARSTICK
GEARWHEEL
GLABELLAR
GLADIATOR
GLADIOLUS
GLADSTONE
GLAIREOUS
GLAMORIZE
GLAMOROUS
GLANDULAR
GLASSWARE
GOALMOUTH
GRACELESS
GRADATION
GRADGRIND
GRADUALLY
GRADUATED
GRAMPIANS
GRANDIOSE
GRANDNESS
GRANDSIRE
GRANULATE
GRANULITE
GRANULOSE
GRAPESHOT
GRAPETREE
GRAPEVINE
GRAPHICAL
GRAPPLING
GRASSLAND
GRATICULE
GRATITUDE
GRAVADLAX
GRAVESEND
GRAVESIDE
GRAVEYARD
GRAVITATE
GUACAMOLE
GUARANTEE
GUARANTOR
GUARDROOM
GUARDSMAN
GUATEMALA
HEADBOARD
HEADCLOTH
HEADDRESS
HEADFIRST
HEADINESS
HEADLIGHT
HEADLINED
HEADSCARF
HEADSTALL
HEADSTONE
HEALTHILY
HEARDSMAN
HEARTACHE
HEARTBEAT
HEARTBURN
HEARTFELT
HEARTHRUG
HEARTLAND
HEARTLESS
HEATHLAND
HEAVINESS
HEAVISIDE
HEAVYDUTY
HOARFROST
HOARHOUND
HOARSTONE
IMAGELESS
IMAGINARY
INABILITY
INAMORATA
INAMORATO
INANIMATE
INANITION
INAUDIBLE
INAUDIBLY
INAUGURAL
IRASCIBLE
ISALLOBAR
ITALICIZE
JEALOUSLY
KHALIFATE
KHANSAMAH
KNACKERED
KNAPSCULL
KNAPSKULL
LEAFMOULD
LEAKPROOF
LEASEHOLD
LEASTWAYS
LEASTWISE
LIABILITY
LOADSTONE
LOAMSHIRE
LOATHSOME
MEANDRIAN
MEANWHILE
MEASURING
MEATBALLS
NIAISERIE
ODALISQUE
ORANGEADE
ORANGEMAN
ORATORIAN
PEACEABLE
PEACEABLY
PEACETIME
PEARLWORT
PEASANTRY
PEASEWEEP
PHACOLITE
PHAGOCYTE
PHALANGER
PHALAROPE
PHANARIOT
PHANSIGAR
PHANTASMA
PHARAMOND
PHARISAIC
PHARSALIA
PIACEVOLE
PLACATORY
PLACEMENT
PLACIDITY
PLAINNESS
PLAINSMAN
PLAINSONG
PLAINTIFF
PLAINTIVE
PLANETARY
PLASTERED
PLASTERER
PLATITUDE
PLATONIST
PLAUSIBLE
PLAUSIBLY
PLAUSTRAL
PLAYFULLY
PLAYGROUP
PLAYHOUSE
PLAYTHING
PRACTICAL
PRACTISED
PRACTOLOL
PRAGMATIC
PRANKSTER
PTARMIGAN
QUADRATIC
QUADRATUS
QUADRILLE
QUADRUPED
QUADRUPLE
QUAILPIPE
QUALIFIED
QUALIFIER
QUANTICAL
QUANTOCKS
QUARENDEN
QUARTERLY
QUARTETTE
QUASIMODO
QUAVERING
REACHABLE
READDRESS
READINESS
READYEARN
READYMADE
REALISTIC
REALITIES
REANIMATE
REARGUARD
REARHORSE
REARMOUSE
REARRANGE
REARWARDS
REASONING
RHAPSODIC
ROADBLOCK
ROADHOUSE
ROADSTEAD
ROADWORKS
SCABLANDS
SCAGLIOLA
SCALARIUM
SCALDFISH
SCALEABLE
SCALLAWAG
SCALLIONS
SCALLOPED
SCALLYWAG
SCAMBLING
SCANSORES
SCANTLING
SCAPEGOAT
SCAPOLITE
SCARECROW
SCARIFIER
SCARLATTI
SCATTERED
SCAVENGER
SEABOTTLE
SEAFARING
SEANNACHY
SEARCHING
SEASONING
SEAWORTHY
SHADINESS
SHAKEDOWN
SHAKINESS
SHAMEFAST
SHAMELESS
SHAMIANAH
SHAPELESS
SHARESMAN
SHARKSKIN
SHARPENER
SHARPNESS
SHASHLICK
SHATTERED
SHAVELING
SLABSTONE
SLACKNESS
SLAMMAKIN
SLANTWISE
SLAPHAPPY
SLAPSTICK
SLAUGHTER
SLAVISHLY
SMALLNESS
SMALLTIME
SMARTNESS
SNAKEWEED
SOAPSTONE
SPACELESS
SPACESHIP
SPACESUIT
SPADASSIN
SPAGHETTI
SPARINGLY
SPARKLERS
SPARKLING
SPARTACUS
SPASMODIC
SPATIALLY
SPATTERED
STABILITY
STABILIZE
STABLEBOY
STABLELAD
STABLEMAN
STAGEHAND
STAGGERED
STAGIRITE
STAGYRITE
STAINLESS
STAIRCASE
STALEMATE
STALENESS

STALWORTH
STAMMERER
STANCHION
STANDARDS
STANDERBY
STANDGALE
STANDPIPE
STANNATOR
STARBOARD
STARGAZER
STARKNESS
STARLIGHT
STARSTONE
STARTLING
STATEHOOD
STATELESS
STATEMENT
STATEROOM
STATESIDE
STATESMAN
STATEWIDE
STATIONED
STATIONER
STATISTIC
STATOLITH
STATUETTE
STATUTORY
STAUNCHLY
STAVANGER
SWADDLING
SWAGGERER
SWANIMOTE
SWANSDOWN
TEACHABLE
TEAKETTLE
TEARFULLY
TEARSHEET
THACKERAY
THALASSIC
THANATISM
THANKLESS
THATCHING
THAUMATIN
TOADSTONE
TOADSTOOL
TOASTRACK
TRACEABLE
TRACHINUS
TRACKLESS
TRACKSUIT
TRACTABLE
TRADEMARK
TRADESMAN
TRADEWIND
TRADITION
TRAFALGAR
TRAGEDIAN
TRAGELAPH
TRAINABLE
TRAMLINES
TRANSCEND
TRANSFORM
TRANSFUSE
TRANSHUME
TRANSIENT
TRANSLATE
TRANSMUTE
TRANSPIRE
TRANSPORT
TRANSPOSE
TRANSSHIP
TRANSVAAL
TRAPEZIAL
TRAPEZIST
TRAPEZIUM
TRAPEZIUS
TRAPEZOID
TRAPPINGS
TRASIMENE
TRATTORIA
TRAUMATIC
TRAVELERS
TRAVELING
TRAVELLER
TSAREVICH
TWAYBLADE
UNABASHED
UNADOPTED
UNALLOYED
UNALTERED
UNANIMITY
UNANIMOUS
UNASHAMED
UPAITHRIC
UPANISHAD
URANISCUS
UVAROVITE
VIABILITY
WEAKENING
WEARINESS
WEARISOME
WHALEBOAT
WHALEBONE
WHALEMEAT
WRANGLERS
WYANDOTTE
ZEALANDER
ALBATROSS
ALBERTINE
AMBERGRIS
AMBIGUITY
AMBIGUOUS
AMBITIOUS
AMBLYOPIA
AMBROSIAL
AMBROSIAN
AMBROTYPE
AMBULANCE
AMBUSCADE
ARBITRAGE
ARBITRARY
ARBITRATE
ARBORETUM
AUBERGINE
AUBRIETIA
BOBSLEIGH
CABALLERO
CABLEGRAM
CABRIOLET
CUBBYHOLE
DEBATABLE
DEBAUCHED
DEBAUCHEE
DEBENTURE
DEBUTANTE
DUBIOUSLY
DUBROVNIK
ELBOWROOM
EMBARRASS
EMBASSADE
EMBASSAGE
EMBATTLED
EMBELLISH
EMBEZZLER
EMBRACERY
EMBRACING
EMBRANGLE
EMBRASURE
EMBROCATE
EMBROGLIO
EMBROIDER
EMBROILED
EMBRYONIC
FABACEOUS
FABRICATE
FABULINUS
FEBRIFUGE
FIBROLINE
FIBROLITE
GABARDINE
GABERDINE
GABIONADE
GIBBERISH
GIBEONITE
GIBRALTAR
GOBETWEEN
HABERDINE
HABERGEON
HABITABLE
HABITUATE
HEBRIDEAN
HIBERNATE
HIBERNIAN
HOBBINOLL
HOBGOBLIN
HOBNAILED
IMBALANCE
IMBRANGLE
IMBRICATE
IMBROCATE
IMBROGLIO
JOBCENTRE
JOBERNOWL
JOBSEEKER
JOBSWORTH
JUBILANCE
KABELJOUW
LABORIOUS
LABOURITE
LABYRINTH
LIBELLOUS
LIBERALLY
LIBERATED
LIBERATOR
LIBERTIES
LIBERTINE
LIBRARIAN
LOBLOLLYS
LOBSCOUSE
LUBAVITCH
LUBRICANT
LUBRICATE
NABATHEAN
NEBBISHER
NOBLENESS
OBBLIGATO
OMBUDSMAN
ORBICULAR
OUBLIETTE
PUBLICIST
PUBLICITY
PUBLICIZE
PUBLISHED
PUBLISHER
REBELLION
REBOATION
RIBBONISM
ROBERTSON
RUBBERIZE
RUBICELLE
SABBATIAN
SEBACEOUS
SEBASTIAN
SIBILANCE
SIBYLLINE
SOBERNESS
SOBRIQUET
SUBALTERN
SUBCELLAR
SUBCORTEX
SUBDIVIDE
SUBDOLOUS
SUBEDITOR
SUBENTIRE
SUBJACENT
SUBJUGATE
SUBLIMATE
SUBLIMELY
SUBMARINE
SUBMERGED
SUBNORMAL
SUBROGATE
SUBSCRIBE
SUBSCRIPT
SUBSIDIZE
SUBSTANCE
SUBSTRATA
SUBSTRATE
SUBTENANT
SUBTITLED
SYBARITIC
TABANIDAE
TABASHEER
TABBOULEH
TABELLION
TABLATURE
TABLELAND
TABLEWARE
TABULATOR
TOBERMORY
TUBBINESS
UMBILICAL
UMBILICUS
UMBRATILE
UNBALANCE
UNBEKNOWN
UNBENDING
UNBIASSED
UNBOUNDED
UNBRIDLED
VIBRATILE
VIBRATION
VIBRATORY
WEBFOOTED
WOBBEGONG
ZIBELLINE
ACCESSION
ACCESSORY
ACCIDENTS
ACCLIMATE
ACCLIVITY
ACCOMPANY
ACCORDANT
ACCORDING
ACCORDION
ACCRETION
ALCHEMIST
ALCOHOLIC
ANCESTRAL
ANCHORAGE
ANCHORITE
ANCHORMAN
ANCILLARY
ANCIPITAL
ARCHANGEL
ARCHETYPE
ARCHIBALD
ARCHITECT
ARCHIVIST
ARCHIVOLT
ARCTOGAEA
ASCENDANT
ASCENDING
ASCENSION
ASCERTAIN
ASCLEPIUS
AUCTORIAL
AYCKBOURN
BACHARACH
BACKBENCH
BACKBITER
BACKCLOTH
BACKPEDAL
BACKSHISH
BACKSLIDE
BACKSPACE
BACKSTAGE
BACKSWORD
BACKTRACK
BACKWARDS
BACKWATER
BACKWOODS
BACTERIAL
BACTERIUM
BECHSTEIN
BECQUEREL
BICYCLIST
BOCCACCIO
BUCCANEER
BUCENTAUR
BUCHAREST
BUCKETFUL
BUCKTEETH
BUCKTHORN
BUCKWHEAT
CACHAEMIA
CACHECTIC
CACOPHONY
COCHINEAL
COCKAIGNE
COCKATIEL
COCKFIGHT

COCKROACH
COCKSCOMB
COCKSFOOT
COCKSWAIN
CUCHULAIN
CYCLAMATE
CYCLOLITH
CYCLORAMA
CYCLOTRON
DACHSHUND
DECACHORD
DECADENCE
DECALITRE
DECALOGUE
DECAMERON
DECASTYLE
DECATHLON
DECEITFUL
DECEMVIRI
DECEPTION
DECEPTIVE
DECESSION
DECIDEDLY
DECIDUOUS
DECILLION
DECKCHAIR
DECLARING
DECLINING
DECLIVITY
DECOCTION
DECOLLATE
DECOMPOSE
DECONTROL
DECORATED
DECORATOR
DECRETALS
DECUMBENT
DECURSIVE
DECUSSATE
DICHOTOMY
DICTATION
DOCTORATE
DOCTRINAL
DOCUMENTS
DUCKBOARD
ECCENTRIC
ENCANTHIS
ENCAUSTIC
ENCELADUS
ENCHANTED
ENCHANTER
ENCHEASON
ENCHILADA
ENCHORIAL
ENCIRCLED
ENCLOSURE
ENCOLPION
ENCOLPIUM
ENCOMPASS
ENCOUNTER
ENCOURAGE
ENCRATITE
ENCUMBENT
ESCALATOR
ESCOPETTE
ESCULENTS
ETCETERAS
EUCHARIST
EUCHLORIC
EUCLIDEAN
EXCALIBUR
EXCAMBION
EXCAVATOR
EXCELLENT
EXCELSIOR
EXCEPTION
EXCESSIVE
EXCHEQUER
EXCIPIENT
EXCISEMAN
EXCITABLE
EXCLAIMED
EXCLUDING
EXCLUSION
EXCLUSIVE
EXCORIATE
EXCREMENT
EXCULPATE
EXCURSION
EXCUSABLE
EXCUSABLY
FACECLOTH
FACETIOUS
FACSIMILE
FACTIONAL
FACTORISE
FACTUALLY
FACUNDITY
FECUNDITY
FICTIONAL
HACKAMORE
HACKNEYED
HACQUETON
HECOGENIN
HECTORING
HOCCAMORE
HUCKABACK
ILCHESTER
INCAPABLE
INCARDINE
INCARNATE
INCAUTION
INCENTIVE
INCEPTION
INCESSANT
INCIDENCE
INCIPIENT
INCITATUS
INCLEMENT
INCLUDING
INCLUSION
INCLUSIVE
INCOGNITO
INCOMINGS
INCOMMODE
INCONDITE
INCORRECT
INCREASED
INCREMENT
INCUBATOR
INCULCATE
INCULPATE
INCUMBENT
INCURABLE
INCURABLY
INCURIOUS
INCURSION
ISCHAEMIC
JACARANDA
JACKKNIFE
JACKSNIPE
JACKSTRAW
JACQUERIE
JOCKSTRAP
JOCKTELEG
JOCULARLY
KICKSHAWS
LACCOLITE
LACERATED
LACHRYMAL
LACINIATE
LACKBEARD
LACONICAL
LACTATION
LECANORAM
LECHEROUS
LICKERISH
LOCALIZED
LOCELLATE
LOCHINVAR
LOCKSMITH
LUCIFERIN
LUCRATIVE
LUCRETIUS
LUCTATION
LUCUBRATE
MACADAMIA
MACARONIC
MACARTHUR
MACDONALD
MACEDOINE
MACEDONIA
MACHINATE
MACHINERY
MACHINING
MACHINIST
MACKENZIE
MACQUARIE
MACROCOSM
MACROLOGY
MACTATION
MECHANICS
MECHANISM
MECHANIZE
MICKLETON
MICROCHIP
MICROCOSM
MICROCYTE
MICROFILM
MICROLITE
MICROLITH
MICROTOME
MICROTONE
MICROWAVE
MOCCASINS
MOCKERNUT
MUCHLOVED
MUCKENDER
MUCORALES
NECESSARY
NECESSITY
NECKVERSE
NECTARINE
NICARAGUA
NICCOLITE
NICKNEVEN
NICODEMUS
NICTITATE
NOCTURNAL
NUCLEOLUS
OBCORDATE
OCCIPITAL
OCCLUSION
OCCULTIST
OCCUPANCY
OCCUPYING
ONCOMETER
ORCHESTRA
OSCILLATE
PACEMAKER
PACHYDERM
PACKAGING
PECKSNIFF
PECULATOR
PECUNIARY
PICKABACK
PICKETING
PICKTHANK
PICNICKER
PICTOGRAM
PICTORIAL
POCKETFUL
POCKMANKY
PUCELLAGE
RACCABOUT
RACCAHOUT
RACEHORSE
RACETRACK
RACIALISM
RACIALIST
RACKETEER
RACKSTRAW
RACONTEUR
RECALLING
RECAPTURE
RECEIVING
RECEPTION
RECEPTIVE
RECESSION
RECESSIVE
RECIPIENT
RECKONING
RECLAIMED
RECLAIMER
RECOGNIZE
RECOLLECT
RECOMMEND
RECONCILE
RECONDITE
RECONVENE
RECORDING
RECORDIST
RECOVERED
RECTANGLE
RECTIFIER
RECTITUDE
RECTORIAL
RECUMBENT
RECURRENT
RECURRING
RECUSANCE
RICERCARE
RICHELIEU
ROCAMBOLE
SACCHARIN
SACKCLOTH
SACKERSON
SACRAMENT
SACRARIUM
SACRIFICE
SACRILEGE
SACRISTAN
SECATEURS
SECESSION
SECLUSION
SECONDARY
SECRETARY
SECRETION
SECRETIVE
SECTARIAN
SECTIONAL
SECTORIAL
SICCATIVE
SICILIANO
SICKENING
SOCIALISM
SOCIALIST
SOCIALITE
SOCIALIZE
SOCIOLECT
SOCIOLOGY
SUCCEEDED
SUCCENTOR
SUCCESSOR
SUCCINATE
SUCCOTASH
SUCCUBINE
SUCCULENT
SUCCURSAL
SYCOPHANT
TACAMAHAC
TACHILITE
TACHYLITE
TACHYLYTE
TACKINESS
TACTFULLY
TACTICIAN
TECHNICAL
TECHNIQUE
TECTIFORM
TECTONICS
TECTORIAL
TICHBORNE
TICTACTOE
TOCCATINA
UNCEASING
UNCERTAIN
UNCHANGED
UNCHARGED
UNCHECKED
UNCHRISOM
UNCLAIMED
UNCLOTHED
UNCLOUDED
UNCONCERN
UNCONFINE
UNCORRECT
UNCOUPLED
UNCOURTLY
UNCOVERED
UNCROSSED
UNCROWNED

UPCOUNTRY
VACCINATE
VACILLATE
VICARIOUS
VICEREGAL
VICEREINE
VICIOUSLY
VICTIMIZE
VICTORIAN
VICTORINE
YACHTSMAN
YACHTSMEN
ZUCCHETTO
ABDOMINAL
ABDUCTION
ADDERWORT
ADDICTION
ADDICTIVE
ADDRESSED
ADDRESSEE
ALDEBARAN
ANDANTINO
ANDROCLES
ANDROMEDA
ARDUOUSLY
AUDACIOUS
BADMINTON
BEDFELLOW
BEDJACKET
BEDRAGGLE
BEDRIDDEN
BEDSITTER
BEDSPREAD
BODYGUARD
BUDGETARY
CADASTRAL
CEDARWOOD
DEDICATED
DEDUCTION
DEDUCTIVE
DIDACTICS
DODDIPOLL
EDDINGTON
EDDYSTONE
EIDERDOWN
EIDOGRAPH
ENDEARING
ENDEAVOUR
ENDECAGON
ENDEICTIC
ENDLESSLY
ENDOCRINE
ENDOMORPH
ENDOSPERM
ENDOWMENT
ENDPAPERS
ENDURABLE
ENDURANCE
EUDAEMONY
FEDUCIARY
FIDUCIARY
GIDDINESS
GODDESSES
GODFATHER
GODLINESS
GODMOTHER
GODOLPHIN
GODPARENT
HADROSAUR
HEDERATED
HEDYPHANE
HIDEBOUND
HIDEOUSLY
HODIERNAL
HODMANDOD
HODOGRAPH
HODOMETER
HYDRANGEA
HYDRAULIC
HYDRAZINE
HYDROFOIL
HYDROPULT
HYDROSTAT
INDECENCY
INDECORUM
INDELIBLE
INDELIBLY
INDEMNIFY
INDEMNITY
INDENTURE
INDICATES
INDICATOR
INDICTION
INDIGENCE
INDIGNANT
INDIGNITY
INDOLENCE
INDONESIA
INDRAUGHT
INDUCTION
INDUCTIVE
INDULGENT
INDWELLER
IODOPHILE
JUDGEMENT
JUDICIARY
JUDICIOUS
KIDNAPPED
KIDNAPPER
LADYSMITH
LODESTONE
LODGEMENT
LUDICROUS
MADARIAGA
MADAROSIS
MADDENING
MADELEINE
MADRASSAH
MADREPORE
MADRESSAH
MADRILENE
MEDALLION
MEDALLIST
MEDIAEVAL
MEDIATION
MEDICALLY
MEDICATED
MEDICINAL
MEDITATOR
MEDMENHAM
MEDRESSEH
MIDDLEMAN
MIDDLESEX
MIDDLETON
MIDDLINGS
MIDIANITE
MIDINETTE
MIDRASHIM
MIDSTREAM
MIDSUMMER
MIDWIFERY
MIDWINTER
MODELLING
MODERATOR
MODERNISM
MODERNIST
MODERNITY
MODERNIZE
MODESTINE
MODILLION
MUDDINESS
NIDDERING
NIDERLING
ODDJOBMAN
ORDINAIRE
ORDINANCE
OUDENARDE
PADEMELON
PEDAGOGUE
PEDERASTY
PEDICULAR
PEDIGREES
PEDOMETER
RADCLIFFE
RADDLEMAN
RADIANTLY
RADIATING
RADIATION
RADICALLY
RADICCHIO
RADIOGRAM
RADIOLOGY
REDBREAST
REDDENDUM
REDEEMING
REDHANDED
REDHEADED
REDINGOTE
REDIVIVUS
REDLETTER
REDOLENCE
REDSTREAK
REDUCIBLE
REDUCTION
REDUNDANT
RIDERHOOD
RIDERLESS
RIDGEBACK
RUDBECKIA
RUDDIGORE
RUDDLEMAN
RUDIMENTS
SADDENING
SADDLEBAG
SEDENTARY
SEDGEMOOR
SEDITIOUS
SEDUCTION
SEDUCTIVE
SIDEBOARD
SIDEBURNS
SIDELIGHT
SIDEROSIS
SIDESWIPE
SIDETRACK
SIDEWARDS
SUDORIFIC
TEDIOSITY
TEDIOUSLY
UNDAMAGED
UNDAUNTED
UNDECIDED
UNDEFILED
UNDEFINED
UNDERBRED
UNDERCAST
UNDERCOAT
UNDERDONE
UNDERFELT
UNDERFOOT
UNDERHAND
UNDERLINE
UNDERLING
UNDERMINE
UNDERMOST
UNDERPAID
UNDERPASS
UNDERRATE
UNDERSEAL
UNDERSELL
UNDERSIDE
UNDERSIGN
UNDERSONG
UNDERTAKE
UNDERTONE
UNDERWALK
UNDERWEAR
UNDERWENT
UNDERWOOD
UNDILUTED
UNDIVIDED
UNDOUBTED
UNDRESSED
VIDELICET
VIDEODISC
VIDEOTAPE
WEDGEWOOD
WEDNESDAY
WIDOWHOOD
WODEHOUSE
ABERNETHY
ABERRANCE
ACETYLENE
ADENOIDAL
ADEPTNESS
ALERTNESS
ALEURITIS
ALEXANDER
ALEXANDRA
AMELAKITE
AMENDMENT
AMENHOTEP
AMERICIUM
ANECDOTAL
ANECDOTES
APENNINES
APERIODIC
APERITIVE
AREOPAGUS
AWESTRUCK
BEEFEATER
BEEFSTEAK
BEEKEEPER
BEELZEBUB
BEESTINGS
BEETHOVEN
BLEACHERS
BLESSINGS
BREADLINE
BREAKABLE
BREAKAGES
BREAKAWAY
BREAKDOWN
BREAKEVEN
BREAKFAST
BREAKNECK
BREATHING
BREECHING
CAESAREAN
CHEAPJACK
CHEAPNESS
CHEAPSIDE
CHECKBOOK
CHECKLIST
CHECKMATE
CHECKROOM
CHEEKBONE
CHEERLESS
CHEMISTRY
CHEONGSAM
CHEQUERED
CHERISHED
CHERNOZEM
CHERUBINI
CHEVALIER
CLEANNESS
CLEANSING
CLEARANCE
CLEARNESS
CLEOPATRA
CLEPSYDRA
CLERGYMAN
CLEVELAND
COELOSTAT
COEMPTION
COENOBITE
COENOBIUM
CREDULITY
CREDULOUS
CREMATION
CREMATORY
CREPITATE
CREPOLINE
CRESCELLE
CRESCENDO
CRETINOUS
CTESIPHON
DAEDALIAN
DEERHOUND
DIETETICS
DIETICIAN
DJELLABAH
DREAMLESS
EDELWEISS
ELECTORAL
ELECTRESS
ELECTRIFY
ELECTRODE
ELECTUARY
ELEGANTLY
ELEMENTAL
ELEVATION

ELEVENSES
EMERGENCE
EMERGENCY
ENERGETIC
ENERGUMEN
ENERINITE
EPEDAPHIC
EPEOLATRY
ESEMPLASY
ETERNALLY
EVENTUATE
EVERGLADE
EVERGREEN
EVERYBODY
EXECRABLE
EXECRABLY
EXECUTANT
EXECUTION
EXECUTIVE
EXECUTRIX
EXEMPLARY
EXEMPLIFY
EXEMPTION
EXEQUATUR
EXERCISED
EXERCISES
EYEBRIGHT
EYELETEER
EYEOPENER
EYESHADOW
EYESPLICE
EYESTRAIN
FEEDSTUFF
FIELDFARE
FIELDSMAN
FIELDWORK
FLECHETTE
FLEDGLING
FLEETWOOD
FLESHLESS
FLESHPOTS
FLEXITIME
FREDERICK
FREEBOARD
FREELANCE
FREEMASON
FREEPHONE
FREESTONE
FREESTYLE
FREEWHEEL
FREIGHTER
FRENCHMAN
FRENCHMEN
FREQUENCY
FRESHENER
FRESHNESS
FRETFULLY
GAELTACHT
GLEANINGS
GLEEFULLY
GLENDOWER
GLENGARRY
GLENLIVET
GMELINITE
GREASEGUN
GREATCOAT
GREATNESS
GREENAWAY
GREENBACK
GREENFEED
GREENGAGE
GREENHEAD
GREENHORN
GREENMAIL
GREENROOM
GREENSAND
GREENWEED
GREENWICH
GREENWOOD
GREENYARD
GREETINGS
GREGARINE
GREGORIAN
GRENADIER
GRENADINE
GRENVILLE
GREYBEARD
GREYHOUND
GREYWACKE
GUERRILLA
GUESSWORK
HAECCEITY
HAEMALOMA
HAEMATITE
HIERARCHY
ICELANDER
ICELANDIC
IDEALOGUE
IDENTICAL
IDENTIKIT
IDEOGRAPH
IDEOPATHY
INEBRIATE
INEFFABLE
INELEGANT
INERTNESS
INERUDITE
KIESERITE
KLEMPERER
KLENDUSIC
KNEECORDS
LAEVULOSE
LIENTERIC
MAELSTROM
MNEMOSYNE
NIEBELUNG
NIETZSCHE
OBEDIENCE
OBEISANCE
OCEANIDES
ODELSTING
OLECRANON
OLENELLUS
OLEOGRAPH
OLEORESIN
OPENENDED
OPENHEART
OPERATING
OPERATION
OPERATIVE
OPERCULUM
OVENPROOF
OVERBLOWN
OVERBOARD
OVERCLOUD
OVERCROWD
OVERDRAFT
OVERDRAWN
OVERDRESS
OVERDRIVE
OVEREXERT
OVERGROWN
OVERHASTY
OVERHEADS
OVERJOYED
OVERLYING
OVERNIGHT
OVERPAINT
OVERPOISE
OVERPOWER
OVERRATED
OVERREACH
OVERREACT
OVERRIDER
OVERSHADE
OVERSHOES
OVERSHOOT
OVERSIGHT
OVERSIZED
OVERSLEEP
OVERSPEND
OVERSPILL
OVERSTATE
OVERSTEER
OVERTHROW
OVERTONES
OVERVALUE
OVERWEIGH
OVERWHELM
PEEVISHLY
PHELLOGEN
PHENACITE
PHENAKISM
PHEROMONE
PIECEMEAL
PIECEWORK
PIEPOWDER
PIERGLASS
PLEASANCE
PLEIOCENE
PLENITUDE
PLENTEOUS
PLENTIFUL
PLETHORIC
PNEUMATIC
PNEUMONIA
POETASTER
PREBENDAL
PRECATORY
PRECEDENT
PRECEDING
PRECENTOR
PRECEPTOR
PRECIEUSE
PRECINCTS
PRECIPICE
PRECISELY
PRECISIAN
PRECISION
PRECISIVE
PRECOCITY
PRECONISE
PRECURSOR
PREDATORY
PREDICANT
PREDICATE
PREDICTOR
PREDIKANT
PREDILECT
PREFATORY
PREFERRED
PREFIGURE
PREGNANCY
PREHALLUX
PREJUDICE
PRELECTOR
PRELUSORY
PREMATURE
PREMONISH
PREMOTION
PREOCCUPY
PREORDAIN
PREPOLLEX
PRESBYTER
PRESCIENT
PRESCRIBE
PRESCUTUM
PRESENTED
PRESENTER
PRESENTLY
PRESERVED
PRESERVER
PRESERVES
PRESHRUNK
PRESIDENT
PRESIDIAL
PRESIDIUM
PRESSGANG
PRETENDER
PRETERITE
PRETERMIT
PREVALENT
PREVERNAL
PSEUDAXIS
PSEUDONYM
PTERIDIUM
PTEROSAUR
PUERILITY
PUERPERAL
QUEERNESS
QUENNELLE
QUERCETIN
QUERCETUS
QUERIMONY
QUERULOUS
REEDINESS
REEXAMINE
RHEOTAXIS
RHEUMATIC
SCELERATE
SCENTLESS
SCEPTICAL
SDEIGNFUL
SEEMINGLY
SHEARLING
SHECHINAH
SHECHITAH
SHEEPFOLD
SHEEPMEAT
SHEEPSKIN
SHEERLEGS
SHEERNESS
SHEFFIELD
SHEIKHDOM
SHELDDUCK
SHELDRAKE
SHELLBACK
SHELLFISH
SHELLSUIT
SHELTERED
SHEMOZZLE
SHENSTONE
SHEPHERDS
SHETLANDS
SHEWBREAD
SIEGFRIED
SKEDADDLE
SKEPTICAL
SKETCHILY
SKETCHMAP
SKETCHPAD
SKEWWHIFF
SLEEKNESS
SLEEPLESS
SLEEPWALK
SNEERWELL
SPEAKEASY
SPEARHEAD
SPEARMINT
SPEARSIDE
SPEARWORT
SPECIALLY
SPECIALTY
SPECIFICS
SPECIFIED
SPECIMENS
SPECTACLE
SPECTATOR
SPECULATE
SPEECHIFY
SPEEDBOAT
SPEEDWELL
SPELDRING
SPELLBIND
SPELUNKER
STEADFAST
STEAMBOAT
STEAMSHIP
STEELHEAD
STEELYARD
STEENBRAS
STEENKIRK
STEEPNESS
STEERSMAN
STEGNOSIS
STEGNOTIC
STEGOSAUR
STEINBECK
STEINBOCK
STENOPAIC
STERADIAN
STERCORAL
STERILITY
STERILIZE
STERNFAST
STERNNESS
STEVEDORE
STEVENSON
SUETONIUS
SWEATBAND
SWEEPINGS
SWEETENER

SWEETMEAT
SWEETNESS
SWEETSHOP
TEESWATER
THECODONT
THELEMITE
THELONIUS
THEOBROMA
THEOCRACY
THEOSOPHY
THERALITE
THERAPIST
THEREFORE
THEREUPON
THERMIDOR
THERSITES
THESAURUS
TIERCERON
TREACHERY
TREADMILL
TREASURER
TREATMENT
TREBIZOND
TREBUCHET
TREDRILLE
TREETRUNK
TREGEAGLE
TREGETOUR
TREILLAGE
TREMATODE
TREMBLING
TREMOLITE
TREMULATE
TREMULOUS
TRENCHANT
TREVELYAN
TWENTIETH
UNEARTHLY
UNEATABLE
UNEQUALED
UNETHICAL
UNEXPOSED
UREDINIAL
VIENTIANE
VIEWPOINT
WHEATGERM
WHEATMEAL
WHEELBASE
WHEREFORE
WHEREUPON
WHERRYMAN
WHETSTONE
WOEBEGONE
WREAKLESS
WRECKFISH
WRESTLING
AFFECTING
AFFECTION
AFFIDAVIT
AFFILIATE
AFFLICTED
AFFLUENCE
AFFRICATE
BIFURCATE
CAFETERIA
CAFETIERE
COFFERDAM
COFFINITE
CUFFLINKS
DEFALCATE
DEFAULTER
DEFEATISM
DEFEATIST
DEFECTION
DEFECTIVE
DEFENDANT
DEFENDERS
DEFENSIVE
DEFERENCE
DEFERMENT
DEFICIENT
DEFINABLE
DEFLATION
DEFLECTOR
DEFOLIANT
DEFOLIATE
DEFORMITY
DIFFERENT
DIFFICULT
DIFFIDENT
DIFFUSION
EFFECTIVE
EFFECTUAL
EFFICIENT
EFFINGHAM
EFFLUENCE
EFFLUVIUM
EFFULGENT
FIFTEENTH
INFANTILE
INFATUATE
INFECTING
INFECTION
INFERENCE
INFERTILE
INFIELDER
INFIRMARY
INFIRMITY
INFLATION
INFLEXION
INFLUENCE
INFLUENZA
INFORMANT
INFURIATE
LAFAYETTE
LEFTOVERS
LIFEGUARD
LIFESTYLE
LOFTINESS
MUFFETTEE
NEFANDOUS
NEFARIOUS
NEFERTITI
OBFUSCATE
OFFCHANCE
OFFCOLOUR
OFFENBACH
OFFENDING
OFFENSIVE
OFFERTORY
OFFICIALS
OFFICIANT
OFFICIATE
OFFICIOUS
OFFSEASON
OFFSPRING
OLFACTORY
PUFFINESS
RAFFINOSE
REFECTION
REFECTORY
REFERENCE
REFERRING
REFINANCE
REFLATION
REFLECTOR
REFLEXION
REFLEXIVE
REFORMIST
REFRACTOR
REFRESHER
REFULGENT
REFURBISH
REFUSENIK
RUFESCENT
RUFFIANLY
SAFEGUARD
SAFFLOWER
SOFTCOVER
SOFTENING
SUFFERING
SUFFOCATE
SUFFRAGAN
SUFFUSION
UNFAILING
UNFEELING
UNFITTING
UNFLEDGED
UNFOUNDED
WAFERTHIN
AGGRAVATE
AGGREGATE
AGGRESSOR
AGGRIEVED
ALGEBRAIC
ALGORITHM
ANGIOGRAM
ANGLICISM
ANGOSTURA
ANGUISHED
ARGENTINA
ARGENTINE
AUGUSTINE
BAGATELLE
BEGINNING
BIGHEADED
CAGOULARD
CIGARETTE
COGNITION
COGNITIVE
COGNIZANT
DEGRADING
DIGASTRIC
DIGESTION
DIGESTIVE
DIGITALIN
DIGITALIS
DIGNIFIED
DIGNITARY
DOGMATISM
DOGMATIZE
EAGERNESS
EAGLEWOOD
EDGEWORTH
EIGHTIETH
EIGHTSOME
ENGARLAND
ENGINEERS
ENGRAINED
ENGRAVING
ENGRENAGE
ENGROSSED
ENGROSSER
ERGATANER
FIGURANTE
FOGGINESS
FOGRAMITE
FUGACIOUS
FUGGINESS
HIGHCLASS
HIGHFLYER
HIGHLANDS
HIGHLIGHT
HIGHSPEED
HYGIENIST
INGENIOUS
INGENUITY
INGENUOUS
INGESTION
INGLENOOK
INGRAINED
INGROWING
JAGGANATH
JIGGUMBOB
LAGNIAPPE
LAGOMORPH
LEGENDARY
LEGIONARY
LEGISLATE
LIGHTFOOT
LIGHTLESS
LIGHTNESS
LIGHTNING
LIGHTSHIP
LIGHTSOME
LOGARITHM
LOGICALLY
LOGISTICS
LOGOGRIPH
LOGOTHETE
MAGDALENE
MAGDEBURG
MAGICALLY
MAGNALIUM
MAGNESIUM
MAGNETISM
MAGNETIZE
MAGNETRON
MAGNIFIER
MAGNITUDE
MEGACYCLE
MEGAHERTZ
MEGAPHONE
MEGASCOPE
MEGASPORE
MIGRATION
MIGRATORY
MOGADISHU
MUGGLETON
MUGLARITE
NEGLECTED
NEGLIGENT
NEGOTIATE
NEGRITUDE
NIGGARDLY
NIGHTCLUB
NIGHTFALL
NIGHTFIRE
NIGHTGOWN
NIGHTMARE
NIGHTTIME
NIGHTWORK
NIGRITUDE
NIGROSINE
ORGANELLE
ORGANICAL
ORGANISED
ORGANISER
ORGANIZED
ORGANIZER
ORGANZINE
ORGIASTIC
ORGILLOUS
OUGHTNESS
PAGEANTRY
PAGLIACCI
PEGMATITE
PIGGYBACK
PIGGYBANK
PIGHEADED
PIGNERATE
PUGNACITY
PYGMALION
REGARDANT
REGARDFUL
REGARDING
REGISSEUR
REGISTRAR
REGRETFUL
REGUERDON
REGULARLY
REGULATOR
RIGHTEOUS
RIGHTHAND
RIGHTNESS
RIGHTWING
RIGMAROLE
RIGOLETTO
RUGGELACH
SAGACIOUS
SAGAPENUM
SAGITTARY
SEGMENTED
SEGREGATE
SIGHTLESS
SIGHTSEER
SIGNALLER
SIGNALMAN
SIGNATORY
SIGNATURE
SIGNBOARD
SOGGINESS
SUGARCANE
TIGHTENER
TIGHTHEAD
TIGHTNESS
TIGHTROPE
UNGUARDED
VAGUENESS
VEGETABLE
VEGETATOR
VIGESIMAL

VIGILANCE
VIGILANTE
WAGENBOOM
WAGHALTER
WAGNERIAN
WAGNERITE
WAGONETTE
WAGONLOAD
YGGDRASIL
ZYGOMATIC
ZYGOSPORE
ABHORRENT
ADHERENCE
ANHYDRIDE
ANHYDRITE
ANHYDROUS
APHRODITE
ASHKENAZI
ASHMOLEAN
ATHEISTIC
ATHELSTAN
ATHENAEUM
ATHLETICS
BEHAVIOUR
COHERENCE
DEHYDRATE
ECHEVERIA
ECHIDNINE
ENHYDRITE
EPHEDRINE
EPHEMERAL
EPHEMERIS
EPHEMERON
EPHESIANS
EPHIALTES
ETHELBERT
ETHEREOUS
ETHIOPIAN
ETHNOLOGY
EUHEMERUS
EXHAUSTED
EXHIBITOR
ICHNEUMON
ICHNOLITE
INHERITED
INHERITOR
INHIBITED
INHUMANLY
IPHIGENIA
JOHANNINE
LEHRJAHRE
LOHENGRIN
MAHARAJAH
MAHARANEE
MAHARISHI
MEHITABEL
OCHLOCRAT
OPHIUCHUS
OTHERWISE
REHEARSAL
SCHEELITE
SCHEHITAH
SCHELLING
SCHEMATIC
SCHIAVONE
SCHILLING
SCHLEMIEL
SCHLEMIHL
SCHLENTER
SCHLIEREN
SCHMALTZY
SCHMIEDER
SCHMUTTER
SCHNAPPER
SCHNAUZER
SCHNECKEN
SCHNITTKE
SCHNITZEL
SCHNORKEL
SCHNORRER
SCHNOZZLE
SCHOLARCH
SCHOLARLY
SCHOLIAST
SCHOOLBOY
SCHOOLING
SCHOOLMAN
SPHACELUS
SPHENDONE
SPHERICAL
SPHINCTER
TAHSILDAR
UNHAPPILY
UNHEALTHY
UNHEEDING
UNHELPFUL
UNHOPEFUL
UPHOLSTER
USHERETTE
VEHEMENCE
VEHICULAR
WAHABIITE
YOHIMBINE
ACIDULATE
ACIDULOUS
AGINCOURT
AGITATION
ALIGNMENT
AMIANTHUS
AMIDSHIPS
ANIMATION
ANIMISTIC
ANIMOSITY
ARISTOTLE
AXIOMATIC
BAINMARIE
BLINDFOLD
BLINDNESS
BLINDSPOT
BLINDWORM
BLINKERED
BLISTERED
BRICKWORK
BRICKYARD
BRIDEWELL
BRIDLEWAY
BRIEFCASE
BRIEFNESS
BRIGADIER
BRIGADOON
BRILLIANT
BRIMSTONE
BRIQUETTE
BRISKNESS
BRISTLING
BRITANNIA
BRITANNIC
BRITSCHKA
CAIRNGORM
CHICANERY
CHICKADEE
CHICKWEED
CHIEFTAIN
CHIHUAHUA
CHILBLAIN
CHILDCARE
CHILDHOOD
CHILDLESS
CHILDLIKE
CHILOPODA
CHINATOWN
CHINOVNIK
CHINSTRAP
CHIPBOARD
CHIPOLATA
CHIPPINGS
CHIROPODY
CHISELLER
CLIENTELE
CLIMACTIC
CLINGFILM
CLINICIAN
CLIPBOARD
COINTREAU
CRIBELLUM
CRICKETER
CRIMINATE
CRINOLINE
CRIPPLING
CRISPNESS
CRITERION
CRITICISM
CRITICIZE
DAIRYMAID
DRIFTWOOD
DRINKABLE
DRIPSTONE
DWINDLING
EDINBURGH
EDITORIAL
ELIMINATE
ELIZABETH
EMINENTLY
ENIGMATIC
EPICEDIUM
EPICENTRE
EPICLESIS
EPICUREAN
EPICYCLIC
EPIDERMIS
EPIGAEOUS
EPILEPTIC
EPINASTIC
EPINICION
EPINIKION
EPIPHRAGM
EPIPHYSIS
EPIPHYTIC
EPIPOLISM
EPISCOPAL
EPISTAXIS
EPISTOLER
EPITHESIS
EPITOMIZE
ERIOMETER
ERISTICAL
ETIOLATED
ETIQUETTE
EVIDENTLY
EVITERNAL
EXISTENCE
FAINTNESS
FAIRYLAND
FAIRYTALE
FAITHLESS
FLINTLOCK
FLIPPANCY
FRICASSEE
FRIESLAND
FRIGATOON
FRIGHTFUL
FRIGIDITY
FRITHBORH
FRIVOLITY
FRIVOLOUS
FRIZZANTE
GAINFULLY
GAINSAYER
GLISSANDO
GRIEVANCE
GRIMALKIN
GRIMINESS
GRINGOLET
GRISAILLE
GUIDEBOOK
GUIDELINE
GUILDHALL
GUILELESS
GUILLEMOT
GUILLOCHE
GUILTLESS
GUINEVERE
GUITARIST
HAILSTONE
HAILSTORM
HAIRBRUSH
HAIRPIECE
HAIRSTYLE
IDIOBLAST
IDIOGRAPH
IDIOMATIC
IDIOPHONE
IDIOPLASM
IDIOTICON
IMITATION
IMITATIVE
INITIALLY
INITIATED
INITIATOR
ISINGLASS
ITINERANT
ITINERARY
ITINERATE
JUICINESS
KLINOSTAT
KNIPHOFIA
LEICESTER
LEISURELY
LEITMOTIF
LEITMOTIV
LOINCLOTH
LOITERING
MAINFRAME
MAINTENON
MOISTNESS
MRIDAMGAM
MRIDANGAM
NEIGHBOUR
NOISELESS
NOISINESS
OLIGARCHY
OLIGOCENE
OLIVENITE
OMINOUSLY
ORICALCHE
ORIENTATE
ORIFLAMME
ORIGENIST
ORIGINATE
OVIPAROUS
OXIDATION
PAILLASSE
PAILLETTE
PAINFULLY
PAINTWORK
PEIRASTIC
PHIGALIAN
PHILANDER
PHILATELY
PHILIPPIC
PHILISTER
PHILLABEG
PHILLIBEG
PHILOLOGY
PHITONIUM
PLIMSOLLS
POIGNANCY
POINTEDLY
POINTLESS
POINTSMAN
POISONING
POISONOUS
PRICELESS
PRIESTESS
PRIESTLEY
PRIMAEVAL
PRIMARILY
PRIMAVERA
PRIMITIAE
PRIMITIVE
PRIMULINE
PRINCETON
PRINCIPAL
PRINCIPLE
PRINTABLE
PRISMATIC
PRIVATEER
PRIVATELY
PRIVATION
PRIVATIZE
PRIVILEGE
PUISSANCE
QUICKLIME
QUICKNESS
QUICKSAND
QUICKSTEP
QUIESCENT
QUIETNESS
QUILLWORT
QUINQUINA
QUINTETTE
QUINTROON

QUINTUPLE
QUITTANCE
QUIVERFUL
QUIVERING
QUIZZICAL
RAINCHECK
RAINGAUGE
RAINSTORM
RAINWATER
REICHSRAT
REICHSTAG
REIMBURSE
REINFORCE
REINSTATE
REISTAFEL
REITERATE
ROISTERER
RUINATION
RUINOUSLY
SAILCLOTH
SAINTFOIN
SAINTHOOD
SCIAMACHY
SCIARIDAE
SCIENTISM
SCIENTIST
SCINTILLA
SCIOMANCY
SCISSORER
SHIELDING
SHIFTLESS
SHIFTWORK
SHILLABER
SHINTOISM
SHIPOWNER
SHIPSHAPE
SHIPWRECK
SHIVERING
SKIAMACHY
SKILFULLY
SKINDIVER
SKINFLINT
SKINTIGHT
SLIGHTEST
SLIMINESS
SLINGBACK
SLINGSHOT
SLIVOVICA
SLIVOVITZ
SPICILEGE
SPICINESS
SPIDERWEB
SPIKENARD
SPILLICAN
SPILLIKIN
SPINDRIER
SPINDRIFT
SPINELESS
SPINNAKER
SPINNERET
SPIRITOUS
SPIRITUAL
STIFFENER
STIFFNESS
STILLBORN
STILLNESS
STILLROOM
STILTBIRD
STIMULANT
STIMULATE
STINGAREE
STINKBIRD
STINKHORN
STINKWOOD
STIPULATE
STIRABOUT
SWIFTNESS
SWINBURNE
SWINEHERD
SWINGEING
TAILBOARD
TAILLEFER
TAILLIGHT
TAILPIECE
TAILPLANE
TEIRESIAS
THICKHEAD
THICKNESS
THIGHBONE
THINGUMMY
THINKABLE
THINNINGS
THIRDSMAN
THIRSTILY
THIRSTING
THIRTIETH
TRIANGLED
TRIATHLON
TRIBALISM
TRIBESMAN
TRIBESMEN
TRIBOLOGY
TRIBUNATE
TRIBUTARY
TRICERION
TRICKLESS
TRICKSTER
TRICLINIC
TRICOLOUR
TRIDYMITE
TRIENNIAL
TRIERARCH
TRIETERIC
TRIFORIUM
TRIHEDRON
TRILITHON
TRILOBITE
TRIMESTER
TRIMMINGS
TRINKETER
TRIPITAKA
TRIPMETER
TRISAGION
TRITENESS
TRITICALE
TRITURATE
TRIUMPHAL
TRIVIALLY
TUILERIES
TUILLETTE
TWINKLING
ULIGINOUS
UNIFORMED
UNIFORMLY
UNINJURED
UNINVITED
UNISEXUAL
UNITARIAN
UNIVALENT
UNIVERSAL
URICONIAN
URINATION
UTICENSIS
VAINGLORY
VEILLEUSE
VOICELESS
WAISTBAND
WAISTCOAT
WAISTLINE
WAITERAGE
WEIGHTING
WEIRDNESS
WHICHEVER
WHIMSICAL
WHINSTONE
WHIPROUND
WHIPSNADE
WHIRLIGIG
WHIRLPOOL
WHIRLWIND
WHISTLING
WHITAKERS
WHITEBAIT
WHITEDAMP
WHITEFISH
WHITEHALL
WHITEHEAD
WHITENESS
WHITENING
WHITEWALL
WHITEWASH
WHITEWING
WHITEWOOD
WHITTAWER
WHITWORTH
WHIZZBANG
ZEITGEIST
ADJECTIVE
ADJOINING
DEJECTION
ENJOYABLE
ENJOYMENT
GUJARATHI
HIJACKING
INJECTION
INJURIOUS
INJUSTICE
MAJORDOMO
MAJORETTE
MAJUSCULE
MUJAHIDIN
OBJECTION
OBJECTIVE
OBJURGATE
REJECTION
REJOICING
REJOINDER
ANKYLOSIS
ARKWRIGHT
AWKWARDLY
BAKEHOUSE
BAKSHEESH
CAKESTAND
ELKOSHITE
MAKESHIFT
MEKOMETER
NAKEDNESS
OCKHAMIST
PAKISTANI
PEKINGESE
PIKESTAFF
TEKNONYMY
UNKNOWING
ABLUTIONS
AFLATOXIN
ALLANTOID
ALLANTOIS
ALLEGEDLY
ALLEGIANT
ALLEMANDE
ALLEVIATE
ALLIGATOR
ALLOCARPY
ALLOGRAPH
ALLOPATHY
ALLOTMENT
ALLOWABLE
ALLOWANCE
ARLINGTON
AYLESBURY
BALACLAVA
BALALAIKA
BALDAQUIN
BALEFULLY
BALLADEER
BALLADIST
BALLERINA
BALLISTIC
BALLPOINT
BALTHAZAR
BALTIMORE
BELATEDLY
BELEAGUER
BELIEVING
BELLICOSE
BELLYACHE
BELLYFLOP
BELONGING
BELVEDERE
BILATERAL
BILINGUAL
BILIRUBIN
BILLABONG
BILLBOARD
BILLIARDS
BILLOWING
BILLYCOCK
BOLIVIANO
BOLOGNESE
BOLSHEVIK
BULGARIAN
BULKINESS
BULLDOZER
BULLFIGHT
BULLFINCH
CALABOOSE
CALABRESE
CALCANEUM
CALCANEUS
CALCINATE
CALCULATE
CALDARIUM
CALEDONIA
CALEMBOUR
CALENDULA
CALENTURE
CALIBRATE
CALLIPERS
CALLOSITY
CALLOUSLY
CALORIFIC
CALPURNIA
CALVANISM
CALVINIST
CALVITIES
CELANDINE
CELEBRANT
CELEBRATE
CELEBRITY
CELESTIAL
CELLARIST
CELLULITE
CELLULOID
CELLULOSE
CHLAMYDES
CILIOLATE
COLCHICUM
COLERIDGE
COLLAPSAR
COLLATION
COLLEAGUE
COLLECTED
COLLECTOR
COLLEGIAN
COLLIGATE
COLLIMATE
COLLISION
COLLOCATE
COLLODION
COLLOIDAL
COLLOTYPE
COLLUSION
COLLUSIVE
COLLYRIUM
COLOMBIAN
COLOMBIER
COLONNADE
COLOPHONY
COLORLESS
COLOSSEUM
COLOSTOMY
COLOSTRUM
COLOURFUL
COLOURING
COLOURIST
COLTSFOOT
COLUMBARY
COLUMBATE
COLUMBIAN
COLUMBINE
COLUMBITE
COLUMBIUM
COLUMELLA
COLUMNIST
CULMINATE
CULTIVATE
DALLIANCE
DALMATIAN
DALTONISM
DELACROIX
DELICIOUS
DELIGHTED

DELINEATE
DELIRIOUS
DELIVERER
DILIGENCE
DOLEFULLY
DOLOMITES
DOLOMITIC
DULCINIST
EALDORMAN
ECLAMPSIA
EGLANTINE
ELLESMERE
ELLINGTON
ENLIGHTEN
ENLIVENED
FALANGIST
FALDSTOOL
FALERNIAN
FALKLANDS
FALLOPIAN
FALSEHOOD
FALSENESS
FILICALES
FILIGRAIN
FILLIPEEN
FILLISTER
FILMMAKER
FILMSTRIP
FILOPLUME
FILOSELLE
FILTERING
FILTERTIP
FOLIOLOSE
FOLKETING
FOLKWEAVE
FOLLOWING
FULLBLOWN
FULLERENE
FULLGROWN
FULLSCALE
FULMINANT
FULMINATE
GALACTOSE
GALANTINE
GALAPAGOS
GALDRAGON
GALENGALE
GALINGALE
GALIONGEE
GALLABEAH
GALLANTLY
GALLANTRY
GALLICISM
GALLINULE
GALLIPOLI
GALLIVANT
GALLOPADE
GALLSTONE
GALLYCROW
GALRAVAGE
GALVANISM
GALVANIZE
GELIGNITE
GILGAMESH
GOLDCREST
GOLDFIELD
GOLDFINCH
GOLDSINNY
GOLDSMITH
HALFBAKED
HALFDOZEN
HALFEMPTY
HALFPENNY
HALFSTAFF
HALITOSIS
HALLOWEEN
HALLOWMAS
HALLSTATT
HALOBIONT
HALOPHILE
HALOTHANE
HELLEBORE
HELPFULLY
HELVELLYN
HILARIOUS
HILLBILLY
HOLDERBAT
HOLINSHED
HOLLERITH
HOLLYHOCK
HOLLYWOOD
HOLOCAUST
HOLOGRAPH
HOLOPHOTE
HOLYSTONE
HYLOBATES
ILLEGALLY
ILLEGIBLE
ILLEGIBLY
ILLGOTTEN
ILLIBERAL
ILLICITLY
ILLOGICAL
ISLAMABAD
JELLYFISH
KALSOMINE
KILDERKIN
KILLARNEY
KILOCYCLE
KILOHERTZ
KILOMETER
KILOMETRE
LILYWHITE
MALACHITE
MALATHION
MALAYSIAN
MALEBOLGE
MALENGINE
MALFORMED
MALICIOUS
MALIGNANT
MALIGNITY
MALLANDER
MALLEABLE
MALLEMUCK
MALLENDER
MALLEOLUS
MELAMPODE
MELANESIA
MELANOTIC
MELBOURNE
MELIORATE
MELODIOUS
MELODRAMA
MELONLIKE
MELPOMENE
MILESTONE
MILITANCY
MILKSHAKE
MILLAMANT
MILLENIAL
MILLENIUM
MILLEPEDE
MILLEPORE
MILLIGRAM
MILLINERY
MILLIONTH
MILLIPEDE
MILLSTONE
MILOMETER
MOLECULAR
MOLESKINS
MOLLITIES
MOLLYMAWK
MULTIFORM
MULTIPLEX
MULTITUDE
NOLLEKENS
OBLIQUELY
OBLIVIOUS
OILTANKER
OWLEGLASS
PALAESTRA
PALAFITTE
PALAMPORE
PALANKEEN
PALANQUIN
PALATABLE
PALEMPORE
PALEOLITH
PALESTINE
PALINURUS
PALLADIAN
PALLADIUM
PALLIASSE
PALMATION
PALMISTRY
PALMITATE
PALOVERDE
PALPATION
PALPEBRAL
PALPITATE
PALSGRAVE
PALUDRINE
PELLAGRIN
PELLITORY
PELMANISM
PHLEBITIS
PILASTERS
PILFERAGE
PILFERING
PILLICOCK
POLEMARCH
POLEMICAL
POLIANITE
POLICEMAN
POLITBURO
POLITESSE
POLITICAL
POLITIQUE
POLLINATE
POLLUTANT
POLLUTION
POLONAISE
POLVERINE
POLYANDRY
POLYESTER
POLYGONAL
POLYGRAPH
POLYNESIA
POLYPHONE
POLYPHONY
POLYTHENE
PULLULATE
PULMONARY
PULPITEER
PULSATION
PULVERIZE
RELATIONS
RELEVANCE
RELIGEUSE
RELIGIOSO
RELIGIOUS
RELIQUARY
RELIQUIAE
RELUCTANT
RILLETTES
SALACIOUS
SALANGANE
SALERATUS
SALESGIRL
SALESLADY
SALICETUM
SALLYPORT
SALLYPOST
SALOPETTE
SALTINESS
SALTPETER
SALTPETRE
SALTWATER
SALUBRITY
SALVARSAN
SALVATION
SCLAUNDER
SCLEROSIS
SCLEROTAL
SELACHION
SELECTING
SELECTION
SELECTIVE
SELFISHLY
SELJUKIAN
SELLOTAPE
SILICOSIS
SILLINESS
SILTSTONE
SILURIDAE
SOLDERING
SOLDIERLY
SOLEMNITY
SOLEMNIZE
SOLFEGGIO
SOLFERINO
SOLFIDIAN
SOLICITOR
SOLILOQUY
SOLIPSISM
SOLITAIRE
SOLLICKER
SPLENDOUR
SPLENETIC
SPLENITIS
SPLINTERS
SPLITTING
SULFUROUS
SULKINESS
SULPHONIC
SULPHURIC
SULTANATE
SYLLABARY
SYLLABLES
SYLLEPSIS
SYLLOGISM
SYLPHLIKE
SYLVANITE
TALKATIVE
TALMUDIST
TELEGRAPH
TELEOLOGY
TELEPATHY
TELEPHONE
TELEPHONY
TELEPHOTO
TELESALES
TELESCOPE
TELESTICH
TELLINGLY
TELLURIAN
TELLURION
TELLURIUM
TOLERABLE
TOLERABLY
TOLERANCE
TOLERATED
TOLLHOUSE
TOLPUDDLE
ULLSWATER
UNLEARNED
UNLIMITED
UNLUCKILY
UPLIFTING
VALDENSES
VALENTINE
VALIANTLY
VALUATION
VALUELESS
VALVASSOR
VELASQUEZ
VELDSKOEN
VELLENAGE
VELLICATE
VELODROME
VELVETEEN
VOLAGEOUS
VOLATIBLE
VOLGOGRAD
VOLKSRAAD
VOLTIGEUR
VOLTINISM
VOLTMETER
VOLTURNUS
VOLUCRINE
VOLUNTARY
VOLUNTEER
VULCANIST
VULCANITE
VULCANIZE
VULGARIAN
VULGARISM
VULGARITY
VULPINITE
WALDENSES

WALDFLUTE
WALDGRAVE
WALKABOUT
WALLABIES
WALLOPING
WALLOWING
WALLPAPER
WALLYDRAG
WALPURGIS
WELCOMING
WELDSTADT
WELLBEING
WELLBUILT
WELLKNOWN
WELSUMMER
WELTGEIST
WILDGEESE
WILLEMITE
WILLESDEN
WILLFULLY
WILLINGLY
WILLOWING
WILLPOWER
WOLFHOUND
WOLLASTON
WOLVERINE
WULFENITE
XYLOPHONE
YELLOWISH
ADMIRABLE
ADMIRABLY
ADMIRALTY
ADMISSION
ADMITTING
ADMIXTURE
ADMONITOR
AIMLESSLY
ALMANDINE
ARMADILLO
ARMAMENTS
ARMISTICE
ARMSTRONG
AXMINSTER
BAMBOOZLE
BIMONTHLY
BOMBARDON
BOMBASINE
BOMBASTIC
BOMBSHELL
BUMBLEBEE
BUMPTIOUS
CAMBODIAN
CAMBRIDGE
CAMBUSCAN
CAMCORDER
CAMEMBERT
CAMERAMAN
CAMPANILE
CAMPANULA
CIMMERIAN
COMBATANT
COMBATIVE
COMFORTER
COMICALLY
COMINFORM
COMINTERN
COMMANDER
COMMENSAL
COMMISSAR
COMMITTAL
COMMITTED
COMMITTEE
COMMODITY
COMMODORE
COMMOTION
COMMUNION
COMMUNISM
COMMUNIST
COMMUNITY
COMPACTLY
COMPANIES
COMPANION
COMPELLED
COMPETENT
COMPETING
COMPLAINT
COMPLIANT
COMPONENT
COMPOSING
COMPOSITE
COMPOSURE
COMPOTIER
COMPUTING
CYMBELINE
CYMBIDIUM
DAMASCENE
DAMBUSTER
DAMNATION
DAMNEDEST
DEMAGOGUE
DEMANDING
DEMARCATE
DEMEANING
DEMEANOUR
DEMETRIUS
DEMITASSE
DEMOCRACY
DEMULCENT
DEMURRAGE
DIMENSION
DOMICILED
DOMINANCE
DOMINICAL
DOMINICAN
DUMBARTON
DUMBFOUND
EMMERDALE
ESMERALDA
EUMENIDES
EUMYCETES
FAMAGUSTA
FOMALHAUT
GOMPHOSIS
GUMSHIELD
GYMNASIUM
GYMNASTIC
HAMADRYAD
HAMBURGER
HAMFATTER
HAMFISTED
HAMMERING
HAMMURABI
HAMPSTEAD
HAMSTRING
HAMSTRUNG
HEMINGWAY
HEMIPTERA
HEMISTICH
HEMITROPE
HEMSTITCH
HIMALAYAN
HIMALAYAS
HIMYARITE
HOMEGROWN
HOMEOPATH
HOMEOWNER
HOMESTEAD
HOMEWARDS
HOMICIDAL
HOMOGRAPH
HOMOPHONE
HOMOPTERA
HUMANKIND
HUMDINGER
HUMILIATE
HUMONGOUS
HUMUNGOUS
IMMANACLE
IMMANENCE
IMMANENCY
IMMEDIACY
IMMEDIATE
IMMELMANN
IMMENSELY
IMMENSITY
IMMERSION
IMMIGRANT
IMMIGRATE
IMMINENCE
IMMODESTY
IMMORALLY
IMMORTALS
IMMOVABLE
IMMOVABLY
IMMUNISER
IMMUTABLE
IMMUTABLY
JAMBALAYA
JAMPACKED
KOMINFORM
LAMARTINE
LAMASERAI
LAMBSWOOL
LAMINATED
LAMPADARY
LAMPADION
LAMPBLACK
LAMPLIGHT
LAMPSHADE
LIMBURGER
LIMEHOUSE
LIMELIGHT
LIMESTONE
LIMITLESS
LIMOUSINE
LIMPIDITY
LOMBARDIC
LUMBERING
LUMBRICUS
LUMINAIRE
LUMINANCE
LYMESWOLD
LYMPHATIC
MAMMALIAN
MEMORABLE
MEMORITER
MOMENTARY
MOMENTOUS
MUMCHANCE
MUMPSIMUS
NAMEPLATE
NOMINALLY
NOMINATOR
NOMOCRACY
NOMOTHETE
NUMBSKULL
NUMERAIRE
NUMERATOR
NUMERICAL
NUMMULITE
ORMANDINE
PEMPHIGUS
PIMPERNEL
POMOERIUM
POMPADOUR
POMPHOLYX
POMPOSITY
PUMMELLED
RAMILLIES
REMAINDER
REMAINING
REMBRANDT
REMINISCE
REMISSION
REMONTANT
REMOULADE
REMOVABLE
SAMARITAN
SEMANTEME
SEMANTICS
SEMANTIDE
SEMANTRON
SEMAPHORE
SEMBLANCE
SEMEIOTIC
SEMIBREVE
SEMICOLON
SEMIFINAL
SEMIOLOGY
SEMIRAMIS
SIMEONITE
SIMILARLY
SIMPLETON
SIMPLISTE
SIMULATED
SIMULATOR
SIMULCAST
SOMASCOPE
SOMEPLACE
SOMETHING
SOMETIMES
SOMEWHERE
SOMMELIER
SOMNOLENT
SUMMARILY
SUMMARIZE
SUMMATION
SUMPTUARY
SUMPTUOUS
SYMBIOSIS
SYMBIOTIC
SYMBOLISM
SYMBOLIST
SYMBOLIZE
SYMMETRIC
SYMPHONIC
SYMPHYSIS
SYMPODIUM
SYMPOSIUM
TAMERLANE
TAMOXIFEN
TEMPERATE
TEMPORARY
TEMPORIZE
TEMPTRESS
TEMULENCE
TIMENOGUY
TIMEPIECE
TIMESHARE
TIMETABLE
TIMOCRACY
TIMPANIST
TOMBSTONE
TOMENTOSE
TUMESCENT
TUMMYACHE
TYMPANIST
UNMARRIED
UNMATCHED
UNMINDFUL
UNMUSICAL
WAMBENGER
WIMBLEDON
WOMANHOOD
WOMANISER
WOMANIZER
WOMANKIND
WOMENFOLK
AINSWORTH
ANNAPOLIS
ANNAPURNA
ANNOTATED
ANNOTATOR
ANNOUNCER
ANNOYANCE
ANNULMENT
BANDALORE
BANDICOOT
BANDOLEER
BANDOLERO
BANDOLIER
BANDOLINE
BANDSTAND
BANDWAGON
BANISTERS
BANQUETTE
BANTERING
BENBECULA
BENCHMARK
BENIGHTED
BINOCULAR
BONAPARTE
BUNDESTAG
CANALETTO
CANAVERAL
CANCEROUS
CANDIDACY
CANDIDATE
CANDLELIT
CANDLEMAS
CANDYTUFT
CANNELURE

CANNONADE
CANONICAL
CANTABILE
CANTHARIS
CANTHARUS
CANTONESE
CANVASSER
CENTAURUS
CENTENARY
CENTERING
CENTIPEDE
CENTRALLY
CENTREING
CENTURION
CINEMATIC
CINERARIA
CINEREOUS
CONCAVITY
CONCEALED
CONCEITED
CONCERNED
CONCERTED
CONCIERGE
CONCISELY
CONCISION
CONCLUDED
CONCORDAT
CONCOURSE
CONCUBINE
CONCUSSED
CONDEMNED
CONDENSER
CONDIMENT
CONDITION
CONDUCIVE
CONDUCTOR
CONDUCTUS
CONDYLOMA
CONFESSED
CONFESSOR
CONFIDANT
CONFIDENT
CONFIRMED
CONFITEOR
CONFLATED
CONFUCIUS
CONFUSING
CONFUSION
CONGENIAL
CONGERIES
CONGESTED
CONGOLESE
CONGRUENT
CONGRUOUS
CONJUGATE
CONJURING
CONNECTED
CONNECTOR
CONNEXION
CONNOTATE
CONNUBIAL
CONQUEROR
CONSCIOUS
CONSCRIPT
CONSENSUS
CONSIGNEE
CONSIGNOR
CONSONANT
CONSTABLE
CONSTANCE
CONSTANCY
CONSTRICT
CONSTRUCT
CONSULATE
CONSUMING
CONTAGION
CONTAINER
CONTEMPER
CONTENDER
CONTENTED
CONTINENT
CONTINUAL
CONTINUUM
CONTRALTO
CONTRIVED
CONTRIVER
CONTUMACY
CONTUMELY
CONTUSION
CONUNDRUM
CONVECTOR
CONVERTED
CONVERTER
CONVINCED
CONVIVIAL
CUNCTATOR
CUNEIFORM
CYNEGETIC
CYNICALLY
DANDELION
DANDIFIED
DANDYPRAT
DANGEROUS
DENIGRATE
DENSENESS
DENTISTRY
DENTITION
DINGINESS
DINNERSET
DONATELLO
DONCASTER
DONIZETTI
DUNDREARY
DUNGAREES
DUNGENESS
DUNGEONER
DUNSINANE
DUNSTABLE
DYNAMITED
ENNERDALE
FANATICAL
FANDANGLE
FANTASIZE
FANTASTIC
FENCIBLES
FENUGREEK
FINANCIAL
FINANCIER
FINGERING
FINGERTIP
FINICKING
FINICKITY
FINISHING
FINLANDIA
FUNDAMENT
FUNGIBLES
FUNGICIDE
FUNICULAR
GANGPLANK
GENEALOGY
GENERALLY
GENERATOR
GENETICAL
GENEVIEVE
GENIALITY
GENITALIA
GENTEELLY
GENTILITY
GENTLEMAN
GENTLEMEN
GENUFLECT
GENUINELY
GINGERADE
GINGLYMUS
GINORMOUS
GONDOLIER
GONGORISM
GONIATITE
GUNCOTTON
GUNPOWDER
GYNOECIUM
HANDBRAKE
HANDCUFFS
HANDINESS
HANDIWORK
HANDPIECE
HANDSHAKE
HANDSPIKE
HANDSTAND
HANKERING
HANSEATIC
HENDIADYS
HENPECKED
HINDEMITH
HINDRANCE
HINDSIGHT
HINGELESS
HONEYCOMB
HONEYMOON
HONKYTONK
HONORABLE
HONORIFIC
HUNCHBACK
HUNDREDTH
HUNGARIAN
HUNKYDORY
IGNESCENT
IGNORAMUS
IGNORANCE
INNERMOST
INNISFAIL
INNISFREE
INNKEEPER
INNOCENCE
INNOCUOUS
INNOVATOR
JANISSARY
JANSENISM
JANSENIST
JENNETING
JUNEBERRY
JUNKETING
KENTIGERN
KENTLEDGE
KINGMAKER
KINGSIZED
KINKCOUGH
KINSWOMAN
KINTLEDGE
KONIMETER
KONISCOPE
LANCASTER
LANCEWOOD
LANCINATE
LANDAULET
LANDDROST
LANDGRAVE
LANDLOPER
LANDOWNER
LANDSCAPE
LANDSLIDE
LANDSMAAL
LANDSTURM
LANDWARDS
LANGOUSTE
LANGRIDGE
LANGSPIEL
LANGUAGES
LANGUEDOC
LANGUETTE
LANGUIDLY
LANKINESS
LANTHANUM
LENGTHILY
LENIENTLY
LENINGRAD
LINDBERGH
LINEAMENT
LINEOLATE
LINGERING
LINGFIELD
LINKLATER
LINTSTOCK
LONDONESE
LONGCHAMP
LONGEDFOR
LONGEVITY
LONGICORN
LONGINGLY
LONGITUDE
LONGLIVED
LONGRANGE
LONGSHORE
LUNCHTIME
MANDATORY
MANDICATE
MANDOLINE
MANDUCATE
MANGANATE
MANGANESE
MANGETOUT
MANGOUSTE
MANHANDLE
MANHATTAN
MANIFESTO
MANLINESS
MANNEQUIN
MANNERING
MANNERISM
MANOEUVRE
MANOMETER
MANSFIELD
MANUBRIUM
MENADIONE
MENAGERIE
MENDACITY
MENDELISM
MENDICANT
MENIPPEAN
MENNONITE
MENOMINEE
MENOPAUSE
MENSHEVIK
MENSTRUAL
MENSTRUUM
MENTALITY
MENTATION
MENTICIDE
MENTIONED
MENUISIER
MINACIOUS
MINCEMEAT
MINEFIELD
MINELAYER
MINIATURE
MINISCULE
MINISKIRT
MINKSTONE
MINNESOTA
MINUSCULE
MINUTEMAN
MONACTINE
MONASTERY
MONASTRAL
MONATOMIC
MONERGISM
MONEYWORT
MONGOLIAN
MONGOLISM
MONKSHOOD
MONOCEROS
MONOCHORD
MONOCOQUE
MONOCULAR
MONODRAMA
MONOGRAPH
MONOLOGUE
MONOMACHY
MONOMANIA
MONOMETER
MONOPLANE
MONOSTICH
MONOTROCH
MONOXYLON
MONSIGNOR
MONSTROUS
MONTACUTE
MONTAIGNE
MONTANISM
MONTANIST
MONTESPAN
MONTEZUMA
MONTICULE
MONZONITE
MUNDUNGUS
MUNICIPAL
MUNIMENTS
MUNITIONS
NANTUCKET
NINEPENCE
NINETIETH
NONENTITY

NONILLION
NONPAREIL
NONPROFIT
NONSMOKER
NUNCUPATE
OBNOXIOUS
OWNERSHIP
PANATELLA
PANCHAYAT
PANDATION
PANDEMIAN
PANDURATE
PANEGOISM
PANEGYRIC
PANELLING
PANELLIST
PANETTONE
PANHANDLE
PANNIKELL
PANORAMIC
PANTAGAMY
PANTALEON
PANTALOON
PANTHEISM
PANTHENOL
PANTOFFLE
PANTOMIME
PANTOUFLE
PENDENNIS
PENDLETON
PENDRAGON
PENDULATE
PENDULOUS
PENETRATE
PENFRIEND
PENILLION
PENINSULA
PENISTONE
PENITENCE
PENNILESS
PENPUSHER
PENSIONER
PENSIVELY
PENTECOST
PENTHOUSE
PENTOSANE
PENURIOUS
PINCHBECK
PINCHCOCK
PINEAPPLE
PINHOOKER
PINKERTON
PINOCCHIO
PINSTRIPE
PONDEROSA
PONDEROUS
PONTLEVIS
PUNCHLINE
PUNCTILIO
PUNCTUATE
PUNGENTLY
PUNISHING
RANCIDITY
RANCOROUS
RANDINESS
RANTIPOLE
RENASCENT
RENCONTRE
RENDERING
RENDITION
RENEWABLE
RENFIERST
RENOVATOR
RENTALLER
RINGFENCE
RINGSIDER
RUNAROUND
RUNCINATE
RUNESTAVE
RUNNYMEDE
SANCTUARY
SANDALLED
SANDARACH
SANDHURST
SANDPAPER
SANDPIPER
SANDSTONE
SANDSTORM
SANGFROID
SANHEDRIM
SANHEDRIN
SANHEDRON
SANNYASIN
SANTAYANA
SENESCENT
SENESCHAL
SENIORITY
SENSATION
SENSELESS
SENSILLUM
SENSITIVE
SENSITIZE
SENSORIUM
SENSUALLY
SENTIENCE
SENTIMENT
SINCERELY
SINCERITY
SINGALESE
SINGAPORE
SINGLESEX
SINGLETON
SINGSPIEL
SINGULTUS
SINKANSEN
SINUOSITY
SINUSITIS
SONGSMITH
SONNETEER
SONOMETER
SUNBATHER
SUNDOWNER
SUNFLOWER
SUNSCREEN
SUNSTROKE
SUNTANNED
SYNAGOGUE
SYNANGIUM
SYNCHYSIS
SYNCOMIUM
SYNCOPATE
SYNDICATE
SYNEDRION
SYNERGIST
SYNIZESIS
SYNOECETE
SYNOVITIS
SYNTACTIC
SYNTHESIS
SYNTHETIC
TANGERINE
TANTALITE
TANTALIZE
TANTARARA
TANZANIAN
TENACIOUS
TENACULUM
TENAILLON
TENDERIZE
TENEBROSE
TENEMENTS
TENNESSEE
TENSENESS
TENTATIVE
TENTORIUM
TENUOUSLY
TINGUAITE
TONBRIDGE
TONOMETER
TONOPLAST
TUNGSTATE
UNNATURAL
UNNERVING
UNNOTICED
VANCOUVER
VANDALISM
VANDALIZE
VANISHING
VANTBRASS
VENERABLE
VENEREOUS
VENEZUELA
VENGEANCE
VENIALITY
VENTIFACT
VENTILATE
VENTRICLE
VENUSBERG
VINDICATE
WANCHANCY
WANDERING
WANWORTHY
WENCESLAS
WINCANTON
WINCOPIPE
WINDBREAK
WINDCHILL
WINDFALLS
WINDHOVER
WINDSCALE
WINDSWEPT
WINEBERRY
WINEGLASS
WINNEBAGO
WONDERFUL
XANTHIPPE
XENOMANIA
XENOPHOBE
ZENOCRATE
ZINFANDEL
ZINKENITE
ABOLITION
ABOMINATE
ABORIGINE
ABOUNDING
ABOUTFACE
ABOUTTURN
ACONCAGUA
ACOUSTICS
ADORATION
ADORNMENT
AFORESAID
AGONIZING
ALONGSIDE
ALOOFNESS
AMOROUSLY
AMORPHOUS
ANOINTING
ANOMALOUS
ANONYMITY
ANONYMOUS
ANOPHELES
APOCRYPHA
APOLLONUS
APOLOGIST
APOLOGIZE
APOPHATIC
APOPHYSIS
APOSTOLIC
ATONEMENT
AVOCATION
AVOIDABLE
AVOIDANCE
BIOGRAPHY
BIOLOGIST
BIOSPHERE
BLOCKHEAD
BLOODBATH
BLOODLESS
BLOODSHED
BLOODSHOT
BLOWTORCH
BOOBYTRAP
BOOKLOVER
BOOKMAKER
BOOKSHELF
BOOKSTALL
BOOKSTAND
BOOKSTORE
BOOMERANG
BOONDOCKS
BOOTLACES
BROADCAST
BROADLOOM
BROADSIDE
BROKERAGE
BRONCHIAL
BROTHERLY
BROUGHTON
CHOCOLATE
CHOLELITH
CHONDRITE
CHONDROID
CHORISTER
CLOAKROOM
CLOCKWISE
CLOCKWORK
CLOISONNÉ
CLOSENESS
CLOUDLESS
COOKHOUSE
COOPERATE
CROCKFORD
CROCODILE
CROISSANT
CROOKBACK
CROOKEDLY
CROQUETTE
CROSSBEAM
CROSSBILL
CROSSBRED
CROSSEYED
CROSSFIRE
CROSSOVER
CROSSWALK
CROSSWIND
CROSSWISE
CROSSWORD
CROTCHETY
CROUSTADE
CROWNLIKE
CROWSBILL
CROWSFOOT
DEODORANT
DEODORIZE
DEOXIDISE
DIOCLETES
DIONYSIAN
DIONYSIUS
DOODLEBUG
DROMEDARY
DROPPINGS
DROPSICAL
DUODECIMO
ECOLOGIST
ECONOMICS
ECONOMIST
ECONOMIZE
ECOSSAISE
ECOSYSTEM
ELOCUTION
ELONGATED
ELOPEMENT
ELOQUENCE
EMOLLIATE
EMOLLIENT
EMOLUMENT
EMOTIONAL
EPONYMOUS
EROGENOUS
EROSTRATE
EROTICISM
ESOPHAGUS
EVOCATION
EVOCATIVE
EVOCATORY
EVOLUTION
EXODERMIS
EXONERATE
EXORATION
EXOSPHERE
EXOSTOSIS
FLOODGATE
FLOORSHOW
FLOPHOUSE
FLORESTAN
FLORIMELL
FLOTATION
FLOURMILL
FLOWCHART
FLOWERBED
FLOWERING

FLOWERPOT
FLOWSTONE
FOODSTORE
FOODSTUFF
FOOLHARDY
FOOLISHLY
FOOLPROOF
FOOTBRAKE
FOOTHILLS
FOOTLOOSE
FOOTPLATE
FOOTPRINT
FOOTSTALL
FOOTSTOOL
FROBISHER
FROGMARCH
FROGMOUTH
FROGSPAWN
FROISSART
FROSTBITE
GEODESIST
GEOGRAPHY
GEOLOGIST
GEOMETRIC
GEOMETRID
GEORGETTE
GLOMERATE
GLOMERULE
GLORIFIED
GLORYHOLE
GOODNIGHT
GOONHILLY
GOOSANDER
GOOSEFOOT
GOOSEHERD
GOOSENECK
GOOSESTEP
GROCERIES
GROSGRAIN
GROSVENOR
GROTESQUE
GROUNDHOG
GROUNDING
GROUNDNUT
GROUNDSEL
HOOLACHAN
INOCULATE
INOPINATE
INORGANIC
IRONSIDES
IRONSTONE
IRONWORKS
ISOCRATES
ISODORIAN
ISOLATION
ISOMERASE
ISOMETRIC
ISOPROPYL
ISOSCELES
ISOTACTIC
ISOTROPIC
KNOBSTICK
KNOCKDOWN
KNOWINGLY
KNOWLEDGE
KROPOTKIN
LAODICEAN
LIONHEART
LOOKALIKE
LOOSEHEAD
LOOSELEAF
LOOSENESS
MOODINESS
MOONLIGHT
MOONRAKER
MOONSHINE
MOONSTONE
NEOLITHIC
NEOLOGISM
NOOSPHERE
ODOURLESS
OMOPHAGIC
ONOMASTIC
OPOBALSAM
OPODELDOC
OROBANCHE
OROGRAPHY
OZOCERITE
OZOKERITE
PHONECARD
PHONETICS
PHONOGRAM
PHONOLITE
PHONOLOGY
PHOSPHATE
PHOSPHENE
PHOTOCOPY
PHOTOGENE
PHOTOSTAT
PLOUGHMAN
POORHOUSE
PROACTIVE
PROBABLES
PROBATION
PROBOSCIS
PROCACITY
PROCEDURE
PROCERITY
PROCESSOR
PROCLITIC
PROCOELUS
PROCONSUL
PROCREATE
PRODROMAL
PRODROMUS
PROFANELY
PROFANITY
PROFESSED
PROFESSOR
PROFITEER
PROFUSELY
PROFUSION
PROGNOSIS
PROGRAMME
PROJECTED
PROJECTOR
PROKARYON
PROKOFIEV
PROLACTIN
PROLAMINE
PROLEPSIS
PROLIXITY
PROLONGED
PROLUSION
PROMACHOS
PROMENADE
PROMINENT
PROMISING
PROMOTION
PROMPTING
PROMUSCIS
PRONGHORN
PRONOUNCE
PROOFREAD
PROPAGATE
PROPELLED
PROPELLER
PROPELLOR
PROPERDIN
PROPHETIC
PROPIONIC
PROPONENT
PROPRIETY
PROPTOSIS
PROPYLENE
PROROGATE
PROSCRIBE
PROSECUTE
PROSELYTE
PROSTRATE
PROTAMINE
PROTECTOR
PROTESTER
PROTHESIS
PROTHORAX
PROTOSTAR
PROTOTYPE
PROUDHORN
PROUSTITE
PROVEDORE
PROVENDER
PROVIDENT
PROVIDING
PROVISION
PROVOKING
PROVOLONE
PROXIMATE
PROXIMITY
PSORIASIS
PYONGYANG
QUODLIBET
QUOTATION
QUOTIDIAN
QUOTITION
RHODESIAN
RHODOLITE
RHODOPSIN
RIOTOUSLY
ROOSEVELT
ROOTSTOCK
SCOLECITE
SCOLIOSIS
SCOLIOTIC
SCONCHEON
SCORBUTIC
SCORBUTUS
SCORCHING
SCORODITE
SCOTCHMAN
SCOUNDREL
SHOEMAKER
SHOESHINE
SHOLOKHOV
SHOPFLOOR
SHOPFRONT
SHORTCAKE
SHORTFALL
SHORTHAND
SHORTHAUL
SHORTHOLD
SHORTHORN
SHORTLIST
SHORTNESS
SHORTSTAY
SHORTSTOP
SHORTTERM
SHOVELFUL
SHOVELLER
SHOWINESS
SHOWPIECE
SLOUGHING
SLOVENIAN
SLOWCOACH
SMOKEFREE
SMOKELESS
SNOWBOUND
SNOWDONIA
SNOWDRIFT
SNOWFLAKE
SNOWSHOES
SNOWSTORM
SNOWWHITE
SOOTERKIN
SPOFFORTH
SPOILSMAN
SPOKESMAN
SPONGEBAG
SPONSORED
SPOONBILL
SPOONFEED
SPOROCARP
SPORTSMAN
SPORTSMEN
SPOTLIGHT
STOCKFISH
STOCKHOLM
STOCKINET
STOCKINGS
STOCKPILE
STOCKROOM
STOCKWORK
STOCKYARD
STOICALLY
STOLIDITY
STOMACHIC
STONEBOAT
STONECHAT
STONECROP
STONEHAND
STONELESS
STONEWALL
STONEWARE
STONEWORK
STONEWORT
STONKERED
STOOLBALL
STOREROOM
STORIATED
STORNAWAY
STORYBOOK
STORYLINE
STOUTNESS
STOVEPIPE
STOWNLINS
SWORDFISH
SWORDPLAY
SWORDSMAN
SWOTHLING
TAOISEACH
THORNBACK
THORNBILL
THORNDYKE
THORNLESS
THOUSANDS
TOOTHACHE
TOOTHCOMB
TOOTHLESS
TOOTHPICK
TOOTHSOME
TROCHILIC
TROCHILUS
TROMPETTE
TRONDHEIM
TROOPSHIP
TROOSTITE
TROPAELIN
TROPARION
TROSSACHS
TROUBADOR
TROUSSEAU
UNOPPOSED
UROKINASE
VIOLATION
VIOLENTLY
VIOLINIST
VOODOOISM
WHODUNNIT
WHOLEFOOD
WHOLEMEAL
WHOLENESS
WHOLESALE
WHOLESOME
WHOSOEVER
WOODBORER
WOODCHUCK
WOODCRAFT
WOODENTOP
WOODHOUSE
WOODLANDS
WOODLOUSE
WOODSHOCK
WOOLINESS
WOOMERANG
WRONGDOER
WRONGFOOT
ZOOLOGIST
ZOOMANTIC
ZOOSCOPIC
AEPYORNIS
ALPENHORN
AMPERSAND
AMPHIBIAN
AMPLIFIER
AMPLITUDE
APPALLING
APPARATUS
APPARITOR
APPEALING
APPENDAGE
APPERTAIN
APPETIZER
APPLEJACK

APPLIANCE
APPLICANT
APPOINTED
APPOINTEE
APPORTION
APPRAISAL
APPREHEND
APPROVING
ASPARAGUS
ASPARTAME
ASPERSION
ASPIRATOR
ASPLENIUM
BAPTISMAL
BIPARTITE
BYPRODUCT
CAPACIOUS
CAPACITOR
CAPARISON
CAPILLARY
CAPITULAR
CAPITULUM
CAPORETTO
CAPRICCIO
CAPRICORN
CAPTAINCY
CAPTIVATE
CAPTIVITY
CIPOLLINO
COPIOUSLY
COPROLITE
COPYRIGHT
CUPRESSUS
DEPARTURE
DEPENDANT
DEPENDENT
DEPENDING
DEPICTION
DEPOSITOR
DEPRAVITY
DEPRECATE
DEPREDATE
DEPRESSED
DIPHTHONG
DIPLOMACY
DUPLICAND
DUPLICATE
DUPLICITY
EMPAESTIC
EMPANOPLY
EMPENNAGE
EMPHASIZE
EMPHLYSIS
EMPHYSEMA
EMPIRICAL
EMPLECTON
EMPLOYEES
EMPTINESS
ERPINGHAM
ESPAGNOLE
ESPERANCE
ESPERANTO
ESPIONAGE
ESPLANADE
EUPHEMISM
EUPHONIUM
EUPHORBIA
EUPHRATES
EXPANSION
EXPANSIVE
EXPATIATE
EXPECTANT
EXPECTING
EXPEDIENT
EXPENSIVE
EXPERTISE
EXPIATION
EXPIATORY
EXPISCATE
EXPLETIVE
EXPLICATE
EXPLOITER
EXPLOSION
EXPLOSIVE
EXPORTING
EXPOSITOR
EXPRESSED
EXPRESSLY
EXPULSION
EXPURGATE
HAPHAZARD
HAPPENING
HAPPINESS
HEPATICAL
HEPATITIS
HIPPOCRAS
HIPPODAME
HIPPOLYTA
HIPPOLYTE
HOPEFULLY
HOPLOLOGY
HOPSCOTCH
HYPALLAGE
HYPERBOLA
HYPERBOLE
HYPHENATE
HYPINOSIS
HYPNOTISM
HYPNOTIST
HYPNOTIZE
HYPOCAUST
HYPOCRISY
HYPOCRITE
IMPACTION
IMPARTIAL
IMPASSION
IMPASSIVE
IMPATIENT
IMPEACHER
IMPEDANCE
IMPELLING
IMPENDING
IMPERATOR
IMPERFECT
IMPERIOUS
IMPETUOUS
IMPLEMENT
IMPLICATE
IMPLUVIUM
IMPOLITIC
IMPORTANT
IMPORTUNE
IMPOSTURE
IMPOTENCE
IMPOUNDER
IMPRECATE
IMPRECISE
IMPRESSED
IMPROBITY
IMPROMPTU
IMPROVING
IMPROVISE
IMPRUDENT
IMPSONITE
IMPUDENCE
IMPULSION
IMPULSIVE
INPATIENT
JEPHTHAHS
KEPLARIAN
LAPLANDER
LAPSTREAK
LEPROSERY
LIPPITUDE
MAPPEMOND
MEPACRINE
NAPIERIAN
NEPHALISM
NEPHALIST
NEPHELINE
NEPHRITIC
NEPHRITIS
NEPTUNIUM
NIPCHEESE
NIPPERKIN
OPPENHEIM
OPPONENTS
OPPORTUNE
OPPRESSED
OPPRESSOR
ORPHANAGE
ORPHARION
ORPINGTON
PAPARAZZI
PAPARAZZO
PAPERBACK
PAPERCLIP
PAPERWORK
PAPILLOTE
PEPPERONI
PEPPERPOT
PIPEDREAM
PIPESTONE
PIPSQUEAK
POPLITEAL
POPPERING
POPPYCOCK
POPULARLY
POPULATED
PUPILLAGE
PUPPETEER
RAPACIOUS
RAPTORIAL
RAPTUROUS
REPAYABLE
REPAYMENT
REPECHAGE
REPELLENT
REPELLING
REPENTANT
REPERCUSS
REPERTORY
REPLACING
REPLENISH
REPLETION
REPLETIVE
REPLICATE
REPORTAGE
REPORTING
REPOSSESS
REPREHEND
REPRESENT
REPRESSED
REPRIMAND
REPROBATE
REPROCESS
REPRODUCE
REPROVING
REPTATION
REPTILIAN
REPUDIATE
REPUGNANT
REPULSION
REPULSIVE
REPUTABLE
REPUTEDLY
RIPIENIST
SAPSUCKER
SEPARABLE
SEPARATED
SEPARATOR
SEPHARDIM
SEPIOLITE
SEPTEMBER
SEPTIMOLE
SEPULCHER
SEPULCHRE
SEPULTURE
SIPHUNCLE
SOPHISTER
SOPHISTIC
SOPHISTRY
SOPHOCLES
SOPHOMORE
SOPORIFIC
SOPPINESS
SUPERETTE
SUPERFINE
SUPERNOVA
SUPERSEDE
SUPERSTAR
SUPERVENE
SUPERVISE
SUPINATOR
SUPPLIANT
SUPPLICAT
SUPPORTER
SUPPOSING
SUPPURATE
SUPREMACY
SUPREMELY
TAPDANCER
TEPHILLIN
TIPPERARY
TIPSINESS
TIPULIDAE
TOPDRAWER
TOPIARIST
TOPICALLY
TYPICALLY
UMPTEENTH
UNPOPULAR
UNPRECISE
UPPERMOST
VAPORETTO
VAPORIZER
WAPENTAKE
WAPINSHAW
ACQUIESCE
ACQUITTAL
ARQUEBUSE
ENQUIRIES
ESQUILINE
EXQUISITE
INQUILINE
INQUINATE
INQUIRING
INQUORATE
JEQUIRITY
LIQUEFIED
LIQUIDATE
LIQUIDITY
LIQUIDIZE
LIQUORICE
LIQUORISH
LOQUACITY
PIQUANTLY
REQUISITE
ROQUEFORT
SEQUESTER
SEQUINNED
SUQUAMISH
ACROBATIC
ACROPHONY
ACROPOLIS
ADRENALIN
AERODROME
AEROPLANE
AEROSPACE
AEROTAXIS
AFRIKAANS
AFRIKANER
AGREEABLE
AGREEABLY
AGREEMENT
AIRCOOLED
AIRSTREAM
ARRESTING
ARRIVISTE
ARROGANCE
ARROWHEAD
ARROWROOT
ATROCIOUS
AURICULAR
BARAGOUIN
BARBARIAN
BARBARITY
BARBAROUS
BARBITONE
BARBOTINE
BARCELONA
BAREBONES
BAREFACED
BARMBRACK
BARMECIDE
BARNABITE
BARNACLES
BARNSTORM
BAROMETER
BARRACUDA
BARRICADE
BARRISTER

BARTENDER
BARTHOLDI
BARTHOLIN
BARYSCOPE
BERGAMASK
BERGANDER
BERGOMASK
BERKELIUM
BERNSTEIN
BERYLLIUM
BIRDBRAIN
BIRDTABLE
BIRTHMARK
BIRTHWORT
BORDEREAU
BORDERING
BORNAGAIN
BORROWING
BURKINABE
BURLESQUE
BURLINESS
BURROUGHS
BURROWING
BURUNDIAN
CARACALLA
CARAMBOLA
CARBAMATE
CARBAMIDE
CARBONADE
CARBONARI
CARBONATE
CARBONIZE
CARBUNCLE
CARCINOMA
CARDBOARD
CAREERIST
CAREFULLY
CARETAKER
CARIBBEAN
CARMELITE
CARNATION
CARNELIAN
CARNIVORE
CARPACCIO
CARPENTER
CARPENTRY
CARPETING
CARTESIAN
CARTHORSE
CARTILAGE
CARTOGRAM
CARTOUCHE
CARTRIDGE
CARTTRACK
CARTULARY
CARTWHEEL
CARYOPSIS
CERATITIS
CERATODUS
CEREBRATE
CEROMANCY
CERTAINLY
CERTAINTY
CERTIFIED
CERTITUDE
CERVANTES
CHRISTIAN
CHRISTMAS
CHROMATIC
CHRONICLE
CHRYSALIS
CIRCADIAN
CIRCINATE
CIRCULATE
CIRRHOSIS
CORALLINE
CORDIALLY
CORDUROYS
CORDYLINE
CORIANDER
CORKSCREW
CORMORANT
CORNBRASH
CORNCRAKE
CORNEILLE
CORNELIAN
CORNERMAN
CORNFIELD
CORNFLOUR
CORNSTALK
COROLLARY
CORPORATE
CORPOREAL
CORPOSANT
CORPULENT
CORPUSCLE
CORRECTED
CORRECTLY
CORRECTOR
CORREGGIO
CORRELATE
CORROSION
CORROSIVE
CORRUGATE
CORRUPTER
CORTISONE
CORUSCATE
CURETTAGE
CURFUFFLE
CURIOSITY
CURIOUSLY
CURRENTLY
CURRYCOMB
CURSORILY
CURTILAGE
CURVATURE
DAREDEVIL
DARTAGNAN
DARTBOARD
DARTMOUTH
DARWINIAN
DERRINGER
DIRECTION
DIRECTIVE
DIRECTORS
DIRECTORY
DIRIGIBLE
DIRTINESS
DORMITION
DORMITORY
EARNESTLY
EARTHFLAX
EARTHLING
EARTHWORK
EARTHWORM
EBRILLADE
EGREGIOUS
EGRESSION
ENRAPTURE
ENROLMENT
ERRONEOUS
EURHYTHMY
EURIPIDES
FARANDOLE
FARMHOUSE
FARMSTEAD
FERACIOUS
FERDINAND
FERINGHEE
FERMENTED
FEROCIOUS
FERRYBOAT
FERTILITY
FERTILIZE
FERVENTLY
FIREBRAND
FIREBREAK
FIREDRAKE
FIREGUARD
FIRELIGHT
FIREPLACE
FIREPROOF
FIRESTONE
FIREWATER
FIREWORKS
FIRMAMENT
FIRSTEVER
FIRSTHAND
FIRSTRATE
FORASMUCH
FORBIDDEN
FORCEMEAT
FOREANENT
FOREBEARS
FORECLOSE
FORECOURT
FOREFRONT
FOREGOING
FOREIGNER
FORESHORE
FORESIGHT
FORESPEAK
FORESPEND
FORESTAGE
FORESTALL
FORESTERS
FORETASTE
FORFEITED
FORFICATE
FORGATHER
FORGETFUL
FORGETIVE
FORGIVING
FORGOTTEN
FORJASKIT
FORJESKIT
FORLORNLY
FORMALIST
FORMALITY
FORMALIZE
FORMATION
FORMATIVE
FORMULATE
FORNICATE
FORSYTHIA
FORTALICE
FORTHWINK
FORTHWITH
FORTILAGE
FORTITUDE
FORTNIGHT
FORTUNATE
FORWANDER
FURACIOUS
FURIOUSLY
FURNIMENT
FURNITURE
FURTIVELY
GARDENING
GARDEROBE
GARGANTUA
GARGARISM
GARIBALDI
GARNISHEE
GARNITURE
GARRULITY
GARRULOUS
GARRYOWEN
GERFALCON
GERIATRIC
GERMANCER
GERMANDER
GERMANITE
GERMANIUM
GERMICIDE
GERMINATE
GERUNDIVE
GIRANDOLE
GIRONDIST
GYROMANCY
GYROSCOPE
HARBINGER
HARDANGER
HARDBOARD
HARDCOVER
HARDIHOOD
HARDINESS
HARDLINER
HARDSHELL
HARESTANE
HARIGALDS
HARIOLATE
HARLEQUIN
HARLESTON
HARMALINE
HARMATTAN
HARMONICA
HARMONIST
HARMONIUM
HARMONIZE
HARMOTOME
HARPOONER
HARQUEBUS
HARROGATE
HARROWING
HARSHNESS
HARTSHORN
HARVESTER
HERBALIST
HERBARIUM
HERBICIDE
HERBIVORE
HERBORIST
HERCULEAN
HEREAFTER
HERETICAL
HERMANDAD
HERMITAGE
HERODOTUS
HERONSHAW
HERPESTES
HIRUNDINE
HORDEOLUM
HOREHOUND
HORNSTONE
HOROSCOPE
HORRIFIED
HORSEBACK
HORSEHAIR
HORSELESS
HORSEPLAY
HORSESHOE
HORSETAIL
HORSEWHIP
HORTATIVE
HORTATORY
HURRICANE
HURRICANO
HURRIEDLY
IPRINDOLE
IRRADIANT
IRRADIATE
IRRAWADDY
IRREGULAR
IRRITABLE
IRRITABLY
IRRITATED
IRRUPTION
ISRAELITE
JARLSBERG
JERAHMEEL
JERKINESS
JERKWATER
JERUSALEM
JORDANIAN
JURIDICAL
KARABINER
KARAKORAM
KARYOTYPE
KERATITIS
KERBSTONE
KERFUFFLE
KERMESITE
LARGENESS
LARGHETTO
LARGITION
LORGNETTE
LURIDNESS
LYRICALLY
MARAUDING
MARCASITE
MARCHPANE
MARGARINE
MARIJUANA
MARKETEER
MARKETING
MARMALADE
MARMOREAL
MARQUESAS
MARQUETRY
MARROWFAT
MARSHLAND

MARSUPIAL
MARSUPIUM
MARTINEAU
MARTINMAS
MARTYRDOM
MARVELOUS
MERCAPTAN
MERCENARY
MERCERIZE
MERCILESS
MERCURIAL
MERESWINE
MERGANSER
MERRIMENT
MIRABELLE
MIRTHLESS
MORATORIA
MORATORIO
MORBIDITY
MORECAMBE
MORGANITE
MORMONISM
MORTALITY
MORTGAGEE
MORTGAGOR
MORTICIAN
MORTIFIED
MORTSTONE
MURDERESS
MURDEROUS
MURKINESS
MURMURING
MYRMECOID
NARCISSUS
NARGHILLY
NARRATION
NARRATIVE
NARROWING
NERITIDAE
NERVOUSLY
NORMALACY
NORMALITY
NORMALIZE
NORMATIVE
NORTHEAST
NORTHERLY
NORTHWARD
NORTHWEST
NORWEGIAN
NUREMBERG
NURSEMAID
OARSWOMAN
OBREPTION
OUROBOROS
OUROBORUS
OURSELVES
PARABASIS
PARABLAST
PARABOLIC
PARACHUTE
PARACLETE
PARACUSIS
PARAGOGUE
PARAGRAPH
PARALYSIS
PARALYTIC
PARAMEDIC
PARAMETER
PARAMOUNT
PARANOIAC
PARANYMPH
PARASCENE
PARASCEVE
PARASITIC
PARATHION
PARATROOP
PARBUCKLE
PARCHEESI
PARCHMENT
PARDALOTE
PAREGORIC
PARENTAGE
PARENTING
PARFLECHE
PARHELION
PARHYPATE
PARNASITE
PARNASSUS
PAROCHIAL
PAROCHINE
PAROTITIS
PARRICIDE
PARSIMONY
PARSONAGE
PARTAKING
PARTHENON
PARTHOLON
PARTIALLY
PARTICLES
PARTITION
PARTRIDGE
PARTTIMER
PERAEOPOD
PERCALINE
PERCHANCE
PERCHERON
PERCOLATE
PERDITION
PEREGRINE
PERENNIAL
PERFECTLY
PERFERVID
PERFORANS
PERFORATE
PERFORMED
PERFORMER
PERFUMERY
PERGAMENE
PERGUNNAH
PERIAKTOS
PERIANDER
PERIBOLOS
PERICLASE
PERICUTIN
PERIMETER
PERIMORPH
PERIODATE
PERIPATUS
PERIPHERY
PERISCIAN
PERISCOPE
PERISHING
PERISTOME
PERISTYLE
PERMANENT
PERMEABLE
PERMITTED
PERPETUAL
PERPLEXED
PERSECUTE
PERSEVERE
PERSIMMON
PERSONAGE
PERSONATE
PERSONIFY
PERSONNEL
PERSUADED
PERTINENT
PERTURBED
PERTUSATE
PERTUSSIS
PERVASION
PERVASIVE
PERVERTED
PHRENETIC
PHRENITIS
PIRATICAL
PIROUETTE
PORBEAGLE
PORCELAIN
PORCUPINE
PORIFERAN
PORPOISES
PORPORATE
PORRINGER
PORTERAGE
PORTFOLIO
PORTRAYAL
PORTREEVE
PURCHASER
PURDONIUM
PURGATIVE
PURGATORY
PURIFYING
PURITANIC
PURPOSELY
PURSUANCE
PURULENCE
PYRAMIDAL
PYRETHRUM
PYROMANCY
PYROMANIA
PYRRHONIC
REREMOUSE
RORSCHACH
SARBACANE
SARCASTIC
SARMENTUM
SARTORIAL
SARTORIUS
SCRAMBLER
SCRAPBOOK
SCRAPINGS
SCRAPPING
SCRATCHED
SCRATCHES
SCREENING
SCREWBALL
SCREWEDUP
SCREWPINE
SCREWTAPE
SCRIMMAGE
SCRIMPING
SCRIMSHAW
SCRIPTURE
SCRIVENER
SCRODDLED
SCROUNGER
SCRUBBING
SCRUFFILY
SCRUMMAGE
SCRUMPING
SCRUTATOR
SERAPHINE
SERASKIER
SERBONIAN
SERENADER
SERENGETI
SERIALIST
SERIALIZE
SERIATION
SERIOUSLY
SERMONIZE
SERRATION
SERREFILE
SERVICING
SERVIETTE
SERVILELY
SERVILITY
SERVITUDE
SHRIMPING
SHRINKAGE
SHRINKING
SHRUBBERY
SIRBONIAN
SORCERESS
SORROWFUL
SORTILEGE
SPRAICKLE
SPRAUCHLE
SPREADING
SPRECHERY
SPRIGHTLY
SPRINGALD
SPRINGBOK
SPRINGLET
SPRINKLER
SPRITEFUL
SPRITSAIL
STRAGGLER
STRAINING
STRANGELY
STRANGLER
STRANGLES
STRANGURY
STRAPHANG
STRAPLESS
STRAPPADO
STRAPPING
STRATAGEM
STRATEGIC
STREAMING
STREETAGE
STREETCAR
STRENUOUS
STRESSFUL
STRETCHED
STRETCHER
STRIATION
STRICTURE
STRIDENCY
STRINGENT
STRINGOPS
STRIPLING
STROBILUS
STROLLING
STROMBOLI
STRONGARM
STRONGYLE
STRONTIUM
STROSSERS
STRUCTURE
STRUMITIS
STRUTTING
SURCHARGE
SURCINGLE
SURFBOARD
SURFEITED
SURLINESS
SURMULLET
SURPRISED
SURQUEDRY
SURREJOIN
SURRENDER
SURROGATE
SURVEYING
SURVIVING
SYRIACISM
SYRPHIDAE
TARANTASS
TARANTULA
TARAXACUM
TARDINESS
TARGETEER
TARMACKED
TARNATION
TARPAULIN
TARRAGONA
TARTAREAN
TEREBINTH
TERMAGANT
TERMAGENT
TERMINATE
TERPINEOL
TERRACING
TERRARIUM
TERRICOLE
TERRIFIED
TERRITORY
TERRORISM
TERRORIST
TERRORIZE
TERSENESS
THRALLDOM
THRASHING
THRASONIC
THREADFIN
THREEFOLD
THREESOME
THRENETIC
THREONINE
THRESHOLD
THRIFTILY
THRILLANT
THRILLING
THROATILY
THROBBING
THRONGING
THROWAWAY
THROWBACK
THROWDOWN
THROWSTER

TIREDNESS
TORBANITE
TORMENTER
TORMENTIL
TORMENTOR
TORMENTUM
TORTELIER
TURBIDITY
TURBINATE
TURBULENT
TURCOPOLE
TURMAGENT
TURNABOUT
TURNBULLS
TURNROUND
TURNSTILE
TURNSTONE
TURNTABLE
TURPITUDE
TURQUOISE
TYRANNIZE
TYRANNOUS
UKRAINIAN
UNREFINED
UNRELATED
UNRUFFLED
VARANGIAN
VARIATION
VARICELLA
VARIEGATE
VARIOLATE
VARIOUSLY
VARISCITE
VERACIOUS
VERATRINE
VERBALIZE
VERBASCUM
VERBERATE
VERBOSITY
VERDIGRIS
VERIDICAL
VERITABLE
VERKAMPTE
VERMIFORM
VERMIFUGE
VERMILION
VERMINOUS
VERSATILE
VERSIFIER
VERSIONAL
VERTEBRAE
VERTEBRAL
VERTIPORT
VERTUMNUS
VIRGINALS
VIRGINIAN
VIRGINITY
VIRGINIUM
VIRGULATE
VIRTUALLY
VIRULENCE
VORACIOUS
VORTICISM
VORTIGERN
WAREHOUSE
WARMONGER
WARTCRESS
WORCESTER
WORDINESS
WORDSMITH
WORKFORCE
WORKHORSE
WORKHOUSE
WORKPLACE
WORKSPACE
WORLDWIDE
WORMEATEN
WORRISOME
WORTHLESS
WURLITZER
XEROPHYTE
XEROSTOMA
YARDSTICK
YORKSHIRE
ZIRCONIUM
ZOROASTER
ABSCONDER
ABSORBENT
ABSORBING
ABSTAINER
ABSTINENT
ABSURDITY
AESCHYLUS
AESTHETIC
AMSTERDAM
ANSCHLUSS
ANSWERING
ARSENICAL
ASSAILANT
ASSERTING
ASSERTION
ASSERTIVE
ASSIDUITY
ASSIDUOUS
ASSISTANT
ASSOCIATE
ASSONANCE
ASSUETUDE
ASSURANCE
ASSUREDLY
AUSTERITY
AUSTRALIA
BASEBOARD
BASECOURT
BASHFULLY
BASICALLY
BASILICAL
BASILICON
BASKETFUL
BASTINADE
BASTINADO
BESPANGLE
BISECTION
BISHOPRIC
BOSPHORUS
BOSSANOVA
BOSSINESS
BOSTONIAN
BYSTANDER
CASHPOINT
CASSANDRA
CASSATION
CASSEROLE
CASSONADE
CASSOULET
CASSOWARY
CASTANETS
CASTIGATE
CASTILIAN
CASTRATED
CASUARINA
CASUISTIC
CASUISTRY
CESSATION
COSMETICS
COSMOGONY
COSMOLOGY
COSMONAUT
COSTUMIER
CUSPIDORE
CUSTODIAL
CUSTODIAN
CUSTOMARY
CUSTOMIZE
DASHBOARD
DASHWHEEL
DASTARDLY
DESCARTES
DESECRATE
DESERTION
DESERVING
DESICCATE
DESIGNATE
DESIGNING
DESIPIENT
DESIRABLE
DESPERADO
DESPERATE
DESPOTISM
DESTITUTE
DESTROYED
DESTROYER
DESUETUDE
DESULTORY
DISABLING
DISAFFIRM
DISAPPEAR
DISARMING
DISBELIEF
DISBURDEN
DISCARDED
DISCHARGE
DISCLOSED
DISCOLOUR
DISCOMFIT
DISCOURSE
DISCOVERT
DISCOVERY
DISCREDIT
DISEMBARK
DISENGAGE
DISENTOMB
DISFAVOUR
DISFIGURE
DISGRACED
DISGUISED
DISGUSTED
DISHCLOTH
DISHONEST
DISHONOUR
DISHWATER
DISINFECT
DISLOCATE
DISMANTLE
DISMEMBER
DISMISSAL
DISOBLIGE
DISORIENT
DISPARAGE
DISPARATE
DISPARITY
DISPENSER
DISPERSAL
DISPERSED
DISPLACED
DISPLAYED
DISPLEASE
DISPUTANT
DISREGARD
DISREPAIR
DISREPUTE
DISSEMBLE
DISSENTER
DISSIDENT
DISSIPATE
DISSOLUTE
DISSOLVED
DISSONANT
DISTANTLY
DISTEMPER
DISTENDED
DISTILLER
DISTORTED
DISTRAINT
DISTURBED
DISUNITED
DOSSHOUSE
DYSENTERY
DYSPEPSIA
DYSPEPTIC
DYSPHAGIA
DYSTROPHY
EASTBOUND
EASTERNER
EASTLINGS
EASTWARDS
EASYGOING
ELSEWHERE
ENSCONCED
ENSHEATHE
ENSORCELL
ENSTATITE
ERSTWHILE
ESSENTIAL
EUSKARIAN
EXSICCATE
FASCINATE
FASHIONED
FASTENING
FASTTRACK
FESTINATE
FESTIVITY
FISHERMAN
FISHGUARD
FISHPLATE
FOSSILISE
FOSSORIAL
FUSILLADE
FUSSINESS
FUSTIGATE
FUSTINESS
GASCONADE
GASHOLDER
GASOMETER
GASPEREAU
GESSAMINE
GESTATION
GOSLARITE
GOSPELLER
GOSSAMERY
GOSSYPINE
GOSSYPIUM
GUSTATION
HASHEMITE
HASTENING
HASTINESS
HESITANCE
HESITANCY
HESPERIAN
HESSONITE
HESTERNAL
HESYCHASM
HESYCHAST
HISTAMINE
HISTOGRAM
HISTOLOGY
HISTORIAN
HOSPITIUM
HOSTILITY
HUSBANDLY
HUSBANDRY
HUSKINESS
HYSTERICS
INSCRIBED
INSELBERG
INSENSATE
INSERTION
INSHALLAH
INSIDIOUS
INSINCERE
INSINUATE
INSIPIENT
INSISTENT
INSOLENCE
INSOLUBLE
INSOLVENT
INSOMNIAC
INSPECTOR
INSPIRING
INSTANTER
INSTANTLY
INSTIGATE
INSTITUTE
INSULATOR
INSULTING
INSURANCE
INSURGENT
INSWINGER
JESSAMINE
JESSERANT
JOSEPHINE
JOSEPHSON
JUSTIFIED
JUSTINIAN
KISSINGER
LASERWORT
LASSITUDE
LASTDITCH
LESTRIGON
LISTENING
LUSTIHOOD
LUSTINESS

LYSIMETER
MASCULINE
MASEFIELD
MASOCHISM
MASOCHIST
MASSINGER
MASSIVELY
MASSORETE
MASSYMORE
MASTERFUL
MASTERMAN
MASTICATE
MESENTERY
MESMERISM
MESMERIZE
MESOBLAST
MESOMORPH
MESSALINA
MESSENGER
MESSIANIC
MISBEHAVE
MISCHANCE
MISCREANT
MISDIRECT
MISERABLE
MISERABLY
MISFALLEN
MISFIRING
MISGIVING
MISGUIDED
MISHANDLE
MISINFORM
MISLOCATE
MISMANAGE
MISOCLERE
MISONEIST
MISPICKEL
MISPLACED
MISSHAPEN
MISSIONER
MISSTROKE
MISTEMPER
MISTIGRIS
MISTINESS
MISTLETOE
MOSCHATEL
MOSKONFYT
MUSCADINE
MUSCARINE
MUSCOVADO
MUSCOVITE
MUSHINESS
MUSHROOMS
MUSICALLY
MUSICHALL
MUSKETEER
MUSKETOON
MUSKOGEAN
MUSSITATE
MUSSOLINI
MUSSULMAN
MUSTINESS
MYSTERIES
MYSTICISM
NASEBERRY
NASHVILLE
NASTINESS
NESCIENCE
NOSEBLEED
NOSTALGIA
NOSTALGIC
NOSTOLOGY
NYSTAGMUS
OASTHOUSE
OBSCENELY
OBSCENITY
OBSCURELY
OBSCURITY
OBSECRATE
OBSEQUIES
OBSERVANT
OBSESSION
OBSESSIVE
OBSTETRIC
OBSTINACY
OBSTINATE
OESTROGEN
ONSLAUGHT
OPSIMATHY
PASSAMENT
PASSENGER
PASSEPIED
PASSERINE
PASSIVELY
PASSIVITY
PASTERNAK
PASTICCIO
PASTORALE
PASTURAGE
PESSIMISM
PESSIMIST
PESTICIDE
PESTILENT
PISTACHIO
PISTAREEN
PISTOLEER
POSSESSED
POSSESSOR
POSSIBLES
POSTCARDS
POSTERIOR
POSTERITY
POSTHOUSE
POSTNATAL
POSTPONED
POSTULANT
POSTULATE
POSTWOMAN
PUSHCHAIR
PUSSYFOOT
RASKOLNIK
RASPATORY
RASPBERRY
RESENTFUL
RESERPINE
RESERVIST
RESERVOIR
RESHUFFLE
RESIDENCE
RESIDENCY
RESIDUARY
RESILIENT
RESISTANT
RESNATRON
RESONANCE
RESONATOR
RESORTING
RESOURCES
RESPECTED
RESPECTER
RESSALDAR
RESTIFORM
RESTITUTE
RESTRAINT
RESULTANT
RESULTING
RESURFACE
RESURGENT
RESURRECT
RISKINESS
ROSCOMMON
ROSEWATER
ROSINANTE
ROSMARINE
ROSMINIAN
ROSTELLUM
RUSHLIGHT
RUSTICATE
RUSTINESS
SASKATOON
SASQUATCH
SASSAFRAS
SASSENACH
SASSOLITE
SISSERARY
SISYPHEAN
SOSTENUTO
SUSCITATE
SUSPECTED
SUSPENDED
SUSPENDER
SUSPENSOR
SUSPICION
SUSTAINED
TASMANIAN
TASSELLED
TASTELESS
TESTAMENT
TESTATRIX
TESTDRIVE
TESTICLES
TESTIFIER
TESTIMONY
TISIPHONE
TOSCANINI
UNSAVOURY
UNSCATHED
UNSECURED
UNSELFISH
UNSETTLED
UNSHACKLE
UNSHEATHE
UNSIGHTLY
UNSINNING
UNSKILLED
UNSPARING
UNSPOILED
UNSULLIED
UPSETTING
VASECTOMY
VESICULAR
VESPASIAN
VESTIBULE
VESTIGIAL
VESTITURE
VESTMENTS
VISAGISTE
VISCOSITY
VISIONARY
VISUALIZE
WASHBASIN
WASHBOARD
WASHCLOTH
WASHERMAN
WASHSTAND
WASPISHLY
WASSERMAN
WASTELAND
WASTWATER
WESTBOUND
WESTERNER
WESTWARDS
WISCONSIN
WISECRACK
WISTFULLY
YESTERDAY
YESTEREVE
ACTUALITY
ACTUARIAL
AFTERCARE
AFTERDAMP
AFTERGLOW
AFTERMATH
AFTERMOST
AFTERNOON
AFTERWORD
AITCHBONE
ALTERABLE
ALTERCATE
ALTERNATE
ALTIMETER
ALTIPLANO
ALTISSIMO
ANTARCTIC
ANTENATAL
ANTHOLOGY
ANTICLINE
ANTIGONUS
ANTIHELIX
ANTIPASTO
ANTIPATHY
ANTIPHONY
ANTIPODES
ANTIQUARY
ANTIQUITY
ANTITOXIC
ANTITOXIN
ANTIVENIN
ANTONINUS
ARTEMISIA
ARTERIOLE
ARTHRITIC
ARTHRITIS
ARTHROPOD
ARTHROSIS
ARTHURIAN
ARTICHOKE
ARTICULAR
ARTIFICER
ARTILLERY
ASTHMATIC
ASTOUNDED
ASTRAGALS
ASTRAKHAN
ASTRODOME
ASTROLABE
ASTROLOGY
ASTRONAUT
ASTRONOMY
ASTROPHEL
ASTROTURF
ASTUCIOUS
ATTACKING
ATTAINDER
ATTEMPTED
ATTENDANT
ATTENTION
ATTENTIVE
ATTENUATE
ATTITUDES
ATTRIBUTE
ATTRITION
ATTUITION
AUTHENTIC
AUTHORESS
AUTHORITY
AUTHORIZE
AUTOCLAVE
AUTOCRACY
AUTOCROSS
AUTOGRAPH
AUTOLATRY
AUTOLYCUS
AUTOLYSIS
AUTOMAKER
AUTOMATED
AUTOMATIC
AUTOMATON
AUTONOMIC
AUTOPILOT
AUTOROUTE
AUTOSCOPY
BATHTOWEL
BATTALION
BATTLEAXE
BETHLEHEM
BETROTHAL
BETROTHED
BETTERTON
BOTANICAL
BOTSWANAN
BOTTLEFUL
BUTTERBUR
BUTTERCUP
BUTTERFLY
BUTTERNUT
CATACLYSM
CATACOMBS
CATALEPSY
CATALOGUE
CATALYSIS
CATALYTIC
CATAMARAN
CATAPLASM
CATAPLEXY
CATARRHAL
CATATONIA
CATATONIC
CATCHCROP
CATCHMENT
CATCHPOLE
CATCHPOLL

CATCHWORD
CATECHISM
CATECHIZE
CATERWAUL
CATHARSIS
CATHARTIC
CATHEDRAL
CATHEPSIN
CATHERINE
CATSKILLS
CATTLEMAN
CATTLEPEN
COTANGENT
COTHURNUS
COTYLEDON
CUTANEOUS
CUTTHROAT
DETECTION
DETECTIVE
DETENTION
DETERGENT
DETERMINE
DETERRENT
DETONATOR
DETRACTOR
DETRIMENT
DETRITION
DITHERING
DITHYRAMB
DOTHEBOYS
DUTIFULLY
ECTOMORPH
ECTOPLASM
ECTROPION
ENTELECHY
ENTERITIS
ENTERTAIN
ENTHYMEME
ENTOPHYTE
ENTOURAGE
ENTRAMMEL
ENTRANCED
ENTRECHAT
ENTRECÔTE
ENTREMETS
ENTROPION
ENTROPIUM
ESTABLISH
ESTAFETTE
ESTAMINET
ESTHETICS
ESTIMABLE
ESTRANGED
ESTRAPADE
ESTRELDID
EUTROPHIC
EXTEMPORE
EXTENSILE
EXTENSION
EXTENSIVE
EXTENUATE
EXTIRPATE
EXTORTION
EXTRACTOR
EXTRADITE
EXTREMELY
EXTREMISM
EXTREMIST
EXTREMITY
EXTRICATE
EXTRINSIC
EXTROVERT
EXTRUSION
FATIDICAL
FATISCENT
FATTENING
FATUOUSLY
GATECRASH
GATESHEAD
GATHERING
GOTHAMITE
GUTENBERG
GUTTERING
HATCHBACK
HATCHMENT
HETERODOX
HETEROSIS
HITCHCOCK
HITCHHIKE
HOTHEADED
HOTTENTOT
HUTTERITE
ICTERIDAE
INTEGRATE
INTEGRITY
INTELLECT
INTENDANT
INTENDING
INTENSELY
INTENSIFY
INTENSITY
INTENSIVE
INTENTION
INTERBRED
INTERCEDE
INTERCEPT
INTERCITY
INTERDICT
INTERFACE
INTERFERE
INTERJECT
INTERLACE
INTERLARD
INTERLOCK
INTERLOPE
INTERLUDE
INTERMENT
INTERNODE
INTERPLAY
INTERPOSE
INTERPRET
INTERRUPT
INTERSECT
INTERVENE
INTERVIEW
INTESTATE
INTESTINE
INTRICACY
INTRICATE
INTRIGUED
INTRIGUER
INTRINSIC
INTRODUCE
INTROITUS
INTROVERT
INTRUSION
INTRUSIVE
INTUITION
INTUITIVE
INTUMESCE
JETSTREAM
JITTERBUG
KITCHENER
KITTENISH
KITTIWAKE
LATECOMER
LATENIGHT
LATERALLY
LATESCENT
LATHYRISM
LATICLAVE
LATRATION
LATTERDAY
LETHARGIC
LETTERBOX
LETTERING
LITERALLY
LITHOCYST
LITHOPONE
LITHUANIA
LITIGIOUS
LUTESCENT
MATCHLESS
MATCHLOCK
MATCHWOOD
MATELASSE
MATERNITY
MATHURINE
MATRIARCH
MATRICIDE
MATRIMONY
MATTAMORE
MATUTINAL
METABASIS
METABOLIC
METALLOID
METALWORK
METAPELET
METEORITE
METEOROID
METHADONE
METHEGLIN
METHODISM
METHODIST
METRICATE
METROLAND
METRONOME
MITHRAISM
MITRAILLE
MOTHBALLS
MOTHEATEN
MOTHERING
MOTOCROSS
MOTORBIKE
MOTORBOAT
MOTORCADE
MOTORISTS
MUTILATED
MUTOSCOPE
MUTTERING
MYTHOLOGY
NATHANIEL
NATHELESS
NATHEMORE
NATROLITE
NATURALLY
NITHSDALE
NOTARIKON
NOTCHBACK
NOTEPAPER
NOTOCHORD
NOTONECTA
NOTORIETY
NOTORIOUS
NUTJOBBER
NUTRIMENT
NUTRITION
NUTRITIVE
OBTAINING
OBTRUSION
OBTRUSIVE
OCTACHORD
OCTAGONAL
OCTASTICH
OCTILLION
OCTOBRIST
ONTHESPOT
ONTOGENCY
OPTICALLY
OPTOMETRY
OPTOPHONE
ORTANIQUE
ORTHODOXY
ORTHOLOGY
ORTHOPTER
ORTHOTONE
OSTEODERM
OSTEOPATH
OSTRACISM
OSTRACIZE
OSTROGOTH
OTTERBURN
OTTRELITE
OUTERMOST
OUTFITTER
OUTGOINGS
OUTGROWTH
OUTNUMBER
OUTOFTOWN
OUTRIGGER
OUTROOPER
OUTSIDERS
OUTSKIRTS
OUTSPOKEN
OUTSPREAD
OUTWARDLY
OUTWORKER
PATCHOULI
PATCHOULY
PATCHWORK
PATERCOVE
PATERNITY
PATHOGENY
PATHOLOGY
PATHTRAIN
PATIENTLY
PATRIARCH
PATRICIAN
PATRICIDE
PATRIMONY
PATRIOTIC
PATROCLUS
PATROLMAN
PATRONAGE
PATRONESS
PATRONIZE
PATTERNED
PETAURIST
PETERSHAM
PETHIDINE
PETILLANT
PETRIFIED
PETROLEUM
PETROLOGY
PETTICOAT
PETTINESS
PETTITOES
PETULANCE
PHTHALATE
PITCHFORK
PITCHPINE
PITCHPOLE
PITCHPOLL
PITIFULLY
PITUITARY
PITUITRIN
POTASSIUM
POTBOILER
POTENTATE
POTENTIAL
POTHOLING
POTHUNTER
POTPOURRI
POTTINGAR
PYTHONESS
RATEPAYER
RATHERIPE
RATHERISH
RATIONALE
RATIONING
RATTLEBAG
RETAILING
RETAINING
RETALIATE
RETENTION
RETENTIVE
RETIARIUS
RETICENCE
RETICULUM
RETINITIS
RETORSION
RETORTION
RETRACTOR
RETRIEVAL
RETRIEVER
RETROCEDE
RETROFLEX
RETROVERT
RETURNING
ROTAPLANE
ROTTERDAM
ROTUNDATE
ROTUNDITY
RUTHENIAN
RUTHENIUM
SATELLITE
SATIATION
SATINWOOD
SATIRICAL
SATISFIED
SATURATED
SATURNIAN

SATURNINE
SATURNISM
SATYRIDAE
SATYRINAE
SETACEOUS
SITUATION
SOTTISIER
TETRAGRAM
TETRALOGY
TETRARCHY
TETTEROUS
TITHEBARN
TITILLATE
TITRATION
TITTLEBAT
TOTALIZER
TOTAQUINE
TOTTENHAM
TUTIORISM
ULTIMATUM
ULTRONEUS
UNTENABLE
UNTIMEOUS
UNTOUCHED
UNTRAINED
UNTREATED
UNTRODDEN
UNTUTORED
UNTYPICAL
URTICARIA
UTTERANCE
UTTERLESS
UTTERMOST
VITASCOPE
VITELLIUS
VITIATION
VITRIOLIC
VITRUVIAN
WATCHWORD
WATERBABY
WATERBUTT
WATERFALL
WATERFORD
WATERFOWL
WATERGATE
WATERHOLE
WATERLESS
WATERLILY
WATERLINE
WATERMARK
WATERMILL
WATERSHED
WATERSIDE
WATERWEED
WITCHETTY
WITHDRAWN
WITHERING
WITHERITE
WITHSTAND
WITHYWIND
WITNESSED
WITTICISM
WITTINGLY
WUTHERING
YTTERBIUM
ABUNDANCE
ACUMINATE
ACUTENESS
ADULATION
ADULTERER
ADULTHOOD
ADUMBRATE
AGUECHEEK
ALUMINIUM
AMUSEMENT
AMUSINGLY
AQUAPLANE
AQUARELLE
AQUILEGIA
AVUNCULAR
BLUEBEARD
BLUEBERRY
BLUEPRINT
BLUESTONE
BLUFFNESS
BLUNDERER
BLUNTNESS
BLUSTERER
BOULEVARD
BOUNDLESS
BOUNTEOUS
BOUNTIFUL
BOURGEOIS
BRUMMAGEM
BRUNHILDE
BRUSHWOOD
BRUSQUELY
BRUTALISM
BRUTALITY
BRUTALIZE
CAUCASIAN
CAUSATION
CAUTERIZE
CHURCHILL
CHURCHMAN
CHURIDARS
CLUBHOUSE
CLUSTERED
COUCHETTE
COUNSELOR
COUNTDOWN
COUNTLESS
COUNTRIES
COURGETTE
COURTELLE
COURTEOUS
COURTESAN
COURTROOM
COURTSHIP
COURTYARD
COUTURIER
CRUCIALLY
CRUDENESS
CRUMBLING
CRUSTACEA
DAUNTLESS
DEUCALION
DEUTERIUM
DOUBTLESS
DOUKHOBOR
DRUGSTORE
DRUMSTICK
DRUNKENLY
EBULLIENT
EDUCATION
EDUCATIVE
ELUCIDATE
ELUTRIATE
EMULATION
ENUCLEATE
ENUMERATE
ENUNCIATE
EPULATION
EQUALIZER
EQUIPMENT
EQUIPOISE
EQUISETUM
EQUITABLE
EQUITABLY
EQUIVOCAL
EQUIVOQUE
ERUCIFORM
ERUDITION
EXUBERANT
EXUDATION
FAULCHION
FAULTLESS
FEUDALISM
FEUDATORY
FEUILLANT
FLUCTUATE
FLUSTERED
FOUNDLING
FOURPENCE
FOURWHEEL
FRUCTIDOR
FRUGALITY
FRUITCAKE
FRUITERER
FRUITLESS
FRUSTRATE
GAUDEAMUS
GAUDINESS
GAULEITER
GAUNTNESS
GLUCINIUM
GLUCOSIDE
GLUTAMINE
GLUTINOUS
GRUBBINOL
GRUELLING
GRUFFNESS
GRUMBLING
HAUGHTILY
HAUTMONDE
HEURISTIC
HOURGLASS
HOURSTONE
HOUSEBOAT
HOUSECOAT
HOUSEHOLD
HOUSEMAID
HOUSEROOM
HOUSEWIFE
HOUSEWORK
HOUYHNHNM
IBUPROFEN
IGUANODON
INUMBRATE
INUNCTION
INUSITATE
JAUNDICED
JOUISANCE
KRUMMHORN
LAUDATION
LAUDATORY
LAUGHABLE
LAUNCELOT
LAUNCHING
LAUNDRESS
LEUCOCYTE
LEUCOTOME
LEUKAEMIA
LJUBLJANA
LOUDMOUTH
LOUISIANA
LOUSEWORT
MAULSTICK
MAURITIAN
MAURITIUS
MAUSOLEUM
MOURNIVAL
MOUSEHOLE
MOUSELIKE
MOUSETRAP
MOUSTACHE
MOUTHLESS
MOUTHWASH
NAUGHTILY
NAUMACHIA
NAUSEATED
NEUCHATEL
NEURALGIA
NEURALGIC
NEUROGLIA
NEUROLOGY
NEUTRALLY
OCULIFORM
OPULENTLY
OVULATION
PAULOWNIA
PAUSANIAS
PLUMBEOUS
PLUMBLINE
PLUMDAMAS
PLUMPNESS
PLUNDERER
PLURALISM
PLURALITY
PLUTOCRAT
PLUTONIUM
POUJADIST
POULTERER
PRUDENTLY
PRURIENCE
RAUCOUSLY
ROUGHCAST
ROUGHNECK
ROUGHNESS
ROUGHSHOD
ROUMANIAN
ROUMANSCH
ROUNCEVAL
ROUNCIVAL
ROUNDBACK
ROUNDELAY
ROUNDFISH
ROUNDHAND
ROUNDHEAD
ROUNDSMAN
ROUSSETTE
ROUTINELY
SAUCEBOAT
SAUCINESS
SAUCISSON
SAUTERNES
SAUVIGNON
SCUDDALER
SCULPTING
SCULPTURE
SCUNCHEON
SCURRIOUR
SHUBUNKIN
SHUFFLING
SHUTTERED
SLUGHORNE
SLUMBERER
SMUGGLING
SOUBRETTE
SOUFRIERE
SOULFULLY
SOUNDBITE
SOUNDLESS
SOUNDNESS
SOURDOUGH
SOUTENEUR
SOUTHDOWN
SOUTHEAST
SOUTHERLY
SOUTHWARD
SOUTHWARK
SOUTHWEST
SOUVLAKIA
SOUWESTER
SPUNCULID
SQUADRONE
SQUALIDLY
SQUATTERS
SQUEAMISH
SQUINANCY
SQUINTING
SQUIREAGE
SQUIRMING
STUMBLING
STUMPWORK
STUPEFIED
STUPIDITY
TAUCHNITZ
TAUTOLOGY
THUMBLING
THUMBNAIL
THUMBTACK
THUNDERER
TOUCHDOWN
TOUCHLINE
TOUCHWOOD
TOUGHNESS
TOURNEDOS
TRUCKLOAD
TRUCULENT
TRUEPENNY
TRUMPEDUP
TRUMPETER
TRUNCATED
TRUNCHEON
TRUTINATE
UNUSUALLY
URUGUAYAN
VOUCHSAFE
WHUNSTANE
YOUNGSTER
ADVANTAGE

ADVECTION
ADVENTIST
ADVENTURE
ADVERBIAL
ADVERSARY
ADVERSELY
ADVERSITY
ADVERTISE
ADVISABLE
ADVISEDLY
ADVOCATED
ALVEOLATE
BEVERIDGE
CAVALCADE
CAVENDISH
CAVERNOUS
CAVORTING
CEVAPCICI
CIVILISED
CIVILIZED
COVALENCY
COVELLITE
COVERDALE
DAVENPORT
DEVASTATE
DEVELOPED
DEVELOPER
DEVIATION
DEVILMENT
DEVIOUSLY
DEVONPORT
DIVERGENT
DIVERGING
DIVERSIFY
DIVERSION
DIVERSITY
DIVERTING
DIVIDENDS
DIVISIBLE
EAVESDROP
ENVERMEIL
FAVORABLE
FAVORABLY
FAVOURITE
GAVELKIND
GOVERNESS
GOVERNING
HAVERSACK
INVECTIVE
INVENTION
INVENTIVE
INVENTORY
INVERNESS
INVERSION
INVERTASE
INVIDIOUS
INVIOLATE
INVISIBLE
INVOICING
INVOLUCRE
IRVINGISM
JOVIALITY
JUVENILIA
LAVOISIER
LEVANTINE
LEVERAGED
LEVIATHAN
LEVITICUS
LIVERPOOL
LIVERWORT
LIVERYMAN
LIVESTOCK
LIVRAISON
MAVOURNIN
NAVIGABLE
NAVIGATOR
NEVERMORE
NOVELETTE
NOVICIATE
NOVITIATE
NOVOCAINE
NOVODAMUS
OBVENTION
OBVIOUSLY
RAVISHING
REVEALING
REVELLING
REVERENCE
REVERSING
REVERSION
REVETMENT
REVICTUAL
REVOLTING
REVOLVING
REVULSION
RIVERSIDE
SAVERNAKE
SEVENTEEN
SEVERALLY
SEVERANCE
SOVENANCE
SOVEREIGN
TAVERNERS
TAVISTOCK
TOVARISCH
UNVARYING
VIVACIOUS
VIVIDNESS
WAVELLITE
COWARDICE
DOWELLING
DOWNGRADE
DOWNRIGHT
DOWNSTAGE
DOWNTREND
DOWNWARDS
EDWARDIAN
GAWKINESS
HAWCUBITE
HAWKSBILL
HAWTHORNE
HOWTOWDIE
JAWBATION
JEWELLERY
LAWMAKING
LAWMONGER
LAWNMOWER
LOWLANDER
LOWLINESS
NEWCASTLE
NEWLYWEDS
NEWMARKET
NEWSAGENT
NEWSFLASH
NEWSHOUND
NEWSPAPER
NEWSPRINT
NEWSSHEET
NEWSSTALL
NEWSSTAND
PAWKINESS
POWELLITE
POWERBOAT
POWERLESS
REWARDING
REWORKING
ROWDINESS
TOWCESTER
TOWELLING
TOWNSFOLK
UNWATERED
UNWELCOME
UNWILLING
UNWITTING
UNWORRIED
UNWRITTEN
ANXIOUSLY
AUXILIARY
BOXWALLAH
COXSACKIE
DEXTERITY
DEXTEROUS
DEXTRORSE
DIXIELAND
HEXAGONAL
HEXAMERON
HEXAMETER
HEXASTICH
HEXATEUCH
JUXTAPOSE
LUXEMBURG
LUXURIANT
LUXURIATE
LUXURIOUS
MAXILLARY
ROXBURGHE
SAXIFRAGE
SAXITOXIN
SAXOPHONE
SEXUALITY
SIXTEENMO
SIXTEENTH
TAXIDERMY
TAXIMETER
TOXOPHILY
VEXATIONS
VEXATIOUS
VEXILLARY
ABYSMALLY
AMYGDALUS
ASYMMETRY
ASYNERGIA
BOYFRIEND
CEYLONESE
CRYOGENIC
CRYOMETER
CRYPTOGAM
DAYSPRING
DRYASDUST
ETYMOLOGY
FLYWEIGHT
GLYCERIDE
GLYCERINE
HAYMAKING
HAYMARKET
HAYRADDIN
HEYPRESTO
HOYDENISH
JAYWALKER
KEYHOLDER
KEYSTROKE
MAYFLOWER
MAYORALTY
MOYGASHEL
PAYCHEQUE
PAYMASTER
PHYLLOPOD
PHYLOGENY
PHYSICIAN
PHYSICIST
PHYTOLITE
PHYTOTRON
PRYTANEUM
PSYCHICAL
PSYCHOSIS
PSYCHOTIC
REYKJAVIK
RHYMESTER
SCYTHEMAN
SKYJACKER
STYLISHLY
STYLISTIC
STYLOBATE
TAYASSUID
THYESTEAN
THYLACINE
THYRATRON
THYRISTOR
TRYPHOEUS
WAYZGOOSE
BIZARRELY
BYZANTINE
DIZZINESS
FUZZINESS
GAZETTEER
HAZARDOUS
HAZELWORT
LAZARETTO
LAZYBONES
LAZZARONE
MEZZANINE
MEZZOTINT
MUZZINESS
PIZZICATO
RAZORBILL
ROZINANTE

9:4

ADVANTAGE
AFLATOXIN
ALBATROSS
ALLANTOID
ALLANTOIS
ALMANDINE
AMIANTHUS
ANDANTINO
ANNAPOLIS
ANNAPURNA
ANTARCTIC
APPALLING
APPARATUS
APPARITOR
AQUAPLANE
AQUARELLE
ARMADILLO
ARMAMENTS
ASPARAGUS
ASPARTAME
ASSAILANT
ATTACKING
ATTAINDER
AUDACIOUS
BAGATELLE
BALACLAVA
BALALAIKA
BARAGOUIN
BEHAVIOUR
BELATEDLY
BILATERAL
BIPARTITE
BIZARRELY
BLEACHERS
BONAPARTE
BOTANICAL
BREADLINE
BREAKABLE
BREAKAGES
BREAKAWAY
BREAKDOWN
BREAKEVEN
BREAKFAST
BREAKNECK
BREATHING
BROADCAST
BROADLOOM
BROADSIDE
BYZANTINE
CABALLERO
CADASTRAL
CALABOOSE
CALABRESE
CANALETTO
CANAVERAL
CAPACIOUS
CAPACITOR
CAPARISON
CARACALLA
CARAMBOLA
CATACLYSM
CATACOMBS
CATALEPSY
CATALOGUE
CATALYSIS
CATALYTIC
CATAMARAN
CATAPLASM
CATAPLEXY
CATARRHAL
CATATONIA
CATATONIC
CAVALCADE
CEDARWOOD
CELANDINE
CERATITIS
CERATODUS
CEVAPCICI
CHEAPJACK
CHEAPNESS
CHEAPSIDE
CHLAMYDES

CIGARETTE
CLEANNESS
CLEANSING
CLEARANCE
CLEARNESS
CLOAKROOM
CORALLINE
COTANGENT
COVALENCY
COWARDICE
CUTANEOUS
DAMASCENE
DEBATABLE
DEBAUCHED
DEBAUCHEE
DECACHORD
DECADENCE
DECALITRE
DECALOGUE
DECAMERON
DECASTYLE
DECATHLON
DEFALCATE
DEFAULTER
DELACROIX
DEMAGOGUE
DEMANDING
DEMARCATE
DEPARTURE
DEVASTATE
DIDACTICS
DIGASTRIC
DISABLING
DISAFFIRM
DISAPPEAR
DISARMING
DONATELLO
DREAMLESS
DRYASDUST
DYNAMITED
ECLAMPSIA
EDWARDIAN
EGLANTINE
EMBARRASS
EMBASSADE
EMBASSAGE
EMBATTLED
EMPAESTIC
EMPANOPLY
ENCANTHIS
ENCAUSTIC
ENGARLAND
ENRAPTURE
EQUALIZER
ERGATANER
ESCALATOR
ESPAGNOLE
ESTABLISH
ESTAFETTE
ESTAMINET
EUDAEMONY
EXCALIBUR
EXCAMBION
EXCAVATOR
EXHAUSTED
EXPANSION
EXPANSIVE
EXPATIATE
FABACEOUS
FALANGIST
FAMAGUSTA
FANATICAL
FARANDOLE
FERACIOUS
FINANCIAL
FINANCIER
FOMALHAUT
FORASMUCH
FUGACIOUS
FURACIOUS
GABARDINE
GALACTOSE
GALANTINE
GALAPAGOS
GIRANDOLE
GLEANINGS
GREASEGUN
GREATCOAT
GREATNESS
GUJARATHI
HAMADRYAD
HAZARDOUS
HEPATICAL
HEPATITIS
HEXAGONAL
HEXAMERON
HEXAMETER
HEXASTICH
HEXATEUCH
HIJACKING
HILARIOUS
HIMALAYAN
HIMALAYAS
HUMANKIND
HYPALLAGE
IDEALOGUE
IGUANODON
IMBALANCE
IMMANACLE
IMMANENCE
IMMANENCY
IMPACTION
IMPARTIAL
IMPASSION
IMPASSIVE
IMPATIENT
INCAPABLE
INCARDINE
INCARNATE
INCAUTION
INFANTILE
INFATUATE
INPATIENT
IRRADIANT
IRRADIATE
IRRAWADDY
ISLAMABAD
ISRAELITE
JACARANDA
JERAHMEEL
JOHANNINE
KARABINER
KARAKORAM
KERATITIS
LAFAYETTE
LAMARTINE
LAMASERAI
LAZARETTO
LECANORAM
LEVANTINE
LOCALIZED
LOGARITHM
LUBAVITCH
MACADAMIA
MACARONIC
MACARTHUR
MADARIAGA
MADAROSIS
MAHARAJAH
MAHARANEE
MAHARISHI
MALACHITE
MALATHION
MALAYSIAN
MARAUDING
MEDALLION
MEDALLIST
MEGACYCLE
MEGAHERTZ
MEGAPHONE
MEGASCOPE
MEGASPORE
MELAMPODE
MELANESIA
MELANOTIC
MENADIONE
MENAGERIE
MEPACRINE
METABASIS
METABOLIC
METALLOID
METALWORK
METAPELET
MINACIOUS
MIRABELLE
MOGADISHU
MONACTINE
MONASTERY
MONASTRAL
MONATOMIC
MORATORIA
MORATORIO
MUJAHIDIN
NABATHEAN
NEFANDOUS
NEFARIOUS
NICARAGUA
NOTARIKON
OBTAINING
OCEANIDES
OCTACHORD
OCTAGONAL
OCTASTICH
OLFACTORY
ORGANELLE
ORGANICAL
ORGANISED
ORGANISER
ORGANIZED
ORGANIZER
ORGANZINE
ORMANDINE
ORTANIQUE
PALAESTRA
PALAFITTE
PALAMPORE
PALANKEEN
PALANQUIN
PALATABLE
PANATELLA
PAPARAZZI
PAPARAZZO
PARABASIS
PARABLAST
PARABOLIC
PARACHUTE
PARACLETE
PARACUSIS
PARAGOGUE
PARAGRAPH
PARALYSIS
PARALYTIC
PARAMEDIC
PARAMETER
PARAMOUNT
PARANOIAC
PARANYMPH
PARASCENE
PARASCEVE
PARASITIC
PARATHION
PARATROOP
PEDAGOGUE
PERAEOPOD
PETAURIST
PILASTERS
PIRATICAL
PLEASANCE
POTASSIUM
PROACTIVE
PYRAMIDAL
RAPACIOUS
RECALLING
RECAPTURE
REGARDANT
REGARDFUL
REGARDING
RELATIONS
REMAINDER
REMAINING
RENASCENT
REPAYABLE
REPAYMENT
RETAILING
RETAINING
RETALIATE
REWARDING
ROCAMBOLE
ROTAPLANE
RUNAROUND
SAGACIOUS
SAGAPENUM
SALACIOUS
SALANGANE
SAMARITAN
SCIAMACHY
SCIARIDAE
SCLAUNDER
SCRAMBLER
SCRAPBOOK
SCRAPINGS
SCRAPPING
SCRATCHED
SCRATCHES
SEBACEOUS
SEBASTIAN
SECATEURS
SELACHION
SEMANTEME
SEMANTICS
SEMANTIDE
SEMANTRON
SEMAPHORE
SEPARABLE
SEPARATED
SEPARATOR
SERAPHINE
SERASKIER
SETACEOUS
SHEARLING
SKIAMACHY
SOMASCOPE
SPEAKEASY
SPEARHEAD
SPEARMINT
SPEARSIDE
SPEARWORT
SPHACELUS
SPRAICKLE
SPRAUCHLE
SQUADRONE
SQUALIDLY
SQUATTERS
STEADFAST
STEAMBOAT
STEAMSHIP
STRAGGLER
STRAINING
STRANGELY
STRANGLER
STRANGLES
STRANGURY
STRAPHANG
STRAPLESS
STRAPPADO
STRAPPING
STRATAGEM
STRATEGIC
SUBALTERN
SUGARCANE
SWEATBAND
SYBARITIC
SYNAGOGUE
SYNANGIUM
TABANIDAE
TABASHEER
TACAMAHAC
TARANTASS
TARANTULA
TARAXACUM
TAYASSUID
TENACIOUS
TENACULUM
TENAILLON
THRALLDOM
THRASHING
THRASONIC
TOTALIZER
TOTAQUINE
TOVARISCH
TREACHERY
TREADMILL

TREASURER
TREATMENT
TRIANGLED
TRIATHLON
TYRANNIZE
TYRANNOUS
UKRAINIAN
UNBALANCE
UNDAMAGED
UNDAUNTED
UNEARTHLY
UNEATABLE
UNFAILING
UNHAPPILY
UNMARRIED
UNMATCHED
UNNATURAL
UNSAVOURY
UNVARYING
UNWATERED
VARANGIAN
VELASQUEZ
VERACIOUS
VERATRINE
VEXATIONS
VEXATIOUS
VICARIOUS
VISAGISTE
VITASCOPE
VIVACIOUS
VOLAGEOUS
VOLATIBLE
VORACIOUS
WAHABIITE
WHEATGERM
WHEATMEAL
WOMANHOOD
WOMANISER
WOMANIZER
WOMANKIND
WREAKLESS
ALABASTER
ANABOLISM
ANABRANCH
ARABESQUE
ARABINOSE
BAMBOOZLE
BARBARIAN
BARBARITY
BARBAROUS
BARBITONE
BARBOTINE
BENBECULA
BOMBARDON
BOMBASINE
BOMBASTIC
BOMBSHELL
BOOBYTRAP
BUMBLEBEE
CAMBODIAN
CAMBRIDGE
CAMBUSCAN
CARBAMATE
CARBAMIDE
CARBONADE
CARBONARI
CARBONATE
CARBONIZE
CARBUNCLE
CHABAZITE
CLUBHOUSE
COMBATANT
COMBATIVE
CRIBELLUM
CUBBYHOLE
CYMBELINE
CYMBIDIUM
DAMBUSTER
DIABLERIE
DISBELIEF
DISBURDEN
DOUBTLESS
DUMBARTON
DUMBFOUND
ELABORATE
EXUBERANT
EYEBRIGHT
FLABELLUM
FORBIDDEN
FROBISHER
GIBBERISH
GLABELLAR
GRUBBINOL
HAMBURGER
HARBINGER
HERBALIST
HERBARIUM
HERBICIDE
HERBIVORE
HERBORIST
HOBBINOLL
HUSBANDLY
HUSBANDRY
INABILITY
INEBRIATE
JAMBALAYA
JAWBATION
KERBSTONE
KNOBSTICK
LAMBSWOOL
LIABILITY
LIMBURGER
LJUBLJANA
LOMBARDIC
LUMBERING
LUMBRICUS
MELBOURNE
MISBEHAVE
MORBIDITY
NEBBISHER
NIEBELUNG
NUMBSKULL
OPOBALSAM
OROBANCHE
PARBUCKLE
PORBEAGLE
POTBOILER
PREBENDAL
PROBABLES
PROBATION
PROBOSCIS
REDBREAST
REMBRANDT
RIBBONISM
ROXBURGHE
RUBBERIZE
RUDBECKIA
SABBATIAN
SARBACANE
SCABLANDS
SEABOTTLE
SEMBLANCE
SERBONIAN
SHUBUNKIN
SIRBONIAN
SLABSTONE
SOUBRETTE
STABILITY
STABILIZE
STABLEBOY
STABLELAD
STABLEMAN
SUNBATHER
SYMBIOSIS
SYMBIOTIC
SYMBOLISM
SYMBOLIST
SYMBOLIZE
TABBOULEH
TOMBSTONE
TONBRIDGE
TORBANITE
TREBIZOND
TREBUCHET
TRIBALISM
TRIBESMAN
TRIBESMEN
TRIBOLOGY
TRIBUNATE
TRIBUTARY
TUBBINESS
TURBIDITY
TURBINATE
TURBULENT
UNABASHED
VERBALIZE
VERBASCUM
VERBERATE
VERBOSITY
VIABILITY
WAMBENGER
WIMBLEDON
WOBBEGONG
WOEBEGONE
ABSCONDER
AESCHYLUS
AIRCOOLED
AITCHBONE
ANECDOTAL
ANECDOTES
ANSCHLUSS
APOCRYPHA
ARACHNOID
AVOCATION
BARCELONA
BEACHHEAD
BEACHWEAR
BENCHMARK
BLACKBALL
BLACKBIRD
BLACKFACE
BLACKFOOT
BLACKHEAD
BLACKJACK
BLACKLEAD
BLACKLIST
BLACKMAIL
BLACKMORE
BLACKNESS
BLACKWOOD
BLOCKHEAD
BOCCACCIO
BRACTEOLE
BRICKWORK
BRICKYARD
BUCCANEER
CALCANEUM
CALCANEUS
CALCINATE
CALCULATE
CAMCORDER
CANCEROUS
CARCINOMA
CATCHCROP
CATCHMENT
CATCHPOLE
CATCHPOLL
CATCHWORD
CAUCASIAN
CHECKBOOK
CHECKLIST
CHECKMATE
CHECKROOM
CHICANERY
CHICKADEE
CHICKWEED
CHOCOLATE
CIRCADIAN
CIRCINATE
CIRCULATE
CLOCKWISE
CLOCKWORK
COACHLOAD
COLCHICUM
CONCAVITY
CONCEALED
CONCEITED
CONCERNED
CONCERTED
CONCIERGE
CONCISELY
CONCISION
CONCLUDED
CONCORDAT
CONCOURSE
CONCUBINE
CONCUSSED
COUCHETTE
CRACKDOWN
CRACKLING
CRACKSMAN
CRACOVIAN
CRICKETER
CROCKFORD
CROCODILE
CRUCIALLY
CUNCTATOR
DEACONESS
DESCARTES
DEUCALION
DIACRITIC
DIOCLETES
DISCARDED
DISCHARGE
DISCLOSED
DISCOLOUR
DISCOMFIT
DISCOURSE
DISCOVERT
DISCOVERY
DISCREDIT
DONCASTER
DRACONIAN
DULCINIST
EDUCATION
EDUCATIVE
EJACULATE
ELECTORAL
ELECTRESS
ELECTRIFY
ELECTRODE
ELECTUARY
ELOCUTION
ELUCIDATE
EMACIATED
ENACTMENT
ENSCONCED
ENUCLEATE
EPICEDIUM
EPICENTRE
EPICLESIS
EPICUREAN
EPICYCLIC
ERUCIFORM
EVOCATION
EVOCATIVE
EVOCATORY
EXACTMENT
EXACTNESS
EXECRABLE
EXECRABLY
EXECUTANT
EXECUTION
EXECUTIVE
EXECUTRIX
FASCINATE
FENCIBLES
FLECHETTE
FLUCTUATE
FORCEMEAT
FRACTIOUS
FRICASSEE
FRUCTIDOR
GASCONADE
GLUCINIUM
GLUCOSIDE
GLYCERIDE
GLYCERINE
GRACELESS
GROCERIES
GUACAMOLE
GUNCOTTON
HAECCEITY
HATCHBACK
HATCHMENT
HAWCUBITE
HERCULEAN
HITCHCOCK
HITCHHIKE
HOCCAMORE
HUNCHBACK
INOCULATE

INSCRIBED
ISOCRATES
JOBCENTRE
JUICINESS
KITCHENER
KNACKERED
KNOCKDOWN
LACCOLITE
LANCASTER
LANCEWOOD
LANCINATE
LEICESTER
LEUCOCYTE
LEUCOTOME
LUNCHTIME
MARCASITE
MARCHPANE
MASCULINE
MATCHLESS
MATCHLOCK
MATCHWOOD
MERCAPTAN
MERCENARY
MERCERIZE
MERCILESS
MERCURIAL
MINCEMEAT
MISCHANCE
MISCREANT
MOCCASINS
MOSCHATEL
MUMCHANCE
MUSCADINE
MUSCARINE
MUSCOVADO
MUSCOVITE
NARCISSUS
NESCIENCE
NEUCHATEL
NEWCASTLE
NICCOLITE
NIPCHEESE
NOTCHBACK
NUNCUPATE
OBSCENELY
OBSCENITY
OBSCURELY
OBSCURITY
OFFCHANCE
OFFCOLOUR
OLECRANON
ORICALCHE
OZOCERITE
PANCHAYAT
PARCHEESI
PARCHMENT
PATCHOULI
PATCHOULY
PATCHWORK
PAYCHEQUE
PEACEABLE
PEACEABLY
PEACETIME
PERCALINE
PERCHANCE
PERCHERON
PERCOLATE
PHACOLITE
PIACEVOLE
PIECEMEAL
PIECEWORK
PINCHBECK
PINCHCOCK
PITCHFORK
PITCHPINE
PITCHPOLE
PITCHPOLL
PLACATORY
PLACEMENT
PLACIDITY
PORCELAIN
PORCUPINE
PRACTICAL
PRACTISED
PRACTOLOL
PRECATORY
PRECEDENT
PRECEDING
PRECENTOR
PRECEPTOR
PRECIEUSE
PRECINCTS
PRECIPICE
PRECISELY
PRECISIAN
PRECISION
PRECISIVE
PRECOCITY
PRECONISE
PRECURSOR
PRICELESS
PROCACITY
PROCEDURE
PROCERITY
PROCESSOR
PROCLITIC
PROCOELUS
PROCONSUL
PROCREATE
PSYCHICAL
PSYCHOSIS
PSYCHOTIC
PUNCHLINE
PUNCTILIO
PUNCTUATE
PURCHASER
QUICKLIME
QUICKNESS
QUICKSAND
QUICKSTEP
RACCABOUT
RACCAHOUT
RADCLIFFE
RANCIDITY
RANCOROUS
RAUCOUSLY
REACHABLE
REICHSRAT
REICHSTAG
RENCONTRE
ROSCOMMON
RUNCINATE
SACCHARIN
SANCTUARY
SARCASTIC
SAUCEBOAT
SAUCINESS
SAUCISSON
SHECHINAH
SHECHITAH
SICCATIVE
SINCERELY
SINCERITY
SLACKNESS
SORCERESS
SPACELESS
SPACESHIP
SPACESUIT
SPECIALLY
SPECIALTY
SPECIFICS
SPECIFIED
SPECIMENS
SPECTACLE
SPECTATOR
SPECULATE
SPICILEGE
SPICINESS
STOCKFISH
STOCKHOLM
STOCKINET
STOCKINGS
STOCKPILE
STOCKROOM
STOCKWORK
STOCKYARD
SUBCELLAR
SUBCORTEX
SUCCEEDED
SUCCENTOR
SUCCESSOR
SUCCINATE
SUCCOTASH
SUCCUBINE
SUCCULENT
SUCCURSAL
SURCHARGE
SURCINGLE
SUSCITATE
SYNCHYSIS
SYNCOMIUM
SYNCOPATE
TAUCHNITZ
TEACHABLE
THACKERAY
THECODONT
THICKHEAD
THICKNESS
TOCCATINA
TOSCANINI
TOUCHDOWN
TOUCHLINE
TOUCHWOOD
TOWCESTER
TRACEABLE
TRACHINUS
TRACKLESS
TRACKSUIT
TRACTABLE
TRICERION
TRICKLESS
TRICKSTER
TRICLINIC
TRICOLOUR
TROCHILIC
TROCHILUS
TRUCKLOAD
TRUCULENT
TURCOPOLE
UNSCATHED
URICONIAN
UTICENSIS
VACCINATE
VANCOUVER
VISCOSITY
VOICELESS
VOUCHSAFE
VULCANIST
VULCANITE
VULCANIZE
WANCHANCY
WATCHWORD
WELCOMING
WENCESLAS
WHICHEVER
WINCANTON
WINCOPIPE
WISCONSIN
WITCHETTY
WORCESTER
WRECKFISH
ZIRCONIUM
ZUCCHETTO
ACADEMIST
ACIDULATE
ACIDULOUS
AMIDSHIPS
BALDAQUIN
BANDALORE
BANDICOOT
BANDOLEER
BANDOLERO
BANDOLIER
BANDOLINE
BANDSTAND
BANDWAGON
BIRDBRAIN
BIRDTABLE
BORDEREAU
BORDERING
BRADLAUGH
BRIDEWELL
BRIDLEWAY
BUNDESTAG
CALDARIUM
CANDIDACY
CANDIDATE
CANDLELIT
CANDLEMAS
CANDYTUFT
CARDBOARD
COADJUTOR
CONDEMNED
CONDENSER
CONDIMENT
CONDITION
CONDUCIVE
CONDUCTOR
CONDUCTUS
CONDYLOMA
CORDIALLY
CORDUROYS
CORDYLINE
CREDULITY
CREDULOUS
CRUDENESS
DAEDALIAN
DANDELION
DANDIFIED
DANDYPRAT
DEADLIGHT
DEODORANT
DEODORIZE
DODDIPOLL
DOODLEBUG
DUNDREARY
DUODECIMO
EALDORMAN
EPEDAPHIC
EPIDERMIS
ERADICATE
ERUDITION
EVIDENTLY
EXODERMIS
EXUDATION
FALDSTOOL
FANDANGLE
FEEDSTUFF
FERDINAND
FEUDALISM
FEUDATORY
FLEDGLING
FOODSTORE
FOODSTUFF
FREDERICK
FUNDAMENT
GALDRAGON
GARDENING
GARDEROBE
GAUDEAMUS
GAUDINESS
GEODESIST
GIDDINESS
GLADIATOR
GLADIOLUS
GLADSTONE
GODDESSES
GOLDCREST
GOLDFIELD
GOLDFINCH
GOLDSINNY
GOLDSMITH
GONDOLIER
GOODNIGHT
GRADATION
GRADGRIND
GRADUALLY
GRADUATED
GUIDEBOOK
GUIDELINE
HANDBRAKE
HANDCUFFS
HANDINESS
HANDIWORK
HANDPIECE
HANDSHAKE
HANDSPIKE
HANDSTAND
HARDANGER
HARDBOARD
HARDCOVER
HARDIHOOD

HARDINESS
HARDLINER
HARDSHELL
HEADBOARD
HEADCLOTH
HEADDRESS
HEADFIRST
HEADINESS
HEADLIGHT
HEADLINED
HEADSCARF
HEADSTALL
HEADSTONE
HENDIADYS
HINDEMITH
HINDRANCE
HINDSIGHT
HOLDERBAT
HORDEOLUM
HOYDENISH
HUMDINGER
HUNDREDTH
ISODORIAN
JORDANIAN
KILDERKIN
LANDAULET
LANDDROST
LANDGRAVE
LANDLOPER
LANDOWNER
LANDSCAPE
LANDSLIDE
LANDSMAAL
LANDSTURM
LANDWARDS
LAODICEAN
LAUDATION
LAUDATORY
LINDBERGH
LOADSTONE
LONDONESE
LOUDMOUTH
MACDONALD
MADDENING
MAGDALENE
MAGDEBURG
MANDATORY
MANDICATE
MANDOLINE
MANDUCATE
MENDACITY
MENDELISM
MENDICANT
MIDDLEMAN
MIDDLESEX
MIDDLETON
MIDDLINGS
MISDIRECT
MOODINESS
MRIDAMGAM
MRIDANGAM
MUDDINESS
MUNDUNGUS
MURDERESS
MURDEROUS
NIDDERING
OBEDIENCE
OPODELDOC
OXIDATION
PANDATION
PANDEMIAN
PANDURATE
PARDALOTE
PENDENNIS
PENDLETON
PENDRAGON
PENDULATE
PENDULOUS
PERDITION
PONDEROSA
PONDEROUS
PREDATORY
PREDICANT
PREDICATE
PREDICTOR
PREDIKANT
PREDILECT
PRODROMAL
PRODROMUS
PRUDENTLY
PURDONIUM
QUADRATIC
QUADRATUS
QUADRILLE
QUADRUPED
QUADRUPLE
QUODLIBET
RADDLEMAN
RANDINESS
READDRESS
READINESS
READYEARN
READYMADE
REDDENDUM
REEDINESS
RENDERING
RENDITION
RHODESIAN
RHODOLITE
RHODOPSIN
ROADBLOCK
ROADHOUSE
ROADSTEAD
ROADWORKS
ROWDINESS
RUDDIGORE
RUDDLEMAN
SADDENING
SADDLEBAG
SANDALLED
SANDARACH
SANDHURST
SANDPAPER
SANDPIPER
SANDSTONE
SANDSTORM
SCUDDALER
SHADINESS
SKEDADDLE
SOLDERING
SOLDIERLY
SPADASSIN
SPIDERWEB
SUBDIVIDE
SUBDOLOUS
SUNDOWNER
SWADDLING
SYNDICATE
TAPDANCER
TARDINESS
TENDERIZE
TOADSTONE
TOADSTOOL
TOPDRAWER
TRADEMARK
TRADESMAN
TRADEWIND
TRADITION
TREDRILLE
TRIDYMITE
UNADOPTED
UREDINIAL
VALDENSES
VANDALISM
VANDALIZE
VELDSKOEN
VERDIGRIS
VINDICATE
VOODOOISM
WALDENSES
WALDFLUTE
WALDGRAVE
WANDERING
WELDSTADT
WHODUNNIT
WILDGEESE
WINDBREAK
WINDCHILL
WINDFALLS
WINDHOVER
WINDSCALE
WINDSWEPT
WONDERFUL
WOODBORER
WOODCHUCK
WOODCRAFT
WOODENTOP
WOODHOUSE
WOODLANDS
WOODLOUSE
WOODSHOCK
WORDINESS
WORDSMITH
YARDSTICK
YGGDRASIL
ACCESSION
ACCESSORY
ADDERWORT
ADHERENCE
ADJECTIVE
ADRENALIN
ADVECTION
ADVENTIST
ADVENTURE
ADVERBIAL
ADVERSARY
ADVERSELY
ADVERSITY
ADVERTISE
AFFECTING
AFFECTION
AFTERCARE
AFTERDAMP
AFTERGLOW
AFTERMATH
AFTERMOST
AFTERNOON
AFTERWORD
AGREEABLE
AGREEABLY
AGREEMENT
AGUECHEEK
ALBERTINE
ALDEBARAN
ALGEBRAIC
ALLEGEDLY
ALLEGIANT
ALLEMANDE
ALLEVIATE
ALPENHORN
ALTERABLE
ALTERCATE
ALTERNATE
ALVEOLATE
AMBERGRIS
AMPERSAND
ANAEROBIC
ANCESTRAL
ANTENATAL
APPEALING
APPENDAGE
APPERTAIN
APPETIZER
ARGENTINA
ARGENTINE
ARRESTING
ARSENICAL
ARTEMISIA
ARTERIOLE
ASCENDANT
ASCENDING
ASCENSION
ASCERTAIN
ASPERSION
ASSERTING
ASSERTION
ASSERTIVE
ATHEISTIC
ATHELSTAN
ATHENAEUM
ATTEMPTED
ATTENDANT
ATTENTION
ATTENTIVE
ATTENUATE
AUBERGINE
AYLESBURY
BAKEHOUSE
BALEFULLY
BAREBONES
BAREFACED
BASEBOARD
BASECOURT
BELEAGUER
BEVERIDGE
BISECTION
BLUEBEARD
BLUEBERRY
BLUEPRINT
BLUESTONE
BREECHING
BRIEFCASE
BRIEFNESS
BUCENTAUR
CAFETERIA
CAFETIERE
CAKESTAND
CALEDONIA
CALEMBOUR
CALENDULA
CALENTURE
CAMEMBERT
CAMERAMAN
CAREERIST
CAREFULLY
CARETAKER
CATECHISM
CATECHIZE
CATERWAUL
CAVENDISH
CAVERNOUS
CELEBRANT
CELEBRATE
CELEBRITY
CELESTIAL
CEREBRATE
CHEEKBONE
CHEERLESS
CHIEFTAIN
CINEMATIC
CINERARIA
CINEREOUS
CLIENTELE
COHERENCE
COLERIDGE
COVELLITE
COVERDALE
CUNEIFORM
CURETTAGE
CYNEGETIC
DAREDEVIL
DAVENPORT
DEBENTURE
DECEITFUL
DECEMVIRI
DECEPTION
DECEPTIVE
DECESSION
DEFEATISM
DEFEATIST
DEFECTION
DEFECTIVE
DEFENDANT
DEFENDERS
DEFENSIVE
DEFERENCE
DEFERMENT
DEJECTION
DEMEANING
DEMEANOUR
DEMETRIUS
DEPENDANT
DEPENDENT
DEPENDING
DESECRATE
DESERTION
DESERVING
DETECTION
DETECTIVE
DETENTION
DETERGENT
DETERMINE

DETERRENT
DEVELOPED
DEVELOPER
DIAERESIS
DIGESTION
DIGESTIVE
DIMENSION
DIRECTION
DIRECTIVE
DIRECTORS
DIRECTORY
DISEMBARK
DISENGAGE
DISENTOMB
DIVERGENT
DIVERGING
DIVERSIFY
DIVERSION
DIVERSITY
DIVERTING
DOLEFULLY
DOWELLING
DYSENTERY
EAGERNESS
EAVESDROP
ECCENTRIC
ECHEVERIA
EDGEWORTH
EFFECTIVE
EFFECTUAL
EGREGIOUS
EGRESSION
EIDERDOWN
ELAEOLITE
ELLESMERE
ELSEWHERE
EMBELLISH
EMBEZZLER
EMMERDALE
EMPENNAGE
ENCELADUS
ENDEARING
ENDEAVOUR
ENDECAGON
ENDEICTIC
ENNERDALE
ENTELECHY
ENTERITIS
ENTERTAIN
ENVERMEIL
EPHEDRINE
EPHEMERAL
EPHEMERIS
EPHEMERON
EPHESIANS
ESMERALDA
ESPERANCE
ESPERANTO
ESSENTIAL
ETCETERAS
ETHELBERT
ETHEREOUS
EUHEMERUS
EUMENIDES
EXCELLENT
EXCELSIOR
EXCEPTION
EXCESSIVE
EXPECTANT
EXPECTING
EXPEDIENT
EXPENSIVE
EXPERTISE
EXTEMPORE
EXTENSILE
EXTENSION
EXTENSIVE
EXTENUATE
FACECLOTH
FACETIOUS
FALERNIAN
FIREBRAND
FIREBREAK
FIREDRAKE
FIREGUARD
FIRELIGHT
FIREPLACE
FIREPROOF
FIRESTONE
FIREWATER
FIREWORKS
FLEETWOOD
FOREANENT
FOREBEARS
FORECLOSE
FORECOURT
FOREFRONT
FOREGOING
FOREIGNER
FORESHORE
FORESIGHT
FORESPEAK
FORESPEND
FORESTAGE
FORESTALL
FORESTERS
FORETASTE
FREEBOARD
FREELANCE
FREEMASON
FREEPHONE
FREESTONE
FREESTYLE
FREEWHEEL
FRIESLAND
GABERDINE
GALENGALE
GATECRASH
GATESHEAD
GAVELKIND
GAZETTEER
GENEALOGY
GENERALLY
GENERATOR
GENETICAL
GENEVIEVE
GIBEONITE
GLEEFULLY
GOBETWEEN
GOVERNESS
GOVERNING
GREENAWAY
GREENBACK
GREENFEED
GREENGAGE
GREENHEAD
GREENHORN
GREENMAIL
GREENROOM
GREENSAND
GREENWEED
GREENWICH
GREENWOOD
GREENYARD
GREETINGS
GRIEVANCE
GRUELLING
GUTENBERG
HABERDINE
HABERGEON
HARESTANE
HAVERSACK
HAZELWORT
HEDERATED
HEREAFTER
HERETICAL
HETERODOX
HETEROSIS
HIBERNATE
HIBERNIAN
HIDEBOUND
HIDEOUSLY
HOMEGROWN
HOMEOPATH
HOMEOWNER
HOMESTEAD
HOMEWARDS
HONEYCOMB
HONEYMOON
HOPEFULLY
HOREHOUND
HYPERBOLA
HYPERBOLE
ICTERIDAE
IGNESCENT
ILLEGALLY
ILLEGIBLE
ILLEGIBLY
IMMEDIACY
IMMEDIATE
IMMELMANN
IMMENSELY
IMMENSITY
IMMERSION
IMPEACHER
IMPEDANCE
IMPELLING
IMPENDING
IMPERATOR
IMPERFECT
IMPERIOUS
IMPETUOUS
INCENTIVE
INCEPTION
INCESSANT
INDECENCY
INDECORUM
INDELIBLE
INDELIBLY
INDEMNIFY
INDEMNITY
INDENTURE
INFECTING
INFECTION
INFERENCE
INFERTILE
INGENIOUS
INGENUITY
INGENUOUS
INGESTION
INHERITED
INHERITOR
INJECTION
INNERMOST
INSELBERG
INSENSATE
INSERTION
INTEGRATE
INTEGRITY
INTELLECT
INTENDANT
INTENDING
INTENSELY
INTENSIFY
INTENSITY
INTENSIVE
INTENTION
INTERBRED
INTERCEDE
INTERCEPT
INTERCITY
INTERDICT
INTERFACE
INTERFERE
INTERJECT
INTERLACE
INTERLARD
INTERLOCK
INTERLOPE
INTERLUDE
INTERMENT
INTERNODE
INTERPLAY
INTERPOSE
INTERPRET
INTERRUPT
INTERSECT
INTERVENE
INTERVIEW
INTESTATE
INTESTINE
INVECTIVE
INVENTION
INVENTIVE
INVENTORY
INVERNESS
INVERSION
INVERTASE
IRREGULAR
JEWELLERY
JOBERNOWL
JOSEPHINE
JOSEPHSON
JUNEBERRY
JUVENILIA
KABELJOUW
KNEECORDS
LACERATED
LASERWORT
LATECOMER
LATENIGHT
LATERALLY
LATESCENT
LEGENDARY
LEVERAGED
LIBELLOUS
LIBERALLY
LIBERATED
LIBERATOR
LIBERTIES
LIBERTINE
LIFEGUARD
LIFESTYLE
LIMEHOUSE
LIMELIGHT
LIMESTONE
LINEAMENT
LINEOLATE
LITERALLY
LIVERPOOL
LIVERWORT
LIVERYMAN
LIVESTOCK
LOCELLATE
LODESTONE
LOHENGRIN
LUTESCENT
LUXEMBURG
LYMESWOLD
MACEDOINE
MACEDONIA
MADELEINE
MAKESHIFT
MALEBOLGE
MALENGINE
MASEFIELD
MATELASSE
MATERNITY
MERESWINE
MESENTERY
METEORITE
METEOROID
MILESTONE
MINEFIELD
MINELAYER
MISERABLE
MISERABLY
MODELLING
MODERATOR
MODERNISM
MODERNIST
MODERNITY
MODERNIZE
MODESTINE
MOLECULAR
MOLESKINS
MOMENTARY
MOMENTOUS
MONERGISM
MONEYWORT
MORECAMBE
NAKEDNESS
NAMEPLATE
NASEBERRY
NECESSARY
NECESSITY
NEFERTITI
NEVERMORE
NIDERLING
NINEPENCE
NINETIETH
NONENTITY

NOSEBLEED
NOTEPAPER
NOVELETTE
NUMERAIRE
NUMERATOR
NUMERICAL
NUREMBERG
OBJECTION
OBJECTIVE
OBREPTION
OBSECRATE
OBSEQUIES
OBSERVANT
OBSESSION
OBSESSIVE
OBVENTION
OFFENBACH
OFFENDING
OFFENSIVE
OFFERTORY
OPPENHEIM
ORIENTATE
OSTEODERM
OSTEOPATH
OTHERWISE
OTTERBURN
OUDENARDE
OUTERMOST
OWLEGLASS
OWNERSHIP
PACEMAKER
PADEMELON
PAGEANTRY
PALEMPORE
PALEOLITH
PALESTINE
PANEGOISM
PANEGYRIC
PANELLING
PANELLIST
PANETTONE
PAPERBACK
PAPERCLIP
PAPERWORK
PAREGORIC
PARENTAGE
PARENTING
PATERCOVE
PATERNITY
PEDERASTY
PENETRATE
PEREGRINE
PERENNIAL
PETERSHAM
PHLEBITIS
PHRENETIC
PHRENITIS
PIKESTAFF
PINEAPPLE
PIPEDREAM
PIPESTONE
POLEMARCH
POLEMICAL
POTENTATE
POTENTIAL
POWELLITE
POWERBOAT
POWERLESS
PRIESTESS
PRIESTLEY
PUCELLAGE
PYRETHRUM
QUEERNESS
QUIESCENT
QUIETNESS
RACEHORSE
RACETRACK
RATEPAYER
REBELLION
RECEIVING
RECEPTION
RECEPTIVE
RECESSION
RECESSIVE
REDEEMING
REFECTION
REFECTORY
REFERENCE
REFERRING
REHEARSAL
REJECTION
RELEVANCE
RENEWABLE
REPECHAGE
REPELLENT
REPELLING
REPENTANT
REPERCUSS
REPERTORY
REREMOUSE
RESENTFUL
RESERPINE
RESERVIST
RESERVOIR
RETENTION
RETENTIVE
REVEALING
REVELLING
REVERENCE
REVERSING
REVERSION
REVETMENT
RICERCARE
RIDERHOOD
RIDERLESS
RIVERSIDE
ROBERTSON
ROSEWATER
RUFESCENT
RUNESTAVE
SAFEGUARD
SALERATUS
SALESGIRL
SALESLADY
SATELLITE
SAVERNAKE
SCHEELITE
SCHEHITAH
SCHELLING
SCHEMATIC
SCIENTISM
SCIENTIST
SCLEROSIS
SCLEROTAL
SCREENING
SCREWBALL
SCREWEDUP
SCREWPINE
SCREWTAPE
SECESSION
SEDENTARY
SELECTING
SELECTION
SELECTIVE
SEMEIOTIC
SENESCENT
SENESCHAL
SERENADER
SERENGETI
SEVENTEEN
SEVERALLY
SEVERANCE
SHEEPFOLD
SHEEPMEAT
SHEEPSKIN
SHEERLEGS
SHEERNESS
SHIELDING
SHOEMAKER
SHOESHINE
SIDEBOARD
SIDEBURNS
SIDELIGHT
SIDEROSIS
SIDESWIPE
SIDETRACK
SIDEWARDS
SIMEONITE
SLEEKNESS
SLEEPLESS
SLEEPWALK
SNEERWELL
SOBERNESS
SOLEMNITY
SOLEMNIZE
SOMEPLACE
SOMETHING
SOMETIMES
SOMEWHERE
SOVENANCE
SOVEREIGN
SPEECHIFY
SPEEDBOAT
SPEEDWELL
SPHENDONE
SPHERICAL
SPLENDOUR
SPLENETIC
SPLENITIS
SPREADING
SPRECHERY
SQUEAMISH
STEELHEAD
STEELYARD
STEENBRAS
STEENKIRK
STEEPNESS
STEERSMAN
STREAMING
STREETAGE
STREETCAR
STRENUOUS
STRESSFUL
STRETCHED
STRETCHER
SUBEDITOR
SUBENTIRE
SUPERETTE
SUPERFINE
SUPERNOVA
SUPERSEDE
SUPERSTAR
SUPERVENE
SUPERVISE
SWEEPINGS
SWEETENER
SWEETMEAT
SWEETNESS
SWEETSHOP
SYNEDRION
SYNERGIST
TABELLION
TAMERLANE
TAVERNERS
TELEGRAPH
TELEOLOGY
TELEPATHY
TELEPHONE
TELEPHONY
TELEPHOTO
TELESALES
TELESCOPE
TELESTICH
TENEBROSE
TENEMENTS
TEREBINTH
THREADFIN
THREEFOLD
THREESOME
THRENETIC
THREONINE
THRESHOLD
THYESTEAN
TIMENOGUY
TIMEPIECE
TIMESHARE
TIMETABLE
TIREDNESS
TOBERMORY
TOLERABLE
TOLERABLY
TOLERANCE
TOLERATED
TOMENTOSE
TOWELLING
TREETRUNK
TRIENNIAL
TRIERARCH
TRIETERIC
TRUEPENNY
TUMESCENT
UNBEKNOWN
UNBENDING
UNCEASING
UNCERTAIN
UNDECIDED
UNDEFILED
UNDEFINED
UNDERBRED
UNDERCAST
UNDERCOAT
UNDERDONE
UNDERFELT
UNDERFOOT
UNDERHAND
UNDERLINE
UNDERLING
UNDERMINE
UNDERMOST
UNDERPAID
UNDERPASS
UNDERRATE
UNDERSEAL
UNDERSELL
UNDERSIDE
UNDERSIGN
UNDERSONG
UNDERTAKE
UNDERTONE
UNDERWALK
UNDERWEAR
UNDERWENT
UNDERWOOD
UNFEELING
UNHEALTHY
UNHEEDING
UNHELPFUL
UNLEARNED
UNNERVING
UNREFINED
UNRELATED
UNSECURED
UNSELFISH
UNSETTLED
UNTENABLE
UNWELCOME
UPPERMOST
UPSETTING
USHERETTE
UTTERANCE
UTTERLESS
UTTERMOST
VALENTINE
VASECTOMY
VEGETABLE
VEGETATOR
VEHEMENCE
VENERABLE
VENEREOUS
VENEZUELA
VICEREGAL
VICEREINE
VIDELICET
VIDEODISC
VIDEOTAPE
VIGESIMAL
VITELLIUS
WAFERTHIN
WAGENBOOM
WAPENTAKE
WAREHOUSE
WATERBABY
WATERBUTT
WATERFALL
WATERFORD
WATERFOWL
WATERGATE
WATERHOLE
WATERLESS
WATERLILY
WATERLINE
WATERMARK

WATERMILL
WATERSHED
WATERSIDE
WATERWEED
WAVELLITE
WHEELBASE
WINEBERRY
WINEGLASS
WISECRACK
WODEHOUSE
WOMENFOLK
YTTERBIUM
ZIBELLINE
BEDFELLOW
BEEFEATER
BEEFSTEAK
BLUFFNESS
BOYFRIEND
CHAFFINCH
COFFERDAM
COFFINITE
COMFORTER
CONFESSED
CONFESSOR
CONFIDANT
CONFIDENT
CONFIRMED
CONFITEOR
CONFLATED
CONFUCIUS
CONFUSING
CONFUSION
CRAFTSMAN
CUFFLINKS
CURFUFFLE
DEAFENING
DIFFERENT
DIFFICULT
DIFFIDENT
DIFFUSION
DISFAVOUR
DISFIGURE
DRAFTSMAN
DRIFTWOOD
FORFEITED
FORFICATE
GERFALCON
GODFATHER
GRUFFNESS
HALFBAKED
HALFDOZEN
HALFEMPTY
HALFPENNY
HALFSTAFF
HAMFATTER
HAMFISTED
INEFFABLE
KERFUFFLE
LEAFMOULD
MALFORMED
MAYFLOWER
MISFALLEN
MISFIRING
MUFFETTEE
ORIFLAMME
OUTFITTER
PARFLECHE
PENFRIEND
PERFECTLY
PERFERVID
PERFORANS
PERFORATE
PERFORMED
PERFORMER
PERFUMERY
PILFERAGE
PILFERING
PREFATORY
PREFERRED
PREFIGURE
PROFANELY
PROFANITY
PROFESSED
PROFESSOR
PROFITEER
PROFUSELY
PROFUSION
PUFFINESS
RAFFINOSE
RENFIERST
RUFFIANLY
SAFFLOWER
SEAFARING
SELFISHLY
SHEFFIELD
SHIFTLESS
SHIFTWORK
SHUFFLING
SOLFEGGIO
SOLFERINO
SOLFIDIAN
SOUFRIERE
SPOFFORTH
STIFFENER
STIFFNESS
SUFFERING
SUFFOCATE
SUFFRAGAN
SUFFUSION
SULFUROUS
SUNFLOWER
SURFBOARD
SURFEITED
SWIFTNESS
TRAFALGAR
TRIFORIUM
UNIFORMED
UNIFORMLY
WEBFOOTED
WOLFHOUND
WULFENITE
ZINFANDEL
ALIGNMENT
AMYGDALUS
ANAGLYPTA
ARAGONITE
BERGAMASK
BERGANDER
BERGOMASK
BIOGRAPHY
BRIGADIER
BRIGADOON
BUDGETARY
BULGARIAN
COAGULANT
COAGULATE
CONGENIAL
CONGERIES
CONGESTED
CONGOLESE
CONGRUENT
CONGRUOUS
DANGEROUS
DIAGNOSIS
DINGINESS
DISGRACED
DISGUISED
DISGUSTED
DRAGONFLY
DRUGSTORE
DUNGAREES
DUNGENESS
DUNGEONER
ELEGANTLY
ENIGMATIC
EPIGAEOUS
EROGENOUS
EVAGATION
FINGERING
FINGERTIP
FLAGELLIN
FLAGELLUM
FLAGEOLET
FLAGITATE
FLAGRANCE
FLAGSTAFF
FLAGSTONE
FOGGINESS
FORGATHER
FORGETFUL
FORGETIVE
FORGIVING
FORGOTTEN
FRAGILITY
FRAGMENTS
FRAGONARD
FRAGRANCE
FRAGRANCY
FRIGATOON
FRIGHTFUL
FRIGIDITY
FROGMARCH
FROGMOUTH
FROGSPAWN
FRUGALITY
FUGGINESS
FUNGIBLES
FUNGICIDE
GANGPLANK
GARGANTUA
GARGARISM
GEOGRAPHY
GILGAMESH
GINGERADE
GINGLYMUS
GONGORISM
GREGARINE
GREGORIAN
HAUGHTILY
HINGELESS
HOBGOBLIN
HUNGARIAN
ILLGOTTEN
IMAGELESS
IMAGINARY
JAGGANATH
JIGGUMBOB
JUDGEMENT
KINGMAKER
KINGSIZED
LANGOUSTE
LANGRIDGE
LANGSPIEL
LANGUAGES
LANGUEDOC
LANGUETTE
LANGUIDLY
LARGENESS
LARGHETTO
LARGITION
LAUGHABLE
LENGTHILY
LINGERING
LINGFIELD
LODGEMENT
LONGCHAMP
LONGEDFOR
LONGEVITY
LONGICORN
LONGINGLY
LONGITUDE
LONGLIVED
LONGRANGE
LONGSHORE
LORGNETTE
MANGANATE
MANGANESE
MANGETOUT
MANGOUSTE
MARGARINE
MERGANSER
MISGIVING
MISGUIDED
MONGOLIAN
MONGOLISM
MORGANITE
MOYGASHEL
MUGGLETON
NARGHILLY
NAUGHTILY
NEIGHBOUR
NIGGARDLY
OLIGARCHY
OLIGOCENE
ORIGENIST
ORIGINATE
OROGRAPHY
OUTGOINGS
OUTGROWTH
PERGAMENE
PERGUNNAH
PHAGOCYTE
PHIGALIAN
PIGGYBACK
PIGGYBANK
POIGNANCY
PRAGMATIC
PREGNANCY
PROGNOSIS
PROGRAMME
PUNGENTLY
PURGATIVE
PURGATORY
RIDGEBACK
RINGFENCE
RINGSIDER
ROUGHCAST
ROUGHNECK
ROUGHNESS
ROUGHSHOD
RUGGELACH
SANGFROID
SCAGLIOLA
SEDGEMOOR
SIEGFRIED
SINGALESE
SINGAPORE
SINGLESEX
SINGLETON
SINGSPIEL
SINGULTUS
SLIGHTEST
SLUGHORNE
SMUGGLING
SOGGINESS
SONGSMITH
SPAGHETTI
STAGEHAND
STAGGERED
STAGIRITE
STAGYRITE
STEGNOSIS
STEGNOTIC
STEGOSAUR
SWAGGERER
TANGERINE
TARGETEER
THIGHBONE
TINGUAITE
TOUGHNESS
TRAGEDIAN
TRAGELAPH
TREGEAGLE
TREGETOUR
TUNGSTATE
ULIGINOUS
URUGUAYAN
VENGEANCE
VIRGINALS
VIRGINIAN
VIRGINITY
VIRGINIUM
VIRGULATE
VOLGOGRAD
VULGARIAN
VULGARISM
VULGARITY
WEDGEWOOD
WEIGHTING
ALCHEMIST
AMPHIBIAN
ANCHORAGE
ANCHORITE
ANCHORMAN
ANTHOLOGY
ARCHANGEL
ARCHETYPE
ARCHIBALD
ARCHITECT
ARCHIVIST
ARCHIVOLT
ARTHRITIC

ARTHRITIS
ARTHROPOD
ARTHROSIS
ARTHURIAN
ASTHMATIC
ATAHUALPA
AUTHENTIC
AUTHORESS
AUTHORITY
AUTHORIZE
BACHARACH
BASHFULLY
BATHTOWEL
BECHSTEIN
BETHLEHEM
BIGHEADED
BISHOPRIC
BUCHAREST
CACHAEMIA
CACHECTIC
CASHPOINT
CATHARSIS
CATHARTIC
CATHEDRAL
CATHEPSIN
CATHERINE
CHIHUAHUA
COCHINEAL
COTHURNUS
CUCHULAIN
DACHSHUND
DASHBOARD
DASHWHEEL
DICHOTOMY
DIPHTHONG
DISHCLOTH
DISHONEST
DISHONOUR
DISHWATER
DITHERING
DITHYRAMB
DOTHEBOYS
EIGHTIETH
EIGHTSOME
EMPHASIZE
EMPHLYSIS
EMPHYSEMA
ENCHANTED
ENCHANTER
ENCHEASON
ENCHILADA
ENCHORIAL
ENSHEATHE
ENTHYMEME
ESTHETICS
EUCHARIST
EUCHLORIC
EUPHEMISM
EUPHONIUM
EUPHORBIA
EUPHRATES
EURHYTHMY
EXCHEQUER
FASHIONED
FISHERMAN
FISHGUARD
FISHPLATE
GASHOLDER
GATHERING
GOTHAMITE
HAPHAZARD
HASHEMITE
HIGHCLASS
HIGHFLYER
HIGHLANDS
HIGHLIGHT
HIGHSPEED
HOTHEADED
HYPHENATE
ILCHESTER
INSHALLAH
ISCHAEMIC
JEPHTHAHS
KEYHOLDER
LACHRYMAL
LATHYRISM
LECHEROUS
LETHARGIC
LIGHTFOOT
LIGHTLESS
LIGHTNESS
LIGHTNING
LIGHTSHIP
LIGHTSOME
LITHOCYST
LITHOPONE
LITHUANIA
LOCHINVAR
MACHINATE
MACHINERY
MACHINING
MACHINIST
MANHANDLE
MANHATTAN
MATHURINE
MECHANICS
MECHANISM
MECHANIZE
METHADONE
METHEGLIN
METHODISM
METHODIST
MISHANDLE
MITHRAISM
MOTHBALLS
MOTHEATEN
MOTHERING
MUCHLOVED
MUSHINESS
MUSHROOMS
MYTHOLOGY
NASHVILLE
NATHANIEL
NATHELESS
NATHEMORE
NEPHALISM
NEPHALIST
NEPHELINE
NEPHRITIC
NEPHRITIS
NIGHTCLUB
NIGHTFALL
NIGHTFIRE
NIGHTGOWN
NIGHTMARE
NIGHTTIME
NIGHTWORK
NITHSDALE
OCKHAMIST
ONTHESPOT
ORCHESTRA
ORPHANAGE
ORPHARION
ORTHODOXY
ORTHOLOGY
ORTHOPTER
ORTHOTONE
OUGHTNESS
PACHYDERM
PANHANDLE
PARHELION
PARHYPATE
PATHOGENY
PATHOLOGY
PATHTRAIN
PETHIDINE
PHTHALATE
PIGHEADED
PINHOOKER
POTHOLING
POTHUNTER
PREHALLUX
PUSHCHAIR
PYTHONESS
RATHERIPE
RATHERISH
REDHANDED
REDHEADED
RESHUFFLE
RICHELIEU
RIGHTEOUS
RIGHTHAND
RIGHTNESS
RIGHTWING
RUSHLIGHT
RUTHENIAN
RUTHENIUM
SANHEDRIM
SANHEDRIN
SANHEDRON
SEPHARDIM
SIGHTLESS
SIGHTSEER
SIPHUNCLE
SOPHISTER
SOPHISTIC
SOPHISTRY
SOPHOCLES
SOPHOMORE
TACHILITE
TACHYLITE
TACHYLYTE
TECHNICAL
TECHNIQUE
TEPHILLIN
TICHBORNE
TIGHTENER
TIGHTHEAD
TIGHTNESS
TIGHTROPE
TITHEBARN
TRIHEDRON
UNCHANGED
UNCHARGED
UNCHECKED
UNCHRISOM
UNSHACKLE
UNSHEATHE
WAGHALTER
WASHBASIN
WASHBOARD
WASHCLOTH
WASHERMAN
WASHSTAND
WITHDRAWN
WITHERING
WITHERITE
WITHSTAND
WITHYWIND
WUTHERING
YACHTSMAN
YACHTSMEN
ACCIDENTS
ADDICTION
ADDICTIVE
ADMIRABLE
ADMIRABLY
ADMIRALTY
ADMISSION
ADMITTING
ADMIXTURE
ADVISABLE
ADVISEDLY
AFFIDAVIT
AFFILIATE
AFRIKAANS
AFRIKANER
ALLIGATOR
ALTIMETER
ALTIPLANO
ALTISSIMO
AMBIGUITY
AMBIGUOUS
AMBITIOUS
ANCILLARY
ANCIPITAL
ANGIOGRAM
ANOINTING
ANTICLINE
ANTIGONUS
ANTIHELIX
ANTIPASTO
ANTIPATHY
ANTIPHONY
ANTIPODES
ANTIQUARY
ANTIQUITY
ANTITOXIC
ANTITOXIN
ANTIVENIN
ANXIOUSLY
AQUILEGIA
ARBITRAGE
ARBITRARY
ARBITRATE
ARLINGTON
ARMISTICE
ARRIVISTE
ARTICHOKE
ARTICULAR
ARTIFICER
ARTILLERY
ASPIRATOR
ASSIDUITY
ASSIDUOUS
ASSISTANT
ATTITUDES
AURICULAR
AUXILIARY
AVAILABLE
AVOIDABLE
AVOIDANCE
AXMINSTER
BANISTERS
BASICALLY
BASILICAL
BASILICON
BEGINNING
BELIEVING
BENIGHTED
BILINGUAL
BILIRUBIN
BOLIVIANO
BRAINCASE
BRAINLESS
BRAINWASH
BRAINWAVE
CALIBRATE
CAPILLARY
CAPITULAR
CAPITULUM
CARIBBEAN
CHAIRLIFT
CHRISTIAN
CHRISTMAS
CILIOLATE
CIVILISED
CIVILIZED
CLOISONNÉ
COMICALLY
COMINFORM
COMINTERN
COPIOUSLY
CORIANDER
CROISSANT
CURIOSITY
CURIOUSLY
CYNICALLY
DECIDEDLY
DECIDUOUS
DECILLION
DEDICATED
DEFICIENT
DEFINABLE
DELICIOUS
DELIGHTED
DELINEATE
DELIRIOUS
DELIVERER
DEMITASSE
DENIGRATE
DEPICTION
DESICCATE
DESIGNATE
DESIGNING
DESIPIENT
DESIRABLE
DEVIATION
DEVILMENT
DEVIOUSLY
DIGITALIN
DIGITALIS

DILIGENCE
DIRIGIBLE
DISINFECT
DIVIDENDS
DIVISIBLE
DIXIELAND
DOMICILED
DOMINANCE
DOMINICAL
DOMINICAN
DONIZETTI
DRAINPIPE
DUBIOUSLY
DUTIFULLY
EBRILLADE
ECHIDNINE
EDDINGTON
EFFICIENT
EFFINGHAM
ELLINGTON
EMPIRICAL
ENCIRCLED
ENGINEERS
ENLIGHTEN
ENLIVENED
EPHIALTES
EQUIPMENT
EQUIPOISE
EQUISETUM
EQUITABLE
EQUITABLY
EQUIVOCAL
EQUIVOQUE
ERPINGHAM
ESPIONAGE
ESTIMABLE
ETHIOPIAN
EURIPIDES
EXCIPIENT
EXCISEMAN
EXCITABLE
EXHIBITOR
EXPIATION
EXPIATORY
EXPISCATE
EXSICCATE
EXTIRPATE
FATIDICAL
FATISCENT
FERINGHEE
FEUILLANT
FILICALES
FILIGRAIN
FINICKING
FINICKITY
FINISHING
FOLIOLOSE
FREIGHTER
FROISSART
FRUITCAKE
FRUITERER
FRUITLESS
FUNICULAR
FURIOUSLY
FUSILLADE
GABIONADE
GALINGALE
GALIONGEE
GARIBALDI
GELIGNITE
GENIALITY
GENITALIA
GERIATRIC
GLAIREOUS
GONIATITE
HABITABLE
HABITUATE
HALITOSIS
HARIGALDS
HARIOLATE
HEMINGWAY
HEMIPTERA
HEMISTICH
HEMITROPE
HESITANCE
HESITANCY
HODIERNAL
HOLINSHED
HOMICIDAL
HUMILIATE
HYGIENIST
HYPINOSIS
ILLIBERAL
ILLICITLY
IMMIGRANT
IMMIGRATE
IMMINENCE
INCIDENCE
INCIPIENT
INCITATUS
INDICATES
INDICATOR
INDICTION
INDIGENCE
INDIGNANT
INDIGNITY
INFIELDER
INFIRMARY
INFIRMITY
INHIBITED
INNISFAIL
INNISFREE
INSIDIOUS
INSINCERE
INSINUATE
INSIPIENT
INSISTENT
INVIDIOUS
INVIOLATE
INVISIBLE
IPHIGENIA
IPRINDOLE
IRRITABLE
IRRITABLY
IRRITATED
IRVINGISM
JANISSARY
JOUISANCE
JOVIALITY
JUBILANCE
JUDICIARY
JUDICIOUS
JURIDICAL
KOMINFORM
KONIMETER
KONISCOPE
LACINIATE
LAMINATED
LATICLAVE
LEGIONARY
LEGISLATE
LENIENTLY
LENINGRAD
LEVIATHAN
LEVITICUS
LIMITLESS
LITIGIOUS
LOGICALLY
LOGISTICS
LOUISIANA
LUCIFERIN
LUDICROUS
LUMINAIRE
LUMINANCE
LURIDNESS
LYRICALLY
LYSIMETER
MAGICALLY
MALICIOUS
MALIGNANT
MALIGNITY
MANIFESTO
MARIJUANA
MAXILLARY
MEDIAEVAL
MEDIATION
MEDICALLY
MEDICATED
MEDICINAL
MEDITATOR
MEHITABEL
MELIORATE
MENIPPEAN
MIDIANITE
MIDINETTE
MILITANCY
MINIATURE
MINISCULE
MINISKIRT
MISINFORM
MODILLION
MUNICIPAL
MUNIMENTS
MUNITIONS
MUSICALLY
MUSICHALL
MUTILATED
NAPIERIAN
NAVIGABLE
NAVIGATOR
NERITIDAE
NIAISERIE
NOMINALLY
NOMINATOR
NONILLION
NOVICIATE
NOVITIATE
OBEISANCE
OBLIQUELY
OBLIVIOUS
OBVIOUSLY
OCCIPITAL
OCTILLION
OFFICIALS
OFFICIANT
OFFICIATE
OFFICIOUS
OPHIUCHUS
OPSIMATHY
OPTICALLY
ORBICULAR
ORDINAIRE
ORDINANCE
ORGIASTIC
ORGILLOUS
ORPINGTON
OSCILLATE
PAKISTANI
PALINURUS
PAPILLOTE
PATIENTLY
PEDICULAR
PEDIGREES
PEKINGESE
PENILLION
PENINSULA
PENISTONE
PENITENCE
PERIAKTOS
PERIANDER
PERIBOLOS
PERICLASE
PERICUTIN
PERIMETER
PERIMORPH
PERIODATE
PERIPATUS
PERIPHERY
PERISCIAN
PERISCOPE
PERISHING
PERISTOME
PERISTYLE
PETILLANT
PITIFULLY
PLAINNESS
PLAINSMAN
PLAINSONG
PLAINTIFF
PLAINTIVE
PLEIOCENE
POLIANITE
POLICEMAN
POLITBURO
POLITESSE
POLITICAL
POLITIQUE
PORIFERAN
PUNISHING
PUPILLAGE
PURIFYING
PURITANIC
QUAILPIPE
RACIALISM
RACIALIST
RADIANTLY
RADIATING
RADIATION
RADICALLY
RADICCHIO
RADIOGRAM
RADIOLOGY
RAMILLIES
RATIONALE
RATIONING
RAVISHING
RECIPIENT
REDINGOTE
REDIVIVUS
REFINANCE
REGISSEUR
REGISTRAR
RELIGEUSE
RELIGIOSO
RELIGIOUS
RELIQUARY
RELIQUIAE
REMINISCE
REMISSION
RESIDENCE
RESIDENCY
RESIDUARY
RESILIENT
RESISTANT
RETIARIUS
RETICENCE
RETICULUM
RETINITIS
REVICTUAL
RIPIENIST
ROSINANTE
ROZINANTE
RUBICELLE
RUDIMENTS
SAGITTARY
SALICETUM
SATIATION
SATINWOOD
SATIRICAL
SATISFIED
SAXIFRAGE
SAXITOXIN
SCHIAVONE
SCHILLING
SCRIMMAGE
SCRIMPING
SCRIMSHAW
SCRIPTURE
SCRIVENER
SDEIGNFUL
SEDITIOUS
SEMIBREVE
SEMICOLON
SEMIFINAL
SEMIOLOGY
SEMIRAMIS
SENIORITY
SEPIOLITE
SERIALIST
SERIALIZE
SERIATION
SERIOUSLY
SHEIKHDOM
SHRIMPING
SHRINKAGE
SHRINKING
SIBILANCE
SICILIANO
SILICOSIS
SIMILARLY
SOCIALISM
SOCIALIST

SOCIALITE
SOCIALIZE
SOCIOLECT
SOCIOLOGY
SOLICITOR
SOLILOQUY
SOLIPSISM
SOLITAIRE
SPHINCTER
SPLINTERS
SPLITTING
SPOILSMAN
SPRIGHTLY
SPRINGALD
SPRINGBOK
SPRINGLET
SPRINKLER
SPRITEFUL
SPRITSAIL
SQUINANCY
SQUINTING
SQUIREAGE
SQUIRMING
STAINLESS
STAIRCASE
STEINBECK
STEINBOCK
STOICALLY
STRIATION
STRICTURE
STRIDENCY
STRINGENT
STRINGOPS
STRIPLING
SUPINATOR
SYNIZESIS
SYRIACISM
TAOISEACH
TAVISTOCK
TAXIDERMY
TAXIMETER
TEDIOSITY
TEDIOUSLY
THRIFTILY
THRILLANT
THRILLING
TISIPHONE
TITILLATE
TOPIARIST
TOPICALLY
TRAINABLE
TREILLAGE
TUTIORISM
TYPICALLY
ULTIMATUM
UMBILICAL
UMBILICUS
UNBIASSED
UNDILUTED
UNDIVIDED
UNFITTING
UNLIMITED
UNMINDFUL
UNSIGHTLY
UNSINNING
UNTIMEOUS
UNWILLING
UNWITTING
UPAITHRIC
UPLIFTING
URTICARIA
VACILLATE
VALIANTLY
VANISHING
VARIATION
VARICELLA
VARIEGATE
VARIOLATE
VARIOUSLY
VARISCITE
VEHICULAR
VENIALITY
VERIDICAL
VERITABLE
VESICULAR
VEXILLARY
VICIOUSLY
VIGILANCE
VIGILANTE
VISIONARY
VITIATION
VIVIDNESS
WAPINSHAW
YOHIMBINE
BEDJACKET
CONJUGATE
CONJURING
FORJASKIT
FORJESKIT
NUTJOBBER
ODDJOBMAN
POUJADIST
PREJUDICE
PROJECTED
PROJECTOR
SELJUKIAN
SKYJACKER
SUBJACENT
SUBJUGATE
ASHKENAZI
AWAKENING
AYCKBOURN
BACKBENCH
BACKBITER
BACKCLOTH
BACKPEDAL
BACKSHISH
BACKSLIDE
BACKSPACE
BACKSTAGE
BACKSWORD
BACKTRACK
BACKWARDS
BACKWATER
BACKWOODS
BASKETFUL
BEEKEEPER
BERKELIUM
BOOKLOVER
BOOKMAKER
BOOKSHELF
BOOKSTALL
BOOKSTAND
BOOKSTORE
BROKERAGE
BUCKETFUL
BUCKTEETH
BUCKTHORN
BUCKWHEAT
BULKINESS
BURKINABE
COCKAIGNE
COCKATIEL
COCKFIGHT
COCKROACH
COCKSCOMB
COCKSFOOT
COCKSWAIN
COOKHOUSE
CORKSCREW
DECKCHAIR
DOUKHOBOR
DUCKBOARD
EUSKARIAN
FALKLANDS
FOLKETING
FOLKWEAVE
GAWKINESS
HACKAMORE
HACKNEYED
HANKERING
HAWKSBILL
HONKYTONK
HUCKABACK
HUNKYDORY
HUSKINESS
INNKEEPER
JACKKNIFE
JACKSNIPE
JACKSTRAW
JERKINESS
JERKWATER
JOCKSTRAP
JOCKTELEG
JUNKETING
KICKSHAWS
KINKCOUGH
LACKBEARD
LANKINESS
LEAKPROOF
LEUKAEMIA
LICKERISH
LINKLATER
LOCKSMITH
LOOKALIKE
MACKENZIE
MARKETEER
MARKETING
MICKLETON
MILKSHAKE
MINKSTONE
MOCKERNUT
MONKSHOOD
MOSKONFYT
MUCKENDER
MURKINESS
MUSKETEER
MUSKETOON
MUSKOGEAN
NECKVERSE
NICKNEVEN
OZOKERITE
PACKAGING
PAWKINESS
PECKSNIFF
PICKABACK
PICKETING
PICKTHANK
PINKERTON
POCKETFUL
POCKMANKY
PROKARYON
PROKOFIEV
RACKETEER
RACKSTRAW
RASKOLNIK
RECKONING
REYKJAVIK
RISKINESS
SACKCLOTH
SACKERSON
SASKATOON
SHAKEDOWN
SHAKINESS
SICKENING
SINKANSEN
SMOKEFREE
SMOKELESS
SNAKEWEED
SPIKENARD
SPOKESMAN
SULKINESS
TACKINESS
TALKATIVE
TEAKETTLE
UNSKILLED
UROKINASE
VERKAMPTE
VOLKSRAAD
WALKABOUT
WEAKENING
WORKFORCE
WORKHORSE
WORKHOUSE
WORKPLACE
WORKSPACE
YORKSHIRE
ZINKENITE
ABOLITION
ACCLIMATE
ACCLIVITY
ADULATION
ADULTERER
ADULTHOOD
AFFLICTED
AFFLUENCE
AGALACTIC
AIMLESSLY
AMBLYOPIA
AMELAKITE
AMPLIFIER
AMPLITUDE
ANALEPTIC
ANALGESIA
ANALGESIC
ANALOGOUS
ANGLICISM
APOLLONUS
APOLOGIST
APOLOGIZE
APPLEJACK
APPLIANCE
APPLICANT
ASCLEPIUS
ASPLENIUM
ATHLETICS
AVALANCHE
BALLADEER
BALLADIST
BALLERINA
BALLISTIC
BALLPOINT
BEELZEBUB
BELLICOSE
BELLYACHE
BELLYFLOP
BILLABONG
BILLBOARD
BILLIARDS
BILLOWING
BILLYCOCK
BIOLOGIST
BOULEVARD
BRILLIANT
BULLDOZER
BULLFIGHT
BULLFINCH
BURLESQUE
BURLINESS
CABLEGRAM
CALLIPERS
CALLOSITY
CALLOUSLY
CELLARIST
CELLULITE
CELLULOID
CELLULOSE
CEYLONESE
CHALAZION
CHALIAPIN
CHALLENGE
CHALUMEAU
CHILBLAIN
CHILDCARE
CHILDHOOD
CHILDLESS
CHILDLIKE
CHILOPODA
CHOLELITH
COALESCED
COALFIELD
COALITION
COALMINER
COELOSTAT
COLLAPSAR
COLLATION
COLLEAGUE
COLLECTED
COLLECTOR
COLLEGIAN
COLLIGATE
COLLIMATE
COLLISION
COLLOCATE
COLLODION
COLLOIDAL
COLLOTYPE
COLLUSION
COLLUSIVE
COLLYRIUM
CYCLAMATE
CYCLOLITH

CYCLORAMA
CYCLOTRON
DALLIANCE
DECLARING
DECLINING
DECLIVITY
DEFLATION
DEFLECTOR
DIALECTAL
DIALECTIC
DIALOGITE
DIPLOMACY
DISLOCATE
DJELLABAH
DUPLICAND
DUPLICATE
DUPLICITY
EAGLEWOOD
EBULLIENT
ECOLOGIST
EDELWEISS
EFFLUENCE
EFFLUVIUM
EMOLLIATE
EMOLLIENT
EMOLUMENT
EMPLECTON
EMPLOYEES
EMULATION
ENCLOSURE
ENDLESSLY
EPILEPTIC
EPULATION
ESPLANADE
EUCLIDEAN
EVOLUTION
EXCLAIMED
EXCLUDING
EXCLUSION
EXCLUSIVE
EXPLETIVE
EXPLICATE
EXPLOITER
EXPLOSION
EXPLOSIVE
EYELETEER
FALLOPIAN
FAULCHION
FAULTLESS
FIELDFARE
FIELDSMAN
FIELDWORK
FILLIPEEN
FILLISTER
FINLANDIA
FOLLOWING
FOOLHARDY
FOOLISHLY
FOOLPROOF
FORLORNLY
FULLBLOWN
FULLERENE
FULLGROWN
FULLSCALE
GAELTACHT
GALLABEAH
GALLANTLY
GALLANTRY
GALLICISM
GALLINULE
GALLIPOLI
GALLIVANT
GALLOPADE
GALLSTONE
GALLYCROW
GAULEITER
GEOLOGIST
GMELINITE
GOALMOUTH
GODLINESS
GOSLARITE
GUILDHALL
GUILELESS
GUILLEMOT
GUILLOCHE
GUILTLESS
HAILSTONE
HAILSTORM
HALLOWEEN
HALLOWMAS
HALLSTATT
HARLEQUIN
HARLESTON
HEALTHILY
HELLEBORE
HILLBILLY
HOLLERITH
HOLLYHOCK
HOLLYWOOD
HOOLACHAN
HOPLOLOGY
ICELANDER
ICELANDIC
IMPLEMENT
IMPLICATE
IMPLUVIUM
INCLEMENT
INCLUDING
INCLUSION
INCLUSIVE
INELEGANT
INFLATION
INFLEXION
INFLUENCE
INFLUENZA
INGLENOOK
ISALLOBAR
ISOLATION
ITALICIZE
JARLSBERG
JEALOUSLY
JELLYFISH
KEPLARIAN
KHALIFATE
KILLARNEY
LAPLANDER
LOBLOLLYS
LOWLANDER
LOWLINESS
MAELSTROM
MALLANDER
MALLEABLE
MALLEMUCK
MALLENDER
MALLEOLUS
MANLINESS
MAULSTICK
MILLAMANT
MILLENIAL
MILLENIUM
MILLEPEDE
MILLEPORE
MILLIGRAM
MILLINERY
MILLIONTH
MILLIPEDE
MILLSTONE
MISLOCATE
MOLLITIES
MOLLYMAWK
MUGLARITE
NEGLECTED
NEGLIGENT
NEOLITHIC
NEOLOGISM
NEWLYWEDS
NOBLENESS
NOLLEKENS
NUCLEOLUS
OBBLIGATO
OCCLUSION
OCHLOCRAT
OCULIFORM
ODALISQUE
ODELSTING
ONSLAUGHT
OPULENTLY
OUBLIETTE
OVULATION
PAGLIACCI
PAILLASSE
PAILLETTE
PALLADIAN
PALLADIUM
PALLIASSE
PAULOWNIA
PELLAGRIN
PELLITORY
PHALANGER
PHALAROPE
PHELLOGEN
PHILANDER
PHILATELY
PHILIPPIC
PHILISTER
PHILLABEG
PHILLIBEG
PHILOLOGY
PHYLLOPOD
PHYLOGENY
PILLICOCK
POLLINATE
POLLUTANT
POLLUTION
POPLITEAL
POULTERER
PRELECTOR
PRELUSORY
PROLACTIN
PROLAMINE
PROLEPSIS
PROLIXITY
PROLONGED
PROLUSION
PUBLICIST
PUBLICITY
PUBLICIZE
PUBLISHED
PUBLISHER
PULLULATE
QUALIFIED
QUALIFIER
QUILLWORT
REALISTIC
REALITIES
RECLAIMED
RECLAIMER
REDLETTER
REFLATION
REFLECTOR
REFLEXION
REFLEXIVE
REPLACING
REPLENISH
REPLETION
REPLETIVE
REPLICATE
RILLETTES
SAILCLOTH
SALLYPORT
SALLYPOST
SCALARIUM
SCALDFISH
SCALEABLE
SCALLAWAG
SCALLIONS
SCALLOPED
SCALLYWAG
SCELERATE
SCHLEMIEL
SCHLEMIHL
SCHLENTER
SCHLIEREN
SCOLECITE
SCOLIOSIS
SCOLIOTIC
SCULPTING
SCULPTURE
SECLUSION
SELLOTAPE
SHELDDUCK
SHELDRAKE
SHELLBACK
SHELLFISH
SHELLSUIT
SHELTERED
SHILLABER
SHOLOKHOV
SILLINESS
SKILFULLY
SMALLNESS
SMALLTIME
SOLLICKER
SOULFULLY
SPELDRING
SPELLBIND
SPELUNKER
SPILLICAN
SPILLIKIN
STALEMATE
STALENESS
STALWORTH
STILLBORN
STILLNESS
STILLROOM
STILTBIRD
STOLIDITY
STYLISHLY
STYLISTIC
STYLOBATE
SUBLIMATE
SUBLIMELY
SURLINESS
SYLLABARY
SYLLABLES
SYLLEPSIS
SYLLOGISM
TABLATURE
TABLELAND
TABLEWARE
TAILBOARD
TAILLEFER
TAILLIGHT
TAILPIECE
TAILPLANE
TELLINGLY
TELLURIAN
TELLURION
TELLURIUM
THALASSIC
THELEMITE
THELONIUS
THYLACINE
TOLLHOUSE
TRILITHON
TRILOBITE
TUILERIES
TUILLETTE
UNALLOYED
UNALTERED
UNCLAIMED
UNCLOTHED
UNCLOUDED
UNFLEDGED
VEILLEUSE
VELLENAGE
VELLICATE
VIOLATION
VIOLENTLY
VIOLINIST
WALLABIES
WALLOPING
WALLOWING
WALLPAPER
WALLYDRAG
WELLBEING
WELLBUILT
WELLKNOWN
WHALEBOAT
WHALEBONE
WHALEMEAT
WHOLEFOOD
WHOLEMEAL
WHOLENESS
WHOLESALE
WHOLESOME
WILLEMITE
WILLESDEN
WILLFULLY
WILLINGLY
WILLOWING
WILLPOWER

WOLLASTON
WOOLINESS
WORLDWIDE
WURLITZER
YELLOWISH
ZEALANDER
ZOOLOGIST
ABOMINATE
ACUMINATE
ADUMBRATE
AGAMEMNON
ALUMINIUM
ANIMATION
ANIMISTIC
ANIMOSITY
ANOMALOUS
ASHMOLEAN
ASYMMETRY
BADMINTON
BARMBRACK
BARMECIDE
BLAMELESS
BOOMERANG
BRAMBLING
BRIMSTONE
BRUMMAGEM
CARMELITE
CHAMELEON
CHAMFRAIN
CHAMINADE
CHAMOMILE
CHAMPAGNE
CHAMPAIGN
CHAMPERTY
CHAMPLAIN
CHAMPLEVÉ
CHEMISTRY
CIMMERIAN
CLAMOROUS
CLAMPDOWN
CLIMACTIC
COEMPTION
COMMANDER
COMMENSAL
COMMISSAR
COMMITTAL
COMMITTED
COMMITTEE
COMMODITY
COMMODORE
COMMOTION
COMMUNION
COMMUNISM
COMMUNIST
COMMUNITY
CORMORANT
COSMETICS
COSMOGONY
COSMOLOGY
COSMONAUT
CREMATION
CREMATORY
CRIMINATE
CRUMBLING
CULMINATE
DALMATIAN
DIAMETRIC
DISMANTLE
DISMEMBER
DISMISSAL
DOGMATISM
DOGMATIZE
DORMITION
DORMITORY
DRAMATICS
DRAMATIST
DRAMATIZE
DROMEDARY
DRUMSTICK
ELEMENTAL
ELIMINATE
ENAMELLED
ENAMOURED
ENUMERATE
ESEMPLASY
ETYMOLOGY
EXEMPLARY
EXEMPLIFY
EXEMPTION
FARMHOUSE
FARMSTEAD
FERMENTED
FILMMAKER
FILMSTRIP
FIRMAMENT
FLAMMABLE
FLAMSTEED
FORMALIST
FORMALITY
FORMALIZE
FORMATION
FORMATIVE
FORMULATE
FRAMBOISE
FRAMEWORK
FULMINANT
FULMINATE
GEOMETRIC
GEOMETRID
GERMANCER
GERMANDER
GERMANITE
GERMANIUM
GERMICIDE
GERMINATE
GLAMORIZE
GLAMOROUS
GLOMERATE
GLOMERULE
GODMOTHER
GRAMPIANS
GRIMALKIN
GRIMINESS
GRUMBLING
HAEMALOMA
HAEMATITE
HAMMERING
HAMMURABI
HARMALINE
HARMATTAN
HARMONICA
HARMONIST
HARMONIUM
HARMONIZE
HARMOTOME
HAYMAKING
HAYMARKET
HERMANDAD
HERMITAGE
HODMANDOD
INAMORATA
INAMORATO
INUMBRATE
ISOMERASE
ISOMETRIC
KERMESITE
KLEMPERER
KRUMMHORN
LAWMAKING
LAWMONGER
LOAMSHIRE
MAMMALIAN
MARMALADE
MARMOREAL
MEDMENHAM
MESMERISM
MESMERIZE
MISMANAGE
MNEMOSYNE
MORMONISM
MURMURING
MYRMECOID
NAUMACHIA
NEWMARKET
NORMALACY
NORMALITY
NORMALIZE
NORMATIVE
NUMMULITE
ONOMASTIC
PALMATION
PALMISTRY
PALMITATE
PAYMASTER
PEGMATITE
PELMANISM
PERMANENT
PERMEABLE
PERMITTED
PLIMSOLLS
PLUMBEOUS
PLUMBLINE
PLUMDAMAS
PLUMPNESS
PREMATURE
PREMONISH
PREMOTION
PRIMAEVAL
PRIMARILY
PRIMAVERA
PRIMITIAE
PRIMITIVE
PRIMULINE
PROMACHOS
PROMENADE
PROMINENT
PROMISING
PROMOTION
PROMPTING
PROMUSCIS
PULMONARY
PUMMELLED
PYGMALION
REIMBURSE
RHYMESTER
RIGMAROLE
ROSMARINE
ROSMINIAN
ROUMANIAN
ROUMANSCH
SARMENTUM
SCAMBLING
SCHMALTZY
SCHMIEDER
SCHMUTTER
SEEMINGLY
SEGMENTED
SERMONIZE
SHAMEFAST
SHAMELESS
SHAMIANAH
SHEMOZZLE
SLAMMAKIN
SLIMINESS
SLUMBERER
SOMMELIER
STAMMERER
STIMULANT
STIMULATE
STOMACHIC
STUMBLING
STUMPWORK
SUBMARINE
SUBMERGED
SUMMARILY
SUMMARIZE
SUMMATION
SURMULLET
SYMMETRIC
TALMUDIST
TARMACKED
TASMANIAN
TERMAGANT
TERMAGENT
TERMINATE
THUMBLING
THUMBNAIL
THUMBTACK
TORMENTER
TORMENTIL
TORMENTOR
TORMENTUM
TRAMLINES
TREMATODE
TREMBLING
TREMOLITE
TREMULATE
TREMULOUS
TRIMESTER
TRIMMINGS
TROMPETTE
TRUMPEDUP
TRUMPETER
TUMMYACHE
TURMAGENT
VERMIFORM
VERMIFUGE
VERMILION
VERMINOUS
WARMONGER
WHIMSICAL
WOOMERANG
WORMEATEN
ZOOMANTIC
ABANDONED
ABANDONEE
ABUNDANCE
ACONCAGUA
ADENOIDAL
AGINCOURT
AGONIZING
ALONGSIDE
AMENDMENT
AMENHOTEP
ANONYMITY
ANONYMOUS
APENNINES
ASYNERGIA
ATONEMENT
AVUNCULAR
BAINMARIE
BARNABITE
BARNACLES
BARNSTORM
BEANFEAST
BERNSTEIN
BLANDNESS
BLINDFOLD
BLINDNESS
BLINDSPOT
BLINDWORM
BLINKERED
BLUNDERER
BLUNTNESS
BOANERGES
BOONDOCKS
BORNAGAIN
BOUNDLESS
BOUNTEOUS
BOUNTIFUL
BRANCHING
BRANDIRON
BRONCHIAL
BRUNHILDE
CANNELURE
CANNONADE
CARNATION
CARNELIAN
CARNIVORE
CHANTEUSE
CHANTILLY
CHINATOWN
CHINOVNIK
CHINSTRAP
CHONDRITE
CHONDROID
CLINGFILM
CLINICIAN
COENOBITE
COENOBIUM
COGNITION
COGNITIVE
COGNIZANT
COINTREAU
CONNECTED
CONNECTOR
CONNEXION
CONNOTATE
CONNUBIAL
CORNBRASH
CORNCRAKE
CORNEILLE

CORNELIAN
CORNERMAN
CORNFIELD
CORNFLOUR
CORNSTALK
COUNSELOR
COUNTDOWN
COUNTLESS
COUNTRIES
CRANBERRY
CRANBORNE
CRINOLINE
DAMNATION
DAMNEDEST
DAUNTLESS
DIANDROUS
DIANETICS
DIANOETIC
DIGNIFIED
DIGNITARY
DINNERSET
DIONYSIAN
DIONYSIUS
DOWNGRADE
DOWNRIGHT
DOWNSTAGE
DOWNTREND
DOWNWARDS
DRINKABLE
DRUNKENLY
DWINDLING
EARNESTLY
ECONOMICS
ECONOMIST
ECONOMIZE
EDINBURGH
ELONGATED
EMANATION
EMINENTLY
ENUNCIATE
EPINASTIC
EPINICION
EPINIKION
EPONYMOUS
ETHNOLOGY
EVANGELIC
EVENTUATE
EXANIMATE
EXANTHEMA
EXONERATE
FAINTNESS
FLINTLOCK
FORNICATE
FOUNDLING
FRANCESCA
FRANCHISE
FRANCOLIN
FRANGLAIS
FRANKNESS
FRENCHMAN
FRENCHMEN
FURNIMENT
FURNITURE
GAINFULLY
GAINSAYER
GARNISHEE
GARNITURE
GAUNTNESS
GLANDULAR
GLENDOWER
GLENGARRY
GLENLIVET
GOONHILLY
GRANDIOSE
GRANDNESS
GRANDSIRE
GRANULATE
GRANULITE
GRANULOSE
GRENADIER
GRENADINE
GRENVILLE
GRINGOLET
GUINEVERE
GYMNASIUM
GYMNASTIC
HOBNAILED
HORNSTONE
HYPNOTISM
HYPNOTIST
HYPNOTIZE
ICHNEUMON
ICHNOLITE
IDENTICAL
IDENTIKIT
INANIMATE
INANITION
INUNCTION
IRONSIDES
IRONSTONE
IRONWORKS
ISINGLASS
ITINERANT
ITINERARY
ITINERATE
JAUNDICED
JENNETING
KHANSAMAH
KIDNAPPED
KIDNAPPER
KLENDUSIC
KLINOSTAT
LAGNIAPPE
LAUNCELOT
LAUNCHING
LAUNDRESS
LAWNMOWER
LIENTERIC
LIONHEART
LOINCLOTH
MAGNALIUM
MAGNESIUM
MAGNETISM
MAGNETIZE
MAGNETRON
MAGNIFIER
MAGNITUDE
MAINFRAME
MAINTENON
MANNEQUIN
MANNERING
MANNERISM
MEANDRIAN
MEANWHILE
MENNONITE
MINNESOTA
MOONLIGHT
MOONRAKER
MOONSHINE
MOONSTONE
OLENELLUS
OMINOUSLY
OPENENDED
OPENHEART
ORANGEADE
ORANGEMAN
OUTNUMBER
OVENPROOF
PAINFULLY
PAINTWORK
PANNIKELL
PARNASITE
PARNASSUS
PENNILESS
PHANARIOT
PHANSIGAR
PHANTASMA
PHENACITE
PHENAKISM
PHONECARD
PHONETICS
PHONOGRAM
PHONOLITE
PHONOLOGY
PICNICKER
PIGNERATE
PLANETARY
PLENITUDE
PLENTEOUS
PLENTIFUL
PLUNDERER
POINTEDLY
POINTLESS
POINTSMAN
PRANKSTER
PRINCETON
PRINCIPAL
PRINCIPLE
PRINTABLE
PRONGHORN
PRONOUNCE
PUGNACITY
PYONGYANG
QUANTICAL
QUANTOCKS
QUENNELLE
QUINQUINA
QUINTETTE
QUINTROON
QUINTUPLE
RAINCHECK
RAINGAUGE
RAINSTORM
RAINWATER
REANIMATE
REINFORCE
REINSTATE
RESNATRON
ROUNCEVAL
ROUNCIVAL
ROUNDBACK
ROUNDELAY
ROUNDFISH
ROUNDHAND
ROUNDHEAD
ROUNDSMAN
RUINATION
RUINOUSLY
RUNNYMEDE
SAINTFOIN
SAINTHOOD
SANNYASIN
SCANSORES
SCANTLING
SCENTLESS
SCHNAPPER
SCHNAUZER
SCHNECKEN
SCHNITTKE
SCHNITZEL
SCHNORKEL
SCHNORRER
SCHNOZZLE
SCINTILLA
SCONCHEON
SCUNCHEON
SEANNACHY
SHENSTONE
SHINTOISM
SIGNALLER
SIGNALMAN
SIGNATORY
SIGNATURE
SIGNBOARD
SKINDIVER
SKINFLINT
SKINTIGHT
SLANTWISE
SLINGBACK
SLINGSHOT
SOMNOLENT
SONNETEER
SOUNDBITE
SOUNDLESS
SOUNDNESS
SPINDRIER
SPINDRIFT
SPINELESS
SPINNAKER
SPINNERET
SPONGEBAG
SPONSORED
SPUNCULID
STANCHION
STANDARDS
STANDERBY
STANDGALE
STANDPIPE
STANNATOR
STENOPAIC
STINGAREE
STINKBIRD
STINKHORN
STINKWOOD
STONEBOAT
STONECHAT
STONECROP
STONEHAND
STONELESS
STONEWALL
STONEWARE
STONEWORK
STONEWORT
STONKERED
SUBNORMAL
SWANIMOTE
SWANSDOWN
SWINBURNE
SWINEHERD
SWINGEING
TARNATION
TEKNONYMY
TENNESSEE
THANATISM
THANKLESS
THINGUMMY
THINKABLE
THINNINGS
THUNDERER
TOWNSFOLK
TRANSCEND
TRANSFORM
TRANSFUSE
TRANSHUME
TRANSIENT
TRANSLATE
TRANSMUTE
TRANSPIRE
TRANSPORT
TRANSPOSE
TRANSSHIP
TRANSVAAL
TRENCHANT
TRINKETER
TRONDHEIM
TRUNCATED
TRUNCHEON
TURNABOUT
TURNBULLS
TURNROUND
TURNSTILE
TURNSTONE
TURNTABLE
TWENTIETH
TWINKLING
UNANIMITY
UNANIMOUS
UNINJURED
UNINVITED
UNKNOWING
UPANISHAD
URANISCUS
URINATION
VAINGLORY
VIENTIANE
WAGNERIAN
WAGNERITE
WEDNESDAY
WHINSTONE
WHUNSTANE
WINNEBAGO
WITNESSED
WRANGLERS
WRONGDOER
WRONGFOOT
WYANDOTTE
YOUNGSTER
ABDOMINAL
ABHORRENT
ABSORBENT
ABSORBING
ACCOMPANY

ACCORDANT
ACCORDING
ACCORDION
ACROBATIC
ACROPHONY
ACROPOLIS
ADJOINING
ADMONITOR
ADVOCATED
AERODROME
AEROPLANE
AEROSPACE
AEROTAXIS
ALCOHOLIC
ALGORITHM
ALLOCARPY
ALLOGRAPH
ALLOPATHY
ALLOTMENT
ALLOWABLE
ALLOWANCE
ALOOFNESS
ANGOSTURA
ANNOTATED
ANNOTATOR
ANNOUNCER
ANNOYANCE
ANTONINUS
APPOINTED
APPOINTEE
APPORTION
ARBORETUM
AREOPAGUS
ARROGANCE
ARROWHEAD
ARROWROOT
ASSOCIATE
ASSONANCE
ASTOUNDED
ATROCIOUS
AUTOCLAVE
AUTOCRACY
AUTOCROSS
AUTOGRAPH
AUTOLATRY
AUTOLYCUS
AUTOLYSIS
AUTOMAKER
AUTOMATED
AUTOMATIC
AUTOMATON
AUTONOMIC
AUTOPILOT
AUTOROUTE
AUTOSCOPY
AXIOMATIC
BAROMETER
BELONGING
BIMONTHLY
BINOCULAR
BLOODBATH
BLOODLESS
BLOODSHED
BLOODSHOT
BOLOGNESE
CACOPHONY
CAGOULARD
CALORIFIC
CANONICAL
CAPORETTO
CAVORTING
CEROMANCY
CHEONGSAM
CHROMATIC
CHRONICLE
CIPOLLINO
CLEOPATRA
COLOMBIAN
COLOMBIER
COLONNADE
COLOPHONY
COLORLESS
COLOSSEUM
COLOSTOMY
COLOSTRUM
COLOURFUL
COLOURING
COLOURIST
COROLLARY
CROOKBACK
CROOKEDLY
CRYOGENIC
CRYOMETER
DECOCTION
DECOLLATE
DECOMPOSE
DECONTROL
DECORATED
DECORATOR
DEFOLIANT
DEFOLIATE
DEFORMITY
DEMOCRACY
DEPOSITOR
DETONATOR
DEVONPORT
DISOBLIGE
DISORIENT
DOLOMITES
DOLOMITIC
ECTOMORPH
ECTOPLASM
EIDOGRAPH
ELBOWROOM
ELKOSHITE
ENCOLPION
ENCOLPIUM
ENCOMPASS
ENCOUNTER
ENCOURAGE
ENDOCRINE
ENDOMORPH
ENDOSPERM
ENDOWMENT
ENJOYABLE
ENJOYMENT
ENROLMENT
ENSORCELL
ENTOPHYTE
ENTOURAGE
EPEOLATRY
ERIOMETER
ERRONEOUS
ESCOPETTE
ETIOLATED
EXCORIATE
EXPORTING
EXPOSITOR
EXTORTION
EYEOPENER
FAVORABLE
FAVORABLY
FAVOURITE
FEROCIOUS
FILOPLUME
FILOSELLE
FLOODGATE
FLOORSHOW
GASOMETER
GINORMOUS
GIRONDIST
GODOLPHIN
GYNOECIUM
GYROMANCY
GYROSCOPE
HALOBIONT
HALOPHILE
HALOTHANE
HECOGENIN
HERODOTUS
HERONSHAW
HODOGRAPH
HODOMETER
HOLOCAUST
HOLOGRAPH
HOLOPHOTE
HOMOGRAPH
HOMOPHONE
HOMOPTERA
HONORABLE
HONORIFIC
HOROSCOPE
HUMONGOUS
HYLOBATES
HYPOCAUST
HYPOCRISY
HYPOCRITE
IDEOGRAPH
IDEOPATHY
IDIOBLAST
IDIOGRAPH
IDIOMATIC
IDIOPHONE
IDIOPLASM
IDIOTICON
IGNORAMUS
IGNORANCE
ILLOGICAL
IMMODESTY
IMMORALLY
IMMORTALS
IMMOVABLE
IMMOVABLY
IMPOLITIC
IMPORTANT
IMPORTUNE
IMPOSTURE
IMPOTENCE
IMPOUNDER
INCOGNITO
INCOMINGS
INCOMMODE
INCONDITE
INCORRECT
INDOLENCE
INDONESIA
INFORMANT
INNOCENCE
INNOCUOUS
INNOVATOR
INSOLENCE
INSOLUBLE
INSOLVENT
INSOMNIAC
INVOICING
INVOLUCRE
IODOPHILE
KILOCYCLE
KILOHERTZ
KILOMETER
KILOMETRE
LABORIOUS
LABOURITE
LACONICAL
LAGOMORPH
LAVOISIER
LIMOUSINE
LOGOGRIPH
LOGOTHETE
MAJORDOMO
MAJORETTE
MANOEUVRE
MANOMETER
MASOCHISM
MASOCHIST
MAVOURNIN
MAYORALTY
MEKOMETER
MELODIOUS
MELODRAMA
MELONLIKE
MEMORABLE
MEMORITER
MENOMINEE
MENOPAUSE
MESOBLAST
MESOMORPH
MILOMETER
MISOCLERE
MISONEIST
MONOCEROS
MONOCHORD
MONOCOQUE
MONOCULAR
MONODRAMA
MONOGRAPH
MONOLOGUE
MONOMACHY
MONOMANIA
MONOMETER
MONOPLANE
MONOSTICH
MONOTROCH
MONOXYLON
MOTOCROSS
MOTORBIKE
MOTORBOAT
MOTORCADE
MOTORISTS
MUCORALES
MUTOSCOPE
NEGOTIATE
NICODEMUS
NOMOCRACY
NOMOTHETE
NOTOCHORD
NOTONECTA
NOTORIETY
NOTORIOUS
NOVOCAINE
NOVODAMUS
OBCORDATE
OBNOXIOUS
OCTOBRIST
OLEOGRAPH
OLEORESIN
ONCOMETER
ONTOGENCY
OPPONENTS
OPPORTUNE
OPTOMETRY
OPTOPHONE
OUROBOROS
OUROBORUS
OUTOFTOWN
PALOVERDE
PANORAMIC
PAROCHIAL
PAROCHINE
PAROTITIS
PEDOMETER
PINOCCHIO
PIROUETTE
POLONAISE
POMOERIUM
PREOCCUPY
PREORDAIN
PROOFREAD
PYROMANCY
PYROMANIA
RACONTEUR
RAZORBILL
REBOATION
RECOGNIZE
RECOLLECT
RECOMMEND
RECONCILE
RECONDITE
RECONVENE
RECORDING
RECORDIST
RECOVERED
REDOLENCE
REFORMIST
REJOICING
REJOINDER
REMONTANT
REMOULADE
REMOVABLE
RENOVATOR
REPORTAGE
REPORTING
REPOSSESS
RESONANCE
RESONATOR
RESORTING
RESOURCES
RETORSION
RETORTION
REVOLTING
REVOLVING
REWORKING

RHEOTAXIS
RIGOLETTO
SALOPETTE
SAXOPHONE
SCHOLARCH
SCHOLARLY
SCHOLIAST
SCHOOLBOY
SCHOOLING
SCHOOLMAN
SCIOMANCY
SCRODDLED
SCROUNGER
SECONDARY
SONOMETER
SOPORIFIC
SPOONBILL
SPOONFEED
STOOLBALL
STROBILUS
STROLLING
STROMBOLI
STRONGARM
STRONGYLE
STRONTIUM
STROSSERS
SUDORIFIC
SYCOPHANT
SYNOECETE
SYNOVITIS
TAMOXIFEN
THEOBROMA
THEOCRACY
THEOSOPHY
THROATILY
THROBBING
THRONGING
THROWAWAY
THROWBACK
THROWDOWN
THROWSTER
TIMOCRACY
TONOMETER
TONOPLAST
TOXOPHILY
TROOPSHIP
TROOSTITE
UNBOUNDED
UNCONCERN
UNCONFINE
UNCORRECT
UNCOUPLED
UNCOURTLY
UNCOVERED
UNDOUBTED
UNFOUNDED
UNHOPEFUL
UNNOTICED
UNPOPULAR
UNTOUCHED
UNWORRIED
UPCOUNTRY
UPHOLSTER
VAPORETTO
VAPORIZER
VELODROME
WAGONETTE
WAGONLOAD
WIDOWHOOD
XENOMANIA
XENOPHOBE
XEROPHYTE
XEROSTOMA
XYLOPHONE
ZENOCRATE
ZOROASTER
ZYGOMATIC
ZYGOSPORE
ADAPTABLE
ADEPTNESS
ANAPLASTY
ANOPHELES
APOPHATIC
APOPHYSIS
BESPANGLE
BOSPHORUS
BUMPTIOUS
CALPURNIA
CAMPANILE
CAMPANULA
CARPACCIO
CARPENTER
CARPENTRY
CARPETING
CHAPARRAL
CHAPERONE
CHIPBOARD
CHIPOLATA
CHIPPINGS
CLAPBOARD
CLEPSYDRA
CLIPBOARD
COMPACTLY
COMPANIES
COMPANION
COMPELLED
COMPETENT
COMPETING
COMPLAINT
COMPLIANT
COMPONENT
COMPOSING
COMPOSITE
COMPOSURE
COMPOTIER
COMPUTING
COOPERATE
CORPORATE
CORPOREAL
CORPOSANT
CORPULENT
CORPUSCLE
CRAPULENT
CRAPULOUS
CREPITATE
CREPOLINE
CRIPPLING
CRYPTOGAM
CUSPIDORE
DESPERADO
DESPERATE
DESPOTISM
DIAPHRAGM
DISPARAGE
DISPARATE
DISPARITY
DISPENSER
DISPERSAL
DISPERSED
DISPLACED
DISPLAYED
DISPLEASE
DISPUTANT
DRIPSTONE
DROPPINGS
DROPSICAL
DYSPEPSIA
DYSPEPTIC
DYSPHAGIA
ELOPEMENT
ENDPAPERS
EPIPHRAGM
EPIPHYSIS
EPIPHYTIC
EPIPOLISM
ESOPHAGUS
EVAPORATE
FLIPPANCY
FLOPHOUSE
GASPEREAU
GODPARENT
GOMPHOSIS
GOSPELLER
GRAPESHOT
GRAPETREE
GRAPEVINE
GRAPHICAL
GRAPPLING
GUNPOWDER
HAMPSTEAD
HAPPENING
HAPPINESS
HARPOONER
HELPFULLY
HENPECKED
HERPESTES
HESPERIAN
HEYPRESTO
HIPPOCRAS
HIPPODAME
HIPPOLYTA
HIPPOLYTE
HOSPITIUM
IBUPROFEN
INOPINATE
INSPECTOR
INSPIRING
ISOPROPYL
JAMPACKED
KNAPSCULL
KNAPSKULL
KNIPHOFIA
KROPOTKIN
LAMPADARY
LAMPADION
LAMPBLACK
LAMPLIGHT
LAMPSHADE
LIMPIDITY
LIPPITUDE
LYMPHATIC
MAPPEMOND
MELPOMENE
MISPICKEL
MISPLACED
MUMPSIMUS
NIPPERKIN
NONPAREIL
NONPROFIT
OMOPHAGIC
OVIPAROUS
PALPATION
PALPEBRAL
PALPITATE
PEMPHIGUS
PENPUSHER
PEPPERONI
PEPPERPOT
PERPETUAL
PERPLEXED
PIEPOWDER
PIMPERNEL
POMPADOUR
POMPHOLYX
POMPOSITY
POPPERING
POPPYCOCK
PORPOISES
PORPORATE
POTPOURRI
PREPOLLEX
PROPAGATE
PROPELLED
PROPELLER
PROPELLOR
PROPERDIN
PROPHETIC
PROPIONIC
PROPONENT
PROPRIETY
PROPTOSIS
PROPYLENE
PULPITEER
PUPPETEER
PURPOSELY
RASPATORY
RASPBERRY
RESPECTED
RESPECTER
RHAPSODIC
SCAPEGOAT
SCAPOLITE
SCEPTICAL
SHAPELESS
SHEPHERDS
SHIPOWNER
SHIPSHAPE
SHIPWRECK
SHOPFLOOR
SHOPFRONT
SIMPLETON
SIMPLISTE
SKEPTICAL
SLAPHAPPY
SLAPSTICK
SOAPSTONE
SOPPINESS
STIPULATE
STUPEFIED
STUPIDITY
SULPHONIC
SULPHURIC
SUMPTUARY
SUMPTUOUS
SUPPLIANT
SUPPLICAT
SUPPORTER
SUPPOSING
SUPPURATE
SURPRISED
SUSPECTED
SUSPENDED
SUSPENDER
SUSPENSOR
SUSPICION
SYLPHLIKE
SYMPHONIC
SYMPHYSIS
SYMPODIUM
SYMPOSIUM
SYRPHIDAE
TARPAULIN
TEMPERATE
TEMPORARY
TEMPORIZE
TEMPTRESS
TERPINEOL
TIMPANIST
TIPPERARY
TOLPUDDLE
TRAPEZIAL
TRAPEZIST
TRAPEZIUM
TRAPEZIUS
TRAPEZOID
TRAPPINGS
TRIPITAKA
TRIPMETER
TROPAELIN
TROPARION
TRYPHOEUS
TURPITUDE
TYMPANIST
UNOPPOSED
UNSPARING
UNSPOILED
VESPASIAN
VULPINITE
WALPURGIS
WASPISHLY
WHIPROUND
WHIPSNADE
BANQUETTE
BECQUEREL
BRIQUETTE
CHEQUERED
CONQUEROR
CROQUETTE
ELOQUENCE
ETIQUETTE
EXEQUATUR
FREQUENCY
HACQUETON
HARQUEBUS
JACQUERIE
MACQUARIE
MARQUESAS
MARQUETRY
SASQUATCH
SURQUEDRY
TURQUOISE
UNEQUALED

ABERNETHY
ABERRANCE
ABORIGINE
ACARIASIS
ACCRETION
ADDRESSED
ADDRESSEE
ADORATION
ADORNMENT
AFFRICATE
AFORESAID
AGGRAVATE
AGGREGATE
AGGRESSOR
AGGRIEVED
ALERTNESS
AMARANTIN
AMARYLLIS
AMBROSIAL
AMBROSIAN
AMBROTYPE
AMERICIUM
AMOROUSLY
AMORPHOUS
ANARCHIST
ANDROCLES
ANDROMEDA
APARTHEID
APARTMENT
APERIODIC
APERITIVE
APHRODITE
APPRAISAL
APPREHEND
APPROVING
ASTRAGALS
ASTRAKHAN
ASTRODOME
ASTROLABE
ASTROLOGY
ASTRONAUT
ASTRONOMY
ASTROPHEL
ASTROTURF
ATTRIBUTE
ATTRITION
AUBRIETIA
AWARENESS
BARRACUDA
BARRICADE
BARRISTER
BEARDLESS
BEARDSLEY
BEDRAGGLE
BEDRIDDEN
BETROTHAL
BETROTHED
BOARDROOM
BOARDWALK
BORROWING
BOURGEOIS
BURROUGHS
BURROWING
BYPRODUCT
CABRIOLET
CAIRNGORM
CAPRICCIO
CAPRICORN
CHARABANC
CHARACTER
CHARGEFUL
CHARIVARI
CHARLATAN
CHARLOTTE
CHAROLAIS
CHARTERED
CHARTREUX
CHARWOMAN
CHARYBDIS
CHERISHED
CHERNOZEM
CHERUBINI
CHIROPODY
CHORISTER
CHURCHILL
CHURCHMAN
CHURIDARS
CIRRHOSIS
CLARENDON
CLARIFIER
CLERGYMAN
COARCTATE
COPROLITE
CORRECTED
CORRECTLY
CORRECTOR
CORREGGIO
CORRELATE
CORROSION
CORROSIVE
CORRUGATE
CORRUPTER
COURGETTE
COURTELLE
COURTEOUS
COURTESAN
COURTROOM
COURTSHIP
COURTYARD
CUPRESSUS
CURRENTLY
CURRYCOMB
DAIRYMAID
DECRETALS
DEERHOUND
DEGRADING
DEPRAVITY
DEPRECATE
DEPREDATE
DEPRESSED
DERRINGER
DETRACTOR
DETRIMENT
DETRITION
DIARRHOEA
DISREGARD
DISREPAIR
DISREPUTE
DUBROVNIK
ECARDINES
ECTROPION
EGAREMENT
EMBRACERY
EMBRACING
EMBRANGLE
EMBRASURE
EMBROCATE
EMBROGLIO
EMBROIDER
EMBROILED
EMBRYONIC
EMERGENCE
EMERGENCY
ENCRATITE
ENERGETIC
ENERGUMEN
ENERINITE
ENGRAINED
ENGRAVING
ENGRENAGE
ENGROSSED
ENGROSSER
ENTRAMMEL
ENTRANCED
ENTRECHAT
ENTRECÔTE
ENTREMETS
ENTROPION
ENTROPIUM
EPARCHATE
ESTRANGED
ESTRAPADE
ESTRELDID
ETERNALLY
EUTROPHIC
EVERGLADE
EVERGREEN
EVERYBODY
EXARATION
EXCREMENT
EXERCISED
EXERCISES
EXORATION
EXPRESSED
EXPRESSLY
EXTRACTOR
EXTRADITE
EXTREMELY
EXTREMISM
EXTREMIST
EXTREMITY
EXTRICATE
EXTRINSIC
EXTROVERT
EXTRUSION
FABRICATE
FAIRYLAND
FAIRYTALE
FEARFULLY
FEBRIFUGE
FERRYBOAT
FIBROLINE
FIBROLITE
FLORESTAN
FLORIMELL
FOGRAMITE
FOURPENCE
FOURWHEEL
GALRAVAGE
GARRULITY
GARRULOUS
GARRYOWEN
GEARLEVER
GEARSHIFT
GEARSTICK
GEARWHEEL
GEORGETTE
GIBRALTAR
GLORIFIED
GLORYHOLE
GUARANTEE
GUARANTOR
GUARDROOM
GUARDSMAN
GUERRILLA
HADROSAUR
HAIRBRUSH
HAIRPIECE
HAIRSTYLE
HARROGATE
HARROWING
HAYRADDIN
HEARDSMAN
HEARTACHE
HEARTBEAT
HEARTBURN
HEARTFELT
HEARTHRUG
HEARTLAND
HEARTLESS
HEBRIDEAN
HEURISTIC
HIERARCHY
HOARFROST
HOARHOUND
HOARSTONE
HORRIFIED
HOURGLASS
HOURSTONE
HURRICANE
HURRICANO
HURRIEDLY
HYDRANGEA
HYDRAULIC
HYDRAZINE
HYDROFOIL
HYDROPULT
HYDROSTAT
IMBRANGLE
IMBRICATE
IMBROCATE
IMBROGLIO
IMPRECATE
IMPRECISE
IMPRESSED
IMPROBITY
IMPROMPTU
IMPROVING
IMPROVISE
IMPRUDENT
INCREASED
INCREMENT
INDRAUGHT
INERTNESS
INERUDITE
INGRAINED
INGROWING
INORGANIC
INTRICACY
INTRICATE
INTRIGUED
INTRIGUER
INTRINSIC
INTRODUCE
INTROITUS
INTROVERT
INTRUSION
INTRUSIVE
LATRATION
LEHRJAHRE
LEPROSERY
LIBRARIAN
LIVRAISON
LUBRICANT
LUBRICATE
LUCRATIVE
LUCRETIUS
MACROCOSM
MACROLOGY
MADRASSAH
MADREPORE
MADRESSAH
MADRILENE
MARROWFAT
MATRIARCH
MATRICIDE
MATRIMONY
MAURITIAN
MAURITIUS
MEDRESSEH
MERRIMENT
METRICATE
METROLAND
METRONOME
MICROCHIP
MICROCOSM
MICROCYTE
MICROFILM
MICROLITE
MICROLITH
MICROTOME
MICROTONE
MICROWAVE
MIDRASHIM
MIGRATION
MIGRATORY
MITRAILLE
MOURNIVAL
NARRATION
NARRATIVE
NARROWING
NATROLITE
NEGRITUDE
NEURALGIA
NEURALGIC
NEUROGLIA
NEUROLOGY
NIGRITUDE
NIGROSINE
NUTRIMENT
NUTRITION
NUTRITIVE
OBTRUSION
OBTRUSIVE
OPERATING
OPERATION
OPERATIVE
OPERCULUM
OPPRESSED
OPPRESSOR
OSTRACISM
OSTRACIZE

OSTROGOTH
OTTRELITE
OUTRIGGER
OUTROOPER
OVERBLOWN
OVERBOARD
OVERCLOUD
OVERCROWD
OVERDRAFT
OVERDRAWN
OVERDRESS
OVERDRIVE
OVEREXERT
OVERGROWN
OVERHASTY
OVERHEADS
OVERJOYED
OVERLYING
OVERNIGHT
OVERPAINT
OVERPOISE
OVERPOWER
OVERRATED
OVERREACH
OVERREACT
OVERRIDER
OVERSHADE
OVERSHOES
OVERSHOOT
OVERSIGHT
OVERSIZED
OVERSLEEP
OVERSPEND
OVERSPILL
OVERSTATE
OVERSTEER
OVERTHROW
OVERTONES
OVERVALUE
OVERWEIGH
OVERWHELM
PARRICIDE
PATRIARCH
PATRICIAN
PATRICIDE
PATRIMONY
PATRIOTIC
PATROCLUS
PATROLMAN
PATRONAGE
PATRONESS
PATRONIZE
PEARLWORT
PEIRASTIC
PETRIFIED
PETROLEUM
PETROLOGY
PHARAMOND
PHARISAIC
PHARSALIA
PHEROMONE
PIERGLASS
PLURALISM
PLURALITY
POORHOUSE
PORRINGER
PROROGATE
PRURIENCE
PSORIASIS
PTARMIGAN
PTERIDIUM
PTEROSAUR
PUERILITY
PUERPERAL
PYRRHONIC
QUARENDEN
QUARTERLY
QUARTETTE
QUERCETIN
QUERCETUS
QUERIMONY
QUERULOUS
REARGUARD
REARHORSE
REARMOUSE
REARRANGE
REARWARDS
REFRACTOR
REFRESHER
REGRETFUL
REPREHEND
REPRESENT
REPRESSED
REPRIMAND
REPROBATE
REPROCESS
REPRODUCE
REPROVING
RETRACTOR
RETRIEVAL
RETRIEVER
RETROCEDE
RETROFLEX
RETROVERT
SACRAMENT
SACRARIUM
SACRIFICE
SACRILEGE
SACRISTAN
SCARECROW
SCARIFIER
SCARLATTI
SCORBUTIC
SCORBUTUS
SCORCHING
SCORODITE
SCURRIOUR
SEARCHING
SECRETARY
SECRETION
SECRETIVE
SEGREGATE
SERRATION
SERREFILE
SHARESMAN
SHARKSKIN
SHARPENER
SHARPNESS
SHORTCAKE
SHORTFALL
SHORTHAND
SHORTHAUL
SHORTHOLD
SHORTHORN
SHORTLIST
SHORTNESS
SHORTSTAY
SHORTSTOP
SHORTTERM
SMARTNESS
SOBRIQUET
SORROWFUL
SOURDOUGH
SPARINGLY
SPARKLERS
SPARKLING
SPARTACUS
SPIRITOUS
SPIRITUAL
SPOROCARP
SPORTSMAN
SPORTSMEN
STARBOARD
STARGAZER
STARKNESS
STARLIGHT
STARSTONE
STARTLING
STERADIAN
STERCORAL
STERILITY
STERILIZE
STERNFAST
STERNNESS
STIRABOUT
STOREROOM
STORIATED
STORNAWAY
STORYBOOK
STORYLINE
SUBROGATE
SUPREMACY
SUPREMELY
SURREJOIN
SURRENDER
SURROGATE
SWORDFISH
SWORDPLAY
SWORDSMAN
TARRAGONA
TEARFULLY
TEARSHEET
TEIRESIAS
TERRACING
TERRARIUM
TERRICOLE
TERRIFIED
TERRITORY
TERRORISM
TERRORIST
TERRORIZE
TETRAGRAM
TETRALOGY
TETRARCHY
THERALITE
THERAPIST
THEREFORE
THEREUPON
THERMIDOR
THERSITES
THIRDSMAN
THIRSTILY
THIRSTING
THIRTIETH
THORNBACK
THORNBILL
THORNDYKE
THORNLESS
THYRATRON
THYRISTOR
TIERCERON
TITRATION
TOURNEDOS
TSAREVICH
ULTRONEUS
UMBRATILE
UNBRIDLED
UNCROSSED
UNCROWNED
UNDRESSED
UNPRECISE
UNTRAINED
UNTREATED
UNTRODDEN
UNWRITTEN
UVAROVITE
VIBRATILE
VIBRATION
VIBRATORY
VITRIOLIC
VITRUVIAN
WEARINESS
WEARISOME
WEIRDNESS
WHEREFORE
WHEREUPON
WHERRYMAN
WHIRLIGIG
WHIRLPOOL
WHIRLWIND
WORRISOME
ABASEMENT
ABYSMALLY
AHASUERUS
AINSWORTH
AIRSTREAM
AMUSEMENT
AMUSINGLY
ANASTASIA
APOSTOLIC
ARISTOTLE
ARMSTRONG
AWESTRUCK
BAKSHEESH
BEDSITTER
BEDSPREAD
BEESTINGS
BIOSPHERE
BLASPHEME
BLASPHEMY
BLESSINGS
BLISTERED
BLUSTERER
BOBSLEIGH
BOLSHEVIK
BOSSANOVA
BOSSINESS
BOTSWANAN
BRASENOSE
BRASSERIE
BRASSICAS
BRASSIERE
BRASSWARE
BRISKNESS
BRISTLING
BRUSHWOOD
BRUSQUELY
CAESAREAN
CASSANDRA
CASSATION
CASSEROLE
CASSONADE
CASSOULET
CASSOWARY
CATSKILLS
CAUSATION
CEASEFIRE
CEASELESS
CESSATION
CHASTENED
CHISELLER
CLASSICAL
CLASSLESS
CLASSMATE
CLASSROOM
CLOSENESS
CLUSTERED
COASTLINE
CONSCIOUS
CONSCRIPT
CONSENSUS
CONSIGNEE
CONSIGNOR
CONSONANT
CONSTABLE
CONSTANCE
CONSTANCY
CONSTRICT
CONSTRUCT
CONSULATE
CONSUMING
COXSACKIE
CRASHLAND
CRESCELLE
CRESCENDO
CRISPNESS
CROSSBEAM
CROSSBILL
CROSSBRED
CROSSEYED
CROSSFIRE
CROSSOVER
CROSSWALK
CROSSWIND
CROSSWISE
CROSSWORD
CRUSTACEA
CTESIPHON
CURSORILY
DAYSPRING
DENSENESS
DIASTASIS
DISSEMBLE
DISSENTER
DISSIDENT
DISSIPATE
DISSOLUTE
DISSOLVED
DISSONANT
DOSSHOUSE
DUNSINANE
DUNSTABLE

ECOSSAISE
ECOSYSTEM
ELASTOMER
EPISCOPAL
EPISTAXIS
EPISTOLER
ERISTICAL
EROSTRATE
EVASIVELY
EXISTENCE
EXOSPHERE
EXOSTOSIS
EYESHADOW
EYESPLICE
EYESTRAIN
FACSIMILE
FALSEHOOD
FALSENESS
FIRSTEVER
FIRSTHAND
FIRSTRATE
FLASHBACK
FLASHBULB
FLASHCUBE
FLESHLESS
FLESHPOTS
FLUSTERED
FORSYTHIA
FOSSILISE
FOSSORIAL
FRESHENER
FRESHNESS
FROSTBITE
FRUSTRATE
FUSSINESS
GESSAMINE
GLASSWARE
GLISSANDO
GOOSANDER
GOOSEFOOT
GOOSEHERD
GOOSENECK
GOOSESTEP
GOSSAMERY
GOSSYPINE
GOSSYPIUM
GRASSLAND
GRISAILLE
GROSGRAIN
GROSVENOR
GUESSWORK
GUMSHIELD
HAMSTRING
HAMSTRUNG
HANSEATIC
HARSHNESS
HEMSTITCH
HESSONITE
HOPSCOTCH
HORSEBACK
HORSEHAIR
HORSELESS
HORSEPLAY
HORSESHOE
HORSETAIL
HORSEWHIP
HOUSEBOAT
HOUSECOAT
HOUSEHOLD
HOUSEMAID
HOUSEROOM
HOUSEWIFE
HOUSEWORK
IMPSONITE
INUSITATE
IRASCIBLE
ISOSCELES
JANSENISM
JANSENIST
JESSAMINE
JESSERANT
JETSTREAM
JOBSEEKER
JOBSWORTH
KALSOMINE
KEYSTROKE
KIESERITE
KINSWOMAN
KISSINGER
LAPSTREAK
LASSITUDE
LEASEHOLD
LEASTWAYS
LEASTWISE
LEISURELY
LOBSCOUSE
LOOSEHEAD
LOOSELEAF
LOOSENESS
LOUSEWORT
MANSFIELD
MARSHLAND
MARSUPIAL
MARSUPIUM
MASSINGER
MASSIVELY
MASSORETE
MASSYMORE
MAUSOLEUM
MEASURING
MENSHEVIK
MENSTRUAL
MENSTRUUM
MESSALINA
MESSENGER
MESSIANIC
MIDSTREAM
MIDSUMMER
MISSHAPEN
MISSIONER
MISSTROKE
MOISTNESS
MONSIGNOR
MONSTROUS
MOUSEHOLE
MOUSELIKE
MOUSETRAP
MOUSTACHE
MUSSITATE
MUSSOLINI
MUSSULMAN
NAUSEATED
NEWSAGENT
NEWSFLASH
NEWSHOUND
NEWSPAPER
NEWSPRINT
NEWSSHEET
NEWSSTALL
NEWSSTAND
NOISELESS
NOISINESS
NONSMOKER
NOOSPHERE
NURSEMAID
OARSWOMAN
OFFSEASON
OFFSPRING
OURSELVES
OUTSIDERS
OUTSKIRTS
OUTSPOKEN
OUTSPREAD
PALSGRAVE
PARSIMONY
PARSONAGE
PASSAMENT
PASSENGER
PASSEPIED
PASSERINE
PASSIVELY
PASSIVITY
PAUSANIAS
PEASANTRY
PEASEWEEP
PENSIONER
PENSIVELY
PERSECUTE
PERSEVERE
PERSIMMON
PERSONAGE
PERSONATE
PERSONIFY
PERSONNEL
PERSUADED
PESSIMISM
PESSIMIST
PHOSPHATE
PHOSPHENE
PHYSICIAN
PHYSICIST
PINSTRIPE
PIPSQUEAK
PLASTERED
PLASTERER
POISONING
POISONOUS
POSSESSED
POSSESSOR
POSSIBLES
PRESBYTER
PRESCIENT
PRESCRIBE
PRESCUTUM
PRESENTED
PRESENTER
PRESENTLY
PRESERVED
PRESERVER
PRESERVES
PRESHRUNK
PRESIDENT
PRESIDIAL
PRESIDIUM
PRESSGANG
PRISMATIC
PROSCRIBE
PROSECUTE
PROSELYTE
PROSTRATE
PUISSANCE
PULSATION
PURSUANCE
PUSSYFOOT
QUASIMODO
REASONING
REDSTREAK
REISTAFEL
RESSALDAR
ROISTERER
ROOSEVELT
RORSCHACH
ROUSSETTE
SAPSUCKER
SASSAFRAS
SASSENACH
SASSOLITE
SCISSORER
SEASONING
SENSATION
SENSELESS
SENSILLUM
SENSITIVE
SENSITIZE
SENSORIUM
SENSUALLY
SHASHLICK
SISSERARY
SPASMODIC
SUBSCRIBE
SUBSCRIPT
SUBSIDIZE
SUBSTANCE
SUBSTRATA
SUBSTRATE
SUNSCREEN
SUNSTROKE
TAHSILDAR
TASSELLED
TEESWATER
TENSENESS
TERSENESS
THESAURUS
TIPSINESS
TOASTRACK
TRASIMENE
TRISAGION
TROSSACHS
ULLSWATER
UNASHAMED
UNISEXUAL
UNUSUALLY
VERSATILE
VERSIFIER
VERSIONAL
WAISTBAND
WAISTCOAT
WAISTLINE
WASSERMAN
WELSUMMER
WHISTLING
WHOSOEVER
WRESTLING
ZOOSCOPIC
ABATEMENT
ABSTAINER
ABSTINENT
ACETYLENE
ACUTENESS
AESTHETIC
AGITATION
AMSTERDAM
ANATOLIAN
ANATOMIST
ANATOMIZE
APATHETIC
ARCTOGAEA
AUCTORIAL
AUSTERITY
AUSTRALIA
AYATOLLAH
BACTERIAL
BACTERIUM
BALTHAZAR
BALTIMORE
BANTERING
BAPTISMAL
BARTENDER
BARTHOLDI
BARTHOLIN
BASTINADE
BASTINADO
BATTALION
BATTLEAXE
BEATITUDE
BEETHOVEN
BETTERTON
BIRTHMARK
BIRTHWORT
BLATANTLY
BOATHOUSE
BOATSWAIN
BOOTLACES
BOSTONIAN
BOTTLEFUL
BRATWURST
BRITANNIA
BRITANNIC
BRITSCHKA
BROTHERLY
BRUTALISM
BRUTALITY
BRUTALIZE
BUTTERBUR
BUTTERCUP
BUTTERFLY
BUTTERNUT
BYSTANDER
CANTABILE
CANTHARIS
CANTHARUS
CANTONESE
CAPTAINCY
CAPTIVATE
CAPTIVITY
CARTESIAN
CARTHORSE
CARTILAGE
CARTOGRAM
CARTOUCHE
CARTRIDGE
CARTTRACK

CARTULARY
CARTWHEEL
CASTANETS
CASTIGATE
CASTILIAN
CASTRATED
CATTLEMAN
CATTLEPEN
CAUTERIZE
CENTAURUS
CENTENARY
CENTERING
CENTIPEDE
CENTRALLY
CENTREING
CENTURION
CERTAINLY
CERTAINTY
CERTIFIED
CERTITUDE
CHATTERER
COLTSFOOT
CONTAGION
CONTAINER
CONTEMPER
CONTENDER
CONTENTED
CONTINENT
CONTINUAL
CONTINUUM
CONTRALTO
CONTRIVED
CONTRIVER
CONTUMACY
CONTUMELY
CONTUSION
CORTISONE
COSTUMIER
COUTURIER
CRETINOUS
CRITERION
CRITICISM
CRITICIZE
CROTCHETY
CULTIVATE
CURTILAGE
CUSTODIAL
CUSTODIAN
CUSTOMARY
CUSTOMIZE
CUTTHROAT
DALTONISM
DARTAGNAN
DARTBOARD
DARTMOUTH
DASTARDLY
DEATHLESS
DEATHTRAP
DENTISTRY
DENTITION
DESTITUTE
DESTROYED
DESTROYER
DEUTERIUM
DEXTERITY
DEXTEROUS
DEXTRORSE
DIATHESIS
DICTATION
DIETETICS
DIETICIAN
DIRTINESS
DISTANTLY
DISTEMPER
DISTENDED
DISTILLER
DISTORTED
DISTRAINT
DISTURBED
DOCTORATE
DOCTRINAL
DYSTROPHY
EARTHFLAX
EARTHLING
EARTHWORK
EARTHWORM
EASTBOUND
EASTERNER
EASTLINGS
EASTWARDS
EDITORIAL
ELATERIUM
ELUTRIATE
EMOTIONAL
EMPTINESS
ENSTATITE
EPITHESIS
EPITOMIZE
EROTICISM
ERSTWHILE
EVITERNAL
FACTIONAL
FACTORISE
FACTUALLY
FAITHLESS
FANTASIZE
FANTASTIC
FASTENING
FASTTRACK
FATTENING
FEATHERED
FERTILITY
FERTILIZE
FESTINATE
FESTIVITY
FICTIONAL
FIFTEENTH
FILTERING
FILTERTIP
FLATTENED
FLATTENER
FLATTERED
FLATTERER
FLATULENT
FLOTATION
FOOTBRAKE
FOOTHILLS
FOOTLOOSE
FOOTPLATE
FOOTPRINT
FOOTSTALL
FOOTSTOOL
FORTALICE
FORTHWINK
FORTHWITH
FORTILAGE
FORTITUDE
FORTNIGHT
FORTUNATE
FRATCHETY
FRATERNAL
FRETFULLY
FRITHBORH
FURTIVELY
FUSTIGATE
FUSTINESS
GENTEELLY
GENTILITY
GENTLEMAN
GENTLEMEN
GESTATION
GLUTAMINE
GLUTINOUS
GRATICULE
GRATITUDE
GROTESQUE
GUATEMALA
GUITARIST
GUSTATION
GUTTERING
HARTSHORN
HASTENING
HASTINESS
HAUTMONDE
HAWTHORNE
HEATHLAND
HECTORING
HESTERNAL
HISTAMINE
HISTOGRAM
HISTOLOGY
HISTORIAN
HORTATIVE
HORTATORY
HOSTILITY
HOTTENTOT
HOWTOWDIE
HUTTERITE
HYSTERICS
IMITATION
IMITATIVE
INITIALLY
INITIATED
INITIATOR
INSTANTER
INSTANTLY
INSTIGATE
INSTITUTE
ISOTACTIC
ISOTROPIC
JITTERBUG
JUSTIFIED
JUSTINIAN
JUXTAPOSE
KENTIGERN
KENTLEDGE
KINTLEDGE
KITTENISH
KITTIWAKE
LACTATION
LANTHANUM
LASTDITCH
LATTERDAY
LEFTOVERS
LEITMOTIF
LEITMOTIV
LESTRIGON
LETTERBOX
LETTERING
LINTSTOCK
LISTENING
LOATHSOME
LOFTINESS
LOITERING
LUCTATION
LUSTIHOOD
LUSTINESS
MACTATION
MARTINEAU
MARTINMAS
MARTYRDOM
MASTERFUL
MASTERMAN
MASTICATE
MATTAMORE
MEATBALLS
MENTALITY
MENTATION
MENTICIDE
MENTIONED
MIRTHLESS
MISTEMPER
MISTIGRIS
MISTINESS
MISTLETOE
MONTACUTE
MONTAIGNE
MONTANISM
MONTANIST
MONTESPAN
MONTEZUMA
MONTICULE
MORTALITY
MORTGAGEE
MORTGAGOR
MORTICIAN
MORTIFIED
MORTSTONE
MOUTHLESS
MOUTHWASH
MULTIFORM
MULTIPLEX
MULTITUDE
MUSTINESS
MUTTERING
MYSTERIES
MYSTICISM
NANTUCKET
NASTINESS
NECTARINE
NEPTUNIUM
NEUTRALLY
NICTITATE
NIETZSCHE
NOCTURNAL
NORTHEAST
NORTHERLY
NORTHWARD
NORTHWEST
NOSTALGIA
NOSTALGIC
NOSTOLOGY
NYSTAGMUS
OASTHOUSE
OBSTETRIC
OBSTINACY
OBSTINATE
OESTROGEN
OILTANKER
ORATORIAN
PANTAGAMY
PANTALEON
PANTALOON
PANTHEISM
PANTHENOL
PANTOFFLE
PANTOMIME
PANTOUFLE
PARTAKING
PARTHENON
PARTHOLON
PARTIALLY
PARTICLES
PARTITION
PARTRIDGE
PARTTIMER
PASTERNAK
PASTICCIO
PASTORALE
PASTURAGE
PATTERNED
PENTECOST
PENTHOUSE
PENTOSANE
PERTINENT
PERTURBED
PERTUSATE
PERTUSSIS
PESTICIDE
PESTILENT
PETTICOAT
PETTINESS
PETTITOES
PHITONIUM
PHOTOCOPY
PHOTOGENE
PHOTOSTAT
PHYTOLITE
PHYTOTRON
PICTOGRAM
PICTORIAL
PISTACHIO
PISTAREEN
PISTOLEER
PLATITUDE
PLATONIST
PLETHORIC
PLUTOCRAT
PLUTONIUM
POETASTER
PONTLEVIS
PORTERAGE
PORTFOLIO
PORTRAYAL
PORTREEVE
POSTCARDS
POSTERIOR
POSTERITY
POSTHOUSE
POSTNATAL
POSTPONED
POSTULANT

POSTULATE
POSTWOMAN
POTTINGAR
PRETENDER
PRETERITE
PRETERMIT
PROTAMINE
PROTECTOR
PROTESTER
PROTHESIS
PROTHORAX
PROTOSTAR
PROTOTYPE
PRYTANEUM
QUITTANCE
QUOTATION
QUOTIDIAN
QUOTITION
RANTIPOLE
RAPTORIAL
RAPTUROUS
RATTLEBAG
RECTANGLE
RECTIFIER
RECTITUDE
RECTORIAL
REITERATE
RENTALLER
REPTATION
REPTILIAN
RESTIFORM
RESTITUTE
RESTRAINT
RIOTOUSLY
ROOTSTOCK
ROSTELLUM
ROTTERDAM
ROUTINELY
RUSTICATE
RUSTINESS
SALTINESS
SALTPETER
SALTPETRE
SALTWATER
SANTAYANA
SARTORIAL
SARTORIUS
SAUTERNES
SCATTERED
SCOTCHMAN
SCYTHEMAN
SECTARIAN
SECTIONAL
SECTORIAL
SENTIENCE
SENTIMENT
SEPTEMBER
SEPTIMOLE
SHATTERED
SHETLANDS
SHUTTERED
SILTSTONE
SIXTEENMO
SIXTEENTH
SKETCHILY
SKETCHMAP
SKETCHPAD
SOFTCOVER
SOFTENING
SOOTERKIN
SORTILEGE
SOSTENUTO
SOTTISIER
SOUTENEUR
SOUTHDOWN
SOUTHEAST
SOUTHERLY
SOUTHWARD
SOUTHWARK
SOUTHWEST
SPATIALLY
SPATTERED
SPOTLIGHT
STATEHOOD
STATELESS
STATEMENT
STATEROOM
STATESIDE
STATESMAN
STATEWIDE
STATIONED
STATIONER
STATISTIC
STATOLITH
STATUETTE
STATUTORY
SUBTENANT
SUBTITLED
SUETONIUS
SULTANATE
SUNTANNED
SUSTAINED
SWOTHLING
SYNTACTIC
SYNTHESIS
SYNTHETIC
TACTFULLY
TACTICIAN
TANTALITE
TANTALIZE
TANTARARA
TARTAREAN
TASTELESS
TAUTOLOGY
TECTIFORM
TECTONICS
TECTORIAL
TENTATIVE
TENTORIUM
TESTAMENT
TESTATRIX
TESTDRIVE
TESTICLES
TESTIFIER
TESTIMONY
TETTEROUS
THATCHING
TICTACTOE
TITTLEBAT
TOOTHACHE
TOOTHCOMB
TOOTHLESS
TOOTHPICK
TOOTHSOME
TORTELIER
TOTTENHAM
TRATTORIA
TRITENESS
TRITICALE
TRITURATE
TRUTINATE
UMPTEENTH
UNETHICAL
UNITARIAN
VANTBRASS
VENTIFACT
VENTILATE
VENTRICLE
VERTEBRAE
VERTEBRAL
VERTIPORT
VERTUMNUS
VESTIBULE
VESTIGIAL
VESTITURE
VESTMENTS
VICTIMIZE
VICTORIAN
VICTORINE
VIRTUALLY
VOLTIGEUR
VOLTINISM
VOLTMETER
VOLTURNUS
VORTICISM
VORTIGERN
WAITERAGE
WARTCRESS
WASTELAND
WASTWATER
WELTGEIST
WESTBOUND
WESTERNER
WESTWARDS
WHETSTONE
WHITAKERS
WHITEBAIT
WHITEDAMP
WHITEFISH
WHITEHALL
WHITEHEAD
WHITENESS
WHITENING
WHITEWALL
WHITEWASH
WHITEWING
WHITEWOOD
WHITTAWER
WHITWORTH
WISTFULLY
WITTICISM
WITTINGLY
WORTHLESS
XANTHIPPE
YESTERDAY
YESTEREVE
ZEITGEIST
ABDUCTION
ABLUTIONS
ABOUNDING
ABOUTFACE
ABOUTTURN
ABSURDITY
ACOUSTICS
ACQUIESCE
ACQUITTAL
ACTUALITY
ACTUARIAL
ALEURITIS
AMAUROSIS
AMBULANCE
AMBUSCADE
ANGUISHED
ANNULMENT
ARAUCARIA
ARDUOUSLY
ARQUEBUSE
ASSUETUDE
ASSURANCE
ASSUREDLY
ASTUCIOUS
ATTUITION
AUGUSTINE
BEAUTEOUS
BEAUTIFUL
BIFURCATE
BROUGHTON
BURUNDIAN
CASUARINA
CASUISTIC
CASUISTRY
CHAUFFEUR
CLOUDLESS
COLUMBARY
COLUMBATE
COLUMBIAN
COLUMBINE
COLUMBITE
COLUMBIUM
COLUMELLA
COLUMNIST
CONUNDRUM
CORUSCATE
CROUSTADE
DEBUTANTE
DECUMBENT
DECURSIVE
DECUSSATE
DEDUCTION
DEDUCTIVE
DEMULCENT
DEMURRAGE
DESUETUDE
DESULTORY
DISUNITED
DOCUMENTS
EFFULGENT
ENCUMBENT
ENDURABLE
ENDURANCE
ENQUIRIES
EPAULETTE
ESCULENTS
ESQUILINE
EXCULPATE
EXCURSION
EXCUSABLE
EXCUSABLY
EXPULSION
EXPURGATE
EXQUISITE
FABULINUS
FACUNDITY
FATUOUSLY
FECUNDITY
FEDUCIARY
FENUGREEK
FIDUCIARY
FIGURANTE
FLOURMILL
GENUFLECT
GENUINELY
GERUNDIVE
GROUNDHOG
GROUNDING
GROUNDNUT
GROUNDSEL
HIRUNDINE
HUMUNGOUS
IMMUNISER
IMMUTABLE
IMMUTABLY
IMPUDENCE
IMPULSION
IMPULSIVE
INAUDIBLE
INAUDIBLY
INAUGURAL
INCUBATOR
INCULCATE
INCULPATE
INCUMBENT
INCURABLE
INCURABLY
INCURIOUS
INCURSION
INDUCTION
INDUCTIVE
INDULGENT
INFURIATE
INHUMANLY
INJURIOUS
INJUSTICE
INQUILINE
INQUINATE
INQUIRING
INQUORATE
INSULATOR
INSULTING
INSURANCE
INSURGENT
INTUITION
INTUITIVE
INTUMESCE
IRRUPTION
JEQUIRITY
JERUSALEM
JOCULARLY
LIQUEFIED
LIQUIDATE
LIQUIDITY
LIQUIDIZE
LIQUORICE
LIQUORISH
LOQUACITY
LUCUBRATE
LUXURIANT
LUXURIATE
LUXURIOUS
MAJUSCULE
MANUBRIUM
MATUTINAL

MENUISIER
MINUSCULE
MINUTEMAN
NATURALLY
OBFUSCATE
OBJURGATE
OCCULTIST
OCCUPANCY
OCCUPYING
ODOURLESS
OMBUDSMAN
PALUDRINE
PECULATOR
PECUNIARY
PENURIOUS
PETULANCE
PIQUANTLY
PITUITARY
PITUITRIN
PLAUSIBLE
PLAUSIBLY
PLAUSTRAL
PLOUGHMAN
PNEUMATIC
PNEUMONIA
POPULARLY
POPULATED
PROUDHORN
PROUSTITE
PSEUDAXIS
PSEUDONYM
PURULENCE
RECUMBENT
RECURRENT
RECURRING
RECUSANCE
REDUCIBLE
REDUCTION
REDUNDANT
REFULGENT
REFURBISH
REFUSENIK
REGUERDON
REGULARLY
REGULATOR
RELUCTANT
REPUDIATE
REPUGNANT
REPULSION
REPULSIVE
REPUTABLE
REPUTEDLY
REQUISITE
RESULTANT
RESULTING
RESURFACE
RESURGENT
RESURRECT
RETURNING
REVULSION
RHEUMATIC
ROQUEFORT
ROTUNDATE
ROTUNDITY
SALUBRITY
SATURATED
SATURNIAN
SATURNINE
SATURNISM
SCOUNDREL
SCRUBBING
SCRUFFILY
SCRUMMAGE
SCRUMPING
SCRUTATOR
SEDUCTION
SEDUCTIVE
SEPULCHER
SEPULCHRE
SEPULTURE
SEQUESTER
SEQUINNED
SEXUALITY
SHRUBBERY
SILURIDAE
SIMULATED
SIMULATOR
SIMULCAST
SINUOSITY
SINUSITIS
SITUATION
SLAUGHTER
SLOUGHING
STAUNCHLY
STOUTNESS
STRUCTURE
STRUMITIS
STRUTTING
SUQUAMISH
TABULATOR
TEMULENCE
TENUOUSLY
THAUMATIN
THOUSANDS
TIPULIDAE
TRAUMATIC
TRIUMPHAL
TROUBADOR
TROUSSEAU
UNGUARDED
UNLUCKILY
UNMUSICAL
UNRUFFLED
UNSULLIED
UNTUTORED
VAGUENESS
VALUATION
VALUELESS
VENUSBERG
VIRULENCE
VISUALIZE
VOLUCRINE
VOLUNTARY
VOLUNTEER
ATAVISTIC
BELVEDERE
CALVANISM
CALVINIST
CALVITIES
CANVASSER
CERVANTES
CHAVENDER
CHEVALIER
CLEVELAND
CONVECTOR
CONVERTED
CONVERTER
CONVINCED
CONVIVIAL
CURVATURE
DRAVIDIAN
ELEVATION
ELEVENSES
FERVENTLY
FLAVORING
FLAVOURED
FRIVOLITY
FRIVOLOUS
GALVANISM
GALVANIZE
GRAVADLAX
GRAVESEND
GRAVESIDE
GRAVEYARD
GRAVITATE
HARVESTER
HEAVINESS
HEAVISIDE
HEAVYDUTY
HELVELLYN
LAEVULOSE
MARVELOUS
NERVOUSLY
OLIVENITE
PEEVISHLY
PERVASION
PERVASIVE
PERVERTED
POLVERINE
PREVALENT
PREVERNAL
PRIVATEER
PRIVATELY
PRIVATION
PRIVATIZE
PRIVILEGE
PROVEDORE
PROVENDER
PROVIDENT
PROVIDING
PROVISION
PROVOKING
PROVOLONE
PULVERIZE
QUAVERING
QUIVERFUL
QUIVERING
SALVARSAN
SALVATION
SAUVIGNON
SCAVENGER
SERVICING
SERVIETTE
SERVILELY
SERVILITY
SERVITUDE
SHAVELING
SHIVERING
SHOVELFUL
SHOVELLER
SLAVISHLY
SLIVOVICA
SLIVOVITZ
SLOVENIAN
SOUVLAKIA
STAVANGER
STEVEDORE
STEVENSON
STOVEPIPE
SURVEYING
SURVIVING
SYLVANITE
TRAVELERS
TRAVELING
TRAVELLER
TREVELYAN
TRIVIALLY
UNIVALENT
UNIVERSAL
VALVASSOR
VELVETEEN
WOLVERINE
ANSWERING
ARKWRIGHT
AWKWARDLY
BLOWTORCH
BOXWALLAH
CHAWBACON
CROWNLIKE
CROWSBILL
CROWSFOOT
DARWINIAN
FLOWCHART
FLOWERBED
FLOWERING
FLOWERPOT
FLOWSTONE
FLYWEIGHT
FORWANDER
INDWELLER
INSWINGER
JAYWALKER
KNOWINGLY
KNOWLEDGE
MIDWIFERY
MIDWINTER
NORWEGIAN
OUTWARDLY
OUTWORKER
SEAWORTHY
SHEWBREAD
SHOWINESS
SHOWPIECE
SKEWWHIFF
SLOWCOACH
SNOWBOUND
SNOWDONIA
SNOWDRIFT
SNOWFLAKE
SNOWSHOES
SNOWSTORM
SNOWWHITE
SOUWESTER
STOWNLINS
VIEWPOINT
WANWORTHY
ALEXANDER
ALEXANDRA
DEOXIDISE
FLEXITIME
PROXIMATE
PROXIMITY
REEXAMINE
UNEXPOSED
AEPYORNIS
ANHYDRIDE
ANHYDRITE
ANHYDROUS
ANKYLOSIS
BARYSCOPE
BERYLLIUM
BICYCLIST
BODYGUARD
CARYOPSIS
CHRYSALIS
COPYRIGHT
COTYLEDON
DEHYDRATE
EASYGOING
EDDYSTONE
ENHYDRITE
EUMYCETES
GREYBEARD
GREYHOUND
GREYWACKE
HEDYPHANE
HESYCHASM
HESYCHAST
HIMYARITE
HOLYSTONE
HOUYHNHNM
KARYOTYPE
LABYRINTH
LADYSMITH
LAZYBONES
LILYWHITE
PLAYFULLY
PLAYGROUP
PLAYHOUSE
PLAYTHING
POLYANDRY
POLYESTER
POLYGONAL
POLYGRAPH
POLYNESIA
POLYPHONE
POLYPHONY
POLYTHENE
SATYRIDAE
SATYRINAE
SIBYLLINE
SISYPHEAN
TWAYBLADE
UNTYPICAL
AMAZEMENT
BRAZILIAN
CRAZINESS
DIAZEUXIS
DIZZINESS
ELIZABETH
FRIZZANTE
FUZZINESS
LAZZARONE
MEZZANINE
MEZZOTINT
MONZONITE
MUZZINESS
PIZZICATO
QUIZZICAL
TANZANIAN
WAYZGOOSE
WHIZZBANG

9:5

ABSTAINER
ACTUALITY
ACTUARIAL
ADORATION
ADULATION
AGALACTIC
AGGRAVATE
AGITATION
ALABASTER
ALEXANDER
ALEXANDRA
AMARANTIN
AMELAKITE
ANIMATION
ANOMALOUS
APPEALING
APPRAISAL
ARCHANGEL
ASTRAGALS
ASTRAKHAN
AVALANCHE
AVOCATION
AWKWARDLY
BACHARACH
BALDAQUIN
BALLADEER
BALLADIST
BANDALORE
BARBARIAN
BARBARITY
BARBAROUS
BARNABITE
BARNACLES
BARRACUDA
BATTALION
BEDJACKET
BEDRAGGLE
BELEAGUER
BERGAMASK
BERGANDER
BESPANGLE
BILLABONG
BLATANTLY
BOCCACCIO
BOMBARDON
BOMBASINE
BOMBASTIC
BORNAGAIN
BOSSANOVA
BOXWALLAH
BRIGADIER
BRIGADOON
BRITANNIA
BRITANNIC
BRUTALISM
BRUTALITY
BRUTALIZE
BUCCANEER
BUCHAREST
BULGARIAN
BYSTANDER
CACHAEMIA
CAESAREAN
CALCANEUM
CALCANEUS
CALDARIUM
CALVANISM
CAMPANILE
CAMPANULA
CANTABILE
CANVASSER
CAPTAINCY
CARBAMATE
CARBAMIDE
CARNATION
CARPACCIO
CASSANDRA
CASSATION
CASTANETS
CASUARINA
CATHARSIS
CATHARTIC
CAUCASIAN
CAUSATION
CELLARIST
CENTAURUS
CERTAINLY
CERTAINTY
CERVANTES
CESSATION
CHABAZITE
CHALAZION
CHAPARRAL
CHARABANC
CHARACTER
CHEVALIER
CHICANERY
CHINATOWN
CIRCADIAN
CLIMACTIC
COCKAIGNE
COCKATIEL
COLLAPSAR
COLLATION
COMBATANT
COMBATIVE
COMMANDER
COMPACTLY
COMPANIES
COMPANION
CONCAVITY
CONTAGION
CONTAINER
CORIANDER
COXSACKIE
CREMATION
CREMATORY
CURVATURE
CYCLAMATE
DAEDALIAN
DALMATIAN
DAMNATION
DARTAGNAN
DASTARDLY
DECLARING
DEFEATISM
DEFEATIST
DEFLATION
DEGRADING
DEMEANING
DEMEANOUR
DEPRAVITY
DESCARTES
DETRACTOR
DEUCALION
DEVIATION
DICTATION
DISCARDED
DISFAVOUR
DISMANTLE
DISPARAGE
DISPARATE
DISPARITY
DISTANTLY
DOGMATISM
DOGMATIZE
DONCASTER
DRAMATICS
DRAMATIST
DRAMATIZE
DUMBARTON
DUNGAREES
EDUCATION
EDUCATIVE
ELEGANTLY
ELEVATION
ELIZABETH
EMANATION
EMBRACERY
EMBRACING
EMBRANGLE
EMBRASURE
EMPHASIZE
EMULATION
ENCHANTED
ENCHANTER
ENCRATITE
ENDEARING
ENDEAVOUR
ENDPAPERS
ENGRAINED
ENGRAVING
ENSTATITE
ENTRAMMEL
ENTRANCED
EPEDAPHIC
EPHIALTES
EPIGAEOUS
EPINASTIC
EPULATION
ESPLANADE
ESTRANGED
ESTRAPADE
EUCHARIST
EUSKARIAN
EVAGATION
EVOCATION
EVOCATIVE
EVOCATORY
EXARATION
EXCLAIMED
EXORATION
EXPIATION
EXPIATORY
EXTRACTOR
EXTRADITE
EXUDATION
FANDANGLE
FANTASIZE
FANTASTIC
FEUDALISM
FEUDATORY
FINLANDIA
FIRMAMENT
FLOTATION
FOGRAMITE
FOREANENT
FORGATHER
FORJASKIT
FORMALIST
FORMALITY
FORMALIZE
FORMATION
FORMATIVE
FORTALICE
FORWANDER
FRICASSEE
FRIGATOON
FRUGALITY
FUNDAMENT
GALLABEAH
GALLANTLY
GALLANTRY
GALRAVAGE
GALVANISM
GALVANIZE
GARGANTUA
GARGARISM
GENEALOGY
GENIALITY
GERFALCON
GERIATRIC
GERMANCER
GERMANDER
GERMANITE
GERMANIUM
GESSAMINE
GESTATION
GIBRALTAR
GILGAMESH
GLUTAMINE
GODFATHER
GODPARENT
GONIATITE
GOOSANDER
GOSLARITE
GOSSAMERY
GOTHAMITE
GRADATION
GRAVADLAX
GREGARINE
GRENADIER
GRENADINE
GRIMALKIN
GRISAILLE
GUACAMOLE
GUARANTEE
GUARANTOR
GUITARIST
GUSTATION
GYMNASIUM
GYMNASTIC
HACKAMORE
HAEMALOMA
HAEMATITE
HAMFATTER
HAPHAZARD
HARDANGER
HARMALINE
HARMATTAN
HAYMAKING
HAYMARKET
HAYRADDIN
HERBALIST
HERBARIUM
HEREAFTER
HERMANDAD
HIERARCHY
HIMYARITE
HISTAMINE
HOBNAILED
HOCCAMORE
HODMANDOD
HOOLACHAN
HORTATIVE
HORTATORY
HUCKABACK
HUNGARIAN
HUSBANDLY
HUSBANDRY
HYDRANGEA
HYDRAULIC
HYDRAZINE
ICELANDER
ICELANDIC
IMBRANGLE
IMITATION
IMITATIVE
IMPEACHER
INDRAUGHT
INFLATION
INGRAINED
INSHALLAH
INSTANTER
INSTANTLY
ISCHAEMIC
ISOLATION
ISOTACTIC
JAGGANATH
JAMBALAYA
JAMPACKED
JAWBATION
JAYWALKER
JESSAMINE
JORDANIAN
JOVIALITY
JUXTAPOSE
KEPLARIAN
KIDNAPPED
KIDNAPPER
KILLARNEY
LACTATION
LAMPADARY
LAMPADION
LANCASTER
LANDAULET
LAPLANDER
LATRATION
LAUDATION
LAUDATORY
LAWMAKING
LAZZARONE
LETHARGIC
LEUKAEMIA
LEVIATHAN
LIBRARIAN
LINEAMENT
LIVRAISON
LOMBARDIC

LOOKALIKE
LOQUACITY
LOWLANDER
LUCRATIVE
LUCTATION
MACTATION
MADRASSAH
MAGDALENE
MAGNALIUM
MALLANDER
MAMMALIAN
MANDATORY
MANGANATE
MANGANESE
MANHANDLE
MANHATTAN
MARCASITE
MARGARINE
MARMALADE
MATTAMORE
MECHANICS
MECHANISM
MECHANIZE
MEDIAEVAL
MEDIATION
MENDACITY
MENTALITY
MENTATION
MERCAPTAN
MERGANSER
MESSALINA
METHADONE
MEZZANINE
MIDIANITE
MIDRASHIM
MIGRATION
MIGRATORY
MILLAMANT
MINIATURE
MISFALLEN
MISHANDLE
MISMANAGE
MITRAILLE
MOCCASINS
MONTACUTE
MONTAIGNE
MONTANISM
MONTANIST
MORGANITE
MORTALITY
MOYGASHEL
MRIDAMGAM
MRIDANGAM
MUGLARITE
MUSCADINE
MUSCARINE
NARRATION

NARRATIVE
NATHANIEL
NAUMACHIA
NECTARINE
NEPHALISM
NEPHALIST
NEURALGIA
NEURALGIC
NEWCASTLE
NEWMARKET
NEWSAGENT
NIGGARDLY
NONPAREIL
NORMALACY
NORMALITY
NORMALIZE
NORMATIVE
NOSTALGIA
NOSTALGIC
NYSTAGMUS
OCKHAMIST
OILTANKER
OLIGARCHY
ONOMASTIC
ONSLAUGHT
OPERATING
OPERATION
OPERATIVE
OPOBALSAM
ORGIASTIC
ORICALCHE
OROBANCHE
ORPHANAGE
ORPHARION
OSTRACISM
OSTRACIZE
OUTWARDLY
OVIPAROUS
OVULATION
OXIDATION
PACKAGING
PAGEANTRY
PALLADIAN
PALLADIUM
PALMATION
PALPATION
PANDATION
PANHANDLE
PANTAGAMY
PANTALEON
PANTALOON
PARDALOTE
PARNASITE
PARNASSUS
PARTAKING
PASSAMENT
PAUSANIAS

PAYMASTER
PEASANTRY
PEGMATITE
PEIRASTIC
PELLAGRIN
PELMANISM
PERCALINE
PERGAMENE
PERIAKTOS
PERIANDER
PERMANENT
PERVASION
PERVASIVE
PHALANGER
PHALAROPE
PHANARIOT
PHARAMOND
PHENACITE
PHENAKISM
PHIGALIAN
PHILANDER
PHILATELY
PHTHALATE
PICKABACK
PINEAPPLE
PIQUANTLY
PISTACHIO
PISTAREEN
PLACATORY
PLURALISM
PLURALITY
POETASTER
POLIANITE
POLYANDRY
POMPADOUR
POUJADIST
PRECATORY
PREDATORY
PREFATORY
PREHALLUX
PREMATURE
PREVALENT
PRIMAEVAL
PRIMARILY
PRIMAVERA
PRIVATEER
PRIVATELY
PRIVATION
PRIVATIZE
PROBABLES
PROBATION
PROCACITY
PROFANELY
PROFANITY
PROKARYON
PROLACTIN
PROLAMINE

PROMACHOS
PROPAGATE
PROTAMINE
PRYTANEUM
PUGNACITY
PULSATION
PURGATIVE
PURGATORY
PYGMALION
QUOTATION
RACCABOUT
RACCAHOUT
RACIALISM
RACIALIST
RADIANTLY
RADIATING
RADIATION
RASPATORY
REBOATION
RECLAIMED
RECLAIMER
RECTANGLE
REDHANDED
REEXAMINE
REFLATION
REFRACTOR
REHEARSAL
RENTALLER
REPLACING
REPTATION
RESNATRON
RESSALDAR
RETIARIUS
RETRACTOR
REVEALING
RIGMAROLE
ROSMARINE
ROUMANIAN
ROUMANSCH
RUINATION
SABBATIAN
SACRAMENT
SACRARIUM
SALVARSAN
SALVATION
SANDALLED
SANDARACH
SANTAYANA
SARBACANE
SARCASTIC
SASKATOON
SASSAFRAS
SATIATION
SCALARIUM
SCHIAVONE
SCHMALTZY
SCHNAPPER

SCHNAUZER
SEAFARING
SECTARIAN
SENSATION
SEPHARDIM
SERIALIST
SERIALIZE
SERIATION
SERRATION
SEXUALITY
SICCATIVE
SIGNALLER
SIGNALMAN
SIGNATORY
SIGNATURE
SINGALESE
SINGAPORE
SINKANSEN
SITUATION
SKEDADDLE
SKYJACKER
SOCIALISM
SOCIALIST
SOCIALITE
SOCIALIZE
SPADASSIN
SPREADING
SQUEAMISH
STAVANGER
STERADIAN
STIRABOUT
STOMACHIC
STREAMING
STRIATION
SUBJACENT
SUBMARINE
SULTANATE
SUMMARILY
SUMMARIZE
SUMMATION
SUNBATHER
SUNTANNED
SUQUAMISH
SUSTAINED
SYLLABARY
SYLLABLES
SYLVANITE
SYNTACTIC
SYRIACISM
TABLATURE
TALKATIVE
TANTALITE
TANTALIZE
TANTARARA
TANZANIAN
TAPDANCER
TARMACKED

TARNATION
TARPAULIN
TARRAGONA
TARTAREAN
TASMANIAN
TENTATIVE
TERMAGANT
TERMAGENT
TERRACING
TERRARIUM
TESTAMENT
TESTATRIX
TETRAGRAM
TETRALOGY
TETRARCHY
THALASSIC
THANATISM
THERALITE
THERAPIST
THESAURUS
THREADFIN
THROATILY
THYLACINE
THYRATRON
TICTACTOE
TIMPANIST
TITRATION
TOCCATINA
TOPIARIST
TORBANITE
TOSCANINI
TRAFALGAR
TREMATODE
TRIBALISM
TRISAGION
TROPAELIN
TROPARION
TURMAGENT
TURNABOUT
TYMPANIST
UMBRATILE
UNABASHED
UNBIASSED
UNCEASING
UNCHANGED
UNCHARGED
UNCLAIMED
UNGUARDED
UNHEALTHY
UNITARIAN
UNIVALENT
UNLEARNED
UNSCATHED
UNSHACKLE
UNSPARING
UNTRAINED
URINATION

VALIANTLY
VALUATION
VALVASSOR
VANDALISM
VANDALIZE
VARIATION
VENIALITY
VERBALIZE
VERBASCUM
VERKAMPTE
VERSATILE
VESPASIAN
VIBRATILE
VIBRATION
VIBRATORY
VIOLATION
VISUALIZE
VITIATION
VULCANIST
VULCANITE
VULCANIZE
VULGARIAN
VULGARISM
VULGARITY
WAGHALTER
WALKABOUT
WALLABIES
WHITAKERS
WINCANTON
WOLLASTON
ZEALANDER
ZINFANDEL
ZOOMANTIC
ZOROASTER
ACROBATIC
ADUMBRATE
ALDEBARAN
ALGEBRAIC
AYCKBOURN
BACKBENCH
BACKBITER
BAREBONES
BARMBRACK
BASEBOARD
BILLBOARD
BIRDBRAIN
BLUEBEARD
BLUEBERRY
BRAMBLING
CALABOOSE
CALABRESE
CALIBRATE
CARDBOARD
CARIBBEAN
CELEBRANT
CELEBRATE
CELEBRITY
CEREBRATE
CHAWBACON
CHILBLAIN
CHIPBOARD
CLAPBOARD
CLIPBOARD
CORNBRASH
CRANBERRY
CRANBORNE
CRUMBLING
DARTBOARD
DASHBOARD
DISABLING
DISOBLIGE
DUCKBOARD
EASTBOUND
EDINBURGH
ESTABLISH
EXHIBITOR
FIREBRAND
FIREBREAK
FOOTBRAKE
FOREBEARS
FRAMBOISE
FREEBOARD
FULLBLOWN
GARIBALDI
GREYBEARD
GRUBBINOL
GRUMBLING
HAIRBRUSH
HALFBAKED
HALOBIONT
HANDBRAKE
HARDBOARD
HEADBOARD
HIDEBOUND
HILLBILLY
HYLOBATES
IDIOBLAST
ILLIBERAL
INCUBATOR
INHIBITED
INUMBRATE
JUNEBERRY
KARABINER
LACKBEARD
LAMPBLACK
LAZYBONES
LINDBERGH
LUCUBRATE
MALEBOLGE
MANUBRIUM
MEATBALLS
MESOBLAST
METABASIS
METABOLIC
MIRABELLE
MOTHBALLS
NASEBERRY
NOSEBLEED
OCTOBRIST
OUROBOROS
OUROBORUS
OVERBLOWN
OVERBOARD
PARABASIS
PARABLAST
PARABOLIC
PERIBOLOS
PHLEBITIS
PLUMBEOUS
PLUMBLINE
PRESBYTER
RASPBERRY
REIMBURSE
ROADBLOCK
SALUBRITY
SCAMBLING
SCORBUTIC
SCORBUTUS
SCRUBBING
SEMIBREVE
SHEWBREAD
SHRUBBERY
SIDEBOARD
SIDEBURNS
SIGNBOARD
SLUMBERER
SNOWBOUND
STARBOARD
STROBILUS
STUMBLING
SURFBOARD
SWINBURNE
TAILBOARD
TENEBROSE
TEREBINTH
THEOBROMA
THROBBING
THUMBLING
THUMBNAIL
THUMBTACK
TICHBORNE
TREMBLING
TROUBADOR
TURNBULLS
TWAYBLADE
VANTBRASS
WAHABIITE
WASHBASIN
WASHBOARD
WELLBEING
WELLBUILT
WESTBOUND
WINDBREAK
WINEBERRY
WOODBORER
ABDUCTION
ACONCAGUA
ADDICTION
ADDICTIVE
ADJECTIVE
ADVECTION
ADVOCATED
AFFECTING
AFFECTION
AGINCOURT
AGUECHEEK
ALLOCARPY
ANARCHIST
ANTICLINE
ARAUCARIA
ARTICHOKE
ARTICULAR
ASSOCIATE
ASTUCIOUS
ATROCIOUS
ATTACKING
AUDACIOUS
AURICULAR
AUTOCLAVE
AUTOCRACY
AUTOCROSS
AVUNCULAR
BACKCLOTH
BALACLAVA
BASECOURT
BASICALLY
BICYCLIST
BINOCULAR
BISECTION
BLEACHERS
BRANCHING
BREECHING
BRONCHIAL
CAPACIOUS
CAPACITOR
CARACALLA
CATACLYSM
CATACOMBS
CATECHISM
CATECHIZE
CHURCHILL
CHURCHMAN
COARCTATE
COMICALLY
CONSCIOUS
CONSCRIPT
CORNCRAKE
CRESCELLE
CRESCENDO
CROTCHETY
CYNICALLY
DECACHORD
DECKCHAIR
DECOCTION
DEDICATED
DEDUCTION
DEDUCTIVE
DEFECTION
DEFECTIVE
DEFICIENT
DEJECTION
DELACROIX
DELICIOUS
DEMOCRACY
DEPICTION
DESECRATE
DESICCATE
DETECTION
DETECTIVE
DIDACTICS
DIRECTION
DIRECTIVE
DIRECTORS
DIRECTORY
DISHCLOTH
DOMICILED
EFFECTIVE
EFFECTUAL
EFFICIENT
ENDECAGON
ENDOCRINE
ENUNCIATE
EPARCHATE
EPISCOPAL
EUMYCETES
EXERCISED
EXERCISES
EXPECTANT
EXPECTING
EXSICCATE
FABACEOUS
FACECLOTH
FAULCHION
FEDUCIARY
FERACIOUS
FEROCIOUS
FIDUCIARY
FILICALES
FINICKING
FINICKITY
FLOWCHART
FORECLOSE
FORECOURT
FRANCESCA
FRANCHISE
FRANCOLIN
FRATCHETY
FRENCHMAN
FRENCHMEN
FUGACIOUS
FUNICULAR
FURACIOUS
GALACTOSE
GATECRASH
GOLDCREST
HAECCEITY
HANDCUFFS
HARDCOVER
HEADCLOTH
HESYCHASM
HESYCHAST
HIGHCLASS
HIJACKING
HOLOCAUST
HOMICIDAL
HOPSCOTCH
HYPOCAUST
HYPOCRISY
HYPOCRITE
ILLICITLY
IMPACTION
INDECENCY
INDECORUM
INDICATES
INDICATOR
INDICTION
INDUCTION
INDUCTIVE
INFECTING
INFECTION
INJECTION
INNOCENCE
INNOCUOUS
INUNCTION
INVECTIVE
IRASCIBLE
ISOSCELES
JUDICIARY
JUDICIOUS
KILOCYCLE
KINKCOUGH
KNEECORDS
LATECOMER
LATICLAVE
LAUNCELOT
LAUNCHING
LOBSCOUSE
LOGICALLY
LOINCLOTH
LONGCHAMP
LUDICROUS
LYRICALLY

MAGICALLY
MALACHITE
MALICIOUS
MASOCHISM
MASOCHIST
MEDICALLY
MEDICATED
MEDICINAL
MEGACYCLE
MEPACRINE
MINACIOUS
MISOCLERE
MOLECULAR
MONACTINE
MONOCEROS
MONOCHORD
MONOCOQUE
MONOCULAR
MORECAMBE
MOTOCROSS
MUNICIPAL
MUSICALLY
MUSICHALL
NOMOCRACY
NOTOCHORD
NOVICIATE
NOVOCAINE
OBJECTION
OBJECTIVE
OBSECRATE
OCTACHORD
OFFICIALS
OFFICIANT
OFFICIATE
OFFICIOUS
OLFACTORY
OPERCULUM
OPTICALLY
ORBICULAR
OVERCLOUD
OVERCROWD
PARACHUTE
PARACLETE
PARACUSIS
PAROCHIAL
PAROCHINE
PEDICULAR
PERICLASE
PERICUTIN
PINOCCHIO
POLICEMAN
POSTCARDS
PREOCCUPY
PRESCIENT
PRESCRIBE
PRESCUTUM
PRINCETON
PRINCIPAL
PRINCIPLE
PROACTIVE
PROSCRIBE
PUSHCHAIR
QUERCETIN
QUERCETUS
RADICALLY
RADICCHIO
RAINCHECK
RAPACIOUS
REDUCIBLE
REDUCTION
REFECTION
REFECTORY
REJECTION
RELUCTANT
REPECHAGE
RETICENCE
RETICULUM
REVICTUAL
RORSCHACH
ROUNCEVAL
ROUNCIVAL
RUBICELLE
SACKCLOTH
SAGACIOUS
SAILCLOTH
SALACIOUS
SALICETUM
SCONCHEON
SCORCHING
SCOTCHMAN
SCUNCHEON
SEARCHING
SEBACEOUS
SEDUCTION
SEDUCTIVE
SELACHION
SELECTING
SELECTION
SELECTIVE
SEMICOLON
SETACEOUS
SILICOSIS
SKETCHILY
SKETCHMAP
SKETCHPAD
SLOWCOACH
SOFTCOVER
SOLICITOR
SPEECHIFY
SPHACELUS
SPRECHERY
SPUNCULID
STANCHION
STERCORAL
STOICALLY
STRICTURE
STRUCTURE
SUBSCRIBE
SUBSCRIPT
SUNSCREEN
TENACIOUS
TENACULUM
THATCHING
THEOCRACY
TIERCERON
TIMOCRACY
TOPICALLY
TREACHERY
TRENCHANT
TRUNCATED
TRUNCHEON
TYPICALLY
UNDECIDED
UNLUCKILY
UNSECURED
URTICARIA
VARICELLA
VASECTOMY
VEHICULAR
VERACIOUS
VESICULAR
VIVACIOUS
VOLUCRINE
VORACIOUS
WARTCRESS
WASHCLOTH
WINDCHILL
WISECRACK
WOODCHUCK
WOODCRAFT
ZENOCRATE
ZOOSCOPIC
ABANDONED
ABANDONEE
ABUNDANCE
ACCIDENTS
AERODROME
AFFIDAVIT
AMENDMENT
AMYGDALUS
ANECDOTAL
ANECDOTES
ANHYDRIDE
ANHYDRITE
ANHYDROUS
ARMADILLO
ASSIDUITY
ASSIDUOUS
AVOIDABLE
AVOIDANCE
BEARDLESS
BEARDSLEY
BLANDNESS
BLINDFOLD
BLINDNESS
BLINDSPOT
BLINDWORM
BLOODBATH
BLOODLESS
BLOODSHED
BLOODSHOT
BLUNDERER
BOARDROOM
BOARDWALK
BOONDOCKS
BOUNDLESS
BRANDIRON
BREADLINE
BROADCAST
BROADLOOM
BROADSIDE
BULLDOZER
CALEDONIA
CHILDCARE
CHILDHOOD
CHILDLESS
CHILDLIKE
CHONDRITE
CHONDROID
CLOUDLESS
DAREDEVIL
DECADENCE
DECIDEDLY
DECIDUOUS
DEHYDRATE
DIANDROUS
DIVIDENDS
DWINDLING
ECARDINES
ECHIDNINE
ENHYDRITE
EPHEDRINE
EXPEDIENT
FATIDICAL
FIELDFARE
FIELDSMAN
FIELDWORK
FIREDRAKE
FLOODGATE
FOUNDLING
GLANDULAR
GLENDOWER
GRANDIOSE
GRANDNESS
GRANDSIRE
GUARDROOM
GUARDSMAN
GUILDHALL
HALFDOZEN
HAMADRYAD
HEADDRESS
HEARDSMAN
HERODOTUS
IMMEDIACY
IMMEDIATE
IMMODESTY
IMPEDANCE
IMPUDENCE
INAUDIBLE
INAUDIBLY
INCIDENCE
INSIDIOUS
INVIDIOUS
IRRADIANT
IRRADIATE
JAUNDICED
JURIDICAL
KLENDUSIC
LANDDROST
LASTDITCH
LAUNDRESS
LURIDNESS
MACADAMIA
MACEDOINE
MACEDONIA
MEANDRIAN
MELODIOUS
MELODRAMA
MENADIONE
MOGADISHU
MONODRAMA
NAKEDNESS
NICODEMUS
NOVODAMUS
OMBUDSMAN
OVERDRAFT
OVERDRAWN
OVERDRESS
OVERDRIVE
PALUDRINE
PIPEDREAM
PLUMDAMAS
PLUNDERER
PROUDHORN
PSEUDAXIS
PSEUDONYM
READDRESS
REPUDIATE
RESIDENCE
RESIDENCY
RESIDUARY
ROUNDBACK
ROUNDELAY
ROUNDFISH
ROUNDHAND
ROUNDHEAD
ROUNDSMAN
SCALDFISH
SCRODDLED
SCUDDALER
SHELDDUCK
SHELDRAKE
SKINDIVER
SNOWDONIA
SNOWDRIFT
SOUNDBITE
SOUNDLESS
SOUNDNESS
SOURDOUGH
SPEEDBOAT
SPEEDWELL
SPELDRING
SPINDRIER
SPINDRIFT
SQUADRONE
STANDARDS
STANDERBY
STANDGALE
STANDPIPE
STEADFAST
STRIDENCY
SUBEDITOR
SWADDLING
SWORDFISH
SWORDPLAY
SWORDSMAN
SYNEDRION
TAXIDERMY
TESTDRIVE
THIRDSMAN
THUNDERER
TIREDNESS
TREADMILL
TRONDHEIM
VELODROME
VERIDICAL
VIVIDNESS
WEIRDNESS
WITHDRAWN
WORLDWIDE
WYANDOTTE
ABASEMENT
ABATEMENT
ACADEMIST
ACCRETION
ACUTENESS
ADDRESSED
ADDRESSEE
AFORESAID
AGAMEMNON
AGGREGATE
AGGRESSOR

AGREEABLE
AGREEABLY
AGREEMENT
AIMLESSLY
ALCHEMIST
AMAZEMENT
AMSTERDAM
AMUSEMENT
ANALEPTIC
ANSWERING
APPLEJACK
APPREHEND
ARABESQUE
ARCHETYPE
ARQUEBUSE
ASCLEPIUS
ASHKENAZI
ASPLENIUM
ASSUETUDE
ASYNERGIA
ATHLETICS
ATONEMENT
AUSTERITY
AUTHENTIC
AWAKENING
AWARENESS
BACTERIAL
BACTERIUM
BALLERINA
BANTERING
BARCELONA
BARMECIDE
BARTENDER
BASKETFUL
BEDFELLOW
BEEFEATER
BEEKEEPER
BELIEVING
BELVEDERE
BENBECULA
BERKELIUM
BETTERTON
BIGHEADED
BLAMELESS
BOANERGES
BOOMERANG
BORDEREAU
BORDERING
BOULEVARD
BRASENOSE
BRIDEWELL
BROKERAGE
BUCKETFUL
BUDGETARY
BUNDESTAG
BURLESQUE
BUTTERBUR
BUTTERCUP
BUTTERFLY
BUTTERNUT
CABLEGRAM
CACHECTIC
CANCEROUS
CANNELURE
CAREERIST
CARMELITE
CARNELIAN
CARPENTER
CARPENTRY
CARPETING
CARTESIAN
CASSEROLE
CATHEDRAL
CATHEPSIN
CATHERINE
CAUTERIZE
CEASEFIRE
CEASELESS
CENTENARY
CENTERING
CHAMELEON
CHAPERONE
CHAVENDER
CHISELLER
CHOLELITH
CIMMERIAN
CLARENDON
CLEVELAND
CLOSENESS
COALESCED
COFFERDAM
COLLEAGUE
COLLECTED
COLLECTOR
COLLEGIAN
COMMENSAL
COMPELLED
COMPETENT
COMPETING
CONCEALED
CONCEITED
CONCERNED
CONCERTED
CONDEMNED
CONDENSER
CONFESSED
CONFESSOR
CONGENIAL
CONGERIES
CONGESTED
CONNECTED
CONNECTOR
CONNEXION
CONSENSUS
CONTEMPER
CONTENDER
CONTENTED
CONVECTOR
CONVERTED
CONVERTER
COOPERATE
CORNEILLE
CORNELIAN
CORNERMAN
CORRECTED
CORRECTLY
CORRECTOR
CORREGGIO
CORRELATE
COSMETICS
CRIBELLUM
CRITERION
CRUDENESS
CUPRESSUS
CURRENTLY
CYMBELINE
DAMNEDEST
DANDELION
DANGEROUS
DEAFENING
DECRETALS
DEFLECTOR
DENSENESS
DEPRECATE
DEPREDATE
DEPRESSED
DESPERADO
DESPERATE
DESUETUDE
DEUTERIUM
DEXTERITY
DEXTEROUS
DIALECTAL
DIALECTIC
DIAMETRIC
DIANETICS
DIAZEUXIS
DIETETICS
DIFFERENT
DINNERSET
DISBELIEF
DISMEMBER
DISPENSER
DISPERSAL
DISPERSED
DISREGARD
DISREPAIR
DISREPUTE
DISSEMBLE
DISSENTER
DISTEMPER
DISTENDED
DITHERING
DIXIELAND
DOTHEBOYS
DROMEDARY
DUNGENESS
DUNGEONER
DUODECIMO
DYSPEPSIA
DYSPEPTIC
EAGLEWOOD
EARNESTLY
EASTERNER
EGAREMENT
ELATERIUM
ELEMENTAL
ELEVENSES
ELOPEMENT
EMINENTLY
EMPAESTIC
EMPLECTON
ENAMELLED
ENCHEASON
ENDLESSLY
ENGRENAGE
ENSHEATHE
ENTRECHAT
ENTRECÔTE
ENTREMETS
ENUMERATE
EPICEDIUM
EPICENTRE
EPIDERMIS
EPILEPTIC
EROGENOUS
ESTHETICS
ESTRELDID
EUDAEMONY
EUPHEMISM
EVIDENTLY
EVITERNAL
EXCHEQUER
EXCREMENT
EXODERMIS
EXONERATE
EXPLETIVE
EXPRESSED
EXPRESSLY
EXTREMELY
EXTREMISM
EXTREMIST
EXTREMITY
EXUBERANT
EYELETEER
FALSEHOOD
FALSENESS
FASTENING
FATTENING
FERMENTED
FERVENTLY
FIFTEENTH
FILTERING
FILTERTIP
FINGERING
FINGERTIP
FISHERMAN
FLABELLUM
FLAGELLIN
FLAGELLUM
FLAGEOLET
FLORESTAN
FLOWERBED
FLOWERING
FLOWERPOT
FLYWEIGHT
FOLKETING
FORCEMEAT
FORFEITED
FORGETFUL
FORGETIVE
FORJESKIT
FRAMEWORK
FRATERNAL
FREDERICK
FULLERENE
GARDENING
GARDEROBE
GASPEREAU
GATHERING
GAUDEAMUS
GAULEITER
GENTEELLY
GEODESIST
GEOMETRIC
GEOMETRID
GIBBERISH
GINGERADE
GLABELLAR
GLOMERATE
GLOMERULE
GLYCERIDE
GLYCERINE
GODDESSES
GOOSEFOOT
GOOSEHERD
GOOSENECK
GOOSESTEP
GOSPELLER
GRACELESS
GRAPESHOT
GRAPETREE
GRAPEVINE
GRAVESEND
GRAVESIDE
GRAVEYARD
GROCERIES
GROTESQUE
GUATEMALA
GUIDEBOOK
GUIDELINE
GUILELESS
GUINEVERE
GUTTERING
GYNOECIUM
HALFEMPTY
HAMMERING
HANKERING
HANSEATIC
HAPPENING
HARLEQUIN
HARLESTON
HARVESTER
HASHEMITE
HASTENING
HELLEBORE
HELVELLYN
HENPECKED
HERPESTES
HESPERIAN
HESTERNAL
HINDEMITH
HINGELESS
HODIERNAL
HOLDERBAT
HOLLERITH
HORDEOLUM
HORSEBACK
HORSEHAIR
HORSELESS
HORSEPLAY
HORSESHOE
HORSETAIL
HORSEWHIP
HOTHEADED
HOTTENTOT
HOUSEBOAT
HOUSECOAT
HOUSEHOLD
HOUSEMAID
HOUSEROOM
HOUSEWIFE
HOUSEWORK
HOYDENISH
HUTTERITE
HYGIENIST
HYPHENATE
HYSTERICS
ICHNEUMON
ILCHESTER
IMAGELESS
IMPLEMENT

IMPRECATE
IMPRECISE
IMPRESSED
INCLEMENT
INCREASED
INCREMENT
INDWELLER
INELEGANT
INFIELDER
INFLEXION
INGLENOOK
INNKEEPER
INSPECTOR
ISOMERASE
ISOMETRIC
ISRAELITE
ITINERANT
ITINERARY
ITINERATE
JANSENISM
JANSENIST
JENNETING
JESSERANT
JITTERBUG
JOBCENTRE
JOBSEEKER
JUDGEMENT
JUNKETING
KERMESITE
KIESERITE
KILDERKIN
KITTENISH
LANCEWOOD
LARGENESS
LATTERDAY
LEASEHOLD
LECHEROUS
LEICESTER
LENIENTLY
LETTERBOX
LETTERING
LICKERISH
LINGERING
LIQUEFIED
LISTENING
LODGEMENT
LOITERING
LONGEDFOR
LONGEVITY
LOOSEHEAD
LOOSELEAF
LOOSENESS
LOUSEWORT
LUCRETIUS
LUMBERING
MACKENZIE
MADDENING

MADREPORE
MADRESSAH
MAGDEBURG
MAGNESIUM
MAGNETISM
MAGNETIZE
MAGNETRON
MALLEABLE
MALLEMUCK
MALLENDER
MALLEOLUS
MANGETOUT
MANNEQUIN
MANNERING
MANNERISM
MANOEUVRE
MAPPEMOND
MARKETEER
MARKETING
MARVELOUS
MASTERFUL
MASTERMAN
MEDMENHAM
MEDRESSEH
MENDELISM
MERCENARY
MERCERIZE
MESMERISM
MESMERIZE
MESSENGER
METHEGLIN
MILLENIAL
MILLENIUM
MILLEPEDE
MILLEPORE
MINCEMEAT
MINNESOTA
MISBEHAVE
MISTEMPER
MOCKERNUT
MONTESPAN
MONTEZUMA
MOTHEATEN
MOTHERING
MOUSEHOLE
MOUSELIKE
MOUSETRAP
MUCKENDER
MUFFETTEE
MURDERESS
MURDEROUS
MUSKETEER
MUSKETOON
MUTTERING
MYRMECOID
MYSTERIES
NAPIERIAN

NATHELESS
NATHEMORE
NAUSEATED
NEGLECTED
NEPHELINE
NIDDERING
NIEBELUNG
NIPPERKIN
NOBLENESS
NOISELESS
NOLLEKENS
NORWEGIAN
NUCLEOLUS
NURSEMAID
OBSCENELY
OBSCENITY
OBSTETRIC
OFFSEASON
OLENELLUS
OLIVENITE
ONTHESPOT
OPENENDED
OPODELDOC
OPPRESSED
OPPRESSOR
OPULENTLY
ORCHESTRA
ORIGENIST
OTTRELITE
OURSELVES
OVEREXERT
OZOCERITE
OZOKERITE
PALAESTRA
PALPEBRAL
PANDEMIAN
PARHELION
PASSENGER
PASSEPIED
PASSERINE
PASTERNAK
PATIENTLY
PATTERNED
PEACEABLE
PEACEABLY
PEACETIME
PEASEWEEP
PENDENNIS
PENTECOST
PEPPERONI
PEPPERPOT
PERAEOPOD
PERFECTLY
PERFERVID
PERMEABLE
PERPETUAL
PERSECUTE

PERSEVERE
PERVERTED
PHONECARD
PHONETICS
PIACEVOLE
PICKETING
PIECEMEAL
PIECEWORK
PIGHEADED
PIGNERATE
PILFERAGE
PILFERING
PIMPERNEL
PINKERTON
PLACEMENT
PLANETARY
POCKETFUL
POLVERINE
POLYESTER
POMOERIUM
PONDEROSA
PONDEROUS
POPPERING
PORBEAGLE
PORCELAIN
PORTERAGE
POSSESSED
POSSESSOR
POSTERIOR
POSTERITY
PREBENDAL
PRECEDENT
PRECEDING
PRECENTOR
PRECEPTOR
PREFERRED
PRELECTOR
PRESENTED
PRESENTER
PRESENTLY
PRESERVED
PRESERVER
PRESERVES
PRETENDER
PRETERITE
PRETERMIT
PREVERNAL
PRICELESS
PROCEDURE
PROCERITY
PROCESSOR
PROFESSED
PROFESSOR
PROJECTED
PROJECTOR
PROLEPSIS
PROMENADE

PROPELLED
PROPELLER
PROPELLOR
PROPERDIN
PROSECUTE
PROSELYTE
PROTECTOR
PROTESTER
PROVEDORE
PROVENDER
PRUDENTLY
PULVERIZE
PUMMELLED
PUNGENTLY
PUPPETEER
QUARENDEN
QUAVERING
QUIVERFUL
QUIVERING
RACKETEER
RATHERIPE
RATHERISH
REDDENDUM
REDEEMING
REDHEADED
REDLETTER
REFLECTOR
REFLEXION
REFLEXIVE
REFRESHER
REGRETFUL
REGUERDON
REITERATE
RENDERING
REPLENISH
REPLETION
REPLETIVE
REPREHEND
REPRESENT
REPRESSED
RESPECTED
RESPECTER
RHODESIAN
RHYMESTER
RICHELIEU
RIDGEBACK
RILLETTES
RIPIENIST
ROOSEVELT
ROQUEFORT
ROSTELLUM
ROTTERDAM
RUBBERIZE
RUDBECKIA
RUGGELACH
RUTHENIAN
RUTHENIUM

SACKERSON
SADDENING
SANHEDRIM
SANHEDRIN
SANHEDRON
SARMENTUM
SASSENACH
SAUCEBOAT
SAUTERNES
SCALEABLE
SCAPEGOAT
SCARECROW
SCAVENGER
SCELERATE
SCHEELITE
SCHLEMIEL
SCHLEMIHL
SCHLENTER
SCHNECKEN
SCOLECITE
SCREENING
SECRETARY
SECRETION
SECRETIVE
SEDGEMOOR
SEGMENTED
SEGREGATE
SENSELESS
SEPTEMBER
SEQUESTER
SERREFILE
SHAKEDOWN
SHAMEFAST
SHAMELESS
SHAPELESS
SHARESMAN
SHAVELING
SHIVERING
SHOVELFUL
SHOVELLER
SICKENING
SINCERELY
SINCERITY
SISSERARY
SIXTEENMO
SIXTEENTH
SLOVENIAN
SMOKEFREE
SMOKELESS
SNAKEWEED
SOFTENING
SOLDERING
SOLFEGGIO
SOLFERINO
SOMMELIER
SONNETEER
SOOTERKIN

SORCERESS
SOSTENUTO
SOUTENEUR
SOUWESTER
SPACELESS
SPACESHIP
SPACESUIT
SPIDERWEB
SPIKENARD
SPINELESS
SPOKESMAN
STAGEHAND
STALEMATE
STALENESS
STATEHOOD
STATELESS
STATEMENT
STATEROOM
STATESIDE
STATESMAN
STATEWIDE
STEVEDORE
STEVENSON
STONEBOAT
STONECHAT
STONECROP
STONEHAND
STONELESS
STONEWALL
STONEWARE
STONEWORK
STONEWORT
STOREROOM
STOVEPIPE
STREETAGE
STREETCAR
STUPEFIED
SUBCELLAR
SUBMERGED
SUBTENANT
SUCCEEDED
SUCCENTOR
SUCCESSOR
SUFFERING
SUPREMACY
SUPREMELY
SURFEITED
SURREJOIN
SURRENDER
SURVEYING
SUSPECTED
SUSPENDED
SUSPENDER
SUSPENSOR
SWINEHERD
SYLLEPSIS
SYMMETRIC
SYNOECETE
TABLELAND
TABLEWARE
TANGERINE
TARGETEER
TASSELLED
TASTELESS
TEAKETTLE
TEIRESIAS
TEMPERATE
TENDERIZE
TENNESSEE
TENSENESS
TERSENESS
TETTEROUS
THELEMITE
THEREFORE
THEREUPON
THREEFOLD
THREESOME
TIPPERARY
TITHEBARN
TORMENTER
TORMENTIL
TORMENTOR
TORMENTUM
TORTELIER
TOTTENHAM
TOWCESTER
TRACEABLE
TRADEMARK
TRADESMAN
TRADEWIND
TRAGEDIAN
TRAGELAPH
TRAPEZIAL
TRAPEZIST
TRAPEZIUM
TRAPEZIUS
TRAPEZOID
TRAVELERS
TRAVELING
TRAVELLER
TREGEAGLE
TREGETOUR
TREVELYAN
TRIBESMAN
TRIBESMEN
TRICERION
TRIHEDRON
TRIMESTER
TRITENESS
TSAREVICH
TUILERIES
UMPTEENTH
UNCHECKED
UNDRESSED
UNFEELING
UNFLEDGED
UNHEEDING
UNISEXUAL
UNIVERSAL
UNPRECISE
UNSHEATHE
UNTREATED
UTICENSIS
VAGUENESS
VALDENSES
VALUELESS
VARIEGATE
VELLENAGE
VELVETEEN
VENGEANCE
VERBERATE
VERTEBRAE
VERTEBRAL
VIOLENTLY
VOICELESS
WAGNERIAN
WAGNERITE
WAITERAGE
WALDENSES
WAMBENGER
WANDERING
WASHERMAN
WASSERMAN
WASTELAND
WEAKENING
WEDGEWOOD
WEDNESDAY
WENCESLAS
WESTERNER
WHALEBOAT
WHALEBONE
WHALEMEAT
WHEREFORE
WHEREUPON
WHITEBAIT
WHITEDAMP
WHITEFISH
WHITEHALL
WHITEHEAD
WHITENESS
WHITENING
WHITEWALL
WHITEWASH
WHITEWING
WHITEWOOD
WHOLEFOOD
WHOLEMEAL
WHOLENESS
WHOLESALE
WHOLESOME
WILLEMITE
WILLESDEN
WINNEBAGO
WITHERING
WITHERITE
WITNESSED
WOBBEGONG
WOEBEGONE
WOLVERINE
WONDERFUL
WOODENTOP
WOOMERANG
WORCESTER
WORMEATEN
WULFENITE
WUTHERING
YESTERDAY
YESTEREVE
ZINKENITE
ALOOFNESS
ARTIFICER
BALEFULLY
BAREFACED
BASHFULLY
BEANFEAST
BLUFFNESS
BRIEFCASE
BRIEFNESS
BULLFIGHT
BULLFINCH
CAREFULLY
CHAFFINCH
CHAMFRAIN
CHAUFFEUR
CHIEFTAIN
COALFIELD
COCKFIGHT
CORNFIELD
CORNFLOUR
DISAFFIRM
DOLEFULLY
DUMBFOUND
DUTIFULLY
ESTAFETTE
FEARFULLY
FOREFRONT
FRETFULLY
GAINFULLY
GENUFLECT
GLEEFULLY
GOLDFIELD
GOLDFINCH
GRUFFNESS
HEADFIRST
HELPFULLY
HIGHFLYER
HOARFROST
HOPEFULLY
INEFFABLE
LINGFIELD
LUCIFERIN
MAINFRAME
MANIFESTO
MANSFIELD
MASEFIELD
MINEFIELD
NEWSFLASH
OUTOFTOWN
PAINFULLY
PALAFITTE
PITIFULLY
PLAYFULLY
PORIFERAN
PORTFOLIO
PROOFREAD
PURIFYING
REINFORCE
RINGFENCE
SANGFROID
SAXIFRAGE
SCRUFFILY
SEMIFINAL
SHEFFIELD
SHOPFLOOR
SHOPFRONT
SHUFFLING
SIEGFRIED
SKILFULLY
SKINFLINT
SNOWFLAKE
SOULFULLY
SPOFFORTH
STIFFENER
STIFFNESS
TACTFULLY
TEARFULLY
THRIFTILY
UNDEFILED
UNDEFINED
UNREFINED
UNRUFFLED
UPLIFTING
WALDFLUTE
WILLFULLY
WINDFALLS
WISTFULLY
WORKFORCE
ALLEGEDLY
ALLEGIANT
ALLIGATOR
ALLOGRAPH
ALONGSIDE
AMBIGUITY
AMBIGUOUS
ANALGESIA
ANALGESIC
ANTIGONUS
ARROGANCE
AUTOGRAPH
BARAGOUIN
BENIGHTED
BODYGUARD
BOLOGNESE
BOURGEOIS
BROUGHTON
CHARGEFUL
CLERGYMAN
CLINGFILM
COURGETTE
CRYOGENIC
CYNEGETIC
DELIGHTED
DEMAGOGUE
DENIGRATE
DESIGNATE
DESIGNING
DILIGENCE
DIRIGIBLE
DOWNGRADE
EASYGOING
EGREGIOUS
EIDOGRAPH
ELONGATED
EMERGENCE
EMERGENCY
ENERGETIC
ENERGUMEN
ENLIGHTEN
ESPAGNOLE
EVANGELIC
EVERGLADE
EVERGREEN
FAMAGUSTA
FENUGREEK
FILIGRAIN
FIREGUARD
FISHGUARD
FLEDGLING
FOREGOING
FRANGLAIS
FREIGHTER
FULLGROWN
GELIGNITE
GEORGETTE
GLENGARRY
GRADGRIND
GRINGOLET
GROSGRAIN
HARIGALDS
HECOGENIN
HEXAGONAL
HODOGRAPH

HOLOGRAPH
HOMEGROWN
HOMOGRAPH
HOURGLASS
IDEOGRAPH
IDIOGRAPH
ILLEGALLY
ILLEGIBLE
ILLEGIBLY
ILLOGICAL
IMMIGRANT
IMMIGRATE
INAUGURAL
INCOGNITO
INDIGENCE
INDIGNANT
INDIGNITY
INORGANIC
INTEGRATE
INTEGRITY
IPHIGENIA
IRREGULAR
ISINGLASS
LANDGRAVE
LIFEGUARD
LITIGIOUS
LOGOGRIPH
MALIGNANT
MALIGNITY
MENAGERIE
MONOGRAPH
MORTGAGEE
MORTGAGOR
NAVIGABLE
NAVIGATOR
OCTAGONAL
OLEOGRAPH
ONTOGENCY
ORANGEADE
ORANGEMAN
OVERGROWN
OWLEGLASS
PALSGRAVE
PANEGOISM
PANEGYRIC
PARAGOGUE
PARAGRAPH
PAREGORIC
PEDAGOGUE
PEDIGREES
PEREGRINE
PIERGLASS
PLAYGROUP
PLOUGHMAN
POLYGONAL
POLYGRAPH
PRONGHORN
PYONGYANG
RAINGAUGE
REARGUARD
RECOGNIZE
RELIGEUSE
RELIGIOSO
RELIGIOUS
REPUGNANT
SAFEGUARD
SDEIGNFUL
SLAUGHTER
SLINGBACK
SLINGSHOT
SLOUGHING
SMUGGLING
SPONGEBAG
SPRIGHTLY
STAGGERED
STARGAZER
STINGAREE
STRAGGLER
SWAGGERER
SWINGEING
SYNAGOGUE
TELEGRAPH
THINGUMMY
UNSIGHTLY
VAINGLORY
VISAGISTE
VOLAGEOUS
WALDGRAVE
WAYZGOOSE
WELTGEIST
WILDGEESE
WINEGLASS
WRANGLERS
WRONGDOER
WRONGFOOT
YOUNGSTER
ZEITGEIST
AESCHYLUS
AESTHETIC
AITCHBONE
ALCOHOLIC
AMENHOTEP
ANOPHELES
ANSCHLUSS
ANTIHELIX
APATHETIC
APOPHATIC
APOPHYSIS
ARACHNOID
BAKEHOUSE
BAKSHEESH
BALTHAZAR
BARTHOLDI
BARTHOLIN
BEACHHEAD
BEACHWEAR
BEETHOVEN
BENCHMARK
BIRTHMARK
BIRTHWORT
BOATHOUSE
BOLSHEVIK
BOSPHORUS
BROTHERLY
BRUNHILDE
BRUSHWOOD
CANTHARIS
CANTHARUS
CARTHORSE
CATCHCROP
CATCHMENT
CATCHPOLE
CATCHPOLL
CATCHWORD
CIRRHOSIS
CLUBHOUSE
COACHLOAD
COLCHICUM
COOKHOUSE
COUCHETTE
CRASHLAND
CUTTHROAT
DEATHLESS
DEATHTRAP
DEERHOUND
DIAPHRAGM
DIATHESIS
DISCHARGE
DOSSHOUSE
DOUKHOBOR
DYSPHAGIA
EARTHFLAX
EARTHLING
EARTHWORK
EARTHWORM
EPIPHRAGM
EPIPHYSIS
EPIPHYTIC
EPITHESIS
ESOPHAGUS
EYESHADOW
FAITHLESS
FARMHOUSE
FEATHERED
FLASHBACK
FLASHBULB
FLASHCUBE
FLECHETTE
FLESHLESS
FLESHPOTS
FLOPHOUSE
FOOLHARDY
FOOTHILLS
FORTHWINK
FORTHWITH
FRESHENER
FRESHNESS
FRIGHTFUL
FRITHBORH
GOMPHOSIS
GOONHILLY
GRAPHICAL
GREYHOUND
GUMSHIELD
HARSHNESS
HATCHBACK
HATCHMENT
HAUGHTILY
HAWTHORNE
HEATHLAND
HITCHCOCK
HITCHHIKE
HOARHOUND
HOREHOUND
HOUYHNHNM
HUNCHBACK
JERAHMEEL
KILOHERTZ
KITCHENER
KNIPHOFIA
LANTHANUM
LARGHETTO
LAUGHABLE
LIMEHOUSE
LIONHEART
LOATHSOME
LUNCHTIME
LYMPHATIC
MARCHPANE
MARSHLAND
MATCHLESS
MATCHLOCK
MATCHWOOD
MEGAHERTZ
MENSHEVIK
MIRTHLESS
MISCHANCE
MISSHAPEN
MOSCHATEL
MOUTHLESS
MOUTHWASH
MUJAHIDIN
MUMCHANCE
NARGHILLY
NAUGHTILY
NEIGHBOUR
NEUCHATEL
NEWSHOUND
NIPCHEESE
NORTHEAST
NORTHERLY
NORTHWARD
NORTHWEST
NOTCHBACK
OASTHOUSE
OFFCHANCE
OMOPHAGIC
OPENHEART
OVERHASTY
OVERHEADS
PANCHAYAT
PANTHEISM
PANTHENOL
PARCHEESI
PARCHMENT
PARTHENON
PARTHOLON
PATCHOULI
PATCHOULY
PATCHWORK
PAYCHEQUE
PEMPHIGUS
PENTHOUSE
PERCHANCE
PERCHERON
PINCHBECK
PINCHCOCK
PITCHFORK
PITCHPINE
PITCHPOLE
PITCHPOLL
PLAYHOUSE
PLETHORIC
POMPHOLYX
POORHOUSE
POSTHOUSE
PRESHRUNK
PROPHETIC
PROTHESIS
PROTHORAX
PSYCHICAL
PSYCHOSIS
PSYCHOTIC
PUNCHLINE
PURCHASER
PYRRHONIC
RACEHORSE
REACHABLE
REARHORSE
REICHSRAT
REICHSTAG
ROADHOUSE
ROUGHCAST
ROUGHNECK
ROUGHNESS
ROUGHSHOD
SACCHARIN
SANDHURST
SCHEHITAH
SCYTHEMAN
SHASHLICK
SHECHINAH
SHECHITAH
SHEPHERDS
SLAPHAPPY
SLIGHTEST
SLUGHORNE
SOUTHDOWN
SOUTHEAST
SOUTHERLY
SOUTHWARD
SOUTHWARK
SOUTHWEST
SPAGHETTI
SULPHONIC
SULPHURIC
SURCHARGE
SWOTHLING
SYLPHLIKE
SYMPHONIC
SYMPHYSIS
SYNCHYSIS
SYNTHESIS
SYNTHETIC
SYRPHIDAE
TAUCHNITZ
TEACHABLE
THIGHBONE
TOLLHOUSE
TOOTHACHE
TOOTHCOMB
TOOTHLESS
TOOTHPICK
TOOTHSOME
TOUCHDOWN
TOUCHLINE
TOUCHWOOD
TOUGHNESS
TRACHINUS
TROCHILIC
TROCHILUS
TRYPHOEUS
UNASHAMED
UNETHICAL
VOUCHSAFE
WANCHANCY
WAREHOUSE
WATCHWORD
WEIGHTING
WHICHEVER
WINDHOVER
WITCHETTY

WODEHOUSE
WOLFHOUND
WOODHOUSE
WORKHORSE
WORKHOUSE
WORTHLESS
XANTHIPPE
ZUCCHETTO
ABOLITION
ABOMINATE
ABORIGINE
ABSTINENT
ACARIASIS
ACCLIMATE
ACCLIVITY
ACQUIESCE
ACQUITTAL
ACUMINATE
ADJOINING
AFFLICTED
AFFRICATE
AGGRIEVED
AGONIZING
ALUMINIUM
AMERICIUM
AMPHIBIAN
AMPLIFIER
AMPLITUDE
AMUSINGLY
ANGLICISM
ANGUISHED
ANIMISTIC
APERIODIC
APERITIVE
APPLIANCE
APPLICANT
APPOINTED
APPOINTEE
ARABINOSE
ARCHIBALD
ARCHITECT
ARCHIVIST
ARCHIVOLT
ASSAILANT
ATAVISTIC
ATHEISTIC
ATTAINDER
ATTRIBUTE
ATTRITION
ATTUITION
AUBRIETIA
BADMINTON
BALLISTIC
BALTIMORE
BANDICOOT
BAPTISMAL
BARBITONE
BARRICADE
BARRISTER
BASTINADE
BASTINADO
BEATITUDE
BEDRIDDEN
BEDSITTER
BELLICOSE
BILLIARDS
BOSSINESS
BRAZILIAN
BULKINESS
BURKINABE
BURLINESS
CABRIOLET
CALCINATE
CALLIPERS
CALVINIST
CALVITIES
CANDIDACY
CANDIDATE
CAPRICCIO
CAPRICORN
CAPTIVATE
CAPTIVITY
CARCINOMA
CARNIVORE
CARTILAGE
CASTIGATE
CASTILIAN
CASUISTIC
CASUISTRY
CENTIPEDE
CERTIFIED
CERTITUDE
CHALIAPIN
CHAMINADE
CHARIVARI
CHEMISTRY
CHERISHED
CHORISTER
CHURIDARS
CIRCINATE
CLARIFIER
CLINICIAN
COALITION
COCHINEAL
COFFINITE
COGNITION
COGNITIVE
COGNIZANT
COLLIGATE
COLLIMATE
COLLISION
COMMISSAR
COMMITTAL
COMMITTED
COMMITTEE
CONCIERGE
CONCISELY
CONCISION
CONDIMENT
CONDITION
CONFIDANT
CONFIDENT
CONFIRMED
CONFITEOR
CONSIGNEE
CONSIGNOR
CONTINENT
CONTINUAL
CONTINUUM
CONVINCED
CONVIVIAL
CORDIALLY
CORTISONE
CRAZINESS
CREPITATE
CRETINOUS
CRIMINATE
CRITICISM
CRITICIZE
CRUCIALLY
CTESIPHON
CULMINATE
CULTIVATE
CUNEIFORM
CURTILAGE
CUSPIDORE
CYMBIDIUM
DALLIANCE
DANDIFIED
DARWINIAN
DECEITFUL
DECLINING
DECLIVITY
DENTISTRY
DENTITION
DEOXIDISE
DERRINGER
DESTITUTE
DETRIMENT
DETRITION
DIETICIAN
DIFFICULT
DIFFIDENT
DIGNIFIED
DIGNITARY
DINGINESS
DIRTINESS
DISFIGURE
DISMISSAL
DISSIDENT
DISSIPATE
DISTILLER
DIZZINESS
DODDIPOLL
DORMITION
DORMITORY
DRAVIDIAN
DULCINIST
DUNSINANE
DUPLICAND
DUPLICATE
DUPLICITY
ELIMINATE
ELUCIDATE
EMACIATED
EMOTIONAL
EMPTINESS
ENCHILADA
ENDEICTIC
ENERINITE
ENQUIRIES
EPINICION
EPINIKION
ERADICATE
EROTICISM
ERUCIFORM
ERUDITION
ESQUILINE
EUCLIDEAN
EVASIVELY
EXANIMATE
EXPLICATE
EXQUISITE
EXTRICATE
EXTRINSIC
FABRICATE
FACSIMILE
FACTIONAL
FASCINATE
FASHIONED
FEBRIFUGE
FENCIBLES
FERDINAND
FERTILITY
FERTILIZE
FESTINATE
FESTIVITY
FICTIONAL
FILLIPEEN
FILLISTER
FLAGITATE
FLEXITIME
FLORIMELL
FOGGINESS
FOOLISHLY
FORBIDDEN
FOREIGNER
FORFICATE
FORGIVING
FORNICATE
FORTILAGE
FORTITUDE
FOSSILISE
FRAGILITY
FRIGIDITY
FROBISHER
FUGGINESS
FULMINANT
FULMINATE
FUNGIBLES
FUNGICIDE
FURNIMENT
FURNITURE
FURTIVELY
FUSSINESS
FUSTIGATE
FUSTINESS
FUZZINESS
GALLICISM
GALLINULE
GALLIPOLI
GALLIVANT
GARNISHEE
GARNITURE
GAUDINESS
GAWKINESS
GENTILITY
GENUINELY
GERMICIDE
GERMINATE
GIDDINESS
GLADIATOR
GLADIOLUS
GLORIFIED
GLUCINIUM
GLUTINOUS
GMELINITE
GODLINESS
GRATICULE
GRATITUDE
GRAVITATE
GRIMINESS
HAMFISTED
HANDINESS
HANDIWORK
HAPPINESS
HARBINGER
HARDIHOOD
HARDINESS
HASTINESS
HEADINESS
HEAVINESS
HEAVISIDE
HEBRIDEAN
HENDIADYS
HERBICIDE
HERBIVORE
HERMITAGE
HEURISTIC
HOBBINOLL
HORRIFIED
HOSPITIUM
HOSTILITY
HUMDINGER
HURRICANE
HURRICANO
HURRIEDLY
HUSKINESS
IMAGINARY
IMBRICATE
IMPLICATE
INABILITY
INANIMATE
INANITION
INITIALLY
INITIATED
INITIATOR
INOPINATE
INQUILINE
INQUINATE
INQUIRING
INSPIRING
INSTIGATE
INSTITUTE
INSWINGER
INTRICACY
INTRICATE
INTRIGUED
INTRIGUER
INTRINSIC
INTUITION
INTUITIVE
INUSITATE
INVOICING
ITALICIZE
JEQUIRITY
JERKINESS
JUICINESS
JUSTIFIED
JUSTINIAN
KENTIGERN
KHALIFATE
KISSINGER
KITTIWAKE
KNOWINGLY
LAGNIAPPE
LANCINATE
LANKINESS
LAODICEAN
LARGITION
LASSITUDE
LAVOISIER

LIABILITY
LIMPIDITY
LIPPITUDE
LIQUIDATE
LIQUIDITY
LIQUIDIZE
LOCHINVAR
LOFTINESS
LONGICORN
LONGINGLY
LONGITUDE
LOWLINESS
LUBRICANT
LUBRICATE
LUSTIHOOD
LUSTINESS
MACHINATE
MACHINERY
MACHINING
MACHINIST
MADRILENE
MAGNIFIER
MAGNITUDE
MANDICATE
MANLINESS
MARTINEAU
MARTINMAS
MASSINGER
MASSIVELY
MASTICATE
MATRIARCH
MATRICIDE
MATRIMONY
MAURITIAN
MAURITIUS
MENDICANT
MENTICIDE
MENTIONED
MENUISIER
MERCILESS
MERRIMENT
MESSIANIC
METRICATE
MIDWIFERY
MIDWINTER
MILLIGRAM
MILLINERY
MILLIONTH
MILLIPEDE
MISDIRECT
MISFIRING
MISGIVING
MISPICKEL
MISSIONER
MISTIGRIS
MISTINESS
MOLLITIES
MONSIGNOR
MONTICULE
MOODINESS
MORBIDITY
MORTICIAN
MORTIFIED
MUDDINESS
MULTIFORM
MULTIPLEX
MULTITUDE
MURKINESS
MUSHINESS
MUSSITATE
MUSTINESS
MUZZINESS
MYSTICISM
NARCISSUS
NASTINESS
NEBBISHER
NEGLIGENT
NEGRITUDE
NEOLITHIC
NESCIENCE
NICTITATE
NIGRITUDE
NOISINESS
NUTRIMENT
NUTRITION
NUTRITIVE
OBBLIGATO
OBEDIENCE
OBSTINACY
OBSTINATE
OBTAINING
OCULIFORM
ODALISQUE
ORIGINATE
OUBLIETTE
OUTFITTER
OUTRIGGER
OUTSIDERS
PAGLIACCI
PALLIASSE
PALMISTRY
PALMITATE
PALPITATE
PANNIKELL
PARRICIDE
PARSIMONY
PARTIALLY
PARTICLES
PARTITION
PASSIVELY
PASSIVITY
PASTICCIO
PATRIARCH
PATRICIAN
PATRICIDE
PATRIMONY
PATRIOTIC
PAWKINESS
PEEVISHLY
PELLITORY
PENNILESS
PENSIONER
PENSIVELY
PERDITION
PERMITTED
PERSIMMON
PERTINENT
PESSIMISM
PESSIMIST
PESTICIDE
PESTILENT
PETHIDINE
PETRIFIED
PETTICOAT
PETTINESS
PETTITOES
PHARISAIC
PHILIPPIC
PHILISTER
PHYSICIAN
PHYSICIST
PICNICKER
PILLICOCK
PITUITARY
PITUITRIN
PIZZICATO
PLACIDITY
PLATITUDE
PLENITUDE
POLLINATE
POPLITEAL
PORRINGER
POSSIBLES
POTTINGAR
PRECIEUSE
PRECINCTS
PRECIPICE
PRECISELY
PRECISIAN
PRECISION
PRECISIVE
PREDICANT
PREDICATE
PREDICTOR
PREDIKANT
PREDILECT
PREFIGURE
PRESIDENT
PRESIDIAL
PRESIDIUM
PRIMITIAE
PRIMITIVE
PRIVILEGE
PROFITEER
PROLIXITY
PROMINENT
PROMISING
PROPIONIC
PROVIDENT
PROVIDING
PROVISION
PROXIMATE
PROXIMITY
PRURIENCE
PSORIASIS
PTERIDIUM
PUBLICIST
PUBLICITY
PUBLICIZE
PUBLISHED
PUBLISHER
PUERILITY
PUFFINESS
PULPITEER
QUALIFIED
QUALIFIER
QUASIMODO
QUERIMONY
QUOTIDIAN
QUOTITION
RAFFINOSE
RANCIDITY
RANDINESS
RANTIPOLE
READINESS
REALISTIC
REALITIES
REANIMATE
RECEIVING
RECTIFIER
RECTITUDE
REEDINESS
REJOICING
REJOINDER
REMAINDER
REMAINING
RENDITION
RENFIERST
REPLICATE
REPRIMAND
REPTILIAN
REQUISITE
RESTIFORM
RESTITUTE
RETAILING
RETAINING
RETRIEVAL
RETRIEVER
RISKINESS
ROSMINIAN
ROUTINELY
ROWDINESS
RUDDIGORE
RUFFIANLY
RUNCINATE
RUSTICATE
RUSTINESS
SACRIFICE
SACRILEGE
SACRISTAN
SALTINESS
SAUCINESS
SAUCISSON
SAUVIGNON
SCARIFIER
SCHLIEREN
SCHMIEDER
SCHNITTKE
SCHNITZEL
SCOLIOSIS
SCOLIOTIC
SECTIONAL
SEEMINGLY
SELFISHLY
SEMEIOTIC
SENSILLUM
SENSITIVE
SENSITIZE
SENTIENCE
SENTIMENT
SEPTIMOLE
SEQUINNED
SERVICING
SERVIETTE
SERVILELY
SERVILITY
SERVITUDE
SHADINESS
SHAKINESS
SHAMIANAH
SHOWINESS
SILLINESS
SLAVISHLY
SLIMINESS
SOBRIQUET
SOGGINESS
SOLDIERLY
SOLFIDIAN
SOLLICKER
SOPHISTER
SOPHISTIC
SOPHISTRY
SOPPINESS
SORTILEGE
SOTTISIER
SPARINGLY
SPATIALLY
SPECIALLY
SPECIALTY
SPECIFICS
SPECIFIED
SPECIMENS
SPICILEGE
SPICINESS
SPIRITOUS
SPIRITUAL
SPRAICKLE
STABILITY
STABILIZE
STAGIRITE
STATIONED
STATIONER
STATISTIC
STERILITY
STERILIZE
STOLIDITY
STORIATED
STRAINING
STUPIDITY
STYLISHLY
STYLISTIC
SUBDIVIDE
SUBLIMATE
SUBLIMELY
SUBSIDIZE
SUBTITLED
SUCCINATE
SULKINESS
SURCINGLE
SURLINESS
SURVIVING
SUSCITATE
SUSPICION
SWANIMOTE
SYMBIOSIS
SYMBIOTIC
SYNDICATE
TACHILITE
TACKINESS
TACTICIAN
TAHSILDAR
TARDINESS
TECTIFORM
TELLINGLY
TENAILLON
TEPHILLIN
TERMINATE
TERPINEOL
TERRICOLE
TERRIFIED
TERRITORY
TESTICLES

TESTIFIER
TESTIMONY
THYRISTOR
TIPSINESS
TRADITION
TRASIMENE
TREBIZOND
TRILITHON
TRIPITAKA
TRITICALE
TRIVIALLY
TRUTINATE
TUBBINESS
TURBIDITY
TURBINATE
TURPITUDE
UKRAINIAN
ULIGINOUS
UNANIMITY
UNANIMOUS
UNBRIDLED
UNFAILING
UNSKILLED
UNWRITTEN
UPANISHAD
URANISCUS
UREDINIAL
UROKINASE
VACCINATE
VELLICATE
VENTIFACT
VENTILATE
VERDIGRIS
VERMIFORM
VERMIFUGE
VERMILION
VERMINOUS
VERSIFIER
VERSIONAL
VERTIPORT
VESTIBULE
VESTIGIAL
VESTITURE
VIABILITY
VICTIMIZE
VINDICATE
VIOLINIST
VIRGINALS
VIRGINIAN
VIRGINITY
VIRGINIUM
VITRIOLIC
VOLTIGEUR
VOLTINISM
VORTICISM
VORTIGERN
VULPINITE
WASPISHLY
WEARINESS
WEARISOME
WILLINGLY
WITTICISM
WITTINGLY
WOOLINESS
WORDINESS
WORRISOME
WURLITZER
COADJUTOR
LEHRJAHRE
MARIJUANA
OVERJOYED
REYKJAVIK
UNINJURED
AFRIKAANS
AFRIKANER
BLACKBALL
BLACKBIRD
BLACKFACE
BLACKFOOT
BLACKHEAD
BLACKJACK
BLACKLEAD
BLACKLIST
BLACKMAIL
BLACKMORE
BLACKNESS
BLACKWOOD
BLINKERED
BLOCKHEAD
BREAKABLE
BREAKAGES
BREAKAWAY
BREAKDOWN
BREAKEVEN
BREAKFAST
BREAKNECK
BRICKWORK
BRICKYARD
BRISKNESS
CATSKILLS
CHECKBOOK
CHECKLIST
CHECKMATE
CHECKROOM
CHEEKBONE
CHICKADEE
CHICKWEED
CLOAKROOM
CLOCKWISE
CLOCKWORK
CRACKDOWN
CRACKLING
CRACKSMAN
CRICKETER
CROCKFORD
CROOKBACK
CROOKEDLY
DRINKABLE
DRUNKENLY
FRANKNESS
JACKKNIFE
KARAKORAM
KNACKERED
KNOCKDOWN
OUTSKIRTS
PRANKSTER
QUICKLIME
QUICKNESS
QUICKSAND
QUICKSTEP
SHARKSKIN
SHEIKHDOM
SLACKNESS
SLEEKNESS
SPARKLERS
SPARKLING
SPEAKEASY
STARKNESS
STINKBIRD
STINKHORN
STINKWOOD
STOCKFISH
STOCKHOLM
STOCKINET
STOCKINGS
STOCKPILE
STOCKROOM
STOCKWORK
STOCKYARD
STONKERED
THACKERAY
THANKLESS
THICKHEAD
THICKNESS
THINKABLE
TRACKLESS
TRACKSUIT
TRICKLESS
TRICKSTER
TRINKETER
TRUCKLOAD
TWINKLING
UNBEKNOWN
WELLKNOWN
WREAKLESS
WRECKFISH
AFFILIATE
AMBULANCE
ANAGLYPTA
ANAPLASTY
ANCILLARY
ANKYLOSIS
ANNULMENT
APOLLONUS
APPALLING
AQUILEGIA
ARTILLERY
ATHELSTAN
AUTOLATRY
AUTOLYCUS
AUTOLYSIS
AUXILIARY
AVAILABLE
BALALAIKA
BASILICAL
BASILICON
BATTLEAXE
BERYLLIUM
BETHLEHEM
BOBSLEIGH
BOOKLOVER
BOOTLACES
BOTTLEFUL
BRADLAUGH
BRIDLEWAY
BRILLIANT
BUMBLEBEE
CABALLERO
CANALETTO
CANDLELIT
CANDLEMAS
CAPILLARY
CATALEPSY
CATALOGUE
CATALYSIS
CATALYTIC
CATTLEMAN
CATTLEPEN
CAVALCADE
CHALLENGE
CHARLATAN
CHARLOTTE
CIPOLLINO
CIVILISED
CIVILIZED
COMPLAINT
COMPLIANT
CONCLUDED
CONFLATED
CORALLINE
COROLLARY
COTYLEDON
COVALENCY
COVELLITE
CUFFLINKS
DEADLIGHT
DECALITRE
DECALOGUE
DECILLION
DECOLLATE
DEFALCATE
DEFOLIANT
DEFOLIATE
DEMULCENT
DESULTORY
DEVELOPED
DEVELOPER
DEVILMENT
DIABLERIE
DIOCLETES
DISCLOSED
DISPLACED
DISPLAYED
DISPLEASE
DJELLABAH
DOODLEBUG
DOWELLING
EASTLINGS
EBRILLADE
EBULLIENT
EFFULGENT
EMBELLISH
EMOLLIATE
EMOLLIENT
EMPHLYSIS
ENCELADUS
ENCOLPION
ENCOLPIUM
ENROLMENT
ENTELECHY
ENUCLEATE
EPAULETTE
EPEOLATRY
EPICLESIS
EQUALIZER
ESCALATOR
ESCULENTS
ETHELBERT
ETIOLATED
EUCHLORIC
EXCALIBUR
EXCELLENT
EXCELSIOR
EXCULPATE
EXPULSION
FABULINUS
FALKLANDS
FEUILLANT
FIRELIGHT
FOMALHAUT
FOOTLOOSE
FREELANCE
FUSILLADE
GAVELKIND
GEARLEVER
GENTLEMAN
GENTLEMEN
GINGLYMUS
GLENLIVET
GODOLPHIN
GRUELLING
GUILLEMOT
GUILLOCHE
HARDLINER
HAZELWORT
HEADLIGHT
HEADLINED
HIGHLANDS
HIGHLIGHT
HIMALAYAN
HIMALAYAS
HUMILIATE
HYPALLAGE
IDEALOGUE
IMBALANCE
IMMELMANN
IMPELLING
IMPOLITIC
IMPULSION
IMPULSIVE
INCULCATE
INCULPATE
INDELIBLE
INDELIBLY
INDOLENCE
INDULGENT
INSELBERG
INSOLENCE
INSOLUBLE
INSOLVENT
INSULATOR
INSULTING
INTELLECT
INVOLUCRE
ISALLOBAR
JEWELLERY
JOCULARLY
JUBILANCE
KABELJOUW
KENTLEDGE
KINTLEDGE
KNOWLEDGE
LAMPLIGHT
LANDLOPER
LIBELLOUS
LIMELIGHT
LINKLATER
LJUBLJANA
LOCALIZED
LOCELLATE
LONGLIVED
MADELEINE

MATELASSE
MAXILLARY
MAYFLOWER
MEDALLION
MEDALLIST
METALLOID
METALWORK
MICKLETON
MIDDLEMAN
MIDDLESEX
MIDDLETON
MIDDLINGS
MINELAYER
MISPLACED
MISTLETOE
MODELLING
MODILLION
MONOLOGUE
MOONLIGHT
MUCHLOVED
MUGGLETON
MUTILATED
NONILLION
NOVELETTE
OCCULTIST
OCTILLION
ORGILLOUS
ORIFLAMME
OSCILLATE
OVERLYING
PAILLASSE
PAILLETTE
PANELLING
PANELLIST
PAPILLOTE
PARALYSIS
PARALYTIC
PARFLECHE
PEARLWORT
PECULATOR
PENDLETON
PENILLION
PERPLEXED
PETILLANT
PETULANCE
PHELLOGEN
PHILLABEG
PHILLIBEG
PHYLLOPOD
PONTLEVIS
POPULARLY
POPULATED
POWELLITE
PROCLITIC
PUCELLAGE
PUPILLAGE
PURULENCE
QUAILPIPE
QUILLWORT
QUODLIBET
RADCLIFFE
RADDLEMAN
RAMILLIES
RATTLEBAG
REBELLION
RECALLING
RECOLLECT
REDOLENCE
REFULGENT
REGULARLY
REGULATOR
REPELLENT
REPELLING
REPULSION
REPULSIVE
RESILIENT
RESULTANT
RESULTING
RETALIATE
REVELLING
REVOLTING
REVOLVING
REVULSION
RIGOLETTO
RUDDLEMAN
RUSHLIGHT
SADDLEBAG
SAFFLOWER
SATELLITE
SCABLANDS
SCAGLIOLA
SCALLAWAG
SCALLIONS
SCALLOPED
SCALLYWAG
SCARLATTI
SCHELLING
SCHILLING
SCHOLARCH
SCHOLARLY
SCHOLIAST
SEMBLANCE
SEPULCHER
SEPULCHRE
SEPULTURE
SHELLBACK
SHELLFISH
SHELLSUIT
SHETLANDS
SHIELDING
SHILLABER
SIBILANCE
SIBYLLINE
SICILIANO
SIDELIGHT
SIMILARLY
SIMPLETON
SIMPLISTE
SIMULATED
SIMULATOR
SIMULCAST
SINGLESEX
SINGLETON
SMALLNESS
SMALLTIME
SOLILOQUY
SOUVLAKIA
SPELLBIND
SPILLICAN
SPILLIKIN
SPOILSMAN
SPOTLIGHT
SQUALIDLY
STABLEBOY
STABLELAD
STABLEMAN
STARLIGHT
STEELHEAD
STEELYARD
STILLBORN
STILLNESS
STILLROOM
STOOLBALL
STROLLING
SUBALTERN
SUNFLOWER
SUPPLIANT
SUPPLICAT
TABELLION
TABULATOR
TAILLEFER
TAILLIGHT
TEMULENCE
THRALLDOM
THRILLANT
THRILLING
TIPULIDAE
TITILLATE
TITTLEBAT
TOTALIZER
TOWELLING
TRAMLINES
TREILLAGE
TRICLINIC
TUILLETTE
UMBILICAL
UMBILICUS
UNALLOYED
UNBALANCE
UNDILUTED
UNHELPFUL
UNRELATED
UNSELFISH
UNSULLIED
UNWELCOME
UNWILLING
UPHOLSTER
VACILLATE
VEILLEUSE
VEXILLARY
VIDELICET
VIGILANCE
VIGILANTE
VIRULENCE
VITELLIUS
WAVELLITE
WHEELBASE
WHIRLIGIG
WHIRLPOOL
WHIRLWIND
WIMBLEDON
WOODLANDS
WOODLOUSE
ZIBELLINE
ABDOMINAL
ABYSMALLY
ACCOMPANY
ALLEMANDE
ALTIMETER
ARMAMENTS
ARTEMISIA
ASTHMATIC
ASYMMETRY
ATTEMPTED
AUTOMAKER
AUTOMATED
AUTOMATIC
AUTOMATON
AXIOMATIC
BAINMARIE
BAROMETER
BOOKMAKER
BRUMMAGEM
CALEMBOUR
CAMEMBERT
CARAMBOLA
CATAMARAN
CEROMANCY
CHLAMYDES
CHROMATIC
CINEMATIC
COALMINER
COLOMBIAN
COLOMBIER
COLUMBARY
COLUMBATE
COLUMBIAN
COLUMBINE
COLUMBITE
COLUMBIUM
COLUMELLA
COLUMNIST
CRYOMETER
DARTMOUTH
DECAMERON
DECEMVIRI
DECOMPOSE
DECUMBENT
DISEMBARK
DOCUMENTS
DOLOMITES
DOLOMITIC
DREAMLESS
DYNAMITED
ECLAMPSIA
ECTOMORPH
ENCOMPASS
ENCUMBENT
ENDOMORPH
ENIGMATIC
EPHEMERAL
EPHEMERIS
EPHEMERON
ERIOMETER
ESTAMINET
ESTIMABLE
EUHEMERUS
EXCAMBION
EXTEMPORE
FILMMAKER
FLAMMABLE
FRAGMENTS
FREEMASON
FROGMARCH
FROGMOUTH
GASOMETER
GOALMOUTH
GYROMANCY
HAUTMONDE
HEXAMERON
HEXAMETER
HODOMETER
IDIOMATIC
INCOMINGS
INCOMMODE
INCUMBENT
INDEMNIFY
INDEMNITY
INHUMANLY
INSOMNIAC
INTUMESCE
ISLAMABAD
KILOMETER
KILOMETRE
KINGMAKER
KONIMETER
KRUMMHORN
LAGOMORPH
LAWNMOWER
LEAFMOULD
LEITMOTIF
LEITMOTIV
LOUDMOUTH
LUXEMBURG
LYSIMETER
MANOMETER
MEKOMETER
MELAMPODE
MENOMINEE
MESOMORPH
MILOMETER
MONOMACHY
MONOMANIA
MONOMETER
MUNIMENTS
NONSMOKER
NUREMBERG
ONCOMETER
OPSIMATHY
OPTOMETRY
PACEMAKER
PADEMELON
PALAMPORE
PALEMPORE
PARAMEDIC
PARAMETER
PARAMOUNT
PEDOMETER
PERIMETER
PERIMORPH
PNEUMATIC
PNEUMONIA
POCKMANKY
POLEMARCH
POLEMICAL
PRAGMATIC
PRISMATIC
PTARMIGAN
PYRAMIDAL
PYROMANCY
PYROMANIA
REARMOUSE
RECOMMEND
RECUMBENT
REREMOUSE
RHEUMATIC
ROCAMBOLE
RUDIMENTS
SCHEMATIC
SCIAMACHY
SCIOMANCY
SCRAMBLER

SCRIMMAGE
SCRIMPING
SCRIMSHAW
SCRUMMAGE
SCRUMPING
SHOEMAKER
SHRIMPING
SKIAMACHY
SLAMMAKIN
SOLEMNITY
SOLEMNIZE
SONOMETER
SPASMODIC
STAMMERER
STEAMBOAT
STEAMSHIP
STROMBOLI
STRUMITIS
TACAMAHAC
TAXIMETER
TENEMENTS
THAUMATIN
THERMIDOR
TONOMETER
TRAUMATIC
TRIMMINGS
TRIPMETER
TRIUMPHAL
ULTIMATUM
UNDAMAGED
UNLIMITED
UNTIMEOUS
VEHEMENCE
VESTMENTS
VOLTMETER
XENOMANIA
YOHIMBINE
ZYGOMATIC
ABERNETHY
ABOUNDING
ADMONITOR
ADORNMENT
ADRENALIN
ADVANTAGE
ADVENTIST
ADVENTURE
ALIGNMENT
ALLANTOID
ALLANTOIS
ALMANDINE
ALPENHORN
AMIANTHUS
ANDANTINO
ANOINTING
ANTENATAL
ANTONINUS
APENNINES
APPENDAGE
ARGENTINA
ARGENTINE
ARLINGTON
ARSENICAL
ASCENDANT
ASCENDING
ASCENSION
ASSONANCE
ATHENAEUM
ATTENDANT
ATTENTION
ATTENTIVE
ATTENUATE
AUTONOMIC
AXMINSTER
BEGINNING
BELONGING
BILINGUAL
BIMONTHLY
BOTANICAL
BRAINCASE
BRAINLESS
BRAINWASH
BRAINWAVE
BUCENTAUR
BURUNDIAN
BYZANTINE
CAIRNGORM
CALENDULA
CALENTURE
CANONICAL
CAVENDISH
CELANDINE
CHEONGSAM
CHERNOZEM
CHRONICLE
CLEANNESS
CLEANSING
CLIENTELE
COLONNADE
COMINFORM
COMINTERN
CONUNDRUM
COTANGENT
CROWNLIKE
CUTANEOUS
DAVENPORT
DEBENTURE
DECONTROL
DEFENDANT
DEFENDERS
DEFENSIVE
DEFINABLE
DELINEATE
DEMANDING
DEPENDANT
DEPENDENT
DEPENDING
DETENTION
DETONATOR
DEVONPORT
DIAGNOSIS
DIMENSION
DISENGAGE
DISENTOMB
DISINFECT
DISUNITED
DOMINANCE
DOMINICAL
DOMINICAN
DRAINPIPE
DYSENTERY
ECCENTRIC
EDDINGTON
EFFINGHAM
EGLANTINE
ELLINGTON
EMPANOPLY
EMPENNAGE
ENCANTHIS
ENGINEERS
ERPINGHAM
ERRONEOUS
ESSENTIAL
ETERNALLY
EUMENIDES
EXPANSION
EXPANSIVE
EXPENSIVE
EXTENSILE
EXTENSION
EXTENSIVE
EXTENUATE
FACUNDITY
FALANGIST
FARANDOLE
FECUNDITY
FERINGHEE
FINANCIAL
FINANCIER
FORTNIGHT
GALANTINE
GALENGALE
GALINGALE
GERUNDIVE
GIRANDOLE
GIRONDIST
GLEANINGS
GOODNIGHT
GREENAWAY
GREENBACK
GREENFEED
GREENGAGE
GREENHEAD
GREENHORN
GREENMAIL
GREENROOM
GREENSAND
GREENWEED
GREENWICH
GREENWOOD
GREENYARD
GROUNDHOG
GROUNDING
GROUNDNUT
GROUNDSEL
GUTENBERG
HACKNEYED
HEMINGWAY
HERONSHAW
HIRUNDINE
HOLINSHED
HUMANKIND
HUMONGOUS
HUMUNGOUS
HYPINOSIS
IGUANODON
IMMANACLE
IMMANENCE
IMMANENCY
IMMENSELY
IMMENSITY
IMMINENCE
IMMUNISER
IMPENDING
INCENTIVE
INCONDITE
INDENTURE
INDONESIA
INFANTILE
INGENIOUS
INGENUITY
INGENUOUS
INSENSATE
INSINCERE
INSINUATE
INTENDANT
INTENDING
INTENSELY
INTENSIFY
INTENSITY
INTENSIVE
INTENTION
INVENTION
INVENTIVE
INVENTORY
IPRINDOLE
IRVINGISM
JOHANNINE
JUVENILIA
KOMINFORM
LACINIATE
LACONICAL
LAMINATED
LATENIGHT
LECANORAM
LEGENDARY
LENINGRAD
LEVANTINE
LOHENGRIN
LORGNETTE
LUMINAIRE
LUMINANCE
MALENGINE
MELANESIA
MELANOTIC
MELONLIKE
MESENTERY
MIDINETTE
MISINFORM
MISONEIST
MOMENTARY
MOMENTOUS
MOURNIVAL
NEFANDOUS
NICKNEVEN
NOMINALLY
NOMINATOR
NONENTITY
NOTONECTA
OBVENTION
OCEANIDES
OFFENBACH
OFFENDING
OFFENSIVE
OPPENHEIM
OPPONENTS
ORDINAIRE
ORDINANCE
ORGANELLE
ORGANICAL
ORGANISED
ORGANISER
ORGANIZED
ORGANIZER
ORGANZINE
ORIENTATE
ORMANDINE
ORPINGTON
ORTANIQUE
OUDENARDE
OVERNIGHT
PALANKEEN
PALANQUIN
PALINURUS
PARANOIAC
PARANYMPH
PARENTAGE
PARENTING
PECUNIARY
PEKINGESE
PENINSULA
PERENNIAL
PHRENETIC
PHRENITIS
PLAINNESS
PLAINSMAN
PLAINSONG
PLAINTIFF
PLAINTIVE
POIGNANCY
POLONAISE
POLYNESIA
POSTNATAL
POTENTATE
POTENTIAL
PREGNANCY
PROGNOSIS
QUENNELLE
RACONTEUR
RECONCILE
RECONDITE
RECONVENE
REDINGOTE
REDUNDANT
REFINANCE
REMINISCE
REMONTANT
REPENTANT
RESENTFUL
RESONANCE
RESONATOR
RETENTION
RETENTIVE
RETINITIS
ROSINANTE
ROTUNDATE
ROTUNDITY
ROZINANTE
SALANGANE
SATINWOOD
SCIENTISM
SCIENTIST
SCOUNDREL
SEANNACHY
SECONDARY
SEDENTARY
SEMANTEME
SEMANTICS
SEMANTIDE
SEMANTRON
SERENADER
SERENGETI
SEVENTEEN

SHRINKAGE
SHRINKING
SOVENANCE
SPHENDONE
SPHINCTER
SPINNAKER
SPINNERET
SPLENDOUR
SPLENETIC
SPLENITIS
SPLINTERS
SPOONBILL
SPOONFEED
SPRINGALD
SPRINGBOK
SPRINGLET
SPRINKLER
SQUINANCY
SQUINTING
STAINLESS
STANNATOR
STAUNCHLY
STEENBRAS
STEENKIRK
STEGNOSIS
STEGNOTIC
STEINBECK
STEINBOCK
STERNFAST
STERNNESS
STORNAWAY
STOWNLINS
STRANGELY
STRANGLER
STRANGLES
STRANGURY
STRENUOUS
STRINGENT
STRINGOPS
STRONGARM
STRONGYLE
STRONTIUM
SUBENTIRE
SUPINATOR
SYNANGIUM
TABANIDAE
TARANTASS
TARANTULA
TECHNICAL
TECHNIQUE
THINNINGS
THORNBACK
THORNBILL
THORNDYKE
THORNLESS
THRENETIC
THRONGING
TIMENOGUY
TOMENTOSE
TOURNEDOS
TRAINABLE
TRIANGLED
TRIENNIAL
TYRANNIZE
TYRANNOUS
UNBENDING
UNCONCERN
UNCONFINE
UNMINDFUL
UNSINNING
UNTENABLE
VALENTINE
VARANGIAN
VOLUNTARY
VOLUNTEER
WAGENBOOM
WAGONETTE
WAGONLOAD
WAPENTAKE
WAPINSHAW
WOMANHOOD
WOMANISER
WOMANIZER
WOMANKIND
WOMENFOLK
ABSCONDER
ADENOIDAL
AEPYORNIS
AIRCOOLED
ALVEOLATE
AMBROSIAL
AMBROSIAN
AMBROTYPE
AMOROUSLY
ANABOLISM
ANALOGOUS
ANATOLIAN
ANATOMIST
ANATOMIZE
ANCHORAGE
ANCHORITE
ANCHORMAN
ANDROCLES
ANDROMEDA
ANGIOGRAM
ANIMOSITY
ANTHOLOGY
ANXIOUSLY
APHRODITE
APOLOGIST
APOLOGIZE
APPROVING
ARAGONITE
ARCTOGAEA
ARDUOUSLY
ASHMOLEAN
ASTRODOME
ASTROLABE
ASTROLOGY
ASTRONAUT
ASTRONOMY
ASTROPHEL
ASTROTURF
AUCTORIAL
AUTHORESS
AUTHORITY
AUTHORIZE
AYATOLLAH
BAMBOOZLE
BANDOLEER
BANDOLERO
BANDOLIER
BANDOLINE
BARBOTINE
BERGOMASK
BETROTHAL
BETROTHED
BILLOWING
BIOLOGIST
BISHOPRIC
BORROWING
BOSTONIAN
BURROUGHS
BURROWING
BYPRODUCT
CALLOSITY
CALLOUSLY
CAMBODIAN
CAMCORDER
CANNONADE
CANTONESE
CARBONADE
CARBONARI
CARBONATE
CARBONIZE
CARTOGRAM
CARTOUCHE
CARYOPSIS
CASSONADE
CASSOULET
CASSOWARY
CEYLONESE
CHAMOMILE
CHAROLAIS
CHILOPODA
CHINOVNIK
CHIPOLATA
CHIROPODY
CHOCOLATE
CILIOLATE
CLAMOROUS
COELOSTAT
COENOBITE
COENOBIUM
COLLOCATE
COLLODION
COLLOIDAL
COLLOTYPE
COMFORTER
COMMODITY
COMMODORE
COMMOTION
COMPONENT
COMPOSING
COMPOSITE
COMPOSURE
COMPOTIER
CONCORDAT
CONCOURSE
CONGOLESE
CONNOTATE
CONSONANT
COPIOUSLY
COPROLITE
CORMORANT
CORPORATE
CORPOREAL
CORPOSANT
CORROSION
CORROSIVE
COSMOGONY
COSMOLOGY
COSMONAUT
CRACOVIAN
CREPOLINE
CRINOLINE
CROCODILE
CURIOSITY
CURIOUSLY
CURSORILY
CUSTODIAL
CUSTODIAN
CUSTOMARY
CUSTOMIZE
CYCLOLITH
CYCLORAMA
CYCLOTRON
DALTONISM
DEACONESS
DEODORANT
DEODORIZE
DESPOTISM
DEVIOUSLY
DIALOGITE
DIANOETIC
DICHOTOMY
DIPLOMACY
DISCOLOUR
DISCOMFIT
DISCOURSE
DISCOVERT
DISCOVERY
DISHONEST
DISHONOUR
DISLOCATE
DISSOLUTE
DISSOLVED
DISSONANT
DISTORTED
DOCTORATE
DRACONIAN
DRAGONFLY
DUBIOUSLY
DUBROVNIK
EALDORMAN
ECOLOGIST
ECONOMICS
ECONOMIST
ECONOMIZE
ECTROPION
EDITORIAL
ELABORATE
ELAEOLITE
EMBROCATE
EMBROGLIO
EMBROIDER
EMBROILED
EMPLOYEES
ENAMOURED
ENCHORIAL
ENCLOSURE
ENGROSSED
ENGROSSER
ENSCONCED
ENTROPION
ENTROPIUM
EPIPOLISM
EPITOMIZE
ESPIONAGE
ETHIOPIAN
ETHNOLOGY
ETYMOLOGY
EUPHONIUM
EUPHORBIA
EUTROPHIC
EVAPORATE
EXPLOITER
EXPLOSION
EXPLOSIVE
EXTROVERT
FACTORISE
FALLOPIAN
FATUOUSLY
FIBROLINE
FIBROLITE
FLAVORING
FLAVOURED
FOLIOLOSE
FOLLOWING
FORGOTTEN
FORLORNLY
FOSSORIAL
FRAGONARD
FRIVOLITY
FRIVOLOUS
FURIOUSLY
GABIONADE
GALIONGEE
GALLOPADE
GASCONADE
GASHOLDER
GEOLOGIST
GIBEONITE
GLAMORIZE
GLAMOROUS
GLUCOSIDE
GODMOTHER
GONDOLIER
GONGORISM
GREGORIAN
GUNCOTTON
GUNPOWDER
HADROSAUR
HALLOWEEN
HALLOWMAS
HARIOLATE
HARMONICA
HARMONIST
HARMONIUM
HARMONIZE
HARMOTOME
HARPOONER
HARROGATE
HARROWING
HECTORING
HERBORIST
HESSONITE
HIDEOUSLY
HIPPOCRAS
HIPPODAME
HIPPOLYTA
HIPPOLYTE
HISTOGRAM
HISTOLOGY
HISTORIAN
HOBGOBLIN
HOMEOPATH
HOMEOWNER
HOPLOLOGY
HOWTOWDIE
HYDROFOIL
HYDROPULT

HYDROSTAT
HYPNOTISM
HYPNOTIST
HYPNOTIZE
ICHNOLITE
ILLGOTTEN
IMBROCATE
IMBROGLIO
IMPROBITY
IMPROMPTU
IMPROVING
IMPROVISE
IMPSONITE
INAMORATA
INAMORATO
INGROWING
INQUORATE
INTRODUCE
INTROITUS
INTROVERT
INVIOLATE
ISODORIAN
JEALOUSLY
KALSOMINE
KARYOTYPE
KEYHOLDER
KLINOSTAT
KROPOTKIN
LACCOLITE
LANDOWNER
LANGOUSTE
LAWMONGER
LEFTOVERS
LEGIONARY
LEPROSERY
LEUCOCYTE
LEUCOTOME
LINEOLATE
LIQUORICE
LIQUORISH
LITHOCYST
LITHOPONE
LOBLOLLYS
LONDONESE
MACDONALD
MACROCOSM
MACROLOGY
MALFORMED
MANDOLINE
MANGOUSTE
MARMOREAL
MARROWFAT
MASSORETE
MAUSOLEUM
MELBOURNE
MELIORATE
MELPOMENE
MENNONITE
METEORITE
METEOROID
METHODISM
METHODIST
METROLAND
METRONOME
MEZZOTINT
MICROCHIP
MICROCOSM
MICROCYTE
MICROFILM
MICROLITE
MICROLITH
MICROTOME
MICROTONE
MICROWAVE
MISLOCATE
MNEMOSYNE
MONGOLIAN
MONGOLISM
MONZONITE
MORMONISM
MOSKONFYT
MUSCOVADO
MUSCOVITE
MUSKOGEAN
MUSSOLINI
MYTHOLOGY
NARROWING
NATROLITE
NEOLOGISM
NERVOUSLY
NEUROGLIA
NEUROLOGY
NICCOLITE
NIGROSINE
NOSTOLOGY
NUTJOBBER
OBVIOUSLY
OCHLOCRAT
ODDJOBMAN
OFFCOLOUR
OLIGOCENE
OMINOUSLY
ORATORIAN
ORTHODOXY
ORTHOLOGY
ORTHOPTER
ORTHOTONE
OSTEODERM
OSTEOPATH
OSTROGOTH
OUTGOINGS
OUTROOPER
OUTWORKER
PALEOLITH
PANTOFFLE
PANTOMIME
PANTOUFLE
PARSONAGE
PASTORALE
PATHOGENY
PATHOLOGY
PATROCLUS
PATROLMAN
PATRONAGE
PATRONESS
PATRONIZE
PAULOWNIA
PENTOSANE
PERCOLATE
PERFORANS
PERFORATE
PERFORMED
PERFORMER
PERIODATE
PERSONAGE
PERSONATE
PERSONIFY
PERSONNEL
PETROLEUM
PETROLOGY
PHACOLITE
PHAGOCYTE
PHEROMONE
PHILOLOGY
PHITONIUM
PHONOGRAM
PHONOLITE
PHONOLOGY
PHOTOCOPY
PHOTOGENE
PHOTOSTAT
PHYLOGENY
PHYTOLITE
PHYTOTRON
PICTOGRAM
PICTORIAL
PIEPOWDER
PINHOOKER
PISTOLEER
PLATONIST
PLEIOCENE
PLUTOCRAT
PLUTONIUM
POISONING
POISONOUS
POMPOSITY
PORPOISES
PORPORATE
POTBOILER
POTHOLING
POTPOURRI
PRECOCITY
PRECONISE
PREMONISH
PREMOTION
PREPOLLEX
PROBOSCIS
PROCOELUS
PROCONSUL
PROKOFIEV
PROLONGED
PROMOTION
PRONOUNCE
PROPONENT
PROROGATE
PROTOSTAR
PROTOTYPE
PROVOKING
PROVOLONE
PTEROSAUR
PULMONARY
PURDONIUM
PURPOSELY
PYTHONESS
RADIOGRAM
RADIOLOGY
RANCOROUS
RAPTORIAL
RASKOLNIK
RATIONALE
RATIONING
RAUCOUSLY
REASONING
RECKONING
RECTORIAL
RENCONTRE
REPROBATE
REPROCESS
REPRODUCE
REPROVING
RETROCEDE
RETROFLEX
RETROVERT
RHODOLITE
RHODOPSIN
RIBBONISM
RIOTOUSLY
ROSCOMMON
RUINOUSLY
SARTORIAL
SARTORIUS
SASSOLITE
SCAPOLITE
SCHNORKEL
SCHNORRER
SCHNOZZLE
SCHOOLBOY
SCHOOLING
SCHOOLMAN
SCORODITE
SEABOTTLE
SEASONING
SEAWORTHY
SECTORIAL
SELLOTAPE
SEMIOLOGY
SENIORITY
SENSORIUM
SEPIOLITE
SERBONIAN
SERIOUSLY
SERMONIZE
SHEMOZZLE
SHIPOWNER
SHOLOKHOV
SIMEONITE
SINUOSITY
SIRBONIAN
SLIVOVICA
SLIVOVITZ
SOCIOLECT
SOCIOLOGY
SOMNOLENT
SOPHOCLES
SOPHOMORE
SORROWFUL
SPOROCARP
STATOLITH
STEGOSAUR
STENOPAIC
STYLOBATE
SUBCORTEX
SUBDOLOUS
SUBNORMAL
SUBROGATE
SUCCOTASH
SUETONIUS
SUFFOCATE
SUNDOWNER
SUPPORTER
SUPPOSING
SURROGATE
SYLLOGISM
SYMBOLISM
SYMBOLIST
SYMBOLIZE
SYMPODIUM
SYMPOSIUM
SYNCOMIUM
SYNCOPATE
TABBOULEH
TAUTOLOGY
TECTONICS
TECTORIAL
TEDIOSITY
TEDIOUSLY
TEKNONYMY
TELEOLOGY
TEMPORARY
TEMPORIZE
TENTORIUM
TENUOUSLY
TERRORISM
TERRORIST
TERRORIZE
THECODONT
THELONIUS
THREONINE
TREMOLITE
TRIBOLOGY
TRICOLOUR
TRIFORIUM
TRILOBITE
TURCOPOLE
TUTIORISM
ULTRONEUS
UNADOPTED
UNCLOTHED
UNCLOUDED
UNCROSSED
UNCROWNED
UNIFORMED
UNIFORMLY
UNKNOWING
UNSPOILED
UNTRODDEN
URICONIAN
UVAROVITE
VANCOUVER
VARIOLATE
VARIOUSLY
VERBOSITY
VICIOUSLY
VICTORIAN
VICTORINE
VIDEODISC
VIDEOTAPE
VISCOSITY
VISIONARY
VOLGOGRAD
VOODOOISM
WALLOPING
WALLOWING
WANWORTHY
WARMONGER
WEBFOOTED
WELCOMING
WHOSOEVER
WILLOWING
WINCOPIPE
WISCONSIN
YELLOWISH

ZIRCONIUM
ZOOLOGIST
ACROPHONY
ACROPOLIS
AEROPLANE
ALLOPATHY
ALTIPLANO
AMORPHOUS
ANCIPITAL
ANNAPOLIS
ANNAPURNA
ANTIPASTO
ANTIPATHY
ANTIPHONY
ANTIPODES
AQUAPLANE
AREOPAGUS
AUTOPILOT
BACKPEDAL
BALLPOINT
BEDSPREAD
BIOSPHERE
BLASPHEME
BLASPHEMY
BLUEPRINT
BONAPARTE
CACOPHONY
CASHPOINT
CATAPLASM
CATAPLEXY
CEVAPCICI
CHAMPAGNE
CHAMPAIGN
CHAMPERTY
CHAMPLAIN
CHAMPLEVÉ
CHEAPJACK
CHEAPNESS
CHEAPSIDE
CHIPPINGS
CLAMPDOWN
CLEOPATRA
COEMPTION
COLOPHONY
CRIPPLING
CRISPNESS
DAYSPRING
DECEPTION
DECEPTIVE
DESIPIENT
DISAPPEAR
DROPPINGS
ECTOPLASM
ENRAPTURE
ENTOPHYTE
EQUIPMENT
EQUIPOISE
ESCOPETTE
ESEMPLASY
EURIPIDES
EXCEPTION
EXCIPIENT
EXEMPLARY
EXEMPLIFY
EXEMPTION
EXOSPHERE
EYEOPENER
EYESPLICE
FILOPLUME
FIREPLACE
FIREPROOF
FISHPLATE
FLIPPANCY
FOOLPROOF
FOOTPLATE
FOOTPRINT
FOURPENCE
FREEPHONE
GALAPAGOS
GANGPLANK
GRAMPIANS
GRAPPLING
HAIRPIECE
HALFPENNY
HALOPHILE
HANDPIECE
HEDYPHANE
HEMIPTERA
HOLOPHOTE
HOMOPHONE
HOMOPTERA
IDEOPATHY
IDIOPHONE
IDIOPLASM
INCAPABLE
INCEPTION
INCIPIENT
INSIPIENT
IODOPHILE
IRRUPTION
JOSEPHINE
JOSEPHSON
KLEMPERER
LEAKPROOF
MEGAPHONE
MENIPPEAN
MENOPAUSE
METAPELET
MONOPLANE
NAMEPLATE
NEWSPAPER
NEWSPRINT
NINEPENCE
NOOSPHERE
NOTEPAPER
OBREPTION
OCCIPITAL
OCCUPANCY
OCCUPYING
OFFSPRING
OPTOPHONE
OUTSPOKEN
OUTSPREAD
OVENPROOF
OVERPAINT
OVERPOISE
OVERPOWER
PERIPATUS
PERIPHERY
PHOSPHATE
PHOSPHENE
PLUMPNESS
POLYPHONE
POLYPHONY
POSTPONED
PROMPTING
PUERPERAL
RATEPAYER
RECAPTURE
RECEPTION
RECEPTIVE
RECIPIENT
ROTAPLANE
SAGAPENUM
SALOPETTE
SALTPETER
SALTPETRE
SANDPAPER
SANDPIPER
SAXOPHONE
SCRAPBOOK
SCRAPINGS
SCRAPPING
SCRIPTURE
SCULPTING
SCULPTURE
SEMAPHORE
SERAPHINE
SHARPENER
SHARPNESS
SHEEPFOLD
SHEEPMEAT
SHEEPSKIN
SHOWPIECE
SISYPHEAN
SLEEPLESS
SLEEPWALK
SOLIPSISM
SOMEPLACE
STEEPNESS
STRAPHANG
STRAPLESS
STRAPPADO
STRAPPING
STRIPLING
STUMPWORK
SWEEPINGS
SYCOPHANT
TAILPIECE
TAILPLANE
TELEPATHY
TELEPHONE
TELEPHONY
TELEPHOTO
TIMEPIECE
TISIPHONE
TONOPLAST
TOXOPHILY
TRAPPINGS
TROMPETTE
TROOPSHIP
TRUEPENNY
TRUMPEDUP
TRUMPETER
UNEXPOSED
UNHAPPILY
UNHOPEFUL
UNOPPOSED
UNPOPULAR
UNTYPICAL
VIEWPOINT
WALLPAPER
WILLPOWER
WORKPLACE
XENOPHOBE
XEROPHYTE
XYLOPHONE
ANTIQUARY
ANTIQUITY
BRUSQUELY
OBLIQUELY
OBSEQUIES
PIPSQUEAK
QUINQUINA
RELIQUARY
RELIQUIAE
TOTAQUINE
ABERRANCE
ABHORRENT
ABSORBENT
ABSORBING
ABSURDITY
ACCORDANT
ACCORDING
ACCORDION
ADDERWORT
ADHERENCE
ADMIRABLE
ADMIRABLY
ADMIRALTY
ADVERBIAL
ADVERSARY
ADVERSELY
ADVERSITY
ADVERTISE
AFTERCARE
AFTERDAMP
AFTERGLOW
AFTERMATH
AFTERMOST
AFTERNOON
AFTERWORD
ALBERTINE
ALEURITIS
ALGORITHM
ALTERABLE
ALTERCATE
ALTERNATE
AMAUROSIS
AMBERGRIS
AMPERSAND
ANABRANCH
ANAEROBIC
ANTARCTIC
APOCRYPHA
APPARATUS
APPARITOR
APPERTAIN
APPORTION
AQUARELLE
ARBORETUM
ARKWRIGHT
ARTERIOLE
ARTHRITIC
ARTHRITIS
ARTHROPOD
ARTHROSIS
ASCERTAIN
ASPARAGUS
ASPARTAME
ASPERSION
ASPIRATOR
ASSERTING
ASSERTION
ASSERTIVE
ASSURANCE
ASSUREDLY
AUBERGINE
AUSTRALIA
AUTOROUTE
BEVERIDGE
BIFURCATE
BILIRUBIN
BIOGRAPHY
BIPARTITE
BIZARRELY
BOYFRIEND
CALORIFIC
CAMBRIDGE
CAMERAMAN
CAPARISON
CAPORETTO
CARTRIDGE
CASTRATED
CATARRHAL
CATERWAUL
CAVERNOUS
CAVORTING
CEDARWOOD
CENTRALLY
CENTREING
CHAIRLIFT
CHEERLESS
CIGARETTE
CINERARIA
CINEREOUS
CLEARANCE
CLEARNESS
COCKROACH
COHERENCE
COLERIDGE
COLORLESS
CONGRUENT
CONGRUOUS
CONTRALTO
CONTRIVED
CONTRIVER
COPYRIGHT
COVERDALE
COWARDICE
DECORATED
DECORATOR
DECURSIVE
DEFERENCE
DEFERMENT
DEFORMITY
DELIRIOUS
DEMARCATE
DEMURRAGE
DEPARTURE
DESERTION
DESERVING
DESIRABLE
DESTROYED
DESTROYER
DETERGENT
DETERMINE
DETERRENT
DEXTRORSE
DIACRITIC
DIAERESIS
DIARRHOEA

DISARMING
DISCREDIT
DISGRACED
DISORIENT
DISTRAINT
DIVERGENT
DIVERGING
DIVERSIFY
DIVERSION
DIVERSITY
DIVERTING
DOCTRINAL
DOWNRIGHT
DUNDREARY
DYSTROPHY
EAGERNESS
EDWARDIAN
EIDERDOWN
ELUTRIATE
EMBARRASS
EMMERDALE
EMPIRICAL
ENCIRCLED
ENDURABLE
ENDURANCE
ENGARLAND
ENNERDALE
ENSORCELL
ENTERITIS
ENTERTAIN
ENVERMEIL
ESMERALDA
ESPERANCE
ESPERANTO
ETHEREOUS
EUPHRATES
EXCORIATE
EXCURSION
EXECRABLE
EXECRABLY
EXPERTISE
EXPORTING
EXPURGATE
EXTIRPATE
EXTORTION
EYEBRIGHT
FALERNIAN
FAVORABLE
FAVORABLY
FIGURANTE
FLAGRANCE
FLOORSHOW
FLOURMILL
FRAGRANCE
FRAGRANCY
GABARDINE
GABERDINE
GALDRAGON
GENERALLY
GENERATOR
GEOGRAPHY
GINORMOUS
GLAIREOUS
GOVERNESS
GOVERNING
GUERRILLA
GUJARATHI
HABERDINE
HABERGEON
HAVERSACK
HAZARDOUS
HEDERATED
HETERODOX
HETEROSIS
HEYPRESTO
HIBERNATE
HIBERNIAN
HILARIOUS
HINDRANCE
HONORABLE
HONORIFIC
HUNDREDTH
HYPERBOLA
HYPERBOLE
IBUPROFEN
ICTERIDAE
IGNORAMUS
IGNORANCE
IMMERSION
IMMORALLY
IMMORTALS
IMPARTIAL
IMPERATOR
IMPERFECT
IMPERIOUS
IMPORTANT
IMPORTUNE
INCARDINE
INCARNATE
INCORRECT
INCURABLE
INCURABLY
INCURIOUS
INCURSION
INEBRIATE
INFERENCE
INFERTILE
INFIRMARY
INFIRMITY
INFORMANT
INFURIATE
INHERITED
INHERITOR
INJURIOUS
INNERMOST
INSCRIBED
INSERTION
INSURANCE
INSURGENT
INTERBRED
INTERCEDE
INTERCEPT
INTERCITY
INTERDICT
INTERFACE
INTERFERE
INTERJECT
INTERLACE
INTERLARD
INTERLOCK
INTERLOPE
INTERLUDE
INTERMENT
INTERNODE
INTERPLAY
INTERPOSE
INTERPRET
INTERRUPT
INTERSECT
INTERVENE
INTERVIEW
INVERNESS
INVERSION
INVERTASE
ISOCRATES
ISOPROPYL
ISOTROPIC
JACARANDA
JOBERNOWL
LABORIOUS
LABYRINTH
LACERATED
LACHRYMAL
LAMARTINE
LANGRIDGE
LASERWORT
LATERALLY
LAZARETTO
LESTRIGON
LEVERAGED
LIBERALLY
LIBERATED
LIBERATOR
LIBERTIES
LIBERTINE
LITERALLY
LIVERPOOL
LIVERWORT
LIVERYMAN
LOGARITHM
LONGRANGE
LUMBRICUS
LUXURIANT
LUXURIATE
LUXURIOUS
MACARONIC
MACARTHUR
MADARIAGA
MADAROSIS
MAHARAJAH
MAHARANEE
MAHARISHI
MAJORDOMO
MAJORETTE
MATERNITY
MAYORALTY
MEMORABLE
MEMORITER
MISCREANT
MISERABLE
MISERABLY
MITHRAISM
MODERATOR
MODERNISM
MODERNIST
MODERNITY
MODERNIZE
MONERGISM
MOONRAKER
MOTORBIKE
MOTORBOAT
MOTORCADE
MOTORISTS
MUCORALES
MUSHROOMS
NATURALLY
NEFARIOUS
NEFERTITI
NEPHRITIC
NEPHRITIS
NEUTRALLY
NEVERMORE
NICARAGUA
NIDERLING
NONPROFIT
NOTARIKON
NOTORIETY
NOTORIOUS
NUMERAIRE
NUMERATOR
NUMERICAL
OBCORDATE
OBJURGATE
OBSERVANT
ODOURLESS
OESTROGEN
OFFERTORY
OLECRANON
OLEORESIN
OPPORTUNE
OROGRAPHY
OTHERWISE
OTTERBURN
OUTERMOST
OUTGROWTH
OVERRATED
OVERREACH
OVERREACT
OVERRIDER
OWNERSHIP
PANORAMIC
PAPARAZZI
PAPARAZZO
PAPERBACK
PAPERCLIP
PAPERWORK
PARTRIDGE
PATERCOVE
PATERNITY
PEDERASTY
PENDRAGON
PENFRIEND
PENURIOUS
PETERSHAM
PORTRAYAL
PORTREEVE
POWERBOAT
POWERLESS
PREORDAIN
PROCREATE
PRODROMAL
PRODROMUS
PROGRAMME
PROPRIETY
QUADRATIC
QUADRATUS
QUADRILLE
QUADRUPED
QUADRUPLE
QUEERNESS
RAZORBILL
REARRANGE
RECORDING
RECORDIST
RECURRENT
RECURRING
REDBREAST
REFERENCE
REFERRING
REFORMIST
REFURBISH
REGARDANT
REGARDFUL
REGARDING
REMBRANDT
REPERCUSS
REPERTORY
REPORTAGE
REPORTING
RESERPINE
RESERVIST
RESERVOIR
RESORTING
RESTRAINT
RESURFACE
RESURGENT
RESURRECT
RETORSION
RETORTION
RETURNING
REVERENCE
REVERSING
REVERSION
REWARDING
REWORKING
RICERCARE
RIDERHOOD
RIDERLESS
RIVERSIDE
ROBERTSON
RUNAROUND
SALERATUS
SAMARITAN
SATIRICAL
SATURATED
SATURNIAN
SATURNINE
SATURNISM
SATYRIDAE
SATYRINAE
SAVERNAKE
SCIARIDAE
SCLEROSIS
SCLEROTAL
SCURRIOUR
SEMIRAMIS
SEPARABLE
SEPARATED
SEPARATOR
SEVERALLY
SEVERANCE
SHEARLING
SHEERLEGS
SHEERNESS
SIDEROSIS
SILURIDAE
SNEERWELL
SOBERNESS
SOPORIFIC
SOUBRETTE
SOUFRIERE
SOVEREIGN

SPEARHEAD
SPEARMINT
SPEARSIDE
SPEARWORT
SPHERICAL
SQUIREAGE
SQUIRMING
STAIRCASE
STEERSMAN
SUDORIFIC
SUFFRAGAN
SUGARCANE
SUPERETTE
SUPERFINE
SUPERNOVA
SUPERSEDE
SUPERSTAR
SUPERVENE
SUPERVISE
SURPRISED
SYBARITIC
SYNERGIST
TAMERLANE
TAVERNERS
TOBERMORY
TOLERABLE
TOLERABLY
TOLERANCE
TOLERATED
TONBRIDGE
TOPDRAWER
TOVARISCH
TREDRILLE
TRIERARCH
TURNROUND
UNCERTAIN
UNCHRISOM
UNCORRECT
UNDERBRED
UNDERCAST
UNDERCOAT
UNDERDONE
UNDERFELT
UNDERFOOT
UNDERHAND
UNDERLINE
UNDERLING
UNDERMINE
UNDERMOST
UNDERPAID
UNDERPASS
UNDERRATE
UNDERSEAL
UNDERSELL
UNDERSIDE
UNDERSIGN
UNDERSONG
UNDERTAKE
UNDERTONE
UNDERWALK
UNDERWEAR
UNDERWENT
UNDERWOOD
UNEARTHLY
UNMARRIED
UNNERVING
UNVARYING
UNWORRIED
UPPERMOST
USHERETTE
UTTERANCE
UTTERLESS
UTTERMOST
VAPORETTO
VAPORIZER
VENERABLE
VENEREOUS
VENTRICLE
VICARIOUS
VICEREGAL
VICEREINE
WAFERTHIN
WATERBABY
WATERBUTT
WATERFALL
WATERFORD
WATERFOWL
WATERGATE
WATERHOLE
WATERLESS
WATERLILY
WATERLINE
WATERMARK
WATERMILL
WATERSHED
WATERSIDE
WATERWEED
WHERRYMAN
WHIPROUND
YGGDRASIL
YTTERBIUM
ACCESSION
ACCESSORY
ACOUSTICS
ADMISSION
ADVISABLE
ADVISEDLY
AEROSPACE
ALTISSIMO
AMBUSCADE
AMIDSHIPS
ANCESTRAL
ANGOSTURA
ARMISTICE
ARRESTING
ASSISTANT
AUGUSTINE
AUTOSCOPY
AYLESBURY
BACKSHISH
BACKSLIDE
BACKSPACE
BACKSTAGE
BACKSWORD
BANDSTAND
BANISTERS
BARNSTORM
BARYSCOPE
BECHSTEIN
BEEFSTEAK
BERNSTEIN
BLESSINGS
BLUESTONE
BOATSWAIN
BOMBSHELL
BOOKSHELF
BOOKSTALL
BOOKSTAND
BOOKSTORE
BRASSERIE
BRASSICAS
BRASSIERE
BRASSWARE
BRIMSTONE
BRITSCHKA
CADASTRAL
CAKESTAND
CELESTIAL
CHINSTRAP
CHRISTIAN
CHRISTMAS
CHRYSALIS
CLASSICAL
CLASSLESS
CLASSMATE
CLASSROOM
CLEPSYDRA
CLOISONNÉ
COCKSCOMB
COCKSFOOT
COCKSWAIN
COLOSSEUM
COLOSTOMY
COLOSTRUM
COLTSFOOT
CORKSCREW
CORNSTALK
CORUSCATE
COUNSELOR
CROISSANT
CROSSBEAM
CROSSBILL
CROSSBRED
CROSSEYED
CROSSFIRE
CROSSOVER
CROSSWALK
CROSSWIND
CROSSWISE
CROSSWORD
CROUSTADE
CROWSBILL
CROWSFOOT
DACHSHUND
DAMASCENE
DECASTYLE
DECESSION
DECUSSATE
DEPOSITOR
DEVASTATE
DIGASTRIC
DIGESTION
DIGESTIVE
DIVISIBLE
DOWNSTAGE
DRIPSTONE
DROPSICAL
DRUGSTORE
DRUMSTICK
DRYASDUST
EAVESDROP
ECOSSAISE
EDDYSTONE
EGRESSION
ELKOSHITE
ELLESMERE
EMBASSADE
EMBASSAGE
ENDOSPERM
EPHESIANS
EQUISETUM
EXCESSIVE
EXCISEMAN
EXCUSABLE
EXCUSABLY
EXPISCATE
EXPOSITOR
FALDSTOOL
FARMSTEAD
FATISCENT
FEEDSTUFF
FILMSTRIP
FILOSELLE
FINISHING
FIRESTONE
FLAGSTAFF
FLAGSTONE
FLAMSTEED
FLOWSTONE
FOODSTORE
FOODSTUFF
FOOTSTALL
FOOTSTOOL
FORASMUCH
FORESHORE
FORESIGHT
FORESPEAK
FORESPEND
FORESTAGE
FORESTALL
FORESTERS
FREESTONE
FREESTYLE
FRIESLAND
FROGSPAWN
FROISSART
FULLSCALE
GAINSAYER
GALLSTONE
GATESHEAD
GEARSHIFT
GEARSTICK
GLADSTONE
GLASSWARE
GLISSANDO
GOLDSINNY
GOLDSMITH
GRASSLAND
GREASEGUN
GUESSWORK
GYROSCOPE
HAILSTONE
HAILSTORM
HAIRSTYLE
HALFSTAFF
HALLSTATT
HAMPSTEAD
HANDSHAKE
HANDSPIKE
HANDSTAND
HARDSHELL
HARESTANE
HARTSHORN
HAWKSBILL
HEADSCARF
HEADSTALL
HEADSTONE
HEMISTICH
HEXASTICH
HIGHSPEED
HINDSIGHT
HOARSTONE
HOLYSTONE
HOMESTEAD
HORNSTONE
HOROSCOPE
HOURSTONE
IGNESCENT
IMPASSION
IMPASSIVE
IMPOSTURE
INCESSANT
INGESTION
INJUSTICE
INNISFAIL
INNISFREE
INSISTENT
INTESTATE
INTESTINE
INVISIBLE
IRONSIDES
IRONSTONE
JACKSNIPE
JACKSTRAW
JANISSARY
JARLSBERG
JERUSALEM
JOCKSTRAP
JOUISANCE
KERBSTONE
KHANSAMAH
KICKSHAWS
KINGSIZED
KNAPSCULL
KNAPSKULL
KNOBSTICK
KONISCOPE
LADYSMITH
LAMASERAI
LAMBSWOOL
LAMPSHADE
LANDSCAPE
LANDSLIDE
LANDSMAAL
LANDSTURM
LANGSPIEL
LATESCENT
LEGISLATE
LIFESTYLE
LIMESTONE
LINTSTOCK
LIVESTOCK
LOADSTONE
LOAMSHIRE
LOCKSMITH
LODESTONE
LOGISTICS
LONGSHORE
LOUISIANA
LUTESCENT
LYMESWOLD
MAELSTROM

MAJUSCULE
MAKESHIFT
MAULSTICK
MEGASCOPE
MEGASPORE
MERESWINE
MILESTONE
MILKSHAKE
MILLSTONE
MINISCULE
MINISKIRT
MINKSTONE
MINUSCULE
MODESTINE
MOLESKINS
MONASTERY
MONASTRAL
MONKSHOOD
MONOSTICH
MOONSHINE
MOONSTONE
MORTSTONE
MUMPSIMUS
MUTOSCOPE
NECESSARY
NECESSITY
NEWSSHEET
NEWSSTALL
NEWSSTAND
NIAISERIE
NITHSDALE
NUMBSKULL
OBEISANCE
OBFUSCATE
OBSESSION
OBSESSIVE
OCTASTICH
ODELSTING
OVERSHADE
OVERSHOES
OVERSHOOT
OVERSIGHT
OVERSIZED
OVERSLEEP
OVERSPEND
OVERSPILL
OVERSTATE
OVERSTEER
PAKISTANI
PALESTINE
PARASCENE
PARASCEVE
PARASITIC
PECKSNIFF
PENISTONE
PERISCIAN
PERISCOPE
PERISHING
PERISTOME
PERISTYLE
PHANSIGAR
PHARSALIA
PIKESTAFF
PILASTERS
PIPESTONE
PLAUSIBLE
PLAUSIBLY
PLAUSTRAL
PLEASANCE
PLIMSOLLS
POTASSIUM
PRESSGANG
PRIESTESS
PRIESTLEY
PROUSTITE
PUISSANCE
PUNISHING
QUIESCENT
RACKSTRAW
RAINSTORM
RAVISHING
RECESSION
RECESSIVE
RECUSANCE
REFUSENIK
REGISSEUR
REGISTRAR
REINSTATE
REMISSION
RENASCENT
REPOSSESS
RESISTANT
RHAPSODIC
RINGSIDER
ROADSTEAD
ROOTSTOCK
ROUSSETTE
RUFESCENT
RUNESTAVE
SALESGIRL
SALESLADY
SANDSTONE
SANDSTORM
SATISFIED
SCANSORES
SCISSORER
SEBASTIAN
SECESSION
SENESCENT
SENESCHAL
SERASKIER
SHENSTONE
SHIPSHAPE
SHOESHINE
SIDESWIPE
SILTSTONE
SINGSPIEL
SINUSITIS
SLABSTONE
SLAPSTICK
SNOWSHOES
SNOWSTORM
SOAPSTONE
SOMASCOPE
SONGSMITH
SPONSORED
STARSTONE
STRESSFUL
STROSSERS
SWANSDOWN
TABASHEER
TAOISEACH
TAVISTOCK
TAYASSUID
TEARSHEET
TELESALES
TELESCOPE
TELESTICH
THEOSOPHY
THERSITES
THIRSTILY
THIRSTING
THOUSANDS
THRASHING
THRASONIC
THRESHOLD
THYESTEAN
TIMESHARE
TOADSTONE
TOADSTOOL
TOMBSTONE
TOWNSFOLK
TRANSCEND
TRANSFORM
TRANSFUSE
TRANSHUME
TRANSIENT
TRANSLATE
TRANSMUTE
TRANSPIRE
TRANSPORT
TRANSPOSE
TRANSSHIP
TRANSVAAL
TREASURER
TROOSTITE
TROSSACHS
TROUSSEAU
TUMESCENT
TUNGSTATE
TURNSTILE
TURNSTONE
UNMUSICAL
VANISHING
VARISCITE
VELASQUEZ
VELDSKOEN
VENUSBERG
VIGESIMAL
VITASCOPE
VOLKSRAAD
WASHSTAND
WELDSTADT
WHETSTONE
WHIMSICAL
WHINSTONE
WHIPSNADE
WHUNSTANE
WINDSCALE
WINDSWEPT
WITHSTAND
WOODSHOCK
WORDSMITH
WORKSPACE
XEROSTOMA
YARDSTICK
YORKSHIRE
ZYGOSPORE
ABLUTIONS
ABOUTFACE
ABOUTTURN
ADAPTABLE
ADEPTNESS
ADMITTING
ADULTERER
ADULTHOOD
AEROTAXIS
AFLATOXIN
AIRSTREAM
ALBATROSS
ALERTNESS
ALLOTMENT
AMBITIOUS
ANASTASIA
ANNOTATED
ANNOTATOR
ANTITOXIC
ANTITOXIN
APARTHEID
APARTMENT
APOSTOLIC
APPETIZER
ARBITRAGE
ARBITRARY
ARBITRATE
ARISTOTLE
ARMSTRONG
ATTITUDES
AWESTRUCK
BACKTRACK
BAGATELLE
BATHTOWEL
BEAUTEOUS
BEAUTIFUL
BEESTINGS
BELATEDLY
BILATERAL
BIRDTABLE
BLISTERED
BLOWTORCH
BLUNTNESS
BLUSTERER
BOUNTEOUS
BOUNTIFUL
BRACTEOLE
BREATHING
BRISTLING
BUCKTEETH
BUCKTHORN
BUMPTIOUS
CAFETERIA
CAFETIERE
CAPITULAR
CAPITULUM
CARETAKER
CARTTRACK
CATATONIA
CATATONIC
CERATITIS
CERATODUS
CHANTEUSE
CHANTILLY
CHARTERED
CHARTREUX
CHASTENED
CHATTERER
CLUSTERED
COASTLINE
COINTREAU
CONSTABLE
CONSTANCE
CONSTANCY
CONSTRICT
CONSTRUCT
COUNTDOWN
COUNTLESS
COUNTRIES
COURTELLE
COURTEOUS
COURTESAN
COURTROOM
COURTSHIP
COURTYARD
CRAFTSMAN
CRUSTACEA
CRYPTOGAM
CUNCTATOR
CURETTAGE
DAUNTLESS
DEBATABLE
DEBUTANTE
DECATHLON
DEMETRIUS
DEMITASSE
DIASTASIS
DIGITALIN
DIGITALIS
DIPHTHONG
DONATELLO
DOUBTLESS
DOWNTREND
DRAFTSMAN
DRIFTWOOD
DUNSTABLE
EIGHTIETH
EIGHTSOME
ELASTOMER
ELECTORAL
ELECTRESS
ELECTRIFY
ELECTRODE
ELECTUARY
EMBATTLED
ENACTMENT
EPISTAXIS
EPISTOLER
EQUITABLE
EQUITABLY
ERGATANER
ERISTICAL
EROSTRATE
ETCETERAS
EVENTUATE
EXACTMENT
EXACTNESS
EXANTHEMA
EXCITABLE
EXISTENCE
EXOSTOSIS
EXPATIATE
EYESTRAIN
FACETIOUS
FAINTNESS
FANATICAL
FASTTRACK
FAULTLESS
FIRSTEVER
FIRSTHAND
FIRSTRATE
FLATTENED
FLATTENER
FLATTERED

FLATTERER
FLEETWOOD
FLINTLOCK
FLUCTUATE
FLUSTERED
FORETASTE
FRACTIOUS
FROSTBITE
FRUCTIDOR
FRUITCAKE
FRUITERER
FRUITLESS
FRUSTRATE
GAELTACHT
GAUNTNESS
GAZETTEER
GENETICAL
GENITALIA
GOBETWEEN
GREATCOAT
GREATNESS
GREETINGS
GUILTLESS
HABITABLE
HABITUATE
HALITOSIS
HALOTHANE
HAMSTRING
HAMSTRUNG
HEALTHILY
HEARTACHE
HEARTBEAT
HEARTBURN
HEARTFELT
HEARTHRUG
HEARTLAND
HEARTLESS
HEMITROPE
HEMSTITCH
HEPATICAL
HEPATITIS
HERETICAL
HESITANCE
HESITANCY
HEXATEUCH
IDENTICAL
IDENTIKIT
IDIOTICON
IMMUTABLE
IMMUTABLY
IMPATIENT
IMPETUOUS
IMPOTENCE
INCITATUS
INERTNESS
INFATUATE
INPATIENT
IRRITABLE
IRRITABLY
IRRITATED
JEPHTHAHS
JETSTREAM
JOCKTELEG
KERATITIS
KEYSTROKE
LAPSTREAK
LEASTWAYS
LEASTWISE
LENGTHILY
LEVITICUS
LIENTERIC
LIGHTFOOT
LIGHTLESS
LIGHTNESS
LIGHTNING
LIGHTSHIP
LIGHTSOME
LIMITLESS
LOGOTHETE
MAINTENON
MALATHION
MATUTINAL
MEDITATOR
MEHITABEL
MENSTRUAL
MENSTRUUM
MIDSTREAM
MILITANCY
MINUTEMAN
MISSTROKE
MOISTNESS
MONATOMIC
MONOTROCH
MONSTROUS
MORATORIA
MORATORIO
MOUSTACHE
MUNITIONS
NABATHEAN
NEGOTIATE
NERITIDAE
NIGHTCLUB
NIGHTFALL
NIGHTFIRE
NIGHTGOWN
NIGHTMARE
NIGHTTIME
NIGHTWORK
NINETIETH
NOMOTHETE
NOVITIATE
OUGHTNESS
OVERTHROW
OVERTONES
PAINTWORK
PALATABLE
PANATELLA
PANETTONE
PARATHION
PARATROOP
PAROTITIS
PARTTIMER
PATHTRAIN
PENETRATE
PENITENCE
PHANTASMA
PICKTHANK
PINSTRIPE
PIRATICAL
PLASTERED
PLASTERER
PLAYTHING
PLENTEOUS
PLENTIFUL
POINTEDLY
POINTLESS
POINTSMAN
POLITBURO
POLITESSE
POLITICAL
POLITIQUE
POLYTHENE
POULTERER
PRACTICAL
PRACTISED
PRACTOLOL
PRINTABLE
PROPTOSIS
PROSTRATE
PUNCTILIO
PUNCTUATE
PURITANIC
PYRETHRUM
QUANTICAL
QUANTOCKS
QUARTERLY
QUARTETTE
QUIETNESS
QUINTETTE
QUINTROON
QUINTUPLE
QUITTANCE
RACETRACK
REDSTREAK
REISTAFEL
RELATIONS
REPUTABLE
REPUTEDLY
REVETMENT
RHEOTAXIS
RIGHTEOUS
RIGHTHAND
RIGHTNESS
RIGHTWING
ROISTERER
SAGITTARY
SAINTFOIN
SAINTHOOD
SANCTUARY
SAXITOXIN
SCANTLING
SCATTERED
SCENTLESS
SCEPTICAL
SCINTILLA
SCRATCHED
SCRATCHES
SCRUTATOR
SECATEURS
SEDITIOUS
SHATTERED
SHELTERED
SHIFTLESS
SHIFTWORK
SHINTOISM
SHORTCAKE
SHORTFALL
SHORTHAND
SHORTHAUL
SHORTHOLD
SHORTHORN
SHORTLIST
SHORTNESS
SHORTSTAY
SHORTSTOP
SHORTTERM
SHUTTERED
SIDETRACK
SIGHTLESS
SIGHTSEER
SKEPTICAL
SKINTIGHT
SLANTWISE
SMARTNESS
SOLITAIRE
SOMETHING
SOMETIMES
SPARTACUS
SPATTERED
SPECTACLE
SPECTATOR
SPLITTING
SPORTSMAN
SPORTSMEN
SPRITEFUL
SPRITSAIL
SQUATTERS
STARTLING
STILTBIRD
STOUTNESS
STRATAGEM
STRATEGIC
STRETCHED
STRETCHER
STRUTTING
SUBSTANCE
SUBSTRATA
SUBSTRATE
SUMPTUARY
SUMPTUOUS
SUNSTROKE
SWEATBAND
SWEETENER
SWEETMEAT
SWEETNESS
SWEETSHOP
SWIFTNESS
TEMPTRESS
THIRTIETH
TIGHTENER
TIGHTHEAD
TIGHTNESS
TIGHTROPE
TIMETABLE
TOASTRACK
TRACTABLE
TRATTORIA
TREATMENT
TREETRUNK
TRIATHLON
TRIETERIC
TURNTABLE
TWENTIETH
UNALTERED
UNEATABLE
UNFITTING
UNMATCHED
UNNATURAL
UNNOTICED
UNSETTLED
UNTUTORED
UNWATERED
UNWITTING
UPAITHRIC
UPSETTING
VEGETABLE
VEGETATOR
VERATRINE
VERITABLE
VEXATIONS
VEXATIOUS
VIENTIANE
VOLATIBLE
WAISTBAND
WAISTCOAT
WAISTLINE
WHEATGERM
WHEATMEAL
WHISTLING
WHITTAWER
WRESTLING
YACHTSMAN
YACHTSMEN
ACIDULATE
ACIDULOUS
AFFLUENCE
AHASUERUS
ANNOUNCER
ARTHURIAN
ASTOUNDED
ATAHUALPA
BANQUETTE
BECQUEREL
BRIQUETTE
CAGOULARD
CALCULATE
CALPURNIA
CAMBUSCAN
CARBUNCLE
CARTULARY
CELLULITE
CELLULOID
CELLULOSE
CENTURION
CHALUMEAU
CHEQUERED
CHERUBINI
CHIHUAHUA
CIRCULATE
COAGULANT
COAGULATE
COLLUSION
COLLUSIVE
COLOURFUL
COLOURING
COLOURIST
COMMUNION
COMMUNISM
COMMUNIST
COMMUNITY
COMPUTING
CONCUBINE
CONCUSSED
CONDUCIVE
CONDUCTOR
CONDUCTUS
CONFUCIUS
CONFUSING
CONFUSION
CONJUGATE
CONJURING
CONNUBIAL

CONQUEROR
CONSULATE
CONSUMING
CONTUMACY
CONTUMELY
CONTUSION
CORDUROYS
CORPULENT
CORPUSCLE
CORRUGATE
CORRUPTER
COSTUMIER
COTHURNUS
COUTURIER
CRAPULENT
CRAPULOUS
CREDULITY
CREDULOUS
CROQUETTE
CUCHULAIN
CURFUFFLE
DAMBUSTER
DEBAUCHED
DEBAUCHEE
DEFAULTER
DIFFUSION
DISBURDEN
DISGUISED
DISGUSTED
DISPUTANT
DISTURBED
EFFLUENCE
EFFLUVIUM
EJACULATE
ELOCUTION
ELOQUENCE
EMOLUMENT
ENCAUSTIC
ENCOUNTER
ENCOURAGE
ENTOURAGE
EPICUREAN
ETIQUETTE
EVOLUTION
EXCLUDING
EXCLUSION
EXCLUSIVE
EXECUTANT
EXECUTION
EXECUTIVE
EXECUTRIX
EXEQUATUR
EXHAUSTED
EXTRUSION
FACTUALLY
FAVOURITE
FLATULENT
FORMULATE
FORTUNATE
FREQUENCY
GARRULITY
GARRULOUS
GRADUALLY
GRADUATED
GRANULATE
GRANULITE
GRANULOSE
HACQUETON
HAMBURGER
HAMMURABI
HARQUEBUS
HAWCUBITE
HERCULEAN
IMPLUVIUM
IMPOUNDER
IMPRUDENT
INCAUTION
INCLUDING
INCLUSION
INCLUSIVE
INERUDITE
INFLUENCE
INFLUENZA
INOCULATE
INTRUSION
INTRUSIVE
JACQUERIE
JIGGUMBOB
KERFUFFLE
LABOURITE
LAEVULOSE
LANGUAGES
LANGUEDOC
LANGUETTE
LANGUIDLY
LEISURELY
LIMBURGER
LIMOUSINE
LITHUANIA
MACQUARIE
MANDUCATE
MARAUDING
MARQUESAS
MARQUETRY
MARSUPIAL
MARSUPIUM
MASCULINE
MATHURINE
MAVOURNIN
MEASURING
MERCURIAL
MIDSUMMER
MISGUIDED
MUNDUNGUS
MURMURING
MUSSULMAN
NANTUCKET
NEPTUNIUM
NOCTURNAL
NUMMULITE
NUNCUPATE
OBSCURELY
OBSCURITY
OBTRUSION
OBTRUSIVE
OCCLUSION
OPHIUCHUS
OUTNUMBER
PANDURATE
PARBUCKLE
PASTURAGE
PENDULATE
PENDULOUS
PENPUSHER
PERFUMERY
PERGUNNAH
PERSUADED
PERTURBED
PERTUSATE
PERTUSSIS
PETAURIST
PIROUETTE
POLLUTANT
POLLUTION
PORCUPINE
POSTULANT
POSTULATE
POTHUNTER
PRECURSOR
PREJUDICE
PRELUSORY
PRIMULINE
PROFUSELY
PROFUSION
PROLUSION
PROMUSCIS
PULLULATE
PURSUANCE
QUERULOUS
RAPTUROUS
REMOULADE
RESHUFFLE
RESOURCES
ROXBURGHE
SAPSUCKER
SASQUATCH
SCHMUTTER
SCLAUNDER
SCROUNGER
SECLUSION
SELJUKIAN
SENSUALLY
SHUBUNKIN
SINGULTUS
SIPHUNCLE
SPECULATE
SPELUNKER
SPRAUCHLE
STATUETTE
STATUTORY
STIMULANT
STIMULATE
STIPULATE
SUBJUGATE
SUCCUBINE
SUCCULENT
SUCCURSAL
SUFFUSION
SULFUROUS
SUPPURATE
SURMULLET
SURQUEDRY
TALMUDIST
TELLURIAN
TELLURION
TELLURIUM
TINGUAITE
TOLPUDDLE
TREBUCHET
TREMULATE
TREMULOUS
TRIBUNATE
TRIBUTARY
TRITURATE
TRUCULENT
TURBULENT
TURQUOISE
UNBOUNDED
UNCOUPLED
UNCOURTLY
UNDAUNTED
UNDOUBTED
UNEQUALED
UNFOUNDED
UNTOUCHED
UNUSUALLY
UPCOUNTRY
URUGUAYAN
VERTUMNUS
VIRGULATE
VIRTUALLY
VITRUVIAN
VOLTURNUS
WALPURGIS
WELSUMMER
WHODUNNIT
ALLEVIATE
ANTIVENIN
ARRIVISTE
BEHAVIOUR
BOLIVIANO
CANAVERAL
DELIVERER
ECHEVERIA
ENLIVENED
EQUIVOCAL
EQUIVOQUE
EXCAVATOR
GENEVIEVE
GRENVILLE
GRIEVANCE
GROSVENOR
IMMOVABLE
IMMOVABLY
INNOVATOR
LUBAVITCH
NASHVILLE
NECKVERSE
OBLIVIOUS
OVERVALUE
PALOVERDE
RECOVERED
REDIVIVUS
RELEVANCE
REMOVABLE
RENOVATOR
SCRIVENER
SYNOVITIS
UNCOVERED
UNDIVIDED
UNINVITED
UNSAVOURY
AINSWORTH
ALLOWABLE
ALLOWANCE
ARROWHEAD
ARROWROOT
BACKWARDS
BACKWATER
BACKWOODS
BANDWAGON
BOTSWANAN
BRATWURST
BUCKWHEAT
CARTWHEEL
CHARWOMAN
DASHWHEEL
DISHWATER
DOWNWARDS
EASTWARDS
EDELWEISS
EDGEWORTH
ELBOWROOM
ELSEWHERE
ENDOWMENT
ERSTWHILE
FIREWATER
FIREWORKS
FOLKWEAVE
FOURWHEEL
FREEWHEEL
GEARWHEEL
GREYWACKE
HOMEWARDS
IRONWORKS
IRRAWADDY
JERKWATER
JOBSWORTH
KINSWOMAN
LANDWARDS
LILYWHITE
MEANWHILE
OARSWOMAN
OVERWEIGH
OVERWHELM
POSTWOMAN
RAINWATER
REARWARDS
RENEWABLE
ROADWORKS
ROSEWATER
SALTWATER
SCREWBALL
SCREWEDUP
SCREWPINE
SCREWTAPE
SHIPWRECK
SIDEWARDS
SKEWWHIFF
SNOWWHITE
SOMEWHERE
STALWORTH
TEESWATER
THROWAWAY
THROWBACK
THROWDOWN
THROWSTER
ULLSWATER
WASTWATER
WESTWARDS
WHITWORTH
WIDOWHOOD
ADMIXTURE
MONOXYLON
OBNOXIOUS
TAMOXIFEN
TARAXACUM
ACETYLENE
AMARYLLIS
AMBLYOPIA
ANNOYANCE
ANONYMITY

ANONYMOUS
BELLYACHE
BELLYFLOP
BILLYCOCK
BOOBYTRAP
CANDYTUFT
CHARYBDIS
COLLYRIUM
CONDYLOMA
CORDYLINE
CUBBYHOLE
CURRYCOMB
DAIRYMAID
DANDYPRAT
DIONYSIAN
DIONYSIUS
DITHYRAMB
ECOSYSTEM
EMBRYONIC
EMPHYSEMA
ENJOYABLE
ENJOYMENT
ENTHYMEME
EPICYCLIC
EPONYMOUS
EURHYTHMY
EVERYBODY
FAIRYLAND
FAIRYTALE
FERRYBOAT
FORSYTHIA
GALLYCROW
GARRYOWEN
GLORYHOLE
GOSSYPINE
GOSSYPIUM
HEAVYDUTY
HOLLYHOCK
HOLLYWOOD
HONEYCOMB
HONEYMOON
HONKYTONK
HUNKYDORY
JELLYFISH
LAFAYETTE
LATHYRISM
MALAYSIAN
MARTYRDOM
MASSYMORE
MOLLYMAWK
MONEYWORT
NEWLYWEDS
PACHYDERM
PARHYPATE
PIGGYBACK
PIGGYBANK
POPPYCOCK
PROPYLENE
PUSSYFOOT
READYEARN
READYMADE
REPAYABLE
REPAYMENT
RUNNYMEDE
SALLYPORT
SALLYPOST
SANNYASIN
STAGYRITE
STORYBOOK
STORYLINE
TACHYLITE
TACHYLYTE
TRIDYMITE
TUMMYACHE
WALLYDRAG
WITHYWIND
BEELZEBUB
DONIZETTI
EMBEZZLER
FRIZZANTE
NIETZSCHE
QUIZZICAL
SYNIZESIS
VENEZUELA
WHIZZBANG

9:6

ABERRANCE
ABUNDANCE
ABYSMALLY
ACARIASIS
ACONCAGUA
ACROBATIC
ADAPTABLE
ADMIRABLE
ADMIRABLY
ADMIRALTY
ADRENALIN
ADVISABLE
ADVOCATED
AEROTAXIS
AFFIDAVIT
AFRIKAANS
AFRIKANER
AGREEABLE
AGREEABLY
ALDEBARAN
ALLEMANDE
ALLIGATOR
ALLOCARPY
ALLOPATHY
ALLOWABLE
ALLOWANCE
ALTERABLE
AMBULANCE
AMYGDALUS
ANABRANCH
ANAPLASTY
ANASTASIA
ANNOTATED
ANNOTATOR
ANNOYANCE
ANTENATAL
ANTIPASTO
ANTIPATHY
APOPHATIC
APPARATUS
APPLIANCE
ARAUCARIA
AREOPAGUS
ARROGANCE
ASPARAGUS
ASPIRATOR
ASSONANCE
ASSURANCE
ASTHMATIC
ATAHUALPA
ATHENAEUM
AUSTRALIA
AUTOLATRY
AUTOMAKER
AUTOMATED
AUTOMATIC
AUTOMATON
AVAILABLE
AVOIDABLE
AVOIDANCE
AXIOMATIC
BACKWARDS
BACKWATER
BAINMARIE
BALALAIKA
BALTHAZAR
BANDWAGON
BAREFACED
BASICALLY
BEEFEATER
BELLYACHE
BIGHEADED
BILLIARDS
BIOGRAPHY
BIRDTABLE
BONAPARTE
BOOKMAKER
BOOTLACES
BOTSWANAN
BRADLAUGH
BREAKABLE
BREAKAGES
BREAKAWAY
BRUMMAGEM
CAMERAMAN
CANTHARIS
CANTHARUS
CARACALLA
CARETAKER
CASTRATED
CATAMARAN
CENTRALLY
CEROMANCY
CHALIAPIN
CHAMPAGNE
CHAMPAIGN
CHARLATAN
CHAWBACON
CHICKADEE
CHIHUAHUA
CHROMATIC
CHRYSALIS
CINEMATIC
CINERARIA
CLEARANCE
CLEOPATRA
COLLEAGUE
COMICALLY
COMPLAINT
CONCEALED
CONFLATED
CONSTABLE
CONSTANCE
CONSTANCY
CONTRALTO
CORDIALLY
CRUCIALLY
CRUSTACEA
CUNCTATOR
CYNICALLY
DALLIANCE
DEBATABLE
DEBUTANTE
DECORATED
DECORATOR
DEDICATED
DEFINABLE
DEMITASSE
DESIRABLE
DETONATOR
DIASTASIS
DIGITALIN
DIGITALIS
DISCHARGE
DISGRACED
DISHWATER
DISPLACED
DISPLAYED
DISTRAINT
DJELLABAH
DOMINANCE
DOWNWARDS
DRINKABLE
DUNSTABLE
DYSPHAGIA
EASTWARDS
ECOSSAISE
ELONGATED
EMACIATED
ENCELADUS
ENCHEASON
ENDECAGON
ENDURABLE
ENDURANCE
ENIGMATIC
ENJOYABLE
ENSHEATHE
EPEOLATRY
EPISTAXIS
EQUITABLE
EQUITABLY
ERGATANER
ESCALATOR
ESMERALDA
ESOPHAGUS
ESPERANCE
ESPERANTO
ESTIMABLE
ETERNALLY
ETIOLATED
EUPHRATES
EXCAVATOR
EXCITABLE
EXCUSABLE
EXCUSABLY
EXECRABLE
EXECRABLY
EXEQUATUR
EYESHADOW
FACTUALLY
FALKLANDS
FAVORABLE
FAVORABLY
FIGURANTE
FILICALES
FILMMAKER
FIREWATER
FLAGRANCE
FLAMMABLE
FLIPPANCY
FOOLHARDY
FORETASTE
FRAGRANCE
FRAGRANCY
FREELANCE
FREEMASON
FRIZZANTE
FROGMARCH
GAELTACHT
GAINSAYER
GALAPAGOS
GALDRAGON
GARIBALDI
GAUDEAMUS
GENERALLY
GENERATOR
GENITALIA
GEOGRAPHY
GLADIATOR
GLENGARRY
GLISSANDO
GRADUALLY
GRADUATED
GREENAWAY
GREYWACKE
GRIEVANCE
GUJARATHI
GYROMANCY
HABITABLE
HALFBAKED
HANSEATIC
HARIGALDS
HEARTACHE
HEDERATED
HENDIADYS
HESITANCE
HESITANCY
HIGHLANDS
HIMALAYAN
HIMALAYAS
HINDRANCE
HOLOCAUST
HOMEWARDS
HONORABLE
HOTHEADED
HYLOBATES
HYPOCAUST
IDEOPATHY
IDIOMATIC
IGNORAMUS
IGNORANCE
ILLEGALLY
IMBALANCE
IMMANACLE
IMMORALLY
IMMOVABLE
IMMOVABLY
IMMUTABLE
IMMUTABLY
IMPEDANCE
IMPERATOR
INCAPABLE
INCITATUS

INCREASED
INCUBATOR
INCURABLE
INCURABLY
INDICATES
INDICATOR
INEFFABLE
INHUMANLY
INITIALLY
INITIATED
INITIATOR
INNOVATOR
INORGANIC
INSULATOR
INSURANCE
IRRAWADDY
IRRITABLE
IRRITABLY
IRRITATED
ISLAMABAD
ISOCRATES
JACARANDA
JERKWATER
JERUSALEM
JOCULARLY
JOUISANCE
JUBILANCE
KHANSAMAH
KINGMAKER
LACERATED
LAGNIAPPE
LAMINATED
LANDWARDS
LANGUAGES
LANTHANUM
LATERALLY
LAUGHABLE
LEHRJAHRE
LEVERAGED
LIBERALLY
LIBERATED
LIBERATOR
LINKLATER
LITERALLY
LITHUANIA
LOGICALLY
LONGRANGE
LUMINAIRE
LUMINANCE
LYMPHATIC
LYRICALLY
MACADAMIA
MACQUARIE
MAGICALLY
MAHARAJAH
MAHARANEE
MALLEABLE
MATELASSE
MATRIARCH
MAYORALTY
MEATBALLS
MEDICALLY
MEDICATED
MEDITATOR
MEHITABEL
MEMORABLE
MENOPAUSE
MESSIANIC
METABASIS
MILITANCY
MINELAYER
MISCHANCE
MISERABLE
MISERABLY
MISPLACED
MISSHAPEN
MITHRAISM
MODERATOR
MONOMACHY
MONOMANIA
MOONRAKER
MORECAMBE
MORTGAGEE
MORTGAGOR
MOSCHATEL
MOTHBALLS
MOTHEATEN
MOUSTACHE
MUCORALES
MUMCHANCE
MUSICALLY
MUTILATED
NATURALLY
NAUSEATED
NAVIGABLE
NAVIGATOR
NEUCHATEL
NEUTRALLY
NEWSPAPER
NICARAGUA
NOMINALLY
NOMINATOR
NOTEPAPER
NOVOCAINE
NOVODAMUS
NUMERAIRE
NUMERATOR
OBEISANCE
OCCUPANCY
OFFCHANCE
OFFSEASON
OLECRANON
OMOPHAGIC
OPSIMATHY
OPTICALLY
ORDINAIRE
ORDINANCE
ORIFLAMME
OROGRAPHY
OUDENARDE
OVERHASTY
OVERPAINT
OVERRATED
OVERVALUE
PACEMAKER
PAGLIACCI
PAILLASSE
PALATABLE
PALLIASSE
PANCHAYAT
PANORAMIC
PAPARAZZI
PAPARAZZO
PARABASIS
PARTIALLY
PATRIARCH
PEACEABLE
PEACEABLY
PECULATOR
PEDERASTY
PENDRAGON
PERCHANCE
PERIPATUS
PERMEABLE
PERSUADED
PETULANCE
PHANTASMA
PHARSALIA
PHILLABEG
PIGHEADED
PLEASANCE
PLUMDAMAS
PNEUMATIC
POCKMANKY
POIGNANCY
POLEMARCH
POLONAISE
POPULARLY
POPULATED
PORBEAGLE
PORTRAYAL
POSTCARDS
POSTNATAL
PRAGMATIC
PREGNANCY
PRINTABLE
PRISMATIC
PROGRAMME
PSEUDAXIS
PSORIASIS
PUISSANCE
PURCHASER
PURITANIC
PURSUANCE
PYROMANCY
PYROMANIA
QUADRATIC
QUADRATUS
QUITTANCE
RADICALLY
RAINGAUGE
RAINWATER
RATEPAYER
REACHABLE
REARRANGE
REARWARDS
RECUSANCE
REDHEADED
REFINANCE
REGULARLY
REGULATOR
REISTAFEL
RELEVANCE
REMBRANDT
REMOVABLE
RENEWABLE
RENOVATOR
REPAYABLE
REPUTABLE
RESONANCE
RESONATOR
RESTRAINT
REYKJAVIK
RHEOTAXIS
RHEUMATIC
ROSEWATER
ROSINANTE
ROZINANTE
RUFFIANLY
SACCHARIN
SALERATUS
SALTWATER
SANDPAPER
SANNYASIN
SASQUATCH
SATURATED
SCABLANDS
SCALEABLE
SCALLAWAG
SCARLATTI
SCHEMATIC
SCHOLARCH
SCHOLARLY
SCIAMACHY
SCIOMANCY
SCRUTATOR
SCUDDALER
SEANNACHY
SEMBLANCE
SEMIRAMIS
SENSUALLY
SEPARABLE
SEPARATED
SEPARATOR
SERENADER
SEVERALLY
SEVERANCE
SHAMIANAH
SHETLANDS
SHILLABER
SHOEMAKER
SIBILANCE
SIDEWARDS
SIMILARLY
SIMULATED
SIMULATOR
SKIAMACHY
SLAMMAKIN
SLAPHAPPY
SOLITAIRE
SOUVLAKIA
SOVENANCE
SPARTACUS
SPATIALLY
SPECIALLY
SPECIALTY
SPECTACLE
SPECTATOR
SPINNAKER
SQUINANCY
STANDARDS
STANNATOR
STARGAZER
STINGAREE
STOICALLY
STORIATED
STORNAWAY
STRATAGEM
SUBSTANCE
SUFFRAGAN
SUPINATOR
SURCHARGE
TABULATOR
TACAMAHAC
TARAXACUM
TEACHABLE
TEESWATER
TELEPATHY
TELESALES
THAUMATIN
THINKABLE
THOUSANDS
THROWAWAY
TIMETABLE
TINGUAITE
TOLERABLE
TOLERABLY
TOLERANCE
TOLERATED
TOOTHACHE
TOPDRAWER
TOPICALLY
TRACEABLE
TRACTABLE
TRAINABLE
TRAUMATIC
TREGEAGLE
TRIERARCH
TRIVIALLY
TROSSACHS
TROUBADOR
TRUNCATED
TUMMYACHE
TURNTABLE
TYPICALLY
ULLSWATER
ULTIMATUM
UNASHAMED
UNBALANCE
UNDAMAGED
UNEATABLE
UNEQUALED
UNRELATED
UNSHEATHE
UNTENABLE
UNTREATED
UNUSUALLY
URTICARIA
URUGUAYAN
UTTERANCE
VEGETABLE
VEGETATOR
VENERABLE
VENGEANCE
VERITABLE
VIGILANCE
VIGILANTE
VIRTUALLY
WALLPAPER
WANCHANCY
WASHBASIN
WASTWATER
WESTWARDS
WHITTAWER
WINDFALLS
WOODLANDS
WORMEATEN
XENOMANIA
YGGDRASIL
ZYGOMATIC
ABSORBENT
ABSORBING

ADVERBIAL
AITCHBONE
AMPHIBIAN
ARCHIBALD
ARQUEBUSE
ATTRIBUTE
AYLESBURY
BARNABITE
BILLABONG
BLACKBALL
BLACKBIRD
BLOODBATH
CALEMBOUR
CAMEMBERT
CANTABILE
CARAMBOLA
CARIBBEAN
CHARABANC
CHARYBDIS
CHECKBOOK
CHEEKBONE
CHERUBINI
COENOBITE
COENOBIUM
COLOMBIAN
COLOMBIER
COLUMBARY
COLUMBATE
COLUMBIAN
COLUMBINE
COLUMBITE
COLUMBIUM
CONCUBINE
CONNUBIAL
CROOKBACK
CROSSBEAM
CROSSBILL
CROSSBRED
CROWSBILL
DECUMBENT
DISEMBARK
DOTHEBOYS
ELIZABETH
ENCUMBENT
ETHELBERT
EVERYBODY
EXCAMBION
FENCIBLES
FERRYBOAT
FLASHBACK
FLASHBULB
FRITHBORH
FROSTBITE
FUNGIBLES
GALLABEAH
GREENBACK
GUIDEBOOK
GUTENBERG
HATCHBACK
HAWCUBITE
HAWKSBILL
HEARTBEAT
HEARTBURN
HELLEBORE
HOBGOBLIN
HORSEBACK
HOUSEBOAT
HUCKABACK
HUNCHBACK
HYPERBOLA
HYPERBOLE
IMPROBITY
INCUMBENT
INSELBERG
INTERBRED
JARLSBERG
LUXEMBURG
MAGDEBURG
MOTORBIKE
MOTORBOAT
NEIGHBOUR
NOTCHBACK
NUREMBERG
NUTJOBBER
ODDJOBMAN
OFFENBACH
OTTERBURN
PALPEBRAL
PAPERBACK
PICKABACK
PIGGYBACK
PIGGYBANK
PINCHBECK
POLITBURO
POSSIBLES
POWERBOAT
PROBABLES
RACCABOUT
RAZORBILL
RECUMBENT
REFURBISH
REPROBATE
RIDGEBACK
ROCAMBOLE
ROUNDBACK
SAUCEBOAT
SCRAMBLER
SCRAPBOOK
SCREWBALL
SCRUBBING
SHELLBACK
SHRUBBERY
SLINGBACK
SOUNDBITE
SPEEDBOAT
SPELLBIND
SPOONBILL
STEAMBOAT
STEENBRAS
STEINBECK
STEINBOCK
STILLBORN
STILTBIRD
STINKBIRD
STIRABOUT
STONEBOAT
STOOLBALL
STORYBOOK
STROMBOLI
STYLOBATE
SUCCUBINE
SWEATBAND
SYLLABARY
SYLLABLES
THIGHBONE
THORNBACK
THORNBILL
THROBBING
THROWBACK
TITHEBARN
TRILOBITE
TURNABOUT
UNDERBRED
UNDOUBTED
VENUSBERG
VERTEBRAE
VERTEBRAL
VESTIBULE
WAGENBOOM
WAISTBAND
WALKABOUT
WALLABIES
WATERBABY
WATERBUTT
WHALEBOAT
WHALEBONE
WHEELBASE
WHITEBAIT
WHIZZBANG
WINNEBAGO
YOHIMBINE
YTTERBIUM
AFFLICTED
AFFRICATE
AFTERCARE
AGALACTIC
ALTERCATE
AMBUSCADE
AMERICIUM
ANDROCLES
ANGLICISM
ANTARCTIC
APPLICANT
AUTOSCOPY
BANDICOOT
BARMECIDE
BARNACLES
BARRACUDA
BARRICADE
BARYSCOPE
BEDJACKET
BELLICOSE
BENBECULA
BIFURCATE
BILLYCOCK
BOCCACCIO
BRAINCASE
BRIEFCASE
BRITSCHKA
BROADCAST
CACHECTIC
CAPRICCIO
CAPRICORN
CARPACCIO
CATCHCROP
CAVALCADE
CEVAPCICI
CHARACTER
CHILDCARE
CLIMACTIC
CLINICIAN
COCKSCOMB
COLLECTED
COLLECTOR
COLLOCATE
COMPACTLY
CONDUCIVE
CONDUCTOR
CONDUCTUS
CONFUCIUS
CONNECTED
CONNECTOR
CONVECTOR
CORKSCREW
CORRECTED
CORRECTLY
CORRECTOR
CORUSCATE
COXSACKIE
CRITICISM
CRITICIZE
CURRYCOMB
DAMASCENE
DEBAUCHED
DEBAUCHEE
DEFALCATE
DEFLECTOR
DEMARCATE
DEMULCENT
DEPRECATE
DESICCATE
DETRACTOR
DIALECTAL
DIALECTIC
DIETICIAN
DIFFICULT
DISLOCATE
DUODECIMO
DUPLICAND
DUPLICATE
DUPLICITY
EMBRACERY
EMBRACING
EMBROCATE
EMPLECTON
ENCIRCLED
ENDEICTIC
ENSORCELL
ENTRECHAT
ENTRECÔTE
EPICYCLIC
EPINICION
ERADICATE
EROTICISM
EXPISCATE
EXPLICATE
EXSICCATE
EXTRACTOR
EXTRICATE
FABRICATE
FATISCENT
FINANCIAL
FINANCIER
FLASHCUBE
FORFICATE
FORNICATE
FRUITCAKE
FULLSCALE
FUNGICIDE
GALLICISM
GALLYCROW
GERMICIDE
GRATICULE
GREATCOAT
GYNOECIUM
GYROSCOPE
HEADSCARF
HENPECKED
HERBICIDE
HIPPOCRAS
HITCHCOCK
HONEYCOMB
HOOLACHAN
HOROSCOPE
HOUSECOAT
HURRICANE
HURRICANO
IGNESCENT
IMBRICATE
IMBROCATE
IMPEACHER
IMPLICATE
IMPRECATE
IMPRECISE
INCULCATE
INSINCERE
INSPECTOR
INTERCEDE
INTERCEPT
INTERCITY
INTRICACY
INTRICATE
INVOICING
ISOTACTIC
ITALICIZE
JAMPACKED
KNAPSCULL
KONISCOPE
LANDSCAPE
LAODICEAN
LATESCENT
LEUCOCYTE
LITHOCYST
LONGICORN
LOQUACITY
LUBRICANT
LUBRICATE
LUTESCENT
MACROCOSM
MAJUSCULE
MANDICATE
MANDUCATE
MASTICATE
MATRICIDE
MEGASCOPE
MENDACITY
MENDICANT
MENTICIDE
METRICATE
MICROCHIP
MICROCOSM
MICROCYTE
MINISCULE
MINUSCULE
MISLOCATE
MISPICKEL
MONTACUTE
MONTICULE
MORTICIAN
MOTORCADE
MUTOSCOPE
MYRMECOID

MYSTICISM
NANTUCKET
NAUMACHIA
NEGLECTED
NIGHTCLUB
OBFUSCATE
OCHLOCRAT
OLIGOCENE
OPHIUCHUS
OSTRACISM
OSTRACIZE
PAPERCLIP
PARASCENE
PARASCEVE
PARBUCKLE
PARRICIDE
PARTICLES
PASTICCIO
PATERCOVE
PATRICIAN
PATRICIDE
PATROCLUS
PENTECOST
PERFECTLY
PERISCIAN
PERISCOPE
PERSECUTE
PESTICIDE
PETTICOAT
PHAGOCYTE
PHENACITE
PHONECARD
PHOTOCOPY
PHYSICIAN
PHYSICIST
PICNICKER
PILLICOCK
PINCHCOCK
PINOCCHIO
PISTACHIO
PIZZICATO
PLEIOCENE
PLUTOCRAT
POPPYCOCK
PRECOCITY
PREDICANT
PREDICATE
PREDICTOR
PRELECTOR
PREOCCUPY
PROCACITY
PROJECTED
PROJECTOR
PROLACTIN
PROMACHOS
PROSECUTE
PROTECTOR
PUBLICIST
PUBLICITY
PUBLICIZE
PUGNACITY
QUIESCENT
RADICCHIO
RECONCILE
REFLECTOR
REFRACTOR
REJOICING
RENASCENT
REPERCUSS
REPLACING
REPLICATE
REPROCESS
RESPECTED
RESPECTER
RETRACTOR
RETROCEDE
RICERCARE
ROUGHCAST
RUDBECKIA
RUFESCENT
RUSTICATE
SAPSUCKER
SARBACANE
SCARECROW
SCHNECKEN
SCOLECITE
SCRATCHED
SCRATCHES
SENESCENT
SENESCHAL
SEPULCHER
SEPULCHRE
SERVICING
SHORTCAKE
SIMULCAST
SKYJACKER
SOLLICKER
SOMASCOPE
SOPHOCLES
SPHINCTER
SPOROCARP
SPRAICKLE
SPRAUCHLE
STAIRCASE
STAUNCHLY
STOMACHIC
STONECHAT
STONECROP
STRETCHED
STRETCHER
SUBJACENT
SUFFOCATE
SUGARCANE
SUSPECTED
SUSPICION
SYNDICATE
SYNOECETE
SYNTACTIC
SYRIACISM
TACTICIAN
TARMACKED
TELESCOPE
TERRACING
TERRICOLE
TESTICLES
THYLACINE
TICTACTOE
TOOTHCOMB
TRANSCEND
TREBUCHET
TRITICALE
TUMESCENT
UNCHECKED
UNCONCERN
UNDERCAST
UNDERCOAT
UNMATCHED
UNPRECISE
UNSHACKLE
UNTOUCHED
UNWELCOME
VARISCITE
VELLICATE
VINDICATE
VITASCOPE
VORTICISM
WAISTCOAT
WINDSCALE
WITTICISM
ABOUNDING
ABSURDITY
ACCORDANT
ACCORDING
ACCORDION
AFTERDAMP
ALMANDINE
APHRODITE
APPENDAGE
ASCENDANT
ASCENDING
ASTRODOME
ATTENDANT
BALLADEER
BALLADIST
BEDRIDDEN
BELVEDERE
BREAKDOWN
BRIGADIER
BRIGADOON
BURUNDIAN
BYPRODUCT
CALENDULA
CAMBODIAN
CANDIDACY
CANDIDATE
CATHEDRAL
CAVENDISH
CELANDINE
CHURIDARS
CIRCADIAN
CLAMPDOWN
COLLODION
COMMODITY
COMMODORE
CONFIDANT
CONFIDENT
CONUNDRUM
COUNTDOWN
COVERDALE
COWARDICE
CRACKDOWN
CROCODILE
CUSPIDORE
CUSTODIAL
CUSTODIAN
CYMBIDIUM
DAMNEDEST
DEFENDANT
DEFENDERS
DEGRADING
DEMANDING
DEOXIDISE
DEPENDANT
DEPENDENT
DEPENDING
DEPREDATE
DIFFIDENT
DISSIDENT
DRAVIDIAN
DROMEDARY
DRYASDUST
EAVESDROP
EDWARDIAN
EIDERDOWN
ELUCIDATE
EMMERDALE
ENNERDALE
EPICEDIUM
EUCLIDEAN
EXCLUDING
EXTRADITE
FACUNDITY
FARANDOLE
FECUNDITY
FORBIDDEN
FRIGIDITY
GABARDINE
GABERDINE
GERUNDIVE
GIRANDOLE
GIRONDIST
GRAVADLAX
GRENADIER
GRENADINE
GROUNDHOG
GROUNDING
GROUNDNUT
GROUNDSEL
HABERDINE
HAYRADDIN
HAZARDOUS
HEAVYDUTY
HEBRIDEAN
HIPPODAME
HIRUNDINE
HUNKYDORY
IMPENDING
IMPRUDENT
INCARDINE
INCLUDING
INCONDITE
INERUDITE
INTENDANT
INTENDING
INTERDICT
INTRODUCE
IPRINDOLE
KNOCKDOWN
LAMPADARY
LAMPADION
LEGENDARY
LIMPIDITY
LIQUIDATE
LIQUIDITY
LIQUIDIZE
LONGEDFOR
MAJORDOMO
MARAUDING
METHADONE
METHODISM
METHODIST
MORBIDITY
MUSCADINE
NEFANDOUS
NITHSDALE
OBCORDATE
OFFENDING
ORMANDINE
ORTHODOXY
OSTEODERM
OUTSIDERS
PACHYDERM
PALLADIAN
PALLADIUM
PERIODATE
PETHIDINE
PLACIDITY
POMPADOUR
POUJADIST
PRECEDENT
PRECEDING
PREJUDICE
PREORDAIN
PRESIDENT
PRESIDIAL
PRESIDIUM
PROCEDURE
PROVEDORE
PROVIDENT
PROVIDING
PTERIDIUM
QUOTIDIAN
RANCIDITY
RECONDITE
RECORDING
RECORDIST
REDUNDANT
REGARDANT
REGARDFUL
REGARDING
REPRODUCE
REWARDING
ROTUNDATE
ROTUNDITY
SANHEDRIM
SANHEDRIN
SANHEDRON
SCORODITE
SCOUNDREL
SCRODDLED
SECONDARY
SHAKEDOWN
SHELDDUCK
SHIELDING
SKEDADDLE
SOLFIDIAN
SOUTHDOWN
SPHENDONE
SPLENDOUR
SPREADING
STERADIAN
STEVEDORE
STOLIDITY
STUPIDITY
SUBSIDIZE
SWANSDOWN
SYMPODIUM
TALMUDIST
THECODONT
THORNDYKE
THREADFIN
THROWDOWN

TOLPUDDLE
TOUCHDOWN
TRAGEDIAN
TRIHEDRON
TURBIDITY
UNBENDING
UNBRIDLED
UNDERDONE
UNFLEDGED
UNHEEDING
UNMINDFUL
UNTRODDEN
VIDEODISC
WALLYDRAG
WHITEDAMP
WRONGDOER
ABERNETHY
ACCIDENTS
ACQUIESCE
ADHERENCE
ADULTERER
ADVISEDLY
AESTHETIC
AFFLUENCE
AGGRIEVED
AHASUERUS
ALLEGEDLY
ALTIMETER
ANALGESIA
ANALGESIC
ANOPHELES
ANTIHELIX
ANTIVENIN
APATHETIC
AQUARELLE
AQUILEGIA
ARBORETUM
ARMAMENTS
ASSUREDLY
ASYMMETRY
AUBRIETIA
BACKBENCH
BACKPEDAL
BAGATELLE
BAKSHEESH
BANQUETTE
BAROMETER
BATTLEAXE
BEANFEAST
BEAUTEOUS
BECQUEREL
BEEKEEPER
BEELZEBUB
BELATEDLY
BETHLEHEM
BILATERAL
BLINKERED
BLISTERED
BLUEBEARD
BLUEBERRY
BLUNDERER
BLUSTERER
BOBSLEIGH
BOLSHEVIK
BOTTLEFUL
BOUNTEOUS
BOURGEOIS
BRACTEOLE
BRASSERIE
BREAKEVEN
BRIDLEWAY
BRIQUETTE
BROTHERLY
BUCKTEETH
BUMBLEBEE
CACHAEMIA
CAFETERIA
CANALETTO
CANAVERAL
CANDLELIT
CANDLEMAS
CAPORETTO
CATALEPSY
CATTLEMAN
CATTLEPEN
CENTREING
CHALLENGE
CHAMPERTY
CHANTEUSE
CHARGEFUL
CHARTERED
CHASTENED
CHATTERER
CHEQUERED
CIGARETTE
CINEREOUS
CLUSTERED
COHERENCE
COLUMELLA
CONCIERGE
CONQUEROR
COTYLEDON
COUCHETTE
COUNSELOR
COURGETTE
COURTELLE
COURTEOUS
COURTESAN
COVALENCY
CRANBERRY
CRESCELLE
CRESCENDO
CRICKETER
CROOKEDLY
CROQUETTE
CROSSEYED
CRYOGENIC
CRYOMETER
CUTANEOUS
CYNEGETIC
DAREDEVIL
DECADENCE
DECAMERON
DECIDEDLY
DEFERENCE
DELINEATE
DELIVERER
DIABLERIE
DIAERESIS
DIANOETIC
DIATHESIS
DILIGENCE
DIOCLETES
DISCREDIT
DISPLEASE
DIVIDENDS
DOCUMENTS
DONATELLO
DONIZETTI
DOODLEBUG
DRUNKENLY
DUNDREARY
ECHEVERIA
EDELWEISS
EFFLUENCE
ELOQUENCE
EMERGENCE
EMERGENCY
ENERGETIC
ENGINEERS
ENLIVENED
ENTELECHY
ENUCLEATE
EPAULETTE
EPHEMERAL
EPHEMERIS
EPHEMERON
EPICLESIS
EPIGAEOUS
EPITHESIS
EQUISETUM
ERIOMETER
ERRONEOUS
ESCOPETTE
ESCULENTS
ESTAFETTE
ETCETERAS
ETHEREOUS
ETIQUETTE
EUHEMERUS
EUMYCETES
EVANGELIC
EXCISEMAN
EXISTENCE
EYEOPENER
FABACEOUS
FEATHERED
FIFTEENTH
FILOSELLE
FIRSTEVER
FLATTENED
FLATTENER
FLATTERED
FLATTERER
FLECHETTE
FLUSTERED
FOLKWEAVE
FOREBEARS
FOURPENCE
FRAGMENTS
FRANCESCA
FREQUENCY
FRESHENER
FRUITERER
GASOMETER
GEARLEVER
GENTEELLY
GENTLEMAN
GENTLEMEN
GEORGETTE
GLAIREOUS
GREASEGUN
GREYBEARD
GROSVENOR
GUILLEMOT
HACKNEYED
HACQUETON
HAECCEITY
HALFPENNY
HARQUEBUS
HECOGENIN
HEXAMERON
HEXAMETER
HEXATEUCH
HEYPRESTO
HODOMETER
HUNDREDTH
HURRIEDLY
ILLIBERAL
IMMANENCE
IMMANENCY
IMMINENCE
IMMODESTY
IMPOTENCE
IMPUDENCE
INCIDENCE
INDECENCY
INDIGENCE
INDOLENCE
INDONESIA
INFERENCE
INFLUENCE
INFLUENZA
INNKEEPER
INNOCENCE
INSOLENCE
INTUMESCE
IPHIGENIA
ISCHAEMIC
ISOSCELES
JACQUERIE
JOBSEEKER
JOCKTELEG
JUNEBERRY
KENTLEDGE
KILOHERTZ
KILOMETER
KILOMETRE
KINTLEDGE
KITCHENER
KLEMPERER
KNACKERED
KNOWLEDGE
KONIMETER
LACKBEARD
LAFAYETTE
LAMASERAI
LANGUEDOC
LANGUETTE
LARGHETTO
LAUNCELOT
LAZARETTO
LEUKAEMIA
LIENTERIC
LINDBERGH
LIONHEART
LORGNETTE
LUCIFERIN
LYSIMETER
MADELEINE
MAINTENON
MAJORETTE
MANIFESTO
MANOMETER
MARQUESAS
MARQUETRY
MEDIAEVAL
MEGAHERTZ
MEKOMETER
MELANESIA
MENAGERIE
MENSHEVIK
METAPELET
MICKLETON
MIDDLEMAN
MIDDLESEX
MIDDLETON
MIDINETTE
MILOMETER
MINUTEMAN
MIRABELLE
MISCREANT
MISONEIST
MISTLETOE
MONOCEROS
MONOMETER
MUGGLETON
MUNIMENTS
NASEBERRY
NECKVERSE
NESCIENCE
NIAISERIE
NICKNEVEN
NICODEMUS
NINEPENCE
NIPCHEESE
NORTHEAST
NORTHERLY
NOTONECTA
NOVELETTE
OBEDIENCE
OLEORESIN
ONCOMETER
ONTOGENCY
OPENHEART
OPPONENTS
OPTOMETRY
ORANGEADE
ORANGEMAN
ORGANELLE
OUBLIETTE
OVERHEADS
OVERREACH
OVERREACT
OVERWEIGH
PADEMELON
PAILLETTE
PALOVERDE
PANATELLA
PANTHEISM
PANTHENOL
PARAMEDIC
PARAMETER
PARCHEESI
PARFLECHE
PARTHENON
PAYCHEQUE
PEDOMETER
PENDLETON
PENITENCE
PERCHERON
PERIMETER

PERPLEXED
PHRENETIC
PIROUETTE
PLASTERED
PLASTERER
PLENTEOUS
PLUMBEOUS
PLUNDERER
POINTEDLY
POLICEMAN
POLITESSE
POLYNESIA
PONTLEVIS
PORIFERAN
PORTREEVE
POULTERER
PRECIEUSE
PRIMAEVAL
PRINCETON
PROCOELUS
PROCREATE
PROPHETIC
PROTHESIS
PRURIENCE
PUERPERAL
PURULENCE
QUARTERLY
QUARTETTE
QUENNELLE
QUERCETIN
QUERCETUS
QUINTETTE
RADDLEMAN
RASPBERRY
RATTLEBAG
READYEARN
RECOVERED
REDBREAST
REDOLENCE
REFERENCE
REFUSENIK
RELIGEUSE
RENFIERST
REPUTEDLY
RESIDENCE
RESIDENCY
RETICENCE
RETRIEVAL
RETRIEVER
REVERENCE
RIGHTEOUS
RIGOLETTO
RINGFENCE
ROISTERER
ROUNCEVAL
ROUNDELAY
ROUSSETTE
RUBICELLE
RUDDLEMAN
RUDIMENTS
SADDLEBAG
SAGAPENUM
SALICETUM
SALOPETTE
SALTPETER
SALTPETRE
SCATTERED
SCHLIEREN
SCHMIEDER
SCREWEDUP
SCRIVENER
SCYTHEMAN
SEBACEOUS
SECATEURS
SENTIENCE
SERVIETTE
SETACEOUS
SHARPENER
SHATTERED
SHELTERED
SHEPHERDS
SHUTTERED
SIMPLETON
SINGLESEX
SINGLETON
SIXTEENMO
SIXTEENTH
SLUMBERER
SOLDIERLY
SONOMETER
SOUBRETTE
SOUTHEAST
SOUTHERLY
SOVEREIGN
SPAGHETTI
SPATTERED
SPEAKEASY
SPHACELUS
SPINNERET
SPLENETIC
SPONGEBAG
SPRITEFUL
SQUIREAGE
STABLEBOY
STABLELAD
STABLEMAN
STAGGERED
STAMMERER
STANDERBY
STATUETTE
STIFFENER
STONKERED
STRATEGIC
STRIDENCY
SUCCEEDED
SUPERETTE
SURQUEDRY
SWAGGERER
SWEETENER
SWINGEING
SYNIZESIS
SYNTHESIS
SYNTHETIC
TAILLEFER
TAOISEACH
TAXIDERMY
TAXIMETER
TEMULENCE
TENEMENTS
THACKERAY
THRENETIC
THUNDERER
TIERCERON
TIGHTENER
TITTLEBAT
TONOMETER
TOURNEDOS
TRIETERIC
TRINKETER
TRIPMETER
TROMPETTE
TROPAELIN
TRUEPENNY
TRUMPEDUP
TRUMPETER
TUILLETTE
UMPTEENTH
UNALTERED
UNCOVERED
UNHOPEFUL
UNTIMEOUS
UNWATERED
USHERETTE
VAPORETTO
VARICELLA
VEHEMENCE
VEILLEUSE
VENEREOUS
VESTMENTS
VICEREGAL
VICEREINE
VIRULENCE
VOLAGEOUS
VOLTMETER
WAGONETTE
WELLBEING
WELTGEIST
WHICHEVER
WHOSOEVER
WILDGEESE
WIMBLEDON
WINEBERRY
WITCHETTY
ZEITGEIST
ZUCCHETTO
ABOUTFACE
AMPLIFIER
BELLYFLOP
BLACKFACE
BLACKFOOT
BLINDFOLD
BREAKFAST
CEASEFIRE
CERTIFIED
CHAUFFEUR
CLARIFIER
CLINGFILM
COCKSFOOT
COLTSFOOT
COMINFORM
CROCKFORD
CROSSFIRE
CROWSFOOT
CUNEIFORM
CURFUFFLE
DANDIFIED
DIGNIFIED
DISAFFIRM
DISINFECT
EARTHFLAX
ERUCIFORM
FEBRIFUGE
FIELDFARE
GLORIFIED
GOOSEFOOT
GREENFEED
HEARTFELT
HEREAFTER
HORRIFIED
HYDROFOIL
IMPERFECT
INNISFAIL
INNISFREE
INTERFACE
INTERFERE
JELLYFISH
JUSTIFIED
KERFUFFLE
KHALIFATE
KOMINFORM
LIGHTFOOT
LIQUEFIED
MAGNIFIER
MICROFILM
MIDWIFERY
MISINFORM
MORTIFIED
MULTIFORM
NIGHTFALL
NIGHTFIRE
OCULIFORM
PANTOFFLE
PETRIFIED
PITCHFORK
PROKOFIEV
PUSSYFOOT
QUALIFIED
QUALIFIER
RECTIFIER
RESHUFFLE
RESTIFORM
RESURFACE
RETROFLEX
ROQUEFORT
ROUNDFISH
SACRIFICE
SAINTFOIN
SASSAFRAS
SATISFIED
SCALDFISH
SCARIFIER
SCRUFFILY
SERREFILE
SHAMEFAST
SHEEPFOLD
SHELLFISH
SHORTFALL
SMOKEFREE
SPECIFICS
SPECIFIED
SPOONFEED
STEADFAST
STERNFAST
STOCKFISH
STUPEFIED
SUPERFINE
SWORDFISH
TECTIFORM
TERRIFIED
TESTIFIER
THEREFORE
THREEFOLD
TOWNSFOLK
TRANSFORM
TRANSFUSE
UNCONFINE
UNDERFELT
UNDERFOOT
UNRUFFLED
UNSELFISH
VENTIFACT
VERMIFORM
VERMIFUGE
VERSIFIER
WATERFALL
WATERFORD
WATERFOWL
WHEREFORE
WHITEFISH
WHOLEFOOD
WOMENFOLK
WRECKFISH
WRONGFOOT
ABORIGINE
AFTERGLOW
AGGREGATE
AMBERGRIS
ANALOGOUS
ANGIOGRAM
APOLOGIST
APOLOGIZE
ARCTOGAEA
ARLINGTON
ASTRAGALS
AUBERGINE
BEDRAGGLE
BELEAGUER
BELONGING
BILINGUAL
BIOLOGIST
BORNAGAIN
CABLEGRAM
CAIRNGORM
CARTOGRAM
CASTIGATE
CHEONGSAM
COLLEGIAN
COLLIGATE
CONJUGATE
CONSIGNEE
CONSIGNOR
CONTAGION
CORREGGIO
CORRUGATE
COSMOGONY
COTANGENT
DARTAGNAN
DETERGENT
DIALOGITE
DISENGAGE
DISFIGURE
DISREGARD
DIVERGENT
DIVERGING
ECOLOGIST
EDDINGTON
EFFINGHAM
EFFULGENT
ELLINGTON
EMBROGLIO
ERPINGHAM
EXPURGATE

FALANGIST
FERINGHEE
FLOODGATE
FOREIGNER
FUSTIGATE
GALENGALE
GALINGALE
GEOLOGIST
GREENGAGE
HABERGEON
HARROGATE
HEMINGWAY
HISTOGRAM
HUMONGOUS
HUMUNGOUS
IMBROGLIO
INDULGENT
INELEGANT
INSTIGATE
INSURGENT
INTRIGUED
INTRIGUER
IRVINGISM
KENTIGERN
LENINGRAD
LOHENGRIN
MALENGINE
METHEGLIN
MILLIGRAM
MISTIGRIS
MONERGISM
MONSIGNOR
MUSKOGEAN
NEGLIGENT
NEOLOGISM
NEUROGLIA
NEWSAGENT
NIGHTGOWN
NORWEGIAN
NYSTAGMUS
OBBLIGATO
OBJURGATE
ORPINGTON
OSTROGOTH
OUTRIGGER
PACKAGING
PANTAGAMY
PATHOGENY
PEKINGESE
PELLAGRIN
PHONOGRAM
PHOTOGENE
PHYLOGENY
PICTOGRAM
PREFIGURE
PRESSGANG
PROPAGATE
PROROGATE
RADIOGRAM
REDINGOTE
REFULGENT
RESURGENT
RUDDIGORE
SALANGANE
SALESGIRL
SAUVIGNON
SCAPEGOAT
SEGREGATE
SERENGETI
SOLFEGGIO
SPRINGALD
SPRINGBOK
SPRINGLET
STANDGALE
STRAGGLER
STRANGELY
STRANGLER
STRANGLES
STRANGURY
STRINGENT
STRINGOPS
STRONGARM
STRONGYLE
SUBJUGATE
SUBROGATE
SURROGATE
SYLLOGISM
SYNANGIUM
SYNERGIST
TARRAGONA
TERMAGANT
TERMAGENT
TETRAGRAM
THRONGING
TRIANGLED
TRISAGION
TURMAGENT
VARANGIAN
VARIEGATE
VERDIGRIS
VESTIGIAL
VOLGOGRAD
VOLTIGEUR
VORTIGERN
WATERGATE
WHEATGERM
WOBBEGONG
WOEBEGONE
ZOOLOGIST
ACROPHONY
ADULTHOOD
AGUECHEEK
ALPENHORN
AMIDSHIPS
AMORPHOUS
ANARCHIST
ANTIPHONY
APARTHEID
APPREHEND
ARROWHEAD
ARTICHOKE
BACKSHISH
BEACHHEAD
BENIGHTED
BIOSPHERE
BLACKHEAD
BLASPHEME
BLASPHEMY
BLEACHERS
BLOCKHEAD
BOMBSHELL
BOOKSHELF
BRANCHING
BREATHING
BREECHING
BRONCHIAL
BROUGHTON
BUCKTHORN
BUCKWHEAT
CACOPHONY
CARTWHEEL
CATECHISM
CATECHIZE
CHILDHOOD
CHURCHILL
CHURCHMAN
COLOPHONY
CROTCHETY
CUBBYHOLE
DACHSHUND
DASHWHEEL
DECACHORD
DECATHLON
DECKCHAIR
DELIGHTED
DIARRHOEA
DIPHTHONG
ELKOSHITE
ELSEWHERE
ENLIGHTEN
ENTOPHYTE
EPARCHATE
ERSTWHILE
EXANTHEMA
EXOSPHERE
FALSEHOOD
FAULCHION
FINISHING
FIRSTHAND
FLOWCHART
FOMALHAUT
FORESHORE
FOURWHEEL
FRANCHISE
FRATCHETY
FREEPHONE
FREEWHEEL
FREIGHTER
FRENCHMAN
FRENCHMEN
GATESHEAD
GEARSHIFT
GEARWHEEL
GLORYHOLE
GOOSEHERD
GREENHEAD
GREENHORN
GUILDHALL
HALOPHILE
HALOTHANE
HANDSHAKE
HARDIHOOD
HARDSHELL
HARTSHORN
HEALTHILY
HEARTHRUG
HEDYPHANE
HESYCHASM
HESYCHAST
HITCHHIKE
HOLLYHOCK
HOLOPHOTE
HOMOPHONE
HORSEHAIR
HOUSEHOLD
IDIOPHONE
IODOPHILE
JEPHTHAHS
JOSEPHINE
JOSEPHSON
KICKSHAWS
KRUMMHORN
LAMPSHADE
LAUNCHING
LEASEHOLD
LENGTHILY
LILYWHITE
LOAMSHIRE
LOGOTHETE
LONGCHAMP
LONGSHORE
LOOSEHEAD
LUSTIHOOD
MAKESHIFT
MALACHITE
MALATHION
MASOCHISM
MASOCHIST
MEANWHILE
MEGAPHONE
MILKSHAKE
MISBEHAVE
MONKSHOOD
MONOCHORD
MOONSHINE
MOUSEHOLE
MUSICHALL
NABATHEAN
NEWSSHEET
NOMOTHETE
NOOSPHERE
NOTOCHORD
OCTACHORD
OPPENHEIM
OPTOPHONE
OVERSHADE
OVERSHOES
OVERSHOOT
OVERTHROW
OVERWHELM
PARACHUTE
PARATHION
PAROCHIAL
PAROCHINE
PERIPHERY
PERISHING
PHOSPHATE
PHOSPHENE
PICKTHANK
PLAYTHING
PLOUGHMAN
POLYPHONE
POLYPHONY
POLYTHENE
PRONGHORN
PROUDHORN
PUNISHING
PUSHCHAIR
PYRETHRUM
RACCAHOUT
RAINCHECK
RAVISHING
REPECHAGE
REPREHEND
RIDERHOOD
RIGHTHAND
RORSCHACH
ROUNDHAND
ROUNDHEAD
SAINTHOOD
SAXOPHONE
SCONCHEON
SCORCHING
SCOTCHMAN
SCUNCHEON
SEARCHING
SELACHION
SEMAPHORE
SERAPHINE
SHEIKHDOM
SHIPSHAPE
SHOESHINE
SHORTHAND
SHORTHAUL
SHORTHOLD
SHORTHORN
SISYPHEAN
SKETCHILY
SKETCHMAP
SKETCHPAD
SKEWWHIFF
SLAUGHTER
SLOUGHING
SNOWSHOES
SNOWWHITE
SOMETHING
SOMEWHERE
SPEARHEAD
SPEECHIFY
SPRECHERY
SPRIGHTLY
STAGEHAND
STANCHION
STATEHOOD
STEELHEAD
STINKHORN
STOCKHOLM
STONEHAND
STRAPHANG
SWINEHERD
SYCOPHANT
TABASHEER
TEARSHEET
TELEPHONE
TELEPHONY
TELEPHOTO
THATCHING
THICKHEAD
THRASHING
THRESHOLD
TIGHTHEAD
TIMESHARE
TISIPHONE
TOXOPHILY
TRANSHUME
TREACHERY
TRENCHANT
TRIATHLON
TRONDHEIM
TRUNCHEON
UNDERHAND
UNSIGHTLY

UPAITHRIC
VANISHING
WATERHOLE
WHITEHALL
WHITEHEAD
WIDOWHOOD
WINDCHILL
WOMANHOOD
WOODCHUCK
WOODSHOCK
XENOPHOBE
XEROPHYTE
XYLOPHONE
YORKSHIRE
ABDOMINAL
ABLUTIONS
ABSTAINER
ADENOIDAL
ADMONITOR
AFFILIATE
ALEURITIS
ALGORITHM
ALLEGIANT
ALLEVIATE
AMBITIOUS
ANCIPITAL
ANTONINUS
APENNINES
APPARITOR
APPETIZER
APPRAISAL
ARKWRIGHT
ARMADILLO
ARRIVISTE
ARSENICAL
ARTEMISIA
ARTERIOLE
ARTHRITIC
ARTHRITIS
ARTIFICER
ASSOCIATE
ASTUCIOUS
ATROCIOUS
AUDACIOUS
AUTOPILOT
AUXILIARY
BACKBITER
BASILICAL
BASILICON
BEAUTIFUL
BEESTINGS
BEHAVIOUR
BEVERIDGE
BLESSINGS
BOLIVIANO
BOTANICAL
BOUNTIFUL
BOYFRIEND
BRANDIRON
BRASSICAS
BRASSIERE
BRILLIANT
BRUNHILDE
BULLFIGHT
BULLFINCH
BUMPTIOUS
CAFETIERE
CALORIFIC
CAMBRIDGE
CANONICAL
CAPACIOUS
CAPACITOR
CAPARISON
CAPTAINCY
CARTRIDGE
CATSKILLS
CERATITIS
CERTAINLY
CERTAINTY
CHAFFINCH
CHANTILLY
CHIPPINGS
CHRONICLE
CIVILISED
CIVILIZED
CLASSICAL
COALFIELD
COALMINER
COCKAIGNE
COCKFIGHT
COLCHICUM
COLERIDGE
COLLOIDAL
COMPLIANT
CONCEITED
CONSCIOUS
CONTAINER
CONTRIVED
CONTRIVER
COPYRIGHT
CORNEILLE
CORNFIELD
CUFFLINKS
DEADLIGHT
DECALITRE
DEFICIENT
DEFOLIANT
DEFOLIATE
DELICIOUS
DELIRIOUS
DEPOSITOR
DESIPIENT
DIACRITIC
DIRIGIBLE
DISGUISED
DISORIENT
DISUNITED
DIVISIBLE
DOCTRINAL
DOLOMITES
DOLOMITIC
DOMICILED
DOMINICAL
DOMINICAN
DOWNRIGHT
DROPPINGS
DROPSICAL
DYNAMITED
EASTLINGS
EBULLIENT
ECARDINES
EFFICIENT
EGREGIOUS
EIGHTIETH
ELUTRIATE
EMBROIDER
EMBROILED
EMOLLIATE
EMOLLIENT
EMPIRICAL
ENGRAINED
ENTERITIS
ENUNCIATE
EPHESIANS
EQUALIZER
ERISTICAL
ESTAMINET
EUMENIDES
EURIPIDES
EXCALIBUR
EXCIPIENT
EXCLAIMED
EXCORIATE
EXERCISED
EXERCISES
EXHIBITOR
EXPATIATE
EXPEDIENT
EXPLOITER
EXPOSITOR
EYEBRIGHT
FABULINUS
FACETIOUS
FANATICAL
FATIDICAL
FEDUCIARY
FERACIOUS
FEROCIOUS
FIDUCIARY
FIRELIGHT
FLYWEIGHT
FOOTHILLS
FORESIGHT
FORFEITED
FORTNIGHT
FRACTIOUS
FRUCTIDOR
FUGACIOUS
FURACIOUS
GAULEITER
GENETICAL
GENEVIEVE
GLEANINGS
GLENLIVET
GOLDFIELD
GOLDFINCH
GOLDSINNY
GOODNIGHT
GOONHILLY
GRAMPIANS
GRANDIOSE
GRAPHICAL
GREETINGS
GRENVILLE
GRISAILLE
GRUBBINOL
GUERRILLA
GUMSHIELD
HAIRPIECE
HALOBIONT
HANDPIECE
HARDLINER
HEADFIRST
HEADLIGHT
HEADLINED
HEMSTITCH
HEPATICAL
HEPATITIS
HERETICAL
HIGHLIGHT
HILARIOUS
HILLBILLY
HINDSIGHT
HOBNAILED
HOMICIDAL
HONORIFIC
HUMILIATE
ICTERIDAE
IDENTICAL
IDENTIKIT
IDIOTICON
ILLEGIBLE
ILLEGIBLY
ILLICITLY
ILLOGICAL
IMMEDIACY
IMMEDIATE
IMMUNISER
IMPATIENT
IMPERIOUS
IMPOLITIC
INAUDIBLE
INAUDIBLY
INCIPIENT
INCOMINGS
INCURIOUS
INDELIBLE
INDELIBLY
INEBRIATE
INFURIATE
INGENIOUS
INGRAINED
INHERITED
INHERITOR
INHIBITED
INJURIOUS
INPATIENT
INSCRIBED
INSIDIOUS
INSIPIENT
INTROITUS
INVIDIOUS
INVISIBLE
IRASCIBLE
IRONSIDES
IRRADIANT
IRRADIATE
JAUNDICED
JUDICIARY
JUDICIOUS
JURIDICAL
JUVENILIA
KARABINER
KERATITIS
KINGSIZED
LABORIOUS
LABYRINTH
LACINIATE
LACONICAL
LAMPLIGHT
LANGRIDGE
LANGUIDLY
LASTDITCH
LATENIGHT
LESTRIGON
LEVITICUS
LIMELIGHT
LINGFIELD
LITIGIOUS
LIVRAISON
LOCALIZED
LOGARITHM
LONGLIVED
LOUISIANA
LUBAVITCH
LUMBRICUS
LUXURIANT
LUXURIATE
LUXURIOUS
MADARIAGA
MAHARISHI
MALICIOUS
MANSFIELD
MASEFIELD
MATUTINAL
MEDICINAL
MELODIOUS
MEMORITER
MENADIONE
MENOMINEE
MIDDLINGS
MINACIOUS
MINEFIELD
MISGUIDED
MITRAILLE
MOGADISHU
MONTAIGNE
MOONLIGHT
MOTORISTS
MOURNIVAL
MUJAHIDIN
MUMPSIMUS
MUNICIPAL
MUNITIONS
NARGHILLY
NASHVILLE
NEFARIOUS
NEGOTIATE
NEPHRITIC
NEPHRITIS
NERITIDAE
NINETIETH
NOTARIKON
NOTORIETY
NOTORIOUS
NOVICIATE
NOVITIATE
NUMERICAL
OBLIVIOUS
OBNOXIOUS
OCCIPITAL
OCEANIDES
OFFICIALS
OFFICIANT
OFFICIATE
OFFICIOUS
ORGANICAL
ORGANISED
ORGANISER
ORGANIZED
ORGANIZER
ORTANIQUE

OUTGOINGS
OUTSKIRTS
OVERNIGHT
OVERRIDER
OVERSIGHT
OVERSIZED
PALAFITTE
PARASITIC
PAROTITIS
PARTRIDGE
PARTTIMER
PECUNIARY
PEMPHIGUS
PENFRIEND
PENURIOUS
PHANSIGAR
PHILLIBEG
PHLEBITIS
PHRENITIS
PIRATICAL
PLAUSIBLE
PLAUSIBLY
PLENTIFUL
POLEMICAL
POLITICAL
POLITIQUE
PORPOISES
POTBOILER
PRACTICAL
PRACTISED
PRESCIENT
PRINCIPAL
PRINCIPLE
PROCLITIC
PROPRIETY
PSYCHICAL
PTARMIGAN
PUNCTILIO
PYRAMIDAL
QUADRILLE
QUANTICAL
QUIZZICAL
QUODLIBET
RADCLIFFE
RAPACIOUS
RECIPIENT
RECLAIMED
RECLAIMER
REDIVIVUS
REDUCIBLE
RELATIONS
RELIGIOSO
RELIGIOUS
REMINISCE
REPUDIATE
RESILIENT
RETALIATE
RETINITIS
RINGSIDER
ROUNCIVAL
RUSHLIGHT
SAGACIOUS
SALACIOUS
SAMARITAN
SANDPIPER
SATIRICAL
SATYRIDAE
SATYRINAE
SCAGLIOLA
SCALLIONS
SCEPTICAL
SCHEHITAH
SCHOLIAST
SCIARIDAE
SCINTILLA
SCRAPINGS
SCURRIOUR
SEDITIOUS
SEMIFINAL
SHECHINAH
SHECHITAH
SHEFFIELD
SHOWPIECE
SICILIANO
SIDELIGHT
SILURIDAE
SIMPLISTE
SINUSITIS
SKEPTICAL
SKINDIVER
SKINTIGHT
SOLICITOR
SOMETIMES
SOPORIFIC
SOUFRIERE
SPHERICAL
SPILLICAN
SPILLIKIN
SPLENITIS
SPOTLIGHT
SQUALIDLY
STARLIGHT
STOCKINET
STOCKINGS
STROBILUS
STRUMITIS
SUBEDITOR
SUDORIFIC
SUPPLIANT
SUPPLICAT
SURFEITED
SURPRISED
SUSTAINED
SWEEPINGS
SYBARITIC
SYNOVITIS
SYRPHIDAE
TABANIDAE
TAILLIGHT
TAILPIECE
TAMOXIFEN
TECHNICAL
TECHNIQUE
TENACIOUS
TEREBINTH
THERMIDOR
THERSITES
THINNINGS
THIRTIETH
TIMEPIECE
TIPULIDAE
TONBRIDGE
TOTALIZER
TOVARISCH
TRACHINUS
TRAMLINES
TRANSIENT
TRAPPINGS
TREDRILLE
TRICLINIC
TRIMMINGS
TROCHILIC
TROCHILUS
TWENTIETH
UMBILICAL
UMBILICUS
UNCHRISOM
UNCLAIMED
UNDECIDED
UNDEFILED
UNDEFINED
UNDIVIDED
UNETHICAL
UNINVITED
UNLIMITED
UNMUSICAL
UNNOTICED
UNREFINED
UNSPOILED
UNTRAINED
UNTYPICAL
VAPORIZER
VENTRICLE
VERACIOUS
VERIDICAL
VEXATIONS
VEXATIOUS
VICARIOUS
VIDELICET
VIENTIANE
VIGESIMAL
VISAGISTE
VIVACIOUS
VOLATIBLE
VORACIOUS
WAHABIITE
WHIMSICAL
WHIRLIGIG
WOMANISER
WOMANIZER
XANTHIPPE
APPLEJACK
BLACKJACK
CHEAPJACK
INTERJECT
KABELJOUW
LJUBLJANA
SURREJOIN
AMELAKITE
ASTRAKHAN
ATTACKING
EPINIKION
FINICKING
FINICKITY
GAVELKIND
HAYMAKING
HIJACKING
HUMANKIND
KNAPSKULL
LAWMAKING
MINISKIRT
MOLESKINS
NOLLEKENS
NUMBSKULL
PALANKEEN
PANNIKELL
PARTAKING
PERIAKTOS
PHENAKISM
PREDIKANT
PROVOKING
REWORKING
SELJUKIAN
SERASKIER
SHOLOKHOV
SHRINKAGE
SHRINKING
SPRINKLER
STEENKIRK
UNLUCKILY
VELDSKOEN
WHITAKERS
WOMANKIND
ACETYLENE
ACIDULATE
ACIDULOUS
ACTUALITY
AEROPLANE
ALTIPLANO
ALVEOLATE
AMARYLLIS
ANABOLISM
ANATOLIAN
ANCILLARY
ANOMALOUS
ANSCHLUSS
ANTHOLOGY
ANTICLINE
APPALLING
APPEALING
AQUAPLANE
ARTILLERY
ASHMOLEAN
ASSAILANT
ASTROLABE
ASTROLOGY
AUTOCLAVE
AYATOLLAH
BACKCLOTH
BACKSLIDE
BALACLAVA
BANDALORE
BANDOLEER
BANDOLERO
BANDOLIER
BANDOLINE
BARCELONA
BATTALION
BEARDLESS
BEDFELLOW
BERKELIUM
BERYLLIUM
BICYCLIST
BLACKLEAD
BLACKLIST
BLAMELESS
BLOODLESS
BOUNDLESS
BOXWALLAH
BRAINLESS
BRAMBLING
BRAZILIAN
BREADLINE
BRISTLING
BROADLOOM
BRUTALISM
BRUTALITY
BRUTALIZE
CABALLERO
CAGOULARD
CALCULATE
CANNELURE
CAPILLARY
CARMELITE
CARNELIAN
CARTILAGE
CARTULARY
CASTILIAN
CATACLYSM
CATAPLASM
CATAPLEXY
CEASELESS
CELLULITE
CELLULOID
CELLULOSE
CHAIRLIFT
CHAMELEON
CHAMPLAIN
CHAMPLEVÉ
CHAROLAIS
CHECKLIST
CHEERLESS
CHEVALIER
CHILBLAIN
CHILDLESS
CHILDLIKE
CHIPOLATA
CHISELLER
CHOCOLATE
CHOLELITH
CILIOLATE
CIPOLLINO
CIRCULATE
CLASSLESS
CLEVELAND
CLOUDLESS
COACHLOAD
COAGULANT
COAGULATE
COASTLINE
COLORLESS
COMPELLED
CONDYLOMA
CONGOLESE
CONSULATE
COPROLITE
CORALLINE
CORDYLINE
CORNELIAN
CORNFLOUR
COROLLARY
CORPULENT
CORRELATE
COSMOLOGY
COUNTLESS
COVELLITE
CRACKLING
CRAPULENT
CRAPULOUS
CRASHLAND
CREDULITY
CREDULOUS

CREPOLINE
CRIBELLUM
CRINOLINE
CRIPPLING
CROWNLIKE
CRUMBLING
CUCHULAIN
CURTILAGE
CYCLOLITH
CYMBELINE
DAEDALIAN
DANDELION
DAUNTLESS
DEATHLESS
DECILLION
DECOLLATE
DEFAULTER
DEUCALION
DISABLING
DISBELIEF
DISCOLOUR
DISHCLOTH
DISOBLIGE
DISSOLUTE
DISSOLVED
DISTILLER
DIXIELAND
DOUBTLESS
DOWELLING
DREAMLESS
DWINDLING
EARTHLING
EBRILLADE
ECTOPLASM
EJACULATE
ELAEOLITE
EMBELLISH
ENAMELLED
ENCHILADA
ENGARLAND
EPHIALTES
EPIPOLISM
ESEMPLASY
ESQUILINE
ESTABLISH
ESTRELDID
ETHNOLOGY
ETYMOLOGY
EVERGLADE
EXCELLENT
EXEMPLARY
EXEMPLIFY
EYESPLICE
FACECLOTH
FAIRYLAND
FAITHLESS
FAULTLESS

FERTILITY
FERTILIZE
FEUDALISM
FEUILLANT
FIBROLINE
FIBROLITE
FILOPLUME
FIREPLACE
FISHPLATE
FLABELLUM
FLAGELLIN
FLAGELLUM
FLATULENT
FLEDGLING
FLESHLESS
FLINTLOCK
FOLIOLOSE
FOOTPLATE
FORECLOSE
FORMALIST
FORMALITY
FORMALIZE
FORMULATE
FORTALICE
FORTILAGE
FOSSILISE
FOUNDLING
FRAGILITY
FRANGLAIS
FRIESLAND
FRIVOLITY
FRIVOLOUS
FRUGALITY
FRUITLESS
FULLBLOWN
FUSILLADE
GANGPLANK
GARRULITY
GARRULOUS
GASHOLDER
GENEALOGY
GENIALITY
GENTILITY
GENUFLECT
GERFALCON
GIBRALTAR
GLABELLAR
GONDOLIER
GOSPELLER
GRACELESS
GRANULATE
GRANULITE
GRANULOSE
GRAPPLING
GRASSLAND
GRIMALKIN
GRUELLING

GRUMBLING
GUIDELINE
GUILELESS
GUILTLESS
HAEMALOMA
HARIOLATE
HARMALINE
HEADCLOTH
HEARTLAND
HEARTLESS
HEATHLAND
HELVELLYN
HERBALIST
HERCULEAN
HIGHCLASS
HIGHFLYER
HINGELESS
HIPPOLYTA
HIPPOLYTE
HISTOLOGY
HOPLOLOGY
HORSELESS
HOSTILITY
HOURGLASS
HYPALLAGE
ICHNOLITE
IDIOBLAST
IDIOPLASM
IMAGELESS
IMPELLING
INABILITY
INDWELLER
INFIELDER
INOCULATE
INQUILINE
INSHALLAH
INTELLECT
INTERLACE
INTERLARD
INTERLOCK
INTERLOPE
INTERLUDE
INVIOLATE
ISINGLASS
ISRAELITE
JAMBALAYA
JAYWALKER
JEWELLERY
JOVIALITY
KEYHOLDER
LACCOLITE
LAEVULOSE
LAMPBLACK
LANDSLIDE
LATICLAVE
LEGISLATE
LIABILITY

LIBELLOUS
LIGHTLESS
LIMITLESS
LINEOLATE
LOBLOLLYS
LOCELLATE
LOINCLOTH
LOOKALIKE
LOOSELEAF
MACROLOGY
MADRILENE
MAGDALENE
MAGNALIUM
MAMMALIAN
MANDOLINE
MARMALADE
MARSHLAND
MARVELOUS
MASCULINE
MATCHLESS
MATCHLOCK
MAUSOLEUM
MAXILLARY
MEDALLION
MEDALLIST
MELONLIKE
MENDELISM
MENTALITY
MERCILESS
MESOBLAST
MESSALINA
METALLOID
METROLAND
MICROLITE
MICROLITH
MIRTHLESS
MISFALLEN
MISOCLERE
MODELLING
MODILLION
MONGOLIAN
MONGOLISM
MONOPLANE
MORTALITY
MOUSELIKE
MOUTHLESS
MUSSOLINI
MUSSULMAN
MYTHOLOGY
NAMEPLATE
NATHELESS
NATROLITE
NEPHALISM
NEPHALIST
NEPHELINE
NEURALGIA
NEURALGIC

NEUROLOGY
NEWSFLASH
NICCOLITE
NIDERLING
NIEBELUNG
NOISELESS
NONILLION
NORMALACY
NORMALITY
NORMALIZE
NOSEBLEED
NOSTALGIA
NOSTALGIC
NOSTOLOGY
NUMMULITE
OCTILLION
ODOURLESS
OFFCOLOUR
OLENELLUS
OPOBALSAM
OPODELDOC
ORGILLOUS
ORICALCHE
ORTHOLOGY
OSCILLATE
OTTRELITE
OURSELVES
OVERBLOWN
OVERCLOUD
OVERSLEEP
OWLEGLASS
PALEOLITH
PANELLING
PANELLIST
PANTALEON
PANTALOON
PAPILLOTE
PARABLAST
PARACLETE
PARDALOTE
PARHELION
PATHOLOGY
PATROLMAN
PENDULATE
PENDULOUS
PENILLION
PENNILESS
PERCALINE
PERCOLATE
PERICLASE
PESTILENT
PETILLANT
PETROLEUM
PETROLOGY
PHACOLITE
PHIGALIAN
PHILOLOGY

PHONOLITE
PHONOLOGY
PHTHALATE
PHYTOLITE
PIERGLASS
PISTOLEER
PLUMBLINE
PLURALISM
PLURALITY
POINTLESS
PORCELAIN
POSTULANT
POSTULATE
POTHOLING
POWELLITE
POWERLESS
PREDILECT
PREHALLUX
PREPOLLEX
PREVALENT
PRICELESS
PRIMULINE
PRIVILEGE
PROPELLED
PROPELLER
PROPELLOR
PROPYLENE
PROSELYTE
PROVOLONE
PUCELLAGE
PUERILITY
PULLULATE
PUMMELLED
PUNCHLINE
PUPILLAGE
PYGMALION
QUERULOUS
QUICKLIME
RACIALISM
RACIALIST
RADIOLOGY
RAMILLIES
RASKOLNIK
REBELLION
RECALLING
RECOLLECT
REMOULADE
RENTALLER
REPELLENT
REPELLING
REPTILIAN
RESSALDAR
RETAILING
REVEALING
REVELLING
RHODOLITE
RICHELIEU

RIDERLESS
ROADBLOCK
ROSTELLUM
ROTAPLANE
RUGGELACH
SACKCLOTH
SACRILEGE
SAILCLOTH
SALESLADY
SANDALLED
SASSOLITE
SATELLITE
SCAMBLING
SCANTLING
SCAPOLITE
SCENTLESS
SCHEELITE
SCHELLING
SCHILLING
SCHMALTZY
SCHOOLBOY
SCHOOLING
SCHOOLMAN
SEMIOLOGY
SENSELESS
SENSILLUM
SEPIOLITE
SERIALIST
SERIALIZE
SERVILELY
SERVILITY
SEXUALITY
SHAMELESS
SHAPELESS
SHASHLICK
SHAVELING
SHEARLING
SHEERLEGS
SHIFTLESS
SHOPFLOOR
SHORTLIST
SHOVELFUL
SHOVELLER
SHUFFLING
SIBYLLINE
SIGHTLESS
SIGNALLER
SIGNALMAN
SINGALESE
SINGULTUS
SKINFLINT
SLEEPLESS
SMOKELESS
SMUGGLING
SNOWFLAKE
SOCIALISM
SOCIALIST
SOCIALITE
SOCIALIZE
SOCIOLECT
SOCIOLOGY
SOMEPLACE
SOMMELIER
SOMNOLENT
SORTILEGE
SOUNDLESS
SPACELESS
SPARKLERS
SPARKLING
SPECULATE
SPICILEGE
SPINELESS
STABILITY
STABILIZE
STAINLESS
STARTLING
STATELESS
STATOLITH
STERILITY
STERILIZE
STIMULANT
STIMULATE
STIPULATE
STONELESS
STORYLINE
STOWNLINS
STRAPLESS
STRIPLING
STROLLING
STUMBLING
SUBCELLAR
SUBDOLOUS
SUCCULENT
SURMULLET
SWADDLING
SWOTHLING
SYLPHLIKE
SYMBOLISM
SYMBOLIST
SYMBOLIZE
TABELLION
TABLELAND
TACHILITE
TACHYLITE
TACHYLYTE
TAHSILDAR
TAILPLANE
TAMERLANE
TANTALITE
TANTALIZE
TASSELLED
TASTELESS
TAUTOLOGY
TELEOLOGY
TENAILLON
TEPHILLIN
TETRALOGY
THANKLESS
THERALITE
THORNLESS
THRALLDOM
THRILLANT
THRILLING
THUMBLING
TITILLATE
TONOPLAST
TOOTHLESS
TORTELIER
TOUCHLINE
TOWELLING
TRACKLESS
TRAFALGAR
TRAGELAPH
TRANSLATE
TRAVELERS
TRAVELING
TRAVELLER
TREILLAGE
TREMBLING
TREMOLITE
TREMULATE
TREMULOUS
TREVELYAN
TRIBALISM
TRIBOLOGY
TRICKLESS
TRICOLOUR
TRUCKLOAD
TRUCULENT
TURBULENT
TWAYBLADE
TWINKLING
UNDERLINE
UNDERLING
UNFAILING
UNFEELING
UNHEALTHY
UNIVALENT
UNSKILLED
UNSULLIED
UNWILLING
UTTERLESS
VACILLATE
VAINGLORY
VALUELESS
VANDALISM
VANDALIZE
VARIOLATE
VENIALITY
VENTILATE
VERBALIZE
VERMILION
VEXILLARY
VIABILITY
VIRGULATE
VISUALIZE
VITELLIUS
VOICELESS
WAGHALTER
WAGONLOAD
WAISTLINE
WALDFLUTE
WASHCLOTH
WASTELAND
WATERLESS
WATERLILY
WATERLINE
WAVELLITE
WHISTLING
WINEGLASS
WORKPLACE
WORTHLESS
WRANGLERS
WREAKLESS
WRESTLING
ZIBELLINE
ABASEMENT
ABATEMENT
ACADEMIST
ACCLIMATE
ADORNMENT
AFTERMATH
AFTERMOST
AGAMEMNON
AGREEMENT
ALCHEMIST
ALIGNMENT
ALLOTMENT
AMAZEMENT
AMENDMENT
AMUSEMENT
ANATOMIST
ANATOMIZE
ANDROMEDA
ANNULMENT
ANONYMITY
ANONYMOUS
APARTMENT
ATONEMENT
BALTIMORE
BENCHMARK
BERGAMASK
BERGOMASK
BIRTHMARK
BLACKMAIL
BLACKMORE
CARBAMATE
CARBAMIDE
CATCHMENT
CHALUMEAU
CHAMOMILE
CHECKMATE
CLASSMATE
COLLIMATE
CONDEMNED
CONDIMENT
CONSUMING
CONTEMPER
CONTUMACY
CONTUMELY
COSTUMIER
CUSTOMARY
CUSTOMIZE
CYCLAMATE
DAIRYMAID
DEFERMENT
DEFORMITY
DETERMINE
DETRIMENT
DEVILMENT
DIPLOMACY
DISARMING
DISCOMFIT
DISMEMBER
DISSEMBLE
DISTEMPER
ECONOMICS
ECONOMIST
ECONOMIZE
EGAREMENT
ELLESMERE
ELOPEMENT
EMOLUMENT
ENACTMENT
ENDOWMENT
ENJOYMENT
ENROLMENT
ENTHYMEME
ENTRAMMEL
ENTREMETS
ENVERMEIL
EPITOMIZE
EPONYMOUS
EQUIPMENT
EUDAEMONY
EUPHEMISM
EXACTMENT
EXANIMATE
EXCREMENT
EXTREMELY
EXTREMISM
EXTREMIST
EXTREMITY
FACSIMILE
FIRMAMENT
FLORIMELL
FLOURMILL
FOGRAMITE
FORASMUCH
FORCEMEAT
FUNDAMENT
FURNIMENT
GESSAMINE
GILGAMESH
GINORMOUS
GLUTAMINE
GOLDSMITH
GOSSAMERY
GOTHAMITE
GREENMAIL
GUACAMOLE
GUATEMALA
HACKAMORE
HALFEMPTY
HASHEMITE
HATCHMENT
HINDEMITH
HISTAMINE
HOCCAMORE
HONEYMOON
HOUSEMAID
IMMELMANN
IMPLEMENT
IMPROMPTU
INANIMATE
INCLEMENT
INCOMMODE
INCREMENT
INFIRMARY
INFIRMITY
INFORMANT
INNERMOST
INTERMENT
JERAHMEEL
JESSAMINE
JIGGUMBOB
JUDGEMENT
KALSOMINE
LADYSMITH
LANDSMAAL
LINEAMENT
LOCKSMITH
LODGEMENT
MALLEMUCK
MAPPEMOND
MASSYMORE
MATRIMONY
MATTAMORE
MELPOMENE
MERRIMENT
MIDSUMMER
MILLAMANT

MINCEMEAT
MISTEMPER
MOLLYMAWK
MRIDAMGAM
NATHEMORE
NEVERMORE
NIGHTMARE
NURSEMAID
NUTRIMENT
OCKHAMIST
OUTERMOST
OUTNUMBER
PANDEMIAN
PANTOMIME
PARCHMENT
PARSIMONY
PASSAMENT
PATRIMONY
PERFUMERY
PERGAMENE
PERSIMMON
PESSIMISM
PESSIMIST
PHARAMOND
PHEROMONE
PIECEMEAL
PLACEMENT
PROLAMINE
PROTAMINE
PROXIMATE
PROXIMITY
QUASIMODO
QUERIMONY
READYMADE
REANIMATE
RECOMMEND
REDEEMING
REEXAMINE
REFORMIST
REPAYMENT
REPRIMAND
REVETMENT
ROSCOMMON
RUNNYMEDE
SACRAMENT
SCHLEMIEL
SCHLEMIHL
SCRIMMAGE
SCRUMMAGE
SEDGEMOOR
SENTIMENT
SEPTEMBER
SEPTIMOLE
SHEEPMEAT
SONGSMITH
SOPHOMORE
SPEARMINT
SPECIMENS
SQUEAMISH
SQUIRMING
STALEMATE
STATEMENT
STREAMING
SUBLIMATE
SUBLIMELY
SUPREMACY
SUPREMELY
SUQUAMISH
SWANIMOTE
SWEETMEAT
SYNCOMIUM
TESTAMENT
TESTIMONY
THELEMITE
TOBERMORY
TRADEMARK
TRANSMUTE
TRASIMENE
TREADMILL
TREATMENT
TRIDYMITE
UNANIMITY
UNANIMOUS
UNDERMINE
UNDERMOST
UPPERMOST
UTTERMOST
VERKAMPTE
VERTUMNUS
VICTIMIZE
WATERMARK
WATERMILL
WELCOMING
WELSUMMER
WHALEMEAT
WHEATMEAL
WHOLEMEAL
WILLEMITE
WORDSMITH
ABOMINATE
ABSCONDER
ABSTINENT
ACUMINATE
ACUTENESS
ADEPTNESS
ADJOINING
AFTERNOON
ALERTNESS
ALEXANDER
ALEXANDRA
ALOOFNESS
ALTERNATE
ALUMINIUM
AMARANTIN
AMUSINGLY
ANNOUNCER
APPOINTED
APPOINTEE
ARABINOSE
ARACHNOID
ARAGONITE
ARCHANGEL
ASHKENAZI
ASPLENIUM
ASTOUNDED
ASTRONAUT
ASTRONOMY
ATTAINDER
AUTHENTIC
AVALANCHE
AWAKENING
AWARENESS
BADMINTON
BARTENDER
BASTINADE
BASTINADO
BEGINNING
BERGANDER
BESPANGLE
BLACKNESS
BLANDNESS
BLATANTLY
BLINDNESS
BLUFFNESS
BLUNTNESS
BOLOGNESE
BOSSANOVA
BOSSINESS
BOSTONIAN
BRASENOSE
BREAKNECK
BRIEFNESS
BRISKNESS
BRITANNIA
BRITANNIC
BUCCANEER
BULKINESS
BURKINABE
BURLINESS
BYSTANDER
CALCANEUM
CALCANEUS
CALCINATE
CALVANISM
CALVINIST
CAMPANILE
CAMPANULA
CANNONADE
CANTONESE
CARBONADE
CARBONARI
CARBONATE
CARBONIZE
CARBUNCLE
CARCINOMA
CARPENTER
CARPENTRY
CASSANDRA
CASSONADE
CASTANETS
CAVERNOUS
CENTENARY
CERVANTES
CEYLONESE
CHAMINADE
CHAVENDER
CHEAPNESS
CHICANERY
CIRCINATE
CLARENDON
CLEANNESS
CLEARNESS
CLOSENESS
COCHINEAL
COFFINITE
COLONNADE
COLUMNIST
COMMANDER
COMMENSAL
COMMUNION
COMMUNISM
COMMUNIST
COMMUNITY
COMPANIES
COMPANION
COMPONENT
CONDENSER
CONGENIAL
CONSENSUS
CONSONANT
CONTENDER
CONTENTED
CONTINENT
CONTINUAL
CONTINUUM
CONVINCED
CORIANDER
COSMONAUT
CRAZINESS
CRETINOUS
CRIMINATE
CRISPNESS
CRUDENESS
CULMINATE
CURRENTLY
DALTONISM
DARWINIAN
DEACONESS
DEAFENING
DECLINING
DEMEANING
DEMEANOUR
DENSENESS
DERRINGER
DESIGNATE
DESIGNING
DINGINESS
DIRTINESS
DISHONEST
DISHONOUR
DISMANTLE
DISPENSER
DISSENTER
DISSONANT
DISTANTLY
DISTENDED
DIZZINESS
DRACONIAN
DRAGONFLY
DULCINIST
DUNGENESS
DUNSINANE
EAGERNESS
ECHIDNINE
ELEGANTLY
ELEMENTAL
ELEVENSES
ELIMINATE
EMBRANGLE
EMINENTLY
EMPENNAGE
EMPTINESS
ENCHANTED
ENCHANTER
ENCOUNTER
ENERINITE
ENGRENAGE
ENSCONCED
ENTRANCED
EPICENTRE
EROGENOUS
ESPAGNOLE
ESPIONAGE
ESPLANADE
ESTRANGED
EUPHONIUM
EVIDENTLY
EXACTNESS
EXTRINSIC
FAINTNESS
FALERNIAN
FALSENESS
FANDANGLE
FASCINATE
FASTENING
FATTENING
FERDINAND
FERMENTED
FERVENTLY
FESTINATE
FINLANDIA
FOGGINESS
FOREANENT
FORTUNATE
FORWANDER
FRAGONARD
FRANKNESS
FRESHNESS
FUGGINESS
FULMINANT
FULMINATE
FUSSINESS
FUSTINESS
FUZZINESS
GABIONADE
GALIONGEE
GALLANTLY
GALLANTRY
GALLINULE
GALVANISM
GALVANIZE
GARDENING
GARGANTUA
GASCONADE
GAUDINESS
GAUNTNESS
GAWKINESS
GELIGNITE
GENUINELY
GERMANCER
GERMANDER
GERMANITE
GERMANIUM
GERMINATE
GIBEONITE
GIDDINESS
GLUCINIUM
GLUTINOUS
GMELINITE
GODLINESS
GOOSANDER
GOOSENECK
GOVERNESS
GOVERNING
GRANDNESS
GREATNESS
GRIMINESS
GRUFFNESS
GUARANTEE
GUARANTOR
HANDINESS
HAPPENING

HAPPINESS
HARBINGER
HARDANGER
HARDINESS
HARMONICA
HARMONIST
HARMONIUM
HARMONIZE
HARSHNESS
HASTENING
HASTINESS
HEADINESS
HEAVINESS
HERMANDAD
HESSONITE
HIBERNATE
HIBERNIAN
HOBBINOLL
HODMANDOD
HOTTENTOT
HOUYHNHNM
HOYDENISH
HUMDINGER
HUSBANDLY
HUSBANDRY
HUSKINESS
HYDRANGEA
HYGIENIST
HYPHENATE
ICELANDER
ICELANDIC
IMAGINARY
IMBRANGLE
IMPOUNDER
IMPSONITE
INCARNATE
INCOGNITO
INDEMNIFY
INDEMNITY
INDIGNANT
INDIGNITY
INERTNESS
INGLENOOK
INOPINATE
INQUINATE
INSOMNIAC
INSTANTER
INSTANTLY
INSWINGER
INTERNODE
INTRINSIC
INVERNESS
JACKKNIFE
JACKSNIPE
JAGGANATH
JANSENISM
JANSENIST
JERKINESS
JOBCENTRE
JOBERNOWL
JOHANNINE
JORDANIAN
JUICINESS
JUSTINIAN
KISSINGER
KITTENISH
KNOWINGLY
LANCINATE
LANKINESS
LAPLANDER
LARGENESS
LAWMONGER
LEGIONARY
LENIENTLY
LIGHTNESS
LIGHTNING
LISTENING
LOCHINVAR
LOFTINESS
LONDONESE
LONGINGLY
LOOSENESS
LOWLANDER
LOWLINESS
LURIDNESS
LUSTINESS
MACDONALD
MACHINATE
MACHINERY
MACHINING
MACHINIST
MACKENZIE
MADDENING
MALIGNANT
MALIGNITY
MALLANDER
MALLENDER
MANGANATE
MANGANESE
MANHANDLE
MANLINESS
MARTINEAU
MARTINMAS
MASSINGER
MATERNITY
MECHANICS
MECHANISM
MECHANIZE
MEDMENHAM
MENNONITE
MERCENARY
MERGANSER
MESSENGER
METRONOME
MEZZANINE
MIDIANITE
MIDWINTER
MILLENIAL
MILLENIUM
MILLINERY
MISHANDLE
MISMANAGE
MISTINESS
MODERNISM
MODERNIST
MODERNITY
MODERNIZE
MOISTNESS
MONTANISM
MONTANIST
MONZONITE
MOODINESS
MORGANITE
MORMONISM
MOSKONFYT
MRIDANGAM
MUCKENDER
MUDDINESS
MUNDUNGUS
MURKINESS
MUSHINESS
MUSTINESS
MUZZINESS
NAKEDNESS
NASTINESS
NATHANIEL
NEPTUNIUM
NOBLENESS
NOISINESS
OBSCENELY
OBSCENITY
OBSTINACY
OBSTINATE
OBTAINING
OILTANKER
OLIVENITE
OPENENDED
OPULENTLY
ORIGENIST
ORIGINATE
OROBANCHE
ORPHANAGE
OUGHTNESS
PAGEANTRY
PANHANDLE
PARSONAGE
PASSENGER
PATERNITY
PATIENTLY
PATRONAGE
PATRONESS
PATRONIZE
PAUSANIAS
PAWKINESS
PEASANTRY
PECKSNIFF
PELMANISM
PENDENNIS
PERENNIAL
PERGUNNAH
PERIANDER
PERMANENT
PERSONAGE
PERSONATE
PERSONIFY
PERSONNEL
PERTINENT
PETTINESS
PHALANGER
PHILANDER
PHITONIUM
PIQUANTLY
PLAINNESS
PLATONIST
PLUMPNESS
PLUTONIUM
POISONING
POISONOUS
POLIANITE
POLLINATE
POLYANDRY
PORRINGER
POTHUNTER
POTTINGAR
PREBENDAL
PRECENTOR
PRECINCTS
PRECONISE
PREMONISH
PRESENTED
PRESENTER
PRESENTLY
PRETENDER
PROCONSUL
PROFANELY
PROFANITY
PROLONGED
PROMENADE
PROMINENT
PROPONENT
PROVENDER
PRUDENTLY
PRYTANEUM
PUFFINESS
PULMONARY
PUNGENTLY
PURDONIUM
PYTHONESS
QUARENDEN
QUEERNESS
QUICKNESS
QUIETNESS
RADIANTLY
RAFFINOSE
RANDINESS
RATIONALE
RATIONING
READINESS
REASONING
RECKONING
RECOGNIZE
RECTANGLE
REDDENDUM
REDHANDED
REEDINESS
REJOINDER
REMAINDER
REMAINING
RENCONTRE
REPLENISH
REPUGNANT
RETAINING
RETURNING
RIBBONISM
RIGHTNESS
RIPIENIST
RISKINESS
ROSMINIAN
ROUGHNECK
ROUGHNESS
ROUMANIAN
ROUMANSCH
ROUTINELY
ROWDINESS
RUNCINATE
RUSTINESS
RUTHENIAN
RUTHENIUM
SADDENING
SALTINESS
SARMENTUM
SASSENACH
SATURNIAN
SATURNINE
SATURNISM
SAUCINESS
SAVERNAKE
SCAVENGER
SCHLENTER
SCLAUNDER
SCREENING
SCROUNGER
SDEIGNFUL
SEASONING
SEEMINGLY
SEGMENTED
SEQUINNED
SERBONIAN
SERMONIZE
SHADINESS
SHAKINESS
SHARPNESS
SHEERNESS
SHORTNESS
SHOWINESS
SHUBUNKIN
SICKENING
SILLINESS
SIMEONITE
SINKANSEN
SIPHUNCLE
SIRBONIAN
SLACKNESS
SLEEKNESS
SLIMINESS
SLOVENIAN
SMALLNESS
SMARTNESS
SOBERNESS
SOFTENING
SOGGINESS
SOLEMNITY
SOLEMNIZE
SOPPINESS
SOSTENUTO
SOUNDNESS
SOUTENEUR
SPARINGLY
SPELUNKER
SPICINESS
SPIKENARD
STALENESS
STARKNESS
STAVANGER
STEEPNESS
STERNNESS
STEVENSON
STIFFNESS
STILLNESS
STOUTNESS
STRAINING
SUBTENANT
SUCCENTOR
SUCCINATE
SUETONIUS
SULKINESS
SULTANATE
SUNTANNED
SUPERNOVA
SURCINGLE
SURLINESS
SURRENDER

SUSPENDED
SUSPENDER
SUSPENSOR
SWEETNESS
SWIFTNESS
SYLVANITE
TACKINESS
TANZANIAN
TAPDANCER
TARDINESS
TASMANIAN
TAUCHNITZ
TAVERNERS
TECTONICS
TEKNONYMY
TELLINGLY
TENSENESS
TERMINATE
TERPINEOL
TERSENESS
THELONIUS
THICKNESS
THREONINE
THUMBNAIL
TIGHTNESS
TIMPANIST
TIPSINESS
TIREDNESS
TORBANITE
TORMENTER
TORMENTIL
TORMENTOR
TORMENTUM
TOSCANINI
TOTTENHAM
TOUGHNESS
TRIBUNATE
TRIENNIAL
TRITENESS
TRUTINATE
TUBBINESS
TURBINATE
TYMPANIST
TYRANNIZE
TYRANNOUS
UKRAINIAN
ULIGINOUS
ULTRONEUS
UNBEKNOWN
UNBOUNDED
UNCHANGED
UNDAUNTED
UNFOUNDED
UNSINNING
UPCOUNTRY
UREDINIAL
URICONIAN
UROKINASE
UTICENSIS
VACCINATE
VAGUENESS
VALDENSES
VALIANTLY
VELLENAGE
VERMINOUS
VIOLENTLY
VIOLINIST
VIRGINALS
VIRGINIAN
VIRGINITY
VIRGINIUM
VISIONARY
VIVIDNESS
VOLTINISM
VULCANIST
VULCANITE
VULCANIZE
VULPINITE
WALDENSES
WAMBENGER
WARMONGER
WEAKENING
WEARINESS
WEIRDNESS
WELLKNOWN
WHIPSNADE
WHITENESS
WHITENING
WHODUNNIT
WHOLENESS
WILLINGLY
WINCANTON
WISCONSIN
WITTINGLY
WOODENTOP
WOOLINESS
WORDINESS
WULFENITE
ZEALANDER
ZINFANDEL
ZINKENITE
ZIRCONIUM
ZOOMANTIC
ABANDONED
ABANDONEE
ACROPOLIS
AFLATOXIN
AGINCOURT
AINSWORTH
AIRCOOLED
ALCOHOLIC
AMAUROSIS
AMBLYOPIA
AMENHOTEP
ANAEROBIC
ANECDOTAL
ANECDOTES
ANKYLOSIS
ANNAPOLIS
ANTIGONUS
ANTIPODES
ANTITOXIC
ANTITOXIN
APERIODIC
APOLLONUS
APOSTOLIC
ARISTOTLE
ARTHROPOD
ARTHROSIS
AUTONOMIC
AUTOROUTE
AYCKBOURN
BACKWOODS
BAKEHOUSE
BALLPOINT
BAMBOOZLE
BARAGOUIN
BAREBONES
BARTHOLDI
BARTHOLIN
BASEBOARD
BASECOURT
BATHTOWEL
BEETHOVEN
BILLBOARD
BLOWTORCH
BOATHOUSE
BOOKLOVER
BOONDOCKS
BOSPHORUS
BULLDOZER
CABRIOLET
CALABOOSE
CALEDONIA
CARDBOARD
CARTHORSE
CASHPOINT
CATACOMBS
CATALOGUE
CATATONIA
CATATONIC
CERATODUS
CHARLOTTE
CHARWOMAN
CHERNOZEM
CHIPBOARD
CIRRHOSIS
CLAPBOARD
CLIPBOARD
CLOISONNÉ
CLUBHOUSE
COCKROACH
COOKHOUSE
CRANBORNE
CROSSOVER
CRYPTOGAM
DARTBOARD
DARTMOUTH
DASHBOARD
DECALOGUE
DEERHOUND
DEMAGOGUE
DESTROYED
DESTROYER
DEVELOPED
DEVELOPER
DEXTRORSE
DIAGNOSIS
DISCLOSED
DOSSHOUSE
DOUKHOBOR
DUCKBOARD
DUMBFOUND
DUNGEONER
DYSTROPHY
EASTBOUND
EASYGOING
ECTOMORPH
EDGEWORTH
ELASTOMER
ELECTORAL
EMBRYONIC
EMOTIONAL
EMPANOPLY
ENDOMORPH
EPISCOPAL
EPISTOLER
EQUIPOISE
EQUIVOCAL
EQUIVOQUE
EUCHLORIC
EXOSTOSIS
FACTIONAL
FARMHOUSE
FASHIONED
FICTIONAL
FIREWORKS
FLAGEOLET
FLOPHOUSE
FOOTLOOSE
FORECOURT
FOREGOING
FRAMBOISE
FRANCOLIN
FREEBOARD
FROGMOUTH
GARRYOWEN
GLADIOLUS
GLENDOWER
GOALMOUTH
GOMPHOSIS
GREYHOUND
GRINGOLET
GUILLOCHE
HALFDOZEN
HALITOSIS
HARDBOARD
HARDCOVER
HARPOONER
HAUTMONDE
HAWTHORNE
HEADBOARD
HERODOTUS
HETERODOX
HETEROSIS
HEXAGONAL
HIDEBOUND
HOARHOUND
HOPSCOTCH
HORDEOLUM
HOREHOUND
HYPINOSIS
IBUPROFEN
IDEALOGUE
IGUANODON
INDECORUM
IRONWORKS
ISALLOBAR
ISOPROPYL
ISOTROPIC
JOBSWORTH
KARAKORAM
KINKCOUGH
KINSWOMAN
KNEECORDS
KNIPHOFIA
LAGOMORPH
LANDLOPER
LATECOMER
LAWNMOWER
LAZYBONES
LEAFMOULD
LECANORAM
LEITMOTIF
LEITMOTIV
LIMEHOUSE
LOBSCOUSE
LOUDMOUTH
MACARONIC
MACEDOINE
MACEDONIA
MADAROSIS
MALEBOLGE
MALLEOLUS
MAYFLOWER
MELANOTIC
MENTIONED
MESOMORPH
METABOLIC
MILLIONTH
MISSIONER
MONATOMIC
MONOCOQUE
MONOLOGUE
MORATORIA
MORATORIO
MUCHLOVED
MUSHROOMS
NEWSHOUND
NONPROFIT
NONSMOKER
NUCLEOLUS
OARSWOMAN
OASTHOUSE
OCTAGONAL
OESTROGEN
OUROBOROS
OUROBORUS
OUTGROWTH
OUTROOPER
OUTSPOKEN
OVERBOARD
OVERJOYED
OVERPOISE
OVERPOWER
OVERTONES
PANEGOISM
PARABOLIC
PARAGOGUE
PARAMOUNT
PARANOIAC
PAREGORIC
PARTHOLON
PATCHOULI
PATCHOULY
PATRIOTIC
PEDAGOGUE
PENSIONER
PENTHOUSE
PERAEOPOD
PERIBOLOS
PERIMORPH
PHELLOGEN
PHYLLOPOD
PINHOOKER
PLAYHOUSE
PLETHORIC
PLIMSOLLS
PNEUMONIA
POLYGONAL
POMPHOLYX
POORHOUSE

PORTFOLIO
POSTHOUSE
POSTPONED
POSTWOMAN
PRACTOLOL
PRODROMAL
PRODROMUS
PROGNOSIS
PROPIONIC
PROPTOSIS
PROTHORAX
PSEUDONYM
PSYCHOSIS
PSYCHOTIC
PYRRHONIC
QUANTOCKS
RACEHORSE
REARHORSE
REARMOUSE
REINFORCE
REREMOUSE
RHAPSODIC
ROADHOUSE
ROADWORKS
RUNAROUND
SAFFLOWER
SAXITOXIN
SCALLOPED
SCANSORES
SCISSORER
SCLEROSIS
SCLEROTAL
SCOLIOSIS
SCOLIOTIC
SECTIONAL
SEMEIOTIC
SEMICOLON
SHINTOISM
SIDEBOARD
SIDEROSIS
SIGNBOARD
SILICOSIS
SLOWCOACH
SLUGHORNE
SNOWBOUND
SNOWDONIA
SOFTCOVER
SOLILOQUY
SOURDOUGH
SPASMODIC
SPOFFORTH
SPONSORED
STALWORTH
STARBOARD
STATIONED
STATIONER
STEGNOSIS
STEGNOTIC
STERCORAL
SULPHONIC
SUNFLOWER
SURFBOARD
SYMBIOSIS
SYMBIOTIC
SYMPHONIC
SYNAGOGUE
TAILBOARD
THEOSOPHY
THRASONIC
TICHBORNE
TIMENOGUY
TOLLHOUSE
TRATTORIA
TRYPHOEUS
TURNROUND
TURQUOISE
UNALLOYED
UNEXPOSED
UNOPPOSED
UNSAVOURY
UNTUTORED
VERSIONAL
VIEWPOINT
VITRIOLIC
VOODOOISM
WAREHOUSE
WASHBOARD
WAYZGOOSE
WEBFOOTED
WESTBOUND
WHIPROUND
WHITWORTH
WILLPOWER
WINDHOVER
WODEHOUSE
WOLFHOUND
WOODBORER
WOODHOUSE
WOODLOUSE
WORKFORCE
WORKHORSE
WORKHOUSE
WYANDOTTE
ZOOSCOPIC
ACCOMPANY
AEROSPACE
ANALEPTIC
ASCLEPIUS
ASTROPHEL
ATTEMPTED
BACKSPACE
BISHOPRIC
CALLIPERS
CARYOPSIS
CATCHPOLE
CATCHPOLL
CATHEPSIN
CENTIPEDE
CHILOPODA
CHIROPODY
COLLAPSAR
CORRUPTER
CTESIPHON
DANDYPRAT
DAVENPORT
DECOMPOSE
DEVONPORT
DISAPPEAR
DISREPAIR
DISREPUTE
DISSIPATE
DODDIPOLL
DRAINPIPE
DYSPEPSIA
DYSPEPTIC
ECLAMPSIA
ECTROPION
ENCOLPION
ENCOLPIUM
ENCOMPASS
ENDOSPERM
ENDPAPERS
ENTROPION
ENTROPIUM
EPEDAPHIC
EPILEPTIC
ESTRAPADE
ETHIOPIAN
EUTROPHIC
EXCULPATE
EXTEMPORE
EXTIRPATE
FALLOPIAN
FILLIPEEN
FLESHPOTS
FORESPEAK
FORESPEND
FROGSPAWN
GALLIPOLI
GALLOPADE
GODOLPHIN
GOSSYPINE
GOSSYPIUM
HANDSPIKE
HIGHSPEED
HOMEOPATH
HORSEPLAY
HYDROPULT
INCULPATE
INTERPLAY
INTERPOSE
INTERPRET
JUXTAPOSE
KIDNAPPED
KIDNAPPER
LANGSPIEL
LITHOPONE
LIVERPOOL
MADREPORE
MARCHPANE
MARSUPIAL
MARSUPIUM
MEGASPORE
MELAMPODE
MENIPPEAN
MERCAPTAN
MILLEPEDE
MILLEPORE
MILLIPEDE
MULTIPLEX
NUNCUPATE
ORTHOPTER
OSTEOPATH
OVERSPEND
OVERSPILL
PALAMPORE
PALEMPORE
PARHYPATE
PASSEPIED
PHILIPPIC
PINEAPPLE
PITCHPINE
PITCHPOLE
PITCHPOLL
PORCUPINE
PRECEPTOR
PRECIPICE
PROLEPSIS
QUAILPIPE
RANTIPOLE
RESERPINE
RHODOPSIN
SALLYPORT
SALLYPOST
SCHNAPPER
SCRAPPING
SCREWPINE
SCRIMPING
SCRUMPING
SHRIMPING
SINGAPORE
SINGSPIEL
STANDPIPE
STENOPAIC
STOCKPILE
STOVEPIPE
STRAPPADO
STRAPPING
SWORDPLAY
SYLLEPSIS
SYNCOPATE
THERAPIST
TOOTHPICK
TRANSPIRE
TRANSPORT
TRANSPOSE
TRIUMPHAL
TURCOPOLE
UNADOPTED
UNCOUPLED
UNDERPAID
UNDERPASS
UNHAPPILY
UNHELPFUL
VERTIPORT
WALLOPING
WHIRLPOOL
WINCOPIPE
WORKSPACE
ZYGOSPORE
BALDAQUIN
EXCHEQUER
HARLEQUIN
MANNEQUIN
PALANQUIN
SOBRIQUET
VELASQUEZ
ABHORRENT
ACTUARIAL
ADUMBRATE
AEPYORNIS
AERODROME
AIRSTREAM
ALBATROSS
ALGEBRAIC
ALLOGRAPH
AMSTERDAM
ANCHORAGE
ANCHORITE
ANCHORMAN
ANHYDRIDE
ANHYDRITE
ANHYDROUS
ANSWERING
ARBITRAGE
ARBITRARY
ARBITRATE
ARMSTRONG
ARROWROOT
ARTHURIAN
ASYNERGIA
AUCTORIAL
AUSTERITY
AUTHORESS
AUTHORITY
AUTHORIZE
AUTOCRACY
AUTOCROSS
AUTOGRAPH
AWESTRUCK
AWKWARDLY
BACHARACH
BACKTRACK
BACTERIAL
BACTERIUM
BALLERINA
BANTERING
BARBARIAN
BARBARITY
BARBAROUS
BARMBRACK
BEDSPREAD
BETTERTON
BIRDBRAIN
BIZARRELY
BLUEPRINT
BOANERGES
BOARDROOM
BOMBARDON
BOOMERANG
BORDEREAU
BORDERING
BROKERAGE
BUCHAREST
BULGARIAN
BUTTERBUR
BUTTERCUP
BUTTERFLY
BUTTERNUT
CAESAREAN
CALABRESE
CALDARIUM
CALIBRATE
CALPURNIA
CAMCORDER
CANCEROUS
CAREERIST
CARTTRACK
CASSEROLE
CASUARINA
CATARRHAL
CATHARSIS
CATHARTIC
CATHERINE
CAUTERIZE
CELEBRANT
CELEBRATE
CELEBRITY
CELLARIST
CENTERING
CENTURION
CEREBRATE

CHAMFRAIN
CHAPARRAL
CHAPERONE
CHARTREUX
CHECKROOM
CHONDRITE
CHONDROID
CIMMERIAN
CLAMOROUS
CLASSROOM
CLOAKROOM
COFFERDAM
COINTREAU
COLLYRIUM
COLOURFUL
COLOURING
COLOURIST
COMFORTER
CONCERNED
CONCERTED
CONCORDAT
CONFIRMED
CONGERIES
CONJURING
CONSCRIPT
CONSTRICT
CONSTRUCT
CONVERTED
CONVERTER
COOPERATE
CORDUROYS
CORMORANT
CORNBRASH
CORNCRAKE
CORNERMAN
CORPORATE
CORPOREAL
COTHURNUS
COUNTRIES
COURTROOM
COUTURIER
CRITERION
CURSORILY
CUTTHROAT
CYCLORAMA
DANGEROUS
DASTARDLY
DAYSPRING
DECLARING
DEHYDRATE
DELACROIX
DEMETRIUS
DEMOCRACY
DEMURRAGE
DENIGRATE
DEODORANT
DEODORIZE
DESCARTES
DESECRATE
DESPERADO
DESPERATE
DETERRENT
DEUTERIUM
DEXTERITY
DEXTEROUS
DIANDROUS
DIAPHRAGM
DIFFERENT
DINNERSET
DISBURDEN
DISCARDED
DISPARAGE
DISPARATE
DISPARITY
DISPERSAL
DISPERSED
DISTORTED
DISTURBED
DITHERING
DITHYRAMB
DOCTORATE
DOWNGRADE
DOWNTREND
DUMBARTON
DUNGAREES
EALDORMAN
EASTERNER
EDITORIAL
EIDOGRAPH
ELABORATE
ELATERIUM
ELBOWROOM
ELECTRESS
ELECTRIFY
ELECTRODE
EMBARRASS
ENCHORIAL
ENCOURAGE
ENDEARING
ENDOCRINE
ENHYDRITE
ENQUIRIES
ENTOURAGE
ENUMERATE
EPHEDRINE
EPICUREAN
EPIDERMIS
EPIPHRAGM
EROSTRATE
EUCHARIST
EUPHORBIA
EUSKARIAN
EVAPORATE
EVERGREEN
EVITERNAL
EXODERMIS
EXONERATE
EXUBERANT
EYESTRAIN
FACTORISE
FASTTRACK
FAVOURITE
FENUGREEK
FILIGRAIN
FILTERING
FILTERTIP
FINGERING
FINGERTIP
FIREBRAND
FIREBREAK
FIREDRAKE
FIREPROOF
FIRSTRATE
FISHERMAN
FLAVORING
FLOWERBED
FLOWERING
FLOWERPOT
FOOLPROOF
FOOTBRAKE
FOOTPRINT
FOREFRONT
FORLORNLY
FOSSORIAL
FRATERNAL
FREDERICK
FRUSTRATE
FULLERENE
FULLGROWN
GARDEROBE
GARGARISM
GASPEREAU
GATECRASH
GATHERING
GIBBERISH
GINGERADE
GLAMORIZE
GLAMOROUS
GLOMERATE
GLOMERULE
GLYCERIDE
GLYCERINE
GODPARENT
GOLDCREST
GONGORISM
GOSLARITE
GRADGRIND
GREENROOM
GREGARINE
GREGORIAN
GROCERIES
GROSGRAIN
GUARDROOM
GUITARIST
GUTTERING
HAIRBRUSH
HAMADRYAD
HAMBURGER
HAMMERING
HAMMURABI
HAMSTRING
HAMSTRUNG
HANDBRAKE
HANKERING
HAYMARKET
HEADDRESS
HECTORING
HEMITROPE
HERBARIUM
HERBORIST
HESPERIAN
HESTERNAL
HIERARCHY
HIMYARITE
HISTORIAN
HOARFROST
HODIERNAL
HODOGRAPH
HOLDERBAT
HOLLERITH
HOLOGRAPH
HOMEGROWN
HOMOGRAPH
HOUSEROOM
HUNGARIAN
HUTTERITE
HYPOCRISY
HYPOCRITE
HYSTERICS
IDEOGRAPH
IDIOGRAPH
IMMIGRANT
IMMIGRATE
INAMORATA
INAMORATO
INCORRECT
INQUIRING
INQUORATE
INSPIRING
INTEGRATE
INTEGRITY
INTERRUPT
INUMBRATE
ISODORIAN
ISOMERASE
ITINERANT
ITINERARY
ITINERATE
JEQUIRITY
JESSERANT
JETSTREAM
JITTERBUG
KEPLARIAN
KEYSTROKE
KIESERITE
KILDERKIN
KILLARNEY
LABOURITE
LANDDROST
LANDGRAVE
LAPSTREAK
LATHYRISM
LATTERDAY
LAUNDRESS
LAZZARONE
LEAKPROOF
LECHEROUS
LEISURELY
LETHARGIC
LETTERBOX
LETTERING
LIBRARIAN
LICKERISH
LIMBURGER
LINGERING
LIQUORICE
LIQUORISH
LOGOGRIPH
LOITERING
LOMBARDIC
LUCUBRATE
LUDICROUS
LUMBERING
MAINFRAME
MALFORMED
MANNERING
MANNERISM
MANUBRIUM
MARGARINE
MARMOREAL
MARTYRDOM
MASSORETE
MASTERFUL
MASTERMAN
MATHURINE
MAVOURNIN
MEANDRIAN
MEASURING
MELIORATE
MELODRAMA
MENSTRUAL
MENSTRUUM
MEPACRINE
MERCERIZE
MERCURIAL
MESMERISM
MESMERIZE
METEORITE
METEOROID
MIDSTREAM
MISDIRECT
MISFIRING
MISSTROKE
MOCKERNUT
MONODRAMA
MONOGRAPH
MONOTROCH
MONSTROUS
MOTHERING
MOTOCROSS
MUGLARITE
MURDERESS
MURDEROUS
MURMURING
MUSCARINE
MUTTERING
MYSTERIES
NAPIERIAN
NECTARINE
NEWMARKET
NEWSPRINT
NIDDERING
NIGGARDLY
NIPPERKIN
NOCTURNAL
NOMOCRACY
NONPAREIL
OBSCURELY
OBSCURITY
OBSECRATE
OCTOBRIST
OFFSPRING
OLEOGRAPH
OLIGARCHY
ORATORIAN
ORPHARION
OUTSPREAD
OUTWARDLY
OUTWORKER
OVENPROOF
OVERCROWD
OVERDRAFT
OVERDRAWN
OVERDRESS
OVERDRIVE
OVERGROWN
OVIPAROUS
OZOCERITE
OZOKERITE
PALSGRAVE
PALUDRINE
PANDURATE

PARAGRAPH
PARATROOP
PASSERINE
PASTERNAK
PASTORALE
PASTURAGE
PATHTRAIN
PATTERNED
PEDIGREES
PENETRATE
PEPPERONI
PEPPERPOT
PEREGRINE
PERFERVID
PERFORANS
PERFORATE
PERFORMED
PERFORMER
PERTURBED
PERVERTED
PETAURIST
PHALAROPE
PHANARIOT
PICTORIAL
PIGNERATE
PILFERAGE
PILFERING
PIMPERNEL
PINKERTON
PINSTRIPE
PIPEDREAM
PISTAREEN
PLAYGROUP
POLVERINE
POLYGRAPH
POMOERIUM
PONDEROSA
PONDEROUS
POPPERING
PORPORATE
PORTERAGE
POSTERIOR
POSTERITY
PRECURSOR
PREFERRED
PRESCRIBE
PRESERVED
PRESERVER
PRESERVES
PRESHRUNK
PRETERITE
PRETERMIT
PREVERNAL
PRIMARILY
PROCERITY
PROKARYON
PROOFREAD
PROPERDIN
PROSCRIBE
PROSTRATE
PULVERIZE
QUAVERING
QUINTROON
QUIVERFUL
QUIVERING
RACETRACK
RANCOROUS
RAPTORIAL
RAPTUROUS
RATHERIPE
RATHERISH
READDRESS
RECTORIAL
RECURRENT
RECURRING
REDSTREAK
REFERRING
REGUERDON
REHEARSAL
REITERATE
RENDERING
RESOURCES
RESURRECT
RETIARIUS
RIGMAROLE
ROSMARINE
ROTTERDAM
ROXBURGHE
RUBBERIZE
SACKERSON
SACRARIUM
SALUBRITY
SALVARSAN
SANDARACH
SANGFROID
SARTORIAL
SARTORIUS
SAUTERNES
SAXIFRAGE
SCALARIUM
SCELERATE
SCHNORKEL
SCHNORRER
SEAFARING
SEAWORTHY
SECTARIAN
SECTORIAL
SEMIBREVE
SENIORITY
SENSORIUM
SEPHARDIM
SHELDRAKE
SHEWBREAD
SHIPWRECK
SHIVERING
SHOPFRONT
SIDETRACK
SIEGFRIED
SINCERELY
SINCERITY
SISSERARY
SNOWDRIFT
SOLDERING
SOLFERINO
SOOTERKIN
SORCERESS
SPELDRING
SPIDERWEB
SPINDRIER
SPINDRIFT
SQUADRONE
STAGIRITE
STAGYRITE
STATEROOM
STILLROOM
STOCKROOM
STOREROOM
SUBCORTEX
SUBMARINE
SUBMERGED
SUBNORMAL
SUBSCRIBE
SUBSCRIPT
SUBSTRATA
SUBSTRATE
SUCCURSAL
SUFFERING
SULFUROUS
SUMMARILY
SUMMARIZE
SUNSCREEN
SUNSTROKE
SUPPORTER
SUPPURATE
SYNEDRION
TANGERINE
TANTARARA
TARTAREAN
TECTORIAL
TELEGRAPH
TELLURIAN
TELLURION
TELLURIUM
TEMPERATE
TEMPORARY
TEMPORIZE
TEMPTRESS
TENDERIZE
TENEBROSE
TENTORIUM
TERRARIUM
TERRORISM
TERRORIST
TERRORIZE
TESTDRIVE
TETRARCHY
TETTEROUS
THEOBROMA
THEOCRACY
TIGHTROPE
TIMOCRACY
TIPPERARY
TOASTRACK
TOPIARIST
TREETRUNK
TRICERION
TRIFORIUM
TRITURATE
TROPARION
TUILERIES
TUTIORISM
UNCHARGED
UNCORRECT
UNCOURTLY
UNDERRATE
UNGUARDED
UNIFORMED
UNIFORMLY
UNITARIAN
UNIVERSAL
UNLEARNED
UNMARRIED
UNSPARING
UNWORRIED
VANTBRASS
VELODROME
VERATRINE
VERBERATE
VICTORIAN
VICTORINE
VOLKSRAAD
VOLTURNUS
VOLUCRINE
VULGARIAN
VULGARISM
VULGARITY
WAGNERIAN
WAGNERITE
WAITERAGE
WALDGRAVE
WALPURGIS
WANDERING
WANWORTHY
WARTCRESS
WASHERMAN
WASSERMAN
WESTERNER
WINDBREAK
WISECRACK
WITHDRAWN
WITHERING
WITHERITE
WOLVERINE
WONDERFUL
WOODCRAFT
WOOMERANG
WUTHERING
YESTERDAY
YESTEREVE
ZENOCRATE
ACCESSION
ACCESSORY
ADDRESSED
ADDRESSEE
ADMISSION
ADVERSARY
ADVERSELY
ADVERSITY
AFORESAID
AGGRESSOR
AIMLESSLY
ALABASTER
ALONGSIDE
ALTISSIMO
AMBROSIAL
AMBROSIAN
AMPERSAND
ANGUISHED
ANIMISTIC
ANIMOSITY
ARABESQUE
ASCENSION
ASPERSION
ATAVISTIC
ATHEISTIC
ATHELSTAN
AXMINSTER
BALLISTIC
BAPTISMAL
BARRISTER
BEARDSLEY
BLINDSPOT
BLOODSHED
BLOODSHOT
BOMBASINE
BOMBASTIC
BROADSIDE
BUNDESTAG
BURLESQUE
CALLOSITY
CAMBUSCAN
CANVASSER
CARTESIAN
CASUISTIC
CASUISTRY
CAUCASIAN
CHEAPSIDE
CHEMISTRY
CHERISHED
CHORISTER
CLEANSING
COALESCED
COELOSTAT
COLLISION
COLLUSION
COLLUSIVE
COLOSSEUM
COMMISSAR
COMPOSING
COMPOSITE
COMPOSURE
CONCISELY
CONCISION
CONCUSSED
CONFESSED
CONFESSOR
CONFUSING
CONFUSION
CONGESTED
CONTUSION
CORPOSANT
CORPUSCLE
CORROSION
CORROSIVE
CORTISONE
COURTSHIP
CRACKSMAN
CRAFTSMAN
CROISSANT
CUPRESSUS
CURIOSITY
DAMBUSTER
DECESSION
DECURSIVE
DECUSSATE
DEFENSIVE
DENTISTRY
DEPRESSED
DIFFUSION
DIMENSION
DIONYSIAN
DIONYSIUS
DISGUSTED
DISMISSAL
DIVERSIFY
DIVERSION
DIVERSITY
DONCASTER
DRAFTSMAN
EARNESTLY
ECOSYSTEM
EGRESSION

EIGHTSOME
EMBASSADE
EMBASSAGE
EMBRASURE
EMPAESTIC
EMPHASIZE
EMPHYSEMA
ENCAUSTIC
ENCLOSURE
ENDLESSLY
ENGROSSED
ENGROSSER
EPINASTIC
EXCELSIOR
EXCESSIVE
EXCLUSION
EXCLUSIVE
EXCURSION
EXHAUSTED
EXPANSION
EXPANSIVE
EXPENSIVE
EXPLOSION
EXPLOSIVE
EXPRESSED
EXPRESSLY
EXPULSION
EXQUISITE
EXTENSILE
EXTENSION
EXTENSIVE
EXTRUSION
FANTASIZE
FANTASTIC
FIELDSMAN
FILLISTER
FLOORSHOW
FLORESTAN
FOOLISHLY
FORJASKIT
FORJESKIT
FRICASSEE
FROBISHER
FROISSART
GARNISHEE
GEODESIST
GLUCOSIDE
GODDESSES
GOOSESTEP
GRANDSIRE
GRAPESHOT
GRAVESEND
GRAVESIDE
GREENSAND
GROTESQUE
GUARDSMAN
GYMNASIUM
GYMNASTIC
HADROSAUR
HAMFISTED
HARLESTON
HARVESTER
HAVERSACK
HEARDSMAN
HEAVISIDE
HERONSHAW
HERPESTES
HEURISTIC
HOLINSHED
HORSESHOE
HYDROSTAT
ILCHESTER
IMMENSELY
IMMENSITY
IMMERSION
IMPASSION
IMPASSIVE
IMPRESSED
IMPULSION
IMPULSIVE
INCESSANT
INCLUSION
INCLUSIVE
INCURSION
INSENSATE
INTENSELY
INTENSIFY
INTENSITY
INTENSIVE
INTERSECT
INTRUSION
INTRUSIVE
INVERSION
JANISSARY
KERMESITE
KLINOSTAT
LANCASTER
LAVOISIER
LEICESTER
LEPROSERY
LIGHTSHIP
LIGHTSOME
LIMOUSINE
LOATHSOME
MADRASSAH
MADRESSAH
MAGNESIUM
MALAYSIAN
MARCASITE
MEDRESSEH
MENUISIER
MIDRASHIM
MINNESOTA
MNEMOSYNE
MOCCASINS
MONTESPAN
MOYGASHEL
NARCISSUS
NEBBISHER
NECESSARY
NECESSITY
NEWCASTLE
NIETZSCHE
NIGROSINE
OBSESSION
OBSESSIVE
OBTRUSION
OBTRUSIVE
OCCLUSION
ODALISQUE
OFFENSIVE
OMBUDSMAN
ONOMASTIC
ONTHESPOT
OPPRESSED
OPPRESSOR
ORCHESTRA
ORGIASTIC
OWNERSHIP
PALAESTRA
PALMISTRY
PARNASITE
PARNASSUS
PAYMASTER
PEEVISHLY
PEIRASTIC
PENINSULA
PENPUSHER
PENTOSANE
PERTUSATE
PERTUSSIS
PERVASION
PERVASIVE
PETERSHAM
PHARISAIC
PHILISTER
PHOTOSTAT
PLAINSMAN
PLAINSONG
POETASTER
POINTSMAN
POLYESTER
POMPOSITY
POSSESSED
POSSESSOR
POTASSIUM
PRANKSTER
PRECISELY
PRECISIAN
PRECISION
PRECISIVE
PRELUSORY
PROBOSCIS
PROCESSOR
PROFESSED
PROFESSOR
PROFUSELY
PROFUSION
PROLUSION
PROMISING
PROMUSCIS
PROTESTER
PROTOSTAR
PROVISION
PTEROSAUR
PUBLISHED
PUBLISHER
PURPOSELY
QUICKSAND
QUICKSTEP
REALISTIC
RECESSION
RECESSIVE
REFRESHER
REGISSEUR
REICHSRAT
REICHSTAG
REMISSION
REPOSSESS
REPRESENT
REPRESSED
REPULSION
REPULSIVE
REQUISITE
RETORSION
REVERSING
REVERSION
REVULSION
RHODESIAN
RHYMESTER
RIVERSIDE
ROUGHSHOD
ROUNDSMAN
SACRISTAN
SARCASTIC
SAUCISSON
SCRIMSHAW
SECESSION
SECLUSION
SELFISHLY
SEQUESTER
SHARESMAN
SHARKSKIN
SHEEPSKIN
SHELLSUIT
SHORTSTAY
SHORTSTOP
SIGHTSEER
SINUOSITY
SLAVISHLY
SLINGSHOT
SOLIPSISM
SOPHISTER
SOPHISTIC
SOPHISTRY
SOTTISIER
SOUWESTER
SPACESHIP
SPACESUIT
SPADASSIN
SPEARSIDE
SPOILSMAN
SPOKESMAN
SPORTSMAN
SPORTSMEN
SPRITSAIL
STATESIDE
STATESMAN
STATISTIC
STEAMSHIP
STEERSMAN
STEGOSAUR
STRESSFUL
STROSSERS
STYLISHLY
STYLISTIC
SUCCESSOR
SUFFUSION
SUPERSEDE
SUPERSTAR
SUPPOSING
SWEETSHOP
SWORDSMAN
SYMPOSIUM
TAYASSUID
TEDIOSITY
TEIRESIAS
TENNESSEE
THALASSIC
THIRDSMAN
THREESOME
THROWSTER
THYRISTOR
TOOTHSOME
TOWCESTER
TRACKSUIT
TRADESMAN
TRANSSHIP
TRIBESMAN
TRIBESMEN
TRICKSTER
TRIMESTER
TROOPSHIP
TROUSSEAU
UNABASHED
UNBIASSED
UNCEASING
UNCROSSED
UNDERSEAL
UNDERSELL
UNDERSIDE
UNDERSIGN
UNDERSONG
UNDRESSED
UPANISHAD
UPHOLSTER
URANISCUS
VALVASSOR
VERBASCUM
VERBOSITY
VESPASIAN
VISCOSITY
VOUCHSAFE
WAPINSHAW
WASPISHLY
WATERSHED
WATERSIDE
WEARISOME
WEDNESDAY
WENCESLAS
WHOLESALE
WHOLESOME
WILLESDEN
WITNESSED
WOLLASTON
WORCESTER
WORRISOME
YACHTSMAN
YACHTSMEN
YOUNGSTER
ZOROASTER
ABDUCTION
ABOLITION
ABOUTTURN
ACCRETION
ACOUSTICS
ACQUITTAL
ADDICTION
ADDICTIVE
ADJECTIVE
ADMITTING
ADMIXTURE
ADORATION
ADULATION
ADVANTAGE
ADVECTION
ADVENTIST
ADVENTURE
ADVERTISE
AFFECTING
AFFECTION
AGITATION

ALBERTINE
ALLANTOID
ALLANTOIS
AMBROTYPE
AMIANTHUS
AMPLITUDE
ANCESTRAL
ANDANTINO
ANGOSTURA
ANIMATION
ANOINTING
APERITIVE
APPERTAIN
APPORTION
ARCHETYPE
ARCHITECT
ARGENTINA
ARGENTINE
ARMISTICE
ARRESTING
ASCERTAIN
ASPARTAME
ASSERTING
ASSERTION
ASSERTIVE
ASSISTANT
ASSUETUDE
ASTROTURF
ATHLETICS
ATTENTION
ATTENTIVE
ATTRITION
ATTUITION
AUGUSTINE
AVOCATION
BACKSTAGE
BANDSTAND
BANISTERS
BARBITONE
BARBOTINE
BARNSTORM
BASKETFUL
BEATITUDE
BECHSTEIN
BEDSITTER
BEEFSTEAK
BERNSTEIN
BETROTHAL
BETROTHED
BIMONTHLY
BIPARTITE
BISECTION
BLUESTONE
BOOBYTRAP
BOOKSTALL
BOOKSTAND
BOOKSTORE
BRIMSTONE
BUCENTAUR
BUCKETFUL
BUDGETARY
BYZANTINE
CADASTRAL
CAKESTAND
CALENTURE
CALVITIES
CANDYTUFT
CARNATION
CARPETING
CASSATION
CAUSATION
CAVORTING
CELESTIAL
CERTITUDE
CESSATION
CHIEFTAIN
CHINATOWN
CHINSTRAP
CHRISTIAN
CHRISTMAS
CLIENTELE
COALITION
COARCTATE
COCKATIEL
COEMPTION
COGNITION
COGNITIVE
COLLATION
COLLOTYPE
COLOSTOMY
COLOSTRUM
COMBATANT
COMBATIVE
COMINTERN
COMMITTAL
COMMITTED
COMMITTEE
COMMOTION
COMPETENT
COMPETING
COMPOTIER
COMPUTING
CONDITION
CONFITEOR
CONNOTATE
CORNSTALK
COSMETICS
CREMATION
CREMATORY
CREPITATE
CROUSTADE
CURETTAGE
CURVATURE
CYCLOTRON
DALMATIAN
DAMNATION
DEATHTRAP
DEBENTURE
DECASTYLE
DECEITFUL
DECEPTION
DECEPTIVE
DECOCTION
DECONTROL
DECRETALS
DEDUCTION
DEDUCTIVE
DEFEATISM
DEFEATIST
DEFECTION
DEFECTIVE
DEFLATION
DEJECTION
DENTITION
DEPARTURE
DEPICTION
DESERTION
DESPOTISM
DESTITUTE
DESUETUDE
DESULTORY
DETECTION
DETECTIVE
DETENTION
DETRITION
DEVASTATE
DEVIATION
DIAMETRIC
DIANETICS
DICHOTOMY
DICTATION
DIDACTICS
DIETETICS
DIGASTRIC
DIGESTION
DIGESTIVE
DIGNITARY
DIRECTION
DIRECTIVE
DIRECTORS
DIRECTORY
DISENTOMB
DISPUTANT
DIVERTING
DOGMATISM
DOGMATIZE
DORMITION
DORMITORY
DOWNSTAGE
DRAMATICS
DRAMATIST
DRAMATIZE
DRIPSTONE
DRUGSTORE
DRUMSTICK
DYSENTERY
ECCENTRIC
EDDYSTONE
EDUCATION
EDUCATIVE
EFFECTIVE
EFFECTUAL
EGLANTINE
ELEVATION
ELOCUTION
EMANATION
EMBATTLED
EMULATION
ENCANTHIS
ENCRATITE
ENRAPTURE
ENSTATITE
ENTERTAIN
EPULATION
ERUDITION
ESSENTIAL
ESTHETICS
EURHYTHMY
EVAGATION
EVOCATION
EVOCATIVE
EVOCATORY
EVOLUTION
EXARATION
EXCEPTION
EXECUTANT
EXECUTION
EXECUTIVE
EXECUTRIX
EXEMPTION
EXORATION
EXPECTANT
EXPECTING
EXPERTISE
EXPIATION
EXPIATORY
EXPLETIVE
EXPORTING
EXTORTION
EXUDATION
EYELETEER
FAIRYTALE
FALDSTOOL
FARMSTEAD
FEEDSTUFF
FEUDATORY
FILMSTRIP
FIRESTONE
FLAGITATE
FLAGSTAFF
FLAGSTONE
FLAMSTEED
FLEXITIME
FLOTATION
FLOWSTONE
FOLKETING
FOODSTORE
FOODSTUFF
FOOTSTALL
FOOTSTOOL
FORESTAGE
FORESTALL
FORESTERS
FORGATHER
FORGETFUL
FORGETIVE
FORGOTTEN
FORMATION
FORMATIVE
FORSYTHIA
FORTITUDE
FREESTONE
FREESTYLE
FRIGATOON
FRIGHTFUL
FURNITURE
GALACTOSE
GALANTINE
GALLSTONE
GARNITURE
GAZETTEER
GEARSTICK
GEOMETRIC
GEOMETRID
GERIATRIC
GESTATION
GLADSTONE
GODFATHER
GODMOTHER
GONIATITE
GRADATION
GRAPETREE
GRATITUDE
GRAVITATE
GUNCOTTON
GUSTATION
HAEMATITE
HAILSTONE
HAILSTORM
HAIRSTYLE
HALFSTAFF
HALLSTATT
HAMFATTER
HAMPSTEAD
HANDSTAND
HARESTANE
HARMATTAN
HARMOTOME
HAUGHTILY
HEADSTALL
HEADSTONE
HEMIPTERA
HEMISTICH
HERMITAGE
HEXASTICH
HOARSTONE
HOLYSTONE
HOMESTEAD
HOMOPTERA
HONKYTONK
HORNSTONE
HORSETAIL
HORTATIVE
HORTATORY
HOSPITIUM
HOURSTONE
HYPNOTISM
HYPNOTIST
HYPNOTIZE
ILLGOTTEN
IMITATION
IMITATIVE
IMMORTALS
IMPACTION
IMPARTIAL
IMPORTANT
IMPORTUNE
IMPOSTURE
INANITION
INCAUTION
INCENTIVE
INCEPTION
INDENTURE
INDICTION
INDUCTION
INDUCTIVE
INFANTILE
INFECTING
INFECTION
INFERTILE
INFLATION
INGESTION
INJECTION
INJUSTICE
INSERTION
INSISTENT
INSTITUTE
INSULTING
INTENTION
INTESTATE
INTESTINE
INTUITION

INUNCTION
INUSITATE
INVECTIVE
INVENTION
INVENTIVE
INVENTORY
INVERTASE
IRONSTONE
IRRUPTION
ISOLATION
ISOMETRIC
JACKSTRAW
JAWBATION
JENNETING
JOCKSTRAP
JUNKETING
KARYOTYPE
KERBSTONE
KNOBSTICK
KROPOTKIN
LACTATION
LAMARTINE
LANDSTURM
LARGITION
LASSITUDE
LATRATION
LAUDATION
LAUDATORY
LEUCOTOME
LEVANTINE
LEVIATHAN
LIBERTIES
LIBERTINE
LIFESTYLE
LIMESTONE
LINTSTOCK
LIPPITUDE
LIVESTOCK
LOADSTONE
LODESTONE
LOGISTICS
LONGITUDE
LUCRATIVE
LUCRETIUS
LUCTATION
LUNCHTIME
MACARTHUR
MACTATION
MAELSTROM
MAGNETISM
MAGNETIZE
MAGNETRON
MAGNITUDE
MANDATORY
MANGETOUT
MANHATTAN
MARKETEER
MARKETING
MAULSTICK
MAURITIAN
MAURITIUS
MEDIATION
MENTATION
MESENTERY
MEZZOTINT
MICROTOME
MICROTONE
MIGRATION
MIGRATORY
MILESTONE
MILLSTONE
MINIATURE
MINKSTONE
MODESTINE
MOLLITIES
MOMENTARY
MOMENTOUS
MONACTINE
MONASTERY
MONASTRAL
MONOSTICH
MOONSTONE
MORTSTONE
MOUSETRAP
MUFFETTEE
MULTITUDE
MUSKETEER
MUSKETOON
MUSSITATE
NARRATION
NARRATIVE
NAUGHTILY
NEFERTITI
NEGRITUDE
NEOLITHIC
NEWSSTALL
NEWSSTAND
NICTITATE
NIGHTTIME
NIGRITUDE
NONENTITY
NORMATIVE
NUTRITION
NUTRITIVE
OBJECTION
OBJECTIVE
OBREPTION
OBSTETRIC
OBVENTION
OCCULTIST
OCTASTICH
ODELSTING
OFFERTORY
OLFACTORY
OPERATING
OPERATION
OPERATIVE
OPPORTUNE
ORIENTATE
ORTHOTONE
OUTFITTER
OUTOFTOWN
OVERSTATE
OVERSTEER
OVULATION
OXIDATION
PAKISTANI
PALESTINE
PALMATION
PALMITATE
PALPATION
PALPITATE
PANDATION
PANETTONE
PARENTAGE
PARENTING
PARTITION
PEACETIME
PEGMATITE
PELLITORY
PENISTONE
PERDITION
PERISTOME
PERISTYLE
PERMITTED
PERPETUAL
PETTITOES
PHILATELY
PHONETICS
PHYTOTRON
PICKETING
PIKESTAFF
PILASTERS
PIPESTONE
PITUITARY
PITUITRIN
PLACATORY
PLAINTIFF
PLAINTIVE
PLANETARY
PLATITUDE
PLAUSTRAL
PLENITUDE
POCKETFUL
POLLUTANT
POLLUTION
POPLITEAL
POTENTATE
POTENTIAL
PRECATORY
PREDATORY
PREFATORY
PREMATURE
PREMOTION
PRIESTESS
PRIESTLEY
PRIMITIAE
PRIMITIVE
PRIVATEER
PRIVATELY
PRIVATION
PRIVATIZE
PROACTIVE
PROBATION
PROFITEER
PROMOTION
PROMPTING
PROTOTYPE
PROUSTITE
PULPITEER
PULSATION
PUPPETEER
PURGATIVE
PURGATORY
QUOTATION
QUOTITION
RACKETEER
RACKSTRAW
RACONTEUR
RADIATING
RADIATION
RAINSTORM
RASPATORY
REALITIES
REBOATION
RECAPTURE
RECEPTION
RECEPTIVE
RECTITUDE
REDLETTER
REDUCTION
REFECTION
REFECTORY
REFLATION
REGISTRAR
REGRETFUL
REINSTATE
REJECTION
RELUCTANT
REMONTANT
RENDITION
REPENTANT
REPERTORY
REPLETION
REPLETIVE
REPORTAGE
REPORTING
REPTATION
RESENTFUL
RESISTANT
RESNATRON
RESORTING
RESTITUTE
RESULTANT
RESULTING
RETENTION
RETENTIVE
RETORTION
REVICTUAL
REVOLTING
RILLETTES
ROADSTEAD
ROBERTSON
ROOTSTOCK
RUINATION
RUNESTAVE
SABBATIAN
SAGITTARY
SALVATION
SANDSTONE
SANDSTORM
SASKATOON
SATIATION
SCHMUTTER
SCHNITTKE
SCHNITZEL
SCIENTISM
SCIENTIST
SCREWTAPE
SCRIPTURE
SCULPTING
SCULPTURE
SEABOTTLE
SEBASTIAN
SECRETARY
SECRETION
SECRETIVE
SEDENTARY
SEDUCTION
SEDUCTIVE
SELECTING
SELECTION
SELECTIVE
SELLOTAPE
SEMANTEME
SEMANTICS
SEMANTIDE
SEMANTRON
SENSATION
SENSITIVE
SENSITIZE
SEPULTURE
SERIATION
SERRATION
SERVITUDE
SEVENTEEN
SHENSTONE
SHORTTERM
SICCATIVE
SIGNATORY
SIGNATURE
SILTSTONE
SITUATION
SLABSTONE
SLAPSTICK
SLIGHTEST
SMALLTIME
SNOWSTORM
SOAPSTONE
SONNETEER
SPIRITOUS
SPIRITUAL
SPLINTERS
SPLITTING
SQUATTERS
SQUINTING
STARSTONE
STATUTORY
STREETAGE
STREETCAR
STRIATION
STRICTURE
STRONTIUM
STRUCTURE
STRUTTING
SUBALTERN
SUBENTIRE
SUBTITLED
SUCCOTASH
SUMMATION
SUNBATHER
SUSCITATE
SYMMETRIC
TABLATURE
TALKATIVE
TARANTASS
TARANTULA
TARGETEER
TARNATION
TAVISTOCK
TEAKETTLE
TELESTICH
TENTATIVE
TERRITORY
TESTATRIX
THANATISM
THIRSTILY
THIRSTING
THRIFTILY
THROATILY
THUMBTACK

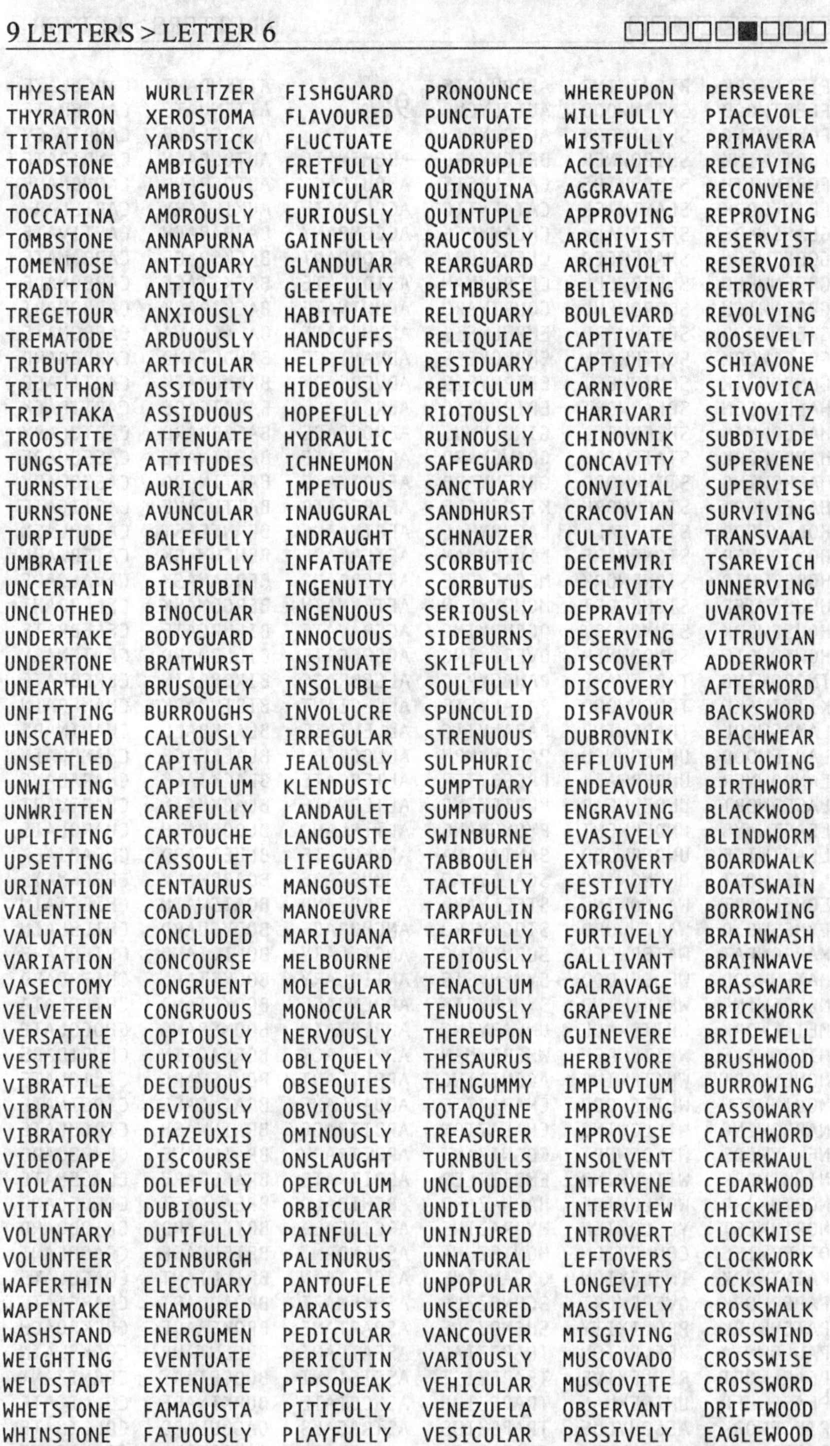

THYESTEAN
THYRATRON
TITRATION
TOADSTONE
TOADSTOOL
TOCCATINA
TOMBSTONE
TOMENTOSE
TRADITION
TREGETOUR
TREMATODE
TRIBUTARY
TRILITHON
TRIPITAKA
TROOSTITE
TUNGSTATE
TURNSTILE
TURNSTONE
TURPITUDE
UMBRATILE
UNCERTAIN
UNCLOTHED
UNDERTAKE
UNDERTONE
UNEARTHLY
UNFITTING
UNSCATHED
UNSETTLED
UNWITTING
UNWRITTEN
UPLIFTING
UPSETTING
URINATION
VALENTINE
VALUATION
VARIATION
VASECTOMY
VELVETEEN
VERSATILE
VESTITURE
VIBRATILE
VIBRATION
VIBRATORY
VIDEOTAPE
VIOLATION
VITIATION
VOLUNTARY
VOLUNTEER
WAFERTHIN
WAPENTAKE
WASHSTAND
WEIGHTING
WELDSTADT
WHETSTONE
WHINSTONE
WHUNSTANE
WITHSTAND
WURLITZER
XEROSTOMA
YARDSTICK
AMBIGUITY
AMBIGUOUS
AMOROUSLY
ANNAPURNA
ANTIQUARY
ANTIQUITY
ANXIOUSLY
ARDUOUSLY
ARTICULAR
ASSIDUITY
ASSIDUOUS
ATTENUATE
ATTITUDES
AURICULAR
AVUNCULAR
BALEFULLY
BASHFULLY
BILIRUBIN
BINOCULAR
BODYGUARD
BRATWURST
BRUSQUELY
BURROUGHS
CALLOUSLY
CAPITULAR
CAPITULUM
CAREFULLY
CARTOUCHE
CASSOULET
CENTAURUS
COADJUTOR
CONCLUDED
CONCOURSE
CONGRUENT
CONGRUOUS
COPIOUSLY
CURIOUSLY
DECIDUOUS
DEVIOUSLY
DIAZEUXIS
DISCOURSE
DOLEFULLY
DUBIOUSLY
DUTIFULLY
EDINBURGH
ELECTUARY
ENAMOURED
ENERGUMEN
EVENTUATE
EXTENUATE
FAMAGUSTA
FATUOUSLY
FEARFULLY
FIREGUARD
FISHGUARD
FLAVOURED
FLUCTUATE
FRETFULLY
FUNICULAR
FURIOUSLY
GAINFULLY
GLANDULAR
GLEEFULLY
HABITUATE
HANDCUFFS
HELPFULLY
HIDEOUSLY
HOPEFULLY
HYDRAULIC
ICHNEUMON
IMPETUOUS
INAUGURAL
INDRAUGHT
INFATUATE
INGENUITY
INGENUOUS
INNOCUOUS
INSINUATE
INSOLUBLE
INVOLUCRE
IRREGULAR
JEALOUSLY
KLENDUSIC
LANDAULET
LANGOUSTE
LIFEGUARD
MANGOUSTE
MANOEUVRE
MARIJUANA
MELBOURNE
MOLECULAR
MONOCULAR
NERVOUSLY
OBLIQUELY
OBSEQUIES
OBVIOUSLY
OMINOUSLY
ONSLAUGHT
OPERCULUM
ORBICULAR
PAINFULLY
PALINURUS
PANTOUFLE
PARACUSIS
PEDICULAR
PERICUTIN
PIPSQUEAK
PITIFULLY
PLAYFULLY
POTPOURRI
PRESCUTUM
PRONOUNCE
PUNCTUATE
QUADRUPED
QUADRUPLE
QUINQUINA
QUINTUPLE
RAUCOUSLY
REARGUARD
REIMBURSE
RELIQUARY
RELIQUIAE
RESIDUARY
RETICULUM
RIOTOUSLY
RUINOUSLY
SAFEGUARD
SANCTUARY
SANDHURST
SCHNAUZER
SCORBUTIC
SCORBUTUS
SERIOUSLY
SIDEBURNS
SKILFULLY
SOULFULLY
SPUNCULID
STRENUOUS
SULPHURIC
SUMPTUARY
SUMPTUOUS
SWINBURNE
TABBOULEH
TACTFULLY
TARPAULIN
TEARFULLY
TEDIOUSLY
TENACULUM
TENUOUSLY
THEREUPON
THESAURUS
THINGUMMY
TOTAQUINE
TREASURER
TURNBULLS
UNCLOUDED
UNDILUTED
UNINJURED
UNNATURAL
UNPOPULAR
UNSECURED
VANCOUVER
VARIOUSLY
VEHICULAR
VENEZUELA
VESICULAR
VICIOUSLY
WELLBUILT
WHEREUPON
WILLFULLY
WISTFULLY
ACCLIVITY
AGGRAVATE
APPROVING
ARCHIVIST
ARCHIVOLT
BELIEVING
BOULEVARD
CAPTIVATE
CAPTIVITY
CARNIVORE
CHARIVARI
CHINOVNIK
CONCAVITY
CONVIVIAL
CRACOVIAN
CULTIVATE
DECEMVIRI
DECLIVITY
DEPRAVITY
DESERVING
DISCOVERT
DISCOVERY
DISFAVOUR
DUBROVNIK
EFFLUVIUM
ENDEAVOUR
ENGRAVING
EVASIVELY
EXTROVERT
FESTIVITY
FORGIVING
FURTIVELY
GALLIVANT
GALRAVAGE
GRAPEVINE
GUINEVERE
HERBIVORE
IMPLUVIUM
IMPROVING
IMPROVISE
INSOLVENT
INTERVENE
INTERVIEW
INTROVERT
LEFTOVERS
LONGEVITY
MASSIVELY
MISGIVING
MUSCOVADO
MUSCOVITE
OBSERVANT
PASSIVELY
PASSIVITY
PENSIVELY
PERSEVERE
PIACEVOLE
PRIMAVERA
RECEIVING
RECONVENE
REPROVING
RESERVIST
RESERVOIR
RETROVERT
REVOLVING
ROOSEVELT
SCHIAVONE
SLIVOVICA
SLIVOVITZ
SUBDIVIDE
SUPERVENE
SUPERVISE
SURVIVING
TRANSVAAL
TSAREVICH
UNNERVING
UVAROVITE
VITRUVIAN
ADDERWORT
AFTERWORD
BACKSWORD
BEACHWEAR
BILLOWING
BIRTHWORT
BLACKWOOD
BLINDWORM
BOARDWALK
BOATSWAIN
BORROWING
BRAINWASH
BRAINWAVE
BRASSWARE
BRICKWORK
BRIDEWELL
BRUSHWOOD
BURROWING
CASSOWARY
CATCHWORD
CATERWAUL
CEDARWOOD
CHICKWEED
CLOCKWISE
CLOCKWORK
COCKSWAIN
CROSSWALK
CROSSWIND
CROSSWISE
CROSSWORD
DRIFTWOOD
EAGLEWOOD
EARTHWORK
EARTHWORM

FIELDWORK
FLEETWOOD
FOLLOWING
FORTHWINK
FORTHWITH
FRAMEWORK
GLASSWARE
GOBETWEEN
GREENWEED
GREENWICH
GREENWOOD
GUESSWORK
GUNPOWDER
HALLOWEEN
HALLOWMAS
HANDIWORK
HARROWING
HAZELWORT
HOLLYWOOD
HOMEOWNER
HORSEWHIP
HOUSEWIFE
HOUSEWORK
HOWTOWDIE
INGROWING
KITTIWAKE
LAMBSWOOL
LANCEWOOD
LANDOWNER
LASERWORT
LEASTWAYS
LEASTWISE
LIVERWORT
LOUSEWORT
LYMESWOLD
MARROWFAT
MATCHWOOD
MERESWINE
METALWORK
MICROWAVE
MONEYWORT
MOUTHWASH
NARROWING
NEWLYWEDS
NIGHTWORK
NORTHWARD
NORTHWEST
OTHERWISE
PAINTWORK
PAPERWORK
PATCHWORK
PAULOWNIA
PEARLWORT
PEASEWEEP
PIECEWORK
PIEPOWDER
QUILLWORT
RIGHTWING
SATINWOOD
SHIFTWORK
SHIPOWNER
SIDESWIPE
SLANTWISE
SLEEPWALK
SNAKEWEED
SNEERWELL
SORROWFUL
SOUTHWARD
SOUTHWARK
SOUTHWEST
SPEARWORT
SPEEDWELL
STATEWIDE
STINKWOOD
STOCKWORK
STONEWALL
STONEWARE
STONEWORK
STONEWORT
STUMPWORK
SUNDOWNER
TABLEWARE
TOUCHWOOD
TRADEWIND
UNCROWNED
UNDERWALK
UNDERWEAR
UNDERWENT
UNDERWOOD
UNKNOWING
WALLOWING
WATCHWORD
WATERWEED
WEDGEWOOD
WHIRLWIND
WHITEWALL
WHITEWASH
WHITEWING
WHITEWOOD
WILLOWING
WINDSWEPT
WITHYWIND
WORLDWIDE
YELLOWISH
CONNEXION
INFLEXION
OVEREXERT
PROLIXITY
REFLEXION
REFLEXIVE
UNISEXUAL
AESCHYLUS
ANAGLYPTA
APOCRYPHA
APOPHYSIS
AUTOLYCUS
AUTOLYSIS
BRICKYARD
CATALYSIS
CATALYTIC
CHLAMYDES
CLEPSYDRA
CLERGYMAN
COURTYARD
EMPHLYSIS
EMPLOYEES
EPIPHYSIS
EPIPHYTIC
GINGLYMUS
GRAVEYARD
GREENYARD
KILOCYCLE
LACHRYMAL
LIVERYMAN
MEGACYCLE
MONOXYLON
OCCUPYING
OVERLYING
PANEGYRIC
PARALYSIS
PARALYTIC
PARANYMPH
PRESBYTER
PURIFYING
PYONGYANG
SANTAYANA
SCALLYWAG
STEELYARD
STOCKYARD
SURVEYING
SYMPHYSIS
SYNCHYSIS
UNVARYING
WHERRYMAN
AGONIZING
CHABAZITE
CHALAZION
COGNIZANT
EMBEZZLER
HAPHAZARD
HYDRAZINE
MONTEZUMA
ORGANZINE
SCHNOZZLE
SHEMOZZLE
TRAPEZIAL
TRAPEZIST
TRAPEZIUM
TRAPEZIUS
TRAPEZOID
TREBIZOND

9:7

ABOMINATE
ABOUTFACE
ACCLIMATE
ACCOMPANY
ACCORDANT
ACIDULATE
ACUMINATE
ADUMBRATE
ADVANTAGE
ADVERSARY
AEROPLANE
AEROSPACE
AFFILIATE
AFFRICATE
AFORESAID
AFRIKAANS
AFTERCARE
AFTERDAMP
AFTERMATH
AGGRAVATE
AGGREGATE
ALGEBRAIC
ALLEGIANT
ALLEVIATE
ALLOGRAPH
ALTERCATE
ALTERNATE
ALTIPLANO
ALVEOLATE
AMBUSCADE
AMPERSAND
ANCHORAGE
ANCILLARY
ANTIQUARY
APPENDAGE
APPERTAIN
APPLEJACK
APPLICANT
AQUAPLANE
ARBITRAGE
ARBITRARY
ARBITRATE
ARCHIBALD
ARCTOGAEA
ASCENDANT
ASCERTAIN
ASHKENAZI
ASPARTAME
ASSAILANT
ASSISTANT
ASSOCIATE
ASTRAGALS
ASTROLABE
ASTRONAUT
ATTENDANT
ATTENUATE
AUTOCLAVE
AUTOCRACY
AUTOGRAPH
AUXILIARY
BACHARACH
BACKSPACE
BACKSTAGE
BACKTRACK
BALACLAVA
BANDSTAND
BARMBRACK
BARRICADE
BASEBOARD
BASTINADE
BASTINADO
BATTLEAXE
BEANFEAST
BENCHMARK
BERGAMASK
BERGOMASK
BIFURCATE
BILLBOARD
BIRDBRAIN
BIRTHMARK
BLACKBALL
BLACKFACE
BLACKJACK
BLACKMAIL
BLOODBATH
BLUEBEARD
BOARDWALK
BOATSWAIN
BODYGUARD
BOLIVIANO
BOOKSTALL
BOOKSTAND
BOOMERANG
BORNAGAIN
BOULEVARD
BRAINCASE
BRAINWASH
BRAINWAVE
BRASSWARE
BREAKFAST
BRICKYARD
BRIEFCASE
BRILLIANT
BROADCAST
BROKERAGE
BUCENTAUR
BUDGETARY
BURKINABE
CAGOULARD
CAKESTAND
CALCINATE
CALCULATE
CALIBRATE
CANDIDACY
CANDIDATE
CANNONADE
CAPILLARY
CAPTIVATE
CARBAMATE
CARBONADE
CARBONARI
CARBONATE
CARDBOARD
CARTILAGE
CARTTRACK
CARTULARY
CASSONADE
CASSOWARY
CASTIGATE
CATAPLASM
CATERWAUL
CAVALCADE
CELEBRANT
CELEBRATE
CENTENARY
CEREBRATE
CHAMFRAIN
CHAMINADE
CHAMPLAIN
CHARABANC
CHARIVARI
CHAROLAIS
CHEAPJACK
CHECKMATE
CHIEFTAIN
CHILBLAIN
CHILDCARE
CHIPBOARD
CHIPOLATA
CHOCOLATE
CHURIDARS
CILIOLATE
CIRCINATE
CIRCULATE
CLAPBOARD
CLASSMATE
CLEVELAND
CLIPBOARD
COAGULANT
COAGULATE
COARCTATE
COCKROACH
COCKSWAIN
COGNIZANT
COLLIGATE
COLLIMATE
COLLOCATE
COLONNADE

COLUMBARY
COLUMBATE
COMBATANT
COMPLIANT
CONFIDANT
CONJUGATE
CONNOTATE
CONSONANT
CONSULATE
CONTUMACY
COOPERATE
CORMORANT
CORNBRASH
CORNCRAKE
CORNSTALK
COROLLARY
CORPORATE
CORPOSANT
CORRELATE
CORRUGATE
CORUSCATE
COSMONAUT
COURTYARD
COVERDALE
CRASHLAND
CREPITATE
CRIMINATE
CROISSANT
CROOKBACK
CROSSWALK
CROUSTADE
CUCHULAIN
CULMINATE
CULTIVATE
CURETTAGE
CURTILAGE
CUSTOMARY
CYCLAMATE
CYCLORAMA
DAIRYMAID
DARTBOARD
DASHBOARD
DECKCHAIR
DECOLLATE
DECRETALS
DECUSSATE
DEFALCATE
DEFENDANT
DEFOLIANT
DEFOLIATE
DEHYDRATE
DELINEATE
DEMARCATE
DEMOCRACY
DEMURRAGE
DENIGRATE
DEODORANT

DEPENDANT
DEPRECATE
DEPREDATE
DESECRATE
DESICCATE
DESIGNATE
DESPERADO
DESPERATE
DEVASTATE
DIAPHRAGM
DIGNITARY
DIPLOMACY
DISEMBARK
DISENGAGE
DISLOCATE
DISPARAGE
DISPARATE
DISPLEASE
DISPUTANT
DISREGARD
DISREPAIR
DISSIPATE
DISSONANT
DITHYRAMB
DIXIELAND
DOCTORATE
DOWNGRADE
DOWNSTAGE
DROMEDARY
DUCKBOARD
DUNDREARY
DUNSINANE
DUPLICAND
DUPLICATE
EBRILLADE
ECTOPLASM
EIDOGRAPH
EJACULATE
ELABORATE
ELECTUARY
ELIMINATE
ELUCIDATE
ELUTRIATE
EMBARRASS
EMBASSADE
EMBASSAGE
EMBROCATE
EMMERDALE
EMOLLIATE
EMPENNAGE
ENCHILADA
ENCOMPASS
ENCOURAGE
ENGARLAND
ENGRENAGE
ENNERDALE
ENTERTAIN

ENTOURAGE
ENUCLEATE
ENUMERATE
ENUNCIATE
EPARCHATE
EPHESIANS
EPIPHRAGM
ERADICATE
EROSTRATE
ESEMPLASY
ESPIONAGE
ESPLANADE
ESTRAPADE
EVAPORATE
EVENTUATE
EVERGLADE
EXANIMATE
EXCORIATE
EXCULPATE
EXECUTANT
EXEMPLARY
EXONERATE
EXPATIATE
EXPECTANT
EXPISCATE
EXPLICATE
EXPURGATE
EXSICCATE
EXTENUATE
EXTIRPATE
EXTRICATE
EXUBERANT
EYESTRAIN
FABRICATE
FAIRYLAND
FAIRYTALE
FASCINATE
FASTTRACK
FEDUCIARY
FERDINAND
FESTINATE
FEUILLANT
FIDUCIARY
FIELDFARE
FILIGRAIN
FIREBRAND
FIREDRAKE
FIREGUARD
FIREPLACE
FIRSTHAND
FIRSTRATE
FISHGUARD
FISHPLATE
FLAGITATE
FLAGSTAFF
FLASHBACK
FLOODGATE

FLOWCHART
FLUCTUATE
FOLKWEAVE
FOMALHAUT
FOOTBRAKE
FOOTPLATE
FOOTSTALL
FOREBEARS
FORESTAGE
FORESTALL
FORFICATE
FORMULATE
FORNICATE
FORTILAGE
FORTUNATE
FRAGONARD
FRANGLAIS
FREEBOARD
FRIESLAND
FROGSPAWN
FROISSART
FRUITCAKE
FRUSTRATE
FULLSCALE
FULMINANT
FULMINATE
FUSILLADE
FUSTIGATE
GABIONADE
GALENGALE
GALINGALE
GALLIVANT
GALLOPADE
GALRAVAGE
GANGPLANK
GASCONADE
GATECRASH
GERMINATE
GINGERADE
GLASSWARE
GLOMERATE
GRAMPIANS
GRANULATE
GRASSLAND
GRAVEYARD
GRAVITATE
GREENBACK
GREENGAGE
GREENMAIL
GREENSAND
GREENYARD
GREYBEARD
GROSGRAIN
GUATEMALA
GUILDHALL
HABITUATE
HADROSAUR

HALFSTAFF
HALLSTATT
HALOTHANE
HAMMURABI
HANDBRAKE
HANDSHAKE
HANDSTAND
HAPHAZARD
HARDBOARD
HARESTANE
HARIOLATE
HARROGATE
HATCHBACK
HAVERSACK
HEADBOARD
HEADSCARF
HEADSTALL
HEARTLAND
HEATHLAND
HEDYPHANE
HERMITAGE
HESYCHASM
HESYCHAST
HIBERNATE
HIGHCLASS
HIPPODAME
HODOGRAPH
HOLOGRAPH
HOMEOPATH
HOMOGRAPH
HORSEBACK
HORSEHAIR
HORSETAIL
HOURGLASS
HOUSEMAID
HUCKABACK
HUMILIATE
HUNCHBACK
HURRICANE
HURRICANO
HYPALLAGE
HYPHENATE
IDEOGRAPH
IDIOBLAST
IDIOGRAPH
IDIOPLASM
IMAGINARY
IMBRICATE
IMBROCATE
IMMEDIACY
IMMEDIATE
IMMELMANN
IMMIGRANT
IMMIGRATE
IMMORTALS
IMPLICATE
IMPORTANT

IMPRECATE
INAMORATA
INAMORATO
INANIMATE
INCARNATE
INCESSANT
INCULCATE
INCULPATE
INDIGNANT
INEBRIATE
INELEGANT
INFATUATE
INFIRMARY
INFORMANT
INFURIATE
INNISFAIL
INOCULATE
INOPINATE
INQUINATE
INQUORATE
INSENSATE
INSINUATE
INSTIGATE
INTEGRATE
INTENDANT
INTERFACE
INTERLACE
INTERLARD
INTESTATE
INTRICACY
INTRICATE
INUMBRATE
INUSITATE
INVERTASE
INVIOLATE
IRRADIANT
IRRADIATE
ISINGLASS
ISOMERASE
ITINERANT
ITINERARY
ITINERATE
JAGGANATH
JAMBALAYA
JANISSARY
JEPHTHAHS
JESSERANT
JUDICIARY
KHALIFATE
KICKSHAWS
KITTIWAKE
LACINIATE
LACKBEARD
LAMPADARY
LAMPBLACK
LAMPSHADE
LANCINATE

LANDGRAVE
LANDSCAPE
LANDSMAAL
LATICLAVE
LEASTWAYS
LEGENDARY
LEGIONARY
LEGISLATE
LIFEGUARD
LINEOLATE
LIONHEART
LIQUIDATE
LJUBLJANA
LOCELLATE
LONGCHAMP
LOUISIANA
LUBRICANT
LUBRICATE
LUCUBRATE
LUXURIANT
LUXURIATE
MACDONALD
MACHINATE
MADARIAGA
MAINFRAME
MALIGNANT
MANDICATE
MANDUCATE
MANGANATE
MARCHPANE
MARIJUANA
MARMALADE
MARSHLAND
MASTICATE
MAXILLARY
MELIORATE
MELODRAMA
MENDICANT
MERCENARY
MESOBLAST
METRICATE
METROLAND
MICROWAVE
MILKSHAKE
MILLAMANT
MISBEHAVE
MISCREANT
MISLOCATE
MISMANAGE
MOLLYMAWK
MOMENTARY
MONODRAMA
MONOGRAPH
MONOPLANE
MOTORCADE
MOUTHWASH
MUSCOVADO
MUSICHALL
MUSSITATE
NAMEPLATE
NECESSARY
NEGOTIATE
NEWSFLASH
NEWSSTALL
NEWSSTAND
NICTITATE
NIGHTFALL
NIGHTMARE
NITHSDALE
NOMOCRACY
NORMALACY
NORTHEAST
NORTHWARD
NOTCHBACK
NOVICIATE
NOVITIATE
NUNCUPATE
NURSEMAID
OBBLIGATO
OBCORDATE
OBFUSCATE
OBJURGATE
OBSECRATE
OBSERVANT
OBSTINACY
OBSTINATE
OFFENBACH
OFFICIALS
OFFICIANT
OFFICIATE
OLEOGRAPH
OPENHEART
ORANGEADE
ORIENTATE
ORIGINATE
ORPHANAGE
OSCILLATE
OSTEOPATH
OVERBOARD
OVERDRAFT
OVERDRAWN
OVERHEADS
OVERREACH
OVERREACT
OVERSHADE
OVERSTATE
OWLEGLASS
PAKISTANI
PALMITATE
PALPITATE
PALSGRAVE
PANDURATE
PANTAGAMY
PAPERBACK
PARABLAST
PARAGRAPH
PARENTAGE
PARHYPATE
PARSONAGE
PASTORALE
PASTURAGE
PATHTRAIN
PATRONAGE
PECUNIARY
PENDULATE
PENETRATE
PENTOSANE
PERCOLATE
PERFORANS
PERFORATE
PERICLASE
PERIODATE
PERSONAGE
PERSONATE
PERTUSATE
PETILLANT
PHARISAIC
PHONECARD
PHOSPHATE
PHTHALATE
PICKABACK
PICKTHANK
PIERGLASS
PIGGYBACK
PIGGYBANK
PIGNERATE
PIKESTAFF
PILFERAGE
PITUITARY
PIZZICATO
PLANETARY
POLLINATE
POLLUTANT
POLYGRAPH
PORCELAIN
PORPORATE
PORTERAGE
POSTULANT
POSTULATE
POTENTATE
PREDICANT
PREDICATE
PREDIKANT
PREORDAIN
PRESSGANG
PROCREATE
PROMENADE
PROPAGATE
PROROGATE
PROSTRATE
PROXIMATE
PTEROSAUR
PUCELLAGE
PULLULATE
PULMONARY
PUNCTUATE
PUPILLAGE
PUSHCHAIR
PYONGYANG
QUICKSAND
RACETRACK
RATIONALE
READYEARN
READYMADE
REANIMATE
REARGUARD
REDBREAST
REDUNDANT
REGARDANT
REINSTATE
REITERATE
RELIQUARY
RELUCTANT
REMONTANT
REMOULADE
REPECHAGE
REPENTANT
REPLICATE
REPORTAGE
REPRIMAND
REPROBATE
REPUDIATE
REPUGNANT
RESIDUARY
RESISTANT
RESULTANT
RESURFACE
RETALIATE
RICERCARE
RIDGEBACK
RIGHTHAND
RORSCHACH
ROTAPLANE
ROTUNDATE
ROUGHCAST
ROUNDBACK
ROUNDHAND
RUGGELACH
RUNCINATE
RUNESTAVE
RUSTICATE
SAFEGUARD
SAGITTARY
SALANGANE
SALESLADY
SANCTUARY
SANDARACH
SANTAYANA
SARBACANE
SASSENACH
SAVERNAKE
SAXIFRAGE
SCELERATE
SCHOLIAST
SCREWBALL
SCREWTAPE
SCRIMMAGE
SCRUMMAGE
SECONDARY
SECRETARY
SEDENTARY
SEGREGATE
SELLOTAPE
SHAMEFAST
SHELDRAKE
SHELLBACK
SHIPSHAPE
SHORTCAKE
SHORTFALL
SHORTHAND
SHORTHAUL
SHRINKAGE
SICILIANO
SIDEBOARD
SIDETRACK
SIGNBOARD
SIMULCAST
SISSERARY
SLEEPWALK
SLINGBACK
SLOWCOACH
SNOWFLAKE
SOMEPLACE
SOUTHEAST
SOUTHWARD
SOUTHWARK
SPEAKEASY
SPECULATE
SPIKENARD
SPOROCARP
SPRINGALD
SPRITSAIL
SQUIREAGE
STAGEHAND
STAIRCASE
STALEMATE
STANDGALE
STARBOARD
STEADFAST
STEELYARD
STEGOSAUR
STENOPAIC
STERNFAST
STIMULANT
STIMULATE
STIPULATE
STOCKYARD
STONEHAND
STONEWALL
STONEWARE
STOOLBALL
STRAPHANG
STRAPPADO
STREETAGE
STRONGARM
STYLOBATE
SUBJUGATE
SUBLIMATE
SUBROGATE
SUBSTRATA
SUBSTRATE
SUBTENANT
SUCCINATE
SUCCOTASH
SUFFOCATE
SUGARCANE
SULTANATE
SUMPTUARY
SUPPLIANT
SUPPURATE
SUPREMACY
SURFBOARD
SURROGATE
SUSCITATE
SWEATBAND
SYCOPHANT
SYLLABARY
SYNCOPATE
SYNDICATE
TABLELAND
TABLEWARE
TAILBOARD
TAILPLANE
TAMERLANE
TANTARARA
TAOISEACH
TARANTASS
TELEGRAPH
TEMPERATE
TEMPORARY
TERMAGANT
TERMINATE
THEOCRACY
THORNBACK
THRILLANT
THROWBACK
THUMBNAIL
THUMBTACK
TIMESHARE
TIMOCRACY
TIPPERARY
TITHEBARN

TITILLATE
TOASTRACK
TONOPLAST
TRADEMARK
TRAGELAPH
TRANSLATE
TRANSVAAL
TREILLAGE
TREMULATE
TRENCHANT
TRIBUNATE
TRIBUTARY
TRIPITAKA
TRITICALE
TRITURATE
TRUTINATE
TUNGSTATE
TURBINATE
TWAYBLADE
UNCERTAIN
UNDERCAST
UNDERHAND
UNDERPAID
UNDERPASS
UNDERRATE
UNDERTAKE
UNDERWALK
UROKINASE
VACCINATE
VACILLATE
VANTBRASS
VARIEGATE
VARIOLATE
VELLENAGE
VELLICATE
VENTIFACT
VENTILATE
VERBERATE
VEXILLARY
VIDEOTAPE
VIENTIANE
VINDICATE
VIRGINALS
VIRGULATE
VISIONARY
VOLKSRAAD
VOLUNTARY
VOUCHSAFE
WAISTBAND
WAITERAGE
WALDGRAVE
WAPENTAKE
WASHBOARD
WASHSTAND
WASTELAND
WATERBABY
WATERFALL
WATERGATE
WATERMARK
WELDSTADT
WHEELBASE
WHIPSNADE
WHITEBAIT
WHITEDAMP
WHITEHALL
WHITEWALL
WHITEWASH
WHIZZBANG
WHOLESALE
WHUNSTANE
WINDSCALE
WINEGLASS
WINNEBAGO
WISECRACK
WITHDRAWN
WITHSTAND
WOODCRAFT
WOOMERANG
WORKPLACE
WORKSPACE
ZENOCRATE
ADAPTABLE
ADMIRABLE
ADMIRABLY
ADVISABLE
AGREEABLE
AGREEABLY
ALLOWABLE
ALTERABLE
ANAEROBIC
AVAILABLE
AVOIDABLE
BEELZEBUB
BILIRUBIN
BIRDTABLE
BREAKABLE
BUMBLEBEE
BUTTERBUR
CONSTABLE
DEBATABLE
DEFINABLE
DESIRABLE
DIRIGIBLE
DISMEMBER
DISSEMBLE
DISTURBED
DIVISIBLE
DJELLABAH
DOODLEBUG
DOUKHOBOR
DRINKABLE
DUNSTABLE
ENDURABLE
ENJOYABLE
EQUITABLE
EQUITABLY
ESTIMABLE
EUPHORBIA
EXCALIBUR
EXCITABLE
EXCUSABLE
EXCUSABLY
EXECRABLE
EXECRABLY
FAVORABLE
FAVORABLY
FLAMMABLE
FLOWERBED
HABITABLE
HARQUEBUS
HOLDERBAT
HONORABLE
ILLEGIBLE
ILLEGIBLY
IMMOVABLE
IMMOVABLY
IMMUTABLE
IMMUTABLY
INAUDIBLE
INAUDIBLY
INCAPABLE
INCURABLE
INCURABLY
INDELIBLE
INDELIBLY
INEFFABLE
INSCRIBED
INSOLUBLE
INVISIBLE
IRASCIBLE
IRRITABLE
IRRITABLY
ISALLOBAR
ISLAMABAD
JIGGUMBOB
JITTERBUG
LAUGHABLE
LETTERBOX
MALLEABLE
MEHITABEL
MEMORABLE
MISERABLE
MISERABLY
NAVIGABLE
NUTJOBBER
OUTNUMBER
PALATABLE
PEACEABLE
PEACEABLY
PERMEABLE
PERTURBED
PHILLABEG
PHILLIBEG
PLAUSIBLE
PLAUSIBLY
PRINTABLE
QUODLIBET
RATTLEBAG
REACHABLE
REDUCIBLE
REMOVABLE
RENEWABLE
REPAYABLE
REPUTABLE
SADDLEBAG
SCALEABLE
SCHOOLBOY
SEPARABLE
SEPTEMBER
SHILLABER
SPONGEBAG
SPRINGBOK
STABLEBOY
TEACHABLE
THINKABLE
TIMETABLE
TITTLEBAT
TOLERABLE
TOLERABLY
TRACEABLE
TRACTABLE
TRAINABLE
TURNTABLE
UNEATABLE
UNTENABLE
VEGETABLE
VENERABLE
VERITABLE
VOLATIBLE
ANNOUNCER
ARSENICAL
ARTIFICER
AUTOLYCUS
AVALANCHE
BAREFACED
BASILICAL
BASILICON
BELLYACHE
BOCCACCIO
BOONDOCKS
BOOTLACES
BOTANICAL
BRASSICAS
BUTTERCUP
CAMBUSCAN
CANONICAL
CAPRICCIO
CARBUNCLE
CARPACCIO
CARTOUCHE
CHAWBACON
CHRONICLE
CLASSICAL
COALESCED
COLCHICUM
CONVINCED
CORPUSCLE
CRUSTACEA
DISGRACED
DISPLACED
DOMINICAL
DOMINICAN
DROPSICAL
EMPIRICAL
ENSCONCED
ENTELECHY
ENTRANCED
EQUIVOCAL
ERISTICAL
FANATICAL
FATIDICAL
GAELTACHT
GENETICAL
GERFALCON
GERMANCER
GRAPHICAL
GREYWACKE
GUILLOCHE
HEARTACHE
HEPATICAL
HERETICAL
HIERARCHY
IDENTICAL
IDIOTICON
ILLOGICAL
IMMANACLE
INVOLUCRE
JAUNDICED
JURIDICAL
KILOCYCLE
LACONICAL
LEVITICUS
LUMBRICUS
MEGACYCLE
MISPLACED
MONOMACHY
MOUSTACHE
NIETZSCHE
NOTONECTA
NUMERICAL
OLIGARCHY
ORGANICAL
ORICALCHE
OROBANCHE
PAGLIACCI
PARFLECHE
PASTICCIO
PIRATICAL
POLEMICAL
POLITICAL
PRACTICAL
PRECINCTS
PROBOSCIS
PROMUSCIS
PSYCHICAL
QUANTICAL
QUANTOCKS
QUIZZICAL
RESOURCES
SATIRICAL
SCEPTICAL
SCIAMACHY
SEANNACHY
SIPHUNCLE
SKEPTICAL
SKIAMACHY
SPARTACUS
SPECTACLE
SPHERICAL
SPILLICAN
STREETCAR
SUPPLICAT
TAPDANCER
TARAXACUM
TECHNICAL
TETRARCHY
TOOTHACHE
TROSSACHS
TUMMYACHE
UMBILICAL
UMBILICUS
UNETHICAL
UNMUSICAL
UNNOTICED
UNTYPICAL
URANISCUS
VENTRICLE
VERBASCUM
VERIDICAL
VIDELICET
WHIMSICAL
ABSCONDER
ADENOIDAL
ADVISEDLY
ALEXANDER
ALEXANDRA
ALLEGEDLY
AMSTERDAM
ANTIPODES
APERIODIC
ASSUREDLY
ASTOUNDED

ATTAINDER
ATTITUDES
AWKWARDLY
BACKPEDAL
BARTENDER
BEDRIDDEN
BELATEDLY
BERGANDER
BEVERIDGE
BIGHEADED
BOMBARDON
BYSTANDER
CAMBRIDGE
CAMCORDER
CARTRIDGE
CASSANDRA
CERATODUS
CHARYBDIS
CHAVENDER
CHICKADEE
CHLAMYDES
CLARENDON
CLEPSYDRA
COFFERDAM
COLERIDGE
COLLOIDAL
COMMANDER
CONCLUDED
CONCORDAT
CONTENDER
CORIANDER
COTYLEDON
CROOKEDLY
DASTARDLY
DECIDEDLY
DISBURDEN
DISCARDED
DISCREDIT
DISTENDED
EMBROIDER
ENCELADUS
ESTRELDID
EUMENIDES
EURIPIDES
EYESHADOW
FINLANDIA
FORBIDDEN
FORWANDER
FRUCTIDOR
GASHOLDER
GERMANDER
GOOSANDER
GUNPOWDER
HAYRADDIN
HENDIADYS
HERMANDAD
HETERODOX
HODMANDOD
HOMICIDAL
HOTHEADED
HOWTOWDIE
HUNDREDTH
HURRIEDLY
HUSBANDLY
HUSBANDRY
ICELANDER
ICELANDIC
ICTERIDAE
IGUANODON
IMPOUNDER
INFIELDER
IRONSIDES
IRRAWADDY
KENTLEDGE
KEYHOLDER
KINTLEDGE
KNOWLEDGE
LANGRIDGE
LANGUEDOC
LANGUIDLY
LAPLANDER
LATTERDAY
LOMBARDIC
LOWLANDER
MALLANDER
MALLENDER
MANHANDLE
MARTYRDOM
MISGUIDED
MISHANDLE
MUCKENDER
MUJAHIDIN
NERITIDAE
NIGGARDLY
OCEANIDES
OPENENDED
OPODELDOC
OUTWARDLY
OVERRIDER
PANHANDLE
PARAMEDIC
PARTRIDGE
PERIANDER
PERSUADED
PHILANDER
PIEPOWDER
PIGHEADED
POINTEDLY
POLYANDRY
PREBENDAL
PRETENDER
PROPERDIN
PROVENDER
PYRAMIDAL
QUARENDEN
REDDENDUM
REDHANDED
REDHEADED
REGUERDON
REJOINDER
REMAINDER
REPUTEDLY
RESSALDAR
RHAPSODIC
RINGSIDER
ROTTERDAM
SATYRIDAE
SCHMIEDER
SCIARIDAE
SCLAUNDER
SCREWEDUP
SEPHARDIM
SERENADER
SHEIKHDOM
SILURIDAE
SKEDADDLE
SPASMODIC
SQUALIDLY
SUCCEEDED
SURQUEDRY
SURRENDER
SUSPENDED
SUSPENDER
SYRPHIDAE
TABANIDAE
TAHSILDAR
THERMIDOR
THRALLDOM
TIPULIDAE
TOLPUDDLE
TONBRIDGE
TOURNEDOS
TROUBADOR
TRUMPEDUP
UNBOUNDED
UNCLOUDED
UNDECIDED
UNDIVIDED
UNFOUNDED
UNGUARDED
UNTRODDEN
WEDNESDAY
WILLESDEN
WIMBLEDON
YESTERDAY
ZEALANDER
ZINFANDEL
ABASEMENT
ABATEMENT
ABHORRENT
ABSORBENT
ABSTINENT
ACETYLENE
ACUTENESS
ADEPTNESS
ADORNMENT
ADVERSELY
AGREEMENT
AGUECHEEK
AIRSTREAM
ALERTNESS
ALIGNMENT
ALLOTMENT
ALOOFNESS
AMAZEMENT
AMENDMENT
AMUSEMENT
ANDROMEDA
ANNULMENT
APARTHEID
APARTMENT
APPREHEND
ARCHITECT
ARROWHEAD
ARTILLERY
ASHMOLEAN
ATHENAEUM
ATONEMENT
AUTHORESS
AWARENESS
BAKSHEESH
BALLADEER
BANDOLEER
BANDOLERO
BANISTERS
BEACHHEAD
BEACHWEAR
BEARDLESS
BECHSTEIN
BEDSPREAD
BEEFSTEAK
BELVEDERE
BERNSTEIN
BIOSPHERE
BIZARRELY
BLACKHEAD
BLACKLEAD
BLACKNESS
BLAMELESS
BLANDNESS
BLASPHEME
BLASPHEMY
BLEACHERS
BLINDNESS
BLOCKHEAD
BLOODLESS
BLUFFNESS
BLUNTNESS
BOLOGNESE
BOMBSHELL
BOOKSHELF
BORDEREAU
BOSSINESS
BOUNDLESS
BOYFRIEND
BRAINLESS
BRASSIERE
BREAKNECK
BRIDEWELL
BRIEFNESS
BRISKNESS
BRUSQUELY
BUCCANEER
BUCHAREST
BUCKTEETH
BUCKWHEAT
BULKINESS
BURLINESS
CABALLERO
CAESAREAN
CAFETIERE
CALABRESE
CALCANEUM
CALCANEUS
CALLIPERS
CAMEMBERT
CANTONESE
CARIBBEAN
CARTWHEEL
CASTANETS
CATAPLEXY
CATCHMENT
CEASELESS
CENTIPEDE
CEYLONESE
CHALUMEAU
CHAMELEON
CHAMPLEVÉ
CHARTREUX
CHAUFFEUR
CHEAPNESS
CHEERLESS
CHICANERY
CHICKWEED
CHILDLESS
CLASSLESS
CLEANNESS
CLEARNESS
CLIENTELE
CLOSENESS
CLOUDLESS
COALFIELD
COCHINEAL
COINTREAU
COLORLESS
COLOSSEUM
COMINTERN
COMPETENT
COMPONENT
CONCISELY
CONDIMENT
CONFIDENT
CONFITEOR
CONGOLESE
CONGRUENT
CONTINENT
CONTUMELY
CORNFIELD
CORPOREAL
CORPULENT
COTANGENT
COUNTLESS
CRAPULENT
CRAZINESS
CRISPNESS
CROSSBEAM
CROTCHETY
CRUDENESS
DAMASCENE
DAMNEDEST
DASHWHEEL
DAUNTLESS
DEACONESS
DEATHLESS
DECUMBENT
DEFENDERS
DEFERMENT
DEFICIENT
DEMULCENT
DENSENESS
DEPENDENT
DESIPIENT
DETERGENT
DETERRENT
DETRIMENT
DEVILMENT
DIFFERENT
DIFFIDENT
DINGINESS
DIRTINESS
DISAPPEAR
DISCOVERT
DISCOVERY
DISHONEST
DISINFECT
DISORIENT
DISSIDENT
DIVERGENT
DIZZINESS
DOUBTLESS
DOWNTREND
DREAMLESS

DUNGAREES
DUNGENESS
DYSENTERY
EAGERNESS
EBULLIENT
EFFICIENT
EFFULGENT
EGAREMENT
EIGHTIETH
ELECTRESS
ELIZABETH
ELLESMERE
ELOPEMENT
ELSEWHERE
EMBRACERY
EMOLLIENT
EMOLUMENT
EMPHYSEMA
EMPLOYEES
EMPTINESS
ENACTMENT
ENCUMBENT
ENDOSPERM
ENDOWMENT
ENDPAPERS
ENGINEERS
ENJOYMENT
ENROLMENT
ENSORCELL
ENTHYMEME
ENTREMETS
ENVERMEIL
EPICUREAN
EQUIPMENT
ETHELBERT
EUCLIDEAN
EVASIVELY
EVERGREEN
EXACTMENT
EXACTNESS
EXANTHEMA
EXCELLENT
EXCIPIENT
EXCREMENT
EXOSPHERE
EXPEDIENT
EXTREMELY
EXTROVERT
EYELETEER
FAINTNESS
FAITHLESS
FALSENESS
FARMSTEAD
FATISCENT
FAULTLESS
FENUGREEK
FILLIPEEN
FIREBREAK
FIRMAMENT
FLAMSTEED
FLATULENT
FLESHLESS
FLORIMELL
FOGGINESS
FORCEMEAT
FOREANENT
FORESPEAK
FORESPEND
FORESTERS
FOURWHEEL
FRANKNESS
FRATCHETY
FREEWHEEL
FRESHNESS
FRUITLESS
FUGGINESS
FULLERENE
FUNDAMENT
FURNIMENT
FURTIVELY
FUSSINESS
FUSTINESS
FUZZINESS
GALLABEAH
GASPEREAU
GATESHEAD
GAUDINESS
GAUNTNESS
GAWKINESS
GAZETTEER
GEARWHEEL
GENEVIEVE
GENUFLECT
GENUINELY
GIDDINESS
GILGAMESH
GOBETWEEN
GODLINESS
GODPARENT
GOLDCREST
GOLDFIELD
GOOSEHERD
GOOSENECK
GOSSAMERY
GOVERNESS
GRACELESS
GRANDNESS
GRAVESEND
GREATNESS
GREENFEED
GREENHEAD
GREENWEED
GRIMINESS
GRUFFNESS
GUILELESS
GUILTLESS
GUINEVERE
GUMSHIELD
GUTENBERG
HABERGEON
HAIRPIECE
HALLOWEEN
HAMPSTEAD
HANDINESS
HANDPIECE
HAPPINESS
HARDINESS
HARDSHELL
HARSHNESS
HASTINESS
HATCHMENT
HEADDRESS
HEADINESS
HEARTBEAT
HEARTFELT
HEARTLESS
HEAVINESS
HEBRIDEAN
HEMIPTERA
HERCULEAN
HIGHSPEED
HINGELESS
HOMESTEAD
HOMOPTERA
HORSELESS
HUSKINESS
IGNESCENT
IMAGELESS
IMMENSELY
IMPATIENT
IMPERFECT
IMPLEMENT
IMPRUDENT
INCIPIENT
INCLEMENT
INCORRECT
INCREMENT
INCUMBENT
INDULGENT
INERTNESS
INPATIENT
INSELBERG
INSINCERE
INSIPIENT
INSISTENT
INSOLVENT
INSURGENT
INTELLECT
INTENSELY
INTERCEDE
INTERCEPT
INTERFERE
INTERJECT
INTERMENT
INTERSECT
INTERVENE
INTROVERT
INVERNESS
JARLSBERG
JERAHMEEL
JERKINESS
JETSTREAM
JEWELLERY
JUDGEMENT
JUICINESS
KENTIGERN
LANKINESS
LAODICEAN
LAPSTREAK
LARGENESS
LATESCENT
LAUNDRESS
LEFTOVERS
LEISURELY
LEPROSERY
LIGHTLESS
LIGHTNESS
LIMITLESS
LINEAMENT
LINGFIELD
LODGEMENT
LOFTINESS
LOGOTHETE
LONDONESE
LOOSEHEAD
LOOSELEAF
LOOSENESS
LOWLINESS
LURIDNESS
LUSTINESS
LUTESCENT
MACHINERY
MADRILENE
MAGDALENE
MANGANESE
MANLINESS
MANSFIELD
MARKETEER
MARMOREAL
MARTINEAU
MASEFIELD
MASSIVELY
MASSORETE
MATCHLESS
MAUSOLEUM
MELPOMENE
MENIPPEAN
MERCILESS
MERRIMENT
MESENTERY
MIDSTREAM
MIDWIFERY
MILLEPEDE
MILLINERY
MILLIPEDE
MINCEMEAT
MINEFIELD
MIRTHLESS
MISDIRECT
MISOCLERE
MISTINESS
MOISTNESS
MONASTERY
MOODINESS
MOUTHLESS
MUDDINESS
MURDERESS
MURKINESS
MUSHINESS
MUSKETEER
MUSKOGEAN
MUSTINESS
MUZZINESS
NABATHEAN
NAKEDNESS
NASTINESS
NATHELESS
NEGLIGENT
NEWLYWEDS
NEWSAGENT
NEWSSHEET
NINETIETH
NIPCHEESE
NOBLENESS
NOISELESS
NOISINESS
NOLLEKENS
NOMOTHETE
NONPAREIL
NOOSPHERE
NORTHWEST
NOSEBLEED
NOTORIETY
NUREMBERG
NUTRIMENT
OBLIQUELY
OBSCENELY
OBSCURELY
ODOURLESS
OLIGOCENE
OPPENHEIM
OSTEODERM
OUGHTNESS
OUTSIDERS
OUTSPREAD
OVERDRESS
OVEREXERT
OVERSLEEP
OVERSPEND
OVERSTEER
OVERWHELM
PACHYDERM
PALANKEEN
PANNIKELL
PANTALEON
PARACLETE
PARASCENE
PARASCEVE
PARCHEESI
PARCHMENT
PASSAMENT
PASSIVELY
PATHOGENY
PATRONESS
PAWKINESS
PEASEWEEP
PEDIGREES
PEKINGESE
PENFRIEND
PENNILESS
PENSIVELY
PERFUMERY
PERGAMENE
PERIPHERY
PERMANENT
PERSEVERE
PERTINENT
PESTILENT
PETROLEUM
PETTINESS
PHILATELY
PHOSPHENE
PHOTOGENE
PHYLOGENY
PIECEMEAL
PILASTERS
PINCHBECK
PIPEDREAM
PIPSQUEAK
PISTAREEN
PISTOLEER
PLACEMENT
PLAINNESS
PLEIOCENE
PLUMPNESS
POINTLESS
POLYTHENE
POPLITEAL
PORTREEVE
POWERLESS
PRECEDENT
PRECISELY

PREDILECT
PRESCIENT
PRESIDENT
PREVALENT
PRICELESS
PRIESTESS
PRIMAVERA
PRIVATEER
PRIVATELY
PRIVILEGE
PROFANELY
PROFITEER
PROFUSELY
PROMINENT
PROOFREAD
PROPONENT
PROPRIETY
PROPYLENE
PROVIDENT
PRYTANEUM
PUFFINESS
PULPITEER
PUPPETEER
PURPOSELY
PYTHONESS
QUEERNESS
QUICKNESS
QUIESCENT
QUIETNESS
RACKETEER
RACONTEUR
RAINCHECK
RANDINESS
READDRESS
READINESS
RECIPIENT
RECOLLECT
RECOMMEND
RECONVENE
RECUMBENT
RECURRENT
REDSTREAK
REEDINESS
REFULGENT
REGISSEUR
RENASCENT
REPAYMENT
REPELLENT
REPOSSESS
REPREHEND
REPRESENT
REPROCESS
RESILIENT
RESURGENT
RESURRECT
RETROCEDE
RETROVERT
REVETMENT
RIDERLESS
RIGHTNESS
RISKINESS
ROADSTEAD
ROOSEVELT
ROUGHNECK
ROUGHNESS
ROUNDHEAD
ROUTINELY
ROWDINESS
RUFESCENT
RUNNYMEDE
RUSTINESS
SACRAMENT
SACRILEGE
SALTINESS
SAUCINESS
SCENTLESS
SCONCHEON
SCUNCHEON
SEMANTEME
SEMIBREVE
SENESCENT
SENSELESS
SENTIMENT
SERENGETI
SERVILELY
SEVENTEEN
SHADINESS
SHAKINESS
SHAMELESS
SHAPELESS
SHARPNESS
SHEEPMEAT
SHEERLEGS
SHEERNESS
SHEFFIELD
SHEWBREAD
SHIFTLESS
SHIPWRECK
SHORTNESS
SHORTTERM
SHOWINESS
SHOWPIECE
SHRUBBERY
SIGHTLESS
SIGHTSEER
SILLINESS
SINCERELY
SINGALESE
SISYPHEAN
SLACKNESS
SLEEKNESS
SLEEPLESS
SLIGHTEST
SLIMINESS
SMALLNESS
SMARTNESS
SMOKELESS
SNAKEWEED
SNEERWELL
SOBERNESS
SOCIOLECT
SOGGINESS
SOMEWHERE
SOMNOLENT
SONNETEER
SOPPINESS
SORCERESS
SORTILEGE
SOUFRIERE
SOUNDLESS
SOUNDNESS
SOUTENEUR
SOUTHWEST
SPACELESS
SPARKLERS
SPEARHEAD
SPECIMENS
SPEEDWELL
SPICILEGE
SPICINESS
SPINELESS
SPLINTERS
SPOONFEED
SPRECHERY
SQUATTERS
STAINLESS
STALENESS
STARKNESS
STATELESS
STATEMENT
STEELHEAD
STEEPNESS
STEINBECK
STERNNESS
STIFFNESS
STILLNESS
STONELESS
STOUTNESS
STRANGELY
STRAPLESS
STRINGENT
STROSSERS
SUBALTERN
SUBJACENT
SUBLIMELY
SUCCULENT
SULKINESS
SUNSCREEN
SUPERSEDE
SUPERVENE
SUPREMELY
SURLINESS
SWEETMEAT
SWEETNESS
SWIFTNESS
SWINEHERD
SYNOECETE
TABASHEER
TACKINESS
TAILPIECE
TARDINESS
TARGETEER
TARTAREAN
TASTELESS
TAVERNERS
TEARSHEET
TEMPTRESS
TENSENESS
TERMAGENT
TERPINEOL
TERSENESS
TESTAMENT
THANKLESS
THICKHEAD
THICKNESS
THIRTIETH
THORNLESS
THYESTEAN
TIGHTHEAD
TIGHTNESS
TIMEPIECE
TIPSINESS
TIREDNESS
TOOTHLESS
TOUGHNESS
TRACKLESS
TRANSCEND
TRANSIENT
TRASIMENE
TRAVELERS
TREACHERY
TREATMENT
TRICKLESS
TRITENESS
TRONDHEIM
TROUSSEAU
TRUCULENT
TRUNCHEON
TRYPHOEUS
TUBBINESS
TUMESCENT
TURBULENT
TURMAGENT
TWENTIETH
ULTRONEUS
UNCONCERN
UNCORRECT
UNDERFELT
UNDERSEAL
UNDERSELL
UNDERWEAR
UNDERWENT
UNIVALENT
UTTERLESS
VAGUENESS
VALUELESS
VELVETEEN
VENEZUELA
VENUSBERG
VIVIDNESS
VOICELESS
VOLTIGEUR
VOLUNTEER
VORTIGERN
WARTCRESS
WATERLESS
WATERWEED
WEARINESS
WEIRDNESS
WHALEMEAT
WHEATGERM
WHEATMEAL
WHITAKERS
WHITEHEAD
WHITENESS
WHOLEMEAL
WHOLENESS
WILDGEESE
WINDBREAK
WINDSWEPT
WOOLINESS
WORDINESS
WORTHLESS
WRANGLERS
WREAKLESS
YESTEREVE
BASKETFUL
BEAUTIFUL
BOTTLEFUL
BOUNTIFUL
BUCKETFUL
BUTTERFLY
CALORIFIC
CHARGEFUL
COLOURFUL
CURFUFFLE
DECEITFUL
DISCOMFIT
DRAGONFLY
FORGETFUL
FRIGHTFUL
HANDCUFFS
HONORIFIC
IBUPROFEN
KERFUFFLE
KNIPHOFIA
LONGEDFOR
MARROWFAT
MASTERFUL
MOSKONFYT
NONPROFIT
PANTOFFLE
PANTOUFLE
PLENTIFUL
POCKETFUL
QUIVERFUL
RADCLIFFE
REGARDFUL
REGRETFUL
REISTAFEL
RESENTFUL
RESHUFFLE
SDEIGNFUL
SHOVELFUL
SOPORIFIC
SORROWFUL
SPRITEFUL
STRESSFUL
SUDORIFIC
TAILLEFER
TAMOXIFEN
THREADFIN
UNHELPFUL
UNHOPEFUL
UNMINDFUL
WONDERFUL
ACONCAGUA
AMUSINGLY
AQUILEGIA
ARCHANGEL
AREOPAGUS
ARKWRIGHT
ASPARAGUS
ASYNERGIA
BANDWAGON
BEDRAGGLE
BESPANGLE
BOANERGES
BREAKAGES
BRUMMAGEM
BULLFIGHT
BURROUGHS
CATALOGUE
CHAMPAGNE
COCKAIGNE
COCKFIGHT
COLLEAGUE
COPYRIGHT
CORREGGIO
CRYPTOGAM
DEADLIGHT
DECALOGUE

DEMAGOGUE
DERRINGER
DOWNRIGHT
DYSPHAGIA
EMBRANGLE
ENDECAGON
ESOPHAGUS
ESTRANGED
EYEBRIGHT
FANDANGLE
FIRELIGHT
FLYWEIGHT
FORESIGHT
FORTNIGHT
GALAPAGOS
GALDRAGON
GALIONGEE
GOODNIGHT
GREASEGUN
HAMBURGER
HARBINGER
HARDANGER
HEADLIGHT
HIGHLIGHT
HINDSIGHT
HUMDINGER
HYDRANGEA
IDEALOGUE
IMBRANGLE
INDRAUGHT
INSWINGER
KISSINGER
KNOWINGLY
LAMPLIGHT
LANGUAGES
LATENIGHT
LAWMONGER
LESTRIGON
LETHARGIC
LEVERAGED
LIMBURGER
LIMELIGHT
LONGINGLY
MASSINGER
MESSENGER
MONOLOGUE
MONTAIGNE
MOONLIGHT
MORTGAGEE
MORTGAGOR
MRIDAMGAM
MRIDANGAM
MUNDUNGUS
NEURALGIA
NEURALGIC
NICARAGUA
NOSTALGIA
NOSTALGIC
OESTROGEN
OMOPHAGIC
ONSLAUGHT
OUTRIGGER
OVERNIGHT
OVERSIGHT
PARAGOGUE
PASSENGER
PEDAGOGUE
PEMPHIGUS
PENDRAGON
PHALANGER
PHANSIGAR
PHELLOGEN
PORBEAGLE
PORRINGER
POTTINGAR
PROLONGED
PTARMIGAN
RECTANGLE
ROXBURGHE
RUSHLIGHT
SCAVENGER
SCROUNGER
SEEMINGLY
SIDELIGHT
SKINTIGHT
SOLFEGGIO
SPARINGLY
SPOTLIGHT
STARLIGHT
STAVANGER
STRATAGEM
STRATEGIC
SUBMERGED
SUFFRAGAN
SURCINGLE
SYNAGOGUE
TAILLIGHT
TELLINGLY
TIMENOGUY
TRAFALGAR
TREGEAGLE
UNCHANGED
UNCHARGED
UNDAMAGED
UNFLEDGED
VICEREGAL
WALPURGIS
WAMBENGER
WARMONGER
WHIRLIGIG
WILLINGLY
WITTINGLY
AMIANTHUS
ANGUISHED
ASTRAKHAN
ASTROPHEL
BETHLEHEM
BETROTHAL
BETROTHED
BIMONTHLY
BLOODSHED
BLOODSHOT
BRITSCHKA
CATARRHAL
CHERISHED
CHIHUAHUA
COURTSHIP
CTESIPHON
DEBAUCHED
DEBAUCHEE
EFFINGHAM
ENCANTHIS
ENTRECHAT
EPEDAPHIC
ERPINGHAM
EURHYTHMY
EUTROPHIC
FERINGHEE
FLOORSHOW
FOOLISHLY
FORGATHER
FORSYTHIA
FROBISHER
GARNISHEE
GODFATHER
GODMOTHER
GODOLPHIN
GRAPESHOT
GROUNDHOG
HERONSHAW
HOLINSHED
HOOLACHAN
HORSESHOE
HORSEWHIP
HOUYHNHNM
IMPEACHER
LEHRJAHRE
LEVIATHAN
LIGHTSHIP
MACARTHUR
MEDMENHAM
MICROCHIP
MIDRASHIM
MOYGASHEL
NAUMACHIA
NEBBISHER
NEOLITHIC
OPHIUCHUS
OWNERSHIP
PEEVISHLY
PENPUSHER
PETERSHAM
PINOCCHIO
PISTACHIO
PROMACHOS
PUBLISHED
PUBLISHER
RADICCHIO
REFRESHER
ROUGHSHOD
SCRATCHED
SCRATCHES
SCRIMSHAW
SELFISHLY
SENESCHAL
SEPULCHER
SEPULCHRE
SHOLOKHOV
SLAVISHLY
SLINGSHOT
SPACESHIP
SPRAUCHLE
STAUNCHLY
STEAMSHIP
STOMACHIC
STONECHAT
STRETCHED
STRETCHER
STYLISHLY
SUNBATHER
SWEETSHOP
TACAMAHAC
TOTTENHAM
TRANSSHIP
TREBUCHET
TRILITHON
TRIUMPHAL
TROOPSHIP
UNABASHED
UNCLOTHED
UNEARTHLY
UNMATCHED
UNSCATHED
UNTOUCHED
UPANISHAD
WAFERTHIN
WAPINSHAW
WASPISHLY
WATERSHED
ABDUCTION
ABOLITION
ABORIGINE
ABOUNDING
ABSORBING
ABSURDITY
ACADEMIST
ACCESSION
ACCLIVITY
ACCORDING
ACCORDION
ACCRETION
ACOUSTICS
ACTUALITY
ACTUARIAL
ADDICTION
ADDICTIVE
ADJECTIVE
ADJOINING
ADMISSION
ADMITTING
ADORATION
ADULATION
ADVECTION
ADVENTIST
ADVERBIAL
ADVERSITY
ADVERTISE
AFFECTING
AFFECTION
AGITATION
AGONIZING
ALBERTINE
ALCHEMIST
ALMANDINE
ALONGSIDE
ALTISSIMO
ALUMINIUM
AMBIGUITY
AMBROSIAL
AMBROSIAN
AMELAKITE
AMERICIUM
AMIDSHIPS
AMPHIBIAN
AMPLIFIER
ANABOLISM
ANARCHIST
ANATOLIAN
ANATOMIST
ANATOMIZE
ANCHORITE
ANDANTINO
ANGLICISM
ANHYDRIDE
ANHYDRITE
ANIMATION
ANIMOSITY
ANOINTING
ANONYMITY
ANSWERING
ANTICLINE
ANTIQUITY
APERITIVE
APHRODITE
APOLOGIST
APOLOGIZE
APPALLING
APPEALING
APPORTION
APPROVING
ARAGONITE
ARCHIVIST
ARGENTINA
ARGENTINE
ARMISTICE
ARRESTING
ARTHURIAN
ASCENDING
ASCENSION
ASCLEPIUS
ASPERSION
ASPLENIUM
ASSERTING
ASSERTION
ASSERTIVE
ASSIDUITY
ATHLETICS
ATTACKING
ATTENTION
ATTENTIVE
ATTRITION
ATTUITION
AUBERGINE
AUCTORIAL
AUGUSTINE
AUSTERITY
AUTHORITY
AUTHORIZE
AVOCATION
AWAKENING
BACKSHISH
BACKSLIDE
BACTERIAL
BACTERIUM
BALALAIKA
BALLADIST
BALLERINA
BALLPOINT
BANDOLIER
BANDOLINE
BANTERING
BARBARIAN
BARBARITY
BARBOTINE
BARMECIDE
BARNABITE
BATTALION
BEGINNING
BELIEVING
BELONGING
BERKELIUM
BERYLLIUM

BICYCLIST
BILLOWING
BIOLOGIST
BIPARTITE
BISECTION
BLACKBIRD
BLACKLIST
BLUEPRINT
BOBSLEIGH
BOMBASINE
BORDERING
BORROWING
BOSTONIAN
BRAMBLING
BRANCHING
BRAZILIAN
BREADLINE
BREATHING
BREECHING
BRIGADIER
BRISTLING
BROADSIDE
BRONCHIAL
BRUTALISM
BRUTALITY
BRUTALIZE
BULGARIAN
BURROWING
BURUNDIAN
BYZANTINE
CALDARIUM
CALLOSITY
CALVANISM
CALVINIST
CALVITIES
CAMBODIAN
CAMPANILE
CANTABILE
CAPTIVITY
CARBAMIDE
CARBONIZE
CAREERIST
CARMELITE
CARNATION
CARNELIAN
CARPETING
CARTESIAN
CASHPOINT
CASSATION
CASTILIAN
CASUARINA
CATECHISM
CATECHIZE
CATHERINE
CAUCASIAN
CAUSATION
CAUTERIZE
CAVENDISH
CAVORTING
CEASEFIRE
CELANDINE
CELEBRITY
CELESTIAL
CELLARIST
CELLULITE
CENTERING
CENTREING
CENTURION
CERTIFIED
CESSATION
CEVAPCICI
CHABAZITE
CHAIRLIFT
CHALAZION
CHAMOMILE
CHAMPAIGN
CHEAPSIDE
CHECKLIST
CHERUBINI
CHEVALIER
CHILDLIKE
CHOLELITH
CHONDRITE
CHRISTIAN
CHURCHILL
CIMMERIAN
CIPOLLINO
CIRCADIAN
CLARIFIER
CLEANSING
CLINGFILM
CLINICIAN
CLOCKWISE
COALITION
COASTLINE
COCKATIEL
COEMPTION
COENOBITE
COENOBIUM
COFFINITE
COGNITION
COGNITIVE
COLLATION
COLLEGIAN
COLLISION
COLLODION
COLLUSION
COLLUSIVE
COLLYRIUM
COLOMBIAN
COLOMBIER
COLOURING
COLOURIST
COLUMBIAN
COLUMBINE
COLUMBITE
COLUMBIUM
COLUMNIST
COMBATIVE
COMMODITY
COMMOTION
COMMUNION
COMMUNISM
COMMUNIST
COMMUNITY
COMPANIES
COMPANION
COMPETING
COMPLAINT
COMPOSING
COMPOSITE
COMPOTIER
COMPUTING
CONCAVITY
CONCISION
CONCUBINE
CONDITION
CONDUCIVE
CONFUCIUS
CONFUSING
CONFUSION
CONGENIAL
CONGERIES
CONJURING
CONNEXION
CONNUBIAL
CONSCRIPT
CONSTRICT
CONSUMING
CONTAGION
CONTUSION
CONVIVIAL
COPROLITE
CORALLINE
CORDYLINE
CORNELIAN
CORROSION
CORROSIVE
COSMETICS
COSTUMIER
COUNTRIES
COUTURIER
COVELLITE
COWARDICE
CRACKLING
CRACOVIAN
CREDULITY
CREMATION
CREPOLINE
CRINOLINE
CRIPPLING
CRITERION
CRITICISM
CRITICIZE
CROCODILE
CROSSBILL
CROSSFIRE
CROSSWIND
CROSSWISE
CROWNLIKE
CROWSBILL
CRUMBLING
CURIOSITY
CURSORILY
CUSTODIAL
CUSTODIAN
CUSTOMIZE
CYCLOLITH
CYMBELINE
CYMBIDIUM
DAEDALIAN
DALMATIAN
DALTONISM
DAMNATION
DANDELION
DANDIFIED
DARWINIAN
DAYSPRING
DEAFENING
DECEMVIRI
DECEPTION
DECEPTIVE
DECESSION
DECILLION
DECLARING
DECLINING
DECLIVITY
DECOCTION
DECURSIVE
DEDUCTION
DEDUCTIVE
DEFEATISM
DEFEATIST
DEFECTION
DEFECTIVE
DEFENSIVE
DEFLATION
DEFORMITY
DEGRADING
DEJECTION
DEMANDING
DEMEANING
DEMETRIUS
DENTITION
DEODORIZE
DEOXIDISE
DEPENDING
DEPICTION
DEPRAVITY
DESERTION
DESERVING
DESIGNING
DESPOTISM
DETECTION
DETECTIVE
DETENTION
DETERMINE
DETRITION
DEUCALION
DEUTERIUM
DEVIATION
DEXTERITY
DIALOGITE
DIANETICS
DICTATION
DIDACTICS
DIETETICS
DIETICIAN
DIFFUSION
DIGESTION
DIGESTIVE
DIGNIFIED
DIMENSION
DIONYSIAN
DIONYSIUS
DIRECTION
DIRECTIVE
DISABLING
DISAFFIRM
DISARMING
DISBELIEF
DISOBLIGE
DISPARITY
DISTRAINT
DITHERING
DIVERGING
DIVERSIFY
DIVERSION
DIVERSITY
DIVERTING
DOGMATISM
DOGMATIZE
DORMITION
DOWELLING
DRACONIAN
DRAINPIPE
DRAMATICS
DRAMATIST
DRAMATIZE
DRAVIDIAN
DRUMSTICK
DULCINIST
DUODECIMO
DUPLICITY
DWINDLING
EARTHLING
EASYGOING
ECHIDNINE
ECOLOGIST
ECONOMICS
ECONOMIST
ECONOMIZE
ECOSSAISE
ECTROPION
EDELWEISS
EDITORIAL
EDUCATION
EDUCATIVE
EDWARDIAN
EFFECTIVE
EFFLUVIUM
EGLANTINE
EGRESSION
ELAEOLITE
ELATERIUM
ELECTRIFY
ELEVATION
ELKOSHITE
ELOCUTION
EMANATION
EMBELLISH
EMBRACING
EMPHASIZE
EMULATION
ENCHORIAL
ENCOLPION
ENCOLPIUM
ENCRATITE
ENDEARING
ENDOCRINE
ENERINITE
ENGRAVING
ENHYDRITE
ENQUIRIES
ENSTATITE
ENTROPION
ENTROPIUM
EPHEDRINE
EPICEDIUM
EPINICION
EPINIKION
EPIPOLISM
EPITOMIZE
EPULATION
EQUIPOISE
EROTICISM
ERSTWHILE
ERUDITION
ESQUILINE
ESSENTIAL
ESTABLISH
ESTHETICS

ETHIOPIAN
EUCHARIST
EUPHEMISM
EUPHONIUM
EUSKARIAN
EVAGATION
EVOCATION
EVOCATIVE
EVOLUTION
EXARATION
EXCAMBION
EXCELSIOR
EXCEPTION
EXCESSIVE
EXCLUDING
EXCLUSION
EXCLUSIVE
EXCURSION
EXECUTION
EXECUTIVE
EXEMPLIFY
EXEMPTION
EXORATION
EXPANSION
EXPANSIVE
EXPECTING
EXPENSIVE
EXPERTISE
EXPIATION
EXPLETIVE
EXPLOSION
EXPLOSIVE
EXPORTING
EXPULSION
EXQUISITE
EXTENSILE
EXTENSION
EXTENSIVE
EXTORTION
EXTRADITE
EXTREMISM
EXTREMIST
EXTREMITY
EXTRUSION
EXUDATION
EYESPLICE
FACSIMILE
FACTORISE
FACUNDITY
FALANGIST
FALERNIAN
FALLOPIAN
FANTASIZE
FASTENING
FATTENING
FAULCHION
FAVOURITE
FECUNDITY
FERTILITY
FERTILIZE
FESTIVITY
FEUDALISM
FIBROLINE
FIBROLITE
FILTERING
FINANCIAL
FINANCIER
FINGERING
FINICKING
FINICKITY
FINISHING
FLAVORING
FLEDGLING
FLEXITIME
FLOTATION
FLOURMILL
FLOWERING
FOGRAMITE
FOLKETING
FOLLOWING
FOOTPRINT
FOREGOING
FORGETIVE
FORGIVING
FORMALIST
FORMALITY
FORMALIZE
FORMATION
FORMATIVE
FORTALICE
FORTHWINK
FORTHWITH
FOSSILISE
FOSSORIAL
FOUNDLING
FRAGILITY
FRAMBOISE
FRANCHISE
FREDERICK
FRIGIDITY
FRIVOLITY
FROSTBITE
FRUGALITY
FUNGICIDE
GABARDINE
GABERDINE
GALANTINE
GALLICISM
GALVANISM
GALVANIZE
GARDENING
GARGARISM
GARRULITY
GATHERING
GAVELKIND
GEARSHIFT
GEARSTICK
GELIGNITE
GENIALITY
GENTILITY
GEODESIST
GEOLOGIST
GERMANITE
GERMANIUM
GERMICIDE
GERUNDIVE
GESSAMINE
GESTATION
GIBBERISH
GIBEONITE
GIRONDIST
GLAMORIZE
GLORIFIED
GLUCINIUM
GLUCOSIDE
GLUTAMINE
GLYCERIDE
GLYCERINE
GMELINITE
GOLDSMITH
GONDOLIER
GONGORISM
GONIATITE
GOSLARITE
GOSSYPINE
GOSSYPIUM
GOTHAMITE
GOVERNING
GRADATION
GRADGRIND
GRANDSIRE
GRANULITE
GRAPEVINE
GRAPPLING
GRAVESIDE
GREENWICH
GREGARINE
GREGORIAN
GRENADIER
GRENADINE
GROCERIES
GROUNDING
GRUELLING
GRUMBLING
GUIDELINE
GUITARIST
GUSTATION
GUTTERING
GYMNASIUM
GYNOECIUM
HABERDINE
HAECCEITY
HAEMATITE
HALOPHILE
HAMMERING
HAMSTRING
HANDSPIKE
HANKERING
HAPPENING
HARMALINE
HARMONICA
HARMONIST
HARMONIUM
HARMONIZE
HARROWING
HASHEMITE
HASTENING
HAUGHTILY
HAWCUBITE
HAWKSBILL
HAYMAKING
HEALTHILY
HEAVISIDE
HECTORING
HEMISTICH
HERBALIST
HERBARIUM
HERBICIDE
HERBORIST
HESPERIAN
HESSONITE
HEXASTICH
HIBERNIAN
HIJACKING
HIMYARITE
HINDEMITH
HIRUNDINE
HISTAMINE
HISTORIAN
HITCHHIKE
HOLLERITH
HORRIFIED
HORTATIVE
HOSPITIUM
HOSTILITY
HOUSEWIFE
HOYDENISH
HUMANKIND
HUNGARIAN
HUTTERITE
HYDRAZINE
HYGIENIST
HYPNOTISM
HYPNOTIST
HYPNOTIZE
HYPOCRISY
HYPOCRITE
HYSTERICS
ICHNOLITE
IMITATION
IMITATIVE
IMMENSITY
IMMERSION
IMPACTION
IMPARTIAL
IMPASSION
IMPASSIVE
IMPELLING
IMPENDING
IMPLUVIUM
IMPRECISE
IMPROBITY
IMPROVING
IMPROVISE
IMPSONITE
IMPULSION
IMPULSIVE
INABILITY
INANITION
INCARDINE
INCAUTION
INCENTIVE
INCEPTION
INCLUDING
INCLUSION
INCLUSIVE
INCOGNITO
INCONDITE
INCURSION
INDEMNIFY
INDEMNITY
INDICTION
INDIGNITY
INDUCTION
INDUCTIVE
INERUDITE
INFANTILE
INFECTING
INFECTION
INFERTILE
INFIRMITY
INFLATION
INFLEXION
INGENUITY
INGESTION
INGROWING
INJECTION
INJUSTICE
INQUILINE
INQUIRING
INSERTION
INSOMNIAC
INSPIRING
INSULTING
INTEGRITY
INTENDING
INTENSIFY
INTENSITY
INTENSIVE
INTENTION
INTERCITY
INTERDICT
INTERVIEW
INTESTINE
INTRUSION
INTRUSIVE
INTUITION
INTUITIVE
INUNCTION
INVECTIVE
INVENTION
INVENTIVE
INVERSION
INVOICING
IODOPHILE
IRRUPTION
IRVINGISM
ISODORIAN
ISOLATION
ISRAELITE
ITALICIZE
JACKKNIFE
JACKSNIPE
JANSENISM
JANSENIST
JAWBATION
JELLYFISH
JENNETING
JEQUIRITY
JESSAMINE
JOHANNINE
JORDANIAN
JOSEPHINE
JOVIALITY
JUNKETING
JUSTIFIED
JUSTINIAN
KALSOMINE
KEPLARIAN
KERMESITE
KIESERITE
KITTENISH
KNOBSTICK
LABOURITE
LACCOLITE
LACTATION
LADYSMITH
LAMARTINE
LAMPADION
LANDSLIDE
LANGSPIEL
LARGITION

LATHYRISM
LATRATION
LAUDATION
LAUNCHING
LAVOISIER
LAWMAKING
LEASTWISE
LENGTHILY
LETTERING
LEVANTINE
LIABILITY
LIBERTIES
LIBERTINE
LIBRARIAN
LICKERISH
LIGHTNING
LILYWHITE
LIMOUSINE
LIMPIDITY
LINGERING
LIQUEFIED
LIQUIDITY
LIQUIDIZE
LIQUORICE
LIQUORISH
LISTENING
LOAMSHIRE
LOCKSMITH
LOGISTICS
LOGOGRIPH
LOITERING
LONGEVITY
LOOKALIKE
LOQUACITY
LUCRATIVE
LUCRETIUS
LUCTATION
LUMBERING
LUMINAIRE
LUNCHTIME
MACEDOINE
MACHINING
MACHINIST
MACTATION
MADDENING
MADELEINE
MAGNALIUM
MAGNESIUM
MAGNETISM
MAGNETIZE
MAGNIFIER
MAKESHIFT
MALACHITE
MALATHION
MALAYSIAN
MALENGINE
MALIGNITY
MAMMALIAN
MANDOLINE
MANNERING
MANNERISM
MANUBRIUM
MARAUDING
MARCASITE
MARGARINE
MARKETING
MARSUPIAL
MARSUPIUM
MASCULINE
MASOCHISM
MASOCHIST
MATERNITY
MATHURINE
MATRICIDE
MAULSTICK
MAURITIAN
MAURITIUS
MEANDRIAN
MEANWHILE
MEASURING
MECHANICS
MECHANISM
MECHANIZE
MEDALLION
MEDALLIST
MEDIATION
MELONLIKE
MENDACITY
MENDELISM
MENNONITE
MENTALITY
MENTATION
MENTICIDE
MENUISIER
MEPACRINE
MERCERIZE
MERCURIAL
MERESWINE
MESMERISM
MESMERIZE
MESSALINA
METEORITE
METHODISM
METHODIST
MEZZANINE
MEZZOTINT
MICROFILM
MICROLITE
MICROLITH
MIDIANITE
MIGRATION
MILLENIAL
MILLENIUM
MINISKIRT
MISFIRING
MISGIVING
MISONEIST
MITHRAISM
MOCCASINS
MODELLING
MODERNISM
MODERNIST
MODERNITY
MODERNIZE
MODESTINE
MODILLION
MOLESKINS
MOLLITIES
MONACTINE
MONERGISM
MONGOLIAN
MONGOLISM
MONOSTICH
MONTANISM
MONTANIST
MONZONITE
MOONSHINE
MORBIDITY
MORGANITE
MORMONISM
MORTALITY
MORTICIAN
MORTIFIED
MOTHERING
MOTORBIKE
MOUSELIKE
MUGLARITE
MURMURING
MUSCADINE
MUSCARINE
MUSCOVITE
MUSSOLINI
MUTTERING
MYSTERIES
MYSTICISM
NAPIERIAN
NARRATION
NARRATIVE
NARROWING
NATHANIEL
NATROLITE
NAUGHTILY
NECESSITY
NECTARINE
NEFERTITI
NEOLOGISM
NEPHALISM
NEPHALIST
NEPHELINE
NEPTUNIUM
NEWSPRINT
NICCOLITE
NIDDERING
NIDERLING
NIGHTFIRE
NIGHTTIME
NIGROSINE
NONENTITY
NONILLION
NORMALITY
NORMALIZE
NORMATIVE
NORWEGIAN
NOVOCAINE
NUMERAIRE
NUMMULITE
NUTRITION
NUTRITIVE
OBJECTION
OBJECTIVE
OBREPTION
OBSCENITY
OBSCURITY
OBSEQUIES
OBSESSION
OBSESSIVE
OBTAINING
OBTRUSION
OBTRUSIVE
OBVENTION
OCCLUSION
OCCULTIST
OCCUPYING
OCKHAMIST
OCTASTICH
OCTILLION
OCTOBRIST
ODELSTING
OFFENDING
OFFENSIVE
OFFSPRING
OLIVENITE
OPERATING
OPERATION
OPERATIVE
ORATORIAN
ORDINAIRE
ORGANZINE
ORIGENIST
ORMANDINE
ORPHARION
OSTRACISM
OSTRACIZE
OTHERWISE
OTTRELITE
OVERDRIVE
OVERLYING
OVERPAINT
OVERPOISE
OVERSPILL
OVERWEIGH
OVULATION
OXIDATION
OZOCERITE
OZOKERITE
PACKAGING
PALEOLITH
PALESTINE
PALLADIAN
PALLADIUM
PALMATION
PALPATION
PALUDRINE
PANDATION
PANDEMIAN
PANEGOISM
PANELLING
PANELLIST
PANTHEISM
PANTOMIME
PARANOIAC
PARATHION
PARENTING
PARHELION
PARNASITE
PAROCHIAL
PAROCHINE
PARRICIDE
PARTAKING
PARTITION
PASSEPIED
PASSERINE
PASSIVITY
PATERNITY
PATRICIAN
PATRICIDE
PATRONIZE
PAUSANIAS
PEACETIME
PECKSNIFF
PEGMATITE
PELMANISM
PENILLION
PERCALINE
PERDITION
PEREGRINE
PERENNIAL
PERISCIAN
PERISHING
PERSONIFY
PERVASION
PERVASIVE
PESSIMISM
PESSIMIST
PESTICIDE
PETAURIST
PETHIDINE
PETRIFIED
PHACOLITE
PHANARIOT
PHENACITE
PHENAKISM
PHIGALIAN
PHITONIUM
PHONETICS
PHONOLITE
PHYSICIAN
PHYSICIST
PHYTOLITE
PICKETING
PICTORIAL
PILFERING
PINSTRIPE
PITCHPINE
PLACIDITY
PLAINTIFF
PLAINTIVE
PLATONIST
PLAYTHING
PLUMBLINE
PLURALISM
PLURALITY
PLUTONIUM
POISONING
POLIANITE
POLLUTION
POLONAISE
POLVERINE
POMOERIUM
POMPOSITY
POPPERING
PORCUPINE
POSTERIOR
POSTERITY
POTASSIUM
POTENTIAL
POTHOLING
POUJADIST
POWELLITE
PRECEDING
PRECIPICE
PRECISIAN
PRECISION
PRECISIVE
PRECOCITY
PRECONISE
PREJUDICE
PREMONISH
PREMOTION
PRESCRIBE
PRESIDIAL
PRESIDIUM

PRETERITE
PRIMARILY
PRIMITIAE
PRIMITIVE
PRIMULINE
PRIVATION
PRIVATIZE
PROACTIVE
PROBATION
PROCACITY
PROCERITY
PROFANITY
PROFUSION
PROKOFIEV
PROLAMINE
PROLIXITY
PROLUSION
PROMISING
PROMOTION
PROMPTING
PROSCRIBE
PROTAMINE
PROUSTITE
PROVIDING
PROVISION
PROVOKING
PROXIMITY
PTERIDIUM
PUBLICIST
PUBLICITY
PUBLICIZE
PUERILITY
PUGNACITY
PULSATION
PULVERIZE
PUNCHLINE
PUNISHING
PURDONIUM
PURGATIVE
PURIFYING
PYGMALION
QUAILPIPE
QUALIFIED
QUALIFIER
QUAVERING
QUICKLIME
QUINQUINA
QUIVERING
QUOTATION
QUOTIDIAN
QUOTITION
RACIALISM
RACIALIST
RADIATING
RADIATION
RAMILLIES
RANCIDITY
RAPTORIAL
RATHERIPE
RATHERISH
RATIONING
RAVISHING
RAZORBILL
REALITIES
REASONING
REBELLION
REBOATION
RECALLING
RECEIVING
RECEPTION
RECEPTIVE
RECESSION
RECESSIVE
RECKONING
RECOGNIZE
RECONCILE
RECONDITE
RECORDING
RECORDIST
RECTIFIER
RECTORIAL
RECURRING
REDEEMING
REDUCTION
REEXAMINE
REFECTION
REFERRING
REFLATION
REFLEXION
REFLEXIVE
REFORMIST
REFURBISH
REGARDING
REJECTION
REJOICING
RELIQUIAE
REMAINING
REMISSION
RENDERING
RENDITION
REPELLING
REPLACING
REPLENISH
REPLETION
REPLETIVE
REPORTING
REPROVING
REPTATION
REPTILIAN
REPULSION
REPULSIVE
REQUISITE
RESERPINE
RESERVIST
RESORTING
RESTRAINT
RESULTING
RETAILING
RETAINING
RETENTION
RETENTIVE
RETIARIUS
RETORSION
RETORTION
RETURNING
REVEALING
REVELLING
REVERSING
REVERSION
REVOLTING
REVOLVING
REVULSION
REWARDING
REWORKING
RHODESIAN
RHODOLITE
RIBBONISM
RICHELIEU
RIGHTWING
RIPIENIST
RIVERSIDE
ROSMARINE
ROSMINIAN
ROTUNDITY
ROUMANIAN
ROUNDFISH
RUBBERIZE
RUINATION
RUTHENIAN
RUTHENIUM
SABBATIAN
SACRARIUM
SACRIFICE
SADDENING
SALESGIRL
SALUBRITY
SALVATION
SARTORIAL
SARTORIUS
SASSOLITE
SATELLITE
SATIATION
SATISFIED
SATURNIAN
SATURNINE
SATURNISM
SCALARIUM
SCALDFISH
SCAMBLING
SCANTLING
SCAPOLITE
SCARIFIER
SCHEELITE
SCHELLING
SCHILLING
SCHLEMIEL
SCHLEMIHL
SCHOOLING
SCIENTISM
SCIENTIST
SCOLECITE
SCORCHING
SCORODITE
SCRAPPING
SCREENING
SCREWPINE
SCRIMPING
SCRUBBING
SCRUFFILY
SCRUMPING
SCULPTING
SEAFARING
SEARCHING
SEASONING
SEBASTIAN
SECESSION
SECLUSION
SECRETION
SECRETIVE
SECTARIAN
SECTORIAL
SEDUCTION
SEDUCTIVE
SELACHION
SELECTING
SELECTION
SELECTIVE
SELJUKIAN
SEMANTICS
SEMANTIDE
SENIORITY
SENSATION
SENSITIVE
SENSITIZE
SENSORIUM
SEPIOLITE
SERAPHINE
SERASKIER
SERBONIAN
SERIALIST
SERIALIZE
SERIATION
SERMONIZE
SERRATION
SERREFILE
SERVICING
SERVILITY
SEXUALITY
SHASHLICK
SHAVELING
SHEARLING
SHELLFISH
SHIELDING
SHINTOISM
SHIVERING
SHOESHINE
SHORTLIST
SHRIMPING
SHRINKING
SHUFFLING
SIBYLLINE
SICCATIVE
SICKENING
SIDESWIPE
SIEGFRIED
SIMEONITE
SINCERITY
SINGSPIEL
SINUOSITY
SIRBONIAN
SITUATION
SKETCHILY
SKEWWHIFF
SKINFLINT
SLANTWISE
SLAPSTICK
SLIVOVICA
SLIVOVITZ
SLOUGHING
SLOVENIAN
SMALLTIME
SMUGGLING
SNOWDRIFT
SNOWWHITE
SOCIALISM
SOCIALIST
SOCIALITE
SOCIALIZE
SOFTENING
SOLDERING
SOLEMNITY
SOLEMNIZE
SOLFERINO
SOLFIDIAN
SOLIPSISM
SOLITAIRE
SOMETHING
SOMMELIER
SONGSMITH
SOTTISIER
SOUNDBITE
SOVEREIGN
SPARKLING
SPEARMINT
SPEARSIDE
SPECIFICS
SPECIFIED
SPEECHIFY
SPELDRING
SPELLBIND
SPINDRIER
SPINDRIFT
SPLITTING
SPOONBILL
SPREADING
SQUEAMISH
SQUINTING
SQUIRMING
STABILITY
STABILIZE
STAGIRITE
STAGYRITE
STANCHION
STANDPIPE
STARTLING
STATESIDE
STATEWIDE
STATOLITH
STEENKIRK
STERADIAN
STERILITY
STERILIZE
STILTBIRD
STINKBIRD
STOCKFISH
STOCKPILE
STOLIDITY
STORYLINE
STOVEPIPE
STOWNLINS
STRAINING
STRAPPING
STREAMING
STRIATION
STRIPLING
STROLLING
STRONTIUM
STRUTTING
STUMBLING
STUPEFIED
STUPIDITY
SUBDIVIDE
SUBENTIRE
SUBMARINE
SUBSCRIBE
SUBSCRIPT
SUBSIDIZE
SUCCUBINE
SUETONIUS
SUFFERING
SUFFUSION
SUMMARILY

SUMMARIZE
SUMMATION
SUPERFINE
SUPERVISE
SUPPOSING
SUQUAMISH
SURVEYING
SURVIVING
SUSPICION
SWADDLING
SWINGEING
SWORDFISH
SWOTHLING
SYLLOGISM
SYLPHLIKE
SYLVANITE
SYMBOLISM
SYMBOLIST
SYMBOLIZE
SYMPODIUM
SYMPOSIUM
SYNANGIUM
SYNCOMIUM
SYNEDRION
SYNERGIST
SYRIACISM
TABELLION
TACHILITE
TACHYLITE
TACTICIAN
TALKATIVE
TALMUDIST
TANGERINE
TANTALITE
TANTALIZE
TANZANIAN
TARNATION
TASMANIAN
TAUCHNITZ
TECTONICS
TECTORIAL
TEDIOSITY
TEIRESIAS
TELESTICH
TELLURIAN
TELLURION
TELLURIUM
TEMPORIZE
TENDERIZE
TENTATIVE
TENTORIUM
TERRACING
TERRARIUM
TERRIFIED
TERRORISM
TERRORIST
TERRORIZE
TESTDRIVE
TESTIFIER
THANATISM
THATCHING
THELEMITE
THELONIUS
THERALITE
THERAPIST
THIRSTILY
THIRSTING
THORNBILL
THRASHING
THREONINE
THRIFTILY
THRILLING
THROATILY
THROBBING
THRONGING
THUMBLING
THYLACINE
TIMPANIST
TINGUAITE
TITRATION
TOCCATINA
TOOTHPICK
TOPIARIST
TORBANITE
TORTELIER
TOSCANINI
TOTAQUINE
TOUCHLINE
TOWELLING
TOXOPHILY
TRADEWIND
TRADITION
TRAGEDIAN
TRANSPIRE
TRAPEZIAL
TRAPEZIST
TRAPEZIUM
TRAPEZIUS
TRAVELING
TREADMILL
TREMBLING
TREMOLITE
TRIBALISM
TRICERION
TRIDYMITE
TRIENNIAL
TRIFORIUM
TRILOBITE
TRISAGION
TROOSTITE
TROPARION
TSAREVICH
TUILERIES
TURBIDITY
TURNSTILE
TURQUOISE
TUTIORISM
TWINKLING
TYMPANIST
TYRANNIZE
UKRAINIAN
UMBRATILE
UNANIMITY
UNBENDING
UNCEASING
UNCONFINE
UNDERLINE
UNDERLING
UNDERMINE
UNDERSIDE
UNDERSIGN
UNFAILING
UNFEELING
UNFITTING
UNHAPPILY
UNHEEDING
UNITARIAN
UNKNOWING
UNLUCKILY
UNMARRIED
UNNERVING
UNPRECISE
UNSELFISH
UNSINNING
UNSPARING
UNSULLIED
UNVARYING
UNWILLING
UNWITTING
UNWORRIED
UPLIFTING
UPSETTING
UREDINIAL
URICONIAN
URINATION
UVAROVITE
VALENTINE
VALUATION
VANDALISM
VANDALIZE
VANISHING
VARANGIAN
VARIATION
VARISCITE
VENIALITY
VERATRINE
VERBALIZE
VERBOSITY
VERMILION
VERSATILE
VERSIFIER
VESPASIAN
VESTIGIAL
VIABILITY
VIBRATILE
VIBRATION
VICEREINE
VICTIMIZE
VICTORIAN
VICTORINE
VIDEODISC
VIEWPOINT
VIOLATION
VIOLINIST
VIRGINIAN
VIRGINITY
VIRGINIUM
VISCOSITY
VISUALIZE
VITELLIUS
VITIATION
VITRUVIAN
VOLTINISM
VOLUCRINE
VOODOOISM
VORTICISM
VULCANIST
VULCANITE
VULCANIZE
VULGARIAN
VULGARISM
VULGARITY
VULPINITE
WAGNERIAN
WAGNERITE
WAHABIITE
WAISTLINE
WALLABIES
WALLOPING
WALLOWING
WANDERING
WATERLILY
WATERLINE
WATERMILL
WATERSIDE
WAVELLITE
WEAKENING
WEIGHTING
WELCOMING
WELLBEING
WELLBUILT
WELTGEIST
WHIRLWIND
WHISTLING
WHITEFISH
WHITENING
WHITEWING
WILLEMITE
WILLOWING
WINCOPIPE
WINDCHILL
WITHERING
WITHERITE
WITHYWIND
WITTICISM
WOLVERINE
WOMANKIND
WORDSMITH
WORLDWIDE
WRECKFISH
WRESTLING
WULFENITE
WUTHERING
YARDSTICK
YELLOWISH
YOHIMBINE
YORKSHIRE
YTTERBIUM
ZEITGEIST
ZIBELLINE
ZINKENITE
ZIRCONIUM
ZOOLOGIST
MAHARAJAH
AUTOMAKER
BEDJACKET
BOOKMAKER
CARETAKER
COXSACKIE
FILMMAKER
FORJASKIT
FORJESKIT
GRIMALKIN
HALFBAKED
HAYMARKET
HENPECKED
IDENTIKIT
JAMPACKED
JAYWALKER
JOBSEEKER
KILDERKIN
KINGMAKER
KROPOTKIN
MISPICKEL
MOONRAKER
NANTUCKET
NEWMARKET
NIPPERKIN
NONSMOKER
NOTARIKON
OILTANKER
OUTSPOKEN
OUTWORKER
PACEMAKER
PARBUCKLE
PICNICKER
PINHOOKER
RUDBECKIA
SAPSUCKER
SCHNECKEN
SCHNORKEL
SHARKSKIN
SHEEPSKIN
SHOEMAKER
SHUBUNKIN
SKYJACKER
SLAMMAKIN
SOLLICKER
SOOTERKIN
SOUVLAKIA
SPELUNKER
SPILLIKIN
SPINNAKER
SPRAICKLE
TARMACKED
UNCHECKED
UNSHACKLE
ABYSMALLY
ACROPOLIS
ADMIRALTY
ADRENALIN
AESCHYLUS
AFTERGLOW
AIRCOOLED
ALCOHOLIC
AMARYLLIS
AMYGDALUS
ANDROCLES
ANNAPOLIS
ANOPHELES
ANTIHELIX
APOSTOLIC
AQUARELLE
ARMADILLO
ARTICULAR
ATAHUALPA
AURICULAR
AUSTRALIA
AUTOPILOT
AVUNCULAR
AYATOLLAH
BAGATELLE
BALEFULLY
BARNACLES
BARTHOLDI
BARTHOLIN
BASHFULLY
BASICALLY
BEARDSLEY
BEDFELLOW
BELLYFLOP
BINOCULAR

BOXWALLAH
BRUNHILDE
CABRIOLET
CANDLELIT
CAPITULAR
CAPITULUM
CARACALLA
CAREFULLY
CASSOULET
CATSKILLS
CENTRALLY
CHANTILLY
CHISELLER
CHRYSALIS
COLUMELLA
COMICALLY
COMPELLED
CONCEALED
CONTRALTO
CORDIALLY
CORNEILLE
COUNSELOR
COURTELLE
CRESCELLE
CRIBELLUM
CRUCIALLY
CYNICALLY
DECATHLON
DIGITALIN
DIGITALIS
DISTILLER
DOLEFULLY
DOMICILED
DONATELLO
DUTIFULLY
EARTHFLAX
EMBATTLED
EMBEZZLER
EMBROGLIO
EMBROILED
ENAMELLED
ENCIRCLED
EPICYCLIC
EPISTOLER
ESMERALDA
ETERNALLY
EVANGELIC
FACTUALLY
FEARFULLY
FENCIBLES
FILICALES
FILOSELLE
FLABELLUM
FLAGELLIN
FLAGELLUM
FLAGEOLET
FOOTHILLS
FRANCOLIN
FRETFULLY
FUNGIBLES
FUNICULAR
GAINFULLY
GARIBALDI
GENERALLY
GENITALIA
GENTEELLY
GLABELLAR
GLADIOLUS
GLANDULAR
GLEEFULLY
GOONHILLY
GOSPELLER
GRADUALLY
GRAVADLAX
GRENVILLE
GRINGOLET
GRISAILLE
GUERRILLA
HARIGALDS
HELPFULLY
HELVELLYN
HILLBILLY
HOBGOBLIN
HOBNAILED
HOPEFULLY
HORDEOLUM
HORSEPLAY
HYDRAULIC
ILLEGALLY
IMBROGLIO
IMMORALLY
INDWELLER
INITIALLY
INSHALLAH
INTERPLAY
IRREGULAR
ISOSCELES
JERUSALEM
JOCKTELEG
JUVENILIA
LANDAULET
LATERALLY
LAUNCELOT
LIBERALLY
LITERALLY
LOBLOLLYS
LOGICALLY
LYRICALLY
MAGICALLY
MALEBOLGE
MALLEOLUS
MAYORALTY
MEATBALLS
MEDICALLY
METABOLIC
METAPELET
METHEGLIN
MIRABELLE
MISFALLEN
MITRAILLE
MOLECULAR
MONOCULAR
MONOXYLON
MOTHBALLS
MUCORALES
MULTIPLEX
MUSICALLY
NARGHILLY
NASHVILLE
NATURALLY
NEUROGLIA
NEUTRALLY
NIGHTCLUB
NOMINALLY
NUCLEOLUS
OLENELLUS
OPERCULUM
OPTICALLY
ORBICULAR
ORGANELLE
OVERVALUE
PADEMELON
PAINFULLY
PANATELLA
PAPERCLIP
PARABOLIC
PARTHOLON
PARTIALLY
PARTICLES
PATROCLUS
PEDICULAR
PERIBOLOS
PHARSALIA
PITIFULLY
PLAYFULLY
PLIMSOLLS
POMPHOLYX
PORTFOLIO
POSSIBLES
POTBOILER
PRACTOLOL
PREHALLUX
PREPOLLEX
PRIESTLEY
PROBABLES
PROCOELUS
PROPELLED
PROPELLER
PROPELLOR
PUMMELLED
PUNCTILIO
QUADRILLE
QUENNELLE
RADICALLY
RENTALLER
RETICULUM
RETROFLEX
ROSTELLUM
ROUNDELAY
RUBICELLE
SANDALLED
SCINTILLA
SCRAMBLER
SCRODDLED
SCUDDALER
SEMICOLON
SENSILLUM
SENSUALLY
SEVERALLY
SHOVELLER
SIGNALLER
SKILFULLY
SOPHOCLES
SOULFULLY
SPATIALLY
SPECIALLY
SPECIALTY
SPHACELUS
SPRINGLET
SPRINKLER
SPUNCULID
STABLELAD
STOICALLY
STRAGGLER
STRANGLER
STRANGLES
STROBILUS
SUBCELLAR
SUBTITLED
SURMULLET
SWORDPLAY
SYLLABLES
TABBOULEH
TACTFULLY
TARPAULIN
TASSELLED
TEARFULLY
TELESALES
TENACULUM
TENAILLON
TEPHILLIN
TESTICLES
TOPICALLY
TRAVELLER
TREDRILLE
TRIANGLED
TRIATHLON
TRIVIALLY
TROCHILIC
TROCHILUS
TROPAELIN
TURNBULLS
TYPICALLY
UNBRIDLED
UNCOUPLED
UNDEFILED
UNEQUALED
UNPOPULAR
UNRUFFLED
UNSETTLED
UNSKILLED
UNSPOILED
UNUSUALLY
VARICELLA
VEHICULAR
VESICULAR
VIRTUALLY
VITRIOLIC
WENCESLAS
WILLFULLY
WINDFALLS
WISTFULLY
ANCHORMAN
AUTONOMIC
BAPTISMAL
CACHAEMIA
CAMERAMAN
CANDLEMAS
CATACOMBS
CATTLEMAN
CHARWOMAN
CHRISTMAS
CHURCHMAN
CLERGYMAN
CONFIRMED
CORNERMAN
CRACKSMAN
CRAFTSMAN
DRAFTSMAN
EALDORMAN
ELASTOMER
ENERGUMEN
ENTRAMMEL
EPIDERMIS
EXCISEMAN
EXCLAIMED
EXODERMIS
FIELDSMAN
FISHERMAN
FRENCHMAN
FRENCHMEN
GAUDEAMUS
GENTLEMAN
GENTLEMEN
GINGLYMUS
GUARDSMAN
GUILLEMOT
HALLOWMAS
HEARDSMAN
ICHNEUMON
IGNORAMUS
ISCHAEMIC
KHANSAMAH
KINSWOMAN
LACHRYMAL
LATECOMER
LEUKAEMIA
LIVERYMAN
MACADAMIA
MALFORMED
MARTINMAS
MASTERMAN
MIDDLEMAN
MIDSUMMER
MINUTEMAN
MONATOMIC
MORECAMBE
MUMPSIMUS
MUSSULMAN
NICODEMUS
NOVODAMUS
NYSTAGMUS
OARSWOMAN
ODDJOBMAN
OMBUDSMAN
ORANGEMAN
ORIFLAMME
PANORAMIC
PARANYMPH
PARTTIMER
PATROLMAN
PERFORMED
PERFORMER
PERSIMMON
PLAINSMAN
PLOUGHMAN
PLUMDAMAS
POINTSMAN
POLICEMAN
POSTWOMAN
PRETERMIT
PRODROMAL
PRODROMUS
PROGRAMME
RADDLEMAN
RECLAIMED
RECLAIMER
ROSCOMMON
ROUNDSMAN
RUDDLEMAN
SCHOOLMAN
SCOTCHMAN

SCYTHEMAN
SEMIRAMIS
SHARESMAN
SIGNALMAN
SKETCHMAP
SOMETIMES
SPOILSMAN
SPOKESMAN
SPORTSMAN
SPORTSMEN
STABLEMAN
STATESMAN
STEERSMAN
SUBNORMAL
SWORDSMAN
THINGUMMY
THIRDSMAN
TRADESMAN
TRIBESMAN
TRIBESMEN
UNASHAMED
UNCLAIMED
UNIFORMED
UNIFORMLY
VIGESIMAL
WASHERMAN
WASSERMAN
WELSUMMER
WHERRYMAN
YACHTSMAN
YACHTSMEN
ABANDONED
ABANDONEE
ABDOMINAL
ABERRANCE
ABSTAINER
ABUNDANCE
ACCIDENTS
ADHERENCE
AEPYORNIS
AFFLUENCE
AFRIKANER
AGAMEMNON
ALLEMANDE
ALLOWANCE
AMBULANCE
ANABRANCH
ANNOYANCE
ANTIGONUS
ANTIVENIN
ANTONINUS
APENNINES
APOLLONUS
APPLIANCE
ARMAMENTS
ARROGANCE
ASSONANCE
ASSURANCE
AVOIDANCE
BACKBENCH
BAREBONES
BEESTINGS
BLESSINGS
BOTSWANAN
BRITANNIA
BRITANNIC
BULLFINCH
BUTTERNUT
CALEDONIA
CALPURNIA
CAPTAINCY
CATATONIA
CATATONIC
CEROMANCY
CERTAINLY
CERTAINTY
CHAFFINCH
CHALLENGE
CHASTENED
CHINOVNIK
CHIPPINGS
CLEARANCE
CLOISONNÉ
COALMINER
COHERENCE
CONCERNED
CONDEMNED
CONSIGNEE
CONSIGNOR
CONSTANCE
CONSTANCY
CONTAINER
COTHURNUS
COVALENCY
CRESCENDO
CRYOGENIC
CUFFLINKS
DALLIANCE
DARTAGNAN
DEBUTANTE
DECADENCE
DEFERENCE
DILIGENCE
DIVIDENDS
DOCTRINAL
DOCUMENTS
DOMINANCE
DROPPINGS
DRUNKENLY
DUBROVNIK
DUNGEONER
EASTERNER
EASTLINGS
ECARDINES
EFFLUENCE
ELOQUENCE
EMBRYONIC
EMERGENCE
EMERGENCY
EMOTIONAL
ENDURANCE
ENGRAINED
ENLIVENED
ERGATANER
ESCULENTS
ESPERANCE
ESPERANTO
ESTAMINET
EVITERNAL
EXISTENCE
EYEOPENER
FABULINUS
FACTIONAL
FALKLANDS
FASHIONED
FICTIONAL
FIFTEENTH
FIGURANTE
FLAGRANCE
FLATTENED
FLATTENER
FLIPPANCY
FOREIGNER
FORLORNLY
FOURPENCE
FRAGMENTS
FRAGRANCE
FRAGRANCY
FRATERNAL
FREELANCE
FREQUENCY
FRESHENER
FRIZZANTE
GLEANINGS
GLISSANDO
GOLDFINCH
GOLDSINNY
GREETINGS
GRIEVANCE
GROSVENOR
GROUNDNUT
GRUBBINOL
GYROMANCY
HALFPENNY
HARDLINER
HARPOONER
HAUTMONDE
HEADLINED
HECOGENIN
HESITANCE
HESITANCY
HESTERNAL
HEXAGONAL
HIGHLANDS
HINDRANCE
HODIERNAL
HOMEOWNER
IGNORANCE
IMBALANCE
IMMANENCE
IMMANENCY
IMMINENCE
IMPEDANCE
IMPOTENCE
IMPUDENCE
INCIDENCE
INCOMINGS
INDECENCY
INDIGENCE
INDOLENCE
INFERENCE
INFLUENCE
INFLUENZA
INGRAINED
INHUMANLY
INNOCENCE
INORGANIC
INSOLENCE
INSURANCE
IPHIGENIA
JACARANDA
JOUISANCE
JUBILANCE
KARABINER
KILLARNEY
KITCHENER
LABYRINTH
LANDOWNER
LANTHANUM
LAZYBONES
LITHUANIA
LONGRANGE
LUMINANCE
MACARONIC
MACEDONIA
MAHARANEE
MAINTENON
MATUTINAL
MAVOURNIN
MEDICINAL
MENOMINEE
MENTIONED
MESSIANIC
MIDDLINGS
MILITANCY
MILLIONTH
MISCHANCE
MISSIONER
MOCKERNUT
MONOMANIA
MONSIGNOR
MUMCHANCE
MUNIMENTS
NESCIENCE
NINEPENCE
NOCTURNAL
OBEDIENCE
OBEISANCE
OCCUPANCY
OCTAGONAL
OFFCHANCE
OLECRANON
ONTOGENCY
OPPONENTS
ORDINANCE
OUTGOINGS
OVERTONES
PANTHENOL
PARTHENON
PASTERNAK
PATTERNED
PAULOWNIA
PENDENNIS
PENITENCE
PENSIONER
PERCHANCE
PERGUNNAH
PERSONNEL
PETULANCE
PIMPERNEL
PLEASANCE
PNEUMONIA
POCKMANKY
POIGNANCY
POLYGONAL
POSTPONED
PREGNANCY
PREVERNAL
PRONOUNCE
PROPIONIC
PRURIENCE
PSEUDONYM
PUISSANCE
PURITANIC
PURSUANCE
PURULENCE
PYROMANCY
PYROMANIA
PYRRHONIC
QUITTANCE
RASKOLNIK
REARRANGE
RECUSANCE
REDOLENCE
REFERENCE
REFINANCE
REFUSENIK
RELEVANCE
REMBRANDT
RESIDENCE
RESIDENCY
RESONANCE
RETICENCE
REVERENCE
RINGFENCE
ROSINANTE
ROZINANTE
RUDIMENTS
RUFFIANLY
SAGAPENUM
SATYRINAE
SAUTERNES
SAUVIGNON
SCABLANDS
SCIOMANCY
SCRAPINGS
SCRIVENER
SECTIONAL
SEMBLANCE
SEMIFINAL
SENTIENCE
SEQUINNED
SEVERANCE
SHAMIANAH
SHARPENER
SHECHINAH
SHETLANDS
SHIPOWNER
SIBILANCE
SIXTEENMO
SIXTEENTH
SNOWDONIA
SOVENANCE
SQUINANCY
STATIONED
STATIONER
STIFFENER
STOCKINET
STOCKINGS
STRIDENCY
SUBSTANCE
SULPHONIC
SUNDOWNER
SUNTANNED
SUSTAINED
SWEEPINGS
SWEETENER
SYMPHONIC
TEMULENCE
TENEMENTS
TEREBINTH
THINNINGS

THOUSANDS
THRASONIC
TIGHTENER
TOLERANCE
TRACHINUS
TRAMLINES
TRAPPINGS
TRICLINIC
TRIMMINGS
TRUEPENNY
UMPTEENTH
UNBALANCE
UNCROWNED
UNDEFINED
UNLEARNED
UNREFINED
UNTRAINED
UTTERANCE
VEHEMENCE
VENGEANCE
VERSIONAL
VERTUMNUS
VESTMENTS
VIGILANCE
VIGILANTE
VIRULENCE
VOLTURNUS
WANCHANCY
WESTERNER
WHODUNNIT
WOODLANDS
XENOMANIA
ABLUTIONS
ACCESSORY
ACIDULOUS
ACROPHONY
ADDERWORT
ADULTHOOD
AERODROME
AFTERMOST
AFTERNOON
AFTERWORD
AITCHBONE
ALBATROSS
ALLANTOID
ALLANTOIS
ALPENHORN
AMBIGUOUS
AMBITIOUS
AMORPHOUS
ANALOGOUS
ANHYDROUS
ANOMALOUS
ANONYMOUS
ANTHOLOGY
ANTIPHONY
ARABINOSE
ARACHNOID
ARCHIVOLT
ARMSTRONG
ARROWROOT
ARTERIOLE
ARTICHOKE
ASSIDUOUS
ASTRODOME
ASTROLOGY
ASTRONOMY
ASTUCIOUS
ATROCIOUS
AUDACIOUS
AUTOCROSS
AUTOSCOPY
BACKCLOTH
BACKSWORD
BACKWOODS
BALTIMORE
BANDALORE
BANDICOOT
BARBAROUS
BARBITONE
BARCELONA
BARNSTORM
BARYSCOPE
BEAUTEOUS
BEHAVIOUR
BELLICOSE
BILLABONG
BILLYCOCK
BIRTHWORT
BLACKFOOT
BLACKMORE
BLACKWOOD
BLINDFOLD
BLINDWORM
BLUESTONE
BOARDROOM
BOOKSTORE
BOSSANOVA
BOUNTEOUS
BOURGEOIS
BRACTEOLE
BRASENOSE
BREAKDOWN
BRICKWORK
BRIGADOON
BRIMSTONE
BROADLOOM
BRUSHWOOD
BUCKTHORN
BUMPTIOUS
CACOPHONY
CAIRNGORM
CALABOOSE
CALEMBOUR
CANCEROUS
CAPACIOUS
CAPRICORN
CARAMBOLA
CARCINOMA
CARNIVORE
CASSEROLE
CATCHPOLE
CATCHPOLL
CATCHWORD
CAVERNOUS
CEDARWOOD
CELLULOID
CELLULOSE
CHAPERONE
CHECKBOOK
CHECKROOM
CHEEKBONE
CHILDHOOD
CHILOPODA
CHINATOWN
CHIROPODY
CHONDROID
CINEREOUS
CLAMOROUS
CLAMPDOWN
CLASSROOM
CLOAKROOM
CLOCKWORK
COACHLOAD
COCKSCOMB
COCKSFOOT
COLOPHONY
COLOSTOMY
COLTSFOOT
COMINFORM
COMMODORE
CONDYLOMA
CONGRUOUS
CONSCIOUS
CORDUROYS
CORNFLOUR
CORTISONE
COSMOGONY
COSMOLOGY
COUNTDOWN
COURTEOUS
COURTROOM
CRACKDOWN
CRAPULOUS
CREDULOUS
CREMATORY
CRETINOUS
CROCKFORD
CROSSWORD
CROWSFOOT
CUBBYHOLE
CUNEIFORM
CURRYCOMB
CUSPIDORE
CUTANEOUS
CUTTHROAT
DANGEROUS
DAVENPORT
DECACHORD
DECIDUOUS
DECOMPOSE
DELACROIX
DELICIOUS
DELIRIOUS
DEMEANOUR
DESULTORY
DEVONPORT
DEXTEROUS
DIANDROUS
DIARRHOEA
DICHOTOMY
DIPHTHONG
DIRECTORS
DIRECTORY
DISCOLOUR
DISENTOMB
DISFAVOUR
DISHCLOTH
DISHONOUR
DODDIPOLL
DORMITORY
DOTHEBOYS
DRIFTWOOD
DRIPSTONE
DRUGSTORE
EAGLEWOOD
EARTHWORK
EARTHWORM
EDDYSTONE
EGREGIOUS
EIDERDOWN
EIGHTSOME
ELBOWROOM
ELECTRODE
ENDEAVOUR
EPIGAEOUS
EPONYMOUS
EROGENOUS
ERRONEOUS
ERUCIFORM
ESPAGNOLE
ETHEREOUS
ETHNOLOGY
ETYMOLOGY
EUDAEMONY
EVERYBODY
EVOCATORY
EXPIATORY
EXTEMPORE
FABACEOUS
FACECLOTH
FACETIOUS
FALDSTOOL
FALSEHOOD
FARANDOLE
FERACIOUS
FEROCIOUS
FERRYBOAT
FEUDATORY
FIELDWORK
FIREPROOF
FIRESTONE
FLAGSTONE
FLEETWOOD
FLESHPOTS
FLINTLOCK
FLOWSTONE
FOLIOLOSE
FOODSTORE
FOOLPROOF
FOOTLOOSE
FOOTSTOOL
FORECLOSE
FOREFRONT
FORESHORE
FRACTIOUS
FRAMEWORK
FREEPHONE
FREESTONE
FRIGATOON
FRITHBORH
FRIVOLOUS
FUGACIOUS
FULLBLOWN
FULLGROWN
FURACIOUS
GALACTOSE
GALLIPOLI
GALLSTONE
GARDEROBE
GARRULOUS
GENEALOGY
GINORMOUS
GIRANDOLE
GLADSTONE
GLAIREOUS
GLAMOROUS
GLORYHOLE
GLUTINOUS
GOOSEFOOT
GRANDIOSE
GRANULOSE
GREATCOAT
GREENHORN
GREENROOM
GREENWOOD
GUACAMOLE
GUARDROOM
GUESSWORK
GUIDEBOOK
GYROSCOPE
HACKAMORE
HAEMALOMA
HAILSTONE
HAILSTORM
HALOBIONT
HANDIWORK
HARDIHOOD
HARMOTOME
HARTSHORN
HAZARDOUS
HAZELWORT
HEADCLOTH
HEADSTONE
HELLEBORE
HEMITROPE
HERBIVORE
HILARIOUS
HISTOLOGY
HITCHCOCK
HOARFROST
HOARSTONE
HOBBINOLL
HOCCAMORE
HOLLYHOCK
HOLLYWOOD
HOLOPHOTE
HOLYSTONE
HOMEGROWN
HOMOPHONE
HONEYCOMB
HONEYMOON
HONKYTONK
HOPLOLOGY
HORNSTONE
HOROSCOPE
HORTATORY
HOURSTONE
HOUSEBOAT
HOUSECOAT
HOUSEHOLD
HOUSEROOM
HOUSEWORK
HUMONGOUS
HUMUNGOUS
HUNKYDORY
HYDROFOIL
HYPERBOLA
HYPERBOLE
IDIOPHONE
IMPERIOUS
IMPETUOUS

INCOMMODE
INCURIOUS
INGENIOUS
INGENUOUS
INGLENOOK
INJURIOUS
INNERMOST
INNOCUOUS
INSIDIOUS
INTERLOCK
INTERLOPE
INTERNODE
INTERPOSE
INVENTORY
INVIDIOUS
IPRINDOLE
IRONSTONE
JOBERNOWL
JUDICIOUS
JUXTAPOSE
KABELJOUW
KERBSTONE
KEYSTROKE
KNOCKDOWN
KOMINFORM
KONISCOPE
KRUMMHORN
LABORIOUS
LAEVULOSE
LAMBSWOOL
LANCEWOOD
LANDDROST
LASERWORT
LAUDATORY
LAZZARONE
LEAKPROOF
LEASEHOLD
LECHEROUS
LEUCOTOME
LIBELLOUS
LIGHTFOOT
LIGHTSOME
LIMESTONE
LINTSTOCK
LITHOPONE
LITIGIOUS
LIVERPOOL
LIVERWORT
LIVESTOCK
LOADSTONE
LOATHSOME
LODESTONE
LOINCLOTH
LONGICORN
LONGSHORE
LOUSEWORT
LUDICROUS
LUSTIHOOD
LUXURIOUS
LYMESWOLD
MACROCOSM
MACROLOGY
MADREPORE
MAJORDOMO
MALICIOUS
MANDATORY
MANGETOUT
MAPPEMOND
MARVELOUS
MASSYMORE
MATCHLOCK
MATCHWOOD
MATRIMONY
MATTAMORE
MEGAPHONE
MEGASCOPE
MEGASPORE
MELAMPODE
MELODIOUS
MENADIONE
METALLOID
METALWORK
METEOROID
METHADONE
METRONOME
MICROCOSM
MICROTOME
MICROTONE
MIGRATORY
MILESTONE
MILLEPORE
MILLSTONE
MINACIOUS
MINKSTONE
MINNESOTA
MISINFORM
MISSTROKE
MOMENTOUS
MONEYWORT
MONKSHOOD
MONOCHORD
MONOTROCH
MONSTROUS
MOONSTONE
MORTSTONE
MOTOCROSS
MOTORBOAT
MOUSEHOLE
MULTIFORM
MUNITIONS
MURDEROUS
MUSHROOMS
MUSKETOON
MUTOSCOPE
MYRMECOID
MYTHOLOGY
NATHEMORE
NEFANDOUS
NEFARIOUS
NEIGHBOUR
NEUROLOGY
NEVERMORE
NIGHTGOWN
NIGHTWORK
NOSTOLOGY
NOTOCHORD
NOTORIOUS
OBLIVIOUS
OBNOXIOUS
OCTACHORD
OCULIFORM
OFFCOLOUR
OFFERTORY
OFFICIOUS
OLFACTORY
OPTOPHONE
ORGILLOUS
ORTHODOXY
ORTHOLOGY
ORTHOTONE
OSTROGOTH
OUTERMOST
OUTOFTOWN
OVENPROOF
OVERBLOWN
OVERCLOUD
OVERCROWD
OVERGROWN
OVERSHOES
OVERSHOOT
OVIPAROUS
PAINTWORK
PALAMPORE
PALEMPORE
PANETTONE
PANTALOON
PAPERWORK
PAPILLOTE
PARATROOP
PARDALOTE
PARSIMONY
PATCHWORK
PATERCOVE
PATHOLOGY
PATRIMONY
PEARLWORT
PELLITORY
PENDULOUS
PENISTONE
PENTECOST
PENURIOUS
PEPPERONI
PERISCOPE
PERISTOME
PETROLOGY
PETTICOAT
PETTITOES
PHALAROPE
PHARAMOND
PHEROMONE
PHILOLOGY
PHONOLOGY
PHOTOCOPY
PIACEVOLE
PIECEWORK
PILLICOCK
PINCHCOCK
PIPESTONE
PITCHFORK
PITCHPOLE
PITCHPOLL
PLACATORY
PLAINSONG
PLAYGROUP
PLENTEOUS
PLUMBEOUS
POISONOUS
POLYPHONE
POLYPHONY
POMPADOUR
PONDEROSA
PONDEROUS
POPPYCOCK
POWERBOAT
PRECATORY
PREDATORY
PREFATORY
PRELUSORY
PRONGHORN
PROUDHORN
PROVEDORE
PROVOLONE
PURGATORY
PUSSYFOOT
QUASIMODO
QUERIMONY
QUERULOUS
QUILLWORT
QUINTROON
RACCABOUT
RACCAHOUT
RADIOLOGY
RAFFINOSE
RAINSTORM
RANCOROUS
RANTIPOLE
RAPACIOUS
RAPTUROUS
RASPATORY
REDINGOTE
REFECTORY
RELATIONS
RELIGIOSO
RELIGIOUS
REPERTORY
RESERVOIR
RESTIFORM
RIDERHOOD
RIGHTEOUS
RIGMAROLE
ROADBLOCK
ROCAMBOLE
ROOTSTOCK
ROQUEFORT
RUDDIGORE
SACKCLOTH
SAGACIOUS
SAILCLOTH
SAINTFOIN
SAINTHOOD
SALACIOUS
SALLYPORT
SALLYPOST
SANDSTONE
SANDSTORM
SANGFROID
SASKATOON
SATINWOOD
SAUCEBOAT
SAXOPHONE
SCAGLIOLA
SCALLIONS
SCAPEGOAT
SCHIAVONE
SCRAPBOOK
SCURRIOUR
SEBACEOUS
SEDGEMOOR
SEDITIOUS
SEMAPHORE
SEMIOLOGY
SEPTIMOLE
SETACEOUS
SHAKEDOWN
SHEEPFOLD
SHENSTONE
SHIFTWORK
SHOPFLOOR
SHOPFRONT
SHORTHOLD
SHORTHORN
SIGNATORY
SILTSTONE
SINGAPORE
SLABSTONE
SNOWSHOES
SNOWSTORM
SOAPSTONE
SOCIOLOGY
SOMASCOPE
SOPHOMORE
SOUTHDOWN
SPEARWORT
SPEEDBOAT
SPHENDONE
SPIRITOUS
SPLENDOUR
SQUADRONE
STARSTONE
STATEHOOD
STATEROOM
STATUTORY
STEAMBOAT
STEINBOCK
STEVEDORE
STILLBORN
STILLROOM
STINKHORN
STINKWOOD
STIRABOUT
STOCKHOLM
STOCKROOM
STOCKWORK
STONEBOAT
STONEWORK
STONEWORT
STOREROOM
STORYBOOK
STRENUOUS
STRINGOPS
STROMBOLI
STUMPWORK
SUBDOLOUS
SULFUROUS
SUMPTUOUS
SUNSTROKE
SUPERNOVA
SURREJOIN
SWANIMOTE
SWANSDOWN
TARRAGONA
TAUTOLOGY
TAVISTOCK
TECTIFORM
TELEOLOGY
TELEPHONE
TELEPHONY
TELEPHOTO
TELESCOPE
TENACIOUS
TENEBROSE
TERRICOLE

TERRITORY
TESTIMONY
TETRALOGY
TETTEROUS
THECODONT
THEOBROMA
THEREFORE
THIGHBONE
THREEFOLD
THREESOME
THRESHOLD
THROWDOWN
TIGHTROPE
TISIPHONE
TOADSTONE
TOADSTOOL
TOBERMORY
TOMBSTONE
TOMENTOSE
TOOTHCOMB
TOOTHSOME
TOUCHDOWN
TOUCHWOOD
TOWNSFOLK
TRANSFORM
TRANSPORT
TRANSPOSE
TRAPEZOID
TREBIZOND
TREGETOUR
TREMATODE
TREMULOUS
TRIBOLOGY
TRICOLOUR
TRUCKLOAD
TURCOPOLE
TURNABOUT
TURNSTONE
TYRANNOUS
ULIGINOUS
UNANIMOUS
UNBEKNOWN
UNDERCOAT
UNDERDONE
UNDERFOOT
UNDERMOST
UNDERSONG
UNDERTONE
UNDERWOOD
UNTIMEOUS
UNWELCOME
UPPERMOST
UTTERMOST
VAINGLORY
VASECTOMY
VELDSKOEN
VELODROME
VENEREOUS
VERACIOUS
VERMIFORM
VERMINOUS
VERTIPORT
VEXATIONS
VEXATIOUS
VIBRATORY
VICARIOUS
VITASCOPE
VIVACIOUS
VOLAGEOUS
VORACIOUS
WAGENBOOM
WAGONLOAD
WAISTCOAT
WALKABOUT
WASHCLOTH
WATCHWORD
WATERFORD
WATERFOWL
WATERHOLE
WAYZGOOSE
WEARISOME
WEDGEWOOD
WELLKNOWN
WHALEBOAT
WHALEBONE
WHEREFORE
WHETSTONE
WHINSTONE
WHIRLPOOL
WHITEWOOD
WHOLEFOOD
WHOLESOME
WIDOWHOOD
WOBBEGONG
WOEBEGONE
WOMANHOOD
WOMENFOLK
WOODSHOCK
WORRISOME
WRONGDOER
WRONGFOOT
XENOPHOBE
XEROSTOMA
XYLOPHONE
ZYGOSPORE
ENTRECÔTE
AMBLYOPIA
ANAGLYPTA
APOCRYPHA
ARTHROPOD
BEEKEEPER
BIOGRAPHY
BLINDSPOT
CATALEPSY
CATTLEPEN
CHALIAPIN
CONTEMPER
DEVELOPED
DEVELOPER
DISTEMPER
DYSTROPHY
EMPANOPLY
EPISCOPAL
FLOWERPOT
GEOGRAPHY
HALFEMPTY
IMPROMPTU
INNKEEPER
ISOPROPYL
ISOTROPIC
KIDNAPPED
KIDNAPPER
LAGNIAPPE
LANDLOPER
MISSHAPEN
MISTEMPER
MONTESPAN
MUNICIPAL
NEWSPAPER
NOTEPAPER
ONTHESPOT
OROGRAPHY
OUTROOPER
PEPPERPOT
PERAEOPOD
PHILIPPIC
PHYLLOPOD
PINEAPPLE
PRINCIPAL
PRINCIPLE
QUADRUPED
QUADRUPLE
QUINTUPLE
SANDPAPER
SANDPIPER
SCALLOPED
SCHNAPPER
SKETCHPAD
SLAPHAPPY
THEOSOPHY
THEREUPON
VERKAMPTE
WALLPAPER
WHEREUPON
XANTHIPPE
ZOOSCOPIC
ARABESQUE
BURLESQUE
EQUIVOQUE
GROTESQUE
MONOCOQUE
ODALISQUE
ORTANIQUE
PAYCHEQUE
POLITIQUE
SOLILOQUY
TECHNIQUE
ADULTERER
AHASUERUS
AINSWORTH
ALDEBARAN
ALLOCARPY
AMBERGRIS
ANCESTRAL
ANGIOGRAM
ANNAPURNA
ARAUCARIA
BACKWARDS
BAINMARIE
BECQUEREL
BILATERAL
BILLIARDS
BISHOPRIC
BLINKERED
BLISTERED
BLOWTORCH
BLUEBERRY
BLUNDERER
BLUSTERER
BONAPARTE
BOOBYTRAP
BOSPHORUS
BRANDIRON
BRASSERIE
BRATWURST
BROTHERLY
CABLEGRAM
CADASTRAL
CAFETERIA
CANAVERAL
CANTHARIS
CANTHARUS
CARTHORSE
CARTOGRAM
CATAMARAN
CATCHCROP
CATHEDRAL
CENTAURUS
CHAMPERTY
CHAPARRAL
CHARTERED
CHATTERER
CHEQUERED
CHINSTRAP
CINERARIA
CLUSTERED
COLOSTRUM
CONCIERGE
CONCOURSE
CONQUEROR
CONUNDRUM
CORKSCREW
CRANBERRY
CRANBORNE
CROSSBRED
CYCLOTRON
DANDYPRAT
DEATHTRAP
DECAMERON
DECONTROL
DELIVERER
DEXTRORSE
DIABLERIE
DIAMETRIC
DIGASTRIC
DISCHARGE
DISCOURSE
DOWNWARDS
EASTWARDS
EAVESDROP
ECCENTRIC
ECHEVERIA
ECTOMORPH
EDGEWORTH
EDINBURGH
ELECTORAL
ENAMOURED
ENDOMORPH
EPHEMERAL
EPHEMERIS
EPHEMERON
ETCETERAS
EUCHLORIC
EUHEMERUS
EXECUTRIX
FEATHERED
FILMSTRIP
FIREWORKS
FLATTERED
FLATTERER
FLAVOURED
FLUSTERED
FOOLHARDY
FROGMARCH
FRUITERER
GALLYCROW
GEOMETRIC
GEOMETRID
GERIATRIC
GLENGARRY
GRAPETREE
HAWTHORNE
HEADFIRST
HEARTHRUG
HEXAMERON
HIPPOCRAS
HISTOGRAM
HOMEWARDS
ILLIBERAL
INAUGURAL
INDECORUM
INNISFREE
INTERBRED
INTERPRET
IRONWORKS
ISOMETRIC
JACKSTRAW
JACQUERIE
JOBSWORTH
JOCKSTRAP
JOCULARLY
JUNEBERRY
KARAKORAM
KILOHERTZ
KLEMPERER
KNACKERED
KNEECORDS
LAGOMORPH
LAMASERAI
LANDWARDS
LECANORAM
LENINGRAD
LIENTERIC
LINDBERGH
LOHENGRIN
LUCIFERIN
MACQUARIE
MAELSTROM
MAGNETRON
MATRIARCH
MEGAHERTZ
MELBOURNE
MENAGERIE
MESOMORPH
MILLIGRAM
MISTIGRIS
MONASTRAL
MONOCEROS
MORATORIA
MORATORIO
MOUSETRAP
NASEBERRY
NECKVERSE
NIAISERIE
NORTHERLY
OBSTETRIC
OCHLOCRAT
OUDENARDE
OUROBOROS
OUROBORUS
OUTSKIRTS
OVERTHROW

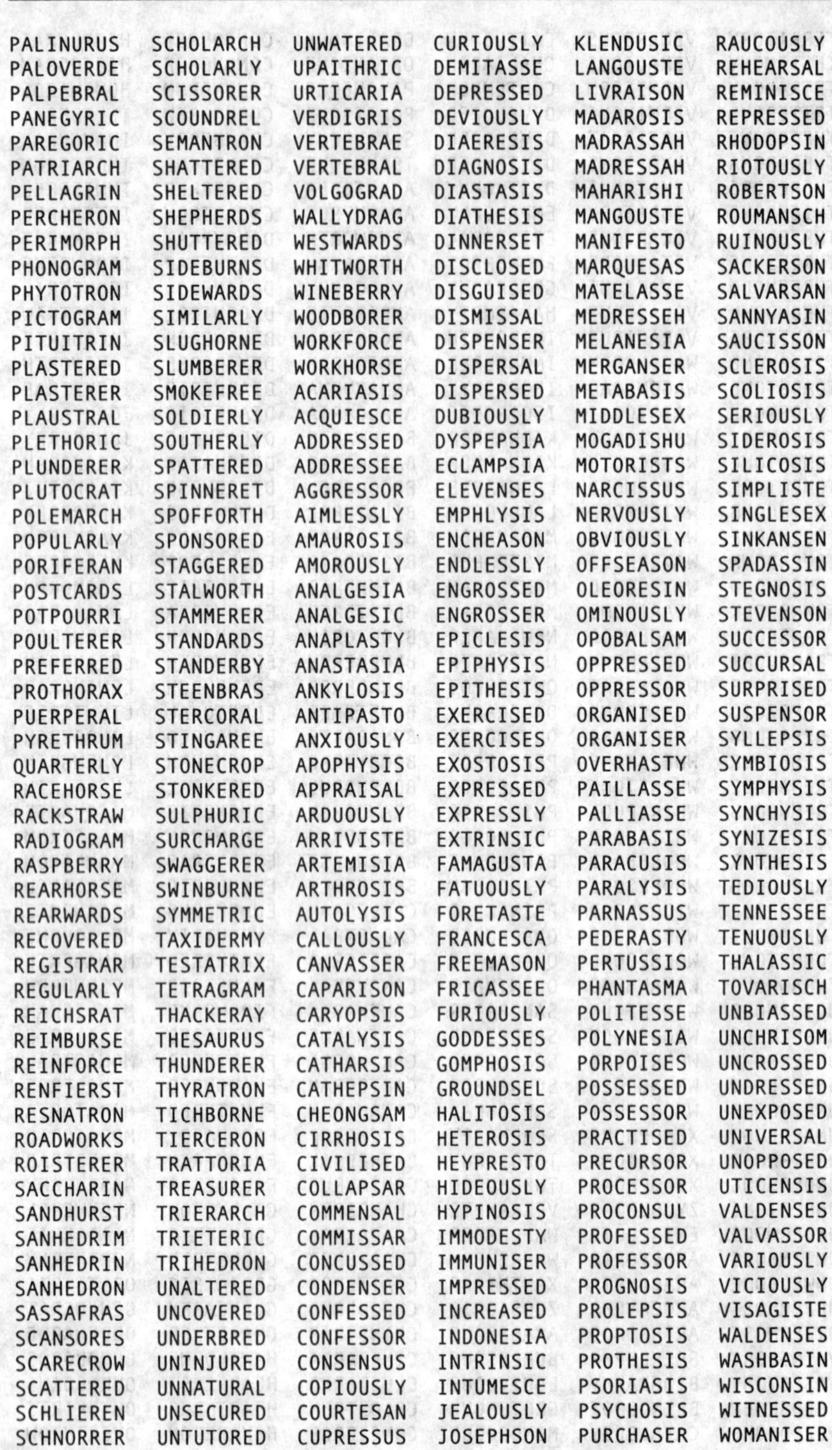

PALINURUS
PALOVERDE
PALPEBRAL
PANEGYRIC
PAREGORIC
PATRIARCH
PELLAGRIN
PERCHERON
PERIMORPH
PHONOGRAM
PHYTOTRON
PICTOGRAM
PITUITRIN
PLASTERED
PLASTERER
PLAUSTRAL
PLETHORIC
PLUNDERER
PLUTOCRAT
POLEMARCH
POPULARLY
PORIFERAN
POSTCARDS
POTPOURRI
POULTERER
PREFERRED
PROTHORAX
PUERPERAL
PYRETHRUM
QUARTERLY
RACEHORSE
RACKSTRAW
RADIOGRAM
RASPBERRY
REARHORSE
REARWARDS
RECOVERED
REGISTRAR
REGULARLY
REICHSRAT
REIMBURSE
REINFORCE
RENFIERST
RESNATRON
ROADWORKS
ROISTERER
SACCHARIN
SANDHURST
SANHEDRIM
SANHEDRIN
SANHEDRON
SASSAFRAS
SCANSORES
SCARECROW
SCATTERED
SCHLIEREN
SCHNORRER
SCHOLARCH
SCHOLARLY
SCISSORER
SCOUNDREL
SEMANTRON
SHATTERED
SHELTERED
SHEPHERDS
SHUTTERED
SIDEBURNS
SIDEWARDS
SIMILARLY
SLUGHORNE
SLUMBERER
SMOKEFREE
SOLDIERLY
SOUTHERLY
SPATTERED
SPINNERET
SPOFFORTH
SPONSORED
STAGGERED
STALWORTH
STAMMERER
STANDARDS
STANDERBY
STEENBRAS
STERCORAL
STINGAREE
STONECROP
STONKERED
SULPHURIC
SURCHARGE
SWAGGERER
SWINBURNE
SYMMETRIC
TAXIDERMY
TESTATRIX
TETRAGRAM
THACKERAY
THESAURUS
THUNDERER
THYRATRON
TICHBORNE
TIERCERON
TRATTORIA
TREASURER
TRIERARCH
TRIETERIC
TRIHEDRON
UNALTERED
UNCOVERED
UNDERBRED
UNINJURED
UNNATURAL
UNSECURED
UNTUTORED
UNWATERED
UPAITHRIC
URTICARIA
VERDIGRIS
VERTEBRAE
VERTEBRAL
VOLGOGRAD
WALLYDRAG
WESTWARDS
WHITWORTH
WINEBERRY
WOODBORER
WORKFORCE
WORKHORSE
ACARIASIS
ACQUIESCE
ADDRESSED
ADDRESSEE
AGGRESSOR
AIMLESSLY
AMAUROSIS
AMOROUSLY
ANALGESIA
ANALGESIC
ANAPLASTY
ANASTASIA
ANKYLOSIS
ANTIPASTO
ANXIOUSLY
APOPHYSIS
APPRAISAL
ARDUOUSLY
ARRIVISTE
ARTEMISIA
ARTHROSIS
AUTOLYSIS
CALLOUSLY
CANVASSER
CAPARISON
CARYOPSIS
CATALYSIS
CATHARSIS
CATHEPSIN
CHEONGSAM
CIRRHOSIS
CIVILISED
COLLAPSAR
COMMENSAL
COMMISSAR
CONCUSSED
CONDENSER
CONFESSED
CONFESSOR
CONSENSUS
COPIOUSLY
COURTESAN
CUPRESSUS
CURIOUSLY
DEMITASSE
DEPRESSED
DEVIOUSLY
DIAERESIS
DIAGNOSIS
DIASTASIS
DIATHESIS
DINNERSET
DISCLOSED
DISGUISED
DISMISSAL
DISPENSER
DISPERSAL
DISPERSED
DUBIOUSLY
DYSPEPSIA
ECLAMPSIA
ELEVENSES
EMPHLYSIS
ENCHEASON
ENDLESSLY
ENGROSSED
ENGROSSER
EPICLESIS
EPIPHYSIS
EPITHESIS
EXERCISED
EXERCISES
EXOSTOSIS
EXPRESSED
EXPRESSLY
EXTRINSIC
FAMAGUSTA
FATUOUSLY
FORETASTE
FRANCESCA
FREEMASON
FRICASSEE
FURIOUSLY
GODDESSES
GOMPHOSIS
GROUNDSEL
HALITOSIS
HETEROSIS
HEYPRESTO
HIDEOUSLY
HYPINOSIS
IMMODESTY
IMMUNISER
IMPRESSED
INCREASED
INDONESIA
INTRINSIC
INTUMESCE
JEALOUSLY
JOSEPHSON
KLENDUSIC
LANGOUSTE
LIVRAISON
MADAROSIS
MADRASSAH
MADRESSAH
MAHARISHI
MANGOUSTE
MANIFESTO
MARQUESAS
MATELASSE
MEDRESSEH
MELANESIA
MERGANSER
METABASIS
MIDDLESEX
MOGADISHU
MOTORISTS
NARCISSUS
NERVOUSLY
OBVIOUSLY
OFFSEASON
OLEORESIN
OMINOUSLY
OPOBALSAM
OPPRESSED
OPPRESSOR
ORGANISED
ORGANISER
OVERHASTY
PAILLASSE
PALLIASSE
PARABASIS
PARACUSIS
PARALYSIS
PARNASSUS
PEDERASTY
PERTUSSIS
PHANTASMA
POLITESSE
POLYNESIA
PORPOISES
POSSESSED
POSSESSOR
PRACTISED
PRECURSOR
PROCESSOR
PROCONSUL
PROFESSED
PROFESSOR
PROGNOSIS
PROLEPSIS
PROPTOSIS
PROTHESIS
PSORIASIS
PSYCHOSIS
PURCHASER
RAUCOUSLY
REHEARSAL
REMINISCE
REPRESSED
RHODOPSIN
RIOTOUSLY
ROBERTSON
ROUMANSCH
RUINOUSLY
SACKERSON
SALVARSAN
SANNYASIN
SAUCISSON
SCLEROSIS
SCOLIOSIS
SERIOUSLY
SIDEROSIS
SILICOSIS
SIMPLISTE
SINGLESEX
SINKANSEN
SPADASSIN
STEGNOSIS
STEVENSON
SUCCESSOR
SUCCURSAL
SURPRISED
SUSPENSOR
SYLLEPSIS
SYMBIOSIS
SYMPHYSIS
SYNCHYSIS
SYNIZESIS
SYNTHESIS
TEDIOUSLY
TENNESSEE
TENUOUSLY
THALASSIC
TOVARISCH
UNBIASSED
UNCHRISOM
UNCROSSED
UNDRESSED
UNEXPOSED
UNIVERSAL
UNOPPOSED
UTICENSIS
VALDENSES
VALVASSOR
VARIOUSLY
VICIOUSLY
VISAGISTE
WALDENSES
WASHBASIN
WISCONSIN
WITNESSED
WOMANISER

YGGDRASIL
ABERNETHY
ACQUITTAL
ACROBATIC
ADMONITOR
ADVOCATED
AESTHETIC
AFFLICTED
AGALACTIC
ALABASTER
ALEURITIS
ALGORITHM
ALLIGATOR
ALLOPATHY
ALTIMETER
AMARANTIN
AMENHOTEP
ANALEPTIC
ANCIPITAL
ANECDOTAL
ANECDOTES
ANIMISTIC
ANNOTATED
ANNOTATOR
ANTARCTIC
ANTENATAL
ANTIPATHY
APATHETIC
APOPHATIC
APPARATUS
APPARITOR
APPOINTED
APPOINTEE
ARBORETUM
ARISTOTLE
ARLINGTON
ARTHRITIC
ARTHRITIS
ASPIRATOR
ASTHMATIC
ASYMMETRY
ATAVISTIC
ATHEISTIC
ATHELSTAN
ATTEMPTED
AUBRIETIA
AUTHENTIC
AUTOLATRY
AUTOMATED
AUTOMATIC
AUTOMATON
AXIOMATIC
AXMINSTER
BACKBITER
BACKWATER
BADMINTON
BALLISTIC
BANQUETTE
BAROMETER
BARRISTER
BEDSITTER
BEEFEATER
BENIGHTED
BETTERTON
BLATANTLY
BOMBASTIC
BRIQUETTE
BROUGHTON
BUNDESTAG
CACHECTIC
CANALETTO
CAPACITOR
CAPORETTO
CARPENTER
CARPENTRY
CASTRATED
CASUISTIC
CASUISTRY
CATALYTIC
CATHARTIC
CERATITIS
CERVANTES
CHARACTER
CHARLATAN
CHARLOTTE
CHEMISTRY
CHORISTER
CHROMATIC
CIGARETTE
CINEMATIC
CLEOPATRA
CLIMACTIC
COADJUTOR
COELOSTAT
COLLECTED
COLLECTOR
COMFORTER
COMMITTAL
COMMITTED
COMMITTEE
COMPACTLY
CONCEITED
CONCERTED
CONDUCTOR
CONDUCTUS
CONFLATED
CONGESTED
CONNECTED
CONNECTOR
CONTENTED
CONVECTOR
CONVERTED
CONVERTER
CORRECTED
CORRECTLY
CORRECTOR
CORRUPTER
COUCHETTE
COURGETTE
CRICKETER
CROQUETTE
CRYOMETER
CUNCTATOR
CURRENTLY
CYNEGETIC
DAMBUSTER
DECALITRE
DECORATED
DECORATOR
DEDICATED
DEFAULTER
DEFLECTOR
DELIGHTED
DENTISTRY
DEPOSITOR
DESCARTES
DETONATOR
DETRACTOR
DIACRITIC
DIALECTAL
DIALECTIC
DIANOETIC
DIOCLETES
DISGUSTED
DISHWATER
DISMANTLE
DISSENTER
DISTANTLY
DISTORTED
DISUNITED
DOLOMITES
DOLOMITIC
DONCASTER
DONIZETTI
DUMBARTON
DYNAMITED
DYSPEPTIC
EARNESTLY
ECOSYSTEM
EDDINGTON
ELEGANTLY
ELEMENTAL
ELLINGTON
ELONGATED
EMACIATED
EMINENTLY
EMPAESTIC
EMPLECTON
ENCAUSTIC
ENCHANTED
ENCHANTER
ENCOUNTER
ENDEICTIC
ENERGETIC
ENIGMATIC
ENLIGHTEN
ENSHEATHE
ENTERITIS
EPAULETTE
EPEOLATRY
EPHIALTES
EPICENTRE
EPILEPTIC
EPINASTIC
EPIPHYTIC
EQUISETUM
ERIOMETER
ESCALATOR
ESCOPETTE
ESTAFETTE
ETIOLATED
ETIQUETTE
EUMYCETES
EUPHRATES
EVIDENTLY
EXCAVATOR
EXEQUATUR
EXHAUSTED
EXHIBITOR
EXPLOITER
EXPOSITOR
EXTRACTOR
FANTASTIC
FERMENTED
FERVENTLY
FILLISTER
FILTERTIP
FINGERTIP
FIREWATER
FLECHETTE
FLORESTAN
FORFEITED
FORGOTTEN
FREIGHTER
GALLANTLY
GALLANTRY
GARGANTUA
GASOMETER
GAULEITER
GENERATOR
GEORGETTE
GIBRALTAR
GLADIATOR
GOOSESTEP
GRADUATED
GUARANTEE
GUARANTOR
GUJARATHI
GUNCOTTON
GYMNASTIC
HACQUETON
HAMFATTER
HAMFISTED
HANSEATIC
HARLESTON
HARMATTAN
HARVESTER
HEDERATED
HEMSTITCH
HEPATITIS
HEREAFTER
HERODOTUS
HERPESTES
HEURISTIC
HEXAMETER
HODOMETER
HOPSCOTCH
HOTTENTOT
HYDROSTAT
HYLOBATES
IDEOPATHY
IDIOMATIC
ILCHESTER
ILLGOTTEN
ILLICITLY
IMPERATOR
IMPOLITIC
INCITATUS
INCUBATOR
INDICATES
INDICATOR
INHERITED
INHERITOR
INHIBITED
INITIATED
INITIATOR
INNOVATOR
INSPECTOR
INSTANTER
INSTANTLY
INSULATOR
INTROITUS
IRRITATED
ISOCRATES
ISOTACTIC
JERKWATER
JOBCENTRE
KERATITIS
KILOMETER
KILOMETRE
KLINOSTAT
KONIMETER
LACERATED
LAFAYETTE
LAMINATED
LANCASTER
LANGUETTE
LARGHETTO
LASTDITCH
LAZARETTO
LEICESTER
LEITMOTIF
LEITMOTIV
LENIENTLY
LIBERATED
LIBERATOR
LINKLATER
LOGARITHM
LORGNETTE
LUBAVITCH
LYMPHATIC
LYSIMETER
MAJORETTE
MANHATTAN
MANOMETER
MARQUETRY
MEDICATED
MEDITATOR
MEKOMETER
MELANOTIC
MEMORITER
MERCAPTAN
MICKLETON
MIDDLETON
MIDINETTE
MIDWINTER
MILOMETER
MISTLETOE
MODERATOR
MONOMETER
MOSCHATEL
MOTHEATEN
MUFFETTEE
MUGGLETON
MUTILATED
NAUSEATED
NAVIGATOR
NEGLECTED
NEPHRITIC
NEPHRITIS
NEUCHATEL
NEWCASTLE
NOMINATOR
NOVELETTE
NUMERATOR
OCCIPITAL
ONCOMETER
ONOMASTIC
OPSIMATHY
OPTOMETRY
OPULENTLY
ORCHESTRA

ORGIASTIC
ORPINGTON
ORTHOPTER
OUBLIETTE
OUTFITTER
OVERRATED
PAGEANTRY
PAILLETTE
PALAESTRA
PALAFITTE
PALMISTRY
PARALYTIC
PARAMETER
PARASITIC
PAROTITIS
PATIENTLY
PATRIOTIC
PAYMASTER
PEASANTRY
PECULATOR
PEDOMETER
PEIRASTIC
PENDLETON
PERFECTLY
PERIAKTOS
PERICUTIN
PERIMETER
PERIPATUS
PERMITTED
PERVERTED
PHILISTER
PHLEBITIS
PHOTOSTAT
PHRENETIC
PHRENITIS
PINKERTON
PIQUANTLY
PIROUETTE
PNEUMATIC
POETASTER
POLYESTER
POPULATED
POSTNATAL
POTHUNTER
PRAGMATIC
PRANKSTER
PRECENTOR
PRECEPTOR
PREDICTOR
PRELECTOR
PRESBYTER
PRESCUTUM
PRESENTED
PRESENTER
PRESENTLY
PRINCETON
PRISMATIC
PROCLITIC
PROJECTED
PROJECTOR
PROLACTIN
PROPHETIC
PROTECTOR
PROTESTER
PROTOSTAR
PRUDENTLY
PSYCHOTIC
PUNGENTLY
QUADRATIC
QUADRATUS
QUARTETTE
QUERCETIN
QUERCETUS
QUICKSTEP
QUINTETTE
RADIANTLY
RAINWATER
REALISTIC
REDLETTER
REFLECTOR
REFRACTOR
REGULATOR
REICHSTAG
RENCONTRE
RENOVATOR
RESONATOR
RESPECTED
RESPECTER
RETINITIS
RETRACTOR
RHEUMATIC
RHYMESTER
RIGOLETTO
RILLETTES
ROSEWATER
ROUSSETTE
SACRISTAN
SALERATUS
SALICETUM
SALOPETTE
SALTPETER
SALTPETRE
SALTWATER
SAMARITAN
SARCASTIC
SARMENTUM
SASQUATCH
SATURATED
SCARLATTI
SCHEHITAH
SCHEMATIC
SCHLENTER
SCHMALTZY
SCHMUTTER
SCHNITTKE
SCLEROTAL
SCOLIOTIC
SCORBUTIC
SCORBUTUS
SCRUTATOR
SEABOTTLE
SEAWORTHY
SEGMENTED
SEMEIOTIC
SEPARATED
SEPARATOR
SEQUESTER
SERVIETTE
SHECHITAH
SHORTSTAY
SHORTSTOP
SIMPLETON
SIMULATED
SIMULATOR
SINGLETON
SINGULTUS
SINUSITIS
SLAUGHTER
SOLICITOR
SONOMETER
SOPHISTER
SOPHISTIC
SOPHISTRY
SOUBRETTE
SOUWESTER
SPAGHETTI
SPECTATOR
SPHINCTER
SPLENETIC
SPLENITIS
SPRIGHTLY
STANNATOR
STATISTIC
STATUETTE
STEGNOTIC
STORIATED
STRUMITIS
STYLISTIC
SUBCORTEX
SUBEDITOR
SUCCENTOR
SUPERETTE
SUPERSTAR
SUPINATOR
SUPPORTER
SURFEITED
SUSPECTED
SYBARITIC
SYMBIOTIC
SYNOVITIS
SYNTACTIC
SYNTHETIC
TABULATOR
TAXIMETER
TEAKETTLE
TEESWATER
TELEPATHY
THAUMATIN
THERSITES
THRENETIC
THROWSTER
THYRISTOR
TICTACTOE
TOLERATED
TONOMETER
TORMENTER
TORMENTIL
TORMENTOR
TORMENTUM
TOWCESTER
TRAUMATIC
TRICKSTER
TRIMESTER
TRINKETER
TRIPMETER
TROMPETTE
TRUMPETER
TRUNCATED
TUILLETTE
ULLSWATER
ULTIMATUM
UNADOPTED
UNCOURTLY
UNDAUNTED
UNDILUTED
UNDOUBTED
UNHEALTHY
UNINVITED
UNLIMITED
UNRELATED
UNSHEATHE
UNSIGHTLY
UNTREATED
UNWRITTEN
UPCOUNTRY
UPHOLSTER
USHERETTE
VALIANTLY
VAPORETTO
VEGETATOR
VIOLENTLY
VOLTMETER
WAGHALTER
WAGONETTE
WANWORTHY
WASTWATER
WEBFOOTED
WINCANTON
WITCHETTY
WOLLASTON
WOODENTOP
WORCESTER
WORMEATEN
WYANDOTTE
YOUNGSTER
ZOOMANTIC
ZOROASTER
ZUCCHETTO
ZYGOMATIC
ABOUTTURN
ADMIXTURE
ADVENTURE
AGINCOURT
AMPLITUDE
ANGOSTURA
ANSCHLUSS
ARQUEBUSE
ASSUETUDE
ASTROTURF
ATTRIBUTE
AUTOROUTE
AWESTRUCK
AYCKBOURN
AYLESBURY
BAKEHOUSE
BALDAQUIN
BARAGOUIN
BARRACUDA
BASECOURT
BEATITUDE
BELEAGUER
BENBECULA
BILINGUAL
BOATHOUSE
BRADLAUGH
BYPRODUCT
CALENDULA
CALENTURE
CAMPANULA
CANDYTUFT
CANNELURE
CERTITUDE
CHANTEUSE
CLUBHOUSE
COMPOSURE
CONSTRUCT
CONTINUAL
CONTINUUM
COOKHOUSE
CURVATURE
DACHSHUND
DARTMOUTH
DEBENTURE
DEERHOUND
DEPARTURE
DESTITUTE
DESUETUDE
DIFFICULT
DISFIGURE
DISREPUTE
DISSOLUTE
DOSSHOUSE
DRYASDUST
DUMBFOUND
EASTBOUND
EFFECTUAL
EMBRASURE
ENCLOSURE
ENRAPTURE
EXCHEQUER
FARMHOUSE
FEBRIFUGE
FEEDSTUFF
FILOPLUME
FLASHBULB
FLASHCUBE
FLOPHOUSE
FOODSTUFF
FORASMUCH
FORECOURT
FORTITUDE
FROGMOUTH
FURNITURE
GALLINULE
GARNITURE
GLOMERULE
GOALMOUTH
GRATICULE
GRATITUDE
GREYHOUND
HAIRBRUSH
HAMSTRUNG
HARLEQUIN
HEARTBURN
HEAVYDUTY
HEXATEUCH
HIDEBOUND
HOARHOUND
HOLOCAUST
HOREHOUND
HYDROPULT
HYPOCAUST
IMPORTUNE
IMPOSTURE
INDENTURE
INSTITUTE
INTERLUDE
INTERRUPT
INTRIGUED
INTRIGUER
INTRODUCE
KINKCOUGH

KNAPSCULL
KNAPSKULL
LANDSTURM
LASSITUDE
LEAFMOULD
LIMEHOUSE
LIPPITUDE
LOBSCOUSE
LONGITUDE
LOUDMOUTH
LUXEMBURG
MAGDEBURG
MAGNITUDE
MAJUSCULE
MALLEMUCK
MANNEQUIN
MENOPAUSE
MENSTRUAL
MENSTRUUM
MINIATURE
MINISCULE
MINUSCULE
MONTACUTE
MONTEZUMA
MONTICULE
MULTITUDE
NEGRITUDE
NEWSHOUND
NIEBELUNG
NIGRITUDE
NUMBSKULL
OASTHOUSE
OPPORTUNE
OTTERBURN
PALANQUIN
PARACHUTE
PARAMOUNT
PATCHOULI
PATCHOULY
PENINSULA
PENTHOUSE
PERPETUAL
PERSECUTE
PLATITUDE
PLAYHOUSE
PLENITUDE
POLITBURO
POORHOUSE
POSTHOUSE
PRECIEUSE
PREFIGURE
PREMATURE
PREOCCUPY
PRESHRUNK
PROCEDURE
PROSECUTE
RAINGAUGE
REARMOUSE
RECAPTURE
RECTITUDE
RELIGEUSE
REPERCUSS
REPRODUCE
REREMOUSE
RESTITUTE
REVICTUAL
ROADHOUSE
RUNAROUND
SCRIPTURE
SCULPTURE
SECATEURS
SEPULTURE
SERVITUDE
SHELDDUCK
SHELLSUIT
SIGNATURE
SNOWBOUND
SOBRIQUET
SOSTENUTO
SOURDOUGH
SPACESUIT
SPIRITUAL
STRANGURY
STRICTURE
STRUCTURE
TABLATURE
TARANTULA
TAYASSUID
TOLLHOUSE
TRACKSUIT
TRANSFUSE
TRANSHUME
TRANSMUTE
TREETRUNK
TURNROUND
TURPITUDE
UNISEXUAL
UNSAVOURY
VEILLEUSE
VELASQUEZ
VERMIFUGE
VESTIBULE
VESTITURE
WALDFLUTE
WAREHOUSE
WATERBUTT
WESTBOUND
WHIPROUND
WODEHOUSE
WOLFHOUND
WOODCHUCK
WOODHOUSE
WOODLOUSE
WORKHOUSE
AFFIDAVIT
AGGRIEVED
BEETHOVEN
BOLSHEVIK
BOOKLOVER
BREAKEVEN
CONTRIVED
CONTRIVER
CROSSOVER
DAREDEVIL
DISSOLVED
FIRSTEVER
GEARLEVER
GLENLIVET
HARDCOVER
LOCHINVAR
LONGLIVED
MANOEUVRE
MEDIAEVAL
MENSHEVIK
MOURNIVAL
MUCHLOVED
NICKNEVEN
OURSELVES
PERFERVID
PONTLEVIS
PRESERVED
PRESERVER
PRESERVES
PRIMAEVAL
REDIVIVUS
RETRIEVAL
RETRIEVER
REYKJAVIK
ROUNCEVAL
ROUNCIVAL
SKINDIVER
SOFTCOVER
VANCOUVER
WHICHEVER
WHOSOEVER
WINDHOVER
BATHTOWEL
BREAKAWAY
BRIDLEWAY
GARRYOWEN
GLENDOWER
GREENAWAY
HEMINGWAY
LAWNMOWER
MAYFLOWER
OUTGROWTH
OVERPOWER
SAFFLOWER
SCALLAWAG
SCALLYWAG
SPIDERWEB
STORNAWAY
SUNFLOWER
THROWAWAY
TOPDRAWER
WHITTAWER
WILLPOWER
AEROTAXIS
AFLATOXIN
ANTITOXIC
ANTITOXIN
DIAZEUXIS
EPISTAXIS
PERPLEXED
PSEUDAXIS
RHEOTAXIS
SAXITOXIN
AMBROTYPE
ARCHETYPE
CATACLYSM
COLLOTYPE
CROSSEYED
DECASTYLE
DESTROYED
DESTROYER
DISPLAYED
ENTOPHYTE
FREESTYLE
GAINSAYER
HACKNEYED
HAIRSTYLE
HAMADRYAD
HIGHFLYER
HIMALAYAN
HIMALAYAS
HIPPOLYTA
HIPPOLYTE
KARYOTYPE
LEUCOCYTE
LIFESTYLE
LITHOCYST
MICROCYTE
MINELAYER
MNEMOSYNE
OVERJOYED
PANCHAYAT
PERISTYLE
PHAGOCYTE
PORTRAYAL
PROKARYON
PROSELYTE
PROTOTYPE
RATEPAYER
STRONGYLE
TACHYLYTE
TEKNONYMY
THORNDYKE
TREVELYAN
UNALLOYED
URUGUAYAN
XEROPHYTE
APPETIZER
BALTHAZAR
BAMBOOZLE
BULLDOZER
CHERNOZEM
CIVILIZED
EQUALIZER
HALFDOZEN
KINGSIZED
LOCALIZED
MACKENZIE
ORGANIZED
ORGANIZER
OVERSIZED
PAPARAZZI
PAPARAZZO
SCHNAUZER
SCHNITZEL
SCHNOZZLE
SHEMOZZLE
STARGAZER
TOTALIZER
VAPORIZER
WOMANIZER
WURLITZER

9:8

ABDOMINAL
ACQUITTAL
ACTUARIAL
ADENOIDAL
ADVERBIAL
AIRSTREAM
ALDEBARAN
AMBROSIAL
AMBROSIAN
AMPHIBIAN
AMSTERDAM
ANATOLIAN
ANCESTRAL
ANCHORMAN
ANCIPITAL
ANECDOTAL
ANGIOGRAM
ANTENATAL
APPRAISAL
ARROWHEAD
ARSENICAL
ARTHURIAN
ARTICULAR
ASHMOLEAN
ASTRAKHAN
ATHELSTAN
AUCTORIAL
AURICULAR
AVUNCULAR
AYATOLLAH
BACKPEDAL
BACTERIAL
BALTHAZAR
BAPTISMAL
BARBARIAN
BASILICAL
BEACHHEAD
BEACHWEAR
BEDSPREAD
BEEFSTEAK
BETROTHAL
BILATERAL
BILINGUAL
BINOCULAR
BLACKHEAD
BLACKLEAD
BLOCKHEAD
BOOBYTRAP
BORDEREAU
BOSTONIAN
BOTANICAL
BOTSWANAN
BOXWALLAH
BRASSICAS
BRAZILIAN
BREAKAWAY
BRIDLEWAY
BRONCHIAL
BUCKWHEAT
BULGARIAN
BUNDESTAG
BURUNDIAN
CABLEGRAM
CADASTRAL
CAESAREAN
CAMBODIAN
CAMBUSCAN
CAMERAMAN
CANAVERAL
CANDLEMAS
CANONICAL
CAPITULAR
CARIBBEAN
CARNELIAN
CARTESIAN
CARTOGRAM
CASTILIAN
CATAMARAN
CATARRHAL
CATHEDRAL
CATTLEMAN
CAUCASIAN

CELESTIAL
CHALUMEAU
CHAPARRAL
CHARLATAN
CHARWOMAN
CHEONGSAM
CHINSTRAP
CHRISTIAN
CHRISTMAS
CHURCHMAN
CIMMERIAN
CIRCADIAN
CLASSICAL
CLERGYMAN
CLINICIAN
COACHLOAD
COCHINEAL
COELOSTAT
COFFERDAM
COINTREAU
COLLAPSAR
COLLEGIAN
COLLOIDAL
COLOMBIAN
COLUMBIAN
COMMENSAL
COMMISSAR
COMMITTAL
CONCORDAT
CONGENIAL
CONNUBIAL
CONTINUAL
CONVIVIAL
CORNELIAN
CORNERMAN
CORPOREAL
COURTESAN
CRACKSMAN
CRACOVIAN
CRAFTSMAN
CROSSBEAM
CRYPTOGAM
CUSTODIAL
CUSTODIAN
CUTTHROAT
DAEDALIAN
DALMATIAN
DANDYPRAT
DARTAGNAN
DARWINIAN
DEATHTRAP
DIALECTAL
DIETICIAN
DIONYSIAN
DISAPPEAR
DISMISSAL
DISPERSAL

DJELLABAH
DOCTRINAL
DOMINICAL
DOMINICAN
DRACONIAN
DRAFTSMAN
DRAVIDIAN
DROPSICAL
EALDORMAN
EARTHFLAX
EDITORIAL
EDWARDIAN
EFFECTUAL
EFFINGHAM
ELECTORAL
ELEMENTAL
EMOTIONAL
EMPIRICAL
ENCHORIAL
ENTRECHAT
EPHEMERAL
EPICUREAN
EPISCOPAL
EQUIVOCAL
ERISTICAL
ERPINGHAM
ESSENTIAL
ETCETERAS
ETHIOPIAN
EUCLIDEAN
EUSKARIAN
EVITERNAL
EXCISEMAN
FACTIONAL
FALERNIAN
FALLOPIAN
FANATICAL
FARMSTEAD
FATIDICAL
FERRYBOAT
FICTIONAL
FIELDSMAN
FINANCIAL
FIREBREAK
FISHERMAN
FLORESTAN
FORCEMEAT
FORESPEAK
FOSSORIAL
FRATERNAL
FRENCHMAN
FUNICULAR
GALLABEAH
GASPEREAU
GATESHEAD
GENETICAL
GENTLEMAN

GIBRALTAR
GLABELLAR
GLANDULAR
GRAPHICAL
GRAVADLAX
GREATCOAT
GREENAWAY
GREENHEAD
GREGORIAN
GUARDSMAN
HALLOWMAS
HAMADRYAD
HAMPSTEAD
HARMATTAN
HEARDSMAN
HEARTBEAT
HEBRIDEAN
HEMINGWAY
HEPATICAL
HERCULEAN
HERETICAL
HERMANDAD
HERONSHAW
HESPERIAN
HESTERNAL
HEXAGONAL
HIBERNIAN
HIMALAYAN
HIMALAYAS
HIPPOCRAS
HISTOGRAM
HISTORIAN
HODIERNAL
HOLDERBAT
HOMESTEAD
HOMICIDAL
HOOLACHAN
HORSEPLAY
HOUSEBOAT
HOUSECOAT
HUNGARIAN
HYDROSTAT
ICTERIDAE
IDENTICAL
ILLIBERAL
ILLOGICAL
IMPARTIAL
INAUGURAL
INSHALLAH
INSOMNIAC
INTERPLAY
IRREGULAR
ISALLOBAR
ISLAMABAD
ISODORIAN
JACKSTRAW
JETSTREAM

JOCKSTRAP
JORDANIAN
JURIDICAL
JUSTINIAN
KARAKORAM
KEPLARIAN
KHANSAMAH
KINSWOMAN
KLINOSTAT
LACHRYMAL
LACONICAL
LAMASERAI
LANDSMAAL
LAODICEAN
LAPSTREAK
LATTERDAY
LECANORAM
LENINGRAD
LEVIATHAN
LIBRARIAN
LIVERYMAN
LOCHINVAR
LOOSEHEAD
LOOSELEAF
MADRASSAH
MADRESSAH
MAHARAJAH
MALAYSIAN
MAMMALIAN
MANHATTAN
MARMOREAL
MARQUESAS
MARROWFAT
MARSUPIAL
MARTINEAU
MARTINMAS
MASTERMAN
MATUTINAL
MAURITIAN
MEANDRIAN
MEDIAEVAL
MEDICINAL
MEDMENHAM
MENIPPEAN
MENSTRUAL
MERCAPTAN
MERCURIAL
MIDDLEMAN
MIDSTREAM
MILLENIAL
MILLIGRAM
MINCEMEAT
MINUTEMAN
MOLECULAR
MONASTRAL
MONGOLIAN
MONOCULAR

MONTESPAN
MORTICIAN
MOTORBOAT
MOURNIVAL
MOUSETRAP
MRIDAMGAM
MRIDANGAM
MUNICIPAL
MUSKOGEAN
MUSSULMAN
NABATHEAN
NAPIERIAN
NERITIDAE
NOCTURNAL
NORWEGIAN
NUMERICAL
OARSWOMAN
OCCIPITAL
OCHLOCRAT
OCTAGONAL
ODDJOBMAN
OMBUDSMAN
OPOBALSAM
ORANGEMAN
ORATORIAN
ORBICULAR
ORGANICAL
OUTSPREAD
PALLADIAN
PALPEBRAL
PANCHAYAT
PANDEMIAN
PARANOIAC
PAROCHIAL
PASTERNAK
PATRICIAN
PATROLMAN
PAUSANIAS
PEDICULAR
PERENNIAL
PERGUNNAH
PERISCIAN
PERPETUAL
PETERSHAM
PETTICOAT
PHANSIGAR
PHIGALIAN
PHONOGRAM
PHOTOSTAT
PHYSICIAN
PICTOGRAM
PICTORIAL
PIECEMEAL
PIPEDREAM
PIPSQUEAK
PIRATICAL
PLAINSMAN

PLAUSTRAL
PLOUGHMAN
PLUMDAMAS
PLUTOCRAT
POINTSMAN
POLEMICAL
POLICEMAN
POLITICAL
POLYGONAL
POPLITEAL
PORIFERAN
PORTRAYAL
POSTNATAL
POSTWOMAN
POTENTIAL
POTTINGAR
POWERBOAT
PRACTICAL
PREBENDAL
PRECISIAN
PRESIDIAL
PREVERNAL
PRIMAEVAL
PRIMITIAE
PRINCIPAL
PRODROMAL
PROOFREAD
PROTHORAX
PROTOSTAR
PSYCHICAL
PTARMIGAN
PUERPERAL
PYRAMIDAL
QUANTICAL
QUIZZICAL
QUOTIDIAN
RACKSTRAW
RADDLEMAN
RADIOGRAM
RAPTORIAL
RATTLEBAG
RECTORIAL
REDSTREAK
REGISTRAR
REHEARSAL
REICHSRAT
REICHSTAG
RELIQUIAE
REPTILIAN
RESSALDAR
RETRIEVAL
REVICTUAL
RHODESIAN
ROADSTEAD
ROSMINIAN
ROTTERDAM
ROUMANIAN

ROUNCEVAL
ROUNCIVAL
ROUNDELAY
ROUNDHEAD
ROUNDSMAN
RUDDLEMAN
RUTHENIAN
SABBATIAN
SACRISTAN
SADDLEBAG
SALVARSAN
SAMARITAN
SARTORIAL
SASSAFRAS
SATIRICAL
SATURNIAN
SATYRIDAE
SATYRINAE
SAUCEBOAT
SCALLAWAG
SCALLYWAG
SCAPEGOAT
SCEPTICAL
SCHEHITAH
SCHOOLMAN
SCIARIDAE
SCLEROTAL
SCOTCHMAN
SCRIMSHAW
SCYTHEMAN
SEBASTIAN
SECTARIAN
SECTIONAL
SECTORIAL
SELJUKIAN
SEMIFINAL
SENESCHAL
SERBONIAN
SHAMIANAH
SHARESMAN
SHECHINAH
SHECHITAH
SHEEPMEAT
SHEWBREAD
SHORTSTAY
SIGNALMAN
SILURIDAE
SIRBONIAN
SISYPHEAN
SKEPTICAL
SKETCHMAP
SKETCHPAD
SLOVENIAN
SOLFIDIAN
SPEARHEAD
SPEEDBOAT
SPHERICAL
SPILLICAN
SPIRITUAL
SPOILSMAN
SPOKESMAN
SPONGEBAG
SPORTSMAN
STABLELAD
STABLEMAN
STATESMAN
STEAMBOAT
STEELHEAD
STEENBRAS
STEERSMAN
STERADIAN
STERCORAL
STONEBOAT
STONECHAT
STORNAWAY
STREETCAR
SUBCELLAR
SUBNORMAL
SUCCURSAL
SUFFRAGAN
SUPERSTAR
SUPPLICAT
SWEETMEAT
SWORDPLAY
SWORDSMAN
SYRPHIDAE
TABANIDAE
TACAMAHAC
TACTICIAN
TAHSILDAR
TANZANIAN
TARTAREAN
TASMANIAN
TECHNICAL
TECTORIAL
TEIRESIAS
TELLURIAN
TETRAGRAM
THACKERAY
THICKHEAD
THIRDSMAN
THROWAWAY
THYESTEAN
TIGHTHEAD
TIPULIDAE
TITTLEBAT
TOTTENHAM
TRADESMAN
TRAFALGAR
TRAGEDIAN
TRANSVAAL
TRAPEZIAL
TREVELYAN
TRIBESMAN
TRIENNIAL
TRIUMPHAL
TROUSSEAU
TRUCKLOAD
UKRAINIAN
UMBILICAL
UNDERCOAT
UNDERSEAL
UNDERWEAR
UNETHICAL
UNISEXUAL
UNITARIAN
UNIVERSAL
UNMUSICAL
UNNATURAL
UNPOPULAR
UNTYPICAL
UPANISHAD
UREDINIAL
URICONIAN
URUGUAYAN
VARANGIAN
VEHICULAR
VERIDICAL
VERSIONAL
VERTEBRAE
VERTEBRAL
VESICULAR
VESPASIAN
VESTIGIAL
VICEREGAL
VICTORIAN
VIGESIMAL
VIRGINIAN
VITRUVIAN
VOLGOGRAD
VOLKSRAAD
VULGARIAN
WAGNERIAN
WAGONLOAD
WAISTCOAT
WALLYDRAG
WAPINSHAW
WASHERMAN
WASSERMAN
WEDNESDAY
WENCESLAS
WHALEBOAT
WHALEMEAT
WHEATMEAL
WHERRYMAN
WHIMSICAL
WHITEHEAD
WHOLEMEAL
WINDBREAK
YACHTSMAN
YESTERDAY
ASTROLABE
BURKINABE
CATACOMBS
FLASHCUBE
GARDEROBE
HAMMURABI
MORECAMBE
PRESCRIBE
PROSCRIBE
STANDERBY
SUBSCRIBE
WATERBABY
XENOPHOBE
ABERRANCE
ABOUTFACE
ABUNDANCE
ACOUSTICS
ACQUIESCE
ADHERENCE
AEROSPACE
AFFLUENCE
ALLOWANCE
AMBULANCE
ANABRANCH
ANNOYANCE
APPLEJACK
APPLIANCE
ARCHITECT
ARMISTICE
ARROGANCE
ASSONANCE
ASSURANCE
ATHLETICS
AUTOCRACY
AVOIDANCE
AWESTRUCK
BACHARACH
BACKBENCH
BACKSPACE
BACKTRACK
BARMBRACK
BILLYCOCK
BLACKFACE
BLACKJACK
BLOWTORCH
BREAKNECK
BULLFINCH
BYPRODUCT
CANDIDACY
CAPTAINCY
CARTTRACK
CEROMANCY
CEVAPCICI
CHAFFINCH
CHEAPJACK
CLEARANCE
COCKROACH
COHERENCE
CONSTANCE
CONSTANCY
CONSTRICT
CONSTRUCT
CONTUMACY
COSMETICS
COVALENCY
COWARDICE
CROOKBACK
DALLIANCE
DECADENCE
DEFERENCE
DEMOCRACY
DIANETICS
DIDACTICS
DIETETICS
DILIGENCE
DIPLOMACY
DISINFECT
DOMINANCE
DRAMATICS
DRUMSTICK
ECONOMICS
EFFLUENCE
ELOQUENCE
EMERGENCE
EMERGENCY
ENDURANCE
ESPERANCE
ESTHETICS
EXISTENCE
EYESPLICE
FASTTRACK
FIREPLACE
FLAGRANCE
FLASHBACK
FLINTLOCK
FLIPPANCY
FORASMUCH
FORTALICE
FOURPENCE
FRAGRANCE
FRAGRANCY
FRANCESCA
FREDERICK
FREELANCE
FREQUENCY
FROGMARCH
GEARSTICK
GENUFLECT
GOLDFINCH
GOOSENECK
GREENBACK
GREENWICH
GRIEVANCE
GYROMANCY
HAIRPIECE
HANDPIECE
HARMONICA
HATCHBACK
HAVERSACK
HEMISTICH
HEMSTITCH
HESITANCE
HESITANCY
HEXASTICH
HEXATEUCH
HINDRANCE
HITCHCOCK
HOLLYHOCK
HOPSCOTCH
HORSEBACK
HUCKABACK
HUNCHBACK
HYSTERICS
IGNORANCE
IMBALANCE
IMMANENCE
IMMANENCY
IMMEDIACY
IMMINENCE
IMPEDANCE
IMPERFECT
IMPOTENCE
IMPUDENCE
INCIDENCE
INCORRECT
INDECENCY
INDIGENCE
INDOLENCE
INFERENCE
INFLUENCE
INJUSTICE
INNOCENCE
INSOLENCE
INSURANCE
INTELLECT
INTERDICT
INTERFACE
INTERJECT
INTERLACE
INTERLOCK
INTERSECT
INTRICACY
INTRODUCE
INTUMESCE
JOUISANCE
JUBILANCE
KNOBSTICK
LAMPBLACK
LASTDITCH
LINTSTOCK
LIQUORICE

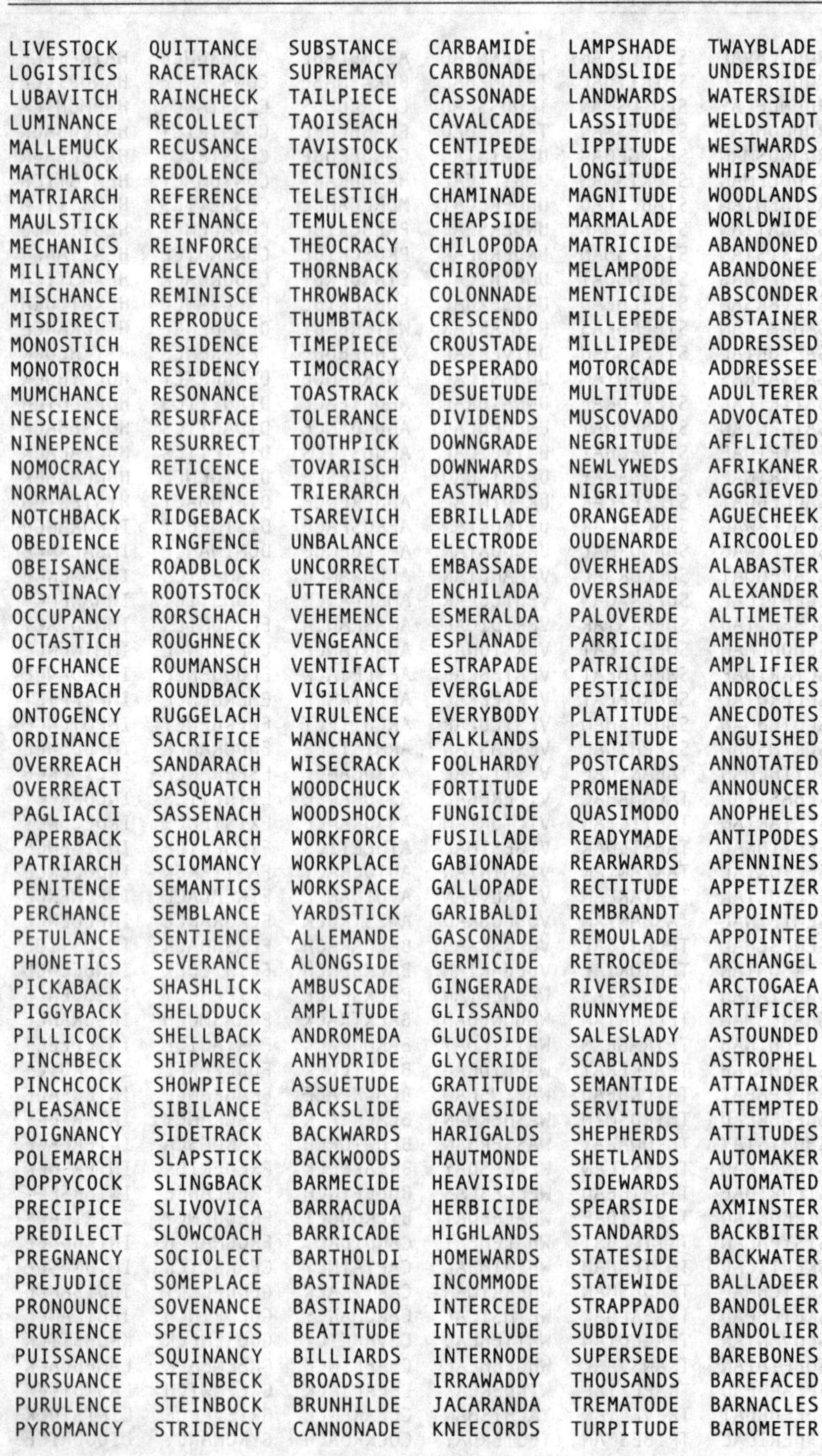

LIVESTOCK
LOGISTICS
LUBAVITCH
LUMINANCE
MALLEMUCK
MATCHLOCK
MATRIARCH
MAULSTICK
MECHANICS
MILITANCY
MISCHANCE
MISDIRECT
MONOSTICH
MONOTROCH
MUMCHANCE
NESCIENCE
NINEPENCE
NOMOCRACY
NORMALACY
NOTCHBACK
OBEDIENCE
OBEISANCE
OBSTINACY
OCCUPANCY
OCTASTICH
OFFCHANCE
OFFENBACH
ONTOGENCY
ORDINANCE
OVERREACH
OVERREACT
PAGLIACCI
PAPERBACK
PATRIARCH
PENITENCE
PERCHANCE
PETULANCE
PHONETICS
PICKABACK
PIGGYBACK
PILLICOCK
PINCHBECK
PINCHCOCK
PLEASANCE
POIGNANCY
POLEMARCH
POPPYCOCK
PRECIPICE
PREDILECT
PREGNANCY
PREJUDICE
PRONOUNCE
PRURIENCE
PUISSANCE
PURSUANCE
PURULENCE
PYROMANCY
QUITTANCE
RACETRACK
RAINCHECK
RECOLLECT
RECUSANCE
REDOLENCE
REFERENCE
REFINANCE
REINFORCE
RELEVANCE
REMINISCE
REPRODUCE
RESIDENCE
RESIDENCY
RESONANCE
RESURFACE
RESURRECT
RETICENCE
REVERENCE
RIDGEBACK
RINGFENCE
ROADBLOCK
ROOTSTOCK
RORSCHACH
ROUGHNECK
ROUMANSCH
ROUNDBACK
RUGGELACH
SACRIFICE
SANDARACH
SASQUATCH
SASSENACH
SCHOLARCH
SCIOMANCY
SEMANTICS
SEMBLANCE
SENTIENCE
SEVERANCE
SHASHLICK
SHELDDUCK
SHELLBACK
SHIPWRECK
SHOWPIECE
SIBILANCE
SIDETRACK
SLAPSTICK
SLINGBACK
SLIVOVICA
SLOWCOACH
SOCIOLECT
SOMEPLACE
SOVENANCE
SPECIFICS
SQUINANCY
STEINBECK
STEINBOCK
STRIDENCY
SUBSTANCE
SUPREMACY
TAILPIECE
TAOISEACH
TAVISTOCK
TECTONICS
TELESTICH
TEMULENCE
THEOCRACY
THORNBACK
THROWBACK
THUMBTACK
TIMEPIECE
TIMOCRACY
TOASTRACK
TOLERANCE
TOOTHPICK
TOVARISCH
TRIERARCH
TSAREVICH
UNBALANCE
UNCORRECT
UTTERANCE
VEHEMENCE
VENGEANCE
VENTIFACT
VIGILANCE
VIRULENCE
WANCHANCY
WISECRACK
WOODCHUCK
WOODSHOCK
WORKFORCE
WORKPLACE
WORKSPACE
YARDSTICK
ALLEMANDE
ALONGSIDE
AMBUSCADE
AMPLITUDE
ANDROMEDA
ANHYDRIDE
ASSUETUDE
BACKSLIDE
BACKWARDS
BACKWOODS
BARMECIDE
BARRACUDA
BARRICADE
BARTHOLDI
BASTINADE
BASTINADO
BEATITUDE
BILLIARDS
BROADSIDE
BRUNHILDE
CANNONADE
CARBAMIDE
CARBONADE
CASSONADE
CAVALCADE
CENTIPEDE
CERTITUDE
CHAMINADE
CHEAPSIDE
CHILOPODA
CHIROPODY
COLONNADE
CRESCENDO
CROUSTADE
DESPERADO
DESUETUDE
DIVIDENDS
DOWNGRADE
DOWNWARDS
EASTWARDS
EBRILLADE
ELECTRODE
EMBASSADE
ENCHILADA
ESMERALDA
ESPLANADE
ESTRAPADE
EVERGLADE
EVERYBODY
FALKLANDS
FOOLHARDY
FORTITUDE
FUNGICIDE
FUSILLADE
GABIONADE
GALLOPADE
GARIBALDI
GASCONADE
GERMICIDE
GINGERADE
GLISSANDO
GLUCOSIDE
GLYCERIDE
GRATITUDE
GRAVESIDE
HARIGALDS
HAUTMONDE
HEAVISIDE
HERBICIDE
HIGHLANDS
HOMEWARDS
INCOMMODE
INTERCEDE
INTERLUDE
INTERNODE
IRRAWADDY
JACARANDA
KNEECORDS
LAMPSHADE
LANDSLIDE
LANDWARDS
LASSITUDE
LIPPITUDE
LONGITUDE
MAGNITUDE
MARMALADE
MATRICIDE
MELAMPODE
MENTICIDE
MILLEPEDE
MILLIPEDE
MOTORCADE
MULTITUDE
MUSCOVADO
NEGRITUDE
NEWLYWEDS
NIGRITUDE
ORANGEADE
OUDENARDE
OVERHEADS
OVERSHADE
PALOVERDE
PARRICIDE
PATRICIDE
PESTICIDE
PLATITUDE
PLENITUDE
POSTCARDS
PROMENADE
QUASIMODO
READYMADE
REARWARDS
RECTITUDE
REMBRANDT
REMOULADE
RETROCEDE
RIVERSIDE
RUNNYMEDE
SALESLADY
SCABLANDS
SEMANTIDE
SERVITUDE
SHEPHERDS
SHETLANDS
SIDEWARDS
SPEARSIDE
STANDARDS
STATESIDE
STATEWIDE
STRAPPADO
SUBDIVIDE
SUPERSEDE
THOUSANDS
TREMATODE
TURPITUDE
TWAYBLADE
UNDERSIDE
WATERSIDE
WELDSTADT
WESTWARDS
WHIPSNADE
WOODLANDS
WORLDWIDE
ABANDONED
ABANDONEE
ABSCONDER
ABSTAINER
ADDRESSED
ADDRESSEE
ADULTERER
ADVOCATED
AFFLICTED
AFRIKANER
AGGRIEVED
AGUECHEEK
AIRCOOLED
ALABASTER
ALEXANDER
ALTIMETER
AMENHOTEP
AMPLIFIER
ANDROCLES
ANECDOTES
ANGUISHED
ANNOTATED
ANNOUNCER
ANOPHELES
ANTIPODES
APENNINES
APPETIZER
APPOINTED
APPOINTEE
ARCHANGEL
ARCTOGAEA
ARTIFICER
ASTOUNDED
ASTROPHEL
ATTAINDER
ATTEMPTED
ATTITUDES
AUTOMAKER
AUTOMATED
AXMINSTER
BACKBITER
BACKWATER
BALLADEER
BANDOLEER
BANDOLIER
BAREBONES
BAREFACED
BARNACLES
BAROMETER

BARRISTER
BARTENDER
BATHTOWEL
BEARDSLEY
BECQUEREL
BEDJACKET
BEDRIDDEN
BEDSITTER
BEEFEATER
BEEKEEPER
BEETHOVEN
BELEAGUER
BENIGHTED
BERGANDER
BETHLEHEM
BETROTHED
BIGHEADED
BLINKERED
BLISTERED
BLOODSHED
BLUNDERER
BLUSTERER
BOANERGES
BOOKLOVER
BOOKMAKER
BOOTLACES
BREAKAGES
BREAKEVEN
BRIGADIER
BRUMMAGEM
BUCCANEER
BULLDOZER
BUMBLEBEE
BYSTANDER
CABRIOLET
CALVITIES
CAMCORDER
CANVASSER
CARETAKER
CARPENTER
CARTWHEEL
CASSOULET
CASTRATED
CATTLEPEN
CERTIFIED
CERVANTES
CHARACTER
CHARTERED
CHASTENED
CHATTERER
CHAVENDER
CHEQUERED
CHERISHED
CHERNOZEM
CHEVALIER
CHICKADEE
CHICKWEED
CHISELLER
CHLAMYDES
CHORISTER
CIVILISED
CIVILIZED
CLARIFIER
CLUSTERED
COALESCED
COALMINER
COCKATIEL
COLLECTED
COLOMBIER
COMFORTER
COMMANDER
COMMITTED
COMMITTEE
COMPANIES
COMPELLED
COMPOTIER
CONCEALED
CONCEITED
CONCERNED
CONCERTED
CONCLUDED
CONCUSSED
CONDEMNED
CONDENSER
CONFESSED
CONFIRMED
CONFLATED
CONGERIES
CONGESTED
CONNECTED
CONSIGNEE
CONTAINER
CONTEMPER
CONTENDER
CONTENTED
CONTRIVED
CONTRIVER
CONVERTED
CONVERTER
CONVINCED
CORIANDER
CORKSCREW
CORRECTED
CORRUPTER
COSTUMIER
COUNTRIES
COUTURIER
CRICKETER
CROSSBRED
CROSSEYED
CROSSOVER
CRUSTACEA
CRYOMETER
DAMBUSTER
DANDIFIED
DASHWHEEL
DEBAUCHED
DEBAUCHEE
DECORATED
DEDICATED
DEFAULTER
DELIGHTED
DELIVERER
DEPRESSED
DERRINGER
DESCARTES
DESTROYED
DESTROYER
DEVELOPED
DEVELOPER
DIARRHOEA
DIGNIFIED
DINNERSET
DIOCLETES
DISBELIEF
DISBURDEN
DISCARDED
DISCLOSED
DISGRACED
DISGUISED
DISGUSTED
DISHWATER
DISMEMBER
DISPENSER
DISPERSED
DISPLACED
DISPLAYED
DISSENTER
DISSOLVED
DISTEMPER
DISTENDED
DISTILLER
DISTORTED
DISTURBED
DISUNITED
DOLOMITES
DOMICILED
DONCASTER
DUNGAREES
DUNGEONER
DYNAMITED
EASTERNER
ECARDINES
ECOSYSTEM
ELASTOMER
ELEVENSES
ELONGATED
EMACIATED
EMBATTLED
EMBEZZLER
EMBROIDER
EMBROILED
EMPLOYEES
ENAMELLED
ENAMOURED
ENCHANTED
ENCHANTER
ENCIRCLED
ENCOUNTER
ENERGUMEN
ENGRAINED
ENGROSSED
ENGROSSER
ENLIGHTEN
ENLIVENED
ENQUIRIES
ENSCONCED
ENTRAMMEL
ENTRANCED
EPHIALTES
EPISTOLER
EQUALIZER
ERGATANER
ERIOMETER
ESTAMINET
ESTRANGED
ETIOLATED
EUMENIDES
EUMYCETES
EUPHRATES
EURIPIDES
EVERGREEN
EXCHEQUER
EXCLAIMED
EXERCISED
EXERCISES
EXHAUSTED
EXPLOITER
EXPRESSED
EYELETEER
EYEOPENER
FASHIONED
FEATHERED
FENCIBLES
FENUGREEK
FERINGHEE
FERMENTED
FILICALES
FILLIPEEN
FILLISTER
FILMMAKER
FINANCIER
FIREWATER
FIRSTEVER
FLAGEOLET
FLAMSTEED
FLATTENED
FLATTENER
FLATTERED
FLATTERER
FLAVOURED
FLOWERBED
FLUSTERED
FORBIDDEN
FOREIGNER
FORFEITED
FORGATHER
FORGOTTEN
FORWANDER
FOURWHEEL
FREEWHEEL
FREIGHTER
FRENCHMEN
FRESHENER
FRICASSEE
FROBISHER
FRUITERER
FUNGIBLES
GAINSAYER
GALIONGEE
GARNISHEE
GARRYOWEN
GASHOLDER
GASOMETER
GAULEITER
GAZETTEER
GEARLEVER
GEARWHEEL
GENTLEMEN
GERMANCER
GERMANDER
GLENDOWER
GLENLIVET
GLORIFIED
GOBETWEEN
GODDESSES
GODFATHER
GODMOTHER
GONDOLIER
GOOSANDER
GOOSESTEP
GOSPELLER
GRADUATED
GRAPETREE
GREENFEED
GREENWEED
GRENADIER
GRINGOLET
GROCERIES
GROUNDSEL
GUARANTEE
GUNPOWDER
HACKNEYED
HALFBAKED
HALFDOZEN
HALLOWEEN
HAMBURGER
HAMFATTER
HAMFISTED
HARBINGER
HARDANGER
HARDCOVER
HARDLINER
HARPOONER
HARVESTER
HAYMARKET
HEADLINED
HEDERATED
HENPECKED
HEREAFTER
HERPESTES
HEXAMETER
HIGHFLYER
HIGHSPEED
HOBNAILED
HODOMETER
HOLINSHED
HOMEOWNER
HORRIFIED
HOTHEADED
HUMDINGER
HYDRANGEA
HYLOBATES
IBUPROFEN
ICELANDER
ILCHESTER
ILLGOTTEN
IMMUNISER
IMPEACHER
IMPOUNDER
IMPRESSED
INCREASED
INDICATES
INDWELLER
INFIELDER
INGRAINED
INHERITED
INHIBITED
INITIATED
INNISFREE
INNKEEPER
INSCRIBED
INSTANTER
INSWINGER
INTERBRED
INTERPRET
INTERVIEW
INTRIGUED
INTRIGUER
IRONSIDES
IRRITATED
ISOCRATES

ISOSCELES
JAMPACKED
JAUNDICED
JAYWALKER
JERAHMEEL
JERKWATER
JERUSALEM
JOBSEEKER
JOCKTELEG
JUSTIFIED
KARABINER
KEYHOLDER
KIDNAPPED
KIDNAPPER
KILLARNEY
KILOMETER
KINGMAKER
KINGSIZED
KISSINGER
KITCHENER
KLEMPERER
KNACKERED
KONIMETER
LACERATED
LAMINATED
LANCASTER
LANDAULET
LANDLOPER
LANDOWNER
LANGSPIEL
LANGUAGES
LAPLANDER
LATECOMER
LAVOISIER
LAWMONGER
LAWNMOWER
LAZYBONES
LEICESTER
LEVERAGED
LIBERATED
LIBERTIES
LIMBURGER
LINKLATER
LIQUEFIED
LOCALIZED
LONGLIVED
LOWLANDER
LYSIMETER
MAGNIFIER
MAHARANEE
MALFORMED
MALLANDER
MALLENDER
MANOMETER
MARKETEER
MASSINGER
MAYFLOWER
MEDICATED
MEDRESSEH
MEHITABEL
MEKOMETER
MEMORITER
MENOMINEE
MENTIONED
MENUISIER
MERGANSER
MESSENGER
METAPELET
MIDDLESEX
MIDSUMMER
MIDWINTER
MILOMETER
MINELAYER
MISFALLEN
MISGUIDED
MISPICKEL
MISPLACED
MISSHAPEN
MISSIONER
MISTEMPER
MOLLITIES
MONOMETER
MOONRAKER
MORTGAGEE
MORTIFIED
MOSCHATEL
MOTHEATEN
MOYGASHEL
MUCHLOVED
MUCKENDER
MUCORALES
MUFFETTEE
MULTIPLEX
MUSKETEER
MUTILATED
MYSTERIES
NANTUCKET
NATHANIEL
NAUSEATED
NEBBISHER
NEGLECTED
NEUCHATEL
NEWMARKET
NEWSPAPER
NEWSSHEET
NICKNEVEN
NONSMOKER
NOSEBLEED
NOTEPAPER
NUTJOBBER
OBSEQUIES
OCEANIDES
OESTROGEN
OILTANKER
ONCOMETER
OPENENDED
OPPRESSED
ORGANISED
ORGANISER
ORGANIZED
ORGANIZER
ORTHOPTER
OURSELVES
OUTFITTER
OUTNUMBER
OUTRIGGER
OUTROOPER
OUTSPOKEN
OUTWORKER
OVERJOYED
OVERPOWER
OVERRATED
OVERRIDER
OVERSHOES
OVERSIZED
OVERSLEEP
OVERSTEER
OVERTONES
PACEMAKER
PALANKEEN
PARAMETER
PARTICLES
PARTTIMER
PASSENGER
PASSEPIED
PATTERNED
PAYMASTER
PEASEWEEP
PEDIGREES
PEDOMETER
PENPUSHER
PENSIONER
PERFORMED
PERFORMER
PERIANDER
PERIMETER
PERMITTED
PERPLEXED
PERSONNEL
PERSUADED
PERTURBED
PERVERTED
PETRIFIED
PETTITOES
PHALANGER
PHELLOGEN
PHILANDER
PHILISTER
PHILLABEG
PHILLIBEG
PICNICKER
PIEPOWDER
PIGHEADED
PIMPERNEL
PINHOOKER
PISTAREEN
PISTOLEER
PLASTERED
PLASTERER
PLUNDERER
POETASTER
POLYESTER
POPULATED
PORPOISES
PORRINGER
POSSESSED
POSSIBLES
POSTPONED
POTBOILER
POTHUNTER
POULTERER
PRACTISED
PRANKSTER
PREFERRED
PREPOLLEX
PRESBYTER
PRESENTED
PRESENTER
PRESERVED
PRESERVER
PRESERVES
PRETENDER
PRIESTLEY
PRIVATEER
PROBABLES
PROFESSED
PROFITEER
PROJECTED
PROKOFIEV
PROLONGED
PROPELLED
PROPELLER
PROTESTER
PROVENDER
PUBLISHED
PUBLISHER
PULPITEER
PUMMELLED
PUPPETEER
PURCHASER
QUADRUPED
QUALIFIED
QUALIFIER
QUARENDEN
QUICKSTEP
QUODLIBET
RACKETEER
RAINWATER
RAMILLIES
RATEPAYER
REALITIES
RECLAIMED
RECLAIMER
RECOVERED
RECTIFIER
REDHANDED
REDHEADED
REDLETTER
REFRESHER
REISTAFEL
REJOINDER
REMAINDER
RENTALLER
REPRESSED
RESOURCES
RESPECTED
RESPECTER
RETRIEVER
RETROFLEX
RHYMESTER
RICHELIEU
RILLETTES
RINGSIDER
ROISTERER
ROSEWATER
SAFFLOWER
SALTPETER
SALTWATER
SANDALLED
SANDPAPER
SANDPIPER
SAPSUCKER
SATISFIED
SATURATED
SAUTERNES
SCALLOPED
SCANSORES
SCARIFIER
SCATTERED
SCAVENGER
SCHLEMIEL
SCHLENTER
SCHLIEREN
SCHMIEDER
SCHMUTTER
SCHNAPPER
SCHNAUZER
SCHNECKEN
SCHNITZEL
SCHNORKEL
SCHNORRER
SCISSORER
SCLAUNDER
SCOUNDREL
SCRAMBLER
SCRATCHED
SCRATCHES
SCRIVENER
SCRODDLED
SCROUNGER
SCUDDALER
SEGMENTED
SEPARATED
SEPTEMBER
SEPULCHER
SEQUESTER
SEQUINNED
SERASKIER
SERENADER
SEVENTEEN
SHARPENER
SHATTERED
SHELTERED
SHILLABER
SHIPOWNER
SHOEMAKER
SHOVELLER
SHUTTERED
SIEGFRIED
SIGHTSEER
SIGNALLER
SIMULATED
SINGLESEX
SINGSPIEL
SINKANSEN
SKINDIVER
SKYJACKER
SLAUGHTER
SLUMBERER
SMOKEFREE
SNAKEWEED
SNOWSHOES
SOBRIQUET
SOFTCOVER
SOLLICKER
SOMETIMES
SOMMELIER
SONNETEER
SONOMETER
SOPHISTER
SOPHOCLES
SOTTISIER
SOUWESTER
SPATTERED
SPECIFIED
SPELUNKER
SPHINCTER
SPIDERWEB
SPINDRIER
SPINNAKER
SPINNERET
SPONSORED

SPOONFEED
SPORTSMEN
SPRINGLET
SPRINKLER
STAGGERED
STAMMERER
STARGAZER
STATIONED
STATIONER
STAVANGER
STIFFENER
STINGAREE
STOCKINET
STONKERED
STORIATED
STRAGGLER
STRANGLER
STRANGLES
STRATAGEM
STRETCHED
STRETCHER
STUPEFIED
SUBCORTEX
SUBMERGED
SUBTITLED
SUCCEEDED
SUNBATHER
SUNDOWNER
SUNFLOWER
SUNSCREEN
SUNTANNED
SUPPORTER
SURFEITED
SURMULLET
SURPRISED
SURRENDER
SUSPECTED
SUSPENDED
SUSPENDER
SUSTAINED
SWAGGERER
SWEETENER
SYLLABLES
TABASHEER
TABBOULEH
TAILLEFER
TAMOXIFEN
TAPDANCER
TARGETEER
TARMACKED
TASSELLED
TAXIMETER
TEARSHEET
TEESWATER
TELESALES
TENNESSEE
TERRIFIED
TESTICLES
TESTIFIER
THERSITES
THROWSTER
THUNDERER
TIGHTENER
TOLERATED
TONOMETER
TOPDRAWER
TORMENTER
TORTELIER
TOTALIZER
TOWCESTER
TRAMLINES
TRAVELLER
TREASURER
TREBUCHET
TRIANGLED
TRIBESMEN
TRICKSTER
TRIMESTER
TRINKETER
TRIPMETER
TRUMPETER
TRUNCATED
TUILERIES
ULLSWATER
UNABASHED
UNADOPTED
UNALLOYED
UNALTERED
UNASHAMED
UNBIASSED
UNBOUNDED
UNBRIDLED
UNCHANGED
UNCHARGED
UNCHECKED
UNCLAIMED
UNCLOTHED
UNCLOUDED
UNCOUPLED
UNCOVERED
UNCROSSED
UNCROWNED
UNDAMAGED
UNDAUNTED
UNDECIDED
UNDEFILED
UNDEFINED
UNDERBRED
UNDILUTED
UNDIVIDED
UNDOUBTED
UNDRESSED
UNEQUALED
UNEXPOSED
UNFLEDGED
UNFOUNDED
UNGUARDED
UNIFORMED
UNINJURED
UNINVITED
UNLEARNED
UNLIMITED
UNMARRIED
UNMATCHED
UNNOTICED
UNOPPOSED
UNREFINED
UNRELATED
UNRUFFLED
UNSCATHED
UNSECURED
UNSETTLED
UNSKILLED
UNSPOILED
UNSULLIED
UNTOUCHED
UNTRAINED
UNTREATED
UNTRODDEN
UNTUTORED
UNWATERED
UNWORRIED
UNWRITTEN
UPHOLSTER
VALDENSES
VANCOUVER
VAPORIZER
VELASQUEZ
VELDSKOEN
VELVETEEN
VERSIFIER
VIDELICET
VOLTMETER
VOLUNTEER
WAGHALTER
WALDENSES
WALLABIES
WALLPAPER
WAMBENGER
WARMONGER
WASTWATER
WATERSHED
WATERWEED
WEBFOOTED
WELSUMMER
WESTERNER
WHICHEVER
WHITTAWER
WHOSOEVER
WILLESDEN
WILLPOWER
WINDHOVER
WITNESSED
WOMANISER
WOMANIZER
WOODBORER
WORCESTER
WORMEATEN
WRONGDOER
WURLITZER
YACHTSMEN
YOUNGSTER
ZEALANDER
ZINFANDEL
ZOROASTER
CANDYTUFT
CHAIRLIFT
DIVERSIFY
ELECTRIFY
EXEMPLIFY
FEEDSTUFF
FLAGSTAFF
FOODSTUFF
GEARSHIFT
HALFSTAFF
HANDCUFFS
HOUSEWIFE
INDEMNIFY
INTENSIFY
JACKKNIFE
MAKESHIFT
OVERDRAFT
PECKSNIFF
PERSONIFY
PIKESTAFF
PLAINTIFF
RADCLIFFE
SKEWWHIFF
SNOWDRIFT
SPEECHIFY
SPINDRIFT
VOUCHSAFE
WOODCRAFT
ADVANTAGE
ANCHORAGE
ANTHOLOGY
APPENDAGE
ARBITRAGE
ASTROLOGY
BACKSTAGE
BEESTINGS
BEVERIDGE
BLESSINGS
BOBSLEIGH
BRADLAUGH
BROKERAGE
CAMBRIDGE
CARTILAGE
CARTRIDGE
CHALLENGE
CHAMPAIGN
CHIPPINGS
COLERIDGE
CONCIERGE
COSMOLOGY
CURETTAGE
CURTILAGE
DEMURRAGE
DIAPHRAGM
DISCHARGE
DISENGAGE
DISOBLIGE
DISPARAGE
DOWNSTAGE
DROPPINGS
EASTLINGS
EDINBURGH
EMBASSAGE
EMPENNAGE
ENCOURAGE
ENGRENAGE
ENTOURAGE
EPIPHRAGM
ESPIONAGE
ETHNOLOGY
ETYMOLOGY
FEBRIFUGE
FORESTAGE
FORTILAGE
GALRAVAGE
GENEALOGY
GLEANINGS
GREENGAGE
GREETINGS
HERMITAGE
HISTOLOGY
HOPLOLOGY
HYPALLAGE
INCOMINGS
KENTLEDGE
KINKCOUGH
KINTLEDGE
KNOWLEDGE
LANGRIDGE
LINDBERGH
LONGRANGE
MACROLOGY
MADARIAGA
MALEBOLGE
MIDDLINGS
MISMANAGE
MYTHOLOGY
NEUROLOGY
NOSTOLOGY
ORPHANAGE
ORTHOLOGY
OUTGOINGS
OVERWEIGH
PARENTAGE
PARSONAGE
PARTRIDGE
PASTURAGE
PATHOLOGY
PATRONAGE
PERSONAGE
PETROLOGY
PHILOLOGY
PHONOLOGY
PILFERAGE
PORTERAGE
PRIVILEGE
PUCELLAGE
PUPILLAGE
RADIOLOGY
RAINGAUGE
REARRANGE
REPECHAGE
REPORTAGE
SACRILEGE
SAXIFRAGE
SCRAPINGS
SCRIMMAGE
SCRUMMAGE
SEMIOLOGY
SHEERLEGS
SHRINKAGE
SOCIOLOGY
SORTILEGE
SOURDOUGH
SOVEREIGN
SPICILEGE
SQUIREAGE
STOCKINGS
STREETAGE
SURCHARGE
SWEEPINGS
TAUTOLOGY
TELEOLOGY
TETRALOGY
THINNINGS
TONBRIDGE
TRAPPINGS
TREILLAGE
TRIBOLOGY
TRIMMINGS
UNDERSIGN
VELLENAGE
VERMIFUGE
WAITERAGE
WINNEBAGO
ABERNETHY
ALGORITHM

ALLOPATHY
ANTIPATHY
APOCRYPHA
ARKWRIGHT
AVALANCHE
BELLYACHE
BIOGRAPHY
BULLFIGHT
BURROUGHS
CARTOUCHE
COCKFIGHT
COPYRIGHT
DEADLIGHT
DOWNRIGHT
DYSTROPHY
ENSHEATHE
ENTELECHY
EYEBRIGHT
FIRELIGHT
FLYWEIGHT
FORESIGHT
FORTNIGHT
GAELTACHT
GEOGRAPHY
GOODNIGHT
GUILLOCHE
GUJARATHI
HEADLIGHT
HEARTACHE
HIERARCHY
HIGHLIGHT
HINDSIGHT
IDEOPATHY
INDRAUGHT
JEPHTHAHS
LAMPLIGHT
LATENIGHT
LIMELIGHT
LOGARITHM
MAHARISHI
MOGADISHU
MONOMACHY
MOONLIGHT
MOUSTACHE
NIETZSCHE
OLIGARCHY
ONSLAUGHT
OPSIMATHY
ORICALCHE
OROBANCHE
OROGRAPHY
OVERNIGHT
OVERSIGHT
PARFLECHE
ROXBURGHE
RUSHLIGHT
SCHLEMIHL

SCIAMACHY
SEANNACHY
SEAWORTHY
SIDELIGHT
SKIAMACHY
SKINTIGHT
SPOTLIGHT
STARLIGHT
TAILLIGHT
TELEPATHY
TETRARCHY
THEOSOPHY
TOOTHACHE
TROSSACHS
TUMMYACHE
UNHEALTHY
UNSHEATHE
WANWORTHY
ACARIASIS
ACROBATIC
ACROPOLIS
ADRENALIN
AEPYORNIS
AEROTAXIS
AESTHETIC
AFFIDAVIT
AFLATOXIN
AFORESAID
AGALACTIC
ALCOHOLIC
ALEURITIS
ALGEBRAIC
ALLANTOID
ALLANTOIS
AMARANTIN
AMARYLLIS
AMAUROSIS
AMBERGRIS
AMBLYOPIA
ANAEROBIC
ANALEPTIC
ANALGESIA
ANALGESIC
ANASTASIA
ANIMISTIC
ANKYLOSIS
ANNAPOLIS
ANTARCTIC
ANTIHELIX
ANTITOXIC
ANTITOXIN
ANTIVENIN
APARTHEID
APATHETIC
APERIODIC
APOPHATIC
APOPHYSIS

APOSTOLIC
APPERTAIN
AQUILEGIA
ARACHNOID
ARAUCARIA
ARTEMISIA
ARTHRITIC
ARTHRITIS
ARTHROSIS
ASCERTAIN
ASTHMATIC
ASYNERGIA
ATAVISTIC
ATHEISTIC
AUBRIETIA
AUSTRALIA
AUTHENTIC
AUTOLYSIS
AUTOMATIC
AUTONOMIC
AXIOMATIC
BAINMARIE
BALDAQUIN
BALLISTIC
BARAGOUIN
BARTHOLIN
BECHSTEIN
BERNSTEIN
BILIRUBIN
BIRDBRAIN
BISHOPRIC
BLACKMAIL
BOATSWAIN
BOCCACCIO
BOLSHEVIK
BOMBASTIC
BORNAGAIN
BOURGEOIS
BRASSERIE
BRITANNIA
BRITANNIC
CACHAEMIA
CACHECTIC
CAFETERIA
CALEDONIA
CALORIFIC
CALPURNIA
CANDLELIT
CANTHARIS
CAPRICCIO
CARPACCIO
CARYOPSIS
CASUISTIC
CATALYSIS
CATALYTIC
CATATONIA
CATATONIC

CATHARSIS
CATHARTIC
CATHEPSIN
CELLULOID
CERATITIS
CHALIAPIN
CHAMFRAIN
CHAMPLAIN
CHAROLAIS
CHARYBDIS
CHIEFTAIN
CHILBLAIN
CHINOVNIK
CHONDROID
CHROMATIC
CHRYSALIS
CINEMATIC
CINERARIA
CIRRHOSIS
CLIMACTIC
COCKSWAIN
CORREGGIO
COURTSHIP
COXSACKIE
CRYOGENIC
CUCHULAIN
CYNEGETIC
DAIRYMAID
DAREDEVIL
DECKCHAIR
DELACROIX
DIABLERIE
DIACRITIC
DIAERESIS
DIAGNOSIS
DIALECTIC
DIAMETRIC
DIANOETIC
DIASTASIS
DIATHESIS
DIAZEUXIS
DIGASTRIC
DIGITALIN
DIGITALIS
DISCOMFIT
DISCREDIT
DISREPAIR
DOLOMITIC
DUBROVNIK
DYSPEPSIA
DYSPEPTIC
DYSPHAGIA
ECCENTRIC
ECHEVERIA
ECLAMPSIA
EMBROGLIO
EMBRYONIC

EMPAESTIC
EMPHLYSIS
ENCANTHIS
ENCAUSTIC
ENDEICTIC
ENERGETIC
ENIGMATIC
ENTERITIS
ENTERTAIN
ENVERMEIL
EPEDAPHIC
EPHEMERIS
EPICLESIS
EPICYCLIC
EPIDERMIS
EPILEPTIC
EPINASTIC
EPIPHYSIS
EPIPHYTIC
EPISTAXIS
EPITHESIS
ESTRELDID
EUCHLORIC
EUPHORBIA
EUTROPHIC
EVANGELIC
EXECUTRIX
EXODERMIS
EXOSTOSIS
EXTRINSIC
EYESTRAIN
FANTASTIC
FILIGRAIN
FILMSTRIP
FILTERTIP
FINGERTIP
FINLANDIA
FLAGELLIN
FORJASKIT
FORJESKIT
FORSYTHIA
FRANCOLIN
FRANGLAIS
GENITALIA
GEOMETRIC
GEOMETRID
GERIATRIC
GODOLPHIN
GOMPHOSIS
GREENMAIL
GRIMALKIN
GROSGRAIN
GYMNASTIC
HALITOSIS
HANSEATIC
HARLEQUIN
HAYRADDIN

HECOGENIN
HEPATITIS
HETEROSIS
HEURISTIC
HOBGOBLIN
HONORIFIC
HORSEHAIR
HORSETAIL
HORSEWHIP
HOUSEMAID
HOWTOWDIE
HYDRAULIC
HYDROFOIL
HYPINOSIS
ICELANDIC
IDENTIKIT
IDIOMATIC
IMBROGLIO
IMPOLITIC
INDONESIA
INNISFAIL
INORGANIC
INTRINSIC
IPHIGENIA
ISCHAEMIC
ISOMETRIC
ISOTACTIC
ISOTROPIC
JACQUERIE
JUVENILIA
KERATITIS
KILDERKIN
KLENDUSIC
KNIPHOFIA
KROPOTKIN
LEITMOTIF
LEITMOTIV
LETHARGIC
LEUKAEMIA
LIENTERIC
LIGHTSHIP
LITHUANIA
LOHENGRIN
LOMBARDIC
LUCIFERIN
LYMPHATIC
MACADAMIA
MACARONIC
MACEDONIA
MACKENZIE
MACQUARIE
MADAROSIS
MANNEQUIN
MAVOURNIN
MELANESIA
MELANOTIC
MENAGERIE

MENSHEVIK
MESSIANIC
METABASIS
METABOLIC
METALLOID
METEOROID
METHEGLIN
MICROCHIP
MIDRASHIM
MISTIGRIS
MONATOMIC
MONOMANIA
MORATORIA
MORATORIO
MUJAHIDIN
MYRMECOID
NAUMACHIA
NEOLITHIC
NEPHRITIC
NEPHRITIS
NEURALGIA
NEURALGIC
NEUROGLIA
NIAISERIE
NIPPERKIN
NONPAREIL
NONPROFIT
NOSTALGIA
NOSTALGIC
NURSEMAID
OBSTETRIC
OLEORESIN
OMOPHAGIC
ONOMASTIC
OPPENHEIM
ORGIASTIC
OWNERSHIP
PALANQUIN
PANEGYRIC
PANORAMIC
PAPERCLIP
PARABASIS
PARABOLIC
PARACUSIS
PARALYSIS
PARALYTIC
PARAMEDIC
PARASITIC
PAREGORIC
PAROTITIS
PASTICCIO
PATHTRAIN
PATRIOTIC
PAULOWNIA
PEIRASTIC
PELLAGRIN
PENDENNIS
PERFERVID
PERICUTIN
PERTUSSIS
PHARISAIC
PHARSALIA
PHILIPPIC
PHLEBITIS
PHRENETIC
PHRENITIS
PINOCCHIO
PISTACHIO
PITUITRIN
PLETHORIC
PNEUMATIC
PNEUMONIA
POLYNESIA
PONTLEVIS
PORCELAIN
PORTFOLIO
PRAGMATIC
PREORDAIN
PRETERMIT
PRISMATIC
PROBOSCIS
PROCLITIC
PROGNOSIS
PROLACTIN
PROLEPSIS
PROMUSCIS
PROPERDIN
PROPHETIC
PROPIONIC
PROPTOSIS
PROTHESIS
PSEUDAXIS
PSORIASIS
PSYCHOSIS
PSYCHOTIC
PUNCTILIO
PURITANIC
PUSHCHAIR
PYROMANIA
PYRRHONIC
QUADRATIC
QUERCETIN
RADICCHIO
RASKOLNIK
REALISTIC
REFUSENIK
RESERVOIR
RETINITIS
REYKJAVIK
RHAPSODIC
RHEOTAXIS
RHEUMATIC
RHODOPSIN
RUDBECKIA
SACCHARIN
SAINTFOIN
SANGFROID
SANHEDRIM
SANHEDRIN
SANNYASIN
SARCASTIC
SAXITOXIN
SCHEMATIC
SCLEROSIS
SCOLIOSIS
SCOLIOTIC
SCORBUTIC
SEMEIOTIC
SEMIRAMIS
SEPHARDIM
SHARKSKIN
SHEEPSKIN
SHELLSUIT
SHUBUNKIN
SIDEROSIS
SILICOSIS
SINUSITIS
SLAMMAKIN
SNOWDONIA
SOLFEGGIO
SOOTERKIN
SOPHISTIC
SOPORIFIC
SOUVLAKIA
SPACESHIP
SPACESUIT
SPADASSIN
SPASMODIC
SPILLIKIN
SPLENETIC
SPLENITIS
SPRITSAIL
SPUNCULID
STATISTIC
STEAMSHIP
STEGNOSIS
STEGNOTIC
STENOPAIC
STOMACHIC
STRATEGIC
STRUMITIS
STYLISTIC
SUDORIFIC
SULPHONIC
SULPHURIC
SURREJOIN
SYBARITIC
SYLLEPSIS
SYMBIOSIS
SYMBIOTIC
SYMMETRIC
SYMPHONIC
SYMPHYSIS
SYNCHYSIS
SYNIZESIS
SYNOVITIS
SYNTACTIC
SYNTHESIS
SYNTHETIC
TARPAULIN
TAYASSUID
TEPHILLIN
TESTATRIX
THALASSIC
THAUMATIN
THRASONIC
THREADFIN
THRENETIC
THUMBNAIL
TORMENTIL
TRACKSUIT
TRANSSHIP
TRAPEZOID
TRATTORIA
TRAUMATIC
TRICLINIC
TRIETERIC
TROCHILIC
TRONDHEIM
TROOPSHIP
TROPAELIN
UNCERTAIN
UNDERPAID
UPAITHRIC
URTICARIA
UTICENSIS
VERDIGRIS
VITRIOLIC
WAFERTHIN
WALPURGIS
WASHBASIN
WHIRLIGIG
WHITEBAIT
WHODUNNIT
WISCONSIN
XENOMANIA
YGGDRASIL
ZOOMANTIC
ZOOSCOPIC
ZYGOMATIC
ARTICHOKE
BALALAIKA
BOONDOCKS
BRITSCHKA
CHILDLIKE
CORNCRAKE
CROWNLIKE
CUFFLINKS
FIREDRAKE
FIREWORKS
FOOTBRAKE
FRUITCAKE
GREYWACKE
HANDBRAKE
HANDSHAKE
HANDSPIKE
HITCHHIKE
IRONWORKS
KEYSTROKE
KITTIWAKE
LOOKALIKE
MELONLIKE
MILKSHAKE
MISSTROKE
MOTORBIKE
MOUSELIKE
POCKMANKY
QUANTOCKS
ROADWORKS
SAVERNAKE
SCHNITTKE
SHELDRAKE
SHORTCAKE
SNOWFLAKE
SUNSTROKE
SYLPHLIKE
THORNDYKE
TRIPITAKA
UNDERTAKE
WAPENTAKE
ABYSMALLY
ADAPTABLE
ADMIRABLE
ADMIRABLY
ADVERSELY
ADVISABLE
ADVISEDLY
AGREEABLE
AGREEABLY
AIMLESSLY
ALLEGEDLY
ALLOWABLE
ALTERABLE
AMOROUSLY
AMUSINGLY
ANXIOUSLY
AQUARELLE
ARCHIBALD
ARCHIVOLT
ARDUOUSLY
ARISTOTLE
ARMADILLO
ARTERIOLE
ASSUREDLY
ASTRAGALS
AVAILABLE
AVOIDABLE
AWKWARDLY
BAGATELLE
BALEFULLY
BAMBOOZLE
BASHFULLY
BASICALLY
BEDRAGGLE
BELATEDLY
BENBECULA
BESPANGLE
BIMONTHLY
BIRDTABLE
BIZARRELY
BLACKBALL
BLATANTLY
BLINDFOLD
BOARDWALK
BOMBSHELL
BOOKSHELF
BOOKSTALL
BRACTEOLE
BREAKABLE
BRIDEWELL
BROTHERLY
BRUSQUELY
BUTTERFLY
CALENDULA
CALLOUSLY
CAMPANILE
CAMPANULA
CANTABILE
CARACALLA
CARAMBOLA
CARBUNCLE
CAREFULLY
CASSEROLE
CATCHPOLE
CATCHPOLL
CATSKILLS
CENTRALLY
CERTAINLY
CHAMOMILE
CHANTILLY
CHRONICLE
CHURCHILL
CLIENTELE
CLINGFILM
COALFIELD
COLUMELLA
COMICALLY
COMPACTLY
CONCISELY
CONSTABLE
CONTUMELY
COPIOUSLY

CORDIALLY
CORNEILLE
CORNFIELD
CORNSTALK
CORPUSCLE
CORRECTLY
COURTELLE
COVERDALE
CRESCELLE
CROCODILE
CROOKEDLY
CROSSBILL
CROSSWALK
CROWSBILL
CRUCIALLY
CUBBYHOLE
CURFUFFLE
CURIOUSLY
CURRENTLY
CURSORILY
CYNICALLY
DASTARDLY
DEBATABLE
DECASTYLE
DECIDEDLY
DECRETALS
DEFINABLE
DESIRABLE
DEVIOUSLY
DIFFICULT
DIRIGIBLE
DISMANTLE
DISSEMBLE
DISTANTLY
DIVISIBLE
DODDIPOLL
DOLEFULLY
DONATELLO
DRAGONFLY
DRINKABLE
DRUNKENLY
DUBIOUSLY
DUNSTABLE
DUTIFULLY
EARNESTLY
ELEGANTLY
EMBRANGLE
EMINENTLY
EMMERDALE
EMPANOPLY
ENDLESSLY
ENDURABLE
ENJOYABLE
ENNERDALE
ENSORCELL
EQUITABLE
EQUITABLY

ERSTWHILE
ESPAGNOLE
ESTIMABLE
ETERNALLY
EVASIVELY
EVIDENTLY
EXCITABLE
EXCUSABLE
EXCUSABLY
EXECRABLE
EXECRABLY
EXPRESSLY
EXTENSILE
EXTREMELY
FACSIMILE
FACTUALLY
FAIRYTALE
FANDANGLE
FARANDOLE
FATUOUSLY
FAVORABLE
FAVORABLY
FEARFULLY
FERVENTLY
FILOSELLE
FLAMMABLE
FLASHBULB
FLORIMELL
FLOURMILL
FOOLISHLY
FOOTHILLS
FOOTSTALL
FORESTALL
FORLORNLY
FREESTYLE
FRETFULLY
FULLSCALE
FURIOUSLY
FURTIVELY
GAINFULLY
GALENGALE
GALINGALE
GALLANTLY
GALLINULE
GALLIPOLI
GENERALLY
GENTEELLY
GENUINELY
GIRANDOLE
GLEEFULLY
GLOMERULE
GLORYHOLE
GOLDFIELD
GOONHILLY
GRADUALLY
GRATICULE
GRENVILLE

GRISAILLE
GUACAMOLE
GUATEMALA
GUERRILLA
GUILDHALL
GUMSHIELD
HABITABLE
HAIRSTYLE
HALOPHILE
HARDSHELL
HAUGHTILY
HAWKSBILL
HEADSTALL
HEALTHILY
HEARTFELT
HELPFULLY
HIDEOUSLY
HILLBILLY
HOBBINOLL
HONORABLE
HOPEFULLY
HOUSEHOLD
HURRIEDLY
HUSBANDLY
HYDROPULT
HYPERBOLA
HYPERBOLE
ILLEGALLY
ILLEGIBLE
ILLEGIBLY
ILLICITLY
IMBRANGLE
IMMANACLE
IMMENSELY
IMMORALLY
IMMORTALS
IMMOVABLE
IMMOVABLY
IMMUTABLE
IMMUTABLY
INAUDIBLE
INAUDIBLY
INCAPABLE
INCURABLE
INCURABLY
INDELIBLE
INDELIBLY
INEFFABLE
INFANTILE
INFERTILE
INHUMANLY
INITIALLY
INSOLUBLE
INSTANTLY
INTENSELY
INVISIBLE
IODOPHILE

IPRINDOLE
IRASCIBLE
IRRITABLE
IRRITABLY
JEALOUSLY
JOCULARLY
KERFUFFLE
KILOCYCLE
KNAPSCULL
KNAPSKULL
KNOWINGLY
LANGUIDLY
LATERALLY
LAUGHABLE
LEAFMOULD
LEASEHOLD
LEISURELY
LENGTHILY
LENIENTLY
LIBERALLY
LIFESTYLE
LINGFIELD
LITERALLY
LOGICALLY
LONGINGLY
LYMESWOLD
LYRICALLY
MACDONALD
MAGICALLY
MAJUSCULE
MALLEABLE
MANHANDLE
MANSFIELD
MASEFIELD
MASSIVELY
MEANWHILE
MEATBALLS
MEDICALLY
MEGACYCLE
MEMORABLE
MICROFILM
MINEFIELD
MINISCULE
MINUSCULE
MIRABELLE
MISERABLE
MISERABLY
MISHANDLE
MITRAILLE
MONTICULE
MOTHBALLS
MOUSEHOLE
MUSICALLY
MUSICHALL
NARGHILLY
NASHVILLE
NATURALLY

NAUGHTILY
NAVIGABLE
NERVOUSLY
NEUTRALLY
NEWCASTLE
NEWSSTALL
NIGGARDLY
NIGHTFALL
NITHSDALE
NOMINALLY
NORTHERLY
NUMBSKULL
OBLIQUELY
OBSCENELY
OBSCURELY
OBVIOUSLY
OFFICIALS
OMINOUSLY
OPTICALLY
OPULENTLY
ORGANELLE
OUTWARDLY
OVERSPILL
OVERWHELM
PAINFULLY
PALATABLE
PANATELLA
PANHANDLE
PANNIKELL
PANTOFFLE
PANTOUFLE
PARBUCKLE
PARTIALLY
PASSIVELY
PASTORALE
PATCHOULI
PATCHOULY
PATIENTLY
PEACEABLE
PEACEABLY
PEEVISHLY
PENINSULA
PENSIVELY
PERFECTLY
PERISTYLE
PERMEABLE
PHILATELY
PIACEVOLE
PINEAPPLE
PIQUANTLY
PITCHPOLE
PITCHPOLL
PITIFULLY
PLAUSIBLE
PLAUSIBLY
PLAYFULLY
PLIMSOLLS

POINTEDLY
POPULARLY
PORBEAGLE
PRECISELY
PRESENTLY
PRIMARILY
PRINCIPLE
PRINTABLE
PRIVATELY
PROFANELY
PROFUSELY
PRUDENTLY
PUNGENTLY
PURPOSELY
QUADRILLE
QUADRUPLE
QUARTERLY
QUENNELLE
QUINTUPLE
RADIANTLY
RADICALLY
RANTIPOLE
RATIONALE
RAUCOUSLY
RAZORBILL
REACHABLE
RECONCILE
RECTANGLE
REDUCIBLE
REGULARLY
REMOVABLE
RENEWABLE
REPAYABLE
REPUTABLE
REPUTEDLY
RESHUFFLE
RIGMAROLE
RIOTOUSLY
ROCAMBOLE
ROOSEVELT
ROUTINELY
RUBICELLE
RUFFIANLY
RUINOUSLY
SCAGLIOLA
SCALEABLE
SCHNOZZLE
SCHOLARLY
SCINTILLA
SCREWBALL
SCRUFFILY
SEABOTTLE
SEEMINGLY
SELFISHLY
SENSUALLY
SEPARABLE
SEPTIMOLE

SERIOUSLY
SERREFILE
SERVILELY
SEVERALLY
SHEEPFOLD
SHEFFIELD
SHEMOZZLE
SHORTFALL
SHORTHOLD
SIMILARLY
SINCERELY
SIPHUNCLE
SKEDADDLE
SKETCHILY
SKILFULLY
SLAVISHLY
SLEEPWALK
SNEERWELL
SOLDIERLY
SOULFULLY
SOUTHERLY
SPARINGLY
SPATIALLY
SPECIALLY
SPECTACLE
SPEEDWELL
SPOONBILL
SPRAICKLE
SPRAUCHLE
SPRIGHTLY
SPRINGALD
SQUALIDLY
STANDGALE
STAUNCHLY
STOCKHOLM
STOCKPILE
STOICALLY
STONEWALL
STOOLBALL
STRANGELY
STROMBOLI
STRONGYLE
STYLISHLY
SUBLIMELY
SUMMARILY
SUPREMELY
SURCINGLE
TACTFULLY
TARANTULA
TEACHABLE
TEAKETTLE
TEARFULLY
TEDIOUSLY
TELLINGLY
TENUOUSLY
TERRICOLE
THINKABLE
THIRSTILY
THORNBILL
THREEFOLD
THRESHOLD
THRIFTILY
THROATILY
TIMETABLE
TOLERABLE
TOLERABLY
TOLPUDDLE
TOPICALLY
TOWNSFOLK
TOXOPHILY
TRACEABLE
TRACTABLE
TRAINABLE
TREADMILL
TREDRILLE
TREGEAGLE
TRITICALE
TRIVIALLY
TURCOPOLE
TURNBULLS
TURNSTILE
TURNTABLE
TYPICALLY
UMBRATILE
UNCOURTLY
UNDERFELT
UNDERSELL
UNDERWALK
UNEARTHLY
UNEATABLE
UNHAPPILY
UNIFORMLY
UNLUCKILY
UNSHACKLE
UNSIGHTLY
UNTENABLE
UNUSUALLY
VALIANTLY
VARICELLA
VARIOUSLY
VEGETABLE
VENERABLE
VENEZUELA
VENTRICLE
VERITABLE
VERSATILE
VESTIBULE
VIBRATILE
VICIOUSLY
VIOLENTLY
VIRGINALS
VIRTUALLY
VOLATIBLE
WASPISHLY
WATERFALL
WATERHOLE
WATERLILY
WATERMILL
WELLBUILT
WHITEHALL
WHITEWALL
WHOLESALE
WILLFULLY
WILLINGLY
WINDCHILL
WINDFALLS
WINDSCALE
WISTFULLY
WITTINGLY
WOMENFOLK
AERODROME
AFTERDAMP
ALTISSIMO
ASPARTAME
ASTRODOME
ASTRONOMY
BLASPHEME
BLASPHEMY
CARCINOMA
COCKSCOMB
COLOSTOMY
CONDYLOMA
CURRYCOMB
CYCLORAMA
DICHOTOMY
DISENTOMB
DITHYRAMB
DUODECIMO
EIGHTSOME
EMPHYSEMA
ENTHYMEME
EURHYTHMY
EXANTHEMA
FILOPLUME
FLEXITIME
HAEMALOMA
HARMOTOME
HIPPODAME
HONEYCOMB
LEUCOTOME
LIGHTSOME
LOATHSOME
LONGCHAMP
LUNCHTIME
MAINFRAME
MAJORDOMO
MELODRAMA
METRONOME
MICROTOME
MONODRAMA
MONTEZUMA
MUSHROOMS
NIGHTTIME
ORIFLAMME
PANTAGAMY
PANTOMIME
PEACETIME
PERISTOME
PHANTASMA
PROGRAMME
QUICKLIME
SEMANTEME
SIXTEENMO
SMALLTIME
TAXIDERMY
TEKNONYMY
THEOBROMA
THINGUMMY
THREESOME
TOOTHCOMB
TOOTHSOME
TRANSHUME
UNWELCOME
VASECTOMY
VELODROME
WEARISOME
WHITEDAMP
WHOLESOME
WORRISOME
XEROSTOMA
ABASEMENT
ABATEMENT
ABHORRENT
ABLUTIONS
ABORIGINE
ABOUNDING
ABSORBENT
ABSORBING
ABSTINENT
ACCOMPANY
ACCORDANT
ACCORDING
ACETYLENE
ACROPHONY
ADJOINING
ADMITTING
ADORNMENT
AEROPLANE
AFFECTING
AFRIKAANS
AGONIZING
AGREEMENT
AITCHBONE
ALBERTINE
ALIGNMENT
ALLEGIANT
ALLOTMENT
ALMANDINE
ALTIPLANO
AMAZEMENT
AMENDMENT
AMPERSAND
AMUSEMENT
ANDANTINO
ANNAPURNA
ANNULMENT
ANOINTING
ANSWERING
ANTICLINE
ANTIPHONY
APARTMENT
APPALLING
APPEALING
APPLICANT
APPREHEND
APPROVING
AQUAPLANE
ARGENTINA
ARGENTINE
ARMSTRONG
ARRESTING
ASCENDANT
ASCENDING
ASSAILANT
ASSERTING
ASSISTANT
ATONEMENT
ATTACKING
ATTENDANT
AUBERGINE
AUGUSTINE
AWAKENING
BALLERINA
BALLPOINT
BANDOLINE
BANDSTAND
BANTERING
BARBITONE
BARBOTINE
BARCELONA
BEGINNING
BELIEVING
BELONGING
BILLABONG
BILLOWING
BLUEPRINT
BLUESTONE
BOLIVIANO
BOMBASINE
BOOKSTAND
BOOMERANG
BORDERING
BORROWING
BOYFRIEND
BRAMBLING
BRANCHING
BREADLINE
BREATHING
BREECHING
BRILLIANT
BRIMSTONE
BRISTLING
BURROWING
BYZANTINE
CACOPHONY
CAKESTAND
CARPETING
CASHPOINT
CASUARINA
CATCHMENT
CATHERINE
CAVORTING
CELANDINE
CELEBRANT
CENTERING
CENTREING
CHAMPAGNE
CHAPERONE
CHARABANC
CHEEKBONE
CHERUBINI
CIPOLLINO
CLEANSING
CLEVELAND
CLOISONNÉ
COAGULANT
COASTLINE
COCKAIGNE
COGNIZANT
COLOPHONY
COLOURING
COLUMBINE
COMBATANT
COMPETENT
COMPETING
COMPLAINT
COMPLIANT
COMPONENT
COMPOSING
COMPUTING
CONCUBINE
CONDIMENT
CONFIDANT
CONFIDENT
CONFUSING
CONGRUENT
CONJURING
CONSONANT
CONSUMING
CONTINENT
CORALLINE
CORDYLINE

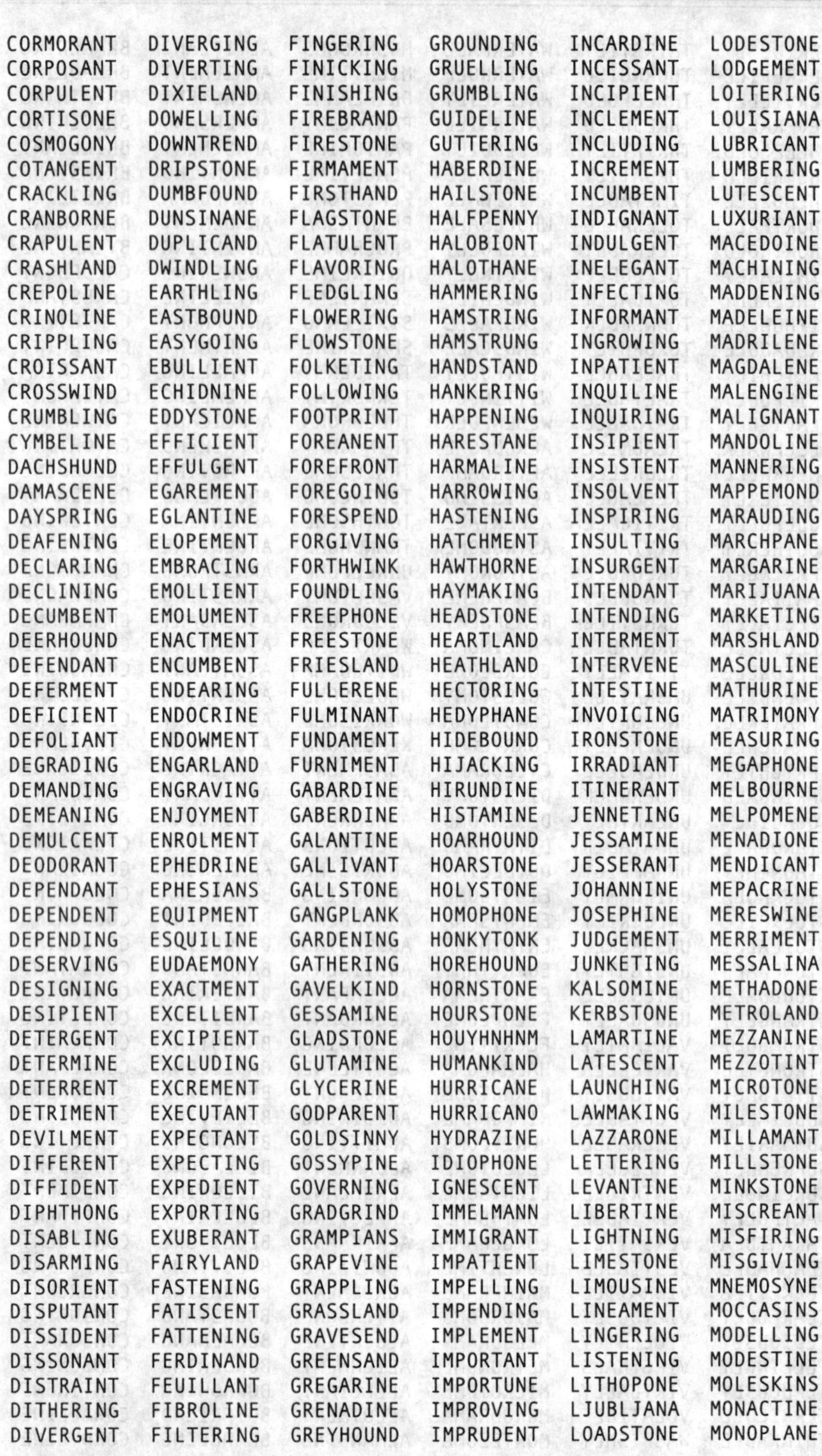

CORMORANT
CORPOSANT
CORPULENT
CORTISONE
COSMOGONY
COTANGENT
CRACKLING
CRANBORNE
CRAPULENT
CRASHLAND
CREPOLINE
CRINOLINE
CRIPPLING
CROISSANT
CROSSWIND
CRUMBLING
CYMBELINE
DACHSHUND
DAMASCENE
DAYSPRING
DEAFENING
DECLARING
DECLINING
DECUMBENT
DEERHOUND
DEFENDANT
DEFERMENT
DEFICIENT
DEFOLIANT
DEGRADING
DEMANDING
DEMEANING
DEMULCENT
DEODORANT
DEPENDANT
DEPENDENT
DEPENDING
DESERVING
DESIGNING
DESIPIENT
DETERGENT
DETERMINE
DETERRENT
DETRIMENT
DEVILMENT
DIFFERENT
DIFFIDENT
DIPHTHONG
DISABLING
DISARMING
DISORIENT
DISPUTANT
DISSIDENT
DISSONANT
DISTRAINT
DITHERING
DIVERGENT
DIVERGING
DIVERTING
DIXIELAND
DOWELLING
DOWNTREND
DRIPSTONE
DUMBFOUND
DUNSINANE
DUPLICAND
DWINDLING
EARTHLING
EASTBOUND
EASYGOING
EBULLIENT
ECHIDNINE
EDDYSTONE
EFFICIENT
EFFULGENT
EGAREMENT
EGLANTINE
ELOPEMENT
EMBRACING
EMOLLIENT
EMOLUMENT
ENACTMENT
ENCUMBENT
ENDEARING
ENDOCRINE
ENDOWMENT
ENGARLAND
ENGRAVING
ENJOYMENT
ENROLMENT
EPHEDRINE
EPHESIANS
EQUIPMENT
ESQUILINE
EUDAEMONY
EXACTMENT
EXCELLENT
EXCIPIENT
EXCLUDING
EXCREMENT
EXECUTANT
EXPECTANT
EXPECTING
EXPEDIENT
EXPORTING
EXUBERANT
FAIRYLAND
FASTENING
FATISCENT
FATTENING
FERDINAND
FEUILLANT
FIBROLINE
FILTERING
FINGERING
FINICKING
FINISHING
FIREBRAND
FIRESTONE
FIRMAMENT
FIRSTHAND
FLAGSTONE
FLATULENT
FLAVORING
FLEDGLING
FLOWERING
FLOWSTONE
FOLKETING
FOLLOWING
FOOTPRINT
FOREANENT
FOREFRONT
FOREGOING
FORESPEND
FORGIVING
FORTHWINK
FOUNDLING
FREEPHONE
FREESTONE
FRIESLAND
FULLERENE
FULMINANT
FUNDAMENT
FURNIMENT
GABARDINE
GABERDINE
GALANTINE
GALLIVANT
GALLSTONE
GANGPLANK
GARDENING
GATHERING
GAVELKIND
GESSAMINE
GLADSTONE
GLUTAMINE
GLYCERINE
GODPARENT
GOLDSINNY
GOSSYPINE
GOVERNING
GRADGRIND
GRAMPIANS
GRAPEVINE
GRAPPLING
GRASSLAND
GRAVESEND
GREENSAND
GREGARINE
GRENADINE
GREYHOUND
GROUNDING
GRUELLING
GRUMBLING
GUIDELINE
GUTTERING
HABERDINE
HAILSTONE
HALFPENNY
HALOBIONT
HALOTHANE
HAMMERING
HAMSTRING
HAMSTRUNG
HANDSTAND
HANKERING
HAPPENING
HARESTANE
HARMALINE
HARROWING
HASTENING
HATCHMENT
HAWTHORNE
HAYMAKING
HEADSTONE
HEARTLAND
HEATHLAND
HECTORING
HEDYPHANE
HIDEBOUND
HIJACKING
HIRUNDINE
HISTAMINE
HOARHOUND
HOARSTONE
HOLYSTONE
HOMOPHONE
HONKYTONK
HOREHOUND
HORNSTONE
HOURSTONE
HOUYHNHNM
HUMANKIND
HURRICANE
HURRICANO
HYDRAZINE
IDIOPHONE
IGNESCENT
IMMELMANN
IMMIGRANT
IMPATIENT
IMPELLING
IMPENDING
IMPLEMENT
IMPORTANT
IMPORTUNE
IMPROVING
IMPRUDENT
INCARDINE
INCESSANT
INCIPIENT
INCLEMENT
INCLUDING
INCREMENT
INCUMBENT
INDIGNANT
INDULGENT
INELEGANT
INFECTING
INFORMANT
INGROWING
INPATIENT
INQUILINE
INQUIRING
INSIPIENT
INSISTENT
INSOLVENT
INSPIRING
INSULTING
INSURGENT
INTENDANT
INTENDING
INTERMENT
INTERVENE
INTESTINE
INVOICING
IRONSTONE
IRRADIANT
ITINERANT
JENNETING
JESSAMINE
JESSERANT
JOHANNINE
JOSEPHINE
JUDGEMENT
JUNKETING
KALSOMINE
KERBSTONE
LAMARTINE
LATESCENT
LAUNCHING
LAWMAKING
LAZZARONE
LETTERING
LEVANTINE
LIBERTINE
LIGHTNING
LIMESTONE
LIMOUSINE
LINEAMENT
LINGERING
LISTENING
LITHOPONE
LJUBLJANA
LOADSTONE
LODESTONE
LODGEMENT
LOITERING
LOUISIANA
LUBRICANT
LUMBERING
LUTESCENT
LUXURIANT
MACEDOINE
MACHINING
MADDENING
MADELEINE
MADRILENE
MAGDALENE
MALENGINE
MALIGNANT
MANDOLINE
MANNERING
MAPPEMOND
MARAUDING
MARCHPANE
MARGARINE
MARIJUANA
MARKETING
MARSHLAND
MASCULINE
MATHURINE
MATRIMONY
MEASURING
MEGAPHONE
MELBOURNE
MELPOMENE
MENADIONE
MENDICANT
MEPACRINE
MERESWINE
MERRIMENT
MESSALINA
METHADONE
METROLAND
MEZZANINE
MEZZOTINT
MICROTONE
MILESTONE
MILLAMANT
MILLSTONE
MINKSTONE
MISCREANT
MISFIRING
MISGIVING
MNEMOSYNE
MOCCASINS
MODELLING
MODESTINE
MOLESKINS
MONACTINE
MONOPLANE

MONTAIGNE
MOONSHINE
MOONSTONE
MORTSTONE
MOTHERING
MUNITIONS
MURMURING
MUSCADINE
MUSCARINE
MUSSOLINI
MUTTERING
NARROWING
NECTARINE
NEGLIGENT
NEPHELINE
NEWSAGENT
NEWSHOUND
NEWSPRINT
NEWSSTAND
NIDDERING
NIDERLING
NIEBELUNG
NIGROSINE
NOLLEKENS
NOVOCAINE
NUTRIMENT
OBSERVANT
OBTAINING
OCCUPYING
ODELSTING
OFFENDING
OFFICIANT
OFFSPRING
OLIGOCENE
OPERATING
OPPORTUNE
OPTOPHONE
ORGANZINE
ORMANDINE
ORTHOTONE
OVERLYING
OVERPAINT
OVERSPEND
PACKAGING
PAKISTANI
PALESTINE
PALUDRINE
PANELLING
PANETTONE
PARAMOUNT
PARASCENE
PARCHMENT
PARENTING
PAROCHINE
PARSIMONY
PARTAKING
PASSAMENT
PASSERINE
PATHOGENY
PATRIMONY
PENFRIEND
PENISTONE
PENTOSANE
PEPPERONI
PERCALINE
PEREGRINE
PERFORANS
PERGAMENE
PERISHING
PERMANENT
PERTINENT
PESTILENT
PETHIDINE
PETILLANT
PHARAMOND
PHEROMONE
PHOSPHENE
PHOTOGENE
PHYLOGENY
PICKETING
PICKTHANK
PIGGYBANK
PILFERING
PIPESTONE
PITCHPINE
PLACEMENT
PLAINSONG
PLAYTHING
PLEIOCENE
PLUMBLINE
POISONING
POLLUTANT
POLVERINE
POLYPHONE
POLYPHONY
POLYTHENE
POPPERING
PORCUPINE
POSTULANT
POTHOLING
PRECEDENT
PRECEDING
PREDICANT
PREDIKANT
PRESCIENT
PRESHRUNK
PRESIDENT
PRESSGANG
PREVALENT
PRIMULINE
PROLAMINE
PROMINENT
PROMISING
PROMPTING
PROPONENT
PROPYLENE
PROTAMINE
PROVIDENT
PROVIDING
PROVOKING
PROVOLONE
PUNCHLINE
PUNISHING
PURIFYING
PYONGYANG
QUAVERING
QUERIMONY
QUICKSAND
QUIESCENT
QUINQUINA
QUIVERING
RADIATING
RATIONING
RAVISHING
REASONING
RECALLING
RECEIVING
RECIPIENT
RECKONING
RECOMMEND
RECONVENE
RECORDING
RECUMBENT
RECURRENT
RECURRING
REDEEMING
REDUNDANT
REEXAMINE
REFERRING
REFULGENT
REGARDANT
REGARDING
REJOICING
RELATIONS
RELUCTANT
REMAINING
REMONTANT
RENASCENT
RENDERING
REPAYMENT
REPELLENT
REPELLING
REPENTANT
REPLACING
REPORTING
REPREHEND
REPRESENT
REPRIMAND
REPROVING
REPUGNANT
RESERPINE
RESILIENT
RESISTANT
RESORTING
RESTRAINT
RESULTANT
RESULTING
RESURGENT
RETAILING
RETAINING
RETURNING
REVEALING
REVELLING
REVERSING
REVETMENT
REVOLTING
REVOLVING
REWARDING
REWORKING
RIGHTHAND
RIGHTWING
ROSMARINE
ROTAPLANE
ROUNDHAND
RUFESCENT
RUNAROUND
SACRAMENT
SADDENING
SALANGANE
SANDSTONE
SANTAYANA
SARBACANE
SATURNINE
SAXOPHONE
SCALLIONS
SCAMBLING
SCANTLING
SCHELLING
SCHIAVONE
SCHILLING
SCHOOLING
SCORCHING
SCRAPPING
SCREENING
SCREWPINE
SCRIMPING
SCRUBBING
SCRUMPING
SCULPTING
SEAFARING
SEARCHING
SEASONING
SELECTING
SENESCENT
SENTIMENT
SERAPHINE
SERVICING
SHAVELING
SHEARLING
SHENSTONE
SHIELDING
SHIVERING
SHOESHINE
SHOPFRONT
SHORTHAND
SHRIMPING
SHRINKING
SHUFFLING
SIBYLLINE
SICILIANO
SICKENING
SIDEBURNS
SILTSTONE
SKINFLINT
SLABSTONE
SLOUGHING
SLUGHORNE
SMUGGLING
SNOWBOUND
SOAPSTONE
SOFTENING
SOLDERING
SOLFERINO
SOMETHING
SOMNOLENT
SPARKLING
SPEARMINT
SPECIMENS
SPELDRING
SPELLBIND
SPHENDONE
SPLITTING
SPREADING
SQUADRONE
SQUINTING
SQUIRMING
STAGEHAND
STARSTONE
STARTLING
STATEMENT
STIMULANT
STONEHAND
STORYLINE
STOWNLINS
STRAINING
STRAPHANG
STRAPPING
STREAMING
STRINGENT
STRIPLING
STROLLING
STRUTTING
STUMBLING
SUBJACENT
SUBMARINE
SUBTENANT
SUCCUBINE
SUCCULENT
SUFFERING
SUGARCANE
SUPERFINE
SUPERVENE
SUPPLIANT
SUPPOSING
SURVEYING
SURVIVING
SWADDLING
SWEATBAND
SWINBURNE
SWINGEING
SWOTHLING
SYCOPHANT
TABLELAND
TAILPLANE
TAMERLANE
TANGERINE
TARRAGONA
TELEPHONE
TELEPHONY
TERMAGANT
TERMAGENT
TERRACING
TESTAMENT
TESTIMONY
THATCHING
THECODONT
THIGHBONE
THIRSTING
THRASHING
THREONINE
THRILLANT
THRILLING
THROBBING
THRONGING
THUMBLING
THYLACINE
TICHBORNE
TISIPHONE
TOADSTONE
TOCCATINA
TOMBSTONE
TOSCANINI
TOTAQUINE
TOUCHLINE
TOWELLING
TRADEWIND
TRANSCEND
TRANSIENT
TRASIMENE
TRAVELING
TREATMENT
TREBIZOND

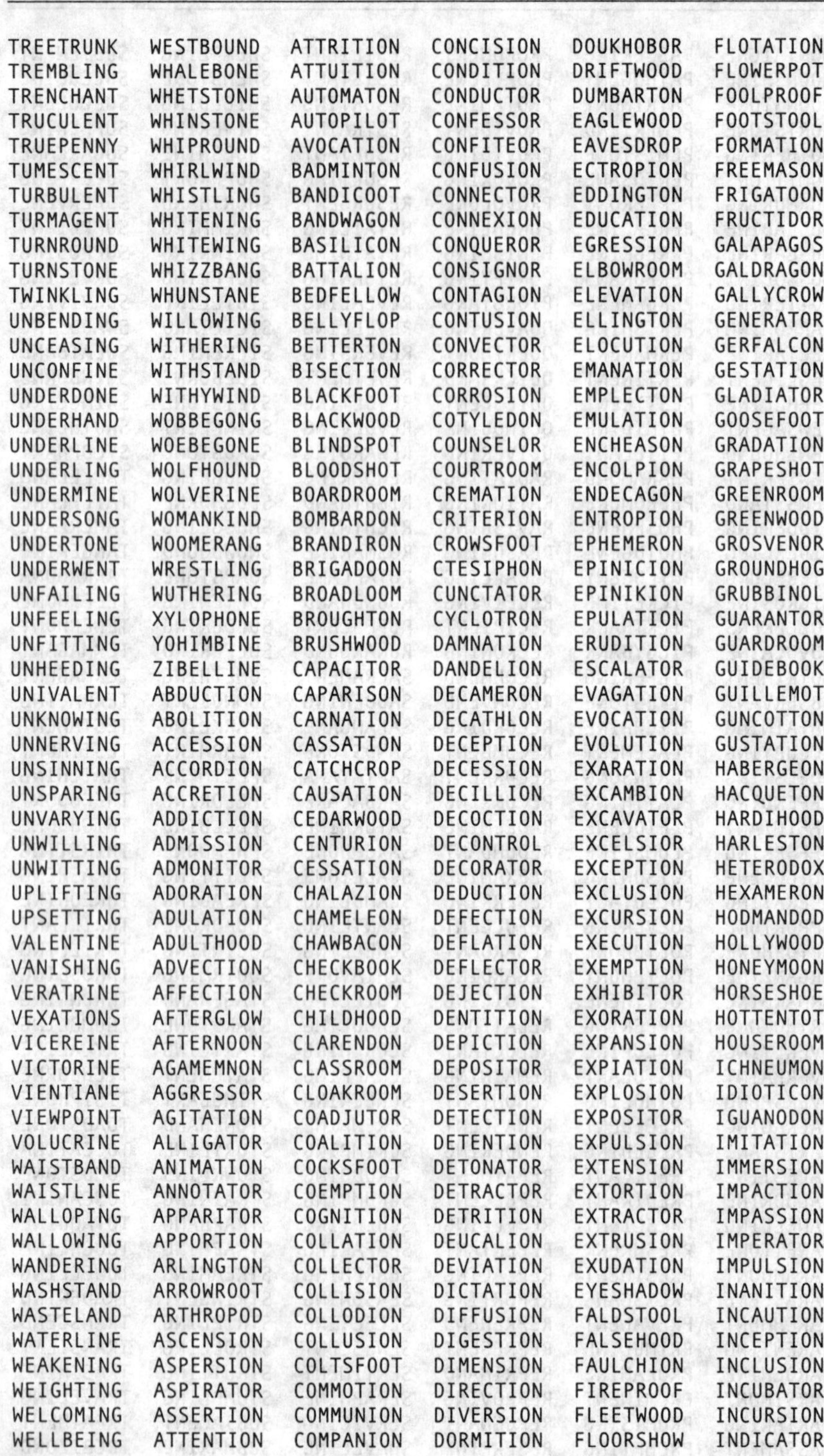

TREETRUNK
TREMBLING
TRENCHANT
TRUCULENT
TRUEPENNY
TUMESCENT
TURBULENT
TURMAGENT
TURNROUND
TURNSTONE
TWINKLING
UNBENDING
UNCEASING
UNCONFINE
UNDERDONE
UNDERHAND
UNDERLINE
UNDERLING
UNDERMINE
UNDERSONG
UNDERTONE
UNDERWENT
UNFAILING
UNFEELING
UNFITTING
UNHEEDING
UNIVALENT
UNKNOWING
UNNERVING
UNSINNING
UNSPARING
UNVARYING
UNWILLING
UNWITTING
UPLIFTING
UPSETTING
VALENTINE
VANISHING
VERATRINE
VEXATIONS
VICEREINE
VICTORINE
VIENTIANE
VIEWPOINT
VOLUCRINE
WAISTBAND
WAISTLINE
WALLOPING
WALLOWING
WANDERING
WASHSTAND
WASTELAND
WATERLINE
WEAKENING
WEIGHTING
WELCOMING
WELLBEING
WESTBOUND
WHALEBONE
WHETSTONE
WHINSTONE
WHIPROUND
WHIRLWIND
WHISTLING
WHITENING
WHITEWING
WHIZZBANG
WHUNSTANE
WILLOWING
WITHERING
WITHSTAND
WITHYWIND
WOBBEGONG
WOEBEGONE
WOLFHOUND
WOLVERINE
WOMANKIND
WOOMERANG
WRESTLING
WUTHERING
XYLOPHONE
YOHIMBINE
ZIBELLINE
ABDUCTION
ABOLITION
ACCESSION
ACCORDION
ACCRETION
ADDICTION
ADMISSION
ADMONITOR
ADORATION
ADULATION
ADULTHOOD
ADVECTION
AFFECTION
AFTERGLOW
AFTERNOON
AGAMEMNON
AGGRESSOR
AGITATION
ALLIGATOR
ANIMATION
ANNOTATOR
APPARITOR
APPORTION
ARLINGTON
ARROWROOT
ARTHROPOD
ASCENSION
ASPERSION
ASPIRATOR
ASSERTION
ATTENTION
ATTRITION
ATTUITION
AUTOMATON
AUTOPILOT
AVOCATION
BADMINTON
BANDICOOT
BANDWAGON
BASILICON
BATTALION
BEDFELLOW
BELLYFLOP
BETTERTON
BISECTION
BLACKFOOT
BLACKWOOD
BLINDSPOT
BLOODSHOT
BOARDROOM
BOMBARDON
BRANDIRON
BRIGADOON
BROADLOOM
BROUGHTON
BRUSHWOOD
CAPACITOR
CAPARISON
CARNATION
CASSATION
CATCHCROP
CAUSATION
CEDARWOOD
CENTURION
CESSATION
CHALAZION
CHAMELEON
CHAWBACON
CHECKBOOK
CHECKROOM
CHILDHOOD
CLARENDON
CLASSROOM
CLOAKROOM
COADJUTOR
COALITION
COCKSFOOT
COEMPTION
COGNITION
COLLATION
COLLECTOR
COLLISION
COLLODION
COLLUSION
COLTSFOOT
COMMOTION
COMMUNION
COMPANION
CONCISION
CONDITION
CONDUCTOR
CONFESSOR
CONFITEOR
CONFUSION
CONNECTOR
CONNEXION
CONQUEROR
CONSIGNOR
CONTAGION
CONTUSION
CONVECTOR
CORRECTOR
CORROSION
COTYLEDON
COUNSELOR
COURTROOM
CREMATION
CRITERION
CROWSFOOT
CTESIPHON
CUNCTATOR
CYCLOTRON
DAMNATION
DANDELION
DECAMERON
DECATHLON
DECEPTION
DECESSION
DECILLION
DECOCTION
DECONTROL
DECORATOR
DEDUCTION
DEFECTION
DEFLATION
DEFLECTOR
DEJECTION
DENTITION
DEPICTION
DEPOSITOR
DESERTION
DETECTION
DETENTION
DETONATOR
DETRACTOR
DETRITION
DEUCALION
DEVIATION
DICTATION
DIFFUSION
DIGESTION
DIMENSION
DIRECTION
DIVERSION
DORMITION
DOUKHOBOR
DRIFTWOOD
DUMBARTON
EAGLEWOOD
EAVESDROP
ECTROPION
EDDINGTON
EDUCATION
EGRESSION
ELBOWROOM
ELEVATION
ELLINGTON
ELOCUTION
EMANATION
EMPLECTON
EMULATION
ENCHEASON
ENCOLPION
ENDECAGON
ENTROPION
EPHEMERON
EPINICION
EPINIKION
EPULATION
ERUDITION
ESCALATOR
EVAGATION
EVOCATION
EVOLUTION
EXARATION
EXCAMBION
EXCAVATOR
EXCELSIOR
EXCEPTION
EXCLUSION
EXCURSION
EXECUTION
EXEMPTION
EXHIBITOR
EXORATION
EXPANSION
EXPIATION
EXPLOSION
EXPOSITOR
EXPULSION
EXTENSION
EXTORTION
EXTRACTOR
EXTRUSION
EXUDATION
EYESHADOW
FALDSTOOL
FALSEHOOD
FAULCHION
FIREPROOF
FLEETWOOD
FLOORSHOW
FLOTATION
FLOWERPOT
FOOLPROOF
FOOTSTOOL
FORMATION
FREEMASON
FRIGATOON
FRUCTIDOR
GALAPAGOS
GALDRAGON
GALLYCROW
GENERATOR
GERFALCON
GESTATION
GLADIATOR
GOOSEFOOT
GRADATION
GRAPESHOT
GREENROOM
GREENWOOD
GROSVENOR
GROUNDHOG
GRUBBINOL
GUARANTOR
GUARDROOM
GUIDEBOOK
GUILLEMOT
GUNCOTTON
GUSTATION
HABERGEON
HACQUETON
HARDIHOOD
HARLESTON
HETERODOX
HEXAMERON
HODMANDOD
HOLLYWOOD
HONEYMOON
HORSESHOE
HOTTENTOT
HOUSEROOM
ICHNEUMON
IDIOTICON
IGUANODON
IMITATION
IMMERSION
IMPACTION
IMPASSION
IMPERATOR
IMPULSION
INANITION
INCAUTION
INCEPTION
INCLUSION
INCUBATOR
INCURSION
INDICATOR

INDICTION
INDUCTION
INFECTION
INFLATION
INFLEXION
INGESTION
INGLENOOK
INHERITOR
INITIATOR
INJECTION
INNOVATOR
INSERTION
INSPECTOR
INSULATOR
INTENTION
INTRUSION
INTUITION
INUNCTION
INVENTION
INVERSION
IRRUPTION
ISOLATION
JAWBATION
JIGGUMBOB
JOSEPHSON
LACTATION
LAMBSWOOL
LAMPADION
LANCEWOOD
LANGUEDOC
LARGITION
LATRATION
LAUDATION
LAUNCELOT
LEAKPROOF
LESTRIGON
LETTERBOX
LIBERATOR
LIGHTFOOT
LIVERPOOL
LIVRAISON
LONGEDFOR
LUCTATION
LUSTIHOOD
MACTATION
MAELSTROM
MAGNETRON
MAINTENON
MALATHION
MARTYRDOM
MATCHWOOD
MEDALLION
MEDIATION
MEDITATOR
MENTATION
MICKLETON
MIDDLETON
MIGRATION
MISTLETOE
MODERATOR
MODILLION
MONKSHOOD
MONOCEROS
MONOXYLON
MONSIGNOR
MORTGAGOR
MUGGLETON
MUSKETOON
NARRATION
NAVIGATOR
NOMINATOR
NONILLION
NOTARIKON
NUMERATOR
NUTRITION
OBJECTION
OBREPTION
OBSESSION
OBTRUSION
OBVENTION
OCCLUSION
OCTILLION
OFFSEASON
OLECRANON
ONTHESPOT
OPERATION
OPODELDOC
OPPRESSOR
ORPHARION
ORPINGTON
OUROBOROS
OVENPROOF
OVERSHOOT
OVERTHROW
OVULATION
OXIDATION
PADEMELON
PALMATION
PALPATION
PANDATION
PANTALEON
PANTALOON
PANTHENOL
PARATHION
PARATROOP
PARHELION
PARTHENON
PARTHOLON
PARTITION
PECULATOR
PENDLETON
PENDRAGON
PENILLION
PEPPERPOT
PERAEOPOD
PERCHERON
PERDITION
PERIAKTOS
PERIBOLOS
PERSIMMON
PERVASION
PHANARIOT
PHYLLOPOD
PHYTOTRON
PINKERTON
POLLUTION
POSSESSOR
POSTERIOR
PRACTOLOL
PRECENTOR
PRECEPTOR
PRECISION
PRECURSOR
PREDICTOR
PRELECTOR
PREMOTION
PRINCETON
PRIVATION
PROBATION
PROCESSOR
PROFESSOR
PROFUSION
PROJECTOR
PROKARYON
PROLUSION
PROMACHOS
PROMOTION
PROPELLOR
PROTECTOR
PROVISION
PULSATION
PUSSYFOOT
PYGMALION
QUINTROON
QUOTATION
QUOTITION
RADIATION
REBELLION
REBOATION
RECEPTION
RECESSION
REDUCTION
REFECTION
REFLATION
REFLECTOR
REFLEXION
REFRACTOR
REGUERDON
REGULATOR
REJECTION
REMISSION
RENDITION
RENOVATOR
REPLETION
REPTATION
REPULSION
RESNATRON
RESONATOR
RETENTION
RETORSION
RETORTION
RETRACTOR
REVERSION
REVULSION
RIDERHOOD
ROBERTSON
ROSCOMMON
ROUGHSHOD
RUINATION
SACKERSON
SAINTHOOD
SALVATION
SANHEDRON
SASKATOON
SATIATION
SATINWOOD
SAUCISSON
SAUVIGNON
SCARECROW
SCHOOLBOY
SCONCHEON
SCRAPBOOK
SCRUTATOR
SCUNCHEON
SECESSION
SECLUSION
SECRETION
SEDGEMOOR
SEDUCTION
SELACHION
SELECTION
SEMANTRON
SEMICOLON
SENSATION
SEPARATOR
SERIATION
SERRATION
SHEIKHDOM
SHOLOKHOV
SHOPFLOOR
SHORTSTOP
SIMPLETON
SIMULATOR
SINGLETON
SITUATION
SLINGSHOT
SOLICITOR
SPECTATOR
SPRINGBOK
STABLEBOY
STANCHION
STANNATOR
STATEHOOD
STATEROOM
STEVENSON
STILLROOM
STINKWOOD
STOCKROOM
STONECROP
STOREROOM
STORYBOOK
STRIATION
SUBEDITOR
SUCCENTOR
SUCCESSOR
SUFFUSION
SUMMATION
SUPINATOR
SUSPENSOR
SUSPICION
SWEETSHOP
SYNEDRION
TABELLION
TABULATOR
TARNATION
TELLURION
TENAILLON
TERPINEOL
THEREUPON
THERMIDOR
THRALLDOM
THYRATRON
THYRISTOR
TICTACTOE
TIERCERON
TITRATION
TOADSTOOL
TORMENTOR
TOUCHWOOD
TOURNEDOS
TRADITION
TRIATHLON
TRICERION
TRIHEDRON
TRILITHON
TRISAGION
TROPARION
TROUBADOR
TRUNCHEON
UNCHRISOM
UNDERFOOT
UNDERWOOD
URINATION
VALUATION
VALVASSOR
VARIATION
VEGETATOR
VERMILION
VIBRATION
VIOLATION
VITIATION
WAGENBOOM
WEDGEWOOD
WHEREUPON
WHIRLPOOL
WHITEWOOD
WHOLEFOOD
WIDOWHOOD
WIMBLEDON
WINCANTON
WOLLASTON
WOMANHOOD
WOODENTOP
WRONGFOOT
ALLOCARPY
ALLOGRAPH
AMBROTYPE
AMIDSHIPS
ARCHETYPE
ATAHUALPA
AUTOGRAPH
AUTOSCOPY
BARYSCOPE
COLLOTYPE
CONSCRIPT
DRAINPIPE
ECTOMORPH
EIDOGRAPH
ENDOMORPH
GYROSCOPE
HEMITROPE
HODOGRAPH
HOLOGRAPH
HOMOGRAPH
HOROSCOPE
IDEOGRAPH
IDIOGRAPH
INTERCEPT
INTERLOPE
INTERRUPT
JACKSNIPE
KARYOTYPE
KONISCOPE
LAGNIAPPE
LAGOMORPH
LANDSCAPE
LOGOGRIPH
MEGASCOPE
MESOMORPH
MONOGRAPH
MUTOSCOPE
OLEOGRAPH

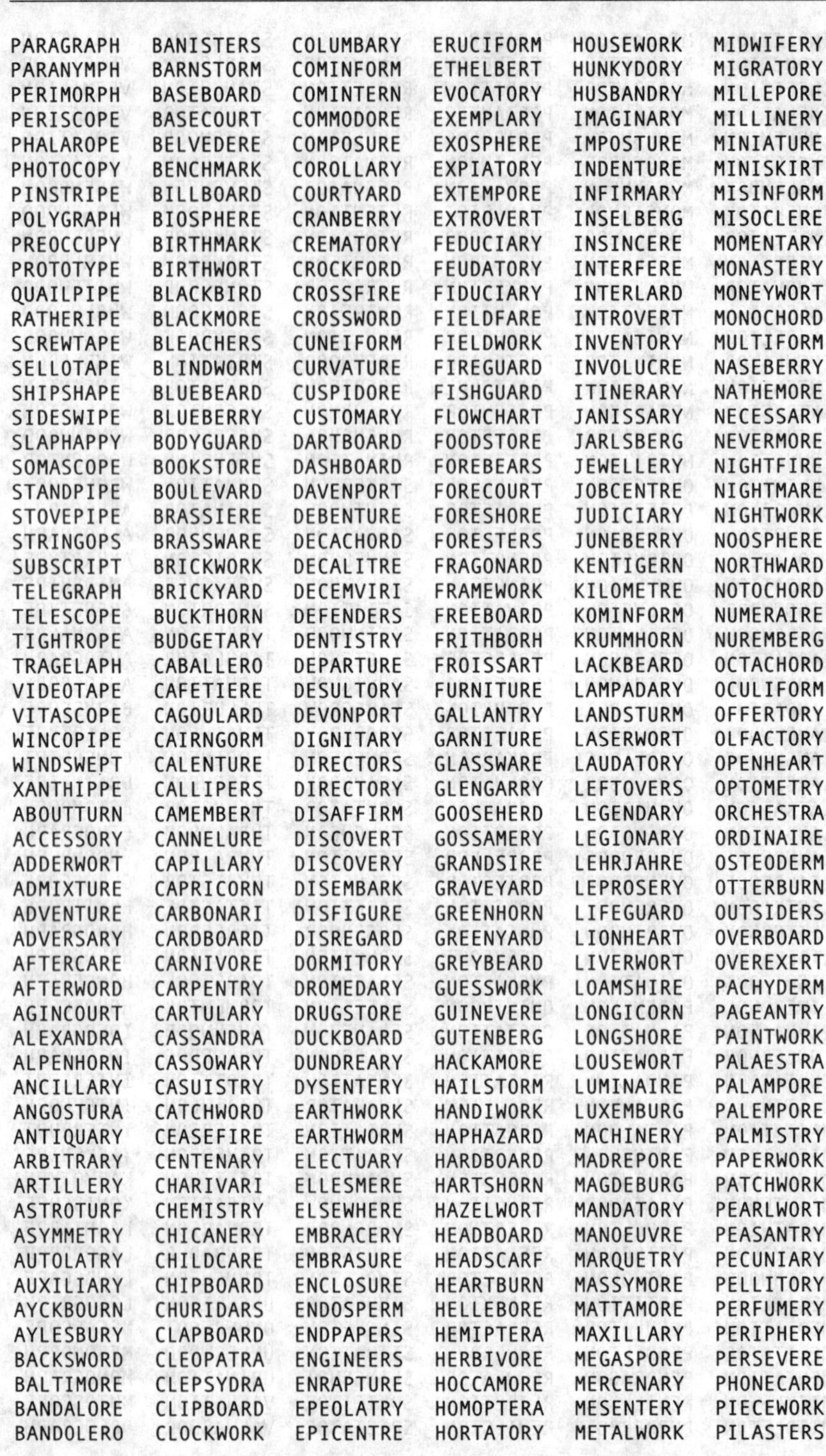

PARAGRAPH
PARANYMPH
PERIMORPH
PERISCOPE
PHALAROPE
PHOTOCOPY
PINSTRIPE
POLYGRAPH
PREOCCUPY
PROTOTYPE
QUAILPIPE
RATHERIPE
SCREWTAPE
SELLOTAPE
SHIPSHAPE
SIDESWIPE
SLAPHAPPY
SOMASCOPE
STANDPIPE
STOVEPIPE
STRINGOPS
SUBSCRIPT
TELEGRAPH
TELESCOPE
TIGHTROPE
TRAGELAPH
VIDEOTAPE
VITASCOPE
WINCOPIPE
WINDSWEPT
XANTHIPPE
ABOUTTURN
ACCESSORY
ADDERWORT
ADMIXTURE
ADVENTURE
ADVERSARY
AFTERCARE
AFTERWORD
AGINCOURT
ALEXANDRA
ALPENHORN
ANCILLARY
ANGOSTURA
ANTIQUARY
ARBITRARY
ARTILLERY
ASTROTURF
ASYMMETRY
AUTOLATRY
AUXILIARY
AYCKBOURN
AYLESBURY
BACKSWORD
BALTIMORE
BANDALORE
BANDOLERO
BANISTERS
BARNSTORM
BASEBOARD
BASECOURT
BELVEDERE
BENCHMARK
BILLBOARD
BIOSPHERE
BIRTHMARK
BIRTHWORT
BLACKBIRD
BLACKMORE
BLEACHERS
BLINDWORM
BLUEBEARD
BLUEBERRY
BODYGUARD
BOOKSTORE
BOULEVARD
BRASSIERE
BRASSWARE
BRICKWORK
BRICKYARD
BUCKTHORN
BUDGETARY
CABALLERO
CAFETIERE
CAGOULARD
CAIRNGORM
CALENTURE
CALLIPERS
CAMEMBERT
CANNELURE
CAPILLARY
CAPRICORN
CARBONARI
CARDBOARD
CARNIVORE
CARPENTRY
CARTULARY
CASSANDRA
CASSOWARY
CASUISTRY
CATCHWORD
CEASEFIRE
CENTENARY
CHARIVARI
CHEMISTRY
CHICANERY
CHILDCARE
CHIPBOARD
CHURIDARS
CLAPBOARD
CLEOPATRA
CLEPSYDRA
CLIPBOARD
CLOCKWORK
COLUMBARY
COMINFORM
COMINTERN
COMMODORE
COMPOSURE
COROLLARY
COURTYARD
CRANBERRY
CREMATORY
CROCKFORD
CROSSFIRE
CROSSWORD
CUNEIFORM
CURVATURE
CUSPIDORE
CUSTOMARY
DARTBOARD
DASHBOARD
DAVENPORT
DEBENTURE
DECACHORD
DECALITRE
DECEMVIRI
DEFENDERS
DENTISTRY
DEPARTURE
DESULTORY
DEVONPORT
DIGNITARY
DIRECTORS
DIRECTORY
DISAFFIRM
DISCOVERT
DISCOVERY
DISEMBARK
DISFIGURE
DISREGARD
DORMITORY
DROMEDARY
DRUGSTORE
DUCKBOARD
DUNDREARY
DYSENTERY
EARTHWORK
EARTHWORM
ELECTUARY
ELLESMERE
ELSEWHERE
EMBRACERY
EMBRASURE
ENCLOSURE
ENDOSPERM
ENDPAPERS
ENGINEERS
ENRAPTURE
EPEOLATRY
EPICENTRE
ERUCIFORM
ETHELBERT
EVOCATORY
EXEMPLARY
EXOSPHERE
EXPIATORY
EXTEMPORE
EXTROVERT
FEDUCIARY
FEUDATORY
FIDUCIARY
FIELDFARE
FIELDWORK
FIREGUARD
FISHGUARD
FLOWCHART
FOODSTORE
FOREBEARS
FORECOURT
FORESHORE
FORESTERS
FRAGONARD
FRAMEWORK
FREEBOARD
FRITHBORH
FROISSART
FURNITURE
GALLANTRY
GARNITURE
GLASSWARE
GLENGARRY
GOOSEHERD
GOSSAMERY
GRANDSIRE
GRAVEYARD
GREENHORN
GREENYARD
GREYBEARD
GUESSWORK
GUINEVERE
GUTENBERG
HACKAMORE
HAILSTORM
HANDIWORK
HAPHAZARD
HARDBOARD
HARTSHORN
HAZELWORT
HEADBOARD
HEADSCARF
HEARTBURN
HELLEBORE
HEMIPTERA
HERBIVORE
HOCCAMORE
HOMOPTERA
HORTATORY
HOUSEWORK
HUNKYDORY
HUSBANDRY
IMAGINARY
IMPOSTURE
INDENTURE
INFIRMARY
INSELBERG
INSINCERE
INTERFERE
INTERLARD
INTROVERT
INVENTORY
INVOLUCRE
ITINERARY
JANISSARY
JARLSBERG
JEWELLERY
JOBCENTRE
JUDICIARY
JUNEBERRY
KENTIGERN
KILOMETRE
KOMINFORM
KRUMMHORN
LACKBEARD
LAMPADARY
LANDSTURM
LASERWORT
LAUDATORY
LEFTOVERS
LEGENDARY
LEGIONARY
LEHRJAHRE
LEPROSERY
LIFEGUARD
LIONHEART
LIVERWORT
LOAMSHIRE
LONGICORN
LONGSHORE
LOUSEWORT
LUMINAIRE
LUXEMBURG
MACHINERY
MADREPORE
MAGDEBURG
MANDATORY
MANOEUVRE
MARQUETRY
MASSYMORE
MATTAMORE
MAXILLARY
MEGASPORE
MERCENARY
MESENTERY
METALWORK
MIDWIFERY
MIGRATORY
MILLEPORE
MILLINERY
MINIATURE
MINISKIRT
MISINFORM
MISOCLERE
MOMENTARY
MONASTERY
MONEYWORT
MONOCHORD
MULTIFORM
NASEBERRY
NATHEMORE
NECESSARY
NEVERMORE
NIGHTFIRE
NIGHTMARE
NIGHTWORK
NOOSPHERE
NORTHWARD
NOTOCHORD
NUMERAIRE
NUREMBERG
OCTACHORD
OCULIFORM
OFFERTORY
OLFACTORY
OPENHEART
OPTOMETRY
ORCHESTRA
ORDINAIRE
OSTEODERM
OTTERBURN
OUTSIDERS
OVERBOARD
OVEREXERT
PACHYDERM
PAGEANTRY
PAINTWORK
PALAESTRA
PALAMPORE
PALEMPORE
PALMISTRY
PAPERWORK
PATCHWORK
PEARLWORT
PEASANTRY
PECUNIARY
PELLITORY
PERFUMERY
PERIPHERY
PERSEVERE
PHONECARD
PIECEWORK
PILASTERS

PITCHFORK
PITUITARY
PLACATORY
PLANETARY
POLITBURO
POLYANDRY
POTPOURRI
PRECATORY
PREDATORY
PREFATORY
PREFIGURE
PRELUSORY
PREMATURE
PRIMAVERA
PROCEDURE
PRONGHORN
PROUDHORN
PROVEDORE
PULMONARY
PURGATORY
QUILLWORT
RAINSTORM
RASPATORY
RASPBERRY
READYEARN
REARGUARD
RECAPTURE
REFECTORY
RELIQUARY
RENCONTRE
REPERTORY
RESIDUARY
RESTIFORM
RETROVERT
RICERCARE
ROQUEFORT
RUDDIGORE
SAFEGUARD
SAGITTARY
SALESGIRL
SALLYPORT
SALTPETRE
SANCTUARY
SANDSTORM
SCRIPTURE
SCULPTURE
SECATEURS
SECONDARY
SECRETARY
SEDENTARY
SEMAPHORE
SEPULCHRE
SEPULTURE
SHIFTWORK
SHORTHORN
SHORTTERM
SHRUBBERY
SIDEBOARD
SIGNATORY
SIGNATURE
SIGNBOARD
SINGAPORE
SISSERARY
SNOWSTORM
SOLITAIRE
SOMEWHERE
SOPHISTRY
SOPHOMORE
SOUFRIERE
SOUTHWARD
SOUTHWARK
SPARKLERS
SPEARWORT
SPIKENARD
SPLINTERS
SPOROCARP
SPRECHERY
SQUATTERS
STARBOARD
STATUTORY
STEELYARD
STEENKIRK
STEVEDORE
STILLBORN
STILTBIRD
STINKBIRD
STINKHORN
STOCKWORK
STOCKYARD
STONEWARE
STONEWORK
STONEWORT
STRANGURY
STRICTURE
STRONGARM
STROSSERS
STRUCTURE
STUMPWORK
SUBALTERN
SUBENTIRE
SUMPTUARY
SURFBOARD
SURQUEDRY
SWINEHERD
SYLLABARY
TABLATURE
TABLEWARE
TAILBOARD
TANTARARA
TAVERNERS
TECTIFORM
TEMPORARY
TERRITORY
THEREFORE
TIMESHARE
TIPPERARY
TITHEBARN
TOBERMORY
TRADEMARK
TRANSFORM
TRANSPIRE
TRANSPORT
TRAVELERS
TREACHERY
TRIBUTARY
UNCONCERN
UNSAVOURY
UPCOUNTRY
VAINGLORY
VENUSBERG
VERMIFORM
VERTIPORT
VESTITURE
VEXILLARY
VIBRATORY
VISIONARY
VOLUNTARY
VORTIGERN
WASHBOARD
WATCHWORD
WATERFORD
WATERMARK
WHEATGERM
WHEREFORE
WHITAKERS
WINEBERRY
WRANGLERS
YORKSHIRE
ZYGOSPORE
ACADEMIST
ACUTENESS
ADEPTNESS
ADVENTIST
ADVERTISE
AFTERMOST
ALBATROSS
ALCHEMIST
ALERTNESS
ALOOFNESS
ANABOLISM
ANARCHIST
ANATOMIST
ANGLICISM
ANSCHLUSS
APOLOGIST
ARABINOSE
ARCHIVIST
ARQUEBUSE
AUTHORESS
AUTOCROSS
AWARENESS
BACKSHISH
BAKEHOUSE
BAKSHEESH
BALLADIST
BEANFEAST
BEARDLESS
BELLICOSE
BERGAMASK
BERGOMASK
BICYCLIST
BIOLOGIST
BLACKLIST
BLACKNESS
BLAMELESS
BLANDNESS
BLINDNESS
BLOODLESS
BLUFFNESS
BLUNTNESS
BOATHOUSE
BOLOGNESE
BOSSINESS
BOUNDLESS
BRAINCASE
BRAINLESS
BRAINWASH
BRASENOSE
BRATWURST
BREAKFAST
BRIEFCASE
BRIEFNESS
BRISKNESS
BROADCAST
BRUTALISM
BUCHAREST
BULKINESS
BURLINESS
CALABOOSE
CALABRESE
CALVANISM
CALVINIST
CANTONESE
CAREERIST
CARTHORSE
CATACLYSM
CATALEPSY
CATAPLASM
CATECHISM
CAVENDISH
CEASELESS
CELLARIST
CELLULOSE
CEYLONESE
CHANTEUSE
CHEAPNESS
CHECKLIST
CHEERLESS
CHILDLESS
CLASSLESS
CLEANNESS
CLEARNESS
CLOCKWISE
CLOSENESS
CLOUDLESS
CLUBHOUSE
COLORLESS
COLOURIST
COLUMNIST
COMMUNISM
COMMUNIST
CONCOURSE
CONGOLESE
COOKHOUSE
CORNBRASH
COUNTLESS
CRAZINESS
CRISPNESS
CRITICISM
CROSSWISE
CRUDENESS
DALTONISM
DAMNEDEST
DAUNTLESS
DEACONESS
DEATHLESS
DECOMPOSE
DEFEATISM
DEFEATIST
DEMITASSE
DENSENESS
DEOXIDISE
DESPOTISM
DEXTRORSE
DINGINESS
DIRTINESS
DISCOURSE
DISHONEST
DISPLEASE
DIZZINESS
DOGMATISM
DOSSHOUSE
DOUBTLESS
DRAMATIST
DREAMLESS
DRYASDUST
DULCINIST
DUNGENESS
EAGERNESS
ECOLOGIST
ECONOMIST
ECOSSAISE
ECTOPLASM
EDELWEISS
ELECTRESS
EMBARRASS
EMBELLISH
EMPTINESS
ENCOMPASS
EPIPOLISM
EQUIPOISE
EROTICISM
ESEMPLASY
ESTABLISH
EUCHARIST
EUPHEMISM
EXACTNESS
EXPERTISE
EXTREMISM
EXTREMIST
FACTORISE
FAINTNESS
FAITHLESS
FALANGIST
FALSENESS
FARMHOUSE
FAULTLESS
FEUDALISM
FLESHLESS
FLOPHOUSE
FOGGINESS
FOLIOLOSE
FOOTLOOSE
FORECLOSE
FORMALIST
FOSSILISE
FRAMBOISE
FRANCHISE
FRANKNESS
FRESHNESS
FRUITLESS
FUGGINESS
FUSSINESS
FUSTINESS
FUZZINESS
GALACTOSE
GALLICISM
GALVANISM
GARGARISM
GATECRASH
GAUDINESS
GAUNTNESS
GAWKINESS
GEODESIST
GEOLOGIST
GIBBERISH
GIDDINESS
GILGAMESH
GIRONDIST
GODLINESS
GOLDCREST
GONGORISM

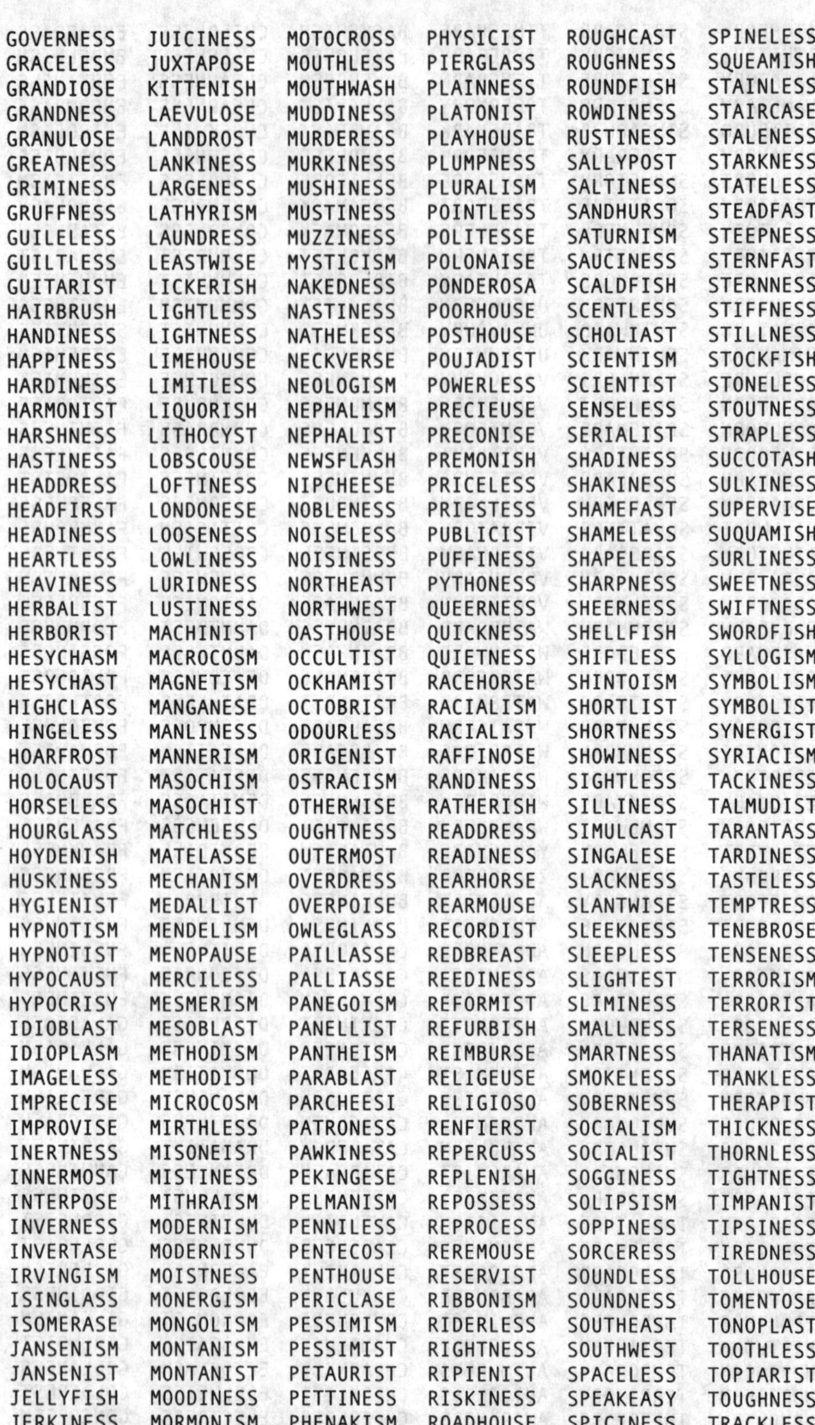

GOVERNESS
GRACELESS
GRANDIOSE
GRANDNESS
GRANULOSE
GREATNESS
GRIMINESS
GRUFFNESS
GUILELESS
GUILTLESS
GUITARIST
HAIRBRUSH
HANDINESS
HAPPINESS
HARDINESS
HARMONIST
HARSHNESS
HASTINESS
HEADDRESS
HEADFIRST
HEADINESS
HEARTLESS
HEAVINESS
HERBALIST
HERBORIST
HESYCHASM
HESYCHAST
HIGHCLASS
HINGELESS
HOARFROST
HOLOCAUST
HORSELESS
HOURGLASS
HOYDENISH
HUSKINESS
HYGIENIST
HYPNOTISM
HYPNOTIST
HYPOCAUST
HYPOCRISY
IDIOBLAST
IDIOPLASM
IMAGELESS
IMPRECISE
IMPROVISE
INERTNESS
INNERMOST
INTERPOSE
INVERNESS
INVERTASE
IRVINGISM
ISINGLASS
ISOMERASE
JANSENISM
JANSENIST
JELLYFISH
JERKINESS
JUICINESS
JUXTAPOSE
KITTENISH
LAEVULOSE
LANDDROST
LANKINESS
LARGENESS
LATHYRISM
LAUNDRESS
LEASTWISE
LICKERISH
LIGHTLESS
LIGHTNESS
LIMEHOUSE
LIMITLESS
LIQUORISH
LITHOCYST
LOBSCOUSE
LOFTINESS
LONDONESE
LOOSENESS
LOWLINESS
LURIDNESS
LUSTINESS
MACHINIST
MACROCOSM
MAGNETISM
MANGANESE
MANLINESS
MANNERISM
MASOCHISM
MASOCHIST
MATCHLESS
MATELASSE
MECHANISM
MEDALLIST
MENDELISM
MENOPAUSE
MERCILESS
MESMERISM
MESOBLAST
METHODISM
METHODIST
MICROCOSM
MIRTHLESS
MISONEIST
MISTINESS
MITHRAISM
MODERNISM
MODERNIST
MOISTNESS
MONERGISM
MONGOLISM
MONTANISM
MONTANIST
MOODINESS
MORMONISM
MOTOCROSS
MOUTHLESS
MOUTHWASH
MUDDINESS
MURDERESS
MURKINESS
MUSHINESS
MUSTINESS
MUZZINESS
MYSTICISM
NAKEDNESS
NASTINESS
NATHELESS
NECKVERSE
NEOLOGISM
NEPHALISM
NEPHALIST
NEWSFLASH
NIPCHEESE
NOBLENESS
NOISELESS
NOISINESS
NORTHEAST
NORTHWEST
OASTHOUSE
OCCULTIST
OCKHAMIST
OCTOBRIST
ODOURLESS
ORIGENIST
OSTRACISM
OTHERWISE
OUGHTNESS
OUTERMOST
OVERDRESS
OVERPOISE
OWLEGLASS
PAILLASSE
PALLIASSE
PANEGOISM
PANELLIST
PANTHEISM
PARABLAST
PARCHEESI
PATRONESS
PAWKINESS
PEKINGESE
PELMANISM
PENNILESS
PENTECOST
PENTHOUSE
PERICLASE
PESSIMISM
PESSIMIST
PETAURIST
PETTINESS
PHENAKISM
PHYSICIST
PIERGLASS
PLAINNESS
PLATONIST
PLAYHOUSE
PLUMPNESS
PLURALISM
POINTLESS
POLITESSE
POLONAISE
PONDEROSA
POORHOUSE
POSTHOUSE
POUJADIST
POWERLESS
PRECIEUSE
PRECONISE
PREMONISH
PRICELESS
PRIESTESS
PUBLICIST
PUFFINESS
PYTHONESS
QUEERNESS
QUICKNESS
QUIETNESS
RACEHORSE
RACIALISM
RACIALIST
RAFFINOSE
RANDINESS
RATHERISH
READDRESS
READINESS
REARHORSE
REARMOUSE
RECORDIST
REDBREAST
REEDINESS
REFORMIST
REFURBISH
REIMBURSE
RELIGEUSE
RELIGIOSO
RENFIERST
REPERCUSS
REPLENISH
REPOSSESS
REPROCESS
REREMOUSE
RESERVIST
RIBBONISM
RIDERLESS
RIGHTNESS
RIPIENIST
RISKINESS
ROADHOUSE
ROUGHCAST
ROUGHNESS
ROUNDFISH
ROWDINESS
RUSTINESS
SALLYPOST
SALTINESS
SANDHURST
SATURNISM
SAUCINESS
SCALDFISH
SCENTLESS
SCHOLIAST
SCIENTISM
SCIENTIST
SENSELESS
SERIALIST
SHADINESS
SHAKINESS
SHAMEFAST
SHAMELESS
SHAPELESS
SHARPNESS
SHEERNESS
SHELLFISH
SHIFTLESS
SHINTOISM
SHORTLIST
SHORTNESS
SHOWINESS
SIGHTLESS
SILLINESS
SIMULCAST
SINGALESE
SLACKNESS
SLANTWISE
SLEEKNESS
SLEEPLESS
SLIGHTEST
SLIMINESS
SMALLNESS
SMARTNESS
SMOKELESS
SOBERNESS
SOCIALISM
SOCIALIST
SOGGINESS
SOLIPSISM
SOPPINESS
SORCERESS
SOUNDLESS
SOUNDNESS
SOUTHEAST
SOUTHWEST
SPACELESS
SPEAKEASY
SPICINESS
SPINELESS
SQUEAMISH
STAINLESS
STAIRCASE
STALENESS
STARKNESS
STATELESS
STEADFAST
STEEPNESS
STERNFAST
STERNNESS
STIFFNESS
STILLNESS
STOCKFISH
STONELESS
STOUTNESS
STRAPLESS
SUCCOTASH
SULKINESS
SUPERVISE
SUQUAMISH
SURLINESS
SWEETNESS
SWIFTNESS
SWORDFISH
SYLLOGISM
SYMBOLISM
SYMBOLIST
SYNERGIST
SYRIACISM
TACKINESS
TALMUDIST
TARANTASS
TARDINESS
TASTELESS
TEMPTRESS
TENEBROSE
TENSENESS
TERRORISM
TERRORIST
TERSENESS
THANATISM
THANKLESS
THERAPIST
THICKNESS
THORNLESS
TIGHTNESS
TIMPANIST
TIPSINESS
TIREDNESS
TOLLHOUSE
TOMENTOSE
TONOPLAST
TOOTHLESS
TOPIARIST
TOUGHNESS
TRACKLESS

TRANSFUSE
TRANSPOSE
TRAPEZIST
TRIBALISM
TRICKLESS
TRITENESS
TUBBINESS
TURQUOISE
TUTIORISM
TYMPANIST
UNDERCAST
UNDERMOST
UNDERPASS
UNPRECISE
UNSELFISH
UPPERMOST
UROKINASE
UTTERLESS
UTTERMOST
VAGUENESS
VALUELESS
VANDALISM
VANTBRASS
VEILLEUSE
VIDEODISC
VIOLINIST
VIVIDNESS
VOICELESS
VOLTINISM
VOODOOISM
VORTICISM
VULCANIST
VULGARISM
WAREHOUSE
WARTCRESS
WATERLESS
WAYZGOOSE
WEARINESS
WEIRDNESS
WELTGEIST
WHEELBASE
WHITEFISH
WHITENESS
WHITEWASH
WHOLENESS
WILDGEESE
WINEGLASS
WITTICISM
WODEHOUSE
WOODHOUSE
WOODLOUSE
WOOLINESS
WORDINESS
WORKHORSE
WORKHOUSE
WORTHLESS
WREAKLESS
WRECKFISH
YELLOWISH
ZEITGEIST
ZOOLOGIST
ABOMINATE
ABSURDITY
ACCIDENTS
ACCLIMATE
ACCLIVITY
ACIDULATE
ACTUALITY
ACUMINATE
ADMIRALTY
ADUMBRATE
ADVERSITY
AFFILIATE
AFFRICATE
AFTERMATH
AGGRAVATE
AGGREGATE
AINSWORTH
ALLEVIATE
ALTERCATE
ALTERNATE
ALVEOLATE
AMBIGUITY
AMELAKITE
ANAGLYPTA
ANAPLASTY
ANCHORITE
ANHYDRITE
ANIMOSITY
ANONYMITY
ANTIPASTO
ANTIQUITY
APHRODITE
ARAGONITE
ARBITRATE
ARMAMENTS
ARRIVISTE
ASSIDUITY
ASSOCIATE
ATTENUATE
ATTRIBUTE
AUSTERITY
AUTHORITY
AUTOROUTE
BACKCLOTH
BANQUETTE
BARBARITY
BARNABITE
BIFURCATE
BIPARTITE
BLOODBATH
BONAPARTE
BRIQUETTE
BRUTALITY
BUCKTEETH
CALCINATE
CALCULATE
CALIBRATE
CALLOSITY
CANALETTO
CANDIDATE
CAPORETTO
CAPTIVATE
CAPTIVITY
CARBAMATE
CARBONATE
CARMELITE
CASTANETS
CASTIGATE
CELEBRATE
CELEBRITY
CELLULITE
CEREBRATE
CERTAINTY
CHABAZITE
CHAMPERTY
CHARLOTTE
CHECKMATE
CHIPOLATA
CHOCOLATE
CHOLELITH
CHONDRITE
CIGARETTE
CILIOLATE
CIRCINATE
CIRCULATE
CLASSMATE
COAGULATE
COARCTATE
COENOBITE
COFFINITE
COLLIGATE
COLLIMATE
COLLOCATE
COLUMBATE
COLUMBITE
COMMODITY
COMMUNITY
COMPOSITE
CONCAVITY
CONJUGATE
CONNOTATE
CONSULATE
CONTRALTO
COOPERATE
COPROLITE
CORPORATE
CORRELATE
CORRUGATE
CORUSCATE
COUCHETTE
COURGETTE
COVELLITE
CREDULITY
CREPITATE
CRIMINATE
CROQUETTE
CROTCHETY
CULMINATE
CULTIVATE
CURIOSITY
CYCLAMATE
CYCLOLITH
DARTMOUTH
DEBUTANTE
DECLIVITY
DECOLLATE
DECUSSATE
DEFALCATE
DEFOLIATE
DEFORMITY
DEHYDRATE
DELINEATE
DEMARCATE
DENIGRATE
DEPRAVITY
DEPRECATE
DEPREDATE
DESECRATE
DESICCATE
DESIGNATE
DESPERATE
DESTITUTE
DEVASTATE
DEXTERITY
DIALOGITE
DISHCLOTH
DISLOCATE
DISPARATE
DISPARITY
DISREPUTE
DISSIPATE
DISSOLUTE
DIVERSITY
DOCTORATE
DOCUMENTS
DONIZETTI
DUPLICATE
DUPLICITY
EDGEWORTH
EIGHTIETH
EJACULATE
ELABORATE
ELAEOLITE
ELIMINATE
ELIZABETH
ELKOSHITE
ELUCIDATE
ELUTRIATE
EMBROCATE
EMOLLIATE
ENCRATITE
ENERINITE
ENHYDRITE
ENSTATITE
ENTOPHYTE
ENTRECÔTE
ENTREMETS
ENUCLEATE
ENUMERATE
ENUNCIATE
EPARCHATE
EPAULETTE
ERADICATE
EROSTRATE
ESCOPETTE
ESCULENTS
ESPERANTO
ESTAFETTE
ETIQUETTE
EVAPORATE
EVENTUATE
EXANIMATE
EXCORIATE
EXCULPATE
EXONERATE
EXPATIATE
EXPISCATE
EXPLICATE
EXPURGATE
EXQUISITE
EXSICCATE
EXTENUATE
EXTIRPATE
EXTRADITE
EXTREMITY
EXTRICATE
FABRICATE
FACECLOTH
FACUNDITY
FAMAGUSTA
FASCINATE
FAVOURITE
FECUNDITY
FERTILITY
FESTINATE
FESTIVITY
FIBROLITE
FIFTEENTH
FIGURANTE
FINICKITY
FIRSTRATE
FISHPLATE
FLAGITATE
FLECHETTE
FLESHPOTS
FLOODGATE
FLUCTUATE
FOGRAMITE
FOOTPLATE
FORETASTE
FORFICATE
FORMALITY
FORMULATE
FORNICATE
FORTHWITH
FORTUNATE
FRAGILITY
FRAGMENTS
FRATCHETY
FRIGIDITY
FRIVOLITY
FRIZZANTE
FROGMOUTH
FROSTBITE
FRUGALITY
FRUSTRATE
FULMINATE
FUSTIGATE
GARRULITY
GELIGNITE
GENIALITY
GENTILITY
GEORGETTE
GERMANITE
GERMINATE
GIBEONITE
GLOMERATE
GMELINITE
GOALMOUTH
GOLDSMITH
GONIATITE
GOSLARITE
GOTHAMITE
GRANULATE
GRANULITE
GRAVITATE
HABITUATE
HAECCEITY
HAEMATITE
HALFEMPTY
HALLSTATT
HARIOLATE
HARROGATE
HASHEMITE
HAWCUBITE
HEADCLOTH
HEAVYDUTY
HESSONITE
HEYPRESTO
HIBERNATE
HIMYARITE

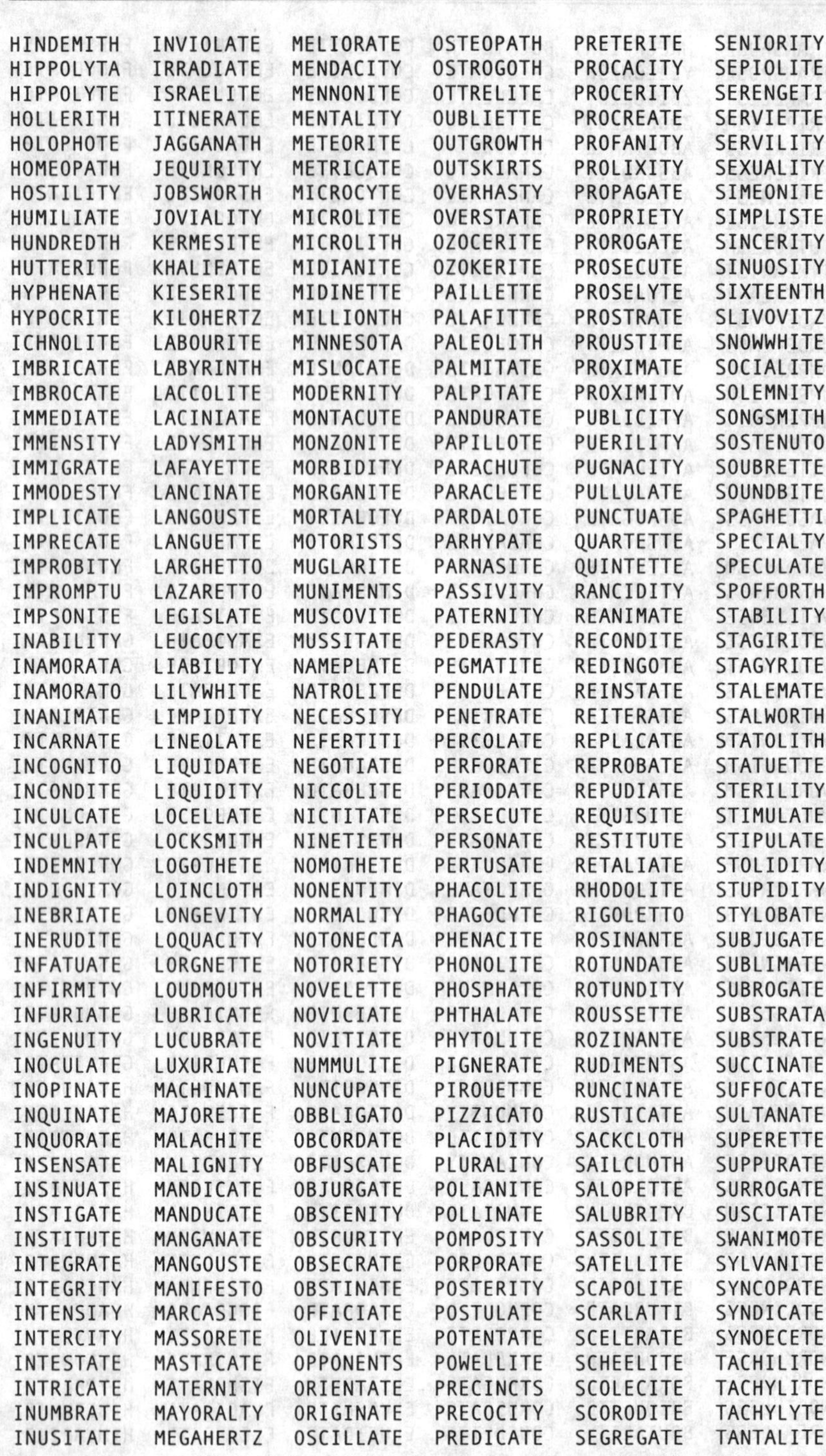

HINDEMITH
HIPPOLYTA
HIPPOLYTE
HOLLERITH
HOLOPHOTE
HOMEOPATH
HOSTILITY
HUMILIATE
HUNDREDTH
HUTTERITE
HYPHENATE
HYPOCRITE
ICHNOLITE
IMBRICATE
IMBROCATE
IMMEDIATE
IMMENSITY
IMMIGRATE
IMMODESTY
IMPLICATE
IMPRECATE
IMPROBITY
IMPROMPTU
IMPSONITE
INABILITY
INAMORATA
INAMORATO
INANIMATE
INCARNATE
INCOGNITO
INCONDITE
INCULCATE
INCULPATE
INDEMNITY
INDIGNITY
INEBRIATE
INERUDITE
INFATUATE
INFIRMITY
INFURIATE
INGENUITY
INOCULATE
INOPINATE
INQUINATE
INQUORATE
INSENSATE
INSINUATE
INSTIGATE
INSTITUTE
INTEGRATE
INTEGRITY
INTENSITY
INTERCITY
INTESTATE
INTRICATE
INUMBRATE
INUSITATE
INVIOLATE
IRRADIATE
ISRAELITE
ITINERATE
JAGGANATH
JEQUIRITY
JOBSWORTH
JOVIALITY
KERMESITE
KHALIFATE
KIESERITE
KILOHERTZ
LABOURITE
LABYRINTH
LACCOLITE
LACINIATE
LADYSMITH
LAFAYETTE
LANCINATE
LANGOUSTE
LANGUETTE
LARGHETTO
LAZARETTO
LEGISLATE
LEUCOCYTE
LIABILITY
LILYWHITE
LIMPIDITY
LINEOLATE
LIQUIDATE
LIQUIDITY
LOCELLATE
LOCKSMITH
LOGOTHETE
LOINCLOTH
LONGEVITY
LOQUACITY
LORGNETTE
LOUDMOUTH
LUBRICATE
LUCUBRATE
LUXURIATE
MACHINATE
MAJORETTE
MALACHITE
MALIGNITY
MANDICATE
MANDUCATE
MANGANATE
MANGOUSTE
MANIFESTO
MARCASITE
MASSORETE
MASTICATE
MATERNITY
MAYORALTY
MEGAHERTZ
MELIORATE
MENDACITY
MENNONITE
MENTALITY
METEORITE
METRICATE
MICROCYTE
MICROLITE
MICROLITH
MIDIANITE
MIDINETTE
MILLIONTH
MINNESOTA
MISLOCATE
MODERNITY
MONTACUTE
MONZONITE
MORBIDITY
MORGANITE
MORTALITY
MOTORISTS
MUGLARITE
MUNIMENTS
MUSCOVITE
MUSSITATE
NAMEPLATE
NATROLITE
NECESSITY
NEFERTITI
NEGOTIATE
NICCOLITE
NICTITATE
NINETIETH
NOMOTHETE
NONENTITY
NORMALITY
NOTONECTA
NOTORIETY
NOVELETTE
NOVICIATE
NOVITIATE
NUMMULITE
NUNCUPATE
OBBLIGATO
OBCORDATE
OBFUSCATE
OBJURGATE
OBSCENITY
OBSCURITY
OBSECRATE
OBSTINATE
OFFICIATE
OLIVENITE
OPPONENTS
ORIENTATE
ORIGINATE
OSCILLATE
OSTEOPATH
OSTROGOTH
OTTRELITE
OUBLIETTE
OUTGROWTH
OUTSKIRTS
OVERHASTY
OVERSTATE
OZOCERITE
OZOKERITE
PAILLETTE
PALAFITTE
PALEOLITH
PALMITATE
PALPITATE
PANDURATE
PAPILLOTE
PARACHUTE
PARACLETE
PARDALOTE
PARHYPATE
PARNASITE
PASSIVITY
PATERNITY
PEDERASTY
PEGMATITE
PENDULATE
PENETRATE
PERCOLATE
PERFORATE
PERIODATE
PERSECUTE
PERSONATE
PERTUSATE
PHACOLITE
PHAGOCYTE
PHENACITE
PHONOLITE
PHOSPHATE
PHTHALATE
PHYTOLITE
PIGNERATE
PIROUETTE
PIZZICATO
PLACIDITY
PLURALITY
POLIANITE
POLLINATE
POMPOSITY
PORPORATE
POSTERITY
POSTULATE
POTENTATE
POWELLITE
PRECINCTS
PRECOCITY
PREDICATE
PRETERITE
PROCACITY
PROCERITY
PROCREATE
PROFANITY
PROLIXITY
PROPAGATE
PROPRIETY
PROROGATE
PROSECUTE
PROSELYTE
PROSTRATE
PROUSTITE
PROXIMATE
PROXIMITY
PUBLICITY
PUERILITY
PUGNACITY
PULLULATE
PUNCTUATE
QUARTETTE
QUINTETTE
RANCIDITY
REANIMATE
RECONDITE
REDINGOTE
REINSTATE
REITERATE
REPLICATE
REPROBATE
REPUDIATE
REQUISITE
RESTITUTE
RETALIATE
RHODOLITE
RIGOLETTO
ROSINANTE
ROTUNDATE
ROTUNDITY
ROUSSETTE
ROZINANTE
RUDIMENTS
RUNCINATE
RUSTICATE
SACKCLOTH
SAILCLOTH
SALOPETTE
SALUBRITY
SASSOLITE
SATELLITE
SCAPOLITE
SCARLATTI
SCELERATE
SCHEELITE
SCOLECITE
SCORODITE
SEGREGATE
SENIORITY
SEPIOLITE
SERENGETI
SERVIETTE
SERVILITY
SEXUALITY
SIMEONITE
SIMPLISTE
SINCERITY
SINUOSITY
SIXTEENTH
SLIVOVITZ
SNOWWHITE
SOCIALITE
SOLEMNITY
SONGSMITH
SOSTENUTO
SOUBRETTE
SOUNDBITE
SPAGHETTI
SPECIALTY
SPECULATE
SPOFFORTH
STABILITY
STAGIRITE
STAGYRITE
STALEMATE
STALWORTH
STATOLITH
STATUETTE
STERILITY
STIMULATE
STIPULATE
STOLIDITY
STUPIDITY
STYLOBATE
SUBJUGATE
SUBLIMATE
SUBROGATE
SUBSTRATA
SUBSTRATE
SUCCINATE
SUFFOCATE
SULTANATE
SUPERETTE
SUPPURATE
SURROGATE
SUSCITATE
SWANIMOTE
SYLVANITE
SYNCOPATE
SYNDICATE
SYNOECETE
TACHILITE
TACHYLITE
TACHYLYTE
TANTALITE

TAUCHNITZ
TEDIOSITY
TELEPHOTO
TEMPERATE
TENEMENTS
TEREBINTH
TERMINATE
THELEMITE
THERALITE
THIRTIETH
TINGUAITE
TITILLATE
TORBANITE
TRANSLATE
TRANSMUTE
TREMOLITE
TREMULATE
TRIBUNATE
TRIDYMITE
TRILOBITE
TRITURATE
TROMPETTE
TROOSTITE
TRUTINATE
TUILLETTE
TUNGSTATE
TURBIDITY
TURBINATE
TWENTIETH
UMPTEENTH
UNANIMITY
UNDERRATE
USHERETTE
UVAROVITE
VACCINATE
VACILLATE
VAPORETTO
VARIEGATE
VARIOLATE
VARISCITE
VELLICATE
VENIALITY
VENTILATE
VERBERATE
VERBOSITY
VERKAMPTE
VESTMENTS
VIABILITY
VIGILANTE
VINDICATE
VIRGINITY
VIRGULATE
VISAGISTE
VISCOSITY
VULCANITE
VULGARITY
VULPINITE
WAGNERITE
WAGONETTE
WAHABIITE
WALDFLUTE
WASHCLOTH
WATERBUTT
WATERGATE
WAVELLITE
WHITWORTH
WILLEMITE
WITCHETTY
WITHERITE
WORDSMITH
WULFENITE
WYANDOTTE
XEROPHYTE
ZENOCRATE
ZINKENITE
ZUCCHETTO
ACIDULOUS
ACONCAGUA
AESCHYLUS
AHASUERUS
ALUMINIUM
AMBIGUOUS
AMBITIOUS
AMERICIUM
AMIANTHUS
AMORPHOUS
AMYGDALUS
ANALOGOUS
ANHYDROUS
ANOMALOUS
ANONYMOUS
ANTIGONUS
ANTONINUS
APOLLONUS
APPARATUS
ARABESQUE
ARBORETUM
AREOPAGUS
ASCLEPIUS
ASPARAGUS
ASPLENIUM
ASSIDUOUS
ASTRONAUT
ASTUCIOUS
ATHENAEUM
ATROCIOUS
AUDACIOUS
AUTOLYCUS
BACTERIUM
BARBAROUS
BASKETFUL
BEAUTEOUS
BEAUTIFUL
BEELZEBUB
BEHAVIOUR
BERKELIUM
BERYLLIUM
BOSPHORUS
BOTTLEFUL
BOUNTEOUS
BOUNTIFUL
BUCENTAUR
BUCKETFUL
BUMPTIOUS
BURLESQUE
BUTTERBUR
BUTTERCUP
BUTTERNUT
CALCANEUM
CALCANEUS
CALDARIUM
CALEMBOUR
CANCEROUS
CANTHARUS
CAPACIOUS
CAPITULUM
CATALOGUE
CATERWAUL
CAVERNOUS
CENTAURUS
CERATODUS
CHARGEFUL
CHARTREUX
CHAUFFEUR
CHIHUAHUA
CINEREOUS
CLAMOROUS
COENOBIUM
COLCHICUM
COLLEAGUE
COLLYRIUM
COLOSSEUM
COLOSTRUM
COLOURFUL
COLUMBIUM
CONDUCTUS
CONFUCIUS
CONGRUOUS
CONSCIOUS
CONSENSUS
CONTINUUM
CONUNDRUM
CORNFLOUR
COSMONAUT
COTHURNUS
COURTEOUS
CRAPULOUS
CREDULOUS
CRETINOUS
CRIBELLUM
CUPRESSUS
CUTANEOUS
CYMBIDIUM
DANGEROUS
DECALOGUE
DECEITFUL
DECIDUOUS
DELICIOUS
DELIRIOUS
DEMAGOGUE
DEMEANOUR
DEMETRIUS
DEUTERIUM
DEXTEROUS
DIANDROUS
DIONYSIUS
DISCOLOUR
DISFAVOUR
DISHONOUR
DOODLEBUG
EFFLUVIUM
EGREGIOUS
ELATERIUM
ENCELADUS
ENCOLPIUM
ENDEAVOUR
ENTROPIUM
EPICEDIUM
EPIGAEOUS
EPONYMOUS
EQUISETUM
EQUIVOQUE
EROGENOUS
ERRONEOUS
ESOPHAGUS
ETHEREOUS
EUHEMERUS
EUPHONIUM
EXCALIBUR
EXEQUATUR
FABACEOUS
FABULINUS
FACETIOUS
FERACIOUS
FEROCIOUS
FLABELLUM
FLAGELLUM
FOMALHAUT
FORGETFUL
FRACTIOUS
FRIGHTFUL
FRIVOLOUS
FUGACIOUS
FURACIOUS
GARGANTUA
GARRULOUS
GAUDEAMUS
GERMANIUM
GINGLYMUS
GINORMOUS
GLADIOLUS
GLAIREOUS
GLAMOROUS
GLUCINIUM
GLUTINOUS
GOSSYPIUM
GREASEGUN
GROTESQUE
GROUNDNUT
GYMNASIUM
GYNOECIUM
HADROSAUR
HARMONIUM
HARQUEBUS
HAZARDOUS
HEARTHRUG
HERBARIUM
HERODOTUS
HILARIOUS
HORDEOLUM
HOSPITIUM
HUMONGOUS
HUMUNGOUS
IDEALOGUE
IGNORAMUS
IMPERIOUS
IMPETUOUS
IMPLUVIUM
INCITATUS
INCURIOUS
INDECORUM
INGENIOUS
INGENUOUS
INJURIOUS
INNOCUOUS
INSIDIOUS
INTROITUS
INVIDIOUS
JITTERBUG
JUDICIOUS
KABELJOUW
LABORIOUS
LANTHANUM
LECHEROUS
LEVITICUS
LIBELLOUS
LITIGIOUS
LUCRETIUS
LUDICROUS
LUMBRICUS
LUXURIOUS
MACARTHUR
MAGNALIUM
MAGNESIUM
MALICIOUS
MALLEOLUS
MANGETOUT
MANUBRIUM
MARSUPIUM
MARVELOUS
MASTERFUL
MAURITIUS
MAUSOLEUM
MELODIOUS
MENSTRUUM
MILLENIUM
MINACIOUS
MOCKERNUT
MOMENTOUS
MONOCOQUE
MONOLOGUE
MONSTROUS
MUMPSIMUS
MUNDUNGUS
MURDEROUS
NARCISSUS
NEFANDOUS
NEFARIOUS
NEIGHBOUR
NEPTUNIUM
NICARAGUA
NICODEMUS
NIGHTCLUB
NOTORIOUS
NOVODAMUS
NUCLEOLUS
NYSTAGMUS
OBLIVIOUS
OBNOXIOUS
ODALISQUE
OFFCOLOUR
OFFICIOUS
OLENELLUS
OPERCULUM
OPHIUCHUS
ORGILLOUS
ORTANIQUE
OUROBORUS
OVERCLOUD
OVERVALUE
OVIPAROUS
PALINURUS
PALLADIUM
PARAGOGUE
PARNASSUS
PATROCLUS
PAYCHEQUE
PEDAGOGUE
PEMPHIGUS
PENDULOUS
PENURIOUS
PERIPATUS

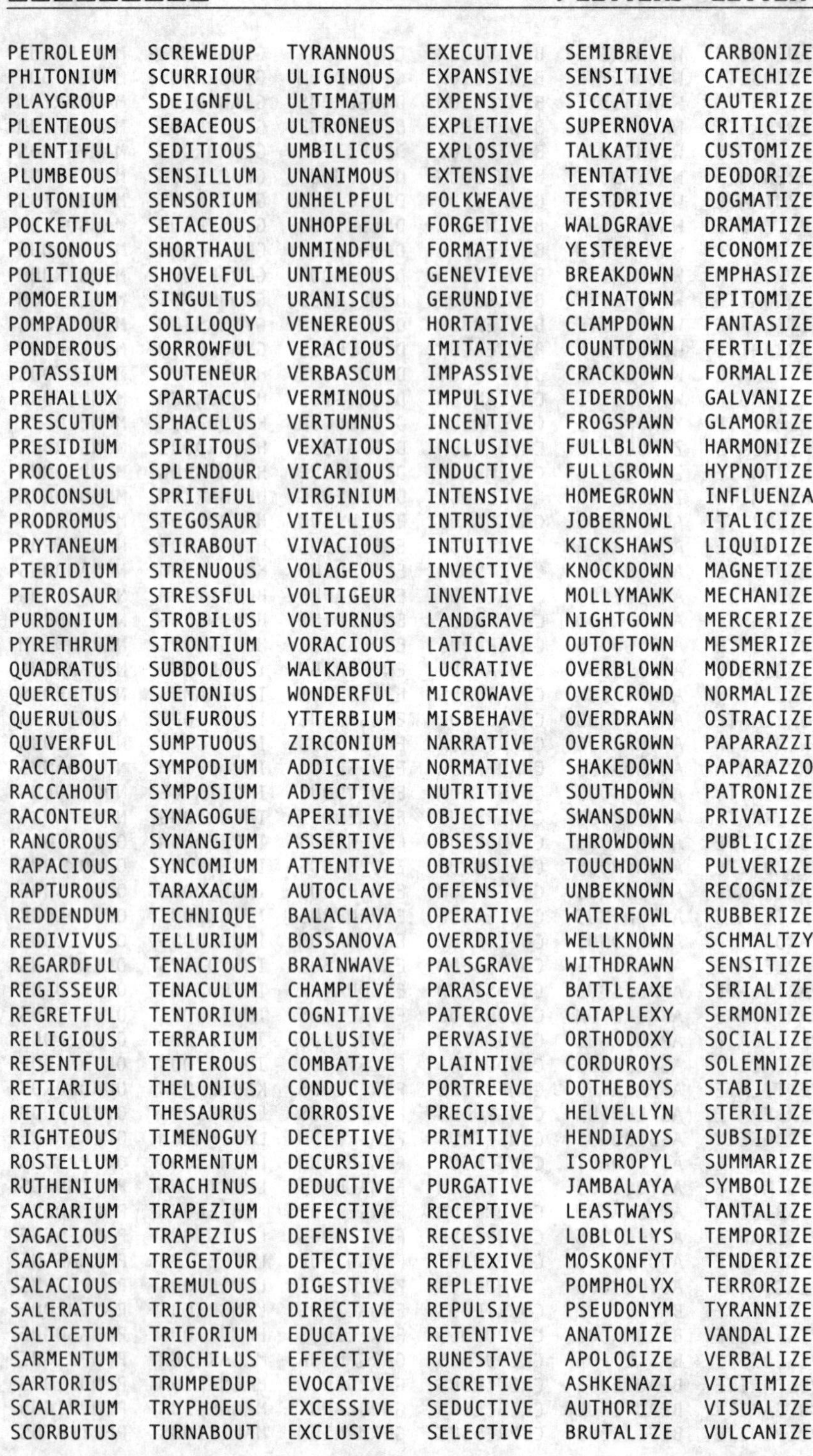

PETROLEUM
PHITONIUM
PLAYGROUP
PLENTEOUS
PLENTIFUL
PLUMBEOUS
PLUTONIUM
POCKETFUL
POISONOUS
POLITIQUE
POMOERIUM
POMPADOUR
PONDEROUS
POTASSIUM
PREHALLUX
PRESCUTUM
PRESIDIUM
PROCOELUS
PROCONSUL
PRODROMUS
PRYTANEUM
PTERIDIUM
PTEROSAUR
PURDONIUM
PYRETHRUM
QUADRATUS
QUERCETUS
QUERULOUS
QUIVERFUL
RACCABOUT
RACCAHOUT
RACONTEUR
RANCOROUS
RAPACIOUS
RAPTUROUS
REDDENDUM
REDIVIVUS
REGARDFUL
REGISSEUR
REGRETFUL
RELIGIOUS
RESENTFUL
RETIARIUS
RETICULUM
RIGHTEOUS
ROSTELLUM
RUTHENIUM
SACRARIUM
SAGACIOUS
SAGAPENUM
SALACIOUS
SALERATUS
SALICETUM
SARMENTUM
SARTORIUS
SCALARIUM
SCORBUTUS
SCREWEDUP
SCURRIOUR
SDEIGNFUL
SEBACEOUS
SEDITIOUS
SENSILLUM
SENSORIUM
SETACEOUS
SHORTHAUL
SHOVELFUL
SINGULTUS
SOLILOQUY
SORROWFUL
SOUTENEUR
SPARTACUS
SPHACELUS
SPIRITOUS
SPLENDOUR
SPRITEFUL
STEGOSAUR
STIRABOUT
STRENUOUS
STRESSFUL
STROBILUS
STRONTIUM
SUBDOLOUS
SUETONIUS
SULFUROUS
SUMPTUOUS
SYMPODIUM
SYMPOSIUM
SYNAGOGUE
SYNANGIUM
SYNCOMIUM
TARAXACUM
TECHNIQUE
TELLURIUM
TENACIOUS
TENACULUM
TENTORIUM
TERRARIUM
TETTEROUS
THELONIUS
THESAURUS
TIMENOGUY
TORMENTUM
TRACHINUS
TRAPEZIUM
TRAPEZIUS
TREGETOUR
TREMULOUS
TRICOLOUR
TRIFORIUM
TROCHILUS
TRUMPEDUP
TRYPHOEUS
TURNABOUT
TYRANNOUS
ULIGINOUS
ULTIMATUM
ULTRONEUS
UMBILICUS
UNANIMOUS
UNHELPFUL
UNHOPEFUL
UNMINDFUL
UNTIMEOUS
URANISCUS
VENEREOUS
VERACIOUS
VERBASCUM
VERMINOUS
VERTUMNUS
VEXATIOUS
VICARIOUS
VIRGINIUM
VITELLIUS
VIVACIOUS
VOLAGEOUS
VOLTIGEUR
VOLTURNUS
VORACIOUS
WALKABOUT
WONDERFUL
YTTERBIUM
ZIRCONIUM
ADDICTIVE
ADJECTIVE
APERITIVE
ASSERTIVE
ATTENTIVE
AUTOCLAVE
BALACLAVA
BOSSANOVA
BRAINWAVE
CHAMPLEVÉ
COGNITIVE
COLLUSIVE
COMBATIVE
CONDUCIVE
CORROSIVE
DECEPTIVE
DECURSIVE
DEDUCTIVE
DEFECTIVE
DEFENSIVE
DETECTIVE
DIGESTIVE
DIRECTIVE
EDUCATIVE
EFFECTIVE
EVOCATIVE
EXCESSIVE
EXCLUSIVE
EXECUTIVE
EXPANSIVE
EXPENSIVE
EXPLETIVE
EXPLOSIVE
EXTENSIVE
FOLKWEAVE
FORGETIVE
FORMATIVE
GENEVIEVE
GERUNDIVE
HORTATIVE
IMITATIVE
IMPASSIVE
IMPULSIVE
INCENTIVE
INCLUSIVE
INDUCTIVE
INTENSIVE
INTRUSIVE
INTUITIVE
INVECTIVE
INVENTIVE
LANDGRAVE
LATICLAVE
LUCRATIVE
MICROWAVE
MISBEHAVE
NARRATIVE
NORMATIVE
NUTRITIVE
OBJECTIVE
OBSESSIVE
OBTRUSIVE
OFFENSIVE
OPERATIVE
OVERDRIVE
PALSGRAVE
PARASCEVE
PATERCOVE
PERVASIVE
PLAINTIVE
PORTREEVE
PRECISIVE
PRIMITIVE
PROACTIVE
PURGATIVE
RECEPTIVE
RECESSIVE
REFLEXIVE
REPLETIVE
REPULSIVE
RETENTIVE
RUNESTAVE
SECRETIVE
SEDUCTIVE
SELECTIVE
SEMIBREVE
SENSITIVE
SICCATIVE
SUPERNOVA
TALKATIVE
TENTATIVE
TESTDRIVE
WALDGRAVE
YESTEREVE
BREAKDOWN
CHINATOWN
CLAMPDOWN
COUNTDOWN
CRACKDOWN
EIDERDOWN
FROGSPAWN
FULLBLOWN
FULLGROWN
HOMEGROWN
JOBERNOWL
KICKSHAWS
KNOCKDOWN
MOLLYMAWK
NIGHTGOWN
OUTOFTOWN
OVERBLOWN
OVERCROWD
OVERDRAWN
OVERGROWN
SHAKEDOWN
SOUTHDOWN
SWANSDOWN
THROWDOWN
TOUCHDOWN
UNBEKNOWN
WATERFOWL
WELLKNOWN
WITHDRAWN
BATTLEAXE
CATAPLEXY
ORTHODOXY
CORDUROYS
DOTHEBOYS
HELVELLYN
HENDIADYS
ISOPROPYL
JAMBALAYA
LEASTWAYS
LOBLOLLYS
MOSKONFYT
POMPHOLYX
PSEUDONYM
ANATOMIZE
APOLOGIZE
ASHKENAZI
AUTHORIZE
BRUTALIZE
CARBONIZE
CATECHIZE
CAUTERIZE
CRITICIZE
CUSTOMIZE
DEODORIZE
DOGMATIZE
DRAMATIZE
ECONOMIZE
EMPHASIZE
EPITOMIZE
FANTASIZE
FERTILIZE
FORMALIZE
GALVANIZE
GLAMORIZE
HARMONIZE
HYPNOTIZE
INFLUENZA
ITALICIZE
LIQUIDIZE
MAGNETIZE
MECHANIZE
MERCERIZE
MESMERIZE
MODERNIZE
NORMALIZE
OSTRACIZE
PAPARAZZI
PAPARAZZO
PATRONIZE
PRIVATIZE
PUBLICIZE
PULVERIZE
RECOGNIZE
RUBBERIZE
SCHMALTZY
SENSITIZE
SERIALIZE
SERMONIZE
SOCIALIZE
SOLEMNIZE
STABILIZE
STERILIZE
SUBSIDIZE
SUMMARIZE
SYMBOLIZE
TANTALIZE
TEMPORIZE
TENDERIZE
TERRORIZE
TYRANNIZE
VANDALIZE
VERBALIZE
VICTIMIZE
VISUALIZE
VULCANIZE

9:9

ACONCAGUA
ALEXANDRA
AMBLYOPIA
ANAGLYPTA
ANALGESIA
ANASTASIA
ANDROMEDA
ANGOSTURA
ANNAPURNA
APOCRYPHA
AQUILEGIA
ARAUCARIA
ARCTOGAEA
ARGENTINA
ARTEMISIA
ASYNERGIA
ATAHUALPA
AUBRIETIA
AUSTRALIA
BALACLAVA
BALALAIKA
BALLERINA
BARCELONA
BARRACUDA
BENBECULA
BOSSANOVA
BRITANNIA
BRITSCHKA
CACHAEMIA
CAFETERIA
CALEDONIA
CALENDULA
CALPURNIA
CAMPANULA
CARACALLA
CARAMBOLA
CARCINOMA
CASSANDRA
CASUARINA
CATATONIA
CHIHUAHUA
CHILOPODA
CHIPOLATA
CINERARIA
CLEOPATRA
CLEPSYDRA
COLUMELLA
CONDYLOMA
CRUSTACEA
CYCLORAMA
DIARRHOEA
DYSPEPSIA
DYSPHAGIA

ECHEVERIA
ECLAMPSIA
EMPHYSEMA
ENCHILADA
ESMERALDA
EUPHORBIA
EXANTHEMA
FAMAGUSTA
FINLANDIA
FORSYTHIA
FRANCESCA
GARGANTUA
GENITALIA
GUATEMALA
GUERRILLA
HAEMALOMA
HARMONICA
HEMIPTERA
HIPPOLYTA
HOMOPTERA
HYDRANGEA
HYPERBOLA
INAMORATA
INDONESIA
INFLUENZA
IPHIGENIA
JACARANDA
JAMBALAYA
JUVENILIA
KNIPHOFIA
LEUKAEMIA
LITHUANIA
LJUBLJANA
LOUISIANA
MACADAMIA
MACEDONIA
MADARIAGA
MARIJUANA
MELANESIA
MELODRAMA
MESSALINA
MINNESOTA
MONODRAMA
MONOMANIA
MONTEZUMA
MORATORIA
NAUMACHIA
NEURALGIA
NEUROGLIA
NICARAGUA
NOSTALGIA
NOTONECTA
ORCHESTRA
PALAESTRA
PANATELLA
PAULOWNIA
PENINSULA

PHANTASMA
PHARSALIA
PNEUMONIA
POLYNESIA
PONDEROSA
PRIMAVERA
PYROMANIA
QUINQUINA
RUDBECKIA
SANTAYANA
SCAGLIOLA
SCINTILLA
SLIVOVICA
SNOWDONIA
SOUVLAKIA
SUBSTRATA
SUPERNOVA
TANTARARA
TARANTULA
TARRAGONA
THEOBROMA
TOCCATINA
TRATTORIA
TRIPITAKA
URTICARIA
VARICELLA
VENEZUELA
XENOMANIA
XEROSTOMA
BEELZEBUB
COCKSCOMB
CURRYCOMB
DISENTOMB
DITHYRAMB
FLASHBULB
HONEYCOMB
JIGGUMBOB
NIGHTCLUB
SPIDERWEB
TOOTHCOMB
ACROBATIC
AESTHETIC
AGALACTIC
ALCOHOLIC
ALGEBRAIC
ANAEROBIC
ANALEPTIC
ANALGESIC
ANIMISTIC
ANTARCTIC
ANTITOXIC
APATHETIC
APERIODIC
APOPHATIC
APOSTOLIC
ARTHRITIC
ASTHMATIC

ATAVISTIC
ATHEISTIC
AUTHENTIC
AUTOMATIC
AUTONOMIC
AXIOMATIC
BALLISTIC
BISHOPRIC
BOMBASTIC
BRITANNIC
CACHECTIC
CALORIFIC
CASUISTIC
CATALYTIC
CATATONIC
CATHARTIC
CHARABANC
CHROMATIC
CINEMATIC
CLIMACTIC
CRYOGENIC
CYNEGETIC
DIACRITIC
DIALECTIC
DIAMETRIC
DIANOETIC
DIGASTRIC
DOLOMITIC
DYSPEPTIC
ECCENTRIC
EMBRYONIC
EMPAESTIC
ENCAUSTIC
ENDEICTIC
ENERGETIC
ENIGMATIC
EPEDAPHIC
EPICYCLIC
EPILEPTIC
EPINASTIC
EPIPHYTIC
EUCHLORIC
EUTROPHIC
EVANGELIC
EXTRINSIC
FANTASTIC
GEOMETRIC
GERIATRIC
GYMNASTIC
HANSEATIC
HEURISTIC
HONORIFIC
HYDRAULIC
ICELANDIC
IDIOMATIC
IMPOLITIC
INORGANIC

INSOMNIAC
INTRINSIC
ISCHAEMIC
ISOMETRIC
ISOTACTIC
ISOTROPIC
KLENDUSIC
LANGUEDOC
LETHARGIC
LIENTERIC
LOMBARDIC
LYMPHATIC
MACARONIC
MELANOTIC
MESSIANIC
METABOLIC
MONATOMIC
NEOLITHIC
NEPHRITIC
NEURALGIC
NOSTALGIC
OBSTETRIC
OMOPHAGIC
ONOMASTIC
OPODELDOC
ORGIASTIC
PANEGYRIC
PANORAMIC
PARABOLIC
PARALYTIC
PARAMEDIC
PARANOIAC
PARASITIC
PAREGORIC
PATRIOTIC
PEIRASTIC
PHARISAIC
PHILIPPIC
PHRENETIC
PLETHORIC
PNEUMATIC
PRAGMATIC
PRISMATIC
PROCLITIC
PROPHETIC
PROPIONIC
PSYCHOTIC
PURITANIC
PYRRHONIC
QUADRATIC
REALISTIC
RHAPSODIC
RHEUMATIC
SARCASTIC
SCHEMATIC
SCOLIOTIC
SCORBUTIC

SEMEIOTIC
SOPHISTIC
SOPORIFIC
SPASMODIC
SPLENETIC
STATISTIC
STEGNOTIC
STENOPAIC
STOMACHIC
STRATEGIC
STYLISTIC
SUDORIFIC
SULPHONIC
SULPHURIC
SYBARITIC
SYMBIOTIC
SYMMETRIC
SYMPHONIC
SYNTACTIC
SYNTHETIC
TACAMAHAC
THALASSIC
THRASONIC
THRENETIC
TRAUMATIC
TRICLINIC
TRIETERIC
TROCHILIC
UPAITHRIC
VIDEODISC
VITRIOLIC
ZOOMANTIC
ZOOSCOPIC
ZYGOMATIC
ABANDONED
ADDRESSED
ADULTHOOD
ADVOCATED
AFFLICTED
AFORESAID
AFTERWORD
AGGRIEVED
AIRCOOLED
ALLANTOID
AMPERSAND
ANGUISHED
ANNOTATED
APARTHEID
APPOINTED
APPREHEND
ARACHNOID
ARCHIBALD
ARROWHEAD
ARTHROPOD
ASTOUNDED
ATTEMPTED
AUTOMATED

BACKSWORD
BANDSTAND
BAREFACED
BASEBOARD
BEACHHEAD
BEDSPREAD
BENIGHTED
BETROTHED
BIGHEADED
BILLBOARD
BLACKBIRD
BLACKHEAD
BLACKLEAD
BLACKWOOD
BLINDFOLD
BLINKERED
BLISTERED
BLOCKHEAD
BLOODSHED
BLUEBEARD
BODYGUARD
BOOKSTAND
BOULEVARD
BOYFRIEND
BRICKYARD
BRUSHWOOD
CAGOULARD
CAKESTAND
CARDBOARD
CASTRATED
CATCHWORD
CEDARWOOD
CELLULOID
CERTIFIED
CHARTERED
CHASTENED
CHEQUERED
CHERISHED
CHICKWEED
CHILDHOOD
CHIPBOARD
CHONDROID
CIVILISED
CIVILIZED
CLAPBOARD
CLEVELAND
CLIPBOARD
CLUSTERED
COACHLOAD
COALESCED
COALFIELD
COLLECTED
COMMITTED
COMPELLED
CONCEALED
CONCEITED
CONCERNED

CONCERTED
CONCLUDED
CONCUSSED
CONDEMNED
CONFESSED
CONFIRMED
CONFLATED
CONGESTED
CONNECTED
CONTENTED
CONTRIVED
CONVERTED
CONVINCED
CORNFIELD
CORRECTED
COURTYARD
CRASHLAND
CROCKFORD
CROSSBRED
CROSSEYED
CROSSWIND
CROSSWORD
DACHSHUND
DAIRYMAID
DANDIFIED
DARTBOARD
DASHBOARD
DEBAUCHED
DECACHORD
DECORATED
DEDICATED
DEERHOUND
DELIGHTED
DEPRESSED
DESTROYED
DEVELOPED
DIGNIFIED
DISCARDED
DISCLOSED
DISGRACED
DISGUISED
DISGUSTED
DISPERSED
DISPLACED
DISPLAYED
DISREGARD
DISSOLVED
DISTENDED
DISTORTED
DISTURBED
DISUNITED
DIXIELAND
DOMICILED
DOWNTREND
DRIFTWOOD
DUCKBOARD
DUMBFOUND

DUPLICAND
DYNAMITED
EAGLEWOOD
EASTBOUND
ELONGATED
EMACIATED
EMBATTLED
EMBROILED
ENAMELLED
ENAMOURED
ENCHANTED
ENCIRCLED
ENGARLAND
ENGRAINED
ENGROSSED
ENLIVENED
ENSCONCED
ENTRANCED
ESTRANGED
ESTRELDID
ETIOLATED
EXCLAIMED
EXERCISED
EXHAUSTED
EXPRESSED
FAIRYLAND
FALSEHOOD
FARMSTEAD
FASHIONED
FEATHERED
FERDINAND
FERMENTED
FIREBRAND
FIREGUARD
FIRSTHAND
FISHGUARD
FLAMSTEED
FLATTENED
FLATTERED
FLAVOURED
FLEETWOOD
FLOWERBED
FLUSTERED
FORESPEND
FORFEITED
FRAGONARD
FREEBOARD
FRIESLAND
GATESHEAD
GAVELKIND
GEOMETRID
GLORIFIED
GOLDFIELD
GOOSEHERD
GRADGRIND
GRADUATED
GRASSLAND

GRAVESEND
GRAVEYARD
GREENFEED
GREENHEAD
GREENSAND
GREENWEED
GREENWOOD
GREENYARD
GREYBEARD
GREYHOUND
GUMSHIELD
HACKNEYED
HALFBAKED
HAMADRYAD
HAMFISTED
HAMPSTEAD
HANDSTAND
HAPHAZARD
HARDBOARD
HARDIHOOD
HEADBOARD
HEADLINED
HEARTLAND
HEATHLAND
HEDERATED
HENPECKED
HERMANDAD
HIDEBOUND
HIGHSPEED
HOARHOUND
HOBNAILED
HODMANDOD
HOLINSHED
HOLLYWOOD
HOMESTEAD
HOREHOUND
HORRIFIED
HOTHEADED
HOUSEHOLD
HOUSEMAID
HUMANKIND
IMPRESSED
INCREASED
INGRAINED
INHERITED
INHIBITED
INITIATED
INSCRIBED
INTERBRED
INTERLARD
INTRIGUED
IRRITATED
ISLAMABAD
JAMPACKED
JAUNDICED
JUSTIFIED
KIDNAPPED

KINGSIZED
KNACKERED
LACERATED
LACKBEARD
LAMINATED
LANCEWOOD
LEAFMOULD
LEASEHOLD
LENINGRAD
LEVERAGED
LIBERATED
LIFEGUARD
LINGFIELD
LIQUEFIED
LOCALIZED
LONGLIVED
LOOSEHEAD
LUSTIHOOD
LYMESWOLD
MACDONALD
MALFORMED
MANSFIELD
MAPPEMOND
MARSHLAND
MASEFIELD
MATCHWOOD
MEDICATED
MENTIONED
METALLOID
METEOROID
METROLAND
MINEFIELD
MISGUIDED
MISPLACED
MONKSHOOD
MONOCHORD
MORTIFIED
MUCHLOVED
MUTILATED
MYRMECOID
NAUSEATED
NEGLECTED
NEWSHOUND
NEWSSTAND
NORTHWARD
NOSEBLEED
NOTOCHORD
NURSEMAID
OCTACHORD
OPENENDED
OPPRESSED
ORGANISED
ORGANIZED
OUTSPREAD
OVERBOARD
OVERCLOUD
OVERCROWD

OVERJOYED
OVERRATED
OVERSIZED
OVERSPEND
PASSEPIED
PATTERNED
PENFRIEND
PERAEOPOD
PERFERVID
PERFORMED
PERMITTED
PERPLEXED
PERSUADED
PERTURBED
PERVERTED
PETRIFIED
PHARAMOND
PHONECARD
PHYLLOPOD
PIGHEADED
PLASTERED
POPULATED
POSSESSED
POSTPONED
PRACTISED
PREFERRED
PRESENTED
PRESERVED
PROFESSED
PROJECTED
PROLONGED
PROOFREAD
PROPELLED
PUBLISHED
PUMMELLED
QUADRUPED
QUALIFIED
QUICKSAND
REARGUARD
RECLAIMED
RECOMMEND
RECOVERED
REDHANDED
REDHEADED
REPREHEND
REPRESSED
REPRIMAND
RESPECTED
RIDERHOOD
RIGHTHAND
ROADSTEAD
ROUGHSHOD
ROUNDHAND
ROUNDHEAD
RUNAROUND
SAFEGUARD
SAINTHOOD

SANDALLED
SANGFROID
SATINWOOD
SATISFIED
SATURATED
SCALLOPED
SCATTERED
SCRATCHED
SCRODDLED
SEGMENTED
SEPARATED
SEQUINNED
SHATTERED
SHEEPFOLD
SHEFFIELD
SHELTERED
SHEWBREAD
SHORTHAND
SHORTHOLD
SHUTTERED
SIDEBOARD
SIEGFRIED
SIGNBOARD
SIMULATED
SKETCHPAD
SNAKEWEED
SNOWBOUND
SOUTHWARD
SPATTERED
SPEARHEAD
SPECIFIED
SPELLBIND
SPIKENARD
SPONSORED
SPOONFEED
SPRINGALD
SPUNCULID
STABLELAD
STAGEHAND
STAGGERED
STARBOARD
STATEHOOD
STATIONED
STEELHEAD
STEELYARD
STILTBIRD
STINKBIRD
STINKWOOD
STOCKYARD
STONEHAND
STONKERED
STORIATED
STRETCHED
STUPEFIED
SUBMERGED
SUBTITLED
SUCCEEDED
SUNTANNED
SURFBOARD
SURFEITED
SURPRISED
SUSPECTED
SUSPENDED
SUSTAINED
SWEATBAND
SWINEHERD
TABLELAND
TAILBOARD
TARMACKED
TASSELLED
TAYASSUID
TERRIFIED
THICKHEAD
THREEFOLD
THRESHOLD
TIGHTHEAD
TOLERATED
TOUCHWOOD
TRADEWIND
TRANSCEND
TRAPEZOID
TREBIZOND
TRIANGLED
TRUCKLOAD
TRUNCATED
TURNROUND
UNABASHED
UNADOPTED
UNALLOYED
UNALTERED
UNASHAMED
UNBIASSED
UNBOUNDED
UNBRIDLED
UNCHANGED
UNCHARGED
UNCHECKED
UNCLAIMED
UNCLOTHED
UNCLOUDED
UNCOUPLED
UNCOVERED
UNCROSSED
UNCROWNED
UNDAMAGED
UNDAUNTED
UNDECIDED
UNDEFILED
UNDEFINED
UNDERBRED
UNDERHAND
UNDERPAID
UNDERWOOD
UNDILUTED
UNDIVIDED
UNDOUBTED
UNDRESSED
UNEQUALED
UNEXPOSED
UNFLEDGED
UNFOUNDED
UNGUARDED
UNIFORMED
UNINJURED
UNINVITED
UNLEARNED
UNLIMITED
UNMARRIED
UNMATCHED
UNNOTICED
UNOPPOSED
UNREFINED
UNRELATED
UNRUFFLED
UNSCATHED
UNSECURED
UNSETTLED
UNSKILLED
UNSPOILED
UNSULLIED
UNTOUCHED
UNTRAINED
UNTREATED
UNTUTORED
UNWATERED
UNWORRIED
UPANISHAD
VOLGOGRAD
VOLKSRAAD
WAGONLOAD
WAISTBAND
WASHBOARD
WASHSTAND
WASTELAND
WATCHWORD
WATERFORD
WATERSHED
WATERWEED
WEBFOOTED
WEDGEWOOD
WESTBOUND
WHIPROUND
WHIRLWIND
WHITEHEAD
WHITEWOOD
WHOLEFOOD
WIDOWHOOD
WITHSTAND
WITHYWIND
WITNESSED
WOLFHOUND
WOMANHOOD
WOMANKIND
ABANDONEE
ABERRANCE
ABOMINATE
ABORIGINE
ABOUTFACE
ABUNDANCE
ACCLIMATE
ACETYLENE
ACIDULATE
ACQUIESCE
ACUMINATE
ADAPTABLE
ADDICTIVE
ADDRESSEE
ADHERENCE
ADJECTIVE
ADMIRABLE
ADMIXTURE
ADUMBRATE
ADVANTAGE
ADVENTURE
ADVERTISE
ADVISABLE
AERODROME
AEROPLANE
AEROSPACE
AFFILIATE
AFFLUENCE
AFFRICATE
AFTERCARE
AGGRAVATE
AGGREGATE
AGREEABLE
AITCHBONE
ALBERTINE
ALLEMANDE
ALLEVIATE
ALLOWABLE
ALLOWANCE
ALMANDINE
ALONGSIDE
ALTERABLE
ALTERCATE
ALTERNATE
ALVEOLATE
AMBROTYPE
AMBULANCE
AMBUSCADE
AMELAKITE
AMPLITUDE
ANATOMIZE
ANCHORAGE
ANCHORITE
ANHYDRIDE
ANHYDRITE
ANNOYANCE
ANTICLINE
APERITIVE
APHRODITE
APOLOGIZE
APPENDAGE
APPLIANCE
APPOINTEE
AQUAPLANE
AQUARELLE
ARABESQUE
ARABINOSE
ARAGONITE
ARBITRAGE
ARBITRATE
ARCHETYPE
ARGENTINE
ARISTOTLE
ARMISTICE
ARQUEBUSE
ARRIVISTE
ARROGANCE
ARTERIOLE
ARTICHOKE
ASPARTAME
ASSERTIVE
ASSOCIATE
ASSONANCE
ASSUETUDE
ASSURANCE
ASTRODOME
ASTROLABE
ATTENTIVE
ATTENUATE
ATTRIBUTE
AUBERGINE
AUGUSTINE
AUTHORIZE
AUTOCLAVE
AUTOROUTE
AVAILABLE
AVALANCHE
AVOIDABLE
AVOIDANCE
BACKSLIDE
BACKSPACE
BACKSTAGE
BAGATELLE
BAINMARIE
BAKEHOUSE
BALTIMORE
BAMBOOZLE
BANDALORE
BANDOLINE
BANQUETTE
BARBITONE
BARBOTINE
BARMECIDE
BARNABITE
BARRICADE
BARYSCOPE
BASTINADE
BATTLEAXE
BEATITUDE
BEDRAGGLE
BELLICOSE
BELLYACHE
BELVEDERE
BESPANGLE
BEVERIDGE
BIFURCATE
BIOSPHERE
BIPARTITE
BIRDTABLE
BLACKFACE
BLACKMORE
BLASPHEME
BLUESTONE
BOATHOUSE
BOLOGNESE
BOMBASINE
BONAPARTE
BOOKSTORE
BRACTEOLE
BRAINCASE
BRAINWAVE
BRASENOSE
BRASSERIE
BRASSIERE
BRASSWARE
BREADLINE
BREAKABLE
BRIEFCASE
BRIMSTONE
BRIQUETTE
BROADSIDE
BROKERAGE
BRUNHILDE
BRUTALIZE
BUMBLEBEE
BURKINABE
BURLESQUE
BYZANTINE
CAFETIERE
CALABOOSE
CALABRESE
CALCINATE
CALCULATE
CALENTURE
CALIBRATE
CAMBRIDGE
CAMPANILE
CANDIDATE
CANNELURE

CANNONADE
CANTABILE
CANTONESE
CAPTIVATE
CARBAMATE
CARBAMIDE
CARBONADE
CARBONATE
CARBONIZE
CARBUNCLE
CARMELITE
CARNIVORE
CARTHORSE
CARTILAGE
CARTOUCHE
CARTRIDGE
CASSEROLE
CASSONADE
CASTIGATE
CATALOGUE
CATCHPOLE
CATECHIZE
CATHERINE
CAUTERIZE
CAVALCADE
CEASEFIRE
CELANDINE
CELEBRATE
CELLULITE
CELLULOSE
CENTIPEDE
CEREBRATE
CERTITUDE
CEYLONESE
CHABAZITE
CHALLENGE
CHAMINADE
CHAMOMILE
CHAMPAGNE
CHANTEUSE
CHAPERONE
CHARLOTTE
CHEAPSIDE
CHECKMATE
CHEEKBONE
CHICKADEE
CHILDCARE
CHILDLIKE
CHOCOLATE
CHONDRITE
CHRONICLE
CIGARETTE
CILIOLATE
CIRCINATE
CIRCULATE
CLASSMATE
CLEARANCE
CLIENTELE
CLOCKWISE
CLUBHOUSE
COAGULATE
COARCTATE
COASTLINE
COCKAIGNE
COENOBITE
COFFINITE
COGNITIVE
COHERENCE
COLERIDGE
COLLEAGUE
COLLIGATE
COLLIMATE
COLLOCATE
COLLOTYPE
COLLUSIVE
COLONNADE
COLUMBATE
COLUMBINE
COLUMBITE
COMBATIVE
COMMITTEE
COMMODORE
COMPOSITE
COMPOSURE
CONCIERGE
CONCOURSE
CONCUBINE
CONDUCIVE
CONGOLESE
CONJUGATE
CONNOTATE
CONSIGNEE
CONSTABLE
CONSTANCE
CONSULATE
COOKHOUSE
COOPERATE
COPROLITE
CORALLINE
CORDYLINE
CORNCRAKE
CORNEILLE
CORPORATE
CORPUSCLE
CORRELATE
CORROSIVE
CORRUGATE
CORTISONE
CORUSCATE
COUCHETTE
COURGETTE
COURTELLE
COVELLITE
COVERDALE
COWARDICE
COXSACKIE
CRANBORNE
CREPITATE
CREPOLINE
CRESCELLE
CRIMINATE
CRINOLINE
CRITICIZE
CROCODILE
CROQUETTE
CROSSFIRE
CROSSWISE
CROUSTADE
CROWNLIKE
CUBBYHOLE
CULMINATE
CULTIVATE
CURETTAGE
CURFUFFLE
CURTILAGE
CURVATURE
CUSPIDORE
CUSTOMIZE
CYCLAMATE
CYMBELINE
DALLIANCE
DAMASCENE
DEBATABLE
DEBAUCHEE
DEBENTURE
DEBUTANTE
DECADENCE
DECALITRE
DECALOGUE
DECASTYLE
DECEPTIVE
DECOLLATE
DECOMPOSE
DECURSIVE
DECUSSATE
DEDUCTIVE
DEFALCATE
DEFECTIVE
DEFENSIVE
DEFERENCE
DEFINABLE
DEFOLIATE
DEHYDRATE
DELINEATE
DEMAGOGUE
DEMARCATE
DEMITASSE
DEMURRAGE
DENIGRATE
DEODORIZE
DEOXIDISE
DEPARTURE
DEPRECATE
DEPREDATE
DESECRATE
DESICCATE
DESIGNATE
DESIRABLE
DESPERATE
DESTITUTE
DESUETUDE
DETECTIVE
DETERMINE
DEVASTATE
DEXTRORSE
DIABLERIE
DIALOGITE
DIGESTIVE
DILIGENCE
DIRECTIVE
DIRIGIBLE
DISCHARGE
DISCOURSE
DISENGAGE
DISFIGURE
DISLOCATE
DISMANTLE
DISOBLIGE
DISPARAGE
DISPARATE
DISPLEASE
DISREPUTE
DISSEMBLE
DISSIPATE
DISSOLUTE
DIVISIBLE
DOCTORATE
DOGMATIZE
DOMINANCE
DOSSHOUSE
DOWNGRADE
DOWNSTAGE
DRAINPIPE
DRAMATIZE
DRINKABLE
DRIPSTONE
DRUGSTORE
DUNSINANE
DUNSTABLE
DUPLICATE
EBRILLADE
ECHIDNINE
ECONOMIZE
ECOSSAISE
EDDYSTONE
EDUCATIVE
EFFECTIVE
EFFLUENCE
EGLANTINE
EIGHTSOME
EJACULATE
ELABORATE
ELAEOLITE
ELECTRODE
ELIMINATE
ELKOSHITE
ELLESMERE
ELOQUENCE
ELSEWHERE
ELUCIDATE
ELUTRIATE
EMBASSADE
EMBASSAGE
EMBRANGLE
EMBRASURE
EMBROCATE
EMERGENCE
EMMERDALE
EMOLLIATE
EMPENNAGE
EMPHASIZE
ENCLOSURE
ENCOURAGE
ENCRATITE
ENDOCRINE
ENDURABLE
ENDURANCE
ENERINITE
ENGRENAGE
ENHYDRITE
ENJOYABLE
ENNERDALE
ENRAPTURE
ENSHEATHE
ENSTATITE
ENTHYMEME
ENTOPHYTE
ENTOURAGE
ENTRECÔTE
ENUCLEATE
ENUMERATE
ENUNCIATE
EPARCHATE
EPAULETTE
EPHEDRINE
EPICENTRE
EPITOMIZE
EQUIPOISE
EQUITABLE
EQUIVOQUE
ERADICATE
EROSTRATE
ERSTWHILE
ESCOPETTE
ESPAGNOLE
ESPERANCE
ESPIONAGE
ESPLANADE
ESQUILINE
ESTAFETTE
ESTIMABLE
ESTRAPADE
ETIQUETTE
EVAPORATE
EVENTUATE
EVERGLADE
EVOCATIVE
EXANIMATE
EXCESSIVE
EXCITABLE
EXCLUSIVE
EXCORIATE
EXCULPATE
EXCUSABLE
EXECRABLE
EXECUTIVE
EXISTENCE
EXONERATE
EXOSPHERE
EXPANSIVE
EXPATIATE
EXPENSIVE
EXPERTISE
EXPISCATE
EXPLETIVE
EXPLICATE
EXPLOSIVE
EXPURGATE
EXQUISITE
EXSICCATE
EXTEMPORE
EXTENSILE
EXTENSIVE
EXTENUATE
EXTIRPATE
EXTRADITE
EXTRICATE
EYESPLICE
FABRICATE
FACSIMILE
FACTORISE
FAIRYTALE
FANDANGLE
FANTASIZE
FARANDOLE
FARMHOUSE
FASCINATE
FAVORABLE
FAVOURITE
FEBRIFUGE
FERINGHEE
FERTILIZE

FESTINATE
FIBROLINE
FIBROLITE
FIELDFARE
FIGURANTE
FILOPLUME
FILOSELLE
FIREDRAKE
FIREPLACE
FIRESTONE
FIRSTRATE
FISHPLATE
FLAGITATE
FLAGRANCE
FLAGSTONE
FLAMMABLE
FLASHCUBE
FLECHETTE
FLEXITIME
FLOODGATE
FLOPHOUSE
FLOWSTONE
FLUCTUATE
FOGRAMITE
FOLIOLOSE
FOLKWEAVE
FOODSTORE
FOOTBRAKE
FOOTLOOSE
FOOTPLATE
FORECLOSE
FORESHORE
FORESTAGE
FORETASTE
FORFICATE
FORGETIVE
FORMALIZE
FORMATIVE
FORMULATE
FORNICATE
FORTALICE
FORTILAGE
FORTITUDE
FORTUNATE
FOSSILISE
FOURPENCE
FRAGRANCE
FRAMBOISE
FRANCHISE
FREELANCE
FREEPHONE
FREESTONE
FREESTYLE
FRICASSEE
FRIZZANTE
FROSTBITE
FRUITCAKE
FRUSTRATE
FULLERENE
FULLSCALE
FULMINATE
FUNGICIDE
FURNITURE
FUSILLADE
FUSTIGATE
GABARDINE
GABERDINE
GABIONADE
GALACTOSE
GALANTINE
GALENGALE
GALINGALE
GALIONGEE
GALLINULE
GALLOPADE
GALLSTONE
GALRAVAGE
GALVANIZE
GARDEROBE
GARNISHEE
GARNITURE
GASCONADE
GELIGNITE
GENEVIEVE
GEORGETTE
GERMANITE
GERMICIDE
GERMINATE
GERUNDIVE
GESSAMINE
GIBEONITE
GINGERADE
GIRANDOLE
GLADSTONE
GLAMORIZE
GLASSWARE
GLOMERATE
GLOMERULE
GLORYHOLE
GLUCOSIDE
GLUTAMINE
GLYCERIDE
GLYCERINE
GMELINITE
GONIATITE
GOSLARITE
GOSSYPINE
GOTHAMITE
GRANDIOSE
GRANDSIRE
GRANULATE
GRANULITE
GRANULOSE
GRAPETREE
GRAPEVINE
GRATICULE
GRATITUDE
GRAVESIDE
GRAVITATE
GREENGAGE
GREGARINE
GRENADINE
GRENVILLE
GREYWACKE
GRIEVANCE
GRISAILLE
GROTESQUE
GUACAMOLE
GUARANTEE
GUIDELINE
GUILLOCHE
GUINEVERE
GYROSCOPE
HABERDINE
HABITABLE
HABITUATE
HACKAMORE
HAEMATITE
HAILSTONE
HAIRPIECE
HAIRSTYLE
HALOPHILE
HALOTHANE
HANDBRAKE
HANDPIECE
HANDSHAKE
HANDSPIKE
HARESTANE
HARIOLATE
HARMALINE
HARMONIZE
HARMOTOME
HARROGATE
HASHEMITE
HAUTMONDE
HAWCUBITE
HAWTHORNE
HEADSTONE
HEARTACHE
HEAVISIDE
HEDYPHANE
HELLEBORE
HEMITROPE
HERBICIDE
HERBIVORE
HERMITAGE
HESITANCE
HESSONITE
HIBERNATE
HIMYARITE
HINDRANCE
HIPPODAME
HIPPOLYTE
HIRUNDINE
HISTAMINE
HITCHHIKE
HOARSTONE
HOCCAMORE
HOLOPHOTE
HOLYSTONE
HOMOPHONE
HONORABLE
HORNSTONE
HOROSCOPE
HORSESHOE
HORTATIVE
HOURSTONE
HOUSEWIFE
HOWTOWDIE
HUMILIATE
HURRICANE
HUTTERITE
HYDRAZINE
HYPALLAGE
HYPERBOLE
HYPHENATE
HYPNOTIZE
HYPOCRITE
ICHNOLITE
ICTERIDAE
IDEALOGUE
IDIOPHONE
IGNORANCE
ILLEGIBLE
IMBALANCE
IMBRANGLE
IMBRICATE
IMBROCATE
IMITATIVE
IMMANACLE
IMMANENCE
IMMEDIATE
IMMIGRATE
IMMINENCE
IMMOVABLE
IMMUTABLE
IMPASSIVE
IMPEDANCE
IMPLICATE
IMPORTUNE
IMPOSTURE
IMPOTENCE
IMPRECATE
IMPRECISE
IMPROVISE
IMPSONITE
IMPUDENCE
IMPULSIVE
INANIMATE
INAUDIBLE
INCAPABLE
INCARDINE
INCARNATE
INCENTIVE
INCIDENCE
INCLUSIVE
INCOMMODE
INCONDITE
INCULCATE
INCULPATE
INCURABLE
INDELIBLE
INDENTURE
INDIGENCE
INDOLENCE
INDUCTIVE
INEBRIATE
INEFFABLE
INERUDITE
INFANTILE
INFATUATE
INFERENCE
INFERTILE
INFLUENCE
INFURIATE
INJUSTICE
INNISFREE
INNOCENCE
INOCULATE
INOPINATE
INQUILINE
INQUINATE
INQUORATE
INSENSATE
INSINCERE
INSINUATE
INSOLENCE
INSOLUBLE
INSTIGATE
INSTITUTE
INSURANCE
INTEGRATE
INTENSIVE
INTERCEDE
INTERFACE
INTERFERE
INTERLACE
INTERLOPE
INTERLUDE
INTERNODE
INTERPOSE
INTERVENE
INTESTATE
INTESTINE
INTRICATE
INTRODUCE
INTRUSIVE
INTUITIVE
INTUMESCE
INUMBRATE
INUSITATE
INVECTIVE
INVENTIVE
INVERTASE
INVIOLATE
INVISIBLE
INVOLUCRE
IODOPHILE
IPRINDOLE
IRASCIBLE
IRONSTONE
IRRADIATE
IRRITABLE
ISOMERASE
ISRAELITE
ITALICIZE
ITINERATE
JACKKNIFE
JACKSNIPE
JACQUERIE
JESSAMINE
JOBCENTRE
JOHANNINE
JOSEPHINE
JOUISANCE
JUBILANCE
JUXTAPOSE
KALSOMINE
KARYOTYPE
KENTLEDGE
KERBSTONE
KERFUFFLE
KERMESITE
KEYSTROKE
KHALIFATE
KIESERITE
KILOCYCLE
KILOMETRE
KINTLEDGE
KITTIWAKE
KNOWLEDGE
KONISCOPE
LABOURITE
LACCOLITE
LACINIATE
LAEVULOSE
LAFAYETTE
LAGNIAPPE
LAMARTINE
LAMPSHADE
LANCINATE
LANDGRAVE

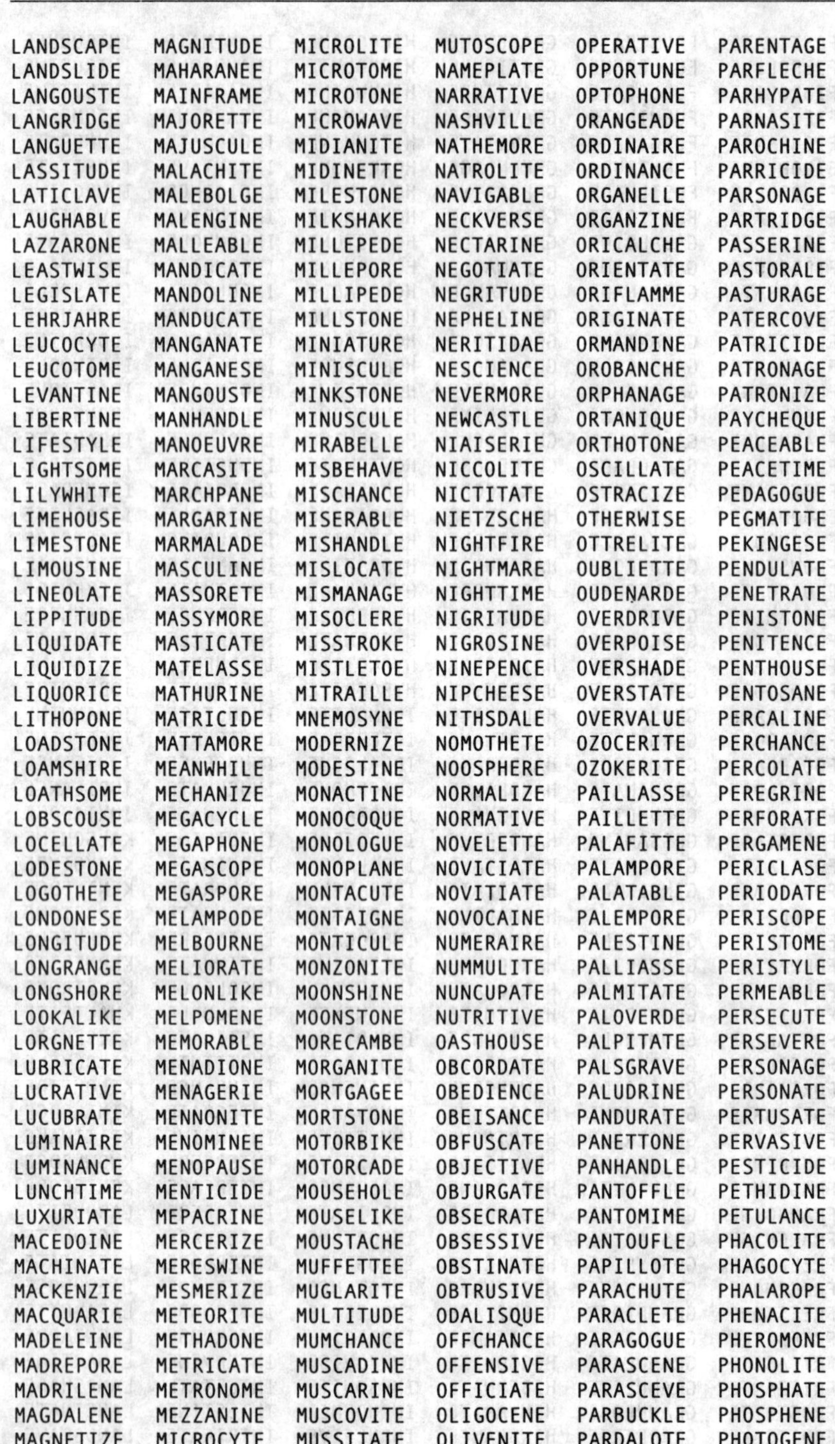

LANDSCAPE
LANDSLIDE
LANGOUSTE
LANGRIDGE
LANGUETTE
LASSITUDE
LATICLAVE
LAUGHABLE
LAZZARONE
LEASTWISE
LEGISLATE
LEHRJAHRE
LEUCOCYTE
LEUCOTOME
LEVANTINE
LIBERTINE
LIFESTYLE
LIGHTSOME
LILYWHITE
LIMEHOUSE
LIMESTONE
LIMOUSINE
LINEOLATE
LIPPITUDE
LIQUIDATE
LIQUIDIZE
LIQUORICE
LITHOPONE
LOADSTONE
LOAMSHIRE
LOATHSOME
LOBSCOUSE
LOCELLATE
LODESTONE
LOGOTHETE
LONDONESE
LONGITUDE
LONGRANGE
LONGSHORE
LOOKALIKE
LORGNETTE
LUBRICATE
LUCRATIVE
LUCUBRATE
LUMINAIRE
LUMINANCE
LUNCHTIME
LUXURIATE
MACEDOINE
MACHINATE
MACKENZIE
MACQUARIE
MADELEINE
MADREPORE
MADRILENE
MAGDALENE
MAGNETIZE
MAGNITUDE
MAHARANEE
MAINFRAME
MAJORETTE
MAJUSCULE
MALACHITE
MALEBOLGE
MALENGINE
MALLEABLE
MANDICATE
MANDOLINE
MANDUCATE
MANGANATE
MANGANESE
MANGOUSTE
MANHANDLE
MANOEUVRE
MARCASITE
MARCHPANE
MARGARINE
MARMALADE
MASCULINE
MASSORETE
MASSYMORE
MASTICATE
MATELASSE
MATHURINE
MATRICIDE
MATTAMORE
MEANWHILE
MECHANIZE
MEGACYCLE
MEGAPHONE
MEGASCOPE
MEGASPORE
MELAMPODE
MELBOURNE
MELIORATE
MELONLIKE
MELPOMENE
MEMORABLE
MENADIONE
MENAGERIE
MENNONITE
MENOMINEE
MENOPAUSE
MENTICIDE
MEPACRINE
MERCERIZE
MERESWINE
MESMERIZE
METEORITE
METHADONE
METRICATE
METRONOME
MEZZANINE
MICROCYTE
MICROLITE
MICROTOME
MICROTONE
MICROWAVE
MIDIANITE
MIDINETTE
MILESTONE
MILKSHAKE
MILLEPEDE
MILLEPORE
MILLIPEDE
MILLSTONE
MINIATURE
MINISCULE
MINKSTONE
MINUSCULE
MIRABELLE
MISBEHAVE
MISCHANCE
MISERABLE
MISHANDLE
MISLOCATE
MISMANAGE
MISOCLERE
MISSTROKE
MISTLETOE
MITRAILLE
MNEMOSYNE
MODERNIZE
MODESTINE
MONACTINE
MONOCOQUE
MONOLOGUE
MONOPLANE
MONTACUTE
MONTAIGNE
MONTICULE
MONZONITE
MOONSHINE
MOONSTONE
MORECAMBE
MORGANITE
MORTGAGEE
MORTSTONE
MOTORBIKE
MOTORCADE
MOUSEHOLE
MOUSELIKE
MOUSTACHE
MUFFETTEE
MUGLARITE
MULTITUDE
MUMCHANCE
MUSCADINE
MUSCARINE
MUSCOVITE
MUSSITATE
MUTOSCOPE
NAMEPLATE
NARRATIVE
NASHVILLE
NATHEMORE
NATROLITE
NAVIGABLE
NECKVERSE
NECTARINE
NEGOTIATE
NEGRITUDE
NEPHELINE
NERITIDAE
NESCIENCE
NEVERMORE
NEWCASTLE
NIAISERIE
NICCOLITE
NICTITATE
NIETZSCHE
NIGHTFIRE
NIGHTMARE
NIGHTTIME
NIGRITUDE
NIGROSINE
NINEPENCE
NIPCHEESE
NITHSDALE
NOMOTHETE
NOOSPHERE
NORMALIZE
NORMATIVE
NOVELETTE
NOVICIATE
NOVITIATE
NOVOCAINE
NUMERAIRE
NUMMULITE
NUNCUPATE
NUTRITIVE
OASTHOUSE
OBCORDATE
OBEDIENCE
OBEISANCE
OBFUSCATE
OBJECTIVE
OBJURGATE
OBSECRATE
OBSESSIVE
OBSTINATE
OBTRUSIVE
ODALISQUE
OFFCHANCE
OFFENSIVE
OFFICIATE
OLIGOCENE
OLIVENITE
OPERATIVE
OPPORTUNE
OPTOPHONE
ORANGEADE
ORDINAIRE
ORDINANCE
ORGANELLE
ORGANZINE
ORICALCHE
ORIENTATE
ORIFLAMME
ORIGINATE
ORMANDINE
OROBANCHE
ORPHANAGE
ORTANIQUE
ORTHOTONE
OSCILLATE
OSTRACIZE
OTHERWISE
OTTRELITE
OUBLIETTE
OUDENARDE
OVERDRIVE
OVERPOISE
OVERSHADE
OVERSTATE
OVERVALUE
OZOCERITE
OZOKERITE
PAILLASSE
PAILLETTE
PALAFITTE
PALAMPORE
PALATABLE
PALEMPORE
PALESTINE
PALLIASSE
PALMITATE
PALOVERDE
PALPITATE
PALSGRAVE
PALUDRINE
PANDURATE
PANETTONE
PANHANDLE
PANTOFFLE
PANTOMIME
PANTOUFLE
PAPILLOTE
PARACHUTE
PARACLETE
PARAGOGUE
PARASCENE
PARASCEVE
PARBUCKLE
PARDALOTE
PARENTAGE
PARFLECHE
PARHYPATE
PARNASITE
PAROCHINE
PARRICIDE
PARSONAGE
PARTRIDGE
PASSERINE
PASTORALE
PASTURAGE
PATERCOVE
PATRICIDE
PATRONAGE
PATRONIZE
PAYCHEQUE
PEACEABLE
PEACETIME
PEDAGOGUE
PEGMATITE
PEKINGESE
PENDULATE
PENETRATE
PENISTONE
PENITENCE
PENTHOUSE
PENTOSANE
PERCALINE
PERCHANCE
PERCOLATE
PEREGRINE
PERFORATE
PERGAMENE
PERICLASE
PERIODATE
PERISCOPE
PERISTOME
PERISTYLE
PERMEABLE
PERSECUTE
PERSEVERE
PERSONAGE
PERSONATE
PERTUSATE
PERVASIVE
PESTICIDE
PETHIDINE
PETULANCE
PHACOLITE
PHAGOCYTE
PHALAROPE
PHENACITE
PHEROMONE
PHONOLITE
PHOSPHATE
PHOSPHENE
PHOTOGENE

PHTHALATE
PHYTOLITE
PIACEVOLE
PIGNERATE
PILFERAGE
PINEAPPLE
PINSTRIPE
PIPESTONE
PIROUETTE
PITCHPINE
PITCHPOLE
PLAINTIVE
PLATITUDE
PLAUSIBLE
PLAYHOUSE
PLEASANCE
PLEIOCENE
PLENITUDE
PLUMBLINE
POLIANITE
POLITESSE
POLITIQUE
POLLINATE
POLONAISE
POLVERINE
POLYPHONE
POLYTHENE
POORHOUSE
PORBEAGLE
PORCUPINE
PORPORATE
PORTERAGE
PORTREEVE
POSTHOUSE
POSTULATE
POTENTATE
POWELLITE
PRECIEUSE
PRECIPICE
PRECISIVE
PRECONISE
PREDICATE
PREFIGURE
PREJUDICE
PREMATURE
PRESCRIBE
PRETERITE
PRIMITIAE
PRIMITIVE
PRIMULINE
PRINCIPLE
PRINTABLE
PRIVATIZE
PRIVILEGE
PROACTIVE
PROCEDURE
PROCREATE
PROGRAMME
PROLAMINE
PROMENADE
PRONOUNCE
PROPAGATE
PROPYLENE
PROROGATE
PROSCRIBE
PROSECUTE
PROSELYTE
PROSTRATE
PROTAMINE
PROTOTYPE
PROUSTITE
PROVEDORE
PROVOLONE
PROXIMATE
PRURIENCE
PUBLICIZE
PUCELLAGE
PUISSANCE
PULLULATE
PULVERIZE
PUNCHLINE
PUNCTUATE
PUPILLAGE
PURGATIVE
PURSUANCE
PURULENCE
QUADRILLE
QUADRUPLE
QUAILPIPE
QUARTETTE
QUENNELLE
QUICKLIME
QUINTETTE
QUINTUPLE
QUITTANCE
RACEHORSE
RADCLIFFE
RAFFINOSE
RAINGAUGE
RANTIPOLE
RATHERIPE
RATIONALE
REACHABLE
READYMADE
REANIMATE
REARHORSE
REARMOUSE
REARRANGE
RECAPTURE
RECEPTIVE
RECESSIVE
RECOGNIZE
RECONCILE
RECONDITE
RECONVENE
RECTANGLE
RECTITUDE
RECUSANCE
REDINGOTE
REDOLENCE
REDUCIBLE
REEXAMINE
REFERENCE
REFINANCE
REFLEXIVE
REIMBURSE
REINFORCE
REINSTATE
REITERATE
RELEVANCE
RELIGEUSE
RELIQUIAE
REMINISCE
REMOULADE
REMOVABLE
RENCONTRE
RENEWABLE
REPAYABLE
REPECHAGE
REPLETIVE
REPLICATE
REPORTAGE
REPROBATE
REPRODUCE
REPUDIATE
REPULSIVE
REPUTABLE
REQUISITE
REREMOUSE
RESERPINE
RESHUFFLE
RESIDENCE
RESONANCE
RESTITUTE
RESURFACE
RETALIATE
RETENTIVE
RETICENCE
RETROCEDE
REVERENCE
RHODOLITE
RICERCARE
RIGMAROLE
RINGFENCE
RIVERSIDE
ROADHOUSE
ROCAMBOLE
ROSINANTE
ROSMARINE
ROTAPLANE
ROTUNDATE
ROUSSETTE
ROXBURGHE
ROZINANTE
RUBBERIZE
RUBICELLE
RUDDIGORE
RUNCINATE
RUNESTAVE
RUNNYMEDE
RUSTICATE
SACRIFICE
SACRILEGE
SALANGANE
SALOPETTE
SALTPETRE
SANDSTONE
SARBACANE
SASSOLITE
SATELLITE
SATURNINE
SATYRIDAE
SATYRINAE
SAVERNAKE
SAXIFRAGE
SAXOPHONE
SCALEABLE
SCAPOLITE
SCELERATE
SCHEELITE
SCHIAVONE
SCHNITTKE
SCHNOZZLE
SCIARIDAE
SCOLECITE
SCORODITE
SCREWPINE
SCREWTAPE
SCRIMMAGE
SCRIPTURE
SCRUMMAGE
SCULPTURE
SEABOTTLE
SECRETIVE
SEDUCTIVE
SEGREGATE
SELECTIVE
SELLOTAPE
SEMANTEME
SEMANTIDE
SEMAPHORE
SEMBLANCE
SEMIBREVE
SENSITIVE
SENSITIZE
SENTIENCE
SEPARABLE
SEPIOLITE
SEPTIMOLE
SEPULCHRE
SEPULTURE
SERAPHINE
SERIALIZE
SERMONIZE
SERREFILE
SERVIETTE
SERVITUDE
SEVERANCE
SHELDRAKE
SHEMOZZLE
SHENSTONE
SHIPSHAPE
SHOESHINE
SHORTCAKE
SHOWPIECE
SHRINKAGE
SIBILANCE
SIBYLLINE
SICCATIVE
SIDESWIPE
SIGNATURE
SILTSTONE
SILURIDAE
SIMEONITE
SIMPLISTE
SINGALESE
SINGAPORE
SIPHUNCLE
SKEDADDLE
SLABSTONE
SLANTWISE
SLUGHORNE
SMALLTIME
SMOKEFREE
SNOWFLAKE
SNOWWHITE
SOAPSTONE
SOCIALITE
SOCIALIZE
SOLEMNIZE
SOLITAIRE
SOMASCOPE
SOMEPLACE
SOMEWHERE
SOPHOMORE
SORTILEGE
SOUBRETTE
SOUFRIERE
SOUNDBITE
SOVENANCE
SPEARSIDE
SPECTACLE
SPECULATE
SPHENDONE
SPICILEGE
SPRAICKLE
SPRAUCHLE
SQUADRONE
SQUIREAGE
STABILIZE
STAGIRITE
STAGYRITE
STAIRCASE
STALEMATE
STANDGALE
STANDPIPE
STARSTONE
STATESIDE
STATEWIDE
STATUETTE
STERILIZE
STEVEDORE
STIMULATE
STINGAREE
STIPULATE
STOCKPILE
STONEWARE
STORYLINE
STOVEPIPE
STREETAGE
STRICTURE
STRONGYLE
STRUCTURE
STYLOBATE
SUBDIVIDE
SUBENTIRE
SUBJUGATE
SUBLIMATE
SUBMARINE
SUBROGATE
SUBSCRIBE
SUBSIDIZE
SUBSTANCE
SUBSTRATE
SUCCINATE
SUCCUBINE
SUFFOCATE
SUGARCANE
SULTANATE
SUMMARIZE
SUNSTROKE
SUPERETTE
SUPERFINE
SUPERSEDE
SUPERVENE
SUPERVISE
SUPPURATE
SURCHARGE
SURCINGLE
SURROGATE
SUSCITATE
SWANIMOTE

SWINBURNE
SYLPHLIKE
SYLVANITE
SYMBOLIZE
SYNAGOGUE
SYNCOPATE
SYNDICATE
SYNOECETE
SYRPHIDAE
TABANIDAE
TABLATURE
TABLEWARE
TACHILITE
TACHYLITE
TACHYLYTE
TAILPIECE
TAILPLANE
TALKATIVE
TAMERLANE
TANGERINE
TANTALITE
TANTALIZE
TEACHABLE
TEAKETTLE
TECHNIQUE
TELEPHONE
TELESCOPE
TEMPERATE
TEMPORIZE
TEMULENCE
TENDERIZE
TENEBROSE
TENNESSEE
TENTATIVE
TERMINATE
TERRICOLE
TERRORIZE
TESTDRIVE
THELEMITE
THERALITE
THEREFORE
THIGHBONE
THINKABLE
THORNDYKE
THREESOME
THREONINE
THYLACINE
TICHBORNE
TICTACTOE
TIGHTROPE
TIMEPIECE
TIMESHARE
TIMETABLE
TINGUAITE
TIPULIDAE
TISIPHONE
TITILLATE
TOADSTONE
TOLERABLE
TOLERANCE
TOLLHOUSE
TOLPUDDLE
TOMBSTONE
TOMENTOSE
TONBRIDGE
TOOTHACHE
TOOTHSOME
TORBANITE
TOTAQUINE
TOUCHLINE
TRACEABLE
TRACTABLE
TRAINABLE
TRANSFUSE
TRANSHUME
TRANSLATE
TRANSMUTE
TRANSPIRE
TRANSPOSE
TRASIMENE
TREDRILLE
TREGEAGLE
TREILLAGE
TREMATODE
TREMOLITE
TREMULATE
TRIBUNATE
TRIDYMITE
TRILOBITE
TRITICALE
TRITURATE
TROMPETTE
TROOSTITE
TRUTINATE
TUILLETTE
TUMMYACHE
TUNGSTATE
TURBINATE
TURCOPOLE
TURNSTILE
TURNSTONE
TURNTABLE
TURPITUDE
TURQUOISE
TWAYBLADE
TYRANNIZE
UMBRATILE
UNBALANCE
UNCONFINE
UNDERDONE
UNDERLINE
UNDERMINE
UNDERRATE
UNDERSIDE
UNDERTAKE
UNDERTONE
UNEATABLE
UNPRECISE
UNSHACKLE
UNSHEATHE
UNTENABLE
UNWELCOME
UROKINASE
USHERETTE
UTTERANCE
UVAROVITE
VACCINATE
VACILLATE
VALENTINE
VANDALIZE
VARIEGATE
VARIOLATE
VARISCITE
VEGETABLE
VEHEMENCE
VEILLEUSE
VELLENAGE
VELLICATE
VELODROME
VENERABLE
VENGEANCE
VENTILATE
VENTRICLE
VERATRINE
VERBALIZE
VERBERATE
VERITABLE
VERKAMPTE
VERMIFUGE
VERSATILE
VERTEBRAE
VESTIBULE
VESTITURE
VIBRATILE
VICEREINE
VICTIMIZE
VICTORINE
VIDEOTAPE
VIENTIANE
VIGILANCE
VIGILANTE
VINDICATE
VIRGULATE
VIRULENCE
VISAGISTE
VISUALIZE
VITASCOPE
VOLATIBLE
VOLUCRINE
VOUCHSAFE
VULCANITE
VULCANIZE
VULPINITE
WAGNERITE
WAGONETTE
WAHABIITE
WAISTLINE
WAITERAGE
WALDFLUTE
WALDGRAVE
WAPENTAKE
WAREHOUSE
WATERGATE
WATERHOLE
WATERLINE
WATERSIDE
WAVELLITE
WAYZGOOSE
WEARISOME
WHALEBONE
WHEELBASE
WHEREFORE
WHETSTONE
WHINSTONE
WHIPSNADE
WHOLESALE
WHOLESOME
WHUNSTANE
WILDGEESE
WILLEMITE
WINCOPIPE
WINDSCALE
WITHERITE
WODEHOUSE
WOEBEGONE
WOLVERINE
WOODHOUSE
WOODLOUSE
WORKFORCE
WORKHORSE
WORKHOUSE
WORKPLACE
WORKSPACE
WORLDWIDE
WORRISOME
WULFENITE
WYANDOTTE
XANTHIPPE
XENOPHOBE
XEROPHYTE
XYLOPHONE
YESTEREVE
YOHIMBINE
YORKSHIRE
ZENOCRATE
ZIBELLINE
ZINKENITE
ZYGOSPORE
CHAMPLEVÉ
CLOISONNÉ
ASTROTURF
BOOKSHELF
DISBELIEF
FEEDSTUFF
FIREPROOF
FLAGSTAFF
FOODSTUFF
FOOLPROOF
HALFSTAFF
HEADSCARF
LEAKPROOF
LEITMOTIF
LOOSELEAF
OVENPROOF
PECKSNIFF
PIKESTAFF
PLAINTIFF
SKEWWHIFF
ABOUNDING
ABSORBING
ACCORDING
ADJOINING
ADMITTING
AFFECTING
AGONIZING
ANOINTING
ANSWERING
APPALLING
APPEALING
APPROVING
ARMSTRONG
ARRESTING
ASCENDING
ASSERTING
ATTACKING
AWAKENING
BANTERING
BEGINNING
BELIEVING
BELONGING
BILLABONG
BILLOWING
BOOMERANG
BORDERING
BORROWING
BRAMBLING
BRANCHING
BREATHING
BREECHING
BRISTLING
BUNDESTAG
BURROWING
CARPETING
CAVORTING
CENTERING
CENTREING
CLEANSING
COLOURING
COMPETING
COMPOSING
COMPUTING
CONFUSING
CONJURING
CONSUMING
CRACKLING
CRIPPLING
CRUMBLING
DAYSPRING
DEAFENING
DECLARING
DECLINING
DEGRADING
DEMANDING
DEMEANING
DEPENDING
DESERVING
DESIGNING
DIPHTHONG
DISABLING
DISARMING
DITHERING
DIVERGING
DIVERTING
DOODLEBUG
DOWELLING
DWINDLING
EARTHLING
EASYGOING
EMBRACING
ENDEARING
ENGRAVING
EXCLUDING
EXPECTING
EXPORTING
FASTENING
FATTENING
FILTERING
FINGERING
FINICKING
FINISHING
FLAVORING
FLEDGLING
FLOWERING
FOLKETING
FOLLOWING
FOREGOING
FORGIVING
FOUNDLING
GARDENING
GATHERING
GOVERNING
GRAPPLING

GROUNDHOG
GROUNDING
GRUELLING
GRUMBLING
GUTENBERG
GUTTERING
HAMMERING
HAMSTRING
HAMSTRUNG
HANKERING
HAPPENING
HARROWING
HASTENING
HAYMAKING
HEARTHRUG
HECTORING
HIJACKING
IMPELLING
IMPENDING
IMPROVING
INCLUDING
INFECTING
INGROWING
INQUIRING
INSELBERG
INSPIRING
INSULTING
INTENDING
INVOICING
JARLSBERG
JENNETING
JITTERBUG
JOCKTELEG
JUNKETING
LAUNCHING
LAWMAKING
LETTERING
LIGHTNING
LINGERING
LISTENING
LOITERING
LUMBERING
LUXEMBURG
MACHINING
MADDENING
MAGDEBURG
MANNERING
MARAUDING
MARKETING
MEASURING
MISFIRING
MISGIVING
MODELLING
MOTHERING
MURMURING
MUTTERING
NARROWING
NIDDERING
NIDERLING
NIEBELUNG
NUREMBERG
OBTAINING
OCCUPYING
ODELSTING
OFFENDING
OFFSPRING
OPERATING
OVERLYING
PACKAGING
PANELLING
PARENTING
PARTAKING
PERISHING
PHILLABEG
PHILLIBEG
PICKETING
PILFERING
PLAINSONG
PLAYTHING
POISONING
POPPERING
POTHOLING
PRECEDING
PRESSGANG
PROMISING
PROMPTING
PROVIDING
PROVOKING
PUNISHING
PURIFYING
PYONGYANG
QUAVERING
QUIVERING
RADIATING
RATIONING
RATTLEBAG
RAVISHING
REASONING
RECALLING
RECEIVING
RECKONING
RECORDING
RECURRING
REDEEMING
REFERRING
REGARDING
REICHSTAG
REJOICING
REMAINING
RENDERING
REPELLING
REPLACING
REPORTING
REPROVING
RESORTING
RESULTING
RETAILING
RETAINING
RETURNING
REVEALING
REVELLING
REVERSING
REVOLTING
REVOLVING
REWARDING
REWORKING
RIGHTWING
SADDENING
SADDLEBAG
SCALLAWAG
SCALLYWAG
SCAMBLING
SCANTLING
SCHELLING
SCHILLING
SCHOOLING
SCORCHING
SCRAPPING
SCREENING
SCRIMPING
SCRUBBING
SCRUMPING
SCULPTING
SEAFARING
SEARCHING
SEASONING
SELECTING
SERVICING
SHAVELING
SHEARLING
SHIELDING
SHIVERING
SHRIMPING
SHRINKING
SHUFFLING
SICKENING
SLOUGHING
SMUGGLING
SOFTENING
SOLDERING
SOMETHING
SPARKLING
SPELDRING
SPLITTING
SPONGEBAG
SPREADING
SQUINTING
SQUIRMING
STARTLING
STRAINING
STRAPHANG
STRAPPING
STREAMING
STRIPLING
STROLLING
STRUTTING
STUMBLING
SUFFERING
SUPPOSING
SURVEYING
SURVIVING
SWADDLING
SWINGEING
SWOTHLING
TERRACING
THATCHING
THIRSTING
THRASHING
THRILLING
THROBBING
THRONGING
THUMBLING
TOWELLING
TRAVELING
TREMBLING
TWINKLING
UNBENDING
UNCEASING
UNDERLING
UNDERSONG
UNFAILING
UNFEELING
UNFITTING
UNHEEDING
UNKNOWING
UNNERVING
UNSINNING
UNSPARING
UNVARYING
UNWILLING
UNWITTING
UPLIFTING
UPSETTING
VANISHING
VENUSBERG
WALLOPING
WALLOWING
WALLYDRAG
WANDERING
WEAKENING
WEIGHTING
WELCOMING
WELLBEING
WHIRLIGIG
WHISTLING
WHITENING
WHITEWING
WHIZZBANG
WILLOWING
WITHERING
WOBBEGONG
WOOMERANG
WRESTLING
WUTHERING
AFTERMATH
AINSWORTH
ALLOGRAPH
ANABRANCH
AUTOGRAPH
AYATOLLAH
BACHARACH
BACKBENCH
BACKCLOTH
BACKSHISH
BAKSHEESH
BLOODBATH
BLOWTORCH
BOBSLEIGH
BOXWALLAH
BRADLAUGH
BRAINWASH
BUCKTEETH
BULLFINCH
CAVENDISH
CHAFFINCH
CHOLELITH
COCKROACH
CORNBRASH
CYCLOLITH
DARTMOUTH
DISHCLOTH
DJELLABAH
ECTOMORPH
EDGEWORTH
EDINBURGH
EIDOGRAPH
EIGHTIETH
ELIZABETH
EMBELLISH
ENDOMORPH
ESTABLISH
FACECLOTH
FIFTEENTH
FORASMUCH
FORTHWITH
FRITHBORH
FROGMARCH
FROGMOUTH
GALLABEAH
GATECRASH
GIBBERISH
GILGAMESH
GOALMOUTH
GOLDFINCH
GOLDSMITH
GREENWICH
HAIRBRUSH
HEADCLOTH
HEMISTICH
HEMSTITCH
HEXASTICH
HEXATEUCH
HINDEMITH
HODOGRAPH
HOLLERITH
HOLOGRAPH
HOMEOPATH
HOMOGRAPH
HOPSCOTCH
HOYDENISH
HUNDREDTH
IDEOGRAPH
IDIOGRAPH
INSHALLAH
JAGGANATH
JELLYFISH
JOBSWORTH
KHANSAMAH
KINKCOUGH
KITTENISH
LABYRINTH
LADYSMITH
LAGOMORPH
LASTDITCH
LICKERISH
LINDBERGH
LIQUORISH
LOCKSMITH
LOGOGRIPH
LOINCLOTH
LOUDMOUTH
LUBAVITCH
MADRASSAH
MADRESSAH
MAHARAJAH
MATRIARCH
MEDRESSEH
MESOMORPH
MICROLITH
MILLIONTH
MONOGRAPH
MONOSTICH
MONOTROCH
MOUTHWASH
NEWSFLASH
NINETIETH
OCTASTICH
OFFENBACH
OLEOGRAPH
OSTEOPATH
OSTROGOTH
OUTGROWTH

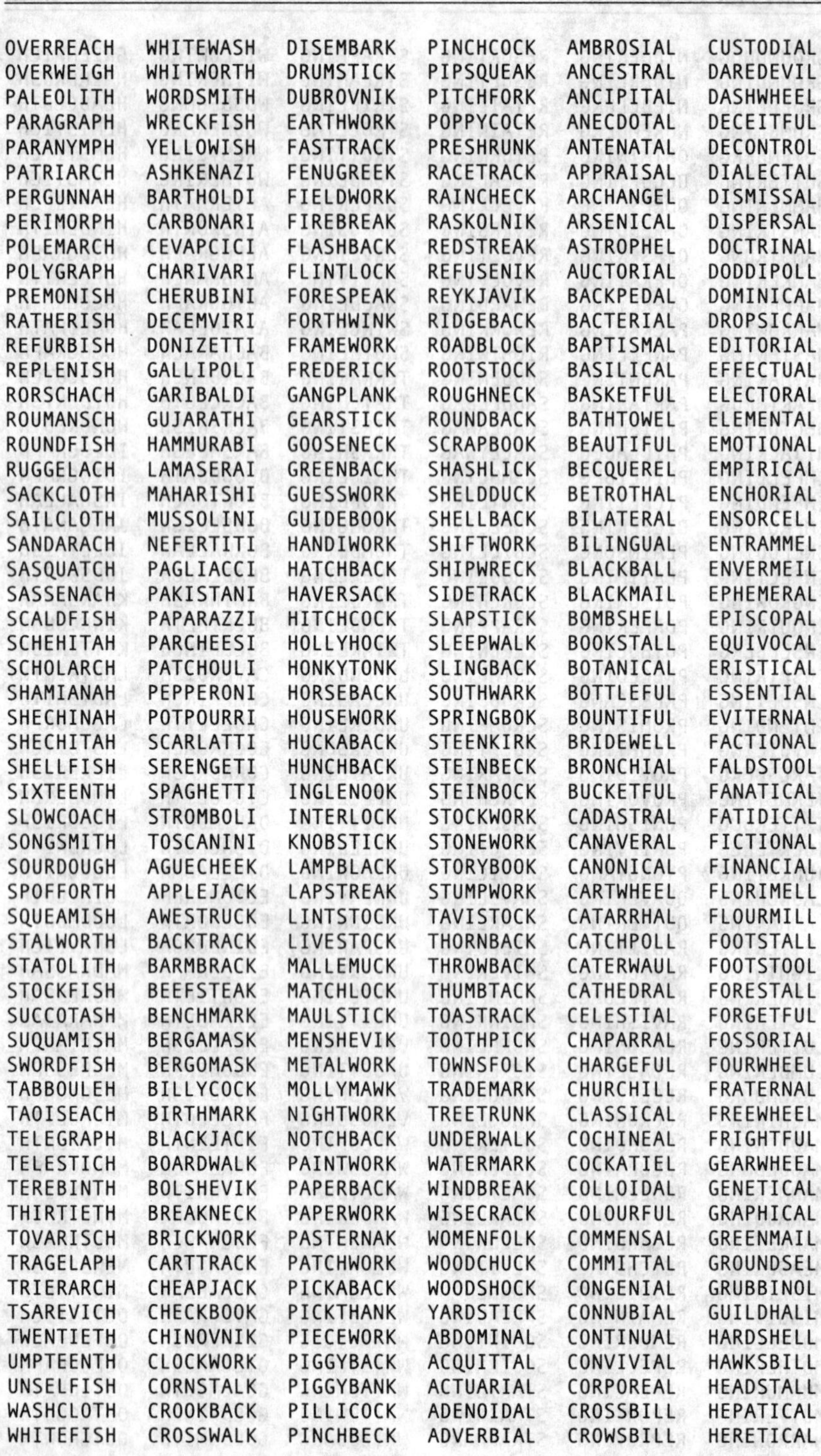

OVERREACH
OVERWEIGH
PALEOLITH
PARAGRAPH
PARANYMPH
PATRIARCH
PERGUNNAH
PERIMORPH
POLEMARCH
POLYGRAPH
PREMONISH
RATHERISH
REFURBISH
REPLENISH
RORSCHACH
ROUMANSCH
ROUNDFISH
RUGGELACH
SACKCLOTH
SAILCLOTH
SANDARACH
SASQUATCH
SASSENACH
SCALDFISH
SCHEHITAH
SCHOLARCH
SHAMIANAH
SHECHINAH
SHECHITAH
SHELLFISH
SIXTEENTH
SLOWCOACH
SONGSMITH
SOURDOUGH
SPOFFORTH
SQUEAMISH
STALWORTH
STATOLITH
STOCKFISH
SUCCOTASH
SUQUAMISH
SWORDFISH
TABBOULEH
TAOISEACH
TELEGRAPH
TELESTICH
TEREBINTH
THIRTIETH
TOVARISCH
TRAGELAPH
TRIERARCH
TSAREVICH
TWENTIETH
UMPTEENTH
UNSELFISH
WASHCLOTH
WHITEFISH
WHITEWASH
WHITWORTH
WORDSMITH
WRECKFISH
YELLOWISH
ASHKENAZI
BARTHOLDI
CARBONARI
CEVAPCICI
CHARIVARI
CHERUBINI
DECEMVIRI
DONIZETTI
GALLIPOLI
GARIBALDI
GUJARATHI
HAMMURABI
LAMASERAI
MAHARISHI
MUSSOLINI
NEFERTITI
PAGLIACCI
PAKISTANI
PAPARAZZI
PARCHEESI
PATCHOULI
PEPPERONI
POTPOURRI
SCARLATTI
SERENGETI
SPAGHETTI
STROMBOLI
TOSCANINI
AGUECHEEK
APPLEJACK
AWESTRUCK
BACKTRACK
BARMBRACK
BEEFSTEAK
BENCHMARK
BERGAMASK
BERGOMASK
BILLYCOCK
BIRTHMARK
BLACKJACK
BOARDWALK
BOLSHEVIK
BREAKNECK
BRICKWORK
CARTTRACK
CHEAPJACK
CHECKBOOK
CHINOVNIK
CLOCKWORK
CORNSTALK
CROOKBACK
CROSSWALK
DISEMBARK
DRUMSTICK
DUBROVNIK
EARTHWORK
FASTTRACK
FENUGREEK
FIELDWORK
FIREBREAK
FLASHBACK
FLINTLOCK
FORESPEAK
FORTHWINK
FRAMEWORK
FREDERICK
GANGPLANK
GEARSTICK
GOOSENECK
GREENBACK
GUESSWORK
GUIDEBOOK
HANDIWORK
HATCHBACK
HAVERSACK
HITCHCOCK
HOLLYHOCK
HONKYTONK
HORSEBACK
HOUSEWORK
HUCKABACK
HUNCHBACK
INGLENOOK
INTERLOCK
KNOBSTICK
LAMPBLACK
LAPSTREAK
LINTSTOCK
LIVESTOCK
MALLEMUCK
MATCHLOCK
MAULSTICK
MENSHEVIK
METALWORK
MOLLYMAWK
NIGHTWORK
NOTCHBACK
PAINTWORK
PAPERBACK
PAPERWORK
PASTERNAK
PATCHWORK
PICKABACK
PICKTHANK
PIECEWORK
PIGGYBACK
PIGGYBANK
PILLICOCK
PINCHBECK
PINCHCOCK
PIPSQUEAK
PITCHFORK
POPPYCOCK
PRESHRUNK
RACETRACK
RAINCHECK
RASKOLNIK
REDSTREAK
REFUSENIK
REYKJAVIK
RIDGEBACK
ROADBLOCK
ROOTSTOCK
ROUGHNECK
ROUNDBACK
SCRAPBOOK
SHASHLICK
SHELDDUCK
SHELLBACK
SHIFTWORK
SHIPWRECK
SIDETRACK
SLAPSTICK
SLEEPWALK
SLINGBACK
SOUTHWARK
SPRINGBOK
STEENKIRK
STEINBECK
STEINBOCK
STOCKWORK
STONEWORK
STORYBOOK
STUMPWORK
TAVISTOCK
THORNBACK
THROWBACK
THUMBTACK
TOASTRACK
TOOTHPICK
TOWNSFOLK
TRADEMARK
TREETRUNK
UNDERWALK
WATERMARK
WINDBREAK
WISECRACK
WOMENFOLK
WOODCHUCK
WOODSHOCK
YARDSTICK
ABDOMINAL
ACQUITTAL
ACTUARIAL
ADENOIDAL
ADVERBIAL
AMBROSIAL
ANCESTRAL
ANCIPITAL
ANECDOTAL
ANTENATAL
APPRAISAL
ARCHANGEL
ARSENICAL
ASTROPHEL
AUCTORIAL
BACKPEDAL
BACTERIAL
BAPTISMAL
BASILICAL
BASKETFUL
BATHTOWEL
BEAUTIFUL
BECQUEREL
BETROTHAL
BILATERAL
BILINGUAL
BLACKBALL
BLACKMAIL
BOMBSHELL
BOOKSTALL
BOTANICAL
BOTTLEFUL
BOUNTIFUL
BRIDEWELL
BRONCHIAL
BUCKETFUL
CADASTRAL
CANAVERAL
CANONICAL
CARTWHEEL
CATARRHAL
CATCHPOLL
CATERWAUL
CATHEDRAL
CELESTIAL
CHAPARRAL
CHARGEFUL
CHURCHILL
CLASSICAL
COCHINEAL
COCKATIEL
COLLOIDAL
COLOURFUL
COMMENSAL
COMMITTAL
CONGENIAL
CONNUBIAL
CONTINUAL
CONVIVIAL
CORPOREAL
CROSSBILL
CROWSBILL
CUSTODIAL
DAREDEVIL
DASHWHEEL
DECEITFUL
DECONTROL
DIALECTAL
DISMISSAL
DISPERSAL
DOCTRINAL
DODDIPOLL
DOMINICAL
DROPSICAL
EDITORIAL
EFFECTUAL
ELECTORAL
ELEMENTAL
EMOTIONAL
EMPIRICAL
ENCHORIAL
ENSORCELL
ENTRAMMEL
ENVERMEIL
EPHEMERAL
EPISCOPAL
EQUIVOCAL
ERISTICAL
ESSENTIAL
EVITERNAL
FACTIONAL
FALDSTOOL
FANATICAL
FATIDICAL
FICTIONAL
FINANCIAL
FLORIMELL
FLOURMILL
FOOTSTALL
FOOTSTOOL
FORESTALL
FORGETFUL
FOSSORIAL
FOURWHEEL
FRATERNAL
FREEWHEEL
FRIGHTFUL
GEARWHEEL
GENETICAL
GRAPHICAL
GREENMAIL
GROUNDSEL
GRUBBINOL
GUILDHALL
HARDSHELL
HAWKSBILL
HEADSTALL
HEPATICAL
HERETICAL

HESTERNAL
HEXAGONAL
HOBBINOLL
HODIERNAL
HOMICIDAL
HORSETAIL
HYDROFOIL
IDENTICAL
ILLIBERAL
ILLOGICAL
IMPARTIAL
INAUGURAL
INNISFAIL
ISOPROPYL
JERAHMEEL
JOBERNOWL
JURIDICAL
KNAPSCULL
KNAPSKULL
LACHRYMAL
LACONICAL
LAMBSWOOL
LANDSMAAL
LANGSPIEL
LIVERPOOL
MARMOREAL
MARSUPIAL
MASTERFUL
MATUTINAL
MEDIAEVAL
MEDICINAL
MEHITABEL
MENSTRUAL
MERCURIAL
MILLENIAL
MISPICKEL
MONASTRAL
MOSCHATEL
MOURNIVAL
MOYGASHEL
MUNICIPAL
MUSICHALL
NATHANIEL
NEUCHATEL
NEWSSTALL
NIGHTFALL
NOCTURNAL
NONPAREIL
NUMBSKULL
NUMERICAL
OCCIPITAL
OCTAGONAL
ORGANICAL
OVERSPILL
PALPEBRAL
PANNIKELL
PANTHENOL
PAROCHIAL
PERENNIAL
PERPETUAL
PERSONNEL
PICTORIAL
PIECEMEAL
PIMPERNEL
PIRATICAL
PITCHPOLL
PLAUSTRAL
PLENTIFUL
POCKETFUL
POLEMICAL
POLITICAL
POLYGONAL
POPLITEAL
PORTRAYAL
POSTNATAL
POTENTIAL
PRACTICAL
PRACTOLOL
PREBENDAL
PRESIDIAL
PREVERNAL
PRIMAEVAL
PRINCIPAL
PROCONSUL
PRODROMAL
PSYCHICAL
PUERPERAL
PYRAMIDAL
QUANTICAL
QUIVERFUL
QUIZZICAL
RAPTORIAL
RAZORBILL
RECTORIAL
REGARDFUL
REGRETFUL
REHEARSAL
REISTAFEL
RESENTFUL
RETRIEVAL
REVICTUAL
ROUNCEVAL
ROUNCIVAL
SALESGIRL
SARTORIAL
SATIRICAL
SCEPTICAL
SCHLEMIEL
SCHLEMIHL
SCHNITZEL
SCHNORKEL
SCLEROTAL
SCOUNDREL
SCREWBALL
SDEIGNFUL
SECTIONAL
SECTORIAL
SEMIFINAL
SENESCHAL
SHORTFALL
SHORTHAUL
SHOVELFUL
SINGSPIEL
SKEPTICAL
SNEERWELL
SORROWFUL
SPEEDWELL
SPHERICAL
SPIRITUAL
SPOONBILL
SPRITEFUL
SPRITSAIL
STERCORAL
STONEWALL
STOOLBALL
STRESSFUL
SUBNORMAL
SUCCURSAL
TECHNICAL
TECTORIAL
TERPINEOL
THORNBILL
THUMBNAIL
TOADSTOOL
TORMENTIL
TRANSVAAL
TRAPEZIAL
TREADMILL
TRIENNIAL
TRIUMPHAL
UMBILICAL
UNDERSEAL
UNDERSELL
UNETHICAL
UNHELPFUL
UNHOPEFUL
UNISEXUAL
UNIVERSAL
UNMINDFUL
UNMUSICAL
UNNATURAL
UNTYPICAL
UREDINIAL
VERIDICAL
VERSIONAL
VERTEBRAL
VESTIGIAL
VICEREGAL
VIGESIMAL
WATERFALL
WATERFOWL
WATERMILL
WHEATMEAL
WHIMSICAL
WHIRLPOOL
WHITEHALL
WHITEWALL
WHOLEMEAL
WINDCHILL
WONDERFUL
YGGDRASIL
ZINFANDEL
AIRSTREAM
ALGORITHM
ALUMINIUM
AMERICIUM
AMSTERDAM
ANABOLISM
ANGIOGRAM
ANGLICISM
ARBORETUM
ASPLENIUM
ATHENAEUM
BACTERIUM
BARNSTORM
BERKELIUM
BERYLLIUM
BETHLEHEM
BLINDWORM
BOARDROOM
BROADLOOM
BRUMMAGEM
BRUTALISM
CABLEGRAM
CAIRNGORM
CALCANEUM
CALDARIUM
CALVANISM
CAPITULUM
CARTOGRAM
CATACLYSM
CATAPLASM
CATECHISM
CHECKROOM
CHEONGSAM
CHERNOZEM
CLASSROOM
CLINGFILM
CLOAKROOM
COENOBIUM
COFFERDAM
COLCHICUM
COLLYRIUM
COLOSSEUM
COLOSTRUM
COLUMBIUM
COMINFORM
COMMUNISM
CONTINUUM
CONUNDRUM
COURTROOM
CRIBELLUM
CRITICISM
CROSSBEAM
CRYPTOGAM
CUNEIFORM
CYMBIDIUM
DALTONISM
DEFEATISM
DESPOTISM
DEUTERIUM
DIAPHRAGM
DISAFFIRM
DOGMATISM
EARTHWORM
ECOSYSTEM
ECTOPLASM
EFFINGHAM
EFFLUVIUM
ELATERIUM
ELBOWROOM
ENCOLPIUM
ENDOSPERM
ENTROPIUM
EPICEDIUM
EPIPHRAGM
EPIPOLISM
EQUISETUM
EROTICISM
ERPINGHAM
ERUCIFORM
EUPHEMISM
EUPHONIUM
EXTREMISM
FEUDALISM
FLABELLUM
FLAGELLUM
GALLICISM
GALVANISM
GARGARISM
GERMANIUM
GLUCINIUM
GONGORISM
GOSSYPIUM
GREENROOM
GUARDROOM
GYMNASIUM
GYNOECIUM
HAILSTORM
HARMONIUM
HERBARIUM
HESYCHASM
HISTOGRAM
HORDEOLUM
HOSPITIUM
HOUSEROOM
HOUYHNHNM
HYPNOTISM
IDIOPLASM
IMPLUVIUM
INDECORUM
IRVINGISM
JANSENISM
JERUSALEM
JETSTREAM
KARAKORAM
KOMINFORM
LANDSTURM
LANTHANUM
LATHYRISM
LECANORAM
LOGARITHM
MACROCOSM
MAELSTROM
MAGNALIUM
MAGNESIUM
MAGNETISM
MANNERISM
MANUBRIUM
MARSUPIUM
MARTYRDOM
MASOCHISM
MAUSOLEUM
MECHANISM
MEDMENHAM
MENDELISM
MENSTRUUM
MESMERISM
METHODISM
MICROCOSM
MICROFILM
MIDRASHIM
MIDSTREAM
MILLENIUM
MILLIGRAM
MISINFORM
MITHRAISM
MODERNISM
MONERGISM
MONGOLISM
MONTANISM
MORMONISM
MRIDAMGAM
MRIDANGAM
MULTIFORM
MYSTICISM
NEOLOGISM
NEPHALISM
NEPTUNIUM
OCULIFORM
OPERCULUM
OPOBALSAM

OPPENHEIM
OSTEODERM
OSTRACISM
OVERWHELM
PACHYDERM
PALLADIUM
PANEGOISM
PANTHEISM
PELMANISM
PESSIMISM
PETERSHAM
PETROLEUM
PHENAKISM
PHITONIUM
PHONOGRAM
PICTOGRAM
PIPEDREAM
PLURALISM
PLUTONIUM
POMOERIUM
POTASSIUM
PRESCUTUM
PRESIDIUM
PRYTANEUM
PSEUDONYM
PTERIDIUM
PURDONIUM
PYRETHRUM
RACIALISM
RADIOGRAM
RAINSTORM
REDDENDUM
RESTIFORM
RETICULUM
RIBBONISM
ROSTELLUM
ROTTERDAM
RUTHENIUM
SACRARIUM
SAGAPENUM
SALICETUM
SANDSTORM
SANHEDRIM
SARMENTUM
SATURNISM
SCALARIUM
SCIENTISM
SENSILLUM
SENSORIUM
SEPHARDIM
SHEIKHDOM
SHINTOISM
SHORTTERM
SNOWSTORM
SOCIALISM
SOLIPSISM
STATEROOM
STILLROOM
STOCKHOLM
STOCKROOM
STOREROOM
STRATAGEM
STRONGARM
STRONTIUM
SYLLOGISM
SYMBOLISM
SYMPODIUM
SYMPOSIUM
SYNANGIUM
SYNCOMIUM
SYRIACISM
TARAXACUM
TECTIFORM
TELLURIUM
TENACULUM
TENTORIUM
TERRARIUM
TERRORISM
TETRAGRAM
THANATISM
THRALLDOM
TORMENTUM
TOTTENHAM
TRANSFORM
TRAPEZIUM
TRIBALISM
TRIFORIUM
TRONDHEIM
TUTIORISM
ULTIMATUM
UNCHRISOM
VANDALISM
VERBASCUM
VERMIFORM
VIRGINIUM
VOLTINISM
VOODOOISM
VORTICISM
VULGARISM
WAGENBOOM
WHEATGERM
WITTICISM
YTTERBIUM
ZIRCONIUM
ABDUCTION
ABOLITION
ABOUTTURN
ACCESSION
ACCORDION
ACCRETION
ADDICTION
ADMISSION
ADORATION
ADRENALIN
ADULATION
ADVECTION
AFFECTION
AFLATOXIN
AFTERNOON
AGAMEMNON
AGITATION
ALDEBARAN
ALPENHORN
AMARANTIN
AMBROSIAN
AMPHIBIAN
ANATOLIAN
ANCHORMAN
ANIMATION
ANTITOXIN
ANTIVENIN
APPERTAIN
APPORTION
ARLINGTON
ARTHURIAN
ASCENSION
ASCERTAIN
ASHMOLEAN
ASPERSION
ASSERTION
ASTRAKHAN
ATHELSTAN
ATTENTION
ATTRITION
ATTUITION
AUTOMATON
AVOCATION
AYCKBOURN
BADMINTON
BALDAQUIN
BANDWAGON
BARAGOUIN
BARBARIAN
BARTHOLIN
BASILICON
BATTALION
BECHSTEIN
BEDRIDDEN
BEETHOVEN
BERNSTEIN
BETTERTON
BILIRUBIN
BIRDBRAIN
BISECTION
BOATSWAIN
BOMBARDON
BORNAGAIN
BOSTONIAN
BOTSWANAN
BRANDIRON
BRAZILIAN
BREAKDOWN
BREAKEVEN
BRIGADOON
BROUGHTON
BUCKTHORN
BULGARIAN
BURUNDIAN
CAESAREAN
CAMBODIAN
CAMBUSCAN
CAMERAMAN
CAPARISON
CAPRICORN
CARIBBEAN
CARNATION
CARNELIAN
CARTESIAN
CASSATION
CASTILIAN
CATAMARAN
CATHEPSIN
CATTLEMAN
CATTLEPEN
CAUCASIAN
CAUSATION
CENTURION
CESSATION
CHALAZION
CHALIAPIN
CHAMELEON
CHAMFRAIN
CHAMPAIGN
CHAMPLAIN
CHARLATAN
CHARWOMAN
CHAWBACON
CHIEFTAIN
CHILBLAIN
CHINATOWN
CHRISTIAN
CHURCHMAN
CIMMERIAN
CIRCADIAN
CLAMPDOWN
CLARENDON
CLERGYMAN
CLINICIAN
COALITION
COCKSWAIN
COEMPTION
COGNITION
COLLATION
COLLEGIAN
COLLISION
COLLODION
COLLUSION
COLOMBIAN
COLUMBIAN
COMINTERN
COMMOTION
COMMUNION
COMPANION
CONCISION
CONDITION
CONFUSION
CONNEXION
CONTAGION
CONTUSION
CORNELIAN
CORNERMAN
CORROSION
COTYLEDON
COUNTDOWN
COURTESAN
CRACKDOWN
CRACKSMAN
CRACOVIAN
CRAFTSMAN
CREMATION
CRITERION
CTESIPHON
CUCHULAIN
CUSTODIAN
CYCLOTRON
DAEDALIAN
DALMATIAN
DAMNATION
DANDELION
DARTAGNAN
DARWINIAN
DECAMERON
DECATHLON
DECEPTION
DECESSION
DECILLION
DECOCTION
DEDUCTION
DEFECTION
DEFLATION
DEJECTION
DENTITION
DEPICTION
DESERTION
DETECTION
DETENTION
DETRITION
DEUCALION
DEVIATION
DICTATION
DIETICIAN
DIFFUSION
DIGESTION
DIGITALIN
DIMENSION
DIONYSIAN
DIRECTION
DISBURDEN
DIVERSION
DOMINICAN
DORMITION
DRACONIAN
DRAFTSMAN
DRAVIDIAN
DUMBARTON
EALDORMAN
ECTROPION
EDDINGTON
EDUCATION
EDWARDIAN
EGRESSION
EIDERDOWN
ELEVATION
ELLINGTON
ELOCUTION
EMANATION
EMPLECTON
EMULATION
ENCHEASON
ENCOLPION
ENDECAGON
ENERGUMEN
ENLIGHTEN
ENTERTAIN
ENTROPION
EPHEMERON
EPICUREAN
EPINICION
EPINIKION
EPULATION
ERUDITION
ETHIOPIAN
EUCLIDEAN
EUSKARIAN
EVAGATION
EVERGREEN
EVOCATION
EVOLUTION
EXARATION
EXCAMBION
EXCEPTION
EXCISEMAN
EXCLUSION
EXCURSION
EXECUTION
EXEMPTION
EXORATION
EXPANSION
EXPIATION
EXPLOSION
EXPULSION
EXTENSION

EXTORTION
EXTRUSION
EXUDATION
EYESTRAIN
FALERNIAN
FALLOPIAN
FAULCHION
FIELDSMAN
FILIGRAIN
FILLIPEEN
FISHERMAN
FLAGELLIN
FLORESTAN
FLOTATION
FORBIDDEN
FORGOTTEN
FORMATION
FRANCOLIN
FREEMASON
FRENCHMAN
FRENCHMEN
FRIGATOON
FROGSPAWN
FULLBLOWN
FULLGROWN
GALDRAGON
GARRYOWEN
GENTLEMAN
GENTLEMEN
GERFALCON
GESTATION
GOBETWEEN
GODOLPHIN
GRADATION
GREASEGUN
GREENHORN
GREGORIAN
GRIMALKIN
GROSGRAIN
GUARDSMAN
GUNCOTTON
GUSTATION
HABERGEON
HACQUETON
HALFDOZEN
HALLOWEEN
HARLEQUIN
HARLESTON
HARMATTAN
HARTSHORN
HAYRADDIN
HEARDSMAN
HEARTBURN
HEBRIDEAN
HECOGENIN
HELVELLYN
HERCULEAN
HESPERIAN
HEXAMERON
HIBERNIAN
HIMALAYAN
HISTORIAN
HOBGOBLIN
HOMEGROWN
HONEYMOON
HOOLACHAN
HUNGARIAN
IBUPROFEN
ICHNEUMON
IDIOTICON
IGUANODON
ILLGOTTEN
IMITATION
IMMELMANN
IMMERSION
IMPACTION
IMPASSION
IMPULSION
INANITION
INCAUTION
INCEPTION
INCLUSION
INCURSION
INDICTION
INDUCTION
INFECTION
INFLATION
INFLEXION
INGESTION
INJECTION
INSERTION
INTENTION
INTRUSION
INTUITION
INUNCTION
INVENTION
INVERSION
IRRUPTION
ISODORIAN
ISOLATION
JAWBATION
JORDANIAN
JOSEPHSON
JUSTINIAN
KENTIGERN
KEPLARIAN
KILDERKIN
KINSWOMAN
KNOCKDOWN
KROPOTKIN
KRUMMHORN
LACTATION
LAMPADION
LAODICEAN
LARGITION
LATRATION
LAUDATION
LESTRIGON
LEVIATHAN
LIBRARIAN
LIVERYMAN
LIVRAISON
LOHENGRIN
LONGICORN
LUCIFERIN
LUCTATION
MACTATION
MAGNETRON
MAINTENON
MALATHION
MALAYSIAN
MAMMALIAN
MANHATTAN
MANNEQUIN
MASTERMAN
MAURITIAN
MAVOURNIN
MEANDRIAN
MEDALLION
MEDIATION
MENIPPEAN
MENTATION
MERCAPTAN
METHEGLIN
MICKLETON
MIDDLEMAN
MIDDLETON
MIGRATION
MINUTEMAN
MISFALLEN
MISSHAPEN
MODILLION
MONGOLIAN
MONOXYLON
MONTESPAN
MORTICIAN
MOTHEATEN
MUGGLETON
MUJAHIDIN
MUSKETOON
MUSKOGEAN
MUSSULMAN
NABATHEAN
NAPIERIAN
NARRATION
NICKNEVEN
NIGHTGOWN
NIPPERKIN
NONILLION
NORWEGIAN
NOTARIKON
NUTRITION
OARSWOMAN
OBJECTION
OBREPTION
OBSESSION
OBTRUSION
OBVENTION
OCCLUSION
OCTILLION
ODDJOBMAN
OESTROGEN
OFFSEASON
OLECRANON
OLEORESIN
OMBUDSMAN
OPERATION
ORANGEMAN
ORATORIAN
ORPHARION
ORPINGTON
OTTERBURN
OUTOFTOWN
OUTSPOKEN
OVERBLOWN
OVERDRAWN
OVERGROWN
OVULATION
OXIDATION
PADEMELON
PALANKEEN
PALANQUIN
PALLADIAN
PALMATION
PALPATION
PANDATION
PANDEMIAN
PANTALEON
PANTALOON
PARATHION
PARHELION
PARTHENON
PARTHOLON
PARTITION
PATHTRAIN
PATRICIAN
PATROLMAN
PELLAGRIN
PENDLETON
PENDRAGON
PENILLION
PERCHERON
PERDITION
PERICUTIN
PERISCIAN
PERSIMMON
PERVASION
PHELLOGEN
PHIGALIAN
PHYSICIAN
PHYTOTRON
PINKERTON
PISTAREEN
PITUITRIN
PLAINSMAN
PLOUGHMAN
POINTSMAN
POLICEMAN
POLLUTION
PORCELAIN
PORIFERAN
POSTWOMAN
PRECISIAN
PRECISION
PREMOTION
PREORDAIN
PRINCETON
PRIVATION
PROBATION
PROFUSION
PROKARYON
PROLACTIN
PROLUSION
PROMOTION
PRONGHORN
PROPERDIN
PROUDHORN
PROVISION
PTARMIGAN
PULSATION
PYGMALION
QUARENDEN
QUERCETIN
QUINTROON
QUOTATION
QUOTIDIAN
QUOTITION
RADDLEMAN
RADIATION
READYEARN
REBELLION
REBOATION
RECEPTION
RECESSION
REDUCTION
REFECTION
REFLATION
REFLEXION
REGUERDON
REJECTION
REMISSION
RENDITION
REPLETION
REPTATION
REPTILIAN
REPULSION
RESNATRON
RETENTION
RETORSION
RETORTION
REVERSION
REVULSION
RHODESIAN
RHODOPSIN
ROBERTSON
ROSCOMMON
ROSMINIAN
ROUMANIAN
ROUNDSMAN
RUDDLEMAN
RUINATION
RUTHENIAN
SABBATIAN
SACCHARIN
SACKERSON
SACRISTAN
SAINTFOIN
SALVARSAN
SALVATION
SAMARITAN
SANHEDRIN
SANHEDRON
SANNYASIN
SASKATOON
SATIATION
SATURNIAN
SAUCISSON
SAUVIGNON
SAXITOXIN
SCHLIEREN
SCHNECKEN
SCHOOLMAN
SCONCHEON
SCOTCHMAN
SCUNCHEON
SCYTHEMAN
SEBASTIAN
SECESSION
SECLUSION
SECRETION
SECTARIAN
SEDUCTION
SELACHION
SELECTION
SELJUKIAN
SEMANTRON
SEMICOLON
SENSATION
SERBONIAN
SERIATION
SERRATION
SEVENTEEN

SHAKEDOWN
SHARESMAN
SHARKSKIN
SHEEPSKIN
SHORTHORN
SHUBUNKIN
SIGNALMAN
SIMPLETON
SINGLETON
SINKANSEN
SIRBONIAN
SISYPHEAN
SITUATION
SLAMMAKIN
SLOVENIAN
SOLFIDIAN
SOOTERKIN
SOUTHDOWN
SOVEREIGN
SPADASSIN
SPILLICAN
SPILLIKIN
SPOILSMAN
SPOKESMAN
SPORTSMAN
SPORTSMEN
STABLEMAN
STANCHION
STATESMAN
STEERSMAN
STERADIAN
STEVENSON
STILLBORN
STINKHORN
STRIATION
SUBALTERN
SUFFRAGAN
SUFFUSION
SUMMATION
SUNSCREEN
SURREJOIN
SUSPICION
SWANSDOWN
SWORDSMAN
SYNEDRION
TABELLION
TACTICIAN
TAMOXIFEN
TANZANIAN
TARNATION
TARPAULIN
TARTAREAN
TASMANIAN
TELLURIAN
TELLURION
TENAILLON
TEPHILLIN
THAUMATIN
THEREUPON
THIRDSMAN
THREADFIN
THROWDOWN
THYESTEAN
THYRATRON
TIERCERON
TITHEBARN
TITRATION
TOUCHDOWN
TRADESMAN
TRADITION
TRAGEDIAN
TREVELYAN
TRIATHLON
TRIBESMAN
TRIBESMEN
TRICERION
TRIHEDRON
TRILITHON
TRISAGION
TROPAELIN
TROPARION
TRUNCHEON
UKRAINIAN
UNBEKNOWN
UNCERTAIN
UNCONCERN
UNDERSIGN
UNITARIAN
UNTRODDEN
UNWRITTEN
URICONIAN
URINATION
URUGUAYAN
VALUATION
VARANGIAN
VARIATION
VELDSKOEN
VELVETEEN
VERMILION
VESPASIAN
VIBRATION
VICTORIAN
VIOLATION
VIRGINIAN
VITIATION
VITRUVIAN
VORTIGERN
VULGARIAN
WAFERTHIN
WAGNERIAN
WASHBASIN
WASHERMAN
WASSERMAN
WELLKNOWN
WHEREUPON
WHERRYMAN
WILLESDEN
WIMBLEDON
WINCANTON
WISCONSIN
WITHDRAWN
WOLLASTON
WORMEATEN
YACHTSMAN
YACHTSMEN
ALTIPLANO
ALTISSIMO
ANDANTINO
ANTIPASTO
ARMADILLO
BANDOLERO
BASTINADO
BOCCACCIO
BOLIVIANO
CABALLERO
CANALETTO
CAPORETTO
CAPRICCIO
CARPACCIO
CIPOLLINO
CONTRALTO
CORREGGIO
CRESCENDO
DESPERADO
DONATELLO
DUODECIMO
EMBROGLIO
ESPERANTO
GLISSANDO
HEYPRESTO
HURRICANO
IMBROGLIO
INAMORATO
INCOGNITO
LARGHETTO
LAZARETTO
MAJORDOMO
MANIFESTO
MORATORIO
MUSCOVADO
OBBLIGATO
PAPARAZZO
PASTICCIO
PINOCCHIO
PISTACHIO
PIZZICATO
POLITBURO
PORTFOLIO
PUNCTILIO
QUASIMODO
RADICCHIO
RELIGIOSO
RIGOLETTO
SICILIANO
SIXTEENMO
SOLFEGGIO
SOLFERINO
SOSTENUTO
STRAPPADO
TELEPHOTO
VAPORETTO
WINNEBAGO
ZUCCHETTO
AFTERDAMP
AMENHOTEP
BELLYFLOP
BOOBYTRAP
BUTTERCUP
CATCHCROP
CHINSTRAP
COURTSHIP
DEATHTRAP
EAVESDROP
FILMSTRIP
FILTERTIP
FINGERTIP
GOOSESTEP
HORSEWHIP
JOCKSTRAP
LIGHTSHIP
LONGCHAMP
MICROCHIP
MOUSETRAP
OVERSLEEP
OWNERSHIP
PAPERCLIP
PARATROOP
PEASEWEEP
PLAYGROUP
QUICKSTEP
SCREWEDUP
SHORTSTOP
SKETCHMAP
SPACESHIP
SPOROCARP
STEAMSHIP
STONECROP
SWEETSHOP
TRANSSHIP
TROOPSHIP
TRUMPEDUP
WHITEDAMP
WOODENTOP
ABSCONDER
ABSTAINER
ADMONITOR
ADULTERER
AFRIKANER
AGGRESSOR
ALABASTER
ALEXANDER
ALLIGATOR
ALTIMETER
AMPLIFIER
ANNOTATOR
ANNOUNCER
APPARITOR
APPETIZER
ARTICULAR
ARTIFICER
ASPIRATOR
ATTAINDER
AURICULAR
AUTOMAKER
AVUNCULAR
AXMINSTER
BACKBITER
BACKWATER
BALLADEER
BALTHAZAR
BANDOLEER
BANDOLIER
BAROMETER
BARRISTER
BARTENDER
BEACHWEAR
BEDSITTER
BEEFEATER
BEEKEEPER
BEHAVIOUR
BELEAGUER
BERGANDER
BINOCULAR
BLUNDERER
BLUSTERER
BOOKLOVER
BOOKMAKER
BRIGADIER
BUCCANEER
BUCENTAUR
BULLDOZER
BUTTERBUR
BYSTANDER
CALEMBOUR
CAMCORDER
CANVASSER
CAPACITOR
CAPITULAR
CARETAKER
CARPENTER
CHARACTER
CHATTERER
CHAUFFEUR
CHAVENDER
CHEVALIER
CHISELLER
CHORISTER
CLARIFIER
COADJUTOR
COALMINER
COLLAPSAR
COLLECTOR
COLOMBIER
COMFORTER
COMMANDER
COMMISSAR
COMPOTIER
CONDENSER
CONDUCTOR
CONFESSOR
CONFITEOR
CONNECTOR
CONQUEROR
CONSIGNOR
CONTAINER
CONTEMPER
CONTENDER
CONTRIVER
CONVECTOR
CONVERTER
CORIANDER
CORNFLOUR
CORRECTOR
CORRUPTER
COSTUMIER
COUNSELOR
COUTURIER
CRICKETER
CROSSOVER
CRYOMETER
CUNCTATOR
DAMBUSTER
DECKCHAIR
DECORATOR
DEFAULTER
DEFLECTOR
DELIVERER
DEMEANOUR
DEPOSITOR
DERRINGER
DESTROYER
DETONATOR
DETRACTOR
DEVELOPER
DISAPPEAR
DISCOLOUR
DISFAVOUR
DISHONOUR
DISHWATER
DISMEMBER
DISPENSER
DISREPAIR

DISSENTER
DISTEMPER
DISTILLER
DONCASTER
DOUKHOBOR
DUNGEONER
EASTERNER
ELASTOMER
EMBEZZLER
EMBROIDER
ENCHANTER
ENCOUNTER
ENDEAVOUR
ENGROSSER
EPISTOLER
EQUALIZER
ERGATANER
ERIOMETER
ESCALATOR
EXCALIBUR
EXCAVATOR
EXCELSIOR
EXCHEQUER
EXEQUATUR
EXHIBITOR
EXPLOITER
EXPOSITOR
EXTRACTOR
EYELETEER
EYEOPENER
FILLISTER
FILMMAKER
FINANCIER
FIREWATER
FIRSTEVER
FLATTENER
FLATTERER
FOREIGNER
FORGATHER
FORWANDER
FREIGHTER
FRESHENER
FROBISHER
FRUCTIDOR
FRUITERER
FUNICULAR
GAINSAYER
GASHOLDER
GASOMETER
GAULEITER
GAZETTEER
GEARLEVER
GENERATOR
GERMANCER
GERMANDER
GIBRALTAR
GLABELLAR
GLADIATOR
GLANDULAR
GLENDOWER
GODFATHER
GODMOTHER
GONDOLIER
GOOSANDER
GOSPELLER
GRENADIER
GROSVENOR
GUARANTOR
GUNPOWDER
HADROSAUR
HAMBURGER
HAMFATTER
HARBINGER
HARDANGER
HARDCOVER
HARDLINER
HARPOONER
HARVESTER
HEREAFTER
HEXAMETER
HIGHFLYER
HODOMETER
HOMEOWNER
HORSEHAIR
HUMDINGER
ICELANDER
ILCHESTER
IMMUNISER
IMPEACHER
IMPERATOR
IMPOUNDER
INCUBATOR
INDICATOR
INDWELLER
INFIELDER
INHERITOR
INITIATOR
INNKEEPER
INNOVATOR
INSPECTOR
INSTANTER
INSULATOR
INSWINGER
INTRIGUER
IRREGULAR
ISALLOBAR
JAYWALKER
JERKWATER
JOBSEEKER
KARABINER
KEYHOLDER
KIDNAPPER
KILOMETER
KINGMAKER
KISSINGER
KITCHENER
KLEMPERER
KONIMETER
LANCASTER
LANDLOPER
LANDOWNER
LAPLANDER
LATECOMER
LAVOISIER
LAWMONGER
LAWNMOWER
LEICESTER
LIBERATOR
LIMBURGER
LINKLATER
LOCHINVAR
LONGEDFOR
LOWLANDER
LYSIMETER
MACARTHUR
MAGNIFIER
MALLANDER
MALLENDER
MANOMETER
MARKETEER
MASSINGER
MAYFLOWER
MEDITATOR
MEKOMETER
MEMORITER
MENUISIER
MERGANSER
MESSENGER
MIDSUMMER
MIDWINTER
MILOMETER
MINELAYER
MISSIONER
MISTEMPER
MODERATOR
MOLECULAR
MONOCULAR
MONOMETER
MONSIGNOR
MOONRAKER
MORTGAGOR
MUCKENDER
MUSKETEER
NAVIGATOR
NEBBISHER
NEIGHBOUR
NEWSPAPER
NOMINATOR
NONSMOKER
NOTEPAPER
NUMERATOR
NUTJOBBER
OFFCOLOUR
OILTANKER
ONCOMETER
OPPRESSOR
ORBICULAR
ORGANISER
ORGANIZER
ORTHOPTER
OUTFITTER
OUTNUMBER
OUTRIGGER
OUTROOPER
OUTWORKER
OVERPOWER
OVERRIDER
OVERSTEER
PACEMAKER
PARAMETER
PARTTIMER
PASSENGER
PAYMASTER
PECULATOR
PEDICULAR
PEDOMETER
PENPUSHER
PENSIONER
PERFORMER
PERIANDER
PERIMETER
PHALANGER
PHANSIGAR
PHILANDER
PHILISTER
PICNICKER
PIEPOWDER
PINHOOKER
PISTOLEER
PLASTERER
PLUNDERER
POETASTER
POLYESTER
POMPADOUR
PORRINGER
POSSESSOR
POSTERIOR
POTBOILER
POTHUNTER
POTTINGAR
POULTERER
PRANKSTER
PRECENTOR
PRECEPTOR
PRECURSOR
PREDICTOR
PRELECTOR
PRESBYTER
PRESENTER
PRESERVER
PRETENDER
PRIVATEER
PROCESSOR
PROFESSOR
PROFITEER
PROJECTOR
PROPELLER
PROPELLOR
PROTECTOR
PROTESTER
PROTOSTAR
PROVENDER
PTEROSAUR
PUBLISHER
PULPITEER
PUPPETEER
PURCHASER
PUSHCHAIR
QUALIFIER
RACKETEER
RACONTEUR
RAINWATER
RATEPAYER
RECLAIMER
RECTIFIER
REDLETTER
REFLECTOR
REFRACTOR
REFRESHER
REGISSEUR
REGISTRAR
REGULATOR
REJOINDER
REMAINDER
RENOVATOR
RENTALLER
RESERVOIR
RESONATOR
RESPECTER
RESSALDAR
RETRACTOR
RETRIEVER
RHYMESTER
RINGSIDER
ROISTERER
ROSEWATER
SAFFLOWER
SALTPETER
SALTWATER
SANDPAPER
SANDPIPER
SAPSUCKER
SCARIFIER
SCAVENGER
SCHLENTER
SCHMIEDER
SCHMUTTER
SCHNAPPER
SCHNAUZER
SCHNORRER
SCISSORER
SCLAUNDER
SCRAMBLER
SCRIVENER
SCROUNGER
SCRUTATOR
SCUDDALER
SCURRIOUR
SEDGEMOOR
SEPARATOR
SEPTEMBER
SEPULCHER
SEQUESTER
SERASKIER
SERENADER
SHARPENER
SHILLABER
SHIPOWNER
SHOEMAKER
SHOPFLOOR
SHOVELLER
SIGHTSEER
SIGNALLER
SIMULATOR
SKINDIVER
SKYJACKER
SLAUGHTER
SLUMBERER
SOFTCOVER
SOLICITOR
SOLLICKER
SOMMELIER
SONNETEER
SONOMETER
SOPHISTER
SOTTISIER
SOUTENEUR
SOUWESTER
SPECTATOR
SPELUNKER
SPHINCTER
SPINDRIER
SPINNAKER
SPLENDOUR
SPRINKLER
STAMMERER
STANNATOR
STARGAZER
STATIONER
STAVANGER
STEGOSAUR
STIFFENER

STRAGGLER
STRANGLER
STREETCAR
STRETCHER
SUBCELLAR
SUBEDITOR
SUCCENTOR
SUCCESSOR
SUNBATHER
SUNDOWNER
SUNFLOWER
SUPERSTAR
SUPINATOR
SUPPORTER
SURRENDER
SUSPENDER
SUSPENSOR
SWAGGERER
SWEETENER
TABASHEER
TABULATOR
TAHSILDAR
TAILLEFER
TAPDANCER
TARGETEER
TAXIMETER
TEESWATER
TESTIFIER
THERMIDOR
THROWSTER
THUNDERER
THYRISTOR
TIGHTENER
TONOMETER
TOPDRAWER
TORMENTER
TORMENTOR
TORTELIER
TOTALIZER
TOWCESTER
TRAFALGAR
TRAVELLER
TREASURER
TREGETOUR
TRICKSTER
TRICOLOUR
TRIMESTER
TRINKETER
TRIPMETER
TROUBADOR
TRUMPETER
ULLSWATER
UNDERWEAR
UNPOPULAR
UPHOLSTER
VALVASSOR
VANCOUVER

VAPORIZER
VEGETATOR
VEHICULAR
VERSIFIER
VESICULAR
VOLTIGEUR
VOLTMETER
VOLUNTEER
WAGHALTER
WALLPAPER
WAMBENGER
WARMONGER
WASTWATER
WELSUMMER
WESTERNER
WHICHEVER
WHITTAWER
WHOSOEVER
WILLPOWER
WINDHOVER
WOMANISER
WOMANIZER
WOODBORER
WORCESTER
WRONGDOER
WURLITZER
YOUNGSTER
ZEALANDER
ZOROASTER
ABLUTIONS
ACARIASIS
ACCIDENTS
ACIDULOUS
ACOUSTICS
ACROPOLIS
ACUTENESS
ADEPTNESS
AEPYORNIS
AEROTAXIS
AESCHYLUS
AFRIKAANS
AHASUERUS
ALBATROSS
ALERTNESS
ALEURITIS
ALLANTOIS
ALOOFNESS
AMARYLLIS
AMAUROSIS
AMBERGRIS
AMBIGUOUS
AMBITIOUS
AMIANTHUS
AMIDSHIPS
AMORPHOUS
AMYGDALUS
ANALOGOUS

ANDROCLES
ANECDOTES
ANHYDROUS
ANKYLOSIS
ANNAPOLIS
ANOMALOUS
ANONYMOUS
ANOPHELES
ANSCHLUSS
ANTIGONUS
ANTIPODES
ANTONINUS
APENNINES
APOLLONUS
APOPHYSIS
APPARATUS
AREOPAGUS
ARMAMENTS
ARTHRITIS
ARTHROSIS
ASCLEPIUS
ASPARAGUS
ASSIDUOUS
ASTRAGALS
ASTUCIOUS
ATHLETICS
ATROCIOUS
ATTITUDES
AUDACIOUS
AUTHORESS
AUTOCROSS
AUTOLYCUS
AUTOLYSIS
AWARENESS
BACKWARDS
BACKWOODS
BANISTERS
BARBAROUS
BAREBONES
BARNACLES
BEARDLESS
BEAUTEOUS
BEESTINGS
BILLIARDS
BLACKNESS
BLAMELESS
BLANDNESS
BLEACHERS
BLESSINGS
BLINDNESS
BLOODLESS
BLUFFNESS
BLUNTNESS
BOANERGES
BOONDOCKS
BOOTLACES
BOSPHORUS

BOSSINESS
BOUNDLESS
BOUNTEOUS
BOURGEOIS
BRAINLESS
BRASSICAS
BREAKAGES
BRIEFNESS
BRISKNESS
BULKINESS
BUMPTIOUS
BURLINESS
BURROUGHS
CALCANEUS
CALLIPERS
CALVITIES
CANCEROUS
CANDLEMAS
CANTHARIS
CANTHARUS
CAPACIOUS
CARYOPSIS
CASTANETS
CATACOMBS
CATALYSIS
CATHARSIS
CATSKILLS
CAVERNOUS
CEASELESS
CENTAURUS
CERATITIS
CERATODUS
CERVANTES
CHAROLAIS
CHARYBDIS
CHEAPNESS
CHEERLESS
CHILDLESS
CHIPPINGS
CHLAMYDES
CHRISTMAS
CHRYSALIS
CHURIDARS
CINEREOUS
CIRRHOSIS
CLAMOROUS
CLASSLESS
CLEANNESS
CLEARNESS
CLOSENESS
CLOUDLESS
COLORLESS
COMPANIES
CONDUCTUS
CONFUCIUS
CONGERIES
CONGRUOUS

CONSCIOUS
CONSENSUS
CORDUROYS
COSMETICS
COTHURNUS
COUNTLESS
COUNTRIES
COURTEOUS
CRAPULOUS
CRAZINESS
CREDULOUS
CRETINOUS
CRISPNESS
CRUDENESS
CUFFLINKS
CUPRESSUS
CUTANEOUS
DANGEROUS
DAUNTLESS
DEACONESS
DEATHLESS
DECIDUOUS
DECRETALS
DEFENDERS
DELICIOUS
DELIRIOUS
DEMETRIUS
DENSENESS
DESCARTES
DEXTEROUS
DIAERESIS
DIAGNOSIS
DIANDROUS
DIANETICS
DIASTASIS
DIATHESIS
DIAZEUXIS
DIDACTICS
DIETETICS
DIGITALIS
DINGINESS
DIOCLETES
DIONYSIUS
DIRECTORS
DIRTINESS
DIVIDENDS
DIZZINESS
DOCUMENTS
DOLOMITES
DOTHEBOYS
DOUBTLESS
DOWNWARDS
DRAMATICS
DREAMLESS
DROPPINGS
DUNGAREES
DUNGENESS

EAGERNESS
EASTLINGS
EASTWARDS
ECARDINES
ECONOMICS
EDELWEISS
EGREGIOUS
ELECTRESS
ELEVENSES
EMBARRASS
EMPHLYSIS
EMPLOYEES
EMPTINESS
ENCANTHIS
ENCELADUS
ENCOMPASS
ENDPAPERS
ENGINEERS
ENQUIRIES
ENTERITIS
ENTREMETS
EPHEMERIS
EPHESIANS
EPHIALTES
EPICLESIS
EPIDERMIS
EPIGAEOUS
EPIPHYSIS
EPISTAXIS
EPITHESIS
EPONYMOUS
EROGENOUS
ERRONEOUS
ESCULENTS
ESOPHAGUS
ESTHETICS
ETCETERAS
ETHEREOUS
EUHEMERUS
EUMENIDES
EUMYCETES
EUPHRATES
EURIPIDES
EXACTNESS
EXERCISES
EXODERMIS
EXOSTOSIS
FABACEOUS
FABULINUS
FACETIOUS
FAINTNESS
FAITHLESS
FALKLANDS
FALSENESS
FAULTLESS
FENCIBLES
FERACIOUS

FEROCIOUS
FILICALES
FIREWORKS
FLESHLESS
FLESHPOTS
FOGGINESS
FOOTHILLS
FOREBEARS
FORESTERS
FRACTIOUS
FRAGMENTS
FRANGLAIS
FRANKNESS
FRESHNESS
FRIVOLOUS
FRUITLESS
FUGACIOUS
FUGGINESS
FUNGIBLES
FURACIOUS
FUSSINESS
FUSTINESS
FUZZINESS
GALAPAGOS
GARRULOUS
GAUDEAMUS
GAUDINESS
GAUNTNESS
GAWKINESS
GIDDINESS
GINGLYMUS
GINORMOUS
GLADIOLUS
GLAIREOUS
GLAMOROUS
GLEANINGS
GLUTINOUS
GODDESSES
GODLINESS
GOMPHOSIS
GOVERNESS
GRACELESS
GRAMPIANS
GRANDNESS
GREATNESS
GREETINGS
GRIMINESS
GROCERIES
GRUFFNESS
GUILELESS
GUILTLESS
HALITOSIS
HALLOWMAS
HANDCUFFS
HANDINESS
HAPPINESS
HARDINESS
HARIGALDS
HARQUEBUS
HARSHNESS
HASTINESS
HAZARDOUS
HEADDRESS
HEADINESS
HEARTLESS
HEAVINESS
HENDIADYS
HEPATITIS
HERODOTUS
HERPESTES
HETEROSIS
HIGHCLASS
HIGHLANDS
HILARIOUS
HIMALAYAS
HINGELESS
HIPPOCRAS
HOMEWARDS
HORSELESS
HOURGLASS
HUMONGOUS
HUMUNGOUS
HUSKINESS
HYLOBATES
HYPINOSIS
HYSTERICS
IGNORAMUS
IMAGELESS
IMMORTALS
IMPERIOUS
IMPETUOUS
INCITATUS
INCOMINGS
INCURIOUS
INDICATES
INERTNESS
INGENIOUS
INGENUOUS
INJURIOUS
INNOCUOUS
INSIDIOUS
INTROITUS
INVERNESS
INVIDIOUS
IRONSIDES
IRONWORKS
ISINGLASS
ISOCRATES
ISOSCELES
JEPHTHAHS
JERKINESS
JUDICIOUS
JUICINESS
KERATITIS
KICKSHAWS
KNEECORDS
LABORIOUS
LANDWARDS
LANGUAGES
LANKINESS
LARGENESS
LAUNDRESS
LAZYBONES
LEASTWAYS
LECHEROUS
LEFTOVERS
LEVITICUS
LIBELLOUS
LIBERTIES
LIGHTLESS
LIGHTNESS
LIMITLESS
LITIGIOUS
LOBLOLLYS
LOFTINESS
LOGISTICS
LOOSENESS
LOWLINESS
LUCRETIUS
LUDICROUS
LUMBRICUS
LURIDNESS
LUSTINESS
LUXURIOUS
MADAROSIS
MALICIOUS
MALLEOLUS
MANLINESS
MARQUESAS
MARTINMAS
MARVELOUS
MATCHLESS
MAURITIUS
MEATBALLS
MECHANICS
MELODIOUS
MERCILESS
METABASIS
MIDDLINGS
MINACIOUS
MIRTHLESS
MISTIGRIS
MISTINESS
MOCCASINS
MOISTNESS
MOLESKINS
MOLLITIES
MOMENTOUS
MONOCEROS
MONSTROUS
MOODINESS
MOTHBALLS
MOTOCROSS
MOTORISTS
MOUTHLESS
MUCORALES
MUDDINESS
MUMPSIMUS
MUNDUNGUS
MUNIMENTS
MUNITIONS
MURDERESS
MURDEROUS
MURKINESS
MUSHINESS
MUSHROOMS
MUSTINESS
MUZZINESS
MYSTERIES
NAKEDNESS
NARCISSUS
NASTINESS
NATHELESS
NEFANDOUS
NEFARIOUS
NEPHRITIS
NEWLYWEDS
NICODEMUS
NOBLENESS
NOISELESS
NOISINESS
NOLLEKENS
NOTORIOUS
NOVODAMUS
NUCLEOLUS
NYSTAGMUS
OBLIVIOUS
OBNOXIOUS
OBSEQUIES
OCEANIDES
ODOURLESS
OFFICIALS
OFFICIOUS
OLENELLUS
OPHIUCHUS
OPPONENTS
ORGILLOUS
OUGHTNESS
OUROBOROS
OUROBORUS
OURSELVES
OUTGOINGS
OUTSIDERS
OUTSKIRTS
OVERDRESS
OVERHEADS
OVERSHOES
OVERTONES
OVIPAROUS
OWLEGLASS
PALINURUS
PARABASIS
PARACUSIS
PARALYSIS
PARNASSUS
PAROTITIS
PARTICLES
PATROCLUS
PATRONESS
PAUSANIAS
PAWKINESS
PEDIGREES
PEMPHIGUS
PENDENNIS
PENDULOUS
PENNILESS
PENURIOUS
PERFORANS
PERIAKTOS
PERIBOLOS
PERIPATUS
PERTUSSIS
PETTINESS
PETTITOES
PHLEBITIS
PHONETICS
PHRENITIS
PIERGLASS
PILASTERS
PLAINNESS
PLENTEOUS
PLIMSOLLS
PLUMBEOUS
PLUMDAMAS
PLUMPNESS
POINTLESS
POISONOUS
PONDEROUS
PONTLEVIS
PORPOISES
POSSIBLES
POSTCARDS
POWERLESS
PRECINCTS
PRESERVES
PRICELESS
PRIESTESS
PROBABLES
PROBOSCIS
PROCOELUS
PRODROMUS
PROGNOSIS
PROLEPSIS
PROMACHOS
PROMUSCIS
PROPTOSIS
PROTHESIS
PSEUDAXIS
PSORIASIS
PSYCHOSIS
PUFFINESS
PYTHONESS
QUADRATUS
QUANTOCKS
QUEERNESS
QUERCETUS
QUERULOUS
QUICKNESS
QUIETNESS
RAMILLIES
RANCOROUS
RANDINESS
RAPACIOUS
RAPTUROUS
READDRESS
READINESS
REALITIES
REARWARDS
REDIVIVUS
REEDINESS
RELATIONS
RELIGIOUS
REPERCUSS
REPOSSESS
REPROCESS
RESOURCES
RETIARIUS
RETINITIS
RHEOTAXIS
RIDERLESS
RIGHTEOUS
RIGHTNESS
RILLETTES
RISKINESS
ROADWORKS
ROUGHNESS
ROWDINESS
RUDIMENTS
RUSTINESS
SAGACIOUS
SALACIOUS
SALERATUS
SALTINESS
SARTORIUS
SASSAFRAS
SAUCINESS
SAUTERNES
SCABLANDS
SCALLIONS
SCANSORES
SCENTLESS
SCLEROSIS

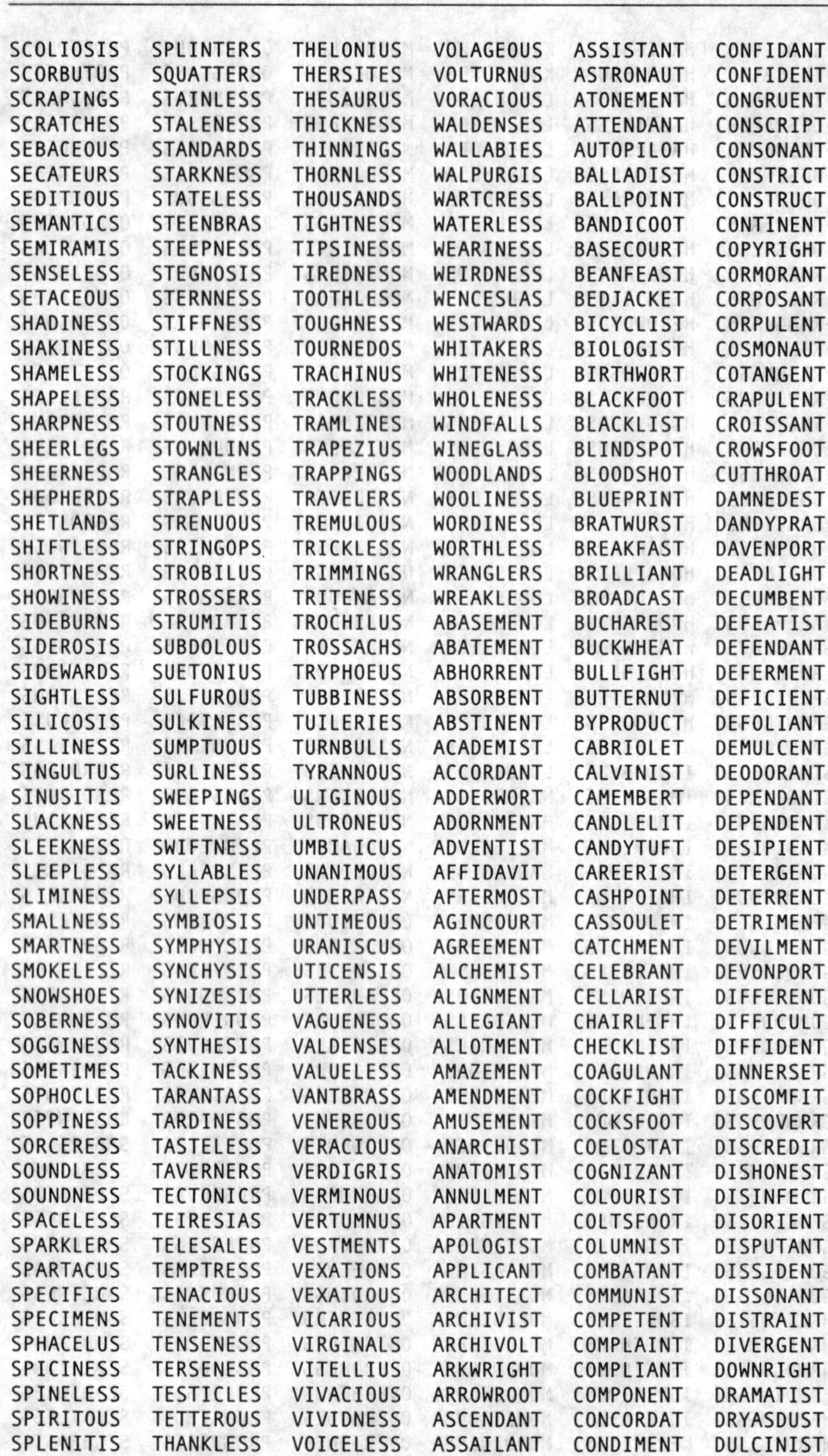

SCOLIOSIS
SCORBUTUS
SCRAPINGS
SCRATCHES
SEBACEOUS
SECATEURS
SEDITIOUS
SEMANTICS
SEMIRAMIS
SENSELESS
SETACEOUS
SHADINESS
SHAKINESS
SHAMELESS
SHAPELESS
SHARPNESS
SHEERLEGS
SHEERNESS
SHEPHERDS
SHETLANDS
SHIFTLESS
SHORTNESS
SHOWINESS
SIDEBURNS
SIDEROSIS
SIDEWARDS
SIGHTLESS
SILICOSIS
SILLINESS
SINGULTUS
SINUSITIS
SLACKNESS
SLEEKNESS
SLEEPLESS
SLIMINESS
SMALLNESS
SMARTNESS
SMOKELESS
SNOWSHOES
SOBERNESS
SOGGINESS
SOMETIMES
SOPHOCLES
SOPPINESS
SORCERESS
SOUNDLESS
SOUNDNESS
SPACELESS
SPARKLERS
SPARTACUS
SPECIFICS
SPECIMENS
SPHACELUS
SPICINESS
SPINELESS
SPIRITOUS
SPLENITIS
SPLINTERS
SQUATTERS
STAINLESS
STALENESS
STANDARDS
STARKNESS
STATELESS
STEENBRAS
STEEPNESS
STEGNOSIS
STERNNESS
STIFFNESS
STILLNESS
STOCKINGS
STONELESS
STOUTNESS
STOWNLINS
STRANGLES
STRAPLESS
STRENUOUS
STRINGOPS
STROBILUS
STROSSERS
STRUMITIS
SUBDOLOUS
SUETONIUS
SULFUROUS
SULKINESS
SUMPTUOUS
SURLINESS
SWEEPINGS
SWEETNESS
SWIFTNESS
SYLLABLES
SYLLEPSIS
SYMBIOSIS
SYMPHYSIS
SYNCHYSIS
SYNIZESIS
SYNOVITIS
SYNTHESIS
TACKINESS
TARANTASS
TARDINESS
TASTELESS
TAVERNERS
TECTONICS
TEIRESIAS
TELESALES
TEMPTRESS
TENACIOUS
TENEMENTS
TENSENESS
TERSENESS
TESTICLES
TETTEROUS
THANKLESS
THELONIUS
THERSITES
THESAURUS
THICKNESS
THINNINGS
THORNLESS
THOUSANDS
TIGHTNESS
TIPSINESS
TIREDNESS
TOOTHLESS
TOUGHNESS
TOURNEDOS
TRACHINUS
TRACKLESS
TRAMLINES
TRAPEZIUS
TRAPPINGS
TRAVELERS
TREMULOUS
TRICKLESS
TRIMMINGS
TRITENESS
TROCHILUS
TROSSACHS
TRYPHOEUS
TUBBINESS
TUILERIES
TURNBULLS
TYRANNOUS
ULIGINOUS
ULTRONEUS
UMBILICUS
UNANIMOUS
UNDERPASS
UNTIMEOUS
URANISCUS
UTICENSIS
UTTERLESS
VAGUENESS
VALDENSES
VALUELESS
VANTBRASS
VENEREOUS
VERACIOUS
VERDIGRIS
VERMINOUS
VERTUMNUS
VESTMENTS
VEXATIONS
VEXATIOUS
VICARIOUS
VIRGINALS
VITELLIUS
VIVACIOUS
VIVIDNESS
VOICELESS
VOLAGEOUS
VOLTURNUS
VORACIOUS
WALDENSES
WALLABIES
WALPURGIS
WARTCRESS
WATERLESS
WEARINESS
WEIRDNESS
WENCESLAS
WESTWARDS
WHITAKERS
WHITENESS
WHOLENESS
WINDFALLS
WINEGLASS
WOODLANDS
WOOLINESS
WORDINESS
WORTHLESS
WRANGLERS
WREAKLESS
ABASEMENT
ABATEMENT
ABHORRENT
ABSORBENT
ABSTINENT
ACADEMIST
ACCORDANT
ADDERWORT
ADORNMENT
ADVENTIST
AFFIDAVIT
AFTERMOST
AGINCOURT
AGREEMENT
ALCHEMIST
ALIGNMENT
ALLEGIANT
ALLOTMENT
AMAZEMENT
AMENDMENT
AMUSEMENT
ANARCHIST
ANATOMIST
ANNULMENT
APARTMENT
APOLOGIST
APPLICANT
ARCHITECT
ARCHIVIST
ARCHIVOLT
ARKWRIGHT
ARROWROOT
ASCENDANT
ASSAILANT
ASSISTANT
ASTRONAUT
ATONEMENT
ATTENDANT
AUTOPILOT
BALLADIST
BALLPOINT
BANDICOOT
BASECOURT
BEANFEAST
BEDJACKET
BICYCLIST
BIOLOGIST
BIRTHWORT
BLACKFOOT
BLACKLIST
BLINDSPOT
BLOODSHOT
BLUEPRINT
BRATWURST
BREAKFAST
BRILLIANT
BROADCAST
BUCHAREST
BUCKWHEAT
BULLFIGHT
BUTTERNUT
BYPRODUCT
CABRIOLET
CALVINIST
CAMEMBERT
CANDLELIT
CANDYTUFT
CAREERIST
CASHPOINT
CASSOULET
CATCHMENT
CELEBRANT
CELLARIST
CHAIRLIFT
CHECKLIST
COAGULANT
COCKFIGHT
COCKSFOOT
COELOSTAT
COGNIZANT
COLOURIST
COLTSFOOT
COLUMNIST
COMBATANT
COMMUNIST
COMPETENT
COMPLAINT
COMPLIANT
COMPONENT
CONCORDAT
CONDIMENT
CONFIDANT
CONFIDENT
CONGRUENT
CONSCRIPT
CONSONANT
CONSTRICT
CONSTRUCT
CONTINENT
COPYRIGHT
CORMORANT
CORPOSANT
CORPULENT
COSMONAUT
COTANGENT
CRAPULENT
CROISSANT
CROWSFOOT
CUTTHROAT
DAMNEDEST
DANDYPRAT
DAVENPORT
DEADLIGHT
DECUMBENT
DEFEATIST
DEFENDANT
DEFERMENT
DEFICIENT
DEFOLIANT
DEMULCENT
DEODORANT
DEPENDANT
DEPENDENT
DESIPIENT
DETERGENT
DETERRENT
DETRIMENT
DEVILMENT
DEVONPORT
DIFFERENT
DIFFICULT
DIFFIDENT
DINNERSET
DISCOMFIT
DISCOVERT
DISCREDIT
DISHONEST
DISINFECT
DISORIENT
DISPUTANT
DISSIDENT
DISSONANT
DISTRAINT
DIVERGENT
DOWNRIGHT
DRAMATIST
DRYASDUST
DULCINIST

EBULLIENT
ECOLOGIST
ECONOMIST
EFFICIENT
EFFULGENT
EGAREMENT
ELOPEMENT
EMOLLIENT
EMOLUMENT
ENACTMENT
ENCUMBENT
ENDOWMENT
ENJOYMENT
ENROLMENT
ENTRECHAT
EQUIPMENT
ESTAMINET
ETHELBERT
EUCHARIST
EXACTMENT
EXCELLENT
EXCIPIENT
EXCREMENT
EXECUTANT
EXPECTANT
EXPEDIENT
EXTREMIST
EXTROVERT
EXUBERANT
EYEBRIGHT
FALANGIST
FATISCENT
FERRYBOAT
FEUILLANT
FIRELIGHT
FIRMAMENT
FLAGEOLET
FLATULENT
FLOWCHART
FLOWERPOT
FLYWEIGHT
FOMALHAUT
FOOTPRINT
FORCEMEAT
FOREANENT
FORECOURT
FOREFRONT
FORESIGHT
FORJASKIT
FORJESKIT
FORMALIST
FORTNIGHT
FROISSART
FULMINANT
FUNDAMENT
FURNIMENT
GAELTACHT
GALLIVANT
GEARSHIFT
GENUFLECT
GEODESIST
GEOLOGIST
GIRONDIST
GLENLIVET
GODPARENT
GOLDCREST
GOODNIGHT
GOOSEFOOT
GRAPESHOT
GREATCOAT
GRINGOLET
GROUNDNUT
GUILLEMOT
GUITARIST
HALLSTATT
HALOBIONT
HARMONIST
HATCHMENT
HAYMARKET
HAZELWORT
HEADFIRST
HEADLIGHT
HEARTBEAT
HEARTFELT
HERBALIST
HERBORIST
HESYCHAST
HIGHLIGHT
HINDSIGHT
HOARFROST
HOLDERBAT
HOLOCAUST
HOTTENTOT
HOUSEBOAT
HOUSECOAT
HYDROPULT
HYDROSTAT
HYGIENIST
HYPNOTIST
HYPOCAUST
IDENTIKIT
IDIOBLAST
IGNESCENT
IMMIGRANT
IMPATIENT
IMPERFECT
IMPLEMENT
IMPORTANT
IMPRUDENT
INCESSANT
INCIPIENT
INCLEMENT
INCORRECT
INCREMENT
INCUMBENT
INDIGNANT
INDRAUGHT
INDULGENT
INELEGANT
INFORMANT
INNERMOST
INPATIENT
INSIPIENT
INSISTENT
INSOLVENT
INSURGENT
INTELLECT
INTENDANT
INTERCEPT
INTERDICT
INTERJECT
INTERMENT
INTERPRET
INTERRUPT
INTERSECT
INTROVERT
IRRADIANT
ITINERANT
JANSENIST
JESSERANT
JUDGEMENT
KLINOSTAT
LAMPLIGHT
LANDAULET
LANDDROST
LASERWORT
LATENIGHT
LATESCENT
LAUNCELOT
LIGHTFOOT
LIMELIGHT
LINEAMENT
LIONHEART
LITHOCYST
LIVERWORT
LODGEMENT
LOUSEWORT
LUBRICANT
LUTESCENT
LUXURIANT
MACHINIST
MAKESHIFT
MALIGNANT
MANGETOUT
MARROWFAT
MASOCHIST
MEDALLIST
MENDICANT
MERRIMENT
MESOBLAST
METAPELET
METHODIST
MEZZOTINT
MILLAMANT
MINCEMEAT
MINISKIRT
MISCREANT
MISDIRECT
MISONEIST
MOCKERNUT
MODERNIST
MONEYWORT
MONTANIST
MOONLIGHT
MOSKONFYT
MOTORBOAT
NANTUCKET
NEGLIGENT
NEPHALIST
NEWMARKET
NEWSAGENT
NEWSPRINT
NEWSSHEET
NONPROFIT
NORTHEAST
NORTHWEST
NUTRIMENT
OBSERVANT
OCCULTIST
OCHLOCRAT
OCKHAMIST
OCTOBRIST
OFFICIANT
ONSLAUGHT
ONTHESPOT
OPENHEART
ORIGENIST
OUTERMOST
OVERDRAFT
OVEREXERT
OVERNIGHT
OVERPAINT
OVERREACT
OVERSHOOT
OVERSIGHT
PANCHAYAT
PANELLIST
PARABLAST
PARAMOUNT
PARCHMENT
PASSAMENT
PEARLWORT
PENTECOST
PEPPERPOT
PERMANENT
PERTINENT
PESSIMIST
PESTILENT
PETAURIST
PETILLANT
PETTICOAT
PHANARIOT
PHOTOSTAT
PHYSICIST
PLACEMENT
PLATONIST
PLUTOCRAT
POLLUTANT
POSTULANT
POUJADIST
POWERBOAT
PRECEDENT
PREDICANT
PREDIKANT
PREDILECT
PRESCIENT
PRESIDENT
PRETERMIT
PREVALENT
PROMINENT
PROPONENT
PROVIDENT
PUBLICIST
PUSSYFOOT
QUIESCENT
QUILLWORT
QUODLIBET
RACCABOUT
RACCAHOUT
RACIALIST
RECIPIENT
RECOLLECT
RECORDIST
RECUMBENT
RECURRENT
REDBREAST
REDUNDANT
REFORMIST
REFULGENT
REGARDANT
REICHSRAT
RELUCTANT
REMBRANDT
REMONTANT
RENASCENT
RENFIERST
REPAYMENT
REPELLENT
REPENTANT
REPRESENT
REPUGNANT
RESERVIST
RESILIENT
RESISTANT
RESTRAINT
RESULTANT
RESURGENT
RESURRECT
RETROVERT
REVETMENT
RIPIENIST
ROOSEVELT
ROQUEFORT
ROUGHCAST
RUFESCENT
RUSHLIGHT
SACRAMENT
SALLYPORT
SALLYPOST
SANDHURST
SAUCEBOAT
SCAPEGOAT
SCHOLIAST
SCIENTIST
SENESCENT
SENTIMENT
SERIALIST
SHAMEFAST
SHEEPMEAT
SHELLSUIT
SHOPFRONT
SHORTLIST
SIDELIGHT
SIMULCAST
SKINFLINT
SKINTIGHT
SLIGHTEST
SLINGSHOT
SNOWDRIFT
SOBRIQUET
SOCIALIST
SOCIOLECT
SOMNOLENT
SOUTHEAST
SOUTHWEST
SPACESUIT
SPEARMINT
SPEARWORT
SPEEDBOAT
SPINDRIFT
SPINNERET
SPOTLIGHT
SPRINGLET
STARLIGHT
STATEMENT
STEADFAST
STEAMBOAT
STERNFAST
STIMULANT
STIRABOUT
STOCKINET
STONEBOAT

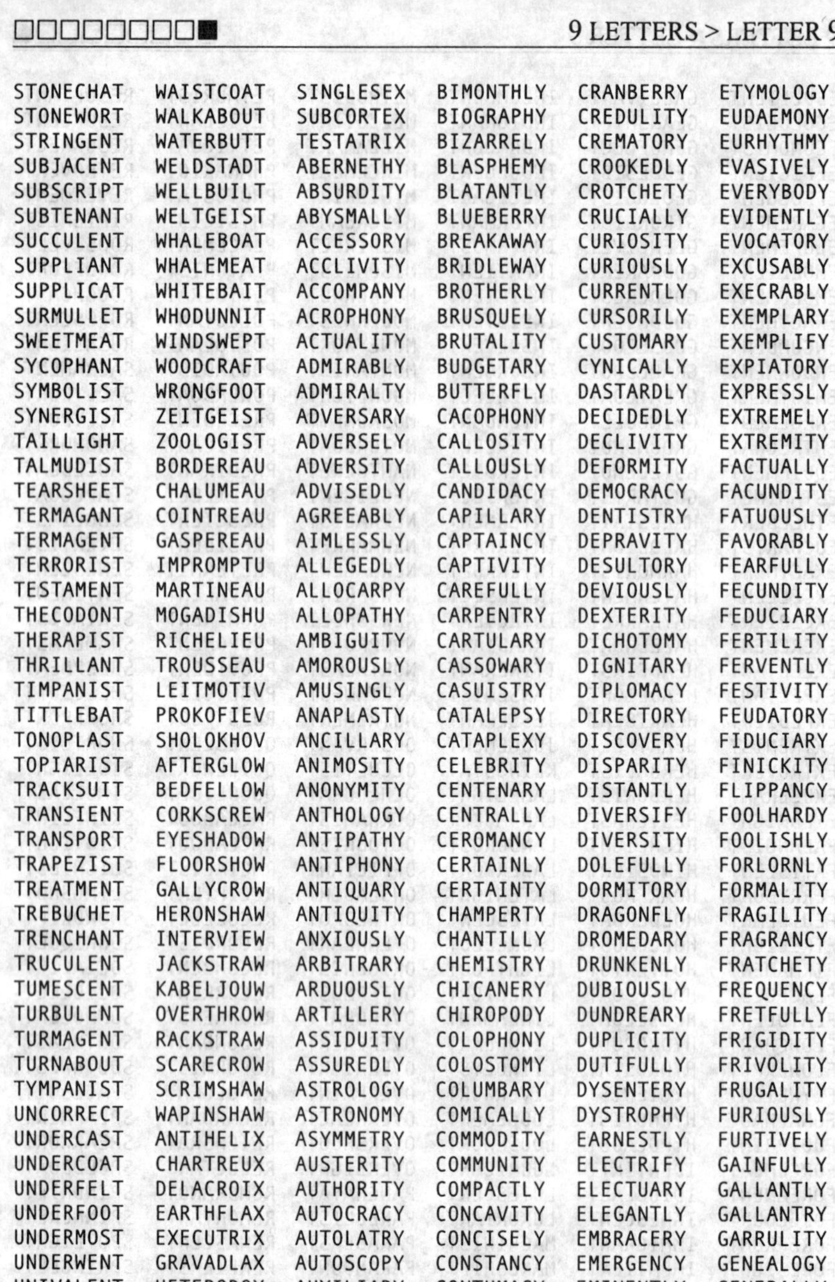

STONECHAT
STONEWORT
STRINGENT
SUBJACENT
SUBSCRIPT
SUBTENANT
SUCCULENT
SUPPLIANT
SUPPLICAT
SURMULLET
SWEETMEAT
SYCOPHANT
SYMBOLIST
SYNERGIST
TAILLIGHT
TALMUDIST
TEARSHEET
TERMAGANT
TERMAGENT
TERRORIST
TESTAMENT
THECODONT
THERAPIST
THRILLANT
TIMPANIST
TITTLEBAT
TONOPLAST
TOPIARIST
TRACKSUIT
TRANSIENT
TRANSPORT
TRAPEZIST
TREATMENT
TREBUCHET
TRENCHANT
TRUCULENT
TUMESCENT
TURBULENT
TURMAGENT
TURNABOUT
TYMPANIST
UNCORRECT
UNDERCAST
UNDERCOAT
UNDERFELT
UNDERFOOT
UNDERMOST
UNDERWENT
UNIVALENT
UPPERMOST
UTTERMOST
VENTIFACT
VERTIPORT
VIDELICET
VIEWPOINT
VIOLINIST
VULCANIST

WAISTCOAT
WALKABOUT
WATERBUTT
WELDSTADT
WELLBUILT
WELTGEIST
WHALEBOAT
WHALEMEAT
WHITEBAIT
WHODUNNIT
WINDSWEPT
WOODCRAFT
WRONGFOOT
ZEITGEIST
ZOOLOGIST
BORDEREAU
CHALUMEAU
COINTREAU
GASPEREAU
IMPROMPTU
MARTINEAU
MOGADISHU
RICHELIEU
TROUSSEAU
LEITMOTIV
PROKOFIEV
SHOLOKHOV
AFTERGLOW
BEDFELLOW
CORKSCREW
EYESHADOW
FLOORSHOW
GALLYCROW
HERONSHAW
INTERVIEW
JACKSTRAW
KABELJOUW
OVERTHROW
RACKSTRAW
SCARECROW
SCRIMSHAW
WAPINSHAW
ANTIHELIX
CHARTREUX
DELACROIX
EARTHFLAX
EXECUTRIX
GRAVADLAX
HETERODOX
LETTERBOX
MIDDLESEX
MULTIPLEX
POMPHOLYX
PREHALLUX
PREPOLLEX
PROTHORAX
RETROFLEX

SINGLESEX
SUBCORTEX
TESTATRIX
ABERNETHY
ABSURDITY
ABYSMALLY
ACCESSORY
ACCLIVITY
ACCOMPANY
ACROPHONY
ACTUALITY
ADMIRABLY
ADMIRALTY
ADVERSARY
ADVERSELY
ADVERSITY
ADVISEDLY
AGREEABLY
AIMLESSLY
ALLEGEDLY
ALLOCARPY
ALLOPATHY
AMBIGUITY
AMOROUSLY
AMUSINGLY
ANAPLASTY
ANCILLARY
ANIMOSITY
ANONYMITY
ANTHOLOGY
ANTIPATHY
ANTIPHONY
ANTIQUARY
ANTIQUITY
ANXIOUSLY
ARBITRARY
ARDUOUSLY
ARTILLERY
ASSIDUITY
ASSUREDLY
ASTROLOGY
ASTRONOMY
ASYMMETRY
AUSTERITY
AUTHORITY
AUTOCRACY
AUTOLATRY
AUTOSCOPY
AUXILIARY
AWKWARDLY
AYLESBURY
BALEFULLY
BARBARITY
BASHFULLY
BASICALLY
BEARDSLEY
BELATEDLY

BIMONTHLY
BIOGRAPHY
BIZARRELY
BLASPHEMY
BLATANTLY
BLUEBERRY
BREAKAWAY
BRIDLEWAY
BROTHERLY
BRUSQUELY
BRUTALITY
BUDGETARY
BUTTERFLY
CACOPHONY
CALLOSITY
CALLOUSLY
CANDIDACY
CAPILLARY
CAPTAINCY
CAPTIVITY
CAREFULLY
CARPENTRY
CARTULARY
CASSOWARY
CASUISTRY
CATALEPSY
CATAPLEXY
CELEBRITY
CENTENARY
CENTRALLY
CEROMANCY
CERTAINLY
CERTAINTY
CHAMPERTY
CHANTILLY
CHEMISTRY
CHICANERY
CHIROPODY
COLOPHONY
COLOSTOMY
COLUMBARY
COMICALLY
COMMODITY
COMMUNITY
COMPACTLY
CONCAVITY
CONCISELY
CONSTANCY
CONTUMACY
CONTUMELY
COPIOUSLY
CORDIALLY
COROLLARY
CORRECTLY
COSMOGONY
COSMOLOGY
COVALENCY

CRANBERRY
CREDULITY
CREMATORY
CROOKEDLY
CROTCHETY
CRUCIALLY
CURIOSITY
CURIOUSLY
CURRENTLY
CURSORILY
CUSTOMARY
CYNICALLY
DASTARDLY
DECIDEDLY
DECLIVITY
DEFORMITY
DEMOCRACY
DENTISTRY
DEPRAVITY
DESULTORY
DEVIOUSLY
DEXTERITY
DICHOTOMY
DIGNITARY
DIPLOMACY
DIRECTORY
DISCOVERY
DISPARITY
DISTANTLY
DIVERSIFY
DIVERSITY
DOLEFULLY
DORMITORY
DRAGONFLY
DROMEDARY
DRUNKENLY
DUBIOUSLY
DUNDREARY
DUPLICITY
DUTIFULLY
DYSENTERY
DYSTROPHY
EARNESTLY
ELECTRIFY
ELECTUARY
ELEGANTLY
EMBRACERY
EMERGENCY
EMINENTLY
EMPANOPLY
ENDLESSLY
ENTELECHY
EPEOLATRY
EQUITABLY
ESEMPLASY
ETERNALLY
ETHNOLOGY

ETYMOLOGY
EUDAEMONY
EURHYTHMY
EVASIVELY
EVERYBODY
EVIDENTLY
EVOCATORY
EXCUSABLY
EXECRABLY
EXEMPLARY
EXEMPLIFY
EXPIATORY
EXPRESSLY
EXTREMELY
EXTREMITY
FACTUALLY
FACUNDITY
FATUOUSLY
FAVORABLY
FEARFULLY
FECUNDITY
FEDUCIARY
FERTILITY
FERVENTLY
FESTIVITY
FEUDATORY
FIDUCIARY
FINICKITY
FLIPPANCY
FOOLHARDY
FOOLISHLY
FORLORNLY
FORMALITY
FRAGILITY
FRAGRANCY
FRATCHETY
FREQUENCY
FRETFULLY
FRIGIDITY
FRIVOLITY
FRUGALITY
FURIOUSLY
FURTIVELY
GAINFULLY
GALLANTLY
GALLANTRY
GARRULITY
GENEALOGY
GENERALLY
GENIALITY
GENTEELLY
GENTILITY
GENUINELY
GEOGRAPHY
GLEEFULLY
GLENGARRY
GOLDSINNY

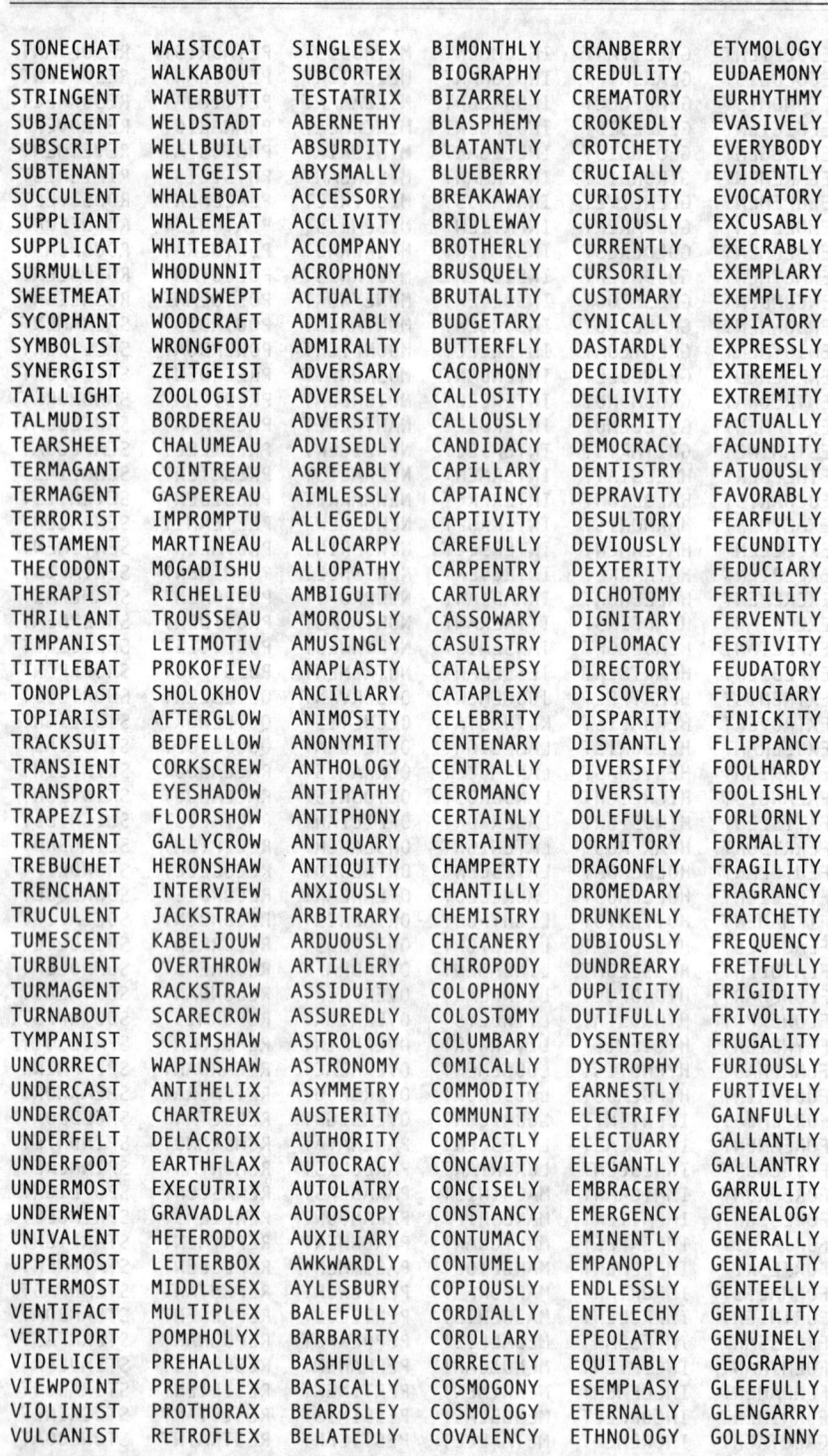

GOONHILLY
GOSSAMERY
GRADUALLY
GREENAWAY
GYROMANCY
HAECCEITY
HALFEMPTY
HALFPENNY
HAUGHTILY
HEALTHILY
HEAVYDUTY
HELPFULLY
HEMINGWAY
HESITANCY
HIDEOUSLY
HIERARCHY
HILLBILLY
HISTOLOGY
HOPEFULLY
HOPLOLOGY
HORSEPLAY
HORTATORY
HOSTILITY
HUNKYDORY
HURRIEDLY
HUSBANDLY
HUSBANDRY
HYPOCRISY
IDEOPATHY
ILLEGALLY
ILLEGIBLY
ILLICITLY
IMAGINARY
IMMANENCY
IMMEDIACY
IMMENSELY
IMMENSITY
IMMODESTY
IMMORALLY
IMMOVABLY
IMMUTABLY
IMPROBITY
INABILITY
INAUDIBLY
INCURABLY
INDECENCY
INDELIBLY
INDEMNIFY
INDEMNITY
INDIGNITY
INFIRMARY
INFIRMITY
INGENUITY
INHUMANLY
INITIALLY
INSTANTLY
INTEGRITY
INTENSELY
INTENSIFY
INTENSITY
INTERCITY
INTERPLAY
INTRICACY
INVENTORY
IRRAWADDY
IRRITABLY
ITINERARY
JANISSARY
JEALOUSLY
JEQUIRITY
JEWELLERY
JOCULARLY
JOVIALITY
JUDICIARY
JUNEBERRY
KILLARNEY
KNOWINGLY
LAMPADARY
LANGUIDLY
LATERALLY
LATTERDAY
LAUDATORY
LEGENDARY
LEGIONARY
LEISURELY
LENGTHILY
LENIENTLY
LEPROSERY
LIABILITY
LIBERALLY
LIMPIDITY
LIQUIDITY
LITERALLY
LOGICALLY
LONGEVITY
LONGINGLY
LOQUACITY
LYRICALLY
MACHINERY
MACROLOGY
MAGICALLY
MALIGNITY
MANDATORY
MARQUETRY
MASSIVELY
MATERNITY
MATRIMONY
MAXILLARY
MAYORALTY
MEDICALLY
MENDACITY
MENTALITY
MERCENARY
MESENTERY
MIDWIFERY
MIGRATORY
MILITANCY
MILLINERY
MISERABLY
MODERNITY
MOMENTARY
MONASTERY
MONOMACHY
MORBIDITY
MORTALITY
MUSICALLY
MYTHOLOGY
NARGHILLY
NASEBERRY
NATURALLY
NAUGHTILY
NECESSARY
NECESSITY
NERVOUSLY
NEUROLOGY
NEUTRALLY
NIGGARDLY
NOMINALLY
NOMOCRACY
NONENTITY
NORMALACY
NORMALITY
NORTHERLY
NOSTOLOGY
NOTORIETY
OBLIQUELY
OBSCENELY
OBSCENITY
OBSCURELY
OBSCURITY
OBSTINACY
OBVIOUSLY
OCCUPANCY
OFFERTORY
OLFACTORY
OLIGARCHY
OMINOUSLY
ONTOGENCY
OPSIMATHY
OPTICALLY
OPTOMETRY
OPULENTLY
OROGRAPHY
ORTHODOXY
ORTHOLOGY
OUTWARDLY
OVERHASTY
PAGEANTRY
PAINFULLY
PALMISTRY
PANTAGAMY
PARSIMONY
PARTIALLY
PASSIVELY
PASSIVITY
PATCHOULY
PATERNITY
PATHOGENY
PATHOLOGY
PATIENTLY
PATRIMONY
PEACEABLY
PEASANTRY
PECUNIARY
PEDERASTY
PEEVISHLY
PELLITORY
PENSIVELY
PERFECTLY
PERFUMERY
PERIPHERY
PERSONIFY
PETROLOGY
PHILATELY
PHILOLOGY
PHONOLOGY
PHOTOCOPY
PHYLOGENY
PIQUANTLY
PITIFULLY
PITUITARY
PLACATORY
PLACIDITY
PLANETARY
PLAUSIBLY
PLAYFULLY
PLURALITY
POCKMANKY
POIGNANCY
POINTEDLY
POLYANDRY
POLYPHONY
POMPOSITY
POPULARLY
POSTERITY
PRECATORY
PRECISELY
PRECOCITY
PREDATORY
PREFATORY
PREGNANCY
PRELUSORY
PREOCCUPY
PRESENTLY
PRIESTLEY
PRIMARILY
PRIVATELY
PROCACITY
PROCERITY
PROFANELY
PROFANITY
PROFUSELY
PROLIXITY
PROPRIETY
PROXIMITY
PRUDENTLY
PUBLICITY
PUERILITY
PUGNACITY
PULMONARY
PUNGENTLY
PURGATORY
PURPOSELY
PYROMANCY
QUARTERLY
QUERIMONY
RADIANTLY
RADICALLY
RADIOLOGY
RANCIDITY
RASPATORY
RASPBERRY
RAUCOUSLY
REFECTORY
REGULARLY
RELIQUARY
REPERTORY
REPUTEDLY
RESIDENCY
RESIDUARY
RIOTOUSLY
ROTUNDITY
ROUNDELAY
ROUTINELY
RUFFIANLY
RUINOUSLY
SAGITTARY
SALESLADY
SALUBRITY
SANCTUARY
SCHMALTZY
SCHOLARLY
SCHOOLBOY
SCIAMACHY
SCIOMANCY
SCRUFFILY
SEANNACHY
SEAWORTHY
SECONDARY
SECRETARY
SEDENTARY
SEEMINGLY
SELFISHLY
SEMIOLOGY
SENIORITY
SENSUALLY
SERIOUSLY
SERVILELY
SERVILITY
SEVERALLY
SEXUALITY
SHORTSTAY
SHRUBBERY
SIGNATORY
SIMILARLY
SINCERELY
SINCERITY
SINUOSITY
SISSERARY
SKETCHILY
SKIAMACHY
SKILFULLY
SLAPHAPPY
SLAVISHLY
SOCIOLOGY
SOLDIERLY
SOLEMNITY
SOLILOQUY
SOPHISTRY
SOULFULLY
SOUTHERLY
SPARINGLY
SPATIALLY
SPEAKEASY
SPECIALLY
SPECIALTY
SPEECHIFY
SPRECHERY
SPRIGHTLY
SQUALIDLY
SQUINANCY
STABILITY
STABLEBOY
STANDERBY
STATUTORY
STAUNCHLY
STERILITY
STOICALLY
STOLIDITY
STORNAWAY
STRANGELY
STRANGURY
STRIDENCY
STUPIDITY
STYLISHLY
SUBLIMELY
SUMMARILY
SUMPTUARY
SUPREMACY
SUPREMELY
SURQUEDRY
SWORDPLAY

SYLLABARY
TACTFULLY
TAUTOLOGY
TAXIDERMY
TEARFULLY
TEDIOSITY
TEDIOUSLY
TEKNONYMY
TELEOLOGY
TELEPATHY
TELEPHONY
TELLINGLY
TEMPORARY
TENUOUSLY
TERRITORY
TESTIMONY
TETRALOGY
TETRARCHY
THACKERAY
THEOCRACY
THEOSOPHY
THINGUMMY
THIRSTILY
THRIFTILY
THROATILY
THROWAWAY
TIMENOGUY
TIMOCRACY
TIPPERARY
TOBERMORY
TOLERABLY
TOPICALLY
TOXOPHILY
TREACHERY
TRIBOLOGY
TRIBUTARY
TRIVIALLY
TRUEPENNY
TURBIDITY
TYPICALLY
UNANIMITY
UNCOURTLY
UNEARTHLY
UNHAPPILY
UNHEALTHY
UNIFORMLY
UNLUCKILY
UNSAVOURY
UNSIGHTLY
UNUSUALLY
UPCOUNTRY
VAINGLORY
VALIANTLY
VARIOUSLY
VASECTOMY
VENIALITY
VERBOSITY
VEXILLARY
VIABILITY
VIBRATORY
VICIOUSLY
VIOLENTLY
VIRGINITY
VIRTUALLY
VISCOSITY
VISIONARY
VOLUNTARY
VULGARITY
WANCHANCY
WANWORTHY
WASPISHLY
WATERBABY
WATERLILY
WEDNESDAY
WILLFULLY
WILLINGLY
WINEBERRY
WISTFULLY
WITCHETTY
WITTINGLY
YESTERDAY
KILOHERTZ
MEGAHERTZ
SLIVOVITZ
TAUCHNITZ
VELASQUEZ

10:1

ABBREVIATE
ABDICATION
ABERDEVINE
ABERGLAUBE
ABERRATION
ABHIDHAMMA
ABHORRENCE
ABITURIENT
ABNORMALLY
ABOMINABLE
ABOMINABLY
ABONNEMENT
ABORIGINAL
ABOVEBOARD
ABRIDGMENT
ABROGATION
ABRUPTNESS
ABSCISSION
ABSOLUTELY
ABSOLUTION
ABSOLUTISM
ABSORPTION
ABSTEMIOUS
ABSTENTION
ABSTINENCE
ABSTRACTED
ABUNDANTLY
ABYSSINIAN
ACANACEOUS
ACCELERATE
ACCENTUATE
ACCESSIBLE
ACCESSIONS
ACCIDENTAL
ACCLIVIOUS
ACCOMPLICE
ACCOMPLISH
ACCORDANCE
ACCOUNTANT
ACCOUNTING
ACCREDITED
ACCUBATION
ACCUMULATE
ACCURATELY
ACCUSATION
ACCUSATIVE
ACCUSINGLY
ACCUSTOMED
ACEPHALOUS
ACETABULAR
ACETABULUM
ACHITOPHEL
ACHROMATIC
ACOLOUTHOS
ACOTYLEDON
ACQUAINTED
ACROAMATIC
ACROBATICS
ACROGENOUS
ACROMEGALY
ACRONYCHAL
ACROTERION
ACTIONABLE
ACTIVITIST
ADAMANTINE
ADAPTATION
ADDITAMENT
ADDITIONAL
ADELANTADO
ADEQUATELY
ADHIBITION
ADIAPHORON
ADJECTIVAL
ADJUDICATE
ADJUSTABLE
ADJUSTMENT
ADMINISTER
ADMIRATION
ADMIRINGLY
ADMISSIBLE
ADMITTANCE
ADMITTEDLY
ADMONITION
ADOLESCENT
ADRAMELECH
ADRENALINE
ADULLAMITE
ADULTERANT
ADULTERATE
ADULTERESS
ADULTERINE
ADULTEROUS
ADVENTURER
ADVERSARIA
ADVERTISER
AERENCHYMA
AEROBATICS
AEROPHAGIA
AERUGINOUS
AESTHETICS
AFFABILITY
AFFETTUOSO
AFFILIATED
AFFLICTION
AFFORDABLE
AFICIONADO
AFRICANDER
AFRORMOSIA
AFTERBIRTH
AFTERHOURS
AFTERPIECE
AFTERSHAVE
AFTERSHOCK
AFTERTASTE
AFTERWARDS
AGAPANTHUS
AGGRANDISE
AGGRESSION
AGGRESSIVE
AGONISTICS
AGRONOMIST
AHITHOPHEL
AIRFREIGHT
ALABANDINE
ALABANDITE
ALBIGENSES
ALCAICERIA
ALCHERINGA
ALCIBIADES
ALCOHOLISM
ALCYONARIA
ALDERMANLY
ALECTORIAN
ALEMBICATE
ALEXANDERS
ALEXANDRIA
ALGOLAGNIA
ALGONQUIAN
ALIENATION
ALIMENTARY
ALKALINITY
ALLEGATION
ALLEGEANCE
ALLEGIANCE
ALLIGATION
ALLOCATION
ALLOCUTION
ALLOSAURUS
ALLOSTERIC
ALLOTROPIC
ALLPURPOSE
ALLUREMENT
ALLYCHOLLY
ALMACANTAR
ALMSGIVING
ALMSHOUSES
ALMUCANTAR
ALPENSTOCK
ALPHONSINE
ALTAZIMUTH
ALTERATION
ALTERNATOR
ALTOGETHER
ALTRUISTIC
ALZHEIMERS
AMALGAMATE
AMANUENSIS
AMARYLLIDS
AMATEURISH
AMBARVALIA
AMBASSADOR
AMBIVALENT
AMBLYOPSIS
AMBLYSTOMA
AMBOCEPTOR
AMBULACRUM
AMBULATORY
AMELIORATE
AMIABILITY
AMMUNITION
AMPELOPSIS
AMPHIBIOUS
AMPHIBRACH
AMPHICTYON
AMPHIGOURI
AMPHIMACER
AMPHIMIXIS
AMPHINEURA
AMPHITRITE
AMPHITRYON
AMPHOTERIC
AMPLEFORTH
AMPUSSYAND
AMPUTATION
AMRITATTVA
AMYGDALOID
ANABAPTIST
ANACARDIUM
ANACHARSIS
ANACLASTIC
ANACOUSTIC
ANACRUSTIC
ANADROMOUS
ANADYOMENE
ANALOGICAL
ANALPHABET
ANALYTICAL
ANARCHICAL
ANASTIGMAT
ANASTROPHE
ANATOMICAL
ANAXIMENES
ANCHORETIC
ANCHYLOSIS
ANCIPITOUS
ANDALUSIAN
ANDALUSITE
ANDROMACHE
ANEMOGRAPH
ANEMOMETER
ANESTHESIA
ANESTHETIC
ANGIOSPERM
ANGLOPHILE
ANGLOPHOBE
ANGUILLULA
ANGURVADEL
ANGWANTIBO
ANHELATION
ANIMADVERT
ANNEXATION
ANNIHILATE
ANNOTATION
ANNUALIZED
ANNUNCIATE
ANSCHAUUNG
ANSWERABLE
ANTAGONISE
ANTAGONISM
ANTAGONIST
ANTAGONIZE
ANTARCTICA
ANTECEDENT
ANTHEOLION
ANTHOCLORE
ANTHRACINE
ANTHRACITE
ANTHROPOID
ANTIADITIS
ANTIBARBUS
ANTIBIOTIC
ANTICHTHON
ANTICIPATE
ANTICLIMAX
ANTIFREEZE
ANTIMASQUE
ANTIMATTER
ANTIMONIAN
ANTINOMIAN
ANTIOCHENE
ANTIOCHIAN
ANTIPHONAL
ANTIPODEAN
ANTIPROTON
ANTIQUATED
ANTISEPSIS
ANTISEPTIC
ANTISOCIAL
ANTISTATIC
ANTITHESIS
ANTITHETIC
ANTITRAGUS
ANTIVENENE
APEMANTHUS
APHAERESIS
APICULTURE
APOCALYPSE
APOCRYPHAL
APOLAUSTIC
APOLLONIAN
APOLLONIUS
APOLOGETIC
APOPEMPTIC
APOPHTHEGM
APOPLECTIC
APOSEMATIC
APOSTROPHE
APOTHECARY
APOTHECIUM
APOTHEOSIS
APOTROPAIC
APPARENTLY
APPARITION
APPEARANCE
APPETITIVE
APPETIZING
APPLICABLE

APPLICATOR
APPOSITION
APPRECIATE
APPRENTICE
APTERYGOTA
AQUAFORTIS
AQUAMANALE
AQUAMANILE
AQUAMARINE
ARACOSTYLE
ARAGONITES
ARAUCANIAN
ARBITRATOR
ARCHBISHOP
ARCHDEACON
ARCHETYPAL
ARCHIMEDES
ARCHITRAVE
AREFACTION
ARENACEOUS
AREOGRAPHY
AREOPAGITE
ARGOLEMONO
ARIMASPIAN
ARISTIPPUS
ARISTOCRAT
ARISTOLOGY
ARISTOTLES
ARITHMETIC
ARMAGEDDON
ARMIPOTENT
ARROGANTLY
ARSMETRICK
ARTHRALGIA
ARTHROMERE
ARTHURIANA
ARTICULATA
ARTICULATE
ARTIFICIAL
ARTOCARPUS
ARUNDELIAN
ARYTAENOID
ASAFOETIDA
ASARABACCA
ASBESTOSIS
ASCENDANCY
ASCENDENCY
ASCETICISM
ASCRIBABLE
ASPARAGINE
ASPERSIONS
ASPHALTITE
ASPHYXIATE
ASPIDISTRA
ASPIRATION
ASSEMBLAGE
ASSEMBLING
ASSESSMENT
ASSEVERATE
ASSIGNABLE

ASSIGNMENT
ASSIMILATE
ASSISTANCE
ASSOCIATED
ASSORTMENT
ASSUMPTION
ASSUMPTIVE
ASTEROIDEA
ASTIGMATIC
ASTOMATOUS
ASTONISHED
ASTOUNDING
ASTRAGALUS
ASTRALAGUS
ASTRINGENT
ASTROLOGER
ASTRONOMER
ASTUTENESS
ASYMMETRIC
ASYNARTETE
ATELEIOSIS
ATHANASIAN
ATMOSPHERE
ATRACURIUM
ATRAMENTAL
ATTACHMENT
ATTAINABLE
ATTAINMENT
ATTENDANCE
ATTRACTION
ATTRACTIVE
AUCTIONEER
AUDIBILITY
AUDITORIUM
AURIFEROUS
AUSPICIOUS
AUSTRALIAN
AUSTRALORP
AUSTRINGER
AUTECOLOGY
AUTHORISED
AUTHORSHIP
AUTOCHTHON
AUTOCRATIC
AUTODIDACT
AUTOGENOUS
AUTOMATION
AUTOMOBILE
AUTOMOTIVE
AUTONOMOUS
AUTOPLASTY
AUTOSTRADA
AVANTGARDE
AVANTURINE
AVARICIOUS
AVENTURINE
AVERRHOISM
AVICULARIA
AVVOGADORE
AXINOMANCY

BABESIASIS
BABIROUSSA
BABYLONIAN
BABYSITTER
BACCHANTES
BACITRACIN
BACKBITING
BACKBLOCKS
BACKGAMMON
BACKGROUND
BACKHANDED
BACKHANDER
BACKPACKER
BACKSLIDER
BACKSTAIRS
BACKSTROKE
BADDERLOCK
BAFFLEMENT
BAGASSOSIS
BAHRAINIAN
BAILIEWICK
BAILLIWICK
BALANCHINE
BALBRIGGAN
BALBUTIENT
BALDERDASH
BALIBUNTAL
BALLISTICS
BALLISTITE
BALLOONING
BALLOONIST
BALNEATION
BALNEOLOGY
BALUSTRADE
BAMBOOZLED
BANDERILLA
BANDERILLO
BANDMASTER
BANGLADESH
BANISHMENT
BANKRUPTCY
BARASINGHA
BARBAROSSA
BARBITURIC
BARCAROLLE
BARCHESTER
BAREFOOTED
BAREHEADED
BARELEGGED
BARGAINING
BARLEYBREE
BARLEYCORN
BARMECIDAL
BARMITZVAH
BAROMETRIC
BARRACKING
BARRACOOTA
BARRACOUTA
BARRAMUNDA
BARRENNESS

BARYSPHERE
BASKETBALL
BASKETWORK
BASSINGTON
BASSOONIST
BATHYSCAPH
BATRACHIAN
BATTAILOUS
BATTENBERG
BATTENBURG
BATTLEDOOR
BATTLEDORE
BATTLEMENT
BATTLESHIP
BAUDELAIRE
BEARGARDEN
BEAUJOLAIS
BEAUTICIAN
BEAUTIFIER
BEAVERSKIN
BEDCHAMBER
BEDCLOTHES
BEDEVILLED
BEDRAGGLED
BEEFBURGER
BEEFEATERS
BEEKEEPING
BEFOREHAND
BEHAVIORAL
BEHINDHAND
BELARUSIAN
BELIEVABLE
BELLADONNA
BELLAMOURE
BELLARMINE
BELLWETHER
BELONGINGS
BELSHAZZAR
BENEDICITE
BENEFACTOR
BENEFICENT
BENEFICIAL
BENEVOLENT
BENTHAMITE
BENZEDRINE
BERMOOTHES
BERNARDINE
BERSAGLIER
BESTIALITY
BESTSELLER
BETACRUCIS
BETELGEUSE
BETELGEUZE
BEWILDERED
BEWITCHING
BIANNUALLY
BICHROMATE
BIENNIALLY
BIJOUTERIE
BILIVERDIN

BINOCULARS
BIOCHEMIST
BIOGRAPHER
BIOLOGICAL
BIOPHYSICS
BIORHYTHMS
BIPARTISAN
BIPINNARIA
BIRKENHEAD
BIRMINGHAM
BIRTHPLACE
BIRTHRIGHT
BISSEXTILE
BITTERLING
BITTERNESS
BITUMINOUS
BLACKBEARD
BLACKBERRY
BLACKBOARD
BLACKBULLY
BLACKENING
BLACKGUARD
BLACKHEART
BLACKSHIRT
BLACKSMITH
BLACKSTONE
BLACKTHORN
BLACKWATER
BLANCMANGE
BLANQUETTE
BLASPHEMER
BLASTOIDEA
BLEARYEYED
BLEPHARISM
BLISSFULLY
BLISTERING
BLITHERING
BLITZKRIEG
BLOCKHOUSE
BLOODHOUND
BLOODSTAIN
BLOODSTOCK
BLOODSTONE
BLOOMSBURY
BLOTTESQUE
BLUEBOTTLE
BLUEMANTLE
BLUETHROAT
BLUNDERING
BOBBYSOXER
BOISTEROUS
BOLLANDIST
BOLSHEVIST
BOMBARDIER
BONDHOLDER
BONDSWOMAN
BONESHAKER
BOOKBINDER
BOOKKEEPER
BOOKMARKER

BOOKMOBILE
BOOKSELLER
BOONDOGGLE
BOOTLEGGER
BOOTLICKER
BOOZINGKEN
BORDERLAND
BORDERLINE
BORDRAGING
BORROWINGS
BOTHERSOME
BOTTICELLI
BOTTLEHEAD
BOTTLENECK
BOTTOMLESS
BOUILLOTTE
BOURIGNIAN
BOUSINGKEN
BOWDLERISE
BOWDLERIZE
BRACHIOPOD
BRADYKININ
BRADYSEISM
BRAGADISME
BRAINCHILD
BRAININESS
BRAINPOWER
BRAINSTORM
BRASSBOUND
BRATISLAVA
BREADFRUIT
BREAKABLES
BREAKWATER
BREASTBONE
BREASTFEED
BREASTWORK
BREATHLESS
BRESSUMMER
BRICKLAYER
BRICKWORKS
BRIDEGROOM
BRIDESMAID
BRIDGEHEAD
BRIDGETOWN
BRIDLEPATH
BRIGANDINE
BRIGANTINE
BRIGHTNESS
BRILLIANCE
BRITISHISM
BROADCLOTH
BROADPIECE
BROADSHEET
BROADSWORD
BROCATELLE
BROKENDOWN
BRONCHITIC
BRONCHITIS
BROOMSTICK
BROWNSTONE
BUCCINATOR
BUCEPHALUS
BUCHMANISM
BUCKINGHAM
BUCKJUMPER
BUDGERIGAR
BUFFLEHEAD
BUFFOONERY
BULLHEADED
BUMFREEZER
BUNDESWEHR
BURDENSOME
BUREAUCRAT
BURGEONING
BURGLARIZE
BURLINGTON
BUSHRANGER
BUTCHERING
BUTTERBAKE
BUTTERBUMP
BUTTERMERE
BUTTERMILK
BUTTONDOWN
BUTTONHOLE
BYELECTION
CACHINNATE
CACODAEMON
CACOGRAPHY
CACOMISTLE
CACUMINOUS
CADAVEROUS
CAERPHILLY
CAESPITOSE
CALAMANDER
CALAMITOUS
CALAMONDIN
CALAVERITE
CALCAREOUS
CALCEDONIO
CALCEOLATE
CALCULABLE
CALCULATED
CALCULATOR
CALEDONIAN
CALEFACTOR
CALESCENCE
CALIFORNIA
CALLIATURE
CALORIFIER
CALUMNIATE
CALYDONIAN
CALYPTRATE
CAMBERWELL
CAMBRENSIS
CAMELOPARD
CAMERLENGO
CAMERLINGO
CAMERONIAN
CAMOUFLAGE
CAMPAIGNER
CAMPANELLA
CAMPARADOR
CAMPERDOWN
CAMPESTRAL
CAMSTEERIE
CANCIONERO
CANCRIZANS
CANDELABRA
CANDELILLA
CANDLEFISH
CANDLEWICK
CANDYFLOSS
CANECUTTER
CANEPHORUS
CANNELLONI
CANNONBALL
CANTABRIAN
CANTALOUPE
CANTATRICE
CANTELOUPE
CANTERBURY
CANTILEVER
CANTILLATE
CANTONMENT
CANVASBACK
CANVASSING
CAOUTCHOUC
CAPABILITY
CAPACITATE
CAPERNAITE
CAPERNOITY
CAPILLAIRE
CAPITALISM
CAPITALIST
CAPITALIZE
CAPITATION
CAPITELLUM
CAPITOLINE
CAPITULARY
CAPITULATE
CAPNOMANCY
CAPODASTRO
CAPPUCCINO
CAPREOLATE
CAPRICIOUS
CAPTIVATED
CARABINEER
CARABINIER
CARACTACUS
CARAMELIZE
CARBURETOR
CARCINOGEN
CARDIOGRAM
CARDIOLOGY
CARELESSLY
CARICATURA
CARICATURE
CARMAGNOLE
CARNASSIAL
CARPATHIAN
CARPENTIER
CARPHOLOGY
CARRAGHEEN
CARTHAMINE
CARTHUSIAN
CARTOMANCY
CARTOONIST
CARYATIDES
CASCARILLA
CASSIABARK
CASSIOPEIA
CASSOLETTE
CASSUMUNAR
CASTRATION
CASUALNESS
CATABOLISM
CATACHUMEN
CATAFALQUE
CATALECTIC
CATALEPTIC
CATALOGUER
CATAPHRACT
CATARRHINE
CATASTASIS
CATAWAMPUS
CATCHPENNY
CATCRACKER
CATECHUMEN
CATEGORISE
CATEGORIZE
CATENACCIO
CATHOLICON
CATHOLICOS
CATTLEGRID
CAUTIONARY
CAUTIOUSLY
CAVALRYMAN
CAVICORNIA
CECIDOMYIA
CELEBRATED
CELESTIALS
CELLOPHANE
CELLULITIS
CENSORIOUS
CENSORSHIP
CENTENNIAL
CENTESIMAL
CENTIGRADE
CENTILITER
CENTILITRE
CENTIMETER
CENTIMETRE
CENTRALIZE
CENTRIFUGE
CENTROSOME
CEPHALOPOD
CEREBELLUM
CEREMONIAL
CEREMONIES
CERTIORARI
CESTRACION
CHAFFERING
CHAIRWOMAN
CHALCEDONY
CHALLENGER
CHALYBEATE
CHAMAEROPS
CHAMBERPOT
CHAMBERTIN
CHAMBRANLE
CHAMPIGNON
CHANCELLOR
CHANDELIER
CHANGEABLE
CHANGELESS
CHANGELING
CHAPARAJOS
CHAPAREJOS
CHAPFALLEN
CHAPLAINCY
CHAPTALISE
CHARDONNAY
CHARGEABLE
CHARGEHAND
CHARIOTEER
CHARITABLE
CHARITABLY
CHAROLLAIS
CHARTREUSE
CHATELAINE
CHATTERBOX
CHATTERTON
CHAUCERIAN
CHAUDFROID
CHAULMUGRA
CHAUTAUQUA
CHAUVINISM
CHAUVINIST
CHEAPSKATE
CHECKLATON
CHECKPOINT
CHEEKINESS
CHEERFULLY
CHEESECAKE
CHEESEWOOD
CHEIRONOMY
CHELTENHAM
CHEMICALLY
CHEMONASTY
CHEQUEBOOK
CHERIMOYER
CHERRYWOOD
CHERSONESE
CHERVONETS
CHESSBOARD
CHESSYLITE
CHESTERTON
CHEVESAILE
CHEVISANCE
CHEVROTAIN

CHICHESTER
CHICKENPOX
CHIFFCHAFF
CHIFFONIER
CHILDBIRTH
CHILDERMAS
CHILDISHLY
CHILLINESS
CHIMBORAZO
CHIMNEYPOT
CHIMPANZEE
CHINAGRAPH
CHINASTONE
CHINCHILLA
CHINQUAPIN
CHIRICAUNE
CHIROMANCY
CHIRONOMIC
CHIROPTERA
CHITARRONE
CHITTAGONG
CHIVALROUS
CHLORINATE
CHLOROFORM
CHOICELESS
CHOLALOGUE
CHOPSTICKS
CHREMATIST
CHRISTIANA
CHROMOSOME
CHRONICLER
CHRONICLES
CHRONOLOGY
CHRYSIPPUS
CHRYSOLITE
CHUCKWALLA
CHURCHGOER
CHURCHYARD
CHURLISHLY
CINDERELLA
CINECAMERA
CINQUEFOIL
CIRCASSIAN
CIRCUITOUS
CIRCUMCISE
CIRCUMFLEX
CIRCUMFUSE
CIRCUMVENT
CIRRHOPODA
CIRRIPEDEA
CIRRIPEDIA
CISLEITHAN
CISPONTINE
CISTERCIAN
CITRONELLA
CLAIRCOLLE
CLAMMINESS
CLAMOURING
CLANSWOMAN
CLARABELLA
CLASPKNIFE
CLASSICISM
CLASSICIST
CLASSIFIED
CLAVICHORD
CLEARSTORY
CLEARWATER
CLEMENCEAU
CLEMENTINE
CLERESTORY
CLEROMANCY
CLEVERNESS
CLINGSTONE
CLINICALLY
CLOCKMAKER
CLODHOPPER
CLOISTERED
CLOMIPHENE
CLOSTRIDIA
CLOUDBERRY
CLOUDBURST
CLOUDINESS
CLUMPERTON
CLUMSINESS
CLYDESDALE
CNIDOBLAST
COADJUTANT
COARSENESS
COASTGUARD
COATHANGER
COCCINEOUS
COCHLEARIA
COCKABULLY
COCKALORUM
COCKATRICE
COCKCHAFER
COCKERNONY
CODSWALLOP
COELACANTH
COETANEOUS
COEXISTENT
COGITATION
COGNISANCE
COGNIZANCE
COHERENTLY
COINCIDENT
COLBERTINE
COLCHESTER
COLCHICINE
COLDSTREAM
COLEOPTERA
COLEORHIZA
COLLAPSING
COLLARBONE
COLLATERAL
COLLECTING
COLLECTION
COLLECTIVE
COLLEGIATE
COLLEMBOLA
COLLIMATOR
COLLIQUATE
COLLOCUTER
COLLOQUIAL
COLONNADED
COLORATION
COLORATURA
COLOSSALLY
COLOURLESS
COLPORTAGE
COLPORTEUR
COLPOSCOPE
COMANCHERO
COMBUSTION
COMEDIENNE
COMESTIBLE
COMFORTING
COMMANDANT
COMMANDEER
COMMANDING
COMMENTARY
COMMENTATE
COMMERCIAL
COMMISSARY
COMMISSION
COMMISSURE
COMMITMENT
COMMIXTURE
COMMODIOUS
COMMONWEAL
COMMUNALLY
COMMUNIQUÉ
COMMUTABLE
COMPARABLE
COMPARATOR
COMPARISON
COMPASSION
COMPATIBLE
COMPATRIOT
COMPELLING
COMPENDIUM
COMPENSATE
COMPETENCE
COMPETITOR
COMPLACENT
COMPLANATE
COMPLEMENT
COMPLETELY
COMPLETION
COMPLEXION
COMPLEXITY
COMPLIANCE
COMPLICATE
COMPLICITY
COMPLIMENT
COMPLUVIUM
COMPOSITOR
COMPOUNDED
COMPRADORE
COMPREHEND
COMPRESSED
COMPRESSOR
COMPROMISE
COMPULSION
COMPULSIVE
COMPULSORY
COMSTOCKER
CONCENTRIC
CONCEPTION
CONCEPTUAL
CONCERNING
CONCERTINA
CONCERVATE
CONCESSION
CONCHIGLIE
CONCHIOLIN
CONCHOLOGY
CONCILIATE
CONCINNITY
CONCINNOUS
CONCLUDING
CONCLUSION
CONCLUSIVE
CONCOCTION
CONCORDANT
CONCRETION
CONCURRENT
CONCUSSION
CONDESCEND
CONDIMENTS
CONDOLENCE
CONDOTTIER
CONDUCTING
CONDUCTION
CONFECTION
CONFEDERAL
CONFERENCE
CONFERVOID
CONFESSION
CONFIDANTE
CONFIDENCE
CONFISCATE
CONFLUENCE
CONFORMIST
CONFORMITY
CONFOUNDED
CONFUSEDLY
CONGENITAL
CONGESTION
CONGREGATE
CONIFEROUS
CONJECTURE
CONNECTING
CONNECTION
CONNECTIVE
CONNIPTION
CONNIVANCE
CONQUERING
CONSCIENCE
CONSECRATE
CONSENSION
CONSEQUENT
CONSIDERED
CONSISTENT
CONSISTORY
CONSONANCE
CONSONANTS
CONSORTIUM
CONSPECTUS
CONSPIRACY
CONSTANTAN
CONSTANTIA
CONSTANTLY
CONSTITUTE
CONSTRAINT
CONSTRINGE
CONSUETUDE
CONSULTANT
CONSULTING
CONSUMMATE
CONTAGIOUS
CONTENTION
CONTESTANT
CONTEXTUAL
CONTIGUITY
CONTIGUOUS
CONTINENCE
CONTINGENT
CONTINUING
CONTINUITY
CONTINUOUS
CONTORTION
CONTRABAND
CONTRACTOR
CONTRADICT
CONTRAFLOW
CONTRAHENT
CONTRARILY
CONTRAVENE
CONTRECOUP
CONTRIBUTE
CONTRITION
CONTROLLER
CONTROVERT
CONVALESCE
CONVECTION
CONVENANCE
CONVENIENT
CONVENTION
CONVERGENT
CONVERSANT
CONVERSELY
CONVERSION
CONVEYABLE
CONVEYANCE
CONVICTION
CONVINCING
CONVOLUTED
CONVOLVUTE
CONVULSION

CONVULSIVE
COORDINATE
COPARCENER
COPENHAGEN
COPERNICUS
COPESETTIC
COPPERHEAD
COPPERNOSE
COPPERSKIN
COPULATION
COPYHOLDER
COPYWRITER
COQUELICOT
COQUETTISH
COQUIMBITE
CORDIALITY
CORDIERITE
CORDILLERA
CORDWAINER
CORINTHIAN
CORNCOCKLE
CORNFLAKES
CORNFLOWER
CORNSTALKS
CORNSTARCH
CORNUCOPIA
COROMANDEL
CORONATION
CORPULENCE
CORRECTING
CORRECTION
CORRECTIVE
CORREGIDOR
CORRESPOND
CORRIGENDA
CORROBOREE
CORRUGATED
CORRUGATOR
CORRUPTING
CORRUPTION
CORTADERIA
CORYBANTES
CORYBANTIC
CORYPHAEUS
COSTLINESS
COTTIERISM
COTTONTAIL
COTTONWOOD
COUNCILLOR
COUNSELING
COUNSELLOR
COUNTERACT
COUNTRYMAN
COURAGEOUS
COURTHOUSE
COUSCOUSOU
COVENANTER
COXCOMICAL
CRAFTINESS
CRAIGFLUKE
CRANKSHAFT
CRAPULENCE
CRAQUETURE
CREATIVITY
CREDENTIAL
CREDITABLE
CREDITABLY
CRENELLATE
CREOPHAGUS
CRETACEOUS
CRICKETING
CRIMINALLY
CRISPBREAD
CRISPINIAN
CRISSCROSS
CRITICALLY
CROCKFORDS
CROSSBREED
CROSSCHECK
CROSSPIECE
CROSSREFER
CROSSROADS
CROTALARIA
CROTALIDAE
CRUIKSHANK
CRUSTACEAN
CRYOGENICS
CRYOPHORUS
CRYPTOGRAM
CTENOPHORA
CUCKOOPINT
CUCULLATED
CUCURBITAL
CUDDLESOME
CUIRASSIER
CUISENAIRE
CULTIVATED
CULTIVATOR
CULVERTAGE
CUMBERLAND
CUMBERSOME
CUMMERBUND
CUMULATIVE
CURMUDGEON
CURMURRING
CURRENCIES
CURRICULUM
CURVACEOUS
CURVETTING
CUSSEDNESS
CUTTLEBONE
CUTTLEFISH
CYBERNETIC
CYCLOPEDIA
CYCLOSTYLE
CYNOMOLGUS
CYSTOSCOPY
DAMSELFISH
DARJEELING
DARKHAIRED
DAYDREAMER
DEACTIVATE
DEADLINESS
DEADNETTLE
DEALERSHIP
DEBASEMENT
DEBATEMENT
DEBAUCHERY
DEBILITATE
DEBOUCHURE
DEBRIEFING
DECAGRAMME
DECAHEDRON
DECAMPMENT
DECAPITATE
DECATHLETE
DECELERATE
DECENNOVAL
DECIMALIZE
DECIPHERED
DECISIVELY
DECLENSION
DECOLLATOR
DECOLORATE
DECOMPOSED
DECORATION
DECORATIVE
DECRESCENT
DEDICATION
DEDUCTIBLE
DEEPFREEZE
DEEPSEATED
DEFACEMENT
DEFAMATION
DEFAMATORY
DEFEASANCE
DEFECATION
DEFENSIBLE
DEFICIENCY
DEFILEMENT
DEFINITELY
DEFINITION
DEFINITIVE
DEFLAGRATE
DEFLECTION
DEFRAYMENT
DEGENERACY
DEGENERATE
DEGRADABLE
DEHISCENCE
DEJECTEDLY
DELCREDERE
DELECTABLE
DELEGATION
DELIBERATE
DELICATELY
DELIGATION
DELIGHTFUL
DELINQUENT
DELIRATION
DELPHINIUM
DELTIOLOGY
DEMOBILISE
DEMOBILIZE
DEMOCRATIC
DEMOCRITUS
DEMOGORGON
DEMOGRAPHY
DEMOISELLE
DEMOLITION
DEMONIACAL
DEMORALISE
DEMORALIZE
DENDROPHIS
DENOUEMENT
DENTIFRICE
DEPARTMENT
DEPARTURES
DEPENDABLE
DEPENDENCE
DEPENDENCY
DEPILATORY
DEPLORABLE
DEPLORABLY
DEPLOYMENT
DEPOPULATE
DEPORTMENT
DEPOSITARY
DEPOSITION
DEPOSITORY
DEPRECIATE
DEPRESSANT
DEPRESSING
DEPRESSION
DEPRESSIVE
DEPUTATION
DERACINATE
DERAILLEUR
DERAILMENT
DEREGULATE
DERIVATION
DERIVATIVE
DERMATITIS
DEROGATORY
DESALINATE
DESBOROUGH
DESCENDANT
DESCENDING
DESCRIBING
DESECRATED
DESERVEDLY
DÉSHABILLÉ
DESICCATED
DESIDERATA
DESOLATION
DESPAIRING
DESPICABLE
DESPITEOUS
DESPONDENT
DESQUAMATE
DESSIATINE
DESSYATINE
DETACHABLE
DETACHMENT
DETAINMENT
DETECTABLE
DETERMINED
DETERRENCE
DETESTABLE
DETONATION
DETRACTION
DETRUNCATE
DEUTOPLASM
DEVANAGARI
DEVASTATED
DEVASTAVIT
DEVELOPING
DEVOLUTION
DEVOTEMENT
DEVOTIONAL
DHARMSHALA
DIABOLICAL
DIACAUSTIC
DIACONICON
DIAGENESIS
DIAGNOSTIC
DIAGONALLY
DIALECTICS
DIAPEDESIS
DIAPHANOUS
DIASKEUAST
DIASTALTIC
DICHROMISM
DICKCISSEL
DICTIONARY
DICTOGRAPH
DICYNODONT
DIDASCALIC
DIDGERIDOO
DIDUNCULUS
DIELECTRIC
DIFFERENCE
DIFFICULTY
DIFFIDENCE
DIGESTIBLE
DIGITORIUM
DIGRESSION
DILAPIDATE
DILATATION
DILETTANTE
DILIGENTLY
DIMINISHED
DIMINUENDO
DIMINUTION
DIMINUTIVE
DINANDERIE
DINNERTIME
DIOPHANTOS
DIPHTHERIA
DIPLODOCUS

DIPLOMATIC
DIPSOMANIA
DIRECTIONS
DIRECTNESS
DIRECTOIRE
DIREMPTION
DISABILITY
DISAPPOINT
DISAPPROVE
DISARRANGE
DISASTROUS
DISBELIEVE
DISBURTHEN
DISCERNING
DISCIPLINE
DISCLAIMER
DISCLOSURE
DISCOBOLUS
DISCOLORED
DISCOMFORT
DISCOMMODE
DISCOMPOSE
DISCONCERT
DISCONNECT
DISCONTENT
DISCOPHORA
DISCORDANT
DISCOURAGE
DISCOVERER
DISCREETLY
DISCREPANT
DISCRETION
DISCURSIVE
DISCUSSING
DISCUSSION
DISDAINFUL
DISEMBOGUE
DISEMBOWEL
DISENCHANT
DISENGAGED
DISENNOBLE
DISFIGURED
DISGRUNTLE
DISGUSTING
DISHABILLE
DISHARMONY
DISHEARTEN
DISHONESTY
DISHWASHER
DISINCLINE
DISINHERIT
DISJOINTED
DISLOYALTY
DISMANTLED
DISMISSIVE
DISORDERED
DISORDERLY
DISPENSARY
DISPENSING
DISPERSION
DISPIRITED
DISPOSABLE
DISPOSSESS
DISPUTABLE
DISQUALIFY
DISQUIETED
DISRESPECT
DISRUPTION
DISRUPTIVE
DISSECTION
DISSELBOOM
DISSEMBLER
DISSENSION
DISSENTING
DISSERTATE
DISSERVICE
DISSIDENCE
DISSILIENT
DISSIMILAR
DISSIPATED
DISSOCIATE
DISSOLVENT
DISSONANCE
DISSUASION
DISTENSION
DISTILLATE
DISTILLERY
DISTILLING
DISTINCTLY
DISTORTION
DISTRACTED
DISTRAUGHT
DISTRESSED
DISTRIBUTE
DISTRINGAS
DISTURBING
DITHIONATE
DIURNALIST
DIVERGENCE
DIVINATION
DIVISIONAL
DOCIMASTIC
DODECANESE
DOGGEDNESS
DOLCEMENTE
DOLICHOLIS
DOLICHOTUS
DOMICILARY
DOMINATING
DOMINATION
DONNYBROOK
DOORKEEPER
DOORTODOOR
DOPPLERITE
DOSTOEVSKY
DOUBLEBASS
DOUBLETALK
DOUBTFULLY
DOVERCOURT
DOWNMARKET
DOWNSIZING
DOWNSTAIRS
DOWNSTREAM
DRACONITES
DRAKESTONE
DRAWBRIDGE
DRAWCANSIR
DRAWSTRING
DREADFULLY
DREADLOCKS
DREAMINESS
DREARINESS
DREARISOME
DREIKANTER
DRESSMAKER
DRINKWATER
DROSOPHILA
DROWSINESS
DRUMBLEDOR
DRUZHINNIK
DUCKBOARDS
DUKKERIPEN
DUMBLEDORE
DUNDERFUNK
DUNDERHEAD
DUNDERPATE
DUNIWASSAL
DUODECIMAL
DUPLICATOR
DURABILITY
DUTCHWOMAN
DUUMVIRATE
DYNAMITARD
DYSCRASITE
DYSPROSIUM
DYSTROPHIC
EARTHQUAKE
EARTHWORKS
EASTERLING
EATANSWILL
EBOULEMENT
EBRACTEATE
EBULLIENCE
ECARDINATE
ECCHYMOSIS
ECCOPROTIC
ECHINODERM
ECHINOIDEA
ECHOPRAXIA
ECOLOGICAL
ECONOMICAL
ECTHLIPSIS
ECUADORIAN
ECUMENICAL
EDULCORATE
EFFACEMENT
EFFECTUATE
EFFEMINACY
EFFEMINATE
EFFERVESCE
EFFICIENCY
EFFLEURAGE
EFFORTLESS
EFFRONTERY
EFFUSIVELY
EGOCENTRIC
EGURGITATE
EIGHTEENTH
EISTEDDFOD
ELACAMPANE
ELASTICATE
ELASTICITY
ELDERBERRY
ELECAMPANE
ELECTORATE
ELECTRICAL
ELECTROMER
ELECTRONIC
ELEGABALUS
ELEMENTARY
ELEUSINIAN
ELIMINATOR
ELLIPTICAL
ELONGATION
ELOQUENTLY
ELYTRIFORM
EMACIATION
EMALANGENI
EMANCIPATE
EMARGINATE
EMASCULATE
EMBANKMENT
EMBERGOOSE
EMBITTERED
EMBLEMATIC
EMBLEMENTS
EMBODIMENT
EMBONPOINT
EMBOUCHURE
EMBROIDERY
EMBRYOLOGY
EMENDATION
EMIGRATION
EMMENTALER
EMMETROPIA
EMOLUMENTS
EMPEDOCLES
EMPFINDUNG
EMPLASTRUM
EMPLOYMENT
EMULSIFIER
ENANTIOSIS
ENCAMPMENT
ENCASEMENT
ENCEPHALON
ENCHANTING
ENCLOISTER
ENCOIGNURE
ENCYCLICAL
ENDEARMENT
ENDOGAMOUS
ENDOSMOSIS
ENGAGEMENT
ENGENDRURE
ENGLISHMAN
ENGLISHMEN
ENGOUEMENT
ENGROSSING
ENHYDRITIC
ENKEPHALIN
ENLACEMENT
ENLÈVEMENT
ENLISTMENT
ENORMOUSLY
ENRAPTURED
ENRICHMENT
ENROLLMENT
ENSANGUINE
ENTEROCELE
ENTERPRISE
ENTHUSIASM
ENTHUSIAST
ENTICEMENT
ENTOMBMENT
ENTOMOLOGY
ENTRANCING
ENTREATING
ENTREMESSE
ENTRENCHED
ENTRYPHONE
EPANOPHORA
EPAULEMENT
EPENTHETIC
EPHRAIMITE
EPICANTHUS
EPIDEICTIC
EPIDENDRUM
EPIDIDYMUS
EPIDIORITE
EPIGENETIC
EPIGLOTTIS
EPILIMNION
EPIMENIDES
EPIMETHEUS
EPIPHONEMA
EPIPLASTRA
EPISCOPATE
EPISPASTIC
EPISTEMICS
EPISTROPHE
EPITHELIUM
EPONYCHIUM
EPROUVETTE
EQUANIMITY
EQUATORIAL
EQUESTRIAN
EQUITATION
EQUIVALENT
EQUIVOCATE
ERGONOMICS

ERIOCAULON
ERUBESCENT
ERUCTATION
ERYMANTHUS
ERYSIPELAS
ESCADRILLE
ESCALATION
ESCAPEMENT
ESCARPMENT
ESCHAROTIC
ESCRITOIRE
ESCULAPIAN
ESCUTCHEON
ESPADRILLE
ESPECIALLY
ESTANCIERO
ESTIMATION
ESTRAMACON
ETEOCRETAN
ETHEOSTOMA
ETHYLAMINE
EUCALYPTUS
EUCHLORINE
EUDIOMETER
EUHEMERISM
EULOGISTIC
EUPHONIOUS
EUPHROSYNE
EUROCHEQUE
EUROCLYDON
EURYPTERUS
EUSTACHIAN
EUTHANASIA
EUTHYNEURA
EUTRAPELIA
EVACUATION
EVALUATION
EVANESCENT
EVANGELIST
EVANGELIZE
EVAPORATED
EVENHANDED
EVENTUALLY
EVERGLADES
EVERYPLACE
EVERYTHING
EVERYWHERE
EVISCERATE
EVITERNITY
EXACERBATE
EXACTITUDE
EXAGGERATE
EXALTATION
EXASPERATE
EXCAVATION
EXCELLENCE
EXCELLENCY
EXCITEMENT
EXCRUCIATE
EXECRATION
EXEMPTNESS
EXENTERATE
EXHALATION
EXHAUSTING
EXHAUSTION
EXHAUSTIVE
EXHIBITION
EXHILARATE
EXHUMATION
EXONERATED
EXORBITANT
EXOTHERMIC
EXOTICALLY
EXPATRIATE
EXPECTANCY
EXPEDIENCE
EXPEDIENCY
EXPEDITION
EXPENDABLE
EXPERIENCE
EXPERIMENT
EXPIRATION
EXPLICABLE
EXPLICITLY
EXPOSITION
EXPOSITORY
EXPOUNDERS
EXPRESSION
EXPRESSIVE
EXPRESSMAN
EXPRESSWAY
EXTENDABLE
EXTENSIBLE
EXTERNALLY
EXTINCTION
EXTINGUISH
EXTRACTION
EXTRANEOUS
EXUBERANCE
EXULTATION
EYEWITNESS
FABULOUSLY
FACESAVING
FACILITATE
FACILITIES
FACTITIOUS
FAHRENHEIT
FAIRGROUND
FAIRHAIRED
FAITHFULLY
FALDISTORY
FALKLANDER
FALLACIOUS
FALLINGOFF
FALSETRUTH
FAMILIARLY
FAMISHMENT
FANATICISM
FANTASTICO
FANTOCCINI
FAREPAYING
FARFETCHED
FARRANDINE
FASCIATION
FASCINATED
FASCINATOR
FASTIDIOUS
FASTIGIATE
FASTMOVING
FATALISTIC
FATALITIES
FATHERLAND
FATHERLESS
FAULTINESS
FAVORITISM
FAVOURABLE
FAVOURABLY
FEARLESSLY
FEARNOUGHT
FEATHERBED
FEDERALISM
FEDERALIST
FEDERATION
FEEBLENESS
FELICITATE
FELICITOUS
FELLOWSHIP
FEMININITY
FENESTELLA
FERNITICLE
FERRANDINE
FERTILISED
FERTILISER
FERTILIZER
FESCENNINE
FETTERLOCK
FETTUCCINE
FEUILLETON
FEVERISHLY
FIANCHETTO
FIBERGLASS
FIBREGLASS
FIBRILLATE
FIBROSITIS
FICKLENESS
FICTITIOUS
FIDDLEWOOD
FIELDMOUSE
FIENDISHLY
FIERCENESS
FIGURATION
FIGURATIVE
FIGUREHEAD
FILIBUSTER
FILLIBRUSH
FILTHINESS
FILTRATION
FINGERLING
FINGERNAIL
FINISTERRE
FIREWALKER
FIREWARDEN
FIRTHSOKEN
FISHMONGER
FISHSELLER
FISTICUFFS
FITZGERALD
FLABBINESS
FLAGELLATE
FLAGITIOUS
FLAGRANTLY
FLAMBOYANT
FLAMEPROOF
FLAMINGANT
FLANCONADE
FLAPDOODLE
FLASHINESS
FLASHLIGHT
FLASHPOINT
FLATTERING
FLATULENCE
FLAVESCENT
FLAVOURING
FLEETINGLY
FLESHINESS
FLICKERING
FLIGHTLESS
FLIMSINESS
FLINDERSIA
FLIPPANTLY
FLIRTATION
FLOCCULATE
FLOCCULENT
FLOODLIGHT
FLOORBOARD
FLOORCLOTH
FLORENTINE
FLORESCENT
FLORIBUNDA
FLOURISHED
FLOWERBEDS
FLUCTUATER
FLUFFINESS
FLUGELHORN
FLUNKEYDOM
FLUTEMOUTH
FLYCATCHER
FONTANELLE
FONTICULUS
FONTINALIS
FOODSTUFFS
FOOTBALLER
FOOTBRIDGE
FOOTLIGHTS
FOOTPRINTS
FORBEARING
FORBIDDING
FORCEFULLY
FOREBITTER
FOREBODING
FORECASTER
FORECASTLE
FOREDAMNED
FOREFATHER
FOREFINGER
FOREGATHER
FOREGROUND
FOREORDAIN
FORERUNNER
FORESHADOW
FOREWARNED
FORFAITING
FORFEITURE
FORFEUCHEN
FORFOUGHEN
FORGIVABLE
FORINSECAL
FORMIDABLE
FORTHRIGHT
FORTINBRAS
FORTISSIMO
FORTUITOUS
FOSSILIZED
FOUDROYANT
FOUNDATION
FOURCHETTE
FOURIERISM
FOURRAGERE
FOURTEENTH
FOXHUNTING
FRACTIONAL
FRAMBOESIA
FRANCHISEE
FRANCHISOR
FRANCISCAN
FRANGIPANE
FRANGIPANI
FRATERETTO
FRATERNISE
FRATERNITY
FRATERNIZE
FRATICELLI
FRATRICIDE
FRAUDULENT
FRAUNHOFER
FRAXINELLA
FREEBOOTER
FREEHANDER
FREEHOLDER
FREELANCER
FREELOADER
FREEMARTIN
FREEMASONS
FREIGHTAGE
FREMESCENT
FRENETICAL
FRENZIEDLY
FREQUENTED
FREQUENTER
FREQUENTLY

FRESHWATER
FRICANDEAU
FRIENDLESS
FRIENDSHIP
FRIGHTENED
FRINGILLID
FRISKINESS
FRITHSOKEN
FRITILLARY
FROGHOPPER
FROLICSOME
FROMANTEEL
FRONTWARDS
FRUITFULLY
FRUSTRATED
FUDDYDUDDY
FULFILMENT
FULIGINOUS
FULLLENGTH
FULLYGROWN
FUMIGATION
FUNCTIONAL
FUNGICIDAL
FURNISHING
FUSTANELLA
FUSTANELLE
FUTURISTIC
GADOLINIUM
GAINGIVING
GAINSTRIVE
GALIMATIAS
GALLABIYAH
GALLABIYEH
GALLIAMBIC
GALRAVITCH
GALSWORTHY
GALUMPHING
GALVANISER
GAMEKEEPER
GANGRENOUS
GARGANTUAN
GARGOUILLE
GARLANDAGE
GARNIERITE
GASCONNADE
GASTEROPOD
GASTRONOME
GASTRONOMY
GAULTHERIA
GELATINOUS
GEMINATION
GENERALISE
GENERALITY
GENERALIZE
GENERATION
GENERATRIX
GENEROSITY
GENEROUSLY
GENETHLIAC
GENEVRETTE
GENICULATE
GENTLEFOLK
GENTLENESS
GEOCENTRIC
GEOGRAPHER
GEOGRAPHIC
GEOLOGICAL
GEOPHYSICS
GEORGETOWN
GEOTHERMAL
GEOTROPISM
GERIATRICS
GERMICIDAL
GESUNDHEIT
GETHSEMANE
GETTYSBURG
GETUPANDGO
GHIBELLINE
GIBBERELLA
GILBERTIAN
GILBERTINE
GILLRAVAGE
GINGERBEER
GINGERSNAP
GINGIVITIS
GIRDLERINK
GIRLFRIEND
GLACIATION
GLAMOURISE
GLASSHOUSE
GLASSINESS
GLAUCONITE
GLEEMAIDEN
GLENDOVEER
GLISTENING
GLITTERAND
GLITTERATI
GLITTERING
GLORIOUSLY
GLOSSINESS
GLOUCESTER
GLUTTONOUS
GNOSTICISM
GOALKEEPER
GOATSUCKER
GOBEMOUCHE
GODPARENTS
GOLDDIGGER
GOLDFINGER
GOLDILOCKS
GOLIATHISE
GONDOLIERS
GONFANONER
GONIOMETER
GONORRHOEA
GOODFELLOW
GOOSEBERRY
GOOSEFLESH
GORGEOUSLY
GORMANDIZE
GOVERNANCE
GOVERNESSY
GOVERNMENT
GRACEFULLY
GRACIOUSLY
GRADUATION
GRAMICIDIN
GRAMMARIAN
GRAMOPHONE
GRANADILLA
GRANDCHILD
GRANDSTAND
GRANGERISM
GRANGERIZE
GRANULATED
GRAPEFRUIT
GRAPHOLOGY
GRAPTOLITE
GRASSLANDS
GRASSROOTS
GRASSWIDOW
GRATEFULLY
GRATIFYING
GRATILLITY
GRATUITOUS
GRAVEOLENT
GRAVESTONE
GREEDINESS
GREENCLOTH
GREENFINCH
GREENHEART
GREENHOUSE
GREENSHANK
GREENSTICK
GREENSWARD
GREGARIOUS
GRENADIERS
GRENADILLA
GREYFRIARS
GRIDIRONER
GRIDLOCKED
GRINDSTONE
GRITTINESS
GROCETERIA
GROUNDBAIT
GROUNDLESS
GROUNDLING
GROUNDSMAN
GROUNDWORK
GROVELLING
GRUBBINESS
GRUMPINESS
GUACHAMOLE
GUARANTEED
GUARNERIUS
GUATEMALAN
GUBERNATOR
GUESTHOUSE
GUIDELINES
GUILLOTINE
GUTTIFERAE
GUTTURALLY
GYMNASTICS
GYMNOSOPHY
GYNECOLOGY
GYPSOPHILA
GYROSCOPIC
HABILITATE
HABITATION
HABITUALLY
HACKBUTEER
HACKMATACK
HAEMANTHUS
HAIRSPRING
HAKENKREUZ
HALFDOLLAR
HALFHOURLY
HALFSISTER
HALFYEARLY
HALIEUTICS
HALLELUJAH
HALLMARKED
HALLOYSITE
HALLUBALOO
HAMESUCKEN
HAMMERHEAD
HAMMERLOCK
HAMSHACKLE
HANDICRAFT
HANDLEBARS
HANDMAIDEN
HANDPICKED
HANDSOMELY
HANDSPRING
HANGGLIDER
HANKYPANKY
HANOVERIAN
HARASSMENT
HARDBOILED
HARDCASTLE
HARMANBECK
HARMONIOUS
HARRINGTON
HARTEBEEST
HARVESTMAN
HATEENOUGH
HAUSTELLUM
HAUSTORIUM
HEADHUNTED
HEADHUNTER
HEADLIGHTS
HEADMASTER
HEADPHONES
HEADSTRONG
HEARTBREAK
HEARTINESS
HEAVENWARD
HECTICALLY
HECTOLITRE
HEDONISTIC
HEEDLESSLY
HEIDELBERG
HELICOPTER
HELIOGRAPH
HELIOLATER
HELIOTROPE
HELLBENDER
HELLESPONT
HELPLESSLY
HEMICHORDA
HEMIHEDRON
HEMIPLEGIA
HEMISPHERE
HEMOGLOBIN
HEMOPHILIA
HEMORRHAGE
HENCEFORTH
HENDECAGON
HEPATOCELE
HEPTAGONAL
HEPTAMERON
HEPTATEUCH
HEPTATHLON
HERBACEOUS
HEREABOUTS
HEREDITARY
HERESIARCH
HEROICALLY
HESITANTLY
HESITATION
HESPERIDES
HETERODOXY
HIERARCHIC
HIEROGLYPH
HIEROMANCY
HIEROPHANT
HIEROSCOPY
HIGHBINDER
HIGHFLYING
HIGHHANDED
HIGHLANDER
HIGHWAYMAN
HILDEBRAND
HINDENBURG
HINDUSTANI
HINTERLAND
HIPPARCHUS
HIPPOCRENE
HIPPODROME
HIPPOGRIFF
HIPPOGRYPH
HIPPOMANES
HISTORICAL
HISTRIONIC
HITCHHIKER
HITHERWARD
HITOPADESA
HITOPODESA
HOARSENESS
HOBBYHORSE

HODGEPODGE
HOLOFERNES
HOLOGRAPHY
HOLOPHOTAL
HOLOSTERIC
HOMECOMING
HOMELINESS
HOMEOPATHY
HOMEOUSIAN
HOMEWORKER
HOMOEOPATH
HOMOGENIZE
HOMOPHOBIA
HOMOPHOBIC
HOMORELAPS
HOMOSEXUAL
HOMUNCULUS
HONEYBUNCH
HONORARIUM
HONOURABLE
HONOURABLY
HONOURLESS
HOODWINKED
HOOTANANNY
HOOTENANNY
HOOTNANNIE
HOPELESSLY
HORIZONTAL
HORNBLENDE
HORNBLOWER
HORNRIMMED
HORRENDOUS
HORRIFYING
HORSEDRAWN
HORSELBERG
HORSEPOWER
HORSERIDER
HORSEWOMAN
HOSPITABLE
HOSPITABLY
HOTCHPOTCH
HOUSEBOUND
HOUSECRAFT
HOUSEMAIDS
HOUSEPROUD
HOVERCRAFT
HOWLEGLASS
HOWSOMEVER
HULLABALOO
HUMANISTIC
HUMANITIES
HUMBLENESS
HUMDUDGEON
HUMIDIFIER
HUMORESQUE
HUMOROUSLY
HUMOURLESS
HUMPBACKED
HUSBANDAGE
HYALOPHANE
HYDRAULICS
HYDROLYSIS
HYDROMETER
HYDROPHANE
HYDROPLANE
HYDROPONIC
HYGROMETER
HYPAETHRAL
HYPAETHRON
HYPERBOLIC
HYPERDULIA
HYPNOTIZED
HYPOCORISM
HYPODERMIC
HYPOGAEOUS
HYPOTENUSE
HYPOTHESIS
HYSTERESIS
HYSTERICAL
IATROGENIC
ICEBREAKER
ICHTHYOSIS
ICONOCLAST
ICONOSCOPE
ICOSANDRIA
ICOSOHEDRA
IDEALISTIC
IGNIMBRITE
IGNORANTLY
ILLADVISED
ILLAQUEATE
ILLEGALITY
ILLITERACY
ILLITERATE
ILLUMINATE
ILLUMINATI
ILLUSTRATE
IMAGINABLE
IMBECILITY
IMBRICATED
IMBROCCATA
IMMACULACY
IMMACULATE
IMMATERIAL
IMMATURITY
IMMEMORIAL
IMMOBILITY
IMMOBILIZE
IMMODERATE
IMMOLATION
IMMORALITY
IMMORTELLE
IMMUNOLOGY
IMPAIRMENT
IMPALPABLE
IMPALUDISM
IMPARLANCE
IMPASSABLE
IMPATIENCE
IMPECCABLE
IMPECCABLY
IMPEDIMENT
IMPENITENT
IMPERATIVE
IMPERSONAL
IMPERVIOUS
IMPLACABLE
IMPLACABLY
IMPLICITLY
IMPOLITELY
IMPORTANCE
IMPOSITION
IMPOSSIBLE
IMPOSSIBLY
IMPOSTHUME
IMPOTENTLY
IMPOVERISH
IMPREGNATE
IMPRESARIO
IMPRESSION
IMPRESSIVE
IMPRIMATUR
IMPROBABLE
IMPROBABLY
IMPROPERLY
IMPROVISED
IMPRUDENCE
IMPUDENTLY
IMPURITIES
IMPUTATION
INACCURACY
INACCURATE
INACTIVITY
INADEQUACY
INADEQUATE
INAPTITUDE
INARTISTIC
INAUGURATE
INBREEDING
INCAPACITY
INCAPARINA
INCAUTIOUS
INCENDIARY
INCESTUOUS
INCIDENTAL
INCINERATE
INCISIVELY
INCITEMENT
INCIVILITY
INCOHERENT
INCOMPLETE
INCONSTANT
INCRASSATE
INCREASING
INCREDIBLE
INCREDIBLY
INCRESCENT
INCUBATION
INCUMBENCY
INCUNABULA
INDAPAMIDE
INDECENTLY
INDECISION
INDECISIVE
INDECOROUS
INDEFINITE
INDELICACY
INDELICATE
INDENTURES
INDICATION
INDICATIVE
INDICOLITE
INDICTABLE
INDICTMENT
INDIGENOUS
INDIGOLITE
INDIRECTLY
INDISCREET
INDISPOSED
INDISTINCT
INDITEMENT
INDIVIDUAL
INDONESIAN
INDUCEMENT
INDUCTANCE
INDULGENCE
INDUMENTUM
INDUSTRIAL
INEBRIATED
INEDUCABLE
INEFFICACY
INELIGIBLE
INEPTITUDE
INEQUALITY
INESCULENT
INEVITABLE
INEVITABLY
INEXORABLE
INFALLIBLE
INFALLIBLY
INFATUATED
INFECTIOUS
INFEFTMENT
INFERNALLY
INFIDELITY
INFIGHTING
INFILTRATE
INFINITELY
INFINITIVE
INFLATABLE
INFLECTION
INFLEXIBLE
INFLEXIBLY
INFLICTION
INFORMALLY
INFRACTION
INFREQUENT
INFURIATED
INGEMINATE
INGENERATE
INGLORIOUS
INGRATIATE
INGREDIENT
INHABITANT
INHALATION
INHERENTLY
INHIBITING
INHIBITION
INHIBITORY
INHUMANITY
INIMITABLE
INIQUITOUS
INITIATION
INITIATIVE
INJUNCTION
INKSLINGER
INNERSPACE
INNOCENTLY
INNOVATION
INNOVATIVE
INOPERABLE
INORDINATE
INOSCULATE
INQUIRENDO
INQUISITOR
INSANITARY
INSATIABLE
INSATIABLY
INSECURELY
INSECURITY
INSEMINATE
INSENSIBLE
INSIPIDITY
INSISTENCE
INSOLENTLY
INSOLVENCY
INSOUCIANT
INSPECTION
INSPISSATE
INSTALMENT
INSTIGATOR
INSTRUCTED
INSTRUCTOR
INSTRUMENT
INSUFFLATE
INSULARITY
INSULATION
INSURGENCY
INTAGLIATE
INTANGIBLE
INTEGRATED
INTEGUMENT
INTELIGENT
INTEMERATE
INTENDMENT
INTENERATE
INTENTNESS
INTERBREED
INTERCEDER
INTERCLUDE

INTERESTED
INTERFERER
INTERFERON
INTERLEAVE
INTERLOPER
INTERMARRY
INTERMEZZO
INTERNALLY
INTERNMENT
INTERNODAL
INTERPHONE
INTERSTATE
INTERSTICE
INTERTRIGO
INTERTWINE
INTERWEAVE
INTERWOVEN
INTESTINAL
INTESTINES
INTIMATELY
INTIMATION
INTIMIDATE
INTINCTION
INTOLERANT
INTONATION
INTOXICANT
INTOXICATE
INTRAURBAN
INTRIGUING
INTROSPECT
INUNDATION
INVALIDATE
INVALIDITY
INVALUABLE
INVARIABLE
INVARIABLY
INVESTMENT
INVETERATE
INVIGILATE
INVIGORATE
INVINCIBLE
INVIOLABLE
INVITATION
INVOCATION
IONOSPHERE
IRIDESCENT
IRISHWOMAN
IRISHWOMEN
IRONICALLY
IRONMONGER
IRRADICATE
IRRATIONAL
IRRELEVANT
IRREMEDIAL
IRRESOLUTE
IRREVERENT
IRRIGATION
IRRITATING
IRRITATION
ISABELLINE
ISOMETRICS
ISONIAZIDE
JABBERWOCK
JACKANAPES
JACKBOOTED
JACKHAMMER
JACKSTONES
JACKSTRAWS
JACULATION
JAGUARONDI
JAGUARUNDI
JAMESONITE
JARDINIERE
JARGONELLE
JAUNTINESS
JAYWALKING
JEISTIECOR
JEOPARDISE
JEOPARDIZE
JERRYBUILT
JIGGAMAREE
JINGOISTIC
JOBSEEKERS
JOCULARITY
JOHNSONIAN
JOLTERHEAD
JOURNALESE
JOURNALISM
JOURNALIST
JOURNEYMAN
JOUYSAUNCE
JUBILANTLY
JUBILATION
JUDICATURE
JUDICIALLY
JUGENDSTIL
JUGGERNAUT
JUSTICIARY
KARMATHIAN
KARTTIKAYA
KATERFELTO
KEMPERYMAN
KENILWORTH
KENSPECKLE
KENTUCKIAN
KERSEYMERE
KESSELRING
KETTLEDRUM
KEYBOARDER
KHIDMUTGAR
KIDNAPPING
KIESELGUHR
KILMARNOCK
KILOMETRES
KIMBERLITE
KINCHINLAY
KINDLINESS
KINGFISHER
KLANGFARBE
KLEBSIELLA
KLOOTCHMAN
KNIFEBOARD
KNIGHTHOOD
KNOBKERRIE
KNOCKABOUT
KOEKSISTER
KOOKABURRA
KRIEGSPIEL
KSHATRIYAS
KUOMINTANG
KURDAITCHA
LABORATORY
LACCADIVES
LACERATION
LACHRYMOSE
LACKADAISY
LACKLUSTER
LACKLUSTRE
LACUSTRINE
LADYKILLER
LAEOTROPIC
LAMARCKISM
LAMBREQUIN
LAMENTABLE
LAMENTABLY
LAMINATION
LANCEOLATE
LANDAMMANN
LANDLOCKED
LANDLOUPER
LANDLUBBER
LANDSTHING
LANGERHANS
LANGUOROUS
LANIGEROUS
LANSQUENET
LANTHANIDE
LARGESCALE
LARYNGITIS
LASCIVIOUS
LASTMINUTE
LATTERMATH
LATTICINIO
LAUDERDALE
LAUNCEGAYE
LAUNCESTON
LAUNDROMAT
LAURDALITE
LAURENTIAN
LAURUSTINE
LAURVIKITE
LAVALLIÈRE
LAVISHNESS
LAWABIDING
LAWBREAKER
LAWRENCIUM
LEADERSHIP
LEAFHOPPER
LEAMINGTON
LEBENSRAUM
LEDERHOSEN
LEFTHANDED
LEFTHANDER
LEFTWINGER
LEGALISTIC
LEGIBILITY
LEGISLATOR
LEGITIMACY
LEGITIMATE
LEGITIMIZE
LEGUMINOUS
LEGWARMERS
LEMNISCATE
LENGTHWAYS
LENGTHWISE
LENOCINIUM
LENTICULAR
LENTIGINES
LEONTIASIS
LEOPARDESS
LEPRECHAUN
LESBIANISM
LETTERHEAD
LEUCHAEMIA
LEVITATION
LHERZOLITE
LIBERALISM
LIBERALITY
LIBERALIZE
LIBERATION
LIBIDINOUS
LIBRETTIST
LIBREVILLE
LICENTIATE
LICENTIOUS
LIEBERMANN
LIEUTENANT
LIGHTERMAN
LIGHTHOUSE
LIGHTINGUP
LIGNOCAINE
LIKELIHOOD
LIKEMINDED
LILYWHITES
LIMBERNECK
LIMBURGITE
LIMITATION
LIMITROPHE
LINEAMENTS
LINEOMYCIN
LINGUISTIC
LINGULELLA
LIPIZZANER
LIQUESCENT
LIQUIDATOR
LIQUIDIZER
LISTLESSLY
LITERATURE
LITHISTADA
LITHOGRAPH
LITHOMARGE
LITHOPHANE
LITHUANIAN
LITIGATION
LITTLENESS
LITURGICAL
LIVELIHOOD
LIVELINESS
LIVERWURST
LOCKERROOM
LOCKKEEPER
LOCOMOTION
LOCOMOTIVE
LOCULAMENT
LOGANBERRY
LOGARITHMS
LOGGERHEAD
LOGISTICAL
LOGORRHOEA
LONELINESS
LONGCHAMPS
LONGFELLOW
LOQUACIOUS
LORDLINESS
LORDOLATRY
LOTOPHAGUS
LOUISIETTE
LOVELINESS
LUGUBRIOUS
LUMBERJACK
LUMINARIST
LUMINOSITY
LUMPSUCKER
LUPERCALIA
LUSITANIAN
LUTESTRING
LUXEMBOURG
LUXURIANCE
LYCHNAPSIA
LYSENKOISM
MABINOGION
MACEDONIAN
MACKINTOSH
MACONOCHIE
MACROBIOTE
MACROCARPA
MADAGASCAN
MADAGASCAR
MAGISTRACY
MAGISTRAND
MAGISTRATE
MAGNIFICAT
MAGNIFYING
MAHAYANALI
MAHOMMEDAN
MAIDENHAIR
MAIDENHOOD
MAINPERNOR
MAINSPRING
MAINSTREAM

MAISONETTE
MAKESYSTEM
MAKEWEIGHT
MAKUNOUCHI
MALACOLOGY
MALAGUETTA
MALAPROPOS
MALAYALAAM
MALCONTENT
MALEFACTOR
MALEVOLENT
MALIGNANCY
MALINGERER
MALLOPHAGA
MALMESBURY
MALODOROUS
MALTHUSIAN
MANAGEABLE
MANAGEMENT
MANAGERESS
MANAGERIAL
MANCHESTER
MANCHINEEL
MANDEVILLE
MANDRAGORA
MANGABEIRA
MANGOSTEEN
MANICHAEAN
MANICURIST
MANIFESTLY
MANIPULATE
MANSERVANT
MANUSCRIPT
MANZANILLA
MAQUILLAGE
MARASCHINO
MARCANTANT
MARCESCENT
MARCIONITE
MARGINALIA
MARGINALLY
MARGUERITE
MARIOLATRY
MARIONETTE
MARKETABLE
MARQUETRIE
MARSHALSEA
MARTINGALE
MARTINIQUE
MARVELLOUS
MARYLEBONE
MASCARPONE
MASKANONGE
MASKINONGE
MASKIROVKA
MASQUERADE
MASSASAUGA
MASTECTOMY
MASTERMIND
MASTERWORT
MASTURBATE
MATCHMAKER
MATCHSTALK
MATCHSTICK
MATELLASSE
MATERIALLY
MATERNALLY
MATRIARCHY
MATTERHORN
MATURATION
MAUPASSANT
MAURITANIA
MAVOURNEEN
MAXIMALIST
MAXIMILIAN
MAYONNAISE
MEADOWPLAN
MEAGERNESS
MEAGRENESS
MEANDERING
MEANINGFUL
MEASURABLE
MECHANICAL
MECHANIZED
MEDDLESOME
MEDICAMENT
MEDICATION
MEDIOCRITY
MEDITATION
MEDITATIVE
MEDIUMTERM
MEERSCHAUM
MEGALITHIC
MEGALOSAUR
MELACONITE
MELANCHOLY
MELANESIAN
MELLOWNESS
MELOCOTOON
MEMBERSHIP
MEMBRANOUS
MEMORANDUM
MENACINGLY
MENDACIOUS
MENECHMIAN
MENINGITIS
MENORRHOEA
MENSTRUATE
MEPERIDINE
MERCANTILE
MERCIFULLY
MERRYMAKER
MESENTERON
MESITYLENE
MESOLITHIC
METABOLISE
METABOLISM
METACARPAL
METACARPUS
METACENTRE
METALEPSIS
METALLURGY
METAPHRASE
METAPLASIS
METASTABLE
METATARSAL
METATARSUS
METATHERIA
METATHESIS
METHEDRINE
METHODICAL
METHOMANIA
METHUSALEH
METHUSELAH
METHYLATED
METICULOUS
METROPOLIS
METTLESOME
MICHAELMAS
MICROFICHE
MICROLIGHT
MICROMETER
MICRONESIA
MICROPHONE
MICROSCOPE
MIDLOTHIAN
MIDSHIPMAN
MIGHTINESS
MIGNONETTE
MILEOMETER
MILITARISM
MILITARIST
MILITIAMAN
MILLEFIORI
MILLIMETER
MILLIMETRE
MIMEOGRAPH
MINDERERUS
MINERALOGY
MINESTRONE
MINEWORKER
MINIMALIST
MINIMARKET
MINISTRATE
MINUTEBOOK
MINUTENESS
MIRACULOUS
MISCELLANY
MISCHMETAL
MISCONDUCT
MISERICORD
MISFORTUNE
MISGIVINGS
MISHGUGGLE
MISHNAYOTH
MISLEADING
MISMATCHED
MISOCAPNIC
MISOGYNIST
MISPRISION
MISSIONARY
MISTAKENLY
MITHRIDATE
MITIGATING
MITIGATION
MIZZENMAST
MODERATELY
MODERATION
MODIFIABLE
MODULATION
MOISTURIZE
MOLENDINAR
MOLYBDENUM
MONARCHIST
MONEGASQUE
MONETARISM
MONETARIST
MONILIASIS
MONILIFORM
MONOCHROME
MONOECIOUS
MONOGAMOUS
MONOLITHIC
MONOPHONIC
MONOPLEGIA
MONOPOLISE
MONOPOLIZE
MONOPTERON
MONOPTEROS
MONOTHEISM
MONOTONOUS
MONSTRANCE
MONTAGNARD
MONTESSORI
MONTEVERDI
MONTEVIDEO
MONTGOMERY
MONTICULUS
MONTRACHET
MONTSERRAT
MONUMENTAL
MORALITIES
MORATORIUM
MORBIDEZZA
MORDACIOUS
MORGANATIC
MORGANETTA
MORIGEROUS
MORISONIAN
MOROSENESS
MORPHOLOGY
MORTADELLA
MOSASAUROS
MOSSBUNKER
MOTHERHOOD
MOTHERLAND
MOTHERLESS
MOTHERLIKE
MOTIONLESS
MOTIVATION
MOTORCYCLE
MOUCHARABY
MOUDIEWART
MOULDINESS
MOULDIWARP
MOUNTEBANK
MOURNFULLY
MOUSEPIECE
MOUSSELINE
MOUSTERIAN
MOUTHORGAN
MOUTHPIECE
MOZAMBIQUE
MOZZARELLA
MUCKRAKING
MUDSKIPPER
MUJAHEDDIN
MULIEBRITY
MULLIGRUBS
MULTIMEDIA
MULTIPLIED
MULTIPLIER
MUMBLENEWS
MUNIFICENT
MUSICOLOGY
MUSKETEERS
MUSSORGSKY
MUTABILITY
MUTILATION
MUTINOUSLY
MUTTONHEAD
MYCORRHIZA
MYRINGITIS
MYRIOSCOPE
MYSTAGOGUE
MYSTAGOGUS
MYSTERIOUS
NAPTHALENE
NARCISSISM
NARCOLEPSY
NARROWBOAT
NARROWDALE
NARROWNESS
NASTURTIUM
NATATORIAL
NATATORIUM
NATHELESSE
NATIONALLY
NATIONWIDE
NATTERJACK
NATURALISM
NATURALIST
NATURALIZE
NATUROPATH
NAUSEATING
NAUSEATIVE
NAVIGATION
NDRANGHETA
NEAPOLITAN
NECROMANCY

NECROPOLIS
NECTABANUS
NEEDLECASE
NEEDLEWORK
NEFANDROUS
NEGATIVELY
NEGLECTFUL
NEGLIGENCE
NEGLIGIBLE
NEGOTIABLE
NEGOTIATOR
NEIGHBORLY
NEMATOCYST
NEOTERICAL
NESSELRODE
NETHERMOST
NETTLERASH
NETTLETREE
NETWORKING
NEURILEMMA
NEUROLEMMA
NEUTRALISE
NEUTRALITY
NEUTRALIZE
NEUTROPHIL
NEWFANGLED
NEWSAGENTS
NEWSCASTER
NEWSLETTER
NEWSMONGER
NEWSPAPERS
NEWSREADER
NEWSWORTHY
NICARAGUAN
NICROSILAL
NIDDERLING
NIGGERHEAD
NIGHTDRESS
NIGHTLIGHT
NIGHTSHADE
NIGHTSHIRT
NIGHTSTICK
NIGRESCENT
NIHILISTIC
NIMBLENESS
NINCOMPOOP
NINETEENTH
NOBLEWOMAN
NOMINALIST
NOMINATION
NOMINATIVE
NONALIGNED
NONCHALANT
NONFICTION
NONONSENSE
NONPAYMENT
NONPLUSSED
NONSMOKING
NONSUCCESS
NONVIOLENT
NORBERTINE
NORMOBLAST
NORTHANGER
NORTHBOUND
NORTHERNER
NORTHSTEAD
NORTHWARDS
NOSOCOMIAL
NOSOPHOBIA
NOTABILITY
NOTEWORTHY
NOTICEABLE
NOTICEABLY
NOTIFIABLE
NOTIONALLY
NOTORYCTES
NOUAKCHOTT
NOURISHING
NOURRITURE
NOVACULITE
NUCLEONICS
NUDIBRANCH
NUMBERLESS
NUMERATION
NUMISMATIC
NURSERYMAN
NUTCRACKER
NUTRITIOUS
NYCTALOPIA
NYMPHOLEPT
OBEDIENTLY
OBFUSCATED
OBJECTLESS
OBLIGATION
OBLIGATORY
OBLIGINGLY
OBLITERATE
OBLOMOVISM
OBSEQUIOUS
OBSERVABLE
OBSERVANCE
OBSIDIONAL
OBSTETRICS
OBTAINABLE
OBTUSENESS
OCCASIONAL
OCCIDENTAL
OCCUPATION
OCCURRENCE
OCEANGOING
OCHLOCRACY
OCTAHEDRON
OCTODECIMO
ODDFELLOWS
ODELSTHING
ODIOUSNESS
ODONTALGIA
ODONTOLITE
ODONTOLOGY
OESOPHAGUS
OFFBALANCE
OFFICIALLY
OFFLICENCE
OFFPUTTING
OFFTHECUFF
OFFTHEWALL
OFTENTIMES
OIREACHTAS
OLEAGINOUS
OLERACEOUS
OMBROMETER
OMBROPHOBE
OMNIPOTENT
OMNISCIENT
OMNIVOROUS
OMOPHORION
ONOMASTICS
OPALESCENT
OPENHANDED
OPENMINDED
OPHICLEIDE
OPHTHALMIC
OPISOMETER
OPOTHERAPY
OPPOSITION
OPPRESSION
OPPRESSIVE
OPPROBRIUM
OPTIMISTIC
ORATORICAL
ORCHESTRAL
ORCHIDEOUS
ORDINARILY
ORDINATION
ORDONNANCE
ORIDINANCE
ORIGINALLY
ORIGINATOR
ORNAMENTAL
OROBRANCHE
OROGENESIS
ORPHEOREON
ORTHOCAINE
ORTHOCLASE
ORTHOGONAL
ORTHOPNOEA
ORTHOPTICS
OSCILLATOR
OSCITATION
OSCULATION
OSCULATORY
OSMETERIUM
OSMIDROSIS
OSTENSIBLE
OSTENSIBLY
OSTEOBLAST
OSTEOCOLLA
OSTEOLEPIS
OSTEOPATHY
OSTEOPHYTE
OSTROGOTHS
OTHERGATES
OTHERGUESS
OUANANICHE
OUGHTLINGS
OUTBALANCE
OUTLANDISH
OUTPATIENT
OUTPERFORM
OUTPOURING
OUTRAGEOUS
OUTSPECKLE
OUVIRANDRA
OVERCHARGE
OVEREATING
OVERLANDER
OVERPRAISE
OVERRIDING
OVERSHADOW
OVERSLAUGH
OVERSPREAD
OVERSTRAIN
OVERSTRUNG
OVERSUPPLY
OVERTHETOP
OVERTHWART
OVERWEIGHT
OVERWORKED
OVIPOSITOR
OWLSPIEGLE
OXYGENATOR
OXYMORONIC
OZYMANDIAS
PACIFICISM
PADAREWSKI
PADDINGTON
PADDYMELON
PAEDIATRIC
PAGINATION
PAINKILLER
PAINLESSLY
PAINTBRUSH
PALAEOTYPE
PALAESTRAL
PALAGONITE
PALATALISE
PALATINATE
PALESTRINA
PALFRENIER
PALIMPSEST
PALINDROME
PALISANDER
PALLBEARER
PALLIATIVE
PALMATIFID
PALMATOZOA
PALMERSTON
PALMERWORM
PALUDAMENT
PALUSTRINE
PANAMANIAN
PANARITIUM
PANCRATIUM
PANJANDRUM
PANNICULUS
PANOPTICON
PANSOPHIST
PANTAGRUEL
PANTALOONS
PANTOGRAPH
PANTOSCOPE
PAPAVERINE
PAPERCHASE
PAPERKNIFE
PAPIAMENTO
PARACELSUS
PARADIDDLE
PARADOXIDE
PARADOXINE
PARAENESIS
PARAGLOSSA
PARAGONITE
PARAGUAYAN
PARALLELED
PARAMARIBO
PARAMETRIC
PARANORMAL
PARAPHILIA
PARAPHONIA
PARAPHRASE
PARAPHYSIS
PARAPLEGIA
PARAPLEGIC
PARAPRAXIS
PARARTHRIA
PARASCENIA
PARASELENE
PARASTATAL
PARATROOPS
PARDONABLE
PARDONABLY
PARENCHYMA
PARENTHOOD
PARENTLESS
PARGETTING
PARISCHANE
PARISIENNE
PARKLEAVES
PARLIAMENT
PARMACITIE
PARNASSIAN
PARNELLISM
PARONYCHIA
PARRAMATTA
PARTHENOPE
PARTIALITY
PARTICIPLE
PARTICULAR
PARTINGALE
PASIGRAPHY

PASQUINADE
PASSAGEWAY
PASSAMEZZO
PASSIONATE
PASTEBOARD
PASTEURISE
PASTEURIZE
PASTORELLA
PATAGONIAN
PATAVINITY
PATCHCOCKE
PATCHINESS
PATERNALLY
PATHFINDER
PATHOGENIC
PATIBULARY
PATISSERIE
PATRIARCHY
PATRIOTISM
PATRONISED
PATRONYMIC
PAWNBROKER
PEACEFULLY
PEACEMAKER
PEACHERINO
PEASHOOTER
PEAUDESOIE
PECCADILLO
PECULATION
PECULIARLY
PEDESTRIAN
PEDIATRICS
PEDICULATE
PEDIMENTAL
PEDIPALPUS
PEELGARLIC
PEJORATIVE
PENELOPHON
PENETRABLE
PENETRALIA
PENICILLIN
PENINSULAR
PENNILLION
PENNISETUM
PENSIEROSO
PENSIONNAT
PENTAGONAL
PENTAMERON
PENTAMETER
PENTATEUCH
PENTATHLON
PENTATONIC
PENTELIKON
PENTETERIC
PENTIMENTO
PENTSTEMON
PEPPERCORN
PEPPERMILL
PEPPERMINT
PEPPERWORT
PERCENTAGE
PERCENTILE
PERCEPTION
PERCEPTIVE
PERCIPIENT
PERCOLATOR
PERCUSSION
PERDENDOSI
PERDITIOUS
PERDURABLE
PEREMPTORY
PERFECTION
PERFICIENT
PERFIDIOUS
PERFORATED
PERFORATOR
PERFORMING
PERIDOTITE
PERIEGESIS
PERIHELION
PERILOUSLY
PERIODICAL
PERIPHERAL
PERISHABLE
PERIWINKLE
PERMAFROST
PERMANENCE
PERMANENCY
PERMEATION
PERMISSION
PERMISSIVE
PERNICIOUS
PERNICKETY
PERORATION
PEROVSKITE
PERPETRATE
PERPETUATE
PERPETUITY
PERPLEXING
PERPLEXITY
PERQUISITE
PERSECUTOR
PERSEPHONE
PERSEPOLIS
PERSICARIA
PERSIENNES
PERSIFLAGE
PERSISTENT
PERSONABLE
PERSONALLY
PERSTRINGE
PERSUADING
PERSUASION
PERSUASIVE
PERTINENCE
PERVERSELY
PERVERSION
PERVERSITY
PESCADORES
PESTALOZZI
PESTILENCE
PETITIONER
PETRARCHAN
PETRIFYING
PETRISSAGE
PETROGLYPH
PETRONELLA
PETTICHAPS
PETTYCHAPS
PETULANTLY
PHAELONIAN
PHAENOTYPE
PHAGEDAENA
PHANTASIME
PHANTASIST
PHARMACIST
PHENOMENAL
PHENOMENON
PHILATELIC
PHILIPPINA
PHILIPPINE
PHILISTINE
PHILLIPINA
PHILLIPINE
PHILLUMENY
PHILOPOENA
PHILOSOPHY
PHILOXENIA
PHLEGETHON
PHLEGMASIA
PHLEGMATIC
PHLOGISTIC
PHLOGISTON
PHLOGOPITE
PHOLIDOSIS
PHONOGRAPH
PHOSPHORUS
PHOTODIODE
PHOTOGENIC
PHOTOGRAPH
PHOTONASTY
PHRENESIAC
PHRENOLOGY
PHYLACTERY
PHYLLIOPOD
PHYSICALLY
PHYSIOCRAT
PHYSIOLOGY
PIANOFORTE
PICARESQUE
PICAYUNISH
PICCADILLY
PICCALILLI
PICCANINNY
PICHICIAGO
PICKPOCKET
PIGEONHOLE
PILEDRIVER
PILGARLICK
PILGRIMAGE
PILLIWINKS
PILLOWCASE
PILLOWSLIP
PINAKOTHEK
PINCHPENNY
PINCUSHION
PINNIPEDIA
PIONEERING
PIRANDELLO
PISTILLATE
PITCHSTONE
PITYRIASIS
PLAGIARISE
PLAGIARISM
PLAGIARIST
PLAGIARIZE
PLANCHETTE
PLANOBLAST
PLANTATION
PLASMODESM
PLASTICINE
PLASTICITY
PLATELAYER
PLATINISED
PLATTELAND
PLAYFELLOW
PLAYGROUND
PLAYWRIGHT
PLEASANTLY
PLEASANTRY
PLEBISCITE
PLEONASTIC
PLEROPHORY
PLESIOSAUR
PLEXIMETER
PLIABILITY
PLIOHIPPUS
PLOUGHBOTE
PLOUGHGATE
PLOUGHWISE
PLUMASSIER
PLUNDERING
PLUPERFECT
PLUTOCRACY
POCAHONTAS
POCKETBOOK
POCKMANTIE
POCKMARKED
POETASTERY
POETICALLY
POGONOTOMY
POHUTUKAWA
POIGNANTLY
POIKILITIC
POINSETTIA
POINTBLANK
POKERFACED
POLIANTHES
POLITENESS
POLITICIAN
POLITICIZE
POLLINATED
POLYANTHUS
POLYCHAETE
POLYCHREST
POLYCHROME
POLYGAMIST
POLYGAMOUS
POLYHEDRON
POLYHYMNIA
POLYMERIZE
POLYNESIAN
POLYPHEMUS
POLYTHEISM
POMERANIAN
PONCHIELLI
PONEROLOGY
PONTEDERIA
PONTEFRACT
PONTICELLO
PONTIFICAL
POPULARITY
POPULARIZE
POPULATION
PORLOCKING
PORNOCRACY
PORRACEOUS
PORTAMENTO
PORTCULLIS
PORTENTOUS
PORTIONIST
PORTMANTLE
PORTMANTUA
PORTSMOUTH
PORTUGUESE
POSITIVELY
POSITIVIST
POSSESSION
POSSESSIVE
POSTCHAISE
POSTHUMOUS
POSTILLATE
POSTILLION
POSTLIMINY
POSTMASTER
POSTSCRIPT
POTENTIATE
POTENTILLA
POURPARLER
POWERHOUSE
POZZUOLANA
PRAEMUNIRE
PRAETORIAN
PRAETORIUM
PRAGMATISM
PRAGMATIST
PRATINCOLE
PRAXITELES
PREARRANGE
PREBENDARY

PRECARIOUS
PRECAUTION
PRECEDENCE
PRECIPITIN
PRECOCIOUS
PRECURSORY
PREDACIOUS
PREDECEASE
PREDESTINE
PREDICTION
PREDISPOSE
PREDNISONE
PREEMINENT
PREFERABLE
PREFERABLY
PREFERENCE
PREFERMENT
PREHENSILE
PREHISTORY
PREJUDICED
PRELECTION
PREMARITAL
PREPARATOR
PREPAYMENT
PREPENSELY
PREPOSITOR
PREPOSSESS
PREPOTENCE
PRESBYOPIA
PRESBYTERY
PRESCIENCE
PRESENTDAY
PRESIDENCY
PRESSURIZE
PRESUMABLY
PRESUPPOSE
PRETENSION
PRETINCOLE
PRETTINESS
PREVAILING
PREVALENCE
PREVENANCY
PREVENTION
PREVENTIVE
PREVIOUSLY
PRICKLOUSE
PRIESTHOOD
PRIMORDIAL
PRINCIPIUM
PRINCIPLED
PRINCIPLES
PRIVATEERS
PRIVILEGED
PRIZEFIGHT
PROAIRESIS
PROCEDURAL
PROCEEDING
PROCESSING
PROCESSION
PROCLIVITY
PROCREATOR
PROCRUSTES
PROCURABLE
PROCURATOR
PRODIGALLY
PRODIGIOUS
PRODUCTION
PRODUCTIVE
PROFESSION
PROFICIENT
PROFITABLE
PROFITABLY
PROFITLESS
PROFLIGACY
PROFLIGATE
PROFOUNDLY
PROFUNDITY
PROGENITOR
PROGESSION
PROGRAMMER
PROHIBITED
PROJECTILE
PROJECTING
PROJECTION
PROMENADER
PROMETHEAN
PROMETHEUS
PROMETHIUM
PROMINENCE
PROMISSORY
PROMONTORY
PROMPTNESS
PROMULGATE
PRONOUNCED
PROPAGANDA
PROPAGATOR
PROPELLANT
PROPENSITY
PROPERTIUS
PROPHETESS
PROPIONATE
PROPITIATE
PROPITIOUS
PROPLITEAL
PROPORTION
PROPOSITUS
PROPRAETOR
PROPRIETOR
PROPULSION
PROPYLAEUM
PROSCENIUM
PROSCIUTTO
PROSCRIBED
PROSECUTOR
PROSERPINA
PROSERPINE
PROSILIENT
PROSPECTOR
PROSPECTUS
PROSPERINA
PROSPERITY
PROSPEROUS
PROSTHESIS
PROSTHETIC
PROSTITUTE
PROTAGORAS
PROTANOPIC
PROTECTION
PROTECTIVE
PROTERVITY
PROTESTANT
PROTOPLASM
PROTRACTED
PROTRACTOR
PROTRUSION
PROVEDITOR
PROVENANCE
PROVERBIAL
PROVIDENCE
PROVINCIAL
PROVISIONS
PRUDENTIAL
PRZEWALSKI
PSALTERIUM
PSAMMOPHIL
PSEPHOLOGY
PSEUDOCARP
PSILOCYBIN
PSOCOPTERA
PSYCHIATRY
PSYCHOLOGY
PSYCHOPATH
PSYCHOPOMP
PTERANODON
PTERYGOTUS
PUBERULENT
PUBESCENCE
PUBLISHING
PUCKERWOOD
PUGNACIOUS
PULSATANCE
PUMMELLING
PUMPHANDLE
PUNCHDRUNK
PUNCTUALLY
PUNCTULATE
PUNDIGRION
PUNICACEAE
PUNISHABLE
PUNISHMENT
PURITANISM
PURPOSEFUL
PURSUIVANT
PUTREFYING
PUTRESCENT
PUZZLEMENT
PYCNOGONID
PYRACANTHA
PYRAGYRITE
PYROGRAPHY
PYROMANIAC
PYROPHORUS
PYTHAGORAS
PYTHOGENIC
QUADRANGLE
QUADRATURA
QUADRICEPS
QUADRIREME
QUAESTUARY
QUAINTNESS
QUARANTINE
QUARRENDER
QUARTERING
QUARTEROON
QUATERNARY
QUEASINESS
QUEENSBURY
QUEENSTOWN
QUENCHLESS
QUERCITRON
QUERSPRUNG
QUESADILLA
QUESTIONER
QUICKSANDS
QUICKTHORN
QUIESCENCE
QUIRINALIA
QUIZMASTER
RABBINICAL
RACECOURSE
RADICALISM
RADIOGRAPH
RADIOLARIA
RAGAMUFFIN
RAILWAYMAN
RAIYATWARI
RAJPRAMUKH
RAMPALLIAN
RAMSHACKLE
RANDLETREE
RANDOMNESS
RANNELTREE
RANNLETREE
RANTLETREE
RANUNCULUS
RAPPORTEUR
RATIONALLY
RATTLETRAP
RAVENOUSLY
RAVENSBILL
RAVENSDUCK
RAVENSTONE
RAWINSONDE
RAWSTHORNE
RAZZMATAZZ
REACTIVATE
READERSHIP
REAMINGBIT
REAPPRAISE
REARMAMENT
REASONABLE
REASONABLY
REASSEMBLE
REASSURING
REBELLIOUS
RECEPTACLE
RECIDIVISM
RECIDIVIST
RECIPROCAL
RECITATION
RECITATIVE
RECITATIVO
RECKLESSLY
RECOGNISED
RECOGNIZED
RECOMMENCE
RECOMPENSE
RECONCILED
RECONSIDER
RECREATION
RECRUDESCE
RECUPERATE
RECURRENCE
REDCURRANT
REDECORATE
REDEMPTION
REDISCOVER
REDRUTHITE
REDUNDANCY
REELECTION
REFERENDUM
REFINEMENT
REFLECTING
REFLECTION
REFLECTIVE
REFRACTION
REFRACTIVE
REFRACTORY
REFRESHING
REFUTATION
REGARDLESS
REGENERATE
REGIMENTAL
REGIMENTED
REGISTERED
REGRESSION
REGRESSIVE
REGULARITY
REGULARIZE
REGULATION
REITERATED
REJONEADOR
REJUVENATE
RELATIVELY
RELATIVITY
RELAXATION
RELAXATIVE
RELEGATION
RELENTLESS
RELINQUISH

RELOCATION
RELUCTANCE
REMARKABLE
REMARKABLY
REMITTANCE
REMONETISE
REMORSEFUL
REMOTENESS
REMUNERATE
RENDEZVOUS
RENOVATION
REORGANIZE
REPAIRABLE
REPARATION
REPATRIATE
REPEATABLE
REPEATEDLY
REPENTANCE
REPERTOIRE
REPETITEUR
REPETITION
REPETITIVE
REPORTEDLY
REPOSITORY
REPRESSION
REPRESSIVE
REPRODUCER
REPUBLICAN
REPUGNANCE
REPUTATION
REQUIESCAT
REREDORTER
RESCHEDULE
RESEARCHER
RESEMBLING
RESENTMENT
RESERVISTS
RESIGNEDLY
RESILIENCE
RESISTANCE
RESOLUTELY
RESOLUTION
RESORCINOL
RESOUNDING
RESPECTFUL
RESPECTING
RESPECTIVE
RESPIRATOR
RESPONDENT
RESPONSIVE
RESTAURANT
RESTLESSLY
RESTRAINED
RESTRICTED
RESUMPTION
RESUPINATE
RESURGENCE
RETINALITE
RETIREMENT
RETRACTION
RETRAINING
RETREATING
RETROGRADE
RETROGRESS
RETROSPECT
RETURNABLE
REVELATION
REVENGEFUL
REVERENTLY
REVERSIBLE
REVITALIZE
REVIVALIST
REVOCATION
REVOLUTION
RHAMPASTOS
RHAPSODISE
RHAPSODIZE
RHEOTROPIC
RHETORICAL
RHEUMATICS
RHEUMATISM
RHEUMATOID
RHINEGRAVE
RHINESTONE
RHINOCEROS
RHINOLALIA
RHINOPHYMA
RHIPIPTERA
RHOEADALES
RHYTHMICAL
RIBOFLAVIN
RICHARDSON
RICHTHOFEN
RIDICULOUS
RIDINGHOOD
RIGELATION
RIGHTFULLY
RIGOROUSLY
RIJSTTAFEL
RINDERPEST
RINGELMANN
RINGLEADER
RINGMASTER
RIPSNORTER
RITORNELLE
RITORNELLO
ROADRUNNER
ROADWORTHY
ROBERDSMAN
ROBERTSMAN
ROBUSTIOUS
ROBUSTNESS
ROCKABILLY
ROCKINGHAM
ROCKSTEADY
ROISTERING
ROLANDSECK
ROLLICKING
ROMANESQUE
ROQUELAURE
ROSANILINE
ROSECHAFER
ROSEMALING
ROTHSCHILD
ROTISSERIE
ROTTWEILER
ROUGHHOUSE
ROUNDABOUT
ROUNDHOUSE
ROUSEABOUT
ROUSTABOUT
ROWDYDOWDY
ROWLANDSON
RUBBERNECK
RUBIGINOUS
RUBINSTEIN
RUDDERLESS
RUDIMENTAL
RUDOLPHINE
RUGGEDNESS
RUMBLOSSOM
RUMBULLION
RUMINANTIA
RUMINATION
RUMINATIVE
RUPESTRIAN
RUPICOLINE
RUTHERFORD
RUTHLESSLY
SABBATICAL
SABRETACHE
SACCHARASE
SACCHARIDE
SACCHARINE
SACCHAROID
SACERDOTAL
SACREDNESS
SACROSANCT
SADDLEBACK
SADDLEBILL
SAGITTARIA
SALAMANDER
SALESWOMAN
SALICORNIA
SALIVATION
SALLENDERS
SALMAGUNDI
SALMANAZAR
SALMONELLA
SALOPETTES
SALPINGIAN
SALTARELLO
SALTIGRADE
SALUBRIOUS
SALUTATION
SAMARSKITE
SAMOTHRACE
SANATORIUM
SANCTIFIED
SANCTITIES
SANCTITUDE
SANDALWOOD
SANDEMANIA
SANDERLING
SANDGROPER
SANDINISTA
SANDWICHES
SANFORISED
SANGUINARY
SANITARIUM
SANITATION
SANNAYASIN
SAPPERMENT
SAPROPHYTE
SARCOCOLLA
SARCOLEMMA
SARMENTOUS
SARSQUATCH
SATISFYING
SATURATION
SATURNALIA
SATYAGRAHA
SAUERKRAUT
SAUROPSIDA
SAVAGENESS
SAVONAROLA
SAXICOLINE
SAXICOLOUS
SBUDDIKINS
SCAMMOZZIS
SCANDALISE
SCANDALIZE
SCANDALOUS
SCANDAROON
SCANDERBEG
SCANTINESS
SCAPEGRACE
SCAPHOPODA
SCARAMOUCH
SCARCEMENT
SCARCENESS
SCARLATINA
SCARLETINA
SCATHELESS
SCATTERING
SCATURIENT
SCEPTICISM
SCHALSTEIN
SCHIPPERKE
SCHISMATIC
SCHLIMAZEL
SCHOLAEMIA
SCHOLASTIC
SCHOOLBOOK
SCHOOLGIRL
SCHOOLMAAM
SCHWARZLOT
SCIENTIFIC
SCLERIASIS
SCOFFINGLY
SCOMBRESOX
SCOOTERIST
SCOPELIDAE
SCORDATURA
SCOREBOARD
SCORNFULLY
SCORZONERA
SCOTODINIA
SCOTSWOMAN
SCREECHING
SCREENPLAY
SCRIBBLING
SCRIMSHANK
SCRIPTURAL
SCRIPTURES
SCROUNGING
SCRUPULOUS
SCRUTINEER
SCRUTINISE
SCRUTINIZE
SCULPTRESS
SCURRILITY
SCURRILOUS
SCUTELLATE
SDRUCCIOLA
SEAMANSHIP
SEAMSTRESS
SEANNACHIE
SEASONABLE
SEASONABLY
SECONDBEST
SECONDHAND
SECONDMENT
SECONDRATE
SECRETAIRE
SECULARIZE
SECURITIES
SEDATENESS
SEDULOUSLY
SEECATCHIE
SEEMLIHEAD
SEERSUCKER
SEGREGATED
SEGUIDILLA
SEISMOLOGY
SELEGILINE
SELFESTEEM
SELFSTYLED
SELLINGERS
SELTZOGENE
SEMICIRCLE
SEMIQUAVER
SENATORIAL
SENEGALESE
SENESCENCE
SENSUALITY
SENSUOUSLY
SEPARATELY
SEPARATION
SEPARATISM

SEPARATIST
SEPARATRIX
SEPTENNIAL
SEPTUAGINT
SEPULCHRAL
SEQUACIOUS
SEQUENTIAL
SERMONICAL
SERPENTINE
SERRADELLA
SERRADILLA
SERRASALMO
SERVICEMAN
SETTERWORT
SETTLEMENT
SEVENTIETH
SEXAGESIMA
SEXOLOGIST
SGANARELLE
SHABBINESS
SHACKLETON
SHADOWLESS
SHAGHAIRED
SHAKUHACHI
SHAMEFACED
SHAMEFULLY
SHAMPOOING
SHANDRYDAN
SHANDYGAFF
SHARAWADGI
SHARAWAGGI
SHATTERING
SHEARWATER
SHECKLATON
SHEEPISHLY
SHEEPSHANK
SHELDONIAN
SHELLSHOCK
SHELLYCOAT
SHENANIGAN
SHERARDISE
SHIBBOLETH
SHIELDRAKE
SHIFTINESS
SHILLELAGH
SHIMMERING
SHISHKEBAB
SHOCKINGLY
SHOCKPROOF
SHODDINESS
SHOESTRING
SHOPKEEPER
SHOPLIFTER
SHOPSOILED
SHOPWALKER
SHORTBREAD
SHORTENING
SHORTLIVED
SHORTRANGE
SHOVELHEAD
SHOVELNOSE
SHOWJUMPER
SHREWDNESS
SHRIEVALTY
SHRILLNESS
SHRIVELLED
SHROVETIDE
SHUDDERING
SICILIENNE
SIDEBOARDS
SIDERATION
SIDEROSTAT
SIDESADDLE
SIDEWINDER
SIGILLARIA
SIGNIFICAT
SIGNORELLI
SILHOUETTE
SILVERBACK
SILVERBILL
SILVERFISH
SILVERSIDE
SILVERSKIN
SILVERWARE
SIMILARITY
SIMILITUDE
SIMILLIMUM
SIMMENTHAL
SIMPLICITY
SIMPLISTIC
SIMULACRUM
SIMULATING
SIMULATION
SINARCHIST
SINARQUIST
SINFULNESS
SINGHALESE
SINGLENESS
SINGULARLY
SINSEMILLA
SISTERHOOD
SKATEBOARD
SKEPTICISM
SKETCHBOOK
SKEUOMORPH
SKILLFULLY
SKINDIVING
SKRIMSHANK
SKUPSHTINA
SKYSCRAPER
SLAMMERKIN
SLANDEROUS
SLATTERNLY
SLEEPINESS
SLEEVELESS
SLIPSTREAM
SLOPPINESS
SLUGGISHLY
SLUMBERING
SMALLSCALE
SMARAGDINE
SMARMINESS
SMATTERING
SMITHEREEN
SMOKESTACK
SMOOTHNESS
SMORREBROD
SNAKEMOUTH
SNAKESTONE
SNAPDRAGON
SNAPHAUNCE
SNAPHAUNCH
SNEEZEWOOD
SNIGGERING
SNOOTINESS
SNORKELING
SNOWCAPPED
SNOWMOBILE
SOBERSIDES
SOFTBOILED
SOGDOLAGER
SOGDOLIGER
SOGDOLOGER
SOLICITOUS
SOLICITUDE
SOLIDARITY
SOLIFIDIAN
SOLIVAGANT
SOLUBILITY
SOMBRERITE
SOMERSAULT
SOMERVILLE
SOMNOLENCE
SONGSTRESS
SONGWRITER
SOOTHINGLY
SOOTHSAYER
SOPHOCLEAN
SOPHOMORIC
SORDIDNESS
SOUBRIQUET
SOUNDPROOF
SOUNDTRACK
SOURDELINE
SOUSAPHONE
SOUTERRAIN
SOUTHBOUND
SOUTHERNER
SOUTHWARDS
SPACECRAFT
SPALLATION
SPARSENESS
SPARTACIST
SPATCHCOCK
SPEAKERINE
SPECIALISE
SPECIALIST
SPECIALITY
SPECIALIZE
SPECIOUSLY
SPECTACLED
SPECTACLES
SPECTATORS
SPECULATOR
SPEECHLESS
SPEEDINESS
SPELEOLOGY
SPELLBOUND
SPENCERIAN
SPENSERIAN
SPERMACETI
SPERRYLITE
SPHACELATE
SPHALERITE
SPIDERWORT
SPIFLICATE
SPILLIKINS
SPINESCENT
SPIRACULUM
SPIRITEDLY
SPIRITLESS
SPIRITUOUS
SPIRKETING
SPISSITUDE
SPITCHCOCK
SPITEFULLY
SPLANCHNIC
SPLENDIDLY
SPLITLEVEL
SPODOMANCY
SPOILSPORT
SPOKESHAVE
SPOLIATION
SPOLIATIVE
SPONGEWARE
SPONGIFORM
SPONSIONAL
SPOONERISM
SPORTINGLY
SPORTSWEAR
SPOTLESSLY
SPREAGHERY
SPRINGBOKS
SPRINGHAAS
SPRINGLESS
SPRINGLIKE
SPRINGTAIL
SPRINGTIME
SPRINKLING
SPRUCENESS
SPURIOUSLY
SQUEEZEBOX
SQUETEAGUE
SQUIREARCH
STABILISER
STABILIZER
STADHOLDER
STAGECOACH
STAGECRAFT
STAGGERING
STAGNATION
STALACTITE
STALAGMITE
STALHELMER
STALLENGER
STALLINGER
STAMMERING
STANDPOINT
STANDSTILL
STANISLAUS
STAPHYLINE
STARVATION
STARVELING
STATECRAFT
STATIONARY
STATIONERY
STATISTICS
STATOCRACY
STATUESQUE
STAUROLITE
STAVESACRE
STEADINESS
STEAKHOUSE
STEALTHILY
STEELINESS
STEELWORKS
STEMWINDER
STENOTYPER
STENTORIAN
STEPFATHER
STEPHANITE
STEPHENSON
STEPLADDER
STEPMOTHER
STEPSISTER
STEREOTOMY
STEREOTYPE
STERILISER
STERILIZER
STERNALGIA
STERTEROUS
STERTOROUS
STEWARDESS
STIACCIATO
STICHARION
STICKINESS
STICKYBEAK
STIGMATISE
STIGMATIZE
STILLBIRTH
STILLICIDE
STILLIFORM
STILLSTAND
STINGINESS
STINGYBARK
STOCHASTIC
STOCKINESS
STOMATOPOD
STONEBRASH
STONEHENGE

STONEMASON
STONYHURST
STOREFRONT
STOREHOUSE
STOUTHERIE
STOUTHRIEF
STRABISMUS
STRABOTOMY
STRACCHINO
STRAGGLING
STRAIGHTEN
STRAITENED
STRAMONIUM
STRAPONTIN
STRASBOURG
STRATEGIST
STRATHSPEY
STRATIOTES
STRATOCRAT
STRATOCYST
STRAVINSKY
STRAWBERRY
STRAWBOARD
STREAMERED
STREAMLINE
STREETLAMP
STREETWISE
STRELITZIA
STRENGTHEN
STREPITANT
STREPITOSO
STRICTNESS
STRIDENTLY
STRIDEWAYS
STRIDULATE
STRIKINGLY
STRINDBERG
STRINGENCY
STRINGENDO
STRINGHALT
STRIPTEASE
STROGANOFF
STRONGHOLD
STRONGROOM
STROPHIOLE
STRUCTURAL
STRULDBERG
STRULDBRUG
STRYCHNINE
STUBBORNLY
STUDIOUSLY
STUFFINESS
STULTIFIED
STUMBLEDOM
STUPEFYING
STUPENDOUS
STURDINESS
STYLISTICS
STYLOPISED
SUAVEOLENT

SUBCOMPACT
SUBHEADING
SUBJECTION
SUBJECTIVE
SUBLIMATER
SUBLIMINAL
SUBMARINER
SUBMEDIANT
SUBMERSION
SUBMISSION
SUBMISSIVE
SUBREPTION
SUBSCRIBER
SUBSECTION
SUBSELLIUM
SUBSEQUENT
SUBSIDENCE
SUBSIDIARY
SUBSISTENT
SUBSTATION
SUBSTITUTE
SUBSTRATUM
SUBTENANCY
SUBTERFUGE
SUBTROPICS
SUBVENTION
SUBVERSION
SUBVERSIVE
SUCCEEDING
SUCCESSFUL
SUCCESSION
SUCCESSIVE
SUCCINCTLY
SUDDENNESS
SUFFERANCE
SUFFICIENT
SUFFRAGIST
SUGARALLIE
SUGGESTION
SUGGESTIVE
SULPHUROUS
SULTRINESS
SUMMERTIME
SUNBATHING
SUNGLASSES
SUPERADDED
SUPERCARGO
SUPERGIANT
SUPERHUMAN
SUPERMODEL
SUPERPOWER
SUPERSONIC
SUPERSTORE
SUPERTONIC
SUPERVISED
SUPERVISOR
SUPERWOMAN
SUPPLEJACK
SUPPLEMENT
SUPPLENESS

SUPPLICANT
SUPPLICATE
SUPPORTING
SUPPORTIVE
SUPPOSEDLY
SUPPRESSED
SUPPRESSOR
SURFRIDING
SURGICALLY
SURINAMESE
SURPASSING
SURPRISING
SURREALISM
SURREALIST
SURROUNDED
SUSPENDERS
SUSPENSION
SUSPICIOUS
SUSTAINING
SUSTENANCE
SUZERAINTY
SVADILFARI
SWAGGERING
SWALLOWING
SWEATSHIRT
SWEDENBORG
SWEEPSTAKE
SWEETBREAD
SWEETENING
SWEETHEART
SWELTERING
SWIMMINGLY
SWITCHBACK
SWORDSTICK
SYMBOLICAL
SYMPATHISE
SYMPATHIZE
SYMPHONIUM
SYNAERESIS
SYNCOPATED
SYNCRETISE
SYNECDOCHE
SYNEIDESIS
SYNONYMOUS
SYNOSTOSIS
SYNTAGMATA
SYNTERESIS
SYNTHESIZE
SYNTHRONUS
SYPHILITIC
SYSTEMATIC
TABERNACLE
TABLANETTE
TABLECLOTH
TABLESPOON
TABULATION
TACHOGRAPH
TACHOMETER
TACTICALLY
TACTLESSLY

TAGLIARINI
TAILGATING
TAILORMADE
TALEBEARER
TALLEYRAND
TAMBERLANE
TAMBOURINE
TAMPERFOOT
TANAGRIDAE
TANGANYIKA
TANGENTIAL
TANGLEFOOT
TANNHAUSER
TANTAMOUNT
TAPDANCING
TAPERECORD
TAPOTEMENT
TARADIDDLE
TARANTELLA
TARDIGRADE
TARPAULING
TARTRAZINE
TASKMASTER
TASTEFULLY
TATPURUSHA
TATTERSALL
TAXONOMIST
TCHOUKBALL
TECHNETIUM
TECHNICIAN
TECHNOCRAT
TECHNOLOGY
TEDDINGTON
TEENYWEENY
TEETOTALER
TEICHOPSIA
TEINOSCOPE
TELEGRAPHY
TELEOSTOME
TELEPATHIC
TELEPHONIC
TELESCOPIC
TELEVISION
TELPHERAGE
TEMPERANCE
TEMPTATION
TENDERFOOT
TENDERLOIN
TENDERNESS
TENDRILLED
TENEBRIFIC
TENNANTITE
TENRECIDAE
TENTERHOOK
TEPIDARIUM
TERMINABLE
TERMINALIA
TERMINALLY
TERNEPLATE
TERRACOTTA

TERREPLEIN
TERRIFYING
TERTIARIES
TESCHENITE
TESTACEOUS
TESTICULAR
THALASSIAN
THALESTRIS
THALICTRUM
THALLIFORM
THANKFULLY
THAUMASITE
THEATRICAL
THELLUSSON
THEMSELVES
THEOCRITUS
THEODOLITE
THEOLOGATE
THEOLOGIAN
THEOLOGISE
THEOLOGIST
THEREAFTER
THEREANENT
THERMIONIC
THERMISTOR
THERMOSTAT
THICKENING
THIMBLEFUL
THIMBLEWIT
THINGUMBOB
THIRTEENTH
THIXOTROPY
THOROUGHLY
THOUGHTFUL
THOUSANDTH
THREADBARE
THREADLIKE
THREADWORM
THREATENED
THREEPENCE
THREEPENNY
THREESCORE
THRENODIAL
THROMBOSIS
THROUGHOUT
THROUGHPUT
THROUGHWAY
THUCYDIDES
THUMBIKINS
THUMBSCREW
THUNDERBOX
THUNDERING
THUNDEROUS
TICKERTAPE
TIEBREAKER
TILLANDSIA
TIMBERYARD
TIMBROLOGY
TIMEKEEPER
TIMELINESS

TIMESAVING
TIMESERVER
TIMESWITCH
TINKERBELL
TINTORETTO
TIRAILLEUR
TIRELESSLY
TIROCINIUM
TITARAKURA
TOCCATELLA
TOCOPHEROL
TOILETRIES
TOILINETTE
TOLERANTLY
TOLERATION
TOLLKEEPER
TOMFOOLERY
TONGUESTER
TOOTHBRUSH
TOOTHPASTE
TOPICALITY
TOPOGRAPHY
TOPOLOGIST
TOPSYTURVY
TORBERNITE
TORCHLIGHT
TORPESCENT
TORQUEMADA
TORRENTIAL
TORRICELLI
TORTELLINI
TORTUOUSLY
TOSSICATED
TOSTICATED
TOUCHANDGO
TOUCHINESS
TOUCHPAPER
TOUCHPIECE
TOUCHSTONE
TOURBILLON
TOURMALINE
TOURNAMENT
TOURNIQUET
TOWNSWOMAN
TOXICOLOGY
TRACHELATE
TRADITIONS
TRAFFICKER
TRAGACANTH
TRAGICALLY
TRAITOROUS
TRAJECTORY
TRAMONTANA
TRAMONTANE
TRAMPOLINE
TRANQUILLY
TRANSCRIBE
TRANSCRIPT
TRANSGRESS
TRANSIENCE
TRANSISTOR
TRANSITION
TRANSITIVE
TRANSITORY
TRANSLATED
TRANSLATOR
TRANSPLANT
TRANSPOSED
TRANSVERSE
TRAUMATIZE
TRAVANCORE
TRAVELATOR
TRAVELLERS
TRAVELLING
TRAVELOGUE
TRAVERTINE
TRAVOLATOR
TRECENTIST
TREKSCHUIT
TREMENDOUS
TRENCHMORE
TRENDINESS
TRESPASSER
TRIACONTER
TRIANGULAR
TRICHOLOGY
TRICKINESS
TRICLINIUM
TRIDENTINE
TRILATERAL
TRILINGUAL
TRIMALCHIO
TRIMSNITCH
TRINACRIAN
TRIPARTITE
TRIPEHOUND
TRIPLICATE
TRIPUDIARY
TRISKELION
TRITANOPIA
TRIUMPHANT
TRIVIALITY
TRIVIALIZE
TROCHANTER
TROCHOTRON
TROCTOLITE
TROGLODYTE
TROMBONIST
TROMOMETER
TROPAEOLUM
TROPHONIUS
TROPOPAUSE
TROPOPHYTE
TROTSKYITE
TROUBADOUR
TROUVAILLE
TRUCULENCE
TRUSTFULLY
TRUTHFULLY
TRYPTOPHAN
TUBERCULAR
TULARAEMIA
TUMBLEDOWN
TUMESCENCE
TUMULTUOUS
TURBULENCE
TURNAROUND
TURPENTINE
TURRITELLA
TURTLEDOVE
TURTLENECK
TUTIVILLUS
TYPESCRIPT
TYPESETTER
TYPEWRITER
TYPOGRAPHY
TYRANNICAL
TYRANNISED
UBERMENSCH
UBIQUITOUS
ULCERATION
ULSTERETTE
ULTIMATELY
ULTRAFICHE
ULTRASONIC
ULTRASOUND
ULTRONEOUS
UMBELLIFER
UNABRIDGED
UNACCENTED
UNAFFECTED
UNANSWERED
UNARGUABLE
UNASSIGNED
UNASSUMING
UNATTACHED
UNATTENDED
UNAVAILING
UNBALANCED
UNBEARABLE
UNBEARABLY
UNBEATABLE
UNBECOMING
UNBELIEVER
UNBLEACHED
UNBLINKING
UNBLUSHING
UNCOMMONLY
UNCONFINED
UNCRITICAL
UNCTUOUSLY
UNCULTURED
UNDECLARED
UNDEFEATED
UNDEFENDED
UNDENIABLE
UNDERBURNT
UNDERCLASS
UNDERCOVER
UNDERCRAFT
UNDERCROFT
UNDERFLOOR
UNDERLEASE
UNDERLINEN
UNDERLYING
UNDERNEATH
UNDERPANTS
UNDERSCORE
UNDERSHIRT
UNDERSIZED
UNDERSKIRT
UNDERSLUNG
UNDERSTAND
UNDERSTATE
UNDERSTEER
UNDERSTOOD
UNDERSTUDY
UNDERTAKER
UNDERVALUE
UNDERWATER
UNDERWORLD
UNDERWRITE
UNDESCRIED
UNDESERVED
UNDETECTED
UNDETERRED
UNDIGESTED
UNDISPUTED
UNDOCTORED
UNDULATING
UNDULATION
UNEASINESS
UNEDIFYING
UNEDUCATED
UNEMPLOYED
UNENVIABLE
UNEQUALLED
UNEVENNESS
UNEVENTFUL
UNEXAMPLED
UNEXPECTED
UNEXPLORED
UNFAITHFUL
UNFAMILIAR
UNFATHOMED
UNFETTERED
UNFINISHED
UNFLAGGING
UNFLAVORED
UNFORESEEN
UNFRIENDLY
UNFRUITFUL
UNGRACIOUS
UNGRATEFUL
UNGROUNDED
UNHAMPERED
UNHEARABLE
UNHERALDED
UNHYGIENIC
UNICAMERAL
UNIFORMITY
UNIGENITUS
UNILATERAL
UNIMPAIRED
UNINFORMED
UNINSPIRED
UNINVITING
UNIQUENESS
UNIVERSITY
UNLADYLIKE
UNLEAVENED
UNLETTERED
UNLICENSED
UNMANNERED
UNMANNERLY
UNNUMBERED
UNOBSERVED
UNOCCUPIED
UNOFFICIAL
UNORIGINAL
UNORTHODOX
UNPLEASANT
UNPREPARED
UNPROMPTED
UNPROVOKED
UNPUNCTUAL
UNREADABLE
UNREASONED
UNREDEEMED
UNRELIABLE
UNRELIEVED
UNREQUITED
UNRESERVED
UNRESOLVED
UNREVEALED
UNRIVALLED
UNROMANTIC
UNRULINESS
UNSALARIED
UNSCHOOLED
UNSCRAMBLE
UNSCRIPTED
UNSEASONED
UNSETTLING
UNSHACKLED
UNSLEEPING
UNSOCIABLE
UNSPECIFIC
UNSUITABLE
UNSWERVING
UNTHINKING
UNTIDINESS
UNTRUTHFUL
UNWORKABLE
UNYIELDING
UPBRINGING
UPHOLSTERY
UPPERCLASS
UPROARIOUS
UPSTANDING

UROPOIESIS
UROSTEGITE
URTICACEAE
USEFULNESS
USQUEBAUGH
USUCAPTION
USURPATION
UTILIZABLE
VALENTINES
VALIDATION
VALLADOLID
VANDERBILT
VARICOSITY
VARIEGATED
VARNISHING
VAUDEVILLE
VEGETABLES
VEGETARIAN
VEGETATION
VEHEMENTLY
VELITATION
VELOCIPEDE
VENERATION
VENEZUELAN
VENTILATOR
VERIFIABLE
VERMICELLI
VERMILLION
VERNACULAR
VERNISSAGE
VERSAILLES
VERTEBRATE
VERTICALLY
VESICULATE
VESTIBULUM
VETERINARY
VIBRACULUM
VIBRAPHONE
VIBRATIONS
VICEGERENT
VICEREGENT
VICTORIANA
VICTORIOUS
VICTUALLER
VIETNAMESE
VIEWFINDER
VIGILANTES
VIGOROUSLY
VILLAINOUS
VILLANELLE
VILLANOVAN
VINDEMIATE
VINDICTIVE
VINEGARISH
VIROLOGIST
VIRTUOSITY
VIRTUOUSLY
VIRULENTLY
VISIBILITY
VISITATION
VITELLICLE
VITUPERATE
VIVANDIÈRE
VIVIPAROUS
VOCABULARY
VOCABULIST
VOCATIONAL
VOCIFERATE
VOCIFEROUS
VOETGANGER
VOLATILITY
VOLLEYBALL
VOLUBILITY
VOLUMINOUS
VOLUPTUARY
VOLUPTUOUS
VOLUTATION
VORAGINOUS
VULCANALIA
VULNERABLE
WAGEEARNER
WAINSCOTED
WALDENSIAN
WALLACHIAN
WALLFLOWER
WAMPUMPEAG
WANCHANCIE
WANDERINGS
WANDERLUST
WANDSWORTH
WANTHRIVEN
WAPENSCHAW
WAPINSCHAW
WAPPENSHAW
WARRANDICE
WASHINGTON
WASSAILING
WASSERMANS
WASTEFULLY
WASTEPAPER
WATCHFULLY
WATCHMAKER
WATCHTOWER
WATERBORNE
WATERBRASH
WATERCOLOR
WATERCRESS
WATERFRONT
WATERLEVEL
WATERMELON
WATERPROOF
WATERSKIER
WATERSPOUT
WATERTIGHT
WATERWHEEL
WATERWINGS
WATERWORKS
WATTLEWORK
WAVELENGTH
WEAPONLESS
WEATHERMAN
WEEDKILLER
WEIGHTLESS
WEIMARANER
WELLEARNED
WELLINGTON
WELLSPRING
WELSHWOMAN
WENTLETRAP
WESTERNIZE
WHARFINGER
WHATSOEVER
WHEATSHEAF
WHEATSTONE
WHEELCHAIR
WHEELHOUSE
WHEEZINESS
WHEWELLITE
WHIGGAMORE
WHILLYWHAW
WHIRLYBIRD
WHISPERING
WHITEHEART
WHITETHORN
WHITEWATER
WHITSTABLE
WHITTERICK
WHOLESALER
WHOLEWHEAT
WICKEDNESS
WICKERWORK
WIDDICOMBE
WIDESPREAD
WILDEBEEST
WILDERNESS
WILDFOWLER
WILLIAMSON
WILLINGDON
WILLOWHERB
WILLYWILLY
WINCEYETTE
WINCHESTER
WINDERMERE
WINDFLOWER
WINDJAMMER
WINDOWSILL
WINDSCREEN
WINDSHIELD
WINDSURFER
WINTERTIME
WISHYWASHY
WITCHCRAFT
WITGATBOOM
WITHDRAWAL
WITSNAPPER
WOFFINGTON
WOLFRAMITE
WONDERLAND
WONDERMENT
WOODENHEAD
WOODPECKER
WOODPIGEON
WOODWORKER
WOOLLYBACK
WOOLLYBUTT
WORDSWORTH
WORKAHOLIC
WORLDCLASS
WORSHIPPER
WORTHINESS
WORTHWHILE
WRAPAROUND
WRETCHEDLY
WRISTWATCH
WRONGDOING
WRONGFULLY
WUNDERKIND
WYCLIFFIAN
XENOPHOBIA
XENOPHOBIC
XEROPHYTIC
XEROSTOMIA
XIPHOPAGUS
YAFFINGALE
YARBOROUGH
YELLOWBACK
YELLOWGIRL
YELLOWJACK
YELLOWROOT
YELLOWWOOD
YESTERWEEK
YESTERYEAR
YGGDRASILL
YOUNGBERRY
YOURSELVES
YTHUNDERED
ZABAGLIONE
ZAPOROGIAN
ZEUGLODONT
ZIMBABWEAN
ZINCOGRAPH
ZOANTHARIA
ZOLLVEREIN
ZOOLOGICAL
ZOOTHAPSIS
ZOOTHERAPY
ZUMBOORUCK
ZWITTERION

10:2

BABESIASIS
BABIROUSSA
BABYLONIAN
BABYSITTER
BACCHANTES
BACITRACIN
BACKBITING
BACKBLOCKS
BACKGAMMON
BACKGROUND
BACKHANDED
BACKHANDER
BACKPACKER
BACKSLIDER
BACKSTAIRS
BACKSTROKE
BADDERLOCK
BAFFLEMENT
BAGASSOSIS
BAHRAINIAN
BAILIEWICK
BAILLIWICK
BALANCHINE
BALBRIGGAN
BALBUTIENT
BALDERDASH
BALIBUNTAL
BALLISTICS
BALLISTITE
BALLOONING
BALLOONIST
BALNEATION
BALNEOLOGY
BALUSTRADE
BAMBOOZLED
BANDERILLA
BANDERILLO
BANDMASTER
BANGLADESH
BANISHMENT
BANKRUPTCY
BARASINGHA
BARBAROSSA
BARBITURIC
BARCAROLLE
BARCHESTER
BAREFOOTED
BAREHEADED
BARELEGGED
BARGAINING
BARLEYBREE
BARLEYCORN
BARMECIDAL
BARMITZVAH
BAROMETRIC
BARRACKING
BARRACOOTA
BARRACOUTA
BARRAMUNDA
BARRENNESS
BARYSPHERE
BASKETBALL
BASKETWORK
BASSINGTON
BASSOONIST
BATHYSCAPH
BATRACHIAN
BATTAILOUS

BATTENBERG
BATTENBURG
BATTLEDOOR
BATTLEDORE
BATTLEMENT
BATTLESHIP
BAUDELAIRE
CACHINNATE
CACODAEMON
CACOGRAPHY
CACOMISTLE
CACUMINOUS
CADAVEROUS
CAERPHILLY
CAESPITOSE
CALAMANDER
CALAMITOUS
CALAMONDIN
CALAVERITE
CALCAREOUS
CALCEDONIO
CALCEOLATE
CALCULABLE
CALCULATED
CALCULATOR
CALEDONIAN
CALEFACTOR
CALESCENCE
CALIFORNIA
CALLIATURE
CALORIFIER
CALUMNIATE
CALYDONIAN
CALYPTRATE
CAMBERWELL
CAMBRENSIS
CAMELOPARD
CAMERLENGO
CAMERLINGO
CAMERONIAN
CAMOUFLAGE
CAMPAIGNER
CAMPANELLA
CAMPARADOR
CAMPERDOWN
CAMPESTRAL
CAMSTEERIE
CANCIONERO
CANCRIZANS
CANDELABRA
CANDELILLA
CANDLEFISH
CANDLEWICK
CANDYFLOSS
CANECUTTER
CANEPHORUS
CANNELLONI
CANNONBALL
CANTABRIAN
CANTALOUPE
CANTATRICE
CANTELOUPE
CANTERBURY
CANTILEVER
CANTILLATE
CANTONMENT
CANVASBACK
CANVASSING
CAOUTCHOUC
CAPABILITY
CAPACITATE
CAPERNAITE
CAPERNOITY
CAPILLAIRE
CAPITALISM
CAPITALIST
CAPITALIZE
CAPITATION
CAPITELLUM
CAPITOLINE
CAPITULARY
CAPITULATE
CAPNOMANCY
CAPODASTRO
CAPPUCCINO
CAPREOLATE
CAPRICIOUS
CAPTIVATED
CARABINEER
CARABINIER
CARACTACUS
CARAMELIZE
CARBURETOR
CARCINOGEN
CARDIOGRAM
CARDIOLOGY
CARELESSLY
CARICATURA
CARICATURE
CARMAGNOLE
CARNASSIAL
CARPATHIAN
CARPENTIER
CARPHOLOGY
CARRAGHEEN
CARTHAMINE
CARTHUSIAN
CARTOMANCY
CARTOONIST
CARYATIDES
CASCARILLA
CASSIABARK
CASSIOPEIA
CASSOLETTE
CASSUMUNAR
CASTRATION
CASUALNESS
CATABOLISM
CATACHUMEN
CATAFALQUE
CATALECTIC
CATALEPTIC
CATALOGUER
CATAPHRACT
CATARRHINE
CATASTASIS
CATAWAMPUS
CATCHPENNY
CATCRACKER
CATECHUMEN
CATEGORISE
CATEGORIZE
CATENACCIO
CATHOLICON
CATHOLICOS
CATTLEGRID
CAUTIONARY
CAUTIOUSLY
CAVALRYMAN
CAVICORNIA
DAMSELFISH
DARJEELING
DARKHAIRED
DAYDREAMER
EARTHQUAKE
EARTHWORKS
EASTERLING
EATANSWILL
FABULOUSLY
FACESAVING
FACILITATE
FACILITIES
FACTITIOUS
FAHRENHEIT
FAIRGROUND
FAIRHAIRED
FAITHFULLY
FALDISTORY
FALKLANDER
FALLACIOUS
FALLINGOFF
FALSETRUTH
FAMILIARLY
FAMISHMENT
FANATICISM
FANTASTICO
FANTOCCINI
FAREPAYING
FARFETCHED
FARRANDINE
FASCIATION
FASCINATED
FASCINATOR
FASTIDIOUS
FASTIGIATE
FASTMOVING
FATALISTIC
FATALITIES
FATHERLAND
FATHERLESS
FAULTINESS
FAVORITISM
FAVOURABLE
FAVOURABLY
GADOLINIUM
GAINGIVING
GAINSTRIVE
GALIMATIAS
GALLABIYAH
GALLABIYEH
GALLIAMBIC
GALRAVITCH
GALSWORTHY
GALUMPHING
GALVANISER
GAMEKEEPER
GANGRENOUS
GARGANTUAN
GARGOUILLE
GARLANDAGE
GARNIERITE
GASCONNADE
GASTEROPOD
GASTRONOME
GASTRONOMY
GAULTHERIA
HABILITATE
HABITATION
HABITUALLY
HACKBUTEER
HACKMATACK
HAEMANTHUS
HAIRSPRING
HAKENKREUZ
HALFDOLLAR
HALFHOURLY
HALFSISTER
HALFYEARLY
HALIEUTICS
HALLELUJAH
HALLMARKED
HALLOYSITE
HALLUBALOO
HAMESUCKEN
HAMMERHEAD
HAMMERLOCK
HAMSHACKLE
HANDICRAFT
HANDLEBARS
HANDMAIDEN
HANDPICKED
HANDSOMELY
HANDSPRING
HANGGLIDER
HANKYPANKY
HANOVERIAN
HARASSMENT
HARDBOILED
HARDCASTLE
HARMANBECK
HARMONIOUS
HARRINGTON
HARTEBEEST
HARVESTMAN
HATEENOUGH
HAUSTELLUM
HAUSTORIUM
IATROGENIC
JABBERWOCK
JACKANAPES
JACKBOOTED
JACKHAMMER
JACKSTONES
JACKSTRAWS
JACULATION
JAGUARONDI
JAGUARUNDI
JAMESONITE
JARDINIERE
JARGONELLE
JAUNTINESS
JAYWALKING
KARMATHIAN
KARTTIKAYA
KATERFELTO
LABORATORY
LACCADIVES
LACERATION
LACHRYMOSE
LACKADAISY
LACKLUSTER
LACKLUSTRE
LACUSTRINE
LADYKILLER
LAEOTROPIC
LAMARCKISM
LAMBREQUIN
LAMENTABLE
LAMENTABLY
LAMINATION
LANCEOLATE
LANDAMMANN
LANDLOCKED
LANDLOUPER
LANDLUBBER
LANDSTHING
LANGERHANS
LANGUOROUS
LANIGEROUS
LANSQUENET
LANTHANIDE
LARGESCALE
LARYNGITIS
LASCIVIOUS
LASTMINUTE
LATTERMATH
LATTICINIO
LAUDERDALE
LAUNCEGAYE
LAUNCESTON

LAUNDROMAT
LAURDALITE
LAURENTIAN
LAURUSTINE
LAURVIKITE
LAVALLIÈRE
LAVISHNESS
LAWABIDING
LAWBREAKER
LAWRENCIUM
MABINOGION
MACEDONIAN
MACKINTOSH
MACONOCHIE
MACROBIOTE
MACROCARPA
MADAGASCAN
MADAGASCAR
MAGISTRACY
MAGISTRAND
MAGISTRATE
MAGNIFICAT
MAGNIFYING
MAHAYANALI
MAHOMMEDAN
MAIDENHAIR
MAIDENHOOD
MAINPERNOR
MAINSPRING
MAINSTREAM
MAISONETTE
MAKESYSTEM
MAKEWEIGHT
MAKUNOUCHI
MALACOLOGY
MALAGUETTA
MALAPROPOS
MALAYALAAM
MALCONTENT
MALEFACTOR
MALEVOLENT
MALIGNANCY
MALINGERER
MALLOPHAGA
MALMESBURY
MALODOROUS
MALTHUSIAN
MANAGEABLE
MANAGEMENT
MANAGERESS
MANAGERIAL
MANCHESTER
MANCHINEEL
MANDEVILLE
MANDRAGORA
MANGABEIRA
MANGOSTEEN
MANICHAEAN
MANICURIST
MANIFESTLY
MANIPULATE
MANSERVANT
MANUSCRIPT
MANZANILLA
MAQUILLAGE
MARASCHINO
MARCANTANT
MARCESCENT
MARCIONITE
MARGINALIA
MARGINALLY
MARGUERITE
MARIOLATRY
MARIONETTE
MARKETABLE
MARQUETRIE
MARSHALSEA
MARTINGALE
MARTINIQUE
MARVELLOUS
MARYLEBONE
MASCARPONE
MASKANONGE
MASKINONGE
MASKIROVKA
MASQUERADE
MASSASAUGA
MASTECTOMY
MASTERMIND
MASTERWORT
MASTURBATE
MATCHMAKER
MATCHSTALK
MATCHSTICK
MATELLASSE
MATERIALLY
MATERNALLY
MATRIARCHY
MATTERHORN
MATURATION
MAUPASSANT
MAURITANIA
MAVOURNEEN
MAXIMALIST
MAXIMILIAN
MAYONNAISE
NAPTHALENE
NARCISSISM
NARCOLEPSY
NARROWBOAT
NARROWDALE
NARROWNESS
NASTURTIUM
NATATORIAL
NATATORIUM
NATHELESSE
NATIONALLY
NATIONWIDE
NATTERJACK
NATURALISM
NATURALIST
NATURALIZE
NATUROPATH
NAUSEATING
NAUSEATIVE
NAVIGATION
PACIFICISM
PADAREWSKI
PADDINGTON
PADDYMELON
PAEDIATRIC
PAGINATION
PAINKILLER
PAINLESSLY
PAINTBRUSH
PALAEOTYPE
PALAESTRAL
PALAGONITE
PALATALISE
PALATINATE
PALESTRINA
PALFRENIER
PALIMPSEST
PALINDROME
PALISANDER
PALLBEARER
PALLIATIVE
PALMATIFID
PALMATOZOA
PALMERSTON
PALMERWORM
PALUDAMENT
PALUSTRINE
PANAMANIAN
PANARITIUM
PANCRATIUM
PANJANDRUM
PANNICULUS
PANOPTICON
PANSOPHIST
PANTAGRUEL
PANTALOONS
PANTOGRAPH
PANTOSCOPE
PAPAVERINE
PAPERCHASE
PAPERKNIFE
PAPIAMENTO
PARACELSUS
PARADIDDLE
PARADOXIDE
PARADOXINE
PARAENESIS
PARAGLOSSA
PARAGONITE
PARAGUAYAN
PARALLELED
PARAMARIBO
PARAMETRIC
PARANORMAL
PARAPHILIA
PARAPHONIA
PARAPHRASE
PARAPHYSIS
PARAPLEGIA
PARAPLEGIC
PARAPRAXIS
PARARTHRIA
PARASCENIA
PARASELENE
PARASTATAL
PARATROOPS
PARDONABLE
PARDONABLY
PARENCHYMA
PARENTHOOD
PARENTLESS
PARGETTING
PARISCHANE
PARISIENNE
PARKLEAVES
PARLIAMENT
PARMACITIE
PARNASSIAN
PARNELLISM
PARONYCHIA
PARRAMATTA
PARTHENOPE
PARTIALITY
PARTICIPLE
PARTICULAR
PARTINGALE
PASIGRAPHY
PASQUINADE
PASSAGEWAY
PASSAMEZZO
PASSIONATE
PASTEBOARD
PASTEURISE
PASTEURIZE
PASTORELLA
PATAGONIAN
PATAVINITY
PATCHCOCKE
PATCHINESS
PATERNALLY
PATHFINDER
PATHOGENIC
PATIBULARY
PATISSERIE
PATRIARCHY
PATRIOTISM
PATRONISED
PATRONYMIC
PAWNBROKER
RABBINICAL
RACECOURSE
RADICALISM
RADIOGRAPH
RADIOLARIA
RAGAMUFFIN
RAILWAYMAN
RAIYATWARI
RAJPRAMUKH
RAMPALLIAN
RAMSHACKLE
RANDLETREE
RANDOMNESS
RANNELTREE
RANNLETREE
RANTLETREE
RANUNCULUS
RAPPORTEUR
RATIONALLY
RATTLETRAP
RAVENOUSLY
RAVENSBILL
RAVENSDUCK
RAVENSTONE
RAWINSONDE
RAWSTHORNE
RAZZMATAZZ
SABBATICAL
SABRETACHE
SACCHARASE
SACCHARIDE
SACCHARINE
SACCHAROID
SACERDOTAL
SACREDNESS
SACROSANCT
SADDLEBACK
SADDLEBILL
SAGITTARIA
SALAMANDER
SALESWOMAN
SALICORNIA
SALIVATION
SALLENDERS
SALMAGUNDI
SALMANAZAR
SALMONELLA
SALOPETTES
SALPINGIAN
SALTARELLO
SALTIGRADE
SALUBRIOUS
SALUTATION
SAMARSKITE
SAMOTHRACE
SANATORIUM
SANCTIFIED
SANCTITIES
SANCTITUDE
SANDALWOOD
SANDEMANIA
SANDERLING
SANDGROPER
SANDINISTA
SANDWICHES

SANFORISED
SANGUINARY
SANITARIUM
SANITATION
SANNAYASIN
SAPPERMENT
SAPROPHYTE
SARCOCOLLA
SARCOLEMMA
SARMENTOUS
SARSQUATCH
SATISFYING
SATURATION
SATURNALIA
SATYAGRAHA
SAUERKRAUT
SAUROPSIDA
SAVAGENESS
SAVONAROLA
SAXICOLINE
SAXICOLOUS
TABERNACLE
TABLANETTE
TABLECLOTH
TABLESPOON
TABULATION
TACHOGRAPH
TACHOMETER
TACTICALLY
TACTLESSLY
TAGLIARINI
TAILGATING
TAILORMADE
TALEBEARER
TALLEYRAND
TAMBERLANE
TAMBOURINE
TAMPERFOOT
TANAGRIDAE
TANGANYIKA
TANGENTIAL
TANGLEFOOT
TANNHAUSER
TANTAMOUNT
TAPDANCING
TAPERECORD
TAPOTEMENT
TARADIDDLE
TARANTELLA
TARDIGRADE
TARPAULING
TARTRAZINE
TASKMASTER
TASTEFULLY
TATPURUSHA
TATTERSALL
TAXONOMIST
VALENTINES
VALIDATION
VALLADOLID
VANDERBILT
VARICOSITY
VARIEGATED
VARNISHING
VAUDEVILLE
WAGEEARNER
WAINSCOTED
WALDENSIAN
WALLACHIAN
WALLFLOWER
WAMPUMPEAG
WANCHANCIE
WANDERINGS
WANDERLUST
WANDSWORTH
WANTHRIVEN
WAPENSCHAW
WAPINSCHAW
WAPPENSHAW
WARRANDICE
WASHINGTON
WASSAILING
WASSERMANS
WASTEFULLY
WASTEPAPER
WATCHFULLY
WATCHMAKER
WATCHTOWER
WATERBORNE
WATERBRASH
WATERCOLOR
WATERCRESS
WATERFRONT
WATERLEVEL
WATERMELON
WATERPROOF
WATERSKIER
WATERSPOUT
WATERTIGHT
WATERWHEEL
WATERWINGS
WATERWORKS
WATTLEWORK
WAVELENGTH
YAFFINGALE
YARBOROUGH
ZABAGLIONE
ZAPOROGIAN
ABBREVIATE
ABDICATION
ABERDEVINE
ABERGLAUBE
ABERRATION
ABHIDHAMMA
ABHORRENCE
ABITURIENT
ABNORMALLY
ABOMINABLE
ABOMINABLY
ABONNEMENT
ABORIGINAL
ABOVEBOARD
ABRIDGMENT
ABROGATION
ABRUPTNESS
ABSCISSION
ABSOLUTELY
ABSOLUTION
ABSOLUTISM
ABSORPTION
ABSTEMIOUS
ABSTENTION
ABSTINENCE
ABSTRACTED
ABUNDANTLY
ABYSSINIAN
EBOULEMENT
EBRACTEATE
EBULLIENCE
OBEDIENTLY
OBFUSCATED
OBJECTLESS
OBLIGATION
OBLIGATORY
OBLIGINGLY
OBLITERATE
OBLOMOVISM
OBSEQUIOUS
OBSERVABLE
OBSERVANCE
OBSIDIONAL
OBSTETRICS
OBTAINABLE
OBTUSENESS
SBUDDIKINS
UBERMENSCH
UBIQUITOUS
ACANACEOUS
ACCELERATE
ACCENTUATE
ACCESSIBLE
ACCESSIONS
ACCIDENTAL
ACCLIVIOUS
ACCOMPLICE
ACCOMPLISH
ACCORDANCE
ACCOUNTANT
ACCOUNTING
ACCREDITED
ACCUBATION
ACCUMULATE
ACCURATELY
ACCUSATION
ACCUSATIVE
ACCUSINGLY
ACCUSTOMED
ACEPHALOUS
ACETABULAR
ACETABULUM
ACHITOPHEL
ACHROMATIC
ACOLOUTHOS
ACOTYLEDON
ACQUAINTED
ACROAMATIC
ACROBATICS
ACROGENOUS
ACROMEGALY
ACRONYCHAL
ACROTERION
ACTIONABLE
ACTIVITIST
ECARDINATE
ECCHYMOSIS
ECCOPROTIC
ECHINODERM
ECHINOIDEA
ECHOPRAXIA
ECOLOGICAL
ECONOMICAL
ECTHLIPSIS
ECUADORIAN
ECUMENICAL
ICEBREAKER
ICHTHYOSIS
ICONOCLAST
ICONOSCOPE
ICOSANDRIA
ICOSOHEDRA
OCCASIONAL
OCCIDENTAL
OCCUPATION
OCCURRENCE
OCEANGOING
OCHLOCRACY
OCTAHEDRON
OCTODECIMO
SCAMMOZZIS
SCANDALISE
SCANDALIZE
SCANDALOUS
SCANDAROON
SCANDERBEG
SCANTINESS
SCAPEGRACE
SCAPHOPODA
SCARAMOUCH
SCARCEMENT
SCARCENESS
SCARLATINA
SCARLETINA
SCATHELESS
SCATTERING
SCATURIENT
SCEPTICISM
SCHALSTEIN
SCHIPPERKE
SCHISMATIC
SCHLIMAZEL
SCHOLAEMIA
SCHOLASTIC
SCHOOLBOOK
SCHOOLGIRL
SCHOOLMAAM
SCHWARZLOT
SCIENTIFIC
SCLERIASIS
SCOFFINGLY
SCOMBRESOX
SCOOTERIST
SCOPELIDAE
SCORDATURA
SCOREBOARD
SCORNFULLY
SCORZONERA
SCOTODINIA
SCOTSWOMAN
SCREECHING
SCREENPLAY
SCRIBBLING
SCRIMSHANK
SCRIPTURAL
SCRIPTURES
SCROUNGING
SCRUPULOUS
SCRUTINEER
SCRUTINISE
SCRUTINIZE
SCULPTRESS
SCURRILITY
SCURRILOUS
SCUTELLATE
TCHOUKBALL
ADAMANTINE
ADAPTATION
ADDITAMENT
ADDITIONAL
ADELANTADO
ADEQUATELY
ADHIBITION
ADIAPHORON
ADJECTIVAL
ADJUDICATE
ADJUSTABLE
ADJUSTMENT
ADMINISTER
ADMIRATION
ADMIRINGLY
ADMISSIBLE
ADMITTANCE
ADMITTEDLY
ADMONITION
ADOLESCENT
ADRAMELECH
ADRENALINE
ADULLAMITE
ADULTERANT
ADULTERATE
ADULTERESS

ADULTERINE
ADULTEROUS
ADVENTURER
ADVERSARIA
ADVERTISER
EDULCORATE
IDEALISTIC
NDRANGHETA
ODDFELLOWS
ODELSTHING
ODIOUSNESS
ODONTALGIA
ODONTOLITE
ODONTOLOGY
SDRUCCIOLA
AERENCHYMA
AEROBATICS
AEROPHAGIA
AERUGINOUS
AESTHETICS
BEARGARDEN
BEAUJOLAIS
BEAUTICIAN
BEAUTIFIER
BEAVERSKIN
BEDCHAMBER
BEDCLOTHES
BEDEVILLED
BEDRAGGLED
BEEFBURGER
BEEFEATERS
BEEKEEPING
BEFOREHAND
BEHAVIORAL
BEHINDHAND
BELARUSIAN
BELIEVABLE
BELLADONNA
BELLAMOURE
BELLARMINE
BELLWETHER
BELONGINGS
BELSHAZZAR
BENEDICITE
BENEFACTOR
BENEFICENT
BENEFICIAL
BENEVOLENT
BENTHAMITE
BENZEDRINE
BERMOOTHES
BERNARDINE
BERSAGLIER
BESTIALITY
BESTSELLER
BETACRUCIS
BETELGEUSE
BETELGEUZE
BEWILDERED
BEWITCHING
CECIDOMYIA
CELEBRATED
CELESTIALS
CELLOPHANE
CELLULITIS
CENSORIOUS
CENSORSHIP
CENTENNIAL
CENTESIMAL
CENTIGRADE
CENTILITER
CENTILITRE
CENTIMETER
CENTIMETRE
CENTRALIZE
CENTRIFUGE
CENTROSOME
CEPHALOPOD
CEREBELLUM
CEREMONIAL
CEREMONIES
CERTIORARI
CESTRACION
DEACTIVATE
DEADLINESS
DEADNETTLE
DEALERSHIP
DEBASEMENT
DEBATEMENT
DEBAUCHERY
DEBILITATE
DEBOUCHURE
DEBRIEFING
DECAGRAMME
DECAHEDRON
DECAMPMENT
DECAPITATE
DECATHLETE
DECELERATE
DECENNOVAL
DECIMALIZE
DECIPHERED
DECISIVELY
DECLENSION
DECOLLATOR
DECOLORATE
DECOMPOSED
DECORATION
DECORATIVE
DECRESCENT
DEDICATION
DEDUCTIBLE
DEEPFREEZE
DEEPSEATED
DEFACEMENT
DEFAMATION
DEFAMATORY
DEFEASANCE
DEFECATION
DEFENSIBLE
DEFICIENCY
DEFILEMENT
DEFINITELY
DEFINITION
DEFINITIVE
DEFLAGRATE
DEFLECTION
DEFRAYMENT
DEGENERACY
DEGENERATE
DEGRADABLE
DEHISCENCE
DEJECTEDLY
DELCREDERE
DELECTABLE
DELEGATION
DELIBERATE
DELICATELY
DELIGATION
DELIGHTFUL
DELINQUENT
DELIRATION
DELPHINIUM
DELTIOLOGY
DEMOBILISE
DEMOBILIZE
DEMOCRATIC
DEMOCRITUS
DEMOGORGON
DEMOGRAPHY
DEMOISELLE
DEMOLITION
DEMONIACAL
DEMORALISE
DEMORALIZE
DENDROPHIS
DENOUEMENT
DENTIFRICE
DEPARTMENT
DEPARTURES
DEPENDABLE
DEPENDENCE
DEPENDENCY
DEPILATORY
DEPLORABLE
DEPLORABLY
DEPLOYMENT
DEPOPULATE
DEPORTMENT
DEPOSITARY
DEPOSITION
DEPOSITORY
DEPRECIATE
DEPRESSANT
DEPRESSING
DEPRESSION
DEPRESSIVE
DEPUTATION
DERACINATE
DERAILLEUR
DERAILMENT
DEREGULATE
DERIVATION
DERIVATIVE
DERMATITIS
DEROGATORY
DESALINATE
DESBOROUGH
DESCENDANT
DESCENDING
DESCRIBING
DESECRATED
DESERVEDLY
DESICCATED
DESIDERATA
DESOLATION
DESPAIRING
DESPICABLE
DESPITEOUS
DESPONDENT
DESQUAMATE
DESSIATINE
DESSYATINE
DETACHABLE
DETACHMENT
DETAINMENT
DETECTABLE
DETERMINED
DETERRENCE
DETESTABLE
DETONATION
DETRACTION
DETRUNCATE
DEUTOPLASM
DEVANAGARI
DEVASTATED
DEVASTAVIT
DEVELOPING
DEVOLUTION
DEVOTEMENT
DEVOTIONAL
FEARLESSLY
FEARNOUGHT
FEATHERBED
FEDERALISM
FEDERALIST
FEDERATION
FEEBLENESS
FELICITATE
FELICITOUS
FELLOWSHIP
FEMININITY
FENESTELLA
FERNITICLE
FERRANDINE
FERTILISED
FERTILISER
FERTILIZER
FESCENNINE
FETTERLOCK
FETTUCCINE
FEUILLETON
FEVERISHLY
GELATINOUS
GEMINATION
GENERALISE
GENERALITY
GENERALIZE
GENERATION
GENERATRIX
GENEROSITY
GENEROUSLY
GENETHLIAC
GENEVRETTE
GENICULATE
GENTLEFOLK
GENTLENESS
GEOCENTRIC
GEOGRAPHER
GEOGRAPHIC
GEOLOGICAL
GEOPHYSICS
GEORGETOWN
GEOTHERMAL
GEOTROPISM
GERIATRICS
GERMICIDAL
GESUNDHEIT
GETHSEMANE
GETTYSBURG
GETUPANDGO
HEADHUNTED
HEADHUNTER
HEADLIGHTS
HEADMASTER
HEADPHONES
HEADSTRONG
HEARTBREAK
HEARTINESS
HEAVENWARD
HECTICALLY
HECTOLITRE
HEDONISTIC
HEEDLESSLY
HEIDELBERG
HELICOPTER
HELIOGRAPH
HELIOLATER
HELIOTROPE
HELLBENDER
HELLESPONT
HELPLESSLY
HEMICHORDA
HEMIHEDRON
HEMIPLEGIA
HEMISPHERE
HEMOGLOBIN
HEMOPHILIA
HEMORRHAGE
HENCEFORTH

HENDECAGON
HEPATOCELE
HEPTAGONAL
HEPTAMERON
HEPTATEUCH
HEPTATHLON
HERBACEOUS
HEREABOUTS
HEREDITARY
HERESIARCH
HEROICALLY
HESITANTLY
HESITATION
HESPERIDES
HETERODOXY
JEISTIECOR
JEOPARDISE
JEOPARDIZE
JERRYBUILT
KEMPERYMAN
KENILWORTH
KENSPECKLE
KENTUCKIAN
KERSEYMERE
KESSELRING
KETTLEDRUM
KEYBOARDER
LEADERSHIP
LEAFHOPPER
LEAMINGTON
LEBENSRAUM
LEDERHOSEN
LEFTHANDED
LEFTHANDER
LEFTWINGER
LEGALISTIC
LEGIBILITY
LEGISLATOR
LEGITIMACY
LEGITIMATE
LEGITIMIZE
LEGUMINOUS
LEGWARMERS
LEMNISCATE
LENGTHWAYS
LENGTHWISE
LENOCINIUM
LENTICULAR
LENTIGINES
LEONTIASIS
LEOPARDESS
LEPRECHAUN
LESBIANISM
LETTERHEAD
LEUCHAEMIA
LEVITATION
MEADOWPLAN
MEAGERNESS
MEAGRENESS
MEANDERING
MEANINGFUL
MEASURABLE
MECHANICAL
MECHANIZED
MEDDLESOME
MEDICAMENT
MEDICATION
MEDIOCRITY
MEDITATION
MEDITATIVE
MEDIUMTERM
MEERSCHAUM
MEGALITHIC
MEGALOSAUR
MELACONITE
MELANCHOLY
MELANESIAN
MELLOWNESS
MELOCOTOON
MEMBERSHIP
MEMBRANOUS
MEMORANDUM
MENACINGLY
MENDACIOUS
MENECHMIAN
MENINGITIS
MENORRHOEA
MENSTRUATE
MEPERIDINE
MERCANTILE
MERCIFULLY
MERRYMAKER
MESENTERON
MESITYLENE
MESOLITHIC
METABOLISE
METABOLISM
METACARPAL
METACARPUS
METACENTRE
METALEPSIS
METALLURGY
METAPHRASE
METAPLASIS
METASTABLE
METATARSAL
METATARSUS
METATHERIA
METATHESIS
METHEDRINE
METHODICAL
METHOMANIA
METHUSALEH
METHUSELAH
METHYLATED
METICULOUS
METROPOLIS
METTLESOME
NEAPOLITAN
NECROMANCY
NECROPOLIS
NECTABANUS
NEEDLECASE
NEEDLEWORK
NEFANDROUS
NEGATIVELY
NEGLECTFUL
NEGLIGENCE
NEGLIGIBLE
NEGOTIABLE
NEGOTIATOR
NEIGHBORLY
NEMATOCYST
NEOTERICAL
NESSELRODE
NETHERMOST
NETTLERASH
NETTLETREE
NETWORKING
NEURILEMMA
NEUROLEMMA
NEUTRALISE
NEUTRALITY
NEUTRALIZE
NEUTROPHIL
NEWFANGLED
NEWSAGENTS
NEWSCASTER
NEWSLETTER
NEWSMONGER
NEWSPAPERS
NEWSREADER
NEWSWORTHY
OESOPHAGUS
PEACEFULLY
PEACEMAKER
PEACHERINO
PEASHOOTER
PEAUDESOIE
PECCADILLO
PECULATION
PECULIARLY
PEDESTRIAN
PEDIATRICS
PEDICULATE
PEDIMENTAL
PEDIPALPUS
PEELGARLIC
PEJORATIVE
PENELOPHON
PENETRABLE
PENETRALIA
PENICILLIN
PENINSULAR
PENNILLION
PENNISETUM
PENSIEROSO
PENSIONNAT
PENTAGONAL
PENTAMERON
PENTAMETER
PENTATEUCH
PENTATHLON
PENTATONIC
PENTELIKON
PENTETERIC
PENTIMENTO
PENTSTEMON
PEPPERCORN
PEPPERMILL
PEPPERMINT
PEPPERWORT
PERCENTAGE
PERCENTILE
PERCEPTION
PERCEPTIVE
PERCIPIENT
PERCOLATOR
PERCUSSION
PERDENDOSI
PERDITIOUS
PERDURABLE
PEREMPTORY
PERFECTION
PERFICIENT
PERFIDIOUS
PERFORATED
PERFORATOR
PERFORMING
PERIDOTITE
PERIEGESIS
PERIHELION
PERILOUSLY
PERIODICAL
PERIPHERAL
PERISHABLE
PERIWINKLE
PERMAFROST
PERMANENCE
PERMANENCY
PERMEATION
PERMISSION
PERMISSIVE
PERNICIOUS
PERNICKETY
PERORATION
PEROVSKITE
PERPETRATE
PERPETUATE
PERPETUITY
PERPLEXING
PERPLEXITY
PERQUISITE
PERSECUTOR
PERSEPHONE
PERSEPOLIS
PERSICARIA
PERSIENNES
PERSIFLAGE
PERSISTENT
PERSONABLE
PERSONALLY
PERSTRINGE
PERSUADING
PERSUASION
PERSUASIVE
PERTINENCE
PERVERSELY
PERVERSION
PERVERSITY
PESCADORES
PESTALOZZI
PESTILENCE
PETITIONER
PETRARCHAN
PETRIFYING
PETRISSAGE
PETROGLYPH
PETRONELLA
PETTICHAPS
PETTYCHAPS
PETULANTLY
REACTIVATE
READERSHIP
REAMINGBIT
REAPPRAISE
REARMAMENT
REASONABLE
REASONABLY
REASSEMBLE
REASSURING
REBELLIOUS
RECEPTACLE
RECIDIVISM
RECIDIVIST
RECIPROCAL
RECITATION
RECITATIVE
RECITATIVO
RECKLESSLY
RECOGNISED
RECOGNIZED
RECOMMENCE
RECOMPENSE
RECONCILED
RECONSIDER
RECREATION
RECRUDESCE
RECUPERATE
RECURRENCE
REDCURRANT
REDECORATE
REDEMPTION
REDISCOVER
REDRUTHITE
REDUNDANCY
REELECTION
REFERENDUM
REFINEMENT
REFLECTING

REFLECTION
REFLECTIVE
REFRACTION
REFRACTIVE
REFRACTORY
REFRESHING
REFUTATION
REGARDLESS
REGENERATE
REGIMENTAL
REGIMENTED
REGISTERED
REGRESSION
REGRESSIVE
REGULARITY
REGULARIZE
REGULATION
REITERATED
REJONEADOR
REJUVENATE
RELATIVELY
RELATIVITY
RELAXATION
RELAXATIVE
RELEGATION
RELENTLESS
RELINQUISH
RELOCATION
RELUCTANCE
REMARKABLE
REMARKABLY
REMITTANCE
REMONETISE
REMORSEFUL
REMOTENESS
REMUNERATE
RENDEZVOUS
RENOVATION
REORGANIZE
REPAIRABLE
REPARATION
REPATRIATE
REPEATABLE
REPEATEDLY
REPENTANCE
REPERTOIRE
REPETITEUR
REPETITION
REPETITIVE
REPORTEDLY
REPOSITORY
REPRESSION
REPRESSIVE
REPRODUCER
REPUBLICAN
REPUGNANCE
REPUTATION
REQUIESCAT
REREDORTER
RESCHEDULE
RESEARCHER
RESEMBLING
RESENTMENT
RESERVISTS
RESIGNEDLY
RESILIENCE
RESISTANCE
RESOLUTELY
RESOLUTION
RESORCINOL
RESOUNDING
RESPECTFUL
RESPECTING
RESPECTIVE
RESPIRATOR
RESPONDENT
RESPONSIVE
RESTAURANT
RESTLESSLY
RESTRAINED
RESTRICTED
RESUMPTION
RESUPINATE
RESURGENCE
RETINALITE
RETIREMENT
RETRACTION
RETRAINING
RETREATING
RETROGRADE
RETROGRESS
RETROSPECT
RETURNABLE
REVELATION
REVENGEFUL
REVERENTLY
REVERSIBLE
REVITALIZE
REVIVALIST
REVOCATION
REVOLUTION
SEAMANSHIP
SEAMSTRESS
SEANNACHIE
SEASONABLE
SEASONABLY
SECONDBEST
SECONDHAND
SECONDMENT
SECONDRATE
SECRETAIRE
SECULARIZE
SECURITIES
SEDATENESS
SEDULOUSLY
SEECATCHIE
SEEMLIHEAD
SEERSUCKER
SEGREGATED
SEGUIDILLA
SEISMOLOGY
SELEGILINE
SELFESTEEM
SELFSTYLED
SELLINGERS
SELTZOGENE
SEMICIRCLE
SEMIQUAVER
SENATORIAL
SENEGALESE
SENESCENCE
SENSUALITY
SENSUOUSLY
SEPARATELY
SEPARATION
SEPARATISM
SEPARATIST
SEPARATRIX
SEPTENNIAL
SEPTUAGINT
SEPULCHRAL
SEQUACIOUS
SEQUENTIAL
SERMONICAL
SERPENTINE
SERRADELLA
SERRADILLA
SERRASALMO
SERVICEMAN
SETTERWORT
SETTLEMENT
SEVENTIETH
SEXAGESIMA
SEXOLOGIST
TECHNETIUM
TECHNICIAN
TECHNOCRAT
TECHNOLOGY
TEDDINGTON
TEENYWEENY
TEETOTALER
TEICHOPSIA
TEINOSCOPE
TELEGRAPHY
TELEOSTOME
TELEPATHIC
TELEPHONIC
TELESCOPIC
TELEVISION
TELPHERAGE
TEMPERANCE
TEMPTATION
TENDERFOOT
TENDERLOIN
TENDERNESS
TENDRILLED
TENEBRIFIC
TENNANTITE
TENRECIDAE
TENTERHOOK
TEPIDARIUM
TERMINABLE
TERMINALIA
TERMINALLY
TERNEPLATE
TERRACOTTA
TERREPLEIN
TERRIFYING
TERTIARIES
TESCHENITE
TESTACEOUS
TESTICULAR
VEGETABLES
VEGETARIAN
VEGETATION
VEHEMENTLY
VELITATION
VELOCIPEDE
VENERATION
VENEZUELAN
VENTILATOR
VERIFIABLE
VERMICELLI
VERMILLION
VERNACULAR
VERNISSAGE
VERSAILLES
VERTEBRATE
VERTICALLY
VESICULATE
VESTIBULUM
VETERINARY
WEAPONLESS
WEATHERMAN
WEEDKILLER
WEIGHTLESS
WEIMARANER
WELLEARNED
WELLINGTON
WELLSPRING
WELSHWOMAN
WENTLETRAP
WESTERNIZE
XENOPHOBIA
XENOPHOBIC
XEROPHYTIC
XEROSTOMIA
YELLOWBACK
YELLOWGIRL
YELLOWJACK
YELLOWROOT
YELLOWWOOD
YESTERWEEK
YESTERYEAR
ZEUGLODONT
DÉSHABILLÉ
AFFABILITY
AFFETTUOSO
AFFILIATED
AFFLICTION
AFFORDABLE
AFICIONADO
AFRICANDER
AFRORMOSIA
AFTERBIRTH
AFTERHOURS
AFTERPIECE
AFTERSHAVE
AFTERSHOCK
AFTERTASTE
AFTERWARDS
EFFACEMENT
EFFECTUATE
EFFEMINACY
EFFEMINATE
EFFERVESCE
EFFICIENCY
EFFLEURAGE
EFFORTLESS
EFFRONTERY
EFFUSIVELY
OFFBALANCE
OFFICIALLY
OFFLICENCE
OFFPUTTING
OFFTHECUFF
OFFTHEWALL
OFTENTIMES
AGAPANTHUS
AGGRANDISE
AGGRESSION
AGGRESSIVE
AGONISTICS
AGRONOMIST
EGOCENTRIC
EGURGITATE
IGNIMBRITE
IGNORANTLY
SGANARELLE
YGGDRASILL
AHITHOPHEL
CHAFFERING
CHAIRWOMAN
CHALCEDONY
CHALLENGER
CHALYBEATE
CHAMAEROPS
CHAMBERPOT
CHAMBERTIN
CHAMBRANLE
CHAMPIGNON
CHANCELLOR
CHANDELIER
CHANGEABLE
CHANGELESS
CHANGELING
CHAPARAJOS
CHAPAREJOS
CHAPFALLEN
CHAPLAINCY

CHAPTALISE
CHARDONNAY
CHARGEABLE
CHARGEHAND
CHARIOTEER
CHARITABLE
CHARITABLY
CHAROLLAIS
CHARTREUSE
CHATELAINE
CHATTERBOX
CHATTERTON
CHAUCERIAN
CHAUDFROID
CHAULMUGRA
CHAUTAUQUA
CHAUVINISM
CHAUVINIST
CHEAPSKATE
CHECKLATON
CHECKPOINT
CHEEKINESS
CHEERFULLY
CHEESECAKE
CHEESEWOOD
CHEIRONOMY
CHELTENHAM
CHEMICALLY
CHEMONASTY
CHEQUEBOOK
CHERIMOYER
CHERRYWOOD
CHERSONESE
CHERVONETS
CHESSBOARD
CHESSYLITE
CHESTERTON
CHEVESAILE
CHEVISANCE
CHEVROTAIN
CHICHESTER
CHICKENPOX
CHIFFCHAFF
CHIFFONIER
CHILDBIRTH
CHILDERMAS
CHILDISHLY
CHILLINESS
CHIMBORAZO
CHIMNEYPOT
CHIMPANZEE
CHINAGRAPH
CHINASTONE
CHINCHILLA
CHINQUAPIN
CHIRICAUNE
CHIROMANCY
CHIRONOMIC
CHIROPTERA
CHITARRONE
CHITTAGONG
CHIVALROUS
CHLORINATE
CHLOROFORM
CHOICELESS
CHOLALOGUE
CHOPSTICKS
CHREMATIST
CHRISTIANA
CHROMOSOME
CHRONICLER
CHRONICLES
CHRONOLOGY
CHRYSIPPUS
CHRYSOLITE
CHUCKWALLA
CHURCHGOER
CHURCHYARD
CHURLISHLY
DHARMSHALA
GHIBELLINE
KHIDMUTGAR
LHERZOLITE
PHAELONIAN
PHAENOTYPE
PHAGEDAENA
PHANTASIME
PHANTASIST
PHARMACIST
PHENOMENAL
PHENOMENON
PHILATELIC
PHILIPPINA
PHILIPPINE
PHILISTINE
PHILLIPINA
PHILLIPINE
PHILLUMENY
PHILOPOENA
PHILOSOPHY
PHILOXENIA
PHLEGETHON
PHLEGMASIA
PHLEGMATIC
PHLOGISTIC
PHLOGISTON
PHLOGOPITE
PHOLIDOSIS
PHONOGRAPH
PHOSPHORUS
PHOTODIODE
PHOTOGENIC
PHOTOGRAPH
PHOTONASTY
PHRENESIAC
PHRENOLOGY
PHYLACTERY
PHYLLIOPOD
PHYSICALLY
PHYSIOCRAT
PHYSIOLOGY
RHAMPASTOS
RHAPSODISE
RHAPSODIZE
RHEOTROPIC
RHETORICAL
RHEUMATICS
RHEUMATISM
RHEUMATOID
RHINEGRAVE
RHINESTONE
RHINOCEROS
RHINOLALIA
RHINOPHYMA
RHIPIPTERA
RHOEADALES
RHYTHMICAL
SHABBINESS
SHACKLETON
SHADOWLESS
SHAGHAIRED
SHAKUHACHI
SHAMEFACED
SHAMEFULLY
SHAMPOOING
SHANDRYDAN
SHANDYGAFF
SHARAWADGI
SHARAWAGGI
SHATTERING
SHEARWATER
SHECKLATON
SHEEPISHLY
SHEEPSHANK
SHELDONIAN
SHELLSHOCK
SHELLYCOAT
SHENANIGAN
SHERARDISE
SHIBBOLETH
SHIELDRAKE
SHIFTINESS
SHILLELAGH
SHIMMERING
SHISHKEBAB
SHOCKINGLY
SHOCKPROOF
SHODDINESS
SHOESTRING
SHOPKEEPER
SHOPLIFTER
SHOPSOILED
SHOPWALKER
SHORTBREAD
SHORTENING
SHORTLIVED
SHORTRANGE
SHOVELHEAD
SHOVELNOSE
SHOWJUMPER
SHREWDNESS
SHRIEVALTY
SHRILLNESS
SHRIVELLED
SHROVETIDE
SHUDDERING
THALASSIAN
THALESTRIS
THALICTRUM
THALLIFORM
THANKFULLY
THAUMASITE
THEATRICAL
THELLUSSON
THEMSELVES
THEOCRITUS
THEODOLITE
THEOLOGATE
THEOLOGIAN
THEOLOGISE
THEOLOGIST
THEREAFTER
THEREANENT
THERMIONIC
THERMISTOR
THERMOSTAT
THICKENING
THIMBLEFUL
THIMBLEWIT
THINGUMBOB
THIRTEENTH
THIXOTROPY
THOROUGHLY
THOUGHTFUL
THOUSANDTH
THREADBARE
THREADLIKE
THREADWORM
THREATENED
THREEPENCE
THREEPENNY
THREESCORE
THRENODIAL
THROMBOSIS
THROUGHOUT
THROUGHPUT
THROUGHWAY
THUCYDIDES
THUMBIKINS
THUMBSCREW
THUNDERBOX
THUNDERING
THUNDEROUS
WHARFINGER
WHATSOEVER
WHEATSHEAF
WHEATSTONE
WHEELCHAIR
WHEELHOUSE
WHEEZINESS
WHEWELLITE
WHIGGAMORE
WHILLYWHAW
WHIRLYBIRD
WHISPERING
WHITEHEART
WHITETHORN
WHITEWATER
WHITSTABLE
WHITTERICK
WHOLESALER
WHOLEWHEAT
AIRFREIGHT
BIANNUALLY
BICHROMATE
BIENNIALLY
BIJOUTERIE
BILIVERDIN
BINOCULARS
BIOCHEMIST
BIOGRAPHER
BIOLOGICAL
BIOPHYSICS
BIORHYTHMS
BIPARTISAN
BIPINNARIA
BIRKENHEAD
BIRMINGHAM
BIRTHPLACE
BIRTHRIGHT
BISSEXTILE
BITTERLING
BITTERNESS
BITUMINOUS
CINDERELLA
CINECAMERA
CINQUEFOIL
CIRCASSIAN
CIRCUITOUS
CIRCUMCISE
CIRCUMFLEX
CIRCUMFUSE
CIRCUMVENT
CIRRHOPODA
CIRRIPEDEA
CIRRIPEDIA
CISLEITHAN
CISPONTINE
CISTERCIAN
CITRONELLA
DIABOLICAL
DIACAUSTIC
DIACONICON
DIAGENESIS
DIAGNOSTIC
DIAGONALLY
DIALECTICS
DIAPEDESIS
DIAPHANOUS
DIASKEUAST

DIASTALTIC
DICHROMISM
DICKCISSEL
DICTIONARY
DICTOGRAPH
DICYNODONT
DIDASCALIC
DIDGERIDOO
DIDUNCULUS
DIELECTRIC
DIFFERENCE
DIFFICULTY
DIFFIDENCE
DIGESTIBLE
DIGITORIUM
DIGRESSION
DILAPIDATE
DILATATION
DILETTANTE
DILIGENTLY
DIMINISHED
DIMINUENDO
DIMINUTION
DIMINUTIVE
DINANDERIE
DINNERTIME
DIOPHANTOS
DIPHTHERIA
DIPLODOCUS
DIPLOMATIC
DIPSOMANIA
DIRECTIONS
DIRECTNESS
DIRECTOIRE
DIREMPTION
DISABILITY
DISAPPOINT
DISAPPROVE
DISARRANGE
DISASTROUS
DISBELIEVE
DISBURTHEN
DISCERNING
DISCIPLINE
DISCLAIMER
DISCLOSURE
DISCOBOLUS
DISCOLORED
DISCOMFORT
DISCOMMODE
DISCOMPOSE
DISCONCERT
DISCONNECT
DISCONTENT
DISCOPHORA
DISCORDANT
DISCOURAGE
DISCOVERER
DISCREETLY
DISCREPANT
DISCRETION
DISCURSIVE
DISCUSSING
DISCUSSION
DISDAINFUL
DISEMBOGUE
DISEMBOWEL
DISENCHANT
DISENGAGED
DISENNOBLE
DISFIGURED
DISGRUNTLE
DISGUSTING
DISHABILLE
DISHARMONY
DISHEARTEN
DISHONESTY
DISHWASHER
DISINCLINE
DISINHERIT
DISJOINTED
DISLOYALTY
DISMANTLED
DISMISSIVE
DISORDERED
DISORDERLY
DISPENSARY
DISPENSING
DISPERSION
DISPIRITED
DISPOSABLE
DISPOSSESS
DISPUTABLE
DISQUALIFY
DISQUIETED
DISRESPECT
DISRUPTION
DISRUPTIVE
DISSECTION
DISSELBOOM
DISSEMBLER
DISSENSION
DISSENTING
DISSERTATE
DISSERVICE
DISSIDENCE
DISSILIENT
DISSIMILAR
DISSIPATED
DISSOCIATE
DISSOLVENT
DISSONANCE
DISSUASION
DISTENSION
DISTILLATE
DISTILLERY
DISTILLING
DISTINCTLY
DISTORTION
DISTRACTED
DISTRAUGHT
DISTRESSED
DISTRIBUTE
DISTRINGAS
DISTURBING
DITHIONATE
DIURNALIST
DIVERGENCE
DIVINATION
DIVISIONAL
EIGHTEENTH
EISTEDDFOD
FIANCHETTO
FIBERGLASS
FIBREGLASS
FIBRILLATE
FIBROSITIS
FICKLENESS
FICTITIOUS
FIDDLEWOOD
FIELDMOUSE
FIENDISHLY
FIERCENESS
FIGURATION
FIGURATIVE
FIGUREHEAD
FILIBUSTER
FILLIBRUSH
FILTHINESS
FILTRATION
FINGERLING
FINGERNAIL
FINISTERRE
FIREWALKER
FIREWARDEN
FIRTHSOKEN
FISHMONGER
FISHSELLER
FISTICUFFS
FITZGERALD
GIBBERELLA
GILBERTIAN
GILBERTINE
GILLRAVAGE
GINGERBEER
GINGERSNAP
GINGIVITIS
GIRDLERINK
GIRLFRIEND
HIERARCHIC
HIEROGLYPH
HIEROMANCY
HIEROPHANT
HIEROSCOPY
HIGHBINDER
HIGHFLYING
HIGHHANDED
HIGHLANDER
HIGHWAYMAN
HILDEBRAND
HINDENBURG
HINDUSTANI
HINTERLAND
HIPPARCHUS
HIPPOCRENE
HIPPODROME
HIPPOGRIFF
HIPPOGRYPH
HIPPOMANES
HISTORICAL
HISTRIONIC
HITCHHIKER
HITHERWARD
HITOPADESA
HITOPODESA
JIGGAMAREE
JINGOISTIC
KIDNAPPING
KIESELGUHR
KILMARNOCK
KILOMETRES
KIMBERLITE
KINCHINLAY
KINDLINESS
KINGFISHER
LIBERALISM
LIBERALITY
LIBERALIZE
LIBERATION
LIBIDINOUS
LIBRETTIST
LIBREVILLE
LICENTIATE
LICENTIOUS
LIEBERMANN
LIEUTENANT
LIGHTERMAN
LIGHTHOUSE
LIGHTINGUP
LIGNOCAINE
LIKELIHOOD
LIKEMINDED
LILYWHITES
LIMBERNECK
LIMBURGITE
LIMITATION
LIMITROPHE
LINEAMENTS
LINEOMYCIN
LINGUISTIC
LINGULELLA
LIPIZZANER
LIQUESCENT
LIQUIDATOR
LIQUIDIZER
LISTLESSLY
LITERATURE
LITHISTADA
LITHOGRAPH
LITHOMARGE
LITHOPHANE
LITHUANIAN
LITIGATION
LITTLENESS
LITURGICAL
LIVELIHOOD
LIVELINESS
LIVERWURST
MICHAELMAS
MICROFICHE
MICROLIGHT
MICROMETER
MICRONESIA
MICROPHONE
MICROSCOPE
MIDLOTHIAN
MIDSHIPMAN
MIGHTINESS
MIGNONETTE
MILEOMETER
MILITARISM
MILITARIST
MILITIAMAN
MILLEFIORI
MILLIMETER
MILLIMETRE
MIMEOGRAPH
MINDERERUS
MINERALOGY
MINESTRONE
MINEWORKER
MINIMALIST
MINIMARKET
MINISTRATE
MINUTEBOOK
MINUTENESS
MIRACULOUS
MISCELLANY
MISCHMETAL
MISCONDUCT
MISERICORD
MISFORTUNE
MISGIVINGS
MISHGUGGLE
MISHNAYOTH
MISLEADING
MISMATCHED
MISOCAPNIC
MISOGYNIST
MISPRISION
MISSIONARY
MISTAKENLY
MITHRIDATE
MITIGATING
MITIGATION
MIZZENMAST
NICARAGUAN
NICROSILAL
NIDDERLING
NIGGERHEAD

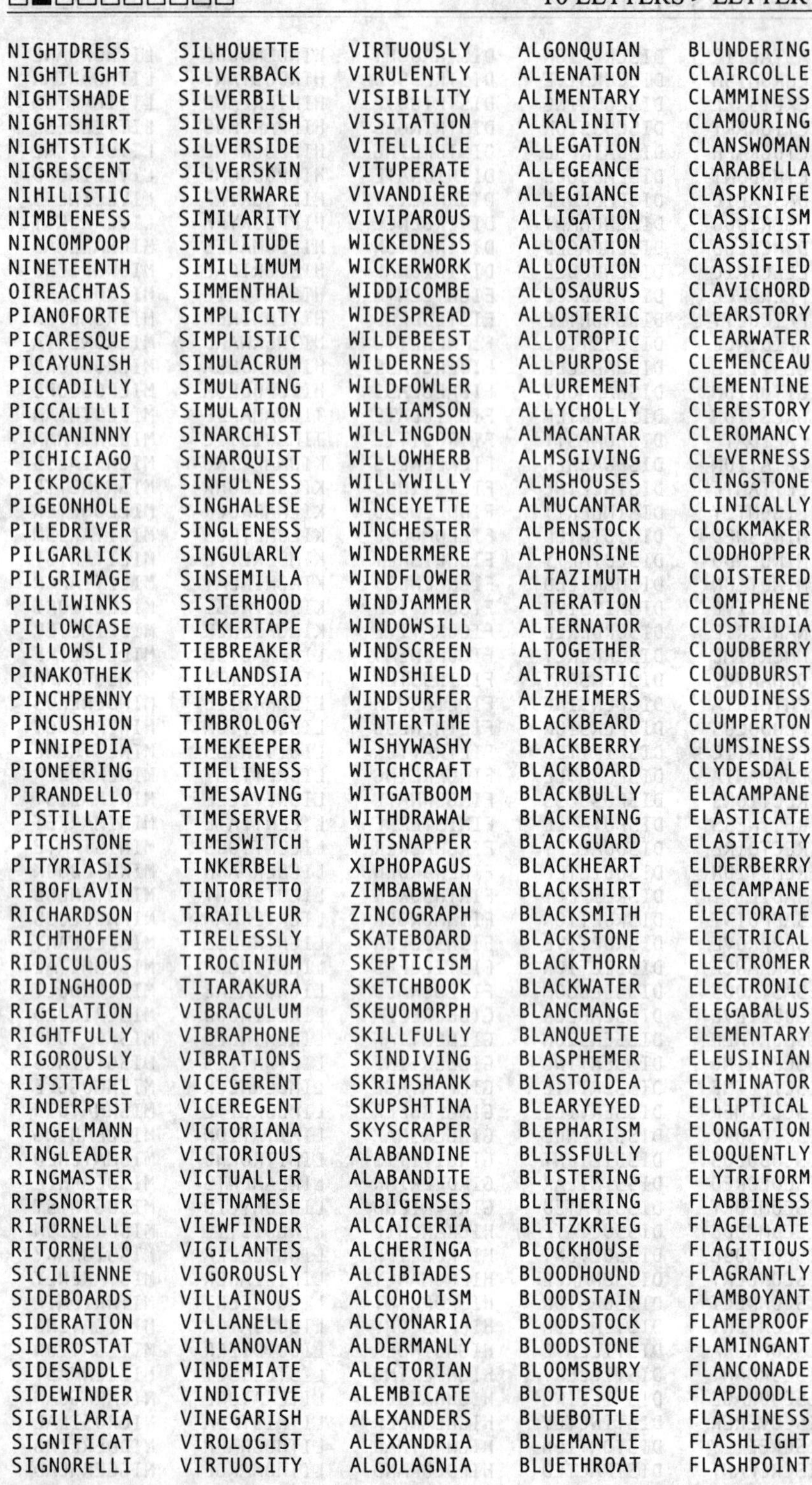

NIGHTDRESS
NIGHTLIGHT
NIGHTSHADE
NIGHTSHIRT
NIGHTSTICK
NIGRESCENT
NIHILISTIC
NIMBLENESS
NINCOMPOOP
NINETEENTH
OIREACHTAS
PIANOFORTE
PICARESQUE
PICAYUNISH
PICCADILLY
PICCALILLI
PICCANINNY
PICHICIAGO
PICKPOCKET
PIGEONHOLE
PILEDRIVER
PILGARLICK
PILGRIMAGE
PILLIWINKS
PILLOWCASE
PILLOWSLIP
PINAKOTHEK
PINCHPENNY
PINCUSHION
PINNIPEDIA
PIONEERING
PIRANDELLO
PISTILLATE
PITCHSTONE
PITYRIASIS
RIBOFLAVIN
RICHARDSON
RICHTHOFEN
RIDICULOUS
RIDINGHOOD
RIGELATION
RIGHTFULLY
RIGOROUSLY
RIJSTTAFEL
RINDERPEST
RINGELMANN
RINGLEADER
RINGMASTER
RIPSNORTER
RITORNELLE
RITORNELLO
SICILIENNE
SIDEBOARDS
SIDERATION
SIDEROSTAT
SIDESADDLE
SIDEWINDER
SIGILLARIA
SIGNIFICAT
SIGNORELLI
SILHOUETTE
SILVERBACK
SILVERBILL
SILVERFISH
SILVERSIDE
SILVERSKIN
SILVERWARE
SIMILARITY
SIMILITUDE
SIMILLIMUM
SIMMENTHAL
SIMPLICITY
SIMPLISTIC
SIMULACRUM
SIMULATING
SIMULATION
SINARCHIST
SINARQUIST
SINFULNESS
SINGHALESE
SINGLENESS
SINGULARLY
SINSEMILLA
SISTERHOOD
TICKERTAPE
TIEBREAKER
TILLANDSIA
TIMBERYARD
TIMBROLOGY
TIMEKEEPER
TIMELINESS
TIMESAVING
TIMESERVER
TIMESWITCH
TINKERBELL
TINTORETTO
TIRAILLEUR
TIRELESSLY
TIROCINIUM
TITARAKURA
VIBRACULUM
VIBRAPHONE
VIBRATIONS
VICEGERENT
VICEREGENT
VICTORIANA
VICTORIOUS
VICTUALLER
VIETNAMESE
VIEWFINDER
VIGILANTES
VIGOROUSLY
VILLAINOUS
VILLANELLE
VILLANOVAN
VINDEMIATE
VINDICTIVE
VINEGARISH
VIROLOGIST
VIRTUOSITY
VIRTUOUSLY
VIRULENTLY
VISIBILITY
VISITATION
VITELLICLE
VITUPERATE
VIVANDIÈRE
VIVIPAROUS
WICKEDNESS
WICKERWORK
WIDDICOMBE
WIDESPREAD
WILDEBEEST
WILDERNESS
WILDFOWLER
WILLIAMSON
WILLINGDON
WILLOWHERB
WILLYWILLY
WINCEYETTE
WINCHESTER
WINDERMERE
WINDFLOWER
WINDJAMMER
WINDOWSILL
WINDSCREEN
WINDSHIELD
WINDSURFER
WINTERTIME
WISHYWASHY
WITCHCRAFT
WITGATBOOM
WITHDRAWAL
WITSNAPPER
XIPHOPAGUS
ZIMBABWEAN
ZINCOGRAPH
SKATEBOARD
SKEPTICISM
SKETCHBOOK
SKEUOMORPH
SKILLFULLY
SKINDIVING
SKRIMSHANK
SKUPSHTINA
SKYSCRAPER
ALABANDINE
ALABANDITE
ALBIGENSES
ALCAICERIA
ALCHERINGA
ALCIBIADES
ALCOHOLISM
ALCYONARIA
ALDERMANLY
ALECTORIAN
ALEMBICATE
ALEXANDERS
ALEXANDRIA
ALGOLAGNIA
ALGONQUIAN
ALIENATION
ALIMENTARY
ALKALINITY
ALLEGATION
ALLEGEANCE
ALLEGIANCE
ALLIGATION
ALLOCATION
ALLOCUTION
ALLOSAURUS
ALLOSTERIC
ALLOTROPIC
ALLPURPOSE
ALLUREMENT
ALLYCHOLLY
ALMACANTAR
ALMSGIVING
ALMSHOUSES
ALMUCANTAR
ALPENSTOCK
ALPHONSINE
ALTAZIMUTH
ALTERATION
ALTERNATOR
ALTOGETHER
ALTRUISTIC
ALZHEIMERS
BLACKBEARD
BLACKBERRY
BLACKBOARD
BLACKBULLY
BLACKENING
BLACKGUARD
BLACKHEART
BLACKSHIRT
BLACKSMITH
BLACKSTONE
BLACKTHORN
BLACKWATER
BLANCMANGE
BLANQUETTE
BLASPHEMER
BLASTOIDEA
BLEARYEYED
BLEPHARISM
BLISSFULLY
BLISTERING
BLITHERING
BLITZKRIEG
BLOCKHOUSE
BLOODHOUND
BLOODSTAIN
BLOODSTOCK
BLOODSTONE
BLOOMSBURY
BLOTTESQUE
BLUEBOTTLE
BLUEMANTLE
BLUETHROAT
BLUNDERING
CLAIRCOLLE
CLAMMINESS
CLAMOURING
CLANSWOMAN
CLARABELLA
CLASPKNIFE
CLASSICISM
CLASSICIST
CLASSIFIED
CLAVICHORD
CLEARSTORY
CLEARWATER
CLEMENCEAU
CLEMENTINE
CLERESTORY
CLEROMANCY
CLEVERNESS
CLINGSTONE
CLINICALLY
CLOCKMAKER
CLODHOPPER
CLOISTERED
CLOMIPHENE
CLOSTRIDIA
CLOUDBERRY
CLOUDBURST
CLOUDINESS
CLUMPERTON
CLUMSINESS
CLYDESDALE
ELACAMPANE
ELASTICATE
ELASTICITY
ELDERBERRY
ELECAMPANE
ELECTORATE
ELECTRICAL
ELECTROMER
ELECTRONIC
ELEGABALUS
ELEMENTARY
ELEUSINIAN
ELIMINATOR
ELLIPTICAL
ELONGATION
ELOQUENTLY
ELYTRIFORM
FLABBINESS
FLAGELLATE
FLAGITIOUS
FLAGRANTLY
FLAMBOYANT
FLAMEPROOF
FLAMINGANT
FLANCONADE
FLAPDOODLE
FLASHINESS
FLASHLIGHT
FLASHPOINT

FLATTERING
FLATULENCE
FLAVESCENT
FLAVOURING
FLEETINGLY
FLESHINESS
FLICKERING
FLIGHTLESS
FLIMSINESS
FLINDERSIA
FLIPPANTLY
FLIRTATION
FLOCCULATE
FLOCCULENT
FLOODLIGHT
FLOORBOARD
FLOORCLOTH
FLORENTINE
FLORESCENT
FLORIBUNDA
FLOURISHED
FLOWERBEDS
FLUCTUATER
FLUFFINESS
FLUGELHORN
FLUNKEYDOM
FLUTEMOUTH
FLYCATCHER
GLACIATION
GLAMOURISE
GLASSHOUSE
GLASSINESS
GLAUCONITE
GLEEMAIDEN
GLENDOVEER
GLISTENING
GLITTERAND
GLITTERATI
GLITTERING
GLORIOUSLY
GLOSSINESS
GLOUCESTER
GLUTTONOUS
ILLADVISED
ILLAQUEATE
ILLEGALITY
ILLITERACY
ILLITERATE
ILLUMINATE
ILLUMINATI
ILLUSTRATE
KLANGFARBE
KLEBSIELLA
KLOOTCHMAN
OLEAGINOUS
OLERACEOUS
PLAGIARISE
PLAGIARISM
PLAGIARIST
PLAGIARIZE
PLANCHETTE
PLANOBLAST
PLANTATION
PLASMODESM
PLASTICINE
PLASTICITY
PLATELAYER
PLATINISED
PLATTELAND
PLAYFELLOW
PLAYGROUND
PLAYWRIGHT
PLEASANTLY
PLEASANTRY
PLEBISCITE
PLEONASTIC
PLEROPHORY
PLESIOSAUR
PLEXIMETER
PLIABILITY
PLIOHIPPUS
PLOUGHBOTE
PLOUGHGATE
PLOUGHWISE
PLUMASSIER
PLUNDERING
PLUPERFECT
PLUTOCRACY
SLAMMERKIN
SLANDEROUS
SLATTERNLY
SLEEPINESS
SLEEVELESS
SLIPSTREAM
SLOPPINESS
SLUGGISHLY
SLUMBERING
ULCERATION
ULSTERETTE
ULTIMATELY
ULTRAFICHE
ULTRASONIC
ULTRASOUND
ULTRONEOUS
AMALGAMATE
AMANUENSIS
AMARYLLIDS
AMATEURISH
AMBARVALIA
AMBASSADOR
AMBIVALENT
AMBLYOPSIS
AMBLYSTOMA
AMBOCEPTOR
AMBULACRUM
AMBULATORY
AMELIORATE
AMIABILITY
AMMUNITION
AMPELOPSIS
AMPHIBIOUS
AMPHIBRACH
AMPHICTYON
AMPHIGOURI
AMPHIMACER
AMPHIMIXIS
AMPHINEURA
AMPHITRITE
AMPHITRYON
AMPHOTERIC
AMPLEFORTH
AMPUSSYAND
AMPUTATION
AMRITATTVA
AMYGDALOID
EMACIATION
EMALANGENI
EMANCIPATE
EMARGINATE
EMASCULATE
EMBANKMENT
EMBERGOOSE
EMBITTERED
EMBLEMATIC
EMBLEMENTS
EMBODIMENT
EMBONPOINT
EMBOUCHURE
EMBROIDERY
EMBRYOLOGY
EMENDATION
EMIGRATION
EMMENTALER
EMMETROPIA
EMOLUMENTS
EMPEDOCLES
EMPFINDUNG
EMPLASTRUM
EMPLOYMENT
EMULSIFIER
IMAGINABLE
IMBECILITY
IMBRICATED
IMBROCCATA
IMMACULACY
IMMACULATE
IMMATERIAL
IMMATURITY
IMMEMORIAL
IMMOBILITY
IMMOBILIZE
IMMODERATE
IMMOLATION
IMMORALITY
IMMORTELLE
IMMUNOLOGY
IMPAIRMENT
IMPALPABLE
IMPALUDISM
IMPARLANCE
IMPASSABLE
IMPATIENCE
IMPECCABLE
IMPECCABLY
IMPEDIMENT
IMPENITENT
IMPERATIVE
IMPERSONAL
IMPERVIOUS
IMPLACABLE
IMPLACABLY
IMPLICITLY
IMPOLITELY
IMPORTANCE
IMPOSITION
IMPOSSIBLE
IMPOSSIBLY
IMPOSTHUME
IMPOTENTLY
IMPOVERISH
IMPREGNATE
IMPRESARIO
IMPRESSION
IMPRESSIVE
IMPRIMATUR
IMPROBABLE
IMPROBABLY
IMPROPERLY
IMPROVISED
IMPRUDENCE
IMPUDENTLY
IMPURITIES
IMPUTATION
OMBROMETER
OMBROPHOBE
OMNIPOTENT
OMNISCIENT
OMNIVOROUS
OMOPHORION
SMALLSCALE
SMARAGDINE
SMARMINESS
SMATTERING
SMITHEREEN
SMOKESTACK
SMOOTHNESS
SMORREBROD
UMBELLIFER
ANABAPTIST
ANACARDIUM
ANACHARSIS
ANACLASTIC
ANACOUSTIC
ANACRUSTIC
ANADROMOUS
ANADYOMENE
ANALOGICAL
ANALPHABET
ANALYTICAL
ANARCHICAL
ANASTIGMAT
ANASTROPHE
ANATOMICAL
ANAXIMENES
ANCHORETIC
ANCHYLOSIS
ANCIPITOUS
ANDALUSIAN
ANDALUSITE
ANDROMACHE
ANEMOGRAPH
ANEMOMETER
ANESTHESIA
ANESTHETIC
ANGIOSPERM
ANGLOPHILE
ANGLOPHOBE
ANGUILLULA
ANGURVADEL
ANGWANTIBO
ANHELATION
ANIMADVERT
ANNEXATION
ANNIHILATE
ANNOTATION
ANNUALIZED
ANNUNCIATE
ANSCHAUUNG
ANSWERABLE
ANTAGONISE
ANTAGONISM
ANTAGONIST
ANTAGONIZE
ANTARCTICA
ANTECEDENT
ANTHEOLION
ANTHOCLORE
ANTHRACINE
ANTHRACITE
ANTHROPOID
ANTIADITIS
ANTIBARBUS
ANTIBIOTIC
ANTICHTHON
ANTICIPATE
ANTICLIMAX
ANTIFREEZE
ANTIMASQUE
ANTIMATTER
ANTIMONIAN
ANTINOMIAN
ANTIOCHENE
ANTIOCHIAN
ANTIPHONAL
ANTIPODEAN
ANTIPROTON
ANTIQUATED
ANTISEPSIS
ANTISEPTIC
ANTISOCIAL

ANTISTATIC
ANTITHESIS
ANTITHETIC
ANTITRAGUS
ANTIVENENE
CNIDOBLAST
ENANTIOSIS
ENCAMPMENT
ENCASEMENT
ENCEPHALON
ENCHANTING
ENCLOISTER
ENCOIGNURE
ENCYCLICAL
ENDEARMENT
ENDOGAMOUS
ENDOSMOSIS
ENGAGEMENT
ENGENDRURE
ENGLISHMAN
ENGLISHMEN
ENGOUEMENT
ENGROSSING
ENHYDRITIC
ENKEPHALIN
ENLACEMENT
ENLÈVEMENT
ENLISTMENT
ENORMOUSLY
ENRAPTURED
ENRICHMENT
ENROLLMENT
ENSANGUINE
ENTEROCELE
ENTERPRISE
ENTHUSIASM
ENTHUSIAST
ENTICEMENT
ENTOMBMENT
ENTOMOLOGY
ENTRANCING
ENTREATING
ENTREMESSE
ENTRENCHED
ENTRYPHONE
GNOSTICISM
INACCURACY
INACCURATE
INACTIVITY
INADEQUACY
INADEQUATE
INAPTITUDE
INARTISTIC
INAUGURATE
INBREEDING
INCAPACITY
INCAPARINA
INCAUTIOUS
INCENDIARY
INCESTUOUS
INCIDENTAL
INCINERATE
INCISIVELY
INCITEMENT
INCIVILITY
INCOHERENT
INCOMPLETE
INCONSTANT
INCRASSATE
INCREASING
INCREDIBLE
INCREDIBLY
INCRESCENT
INCUBATION
INCUMBENCY
INCUNABULA
INDAPAMIDE
INDECENTLY
INDECISION
INDECISIVE
INDECOROUS
INDEFINITE
INDELICACY
INDELICATE
INDENTURES
INDICATION
INDICATIVE
INDICOLITE
INDICTABLE
INDICTMENT
INDIGENOUS
INDIGOLITE
INDIRECTLY
INDISCREET
INDISPOSED
INDISTINCT
INDITEMENT
INDIVIDUAL
INDONESIAN
INDUCEMENT
INDUCTANCE
INDULGENCE
INDUMENTUM
INDUSTRIAL
INEBRIATED
INEDUCABLE
INEFFICACY
INELIGIBLE
INEPTITUDE
INEQUALITY
INESCULENT
INEVITABLE
INEVITABLY
INEXORABLE
INFALLIBLE
INFALLIBLY
INFATUATED
INFECTIOUS
INFEFTMENT
INFERNALLY
INFIDELITY
INFIGHTING
INFILTRATE
INFINITELY
INFINITIVE
INFLATABLE
INFLECTION
INFLEXIBLE
INFLEXIBLY
INFLICTION
INFORMALLY
INFRACTION
INFREQUENT
INFURIATED
INGEMINATE
INGENERATE
INGLORIOUS
INGRATIATE
INGREDIENT
INHABITANT
INHALATION
INHERENTLY
INHIBITING
INHIBITION
INHIBITORY
INHUMANITY
INIMITABLE
INIQUITOUS
INITIATION
INITIATIVE
INJUNCTION
INKSLINGER
INNERSPACE
INNOCENTLY
INNOVATION
INNOVATIVE
INOPERABLE
INORDINATE
INOSCULATE
INQUIRENDO
INQUISITOR
INSANITARY
INSATIABLE
INSATIABLY
INSECURELY
INSECURITY
INSEMINATE
INSENSIBLE
INSIPIDITY
INSISTENCE
INSOLENTLY
INSOLVENCY
INSOUCIANT
INSPECTION
INSPISSATE
INSTALMENT
INSTIGATOR
INSTRUCTED
INSTRUCTOR
INSTRUMENT
INSUFFLATE
INSULARITY
INSULATION
INSURGENCY
INTAGLIATE
INTANGIBLE
INTEGRATED
INTEGUMENT
INTELIGENT
INTEMERATE
INTENDMENT
INTENERATE
INTENTNESS
INTERBREED
INTERCEDER
INTERCLUDE
INTERESTED
INTERFERER
INTERFERON
INTERLEAVE
INTERLOPER
INTERMARRY
INTERMEZZO
INTERNALLY
INTERNMENT
INTERNODAL
INTERPHONE
INTERSTATE
INTERSTICE
INTERTRIGO
INTERTWINE
INTERWEAVE
INTERWOVEN
INTESTINAL
INTESTINES
INTIMATELY
INTIMATION
INTIMIDATE
INTINCTION
INTOLERANT
INTONATION
INTOXICANT
INTOXICATE
INTRAURBAN
INTRIGUING
INTROSPECT
INUNDATION
INVALIDATE
INVALIDITY
INVALUABLE
INVARIABLE
INVARIABLY
INVESTMENT
INVETERATE
INVIGILATE
INVIGORATE
INVINCIBLE
INVIOLABLE
INVITATION
INVOCATION
KNIFEBOARD
KNIGHTHOOD
KNOBKERRIE
KNOCKABOUT
ONOMASTICS
SNAKEMOUTH
SNAKESTONE
SNAPDRAGON
SNAPHAUNCE
SNAPHAUNCH
SNEEZEWOOD
SNIGGERING
SNOOTINESS
SNORKELING
SNOWCAPPED
SNOWMOBILE
UNABRIDGED
UNACCENTED
UNAFFECTED
UNANSWERED
UNARGUABLE
UNASSIGNED
UNASSUMING
UNATTACHED
UNATTENDED
UNAVAILING
UNBALANCED
UNBEARABLE
UNBEARABLY
UNBEATABLE
UNBECOMING
UNBELIEVER
UNBLEACHED
UNBLINKING
UNBLUSHING
UNCOMMONLY
UNCONFINED
UNCRITICAL
UNCTUOUSLY
UNCULTURED
UNDECLARED
UNDEFEATED
UNDEFENDED
UNDENIABLE
UNDERBURNT
UNDERCLASS
UNDERCOVER
UNDERCRAFT
UNDERCROFT
UNDERFLOOR
UNDERLEASE
UNDERLINEN
UNDERLYING
UNDERNEATH
UNDERPANTS
UNDERSCORE
UNDERSHIRT
UNDERSIZED
UNDERSKIRT
UNDERSLUNG

UNDERSTAND
UNDERSTATE
UNDERSTEER
UNDERSTOOD
UNDERSTUDY
UNDERTAKER
UNDERVALUE
UNDERWATER
UNDERWORLD
UNDERWRITE
UNDESCRIED
UNDESERVED
UNDETECTED
UNDETERRED
UNDIGESTED
UNDISPUTED
UNDOCTORED
UNDULATING
UNDULATION
UNEASINESS
UNEDIFYING
UNEDUCATED
UNEMPLOYED
UNENVIABLE
UNEQUALLED
UNEVENNESS
UNEVENTFUL
UNEXAMPLED
UNEXPECTED
UNEXPLORED
UNFAITHFUL
UNFAMILIAR
UNFATHOMED
UNFETTERED
UNFINISHED
UNFLAGGING
UNFLAVORED
UNFORESEEN
UNFRIENDLY
UNFRUITFUL
UNGRACIOUS
UNGRATEFUL
UNGROUNDED
UNHAMPERED
UNHEARABLE
UNHERALDED
UNHYGIENIC
UNICAMERAL
UNIFORMITY
UNIGENITUS
UNILATERAL
UNIMPAIRED
UNINFORMED
UNINSPIRED
UNINVITING
UNIQUENESS
UNIVERSITY
UNLADYLIKE
UNLEAVENED
UNLETTERED
UNLICENSED
UNMANNERED
UNMANNERLY
UNNUMBERED
UNOBSERVED
UNOCCUPIED
UNOFFICIAL
UNORIGINAL
UNORTHODOX
UNPLEASANT
UNPREPARED
UNPROMPTED
UNPROVOKED
UNPUNCTUAL
UNREADABLE
UNREASONED
UNREDEEMED
UNRELIABLE
UNRELIEVED
UNREQUITED
UNRESERVED
UNRESOLVED
UNREVEALED
UNRIVALLED
UNROMANTIC
UNRULINESS
UNSALARIED
UNSCHOOLED
UNSCRAMBLE
UNSCRIPTED
UNSEASONED
UNSETTLING
UNSHACKLED
UNSLEEPING
UNSOCIABLE
UNSPECIFIC
UNSUITABLE
UNSWERVING
UNTHINKING
UNTIDINESS
UNTRUTHFUL
UNWORKABLE
UNYIELDING
BOBBYSOXER
BOISTEROUS
BOLLANDIST
BOLSHEVIST
BOMBARDIER
BONDHOLDER
BONDSWOMAN
BONESHAKER
BOOKBINDER
BOOKKEEPER
BOOKMARKER
BOOKMOBILE
BOOKSELLER
BOONDOGGLE
BOOTLEGGER
BOOTLICKER
BOOZINGKEN
BORDERLAND
BORDERLINE
BORDRAGING
BORROWINGS
BOTHERSOME
BOTTICELLI
BOTTLEHEAD
BOTTLENECK
BOTTOMLESS
BOUILLOTTE
BOURIGNIAN
BOUSINGKEN
BOWDLERISE
BOWDLERIZE
COADJUTANT
COARSENESS
COASTGUARD
COATHANGER
COCCINEOUS
COCHLEARIA
COCKABULLY
COCKALORUM
COCKATRICE
COCKCHAFER
COCKERNONY
CODSWALLOP
COELACANTH
COETANEOUS
COEXISTENT
COGITATION
COGNISANCE
COGNIZANCE
COHERENTLY
COINCIDENT
COLBERTINE
COLCHESTER
COLCHICINE
COLDSTREAM
COLEOPTERA
COLEORHIZA
COLLAPSING
COLLARBONE
COLLATERAL
COLLECTING
COLLECTION
COLLECTIVE
COLLEGIATE
COLLEMBOLA
COLLIMATOR
COLLIQUATE
COLLOCUTER
COLLOQUIAL
COLONNADED
COLORATION
COLORATURA
COLOSSALLY
COLOURLESS
COLPORTAGE
COLPORTEUR
COLPOSCOPE
COMANCHERO
COMBUSTION
COMEDIENNE
COMESTIBLE
COMFORTING
COMMANDANT
COMMANDEER
COMMANDING
COMMENTARY
COMMENTATE
COMMERCIAL
COMMISSARY
COMMISSION
COMMISSURE
COMMITMENT
COMMIXTURE
COMMODIOUS
COMMONWEAL
COMMUNALLY
COMMUNIQUÉ
COMMUTABLE
COMPARABLE
COMPARATOR
COMPARISON
COMPASSION
COMPATIBLE
COMPATRIOT
COMPELLING
COMPENDIUM
COMPENSATE
COMPETENCE
COMPETITOR
COMPLACENT
COMPLANATE
COMPLEMENT
COMPLETELY
COMPLETION
COMPLEXION
COMPLEXITY
COMPLIANCE
COMPLICATE
COMPLICITY
COMPLIMENT
COMPLUVIUM
COMPOSITOR
COMPOUNDED
COMPRADORE
COMPREHEND
COMPRESSED
COMPRESSOR
COMPROMISE
COMPULSION
COMPULSIVE
COMPULSORY
COMSTOCKER
CONCENTRIC
CONCEPTION
CONCEPTUAL
CONCERNING
CONCERTINA
CONCERVATE
CONCESSION
CONCHIGLIE
CONCHIOLIN
CONCHOLOGY
CONCILIATE
CONCINNITY
CONCINNOUS
CONCLUDING
CONCLUSION
CONCLUSIVE
CONCOCTION
CONCORDANT
CONCRETION
CONCURRENT
CONCUSSION
CONDESCEND
CONDIMENTS
CONDOLENCE
CONDOTTIER
CONDUCTING
CONDUCTION
CONFECTION
CONFEDERAL
CONFERENCE
CONFERVOID
CONFESSION
CONFIDANTE
CONFIDENCE
CONFISCATE
CONFLUENCE
CONFORMIST
CONFORMITY
CONFOUNDED
CONFUSEDLY
CONGENITAL
CONGESTION
CONGREGATE
CONIFEROUS
CONJECTURE
CONNECTING
CONNECTION
CONNECTIVE
CONNIPTION
CONNIVANCE
CONQUERING
CONSCIENCE
CONSECRATE
CONSENSION
CONSEQUENT
CONSIDERED
CONSISTENT
CONSISTORY
CONSONANCE
CONSONANTS
CONSORTIUM
CONSPECTUS
CONSPIRACY
CONSTANTAN
CONSTANTIA

CONSTANTLY
CONSTITUTE
CONSTRAINT
CONSTRINGE
CONSUETUDE
CONSULTANT
CONSULTING
CONSUMMATE
CONTAGIOUS
CONTENTION
CONTESTANT
CONTEXTUAL
CONTIGUITY
CONTIGUOUS
CONTINENCE
CONTINGENT
CONTINUING
CONTINUITY
CONTINUOUS
CONTORTION
CONTRABAND
CONTRACTOR
CONTRADICT
CONTRAFLOW
CONTRAHENT
CONTRARILY
CONTRAVENE
CONTRECOUP
CONTRIBUTE
CONTRITION
CONTROLLER
CONTROVERT
CONVALESCE
CONVECTION
CONVENANCE
CONVENIENT
CONVENTION
CONVERGENT
CONVERSANT
CONVERSELY
CONVERSION
CONVEYABLE
CONVEYANCE
CONVICTION
CONVINCING
CONVOLUTED
CONVOLVUTE
CONVULSION
CONVULSIVE
COORDINATE
COPARCENER
COPENHAGEN
COPERNICUS
COPESETTIC
COPPERHEAD
COPPERNOSE
COPPERSKIN
COPULATION
COPYHOLDER
COPYWRITER
COQUELICOT
COQUETTISH
COQUIMBITE
CORDIALITY
CORDIERITE
CORDILLERA
CORDWAINER
CORINTHIAN
CORNCOCKLE
CORNFLAKES
CORNFLOWER
CORNSTALKS
CORNSTARCH
CORNUCOPIA
COROMANDEL
CORONATION
CORPULENCE
CORRECTING
CORRECTION
CORRECTIVE
CORREGIDOR
CORRESPOND
CORRIGENDA
CORROBOREE
CORRUGATED
CORRUGATOR
CORRUPTING
CORRUPTION
CORTADERIA
CORYBANTES
CORYBANTIC
CORYPHAEUS
COSTLINESS
COTTIERISM
COTTONTAIL
COTTONWOOD
COUNCILLOR
COUNSELING
COUNSELLOR
COUNTERACT
COUNTRYMAN
COURAGEOUS
COURTHOUSE
COUSCOUSOU
COVENANTER
COXCOMICAL
DOCIMASTIC
DODECANESE
DOGGEDNESS
DOLCEMENTE
DOLICHOLIS
DOLICHOTUS
DOMICILARY
DOMINATING
DOMINATION
DONNYBROOK
DOORKEEPER
DOORTODOOR
DOPPLERITE
DOSTOEVSKY
DOUBLEBASS
DOUBLETALK
DOUBTFULLY
DOVERCOURT
DOWNMARKET
DOWNSIZING
DOWNSTAIRS
DOWNSTREAM
FONTANELLE
FONTICULUS
FONTINALIS
FOODSTUFFS
FOOTBALLER
FOOTBRIDGE
FOOTLIGHTS
FOOTPRINTS
FORBEARING
FORBIDDING
FORCEFULLY
FOREBITTER
FOREBODING
FORECASTER
FORECASTLE
FOREDAMNED
FOREFATHER
FOREFINGER
FOREGATHER
FOREGROUND
FOREORDAIN
FORERUNNER
FORESHADOW
FOREWARNED
FORFAITING
FORFEITURE
FORFEUCHEN
FORFOUGHEN
FORGIVABLE
FORINSECAL
FORMIDABLE
FORTHRIGHT
FORTINBRAS
FORTISSIMO
FORTUITOUS
FOSSILIZED
FOUDROYANT
FOUNDATION
FOURCHETTE
FOURIERISM
FOURRAGERE
FOURTEENTH
FOXHUNTING
GOALKEEPER
GOATSUCKER
GOBEMOUCHE
GODPARENTS
GOLDDIGGER
GOLDFINGER
GOLDILOCKS
GOLIATHISE
GONDOLIERS
GONFANONER
GONIOMETER
GONORRHOEA
GOODFELLOW
GOOSEBERRY
GOOSEFLESH
GORGEOUSLY
GORMANDIZE
GOVERNANCE
GOVERNESSY
GOVERNMENT
HOARSENESS
HOBBYHORSE
HODGEPODGE
HOLOFERNES
HOLOGRAPHY
HOLOPHOTAL
HOLOSTERIC
HOMECOMING
HOMELINESS
HOMEOPATHY
HOMEOUSIAN
HOMEWORKER
HOMOEOPATH
HOMOGENIZE
HOMOPHOBIA
HOMOPHOBIC
HOMORELAPS
HOMOSEXUAL
HOMUNCULUS
HONEYBUNCH
HONORARIUM
HONOURABLE
HONOURABLY
HONOURLESS
HOODWINKED
HOOTANANNY
HOOTENANNY
HOOTNANNIE
HOPELESSLY
HORIZONTAL
HORNBLENDE
HORNBLOWER
HORNRIMMED
HORRENDOUS
HORRIFYING
HORSEDRAWN
HORSELBERG
HORSEPOWER
HORSERIDER
HORSEWOMAN
HOSPITABLE
HOSPITABLY
HOTCHPOTCH
HOUSEBOUND
HOUSECRAFT
HOUSEMAIDS
HOUSEPROUD
HOVERCRAFT
HOWLEGLASS
HOWSOMEVER
IONOSPHERE
JOBSEEKERS
JOCULARITY
JOHNSONIAN
JOLTERHEAD
JOURNALESE
JOURNALISM
JOURNALIST
JOURNEYMAN
JOUYSAUNCE
KOEKSISTER
KOOKABURRA
LOCKERROOM
LOCKKEEPER
LOCOMOTION
LOCOMOTIVE
LOCULAMENT
LOGANBERRY
LOGARITHMS
LOGGERHEAD
LOGISTICAL
LOGORRHOEA
LONELINESS
LONGCHAMPS
LONGFELLOW
LOQUACIOUS
LORDLINESS
LORDOLATRY
LOTOPHAGUS
LOUISIETTE
LOVELINESS
MODERATELY
MODERATION
MODIFIABLE
MODULATION
MOISTURIZE
MOLENDINAR
MOLYBDENUM
MONARCHIST
MONEGASQUE
MONETARISM
MONETARIST
MONILIASIS
MONILIFORM
MONOCHROME
MONOECIOUS
MONOGAMOUS
MONOLITHIC
MONOPHONIC
MONOPLEGIA
MONOPOLISE
MONOPOLIZE
MONOPTERON
MONOPTEROS
MONOTHEISM
MONOTONOUS
MONSTRANCE
MONTAGNARD
MONTESSORI

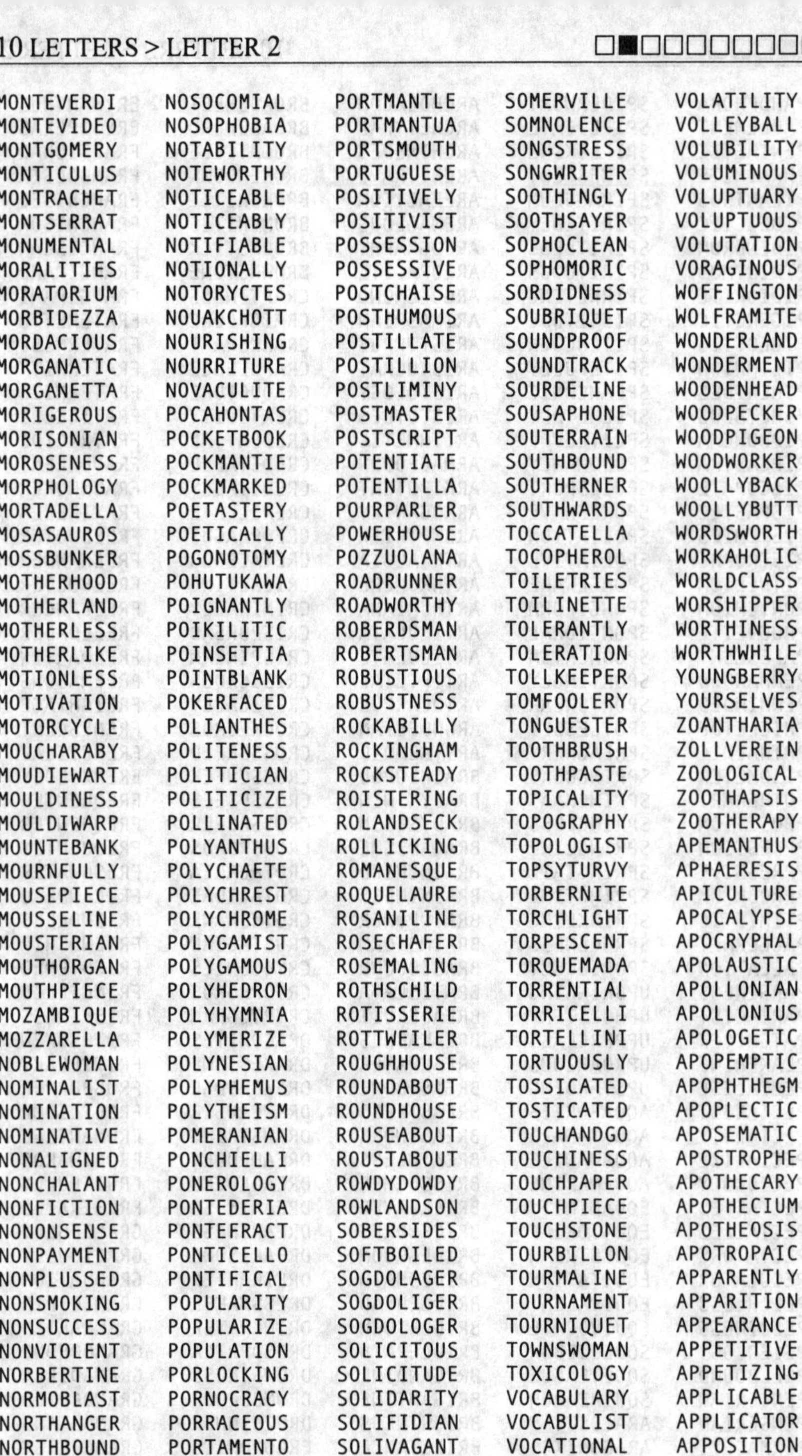

MONTEVERDI
MONTEVIDEO
MONTGOMERY
MONTICULUS
MONTRACHET
MONTSERRAT
MONUMENTAL
MORALITIES
MORATORIUM
MORBIDEZZA
MORDACIOUS
MORGANATIC
MORGANETTA
MORIGEROUS
MORISONIAN
MOROSENESS
MORPHOLOGY
MORTADELLA
MOSASAUROS
MOSSBUNKER
MOTHERHOOD
MOTHERLAND
MOTHERLESS
MOTHERLIKE
MOTIONLESS
MOTIVATION
MOTORCYCLE
MOUCHARABY
MOUDIEWART
MOULDINESS
MOULDIWARP
MOUNTEBANK
MOURNFULLY
MOUSEPIECE
MOUSSELINE
MOUSTERIAN
MOUTHORGAN
MOUTHPIECE
MOZAMBIQUE
MOZZARELLA
NOBLEWOMAN
NOMINALIST
NOMINATION
NOMINATIVE
NONALIGNED
NONCHALANT
NONFICTION
NONONSENSE
NONPAYMENT
NONPLUSSED
NONSMOKING
NONSUCCESS
NONVIOLENT
NORBERTINE
NORMOBLAST
NORTHANGER
NORTHBOUND
NORTHERNER
NORTHSTEAD
NORTHWARDS
NOSOCOMIAL
NOSOPHOBIA
NOTABILITY
NOTEWORTHY
NOTICEABLE
NOTICEABLY
NOTIFIABLE
NOTIONALLY
NOTORYCTES
NOUAKCHOTT
NOURISHING
NOURRITURE
NOVACULITE
POCAHONTAS
POCKETBOOK
POCKMANTIE
POCKMARKED
POETASTERY
POETICALLY
POGONOTOMY
POHUTUKAWA
POIGNANTLY
POIKILITIC
POINSETTIA
POINTBLANK
POKERFACED
POLIANTHES
POLITENESS
POLITICIAN
POLITICIZE
POLLINATED
POLYANTHUS
POLYCHAETE
POLYCHREST
POLYCHROME
POLYGAMIST
POLYGAMOUS
POLYHEDRON
POLYHYMNIA
POLYMERIZE
POLYNESIAN
POLYPHEMUS
POLYTHEISM
POMERANIAN
PONCHIELLI
PONEROLOGY
PONTEDERIA
PONTEFRACT
PONTICELLO
PONTIFICAL
POPULARITY
POPULARIZE
POPULATION
PORLOCKING
PORNOCRACY
PORRACEOUS
PORTAMENTO
PORTCULLIS
PORTENTOUS
PORTIONIST
PORTMANTLE
PORTMANTUA
PORTSMOUTH
PORTUGUESE
POSITIVELY
POSITIVIST
POSSESSION
POSSESSIVE
POSTCHAISE
POSTHUMOUS
POSTILLATE
POSTILLION
POSTLIMINY
POSTMASTER
POSTSCRIPT
POTENTIATE
POTENTILLA
POURPARLER
POWERHOUSE
POZZUOLANA
ROADRUNNER
ROADWORTHY
ROBERDSMAN
ROBERTSMAN
ROBUSTIOUS
ROBUSTNESS
ROCKABILLY
ROCKINGHAM
ROCKSTEADY
ROISTERING
ROLANDSECK
ROLLICKING
ROMANESQUE
ROQUELAURE
ROSANILINE
ROSECHAFER
ROSEMALING
ROTHSCHILD
ROTISSERIE
ROTTWEILER
ROUGHHOUSE
ROUNDABOUT
ROUNDHOUSE
ROUSEABOUT
ROUSTABOUT
ROWDYDOWDY
ROWLANDSON
SOBERSIDES
SOFTBOILED
SOGDOLAGER
SOGDOLIGER
SOGDOLOGER
SOLICITOUS
SOLICITUDE
SOLIDARITY
SOLIFIDIAN
SOLIVAGANT
SOLUBILITY
SOMBRERITE
SOMERSAULT
SOMERVILLE
SOMNOLENCE
SONGSTRESS
SONGWRITER
SOOTHINGLY
SOOTHSAYER
SOPHOCLEAN
SOPHOMORIC
SORDIDNESS
SOUBRIQUET
SOUNDPROOF
SOUNDTRACK
SOURDELINE
SOUSAPHONE
SOUTERRAIN
SOUTHBOUND
SOUTHERNER
SOUTHWARDS
TOCCATELLA
TOCOPHEROL
TOILETRIES
TOILINETTE
TOLERANTLY
TOLERATION
TOLLKEEPER
TOMFOOLERY
TONGUESTER
TOOTHBRUSH
TOOTHPASTE
TOPICALITY
TOPOGRAPHY
TOPOLOGIST
TOPSYTURVY
TORBERNITE
TORCHLIGHT
TORPESCENT
TORQUEMADA
TORRENTIAL
TORRICELLI
TORTELLINI
TORTUOUSLY
TOSSICATED
TOSTICATED
TOUCHANDGO
TOUCHINESS
TOUCHPAPER
TOUCHPIECE
TOUCHSTONE
TOURBILLON
TOURMALINE
TOURNAMENT
TOURNIQUET
TOWNSWOMAN
TOXICOLOGY
VOCABULARY
VOCABULIST
VOCATIONAL
VOCIFERATE
VOCIFEROUS
VOETGANGER
VOLATILITY
VOLLEYBALL
VOLUBILITY
VOLUMINOUS
VOLUPTUARY
VOLUPTUOUS
VOLUTATION
VORAGINOUS
WOFFINGTON
WOLFRAMITE
WONDERLAND
WONDERMENT
WOODENHEAD
WOODPECKER
WOODPIGEON
WOODWORKER
WOOLLYBACK
WOOLLYBUTT
WORDSWORTH
WORKAHOLIC
WORLDCLASS
WORSHIPPER
WORTHINESS
WORTHWHILE
YOUNGBERRY
YOURSELVES
ZOANTHARIA
ZOLLVEREIN
ZOOLOGICAL
ZOOTHAPSIS
ZOOTHERAPY
APEMANTHUS
APHAERESIS
APICULTURE
APOCALYPSE
APOCRYPHAL
APOLAUSTIC
APOLLONIAN
APOLLONIUS
APOLOGETIC
APOPEMPTIC
APOPHTHEGM
APOPLECTIC
APOSEMATIC
APOSTROPHE
APOTHECARY
APOTHECIUM
APOTHEOSIS
APOTROPAIC
APPARENTLY
APPARITION
APPEARANCE
APPETITIVE
APPETIZING
APPLICABLE
APPLICATOR
APPOSITION
APPRECIATE
APPRENTICE
APTERYGOTA

EPANOPHORA
EPAULEMENT
EPENTHETIC
EPHRAIMITE
EPICANTHUS
EPIDEICTIC
EPIDENDRUM
EPIDIDYMUS
EPIDIORITE
EPIGENETIC
EPIGLOTTIS
EPILIMNION
EPIMENIDES
EPIMETHEUS
EPIPHONEMA
EPIPLASTRA
EPISCOPATE
EPISPASTIC
EPISTEMICS
EPISTROPHE
EPITHELIUM
EPONYCHIUM
EPROUVETTE
OPALESCENT
OPENHANDED
OPENMINDED
OPHICLEIDE
OPHTHALMIC
OPISOMETER
OPOTHERAPY
OPPOSITION
OPPRESSION
OPPRESSIVE
OPPROBRIUM
OPTIMISTIC
SPACECRAFT
SPALLATION
SPARSENESS
SPARTACIST
SPATCHCOCK
SPEAKERINE
SPECIALISE
SPECIALIST
SPECIALITY
SPECIALIZE
SPECIOUSLY
SPECTACLED
SPECTACLES
SPECTATORS
SPECULATOR
SPEECHLESS
SPEEDINESS
SPELEOLOGY
SPELLBOUND
SPENCERIAN
SPENSERIAN
SPERMACETI
SPERRYLITE
SPHACELATE
SPHALERITE
SPIDERWORT
SPIFLICATE
SPILLIKINS
SPINESCENT
SPIRACULUM
SPIRITEDLY
SPIRITLESS
SPIRITUOUS
SPIRKETING
SPISSITUDE
SPITCHCOCK
SPITEFULLY
SPLANCHNIC
SPLENDIDLY
SPLITLEVEL
SPODOMANCY
SPOILSPORT
SPOKESHAVE
SPOLIATION
SPOLIATIVE
SPONGEWARE
SPONGIFORM
SPONSIONAL
SPOONERISM
SPORTINGLY
SPORTSWEAR
SPOTLESSLY
SPREAGHERY
SPRINGBOKS
SPRINGHAAS
SPRINGLESS
SPRINGLIKE
SPRINGTAIL
SPRINGTIME
SPRINKLING
SPRUCENESS
SPURIOUSLY
UPBRINGING
UPHOLSTERY
UPPERCLASS
UPROARIOUS
UPSTANDING
AQUAFORTIS
AQUAMANALE
AQUAMANILE
AQUAMARINE
EQUANIMITY
EQUATORIAL
EQUESTRIAN
EQUITATION
EQUIVALENT
EQUIVOCATE
SQUEEZEBOX
SQUETEAGUE
SQUIREARCH
ARACOSTYLE
ARAGONITES
ARAUCANIAN
ARBITRATOR
ARCHBISHOP
ARCHDEACON
ARCHETYPAL
ARCHIMEDES
ARCHITRAVE
AREFACTION
ARENACEOUS
AREOGRAPHY
AREOPAGITE
ARGOLEMONO
ARIMASPIAN
ARISTIPPUS
ARISTOCRAT
ARISTOLOGY
ARISTOTLES
ARITHMETIC
ARMAGEDDON
ARMIPOTENT
ARROGANTLY
ARSMETRICK
ARTHRALGIA
ARTHROMERE
ARTHURIANA
ARTICULATA
ARTICULATE
ARTIFICIAL
ARTOCARPUS
ARUNDELIAN
ARYTAENOID
BRACHIOPOD
BRADYKININ
BRADYSEISM
BRAGADISME
BRAINCHILD
BRAININESS
BRAINPOWER
BRAINSTORM
BRASSBOUND
BRATISLAVA
BREADFRUIT
BREAKABLES
BREAKWATER
BREASTBONE
BREASTFEED
BREASTWORK
BREATHLESS
BRESSUMMER
BRICKLAYER
BRICKWORKS
BRIDEGROOM
BRIDESMAID
BRIDGEHEAD
BRIDGETOWN
BRIDLEPATH
BRIGANDINE
BRIGANTINE
BRIGHTNESS
BRILLIANCE
BRITISHISM
BROADCLOTH
BROADPIECE
BROADSHEET
BROADSWORD
BROCATELLE
BROKENDOWN
BRONCHITIC
BRONCHITIS
BROOMSTICK
BROWNSTONE
CRAFTINESS
CRAIGFLUKE
CRANKSHAFT
CRAPULENCE
CRAQUETURE
CREATIVITY
CREDENTIAL
CREDITABLE
CREDITABLY
CRENELLATE
CREOPHAGUS
CRETACEOUS
CRICKETING
CRIMINALLY
CRISPBREAD
CRISPINIAN
CRISSCROSS
CRITICALLY
CROCKFORDS
CROSSBREED
CROSSCHECK
CROSSPIECE
CROSSREFER
CROSSROADS
CROTALARIA
CROTALIDAE
CRUIKSHANK
CRUSTACEAN
CRYOGENICS
CRYOPHORUS
CRYPTOGRAM
DRACONITES
DRAKESTONE
DRAWBRIDGE
DRAWCANSIR
DRAWSTRING
DREADFULLY
DREADLOCKS
DREAMINESS
DREARINESS
DREARISOME
DREIKANTER
DRESSMAKER
DRINKWATER
DROSOPHILA
DROWSINESS
DRUMBLEDOR
DRUZHINNIK
ERGONOMICS
ERIOCAULON
ERUBESCENT
ERUCTATION
ERYMANTHUS
ERYSIPELAS
FRACTIONAL
FRAMBOESIA
FRANCHISEE
FRANCHISOR
FRANCISCAN
FRANGIPANE
FRANGIPANI
FRATERETTO
FRATERNISE
FRATERNITY
FRATERNIZE
FRATICELLI
FRATRICIDE
FRAUDULENT
FRAUNHOFER
FRAXINELLA
FREEBOOTER
FREEHANDER
FREEHOLDER
FREELANCER
FREELOADER
FREEMARTIN
FREEMASONS
FREIGHTAGE
FREMESCENT
FRENETICAL
FRENZIEDLY
FREQUENTED
FREQUENTER
FREQUENTLY
FRESHWATER
FRICANDEAU
FRIENDLESS
FRIENDSHIP
FRIGHTENED
FRINGILLID
FRISKINESS
FRITHSOKEN
FRITILLARY
FROGHOPPER
FROLICSOME
FROMANTEEL
FRONTWARDS
FRUITFULLY
FRUSTRATED
GRACEFULLY
GRACIOUSLY
GRADUATION
GRAMICIDIN
GRAMMARIAN
GRAMOPHONE
GRANADILLA
GRANDCHILD
GRANDSTAND
GRANGERISM
GRANGERIZE
GRANULATED
GRAPEFRUIT

GRAPHOLOGY
GRAPTOLITE
GRASSLANDS
GRASSROOTS
GRASSWIDOW
GRATEFULLY
GRATIFYING
GRATILLITY
GRATUITOUS
GRAVEOLENT
GRAVESTONE
GREEDINESS
GREENCLOTH
GREENFINCH
GREENHEART
GREENHOUSE
GREENSHANK
GREENSTICK
GREENSWARD
GREGARIOUS
GRENADIERS
GRENADILLA
GREYFRIARS
GRIDIRONER
GRIDLOCKED
GRINDSTONE
GRITTINESS
GROCETERIA
GROUNDBAIT
GROUNDLESS
GROUNDLING
GROUNDSMAN
GROUNDWORK
GROVELLING
GRUBBINESS
GRUMPINESS
IRIDESCENT
IRISHWOMAN
IRISHWOMEN
IRONICALLY
IRONMONGER
IRRADICATE
IRRATIONAL
IRRELEVANT
IRREMEDIAL
IRRESOLUTE
IRREVERENT
IRRIGATION
IRRITATING
IRRITATION
KRIEGSPIEL
ORATORICAL
ORCHESTRAL
ORCHIDEOUS
ORDINARILY
ORDINATION
ORDONNANCE
ORIDINANCE
ORIGINALLY
ORIGINATOR
ORNAMENTAL
OROBRANCHE
OROGENESIS
ORPHEOREON
ORTHOCAINE
ORTHOCLASE
ORTHOGONAL
ORTHOPNOEA
ORTHOPTICS
PRAEMUNIRE
PRAETORIAN
PRAETORIUM
PRAGMATISM
PRAGMATIST
PRATINCOLE
PRAXITELES
PREARRANGE
PREBENDARY
PRECARIOUS
PRECAUTION
PRECEDENCE
PRECIPITIN
PRECOCIOUS
PRECURSORY
PREDACIOUS
PREDECEASE
PREDESTINE
PREDICTION
PREDISPOSE
PREDNISONE
PREEMINENT
PREFERABLE
PREFERABLY
PREFERENCE
PREFERMENT
PREHENSILE
PREHISTORY
PREJUDICED
PRELECTION
PREMARITAL
PREPARATOR
PREPAYMENT
PREPENSELY
PREPOSITOR
PREPOSSESS
PREPOTENCE
PRESBYOPIA
PRESBYTERY
PRESCIENCE
PRESENTDAY
PRESIDENCY
PRESSURIZE
PRESUMABLY
PRESUPPOSE
PRETENSION
PRETINCOLE
PRETTINESS
PREVAILING
PREVALENCE
PREVENANCY
PREVENTION
PREVENTIVE
PREVIOUSLY
PRICKLOUSE
PRIESTHOOD
PRIMORDIAL
PRINCIPIUM
PRINCIPLED
PRINCIPLES
PRIVATEERS
PRIVILEGED
PRIZEFIGHT
PROAIRESIS
PROCEDURAL
PROCEEDING
PROCESSING
PROCESSION
PROCLIVITY
PROCREATOR
PROCRUSTES
PROCURABLE
PROCURATOR
PRODIGALLY
PRODIGIOUS
PRODUCTION
PRODUCTIVE
PROFESSION
PROFICIENT
PROFITABLE
PROFITABLY
PROFITLESS
PROFLIGACY
PROFLIGATE
PROFOUNDLY
PROFUNDITY
PROGENITOR
PROGESSION
PROGRAMMER
PROHIBITED
PROJECTILE
PROJECTING
PROJECTION
PROMENADER
PROMETHEAN
PROMETHEUS
PROMETHIUM
PROMINENCE
PROMISSORY
PROMONTORY
PROMPTNESS
PROMULGATE
PRONOUNCED
PROPAGANDA
PROPAGATOR
PROPELLANT
PROPENSITY
PROPERTIUS
PROPHETESS
PROPIONATE
PROPITIATE
PROPITIOUS
PROPLITEAL
PROPORTION
PROPOSITUS
PROPRAETOR
PROPRIETOR
PROPULSION
PROPYLAEUM
PROSCENIUM
PROSCIUTTO
PROSCRIBED
PROSECUTOR
PROSERPINA
PROSERPINE
PROSILIENT
PROSPECTOR
PROSPECTUS
PROSPERINA
PROSPERITY
PROSPEROUS
PROSTHESIS
PROSTHETIC
PROSTITUTE
PROTAGORAS
PROTANOPIC
PROTECTION
PROTECTIVE
PROTERVITY
PROTESTANT
PROTOPLASM
PROTRACTED
PROTRACTOR
PROTRUSION
PROVEDITOR
PROVENANCE
PROVERBIAL
PROVIDENCE
PROVINCIAL
PROVISIONS
PRUDENTIAL
PRZEWALSKI
TRACHELATE
TRADITIONS
TRAFFICKER
TRAGACANTH
TRAGICALLY
TRAITOROUS
TRAJECTORY
TRAMONTANA
TRAMONTANE
TRAMPOLINE
TRANQUILLY
TRANSCRIBE
TRANSCRIPT
TRANSGRESS
TRANSIENCE
TRANSISTOR
TRANSITION
TRANSITIVE
TRANSITORY
TRANSLATED
TRANSLATOR
TRANSPLANT
TRANSPOSED
TRANSVERSE
TRAUMATIZE
TRAVANCORE
TRAVELATOR
TRAVELLERS
TRAVELLING
TRAVELOGUE
TRAVERTINE
TRAVOLATOR
TRECENTIST
TREKSCHUIT
TREMENDOUS
TRENCHMORE
TRENDINESS
TRESPASSER
TRIACONTER
TRIANGULAR
TRICHOLOGY
TRICKINESS
TRICLINIUM
TRIDENTINE
TRILATERAL
TRILINGUAL
TRIMALCHIO
TRIMSNITCH
TRINACRIAN
TRIPARTITE
TRIPEHOUND
TRIPLICATE
TRIPUDIARY
TRISKELION
TRITANOPIA
TRIUMPHANT
TRIVIALITY
TRIVIALIZE
TROCHANTER
TROCHOTRON
TROCTOLITE
TROGLODYTE
TROMBONIST
TROMOMETER
TROPAEOLUM
TROPHONIUS
TROPOPAUSE
TROPOPHYTE
TROTSKYITE
TROUBADOUR
TROUVAILLE
TRUCULENCE
TRUSTFULLY
TRUTHFULLY
TRYPTOPHAN
UROPOIESIS
UROSTEGITE
URTICACEAE
WRAPAROUND

WRETCHEDLY
WRISTWATCH
WRONGDOING
WRONGFULLY
ASAFOETIDA
ASARABACCA
ASBESTOSIS
ASCENDANCY
ASCENDENCY
ASCETICISM
ASCRIBABLE
ASPARAGINE
ASPERSIONS
ASPHALTITE
ASPHYXIATE
ASPIDISTRA
ASPIRATION
ASSEMBLAGE
ASSEMBLING
ASSESSMENT
ASSEVERATE
ASSIGNABLE
ASSIGNMENT
ASSIMILATE
ASSISTANCE
ASSOCIATED
ASSORTMENT
ASSUMPTION
ASSUMPTIVE
ASTEROIDEA
ASTIGMATIC
ASTOMATOUS
ASTONISHED
ASTOUNDING
ASTRAGALUS
ASTRALAGUS
ASTRINGENT
ASTROLOGER
ASTRONOMER
ASTUTENESS
ASYMMETRIC
ASYNARTETE
ESCADRILLE
ESCALATION
ESCAPEMENT
ESCARPMENT
ESCHAROTIC
ESCRITOIRE
ESCULAPIAN
ESCUTCHEON
ESPADRILLE
ESPECIALLY
ESTANCIERO
ESTIMATION
ESTRAMACON
ISABELLINE
ISOMETRICS
ISONIAZIDE
KSHATRIYAS
OSCILLATOR

OSCITATION
OSCULATION
OSCULATORY
OSMETERIUM
OSMIDROSIS
OSTENSIBLE
OSTENSIBLY
OSTEOBLAST
OSTEOCOLLA
OSTEOLEPIS
OSTEOPATHY
OSTEOPHYTE
OSTROGOTHS
PSALTERIUM
PSAMMOPHIL
PSEPHOLOGY
PSEUDOCARP
PSILOCYBIN
PSOCOPTERA
PSYCHIATRY
PSYCHOLOGY
PSYCHOPATH
PSYCHOPOMP
USEFULNESS
USQUEBAUGH
USUCAPTION
USURPATION
ATELEIOSIS
ATHANASIAN
ATMOSPHERE
ATRACURIUM
ATRAMENTAL
ATTACHMENT
ATTAINABLE
ATTAINMENT
ATTENDANCE
ATTRACTION
ATTRACTIVE
CTENOPHORA
ETEOCRETAN
ETHEOSTOMA
ETHYLAMINE
OTHERGATES
OTHERGUESS
PTERANODON
PTERYGOTUS
STABILISER
STABILIZER
STADHOLDER
STAGECOACH
STAGECRAFT
STAGGERING
STAGNATION
STALACTITE
STALAGMITE
STALHELMER
STALLENGER
STALLINGER
STAMMERING
STANDPOINT

STANDSTILL
STANISLAUS
STAPHYLINE
STARVATION
STARVELING
STATECRAFT
STATIONARY
STATIONERY
STATISTICS
STATOCRACY
STATUESQUE
STAUROLITE
STAVESACRE
STEADINESS
STEAKHOUSE
STEALTHILY
STEELINESS
STEELWORKS
STEMWINDER
STENOTYPER
STENTORIAN
STEPFATHER
STEPHANITE
STEPHENSON
STEPLADDER
STEPMOTHER
STEPSISTER
STEREOTOMY
STEREOTYPE
STERILISER
STERILIZER
STERNALGIA
STERTEROUS
STERTOROUS
STEWARDESS
STIACCIATO
STICHARION
STICKINESS
STICKYBEAK
STIGMATISE
STIGMATIZE
STILLBIRTH
STILLICIDE
STILLIFORM
STILLSTAND
STINGINESS
STINGYBARK
STOCHASTIC
STOCKINESS
STOMATOPOD
STONEBRASH
STONEHENGE
STONEMASON
STONYHURST
STOREFRONT
STOREHOUSE
STOUTHERIE
STOUTHRIEF
STRABISMUS
STRABOTOMY

STRACCHINO
STRAGGLING
STRAIGHTEN
STRAITENED
STRAMONIUM
STRAPONTIN
STRASBOURG
STRATEGIST
STRATHSPEY
STRATIOTES
STRATOCRAT
STRATOCYST
STRAVINSKY
STRAWBERRY
STRAWBOARD
STREAMERED
STREAMLINE
STREETLAMP
STREETWISE
STRELITZIA
STRENGTHEN
STREPITANT
STREPITOSO
STRICTNESS
STRIDENTLY
STRIDEWAYS
STRIDULATE
STRIKINGLY
STRINDBERG
STRINGENCY
STRINGENDO
STRINGHALT
STRIPTEASE
STROGANOFF
STRONGHOLD
STRONGROOM
STROPHIOLE
STRUCTURAL
STRULDBERG
STRULDBRUG
STRYCHNINE
STUBBORNLY
STUDIOUSLY
STUFFINESS
STULTIFIED
STUMBLEDOM
STUPEFYING
STUPENDOUS
STURDINESS
STYLISTICS
STYLOPISED
UTILIZABLE
YTHUNDERED
AUCTIONEER
AUDIBILITY
AUDITORIUM
AURIFEROUS
AUSPICIOUS
AUSTRALIAN
AUSTRALORP

AUSTRINGER
AUTECOLOGY
AUTHORISED
AUTHORSHIP
AUTOCHTHON
AUTOCRATIC
AUTODIDACT
AUTOGENOUS
AUTOMATION
AUTOMOBILE
AUTOMOTIVE
AUTONOMOUS
AUTOPLASTY
AUTOSTRADA
BUCCINATOR
BUCEPHALUS
BUCHMANISM
BUCKINGHAM
BUCKJUMPER
BUDGERIGAR
BUFFLEHEAD
BUFFOONERY
BULLHEADED
BUMFREEZER
BUNDESWEHR
BURDENSOME
BUREAUCRAT
BURGEONING
BURGLARIZE
BURLINGTON
BUSHRANGER
BUTCHERING
BUTTERBAKE
BUTTERBUMP
BUTTERMERE
BUTTERMILK
BUTTONDOWN
BUTTONHOLE
CUCKOOPINT
CUCULLATED
CUCURBITAL
CUDDLESOME
CUIRASSIER
CUISENAIRE
CULTIVATED
CULTIVATOR
CULVERTAGE
CUMBERLAND
CUMBERSOME
CUMMERBUND
CUMULATIVE
CURMUDGEON
CURMURRING
CURRENCIES
CURRICULUM
CURVACEOUS
CURVETTING
CUSSEDNESS
CUTTLEBONE
CUTTLEFISH

DUCKBOARDS
DUKKERIPEN
DUMBLEDORE
DUNDERFUNK
DUNDERHEAD
DUNDERPATE
DUNIWASSAL
DUODECIMAL
DUPLICATOR
DURABILITY
DUTCHWOMAN
DUUMVIRATE
EUCALYPTUS
EUCHLORINE
EUDIOMETER
EUHEMERISM
EULOGISTIC
EUPHONIOUS
EUPHROSYNE
EUROCHEQUE
EUROCLYDON
EURYPTERUS
EUSTACHIAN
EUTHANASIA
EUTHYNEURA
EUTRAPELIA
FUDDYDUDDY
FULFILMENT
FULIGINOUS
FULLLENGTH
FULLYGROWN
FUMIGATION
FUNCTIONAL
FUNGICIDAL
FURNISHING
FUSTANELLA
FUSTANELLE
FUTURISTIC
GUACHAMOLE
GUARANTEED
GUARNERIUS
GUATEMALAN
GUBERNATOR
GUESTHOUSE
GUIDELINES
GUILLOTINE
GUTTIFERAE
GUTTURALLY
HULLABALOO
HUMANISTIC
HUMANITIES
HUMBLENESS
HUMDUDGEON
HUMIDIFIER
HUMORESQUE
HUMOROUSLY
HUMOURLESS
HUMPBACKED
HUSBANDAGE
JUBILANTLY
JUBILATION
JUDICATURE
JUDICIALLY
JUGENDSTIL
JUGGERNAUT
JUSTICIARY
KUOMINTANG
KURDAITCHA
LUGUBRIOUS
LUMBERJACK
LUMINARIST
LUMINOSITY
LUMPSUCKER
LUPERCALIA
LUSITANIAN
LUTESTRING
LUXEMBOURG
LUXURIANCE
MUCKRAKING
MUDSKIPPER
MUJAHEDDIN
MULIEBRITY
MULLIGRUBS
MULTIMEDIA
MULTIPLIED
MULTIPLIER
MUMBLENEWS
MUNIFICENT
MUSICOLOGY
MUSKETEERS
MUSSORGSKY
MUTABILITY
MUTILATION
MUTINOUSLY
MUTTONHEAD
NUCLEONICS
NUDIBRANCH
NUMBERLESS
NUMERATION
NUMISMATIC
NURSERYMAN
NUTCRACKER
NUTRITIOUS
OUANANICHE
OUGHTLINGS
OUTBALANCE
OUTLANDISH
OUTPATIENT
OUTPERFORM
OUTPOURING
OUTRAGEOUS
OUTSPECKLE
OUVIRANDRA
PUBERULENT
PUBESCENCE
PUBLISHING
PUCKERWOOD
PUGNACIOUS
PULSATANCE
PUMMELLING
PUMPHANDLE
PUNCHDRUNK
PUNCTUALLY
PUNCTULATE
PUNDIGRION
PUNICACEAE
PUNISHABLE
PUNISHMENT
PURITANISM
PURPOSEFUL
PURSUIVANT
PUTREFYING
PUTRESCENT
PUZZLEMENT
QUADRANGLE
QUADRATURA
QUADRICEPS
QUADRIREME
QUAESTUARY
QUAINTNESS
QUARANTINE
QUARRENDER
QUARTERING
QUARTEROON
QUATERNARY
QUEASINESS
QUEENSBURY
QUEENSTOWN
QUENCHLESS
QUERCITRON
QUERSPRUNG
QUESADILLA
QUESTIONER
QUICKSANDS
QUICKTHORN
QUIESCENCE
QUIRINALIA
QUIZMASTER
RUBBERNECK
RUBIGINOUS
RUBINSTEIN
RUDDERLESS
RUDIMENTAL
RUDOLPHINE
RUGGEDNESS
RUMBLOSSOM
RUMBULLION
RUMINANTIA
RUMINATION
RUMINATIVE
RUPESTRIAN
RUPICOLINE
RUTHERFORD
RUTHLESSLY
SUAVEOLENT
SUBCOMPACT
SUBHEADING
SUBJECTION
SUBJECTIVE
SUBLIMATER
SUBLIMINAL
SUBMARINER
SUBMEDIANT
SUBMERSION
SUBMISSION
SUBMISSIVE
SUBREPTION
SUBSCRIBER
SUBSECTION
SUBSELLIUM
SUBSEQUENT
SUBSIDENCE
SUBSIDIARY
SUBSISTENT
SUBSTATION
SUBSTITUTE
SUBSTRATUM
SUBTENANCY
SUBTERFUGE
SUBTROPICS
SUBVENTION
SUBVERSION
SUBVERSIVE
SUCCEEDING
SUCCESSFUL
SUCCESSION
SUCCESSIVE
SUCCINCTLY
SUDDENNESS
SUFFERANCE
SUFFICIENT
SUFFRAGIST
SUGARALLIE
SUGGESTION
SUGGESTIVE
SULPHUROUS
SULTRINESS
SUMMERTIME
SUNBATHING
SUNGLASSES
SUPERADDED
SUPERCARGO
SUPERGIANT
SUPERHUMAN
SUPERMODEL
SUPERPOWER
SUPERSONIC
SUPERSTORE
SUPERTONIC
SUPERVISED
SUPERVISOR
SUPERWOMAN
SUPPLEJACK
SUPPLEMENT
SUPPLENESS
SUPPLICANT
SUPPLICATE
SUPPORTING
SUPPORTIVE
SUPPOSEDLY
SUPPRESSED
SUPPRESSOR
SURFRIDING
SURGICALLY
SURINAMESE
SURPASSING
SURPRISING
SURREALISM
SURREALIST
SURROUNDED
SUSPENDERS
SUSPENSION
SUSPICIOUS
SUSTAINING
SUSTENANCE
SUZERAINTY
TUBERCULAR
TULARAEMIA
TUMBLEDOWN
TUMESCENCE
TUMULTUOUS
TURBULENCE
TURNAROUND
TURPENTINE
TURRITELLA
TURTLEDOVE
TURTLENECK
TUTIVILLUS
VULCANALIA
VULNERABLE
WUNDERKIND
ZUMBOORUCK
AVANTGARDE
AVANTURINE
AVARICIOUS
AVENTURINE
AVERRHOISM
AVICULARIA
AVVOGADORE
EVACUATION
EVALUATION
EVANESCENT
EVANGELIST
EVANGELIZE
EVAPORATED
EVENHANDED
EVENTUALLY
EVERGLADES
EVERYPLACE
EVERYTHING
EVERYWHERE
EVISCERATE
EVITERNITY
OVERCHARGE
OVEREATING
OVERLANDER
OVERPRAISE
OVERRIDING
OVERSHADOW
OVERSLAUGH

OVERSPREAD
OVERSTRAIN
OVERSTRUNG
OVERSUPPLY
OVERTHETOP
OVERTHWART
OVERWEIGHT
OVERWORKED
OVIPOSITOR
SVADILFARI
OWLSPIEGLE
SWAGGERING
SWALLOWING
SWEATSHIRT
SWEDENBORG
SWEEPSTAKE
SWEETBREAD
SWEETENING
SWEETHEART
SWELTERING
SWIMMINGLY
SWITCHBACK
SWORDSTICK
ZWITTERION
AXINOMANCY
EXACERBATE
EXACTITUDE
EXAGGERATE
EXALTATION
EXASPERATE
EXCAVATION
EXCELLENCE
EXCELLENCY
EXCITEMENT
EXCRUCIATE
EXECRATION
EXEMPTNESS
EXENTERATE
EXHALATION
EXHAUSTING
EXHAUSTION
EXHAUSTIVE
EXHIBITION
EXHILARATE
EXHUMATION
EXONERATED
EXORBITANT
EXOTHERMIC
EXOTICALLY
EXPATRIATE
EXPECTANCY
EXPEDIENCE
EXPEDIENCY
EXPEDITION
EXPENDABLE
EXPERIENCE
EXPERIMENT
EXPIRATION
EXPLICABLE
EXPLICITLY
EXPOSITION
EXPOSITORY
EXPOUNDERS
EXPRESSION
EXPRESSIVE
EXPRESSMAN
EXPRESSWAY
EXTENDABLE
EXTENSIBLE
EXTERNALLY
EXTINCTION
EXTINGUISH
EXTRACTION
EXTRANEOUS
EXUBERANCE
EXULTATION
OXYGENATOR
OXYMORONIC
BYELECTION
CYBERNETIC
CYCLOPEDIA
CYCLOSTYLE
CYNOMOLGUS
CYSTOSCOPY
DYNAMITARD
DYSCRASITE
DYSPROSIUM
DYSTROPHIC
EYEWITNESS
GYMNASTICS
GYMNOSOPHY
GYNECOLOGY
GYPSOPHILA
GYROSCOPIC
HYALOPHANE
HYDRAULICS
HYDROLYSIS
HYDROMETER
HYDROPHANE
HYDROPLANE
HYDROPONIC
HYGROMETER
HYPAETHRAL
HYPAETHRON
HYPERBOLIC
HYPERDULIA
HYPNOTIZED
HYPOCORISM
HYPODERMIC
HYPOGAEOUS
HYPOTENUSE
HYPOTHESIS
HYSTERESIS
HYSTERICAL
LYCHNAPSIA
LYSENKOISM
MYCORRHIZA
MYRINGITIS
MYRIOSCOPE
MYSTAGOGUE
MYSTAGOGUS
MYSTERIOUS
NYCTALOPIA
NYMPHOLEPT
PYCNOGONID
PYRACANTHA
PYRAGYRITE
PYROGRAPHY
PYROMANIAC
PYROPHORUS
PYTHAGORAS
PYTHOGENIC
SYMBOLICAL
SYMPATHISE
SYMPATHIZE
SYMPHONIUM
SYNAERESIS
SYNCOPATED
SYNCRETISE
SYNECDOCHE
SYNEIDESIS
SYNONYMOUS
SYNOSTOSIS
SYNTAGMATA
SYNTERESIS
SYNTHESIZE
SYNTHRONUS
SYPHILITIC
SYSTEMATIC
TYPESCRIPT
TYPESETTER
TYPEWRITER
TYPOGRAPHY
TYRANNICAL
TYRANNISED
WYCLIFFIAN
OZYMANDIAS

10:3

ACANACEOUS
ADAMANTINE
ADAPTATION
AGAPANTHUS
ALABANDINE
ALABANDITE
AMALGAMATE
AMANUENSIS
AMARYLLIDS
AMATEURISH
ANABAPTIST
ANACARDIUM
ANACHARSIS
ANACLASTIC
ANACOUSTIC
ANACRUSTIC
ANADROMOUS
ANADYOMENE
ANALOGICAL
ANALPHABET
ANALYTICAL
ANARCHICAL
ANASTIGMAT
ANASTROPHE
ANATOMICAL
ANAXIMENES
ARACOSTYLE
ARAGONITES
ARAUCANIAN
ASAFOETIDA
ASARABACCA
AVANTGARDE
AVANTURINE
AVARICIOUS
BEARGARDEN
BEAUJOLAIS
BEAUTICIAN
BEAUTIFIER
BEAVERSKIN
BIANNUALLY
BLACKBEARD
BLACKBERRY
BLACKBOARD
BLACKBULLY
BLACKENING
BLACKGUARD
BLACKHEART
BLACKSHIRT
BLACKSMITH
BLACKSTONE
BLACKTHORN
BLACKWATER
BLANCMANGE
BLANQUETTE
BLASPHEMER
BLASTOIDEA
BRACHIOPOD
BRADYKININ
BRADYSEISM
BRAGADISME
BRAINCHILD
BRAININESS
BRAINPOWER
BRAINSTORM
BRASSBOUND
BRATISLAVA
CHAFFERING
CHAIRWOMAN
CHALCEDONY
CHALLENGER
CHALYBEATE
CHAMAEROPS
CHAMBERPOT
CHAMBERTIN
CHAMBRANLE
CHAMPIGNON
CHANCELLOR
CHANDELIER
CHANGEABLE
CHANGELESS
CHANGELING
CHAPARAJOS
CHAPAREJOS
CHAPFALLEN
CHAPLAINCY
CHAPTALISE
CHARDONNAY
CHARGEABLE
CHARGEHAND
CHARIOTEER
CHARITABLE
CHARITABLY
CHAROLLAIS
CHARTREUSE
CHATELAINE
CHATTERBOX
CHATTERTON
CHAUCERIAN
CHAUDFROID
CHAULMUGRA
CHAUTAUQUA
CHAUVINISM
CHAUVINIST
CLAIRCOLLE
CLAMMINESS
CLAMOURING
CLANSWOMAN
CLARABELLA
CLASPKNIFE
CLASSICISM
CLASSICIST
CLASSIFIED
CLAVICHORD
COADJUTANT
COARSENESS
COASTGUARD
COATHANGER
CRAFTINESS
CRAIGFLUKE
CRANKSHAFT
CRAPULENCE
CRAQUETURE
DEACTIVATE
DEADLINESS
DEADNETTLE
DEALERSHIP
DHARMSHALA
DIABOLICAL
DIACAUSTIC
DIACONICON
DIAGENESIS
DIAGNOSTIC
DIAGONALLY
DIALECTICS
DIAPEDESIS
DIAPHANOUS
DIASKEUAST
DIASTALTIC
DRACONITES

DRAKESTONE
DRAWBRIDGE
DRAWCANSIR
DRAWSTRING
ECARDINATE
ELACAMPANE
ELASTICATE
ELASTICITY
EMACIATION
EMALANGENI
EMANCIPATE
EMARGINATE
EMASCULATE
ENANTIOSIS
EPANOPHORA
EPAULEMENT
EVACUATION
EVALUATION
EVANESCENT
EVANGELIST
EVANGELIZE
EVAPORATED
EXACERBATE
EXACTITUDE
EXAGGERATE
EXALTATION
EXASPERATE
FEARLESSLY
FEARNOUGHT
FEATHERBED
FIANCHETTO
FLABBINESS
FLAGELLATE
FLAGITIOUS
FLAGRANTLY
FLAMBOYANT
FLAMEPROOF
FLAMINGANT
FLANCONADE
FLAPDOODLE
FLASHINESS
FLASHLIGHT
FLASHPOINT
FLATTERING
FLATULENCE
FLAVESCENT
FLAVOURING
FRACTIONAL
FRAMBOESIA
FRANCHISEE
FRANCHISOR
FRANCISCAN
FRANGIPANE
FRANGIPANI
FRATERETTO
FRATERNISE
FRATERNITY
FRATERNIZE
FRATICELLI
FRATRICIDE
FRAUDULENT
FRAUNHOFER
FRAXINELLA
GLACIATION
GLAMOURISE
GLASSHOUSE
GLASSINESS
GLAUCONITE
GOALKEEPER
GOATSUCKER
GRACEFULLY
GRACIOUSLY
GRADUATION
GRAMICIDIN
GRAMMARIAN
GRAMOPHONE
GRANADILLA
GRANDCHILD
GRANDSTAND
GRANGERISM
GRANGERIZE
GRANULATED
GRAPEFRUIT
GRAPHOLOGY
GRAPTOLITE
GRASSLANDS
GRASSROOTS
GRASSWIDOW
GRATEFULLY
GRATIFYING
GRATILLITY
GRATUITOUS
GRAVEOLENT
GRAVESTONE
GUACHAMOLE
GUARANTEED
GUARNERIUS
GUATEMALAN
HEADHUNTED
HEADHUNTER
HEADLIGHTS
HEADMASTER
HEADPHONES
HEADSTRONG
HEARTBREAK
HEARTINESS
HEAVENWARD
HOARSENESS
HYALOPHANE
IMAGINABLE
INACCURACY
INACCURATE
INACTIVITY
INADEQUACY
INADEQUATE
INAPTITUDE
INARTISTIC
INAUGURATE
ISABELLINE
KLANGFARBE
LEADERSHIP
LEAFHOPPER
LEAMINGTON
MEADOWPLAN
MEAGERNESS
MEAGRENESS
MEANDERING
MEANINGFUL
MEASURABLE
NEAPOLITAN
OPALESCENT
ORATORICAL
OUANANICHE
PEACEFULLY
PEACEMAKER
PEACHERINO
PEASHOOTER
PEAUDESOIE
PHAELONIAN
PHAENOTYPE
PHAGEDAENA
PHANTASIME
PHANTASIST
PHARMACIST
PIANOFORTE
PLAGIARISE
PLAGIARISM
PLAGIARIST
PLAGIARIZE
PLANCHETTE
PLANOBLAST
PLANTATION
PLASMODESM
PLASTICINE
PLASTICITY
PLATELAYER
PLATINISED
PLATTELAND
PLAYFELLOW
PLAYGROUND
PLAYWRIGHT
PRAEMUNIRE
PRAETORIAN
PRAETORIUM
PRAGMATISM
PRAGMATIST
PRATINCOLE
PRAXITELES
PSALTERIUM
PSAMMOPHIL
QUADRANGLE
QUADRATURA
QUADRICEPS
QUADRIREME
QUAESTUARY
QUAINTNESS
QUARANTINE
QUARRENDER
QUARTERING
QUARTEROON
QUATERNARY
REACTIVATE
READERSHIP
REAMINGBIT
REAPPRAISE
REARMAMENT
REASONABLE
REASONABLY
REASSEMBLE
REASSURING
RHAMPASTOS
RHAPSODISE
RHAPSODIZE
ROADRUNNER
ROADWORTHY
SCAMMOZZIS
SCANDALISE
SCANDALIZE
SCANDALOUS
SCANDAROON
SCANDERBEG
SCANTINESS
SCAPEGRACE
SCAPHOPODA
SCARAMOUCH
SCARCEMENT
SCARCENESS
SCARLATINA
SCARLETINA
SCATHELESS
SCATTERING
SCATURIENT
SEAMANSHIP
SEAMSTRESS
SEANNACHIE
SEASONABLE
SEASONABLY
SGANARELLE
SHABBINESS
SHACKLETON
SHADOWLESS
SHAGHAIRED
SHAKUHACHI
SHAMEFACED
SHAMEFULLY
SHAMPOOING
SHANDRYDAN
SHANDYGAFF
SHARAWADGI
SHARAWAGGI
SHATTERING
SKATEBOARD
SLAMMERKIN
SLANDEROUS
SLATTERNLY
SMALLSCALE
SMARAGDINE
SMARMINESS
SMATTERING
SNAKEMOUTH
SNAKESTONE
SNAPDRAGON
SNAPHAUNCE
SNAPHAUNCH
SPACECRAFT
SPALLATION
SPARSENESS
SPARTACIST
SPATCHCOCK
STABILISER
STABILIZER
STADHOLDER
STAGECOACH
STAGECRAFT
STAGGERING
STAGNATION
STALACTITE
STALAGMITE
STALHELMER
STALLENGER
STALLINGER
STAMMERING
STANDPOINT
STANDSTILL
STANISLAUS
STAPHYLINE
STARVATION
STARVELING
STATECRAFT
STATIONARY
STATIONERY
STATISTICS
STATOCRACY
STATUESQUE
STAUROLITE
STAVESACRE
SUAVEOLENT
SVADILFARI
SWAGGERING
SWALLOWING
THALASSIAN
THALESTRIS
THALICTRUM
THALLIFORM
THANKFULLY
THAUMASITE
TRACHELATE
TRADITIONS
TRAFFICKER
TRAGACANTH
TRAGICALLY
TRAITOROUS
TRAJECTORY
TRAMONTANA
TRAMONTANE
TRAMPOLINE
TRANQUILLY
TRANSCRIBE
TRANSCRIPT
TRANSGRESS

TRANSIENCE
TRANSISTOR
TRANSITION
TRANSITIVE
TRANSITORY
TRANSLATED
TRANSLATOR
TRANSPLANT
TRANSPOSED
TRANSVERSE
TRAUMATIZE
TRAVANCORE
TRAVELATOR
TRAVELLERS
TRAVELLING
TRAVELOGUE
TRAVERTINE
TRAVOLATOR
UNABRIDGED
UNACCENTED
UNAFFECTED
UNANSWERED
UNARGUABLE
UNASSIGNED
UNASSUMING
UNATTACHED
UNATTENDED
UNAVAILING
WEAPONLESS
WEATHERMAN
WHARFINGER
WHATSOEVER
WRAPAROUND
ZOANTHARIA
ABBREVIATE
ALBIGENSES
AMBARVALIA
AMBASSADOR
AMBIVALENT
AMBLYOPSIS
AMBLYSTOMA
AMBOCEPTOR
AMBULACRUM
AMBULATORY
ARBITRATOR
ASBESTOSIS
BABESIASIS
BABIROUSSA
BABYLONIAN
BABYSITTER
BOBBYSOXER
CYBERNETIC
DEBASEMENT
DEBATEMENT
DEBAUCHERY
DEBILITATE
DEBOUCHURE
DEBRIEFING
EMBANKMENT
EMBERGOOSE
EMBITTERED
EMBLEMATIC
EMBLEMENTS
EMBODIMENT
EMBONPOINT
EMBOUCHURE
EMBROIDERY
EMBRYOLOGY
FABULOUSLY
FIBERGLASS
FIBREGLASS
FIBRILLATE
FIBROSITIS
GIBBERELLA
GOBEMOUCHE
GUBERNATOR
HABILITATE
HABITATION
HABITUALLY
HOBBYHORSE
IMBECILITY
IMBRICATED
IMBROCCATA
INBREEDING
JABBERWOCK
JOBSEEKERS
JUBILANTLY
JUBILATION
LABORATORY
LEBENSRAUM
LIBERALISM
LIBERALITY
LIBERALIZE
LIBERATION
LIBIDINOUS
LIBRETTIST
LIBREVILLE
MABINOGION
NOBLEWOMAN
OMBROMETER
OMBROPHOBE
PUBERULENT
PUBESCENCE
PUBLISHING
RABBINICAL
REBELLIOUS
RIBOFLAVIN
ROBERDSMAN
ROBERTSMAN
ROBUSTIOUS
ROBUSTNESS
RUBBERNECK
RUBIGINOUS
RUBINSTEIN
SABBATICAL
SABRETACHE
SOBERSIDES
SUBCOMPACT
SUBHEADING
SUBJECTION
SUBJECTIVE
SUBLIMATER
SUBLIMINAL
SUBMARINER
SUBMEDIANT
SUBMERSION
SUBMISSION
SUBMISSIVE
SUBREPTION
SUBSCRIBER
SUBSECTION
SUBSELLIUM
SUBSEQUENT
SUBSIDENCE
SUBSIDIARY
SUBSISTENT
SUBSTATION
SUBSTITUTE
SUBSTRATUM
SUBTENANCY
SUBTERFUGE
SUBTROPICS
SUBVENTION
SUBVERSION
SUBVERSIVE
TABERNACLE
TABLANETTE
TABLECLOTH
TABLESPOON
TABULATION
TUBERCULAR
UMBELLIFER
UNBALANCED
UNBEARABLE
UNBEARABLY
UNBEATABLE
UNBECOMING
UNBELIEVER
UNBLEACHED
UNBLINKING
UNBLUSHING
UPBRINGING
VIBRACULUM
VIBRAPHONE
VIBRATIONS
ZABAGLIONE
ACCELERATE
ACCENTUATE
ACCESSIBLE
ACCESSIONS
ACCIDENTAL
ACCLIVIOUS
ACCOMPLICE
ACCOMPLISH
ACCORDANCE
ACCOUNTANT
ACCOUNTING
ACCREDITED
ACCUBATION
ACCUMULATE
ACCURATELY
ACCUSATION
ACCUSATIVE
ACCUSINGLY
ACCUSTOMED
ALCAICERIA
ALCHERINGA
ALCIBIADES
ALCOHOLISM
ALCYONARIA
ANCHORETIC
ANCHYLOSIS
ANCIPITOUS
ARCHBISHOP
ARCHDEACON
ARCHETYPAL
ARCHIMEDES
ARCHITRAVE
ASCENDANCY
ASCENDENCY
ASCETICISM
ASCRIBABLE
AUCTIONEER
BACCHANTES
BACITRACIN
BACKBITING
BACKBLOCKS
BACKGAMMON
BACKGROUND
BACKHANDED
BACKHANDER
BACKPACKER
BACKSLIDER
BACKSTAIRS
BACKSTROKE
BICHROMATE
BUCCINATOR
BUCEPHALUS
BUCHMANISM
BUCKINGHAM
BUCKJUMPER
CACHINNATE
CACODAEMON
CACOGRAPHY
CACOMISTLE
CACUMINOUS
CECIDOMYIA
COCCINEOUS
COCHLEARIA
COCKABULLY
COCKALORUM
COCKATRICE
COCKCHAFER
COCKERNONY
CUCKOOPINT
CUCULLATED
CUCURBITAL
CYCLOPEDIA
CYCLOSTYLE
DECAGRAMME
DECAHEDRON
DECAMPMENT
DECAPITATE
DECATHLETE
DECELERATE
DECENNOVAL
DECIMALIZE
DECIPHERED
DECISIVELY
DECLENSION
DECOLLATOR
DECOLORATE
DECOMPOSED
DECORATION
DECORATIVE
DECRESCENT
DICHROMISM
DICKCISSEL
DICTIONARY
DICTOGRAPH
DICYNODONT
DOCIMASTIC
DUCKBOARDS
ECCHYMOSIS
ECCOPROTIC
ENCAMPMENT
ENCASEMENT
ENCEPHALON
ENCHANTING
ENCLOISTER
ENCOIGNURE
ENCYCLICAL
ESCADRILLE
ESCALATION
ESCAPEMENT
ESCARPMENT
ESCHAROTIC
ESCRITOIRE
ESCULAPIAN
ESCUTCHEON
EUCALYPTUS
EUCHLORINE
EXCAVATION
EXCELLENCE
EXCELLENCY
EXCITEMENT
EXCRUCIATE
FACESAVING
FACILITATE
FACILITIES
FACTITIOUS
FICKLENESS
FICTITIOUS
HACKBUTEER
HACKMATACK
HECTICALLY
HECTOLITRE
INCAPACITY
INCAPARINA
INCAUTIOUS

INCENDIARY
INCESTUOUS
INCIDENTAL
INCINERATE
INCISIVELY
INCITEMENT
INCIVILITY
INCOHERENT
INCOMPLETE
INCONSTANT
INCRASSATE
INCREASING
INCREDIBLE
INCREDIBLY
INCRESCENT
INCUBATION
INCUMBENCY
INCUNABULA
JACKANAPES
JACKBOOTED
JACKHAMMER
JACKSTONES
JACKSTRAWS
JACULATION
JOCULARITY
LACCADIVES
LACERATION
LACHRYMOSE
LACKADAISY
LACKLUSTER
LACKLUSTRE
LACUSTRINE
LICENTIATE
LICENTIOUS
LOCKERROOM
LOCKKEEPER
LOCOMOTION
LOCOMOTIVE
LOCULAMENT
LYCHNAPSIA
MACEDONIAN
MACKINTOSH
MACONOCHIE
MACROBIOTE
MACROCARPA
MECHANICAL
MECHANIZED
MICHAELMAS
MICROFICHE
MICROLIGHT
MICROMETER
MICRONESIA
MICROPHONE
MICROSCOPE
MUCKRAKING
MYCORRHIZA
NECROMANCY
NECROPOLIS
NECTABANUS
NICARAGUAN
NICROSILAL
NUCLEONICS
NYCTALOPIA
OCCASIONAL
OCCIDENTAL
OCCUPATION
OCCURRENCE
ORCHESTRAL
ORCHIDEOUS
OSCILLATOR
OSCITATION
OSCULATION
OSCULATORY
PACIFICISM
PECCADILLO
PECULATION
PECULIARLY
PICARESQUE
PICAYUNISH
PICCADILLY
PICCALILLI
PICCANINNY
PICHICIAGO
PICKPOCKET
POCAHONTAS
POCKETBOOK
POCKMANTIE
POCKMARKED
PUCKERWOOD
PYCNOGONID
RACECOURSE
RECEPTACLE
RECIDIVISM
RECIDIVIST
RECIPROCAL
RECITATION
RECITATIVE
RECITATIVO
RECKLESSLY
RECOGNISED
RECOGNIZED
RECOMMENCE
RECOMPENSE
RECONCILED
RECONSIDER
RECREATION
RECRUDESCE
RECUPERATE
RECURRENCE
RICHARDSON
RICHTHOFEN
ROCKABILLY
ROCKINGHAM
ROCKSTEADY
SACCHARASE
SACCHARIDE
SACCHARINE
SACCHAROID
SACERDOTAL
SACREDNESS
SACROSANCT
SECONDBEST
SECONDHAND
SECONDMENT
SECONDRATE
SECRETAIRE
SECULARIZE
SECURITIES
SICILIENNE
SUCCEEDING
SUCCESSFUL
SUCCESSION
SUCCESSIVE
SUCCINCTLY
TACHOGRAPH
TACHOMETER
TACTICALLY
TACTLESSLY
TECHNETIUM
TECHNICIAN
TECHNOCRAT
TECHNOLOGY
TICKERTAPE
TOCCATELLA
TOCOPHEROL
ULCERATION
UNCOMMONLY
UNCONFINED
UNCRITICAL
UNCTUOUSLY
UNCULTURED
VICEGERENT
VICEREGENT
VICTORIANA
VICTORIOUS
VICTUALLER
VOCABULARY
VOCABULIST
VOCATIONAL
VOCIFERATE
VOCIFEROUS
WICKEDNESS
WICKERWORK
WYCLIFFIAN
ABDICATION
ADDITAMENT
ADDITIONAL
ALDERMANLY
ANDALUSIAN
ANDALUSITE
ANDROMACHE
AUDIBILITY
AUDITORIUM
BADDERLOCK
BEDCHAMBER
BEDCLOTHES
BEDEVILLED
BEDRAGGLED
BUDGERIGAR
CADAVEROUS
CODSWALLOP
CUDDLESOME
DEDICATION
DEDUCTIBLE
DIDASCALIC
DIDGERIDOO
DIDUNCULUS
DODECANESE
ELDERBERRY
ENDEARMENT
ENDOGAMOUS
ENDOSMOSIS
EUDIOMETER
FEDERALISM
FEDERALIST
FEDERATION
FIDDLEWOOD
FUDDYDUDDY
GADOLINIUM
GODPARENTS
HEDONISTIC
HODGEPODGE
HYDRAULICS
HYDROLYSIS
HYDROMETER
HYDROPHANE
HYDROPLANE
HYDROPONIC
INDAPAMIDE
INDECENTLY
INDECISION
INDECISIVE
INDECOROUS
INDEFINITE
INDELICACY
INDELICATE
INDENTURES
INDICATION
INDICATIVE
INDICOLITE
INDICTABLE
INDICTMENT
INDIGENOUS
INDIGOLITE
INDIRECTLY
INDISCREET
INDISPOSED
INDISTINCT
INDITEMENT
INDIVIDUAL
INDONESIAN
INDUCEMENT
INDUCTANCE
INDULGENCE
INDUMENTUM
INDUSTRIAL
JUDICATURE
JUDICIALLY
KIDNAPPING
LADYKILLER
LEDERHOSEN
MADAGASCAN
MADAGASCAR
MEDDLESOME
MEDICAMENT
MEDICATION
MEDIOCRITY
MEDITATION
MEDITATIVE
MEDIUMTERM
MIDLOTHIAN
MIDSHIPMAN
MODERATELY
MODERATION
MODIFIABLE
MODULATION
MUDSKIPPER
NIDDERLING
NUDIBRANCH
ODDFELLOWS
ORDINARILY
ORDINATION
ORDONNANCE
PADAREWSKI
PADDINGTON
PADDYMELON
PEDESTRIAN
PEDIATRICS
PEDICULATE
PEDIMENTAL
PEDIPALPUS
RADICALISM
RADIOGRAPH
RADIOLARIA
REDCURRANT
REDECORATE
REDEMPTION
REDISCOVER
REDRUTHITE
REDUNDANCY
RIDICULOUS
RIDINGHOOD
RUDDERLESS
RUDIMENTAL
RUDOLPHINE
SADDLEBACK
SADDLEBILL
SEDATENESS
SEDULOUSLY
SIDEBOARDS
SIDERATION
SIDEROSTAT
SIDESADDLE
SIDEWINDER
SUDDENNESS
TEDDINGTON
UNDECLARED
UNDEFEATED
UNDEFENDED
UNDENIABLE

UNDERBURNT
UNDERCLASS
UNDERCOVER
UNDERCRAFT
UNDERCROFT
UNDERFLOOR
UNDERLEASE
UNDERLINEN
UNDERLYING
UNDERNEATH
UNDERPANTS
UNDERSCORE
UNDERSHIRT
UNDERSIZED
UNDERSKIRT
UNDERSLUNG
UNDERSTAND
UNDERSTATE
UNDERSTEER
UNDERSTOOD
UNDERSTUDY
UNDERTAKER
UNDERVALUE
UNDERWATER
UNDERWORLD
UNDERWRITE
UNDESCRIED
UNDESERVED
UNDETECTED
UNDETERRED
UNDIGESTED
UNDISPUTED
UNDOCTORED
UNDULATING
UNDULATION
WIDDICOMBE
WIDESPREAD
ABERDEVINE
ABERGLAUBE
ABERRATION
ACEPHALOUS
ACETABULAR
ACETABULUM
ADELANTADO
ADEQUATELY
ALECTORIAN
ALEMBICATE
ALEXANDERS
ALEXANDRIA
AMELIORATE
ANEMOGRAPH
ANEMOMETER
ANESTHESIA
ANESTHETIC
APEMANTHUS
AREFACTION
ARENACEOUS
AREOGRAPHY
AREOPAGITE
ATELEIOSIS
AVENTURINE
AVERRHOISM
BEEFBURGER
BEEFEATERS
BEEKEEPING
BIENNIALLY
BLEARYEYED
BLEPHARISM
BREADFRUIT
BREAKABLES
BREAKWATER
BREASTBONE
BREASTFEED
BREASTWORK
BREATHLESS
BRESSUMMER
BYELECTION
CAERPHILLY
CAESPITOSE
CHEAPSKATE
CHECKLATON
CHECKPOINT
CHEEKINESS
CHEERFULLY
CHEESECAKE
CHEESEWOOD
CHEIRONOMY
CHELTENHAM
CHEMICALLY
CHEMONASTY
CHEQUEBOOK
CHERIMOYER
CHERRYWOOD
CHERSONESE
CHERVONETS
CHESSBOARD
CHESSYLITE
CHESTERTON
CHEVESAILE
CHEVISANCE
CHEVROTAIN
CLEARSTORY
CLEARWATER
CLEMENCEAU
CLEMENTINE
CLERESTORY
CLEROMANCY
CLEVERNESS
COELACANTH
COETANEOUS
COEXISTENT
CREATIVITY
CREDENTIAL
CREDITABLE
CREDITABLY
CRENELLATE
CREOPHAGUS
CRETACEOUS
CTENOPHORA
DEEPFREEZE
DEEPSEATED
DIELECTRIC
DREADFULLY
DREADLOCKS
DREAMINESS
DREARINESS
DREARISOME
DREIKANTER
DRESSMAKER
ELECAMPANE
ELECTORATE
ELECTRICAL
ELECTROMER
ELECTRONIC
ELEGABALUS
ELEMENTARY
ELEUSINIAN
EMENDATION
EPENTHETIC
ETEOCRETAN
EVENHANDED
EVENTUALLY
EVERGLADES
EVERYPLACE
EVERYTHING
EVERYWHERE
EXECRATION
EXEMPTNESS
EXENTERATE
EYEWITNESS
FEEBLENESS
FIELDMOUSE
FIENDISHLY
FIERCENESS
FLEETINGLY
FLESHINESS
FREEBOOTER
FREEHANDER
FREEHOLDER
FREELANCER
FREELOADER
FREEMARTIN
FREEMASONS
FREIGHTAGE
FREMESCENT
FRENETICAL
FRENZIEDLY
FREQUENTED
FREQUENTER
FREQUENTLY
FRESHWATER
GLEEMAIDEN
GLENDOVEER
GREEDINESS
GREENCLOTH
GREENFINCH
GREENHEART
GREENHOUSE
GREENSHANK
GREENSTICK
GREENSWARD
GREGARIOUS
GRENADIERS
GRENADILLA
GREYFRIARS
GUESTHOUSE
HAEMANTHUS
HEEDLESSLY
HIERARCHIC
HIEROGLYPH
HIEROMANCY
HIEROPHANT
HIEROSCOPY
ICEBREAKER
IDEALISTIC
INEBRIATED
INEDUCABLE
INEFFICACY
INELIGIBLE
INEPTITUDE
INEQUALITY
INESCULENT
INEVITABLE
INEVITABLY
INEXORABLE
KIESELGUHR
KLEBSIELLA
KOEKSISTER
LAEOTROPIC
LHERZOLITE
LIEBERMANN
LIEUTENANT
MEERSCHAUM
NEEDLECASE
NEEDLEWORK
OBEDIENTLY
OCEANGOING
ODELSTHING
OLEAGINOUS
OLERACEOUS
OPENHANDED
OPENMINDED
OVERCHARGE
OVEREATING
OVERLANDER
OVERPRAISE
OVERRIDING
OVERSHADOW
OVERSLAUGH
OVERSPREAD
OVERSTRAIN
OVERSTRUNG
OVERSUPPLY
OVERTHETOP
OVERTHWART
OVERWEIGHT
OVERWORKED
PAEDIATRIC
PEELGARLIC
PHENOMENAL
PHENOMENON
PLEASANTLY
PLEASANTRY
PLEBISCITE
PLEONASTIC
PLEROPHORY
PLESIOSAUR
PLEXIMETER
POETASTERY
POETICALLY
PREARRANGE
PREBENDARY
PRECARIOUS
PRECAUTION
PRECEDENCE
PRECIPITIN
PRECOCIOUS
PRECURSORY
PREDACIOUS
PREDECEASE
PREDESTINE
PREDICTION
PREDISPOSE
PREDNISONE
PREEMINENT
PREFERABLE
PREFERABLY
PREFERENCE
PREFERMENT
PREHENSILE
PREHISTORY
PREJUDICED
PRELECTION
PREMARITAL
PREPARATOR
PREPAYMENT
PREPENSELY
PREPOSITOR
PREPOSSESS
PREPOTENCE
PRESBYOPIA
PRESBYTERY
PRESCIENCE
PRESENTDAY
PRESIDENCY
PRESSURIZE
PRESUMABLY
PRESUPPOSE
PRETENSION
PRETINCOLE
PRETTINESS
PREVAILING
PREVALENCE
PREVENANCY
PREVENTION
PREVENTIVE
PREVIOUSLY
PSEPHOLOGY
PSEUDOCARP
PTERANODON

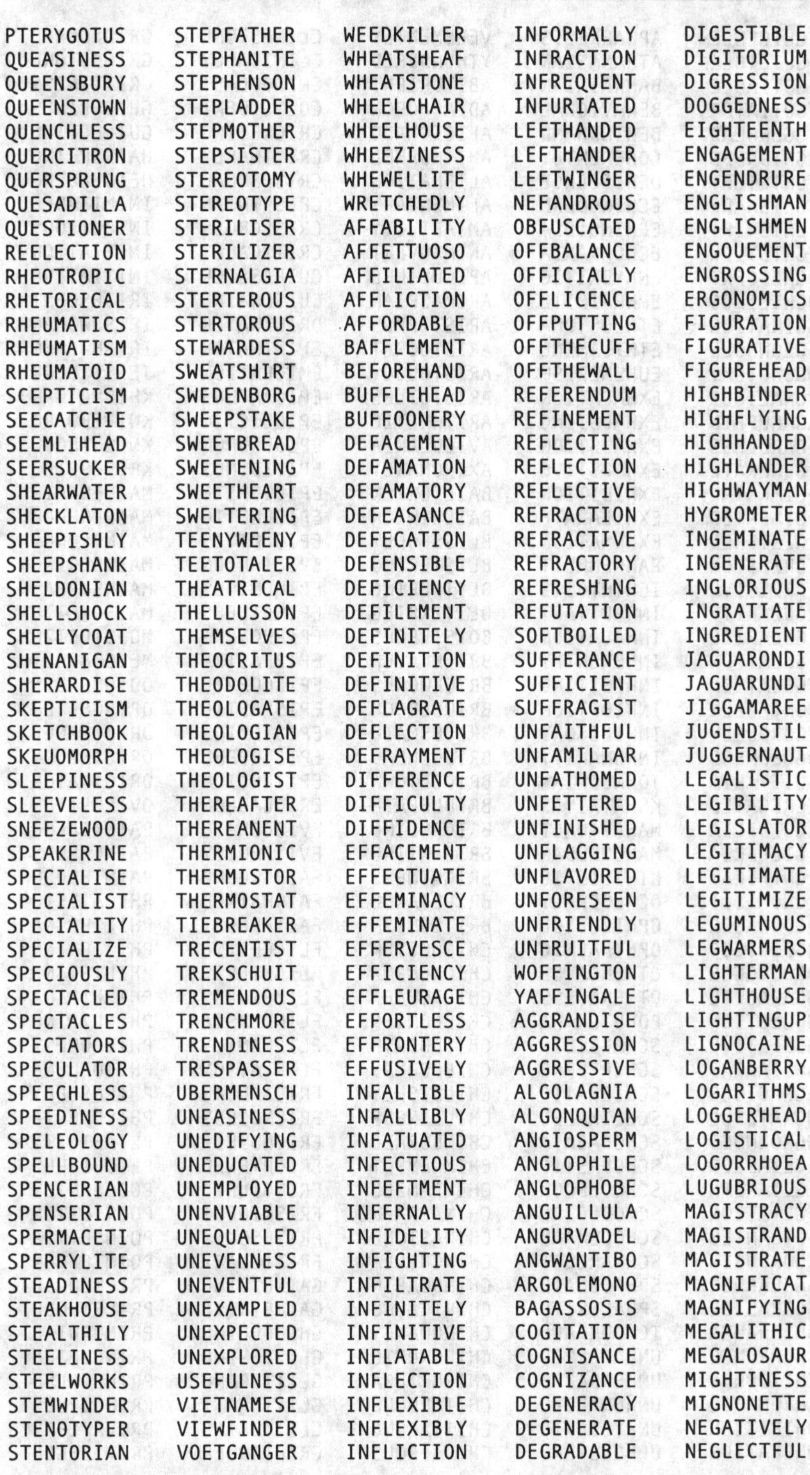

PTERYGOTUS
QUEASINESS
QUEENSBURY
QUEENSTOWN
QUENCHLESS
QUERCITRON
QUERSPRUNG
QUESADILLA
QUESTIONER
REELECTION
RHEOTROPIC
RHETORICAL
RHEUMATICS
RHEUMATISM
RHEUMATOID
SCEPTICISM
SEECATCHIE
SEEMLIHEAD
SEERSUCKER
SHEARWATER
SHECKLATON
SHEEPISHLY
SHEEPSHANK
SHELDONIAN
SHELLSHOCK
SHELLYCOAT
SHENANIGAN
SHERARDISE
SKEPTICISM
SKETCHBOOK
SKEUOMORPH
SLEEPINESS
SLEEVELESS
SNEEZEWOOD
SPEAKERINE
SPECIALISE
SPECIALIST
SPECIALITY
SPECIALIZE
SPECIOUSLY
SPECTACLED
SPECTACLES
SPECTATORS
SPECULATOR
SPEECHLESS
SPEEDINESS
SPELEOLOGY
SPELLBOUND
SPENCERIAN
SPENSERIAN
SPERMACETI
SPERRYLITE
STEADINESS
STEAKHOUSE
STEALTHILY
STEELINESS
STEELWORKS
STEMWINDER
STENOTYPER
STENTORIAN
STEPFATHER
STEPHANITE
STEPHENSON
STEPLADDER
STEPMOTHER
STEPSISTER
STEREOTOMY
STEREOTYPE
STERILISER
STERILIZER
STERNALGIA
STERTEROUS
STERTOROUS
STEWARDESS
SWEATSHIRT
SWEDENBORG
SWEEPSTAKE
SWEETBREAD
SWEETENING
SWEETHEART
SWELTERING
TEENYWEENY
TEETOTALER
THEATRICAL
THELLUSSON
THEMSELVES
THEOCRITUS
THEODOLITE
THEOLOGATE
THEOLOGIAN
THEOLOGISE
THEOLOGIST
THEREAFTER
THEREANENT
THERMIONIC
THERMISTOR
THERMOSTAT
TIEBREAKER
TRECENTIST
TREKSCHUIT
TREMENDOUS
TRENCHMORE
TRENDINESS
TRESPASSER
UBERMENSCH
UNEASINESS
UNEDIFYING
UNEDUCATED
UNEMPLOYED
UNENVIABLE
UNEQUALLED
UNEVENNESS
UNEVENTFUL
UNEXAMPLED
UNEXPECTED
UNEXPLORED
USEFULNESS
VIETNAMESE
VIEWFINDER
VOETGANGER
WEEDKILLER
WHEATSHEAF
WHEATSTONE
WHEELCHAIR
WHEELHOUSE
WHEEZINESS
WHEWELLITE
WRETCHEDLY
AFFABILITY
AFFETTUOSO
AFFILIATED
AFFLICTION
AFFORDABLE
BAFFLEMENT
BEFOREHAND
BUFFLEHEAD
BUFFOONERY
DEFACEMENT
DEFAMATION
DEFAMATORY
DEFEASANCE
DEFECATION
DEFENSIBLE
DEFICIENCY
DEFILEMENT
DEFINITELY
DEFINITION
DEFINITIVE
DEFLAGRATE
DEFLECTION
DEFRAYMENT
DIFFERENCE
DIFFICULTY
DIFFIDENCE
EFFACEMENT
EFFECTUATE
EFFEMINACY
EFFEMINATE
EFFERVESCE
EFFICIENCY
EFFLEURAGE
EFFORTLESS
EFFRONTERY
EFFUSIVELY
INFALLIBLE
INFALLIBLY
INFATUATED
INFECTIOUS
INFEFTMENT
INFERNALLY
INFIDELITY
INFIGHTING
INFILTRATE
INFINITELY
INFINITIVE
INFLATABLE
INFLECTION
INFLEXIBLE
INFLEXIBLY
INFLICTION
INFORMALLY
INFRACTION
INFREQUENT
INFURIATED
LEFTHANDED
LEFTHANDER
LEFTWINGER
NEFANDROUS
OBFUSCATED
OFFBALANCE
OFFICIALLY
OFFLICENCE
OFFPUTTING
OFFTHECUFF
OFFTHEWALL
REFERENDUM
REFINEMENT
REFLECTING
REFLECTION
REFLECTIVE
REFRACTION
REFRACTIVE
REFRACTORY
REFRESHING
REFUTATION
SOFTBOILED
SUFFERANCE
SUFFICIENT
SUFFRAGIST
UNFAITHFUL
UNFAMILIAR
UNFATHOMED
UNFETTERED
UNFINISHED
UNFLAGGING
UNFLAVORED
UNFORESEEN
UNFRIENDLY
UNFRUITFUL
WOFFINGTON
YAFFINGALE
AGGRANDISE
AGGRESSION
AGGRESSIVE
ALGOLAGNIA
ALGONQUIAN
ANGIOSPERM
ANGLOPHILE
ANGLOPHOBE
ANGUILLULA
ANGURVADEL
ANGWANTIBO
ARGOLEMONO
BAGASSOSIS
COGITATION
COGNISANCE
COGNIZANCE
DEGENERACY
DEGENERATE
DEGRADABLE
DIGESTIBLE
DIGITORIUM
DIGRESSION
DOGGEDNESS
EIGHTEENTH
ENGAGEMENT
ENGENDRURE
ENGLISHMAN
ENGLISHMEN
ENGOUEMENT
ENGROSSING
ERGONOMICS
FIGURATION
FIGURATIVE
FIGUREHEAD
HIGHBINDER
HIGHFLYING
HIGHHANDED
HIGHLANDER
HIGHWAYMAN
HYGROMETER
INGEMINATE
INGENERATE
INGLORIOUS
INGRATIATE
INGREDIENT
JAGUARONDI
JAGUARUNDI
JIGGAMAREE
JUGENDSTIL
JUGGERNAUT
LEGALISTIC
LEGIBILITY
LEGISLATOR
LEGITIMACY
LEGITIMATE
LEGITIMIZE
LEGUMINOUS
LEGWARMERS
LIGHTERMAN
LIGHTHOUSE
LIGHTINGUP
LIGNOCAINE
LOGANBERRY
LOGARITHMS
LOGGERHEAD
LOGISTICAL
LOGORRHOEA
LUGUBRIOUS
MAGISTRACY
MAGISTRAND
MAGISTRATE
MAGNIFICAT
MAGNIFYING
MEGALITHIC
MEGALOSAUR
MIGHTINESS
MIGNONETTE
NEGATIVELY
NEGLECTFUL

NEGLIGENCE
NEGLIGIBLE
NEGOTIABLE
NEGOTIATOR
NIGGERHEAD
NIGHTDRESS
NIGHTLIGHT
NIGHTSHADE
NIGHTSHIRT
NIGHTSTICK
NIGRESCENT
OUGHTLINGS
PAGINATION
PIGEONHOLE
POGONOTOMY
PUGNACIOUS
RAGAMUFFIN
REGARDLESS
REGENERATE
REGIMENTAL
REGIMENTED
REGISTERED
REGRESSION
REGRESSIVE
REGULARITY
REGULARIZE
REGULATION
RIGELATION
RIGHTFULLY
RIGOROUSLY
RUGGEDNESS
SAGITTARIA
SEGREGATED
SEGUIDILLA
SIGILLARIA
SIGNIFICAT
SIGNORELLI
SOGDOLAGER
SOGDOLIGER
SOGDOLOGER
SUGARALLIE
SUGGESTION
SUGGESTIVE
TAGLIARINI
UNGRACIOUS
UNGRATEFUL
UNGROUNDED
VEGETABLES
VEGETARIAN
VEGETATION
VIGILANTES
VIGOROUSLY
WAGEEARNER
YGGDRASILL
ABHIDHAMMA
ABHORRENCE
ACHITOPHEL
ACHROMATIC
ADHIBITION
ANHELATION
APHAERESIS
ATHANASIAN
BAHRAINIAN
BEHAVIORAL
BEHINDHAND
COHERENTLY
DEHISCENCE
ECHINODERM
ECHINOIDEA
ECHOPRAXIA
ENHYDRITIC
EPHRAIMITE
ETHEOSTOMA
ETHYLAMINE
EUHEMERISM
EXHALATION
EXHAUSTING
EXHAUSTION
EXHAUSTIVE
EXHIBITION
EXHILARATE
EXHUMATION
FAHRENHEIT
ICHTHYOSIS
INHABITANT
INHALATION
INHERENTLY
INHIBITING
INHIBITION
INHIBITORY
INHUMANITY
JOHNSONIAN
KSHATRIYAS
MAHAYANALI
MAHOMMEDAN
NIHILISTIC
OCHLOCRACY
OPHICLEIDE
OPHTHALMIC
OTHERGATES
OTHERGUESS
POHUTUKAWA
SCHALSTEIN
SCHIPPERKE
SCHISMATIC
SCHLIMAZEL
SCHOLAEMIA
SCHOLASTIC
SCHOOLBOOK
SCHOOLGIRL
SCHOOLMAAM
SCHWARZLOT
SPHACELATE
SPHALERITE
TCHOUKBALL
UNHAMPERED
UNHEARABLE
UNHERALDED
UNHYGIENIC
UPHOLSTERY
VEHEMENTLY
YTHUNDERED
ABITURIENT
ADIAPHORON
AFICIONADO
AHITHOPHEL
ALIENATION
ALIMENTARY
AMIABILITY
ANIMADVERT
APICULTURE
ARIMASPIAN
ARISTIPPUS
ARISTOCRAT
ARISTOLOGY
ARISTOTLES
ARITHMETIC
AVICULARIA
AXINOMANCY
BAILIEWICK
BAILLIWICK
BLISSFULLY
BLISTERING
BLITHERING
BLITZKRIEG
BOISTEROUS
BRICKLAYER
BRICKWORKS
BRIDEGROOM
BRIDESMAID
BRIDGEHEAD
BRIDGETOWN
BRIDLEPATH
BRIGANDINE
BRIGANTINE
BRIGHTNESS
BRILLIANCE
BRITISHISM
CHICHESTER
CHICKENPOX
CHIFFCHAFF
CHIFFONIER
CHILDBIRTH
CHILDERMAS
CHILDISHLY
CHILLINESS
CHIMBORAZO
CHIMNEYPOT
CHIMPANZEE
CHINAGRAPH
CHINASTONE
CHINCHILLA
CHINQUAPIN
CHIRICAUNE
CHIROMANCY
CHIRONOMIC
CHIROPTERA
CHITARRONE
CHITTAGONG
CHIVALROUS
CLINGSTONE
CLINICALLY
CNIDOBLAST
COINCIDENT
CRICKETING
CRIMINALLY
CRISPBREAD
CRISPINIAN
CRISSCROSS
CRITICALLY
CUIRASSIER
CUISENAIRE
DRINKWATER
ELIMINATOR
EMIGRATION
EPICANTHUS
EPIDEICTIC
EPIDENDRUM
EPIDIDYMUS
EPIDIORITE
EPIGENETIC
EPIGLOTTIS
EPILIMNION
EPIMENIDES
EPIMETHEUS
EPIPHONEMA
EPIPLASTRA
EPISCOPATE
EPISPASTIC
EPISTEMICS
EPISTROPHE
EPITHELIUM
ERIOCAULON
EVISCERATE
EVITERNITY
FAIRGROUND
FAIRHAIRED
FAITHFULLY
FLICKERING
FLIGHTLESS
FLIMSINESS
FLINDERSIA
FLIPPANTLY
FLIRTATION
FRICANDEAU
FRIENDLESS
FRIENDSHIP
FRIGHTENED
FRINGILLID
FRISKINESS
FRITHSOKEN
FRITILLARY
GAINGIVING
GAINSTRIVE
GHIBELLINE
GLISTENING
GLITTERAND
GLITTERATI
GLITTERING
GRIDIRONER
GRIDLOCKED
GRINDSTONE
GRITTINESS
GUIDELINES
GUILLOTINE
HAIRSPRING
HEIDELBERG
INIMITABLE
INIQUITOUS
INITIATION
INITIATIVE
IRIDESCENT
IRISHWOMAN
IRISHWOMEN
JEISTIECOR
KHIDMUTGAR
KNIFEBOARD
KNIGHTHOOD
KRIEGSPIEL
MAIDENHAIR
MAIDENHOOD
MAINPERNOR
MAINSPRING
MAINSTREAM
MAISONETTE
MOISTURIZE
NEIGHBORLY
ODIOUSNESS
OPISOMETER
ORIDINANCE
ORIGINALLY
ORIGINATOR
OVIPOSITOR
PAINKILLER
PAINLESSLY
PAINTBRUSH
PHILATELIC
PHILIPPINA
PHILIPPINE
PHILISTINE
PHILLIPINA
PHILLIPINE
PHILLUMENY
PHILOPOENA
PHILOSOPHY
PHILOXENIA
PLIABILITY
PLIOHIPPUS
POIGNANTLY
POIKILITIC
POINSETTIA
POINTBLANK
PRICKLOUSE
PRIESTHOOD
PRIMORDIAL
PRINCIPIUM
PRINCIPLED
PRINCIPLES
PRIVATEERS
PRIVILEGED

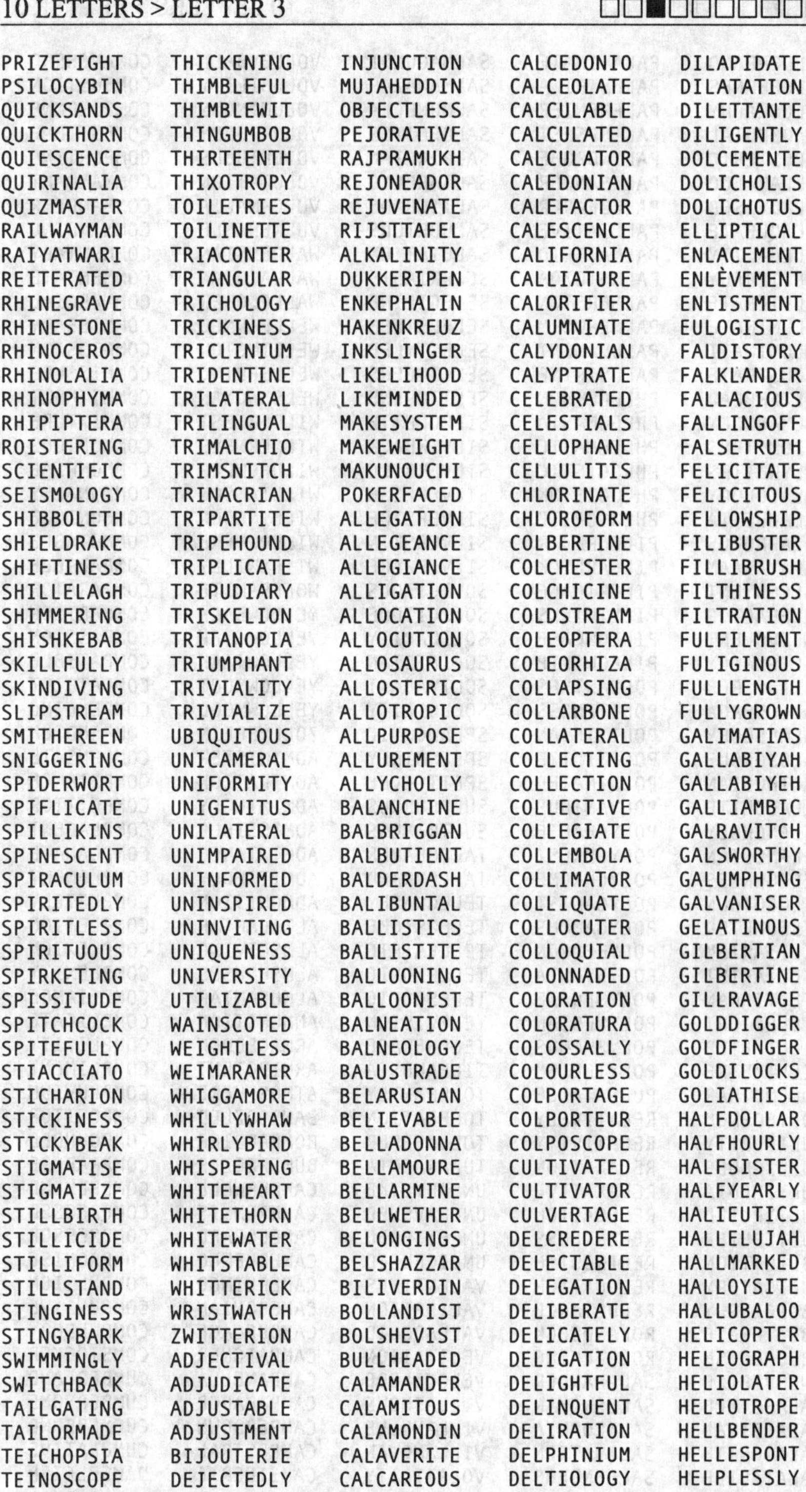

PRIZEFIGHT
PSILOCYBIN
QUICKSANDS
QUICKTHORN
QUIESCENCE
QUIRINALIA
QUIZMASTER
RAILWAYMAN
RAIYATWARI
REITERATED
RHINEGRAVE
RHINESTONE
RHINOCEROS
RHINOLALIA
RHINOPHYMA
RHIPIPTERA
ROISTERING
SCIENTIFIC
SEISMOLOGY
SHIBBOLETH
SHIELDRAKE
SHIFTINESS
SHILLELAGH
SHIMMERING
SHISHKEBAB
SKILLFULLY
SKINDIVING
SLIPSTREAM
SMITHEREEN
SNIGGERING
SPIDERWORT
SPIFLICATE
SPILLIKINS
SPINESCENT
SPIRACULUM
SPIRITEDLY
SPIRITLESS
SPIRITUOUS
SPIRKETING
SPISSITUDE
SPITCHCOCK
SPITEFULLY
STIACCIATO
STICHARION
STICKINESS
STICKYBEAK
STIGMATISE
STIGMATIZE
STILLBIRTH
STILLICIDE
STILLIFORM
STILLSTAND
STINGINESS
STINGYBARK
SWIMMINGLY
SWITCHBACK
TAILGATING
TAILORMADE
TEICHOPSIA
TEINOSCOPE
THICKENING
THIMBLEFUL
THIMBLEWIT
THINGUMBOB
THIRTEENTH
THIXOTROPY
TOILETRIES
TOILINETTE
TRIACONTER
TRIANGULAR
TRICHOLOGY
TRICKINESS
TRICLINIUM
TRIDENTINE
TRILATERAL
TRILINGUAL
TRIMALCHIO
TRIMSNITCH
TRINACRIAN
TRIPARTITE
TRIPEHOUND
TRIPLICATE
TRIPUDIARY
TRISKELION
TRITANOPIA
TRIUMPHANT
TRIVIALITY
TRIVIALIZE
UBIQUITOUS
UNICAMERAL
UNIFORMITY
UNIGENITUS
UNILATERAL
UNIMPAIRED
UNINFORMED
UNINSPIRED
UNINVITING
UNIQUENESS
UNIVERSITY
UTILIZABLE
WAINSCOTED
WEIGHTLESS
WEIMARANER
WHIGGAMORE
WHILLYWHAW
WHIRLYBIRD
WHISPERING
WHITEHEART
WHITETHORN
WHITEWATER
WHITSTABLE
WHITTERICK
WRISTWATCH
ZWITTERION
ADJECTIVAL
ADJUDICATE
ADJUSTABLE
ADJUSTMENT
BIJOUTERIE
DEJECTEDLY
INJUNCTION
MUJAHEDDIN
OBJECTLESS
PEJORATIVE
RAJPRAMUKH
REJONEADOR
REJUVENATE
RIJSTTAFEL
ALKALINITY
DUKKERIPEN
ENKEPHALIN
HAKENKREUZ
INKSLINGER
LIKELIHOOD
LIKEMINDED
MAKESYSTEM
MAKEWEIGHT
MAKUNOUCHI
POKERFACED
ALLEGATION
ALLEGEANCE
ALLEGIANCE
ALLIGATION
ALLOCATION
ALLOCUTION
ALLOSAURUS
ALLOSTERIC
ALLOTROPIC
ALLPURPOSE
ALLUREMENT
ALLYCHOLLY
BALANCHINE
BALBRIGGAN
BALBUTIENT
BALDERDASH
BALIBUNTAL
BALLISTICS
BALLISTITE
BALLOONING
BALLOONIST
BALNEATION
BALNEOLOGY
BALUSTRADE
BELARUSIAN
BELIEVABLE
BELLADONNA
BELLAMOURE
BELLARMINE
BELLWETHER
BELONGINGS
BELSHAZZAR
BILIVERDIN
BOLLANDIST
BOLSHEVIST
BULLHEADED
CALAMANDER
CALAMITOUS
CALAMONDIN
CALAVERITE
CALCAREOUS
CALCEDONIO
CALCEOLATE
CALCULABLE
CALCULATED
CALCULATOR
CALEDONIAN
CALEFACTOR
CALESCENCE
CALIFORNIA
CALLIATURE
CALORIFIER
CALUMNIATE
CALYDONIAN
CALYPTRATE
CELEBRATED
CELESTIALS
CELLOPHANE
CELLULITIS
CHLORINATE
CHLOROFORM
COLBERTINE
COLCHESTER
COLCHICINE
COLDSTREAM
COLEOPTERA
COLEORHIZA
COLLAPSING
COLLARBONE
COLLATERAL
COLLECTING
COLLECTION
COLLECTIVE
COLLEGIATE
COLLEMBOLA
COLLIMATOR
COLLIQUATE
COLLOCUTER
COLLOQUIAL
COLONNADED
COLORATION
COLORATURA
COLOSSALLY
COLOURLESS
COLPORTAGE
COLPORTEUR
COLPOSCOPE
CULTIVATED
CULTIVATOR
CULVERTAGE
DELCREDERE
DELECTABLE
DELEGATION
DELIBERATE
DELICATELY
DELIGATION
DELIGHTFUL
DELINQUENT
DELIRATION
DELPHINIUM
DELTIOLOGY
DILAPIDATE
DILATATION
DILETTANTE
DILIGENTLY
DOLCEMENTE
DOLICHOLIS
DOLICHOTUS
ELLIPTICAL
ENLACEMENT
ENLÈVEMENT
ENLISTMENT
EULOGISTIC
FALDISTORY
FALKLANDER
FALLACIOUS
FALLINGOFF
FALSETRUTH
FELICITATE
FELICITOUS
FELLOWSHIP
FILIBUSTER
FILLIBRUSH
FILTHINESS
FILTRATION
FULFILMENT
FULIGINOUS
FULLLENGTH
FULLYGROWN
GALIMATIAS
GALLABIYAH
GALLABIYEH
GALLIAMBIC
GALRAVITCH
GALSWORTHY
GALUMPHING
GALVANISER
GELATINOUS
GILBERTIAN
GILBERTINE
GILLRAVAGE
GOLDDIGGER
GOLDFINGER
GOLDILOCKS
GOLIATHISE
HALFDOLLAR
HALFHOURLY
HALFSISTER
HALFYEARLY
HALIEUTICS
HALLELUJAH
HALLMARKED
HALLOYSITE
HALLUBALOO
HELICOPTER
HELIOGRAPH
HELIOLATER
HELIOTROPE
HELLBENDER
HELLESPONT
HELPLESSLY

HILDEBRAND
HOLOFERNES
HOLOGRAPHY
HOLOPHOTAL
HOLOSTERIC
HULLABALOO
ILLADVISED
ILLAQUEATE
ILLEGALITY
ILLITERACY
ILLITERATE
ILLUMINATE
ILLUMINATI
ILLUSTRATE
JOLTERHEAD
KILMARNOCK
KILOMETRES
LILYWHITES
MALACOLOGY
MALAGUETTA
MALAPROPOS
MALAYALAAM
MALCONTENT
MALEFACTOR
MALEVOLENT
MALIGNANCY
MALINGERER
MALLOPHAGA
MALMESBURY
MALODOROUS
MALTHUSIAN
MELACONITE
MELANCHOLY
MELANESIAN
MELLOWNESS
MELOCOTOON
MILEOMETER
MILITARISM
MILITARIST
MILITIAMAN
MILLEFIORI
MILLIMETER
MILLIMETRE
MOLENDINAR
MOLYBDENUM
MULIEBRITY
MULLIGRUBS
MULTIMEDIA
MULTIPLIED
MULTIPLIER
OBLIGATION
OBLIGATORY
OBLIGINGLY
OBLITERATE
OBLOMOVISM
OWLSPIEGLE
PALAEOTYPE
PALAESTRAL
PALAGONITE
PALATALISE

PALATINATE
PALESTRINA
PALFRENIER
PALIMPSEST
PALINDROME
PALISANDER
PALLBEARER
PALLIATIVE
PALMATIFID
PALMATOZOA
PALMERSTON
PALMERWORM
PALUDAMENT
PALUSTRINE
PHLEGETHON
PHLEGMASIA
PHLEGMATIC
PHLOGISTIC
PHLOGISTON
PHLOGOPITE
PILEDRIVER
PILGARLICK
PILGRIMAGE
PILLIWINKS
PILLOWCASE
PILLOWSLIP
POLIANTHES
POLITENESS
POLITICIAN
POLITICIZE
POLLINATED
POLYANTHUS
POLYCHAETE
POLYCHREST
POLYCHROME
POLYGAMIST
POLYGAMOUS
POLYHEDRON
POLYHYMNIA
POLYMERIZE
POLYNESIAN
POLYPHEMUS
POLYTHEISM
PULSATANCE
RELATIVELY
RELATIVITY
RELAXATION
RELAXATIVE
RELEGATION
RELENTLESS
RELINQUISH
RELOCATION
RELUCTANCE
ROLANDSECK
ROLLICKING
SALAMANDER
SALESWOMAN
SALICORNIA
SALIVATION
SALLENDERS

SALMAGUNDI
SALMANAZAR
SALMONELLA
SALOPETTES
SALPINGIAN
SALTARELLO
SALTIGRADE
SALUBRIOUS
SALUTATION
SCLERIASIS
SELEGILINE
SELFESTEEM
SELFSTYLED
SELLINGERS
SELTZOGENE
SILHOUETTE
SILVERBACK
SILVERBILL
SILVERFISH
SILVERSIDE
SILVERSKIN
SILVERWARE
SOLICITOUS
SOLICITUDE
SOLIDARITY
SOLIFIDIAN
SOLIVAGANT
SOLUBILITY
SPLANCHNIC
SPLENDIDLY
SPLITLEVEL
SULPHUROUS
SULTRINESS
TALEBEARER
TALLEYRAND
TELEGRAPHY
TELEOSTOME
TELEPATHIC
TELEPHONIC
TELESCOPIC
TELEVISION
TELPHERAGE
TILLANDSIA
TOLERANTLY
TOLERATION
TOLLKEEPER
TULARAEMIA
UNLADYLIKE
UNLEAVENED
UNLETTERED
UNLICENSED
VALENTINES
VALIDATION
VALLADOLID
VELITATION
VELOCIPEDE
VILLAINOUS
VILLANELLE
VILLANOVAN
VOLATILITY

VOLLEYBALL
VOLUBILITY
VOLUMINOUS
VOLUPTUARY
VOLUPTUOUS
VOLUTATION
VULCANALIA
VULNERABLE
WALDENSIAN
WALLACHIAN
WALLFLOWER
WELLEARNED
WELLINGTON
WELLSPRING
WELSHWOMAN
WILDEBEEST
WILDERNESS
WILDFOWLER
WILLIAMSON
WILLINGDON
WILLOWHERB
WILLYWILLY
WOLFRAMITE
YELLOWBACK
YELLOWGIRL
YELLOWJACK
YELLOWROOT
YELLOWWOOD
ZOLLVEREIN
ADMINISTER
ADMIRATION
ADMIRINGLY
ADMISSIBLE
ADMITTANCE
ADMITTEDLY
ADMONITION
ALMACANTAR
ALMSGIVING
ALMSHOUSES
ALMUCANTAR
AMMUNITION
ARMAGEDDON
ARMIPOTENT
ATMOSPHERE
BAMBOOZLED
BOMBARDIER
BUMFREEZER
CAMBERWELL
CAMBRENSIS
CAMELOPARD
CAMERLENGO
CAMERLINGO
CAMERONIAN
CAMOUFLAGE
CAMPAIGNER
CAMPANELLA
CAMPARADOR
CAMPERDOWN
CAMPESTRAL
CAMSTEERIE

COMANCHERO
COMBUSTION
COMEDIENNE
COMESTIBLE
COMFORTING
COMMANDANT
COMMANDEER
COMMANDING
COMMENTARY
COMMENTATE
COMMERCIAL
COMMISSARY
COMMISSION
COMMISSURE
COMMITMENT
COMMIXTURE
COMMODIOUS
COMMONWEAL
COMMUNALLY
COMMUNIQUÉ
COMMUTABLE
COMPARABLE
COMPARATOR
COMPARISON
COMPASSION
COMPATIBLE
COMPATRIOT
COMPELLING
COMPENDIUM
COMPENSATE
COMPETENCE
COMPETITOR
COMPLACENT
COMPLANATE
COMPLEMENT
COMPLETELY
COMPLETION
COMPLEXION
COMPLEXITY
COMPLIANCE
COMPLICATE
COMPLICITY
COMPLIMENT
COMPLUVIUM
COMPOSITOR
COMPOUNDED
COMPRADORE
COMPREHEND
COMPRESSED
COMPRESSOR
COMPROMISE
COMPULSION
COMPULSIVE
COMPULSORY
COMSTOCKER
CUMBERLAND
CUMBERSOME
CUMMERBUND
CUMULATIVE
DAMSELFISH

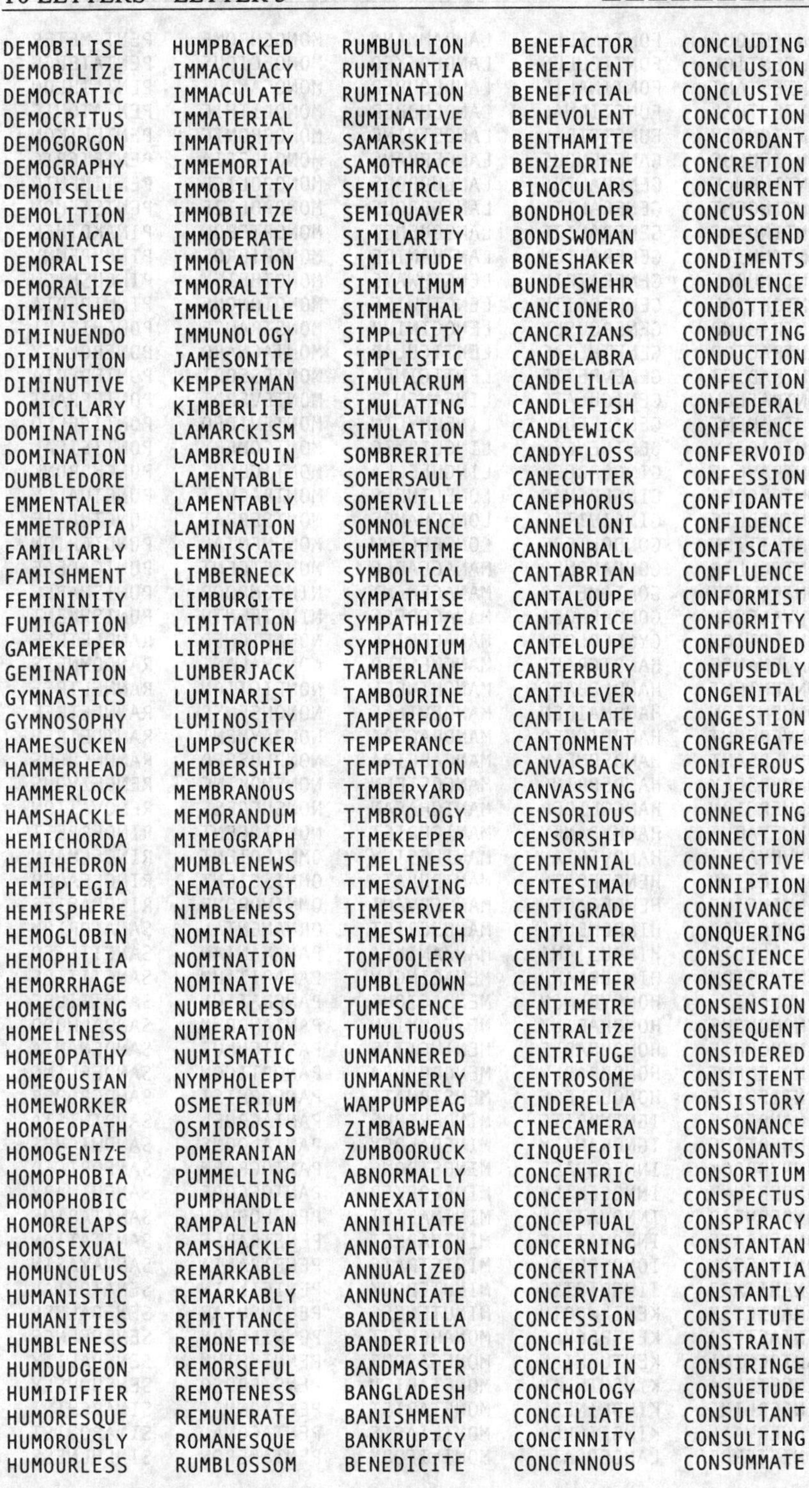

DEMOBILISE
DEMOBILIZE
DEMOCRATIC
DEMOCRITUS
DEMOGORGON
DEMOGRAPHY
DEMOISELLE
DEMOLITION
DEMONIACAL
DEMORALISE
DEMORALIZE
DIMINISHED
DIMINUENDO
DIMINUTION
DIMINUTIVE
DOMICILARY
DOMINATING
DOMINATION
DUMBLEDORE
EMMENTALER
EMMETROPIA
FAMILIARLY
FAMISHMENT
FEMININITY
FUMIGATION
GAMEKEEPER
GEMINATION
GYMNASTICS
GYMNOSOPHY
HAMESUCKEN
HAMMERHEAD
HAMMERLOCK
HAMSHACKLE
HEMICHORDA
HEMIHEDRON
HEMIPLEGIA
HEMISPHERE
HEMOGLOBIN
HEMOPHILIA
HEMORRHAGE
HOMECOMING
HOMELINESS
HOMEOPATHY
HOMEOUSIAN
HOMEWORKER
HOMOEOPATH
HOMOGENIZE
HOMOPHOBIA
HOMOPHOBIC
HOMORELAPS
HOMOSEXUAL
HOMUNCULUS
HUMANISTIC
HUMANITIES
HUMBLENESS
HUMDUDGEON
HUMIDIFIER
HUMORESQUE
HUMOROUSLY
HUMOURLESS
HUMPBACKED
IMMACULACY
IMMACULATE
IMMATERIAL
IMMATURITY
IMMEMORIAL
IMMOBILITY
IMMOBILIZE
IMMODERATE
IMMOLATION
IMMORALITY
IMMORTELLE
IMMUNOLOGY
JAMESONITE
KEMPERYMAN
KIMBERLITE
LAMARCKISM
LAMBREQUIN
LAMENTABLE
LAMENTABLY
LAMINATION
LEMNISCATE
LIMBERNECK
LIMBURGITE
LIMITATION
LIMITROPHE
LUMBERJACK
LUMINARIST
LUMINOSITY
LUMPSUCKER
MEMBERSHIP
MEMBRANOUS
MEMORANDUM
MIMEOGRAPH
MUMBLENEWS
NEMATOCYST
NIMBLENESS
NOMINALIST
NOMINATION
NOMINATIVE
NUMBERLESS
NUMERATION
NUMISMATIC
NYMPHOLEPT
OSMETERIUM
OSMIDROSIS
POMERANIAN
PUMMELLING
PUMPHANDLE
RAMPALLIAN
RAMSHACKLE
REMARKABLE
REMARKABLY
REMITTANCE
REMONETISE
REMORSEFUL
REMOTENESS
REMUNERATE
ROMANESQUE
RUMBLOSSOM
RUMBULLION
RUMINANTIA
RUMINATION
RUMINATIVE
SAMARSKITE
SAMOTHRACE
SEMICIRCLE
SEMIQUAVER
SIMILARITY
SIMILITUDE
SIMILLIMUM
SIMMENTHAL
SIMPLICITY
SIMPLISTIC
SIMULACRUM
SIMULATING
SIMULATION
SOMBRERITE
SOMERSAULT
SOMERVILLE
SOMNOLENCE
SUMMERTIME
SYMBOLICAL
SYMPATHISE
SYMPATHIZE
SYMPHONIUM
TAMBERLANE
TAMBOURINE
TAMPERFOOT
TEMPERANCE
TEMPTATION
TIMBERYARD
TIMBROLOGY
TIMEKEEPER
TIMELINESS
TIMESAVING
TIMESERVER
TIMESWITCH
TOMFOOLERY
TUMBLEDOWN
TUMESCENCE
TUMULTUOUS
UNMANNERED
UNMANNERLY
WAMPUMPEAG
ZIMBABWEAN
ZUMBOORUCK
ABNORMALLY
ANNEXATION
ANNIHILATE
ANNOTATION
ANNUALIZED
ANNUNCIATE
BANDERILLA
BANDERILLO
BANDMASTER
BANGLADESH
BANISHMENT
BANKRUPTCY
BENEDICITE
BENEFACTOR
BENEFICENT
BENEFICIAL
BENEVOLENT
BENTHAMITE
BENZEDRINE
BINOCULARS
BONDHOLDER
BONDSWOMAN
BONESHAKER
BUNDESWEHR
CANCIONERO
CANCRIZANS
CANDELABRA
CANDELILLA
CANDLEFISH
CANDLEWICK
CANDYFLOSS
CANECUTTER
CANEPHORUS
CANNELLONI
CANNONBALL
CANTABRIAN
CANTALOUPE
CANTATRICE
CANTELOUPE
CANTERBURY
CANTILEVER
CANTILLATE
CANTONMENT
CANVASBACK
CANVASSING
CENSORIOUS
CENSORSHIP
CENTENNIAL
CENTESIMAL
CENTIGRADE
CENTILITER
CENTILITRE
CENTIMETER
CENTIMETRE
CENTRALIZE
CENTRIFUGE
CENTROSOME
CINDERELLA
CINECAMERA
CINQUEFOIL
CONCENTRIC
CONCEPTION
CONCEPTUAL
CONCERNING
CONCERTINA
CONCERVATE
CONCESSION
CONCHIGLIE
CONCHIOLIN
CONCHOLOGY
CONCILIATE
CONCINNITY
CONCINNOUS
CONCLUDING
CONCLUSION
CONCLUSIVE
CONCOCTION
CONCORDANT
CONCRETION
CONCURRENT
CONCUSSION
CONDESCEND
CONDIMENTS
CONDOLENCE
CONDOTTIER
CONDUCTING
CONDUCTION
CONFECTION
CONFEDERAL
CONFERENCE
CONFERVOID
CONFESSION
CONFIDANTE
CONFIDENCE
CONFISCATE
CONFLUENCE
CONFORMIST
CONFORMITY
CONFOUNDED
CONFUSEDLY
CONGENITAL
CONGESTION
CONGREGATE
CONIFEROUS
CONJECTURE
CONNECTING
CONNECTION
CONNECTIVE
CONNIPTION
CONNIVANCE
CONQUERING
CONSCIENCE
CONSECRATE
CONSENSION
CONSEQUENT
CONSIDERED
CONSISTENT
CONSISTORY
CONSONANCE
CONSONANTS
CONSORTIUM
CONSPECTUS
CONSPIRACY
CONSTANTAN
CONSTANTIA
CONSTANTLY
CONSTITUTE
CONSTRAINT
CONSTRINGE
CONSUETUDE
CONSULTANT
CONSULTING
CONSUMMATE

CONTAGIOUS
CONTENTION
CONTESTANT
CONTEXTUAL
CONTIGUITY
CONTIGUOUS
CONTINENCE
CONTINGENT
CONTINUING
CONTINUITY
CONTINUOUS
CONTORTION
CONTRABAND
CONTRACTOR
CONTRADICT
CONTRAFLOW
CONTRAHENT
CONTRARILY
CONTRAVENE
CONTRECOUP
CONTRIBUTE
CONTRITION
CONTROLLER
CONTROVERT
CONVALESCE
CONVECTION
CONVENANCE
CONVENIENT
CONVENTION
CONVERGENT
CONVERSANT
CONVERSELY
CONVERSION
CONVEYABLE
CONVEYANCE
CONVICTION
CONVINCING
CONVOLUTED
CONVOLVUTE
CONVULSION
CONVULSIVE
CYNOMOLGUS
DENDROPHIS
DENOUEMENT
DENTIFRICE
DINANDERIE
DINNERTIME
DONNYBROOK
DUNDERFUNK
DUNDERHEAD
DUNDERPATE
DUNIWASSAL
DYNAMITARD
FANATICISM
FANTASTICO
FANTOCCINI
FENESTELLA
FINGERLING
FINGERNAIL
FINISTERRE
FONTANELLE
FONTICULUS
FONTINALIS
FUNCTIONAL
FUNGICIDAL
GANGRENOUS
GENERALISE
GENERALITY
GENERALIZE
GENERATION
GENERATRIX
GENEROSITY
GENEROUSLY
GENETHLIAC
GENEVRETTE
GENICULATE
GENTLEFOLK
GENTLENESS
GINGERBEER
GINGERSNAP
GINGIVITIS
GONDOLIERS
GONFANONER
GONIOMETER
GONORRHOEA
GYNECOLOGY
HANDICRAFT
HANDLEBARS
HANDMAIDEN
HANDPICKED
HANDSOMELY
HANDSPRING
HANGGLIDER
HANKYPANKY
HANOVERIAN
HENCEFORTH
HENDECAGON
HINDENBURG
HINDUSTANI
HINTERLAND
HONEYBUNCH
HONORARIUM
HONOURABLE
HONOURABLY
HONOURLESS
IGNIMBRITE
IGNORANTLY
INNERSPACE
INNOCENTLY
INNOVATION
INNOVATIVE
IONOSPHERE
JINGOISTIC
KENILWORTH
KENSPECKLE
KENTUCKIAN
KINCHINLAY
KINDLINESS
KINGFISHER
LANCEOLATE
LANDAMMANN
LANDLOCKED
LANDLOUPER
LANDLUBBER
LANDSTHING
LANGERHANS
LANGUOROUS
LANIGEROUS
LANSQUENET
LANTHANIDE
LENGTHWAYS
LENGTHWISE
LENOCINIUM
LENTICULAR
LENTIGINES
LINEAMENTS
LINEOMYCIN
LINGUISTIC
LINGULELLA
LONELINESS
LONGCHAMPS
LONGFELLOW
MANAGEABLE
MANAGEMENT
MANAGERESS
MANAGERIAL
MANCHESTER
MANCHINEEL
MANDEVILLE
MANDRAGORA
MANGABEIRA
MANGOSTEEN
MANICHAEAN
MANICURIST
MANIFESTLY
MANIPULATE
MANSERVANT
MANUSCRIPT
MANZANILLA
MENACINGLY
MENDACIOUS
MENECHMIAN
MENINGITIS
MENORRHOEA
MENSTRUATE
MINDERERUS
MINERALOGY
MINESTRONE
MINEWORKER
MINIMALIST
MINIMARKET
MINISTRATE
MINUTEBOOK
MINUTENESS
MONARCHIST
MONEGASQUE
MONETARISM
MONETARIST
MONILIASIS
MONILIFORM
MONOCHROME
MONOECIOUS
MONOGAMOUS
MONOLITHIC
MONOPHONIC
MONOPLEGIA
MONOPOLISE
MONOPOLIZE
MONOPTERON
MONOPTEROS
MONOTHEISM
MONOTONOUS
MONSTRANCE
MONTAGNARD
MONTESSORI
MONTEVERDI
MONTEVIDEO
MONTGOMERY
MONTICULUS
MONTRACHET
MONTSERRAT
MONUMENTAL
MUNIFICENT
NINCOMPOOP
NINETEENTH
NONALIGNED
NONCHALANT
NONFICTION
NONONSENSE
NONPAYMENT
NONPLUSSED
NONSMOKING
NONSUCCESS
NONVIOLENT
OMNIPOTENT
OMNISCIENT
OMNIVOROUS
ORNAMENTAL
PANAMANIAN
PANARITIUM
PANCRATIUM
PANJANDRUM
PANNICULUS
PANOPTICON
PANSOPHIST
PANTAGRUEL
PANTALOONS
PANTOGRAPH
PANTOSCOPE
PENELOPHON
PENETRABLE
PENETRALIA
PENICILLIN
PENINSULAR
PENNILLION
PENNISETUM
PENSIEROSO
PENSIONNAT
PENTAGONAL
PENTAMERON
PENTAMETER
PENTATEUCH
PENTATHLON
PENTATONIC
PENTELIKON
PENTETERIC
PENTIMENTO
PENTSTEMON
PINAKOTHEK
PINCHPENNY
PINCUSHION
PINNIPEDIA
PONCHIELLI
PONEROLOGY
PONTEDERIA
PONTEFRACT
PONTICELLO
PONTIFICAL
PUNCHDRUNK
PUNCTUALLY
PUNCTULATE
PUNDIGRION
PUNICACEAE
PUNISHABLE
PUNISHMENT
RANDLETREE
RANDOMNESS
RANNELTREE
RANNLETREE
RANTLETREE
RANUNCULUS
RENDEZVOUS
RENOVATION
RINDERPEST
RINGELMANN
RINGLEADER
RINGMASTER
SANATORIUM
SANCTIFIED
SANCTITIES
SANCTITUDE
SANDALWOOD
SANDEMANIA
SANDERLING
SANDGROPER
SANDINISTA
SANDWICHES
SANFORISED
SANGUINARY
SANITARIUM
SANITATION
SANNAYASIN
SENATORIAL
SENEGALESE
SENESCENCE
SENSUALITY
SENSUOUSLY
SINARCHIST
SINARQUIST
SINFULNESS

SINGHALESE
SINGLENESS
SINGULARLY
SINSEMILLA
SONGSTRESS
SONGWRITER
SUNBATHING
SUNGLASSES
SYNAERESIS
SYNCOPATED
SYNCRETISE
SYNECDOCHE
SYNEIDESIS
SYNONYMOUS
SYNOSTOSIS
SYNTAGMATA
SYNTERESIS
SYNTHESIZE
SYNTHRONUS
TANAGRIDAE
TANGANYIKA
TANGENTIAL
TANGLEFOOT
TANNHAUSER
TANTAMOUNT
TENDERFOOT
TENDERLOIN
TENDERNESS
TENDRILLED
TENEBRIFIC
TENNANTITE
TENRECIDAE
TENTERHOOK
TINKERBELL
TINTORETTO
TONGUESTER
UNNUMBERED
VANDERBILT
VENERATION
VENEZUELAN
VENTILATOR
VINDEMIATE
VINDICTIVE
VINEGARISH
WANCHANCIE
WANDERINGS
WANDERLUST
WANDSWORTH
WANTHRIVEN
WENTLETRAP
WINCEYETTE
WINCHESTER
WINDERMERE
WINDFLOWER
WINDJAMMER
WINDOWSILL
WINDSCREEN
WINDSHIELD
WINDSURFER
WINTERTIME
WONDERLAND
WONDERMENT
WUNDERKIND
XENOPHOBIA
XENOPHOBIC
ZINCOGRAPH
ABOMINABLE
ABOMINABLY
ABONNEMENT
ABORIGINAL
ABOVEBOARD
ACOLOUTHOS
ACOTYLEDON
ADOLESCENT
AGONISTICS
APOCALYPSE
APOCRYPHAL
APOLAUSTIC
APOLLONIAN
APOLLONIUS
APOLOGETIC
APOPEMPTIC
APOPHTHEGM
APOPLECTIC
APOSEMATIC
APOSTROPHE
APOTHECARY
APOTHECIUM
APOTHEOSIS
APOTROPAIC
BIOCHEMIST
BIOGRAPHER
BIOLOGICAL
BIOPHYSICS
BIORHYTHMS
BLOCKHOUSE
BLOODHOUND
BLOODSTAIN
BLOODSTOCK
BLOODSTONE
BLOOMSBURY
BLOTTESQUE
BOOKBINDER
BOOKKEEPER
BOOKMARKER
BOOKMOBILE
BOOKSELLER
BOONDOGGLE
BOOTLEGGER
BOOTLICKER
BOOZINGKEN
BROADCLOTH
BROADPIECE
BROADSHEET
BROADSWORD
BROCATELLE
BROKENDOWN
BRONCHITIC
BRONCHITIS
BROOMSTICK
BROWNSTONE
CAOUTCHOUC
CHOICELESS
CHOLALOGUE
CHOPSTICKS
CLOCKMAKER
CLODHOPPER
CLOISTERED
CLOMIPHENE
CLOSTRIDIA
CLOUDBERRY
CLOUDBURST
CLOUDINESS
COORDINATE
CROCKFORDS
CROSSBREED
CROSSCHECK
CROSSPIECE
CROSSREFER
CROSSROADS
CROTALARIA
CROTALIDAE
DIOPHANTOS
DOORKEEPER
DOORTODOOR
DROSOPHILA
DROWSINESS
DUODECIMAL
EBOULEMENT
ECOLOGICAL
ECONOMICAL
EGOCENTRIC
ELONGATION
ELOQUENTLY
EMOLUMENTS
ENORMOUSLY
EPONYCHIUM
EXONERATED
EXORBITANT
EXOTHERMIC
EXOTICALLY
FLOCCULATE
FLOCCULENT
FLOODLIGHT
FLOORBOARD
FLOORCLOTH
FLORENTINE
FLORESCENT
FLORIBUNDA
FLOURISHED
FLOWERBEDS
FOODSTUFFS
FOOTBALLER
FOOTBRIDGE
FOOTLIGHTS
FOOTPRINTS
FROGHOPPER
FROLICSOME
FROMANTEEL
FRONTWARDS
GEOCENTRIC
GEOGRAPHER
GEOGRAPHIC
GEOLOGICAL
GEOPHYSICS
GEORGETOWN
GEOTHERMAL
GEOTROPISM
GLORIOUSLY
GLOSSINESS
GLOUCESTER
GNOSTICISM
GOODFELLOW
GOOSEBERRY
GOOSEFLESH
GROCETERIA
GROUNDBAIT
GROUNDLESS
GROUNDLING
GROUNDSMAN
GROUNDWORK
GROVELLING
HOODWINKED
HOOTANANNY
HOOTENANNY
HOOTNANNIE
ICONOCLAST
ICONOSCOPE
ICOSANDRIA
ICOSOHEDRA
INOPERABLE
INORDINATE
INOSCULATE
IRONICALLY
IRONMONGER
ISOMETRICS
ISONIAZIDE
JEOPARDISE
JEOPARDIZE
KLOOTCHMAN
KNOBKERRIE
KNOCKABOUT
KOOKABURRA
KUOMINTANG
LEONTIASIS
LEOPARDESS
NEOTERICAL
ODONTALGIA
ODONTOLITE
ODONTOLOGY
OMOPHORION
ONOMASTICS
OPOTHERAPY
OROBRANCHE
OROGENESIS
PHOLIDOSIS
PHONOGRAPH
PHOSPHORUS
PHOTODIODE
PHOTOGENIC
PHOTOGRAPH
PHOTONASTY
PIONEERING
PLOUGHBOTE
PLOUGHGATE
PLOUGHWISE
PROAIRESIS
PROCEDURAL
PROCEEDING
PROCESSING
PROCESSION
PROCLIVITY
PROCREATOR
PROCRUSTES
PROCURABLE
PROCURATOR
PRODIGALLY
PRODIGIOUS
PRODUCTION
PRODUCTIVE
PROFESSION
PROFICIENT
PROFITABLE
PROFITABLY
PROFITLESS
PROFLIGACY
PROFLIGATE
PROFOUNDLY
PROFUNDITY
PROGENITOR
PROGESSION
PROGRAMMER
PROHIBITED
PROJECTILE
PROJECTING
PROJECTION
PROMENADER
PROMETHEAN
PROMETHEUS
PROMETHIUM
PROMINENCE
PROMISSORY
PROMONTORY
PROMPTNESS
PROMULGATE
PRONOUNCED
PROPAGANDA
PROPAGATOR
PROPELLANT
PROPENSITY
PROPERTIUS
PROPHETESS
PROPIONATE
PROPITIATE
PROPITIOUS
PROPLITEAL
PROPORTION
PROPOSITUS
PROPRAETOR
PROPRIETOR

PROPULSION
PROPYLAEUM
PROSCENIUM
PROSCIUTTO
PROSCRIBED
PROSECUTOR
PROSERPINA
PROSERPINE
PROSILIENT
PROSPECTOR
PROSPECTUS
PROSPERINA
PROSPERITY
PROSPEROUS
PROSTHESIS
PROSTHETIC
PROSTITUTE
PROTAGORAS
PROTANOPIC
PROTECTION
PROTECTIVE
PROTERVITY
PROTESTANT
PROTOPLASM
PROTRACTED
PROTRACTOR
PROTRUSION
PROVEDITOR
PROVENANCE
PROVERBIAL
PROVIDENCE
PROVINCIAL
PROVISIONS
PSOCOPTERA
REORGANIZE
RHOEADALES
SCOFFINGLY
SCOMBRESOX
SCOOTERIST
SCOPELIDAE
SCORDATURA
SCOREBOARD
SCORNFULLY
SCORZONERA
SCOTODINIA
SCOTSWOMAN
SHOCKINGLY
SHOCKPROOF
SHODDINESS
SHOESTRING
SHOPKEEPER
SHOPLIFTER
SHOPSOILED
SHOPWALKER
SHORTBREAD
SHORTENING
SHORTLIVED
SHORTRANGE
SHOVELHEAD
SHOVELNOSE
SHOWJUMPER
SLOPPINESS
SMOKESTACK
SMOOTHNESS
SMORREBROD
SNOOTINESS
SNORKELING
SNOWCAPPED
SNOWMOBILE
SOOTHINGLY
SOOTHSAYER
SPODOMANCY
SPOILSPORT
SPOKESHAVE
SPOLIATION
SPOLIATIVE
SPONGEWARE
SPONGIFORM
SPONSIONAL
SPOONERISM
SPORTINGLY
SPORTSWEAR
SPOTLESSLY
STOCHASTIC
STOCKINESS
STOMATOPOD
STONEBRASH
STONEHENGE
STONEMASON
STONYHURST
STOREFRONT
STOREHOUSE
STOUTHERIE
STOUTHRIEF
SWORDSTICK
THOROUGHLY
THOUGHTFUL
THOUSANDTH
TOOTHBRUSH
TOOTHPASTE
TROCHANTER
TROCHOTRON
TROCTOLITE
TROGLODYTE
TROMBONIST
TROMOMETER
TROPAEOLUM
TROPHONIUS
TROPOPAUSE
TROPOPHYTE
TROTSKYITE
TROUBADOUR
TROUVAILLE
UNOBSERVED
UNOCCUPIED
UNOFFICIAL
UNORIGINAL
UNORTHODOX
UROPOIESIS
UROSTEGITE
WHOLESALER
WHOLEWHEAT
WOODENHEAD
WOODPECKER
WOODPIGEON
WOODWORKER
WOOLLYBACK
WOOLLYBUTT
WRONGDOING
WRONGFULLY
ZOOLOGICAL
ZOOTHAPSIS
ZOOTHERAPY
ALPENSTOCK
ALPHONSINE
AMPELOPSIS
AMPHIBIOUS
AMPHIBRACH
AMPHICTYON
AMPHIGOURI
AMPHIMACER
AMPHIMIXIS
AMPHINEURA
AMPHITRITE
AMPHITRYON
AMPHOTERIC
AMPLEFORTH
AMPUSSYAND
AMPUTATION
APPARENTLY
APPARITION
APPEARANCE
APPETITIVE
APPETIZING
APPLICABLE
APPLICATOR
APPOSITION
APPRECIATE
APPRENTICE
ASPARAGINE
ASPERSIONS
ASPHALTITE
ASPHYXIATE
ASPIDISTRA
ASPIRATION
BIPARTISAN
BIPINNARIA
CAPABILITY
CAPACITATE
CAPERNAITE
CAPERNOITY
CAPILLAIRE
CAPITALISM
CAPITALIST
CAPITALIZE
CAPITATION
CAPITELLUM
CAPITOLINE
CAPITULARY
CAPITULATE
CAPNOMANCY
CAPODASTRO
CAPPUCCINO
CAPREOLATE
CAPRICIOUS
CAPTIVATED
CEPHALOPOD
COPARCENER
COPENHAGEN
COPERNICUS
COPESETTIC
COPPERHEAD
COPPERNOSE
COPPERSKIN
COPULATION
COPYHOLDER
COPYWRITER
DEPARTMENT
DEPARTURES
DEPENDABLE
DEPENDENCE
DEPENDENCY
DEPILATORY
DEPLORABLE
DEPLORABLY
DEPLOYMENT
DEPOPULATE
DEPORTMENT
DEPOSITARY
DEPOSITION
DEPOSITORY
DEPRECIATE
DEPRESSANT
DEPRESSING
DEPRESSION
DEPRESSIVE
DEPUTATION
DIPHTHERIA
DIPLODOCUS
DIPLOMATIC
DIPSOMANIA
DOPPLERITE
DUPLICATOR
EMPEDOCLES
EMPFINDUNG
EMPLASTRUM
EMPLOYMENT
ESPADRILLE
ESPECIALLY
EUPHONIOUS
EUPHROSYNE
EXPATRIATE
EXPECTANCY
EXPEDIENCE
EXPEDIENCY
EXPEDITION
EXPENDABLE
EXPERIENCE
EXPERIMENT
EXPIRATION
EXPLICABLE
EXPLICITLY
EXPOSITION
EXPOSITORY
EXPOUNDERS
EXPRESSION
EXPRESSIVE
EXPRESSMAN
EXPRESSWAY
GYPSOPHILA
HEPATOCELE
HEPTAGONAL
HEPTAMERON
HEPTATEUCH
HEPTATHLON
HIPPARCHUS
HIPPOCRENE
HIPPODROME
HIPPOGRIFF
HIPPOGRYPH
HIPPOMANES
HOPELESSLY
HYPAETHRAL
HYPAETHRON
HYPERBOLIC
HYPERDULIA
HYPNOTIZED
HYPOCORISM
HYPODERMIC
HYPOGAEOUS
HYPOTENUSE
HYPOTHESIS
IMPAIRMENT
IMPALPABLE
IMPALUDISM
IMPARLANCE
IMPASSABLE
IMPATIENCE
IMPECCABLE
IMPECCABLY
IMPEDIMENT
IMPENITENT
IMPERATIVE
IMPERSONAL
IMPERVIOUS
IMPLACABLE
IMPLACABLY
IMPLICITLY
IMPOLITELY
IMPORTANCE
IMPOSITION
IMPOSSIBLE
IMPOSSIBLY
IMPOSTHUME
IMPOTENTLY
IMPOVERISH
IMPREGNATE
IMPRESARIO
IMPRESSION
IMPRESSIVE

IMPRIMATUR
IMPROBABLE
IMPROBABLY
IMPROPERLY
IMPROVISED
IMPRUDENCE
IMPUDENTLY
IMPURITIES
IMPUTATION
LEPRECHAUN
LIPIZZANER
LUPERCALIA
MEPERIDINE
NAPTHALENE
OPPOSITION
OPPRESSION
OPPRESSIVE
OPPROBRIUM
ORPHEOREON
PAPAVERINE
PAPERCHASE
PAPERKNIFE
PAPIAMENTO
PEPPERCORN
PEPPERMILL
PEPPERMINT
PEPPERWORT
POPULARITY
POPULARIZE
POPULATION
RAPPORTEUR
REPAIRABLE
REPARATION
REPATRIATE
REPEATABLE
REPEATEDLY
REPENTANCE
REPERTOIRE
REPETITEUR
REPETITION
REPETITIVE
REPORTEDLY
REPOSITORY
REPRESSION
REPRESSIVE
REPRODUCER
REPUBLICAN
REPUGNANCE
REPUTATION
RIPSNORTER
RUPESTRIAN
RUPICOLINE
SAPPERMENT
SAPROPHYTE
SEPARATELY
SEPARATION
SEPARATISM
SEPARATIST
SEPARATRIX
SEPTENNIAL
SEPTUAGINT
SEPULCHRAL
SOPHOCLEAN
SOPHOMORIC
SUPERADDED
SUPERCARGO
SUPERGIANT
SUPERHUMAN
SUPERMODEL
SUPERPOWER
SUPERSONIC
SUPERSTORE
SUPERTONIC
SUPERVISED
SUPERVISOR
SUPERWOMAN
SUPPLEJACK
SUPPLEMENT
SUPPLENESS
SUPPLICANT
SUPPLICATE
SUPPORTING
SUPPORTIVE
SUPPOSEDLY
SUPPRESSED
SUPPRESSOR
SYPHILITIC
TAPDANCING
TAPERECORD
TAPOTEMENT
TEPIDARIUM
TOPICALITY
TOPOGRAPHY
TOPOLOGIST
TOPSYTURVY
TYPESCRIPT
TYPESETTER
TYPEWRITER
TYPOGRAPHY
UNPLEASANT
UNPREPARED
UNPROMPTED
UNPROVOKED
UNPUNCTUAL
UPPERCLASS
WAPENSCHAW
WAPINSCHAW
WAPPENSHAW
XIPHOPAGUS
ZAPOROGIAN
ACQUAINTED
COQUELICOT
COQUETTISH
COQUIMBITE
INQUIRENDO
INQUISITOR
LIQUESCENT
LIQUIDATOR
LIQUIDIZER
LOQUACIOUS
MAQUILLAGE
REQUIESCAT
ROQUELAURE
SEQUACIOUS
SEQUENTIAL
USQUEBAUGH
ABRIDGMENT
ABROGATION
ABRUPTNESS
ACROAMATIC
ACROBATICS
ACROGENOUS
ACROMEGALY
ACRONYCHAL
ACROTERION
ADRAMELECH
ADRENALINE
AERENCHYMA
AEROBATICS
AEROPHAGIA
AERUGINOUS
AFRICANDER
AFRORMOSIA
AGRONOMIST
AIRFREIGHT
AMRITATTVA
ARROGANTLY
ATRACURIUM
ATRAMENTAL
AURIFEROUS
BARASINGHA
BARBAROSSA
BARBITURIC
BARCAROLLE
BARCHESTER
BAREFOOTED
BAREHEADED
BARELEGGED
BARGAINING
BARLEYBREE
BARLEYCORN
BARMECIDAL
BARMITZVAH
BAROMETRIC
BARRACKING
BARRACOOTA
BARRACOUTA
BARRAMUNDA
BARRENNESS
BARYSPHERE
BERMOOTHES
BERNARDINE
BERSAGLIER
BIRKENHEAD
BIRMINGHAM
BIRTHPLACE
BIRTHRIGHT
BORDERLAND
BORDERLINE
BORDRAGING
BORROWINGS
BURDENSOME
BUREAUCRAT
BURGEONING
BURGLARIZE
BURLINGTON
CARABINEER
CARABINIER
CARACTACUS
CARAMELIZE
CARBURETOR
CARCINOGEN
CARDIOGRAM
CARDIOLOGY
CARELESSLY
CARICATURA
CARICATURE
CARMAGNOLE
CARNASSIAL
CARPATHIAN
CARPENTIER
CARPHOLOGY
CARRAGHEEN
CARTHAMINE
CARTHUSIAN
CARTOMANCY
CARTOONIST
CARYATIDES
CEREBELLUM
CEREMONIAL
CEREMONIES
CERTIORARI
CHREMATIST
CHRISTIANA
CHROMOSOME
CHRONICLER
CHRONICLES
CHRONOLOGY
CHRYSIPPUS
CHRYSOLITE
CIRCASSIAN
CIRCUITOUS
CIRCUMCISE
CIRCUMFLEX
CIRCUMFUSE
CIRCUMVENT
CIRRHOPODA
CIRRIPEDEA
CIRRIPEDIA
CORDIALITY
CORDIERITE
CORDILLERA
CORDWAINER
CORINTHIAN
CORNCOCKLE
CORNFLAKES
CORNFLOWER
CORNSTALKS
CORNSTARCH
CORNUCOPIA
COROMANDEL
CORONATION
CORPULENCE
CORRECTING
CORRECTION
CORRECTIVE
CORREGIDOR
CORRESPOND
CORRIGENDA
CORROBOREE
CORRUGATED
CORRUGATOR
CORRUPTING
CORRUPTION
CORTADERIA
CORYBANTES
CORYBANTIC
CORYPHAEUS
CURMUDGEON
CURMURRING
CURRENCIES
CURRICULUM
CURVACEOUS
CURVETTING
DARJEELING
DARKHAIRED
DERACINATE
DERAILLEUR
DERAILMENT
DEREGULATE
DERIVATION
DERIVATIVE
DERMATITIS
DEROGATORY
DIRECTIONS
DIRECTNESS
DIRECTOIRE
DIREMPTION
DURABILITY
EARTHQUAKE
EARTHWORKS
EBRACTEATE
ENRAPTURED
ENRICHMENT
ENROLLMENT
EPROUVETTE
EUROCHEQUE
EUROCLYDON
EURYPTERUS
FAREPAYING
FARFETCHED
FARRANDINE
FERNITICLE
FERRANDINE
FERTILISED
FERTILISER
FERTILIZER
FIREWALKER
FIREWARDEN
FIRTHSOKEN

FORBEARING
FORBIDDING
FORCEFULLY
FOREBITTER
FOREBODING
FORECASTER
FORECASTLE
FOREDAMNED
FOREFATHER
FOREFINGER
FOREGATHER
FOREGROUND
FOREORDAIN
FORERUNNER
FORESHADOW
FOREWARNED
FORFAITING
FORFEITURE
FORFEUCHEN
FORFOUGHEN
FORGIVABLE
FORINSECAL
FORMIDABLE
FORTHRIGHT
FORTINBRAS
FORTISSIMO
FORTUITOUS
FURNISHING
GARGANTUAN
GARGOUILLE
GARLANDAGE
GARNIERITE
GERIATRICS
GERMICIDAL
GIRDLERINK
GIRLFRIEND
GORGEOUSLY
GORMANDIZE
GYROSCOPIC
HARASSMENT
HARDBOILED
HARDCASTLE
HARMANBECK
HARMONIOUS
HARRINGTON
HARTEBEEST
HARVESTMAN
HERBACEOUS
HEREABOUTS
HEREDITARY
HERESIARCH
HEROICALLY
HORIZONTAL
HORNBLENDE
HORNBLOWER
HORNRIMMED
HORRENDOUS
HORRIFYING
HORSEDRAWN
HORSELBERG
HORSEPOWER
HORSERIDER
HORSEWOMAN
IRRADICATE
IRRATIONAL
IRRELEVANT
IRREMEDIAL
IRRESOLUTE
IRREVERENT
IRRIGATION
IRRITATING
IRRITATION
JARDINIERE
JARGONELLE
JERRYBUILT
KARMATHIAN
KARTTIKAYA
KERSEYMERE
KURDAITCHA
LARGESCALE
LARYNGITIS
LORDLINESS
LORDOLATRY
MARASCHINO
MARCANTANT
MARCESCENT
MARCIONITE
MARGINALIA
MARGINALLY
MARGUERITE
MARIOLATRY
MARIONETTE
MARKETABLE
MARQUETRIE
MARSHALSEA
MARTINGALE
MARTINIQUE
MARVELLOUS
MARYLEBONE
MERCANTILE
MERCIFULLY
MERRYMAKER
MIRACULOUS
MORALITIES
MORATORIUM
MORBIDEZZA
MORDACIOUS
MORGANATIC
MORGANETTA
MORIGEROUS
MORISONIAN
MOROSENESS
MORPHOLOGY
MORTADELLA
MYRINGITIS
MYRIOSCOPE
NARCISSISM
NARCOLEPSY
NARROWBOAT
NARROWDALE
NARROWNESS
NDRANGHETA
NORBERTINE
NORMOBLAST
NORTHANGER
NORTHBOUND
NORTHERNER
NORTHSTEAD
NORTHWARDS
NURSERYMAN
OIREACHTAS
PARACELSUS
PARADIDDLE
PARADOXIDE
PARADOXINE
PARAENESIS
PARAGLOSSA
PARAGONITE
PARAGUAYAN
PARALLELED
PARAMARIBO
PARAMETRIC
PARANORMAL
PARAPHILIA
PARAPHONIA
PARAPHRASE
PARAPHYSIS
PARAPLEGIA
PARAPLEGIC
PARAPRAXIS
PARARTHRIA
PARASCENIA
PARASELENE
PARASTATAL
PARATROOPS
PARDONABLE
PARDONABLY
PARENCHYMA
PARENTHOOD
PARENTLESS
PARGETTING
PARISCHANE
PARISIENNE
PARKLEAVES
PARLIAMENT
PARMACITIE
PARNASSIAN
PARNELLISM
PARONYCHIA
PARRAMATTA
PARTHENOPE
PARTIALITY
PARTICIPLE
PARTICULAR
PARTINGALE
PERCENTAGE
PERCENTILE
PERCEPTION
PERCEPTIVE
PERCIPIENT
PERCOLATOR
PERCUSSION
PERDENDOSI
PERDITIOUS
PERDURABLE
PEREMPTORY
PERFECTION
PERFICIENT
PERFIDIOUS
PERFORATED
PERFORATOR
PERFORMING
PERIDOTITE
PERIEGESIS
PERIHELION
PERILOUSLY
PERIODICAL
PERIPHERAL
PERISHABLE
PERIWINKLE
PERMAFROST
PERMANENCE
PERMANENCY
PERMEATION
PERMISSION
PERMISSIVE
PERNICIOUS
PERNICKETY
PERORATION
PEROVSKITE
PERPETRATE
PERPETUATE
PERPETUITY
PERPLEXING
PERPLEXITY
PERQUISITE
PERSECUTOR
PERSEPHONE
PERSEPOLIS
PERSICARIA
PERSIENNES
PERSIFLAGE
PERSISTENT
PERSONABLE
PERSONALLY
PERSTRINGE
PERSUADING
PERSUASION
PERSUASIVE
PERTINENCE
PERVERSELY
PERVERSION
PERVERSITY
PHRENESIAC
PHRENOLOGY
PIRANDELLO
PORLOCKING
PORNOCRACY
PORRACEOUS
PORTAMENTO
PORTCULLIS
PORTENTOUS
PORTIONIST
PORTMANTLE
PORTMANTUA
PORTSMOUTH
PORTUGUESE
PURITANISM
PURPOSEFUL
PURSUIVANT
PYRACANTHA
PYRAGYRITE
PYROGRAPHY
PYROMANIAC
PYROPHORUS
REREDORTER
SARCOCOLLA
SARCOLEMMA
SARMENTOUS
SARSQUATCH
SCREECHING
SCREENPLAY
SCRIBBLING
SCRIMSHANK
SCRIPTURAL
SCRIPTURES
SCROUNGING
SCRUPULOUS
SCRUTINEER
SCRUTINISE
SCRUTINIZE
SDRUCCIOLA
SERMONICAL
SERPENTINE
SERRADELLA
SERRADILLA
SERRASALMO
SERVICEMAN
SHREWDNESS
SHRIEVALTY
SHRILLNESS
SHRIVELLED
SHROVETIDE
SKRIMSHANK
SORDIDNESS
SPREAGHERY
SPRINGBOKS
SPRINGHAAS
SPRINGLESS
SPRINGLIKE
SPRINGTAIL
SPRINGTIME
SPRINKLING
SPRUCENESS
STRABISMUS
STRABOTOMY
STRACCHINO
STRAGGLING
STRAIGHTEN
STRAITENED

STRAMONIUM
STRAPONTIN
STRASBOURG
STRATEGIST
STRATHSPEY
STRATIOTES
STRATOCRAT
STRATOCYST
STRAVINSKY
STRAWBERRY
STRAWBOARD
STREAMERED
STREAMLINE
STREETLAMP
STREETWISE
STRELITZIA
STRENGTHEN
STREPITANT
STREPITOSO
STRICTNESS
STRIDENTLY
STRIDEWAYS
STRIDULATE
STRIKINGLY
STRINDBERG
STRINGENCY
STRINGENDO
STRINGHALT
STRIPTEASE
STROGANOFF
STRONGHOLD
STRONGROOM
STROPHIOLE
STRUCTURAL
STRULDBERG
STRULDBRUG
STRYCHNINE
SURFRIDING
SURGICALLY
SURINAMESE
SURPASSING
SURPRISING
SURREALISM
SURREALIST
SURROUNDED
TARADIDDLE
TARANTELLA
TARDIGRADE
TARPAULING
TARTRAZINE
TERMINABLE
TERMINALIA
TERMINALLY
TERNEPLATE
TERRACOTTA
TERREPLEIN
TERRIFYING
TERTIARIES
THREADBARE
THREADLIKE
THREADWORM
THREATENED
THREEPENCE
THREEPENNY
THREESCORE
THRENODIAL
THROMBOSIS
THROUGHOUT
THROUGHPUT
THROUGHWAY
TIRAILLEUR
TIRELESSLY
TIROCINIUM
TORBERNITE
TORCHLIGHT
TORPESCENT
TORQUEMADA
TORRENTIAL
TORRICELLI
TORTELLINI
TORTUOUSLY
TURBULENCE
TURNAROUND
TURPENTINE
TURRITELLA
TURTLEDOVE
TURTLENECK
TYRANNICAL
TYRANNISED
UNREADABLE
UNREASONED
UNREDEEMED
UNRELIABLE
UNRELIEVED
UNREQUITED
UNRESERVED
UNRESOLVED
UNREVEALED
UNRIVALLED
UNROMANTIC
UNRULINESS
UPROARIOUS
VARICOSITY
VARIEGATED
VARNISHING
VERIFIABLE
VERMICELLI
VERMILLION
VERNACULAR
VERNISSAGE
VERSAILLES
VERTEBRATE
VERTICALLY
VIROLOGIST
VIRTUOSITY
VIRTUOUSLY
VIRULENTLY
VORAGINOUS
WARRANDICE
WORDSWORTH
WORKAHOLIC
WORLDCLASS
WORSHIPPER
WORTHINESS
WORTHWHILE
XEROPHYTIC
XEROSTOMIA
YARBOROUGH
ABSCISSION
ABSOLUTELY
ABSOLUTION
ABSOLUTISM
ABSORPTION
ABSTEMIOUS
ABSTENTION
ABSTINENCE
ABSTRACTED
AESTHETICS
ANSCHAUUNG
ANSWERABLE
ARSMETRICK
ASSEMBLAGE
ASSEMBLING
ASSESSMENT
ASSEVERATE
ASSIGNABLE
ASSIGNMENT
ASSIMILATE
ASSISTANCE
ASSOCIATED
ASSORTMENT
ASSUMPTION
ASSUMPTIVE
AUSPICIOUS
AUSTRALIAN
AUSTRALORP
AUSTRINGER
BASKETBALL
BASKETWORK
BASSINGTON
BASSOONIST
BESTIALITY
BESTSELLER
BISSEXTILE
BUSHRANGER
CASCARILLA
CASSIABARK
CASSIOPEIA
CASSOLETTE
CASSUMUNAR
CASTRATION
CASUALNESS
CESTRACION
CISLEITHAN
CISPONTINE
CISTERCIAN
COSTLINESS
CUSSEDNESS
CYSTOSCOPY
DESALINATE
DESBOROUGH
DESCENDANT
DESCENDING
DESCRIBING
DESECRATED
DESERVEDLY
DÉSHABILLÉ
DESICCATED
DESIDERATA
DESOLATION
DESPAIRING
DESPICABLE
DESPITEOUS
DESPONDENT
DESQUAMATE
DESSIATINE
DESSYATINE
DISABILITY
DISAPPOINT
DISAPPROVE
DISARRANGE
DISASTROUS
DISBELIEVE
DISBURTHEN
DISCERNING
DISCIPLINE
DISCLAIMER
DISCLOSURE
DISCOBOLUS
DISCOLORED
DISCOMFORT
DISCOMMODE
DISCOMPOSE
DISCONCERT
DISCONNECT
DISCONTENT
DISCOPHORA
DISCORDANT
DISCOURAGE
DISCOVERER
DISCREETLY
DISCREPANT
DISCRETION
DISCURSIVE
DISCUSSING
DISCUSSION
DISDAINFUL
DISEMBOGUE
DISEMBOWEL
DISENCHANT
DISENGAGED
DISENNOBLE
DISFIGURED
DISGRUNTLE
DISGUSTING
DISHABILLE
DISHARMONY
DISHEARTEN
DISHONESTY
DISHWASHER
DISINCLINE
DISINHERIT
DISJOINTED
DISLOYALTY
DISMANTLED
DISMISSIVE
DISORDERED
DISORDERLY
DISPENSARY
DISPENSING
DISPERSION
DISPIRITED
DISPOSABLE
DISPOSSESS
DISPUTABLE
DISQUALIFY
DISQUIETED
DISRESPECT
DISRUPTION
DISRUPTIVE
DISSECTION
DISSELBOOM
DISSEMBLER
DISSENSION
DISSENTING
DISSERTATE
DISSERVICE
DISSIDENCE
DISSILIENT
DISSIMILAR
DISSIPATED
DISSOCIATE
DISSOLVENT
DISSONANCE
DISSUASION
DISTENSION
DISTILLATE
DISTILLERY
DISTILLING
DISTINCTLY
DISTORTION
DISTRACTED
DISTRAUGHT
DISTRESSED
DISTRIBUTE
DISTRINGAS
DISTURBING
DOSTOEVSKY
DYSCRASITE
DYSPROSIUM
DYSTROPHIC
EASTERLING
EISTEDDFOD
ENSANGUINE
EUSTACHIAN
FASCIATION
FASCINATED
FASCINATOR
FASTIDIOUS
FASTIGIATE

FASTMOVING
FESCENNINE
FISHMONGER
FISHSELLER
FISTICUFFS
FOSSILIZED
FUSTANELLA
FUSTANELLE
GASCONNADE
GASTEROPOD
GASTRONOME
GASTRONOMY
GESUNDHEIT
HESITANTLY
HESITATION
HESPERIDES
HISTORICAL
HISTRIONIC
HOSPITABLE
HOSPITABLY
HUSBANDAGE
HYSTERESIS
HYSTERICAL
INSANITARY
INSATIABLE
INSATIABLY
INSECURELY
INSECURITY
INSEMINATE
INSENSIBLE
INSIPIDITY
INSISTENCE
INSOLENTLY
INSOLVENCY
INSOUCIANT
INSPECTION
INSPISSATE
INSTALMENT
INSTIGATOR
INSTRUCTED
INSTRUCTOR
INSTRUMENT
INSUFFLATE
INSULARITY
INSULATION
INSURGENCY
JUSTICIARY
KESSELRING
LASCIVIOUS
LASTMINUTE
LESBIANISM
LISTLESSLY
LUSITANIAN
LYSENKOISM
MASCARPONE
MASKANONGE
MASKINONGE
MASKIROVKA
MASQUERADE
MASSASAUGA
MASTECTOMY
MASTERMIND
MASTERWORT
MASTURBATE
MESENTERON
MESITYLENE
MESOLITHIC
MISCELLANY
MISCHMETAL
MISCONDUCT
MISERICORD
MISFORTUNE
MISGIVINGS
MISHGUGGLE
MISHNAYOTH
MISLEADING
MISMATCHED
MISOCAPNIC
MISOGYNIST
MISPRISION
MISSIONARY
MISTAKENLY
MOSASAUROS
MOSSBUNKER
MUSICOLOGY
MUSKETEERS
MUSSORGSKY
MYSTAGOGUE
MYSTAGOGUS
MYSTERIOUS
NASTURTIUM
NESSELRODE
NOSOCOMIAL
NOSOPHOBIA
OBSEQUIOUS
OBSERVABLE
OBSERVANCE
OBSIDIONAL
OBSTETRICS
OESOPHAGUS
PASIGRAPHY
PASQUINADE
PASSAGEWAY
PASSAMEZZO
PASSIONATE
PASTEBOARD
PASTEURISE
PASTEURIZE
PASTORELLA
PESCADORES
PESTALOZZI
PESTILENCE
PISTILLATE
POSITIVELY
POSITIVIST
POSSESSION
POSSESSIVE
POSTCHAISE
POSTHUMOUS
POSTILLATE
POSTILLION
POSTLIMINY
POSTMASTER
POSTSCRIPT
RESCHEDULE
RESEARCHER
RESEMBLING
RESENTMENT
RESERVISTS
RESIGNEDLY
RESILIENCE
RESISTANCE
RESOLUTELY
RESOLUTION
RESORCINOL
RESOUNDING
RESPECTFUL
RESPECTING
RESPECTIVE
RESPIRATOR
RESPONDENT
RESPONSIVE
RESTAURANT
RESTLESSLY
RESTRAINED
RESTRICTED
RESUMPTION
RESUPINATE
RESURGENCE
ROSANILINE
ROSECHAFER
ROSEMALING
SISTERHOOD
SUSPENDERS
SUSPENSION
SUSPICIOUS
SUSTAINING
SUSTENANCE
SYSTEMATIC
TASKMASTER
TASTEFULLY
TESCHENITE
TESTACEOUS
TESTICULAR
TOSSICATED
TOSTICATED
ULSTERETTE
UNSALARIED
UNSCHOOLED
UNSCRAMBLE
UNSCRIPTED
UNSEASONED
UNSETTLING
UNSHACKLED
UNSLEEPING
UNSOCIABLE
UNSPECIFIC
UNSUITABLE
UNSWERVING
UPSTANDING
VESICULATE
VESTIBULUM
VISIBILITY
VISITATION
WASHINGTON
WASSAILING
WASSERMANS
WASTEFULLY
WASTEPAPER
WESTERNIZE
WISHYWASHY
YESTERWEEK
YESTERYEAR
ACTIONABLE
ACTIVITIST
AFTERBIRTH
AFTERHOURS
AFTERPIECE
AFTERSHAVE
AFTERSHOCK
AFTERTASTE
AFTERWARDS
ALTAZIMUTH
ALTERATION
ALTERNATOR
ALTOGETHER
ALTRUISTIC
ANTAGONISE
ANTAGONISM
ANTAGONIST
ANTAGONIZE
ANTARCTICA
ANTECEDENT
ANTHEOLION
ANTHOCLORE
ANTHRACINE
ANTHRACITE
ANTHROPOID
ANTIADITIS
ANTIBARBUS
ANTIBIOTIC
ANTICHTHON
ANTICIPATE
ANTICLIMAX
ANTIFREEZE
ANTIMASQUE
ANTIMATTER
ANTIMONIAN
ANTINOMIAN
ANTIOCHENE
ANTIOCHIAN
ANTIPHONAL
ANTIPODEAN
ANTIPROTON
ANTIQUATED
ANTISEPSIS
ANTISEPTIC
ANTISOCIAL
ANTISTATIC
ANTITHESIS
ANTITHETIC
ANTITRAGUS
ANTIVENENE
APTERYGOTA
ARTHRALGIA
ARTHROMERE
ARTHURIANA
ARTICULATA
ARTICULATE
ARTIFICIAL
ARTOCARPUS
ASTEROIDEA
ASTIGMATIC
ASTOMATOUS
ASTONISHED
ASTOUNDING
ASTRAGALUS
ASTRALAGUS
ASTRINGENT
ASTROLOGER
ASTRONOMER
ASTUTENESS
ATTACHMENT
ATTAINABLE
ATTAINMENT
ATTENDANCE
ATTRACTION
ATTRACTIVE
AUTECOLOGY
AUTHORISED
AUTHORSHIP
AUTOCHTHON
AUTOCRATIC
AUTODIDACT
AUTOGENOUS
AUTOMATION
AUTOMOBILE
AUTOMOTIVE
AUTONOMOUS
AUTOPLASTY
AUTOSTRADA
BATHYSCAPH
BATRACHIAN
BATTAILOUS
BATTENBERG
BATTENBURG
BATTLEDOOR
BATTLEDORE
BATTLEMENT
BATTLESHIP
BETACRUCIS
BETELGEUSE
BETELGEUZE
BITTERLING
BITTERNESS
BITUMINOUS
BOTHERSOME
BOTTICELLI
BOTTLEHEAD
BOTTLENECK

BOTTOMLESS
BUTCHERING
BUTTERBAKE
BUTTERBUMP
BUTTERMERE
BUTTERMILK
BUTTONDOWN
BUTTONHOLE
CATABOLISM
CATACHUMEN
CATAFALQUE
CATALECTIC
CATALEPTIC
CATALOGUER
CATAPHRACT
CATARRHINE
CATASTASIS
CATAWAMPUS
CATCHPENNY
CATCRACKER
CATECHUMEN
CATEGORISE
CATEGORIZE
CATENACCIO
CATHOLICON
CATHOLICOS
CATTLEGRID
CITRONELLA
COTTIERISM
COTTONTAIL
COTTONWOOD
CUTTLEBONE
CUTTLEFISH
DETACHABLE
DETACHMENT
DETAINMENT
DETECTABLE
DETERMINED
DETERRENCE
DETESTABLE
DETONATION
DETRACTION
DETRUNCATE
DITHIONATE
DUTCHWOMAN
EATANSWILL
ECTHLIPSIS
ENTEROCELE
ENTERPRISE
ENTHUSIASM
ENTHUSIAST
ENTICEMENT
ENTOMBMENT
ENTOMOLOGY
ENTRANCING
ENTREATING
ENTREMESSE
ENTRENCHED
ENTRYPHONE
ESTANCIERO
ESTIMATION
ESTRAMACON
EUTHANASIA
EUTHYNEURA
EUTRAPELIA
EXTENDABLE
EXTENSIBLE
EXTERNALLY
EXTINCTION
EXTINGUISH
EXTRACTION
EXTRANEOUS
FATALISTIC
FATALITIES
FATHERLAND
FATHERLESS
FETTERLOCK
FETTUCCINE
FITZGERALD
FUTURISTIC
GETHSEMANE
GETTYSBURG
GETUPANDGO
GUTTIFERAE
GUTTURALLY
HATEENOUGH
HETERODOXY
HITCHHIKER
HITHERWARD
HITOPADESA
HITOPODESA
HOTCHPOTCH
IATROGENIC
INTAGLIATE
INTANGIBLE
INTEGRATED
INTEGUMENT
INTELIGENT
INTEMERATE
INTENDMENT
INTENERATE
INTENTNESS
INTERBREED
INTERCEDER
INTERCLUDE
INTERESTED
INTERFERER
INTERFERON
INTERLEAVE
INTERLOPER
INTERMARRY
INTERMEZZO
INTERNALLY
INTERNMENT
INTERNODAL
INTERPHONE
INTERSTATE
INTERSTICE
INTERTRIGO
INTERTWINE
INTERWEAVE
INTERWOVEN
INTESTINAL
INTESTINES
INTIMATELY
INTIMATION
INTIMIDATE
INTINCTION
INTOLERANT
INTONATION
INTOXICANT
INTOXICATE
INTRAURBAN
INTRIGUING
INTROSPECT
KATERFELTO
KETTLEDRUM
LATTERMATH
LATTICINIO
LETTERHEAD
LITERATURE
LITHISTADA
LITHOGRAPH
LITHOMARGE
LITHOPHANE
LITHUANIAN
LITIGATION
LITTLENESS
LITURGICAL
LOTOPHAGUS
LUTESTRING
MATCHMAKER
MATCHSTALK
MATCHSTICK
MATELLASSE
MATERIALLY
MATERNALLY
MATRIARCHY
MATTERHORN
MATURATION
METABOLISE
METABOLISM
METACARPAL
METACARPUS
METACENTRE
METALEPSIS
METALLURGY
METAPHRASE
METAPLASIS
METASTABLE
METATARSAL
METATARSUS
METATHERIA
METATHESIS
METHEDRINE
METHODICAL
METHOMANIA
METHUSALEH
METHUSELAH
METHYLATED
METICULOUS
METROPOLIS
METTLESOME
MITHRIDATE
MITIGATING
MITIGATION
MOTHERHOOD
MOTHERLAND
MOTHERLESS
MOTHERLIKE
MOTIONLESS
MOTIVATION
MOTORCYCLE
MUTABILITY
MUTILATION
MUTINOUSLY
MUTTONHEAD
NATATORIAL
NATATORIUM
NATHELESSE
NATIONALLY
NATIONWIDE
NATTERJACK
NATURALISM
NATURALIST
NATURALIZE
NATUROPATH
NETHERMOST
NETTLERASH
NETTLETREE
NETWORKING
NOTABILITY
NOTEWORTHY
NOTICEABLE
NOTICEABLY
NOTIFIABLE
NOTIONALLY
NOTORYCTES
NUTCRACKER
NUTRITIOUS
OBTAINABLE
OBTUSENESS
OCTAHEDRON
OCTODECIMO
OFTENTIMES
OPTIMISTIC
ORTHOCAINE
ORTHOCLASE
ORTHOGONAL
ORTHOPNOEA
ORTHOPTICS
OSTENSIBLE
OSTENSIBLY
OSTEOBLAST
OSTEOCOLLA
OSTEOLEPIS
OSTEOPATHY
OSTEOPHYTE
OSTROGOTHS
OUTBALANCE
OUTLANDISH
OUTPATIENT
OUTPERFORM
OUTPOURING
OUTRAGEOUS
OUTSPECKLE
PATAGONIAN
PATAVINITY
PATCHCOCKE
PATCHINESS
PATERNALLY
PATHFINDER
PATHOGENIC
PATIBULARY
PATISSERIE
PATRIARCHY
PATRIOTISM
PATRONISED
PATRONYMIC
PETITIONER
PETRARCHAN
PETRIFYING
PETRISSAGE
PETROGLYPH
PETRONELLA
PETTICHAPS
PETTYCHAPS
PETULANTLY
PITCHSTONE
PITYRIASIS
POTENTIATE
POTENTILLA
PUTREFYING
PUTRESCENT
PYTHAGORAS
PYTHOGENIC
RATIONALLY
RATTLETRAP
RETINALITE
RETIREMENT
RETRACTION
RETRAINING
RETREATING
RETROGRADE
RETROGRESS
RETROSPECT
RETURNABLE
RITORNELLE
RITORNELLO
ROTHSCHILD
ROTISSERIE
ROTTWEILER
RUTHERFORD
RUTHLESSLY
SATISFYING
SATURATION
SATURNALIA
SATYAGRAHA
SETTERWORT
SETTLEMENT

TATPURUSHA
TATTERSALL
TITARAKURA
TUTIVILLUS
ULTIMATELY
ULTRAFICHE
ULTRASONIC
ULTRASOUND
ULTRONEOUS
UNTHINKING
UNTIDINESS
UNTRUTHFUL
URTICACEAE
VETERINARY
VITELLICLE
VITUPERATE
WATCHFULLY
WATCHMAKER
WATCHTOWER
WATERBORNE
WATERBRASH
WATERCOLOR
WATERCRESS
WATERFRONT
WATERLEVEL
WATERMELON
WATERPROOF
WATERSKIER
WATERSPOUT
WATERTIGHT
WATERWHEEL
WATERWINGS
WATERWORKS
WATTLEWORK
WITCHCRAFT
WITGATBOOM
WITHDRAWAL
WITSNAPPER
ABUNDANTLY
ADULLAMITE
ADULTERANT
ADULTERATE
ADULTERESS
ADULTERINE
ADULTEROUS
AQUAFORTIS
AQUAMANALE
AQUAMANILE
AQUAMARINE
ARUNDELIAN
BAUDELAIRE
BLUEBOTTLE
BLUEMANTLE
BLUETHROAT
BLUNDERING
BOUILLOTTE
BOURIGNIAN
BOUSINGKEN
CAUTIONARY
CAUTIOUSLY
CHUCKWALLA
CHURCHGOER
CHURCHYARD
CHURLISHLY
CLUMPERTON
CLUMSINESS
COUNCILLOR
COUNSELING
COUNSELLOR
COUNTERACT
COUNTRYMAN
COURAGEOUS
COURTHOUSE
COUSCOUSOU
CRUIKSHANK
CRUSTACEAN
DEUTOPLASM
DIURNALIST
DOUBLEBASS
DOUBLETALK
DOUBTFULLY
DRUMBLEDOR
DRUZHINNIK
DUUMVIRATE
EBULLIENCE
ECUADORIAN
ECUMENICAL
EDULCORATE
EGURGITATE
EMULSIFIER
EQUANIMITY
EQUATORIAL
EQUESTRIAN
EQUITATION
EQUIVALENT
EQUIVOCATE
ERUBESCENT
ERUCTATION
EXUBERANCE
EXULTATION
FAULTINESS
FEUILLETON
FLUCTUATER
FLUFFINESS
FLUGELHORN
FLUNKEYDOM
FLUTEMOUTH
FOUDROYANT
FOUNDATION
FOURCHETTE
FOURIERISM
FOURRAGERE
FOURTEENTH
FRUITFULLY
FRUSTRATED
GAULTHERIA
GLUTTONOUS
GRUBBINESS
GRUMPINESS
HAUSTELLUM
HAUSTORIUM
HOUSEBOUND
HOUSECRAFT
HOUSEMAIDS
HOUSEPROUD
INUNDATION
JAUNTINESS
JOURNALESE
JOURNALISM
JOURNALIST
JOURNEYMAN
JOUYSAUNCE
LAUDERDALE
LAUNCEGAYE
LAUNCESTON
LAUNDROMAT
LAURDALITE
LAURENTIAN
LAURUSTINE
LAURVIKITE
LEUCHAEMIA
LOUISIETTE
MAUPASSANT
MAURITANIA
MOUCHARABY
MOUDIEWART
MOULDINESS
MOULDIWARP
MOUNTEBANK
MOURNFULLY
MOUSEPIECE
MOUSSELINE
MOUSTERIAN
MOUTHORGAN
MOUTHPIECE
NAUSEATING
NAUSEATIVE
NEURILEMMA
NEUROLEMMA
NEUTRALISE
NEUTRALITY
NEUTRALIZE
NEUTROPHIL
NOUAKCHOTT
NOURISHING
NOURRITURE
PLUMASSIER
PLUNDERING
PLUPERFECT
PLUTOCRACY
POURPARLER
PRUDENTIAL
ROUGHHOUSE
ROUNDABOUT
ROUNDHOUSE
ROUSEABOUT
ROUSTABOUT
SAUERKRAUT
SAUROPSIDA
SBUDDIKINS
SCULPTRESS
SCURRILITY
SCURRILOUS
SCUTELLATE
SHUDDERING
SKUPSHTINA
SLUGGISHLY
SLUMBERING
SOUBRIQUET
SOUNDPROOF
SOUNDTRACK
SOURDELINE
SOUSAPHONE
SOUTERRAIN
SOUTHBOUND
SOUTHERNER
SOUTHWARDS
SPURIOUSLY
SQUEEZEBOX
SQUETEAGUE
SQUIREARCH
STUBBORNLY
STUDIOUSLY
STUFFINESS
STULTIFIED
STUMBLEDOM
STUPEFYING
STUPENDOUS
STURDINESS
THUCYDIDES
THUMBIKINS
THUMBSCREW
THUNDERBOX
THUNDERING
THUNDEROUS
TOUCHANDGO
TOUCHINESS
TOUCHPAPER
TOUCHPIECE
TOUCHSTONE
TOURBILLON
TOURMALINE
TOURNAMENT
TOURNIQUET
TRUCULENCE
TRUSTFULLY
TRUTHFULLY
USUCAPTION
USURPATION
VAUDEVILLE
YOUNGBERRY
YOURSELVES
ZEUGLODONT
ADVENTURER
ADVERSARIA
ADVERTISER
AVVOGADORE
CAVALRYMAN
CAVICORNIA
COVENANTER
DEVANAGARI
DEVASTATED
DEVASTAVIT
DEVELOPING
DEVOLUTION
DEVOTEMENT
DEVOTIONAL
DIVERGENCE
DIVINATION
DIVISIONAL
DOVERCOURT
FAVORITISM
FAVOURABLE
FAVOURABLY
FEVERISHLY
GOVERNANCE
GOVERNESSY
GOVERNMENT
HOVERCRAFT
INVALIDATE
INVALIDITY
INVALUABLE
INVARIABLE
INVARIABLY
INVESTMENT
INVETERATE
INVIGILATE
INVIGORATE
INVINCIBLE
INVIOLABLE
INVITATION
INVOCATION
LAVALLIÈRE
LAVISHNESS
LEVITATION
LIVELIHOOD
LIVELINESS
LIVERWURST
LOVELINESS
MAVOURNEEN
NAVIGATION
NOVACULITE
OUVIRANDRA
RAVENOUSLY
RAVENSBILL
RAVENSDUCK
RAVENSTONE
REVELATION
REVENGEFUL
REVERENTLY
REVERSIBLE
REVITALIZE
REVIVALIST
REVOCATION
REVOLUTION
SAVAGENESS
SAVONAROLA
SEVENTIETH
VIVANDIÈRE
VIVIPAROUS

WAVELENGTH
BEWILDERED
BEWITCHING
BOWDLERISE
BOWDLERIZE
DOWNMARKET
DOWNSIZING
DOWNSTAIRS
DOWNSTREAM
HOWLEGLASS
HOWSOMEVER
LAWABIDING
LAWBREAKER
LAWRENCIUM
NEWFANGLED
NEWSAGENTS
NEWSCASTER
NEWSLETTER
NEWSMONGER
NEWSPAPERS
NEWSREADER
NEWSWORTHY
PAWNBROKER
POWERHOUSE
RAWINSONDE
RAWSTHORNE
ROWDYDOWDY
ROWLANDSON
TOWNSWOMAN
UNWORKABLE
COXCOMICAL
FOXHUNTING
LUXEMBOURG
LUXURIANCE
MAXIMALIST
MAXIMILIAN
SAXICOLINE
SAXICOLOUS
SEXAGESIMA
SEXOLOGIST
TAXONOMIST
TOXICOLOGY
ABYSSINIAN
AMYGDALOID
ARYTAENOID
ASYMMETRIC
ASYNARTETE
CLYDESDALE
CRYOGENICS
CRYOPHORUS
CRYPTOGRAM
DAYDREAMER
ELYTRIFORM
ERYMANTHUS
ERYSIPELAS
FLYCATCHER
JAYWALKING
KEYBOARDER
MAYONNAISE
OXYGENATOR
OXYMORONIC
OZYMANDIAS
PHYLACTERY
PHYLLIOPOD
PHYSICALLY
PHYSIOCRAT
PHYSIOLOGY
PSYCHIATRY
PSYCHOLOGY
PSYCHOPATH
PSYCHOPOMP
RHYTHMICAL
SKYSCRAPER
STYLISTICS
STYLOPISED
TRYPTOPHAN
UNYIELDING
ALZHEIMERS
MIZZENMAST
MOZAMBIQUE
MOZZARELLA
POZZUOLANA
PRZEWALSKI
PUZZLEMENT
RAZZMATAZZ
SUZERAINTY

10:4

ADIAPHORON
ADRAMELECH
AFFABILITY
ALCAICERIA
ALKALINITY
ALMACANTAR
ALTAZIMUTH
AMBARVALIA
AMBASSADOR
AMIABILITY
ANDALUSIAN
ANDALUSITE
ANTAGONISE
ANTAGONISM
ANTAGONIST
ANTAGONIZE
ANTARCTICA
APHAERESIS
APPARENTLY
APPARITION
AQUAFORTIS
AQUAMANALE
AQUAMANILE
AQUAMARINE
ARMAGEDDON
ASPARAGINE
ATHANASIAN
ATRACURIUM
ATRAMENTAL
ATTACHMENT
ATTAINABLE
ATTAINMENT
BAGASSOSIS
BALANCHINE
BARASINGHA
BEHAVIORAL
BELARUSIAN
BETACRUCIS
BIPARTISAN
BLEARYEYED
BREADFRUIT
BREAKABLES
BREAKWATER
BREASTBONE
BREASTFEED
BREASTWORK
BREATHLESS
BROADCLOTH
BROADPIECE
BROADSHEET
BROADSWORD
CADAVEROUS
CALAMANDER
CALAMITOUS
CALAMONDIN
CALAVERITE
CAPABILITY
CAPACITATE
CARABINEER
CARABINIER
CARACTACUS
CARAMELIZE
CATABOLISM
CATACHUMEN
CATAFALQUE
CATALECTIC
CATALEPTIC
CATALOGUER
CATAPHRACT
CATARRHINE
CATASTASIS
CATAWAMPUS
CAVALRYMAN
CHEAPSKATE
CLEARSTORY
CLEARWATER
COMANCHERO
COPARCENER
CREATIVITY
DEBASEMENT
DEBATEMENT
DEBAUCHERY
DECAGRAMME
DECAHEDRON
DECAMPMENT
DECAPITATE
DECATHLETE
DEFACEMENT
DEFAMATION
DEFAMATORY
DEPARTMENT
DEPARTURES
DERACINATE
DERAILLEUR
DERAILMENT
DESALINATE
DETACHABLE
DETACHMENT
DETAINMENT
DEVANAGARI
DEVASTATED
DEVASTAVIT
DIDASCALIC
DILAPIDATE
DILATATION
DINANDERIE
DISABILITY
DISAPPOINT
DISAPPROVE
DISARRANGE
DISASTROUS
DREADFULLY
DREADLOCKS
DREAMINESS
DREARINESS
DREARISOME
DURABILITY
DYNAMITARD
EATANSWILL
EBRACTEATE
ECUADORIAN
EFFACEMENT
EMBANKMENT
ENCAMPMENT
ENCASEMENT
ENGAGEMENT
ENLACEMENT
ENRAPTURED
ENSANGUINE
EQUANIMITY
EQUATORIAL
ESCADRILLE
ESCALATION
ESCAPEMENT
ESCARPMENT
ESPADRILLE
ESTANCIERO
EUCALYPTUS
EXCAVATION
EXHALATION
EXHAUSTING
EXHAUSTION
EXHAUSTIVE
EXPATRIATE
FANATICISM
FATALISTIC
FATALITIES
GELATINOUS
HARASSMENT
HEPATOCELE
HUMANISTIC
HUMANITIES
HYPAETHRAL
HYPAETHRON
IDEALISTIC
ILLADVISED
ILLAQUEATE
IMMACULACY
IMMACULATE
IMMATERIAL
IMMATURITY
IMPAIRMENT
IMPALPABLE
IMPALUDISM
IMPARLANCE
IMPASSABLE
IMPATIENCE
INCAPACITY
INCAPARINA
INCAUTIOUS
INDAPAMIDE
INFALLIBLE
INFALLIBLY
INFATUATED
INHABITANT
INHALATION
INSANITARY
INSATIABLE
INSATIABLY
INTAGLIATE
INTANGIBLE
INVALIDATE
INVALIDITY
INVALUABLE
INVARIABLE
INVARIABLY
IRRADICATE
IRRATIONAL
KSHATRIYAS
LAMARCKISM
LAVALLIÈRE
LAWABIDING
LEGALISTIC
LOGANBERRY
LOGARITHMS
MADAGASCAN
MADAGASCAR
MAHAYANALI
MALACOLOGY
MALAGUETTA
MALAPROPOS
MALAYALAAM
MANAGEABLE
MANAGEMENT
MANAGERESS
MANAGERIAL
MARASCHINO
MEGALITHIC
MEGALOSAUR
MELACONITE

MELANCHOLY
MELANESIAN
MENACINGLY
METABOLISE
METABOLISM
METACARPAL
METACARPUS
METACENTRE
METALEPSIS
METALLURGY
METAPHRASE
METAPLASIS
METASTABLE
METATARSAL
METATARSUS
METATHERIA
METATHESIS
MIRACULOUS
MONARCHIST
MORALITIES
MORATORIUM
MOSASAUROS
MOZAMBIQUE
MUJAHEDDIN
MUTABILITY
NATATORIAL
NATATORIUM
NDRANGHETA
NEFANDROUS
NEGATIVELY
NEMATOCYST
NICARAGUAN
NONALIGNED
NOTABILITY
NOUAKCHOTT
NOVACULITE
OBTAINABLE
OCCASIONAL
OCEANGOING
OCTAHEDRON
OLEAGINOUS
ORNAMENTAL
PADAREWSKI
PALAEOTYPE
PALAESTRAL
PALAGONITE
PALATALISE
PALATINATE
PANAMANIAN
PANARITIUM
PAPAVERINE
PARACELSUS
PARADIDDLE
PARADOXIDE
PARADOXINE
PARAENESIS
PARAGLOSSA
PARAGONITE
PARAGUAYAN
PARALLELED
PARAMARIBO
PARAMETRIC
PARANORMAL
PARAPHILIA
PARAPHONIA
PARAPHRASE
PARAPHYSIS
PARAPLEGIA
PARAPLEGIC
PARAPRAXIS
PARARTHRIA
PARASCENIA
PARASELENE
PARASTATAL
PARATROOPS
PATAGONIAN
PATAVINITY
PICARESQUE
PICAYUNISH
PINAKOTHEK
PIRANDELLO
PLEASANTLY
PLEASANTRY
PLIABILITY
POCAHONTAS
PREARRANGE
PROAIRESIS
PYRACANTHA
PYRAGYRITE
QUEASINESS
RAGAMUFFIN
REGARDLESS
RELATIVELY
RELATIVITY
RELAXATION
RELAXATIVE
REMARKABLE
REMARKABLY
REPAIRABLE
REPARATION
REPATRIATE
ROLANDSECK
ROMANESQUE
ROSANILINE
SALAMANDER
SAMARSKITE
SANATORIUM
SAVAGENESS
SCHALSTEIN
SEDATENESS
SENATORIAL
SEPARATELY
SEPARATION
SEPARATISM
SEPARATIST
SEPARATRIX
SEXAGESIMA
SHEARWATER
SINARCHIST
SINARQUIST
SPEAKERINE
SPHACELATE
SPHALERITE
SPLANCHNIC
STEADINESS
STEAKHOUSE
STEALTHILY
STIACCIATO
STRABISMUS
STRABOTOMY
STRACCHINO
STRAGGLING
STRAIGHTEN
STRAITENED
STRAMONIUM
STRAPONTIN
STRASBOURG
STRATEGIST
STRATHSPEY
STRATIOTES
STRATOCRAT
STRATOCYST
STRAVINSKY
STRAWBERRY
STRAWBOARD
SUGARALLIE
SWEATSHIRT
SYNAERESIS
TANAGRIDAE
TARADIDDLE
TARANTELLA
THEATRICAL
TIRAILLEUR
TITARAKURA
TRIACONTER
TRIANGULAR
TULARAEMIA
TYRANNICAL
TYRANNISED
UNBALANCED
UNEASINESS
UNFAITHFUL
UNFAMILIAR
UNFATHOMED
UNHAMPERED
UNLADYLIKE
UNMANNERED
UNMANNERLY
UNSALARIED
VIVANDIÈRE
VOCABULARY
VOCABULIST
VOCATIONAL
VOLATILITY
VORAGINOUS
WHEATSHEAF
WHEATSTONE
ZABAGLIONE
ALABANDINE
ALABANDITE
ANABAPTIST
BALBRIGGAN
BALBUTIENT
BAMBOOZLED
BARBAROSSA
BARBITURIC
BOBBYSOXER
BOMBARDIER
CAMBERWELL
CAMBRENSIS
CARBURETOR
COLBERTINE
COMBUSTION
CUMBERLAND
CUMBERSOME
DESBOROUGH
DIABOLICAL
DISBELIEVE
DISBURTHEN
DOUBLEBASS
DOUBLETALK
DOUBTFULLY
DUMBLEDORE
ERUBESCENT
EXUBERANCE
FEEBLENESS
FLABBINESS
FORBEARING
FORBIDDING
GHIBELLINE
GIBBERELLA
GILBERTIAN
GILBERTINE
GRUBBINESS
HERBACEOUS
HOBBYHORSE
HUMBLENESS
HUSBANDAGE
ICEBREAKER
INEBRIATED
ISABELLINE
JABBERWOCK
KEYBOARDER
KIMBERLITE
KLEBSIELLA
KNOBKERRIE
LAMBREQUIN
LAWBREAKER
LESBIANISM
LIEBERMANN
LIMBERNECK
LIMBURGITE
LUMBERJACK
MEMBERSHIP
MEMBRANOUS
MORBIDEZZA
MUMBLENEWS
NIMBLENESS
NORBERTINE
NUMBERLESS
OFFBALANCE
OROBRANCHE
OUTBALANCE
PLEBISCITE
PREBENDARY
RABBINICAL
RUBBERNECK
RUMBLOSSOM
RUMBULLION
SABBATICAL
SHABBINESS
SHIBBOLETH
SOMBRERITE
SOUBRIQUET
STABILISER
STABILIZER
STUBBORNLY
SUNBATHING
SYMBOLICAL
TAMBERLANE
TAMBOURINE
TIEBREAKER
TIMBERYARD
TIMBROLOGY
TORBERNITE
TUMBLEDOWN
TURBULENCE
UNABRIDGED
UNOBSERVED
YARBOROUGH
ZIMBABWEAN
ZUMBOORUCK
ABSCISSION
AFICIONADO
ALECTORIAN
ANACARDIUM
ANACHARSIS
ANACLASTIC
ANACOUSTIC
ANACRUSTIC
ANSCHAUUNG
APICULTURE
APOCALYPSE
APOCRYPHAL
ARACOSTYLE
AVICULARIA
BACCHANTES
BARCAROLLE
BARCHESTER
BEDCHAMBER
BEDCLOTHES
BIOCHEMIST
BLACKBEARD
BLACKBERRY
BLACKBOARD
BLACKBULLY
BLACKENING
BLACKGUARD
BLACKHEART
BLACKSHIRT

BLACKSMITH
BLACKSTONE
BLACKTHORN
BLACKWATER
BLOCKHOUSE
BRACHIOPOD
BRICKLAYER
BRICKWORKS
BROCATELLE
BUCCINATOR
BUTCHERING
CALCAREOUS
CALCEDONIO
CALCEOLATE
CALCULABLE
CALCULATED
CALCULATOR
CANCIONERO
CANCRIZANS
CARCINOGEN
CASCARILLA
CATCHPENNY
CATCRACKER
CHECKLATON
CHECKPOINT
CHICHESTER
CHICKENPOX
CHUCKWALLA
CIRCASSIAN
CIRCUITOUS
CIRCUMCISE
CIRCUMFLEX
CIRCUMFUSE
CIRCUMVENT
CLOCKMAKER
COCCINEOUS
COLCHESTER
COLCHICINE
CONCENTRIC
CONCEPTION
CONCEPTUAL
CONCERNING
CONCERTINA
CONCERVATE
CONCESSION
CONCHIGLIE
CONCHIOLIN
CONCHOLOGY
CONCILIATE
CONCINNITY
CONCINNOUS
CONCLUDING
CONCLUSION
CONCLUSIVE
CONCOCTION
CONCORDANT
CONCRETION
CONCURRENT
CONCUSSION
COXCOMICAL
CRICKETING
CROCKFORDS
DEACTIVATE
DELCREDERE
DESCENDANT
DESCENDING
DESCRIBING
DIACAUSTIC
DIACONICON
DISCERNING
DISCIPLINE
DISCLAIMER
DISCLOSURE
DISCOBOLUS
DISCOLORED
DISCOMFORT
DISCOMMODE
DISCOMPOSE
DISCONCERT
DISCONNECT
DISCONTENT
DISCOPHORA
DISCORDANT
DISCOURAGE
DISCOVERER
DISCREETLY
DISCREPANT
DISCRETION
DISCURSIVE
DISCUSSING
DISCUSSION
DOLCEMENTE
DRACONITES
DUTCHWOMAN
DYSCRASITE
EGOCENTRIC
ELACAMPANE
ELECAMPANE
ELECTORATE
ELECTRICAL
ELECTROMER
ELECTRONIC
EMACIATION
EPICANTHUS
ERUCTATION
EVACUATION
EXACERBATE
EXACTITUDE
EXECRATION
FASCIATION
FASCINATED
FASCINATOR
FESCENNINE
FLICKERING
FLOCCULATE
FLOCCULENT
FLUCTUATER
FLYCATCHER
FORCEFULLY
FRACTIONAL
FRICANDEAU
FUNCTIONAL
GASCONNADE
GEOCENTRIC
GLACIATION
GRACEFULLY
GRACIOUSLY
GROCETERIA
GUACHAMOLE
HENCEFORTH
HITCHHIKER
HOTCHPOTCH
INACCURACY
INACCURATE
INACTIVITY
KINCHINLAY
KNOCKABOUT
LACCADIVES
LANCEOLATE
LASCIVIOUS
LEUCHAEMIA
MALCONTENT
MANCHESTER
MANCHINEEL
MARCANTANT
MARCESCENT
MARCIONITE
MASCARPONE
MATCHMAKER
MATCHSTALK
MATCHSTICK
MERCANTILE
MERCIFULLY
MISCELLANY
MISCHMETAL
MISCONDUCT
MOUCHARABY
NARCISSISM
NARCOLEPSY
NINCOMPOOP
NONCHALANT
NUTCRACKER
PANCRATIUM
PATCHCOCKE
PATCHINESS
PEACEFULLY
PEACEMAKER
PEACHERINO
PECCADILLO
PERCENTAGE
PERCENTILE
PERCEPTION
PERCEPTIVE
PERCIPIENT
PERCOLATOR
PERCUSSION
PESCADORES
PICCADILLY
PICCALILLI
PICCANINNY
PINCHPENNY
PINCUSHION
PITCHSTONE
PONCHIELLI
PRECARIOUS
PRECAUTION
PRECEDENCE
PRECIPITIN
PRECOCIOUS
PRECURSORY
PRICKLOUSE
PROCEDURAL
PROCEEDING
PROCESSING
PROCESSION
PROCLIVITY
PROCREATOR
PROCRUSTES
PROCURABLE
PROCURATOR
PSOCOPTERA
PSYCHIATRY
PSYCHOLOGY
PSYCHOPATH
PSYCHOPOMP
PUNCHDRUNK
PUNCTUALLY
PUNCTULATE
QUICKSANDS
QUICKTHORN
REACTIVATE
REDCURRANT
RESCHEDULE
SACCHARASE
SACCHARIDE
SACCHARINE
SACCHAROID
SANCTIFIED
SANCTITIES
SANCTITUDE
SARCOCOLLA
SARCOLEMMA
SEECATCHIE
SHACKLETON
SHECKLATON
SHOCKINGLY
SHOCKPROOF
SPACECRAFT
SPECIALISE
SPECIALIST
SPECIALITY
SPECIALIZE
SPECIOUSLY
SPECTACLED
SPECTACLES
SPECTATORS
SPECULATOR
STICHARION
STICKINESS
STICKYBEAK
STOCHASTIC
STOCKINESS
SUBCOMPACT
SUCCEEDING
SUCCESSFUL
SUCCESSION
SUCCESSIVE
SUCCINCTLY
SYNCOPATED
SYNCRETISE
TEICHOPSIA
TESCHENITE
THICKENING
THUCYDIDES
TOCCATELLA
TORCHLIGHT
TOUCHANDGO
TOUCHINESS
TOUCHPAPER
TOUCHPIECE
TOUCHSTONE
TRACHELATE
TRECENTIST
TRICHOLOGY
TRICKINESS
TRICLINIUM
TROCHANTER
TROCHOTRON
TROCTOLITE
TRUCULENCE
UNACCENTED
UNICAMERAL
UNOCCUPIED
UNSCHOOLED
UNSCRAMBLE
UNSCRIPTED
USUCAPTION
VULCANALIA
WANCHANCIE
WATCHFULLY
WATCHMAKER
WATCHTOWER
WINCEYETTE
WINCHESTER
WITCHCRAFT
ZINCOGRAPH
ANADROMOUS
ANADYOMENE
BADDERLOCK
BALDERDASH
BANDERILLA
BANDERILLO
BANDMASTER
BAUDELAIRE
BONDHOLDER
BONDSWOMAN
BORDERLAND
BORDERLINE
BORDRAGING
BOWDLERISE

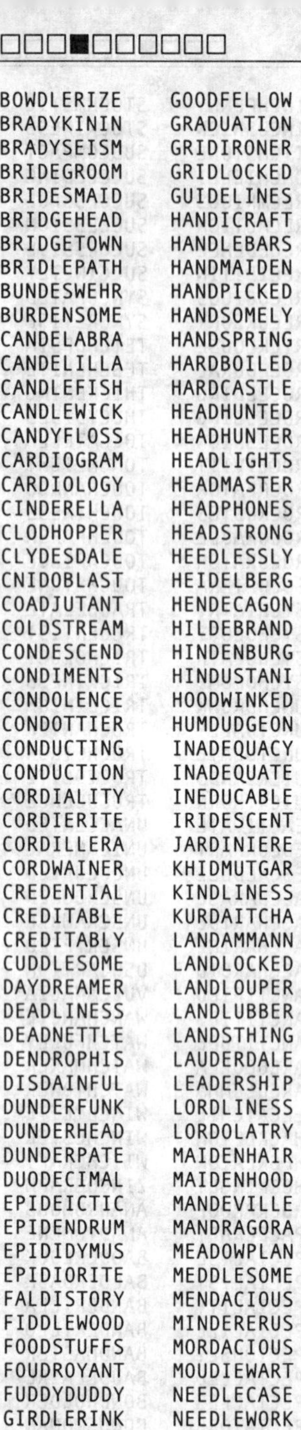

BOWDLERIZE
BRADYKININ
BRADYSEISM
BRIDEGROOM
BRIDESMAID
BRIDGEHEAD
BRIDGETOWN
BRIDLEPATH
BUNDESWEHR
BURDENSOME
CANDELABRA
CANDELILLA
CANDLEFISH
CANDLEWICK
CANDYFLOSS
CARDIOGRAM
CARDIOLOGY
CINDERELLA
CLODHOPPER
CLYDESDALE
CNIDOBLAST
COADJUTANT
COLDSTREAM
CONDESCEND
CONDIMENTS
CONDOLENCE
CONDOTTIER
CONDUCTING
CONDUCTION
CORDIALITY
CORDIERITE
CORDILLERA
CORDWAINER
CREDENTIAL
CREDITABLE
CREDITABLY
CUDDLESOME
DAYDREAMER
DEADLINESS
DEADNETTLE
DENDROPHIS
DISDAINFUL
DUNDERFUNK
DUNDERHEAD
DUNDERPATE
DUODECIMAL
EPIDEICTIC
EPIDENDRUM
EPIDIDYMUS
EPIDIORITE
FALDISTORY
FIDDLEWOOD
FOODSTUFFS
FOUDROYANT
FUDDYDUDDY
GIRDLERINK
GOLDDIGGER
GOLDFINGER
GOLDILOCKS
GONDOLIERS
GOODFELLOW
GRADUATION
GRIDIRONER
GRIDLOCKED
GUIDELINES
HANDICRAFT
HANDLEBARS
HANDMAIDEN
HANDPICKED
HANDSOMELY
HANDSPRING
HARDBOILED
HARDCASTLE
HEADHUNTED
HEADHUNTER
HEADLIGHTS
HEADMASTER
HEADPHONES
HEADSTRONG
HEEDLESSLY
HEIDELBERG
HENDECAGON
HILDEBRAND
HINDENBURG
HINDUSTANI
HOODWINKED
HUMDUDGEON
INADEQUACY
INADEQUATE
INEDUCABLE
IRIDESCENT
JARDINIERE
KHIDMUTGAR
KINDLINESS
KURDAITCHA
LANDAMMANN
LANDLOCKED
LANDLOUPER
LANDLUBBER
LANDSTHING
LAUDERDALE
LEADERSHIP
LORDLINESS
LORDOLATRY
MAIDENHAIR
MAIDENHOOD
MANDEVILLE
MANDRAGORA
MEADOWPLAN
MEDDLESOME
MENDACIOUS
MINDERERUS
MORDACIOUS
MOUDIEWART
NEEDLECASE
NEEDLEWORK
NIDDERLING
OBEDIENTLY
ORIDINANCE
PADDINGTON
PADDYMELON
PAEDIATRIC
PARDONABLE
PARDONABLY
PERDENDOSI
PERDITIOUS
PERDURABLE
PREDACIOUS
PREDECEASE
PREDESTINE
PREDICTION
PREDISPOSE
PREDNISONE
PRODIGALLY
PRODIGIOUS
PRODUCTION
PRODUCTIVE
PRUDENTIAL
PUNDIGRION
QUADRANGLE
QUADRATURA
QUADRICEPS
QUADRIREME
RANDLETREE
RANDOMNESS
READERSHIP
RENDEZVOUS
RINDERPEST
ROADRUNNER
ROADWORTHY
ROWDYDOWDY
RUDDERLESS
SADDLEBACK
SADDLEBILL
SANDALWOOD
SANDEMANIA
SANDERLING
SANDGROPER
SANDINISTA
SANDWICHES
SBUDDIKINS
SHADOWLESS
SHODDINESS
SHUDDERING
SOGDOLAGER
SOGDOLIGER
SOGDOLOGER
SORDIDNESS
SPIDERWORT
SPODOMANCY
STADHOLDER
STUDIOUSLY
SUDDENNESS
SVADILFARI
SWEDENBORG
TAPDANCING
TARDIGRADE
TEDDINGTON
TENDERFOOT
TENDERLOIN
TENDERNESS
TENDRILLED
TRADITIONS
TRIDENTINE
UNEDIFYING
UNEDUCATED
VANDERBILT
VAUDEVILLE
VINDEMIATE
VINDICTIVE
WALDENSIAN
WANDERINGS
WANDERLUST
WANDSWORTH
WEEDKILLER
WIDDICOMBE
WILDEBEEST
WILDERNESS
WILDFOWLER
WINDERMERE
WINDFLOWER
WINDJAMMER
WINDOWSILL
WINDSCREEN
WINDSHIELD
WINDSURFER
WONDERLAND
WONDERMENT
WOODENHEAD
WOODPECKER
WOODPIGEON
WOODWORKER
WORDSWORTH
WUNDERKIND
YGGDRASILL
ACCELERATE
ACCENTUATE
ACCESSIBLE
ACCESSIONS
ADJECTIVAL
ADRENALINE
ADVENTURER
ADVERSARIA
ADVERTISER
AERENCHYMA
AFFETTUOSO
AFTERBIRTH
AFTERHOURS
AFTERPIECE
AFTERSHAVE
AFTERSHOCK
AFTERTASTE
AFTERWARDS
ALDERMANLY
ALIENATION
ALLEGATION
ALLEGEANCE
ALLEGIANCE
ALPENSTOCK
ALTERATION
ALTERNATOR
AMPELOPSIS
ANHELATION
ANNEXATION
ANTECEDENT
APPEARANCE
APPETITIVE
APPETIZING
APTERYGOTA
ASBESTOSIS
ASCENDANCY
ASCENDENCY
ASCETICISM
ASPERSIONS
ASSEMBLAGE
ASSEMBLING
ASSESSMENT
ASSEVERATE
ASTEROIDEA
ATTENDANCE
AUTECOLOGY
BABESIASIS
BAREFOOTED
BAREHEADED
BARELEGGED
BEDEVILLED
BENEDICITE
BENEFACTOR
BENEFICENT
BENEFICIAL
BENEVOLENT
BETELGEUSE
BETELGEUZE
BLUEBOTTLE
BLUEMANTLE
BLUETHROAT
BONESHAKER
BUCEPHALUS
BUREAUCRAT
CALEDONIAN
CALEFACTOR
CALESCENCE
CAMELOPARD
CAMERLENGO
CAMERLINGO
CAMERONIAN
CANECUTTER
CANEPHORUS
CAPERNAITE
CAPERNOITY
CARELESSLY
CATECHUMEN
CATEGORISE
CATEGORIZE
CATENACCIO
CELEBRATED
CELESTIALS
CEREBELLUM
CEREMONIAL
CEREMONIES

CHEEKINESS
CHEERFULLY
CHEESECAKE
CHEESEWOOD
CHREMATIST
CINECAMERA
COHERENTLY
COLEOPTERA
COLEORHIZA
COMEDIENNE
COMESTIBLE
COPENHAGEN
COPERNICUS
COPESETTIC
COVENANTER
CYBERNETIC
DECELERATE
DECENNOVAL
DEFEASANCE
DEFECATION
DEFENSIBLE
DEGENERACY
DEGENERATE
DEJECTEDLY
DELECTABLE
DELEGATION
DEPENDABLE
DEPENDENCE
DEPENDENCY
DEREGULATE
DESECRATED
DESERVEDLY
DETECTABLE
DETERMINED
DETERRENCE
DETESTABLE
DEVELOPING
DIGESTIBLE
DILETTANTE
DIRECTIONS
DIRECTNESS
DIRECTOIRE
DIREMPTION
DISEMBOGUE
DISEMBOWEL
DISENCHANT
DISENGAGED
DISENNOBLE
DIVERGENCE
DODECANESE
DOVERCOURT
EFFECTUATE
EFFEMINACY
EFFEMINATE
EFFERVESCE
ELDERBERRY
EMBERGOOSE
EMMENTALER
EMMETROPIA
EMPEDOCLES
ENCEPHALON
ENDEARMENT
ENGENDRURE
ENKEPHALIN
ENTEROCELE
ENTERPRISE
EQUESTRIAN
ESPECIALLY
ETHEOSTOMA
EUHEMERISM
EXCELLENCE
EXCELLENCY
EXPECTANCY
EXPEDIENCE
EXPEDIENCY
EXPEDITION
EXPENDABLE
EXPERIENCE
EXPERIMENT
EXTENDABLE
EXTENSIBLE
EXTERNALLY
FACESAVING
FAREPAYING
FEDERALISM
FEDERALIST
FEDERATION
FENESTELLA
FEVERISHLY
FIBERGLASS
FIREWALKER
FIREWARDEN
FLEETINGLY
FOREBITTER
FOREBODING
FORECASTER
FORECASTLE
FOREDAMNED
FOREFATHER
FOREFINGER
FOREGATHER
FOREGROUND
FOREORDAIN
FORERUNNER
FORESHADOW
FOREWARNED
FREEBOOTER
FREEHANDER
FREEHOLDER
FREELANCER
FREELOADER
FREEMARTIN
FREEMASONS
FRIENDLESS
FRIENDSHIP
GAMEKEEPER
GENERALISE
GENERALITY
GENERALIZE
GENERATION
GENERATRIX
GENEROSITY
GENEROUSLY
GENETHLIAC
GENEVRETTE
GLEEMAIDEN
GOBEMOUCHE
GOVERNANCE
GOVERNESSY
GOVERNMENT
GREEDINESS
GREENCLOTH
GREENFINCH
GREENHEART
GREENHOUSE
GREENSHANK
GREENSTICK
GREENSWARD
GUBERNATOR
GYNECOLOGY
HAKENKREUZ
HAMESUCKEN
HATEENOUGH
HEREABOUTS
HEREDITARY
HERESIARCH
HETERODOXY
HOMECOMING
HOMELINESS
HOMEOPATHY
HOMEOUSIAN
HOMEWORKER
HONEYBUNCH
HOPELESSLY
HOVERCRAFT
HYPERBOLIC
HYPERDULIA
ILLEGALITY
IMBECILITY
IMMEMORIAL
IMPECCABLE
IMPECCABLY
IMPEDIMENT
IMPENITENT
IMPERATIVE
IMPERSONAL
IMPERVIOUS
INCENDIARY
INCESTUOUS
INDECENTLY
INDECISION
INDECISIVE
INDECOROUS
INDEFINITE
INDELICACY
INDELICATE
INDENTURES
INFECTIOUS
INFEFTMENT
INFERNALLY
INGEMINATE
INGENERATE
INHERENTLY
INNERSPACE
INSECURELY
INSECURITY
INSEMINATE
INSENSIBLE
INTEGRATED
INTEGUMENT
INTELIGENT
INTEMERATE
INTENDMENT
INTENERATE
INTENTNESS
INTERBREED
INTERCEDER
INTERCLUDE
INTERESTED
INTERFERER
INTERFERON
INTERLEAVE
INTERLOPER
INTERMARRY
INTERMEZZO
INTERNALLY
INTERNMENT
INTERNODAL
INTERPHONE
INTERSTATE
INTERSTICE
INTERTRIGO
INTERTWINE
INTERWEAVE
INTERWOVEN
INTESTINAL
INTESTINES
INVESTMENT
INVETERATE
IRRELEVANT
IRREMEDIAL
IRRESOLUTE
IRREVERENT
JAMESONITE
JUGENDSTIL
KATERFELTO
KRIEGSPIEL
LACERATION
LAMENTABLE
LAMENTABLY
LEBENSRAUM
LEDERHOSEN
LIBERALISM
LIBERALITY
LIBERALIZE
LIBERATION
LICENTIATE
LICENTIOUS
LIKELIHOOD
LIKEMINDED
LINEAMENTS
LINEOMYCIN
LITERATURE
LIVELIHOOD
LIVELINESS
LIVERWURST
LONELINESS
LOVELINESS
LUPERCALIA
LUTESTRING
LUXEMBOURG
LYSENKOISM
MACEDONIAN
MAKESYSTEM
MAKEWEIGHT
MALEFACTOR
MALEVOLENT
MATELLASSE
MATERIALLY
MATERNALLY
MENECHMIAN
MEPERIDINE
MESENTERON
MILEOMETER
MIMEOGRAPH
MINERALOGY
MINESTRONE
MINEWORKER
MISERICORD
MODERATELY
MODERATION
MOLENDINAR
MONEGASQUE
MONETARISM
MONETARIST
NINETEENTH
NOTEWORTHY
NUMERATION
OBJECTLESS
OBSEQUIOUS
OBSERVABLE
OBSERVANCE
OFTENTIMES
OIREACHTAS
OSMETERIUM
OSTENSIBLE
OSTENSIBLY
OSTEOBLAST
OSTEOCOLLA
OSTEOLEPIS
OSTEOPATHY
OSTEOPHYTE
OTHERGATES
OTHERGUESS
PALESTRINA
PAPERCHASE
PAPERKNIFE
PARENCHYMA
PARENTHOOD
PARENTLESS

PATERNALLY
PEDESTRIAN
PENELOPHON
PENETRABLE
PENETRALIA
PEREMPTORY
PHAELONIAN
PHAENOTYPE
PHLEGETHON
PHLEGMASIA
PHLEGMATIC
PHRENESIAC
PHRENOLOGY
PIGEONHOLE
PILEDRIVER
POKERFACED
POMERANIAN
PONEROLOGY
POTENTIATE
POTENTILLA
POWERHOUSE
PRAEMUNIRE
PRAETORIAN
PRAETORIUM
PREEMINENT
PRIESTHOOD
PRZEWALSKI
PUBERULENT
PUBESCENCE
QUAESTUARY
QUEENSBURY
QUEENSTOWN
QUIESCENCE
RACECOURSE
RAVENOUSLY
RAVENSBILL
RAVENSDUCK
RAVENSTONE
REBELLIOUS
RECEPTACLE
REDECORATE
REDEMPTION
REFERENDUM
REGENERATE
RELEGATION
RELENTLESS
REPEATABLE
REPEATEDLY
REPENTANCE
REPERTOIRE
REPETITEUR
REPETITION
REPETITIVE
REREDORTER
RESEARCHER
RESEMBLING
RESENTMENT
RESERVISTS
REVELATION
REVENGEFUL
REVERENTLY
REVERSIBLE
RHOEADALES
RIGELATION
ROBERDSMAN
ROBERTSMAN
ROSECHAFER
ROSEMALING
RUPESTRIAN
SACERDOTAL
SALESWOMAN
SAUERKRAUT
SCIENTIFIC
SCLERIASIS
SCREECHING
SCREENPLAY
SELEGILINE
SENEGALESE
SENESCENCE
SEVENTIETH
SHEEPISHLY
SHEEPSHANK
SHIELDRAKE
SHOESTRING
SHREWDNESS
SIDEBOARDS
SIDERATION
SIDEROSTAT
SIDESADDLE
SIDEWINDER
SLEEPINESS
SLEEVELESS
SNEEZEWOOD
SOBERSIDES
SOMERSAULT
SOMERVILLE
SPEECHLESS
SPEEDINESS
SPLENDIDLY
SPREAGHERY
SQUEEZEBOX
SQUETEAGUE
STEELINESS
STEELWORKS
STREAMERED
STREAMLINE
STREETLAMP
STREETWISE
STRELITZIA
STRENGTHEN
STREPITANT
STREPITOSO
SUPERADDED
SUPERCARGO
SUPERGIANT
SUPERHUMAN
SUPERMODEL
SUPERPOWER
SUPERSONIC
SUPERSTORE
SUPERTONIC
SUPERVISED
SUPERVISOR
SUPERWOMAN
SUZERAINTY
SWEEPSTAKE
SWEETBREAD
SWEETENING
SWEETHEART
SYNECDOCHE
SYNEIDESIS
TABERNACLE
TALEBEARER
TAPERECORD
TELEGRAPHY
TELEOSTOME
TELEPATHIC
TELEPHONIC
TELESCOPIC
TELEVISION
TENEBRIFIC
THREADBARE
THREADLIKE
THREADWORM
THREATENED
THREEPENCE
THREEPENNY
THREESCORE
THRENODIAL
TIMEKEEPER
TIMELINESS
TIMESAVING
TIMESERVER
TIMESWITCH
TIRELESSLY
TOLERANTLY
TOLERATION
TUBERCULAR
TUMESCENCE
TYPESCRIPT
TYPESETTER
TYPEWRITER
ULCERATION
UMBELLIFER
UNBEARABLE
UNBEARABLY
UNBEATABLE
UNBECOMING
UNBELIEVER
UNDECLARED
UNDEFEATED
UNDEFENDED
UNDENIABLE
UNDERBURNT
UNDERCLASS
UNDERCOVER
UNDERCRAFT
UNDERCROFT
UNDERFLOOR
UNDERLEASE
UNDERLINEN
UNDERLYING
UNDERNEATH
UNDERPANTS
UNDERSCORE
UNDERSHIRT
UNDERSIZED
UNDERSKIRT
UNDERSLUNG
UNDERSTAND
UNDERSTATE
UNDERSTEER
UNDERSTOOD
UNDERSTUDY
UNDERTAKER
UNDERVALUE
UNDERWATER
UNDERWORLD
UNDERWRITE
UNDESCRIED
UNDESERVED
UNDETECTED
UNDETERRED
UNFETTERED
UNHEARABLE
UNHERALDED
UNLEAVENED
UNLETTERED
UNREADABLE
UNREASONED
UNREDEEMED
UNRELIABLE
UNRELIEVED
UNREQUITED
UNRESERVED
UNRESOLVED
UNREVEALED
UNSEASONED
UNSETTLING
UPPERCLASS
VALENTINES
VEGETABLES
VEGETARIAN
VEGETATION
VEHEMENTLY
VENERATION
VENEZUELAN
VETERINARY
VICEGERENT
VICEREGENT
VINEGARISH
VITELLICLE
WAGEEARNER
WAPENSCHAW
WATERBORNE
WATERBRASH
WATERCOLOR
WATERCRESS
WATERFRONT
WATERLEVEL
WATERMELON
WATERPROOF
WATERSKIER
WATERSPOUT
WATERTIGHT
WATERWHEEL
WATERWINGS
WATERWORKS
WAVELENGTH
WHEELCHAIR
WHEELHOUSE
WHEEZINESS
WIDESPREAD
ENLÈVEMENT
AIRFREIGHT
AREFACTION
ASAFOETIDA
BAFFLEMENT
BEEFBURGER
BEEFEATERS
BUFFLEHEAD
BUFFOONERY
BUMFREEZER
CHAFFERING
CHIFFCHAFF
CHIFFONIER
COMFORTING
CONFECTION
CONFEDERAL
CONFERENCE
CONFERVOID
CONFESSION
CONFIDANTE
CONFIDENCE
CONFISCATE
CONFLUENCE
CONFORMIST
CONFORMITY
CONFOUNDED
CONFUSEDLY
CRAFTINESS
DIFFERENCE
DIFFICULTY
DIFFIDENCE
DISFIGURED
EMPFINDUNG
FARFETCHED
FLUFFINESS
FORFAITING
FORFEITURE
FORFEUCHEN
FORFOUGHEN
FULFILMENT
GONFANONER
HALFDOLLAR
HALFHOURLY
HALFSISTER
HALFYEARLY
INEFFICACY
KNIFEBOARD

LEAFHOPPER
MISFORTUNE
NEWFANGLED
NONFICTION
ODDFELLOWS
PALFRENIER
PERFECTION
PERFICIENT
PERFIDIOUS
PERFORATED
PERFORATOR
PERFORMING
PREFERABLE
PREFERABLY
PREFERENCE
PREFERMENT
PROFESSION
PROFICIENT
PROFITABLE
PROFITABLY
PROFITLESS
PROFLIGACY
PROFLIGATE
PROFOUNDLY
PROFUNDITY
SANFORISED
SCOFFINGLY
SELFESTEEM
SELFSTYLED
SHIFTINESS
SINFULNESS
SPIFLICATE
STUFFINESS
SUFFERANCE
SUFFICIENT
SUFFRAGIST
SURFRIDING
TOMFOOLERY
TRAFFICKER
UNAFFECTED
UNIFORMITY
UNOFFICIAL
USEFULNESS
WOFFINGTON
WOLFRAMITE
YAFFINGALE
AMYGDALOID
ARAGONITES
BANGLADESH
BARGAINING
BIOGRAPHER
BRAGADISME
BRIGANDINE
BRIGANTINE
BRIGHTNESS
BUDGERIGAR
BURGEONING
BURGLARIZE
CONGENITAL
CONGESTION
CONGREGATE
DIAGENESIS
DIAGNOSTIC
DIAGONALLY
DIDGERIDOO
DISGRUNTLE
DISGUSTING
DOGGEDNESS
ELEGABALUS
EMIGRATION
EPIGENETIC
EPIGLOTTIS
EXAGGERATE
FINGERLING
FINGERNAIL
FLAGELLATE
FLAGITIOUS
FLAGRANTLY
FLIGHTLESS
FLUGELHORN
FORGIVABLE
FRIGHTENED
FROGHOPPER
FUNGICIDAL
GANGRENOUS
GARGANTUAN
GARGOUILLE
GEOGRAPHER
GEOGRAPHIC
GINGERBEER
GINGERSNAP
GINGIVITIS
GORGEOUSLY
GREGARIOUS
HANGGLIDER
HODGEPODGE
IMAGINABLE
JARGONELLE
JIGGAMAREE
JINGOISTIC
JUGGERNAUT
KINGFISHER
KNIGHTHOOD
LANGERHANS
LANGUOROUS
LARGESCALE
LENGTHWAYS
LENGTHWISE
LINGUISTIC
LINGULELLA
LOGGERHEAD
LONGCHAMPS
LONGFELLOW
MANGABEIRA
MANGOSTEEN
MARGINALIA
MARGINALLY
MARGUERITE
MEAGERNESS
MEAGRENESS
MISGIVINGS
MORGANATIC
MORGANETTA
NEIGHBORLY
NIGGERHEAD
ORIGINALLY
ORIGINATOR
OROGENESIS
OXYGENATOR
PARGETTING
PHAGEDAENA
PILGARLICK
PILGRIMAGE
PLAGIARISE
PLAGIARISM
PLAGIARIST
PLAGIARIZE
POIGNANTLY
PRAGMATISM
PRAGMATIST
PROGENITOR
PROGESSION
PROGRAMMER
RINGELMANN
RINGLEADER
RINGMASTER
ROUGHHOUSE
RUGGEDNESS
SANGUINARY
SHAGHAIRED
SINGHALESE
SINGLENESS
SINGULARLY
SLUGGISHLY
SNIGGERING
SONGSTRESS
SONGWRITER
STAGECOACH
STAGECRAFT
STAGGERING
STAGNATION
STIGMATISE
STIGMATIZE
SUGGESTION
SUGGESTIVE
SUNGLASSES
SURGICALLY
SWAGGERING
TANGANYIKA
TANGENTIAL
TANGLEFOOT
TONGUESTER
TRAGACANTH
TRAGICALLY
TROGLODYTE
UNIGENITUS
WEIGHTLESS
WHIGGAMORE
WITGATBOOM
ZEUGLODONT
ALCHERINGA
ALPHONSINE
ALZHEIMERS
AMPHIBIOUS
AMPHIBRACH
AMPHICTYON
AMPHIGOURI
AMPHIMACER
AMPHIMIXIS
AMPHINEURA
AMPHITRITE
AMPHITRYON
AMPHOTERIC
ANCHORETIC
ANCHYLOSIS
ANTHEOLION
ANTHOCLORE
ANTHRACINE
ANTHRACITE
ANTHROPOID
ARCHBISHOP
ARCHDEACON
ARCHETYPAL
ARCHIMEDES
ARCHITRAVE
ARTHRALGIA
ARTHROMERE
ARTHURIANA
ASPHALTITE
ASPHYXIATE
AUTHORISED
AUTHORSHIP
BATHYSCAPH
BICHROMATE
BOTHERSOME
BUCHMANISM
BUSHRANGER
CACHINNATE
CATHOLICON
CATHOLICOS
CEPHALOPOD
COCHLEARIA
DÉSHABILLÉ
DICHROMISM
DIPHTHERIA
DISHABILLE
DISHARMONY
DISHEARTEN
DISHONESTY
DISHWASHER
DITHIONATE
ECCHYMOSIS
ECTHLIPSIS
EIGHTEENTH
ENCHANTING
ENTHUSIASM
ENTHUSIAST
ESCHAROTIC
EUCHLORINE
EUPHONIOUS
EUPHROSYNE
EUTHANASIA
EUTHYNEURA
FATHERLAND
FATHERLESS
FISHMONGER
FISHSELLER
FOXHUNTING
GETHSEMANE
HIGHBINDER
HIGHFLYING
HIGHHANDED
HIGHLANDER
HIGHWAYMAN
HITHERWARD
LACHRYMOSE
LIGHTERMAN
LIGHTHOUSE
LIGHTINGUP
LITHISTADA
LITHOGRAPH
LITHOMARGE
LITHOPHANE
LITHUANIAN
LYCHNAPSIA
MECHANICAL
MECHANIZED
METHEDRINE
METHODICAL
METHOMANIA
METHUSALEH
METHUSELAH
METHYLATED
MICHAELMAS
MIGHTINESS
MISHGUGGLE
MISHNAYOTH
MITHRIDATE
MOTHERHOOD
MOTHERLAND
MOTHERLESS
MOTHERLIKE
NATHELESSE
NETHERMOST
NIGHTDRESS
NIGHTLIGHT
NIGHTSHADE
NIGHTSHIRT
NIGHTSTICK
ORCHESTRAL
ORCHIDEOUS
ORPHEOREON
ORTHOCAINE
ORTHOCLASE
ORTHOGONAL
ORTHOPNOEA
ORTHOPTICS
OUGHTLINGS
PATHFINDER
PATHOGENIC

PICHICIAGO
PREHENSILE
PREHISTORY
PROHIBITED
PYTHAGORAS
PYTHOGENIC
RICHARDSON
RICHTHOFEN
RIGHTFULLY
ROTHSCHILD
RUTHERFORD
RUTHLESSLY
SILHOUETTE
SOPHOCLEAN
SOPHOMORIC
SUBHEADING
SYPHILITIC
TACHOGRAPH
TACHOMETER
TECHNETIUM
TECHNICIAN
TECHNOCRAT
TECHNOLOGY
UNSHACKLED
UNTHINKING
WASHINGTON
WISHYWASHY
WITHDRAWAL
XIPHOPAGUS
ABDICATION
ABHIDHAMMA
ABRIDGMENT
ACCIDENTAL
ACHITOPHEL
ACTIONABLE
ACTIVITIST
ADDITAMENT
ADDITIONAL
ADHIBITION
ADMINISTER
ADMIRATION
ADMIRINGLY
ADMISSIBLE
ADMITTANCE
ADMITTEDLY
AFFILIATED
AFRICANDER
ALBIGENSES
ALCIBIADES
ALLIGATION
AMBIVALENT
AMRITATTVA
ANCIPITOUS
ANGIOSPERM
ANNIHILATE
ANTIADITIS
ANTIBARBUS
ANTIBIOTIC
ANTICHTHON
ANTICIPATE
ANTICLIMAX
ANTIFREEZE
ANTIMASQUE
ANTIMATTER
ANTIMONIAN
ANTINOMIAN
ANTIOCHENE
ANTIOCHIAN
ANTIPHONAL
ANTIPODEAN
ANTIPROTON
ANTIQUATED
ANTISEPSIS
ANTISEPTIC
ANTISOCIAL
ANTISTATIC
ANTITHESIS
ANTITHETIC
ANTITRAGUS
ANTIVENENE
ARBITRATOR
ARMIPOTENT
ARTICULATA
ARTICULATE
ARTIFICIAL
ASPIDISTRA
ASPIRATION
ASSIGNABLE
ASSIGNMENT
ASSIMILATE
ASSISTANCE
ASTIGMATIC
AUDIBILITY
AUDITORIUM
AURIFEROUS
BABIROUSSA
BACITRACIN
BALIBUNTAL
BANISHMENT
BEHINDHAND
BELIEVABLE
BEWILDERED
BEWITCHING
BILIVERDIN
BIPINNARIA
BOUILLOTTE
BRAINCHILD
BRAININESS
BRAINPOWER
BRAINSTORM
CALIFORNIA
CAPILLAIRE
CAPITALISM
CAPITALIST
CAPITALIZE
CAPITATION
CAPITELLUM
CAPITOLINE
CAPITULARY
CAPITULATE
CARICATURA
CARICATURE
CAVICORNIA
CECIDOMYIA
CHAIRWOMAN
CHEIRONOMY
CHOICELESS
CHRISTIANA
CLAIRCOLLE
CLOISTERED
COGITATION
CONIFEROUS
CORINTHIAN
CRAIGFLUKE
CRUIKSHANK
DEBILITATE
DECIMALIZE
DECIPHERED
DECISIVELY
DEDICATION
DEFICIENCY
DEFILEMENT
DEFINITELY
DEFINITION
DEFINITIVE
DEHISCENCE
DELIBERATE
DELICATELY
DELIGATION
DELIGHTFUL
DELINQUENT
DELIRATION
DEPILATORY
DERIVATION
DERIVATIVE
DESICCATED
DESIDERATA
DIGITORIUM
DILIGENTLY
DIMINISHED
DIMINUENDO
DIMINUTION
DIMINUTIVE
DISINCLINE
DISINHERIT
DIVINATION
DIVISIONAL
DOCIMASTIC
DOLICHOLIS
DOLICHOTUS
DOMICILARY
DOMINATING
DOMINATION
DREIKANTER
DUNIWASSAL
ECHINODERM
ECHINOIDEA
EFFICIENCY
ELLIPTICAL
EMBITTERED
ENLISTMENT
ENRICHMENT
ENTICEMENT
EQUITATION
EQUIVALENT
EQUIVOCATE
ESTIMATION
EUDIOMETER
EXCITEMENT
EXHIBITION
EXHILARATE
EXPIRATION
EXTINCTION
EXTINGUISH
FACILITATE
FACILITIES
FAMILIARLY
FAMISHMENT
FELICITATE
FELICITOUS
FEMININITY
FEUILLETON
FILIBUSTER
FINISTERRE
FORINSECAL
FREIGHTAGE
FRUITFULLY
FULIGINOUS
FUMIGATION
GALIMATIAS
GEMINATION
GENICULATE
GERIATRICS
GOLIATHISE
GONIOMETER
HABILITATE
HABITATION
HABITUALLY
HALIEUTICS
HELICOPTER
HELIOGRAPH
HELIOLATER
HELIOTROPE
HEMICHORDA
HEMIHEDRON
HEMIPLEGIA
HEMISPHERE
HESITANTLY
HESITATION
HORIZONTAL
HUMIDIFIER
IGNIMBRITE
ILLITERACY
ILLITERATE
INCIDENTAL
INCINERATE
INCISIVELY
INCITEMENT
INCIVILITY
INDICATION
INDICATIVE
INDICOLITE
INDICTABLE
INDICTMENT
INDIGENOUS
INDIGOLITE
INDIRECTLY
INDISCREET
INDISPOSED
INDISTINCT
INDITEMENT
INDIVIDUAL
INFIDELITY
INFIGHTING
INFILTRATE
INFINITELY
INFINITIVE
INHIBITING
INHIBITION
INHIBITORY
INSIPIDITY
INSISTENCE
INTIMATELY
INTIMATION
INTIMIDATE
INTINCTION
INVIGILATE
INVIGORATE
INVINCIBLE
INVIOLABLE
INVITATION
IRRIGATION
IRRITATING
IRRITATION
JUBILANTLY
JUBILATION
JUDICATURE
JUDICIALLY
KENILWORTH
LAMINATION
LANIGEROUS
LAVISHNESS
LEGIBILITY
LEGISLATOR
LEGITIMACY
LEGITIMATE
LEGITIMIZE
LEVITATION
LIBIDINOUS
LIMITATION
LIMITROPHE
LIPIZZANER
LITIGATION
LOGISTICAL
LOUISIETTE
LUMINARIST
LUMINOSITY
LUSITANIAN
MABINOGION
MAGISTRACY

MAGISTRAND
MAGISTRATE
MALIGNANCY
MALINGERER
MANICHAEAN
MANICURIST
MANIFESTLY
MANIPULATE
MARIOLATRY
MARIONETTE
MAXIMALIST
MAXIMILIAN
MEDICAMENT
MEDICATION
MEDIOCRITY
MEDITATION
MEDITATIVE
MEDIUMTERM
MENINGITIS
MESITYLENE
METICULOUS
MILITARISM
MILITARIST
MILITIAMAN
MINIMALIST
MINIMARKET
MINISTRATE
MITIGATING
MITIGATION
MODIFIABLE
MONILIASIS
MONILIFORM
MORIGEROUS
MORISONIAN
MOTIONLESS
MOTIVATION
MULIEBRITY
MUNIFICENT
MUSICOLOGY
MUTILATION
MUTINOUSLY
MYRINGITIS
MYRIOSCOPE
NATIONALLY
NATIONWIDE
NAVIGATION
NIHILISTIC
NOMINALIST
NOMINATION
NOMINATIVE
NOTICEABLE
NOTICEABLY
NOTIFIABLE
NOTIONALLY
NUDIBRANCH
NUMISMATIC
OBLIGATION
OBLIGATORY
OBLIGINGLY
OBLITERATE
OBSIDIONAL
OCCIDENTAL
OFFICIALLY
OMNIPOTENT
OMNISCIENT
OMNIVOROUS
OPHICLEIDE
OPTIMISTIC
ORDINARILY
ORDINATION
OSCILLATOR
OSCITATION
OSMIDROSIS
OUVIRANDRA
PACIFICISM
PAGINATION
PALIMPSEST
PALINDROME
PALISANDER
PAPIAMENTO
PARISCHANE
PARISIENNE
PASIGRAPHY
PATIBULARY
PATISSERIE
PEDIATRICS
PEDICULATE
PEDIMENTAL
PEDIPALPUS
PENICILLIN
PENINSULAR
PERIDOTITE
PERIEGESIS
PERIHELION
PERILOUSLY
PERIODICAL
PERIPHERAL
PERISHABLE
PERIWINKLE
PETITIONER
POLIANTHES
POLITENESS
POLITICIAN
POLITICIZE
POSITIVELY
POSITIVIST
PUNICACEAE
PUNISHABLE
PUNISHMENT
PURITANISM
QUAINTNESS
RADICALISM
RADIOGRAPH
RADIOLARIA
RATIONALLY
RAWINSONDE
RECIDIVISM
RECIDIVIST
RECIPROCAL
RECITATION
RECITATIVE
RECITATIVO
REDISCOVER
REFINEMENT
REGIMENTAL
REGIMENTED
REGISTERED
RELINQUISH
REMITTANCE
RESIGNEDLY
RESILIENCE
RESISTANCE
RETINALITE
RETIREMENT
REVITALIZE
REVIVALIST
RIDICULOUS
RIDINGHOOD
ROTISSERIE
RUBIGINOUS
RUBINSTEIN
RUDIMENTAL
RUMINANTIA
RUMINATION
RUMINATIVE
RUPICOLINE
SAGITTARIA
SALICORNIA
SALIVATION
SANITARIUM
SANITATION
SATISFYING
SAXICOLINE
SAXICOLOUS
SCHIPPERKE
SCHISMATIC
SCRIBBLING
SCRIMSHANK
SCRIPTURAL
SCRIPTURES
SEMICIRCLE
SEMIQUAVER
SHRIEVALTY
SHRILLNESS
SHRIVELLED
SICILIENNE
SIGILLARIA
SIMILARITY
SIMILITUDE
SIMILLIMUM
SKRIMSHANK
SOLICITOUS
SOLICITUDE
SOLIDARITY
SOLIFIDIAN
SOLIVAGANT
SPLITLEVEL
SPOILSPORT
SPRINGBOKS
SPRINGHAAS
SPRINGLESS
SPRINGLIKE
SPRINGTAIL
SPRINGTIME
SPRINKLING
SQUIREARCH
STRICTNESS
STRIDENTLY
STRIDEWAYS
STRIDULATE
STRIKINGLY
STRINDBERG
STRINGENCY
STRINGENDO
STRINGHALT
STRIPTEASE
SURINAMESE
TEPIDARIUM
TOPICALITY
TOXICOLOGY
TRAITOROUS
TUTIVILLUS
ULTIMATELY
UNDIGESTED
UNDISPUTED
UNFINISHED
UNLICENSED
UNRIVALLED
UNTIDINESS
UNYIELDING
URTICACEAE
VALIDATION
VARICOSITY
VARIEGATED
VELITATION
VERIFIABLE
VESICULATE
VIGILANTES
VISIBILITY
VISITATION
VIVIPAROUS
VOCIFERATE
VOCIFEROUS
WAPINSCHAW
CONJECTURE
DARJEELING
DISJOINTED
PANJANDRUM
PREJUDICED
PROJECTILE
PROJECTING
PROJECTION
SUBJECTION
SUBJECTIVE
TRAJECTORY
BACKBITING
BACKBLOCKS
BACKGAMMON
BACKGROUND
BACKHANDED
BACKHANDER
BACKPACKER
BACKSLIDER
BACKSTAIRS
BACKSTROKE
BANKRUPTCY
BASKETBALL
BASKETWORK
BEEKEEPING
BIRKENHEAD
BOOKBINDER
BOOKKEEPER
BOOKMARKER
BOOKMOBILE
BOOKSELLER
BROKENDOWN
BUCKINGHAM
BUCKJUMPER
COCKABULLY
COCKALORUM
COCKATRICE
COCKCHAFER
COCKERNONY
CUCKOOPINT
DARKHAIRED
DICKCISSEL
DRAKESTONE
DUCKBOARDS
DUKKERIPEN
FALKLANDER
FICKLENESS
HACKBUTEER
HACKMATACK
HANKYPANKY
JACKANAPES
JACKBOOTED
JACKHAMMER
JACKSTONES
JACKSTRAWS
KOEKSISTER
KOOKABURRA
LACKADAISY
LACKLUSTER
LACKLUSTRE
LOCKERROOM
LOCKKEEPER
MACKINTOSH
MARKETABLE
MASKANONGE
MASKINONGE
MASKIROVKA
MUCKRAKING
MUSKETEERS
PARKLEAVES
PICKPOCKET
POCKETBOOK
POCKMANTIE
POCKMARKED
POIKILITIC
PUCKERWOOD

RECKLESSLY
ROCKABILLY
ROCKINGHAM
ROCKSTEADY
SHAKUHACHI
SMOKESTACK
SNAKEMOUTH
SNAKESTONE
SPOKESHAVE
TASKMASTER
TICKERTAPE
TINKERBELL
TREKSCHUIT
WICKEDNESS
WICKERWORK
WORKAHOLIC
ACCLIVIOUS
ACOLOUTHOS
ADELANTADO
ADOLESCENT
ADULLAMITE
ADULTERANT
ADULTERATE
ADULTERESS
ADULTERINE
ADULTEROUS
AFFLICTION
AMALGAMATE
AMBLYOPSIS
AMBLYSTOMA
AMELIORATE
AMPLEFORTH
ANALOGICAL
ANALPHABET
ANALYTICAL
ANGLOPHILE
ANGLOPHOBE
APOLAUSTIC
APOLLONIAN
APOLLONIUS
APOLOGETIC
APPLICABLE
APPLICATOR
ATELEIOSIS
BAILIEWICK
BAILLIWICK
BALLISTICS
BALLISTITE
BALLOONING
BALLOONIST
BARLEYBREE
BARLEYCORN
BELLADONNA
BELLAMOURE
BELLARMINE
BELLWETHER
BIOLOGICAL
BOLLANDIST
BRILLIANCE
BULLHEADED
BURLINGTON
BYELECTION
CALLIATURE
CELLOPHANE
CELLULITIS
CHALCEDONY
CHALLENGER
CHALYBEATE
CHELTENHAM
CHILDBIRTH
CHILDERMAS
CHILDISHLY
CHILLINESS
CHOLALOGUE
CISLEITHAN
COELACANTH
COLLAPSING
COLLARBONE
COLLATERAL
COLLECTING
COLLECTION
COLLECTIVE
COLLEGIATE
COLLEMBOLA
COLLIMATOR
COLLIQUATE
COLLOCUTER
COLLOQUIAL
CYCLOPEDIA
CYCLOSTYLE
DEALERSHIP
DECLENSION
DEFLAGRATE
DEFLECTION
DEPLORABLE
DEPLORABLY
DEPLOYMENT
DIALECTICS
DIELECTRIC
DIPLODOCUS
DIPLOMATIC
DISLOYALTY
DUPLICATOR
EBULLIENCE
ECOLOGICAL
EDULCORATE
EFFLEURAGE
EMALANGENI
EMBLEMATIC
EMBLEMENTS
EMOLUMENTS
EMPLASTRUM
EMPLOYMENT
EMULSIFIER
ENCLOISTER
ENGLISHMAN
ENGLISHMEN
EPILIMNION
EVALUATION
EXALTATION
EXPLICABLE
EXPLICITLY
EXULTATION
FALLACIOUS
FALLINGOFF
FAULTINESS
FELLOWSHIP
FIELDMOUSE
FILLIBRUSH
FROLICSOME
FULLLENGTH
FULLYGROWN
GALLABIYAH
GALLABIYEH
GALLIAMBIC
GARLANDAGE
GAULTHERIA
GEOLOGICAL
GILLRAVAGE
GIRLFRIEND
GOALKEEPER
GUILLOTINE
HALLELUJAH
HALLMARKED
HALLOYSITE
HALLUBALOO
HELLBENDER
HELLESPONT
HOWLEGLASS
HULLABALOO
HYALOPHANE
IMPLACABLE
IMPLACABLY
IMPLICITLY
INELIGIBLE
INFLATABLE
INFLECTION
INFLEXIBLE
INFLEXIBLY
INFLICTION
INGLORIOUS
MALLOPHAGA
MELLOWNESS
MIDLOTHIAN
MILLEFIORI
MILLIMETER
MILLIMETRE
MISLEADING
MOULDINESS
MOULDIWARP
MULLIGRUBS
NEGLECTFUL
NEGLIGENCE
NEGLIGIBLE
NOBLEWOMAN
NUCLEONICS
OCHLOCRACY
ODELSTHING
OFFLICENCE
OPALESCENT
OUTLANDISH
PALLBEARER
PALLIATIVE
PARLIAMENT
PEELGARLIC
PHILATELIC
PHILIPPINA
PHILIPPINE
PHILISTINE
PHILLIPINA
PHILLIPINE
PHILLUMENY
PHILOPOENA
PHILOSOPHY
PHILOXENIA
PHOLIDOSIS
PHYLACTERY
PHYLLIOPOD
PILLIWINKS
PILLOWCASE
PILLOWSLIP
POLLINATED
PORLOCKING
PRELECTION
PSALTERIUM
PSILOCYBIN
PUBLISHING
RAILWAYMAN
REELECTION
REFLECTING
REFLECTION
REFLECTIVE
ROLLICKING
ROWLANDSON
SALLENDERS
SCHLIMAZEL
SCULPTRESS
SELLINGERS
SHELDONIAN
SHELLSHOCK
SHELLYCOAT
SHILLELAGH
SKILLFULLY
SMALLSCALE
SPALLATION
SPELEOLOGY
SPELLBOUND
SPILLIKINS
SPOLIATION
SPOLIATIVE
STALACTITE
STALAGMITE
STALHELMER
STALLENGER
STALLINGER
STILLBIRTH
STILLICIDE
STILLIFORM
STILLSTAND
STULTIFIED
STYLISTICS
STYLOPISED
SUBLIMATER
SUBLIMINAL
SWALLOWING
SWELTERING
TABLANETTE
TABLECLOTH
TABLESPOON
TAGLIARINI
TAILGATING
TAILORMADE
TALLEYRAND
THALASSIAN
THALESTRIS
THALICTRUM
THALLIFORM
THELLUSSON
TILLANDSIA
TOILETRIES
TOILINETTE
TOLLKEEPER
TRILATERAL
TRILINGUAL
UNBLEACHED
UNBLINKING
UNBLUSHING
UNFLAGGING
UNFLAVORED
UNILATERAL
UNPLEASANT
UNSLEEPING
UTILIZABLE
VALLADOLID
VILLAINOUS
VILLANELLE
VILLANOVAN
VOLLEYBALL
WALLACHIAN
WALLFLOWER
WELLEARNED
WELLINGTON
WELLSPRING
WHILLYWHAW
WHOLESALER
WHOLEWHEAT
WILLIAMSON
WILLINGDON
WILLOWHERB
WILLYWILLY
WOOLLYBACK
WOOLLYBUTT
WORLDCLASS
WYCLIFFIAN
YELLOWBACK
YELLOWGIRL
YELLOWJACK
YELLOWROOT
YELLOWWOOD
ZOLLVEREIN

ZOOLOGICAL
ABOMINABLE
ABOMINABLY
ADAMANTINE
ALEMBICATE
ALIMENTARY
ANEMOGRAPH
ANEMOMETER
ANIMADVERT
APEMANTHUS
ARIMASPIAN
ARSMETRICK
ASYMMETRIC
BARMECIDAL
BARMITZVAH
BERMOOTHES
BIRMINGHAM
CARMAGNOLE
CHAMAEROPS
CHAMBERPOT
CHAMBERTIN
CHAMBRANLE
CHAMPIGNON
CHEMICALLY
CHEMONASTY
CHIMBORAZO
CHIMNEYPOT
CHIMPANZEE
CLAMMINESS
CLAMOURING
CLEMENCEAU
CLEMENTINE
CLOMIPHENE
CLUMPERTON
CLUMSINESS
COMMANDANT
COMMANDEER
COMMANDING
COMMENTARY
COMMENTATE
COMMERCIAL
COMMISSARY
COMMISSION
COMMISSURE
COMMITMENT
COMMIXTURE
COMMODIOUS
COMMONWEAL
COMMUNALLY
COMMUNIQUÉ
COMMUTABLE
CRIMINALLY
CUMMERBUND
CURMUDGEON
CURMURRING
DERMATITIS
DISMANTLED
DISMISSIVE
DRUMBLEDOR
DUUMVIRATE
ECUMENICAL
ELEMENTARY
ELIMINATOR
EPIMENIDES
EPIMETHEUS
ERYMANTHUS
EXEMPTNESS
FLAMBOYANT
FLAMEPROOF
FLAMINGANT
FLIMSINESS
FORMIDABLE
FRAMBOESIA
FREMESCENT
FROMANTEEL
GERMICIDAL
GLAMOURISE
GORMANDIZE
GRAMICIDIN
GRAMMARIAN
GRAMOPHONE
GRUMPINESS
HAEMANTHUS
HAMMERHEAD
HAMMERLOCK
HARMANBECK
HARMONIOUS
INIMITABLE
ISOMETRICS
KARMATHIAN
KILMARNOCK
KUOMINTANG
LEAMINGTON
MALMESBURY
MISMATCHED
NORMOBLAST
ONOMASTICS
OXYMORONIC
OZYMANDIAS
PALMATIFID
PALMATOZOA
PALMERSTON
PALMERWORM
PARMACITIE
PERMAFROST
PERMANENCE
PERMANENCY
PERMEATION
PERMISSION
PERMISSIVE
PLUMASSIER
PREMARITAL
PRIMORDIAL
PROMENADER
PROMETHEAN
PROMETHEUS
PROMETHIUM
PROMINENCE
PROMISSORY
PROMONTORY
PROMPTNESS
PROMULGATE
PSAMMOPHIL
PUMMELLING
REAMINGBIT
RHAMPASTOS
SALMAGUNDI
SALMANAZAR
SALMONELLA
SARMENTOUS
SCAMMOZZIS
SCOMBRESOX
SEAMANSHIP
SEAMSTRESS
SEEMLIHEAD
SERMONICAL
SHAMEFACED
SHAMEFULLY
SHAMPOOING
SHIMMERING
SIMMENTHAL
SLAMMERKIN
SLUMBERING
STAMMERING
STEMWINDER
STOMATOPOD
STUMBLEDOM
SUBMARINER
SUBMEDIANT
SUBMERSION
SUBMISSION
SUBMISSIVE
SUMMERTIME
SWIMMINGLY
TERMINABLE
TERMINALIA
TERMINALLY
THEMSELVES
THIMBLEFUL
THIMBLEWIT
THUMBIKINS
THUMBSCREW
TRAMONTANA
TRAMONTANE
TRAMPOLINE
TREMENDOUS
TRIMALCHIO
TRIMSNITCH
TROMBONIST
TROMOMETER
UNEMPLOYED
UNIMPAIRED
VERMICELLI
VERMILLION
WEIMARANER
ABONNEMENT
ABUNDANTLY
ACANACEOUS
AGONISTICS
AMANUENSIS
ARENACEOUS
ARUNDELIAN
ASYNARTETE
AVANTGARDE
AVANTURINE
AVENTURINE
AXINOMANCY
BALNEATION
BALNEOLOGY
BERNARDINE
BIANNUALLY
BIENNIALLY
BLANCMANGE
BLANQUETTE
BLUNDERING
BOONDOGGLE
BRONCHITIC
BRONCHITIS
CANNELLONI
CANNONBALL
CAPNOMANCY
CARNASSIAL
CHANCELLOR
CHANDELIER
CHANGEABLE
CHANGELESS
CHANGELING
CHINAGRAPH
CHINASTONE
CHINCHILLA
CHINQUAPIN
CLANSWOMAN
CLINGSTONE
CLINICALLY
COGNISANCE
COGNIZANCE
COINCIDENT
CONNECTING
CONNECTION
CONNECTIVE
CONNIPTION
CONNIVANCE
CORNCOCKLE
CORNFLAKES
CORNFLOWER
CORNSTALKS
CORNSTARCH
CORNUCOPIA
COUNCILLOR
COUNSELING
COUNSELLOR
COUNTERACT
COUNTRYMAN
CRANKSHAFT
CRENELLATE
CTENOPHORA
DINNERTIME
DONNYBROOK
DOWNMARKET
DOWNSIZING
DOWNSTAIRS
DOWNSTREAM
DRINKWATER
ECONOMICAL
ELONGATION
EMANCIPATE
EMENDATION
ENANTIOSIS
EPANOPHORA
EPENTHETIC
EPONYCHIUM
EVANESCENT
EVANGELIST
EVANGELIZE
EVENHANDED
EVENTUALLY
EXENTERATE
EXONERATED
FERNITICLE
FIANCHETTO
FIENDISHLY
FLANCONADE
FLINDERSIA
FLUNKEYDOM
FOUNDATION
FRANCHISEE
FRANCHISOR
FRANCISCAN
FRANGIPANE
FRANGIPANI
FRENETICAL
FRENZIEDLY
FRINGILLID
FRONTWARDS
FURNISHING
GAINGIVING
GAINSTRIVE
GARNIERITE
GLENDOVEER
GRANADILLA
GRANDCHILD
GRANDSTAND
GRANGERISM
GRANGERIZE
GRANULATED
GRENADIERS
GRENADILLA
GRINDSTONE
GYMNASTICS
GYMNOSOPHY
HORNBLENDE
HORNBLOWER
HORNRIMMED
HYPNOTIZED
ICONOCLAST
ICONOSCOPE
INUNDATION
IRONICALLY
IRONMONGER
ISONIAZIDE

JAUNTINESS
JOHNSONIAN
KIDNAPPING
KLANGFARBE
LAUNCEGAYE
LAUNCESTON
LAUNDROMAT
LEMNISCATE
LEONTIASIS
LIGNOCAINE
MAGNIFICAT
MAGNIFYING
MAINPERNOR
MAINSPRING
MAINSTREAM
MEANDERING
MEANINGFUL
MIGNONETTE
MOUNTEBANK
ODONTALGIA
ODONTOLITE
ODONTOLOGY
OPENHANDED
OPENMINDED
OUANANICHE
PAINKILLER
PAINLESSLY
PAINTBRUSH
PANNICULUS
PARNASSIAN
PARNELLISM
PAWNBROKER
PENNILLION
PENNISETUM
PERNICIOUS
PERNICKETY
PHANTASIME
PHANTASIST
PHENOMENAL
PHENOMENON
PHONOGRAPH
PIANOFORTE
PINNIPEDIA
PIONEERING
PLANCHETTE
PLANOBLAST
PLANTATION
PLUNDERING
POINSETTIA
POINTBLANK
PORNOCRACY
PRINCIPIUM
PRINCIPLED
PRINCIPLES
PRONOUNCED
PUGNACIOUS
PYCNOGONID
QUENCHLESS
RANNELTREE
RANNLETREE
RHINEGRAVE
RHINESTONE
RHINOCEROS
RHINOLALIA
RHINOPHYMA
ROUNDABOUT
ROUNDHOUSE
SANNAYASIN
SCANDALISE
SCANDALIZE
SCANDALOUS
SCANDAROON
SCANDERBEG
SCANTINESS
SEANNACHIE
SGANARELLE
SHANDRYDAN
SHANDYGAFF
SHENANIGAN
SIGNIFICAT
SIGNORELLI
SKINDIVING
SLANDEROUS
SOMNOLENCE
SOUNDPROOF
SOUNDTRACK
SPENCERIAN
SPENSERIAN
SPINESCENT
SPONGEWARE
SPONGIFORM
SPONSIONAL
STANDPOINT
STANDSTILL
STANISLAUS
STENOTYPER
STENTORIAN
STINGINESS
STINGYBARK
STONEBRASH
STONEHENGE
STONEMASON
STONYHURST
TANNHAUSER
TEENYWEENY
TEINOSCOPE
TENNANTITE
TERNEPLATE
THANKFULLY
THINGUMBOB
THUNDERBOX
THUNDERING
THUNDEROUS
TOWNSWOMAN
TRANQUILLY
TRANSCRIBE
TRANSCRIPT
TRANSGRESS
TRANSIENCE
TRANSISTOR
TRANSITION
TRANSITIVE
TRANSITORY
TRANSLATED
TRANSLATOR
TRANSPLANT
TRANSPOSED
TRANSVERSE
TRENCHMORE
TRENDINESS
TRINACRIAN
TURNAROUND
UNANSWERED
UNENVIABLE
UNINFORMED
UNINSPIRED
UNINVITING
VARNISHING
VERNACULAR
VERNISSAGE
VULNERABLE
WAINSCOTED
WRONGDOING
WRONGFULLY
YOUNGBERRY
ZOANTHARIA
ABHORRENCE
ABNORMALLY
ABROGATION
ABSOLUTELY
ABSOLUTION
ABSOLUTISM
ABSORPTION
ACCOMPLICE
ACCOMPLISH
ACCORDANCE
ACCOUNTANT
ACCOUNTING
ACROAMATIC
ACROBATICS
ACROGENOUS
ACROMEGALY
ACRONYCHAL
ACROTERION
ADMONITION
AEROBATICS
AEROPHAGIA
AFFORDABLE
AFRORMOSIA
AGRONOMIST
ALCOHOLISM
ALGOLAGNIA
ALGONQUIAN
ALLOCATION
ALLOCUTION
ALLOSAURUS
ALLOSTERIC
ALLOTROPIC
ALTOGETHER
AMBOCEPTOR
ANNOTATION
APPOSITION
AREOGRAPHY
AREOPAGITE
ARGOLEMONO
ARROGANTLY
ARTOCARPUS
ASSOCIATED
ASSORTMENT
ASTOMATOUS
ASTONISHED
ASTOUNDING
ATMOSPHERE
AUTOCHTHON
AUTOCRATIC
AUTODIDACT
AUTOGENOUS
AUTOMATION
AUTOMOBILE
AUTOMOTIVE
AUTONOMOUS
AUTOPLASTY
AUTOSTRADA
AVVOGADORE
BAROMETRIC
BEFOREHAND
BELONGINGS
BIJOUTERIE
BINOCULARS
BLOODHOUND
BLOODSTAIN
BLOODSTOCK
BLOODSTONE
BLOOMSBURY
BROOMSTICK
CACODAEMON
CACOGRAPHY
CACOMISTLE
CALORIFIER
CAMOUFLAGE
CAPODASTRO
CHLORINATE
CHLOROFORM
CHROMOSOME
CHRONICLER
CHRONICLES
CHRONOLOGY
COLONNADED
COLORATION
COLORATURA
COLOSSALLY
COLOURLESS
COROMANDEL
CORONATION
CREOPHAGUS
CRYOGENICS
CRYOPHORUS
CYNOMOLGUS
DEBOUCHURE
DECOLLATOR
DECOLORATE
DECOMPOSED
DECORATION
DECORATIVE
DEMOBILISE
DEMOBILIZE
DEMOCRATIC
DEMOCRITUS
DEMOGORGON
DEMOGRAPHY
DEMOISELLE
DEMOLITION
DEMONIACAL
DEMORALISE
DEMORALIZE
DENOUEMENT
DEPOPULATE
DEPORTMENT
DEPOSITARY
DEPOSITION
DEPOSITORY
DEROGATORY
DESOLATION
DETONATION
DEVOLUTION
DEVOTEMENT
DEVOTIONAL
DISORDERED
DISORDERLY
ECCOPROTIC
ECHOPRAXIA
EFFORTLESS
EMBODIMENT
EMBONPOINT
EMBOUCHURE
ENCOIGNURE
ENDOGAMOUS
ENDOSMOSIS
ENGOUEMENT
ENROLLMENT
ENTOMBMENT
ENTOMOLOGY
EPROUVETTE
ERGONOMICS
ERIOCAULON
ETEOCRETAN
EULOGISTIC
EUROCHEQUE
EUROCLYDON
EXPOSITION
EXPOSITORY
EXPOUNDERS
FAVORITISM
FAVOURABLE
FAVOURABLY
FLOODLIGHT
FLOORBOARD
FLOORCLOTH
GADOLINIUM
GONORRHOEA

GYROSCOPIC
HANOVERIAN
HEDONISTIC
HEMOGLOBIN
HEMOPHILIA
HEMORRHAGE
HEROICALLY
HITOPADESA
HITOPODESA
HOLOFERNES
HOLOGRAPHY
HOLOPHOTAL
HOLOSTERIC
HOMOEOPATH
HOMOGENIZE
HOMOPHOBIA
HOMOPHOBIC
HOMORELAPS
HOMOSEXUAL
HONORARIUM
HONOURABLE
HONOURABLY
HONOURLESS
HUMORESQUE
HUMOROUSLY
HUMOURLESS
HYPOCORISM
HYPODERMIC
HYPOGAEOUS
HYPOTENUSE
HYPOTHESIS
IGNORANTLY
IMMOBILITY
IMMOBILIZE
IMMODERATE
IMMOLATION
IMMORALITY
IMMORTELLE
IMPOLITELY
IMPORTANCE
IMPOSITION
IMPOSSIBLE
IMPOSSIBLY
IMPOSTHUME
IMPOTENTLY
IMPOVERISH
INCOHERENT
INCOMPLETE
INCONSTANT
INDONESIAN
INFORMALLY
INNOCENTLY
INNOVATION
INNOVATIVE
INSOLENTLY
INSOLVENCY
INSOUCIANT
INTOLERANT
INTONATION
INTOXICANT
INTOXICATE
INVOCATION
IONOSPHERE
KILOMETRES
KLOOTCHMAN
LABORATORY
LAEOTROPIC
LENOCINIUM
LOCOMOTION
LOCOMOTIVE
LOGORRHOEA
LOTOPHAGUS
MACONOCHIE
MAHOMMEDAN
MALODOROUS
MAVOURNEEN
MAYONNAISE
MELOCOTOON
MEMORANDUM
MENORRHOEA
MESOLITHIC
MISOCAPNIC
MISOGYNIST
MONOCHROME
MONOECIOUS
MONOGAMOUS
MONOLITHIC
MONOPHONIC
MONOPLEGIA
MONOPOLISE
MONOPOLIZE
MONOPTERON
MONOPTEROS
MONOTHEISM
MONOTONOUS
MOROSENESS
MOTORCYCLE
MYCORRHIZA
NEGOTIABLE
NEGOTIATOR
NONONSENSE
NOSOCOMIAL
NOSOPHOBIA
NOTORYCTES
OBLOMOVISM
OCTODECIMO
ODIOUSNESS
OESOPHAGUS
OPPOSITION
ORDONNANCE
PANOPTICON
PARONYCHIA
PEJORATIVE
PERORATION
PEROVSKITE
PHLOGISTIC
PHLOGISTON
PHLOGOPITE
PLEONASTIC
PLIOHIPPUS
POGONOTOMY
PYROGRAPHY
PYROMANIAC
PYROPHORUS
RECOGNISED
RECOGNIZED
RECOMMENCE
RECOMPENSE
RECONCILED
RECONSIDER
REJONEADOR
RELOCATION
REMONETISE
REMORSEFUL
REMOTENESS
RENOVATION
REPORTEDLY
REPOSITORY
RESOLUTELY
RESOLUTION
RESORCINOL
RESOUNDING
REVOCATION
REVOLUTION
RHEOTROPIC
RIBOFLAVIN
RIGOROUSLY
RITORNELLE
RITORNELLO
RUDOLPHINE
SALOPETTES
SAMOTHRACE
SAVONAROLA
SCHOLAEMIA
SCHOLASTIC
SCHOOLBOOK
SCHOOLGIRL
SCHOOLMAAM
SCOOTERIST
SCROUNGING
SECONDBEST
SECONDHAND
SECONDMENT
SECONDRATE
SEXOLOGIST
SHROVETIDE
SMOOTHNESS
SNOOTINESS
SPOONERISM
STROGANOFF
STRONGHOLD
STRONGROOM
STROPHIOLE
SYNONYMOUS
SYNOSTOSIS
TAPOTEMENT
TAXONOMIST
TCHOUKBALL
THEOCRITUS
THEODOLITE
THEOLOGATE
THEOLOGIAN
THEOLOGISE
THEOLOGIST
THROMBOSIS
THROUGHOUT
THROUGHPUT
THROUGHWAY
TIROCINIUM
TOCOPHEROL
TOPOGRAPHY
TOPOLOGIST
TYPOGRAPHY
UNCOMMONLY
UNCONFINED
UNDOCTORED
UNFORESEEN
UNROMANTIC
UNSOCIABLE
UNWORKABLE
UPHOLSTERY
UPROARIOUS
VELOCIPEDE
VIGOROUSLY
VIROLOGIST
XENOPHOBIA
XENOPHOBIC
XEROPHYTIC
XEROSTOMIA
ZAPOROGIAN
ACEPHALOUS
ADAPTATION
AGAPANTHUS
ALLPURPOSE
APOPEMPTIC
APOPHTHEGM
APOPLECTIC
AUSPICIOUS
BIOPHYSICS
BLEPHARISM
CAMPAIGNER
CAMPANELLA
CAMPARADOR
CAMPERDOWN
CAMPESTRAL
CAPPUCCINO
CARPATHIAN
CARPENTIER
CARPHOLOGY
CHAPARAJOS
CHAPAREJOS
CHAPFALLEN
CHAPLAINCY
CHAPTALISE
CHOPSTICKS
CISPONTINE
COLPORTAGE
COLPORTEUR
COLPOSCOPE
COMPARABLE
COMPARATOR
COMPARISON
COMPASSION
COMPATIBLE
COMPATRIOT
COMPELLING
COMPENDIUM
COMPENSATE
COMPETENCE
COMPETITOR
COMPLACENT
COMPLANATE
COMPLEMENT
COMPLETELY
COMPLETION
COMPLEXION
COMPLEXITY
COMPLIANCE
COMPLICATE
COMPLICITY
COMPLIMENT
COMPLUVIUM
COMPOSITOR
COMPOUNDED
COMPRADORE
COMPREHEND
COMPRESSED
COMPRESSOR
COMPROMISE
COMPULSION
COMPULSIVE
COMPULSORY
COPPERHEAD
COPPERNOSE
COPPERSKIN
CORPULENCE
CRAPULENCE
CRYPTOGRAM
DEEPFREEZE
DEEPSEATED
DELPHINIUM
DESPAIRING
DESPICABLE
DESPITEOUS
DESPONDENT
DIAPEDESIS
DIAPHANOUS
DIOPHANTOS
DISPENSARY
DISPENSING
DISPERSION
DISPIRITED
DISPOSABLE
DISPOSSESS
DISPUTABLE
DOPPLERITE
DYSPROSIUM
EPIPHONEMA
EPIPLASTRA
EVAPORATED

FLAPDOODLE
FLIPPANTLY
GEOPHYSICS
GODPARENTS
GRAPEFRUIT
GRAPHOLOGY
GRAPTOLITE
HELPLESSLY
HESPERIDES
HIPPARCHUS
HIPPOCRENE
HIPPODROME
HIPPOGRIFF
HIPPOGRYPH
HIPPOMANES
HOSPITABLE
HOSPITABLY
HUMPBACKED
INAPTITUDE
INEPTITUDE
INOPERABLE
INSPECTION
INSPISSATE
JEOPARDISE
JEOPARDIZE
KEMPERYMAN
LEOPARDESS
LUMPSUCKER
MAUPASSANT
MISPRISION
MORPHOLOGY
NEAPOLITAN
NONPAYMENT
NONPLUSSED
NYMPHOLEPT
OFFPUTTING
OMOPHORION
OUTPATIENT
OUTPERFORM
OUTPOURING
OVIPOSITOR
PEPPERCORN
PEPPERMILL
PEPPERMINT
PEPPERWORT
PERPETRATE
PERPETUATE
PERPETUITY
PERPLEXING
PERPLEXITY
PLUPERFECT
PREPARATOR
PREPAYMENT
PREPENSELY
PREPOSITOR
PREPOSSESS
PREPOTENCE
PROPAGANDA
PROPAGATOR
PROPELLANT
PROPENSITY
PROPERTIUS
PROPHETESS
PROPIONATE
PROPITIATE
PROPITIOUS
PROPLITEAL
PROPORTION
PROPOSITUS
PROPRAETOR
PROPRIETOR
PROPULSION
PROPYLAEUM
PSEPHOLOGY
PUMPHANDLE
PURPOSEFUL
RAJPRAMUKH
RAMPALLIAN
RAPPORTEUR
REAPPRAISE
RESPECTFUL
RESPECTING
RESPECTIVE
RESPIRATOR
RESPONDENT
RESPONSIVE
RHAPSODISE
RHAPSODIZE
RHIPIPTERA
SALPINGIAN
SAPPERMENT
SCAPEGRACE
SCAPHOPODA
SCEPTICISM
SCOPELIDAE
SERPENTINE
SHOPKEEPER
SHOPLIFTER
SHOPSOILED
SHOPWALKER
SIMPLICITY
SIMPLISTIC
SKEPTICISM
SKUPSHTINA
SLIPSTREAM
SLOPPINESS
SNAPDRAGON
SNAPHAUNCE
SNAPHAUNCH
STAPHYLINE
STEPFATHER
STEPHANITE
STEPHENSON
STEPLADDER
STEPMOTHER
STEPSISTER
STUPEFYING
STUPENDOUS
SULPHUROUS
SUPPLEJACK
SUPPLEMENT
SUPPLENESS
SUPPLICANT
SUPPLICATE
SUPPORTING
SUPPORTIVE
SUPPOSEDLY
SUPPRESSED
SUPPRESSOR
SURPASSING
SURPRISING
SUSPENDERS
SUSPENSION
SUSPICIOUS
SYMPATHISE
SYMPATHIZE
SYMPHONIUM
TAMPERFOOT
TARPAULING
TATPURUSHA
TELPHERAGE
TEMPERANCE
TEMPTATION
TORPESCENT
TRIPARTITE
TRIPEHOUND
TRIPLICATE
TRIPUDIARY
TROPAEOLUM
TROPHONIUS
TROPOPAUSE
TROPOPHYTE
TRYPTOPHAN
TURPENTINE
UNSPECIFIC
UROPOIESIS
WAMPUMPEAG
WAPPENSHAW
WEAPONLESS
WRAPAROUND
ADEQUATELY
CHEQUEBOOK
CINQUEFOIL
CONQUERING
CRAQUETURE
DESQUAMATE
DISQUALIFY
DISQUIETED
ELOQUENTLY
FREQUENTED
FREQUENTER
FREQUENTLY
INEQUALITY
INIQUITOUS
MARQUETRIE
MASQUERADE
PASQUINADE
PERQUISITE
TORQUEMADA
UBIQUITOUS
UNEQUALLED
UNIQUENESS
ABBREVIATE
ABERDEVINE
ABERGLAUBE
ABERRATION
ABORIGINAL
ACCREDITED
ACHROMATIC
AGGRANDISE
AGGRESSION
AGGRESSIVE
ALTRUISTIC
AMARYLLIDS
ANARCHICAL
ANDROMACHE
APPRECIATE
APPRENTICE
ASARABACCA
ASCRIBABLE
ASTRAGALUS
ASTRALAGUS
ASTRINGENT
ASTROLOGER
ASTRONOMER
ATTRACTION
ATTRACTIVE
AVARICIOUS
AVERRHOISM
BAHRAINIAN
BARRACKING
BARRACOOTA
BARRACOUTA
BARRAMUNDA
BARRENNESS
BATRACHIAN
BEARGARDEN
BEDRAGGLED
BIORHYTHMS
BORROWINGS
BOURIGNIAN
CAERPHILLY
CAPREOLATE
CAPRICIOUS
CARRAGHEEN
CHARDONNAY
CHARGEABLE
CHARGEHAND
CHARIOTEER
CHARITABLE
CHARITABLY
CHAROLLAIS
CHARTREUSE
CHERIMOYER
CHERRYWOOD
CHERSONESE
CHERVONETS
CHIRICAUNE
CHIROMANCY
CHIRONOMIC
CHIROPTERA
CHURCHGOER
CHURCHYARD
CHURLISHLY
CIRRHOPODA
CIRRIPEDEA
CIRRIPEDIA
CITRONELLA
CLARABELLA
CLERESTORY
CLEROMANCY
COARSENESS
COORDINATE
CORRECTING
CORRECTION
CORRECTIVE
CORREGIDOR
CORRESPOND
CORRIGENDA
CORROBOREE
CORRUGATED
CORRUGATOR
CORRUPTING
CORRUPTION
COURAGEOUS
COURTHOUSE
CUIRASSIER
CURRENCIES
CURRICULUM
DEBRIEFING
DECRESCENT
DEFRAYMENT
DEGRADABLE
DEPRECIATE
DEPRESSANT
DEPRESSING
DEPRESSION
DEPRESSIVE
DETRACTION
DETRUNCATE
DHARMSHALA
DIGRESSION
DISRESPECT
DISRUPTION
DISRUPTIVE
DIURNALIST
DOORKEEPER
DOORTODOOR
ECARDINATE
EFFRONTERY
EGURGITATE
EMARGINATE
EMBROIDERY
EMBRYOLOGY
ENGROSSING
ENORMOUSLY
ENTRANCING
ENTREATING
ENTREMESSE
ENTRENCHED

ENTRYPHONE
EPHRAIMITE
ESCRITOIRE
ESTRAMACON
EUTRAPELIA
EVERGLADES
EVERYPLACE
EVERYTHING
EVERYWHERE
EXCRUCIATE
EXORBITANT
EXPRESSION
EXPRESSIVE
EXPRESSMAN
EXPRESSWAY
EXTRACTION
EXTRANEOUS
FAHRENHEIT
FAIRGROUND
FAIRHAIRED
FARRANDINE
FEARLESSLY
FEARNOUGHT
FERRANDINE
FIBREGLASS
FIBRILLATE
FIBROSITIS
FIERCENESS
FLIRTATION
FLORENTINE
FLORESCENT
FLORIBUNDA
FOURCHETTE
FOURIERISM
FOURRAGERE
FOURTEENTH
GALRAVITCH
GEORGETOWN
GLORIOUSLY
GUARANTEED
GUARNERIUS
HAIRSPRING
HARRINGTON
HEARTBREAK
HEARTINESS
HIERARCHIC
HIEROGLYPH
HIEROMANCY
HIEROPHANT
HIEROSCOPY
HOARSENESS
HORRENDOUS
HORRIFYING
HYDRAULICS
HYDROLYSIS
HYDROMETER
HYDROPHANE
HYDROPLANE
HYDROPONIC
HYGROMETER

IATROGENIC
IMBRICATED
IMBROCCATA
IMPREGNATE
IMPRESARIO
IMPRESSION
IMPRESSIVE
IMPRIMATUR
IMPROBABLE
IMPROBABLY
IMPROPERLY
IMPROVISED
IMPRUDENCE
INARTISTIC
INBREEDING
INCRASSATE
INCREASING
INCREDIBLE
INCREDIBLY
INCRESCENT
INFRACTION
INFREQUENT
INGRATIATE
INGREDIENT
INORDINATE
INTRAURBAN
INTRIGUING
INTROSPECT
JERRYBUILT
JOURNALESE
JOURNALISM
JOURNALIST
JOURNEYMAN
LAURDALITE
LAURENTIAN
LAURUSTINE
LAURVIKITE
LAWRENCIUM
LEPRECHAUN
LHERZOLITE
LIBRETTIST
LIBREVILLE
MACROBIOTE
MACROCARPA
MATRIARCHY
MAURITANIA
MEERSCHAUM
MERRYMAKER
METROPOLIS
MICROFICHE
MICROLIGHT
MICROMETER
MICRONESIA
MICROPHONE
MICROSCOPE
MOURNFULLY
NARROWBOAT
NARROWDALE
NARROWNESS
NECROMANCY

NECROPOLIS
NEURILEMMA
NEUROLEMMA
NICROSILAL
NIGRESCENT
NOURISHING
NOURRITURE
NUTRITIOUS
OLERACEOUS
OMBROMETER
OMBROPHOBE
OPPRESSION
OPPRESSIVE
OPPROBRIUM
OSTROGOTHS
OUTRAGEOUS
OVERCHARGE
OVEREATING
OVERLANDER
OVERPRAISE
OVERRIDING
OVERSHADOW
OVERSLAUGH
OVERSPREAD
OVERSTRAIN
OVERSTRUNG
OVERSUPPLY
OVERTHETOP
OVERTHWART
OVERWEIGHT
OVERWORKED
PARRAMATTA
PATRIARCHY
PATRIOTISM
PATRONISED
PATRONYMIC
PETRARCHAN
PETRIFYING
PETRISSAGE
PETROGLYPH
PETRONELLA
PHARMACIST
PLEROPHORY
PORRACEOUS
POURPARLER
PTERANODON
PTERYGOTUS
PUTREFYING
PUTRESCENT
QUARANTINE
QUARRENDER
QUARTERING
QUARTEROON
QUERCITRON
QUERSPRUNG
QUIRINALIA
REARMAMENT
RECREATION
RECRUDESCE
REDRUTHITE

REFRACTION
REFRACTIVE
REFRACTORY
REFRESHING
REGRESSION
REGRESSIVE
REORGANIZE
REPRESSION
REPRESSIVE
REPRODUCER
RETRACTION
RETRAINING
RETREATING
RETROGRADE
RETROGRESS
RETROSPECT
SABRETACHE
SACREDNESS
SACROSANCT
SAPROPHYTE
SAUROPSIDA
SCARAMOUCH
SCARCEMENT
SCARCENESS
SCARLATINA
SCARLETINA
SCORDATURA
SCOREBOARD
SCORNFULLY
SCORZONERA
SCURRILITY
SCURRILOUS
SECRETAIRE
SEERSUCKER
SEGREGATED
SERRADELLA
SERRADILLA
SERRASALMO
SHARAWADGI
SHARAWAGGI
SHERARDISE
SHORTBREAD
SHORTENING
SHORTLIVED
SHORTRANGE
SMARAGDINE
SMARMINESS
SMORREBROD
SNORKELING
SOURDELINE
SPARSENESS
SPARTACIST
SPERMACETI
SPERRYLITE
SPIRACULUM
SPIRITEDLY
SPIRITLESS
SPIRITUOUS
SPIRKETING
SPORTINGLY

SPORTSWEAR
SPURIOUSLY
STARVATION
STARVELING
STEREOTOMY
STEREOTYPE
STERILISER
STERILIZER
STERNALGIA
STERTEROUS
STERTOROUS
STOREFRONT
STOREHOUSE
STURDINESS
SUBREPTION
SURREALISM
SURREALIST
SURROUNDED
SWORDSTICK
TENRECIDAE
TERRACOTTA
TERREPLEIN
TERRIFYING
THEREAFTER
THEREANENT
THERMIONIC
THERMISTOR
THERMOSTAT
THIRTEENTH
THOROUGHLY
TORRENTIAL
TORRICELLI
TOURBILLON
TOURMALINE
TOURNAMENT
TOURNIQUET
TURRITELLA
UBERMENSCH
ULTRAFICHE
ULTRASONIC
ULTRASOUND
ULTRONEOUS
UNARGUABLE
UNCRITICAL
UNFRIENDLY
UNFRUITFUL
UNGRACIOUS
UNGRATEFUL
UNGROUNDED
UNORIGINAL
UNORTHODOX
UNPREPARED
UNPROMPTED
UNPROVOKED
UNTRUTHFUL
UPBRINGING
USURPATION
VIBRACULUM
VIBRAPHONE
VIBRATIONS

WARRANDICE
WHARFINGER
WHIRLYBIRD
YOURSELVES
ABYSSINIAN
ALMSGIVING
ALMSHOUSES
ANASTIGMAT
ANASTROPHE
ANESTHESIA
ANESTHETIC
APOSEMATIC
APOSTROPHE
ARISTIPPUS
ARISTOCRAT
ARISTOLOGY
ARISTOTLES
BASSINGTON
BASSOONIST
BELSHAZZAR
BERSAGLIER
BISSEXTILE
BLASPHEMER
BLASTOIDEA
BLISSFULLY
BLISTERING
BOISTEROUS
BOLSHEVIST
BOUSINGKEN
BRASSBOUND
BRESSUMMER
CAESPITOSE
CAMSTEERIE
CASSIABARK
CASSIOPEIA
CASSOLETTE
CASSUMUNAR
CENSORIOUS
CENSORSHIP
CHESSBOARD
CHESSYLITE
CHESTERTON
CLASPKNIFE
CLASSICISM
CLASSICIST
CLASSIFIED
CLOSTRIDIA
COASTGUARD
CODSWALLOP
COMSTOCKER
CONSCIENCE
CONSECRATE
CONSENSION
CONSEQUENT
CONSIDERED
CONSISTENT
CONSISTORY
CONSONANCE
CONSONANTS
CONSORTIUM
CONSPECTUS
CONSPIRACY
CONSTANTAN
CONSTANTIA
CONSTANTLY
CONSTITUTE
CONSTRAINT
CONSTRINGE
CONSUETUDE
CONSULTANT
CONSULTING
CONSUMMATE
COUSCOUSOU
CRISPBREAD
CRISPINIAN
CRISSCROSS
CROSSBREED
CROSSCHECK
CROSSPIECE
CROSSREFER
CROSSROADS
CRUSTACEAN
CUISENAIRE
CUSSEDNESS
DAMSELFISH
DESSIATINE
DESSYATINE
DIASKEUAST
DIASTALTIC
DIPSOMANIA
DISSECTION
DISSELBOOM
DISSEMBLER
DISSENSION
DISSENTING
DISSERTATE
DISSERVICE
DISSIDENCE
DISSILIENT
DISSIMILAR
DISSIPATED
DISSOCIATE
DISSOLVENT
DISSONANCE
DISSUASION
DRESSMAKER
DROSOPHILA
ELASTICATE
ELASTICITY
EMASCULATE
EPISCOPATE
EPISPASTIC
EPISTEMICS
EPISTROPHE
ERYSIPELAS
EVISCERATE
EXASPERATE
FALSETRUTH
FLASHINESS
FLASHLIGHT
FLASHPOINT
FLESHINESS
FOSSILIZED
FRESHWATER
FRISKINESS
FRUSTRATED
GALSWORTHY
GLASSHOUSE
GLASSINESS
GLISTENING
GLOSSINESS
GNOSTICISM
GOOSEBERRY
GOOSEFLESH
GRASSLANDS
GRASSROOTS
GRASSWIDOW
GUESTHOUSE
GYPSOPHILA
HAMSHACKLE
HAUSTELLUM
HAUSTORIUM
HORSEDRAWN
HORSELBERG
HORSEPOWER
HORSERIDER
HORSEWOMAN
HOUSEBOUND
HOUSECRAFT
HOUSEMAIDS
HOUSEPROUD
HOWSOMEVER
ICOSANDRIA
ICOSOHEDRA
INESCULENT
INKSLINGER
INOSCULATE
IRISHWOMAN
IRISHWOMEN
JEISTIECOR
JOBSEEKERS
KENSPECKLE
KERSEYMERE
KESSELRING
KIESELGUHR
LANSQUENET
MAISONETTE
MANSERVANT
MARSHALSEA
MASSASAUGA
MEASURABLE
MENSTRUATE
MIDSHIPMAN
MISSIONARY
MOISTURIZE
MONSTRANCE
MOSSBUNKER
MOUSEPIECE
MOUSSELINE
MOUSTERIAN
MUDSKIPPER
MUSSORGSKY
NAUSEATING
NAUSEATIVE
NESSELRODE
NEWSAGENTS
NEWSCASTER
NEWSLETTER
NEWSMONGER
NEWSPAPERS
NEWSREADER
NEWSWORTHY
NONSMOKING
NONSUCCESS
NURSERYMAN
OPISOMETER
OUTSPECKLE
OWLSPIEGLE
PANSOPHIST
PASSAGEWAY
PASSAMEZZO
PASSIONATE
PEASHOOTER
PENSIEROSO
PENSIONNAT
PERSECUTOR
PERSEPHONE
PERSEPOLIS
PERSICARIA
PERSIENNES
PERSIFLAGE
PERSISTENT
PERSONABLE
PERSONALLY
PERSTRINGE
PERSUADING
PERSUASION
PERSUASIVE
PHOSPHORUS
PHYSICALLY
PHYSIOCRAT
PHYSIOLOGY
PLASMODESM
PLASTICINE
PLASTICITY
PLESIOSAUR
POSSESSION
POSSESSIVE
PRESBYOPIA
PRESBYTERY
PRESCIENCE
PRESENTDAY
PRESIDENCY
PRESSURIZE
PRESUMABLY
PRESUPPOSE
PROSCENIUM
PROSCIUTTO
PROSCRIBED
PROSECUTOR
PROSERPINA
PROSERPINE
PROSILIENT
PROSPECTOR
PROSPECTUS
PROSPERINA
PROSPERITY
PROSPEROUS
PROSTHESIS
PROSTHETIC
PROSTITUTE
PULSATANCE
PURSUIVANT
QUESADILLA
QUESTIONER
RAMSHACKLE
RAWSTHORNE
REASONABLE
REASONABLY
REASSEMBLE
REASSURING
RIJSTTAFEL
RIPSNORTER
ROISTERING
ROUSEABOUT
ROUSTABOUT
SARSQUATCH
SEASONABLE
SEASONABLY
SEISMOLOGY
SENSUALITY
SENSUOUSLY
SHISHKEBAB
SINSEMILLA
SKYSCRAPER
SOUSAPHONE
SPISSITUDE
SUBSCRIBER
SUBSECTION
SUBSELLIUM
SUBSEQUENT
SUBSIDENCE
SUBSIDIARY
SUBSISTENT
SUBSTATION
SUBSTITUTE
SUBSTRATUM
TOPSYTURVY
TOSSICATED
TRESPASSER
TRISKELION
TRUSTFULLY
UNASSIGNED
UNASSUMING
UROSTEGITE
VERSAILLES
WASSAILING
WASSERMANS
WELSHWOMAN
WHISPERING

WITSNAPPER
WORSHIPPER
WRISTWATCH
ABITURIENT
ABSTEMIOUS
ABSTENTION
ABSTINENCE
ABSTRACTED
ACETABULAR
ACETABULUM
ACOTYLEDON
AESTHETICS
AHITHOPHEL
AMATEURISH
ANATOMICAL
APOTHECARY
APOTHECIUM
APOTHEOSIS
APOTROPAIC
ARITHMETIC
ARYTAENOID
AUCTIONEER
AUSTRALIAN
AUSTRALORP
AUSTRINGER
BATTAILOUS
BATTENBERG
BATTENBURG
BATTLEDOOR
BATTLEDORE
BATTLEMENT
BATTLESHIP
BENTHAMITE
BESTIALITY
BESTSELLER
BIRTHPLACE
BIRTHRIGHT
BITTERLING
BITTERNESS
BLITHERING
BLITZKRIEG
BLOTTESQUE
BOOTLEGGER
BOOTLICKER
BOTTICELLI
BOTTLEHEAD
BOTTLENECK
BOTTOMLESS
BRATISLAVA
BRITISHISM
BUTTERBAKE
BUTTERBUMP
BUTTERMERE
BUTTERMILK
BUTTONDOWN
BUTTONHOLE
CANTABRIAN
CANTALOUPE
CANTATRICE
CANTELOUPE
CANTERBURY
CANTILEVER
CANTILLATE
CANTONMENT
CAPTIVATED
CARTHAMINE
CARTHUSIAN
CARTOMANCY
CARTOONIST
CASTRATION
CATTLEGRID
CAUTIONARY
CAUTIOUSLY
CENTENNIAL
CENTESIMAL
CENTIGRADE
CENTILITER
CENTILITRE
CENTIMETER
CENTIMETRE
CENTRALIZE
CENTRIFUGE
CENTROSOME
CERTIORARI
CESTRACION
CHATELAINE
CHATTERBOX
CHATTERTON
CHITARRONE
CHITTAGONG
CISTERCIAN
COATHANGER
COETANEOUS
CONTAGIOUS
CONTENTION
CONTESTANT
CONTEXTUAL
CONTIGUITY
CONTIGUOUS
CONTINENCE
CONTINGENT
CONTINUING
CONTINUITY
CONTINUOUS
CONTORTION
CONTRABAND
CONTRACTOR
CONTRADICT
CONTRAFLOW
CONTRAHENT
CONTRARILY
CONTRAVENE
CONTRECOUP
CONTRIBUTE
CONTRITION
CONTROLLER
CONTROVERT
CORTADERIA
COSTLINESS
COTTIERISM
COTTONTAIL
COTTONWOOD
CRETACEOUS
CRITICALLY
CROTALARIA
CROTALIDAE
CULTIVATED
CULTIVATOR
CUTTLEBONE
CUTTLEFISH
CYSTOSCOPY
DELTIOLOGY
DENTIFRICE
DEUTOPLASM
DICTIONARY
DICTOGRAPH
DISTENSION
DISTILLATE
DISTILLERY
DISTILLING
DISTINCTLY
DISTORTION
DISTRACTED
DISTRAUGHT
DISTRESSED
DISTRIBUTE
DISTRINGAS
DISTURBING
DOSTOEVSKY
DYSTROPHIC
EARTHQUAKE
EARTHWORKS
EASTERLING
EISTEDDFOD
ELYTRIFORM
EPITHELIUM
EUSTACHIAN
EVITERNITY
EXOTHERMIC
EXOTICALLY
FACTITIOUS
FAITHFULLY
FANTASTICO
FANTOCCINI
FASTIDIOUS
FASTIGIATE
FASTMOVING
FEATHERBED
FERTILISED
FERTILISER
FERTILIZER
FETTERLOCK
FETTUCCINE
FICTITIOUS
FILTHINESS
FILTRATION
FIRTHSOKEN
FISTICUFFS
FLATTERING
FLATULENCE
FLUTEMOUTH
FONTANELLE
FONTICULUS
FONTINALIS
FOOTBALLER
FOOTBRIDGE
FOOTLIGHTS
FOOTPRINTS
FORTHRIGHT
FORTINBRAS
FORTISSIMO
FORTUITOUS
FRATERETTO
FRATERNISE
FRATERNITY
FRATERNIZE
FRATICELLI
FRATRICIDE
FRITHSOKEN
FRITILLARY
FUSTANELLA
FUSTANELLE
GASTEROPOD
GASTRONOME
GASTRONOMY
GENTLEFOLK
GENTLENESS
GEOTHERMAL
GEOTROPISM
GETTYSBURG
GLITTERAND
GLITTERATI
GLITTERING
GLUTTONOUS
GOATSUCKER
GRATEFULLY
GRATIFYING
GRATILLITY
GRATUITOUS
GRITTINESS
GUATEMALAN
GUTTIFERAE
GUTTURALLY
HARTEBEEST
HECTICALLY
HECTOLITRE
HEPTAGONAL
HEPTAMERON
HEPTATEUCH
HEPTATHLON
HINTERLAND
HISTORICAL
HISTRIONIC
HOOTANANNY
HOOTENANNY
HOOTNANNIE
HYSTERESIS
HYSTERICAL
ICHTHYOSIS
INITIATION
INITIATIVE
INSTALMENT
INSTIGATOR
INSTRUCTED
INSTRUCTOR
INSTRUMENT
JOLTERHEAD
JUSTICIARY
KARTTIKAYA
KENTUCKIAN
KETTLEDRUM
LANTHANIDE
LASTMINUTE
LATTERMATH
LATTICINIO
LEFTHANDED
LEFTHANDER
LEFTWINGER
LENTICULAR
LENTIGINES
LETTERHEAD
LISTLESSLY
LITTLENESS
MALTHUSIAN
MARTINGALE
MARTINIQUE
MASTECTOMY
MASTERMIND
MASTERWORT
MASTURBATE
MATTERHORN
METTLESOME
MISTAKENLY
MONTAGNARD
MONTESSORI
MONTEVERDI
MONTEVIDEO
MONTGOMERY
MONTICULUS
MONTRACHET
MONTSERRAT
MORTADELLA
MOUTHORGAN
MOUTHPIECE
MULTIMEDIA
MULTIPLIED
MULTIPLIER
MUTTONHEAD
MYSTAGOGUE
MYSTAGOGUS
MYSTERIOUS
NAPTHALENE
NASTURTIUM
NATTERJACK
NECTABANUS
NEOTERICAL
NETTLERASH
NETTLETREE
NEUTRALISE
NEUTRALITY

NEUTRALIZE
NEUTROPHIL
NORTHANGER
NORTHBOUND
NORTHERNER
NORTHSTEAD
NORTHWARDS
NYCTALOPIA
OBSTETRICS
OFFTHECUFF
OFFTHEWALL
OPHTHALMIC
OPOTHERAPY
ORATORICAL
PANTAGRUEL
PANTALOONS
PANTOGRAPH
PANTOSCOPE
PARTHENOPE
PARTIALITY
PARTICIPLE
PARTICULAR
PARTINGALE
PASTEBOARD
PASTEURISE
PASTEURIZE
PASTORELLA
PENTAGONAL
PENTAMERON
PENTAMETER
PENTATEUCH
PENTATHLON
PENTATONIC
PENTELIKON
PENTETERIC
PENTIMENTO
PENTSTEMON
PERTINENCE
PESTALOZZI
PESTILENCE
PETTICHAPS
PETTYCHAPS
PHOTODIODE
PHOTOGENIC
PHOTOGRAPH
PHOTONASTY
PISTILLATE
PLATELAYER
PLATINISED
PLATTELAND
PLUTOCRACY
POETASTERY
POETICALLY
PONTEDERIA
PONTEFRACT
PONTICELLO
PONTIFICAL
PORTAMENTO
PORTCULLIS
PORTENTOUS
PORTIONIST
PORTMANTLE
PORTMANTUA
PORTSMOUTH
PORTUGUESE
POSTCHAISE
POSTHUMOUS
POSTILLATE
POSTILLION
POSTLIMINY
POSTMASTER
POSTSCRIPT
PRATINCOLE
PRETENSION
PRETINCOLE
PRETTINESS
PROTAGORAS
PROTANOPIC
PROTECTION
PROTECTIVE
PROTERVITY
PROTESTANT
PROTOPLASM
PROTRACTED
PROTRACTOR
PROTRUSION
QUATERNARY
RANTLETREE
RATTLETRAP
REITERATED
RESTAURANT
RESTLESSLY
RESTRAINED
RESTRICTED
RHETORICAL
RHYTHMICAL
ROTTWEILER
SALTARELLO
SALTIGRADE
SCATHELESS
SCATTERING
SCATURIENT
SCOTODINIA
SCOTSWOMAN
SCUTELLATE
SELTZOGENE
SEPTENNIAL
SEPTUAGINT
SETTERWORT
SETTLEMENT
SHATTERING
SISTERHOOD
SKATEBOARD
SKETCHBOOK
SLATTERNLY
SMATTERING
SMITHEREEN
SOFTBOILED
SOOTHINGLY
SOOTHSAYER
SOUTERRAIN
SOUTHBOUND
SOUTHERNER
SOUTHWARDS
SPATCHCOCK
SPITCHCOCK
SPITEFULLY
SPOTLESSLY
STATECRAFT
STATIONARY
STATIONERY
STATISTICS
STATOCRACY
STATUESQUE
SUBTENANCY
SUBTERFUGE
SUBTROPICS
SULTRINESS
SUSTAINING
SUSTENANCE
SWITCHBACK
SYNTAGMATA
SYNTERESIS
SYNTHESIZE
SYNTHRONUS
SYSTEMATIC
TACTICALLY
TACTLESSLY
TANTAMOUNT
TARTRAZINE
TASTEFULLY
TATTERSALL
TEETOTALER
TENTERHOOK
TERTIARIES
TESTACEOUS
TESTICULAR
TINTORETTO
TOOTHBRUSH
TOOTHPASTE
TORTELLINI
TORTUOUSLY
TOSTICATED
TRITANOPIA
TROTSKYITE
TRUTHFULLY
TURTLEDOVE
TURTLENECK
ULSTERETTE
UNATTACHED
UNATTENDED
UNCTUOUSLY
UPSTANDING
VENTILATOR
VERTEBRATE
VERTICALLY
VESTIBULUM
VICTORIANA
VICTORIOUS
VICTUALLER
VIETNAMESE
VIRTUOSITY
VIRTUOUSLY
VOETGANGER
WANTHRIVEN
WASTEFULLY
WASTEPAPER
WATTLEWORK
WEATHERMAN
WENTLETRAP
WESTERNIZE
WHATSOEVER
WHITEHEART
WHITETHORN
WHITEWATER
WHITSTABLE
WHITTERICK
WINTERTIME
WORTHINESS
WORTHWHILE
WRETCHEDLY
YESTERWEEK
YESTERYEAR
ZOOTHAPSIS
ZOOTHERAPY
ZWITTERION
ABRUPTNESS
ACCUBATION
ACCUMULATE
ACCURATELY
ACCUSATION
ACCUSATIVE
ACCUSINGLY
ACCUSTOMED
ACQUAINTED
ADJUDICATE
ADJUSTABLE
ADJUSTMENT
AERUGINOUS
ALLUREMENT
ALMUCANTAR
AMBULACRUM
AMBULATORY
AMMUNITION
AMPUSSYAND
AMPUTATION
ANGUILLULA
ANGURVADEL
ANNUALIZED
ANNUNCIATE
ARAUCANIAN
ASSUMPTION
ASSUMPTIVE
ASTUTENESS
BALUSTRADE
BEAUJOLAIS
BEAUTICIAN
BEAUTIFIER
BITUMINOUS
CACUMINOUS
CALUMNIATE
CAOUTCHOUC
CASUALNESS
CHAUCERIAN
CHAUDFROID
CHAULMUGRA
CHAUTAUQUA
CHAUVINISM
CHAUVINIST
CLOUDBERRY
CLOUDBURST
CLOUDINESS
COPULATION
COQUELICOT
COQUETTISH
COQUIMBITE
CUCULLATED
CUCURBITAL
CUMULATIVE
DEDUCTIBLE
DEPUTATION
DIDUNCULUS
EBOULEMENT
EFFUSIVELY
ELEUSINIAN
EPAULEMENT
ESCULAPIAN
ESCUTCHEON
EXHUMATION
FABULOUSLY
FIGURATION
FIGURATIVE
FIGUREHEAD
FLOURISHED
FRAUDULENT
FRAUNHOFER
FUTURISTIC
GALUMPHING
GESUNDHEIT
GETUPANDGO
GLAUCONITE
GLOUCESTER
GROUNDBAIT
GROUNDLESS
GROUNDLING
GROUNDSMAN
GROUNDWORK
HOMUNCULUS
ILLUMINATE
ILLUMINATI
ILLUSTRATE
IMMUNOLOGY
IMPUDENTLY
IMPURITIES
IMPUTATION
INAUGURATE
INCUBATION
INCUMBENCY
INCUNABULA
INDUCEMENT

INDUCTANCE
INDULGENCE
INDUMENTUM
INDUSTRIAL
INFURIATED
INHUMANITY
INJUNCTION
INQUIRENDO
INQUISITOR
INSUFFLATE
INSULARITY
INSULATION
INSURGENCY
JACULATION
JAGUARONDI
JAGUARUNDI
JOCULARITY
LACUSTRINE
LEGUMINOUS
LIEUTENANT
LIQUESCENT
LIQUIDATOR
LIQUIDIZER
LITURGICAL
LOCULAMENT
LOQUACIOUS
LUGUBRIOUS
LUXURIANCE
MAKUNOUCHI
MANUSCRIPT
MAQUILLAGE
MATURATION
MINUTEBOOK
MINUTENESS
MODULATION
MONUMENTAL
NATURALISM
NATURALIST
NATURALIZE
NATUROPATH
OBFUSCATED
OBTUSENESS
OCCUPATION
OCCURRENCE
OSCULATION
OSCULATORY
PALUDAMENT
PALUSTRINE
PEAUDESOIE
PECULATION
PECULIARLY
PETULANTLY
PLOUGHBOTE
PLOUGHGATE
PLOUGHWISE
POHUTUKAWA
POPULARITY
POPULARIZE
POPULATION
PSEUDOCARP
RANUNCULUS
RECUPERATE
RECURRENCE
REDUNDANCY
REFUTATION
REGULARITY
REGULARIZE
REGULATION
REJUVENATE
RELUCTANCE
REMUNERATE
REPUBLICAN
REPUGNANCE
REPUTATION
REQUIESCAT
RESUMPTION
RESUPINATE
RESURGENCE
RETURNABLE
RHEUMATICS
RHEUMATISM
RHEUMATOID
ROBUSTIOUS
ROBUSTNESS
ROQUELAURE
SALUBRIOUS
SALUTATION
SATURATION
SATURNALIA
SCRUPULOUS
SCRUTINEER
SCRUTINISE
SCRUTINIZE
SDRUCCIOLA
SECULARIZE
SECURITIES
SEDULOUSLY
SEGUIDILLA
SEPULCHRAL
SEQUACIOUS
SEQUENTIAL
SIMULACRUM
SIMULATING
SIMULATION
SKEUOMORPH
SOLUBILITY
SPRUCENESS
STAUROLITE
STOUTHERIE
STOUTHRIEF
STRUCTURAL
STRULDBERG
STRULDBRUG
TABULATION
THAUMASITE
THOUGHTFUL
THOUSANDTH
TRAUMATIZE
TRIUMPHANT
TROUBADOUR
TROUVAILLE
TUMULTUOUS
UNCULTURED
UNDULATING
UNDULATION
UNNUMBERED
UNPUNCTUAL
UNRULINESS
UNSUITABLE
USQUEBAUGH
VIRULENTLY
VITUPERATE
VOLUBILITY
VOLUMINOUS
VOLUPTUARY
VOLUPTUOUS
VOLUTATION
YTHUNDERED
ABOVEBOARD
BEAVERSKIN
CANVASBACK
CANVASSING
CHEVESAILE
CHEVISANCE
CHEVROTAIN
CHIVALROUS
CLAVICHORD
CLEVERNESS
CONVALESCE
CONVECTION
CONVENANCE
CONVENIENT
CONVENTION
CONVERGENT
CONVERSANT
CONVERSELY
CONVERSION
CONVEYABLE
CONVEYANCE
CONVICTION
CONVINCING
CONVOLUTED
CONVOLVUTE
CONVULSION
CONVULSIVE
CULVERTAGE
CURVACEOUS
CURVETTING
FLAVESCENT
FLAVOURING
GALVANISER
GRAVEOLENT
GRAVESTONE
GROVELLING
HARVESTMAN
HEAVENWARD
INEVITABLE
INEVITABLY
MARVELLOUS
NONVIOLENT
PERVERSELY
PERVERSION
PERVERSITY
PREVAILING
PREVALENCE
PREVENANCY
PREVENTION
PREVENTIVE
PREVIOUSLY
PRIVATEERS
PRIVILEGED
PROVEDITOR
PROVENANCE
PROVERBIAL
PROVIDENCE
PROVINCIAL
PROVISIONS
SERVICEMAN
SHOVELHEAD
SHOVELNOSE
SILVERBACK
SILVERBILL
SILVERFISH
SILVERSIDE
SILVERSKIN
SILVERWARE
STAVESACRE
SUAVEOLENT
SUBVENTION
SUBVERSION
SUBVERSIVE
TRAVANCORE
TRAVELATOR
TRAVELLERS
TRAVELLING
TRAVELOGUE
TRAVERTINE
TRAVOLATOR
TRIVIALITY
TRIVIALIZE
UNAVAILING
UNEVENNESS
UNEVENTFUL
UNIVERSITY
ANGWANTIBO
ANSWERABLE
BROWNSTONE
DRAWBRIDGE
DRAWCANSIR
DRAWSTRING
DROWSINESS
EYEWITNESS
FLOWERBEDS
JAYWALKING
LEGWARMERS
NETWORKING
SCHWARZLOT
SHOWJUMPER
SNOWCAPPED
SNOWMOBILE
STEWARDESS
UNSWERVING
VIEWFINDER
WHEWELLITE
ALEXANDERS
ALEXANDRIA
ANAXIMENES
COEXISTENT
FRAXINELLA
INEXORABLE
PLEXIMETER
PRAXITELES
THIXOTROPY
UNEXAMPLED
UNEXPECTED
UNEXPLORED
ALCYONARIA
ALLYCHOLLY
BABYLONIAN
BABYSITTER
BARYSPHERE
CALYDONIAN
CALYPTRATE
CARYATIDES
CHRYSIPPUS
CHRYSOLITE
COPYHOLDER
COPYWRITER
CORYBANTES
CORYBANTIC
CORYPHAEUS
DICYNODONT
ENCYCLICAL
ENHYDRITIC
ETHYLAMINE
EURYPTERUS
GREYFRIARS
JOUYSAUNCE
LADYKILLER
LARYNGITIS
LILYWHITES
MARYLEBONE
MOLYBDENUM
PITYRIASIS
PLAYFELLOW
PLAYGROUND
PLAYWRIGHT
POLYANTHUS
POLYCHAETE
POLYCHREST
POLYCHROME
POLYGAMIST
POLYGAMOUS
POLYHEDRON
POLYHYMNIA
POLYMERIZE
POLYNESIAN
POLYPHEMUS
POLYTHEISM
RAIYATWARI

SATYAGRAHA
STRYCHNINE
UNHYGIENIC
BENZEDRINE
BOOZINGKEN
DRUZHINNIK
FITZGERALD
MANZANILLA
MIZZENMAST
MOZZARELLA
POZZUOLANA
PRIZEFIGHT
PUZZLEMENT
QUIZMASTER
RAZZMATAZZ

10:5

ACANACEOUS
ACETABULAR
ACETABULUM
ACQUAINTED
ACROAMATIC
ADAMANTINE
ADELANTADO
AGAPANTHUS
AGGRANDISE
ALABANDINE
ALABANDITE
ALEXANDERS
ALEXANDRIA
ANABAPTIST
ANACARDIUM
ANGWANTIBO
ANIMADVERT
ANNUALIZED
ANTIADITIS
APEMANTHUS
APOCALYPSE
APOLAUSTIC
APPEARANCE
AREFACTION
ARENACEOUS
ARIMASPIAN
ARYTAENOID
ASARABACCA
ASPHALTITE
ASTRAGALUS
ASTRALAGUS
ASYNARTETE
ATTRACTION
ATTRACTIVE
BAHRAINIAN
BARBAROSSA
BARCAROLLE
BARGAINING
BARRACKING
BARRACOOTA
BARRACOUTA
BARRAMUNDA
BATRACHIAN
BATTAILOUS
BEDRAGGLED
BELLADONNA
BELLAMOURE
BELLARMINE
BERNARDINE
BERSAGLIER
BOLLANDIST
BOMBARDIER
BRAGADISME
BRIGANDINE
BRIGANTINE
BROCATELLE
BUREAUCRAT
CALCAREOUS
CAMPAIGNER
CAMPANELLA
CAMPARADOR
CANTABRIAN
CANTALOUPE
CANTATRICE
CANVASBACK
CANVASSING
CARMAGNOLE
CARNASSIAL
CARPATHIAN
CARRAGHEEN
CARYATIDES
CASCARILLA
CASUALNESS
CEPHALOPOD
CHAMAEROPS
CHAPARAJOS
CHAPAREJOS
CHINAGRAPH
CHINASTONE
CHITARRONE
CHIVALROUS
CHOLALOGUE
CIRCASSIAN
CLARABELLA
COCKABULLY
COCKALORUM
COCKATRICE
COELACANTH
COETANEOUS
COLLAPSING
COLLARBONE
COLLATERAL
COMMANDANT
COMMANDEER
COMMANDING
COMPARABLE
COMPARATOR
COMPARISON
COMPASSION
COMPATIBLE
COMPATRIOT
CONTAGIOUS
CONVALESCE
CORTADERIA
COURAGEOUS
CRETACEOUS
CROTALARIA
CROTALIDAE
CUIRASSIER
CURVACEOUS
DEFEASANCE
DEFLAGRATE
DEFRAYMENT
DEGRADABLE
DERMATITIS
DÉSHABILLÉ
DESPAIRING
DETRACTION
DIACAUSTIC
DISDAINFUL
DISHABILLE
DISHARMONY
DISMANTLED
ELACAMPANE
ELECAMPANE
ELEGABALUS
EMALANGENI
EMPLASTRUM
ENCHANTING
ENDEARMENT
ENTRANCING
EPHRAIMITE
EPICANTHUS
ERYMANTHUS
ESCHAROTIC
ESTRAMACON
EUSTACHIAN
EUTHANASIA
EUTRAPELIA
EXTRACTION
EXTRANEOUS
FALLACIOUS
FANTASTICO
FARRANDINE
FERRANDINE
FLYCATCHER
FONTANELLE
FORFAITING
FRICANDEAU
FROMANTEEL
FUSTANELLA
FUSTANELLE
GALLABIYAH
GALLABIYEH
GALRAVITCH
GALVANISER
GARGANTUAN
GARLANDAGE
GERIATRICS
GODPARENTS
GOLIATHISE
GONFANONER
GORMANDIZE
GRANADILLA
GREGARIOUS
GRENADIERS
GRENADILLA
GUARANTEED
GYMNASTICS
HAEMANTHUS
HARMANBECK
HEPTAGONAL
HEPTAMERON
HEPTATEUCH
HEPTATHLON
HERBACEOUS
HEREABOUTS
HIERARCHIC
HIPPARCHUS
HOOTANANNY
HULLABALOO
HUSBANDAGE
HYDRAULICS
ICOSANDRIA
IMPLACABLE
IMPLACABLY
INCRASSATE
INFLATABLE
INFRACTION
INGRATIATE
INSTALMENT
INTRAURBAN
JACKANAPES
JAGUARONDI
JAGUARUNDI
JAYWALKING
JEOPARDISE
JEOPARDIZE
JIGGAMAREE
KARMATHIAN
KIDNAPPING
KILMARNOCK
KOOKABURRA
KURDAITCHA
LACCADIVES
LACKADAISY
LANDAMMANN
LEGWARMERS
LEOPARDESS
LINEAMENTS
LOQUACIOUS
MANGABEIRA
MANZANILLA
MARCANTANT
MASCARPONE
MASKANONGE
MASSASAUGA
MAUPASSANT
MECHANICAL
MECHANIZED
MENDACIOUS
MERCANTILE
MICHAELMAS
MISMATCHED
MISTAKENLY
MONTAGNARD
MORDACIOUS
MORGANATIC
MORGANETTA
MORTADELLA
MOZZARELLA
MYSTAGOGUE
MYSTAGOGUS
NECTABANUS
NEWFANGLED
NEWSAGENTS
NONPAYMENT
NYCTALOPIA
OFFBALANCE
OIREACHTAS
OLERACEOUS
ONOMASTICS
OUANANICHE
OUTBALANCE
OUTLANDISH
OUTPATIENT
OUTRAGEOUS
OZYMANDIAS
PALMATIFID
PALMATOZOA
PANJANDRUM
PANTAGRUEL
PANTALOONS
PAPIAMENTO
PARMACITIE
PARNASSIAN
PARRAMATTA
PASSAGEWAY
PASSAMEZZO
PECCADILLO
PEDIATRICS
PENTAGONAL
PENTAMERON
PENTAMETER
PENTATEUCH
PENTATHLON
PENTATONIC
PERMAFROST
PERMANENCE
PERMANENCY
PESCADORES
PESTALOZZI
PETRARCHAN
PHILATELIC
PHYLACTERY
PICCADILLY
PICCALILLI
PICCANINNY
PILGARLICK
PLUMASSIER
POETASTERY

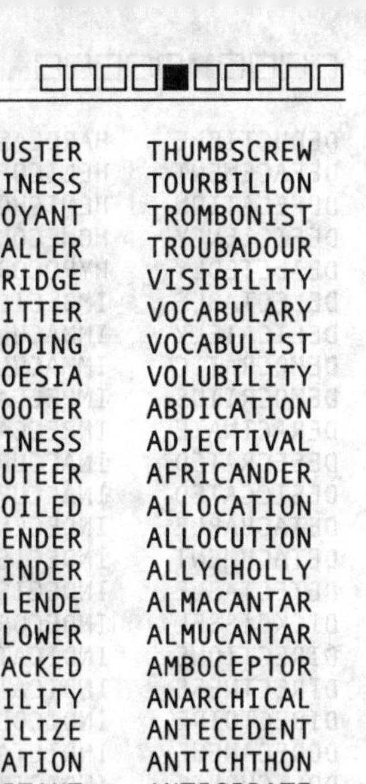

POLIANTHES
POLYANTHUS
PORRACEOUS
PORTAMENTO
PRECARIOUS
PRECAUTION
PREDACIOUS
PREMARITAL
PREPARATOR
PREPAYMENT
PREVAILING
PREVALENCE
PRIVATEERS
PROPAGANDA
PROPAGATOR
PROTAGORAS
PROTANOPIC
PTERANODON
PUGNACIOUS
PULSATANCE
PYTHAGORAS
QUARANTINE
QUESADILLA
RAIYATWARI
RAMPALLIAN
REFRACTION
REFRACTIVE
REFRACTORY
REPEATABLE
REPEATEDLY
RESEARCHER
RESTAURANT
RETRACTION
RETRAINING
RHOEADALES
RICHARDSON
ROCKABILLY
ROWLANDSON
SABBATICAL
SALMAGUNDI
SALMANAZAR
SALTARELLO
SANDALWOOD
SANNAYASIN
SATYAGRAHA
SCARAMOUCH
SCHWARZLOT
SEAMANSHIP
SEECATCHIE
SEQUACIOUS
SERRADELLA
SERRADILLA
SERRASALMO
SGANARELLE
SHARAWADGI
SHARAWAGGI
SHENANIGAN
SHERARDISE
SMARAGDINE
SOUSAPHONE
SPIRACULUM
SPREAGHERY
STALACTITE
STALAGMITE
STEWARDESS
STOMATOPOD
STREAMERED
STREAMLINE
SUBMARINER
SUNBATHING
SURPASSING
SUSTAINING
SYMPATHISE
SYMPATHIZE
SYNTAGMATA
TABLANETTE
TANGANYIKA
TANTAMOUNT
TAPDANCING
TARPAULING
TENNANTITE
TERRACOTTA
TESTACEOUS
THALASSIAN
THREADBARE
THREADLIKE
THREADWORM
THREATENED
TILLANDSIA
TOCCATELLA
TRAGACANTH
TRAVANCORE
TRILATERAL
TRIMALCHIO
TRINACRIAN
TRIPARTITE
TRITANOPIA
TROPAEOLUM
TURNAROUND
ULTRAFICHE
ULTRASONIC
ULTRASOUND
UNAVAILING
UNBEARABLE
UNBEARABLY
UNBEATABLE
UNEXAMPLED
UNFLAGGING
UNFLAVORED
UNGRACIOUS
UNGRATEFUL
UNHEARABLE
UNICAMERAL
UNILATERAL
UNLEAVENED
UNREADABLE
UNREASONED
UNSEASONED
UNSHACKLED
UPROARIOUS
UPSTANDING
USUCAPTION
VALLADOLID
VERNACULAR
VERSAILLES
VIBRACULUM
VIBRAPHONE
VIBRATIONS
VILLAINOUS
VILLANELLE
VILLANOVAN
VULCANALIA
WALLACHIAN
WARRANDICE
WASSAILING
WEIMARANER
WITGATBOOM
WORKAHOLIC
WRAPAROUND
ZIMBABWEAN
ACCUBATION
ACROBATICS
ADHIBITION
AEROBATICS
AFFABILITY
ALCIBIADES
ALEMBICATE
AMIABILITY
ANTIBARBUS
ANTIBIOTIC
ARCHBISHOP
AUDIBILITY
BACKBITING
BACKBLOCKS
BALIBUNTAL
BEEFBURGER
BLUEBOTTLE
BOOKBINDER
CAPABILITY
CARABINEER
CARABINIER
CATABOLISM
CELEBRATED
CEREBELLUM
CHAMBERPOT
CHAMBERTIN
CHAMBRANLE
CHIMBORAZO
CORYBANTES
CORYBANTIC
DELIBERATE
DEMOBILISE
DEMOBILIZE
DISABILITY
DRAWBRIDGE
DRUMBLEDOR
DUCKBOARDS
DURABILITY
EXHIBITION
EXORBITANT
FILIBUSTER
FLABBINESS
FLAMBOYANT
FOOTBALLER
FOOTBRIDGE
FOREBITTER
FOREBODING
FRAMBOESIA
FREEBOOTER
GRUBBINESS
HACKBUTEER
HARDBOILED
HELLBENDER
HIGHBINDER
HORNBLENDE
HORNBLOWER
HUMPBACKED
IMMOBILITY
IMMOBILIZE
INCUBATION
INHABITANT
INHIBITING
INHIBITION
INHIBITORY
JACKBOOTED
LAWABIDING
LEGIBILITY
LUGUBRIOUS
METABOLISE
METABOLISM
MOLYBDENUM
MOSSBUNKER
MUTABILITY
NOTABILITY
NUDIBRANCH
PALLBEARER
PATIBULARY
PAWNBROKER
PLIABILITY
PRESBYOPIA
PRESBYTERY
REPUBLICAN
SALUBRIOUS
SCOMBRESOX
SCRIBBLING
SHABBINESS
SHIBBOLETH
SIDEBOARDS
SLUMBERING
SOFTBOILED
SOLUBILITY
STRABISMUS
STRABOTOMY
STUBBORNLY
STUMBLEDOM
TALEBEARER
TENEBRIFIC
THIMBLEFUL
THIMBLEWIT
THUMBIKINS
THUMBSCREW
TOURBILLON
TROMBONIST
TROUBADOUR
VISIBILITY
VOCABULARY
VOCABULIST
VOLUBILITY
ABDICATION
ADJECTIVAL
AFRICANDER
ALLOCATION
ALLOCUTION
ALLYCHOLLY
ALMACANTAR
ALMUCANTAR
AMBOCEPTOR
ANARCHICAL
ANTECEDENT
ANTICHTHON
ANTICIPATE
ANTICLIMAX
ARAUCANIAN
ARTICULATA
ARTICULATE
ARTOCARPUS
ASSOCIATED
ATRACURIUM
ATTACHMENT
AUTECOLOGY
AUTOCHTHON
AUTOCRATIC
BETACRUCIS
BINOCULARS
BLANCMANGE
BRONCHITIC
BRONCHITIS
CANECUTTER
CAPACITATE
CARACTACUS
CARICATURA
CARICATURE
CATACHUMEN
CATECHUMEN
CAVICORNIA
CHALCEDONY
CHANCELLOR
CHAUCERIAN
CHINCHILLA
CHOICELESS
CHURCHGOER
CHURCHYARD
CINECAMERA
COCKCHAFER
COINCIDENT
CONSCIENCE
CORNCOCKLE
COUNCILLOR
COUSCOUSOU
DEDICATION

DEDUCTIBLE
DEFACEMENT
DEFECATION
DEFICIENCY
DEJECTEDLY
DELECTABLE
DELICATELY
DEMOCRATIC
DEMOCRITUS
DERACINATE
DESECRATED
DESICCATED
DETACHABLE
DETACHMENT
DETECTABLE
DICKCISSEL
DIRECTIONS
DIRECTNESS
DIRECTOIRE
DODECANESE
DOLICHOLIS
DOLICHOTUS
DOMICILARY
DRAWCANSIR
EBRACTEATE
EDULCORATE
EFFACEMENT
EFFECTUATE
EFFICIENCY
EMANCIPATE
EMASCULATE
ENCYCLICAL
ENLACEMENT
ENRICHMENT
ENTICEMENT
EPISCOPATE
ERIOCAULON
ESPECIALLY
ETEOCRETAN
EUROCHEQUE
EUROCLYDON
EVISCERATE
EXPECTANCY
FELICITATE
FELICITOUS
FIANCHETTO
FIERCENESS
FLANCONADE
FLOCCULATE
FLOCCULENT
FORECASTER
FORECASTLE
FOURCHETTE
FRANCHISEE
FRANCHISOR
FRANCISCAN
GENICULATE
GLAUCONITE
GLOUCESTER
GYNECOLOGY
HARDCASTLE
HELICOPTER
HEMICHORDA
HOMECOMING
HYPOCORISM
IMBECILITY
IMMACULACY
IMMACULATE
IMPECCABLE
IMPECCABLY
INACCURACY
INACCURATE
INDECENTLY
INDECISION
INDECISIVE
INDECOROUS
INDICATION
INDICATIVE
INDICOLITE
INDICTABLE
INDICTMENT
INDUCEMENT
INDUCTANCE
INESCULENT
INFECTIOUS
INNOCENTLY
INOSCULATE
INSECURELY
INSECURITY
INVOCATION
JUDICATURE
JUDICIALLY
LAUNCEGAYE
LAUNCESTON
LENOCINIUM
LONGCHAMPS
MALACOLOGY
MANICHAEAN
MANICURIST
MEDICAMENT
MEDICATION
MELACONITE
MELOCOTOON
MENACINGLY
MENECHMIAN
METACARPAL
METACARPUS
METACENTRE
METICULOUS
MIRACULOUS
MISOCAPNIC
MONOCHROME
MUSICOLOGY
NEWSCASTER
NOSOCOMIAL
NOTICEABLE
NOTICEABLY
NOVACULITE
OBJECTLESS
OFFICIALLY
OPHICLEIDE
OVERCHARGE
PARACELSUS
PEDICULATE
PENICILLIN
PLANCHETTE
POLYCHAETE
POLYCHREST
POLYCHROME
PORTCULLIS
POSTCHAISE
PRESCIENCE
PRINCIPIUM
PRINCIPLED
PRINCIPLES
PROSCENIUM
PROSCIUTTO
PROSCRIBED
PUNICACEAE
PYRACANTHA
QUENCHLESS
QUERCITRON
RACECOURSE
RADICALISM
REDECORATE
RELOCATION
RELUCTANCE
REVOCATION
RIDICULOUS
ROSECHAFER
RUPICOLINE
SALICORNIA
SAXICOLINE
SAXICOLOUS
SCARCEMENT
SCARCENESS
SDRUCCIOLA
SEMICIRCLE
SKETCHBOOK
SKYSCRAPER
SNOWCAPPED
SOLICITOUS
SOLICITUDE
SPATCHCOCK
SPEECHLESS
SPENCERIAN
SPHACELATE
SPITCHCOCK
SPRUCENESS
STIACCIATO
STRACCHINO
STRICTNESS
STRUCTURAL
STRYCHNINE
SUBSCRIBER
SWITCHBACK
SYNECDOCHE
THEOCRITUS
TIROCINIUM
TOPICALITY
TOXICOLOGY
TRENCHMORE
TRIACONTER
UNACCENTED
UNBECOMING
UNDECLARED
UNDOCTORED
UNLICENSED
UNOCCUPIED
UNSOCIABLE
URTICACEAE
VARICOSITY
VELOCIPEDE
VESICULATE
WRETCHEDLY
ABERDEVINE
ABHIDHAMMA
ABRIDGMENT
ABUNDANTLY
ACCIDENTAL
ADJUDICATE
AMYGDALOID
ARCHDEACON
ARUNDELIAN
ASPIDISTRA
AUTODIDACT
BENEDICITE
BLOODHOUND
BLOODSTAIN
BLOODSTOCK
BLOODSTONE
BLUNDERING
BOONDOGGLE
BREADFRUIT
BROADCLOTH
BROADPIECE
BROADSHEET
BROADSWORD
CACODAEMON
CALEDONIAN
CALYDONIAN
CAPODASTRO
CECIDOMYIA
CHANDELIER
CHARDONNAY
CHAUDFROID
CHILDBIRTH
CHILDERMAS
CHILDISHLY
CLOUDBERRY
CLOUDBURST
CLOUDINESS
COMEDIENNE
COORDINATE
DESIDERATA
DREADFULLY
DREADLOCKS
ECARDINATE
ECUADORIAN
EMBODIMENT
EMENDATION
EMPEDOCLES
ENHYDRITIC
ESCADRILLE
ESPADRILLE
EXPEDIENCE
EXPEDIENCY
EXPEDITION
FIELDMOUSE
FIENDISHLY
FLAPDOODLE
FLINDERSIA
FLOODLIGHT
FOREDAMNED
FOUNDATION
FRAUDULENT
GLENDOVEER
GOLDDIGGER
GRANDCHILD
GRANDSTAND
GREEDINESS
GRINDSTONE
HALFDOLLAR
HEREDITARY
HUMIDIFIER
HYPODERMIC
ILLADVISED
IMMODERATE
IMPEDIMENT
IMPUDENTLY
INCIDENTAL
INFIDELITY
INORDINATE
INUNDATION
IRRADICATE
LAUNDROMAT
LAURDALITE
LIBIDINOUS
MACEDONIAN
MALODOROUS
MEANDERING
MOULDINESS
MOULDIWARP
OBSIDIONAL
OCCIDENTAL
OCTODECIMO
OSMIDROSIS
PALUDAMENT
PARADIDDLE
PARADOXIDE
PARADOXINE
PEAUDESOIE
PERIDOTITE
PILEDRIVER
PLUNDERING
PSEUDOCARP
RECIDIVISM
RECIDIVIST
REREDORTER
ROUNDABOUT

ROUNDHOUSE
SBUDDIKINS
SCANDALISE
SCANDALIZE
SCANDALOUS
SCANDAROON
SCANDERBEG
SCORDATURA
SHANDRYDAN
SHANDYGAFF
SHELDONIAN
SHODDINESS
SHUDDERING
SKINDIVING
SLANDEROUS
SNAPDRAGON
SOLIDARITY
SOUNDPROOF
SOUNDTRACK
SOURDELINE
SPEEDINESS
STANDPOINT
STANDSTILL
STEADINESS
STRIDENTLY
STRIDEWAYS
STRIDULATE
STURDINESS
SWORDSTICK
TARADIDDLE
TEPIDARIUM
THEODOLITE
THUNDERBOX
THUNDERING
THUNDEROUS
TRENDINESS
UNLADYLIKE
UNREDEEMED
UNTIDINESS
VALIDATION
WITHDRAWAL
WORLDCLASS
ABBREVIATE
ABOVEBOARD
ABSTEMIOUS
ABSTENTION
ACCREDITED
ADOLESCENT
AGGRESSION
AGGRESSIVE
ALCHERINGA
ALIMENTARY
ALZHEIMERS
AMATEURISH
AMPLEFORTH
ANSWERABLE
ANTHEOLION
APHAERESIS
APOPEMPTIC
APOSEMATIC

APPRECIATE
APPRENTICE
ARCHETYPAL
ARSMETRICK
ATELEIOSIS
BADDERLOCK
BALDERDASH
BALNEATION
BALNEOLOGY
BANDERILLA
BANDERILLO
BARLEYBREE
BARLEYCORN
BARMECIDAL
BARRENNESS
BASKETBALL
BASKETWORK
BATTENBERG
BATTENBURG
BAUDELAIRE
BEAVERSKIN
BEEFEATERS
BEEKEEPING
BELIEVABLE
BENZEDRINE
BIRKENHEAD
BISSEXTILE
BITTERLING
BITTERNESS
BORDERLAND
BORDERLINE
BOTHERSOME
BRIDEGROOM
BRIDESMAID
BROKENDOWN
BUDGERIGAR
BUNDESWEHR
BURDENSOME
BURGEONING
BUTTERBAKE
BUTTERBUMP
BUTTERMERE
BUTTERMILK
BYELECTION
CALCEDONIO
CALCEOLATE
CAMBERWELL
CAMPERDOWN
CAMPESTRAL
CANDELABRA
CANDELILLA
CANNELLONI
CANTELOUPE
CANTERBURY
CAPREOLATE
CARPENTIER
CENTENNIAL
CENTESIMAL
CHATELAINE
CHEVESAILE

CINDERELLA
CISLEITHAN
CISTERCIAN
CLEMENCEAU
CLEMENTINE
CLERESTORY
CLEVERNESS
CLYDESDALE
COCKERNONY
COLBERTINE
COLLECTING
COLLECTION
COLLECTIVE
COLLEGIATE
COLLEMBOLA
COMMENTARY
COMMENTATE
COMMERCIAL
COMPELLING
COMPENDIUM
COMPENSATE
COMPETENCE
COMPETITOR
CONCENTRIC
CONCEPTION
CONCEPTUAL
CONCERNING
CONCERTINA
CONCERVATE
CONCESSION
CONDESCEND
CONFECTION
CONFEDERAL
CONFERENCE
CONFERVOID
CONFESSION
CONGENITAL
CONGESTION
CONJECTURE
CONNECTING
CONNECTION
CONNECTIVE
CONSECRATE
CONSENSION
CONSEQUENT
CONTENTION
CONTESTANT
CONTEXTUAL
CONVECTION
CONVENANCE
CONVENIENT
CONVENTION
CONVERGENT
CONVERSANT
CONVERSELY
CONVERSION
CONVEYABLE
CONVEYANCE
COPPERHEAD
COPPERNOSE

COPPERSKIN
COQUELICOT
COQUETTISH
CORRECTING
CORRECTION
CORRECTIVE
CORREGIDOR
CORRESPOND
CREDENTIAL
CRENELLATE
CUISENAIRE
CULVERTAGE
CUMBERLAND
CUMBERSOME
CUMMERBUND
CURRENCIES
CURVETTING
CUSSEDNESS
DAMSELFISH
DARJEELING
DEALERSHIP
DECLENSION
DECRESCENT
DEFLECTION
DEPRECIATE
DEPRESSANT
DEPRESSING
DEPRESSION
DEPRESSIVE
DESCENDANT
DESCENDING
DIAGENESIS
DIALECTICS
DIAPEDESIS
DIDGERIDOO
DIELECTRIC
DIFFERENCE
DIGRESSION
DINNERTIME
DISBELIEVE
DISCERNING
DISHEARTEN
DISPENSARY
DISPENSING
DISPERSION
DISRESPECT
DISSECTION
DISSELBOOM
DISSEMBLER
DISSENSION
DISSENTING
DISSERTATE
DISSERVICE
DISTENSION
DOGGEDNESS
DOLCEMENTE
DRAKESTONE
DUKKERIPEN
DUNDERFUNK
DUNDERHEAD

DUND
DUODE
EASTE
ECUME
EFFLE
EGOCEN
EISTED
ELEMENT
EMBLEMA
EMBLEME
ENTREATI
ENTREMES
ENTRENCHE
EPIDEICTI
EPIDENDRU
EPIGENETI
EPIMENIDES
EPIMETHEUS
ERUBESCENT
EVANESCENT
EVITERNITY
EXACERBATE
EXONERATED
EXPRESSION
EXPRESSIVE
EXPRESSMAN
EXPRESSWAY
EXUBERANCE
FAHRENHEIT
FALSETRUTH
FARFETCHED
FATHERLAND
FATHERLESS
FESCENNINE
FETTERLOCK
FIBREGLASS
FINGERLING
FINGERNAIL
FLAGELLATE
FLAMEPROOF
FLAVESCENT
FLORENTINE
FLORESCENT
FLOWERBEDS
FLUGELHORN
FLUTEMOUTH
FORBEARING
FORCEFULLY
FORFEITURE
FORFEUCHEN
FRATERETTO
FRATERNISE
FRATERNITY
FRATERNIZE
FREMESCENT
FRENETICAL
GASTEROPOD
GEOCENTRIC
GHIBELLINE
GIBBERELLA

ILBERTIAN
ILBERTINE
INGERBEER
INGERSNAP
OOSEBERRY
OOSEFLESH
GORGEOUSLY
GRACEFULLY
GRAPEFRUIT
GRATEFULLY
GRAVEOLENT
GRAVESTONE
GROCETERIA
GROVELLING
GUATEMALAN
GUIDELINES
HALIEUTICS
HALLELUJAH
HAMMERHEAD
HAMMERLOCK
HARTEBEEST
HARVESTMAN
HATEENOUGH
HEAVENWARD
HEIDELBERG
HELLESPONT
HENCEFORTH
HENDECAGON
HESPERIDES
HILDEBRAND
HINDENBURG
HINTERLAND
HITHERWARD
HODGEPODGE
HOMOEOPATH
HOOTENANNY
HORRENDOUS
HORSEDRAWN
HORSELBERG
HORSEPOWER
HORSERIDER
HORSEWOMAN
HOUSEBOUND
HOUSECRAFT
HOUSEMAIDS
HOUSEPROUD
HOWLEGLASS
HYPAETHRAL
HYPAETHRON
HYSTERESIS
HYSTERICAL
IMPREGNATE
IMPRESARIO
IMPRESSION
IMPRESSIVE
INADEQUACY
INADEQUATE
INBREEDING
INCREASING
INCREDIBLE
INCREDIBLY
INCRESCENT
INFLECTION
INFLEXIBLE
INFLEXIBLY
INFREQUENT
INGREDIENT
INOPERABLE
INSPECTION
IRIDESCENT
ISABELLINE
ISOMETRICS
JABBERWOCK
JOBSEEKERS
JOLTERHEAD
JUGGERNAUT
KEMPERYMAN
KERSEYMERE
KESSELRING
KIESELGUHR
KIMBERLITE
KNIFEBOARD
LANCEOLATE
LANGERHANS
LARGESCALE
LATTERMATH
LAUDERDALE
LAURENTIAN
LAWRENCIUM
LEADERSHIP
LEPRECHAUN
LETTERHEAD
LIBRETTIST
LIBREVILLE
LIEBERMANN
LIMBERNECK
LIQUESCENT
LOCKERROOM
LOGGERHEAD
LUMBERJACK
MAIDENHAIR
MAIDENHOOD
MALMESBURY
MANDEVILLE
MANSERVANT
MARCESCENT
MARKETABLE
MARVELLOUS
MASTECTOMY
MASTERMIND
MASTERWORT
MATTERHORN
MEAGERNESS
MEMBERSHIP
METHEDRINE
MILLEFIORI
MINDERERUS
MISCELLANY
MISLEADING
MIZZENMAST
MONOECIOUS
MONTESSORI
MONTEVERDI
MONTEVIDEO
MOTHERHOOD
MOTHERLAND
MOTHERLESS
MOTHERLIKE
MOUSEPIECE
MULIEBRITY
MUSKETEERS
MYSTERIOUS
NATHELESSE
NATTERJACK
NAUSEATING
NAUSEATIVE
NEGLECTFUL
NEOTERICAL
NESSELRODE
NETHERMOST
NIDDERLING
NIGGERHEAD
NIGRESCENT
NOBLEWOMAN
NORBERTINE
NUCLEONICS
NUMBERLESS
NURSERYMAN
OBSTETRICS
ODDFELLOWS
OPALESCENT
OPPRESSION
OPPRESSIVE
ORCHESTRAL
OROGENESIS
ORPHEOREON
OUTPERFORM
OVEREATING
OXYGENATOR
PALAEOTYPE
PALAESTRAL
PALMERSTON
PALMERWORM
PARAENESIS
PARGETTING
PARNELLISM
PASTEBOARD
PASTEURISE
PASTEURIZE
PEACEFULLY
PEACEMAKER
PENTELIKON
PENTETERIC
PEPPERCORN
PEPPERMILL
PEPPERMINT
PEPPERWORT
PERCENTAGE
PERCENTILE
PERCEPTION
PERCEPTIVE
PERDENDOSI
PERFECTION
PERIEGESIS
PERMEATION
PERPETRATE
PERPETUATE
PERPETUITY
PERSECUTOR
PERSEPHONE
PERSEPOLIS
PERVERSELY
PERVERSION
PERVERSITY
PHAGEDAENA
PIONEERING
PLATELAYER
PLUPERFECT
POCKETBOOK
PONTEDERIA
PONTEFRACT
PORTENTOUS
POSSESSION
POSSESSIVE
PREBENDARY
PRECEDENCE
PREDECEASE
PREDESTINE
PREFERABLE
PREFERABLY
PREFERENCE
PREFERMENT
PREHENSILE
PRELECTION
PREPENSELY
PRESENTDAY
PRETENSION
PREVENANCY
PREVENTION
PREVENTIVE
PRIZEFIGHT
PROCEDURAL
PROCEEDING
PROCESSING
PROCESSION
PROFESSION
PROGENITOR
PROGESSION
PROJECTILE
PROJECTING
PROJECTION
PROMENADER
PROMETHEAN
PROMETHEUS
PROMETHIUM
PROPELLANT
PROPENSITY
PROPERTIUS
PROSECUTOR
PROSERPINA
PROSERPINE
PROTECTION
PROTECTIVE
PROTERVITY
PROTESTANT
PROVEDITOR
PROVENANCE
PROVERBIAL
PRUDENTIAL
PUCKERWOOD
PUMMELLING
PUTREFYING
PUTRESCENT
QUATERNARY
RANNELTREE
READERSHIP
RECREATION
REELECTION
REFLECTING
REFLECTION
REFLECTIVE
REFRESHING
REGRESSION
REGRESSIVE
REITERATED
RENDEZVOUS
REPRESSION
REPRESSIVE
RESPECTFUL
RESPECTING
RESPECTIVE
RETREATING
RHINEGRAVE
RHINESTONE
RINDERPEST
RINGELMANN
ROQUELAURE
ROUSEABOUT
RUBBERNECK
RUDDERLESS
RUGGEDNESS
RUTHERFORD
SABRETACHE
SACREDNESS
SALLENDERS
SANDEMANIA
SANDERLING
SAPPERMENT
SARMENTOUS
SCAPEGRACE
SCOPELIDAE
SCOREBOARD
SCREECHING
SCREENPLAY
SCUTELLATE
SECRETAIRE
SEGREGATED
SELFESTEEM
SEPTENNIAL
SEQUENTIAL

SERPENTINE
SETTERWORT
SHAMEFACED
SHAMEFULLY
SHOVELHEAD
SHOVELNOSE
SHRIEVALTY
SILVERBACK
SILVERBILL
SILVERFISH
SILVERSIDE
SILVERSKIN
SILVERWARE
SIMMENTHAL
SINSEMILLA
SISTERHOOD
SKATEBOARD
SMOKESTACK
SNAKEMOUTH
SNAKESTONE
SOUTERRAIN
SPACECRAFT
SPELEOLOGY
SPIDERWORT
SPINESCENT
SPITEFULLY
SPOKESHAVE
SQUEEZEBOX
STAGECOACH
STAGECRAFT
STATECRAFT
STAVESACRE
STEREOTOMY
STEREOTYPE
STONEBRASH
STONEHENGE
STONEMASON
STOREFRONT
STOREHOUSE
STREETLAMP
STREETWISE
STUPEFYING
STUPENDOUS
SUAVEOLENT
SUBHEADING
SUBJECTION
SUBJECTIVE
SUBMEDIANT
SUBMERSION
SUBREPTION
SUBSECTION
SUBSELLIUM
SUBSEQUENT
SUBTENANCY
SUBTERFUGE
SUBVENTION
SUBVERSION
SUBVERSIVE
SUCCEEDING
SUCCESSFUL
SUCCESSION
SUCCESSIVE
SUDDENNESS
SUFFERANCE
SUGGESTION
SUGGESTIVE
SUMMERTIME
SURREALISM
SURREALIST
SUSPENDERS
SUSPENSION
SUSTENANCE
SWEDENBORG
SYNAERESIS
SYNTERESIS
SYSTEMATIC
TABLECLOTH
TABLESPOON
TALLEYRAND
TAMBERLANE
TAMPERFOOT
TANGENTIAL
TASTEFULLY
TATTERSALL
TEMPERANCE
TENDERFOOT
TENDERLOIN
TENDERNESS
TENRECIDAE
TENTERHOOK
TERNEPLATE
TERREPLEIN
THALESTRIS
THEREAFTER
THEREANENT
THREEPENCE
THREEPENNY
THREESCORE
TICKERTAPE
TIMBERYARD
TINKERBELL
TOILETRIES
TORBERNITE
TORPESCENT
TORRENTIAL
TORTELLINI
TRAJECTORY
TRAVELATOR
TRAVELLERS
TRAVELLING
TRAVELOGUE
TRAVERTINE
TRECENTIST
TREMENDOUS
TRIDENTINE
TRIPEHOUND
TURPENTINE
ULSTERETTE
UNBLEACHED
UNEVENNESS
UNEVENTFUL
UNIGENITUS
UNIVERSITY
UNPLEASANT
UNPREPARED
UNSLEEPING
UNSPECIFIC
UNSWERVING
UNYIELDING
USQUEBAUGH
VANDERBILT
VARIEGATED
VAUDEVILLE
VERTEBRATE
VINDEMIATE
VOLLEYBALL
VULNERABLE
WAGEEARNER
WALDENSIAN
WANDERINGS
WANDERLUST
WAPPENSHAW
WASSERMANS
WASTEFULLY
WASTEPAPER
WELLEARNED
WESTERNIZE
WHEWELLITE
WHITEHEART
WHITETHORN
WHITEWATER
WHOLESALER
WHOLEWHEAT
WICKEDNESS
WICKERWORK
WILDEBEEST
WILDERNESS
WINCEYETTE
WINDERMERE
WINTERTIME
WONDERLAND
WONDERMENT
WOODENHEAD
WUNDERKIND
YESTERWEEK
YESTERYEAR
ANTIFREEZE
AQUAFORTIS
ARTIFICIAL
AURIFEROUS
BAREFOOTED
BENEFACTOR
BENEFICENT
BENEFICIAL
CALEFACTOR
CALIFORNIA
CATAFALQUE
CHAFFERING
CHAPFALLEN
CHIFFCHAFF
CHIFFONIER
CONIFEROUS
CORNFLAKES
CORNFLOWER
DEEPFREEZE
FLUFFINESS
FOREFATHER
FOREFINGER
GIRLFRIEND
GOLDFINGER
GOODFELLOW
GREYFRIARS
HIGHFLYING
HOLOFERNES
INDEFINITE
INEFFICACY
INFEFTMENT
INSUFFLATE
KINGFISHER
LONGFELLOW
MALEFACTOR
MANIFESTLY
MODIFIABLE
MUNIFICENT
NOTIFIABLE
PACIFICISM
PATHFINDER
PLAYFELLOW
RIBOFLAVIN
SCOFFINGLY
SOLIFIDIAN
STEPFATHER
STUFFINESS
TRAFFICKER
UNAFFECTED
UNDEFEATED
UNDEFENDED
UNINFORMED
UNOFFICIAL
VERIFIABLE
VIEWFINDER
VOCIFERATE
VOCIFEROUS
WALLFLOWER
WHARFINGER
WILDFOWLER
WINDFLOWER
ABERGLAUBE
ABROGATION
ACROGENOUS
AERUGINOUS
ALBIGENSES
ALLEGATION
ALLEGEANCE
ALLEGIANCE
ALLIGATION
ALMSGIVING
ALTOGETHER
AMALGAMATE
ANTAGONISE
ANTAGONISM
ANTAGONIST
ANTAGONIZE
AREOGRAPHY
ARMAGEDDON
ARROGANTLY
ASSIGNABLE
ASSIGNMENT
ASTIGMATIC
AUTOGENOUS
AVVOGADORE
BACKGAMMON
BACKGROUND
BEARGARDEN
BRIDGEHEAD
BRIDGETOWN
CACOGRAPHY
CATEGORISE
CATEGORIZE
CHANGEABLE
CHANGELESS
CHANGELING
CHARGEABLE
CHARGEHAND
CLINGSTONE
CRAIGFLUKE
CRYOGENICS
DECAGRAMME
DELEGATION
DELIGATION
DELIGHTFUL
DEMOGORGON
DEMOGRAPHY
DEREGULATE
DEROGATORY
DILIGENTLY
EGURGITATE
ELONGATION
EMARGINATE
ENDOGAMOUS
ENGAGEMENT
EULOGISTIC
EVANGELIST
EVANGELIZE
EVERGLADES
EXAGGERATE
FAIRGROUND
FITZGERALD
FOREGATHER
FOREGROUND
FRANGIPANE
FRANGIPANI
FREIGHTAGE
FRINGILLID
FULIGINOUS
FUMIGATION
GAINGIVING
GEORGETOWN
GRANGERISM
GRANGERIZE

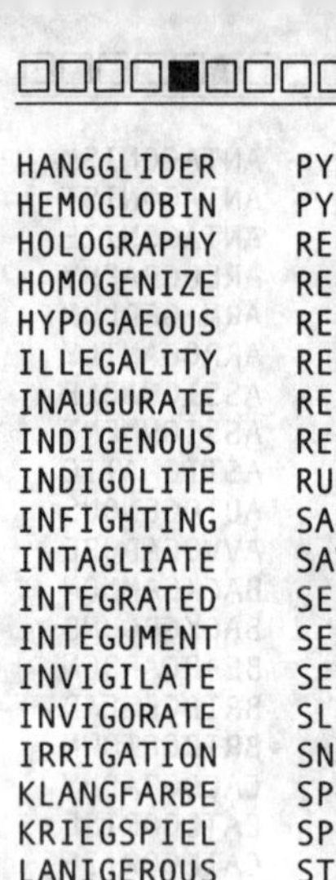

HANGGLIDER
HEMOGLOBIN
HOLOGRAPHY
HOMOGENIZE
HYPOGAEOUS
ILLEGALITY
INAUGURATE
INDIGENOUS
INDIGOLITE
INFIGHTING
INTAGLIATE
INTEGRATED
INTEGUMENT
INVIGILATE
INVIGORATE
IRRIGATION
KLANGFARBE
KRIEGSPIEL
LANIGEROUS
LITIGATION
MADAGASCAN
MADAGASCAR
MALAGUETTA
MALIGNANCY
MANAGEABLE
MANAGEMENT
MANAGERESS
MANAGERIAL
MISHGUGGLE
MISOGYNIST
MITIGATING
MITIGATION
MONEGASQUE
MONOGAMOUS
MONTGOMERY
MORIGEROUS
NAVIGATION
OBLIGATION
OBLIGATORY
OBLIGINGLY
OLEAGINOUS
PALAGONITE
PARAGLOSSA
PARAGONITE
PARAGUAYAN
PASIGRAPHY
PATAGONIAN
PEELGARLIC
PHLEGETHON
PHLEGMASIA
PHLEGMATIC
PHLOGISTIC
PHLOGISTON
PHLOGOPITE
PLAYGROUND
PLOUGHBOTE
PLOUGHGATE
PLOUGHWISE
POLYGAMIST
POLYGAMOUS
PYRAGYRITE
PYROGRAPHY
RECOGNISED
RECOGNIZED
RELEGATION
REORGANIZE
REPUGNANCE
RESIGNEDLY
RUBIGINOUS
SANDGROPER
SAVAGENESS
SELEGILINE
SENEGALESE
SEXAGESIMA
SLUGGISHLY
SNIGGERING
SPONGEWARE
SPONGIFORM
STAGGERING
STINGINESS
STINGYBARK
STRAGGLING
STROGANOFF
SWAGGERING
TAILGATING
TANAGRIDAE
TELEGRAPHY
THINGUMBOB
THOUGHTFUL
TOPOGRAPHY
TYPOGRAPHY
UNARGUABLE
UNDIGESTED
UNHYGIENIC
VICEGERENT
VINEGARISH
VOETGANGER
VORAGINOUS
WHIGGAMORE
WRONGDOING
WRONGFULLY
YOUNGBERRY
ZABAGLIONE
ACEPHALOUS
AESTHETICS
AHITHOPHEL
ALCOHOLISM
ALMSHOUSES
ANACHARSIS
ANNIHILATE
ANSCHAUUNG
APOPHTHEGM
APOTHECARY
APOTHECIUM
APOTHEOSIS
ARITHMETIC
BACCHANTES
BACKHANDED
BACKHANDER
BARCHESTER
BAREHEADED
BEDCHAMBER
BELSHAZZAR
BENTHAMITE
BIOCHEMIST
BIOPHYSICS
BIORHYTHMS
BIRTHPLACE
BIRTHRIGHT
BLEPHARISM
BLITHERING
BOLSHEVIST
BONDHOLDER
BRACHIOPOD
BRIGHTNESS
BULLHEADED
BUTCHERING
CARPHOLOGY
CARTHAMINE
CARTHUSIAN
CATCHPENNY
CHICHESTER
CIRRHOPODA
CLODHOPPER
COATHANGER
COLCHESTER
COLCHICINE
CONCHIGLIE
CONCHIOLIN
CONCHOLOGY
COPYHOLDER
DARKHAIRED
DECAHEDRON
DELPHINIUM
DIAPHANOUS
DIOPHANTOS
DRUZHINNIK
DUTCHWOMAN
EARTHQUAKE
EARTHWORKS
EPIPHONEMA
EPITHELIUM
EVENHANDED
EXOTHERMIC
FAIRHAIRED
FAITHFULLY
FEATHERBED
FILTHINESS
FIRTHSOKEN
FLASHINESS
FLASHLIGHT
FLASHPOINT
FLESHINESS
FLIGHTLESS
FORTHRIGHT
FREEHANDER
FREEHOLDER
FRESHWATER
FRIGHTENED
FRITHSOKEN
FROGHOPPER
GEOPHYSICS
GEOTHERMAL
GRAPHOLOGY
GUACHAMOLE
HALFHOURLY
HAMSHACKLE
HEADHUNTED
HEADHUNTER
HEMIHEDRON
HIGHHANDED
HITCHHIKER
HOTCHPOTCH
ICHTHYOSIS
INCOHERENT
IRISHWOMAN
IRISHWOMEN
JACKHAMMER
KINCHINLAY
KNIGHTHOOD
LANTHANIDE
LEAFHOPPER
LEFTHANDED
LEFTHANDER
LEUCHAEMIA
MALTHUSIAN
MANCHESTER
MANCHINEEL
MARSHALSEA
MATCHMAKER
MATCHSTALK
MATCHSTICK
MIDSHIPMAN
MISCHMETAL
MORPHOLOGY
MOUCHARABY
MOUTHORGAN
MOUTHPIECE
MUJAHEDDIN
NAPTHALENE
NEIGHBORLY
NONCHALANT
NORTHANGER
NORTHBOUND
NORTHERNER
NORTHSTEAD
NORTHWARDS
NYMPHOLEPT
OCTAHEDRON
OFFTHECUFF
OFFTHEWALL
OMOPHORION
OPENHANDED
OPHTHALMIC
OPOTHERAPY
PARTHENOPE
PATCHCOCKE
PATCHINESS
PEACHERINO
PEASHOOTER
PERIHELION
PINCHPENNY
PITCHSTONE
PLIOHIPPUS
POCAHONTAS
POLYHEDRON
POLYHYMNIA
PONCHIELLI
POSTHUMOUS
PROPHETESS
PSEPHOLOGY
PSYCHIATRY
PSYCHOLOGY
PSYCHOPATH
PSYCHOPOMP
PUMPHANDLE
PUNCHDRUNK
RAMSHACKLE
RESCHEDULE
RHYTHMICAL
ROUGHHOUSE
SACCHARASE
SACCHARIDE
SACCHARINE
SACCHAROID
SCAPHOPODA
SCATHELESS
SHAGHAIRED
SHISHKEBAB
SINGHALESE
SMITHEREEN
SNAPHAUNCE
SNAPHAUNCH
SOOTHINGLY
SOOTHSAYER
SOUTHBOUND
SOUTHERNER
SOUTHWARDS
STADHOLDER
STALHELMER
STAPHYLINE
STEPHANITE
STEPHENSON
STICHARION
STOCHASTIC
SULPHUROUS
SYMPHONIUM
SYNTHESIZE
SYNTHRONUS
TANNHAUSER
TEICHOPSIA
TELPHERAGE
TESCHENITE
TOOTHBRUSH
TOOTHPASTE
TORCHLIGHT
TOUCHANDGO
TOUCHINESS
TOUCHPAPER
TOUCHPIECE

TOUCHSTONE
TRACHELATE
TRICHOLOGY
TROCHANTER
TROCHOTRON
TROPHONIUS
TRUTHFULLY
UNSCHOOLED
WANCHANCIE
WANTHRIVEN
WATCHFULLY
WATCHMAKER
WATCHTOWER
WEATHERMAN
WEIGHTLESS
WELSHWOMAN
WINCHESTER
WITCHCRAFT
WORSHIPPER
WORTHINESS
WORTHWHILE
ZOOTHAPSIS
ZOOTHERAPY
ABOMINABLE
ABOMINABLY
ABORIGINAL
ABSCISSION
ABSTINENCE
ACCLIVIOUS
AFFLICTION
AFICIONADO
AGONISTICS
ALCAICERIA
AMELIORATE
AMPHIBIOUS
AMPHIBRACH
AMPHICTYON
AMPHIGOURI
AMPHIMACER
AMPHIMIXIS
AMPHINEURA
AMPHITRITE
AMPHITRYON
ANAXIMENES
ANGUILLULA
APPLICABLE
APPLICATOR
ARCHIMEDES
ARCHITRAVE
ASCRIBABLE
ASTRINGENT
ATTAINABLE
ATTAINMENT
AUCTIONEER
AUSPICIOUS
AVARICIOUS
BAILIEWICK
BALLISTICS
BALLISTITE
BARBITURIC
BARMITZVAH
BASSINGTON
BESTIALITY
BIRMINGHAM
BOOZINGKEN
BOTTICELLI
BOURIGNIAN
BOUSINGKEN
BRATISLAVA
BRITISHISM
BUCCINATOR
BUCKINGHAM
BURLINGTON
CACHINNATE
CALLIATURE
CANCIONERO
CANTILEVER
CANTILLATE
CAPRICIOUS
CAPTIVATED
CARCINOGEN
CARDIOGRAM
CARDIOLOGY
CASSIABARK
CASSIOPEIA
CAUTIONARY
CAUTIOUSLY
CENTIGRADE
CENTILITER
CENTILITRE
CENTIMETER
CENTIMETRE
CERTIORARI
CHARIOTEER
CHARITABLE
CHARITABLY
CHEMICALLY
CHERIMOYER
CHEVISANCE
CHIRICAUNE
CIRRIPEDEA
CIRRIPEDIA
CLAVICHORD
CLINICALLY
CLOMIPHENE
COCCINEOUS
COEXISTENT
COGNISANCE
COGNIZANCE
COLLIMATOR
COLLIQUATE
COMMISSARY
COMMISSION
COMMISSURE
COMMITMENT
COMMIXTURE
CONCILIATE
CONCINNITY
CONCINNOUS
CONDIMENTS
CONFIDANTE
CONFIDENCE
CONFISCATE
CONNIPTION
CONNIVANCE
CONSIDERED
CONSISTENT
CONSISTORY
CONTIGUITY
CONTIGUOUS
CONTINENCE
CONTINGENT
CONTINUING
CONTINUITY
CONTINUOUS
CONVICTION
CONVINCING
COQUIMBITE
CORDIALITY
CORDIERITE
CORDILLERA
CORRIGENDA
COTTIERISM
CREDITABLE
CREDITABLY
CRIMINALLY
CRITICALLY
CULTIVATED
CULTIVATOR
CURRICULUM
DEBRIEFING
DELTIOLOGY
DEMOISELLE
DENTIFRICE
DERAILLEUR
DERAILMENT
DESPICABLE
DESPITEOUS
DESSIATINE
DETAINMENT
DICTIONARY
DIFFICULTY
DIFFIDENCE
DISCIPLINE
DISFIGURED
DISMISSIVE
DISPIRITED
DISSIDENCE
DISSILIENT
DISSIMILAR
DISSIPATED
DISTILLATE
DISTILLERY
DISTILLING
DISTINCTLY
DITHIONATE
DUPLICATOR
ELIMINATOR
EMACIATION
EMPFINDUNG
ENCOIGNURE
ENGLISHMAN
ENGLISHMEN
EPIDIDYMUS
EPIDIORITE
EPILIMNION
ERYSIPELAS
ESCRITOIRE
EXOTICALLY
EXPLICABLE
EXPLICITLY
EYEWITNESS
FACTITIOUS
FALDISTORY
FALLINGOFF
FASCIATION
FASCINATED
FASCINATOR
FASTIDIOUS
FASTIGIATE
FERNITICLE
FERTILISED
FERTILISER
FERTILIZER
FIBRILLATE
FICTITIOUS
FILLIBRUSH
FISTICUFFS
FLAGITIOUS
FLAMINGANT
FLORIBUNDA
FONTICULUS
FONTINALIS
FORBIDDING
FORGIVABLE
FORMIDABLE
FORTINBRAS
FORTISSIMO
FOSSILIZED
FOURIERISM
FRATICELLI
FRAXINELLA
FRITILLARY
FROLICSOME
FULFILMENT
FUNGICIDAL
FURNISHING
GALLIAMBIC
GARNIERITE
GERMICIDAL
GINGIVITIS
GLACIATION
GLORIOUSLY
GOLDILOCKS
GRACIOUSLY
GRAMICIDIN
GRATIFYING
GRATILLITY
GRIDIRONER
GUTTIFERAE
HANDICRAFT
HARRINGTON
HECTICALLY
HEROICALLY
HORRIFYING
HOSPITABLE
HOSPITABLY
IMAGINABLE
IMBRICATED
IMPAIRMENT
IMPLICITLY
IMPRIMATUR
INELIGIBLE
INEVITABLE
INEVITABLY
INFLICTION
INIMITABLE
INITIATION
INITIATIVE
INQUIRENDO
INQUISITOR
INSPISSATE
INSTIGATOR
INTRIGUING
IRONICALLY
ISONIAZIDE
JARDINIERE
JUSTICIARY
KUOMINTANG
LASCIVIOUS
LATTICINIO
LEAMINGTON
LEMNISCATE
LENTICULAR
LENTIGINES
LESBIANISM
LIQUIDATOR
LIQUIDIZER
LITHISTADA
MACKINTOSH
MAGNIFICAT
MAGNIFYING
MAQUILLAGE
MARCIONITE
MARGINALIA
MARGINALLY
MARTINGALE
MARTINIQUE
MASKINONGE
MASKIROVKA
MATRIARCHY
MAURITANIA
MEANINGFUL
MERCIFULLY
MILLIMETER
MILLIMETRE
MISGIVINGS
MISSIONARY
MONTICULUS
MORBIDEZZA

MOUDIEWART
MULLIGRUBS
MULTIMEDIA
MULTIPLIED
MULTIPLIER
NARCISSISM
NEGLIGENCE
NEGLIGIBLE
NEURILEMMA
NONFICTION
NONVIOLENT
NOURISHING
NUTRITIOUS
OBEDIENTLY
OBTAINABLE
OFFLICENCE
ORCHIDEOUS
ORIDINANCE
ORIGINALLY
ORIGINATOR
PADDINGTON
PAEDIATRIC
PALLIATIVE
PANNICULUS
PARLIAMENT
PARTIALITY
PARTICIPLE
PARTICULAR
PARTINGALE
PASSIONATE
PATRIARCHY
PATRIOTISM
PENNILLION
PENNISETUM
PENSIEROSO
PENSIONNAT
PENTIMENTO
PERCIPIENT
PERDITIOUS
PERFICIENT
PERFIDIOUS
PERMISSION
PERMISSIVE
PERNICIOUS
PERNICKETY
PERSICARIA
PERSIENNES
PERSIFLAGE
PERSISTENT
PERTINENCE
PESTILENCE
PETRIFYING
PETRISSAGE
PETTICHAPS
PHILIPPINA
PHILIPPINE
PHILISTINE
PHOLIDOSIS
PHYSICALLY
PHYSIOCRAT

PHYSIOLOGY
PICHICIAGO
PILLIWINKS
PINNIPEDIA
PISTILLATE
PLAGIARISE
PLAGIARISM
PLAGIARIST
PLAGIARIZE
PLATINISED
PLEBISCITE
PLESIOSAUR
PLEXIMETER
POETICALLY
POIKILITIC
POLLINATED
PONTICELLO
PONTIFICAL
PORTIONIST
POSTILLATE
POSTILLION
PRATINCOLE
PRAXITELES
PRECIPITIN
PREDICTION
PREDISPOSE
PREHISTORY
PRESIDENCY
PRETINCOLE
PREVIOUSLY
PRIVILEGED
PROAIRESIS
PRODIGALLY
PRODIGIOUS
PROFICIENT
PROFITABLE
PROFITABLY
PROFITLESS
PROHIBITED
PROMINENCE
PROMISSORY
PROPIONATE
PROPITIATE
PROPITIOUS
PROSILIENT
PROVIDENCE
PROVINCIAL
PROVISIONS
PUBLISHING
PUNDIGRION
QUIRINALIA
RABBINICAL
REAMINGBIT
REPAIRABLE
REQUIESCAT
RESPIRATOR
RHIPIPTERA
ROCKINGHAM
ROLLICKING
SALPINGIAN

SALTIGRADE
SANDINISTA
SCHLIMAZEL
SEGUIDILLA
SELLINGERS
SERVICEMAN
SIGNIFICAT
SORDIDNESS
SPECIALISE
SPECIALIST
SPECIALITY
SPECIALIZE
SPECIOUSLY
SPIRITEDLY
SPIRITLESS
SPIRITUOUS
SPOLIATION
SPOLIATIVE
SPURIOUSLY
STABILISER
STABILIZER
STANISLAUS
STATIONARY
STATIONERY
STATISTICS
STERILISER
STERILIZER
STRAIGHTEN
STRAITENED
STUDIOUSLY
STYLISTICS
SUBLIMATER
SUBLIMINAL
SUBMISSION
SUBMISSIVE
SUBSIDENCE
SUBSIDIARY
SUBSISTENT
SUCCINCTLY
SUFFICIENT
SURGICALLY
SUSPICIOUS
SVADILFARI
SYNEIDESIS
SYPHILITIC
TACTICALLY
TAGLIARINI
TARDIGRADE
TEDDINGTON
TERMINABLE
TERMINALIA
TERMINALLY
TERRIFYING
TERTIARIES
TESTICULAR
THALICTRUM
TIRAILLEUR
TOILINETTE
TORRICELLI
TOSSICATED

TOSTICATED
TRADITIONS
TRAGICALLY
TRILINGUAL
TRIVIALITY
TRIVIALIZE
TURRITELLA
UNBLINKING
UNCRITICAL
UNEDIFYING
UNFAITHFUL
UNFRIENDLY
UNORIGINAL
UNSUITABLE
UNTHINKING
UPBRINGING
UTILIZABLE
VARNISHING
VENTILATOR
VERMICELLI
VERMILLION
VERNISSAGE
VERTICALLY
VESTIBULUM
VINDICTIVE
WASHINGTON
WELLINGTON
WIDDICOMBE
WILLIAMSON
WILLINGDON
WOFFINGTON
WYCLIFFIAN
YAFFINGALE
BEAUJOLAIS
BUCKJUMPER
COADJUTANT
SHOWJUMPER
WINDJAMMER
BLACKBEARD
BLACKBERRY
BLACKBOARD
BLACKBULLY
BLACKENING
BLACKGUARD
BLACKHEART
BLACKSHIRT
BLACKSMITH
BLACKSTONE
BLACKTHORN
BLACKWATER
BLOCKHOUSE
BOOKKEEPER
BREAKABLES
BREAKWATER
BRICKLAYER
BRICKWORKS
CHECKLATON
CHECKPOINT
CHEEKINESS
CHICKENPOX

CHUCKWALLA
CLOCKMAKER
CRANKSHAFT
CRICKETING
CROCKFORDS
CRUIKSHANK
DIASKEUAST
DOORKEEPER
DREIKANTER
DRINKWATER
FLICKERING
FLUNKEYDOM
FRISKINESS
GAMEKEEPER
GOALKEEPER
KNOBKERRIE
KNOCKABOUT
LADYKILLER
LOCKKEEPER
MUDSKIPPER
NOUAKCHOTT
PAINKILLER
PINAKOTHEK
PRICKLOUSE
QUICKSANDS
QUICKTHORN
SHACKLETON
SHECKLATON
SHOCKINGLY
SHOCKPROOF
SHOPKEEPER
SNORKELING
SPEAKERINE
SPIRKETING
STEAKHOUSE
STICKINESS
STICKYBEAK
STOCKINESS
STRIKINGLY
THANKFULLY
THICKENING
TIMEKEEPER
TOLLKEEPER
TRICKINESS
TRISKELION
WEEDKILLER
ABSOLUTELY
ABSOLUTION
ABSOLUTISM
ACCELERATE
ADULLAMITE
AFFILIATED
ALGOLAGNIA
ALKALINITY
AMBULACRUM
AMBULATORY
AMPELOPSIS
ANACLASTIC
ANDALUSIAN
ANDALUSITE

ANHELATION
APOLLONIAN
APOLLONIUS
APOPLECTIC
ARGOLEMONO
BABYLONIAN
BAFFLEMENT
BAILLIWICK
BANGLADESH
BARELEGGED
BATTLEDOOR
BATTLEDORE
BATTLEMENT
BATTLESHIP
BEDCLOTHES
BETELGEUSE
BETELGEUZE
BEWILDERED
BOOTLEGGER
BOOTLICKER
BOTTLEHEAD
BOTTLENECK
BOUILLOTTE
BOWDLERISE
BOWDLERIZE
BRIDLEPATH
BRILLIANCE
BUFFLEHEAD
BURGLARIZE
CAMELOPARD
CANDLEFISH
CANDLEWICK
CAPILLAIRE
CARELESSLY
CATALECTIC
CATALEPTIC
CATALOGUER
CATTLEGRID
CAVALRYMAN
CHALLENGER
CHAPLAINCY
CHAULMUGRA
CHILLINESS
CHURLISHLY
COCHLEARIA
COMPLACENT
COMPLANATE
COMPLEMENT
COMPLETELY
COMPLETION
COMPLEXION
COMPLEXITY
COMPLIANCE
COMPLICATE
COMPLICITY
COMPLIMENT
COMPLUVIUM
CONCLUDING
CONCLUSION
CONCLUSIVE
CONFLUENCE
COPULATION
COSTLINESS
CUCULLATED
CUDDLESOME
CUMULATIVE
CUTTLEBONE
CUTTLEFISH
DEADLINESS
DEBILITATE
DECELERATE
DECOLLATOR
DECOLORATE
DEFILEMENT
DEMOLITION
DEPILATORY
DESALINATE
DESOLATION
DEVELOPING
DEVOLUTION
DISCLAIMER
DISCLOSURE
DOPPLERITE
DOUBLEBASS
DOUBLETALK
DUMBLEDORE
EBOULEMENT
EBULLIENCE
ECTHLIPSIS
ENROLLMENT
EPAULEMENT
EPIGLOTTIS
EPIPLASTRA
ESCALATION
ESCULAPIAN
ETHYLAMINE
EUCALYPTUS
EUCHLORINE
EXCELLENCE
EXCELLENCY
EXHALATION
EXHILARATE
FABULOUSLY
FACILITATE
FACILITIES
FALKLANDER
FAMILIARLY
FATALISTIC
FATALITIES
FEARLESSLY
FEEBLENESS
FEUILLETON
FICKLENESS
FIDDLEWOOD
FOOTLIGHTS
FREELANCER
FREELOADER
FULLLENGTH
GADOLINIUM
GENTLEFOLK
GENTLENESS
GIRDLERINK
GRIDLOCKED
GUILLOTINE
HABILITATE
HANDLEBARS
HEADLIGHTS
HEEDLESSLY
HELPLESSLY
HIGHLANDER
HOMELINESS
HOPELESSLY
HUMBLENESS
IDEALISTIC
IMMOLATION
IMPALPABLE
IMPALUDISM
IMPOLITELY
INDELICACY
INDELICATE
INDULGENCE
INFALLIBLE
INFALLIBLY
INFILTRATE
INHALATION
INKSLINGER
INSOLENTLY
INSOLVENCY
INSULARITY
INSULATION
INTELIGENT
INTOLERANT
INVALIDATE
INVALIDITY
INVALUABLE
IRRELEVANT
JACULATION
JOCULARITY
JUBILANTLY
JUBILATION
KENILWORTH
KETTLEDRUM
KINDLINESS
LACKLUSTER
LACKLUSTRE
LANDLOCKED
LANDLOUPER
LANDLUBBER
LAVALLIÈRE
LEGALISTIC
LIKELIHOOD
LISTLESSLY
LITTLENESS
LIVELIHOOD
LIVELINESS
LOCULAMENT
LONELINESS
LORDLINESS
LOVELINESS
MARYLEBONE
MATELLASSE
MEDDLESOME
MEGALITHIC
MEGALOSAUR
MESOLITHIC
METALEPSIS
METALLURGY
METTLESOME
MODULATION
MONILIASIS
MONILIFORM
MONOLITHIC
MORALITIES
MUMBLENEWS
MUTILATION
NEEDLECASE
NEEDLEWORK
NETTLERASH
NETTLETREE
NEWSLETTER
NIHILISTIC
NIMBLENESS
NONALIGNED
NONPLUSSED
OSCILLATOR
OSCULATION
OSCULATORY
OVERLANDER
PAINLESSLY
PARALLELED
PARKLEAVES
PECULATION
PECULIARLY
PENELOPHON
PERILOUSLY
PERPLEXING
PERPLEXITY
PETULANTLY
PHAELONIAN
PHILLIPINA
PHILLIPINE
PHILLUMENY
PHYLLIOPOD
POPULARITY
POPULARIZE
POPULATION
POSTLIMINY
PROCLIVITY
PROFLIGACY
PROFLIGATE
PROPLITEAL
PUZZLEMENT
RANDLETREE
RANNLETREE
RANTLETREE
RATTLETRAP
REBELLIOUS
RECKLESSLY
REGULARITY
REGULARIZE
REGULATION
RESILIENCE
RESOLUTELY
RESOLUTION
RESTLESSLY
REVELATION
REVOLUTION
RIGELATION
RINGLEADER
RUDOLPHINE
RUMBLOSSOM
RUTHLESSLY
SADDLEBACK
SADDLEBILL
SCARLATINA
SCARLETINA
SCHALSTEIN
SCHOLAEMIA
SCHOLASTIC
SECULARIZE
SEDULOUSLY
SEEMLIHEAD
SEPULCHRAL
SETTLEMENT
SEXOLOGIST
SHELLSHOCK
SHELLYCOAT
SHIELDRAKE
SHILLELAGH
SHOPLIFTER
SHRILLNESS
SICILIENNE
SIGILLARIA
SIMILARITY
SIMILITUDE
SIMILLIMUM
SIMPLICITY
SIMPLISTIC
SIMULACRUM
SIMULATING
SIMULATION
SINGLENESS
SKILLFULLY
SMALLSCALE
SPALLATION
SPELLBOUND
SPHALERITE
SPIFLICATE
SPILLIKINS
SPOILSPORT
SPOTLESSLY
STALLENGER
STALLINGER
STEALTHILY
STEELINESS
STEELWORKS
STEPLADDER
STILLBIRTH
STILLICIDE
STILLIFORM

STILLSTAND
STRELITZIA
STRULDBERG
STRULDBRUG
SUNGLASSES
SUPPLEJACK
SUPPLEMENT
SUPPLENESS
SUPPLICANT
SUPPLICATE
SWALLOWING
TABULATION
TACTLESSLY
TANGLEFOOT
THALLIFORM
THELLUSSON
THEOLOGATE
THEOLOGIAN
THEOLOGISE
THEOLOGIST
TIMELINESS
TIRELESSLY
TOPOLOGIST
TRICLINIUM
TRIPLICATE
TROGLODYTE
TUMBLEDOWN
TUMULTUOUS
TURTLEDOVE
TURTLENECK
UMBELLIFER
UNBALANCED
UNBELIEVER
UNCULTURED
UNDULATING
UNDULATION
UNRELIABLE
UNRELIEVED
UNRULINESS
UNSALARIED
UPHOLSTERY
VIGILANTES
VIROLOGIST
VIRULENTLY
VITELLICLE
WATTLEWORK
WAVELENGTH
WENTLETRAP
WHEELCHAIR
WHEELHOUSE
WHILLYWHAW
WHIRLYBIRD
WOOLLYBACK
WOOLLYBUTT
ZEUGLODONT
ACCOMPLICE
ACCOMPLISH
ACCUMULATE
ACROMEGALY
ADRAMELECH
ANTIMASQUE
ANTIMATTER
ANTIMONIAN
AQUAMANALE
AQUAMANILE
AQUAMARINE
ASSEMBLAGE
ASSEMBLING
ASSIMILATE
ASSUMPTION
ASSUMPTIVE
ASTOMATOUS
ASYMMETRIC
ATRAMENTAL
AUTOMATION
AUTOMOBILE
AUTOMOTIVE
BANDMASTER
BAROMETRIC
BITUMINOUS
BLOOMSBURY
BLUEMANTLE
BOOKMARKER
BOOKMOBILE
BROOMSTICK
BUCHMANISM
CACOMISTLE
CACUMINOUS
CALAMANDER
CALAMITOUS
CALAMONDIN
CALUMNIATE
CARAMELIZE
CEREMONIAL
CEREMONIES
CHREMATIST
CHROMOSOME
CLAMMINESS
COROMANDEL
CYNOMOLGUS
DECAMPMENT
DECIMALIZE
DECOMPOSED
DEFAMATION
DEFAMATORY
DHARMSHALA
DIREMPTION
DISEMBOGUE
DISEMBOWEL
DOCIMASTIC
DOWNMARKET
DREAMINESS
DYNAMITARD
EFFEMINACY
EFFEMINATE
ENCAMPMENT
ENORMOUSLY
ENTOMBMENT
ENTOMOLOGY
ESTIMATION
EUHEMERISM
EXHUMATION
FASTMOVING
FISHMONGER
FREEMARTIN
FREEMASONS
GALIMATIAS
GALUMPHING
GLEEMAIDEN
GOBEMOUCHE
GRAMMARIAN
HACKMATACK
HALLMARKED
HANDMAIDEN
HEADMASTER
IGNIMBRITE
ILLUMINATE
ILLUMINATI
IMMEMORIAL
INCOMPLETE
INCUMBENCY
INDUMENTUM
INGEMINATE
INHUMANITY
INSEMINATE
INTEMERATE
INTIMATELY
INTIMATION
INTIMIDATE
IRONMONGER
IRREMEDIAL
KHIDMUTGAR
KILOMETRES
LASTMINUTE
LEGUMINOUS
LIKEMINDED
LOCOMOTION
LOCOMOTIVE
LUXEMBOURG
MAHOMMEDAN
MAXIMALIST
MAXIMILIAN
MINIMALIST
MINIMARKET
MONUMENTAL
MOZAMBIQUE
NEWSMONGER
NONSMOKING
OBLOMOVISM
OPENMINDED
OPTIMISTIC
ORNAMENTAL
PALIMPSEST
PANAMANIAN
PARAMARIBO
PARAMETRIC
PEDIMENTAL
PEREMPTORY
PHARMACIST
PLASMODESM
POCKMANTIE
POCKMARKED
POLYMERIZE
PORTMANTLE
PORTMANTUA
POSTMASTER
PRAEMUNIRE
PRAGMATISM
PRAGMATIST
PREEMINENT
PSAMMOPHIL
PYROMANIAC
QUIZMASTER
RAGAMUFFIN
RAZZMATAZZ
REARMAMENT
RECOMMENCE
RECOMPENSE
REDEMPTION
REGIMENTAL
REGIMENTED
RESEMBLING
RESUMPTION
RHEUMATICS
RHEUMATISM
RHEUMATOID
RINGMASTER
ROSEMALING
RUDIMENTAL
SALAMANDER
SCAMMOZZIS
SCRIMSHANK
SEISMOLOGY
SHIMMERING
SKRIMSHANK
SLAMMERKIN
SMARMINESS
SNOWMOBILE
SPERMACETI
STAMMERING
STEPMOTHER
STIGMATISE
STIGMATIZE
STRAMONIUM
SWIMMINGLY
TASKMASTER
THAUMASITE
THERMIONIC
THERMISTOR
THERMOSTAT
THROMBOSIS
TOURMALINE
TRAUMATIZE
TRIUMPHANT
UBERMENSCH
ULTIMATELY
UNCOMMONLY
UNFAMILIAR
UNHAMPERED
UNNUMBERED
UNROMANTIC
VEHEMENTLY
VOLUMINOUS
ABONNEMENT
ACCENTUATE
ACRONYCHAL
ADMINISTER
ADMONITION
ADRENALINE
ADVENTURER
AERENCHYMA
AGRONOMIST
ALGONQUIAN
ALIENATION
ALPENSTOCK
AMMUNITION
ANNUNCIATE
ANTINOMIAN
ASCENDANCY
ASCENDENCY
ASTONISHED
ATHANASIAN
ATTENDANCE
AUTONOMOUS
BALANCHINE
BEHINDHAND
BELONGINGS
BIANNUALLY
BIENNIALLY
BIPINNARIA
BRAINCHILD
BRAININESS
BRAINPOWER
BRAINSTORM
BROWNSTONE
CATENACCIO
CHIMNEYPOT
CHRONICLER
CHRONICLES
CHRONOLOGY
COLONNADED
COMANCHERO
COPENHAGEN
CORINTHIAN
CORONATION
COVENANTER
DEADNETTLE
DECENNOVAL
DEFENSIBLE
DEFINITELY
DEFINITION
DEFINITIVE
DEGENERACY
DEGENERATE
DELINQUENT
DEMONIACAL
DEPENDABLE
DEPENDENCE
DEPENDENCY
DETONATION

DEVANAGARI
DIAGNOSTIC
DICYNODONT
DIDUNCULUS
DIMINISHED
DIMINUENDO
DIMINUTION
DIMINUTIVE
DINANDERIE
DISENCHANT
DISENGAGED
DISENNOBLE
DISINCLINE
DISINHERIT
DIURNALIST
DIVINATION
DOMINATING
DOMINATION
EATANSWILL
ECHINODERM
ECHINOIDEA
EMBANKMENT
EMBONPOINT
EMMENTALER
ENGENDRURE
ENSANGUINE
EQUANIMITY
ERGONOMICS
ESTANCIERO
EXPENDABLE
EXTENDABLE
EXTENSIBLE
EXTINCTION
EXTINGUISH
FEARNOUGHT
FEMININITY
FORINSECAL
FRAUNHOFER
FRIENDLESS
FRIENDSHIP
GEMINATION
GESUNDHEIT
GREENCLOTH
GREENFINCH
GREENHEART
GREENHOUSE
GREENSHANK
GREENSTICK
GREENSWARD
GROUNDBAIT
GROUNDLESS
GROUNDLING
GROUNDSMAN
GROUNDWORK
GUARNERIUS
HAKENKREUZ
HEDONISTIC
HOMUNCULUS
HOOTNANNIE
HUMANISTIC
HUMANITIES
IMMUNOLOGY
IMPENITENT
INCENDIARY
INCINERATE
INCONSTANT
INCUNABULA
INDENTURES
INDONESIAN
INFINITELY
INFINITIVE
INGENERATE
INJUNCTION
INSANITARY
INSENSIBLE
INTANGIBLE
INTENDMENT
INTENERATE
INTENTNESS
INTINCTION
INTONATION
INVINCIBLE
JOURNALESE
JOURNALISM
JOURNALIST
JOURNEYMAN
JUGENDSTIL
LAMENTABLE
LAMENTABLY
LAMINATION
LARYNGITIS
LEBENSRAUM
LICENTIATE
LICENTIOUS
LOGANBERRY
LUMINARIST
LUMINOSITY
LYCHNAPSIA
LYSENKOISM
MABINOGION
MACONOCHIE
MAKUNOUCHI
MALINGERER
MAYONNAISE
MELANCHOLY
MELANESIAN
MENINGITIS
MESENTERON
MISHNAYOTH
MOLENDINAR
MOURNFULLY
MUTINOUSLY
MYRINGITIS
NDRANGHETA
NEFANDROUS
NOMINALIST
NOMINATION
NOMINATIVE
NONONSENSE
OCEANGOING
OFTENTIMES
ORDINARILY
ORDINATION
ORDONNANCE
OSTENSIBLE
OSTENSIBLY
PAGINATION
PALINDROME
PARANORMAL
PARENCHYMA
PARENTHOOD
PARENTLESS
PARONYCHIA
PENINSULAR
PHAENOTYPE
PHRENESIAC
PHRENOLOGY
PIRANDELLO
PLEONASTIC
POGONOTOMY
POIGNANTLY
POLYNESIAN
POTENTIATE
POTENTILLA
PREDNISONE
QUAINTNESS
QUEENSBURY
QUEENSTOWN
RANUNCULUS
RAVENOUSLY
RAVENSBILL
RAVENSDUCK
RAVENSTONE
RAWINSONDE
RECONCILED
RECONSIDER
REDUNDANCY
REFINEMENT
REGENERATE
REJONEADOR
RELENTLESS
RELINQUISH
REMONETISE
REMUNERATE
REPENTANCE
RESENTMENT
RETINALITE
REVENGEFUL
RIDINGHOOD
RIPSNORTER
ROLANDSECK
ROMANESQUE
ROSANILINE
RUBINSTEIN
RUMINANTIA
RUMINATION
RUMINATIVE
SAVONAROLA
SCIENTIFIC
SCORNFULLY
SEANNACHIE
SECONDBEST
SECONDHAND
SECONDMENT
SECONDRATE
SEVENTIETH
SPLANCHNIC
SPLENDIDLY
SPOONERISM
SPRINGBOKS
SPRINGHAAS
SPRINGLESS
SPRINGLIKE
SPRINGTAIL
SPRINGTIME
SPRINKLING
STAGNATION
STERNALGIA
STRENGTHEN
STRINDBERG
STRINGENCY
STRINGENDO
STRINGHALT
STRONGHOLD
STRONGROOM
SURINAMESE
SYNONYMOUS
TARANTELLA
TAXONOMIST
TECHNETIUM
TECHNICIAN
TECHNOCRAT
TECHNOLOGY
THRENODIAL
TOURNAMENT
TOURNIQUET
TRIANGULAR
TYRANNICAL
TYRANNISED
UNCONFINED
UNDENIABLE
UNFINISHED
UNMANNERED
UNMANNERLY
UNPUNCTUAL
VALENTINES
VIETNAMESE
VIVANDIÈRE
WAPENSCHAW
WAPINSCHAW
WITSNAPPER
YTHUNDERED
ACHROMATIC
ACOLOUTHOS
ACTIONABLE
ALCYONARIA
ALPHONSINE
AMPHOTERIC
ANACOUSTIC
ANALOGICAL
ANATOMICAL
ANCHORETIC
ANDROMACHE
ANEMOGRAPH
ANEMOMETER
ANGIOSPERM
ANGLOPHILE
ANGLOPHOBE
ANTHOCLORE
ANTIOCHENE
ANTIOCHIAN
APOLOGETIC
ARACOSTYLE
ARAGONITES
ASAFOETIDA
ASTROLOGER
ASTRONOMER
AUTHORISED
AUTHORSHIP
AXINOMANCY
BALLOONING
BALLOONIST
BAMBOOZLED
BASSOONIST
BERMOOTHES
BIOLOGICAL
BORROWINGS
BOTTOMLESS
BUFFOONERY
BUTTONDOWN
BUTTONHOLE
CANNONBALL
CANTONMENT
CAPNOMANCY
CARTOMANCY
CARTOONIST
CASSOLETTE
CATHOLICON
CATHOLICOS
CELLOPHANE
CENSORIOUS
CENSORSHIP
CHAROLLAIS
CHEMONASTY
CHIROMANCY
CHIRONOMIC
CHIROPTERA
CISPONTINE
CITRONELLA
CLAMOURING
CLEROMANCY
CNIDOBLAST
COLEOPTERA
COLEORHIZA
COLLOCUTER
COLLOQUIAL
COLPORTAGE
COLPORTEUR
COLPOSCOPE
COMFORTING

COMMODIOUS
COMMONWEAL
COMPOSITOR
COMPOUNDED
CONCOCTION
CONCORDANT
CONDOLENCE
CONDOTTIER
CONFORMIST
CONFORMITY
CONFOUNDED
CONSONANCE
CONSONANTS
CONSORTIUM
CONTORTION
CONVOLUTED
CONVOLVUTE
CORROBOREE
COTTONTAIL
COTTONWOOD
COXCOMICAL
CTENOPHORA
CUCKOOPINT
CYCLOPEDIA
CYCLOSTYLE
CYSTOSCOPY
DEPLORABLE
DEPLORABLY
DEPLOYMENT
DESBOROUGH
DESPONDENT
DEUTOPLASM
DIABOLICAL
DIACONICON
DIAGONALLY
DICTOGRAPH
DIPLODOCUS
DIPLOMATIC
DIPSOMANIA
DISCOBOLUS
DISCOLORED
DISCOMFORT
DISCOMMODE
DISCOMPOSE
DISCONCERT
DISCONNECT
DISCONTENT
DISCOPHORA
DISCORDANT
DISCOURAGE
DISCOVERER
DISHONESTY
DISJOINTED
DISLOYALTY
DISPOSABLE
DISPOSSESS
DISSOCIATE
DISSOLVENT
DISSONANCE
DISTORTION
DOSTOEVSKY
DRACONITES
DROSOPHILA
ECOLOGICAL
ECONOMICAL
EFFRONTERY
EMBROIDERY
EMPLOYMENT
ENCLOISTER
ENGROSSING
EPANOPHORA
ETHEOSTOMA
EUDIOMETER
EUPHONIOUS
EVAPORATED
FANTOCCINI
FELLOWSHIP
FIBROSITIS
FLAVOURING
FOREORDAIN
FORFOUGHEN
GARGOUILLE
GASCONNADE
GEOLOGICAL
GLAMOURISE
GONDOLIERS
GONIOMETER
GRAMOPHONE
GYMNOSOPHY
GYPSOPHILA
HALLOYSITE
HARMONIOUS
HECTOLITRE
HELIOGRAPH
HELIOLATER
HELIOTROPE
HIEROGLYPH
HIEROMANCY
HIEROPHANT
HIEROSCOPY
HIPPOCRENE
HIPPODROME
HIPPOGRIFF
HIPPOGRYPH
HIPPOMANES
HISTORICAL
HOMEOPATHY
HOMEOUSIAN
HOWSOMEVER
HYALOPHANE
HYDROLYSIS
HYDROMETER
HYDROPHANE
HYDROPLANE
HYDROPONIC
HYGROMETER
HYPNOTIZED
IATROGENIC
ICONOCLAST
ICONOSCOPE
ICOSOHEDRA
IMBROCCATA
IMPROBABLE
IMPROBABLY
IMPROPERLY
IMPROVISED
INEXORABLE
INGLORIOUS
INTROSPECT
INVIOLABLE
JARGONELLE
JINGOISTIC
KEYBOARDER
LIGNOCAINE
LINEOMYCIN
LITHOGRAPH
LITHOMARGE
LITHOPHANE
LORDOLATRY
MACROBIOTE
MACROCARPA
MAISONETTE
MALCONTENT
MALLOPHAGA
MANGOSTEEN
MARIOLATRY
MARIONETTE
MEADOWPLAN
MEDIOCRITY
MELLOWNESS
METHODICAL
METHOMANIA
METROPOLIS
MICROFICHE
MICROLIGHT
MICROMETER
MICRONESIA
MICROPHONE
MICROSCOPE
MIDLOTHIAN
MIGNONETTE
MILEOMETER
MIMEOGRAPH
MISCONDUCT
MISFORTUNE
MOTIONLESS
MUSSORGSKY
MUTTONHEAD
MYRIOSCOPE
NARCOLEPSY
NARROWBOAT
NARROWDALE
NARROWNESS
NATIONALLY
NATIONWIDE
NEAPOLITAN
NECROMANCY
NECROPOLIS
NETWORKING
NEUROLEMMA
NICROSILAL
NINCOMPOOP
NORMOBLAST
NOTIONALLY
OCHLOCRACY
OMBROMETER
OMBROPHOBE
OPISOMETER
OPPROBRIUM
ORATORICAL
ORTHOCAINE
ORTHOCLASE
ORTHOGONAL
ORTHOPNOEA
ORTHOPTICS
OSTEOBLAST
OSTEOCOLLA
OSTEOLEPIS
OSTEOPATHY
OSTEOPHYTE
OSTROGOTHS
OUTPOURING
OVIPOSITOR
OXYMORONIC
PANSOPHIST
PANTOGRAPH
PANTOSCOPE
PARDONABLE
PARDONABLY
PASTORELLA
PATHOGENIC
PATRONISED
PATRONYMIC
PERCOLATOR
PERFORATED
PERFORATOR
PERFORMING
PERIODICAL
PERSONABLE
PERSONALLY
PETROGLYPH
PETRONELLA
PHENOMENAL
PHENOMENON
PHILOPOENA
PHILOSOPHY
PHILOXENIA
PHONOGRAPH
PHOTODIODE
PHOTOGENIC
PHOTOGRAPH
PHOTONASTY
PIANOFORTE
PIGEONHOLE
PILLOWCASE
PILLOWSLIP
PLANOBLAST
PLEROPHORY
PLUTOCRACY
PORLOCKING
PORNOCRACY
PRECOCIOUS
PREPOSITOR
PREPOSSESS
PREPOTENCE
PRIMORDIAL
PROFOUNDLY
PROMONTORY
PRONOUNCED
PROPORTION
PROPOSITUS
PROTOPLASM
PSILOCYBIN
PSOCOPTERA
PURPOSEFUL
PYCNOGONID
PYTHOGENIC
RADIOGRAPH
RADIOLARIA
RANDOMNESS
RAPPORTEUR
RATIONALLY
REASONABLE
REASONABLY
REPRODUCER
RESPONDENT
RESPONSIVE
RETROGRADE
RETROGRESS
RETROSPECT
RHETORICAL
RHINOCEROS
RHINOLALIA
RHINOPHYMA
SACROSANCT
SALMONELLA
SANFORISED
SAPROPHYTE
SARCOCOLLA
SARCOLEMMA
SAUROPSIDA
SCHOOLBOOK
SCHOOLGIRL
SCHOOLMAAM
SCOTODINIA
SEASONABLE
SEASONABLY
SERMONICAL
SHADOWLESS
SIGNORELLI
SILHOUETTE
SKEUOMORPH
SOGDOLAGER
SOGDOLIGER
SOGDOLOGER
SOMNOLENCE
SOPHOCLEAN
SOPHOMORIC
SPODOMANCY
STATOCRACY

STENOTYPER
STYLOPISED
SUBCOMPACT
SUPPORTING
SUPPORTIVE
SUPPOSEDLY
SURROUNDED
SYMBOLICAL
SYNCOPATED
TACHOGRAPH
TACHOMETER
TAILORMADE
TAMBOURINE
TEETOTALER
TEINOSCOPE
TELEOSTOME
THIXOTROPY
THOROUGHLY
TINTORETTO
TOMFOOLERY
TRAMONTANA
TRAMONTANE
TRAVOLATOR
TROMOMETER
TROPOPAUSE
TROPOPHYTE
ULTRONEOUS
UNGROUNDED
UNIFORMITY
UNPROMPTED
UNPROVOKED
UROPOIESIS
VICTORIANA
VICTORIOUS
WEAPONLESS
WILLOWHERB
WINDOWSILL
XIPHOPAGUS
YARBOROUGH
YELLOWBACK
YELLOWGIRL
YELLOWJACK
YELLOWROOT
YELLOWWOOD
ZINCOGRAPH
ZOOLOGICAL
ZUMBOORUCK
ABRUPTNESS
ADIAPHORON
AEROPHAGIA
ANALPHABET
ANCIPITOUS
ANTIPHONAL
ANTIPODEAN
ANTIPROTON
AREOPAGITE
ARMIPOTENT
AUTOPLASTY
BACKPACKER
BLASPHEMER
BUCEPHALUS
CAERPHILLY
CAESPITOSE
CALYPTRATE
CANEPHORUS
CATAPHRACT
CHAMPIGNON
CHEAPSKATE
CHIMPANZEE
CLASPKNIFE
CLUMPERTON
CONSPECTUS
CONSPIRACY
CORYPHAEUS
CREOPHAGUS
CRISPBREAD
CRISPINIAN
CRYOPHORUS
DECAPITATE
DECIPHERED
DEPOPULATE
DILAPIDATE
DISAPPOINT
DISAPPROVE
ECCOPROTIC
ECHOPRAXIA
ELLIPTICAL
ENCEPHALON
ENKEPHALIN
ENRAPTURED
EPISPASTIC
ESCAPEMENT
EURYPTERUS
EXASPERATE
EXEMPTNESS
FAREPAYING
FLIPPANTLY
FOOTPRINTS
GETUPANDGO
GRUMPINESS
HANDPICKED
HEADPHONES
HEMIPLEGIA
HEMOPHILIA
HITOPADESA
HITOPODESA
HOLOPHOTAL
HOMOPHOBIA
HOMOPHOBIC
INCAPACITY
INCAPARINA
INDAPAMIDE
INSIPIDITY
KENSPECKLE
LOTOPHAGUS
MAINPERNOR
MALAPROPOS
MANIPULATE
METAPHRASE
METAPLASIS
MONOPHONIC
MONOPLEGIA
MONOPOLISE
MONOPOLIZE
MONOPTERON
MONOPTEROS
NEWSPAPERS
NOSOPHOBIA
OCCUPATION
OESOPHAGUS
OMNIPOTENT
OUTSPECKLE
OVERPRAISE
OWLSPIEGLE
PANOPTICON
PARAPHILIA
PARAPHONIA
PARAPHRASE
PARAPHYSIS
PARAPLEGIA
PARAPLEGIC
PARAPRAXIS
PEDIPALPUS
PERIPHERAL
PHOSPHORUS
PICKPOCKET
POLYPHEMUS
POURPARLER
PROMPTNESS
PROSPECTOR
PROSPECTUS
PROSPERINA
PROSPERITY
PROSPEROUS
PYROPHORUS
REAPPRAISE
RECEPTACLE
RECIPROCAL
RECUPERATE
RESUPINATE
RHAMPASTOS
SALOPETTES
SCHIPPERKE
SCRIPTURAL
SCRIPTURES
SCRUPULOUS
SCULPTRESS
SHAMPOOING
SHEEPISHLY
SHEEPSHANK
SLEEPINESS
SLOPPINESS
STRAPONTIN
STREPITANT
STREPITOSO
STRIPTEASE
STROPHIOLE
SWEEPSTAKE
TELEPATHIC
TELEPHONIC
TOCOPHEROL
TRAMPOLINE
TRESPASSER
UNEMPLOYED
UNEXPECTED
UNEXPLORED
UNIMPAIRED
USURPATION
VITUPERATE
VIVIPAROUS
VOLUPTUARY
VOLUPTUOUS
WHISPERING
WOODPECKER
WOODPIGEON
XENOPHOBIA
XENOPHOBIC
XEROPHYTIC
ANTIQUATED
BLANQUETTE
CHINQUAPIN
ILLAQUEATE
LANSQUENET
OBSEQUIOUS
SARSQUATCH
SEMIQUAVER
TRANQUILLY
UNREQUITED
ABERRATION
ABHORRENCE
ABNORMALLY
ABSORPTION
ABSTRACTED
ACCORDANCE
ACCURATELY
ADMIRATION
ADMIRINGLY
ADVERSARIA
ADVERTISER
AFFORDABLE
AFRORMOSIA
AFTERBIRTH
AFTERHOURS
AFTERPIECE
AFTERSHAVE
AFTERSHOCK
AFTERTASTE
AFTERWARDS
AIRFREIGHT
ALDERMANLY
ALLUREMENT
ALTERATION
ALTERNATOR
AMBARVALIA
ANACRUSTIC
ANADROMOUS
ANGURVADEL
ANTARCTICA
ANTHRACINE
ANTHRACITE
ANTHROPOID
APOCRYPHAL
APOTROPAIC
APPARENTLY
APPARITION
APTERYGOTA
ARTHRALGIA
ARTHROMERE
ASPARAGINE
ASPERSIONS
ASPIRATION
ASSORTMENT
ASTEROIDEA
AUSTRALIAN
AUSTRALORP
AUSTRINGER
AVERRHOISM
BABIROUSSA
BALBRIGGAN
BANKRUPTCY
BEFOREHAND
BELARUSIAN
BICHROMATE
BIOGRAPHER
BIPARTISAN
BLEARYEYED
BORDRAGING
BUMFREEZER
BUSHRANGER
CALORIFIER
CAMBRENSIS
CAMERLENGO
CAMERLINGO
CAMERONIAN
CANCRIZANS
CAPERNAITE
CAPERNOITY
CASTRATION
CATARRHINE
CATCRACKER
CENTRALIZE
CENTRIFUGE
CENTROSOME
CESTRACION
CHAIRWOMAN
CHEERFULLY
CHEIRONOMY
CHERRYWOOD
CHEVROTAIN
CHLORINATE
CHLOROFORM
CLAIRCOLLE
CLEARSTORY
CLEARWATER
COHERENTLY
COLORATION
COLORATURA
COMPRADORE
COMPREHEND
COMPRESSED

COMPRESSOR
COMPROMISE
CONCRETION
CONGREGATE
CONTRABAND
CONTRACTOR
CONTRADICT
CONTRAFLOW
CONTRAHENT
CONTRARILY
CONTRAVENE
CONTRECOUP
CONTRIBUTE
CONTRITION
CONTROLLER
CONTROVERT
COPARCENER
COPERNICUS
CUCURBITAL
CYBERNETIC
DAYDREAMER
DECORATION
DECORATIVE
DELCREDERE
DELIRATION
DEMORALISE
DEMORALIZE
DENDROPHIS
DEPARTMENT
DEPARTURES
DEPORTMENT
DESCRIBING
DESERVEDLY
DETERMINED
DETERRENCE
DICHROMISM
DISARRANGE
DISCREETLY
DISCREPANT
DISCRETION
DISGRUNTLE
DISORDERED
DISORDERLY
DISTRACTED
DISTRAUGHT
DISTRESSED
DISTRIBUTE
DISTRINGAS
DIVERGENCE
DOVERCOURT
DREARINESS
DREARISOME
DYSCRASITE
DYSPROSIUM
DYSTROPHIC
EFFERVESCE
EFFORTLESS
ELDERBERRY
ELYTRIFORM
EMBERGOOSE
EMIGRATION
ENTEROCELE
ENTERPRISE
ESCARPMENT
EUPHROSYNE
EXECRATION
EXPERIENCE
EXPERIMENT
EXPIRATION
EXTERNALLY
FAVORITISM
FEDERALISM
FEDERALIST
FEDERATION
FEVERISHLY
FIBERGLASS
FIGURATION
FIGURATIVE
FIGUREHEAD
FILTRATION
FLAGRANTLY
FLOORBOARD
FLOORCLOTH
FLOURISHED
FORERUNNER
FOUDROYANT
FOURRAGERE
FRATRICIDE
FUTURISTIC
GANGRENOUS
GASTRONOME
GASTRONOMY
GENERALISE
GENERALITY
GENERALIZE
GENERATION
GENERATRIX
GENEROSITY
GENEROUSLY
GEOGRAPHER
GEOGRAPHIC
GEOTROPISM
GILLRAVAGE
GONORRHOEA
GOVERNANCE
GOVERNESSY
GOVERNMENT
GUBERNATOR
HEMORRHAGE
HETERODOXY
HISTRIONIC
HOMORELAPS
HONORARIUM
HORNRIMMED
HOVERCRAFT
HUMORESQUE
HUMOROUSLY
HYPERBOLIC
HYPERDULIA
ICEBREAKER
IGNORANTLY
IMMORALITY
IMMORTELLE
IMPARLANCE
IMPERATIVE
IMPERSONAL
IMPERVIOUS
IMPORTANCE
IMPURITIES
INDIRECTLY
INEBRIATED
INFERNALLY
INFORMALLY
INFURIATED
INHERENTLY
INNERSPACE
INSTRUCTED
INSTRUCTOR
INSTRUMENT
INSURGENCY
INTERBREED
INTERCEDER
INTERCLUDE
INTERESTED
INTERFERER
INTERFERON
INTERLEAVE
INTERLOPER
INTERMARRY
INTERMEZZO
INTERNALLY
INTERNMENT
INTERNODAL
INTERPHONE
INTERSTATE
INTERSTICE
INTERTRIGO
INTERTWINE
INTERWEAVE
INTERWOVEN
INVARIABLE
INVARIABLY
KATERFELTO
LABORATORY
LACERATION
LACHRYMOSE
LAMARCKISM
LAMBREQUIN
LAWBREAKER
LEDERHOSEN
LIBERALISM
LIBERALITY
LIBERALIZE
LIBERATION
LITERATURE
LITURGICAL
LIVERWURST
LOGARITHMS
LOGORRHOEA
LUPERCALIA
LUXURIANCE
MANDRAGORA
MATERIALLY
MATERNALLY
MATURATION
MEAGRENESS
MEMBRANOUS
MEMORANDUM
MENORRHOEA
MEPERIDINE
MINERALOGY
MISERICORD
MISPRISION
MITHRIDATE
MODERATELY
MODERATION
MONARCHIST
MONTRACHET
MOTORCYCLE
MUCKRAKING
MYCORRHIZA
NATURALISM
NATURALIST
NATURALIZE
NATUROPATH
NEUTRALISE
NEUTRALITY
NEUTRALIZE
NEUTROPHIL
NEWSREADER
NICARAGUAN
NOTORYCTES
NOURRITURE
NUMERATION
NUTCRACKER
OBSERVABLE
OBSERVANCE
OCCURRENCE
OROBRANCHE
OTHERGATES
OTHERGUESS
OUVIRANDRA
OVERRIDING
PADAREWSKI
PALFRENIER
PANARITIUM
PANCRATIUM
PAPERCHASE
PAPERKNIFE
PARARTHRIA
PATERNALLY
PEJORATIVE
PERORATION
PICARESQUE
PILGRIMAGE
PITYRIASIS
POKERFACED
POMERANIAN
PONEROLOGY
POWERHOUSE
PREARRANGE
PROCREATOR
PROCRUSTES
PROGRAMMER
PROPRAETOR
PROPRIETOR
PROTRACTED
PROTRACTOR
PROTRUSION
PUBERULENT
QUADRANGLE
QUADRATURA
QUADRICEPS
QUADRIREME
QUARRENDER
RAJPRAMUKH
RECURRENCE
REFERENDUM
REGARDLESS
REMARKABLE
REMARKABLY
REMORSEFUL
REPARATION
REPERTOIRE
REPORTEDLY
RESERVISTS
RESORCINOL
RESTRAINED
RESTRICTED
RESURGENCE
RETIREMENT
RETURNABLE
REVERENTLY
REVERSIBLE
RIGOROUSLY
RITORNELLE
RITORNELLO
ROADRUNNER
ROBERDSMAN
ROBERTSMAN
SACERDOTAL
SAMARSKITE
SATURATION
SATURNALIA
SAUERKRAUT
SCLERIASIS
SCURRILITY
SCURRILOUS
SECURITIES
SEPARATELY
SEPARATION
SEPARATISM
SEPARATIST
SEPARATRIX
SHEARWATER
SIDERATION
SIDEROSTAT
SINARCHIST
SINARQUIST
SMORREBROD

SOBERSIDES
SOMBRERITE
SOMERSAULT
SOMERVILLE
SOUBRIQUET
SPERRYLITE
SQUIREARCH
STAUROLITE
SUBTROPICS
SUFFRAGIST
SUGARALLIE
SULTRINESS
SUPERADDED
SUPERCARGO
SUPERGIANT
SUPERHUMAN
SUPERMODEL
SUPERPOWER
SUPERSONIC
SUPERSTORE
SUPERTONIC
SUPERVISED
SUPERVISOR
SUPERWOMAN
SUPPRESSED
SUPPRESSOR
SURFRIDING
SURPRISING
SUZERAINTY
SYNCRETISE
TABERNACLE
TAPERECORD
TARTRAZINE
TENDRILLED
TIEBREAKER
TIMBROLOGY
TITARAKURA
TOLERANTLY
TOLERATION
TUBERCULAR
TULARAEMIA
ULCERATION
UNABRIDGED
UNDERBURNT
UNDERCLASS
UNDERCOVER
UNDERCRAFT
UNDERCROFT
UNDERFLOOR
UNDERLEASE
UNDERLINEN
UNDERLYING
UNDERNEATH
UNDERPANTS
UNDERSCORE
UNDERSHIRT
UNDERSIZED
UNDERSKIRT
UNDERSLUNG
UNDERSTAND
UNDERSTATE
UNDERSTEER
UNDERSTOOD
UNDERSTUDY
UNDERTAKER
UNDERVALUE
UNDERWATER
UNDERWORLD
UNDERWRITE
UNFORESEEN
UNHERALDED
UNSCRAMBLE
UNSCRIPTED
UNWORKABLE
UPPERCLASS
VENERATION
VETERINARY
VICEREGENT
VIGOROUSLY
WATERBORNE
WATERBRASH
WATERCOLOR
WATERCRESS
WATERFRONT
WATERLEVEL
WATERMELON
WATERPROOF
WATERSKIER
WATERSPOUT
WATERTIGHT
WATERWHEEL
WATERWINGS
WATERWORKS
WOLFRAMITE
YGGDRASILL
ZAPOROGIAN
ABYSSINIAN
ACCESSIBLE
ACCESSIONS
ACCUSATION
ACCUSATIVE
ACCUSINGLY
ACCUSTOMED
ADJUSTABLE
ADJUSTMENT
ADMISSIBLE
ALLOSAURUS
ALLOSTERIC
AMBASSADOR
AMPUSSYAND
ANTISEPSIS
ANTISEPTIC
ANTISOCIAL
ANTISTATIC
APPOSITION
ASBESTOSIS
ASSESSMENT
ASSISTANCE
ATMOSPHERE
AUTOSTRADA
BABESIASIS
BABYSITTER
BACKSLIDER
BACKSTAIRS
BACKSTROKE
BAGASSOSIS
BALUSTRADE
BANISHMENT
BARASINGHA
BARYSPHERE
BESTSELLER
BLISSFULLY
BONDSWOMAN
BONESHAKER
BOOKSELLER
BRASSBOUND
BREASTBONE
BREASTFEED
BREASTWORK
BRESSUMMER
CALESCENCE
CATASTASIS
CELESTIALS
CHEESECAKE
CHEESEWOOD
CHERSONESE
CHESSBOARD
CHESSYLITE
CHOPSTICKS
CHRISTIANA
CHRYSIPPUS
CHRYSOLITE
CLANSWOMAN
CLASSICISM
CLASSICIST
CLASSIFIED
CLOISTERED
CLUMSINESS
COARSENESS
COLDSTREAM
COLOSSALLY
COMESTIBLE
COPESETTIC
CORNSTALKS
CORNSTARCH
COUNSELING
COUNSELLOR
CRISSCROSS
CROSSBREED
CROSSCHECK
CROSSPIECE
CROSSREFER
CROSSROADS
DEBASEMENT
DECISIVELY
DEEPSEATED
DEHISCENCE
DEPOSITARY
DEPOSITION
DEPOSITORY
DETESTABLE
DEVASTATED
DEVASTAVIT
DIDASCALIC
DIGESTIBLE
DISASTROUS
DIVISIONAL
DOWNSIZING
DOWNSTAIRS
DOWNSTREAM
DRAWSTRING
DRESSMAKER
DROWSINESS
EFFUSIVELY
ELEUSINIAN
EMULSIFIER
ENCASEMENT
ENDOSMOSIS
ENLISTMENT
EQUESTRIAN
EXPOSITION
EXPOSITORY
FACESAVING
FAMISHMENT
FENESTELLA
FINISTERRE
FISHSELLER
FLIMSINESS
FOODSTUFFS
FORESHADOW
GAINSTRIVE
GETHSEMANE
GLASSHOUSE
GLASSINESS
GLOSSINESS
GOATSUCKER
GRASSLANDS
GRASSROOTS
GRASSWIDOW
GYROSCOPIC
HAIRSPRING
HALFSISTER
HAMESUCKEN
HANDSOMELY
HANDSPRING
HARASSMENT
HEADSTRONG
HEMISPHERE
HERESIARCH
HOARSENESS
HOLOSTERIC
HOMOSEXUAL
ILLUSTRATE
IMPASSABLE
IMPOSITION
IMPOSSIBLE
IMPOSSIBLY
IMPOSTHUME
INCESTUOUS
INCISIVELY
INDISCREET
INDISPOSED
INDISTINCT
INDUSTRIAL
INSISTENCE
INTESTINAL
INTESTINES
INVESTMENT
IONOSPHERE
IRRESOLUTE
JACKSTONES
JACKSTRAWS
JAMESONITE
JOHNSONIAN
JOUYSAUNCE
KLEBSIELLA
KOEKSISTER
LACUSTRINE
LANDSTHING
LAVISHNESS
LEGISLATOR
LOGISTICAL
LOUISIETTE
LUMPSUCKER
LUTESTRING
MAGISTRACY
MAGISTRAND
MAGISTRATE
MAINSPRING
MAINSTREAM
MAKESYSTEM
MANUSCRIPT
MARASCHINO
MEERSCHAUM
METASTABLE
MINESTRONE
MINISTRATE
MONTSERRAT
MORISONIAN
MOROSENESS
MOSASAUROS
MOUSSELINE
NUMISMATIC
OBFUSCATED
OBTUSENESS
OCCASIONAL
ODELSTHING
OMNISCIENT
OPPOSITION
OVERSHADOW
OVERSLAUGH
OVERSPREAD
OVERSTRAIN
OVERSTRUNG
OVERSUPPLY
PALESTRINA
PALISANDER
PALUSTRINE
PARASCENIA
PARASELENE

PARASTATAL
PARISCHANE
PARISIENNE
PATISSERIE
PEDESTRIAN
PENTSTEMON
PERISHABLE
PLEASANTLY
PLEASANTRY
POINSETTIA
PORTSMOUTH
POSTSCRIPT
PRESSURIZE
PRIESTHOOD
PUBESCENCE
PUNISHABLE
PUNISHMENT
QUAESTUARY
QUEASINESS
QUERSPRUNG
QUIESCENCE
REASSEMBLE
REASSURING
REDISCOVER
REGISTERED
REPOSITORY
RESISTANCE
RHAPSODISE
RHAPSODIZE
ROBUSTIOUS
ROBUSTNESS
ROCKSTEADY
ROTHSCHILD
ROTISSERIE
RUPESTRIAN
SALESWOMAN
SATISFYING
SCHISMATIC
SCOTSWOMAN
SEAMSTRESS
SEERSUCKER
SELFSTYLED
SENESCENCE
SHOESTRING
SHOPSOILED
SIDESADDLE
SKUPSHTINA
SLIPSTREAM
SONGSTRESS
SPARSENESS
SPENSERIAN
SPISSITUDE
SPONSIONAL
STEPSISTER
STRASBOURG
SYNOSTOSIS
TELESCOPIC
THEMSELVES
THOUSANDTH
TIMESAVING
TIMESERVER
TIMESWITCH
TOWNSWOMAN
TRANSCRIBE
TRANSCRIPT
TRANSGRESS
TRANSIENCE
TRANSISTOR
TRANSITION
TRANSITIVE
TRANSITORY
TRANSLATED
TRANSLATOR
TRANSPLANT
TRANSPOSED
TRANSVERSE
TREKSCHUIT
TRIMSNITCH
TROTSKYITE
TUMESCENCE
TYPESCRIPT
TYPESETTER
UNANSWERED
UNASSIGNED
UNASSUMING
UNDESCRIED
UNDESERVED
UNDISPUTED
UNEASINESS
UNINSPIRED
UNOBSERVED
UNRESERVED
UNRESOLVED
WAINSCOTED
WANDSWORTH
WELLSPRING
WHATSOEVER
WHITSTABLE
WIDESPREAD
WINDSCREEN
WINDSHIELD
WINDSURFER
WORDSWORTH
XEROSTOMIA
YOURSELVES
ACHITOPHEL
ACROTERION
ADAPTATION
ADDITAMENT
ADDITIONAL
ADMITTANCE
ADMITTEDLY
ADULTERANT
ADULTERATE
ADULTERESS
ADULTERINE
ADULTEROUS
AFFETTUOSO
ALECTORIAN
ALLOTROPIC
AMPUTATION
AMRITATTVA
ANASTIGMAT
ANASTROPHE
ANESTHESIA
ANESTHETIC
ANNOTATION
ANTITHESIS
ANTITHETIC
ANTITRAGUS
APOSTROPHE
APPETITIVE
APPETIZING
ARBITRATOR
ARISTIPPUS
ARISTOCRAT
ARISTOLOGY
ARISTOTLES
ASCETICISM
ASTUTENESS
AUDITORIUM
AVANTGARDE
AVANTURINE
AVENTURINE
BACITRACIN
BEAUTICIAN
BEAUTIFIER
BEWITCHING
BLASTOIDEA
BLISTERING
BLOTTESQUE
BLUETHROAT
BOISTEROUS
BREATHLESS
CAMSTEERIE
CAOUTCHOUC
CAPITALISM
CAPITALIST
CAPITALIZE
CAPITATION
CAPITELLUM
CAPITOLINE
CAPITULARY
CAPITULATE
CHAPTALISE
CHARTREUSE
CHATTERBOX
CHATTERTON
CHAUTAUQUA
CHELTENHAM
CHESTERTON
CHITTAGONG
CLOSTRIDIA
COASTGUARD
COGITATION
COMSTOCKER
CONSTANTAN
CONSTANTIA
CONSTANTLY
CONSTITUTE
CONSTRAINT
CONSTRINGE
COUNTERACT
COUNTRYMAN
COURTHOUSE
CRAFTINESS
CREATIVITY
CRUSTACEAN
CRYPTOGRAM
DEACTIVATE
DEBATEMENT
DECATHLETE
DEPUTATION
DEVOTEMENT
DEVOTIONAL
DIASTALTIC
DIGITORIUM
DILATATION
DILETTANTE
DIPHTHERIA
DOORTODOOR
DOUBTFULLY
EIGHTEENTH
ELASTICATE
ELASTICITY
ELECTORATE
ELECTRICAL
ELECTROMER
ELECTRONIC
EMBITTERED
EMMETROPIA
ENANTIOSIS
EPENTHETIC
EPISTEMICS
EPISTROPHE
EQUATORIAL
EQUITATION
ERUCTATION
ESCUTCHEON
EVENTUALLY
EXACTITUDE
EXALTATION
EXCITEMENT
EXENTERATE
EXPATRIATE
EXULTATION
FANATICISM
FAULTINESS
FLATTERING
FLEETINGLY
FLIRTATION
FLUCTUATER
FOURTEENTH
FRACTIONAL
FRONTWARDS
FRUITFULLY
FRUSTRATED
FUNCTIONAL
GAULTHERIA
GELATINOUS
GENETHLIAC
GLISTENING
GLITTERAND
GLITTERATI
GLITTERING
GLUTTONOUS
GNOSTICISM
GRAPTOLITE
GRITTINESS
GUESTHOUSE
HABITATION
HABITUALLY
HAUSTELLUM
HAUSTORIUM
HEARTBREAK
HEARTINESS
HEPATOCELE
HESITANTLY
HESITATION
HYPOTENUSE
HYPOTHESIS
ILLITERACY
ILLITERATE
IMMATERIAL
IMMATURITY
IMPATIENCE
IMPOTENTLY
IMPUTATION
INACTIVITY
INAPTITUDE
INARTISTIC
INCITEMENT
INDITEMENT
INEPTITUDE
INFATUATED
INSATIABLE
INSATIABLY
INVETERATE
INVITATION
IRRATIONAL
IRRITATING
IRRITATION
JAUNTINESS
JEISTIECOR
KARTTIKAYA
KLOOTCHMAN
KSHATRIYAS
LAEOTROPIC
LEGITIMACY
LEGITIMATE
LEGITIMIZE
LENGTHWAYS
LENGTHWISE
LEONTIASIS
LEVITATION
LIEUTENANT
LIGHTERMAN
LIGHTHOUSE
LIGHTINGUP
LIMITATION

LIMITROPHE
LUSITANIAN
MEDITATION
MEDITATIVE
MENSTRUATE
MESITYLENE
METATARSAL
METATARSUS
METATHERIA
METATHESIS
MIGHTINESS
MILITARISM
MILITARIST
MILITIAMAN
MINUTEBOOK
MINUTENESS
MOISTURIZE
MONETARISM
MONETARIST
MONOTHEISM
MONOTONOUS
MONSTRANCE
MORATORIUM
MOUNTEBANK
MOUSTERIAN
NATATORIAL
NATATORIUM
NEGATIVELY
NEGOTIABLE
NEGOTIATOR
NEMATOCYST
NIGHTDRESS
NIGHTLIGHT
NIGHTSHADE
NIGHTSHIRT
NIGHTSTICK
NINETEENTH
OBLITERATE
ODONTALGIA
ODONTOLITE
ODONTOLOGY
OSCITATION
OSMETERIUM
OUGHTLINGS
OVERTHETOP
OVERTHWART
PAINTBRUSH
PALATALISE
PALATINATE
PARATROOPS
PENETRABLE
PENETRALIA
PERSTRINGE
PETITIONER
PHANTASIME
PHANTASIST
PLANTATION
PLASTICINE
PLASTICITY
PLATTELAND
POHUTUKAWA
POINTBLANK
POLITENESS
POLITICIAN
POLITICIZE
POLYTHEISM
POSITIVELY
POSITIVIST
PRAETORIAN
PRAETORIUM
PRETTINESS
PROSTHESIS
PROSTHETIC
PROSTITUTE
PSALTERIUM
PUNCTUALLY
PUNCTULATE
PURITANISM
QUARTERING
QUARTEROON
QUESTIONER
RAWSTHORNE
REACTIVATE
RECITATION
RECITATIVE
RECITATIVO
REFUTATION
RELATIVELY
RELATIVITY
REMITTANCE
REMOTENESS
REPATRIATE
REPETITEUR
REPETITION
REPETITIVE
REPUTATION
REVITALIZE
RHEOTROPIC
RICHTHOFEN
RIGHTFULLY
RIJSTTAFEL
ROISTERING
ROUSTABOUT
SAGITTARIA
SALUTATION
SAMOTHRACE
SANATORIUM
SANCTIFIED
SANCTITIES
SANCTITUDE
SANITARIUM
SANITATION
SCANTINESS
SCATTERING
SCEPTICISM
SCOOTERIST
SCRUTINEER
SCRUTINISE
SCRUTINIZE
SEDATENESS
SENATORIAL
SHATTERING
SHIFTINESS
SHORTBREAD
SHORTENING
SHORTLIVED
SHORTRANGE
SKEPTICISM
SLATTERNLY
SMATTERING
SMOOTHNESS
SNOOTINESS
SPARTACIST
SPECTACLED
SPECTACLES
SPECTATORS
SPLITLEVEL
SPORTINGLY
SPORTSWEAR
SQUETEAGUE
STENTORIAN
STERTEROUS
STERTOROUS
STOUTHERIE
STOUTHRIEF
STRATEGIST
STRATHSPEY
STRATIOTES
STRATOCRAT
STRATOCYST
STULTIFIED
SUBSTATION
SUBSTITUTE
SUBSTRATUM
SWEATSHIRT
SWEETBREAD
SWEETENING
SWEETHEART
SWELTERING
TAPOTEMENT
TEMPTATION
THEATRICAL
THIRTEENTH
TRAITOROUS
TROCTOLITE
TRUSTFULLY
TRYPTOPHAN
UNATTACHED
UNATTENDED
UNDETECTED
UNDETERRED
UNFATHOMED
UNFETTERED
UNLETTERED
UNORTHODOX
UNSETTLING
UROSTEGITE
VEGETABLES
VEGETARIAN
VEGETATION
VELITATION
VISITATION
VOCATIONAL
VOLATILITY
VOLUTATION
WHEATSHEAF
WHEATSTONE
WHITTERICK
WRISTWATCH
ZOANTHARIA
ZWITTERION
ABITURIENT
ACCOUNTANT
ACCOUNTING
ADEQUATELY
ALLPURPOSE
ALTRUISTIC
AMANUENSIS
APICULTURE
ARTHURIANA
ASTOUNDING
AVICULARIA
BALBUTIENT
BIJOUTERIE
CALCULABLE
CALCULATED
CALCULATOR
CAMOUFLAGE
CAPPUCCINO
CARBURETOR
CASSUMUNAR
CELLULITIS
CHEQUEBOOK
CINQUEFOIL
CIRCUITOUS
CIRCUMCISE
CIRCUMFLEX
CIRCUMFUSE
CIRCUMVENT
COLOURLESS
COMBUSTION
COMMUNALLY
COMMUNIQUÉ
COMMUTABLE
COMPULSION
COMPULSIVE
COMPULSORY
CONCURRENT
CONCUSSION
CONDUCTING
CONDUCTION
CONFUSEDLY
CONQUERING
CONSUETUDE
CONSULTANT
CONSULTING
CONSUMMATE
CONVULSION
CONVULSIVE
CORNUCOPIA
CORPULENCE
CORRUGATED
CORRUGATOR
CORRUPTING
CORRUPTION
CRAPULENCE
CRAQUETURE
CURMUDGEON
CURMURRING
DEBAUCHERY
DEBOUCHURE
DENOUEMENT
DESQUAMATE
DETRUNCATE
DISBURTHEN
DISCURSIVE
DISCUSSING
DISCUSSION
DISGUSTING
DISPUTABLE
DISQUALIFY
DISQUIETED
DISRUPTION
DISRUPTIVE
DISSUASION
DISTURBING
ELOQUENTLY
EMBOUCHURE
EMOLUMENTS
ENGOUEMENT
ENTHUSIASM
ENTHUSIAST
EPROUVETTE
EVACUATION
EVALUATION
EXCRUCIATE
EXHAUSTING
EXHAUSTION
EXHAUSTIVE
EXPOUNDERS
FAVOURABLE
FAVOURABLY
FETTUCCINE
FLATULENCE
FORTUITOUS
FOXHUNTING
FREQUENTED
FREQUENTER
FREQUENTLY
GRADUATION
GRANULATED
GRATUITOUS
GUTTURALLY
HALLUBALOO
HINDUSTANI
HONOURABLE
HONOURABLY
HONOURLESS
HUMDUDGEON
HUMOURLESS

IMPRUDENCE
INCAUTIOUS
INEDUCABLE
INEQUALITY
INIQUITOUS
INSOUCIANT
KENTUCKIAN
LANGUOROUS
LAURUSTINE
LIMBURGITE
LINGUISTIC
LINGULELLA
LITHUANIAN
MARGUERITE
MARQUETRIE
MASQUERADE
MASTURBATE
MAVOURNEEN
MEASURABLE
MEDIUMTERM
METHUSALEH
METHUSELAH
NASTURTIUM
NONSUCCESS
ODIOUSNESS
OFFPUTTING
PASQUINADE
PERCUSSION
PERDURABLE
PERQUISITE
PERSUADING
PERSUASION
PERSUASIVE
PINCUSHION
PORTUGUESE
POZZUOLANA
PRECURSORY
PREJUDICED
PRESUMABLY
PRESUPPOSE
PROCURABLE
PROCURATOR
PRODUCTION
PRODUCTIVE
PROFUNDITY
PROMULGATE
PROPULSION
PURSUIVANT
RECRUDESCE
REDCURRANT
REDRUTHITE
RESOUNDING
RUMBULLION
SANGUINARY
SCATURIENT
SCROUNGING
SENSUALITY
SENSUOUSLY
SEPTUAGINT
SHAKUHACHI

SINFULNESS
SINGULARLY
SPECULATOR
STATUESQUE
TATPURUSHA
TCHOUKBALL
THROUGHOUT
THROUGHPUT
THROUGHWAY
TONGUESTER
TORQUEMADA
TORTUOUSLY
TRIPUDIARY
TRUCULENCE
TURBULENCE
UBIQUITOUS
UNBLUSHING
UNCTUOUSLY
UNEDUCATED
UNEQUALLED
UNFRUITFUL
UNIQUENESS
UNTRUTHFUL
USEFULNESS
VICTUALLER
VIRTUOSITY
VIRTUOUSLY
WAMPUMPEAG
ACTIVITIST
AMBIVALENT
ANTIVENENE
ASSEVERATE
BEDEVILLED
BEHAVIORAL
BENEVOLENT
BILIVERDIN
CADAVEROUS
CALAVERITE
CHAUVINISM
CHAUVINIST
CHERVONETS
DERIVATION
DERIVATIVE
DUUMVIRATE
ENLÈVEMENT
EQUIVALENT
EQUIVOCATE
EXCAVATION
GENEVRETTE
HANOVERIAN
IMPOVERISH
INCIVILITY
INDIVIDUAL
INNOVATION
INNOVATIVE
IRREVERENT
LAURVIKITE
MALEVOLENT
MOTIVATION
OMNIVOROUS

PAPAVERINE
PATAVINITY
PEROVSKITE
REJUVENATE
RENOVATION
REVIVALIST
SALIVATION
SHRIVELLED
SHROVETIDE
SLEEVELESS
SOLIVAGANT
STARVATION
STARVELING
STRAVINSKY
TELEVISION
TROUVAILLE
TUTIVILLUS
UNENVIABLE
UNINVITING
UNREVEALED
UNRIVALLED
ZOLLVEREIN
BELLWETHER
CATAWAMPUS
CODSWALLOP
COPYWRITER
CORDWAINER
DISHWASHER
DUNIWASSAL
FIREWALKER
FIREWARDEN
FOREWARNED
GALSWORTHY
HIGHWAYMAN
HOMEWORKER
HOODWINKED
LEFTWINGER
LILYWHITES
MAKEWEIGHT
MINEWORKER
NEWSWORTHY
NOTEWORTHY
OVERWEIGHT
OVERWORKED
PERIWINKLE
PLAYWRIGHT
PRZEWALSKI
RAILWAYMAN
ROADWORTHY
ROTTWEILER
SANDWICHES
SHOPWALKER
SHREWDNESS
SIDEWINDER
SONGWRITER
STEMWINDER
STRAWBERRY
STRAWBOARD
TYPEWRITER
WOODWORKER

ANNEXATION
INTOXICANT
INTOXICATE
RELAXATION
RELAXATIVE
ACOTYLEDON
AMARYLLIDS
AMBLYOPSIS
AMBLYSTOMA
ANADYOMENE
ANALYTICAL
ANCHYLOSIS
ASPHYXIATE
BATHYSCAPH
BOBBYSOXER
BRADYKININ
BRADYSEISM
CANDYFLOSS
CHALYBEATE
DESSYATINE
DONNYBROOK
ECCHYMOSIS
EMBRYOLOGY
ENTRYPHONE
EPONYCHIUM
EUTHYNEURA
EVERYPLACE
EVERYTHING
EVERYWHERE
FUDDYDUDDY
FULLYGROWN
GETTYSBURG
HALFYEARLY
HANKYPANKY
HOBBYHORSE
HONEYBUNCH
JERRYBUILT
MAHAYANALI
MALAYALAAM
MERRYMAKER
METHYLATED
PADDYMELON
PETTYCHAPS
PICAYUNISH
PROPYLAEUM
PTERYGOTUS
ROWDYDOWDY
STONYHURST
TEENYWEENY
THUCYDIDES
TOPSYTURVY
WILLYWILLY
WISHYWASHY
ALTAZIMUTH
BLITZKRIEG
FRENZIEDLY
HORIZONTAL
LHERZOLITE
LIPIZZANER
SCORZONERA

SELTZOGENE
SNEEZEWOOD
VENEZUELAN
WHEEZINESS

10:6

ABDICATION
ABERRATION
ABROGATION
ABSTRACTED
ABUNDANTLY
ACCUBATION
ACCURATELY
ACCUSATION
ACCUSATIVE
ACEPHALOUS
ACROBATICS
ADAPTATION
ADDITAMENT
ADEQUATELY
ADMIRATION
ADRENALINE
ADULLAMITE
AEROBATICS
AFRICANDER
ALGOLAGNIA
ALIENATION
ALLEGATION
ALLIGATION
ALLOCATION
ALLOSAURUS
ALMACANTAR
ALMUCANTAR
ALTERATION
AMALGAMATE
AMBIVALENT
AMBULACRUM
AMBULATORY
AMPUTATION
AMRITATTVA
AMYGDALOID
ANACHARSIS
ANACLASTIC
ANHELATION
ANNEXATION
ANNOTATION
ANSCHAUUNG
ANTHRACINE
ANTHRACITE
ANTIBARBUS
ANTIMASQUE
ANTIMATTER
AQUAMANALE
AQUAMANILE
AQUAMARINE
ARAUCANIAN
AREOPAGITE
ARROGANTLY

ARTHRALGIA
ARTOCARPUS
ASPARAGINE
ASPIRATION
ASTOMATOUS
ATHANASIAN
AUSTRALIAN
AUSTRALORP
AUTOMATION
AVVOGADORE
BACCHANTES
BACKGAMMON
BACKHANDED
BACKHANDER
BACKPACKER
BALNEATION
BANDMASTER
BANGLADESH
BEARGARDEN
BEDCHAMBER
BEEFEATERS
BELSHAZZAR
BENEFACTOR
BENTHAMITE
BESTIALITY
BIOGRAPHER
BLEPHARISM
BLUEMANTLE
BOOKMARKER
BORDRAGING
BREAKABLES
BUCHMANISM
BURGLARIZE
BUSHRANGER
CACODAEMON
CALAMANDER
CALEFACTOR
CALLIATURE
CAPITALISM
CAPITALIST
CAPITALIZE
CAPITATION
CAPODASTRO
CARICATURA
CARICATURE
CARTHAMINE
CASSIABARK
CASTRATION
CATAFALQUE
CATAWAMPUS
CATCRACKER
CATENACCIO
CENTRALIZE
CESTRACION
CHAPFALLEN
CHAPLAINCY
CHAPTALISE
CHAUTAUQUA
CHIMPANZEE
CHITTAGONG
CHREMATIST
CINECAMERA
COATHANGER
CODSWALLOP
COGITATION
COLORATION
COLORATURA
COMPLACENT
COMPLANATE
COMPRADORE
CONSTANTAN
CONSTANTIA
CONSTANTLY
CONTRABAND
CONTRACTOR
CONTRADICT
CONTRAFLOW
CONTRAHENT
CONTRARILY
CONTRAVENE
COPULATION
CORDIALITY
CORDWAINER
COROMANDEL
CORONATION
CORYBANTES
CORYBANTIC
COVENANTER
CRUSTACEAN
CUMULATIVE
DARKHAIRED
DECIMALIZE
DECORATION
DECORATIVE
DEDICATION
DEFAMATION
DEFAMATORY
DEFECATION
DELEGATION
DELICATELY
DELIGATION
DELIRATION
DEMORALISE
DEMORALIZE
DEPILATORY
DEPUTATION
DERIVATION
DERIVATIVE
DEROGATORY
DESOLATION
DESQUAMATE
DESSIATINE
DESSYATINE
DETONATION
DEVANAGARI
DIAPHANOUS
DIASTALTIC
DILATATION
DIOPHANTOS
DISCLAIMER
DISHEARTEN
DISHWASHER
DISQUALIFY
DISSUASION
DISTRACTED
DISTRAUGHT
DIURNALIST
DIVINATION
DOCIMASTIC
DODECANESE
DOMINATING
DOMINATION
DOWNMARKET
DRAWCANSIR
DREIKANTER
DUNIWASSAL
DYSCRASITE
ELONGATION
EMACIATION
EMENDATION
EMIGRATION
ENDOGAMOUS
ENTREATING
EPIPLASTRA
EPISPASTIC
EQUITATION
EQUIVALENT
ERIOCAULON
ERUCTATION
ESCALATION
ESCULAPIAN
ESTIMATION
ETHYLAMINE
EVACUATION
EVALUATION
EVENHANDED
EXALTATION
EXCAVATION
EXECRATION
EXHALATION
EXHILARATE
EXHUMATION
EXPIRATION
EXULTATION
FACESAVING
FAIRHAIRED
FALKLANDER
FAREPAYING
FASCIATION
FEDERALISM
FEDERALIST
FEDERATION
FIGURATION
FIGURATIVE
FILTRATION
FIREWALKER
FIREWARDEN
FLAGRANTLY
FLIPPANTLY
FLIRTATION
FOOTBALLER
FORBEARING
FORECASTER
FORECASTLE
FOREDAMNED
FOREFATHER
FOREGATHER
FOREWARNED
FOUNDATION
FOURRAGERE
FREEHANDER
FREELANCER
FREEMARTIN
FREEMASONS
FUMIGATION
GALIMATIAS
GALLIAMBIC
GEMINATION
GENERALISE
GENERALITY
GENERALIZE
GENERATION
GENERATRIX
GEOGRAPHER
GEOGRAPHIC
GETUPANDGO
GILLRAVAGE
GLACIATION
GLEEMAIDEN
GRADUATION
GRAMMARIAN
GUACHAMOLE
HABITATION
HACKMATACK
HALLMARKED
HAMSHACKLE
HANDMAIDEN
HARDCASTLE
HEADMASTER
HESITANTLY
HESITATION
HIGHHANDED
HIGHLANDER
HIGHWAYMAN
HITOPADESA
HONORARIUM
HOOTNANNIE
HUMPBACKED
HYPOGAEOUS
IGNORANTLY
ILLEGALITY
IMMOLATION
IMMORALITY
IMPERATIVE
IMPUTATION
INCAPACITY
INCAPARINA
INCREASING
INCUBATION
INCUNABULA
INDAPAMIDE
INDICATION
INDICATIVE
INEQUALITY
INHALATION
INHUMANITY
INITIATION
INITIATIVE
INNOVATION
INNOVATIVE
INSULARITY
INSULATION
INTIMATELY
INTIMATION
INTONATION
INUNDATION
INVITATION
INVOCATION
IRRIGATION
IRRITATING
IRRITATION
ISONIAZIDE
JACKHAMMER
JACULATION
JOCULARITY
JOURNALESE
JOURNALISM
JOURNALIST
JOUYSAUNCE
JUBILANTLY
JUBILATION
JUDICATURE
KEYBOARDER
KNOCKABOUT
LABORATORY
LACERATION
LAMINATION
LANTHANIDE
LAURDALITE
LEFTHANDED
LEFTHANDER
LESBIANISM
LEUCHAEMIA
LEVITATION
LIBERALISM
LIBERALITY
LIBERALIZE
LIBERATION
LIMITATION
LITERATURE
LITHUANIAN
LITIGATION
LOCULAMENT
LUMINARIST
LUSITANIAN
LYCHNAPSIA
MADAGASCAN
MADAGASCAR
MAHAYANALI
MALAYALAAM

MALEFACTOR
MANDRAGORA
MARSHALSEA
MATRIARCHY
MATURATION
MAXIMALIST
MEDICAMENT
MEDICATION
MEDITATION
MEDITATIVE
MEMBRANOUS
MEMORANDUM
METACARPAL
METACARPUS
METATARSAL
METATARSUS
MILITARISM
MILITARIST
MINERALOGY
MINIMALIST
MINIMARKET
MISHNAYOTH
MISLEADING
MISOCAPNIC
MITIGATING
MITIGATION
MODERATELY
MODERATION
MODULATION
MONEGASQUE
MONETARISM
MONETARIST
MONOGAMOUS
MONTRACHET
MOSASAUROS
MOTIVATION
MOUCHARABY
MUCKRAKING
MUTILATION
NAPTHALENE
NATURALISM
NATURALIST
NATURALIZE
NAUSEATING
NAUSEATIVE
NAVIGATION
NEUTRALISE
NEUTRALITY
NEUTRALIZE
NEWSCASTER
NEWSPAPERS
NICARAGUAN
NOMINALIST
NOMINATION
NOMINATIVE
NONCHALANT
NORTHANGER
NUMERATION
NUTCRACKER
OBLIGATION
OBLIGATORY
OCCUPATION
ODONTALGIA
OPENHANDED
OPHTHALMIC
ORDINARILY
ORDINATION
OROBRANCHE
OSCITATION
OSCULATION
OSCULATORY
OUVIRANDRA
OVEREATING
OVERLANDER
PAEDIATRIC
PAGINATION
PALATALISE
PALISANDER
PALLIATIVE
PALUDAMENT
PANAMANIAN
PANCRATIUM
PARAMARIBO
PARLIAMENT
PARTIALITY
PATRIARCHY
PECULATION
PEDIPALPUS
PEELGARLIC
PEJORATIVE
PERMEATION
PERORATION
PERSUADING
PERSUASION
PERSUASIVE
PETULANTLY
PHANTASIME
PHANTASIST
PHARMACIST
PLAGIARISE
PLAGIARISM
PLAGIARIST
PLAGIARIZE
PLANTATION
PLEASANTLY
PLEASANTRY
PLEONASTIC
POCKMANTIE
POCKMARKED
POIGNANTLY
POLYGAMIST
POLYGAMOUS
POMERANIAN
POPULARITY
POPULARIZE
POPULATION
PORTMANTLE
PORTMANTUA
POSTMASTER
POURPARLER
PRAGMATISM
PRAGMATIST
PROGRAMMER
PROPRAETOR
PROTRACTED
PROTRACTOR
PRZEWALSKI
PUMPHANDLE
PUNICACEAE
PURITANISM
PYRACANTHA
PYROMANIAC
QUADRANGLE
QUADRATURA
QUIZMASTER
RADICALISM
RAILWAYMAN
RAJPRAMUKH
RAMSHACKLE
RAZZMATAZZ
REARMAMENT
RECITATION
RECITATIVE
RECITATIVO
RECREATION
REFUTATION
REGULARITY
REGULARIZE
REGULATION
RELAXATION
RELAXATIVE
RELEGATION
RELOCATION
RENOVATION
REORGANIZE
REPARATION
REPUTATION
RESTRAINED
RETINALITE
RETREATING
REVELATION
REVITALIZE
REVIVALIST
REVOCATION
RHAMPASTOS
RHEUMATICS
RHEUMATISM
RHEUMATOID
RIGELATION
RINGMASTER
ROSEMALING
ROUNDABOUT
ROUSEABOUT
ROUSTABOUT
RUMINANTIA
RUMINATION
RUMINATIVE
SACCHARASE
SACCHARIDE
SACCHARINE
SACCHAROID
SALAMANDER
SALIVATION
SALUTATION
SANITARIUM
SANITATION
SATURATION
SAVONAROLA
SCANDALISE
SCANDALIZE
SCANDALOUS
SCANDAROON
SCARLATINA
SCHOLAEMIA
SCHOLASTIC
SCORDATURA
SEANNACHIE
SECULARIZE
SENEGALESE
SENSUALITY
SEPARATELY
SEPARATION
SEPARATISM
SEPARATIST
SEPARATRIX
SEPTUAGINT
SHAGHAIRED
SHOPWALKER
SIDERATION
SIDESADDLE
SIMILARITY
SIMULACRUM
SIMULATING
SIMULATION
SINGHALESE
SNAPHAUNCE
SNAPHAUNCH
SNOWCAPPED
SOLIDARITY
SOLIVAGANT
SPALLATION
SPARTACIST
SPECIALISE
SPECIALIST
SPECIALITY
SPECIALIZE
SPECTACLED
SPECTACLES
SPECTATORS
SPERMACETI
SPOLIATION
SPOLIATIVE
STAGNATION
STARVATION
STEPFATHER
STEPHANITE
STEPLADDER
STERNALGIA
STICHARION
STIGMATISE
STIGMATIZE
STOCHASTIC
STROGANOFF
SUBHEADING
SUBSTATION
SUFFRAGIST
SUGARALLIE
SUNGLASSES
SUPERADDED
SURINAMESE
SURREALISM
SURREALIST
SUZERAINTY
TABULATION
TAGLIARINI
TAILGATING
TANNHAUSER
TARTRAZINE
TASKMASTER
TELEPATHIC
TEMPTATION
TEPIDARIUM
TERTIARIES
THAUMASITE
THEREAFTER
THEREANENT
THOUSANDTH
TIMESAVING
TITARAKURA
TOLERANTLY
TOLERATION
TOPICALITY
TOUCHANDGO
TOURMALINE
TOURNAMENT
TRAUMATIZE
TRESPASSER
TRIVIALITY
TRIVIALIZE
TROCHANTER
TROUBADOUR
TROUVAILLE
TULARAEMIA
ULCERATION
ULTIMATELY
UNATTACHED
UNBALANCED
UNBLEACHED
UNDULATING
UNDULATION
UNEQUALLED
UNHERALDED
UNIMPAIRED
UNPLEASANT
UNRIVALLED
UNROMANTIC
UNSALARIED
UNSCRAMBLE
URTICACEAE
USURPATION

VALIDATION
VEGETABLES
VEGETARIAN
VEGETATION
VELITATION
VENERATION
VICTUALLER
VIETNAMESE
VIGILANTES
VINEGARISH
VISITATION
VIVIPAROUS
VOETGANGER
VOLUTATION
WAGEEARNER
WANCHANCIE
WELLEARNED
WHIGGAMORE
WILLIAMSON
WINDJAMMER
WITSNAPPER
WOLFRAMITE
YGGDRASILL
ZOOTHAPSIS
ABOVEBOARD
ACETABULAR
ACETABULUM
AFTERBIRTH
AMPHIBIOUS
AMPHIBRACH
ASARABACCA
ASCRIBABLE
ASSEMBLAGE
ASSEMBLING
BLACKBEARD
BLACKBERRY
BLACKBOARD
BLACKBULLY
BRASSBOUND
CANTABRIAN
CHALYBEATE
CHESSBOARD
CHILDBIRTH
CLARABELLA
CLOUDBERRY
CLOUDBURST
CNIDOBLAST
COCKABULLY
CORROBOREE
CRISPBREAD
CROSSBREED
CUCURBITAL
DÉSHABILLÉ
DISCOBOLUS
DISEMBOGUE
DISEMBOWEL
DISHABILLE
DONNYBROOK
ELDERBERRY
ELEGABALUS
ENTOMBMENT
FILLIBRUSH
FLOORBOARD
FLORIBUNDA
GALLABIYAH
GALLABIYEH
GOOSEBERRY
HALLUBALOO
HARTEBEEST
HEARTBREAK
HEREABOUTS
HILDEBRAND
HONEYBUNCH
HOUSEBOUND
HULLABALOO
HYPERBOLIC
IGNIMBRITE
IMPROBABLE
IMPROBABLY
INCUMBENCY
INTERBREED
JERRYBUILT
KNIFEBOARD
KOOKABURRA
LOGANBERRY
LUXEMBOURG
MACROBIOTE
MANGABEIRA
MOZAMBIQUE
MULIEBRITY
NECTABANUS
NEIGHBORLY
NORMOBLAST
NORTHBOUND
OPPROBRIUM
OSTEOBLAST
PAINTBRUSH
PASTEBOARD
PLANOBLAST
POINTBLANK
PROHIBITED
RESEMBLING
ROCKABILLY
SCOREBOARD
SCRIBBLING
SHORTBREAD
SKATEBOARD
SOUTHBOUND
SPELLBOUND
STILLBIRTH
STONEBRASH
STRASBOURG
STRAWBERRY
STRAWBOARD
SWEETBREAD
THROMBOSIS
TOOTHBRUSH
UNDERBURNT
UNNUMBERED
USQUEBAUGH
VERTEBRATE
VESTIBULUM
WATERBORNE
WATERBRASH
WILDEBEEST
YOUNGBERRY
ZIMBABWEAN
ACANACEOUS
AERENCHYMA
AFFLICTION
ALCAICERIA
AMPHICTYON
ANNUNCIATE
ANTARCTICA
ANTHOCLORE
ANTIOCHENE
ANTIOCHIAN
APPLICABLE
APPLICATOR
APPRECIATE
AREFACTION
ARENACEOUS
ATTRACTION
ATTRACTIVE
AUSPICIOUS
AVARICIOUS
BALANCHINE
BARMECIDAL
BARRACKING
BARRACOOTA
BARRACOUTA
BATRACHIAN
BEWITCHING
BOTTICELLI
BRAINCHILD
BROADCLOTH
BYELECTION
CALESCENCE
CAOUTCHOUC
CAPPUCCINO
CAPRICIOUS
CHEMICALLY
CHIFFCHAFF
CHIRICAUNE
CLAIRCOLLE
CLAVICHORD
CLINICALLY
COELACANTH
COLLECTING
COLLECTION
COLLECTIVE
COLLOCUTER
COMANCHERO
CONCOCTION
CONDUCTING
CONDUCTION
CONFECTION
CONJECTURE
CONNECTING
CONNECTION
CONNECTIVE
CONSECRATE
CONVECTION
CONVICTION
COPARCENER
CORNUCOPIA
CORRECTING
CORRECTION
CORRECTIVE
CRETACEOUS
CRISSCROSS
CRITICALLY
CROSSCHECK
CURRICULUM
CURVACEOUS
DEBAUCHERY
DEBOUCHURE
DEFLECTION
DEHISCENCE
DEPRECIATE
DESICCATED
DESPICABLE
DETRACTION
DIALECTICS
DIDASCALIC
DIDUNCULUS
DIELECTRIC
DIFFICULTY
DISENCHANT
DISINCLINE
DISSECTION
DISSOCIATE
DOVERCOURT
DUODECIMAL
DUPLICATOR
EMBOUCHURE
EPONYCHIUM
ESCUTCHEON
ESTANCIERO
EUSTACHIAN
EXCRUCIATE
EXOTICALLY
EXPLICABLE
EXPLICITLY
EXTINCTION
EXTRACTION
FALLACIOUS
FANTOCCINI
FETTUCCINE
FISTICUFFS
FLOORCLOTH
FONTICULUS
FRATICELLI
FROLICSOME
FUNGICIDAL
GERMICIDAL
GRAMICIDIN
GRANDCHILD
GREENCLOTH
GYROSCOPIC
HANDICRAFT
HECTICALLY
HENDECAGON
HERBACEOUS
HEROICALLY
HIPPOCRENE
HOMUNCULUS
HOUSECRAFT
HOVERCRAFT
ICONOCLAST
IMBRICATED
IMBROCCATA
IMPECCABLE
IMPECCABLY
IMPLACABLE
IMPLACABLY
IMPLICITLY
INDISCREET
INEDUCABLE
INFLECTION
INFLICTION
INFRACTION
INJUNCTION
INSOUCIANT
INSPECTION
INTERCEDER
INTERCLUDE
INTINCTION
INVINCIBLE
IRONICALLY
JUSTICIARY
KENTUCKIAN
KLOOTCHMAN
LAMARCKISM
LATTICINIO
LENTICULAR
LEPRECHAUN
LIGNOCAINE
LOQUACIOUS
LUPERCALIA
MACROCARPA
MANUSCRIPT
MARASCHINO
MASTECTOMY
MEDIOCRITY
MEERSCHAUM
MELANCHOLY
MENDACIOUS
MONARCHIST
MONOECIOUS
MONTICULUS
MORDACIOUS
MOTORCYCLE
NEGLECTFUL
NONFICTION
NONSUCCESS
NOUAKCHOTT
OBFUSCATED
OCHLOCRACY
OFFLICENCE

OIREACHTAS
OLERACEOUS
OMNISCIENT
ORTHOCAINE
ORTHOCLASE
OSTEOCOLLA
PANNICULUS
PAPERCHASE
PARASCENIA
PARENCHYMA
PARISCHANE
PARMACITIE
PARTICIPLE
PARTICULAR
PATCHCOCKE
PERFECTION
PERFICIENT
PERNICIOUS
PERNICKETY
PERSECUTOR
PERSICARIA
PETTICHAPS
PETTYCHAPS
PHYLACTERY
PHYSICALLY
PICHICIAGO
PLUTOCRACY
POETICALLY
PONTICELLO
PORLOCKING
PORNOCRACY
PORRACEOUS
POSTSCRIPT
PRECOCIOUS
PREDACIOUS
PREDECEASE
PREDICTION
PRELECTION
PRODUCTION
PRODUCTIVE
PROFICIENT
PROJECTILE
PROJECTING
PROJECTION
PROSECUTOR
PROTECTION
PROTECTIVE
PSILOCYBIN
PUBESCENCE
PUGNACIOUS
QUIESCENCE
RANUNCULUS
RECONCILED
REDISCOVER
REELECTION
REFLECTING
REFLECTION
REFLECTIVE
REFRACTION
REFRACTIVE

REFRACTORY
RESORCINOL
RESPECTFUL
RESPECTING
RESPECTIVE
RETRACTION
RHINOCEROS
ROLLICKING
ROTHSCHILD
SARCOCOLLA
SCREECHING
SDRUCCIOLA
SENESCENCE
SEPULCHRAL
SEQUACIOUS
SERVICEMAN
SINARCHIST
SOPHOCLEAN
SPACECRAFT
SPIRACULUM
SPLANCHNIC
STAGECOACH
STAGECRAFT
STALACTITE
STATECRAFT
STATOCRACY
STIACCIATO
STRACCHINO
SUBJECTION
SUBJECTIVE
SUBSECTION
SUFFICIENT
SUPERCARGO
SURGICALLY
SUSPICIOUS
TABLECLOTH
TACTICALLY
TELESCOPIC
TENRECIDAE
TERRACOTTA
TESTACEOUS
TESTICULAR
THALICTRUM
TORRICELLI
TOSSICATED
TOSTICATED
TRAGACANTH
TRAGICALLY
TRAJECTORY
TRANSCRIBE
TRANSCRIPT
TREKSCHUIT
TRINACRIAN
TUBERCULAR
TUMESCENCE
TYPESCRIPT
UNDERCLASS
UNDERCOVER
UNDERCRAFT
UNDERCROFT

UNDESCRIED
UNEDUCATED
UNGRACIOUS
UNPUNCTUAL
UNSHACKLED
UNSPECIFIC
UPPERCLASS
VERMICELLI
VERNACULAR
VERTICALLY
VIBRACULUM
VINDICTIVE
WAINSCOTED
WALLACHIAN
WATERCOLOR
WATERCRESS
WHEELCHAIR
WIDDICOMBE
WINDSCREEN
WITCHCRAFT
WORLDCLASS
ACCORDANCE
ACCREDITED
AFFORDABLE
ANIMADVERT
ANTIADITIS
ASCENDANCY
ASCENDENCY
ATTENDANCE
BEHINDHAND
BELLADONNA
BENZEDRINE
BEWILDERED
BRAGADISME
CALCEDONIO
COMMODIOUS
CONFEDERAL
CONFIDANTE
CONFIDENCE
CONSIDERED
CORTADERIA
CURMUDGEON
CUSSEDNESS
DEGRADABLE
DEPENDABLE
DEPENDENCE
DEPENDENCY
DIAPEDESIS
DIFFIDENCE
DINANDERIE
DIPLODOCUS
DISORDERED
DISORDERLY
DISSIDENCE
DOGGEDNESS
EISTEDDFOD
ENGENDRURE
EPIDIDYMUS
EXPENDABLE
EXTENDABLE

FASTIDIOUS
FORBIDDING
FORMIDABLE
FRIENDLESS
FRIENDSHIP
FUDDYDUDDY
GESUNDHEIT
GRANADILLA
GRENADIERS
GRENADILLA
GROUNDBAIT
GROUNDLESS
GROUNDLING
GROUNDSMAN
GROUNDWORK
HIPPODROME
HORSEDRAWN
HUMDUDGEON
HYPERDULIA
IMPRUDENCE
INCENDIARY
INCREDIBLE
INCREDIBLY
INGREDIENT
INTENDMENT
JUGENDSTIL
LACCADIVES
LACKADAISY
LIQUIDATOR
LIQUIDIZER
METHEDRINE
METHODICAL
MOLENDINAR
MOLYBDENUM
MORBIDEZZA
MORTADELLA
NEFANDROUS
NIGHTDRESS
ORCHIDEOUS
PALINDROME
PECCADILLO
PERFIDIOUS
PERIODICAL
PESCADORES
PHAGEDAENA
PHOLIDOSIS
PHOTODIODE
PICCADILLY
PIRANDELLO
PONTEDERIA
PRECEDENCE
PREJUDICED
PRESIDENCY
PROCEDURAL
PROVEDITOR
PROVIDENCE
PUNCHDRUNK
QUESADILLA
RECRUDESCE
REDUNDANCY

REGARDLESS
REPRODUCER
RHOEADALES
ROBERDSMAN
ROLANDSECK
ROWDYDOWDY
RUGGEDNESS
SACERDOTAL
SACREDNESS
SCOTODINIA
SECONDBEST
SECONDHAND
SECONDMENT
SECONDRATE
SEGUIDILLA
SERRADELLA
SERRADILLA
SHIELDRAKE
SHREWDNESS
SORDIDNESS
SPLENDIDLY
STRINDBERG
STRULDBERG
STRULDBRUG
SUBMEDIANT
SUBSIDENCE
SUBSIDIARY
SYNECDOCHE
SYNEIDESIS
THREADBARE
THREADLIKE
THREADWORM
THUCYDIDES
TRIPUDIARY
UNREADABLE
VALLADOLID
VIVANDIÈRE
WICKEDNESS
WRONGDOING
YTHUNDERED
ABERDEVINE
ABONNEMENT
ACCELERATE
ACCIDENTAL
ACROGENOUS
ACROMEGALY
ACROTERION
ADRAMELECH
ADULTERANT
ADULTERATE
ADULTERESS
ADULTERINE
ADULTEROUS
AESTHETICS
AIRFREIGHT
ALBIGENSES
ALLEGEANCE
ALLUREMENT
ALTOGETHER
AMANUENSIS

AMBOCEPTOR
ANTECEDENT
ANTISEPSIS
ANTISEPTIC
ANTIVENENE
APOPLECTIC
APOTHECARY
APOTHECIUM
APOTHEOSIS
APPARENTLY
ARCHDEACON
ARGOLEMONO
ARMAGEDDON
ARUNDELIAN
ARYTAENOID
ASAFOETIDA
ASSEVERATE
ASTUTENESS
ASYMMETRIC
ATRAMENTAL
AURIFEROUS
AUTOGENOUS
BAFFLEMENT
BAILIEWICK
BARCHESTER
BAREHEADED
BARELEGGED
BAROMETRIC
BATTLEDOOR
BATTLEDORE
BATTLEMENT
BATTLESHIP
BEEKEEPING
BEFOREHAND
BELLWETHER
BESTSELLER
BILIVERDIN
BIOCHEMIST
BLACKENING
BLISTERING
BLITHERING
BLOTTESQUE
BLUNDERING
BOISTEROUS
BOLSHEVIST
BOOKKEEPER
BOOKSELLER
BOOTLEGGER
BOTTLEHEAD
BOTTLENECK
BOWDLERISE
BOWDLERIZE
BRIDGEHEAD
BRIDGETOWN
BRIDLEPATH
BUFFLEHEAD
BULLHEADED
BUMFREEZER
BUTCHERING
CADAVEROUS
CALAVERITE
CAMBRENSIS
CAMSTEERIE
CANDLEFISH
CANDLEWICK
CAPITELLUM
CARAMELIZE
CARELESSLY
CATALECTIC
CATALEPTIC
CATTLEGRID
CEREBELLUM
CHAFFERING
CHALCEDONY
CHALLENGER
CHAMAEROPS
CHAMBERPOT
CHAMBERTIN
CHANCELLOR
CHANDELIER
CHANGEABLE
CHANGELESS
CHANGELING
CHARGEABLE
CHARGEHAND
CHATTERBOX
CHATTERTON
CHAUCERIAN
CHEESECAKE
CHEESEWOOD
CHELTENHAM
CHEQUEBOOK
CHESTERTON
CHICHESTER
CHICKENPOX
CHILDERMAS
CHIMNEYPOT
CHOICELESS
CINQUEFOIL
CLUMPERTON
COARSENESS
COCHLEARIA
COHERENTLY
COLCHESTER
COMPLEMENT
COMPLETELY
COMPLETION
COMPLEXION
COMPLEXITY
COMPREHEND
COMPRESSED
COMPRESSOR
CONCRETION
CONGREGATE
CONIFEROUS
CONQUERING
CONSPECTUS
CONSUETUDE
CONTRECOUP
COPESETTIC
CORDIERITE
COTTIERISM
COUNSELING
COUNSELLOR
COUNTERACT
CRAQUETURE
CRICKETING
CRYOGENICS
CUDDLESOME
CUTTLEBONE
CUTTLEFISH
DARJEELING
DAYDREAMER
DEADNETTLE
DEBASEMENT
DEBATEMENT
DEBRIEFING
DECAHEDRON
DECELERATE
DEEPSEATED
DEFACEMENT
DEFILEMENT
DEGENERACY
DEGENERATE
DELCREDERE
DELIBERATE
DENOUEMENT
DESIDERATA
DEVOTEMENT
DIASKEUAST
DILIGENTLY
DISCREETLY
DISCREPANT
DISCRETION
DISTRESSED
DOORKEEPER
DOPPLERITE
DOSTOEVSKY
DOUBLEBASS
DOUBLETALK
DUMBLEDORE
EBOULEMENT
EFFACEMENT
EIGHTEENTH
ELOQUENTLY
ENCASEMENT
ENGAGEMENT
ENGOUEMENT
ENLACEMENT
ENLÈVEMENT
ENTICEMENT
EPAULEMENT
EPISTEMICS
EPITHELIUM
ESCAPEMENT
EUHEMERISM
EVANGELIST
EVANGELIZE
EVISCERATE
EXAGGERATE
EXASPERATE
EXCITEMENT
EXENTERATE
EXOTHERMIC
FEARLESSLY
FEATHERBED
FEEBLENESS
FICKLENESS
FIDDLEWOOD
FIERCENESS
FIGUREHEAD
FISHSELLER
FITZGERALD
FLATTERING
FLICKERING
FLINDERSIA
FLUNKEYDOM
FOURIERISM
FOURTEENTH
FREQUENTED
FREQUENTER
FREQUENTLY
FULLLENGTH
GAMEKEEPER
GANGRENOUS
GARNIERITE
GENTLEFOLK
GENTLENESS
GEORGETOWN
GEOTHERMAL
GETHSEMANE
GIRDLERINK
GLISTENING
GLITTERAND
GLITTERATI
GLITTERING
GLOUCESTER
GOALKEEPER
GOODFELLOW
GRANGERISM
GRANGERIZE
GUARNERIUS
HALFYEARLY
HANDLEBARS
HANOVERIAN
HAUSTELLUM
HEEDLESSLY
HELLBENDER
HELPLESSLY
HEMIHEDRON
HOARSENESS
HOLOFERNES
HOMOGENIZE
HOMORELAPS
HOMOSEXUAL
HOPELESSLY
HUMBLENESS
HUMORESQUE
HYPODERMIC
HYPOTENUSE
ICEBREAKER
ILLITERACY
ILLITERATE
IMMATERIAL
IMMODERATE
IMPOTENTLY
IMPOVERISH
IMPUDENTLY
INBREEDING
INCIDENTAL
INCINERATE
INCITEMENT
INCOHERENT
INDECENTLY
INDIGENOUS
INDIRECTLY
INDITEMENT
INDONESIAN
INDUCEMENT
INDUMENTUM
INFIDELITY
INGENERATE
INHERENTLY
INNOCENTLY
INSOLENTLY
INTEMERATE
INTENERATE
INTERESTED
INTOLERANT
INVETERATE
IRRELEVANT
IRREMEDIAL
IRREVERENT
JOBSEEKERS
JOURNEYMAN
KENSPECKLE
KETTLEDRUM
KILOMETRES
KNOBKERRIE
LAMBREQUIN
LANIGEROUS
LAUNCEGAYE
LAUNCESTON
LAWBREAKER
LIEUTENANT
LIGHTERMAN
LISTLESSLY
LITTLENESS
LOCKKEEPER
LONGFELLOW
MAINPERNOR
MAKEWEIGHT
MANAGEABLE
MANAGEMENT
MANAGERESS
MANAGERIAL
MANCHESTER
MANIFESTLY
MARGUERITE
MARQUETRIE

MARYLEBONE
MASQUERADE
MEAGRENESS
MEANDERING
MEDDLESOME
MELANESIAN
METACENTRE
METALEPSIS
METTLESOME
MICHAELMAS
MINUTEBOOK
MINUTENESS
MONTSERRAT
MONUMENTAL
MORIGEROUS
MOROSENESS
MOUDIEWART
MOUNTEBANK
MOUSSELINE
MOUSTERIAN
MUJAHEDDIN
MUMBLENEWS
NEEDLECASE
NEEDLEWORK
NETTLERASH
NETTLETREE
NEWSLETTER
NEWSREADER
NIMBLENESS
NINETEENTH
NORTHERNER
NOTICEABLE
NOTICEABLY
OBEDIENTLY
OBLITERATE
OBTUSENESS
OCCIDENTAL
OCTAHEDRON
OCTODECIMO
OFFTHECUFF
OFFTHEWALL
OPOTHERAPY
ORNAMENTAL
OSMETERIUM
OUTSPECKLE
OVERWEIGHT
PADAREWSKI
PAINLESSLY
PALFRENIER
PALLBEARER
PAPAVERINE
PARACELSUS
PARAMETRIC
PARASELENE
PARKLEAVES
PARTHENOPE
PEACHERINO
PEAUDESOIE
PEDIMENTAL
PENSIEROSO
PERIHELION
PERPLEXING
PERPLEXITY
PERSIENNES
PHLEGETHON
PHRENESIAC
PICARESQUE
PIONEERING
PLATTELAND
PLAYFELLOW
PLUNDERING
POINSETTIA
POLITENESS
POLYHEDRON
POLYMERIZE
POLYNESIAN
PROCEEDING
PROCREATOR
PROPHETESS
PROSCENIUM
PROSPECTOR
PROSPECTUS
PROSPERINA
PROSPERITY
PROSPEROUS
PSALTERIUM
PUZZLEMENT
QUARRENDER
QUARTERING
QUARTEROON
RANDLETREE
RANNLETREE
RANTLETREE
RATTLETRAP
REASSEMBLE
RECKLESSLY
RECUPERATE
REFERENDUM
REFINEMENT
REGENERATE
REGIMENTAL
REGIMENTED
REJONEADOR
REJUVENATE
REMONETISE
REMOTENESS
REMUNERATE
REQUIESCAT
RESCHEDULE
RESTLESSLY
RETIREMENT
REVERENTLY
RINGLEADER
ROISTERING
ROMANESQUE
ROTTWEILER
RUDIMENTAL
RUTHLESSLY
SADDLEBACK
SADDLEBILL
SALOPETTES
SAVAGENESS
SCANDERBEG
SCARCEMENT
SCARCENESS
SCARLETINA
SCATHELESS
SCATTERING
SCOOTERIST
SEDATENESS
SETTLEMENT
SEXAGESIMA
SHATTERING
SHILLELAGH
SHIMMERING
SHOPKEEPER
SHORTENING
SHRIVELLED
SHROVETIDE
SHUDDERING
SINGLENESS
SLAMMERKIN
SLANDEROUS
SLATTERNLY
SLEEVELESS
SLUMBERING
SMATTERING
SMITHEREEN
SMORREBROD
SNEEZEWOOD
SNIGGERING
SNORKELING
SOMBRERITE
SOURDELINE
SOUTHERNER
SPARSENESS
SPEAKERINE
SPENCERIAN
SPENSERIAN
SPHACELATE
SPHALERITE
SPIRKETING
SPONGEWARE
SPOONERISM
SPOTLESSLY
SPRUCENESS
SQUETEAGUE
SQUIREARCH
STAGGERING
STALHELMER
STALLENGER
STAMMERING
STARVELING
STATUESQUE
STEPHENSON
STERTEROUS
STRATEGIST
STRIDENTLY
STRIDEWAYS
SUCCEEDING
SUPPLEJACK
SUPPLEMENT
SUPPLENESS
SUPPRESSED
SUPPRESSOR
SWAGGERING
SWEETENING
SWELTERING
SYNCRETISE
SYNTHESIZE
TACTLESSLY
TALEBEARER
TANGLEFOOT
TAPERECORD
TAPOTEMENT
TECHNETIUM
TELPHERAGE
TESCHENITE
THEMSELVES
THICKENING
THIRTEENTH
THUNDERBOX
THUNDERING
THUNDEROUS
TIEBREAKER
TIMEKEEPER
TIMESERVER
TIRELESSLY
TOLLKEEPER
TONGUESTER
TORQUEMADA
TRACHELATE
TRISKELION
TROPAEOLUM
TUMBLEDOWN
TURTLEDOVE
TURTLENECK
TYPESETTER
UBERMENSCH
UNACCENTED
UNAFFECTED
UNATTENDED
UNDEFEATED
UNDEFENDED
UNDESERVED
UNDETECTED
UNDETERRED
UNDIGESTED
UNEXPECTED
UNFORESEEN
UNFRIENDLY
UNIQUENESS
UNLICENSED
UNOBSERVED
UNREDEEMED
UNRESERVED
UNREVEALED
UNSLEEPING
UROSTEGITE
VEHEMENTLY
VICEGERENT
VICEREGENT
VIRULENTLY
VITUPERATE
VOCIFERATE
VOCIFEROUS
WATTLEWORK
WAVELENGTH
WEATHERMAN
WENTLETRAP
WHISPERING
WHITTERICK
WINCHESTER
WOODPECKER
YOURSELVES
ZOLLVEREIN
ZOOTHERAPY
ZWITTERION
AMPLEFORTH
BLISSFULLY
BREADFRUIT
CAMOUFLAGE
CANDYFLOSS
CHAUDFROID
CHEERFULLY
CRAIGFLUKE
CROCKFORDS
DENTIFRICE
DOUBTFULLY
DREADFULLY
FAITHFULLY
FORCEFULLY
FRUITFULLY
GOOSEFLESH
GRACEFULLY
GRAPEFRUIT
GRATEFULLY
GRATIFYING
GREENFINCH
GUTTIFERAE
HENCEFORTH
HORRIFYING
INSUFFLATE
INTERFERER
INTERFERON
KATERFELTO
KLANGFARBE
MAGNIFICAT
MAGNIFYING
MERCIFULLY
MICROFICHE
MILLEFIORI
MOURNFULLY
PEACEFULLY
PERMAFROST
PERSIFLAGE
PETRIFYING
PIANOFORTE
POKERFACED
PONTEFRACT

PONTIFICAL
PRIZEFIGHT
PUTREFYING
RIGHTFULLY
SATISFYING
SCORNFULLY
SHAMEFACED
SHAMEFULLY
SIGNIFICAT
SKILLFULLY
SPITEFULLY
STOREFRONT
STUPEFYING
TASTEFULLY
TERRIFYING
THANKFULLY
TRUSTFULLY
TRUTHFULLY
ULTRAFICHE
UNCONFINED
UNDERFLOOR
UNEDIFYING
WASTEFULLY
WATCHFULLY
WATERFRONT
WRONGFULLY
WYCLIFFIAN
ABORIGINAL
ABRIDGMENT
AMPHIGOURI
ANALOGICAL
ANEMOGRAPH
APOLOGETIC
ASTRAGALUS
AVANTGARDE
BEDRAGGLED
BELONGINGS
BERSAGLIER
BETELGEUSE
BETELGEUZE
BIOLOGICAL
BLACKGUARD
BOURIGNIAN
BRIDEGROOM
CARMAGNOLE
CARRAGHEEN
CENTIGRADE
CHINAGRAPH
COASTGUARD
COLLEGIATE
CONTAGIOUS
CONTIGUITY
CONTIGUOUS
CORREGIDOR
CORRIGENDA
CORRUGATED
CORRUGATOR
COURAGEOUS
DEFLAGRATE
DICTOGRAPH
DISENGAGED
DISFIGURED
DIVERGENCE
ECOLOGICAL
EMBERGOOSE
ENCOIGNURE
ENSANGUINE
EXTINGUISH
FASTIGIATE
FIBERGLASS
FIBREGLASS
FULLYGROWN
GEOLOGICAL
HELIOGRAPH
HEPTAGONAL
HIEROGLYPH
HIPPOGRIFF
HIPPOGRYPH
HOWLEGLASS
IATROGENIC
IMPREGNATE
INDULGENCE
INELIGIBLE
INSTIGATOR
INSURGENCY
INTANGIBLE
INTRIGUING
LARYNGITIS
LENTIGINES
LITHOGRAPH
LITURGICAL
MALINGERER
MENINGITIS
MIMEOGRAPH
MONTAGNARD
MULLIGRUBS
MYRINGITIS
MYSTAGOGUE
MYSTAGOGUS
NDRANGHETA
NEGLIGENCE
NEGLIGIBLE
NEWSAGENTS
OCEANGOING
ORTHOGONAL
OSTROGOTHS
OTHERGATES
OTHERGUESS
OUTRAGEOUS
PANTAGRUEL
PANTOGRAPH
PASSAGEWAY
PATHOGENIC
PENTAGONAL
PERIEGESIS
PETROGLYPH
PHONOGRAPH
PHOTOGENIC
PHOTOGRAPH
PORTUGUESE
PRODIGALLY
PRODIGIOUS
PROPAGANDA
PROPAGATOR
PROTAGORAS
PTERYGOTUS
PUNDIGRION
PYCNOGONID
PYTHAGORAS
PYTHOGENIC
RADIOGRAPH
RESURGENCE
RETROGRADE
RETROGRESS
REVENGEFUL
RHINEGRAVE
RIDINGHOOD
SALMAGUNDI
SALTIGRADE
SATYAGRAHA
SCAPEGRACE
SEGREGATED
SMARAGDINE
SPREAGHERY
SPRINGBOKS
SPRINGHAAS
SPRINGLESS
SPRINGLIKE
SPRINGTAIL
SPRINGTIME
STALAGMITE
STRAGGLING
STRAIGHTEN
STRENGTHEN
STRINGENCY
STRINGENDO
STRINGHALT
STRONGHOLD
STRONGROOM
SUPERGIANT
SYNTAGMATA
TACHOGRAPH
TARDIGRADE
THROUGHOUT
THROUGHPUT
THROUGHWAY
TRANSGRESS
TRIANGULAR
UNFLAGGING
UNORIGINAL
VARIEGATED
ZINCOGRAPH
ZOOLOGICAL
ABHIDHAMMA
ADIAPHORON
AEROPHAGIA
AFTERHOURS
ALLYCHOLLY
ANALPHABET
ANARCHICAL
ANESTHESIA
ANESTHETIC
ANTICHTHON
ANTIPHONAL
ANTITHESIS
ANTITHETIC
ATTACHMENT
AUTOCHTHON
AVERRHOISM
BANISHMENT
BLACKHEART
BLASPHEMER
BLOCKHOUSE
BLOODHOUND
BLUETHROAT
BONESHAKER
BREATHLESS
BRONCHITIC
BRONCHITIS
BUCEPHALUS
CAERPHILLY
CANEPHORUS
CATACHUMEN
CATAPHRACT
CATECHUMEN
CHINCHILLA
CHURCHGOER
CHURCHYARD
COCKCHAFER
COPENHAGEN
CORYPHAEUS
COURTHOUSE
CREOPHAGUS
CRYOPHORUS
DECATHLETE
DECIPHERED
DELIGHTFUL
DETACHABLE
DETACHMENT
DIPHTHERIA
DISINHERIT
DOLICHOLIS
DOLICHOTUS
ENCEPHALON
ENKEPHALIN
ENRICHMENT
EPENTHETIC
EUROCHEQUE
FAMISHMENT
FIANCHETTO
FORESHADOW
FOURCHETTE
FRANCHISEE
FRANCHISOR
FRAUNHOFER
FREIGHTAGE
GAULTHERIA
GENETHLIAC
GLASSHOUSE
GREENHEART
GREENHOUSE
GUESTHOUSE
HEADPHONES
HEMICHORDA
HEMOPHILIA
HITCHHIKER
HOBBYHORSE
HOLOPHOTAL
HOMOPHOBIA
HOMOPHOBIC
HYPOTHESIS
ICOSOHEDRA
INFIGHTING
LAVISHNESS
LEDERHOSEN
LENGTHWAYS
LENGTHWISE
LIGHTHOUSE
LILYWHITES
LONGCHAMPS
LOTOPHAGUS
MANICHAEAN
MENECHMIAN
METAPHRASE
METATHERIA
METATHESIS
MONOCHROME
MONOPHONIC
MONOTHEISM
NOSOPHOBIA
OESOPHAGUS
OVERCHARGE
OVERSHADOW
OVERTHETOP
OVERTHWART
PARAPHILIA
PARAPHONIA
PARAPHRASE
PARAPHYSIS
PERIPHERAL
PERISHABLE
PHOSPHORUS
PLANCHETTE
PLOUGHBOTE
PLOUGHGATE
PLOUGHWISE
POLYCHAETE
POLYCHREST
POLYCHROME
POLYPHEMUS
POLYTHEISM
POSTCHAISE
POWERHOUSE
PROSTHESIS
PROSTHETIC
PUNISHABLE
PUNISHMENT
PYROPHORUS
QUENCHLESS
RAWSTHORNE

RICHTHOFEN
ROSECHAFER
ROUGHHOUSE
ROUNDHOUSE
SAMOTHRACE
SHAKUHACHI
SKETCHBOOK
SKUPSHTINA
SMOOTHNESS
SPATCHCOCK
SPEECHLESS
SPITCHCOCK
STEAKHOUSE
STONEHENGE
STONYHURST
STOREHOUSE
STOUTHERIE
STOUTHRIEF
STRATHSPEY
STROPHIOLE
STRYCHNINE
SUPERHUMAN
SWEETHEART
SWITCHBACK
TELEPHONIC
THOUGHTFUL
TOCOPHEROL
TRENCHMORE
TRIPEHOUND
UNFATHOMED
UNORTHODOX
WHEELHOUSE
WHITEHEART
WINDSHIELD
WORKAHOLIC
WRETCHEDLY
XENOPHOBIA
XENOPHOBIC
XEROPHYTIC
ZOANTHARIA
ABYSSINIAN
ACCUSINGLY
ACQUAINTED
ACTIVITIST
ADDITIONAL
ADHIBITION
ADJUDICATE
ADMINISTER
ADMIRINGLY
ADMONITION
AERUGINOUS
AFFABILITY
AFFILIATED
ALCIBIADES
ALEMBICATE
ALKALINITY
ALLEGIANCE
ALMSGIVING
ALTAZIMUTH
ALTRUISTIC
ALZHEIMERS
AMIABILITY
AMMUNITION
ANASTIGMAT
ANCIPITOUS
ANNIHILATE
ANTIBIOTIC
ANTICIPATE
APPARITION
APPETITIVE
APPETIZING
APPOSITION
ARCHBISHOP
ARISTIPPUS
ARTIFICIAL
ASCETICISM
ASPIDISTRA
ASSIMILATE
ASSOCIATED
ASTONISHED
ATELEIOSIS
AUDIBILITY
AUSTRINGER
AUTODIDACT
BABESIASIS
BABYSITTER
BACKBITING
BAHRAINIAN
BAILLIWICK
BALBRIGGAN
BARASINGHA
BARGAINING
BATTAILOUS
BEAUTICIAN
BEAUTIFIER
BEDEVILLED
BEHAVIORAL
BENEDICITE
BENEFICENT
BENEFICIAL
BIENNIALLY
BITUMINOUS
BOOKBINDER
BOOTLICKER
BRACHIOPOD
BRAININESS
BRILLIANCE
CACOMISTLE
CACUMINOUS
CAESPITOSE
CALAMITOUS
CALORIFIER
CAMPAIGNER
CANCRIZANS
CAPABILITY
CAPACITATE
CARABINEER
CARABINIER
CENTRIFUGE
CHAMPIGNON
CHAUVINISM
CHAUVINIST
CHEEKINESS
CHILDISHLY
CHILLINESS
CHLORINATE
CHRONICLER
CHRONICLES
CHRYSIPPUS
CHURLISHLY
CIRCUITOUS
CISLEITHAN
CLAMMINESS
CLASSICISM
CLASSICIST
CLASSIFIED
CLOUDINESS
CLUMSINESS
COINCIDENT
COLCHICINE
COMEDIENNE
COMPLIANCE
COMPLICATE
COMPLICITY
COMPLIMENT
CONCHIGLIE
CONCHIOLIN
CONSCIENCE
CONSPIRACY
CONSTITUTE
CONTRIBUTE
CONTRITION
COORDINATE
COSTLINESS
COUNCILLOR
CRAFTINESS
CREATIVITY
CRISPINIAN
DEACTIVATE
DEADLINESS
DEBILITATE
DECAPITATE
DECISIVELY
DEFICIENCY
DEFINITELY
DEFINITION
DEFINITIVE
DELPHINIUM
DEMOBILISE
DEMOBILIZE
DEMOLITION
DEMONIACAL
DEPOSITARY
DEPOSITION
DEPOSITORY
DERACINATE
DESALINATE
DESCRIBING
DESPAIRING
DEVOTIONAL
DICKCISSEL
DILAPIDATE
DIMINISHED
DISABILITY
DISDAINFUL
DISJOINTED
DISQUIETED
DISTRIBUTE
DISTRINGAS
DIVISIONAL
DOMICILARY
DOWNSIZING
DREAMINESS
DREARINESS
DREARISOME
DROWSINESS
DRUZHINNIK
DURABILITY
DUUMVIRATE
DYNAMITARD
EBULLIENCE
ECARDINATE
ECTHLIPSIS
EFFEMINACY
EFFEMINATE
EFFICIENCY
EFFUSIVELY
EGURGITATE
ELASTICATE
ELASTICITY
ELEUSINIAN
ELYTRIFORM
EMANCIPATE
EMARGINATE
EMBODIMENT
EMBROIDERY
EMULSIFIER
ENANTIOSIS
ENCLOISTER
EPHRAIMITE
EPIDEICTIC
EQUANIMITY
ESPECIALLY
EULOGISTIC
EXACTITUDE
EXHIBITION
EXORBITANT
EXPEDIENCE
EXPEDIENCY
EXPEDITION
EXPERIENCE
EXPERIMENT
EXPOSITION
EXPOSITORY
FACILITATE
FACILITIES
FAMILIARLY
FANATICISM
FATALISTIC
FATALITIES
FAULTINESS
FAVORITISM
FELICITATE
FELICITOUS
FEMININITY
FEVERISHLY
FIENDISHLY
FILTHINESS
FLABBINESS
FLASHINESS
FLEETINGLY
FLESHINESS
FLIMSINESS
FLOURISHED
FLUFFINESS
FOOTLIGHTS
FOREBITTER
FOREFINGER
FORFAITING
FORFEITURE
FORTUITOUS
FRACTIONAL
FRANCISCAN
FRANGIPANE
FRANGIPANI
FRATRICIDE
FRENZIEDLY
FRINGILLID
FRISKINESS
FULIGINOUS
FUNCTIONAL
FUTURISTIC
GADOLINIUM
GAINGIVING
GELATINOUS
GLASSINESS
GLOSSINESS
GNOSTICISM
GOLDDIGGER
GOLDFINGER
GRATUITOUS
GREEDINESS
GRITTINESS
GRUBBINESS
GRUMPINESS
HABILITATE
HALFSISTER
HANDPICKED
HEADLIGHTS
HEARTINESS
HEDONISTIC
HEREDITARY
HERESIARCH
HIGHBINDER
HISTRIONIC
HOMELINESS
HOODWINKED
HORNRIMMED
HUMANISTIC
HUMANITIES

HUMIDIFIER
IDEALISTIC
ILLUMINATE
ILLUMINATI
IMBECILITY
IMMOBILITY
IMMOBILIZE
IMPATIENCE
IMPEDIMENT
IMPENITENT
IMPOLITELY
IMPOSITION
IMPURITIES
INACTIVITY
INAPTITUDE
INARTISTIC
INCISIVELY
INCIVILITY
INDECISION
INDECISIVE
INDEFINITE
INDELICACY
INDELICATE
INDIVIDUAL
INEBRIATED
INEFFICACY
INEPTITUDE
INFINITELY
INFINITIVE
INFURIATED
INGEMINATE
INHABITANT
INHIBITING
INHIBITION
INHIBITORY
INIQUITOUS
INKSLINGER
INORDINATE
INSANITARY
INSATIABLE
INSATIABLY
INSEMINATE
INSIPIDITY
INTELIGENT
INTIMIDATE
INTOXICANT
INTOXICATE
INVALIDATE
INVALIDITY
INVARIABLE
INVARIABLY
INVIGILATE
IRRADICATE
IRRATIONAL
JAUNTINESS
JEISTIECOR
JINGOISTIC
JUDICIALLY
KARTTIKAYA
KINCHINLAY
KINDLINESS
KINGFISHER
KLEBSIELLA
KOEKSISTER
KURDAITCHA
LADYKILLER
LASTMINUTE
LAURVIKITE
LAWABIDING
LEFTWINGER
LEGALISTIC
LEGIBILITY
LEGITIMACY
LEGITIMATE
LEGITIMIZE
LEGUMINOUS
LENOCINIUM
LEONTIASIS
LIBIDINOUS
LIGHTINGUP
LIKELIHOOD
LIKEMINDED
LINGUISTIC
LIVELIHOOD
LIVELINESS
LOGARITHMS
LONELINESS
LORDLINESS
LOUISIETTE
LOVELINESS
LUXURIANCE
MANCHINEEL
MATERIALLY
MAXIMILIAN
MEGALITHIC
MENACINGLY
MEPERIDINE
MESOLITHIC
MIDSHIPMAN
MIGHTINESS
MILITIAMAN
MISERICORD
MISPRISION
MITHRIDATE
MODIFIABLE
MONILIASIS
MONILIFORM
MONOLITHIC
MORALITIES
MOULDINESS
MOULDIWARP
MUDSKIPPER
MUNIFICENT
MUTABILITY
NEGATIVELY
NEGOTIABLE
NEGOTIATOR
NIHILISTIC
NONALIGNED
NOTABILITY
NOTIFIABLE
NOURRITURE
OBLIGINGLY
OBSIDIONAL
OCCASIONAL
OFFICIALLY
OLEAGINOUS
OPENMINDED
OPPOSITION
OPTIMISTIC
OVERRIDING
OWLSPIEGLE
PACIFICISM
PAINKILLER
PALATINATE
PANARITIUM
PARADIDDLE
PARISIENNE
PASQUINADE
PATAVINITY
PATCHINESS
PATHFINDER
PECULIARLY
PENICILLIN
PERIWINKLE
PERQUISITE
PETITIONER
PHILLIPINA
PHILLIPINE
PHLOGISTIC
PHLOGISTON
PHYLLIOPOD
PILGRIMAGE
PITYRIASIS
PLASTICINE
PLASTICITY
PLIABILITY
PLIOHIPPUS
POLITICIAN
POLITICIZE
PONCHIELLI
POSITIVELY
POSITIVIST
POSTLIMINY
PREDNISONE
PREEMINENT
PRESCIENCE
PRETTINESS
PREVAILING
PRINCIPIUM
PRINCIPLED
PRINCIPLES
PROCLIVITY
PROFLIGACY
PROFLIGATE
PROPLITEAL
PROPRIETOR
PROSCIUTTO
PROSTITUTE
PSYCHIATRY
PURSUIVANT
QUADRICEPS
QUADRIREME
QUEASINESS
QUERCITRON
QUESTIONER
REACTIVATE
RECIDIVISM
RECIDIVIST
RELATIVELY
RELATIVITY
REPETITEUR
REPETITION
REPETITIVE
REPOSITORY
RESILIENCE
RESTRICTED
RESUPINATE
RETRAINING
ROSANILINE
RUBIGINOUS
SANCTIFIED
SANCTITIES
SANCTITUDE
SANDWICHES
SANGUINARY
SBUDDIKINS
SCANTINESS
SCEPTICISM
SCLERIASIS
SCOFFINGLY
SCRUTINEER
SCRUTINISE
SCRUTINIZE
SCURRILITY
SCURRILOUS
SECURITIES
SEEMLIHEAD
SELEGILINE
SEMICIRCLE
SHABBINESS
SHEEPISHLY
SHIFTINESS
SHOCKINGLY
SHODDINESS
SHOPLIFTER
SICILIENNE
SIDEWINDER
SIMILITUDE
SIMPLICITY
SIMPLISTIC
SKEPTICISM
SKINDIVING
SLEEPINESS
SLOPPINESS
SLUGGISHLY
SMARMINESS
SNOOTINESS
SOLICITOUS
SOLICITUDE
SOLIFIDIAN
SOLUBILITY
SOOTHINGLY
SOUBRIQUET
SPEEDINESS
SPIFLICATE
SPILLIKINS
SPISSITUDE
SPONGIFORM
SPONSIONAL
SPORTINGLY
STALLINGER
STEADINESS
STEELINESS
STEMWINDER
STEPSISTER
STICKINESS
STILLICIDE
STILLIFORM
STINGINESS
STOCKINESS
STRABISMUS
STRATIOTES
STRAVINSKY
STRELITZIA
STREPITANT
STREPITOSO
STRIKINGLY
STUFFINESS
STULTIFIED
STURDINESS
SUBSTITUTE
SULTRINESS
SUPPLICANT
SUPPLICATE
SURFRIDING
SURPRISING
SUSTAINING
SWIMMINGLY
TARADIDDLE
TECHNICIAN
TELEVISION
TENDRILLED
THALLIFORM
THERMIONIC
THERMISTOR
THUMBIKINS
TIMELINESS
TIROCINIUM
TOUCHINESS
TOURBILLON
TOURNIQUET
TRAFFICKER
TRANSIENCE
TRANSISTOR
TRANSITION
TRANSITIVE
TRANSITORY
TRENDINESS
TRICKINESS

TRICLINIUM
TRIPLICATE
TUTIVILLUS
UBIQUITOUS
UNABRIDGED
UNASSIGNED
UNAVAILING
UNBELIEVER
UNDENIABLE
UNEASINESS
UNENVIABLE
UNFAMILIAR
UNFINISHED
UNFRUITFUL
UNHYGIENIC
UNINVITING
UNOFFICIAL
UNRELIABLE
UNRELIEVED
UNRULINESS
UNSCRIPTED
UNSOCIABLE
UNTIDINESS
UROPOIESIS
VELOCIPEDE
VERIFIABLE
VERSAILLES
VETERINARY
VIEWFINDER
VILLAINOUS
VISIBILITY
VOCATIONAL
VOLATILITY
VOLUBILITY
VOLUMINOUS
VORAGINOUS
WASSAILING
WEEDKILLER
WHARFINGER
WHEEZINESS
WOODPIGEON
WORSHIPPER
WORTHINESS
BLITZKRIEG
BRADYKININ
CLASPKNIFE
EMBANKMENT
HAKENKREUZ
LYSENKOISM
MISTAKENLY
PAPERKNIFE
REMARKABLE
REMARKABLY
SAUERKRAUT
SHISHKEBAB
SPRINKLING
TCHOUKBALL
TROTSKYITE
UNWORKABLE
ABERGLAUBE
ACOTYLEDON
AMARYLLIDS
ANCHYLOSIS
ANGUILLULA
ANNUALIZED
ANTICLIMAX
APICULTURE
APOCALYPSE
ASPHALTITE
ASTRALAGUS
ASTROLOGER
AUTOPLASTY
AVICULARIA
BACKBLOCKS
BACKSLIDER
BAUDELAIRE
BOUILLOTTE
BRICKLAYER
CALCULABLE
CALCULATED
CALCULATOR
CAMERLENGO
CAMERLINGO
CANDELABRA
CANDELILLA
CANNELLONI
CANTALOUPE
CANTELOUPE
CANTILEVER
CANTILLATE
CAPILLAIRE
CASSOLETTE
CASUALNESS
CATHOLICON
CATHOLICOS
CELLULITIS
CENTILITER
CENTILITRE
CEPHALOPOD
CHAROLLAIS
CHATELAINE
CHECKLATON
CHIVALROUS
CHOLALOGUE
COCKALORUM
COMPELLING
COMPULSION
COMPULSIVE
COMPULSORY
CONCILIATE
CONDOLENCE
CONSULTANT
CONSULTING
CONVALESCE
CONVOLUTED
CONVOLVUTE
CONVULSION
CONVULSIVE
COQUELICOT
CORDILLERA
CORNFLAKES
CORNFLOWER
CORPULENCE
CRAPULENCE
CRENELLATE
CROTALARIA
CROTALIDAE
CUCULLATED
DAMSELFISH
DECOLLATOR
DERAILLEUR
DERAILMENT
DIABOLICAL
DISBELIEVE
DISCOLORED
DISSELBOOM
DISSILIENT
DISSOLVENT
DISTILLATE
DISTILLERY
DISTILLING
DREADLOCKS
DRUMBLEDOR
ENCYCLICAL
ENROLLMENT
EUROCLYDON
EVERGLADES
EXCELLENCE
EXCELLENCY
FERTILISED
FERTILISER
FERTILIZER
FEUILLETON
FIBRILLATE
FLAGELLATE
FLASHLIGHT
FLATULENCE
FLOODLIGHT
FLUGELHORN
FOSSILIZED
FRITILLARY
FULFILMENT
GHIBELLINE
GOLDILOCKS
GONDOLIERS
GRANULATED
GRASSLANDS
GRATILLITY
GROVELLING
GUIDELINES
HALLELUJAH
HANGGLIDER
HECTOLITRE
HEIDELBERG
HELIOLATER
HEMIPLEGIA
HEMOGLOBIN
HIGHFLYING
HORNBLENDE
HORNBLOWER
HORSELBERG
HYDROLYSIS
IMPARLANCE
INFALLIBLE
INFALLIBLY
INSTALMENT
INTAGLIATE
INTERLEAVE
INTERLOPER
INVIOLABLE
ISABELLINE
JAYWALKING
KESSELRING
KIESELGUHR
LAVALLIÈRE
LEGISLATOR
LINGULELLA
LORDOLATRY
MAQUILLAGE
MARIOLATRY
MARVELLOUS
MATELLASSE
METALLURGY
METAPLASIS
METHYLATED
MICROLIGHT
MISCELLANY
MONOPLEGIA
NARCOLEPSY
NATHELESSE
NEAPOLITAN
NESSELRODE
NEURILEMMA
NEUROLEMMA
NIGHTLIGHT
NYCTALOPIA
ODDFELLOWS
OFFBALANCE
OPHICLEIDE
OSCILLATOR
OSTEOLEPIS
OUGHTLINGS
OUTBALANCE
OVERSLAUGH
PANTALOONS
PARAGLOSSA
PARALLELED
PARAPLEGIA
PARAPLEGIC
PARNELLISM
PENNILLION
PENTELIKON
PERCOLATOR
PESTALOZZI
PESTILENCE
PICCALILLI
PISTILLATE
PLATELAYER
POIKILITIC
POSTILLATE
POSTILLION
PREVALENCE
PRICKLOUSE
PRIVILEGED
PROMULGATE
PROPELLANT
PROPULSION
PROPYLAEUM
PROSILIENT
PUMMELLING
RADIOLARIA
RAMPALLIAN
RANNELTREE
REBELLIOUS
REPUBLICAN
RHINOLALIA
RIBOFLAVIN
RINGELMANN
ROQUELAURE
RUMBULLION
SANDALWOOD
SARCOLEMMA
SCHOOLBOOK
SCHOOLGIRL
SCHOOLMAAM
SCOPELIDAE
SCUTELLATE
SHACKLETON
SHECKLATON
SHORTLIVED
SHOVELHEAD
SHOVELNOSE
SHRILLNESS
SIGILLARIA
SIMILLIMUM
SINFULNESS
SINGULARLY
SOGDOLAGER
SOGDOLIGER
SOGDOLOGER
SOMNOLENCE
SPECULATOR
SPLITLEVEL
STABILISER
STABILIZER
STERILISER
STERILIZER
STUMBLEDOM
SUBSELLIUM
SVADILFARI
SYMBOLICAL
SYPHILITIC
THIMBLEFUL
THIMBLEWIT
TIRAILLEUR
TORCHLIGHT
TORTELLINI
TRANSLATED
TRANSLATOR
TRAVELATOR

TRAVELLERS
TRAVELLING
TRAVELOGUE
TRAVOLATOR
TRIMALCHIO
TRUCULENCE
TURBULENCE
UMBELLIFER
UNDECLARED
UNDERLEASE
UNDERLINEN
UNDERLYING
UNEMPLOYED
UNEXPLORED
UNYIELDING
USEFULNESS
VENTILATOR
VERMILLION
VITELLICLE
WALLFLOWER
WATERLEVEL
WHEWELLITE
WINDFLOWER
ZABAGLIONE
ABNORMALLY
ABSTEMIOUS
ACHROMATIC
ACROAMATIC
AFRORMOSIA
ALDERMANLY
AMPHIMACER
AMPHIMIXIS
ANATOMICAL
ANAXIMENES
ANDROMACHE
ANEMOMETER
APOPEMPTIC
APOSEMATIC
ARCHIMEDES
ARITHMETIC
ASTIGMATIC
AXINOMANCY
BARRAMUNDA
BELLAMOURE
BLANCMANGE
BOTTOMLESS
CAPNOMANCY
CARTOMANCY
CASSUMUNAR
CENTIMETER
CENTIMETRE
CHAULMUGRA
CHERIMOYER
CHIROMANCY
CIRCUMCISE
CIRCUMFLEX
CIRCUMFUSE
CIRCUMVENT
CLEROMANCY
CLOCKMAKER
COLLEMBOLA
COLLIMATOR
CONDIMENTS
CONSUMMATE
COQUIMBITE
COXCOMICAL
DETERMINED
DIPLOMATIC
DIPSOMANIA
DISCOMFORT
DISCOMMODE
DISCOMPOSE
DISSEMBLER
DISSIMILAR
DOLCEMENTE
DRESSMAKER
ECCHYMOSIS
ECONOMICAL
ELACAMPANE
ELECAMPANE
EMBLEMATIC
EMBLEMENTS
EMOLUMENTS
ENDOSMOSIS
ENTREMESSE
EPILIMNION
ESTRAMACON
EUDIOMETER
FIELDMOUSE
FLUTEMOUTH
GONIOMETER
GUATEMALAN
HEPTAMERON
HIEROMANCY
HIPPOMANES
HOUSEMAIDS
HOWSOMEVER
HYDROMETER
HYGROMETER
IMPRIMATUR
INFORMALLY
INTERMARRY
INTERMEZZO
JIGGAMAREE
LANDAMMANN
LINEAMENTS
LINEOMYCIN
LITHOMARGE
MAHOMMEDAN
MATCHMAKER
MEDIUMTERM
MERRYMAKER
METHOMANIA
MICROMETER
MILEOMETER
MILLIMETER
MILLIMETRE
MISCHMETAL
MULTIMEDIA
NECROMANCY
NINCOMPOOP
NUMISMATIC
OMBROMETER
OPISOMETER
PADDYMELON
PAPIAMENTO
PARRAMATTA
PASSAMEZZO
PEACEMAKER
PENTAMERON
PENTAMETER
PENTIMENTO
PHENOMENAL
PHENOMENON
PHLEGMASIA
PHLEGMATIC
PLEXIMETER
PORTAMENTO
PORTSMOUTH
PRESUMABLY
RANDOMNESS
RECOMMENCE
RHYTHMICAL
SANDEMANIA
SCARAMOUCH
SCHISMATIC
SCHLIMAZEL
SINSEMILLA
SKEUOMORPH
SNAKEMOUTH
SOPHOMORIC
SPODOMANCY
STONEMASON
STREAMERED
STREAMLINE
SUBCOMPACT
SUBLIMATER
SUBLIMINAL
SUPERMODEL
SYSTEMATIC
TACHOMETER
TANTAMOUNT
TROMOMETER
UNCOMMONLY
UNEXAMPLED
UNICAMERAL
UNPROMPTED
VINDEMIATE
WAMPUMPEAG
WATCHMAKER
WATERMELON
ABOMINABLE
ABOMINABLY
ABSTENTION
ABSTINENCE
ACCOUNTANT
ACCOUNTING
ACTIONABLE
ADAMANTINE
ADELANTADO
AGAPANTHUS
AGGRANDISE
ALABANDINE
ALABANDITE
ALCYONARIA
ALEXANDERS
ALEXANDRIA
ALIMENTARY
ALPHONSINE
ALTERNATOR
AMPHINEURA
ANGWANTIBO
APEMANTHUS
APPRENTICE
ARAGONITES
ASSIGNABLE
ASSIGNMENT
ASTOUNDING
ASTRINGENT
ASTRONOMER
ATTAINABLE
ATTAINMENT
BARRENNESS
BASSINGTON
BATTENBERG
BATTENBURG
BIPINNARIA
BIRKENHEAD
BIRMINGHAM
BOLLANDIST
BOOZINGKEN
BOUSINGKEN
BRIGANDINE
BRIGANTINE
BROKENDOWN
BUCCINATOR
BUCKINGHAM
BURDENSOME
BURLINGTON
BUTTONDOWN
BUTTONHOLE
CACHINNATE
CALUMNIATE
CAMPANELLA
CANNONBALL
CANTONMENT
CAPERNAITE
CAPERNOITY
CARCINOGEN
CARPENTIER
CENTENNIAL
CHEMONASTY
CHIRONOMIC
CISPONTINE
CITRONELLA
CLEMENCEAU
CLEMENTINE
COCCINEOUS
COETANEOUS
COLONNADED
COMMANDANT
COMMANDEER
COMMANDING
COMMENTARY
COMMENTATE
COMMONWEAL
COMMUNALLY
COMMUNIQUÉ
COMPENDIUM
COMPENSATE
CONCENTRIC
CONCINNITY
CONCINNOUS
CONGENITAL
CONSENSION
CONSONANCE
CONSONANTS
CONTENTION
CONTINENCE
CONTINGENT
CONTINUING
CONTINUITY
CONTINUOUS
CONVENANCE
CONVENIENT
CONVENTION
CONVINCING
COPERNICUS
COTTONTAIL
COTTONWOOD
CREDENTIAL
CRIMINALLY
CUISENAIRE
CURRENCIES
CYBERNETIC
DECENNOVAL
DECLENSION
DESCENDANT
DESCENDING
DESPONDENT
DETAINMENT
DETRUNCATE
DIACONICON
DIAGENESIS
DIAGONALLY
DISCONCERT
DISCONNECT
DISCONTENT
DISENNOBLE
DISHONESTY
DISMANTLED
DISPENSARY
DISPENSING
DISSENSION
DISSENTING
DISSONANCE
DISTENSION
DISTINCTLY
DRACONITES
ECUMENICAL

EFFRONTERY
EGOCENTRIC
ELEMENTARY
ELIMINATOR
EMALANGENI
EMPFINDUNG
ENCHANTING
ENTRANCING
ENTRENCHED
EPICANTHUS
EPIDENDRUM
EPIGENETIC
EPIMENIDES
ERYMANTHUS
EUPHONIOUS
EUTHANASIA
EUTHYNEURA
EXPOUNDERS
EXTERNALLY
EXTRANEOUS
FAHRENHEIT
FALLINGOFF
FARRANDINE
FASCINATED
FASCINATOR
FERRANDINE
FESCENNINE
FLAMINGANT
FLORENTINE
FONTANELLE
FONTINALIS
FORTINBRAS
FOXHUNTING
FRAXINELLA
FRICANDEAU
FROMANTEEL
FUSTANELLA
FUSTANELLE
GALVANISER
GARGANTUAN
GARLANDAGE
GASCONNADE
GEOCENTRIC
GONFANONER
GORMANDIZE
GOVERNANCE
GOVERNESSY
GOVERNMENT
GUARANTEED
GUBERNATOR
HAEMANTHUS
HARMANBECK
HARMONIOUS
HARRINGTON
HATEENOUGH
HEAVENWARD
HINDENBURG
HOOTANANNY
HOOTENANNY
HORRENDOUS
HUSBANDAGE
ICOSANDRIA
IMAGINABLE
INFERNALLY
INTERNALLY
INTERNMENT
INTERNODAL
JACKANAPES
JARDINIERE
JARGONELLE
KUOMINTANG
LAURENTIAN
LAWRENCIUM
LEAMINGTON
MACKINTOSH
MAIDENHAIR
MAIDENHOOD
MAISONETTE
MALCONTENT
MALIGNANCY
MANZANILLA
MARCANTANT
MARGINALIA
MARGINALLY
MARIONETTE
MARTINGALE
MARTINIQUE
MASKANONGE
MASKINONGE
MATERNALLY
MAYONNAISE
MEANINGFUL
MECHANICAL
MECHANIZED
MERCANTILE
MICRONESIA
MIGNONETTE
MISCONDUCT
MIZZENMAST
MORGANATIC
MORGANETTA
MOTIONLESS
MUTTONHEAD
NATIONALLY
NATIONWIDE
NEWFANGLED
NOTIONALLY
OBTAINABLE
ORDONNANCE
ORIDINANCE
ORIGINALLY
ORIGINATOR
OROGENESIS
OUANANICHE
OUTLANDISH
OXYGENATOR
OZYMANDIAS
PADDINGTON
PANJANDRUM
PARAENESIS
PARDONABLE
PARDONABLY
PARTINGALE
PATERNALLY
PATRONISED
PATRONYMIC
PERCENTAGE
PERCENTILE
PERDENDOSI
PERMANENCE
PERMANENCY
PERSONABLE
PERSONALLY
PERTINENCE
PETRONELLA
PHOTONASTY
PICCANINNY
PIGEONHOLE
PLATINISED
POLIANTHES
POLLINATED
POLYANTHUS
PORTENTOUS
PRATINCOLE
PREBENDARY
PREHENSILE
PREPENSELY
PRESENTDAY
PRETENSION
PRETINCOLE
PREVENANCY
PREVENTION
PREVENTIVE
PROFUNDITY
PROGENITOR
PROMENADER
PROMINENCE
PROMONTORY
PROPENSITY
PROTANOPIC
PROVENANCE
PROVINCIAL
PRUDENTIAL
PTERANODON
QUARANTINE
QUIRINALIA
RABBINICAL
RATIONALLY
REAMINGBIT
REASONABLE
REASONABLY
RECOGNISED
RECOGNIZED
REPUGNANCE
RESIGNEDLY
RESOUNDING
RESPONDENT
RESPONSIVE
RETURNABLE
RITORNELLE
RITORNELLO
ROCKINGHAM
ROWLANDSON
SALLENDERS
SALMANAZAR
SALMONELLA
SALPINGIAN
SANDINISTA
SARMENTOUS
SATURNALIA
SCREENPLAY
SCROUNGING
SEAMANSHIP
SEASONABLE
SEASONABLY
SELLINGERS
SEPTENNIAL
SEQUENTIAL
SERMONICAL
SERPENTINE
SHENANIGAN
SIMMENTHAL
STUPENDOUS
SUBTENANCY
SUBVENTION
SUCCINCTLY
SUDDENNESS
SUSPENDERS
SUSPENSION
SUSTENANCE
SWEDENBORG
TABERNACLE
TABLANETTE
TANGANYIKA
TANGENTIAL
TAPDANCING
TEDDINGTON
TENNANTITE
TERMINABLE
TERMINALIA
TERMINALLY
TILLANDSIA
TOILINETTE
TORRENTIAL
TRAMONTANA
TRAMONTANE
TRAVANCORE
TRECENTIST
TREMENDOUS
TRIDENTINE
TRILINGUAL
TRIMSNITCH
TRITANOPIA
TURPENTINE
TYRANNICAL
TYRANNISED
ULTRONEOUS
UNBLINKING
UNDERNEATH
UNEVENNESS
UNEVENTFUL
UNIGENITUS
UNMANNERED
UNMANNERLY
UNTHINKING
UPBRINGING
UPSTANDING
VILLANELLE
VILLANOVAN
VULCANALIA
WALDENSIAN
WAPPENSHAW
WARRANDICE
WASHINGTON
WEAPONLESS
WELLINGTON
WILLINGDON
WOFFINGTON
WOODENHEAD
YAFFINGALE
ACHITOPHEL
AFICIONADO
AGRONOMIST
AHITHOPHEL
ALCOHOLISM
ALECTORIAN
ALMSHOUSES
AMBLYOPSIS
AMELIORATE
AMPELOPSIS
ANADROMOUS
ANADYOMENE
ANTAGONISE
ANTAGONISM
ANTAGONIST
ANTAGONIZE
ANTHEOLION
ANTHROPOID
ANTIMONIAN
ANTINOMIAN
ANTIPODEAN
ANTISOCIAL
APOLLONIAN
APOLLONIUS
APOTROPAIC
AQUAFORTIS
ARISTOCRAT
ARISTOLOGY
ARISTOTLES
ARMIPOTENT
ARTHROMERE
ASTEROIDEA
AUCTIONEER
AUDITORIUM
AUTECOLOGY
AUTOMOBILE
AUTOMOTIVE
AUTONOMOUS
BABIROUSSA
BABYLONIAN

BALLOONING
BALLOONIST
BALNEOLOGY
BAMBOOZLED
BAREFOOTED
BASSOONIST
BEAUJOLAIS
BEDCLOTHES
BENEVOLENT
BERMOOTHES
BICHROMATE
BLASTOIDEA
BLUEBOTTLE
BONDHOLDER
BOOKMOBILE
BOONDOGGLE
BUFFOONERY
BURGEONING
CALAMONDIN
CALCEOLATE
CALEDONIAN
CALIFORNIA
CALYDONIAN
CAMELOPARD
CAMERONIAN
CANCIONERO
CAPITOLINE
CAPREOLATE
CARDIOGRAM
CARDIOLOGY
CARPHOLOGY
CARTOONIST
CASSIOPEIA
CATABOLISM
CATALOGUER
CATEGORISE
CATEGORIZE
CAUTIONARY
CAUTIOUSLY
CAVICORNIA
CECIDOMYIA
CENTROSOME
CEREMONIAL
CEREMONIES
CERTIORARI
CHARDONNAY
CHARIOTEER
CHEIRONOMY
CHERSONESE
CHERVONETS
CHEVROTAIN
CHIFFONIER
CHIMBORAZO
CHLOROFORM
CHROMOSOME
CHRONOLOGY
CHRYSOLITE
CIRRHOPODA
CLODHOPPER
COMPROMISE
COMSTOCKER
CONCHOLOGY
CONTROLLER
CONTROVERT
COPYHOLDER
CORNCOCKLE
COUSCOUSOU
CRYPTOGRAM
CUCKOOPINT
CYNOMOLGUS
DECOLORATE
DELTIOLOGY
DEMOGORGON
DENDROPHIS
DEVELOPING
DIAGNOSTIC
DICHROMISM
DICTIONARY
DICYNODONT
DIGITORIUM
DISCLOSURE
DITHIONATE
DOORTODOOR
DUCKBOARDS
DYSPROSIUM
DYSTROPHIC
ECHINODERM
ECHINOIDEA
ECUADORIAN
EDULCORATE
ELECTORATE
EMBRYOLOGY
EMPEDOCLES
ENORMOUSLY
ENTEROCELE
ENTOMOLOGY
EPIDIORITE
EPIGLOTTIS
EPIPHONEMA
EPISCOPATE
EQUATORIAL
EQUIVOCATE
ERGONOMICS
EUCHLORINE
EUPHROSYNE
FABULOUSLY
FASTMOVING
FEARNOUGHT
FISHMONGER
FLAMBOYANT
FLANCONADE
FLAPDOODLE
FOREBODING
FOUDROYANT
FRAMBOESIA
FREEBOOTER
FREEHOLDER
FREELOADER
FROGHOPPER
GALSWORTHY
GASTRONOME
GASTRONOMY
GENEROSITY
GENEROUSLY
GEOTROPISM
GLAUCONITE
GLENDOVEER
GLORIOUSLY
GLUTTONOUS
GOBEMOUCHE
GORGEOUSLY
GRACIOUSLY
GRAPHOLOGY
GRAPTOLITE
GRAVEOLENT
GRIDLOCKED
GUILLOTINE
GYNECOLOGY
HALFDOLLAR
HALFHOURLY
HANDSOMELY
HARDBOILED
HAUSTORIUM
HELICOPTER
HEPATOCELE
HETERODOXY
HITOPODESA
HOMECOMING
HOMEWORKER
HOMOEOPATH
HORIZONTAL
HUMOROUSLY
HYPOCORISM
IMMEMORIAL
IMMUNOLOGY
INDECOROUS
INDICOLITE
INDIGOLITE
INVIGORATE
IRONMONGER
IRRESOLUTE
JACKBOOTED
JAMESONITE
JOHNSONIAN
LANCEOLATE
LANDLOCKED
LANDLOUPER
LANGUOROUS
LEAFHOPPER
LHERZOLITE
LOCOMOTION
LOCOMOTIVE
LUMINOSITY
MABINOGION
MACEDONIAN
MACONOCHIE
MAKUNOUCHI
MALACOLOGY
MALEVOLENT
MALODOROUS
MARCIONITE
MEGALOSAUR
MELACONITE
MELOCOTOON
METABOLISE
METABOLISM
MINEWORKER
MISSIONARY
MONOPOLISE
MONOPOLIZE
MONOTONOUS
MONTGOMERY
MORATORIUM
MORISONIAN
MORPHOLOGY
MOUTHORGAN
MUSICOLOGY
MUTINOUSLY
NATATORIAL
NATATORIUM
NATUROPATH
NEMATOCYST
NEUTROPHIL
NEWSMONGER
NEWSWORTHY
NONSMOKING
NONVIOLENT
NOSOCOMIAL
NOTEWORTHY
NUCLEONICS
NYMPHOLEPT
OBLOMOVISM
ODONTOLITE
ODONTOLOGY
OMNIPOTENT
OMNIVOROUS
OMOPHORION
ORPHEOREON
OVERWORKED
PALAEOTYPE
PALAGONITE
PARADOXIDE
PARADOXINE
PARAGONITE
PARANORMAL
PASSIONATE
PATAGONIAN
PATRIOTISM
PEASHOOTER
PENELOPHON
PENSIONNAT
PERIDOTITE
PERILOUSLY
PHAELONIAN
PHAENOTYPE
PHLOGOPITE
PHRENOLOGY
PHYSIOCRAT
PHYSIOLOGY
PICKPOCKET
PINAKOTHEK
PLASMODESM
PLESIOSAUR
POCAHONTAS
POGONOTOMY
PONEROLOGY
PORTIONIST
POZZUOLANA
PRAETORIAN
PRAETORIUM
PREVIOUSLY
PROPIONATE
PSAMMOPHIL
PSEPHOLOGY
PSEUDOCARP
PSYCHOLOGY
PSYCHOPATH
PSYCHOPOMP
RACECOURSE
RAVENOUSLY
REDECORATE
REREDORTER
RHAPSODISE
RHAPSODIZE
RIGOROUSLY
RIPSNORTER
ROADWORTHY
RUMBLOSSOM
RUPICOLINE
SALICORNIA
SANATORIUM
SAXICOLINE
SAXICOLOUS
SCAMMOZZIS
SCAPHOPODA
SCORZONERA
SEDULOUSLY
SEISMOLOGY
SELTZOGENE
SENATORIAL
SENSUOUSLY
SEXOLOGIST
SHAMPOOING
SHELDONIAN
SHIBBOLETH
SHOPSOILED
SIDEBOARDS
SIDEROSTAT
SNOWMOBILE
SOFTBOILED
SPECIOUSLY
SPELEOLOGY
SPURIOUSLY
STADHOLDER
STATIONARY
STATIONERY
STAUROLITE
STENTORIAN
STEPMOTHER
STEREOTOMY

STEREOTYPE
STERTOROUS
STRABOTOMY
STRAMONIUM
STRAPONTIN
STRATOCRAT
STRATOCYST
STUBBORNLY
STUDIOUSLY
SUAVEOLENT
SUBTROPICS
SWALLOWING
SYMPHONIUM
TAXONOMIST
TECHNOCRAT
TECHNOLOGY
TEICHOPSIA
THEODOLITE
THEOLOGATE
THEOLOGIAN
THEOLOGISE
THEOLOGIST
THERMOSTAT
THRENODIAL
TIMBROLOGY
TOMFOOLERY
TOPOLOGIST
TORTUOUSLY
TOXICOLOGY
TRAITOROUS
TRAMPOLINE
TRIACONTER
TRICHOLOGY
TROCHOTRON
TROCTOLITE
TROGLODYTE
TROMBONIST
TROPHONIUS
TRYPTOPHAN
UNBECOMING
UNCTUOUSLY
UNINFORMED
UNRESOLVED
UNSCHOOLED
VARICOSITY
VIGOROUSLY
VIROLOGIST
VIRTUOSITY
VIRTUOUSLY
WHATSOEVER
WILDFOWLER
WOODWORKER
ZAPOROGIAN
ZEUGLODONT
ZUMBOORUCK
ABSORPTION
ACCOMPLICE
ACCOMPLISH
AFTERPIECE
ANABAPTIST
ANGLOPHILE
ANGLOPHOBE
ASSUMPTION
ASSUMPTIVE
ATMOSPHERE
BARYSPHERE
BIRTHPLACE
BRAINPOWER
BROADPIECE
CATCHPENNY
CELLOPHANE
CHECKPOINT
CHIROPTERA
CIRRIPEDEA
CIRRIPEDIA
CLOMIPHENE
COLEOPTERA
COLLAPSING
CONCEPTION
CONCEPTUAL
CONNIPTION
CORRUPTING
CORRUPTION
CROSSPIECE
CTENOPHORA
CYCLOPEDIA
DECAMPMENT
DECOMPOSED
DEUTOPLASM
DIREMPTION
DISAPPOINT
DISAPPROVE
DISCIPLINE
DISCOPHORA
DISRUPTION
DISRUPTIVE
DISSIPATED
DROSOPHILA
EMBONPOINT
ENCAMPMENT
ENTERPRISE
ENTRYPHONE
EPANOPHORA
ERYSIPELAS
ESCARPMENT
EUTRAPELIA
EVERYPLACE
FLAMEPROOF
FLASHPOINT
GALUMPHING
GRAMOPHONE
GYPSOPHILA
HAIRSPRING
HANDSPRING
HANKYPANKY
HEMISPHERE
HIEROPHANT
HODGEPODGE
HOMEOPATHY
HORSEPOWER
HOTCHPOTCH
HOUSEPROUD
HYALOPHANE
HYDROPHANE
HYDROPLANE
HYDROPONIC
IMPALPABLE
IMPROPERLY
INCOMPLETE
INDISPOSED
INTERPHONE
IONOSPHERE
KIDNAPPING
LITHOPHANE
MAINSPRING
MALLOPHAGA
METROPOLIS
MICROPHONE
MOUSEPIECE
MOUTHPIECE
MULTIPLIED
MULTIPLIER
NECROPOLIS
OMBROPHOBE
ORTHOPNOEA
ORTHOPTICS
OSTEOPATHY
OSTEOPHYTE
OVERSPREAD
PALIMPSEST
PANSOPHIST
PERCEPTION
PERCEPTIVE
PERCIPIENT
PEREMPTORY
PERSEPHONE
PERSEPOLIS
PHILIPPINA
PHILIPPINE
PHILOPOENA
PINCHPENNY
PINNIPEDIA
PLEROPHORY
PRECIPITIN
PRESUPPOSE
PROTOPLASM
PSOCOPTERA
QUERSPRUNG
RECOMPENSE
REDEMPTION
RESUMPTION
RHINOPHYMA
RHIPIPTERA
RUDOLPHINE
SAPROPHYTE
SAUROPSIDA
SCHIPPERKE
SHOCKPROOF
SOUNDPROOF
SOUSAPHONE
STANDPOINT
STYLOPISED
SUBREPTION
SUPERPOWER
SYNCOPATED
TERNEPLATE
TERREPLEIN
THREEPENCE
THREEPENNY
TOOTHPASTE
TOUCHPAPER
TOUCHPIECE
TRANSPLANT
TRANSPOSED
TRIUMPHANT
TROPOPAUSE
TROPOPHYTE
UNDERPANTS
UNDISPUTED
UNHAMPERED
UNINSPIRED
UNPREPARED
USUCAPTION
VIBRAPHONE
WASTEPAPER
WATERPROOF
WELLSPRING
WIDESPREAD
XIPHOPAGUS
ALGONQUIAN
COLLIQUATE
COLLOQUIAL
CONSEQUENT
DELINQUENT
EARTHQUAKE
INADEQUACY
INADEQUATE
INFREQUENT
RELINQUISH
SINARQUIST
SUBSEQUENT
ABHORRENCE
ABITURIENT
ALCHERINGA
ALLOTROPIC
ALLPURPOSE
ANACARDIUM
ANASTROPHE
ANCHORETIC
ANSWERABLE
ANTIFREEZE
ANTIPROTON
ANTITRAGUS
APHAERESIS
APOSTROPHE
APPEARANCE
ARBITRATOR
AREOGRAPHY
ARTHURIANA
ASYNARTETE
AUTHORISED
AUTHORSHIP
AUTOCRATIC
BACITRACIN
BACKGROUND
BADDERLOCK
BALDERDASH
BANDERILLA
BANDERILLO
BARBAROSSA
BARCAROLLE
BEAVERSKIN
BELLARMINE
BERNARDINE
BETACRUCIS
BIRTHRIGHT
BITTERLING
BITTERNESS
BOMBARDIER
BORDERLAND
BORDERLINE
BOTHERSOME
BUDGERIGAR
BUTTERBAKE
BUTTERBUMP
BUTTERMERE
BUTTERMILK
CACOGRAPHY
CALCAREOUS
CAMBERWELL
CAMPARADOR
CAMPERDOWN
CANTERBURY
CARBURETOR
CASCARILLA
CATARRHINE
CAVALRYMAN
CELEBRATED
CENSORIOUS
CENSORSHIP
CHAMBRANLE
CHAPARAJOS
CHAPAREJOS
CHARTREUSE
CHITARRONE
CINDERELLA
CISTERCIAN
CLEVERNESS
CLOSTRIDIA
COCKERNONY
COLBERTINE
COLEORHIZA
COLLARBONE
COLOURLESS
COLPORTAGE
COLPORTEUR
COMFORTING
COMMERCIAL
COMPARABLE
COMPARATOR

COMPARISON
CONCERNING
CONCERTINA
CONCERVATE
CONCORDANT
CONCURRENT
CONFERENCE
CONFERVOID
CONFORMIST
CONFORMITY
CONSORTIUM
CONSTRAINT
CONSTRINGE
CONTORTION
CONVERGENT
CONVERSANT
CONVERSELY
CONVERSION
COPPERHEAD
COPPERNOSE
COPPERSKIN
COPYWRITER
COUNTRYMAN
CROSSREFER
CROSSROADS
CULVERTAGE
CUMBERLAND
CUMBERSOME
CUMMERBUND
CURMURRING
DEALERSHIP
DECAGRAMME
DEEPFREEZE
DEMOCRATIC
DEMOCRITUS
DEMOGRAPHY
DEPLORABLE
DEPLORABLY
DESBOROUGH
DESECRATED
DETERRENCE
DIDGERIDOO
DIFFERENCE
DINNERTIME
DISARRANGE
DISBURTHEN
DISCERNING
DISCORDANT
DISCURSIVE
DISHARMONY
DISPERSION
DISPIRITED
DISSERTATE
DISSERVICE
DISTORTION
DISTURBING
DRAWBRIDGE
DUKKERIPEN
DUNDERFUNK
DUNDERHEAD

DUNDERPATE
EASTERLING
ECCOPROTIC
ECHOPRAXIA
ELECTRICAL
ELECTROMER
ELECTRONIC
EMMETROPIA
ENDEARMENT
ENHYDRITIC
EPISTROPHE
ESCADRILLE
ESCHAROTIC
ESPADRILLE
ETEOCRETAN
EVAPORATED
EVITERNITY
EXACERBATE
EXONERATED
EXPATRIATE
EXUBERANCE
FAIRGROUND
FATHERLAND
FATHERLESS
FAVOURABLE
FAVOURABLY
FETTERLOCK
FINGERLING
FINGERNAIL
FLOWERBEDS
FOOTBRIDGE
FOOTPRINTS
FOREGROUND
FOREORDAIN
FORTHRIGHT
FRATERETTO
FRATERNISE
FRATERNITY
FRATERNIZE
FRUSTRATED
GASTEROPOD
GENEVRETTE
GIBBERELLA
GILBERTIAN
GILBERTINE
GINGERBEER
GINGERSNAP
GIRLFRIEND
GODPARENTS
GONORRHOEA
GRASSROOTS
GREGARIOUS
GREYFRIARS
GRIDIRONER
GUTTURALLY
HAMMERHEAD
HAMMERLOCK
HEMORRHAGE
HESPERIDES
HIERARCHIC

HINTERLAND
HIPPARCHUS
HISTORICAL
HITHERWARD
HOLOGRAPHY
HONOURABLE
HONOURABLY
HONOURLESS
HORSERIDER
HUMOURLESS
HYSTERESIS
HYSTERICAL
IMPAIRMENT
INEXORABLE
INGLORIOUS
INOPERABLE
INQUIRENDO
INTEGRATED
JABBERWOCK
JAGUARONDI
JAGUARUNDI
JEOPARDISE
JEOPARDIZE
JOLTERHEAD
JUGGERNAUT
KEMPERYMAN
KILMARNOCK
KIMBERLITE
KSHATRIYAS
LAEOTROPIC
LANGERHANS
LATTERMATH
LAUDERDALE
LAUNDROMAT
LEADERSHIP
LEGWARMERS
LEOPARDESS
LETTERHEAD
LIEBERMANN
LIMBERNECK
LIMBURGITE
LIMITROPHE
LOCKERROOM
LOGGERHEAD
LOGORRHOEA
LUGUBRIOUS
LUMBERJACK
MALAPROPOS
MANSERVANT
MASCARPONE
MASKIROVKA
MASTERMIND
MASTERWORT
MASTURBATE
MATTERHORN
MAVOURNEEN
MEAGERNESS
MEASURABLE
MEMBERSHIP
MENORRHOEA

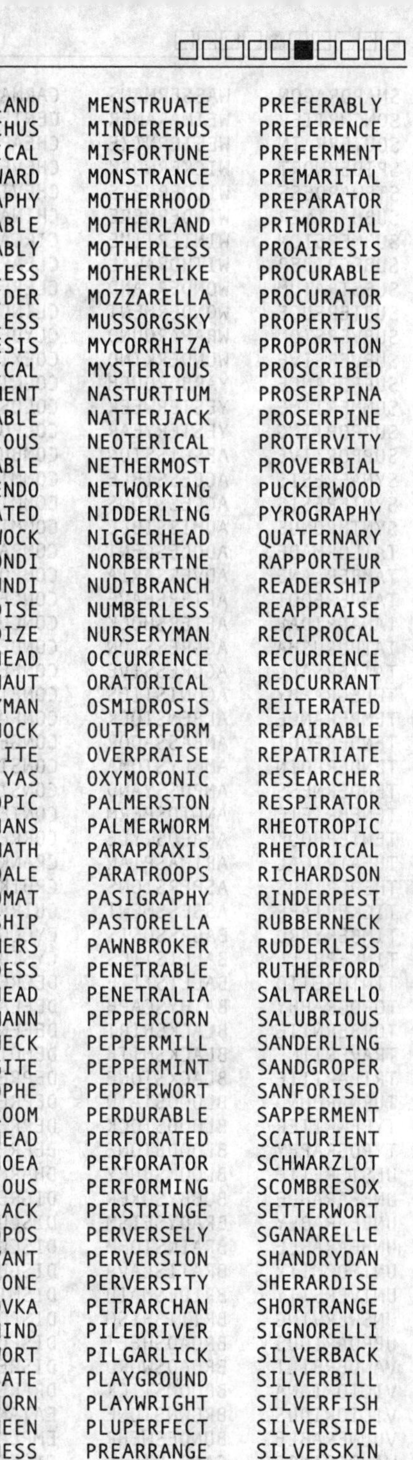

MENSTRUATE
MINDERERUS
MISFORTUNE
MONSTRANCE
MOTHERHOOD
MOTHERLAND
MOTHERLESS
MOTHERLIKE
MOZZARELLA
MUSSORGSKY
MYCORRHIZA
MYSTERIOUS
NASTURTIUM
NATTERJACK
NEOTERICAL
NETHERMOST
NETWORKING
NIDDERLING
NIGGERHEAD
NORBERTINE
NUDIBRANCH
NUMBERLESS
NURSERYMAN
OCCURRENCE
ORATORICAL
OSMIDROSIS
OUTPERFORM
OVERPRAISE
OXYMORONIC
PALMERSTON
PALMERWORM
PARAPRAXIS
PARATROOPS
PASIGRAPHY
PASTORELLA
PAWNBROKER
PENETRABLE
PENETRALIA
PEPPERCORN
PEPPERMILL
PEPPERMINT
PEPPERWORT
PERDURABLE
PERFORATED
PERFORATOR
PERFORMING
PERSTRINGE
PERVERSELY
PERVERSION
PERVERSITY
PETRARCHAN
PILEDRIVER
PILGARLICK
PLAYGROUND
PLAYWRIGHT
PLUPERFECT
PREARRANGE
PRECARIOUS
PRECURSORY
PREFERABLE

PREFERABLY
PREFERENCE
PREFERMENT
PREMARITAL
PREPARATOR
PRIMORDIAL
PROAIRESIS
PROCURABLE
PROCURATOR
PROPERTIUS
PROPORTION
PROSCRIBED
PROSERPINA
PROSERPINE
PROTERVITY
PROVERBIAL
PUCKERWOOD
PYROGRAPHY
QUATERNARY
RAPPORTEUR
READERSHIP
REAPPRAISE
RECIPROCAL
RECURRENCE
REDCURRANT
REITERATED
REPAIRABLE
REPATRIATE
RESEARCHER
RESPIRATOR
RHEOTROPIC
RHETORICAL
RICHARDSON
RINDERPEST
RUBBERNECK
RUDDERLESS
RUTHERFORD
SALTARELLO
SALUBRIOUS
SANDERLING
SANDGROPER
SANFORISED
SAPPERMENT
SCATURIENT
SCHWARZLOT
SCOMBRESOX
SETTERWORT
SGANARELLE
SHANDRYDAN
SHERARDISE
SHORTRANGE
SIGNORELLI
SILVERBACK
SILVERBILL
SILVERFISH
SILVERSIDE
SILVERSKIN
SILVERWARE
SISTERHOOD
SKYSCRAPER

SNAPDRAGON
SONGWRITER
SOUTERRAIN
SPIDERWORT
STEWARDESS
SUBMARINER
SUBMERSION
SUBSCRIBER
SUBSTRATUM
SUBTERFUGE
SUBVERSION
SUBVERSIVE
SUFFERANCE
SUMMERTIME
SUPPORTING
SUPPORTIVE
SYNAERESIS
SYNTERESIS
SYNTHRONUS
TAILORMADE
TAMBERLANE
TAMPERFOOT
TANAGRIDAE
TATPURUSHA
TATTERSALL
TELEGRAPHY
TEMPERANCE
TENDERFOOT
TENDERLOIN
TENDERNESS
TENEBRIFIC
TENTERHOOK
THEATRICAL
THEOCRITUS
TICKERTAPE
TIMBERYARD
TINKERBELL
TINTORETTO
TOPOGRAPHY
TORBERNITE
TRAVERTINE
TRIPARTITE
TURNAROUND
TYPEWRITER
TYPOGRAPHY
ULSTERETTE
UNBEARABLE
UNBEARABLY
UNHEARABLE
UNIFORMITY
UNIVERSITY
UNSWERVING
UPROARIOUS
VANDERBILT
VICTORIANA
VICTORIOUS
VULNERABLE
WANDERINGS
WANDERLUST
WANTHRIVEN
WASSERMANS
WEIMARANER
WESTERNIZE
WICKERWORK
WILDERNESS
WINDERMERE
WINTERTIME
WITHDRAWAL
WONDERLAND
WONDERMENT
WRAPAROUND
WUNDERKIND
YARBOROUGH
YESTERWEEK
YESTERYEAR
ABSCISSION
ACCESSIBLE
ACCESSIONS
ADMISSIBLE
ADOLESCENT
ADVERSARIA
AFTERSHAVE
AFTERSHOCK
AGGRESSION
AGGRESSIVE
AGONISTICS
ALPENSTOCK
AMBASSADOR
AMBLYSTOMA
AMPUSSYAND
ANGIOSPERM
ARACOSTYLE
ARIMASPIAN
ASPERSIONS
ASSESSMENT
BAGASSOSIS
BALLISTICS
BALLISTITE
BATHYSCAPH
BLACKSHIRT
BLACKSMITH
BLACKSTONE
BLOODSTAIN
BLOODSTOCK
BLOODSTONE
BLOOMSBURY
BOBBYSOXER
BRADYSEISM
BRAINSTORM
BRATISLAVA
BRIDESMAID
BRITISHISM
BROADSHEET
BROADSWORD
BROOMSTICK
BROWNSTONE
BUNDESWEHR
CAMPESTRAL
CANVASBACK
CANVASSING
CARNASSIAL
CENTESIMAL
CHEAPSKATE
CHEVESAILE
CHEVISANCE
CHINASTONE
CIRCASSIAN
CLEARSTORY
CLERESTORY
CLINGSTONE
CLYDESDALE
COEXISTENT
COGNISANCE
COLOSSALLY
COLPOSCOPE
COMBUSTION
COMMISSARY
COMMISSION
COMMISSURE
COMPASSION
COMPOSITOR
CONCESSION
CONCUSSION
CONDESCEND
CONFESSION
CONFISCATE
CONFUSEDLY
CONGESTION
CONSISTENT
CONSISTORY
CONTESTANT
CORRESPOND
CRANKSHAFT
CRUIKSHANK
CUIRASSIER
CYCLOSTYLE
CYSTOSCOPY
DECRESCENT
DEFEASANCE
DEFENSIBLE
DEMOISELLE
DEPRESSANT
DEPRESSING
DEPRESSION
DEPRESSIVE
DHARMSHALA
DIGRESSION
DISCUSSING
DISCUSSION
DISGUSTING
DISMISSIVE
DISPOSABLE
DISPOSSESS
DISRESPECT
DRAKESTONE
EATANSWILL
EMPLASTRUM
ENGLISHMAN
ENGLISHMEN
ENGROSSING
ENTHUSIASM
ENTHUSIAST
ERUBESCENT
ETHEOSTOMA
EVANESCENT
EXHAUSTING
EXHAUSTION
EXHAUSTIVE
EXPRESSION
EXPRESSIVE
EXPRESSMAN
EXPRESSWAY
EXTENSIBLE
FALDISTORY
FANTASTICO
FIBROSITIS
FIRTHSOKEN
FLAVESCENT
FLORESCENT
FORINSECAL
FORTISSIMO
FREMESCENT
FRITHSOKEN
FURNISHING
GETTYSBURG
GRANDSTAND
GRAVESTONE
GREENSHANK
GREENSTICK
GREENSWARD
GRINDSTONE
GYMNASTICS
GYMNOSOPHY
HARASSMENT
HARVESTMAN
HELLESPONT
HIEROSCOPY
HINDUSTANI
ICONOSCOPE
IMPASSABLE
IMPERSONAL
IMPOSSIBLE
IMPOSSIBLY
IMPRESARIO
IMPRESSION
IMPRESSIVE
INCONSTANT
INCRASSATE
INCRESCENT
INNERSPACE
INQUISITOR
INSENSIBLE
INSPISSATE
INTERSTATE
INTERSTICE
INTROSPECT
IRIDESCENT
KRIEGSPIEL
LARGESCALE
LAURUSTINE
LEBENSRAUM
LEMNISCATE
LIQUESCENT
LITHISTADA
MALMESBURY
MANGOSTEEN
MARCESCENT
MASSASAUGA
MATCHSTALK
MATCHSTICK
MAUPASSANT
METHUSALEH
METHUSELAH
MICROSCOPE
MONTESSORI
MYRIOSCOPE
NARCISSISM
NICROSILAL
NIGHTSHADE
NIGHTSHIRT
NIGHTSTICK
NIGRESCENT
NONONSENSE
NORTHSTEAD
NOURISHING
ODIOUSNESS
ONOMASTICS
OPALESCENT
OPPRESSION
OPPRESSIVE
ORCHESTRAL
OSTENSIBLE
OSTENSIBLY
OVIPOSITOR
PALAESTRAL
PANTOSCOPE
PARNASSIAN
PATISSERIE
PENINSULAR
PENNISETUM
PERCUSSION
PERMISSION
PERMISSIVE
PEROVSKITE
PERSISTENT
PETRISSAGE
PHILISTINE
PHILOSOPHY
PINCUSHION
PITCHSTONE
PLEBISCITE
PLUMASSIER
POETASTERY
POSSESSION
POSSESSIVE
PREDESTINE
PREDISPOSE
PREHISTORY
PREPOSITOR
PREPOSSESS

PROCESSING
PROCESSION
PROFESSION
PROGESSION
PROMISSORY
PROPOSITUS
PROTESTANT
PROVISIONS
PUBLISHING
PURPOSEFUL
PUTRESCENT
QUEENSBURY
QUEENSTOWN
QUICKSANDS
RAVENSBILL
RAVENSDUCK
RAVENSTONE
RAWINSONDE
RECONSIDER
REFRESHING
REGRESSION
REGRESSIVE
REMORSEFUL
REPRESSION
REPRESSIVE
RETROSPECT
REVERSIBLE
RHINESTONE
ROTISSERIE
RUBINSTEIN
SACROSANCT
SAMARSKITE
SCHALSTEIN
SCRIMSHANK
SELFESTEEM
SERRASALMO
SHEEPSHANK
SHELLSHOCK
SKRIMSHANK
SMALLSCALE
SMOKESTACK
SNAKESTONE
SOBERSIDES
SOMERSAULT
SOOTHSAYER
SPINESCENT
SPOILSPORT
SPOKESHAVE
SPORTSWEAR
STANDSTILL
STANISLAUS
STATISTICS
STAVESACRE
STILLSTAND
STYLISTICS
SUBMISSION
SUBMISSIVE
SUBSISTENT
SUCCESSFUL
SUCCESSION
SUCCESSIVE
SUGGESTION
SUGGESTIVE
SUPERSONIC
SUPERSTORE
SUPPOSEDLY
SURPASSING
SWEATSHIRT
SWEEPSTAKE
SWORDSTICK
TABLESPOON
TEINOSCOPE
TELEOSTOME
THALASSIAN
THALESTRIS
THREESCORE
THUMBSCREW
TORPESCENT
TOUCHSTONE
ULTRASONIC
ULTRASOUND
UNBLUSHING
UNDERSCORE
UNDERSHIRT
UNDERSIZED
UNDERSKIRT
UNDERSLUNG
UNDERSTAND
UNDERSTATE
UNDERSTEER
UNDERSTOOD
UNDERSTUDY
UNREASONED
UNSEASONED
UPHOLSTERY
VARNISHING
VERNISSAGE
WAPENSCHAW
WAPINSCHAW
WATERSKIER
WATERSPOUT
WHEATSHEAF
WHEATSTONE
WHOLESALER
ABRUPTNESS
ACCENTUATE
ACCUSTOMED
ADJECTIVAL
ADJUSTABLE
ADJUSTMENT
ADMITTANCE
ADMITTEDLY
ADVENTURER
ADVERTISER
AFFETTUOSO
AFTERTASTE
ALLOSTERIC
AMPHITRITE
AMPHITRYON
AMPHOTERIC
ANALYTICAL
ANTISTATIC
APOPHTHEGM
ARCHETYPAL
ARCHITRAVE
ARSMETRICK
ASBESTOSIS
ASSISTANCE
ASSORTMENT
AUTOSTRADA
BACKSTAIRS
BACKSTROKE
BALBUTIENT
BALUSTRADE
BARBITURIC
BARMITZVAH
BASKETBALL
BASKETWORK
BIJOUTERIE
BIPARTISAN
BLACKTHORN
BREASTBONE
BREASTFEED
BREASTWORK
BRIGHTNESS
BROCATELLE
CALYPTRATE
CANTATRICE
CARACTACUS
CARPATHIAN
CARYATIDES
CATASTASIS
CELESTIALS
CHARITABLE
CHARITABLY
CHOPSTICKS
CHRISTIANA
CLOISTERED
COCKATRICE
COLDSTREAM
COLLATERAL
COMESTIBLE
COMMITMENT
COMMUTABLE
COMPATIBLE
COMPATRIOT
COMPETENCE
COMPETITOR
CONDOTTIER
COQUETTISH
CORINTHIAN
CORNSTALKS
CORNSTARCH
CREDITABLE
CREDITABLY
CURVETTING
DEDUCTIBLE
DEJECTEDLY
DELECTABLE
DEPARTMENT
DEPARTURES
DEPORTMENT
DERMATITIS
DESPITEOUS
DETECTABLE
DETESTABLE
DEVASTATED
DEVASTAVIT
DIGESTIBLE
DILETTANTE
DIRECTIONS
DIRECTNESS
DIRECTOIRE
DISASTROUS
DISPUTABLE
DOWNSTAIRS
DOWNSTREAM
DRAWSTRING
EBRACTEATE
EFFECTUATE
EFFORTLESS
ELLIPTICAL
EMBITTERED
EMMENTALER
ENLISTMENT
ENRAPTURED
EPIMETHEUS
EQUESTRIAN
ESCRITOIRE
EURYPTERUS
EVERYTHING
EXEMPTNESS
EXPECTANCY
EYEWITNESS
FACTITIOUS
FALSETRUTH
FARFETCHED
FENESTELLA
FERNITICLE
FICTITIOUS
FINISTERRE
FLAGITIOUS
FLIGHTLESS
FLYCATCHER
FOODSTUFFS
FRENETICAL
FRIGHTENED
GAINSTRIVE
GERIATRICS
GOLIATHISE
GROCETERIA
HEADSTRONG
HELIOTROPE
HEPTATEUCH
HEPTATHLON
HOLOSTERIC
HOSPITABLE
HOSPITABLY
HYPAETHRAL
HYPAETHRON
HYPNOTIZED
ILLUSTRATE
IMMORTELLE
IMPORTANCE
IMPOSTHUME
INCAUTIOUS
INCESTUOUS
INDENTURES
INDICTABLE
INDICTMENT
INDISTINCT
INDUCTANCE
INDUSTRIAL
INEVITABLE
INEVITABLY
INFECTIOUS
INFEFTMENT
INFILTRATE
INFLATABLE
INGRATIATE
INIMITABLE
INSISTENCE
INTENTNESS
INTERTRIGO
INTERTWINE
INTESTINAL
INTESTINES
INVESTMENT
ISOMETRICS
JACKSTONES
JACKSTRAWS
KARMATHIAN
KNIGHTHOOD
LACUSTRINE
LAMENTABLE
LAMENTABLY
LANDSTHING
LIBRETTIST
LICENTIATE
LICENTIOUS
LOGISTICAL
LUTESTRING
MAGISTRACY
MAGISTRAND
MAGISTRATE
MAINSTREAM
MARKETABLE
MAURITANIA
MESENTERON
METASTABLE
MIDLOTHIAN
MINESTRONE
MINISTRATE
MISMATCHED
MONOPTERON
MONOPTEROS
MUSKETEERS
NUTRITIOUS
OBJECTLESS
OBSTETRICS

ODELSTHING
OFFPUTTING
OFTENTIMES
OUTPATIENT
OVERSTRAIN
OVERSTRUNG
PALESTRINA
PALMATIFID
PALMATOZOA
PALUSTRINE
PANOPTICON
PARARTHRIA
PARASTATAL
PARENTHOOD
PARENTLESS
PARGETTING
PEDESTRIAN
PEDIATRICS
PENTATEUCH
PENTATHLON
PENTATONIC
PENTETERIC
PENTSTEMON
PERDITIOUS
PERPETRATE
PERPETUATE
PERPETUITY
PHILATELIC
POCKETBOOK
POTENTIATE
POTENTILLA
PRAXITELES
PREPOTENCE
PRIESTHOOD
PRIVATEERS
PROFITABLE
PROFITABLY
PROFITLESS
PROMETHEAN
PROMETHEUS
PROMETHIUM
PROMPTNESS
PROPITIATE
PROPITIOUS
PULSATANCE
QUAESTUARY
QUAINTNESS
QUICKTHORN
RAIYATWARI
RECEPTACLE
REDRUTHITE
REGISTERED
RELENTLESS
RELUCTANCE
REMITTANCE
REPEATABLE
REPEATEDLY
REPENTANCE
REPERTOIRE
REPORTEDLY
RESENTMENT
RESISTANCE
RIJSTTAFEL
ROBERTSMAN
ROBUSTIOUS
ROBUSTNESS
ROCKSTEADY
RUPESTRIAN
SABBATICAL
SABRETACHE
SAGITTARIA
SCIENTIFIC
SCRIPTURAL
SCRIPTURES
SCULPTRESS
SEAMSTRESS
SECRETAIRE
SEECATCHIE
SELFSTYLED
SEVENTIETH
SHOESTRING
SLIPSTREAM
SONGSTRESS
SOUNDTRACK
SPIRITEDLY
SPIRITLESS
SPIRITUOUS
STEALTHILY
STENOTYPER
STOMATOPOD
STRAITENED
STREETLAMP
STREETWISE
STRICTNESS
STRIPTEASE
STRUCTURAL
SUNBATHING
SUPERTONIC
SYMPATHISE
SYMPATHIZE
SYNOSTOSIS
TARANTELLA
TEETOTALER
THIXOTROPY
THREATENED
TOCCATELLA
TOILETRIES
TOPSYTURVY
TRADITIONS
TRILATERAL
TUMULTUOUS
TURRITELLA
UNBEATABLE
UNCRITICAL
UNCULTURED
UNDERTAKER
UNDOCTORED
UNFAITHFUL
UNFETTERED
UNGRATEFUL
UNILATERAL
UNLETTERED
UNSETTLING
UNSUITABLE
UNTRUTHFUL
VALENTINES
VIBRATIONS
VOLUPTUARY
VOLUPTUOUS
WATCHTOWER
WATERTIGHT
WEIGHTLESS
WHITETHORN
WHITSTABLE
WITGATBOOM
XEROSTOMIA
ABSOLUTELY
ABSOLUTION
ABSOLUTISM
ACCUMULATE
ACOLOUTHOS
ALLOCUTION
AMATEURISH
ANACOUSTIC
ANACRUSTIC
ANDALUSIAN
ANDALUSITE
ANTIQUATED
APOLAUSTIC
ARTICULATA
ARTICULATE
ATRACURIUM
AVANTURINE
AVENTURINE
BALIBUNTAL
BANKRUPTCY
BEEFBURGER
BELARUSIAN
BIANNUALLY
BINOCULARS
BLANQUETTE
BRESSUMMER
BUCKJUMPER
BUREAUCRAT
CANECUTTER
CAPITULARY
CAPITULATE
CARTHUSIAN
CHINQUAPIN
CLAMOURING
COADJUTANT
COMPLUVIUM
COMPOUNDED
CONCLUDING
CONCLUSION
CONCLUSIVE
CONFLUENCE
CONFOUNDED
DEPOPULATE
DEREGULATE
DEVOLUTION
DIACAUSTIC
DIMINUENDO
DIMINUTION
DIMINUTIVE
DISCOURAGE
DISGRUNTLE
EFFLEURAGE
EMASCULATE
EVENTUALLY
FILIBUSTER
FLAVOURING
FLOCCULATE
FLOCCULENT
FLUCTUATER
FORERUNNER
FORFEUCHEN
FORFOUGHEN
FRAUDULENT
GARGOUILLE
GENICULATE
GLAMOURISE
GOATSUCKER
HABITUALLY
HACKBUTEER
HALIEUTICS
HAMESUCKEN
HEADHUNTED
HEADHUNTER
HOMEOUSIAN
HYDRAULICS
ILLAQUEATE
IMMACULACY
IMMACULATE
IMMATURITY
IMPALUDISM
INACCURACY
INACCURATE
INAUGURATE
INESCULENT
INFATUATED
INOSCULATE
INSECURELY
INSECURITY
INSTRUCTED
INSTRUCTOR
INSTRUMENT
INTEGUMENT
INTRAURBAN
INVALUABLE
KHIDMUTGAR
LACKLUSTER
LACKLUSTRE
LANDLUBBER
LANSQUENET
LUMPSUCKER
MALAGUETTA
MALTHUSIAN
MANICURIST
MANIPULATE
METICULOUS
MIRACULOUS
MISHGUGGLE
MOISTURIZE
MOSSBUNKER
NONPLUSSED
NOVACULITE
OBSEQUIOUS
OUTPOURING
OVERSUPPLY
PARAGUAYAN
PASTEURISE
PASTEURIZE
PATIBULARY
PEDICULATE
PHILLUMENY
PICAYUNISH
POHUTUKAWA
PORTCULLIS
POSTHUMOUS
PRAEMUNIRE
PRECAUTION
PRESSURIZE
PROCRUSTES
PROFOUNDLY
PRONOUNCED
PROTRUSION
PUBERULENT
PUNCTUALLY
PUNCTULATE
RAGAMUFFIN
REASSURING
RESOLUTELY
RESOLUTION
RESTAURANT
REVOLUTION
RIDICULOUS
ROADRUNNER
SARSQUATCH
SCRUPULOUS
SEERSUCKER
SEMIQUAVER
SHOWJUMPER
SILHOUETTE
STRIDULATE
SULPHUROUS
SURROUNDED
TAMBOURINE
TARPAULING
THELLUSSON
THINGUMBOB
THOROUGHLY
TRANQUILLY
UNARGUABLE
UNASSUMING
UNGROUNDED
UNOCCUPIED
UNREQUITED
VENEZUELAN
VESICULATE

VOCABULARY
VOCABULIST
WINDSURFER
ABBREVIATE
ACCLIVIOUS
AMBARVALIA
ANGURVADEL
BELIEVABLE
CAPTIVATED
CONNIVANCE
CULTIVATED
CULTIVATOR
DESERVEDLY
DISCOVERER
EFFERVESCE
EPROUVETTE
FORGIVABLE
GALRAVITCH
GINGIVITIS
ILLADVISED
IMPERVIOUS
IMPROVISED
INSOLVENCY
LASCIVIOUS
LIBREVILLE
MANDEVILLE
MISGIVINGS
MONTEVERDI
MONTEVIDEO
OBSERVABLE
OBSERVANCE
RESERVISTS
SHRIEVALTY
SOMERVILLE
SUPERVISED
SUPERVISOR
TRANSVERSE
UNDERVALUE
UNFLAVORED
UNLEAVENED
UNPROVOKED
VAUDEVILLE
AFTERWARDS
BLACKWATER
BONDSWOMAN
BORROWINGS
BREAKWATER
BRICKWORKS
CHAIRWOMAN
CHUCKWALLA
CLANSWOMAN
CLEARWATER
DRINKWATER
DUTCHWOMAN
EARTHWORKS
EVERYWHERE
FELLOWSHIP
FRESHWATER
FRONTWARDS
GRASSWIDOW
HORSEWOMAN
INTERWEAVE
INTERWOVEN
IRISHWOMAN
IRISHWOMEN
KENILWORTH
LIVERWURST
MEADOWPLAN
MELLOWNESS
NARROWBOAT
NARROWDALE
NARROWNESS
NOBLEWOMAN
NORTHWARDS
PILLIWINKS
PILLOWCASE
PILLOWSLIP
SALESWOMAN
SCOTSWOMAN
SHADOWLESS
SHARAWADGI
SHARAWAGGI
SHEARWATER
SOUTHWARDS
STEELWORKS
SUPERWOMAN
TEENYWEENY
TIMESWITCH
TOWNSWOMAN
UNANSWERED
UNDERWATER
UNDERWORLD
UNDERWRITE
WANDSWORTH
WATERWHEEL
WATERWINGS
WATERWORKS
WELSHWOMAN
WHITEWATER
WHOLEWHEAT
WILLOWHERB
WILLYWILLY
WINDOWSILL
WISHYWASHY
WORDSWORTH
WORTHWHILE
WRISTWATCH
YELLOWBACK
YELLOWGIRL
YELLOWJACK
YELLOWROOT
YELLOWWOOD
ASPHYXIATE
BISSEXTILE
COMMIXTURE
CONTEXTUAL
INFLEXIBLE
INFLEXIBLY
PHILOXENIA
ACRONYCHAL
APOCRYPHAL
APTERYGOTA
BARLEYBREE
BARLEYCORN
BIOPHYSICS
BIORHYTHMS
BLEARYEYED
CHERRYWOOD
CHESSYLITE
CONVEYABLE
CONVEYANCE
DEFRAYMENT
DEPLOYMENT
DISLOYALTY
EMPLOYMENT
EUCALYPTUS
GEOPHYSICS
HALLOYSITE
ICHTHYOSIS
KERSEYMERE
LACHRYMOSE
MAKESYSTEM
MESITYLENE
MISOGYNIST
NONPAYMENT
NOTORYCTES
PARONYCHIA
POLYHYMNIA
PREPAYMENT
PRESBYOPIA
PRESBYTERY
PYRAGYRITE
SANNAYASIN
SHANDYGAFF
SHELLYCOAT
SPERRYLITE
STAPHYLINE
STICKYBEAK
STINGYBARK
SYNONYMOUS
TALLEYRAND
UNLADYLIKE
VOLLEYBALL
WHILLYWHAW
WHIRLYBIRD
WINCEYETTE
WOOLLYBACK
WOOLLYBUTT
COGNIZANCE
LIPIZZANER
RENDEZVOUS
SQUEEZEBOX
UTILIZABLE

10:7

ABERGLAUBE
ABHIDHAMMA
ABNORMALLY
ABOMINABLE
ABOMINABLY
ACCORDANCE
ACHROMATIC
ACROAMATIC
ACTIONABLE
ADJUSTABLE
ADMITTANCE
ADVERSARIA
AEROPHAGIA
AFFILIATED
AFFORDABLE
AFTERTASTE
AFTERWARDS
ALCIBIADES
ALCYONARIA
ALDERMANLY
ALLEGEANCE
ALLEGIANCE
ALTERNATOR
AMBARVALIA
AMBASSADOR
AMPHIMACER
ANALPHABET
ANDROMACHE
ANGURVADEL
ANSWERABLE
ANTIQUATED
ANTISTATIC
ANTITRAGUS
APOSEMATIC
APPEARANCE
APPLICABLE
APPLICATOR
ARBITRATOR
ARCHDEACON
AREOGRAPHY
ASARABACCA
ASCENDANCY
ASCRIBABLE
ASSIGNABLE
ASSISTANCE
ASSOCIATED
ASTIGMATIC
ASTRAGALUS
ASTRALAGUS
ATTAINABLE
ATTENDANCE
AUTOCRATIC
AUTOPLASTY
AVANTGARDE
AVICULARIA
AXINOMANCY
BABESIASIS
BACITRACIN
BACKSTAIRS
BAREHEADED
BAUDELAIRE
BELIEVABLE
BIANNUALLY
BIENNIALLY
BIPINNARIA
BLACKWATER
BLANCMANGE
BONESHAKER
BREAKWATER
BRICKLAYER
BRILLIANCE
BUCCINATOR
BUCEPHALUS
BULLHEADED
CACOGRAPHY
CALCULABLE
CALCULATED
CALCULATOR
CAMPARADOR
CANDELABRA
CAPERNAITE
CAPILLAIRE
CAPNOMANCY
CAPTIVATED
CARACTACUS
CARTOMANCY
CATASTASIS
CELEBRATED
CHAMBRANLE
CHANGEABLE
CHAPARAJOS
CHARGEABLE
CHARITABLE
CHARITABLY
CHATELAINE
CHECKLATON
CHEMICALLY
CHEMONASTY
CHEVESAILE
CHEVISANCE
CHINQUAPIN
CHIRICAUNE
CHIROMANCY
CHUCKWALLA
CLEARWATER
CLEROMANCY
CLINICALLY
CLOCKMAKER
COCHLEARIA
COCKCHAFER
COELACANTH
COGNISANCE
COGNIZANCE
COLLIMATOR
COLONNADED
COLOSSALLY
COMMUNALLY
COMMUTABLE
COMPARABLE
COMPARATOR
COMPLIANCE
CONFIDANTE
CONNIVANCE

CONSONANCE
CONSONANTS
CONSTRAINT
CONVENANCE
CONVEYABLE
CONVEYANCE
COPENHAGEN
CORNFLAKES
CORNSTALKS
CORNSTARCH
CORRUGATED
CORRUGATOR
CORYPHAEUS
CREDITABLE
CREDITABLY
CREOPHAGUS
CRIMINALLY
CRITICALLY
CROTALARIA
CUCULLATED
CUISENAIRE
CULTIVATED
CULTIVATOR
DAYDREAMER
DECAGRAMME
DECOLLATOR
DEEPSEATED
DEFEASANCE
DEGRADABLE
DELECTABLE
DEMOCRATIC
DEMOGRAPHY
DEMONIACAL
DEPENDABLE
DEPLORABLE
DEPLORABLY
DESECRATED
DESICCATED
DESPICABLE
DETACHABLE
DETECTABLE
DETESTABLE
DEVASTATED
DEVASTAVIT
DIAGONALLY
DIDASCALIC
DILETTANTE
DIPLOMATIC
DIPSOMANIA
DISARRANGE
DISENGAGED
DISLOYALTY
DISPOSABLE
DISPUTABLE
DISSIPATED
DISSONANCE
DOWNSTAIRS
DRESSMAKER
DRINKWATER
DUCKBOARDS
DUPLICATOR
ECHOPRAXIA
ELEGABALUS
ELIMINATOR
EMBLEMATIC
EMMENTALER
ENCEPHALON
ENKEPHALIN
ESPECIALLY
ESTRAMACON
EUTHANASIA
EVAPORATED
EVENTUALLY
EVERGLADES
EXONERATED
EXOTICALLY
EXPECTANCY
EXPENDABLE
EXPLICABLE
EXTENDABLE
EXTERNALLY
EXUBERANCE
FAMILIARLY
FASCINATED
FASCINATOR
FAVOURABLE
FAVOURABLY
FLUCTUATER
FONTINALIS
FORESHADOW
FORGIVABLE
FORMIDABLE
FREELOADER
FRESHWATER
FRONTWARDS
FRUSTRATED
GOVERNANCE
GRANULATED
GRASSLANDS
GUATEMALAN
GUBERNATOR
GUTTURALLY
HABITUALLY
HALFYEARLY
HALLUBALOO
HANKYPANKY
HECTICALLY
HELIOLATER
HENDECAGON
HERESIARCH
HEROICALLY
HIEROMANCY
HIPPOMANES
HOLOGRAPHY
HOMEOPATHY
HONOURABLE
HONOURABLY
HOOTANANNY
HOOTENANNY
HOSPITABLE
HOSPITABLY
HOUSEMAIDS
HULLABALOO
ICEBREAKER
IMAGINABLE
IMBRICATED
IMPALPABLE
IMPARLANCE
IMPASSABLE
IMPECCABLE
IMPECCABLY
IMPLACABLE
IMPLACABLY
IMPORTANCE
IMPRESARIO
IMPRIMATUR
IMPROBABLE
IMPROBABLY
INDICTABLE
INDUCTANCE
INEBRIATED
INEDUCABLE
INEVITABLE
INEVITABLY
INEXORABLE
INFATUATED
INFERNALLY
INFLATABLE
INFORMALLY
INFURIATED
INIMITABLE
INOPERABLE
INSATIABLE
INSATIABLY
INSTIGATOR
INTEGRATED
INTERMARRY
INTERNALLY
INVALUABLE
INVARIABLE
INVARIABLY
INVIOLABLE
IRONICALLY
JACKANAPES
JIGGAMAREE
JUDICIALLY
KLANGFARBE
LACKADAISY
LAMENTABLE
LAMENTABLY
LAWBREAKER
LEGISLATOR
LEONTIASIS
LIGNOCAINE
LIPIZZANER
LIQUIDATOR
LITHOMARGE
LONGCHAMPS
LORDOLATRY
LOTOPHAGUS
LUPERCALIA
LUXURIANCE
MACROCARPA
MALIGNANCY
MANAGEABLE
MANICHAEAN
MARGINALIA
MARGINALLY
MARIOLATRY
MARKETABLE
MASSASAUGA
MATCHMAKER
MATELLASSE
MATERIALLY
MATERNALLY
MAURITANIA
MAYONNAISE
MEASURABLE
MERRYMAKER
METAPLASIS
METASTABLE
METHOMANIA
METHUSALEH
METHYLATED
MILITIAMAN
MODIFIABLE
MONILIASIS
MONSTRANCE
MORGANATIC
NATIONALLY
NECROMANCY
NECTABANUS
NEGOTIABLE
NEGOTIATOR
NEWSREADER
NORTHWARDS
NOTICEABLE
NOTICEABLY
NOTIFIABLE
NOTIONALLY
NUDIBRANCH
NUMISMATIC
OBFUSCATED
OBSERVABLE
OBSERVANCE
OBTAINABLE
OESOPHAGUS
OFFBALANCE
OFFICIALLY
ORDONNANCE
ORIDINANCE
ORIGINALLY
ORIGINATOR
ORTHOCAINE
OSCILLATOR
OSTEOPATHY
OTHERGATES
OUTBALANCE
OVERCHARGE
OVERPRAISE
OVERSHADOW
OVERSLAUGH
OXYGENATOR
PALLBEARER
PARAGUAYAN
PARAPRAXIS
PARASTATAL
PARDONABLE
PARDONABLY
PARKLEAVES
PARRAMATTA
PASIGRAPHY
PATERNALLY
PEACEMAKER
PECULIARLY
PENETRABLE
PENETRALIA
PERCOLATOR
PERDURABLE
PERFORATED
PERFORATOR
PERISHABLE
PERSICARIA
PERSONABLE
PERSONALLY
PHAGEDAENA
PHLEGMASIA
PHLEGMATIC
PHOTONASTY
PHYSICALLY
PITYRIASIS
PLATELAYER
POETICALLY
POKERFACED
POLLINATED
POLYCHAETE
POSTCHAISE
PREARRANGE
PREFERABLE
PREFERABLY
PREPARATOR
PRESUMABLY
PREVENANCY
PROCREATOR
PROCURABLE
PROCURATOR
PRODIGALLY
PROFITABLE
PROFITABLY
PROMENADER
PROPAGANDA
PROPAGATOR
PROPYLAEUM
PROVENANCE
PSYCHIATRY
PULSATANCE
PUNCTUALLY
PUNISHABLE
PYROGRAPHY
QUICKSANDS

QUIRINALIA
RADIOLARIA
RATIONALLY
REAPPRAISE
REASONABLE
REASONABLY
RECEPTACLE
REDUNDANCY
REITERATED
REJONEADOR
RELUCTANCE
REMARKABLE
REMARKABLY
REMITTANCE
REPAIRABLE
REPEATABLE
REPENTANCE
REPUGNANCE
RESISTANCE
RESPIRATOR
RETURNABLE
RHINOLALIA
RHOEADALES
RIBOFLAVIN
RIJSTTAFEL
RINGLEADER
ROQUELAURE
ROSECHAFER
SABRETACHE
SACROSANCT
SAGITTARIA
SALMANAZAR
SANDEMANIA
SANNAYASIN
SARSQUATCH
SATURNALIA
SCHISMATIC
SCHLIMAZEL
SCLERIASIS
SEASONABLE
SEASONABLY
SECRETAIRE
SEGREGATED
SEMIQUAVER
SERRASALMO
SHAKUHACHI
SHAMEFACED
SHARAWADGI
SHARAWAGGI
SHEARWATER
SHECKLATON
SHORTRANGE
SHRIEVALTY
SIDEBOARDS
SIGILLARIA
SINGULARLY
SKYSCRAPER
SNAPDRAGON
SOGDOLAGER
SOMERSAULT
SOOTHSAYER
SOUTHWARDS
SPECULATOR
SPODOMANCY
SQUETEAGUE
SQUIREARCH
STAVESACRE
STONEMASON
SUBLIMATER
SUBSTRATUM
SUBTENANCY
SUFFERANCE
SUPERCARGO
SURGICALLY
SUSTENANCE
SYNCOPATED
SYSTEMATIC
TABERNACLE
TACTICALLY
TALEBEARER
TEETOTALER
TELEGRAPHY
TEMPERANCE
TERMINABLE
TERMINALIA
TERMINALLY
TIEBREAKER
TOOTHPASTE
TOPOGRAPHY
TOSSICATED
TOSTICATED
TOUCHPAPER
TRAGACANTH
TRAGICALLY
TRANSLATED
TRANSLATOR
TRAVELATOR
TRAVOLATOR
TROPOPAUSE
TYPOGRAPHY
UNARGUABLE
UNBEARABLE
UNBEARABLY
UNBEATABLE
UNDECLARED
UNDEFEATED
UNDENIABLE
UNDERPANTS
UNDERTAKER
UNDERVALUE
UNDERWATER
UNEDUCATED
UNENVIABLE
UNHEARABLE
UNPREPARED
UNREADABLE
UNRELIABLE
UNREVEALED
UNSOCIABLE
UNSUITABLE
UNWORKABLE
USQUEBAUGH
UTILIZABLE
VARIEGATED
VENTILATOR
VERIFIABLE
VERTICALLY
VULCANALIA
VULNERABLE
WASTEPAPER
WATCHMAKER
WEIMARANER
WHITEWATER
WHITSTABLE
WHOLESALER
WISHYWASHY
WITHDRAWAL
WRISTWATCH
XIPHOPAGUS
ZOANTHARIA
AUTOMOBILE
BARLEYBREE
BASKETBALL
BATTENBERG
BATTENBURG
BLOOMSBURY
BOOKMOBILE
BREAKABLES
BREASTBONE
BUTTERBAKE
BUTTERBUMP
CANNONBALL
CANTERBURY
CANVASBACK
CASSIABARK
CHEQUEBOOK
COLLARBONE
COLLEMBOLA
CONTRABAND
CONTRIBUTE
COQUIMBITE
CUMMERBUND
CUTTLEBONE
DESCRIBING
DISSELBOOM
DISSEMBLER
DISTRIBUTE
DISTURBING
DOUBLEBASS
EXACERBATE
FLOWERBEDS
FORTINBRAS
GETTYSBURG
GINGERBEER
GROUNDBAIT
HANDLEBARS
HARMANBECK
HEIDELBERG
HINDENBURG
HORSELBERG
INCUNABULA
KNOCKABOUT
LANDLUBBER
MALMESBURY
MARYLEBONE
MASTURBATE
MINUTEBOOK
MOUNTEBANK
NARROWBOAT
PLOUGHBOTE
POCKETBOOK
PROVERBIAL
QUEENSBURY
RAVENSBILL
ROUNDABOUT
ROUSEABOUT
ROUSTABOUT
SADDLEBACK
SADDLEBILL
SCHOOLBOOK
SECONDBEST
SILVERBACK
SILVERBILL
SKETCHBOOK
SMORREBROD
SNOWMOBILE
SPRINGBOKS
STICKYBEAK
STINGYBARK
STRINDBERG
STRULDBERG
STRULDBRUG
SWEDENBORG
SWITCHBACK
TCHOUKBALL
THREADBARE
TINKERBELL
VANDERBILT
VEGETABLES
VOLLEYBALL
WHIRLYBIRD
WITGATBOOM
WOOLLYBACK
WOOLLYBUTT
YELLOWBACK
ABSTRACTED
ACRONYCHAL
ADJUDICATE
ADOLESCENT
ALEMBICATE
AMBULACRUM
ANTHRACINE
ANTHRACITE
ANTISOCIAL
APOPLECTIC
APOTHECARY
APOTHECIUM
ARISTOCRAT
ARTIFICIAL
ASCETICISM
BACKPACKER
BARLEYCORN
BATHYSCAPH
BEAUTICIAN
BENEDICITE
BENEFACTOR
BENEFICENT
BENEFICIAL
BOOTLICKER
BUREAUCRAT
CALEFACTOR
CAPPUCCINO
CATALECTIC
CATCRACKER
CATENACCIO
CESTRACION
CHEESECAKE
CHRONICLER
CHRONICLES
CIRCUMCISE
CISTERCIAN
CLASSICISM
CLASSICIST
CLEMENCEAU
COLCHICINE
COLPOSCOPE
COMMERCIAL
COMPLACENT
COMPLICATE
COMPLICITY
COMSTOCKER
CONDESCEND
CONFISCATE
CONSPECTUS
CONTRACTOR
CONTRECOUP
CONVINCING
CORNCOCKLE
CRUSTACEAN
CURRENCIES
CYSTOSCOPY
DECRESCENT
DETRUNCATE
DISCONCERT
DISTINCTLY
DISTRACTED
ELASTICATE
ELASTICITY
EMPEDOCLES
ENTEROCELE
ENTRANCING
ENTRENCHED
EPIDEICTIC
EQUIVOCATE
ERUBESCENT
EVANESCENT
FANATICISM
FANTOCCINI
FARFETCHED
FETTUCCINE

FLAVESCENT
FLORESCENT
FLYCATCHER
FORFEUCHEN
FRATRICIDE
FREMESCENT
GNOSTICISM
GOATSUCKER
GRIDLOCKED
HAMESUCKEN
HAMSHACKLE
HANDPICKED
HEPATOCELE
HIERARCHIC
HIEROSCOPY
HIPPARCHUS
HUMPBACKED
ICONOSCOPE
IMBROCCATA
INCAPACITY
INCRESCENT
INDELICACY
INDELICATE
INDIRECTLY
INEFFICACY
INSTRUCTED
INSTRUCTOR
INTOXICANT
INTOXICATE
IRIDESCENT
IRRADICATE
KENSPECKLE
LANDLOCKED
LARGESCALE
LAWRENCIUM
LEMNISCATE
LIQUESCENT
LUMPSUCKER
MACONOCHIE
MALEFACTOR
MARCESCENT
MICROSCOPE
MISERICORD
MISMATCHED
MONTRACHET
MUNIFICENT
MYRIOSCOPE
NEEDLECASE
NEMATOCYST
NIGRESCENT
NONSUCCESS
NOTORYCTES
NUTCRACKER
OCTODECIMO
OFFTHECUFF
OPALESCENT
OUTSPECKLE
PACIFICISM
PANTOSCOPE
PARONYCHIA
PEPPERCORN
PETRARCHAN
PHARMACIST
PHYSIOCRAT
PICKPOCKET
PILLOWCASE
PLASTICINE
PLASTICITY
PLEBISCITE
POLITICIAN
POLITICIZE
PRATINCOLE
PRETINCOLE
PROSPECTOR
PROSPECTUS
PROTRACTED
PROTRACTOR
PROVINCIAL
PSEUDOCARP
PUNICACEAE
PUTRESCENT
QUADRICEPS
RAMSHACKLE
RESEARCHER
RESTRICTED
SANDWICHES
SCEPTICISM
SEANNACHIE
SEECATCHIE
SEERSUCKER
SHELLYCOAT
SIMPLICITY
SIMULACRUM
SKEPTICISM
SMALLSCALE
SPARTACIST
SPATCHCOCK
SPECTACLED
SPECTACLES
SPERMACETI
SPIFLICATE
SPINESCENT
SPITCHCOCK
STILLICIDE
STRATOCRAT
STRATOCYST
SUCCINCTLY
SUPPLICANT
SUPPLICATE
TAPDANCING
TAPERECORD
TECHNICIAN
TECHNOCRAT
TEINOSCOPE
THREESCORE
THUMBSCREW
TORPESCENT
TRAFFICKER
TRAVANCORE
TRIMALCHIO
TRIPLICATE
UNAFFECTED
UNATTACHED
UNBLEACHED
UNDERSCORE
UNDETECTED
UNEXPECTED
UNOFFICIAL
URTICACEAE
WAPENSCHAW
WAPINSCHAW
WOODPECKER
AGGRANDISE
ALABANDINE
ALABANDITE
ALEXANDERS
ALEXANDRIA
ANACARDIUM
ANTECEDENT
ANTIPODEAN
ARMAGEDDON
ASTOUNDING
AUTODIDACT
AVVOGADORE
BALDERDASH
BANGLADESH
BATTLEDOOR
BATTLEDORE
BERNARDINE
BOLLANDIST
BOMBARDIER
BRIGANDINE
BROKENDOWN
BUTTONDOWN
CAMPERDOWN
CHALCEDONY
CLYDESDALE
COINCIDENT
COMMANDANT
COMMANDEER
COMMANDING
COMPENDIUM
COMPRADORE
CONCLUDING
CONCORDANT
CONTRADICT
DECAHEDRON
DELCREDERE
DESCENDANT
DESCENDING
DESPONDENT
DICYNODONT
DILAPIDATE
DISCORDANT
DOORTODOOR
DUMBLEDORE
ECHINODERM
EISTEDDFOD
EMBROIDERY
EMPFINDUNG
EPIDENDRUM
EXPOUNDERS
FARRANDINE
FERRANDINE
FORBIDDING
FOREBODING
FOREORDAIN
FRICANDEAU
GARLANDAGE
GORMANDIZE
HEMIHEDRON
HETERODOXY
HITOPADESA
HITOPODESA
HORRENDOUS
HUSBANDAGE
ICOSANDRIA
IMPALUDISM
INBREEDING
INDIVIDUAL
INSIPIDITY
INTIMIDATE
INVALIDATE
INVALIDITY
IRREMEDIAL
JEOPARDISE
JEOPARDIZE
KETTLEDRUM
LAUDERDALE
LAWABIDING
LEOPARDESS
MEPERIDINE
MISCONDUCT
MISLEADING
MITHRIDATE
MUJAHEDDIN
NARROWDALE
OCTAHEDRON
OUTLANDISH
OVERRIDING
OZYMANDIAS
PANJANDRUM
PARADIDDLE
PERDENDOSI
PERSUADING
PLASMODESM
POLYHEDRON
PREBENDARY
PRIMORDIAL
PROCEEDING
PROFUNDITY
RAVENSDUCK
RESCHEDULE
RESOUNDING
RESPONDENT
RHAPSODISE
RHAPSODIZE
RICHARDSON
ROWLANDSON
SALLENDERS
SHERARDISE
SIDESADDLE
SMARAGDINE
SOLIFIDIAN
STEPLADDER
STEWARDESS
STUPENDOUS
SUBHEADING
SUCCEEDING
SUPERADDED
SURFRIDING
SUSPENDERS
TARADIDDLE
THRENODIAL
TILLANDSIA
TREMENDOUS
TROGLODYTE
TROUBADOUR
TUMBLEDOWN
TURTLEDOVE
UNABRIDGED
UNYIELDING
UPSTANDING
WARRANDICE
ZEUGLODONT
ABHORRENCE
ABSTINENCE
ACANACEOUS
ACOTYLEDON
ADMITTEDLY
ALCAICERIA
ALLOSTERIC
AMPHINEURA
AMPHOTERIC
ANAXIMENES
ANCHORETIC
ANEMOMETER
ANESTHESIA
ANESTHETIC
ANTIFREEZE
ANTITHESIS
ANTITHETIC
APHAERESIS
APOLOGETIC
ARCHIMEDES
ARENACEOUS
ARITHMETIC
ASCENDENCY
BETELGEUSE
BETELGEUZE
BEWILDERED
BIJOUTERIE
BLACKBEARD
BLACKBERRY
BLACKHEART
BLANQUETTE
BLASPHEMER
BLEARYEYED
BOOKKEEPER
BOTTICELLI

BRADYSEISM
BROCATELLE
BUMFREEZER
CACODAEMON
CALCAREOUS
CALESCENCE
CAMERLENGO
CAMPANELLA
CAMSTEERIE
CANTILEVER
CARBURETOR
CASSOLETTE
CATCHPENNY
CENTIMETER
CENTIMETRE
CHALYBEATE
CHAPAREJOS
CHARTREUSE
CINDERELLA
CIRRIPEDEA
CIRRIPEDIA
CITRONELLA
CLARABELLA
CLOISTERED
CLOUDBERRY
COCCINEOUS
COETANEOUS
COLLATERAL
COMEDIENNE
COMPETENCE
CONDIMENTS
CONDOLENCE
CONFEDERAL
CONFERENCE
CONFIDENCE
CONFLUENCE
CONFUSEDLY
CONSCIENCE
CONSIDERED
CONTINENCE
CONVALESCE
COPARCENER
CORPULENCE
CORRIGENDA
CORTADERIA
COURAGEOUS
CRAPULENCE
CRETACEOUS
CROSSREFER
CURVACEOUS
CYBERNETIC
CYCLOPEDIA
DECIPHERED
DEEPFREEZE
DEFICIENCY
DEHISCENCE
DEJECTEDLY
DEMOISELLE
DEPENDENCE
DEPENDENCY

DESERVEDLY
DESPITEOUS
DETERRENCE
DIAGENESIS
DIAPEDESIS
DIFFERENCE
DIFFIDENCE
DIMINUENDO
DINANDERIE
DIPHTHERIA
DISCOVERER
DISCREETLY
DISHONESTY
DISINHERIT
DISORDERED
DISORDERLY
DISQUIETED
DISSIDENCE
DIVERGENCE
DOLCEMENTE
DOORKEEPER
DRUMBLEDOR
EBRACTEATE
EBULLIENCE
EFFERVESCE
EFFICIENCY
EIGHTEENTH
ELDERBERRY
EMBITTERED
EMBLEMENTS
EMOLUMENTS
ENTREMESSE
EPENTHETIC
EPIGENETIC
EPROUVETTE
ERYSIPELAS
ETEOCRETAN
EUDIOMETER
EUROCHEQUE
EURYPTERUS
EUTHYNEURA
EUTRAPELIA
EXCELLENCE
EXCELLENCY
EXPEDIENCE
EXPEDIENCY
EXPERIENCE
EXTRANEOUS
FENESTELLA
FEUILLETON
FIANCHETTO
FINISTERRE
FLATULENCE
FONTANELLE
FORINSECAL
FOURCHETTE
FOURTEENTH
FRAMBOESIA
FRATERETTO
FRATICELLI

FRAXINELLA
FRENZIEDLY
FRIGHTENED
FUSTANELLA
FUSTANELLE
GAMEKEEPER
GAULTHERIA
GENEVRETTE
GIBBERELLA
GOALKEEPER
GODPARENTS
GONIOMETER
GOOSEBERRY
GOVERNESSY
GREENHEART
GROCETERIA
GUTTIFERAE
HARTEBEEST
HEMIPLEGIA
HEPTAMERON
HEPTATEUCH
HERBACEOUS
HOLOSTERIC
HORNBLENDE
HOWSOMEVER
HYDROMETER
HYGROMETER
HYPOGAEOUS
HYPOTHESIS
HYSTERESIS
IATROGENIC
ICOSOHEDRA
ILLAQUEATE
IMMORTELLE
IMPATIENCE
IMPROPERLY
IMPRUDENCE
INCUMBENCY
INDULGENCE
INQUIRENDO
INSISTENCE
INSOLVENCY
INSURGENCY
INTERCEDER
INTERFERER
INTERFERON
INTERLEAVE
INTERMEZZO
INTERWEAVE
JARGONELLE
JEISTIECOR
KATERFELTO
KLEBSIELLA
LANSQUENET
LEUCHAEMIA
LINEAMENTS
LINGULELLA
LOCKKEEPER
LOGANBERRY
LOUISIETTE

MAHOMMEDAN
MAISONETTE
MALAGUETTA
MALINGERER
MANGABEIRA
MARIONETTE
MESENTERON
METATHERIA
METATHESIS
METHUSELAH
MICROMETER
MICRONESIA
MIGNONETTE
MILEOMETER
MILLIMETER
MILLIMETRE
MINDERERUS
MISCHMETAL
MISTAKENLY
MOLYBDENUM
MONOPLEGIA
MONOPTERON
MONOPTEROS
MONOTHEISM
MONTEVERDI
MORBIDEZZA
MORGANETTA
MORTADELLA
MOZZARELLA
MULTIMEDIA
MUSKETEERS
NARCOLEPSY
NATHELESSE
NEGLIGENCE
NEURILEMMA
NEUROLEMMA
NEWSAGENTS
NINETEENTH
NONONSENSE
OCCURRENCE
OFFLICENCE
OLERACEOUS
OMBROMETER
OPHICLEIDE
OPISOMETER
ORCHIDEOUS
OROGENESIS
OSTEOLEPIS
OUTRAGEOUS
OVERTHETOP
OWLSPIEGLE
PADDYMELON
PAPIAMENTO
PARAENESIS
PARALLELED
PARAPLEGIA
PARAPLEGIC
PARASCENIA
PARISIENNE
PASSAGEWAY

PASSAMEZZO
PASTORELLA
PATHOGENIC
PATISSERIE
PENNISETUM
PENTAMERON
PENTAMETER
PENTATEUCH
PENTETERIC
PENTIMENTO
PENTSTEMON
PERIEGESIS
PERIPHERAL
PERMANENCE
PERMANENCY
PERTINENCE
PESTILENCE
PETRONELLA
PHENOMENAL
PHENOMENON
PHILATELIC
PHILOXENIA
PHOTOGENIC
PINCHPENNY
PINNIPEDIA
PIRANDELLO
PLANCHETTE
PLEXIMETER
POLYPHEMUS
POLYTHEISM
PONCHIELLI
PONTEDERIA
PONTICELLO
PORRACEOUS
PORTAMENTO
PRAXITELES
PRECEDENCE
PREDECEASE
PREFERENCE
PREPOTENCE
PRESCIENCE
PRESIDENCY
PREVALENCE
PRIVATEERS
PRIVILEGED
PROAIRESIS
PROMINENCE
PROPRAETOR
PROPRIETOR
PROSTHESIS
PROSTHETIC
PROVIDENCE
PUBESCENCE
PURPOSEFUL
PYTHOGENIC
QUIESCENCE
RECOMMENCE
RECOMPENSE
RECRUDESCE
RECURRENCE

REGISTERED
REMORSEFUL
REPEATEDLY
REPORTEDLY
RESIGNEDLY
RESILIENCE
RESURGENCE
REVENGEFUL
RHINOCEROS
RITORNELLE
RITORNELLO
ROCKSTEADY
ROTISSERIE
SALMONELLA
SALTARELLO
SARCOLEMMA
SCHIPPERKE
SCHOLAEMIA
SCOMBRESOX
SENESCENCE
SERRADELLA
SERVICEMAN
SGANARELLE
SHACKLETON
SHISHKEBAB
SHOPKEEPER
SICILIENNE
SIGNORELLI
SILHOUETTE
SOMNOLENCE
SPIRITEDLY
SPLITLEVEL
SQUEEZEBOX
STONEHENGE
STOUTHERIE
STRAITENED
STRAWBERRY
STREAMERED
STRINGENCY
STRINGENDO
STRIPTEASE
STUMBLEDOM
SUBSIDENCE
SUPPOSEDLY
SWEETHEART
SYNAERESIS
SYNEIDESIS
SYNTERESIS
TABLANETTE
TACHOMETER
TARANTELLA
TEENYWEENY
TESTACEOUS
THIMBLEFUL
THIMBLEWIT
THIRTEENTH
THREATENED
THREEPENCE
THREEPENNY
TIMEKEEPER

TINTORETTO
TOCCATELLA
TOCOPHEROL
TOILINETTE
TOLLKEEPER
TORRICELLI
TRANSIENCE
TRANSVERSE
TRILATERAL
TROMOMETER
TRUCULENCE
TULARAEMIA
TUMESCENCE
TURBULENCE
TURRITELLA
ULSTERETTE
ULTRONEOUS
UNANSWERED
UNBELIEVER
UNDERLEASE
UNDERNEATH
UNFETTERED
UNGRATEFUL
UNHAMPERED
UNHYGIENIC
UNICAMERAL
UNILATERAL
UNLEAVENED
UNLETTERED
UNMANNERED
UNMANNERLY
UNNUMBERED
UNREDEEMED
UNRELIEVED
UROPOIESIS
VENEZUELAN
VERMICELLI
VILLANELLE
WATERLEVEL
WATERMELON
WHATSOEVER
WHITEHEART
WILDEBEEST
WINCEYETTE
WRETCHEDLY
YOUNGBERRY
YTHUNDERED
BEAUTIFIER
BREASTFEED
CALORIFIER
CANDLEFISH
CENTRIFUGE
CHLOROFORM
CINQUEFOIL
CIRCUMFLEX
CIRCUMFUSE
CLASSIFIED
CONTRAFLOW
CUTTLEFISH
DAMSELFISH

DEBRIEFING
DISCOMFORT
DUNDERFUNK
ELYTRIFORM
EMULSIFIER
GENTLEFOLK
HUMIDIFIER
MONILIFORM
OUTPERFORM
PLUPERFECT
RAGAMUFFIN
RUTHERFORD
SANCTIFIED
SHOPLIFTER
SILVERFISH
SPONGIFORM
STILLIFORM
STULTIFIED
SUBTERFUGE
SVADILFARI
TAMPERFOOT
TANGLEFOOT
TENDERFOOT
THALLIFORM
THEREAFTER
WYCLIFFIAN
ACROMEGALY
ALGOLAGNIA
ANASTIGMAT
APTERYGOTA
AREOPAGITE
ASPARAGINE
ASTRINGENT
BALBRIGGAN
BARELEGGED
BASSINGTON
BEDRAGGLED
BIRMINGHAM
BOONDOGGLE
BOOTLEGGER
BOOZINGKEN
BORDRAGING
BOUSINGKEN
BUCKINGHAM
BURLINGTON
CAMPAIGNER
CARDIOGRAM
CATALOGUER
CATTLEGRID
CHAMPIGNON
CHITTAGONG
CHURCHGOER
CONCHIGLIE
CONGREGATE
CONTINGENT
CONVERGENT
CRYPTOGRAM
CURMUDGEON
DEVANAGARI
EMALANGENI

FALLINGOFF
FLAMINGANT
FOOTLIGHTS
FORFOUGHEN
FOURRAGERE
GOLDDIGGER
HARRINGTON
HEADLIGHTS
HUMDUDGEON
INTELIGENT
KIESELGUHR
LAUNCEGAYE
LEAMINGTON
LIMBURGITE
MABINOGION
MANDRAGORA
MARTINGALE
MEANINGFUL
MISHGUGGLE
MUSSORGSKY
NEWFANGLED
NICARAGUAN
NONALIGNED
PADDINGTON
PARTINGALE
PLOUGHGATE
PROFLIGACY
PROFLIGATE
PROMULGATE
REAMINGBIT
ROCKINGHAM
SALPINGIAN
SCHOOLGIRL
SCROUNGING
SELLINGERS
SELTZOGENE
SEPTUAGINT
SEXOLOGIST
SHANDYGAFF
SOLIVAGANT
STRATEGIST
SUFFRAGIST
TEDDINGTON
THEOLOGATE
THEOLOGIAN
THEOLOGISE
THEOLOGIST
THOROUGHLY
TOPOLOGIST
TRILINGUAL
UNASSIGNED
UNFLAGGING
UPBRINGING
UROSTEGITE
VICEREGENT
VIROLOGIST
WASHINGTON
WELLINGTON
WILLINGDON
WOFFINGTON

WOODPIGEON
YAFFINGALE
YELLOWGIRL
ZAPOROGIAN
AERENCHYMA
AFTERSHAVE
AFTERSHOCK
ANGLOPHILE
ANGLOPHOBE
ANTIOCHENE
ANTIOCHIAN
APOPHTHEGM
ATMOSPHERE
BALANCHINE
BARYSPHERE
BATRACHIAN
BEFOREHAND
BEHINDHAND
BEWITCHING
BIRKENHEAD
BLACKSHIRT
BLACKTHORN
BOTTLEHEAD
BRAINCHILD
BRIDGEHEAD
BRITISHISM
BROADSHEET
BUFFLEHEAD
BUTTONHOLE
CAOUTCHOUC
CARPATHIAN
CARRAGHEEN
CATARRHINE
CELLOPHANE
CHARGEHAND
CHIFFCHAFF
CLAVICHORD
CLOMIPHENE
COLEORHIZA
COMANCHERO
COMPREHEND
CONTRAHENT
COPPERHEAD
CORINTHIAN
CRANKSHAFT
CROSSCHECK
CRUIKSHANK
CTENOPHORA
DEBAUCHERY
DEBOUCHURE
DHARMSHALA
DISCOPHORA
DISENCHANT
DROSOPHILA
DUNDERHEAD
EMBOUCHURE
ENGLISHMAN
ENGLISHMEN
ENTRYPHONE
EPANOPHORA

EPIMETHEUS
EPONYCHIUM
ESCUTCHEON
EUSTACHIAN
EVERYTHING
EVERYWHERE
FAHRENHEIT
FIGUREHEAD
FLUGELHORN
FURNISHING
GALUMPHING
GESUNDHEIT
GOLIATHISE
GONORRHOEA
GRAMOPHONE
GRANDCHILD
GREENSHANK
GYPSOPHILA
HAMMERHEAD
HEMISPHERE
HEMORRHAGE
HEPTATHLON
HIEROPHANT
HYALOPHANE
HYDROPHANE
HYPAETHRAL
HYPAETHRON
IMPOSTHUME
INTERPHONE
IONOSPHERE
JOLTERHEAD
KARMATHIAN
KLOOTCHMAN
KNIGHTHOOD
LANDSTHING
LANGERHANS
LEPRECHAUN
LETTERHEAD
LIKELIHOOD
LITHOPHANE
LIVELIHOOD
LOGGERHEAD
LOGORRHOEA
MAIDENHAIR
MAIDENHOOD
MALLOPHAGA
MARASCHINO
MATTERHORN
MEERSCHAUM
MELANCHOLY
MENORRHOEA
MICROPHONE
MIDLOTHIAN
MONARCHIST
MOTHERHOOD
MUTTONHEAD
MYCORRHIZA
NDRANGHETA
NIGGERHEAD
NIGHTSHADE
NIGHTSHIRT
NOUAKCHOTT
NOURISHING
ODELSTHING
OIREACHTAS
OMBROPHOBE
OSTEOPHYTE
PANSOPHIST
PAPERCHASE
PARARTHRIA
PARENCHYMA
PARENTHOOD
PARISCHANE
PENTATHLON
PERSEPHONE
PETTICHAPS
PETTYCHAPS
PIGEONHOLE
PINCUSHION
PLEROPHORY
PRIESTHOOD
PROMETHEAN
PROMETHEUS
PROMETHIUM
PUBLISHING
QUICKTHORN
REDRUTHITE
REFRESHING
RHINOPHYMA
RIDINGHOOD
ROTHSCHILD
RUDOLPHINE
SAPROPHYTE
SCREECHING
SCRIMSHANK
SECONDHAND
SEEMLIHEAD
SEPULCHRAL
SHEEPSHANK
SHELLSHOCK
SHOVELHEAD
SINARCHIST
SISTERHOOD
SKRIMSHANK
SOUSAPHONE
SPLANCHNIC
SPOKESHAVE
SPREAGHERY
SPRINGHAAS
STEALTHILY
STRACCHINO
STRAIGHTEN
STRINGHALT
STRONGHOLD
SUNBATHING
SWEATSHIRT
SYMPATHISE
SYMPATHIZE
TENTERHOOK
THROUGHOUT
THROUGHPUT
THROUGHWAY
TREKSCHUIT
TRIUMPHANT
TROPOPHYTE
UNBLUSHING
UNDERSHIRT
UNFAITHFUL
UNTRUTHFUL
VARNISHING
VIBRAPHONE
WALLACHIAN
WATERWHEEL
WHEATSHEAF
WHEELCHAIR
WHITETHORN
WHOLEWHEAT
WILLOWHERB
WOODENHEAD
WORTHWHILE
ABBREVIATE
ABITURIENT
ABORIGINAL
ABSTEMIOUS
ACCESSIBLE
ACCESSIONS
ACCLIVIOUS
ACCREDITED
ADJECTIVAL
ADMISSIBLE
ADVERTISER
AFTERBIRTH
AFTERPIECE
AIRFREIGHT
ALCHERINGA
AMPHIBIOUS
AMPHIMIXIS
ANALOGICAL
ANALYTICAL
ANARCHICAL
ANATOMICAL
ANNUALIZED
ANNUNCIATE
ANTIADITIS
ANTICLIMAX
APPRECIATE
ARAGONITES
ARTHURIANA
ASPERSIONS
ASPHYXIATE
ASTEROIDEA
AUSPICIOUS
AUTHORISED
AVARICIOUS
BACKSLIDER
BALBUTIENT
BANDERILLA
BANDERILLO
BARMECIDAL
BELONGINGS
BIOLOGICAL
BIPARTISAN
BIRTHRIGHT
BLASTOIDEA
BORROWINGS
BRADYKININ
BRAGADISME
BROADPIECE
BRONCHITIC
BRONCHITIS
BUDGERIGAR
CAERPHILLY
CALUMNIATE
CAMERLINGO
CANDELILLA
CAPRICIOUS
CARYATIDES
CASCARILLA
CATHOLICON
CATHOLICOS
CELESTIALS
CELLULITIS
CENSORIOUS
CENTESIMAL
CENTILITER
CENTILITRE
CHAPLAINCY
CHILDBIRTH
CHINCHILLA
CHOPSTICKS
CHRISTIANA
CLOSTRIDIA
COLLEGIATE
COMESTIBLE
COMMODIOUS
COMMUNIQUÉ
COMPARISON
COMPATIBLE
COMPETITOR
COMPOSITOR
CONCILIATE
CONGENITAL
CONSTRINGE
CONTAGIOUS
CONVENIENT
COPERNICUS
COPYWRITER
COQUELICOT
CORDWAINER
CORREGIDOR
COXCOMICAL
CROSSPIECE
CROTALIDAE
CUCURBITAL
DARKHAIRED
DEDUCTIBLE
DEFENSIBLE
DEMOCRITUS
DEPRECIATE
DERMATITIS
DÉSHABILLÉ
DETERMINED
DIABOLICAL
DIACONICON
DIDGERIDOO
DIGESTIBLE
DIRECTIONS
DISBELIEVE
DISCLAIMER
DISHABILLE
DISPIRITED
DISSILIENT
DISSIMILAR
DISSOCIATE
DRACONITES
DRAWBRIDGE
DUKKERIPEN
DUODECIMAL
ECHINOIDEA
ECOLOGICAL
ECONOMICAL
ECUMENICAL
ELECTRICAL
ELLIPTICAL
ENCYCLICAL
ENHYDRITIC
ENTHUSIASM
ENTHUSIAST
EPIMENIDES
ESCADRILLE
ESPADRILLE
ESTANCIERO
EUPHONIOUS
EXCRUCIATE
EXPATRIATE
EXPLICITLY
EXTENSIBLE
FACTITIOUS
FAIRHAIRED
FALLACIOUS
FASTIDIOUS
FASTIGIATE
FERNITICLE
FERTILISED
FERTILISER
FERTILIZER
FIBROSITIS
FICTITIOUS
FLAGITIOUS
FLASHLIGHT
FLOODLIGHT
FOOTBRIDGE
FOOTPRINTS
FORTHRIGHT
FOSSILIZED
FRANCHISEE
FRANCHISOR
FRENETICAL
FUNGICIDAL
GALLABIYAH

GALLABIYEH
GALRAVITCH
GALVANISER
GARGOUILLE
GEOLOGICAL
GERMICIDAL
GINGIVITIS
GIRLFRIEND
GLEEMAIDEN
GONDOLIERS
GRAMICIDIN
GRANADILLA
GRASSWIDOW
GREENFINCH
GREGARIOUS
GRENADIERS
GRENADILLA
GREYFRIARS
GUIDELINES
HANDMAIDEN
HANGGLIDER
HARDBOILED
HARMONIOUS
HECTOLITRE
HEMOPHILIA
HESPERIDES
HISTORICAL
HITCHHIKER
HORSERIDER
HYPNOTIZED
HYSTERICAL
ILLADVISED
IMPERVIOUS
IMPLICITLY
IMPOSSIBLE
IMPOSSIBLY
IMPROVISED
INCAUTIOUS
INCENDIARY
INCREDIBLE
INCREDIBLY
INDISTINCT
INELIGIBLE
INFALLIBLE
INFALLIBLY
INFECTIOUS
INFLEXIBLE
INFLEXIBLY
INGLORIOUS
INGRATIATE
INGREDIENT
INQUISITOR
INSENSIBLE
INSOUCIANT
INTAGLIATE
INTANGIBLE
INTESTINAL
INTESTINES
INVINCIBLE
JARDINIERE

JUSTICIARY
KSHATRIYAS
LACCADIVES
LARYNGITIS
LASCIVIOUS
LATTICINIO
LAVALLIÈRE
LENTIGINES
LIBREVILLE
LICENTIATE
LICENTIOUS
LILYWHITES
LIQUIDIZER
LITURGICAL
LOGISTICAL
LOQUACIOUS
LUGUBRIOUS
MACROBIOTE
MAGNIFICAT
MAKEWEIGHT
MANDEVILLE
MANZANILLA
MARTINIQUE
MECHANICAL
MECHANIZED
MENDACIOUS
MENINGITIS
METHODICAL
MICROFICHE
MICROLIGHT
MILLEFIORI
MISGIVINGS
MOLENDINAR
MONOECIOUS
MONTEVIDEO
MORDACIOUS
MOUSEPIECE
MOUTHPIECE
MOZAMBIQUE
MYRINGITIS
MYSTERIOUS
NEAPOLITAN
NEGLIGIBLE
NEOTERICAL
NICROSILAL
NIGHTLIGHT
NUTRITIOUS
OBSEQUIOUS
OFTENTIMES
OMNISCIENT
ORATORICAL
OSTENSIBLE
OSTENSIBLY
OUANANICHE
OUGHTLINGS
OUTPATIENT
OVERWEIGHT
OVIPOSITOR
PALMATIFID
PANOPTICON

PARAPHILIA
PARMACITIE
PARTICIPLE
PATRONISED
PECCADILLO
PENTELIKON
PERCIPIENT
PERDITIOUS
PERFICIENT
PERFIDIOUS
PERIODICAL
PERNICIOUS
PERSTRINGE
PHOTODIODE
PICCADILLY
PICCALILLI
PICCANINNY
PICHICIAGO
PILEDRIVER
PILLIWINKS
PLATINISED
PLAYWRIGHT
POIKILITIC
PONTIFICAL
POTENTIATE
POTENTILLA
PRECARIOUS
PRECIPITIN
PRECOCIOUS
PREDACIOUS
PREJUDICED
PREMARITAL
PREPOSITOR
PRIZEFIGHT
PRODIGIOUS
PROFICIENT
PROGENITOR
PROHIBITED
PROPITIATE
PROPITIOUS
PROPOSITUS
PROSCRIBED
PROSILIENT
PROVEDITOR
PROVISIONS
PUGNACIOUS
QUESADILLA
RABBINICAL
REBELLIOUS
RECOGNISED
RECOGNIZED
RECONCILED
RECONSIDER
REPATRIATE
REPUBLICAN
RESERVISTS
RESORCINOL
RESTRAINED
REVERSIBLE
RHETORICAL

RHYTHMICAL
ROBUSTIOUS
ROCKABILLY
ROTTWEILER
SABBATICAL
SALUBRIOUS
SANDINISTA
SANFORISED
SCATURIENT
SCIENTIFIC
SCOPELIDAE
SCOTODINIA
SDRUCCIOLA
SEGUIDILLA
SEQUACIOUS
SERMONICAL
SERRADILLA
SEVENTIETH
SHAGHAIRED
SHENANIGAN
SHOPSOILED
SHORTLIVED
SIGNIFICAT
SIMILLIMUM
SINSEMILLA
SOBERSIDES
SOFTBOILED
SOGDOLIGER
SOMERVILLE
SONGWRITER
SPLENDIDLY
STABILISER
STABILIZER
STERILISER
STERILIZER
STIACCIATO
STILLBIRTH
STROPHIOLE
STYLOPISED
SUBLIMINAL
SUBMARINER
SUBMEDIANT
SUBSCRIBER
SUBSIDIARY
SUFFICIENT
SUPERGIANT
SUPERVISED
SUPERVISOR
SUSPICIOUS
SUZERAINTY
SYMBOLICAL
SYPHILITIC
TANAGRIDAE
TENEBRIFIC
TENRECIDAE
THEATRICAL
THEOCRITUS
THUCYDIDES
TIMESWITCH
TORCHLIGHT

TOUCHPIECE
TRADITIONS
TRANQUILLY
TRIMSNITCH
TRIPUDIARY
TROUVAILLE
TYPEWRITER
TYRANNICAL
TYRANNISED
ULTRAFICHE
UMBELLIFER
UNCONFINED
UNCRITICAL
UNDERLINEN
UNDERSIZED
UNGRACIOUS
UNIGENITUS
UNIMPAIRED
UNINSPIRED
UNORIGINAL
UNREQUITED
UNSPECIFIC
UPROARIOUS
VALENTINES
VAUDEVILLE
VIBRATIONS
VICTORIANA
VICTORIOUS
VINDEMIATE
VITELLICLE
VIVANDIÈRE
WANDERINGS
WANTHRIVEN
WATERTIGHT
WATERWINGS
WILLYWILLY
WINDSHIELD
ZABAGLIONE
ZOOLOGICAL
LUMBERJACK
NATTERJACK
SUPPLEJACK
YELLOWJACK
BARRACKING
CHEAPSKATE
JAYWALKING
JOBSEEKERS
KARTTIKAYA
KENTUCKIAN
LAMARCKISM
LAURVIKITE
MUCKRAKING
NETWORKING
NONSMOKING
PERNICKETY
PEROVSKITE
POHUTUKAWA
PORLOCKING
ROLLICKING
SAMARSKITE

SBUDDIKINS
SPILLIKINS
THUMBIKINS
TITARAKURA
UNBLINKING
UNDERSKIRT
UNSHACKLED
UNTHINKING
WATERSKIER
WUNDERKIND
ACCOMPLICE
ACCOMPLISH
ACCUMULATE
ACEPHALOUS
ADRAMELECH
ADRENALINE
AFFABILITY
ALCOHOLISM
AMARYLLIDS
AMBIVALENT
AMIABILITY
AMYGDALOID
ANGUILLULA
ANNIHILATE
ANTHEOLION
ANTHOCLORE
ARISTOLOGY
ARTHRALGIA
ARTICULATA
ARTICULATE
ARUNDELIAN
ASSEMBLAGE
ASSEMBLING
ASSIMILATE
AUDIBILITY
AUSTRALIAN
AUSTRALORP
AUTECOLOGY
BADDERLOCK
BALNEOLOGY
BATTAILOUS
BEAUJOLAIS
BEDEVILLED
BENEVOLENT
BERSAGLIER
BESTIALITY
BESTSELLER
BINOCULARS
BIRTHPLACE
BITTERLING
BONDHOLDER
BOOKSELLER
BORDERLAND
BORDERLINE
BOTTOMLESS
BRATISLAVA
BREATHLESS
BROADCLOTH
CALCEOLATE
CAMOUFLAGE
CANDYFLOSS
CANNELLONI
CANTILLATE
CAPABILITY
CAPITALISM
CAPITALIST
CAPITALIZE
CAPITELLUM
CAPITOLINE
CAPITULARY
CAPITULATE
CAPREOLATE
CARAMELIZE
CARDIOLOGY
CARPHOLOGY
CATABOLISM
CATAFALQUE
CENTRALIZE
CEREBELLUM
CHANCELLOR
CHANDELIER
CHANGELESS
CHANGELING
CHAPFALLEN
CHAPTALISE
CHAROLLAIS
CHESSYLITE
CHOICELESS
CHRONOLOGY
CHRYSOLITE
CNIDOBLAST
CODSWALLOP
COLOURLESS
COMPELLING
CONCHOLOGY
CONTROLLER
COPYHOLDER
CORDIALITY
CORDILLERA
COUNCILLOR
COUNSELING
COUNSELLOR
CRAIGFLUKE
CRENELLATE
CUMBERLAND
CYNOMOLGUS
DARJEELING
DECATHLETE
DECIMALIZE
DELTIOLOGY
DEMOBILISE
DEMOBILIZE
DEMORALISE
DEMORALIZE
DEPOPULATE
DERAILLEUR
DEREGULATE
DEUTOPLASM
DIASTALTIC
DISABILITY
DISCIPLINE
DISINCLINE
DISQUALIFY
DISTILLATE
DISTILLERY
DISTILLING
DIURNALIST
DOMICILIARY
DURABILITY
EASTERLING
EFFORTLESS
EMASCULATE
EMBRYOLOGY
ENTOMOLOGY
EPITHELIUM
EQUIVALENT
EVANGELIST
EVANGELIZE
EVERYPLACE
FATHERLAND
FATHERLESS
FEDERALISM
FEDERALIST
FETTERLOCK
FIBERGLASS
FIBREGLASS
FIBRILLATE
FINGERLING
FIREWALKER
FISHSELLER
FLAGELLATE
FLIGHTLESS
FLOCCULATE
FLOCCULENT
FLOORCLOTH
FOOTBALLER
FRAUDULENT
FREEHOLDER
FRIENDLESS
FRINGILLID
FRITILLARY
GENERALISE
GENERALITY
GENERALIZE
GENETHLIAC
GENICULATE
GHIBELLINE
GOODFELLOW
GOOSEFLESH
GRAPHOLOGY
GRAPTOLITE
GRATILLITY
GRAVEOLENT
GREENCLOTH
GROUNDLESS
GROUNDLING
GROVELLING
GYNECOLOGY
HALFDOLLAR
HAMMERLOCK
HAUSTELLUM
HIEROGLYPH
HINTERLAND
HOMORELAPS
HONOURLESS
HOWLEGLASS
HUMOURLESS
HYDRAULICS
HYDROPLANE
ICONOCLAST
ILLEGALITY
IMBECILITY
IMMACULACY
IMMACULATE
IMMOBILITY
IMMOBILIZE
IMMORALITY
IMMUNOLOGY
INCIVILITY
INCOMPLETE
INDICOLITE
INDIGOLITE
INEQUALITY
INESCULENT
INFIDELITY
INOSCULATE
INSUFFLATE
INTERCLUDE
INVIGILATE
IRRESOLUTE
ISABELLINE
JOURNALESE
JOURNALISM
JOURNALIST
KIMBERLITE
LADYKILLER
LANCEOLATE
LAURDALITE
LEGIBILITY
LHERZOLITE
LIBERALISM
LIBERALITY
LIBERALIZE
LONGFELLOW
MALACOLOGY
MALAYALAAM
MALEVOLENT
MANIPULATE
MAQUILLAGE
MARSHALSEA
MARVELLOUS
MAXIMALIST
MAXIMILIAN
MESITYLENE
METABOLISE
METABOLISM
METICULOUS
MICHAELMAS
MINERALOGY
MINIMALIST
MIRACULOUS
MISCELLANY
MONOPOLISE
MONOPOLIZE
MORPHOLOGY
MOTHERLAND
MOTHERLESS
MOTHERLIKE
MOTIONLESS
MOUSSELINE
MULTIPLIED
MULTIPLIER
MUSICOLOGY
MUTABILITY
NAPTHALENE
NATURALISM
NATURALIST
NATURALIZE
NEUTRALISE
NEUTRALITY
NEUTRALIZE
NIDDERLING
NOMINALIST
NONCHALANT
NONVIOLENT
NORMOBLAST
NOTABILITY
NOVACULITE
NUMBERLESS
NYMPHOLEPT
OBJECTLESS
ODDFELLOWS
ODONTALGIA
ODONTOLITE
ODONTOLOGY
OPHTHALMIC
ORTHOCLASE
OSTEOBLAST
PAINKILLER
PALATALISE
PARACELSUS
PARASELENE
PARENTLESS
PARNELLISM
PARTIALITY
PATIBULARY
PEDICULATE
PEDIPALPUS
PENICILLIN
PENNILLION
PERIHELION
PERSIFLAGE
PETROGLYPH
PHRENOLOGY
PHYSIOLOGY
PILGARLICK
PISTILLATE
PLANOBLAST
PLATTELAND
PLAYFELLOW

PLIABILITY
POINTBLANK
PONEROLOGY
PORTCULLIS
POSTILLATE
POSTILLION
POZZUOLANA
PREVAILING
PROFITLESS
PROPELLANT
PROTOPLASM
PRZEWALSKI
PSEPHOLOGY
PSYCHOLOGY
PUBERULENT
PUMMELLING
PUNCTULATE
QUENCHLESS
RADICALISM
RAMPALLIAN
REGARDLESS
RELENTLESS
RESEMBLING
RETINALITE
REVITALIZE
REVIVALIST
RIDICULOUS
ROSANILINE
ROSEMALING
RUDDERLESS
RUMBULLION
RUPICOLINE
SANDERLING
SAXICOLINE
SAXICOLOUS
SCANDALISE
SCANDALIZE
SCANDALOUS
SCATHELESS
SCRIBBLING
SCRUPULOUS
SCURRILITY
SCURRILOUS
SCUTELLATE
SEISMOLOGY
SELEGILINE
SENEGALESE
SENSUALITY
SHADOWLESS
SHIBBOLETH
SHILLELAGH
SHOPWALKER
SHRIVELLED
SINGHALESE
SLEEVELESS
SNORKELING
SOLUBILITY
SOPHOCLEAN
SOURDELINE
SPECIALISE
SPECIALIST
SPECIALITY
SPECIALIZE
SPEECHLESS
SPELEOLOGY
SPERRYLITE
SPHACELATE
SPIRITLESS
SPRINGLESS
SPRINGLIKE
SPRINKLING
STADHOLDER
STALHELMER
STANISLAUS
STAPHYLINE
STARVELING
STAUROLITE
STERNALGIA
STRAGGLING
STREAMLINE
STREETLAMP
STRIDULATE
SUAVEOLENT
SUBSELLIUM
SUGARALLIE
SURREALISM
SURREALIST
TABLECLOTH
TAMBERLANE
TARPAULING
TECHNOLOGY
TENDERLOIN
TENDRILLED
TERNEPLATE
TERREPLEIN
THEMSELVES
THEODOLITE
THREADLIKE
TIMBROLOGY
TIRAILLEUR
TOMFOOLERY
TOPICALITY
TORTELLINI
TOURBILLON
TOURMALINE
TOXICOLOGY
TRACHELATE
TRAMPOLINE
TRANSPLANT
TRAVELLERS
TRAVELLING
TRICHOLOGY
TRISKELION
TRIVIALITY
TRIVIALIZE
TROCTOLITE
TUTIVILLUS
UNAVAILING
UNDERCLASS
UNDERFLOOR
UNDERSLUNG
UNEQUALLED
UNFAMILIAR
UNHERALDED
UNLADYLIKE
UNRESOLVED
UNRIVALLED
UNSETTLING
UPPERCLASS
VERMILLION
VERSAILLES
VESICULATE
VICTUALLER
VISIBILITY
VOCABULARY
VOCABULIST
VOLATILITY
VOLUBILITY
WANDERLUST
WASSAILING
WEAPONLESS
WEEDKILLER
WEIGHTLESS
WHEWELLITE
WONDERLAND
WORLDCLASS
YOURSELVES
ABONNEMENT
ABRIDGMENT
ADDITAMENT
ADJUSTMENT
ADULLAMITE
AGRONOMIST
ALLUREMENT
ALTAZIMUTH
ALZHEIMERS
AMALGAMATE
ANADROMOUS
ANADYOMENE
ANTINOMIAN
ARGOLEMONO
ARTHROMERE
ASSESSMENT
ASSIGNMENT
ASSORTMENT
ATTACHMENT
ATTAINMENT
AUTONOMOUS
BACKGAMMON
BAFFLEMENT
BANISHMENT
BATTLEMENT
BEDCHAMBER
BELLARMINE
BENTHAMITE
BICHROMATE
BIOCHEMIST
BLACKSMITH
BRESSUMMER
BRIDESMAID
BUCKJUMPER
BUTTERMERE
BUTTERMILK
CANTONMENT
CARTHAMINE
CATAWAMPUS
CECIDOMYIA
CINECAMERA
COMMITMENT
COMPLEMENT
COMPLIMENT
COMPROMISE
CONFORMIST
CONFORMITY
CONSUMMATE
DEBASEMENT
DEBATEMENT
DECAMPMENT
DEFACEMENT
DEFILEMENT
DEFRAYMENT
DENOUEMENT
DEPARTMENT
DEPLOYMENT
DEPORTMENT
DERAILMENT
DESQUAMATE
DETACHMENT
DETAINMENT
DEVOTEMENT
DICHROMISM
DISCOMMODE
DISHARMONY
EBOULEMENT
EFFACEMENT
EMBANKMENT
EMBODIMENT
EMPLOYMENT
ENCAMPMENT
ENCASEMENT
ENDEARMENT
ENDOGAMOUS
ENGAGEMENT
ENGOUEMENT
ENLACEMENT
ENLÈVEMENT
ENLISTMENT
ENRICHMENT
ENROLLMENT
ENTICEMENT
ENTOMBMENT
EPAULEMENT
EPHRAIMITE
EPISTEMICS
EQUANIMITY
ERGONOMICS
ESCAPEMENT
ESCARPMENT
ETHYLAMINE
EXCITEMENT
EXPERIMENT
FAMISHMENT
FOREDAMNED
FULFILMENT
GALLIAMBIC
GETHSEMANE
GOVERNMENT
GUACHAMOLE
HANDSOMELY
HARASSMENT
HOMECOMING
HORNRIMMED
IMPAIRMENT
IMPEDIMENT
INCITEMENT
INDAPAMIDE
INDICTMENT
INDITEMENT
INDUCEMENT
INFEFTMENT
INSTALMENT
INSTRUMENT
INTEGUMENT
INTENDMENT
INTERNMENT
INVESTMENT
JACKHAMMER
KERSEYMERE
LACHRYMOSE
LANDAMMANN
LATTERMATH
LEGITIMACY
LEGITIMATE
LEGITIMIZE
LEGWARMERS
LIEBERMANN
LOCULAMENT
MANAGEMENT
MASTERMIND
MEDICAMENT
MENECHMIAN
MIZZENMAST
MONOGAMOUS
MONTGOMERY
NETHERMOST
NONPAYMENT
NOSOCOMIAL
PALUDAMENT
PARLIAMENT
PEPPERMILL
PEPPERMINT
PERFORMING
PHILLUMENY
PILGRIMAGE
POLYGAMIST
POLYGAMOUS
POLYHYMNIA
POSTHUMOUS
POSTLIMINY
PREFERMENT

PREPAYMENT
PROGRAMMER
PUNISHMENT
PUZZLEMENT
RAJPRAMUKH
REARMAMENT
REASSEMBLE
REFINEMENT
RESENTMENT
RETIREMENT
RINGELMANN
SAPPERMENT
SCARCEMENT
SCHOOLMAAM
SECONDMENT
SETTLEMENT
SHOWJUMPER
STALAGMITE
SUPPLEMENT
SURINAMESE
SYNONYMOUS
SYNTAGMATA
TAILORMADE
TAPOTEMENT
TAXONOMIST
THINGUMBOB
TORQUEMADA
TOURNAMENT
TRENCHMORE
UNASSUMING
UNBECOMING
UNIFORMITY
UNSCRAMBLE
VIETNAMESE
WASSERMANS
WHIGGAMORE
WILLIAMSON
WINDERMERE
WINDJAMMER
WOLFRAMITE
WONDERMENT
ABRUPTNESS
ABUNDANTLY
ABYSSINIAN
ACCIDENTAL
ACCUSINGLY
ACQUAINTED
ACROGENOUS
ADMIRINGLY
AERUGINOUS
AFICIONADO
AFRICANDER
ALBIGENSES
ALKALINITY
ALMACANTAR
ALMUCANTAR
AMANUENSIS
ANTAGONISE
ANTAGONISM
ANTAGONIST

ANTAGONIZE
ANTIMONIAN
ANTIVENENE
APOLLONIAN
APOLLONIUS
APPARENTLY
AQUAMANALE
AQUAMANILE
ARAUCANIAN
ARROGANTLY
ARYTAENOID
ASTUTENESS
ATRAMENTAL
AUCTIONEER
AUSTRINGER
AUTOGENOUS
BABYLONIAN
BACCHANTES
BACKHANDED
BACKHANDER
BAHRAINIAN
BALIBUNTAL
BALLOONING
BALLOONIST
BARASINGHA
BARGAINING
BARRENNESS
BASSOONIST
BITTERNESS
BITUMINOUS
BLACKENING
BLUEMANTLE
BOOKBINDER
BOTTLENECK
BOURIGNIAN
BRAININESS
BRIGHTNESS
BUCHMANISM
BUFFOONERY
BURGEONING
BUSHRANGER
CACHINNATE
CACUMINOUS
CALAMANDER
CALAMONDIN
CALEDONIAN
CALYDONIAN
CAMBRENSIS
CAMERONIAN
CANCIONERO
CARABINEER
CARABINIER
CARMAGNOLE
CARTOONIST
CASUALNESS
CAUTIONARY
CENTENNIAL
CEREMONIAL
CEREMONIES
CHALLENGER

CHARDONNAY
CHAUVINISM
CHAUVINIST
CHEEKINESS
CHEIRONOMY
CHELTENHAM
CHERSONESE
CHERVONETS
CHICKENPOX
CHIFFONIER
CHILLINESS
CHIMPANZEE
CHLORINATE
CLAMMINESS
CLASPKNIFE
CLEVERNESS
CLOUDINESS
CLUMSINESS
COARSENESS
COATHANGER
COCKERNONY
COHERENTLY
COMPLANATE
COMPOUNDED
CONCERNING
CONCINNITY
CONCINNOUS
CONFOUNDED
CONSTANTAN
CONSTANTIA
CONSTANTLY
COORDINATE
COPPERNOSE
COROMANDEL
CORYBANTES
CORYBANTIC
COSTLINESS
COVENANTER
CRAFTINESS
CRISPINIAN
CRYOGENICS
CUSSEDNESS
DEADLINESS
DELPHINIUM
DERACINATE
DESALINATE
DIAPHANOUS
DICTIONARY
DILIGENTLY
DIOPHANTOS
DIRECTNESS
DISCERNING
DISCONNECT
DISDAINFUL
DISGRUNTLE
DISJOINTED
DISTRINGAS
DITHIONATE
DODECANESE
DOGGEDNESS

DRAWCANSIR
DREAMINESS
DREARINESS
DREIKANTER
DROWSINESS
DRUZHINNIK
ECARDINATE
EFFEMINACY
EFFEMINATE
ELEUSINIAN
ELOQUENTLY
EMARGINATE
ENCOIGNURE
EPILIMNION
EPIPHONEMA
EVENHANDED
EVITERNITY
EXEMPTNESS
EYEWITNESS
FALKLANDER
FAULTINESS
FEEBLENESS
FEMININITY
FESCENNINE
FICKLENESS
FIERCENESS
FILTHINESS
FINGERNAIL
FISHMONGER
FLABBINESS
FLAGRANTLY
FLANCONADE
FLASHINESS
FLEETINGLY
FLESHINESS
FLIMSINESS
FLIPPANTLY
FLUFFINESS
FOREFINGER
FORERUNNER
FRATERNISE
FRATERNITY
FRATERNIZE
FREEHANDER
FREELANCER
FREQUENTED
FREQUENTER
FREQUENTLY
FRISKINESS
FULIGINOUS
FULLLENGTH
GADOLINIUM
GANGRENOUS
GASCONNADE
GASTRONOME
GASTRONOMY
GELATINOUS
GENTLENESS
GETUPANDGO
GLASSINESS

GLAUCONITE
GLISTENING
GLOSSINESS
GLUTTONOUS
GOLDFINGER
GREEDINESS
GRITTINESS
GRUBBINESS
GRUMPINESS
HEADHUNTED
HEADHUNTER
HEARTINESS
HELLBENDER
HESITANTLY
HIGHBINDER
HIGHHANDED
HIGHLANDER
HOARSENESS
HOMELINESS
HOMOGENIZE
HOODWINKED
HOOTNANNIE
HORIZONTAL
HUMBLENESS
HYPOTENUSE
IGNORANTLY
ILLUMINATE
ILLUMINATI
IMPOTENTLY
IMPREGNATE
IMPUDENTLY
INCIDENTAL
INDECENTLY
INDEFINITE
INDIGENOUS
INDUMENTUM
INGEMINATE
INHERENTLY
INHUMANITY
INKSLINGER
INNOCENTLY
INORDINATE
INSEMINATE
INSOLENTLY
INTENTNESS
IRONMONGER
JAMESONITE
JAUNTINESS
JOHNSONIAN
JUBILANTLY
JUGGERNAUT
KILMARNOCK
KINCHINLAY
KINDLINESS
LANTHANIDE
LASTMINUTE
LAVISHNESS
LEFTHANDED
LEFTHANDER
LEFTWINGER

LEGUMINOUS
LENOCINIUM
LESBIANISM
LIBIDINOUS
LIEUTENANT
LIGHTINGUP
LIKEMINDED
LIMBERNECK
LITHUANIAN
LITTLENESS
LIVELINESS
LONELINESS
LORDLINESS
LOVELINESS
LUSITANIAN
MACEDONIAN
MAHAYANALI
MANCHINEEL
MARCIONITE
MAVOURNEEN
MEAGERNESS
MEAGRENESS
MELACONITE
MELLOWNESS
MEMBRANOUS
MEMORANDUM
MENACINGLY
METACENTRE
MIGHTINESS
MINUTENESS
MISOGYNIST
MISSIONARY
MONOTONOUS
MONTAGNARD
MONUMENTAL
MORISONIAN
MOROSENESS
MOSSBUNKER
MOULDINESS
MUMBLENEWS
NARROWNESS
NEWSMONGER
NIMBLENESS
NORTHANGER
NUCLEONICS
OBEDIENTLY
OBLIGINGLY
OBTUSENESS
OCCIDENTAL
ODIOUSNESS
OLEAGINOUS
OPENHANDED
OPENMINDED
ORNAMENTAL
OROBRANCHE
ORTHOPNOEA
OUVIRANDRA
OVERLANDER
PALAGONITE
PALATINATE
PALFRENIER
PALISANDER
PANAMANIAN
PAPERKNIFE
PARAGONITE
PARTHENOPE
PASQUINADE
PASSIONATE
PATAGONIAN
PATAVINITY
PATCHINESS
PATHFINDER
PEDIMENTAL
PENSIONNAT
PERIWINKLE
PERSIENNES
PETULANTLY
PHAELONIAN
PICAYUNISH
PLEASANTLY
PLEASANTRY
POCAHONTAS
POCKMANTIE
POIGNANTLY
POLITENESS
POMERANIAN
PORTIONIST
PORTMANTLE
PORTMANTUA
PRAEMUNIRE
PREEMINENT
PRETTINESS
PROFOUNDLY
PROMPTNESS
PRONOUNCED
PROPIONATE
PROSCENIUM
PUMPHANDLE
PURITANISM
PYRACANTHA
PYROMANIAC
QUADRANGLE
QUAINTNESS
QUARRENDER
QUATERNARY
QUEASINESS
RANDOMNESS
REFERENDUM
REGIMENTAL
REGIMENTED
REJUVENATE
REMOTENESS
REORGANIZE
RESUPINATE
RETRAINING
REVERENTLY
ROADRUNNER
ROBUSTNESS
RUBBERNECK
RUBIGINOUS
RUDIMENTAL
RUGGEDNESS
RUMINANTIA
SACREDNESS
SALAMANDER
SANGUINARY
SAVAGENESS
SCANTINESS
SCARCENESS
SCOFFINGLY
SCORZONERA
SCRUTINEER
SCRUTINISE
SCRUTINIZE
SEDATENESS
SEPTENNIAL
SHABBINESS
SHELDONIAN
SHIFTINESS
SHOCKINGLY
SHODDINESS
SHORTENING
SHOVELNOSE
SHREWDNESS
SHRILLNESS
SIDEWINDER
SINFULNESS
SINGLENESS
SLEEPINESS
SLOPPINESS
SMARMINESS
SMOOTHNESS
SNOOTINESS
SOOTHINGLY
SORDIDNESS
SPARSENESS
SPEEDINESS
SPORTINGLY
SPRUCENESS
STALLENGER
STALLINGER
STATIONARY
STATIONERY
STEADINESS
STEELINESS
STEMWINDER
STEPHANITE
STEPHENSON
STICKINESS
STINGINESS
STOCKINESS
STRAMONIUM
STRAPONTIN
STRAVINSKY
STRICTNESS
STRIDENTLY
STRIKINGLY
STROGANOFF
STRYCHNINE
STUFFINESS
STURDINESS
SUDDENNESS
SULTRINESS
SUPPLENESS
SURROUNDED
SUSTAINING
SWEETENING
SWIMMINGLY
SYMPHONIUM
TENDERNESS
TESCHENITE
THEREANENT
THICKENING
THOUSANDTH
TIMELINESS
TIROCINIUM
TOLERANTLY
TORBERNITE
TOUCHANDGO
TOUCHINESS
TRENDINESS
TRIACONTER
TRICKINESS
TRICLINIUM
TROCHANTER
TROMBONIST
TROPHONIUS
TURTLENECK
UBERMENSCH
UNACCENTED
UNATTENDED
UNBALANCED
UNDEFENDED
UNEASINESS
UNEVENNESS
UNFRIENDLY
UNGROUNDED
UNIQUENESS
UNLICENSED
UNROMANTIC
UNRULINESS
UNTIDINESS
USEFULNESS
VEHEMENTLY
VETERINARY
VIEWFINDER
VIGILANTES
VILLAINOUS
VIRULENTLY
VOETGANGER
VOLUMINOUS
VORAGINOUS
WANCHANCIE
WAVELENGTH
WESTERNIZE
WHARFINGER
WHEEZINESS
WICKEDNESS
WILDERNESS
WORTHINESS
ABOVEBOARD
ACCUSTOMED
ADDITIONAL
ADIAPHORON
AFRORMOSIA
AFTERHOURS
ALLOTROPIC
ALLYCHOLLY
AMPHIGOURI
AMPLEFORTH
ANASTROPHE
ANCHYLOSIS
ANTIBIOTIC
ANTIPHONAL
ANTIPROTON
APOSTROPHE
APOTHEOSIS
ASBESTOSIS
ASTROLOGER
ASTRONOMER
ATELEIOSIS
AVERRHOISM
BACKBLOCKS
BACKGROUND
BAGASSOSIS
BARBAROSSA
BARCAROLLE
BAREFOOTED
BARRACOOTA
BARRACOUTA
BEHAVIORAL
BELLADONNA
BELLAMOURE
BLACKBOARD
BLOCKHOUSE
BLOODHOUND
BOBBYSOXER
BONDSWOMAN
BOUILLOTTE
BRACHIOPOD
BRAINPOWER
BRASSBOUND
BRICKWORKS
CALCEDONIO
CANEPHORUS
CANTALOUPE
CANTELOUPE
CAPERNOITY
CARCINOGEN
CEPHALOPOD
CHAIRWOMAN
CHECKPOINT
CHERIMOYER
CHESSBOARD
CHIRONOMIC
CHOLALOGUE
CLAIRCOLLE
CLANSWOMAN
COCKALORUM
CONCHIOLIN

CORNFLOWER
CORNUCOPIA
CORROBOREE
COURTHOUSE
CROCKFORDS
CROSSROADS
CRYOPHORUS
DECENNOVAL
DECOMPOSED
DESBOROUGH
DEVOTIONAL
DIPLODOCUS
DIRECTOIRE
DISAPPOINT
DISCOBOLUS
DISCOLORED
DISEMBOGUE
DISEMBOWEL
DISENNOBLE
DIVISIONAL
DOLICHOLIS
DOLICHOTUS
DOVERCOURT
DREADLOCKS
DUTCHWOMAN
EARTHWORKS
ECCHYMOSIS
ECCOPROTIC
ELECTROMER
ELECTRONIC
EMBERGOOSE
EMBONPOINT
EMMETROPIA
ENANTIOSIS
ENDOSMOSIS
EPISTROPHE
ESCHAROTIC
ESCRITOIRE
FAIRGROUND
FIELDMOUSE
FIRTHSOKEN
FLAPDOODLE
FLASHPOINT
FLOORBOARD
FLUTEMOUTH
FOREGROUND
FRACTIONAL
FRAUNHOFER
FREEBOOTER
FRITHSOKEN
FUNCTIONAL
GASTEROPOD
GLASSHOUSE
GOLDILOCKS
GONFANONER
GRASSROOTS
GREENHOUSE
GRIDIRONER
GUESTHOUSE
GYMNOSOPHY
GYROSCOPIC
HATEENOUGH
HEADPHONES
HEMICHORDA
HEMOGLOBIN
HENCEFORTH
HEPTAGONAL
HEREABOUTS
HISTRIONIC
HOBBYHORSE
HODGEPODGE
HOLOPHOTAL
HOMOPHOBIA
HOMOPHOBIC
HORNBLOWER
HORSEPOWER
HORSEWOMAN
HOTCHPOTCH
HOUSEBOUND
HYDROPONIC
HYPERBOLIC
ICHTHYOSIS
IMPERSONAL
INDISPOSED
INTERLOPER
INTERNODAL
INTERWOVEN
IRISHWOMAN
IRISHWOMEN
IRRATIONAL
JACKBOOTED
JACKSTONES
JAGUARONDI
KENILWORTH
KNIFEBOARD
LAEOTROPIC
LAUNDROMAT
LEDERHOSEN
LIGHTHOUSE
LIMITROPHE
LUXEMBOURG
LYSENKOISM
MALAPROPOS
MASKANONGE
MASKINONGE
MASKIROVKA
METROPOLIS
MONOPHONIC
MYSTAGOGUE
MYSTAGOGUS
NECROPOLIS
NEIGHBORLY
NOBLEWOMAN
NORTHBOUND
NOSOPHOBIA
NYCTALOPIA
OBSIDIONAL
OCCASIONAL
OCEANGOING
ORTHOGONAL
OSMIDROSIS
OSTEOCOLLA
OSTROGOTHS
OXYMORONIC
PALMATOZOA
PANTALOONS
PARAGLOSSA
PARAPHONIA
PARATROOPS
PASTEBOARD
PATCHCOCKE
PAWNBROKER
PEASHOOTER
PENTAGONAL
PENTATONIC
PERSEPOLIS
PESCADORES
PESTALOZZI
PETITIONER
PHILOPOENA
PHILOSOPHY
PHOLIDOSIS
PHOSPHORUS
PHYLLIOPOD
PIANOFORTE
PLAYGROUND
PORTSMOUTH
POWERHOUSE
PRESBYOPIA
PRICKLOUSE
PROTAGORAS
PROTANOPIC
PTERANODON
PTERYGOTUS
PYCNOGONID
PYROPHORUS
PYTHAGORAS
QUESTIONER
RAWINSONDE
RAWSTHORNE
RECIPROCAL
REDISCOVER
REPERTOIRE
RHEOTROPIC
RICHTHOFEN
ROUGHHOUSE
ROUNDHOUSE
ROWDYDOWDY
SACERDOTAL
SALESWOMAN
SANDGROPER
SARCOCOLLA
SCARAMOUCH
SCOREBOARD
SCOTSWOMAN
SHAMPOOING
SKATEBOARD
SKEUOMORPH
SNAKEMOUTH
SOGDOLOGER
SOPHOMORIC
SOUTHBOUND
SPELLBOUND
SPONSIONAL
STAGECOACH
STANDPOINT
STEAKHOUSE
STEELWORKS
STOMATOPOD
STOREHOUSE
STRASBOURG
STRATIOTES
STRAWBOARD
SUPERMODEL
SUPERPOWER
SUPERSONIC
SUPERTONIC
SUPERWOMAN
SYNECDOCHE
SYNOSTOSIS
SYNTHRONUS
TANTAMOUNT
TELEPHONIC
TELESCOPIC
TERRACOTTA
THERMIONIC
THROMBOSIS
TOWNSWOMAN
TRANSPOSED
TRAVELOGUE
TRIPEHOUND
TRITANOPIA
TROPAEOLUM
TURNAROUND
ULTRASONIC
ULTRASOUND
UNCOMMONLY
UNDERCOVER
UNDERWORLD
UNDOCTORED
UNEMPLOYED
UNEXPLORED
UNFATHOMED
UNFLAVORED
UNORTHODOX
UNPROVOKED
UNREASONED
UNSCHOOLED
UNSEASONED
VALLADOLID
VILLANOVAN
VOCATIONAL
WAINSCOTED
WALLFLOWER
WANDSWORTH
WATCHTOWER
WATERBORNE
WATERCOLOR
WATERWORKS
WELSHWOMAN
WHEELHOUSE
WIDDICOMBE
WINDFLOWER
WORDSWORTH
WORKAHOLIC
WRAPAROUND
WRONGDOING
XENOPHOBIA
XENOPHOBIC
XEROSTOMIA
YARBOROUGH
ACHITOPHEL
AHITHOPHEL
ALLPURPOSE
AMBLYOPSIS
AMBOCEPTOR
AMPELOPSIS
ANGIOSPERM
ANTHROPOID
ANTICIPATE
ANTISEPSIS
ANTISEPTIC
APOCRYPHAL
APOPEMPTIC
APOTROPAIC
ARIMASPIAN
ARISTIPPUS
BANKRUPTCY
BEEKEEPING
BIOGRAPHER
BRIDLEPATH
CAMELOPARD
CASSIOPEIA
CATALEPTIC
CHRYSIPPUS
CIRRHOPODA
CLODHOPPER
CORRESPOND
CUCKOOPINT
DENDROPHIS
DEVELOPING
DISCOMPOSE
DISCREPANT
DISRESPECT
DUNDERPATE
DYSTROPHIC
ECTHLIPSIS
ELACAMPANE
ELECAMPANE
EMANCIPATE
EPISCOPATE
ESCULAPIAN
EUCALYPTUS
FRANGIPANE
FRANGIPANI
FROGHOPPER
GEOGRAPHER
GEOGRAPHIC
GEOTROPISM
HELICOPTER

HELLESPONT
HOMOEOPATH
INNERSPACE
INTROSPECT
KIDNAPPING
KRIEGSPIEL
LEAFHOPPER
LYCHNAPSIA
MASCARPONE
MEADOWPLAN
METALEPSIS
MIDSHIPMAN
MISOCAPNIC
MUDSKIPPER
NATUROPATH
NEUTROPHIL
NEWSPAPERS
NINCOMPOOP
OVERSUPPLY
PENELOPHON
PHILIPPINA
PHILIPPINE
PHILLIPINA
PHILLIPINE
PHLOGOPITE
PLIOHIPPUS
PREDISPOSE
PRESUPPOSE
PRINCIPIUM
PRINCIPLED
PRINCIPLES
PROSERPINA
PROSERPINE
PSAMMOPHIL
PSYCHOPATH
PSYCHOPOMP
RETROSPECT
RINDERPEST
SCAPHOPODA
SCREENPLAY
SNOWCAPPED
SPOILSPORT
SUBCOMPACT
SUBTROPICS
TABLESPOON
TEICHOPSIA
TRYPTOPHAN
UNEXAMPLED
UNOCCUPIED
UNPROMPTED
UNSCRIPTED
UNSLEEPING
VELOCIPEDE
WAMPUMPEAG
WATERSPOUT
WITSNAPPER
WORSHIPPER
ZOOTHAPSIS
LAMBREQUIN
SOUBRIQUET
TOURNIQUET
ACCELERATE
ACROTERION
ADULTERANT
ADULTERATE
ADULTERESS
ADULTERINE
ADULTEROUS
ALECTORIAN
AMATEURISH
AMELIORATE
AMPHIBRACH
AMPHITRITE
AMPHITRYON
ANACHARSIS
ANEMOGRAPH
ANTIBARBUS
AQUAFORTIS
AQUAMARINE
ARCHITRAVE
ARSMETRICK
ARTOCARPUS
ASSEVERATE
ATRACURIUM
AUDITORIUM
AURIFEROUS
AUTOSTRADA
AVANTURINE
AVENTURINE
BACKSTROKE
BALUSTRADE
BEARGARDEN
BEEFBURGER
BENZEDRINE
BILIVERDIN
BLEPHARISM
BLISTERING
BLITHERING
BLITZKRIEG
BLUETHROAT
BLUNDERING
BOISTEROUS
BOOKMARKER
BOWDLERISE
BOWDLERIZE
BREADFRUIT
BRIDEGROOM
BURGLARIZE
BUTCHERING
CADAVEROUS
CALAVERITE
CALIFORNIA
CALYPTRATE
CANTABRIAN
CANTATRICE
CATAPHRACT
CATEGORISE
CATEGORIZE
CAVICORNIA
CENTIGRADE
CERTIORARI
CHAFFERING
CHAMAEROPS
CHAMBERPOT
CHAMBERTIN
CHATTERBOX
CHATTERTON
CHAUCERIAN
CHAUDFROID
CHESTERTON
CHILDERMAS
CHIMBORAZO
CHINAGRAPH
CHITARRONE
CHIVALROUS
CLAMOURING
CLUMPERTON
COCKATRICE
COLDSTREAM
COMPATRIOT
CONCURRENT
CONIFEROUS
CONQUERING
CONSECRATE
CONSPIRACY
CONTRARILY
CORDIERITE
COTTIERISM
COUNTERACT
CRISPBREAD
CRISSCROSS
CROSSBREED
CURMURRING
DECELERATE
DECOLORATE
DEFLAGRATE
DEGENERACY
DEGENERATE
DELIBERATE
DEMOGORGON
DENTIFRICE
DESIDERATA
DESPAIRING
DICTOGRAPH
DIGITORIUM
DISAPPROVE
DISASTROUS
DISCOURAGE
DISHEARTEN
DONNYBROOK
DOPPLERITE
DOWNMARKET
DOWNSTREAM
DRAWSTRING
DUUMVIRATE
ECUADORIAN
EDULCORATE
EFFLEURAGE
ELECTORATE
ENGENDRURE
ENTERPRISE
EPIDIORITE
EQUATORIAL
EQUESTRIAN
EUCHLORINE
EUHEMERISM
EVISCERATE
EXAGGERATE
EXASPERATE
EXENTERATE
EXHILARATE
EXOTHERMIC
FALSETRUTH
FEATHERBED
FILLIBRUSH
FIREWARDEN
FITZGERALD
FLAMEPROOF
FLATTERING
FLAVOURING
FLICKERING
FLINDERSIA
FORBEARING
FOREWARNED
FOURIERISM
FREEMARTIN
FULLYGROWN
GAINSTRIVE
GALSWORTHY
GARNIERITE
GEOTHERMAL
GERIATRICS
GIRDLERINK
GLAMOURISE
GLITTERAND
GLITTERATI
GLITTERING
GRAMMARIAN
GRANGERISM
GRANGERIZE
GRAPEFRUIT
GUARNERIUS
HAIRSPRING
HAKENKREUZ
HALLMARKED
HANDICRAFT
HANDSPRING
HANOVERIAN
HAUSTORIUM
HEADSTRONG
HEARTBREAK
HELIOGRAPH
HELIOTROPE
HILDEBRAND
HIPPOCRENE
HIPPODROME
HIPPOGRIFF
HIPPOGRYPH
HOLOFERNES
HOMEWORKER
HONORARIUM
HORSEDRAWN
HOUSECRAFT
HOUSEPROUD
HOVERCRAFT
HYPOCORISM
HYPODERMIC
IGNIMBRITE
ILLITERACY
ILLITERATE
ILLUSTRATE
IMMATERIAL
IMMATURITY
IMMEMORIAL
IMMODERATE
IMPOVERISH
INACCURACY
INACCURATE
INAUGURATE
INCAPARINA
INCINERATE
INCOHERENT
INDECOROUS
INDISCREET
INDUSTRIAL
INFILTRATE
INGENERATE
INSECURELY
INSECURITY
INSULARITY
INTEMERATE
INTENERATE
INTERBREED
INTERTRIGO
INTOLERANT
INTRAURBAN
INVETERATE
INVIGORATE
IRREVERENT
ISOMETRICS
JACKSTRAWS
JOCULARITY
KESSELRING
KEYBOARDER
KNOBKERRIE
LACUSTRINE
LANGUOROUS
LANIGEROUS
LEBENSRAUM
LIGHTERMAN
LITHOGRAPH
LOCKERROOM
LUMINARIST
LUTESTRING
MAGISTRACY
MAGISTRAND
MAGISTRATE
MAINPERNOR
MAINSPRING
MAINSTREAM

MALODOROUS
MANAGERESS
MANAGERIAL
MANICURIST
MANUSCRIPT
MARGUERITE
MASQUERADE
MATRIARCHY
MEANDERING
MEDIOCRITY
METACARPAL
METACARPUS
METAPHRASE
METATARSAL
METATARSUS
METHEDRINE
MILITARISM
MILITARIST
MIMEOGRAPH
MINESTRONE
MINEWORKER
MINIMARKET
MINISTRATE
MOISTURIZE
MONETARISM
MONETARIST
MONOCHROME
MONTSERRAT
MORATORIUM
MORIGEROUS
MOUCHARABY
MOUSTERIAN
MOUTHORGAN
MULIEBRITY
MULLIGRUBS
NATATORIAL
NATATORIUM
NEFANDROUS
NESSELRODE
NETTLERASH
NEWSWORTHY
NIGHTDRESS
NORTHERNER
NOTEWORTHY
OBLITERATE
OBSTETRICS
OCHLOCRACY
OMNIVOROUS
OMOPHORION
OPOTHERAPY
OPPROBRIUM
ORDINARILY
ORPHEOREON
OSMETERIUM
OUTPOURING
OVERSPREAD
OVERSTRAIN
OVERSTRUNG
OVERWORKED
PAINTBRUSH
PALESTRINA
PALINDROME
PALUSTRINE
PANTAGRUEL
PANTOGRAPH
PAPAVERINE
PARAMARIBO
PARANORMAL
PARAPHRASE
PASTEURISE
PASTEURIZE
PATRIARCHY
PEACHERINO
PEDESTRIAN
PEDIATRICS
PEELGARLIC
PENSIEROSO
PERMAFROST
PERPETRATE
PHONOGRAPH
PHOTOGRAPH
PIONEERING
PLAGIARISE
PLAGIARISM
PLAGIARIST
PLAGIARIZE
PLUNDERING
PLUTOCRACY
POCKMARKED
POLYCHREST
POLYCHROME
POLYMERIZE
PONTEFRACT
POPULARITY
POPULARIZE
PORNOCRACY
POSTSCRIPT
POURPARLER
PRAETORIAN
PRAETORIUM
PRESSURIZE
PROSPERINA
PROSPERITY
PROSPEROUS
PSALTERIUM
PUNCHDRUNK
PUNDIGRION
PYRAGYRITE
QUADRIREME
QUARTERING
QUARTEROON
QUERSPRUNG
RADIOGRAPH
REASSURING
RECUPERATE
REDCURRANT
REDECORATE
REGENERATE
REGULARITY
REGULARIZE
REMUNERATE
REREDORTER
RESTAURANT
RETROGRADE
RETROGRESS
RHINEGRAVE
RIPSNORTER
ROADWORTHY
ROISTERING
RUPESTRIAN
SACCHARASE
SACCHARIDE
SACCHARINE
SACCHAROID
SALICORNIA
SALTIGRADE
SAMOTHRACE
SANATORIUM
SANITARIUM
SATYAGRAHA
SAUERKRAUT
SAVONAROLA
SCANDAROON
SCANDERBEG
SCAPEGRACE
SCATTERING
SCOOTERIST
SCULPTRESS
SEAMSTRESS
SECONDRATE
SECULARIZE
SEMICIRCLE
SENATORIAL
SHATTERING
SHIELDRAKE
SHIMMERING
SHOCKPROOF
SHOESTRING
SHORTBREAD
SHUDDERING
SIMILARITY
SLAMMERKIN
SLANDEROUS
SLATTERNLY
SLIPSTREAM
SLUMBERING
SMATTERING
SMITHEREEN
SNIGGERING
SOLIDARITY
SOMBRERITE
SONGSTRESS
SOUNDPROOF
SOUNDTRACK
SOUTERRAIN
SOUTHERNER
SPACECRAFT
SPEAKERINE
SPENCERIAN
SPENSERIAN
SPHALERITE
SPOONERISM
STAGECRAFT
STAGGERING
STAMMERING
STATECRAFT
STATOCRACY
STENTORIAN
STERTEROUS
STERTOROUS
STICHARION
STONEBRASH
STOREFRONT
STOUTHRIEF
STRONGROOM
STUBBORNLY
SULPHUROUS
SWAGGERING
SWEETBREAD
SWELTERING
TACHOGRAPH
TAGLIARINI
TALLEYRAND
TAMBOURINE
TARDIGRADE
TELPHERAGE
TEPIDARIUM
TERTIARIES
THIXOTROPY
THUNDERBOX
THUNDERING
THUNDEROUS
TIMESERVER
TOILETRIES
TOOTHBRUSH
TRAITOROUS
TRANSCRIBE
TRANSCRIPT
TRANSGRESS
TRINACRIAN
TYPESCRIPT
UNDERCRAFT
UNDERCROFT
UNDERWRITE
UNDESCRIED
UNDESERVED
UNDETERRED
UNINFORMED
UNOBSERVED
UNRESERVED
UNSALARIED
VEGETARIAN
VERTEBRATE
VICEGERENT
VINEGARISH
VITUPERATE
VIVIPAROUS
VOCIFERATE
VOCIFEROUS
WAGEEARNER
WATERBRASH
WATERCRESS
WATERFRONT
WATERPROOF
WEATHERMAN
WELLEARNED
WELLSPRING
WHISPERING
WHITTERICK
WIDESPREAD
WINDSCREEN
WINDSURFER
WITCHCRAFT
WOODWORKER
YELLOWROOT
ZINCOGRAPH
ZOLLVEREIN
ZOOTHERAPY
ZUMBOORUCK
ZWITTERION
ABSCISSION
ADMINISTER
AGGRESSION
AGGRESSIVE
ALPHONSINE
ALTRUISTIC
ANACLASTIC
ANACOUSTIC
ANACRUSTIC
ANDALUSIAN
ANDALUSITE
ANTIMASQUE
APOLAUSTIC
ARCHBISHOP
ASPIDISTRA
ASTONISHED
ATHANASIAN
AUTHORSHIP
BANDMASTER
BARCHESTER
BATTLESHIP
BEAVERSKIN
BELARUSIAN
BIOPHYSICS
BLOTTESQUE
BOTHERSOME
BURDENSOME
CACOMISTLE
CANVASSING
CAPODASTRO
CARELESSLY
CARNASSIAL
CARTHUSIAN
CENSORSHIP
CENTROSOME
CHICHESTER
CHILDISHLY
CHROMOSOME
CHURLISHLY
CIRCASSIAN

COLCHESTER
COLLAPSING
COMMISSARY
COMMISSION
COMMISSURE
COMPASSION
COMPENSATE
COMPRESSED
COMPRESSOR
COMPULSION
COMPULSIVE
COMPULSORY
CONCESSION
CONCLUSION
CONCLUSIVE
CONCUSSION
CONFESSION
CONSENSION
CONVERSANT
CONVERSELY
CONVERSION
CONVULSION
CONVULSIVE
COPPERSKIN
CUDDLESOME
CUIRASSIER
CUMBERSOME
DEALERSHIP
DECLENSION
DEPRESSANT
DEPRESSING
DEPRESSION
DEPRESSIVE
DIACAUSTIC
DIAGNOSTIC
DICKCISSEL
DIGRESSION
DIMINISHED
DISCLOSURE
DISCURSIVE
DISCUSSING
DISCUSSION
DISHWASHER
DISMISSIVE
DISPENSARY
DISPENSING
DISPERSION
DISPOSSESS
DISSENSION
DISSUASION
DISTENSION
DISTRESSED
DOCIMASTIC
DREARISOME
DUNIWASSAL
DYSCRASITE
DYSPROSIUM
ENCLOISTER
ENGROSSING
EPIPLASTRA
EPISPASTIC
EULOGISTIC
EUPHROSYNE
EXPRESSION
EXPRESSIVE
EXPRESSMAN
EXPRESSWAY
FATALISTIC
FEARLESSLY
FELLOWSHIP
FEVERISHLY
FIENDISHLY
FILIBUSTER
FLOURISHED
FORECASTER
FORECASTLE
FORTISSIMO
FRANCISCAN
FREEMASONS
FRIENDSHIP
FROLICSOME
FUTURISTIC
GENEROSITY
GEOPHYSICS
GINGERSNAP
GLOUCESTER
GROUNDSMAN
HALFSISTER
HALLOYSITE
HARDCASTLE
HEADMASTER
HEDONISTIC
HEEDLESSLY
HELPLESSLY
HOMEOUSIAN
HOPELESSLY
HUMANISTIC
HUMORESQUE
IDEALISTIC
IMPRESSION
IMPRESSIVE
INARTISTIC
INCRASSATE
INCREASING
INDECISION
INDECISIVE
INDONESIAN
INSPISSATE
INTERESTED
JINGOISTIC
JUGENDSTIL
KINGFISHER
KOEKSISTER
LACKLUSTER
LACKLUSTRE
LAUNCESTON
LEADERSHIP
LEGALISTIC
LINGUISTIC
LISTLESSLY
LUMINOSITY
MADAGASCAN
MADAGASCAR
MAKESYSTEM
MALTHUSIAN
MANCHESTER
MANIFESTLY
MAUPASSANT
MEDDLESOME
MEGALOSAUR
MELANESIAN
MEMBERSHIP
METTLESOME
MISPRISION
MONEGASQUE
MONTESSORI
NARCISSISM
NEWSCASTER
NIHILISTIC
NONPLUSSED
OPPRESSION
OPPRESSIVE
OPTIMISTIC
PAINLESSLY
PALIMPSEST
PALMERSTON
PARNASSIAN
PEAUDESOIE
PERCUSSION
PERMISSION
PERMISSIVE
PERQUISITE
PERSUASION
PERSUASIVE
PERVERSELY
PERVERSION
PERVERSITY
PETRISSAGE
PHANTASIME
PHANTASIST
PHLOGISTIC
PHLOGISTON
PHRENESIAC
PICARESQUE
PILLOWSLIP
PLEONASTIC
PLESIOSAUR
PLUMASSIER
POLYNESIAN
POSSESSION
POSSESSIVE
POSTMASTER
PRECURSORY
PREDNISONE
PREHENSILE
PREPENSELY
PREPOSSESS
PRETENSION
PROCESSING
PROCESSION
PROCRUSTES
PROFESSION
PROGESSION
PROMISSORY
PROPENSITY
PROPULSION
PROTRUSION
QUIZMASTER
READERSHIP
RECKLESSLY
REGRESSION
REGRESSIVE
REPRESSION
REPRESSIVE
REQUIESCAT
RESPONSIVE
RESTLESSLY
RHAMPASTOS
RINGMASTER
ROBERDSMAN
ROBERTSMAN
ROLANDSECK
ROMANESQUE
RUMBLOSSOM
RUTHLESSLY
SAUROPSIDA
SCHOLASTIC
SEAMANSHIP
SEXAGESIMA
SHEEPISHLY
SIDEROSTAT
SILVERSIDE
SILVERSKIN
SIMPLISTIC
SLUGGISHLY
SPOTLESSLY
STATUESQUE
STEPSISTER
STOCHASTIC
STRABISMUS
STRATHSPEY
SUBMERSION
SUBMISSION
SUBMISSIVE
SUBVERSION
SUBVERSIVE
SUCCESSFUL
SUCCESSION
SUCCESSIVE
SUNGLASSES
SUPPRESSED
SUPPRESSOR
SURPASSING
SURPRISING
SUSPENSION
SYNTHESIZE
TACTLESSLY
TASKMASTER
TATTERSALL
TELEVISION
THALASSIAN
THAUMASITE
THELLUSSON
THERMISTOR
THERMOSTAT
TIRELESSLY
TONGUESTER
TRANSISTOR
TRESPASSER
UNDIGESTED
UNFINISHED
UNFORESEEN
UNIVERSITY
UNPLEASANT
VARICOSITY
VERNISSAGE
VIRTUOSITY
WALDENSIAN
WAPPENSHAW
WINCHESTER
WINDOWSILL
YGGDRASILL
ABDICATION
ABERRATION
ABROGATION
ABSOLUTELY
ABSOLUTION
ABSOLUTISM
ABSORPTION
ABSTENTION
ACCOUNTANT
ACCOUNTING
ACCUBATION
ACCURATELY
ACCUSATION
ACCUSATIVE
ACOLOUTHOS
ACROBATICS
ACTIVITIST
ADAMANTINE
ADAPTATION
ADELANTADO
ADEQUATELY
ADHIBITION
ADMIRATION
ADMONITION
AEROBATICS
AESTHETICS
AFFLICTION
AGAPANTHUS
AGONISTICS
ALIENATION
ALIMENTARY
ALLEGATION
ALLIGATION
ALLOCATION
ALLOCUTION
ALPENSTOCK
ALTERATION
ALTOGETHER

AMBLYSTOMA
AMBULATORY
AMMUNITION
AMPHICTYON
AMPUTATION
AMRITATTVA
ANABAPTIST
ANCIPITOUS
ANGWANTIBO
ANHELATION
ANNEXATION
ANNOTATION
ANTARCTICA
ANTICHTHON
ANTIMATTER
APEMANTHUS
APICULTURE
APPARITION
APPETITIVE
APPOSITION
APPRENTICE
ARACOSTYLE
AREFACTION
ARISTOTLES
ARMIPOTENT
ASAFOETIDA
ASPHALTITE
ASPIRATION
ASSUMPTION
ASSUMPTIVE
ASTOMATOUS
ASYMMETRIC
ASYNARTETE
ATTRACTION
ATTRACTIVE
AUTOCHTHON
AUTOMATION
AUTOMOTIVE
BABYSITTER
BACKBITING
BALLISTICS
BALLISTITE
BALNEATION
BAROMETRIC
BEDCLOTHES
BEEFEATERS
BELLWETHER
BERMOOTHES
BIORHYTHMS
BISSEXTILE
BLACKSTONE
BLOODSTAIN
BLOODSTOCK
BLOODSTONE
BLUEBOTTLE
BRAINSTORM
BRIDGETOWN
BRIGANTINE
BROOMSTICK
BROWNSTONE
BYELECTION
CAESPITOSE
CALAMITOUS
CALLIATURE
CAMPESTRAL
CANECUTTER
CAPACITATE
CAPITATION
CARICATURA
CARICATURE
CARPENTIER
CASTRATION
CHARIOTEER
CHEVROTAIN
CHINASTONE
CHIROPTERA
CHREMATIST
CIRCUITOUS
CISLEITHAN
CISPONTINE
CLEARSTORY
CLEMENTINE
CLERESTORY
CLINGSTONE
COADJUTANT
COEXISTENT
COGITATION
COLBERTINE
COLEOPTERA
COLLECTING
COLLECTION
COLLECTIVE
COLORATION
COLORATURA
COLPORTAGE
COLPORTEUR
COMBUSTION
COMFORTING
COMMENTARY
COMMENTATE
COMMIXTURE
COMPLETELY
COMPLETION
CONCENTRIC
CONCEPTION
CONCEPTUAL
CONCERTINA
CONCOCTION
CONCRETION
CONDOTTIER
CONDUCTING
CONDUCTION
CONFECTION
CONGESTION
CONJECTURE
CONNECTING
CONNECTION
CONNECTIVE
CONNIPTION
CONSISTENT
CONSISTORY
CONSORTIUM
CONSTITUTE
CONSUETUDE
CONSULTANT
CONSULTING
CONTENTION
CONTESTANT
CONTEXTUAL
CONTORTION
CONTRITION
CONVECTION
CONVENTION
CONVICTION
COPESETTIC
COPULATION
COQUETTISH
CORONATION
CORRECTING
CORRECTION
CORRECTIVE
CORRUPTING
CORRUPTION
COTTONTAIL
CRAQUETURE
CREDENTIAL
CRICKETING
CULVERTAGE
CUMULATIVE
CURVETTING
CYCLOSTYLE
DEADNETTLE
DEBILITATE
DECAPITATE
DECORATION
DECORATIVE
DEDICATION
DEFAMATION
DEFAMATORY
DEFECATION
DEFINITELY
DEFINITION
DEFINITIVE
DEFLECTION
DELEGATION
DELICATELY
DELIGATION
DELIGHTFUL
DELIRATION
DEMOLITION
DEPILATORY
DEPOSITARY
DEPOSITION
DEPOSITORY
DEPUTATION
DERIVATION
DERIVATIVE
DEROGATORY
DESOLATION
DESSIATINE
DESSYATINE
DETONATION
DETRACTION
DEVOLUTION
DIALECTICS
DIELECTRIC
DILATATION
DIMINUTION
DIMINUTIVE
DINNERTIME
DIREMPTION
DISBURTHEN
DISCONTENT
DISCRETION
DISGUSTING
DISMANTLED
DISRUPTION
DISRUPTIVE
DISSECTION
DISSENTING
DISSERTATE
DISTORTION
DIVINATION
DOMINATING
DOMINATION
DOUBLETALK
DRAKESTONE
DYNAMITARD
EFFRONTERY
EGOCENTRIC
EGURGITATE
ELEMENTARY
ELONGATION
EMACIATION
EMENDATION
EMIGRATION
EMPLASTRUM
ENCHANTING
ENTREATING
EPICANTHUS
EPIGLOTTIS
EQUITATION
ERUCTATION
ERYMANTHUS
ESCALATION
ESTIMATION
ETHEOSTOMA
EVACUATION
EVALUATION
EXACTITUDE
EXALTATION
EXCAVATION
EXECRATION
EXHALATION
EXHAUSTING
EXHAUSTION
EXHAUSTIVE
EXHIBITION
EXHUMATION
EXORBITANT
EXPEDITION
EXPIRATION
EXPOSITION
EXPOSITORY
EXTINCTION
EXTRACTION
EXULTATION
FACILITATE
FACILITIES
FALDISTORY
FANTASTICO
FASCIATION
FATALITIES
FAVORITISM
FEDERATION
FELICITATE
FELICITOUS
FIGURATION
FIGURATIVE
FILTRATION
FLIRTATION
FLORENTINE
FOREBITTER
FOREFATHER
FOREGATHER
FORFAITING
FORFEITURE
FORTUITOUS
FOUNDATION
FOXHUNTING
FREIGHTAGE
FROMANTEEL
FUMIGATION
GALIMATIAS
GARGANTUAN
GEMINATION
GENERATION
GENERATRIX
GEOCENTRIC
GEORGETOWN
GILBERTIAN
GILBERTINE
GLACIATION
GRADUATION
GRANDSTAND
GRATUITOUS
GRAVESTONE
GREENSTICK
GRINDSTONE
GUARANTEED
GUILLOTINE
GYMNASTICS
HABILITATE
HABITATION
HACKBUTEER
HACKMATACK
HAEMANTHUS
HALIEUTICS
HARVESTMAN
HEREDITARY

HESITATION
HINDUSTANI
HUMANITIES
IMMOLATION
IMPENITENT
IMPERATIVE
IMPOLITELY
IMPOSITION
IMPURITIES
IMPUTATION
INAPTITUDE
INCONSTANT
INCUBATION
INDICATION
INDICATIVE
INEPTITUDE
INFIGHTING
INFINITELY
INFINITIVE
INFLECTION
INFLICTION
INFRACTION
INHABITANT
INHALATION
INHIBITING
INHIBITION
INHIBITORY
INIQUITOUS
INITIATION
INITIATIVE
INJUNCTION
INNOVATION
INNOVATIVE
INSANITARY
INSPECTION
INSULATION
INTERSTATE
INTERSTICE
INTIMATELY
INTIMATION
INTINCTION
INTONATION
INUNDATION
INVITATION
INVOCATION
IRRIGATION
IRRITATING
IRRITATION
JACULATION
JUBILATION
JUDICATURE
KHIDMUTGAR
KILOMETRES
KUOMINTANG
KURDAITCHA
LABORATORY
LACERATION
LAMINATION
LAURENTIAN
LAURUSTINE
LEVITATION
LIBERATION
LIBRETTIST
LIMITATION
LITERATURE
LITHISTADA
LITIGATION
LOCOMOTION
LOCOMOTIVE
LOGARITHMS
MACKINTOSH
MALCONTENT
MANGOSTEEN
MARCANTANT
MARQUETRIE
MASTECTOMY
MATCHSTALK
MATCHSTICK
MATURATION
MEDICATION
MEDITATION
MEDITATIVE
MEDIUMTERM
MEGALITHIC
MELOCOTOON
MERCANTILE
MESOLITHIC
MISFORTUNE
MITIGATING
MITIGATION
MODERATELY
MODERATION
MODULATION
MONOLITHIC
MORALITIES
MOTIVATION
MUTILATION
NASTURTIUM
NAUSEATING
NAUSEATIVE
NAVIGATION
NEGLECTFUL
NETTLETREE
NEWSLETTER
NIGHTSTICK
NOMINATION
NOMINATIVE
NONFICTION
NORBERTINE
NORTHSTEAD
NOURRITURE
NUMERATION
OBLIGATION
OBLIGATORY
OCCUPATION
OFFPUTTING
OMNIPOTENT
ONOMASTICS
OPPOSITION
ORCHESTRAL
ORDINATION
ORTHOPTICS
OSCITATION
OSCULATION
OSCULATORY
OVEREATING
PAEDIATRIC
PAGINATION
PALAEOTYPE
PALAESTRAL
PALLIATIVE
PANARITIUM
PANCRATIUM
PARAMETRIC
PARGETTING
PATRIOTISM
PECULATION
PEJORATIVE
PERCENTAGE
PERCENTILE
PERCEPTION
PERCEPTIVE
PEREMPTORY
PERFECTION
PERIDOTITE
PERMEATION
PERORATION
PERSISTENT
PHAENOTYPE
PHILISTINE
PHLEGETHON
PHYLACTERY
PINAKOTHEK
PITCHSTONE
PLANTATION
POETASTERY
POGONOTOMY
POINSETTIA
POLIANTHES
POLYANTHUS
POPULATION
PORTENTOUS
PRAGMATISM
PRAGMATIST
PRECAUTION
PREDESTINE
PREDICTION
PREHISTORY
PRELECTION
PRESBYTERY
PRESENTDAY
PREVENTION
PREVENTIVE
PRODUCTION
PRODUCTIVE
PROJECTILE
PROJECTING
PROJECTION
PROMONTORY
PROPERTIUS
PROPHETESS
PROPLITEAL
PROPORTION
PROSTITUTE
PROTECTION
PROTECTIVE
PROTESTANT
PRUDENTIAL
PSOCOPTERA
QUADRATURA
QUARANTINE
QUEENSTOWN
QUERCITRON
RANDLETREE
RANNELTREE
RANNLETREE
RANTLETREE
RAPPORTEUR
RATTLETRAP
RAVENSTONE
RAZZMATAZZ
RECITATION
RECITATIVE
RECITATIVO
RECREATION
REDEMPTION
REELECTION
REFLECTING
REFLECTION
REFLECTIVE
REFRACTION
REFRACTIVE
REFRACTORY
REFUTATION
REGULATION
RELAXATION
RELAXATIVE
RELEGATION
RELOCATION
REMONETISE
RENOVATION
REPARATION
REPETITEUR
REPETITION
REPETITIVE
REPOSITORY
REPUTATION
RESOLUTELY
RESOLUTION
RESPECTFUL
RESPECTING
RESPECTIVE
RESUMPTION
RETRACTION
RETREATING
REVELATION
REVOCATION
REVOLUTION
RHEUMATICS
RHEUMATISM
RHEUMATOID
RHINESTONE
RHIPIPTERA
RIGELATION
RUBINSTEIN
RUMINATION
RUMINATIVE
SALIVATION
SALOPETTES
SALUTATION
SANCTITIES
SANCTITUDE
SANITATION
SARMENTOUS
SATURATION
SCARLATINA
SCARLETINA
SCHALSTEIN
SCORDATURA
SECURITIES
SELFESTEEM
SEPARATELY
SEPARATION
SEPARATISM
SEPARATIST
SEPARATRIX
SEQUENTIAL
SERPENTINE
SHROVETIDE
SIDERATION
SIMILITUDE
SIMMENTHAL
SIMULATING
SIMULATION
SKUPSHTINA
SMOKESTACK
SNAKESTONE
SOLICITOUS
SOLICITUDE
SPALLATION
SPECTATORS
SPIRKETING
SPISSITUDE
SPOLIATION
SPOLIATIVE
SPRINGTAIL
SPRINGTIME
STAGNATION
STALACTITE
STANDSTILL
STARVATION
STATISTICS
STEPFATHER
STEPMOTHER
STEREOTOMY
STEREOTYPE
STIGMATISE
STIGMATIZE
STILLSTAND
STRABOTOMY

STRELITZIA
STRENGTHEN
STREPITANT
STREPITOSO
STYLISTICS
SUBJECTION
SUBJECTIVE
SUBREPTION
SUBSECTION
SUBSISTENT
SUBSTATION
SUBSTITUTE
SUBVENTION
SUGGESTION
SUGGESTIVE
SUMMERTIME
SUPERSTORE
SUPPORTING
SUPPORTIVE
SWEEPSTAKE
SWORDSTICK
SYNCRETISE
TABULATION
TAILGATING
TANGENTIAL
TECHNETIUM
TELEOSTOME
TELEPATHIC
TEMPTATION
TENNANTITE
THALESTRIS
THALICTRUM
THOUGHTFUL
TICKERTAPE
TOLERATION
TORRENTIAL
TOUCHSTONE
TRAJECTORY
TRAMONTANA
TRAMONTANE
TRANSITION
TRANSITIVE
TRANSITORY
TRAUMATIZE
TRAVERTINE
TRECENTIST
TRIDENTINE
TRIPARTITE
TROCHOTRON
TURPENTINE
TYPESETTER
UBIQUITOUS
ULCERATION
ULTIMATELY
UNDERSTAND
UNDERSTATE
UNDERSTEER
UNDERSTOOD
UNDERSTUDY
UNDULATING

UNDULATION
UNEVENTFUL
UNFRUITFUL
UNINVITING
UNPUNCTUAL
UPHOLSTERY
USUCAPTION
USURPATION
VALIDATION
VEGETATION
VELITATION
VENERATION
VINDICTIVE
VISITATION
VOLUTATION
WENTLETRAP
WHEATSTONE
WINTERTIME
ACCENTUATE
ACETABULAR
ACETABULUM
ADVENTURER
AFFETTUOSO
ALGONQUIAN
ALLOSAURUS
ALMSHOUSES
ANSCHAUUNG
BABIROUSSA
BARBITURIC
BARRAMUNDA
BETACRUCIS
BLACKBULLY
BLACKGUARD
BLISSFULLY
CASSUMUNAR
CATACHUMEN
CATECHUMEN
CAUTIOUSLY
CHAULMUGRA
CHAUTAUQUA
CHEERFULLY
CLOUDBURST
COASTGUARD
COCKABULLY
COLLIQUATE
COLLOCUTER
COLLOQUIAL
CONSEQUENT
CONTIGUITY
CONTIGUOUS
CONTINUING
CONTINUITY
CONTINUOUS
CONVOLUTED
COUSCOUSOU
CURRICULUM
DELINQUENT
DEPARTURES
DIASKEUAST
DIDUNCULUS

DIFFICULTY
DISFIGURED
DISTRAUGHT
DOUBTFULLY
DREADFULLY
EARTHQUAKE
EFFECTUATE
ENORMOUSLY
ENRAPTURED
ENSANGUINE
ERIOCAULON
EXTINGUISH
FABULOUSLY
FAITHFULLY
FEARNOUGHT
FISTICUFFS
FLORIBUNDA
FONTICULUS
FOODSTUFFS
FORCEFULLY
FRUITFULLY
FUDDYDUDDY
GENEROUSLY
GLORIOUSLY
GOBEMOUCHE
GORGEOUSLY
GRACEFULLY
GRACIOUSLY
GRATEFULLY
HALFHOURLY
HALLELUJAH
HOMUNCULUS
HONEYBUNCH
HUMOROUSLY
HYPERDULIA
INADEQUACY
INADEQUATE
INCESTUOUS
INDENTURES
INFREQUENT
INTRIGUING
JAGUARUNDI
JERRYBUILT
JOUYSAUNCE
KOOKABURRA
LANDLOUPER
LENTICULAR
LIVERWURST
MAKUNOUCHI
MENSTRUATE
MERCIFULLY
METALLURGY
MONTICULUS
MOSASAUROS
MOURNFULLY
MUTINOUSLY
OTHERGUESS
PANNICULUS
PARTICULAR
PEACEFULLY

PENINSULAR
PERILOUSLY
PERPETUATE
PERPETUITY
PERSECUTOR
PORTUGUESE
PREVIOUSLY
PROCEDURAL
PROSCIUTTO
PROSECUTOR
QUAESTUARY
RACECOURSE
RANUNCULUS
RAVENOUSLY
RELINQUISH
REPRODUCER
RIGHTFULLY
RIGOROUSLY
SALMAGUNDI
SCORNFULLY
SCRIPTURAL
SCRIPTURES
SEDULOUSLY
SENSUOUSLY
SHAMEFULLY
SINARQUIST
SKILLFULLY
SNAPHAUNCE
SNAPHAUNCH
SPECIOUSLY
SPIRACULUM
SPIRITUOUS
SPITEFULLY
SPURIOUSLY
STONYHURST
STRUCTURAL
STUDIOUSLY
SUBSEQUENT
SUPERHUMAN
TANNHAUSER
TASTEFULLY
TATPURUSHA
TESTICULAR
THANKFULLY
TOPSYTURVY
TORTUOUSLY
TRIANGULAR
TRUSTFULLY
TRUTHFULLY
TUBERCULAR
TUMULTUOUS
UNCTUOUSLY
UNCULTURED
UNDERBURNT
UNDISPUTED
VERNACULAR
VESTIBULUM
VIBRACULUM
VIGOROUSLY
VIRTUOUSLY

VOLUPTUARY
VOLUPTUOUS
WASTEFULLY
WATCHFULLY
WRONGFULLY
ABERDEVINE
ALMSGIVING
ANIMADVERT
BOLSHEVIST
CIRCUMVENT
COMPLUVIUM
CONCERVATE
CONFERVOID
CONTRAVENE
CONTROVERT
CONVOLVUTE
CREATIVITY
DEACTIVATE
DECISIVELY
DISSERVICE
DISSOLVENT
DOSTOEVSKY
EFFUSIVELY
FACESAVING
FASTMOVING
GAINGIVING
GILLRAVAGE
GLENDOVEER
INACTIVITY
INCISIVELY
IRRELEVANT
MANSERVANT
NEGATIVELY
OBLOMOVISM
POSITIVELY
POSITIVIST
PROCLIVITY
PROTERVITY
PURSUIVANT
REACTIVATE
RECIDIVISM
RECIDIVIST
RELATIVELY
RELATIVITY
RENDEZVOUS
SKINDIVING
TIMESAVING
UNSWERVING
BAILIEWICK
BAILLIWICK
BASKETWORK
BREASTWORK
BROADSWORD
BUNDESWEHR
CAMBERWELL
CANDLEWICK
CHEESEWOOD
CHERRYWOOD
COMMONWEAL
COTTONWOOD

EATANSWILL
FIDDLEWOOD
GREENSWARD
GROUNDWORK
HEAVENWARD
HITHERWARD
INTERTWINE
JABBERWOCK
LENGTHWAYS
LENGTHWISE
MASTERWORT
MOUDIEWART
MOULDIWARP
NATIONWIDE
NEEDLEWORK
OFFTHEWALL
OVERTHWART
PADAREWSKI
PALMERWORM
PEPPERWORT
PLOUGHWISE
PUCKERWOOD
RAIYATWARI
SANDALWOOD
SETTERWORT
SILVERWARE
SNEEZEWOOD
SPIDERWORT
SPONGEWARE
SPORTSWEAR
STREETWISE
STRIDEWAYS
SWALLOWING
THREADWORM
WATTLEWORK
WHILLYWHAW
WICKERWORK
WILDFOWLER
YELLOWWOOD
YESTERWEEK
ZIMBABWEAN
COMPLEXION
COMPLEXITY
HOMOSEXUAL
PARADOXIDE
PARADOXINE
PERPLEXING
PERPLEXITY
AMPUSSYAND
APOCALYPSE
ARCHETYPAL
CAVALRYMAN
CHIMNEYPOT
CHURCHYARD
COUNTRYMAN
EPIDIDYMUS
EUROCLYDON
FAREPAYING
FLAMBOYANT
FLUNKEYDOM
FOUDROYANT
GRATIFYING
HIGHFLYING
HIGHWAYMAN
HORRIFYING
HYDROLYSIS
JOURNEYMAN
KEMPERYMAN
LINEOMYCIN
MAGNIFYING
MISHNAYOTH
MOTORCYCLE
NURSERYMAN
PARAPHYSIS
PATRONYMIC
PETRIFYING
PSILOCYBIN
PUTREFYING
RAILWAYMAN
SATISFYING
SELFSTYLED
SHANDRYDAN
STENOTYPER
STUPEFYING
TANGANYIKA
TERRIFYING
TIMBERYARD
TROTSKYITE
UNDERLYING
UNEDIFYING
XEROPHYTIC
YESTERYEAR
APPETIZING
BAMBOOZLED
BARMITZVAH
BELSHAZZAR
CANCRIZANS
DOWNSIZING
ISONIAZIDE
SCAMMOZZIS
SCHWARZLOT
TARTRAZINE

10:8

ABBREVIATE
ABOVEBOARD
ACCELERATE
ACCENTUATE
ACCOUNTANT
ACCUMULATE
ACROMEGALY
ADELANTADO
ADJUDICATE
ADULTERANT
ADULTERATE
AFICIONADO
AFTERSHAVE
ALEMBICATE
ALIMENTARY
AMALGAMATE
AMELIORATE
AMPHIBRACH
AMPUSSYAND
ANEMOGRAPH
ANNIHILATE
ANNUNCIATE
ANTICIPATE
APOTHECARY
APOTROPAIC
APPRECIATE
AQUAMANALE
ARCHITRAVE
ARTHURIANA
ARTICULATA
ARTICULATE
ASPHYXIATE
ASSEMBLAGE
ASSEVERATE
ASSIMILATE
AUTODIDACT
AUTOSTRADA
BALDERDASH
BALUSTRADE
BASKETBALL
BATHYSCAPH
BEAUJOLAIS
BEFOREHAND
BEHINDHAND
BICHROMATE
BINOCULARS
BIRTHPLACE
BLACKBEARD
BLACKBOARD
BLACKGUARD
BLACKHEART
BLOODSTAIN
BORDERLAND
BRATISLAVA
BRIDESMAID
BRIDLEPATH
BUTTERBAKE
CACHINNATE
CALCEOLATE
CALUMNIATE
CALYPTRATE
CAMELOPARD
CAMOUFLAGE
CANCRIZANS
CANNONBALL
CANTILLATE
CANVASBACK
CAPACITATE
CAPITULARY
CAPITULATE
CAPREOLATE
CASSIABARK
CATAPHRACT
CAUTIONARY
CELESTIALS
CELLOPHANE
CENTIGRADE
CERTIORARI
CHALYBEATE
CHARGEHAND
CHAROLLAIS
CHEAPSKATE
CHEESECAKE
CHESSBOARD
CHEVROTAIN
CHIFFCHAFF
CHIMBORAZO
CHINAGRAPH
CHLORINATE
CHRISTIANA
CHURCHYARD
CLYDESDALE
CNIDOBLAST
COADJUTANT
COASTGUARD
COLLEGIATE
COLLIQUATE
COLPORTAGE
COMMANDANT
COMMENTARY
COMMENTATE
COMMISSARY
COMPENSATE
COMPLANATE
COMPLICATE
CONCERVATE
CONCILIATE
CONCORDANT
CONFISCATE
CONGREGATE
CONSECRATE
CONSPIRACY
CONSULTANT
CONSUMMATE
CONTESTANT
CONTRABAND
CONVERSANT
COORDINATE
COTTONTAIL
COUNTERACT
CRANKSHAFT
CRENELLATE
CROSSROADS
CRUIKSHANK
CULVERTAGE
CUMBERLAND
DEACTIVATE
DEBILITATE
DECAPITATE
DECELERATE
DECOLORATE
DEFLAGRATE
DEGENERACY
DEGENERATE
DELIBERATE
DEPOPULATE
DEPOSITARY
DEPRECIATE
DEPRESSANT
DERACINATE
DEREGULATE
DESALINATE
DESCENDANT
DESIDERATA
DESQUAMATE
DETRUNCATE
DEUTOPLASM
DEVANAGARI
DHARMSHALA
DIASKEUAST
DICTIONARY
DICTOGRAPH
DILAPIDATE
DISCORDANT
DISCOURAGE
DISCREPANT
DISENCHANT
DISPENSARY
DISSERTATE
DISSOCIATE
DISTILLATE
DITHIONATE
DOMICILIARY
DOUBLEBASS
DOUBLETALK
DUNDERPATE
DUUMVIRATE
DYNAMITARD
EARTHQUAKE
EBRACTEATE
ECARDINATE
EDULCORATE
EFFECTUATE
EFFEMINACY
EFFEMINATE
EFFLEURAGE
EGURGITATE
ELACAMPANE
ELASTICATE
ELECAMPANE
ELECTORATE
ELEMENTARY
EMANCIPATE
EMARGINATE
EMASCULATE
ENTHUSIASM
ENTHUSIAST
EPISCOPATE
EQUIVOCATE
EVERYPLACE
EVISCERATE
EXACERBATE
EXAGGERATE
EXASPERATE

EXCRUCIATE
EXENTERATE
EXHILARATE
EXORBITANT
EXPATRIATE
FACILITATE
FASTIGIATE
FATHERLAND
FELICITATE
FIBERGLASS
FIBREGLASS
FIBRILLATE
FINGERNAIL
FITZGERALD
FLAGELLATE
FLAMBOYANT
FLAMINGANT
FLANCONADE
FLOCCULATE
FLOORBOARD
FOREORDAIN
FOUDROYANT
FRANGIPANE
FRANGIPANI
FREIGHTAGE
FRITILLARY
GARLANDAGE
GASCONNADE
GENICULATE
GETHSEMANE
GILLRAVAGE
GLITTERAND
GLITTERATI
GRANDSTAND
GREENHEART
GREENSHANK
GREENSWARD
GREYFRIARS
GROUNDBAIT
HABILITATE
HACKMATACK
HANDICRAFT
HANDLEBARS
HEAVENWARD
HELIOGRAPH
HEMORRHAGE
HEREDITARY
HIEROPHANT
HILDEBRAND
HINDUSTANI
HINTERLAND
HITHERWARD
HOMOEOPATH
HOMORELAPS
HORSEDRAWN
HOUSECRAFT
HOVERCRAFT
HOWLEGLASS
HUSBANDAGE
HYALOPHANE
HYDROPHANE
HYDROPLANE
ICONOCLAST
ILLAQUEATE
ILLITERACY
ILLITERATE
ILLUMINATE
ILLUMINATI
ILLUSTRATE
IMBROCCATA
IMMACULACY
IMMACULATE
IMMODERATE
IMPREGNATE
INACCURACY
INACCURATE
INADEQUACY
INADEQUATE
INAUGURATE
INCENDIARY
INCINERATE
INCONSTANT
INCRASSATE
INDELICACY
INDELICATE
INEFFICACY
INFILTRATE
INGEMINATE
INGENERATE
INGRATIATE
INHABITANT
INNERSPACE
INORDINATE
INOSCULATE
INSANITARY
INSEMINATE
INSOUCIANT
INSPISSATE
INSUFFLATE
INTAGLIATE
INTEMERATE
INTENERATE
INTERLEAVE
INTERSTATE
INTERWEAVE
INTIMIDATE
INTOLERANT
INTOXICANT
INTOXICATE
INVALIDATE
INVETERATE
INVIGILATE
INVIGORATE
IRRADICATE
IRRELEVANT
JACKSTRAWS
JUGGERNAUT
JUSTICIARY
KARTTIKAYA
KNIFEBOARD
KUOMINTANG
LANCEOLATE
LANDAMMANN
LANGERHANS
LARGESCALE
LATTERMATH
LAUDERDALE
LAUNCEGAYE
LEBENSRAUM
LEGITIMACY
LEGITIMATE
LEMNISCATE
LENGTHWAYS
LEPRECHAUN
LICENTIATE
LIEBERMANN
LIEUTENANT
LITHISTADA
LITHOGRAPH
LITHOPHANE
LUMBERJACK
MAGISTRACY
MAGISTRAND
MAGISTRATE
MAHAYANALI
MAIDENHAIR
MALAYALAAM
MALLOPHAGA
MANIPULATE
MANSERVANT
MAQUILLAGE
MARCANTANT
MARTINGALE
MASQUERADE
MASTURBATE
MATCHSTALK
MAUPASSANT
MEERSCHAUM
MEGALOSAUR
MENSTRUATE
METAPHRASE
MIMEOGRAPH
MINISTRATE
MISCELLANY
MISSIONARY
MITHRIDATE
MIZZENMAST
MONTAGNARD
MOTHERLAND
MOUCHARABY
MOUDIEWART
MOULDIWARP
MOUNTEBANK
NARROWDALE
NATTERJACK
NATUROPATH
NEEDLECASE
NETTLERASH
NIGHTSHADE
NONCHALANT
NORMOBLAST
OBLITERATE
OCHLOCRACY
OFFTHEWALL
OPOTHERAPY
ORTHOCLASE
OSTEOBLAST
OVERSTRAIN
OVERTHWART
PALATINATE
PANTOGRAPH
PAPERCHASE
PARAPHRASE
PARISCHANE
PARTINGALE
PASQUINADE
PASSIONATE
PASTEBOARD
PATIBULARY
PEDICULATE
PERCENTAGE
PERPETRATE
PERPETUATE
PERSIFLAGE
PETRISSAGE
PETTICHAPS
PETTYCHAPS
PHONOGRAPH
PHOTOGRAPH
PICHICIAGO
PILGRIMAGE
PILLOWCASE
PISTILLATE
PLANOBLAST
PLATTELAND
PLESIOSAUR
PLOUGHGATE
PLUTOCRACY
POHUTUKAWA
POINTBLANK
PONTEFRACT
PORNOCRACY
POSTILLATE
POTENTIATE
POZZUOLANA
PREBENDARY
PREDECEASE
PROFLIGACY
PROFLIGATE
PROMULGATE
PROPELLANT
PROPIONATE
PROPITIATE
PROTESTANT
PROTOPLASM
PSEUDOCARP
PSYCHOPATH
PUNCTULATE
PURSUIVANT
QUAESTUARY
QUATERNARY
RADIOGRAPH
RAIYATWARI
RAZZMATAZZ
REACTIVATE
RECUPERATE
REDCURRANT
REDECORATE
REGENERATE
REJUVENATE
REMUNERATE
REPATRIATE
RESTAURANT
RESUPINATE
RETROGRADE
RHINEGRAVE
RINGELMANN
ROCKSTEADY
SACCHARASE
SADDLEBACK
SALTIGRADE
SAMOTHRACE
SANGUINARY
SATYAGRAHA
SAUERKRAUT
SCAPEGRACE
SCHOOLMAAM
SCOREBOARD
SCRIMSHANK
SCUTELLATE
SECONDHAND
SECONDRATE
SHANDYGAFF
SHEEPSHANK
SHIELDRAKE
SHILLELAGH
SILVERBACK
SILVERWARE
SKATEBOARD
SKRIMSHANK
SMALLSCALE
SMOKESTACK
SOLIVAGANT
SOUNDTRACK
SOUTERRAIN
SPACECRAFT
SPHACELATE
SPIFLICATE
SPOKESHAVE
SPONGEWARE
SPRINGHAAS
SPRINGTAIL
STAGECOACH
STAGECRAFT
STANISLAUS
STATECRAFT
STATIONARY
STATOCRACY
STIACCIATO
STILLSTAND

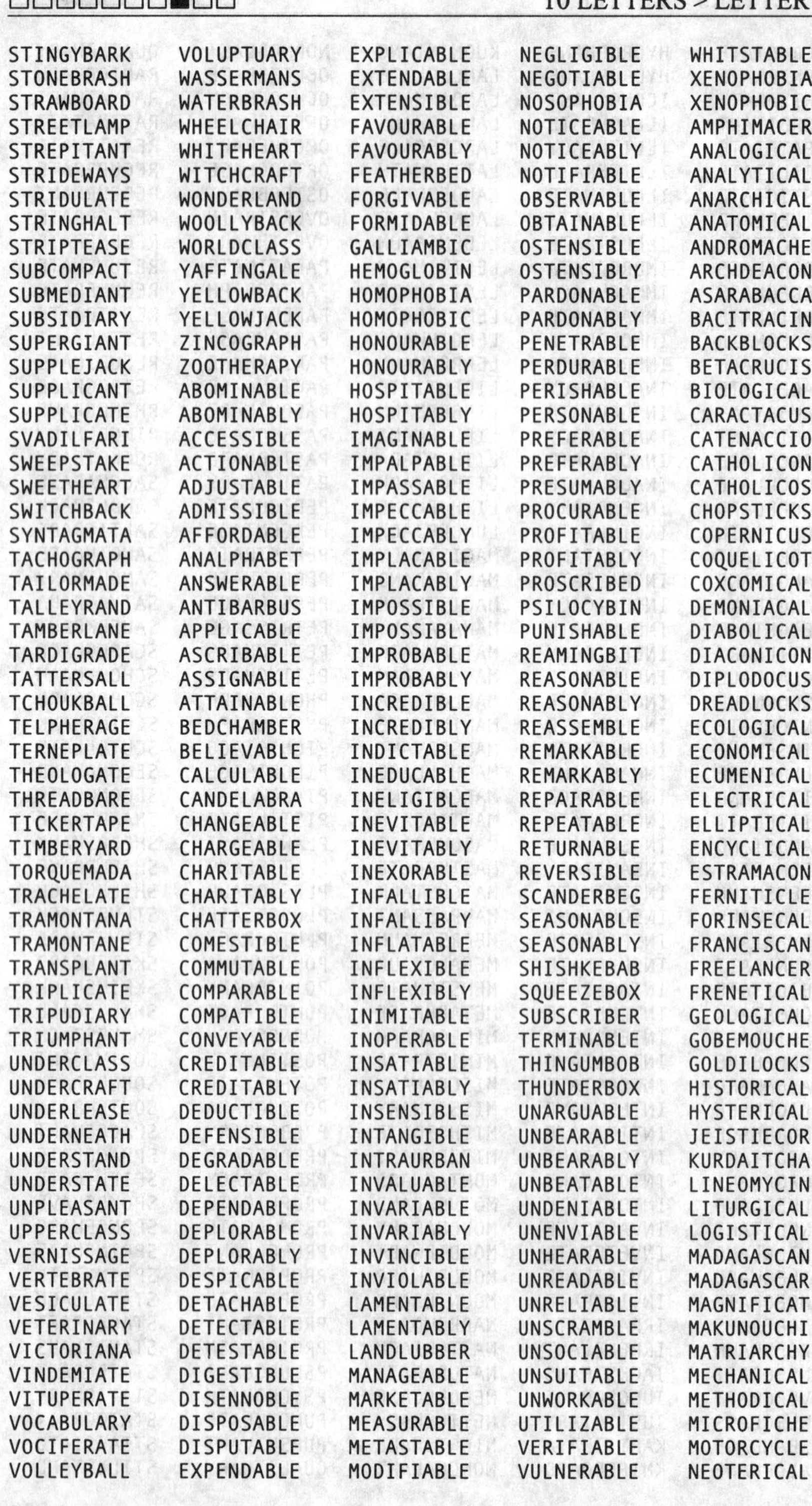

STINGYBARK
STONEBRASH
STRAWBOARD
STREETLAMP
STREPITANT
STRIDEWAYS
STRIDULATE
STRINGHALT
STRIPTEASE
SUBCOMPACT
SUBMEDIANT
SUBSIDIARY
SUPERGIANT
SUPPLEJACK
SUPPLICANT
SUPPLICATE
SVADILFARI
SWEEPSTAKE
SWEETHEART
SWITCHBACK
SYNTAGMATA
TACHOGRAPH
TAILORMADE
TALLEYRAND
TAMBERLANE
TARDIGRADE
TATTERSALL
TCHOUKBALL
TELPHERAGE
TERNEPLATE
THEOLOGATE
THREADBARE
TICKERTAPE
TIMBERYARD
TORQUEMADA
TRACHELATE
TRAMONTANA
TRAMONTANE
TRANSPLANT
TRIPLICATE
TRIPUDIARY
TRIUMPHANT
UNDERCLASS
UNDERCRAFT
UNDERLEASE
UNDERNEATH
UNDERSTAND
UNDERSTATE
UNPLEASANT
UPPERCLASS
VERNISSAGE
VERTEBRATE
VESICULATE
VETERINARY
VICTORIANA
VINDEMIATE
VITUPERATE
VOCABULARY
VOCIFERATE
VOLLEYBALL
VOLUPTUARY
WASSERMANS
WATERBRASH
WHEELCHAIR
WHITEHEART
WITCHCRAFT
WONDERLAND
WOOLLYBACK
WORLDCLASS
YAFFINGALE
YELLOWBACK
YELLOWJACK
ZINCOGRAPH
ZOOTHERAPY
ABOMINABLE
ABOMINABLY
ACCESSIBLE
ACTIONABLE
ADJUSTABLE
ADMISSIBLE
AFFORDABLE
ANALPHABET
ANSWERABLE
ANTIBARBUS
APPLICABLE
ASCRIBABLE
ASSIGNABLE
ATTAINABLE
BEDCHAMBER
BELIEVABLE
CALCULABLE
CANDELABRA
CHANGEABLE
CHARGEABLE
CHARITABLE
CHARITABLY
CHATTERBOX
COMESTIBLE
COMMUTABLE
COMPARABLE
COMPATIBLE
CONVEYABLE
CREDITABLE
CREDITABLY
DEDUCTIBLE
DEFENSIBLE
DEGRADABLE
DELECTABLE
DEPENDABLE
DEPLORABLE
DEPLORABLY
DESPICABLE
DETACHABLE
DETECTABLE
DETESTABLE
DIGESTIBLE
DISENNOBLE
DISPOSABLE
DISPUTABLE
EXPENDABLE
EXPLICABLE
EXTENDABLE
EXTENSIBLE
FAVOURABLE
FAVOURABLY
FEATHERBED
FORGIVABLE
FORMIDABLE
GALLIAMBIC
HEMOGLOBIN
HOMOPHOBIA
HOMOPHOBIC
HONOURABLE
HONOURABLY
HOSPITABLE
HOSPITABLY
IMAGINABLE
IMPALPABLE
IMPASSABLE
IMPECCABLE
IMPECCABLY
IMPLACABLE
IMPLACABLY
IMPOSSIBLE
IMPOSSIBLY
IMPROBABLE
IMPROBABLY
INCREDIBLE
INCREDIBLY
INDICTABLE
INEDUCABLE
INELIGIBLE
INEVITABLE
INEVITABLY
INEXORABLE
INFALLIBLE
INFALLIBLY
INFLATABLE
INFLEXIBLE
INFLEXIBLY
INIMITABLE
INOPERABLE
INSATIABLE
INSATIABLY
INSENSIBLE
INTANGIBLE
INTRAURBAN
INVALUABLE
INVARIABLE
INVARIABLY
INVINCIBLE
INVIOLABLE
LAMENTABLE
LAMENTABLY
LANDLUBBER
MANAGEABLE
MARKETABLE
MEASURABLE
METASTABLE
MODIFIABLE
NEGLIGIBLE
NEGOTIABLE
NOSOPHOBIA
NOTICEABLE
NOTICEABLY
NOTIFIABLE
OBSERVABLE
OBTAINABLE
OSTENSIBLE
OSTENSIBLY
PARDONABLE
PARDONABLY
PENETRABLE
PERDURABLE
PERISHABLE
PERSONABLE
PREFERABLE
PREFERABLY
PRESUMABLY
PROCURABLE
PROFITABLE
PROFITABLY
PROSCRIBED
PSILOCYBIN
PUNISHABLE
REAMINGBIT
REASONABLE
REASONABLY
REASSEMBLE
REMARKABLE
REMARKABLY
REPAIRABLE
REPEATABLE
RETURNABLE
REVERSIBLE
SCANDERBEG
SEASONABLE
SEASONABLY
SHISHKEBAB
SQUEEZEBOX
SUBSCRIBER
TERMINABLE
THINGUMBOB
THUNDERBOX
UNARGUABLE
UNBEARABLE
UNBEARABLY
UNBEATABLE
UNDENIABLE
UNENVIABLE
UNHEARABLE
UNREADABLE
UNRELIABLE
UNSCRAMBLE
UNSOCIABLE
UNSUITABLE
UNWORKABLE
UTILIZABLE
VERIFIABLE
VULNERABLE
WHITSTABLE
XENOPHOBIA
XENOPHOBIC
AMPHIMACER
ANALOGICAL
ANALYTICAL
ANARCHICAL
ANATOMICAL
ANDROMACHE
ARCHDEACON
ASARABACCA
BACITRACIN
BACKBLOCKS
BETACRUCIS
BIOLOGICAL
CARACTACUS
CATENACCIO
CATHOLICON
CATHOLICOS
CHOPSTICKS
COPERNICUS
COQUELICOT
COXCOMICAL
DEMONIACAL
DIABOLICAL
DIACONICON
DIPLODOCUS
DREADLOCKS
ECOLOGICAL
ECONOMICAL
ECUMENICAL
ELECTRICAL
ELLIPTICAL
ENCYCLICAL
ESTRAMACON
FERNITICLE
FORINSECAL
FRANCISCAN
FREELANCER
FRENETICAL
GEOLOGICAL
GOBEMOUCHE
GOLDILOCKS
HISTORICAL
HYSTERICAL
JEISTIECOR
KURDAITCHA
LINEOMYCIN
LITURGICAL
LOGISTICAL
MADAGASCAN
MADAGASCAR
MAGNIFICAT
MAKUNOUCHI
MATRIARCHY
MECHANICAL
METHODICAL
MICROFICHE
MOTORCYCLE
NEOTERICAL

ORATORICAL
OROBRANCHE
OUANANICHE
PANOPTICON
PATCHCOCKE
PATRIARCHY
PERIODICAL
POKERFACED
PONTIFICAL
PREJUDICED
PRONOUNCED
RABBINICAL
RECEPTACLE
RECIPROCAL
REPRODUCER
REPUBLICAN
REQUIESCAT
RHETORICAL
RHYTHMICAL
SABBATICAL
SABRETACHE
SEMICIRCLE
SERMONICAL
SHAKUHACHI
SHAMEFACED
SIGNIFICAT
STAVESACRE
SYMBOLICAL
SYNECDOCHE
TABERNACLE
THEATRICAL
TYRANNICAL
ULTRAFICHE
UNBALANCED
UNCRITICAL
VITELLICLE
WANCHANCIE
ZOOLOGICAL
ACOTYLEDON
ADMITTEDLY
AFRICANDER
ALCIBIADES
AMBASSADOR
ANGURVADEL
ARCHIMEDES
ARMAGEDDON
ASTEROIDEA
BACKHANDED
BACKHANDER
BACKSLIDER
BAREHEADED
BARMECIDAL
BEARGARDEN
BILIVERDIN
BLASTOIDEA
BONDHOLDER
BOOKBINDER
BULLHEADED
CALAMANDER
CALAMONDIN
CAMPARADOR
CARYATIDES
CIRRIPEDEA
CIRRIPEDIA
CLOSTRIDIA
COLONNADED
COMPOUNDED
CONFOUNDED
CONFUSEDLY
COPYHOLDER
COROMANDEL
CORREGIDOR
CROTALIDAE
CYCLOPEDIA
DEJECTEDLY
DESERVEDLY
DIDGERIDOO
DRAWBRIDGE
DRUMBLEDOR
ECHINOIDEA
EPIMENIDES
EUROCLYDON
EVENHANDED
EVERGLADES
FALKLANDER
FIREWARDEN
FLAPDOODLE
FLUNKEYDOM
FOOTBRIDGE
FORESHADOW
FREEHANDER
FREEHOLDER
FREELOADER
FRENZIEDLY
FUDDYDUDDY
FUNGICIDAL
GERMICIDAL
GETUPANDGO
GLEEMAIDEN
GRAMICIDIN
GRASSWIDOW
HANDMAIDEN
HANGGLIDER
HELLBENDER
HESPERIDES
HIGHBINDER
HIGHHANDED
HIGHLANDER
HODGEPODGE
HORSERIDER
ICOSOHEDRA
INTERCEDER
INTERNODAL
KEYBOARDER
LEFTHANDED
LEFTHANDER
LIKEMINDED
MAHOMMEDAN
MEMORANDUM
MONTEVIDEO
MUJAHEDDIN
MULTIMEDIA
NEWSREADER
OPENHANDED
OPENMINDED
OUVIRANDRA
OVERLANDER
OVERSHADOW
PALISANDER
PARADIDDLE
PATHFINDER
PINNIPEDIA
PRESENTDAY
PROFOUNDLY
PROMENADER
PTERANODON
PUMPHANDLE
QUARRENDER
RECONSIDER
REFERENDUM
REJONEADOR
REPEATEDLY
REPORTEDLY
RESIGNEDLY
RINGLEADER
SALAMANDER
SCOPELIDAE
SHANDRYDAN
SHARAWADGI
SIDESADDLE
SIDEWINDER
SOBERSIDES
SPIRITEDLY
SPLENDIDLY
STADHOLDER
STEMWINDER
STEPLADDER
STUMBLEDOM
SUPERADDED
SUPERMODEL
SUPPOSEDLY
SURROUNDED
TANAGRIDAE
TARADIDDLE
TENRECIDAE
THOUSANDTH
THUCYDIDES
TOUCHANDGO
UNATTENDED
UNDEFENDED
UNFRIENDLY
UNGROUNDED
UNHERALDED
UNORTHODOX
VIEWFINDER
WILLINGDON
WRETCHEDLY
ABITURIENT
ABONNEMENT
ABRIDGMENT
ABRUPTNESS
ABSOLUTELY
ACCURATELY
ADDITAMENT
ADEQUATELY
ADJUSTMENT
ADOLESCENT
ADRAMELECH
ADULTERESS
AFTERPIECE
ALEXANDERS
ALLUREMENT
ALZHEIMERS
AMBIVALENT
ANADYOMENE
ANGIOSPERM
ANIMADVERT
ANTECEDENT
ANTIFREEZE
ANTIOCHENE
ANTIPODEAN
ANTIVENENE
APOPHTHEGM
ARMIPOTENT
ARTHROMERE
ASSESSMENT
ASSIGNMENT
ASSORTMENT
ASTRINGENT
ASTUTENESS
ASYNARTETE
ATMOSPHERE
ATTACHMENT
ATTAINMENT
AUCTIONEER
BAFFLEMENT
BALBUTIENT
BANGLADESH
BANISHMENT
BARRENNESS
BARYSPHERE
BATTENBERG
BATTLEMENT
BEEFEATERS
BENEFICENT
BENEVOLENT
BIRKENHEAD
BITTERNESS
BOTTLEHEAD
BOTTLENECK
BOTTOMLESS
BRAININESS
BREASTFEED
BREATHLESS
BRIDGEHEAD
BRIGHTNESS
BROADPIECE
BROADSHEET
BUFFLEHEAD
BUFFOONERY
BUNDESWEHR
BUTTERMERE
CAMBERWELL
CANCIONERO
CANTONMENT
CARABINEER
CARRAGHEEN
CASSIOPEIA
CASUALNESS
CHANGELESS
CHARIOTEER
CHEEKINESS
CHERSONESE
CHERVONETS
CHILLINESS
CHIROPTERA
CHOICELESS
CINECAMERA
CIRCUMVENT
CLAMMINESS
CLEMENCEAU
CLEVERNESS
CLOMIPHENE
CLOUDINESS
CLUMSINESS
COARSENESS
COEXISTENT
COINCIDENT
COLDSTREAM
COLEOPTERA
COLOURLESS
COLPORTEUR
COMANCHERO
COMMANDEER
COMMITMENT
COMMONWEAL
COMPLACENT
COMPLEMENT
COMPLETELY
COMPLIMENT
COMPREHEND
CONCURRENT
CONDESCEND
CONSEQUENT
CONSISTENT
CONTINGENT
CONTRAHENT
CONTRAVENE
CONTROVERT
CONVENIENT
CONVERGENT
CONVERSELY
COPPERHEAD
CORDILLERA
CORYPHAEUS
COSTLINESS
CRAFTINESS
CRISPBREAD
CROSSBREED
CROSSCHECK

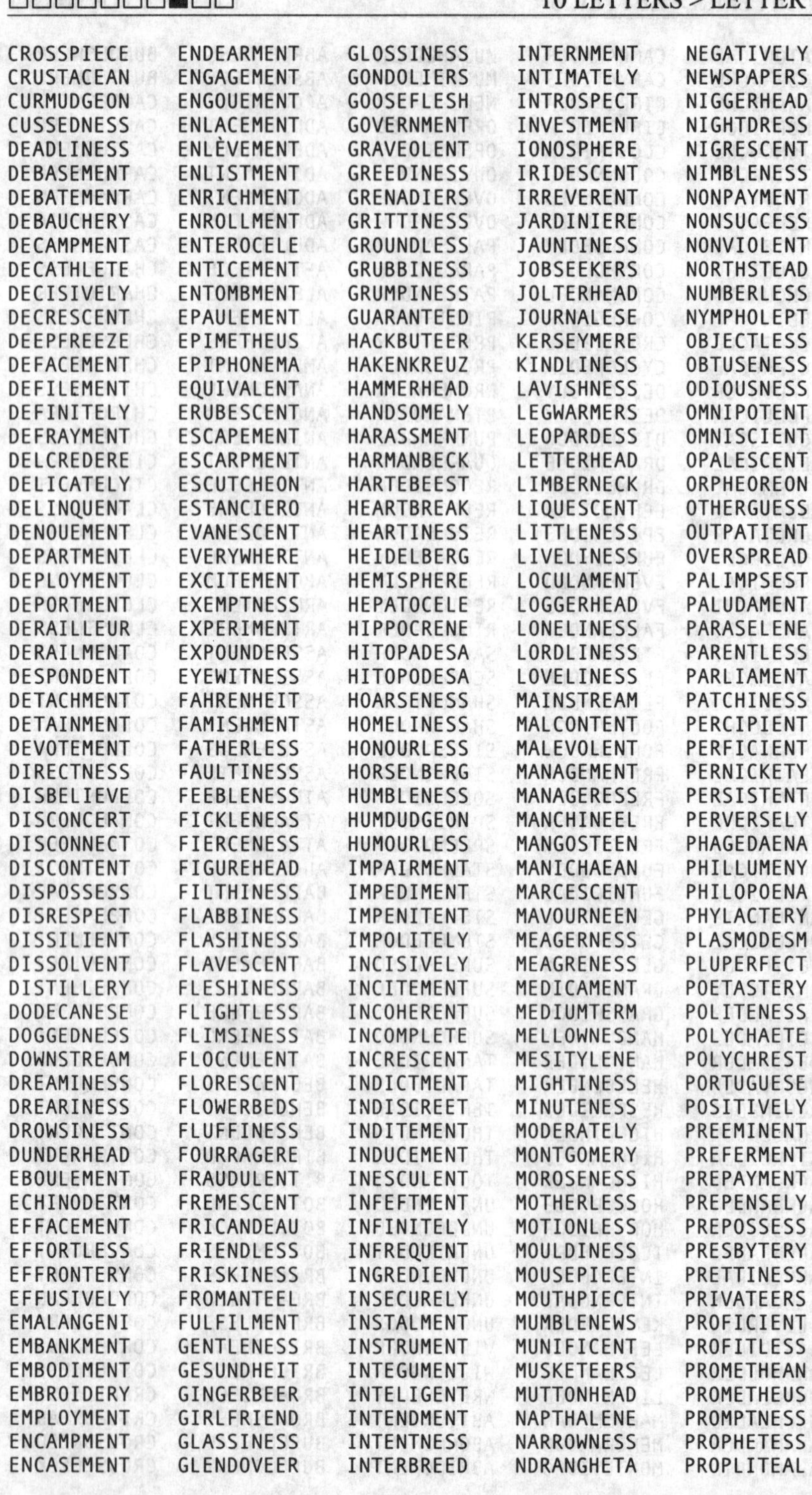

CROSSPIECE
CRUSTACEAN
CURMUDGEON
CUSSEDNESS
DEADLINESS
DEBASEMENT
DEBATEMENT
DEBAUCHERY
DECAMPMENT
DECATHLETE
DECISIVELY
DECRESCENT
DEEPFREEZE
DEFACEMENT
DEFILEMENT
DEFINITELY
DEFRAYMENT
DELCREDERE
DELICATELY
DELINQUENT
DENOUEMENT
DEPARTMENT
DEPLOYMENT
DEPORTMENT
DERAILLEUR
DERAILMENT
DESPONDENT
DETACHMENT
DETAINMENT
DEVOTEMENT
DIRECTNESS
DISBELIEVE
DISCONCERT
DISCONNECT
DISCONTENT
DISPOSSESS
DISRESPECT
DISSILIENT
DISSOLVENT
DISTILLERY
DODECANESE
DOGGEDNESS
DOWNSTREAM
DREAMINESS
DREARINESS
DROWSINESS
DUNDERHEAD
EBOULEMENT
ECHINODERM
EFFACEMENT
EFFORTLESS
EFFRONTERY
EFFUSIVELY
EMALANGENI
EMBANKMENT
EMBODIMENT
EMBROIDERY
EMPLOYMENT
ENCAMPMENT
ENCASEMENT
ENDEARMENT
ENGAGEMENT
ENGOUEMENT
ENLACEMENT
ENLÈVEMENT
ENLISTMENT
ENRICHMENT
ENROLLMENT
ENTEROCELE
ENTICEMENT
ENTOMBMENT
EPAULEMENT
EPIMETHEUS
EPIPHONEMA
EQUIVALENT
ERUBESCENT
ESCAPEMENT
ESCARPMENT
ESCUTCHEON
ESTANCIERO
EVANESCENT
EVERYWHERE
EXCITEMENT
EXEMPTNESS
EXPERIMENT
EXPOUNDERS
EYEWITNESS
FAHRENHEIT
FAMISHMENT
FATHERLESS
FAULTINESS
FEEBLENESS
FICKLENESS
FIERCENESS
FIGUREHEAD
FILTHINESS
FLABBINESS
FLASHINESS
FLAVESCENT
FLESHINESS
FLIGHTLESS
FLIMSINESS
FLOCCULENT
FLORESCENT
FLOWERBEDS
FLUFFINESS
FOURRAGERE
FRAUDULENT
FREMESCENT
FRICANDEAU
FRIENDLESS
FRISKINESS
FROMANTEEL
FULFILMENT
GENTLENESS
GESUNDHEIT
GINGERBEER
GIRLFRIEND
GLASSINESS
GLENDOVEER
GLOSSINESS
GONDOLIERS
GOOSEFLESH
GOVERNMENT
GRAVEOLENT
GREEDINESS
GRENADIERS
GRITTINESS
GROUNDLESS
GRUBBINESS
GRUMPINESS
GUARANTEED
HACKBUTEER
HAKENKREUZ
HAMMERHEAD
HANDSOMELY
HARASSMENT
HARMANBECK
HARTEBEEST
HEARTBREAK
HEARTINESS
HEIDELBERG
HEMISPHERE
HEPATOCELE
HIPPOCRENE
HITOPADESA
HITOPODESA
HOARSENESS
HOMELINESS
HONOURLESS
HORSELBERG
HUMBLENESS
HUMDUDGEON
HUMOURLESS
IMPAIRMENT
IMPEDIMENT
IMPENITENT
IMPOLITELY
INCISIVELY
INCITEMENT
INCOHERENT
INCOMPLETE
INCRESCENT
INDICTMENT
INDISCREET
INDITEMENT
INDUCEMENT
INESCULENT
INFEFTMENT
INFINITELY
INFREQUENT
INGREDIENT
INSECURELY
INSTALMENT
INSTRUMENT
INTEGUMENT
INTELIGENT
INTENDMENT
INTENTNESS
INTERBREED
INTERNMENT
INTIMATELY
INTROSPECT
INVESTMENT
IONOSPHERE
IRIDESCENT
IRREVERENT
JARDINIERE
JAUNTINESS
JOBSEEKERS
JOLTERHEAD
JOURNALESE
KERSEYMERE
KINDLINESS
LAVISHNESS
LEGWARMERS
LEOPARDESS
LETTERHEAD
LIMBERNECK
LIQUESCENT
LITTLENESS
LIVELINESS
LOCULAMENT
LOGGERHEAD
LONELINESS
LORDLINESS
LOVELINESS
MAINSTREAM
MALCONTENT
MALEVOLENT
MANAGEMENT
MANAGERESS
MANCHINEEL
MANGOSTEEN
MANICHAEAN
MARCESCENT
MAVOURNEEN
MEAGERNESS
MEAGRENESS
MEDICAMENT
MEDIUMTERM
MELLOWNESS
MESITYLENE
MIGHTINESS
MINUTENESS
MODERATELY
MONTGOMERY
MOROSENESS
MOTHERLESS
MOTIONLESS
MOULDINESS
MOUSEPIECE
MOUTHPIECE
MUMBLENEWS
MUNIFICENT
MUSKETEERS
MUTTONHEAD
NAPTHALENE
NARROWNESS
NDRANGHETA
NEGATIVELY
NEWSPAPERS
NIGGERHEAD
NIGHTDRESS
NIGRESCENT
NIMBLENESS
NONPAYMENT
NONSUCCESS
NONVIOLENT
NORTHSTEAD
NUMBERLESS
NYMPHOLEPT
OBJECTLESS
OBTUSENESS
ODIOUSNESS
OMNIPOTENT
OMNISCIENT
OPALESCENT
ORPHEOREON
OTHERGUESS
OUTPATIENT
OVERSPREAD
PALIMPSEST
PALUDAMENT
PARASELENE
PARENTLESS
PARLIAMENT
PATCHINESS
PERCIPIENT
PERFICIENT
PERNICKETY
PERSISTENT
PERVERSELY
PHAGEDAENA
PHILLUMENY
PHILOPOENA
PHYLACTERY
PLASMODESM
PLUPERFECT
POETASTERY
POLITENESS
POLYCHAETE
POLYCHREST
PORTUGUESE
POSITIVELY
PREEMINENT
PREFERMENT
PREPAYMENT
PREPENSELY
PREPOSSESS
PRESBYTERY
PRETTINESS
PRIVATEERS
PROFICIENT
PROFITLESS
PROMETHEAN
PROMETHEUS
PROMPTNESS
PROPHETESS
PROPLITEAL

PROPYLAEUM
PROSILIENT
PSOCOPTERA
PUBERULENT
PUNICACEAE
PUNISHMENT
PUTRESCENT
PUZZLEMENT
QUADRICEPS
QUADRIREME
QUAINTNESS
QUEASINESS
QUENCHLESS
RANDOMNESS
RAPPORTEUR
REARMAMENT
REFINEMENT
REGARDLESS
RELATIVELY
RELENTLESS
REMOTENESS
REPETITEUR
RESENTMENT
RESOLUTELY
RESPONDENT
RETIREMENT
RETROGRESS
RETROSPECT
RHIPIPTERA
RINDERPEST
ROBUSTNESS
ROLANDSECK
RUBBERNECK
RUBINSTEIN
RUDDERLESS
RUGGEDNESS
SACREDNESS
SALLENDERS
SAPPERMENT
SAVAGENESS
SCANTINESS
SCARCEMENT
SCARCENESS
SCATHELESS
SCATURIENT
SCHALSTEIN
SCORZONERA
SCRUTINEER
SCULPTRESS
SEAMSTRESS
SECONDBEST
SECONDMENT
SEDATENESS
SEEMLIHEAD
SELFESTEEM
SELLINGERS
SELTZOGENE
SENEGALESE
SEPARATELY
SETTLEMENT
SEVENTIETH
SHABBINESS
SHADOWLESS
SHIBBOLETH
SHIFTINESS
SHODDINESS
SHORTBREAD
SHOVELHEAD
SHREWDNESS
SHRILLNESS
SINFULNESS
SINGHALESE
SINGLENESS
SLEEPINESS
SLEEVELESS
SLIPSTREAM
SLOPPINESS
SMARMINESS
SMITHEREEN
SMOOTHNESS
SNOOTINESS
SONGSTRESS
SOPHOCLEAN
SORDIDNESS
SPARSENESS
SPEECHLESS
SPEEDINESS
SPERMACETI
SPINESCENT
SPIRITLESS
SPORTSWEAR
SPREAGHERY
SPRINGLESS
SPRUCENESS
STATIONERY
STEADINESS
STEELINESS
STEWARDESS
STICKINESS
STICKYBEAK
STINGINESS
STOCKINESS
STRICTNESS
STRINDBERG
STRULDBERG
STUFFINESS
STURDINESS
SUAVEOLENT
SUBSEQUENT
SUBSISTENT
SUDDENNESS
SUFFICIENT
SULTRINESS
SUPPLEMENT
SUPPLENESS
SURINAMESE
SUSPENDERS
SWEETBREAD
TAPOTEMENT
TEENYWEENY
TENDERNESS
TERREPLEIN
THEREANENT
TIMELINESS
TINKERBELL
TIRAILLEUR
TOMFOOLERY
TORPESCENT
TOUCHINESS
TOUCHPIECE
TOURNAMENT
TRANSGRESS
TRAVELLERS
TRENDINESS
TRICKINESS
TURTLENECK
ULTIMATELY
UNDERSTEER
UNEASINESS
UNEVENNESS
UNFORESEEN
UNIQUENESS
UNRULINESS
UNTIDINESS
UPHOLSTERY
URTICACEAE
USEFULNESS
VELOCIPEDE
VICEGERENT
VICEREGENT
VIETNAMESE
WAMPUMPEAG
WATERCRESS
WATERWHEEL
WEAPONLESS
WEIGHTLESS
WHEATSHEAF
WHEEZINESS
WHOLEWHEAT
WICKEDNESS
WIDESPREAD
WILDEBEEST
WILDERNESS
WILLOWHERB
WINDERMERE
WINDSCREEN
WINDSHIELD
WONDERMENT
WOODENHEAD
WOODPIGEON
WORTHINESS
YESTERWEEK
YESTERYEAR
ZIMBABWEAN
ZOLLVEREIN
LAVALLIÈRE
VIVANDIÈRE
COCKCHAFER
CROSSREFER
DELIGHTFUL
DISDAINFUL
EISTEDDFOD
FISTICUFFS
FOODSTUFFS
FRAUNHOFER
MEANINGFUL
NEGLECTFUL
PALMATIFID
PURPOSEFUL
RAGAMUFFIN
REMORSEFUL
RESPECTFUL
REVENGEFUL
RICHTHOFEN
RIJSTTAFEL
ROSECHAFER
SCIENTIFIC
SUCCESSFUL
TENEBRIFIC
THIMBLEFUL
THOUGHTFUL
UMBELLIFER
UNEVENTFUL
UNFAITHFUL
UNFRUITFUL
UNGRATEFUL
UNSPECIFIC
UNTRUTHFUL
WINDSURFER
ACCUSINGLY
ADMIRINGLY
AEROPHAGIA
AIRFREIGHT
ANTITRAGUS
ARTHRALGIA
ASTRALAGUS
ASTROLOGER
AUSTRINGER
BALBRIGGAN
BARASINGHA
BARELEGGED
BEEFBURGER
BIRTHRIGHT
BOONDOGGLE
BOOTLEGGER
BUDGERIGAR
BUSHRANGER
CARCINOGEN
CHALLENGER
CHAULMUGRA
CHOLALOGUE
COATHANGER
COPENHAGEN
CREOPHAGUS
CYNOMOLGUS
DEMOGORGON
DISEMBOGUE
DISENGAGED
DISTRAUGHT
DISTRINGAS
FEARNOUGHT
FISHMONGER
FLASHLIGHT
FLEETINGLY
FLOODLIGHT
FOREFINGER
FORTHRIGHT
FULLLENGTH
GOLDDIGGER
GOLDFINGER
HEMIPLEGIA
HENDECAGON
INKSLINGER
IRONMONGER
KHIDMUTGAR
LEFTWINGER
LIGHTINGUP
LOTOPHAGUS
MAKEWEIGHT
MENACINGLY
MICROLIGHT
MISHGUGGLE
MONOPLEGIA
MOUTHORGAN
MYSTAGOGUE
MYSTAGOGUS
NEWSMONGER
NIGHTLIGHT
NORTHANGER
OBLIGINGLY
ODONTALGIA
OESOPHAGUS
OVERWEIGHT
OWLSPIEGLE
PARAPLEGIA
PARAPLEGIC
PLAYWRIGHT
PRIVILEGED
PRIZEFIGHT
QUADRANGLE
SCOFFINGLY
SHARAWAGGI
SHENANIGAN
SHOCKINGLY
SNAPDRAGON
SOGDOLAGER
SOGDOLIGER
SOGDOLOGER
SOOTHINGLY
SPORTINGLY
SQUETEAGUE
STALLENGER
STALLINGER
STERNALGIA
STRIKINGLY
SWIMMINGLY
TORCHLIGHT
TRAVELOGUE
UNABRIDGED
VOETGANGER

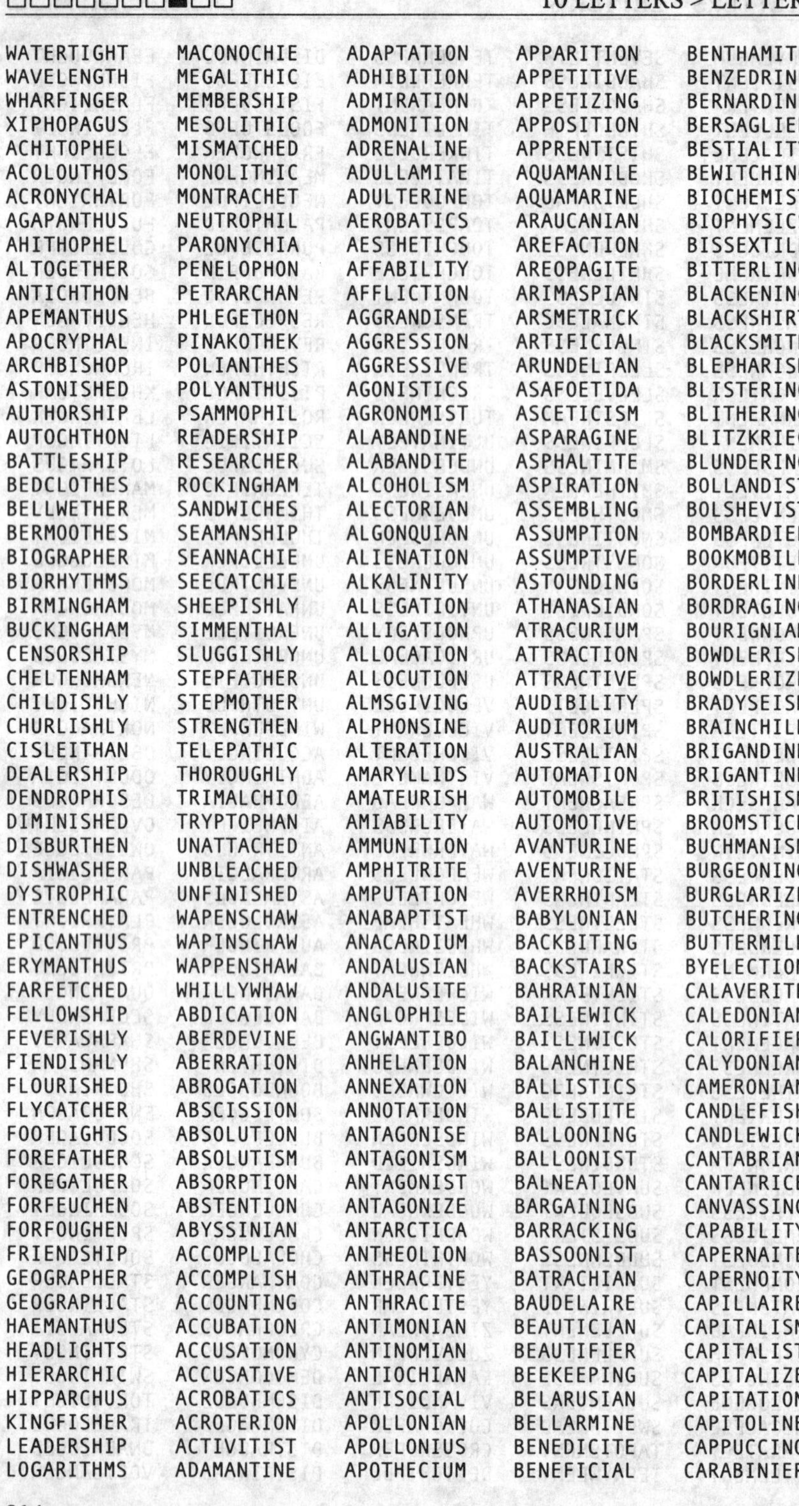

WATERTIGHT
WAVELENGTH
WHARFINGER
XIPHOPAGUS
ACHITOPHEL
ACOLOUTHOS
ACRONYCHAL
AGAPANTHUS
AHITHOPHEL
ALTOGETHER
ANTICHTHON
APEMANTHUS
APOCRYPHAL
ARCHBISHOP
ASTONISHED
AUTHORSHIP
AUTOCHTHON
BATTLESHIP
BEDCLOTHES
BELLWETHER
BERMOOTHES
BIOGRAPHER
BIORHYTHMS
BIRMINGHAM
BUCKINGHAM
CENSORSHIP
CHELTENHAM
CHILDISHLY
CHURLISHLY
CISLEITHAN
DEALERSHIP
DENDROPHIS
DIMINISHED
DISBURTHEN
DISHWASHER
DYSTROPHIC
ENTRENCHED
EPICANTHUS
ERYMANTHUS
FARFETCHED
FELLOWSHIP
FEVERISHLY
FIENDISHLY
FLOURISHED
FLYCATCHER
FOOTLIGHTS
FOREFATHER
FOREGATHER
FORFEUCHEN
FORFOUGHEN
FRIENDSHIP
GEOGRAPHER
GEOGRAPHIC
HAEMANTHUS
HEADLIGHTS
HIERARCHIC
HIPPARCHUS
KINGFISHER
LEADERSHIP
LOGARITHMS
MACONOCHIE
MEGALITHIC
MEMBERSHIP
MESOLITHIC
MISMATCHED
MONOLITHIC
MONTRACHET
NEUTROPHIL
PARONYCHIA
PENELOPHON
PETRARCHAN
PHLEGETHON
PINAKOTHEK
POLIANTHES
POLYANTHUS
PSAMMOPHIL
READERSHIP
RESEARCHER
ROCKINGHAM
SANDWICHES
SEAMANSHIP
SEANNACHIE
SEECATCHIE
SHEEPISHLY
SIMMENTHAL
SLUGGISHLY
STEPFATHER
STEPMOTHER
STRENGTHEN
TELEPATHIC
THOROUGHLY
TRIMALCHIO
TRYPTOPHAN
UNATTACHED
UNBLEACHED
UNFINISHED
WAPENSCHAW
WAPINSCHAW
WAPPENSHAW
WHILLYWHAW
ABDICATION
ABERDEVINE
ABERRATION
ABROGATION
ABSCISSION
ABSOLUTION
ABSOLUTISM
ABSORPTION
ABSTENTION
ABYSSINIAN
ACCOMPLICE
ACCOMPLISH
ACCOUNTING
ACCUBATION
ACCUSATION
ACCUSATIVE
ACROBATICS
ACROTERION
ACTIVITIST
ADAMANTINE
ADAPTATION
ADHIBITION
ADMIRATION
ADMONITION
ADRENALINE
ADULLAMITE
ADULTERINE
AEROBATICS
AESTHETICS
AFFABILITY
AFFLICTION
AGGRANDISE
AGGRESSION
AGGRESSIVE
AGONISTICS
AGRONOMIST
ALABANDINE
ALABANDITE
ALCOHOLISM
ALECTORIAN
ALGONQUIAN
ALIENATION
ALKALINITY
ALLEGATION
ALLIGATION
ALLOCATION
ALLOCUTION
ALMSGIVING
ALPHONSINE
ALTERATION
AMARYLLIDS
AMATEURISH
AMIABILITY
AMMUNITION
AMPHITRITE
AMPUTATION
ANABAPTIST
ANACARDIUM
ANDALUSIAN
ANDALUSITE
ANGLOPHILE
ANGWANTIBO
ANHELATION
ANNEXATION
ANNOTATION
ANTAGONISE
ANTAGONISM
ANTAGONIST
ANTAGONIZE
ANTARCTICA
ANTHEOLION
ANTHRACINE
ANTHRACITE
ANTIMONIAN
ANTINOMIAN
ANTIOCHIAN
ANTISOCIAL
APOLLONIAN
APOLLONIUS
APOTHECIUM
APPARITION
APPETITIVE
APPETIZING
APPOSITION
APPRENTICE
AQUAMANILE
AQUAMARINE
ARAUCANIAN
AREFACTION
AREOPAGITE
ARIMASPIAN
ARSMETRICK
ARTIFICIAL
ARUNDELIAN
ASAFOETIDA
ASCETICISM
ASPARAGINE
ASPHALTITE
ASPIRATION
ASSEMBLING
ASSUMPTION
ASSUMPTIVE
ASTOUNDING
ATHANASIAN
ATRACURIUM
ATTRACTION
ATTRACTIVE
AUDIBILITY
AUDITORIUM
AUSTRALIAN
AUTOMATION
AUTOMOBILE
AUTOMOTIVE
AVANTURINE
AVENTURINE
AVERRHOISM
BABYLONIAN
BACKBITING
BACKSTAIRS
BAHRAINIAN
BAILIEWICK
BAILLIWICK
BALANCHINE
BALLISTICS
BALLISTITE
BALLOONING
BALLOONIST
BALNEATION
BARGAINING
BARRACKING
BASSOONIST
BATRACHIAN
BAUDELAIRE
BEAUTICIAN
BEAUTIFIER
BEEKEEPING
BELARUSIAN
BELLARMINE
BENEDICITE
BENEFICIAL
BENTHAMITE
BENZEDRINE
BERNARDINE
BERSAGLIER
BESTIALITY
BEWITCHING
BIOCHEMIST
BIOPHYSICS
BISSEXTILE
BITTERLING
BLACKENING
BLACKSHIRT
BLACKSMITH
BLEPHARISM
BLISTERING
BLITHERING
BLITZKRIEG
BLUNDERING
BOLLANDIST
BOLSHEVIST
BOMBARDIER
BOOKMOBILE
BORDERLINE
BORDRAGING
BOURIGNIAN
BOWDLERISE
BOWDLERIZE
BRADYSEISM
BRAINCHILD
BRIGANDINE
BRIGANTINE
BRITISHISM
BROOMSTICK
BUCHMANISM
BURGEONING
BURGLARIZE
BUTCHERING
BUTTERMILK
BYELECTION
CALAVERITE
CALEDONIAN
CALORIFIER
CALYDONIAN
CAMERONIAN
CANDLEFISH
CANDLEWICK
CANTABRIAN
CANTATRICE
CANVASSING
CAPABILITY
CAPERNAITE
CAPERNOITY
CAPILLAIRE
CAPITALISM
CAPITALIST
CAPITALIZE
CAPITATION
CAPITOLINE
CAPPUCCINO
CARABINIER

CARAMELIZE
CARNASSIAL
CARPATHIAN
CARPENTIER
CARTHAMINE
CARTHUSIAN
CARTOONIST
CASTRATION
CATABOLISM
CATARRHINE
CATEGORISE
CATEGORIZE
CENTENNIAL
CENTRALIZE
CEREMONIAL
CEREMONIES
CESTRACION
CHAFFERING
CHANDELIER
CHANGELING
CHAPTALISE
CHATELAINE
CHAUCERIAN
CHAUVINISM
CHAUVINIST
CHECKPOINT
CHESSYLITE
CHEVESAILE
CHIFFONIER
CHREMATIST
CHRYSOLITE
CIRCASSIAN
CIRCUMCISE
CISPONTINE
CISTERCIAN
CLAMOURING
CLASPKNIFE
CLASSICISM
CLASSICIST
CLASSIFIED
CLEMENTINE
COCKATRICE
COGITATION
COLBERTINE
COLCHICINE
COLEORHIZA
COLLAPSING
COLLECTING
COLLECTION
COLLECTIVE
COLLOQUIAL
COLORATION
COMBUSTION
COMFORTING
COMMANDING
COMMERCIAL
COMMISSION
COMPASSION
COMPATRIOT
COMPELLING
COMPENDIUM
COMPLETION
COMPLEXION
COMPLEXITY
COMPLICITY
COMPLUVIUM
COMPROMISE
COMPULSION
COMPULSIVE
CONCEPTION
CONCERNING
CONCERTINA
CONCESSION
CONCINNITY
CONCLUDING
CONCLUSION
CONCLUSIVE
CONCOCTION
CONCRETION
CONCUSSION
CONDOTTIER
CONDUCTING
CONDUCTION
CONFECTION
CONFESSION
CONFORMIST
CONFORMITY
CONGESTION
CONNECTING
CONNECTION
CONNECTIVE
CONNIPTION
CONQUERING
CONSENSION
CONSORTIUM
CONSTRAINT
CONSULTING
CONTENTION
CONTIGUITY
CONTINUING
CONTINUITY
CONTORTION
CONTRADICT
CONTRARILY
CONTRITION
CONVECTION
CONVENTION
CONVERSION
CONVICTION
CONVINCING
CONVULSION
CONVULSIVE
COPULATION
COQUETTISH
COQUIMBITE
CORDIALITY
CORDIERITE
CORINTHIAN
CORONATION
CORRECTING
CORRECTION
CORRECTIVE
CORRUPTING
CORRUPTION
COTTIERISM
COUNSELING
CREATIVITY
CREDENTIAL
CRICKETING
CRISPINIAN
CRYOGENICS
CUCKOOPINT
CUIRASSIER
CUISENAIRE
CUMULATIVE
CURMURRING
CURRENCIES
CURVETTING
CUTTLEFISH
DAMSELFISH
DARJEELING
DEBRIEFING
DECIMALIZE
DECLENSION
DECORATION
DECORATIVE
DEDICATION
DEFAMATION
DEFECATION
DEFINITION
DEFINITIVE
DEFLECTION
DELEGATION
DELIGATION
DELIRATION
DELPHINIUM
DEMOBILISE
DEMOBILIZE
DEMOLITION
DEMORALISE
DEMORALIZE
DENTIFRICE
DEPOSITION
DEPRESSING
DEPRESSION
DEPRESSIVE
DEPUTATION
DERIVATION
DERIVATIVE
DESCENDING
DESCRIBING
DESOLATION
DESPAIRING
DESSIATINE
DESSYATINE
DETONATION
DETRACTION
DEVELOPING
DEVOLUTION
DIALECTICS
DICHROMISM
DIGITORIUM
DIGRESSION
DILATATION
DIMINUTION
DIMINUTIVE
DINNERTIME
DIRECTOIRE
DIREMPTION
DISABILITY
DISAPPOINT
DISCERNING
DISCIPLINE
DISCRETION
DISCURSIVE
DISCUSSING
DISCUSSION
DISGUSTING
DISINCLINE
DISMISSIVE
DISPENSING
DISPERSION
DISQUALIFY
DISRUPTION
DISRUPTIVE
DISSECTION
DISSENSION
DISSENTING
DISSERVICE
DISSUASION
DISTENSION
DISTILLING
DISTORTION
DISTURBING
DIURNALIST
DIVINATION
DOMINATING
DOMINATION
DOPPLERITE
DOWNSIZING
DOWNSTAIRS
DRAWSTRING
DROSOPHILA
DURABILITY
DYSCRASITE
DYSPROSIUM
EASTERLING
EATANSWILL
ECUADORIAN
ELASTICITY
ELEUSINIAN
ELONGATION
EMACIATION
EMBONPOINT
EMENDATION
EMIGRATION
EMULSIFIER
ENCHANTING
ENGROSSING
ENSANGUINE
ENTERPRISE
ENTRANCING
ENTREATING
EPHRAIMITE
EPIDIORITE
EPILIMNION
EPISTEMICS
EPITHELIUM
EPONYCHIUM
EQUANIMITY
EQUATORIAL
EQUESTRIAN
EQUITATION
ERGONOMICS
ERUCTATION
ESCALATION
ESCRITOIRE
ESCULAPIAN
ESTIMATION
ETHYLAMINE
EUCHLORINE
EUHEMERISM
EUSTACHIAN
EVACUATION
EVALUATION
EVANGELIST
EVANGELIZE
EVERYTHING
EVITERNITY
EXALTATION
EXCAVATION
EXECRATION
EXHALATION
EXHAUSTING
EXHAUSTION
EXHAUSTIVE
EXHIBITION
EXHUMATION
EXPEDITION
EXPIRATION
EXPOSITION
EXPRESSION
EXPRESSIVE
EXTINCTION
EXTINGUISH
EXTRACTION
EXULTATION
FACESAVING
FACILITIES
FANATICISM
FANTASTICO
FANTOCCINI
FAREPAYING
FARRANDINE
FASCIATION
FASTMOVING
FATALITIES
FAVORITISM
FEDERALISM
FEDERALIST

FEDERATION
FEMININITY
FERRANDINE
FESCENNINE
FETTUCCINE
FIGURATION
FIGURATIVE
FILTRATION
FINGERLING
FLASHPOINT
FLATTERING
FLAVOURING
FLICKERING
FLIRTATION
FLORENTINE
FORBEARING
FORBIDDING
FOREBODING
FORFAITING
FORTISSIMO
FOUNDATION
FOURIERISM
FOXHUNTING
FRATERNISE
FRATERNITY
FRATERNIZE
FRATRICIDE
FUMIGATION
FURNISHING
GADOLINIUM
GAINGIVING
GAINSTRIVE
GALIMATIAS
GALUMPHING
GARNIERITE
GEMINATION
GENERALISE
GENERALITY
GENERALIZE
GENERATION
GENEROSITY
GENETHLIAC
GEOPHYSICS
GEOTROPISM
GERIATRICS
GHIBELLINE
GILBERTIAN
GILBERTINE
GIRDLERINK
GLACIATION
GLAMOURISE
GLAUCONITE
GLISTENING
GLITTERING
GNOSTICISM
GOLIATHISE
GORMANDIZE
GRADUATION
GRAMMARIAN
GRANDCHILD
GRANGERISM
GRANGERIZE
GRAPTOLITE
GRATIFYING
GRATILLITY
GREENSTICK
GROUNDLING
GROVELLING
GUARNERIUS
GUILLOTINE
GYMNASTICS
GYPSOPHILA
HABITATION
HAIRSPRING
HALIEUTICS
HALLOYSITE
HANDSPRING
HANOVERIAN
HAUSTORIUM
HESITATION
HIGHFLYING
HIPPOGRIFF
HOMECOMING
HOMEOUSIAN
HOMOGENIZE
HONORARIUM
HORRIFYING
HOUSEMAIDS
HUMANITIES
HUMIDIFIER
HYDRAULICS
HYPOCORISM
IGNIMBRITE
ILLEGALITY
IMBECILITY
IMMATERIAL
IMMATURITY
IMMEMORIAL
IMMOBILITY
IMMOBILIZE
IMMOLATION
IMMORALITY
IMPALUDISM
IMPERATIVE
IMPOSITION
IMPOVERISH
IMPRESSION
IMPRESSIVE
IMPURITIES
IMPUTATION
INACTIVITY
INBREEDING
INCAPACITY
INCAPARINA
INCIVILITY
INCREASING
INCUBATION
INDAPAMIDE
INDECISION
INDECISIVE
INDEFINITE
INDICATION
INDICATIVE
INDICOLITE
INDIGOLITE
INDONESIAN
INDUSTRIAL
INEQUALITY
INFIDELITY
INFIGHTING
INFINITIVE
INFLECTION
INFLICTION
INFRACTION
INHALATION
INHIBITING
INHIBITION
INHUMANITY
INITIATION
INITIATIVE
INJUNCTION
INNOVATION
INNOVATIVE
INSECURITY
INSIPIDITY
INSPECTION
INSULARITY
INSULATION
INTERSTICE
INTERTRIGO
INTERTWINE
INTIMATION
INTINCTION
INTONATION
INTRIGUING
INUNDATION
INVALIDITY
INVITATION
INVOCATION
IRREMEDIAL
IRRIGATION
IRRITATING
IRRITATION
ISABELLINE
ISOMETRICS
ISONIAZIDE
JACULATION
JAMESONITE
JAYWALKING
JEOPARDISE
JEOPARDIZE
JERRYBUILT
JOCULARITY
JOHNSONIAN
JOURNALISM
JOURNALIST
JUBILATION
KARMATHIAN
KENTUCKIAN
KESSELRING
KIDNAPPING
KIMBERLITE
KRIEGSPIEL
LACERATION
LACKADAISY
LACUSTRINE
LAMARCKISM
LAMINATION
LANDSTHING
LANTHANIDE
LAURDALITE
LAURENTIAN
LAURUSTINE
LAURVIKITE
LAWABIDING
LAWRENCIUM
LEGIBILITY
LEGITIMIZE
LENGTHWISE
LENOCINIUM
LESBIANISM
LEVITATION
LHERZOLITE
LIBERALISM
LIBERALITY
LIBERALIZE
LIBERATION
LIBRETTIST
LIGNOCAINE
LIMBURGITE
LIMITATION
LITHUANIAN
LITIGATION
LOCOMOTION
LOCOMOTIVE
LUMINARIST
LUMINOSITY
LUSITANIAN
LUTESTRING
LYSENKOISM
MABINOGION
MACEDONIAN
MAGNIFYING
MAINSPRING
MALTHUSIAN
MANAGERIAL
MANGABEIRA
MANICURIST
MANUSCRIPT
MARASCHINO
MARCIONITE
MARGUERITE
MASTERMIND
MATCHSTICK
MATURATION
MAXIMALIST
MAXIMILIAN
MAYONNAISE
MEANDERING
MEDICATION
MEDIOCRITY
MEDITATION
MEDITATIVE
MELACONITE
MELANESIAN
MENECHMIAN
MEPERIDINE
MERCANTILE
METABOLISE
METABOLISM
METHEDRINE
MIDLOTHIAN
MILITARISM
MILITARIST
MINIMALIST
MISLEADING
MISOGYNIST
MISPRISION
MITIGATING
MITIGATION
MODERATION
MODULATION
MOISTURIZE
MONARCHIST
MONETARISM
MONETARIST
MONOPOLISE
MONOPOLIZE
MONOTHEISM
MORALITIES
MORATORIUM
MORISONIAN
MOTHERLIKE
MOTIVATION
MOUSSELINE
MOUSTERIAN
MUCKRAKING
MULIEBRITY
MULTIPLIED
MULTIPLIER
MUTABILITY
MUTILATION
MYCORRHIZA
NARCISSISM
NASTURTIUM
NATATORIAL
NATATORIUM
NATIONWIDE
NATURALISM
NATURALIST
NATURALIZE
NAUSEATING
NAUSEATIVE
NAVIGATION
NETWORKING
NEUTRALISE
NEUTRALITY
NEUTRALIZE
NIDDERLING
NIGHTSHIRT

NIGHTSTICK
NOMINALIST
NOMINATION
NOMINATIVE
NONFICTION
NONSMOKING
NORBERTINE
NOSOCOMIAL
NOTABILITY
NOURISHING
NOVACULITE
NUCLEONICS
NUMERATION
OBLIGATION
OBLOMOVISM
OBSTETRICS
OCCUPATION
OCEANGOING
OCTODECIMO
ODELSTHING
ODONTOLITE
OFFPUTTING
OMOPHORION
ONOMASTICS
OPHICLEIDE
OPPOSITION
OPPRESSION
OPPRESSIVE
OPPROBRIUM
ORDINARILY
ORDINATION
ORTHOCAINE
ORTHOPTICS
OSCITATION
OSCULATION
OSMETERIUM
OUTLANDISH
OUTPOURING
OVEREATING
OVERPRAISE
OVERRIDING
OZYMANDIAS
PACIFICISM
PAGINATION
PALAGONITE
PALATALISE
PALESTRINA
PALFRENIER
PALLIATIVE
PALUSTRINE
PANAMANIAN
PANARITIUM
PANCRATIUM
PANSOPHIST
PAPAVERINE
PAPERKNIFE
PARADOXIDE
PARADOXINE
PARAGONITE
PARAMARIBO
PARGETTING
PARNASSIAN
PARNELLISM
PARTIALITY
PASTEURISE
PASTEURIZE
PATAGONIAN
PATAVINITY
PATRIOTISM
PEACHERINO
PECULATION
PEDESTRIAN
PEDIATRICS
PEJORATIVE
PENNILLION
PEPPERMILL
PEPPERMINT
PERCENTILE
PERCEPTION
PERCEPTIVE
PERCUSSION
PERFECTION
PERFORMING
PERIDOTITE
PERIHELION
PERMEATION
PERMISSION
PERMISSIVE
PERORATION
PEROVSKITE
PERPETUITY
PERPLEXING
PERPLEXITY
PERQUISITE
PERSUADING
PERSUASION
PERSUASIVE
PERVERSION
PERVERSITY
PETRIFYING
PHAELONIAN
PHANTASIME
PHANTASIST
PHARMACIST
PHILIPPINA
PHILIPPINE
PHILISTINE
PHILLIPINA
PHILLIPINE
PHLOGOPITE
PHRENESIAC
PICAYUNISH
PILGARLICK
PINCUSHION
PIONEERING
PLAGIARISE
PLAGIARISM
PLAGIARIST
PLAGIARIZE
PLANTATION
PLASTICINE
PLASTICITY
PLEBISCITE
PLIABILITY
PLOUGHWISE
PLUMASSIER
PLUNDERING
POLITICIAN
POLITICIZE
POLYGAMIST
POLYMERIZE
POLYNESIAN
POLYTHEISM
POMERANIAN
POPULARITY
POPULARIZE
POPULATION
PORLOCKING
PORTIONIST
POSITIVIST
POSSESSION
POSSESSIVE
POSTCHAISE
POSTILLION
POSTLIMINY
POSTSCRIPT
PRAEMUNIRE
PRAETORIAN
PRAETORIUM
PRAGMATISM
PRAGMATIST
PRECAUTION
PREDESTINE
PREDICTION
PREHENSILE
PRELECTION
PRESSURIZE
PRETENSION
PREVAILING
PREVENTION
PREVENTIVE
PRIMORDIAL
PRINCIPIUM
PROCEEDING
PROCESSING
PROCESSION
PROCLIVITY
PRODUCTION
PRODUCTIVE
PROFESSION
PROFUNDITY
PROGESSION
PROJECTILE
PROJECTING
PROJECTION
PROMETHIUM
PROPENSITY
PROPERTIUS
PROPORTION
PROPULSION
PROSCENIUM
PROSERPINA
PROSERPINE
PROSPERINA
PROSPERITY
PROTECTION
PROTECTIVE
PROTERVITY
PROTRUSION
PROVERBIAL
PROVINCIAL
PRUDENTIAL
PSALTERIUM
PUBLISHING
PUMMELLING
PUNDIGRION
PURITANISM
PUTREFYING
PYRAGYRITE
PYROMANIAC
QUARANTINE
QUARTERING
RADICALISM
RAMPALLIAN
RAVENSBILL
REAPPRAISE
REASSURING
RECIDIVISM
RECIDIVIST
RECITATION
RECITATIVE
RECITATIVO
RECREATION
REDEMPTION
REDRUTHITE
REELECTION
REFLECTING
REFLECTION
REFLECTIVE
REFRACTION
REFRACTIVE
REFRESHING
REFUTATION
REGRESSION
REGRESSIVE
REGULARITY
REGULARIZE
REGULATION
RELATIVITY
RELAXATION
RELAXATIVE
RELEGATION
RELINQUISH
RELOCATION
REMONETISE
RENOVATION
REORGANIZE
REPARATION
REPERTOIRE
REPETITION
REPETITIVE
REPRESSION
REPRESSIVE
REPUTATION
RESEMBLING
RESOLUTION
RESOUNDING
RESPECTING
RESPECTIVE
RESPONSIVE
RESUMPTION
RETINALITE
RETRACTION
RETRAINING
RETREATING
REVELATION
REVITALIZE
REVIVALIST
REVOCATION
REVOLUTION
RHAPSODISE
RHAPSODIZE
RHEUMATICS
RHEUMATISM
RIGELATION
ROISTERING
ROLLICKING
ROSANILINE
ROSEMALING
ROTHSCHILD
RUDOLPHINE
RUMBULLION
RUMINATION
RUMINATIVE
RUPESTRIAN
RUPICOLINE
SACCHARIDE
SACCHARINE
SADDLEBILL
SALIVATION
SALPINGIAN
SALUTATION
SAMARSKITE
SANATORIUM
SANCTIFIED
SANCTITIES
SANDERLING
SANITARIUM
SANITATION
SATISFYING
SATURATION
SAUROPSIDA
SAXICOLINE
SBUDDIKINS
SCANDALISE
SCANDALIZE
SCARLATINA
SCARLETINA
SCATTERING
SCEPTICISM

SCHOOLGIRL
SCOOTERIST
SCREECHING
SCRIBBLING
SCROUNGING
SCRUTINISE
SCRUTINIZE
SCURRILITY
SECRETAIRE
SECULARIZE
SECURITIES
SELEGILINE
SENATORIAL
SENSUALITY
SEPARATION
SEPARATISM
SEPARATIST
SEPTENNIAL
SEPTUAGINT
SEQUENTIAL
SERPENTINE
SEXAGESIMA
SEXOLOGIST
SHAMPOOING
SHATTERING
SHELDONIAN
SHERARDISE
SHIMMERING
SHOESTRING
SHORTENING
SHROVETIDE
SHUDDERING
SIDERATION
SILVERBILL
SILVERFISH
SILVERSIDE
SIMILARITY
SIMPLICITY
SIMULATING
SIMULATION
SINARCHIST
SINARQUIST
SKEPTICISM
SKINDIVING
SKUPSHTINA
SLUMBERING
SMARAGDINE
SMATTERING
SNIGGERING
SNORKELING
SNOWMOBILE
SOLIDARITY
SOLIFIDIAN
SOLUBILITY
SOMBRERITE
SOURDELINE
SPALLATION
SPARTACIST
SPEAKERINE
SPECIALISE
SPECIALIST
SPECIALITY
SPECIALIZE
SPENCERIAN
SPENSERIAN
SPERRYLITE
SPHALERITE
SPILLIKINS
SPIRKETING
SPOLIATION
SPOLIATIVE
SPOONERISM
SPRINGLIKE
SPRINGTIME
SPRINKLING
STAGGERING
STAGNATION
STALACTITE
STALAGMITE
STAMMERING
STANDPOINT
STANDSTILL
STAPHYLINE
STARVATION
STARVELING
STATISTICS
STAUROLITE
STEALTHILY
STENTORIAN
STEPHANITE
STICHARION
STIGMATISE
STIGMATIZE
STILLICIDE
STOUTHRIEF
STRACCHINO
STRAGGLING
STRAMONIUM
STRATEGIST
STREAMLINE
STREETWISE
STRYCHNINE
STULTIFIED
STUPEFYING
STYLISTICS
SUBHEADING
SUBJECTION
SUBJECTIVE
SUBMERSION
SUBMISSION
SUBMISSIVE
SUBREPTION
SUBSECTION
SUBSELLIUM
SUBSTATION
SUBTROPICS
SUBVENTION
SUBVERSION
SUBVERSIVE
SUCCEEDING
SUCCESSION
SUCCESSIVE
SUFFRAGIST
SUGGESTION
SUGGESTIVE
SUMMERTIME
SUNBATHING
SUPPORTING
SUPPORTIVE
SURFRIDING
SURPASSING
SURPRISING
SURREALISM
SURREALIST
SUSPENSION
SUSTAINING
SWAGGERING
SWALLOWING
SWEATSHIRT
SWEETENING
SWELTERING
SWORDSTICK
SYMPATHISE
SYMPATHIZE
SYMPHONIUM
SYNCRETISE
SYNTHESIZE
TABULATION
TAGLIARINI
TAILGATING
TAMBOURINE
TANGANYIKA
TANGENTIAL
TAPDANCING
TARPAULING
TARTRAZINE
TAXONOMIST
TECHNETIUM
TECHNICIAN
TELEVISION
TEMPTATION
TENNANTITE
TEPIDARIUM
TERRIFYING
TERTIARIES
TESCHENITE
THALASSIAN
THAUMASITE
THEODOLITE
THEOLOGIAN
THEOLOGISE
THEOLOGIST
THICKENING
THREADLIKE
THRENODIAL
THUMBIKINS
THUNDERING
TIMESAVING
TIROCINIUM
TOILETRIES
TOLERATION
TOPICALITY
TOPOLOGIST
TORBERNITE
TORRENTIAL
TORTELLINI
TOURMALINE
TRAMPOLINE
TRANSCRIBE
TRANSCRIPT
TRANSITION
TRANSITIVE
TRAUMATIZE
TRAVELLING
TRAVERTINE
TRECENTIST
TRICLINIUM
TRIDENTINE
TRINACRIAN
TRIPARTITE
TRISKELION
TRIVIALITY
TRIVIALIZE
TROCTOLITE
TROMBONIST
TROPHONIUS
TROTSKYITE
TURPENTINE
TYPESCRIPT
ULCERATION
UNASSUMING
UNAVAILING
UNBECOMING
UNBLINKING
UNBLUSHING
UNDERLYING
UNDERSHIRT
UNDERSKIRT
UNDERWRITE
UNDESCRIED
UNDULATING
UNDULATION
UNEDIFYING
UNFAMILIAR
UNFLAGGING
UNIFORMITY
UNINVITING
UNIVERSITY
UNLADYLIKE
UNOCCUPIED
UNOFFICIAL
UNSALARIED
UNSETTLING
UNSLEEPING
UNSWERVING
UNTHINKING
UNYIELDING
UPBRINGING
UPSTANDING
UROSTEGITE
USUCAPTION
USURPATION
VALIDATION
VANDERBILT
VARICOSITY
VARNISHING
VEGETARIAN
VEGETATION
VELITATION
VENERATION
VERMILLION
VINDICTIVE
VINEGARISH
VIROLOGIST
VIRTUOSITY
VISIBILITY
VISITATION
VOCABULIST
VOLATILITY
VOLUBILITY
VOLUTATION
WALDENSIAN
WALLACHIAN
WARRANDICE
WASSAILING
WATERSKIER
WELLSPRING
WESTERNIZE
WHEWELLITE
WHIRLYBIRD
WHISPERING
WHITTERICK
WINDOWSILL
WINTERTIME
WOLFRAMITE
WORTHWHILE
WRONGDOING
WUNDERKIND
WYCLIFFIAN
YELLOWGIRL
YGGDRASILL
ZAPOROGIAN
ZWITTERION
CHAPARAJOS
CHAPAREJOS
HALLELUJAH
BACKPACKER
BEAVERSKIN
BONESHAKER
BOOKMARKER
BOOTLICKER
BOOZINGKEN
BOUSINGKEN
CATCRACKER
CLOCKMAKER
COMSTOCKER
COPPERSKIN
CORNCOCKLE
CORNFLAKES
DOWNMARKET

DRESSMAKER
FIREWALKER
FIRTHSOKEN
FRITHSOKEN
GOATSUCKER
GRIDLOCKED
HALLMARKED
HAMESUCKEN
HAMSHACKLE
HANDPICKED
HITCHHIKER
HOMEWORKER
HOODWINKED
HUMPBACKED
ICEBREAKER
KENSPECKLE
LANDLOCKED
LAWBREAKER
LUMPSUCKER
MATCHMAKER
MERRYMAKER
MINEWORKER
MINIMARKET
MOSSBUNKER
NUTCRACKER
OUTSPECKLE
OVERWORKED
PAWNBROKER
PEACEMAKER
PENTELIKON
PERIWINKLE
PICKPOCKET
POCKMARKED
RAMSHACKLE
SEERSUCKER
SHOPWALKER
SILVERSKIN
SLAMMERKIN
TIEBREAKER
TRAFFICKER
UNDERTAKER
UNPROVOKED
WATCHMAKER
WOODPECKER
WOODWORKER
ABNORMALLY
ACETABULAR
ACETABULUM
ALLYCHOLLY
AMBARVALIA
ARISTOTLES
ASTRAGALUS
BAMBOOZLED
BANDERILLA
BANDERILLO
BARCAROLLE
BEDEVILLED
BEDRAGGLED
BESTSELLER
BIANNUALLY
BIENNIALLY
BLACKBULLY
BLISSFULLY
BOOKSELLER
BOTTICELLI
BREAKABLES
BROCATELLE
BUCEPHALUS
CAERPHILLY
CAMPANELLA
CANDELILLA
CAPITELLUM
CASCARILLA
CEREBELLUM
CHANCELLOR
CHAPFALLEN
CHEERFULLY
CHEMICALLY
CHINCHILLA
CHRONICLER
CHRONICLES
CHUCKWALLA
CINDERELLA
CIRCUMFLEX
CITRONELLA
CLAIRCOLLE
CLARABELLA
CLINICALLY
COCKABULLY
CODSWALLOP
COLOSSALLY
COMMUNALLY
CONCHIGLIE
CONCHIOLIN
CONTRAFLOW
CONTROLLER
CORNSTALKS
COUNCILLOR
COUNSELLOR
CRIMINALLY
CRITICALLY
CURRICULUM
DEMOISELLE
DÉSHABILLÉ
DIAGONALLY
DIDASCALIC
DIDUNCULUS
DIFFICULTY
DISCOBOLUS
DISHABILLE
DISLOYALTY
DISMANTLED
DISSEMBLER
DISSIMILAR
DOLICHOLIS
DOUBTFULLY
DREADFULLY
ELEGABALUS
EMMENTALER
EMPEDOCLES
ENCEPHALON
ENKEPHALIN
ERIOCAULON
ERYSIPELAS
ESCADRILLE
ESPADRILLE
ESPECIALLY
EUTRAPELIA
EVENTUALLY
EXOTICALLY
EXTERNALLY
FAITHFULLY
FENESTELLA
FISHSELLER
FONTANELLE
FONTICULUS
FONTINALIS
FOOTBALLER
FORCEFULLY
FRATICELLI
FRAXINELLA
FRINGILLID
FRUITFULLY
FUSTANELLA
FUSTANELLE
GARGOUILLE
GIBBERELLA
GOODFELLOW
GRACEFULLY
GRANADILLA
GRATEFULLY
GRENADILLA
GUATEMALAN
GUTTURALLY
HABITUALLY
HALFDOLLAR
HALLUBALOO
HARDBOILED
HAUSTELLUM
HECTICALLY
HEMOPHILIA
HEPTATHLON
HEROICALLY
HOMUNCULUS
HULLABALOO
HYPERBOLIC
HYPERDULIA
IMMORTELLE
INFERNALLY
INFORMALLY
INTERNALLY
IRONICALLY
JARGONELLE
JUDICIALLY
KATERFELTO
KINCHINLAY
KLEBSIELLA
LADYKILLER
LENTICULAR
LIBREVILLE
LINGULELLA
LONGFELLOW
LUPERCALIA
MANDEVILLE
MANZANILLA
MARGINALIA
MARGINALLY
MATERIALLY
MATERNALLY
MEADOWPLAN
MERCIFULLY
METHUSALEH
METHUSELAH
METROPOLIS
MONTICULUS
MORTADELLA
MOURNFULLY
MOZZARELLA
NATIONALLY
NECROPOLIS
NEWFANGLED
NICROSILAL
NOTIONALLY
OFFICIALLY
ORIGINALLY
OSTEOCOLLA
PADDYMELON
PAINKILLER
PANNICULUS
PARALLELED
PARAPHILIA
PARTICULAR
PASTORELLA
PATERNALLY
PEACEFULLY
PECCADILLO
PEELGARLIC
PENETRALIA
PENICILLIN
PENINSULAR
PENTATHLON
PERSEPOLIS
PERSONALLY
PETRONELLA
PHILATELIC
PHYSICALLY
PICCADILLY
PICCALILLI
PILLOWSLIP
PIRANDELLO
PLAYFELLOW
POETICALLY
PONCHIELLI
PONTICELLO
PORTCULLIS
POTENTILLA
POURPARLER
PRAXITELES
PRINCIPLED
PRINCIPLES
PRODIGALLY
PUNCTUALLY
QUESADILLA
QUIRINALIA
RANUNCULUS
RATIONALLY
RECONCILED
RHINOLALIA
RHOEADALES
RIGHTFULLY
RITORNELLE
RITORNELLO
ROCKABILLY
ROTTWEILER
SALMONELLA
SALTARELLO
SARCOCOLLA
SATURNALIA
SCHWARZLOT
SCORNFULLY
SCREENPLAY
SEGUIDILLA
SELFSTYLED
SERRADELLA
SERRADILLA
SERRASALMO
SGANARELLE
SHAMEFULLY
SHOPSOILED
SHRIEVALTY
SHRIVELLED
SIGNORELLI
SINSEMILLA
SKILLFULLY
SOFTBOILED
SOMERVILLE
SPECTACLED
SPECTACLES
SPIRACULUM
SPITEFULLY
SUGARALLIE
SURGICALLY
TACTICALLY
TARANTELLA
TASTEFULLY
TEETOTALER
TENDRILLED
TERMINALIA
TERMINALLY
TESTICULAR
THANKFULLY
TOCCATELLA
TORRICELLI
TOURBILLON
TRAGICALLY
TRANQUILLY
TRIANGULAR
TROPAEOLUM
TROUVAILLE
TRUSTFULLY

TRUTHFULLY
TUBERCULAR
TURRITELLA
TUTIVILLUS
UNDERVALUE
UNEQUALLED
UNEXAMPLED
UNREVEALED
UNRIVALLED
UNSCHOOLED
UNSHACKLED
VALLADOLID
VAUDEVILLE
VEGETABLES
VENEZUELAN
VERMICELLI
VERNACULAR
VERSAILLES
VERTICALLY
VESTIBULUM
VIBRACULUM
VICTUALLER
VILLANELLE
VULCANALIA
WASTEFULLY
WATCHFULLY
WATERCOLOR
WATERMELON
WEEDKILLER
WHOLESALER
WILDFOWLER
WILLYWILLY
WORKAHOLIC
WRONGFULLY
ABHIDHAMMA
ACCUSTOMED
ANASTIGMAT
ANTICLIMAX
ASTRONOMER
BACKGAMMON
BLASPHEMER
BONDSWOMAN
BRESSUMMER
CACODAEMON
CATACHUMEN
CATECHUMEN
CAVALRYMAN
CENTESIMAL
CHAIRWOMAN
CHILDERMAS
CHIRONOMIC
CLANSWOMAN
COUNTRYMAN
DAYDREAMER
DECAGRAMME
DISCLAIMER
DUODECIMAL
DUTCHWOMAN
ELECTROMER
ENGLISHMAN
ENGLISHMEN
EPIDIDYMUS
EXOTHERMIC
EXPRESSMAN
GEOTHERMAL
GROUNDSMAN
HARVESTMAN
HIGHWAYMAN
HORNRIMMED
HORSEWOMAN
HYPODERMIC
IRISHWOMAN
IRISHWOMEN
JACKHAMMER
JOURNEYMAN
KEMPERYMAN
KLOOTCHMAN
LAUNDROMAT
LEUCHAEMIA
LIGHTERMAN
LONGCHAMPS
MICHAELMAS
MIDSHIPMAN
MILITIAMAN
NEURILEMMA
NEUROLEMMA
NOBLEWOMAN
NURSERYMAN
OFTENTIMES
OPHTHALMIC
PARANORMAL
PATRONYMIC
PENTSTEMON
POLYPHEMUS
PROGRAMMER
RAILWAYMAN
ROBERDSMAN
ROBERTSMAN
SALESWOMAN
SARCOLEMMA
SCHOLAEMIA
SCOTSWOMAN
SERVICEMAN
SIMILLIMUM
STALHELMER
STRABISMUS
SUPERHUMAN
SUPERWOMAN
TOWNSWOMAN
TULARAEMIA
UNFATHOMED
UNINFORMED
UNREDEEMED
WEATHERMAN
WELSHWOMAN
WIDDICOMBE
WINDJAMMER
XEROSTOMIA
ABHORRENCE
ABORIGINAL
ABSTINENCE
ACCORDANCE
ADDITIONAL
ADMITTANCE
ALCHERINGA
ALDERMANLY
ALGOLAGNIA
ALLEGEANCE
ALLEGIANCE
ANAXIMENES
ANTIPHONAL
APPEARANCE
ASCENDANCY
ASCENDENCY
ASSISTANCE
ATTENDANCE
AXINOMANCY
BARRAMUNDA
BELLADONNA
BELONGINGS
BLANCMANGE
BORROWINGS
BRADYKININ
BRILLIANCE
CALCEDONIO
CALESCENCE
CALIFORNIA
CAMERLENGO
CAMERLINGO
CAMPAIGNER
CAPNOMANCY
CARTOMANCY
CASSUMUNAR
CATCHPENNY
CAVICORNIA
CHAMBRANLE
CHAMPIGNON
CHAPLAINCY
CHARDONNAY
CHEVISANCE
CHIROMANCY
CLEROMANCY
COELACANTH
COGNISANCE
COGNIZANCE
COMEDIENNE
COMPETENCE
COMPLIANCE
CONDIMENTS
CONDOLENCE
CONFERENCE
CONFIDANTE
CONFIDENCE
CONFLUENCE
CONNIVANCE
CONSCIENCE
CONSONANCE
CONSONANTS
CONSTRINGE
CONTINENCE
CONVENANCE
CONVEYANCE
COPARCENER
CORDWAINER
CORPULENCE
CORRIGENDA
CRAPULENCE
DEFEASANCE
DEFICIENCY
DEHISCENCE
DEPENDENCE
DEPENDENCY
DETERMINED
DETERRENCE
DEVOTIONAL
DIFFERENCE
DIFFIDENCE
DILETTANTE
DIMINUENDO
DIPSOMANIA
DISARRANGE
DISSIDENCE
DISSONANCE
DIVERGENCE
DIVISIONAL
DOLCEMENTE
DRUZHINNIK
EBULLIENCE
EFFICIENCY
EIGHTEENTH
ELECTRONIC
EMBLEMENTS
EMOLUMENTS
EXCELLENCE
EXCELLENCY
EXPECTANCY
EXPEDIENCE
EXPEDIENCY
EXPERIENCE
EXUBERANCE
FLATULENCE
FLORIBUNDA
FOOTPRINTS
FOREDAMNED
FORERUNNER
FOREWARNED
FOURTEENTH
FRACTIONAL
FRIGHTENED
FUNCTIONAL
GINGERSNAP
GODPARENTS
GONFANONER
GOVERNANCE
GRASSLANDS
GREENFINCH
GRIDIRONER
GUIDELINES
HANKYPANKY
HEADPHONES
HEPTAGONAL
HIEROMANCY
HIPPOMANES
HISTRIONIC
HOLOFERNES
HONEYBUNCH
HOOTANANNY
HOOTENANNY
HOOTNANNIE
HORNBLENDE
HYDROPONIC
IATROGENIC
IMPARLANCE
IMPATIENCE
IMPERSONAL
IMPORTANCE
IMPRUDENCE
INCUMBENCY
INDISTINCT
INDUCTANCE
INDULGENCE
INQUIRENDO
INSISTENCE
INSOLVENCY
INSURGENCY
INTESTINAL
INTESTINES
IRRATIONAL
JACKSTONES
JAGUARONDI
JAGUARUNDI
JOUYSAUNCE
LANSQUENET
LATTICINIO
LENTIGINES
LINEAMENTS
LIPIZZANER
LUXURIANCE
MAINPERNOR
MALIGNANCY
MASKANONGE
MASKINONGE
MAURITANIA
METHOMANIA
MISGIVINGS
MISOCAPNIC
MISTAKENLY
MOLENDINAR
MOLYBDENUM
MONOPHONIC
MONSTRANCE
NECROMANCY
NECTABANUS
NEGLIGENCE
NEWSAGENTS
NINETEENTH
NONALIGNED
NONONSENSE
NORTHERNER
NUDIBRANCH

OBSERVANCE
OBSIDIONAL
OCCASIONAL
OCCURRENCE
OFFBALANCE
OFFLICENCE
ORDONNANCE
ORIDINANCE
ORTHOGONAL
OUGHTLINGS
OUTBALANCE
OXYMORONIC
PAPIAMENTO
PARAPHONIA
PARASCENIA
PARISIENNE
PATHOGENIC
PENSIONNAT
PENTAGONAL
PENTATONIC
PENTIMENTO
PERMANENCE
PERMANENCY
PERSIENNES
PERSTRINGE
PERTINENCE
PESTILENCE
PETITIONER
PHENOMENAL
PHENOMENON
PHILOXENIA
PHOTOGENIC
PICCANINNY
PILLIWINKS
PINCHPENNY
POLYHYMNIA
PORTAMENTO
PREARRANGE
PRECEDENCE
PREFERENCE
PREPOTENCE
PRESCIENCE
PRESIDENCY
PREVALENCE
PREVENANCY
PROMINENCE
PROPAGANDA
PROVENANCE
PROVIDENCE
PUBESCENCE
PULSATANCE
PYCNOGONID
PYTHOGENIC
QUESTIONER
QUICKSANDS
QUIESCENCE
RAWINSONDE
RECOMMENCE
RECOMPENSE
RECURRENCE
REDUNDANCY
RELUCTANCE
REMITTANCE
REPENTANCE
REPUGNANCE
RESILIENCE
RESISTANCE
RESORCINOL
RESTRAINED
RESURGENCE
ROADRUNNER
SACROSANCT
SALICORNIA
SALMAGUNDI
SANDEMANIA
SCOTODINIA
SENESCENCE
SHORTRANGE
SICILIENNE
SLATTERNLY
SNAPHAUNCE
SNAPHAUNCH
SOMNOLENCE
SOUTHERNER
SPLANCHNIC
SPODOMANCY
SPONSIONAL
STONEHENGE
STRAITENED
STRINGENCY
STRINGENDO
STUBBORNLY
SUBLIMINAL
SUBMARINER
SUBSIDENCE
SUBTENANCY
SUFFERANCE
SUPERSONIC
SUPERTONIC
SUSTENANCE
SUZERAINTY
SYNTHRONUS
TELEPHONIC
TEMPERANCE
THERMIONIC
THIRTEENTH
THREATENED
THREEPENCE
THREEPENNY
TRAGACANTH
TRANSIENCE
TRUCULENCE
TUMESCENCE
TURBULENCE
ULTRASONIC
UNASSIGNED
UNCOMMONLY
UNCONFINED
UNDERLINEN
UNDERPANTS
UNHYGIENIC
UNLEAVENED
UNORIGINAL
UNREASONED
UNSEASONED
VALENTINES
VOCATIONAL
WAGEEARNER
WANDERINGS
WATERWINGS
WEIMARANER
WELLEARNED
ABSTEMIOUS
ACANACEOUS
ACCESSIONS
ACCLIVIOUS
ACEPHALOUS
ACROGENOUS
ADULTEROUS
AERUGINOUS
AFFETTUOSO
AFTERSHOCK
ALLPURPOSE
ALPENSTOCK
AMBLYSTOMA
AMBULATORY
AMPHIBIOUS
AMYGDALOID
ANADROMOUS
ANCIPITOUS
ANGLOPHOBE
ANTHOCLORE
ANTHROPOID
APTERYGOTA
ARENACEOUS
ARGOLEMONO
ARISTOLOGY
ARYTAENOID
ASPERSIONS
ASTOMATOUS
AURIFEROUS
AUSPICIOUS
AUSTRALORP
AUTECOLOGY
AUTOGENOUS
AUTONOMOUS
AVARICIOUS
AVVOGADORE
BACKSTROKE
BADDERLOCK
BALNEOLOGY
BARLEYCORN
BARRACOOTA
BASKETWORK
BATTAILOUS
BATTLEDOOR
BATTLEDORE
BITUMINOUS
BLACKSTONE
BLACKTHORN
BLOODSTOCK
BLOODSTONE
BLUETHROAT
BOISTEROUS
BOTHERSOME
BRAINSTORM
BREASTBONE
BREASTWORK
BRIDEGROOM
BRIDGETOWN
BROADCLOTH
BROADSWORD
BROKENDOWN
BROWNSTONE
BURDENSOME
BUTTONDOWN
BUTTONHOLE
CACUMINOUS
CADAVEROUS
CAESPITOSE
CALAMITOUS
CALCAREOUS
CAMPERDOWN
CANDYFLOSS
CANNELLONI
CAOUTCHOUC
CAPRICIOUS
CARDIOLOGY
CARMAGNOLE
CARPHOLOGY
CENSORIOUS
CENTROSOME
CHALCEDONY
CHAMAEROPS
CHAUDFROID
CHEESEWOOD
CHEIRONOMY
CHEQUEBOOK
CHERRYWOOD
CHINASTONE
CHITARRONE
CHITTAGONG
CHIVALROUS
CHLOROFORM
CHROMOSOME
CHRONOLOGY
CHURCHGOER
CINQUEFOIL
CIRCUITOUS
CIRRHOPODA
CLAVICHORD
CLEARSTORY
CLERESTORY
CLINGSTONE
COCCINEOUS
COCKERNONY
COETANEOUS
COLLARBONE
COLLEMBOLA
COLPOSCOPE
COMMODIOUS
COMPRADORE
COMPULSORY
CONCHOLOGY
CONCINNOUS
CONFERVOID
CONIFEROUS
CONSISTORY
CONTAGIOUS
CONTIGUOUS
CONTINUOUS
CONTRECOUP
COPPERNOSE
CORRESPOND
COTTONWOOD
COURAGEOUS
CRETACEOUS
CRISSCROSS
CTENOPHORA
CUDDLESOME
CUMBERSOME
CURVACEOUS
CUTTLEBONE
CYSTOSCOPY
DEFAMATORY
DELTIOLOGY
DEPILATORY
DEPOSITORY
DEROGATORY
DESPITEOUS
DIAPHANOUS
DICYNODONT
DIRECTIONS
DISAPPROVE
DISASTROUS
DISCOMFORT
DISCOMMODE
DISCOMPOSE
DISCOPHORA
DISHARMONY
DISSELBOOM
DONNYBROOK
DOORTODOOR
DRAKESTONE
DREARISOME
DUMBLEDORE
ELYTRIFORM
EMBERGOOSE
EMBRYOLOGY
ENDOGAMOUS
ENTOMOLOGY
ENTRYPHONE
EPANOPHORA
ETHEOSTOMA
EUPHONIOUS
EXPOSITORY
EXTRANEOUS
FACTITIOUS
FALDISTORY
FALLACIOUS

FALLINGOFF
FASTIDIOUS
FELICITOUS
FETTERLOCK
FICTITIOUS
FIDDLEWOOD
FLAGITIOUS
FLAMEPROOF
FLOORCLOTH
FLUGELHORN
FORTUITOUS
FREEMASONS
FROLICSOME
FULIGINOUS
FULLYGROWN
GANGRENOUS
GASTRONOME
GASTRONOMY
GELATINOUS
GENTLEFOLK
GEORGETOWN
GLUTTONOUS
GONORRHOEA
GRAMOPHONE
GRAPHOLOGY
GRASSROOTS
GRATUITOUS
GRAVESTONE
GREENCLOTH
GREGARIOUS
GRINDSTONE
GROUNDWORK
GUACHAMOLE
GYNECOLOGY
HAMMERLOCK
HARMONIOUS
HEADSTRONG
HELIOTROPE
HELLESPONT
HERBACEOUS
HETERODOXY
HIEROSCOPY
HIPPODROME
HORRENDOUS
HOUSEPROUD
HYPOGAEOUS
ICONOSCOPE
IMMUNOLOGY
IMPERVIOUS
INCAUTIOUS
INCESTUOUS
INDECOROUS
INDIGENOUS
INFECTIOUS
INGLORIOUS
INHIBITORY
INIQUITOUS
INTERPHONE
JABBERWOCK
KILMARNOCK
KNIGHTHOOD
KNOCKABOUT
LABORATORY
LACHRYMOSE
LANGUOROUS
LANIGEROUS
LASCIVIOUS
LEGUMINOUS
LIBIDINOUS
LICENTIOUS
LIKELIHOOD
LIVELIHOOD
LOCKERROOM
LOGORRHOEA
LOQUACIOUS
LUGUBRIOUS
MACKINTOSH
MACROBIOTE
MAIDENHOOD
MALACOLOGY
MALODOROUS
MANDRAGORA
MARVELLOUS
MARYLEBONE
MASCARPONE
MASTECTOMY
MASTERWORT
MATTERHORN
MEDDLESOME
MELANCHOLY
MELOCOTOON
MEMBRANOUS
MENDACIOUS
MENORRHOEA
METICULOUS
METTLESOME
MICROPHONE
MICROSCOPE
MILLEFIORI
MINERALOGY
MINESTRONE
MINUTEBOOK
MIRACULOUS
MISERICORD
MISHNAYOTH
MONILIFORM
MONOCHROME
MONOECIOUS
MONOGAMOUS
MONOTONOUS
MONTESSORI
MORDACIOUS
MORIGEROUS
MORPHOLOGY
MOTHERHOOD
MUSICOLOGY
MYRIOSCOPE
MYSTERIOUS
NARROWBOAT
NEEDLEWORK
NEFANDROUS
NESSELRODE
NETHERMOST
NINCOMPOOP
NOUAKCHOTT
NUTRITIOUS
OBLIGATORY
OBSEQUIOUS
ODDFELLOWS
ODONTOLOGY
OLEAGINOUS
OLERACEOUS
OMBROPHOBE
OMNIVOROUS
ORCHIDEOUS
ORTHOPNOEA
OSCULATORY
OUTPERFORM
OUTRAGEOUS
PALINDROME
PALMERWORM
PANTALOONS
PANTOSCOPE
PARATROOPS
PARENTHOOD
PARTHENOPE
PEAUDESOIE
PENSIEROSO
PEPPERCORN
PEPPERWORT
PERDENDOSI
PERDITIOUS
PEREMPTORY
PERFIDIOUS
PERMAFROST
PERNICIOUS
PERSEPHONE
PHOTODIODE
PHRENOLOGY
PHYSIOLOGY
PIGEONHOLE
PITCHSTONE
PLEROPHORY
PLOUGHBOTE
POCKETBOOK
POGONOTOMY
POLYCHROME
POLYGAMOUS
PONEROLOGY
PORRACEOUS
PORTENTOUS
POSTHUMOUS
PRATINCOLE
PRECARIOUS
PRECOCIOUS
PRECURSORY
PREDACIOUS
PREDISPOSE
PREDNISONE
PREHISTORY
PRESUPPOSE
PRETINCOLE
PRIESTHOOD
PRODIGIOUS
PROMISSORY
PROMONTORY
PROPITIOUS
PROSPEROUS
PROVISIONS
PSEPHOLOGY
PSYCHOLOGY
PSYCHOPOMP
PUCKERWOOD
PUGNACIOUS
QUARTEROON
QUEENSTOWN
QUICKTHORN
RAVENSTONE
REBELLIOUS
REFRACTORY
RENDEZVOUS
REPOSITORY
RHEUMATOID
RHINESTONE
RIDICULOUS
RIDINGHOOD
ROBUSTIOUS
ROUNDABOUT
ROUSEABOUT
ROUSTABOUT
RUBIGINOUS
RUTHERFORD
SACCHAROID
SALUBRIOUS
SANDALWOOD
SARMENTOUS
SAVONAROLA
SAXICOLOUS
SCANDALOUS
SCANDAROON
SCAPHOPODA
SCHOOLBOOK
SCRUPULOUS
SCURRILOUS
SDRUCCIOLA
SEISMOLOGY
SEQUACIOUS
SETTERWORT
SHELLSHOCK
SHELLYCOAT
SHOCKPROOF
SHOVELNOSE
SISTERHOOD
SKETCHBOOK
SLANDEROUS
SNAKESTONE
SNEEZEWOOD
SOLICITOUS
SOUNDPROOF
SOUSAPHONE
SPATCHCOCK
SPECTATORS
SPELEOLOGY
SPIDERWORT
SPIRITUOUS
SPITCHCOCK
SPOILSPORT
SPONGIFORM
SPRINGBOKS
STEREOTOMY
STERTEROUS
STERTOROUS
STILLIFORM
STOREFRONT
STRABOTOMY
STREPITOSO
STROGANOFF
STRONGHOLD
STRONGROOM
STROPHIOLE
STUPENDOUS
SULPHUROUS
SUPERSTORE
SUSPICIOUS
SWEDENBORG
SYNONYMOUS
TABLECLOTH
TABLESPOON
TAMPERFOOT
TANGLEFOOT
TAPERECORD
TECHNOLOGY
TEINOSCOPE
TELEOSTOME
TENDERFOOT
TENDERLOIN
TENTERHOOK
TESTACEOUS
THALLIFORM
THIXOTROPY
THREADWORM
THREESCORE
THROUGHOUT
THUNDEROUS
TIMBROLOGY
TOUCHSTONE
TOXICOLOGY
TRADITIONS
TRAITOROUS
TRAJECTORY
TRANSITORY
TRAVANCORE
TREMENDOUS
TRENCHMORE
TRICHOLOGY
TROUBADOUR
TUMBLEDOWN
TUMULTUOUS
TURTLEDOVE
UBIQUITOUS

ULTRONEOUS
UNDERCROFT
UNDERFLOOR
UNDERSCORE
UNDERSTOOD
UNGRACIOUS
UPROARIOUS
VIBRAPHONE
VIBRATIONS
VICTORIOUS
VILLAINOUS
VIVIPAROUS
VOCIFEROUS
VOLUMINOUS
VOLUPTUOUS
VORAGINOUS
WATERFRONT
WATERPROOF
WATERSPOUT
WATTLEWORK
WHEATSTONE
WHIGGAMORE
WHITETHORN
WICKERWORK
WITGATBOOM
YELLOWROOT
YELLOWWOOD
ZABAGLIONE
ZEUGLODONT
ALLOTROPIC
ANASTROPHE
APOCALYPSE
APOSTROPHE
ARCHETYPAL
AREOGRAPHY
ARISTIPPUS
ARTOCARPUS
BOOKKEEPER
BRACHIOPOD
BUCKJUMPER
CACOGRAPHY
CATAWAMPUS
CEPHALOPOD
CHAMBERPOT
CHICKENPOX
CHIMNEYPOT
CHINQUAPIN
CHRYSIPPUS
CLODHOPPER
CORNUCOPIA
DEMOGRAPHY
DOORKEEPER
DUKKERIPEN
EMMETROPIA
EPISTROPHE
FROGHOPPER
GAMEKEEPER
GASTEROPOD
GOALKEEPER
GYMNOSOPHY
GYROSCOPIC
HOLOGRAPHY
INTERLOPER
JACKANAPES
LAEOTROPIC
LANDLOUPER
LEAFHOPPER
LIMITROPHE
LOCKKEEPER
MALAPROPOS
METACARPAL
METACARPUS
MUDSKIPPER
NARCOLEPSY
NYCTALOPIA
OSTEOLEPIS
OVERSUPPLY
PARTICIPLE
PASIGRAPHY
PEDIPALPUS
PHILOSOPHY
PHYLLIOPOD
PLIOHIPPUS
PRESBYOPIA
PROTANOPIC
PYROGRAPHY
RHEOTROPIC
SANDGROPER
SHOPKEEPER
SHOWJUMPER
SKYSCRAPER
SNOWCAPPED
STENOTYPER
STOMATOPOD
STRATHSPEY
TELEGRAPHY
TELESCOPIC
THROUGHPUT
TIMEKEEPER
TOLLKEEPER
TOPOGRAPHY
TOUCHPAPER
TRITANOPIA
TYPOGRAPHY
WASTEPAPER
WITSNAPPER
WORSHIPPER
ANTIMASQUE
BLOTTESQUE
CATAFALQUE
CHAUTAUQUA
COMMUNIQUÉ
EUROCHEQUE
HUMORESQUE
MARTINIQUE
MONEGASQUE
MOZAMBIQUE
PICARESQUE
ROMANESQUE
STATUESQUE
ADIAPHORON
ADVENTURER
ADVERSARIA
AFTERBIRTH
AFTERWARDS
ALCAICERIA
ALCYONARIA
ALEXANDRIA
ALLOSAURUS
ALLOSTERIC
AMBULACRUM
AMPHOTERIC
AMPLEFORTH
ARISTOCRAT
ASYMMETRIC
AVANTGARDE
AVICULARIA
BARBITURIC
BARLEYBREE
BAROMETRIC
BEHAVIORAL
BEWILDERED
BIJOUTERIE
BIPINNARIA
BLACKBERRY
BRICKWORKS
BUREAUCRAT
CAMPESTRAL
CAMSTEERIE
CANEPHORUS
CARDIOGRAM
CATTLEGRID
CHILDBIRTH
CLOISTERED
CLOUDBERRY
CLOUDBURST
COCHLEARIA
COCKALORUM
COLLATERAL
CONCENTRIC
CONFEDERAL
CONSIDERED
CORNSTARCH
CORROBOREE
CORTADERIA
CROCKFORDS
CROTALARIA
CRYOPHORUS
CRYPTOGRAM
DARKHAIRED
DECAHEDRON
DECIPHERED
DEPARTURES
DIELECTRIC
DINANDERIE
DIPHTHERIA
DISCOLORED
DISCOVERER
DISFIGURED
DISINHERIT
DISORDERED
DISORDERLY
DUCKBOARDS
EARTHWORKS
EGOCENTRIC
ELDERBERRY
EMBITTERED
EMPLASTRUM
ENRAPTURED
EPIDENDRUM
EURYPTERUS
FAIRHAIRED
FAMILIARLY
FINISTERRE
FORTINBRAS
FRONTWARDS
GAULTHERIA
GENERATRIX
GEOCENTRIC
GOOSEBERRY
GROCETERIA
GUTTIFERAE
HALFHOURLY
HALFYEARLY
HEMICHORDA
HEMIHEDRON
HENCEFORTH
HEPTAMERON
HERESIARCH
HOBBYHORSE
HOLOSTERIC
HYPAETHRAL
HYPAETHRON
ICOSANDRIA
IMPRESARIO
IMPROPERLY
INDENTURES
INTERFERER
INTERFERON
INTERMARRY
JIGGAMAREE
KENILWORTH
KETTLEDRUM
KILOMETRES
KLANGFARBE
KNOBKERRIE
KOOKABURRA
LITHOMARGE
LIVERWURST
LOGANBERRY
MACROCARPA
MALINGERER
MARQUETRIE
MESENTERON
METALLURGY
METATHERIA
MINDERERUS
MONOPTERON
MONOPTEROS
MONTEVERDI
MONTSERRAT
MOSASAUROS
NEIGHBORLY
NETTLETREE
NORTHWARDS
OCTAHEDRON
ORCHESTRAL
OVERCHARGE
PAEDIATRIC
PALAESTRAL
PALLBEARER
PANJANDRUM
PARAMETRIC
PARARTHRIA
PATISSERIE
PECULIARLY
PENTAMERON
PENTETERIC
PERIPHERAL
PERSICARIA
PESCADORES
PHOSPHORUS
PHYSIOCRAT
PIANOFORTE
POLYHEDRON
PONTEDERIA
PROCEDURAL
PROTAGORAS
PYROPHORUS
PYTHAGORAS
QUERCITRON
RACECOURSE
RADIOLARIA
RANDLETREE
RANNELTREE
RANNLETREE
RANTLETREE
RATTLETRAP
RAWSTHORNE
REGISTERED
RHINOCEROS
ROTISSERIE
SAGITTARIA
SCHIPPERKE
SCRIPTURAL
SCRIPTURES
SEPARATRIX
SEPULCHRAL
SHAGHAIRED
SIDEBOARDS
SIGILLARIA
SIMULACRUM
SINGULARLY
SKEUOMORPH
SMORREBROD
SOPHOMORIC
SOUTHWARDS
SQUIREARCH
STEELWORKS
STILLBIRTH

STONYHURST
STOUTHERIE
STRATOCRAT
STRAWBERRY
STREAMERED
STRUCTURAL
STRULDBRUG
SUPERCARGO
TALEBEARER
TECHNOCRAT
THALESTRIS
THALICTRUM
THUMBSCREW
TOCOPHEROL
TOPSYTURVY
TRANSVERSE
TRILATERAL
TROCHOTRON
UNANSWERED
UNCULTURED
UNDECLARED
UNDERBURNT
UNDERWORLD
UNDETERRED
UNDOCTORED
UNEXPLORED
UNFETTERED
UNFLAVORED
UNHAMPERED
UNICAMERAL
UNILATERAL
UNIMPAIRED
UNINSPIRED
UNLETTERED
UNMANNERED
UNMANNERLY
UNNUMBERED
UNPREPARED
WANDSWORTH
WATERBORNE
WATERWORKS
WENTLETRAP
WORDSWORTH
YOUNGBERRY
YTHUNDERED
ZOANTHARIA
ADVERTISER
AFRORMOSIA
AFTERTASTE
ALBIGENSES
ALMSHOUSES
AMANUENSIS
AMBLYOPSIS
AMPELOPSIS
ANACHARSIS
ANCHYLOSIS
ANESTHESIA
ANTISEPSIS
ANTITHESIS
APHAERESIS
APOTHEOSIS
ASBESTOSIS
ATELEIOSIS
AUTHORISED
AUTOPLASTY
BABESIASIS
BABIROUSSA
BAGASSOSIS
BARBAROSSA
BIPARTISAN
BRAGADISME
CAMBRENSIS
CARELESSLY
CATASTASIS
CAUTIOUSLY
CHEMONASTY
COMPARISON
COMPRESSED
COMPRESSOR
CONVALESCE
COUSCOUSOU
DECOMPOSED
DIAGENESIS
DIAPEDESIS
DICKCISSEL
DISHONESTY
DISTRESSED
DOSTOEVSKY
DRAWCANSIR
DUNIWASSAL
ECCHYMOSIS
ECTHLIPSIS
EFFERVESCE
ENANTIOSIS
ENDOSMOSIS
ENORMOUSLY
ENTREMESSE
EUTHANASIA
FABULOUSLY
FEARLESSLY
FERTILISED
FERTILISER
FLINDERSIA
FRAMBOESIA
FRANCHISEE
FRANCHISOR
GALVANISER
GENEROUSLY
GLORIOUSLY
GORGEOUSLY
GOVERNESSY
GRACIOUSLY
HEEDLESSLY
HELPLESSLY
HOPELESSLY
HUMOROUSLY
HYDROLYSIS
HYPOTHESIS
HYSTERESIS
ICHTHYOSIS
ILLADVISED
IMPROVISED
INDISPOSED
LEDERHOSEN
LEONTIASIS
LISTLESSLY
LYCHNAPSIA
MARSHALSEA
MATELLASSE
METALEPSIS
METAPLASIS
METATARSAL
METATARSUS
METATHESIS
MICRONESIA
MONILIASIS
MUSSORGSKY
MUTINOUSLY
NATHELESSE
NONPLUSSED
OROGENESIS
OSMIDROSIS
PADAREWSKI
PAINLESSLY
PARACELSUS
PARAENESIS
PARAGLOSSA
PARAPHYSIS
PATRONISED
PERIEGESIS
PERILOUSLY
PHLEGMASIA
PHOLIDOSIS
PHOTONASTY
PITYRIASIS
PLATINISED
PREVIOUSLY
PROAIRESIS
PROSTHESIS
PRZEWALSKI
RAVENOUSLY
RECKLESSLY
RECOGNISED
RECRUDESCE
RESERVISTS
RESTLESSLY
RICHARDSON
RIGOROUSLY
ROWLANDSON
RUMBLOSSOM
RUTHLESSLY
SANDINISTA
SANFORISED
SANNAYASIN
SCLERIASIS
SCOMBRESOX
SEDULOUSLY
SENSUOUSLY
SPECIOUSLY
SPOTLESSLY
SPURIOUSLY
STABILISER
STEPHENSON
STERILISER
STONEMASON
STRAVINSKY
STUDIOUSLY
STYLOPISED
SUNGLASSES
SUPERVISED
SUPERVISOR
SUPPRESSED
SUPPRESSOR
SYNAERESIS
SYNEIDESIS
SYNOSTOSIS
SYNTERESIS
TACTLESSLY
TANNHAUSER
TATPURUSHA
TEICHOPSIA
THELLUSSON
THROMBOSIS
TILLANDSIA
TIRELESSLY
TOOTHPASTE
TORTUOUSLY
TRANSPOSED
TRESPASSER
TYRANNISED
UBERMENSCH
UNCTUOUSLY
UNLICENSED
UROPOIESIS
VIGOROUSLY
VIRTUOUSLY
WILLIAMSON
WISHYWASHY
ZOOTHAPSIS
ABSTRACTED
ABUNDANTLY
ACCIDENTAL
ACCREDITED
ACHROMATIC
ACQUAINTED
ACROAMATIC
ADMINISTER
AFFILIATED
ALMACANTAR
ALMUCANTAR
ALTERNATOR
ALTRUISTIC
AMBOCEPTOR
AMRITATTVA
ANACLASTIC
ANACOUSTIC
ANACRUSTIC
ANCHORETIC
ANEMOMETER
ANESTHETIC
ANTIADITIS
ANTIBIOTIC
ANTIMATTER
ANTIPROTON
ANTIQUATED
ANTISEPTIC
ANTISTATIC
ANTITHETIC
APOLAUSTIC
APOLOGETIC
APOPEMPTIC
APOPLECTIC
APOSEMATIC
APPARENTLY
APPLICATOR
AQUAFORTIS
ARAGONITES
ARBITRATOR
ARITHMETIC
ARROGANTLY
ASPIDISTRA
ASSOCIATED
ASTIGMATIC
ATRAMENTAL
AUTOCRATIC
BABYSITTER
BACCHANTES
BALIBUNTAL
BANDMASTER
BANKRUPTCY
BARCHESTER
BAREFOOTED
BASSINGTON
BENEFACTOR
BLACKWATER
BLANQUETTE
BLUEBOTTLE
BLUEMANTLE
BOUILLOTTE
BREAKWATER
BRONCHITIC
BRONCHITIS
BUCCINATOR
BURLINGTON
CACOMISTLE
CALCULATED
CALCULATOR
CALEFACTOR
CANECUTTER
CAPODASTRO
CAPTIVATED
CARBURETOR
CASSOLETTE
CATALECTIC
CATALEPTIC
CELEBRATED
CELLULITIS
CENTILITER
CENTILITRE
CENTIMETER

CENTIMETRE
CHAMBERTIN
CHATTERTON
CHECKLATON
CHESTERTON
CHICHESTER
CLEARWATER
CLUMPERTON
COHERENTLY
COLCHESTER
COLLIMATOR
COLLOCUTER
COMPARATOR
COMPETITOR
COMPOSITOR
CONGENITAL
CONSPECTUS
CONSTANTAN
CONSTANTIA
CONSTANTLY
CONTRACTOR
CONVOLUTED
COPESETTIC
COPYWRITER
CORRUGATED
CORRUGATOR
CORYBANTES
CORYBANTIC
COVENANTER
CUCULLATED
CUCURBITAL
CULTIVATED
CULTIVATOR
CYBERNETIC
DEADNETTLE
DECOLLATOR
DEEPSEATED
DEMOCRATIC
DEMOCRITUS
DERMATITIS
DESECRATED
DESICCATED
DEVASTATED
DIACAUSTIC
DIAGNOSTIC
DIASTALTIC
DILIGENTLY
DIOPHANTOS
DIPLOMATIC
DISCREETLY
DISGRUNTLE
DISHEARTEN
DISJOINTED
DISPIRITED
DISQUIETED
DISSIPATED
DISTINCTLY
DISTRACTED
DOCIMASTIC
DOLICHOTUS
DRACONITES
DREIKANTER
DRINKWATER
DUPLICATOR
ECCOPROTIC
ELIMINATOR
ELOQUENTLY
EMBLEMATIC
ENCLOISTER
ENHYDRITIC
EPENTHETIC
EPIDEICTIC
EPIGENETIC
EPIGLOTTIS
EPIPLASTRA
EPISPASTIC
EPROUVETTE
ESCHAROTIC
ETEOCRETAN
EUCALYPTUS
EUDIOMETER
EULOGISTIC
EVAPORATED
EXONERATED
EXPLICITLY
FASCINATED
FASCINATOR
FATALISTIC
FEUILLETON
FIANCHETTO
FIBROSITIS
FILIBUSTER
FLAGRANTLY
FLIPPANTLY
FLUCTUATER
FOREBITTER
FORECASTER
FORECASTLE
FOURCHETTE
FRATERETTO
FREEBOOTER
FREEMARTIN
FREQUENTED
FREQUENTER
FREQUENTLY
FRESHWATER
FRUSTRATED
FUTURISTIC
GALRAVITCH
GALSWORTHY
GENEVRETTE
GINGIVITIS
GLOUCESTER
GONIOMETER
GRANULATED
GUBERNATOR
HALFSISTER
HARDCASTLE
HARRINGTON
HEADHUNTED
HEADHUNTER
HEADMASTER
HECTOLITRE
HEDONISTIC
HELICOPTER
HELIOLATER
HESITANTLY
HOLOPHOTAL
HOMEOPATHY
HORIZONTAL
HOTCHPOTCH
HUMANISTIC
HYDROMETER
HYGROMETER
IDEALISTIC
IGNORANTLY
IMBRICATED
IMPLICITLY
IMPOTENTLY
IMPRIMATUR
IMPUDENTLY
INARTISTIC
INCIDENTAL
INDECENTLY
INDIRECTLY
INDUMENTUM
INEBRIATED
INFATUATED
INFURIATED
INHERENTLY
INNOCENTLY
INQUISITOR
INSOLENTLY
INSTIGATOR
INSTRUCTED
INSTRUCTOR
INTEGRATED
INTERESTED
JACKBOOTED
JINGOISTIC
JUBILANTLY
JUGENDSTIL
KOEKSISTER
LACKLUSTER
LACKLUSTRE
LARYNGITIS
LAUNCESTON
LEAMINGTON
LEGALISTIC
LEGISLATOR
LILYWHITES
LINGUISTIC
LIQUIDATOR
LORDOLATRY
LOUISIETTE
MAISONETTE
MAKESYSTEM
MALAGUETTA
MALEFACTOR
MANCHESTER
MANIFESTLY
MARIOLATRY
MARIONETTE
MENINGITIS
METACENTRE
METHYLATED
MICROMETER
MIGNONETTE
MILEOMETER
MILLIMETER
MILLIMETRE
MISCHMETAL
MONUMENTAL
MORGANATIC
MORGANETTA
MYRINGITIS
NEAPOLITAN
NEGOTIATOR
NEWSCASTER
NEWSLETTER
NEWSWORTHY
NIHILISTIC
NOTEWORTHY
NOTORYCTES
NUMISMATIC
OBEDIENTLY
OBFUSCATED
OCCIDENTAL
OIREACHTAS
OMBROMETER
OPISOMETER
OPTIMISTIC
ORIGINATOR
ORNAMENTAL
OSCILLATOR
OSTEOPATHY
OSTROGOTHS
OTHERGATES
OVERTHETOP
OVIPOSITOR
OXYGENATOR
PADDINGTON
PALMERSTON
PARASTATAL
PARMACITIE
PARRAMATTA
PEASHOOTER
PEDIMENTAL
PENNISETUM
PENTAMETER
PERCOLATOR
PERFORATED
PERFORATOR
PERSECUTOR
PETULANTLY
PHLEGMATIC
PHLOGISTIC
PHLOGISTON
PLANCHETTE
PLEASANTLY
PLEASANTRY
PLEONASTIC
PLEXIMETER
POCAHONTAS
POCKMANTIE
POIGNANTLY
POIKILITIC
POINSETTIA
POLLINATED
PORTMANTLE
PORTMANTUA
POSTMASTER
PRECIPITIN
PREMARITAL
PREPARATOR
PREPOSITOR
PROCREATOR
PROCRUSTES
PROCURATOR
PROGENITOR
PROHIBITED
PROPAGATOR
PROPOSITUS
PROPRAETOR
PROPRIETOR
PROSCIUTTO
PROSECUTOR
PROSPECTOR
PROSPECTUS
PROSTHETIC
PROTRACTED
PROTRACTOR
PROVEDITOR
PSYCHIATRY
PTERYGOTUS
PYRACANTHA
QUIZMASTER
REGIMENTAL
REGIMENTED
REITERATED
REREDORTER
RESPIRATOR
RESTRICTED
REVERENTLY
RHAMPASTOS
RINGMASTER
RIPSNORTER
ROADWORTHY
RUDIMENTAL
RUMINANTIA
SACERDOTAL
SALOPETTES
SARSQUATCH
SCHISMATIC
SCHOLASTIC
SEGREGATED
SHACKLETON
SHEARWATER
SHECKLATON
SHOPLIFTER

SIDEROSTAT
SILHOUETTE
SIMPLISTIC
SONGWRITER
SPECULATOR
STEPSISTER
STOCHASTIC
STRAIGHTEN
STRAPONTIN
STRATIOTES
STRIDENTLY
SUBLIMATER
SUBSTRATUM
SUCCINCTLY
SYNCOPATED
SYPHILITIC
SYSTEMATIC
TABLANETTE
TACHOMETER
TASKMASTER
TEDDINGTON
TERRACOTTA
THEOCRITUS
THEREAFTER
THERMISTOR
THERMOSTAT
TIMESWITCH
TINTORETTO
TOILINETTE
TOLERANTLY
TONGUESTER
TOSSICATED
TOSTICATED
TRANSISTOR
TRANSLATED
TRANSLATOR
TRAVELATOR
TRAVOLATOR
TRIACONTER
TRIMSNITCH
TROCHANTER
TROMOMETER
TYPESETTER
TYPEWRITER
ULSTERETTE
UNACCENTED
UNAFFECTED
UNDEFEATED
UNDERWATER
UNDETECTED
UNDIGESTED
UNDISPUTED
UNEDUCATED
UNEXPECTED
UNIGENITUS
UNPROMPTED
UNREQUITED
UNROMANTIC
UNSCRIPTED
VARIEGATED
VEHEMENTLY
VENTILATOR
VIGILANTES
VIRULENTLY
WAINSCOTED
WASHINGTON
WELLINGTON
WHITEWATER
WINCEYETTE
WINCHESTER
WOFFINGTON
WRISTWATCH
XEROPHYTIC
ABERGLAUBE
AFTERHOURS
ALTAZIMUTH
AMPHIGOURI
AMPHINEURA
ANGUILLULA
ANSCHAUUNG
APICULTURE
BACKGROUND
BARRACOUTA
BATTENBURG
BELLAMOURE
BETELGEUSE
BETELGEUZE
BLOCKHOUSE
BLOODHOUND
BLOOMSBURY
BRASSBOUND
BREADFRUIT
BUTTERBUMP
CALLIATURE
CANTALOUPE
CANTELOUPE
CANTERBURY
CARICATURA
CARICATURE
CATALOGUER
CENTRIFUGE
CHARTREUSE
CHIRICAUNE
CIRCUMFUSE
COLORATURA
COMMISSURE
COMMIXTURE
CONCEPTUAL
CONJECTURE
CONSTITUTE
CONSUETUDE
CONTEXTUAL
CONTRIBUTE
CONVOLVUTE
COURTHOUSE
CRAIGFLUKE
CRAQUETURE
CUMMERBUND
DEBOUCHURE
DESBOROUGH
DISCLOSURE
DISTRIBUTE
DOVERCOURT
DUNDERFUNK
EMBOUCHURE
EMPFINDUNG
ENCOIGNURE
ENGENDRURE
EUTHYNEURA
EXACTITUDE
FAIRGROUND
FALSETRUTH
FIELDMOUSE
FILLIBRUSH
FLUTEMOUTH
FOREGROUND
FORFEITURE
GARGANTUAN
GETTYSBURG
GLASSHOUSE
GRAPEFRUIT
GREENHOUSE
GUESTHOUSE
HATEENOUGH
HEPTATEUCH
HEREABOUTS
HINDENBURG
HOMOSEXUAL
HOUSEBOUND
HYPOTENUSE
IMPOSTHUME
INAPTITUDE
INCUNABULA
INDIVIDUAL
INEPTITUDE
INTERCLUDE
IRRESOLUTE
JUDICATURE
KIESELGUHR
LAMBREQUIN
LASTMINUTE
LIGHTHOUSE
LITERATURE
LUXEMBOURG
MALMESBURY
MASSASAUGA
MISCONDUCT
MISFORTUNE
MULLIGRUBS
NICARAGUAN
NORTHBOUND
NOURRITURE
OFFTHECUFF
OVERSLAUGH
OVERSTRUNG
PAINTBRUSH
PANTAGRUEL
PENTATEUCH
PLAYGROUND
PORTSMOUTH
POWERHOUSE
PRICKLOUSE
PROSTITUTE
PUNCHDRUNK
QUADRATURA
QUEENSBURY
QUERSPRUNG
RAJPRAMUKH
RAVENSDUCK
RESCHEDULE
ROQUELAURE
ROUGHHOUSE
ROUNDHOUSE
SANCTITUDE
SCARAMOUCH
SCORDATURA
SIMILITUDE
SNAKEMOUTH
SOLICITUDE
SOMERSAULT
SOUBRIQUET
SOUTHBOUND
SPELLBOUND
SPISSITUDE
STEAKHOUSE
STOREHOUSE
STRASBOURG
SUBSTITUTE
SUBTERFUGE
TANTAMOUNT
TITARAKURA
TOOTHBRUSH
TOURNIQUET
TREKSCHUIT
TRILINGUAL
TRIPEHOUND
TROPOPAUSE
TURNAROUND
ULTRASOUND
UNDERSLUNG
UNDERSTUDY
UNPUNCTUAL
USQUEBAUGH
WANDERLUST
WHEELHOUSE
WOOLLYBUTT
WRAPAROUND
YARBOROUGH
ZUMBOORUCK
ADJECTIVAL
BARMITZVAH
CANTILEVER
DECENNOVAL
DEVASTAVIT
HOWSOMEVER
INTERWOVEN
LACCADIVES
MASKIROVKA
PARKLEAVES
PILEDRIVER
REDISCOVER
RIBOFLAVIN
SEMIQUAVER
SHORTLIVED
SPLITLEVEL
THEMSELVES
TIMESERVER
UNBELIEVER
UNDERCOVER
UNDESERVED
UNOBSERVED
UNRELIEVED
UNRESERVED
UNRESOLVED
VILLANOVAN
WANTHRIVEN
WATERLEVEL
WHATSOEVER
YOURSELVES
BRAINPOWER
CORNFLOWER
DISEMBOWEL
EXPRESSWAY
HORNBLOWER
HORSEPOWER
PASSAGEWAY
ROWDYDOWDY
SUPERPOWER
THIMBLEWIT
THROUGHWAY
WALLFLOWER
WATCHTOWER
WINDFLOWER
WITHDRAWAL
AMPHIMIXIS
BOBBYSOXER
ECHOPRAXIA
PARAPRAXIS
AERENCHYMA
AMPHICTYON
AMPHITRYON
ARACOSTYLE
BLEARYEYED
BRICKLAYER
CECIDOMYIA
CHERIMOYER
CYCLOSTYLE
EUPHROSYNE
GALLABIYAH
GALLABIYEH
HIEROGLYPH
HIPPOGRYPH
KSHATRIYAS
NEMATOCYST
OSTEOPHYTE
PALAEOTYPE
PARAGUAYAN
PARENCHYMA
PETROGLYPH
PHAENOTYPE

PLATELAYER
RHINOPHYMA
SAPROPHYTE
SOOTHSAYER
STEREOTYPE
STRATOCYST
TROGLODYTE
TROPOPHYTE
UNEMPLOYED
ANNUALIZED
BELSHAZZAR
BUMFREEZER
CHIMPANZEE
FERTILIZER
FOSSILIZED
HYPNOTIZED
INTERMEZZO
LIQUIDIZER
MECHANIZED
MORBIDEZZA
PALMATOZOA
PASSAMEZZO
PESTALOZZI
RECOGNIZED
SALMANAZAR
SCAMMOZZIS
SCHLIMAZEL
STABILIZER
STERILIZER
STRELITZIA
UNDERSIZED

10:9

ABORIGINAL
ABYSSINIAN
ACCIDENTAL
ACETABULAR
ACRONYCHAL
ADDITIONAL
ADJECTIVAL
ALECTORIAN
ALGONQUIAN
ALMACANTAR
ALMUCANTAR
ANALOGICAL
ANALYTICAL
ANARCHICAL
ANASTIGMAT
ANATOMICAL
ANDALUSIAN
ANTICLIMAX
ANTIMONIAN
ANTINOMIAN
ANTIOCHIAN
ANTIPHONAL
ANTIPODEAN
ANTISOCIAL
APOCRYPHAL
APOLLONIAN
ARAUCANIAN
ARCHETYPAL
ARIMASPIAN
ARISTOCRAT
ARTIFICIAL
ARUNDELIAN
ATHANASIAN
ATRAMENTAL
AUSTRALIAN
BABYLONIAN
BAHRAINIAN
BALBRIGGAN
BALIBUNTAL
BARMECIDAL
BARMITZVAH
BATRACHIAN
BEAUTICIAN
BEHAVIORAL
BELARUSIAN
BELSHAZZAR
BENEFICIAL
BIOLOGICAL
BIPARTISAN
BIRKENHEAD
BIRMINGHAM
BLUETHROAT
BONDSWOMAN
BOTTLEHEAD
BOURIGNIAN
BRIDGEHEAD
BUCKINGHAM
BUDGERIGAR
BUFFLEHEAD
BUREAUCRAT
CALEDONIAN
CALYDONIAN
CAMERONIAN
CAMPESTRAL
CANTABRIAN
CARDIOGRAM
CARNASSIAL
CARPATHIAN
CARTHUSIAN
CASSUMUNAR
CAVALRYMAN
CENTENNIAL
CENTESIMAL
CEREMONIAL
CHAIRWOMAN
CHARDONNAY
CHAUCERIAN
CHELTENHAM
CHILDERMAS
CIRCASSIAN
CISLEITHAN
CISTERCIAN
CLANSWOMAN
CLEMENCEAU
COLDSTREAM
COLLATERAL
COLLOQUIAL
COMMERCIAL
COMMONWEAL
CONCEPTUAL
CONFEDERAL
CONGENITAL
CONSTANTAN
CONTEXTUAL
COPPERHEAD
CORINTHIAN
COUNTRYMAN
COXCOMICAL
CREDENTIAL
CRISPBREAD
CRISPINIAN
CROTALIDAE
CRUSTACEAN
CRYPTOGRAM
CUCURBITAL
DECENNOVAL
DEMONIACAL
DEVOTIONAL
DIABOLICAL
DISSIMILAR
DISTRINGAS
DIVISIONAL
DOWNSTREAM
DUNDERHEAD
DUNIWASSAL
DUODECIMAL
DUTCHWOMAN
ECOLOGICAL
ECONOMICAL
ECUADORIAN
ECUMENICAL
ELECTRICAL
ELEUSINIAN
ELLIPTICAL
ENCYCLICAL
ENGLISHMAN
EQUATORIAL
EQUESTRIAN
ERYSIPELAS
ESCULAPIAN
ETEOCRETAN
EUSTACHIAN
EXPRESSMAN
EXPRESSWAY
FIGUREHEAD
FORINSECAL
FORTINBRAS
FRACTIONAL
FRANCISCAN
FRENETICAL
FRICANDEAU
FUNCTIONAL
FUNGICIDAL
GALIMATIAS
GALLABIYAH
GARGANTUAN
GENETHLIAC
GEOLOGICAL
GEOTHERMAL
GERMICIDAL
GILBERTIAN
GINGERSNAP
GRAMMARIAN
GROUNDSMAN
GUATEMALAN
GUTTIFERAE
HALFDOLLAR
HALLELUJAH
HAMMERHEAD
HANOVERIAN
HARVESTMAN
HEARTBREAK
HEPTAGONAL
HIGHWAYMAN
HISTORICAL
HOLOPHOTAL
HOMEOUSIAN
HOMOSEXUAL
HORIZONTAL
HORSEWOMAN
HYPAETHRAL
HYSTERICAL
IMMATERIAL
IMMEMORIAL
IMPERSONAL
INCIDENTAL
INDIVIDUAL
INDONESIAN
INDUSTRIAL
INTERNODAL
INTESTINAL
INTRAURBAN
IRISHWOMAN
IRRATIONAL
IRREMEDIAL
JOHNSONIAN
JOLTERHEAD
JOURNEYMAN
KARMATHIAN
KEMPERYMAN
KENTUCKIAN
KHIDMUTGAR
KINCHINLAY
KLOOTCHMAN
KSHATRIYAS
LAUNDROMAT
LAURENTIAN
LENTICULAR
LETTERHEAD
LIGHTERMAN
LITHUANIAN
LITURGICAL
LOGGERHEAD
LOGISTICAL
LUSITANIAN
MACEDONIAN
MADAGASCAN
MADAGASCAR
MAGNIFICAT
MAHOMMEDAN
MAINSTREAM
MALAYALAAM
MALTHUSIAN
MANAGERIAL
MANICHAEAN
MAXIMILIAN
MEADOWPLAN
MECHANICAL
MELANESIAN
MENECHMIAN
METACARPAL
METATARSAL
METHODICAL
METHUSELAH
MICHAELMAS
MIDLOTHIAN
MIDSHIPMAN
MILITIAMAN
MISCHMETAL
MOLENDINAR
MONTSERRAT
MONUMENTAL
MORISONIAN
MOUSTERIAN
MOUTHORGAN
MUTTONHEAD
NARROWBOAT
NATATORIAL
NEAPOLITAN
NEOTERICAL
NICARAGUAN
NICROSILAL
NIGGERHEAD
NOBLEWOMAN
NORTHSTEAD
NOSOCOMIAL
NURSERYMAN
OBSIDIONAL
OCCASIONAL
OCCIDENTAL
OIREACHTAS
ORATORICAL
ORCHESTRAL
ORNAMENTAL
ORTHOGONAL
OVERSPREAD
OZYMANDIAS
PALAESTRAL
PANAMANIAN
PARAGUAYAN
PARANORMAL
PARASTATAL
PARNASSIAN
PARTICULAR
PASSAGEWAY

PATAGONIAN
PEDESTRIAN
PEDIMENTAL
PENINSULAR
PENSIONNAT
PENTAGONAL
PERIODICAL
PERIPHERAL
PETRARCHAN
PHAELONIAN
PHENOMENAL
PHRENESIAC
PHYSIOCRAT
POCAHONTAS
POLITICIAN
POLYNESIAN
POMERANIAN
PONTIFICAL
PRAETORIAN
PREMARITAL
PRESENTDAY
PRIMORDIAL
PROCEDURAL
PROMETHEAN
PROPLITEAL
PROTAGORAS
PROVERBIAL
PROVINCIAL
PRUDENTIAL
PUNICACEAE
PYROMANIAC
PYTHAGORAS
RABBINICAL
RAILWAYMAN
RAMPALLIAN
RATTLETRAP
RECIPROCAL
REGIMENTAL
REPUBLICAN
REQUIESCAT
RHETORICAL
RHYTHMICAL
ROBERDSMAN
ROBERTSMAN
ROCKINGHAM
RUDIMENTAL
RUPESTRIAN
SABBATICAL
SACERDOTAL
SALESWOMAN
SALMANAZAR
SALPINGIAN
SCHOOLMAAM
SCOPELIDAE
SCOTSWOMAN
SCREENPLAY
SCRIPTURAL
SEEMLIHEAD
SENATORIAL
SEPTENNIAL
SEPULCHRAL
SEQUENTIAL
SERMONICAL
SERVICEMAN
SHANDRYDAN
SHELDONIAN
SHELLYCOAT
SHENANIGAN
SHISHKEBAB
SHORTBREAD
SHOVELHEAD
SIDEROSTAT
SIGNIFICAT
SIMMENTHAL
SLIPSTREAM
SOLIFIDIAN
SOPHOCLEAN
SPENCERIAN
SPENSERIAN
SPONSIONAL
SPORTSWEAR
SPRINGHAAS
STENTORIAN
STICKYBEAK
STRATOCRAT
STRUCTURAL
SUBLIMINAL
SUPERHUMAN
SUPERWOMAN
SWEETBREAD
SYMBOLICAL
TANAGRIDAE
TANGENTIAL
TECHNICIAN
TECHNOCRAT
TENRECIDAE
TESTICULAR
THALASSIAN
THEATRICAL
THEOLOGIAN
THERMOSTAT
THRENODIAL
THROUGHWAY
TORRENTIAL
TOWNSWOMAN
TRIANGULAR
TRILATERAL
TRILINGUAL
TRINACRIAN
TRYPTOPHAN
TUBERCULAR
TYRANNICAL
UNCRITICAL
UNFAMILIAR
UNICAMERAL
UNILATERAL
UNOFFICIAL
UNORIGINAL
UNPUNCTUAL
URTICACEAE
VEGETARIAN
VENEZUELAN
VERNACULAR
VILLANOVAN
VOCATIONAL
WALDENSIAN
WALLACHIAN
WAMPUMPEAG
WAPENSCHAW
WAPINSCHAW
WAPPENSHAW
WEATHERMAN
WELSHWOMAN
WENTLETRAP
WHEATSHEAF
WHILLYWHAW
WHOLEWHEAT
WIDESPREAD
WITHDRAWAL
WOODENHEAD
WYCLIFFIAN
YESTERYEAR
ZAPOROGIAN
ZIMBABWEAN
ZOOLOGICAL
ABERGLAUBE
ANGLOPHOBE
ANGWANTIBO
KLANGFARBE
MOUCHARABY
MULLIGRUBS
OMBROPHOBE
PARAMARIBO
TRANSCRIBE
WIDDICOMBE
ABHORRENCE
ABSTINENCE
ACCOMPLICE
ACCORDANCE
ACROBATICS
ADMITTANCE
ADRAMELECH
AEROBATICS
AESTHETICS
AFTERPIECE
AFTERSHOCK
AGONISTICS
ALLEGEANCE
ALLEGIANCE
ALPENSTOCK
AMPHIBRACH
ANTARCTICA
APPEARANCE
APPRENTICE
ARSMETRICK
ASARABACCA
ASCENDANCY
ASCENDENCY
ASSISTANCE
ATTENDANCE
AUTODIDACT
AXINOMANCY
BADDERLOCK
BAILIEWICK
BAILLIWICK
BALLISTICS
BANKRUPTCY
BIOPHYSICS
BIRTHPLACE
BLOODSTOCK
BOTTLENECK
BRILLIANCE
BROADPIECE
BROOMSTICK
CALESCENCE
CANDLEWICK
CANTATRICE
CANVASBACK
CAPNOMANCY
CARTOMANCY
CATAPHRACT
CHAPLAINCY
CHEVISANCE
CHIROMANCY
CLEROMANCY
COCKATRICE
COGNISANCE
COGNIZANCE
COMPETENCE
COMPLIANCE
CONDOLENCE
CONFERENCE
CONFIDENCE
CONFLUENCE
CONNIVANCE
CONSCIENCE
CONSONANCE
CONSPIRACY
CONTINENCE
CONTRADICT
CONVALESCE
CONVENANCE
CONVEYANCE
CORNSTARCH
CORPULENCE
COUNTERACT
CRAPULENCE
CROSSCHECK
CROSSPIECE
CRYOGENICS
DEFEASANCE
DEFICIENCY
DEGENERACY
DEHISCENCE
DENTIFRICE
DEPENDENCE
DEPENDENCY
DETERRENCE
DIALECTICS
DIFFERENCE
DIFFIDENCE
DISCONNECT
DISRESPECT
DISSERVICE
DISSIDENCE
DISSONANCE
DIVERGENCE
EBULLIENCE
EFFEMINACY
EFFERVESCE
EFFICIENCY
EPISTEMICS
ERGONOMICS
EVERYPLACE
EXCELLENCE
EXCELLENCY
EXPECTANCY
EXPEDIENCE
EXPEDIENCY
EXPERIENCE
EXUBERANCE
FANTASTICO
FETTERLOCK
FLATULENCE
GALRAVITCH
GEOPHYSICS
GERIATRICS
GOVERNANCE
GREENFINCH
GREENSTICK
GYMNASTICS
HACKMATACK
HALIEUTICS
HAMMERLOCK
HARMANBECK
HEPTATEUCH
HERESIARCH
HIEROMANCY
HONEYBUNCH
HOTCHPOTCH
HYDRAULICS
ILLITERACY
IMMACULACY
IMPARLANCE
IMPATIENCE
IMPORTANCE
IMPRUDENCE
INACCURACY
INADEQUACY
INCUMBENCY
INDELICACY
INDISTINCT
INDUCTANCE
INDULGENCE
INEFFICACY
INNERSPACE
INSISTENCE
INSOLVENCY
INSURGENCY
INTERSTICE

INTROSPECT
ISOMETRICS
JABBERWOCK
JOUYSAUNCE
KILMARNOCK
LEGITIMACY
LIMBERNECK
LUMBERJACK
LUXURIANCE
MAGISTRACY
MALIGNANCY
MATCHSTICK
MISCONDUCT
MONSTRANCE
MOUSEPIECE
MOUTHPIECE
NATTERJACK
NECROMANCY
NEGLIGENCE
NIGHTSTICK
NUCLEONICS
NUDIBRANCH
OBSERVANCE
OBSTETRICS
OCCURRENCE
OCHLOCRACY
OFFBALANCE
OFFLICENCE
ONOMASTICS
ORDONNANCE
ORIDINANCE
ORTHOPTICS
OUTBALANCE
PEDIATRICS
PENTATEUCH
PERMANENCE
PERMANENCY
PERTINENCE
PESTILENCE
PILGARLICK
PLUPERFECT
PLUTOCRACY
PONTEFRACT
PORNOCRACY
PRECEDENCE
PREFERENCE
PREPOTENCE
PRESCIENCE
PRESIDENCY
PREVALENCE
PREVENANCY
PROFLIGACY
PROMINENCE
PROVENANCE
PROVIDENCE
PUBESCENCE
PULSATANCE
QUIESCENCE
RAVENSDUCK
RECOMMENCE
RECRUDESCE
RECURRENCE
REDUNDANCY
RELUCTANCE
REMITTANCE
REPENTANCE
REPUGNANCE
RESILIENCE
RESISTANCE
RESURGENCE
RETROSPECT
RHEUMATICS
ROLANDSECK
RUBBERNECK
SACROSANCT
SADDLEBACK
SAMOTHRACE
SARSQUATCH
SCAPEGRACE
SCARAMOUCH
SENESCENCE
SHELLSHOCK
SILVERBACK
SMOKESTACK
SNAPHAUNCE
SNAPHAUNCH
SOMNOLENCE
SOUNDTRACK
SPATCHCOCK
SPITCHCOCK
SPODOMANCY
SQUIREARCH
STAGECOACH
STATISTICS
STATOCRACY
STRINGENCY
STYLISTICS
SUBCOMPACT
SUBSIDENCE
SUBTENANCY
SUBTROPICS
SUFFERANCE
SUPPLEJACK
SUSTENANCE
SWITCHBACK
SWORDSTICK
TEMPERANCE
THREEPENCE
TIMESWITCH
TOUCHPIECE
TRANSIENCE
TRIMSNITCH
TRUCULENCE
TUMESCENCE
TURBULENCE
TURTLENECK
UBERMENSCH
WARRANDICE
WHITTERICK
WOOLLYBACK
WRISTWATCH
YELLOWBACK
YELLOWJACK
ZUMBOORUCK
ADELANTADO
AFICIONADO
AFTERWARDS
AMARYLLIDS
ASAFOETIDA
AUTOSTRADA
AVANTGARDE
BALUSTRADE
BARRAMUNDA
CENTIGRADE
CIRRHOPODA
CONSUETUDE
CORRIGENDA
CROCKFORDS
CROSSROADS
DIMINUENDO
DISCOMMODE
DUCKBOARDS
EXACTITUDE
FLANCONADE
FLORIBUNDA
FLOWERBEDS
FRATRICIDE
FRONTWARDS
FUDDYDUDDY
GASCONNADE
GRASSLANDS
HEMICHORDA
HORNBLENDE
HOUSEMAIDS
INAPTITUDE
INDAPAMIDE
INEPTITUDE
INQUIRENDO
INTERCLUDE
ISONIAZIDE
JAGUARONDI
JAGUARUNDI
LANTHANIDE
LITHISTADA
MASQUERADE
MONTEVERDI
NATIONWIDE
NESSELRODE
NIGHTSHADE
NORTHWARDS
OPHICLEIDE
PARADOXIDE
PASQUINADE
PHOTODIODE
PROPAGANDA
QUICKSANDS
RAWINSONDE
RETROGRADE
ROCKSTEADY
ROWDYDOWDY
SACCHARIDE
SALMAGUNDI
SALTIGRADE
SANCTITUDE
SAUROPSIDA
SCAPHOPODA
SHROVETIDE
SIDEBOARDS
SILVERSIDE
SIMILITUDE
SOLICITUDE
SOUTHWARDS
SPISSITUDE
STILLICIDE
STRINGENDO
TAILORMADE
TARDIGRADE
TORQUEMADA
UNDERSTUDY
VELOCIPEDE
ABSTRACTED
ACCREDITED
ACCUSTOMED
ACHITOPHEL
ACQUAINTED
ADMINISTER
ADVENTURER
ADVERTISER
AFFILIATED
AFRICANDER
AHITHOPHEL
ALBIGENSES
ALCIBIADES
ALMSHOUSES
ALTOGETHER
AMPHIMACER
ANALPHABET
ANAXIMENES
ANEMOMETER
ANGURVADEL
ANNUALIZED
ANTIMATTER
ANTIQUATED
ARAGONITES
ARCHIMEDES
ARISTOTLES
ASSOCIATED
ASTEROIDEA
ASTONISHED
ASTROLOGER
ASTRONOMER
AUCTIONEER
AUSTRINGER
AUTHORISED
BABYSITTER
BACCHANTES
BACKHANDED
BACKHANDER
BACKPACKER
BACKSLIDER
BAMBOOZLED
BANDMASTER
BARCHESTER
BAREFOOTED
BAREHEADED
BARELEGGED
BARLEYBREE
BEARGARDEN
BEAUTIFIER
BEDCHAMBER
BEDCLOTHES
BEDEVILLED
BEDRAGGLED
BEEFBURGER
BELLWETHER
BERMOOTHES
BERSAGLIER
BESTSELLER
BEWILDERED
BIOGRAPHER
BLACKWATER
BLASPHEMER
BLASTOIDEA
BLEARYEYED
BLITZKRIEG
BOBBYSOXER
BOMBARDIER
BONDHOLDER
BONESHAKER
BOOKBINDER
BOOKKEEPER
BOOKMARKER
BOOKSELLER
BOOTLEGGER
BOOTLICKER
BOOZINGKEN
BOUSINGKEN
BRAINPOWER
BREAKABLES
BREAKWATER
BREASTFEED
BRESSUMMER
BRICKLAYER
BROADSHEET
BUCKJUMPER
BULLHEADED
BUMFREEZER
BUSHRANGER
CALAMANDER
CALCULATED
CALORIFIER
CAMPAIGNER
CANECUTTER
CANTILEVER
CAPTIVATED
CARABINEER
CARABINIER
CARCINOGEN
CARPENTIER
CARRAGHEEN

CARYATIDES
CATACHUMEN
CATALOGUER
CATCRACKER
CATECHUMEN
CELEBRATED
CENTILITER
CENTIMETER
CEREMONIES
CHALLENGER
CHANDELIER
CHAPFALLEN
CHARIOTEER
CHERIMOYER
CHICHESTER
CHIFFONIER
CHIMPANZEE
CHRONICLER
CHRONICLES
CHURCHGOER
CIRCUMFLEX
CIRRIPEDEA
CLASSIFIED
CLEARWATER
CLOCKMAKER
CLODHOPPER
CLOISTERED
COATHANGER
COCKCHAFER
COLCHESTER
COLLOCUTER
COLONNADED
COMMANDEER
COMPOUNDED
COMPRESSED
COMSTOCKER
CONDOTTIER
CONFOUNDED
CONSIDERED
CONTROLLER
CONVOLUTED
COPARCENER
COPENHAGEN
COPYHOLDER
COPYWRITER
CORDWAINER
CORNFLAKES
CORNFLOWER
COROMANDEL
CORROBOREE
CORRUGATED
CORYBANTES
COVENANTER
CROSSBREED
CROSSREFER
CUCULLATED
CUIRASSIER
CULTIVATED
CURRENCIES
DARKHAIRED
DAYDREAMER
DECIPHERED
DECOMPOSED
DEEPSEATED
DEPARTURES
DESECRATED
DESICCATED
DETERMINED
DEVASTATED
DICKCISSEL
DIMINISHED
DISBURTHEN
DISCLAIMER
DISCOLORED
DISCOVERER
DISEMBOWEL
DISENGAGED
DISFIGURED
DISHEARTEN
DISHWASHER
DISJOINTED
DISMANTLED
DISORDERED
DISPIRITED
DISQUIETED
DISSEMBLER
DISSIPATED
DISTRACTED
DISTRESSED
DOORKEEPER
DOWNMARKET
DRACONITES
DREIKANTER
DRESSMAKER
DRINKWATER
DUKKERIPEN
ECHINOIDEA
ELECTROMER
EMBITTERED
EMMENTALER
EMPEDOCLES
EMULSIFIER
ENCLOISTER
ENGLISHMEN
ENRAPTURED
ENTRENCHED
EPIMENIDES
EUDIOMETER
EVAPORATED
EVENHANDED
EVERGLADES
EXONERATED
FACILITIES
FAIRHAIRED
FALKLANDER
FARFETCHED
FASCINATED
FATALITIES
FEATHERBED
FERTILISED
FERTILISER
FERTILIZER
FILIBUSTER
FIREWALKER
FIREWARDEN
FIRTHSOKEN
FISHMONGER
FISHSELLER
FLOURISHED
FLUCTUATER
FLYCATCHER
FOOTBALLER
FOREBITTER
FORECASTER
FOREDAMNED
FOREFATHER
FOREFINGER
FOREGATHER
FORERUNNER
FOREWARNED
FORFEUCHEN
FORFOUGHEN
FOSSILIZED
FRANCHISEE
FRAUNHOFER
FREEBOOTER
FREEHANDER
FREEHOLDER
FREELANCER
FREELOADER
FREQUENTED
FREQUENTER
FRESHWATER
FRIGHTENED
FRITHSOKEN
FROGHOPPER
FROMANTEEL
FRUSTRATED
GALLABIYEH
GALVANISER
GAMEKEEPER
GEOGRAPHER
GINGERBEER
GLEEMAIDEN
GLENDOVEER
GLOUCESTER
GOALKEEPER
GOATSUCKER
GOLDDIGGER
GOLDFINGER
GONFANONER
GONIOMETER
GONORRHOEA
GRANULATED
GRIDIRONER
GRIDLOCKED
GUARANTEED
GUIDELINES
HACKBUTEER
HALFSISTER
HALLMARKED
HAMESUCKEN
HANDMAIDEN
HANDPICKED
HANGGLIDER
HARDBOILED
HEADHUNTED
HEADHUNTER
HEADMASTER
HEADPHONES
HELICOPTER
HELIOLATER
HELLBENDER
HESPERIDES
HIGHBINDER
HIGHHANDED
HIGHLANDER
HIPPOMANES
HITCHHIKER
HOLOFERNES
HOMEWORKER
HOODWINKED
HORNBLOWER
HORNRIMMED
HORSEPOWER
HORSERIDER
HOWSOMEVER
HUMANITIES
HUMIDIFIER
HUMPBACKED
HYDROMETER
HYGROMETER
HYPNOTIZED
ICEBREAKER
ILLADVISED
IMBRICATED
IMPROVISED
IMPURITIES
INDENTURES
INDISCREET
INDISPOSED
INEBRIATED
INFATUATED
INFURIATED
INKSLINGER
INSTRUCTED
INTEGRATED
INTERBREED
INTERCEDER
INTERESTED
INTERFERER
INTERLOPER
INTERWOVEN
INTESTINES
IRISHWOMEN
IRONMONGER
JACKANAPES
JACKBOOTED
JACKHAMMER
JACKSTONES
JIGGAMAREE
KEYBOARDER
KILOMETRES
KINGFISHER
KOEKSISTER
KRIEGSPIEL
LACCADIVES
LACKLUSTER
LADYKILLER
LANDLOCKED
LANDLOUPER
LANDLUBBER
LANSQUENET
LAWBREAKER
LEAFHOPPER
LEDERHOSEN
LEFTHANDED
LEFTHANDER
LEFTWINGER
LENTIGINES
LIKEMINDED
LILYWHITES
LIPIZZANER
LIQUIDIZER
LOCKKEEPER
LOGORRHOEA
LUMPSUCKER
MAKESYSTEM
MALINGERER
MANCHESTER
MANCHINEEL
MANGOSTEEN
MARSHALSEA
MATCHMAKER
MAVOURNEEN
MECHANIZED
MENORRHOEA
MERRYMAKER
METHUSALEH
METHYLATED
MICROMETER
MILEOMETER
MILLIMETER
MINEWORKER
MINIMARKET
MISMATCHED
MONTEVIDEO
MONTRACHET
MORALITIES
MOSSBUNKER
MUDSKIPPER
MULTIPLIED
MULTIPLIER
NETTLETREE
NEWFANGLED
NEWSCASTER
NEWSLETTER
NEWSMONGER
NEWSREADER
NONALIGNED

NONPLUSSED
NORTHANGER
NORTHERNER
NOTORYCTES
NUTCRACKER
OBFUSCATED
OFTENTIMES
OMBROMETER
OPENHANDED
OPENMINDED
OPISOMETER
ORTHOPNOEA
OTHERGATES
OVERLANDER
OVERWORKED
PAINKILLER
PALFRENIER
PALISANDER
PALLBEARER
PANTAGRUEL
PARALLELED
PARKLEAVES
PATHFINDER
PATRONISED
PAWNBROKER
PEACEMAKER
PEASHOOTER
PENTAMETER
PERFORATED
PERSIENNES
PESCADORES
PETITIONER
PICKPOCKET
PILEDRIVER
PINAKOTHEK
PLATELAYER
PLATINISED
PLEXIMETER
PLUMASSIER
POCKMARKED
POKERFACED
POLIANTHES
POLLINATED
POSTMASTER
POURPARLER
PRAXITELES
PREJUDICED
PRINCIPLED
PRINCIPLES
PRIVILEGED
PROCRUSTES
PROGRAMMER
PROHIBITED
PROMENADER
PRONOUNCED
PROSCRIBED
PROTRACTED
QUARRENDER
QUESTIONER
QUIZMASTER
RANDLETREE
RANNELTREE
RANNLETREE
RANTLETREE
RECOGNISED
RECOGNIZED
RECONCILED
RECONSIDER
REDISCOVER
REGIMENTED
REGISTERED
REITERATED
REPRODUCER
REREDORTER
RESEARCHER
RESTRAINED
RESTRICTED
RHOEADALES
RICHTHOFEN
RIJSTTAFEL
RINGLEADER
RINGMASTER
RIPSNORTER
ROADRUNNER
ROSECHAFER
ROTTWEILER
SALAMANDER
SALOPETTES
SANCTIFIED
SANCTITIES
SANDGROPER
SANDWICHES
SANFORISED
SCANDERBEG
SCHLIMAZEL
SCRIPTURES
SCRUTINEER
SECURITIES
SEERSUCKER
SEGREGATED
SELFESTEEM
SELFSTYLED
SEMIQUAVER
SHAGHAIRED
SHAMEFACED
SHEARWATER
SHOPKEEPER
SHOPLIFTER
SHOPSOILED
SHOPWALKER
SHORTLIVED
SHOWJUMPER
SHRIVELLED
SIDEWINDER
SKYSCRAPER
SMITHEREEN
SNOWCAPPED
SOBERSIDES
SOFTBOILED
SOGDOLAGER
SOGDOLIGER
SOGDOLOGER
SONGWRITER
SOOTHSAYER
SOUBRIQUET
SOUTHERNER
SPECTACLED
SPECTACLES
SPLITLEVEL
STABILISER
STABILIZER
STADHOLDER
STALHELMER
STALLENGER
STALLINGER
STEMWINDER
STENOTYPER
STEPFATHER
STEPLADDER
STEPMOTHER
STEPSISTER
STERILISER
STERILIZER
STOUTHRIEF
STRAIGHTEN
STRAITENED
STRATHSPEY
STRATIOTES
STREAMERED
STRENGTHEN
STULTIFIED
STYLOPISED
SUBLIMATER
SUBMARINER
SUBSCRIBER
SUNGLASSES
SUPERADDED
SUPERMODEL
SUPERPOWER
SUPERVISED
SUPPRESSED
SURROUNDED
SYNCOPATED
TACHOMETER
TALEBEARER
TANNHAUSER
TASKMASTER
TEETOTALER
TENDRILLED
TERTIARIES
THEMSELVES
THEREAFTER
THREATENED
THUCYDIDES
THUMBSCREW
TIEBREAKER
TIMEKEEPER
TIMESERVER
TOILETRIES
TOLLKEEPER
TONGUESTER
TOSSICATED
TOSTICATED
TOUCHPAPER
TOURNIQUET
TRAFFICKER
TRANSLATED
TRANSPOSED
TRESPASSER
TRIACONTER
TROCHANTER
TROMOMETER
TYPESETTER
TYPEWRITER
TYRANNISED
UMBELLIFER
UNABRIDGED
UNACCENTED
UNAFFECTED
UNANSWERED
UNASSIGNED
UNATTACHED
UNATTENDED
UNBALANCED
UNBELIEVER
UNBLEACHED
UNCONFINED
UNCULTURED
UNDECLARED
UNDEFEATED
UNDEFENDED
UNDERCOVER
UNDERLINEN
UNDERSIZED
UNDERSTEER
UNDERTAKER
UNDERWATER
UNDESCRIED
UNDESERVED
UNDETECTED
UNDETERRED
UNDIGESTED
UNDISPUTED
UNDOCTORED
UNEDUCATED
UNEMPLOYED
UNEQUALLED
UNEXAMPLED
UNEXPECTED
UNEXPLORED
UNFATHOMED
UNFETTERED
UNFINISHED
UNFLAVORED
UNFORESEEN
UNGROUNDED
UNHAMPERED
UNHERALDED
UNIMPAIRED
UNINFORMED
UNINSPIRED
UNLEAVENED
UNLETTERED
UNLICENSED
UNMANNERED
UNNUMBERED
UNOBSERVED
UNOCCUPIED
UNPREPARED
UNPROMPTED
UNPROVOKED
UNREASONED
UNREDEEMED
UNRELIEVED
UNREQUITED
UNRESERVED
UNRESOLVED
UNREVEALED
UNRIVALLED
UNSALARIED
UNSCHOOLED
UNSCRIPTED
UNSEASONED
UNSHACKLED
VALENTINES
VARIEGATED
VEGETABLES
VERSAILLES
VICTUALLER
VIEWFINDER
VIGILANTES
VOETGANGER
WAGEEARNER
WAINSCOTED
WALLFLOWER
WANTHRIVEN
WASTEPAPER
WATCHMAKER
WATCHTOWER
WATERLEVEL
WATERSKIER
WATERWHEEL
WEEDKILLER
WEIMARANER
WELLEARNED
WHARFINGER
WHATSOEVER
WHITEWATER
WHOLESALER
WILDFOWLER
WINCHESTER
WINDFLOWER
WINDJAMMER
WINDSCREEN
WINDSURFER
WITSNAPPER
WOODPECKER
WOODWORKER
WORSHIPPER
YESTERWEEK

YOURSELVES
YTHUNDERED
CHIFFCHAFF
CLASPKNIFE
CRANKSHAFT
DISQUALIFY
FALLINGOFF
FISTICUFFS
FOODSTUFFS
HANDICRAFT
HIPPOGRIFF
HOUSECRAFT
HOVERCRAFT
OFFTHECUFF
PAPERKNIFE
SHANDYGAFF
SPACECRAFT
STAGECRAFT
STATECRAFT
STROGANOFF
UNDERCRAFT
UNDERCROFT
WITCHCRAFT
ALCHERINGA
APOPHTHEGM
ARISTOLOGY
ASSEMBLAGE
AUTECOLOGY
BALNEOLOGY
BELONGINGS
BLANCMANGE
BORROWINGS
CAMERLENGO
CAMERLINGO
CAMOUFLAGE
CARDIOLOGY
CARPHOLOGY
CENTRIFUGE
CHRONOLOGY
COLPORTAGE
CONCHOLOGY
CONSTRINGE
CULVERTAGE
DELTIOLOGY
DESBOROUGH
DISARRANGE
DISCOURAGE
DRAWBRIDGE
EFFLEURAGE
EMBRYOLOGY
ENTOMOLOGY
FOOTBRIDGE
FREIGHTAGE
GARLANDAGE
GETUPANDGO
GILLRAVAGE
GRAPHOLOGY
GYNECOLOGY
HATEENOUGH
HEMORRHAGE
HODGEPODGE
HUSBANDAGE
IMMUNOLOGY
INTERTRIGO
LITHOMARGE
MALACOLOGY
MALLOPHAGA
MAQUILLAGE
MASKANONGE
MASKINONGE
MASSASAUGA
METALLURGY
MINERALOGY
MISGIVINGS
MORPHOLOGY
MUSICOLOGY
ODONTOLOGY
OUGHTLINGS
OVERCHARGE
OVERSLAUGH
PERCENTAGE
PERSIFLAGE
PERSTRINGE
PETRISSAGE
PHRENOLOGY
PHYSIOLOGY
PICHICIAGO
PILGRIMAGE
PONEROLOGY
PREARRANGE
PSEPHOLOGY
PSYCHOLOGY
SEISMOLOGY
SHARAWADGI
SHARAWAGGI
SHILLELAGH
SHORTRANGE
SPELEOLOGY
STONEHENGE
SUBTERFUGE
SUPERCARGO
TECHNOLOGY
TELPHERAGE
TIMBROLOGY
TOUCHANDGO
TOXICOLOGY
TRICHOLOGY
USQUEBAUGH
VERNISSAGE
WANDERINGS
WATERWINGS
YARBOROUGH
AIRFREIGHT
ANASTROPHE
ANDROMACHE
APOSTROPHE
AREOGRAPHY
BARASINGHA
BIRTHRIGHT
BUNDESWEHR
CACOGRAPHY
DEMOGRAPHY
DISTRAUGHT
EPISTROPHE
FEARNOUGHT
FLASHLIGHT
FLOODLIGHT
FORTHRIGHT
GALSWORTHY
GOBEMOUCHE
GYMNOSOPHY
HOLOGRAPHY
HOMEOPATHY
KIESELGUHR
KURDAITCHA
LIMITROPHE
MAKEWEIGHT
MAKUNOUCHI
MATRIARCHY
MICROFICHE
MICROLIGHT
NEWSWORTHY
NIGHTLIGHT
NOTEWORTHY
OROBRANCHE
OSTEOPATHY
OSTROGOTHS
OUANANICHE
OVERWEIGHT
PASIGRAPHY
PATRIARCHY
PHILOSOPHY
PLAYWRIGHT
PRIZEFIGHT
PYRACANTHA
PYROGRAPHY
ROADWORTHY
SABRETACHE
SATYAGRAHA
SHAKUHACHI
SYNECDOCHE
TATPURUSHA
TELEGRAPHY
TOPOGRAPHY
TORCHLIGHT
TYPOGRAPHY
ULTRAFICHE
WATERTIGHT
WISHYWASHY
ACHROMATIC
ACROAMATIC
ADVERSARIA
AEROPHAGIA
AFRORMOSIA
ALCAICERIA
ALCYONARIA
ALEXANDRIA
ALGOLAGNIA
ALLOSTERIC
ALLOTROPIC
ALTRUISTIC
AMANUENSIS
AMBARVALIA
AMBLYOPSIS
AMPELOPSIS
AMPHIMIXIS
AMPHOTERIC
AMYGDALOID
ANACHARSIS
ANACLASTIC
ANACOUSTIC
ANACRUSTIC
ANCHORETIC
ANCHYLOSIS
ANESTHESIA
ANESTHETIC
ANTHROPOID
ANTIADITIS
ANTIBIOTIC
ANTISEPSIS
ANTISEPTIC
ANTISTATIC
ANTITHESIS
ANTITHETIC
APHAERESIS
APOLAUSTIC
APOLOGETIC
APOPEMPTIC
APOPLECTIC
APOSEMATIC
APOTHEOSIS
APOTROPAIC
AQUAFORTIS
ARITHMETIC
ARTHRALGIA
ARYTAENOID
ASBESTOSIS
ASTIGMATIC
ASYMMETRIC
ATELEIOSIS
AUTHORSHIP
AUTOCRATIC
AVICULARIA
BABESIASIS
BACITRACIN
BAGASSOSIS
BARBITURIC
BAROMETRIC
BATTLESHIP
BEAUJOLAIS
BEAVERSKIN
BETACRUCIS
BIJOUTERIE
BILIVERDIN
BIPINNARIA
BLOODSTAIN
BRADYKININ
BREADFRUIT
BRIDESMAID
BRONCHITIC
BRONCHITIS
CALAMONDIN
CALCEDONIO
CALIFORNIA
CAMBRENSIS
CAMSTEERIE
CASSIOPEIA
CATALECTIC
CATALEPTIC
CATASTASIS
CATENACCIO
CATTLEGRID
CAVICORNIA
CECIDOMYIA
CELLULITIS
CENSORSHIP
CHAMBERTIN
CHAROLLAIS
CHAUDFROID
CHEVROTAIN
CHINQUAPIN
CHIRONOMIC
CINQUEFOIL
CIRRIPEDIA
CLOSTRIDIA
COCHLEARIA
CONCENTRIC
CONCHIGLIE
CONCHIOLIN
CONFERVOID
CONSTANTIA
COPESETTIC
COPPERSKIN
CORNUCOPIA
CORTADERIA
CORYBANTIC
COTTONTAIL
CROTALARIA
CYBERNETIC
CYCLOPEDIA
DEALERSHIP
DEMOCRATIC
DENDROPHIS
DERMATITIS
DEVASTAVIT
DIACAUSTIC
DIAGENESIS
DIAGNOSTIC
DIAPEDESIS
DIASTALTIC
DIDASCALIC
DIELECTRIC
DINANDERIE
DIPHTHERIA
DIPLOMATIC
DIPSOMANIA
DISINHERIT
DOCIMASTIC
DOLICHOLIS
DRAWCANSIR

DRUZHINNIK
DYSTROPHIC
ECCHYMOSIS
ECCOPROTIC
ECHOPRAXIA
ECTHLIPSIS
EGOCENTRIC
ELECTRONIC
EMBLEMATIC
EMMETROPIA
ENANTIOSIS
ENDOSMOSIS
ENHYDRITIC
ENKEPHALIN
EPENTHETIC
EPIDEICTIC
EPIGENETIC
EPIGLOTTIS
EPISPASTIC
ESCHAROTIC
EULOGISTIC
EUTHANASIA
EUTRAPELIA
EXOTHERMIC
FAHRENHEIT
FATALISTIC
FELLOWSHIP
FIBROSITIS
FINGERNAIL
FLINDERSIA
FONTINALIS
FOREORDAIN
FRAMBOESIA
FREEMARTIN
FRIENDSHIP
FRINGILLID
FUTURISTIC
GALLIAMBIC
GAULTHERIA
GENERATRIX
GEOCENTRIC
GEOGRAPHIC
GESUNDHEIT
GINGIVITIS
GRAMICIDIN
GRAPEFRUIT
GROCETERIA
GROUNDBAIT
GYROSCOPIC
HEDONISTIC
HEMIPLEGIA
HEMOGLOBIN
HEMOPHILIA
HIERARCHIC
HISTRIONIC
HOLOSTERIC
HOMOPHOBIA
HOMOPHOBIC
HOOTNANNIE
HUMANISTIC

HYDROLYSIS
HYDROPONIC
HYPERBOLIC
HYPERDULIA
HYPODERMIC
HYPOTHESIS
HYSTERESIS
IATROGENIC
ICHTHYOSIS
ICOSANDRIA
IDEALISTIC
IMPRESARIO
INARTISTIC
JINGOISTIC
JUGENDSTIL
KNOBKERRIE
LAEOTROPIC
LAMBREQUIN
LARYNGITIS
LATTICINIO
LEADERSHIP
LEGALISTIC
LEONTIASIS
LEUCHAEMIA
LINEOMYCIN
LINGUISTIC
LUPERCALIA
LYCHNAPSIA
MACONOCHIE
MAIDENHAIR
MARGINALIA
MARQUETRIE
MAURITANIA
MEGALITHIC
MEMBERSHIP
MENINGITIS
MESOLITHIC
METALEPSIS
METAPLASIS
METATHERIA
METATHESIS
METHOMANIA
METROPOLIS
MICRONESIA
MISOCAPNIC
MONILIASIS
MONOLITHIC
MONOPHONIC
MONOPLEGIA
MORGANATIC
MUJAHEDDIN
MULTIMEDIA
MYRINGITIS
NECROPOLIS
NEUTROPHIL
NIHILISTIC
NOSOPHOBIA
NUMISMATIC
NYCTALOPIA
ODONTALGIA

OPHTHALMIC
OPTIMISTIC
OROGENESIS
OSMIDROSIS
OSTEOLEPIS
OVERSTRAIN
OXYMORONIC
PAEDIATRIC
PALMATIFID
PARAENESIS
PARAMETRIC
PARAPHILIA
PARAPHONIA
PARAPHYSIS
PARAPLEGIA
PARAPLEGIC
PARAPRAXIS
PARARTHRIA
PARASCENIA
PARMACITIE
PARONYCHIA
PATHOGENIC
PATISSERIE
PATRONYMIC
PEAUDESOIE
PEELGARLIC
PENETRALIA
PENICILLIN
PENTATONIC
PENTETERIC
PERIEGESIS
PERSEPOLIS
PERSICARIA
PHILATELIC
PHILOXENIA
PHLEGMASIA
PHLEGMATIC
PHLOGISTIC
PHOLIDOSIS
PHOTOGENIC
PILLOWSLIP
PINNIPEDIA
PITYRIASIS
PLEONASTIC
POCKMANTIE
POIKILITIC
POINSETTIA
POLYHYMNIA
PONTEDERIA
PORTCULLIS
PRECIPITIN
PRESBYOPIA
PROAIRESIS
PROSTHESIS
PROSTHETIC
PROTANOPIC
PSAMMOPHIL
PSILOCYBIN
PYCNOGONID
PYTHOGENIC

QUIRINALIA
RADIOLARIA
RAGAMUFFIN
READERSHIP
REAMINGBIT
RHEOTROPIC
RHEUMATOID
RHINOLALIA
RIBOFLAVIN
ROTISSERIE
RUBINSTEIN
RUMINANTIA
SACCHAROID
SAGITTARIA
SALICORNIA
SANDEMANIA
SANNAYASIN
SATURNALIA
SCAMMOZZIS
SCHALSTEIN
SCHISMATIC
SCHOLAEMIA
SCHOLASTIC
SCIENTIFIC
SCLERIASIS
SCOTODINIA
SEAMANSHIP
SEANNACHIE
SEECATCHIE
SEPARATRIX
SIGILLARIA
SILVERSKIN
SIMPLISTIC
SLAMMERKIN
SOPHOMORIC
SOUTERRAIN
SPLANCHNIC
SPRINGTAIL
STERNALGIA
STOCHASTIC
STOUTHERIE
STRAPONTIN
STRELITZIA
SUGARALLIE
SUPERSONIC
SUPERTONIC
SYNAERESIS
SYNEIDESIS
SYNOSTOSIS
SYNTERESIS
SYPHILITIC
SYSTEMATIC
TEICHOPSIA
TELEPATHIC
TELEPHONIC
TELESCOPIC
TENDERLOIN
TENEBRIFIC
TERMINALIA
TERREPLEIN

THALESTRIS
THERMIONIC
THIMBLEWIT
THROMBOSIS
TILLANDSIA
TREKSCHUIT
TRIMALCHIO
TRITANOPIA
TULARAEMIA
ULTRASONIC
UNHYGIENIC
UNROMANTIC
UNSPECIFIC
UROPOIESIS
VALLADOLID
VULCANALIA
WANCHANCIE
WHEELCHAIR
WORKAHOLIC
XENOPHOBIA
XENOPHOBIC
XEROPHYTIC
XEROSTOMIA
ZOANTHARIA
ZOLLVEREIN
ZOOTHAPSIS
BACKBLOCKS
BACKSTROKE
BRICKWORKS
BUTTERBAKE
CHEESECAKE
CHOPSTICKS
CORNSTALKS
CRAIGFLUKE
DOSTOEVSKY
DREADLOCKS
EARTHQUAKE
EARTHWORKS
GOLDILOCKS
HANKYPANKY
MASKIROVKA
MOTHERLIKE
MUSSORGSKY
PADAREWSKI
PATCHCOCKE
PILLIWINKS
PRZEWALSKI
RAJPRAMUKH
SCHIPPERKE
SHIELDRAKE
SPRINGBOKS
SPRINGLIKE
STEELWORKS
STRAVINSKY
SWEEPSTAKE
TANGANYIKA
THREADLIKE
UNLADYLIKE
WATERWORKS
ABNORMALLY

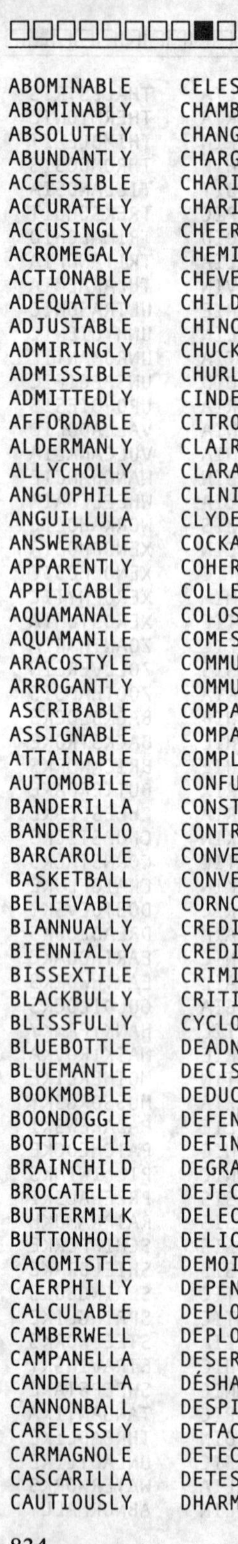

ABOMINABLE
ABOMINABLY
ABSOLUTELY
ABUNDANTLY
ACCESSIBLE
ACCURATELY
ACCUSINGLY
ACROMEGALY
ACTIONABLE
ADEQUATELY
ADJUSTABLE
ADMIRINGLY
ADMISSIBLE
ADMITTEDLY
AFFORDABLE
ALDERMANLY
ALLYCHOLLY
ANGLOPHILE
ANGUILLULA
ANSWERABLE
APPARENTLY
APPLICABLE
AQUAMANALE
AQUAMANILE
ARACOSTYLE
ARROGANTLY
ASCRIBABLE
ASSIGNABLE
ATTAINABLE
AUTOMOBILE
BANDERILLA
BANDERILLO
BARCAROLLE
BASKETBALL
BELIEVABLE
BIANNUALLY
BIENNIALLY
BISSEXTILE
BLACKBULLY
BLISSFULLY
BLUEBOTTLE
BLUEMANTLE
BOOKMOBILE
BOONDOGGLE
BOTTICELLI
BRAINCHILD
BROCATELLE
BUTTERMILK
BUTTONHOLE
CACOMISTLE
CAERPHILLY
CALCULABLE
CAMBERWELL
CAMPANELLA
CANDELILLA
CANNONBALL
CARELESSLY
CARMAGNOLE
CASCARILLA
CAUTIOUSLY
CELESTIALS
CHAMBRANLE
CHANGEABLE
CHARGEABLE
CHARITABLE
CHARITABLY
CHEERFULLY
CHEMICALLY
CHEVESAILE
CHILDISHLY
CHINCHILLA
CHUCKWALLA
CHURLISHLY
CINDERELLA
CITRONELLA
CLAIRCOLLE
CLARABELLA
CLINICALLY
CLYDESDALE
COCKABULLY
COHERENTLY
COLLEMBOLA
COLOSSALLY
COMESTIBLE
COMMUNALLY
COMMUTABLE
COMPARABLE
COMPATIBLE
COMPLETELY
CONFUSEDLY
CONSTANTLY
CONTRARILY
CONVERSELY
CONVEYABLE
CORNCOCKLE
CREDITABLE
CREDITABLY
CRIMINALLY
CRITICALLY
CYCLOSTYLE
DEADNETTLE
DECISIVELY
DEDUCTIBLE
DEFENSIBLE
DEFINITELY
DEGRADABLE
DEJECTEDLY
DELECTABLE
DELICATELY
DEMOISELLE
DEPENDABLE
DEPLORABLE
DEPLORABLY
DESERVEDLY
DÉSHABILLÉ
DESPICABLE
DETACHABLE
DETECTABLE
DETESTABLE
DHARMSHALA
DIAGONALLY
DIGESTIBLE
DILIGENTLY
DISCREETLY
DISENNOBLE
DISGRUNTLE
DISHABILLE
DISORDERLY
DISPOSABLE
DISPUTABLE
DISTINCTLY
DOUBLETALK
DOUBTFULLY
DREADFULLY
DROSOPHILA
EATANSWILL
EFFUSIVELY
ELOQUENTLY
ENORMOUSLY
ENTEROCELE
ESCADRILLE
ESPADRILLE
ESPECIALLY
EVENTUALLY
EXOTICALLY
EXPENDABLE
EXPLICABLE
EXPLICITLY
EXTENDABLE
EXTENSIBLE
EXTERNALLY
FABULOUSLY
FAITHFULLY
FAMILIARLY
FAVOURABLE
FAVOURABLY
FEARLESSLY
FENESTELLA
FERNITICLE
FEVERISHLY
FIENDISHLY
FITZGERALD
FLAGRANTLY
FLAPDOODLE
FLEETINGLY
FLIPPANTLY
FONTANELLE
FORCEFULLY
FORECASTLE
FORGIVABLE
FORMIDABLE
FRATICELLI
FRAXINELLA
FRENZIEDLY
FREQUENTLY
FRUITFULLY
FUSTANELLA
FUSTANELLE
GARGOUILLE
GENEROUSLY
GENTLEFOLK
GIBBERELLA
GLORIOUSLY
GORGEOUSLY
GRACEFULLY
GRACIOUSLY
GRANADILLA
GRANDCHILD
GRATEFULLY
GRENADILLA
GUACHAMOLE
GUTTURALLY
GYPSOPHILA
HABITUALLY
HALFHOURLY
HALFYEARLY
HAMSHACKLE
HANDSOMELY
HARDCASTLE
HECTICALLY
HEEDLESSLY
HELPLESSLY
HEPATOCELE
HEROICALLY
HESITANTLY
HONOURABLE
HONOURABLY
HOPELESSLY
HOSPITABLE
HOSPITABLY
HUMOROUSLY
IGNORANTLY
IMAGINABLE
IMMORTELLE
IMPALPABLE
IMPASSABLE
IMPECCABLE
IMPECCABLY
IMPLACABLE
IMPLACABLY
IMPLICITLY
IMPOLITELY
IMPOSSIBLE
IMPOSSIBLY
IMPOTENTLY
IMPROBABLE
IMPROBABLY
IMPROPERLY
IMPUDENTLY
INCISIVELY
INCREDIBLE
INCREDIBLY
INCUNABULA
INDECENTLY
INDICTABLE
INDIRECTLY
INEDUCABLE
INELIGIBLE
INEVITABLE
INEVITABLY
INEXORABLE
INFALLIBLE
INFALLIBLY
INFERNALLY
INFINITELY
INFLATABLE
INFLEXIBLE
INFLEXIBLY
INFORMALLY
INHERENTLY
INIMITABLE
INNOCENTLY
INOPERABLE
INSATIABLE
INSATIABLY
INSECURELY
INSENSIBLE
INSOLENTLY
INTANGIBLE
INTERNALLY
INTIMATELY
INVALUABLE
INVARIABLE
INVARIABLY
INVINCIBLE
INVIOLABLE
IRONICALLY
JARGONELLE
JERRYBUILT
JUBILANTLY
JUDICIALLY
KENSPECKLE
KLEBSIELLA
LAMENTABLE
LAMENTABLY
LARGESCALE
LAUDERDALE
LIBREVILLE
LINGULELLA
LISTLESSLY
MAHAYANALI
MANAGEABLE
MANDEVILLE
MANIFESTLY
MANZANILLA
MARGINALLY
MARKETABLE
MARTINGALE
MATCHSTALK
MATERIALLY
MATERNALLY
MEASURABLE
MELANCHOLY
MENACINGLY
MERCANTILE
MERCIFULLY
METASTABLE
MISHGUGGLE
MISTAKENLY
MODERATELY

MODIFIABLE
MORTADELLA
MOTORCYCLE
MOURNFULLY
MOZZARELLA
MUTINOUSLY
NARROWDALE
NATIONALLY
NEGATIVELY
NEGLIGIBLE
NEGOTIABLE
NEIGHBORLY
NOTICEABLE
NOTICEABLY
NOTIFIABLE
NOTIONALLY
OBEDIENTLY
OBLIGINGLY
OBSERVABLE
OBTAINABLE
OFFICIALLY
OFFTHEWALL
ORDINARILY
ORIGINALLY
OSTENSIBLE
OSTENSIBLY
OSTEOCOLLA
OUTSPECKLE
OVERSUPPLY
OWLSPIEGLE
PAINLESSLY
PARADIDDLE
PARDONABLE
PARDONABLY
PARTICIPLE
PARTINGALE
PASTORELLA
PATERNALLY
PEACEFULLY
PECCADILLO
PECULIARLY
PENETRABLE
PEPPERMILL
PERCENTILE
PERDURABLE
PERILOUSLY
PERISHABLE
PERIWINKLE
PERSONABLE
PERSONALLY
PERVERSELY
PETRONELLA
PETULANTLY
PHYSICALLY
PICCADILLY
PICCALILLI
PIGEONHOLE
PIRANDELLO
PLEASANTLY
POETICALLY
POIGNANTLY
PONCHIELLI
PONTICELLO
PORTMANTLE
POSITIVELY
POTENTILLA
PRATINCOLE
PREFERABLE
PREFERABLY
PREHENSILE
PREPENSELY
PRESUMABLY
PRETINCOLE
PREVIOUSLY
PROCURABLE
PRODIGALLY
PROFITABLE
PROFITABLY
PROFOUNDLY
PROJECTILE
PUMPHANDLE
PUNCTUALLY
PUNISHABLE
QUADRANGLE
QUESADILLA
RAMSHACKLE
RATIONALLY
RAVENOUSLY
RAVENSBILL
REASONABLE
REASONABLY
REASSEMBLE
RECEPTACLE
RECKLESSLY
RELATIVELY
REMARKABLE
REMARKABLY
REPAIRABLE
REPEATABLE
REPEATEDLY
REPORTEDLY
RESCHEDULE
RESIGNEDLY
RESOLUTELY
RESTLESSLY
RETURNABLE
REVERENTLY
REVERSIBLE
RIGHTFULLY
RIGOROUSLY
RITORNELLE
RITORNELLO
ROCKABILLY
ROTHSCHILD
RUTHLESSLY
SADDLEBILL
SALMONELLA
SALTARELLO
SARCOCOLLA
SAVONAROLA
SCOFFINGLY
SCORNFULLY
SDRUCCIOLA
SEASONABLE
SEASONABLY
SEDULOUSLY
SEGUIDILLA
SEMICIRCLE
SENSUOUSLY
SEPARATELY
SERRADELLA
SERRADILLA
SGANARELLE
SHAMEFULLY
SHEEPISHLY
SHOCKINGLY
SIDESADDLE
SIGNORELLI
SILVERBILL
SINGULARLY
SINSEMILLA
SKILLFULLY
SLATTERNLY
SLUGGISHLY
SMALLSCALE
SNOWMOBILE
SOMERSAULT
SOMERVILLE
SOOTHINGLY
SPECIOUSLY
SPIRITEDLY
SPITEFULLY
SPLENDIDLY
SPORTINGLY
SPOTLESSLY
SPURIOUSLY
STANDSTILL
STEALTHILY
STRIDENTLY
STRIKINGLY
STRINGHALT
STRONGHOLD
STROPHIOLE
STUBBORNLY
STUDIOUSLY
SUCCINCTLY
SUPPOSEDLY
SURGICALLY
SWIMMINGLY
TABERNACLE
TACTICALLY
TACTLESSLY
TARADIDDLE
TARANTELLA
TASTEFULLY
TATTERSALL
TCHOUKBALL
TERMINABLE
TERMINALLY
THANKFULLY
THOROUGHLY
TINKERBELL
TIRELESSLY
TOCCATELLA
TOLERANTLY
TORRICELLI
TORTUOUSLY
TRAGICALLY
TRANQUILLY
TROUVAILLE
TRUSTFULLY
TRUTHFULLY
TURRITELLA
ULTIMATELY
UNARGUABLE
UNBEARABLE
UNBEARABLY
UNBEATABLE
UNCOMMONLY
UNCTUOUSLY
UNDENIABLE
UNDERWORLD
UNENVIABLE
UNFRIENDLY
UNHEARABLE
UNMANNERLY
UNREADABLE
UNRELIABLE
UNSCRAMBLE
UNSOCIABLE
UNSUITABLE
UNWORKABLE
UTILIZABLE
VANDERBILT
VAUDEVILLE
VEHEMENTLY
VERIFIABLE
VERMICELLI
VERTICALLY
VIGOROUSLY
VILLANELLE
VIRTUOUSLY
VIRULENTLY
VITELLICLE
VOLLEYBALL
VULNERABLE
WASTEFULLY
WATCHFULLY
WHITSTABLE
WILLYWILLY
WINDOWSILL
WINDSHIELD
WORTHWHILE
WRETCHEDLY
WRONGFULLY
YAFFINGALE
YGGDRASILL
ABHIDHAMMA
AERENCHYMA
AMBLYSTOMA
BIORHYTHMS
BOTHERSOME
BRAGADISME
BURDENSOME
BUTTERBUMP
CENTROSOME
CHEIRONOMY
CHROMOSOME
CUDDLESOME
CUMBERSOME
DECAGRAMME
DINNERTIME
DREARISOME
EPIPHONEMA
ETHEOSTOMA
FORTISSIMO
FROLICSOME
GASTRONOME
GASTRONOMY
HIPPODROME
IMPOSTHUME
LOGARITHMS
MASTECTOMY
MEDDLESOME
METTLESOME
MONOCHROME
NEURILEMMA
NEUROLEMMA
OCTODECIMO
PALINDROME
PARENCHYMA
PHANTASIME
POGONOTOMY
POLYCHROME
PSYCHOPOMP
QUADRIREME
RHINOPHYMA
SARCOLEMMA
SERRASALMO
SEXAGESIMA
SPRINGTIME
STEREOTOMY
STRABOTOMY
STREETLAMP
SUMMERTIME
TELEOSTOME
WINTERTIME
ABERDEVINE
ABITURIENT
ABONNEMENT
ABRIDGMENT
ACCESSIONS
ACCOUNTANT
ACCOUNTING
ADAMANTINE
ADDITAMENT
ADJUSTMENT
ADOLESCENT
ADRENALINE
ADULTERANT

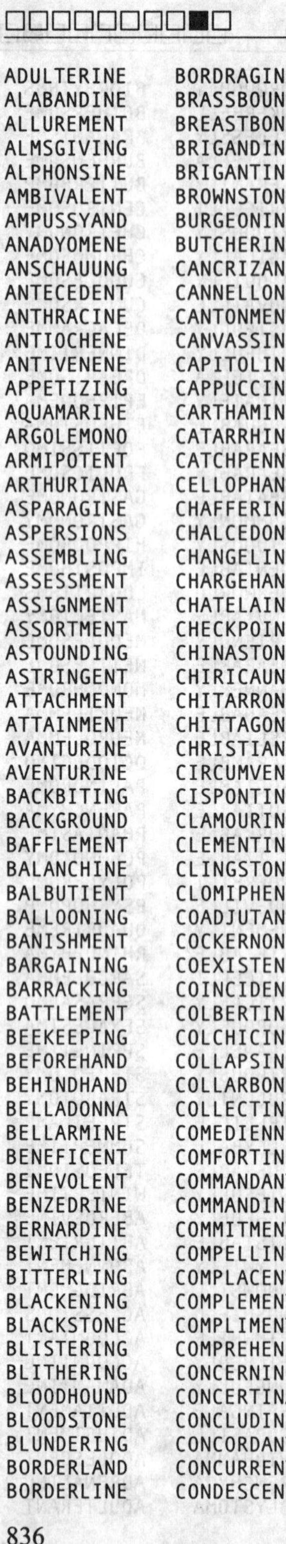

ADULTERINE
ALABANDINE
ALLUREMENT
ALMSGIVING
ALPHONSINE
AMBIVALENT
AMPUSSYAND
ANADYOMENE
ANSCHAUUNG
ANTECEDENT
ANTHRACINE
ANTIOCHENE
ANTIVENENE
APPETIZING
AQUAMARINE
ARGOLEMONO
ARMIPOTENT
ARTHURIANA
ASPARAGINE
ASPERSIONS
ASSEMBLING
ASSESSMENT
ASSIGNMENT
ASSORTMENT
ASTOUNDING
ASTRINGENT
ATTACHMENT
ATTAINMENT
AVANTURINE
AVENTURINE
BACKBITING
BACKGROUND
BAFFLEMENT
BALANCHINE
BALBUTIENT
BALLOONING
BANISHMENT
BARGAINING
BARRACKING
BATTLEMENT
BEEKEEPING
BEFOREHAND
BEHINDHAND
BELLADONNA
BELLARMINE
BENEFICENT
BENEVOLENT
BENZEDRINE
BERNARDINE
BEWITCHING
BITTERLING
BLACKENING
BLACKSTONE
BLISTERING
BLITHERING
BLOODHOUND
BLOODSTONE
BLUNDERING
BORDERLAND
BORDERLINE
BORDRAGING
BRASSBOUND
BREASTBONE
BRIGANDINE
BRIGANTINE
BROWNSTONE
BURGEONING
BUTCHERING
CANCRIZANS
CANNELLONI
CANTONMENT
CANVASSING
CAPITOLINE
CAPPUCCINO
CARTHAMINE
CATARRHINE
CATCHPENNY
CELLOPHANE
CHAFFERING
CHALCEDONY
CHANGELING
CHARGEHAND
CHATELAINE
CHECKPOINT
CHINASTONE
CHIRICAUNE
CHITARRONE
CHITTAGONG
CHRISTIANA
CIRCUMVENT
CISPONTINE
CLAMOURING
CLEMENTINE
CLINGSTONE
CLOMIPHENE
COADJUTANT
COCKERNONY
COEXISTENT
COINCIDENT
COLBERTINE
COLCHICINE
COLLAPSING
COLLARBONE
COLLECTING
COMEDIENNE
COMFORTING
COMMANDANT
COMMANDING
COMMITMENT
COMPELLING
COMPLACENT
COMPLEMENT
COMPLIMENT
COMPREHEND
CONCERNING
CONCERTINA
CONCLUDING
CONCORDANT
CONCURRENT
CONDESCEND
CONDUCTING
CONNECTING
CONQUERING
CONSEQUENT
CONSISTENT
CONSTRAINT
CONSULTANT
CONSULTING
CONTESTANT
CONTINGENT
CONTINUING
CONTRABAND
CONTRAHENT
CONTRAVENE
CONVENIENT
CONVERGENT
CONVERSANT
CONVINCING
CORRECTING
CORRESPOND
CORRUPTING
COUNSELING
CRICKETING
CRUIKSHANK
CUCKOOPINT
CUMBERLAND
CUMMERBUND
CURMURRING
CURVETTING
CUTTLEBONE
DARJEELING
DEBASEMENT
DEBATEMENT
DEBRIEFING
DECAMPMENT
DECRESCENT
DEFACEMENT
DEFILEMENT
DEFRAYMENT
DELINQUENT
DENOUEMENT
DEPARTMENT
DEPLOYMENT
DEPORTMENT
DEPRESSANT
DEPRESSING
DERAILMENT
DESCENDANT
DESCENDING
DESCRIBING
DESPAIRING
DESPONDENT
DESSIATINE
DESSYATINE
DETACHMENT
DETAINMENT
DEVELOPING
DEVOTEMENT
DICYNODONT
DIRECTIONS
DISAPPOINT
DISCERNING
DISCIPLINE
DISCONTENT
DISCORDANT
DISCREPANT
DISCUSSING
DISENCHANT
DISGUSTING
DISHARMONY
DISINCLINE
DISPENSING
DISSENTING
DISSILIENT
DISSOLVENT
DISTILLING
DISTURBING
DOMINATING
DOWNSIZING
DRAKESTONE
DRAWSTRING
DUNDERFUNK
EASTERLING
EBOULEMENT
EFFACEMENT
ELACAMPANE
ELECAMPANE
EMALANGENI
EMBANKMENT
EMBODIMENT
EMBONPOINT
EMPFINDUNG
EMPLOYMENT
ENCAMPMENT
ENCASEMENT
ENCHANTING
ENDEARMENT
ENGAGEMENT
ENGOUEMENT
ENGROSSING
ENLACEMENT
ENLÈVEMENT
ENLISTMENT
ENRICHMENT
ENROLLMENT
ENSANGUINE
ENTICEMENT
ENTOMBMENT
ENTRANCING
ENTREATING
ENTRYPHONE
EPAULEMENT
EQUIVALENT
ERUBESCENT
ESCAPEMENT
ESCARPMENT
ETHYLAMINE
EUCHLORINE
EUPHROSYNE
EVANESCENT
EVERYTHING
EXCITEMENT
EXHAUSTING
EXORBITANT
EXPERIMENT
FACESAVING
FAIRGROUND
FAMISHMENT
FANTOCCINI
FAREPAYING
FARRANDINE
FASTMOVING
FATHERLAND
FERRANDINE
FESCENNINE
FETTUCCINE
FINGERLING
FLAMBOYANT
FLAMINGANT
FLASHPOINT
FLATTERING
FLAVESCENT
FLAVOURING
FLICKERING
FLOCCULENT
FLORENTINE
FLORESCENT
FORBEARING
FORBIDDING
FOREBODING
FOREGROUND
FORFAITING
FOUDROYANT
FOXHUNTING
FRANGIPANE
FRANGIPANI
FRAUDULENT
FREEMASONS
FREMESCENT
FULFILMENT
FURNISHING
GAINGIVING
GALUMPHING
GETHSEMANE
GHIBELLINE
GILBERTINE
GIRDLERINK
GIRLFRIEND
GLISTENING
GLITTERAND
GLITTERING
GOVERNMENT
GRAMOPHONE
GRANDSTAND
GRATIFYING
GRAVEOLENT
GRAVESTONE
GREENSHANK
GRINDSTONE
GROUNDLING

GROVELLING
GUILLOTINE
HAIRSPRING
HANDSPRING
HARASSMENT
HEADSTRONG
HELLESPONT
HIEROPHANT
HIGHFLYING
HILDEBRAND
HINDUSTANI
HINTERLAND
HIPPOCRENE
HOMECOMING
HOOTANANNY
HOOTENANNY
HORRIFYING
HOUSEBOUND
HYALOPHANE
HYDROPHANE
HYDROPLANE
IMPAIRMENT
IMPEDIMENT
IMPENITENT
INBREEDING
INCAPARINA
INCITEMENT
INCOHERENT
INCONSTANT
INCREASING
INCRESCENT
INDICTMENT
INDITEMENT
INDUCEMENT
INESCULENT
INFEFTMENT
INFIGHTING
INFREQUENT
INGREDIENT
INHABITANT
INHIBITING
INSOUCIANT
INSTALMENT
INSTRUMENT
INTEGUMENT
INTELIGENT
INTENDMENT
INTERNMENT
INTERPHONE
INTERTWINE
INTOLERANT
INTOXICANT
INTRIGUING
INVESTMENT
IRIDESCENT
IRRELEVANT
IRREVERENT
IRRITATING
ISABELLINE
JAYWALKING
KESSELRING
KIDNAPPING
KUOMINTANG
LACUSTRINE
LANDAMMANN
LANDSTHING
LANGERHANS
LAURUSTINE
LAWABIDING
LIEBERMANN
LIEUTENANT
LIGNOCAINE
LIQUESCENT
LITHOPHANE
LOCULAMENT
LUTESTRING
MAGISTRAND
MAGNIFYING
MAINSPRING
MALCONTENT
MALEVOLENT
MANAGEMENT
MANSERVANT
MARASCHINO
MARCANTANT
MARCESCENT
MARYLEBONE
MASCARPONE
MASTERMIND
MAUPASSANT
MEANDERING
MEDICAMENT
MEPERIDINE
MESITYLENE
METHEDRINE
MICROPHONE
MINESTRONE
MISCELLANY
MISFORTUNE
MISLEADING
MITIGATING
MOTHERLAND
MOUNTEBANK
MOUSSELINE
MUCKRAKING
MUNIFICENT
NAPTHALENE
NAUSEATING
NETWORKING
NIDDERLING
NIGRESCENT
NONCHALANT
NONPAYMENT
NONSMOKING
NONVIOLENT
NORBERTINE
NORTHBOUND
NOURISHING
OCEANGOING
ODELSTHING
OFFPUTTING
OMNIPOTENT
OMNISCIENT
OPALESCENT
ORTHOCAINE
OUTPATIENT
OUTPOURING
OVEREATING
OVERRIDING
OVERSTRUNG
PALESTRINA
PALUDAMENT
PALUSTRINE
PANTALOONS
PAPAVERINE
PARADOXINE
PARASELENE
PARGETTING
PARISCHANE
PARISIENNE
PARLIAMENT
PEACHERINO
PEPPERMINT
PERCIPIENT
PERFICIENT
PERFORMING
PERPLEXING
PERSEPHONE
PERSISTENT
PERSUADING
PETRIFYING
PHAGEDAENA
PHILIPPINA
PHILIPPINE
PHILISTINE
PHILLIPINA
PHILLIPINE
PHILLUMENY
PHILOPOENA
PICCANINNY
PINCHPENNY
PIONEERING
PITCHSTONE
PLASTICINE
PLATTELAND
PLAYGROUND
PLUNDERING
POINTBLANK
PORLOCKING
POSTLIMINY
POZZUOLANA
PREDESTINE
PREDNISONE
PREEMINENT
PREFERMENT
PREPAYMENT
PREVAILING
PROCEEDING
PROCESSING
PROFICIENT
PROJECTING
PROPELLANT
PROSERPINA
PROSERPINE
PROSILIENT
PROSPERINA
PROTESTANT
PROVISIONS
PUBERULENT
PUBLISHING
PUMMELLING
PUNCHDRUNK
PUNISHMENT
PURSUIVANT
PUTREFYING
PUTRESCENT
PUZZLEMENT
QUARANTINE
QUARTERING
QUERSPRUNG
RAVENSTONE
RAWSTHORNE
REARMAMENT
REASSURING
REDCURRANT
REFINEMENT
REFLECTING
REFRESHING
RESEMBLING
RESENTMENT
RESOUNDING
RESPECTING
RESPONDENT
RESTAURANT
RETIREMENT
RETRAINING
RETREATING
RHINESTONE
RINGELMANN
ROISTERING
ROLLICKING
ROSANILINE
ROSEMALING
RUDOLPHINE
RUPICOLINE
SACCHARINE
SANDERLING
SAPPERMENT
SATISFYING
SAXICOLINE
SBUDDIKINS
SCARCEMENT
SCARLATINA
SCARLETINA
SCATTERING
SCATURIENT
SCREECHING
SCRIBBLING
SCRIMSHANK
SCROUNGING
SECONDHAND
SECONDMENT
SELEGILINE
SELTZOGENE
SEPTUAGINT
SERPENTINE
SETTLEMENT
SHAMPOOING
SHATTERING
SHEEPSHANK
SHIMMERING
SHOESTRING
SHORTENING
SHUDDERING
SICILIENNE
SIMULATING
SKINDIVING
SKRIMSHANK
SKUPSHTINA
SLUMBERING
SMARAGDINE
SMATTERING
SNAKESTONE
SNIGGERING
SNORKELING
SOLIVAGANT
SOURDELINE
SOUSAPHONE
SOUTHBOUND
SPEAKERINE
SPELLBOUND
SPILLIKINS
SPINESCENT
SPIRKETING
SPRINKLING
STAGGERING
STAMMERING
STANDPOINT
STAPHYLINE
STARVELING
STILLSTAND
STOREFRONT
STRACCHINO
STRAGGLING
STREAMLINE
STREPITANT
STRYCHNINE
STUPEFYING
SUAVEOLENT
SUBHEADING
SUBMEDIANT
SUBSEQUENT
SUBSISTENT
SUCCEEDING
SUFFICIENT
SUNBATHING
SUPERGIANT
SUPPLEMENT
SUPPLICANT
SUPPORTING

SURFRIDING
SURPASSING
SURPRISING
SUSTAINING
SWAGGERING
SWALLOWING
SWEETENING
SWELTERING
TAGLIARINI
TAILGATING
TALLEYRAND
TAMBERLANE
TAMBOURINE
TANTAMOUNT
TAPDANCING
TAPOTEMENT
TARPAULING
TARTRAZINE
TEENYWEENY
TERRIFYING
THEREANENT
THICKENING
THREEPENNY
THUMBIKINS
THUNDERING
TIMESAVING
TORPESCENT
TORTELLINI
TOUCHSTONE
TOURMALINE
TOURNAMENT
TRADITIONS
TRAMONTANA
TRAMONTANE
TRAMPOLINE
TRANSPLANT
TRAVELLING
TRAVERTINE
TRIDENTINE
TRIPEHOUND
TRIUMPHANT
TURNAROUND
TURPENTINE
ULTRASOUND
UNASSUMING
UNAVAILING
UNBECOMING
UNBLINKING
UNBLUSHING
UNDERBURNT
UNDERLYING
UNDERSLUNG
UNDERSTAND
UNDULATING
UNEDIFYING
UNFLAGGING
UNINVITING
UNPLEASANT
UNSETTLING
UNSLEEPING
UNSWERVING
UNTHINKING
UNYIELDING
UPBRINGING
UPSTANDING
VARNISHING
VIBRAPHONE
VIBRATIONS
VICEGERENT
VICEREGENT
VICTORIANA
WASSAILING
WASSERMANS
WATERBORNE
WATERFRONT
WELLSPRING
WHEATSTONE
WHISPERING
WONDERLAND
WONDERMENT
WRAPAROUND
WRONGDOING
WUNDERKIND
ZABAGLIONE
ZEUGLODONT
ABDICATION
ABERRATION
ABROGATION
ABSCISSION
ABSOLUTION
ABSORPTION
ABSTENTION
ACCUBATION
ACCUSATION
ACOLOUTHOS
ACOTYLEDON
ACROTERION
ADAPTATION
ADHIBITION
ADIAPHORON
ADMIRATION
ADMONITION
AFFLICTION
AGGRESSION
ALIENATION
ALLEGATION
ALLIGATION
ALLOCATION
ALLOCUTION
ALTERATION
ALTERNATOR
AMBASSADOR
AMBOCEPTOR
AMMUNITION
AMPHICTYON
AMPHITRYON
AMPUTATION
ANHELATION
ANNEXATION
ANNOTATION
ANTHEOLION
ANTICHTHON
ANTIPROTON
APPARITION
APPLICATOR
APPOSITION
ARBITRATOR
ARCHBISHOP
ARCHDEACON
AREFACTION
ARMAGEDDON
ASPIRATION
ASSUMPTION
ATTRACTION
AUTOCHTHON
AUTOMATION
BACKGAMMON
BALNEATION
BASSINGTON
BATTLEDOOR
BENEFACTOR
BRACHIOPOD
BRIDEGROOM
BUCCINATOR
BURLINGTON
BYELECTION
CACODAEMON
CALCULATOR
CALEFACTOR
CAMPARADOR
CAPITATION
CARBURETOR
CASTRATION
CATHOLICON
CATHOLICOS
CEPHALOPOD
CESTRACION
CHAMBERPOT
CHAMPIGNON
CHANCELLOR
CHAPARAJOS
CHAPAREJOS
CHATTERBOX
CHATTERTON
CHECKLATON
CHEESEWOOD
CHEQUEBOOK
CHERRYWOOD
CHESTERTON
CHICKENPOX
CHIMNEYPOT
CLUMPERTON
CODSWALLOP
COGITATION
COLLECTION
COLLIMATOR
COLORATION
COMBUSTION
COMMISSION
COMPARATOR
COMPARISON
COMPASSION
COMPATRIOT
COMPETITOR
COMPLETION
COMPLEXION
COMPOSITOR
COMPRESSOR
COMPULSION
CONCEPTION
CONCESSION
CONCLUSION
CONCOCTION
CONCRETION
CONCUSSION
CONDUCTION
CONFECTION
CONFESSION
CONGESTION
CONNECTION
CONNIPTION
CONSENSION
CONTENTION
CONTORTION
CONTRACTOR
CONTRAFLOW
CONTRITION
CONVECTION
CONVENTION
CONVERSION
CONVICTION
CONVULSION
COPULATION
COQUELICOT
CORONATION
CORRECTION
CORREGIDOR
CORRUGATOR
CORRUPTION
COTTONWOOD
COUNCILLOR
COUNSELLOR
COUSCOUSOU
CULTIVATOR
CURMUDGEON
DECAHEDRON
DECLENSION
DECOLLATOR
DECORATION
DEDICATION
DEFAMATION
DEFECATION
DEFINITION
DEFLECTION
DELEGATION
DELIGATION
DELIRATION
DEMOGORGON
DEMOLITION
DEPOSITION
DEPRESSION
DEPUTATION
DERIVATION
DESOLATION
DETONATION
DETRACTION
DEVOLUTION
DIACONICON
DIDGERIDOO
DIGRESSION
DILATATION
DIMINUTION
DIOPHANTOS
DIREMPTION
DISCRETION
DISCUSSION
DISPERSION
DISRUPTION
DISSECTION
DISSELBOOM
DISSENSION
DISSUASION
DISTENSION
DISTORTION
DIVINATION
DOMINATION
DONNYBROOK
DOORTODOOR
DRUMBLEDOR
DUPLICATOR
EISTEDDFOD
ELIMINATOR
ELONGATION
EMACIATION
EMENDATION
EMIGRATION
ENCEPHALON
EPILIMNION
EQUITATION
ERIOCAULON
ERUCTATION
ESCALATION
ESCUTCHEON
ESTIMATION
ESTRAMACON
EUROCLYDON
EVACUATION
EVALUATION
EXALTATION
EXCAVATION
EXECRATION
EXHALATION
EXHAUSTION
EXHIBITION
EXHUMATION
EXPEDITION
EXPIRATION
EXPOSITION
EXPRESSION
EXTINCTION

EXTRACTION
EXULTATION
FASCIATION
FASCINATOR
FEDERATION
FEUILLETON
FIDDLEWOOD
FIGURATION
FILTRATION
FLAMEPROOF
FLIRTATION
FLUNKEYDOM
FORESHADOW
FOUNDATION
FRANCHISOR
FUMIGATION
GASTEROPOD
GEMINATION
GENERATION
GLACIATION
GOODFELLOW
GRADUATION
GRASSWIDOW
GUBERNATOR
HABITATION
HALLUBALOO
HARRINGTON
HEMIHEDRON
HENDECAGON
HEPTAMERON
HEPTATHLON
HESITATION
HULLABALOO
HUMDUDGEON
HYPAETHRON
IMMOLATION
IMPOSITION
IMPRESSION
IMPUTATION
INCUBATION
INDECISION
INDICATION
INFLECTION
INFLICTION
INFRACTION
INHALATION
INHIBITION
INITIATION
INJUNCTION
INNOVATION
INQUISITOR
INSPECTION
INSTIGATOR
INSTRUCTOR
INSULATION
INTERFERON
INTIMATION
INTINCTION
INTONATION
INUNDATION
INVITATION
INVOCATION
IRRIGATION
IRRITATION
JACULATION
JEISTIECOR
JUBILATION
KNIGHTHOOD
LACERATION
LAMINATION
LAUNCESTON
LEAMINGTON
LEGISLATOR
LEVITATION
LIBERATION
LIKELIHOOD
LIMITATION
LIQUIDATOR
LITIGATION
LIVELIHOOD
LOCKERROOM
LOCOMOTION
LONGFELLOW
MABINOGION
MAIDENHOOD
MAINPERNOR
MALAPROPOS
MALEFACTOR
MATURATION
MEDICATION
MEDITATION
MELOCOTOON
MESENTERON
MINUTEBOOK
MISPRISION
MITIGATION
MODERATION
MODULATION
MONOPTERON
MONOPTEROS
MOSASAUROS
MOTHERHOOD
MOTIVATION
MUTILATION
NAVIGATION
NEGOTIATOR
NINCOMPOOP
NOMINATION
NONFICTION
NUMERATION
OBLIGATION
OCCUPATION
OCTAHEDRON
OMOPHORION
OPPOSITION
OPPRESSION
ORDINATION
ORIGINATOR
ORPHEOREON
OSCILLATOR
OSCITATION
OSCULATION
OVERSHADOW
OVERTHETOP
OVIPOSITOR
OXYGENATOR
PADDINGTON
PADDYMELON
PAGINATION
PALMATOZOA
PALMERSTON
PANOPTICON
PARENTHOOD
PECULATION
PENELOPHON
PENNILLION
PENTAMERON
PENTATHLON
PENTELIKON
PENTSTEMON
PERCEPTION
PERCOLATOR
PERCUSSION
PERFECTION
PERFORATOR
PERIHELION
PERMEATION
PERMISSION
PERORATION
PERSECUTOR
PERSUASION
PERVERSION
PHENOMENON
PHLEGETHON
PHLOGISTON
PHYLLIOPOD
PINCUSHION
PLANTATION
PLAYFELLOW
POCKETBOOK
POLYHEDRON
POPULATION
POSSESSION
POSTILLION
PRECAUTION
PREDICTION
PRELECTION
PREPARATOR
PREPOSITOR
PRETENSION
PREVENTION
PRIESTHOOD
PROCESSION
PROCREATOR
PROCURATOR
PRODUCTION
PROFESSION
PROGENITOR
PROGESSION
PROJECTION
PROPAGATOR
PROPORTION
PROPRAETOR
PROPRIETOR
PROPULSION
PROSECUTOR
PROSPECTOR
PROTECTION
PROTRACTOR
PROTRUSION
PROVEDITOR
PTERANODON
PUCKERWOOD
PUNDIGRION
QUARTEROON
QUERCITRON
RECITATION
RECREATION
REDEMPTION
REELECTION
REFLECTION
REFRACTION
REFUTATION
REGRESSION
REGULATION
REJONEADOR
RELAXATION
RELEGATION
RELOCATION
RENOVATION
REPARATION
REPETITION
REPRESSION
REPUTATION
RESOLUTION
RESORCINOL
RESPIRATOR
RESUMPTION
RETRACTION
REVELATION
REVOCATION
REVOLUTION
RHAMPASTOS
RHINOCEROS
RICHARDSON
RIDINGHOOD
RIGELATION
ROWLANDSON
RUMBLOSSOM
RUMBULLION
RUMINATION
SALIVATION
SALUTATION
SANDALWOOD
SANITATION
SATURATION
SCANDAROON
SCHOOLBOOK
SCHWARZLOT
SCOMBRESOX
SEPARATION
SHACKLETON
SHECKLATON
SHOCKPROOF
SIDERATION
SIMULATION
SISTERHOOD
SKETCHBOOK
SMORREBROD
SNAPDRAGON
SNEEZEWOOD
SOUNDPROOF
SPALLATION
SPECULATOR
SPOLIATION
SQUEEZEBOX
STAGNATION
STARVATION
STEPHENSON
STICHARION
STOMATOPOD
STONEMASON
STRONGROOM
STUMBLEDOM
SUBJECTION
SUBMERSION
SUBMISSION
SUBREPTION
SUBSECTION
SUBSTATION
SUBVENTION
SUBVERSION
SUCCESSION
SUGGESTION
SUPERVISOR
SUPPRESSOR
SUSPENSION
TABLESPOON
TABULATION
TAMPERFOOT
TANGLEFOOT
TEDDINGTON
TELEVISION
TEMPTATION
TENDERFOOT
TENTERHOOK
THELLUSSON
THERMISTOR
THINGUMBOB
THUNDERBOX
TOCOPHEROL
TOLERATION
TOURBILLON
TRANSISTOR
TRANSITION
TRANSLATOR
TRAVELATOR
TRAVOLATOR
TRISKELION
TROCHOTRON

ULCERATION
UNDERFLOOR
UNDERSTOOD
UNDULATION
UNORTHODOX
USUCAPTION
USURPATION
VALIDATION
VEGETATION
VELITATION
VENERATION
VENTILATOR
VERMILLION
VISITATION
VOLUTATION
WASHINGTON
WATERCOLOR
WATERMELON
WATERPROOF
WELLINGTON
WILLIAMSON
WILLINGDON
WITGATBOOM
WOFFINGTON
WOODPIGEON
YELLOWROOT
YELLOWWOOD
ZWITTERION
ANEMOGRAPH
BATHYSCAPH
CANTALOUPE
CANTELOUPE
CHAMAEROPS
CHINAGRAPH
COLPOSCOPE
CYSTOSCOPY
DICTOGRAPH
HELIOGRAPH
HELIOTROPE
HIEROGLYPH
HIEROSCOPY
HIPPOGRYPH
HOMORELAPS
ICONOSCOPE
LITHOGRAPH
LONGCHAMPS
MACROCARPA
MANUSCRIPT
MICROSCOPE
MIMEOGRAPH
MYRIOSCOPE
NYMPHOLEPT
OPOTHERAPY
PALAEOTYPE
PANTOGRAPH
PANTOSCOPE
PARATROOPS
PARTHENOPE
PETROGLYPH
PETTICHAPS
PETTYCHAPS
PHAENOTYPE
PHONOGRAPH
PHOTOGRAPH
POSTSCRIPT
QUADRICEPS
RADIOGRAPH
SKEUOMORPH
STEREOTYPE
TACHOGRAPH
TEINOSCOPE
THIXOTROPY
TICKERTAPE
TRANSCRIPT
TYPESCRIPT
ZINCOGRAPH
ZOOTHERAPY
ABOVEBOARD
AFTERHOURS
ALEXANDERS
ALIMENTARY
ALZHEIMERS
AMBULATORY
AMPHIGOURI
AMPHINEURA
ANGIOSPERM
ANIMADVERT
ANTHOCLORE
APICULTURE
APOTHECARY
ARTHROMERE
ASPIDISTRA
ATMOSPHERE
AUSTRALORP
AVVOGADORE
BACKSTAIRS
BARLEYCORN
BARYSPHERE
BASKETWORK
BATTENBERG
BATTENBURG
BATTLEDORE
BAUDELAIRE
BEEFEATERS
BELLAMOURE
BINOCULARS
BLACKBEARD
BLACKBERRY
BLACKBOARD
BLACKGUARD
BLACKHEART
BLACKSHIRT
BLACKTHORN
BLOOMSBURY
BRAINSTORM
BREASTWORK
BROADSWORD
BUFFOONERY
BUTTERMERE
CALLIATURE
CAMELOPARD
CANCIONERO
CANDELABRA
CANTERBURY
CAPILLAIRE
CAPITULARY
CAPODASTRO
CARICATURA
CARICATURE
CASSIABARK
CAUTIONARY
CENTILITRE
CENTIMETRE
CERTIORARI
CHAULMUGRA
CHESSBOARD
CHIROPTERA
CHLOROFORM
CHURCHYARD
CINECAMERA
CLAVICHORD
CLEARSTORY
CLERESTORY
CLOUDBERRY
COASTGUARD
COLEOPTERA
COLORATURA
COMANCHERO
COMMENTARY
COMMISSARY
COMMISSURE
COMMIXTURE
COMPRADORE
COMPULSORY
CONJECTURE
CONSISTORY
CONTROVERT
CORDILLERA
CRAQUETURE
CTENOPHORA
CUISENAIRE
DEBAUCHERY
DEBOUCHURE
DEFAMATORY
DELCREDERE
DEPILATORY
DEPOSITARY
DEPOSITORY
DEROGATORY
DEVANAGARI
DICTIONARY
DIRECTOIRE
DISCLOSURE
DISCOMFORT
DISCONCERT
DISCOPHORA
DISPENSARY
DISTILLERY
DOMICILARY
DOVERCOURT
DOWNSTAIRS
DUMBLEDORE
DYNAMITARD
ECHINODERM
EFFRONTERY
ELDERBERRY
ELEMENTARY
ELYTRIFORM
EMBOUCHURE
EMBROIDERY
ENCOIGNURE
ENGENDRURE
EPANOPHORA
EPIPLASTRA
ESCRITOIRE
ESTANCIERO
EUTHYNEURA
EVERYWHERE
EXPOSITORY
EXPOUNDERS
FALDISTORY
FINISTERRE
FLOORBOARD
FLUGELHORN
FORFEITURE
FOURRAGERE
FRITILLARY
GETTYSBURG
GONDOLIERS
GOOSEBERRY
GREENHEART
GREENSWARD
GRENADIERS
GREYFRIARS
GROUNDWORK
HANDLEBARS
HEAVENWARD
HECTOLITRE
HEIDELBERG
HEMISPHERE
HEREDITARY
HINDENBURG
HITHERWARD
HORSELBERG
ICOSOHEDRA
INCENDIARY
INHIBITORY
INSANITARY
INTERMARRY
IONOSPHERE
JARDINIERE
JOBSEEKERS
JUDICATURE
JUSTICIARY
KERSEYMERE
KNIFEBOARD
KOOKABURRA
LABORATORY
LACKLUSTRE
LAVALLIÈRE
LEGWARMERS
LITERATURE
LOGANBERRY
LORDOLATRY
LUXEMBOURG
MALMESBURY
MANDRAGORA
MANGABEIRA
MARIOLATRY
MASTERWORT
MATTERHORN
MEDIUMTERM
METACENTRE
MILLEFIORI
MILLIMETRE
MISERICORD
MISSIONARY
MONILIFORM
MONTAGNARD
MONTESSORI
MONTGOMERY
MOUDIEWART
MOULDIWARP
MUSKETEERS
NEEDLEWORK
NEWSPAPERS
NIGHTSHIRT
NOURRITURE
OBLIGATORY
OSCULATORY
OUTPERFORM
OUVIRANDRA
OVERTHWART
PALMERWORM
PASTEBOARD
PATIBULARY
PEPPERCORN
PEPPERWORT
PEREMPTORY
PHYLACTERY
PLEASANTRY
PLEROPHORY
POETASTERY
PRAEMUNIRE
PREBENDARY
PRECURSORY
PREHISTORY
PRESBYTERY
PRIVATEERS
PROMISSORY
PROMONTORY
PSEUDOCARP
PSOCOPTERA
PSYCHIATRY
QUADRATURA
QUAESTUARY
QUATERNARY
QUEENSBURY
QUICKTHORN
RAIYATWARI

REFRACTORY
REPERTOIRE
REPOSITORY
RHIPIPTERA
ROQUELAURE
RUTHERFORD
SALLENDERS
SANGUINARY
SCHOOLGIRL
SCORDATURA
SCOREBOARD
SCORZONERA
SECRETAIRE
SELLINGERS
SETTERWORT
SILVERWARE
SKATEBOARD
SPECTATORS
SPIDERWORT
SPOILSPORT
SPONGEWARE
SPONGIFORM
SPREAGHERY
STATIONARY
STATIONERY
STAVESACRE
STILLIFORM
STINGYBARK
STRASBOURG
STRAWBERRY
STRAWBOARD
STRINDBERG
STRULDBERG
SUBSIDIARY
SUPERSTORE
SUSPENDERS
SVADILFARI
SWEATSHIRT
SWEDENBORG
SWEETHEART
TAPERECORD
THALLIFORM
THREADBARE
THREADWORM
THREESCORE
TIMBERYARD
TITARAKURA
TOMFOOLERY
TRAJECTORY
TRANSITORY
TRAVANCORE
TRAVELLERS
TRENCHMORE
TRIPUDIARY
UNDERSCORE
UNDERSHIRT
UNDERSKIRT
UPHOLSTERY
VETERINARY
VIVANDIÈRE
VOCABULARY
VOLUPTUARY
WATTLEWORK
WHIGGAMORE
WHIRLYBIRD
WHITEHEART
WHITETHORN
WICKERWORK
WILLOWHERB
WINDERMERE
YELLOWGIRL
YOUNGBERRY
ABRUPTNESS
ABSOLUTISM
ACCOMPLISH
ACTIVITIST
ADULTERESS
AFFETTUOSO
AGGRANDISE
AGRONOMIST
ALCOHOLISM
ALLPURPOSE
AMATEURISH
ANABAPTIST
ANTAGONISE
ANTAGONISM
ANTAGONIST
APOCALYPSE
ASCETICISM
ASTUTENESS
AVERRHOISM
BABIROUSSA
BALDERDASH
BALLOONIST
BANGLADESH
BARBAROSSA
BARRENNESS
BASSOONIST
BETELGEUSE
BIOCHEMIST
BITTERNESS
BLEPHARISM
BLOCKHOUSE
BOLLANDIST
BOLSHEVIST
BOTTOMLESS
BOWDLERISE
BRADYSEISM
BRAININESS
BREATHLESS
BRIGHTNESS
BRITISHISM
BUCHMANISM
CAESPITOSE
CANDLEFISH
CANDYFLOSS
CAPITALISM
CAPITALIST
CARTOONIST
CASUALNESS
CATABOLISM
CATEGORISE
CHANGELESS
CHAPTALISE
CHARTREUSE
CHAUVINISM
CHAUVINIST
CHEEKINESS
CHERSONESE
CHILLINESS
CHOICELESS
CHREMATIST
CIRCUMCISE
CIRCUMFUSE
CLAMMINESS
CLASSICISM
CLASSICIST
CLEVERNESS
CLOUDBURST
CLOUDINESS
CLUMSINESS
CNIDOBLAST
COARSENESS
COLOURLESS
COMPROMISE
CONFORMIST
COPPERNOSE
COQUETTISH
COSTLINESS
COTTIERISM
COURTHOUSE
CRAFTINESS
CRISSCROSS
CUSSEDNESS
CUTTLEFISH
DAMSELFISH
DEADLINESS
DEMOBILISE
DEMORALISE
DEUTOPLASM
DIASKEUAST
DICHROMISM
DIRECTNESS
DISCOMPOSE
DISPOSSESS
DIURNALIST
DODECANESE
DOGGEDNESS
DOUBLEBASS
DREAMINESS
DREARINESS
DROWSINESS
EFFORTLESS
EMBERGOOSE
ENTERPRISE
ENTHUSIASM
ENTHUSIAST
ENTREMESSE
EUHEMERISM
EVANGELIST
EXEMPTNESS
EXTINGUISH
EYEWITNESS
FANATICISM
FATHERLESS
FAULTINESS
FAVORITISM
FEDERALISM
FEDERALIST
FEEBLENESS
FIBERGLASS
FIBREGLASS
FICKLENESS
FIELDMOUSE
FIERCENESS
FILLIBRUSH
FILTHINESS
FLABBINESS
FLASHINESS
FLESHINESS
FLIGHTLESS
FLIMSINESS
FLUFFINESS
FOURIERISM
FRATERNISE
FRIENDLESS
FRISKINESS
GENERALISE
GENTLENESS
GEOTROPISM
GLAMOURISE
GLASSHOUSE
GLASSINESS
GLOSSINESS
GNOSTICISM
GOLIATHISE
GOOSEFLESH
GOVERNESSY
GRANGERISM
GREEDINESS
GREENHOUSE
GRITTINESS
GROUNDLESS
GRUBBINESS
GRUMPINESS
GUESTHOUSE
HARTEBEEST
HEARTINESS
HITOPADESA
HITOPODESA
HOARSENESS
HOBBYHORSE
HOMELINESS
HONOURLESS
HOWLEGLASS
HUMBLENESS
HUMOURLESS
HYPOCORISM
HYPOTENUSE
ICONOCLAST
IMPALUDISM
IMPOVERISH
INTENTNESS
JAUNTINESS
JEOPARDISE
JOURNALESE
JOURNALISM
JOURNALIST
KINDLINESS
LACHRYMOSE
LACKADAISY
LAMARCKISM
LAVISHNESS
LENGTHWISE
LEOPARDESS
LESBIANISM
LIBERALISM
LIBRETTIST
LIGHTHOUSE
LITTLENESS
LIVELINESS
LIVERWURST
LONELINESS
LORDLINESS
LOVELINESS
LUMINARIST
LYSENKOISM
MACKINTOSH
MANAGERESS
MANICURIST
MATELLASSE
MAXIMALIST
MAYONNAISE
MEAGERNESS
MEAGRENESS
MELLOWNESS
METABOLISE
METABOLISM
METAPHRASE
MIGHTINESS
MILITARISM
MILITARIST
MINIMALIST
MINUTENESS
MISOGYNIST
MIZZENMAST
MONARCHIST
MONETARISM
MONETARIST
MONOPOLISE
MONOTHEISM
MOROSENESS
MOTHERLESS
MOTIONLESS
MOULDINESS
NARCISSISM
NARCOLEPSY
NARROWNESS
NATHELESSE
NATURALISM

NATURALIST
NEEDLECASE
NEMATOCYST
NETHERMOST
NETTLERASH
NEUTRALISE
NIGHTDRESS
NIMBLENESS
NOMINALIST
NONONSENSE
NONSUCCESS
NORMOBLAST
NUMBERLESS
OBJECTLESS
OBLOMOVISM
OBTUSENESS
ODIOUSNESS
ORTHOCLASE
OSTEOBLAST
OTHERGUESS
OUTLANDISH
OVERPRAISE
PACIFICISM
PAINTBRUSH
PALATALISE
PALIMPSEST
PANSOPHIST
PAPERCHASE
PARAGLOSSA
PARAPHRASE
PARENTLESS
PARNELLISM
PASTEURISE
PATCHINESS
PATRIOTISM
PENSIEROSO
PERDENDOSI
PERMAFROST
PHANTASIST
PHARMACIST
PICAYUNISH
PILLOWCASE
PLAGIARISE
PLAGIARISM
PLAGIARIST
PLANOBLAST
PLASMODESM
PLOUGHWISE
POLITENESS
POLYCHREST
POLYGAMIST
POLYTHEISM
PORTIONIST
PORTUGUESE
POSITIVIST
POSTCHAISE
POWERHOUSE
PRAGMATISM
PRAGMATIST
PREDECEASE
PREDISPOSE
PREPOSSESS
PRESUPPOSE
PRETTINESS
PRICKLOUSE
PROFITLESS
PROMPTNESS
PROPHETESS
PROTOPLASM
PURITANISM
QUAINTNESS
QUEASINESS
QUENCHLESS
RACECOURSE
RADICALISM
RANDOMNESS
REAPPRAISE
RECIDIVISM
RECIDIVIST
RECOMPENSE
REGARDLESS
RELENTLESS
RELINQUISH
REMONETISE
REMOTENESS
RETROGRESS
REVIVALIST
RHAPSODISE
RHEUMATISM
RINDERPEST
ROBUSTNESS
ROUGHHOUSE
ROUNDHOUSE
RUDDERLESS
RUGGEDNESS
SACCHARASE
SACREDNESS
SAVAGENESS
SCANDALISE
SCANTINESS
SCARCENESS
SCATHELESS
SCEPTICISM
SCOOTERIST
SCRUTINISE
SCULPTRESS
SEAMSTRESS
SECONDBEST
SEDATENESS
SENEGALESE
SEPARATISM
SEPARATIST
SEXOLOGIST
SHABBINESS
SHADOWLESS
SHERARDISE
SHIFTINESS
SHODDINESS
SHOVELNOSE
SHREWDNESS
SHRILLNESS
SILVERFISH
SINARCHIST
SINARQUIST
SINFULNESS
SINGHALESE
SINGLENESS
SKEPTICISM
SLEEPINESS
SLEEVELESS
SLOPPINESS
SMARMINESS
SMOOTHNESS
SNOOTINESS
SONGSTRESS
SORDIDNESS
SPARSENESS
SPARTACIST
SPECIALISE
SPECIALIST
SPEECHLESS
SPEEDINESS
SPIRITLESS
SPOONERISM
SPRINGLESS
SPRUCENESS
STEADINESS
STEAKHOUSE
STEELINESS
STEWARDESS
STICKINESS
STIGMATISE
STINGINESS
STOCKINESS
STONEBRASH
STONYHURST
STOREHOUSE
STRATEGIST
STRATOCYST
STREETWISE
STREPITOSO
STRICTNESS
STRIPTEASE
STUFFINESS
STURDINESS
SUDDENNESS
SUFFRAGIST
SULTRINESS
SUPPLENESS
SURINAMESE
SURREALISM
SURREALIST
SYMPATHISE
SYNCRETISE
TAXONOMIST
TENDERNESS
THEOLOGISE
THEOLOGIST
TIMELINESS
TOOTHBRUSH
TOPOLOGIST
TOUCHINESS
TRANSGRESS
TRANSVERSE
TRECENTIST
TRENDINESS
TRICKINESS
TROMBONIST
TROPOPAUSE
UNDERCLASS
UNDERLEASE
UNEASINESS
UNEVENNESS
UNIQUENESS
UNRULINESS
UNTIDINESS
UPPERCLASS
USEFULNESS
VIETNAMESE
VINEGARISH
VIROLOGIST
VOCABULIST
WANDERLUST
WATERBRASH
WATERCRESS
WEAPONLESS
WEIGHTLESS
WHEELHOUSE
WHEEZINESS
WICKEDNESS
WILDEBEEST
WILDERNESS
WORLDCLASS
WORTHINESS
ABBREVIATE
ACCELERATE
ACCENTUATE
ACCUMULATE
ADJUDICATE
ADULLAMITE
ADULTERATE
AFFABILITY
AFTERBIRTH
AFTERTASTE
ALABANDITE
ALEMBICATE
ALKALINITY
ALTAZIMUTH
AMALGAMATE
AMELIORATE
AMIABILITY
AMPHITRITE
AMPLEFORTH
ANDALUSITE
ANNIHILATE
ANNUNCIATE
ANTHRACITE
ANTICIPATE
APPRECIATE
APTERYGOTA
AREOPAGITE
ARTICULATA
ARTICULATE
ASPHALTITE
ASPHYXIATE
ASSEVERATE
ASSIMILATE
ASYNARTETE
AUDIBILITY
AUTOPLASTY
BALLISTITE
BARRACOOTA
BARRACOUTA
BENEDICITE
BENTHAMITE
BESTIALITY
BICHROMATE
BLACKSMITH
BLANQUETTE
BOUILLOTTE
BRIDLEPATH
BROADCLOTH
CACHINNATE
CALAVERITE
CALCEOLATE
CALUMNIATE
CALYPTRATE
CANTILLATE
CAPABILITY
CAPACITATE
CAPERNAITE
CAPERNOITY
CAPITULATE
CAPREOLATE
CASSOLETTE
CHALYBEATE
CHEAPSKATE
CHEMONASTY
CHERVONETS
CHESSYLITE
CHILDBIRTH
CHLORINATE
CHRYSOLITE
COELACANTH
COLLEGIATE
COLLIQUATE
COMMENTATE
COMPENSATE
COMPLANATE
COMPLEXITY
COMPLICATE
COMPLICITY
CONCERVATE
CONCILIATE
CONCINNITY
CONDIMENTS
CONFIDANTE
CONFISCATE
CONFORMITY
CONGREGATE

CONSECRATE
CONSONANTS
CONSTITUTE
CONSUMMATE
CONTIGUITY
CONTINUITY
CONTRIBUTE
CONVOLVUTE
COORDINATE
COQUIMBITE
CORDIALITY
CORDIERITE
CREATIVITY
CRENELLATE
DEACTIVATE
DEBILITATE
DECAPITATE
DECATHLETE
DECELERATE
DECOLORATE
DEFLAGRATE
DEGENERATE
DELIBERATE
DEPOPULATE
DEPRECIATE
DERACINATE
DEREGULATE
DESALINATE
DESIDERATA
DESQUAMATE
DETRUNCATE
DIFFICULTY
DILAPIDATE
DILETTANTE
DISABILITY
DISHONESTY
DISLOYALTY
DISSERTATE
DISSOCIATE
DISTILLATE
DISTRIBUTE
DITHIONATE
DOLCEMENTE
DOPPLERITE
DUNDERPATE
DURABILITY
DUUMVIRATE
DYSCRASITE
EBRACTEATE
ECARDINATE
EDULCORATE
EFFECTUATE
EFFEMINATE
EGURGITATE
EIGHTEENTH
ELASTICATE
ELASTICITY
ELECTORATE
EMANCIPATE
EMARGINATE
EMASCULATE
EMBLEMENTS
EMOLUMENTS
EPHRAIMITE
EPIDIORITE
EPISCOPATE
EPROUVETTE
EQUANIMITY
EQUIVOCATE
EVISCERATE
EVITERNITY
EXACERBATE
EXAGGERATE
EXASPERATE
EXCRUCIATE
EXENTERATE
EXHILARATE
EXPATRIATE
FACILITATE
FALSETRUTH
FASTIGIATE
FELICITATE
FEMININITY
FIANCHETTO
FIBRILLATE
FLAGELLATE
FLOCCULATE
FLOORCLOTH
FLUTEMOUTH
FOOTLIGHTS
FOOTPRINTS
FOURCHETTE
FOURTEENTH
FRATERETTO
FRATERNITY
FULLLENGTH
GARNIERITE
GENERALITY
GENEROSITY
GENEVRETTE
GENICULATE
GLAUCONITE
GLITTERATI
GODPARENTS
GRAPTOLITE
GRASSROOTS
GRATILLITY
GREENCLOTH
HABILITATE
HALLOYSITE
HEADLIGHTS
HENCEFORTH
HEREABOUTS
HOMOEOPATH
IGNIMBRITE
ILLAQUEATE
ILLEGALITY
ILLITERATE
ILLUMINATE
ILLUMINATI
ILLUSTRATE
IMBECILITY
IMBROCCATA
IMMACULATE
IMMATURITY
IMMOBILITY
IMMODERATE
IMMORALITY
IMPREGNATE
INACCURATE
INACTIVITY
INADEQUATE
INAUGURATE
INCAPACITY
INCINERATE
INCIVILITY
INCOMPLETE
INCRASSATE
INDEFINITE
INDELICATE
INDICOLITE
INDIGOLITE
INEQUALITY
INFIDELITY
INFILTRATE
INGEMINATE
INGENERATE
INGRATIATE
INHUMANITY
INORDINATE
INOSCULATE
INSECURITY
INSEMINATE
INSIPIDITY
INSPISSATE
INSUFFLATE
INSULARITY
INTAGLIATE
INTEMERATE
INTENERATE
INTERSTATE
INTIMIDATE
INTOXICATE
INVALIDATE
INVALIDITY
INVETERATE
INVIGILATE
INVIGORATE
IRRADICATE
IRRESOLUTE
JAMESONITE
JOCULARITY
KATERFELTO
KENILWORTH
KIMBERLITE
LANCEOLATE
LASTMINUTE
LATTERMATH
LAURDALITE
LAURVIKITE
LEGIBILITY
LEGITIMATE
LEMNISCATE
LHERZOLITE
LIBERALITY
LICENTIATE
LIMBURGITE
LINEAMENTS
LOUISIETTE
LUMINOSITY
MACROBIOTE
MAGISTRATE
MAISONETTE
MALAGUETTA
MANIPULATE
MARCIONITE
MARGUERITE
MARIONETTE
MASTURBATE
MEDIOCRITY
MELACONITE
MENSTRUATE
MIGNONETTE
MINISTRATE
MISHNAYOTH
MITHRIDATE
MORGANETTA
MULIEBRITY
MUTABILITY
NATUROPATH
NDRANGHETA
NEUTRALITY
NEWSAGENTS
NINETEENTH
NOTABILITY
NOUAKCHOTT
NOVACULITE
OBLITERATE
ODONTOLITE
OSTEOPHYTE
PALAGONITE
PALATINATE
PAPIAMENTO
PARAGONITE
PARRAMATTA
PARTIALITY
PASSIONATE
PATAVINITY
PEDICULATE
PENTIMENTO
PERIDOTITE
PERNICKETY
PEROVSKITE
PERPETRATE
PERPETUATE
PERPETUITY
PERPLEXITY
PERQUISITE
PERVERSITY
PHLOGOPITE
PHOTONASTY
PIANOFORTE
PISTILLATE
PLANCHETTE
PLASTICITY
PLEBISCITE
PLIABILITY
PLOUGHBOTE
PLOUGHGATE
POLYCHAETE
POPULARITY
PORTAMENTO
PORTSMOUTH
POSTILLATE
POTENTIATE
PROCLIVITY
PROFLIGATE
PROFUNDITY
PROMULGATE
PROPENSITY
PROPIONATE
PROPITIATE
PROSCIUTTO
PROSPERITY
PROSTITUTE
PROTERVITY
PSYCHOPATH
PUNCTULATE
PYRAGYRITE
REACTIVATE
RECUPERATE
REDECORATE
REDRUTHITE
REGENERATE
REGULARITY
REJUVENATE
RELATIVITY
REMUNERATE
REPATRIATE
RESERVISTS
RESUPINATE
RETINALITE
SAMARSKITE
SANDINISTA
SAPROPHYTE
SCURRILITY
SCUTELLATE
SECONDRATE
SENSUALITY
SEVENTIETH
SHIBBOLETH
SHRIEVALTY
SILHOUETTE
SIMILARITY
SIMPLICITY
SNAKEMOUTH
SOLIDARITY
SOLUBILITY
SOMBRERITE
SPECIALITY

SPERMACETI
SPERRYLITE
SPHACELATE
SPHALERITE
SPIFLICATE
STALACTITE
STALAGMITE
STAUROLITE
STEPHANITE
STIACCIATO
STILLBIRTH
STRIDULATE
SUBSTITUTE
SUPPLICATE
SUZERAINTY
SYNTAGMATA
TABLANETTE
TABLECLOTH
TENNANTITE
TERNEPLATE
TERRACOTTA
TESCHENITE
THAUMASITE
THEODOLITE
THEOLOGATE
THIRTEENTH
THOUSANDTH
TINTORETTO
TOILINETTE
TOOTHPASTE
TOPICALITY
TORBERNITE
TRACHELATE
TRAGACANTH
TRIPARTITE
TRIPLICATE
TRIVIALITY
TROCTOLITE
TROGLODYTE
TROPOPHYTE
TROTSKYITE
ULSTERETTE
UNDERNEATH
UNDERPANTS
UNDERSTATE
UNDERWRITE
UNIFORMITY
UNIVERSITY
UROSTEGITE
VARICOSITY
VERTEBRATE
VESICULATE
VINDEMIATE
VIRTUOSITY
VISIBILITY
VITUPERATE
VOCIFERATE
VOLATILITY
VOLUBILITY
WANDSWORTH
WAVELENGTH
WHEWELLITE
WINCEYETTE
WOLFRAMITE
WOOLLYBUTT
WORDSWORTH
ABSTEMIOUS
ACANACEOUS
ACCLIVIOUS
ACEPHALOUS
ACETABULUM
ACROGENOUS
ADULTEROUS
AERUGINOUS
AGAPANTHUS
ALLOSAURUS
AMBULACRUM
AMPHIBIOUS
ANACARDIUM
ANADROMOUS
ANCIPITOUS
ANTIBARBUS
ANTIMASQUE
ANTITRAGUS
APEMANTHUS
APOLLONIUS
APOTHECIUM
ARENACEOUS
ARISTIPPUS
ARTOCARPUS
ASTOMATOUS
ASTRAGALUS
ASTRALAGUS
ATRACURIUM
AUDITORIUM
AURIFEROUS
AUSPICIOUS
AUTOGENOUS
AUTONOMOUS
AVARICIOUS
BATTAILOUS
BITUMINOUS
BLOTTESQUE
BOISTEROUS
BUCEPHALUS
CACUMINOUS
CADAVEROUS
CALAMITOUS
CALCAREOUS
CANEPHORUS
CAOUTCHOUC
CAPITELLUM
CAPRICIOUS
CARACTACUS
CATAFALQUE
CATAWAMPUS
CENSORIOUS
CEREBELLUM
CHAUTAUQUA
CHIVALROUS
CHOLALOGUE
CHRYSIPPUS
CIRCUITOUS
COCCINEOUS
COCKALORUM
COETANEOUS
COLPORTEUR
COMMODIOUS
COMMUNIQUÉ
COMPENDIUM
COMPLUVIUM
CONCINNOUS
CONIFEROUS
CONSORTIUM
CONSPECTUS
CONTAGIOUS
CONTIGUOUS
CONTINUOUS
CONTRECOUP
COPERNICUS
CORYPHAEUS
COURAGEOUS
CREOPHAGUS
CRETACEOUS
CRYOPHORUS
CURRICULUM
CURVACEOUS
CYNOMOLGUS
DELIGHTFUL
DELPHINIUM
DEMOCRITUS
DERAILLEUR
DESPITEOUS
DIAPHANOUS
DIDUNCULUS
DIGITORIUM
DIPLODOCUS
DISASTROUS
DISCOBOLUS
DISDAINFUL
DISEMBOGUE
DOLICHOTUS
DYSPROSIUM
ELEGABALUS
EMPLASTRUM
ENDOGAMOUS
EPICANTHUS
EPIDENDRUM
EPIDIDYMUS
EPIMETHEUS
EPITHELIUM
EPONYCHIUM
ERYMANTHUS
EUCALYPTUS
EUPHONIOUS
EUROCHEQUE
EURYPTERUS
EXTRANEOUS
FACTITIOUS
FALLACIOUS
FASTIDIOUS
FELICITOUS
FICTITIOUS
FLAGITIOUS
FONTICULUS
FORTUITOUS
FULIGINOUS
GADOLINIUM
GANGRENOUS
GELATINOUS
GLUTTONOUS
GRATUITOUS
GREGARIOUS
GUARNERIUS
HAEMANTHUS
HAKENKREUZ
HARMONIOUS
HAUSTELLUM
HAUSTORIUM
HERBACEOUS
HIPPARCHUS
HOMUNCULUS
HONORARIUM
HORRENDOUS
HOUSEPROUD
HUMORESQUE
HYPOGAEOUS
IMPERVIOUS
IMPRIMATUR
INCAUTIOUS
INCESTUOUS
INDECOROUS
INDIGENOUS
INDUMENTUM
INFECTIOUS
INGLORIOUS
INIQUITOUS
JUGGERNAUT
KETTLEDRUM
KNOCKABOUT
LANGUOROUS
LANIGEROUS
LASCIVIOUS
LAWRENCIUM
LEBENSRAUM
LEGUMINOUS
LENOCINIUM
LEPRECHAUN
LIBIDINOUS
LICENTIOUS
LIGHTINGUP
LOQUACIOUS
LOTOPHAGUS
LUGUBRIOUS
MALODOROUS
MARTINIQUE
MARVELLOUS
MEANINGFUL
MEERSCHAUM
MEGALOSAUR
MEMBRANOUS
MEMORANDUM
MENDACIOUS
METACARPUS
METATARSUS
METICULOUS
MINDERERUS
MIRACULOUS
MOLYBDENUM
MONEGASQUE
MONOECIOUS
MONOGAMOUS
MONOTONOUS
MONTICULUS
MORATORIUM
MORDACIOUS
MORIGEROUS
MOZAMBIQUE
MYSTAGOGUE
MYSTAGOGUS
MYSTERIOUS
NASTURTIUM
NATATORIUM
NECTABANUS
NEFANDROUS
NEGLECTFUL
NUTRITIOUS
OBSEQUIOUS
OESOPHAGUS
OLEAGINOUS
OLERACEOUS
OMNIVOROUS
OPPROBRIUM
ORCHIDEOUS
OSMETERIUM
OUTRAGEOUS
PANARITIUM
PANCRATIUM
PANJANDRUM
PANNICULUS
PARACELSUS
PEDIPALPUS
PENNISETUM
PERDITIOUS
PERFIDIOUS
PERNICIOUS
PHOSPHORUS
PICARESQUE
PLESIOSAUR
PLIOHIPPUS
POLYANTHUS
POLYGAMOUS
POLYPHEMUS
PORRACEOUS
PORTENTOUS
PORTMANTUA
POSTHUMOUS
PRAETORIUM
PRECARIOUS
PRECOCIOUS

PREDACIOUS
PRINCIPIUM
PRODIGIOUS
PROMETHEUS
PROMETHIUM
PROPERTIUS
PROPITIOUS
PROPOSITUS
PROPYLAEUM
PROSCENIUM
PROSPECTUS
PROSPEROUS
PSALTERIUM
PTERYGOTUS
PUGNACIOUS
PURPOSEFUL
PYROPHORUS
RANUNCULUS
RAPPORTEUR
REBELLIOUS
REFERENDUM
REMORSEFUL
RENDEZVOUS
REPETITEUR
RESPECTFUL
REVENGEFUL
RIDICULOUS
ROBUSTIOUS
ROMANESQUE
ROUNDABOUT
ROUSEABOUT
ROUSTABOUT
RUBIGINOUS
SALUBRIOUS
SANATORIUM
SANITARIUM
SARMENTOUS
SAUERKRAUT
SAXICOLOUS
SCANDALOUS
SCRUPULOUS
SCURRILOUS
SEQUACIOUS
SIMILLIMUM
SIMULACRUM
SLANDEROUS
SOLICITOUS
SPIRACULUM
SPIRITUOUS
SQUETEAGUE
STANISLAUS
STATUESQUE
STERTEROUS
STERTOROUS
STRABISMUS
STRAMONIUM
STRULDBRUG
STUPENDOUS
SUBSELLIUM
SUBSTRATUM
SUCCESSFUL
SULPHUROUS
SUSPICIOUS
SYMPHONIUM
SYNONYMOUS
SYNTHRONUS
TECHNETIUM
TEPIDARIUM
TESTACEOUS
THALICTRUM
THEOCRITUS
THIMBLEFUL
THOUGHTFUL
THROUGHOUT
THROUGHPUT
THUNDEROUS
TIRAILLEUR
TIROCINIUM
TRAITOROUS
TRAVELOGUE
TREMENDOUS
TRICLINIUM
TROPAEOLUM
TROPHONIUS
TROUBADOUR
TUMULTUOUS
TUTIVILLUS
UBIQUITOUS
ULTRONEOUS
UNDERVALUE
UNEVENTFUL
UNFAITHFUL
UNFRUITFUL
UNGRACIOUS
UNGRATEFUL
UNIGENITUS
UNTRUTHFUL
UPROARIOUS
VESTIBULUM
VIBRACULUM
VICTORIOUS
VILLAINOUS
VIVIPAROUS
VOCIFEROUS
VOLUMINOUS
VOLUPTUOUS
VORAGINOUS
WATERSPOUT
XIPHOPAGUS
ACCUSATIVE
AFTERSHAVE
AGGRESSIVE
AMRITATTVA
APPETITIVE
ARCHITRAVE
ASSUMPTIVE
ATTRACTIVE
AUTOMOTIVE
BRATISLAVA
COLLECTIVE
COMPULSIVE
CONCLUSIVE
CONNECTIVE
CONVULSIVE
CORRECTIVE
CUMULATIVE
DECORATIVE
DEFINITIVE
DEPRESSIVE
DERIVATIVE
DIMINUTIVE
DISAPPROVE
DISBELIEVE
DISCURSIVE
DISMISSIVE
DISRUPTIVE
EXHAUSTIVE
EXPRESSIVE
FIGURATIVE
GAINSTRIVE
IMPERATIVE
IMPRESSIVE
INDECISIVE
INDICATIVE
INFINITIVE
INITIATIVE
INNOVATIVE
INTERLEAVE
INTERWEAVE
LOCOMOTIVE
MEDITATIVE
NAUSEATIVE
NOMINATIVE
OPPRESSIVE
PALLIATIVE
PEJORATIVE
PERCEPTIVE
PERMISSIVE
PERSUASIVE
POSSESSIVE
PREVENTIVE
PRODUCTIVE
PROTECTIVE
RECITATIVE
RECITATIVO
REFLECTIVE
REFRACTIVE
REGRESSIVE
RELAXATIVE
REPETITIVE
REPRESSIVE
RESPECTIVE
RESPONSIVE
RHINEGRAVE
RUMINATIVE
SPOKESHAVE
SPOLIATIVE
SUBJECTIVE
SUBMISSIVE
SUBVERSIVE
SUCCESSIVE
SUGGESTIVE
SUPPORTIVE
TOPSYTURVY
TRANSITIVE
TURTLEDOVE
VINDICTIVE
BRIDGETOWN
BROKENDOWN
BUTTONDOWN
CAMPERDOWN
FULLYGROWN
GEORGETOWN
HORSEDRAWN
JACKSTRAWS
MUMBLENEWS
ODDFELLOWS
POHUTUKAWA
QUEENSTOWN
TUMBLEDOWN
HETERODOXY
KARTTIKAYA
LAUNCEGAYE
LENGTHWAYS
STRIDEWAYS
ANTAGONIZE
ANTIFREEZE
BETELGEUZE
BOWDLERIZE
BURGLARIZE
CAPITALIZE
CARAMELIZE
CATEGORIZE
CENTRALIZE
CHIMBORAZO
COLEORHIZA
DECIMALIZE
DEEPFREEZE
DEMOBILIZE
DEMORALIZE
EVANGELIZE
FRATERNIZE
GENERALIZE
GORMANDIZE
GRANGERIZE
HOMOGENIZE
IMMOBILIZE
INTERMEZZO
JEOPARDIZE
LEGITIMIZE
LIBERALIZE
MOISTURIZE
MONOPOLIZE
MORBIDEZZA
MYCORRHIZA
NATURALIZE
NEUTRALIZE
PASSAMEZZO
PASTEURIZE
PESTALOZZI
PLAGIARIZE
POLITICIZE
POLYMERIZE
POPULARIZE
PRESSURIZE
RAZZMATAZZ
REGULARIZE
REORGANIZE
REVITALIZE
RHAPSODIZE
SCANDALIZE
SCRUTINIZE
SECULARIZE
SPECIALIZE
STIGMATIZE
SYMPATHIZE
SYNTHESIZE
TRAUMATIZE
TRIVIALIZE
WESTERNIZE

10:10

ABHIDHAMMA
ADVERSARIA
AERENCHYMA
AEROPHAGIA
AFRORMOSIA
ALCAICERIA
ALCHERINGA
ALCYONARIA
ALEXANDRIA
ALGOLAGNIA
AMBARVALIA
AMBLYSTOMA
AMPHINEURA
AMRITATTVA
ANESTHESIA
ANGUILLULA
ANTARCTICA
APTERYGOTA
ARTHRALGIA
ARTHURIANA
ARTICULATA
ASAFOETIDA
ASARABACCA
ASPIDISTRA
ASTEROIDEA
AUTOSTRADA
AVICULARIA
BABIROUSSA
BANDERILLA
BARASINGHA
BARBAROSSA
BARRACOOTA
BARRACOUTA
BARRAMUNDA
BELLADONNA
BIPINNARIA

BLASTOIDEA
BRATISLAVA
CALIFORNIA
CAMPANELLA
CANDELABRA
CANDELILLA
CARICATURA
CASCARILLA
CASSIOPEIA
CAVICORNIA
CECIDOMYIA
CHAULMUGRA
CHAUTAUQUA
CHINCHILLA
CHIROPTERA
CHRISTIANA
CHUCKWALLA
CINDERELLA
CINECAMERA
CIRRHOPODA
CIRRIPEDEA
CIRRIPEDIA
CITRONELLA
CLARABELLA
CLOSTRIDIA
COCHLEARIA
COLEOPTERA
COLEORHIZA
COLLEMBOLA
COLORATURA
CONCERTINA
CONSTANTIA
CORDILLERA
CORNUCOPIA
CORRIGENDA
CORTADERIA
CROTALARIA
CTENOPHORA
CYCLOPEDIA
DESIDERATA
DHARMSHALA
DIPHTHERIA
DIPSOMANIA
DISCOPHORA
DROSOPHILA
ECHINOIDEA
ECHOPRAXIA
EMMETROPIA
EPANOPHORA
EPIPHONEMA
EPIPLASTRA
ETHEOSTOMA
EUTHANASIA
EUTHYNEURA
EUTRAPELIA
FENESTELLA
FLINDERSIA
FLORIBUNDA
FRAMBOESIA
FRAXINELLA
FUSTANELLA
GAULTHERIA
GIBBERELLA
GONORRHOEA
GRANADILLA
GRENADILLA
GROCETERIA
GYPSOPHILA
HEMICHORDA
HEMIPLEGIA
HEMOPHILIA
HITOPADESA
HITOPODESA
HOMOPHOBIA
HYPERDULIA
ICOSANDRIA
ICOSOHEDRA
IMBROCCATA
INCAPARINA
INCUNABULA
KARTTIKAYA
KLEBSIELLA
KOOKABURRA
KURDAITCHA
LEUCHAEMIA
LINGULELLA
LITHISTADA
LOGORRHOEA
LUPERCALIA
LYCHNAPSIA
MACROCARPA
MALAGUETTA
MALLOPHAGA
MANDRAGORA
MANGABEIRA
MANZANILLA
MARGINALIA
MARSHALSEA
MASKIROVKA
MASSASAUGA
MAURITANIA
MENORRHOEA
METATHERIA
METHOMANIA
MICRONESIA
MONOPLEGIA
MORBIDEZZA
MORGANETTA
MORTADELLA
MOZZARELLA
MULTIMEDIA
MYCORRHIZA
NDRANGHETA
NEURILEMMA
NEUROLEMMA
NOSOPHOBIA
NYCTALOPIA
ODONTALGIA
ORTHOPNOEA
OSTEOCOLLA
OUVIRANDRA
PALESTRINA
PALMATOZOA
PARAGLOSSA
PARAPHILIA
PARAPHONIA
PARAPLEGIA
PARARTHRIA
PARASCENIA
PARENCHYMA
PARONYCHIA
PARRAMATTA
PASTORELLA
PENETRALIA
PERSICARIA
PETRONELLA
PHAGEDAENA
PHILIPPINA
PHILLIPINA
PHILOPOENA
PHILOXENIA
PHLEGMASIA
PINNIPEDIA
POHUTUKAWA
POINSETTIA
POLYHYMNIA
PONTEDERIA
PORTMANTUA
POTENTILLA
POZZUOLANA
PRESBYOPIA
PROPAGANDA
PROSERPINA
PROSPERINA
PSOCOPTERA
PYRACANTHA
QUADRATURA
QUESADILLA
QUIRINALIA
RADIOLARIA
RHINOLALIA
RHINOPHYMA
RHIPIPTERA
RUMINANTIA
SAGITTARIA
SALICORNIA
SALMONELLA
SANDEMANIA
SANDINISTA
SARCOCOLLA
SARCOLEMMA
SATURNALIA
SATYAGRAHA
SAUROPSIDA
SAVONAROLA
SCAPHOPODA
SCARLATINA
SCARLETINA
SCHOLAEMIA
SCORDATURA
SCORZONERA
SCOTODINIA
SDRUCCIOLA
SEGUIDILLA
SERRADELLA
SERRADILLA
SEXAGESIMA
SIGILLARIA
SINSEMILLA
SKUPSHTINA
STERNALGIA
STRELITZIA
SYNTAGMATA
TANGANYIKA
TARANTELLA
TATPURUSHA
TEICHOPSIA
TERMINALIA
TERRACOTTA
TILLANDSIA
TITARAKURA
TOCCATELLA
TORQUEMADA
TRAMONTANA
TRITANOPIA
TULARAEMIA
TURRITELLA
VICTORIANA
VULCANALIA
XENOPHOBIA
XEROSTOMIA
ZOANTHARIA
SHISHKEBAB
THINGUMBOB
WILLOWHERB
ACHROMATIC
ACROAMATIC
ALLOSTERIC
ALLOTROPIC
ALTRUISTIC
AMPHOTERIC
ANACLASTIC
ANACOUSTIC
ANACRUSTIC
ANCHORETIC
ANESTHETIC
ANTIBIOTIC
ANTISEPTIC
ANTISTATIC
ANTITHETIC
APOLAUSTIC
APOLOGETIC
APOPEMPTIC
APOPLECTIC
APOSEMATIC
APOTROPAIC
ARITHMETIC
ASTIGMATIC
ASYMMETRIC
AUTOCRATIC
BARBITURIC
BAROMETRIC
BRONCHITIC
CAOUTCHOUC
CATALECTIC
CATALEPTIC
CHIRONOMIC
CONCENTRIC
COPESETTIC
CORYBANTIC
CYBERNETIC
DEMOCRATIC
DIACAUSTIC
DIAGNOSTIC
DIASTALTIC
DIDASCALIC
DIELECTRIC
DIPLOMATIC
DOCIMASTIC
DYSTROPHIC
ECCOPROTIC
EGOCENTRIC
ELECTRONIC
EMBLEMATIC
ENHYDRITIC
EPENTHETIC
EPIDEICTIC
EPIGENETIC
EPISPASTIC
ESCHAROTIC
EULOGISTIC
EXOTHERMIC
FATALISTIC
FUTURISTIC
GALLIAMBIC
GENETHLIAC
GEOCENTRIC
GEOGRAPHIC
GYROSCOPIC
HEDONISTIC
HIERARCHIC
HISTRIONIC
HOLOSTERIC
HOMOPHOBIC
HUMANISTIC
HYDROPONIC
HYPERBOLIC
HYPODERMIC
IATROGENIC
IDEALISTIC
INARTISTIC
JINGOISTIC
LAEOTROPIC
LEGALISTIC
LINGUISTIC
MEGALITHIC
MESOLITHIC
MISOCAPNIC
MONOLITHIC
MONOPHONIC

MORGANATIC
NIHILISTIC
NUMISMATIC
OPHTHALMIC
OPTIMISTIC
OXYMORONIC
PAEDIATRIC
PARAMETRIC
PARAPLEGIC
PATHOGENIC
PATRONYMIC
PEELGARLIC
PENTATONIC
PENTETERIC
PHILATELIC
PHLEGMATIC
PHLOGISTIC
PHOTOGENIC
PHRENESIAC
PLEONASTIC
POIKILITIC
PROSTHETIC
PROTANOPIC
PYROMANIAC
PYTHOGENIC
RHEOTROPIC
SCHISMATIC
SCHOLASTIC
SCIENTIFIC
SIMPLISTIC
SOPHOMORIC
SPLANCHNIC
STOCHASTIC
SUPERSONIC
SUPERTONIC
SYPHILITIC
SYSTEMATIC
TELEPATHIC
TELEPHONIC
TELESCOPIC
TENEBRIFIC
THERMIONIC
ULTRASONIC
UNHYGIENIC
UNROMANTIC
UNSPECIFIC
WORKAHOLIC
XENOPHOBIC
XEROPHYTIC
ABOVEBOARD
ABSTRACTED
ACCREDITED
ACCUSTOMED
ACQUAINTED
AFFILIATED
AMPUSSYAND
AMYGDALOID
ANNUALIZED
ANTHROPOID
ANTIQUATED
ARYTAENOID
ASSOCIATED
ASTONISHED
AUTHORISED
BACKGROUND
BACKHANDED
BAMBOOZLED
BAREFOOTED
BAREHEADED
BARELEGGED
BEDEVILLED
BEDRAGGLED
BEFOREHAND
BEHINDHAND
BEWILDERED
BIRKENHEAD
BLACKBEARD
BLACKBOARD
BLACKGUARD
BLEARYEYED
BLOODHOUND
BORDERLAND
BOTTLEHEAD
BRACHIOPOD
BRAINCHILD
BRASSBOUND
BREASTFEED
BRIDESMAID
BRIDGEHEAD
BROADSWORD
BUFFLEHEAD
BULLHEADED
CALCULATED
CAMELOPARD
CAPTIVATED
CATTLEGRID
CELEBRATED
CEPHALOPOD
CHARGEHAND
CHAUDFROID
CHEESEWOOD
CHERRYWOOD
CHESSBOARD
CHURCHYARD
CLASSIFIED
CLAVICHORD
CLOISTERED
COASTGUARD
COLONNADED
COMPOUNDED
COMPREHEND
COMPRESSED
CONDESCEND
CONFERVOID
CONFOUNDED
CONSIDERED
CONTRABAND
CONVOLUTED
COPPERHEAD
CORRESPOND
CORRUGATED
COTTONWOOD
CRISPBREAD
CROSSBREED
CUCULLATED
CULTIVATED
CUMBERLAND
CUMMERBUND
DARKHAIRED
DECIPHERED
DECOMPOSED
DEEPSEATED
DESECRATED
DESICCATED
DETERMINED
DEVASTATED
DIMINISHED
DISCOLORED
DISENGAGED
DISFIGURED
DISJOINTED
DISMANTLED
DISORDERED
DISPIRITED
DISQUIETED
DISSIPATED
DISTRACTED
DISTRESSED
DUNDERHEAD
DYNAMITARD
EISTEDDFOD
EMBITTERED
ENRAPTURED
ENTRENCHED
EVAPORATED
EVENHANDED
EXONERATED
FAIRGROUND
FAIRHAIRED
FARFETCHED
FASCINATED
FATHERLAND
FEATHERBED
FERTILISED
FIDDLEWOOD
FIGUREHEAD
FITZGERALD
FLOORBOARD
FLOURISHED
FOREDAMNED
FOREGROUND
FOREWARNED
FOSSILIZED
FREQUENTED
FRIGHTENED
FRINGILLID
FRUSTRATED
GASTEROPOD
GIRLFRIEND
GLITTERAND
GRANDCHILD
GRANDSTAND
GRANULATED
GREENSWARD
GRIDLOCKED
GUARANTEED
HALLMARKED
HAMMERHEAD
HANDPICKED
HARDBOILED
HEADHUNTED
HEAVENWARD
HIGHHANDED
HILDEBRAND
HINTERLAND
HITHERWARD
HOODWINKED
HORNRIMMED
HOUSEBOUND
HOUSEPROUD
HUMPBACKED
HYPNOTIZED
ILLADVISED
IMBRICATED
IMPROVISED
INDISPOSED
INEBRIATED
INFATUATED
INFURIATED
INSTRUCTED
INTEGRATED
INTERBREED
INTERESTED
JACKBOOTED
JOLTERHEAD
KNIFEBOARD
KNIGHTHOOD
LANDLOCKED
LEFTHANDED
LETTERHEAD
LIKELIHOOD
LIKEMINDED
LIVELIHOOD
LOGGERHEAD
MAGISTRAND
MAIDENHOOD
MASTERMIND
MECHANIZED
METHYLATED
MISERICORD
MISMATCHED
MONTAGNARD
MOTHERHOOD
MOTHERLAND
MULTIPLIED
MUTTONHEAD
NEWFANGLED
NIGGERHEAD
NONALIGNED
NONPLUSSED
NORTHBOUND
NORTHSTEAD
OBFUSCATED
OPENHANDED
OPENMINDED
OVERSPREAD
OVERWORKED
PALMATIFID
PARALLELED
PARENTHOOD
PASTEBOARD
PATRONISED
PERFORATED
PHYLLIOPOD
PLATINISED
PLATTELAND
PLAYGROUND
POCKMARKED
POKERFACED
POLLINATED
PREJUDICED
PRIESTHOOD
PRINCIPLED
PRIVILEGED
PROHIBITED
PRONOUNCED
PROSCRIBED
PROTRACTED
PUCKERWOOD
PYCNOGONID
RECOGNISED
RECOGNIZED
RECONCILED
REGIMENTED
REGISTERED
REITERATED
RESTRAINED
RESTRICTED
RHEUMATOID
RIDINGHOOD
ROTHSCHILD
RUTHERFORD
SACCHAROID
SANCTIFIED
SANDALWOOD
SANFORISED
SCOREBOARD
SECONDHAND
SEEMLIHEAD
SEGREGATED
SELFSTYLED
SHAGHAIRED
SHAMEFACED
SHOPSOILED
SHORTBREAD
SHORTLIVED
SHOVELHEAD
SHRIVELLED
SISTERHOOD
SKATEBOARD

SMORREBROD
SNEEZEWOOD
SNOWCAPPED
SOFTBOILED
SOUTHBOUND
SPECTACLED
SPELLBOUND
STILLSTAND
STOMATOPOD
STRAITENED
STRAWBOARD
STREAMERED
STRONGHOLD
STULTIFIED
STYLOPISED
SUPERADDED
SUPERVISED
SUPPRESSED
SURROUNDED
SWEETBREAD
SYNCOPATED
TALLEYRAND
TAPERECORD
TENDRILLED
THREATENED
TIMBERYARD
TOSSICATED
TOSTICATED
TRANSLATED
TRANSPOSED
TRIPEHOUND
TURNAROUND
TYRANNISED
ULTRASOUND
UNABRIDGED
UNACCENTED
UNAFFECTED
UNANSWERED
UNASSIGNED
UNATTACHED
UNATTENDED
UNBALANCED
UNBLEACHED
UNCONFINED
UNCULTURED
UNDECLARED
UNDEFEATED
UNDEFENDED
UNDERSIZED
UNDERSTAND
UNDERSTOOD
UNDERWORLD
UNDESCRIED
UNDESERVED
UNDETECTED
UNDETERRED
UNDIGESTED
UNDISPUTED
UNDOCTORED
UNEDUCATED
UNEMPLOYED
UNEQUALLED
UNEXAMPLED
UNEXPECTED
UNEXPLORED
UNFATHOMED
UNFETTERED
UNFINISHED
UNFLAVORED
UNGROUNDED
UNHAMPERED
UNHERALDED
UNIMPAIRED
UNINFORMED
UNINSPIRED
UNLEAVENED
UNLETTERED
UNLICENSED
UNMANNERED
UNNUMBERED
UNOBSERVED
UNOCCUPIED
UNPREPARED
UNPROMPTED
UNPROVOKED
UNREASONED
UNREDEEMED
UNRELIEVED
UNREQUITED
UNRESERVED
UNRESOLVED
UNREVEALED
UNRIVALLED
UNSALARIED
UNSCHOOLED
UNSCRIPTED
UNSEASONED
UNSHACKLED
VALLADOLID
VARIEGATED
WAINSCOTED
WELLEARNED
WHIRLYBIRD
WIDESPREAD
WINDSHIELD
WONDERLAND
WOODENHEAD
WRAPAROUND
WUNDERKIND
YELLOWWOOD
YTHUNDERED
ABBREVIATE
ABERDEVINE
ABERGLAUBE
ABHORRENCE
ABOMINABLE
ABSTINENCE
ACCELERATE
ACCENTUATE
ACCESSIBLE
ACCOMPLICE
ACCORDANCE
ACCUMULATE
ACCUSATIVE
ACTIONABLE
ADAMANTINE
ADJUDICATE
ADJUSTABLE
ADMISSIBLE
ADMITTANCE
ADRENALINE
ADULLAMITE
ADULTERATE
ADULTERINE
AFFORDABLE
AFTERPIECE
AFTERSHAVE
AFTERTASTE
AGGRANDISE
AGGRESSIVE
ALABANDINE
ALABANDITE
ALEMBICATE
ALLEGEANCE
ALLEGIANCE
ALLPURPOSE
ALPHONSINE
AMALGAMATE
AMELIORATE
AMPHITRITE
ANADYOMENE
ANASTROPHE
ANDALUSITE
ANDROMACHE
ANGLOPHILE
ANGLOPHOBE
ANNIHILATE
ANNUNCIATE
ANSWERABLE
ANTAGONISE
ANTAGONIZE
ANTHOCLORE
ANTHRACINE
ANTHRACITE
ANTICIPATE
ANTIFREEZE
ANTIMASQUE
ANTIOCHENE
ANTIVENENE
APICULTURE
APOCALYPSE
APOSTROPHE
APPEARANCE
APPETITIVE
APPLICABLE
APPRECIATE
APPRENTICE
AQUAMANALE
AQUAMANILE
AQUAMARINE
ARACOSTYLE
ARCHITRAVE
AREOPAGITE
ARTHROMERE
ARTICULATE
ASCRIBABLE
ASPARAGINE
ASPHALTITE
ASPHYXIATE
ASSEMBLAGE
ASSEVERATE
ASSIGNABLE
ASSIMILATE
ASSISTANCE
ASSUMPTIVE
ASYNARTETE
ATMOSPHERE
ATTAINABLE
ATTENDANCE
ATTRACTIVE
AUTOMOBILE
AUTOMOTIVE
AVANTGARDE
AVANTURINE
AVENTURINE
AVVOGADORE
BACKSTROKE
BALANCHINE
BALLISTITE
BALUSTRADE
BARCAROLLE
BARLEYBREE
BARYSPHERE
BATTLEDORE
BAUDELAIRE
BELIEVABLE
BELLAMOURE
BELLARMINE
BENEDICITE
BENTHAMITE
BENZEDRINE
BERNARDINE
BETELGEUSE
BETELGEUZE
BICHROMATE
BIJOUTERIE
BIRTHPLACE
BISSEXTILE
BLACKSTONE
BLANCMANGE
BLANQUETTE
BLOCKHOUSE
BLOODSTONE
BLOTTESQUE
BLUEBOTTLE
BLUEMANTLE
BOOKMOBILE
BOONDOGGLE
BORDERLINE
BOTHERSOME
BOUILLOTTE
BOWDLERISE
BOWDLERIZE
BRAGADISME
BREASTBONE
BRIGANDINE
BRIGANTINE
BRILLIANCE
BROADPIECE
BROCATELLE
BROWNSTONE
BURDENSOME
BURGLARIZE
BUTTERBAKE
BUTTERMERE
BUTTONHOLE
CACHINNATE
CACOMISTLE
CAESPITOSE
CALAVERITE
CALCEOLATE
CALCULABLE
CALESCENCE
CALLIATURE
CALUMNIATE
CALYPTRATE
CAMOUFLAGE
CAMSTEERIE
CANTALOUPE
CANTATRICE
CANTELOUPE
CANTILLATE
CAPACITATE
CAPERNAITE
CAPILLAIRE
CAPITALIZE
CAPITOLINE
CAPITULATE
CAPREOLATE
CARAMELIZE
CARICATURE
CARMAGNOLE
CARTHAMINE
CASSOLETTE
CATAFALQUE
CATARRHINE
CATEGORISE
CATEGORIZE
CELLOPHANE
CENTIGRADE
CENTILITRE
CENTIMETRE
CENTRALIZE
CENTRIFUGE
CENTROSOME
CHALYBEATE
CHAMBRANLE
CHANGEABLE
CHAPTALISE
CHARGEABLE

CHARITABLE
CHARTREUSE
CHATELAINE
CHEAPSKATE
CHEESECAKE
CHERSONESE
CHESSYLITE
CHEVESAILE
CHEVISANCE
CHIMPANZEE
CHINASTONE
CHIRICAUNE
CHITARRONE
CHLORINATE
CHOLALOGUE
CHROMOSOME
CHRYSOLITE
CIRCUMCISE
CIRCUMFUSE
CISPONTINE
CLAIRCOLLE
CLASPKNIFE
CLEMENTINE
CLINGSTONE
CLOMIPHENE
CLYDESDALE
COCKATRICE
COGNISANCE
COGNIZANCE
COLBERTINE
COLCHICINE
COLLARBONE
COLLECTIVE
COLLEGIATE
COLLIQUATE
COLPORTAGE
COLPOSCOPE
COMEDIENNE
COMESTIBLE
COMMENTATE
COMMISSURE
COMMIXTURE
COMMUTABLE
COMPARABLE
COMPATIBLE
COMPENSATE
COMPETENCE
COMPLANATE
COMPLIANCE
COMPLICATE
COMPRADORE
COMPROMISE
COMPULSIVE
CONCERVATE
CONCHIGLIE
CONCILIATE
CONCLUSIVE
CONDOLENCE
CONFERENCE
CONFIDANTE

CONFIDENCE
CONFISCATE
CONFLUENCE
CONGREGATE
CONJECTURE
CONNECTIVE
CONNIVANCE
CONSCIENCE
CONSECRATE
CONSONANCE
CONSTITUTE
CONSTRINGE
CONSUETUDE
CONSUMMATE
CONTINENCE
CONTRAVENE
CONTRIBUTE
CONVALESCE
CONVENANCE
CONVEYABLE
CONVEYANCE
CONVOLVUTE
CONVULSIVE
COORDINATE
COPPERNOSE
COQUIMBITE
CORDIERITE
CORNCOCKLE
CORPULENCE
CORRECTIVE
CORROBOREE
COURTHOUSE
CRAIGFLUKE
CRAPULENCE
CRAQUETURE
CREDITABLE
CRENELLATE
CROSSPIECE
CROTALIDAE
CUDDLESOME
CUISENAIRE
CULVERTAGE
CUMBERSOME
CUMULATIVE
CUTTLEBONE
CYCLOSTYLE
DEACTIVATE
DEADNETTLE
DEBILITATE
DEBOUCHURE
DECAGRAMME
DECAPITATE
DECATHLETE
DECELERATE
DECIMALIZE
DECOLORATE
DECORATIVE
DEDUCTIBLE
DEEPFREEZE
DEFEASANCE

DEFENSIBLE
DEFINITIVE
DEFLAGRATE
DEGENERATE
DEGRADABLE
DEHISCENCE
DELCREDERE
DELECTABLE
DELIBERATE
DEMOBILISE
DEMOBILIZE
DEMOISELLE
DEMORALISE
DEMORALIZE
DENTIFRICE
DEPENDABLE
DEPENDENCE
DEPLORABLE
DEPOPULATE
DEPRECIATE
DEPRESSIVE
DERACINATE
DEREGULATE
DERIVATIVE
DESALINATE
DESPICABLE
DESQUAMATE
DESSIATINE
DESSYATINE
DETACHABLE
DETECTABLE
DETERRENCE
DETESTABLE
DETRUNCATE
DIFFERENCE
DIFFIDENCE
DIGESTIBLE
DILAPIDATE
DILETTANTE
DIMINUTIVE
DINANDERIE
DINNERTIME
DIRECTOIRE
DISAPPROVE
DISARRANGE
DISBELIEVE
DISCIPLINE
DISCLOSURE
DISCOMMODE
DISCOMPOSE
DISCOURAGE
DISCURSIVE
DISEMBOGUE
DISENNOBLE
DISGRUNTLE
DISHABILLE
DISINCLINE
DISMISSIVE
DISPOSABLE
DISPUTABLE

DISRUPTIVE
DISSERTATE
DISSERVICE
DISSIDENCE
DISSOCIATE
DISSONANCE
DISTILLATE
DISTRIBUTE
DITHIONATE
DIVERGENCE
DODECANESE
DOLCEMENTE
DOPPLERITE
DRAKESTONE
DRAWBRIDGE
DREARISOME
DUMBLEDORE
DUNDERPATE
DUUMVIRATE
DYSCRASITE
EARTHQUAKE
EBRACTEATE
EBULLIENCE
ECARDINATE
EDULCORATE
EFFECTUATE
EFFEMINATE
EFFERVESCE
EFFLEURAGE
EGURGITATE
ELACAMPANE
ELASTICATE
ELECAMPANE
ELECTORATE
EMANCIPATE
EMARGINATE
EMASCULATE
EMBERGOOSE
EMBOUCHURE
ENCOIGNURE
ENGENDRURE
ENSANGUINE
ENTEROCELE
ENTERPRISE
ENTREMESSE
ENTRYPHONE
EPHRAIMITE
EPIDIORITE
EPISCOPATE
EPISTROPHE
EPROUVETTE
EQUIVOCATE
ESCADRILLE
ESCRITOIRE
ESPADRILLE
ETHYLAMINE
EUCHLORINE
EUPHROSYNE
EUROCHEQUE
EVANGELIZE

EVERYPLACE
EVERYWHERE
EVISCERATE
EXACERBATE
EXACTITUDE
EXAGGERATE
EXASPERATE
EXCELLENCE
EXCRUCIATE
EXENTERATE
EXHAUSTIVE
EXHILARATE
EXPATRIATE
EXPEDIENCE
EXPENDABLE
EXPERIENCE
EXPLICABLE
EXPRESSIVE
EXTENDABLE
EXTENSIBLE
EXUBERANCE
FACILITATE
FARRANDINE
FASTIGIATE
FAVOURABLE
FELICITATE
FERNITICLE
FERRANDINE
FESCENNINE
FETTUCCINE
FIBRILLATE
FIELDMOUSE
FIGURATIVE
FINISTERRE
FLAGELLATE
FLANCONADE
FLAPDOODLE
FLATULENCE
FLOCCULATE
FLORENTINE
FONTANELLE
FOOTBRIDGE
FORECASTLE
FORFEITURE
FORGIVABLE
FORMIDABLE
FOURCHETTE
FOURRAGERE
FRANCHISEE
FRANGIPANE
FRATERNISE
FRATERNIZE
FRATRICIDE
FREIGHTAGE
FROLICSOME
FUSTANELLE
GAINSTRIVE
GARGOUILLE
GARLANDAGE
GARNIERITE

GASCONNADE
GASTRONOME
GENERALISE
GENERALIZE
GENEVRETTE
GENICULATE
GETHSEMANE
GHIBELLINE
GILBERTINE
GILLRAVAGE
GLAMOURISE
GLASSHOUSE
GLAUCONITE
GOBEMOUCHE
GOLIATHISE
GORMANDIZE
GOVERNANCE
GRAMOPHONE
GRANGERIZE
GRAPTOLITE
GRAVESTONE
GREENHOUSE
GRINDSTONE
GUACHAMOLE
GUESTHOUSE
GUILLOTINE
GUTTIFERAE
HABILITATE
HALLOYSITE
HAMSHACKLE
HARDCASTLE
HECTOLITRE
HELIOTROPE
HEMISPHERE
HEMORRHAGE
HEPATOCELE
HIPPOCRENE
HIPPODROME
HOBBYHORSE
HODGEPODGE
HOMOGENIZE
HONOURABLE
HOOTNANNIE
HORNBLENDE
HOSPITABLE
HUMORESQUE
HUSBANDAGE
HYALOPHANE
HYDROPHANE
HYDROPLANE
HYPOTENUSE
ICONOSCOPE
IGNIMBRITE
ILLAQUEATE
ILLITERATE
ILLUMINATE
ILLUSTRATE
IMAGINABLE
IMMACULATE
IMMOBILIZE
IMMODERATE
IMMORTELLE
IMPALPABLE
IMPARLANCE
IMPASSABLE
IMPATIENCE
IMPECCABLE
IMPERATIVE
IMPLACABLE
IMPORTANCE
IMPOSSIBLE
IMPOSTHUME
IMPREGNATE
IMPRESSIVE
IMPROBABLE
IMPRUDENCE
INACCURATE
INADEQUATE
INAPTITUDE
INAUGURATE
INCINERATE
INCOMPLETE
INCRASSATE
INCREDIBLE
INDAPAMIDE
INDECISIVE
INDEFINITE
INDELICATE
INDICATIVE
INDICOLITE
INDICTABLE
INDIGOLITE
INDUCTANCE
INDULGENCE
INEDUCABLE
INELIGIBLE
INEPTITUDE
INEVITABLE
INEXORABLE
INFALLIBLE
INFILTRATE
INFINITIVE
INFLATABLE
INFLEXIBLE
INGEMINATE
INGENERATE
INGRATIATE
INIMITABLE
INITIATIVE
INNERSPACE
INNOVATIVE
INOPERABLE
INORDINATE
INOSCULATE
INSATIABLE
INSEMINATE
INSENSIBLE
INSISTENCE
INSPISSATE
INSUFFLATE
INTAGLIATE
INTANGIBLE
INTEMERATE
INTENERATE
INTERCLUDE
INTERLEAVE
INTERPHONE
INTERSTATE
INTERSTICE
INTERTWINE
INTERWEAVE
INTIMIDATE
INTOXICATE
INVALIDATE
INVALUABLE
INVARIABLE
INVETERATE
INVIGILATE
INVIGORATE
INVINCIBLE
INVIOLABLE
IONOSPHERE
IRRADICATE
IRRESOLUTE
ISABELLINE
ISONIAZIDE
JAMESONITE
JARDINIERE
JARGONELLE
JEOPARDISE
JEOPARDIZE
JIGGAMAREE
JOURNALESE
JOUYSAUNCE
JUDICATURE
KENSPECKLE
KERSEYMERE
KIMBERLITE
KLANGFARBE
KNOBKERRIE
LACHRYMOSE
LACKLUSTRE
LACUSTRINE
LAMENTABLE
LANCEOLATE
LANTHANIDE
LARGESCALE
LASTMINUTE
LAUDERDALE
LAUNCEGAYE
LAURDALITE
LAURUSTINE
LAURVIKITE
LAVALLIÈRE
LEGITIMATE
LEGITIMIZE
LEMNISCATE
LENGTHWISE
LHERZOLITE
LIBERALIZE
LIBREVILLE
LICENTIATE
LIGHTHOUSE
LIGNOCAINE
LIMBURGITE
LIMITROPHE
LITERATURE
LITHOMARGE
LITHOPHANE
LOCOMOTIVE
LOUISIETTE
LUXURIANCE
MACONOCHIE
MACROBIOTE
MAGISTRATE
MAISONETTE
MANAGEABLE
MANDEVILLE
MANIPULATE
MAQUILLAGE
MARCIONITE
MARGUERITE
MARIONETTE
MARKETABLE
MARQUETRIE
MARTINGALE
MARTINIQUE
MARYLEBONE
MASCARPONE
MASKANONGE
MASKINONGE
MASQUERADE
MASTURBATE
MATELLASSE
MAYONNAISE
MEASURABLE
MEDDLESOME
MEDITATIVE
MELACONITE
MENSTRUATE
MEPERIDINE
MERCANTILE
MESITYLENE
METABOLISE
METACENTRE
METAPHRASE
METASTABLE
METHEDRINE
METTLESOME
MICROFICHE
MICROPHONE
MICROSCOPE
MIGNONETTE
MILLIMETRE
MINESTRONE
MINISTRATE
MISFORTUNE
MISHGUGGLE
MITHRIDATE
MODIFIABLE
MOISTURIZE
MONEGASQUE
MONOCHROME
MONOPOLISE
MONOPOLIZE
MONSTRANCE
MOTHERLIKE
MOTORCYCLE
MOUSEPIECE
MOUSSELINE
MOUTHPIECE
MOZAMBIQUE
MYRIOSCOPE
MYSTAGOGUE
NAPTHALENE
NARROWDALE
NATHELESSE
NATIONWIDE
NATURALIZE
NAUSEATIVE
NEEDLECASE
NEGLIGENCE
NEGLIGIBLE
NEGOTIABLE
NESSELRODE
NETTLETREE
NEUTRALISE
NEUTRALIZE
NIGHTSHADE
NOMINATIVE
NONONSENSE
NORBERTINE
NOTICEABLE
NOTIFIABLE
NOURRITURE
NOVACULITE
OBLITERATE
OBSERVABLE
OBSERVANCE
OBTAINABLE
OCCURRENCE
ODONTOLITE
OFFBALANCE
OFFLICENCE
OMBROPHOBE
OPHICLEIDE
OPPRESSIVE
ORDONNANCE
ORIDINANCE
OROBRANCHE
ORTHOCAINE
ORTHOCLASE
OSTENSIBLE
OSTEOPHYTE
OUANANICHE
OUTBALANCE
OUTSPECKLE
OVERCHARGE
OVERPRAISE
OWLSPIEGLE

PALAEOTYPE
PALAGONITE
PALATALISE
PALATINATE
PALINDROME
PALLIATIVE
PALUSTRINE
PANTOSCOPE
PAPAVERINE
PAPERCHASE
PAPERKNIFE
PARADIDDLE
PARADOXIDE
PARADOXINE
PARAGONITE
PARAPHRASE
PARASELENE
PARDONABLE
PARISCHANE
PARISIENNE
PARMACITIE
PARTHENOPE
PARTICIPLE
PARTINGALE
PASQUINADE
PASSIONATE
PASTEURISE
PASTEURIZE
PATCHCOCKE
PATISSERIE
PEAUDESOIE
PEDICULATE
PEJORATIVE
PENETRABLE
PERCENTAGE
PERCENTILE
PERCEPTIVE
PERDURABLE
PERIDOTITE
PERISHABLE
PERIWINKLE
PERMANENCE
PERMISSIVE
PEROVSKITE
PERPETRATE
PERPETUATE
PERQUISITE
PERSEPHONE
PERSIFLAGE
PERSONABLE
PERSTRINGE
PERSUASIVE
PERTINENCE
PESTILENCE
PETRISSAGE
PHAENOTYPE
PHANTASIME
PHILIPPINE
PHILISTINE
PHILLIPINE
PHLOGOPITE
PHOTODIODE
PIANOFORTE
PICARESQUE
PIGEONHOLE
PILGRIMAGE
PILLOWCASE
PISTILLATE
PITCHSTONE
PLAGIARISE
PLAGIARIZE
PLANCHETTE
PLASTICINE
PLEBISCITE
PLOUGHBOTE
PLOUGHGATE
PLOUGHWISE
POCKMANTIE
POLITICIZE
POLYCHAETE
POLYCHROME
POLYMERIZE
POPULARIZE
PORTMANTLE
PORTUGUESE
POSSESSIVE
POSTCHAISE
POSTILLATE
POTENTIATE
POWERHOUSE
PRAEMUNIRE
PRATINCOLE
PREARRANGE
PRECEDENCE
PREDECEASE
PREDESTINE
PREDISPOSE
PREDNISONE
PREFERABLE
PREFERENCE
PREHENSILE
PREPOTENCE
PRESCIENCE
PRESSURIZE
PRESUPPOSE
PRETINCOLE
PREVALENCE
PREVENTIVE
PRICKLOUSE
PROCURABLE
PRODUCTIVE
PROFITABLE
PROFLIGATE
PROJECTILE
PROMINENCE
PROMULGATE
PROPIONATE
PROPITIATE
PROSERPINE
PROSTITUTE
PROTECTIVE
PROVENANCE
PROVIDENCE
PUBESCENCE
PULSATANCE
PUMPHANDLE
PUNCTULATE
PUNICACEAE
PUNISHABLE
PYRAGYRITE
QUADRANGLE
QUADRIREME
QUARANTINE
QUIESCENCE
RACECOURSE
RAMSHACKLE
RANDLETREE
RANNELTREE
RANNLETREE
RANTLETREE
RAVENSTONE
RAWINSONDE
RAWSTHORNE
REACTIVATE
REAPPRAISE
REASONABLE
REASSEMBLE
RECEPTACLE
RECITATIVE
RECOMMENCE
RECOMPENSE
RECRUDESCE
RECUPERATE
RECURRENCE
REDECORATE
REDRUTHITE
REFLECTIVE
REFRACTIVE
REGENERATE
REGRESSIVE
REGULARIZE
REJUVENATE
RELAXATIVE
RELUCTANCE
REMARKABLE
REMITTANCE
REMONETISE
REMUNERATE
REORGANIZE
REPAIRABLE
REPATRIATE
REPEATABLE
REPENTANCE
REPERTOIRE
REPETITIVE
REPRESSIVE
REPUGNANCE
RESCHEDULE
RESILIENCE
RESISTANCE
RESPECTIVE
RESPONSIVE
RESUPINATE
RESURGENCE
RETINALITE
RETROGRADE
RETURNABLE
REVERSIBLE
REVITALIZE
RHAPSODISE
RHAPSODIZE
RHINEGRAVE
RHINESTONE
RITORNELLE
ROMANESQUE
ROQUELAURE
ROSANILINE
ROTISSERIE
ROUGHHOUSE
ROUNDHOUSE
RUDOLPHINE
RUMINATIVE
RUPICOLINE
SABRETACHE
SACCHARASE
SACCHARIDE
SACCHARINE
SALTIGRADE
SAMARSKITE
SAMOTHRACE
SANCTITUDE
SAPROPHYTE
SAXICOLINE
SCANDALISE
SCANDALIZE
SCAPEGRACE
SCHIPPERKE
SCOPELIDAE
SCRUTINISE
SCRUTINIZE
SCUTELLATE
SEANNACHIE
SEASONABLE
SECONDRATE
SECRETAIRE
SECULARIZE
SEECATCHIE
SELEGILINE
SELTZOGENE
SEMICIRCLE
SENEGALESE
SENESCENCE
SERPENTINE
SGANARELLE
SHERARDISE
SHIELDRAKE
SHORTRANGE
SHOVELNOSE
SHROVETIDE
SICILIENNE
SIDESADDLE
SILHOUETTE
SILVERSIDE
SILVERWARE
SIMILITUDE
SINGHALESE
SMALLSCALE
SMARAGDINE
SNAKESTONE
SNAPHAUNCE
SNOWMOBILE
SOLICITUDE
SOMBRERITE
SOMERVILLE
SOMNOLENCE
SOURDELINE
SOUSAPHONE
SPEAKERINE
SPECIALISE
SPECIALIZE
SPERRYLITE
SPHACELATE
SPHALERITE
SPIFLICATE
SPISSITUDE
SPOKESHAVE
SPOLIATIVE
SPONGEWARE
SPRINGLIKE
SPRINGTIME
SQUETEAGUE
STALACTITE
STALAGMITE
STAPHYLINE
STATUESQUE
STAUROLITE
STAVESACRE
STEAKHOUSE
STEPHANITE
STEREOTYPE
STIGMATISE
STIGMATIZE
STILLICIDE
STONEHENGE
STOREHOUSE
STOUTHERIE
STREAMLINE
STREETWISE
STRIDULATE
STRIPTEASE
STROPHIOLE
STRYCHNINE
SUBJECTIVE
SUBMISSIVE
SUBSIDENCE
SUBSTITUTE
SUBTERFUGE
SUBVERSIVE
SUCCESSIVE
SUFFERANCE

SUGARALLIE
SUGGESTIVE
SUMMERTIME
SUPERSTORE
SUPPLICATE
SUPPORTIVE
SURINAMESE
SUSTENANCE
SWEEPSTAKE
SYMPATHISE
SYMPATHIZE
SYNCRETISE
SYNECDOCHE
SYNTHESIZE
TABERNACLE
TABLANETTE
TAILORMADE
TAMBERLANE
TAMBOURINE
TANAGRIDAE
TARADIDDLE
TARDIGRADE
TARTRAZINE
TEINOSCOPE
TELEOSTOME
TELPHERAGE
TEMPERANCE
TENNANTITE
TENRECIDAE
TERMINABLE
TERNEPLATE
TESCHENITE
THAUMASITE
THEODOLITE
THEOLOGATE
THEOLOGISE
THREADBARE
THREADLIKE
THREEPENCE
THREESCORE
TICKERTAPE
TOILINETTE
TOOTHPASTE
TORBERNITE
TOUCHPIECE
TOUCHSTONE
TOURMALINE
TRACHELATE
TRAMONTANE
TRAMPOLINE
TRANSCRIBE
TRANSIENCE
TRANSITIVE
TRANSVERSE
TRAUMATIZE
TRAVANCORE
TRAVELOGUE
TRAVERTINE
TRENCHMORE
TRIDENTINE
TRIPARTITE
TRIPLICATE
TRIVIALIZE
TROCTOLITE
TROGLODYTE
TROPOPAUSE
TROPOPHYTE
TROTSKYITE
TROUVAILLE
TRUCULENCE
TUMESCENCE
TURBULENCE
TURPENTINE
TURTLEDOVE
ULSTERETTE
ULTRAFICHE
UNARGUABLE
UNBEARABLE
UNBEATABLE
UNDENIABLE
UNDERLEASE
UNDERSCORE
UNDERSTATE
UNDERVALUE
UNDERWRITE
UNENVIABLE
UNHEARABLE
UNLADYLIKE
UNREADABLE
UNRELIABLE
UNSCRAMBLE
UNSOCIABLE
UNSUITABLE
UNWORKABLE
UROSTEGITE
URTICACEAE
UTILIZABLE
VAUDEVILLE
VELOCIPEDE
VERIFIABLE
VERNISSAGE
VERTEBRATE
VESICULATE
VIBRAPHONE
VIETNAMESE
VILLANELLE
VINDEMIATE
VINDICTIVE
VITELLICLE
VITUPERATE
VIVANDIÈRE
VOCIFERATE
VULNERABLE
WANCHANCIE
WARRANDICE
WATERBORNE
WESTERNIZE
WHEATSTONE
WHEELHOUSE
WHEWELLITE
WHIGGAMORE
WHITSTABLE
WIDDICOMBE
WINCEYETTE
WINDERMERE
WINTERTIME
WOLFRAMITE
WORTHWHILE
YAFFINGALE
ZABAGLIONE
COMMUNIQUÉ
DÉSHABILLÉ
CHIFFCHAFF
FALLINGOFF
FLAMEPROOF
HIPPOGRIFF
OFFTHECUFF
SHANDYGAFF
SHOCKPROOF
SOUNDPROOF
STOUTHRIEF
STROGANOFF
WATERPROOF
WHEATSHEAF
ACCOUNTING
ALMSGIVING
ANSCHAUUNG
APPETIZING
ASSEMBLING
ASTOUNDING
BACKBITING
BALLOONING
BARGAINING
BARRACKING
BATTENBERG
BATTENBURG
BEEKEEPING
BEWITCHING
BITTERLING
BLACKENING
BLISTERING
BLITHERING
BLITZKRIEG
BLUNDERING
BORDRAGING
BURGEONING
BUTCHERING
CANVASSING
CHAFFERING
CHANGELING
CHITTAGONG
CLAMOURING
COLLAPSING
COLLECTING
COMFORTING
COMMANDING
COMPELLING
CONCERNING
CONCLUDING
CONDUCTING
CONNECTING
CONQUERING
CONSULTING
CONTINUING
CONVINCING
CORRECTING
CORRUPTING
COUNSELING
CRICKETING
CURMURRING
CURVETTING
DARJEELING
DEBRIEFING
DEPRESSING
DESCENDING
DESCRIBING
DESPAIRING
DEVELOPING
DISCERNING
DISCUSSING
DISGUSTING
DISPENSING
DISSENTING
DISTILLING
DISTURBING
DOMINATING
DOWNSIZING
DRAWSTRING
EASTERLING
EMPFINDUNG
ENCHANTING
ENGROSSING
ENTRANCING
ENTREATING
EVERYTHING
EXHAUSTING
FACESAVING
FAREPAYING
FASTMOVING
FINGERLING
FLATTERING
FLAVOURING
FLICKERING
FORBEARING
FORBIDDING
FOREBODING
FORFAITING
FOXHUNTING
FURNISHING
GAINGIVING
GALUMPHING
GETTYSBURG
GLISTENING
GLITTERING
GRATIFYING
GROUNDLING
GROVELLING
HAIRSPRING
HANDSPRING
HEADSTRONG
HEIDELBERG
HIGHFLYING
HINDENBURG
HOMECOMING
HORRIFYING
HORSELBERG
INBREEDING
INCREASING
INFIGHTING
INHIBITING
INTRIGUING
IRRITATING
JAYWALKING
KESSELRING
KIDNAPPING
KUOMINTANG
LANDSTHING
LAWABIDING
LUTESTRING
LUXEMBOURG
MAGNIFYING
MAINSPRING
MEANDERING
MISLEADING
MITIGATING
MUCKRAKING
NAUSEATING
NETWORKING
NIDDERLING
NONSMOKING
NOURISHING
OCEANGOING
ODELSTHING
OFFPUTTING
OUTPOURING
OVEREATING
OVERRIDING
OVERSTRUNG
PARGETTING
PERFORMING
PERPLEXING
PERSUADING
PETRIFYING
PIONEERING
PLUNDERING
PORLOCKING
PREVAILING
PROCEEDING
PROCESSING
PROJECTING
PUBLISHING
PUMMELLING
PUTREFYING
QUARTERING
QUERSPRUNG
REASSURING
REFLECTING
REFRESHING
RESEMBLING
RESOUNDING

RESPECTING
RETRAINING
RETREATING
ROISTERING
ROLLICKING
ROSEMALING
SANDERLING
SATISFYING
SCANDERBEG
SCATTERING
SCREECHING
SCRIBBLING
SCROUNGING
SHAMPOOING
SHATTERING
SHIMMERING
SHOESTRING
SHORTENING
SHUDDERING
SIMULATING
SKINDIVING
SLUMBERING
SMATTERING
SNIGGERING
SNORKELING
SPIRKETING
SPRINKLING
STAGGERING
STAMMERING
STARVELING
STRAGGLING
STRASBOURG
STRINDBERG
STRULDBERG
STRULDBRUG
STUPEFYING
SUBHEADING
SUCCEEDING
SUNBATHING
SUPPORTING
SURFRIDING
SURPASSING
SURPRISING
SUSTAINING
SWAGGERING
SWALLOWING
SWEDENBORG
SWEETENING
SWELTERING
TAILGATING
TAPDANCING
TARPAULING
TERRIFYING
THICKENING
THUNDERING
TIMESAVING
TRAVELLING
UNASSUMING
UNAVAILING
UNBECOMING
UNBLINKING
UNBLUSHING
UNDERLYING
UNDERSLUNG
UNDULATING
UNEDIFYING
UNFLAGGING
UNINVITING
UNSETTLING
UNSLEEPING
UNSWERVING
UNTHINKING
UNYIELDING
UPBRINGING
UPSTANDING
VARNISHING
WAMPUMPEAG
WASSAILING
WELLSPRING
WHISPERING
WRONGDOING
ACCOMPLISH
ADRAMELECH
AFTERBIRTH
ALTAZIMUTH
AMATEURISH
AMPHIBRACH
AMPLEFORTH
ANEMOGRAPH
BALDERDASH
BANGLADESH
BARMITZVAH
BATHYSCAPH
BLACKSMITH
BRIDLEPATH
BROADCLOTH
CANDLEFISH
CHILDBIRTH
CHINAGRAPH
COELACANTH
COQUETTISH
CORNSTARCH
CUTTLEFISH
DAMSELFISH
DESBOROUGH
DICTOGRAPH
EIGHTEENTH
EXTINGUISH
FALSETRUTH
FILLIBRUSH
FLOORCLOTH
FLUTEMOUTH
FOURTEENTH
FULLLENGTH
GALLABIYAH
GALLABIYEH
GALRAVITCH
GOOSEFLESH
GREENCLOTH
GREENFINCH
HALLELUJAH
HATEENOUGH
HELIOGRAPH
HENCEFORTH
HEPTATEUCH
HERESIARCH
HIEROGLYPH
HIPPOGRYPH
HOMOEOPATH
HONEYBUNCH
HOTCHPOTCH
IMPOVERISH
KENILWORTH
LATTERMATH
LITHOGRAPH
MACKINTOSH
METHUSALEH
METHUSELAH
MIMEOGRAPH
MISHNAYOTH
NATUROPATH
NETTLERASH
NINETEENTH
NUDIBRANCH
OUTLANDISH
OVERSLAUGH
PAINTBRUSH
PANTOGRAPH
PENTATEUCH
PETROGLYPH
PHONOGRAPH
PHOTOGRAPH
PICAYUNISH
PORTSMOUTH
PSYCHOPATH
RADIOGRAPH
RAJPRAMUKH
RELINQUISH
SARSQUATCH
SCARAMOUCH
SEVENTIETH
SHIBBOLETH
SHILLELAGH
SILVERFISH
SKEUOMORPH
SNAKEMOUTH
SNAPHAUNCH
SQUIREARCH
STAGECOACH
STILLBIRTH
STONEBRASH
TABLECLOTH
TACHOGRAPH
THIRTEENTH
THOUSANDTH
TIMESWITCH
TOOTHBRUSH
TRAGACANTH
TRIMSNITCH
UBERMENSCH
UNDERNEATH
USQUEBAUGH
VINEGARISH
WANDSWORTH
WATERBRASH
WAVELENGTH
WORDSWORTH
WRISTWATCH
YARBOROUGH
ZINCOGRAPH
AMPHIGOURI
BOTTICELLI
CANNELLONI
CERTIORARI
DEVANAGARI
EMALANGENI
FANTOCCINI
FRANGIPANI
FRATICELLI
GLITTERATI
HINDUSTANI
ILLUMINATI
JAGUARONDI
JAGUARUNDI
MAHAYANALI
MAKUNOUCHI
MILLEFIORI
MONTESSORI
MONTEVERDI
PADAREWSKI
PERDENDOSI
PESTALOZZI
PICCALILLI
PONCHIELLI
PRZEWALSKI
RAIYATWARI
SALMAGUNDI
SHAKUHACHI
SHARAWADGI
SHARAWAGGI
SIGNORELLI
SPERMACETI
SVADILFARI
TAGLIARINI
TORRICELLI
TORTELLINI
VERMICELLI
AFTERSHOCK
ALPENSTOCK
ARSMETRICK
BADDERLOCK
BAILIEWICK
BAILLIWICK
BASKETWORK
BLOODSTOCK
BOTTLENECK
BREASTWORK
BROOMSTICK
BUTTERMILK
CANDLEWICK
CANVASBACK
CASSIABARK
CHEQUEBOOK
CROSSCHECK
CRUIKSHANK
DONNYBROOK
DOUBLETALK
DRUZHINNIK
DUNDERFUNK
FETTERLOCK
GENTLEFOLK
GIRDLERINK
GREENSHANK
GREENSTICK
GROUNDWORK
HACKMATACK
HAMMERLOCK
HARMANBECK
HEARTBREAK
JABBERWOCK
KILMARNOCK
LIMBERNECK
LUMBERJACK
MATCHSTALK
MATCHSTICK
MINUTEBOOK
MOUNTEBANK
NATTERJACK
NEEDLEWORK
NIGHTSTICK
PILGARLICK
PINAKOTHEK
POCKETBOOK
POINTBLANK
PUNCHDRUNK
RAVENSDUCK
ROLANDSECK
RUBBERNECK
SADDLEBACK
SCHOOLBOOK
SCRIMSHANK
SHEEPSHANK
SHELLSHOCK
SILVERBACK
SKETCHBOOK
SKRIMSHANK
SMOKESTACK
SOUNDTRACK
SPATCHCOCK
SPITCHCOCK
STICKYBEAK
STINGYBARK
SUPPLEJACK
SWITCHBACK
SWORDSTICK
TENTERHOOK
TURTLENECK
WATTLEWORK
WHITTERICK
WICKERWORK

WOOLLYBACK
YELLOWBACK
YELLOWJACK
YESTERWEEK
ZUMBOORUCK
ABORIGINAL
ACCIDENTAL
ACHITOPHEL
ACRONYCHAL
ADDITIONAL
ADJECTIVAL
AHITHOPHEL
ANALOGICAL
ANALYTICAL
ANARCHICAL
ANATOMICAL
ANGURVADEL
ANTIPHONAL
ANTISOCIAL
APOCRYPHAL
ARCHETYPAL
ARTIFICIAL
ATRAMENTAL
BALIBUNTAL
BARMECIDAL
BASKETBALL
BEHAVIORAL
BENEFICIAL
BIOLOGICAL
CAMBERWELL
CAMPESTRAL
CANNONBALL
CARNASSIAL
CENTENNIAL
CENTESIMAL
CEREMONIAL
CINQUEFOIL
COLLATERAL
COLLOQUIAL
COMMERCIAL
COMMONWEAL
CONCEPTUAL
CONFEDERAL
CONGENITAL
CONTEXTUAL
COROMANDEL
COTTONTAIL
COXCOMICAL
CREDENTIAL
CUCURBITAL
DECENNOVAL
DELIGHTFUL
DEMONIACAL
DEVOTIONAL
DIABOLICAL
DICKCISSEL
DISDAINFUL
DISEMBOWEL
DIVISIONAL
DUNIWASSAL
DUODECIMAL
EATANSWILL
ECOLOGICAL
ECONOMICAL
ECUMENICAL
ELECTRICAL
ELLIPTICAL
ENCYCLICAL
EQUATORIAL
FINGERNAIL
FORINSECAL
FRACTIONAL
FRENETICAL
FROMANTEEL
FUNCTIONAL
FUNGICIDAL
GEOLOGICAL
GEOTHERMAL
GERMICIDAL
HEPTAGONAL
HISTORICAL
HOLOPHOTAL
HOMOSEXUAL
HORIZONTAL
HYPAETHRAL
HYSTERICAL
IMMATERIAL
IMMEMORIAL
IMPERSONAL
INCIDENTAL
INDIVIDUAL
INDUSTRIAL
INTERNODAL
INTESTINAL
IRRATIONAL
IRREMEDIAL
JUGENDSTIL
KRIEGSPIEL
LITURGICAL
LOGISTICAL
MANAGERIAL
MANCHINEEL
MEANINGFUL
MECHANICAL
METACARPAL
METATARSAL
METHODICAL
MISCHMETAL
MONUMENTAL
NATATORIAL
NEGLECTFUL
NEOTERICAL
NEUTROPHIL
NICROSILAL
NOSOCOMIAL
OBSIDIONAL
OCCASIONAL
OCCIDENTAL
OFFTHEWALL
ORATORICAL
ORCHESTRAL
ORNAMENTAL
ORTHOGONAL
PALAESTRAL
PANTAGRUEL
PARANORMAL
PARASTATAL
PEDIMENTAL
PENTAGONAL
PEPPERMILL
PERIODICAL
PERIPHERAL
PHENOMENAL
PONTIFICAL
PREMARITAL
PRIMORDIAL
PROCEDURAL
PROPLITEAL
PROVERBIAL
PROVINCIAL
PRUDENTIAL
PSAMMOPHIL
PURPOSEFUL
RABBINICAL
RAVENSBILL
RECIPROCAL
REGIMENTAL
REMORSEFUL
RESORCINOL
RESPECTFUL
REVENGEFUL
RHETORICAL
RHYTHMICAL
RIJSTTAFEL
RUDIMENTAL
SABBATICAL
SACERDOTAL
SADDLEBILL
SCHLIMAZEL
SCHOOLGIRL
SCRIPTURAL
SENATORIAL
SEPTENNIAL
SEPULCHRAL
SEQUENTIAL
SERMONICAL
SILVERBILL
SIMMENTHAL
SPLITLEVEL
SPONSIONAL
SPRINGTAIL
STANDSTILL
STRUCTURAL
SUBLIMINAL
SUCCESSFUL
SUPERMODEL
SYMBOLICAL
TANGENTIAL
TATTERSALL
TCHOUKBALL
THEATRICAL
THIMBLEFUL
THOUGHTFUL
THRENODIAL
TINKERBELL
TOCOPHEROL
TORRENTIAL
TRILATERAL
TRILINGUAL
TYRANNICAL
UNCRITICAL
UNEVENTFUL
UNFAITHFUL
UNFRUITFUL
UNGRATEFUL
UNICAMERAL
UNILATERAL
UNOFFICIAL
UNORIGINAL
UNPUNCTUAL
UNTRUTHFUL
VOCATIONAL
VOLLEYBALL
WATERLEVEL
WATERWHEEL
WINDOWSILL
WITHDRAWAL
YELLOWGIRL
YGGDRASILL
ZOOLOGICAL
ABSOLUTISM
ACETABULUM
ALCOHOLISM
AMBULACRUM
ANACARDIUM
ANGIOSPERM
ANTAGONISM
APOPHTHEGM
APOTHECIUM
ASCETICISM
ATRACURIUM
AUDITORIUM
AVERRHOISM
BIRMINGHAM
BLEPHARISM
BRADYSEISM
BRAINSTORM
BRIDEGROOM
BRITISHISM
BUCHMANISM
BUCKINGHAM
CAPITALISM
CAPITELLUM
CARDIOGRAM
CATABOLISM
CEREBELLUM
CHAUVINISM
CHELTENHAM
CHLOROFORM
CLASSICISM
COCKALORUM
COLDSTREAM
COMPENDIUM
COMPLUVIUM
CONSORTIUM
COTTIERISM
CRYPTOGRAM
CURRICULUM
DELPHINIUM
DEUTOPLASM
DICHROMISM
DIGITORIUM
DISSELBOOM
DOWNSTREAM
DYSPROSIUM
ECHINODERM
ELYTRIFORM
EMPLASTRUM
ENTHUSIASM
EPIDENDRUM
EPITHELIUM
EPONYCHIUM
EUHEMERISM
FANATICISM
FAVORITISM
FEDERALISM
FLUNKEYDOM
FOURIERISM
GADOLINIUM
GEOTROPISM
GNOSTICISM
GRANGERISM
HAUSTELLUM
HAUSTORIUM
HONORARIUM
HYPOCORISM
IMPALUDISM
INDUMENTUM
JOURNALISM
KETTLEDRUM
LAMARCKISM
LAWRENCIUM
LEBENSRAUM
LENOCINIUM
LESBIANISM
LIBERALISM
LOCKERROOM
LYSENKOISM
MAINSTREAM
MAKESYSTEM
MALAYALAAM
MEDIUMTERM
MEERSCHAUM
MEMORANDUM
METABOLISM
MILITARISM
MOLYBDENUM
MONETARISM
MONILIFORM
MONOTHEISM

MORATORIUM
NARCISSISM
NASTURTIUM
NATATORIUM
NATURALISM
OBLOMOVISM
OPPROBRIUM
OSMETERIUM
OUTPERFORM
PACIFICISM
PALMERWORM
PANARITIUM
PANCRATIUM
PANJANDRUM
PARNELLISM
PATRIOTISM
PENNISETUM
PLAGIARISM
PLASMODESM
POLYTHEISM
PRAETORIUM
PRAGMATISM
PRINCIPIUM
PROMETHIUM
PROPYLAEUM
PROSCENIUM
PROTOPLASM
PSALTERIUM
PURITANISM
RADICALISM
RECIDIVISM
REFERENDUM
RHEUMATISM
ROCKINGHAM
RUMBLOSSOM
SANATORIUM
SANITARIUM
SCEPTICISM
SCHOOLMAAM
SELFESTEEM
SEPARATISM
SIMILLIMUM
SIMULACRUM
SKEPTICISM
SLIPSTREAM
SPIRACULUM
SPONGIFORM
SPOONERISM
STILLIFORM
STRAMONIUM
STRONGROOM
STUMBLEDOM
SUBSELLIUM
SUBSTRATUM
SURREALISM
SYMPHONIUM
TECHNETIUM
TEPIDARIUM
THALICTRUM
THALLIFORM
THREADWORM
TIROCINIUM
TRICLINIUM
TROPAEOLUM
VESTIBULUM
VIBRACULUM
WITGATBOOM
ABDICATION
ABERRATION
ABROGATION
ABSCISSION
ABSOLUTION
ABSORPTION
ABSTENTION
ABYSSINIAN
ACCUBATION
ACCUSATION
ACOTYLEDON
ACROTERION
ADAPTATION
ADHIBITION
ADIAPHORON
ADMIRATION
ADMONITION
AFFLICTION
AGGRESSION
ALECTORIAN
ALGONQUIAN
ALIENATION
ALLEGATION
ALLIGATION
ALLOCATION
ALLOCUTION
ALTERATION
AMMUNITION
AMPHICTYON
AMPHITRYON
AMPUTATION
ANDALUSIAN
ANHELATION
ANNEXATION
ANNOTATION
ANTHEOLION
ANTICHTHON
ANTIMONIAN
ANTINOMIAN
ANTIOCHIAN
ANTIPODEAN
ANTIPROTON
APOLLONIAN
APPARITION
APPOSITION
ARAUCANIAN
ARCHDEACON
AREFACTION
ARIMASPIAN
ARMAGEDDON
ARUNDELIAN
ASPIRATION
ASSUMPTION
ATHANASIAN
ATTRACTION
AUSTRALIAN
AUTOCHTHON
AUTOMATION
BABYLONIAN
BACITRACIN
BACKGAMMON
BAHRAINIAN
BALBRIGGAN
BALNEATION
BARLEYCORN
BASSINGTON
BATRACHIAN
BEARGARDEN
BEAUTICIAN
BEAVERSKIN
BELARUSIAN
BILIVERDIN
BIPARTISAN
BLACKTHORN
BLOODSTAIN
BONDSWOMAN
BOOZINGKEN
BOURIGNIAN
BOUSINGKEN
BRADYKININ
BRIDGETOWN
BROKENDOWN
BURLINGTON
BUTTONDOWN
BYELECTION
CACODAEMON
CALAMONDIN
CALEDONIAN
CALYDONIAN
CAMERONIAN
CAMPERDOWN
CANTABRIAN
CAPITATION
CARCINOGEN
CARPATHIAN
CARRAGHEEN
CARTHUSIAN
CASTRATION
CATACHUMEN
CATECHUMEN
CATHOLICON
CAVALRYMAN
CESTRACION
CHAIRWOMAN
CHAMBERTIN
CHAMPIGNON
CHAPFALLEN
CHATTERTON
CHAUCERIAN
CHECKLATON
CHESTERTON
CHEVROTAIN
CHINQUAPIN
CIRCASSIAN
CISLEITHAN
CISTERCIAN
CLANSWOMAN
CLUMPERTON
COGITATION
COLLECTION
COLORATION
COMBUSTION
COMMISSION
COMPARISON
COMPASSION
COMPLETION
COMPLEXION
COMPULSION
CONCEPTION
CONCESSION
CONCHIOLIN
CONCLUSION
CONCOCTION
CONCRETION
CONCUSSION
CONDUCTION
CONFECTION
CONFESSION
CONGESTION
CONNECTION
CONNIPTION
CONSENSION
CONSTANTAN
CONTENTION
CONTORTION
CONTRITION
CONVECTION
CONVENTION
CONVERSION
CONVICTION
CONVULSION
COPENHAGEN
COPPERSKIN
COPULATION
CORINTHIAN
CORONATION
CORRECTION
CORRUPTION
COUNTRYMAN
CRISPINIAN
CRUSTACEAN
CURMUDGEON
DECAHEDRON
DECLENSION
DECORATION
DEDICATION
DEFAMATION
DEFECATION
DEFINITION
DEFLECTION
DELEGATION
DELIGATION
DELIRATION
DEMOGORGON
DEMOLITION
DEPOSITION
DEPRESSION
DEPUTATION
DERIVATION
DESOLATION
DETONATION
DETRACTION
DEVOLUTION
DIACONICON
DIGRESSION
DILATATION
DIMINUTION
DIREMPTION
DISBURTHEN
DISCRETION
DISCUSSION
DISHEARTEN
DISPERSION
DISRUPTION
DISSECTION
DISSENSION
DISSUASION
DISTENSION
DISTORTION
DIVINATION
DOMINATION
DUKKERIPEN
DUTCHWOMAN
ECUADORIAN
ELEUSINIAN
ELONGATION
EMACIATION
EMENDATION
EMIGRATION
ENCEPHALON
ENGLISHMAN
ENGLISHMEN
ENKEPHALIN
EPILIMNION
EQUESTRIAN
EQUITATION
ERIOCAULON
ERUCTATION
ESCALATION
ESCULAPIAN
ESCUTCHEON
ESTIMATION
ESTRAMACON
ETEOCRETAN
EUROCLYDON
EUSTACHIAN
EVACUATION
EVALUATION
EXALTATION
EXCAVATION
EXECRATION
EXHALATION
EXHAUSTION

EXHIBITION
EXHUMATION
EXPEDITION
EXPIRATION
EXPOSITION
EXPRESSION
EXPRESSMAN
EXTINCTION
EXTRACTION
EXULTATION
FASCIATION
FEDERATION
FEUILLETON
FIGURATION
FILTRATION
FIREWARDEN
FIRTHSOKEN
FLIRTATION
FLUGELHORN
FOREORDAIN
FORFEUCHEN
FORFOUGHEN
FOUNDATION
FRANCISCAN
FREEMARTIN
FRITHSOKEN
FULLYGROWN
FUMIGATION
GARGANTUAN
GEMINATION
GENERATION
GEORGETOWN
GILBERTIAN
GLACIATION
GLEEMAIDEN
GRADUATION
GRAMICIDIN
GRAMMARIAN
GROUNDSMAN
GUATEMALAN
HABITATION
HAMESUCKEN
HANDMAIDEN
HANOVERIAN
HARRINGTON
HARVESTMAN
HEMIHEDRON
HEMOGLOBIN
HENDECAGON
HEPTAMERON
HEPTATHLON
HESITATION
HIGHWAYMAN
HOMEOUSIAN
HORSEDRAWN
HORSEWOMAN
HUMDUDGEON
HYPAETHRON
IMMOLATION
IMPOSITION
IMPRESSION
IMPUTATION
INCUBATION
INDECISION
INDICATION
INDONESIAN
INFLECTION
INFLICTION
INFRACTION
INHALATION
INHIBITION
INITIATION
INJUNCTION
INNOVATION
INSPECTION
INSULATION
INTERFERON
INTERWOVEN
INTIMATION
INTINCTION
INTONATION
INTRAURBAN
INUNDATION
INVITATION
INVOCATION
IRISHWOMAN
IRISHWOMEN
IRRIGATION
IRRITATION
JACULATION
JOHNSONIAN
JOURNEYMAN
JUBILATION
KARMATHIAN
KEMPERYMAN
KENTUCKIAN
KLOOTCHMAN
LACERATION
LAMBREQUIN
LAMINATION
LANDAMMANN
LAUNCESTON
LAURENTIAN
LEAMINGTON
LEDERHOSEN
LEPRECHAUN
LEVITATION
LIBERATION
LIEBERMANN
LIGHTERMAN
LIMITATION
LINEOMYCIN
LITHUANIAN
LITIGATION
LOCOMOTION
LUSITANIAN
MABINOGION
MACEDONIAN
MADAGASCAN
MAHOMMEDAN
MALTHUSIAN
MANGOSTEEN
MANICHAEAN
MATTERHORN
MATURATION
MAVOURNEEN
MAXIMILIAN
MEADOWPLAN
MEDICATION
MEDITATION
MELANESIAN
MELOCOTOON
MENECHMIAN
MESENTERON
MIDLOTHIAN
MIDSHIPMAN
MILITIAMAN
MISPRISION
MITIGATION
MODERATION
MODULATION
MONOPTERON
MORISONIAN
MOTIVATION
MOUSTERIAN
MOUTHORGAN
MUJAHEDDIN
MUTILATION
NAVIGATION
NEAPOLITAN
NICARAGUAN
NOBLEWOMAN
NOMINATION
NONFICTION
NUMERATION
NURSERYMAN
OBLIGATION
OCCUPATION
OCTAHEDRON
OMOPHORION
OPPOSITION
OPPRESSION
ORDINATION
ORPHEOREON
OSCITATION
OSCULATION
OVERSTRAIN
PADDINGTON
PADDYMELON
PAGINATION
PALMERSTON
PANAMANIAN
PANOPTICON
PARAGUAYAN
PARNASSIAN
PATAGONIAN
PECULATION
PEDESTRIAN
PENELOPHON
PENICILLIN
PENNILLION
PENTAMERON
PENTATHLON
PENTELIKON
PENTSTEMON
PEPPERCORN
PERCEPTION
PERCUSSION
PERFECTION
PERIHELION
PERMEATION
PERMISSION
PERORATION
PERSUASION
PERVERSION
PETRARCHAN
PHAELONIAN
PHENOMENON
PHLEGETHON
PHLOGISTON
PINCUSHION
PLANTATION
POLITICIAN
POLYHEDRON
POLYNESIAN
POMERANIAN
POPULATION
POSSESSION
POSTILLION
PRAETORIAN
PRECAUTION
PRECIPITIN
PREDICTION
PRELECTION
PRETENSION
PREVENTION
PROCESSION
PRODUCTION
PROFESSION
PROGESSION
PROJECTION
PROMETHEAN
PROPORTION
PROPULSION
PROTECTION
PROTRUSION
PSILOCYBIN
PTERANODON
PUNDIGRION
QUARTEROON
QUEENSTOWN
QUERCITRON
QUICKTHORN
RAGAMUFFIN
RAILWAYMAN
RAMPALLIAN
RECITATION
RECREATION
REDEMPTION
REELECTION
REFLECTION
REFRACTION
REFUTATION
REGRESSION
REGULATION
RELAXATION
RELEGATION
RELOCATION
RENOVATION
REPARATION
REPETITION
REPRESSION
REPUBLICAN
REPUTATION
RESOLUTION
RESUMPTION
RETRACTION
REVELATION
REVOCATION
REVOLUTION
RIBOFLAVIN
RICHARDSON
RICHTHOFEN
RIGELATION
RINGELMANN
ROBERDSMAN
ROBERTSMAN
ROWLANDSON
RUBINSTEIN
RUMBULLION
RUMINATION
RUPESTRIAN
SALESWOMAN
SALIVATION
SALPINGIAN
SALUTATION
SANITATION
SANNAYASIN
SATURATION
SCANDAROON
SCHALSTEIN
SCOTSWOMAN
SEPARATION
SERVICEMAN
SHACKLETON
SHANDRYDAN
SHECKLATON
SHELDONIAN
SHENANIGAN
SIDERATION
SILVERSKIN
SIMULATION
SLAMMERKIN
SMITHEREEN
SNAPDRAGON
SOLIFIDIAN
SOPHOCLEAN
SOUTERRAIN
SPALLATION
SPENCERIAN

SPENSERIAN
SPOLIATION
STAGNATION
STARVATION
STENTORIAN
STEPHENSON
STICHARION
STONEMASON
STRAIGHTEN
STRAPONTIN
STRENGTHEN
SUBJECTION
SUBMERSION
SUBMISSION
SUBREPTION
SUBSECTION
SUBSTATION
SUBVENTION
SUBVERSION
SUCCESSION
SUGGESTION
SUPERHUMAN
SUPERWOMAN
SUSPENSION
TABLESPOON
TABULATION
TECHNICIAN
TEDDINGTON
TELEVISION
TEMPTATION
TENDERLOIN
TERREPLEIN
THALASSIAN
THELLUSSON
THEOLOGIAN
TOLERATION
TOURBILLON
TOWNSWOMAN
TRANSITION
TRINACRIAN
TRISKELION
TROCHOTRON
TRYPTOPHAN
TUMBLEDOWN
ULCERATION
UNDERLINEN
UNDULATION
UNFORESEEN
USUCAPTION
USURPATION
VALIDATION
VEGETARIAN
VEGETATION
VELITATION
VENERATION
VENEZUELAN
VERMILLION
VILLANOVAN
VISITATION
VOLUTATION
WALDENSIAN
WALLACHIAN
WANTHRIVEN
WASHINGTON
WATERMELON
WEATHERMAN
WELLINGTON
WELSHWOMAN
WHITETHORN
WILLIAMSON
WILLINGDON
WINDSCREEN
WOFFINGTON
WOODPIGEON
WYCLIFFIAN
ZAPOROGIAN
ZIMBABWEAN
ZOLLVEREIN
ZWITTERION
ADELANTADO
AFFETTUOSO
AFICIONADO
ANGWANTIBO
ARGOLEMONO
BANDERILLO
CALCEDONIO
CAMERLENGO
CAMERLINGO
CANCIONERO
CAPODASTRO
CAPPUCCINO
CATENACCIO
CHIMBORAZO
COMANCHERO
DIDGERIDOO
DIMINUENDO
ESTANCIERO
FANTASTICO
FIANCHETTO
FORTISSIMO
FRATERETTO
GETUPANDGO
HALLUBALOO
HULLABALOO
IMPRESARIO
INQUIRENDO
INTERMEZZO
INTERTRIGO
KATERFELTO
LATTICINIO
MARASCHINO
MONTEVIDEO
OCTODECIMO
PAPIAMENTO
PARAMARIBO
PASSAMEZZO
PEACHERINO
PECCADILLO
PENSIEROSO
PENTIMENTO
PICHICIAGO
PIRANDELLO
PONTICELLO
PORTAMENTO
PROSCIUTTO
RECITATIVO
RITORNELLO
SALTARELLO
SERRASALMO
STIACCIATO
STRACCHINO
STREPITOSO
STRINGENDO
SUPERCARGO
TINTORETTO
TOUCHANDGO
TRIMALCHIO
ARCHBISHOP
AUSTRALORP
AUTHORSHIP
BATTLESHIP
BUTTERBUMP
CENSORSHIP
CODSWALLOP
CONTRECOUP
DEALERSHIP
FELLOWSHIP
FRIENDSHIP
GINGERSNAP
LEADERSHIP
LIGHTINGUP
MEMBERSHIP
MOULDIWARP
NINCOMPOOP
OVERTHETOP
PILLOWSLIP
PSEUDOCARP
PSYCHOPOMP
RATTLETRAP
READERSHIP
SEAMANSHIP
STREETLAMP
WENTLETRAP
ACETABULAR
ADMINISTER
ADVENTURER
ADVERTISER
AFRICANDER
ALMACANTAR
ALMUCANTAR
ALTERNATOR
ALTOGETHER
AMBASSADOR
AMBOCEPTOR
AMPHIMACER
ANEMOMETER
ANTIMATTER
APPLICATOR
ARBITRATOR
ASTROLOGER
ASTRONOMER
AUCTIONEER
AUSTRINGER
BABYSITTER
BACKHANDER
BACKPACKER
BACKSLIDER
BANDMASTER
BARCHESTER
BATTLEDOOR
BEAUTIFIER
BEDCHAMBER
BEEFBURGER
BELLWETHER
BELSHAZZAR
BENEFACTOR
BERSAGLIER
BESTSELLER
BIOGRAPHER
BLACKWATER
BLASPHEMER
BOBBYSOXER
BOMBARDIER
BONDHOLDER
BONESHAKER
BOOKBINDER
BOOKKEEPER
BOOKMARKER
BOOKSELLER
BOOTLEGGER
BOOTLICKER
BRAINPOWER
BREAKWATER
BRESSUMMER
BRICKLAYER
BUCCINATOR
BUCKJUMPER
BUDGERIGAR
BUMFREEZER
BUNDESWEHR
BUSHRANGER
CALAMANDER
CALCULATOR
CALEFACTOR
CALORIFIER
CAMPAIGNER
CAMPARADOR
CANECUTTER
CANTILEVER
CARABINEER
CARABINIER
CARBURETOR
CARPENTIER
CASSUMUNAR
CATALOGUER
CATCRACKER
CENTILITER
CENTIMETER
CHALLENGER
CHANCELLOR
CHANDELIER
CHARIOTEER
CHERIMOYER
CHICHESTER
CHIFFONIER
CHRONICLER
CHURCHGOER
CLEARWATER
CLOCKMAKER
CLODHOPPER
COATHANGER
COCKCHAFER
COLCHESTER
COLLIMATOR
COLLOCUTER
COLPORTEUR
COMMANDEER
COMPARATOR
COMPETITOR
COMPOSITOR
COMPRESSOR
COMSTOCKER
CONDOTTIER
CONTRACTOR
CONTROLLER
COPARCENER
COPYHOLDER
COPYWRITER
CORDWAINER
CORNFLOWER
CORREGIDOR
CORRUGATOR
COUNCILLOR
COUNSELLOR
COVENANTER
CROSSREFER
CUIRASSIER
CULTIVATOR
DAYDREAMER
DECOLLATOR
DERAILLEUR
DISCLAIMER
DISCOVERER
DISHWASHER
DISSEMBLER
DISSIMILAR
DOORKEEPER
DOORTODOOR
DRAWCANSIR
DREIKANTER
DRESSMAKER
DRINKWATER
DRUMBLEDOR
DUPLICATOR
ELECTROMER
ELIMINATOR
EMMENTALER
EMULSIFIER
ENCLOISTER
EUDIOMETER

FALKLANDER
FASCINATOR
FERTILISER
FERTILIZER
FILIBUSTER
FIREWALKER
FISHMONGER
FISHSELLER
FLUCTUATER
FLYCATCHER
FOOTBALLER
FOREBITTER
FORECASTER
FOREFATHER
FOREFINGER
FOREGATHER
FORERUNNER
FRANCHISOR
FRAUNHOFER
FREEBOOTER
FREEHANDER
FREEHOLDER
FREELANCER
FREELOADER
FREQUENTER
FRESHWATER
FROGHOPPER
GALVANISER
GAMEKEEPER
GEOGRAPHER
GINGERBEER
GLENDOVEER
GLOUCESTER
GOALKEEPER
GOATSUCKER
GOLDDIGGER
GOLDFINGER
GONFANONER
GONIOMETER
GRIDIRONER
GUBERNATOR
HACKBUTEER
HALFDOLLAR
HALFSISTER
HANGGLIDER
HEADHUNTER
HEADMASTER
HELICOPTER
HELIOLATER
HELLBENDER
HIGHBINDER
HIGHLANDER
HITCHHIKER
HOMEWORKER
HORNBLOWER
HORSEPOWER
HORSERIDER
HOWSOMEVER
HUMIDIFIER
HYDROMETER
HYGROMETER
ICEBREAKER
IMPRIMATUR
INKSLINGER
INQUISITOR
INSTIGATOR
INSTRUCTOR
INTERCEDER
INTERFERER
INTERLOPER
IRONMONGER
JACKHAMMER
JEISTIECOR
KEYBOARDER
KHIDMUTGAR
KIESELGUHR
KINGFISHER
KOEKSISTER
LACKLUSTER
LADYKILLER
LANDLOUPER
LANDLUBBER
LAWBREAKER
LEAFHOPPER
LEFTHANDER
LEFTWINGER
LEGISLATOR
LENTICULAR
LIPIZZANER
LIQUIDATOR
LIQUIDIZER
LOCKKEEPER
LUMPSUCKER
MADAGASCAR
MAIDENHAIR
MAINPERNOR
MALEFACTOR
MALINGERER
MANCHESTER
MATCHMAKER
MEGALOSAUR
MERRYMAKER
MICROMETER
MILEOMETER
MILLIMETER
MINEWORKER
MOLENDINAR
MOSSBUNKER
MUDSKIPPER
MULTIPLIER
NEGOTIATOR
NEWSCASTER
NEWSLETTER
NEWSMONGER
NEWSREADER
NORTHANGER
NORTHERNER
NUTCRACKER
OMBROMETER
OPISOMETER
ORIGINATOR
OSCILLATOR
OVERLANDER
OVIPOSITOR
OXYGENATOR
PAINKILLER
PALFRENIER
PALISANDER
PALLBEARER
PARTICULAR
PATHFINDER
PAWNBROKER
PEACEMAKER
PEASHOOTER
PENINSULAR
PENTAMETER
PERCOLATOR
PERFORATOR
PERSECUTOR
PETITIONER
PILEDRIVER
PLATELAYER
PLESIOSAUR
PLEXIMETER
PLUMASSIER
POSTMASTER
POURPARLER
PREPARATOR
PREPOSITOR
PROCREATOR
PROCURATOR
PROGENITOR
PROGRAMMER
PROMENADER
PROPAGATOR
PROPRAETOR
PROPRIETOR
PROSECUTOR
PROSPECTOR
PROTRACTOR
PROVEDITOR
QUARRENDER
QUESTIONER
QUIZMASTER
RAPPORTEUR
RECONSIDER
REDISCOVER
REJONEADOR
REPETITEUR
REPRODUCER
REREDORTER
RESEARCHER
RESPIRATOR
RINGLEADER
RINGMASTER
RIPSNORTER
ROADRUNNER
ROSECHAFER
ROTTWEILER
SALAMANDER
SALMANAZAR
SANDGROPER
SCRUTINEER
SEERSUCKER
SEMIQUAVER
SHEARWATER
SHOPKEEPER
SHOPLIFTER
SHOPWALKER
SHOWJUMPER
SIDEWINDER
SKYSCRAPER
SOGDOLAGER
SOGDOLIGER
SOGDOLOGER
SONGWRITER
SOOTHSAYER
SOUTHERNER
SPECULATOR
SPORTSWEAR
STABILISER
STABILIZER
STADHOLDER
STALHELMER
STALLENGER
STALLINGER
STEMWINDER
STENOTYPER
STEPFATHER
STEPLADDER
STEPMOTHER
STEPSISTER
STERILISER
STERILIZER
SUBLIMATER
SUBMARINER
SUBSCRIBER
SUPERPOWER
SUPERVISOR
SUPPRESSOR
TACHOMETER
TALEBEARER
TANNHAUSER
TASKMASTER
TEETOTALER
TESTICULAR
THEREAFTER
THERMISTOR
TIEBREAKER
TIMEKEEPER
TIMESERVER
TIRAILLEUR
TOLLKEEPER
TONGUESTER
TOUCHPAPER
TRAFFICKER
TRANSISTOR
TRANSLATOR
TRAVELATOR
TRAVOLATOR
TRESPASSER
TRIACONTER
TRIANGULAR
TROCHANTER
TROMOMETER
TROUBADOUR
TUBERCULAR
TYPESETTER
TYPEWRITER
UMBELLIFER
UNBELIEVER
UNDERCOVER
UNDERFLOOR
UNDERSTEER
UNDERTAKER
UNDERWATER
UNFAMILIAR
VENTILATOR
VERNACULAR
VICTUALLER
VIEWFINDER
VOETGANGER
WAGEEARNER
WALLFLOWER
WASTEPAPER
WATCHMAKER
WATCHTOWER
WATERCOLOR
WATERSKIER
WEEDKILLER
WEIMARANER
WHARFINGER
WHATSOEVER
WHEELCHAIR
WHITEWATER
WHOLESALER
WILDFOWLER
WINCHESTER
WINDFLOWER
WINDJAMMER
WINDSURFER
WITSNAPPER
WOODPECKER
WOODWORKER
WORSHIPPER
YESTERYEAR
ABRUPTNESS
ABSTEMIOUS
ACANACEOUS
ACCESSIONS
ACCLIVIOUS
ACEPHALOUS
ACOLOUTHOS
ACROBATICS
ACROGENOUS
ADULTERESS
ADULTEROUS
AEROBATICS
AERUGINOUS
AESTHETICS

AFTERHOURS
AFTERWARDS
AGAPANTHUS
AGONISTICS
ALBIGENSES
ALCIBIADES
ALEXANDERS
ALLOSAURUS
ALMSHOUSES
ALZHEIMERS
AMANUENSIS
AMARYLLIDS
AMBLYOPSIS
AMPELOPSIS
AMPHIBIOUS
AMPHIMIXIS
ANACHARSIS
ANADROMOUS
ANAXIMENES
ANCHYLOSIS
ANCIPITOUS
ANTIADITIS
ANTIBARBUS
ANTISEPSIS
ANTITHESIS
ANTITRAGUS
APEMANTHUS
APHAERESIS
APOLLONIUS
APOTHEOSIS
AQUAFORTIS
ARAGONITES
ARCHIMEDES
ARENACEOUS
ARISTIPPUS
ARISTOTLES
ARTOCARPUS
ASBESTOSIS
ASPERSIONS
ASTOMATOUS
ASTRAGALUS
ASTRALAGUS
ASTUTENESS
ATELEIOSIS
AURIFEROUS
AUSPICIOUS
AUTOGENOUS
AUTONOMOUS
AVARICIOUS
BABESIASIS
BACCHANTES
BACKBLOCKS
BACKSTAIRS
BAGASSOSIS
BALLISTICS
BARRENNESS
BATTAILOUS
BEAUJOLAIS
BEDCLOTHES
BEEFEATERS
BELONGINGS
BERMOOTHES
BETACRUCIS
BINOCULARS
BIOPHYSICS
BIORHYTHMS
BITTERNESS
BITUMINOUS
BOISTEROUS
BORROWINGS
BOTTOMLESS
BRAININESS
BREAKABLES
BREATHLESS
BRICKWORKS
BRIGHTNESS
BRONCHITIS
BUCEPHALUS
CACUMINOUS
CADAVEROUS
CALAMITOUS
CALCAREOUS
CAMBRENSIS
CANCRIZANS
CANDYFLOSS
CANEPHORUS
CAPRICIOUS
CARACTACUS
CARYATIDES
CASUALNESS
CATASTASIS
CATAWAMPUS
CATHOLICOS
CELESTIALS
CELLULITIS
CENSORIOUS
CEREMONIES
CHAMAEROPS
CHANGELESS
CHAPARAJOS
CHAPAREJOS
CHAROLLAIS
CHEEKINESS
CHERVONETS
CHILDERMAS
CHILLINESS
CHIVALROUS
CHOICELESS
CHOPSTICKS
CHRONICLES
CHRYSIPPUS
CIRCUITOUS
CLAMMINESS
CLEVERNESS
CLOUDINESS
CLUMSINESS
COARSENESS
COCCINEOUS
COETANEOUS
COLOURLESS
COMMODIOUS
CONCINNOUS
CONDIMENTS
CONIFEROUS
CONSONANTS
CONSPECTUS
CONTAGIOUS
CONTIGUOUS
CONTINUOUS
COPERNICUS
CORNFLAKES
CORNSTALKS
CORYBANTES
CORYPHAEUS
COSTLINESS
COURAGEOUS
CRAFTINESS
CREOPHAGUS
CRETACEOUS
CRISSCROSS
CROCKFORDS
CROSSROADS
CRYOGENICS
CRYOPHORUS
CURRENCIES
CURVACEOUS
CUSSEDNESS
CYNOMOLGUS
DEADLINESS
DEMOCRITUS
DENDROPHIS
DEPARTURES
DERMATITIS
DESPITEOUS
DIAGENESIS
DIALECTICS
DIAPEDESIS
DIAPHANOUS
DIDUNCULUS
DIOPHANTOS
DIPLODOCUS
DIRECTIONS
DIRECTNESS
DISASTROUS
DISCOBOLUS
DISPOSSESS
DISTRINGAS
DOGGEDNESS
DOLICHOLIS
DOLICHOTUS
DOUBLEBASS
DOWNSTAIRS
DRACONITES
DREADLOCKS
DREAMINESS
DREARINESS
DROWSINESS
DUCKBOARDS
EARTHWORKS
ECCHYMOSIS
ECTHLIPSIS
EFFORTLESS
ELEGABALUS
EMBLEMENTS
EMOLUMENTS
EMPEDOCLES
ENANTIOSIS
ENDOGAMOUS
ENDOSMOSIS
EPICANTHUS
EPIDIDYMUS
EPIGLOTTIS
EPIMENIDES
EPIMETHEUS
EPISTEMICS
ERGONOMICS
ERYMANTHUS
ERYSIPELAS
EUCALYPTUS
EUPHONIOUS
EURYPTERUS
EVERGLADES
EXEMPTNESS
EXPOUNDERS
EXTRANEOUS
EYEWITNESS
FACILITIES
FACTITIOUS
FALLACIOUS
FASTIDIOUS
FATALITIES
FATHERLESS
FAULTINESS
FEEBLENESS
FELICITOUS
FIBERGLASS
FIBREGLASS
FIBROSITIS
FICKLENESS
FICTITIOUS
FIERCENESS
FILTHINESS
FISTICUFFS
FLABBINESS
FLAGITIOUS
FLASHINESS
FLESHINESS
FLIGHTLESS
FLIMSINESS
FLOWERBEDS
FLUFFINESS
FONTICULUS
FONTINALIS
FOODSTUFFS
FOOTLIGHTS
FOOTPRINTS
FORTINBRAS
FORTUITOUS
FREEMASONS
FRIENDLESS
FRISKINESS
FRONTWARDS
FULIGINOUS
GALIMATIAS
GANGRENOUS
GELATINOUS
GENTLENESS
GEOPHYSICS
GERIATRICS
GINGIVITIS
GLASSINESS
GLOSSINESS
GLUTTONOUS
GODPARENTS
GOLDILOCKS
GONDOLIERS
GRASSLANDS
GRASSROOTS
GRATUITOUS
GREEDINESS
GREGARIOUS
GRENADIERS
GREYFRIARS
GRITTINESS
GROUNDLESS
GRUBBINESS
GRUMPINESS
GUARNERIUS
GUIDELINES
GYMNASTICS
HAEMANTHUS
HALIEUTICS
HANDLEBARS
HARMONIOUS
HEADLIGHTS
HEADPHONES
HEARTINESS
HERBACEOUS
HEREABOUTS
HESPERIDES
HIPPARCHUS
HIPPOMANES
HOARSENESS
HOLOFERNES
HOMELINESS
HOMORELAPS
HOMUNCULUS
HONOURLESS
HORRENDOUS
HOUSEMAIDS
HOWLEGLASS
HUMANITIES
HUMBLENESS
HUMOURLESS
HYDRAULICS
HYDROLYSIS
HYPOGAEOUS
HYPOTHESIS
HYSTERESIS
ICHTHYOSIS

IMPERVIOUS
IMPURITIES
INCAUTIOUS
INCESTUOUS
INDECOROUS
INDENTURES
INDIGENOUS
INFECTIOUS
INGLORIOUS
INIQUITOUS
INTENTNESS
INTESTINES
ISOMETRICS
JACKANAPES
JACKSTONES
JACKSTRAWS
JAUNTINESS
JOBSEEKERS
KILOMETRES
KINDLINESS
KSHATRIYAS
LACCADIVES
LANGERHANS
LANGUOROUS
LANIGEROUS
LARYNGITIS
LASCIVIOUS
LAVISHNESS
LEGUMINOUS
LEGWARMERS
LENGTHWAYS
LENTIGINES
LEONTIASIS
LEOPARDESS
LIBIDINOUS
LICENTIOUS
LILYWHITES
LINEAMENTS
LITTLENESS
LIVELINESS
LOGARITHMS
LONELINESS
LONGCHAMPS
LOQUACIOUS
LORDLINESS
LOTOPHAGUS
LOVELINESS
LUGUBRIOUS
MALAPROPOS
MALODOROUS
MANAGERESS
MARVELLOUS
MEAGERNESS
MEAGRENESS
MELLOWNESS
MEMBRANOUS
MENDACIOUS
MENINGITIS
METACARPUS
METALEPSIS
METAPLASIS
METATARSUS
METATHESIS
METICULOUS
METROPOLIS
MICHAELMAS
MIGHTINESS
MINDERERUS
MINUTENESS
MIRACULOUS
MISGIVINGS
MONILIASIS
MONOECIOUS
MONOGAMOUS
MONOPTEROS
MONOTONOUS
MONTICULUS
MORALITIES
MORDACIOUS
MORIGEROUS
MOROSENESS
MOSASAUROS
MOTHERLESS
MOTIONLESS
MOULDINESS
MULLIGRUBS
MUMBLENEWS
MUSKETEERS
MYRINGITIS
MYSTAGOGUS
MYSTERIOUS
NARROWNESS
NECROPOLIS
NECTABANUS
NEFANDROUS
NEWSAGENTS
NEWSPAPERS
NIGHTDRESS
NIMBLENESS
NONSUCCESS
NORTHWARDS
NOTORYCTES
NUCLEONICS
NUMBERLESS
NUTRITIOUS
OBJECTLESS
OBSEQUIOUS
OBSTETRICS
OBTUSENESS
ODDFELLOWS
ODIOUSNESS
OESOPHAGUS
OFTENTIMES
OIREACHTAS
OLEAGINOUS
OLERACEOUS
OMNIVOROUS
ONOMASTICS
ORCHIDEOUS
OROGENESIS
ORTHOPTICS
OSMIDROSIS
OSTEOLEPIS
OSTROGOTHS
OTHERGATES
OTHERGUESS
OUGHTLINGS
OUTRAGEOUS
OZYMANDIAS
PANNICULUS
PANTALOONS
PARACELSUS
PARAENESIS
PARAPHYSIS
PARAPRAXIS
PARATROOPS
PARENTLESS
PARKLEAVES
PATCHINESS
PEDIATRICS
PEDIPALPUS
PERDITIOUS
PERFIDIOUS
PERIEGESIS
PERNICIOUS
PERSEPOLIS
PERSIENNES
PESCADORES
PETTICHAPS
PETTYCHAPS
PHOLIDOSIS
PHOSPHORUS
PILLIWINKS
PITYRIASIS
PLIOHIPPUS
POCAHONTAS
POLIANTHES
POLITENESS
POLYANTHUS
POLYGAMOUS
POLYPHEMUS
PORRACEOUS
PORTCULLIS
PORTENTOUS
POSTHUMOUS
PRAXITELES
PRECARIOUS
PRECOCIOUS
PREDACIOUS
PREPOSSESS
PRETTINESS
PRINCIPLES
PRIVATEERS
PROAIRESIS
PROCRUSTES
PRODIGIOUS
PROFITLESS
PROMETHEUS
PROMPTNESS
PROPERTIUS
PROPHETESS
PROPITIOUS
PROPOSITUS
PROSPECTUS
PROSPEROUS
PROSTHESIS
PROTAGORAS
PROVISIONS
PTERYGOTUS
PUGNACIOUS
PYROPHORUS
PYTHAGORAS
QUADRICEPS
QUAINTNESS
QUEASINESS
QUENCHLESS
QUICKSANDS
RANDOMNESS
RANUNCULUS
REBELLIOUS
REGARDLESS
RELENTLESS
REMOTENESS
RENDEZVOUS
RESERVISTS
RETROGRESS
RHAMPASTOS
RHEUMATICS
RHINOCEROS
RHOEADALES
RIDICULOUS
ROBUSTIOUS
ROBUSTNESS
RUBIGINOUS
RUDDERLESS
RUGGEDNESS
SACREDNESS
SALLENDERS
SALOPETTES
SALUBRIOUS
SANCTITIES
SANDWICHES
SARMENTOUS
SAVAGENESS
SAXICOLOUS
SBUDDIKINS
SCAMMOZZIS
SCANDALOUS
SCANTINESS
SCARCENESS
SCATHELESS
SCLERIASIS
SCRIPTURES
SCRUPULOUS
SCULPTRESS
SCURRILOUS
SEAMSTRESS
SECURITIES
SEDATENESS
SELLINGERS
SEQUACIOUS
SHABBINESS
SHADOWLESS
SHIFTINESS
SHODDINESS
SHREWDNESS
SHRILLNESS
SIDEBOARDS
SINFULNESS
SINGLENESS
SLANDEROUS
SLEEPINESS
SLEEVELESS
SLOPPINESS
SMARMINESS
SMOOTHNESS
SNOOTINESS
SOBERSIDES
SOLICITOUS
SONGSTRESS
SORDIDNESS
SOUTHWARDS
SPARSENESS
SPECTACLES
SPECTATORS
SPEECHLESS
SPEEDINESS
SPILLIKINS
SPIRITLESS
SPIRITUOUS
SPRINGBOKS
SPRINGHAAS
SPRINGLESS
SPRUCENESS
STANISLAUS
STATISTICS
STEADINESS
STEELINESS
STEELWORKS
STERTEROUS
STERTOROUS
STEWARDESS
STICKINESS
STINGINESS
STOCKINESS
STRABISMUS
STRATIOTES
STRICTNESS
STRIDEWAYS
STUFFINESS
STUPENDOUS
STURDINESS
STYLISTICS
SUBTROPICS
SUDDENNESS
SULPHUROUS
SULTRINESS
SUNGLASSES
SUPPLENESS
SUSPENDERS

SUSPICIOUS
SYNAERESIS
SYNEIDESIS
SYNONYMOUS
SYNOSTOSIS
SYNTERESIS
SYNTHRONUS
TENDERNESS
TERTIARIES
TESTACEOUS
THALESTRIS
THEMSELVES
THEOCRITUS
THROMBOSIS
THUCYDIDES
THUMBIKINS
THUNDEROUS
TIMELINESS
TOILETRIES
TOUCHINESS
TRADITIONS
TRAITOROUS
TRANSGRESS
TRAVELLERS
TREMENDOUS
TRENDINESS
TRICKINESS
TROPHONIUS
TUMULTUOUS
TUTIVILLUS
UBIQUITOUS
ULTRONEOUS
UNDERCLASS
UNDERPANTS
UNEASINESS
UNEVENNESS
UNGRACIOUS
UNIGENITUS
UNIQUENESS
UNRULINESS
UNTIDINESS
UPPERCLASS
UPROARIOUS
UROPOIESIS
USEFULNESS
VALENTINES
VEGETABLES
VERSAILLES
VIBRATIONS
VICTORIOUS
VIGILANTES
VILLAINOUS
VIVIPAROUS
VOCIFEROUS
VOLUMINOUS
VOLUPTUOUS
VORAGINOUS
WANDERINGS
WASSERMANS
WATERCRESS

WATERWINGS
WATERWORKS
WEAPONLESS
WEIGHTLESS
WHEEZINESS
WICKEDNESS
WILDERNESS
WORLDCLASS
WORTHINESS
XIPHOPAGUS
YOURSELVES
ZOOTHAPSIS
ABITURIENT
ABONNEMENT
ABRIDGMENT
ACCOUNTANT
ACTIVITIST
ADDITAMENT
ADJUSTMENT
ADOLESCENT
ADULTERANT
AGRONOMIST
AIRFREIGHT
ALLUREMENT
AMBIVALENT
ANABAPTIST
ANALPHABET
ANASTIGMAT
ANIMADVERT
ANTAGONIST
ANTECEDENT
ARISTOCRAT
ARMIPOTENT
ASSESSMENT
ASSIGNMENT
ASSORTMENT
ASTRINGENT
ATTACHMENT
ATTAINMENT
AUTODIDACT
BAFFLEMENT
BALBUTIENT
BALLOONIST
BANISHMENT
BASSOONIST
BATTLEMENT
BENEFICENT
BENEVOLENT
BIOCHEMIST
BIRTHRIGHT
BLACKHEART
BLACKSHIRT
BLUETHROAT
BOLLANDIST
BOLSHEVIST
BREADFRUIT
BROADSHEET
BUREAUCRAT
CANTONMENT
CAPITALIST

CARTOONIST
CATAPHRACT
CHAMBERPOT
CHAUVINIST
CHECKPOINT
CHIMNEYPOT
CHREMATIST
CIRCUMVENT
CLASSICIST
CLOUDBURST
CNIDOBLAST
COADJUTANT
COEXISTENT
COINCIDENT
COMMANDANT
COMMITMENT
COMPATRIOT
COMPLACENT
COMPLEMENT
COMPLIMENT
CONCORDANT
CONCURRENT
CONFORMIST
CONSEQUENT
CONSISTENT
CONSTRAINT
CONSULTANT
CONTESTANT
CONTINGENT
CONTRADICT
CONTRAHENT
CONTROVERT
CONVENIENT
CONVERGENT
CONVERSANT
COQUELICOT
COUNTERACT
CRANKSHAFT
CUCKOOPINT
DEBASEMENT
DEBATEMENT
DECAMPMENT
DECRESCENT
DEFACEMENT
DEFILEMENT
DEFRAYMENT
DELINQUENT
DENOUEMENT
DEPARTMENT
DEPLOYMENT
DEPORTMENT
DEPRESSANT
DERAILMENT
DESCENDANT
DESPONDENT
DETACHMENT
DETAINMENT
DEVASTAVIT
DEVOTEMENT
DIASKEUAST

DICYNODONT
DISAPPOINT
DISCOMFORT
DISCONCERT
DISCONNECT
DISCONTENT
DISCORDANT
DISCREPANT
DISENCHANT
DISINHERIT
DISRESPECT
DISSILIENT
DISSOLVENT
DISTRAUGHT
DIURNALIST
DOVERCOURT
DOWNMARKET
EBOULEMENT
EFFACEMENT
EMBANKMENT
EMBODIMENT
EMBONPOINT
EMPLOYMENT
ENCAMPMENT
ENCASEMENT
ENDEARMENT
ENGAGEMENT
ENGOUEMENT
ENLACEMENT
ENLÈVEMENT
ENLISTMENT
ENRICHMENT
ENROLLMENT
ENTHUSIAST
ENTICEMENT
ENTOMBMENT
EPAULEMENT
EQUIVALENT
ERUBESCENT
ESCAPEMENT
ESCARPMENT
EVANESCENT
EVANGELIST
EXCITEMENT
EXORBITANT
EXPERIMENT
FAHRENHEIT
FAMISHMENT
FEARNOUGHT
FEDERALIST
FLAMBOYANT
FLAMINGANT
FLASHLIGHT
FLASHPOINT
FLAVESCENT
FLOCCULENT
FLOODLIGHT
FLORESCENT
FORTHRIGHT
FOUDROYANT

FRAUDULENT
FREMESCENT
FULFILMENT
GESUNDHEIT
GOVERNMENT
GRAPEFRUIT
GRAVEOLENT
GREENHEART
GROUNDBAIT
HANDICRAFT
HARASSMENT
HARTEBEEST
HELLESPONT
HIEROPHANT
HOUSECRAFT
HOVERCRAFT
ICONOCLAST
IMPAIRMENT
IMPEDIMENT
IMPENITENT
INCITEMENT
INCOHERENT
INCONSTANT
INCRESCENT
INDICTMENT
INDISCREET
INDISTINCT
INDITEMENT
INDUCEMENT
INESCULENT
INFEFTMENT
INFREQUENT
INGREDIENT
INHABITANT
INSOUCIANT
INSTALMENT
INSTRUMENT
INTEGUMENT
INTELIGENT
INTENDMENT
INTERNMENT
INTOLERANT
INTOXICANT
INTROSPECT
INVESTMENT
IRIDESCENT
IRRELEVANT
IRREVERENT
JERRYBUILT
JOURNALIST
JUGGERNAUT
KNOCKABOUT
LANSQUENET
LAUNDROMAT
LIBRETTIST
LIEUTENANT
LIQUESCENT
LIVERWURST
LOCULAMENT
LUMINARIST

MAGNIFICAT
MAKEWEIGHT
MALCONTENT
MALEVOLENT
MANAGEMENT
MANICURIST
MANSERVANT
MANUSCRIPT
MARCANTANT
MARCESCENT
MASTERWORT
MAUPASSANT
MAXIMALIST
MEDICAMENT
MICROLIGHT
MILITARIST
MINIMALIST
MINIMARKET
MISCONDUCT
MISOGYNIST
MIZZENMAST
MONARCHIST
MONETARIST
MONTRACHET
MONTSERRAT
MOUDIEWART
MUNIFICENT
NARROWBOAT
NATURALIST
NEMATOCYST
NETHERMOST
NIGHTLIGHT
NIGHTSHIRT
NIGRESCENT
NOMINALIST
NONCHALANT
NONPAYMENT
NONVIOLENT
NORMOBLAST
NOUAKCHOTT
NYMPHOLEPT
OMNIPOTENT
OMNISCIENT
OPALESCENT
OSTEOBLAST
OUTPATIENT
OVERTHWART
OVERWEIGHT
PALIMPSEST
PALUDAMENT
PANSOPHIST
PARLIAMENT
PENSIONNAT
PEPPERMINT
PEPPERWORT
PERCIPIENT
PERFICIENT
PERMAFROST
PERSISTENT
PHANTASIST
PHARMACIST
PHYSIOCRAT
PICKPOCKET
PLAGIARIST
PLANOBLAST
PLAYWRIGHT
PLUPERFECT
POLYCHREST
POLYGAMIST
PONTEFRACT
PORTIONIST
POSITIVIST
POSTSCRIPT
PRAGMATIST
PREEMINENT
PREFERMENT
PREPAYMENT
PRIZEFIGHT
PROFICIENT
PROPELLANT
PROSILIENT
PROTESTANT
PUBERULENT
PUNISHMENT
PURSUIVANT
PUTRESCENT
PUZZLEMENT
REAMINGBIT
REARMAMENT
RECIDIVIST
REDCURRANT
REFINEMENT
REQUIESCAT
RESENTMENT
RESPONDENT
RESTAURANT
RETIREMENT
RETROSPECT
REVIVALIST
RINDERPEST
ROUNDABOUT
ROUSEABOUT
ROUSTABOUT
SACROSANCT
SAPPERMENT
SAUERKRAUT
SCARCEMENT
SCATURIENT
SCHWARZLOT
SCOOTERIST
SECONDBEST
SECONDMENT
SEPARATIST
SEPTUAGINT
SETTERWORT
SETTLEMENT
SEXOLOGIST
SHELLYCOAT
SIDEROSTAT
SIGNIFICAT
SINARCHIST
SINARQUIST
SOLIVAGANT
SOMERSAULT
SOUBRIQUET
SPACECRAFT
SPARTACIST
SPECIALIST
SPIDERWORT
SPINESCENT
SPOILSPORT
STAGECRAFT
STANDPOINT
STATECRAFT
STONYHURST
STOREFRONT
STRATEGIST
STRATOCRAT
STRATOCYST
STREPITANT
STRINGHALT
SUAVEOLENT
SUBCOMPACT
SUBMEDIANT
SUBSEQUENT
SUBSISTENT
SUFFICIENT
SUFFRAGIST
SUPERGIANT
SUPPLEMENT
SUPPLICANT
SURREALIST
SWEATSHIRT
SWEETHEART
TAMPERFOOT
TANGLEFOOT
TANTAMOUNT
TAPOTEMENT
TAXONOMIST
TECHNOCRAT
TENDERFOOT
THEOLOGIST
THEREANENT
THERMOSTAT
THIMBLEWIT
THROUGHOUT
THROUGHPUT
TOPOLOGIST
TORCHLIGHT
TORPESCENT
TOURNAMENT
TOURNIQUET
TRANSCRIPT
TRANSPLANT
TRECENTIST
TREKSCHUIT
TRIUMPHANT
TROMBONIST
TYPESCRIPT
UNDERBURNT
UNDERCRAFT
UNDERCROFT
UNDERSHIRT
UNDERSKIRT
UNPLEASANT
VANDERBILT
VICEGERENT
VICEREGENT
VIROLOGIST
VOCABULIST
WANDERLUST
WATERFRONT
WATERSPOUT
WATERTIGHT
WHITEHEART
WHOLEWHEAT
WILDEBEEST
WITCHCRAFT
WONDERMENT
WOOLLYBUTT
YELLOWROOT
ZEUGLODONT
CLEMENCEAU
COUSCOUSOU
FRICANDEAU
CONTRAFLOW
FORESHADOW
GOODFELLOW
GRASSWIDOW
LONGFELLOW
OVERSHADOW
PLAYFELLOW
THUMBSCREW
WAPENSCHAW
WAPINSCHAW
WAPPENSHAW
WHILLYWHAW
ANTICLIMAX
CHATTERBOX
CHICKENPOX
CIRCUMFLEX
GENERATRIX
SCOMBRESOX
SEPARATRIX
SQUEEZEBOX
THUNDERBOX
UNORTHODOX
ABNORMALLY
ABOMINABLY
ABSOLUTELY
ABUNDANTLY
ACCURATELY
ACCUSINGLY
ACROMEGALY
ADEQUATELY
ADMIRINGLY
ADMITTEDLY
AFFABILITY
ALDERMANLY
ALIMENTARY
ALKALINITY
ALLYCHOLLY
AMBULATORY
AMIABILITY
APOTHECARY
APPARENTLY
AREOGRAPHY
ARISTOLOGY
ARROGANTLY
ASCENDANCY
ASCENDENCY
AUDIBILITY
AUTECOLOGY
AUTOPLASTY
AXINOMANCY
BALNEOLOGY
BANKRUPTCY
BESTIALITY
BIANNUALLY
BIENNIALLY
BLACKBERRY
BLACKBULLY
BLISSFULLY
BLOOMSBURY
BUFFOONERY
CACOGRAPHY
CAERPHILLY
CANTERBURY
CAPABILITY
CAPERNOITY
CAPITULARY
CAPNOMANCY
CARDIOLOGY
CARELESSLY
CARPHOLOGY
CARTOMANCY
CATCHPENNY
CAUTIONARY
CAUTIOUSLY
CHALCEDONY
CHAPLAINCY
CHARDONNAY
CHARITABLY
CHEERFULLY
CHEIRONOMY
CHEMICALLY
CHEMONASTY
CHILDISHLY
CHIROMANCY
CHRONOLOGY
CHURLISHLY
CLEARSTORY
CLERESTORY
CLEROMANCY
CLINICALLY
CLOUDBERRY
COCKABULLY
COCKERNONY
COHERENTLY
COLOSSALLY

COMMENTARY
COMMISSARY
COMMUNALLY
COMPLETELY
COMPLEXITY
COMPLICITY
COMPULSORY
CONCHOLOGY
CONCINNITY
CONFORMITY
CONFUSEDLY
CONSISTORY
CONSPIRACY
CONSTANTLY
CONTIGUITY
CONTINUITY
CONTRARILY
CONVERSELY
CORDIALITY
CREATIVITY
CREDITABLY
CRIMINALLY
CRITICALLY
CYSTOSCOPY
DEBAUCHERY
DECISIVELY
DEFAMATORY
DEFICIENCY
DEFINITELY
DEGENERACY
DEJECTEDLY
DELICATELY
DELTIOLOGY
DEMOGRAPHY
DEPENDENCY
DEPILATORY
DEPLORABLY
DEPOSITARY
DEPOSITORY
DEROGATORY
DESERVEDLY
DIAGONALLY
DICTIONARY
DIFFICULTY
DILIGENTLY
DISABILITY
DISCREETLY
DISHARMONY
DISHONESTY
DISLOYALTY
DISORDERLY
DISPENSARY
DISQUALIFY
DISTILLERY
DISTINCTLY
DOMICILARY
DOSTOEVSKY
DOUBTFULLY
DREADFULLY
DURABILITY
EFFEMINACY
EFFICIENCY
EFFRONTERY
EFFUSIVELY
ELASTICITY
ELDERBERRY
ELEMENTARY
ELOQUENTLY
EMBROIDERY
EMBRYOLOGY
ENORMOUSLY
ENTOMOLOGY
EQUANIMITY
ESPECIALLY
EVENTUALLY
EVITERNITY
EXCELLENCY
EXOTICALLY
EXPECTANCY
EXPEDIENCY
EXPLICITLY
EXPOSITORY
EXPRESSWAY
EXTERNALLY
FABULOUSLY
FAITHFULLY
FALDISTORY
FAMILIARLY
FAVOURABLY
FEARLESSLY
FEMININITY
FEVERISHLY
FIENDISHLY
FLAGRANTLY
FLEETINGLY
FLIPPANTLY
FORCEFULLY
FRATERNITY
FRENZIEDLY
FREQUENTLY
FRITILLARY
FRUITFULLY
FUDDYDUDDY
GALSWORTHY
GASTRONOMY
GENERALITY
GENEROSITY
GENEROUSLY
GLORIOUSLY
GOOSEBERRY
GORGEOUSLY
GOVERNESSY
GRACEFULLY
GRACIOUSLY
GRAPHOLOGY
GRATEFULLY
GRATILLITY
GUTTURALLY
GYMNOSOPHY
GYNECOLOGY
HABITUALLY
HALFHOURLY
HALFYEARLY
HANDSOMELY
HANKYPANKY
HECTICALLY
HEEDLESSLY
HELPLESSLY
HEREDITARY
HEROICALLY
HESITANTLY
HETERODOXY
HIEROMANCY
HIEROSCOPY
HOLOGRAPHY
HOMEOPATHY
HONOURABLY
HOOTANANNY
HOOTENANNY
HOPELESSLY
HOSPITABLY
HUMOROUSLY
IGNORANTLY
ILLEGALITY
ILLITERACY
IMBECILITY
IMMACULACY
IMMATURITY
IMMOBILITY
IMMORALITY
IMMUNOLOGY
IMPECCABLY
IMPLACABLY
IMPLICITLY
IMPOLITELY
IMPOSSIBLY
IMPOTENTLY
IMPROBABLY
IMPROPERLY
IMPUDENTLY
INACCURACY
INACTIVITY
INADEQUACY
INCAPACITY
INCENDIARY
INCISIVELY
INCIVILITY
INCREDIBLY
INCUMBENCY
INDECENTLY
INDELICACY
INDIRECTLY
INEFFICACY
INEQUALITY
INEVITABLY
INFALLIBLY
INFERNALLY
INFIDELITY
INFINITELY
INFLEXIBLY
INFORMALLY
INHERENTLY
INHIBITORY
INHUMANITY
INNOCENTLY
INSANITARY
INSATIABLY
INSECURELY
INSECURITY
INSIPIDITY
INSOLENTLY
INSOLVENCY
INSULARITY
INSURGENCY
INTERMARRY
INTERNALLY
INTIMATELY
INVALIDITY
INVARIABLY
IRONICALLY
JOCULARITY
JUBILANTLY
JUDICIALLY
JUSTICIARY
KINCHINLAY
LABORATORY
LACKADAISY
LAMENTABLY
LEGIBILITY
LEGITIMACY
LIBERALITY
LISTLESSLY
LOGANBERRY
LORDOLATRY
LUMINOSITY
MAGISTRACY
MALACOLOGY
MALIGNANCY
MALMESBURY
MANIFESTLY
MARGINALLY
MARIOLATRY
MASTECTOMY
MATERIALLY
MATERNALLY
MATRIARCHY
MEDIOCRITY
MELANCHOLY
MENACINGLY
MERCIFULLY
METALLURGY
MINERALOGY
MISCELLANY
MISSIONARY
MISTAKENLY
MODERATELY
MONTGOMERY
MORPHOLOGY
MOUCHARABY
MOURNFULLY
MULIEBRITY
MUSICOLOGY
MUSSORGSKY
MUTABILITY
MUTINOUSLY
NARCOLEPSY
NATIONALLY
NECROMANCY
NEGATIVELY
NEIGHBORLY
NEUTRALITY
NEWSWORTHY
NOTABILITY
NOTEWORTHY
NOTICEABLY
NOTIONALLY
OBEDIENTLY
OBLIGATORY
OBLIGINGLY
OCHLOCRACY
ODONTOLOGY
OFFICIALLY
OPOTHERAPY
ORDINARILY
ORIGINALLY
OSCULATORY
OSTENSIBLY
OSTEOPATHY
OVERSUPPLY
PAINLESSLY
PARDONABLY
PARTIALITY
PASIGRAPHY
PASSAGEWAY
PATAVINITY
PATERNALLY
PATIBULARY
PATRIARCHY
PEACEFULLY
PECULIARLY
PEREMPTORY
PERILOUSLY
PERMANENCY
PERNICKETY
PERPETUITY
PERPLEXITY
PERSONALLY
PERVERSELY
PERVERSITY
PETULANTLY
PHILLUMENY
PHILOSOPHY
PHOTONASTY
PHRENOLOGY
PHYLACTERY
PHYSICALLY
PHYSIOLOGY
PICCADILLY
PICCANINNY
PINCHPENNY

PLASTICITY
PLEASANTLY
PLEASANTRY
PLEROPHORY
PLIABILITY
PLUTOCRACY
POETASTERY
POETICALLY
POGONOTOMY
POIGNANTLY
PONEROLOGY
POPULARITY
PORNOCRACY
POSITIVELY
POSTLIMINY
PREBENDARY
PRECURSORY
PREFERABLY
PREHISTORY
PREPENSELY
PRESBYTERY
PRESENTDAY
PRESIDENCY
PRESUMABLY
PREVENANCY
PREVIOUSLY
PROCLIVITY
PRODIGALLY
PROFITABLY
PROFLIGACY
PROFOUNDLY
PROFUNDITY
PROMISSORY
PROMONTORY
PROPENSITY
PROSPERITY
PROTERVITY
PSEPHOLOGY
PSYCHIATRY
PSYCHOLOGY
PUNCTUALLY
PYROGRAPHY
QUAESTUARY
QUATERNARY
QUEENSBURY
RATIONALLY
RAVENOUSLY
REASONABLY
RECKLESSLY
REDUNDANCY
REFRACTORY
REGULARITY
RELATIVELY
RELATIVITY
REMARKABLY
REPEATEDLY
REPORTEDLY
REPOSITORY
RESIGNEDLY
RESOLUTELY
RESTLESSLY
REVERENTLY
RIGHTFULLY
RIGOROUSLY
ROADWORTHY
ROCKABILLY
ROCKSTEADY
ROWDYDOWDY
RUTHLESSLY
SANGUINARY
SCOFFINGLY
SCORNFULLY
SCREENPLAY
SCURRILITY
SEASONABLY
SEDULOUSLY
SEISMOLOGY
SENSUALITY
SENSUOUSLY
SEPARATELY
SHAMEFULLY
SHEEPISHLY
SHOCKINGLY
SHRIEVALTY
SIMILARITY
SIMPLICITY
SINGULARLY
SKILLFULLY
SLATTERNLY
SLUGGISHLY
SOLIDARITY
SOLUBILITY
SOOTHINGLY
SPECIALITY
SPECIOUSLY
SPELEOLOGY
SPIRITEDLY
SPITEFULLY
SPLENDIDLY
SPODOMANCY
SPORTINGLY
SPOTLESSLY
SPREAGHERY
SPURIOUSLY
STATIONARY
STATIONERY
STATOCRACY
STEALTHILY
STEREOTOMY
STRABOTOMY
STRATHSPEY
STRAVINSKY
STRAWBERRY
STRIDENTLY
STRIKINGLY
STRINGENCY
STUBBORNLY
STUDIOUSLY
SUBSIDIARY
SUBTENANCY
SUCCINCTLY
SUPPOSEDLY
SURGICALLY
SUZERAINTY
SWIMMINGLY
TACTICALLY
TACTLESSLY
TASTEFULLY
TECHNOLOGY
TEENYWEENY
TELEGRAPHY
TERMINALLY
THANKFULLY
THIXOTROPY
THOROUGHLY
THREEPENNY
THROUGHWAY
TIMBROLOGY
TIRELESSLY
TOLERANTLY
TOMFOOLERY
TOPICALITY
TOPOGRAPHY
TOPSYTURVY
TORTUOUSLY
TOXICOLOGY
TRAGICALLY
TRAJECTORY
TRANQUILLY
TRANSITORY
TRICHOLOGY
TRIPUDIARY
TRIVIALITY
TRUSTFULLY
TRUTHFULLY
TYPOGRAPHY
ULTIMATELY
UNBEARABLY
UNCOMMONLY
UNCTUOUSLY
UNDERSTUDY
UNFRIENDLY
UNIFORMITY
UNIVERSITY
UNMANNERLY
UPHOLSTERY
VARICOSITY
VEHEMENTLY
VERTICALLY
VETERINARY
VIGOROUSLY
VIRTUOSITY
VIRTUOUSLY
VIRULENTLY
VISIBILITY
VOCABULARY
VOLATILITY
VOLUBILITY
VOLUPTUARY
WASTEFULLY
WATCHFULLY
WILLYWILLY
WISHYWASHY
WRETCHEDLY
WRONGFULLY
YOUNGBERRY
ZOOTHERAPY
HAKENKREUZ
RAZZMATAZZ

11:1

ABANDONMENT
ABBREVIATED
ABECEDARIAN
ABIOGENETIC
ABLACTATION
ABNORMALITY
ABOMINATION
ABORTIONIST
ABRACADABRA
ABRIDGEMENT
ABSENTEEISM
ABSTRACTION
ACADEMICIAN
ACATALECTIC
ACCELERATOR
ACCESSORIES
ACCIPITRINE
ACCLAMATION
ACCLIMATION
ACCLIMATISE
ACCLIMATIZE
ACCOMMODATE
ACCOMPANIST
ACCORDINGLY
ACCOUNTABLE
ACCOUNTANCY
ACCRESCENCE
ACCUMULATOR
ACHIEVEMENT
ACINACIFORM
ACKNOWLEDGE
ACOLOUTHITE
ACQUIESCENT
ACQUISITION
ACQUISITIVE
ACRIFLAVINE
ACRIMONIOUS
ACTUALITIES
ACUPUNCTURE
ADJOURNMENT
ADJUDICATOR
ADOLESCENCE
ADOPTIANISM
ADOPTIONISM
ADULLAMITES
ADULTERATED
ADUMBRATION
ADVANCEMENT
ADVENTURESS
ADVENTUROUS
ADVERBIALLY
ADVERTISING
AERODYNAMIC
AERONAUTICS
AESCULAPIAN
AESCULAPIUS
AFFECTATION
AFFILIATION
AFFIRMATION
AFFIRMATIVE
AFFLIICTION
AFGHANISTAN
AFTERSCHOOL
AGGLOMERATE
AGGLUTINANT
AGGLUTINATE
AGGRAVATING
AGGRAVATION
AGGREGATION
AGNOSTICISM
AGONOTHETES
AGORAPHOBIA
AGRICULTURE
AGROSTOLOGY
AGUARDIENTE
AIGUILLETTE
AILUROPHILE
AIRCRAFTMAN
AIRSICKNESS
ALBIGENSIAN
ALBUGINEOUS
ALCYONARIAN
ALEXANDRINE
ALEXANDRITE
ALIFANFARON
ALLEGORICAL
ALLELOMORPH
ALLEVIATION
ALPHABETIZE
ALTERCATION
ALTERNATELY
ALTERNATING
ALTERNATION
ALTERNATIVE
AMBIVALENCE
AMELANCHIER
AMERCIAMENT
AMERICANISM
AMINOBUTENE
AMMOPHILOUS
AMONTILLADO
AMPHETAMINE
AMPHIBOLOGY
AMPHISBAENA
AMPHISBOENA
AMPLEXICAUL
ANACHRONISM
ANACOLUTHIA
ANACREONTIC
ANADIPLOSIS
ANAESTHESIA
ANAESTHETIC
ANAGNORISIS
ANAPHYLAXIS
ANAPLEROSIS
ANAPLEROTIC
ANASTOMOSIS
ANAXIMANDER
ANDROGENOUS
ANENCEPHALY
ANESTHETIST
ANESTHETIZE
ANFRACTUOUS
ANGELOLATRY
ANISOCERCAL
ANNABERGITE
ANNIVERSARY
ANONYMOUSLY
ANTECEDENCE
ANTECHAMBER
ANTEPENDIUM
ANTHESTERIA
ANTHOCYANIN
ANTHOLOGIZE
ANTHONOMOUS
ANTIBURGHER
ANTICYCLONE
ANTINEUTRON
ANTIPHRASIS
ANTIPYRETIC
ANTIQUARIAN
ANTIRRHINUM
ANTISTHENES
ANTISTROPHE
ANTONOMASIA
APATOSAURUS
APHANIPTERA
APHRODISIAC
APLANOSPORE
APOCALYPTIC
APODYTERIUM
APOLLINARIS
APOLLONICON
APOMORPHINE
APONEUROSIS
APOPHYLLITE
APOSIOPESIS
APOSTROPHUS
APPALLINGLY
APPARATCHIK
APPEARANCES
APPEASEMENT
APPELLATION
APPELLATIVE
APPLICATION
APPOINTMENT
APPRECIABLE
APPRECIABLY
APPRENTICED
APPROACHING
APPROBATION
APPROPRIATE
APPROVINGLY
APPROXIMATE
APPURTENANT
ARBITRAGEUR
ARBITRAMENT
ARBITRARILY
ARBITRATION
ARCHAEOLOGY
ARCHEGONIAL
ARCHEGONIUM
ARCHENTERON
ARCHILOCHUS
ARCHIPELAGO
ARGATHELIAN
ARGENTINIAN
ARISTOCRACY
ARQUEBUSIER
ARRANGEMENT
ARRHENOTOKY
ARRIVEDERCI
ARTHRAPODAL
ARTHRODESIS
ARTHROSPORE
ARTICULATED
ARTILLERIST
ARTIODACTYL
ASCLEPIADES
ASPERGILLUM
ASPERGILLUS
ASPERSORIUM
ASPHETERISM
ASSASSINATE
ASSEMBLYMAN
ASSIDUOUSLY
ASSIGNATION
ASSIMILATED
ASSOCIATION
ASSYTHEMENT
ASTIGMATISM
ASTONISHING
ASTRINGENCY
ATHARVAVEDA
ATHERINIDAE
ATHERMANOUS
ATMOSPHERIC
ATRABILIOUS
ATROCIOUSLY
ATTENTIVELY
ATTENUATION
ATTESTATION
ATTRIBUTION
ATTRIBUTIVE
AUDACIOUSLY
AUDIOVISUAL
AUGUSTINIAN
AURIGNACIAN
AUXANOMETER
AVERRUNCATE
AVOIRDUPOIS
AWKWARDNESS
AXEROPHTHOL
AZOTOBACTER
BACCHANALIA
BACKBENCHER
BACKFIELDER
BACKPACKING
BACKSLIDING
BADDELEYITE
BADTEMPERED
BALISTRARIA
BALLBEARING
BANDEIRANTE
BANGLADESHI
BANNOCKBURN
BARBASTELLE
BARBITURATE
BARNSTORMER
BARTHOLOMEW
BARYCENTRIC
BASHFULNESS
BASKERVILLE
BATHYSPHERE
BATTLEDRESS
BATTLEFIELD
BATTLEFRONT
BATTLEMENTS
BEACHCOMBER
BEASTLINESS
BEAUMONTAGE
BEAUTIFULLY
BEHAVIOURAL
BELEAGUERED
BELLEROPHON
BELLETTRIST
BELLIGERENT
BELLYTIMBER
BELORUSSIAN
BENEDICTINE
BENEDICTION
BENEFICIARY
BENEFICIATE
BENEVOLENCE
BEREAVEMENT
BERGSCHRUND
BESIEGEMENT
BESSARABIAN
BESTSELLING
BEWILDERING
BIBLIOPHILE
BICARBONATE
BICENTENARY
BIELORUSSIA
BIFURCATION
BILIOUSNESS
BILLIONAIRE
BIOCHEMICAL
BIRDWATCHER
BITTERSWEET
BLACKFELLOW
BLACKMAILER
BLADDERWORT
BLAMEWORTHY
BLANKURSINE
BLASPHEMOUS
BLESSEDNESS

BLOCKBUSTER
BLOODSPORTS
BLOODSTREAM
BLOODSUCKER
BLUNDERBORE
BODHISATTVA
BOMBARDMENT
BOOKBINDING
BOOKKEEPING
BOOKSELLERS
BORBORYGMUS
BOTANOMANCY
BOURGEOISIE
BOUTONNIERE
BOYSENBERRY
BRAGGADOCIO
BRANDENBURG
BRAZZAVILLE
BREADCRUMBS
BREADWINNER
BREASTPLATE
BREATHALYSE
BRILLIANTLY
BRISTLECONE
BRITTLENESS
BROADCASTER
BROADMINDED
BROBDINGNAG
BROTHERHOOD
BRUCELLOSIS
BULLFIGHTER
BUMBERSHOOT
BUPRESTIDAE
BUREAUCRACY
BURGOMASTER
BUSHWHACKER
BUSINESSMAN
CABBALISTIC
CACOGASTRIC
CACOPHONOUS
CALCEOLARIA
CALCULATING
CALCULATION
CALEFACIENT
CALENDERING
CALIBRATION
CALIFORNIUM
CALLANETICS
CALLIGRAPHY
CALLISTEMON
CALLITRICHE
CALLOUSNESS
CAMALDOLITE
CAMARADERIE
CAMEROONIAN
CAMOUFLAGED
CAMPANOLOGY
CAMPESTRIAN
CAMPHORATED
CANDESCENCE
CANDIDATURE
CANDLELIGHT
CANDLESTICK
CANNIBALISM
CANNIBALIZE
CAPACITANCE
CAPACITATOR
CAPERNOITED
CAPERNOITIE
CAPRICCIOSO
CAPTIVATING
CAPTIVATION
CARABINIERE
CARAVANNING
CARBORUNDUM
CARBURETTOR
CARDIOGRAPH
CARDOPHAGUS
CAREFULNESS
CARMINATIVE
CARNAPTIOUS
CARNIVOROUS
CAROLINGIAN
CARRIAGEWAY
CARSICKNESS
CARTOGRAPHY
CASSITERITE
CASTELLATED
CATACAUSTIC
CATACHRESIS
CATACLYSMIC
CATALLACTIC
CATASTROPHE
CATCHPHRASE
CATEGORICAL
CATERPILLAR
CATHOLICISM
CAULIFLOWER
CAUSTICALLY
CEASELESSLY
CELEBRATION
CENTENARIAN
CENTERPIECE
CENTREBOARD
CENTREPIECE
CENTRIFUGAL
CENTRIPETAL
CENTUMVIRUS
CENTURIATOR
CERARGYRITE
CEREBRATION
CEREMONIOUS
CERTIFIABLE
CERTIFICATE
CESAREWITCH
CHAIRPERSON
CHALLENGING
CHAMBERLAIN
CHAMBERMAID
CHANCELLERY
CHANTARELLE
CHANTERELLE
CHANTICLEER
CHARACINOID
CHARGEPAYER
CHARISMATIC
CHARLEMAGNE
CHAULMOOGRA
CHAULMOUGRA
CHEERLEADER
CHEESECLOTH
CHEIROGNOMY
CHIAROSCURO
CHIASTOLITE
CHICHEVACHE
CHICKENFEED
CHILDMINDER
CHILLINGHAM
CHINOISERIE
CHIPPENDALE
CHIROGRAPHY
CHIROPODIST
CHITTERLING
CHLOROPHYLL
CHOCKABLOCK
CHOIRMASTER
CHOLESTEROL
CHONDROSTEI
CHORDOPHONE
CHOROGRAPHY
CHRISTENING
CHRISTMASSY
CHRISTOPHER
CHRONICALLY
CHRONOMETER
CHRYSAROBIN
CHRYSOPRASE
CILOFIBRATE
CINQUECENTO
CIRCULARIZE
CIRCULATING
CIRCULATION
CIRCULATORY
CIRCUMCISER
CIRCUMFLECT
CIRCUMSPECT
CIRRHIPEDEA
CIRRHIPEDIA
CITIZENSHIP
CITLALEPETL
CLADOSPORUM
CLAIRSCHACH
CLAIRVOYANT
CLANDESTINE
CLANJAMFRAY
CLAPPERCLAW
CLARENCIEUX
CLEANLINESS
CLEANSHAVEN
CLIFFHANGER
CLIMACTERIC
CLIMATOLOGY
CLINOCHLORE
CLIOMETRICS
COACHFELLOW
COAGULATION
COALESCENCE
COBBLESTONE
COCKLESHELL
COEFFICIENT
COENOBITISM
COEXISTENCE
COGNOSCENTE
COGNOSCENTI
COHORTATIVE
COINCIDENCE
COLDBLOODED
COLEORRHIZA
COLLABORATE
COLLAPSIBLE
COLLECTANEA
COLLENCHYMA
COLLOCATION
COLONIALISM
COLONIALIST
COLOURBLIND
COLUMBARIUM
COMBINATION
COMBUSTIBLE
COMESTIBLES
COMEUPPANCE
COMFORTABLE
COMFORTABLY
COMFORTLESS
COMMANDMENT
COMMEMORATE
COMMENDABLE
COMMENDABLY
COMMENTATOR
COMMINATION
COMMISERATE
COMMONPLACE
COMMONSENSE
COMMUNICANT
COMMUNICATE
COMMUTATION
COMPARATIVE
COMPARTMENT
COMPENDIOUS
COMPETENTLY
COMPETITION
COMPETITIVE
COMPILATION
COMPILEMENT
COMPLACENCY
COMPLAISANT
COMPLICATED
COMPLIMENTS
COMPOSITION
COMPOTATION
COMPRIMARIO
COMPTROLLER
COMPUNCTION
COMPUTATION
COMPUTERIZE
COMRADESHIP
COMSTOCKERY
CONCEALMENT
CONCEIVABLE
CONCEIVABLY
CONCENTRATE
CONCEPTICLE
CONCILIATOR
CONCISENESS
CONCOMITANT
CONCORDANCE
CONCURRENCE
CONDITIONAL
CONDITIONER
CONDOLENCES
CONDOMINIUM
CONDOTTIERE
CONDOTTIORE
CONDUCTRESS
CONFABULATE
CONFARREATE
CONFEDERACY
CONFEDERATE
CONFIDENTLY
CONFINEMENT
CONFUTATION
CONGRESSMAN
CONJECTURAL
CONJUGATION
CONJUNCTION
CONJUNCTURE
CONNECTICUT
CONNOISSEUR
CONNOTATION
CONSCIOUSLY
CONSECUTIVE
CONSEQUENCE
CONSERVANCY
CONSIDERATE
CONSIDERING
CONSIGNMENT
CONSILIENCE
CONSISTENCE
CONSISTENCY
CONSOLATION
CONSOLIDATE
CONSPICUOUS
CONSPIRATOR
CONSTANTINE
CONSTELLATE
CONSTERNATE
CONSTIPATED
CONSTITUENT
CONSTRAINED
CONSTRICTED

CONSTRICTOR
CONSTRUCTOR
CONSTUPRATE
CONSULTANCY
CONSUMABLES
CONSUMERISM
CONSUMPTION
CONSUMPTIVE
CONTAINMENT
CONTAMINANT
CONTAMINATE
CONTEMPLANT
CONTEMPLATE
CONTENEMENT
CONTENTEDLY
CONTENTIOUS
CONTENTMENT
CONTINENTAL
CONTINGENCE
CONTINGENCY
CONTINUALLY
CONTINUANCE
CONTRACTION
CONTRACTUAL
CONTRAPTION
CONTRASTING
CONTRAYERVA
CONTRETEMPS
CONTRIBUTOR
CONTRIVANCE
CONTROVERSY
CONTUBERNAL
CONURBATION
CONVALLARIA
CONVENIENCE
CONVENTICLE
CONVERGENCE
CONVERTIBLE
CONVOCATION
CONVOLUTION
CONVOLVULUS
CONVULSIONS
COOPERATION
COOPERATIVE
COORDINATED
COORDINATES
COPPERPLATE
COPROPHAGAN
COPROSTEROL
CORDWAINERS
CORINTHIANS
CORNERSTONE
CORPORATION
CORRECTNESS
CORRELATION
CORROBORATE
CORRUGATION
CORRUPTIBLE
COTTONMOUTH
COULOMMIERS
COUNSELLING
COUNTENANCE
COUNTERFEIT
COUNTERFOIL
COUNTERFORT
COUNTERGLOW
COUNTERHAND
COUNTERMAND
COUNTERPANE
COUNTERPART
COUNTERSIGN
COUNTERSINK
COUNTRIFIED
COUNTRYSIDE
COURTEOUSLY
COURTLINESS
COXWAINLESS
CRACKERJACK
CRACKHALTER
CRACOVIENNE
CRATERELLUS
CREDENTIALS
CREDIBILITY
CREDULOUSLY
CRÉMAILLÈRE
CREMATORIUM
CRENELLATED
CREPITATION
CREPUSCULAR
CRESCENTADE
CRESTFALLEN
CRIMINOLOGY
CRITHOMANCY
CRITICASTER
CROCIDOLITE
CROMWELLIAN
CROOKEDNESS
CROSSLEGGED
CRUCIFIXION
CRYSTALLINE
CRYSTALLISE
CRYSTALLIZE
CULMINATION
CULPABILITY
CULTIVATION
CULVERINEER
CURNAPTIOUS
CURTAILMENT
CUSTOMARILY
CYBERNETICS
CYCLOSTYLED
CYLINDRICAL
CYMOPHANOUS
DACTYLOGRAM
DANGEROUSLY
DARDANELLES
DEBILITATED
DECAPITATED
DECARBONIZE
DECEITFULLY
DECEPTIVELY
DECLAMATION
DECLAMATORY
DECLARATION
DECONSTRUCT
DECORATIONS
DECORTICATE
DECREPITATE
DECREPITUDE
DEERSTALKER
DEFENCELESS
DEFENSELESS
DEFENSIVELY
DEFERENTIAL
DEFOLIATION
DEFORMATION
DEGLUTINATE
DEGLUTITION
DEGRADATION
DEGRINGOLER
DEHORTATIVE
DEHYDRATION
DEIFICATION
DELECTATION
DELETERIOUS
DELICIOUSLY
DELICTATION
DELINEATION
DELINQUENCY
DELITESCENT
DELIVERANCE
DEMAGOGUERY
DEMARCATION
DEMIBASTION
DEMOGRAPHIC
DEMONOMANIA
DEMONSTRATE
DEMORALIZED
DEMOSTHENES
DEMOSTHENIC
DENDRACHATE
DENOMINATOR
DEPARTEMENT
DEPHLEGMATE
DEPORTATION
DEPREDATION
DEPRIVATION
DERANGEMENT
DERELICTION
DERMATOLOGY
DESCENDANTS
DESCRIPTION
DESCRIPTIVE
DESECRATION
DESEGREGATE
DESELECTION
DESERPIDINE
DESICCATION
DESIGNATION
DESPERATELY
DESPERATION
DESPONDENCY
DESTABILIZE
DESTINATION
DESTITUTION
DESTRUCTION
DESTRUCTIVE
DETERIORATE
DETERMINANT
DETERMINING
DETESTATION
DETRIMENTAL
DEUTERONOMY
DEUTSCHMARK
DEVALUATION
DEVASTATING
DEVASTATION
DEVELOPMENT
DEVIOUSNESS
DEVITRIFIED
DIAGNOSTICS
DIAMONDBACK
DIAPHORESIS
DIAPHORETIC
DIARTHROSIS
DIASCORDIUM
DIATESSARON
DIATESSERON
DICEPHALOUS
DICOTYLEDON
DICTATORIAL
DIFFERENTLY
DIFFIDENTLY
DIFFRACTION
DILAPIDATED
DIMENSIONAL
DINNYHAUSER
DINNYHAYSER
DIORTHORTIC
DIPHYCERCAL
DIPLOMATICS
DIPLOMATIST
DIPROTODONT
DIPSOMANIAC
DIPTEROCARP
DIRECTIONAL
DIRECTORATE
DISABLEMENT
DISAFFECTED
DISAGREEING
DISAPPROVAL
DISARMAMENT
DISBELIEVER
DISCERNIBLE
DISCERNMENT
DISCIPLINED
DISCOLOURED
DISCONTINUE
DISCOTHEQUE
DISCOURTESY
DISCREPANCY
DISEMBODIED
DISENCUMBER
DISENTANGLE
DISFIGURING
DISGRACEFUL
DISGRUNTLED
DISHEVELLED
DISHONESTLY
DISILLUSION
DISIMPRISON
DISINCLINED
DISJUNCTION
DISLOCATION
DISOBEDIENT
DISORGANIZE
DISORIENTED
DISPARAGING
DISPENSABLE
DISPERSABLE
DISPLEASURE
DISPOSITION
DISPUTATION
DISQUIETING
DISREGARDED
DISSEMINATE
DISSEPIMENT
DISSERTATOR
DISSIMULATE
DISSIPATION
DISSOLUTION
DISTASTEFUL
DISTINCTION
DISTINCTIVE
DISTINGUISH
DISTRACTION
DISTRESSING
DISTRIBUTED
DISTRIBUTOR
DISTRUSTFUL
DISTURBANCE
DITHELETISM
DITTOGRAPHY
DIVORCEMENT
DOCTRINAIRE
DOCUMENTARY
DODECASTYLE
DOLABRIFORM
DOMESTICATE
DOMESTICITY
DOMINEERING
DOUBLECHECK
DOUBLECROSS
DOUROUCOULI
DOWNHEARTED
DOWNTRODDEN
DRACUNCULUS
DRAGGLETAIL
DRAGONNADES
DRASTICALLY

DRAUGHTSMAN
DREADLOCKED
DREADNOUGHT
DRESSMAKING
DRINKDRIVER
DRUNKENNESS
DRYCLEANERS
DRYCLEANING
DUBIOUSNESS
DUMBFOUNDED
DUNIEWASSAL
DUPLICATING
DUPLICATION
DUSTWRAPPER
DYAESTHESIA
DYSFUNCTION
DYSLOGISTIC
EARNESTNESS
EARTHENWARE
EARTHSHAKER
EASTERNMOST
ECCALEOBION
EDIFICATION
EDUCATIONAL
EFFECTIVELY
EFFECTUALLY
EFFICACIOUS
EFFICIENTLY
EGALITARIAN
EGOTISTICAL
EINSTEINIUM
EJACULATION
ELABORATELY
ELABORATION
ELASTOPLAST
ELECTRICIAN
ELECTRICITY
ELECTROCUTE
ELECTROLIER
ELECTROLYTE
ELECTRONICS
ELECTROTINT
ELEPHANTINE
ELEUTHERIAN
ELIGIBILITY
ELIMINATION
ELIZABETHAN
ELUCIDATION
EMBARKATION
EMBARRASSED
EMBELLISHED
EMBOÎTEMENT
EMBROCATION
EMMENAGOGUE
EMMENTHALER
EMOTIONALLY
EMPHYTEUSIS
EMPIECEMENT
EMPIRICUTIC
EMPLACEMENT
EMPOWERMENT
EMPTYHANDED
EMPYROMANCY
ENARTHROSIS
ENCAPSULATE
ENCEPHALOMA
ENCHANTMENT
ENCHANTRESS
ENCHIRIDION
ENCHONDROMA
ENCOURAGING
ENCROACHING
ENCUMBRANCE
ENDOCARDIUM
ENDORSEMENT
ENDOTHERMIC
ENFEOFFMENT
ENFORCEABLE
ENFORCEMENT
ENFOULDERED
ENFRANCHISE
ENGHALSKRUG
ENGINEERING
ENHANCEMENT
ENJAMBEMENT
ENKEPHALINE
ENLARGEMENT
ENLIGHTENED
ENNEAHEDRON
ENSLAVEMENT
ENTABLATURE
ENTABLEMENT
ENTERTAINER
ENTHRALLING
ENTITLEMENT
ENUMERATION
ENUNCIATION
ENVIRONMENT
EOANTHROPUS
EPAMINONDAS
EPANALEPSIS
EPICHEIREMA
EPIDIASCOPE
EPIGENESIST
EPINEPHRINE
EPITHYMETIC
EPOCHMAKING
EQUIDISTANT
EQUILATERAL
EQUILIBRIST
EQUILIBRIUM
EQUINOCTIAL
EQUIPOLLENT
EQUIVALENCE
EQUIVOCALLY
ERADICATION
EREMACAUSIS
ERIODENDRON
ERRATICALLY
ERRONEOUSLY
ERYMANTHIAN
ERYTHROCYTE
ESCARMOUCHE
ESCHATOLOGY
ESCHERICHIA
ESPIEGLERIE
ESSENTIALLY
ESTABLISHED
ESTABLISHER
ESTRAMAZONE
ESTRANGHELO
ETHNOGRAPHY
ETHNOLOGIST
ETYMOLOGIST
EUCALYPTOLE
EUCHARISTIC
EUPHEMISTIC
EURHYTHMICS
EVANGELICAL
EVAPORATION
EVASIVENESS
EVENTRATION
EVENTUALITY
EVERLASTING
EVISCERATED
EXAGGERATED
EXAMINATION
EXANTHEMATA
EXASPERATED
EXCEEDINGLY
EXCEPTIONAL
EXCESSIVELY
EXCLAMATION
EXCLUSIVELY
EXCRESCENCE
EXECUTIONER
EXHILARATED
EXHORTATION
EXONERATION
EXORBITANCE
EXOSKELETON
EXPECTANTLY
EXPECTATION
EXPECTORANT
EXPECTORATE
EXPEDITIOUS
EXPENDITURE
EXPERIENCED
EXPLANATION
EXPLANATORY
EXPLORATION
EXPLORATORY
EXPONENTIAL
EXPOSTULATE
EXPROPRIATE
EXPURGATION
EXQUISITELY
EXTEMPORISE
EXTEMPORIZE
EXTENSIVELY
EXTENUATING
EXTENUATION
EXTERMINATE
EXTORTIONER
EXTRADITION
EXTRAPOLATE
EXTRAVAGANT
EXTROGENOUS
EXTROVERTED
EYECATCHING
FABRICATION
FACETIOUSLY
FACTFINDING
FAIRWEATHER
FALLIBILITY
FAMILIARISE
FAMILIARITY
FAMILIARIZE
FANATICALLY
FANFARONADE
FARINACEOUS
FARRAGINOUS
FARREACHING
FARTHERMOST
FARTHINGALE
FASCINATING
FASCINATION
FASHIONABLE
FASHIONABLY
FATUOUSNESS
FAULTFINDER
FAULTLESSLY
FAUXBOURDON
FAVOURITISM
FEASIBILITY
FEATURELESS
FEHMGERICHT
FERNITICKLE
FEROCIOUSLY
FERRONNIÈRE
FESTINATELY
FESTSCHRIFT
FIDDLEDEDEE
FIELDWORKER
FILAMENTOUS
FILLIBUSTER
FINANCIALLY
FINGERPRINT
FINGERSTALL
FIRELIGHTER
FISHANDCHIP
FISHMONGERS
FITZWILLIAM
FLABBERGAST
FLAMBOYANCE
FLAMBOYANTE
FLANNELETTE
FLAVOURSOME
FLEXIBILITY
FLICKERTAIL
FLIRTATIOUS
FLORILEGIUM
FLOURISHING
FLUCTUATING
FLUCTUATION
FLUORESCENT
FOMENTATION
FOOLISHNESS
FOOTBALLING
FOOTWASHING
FORAMINIFER
FORBEARANCE
FORBIDDANCE
FORECASTING
FORECLOSURE
FOREFATHERS
FORESEEABLE
FORESHORTEN
FORESTATION
FORETHOUGHT
FOREWARNING
FORFOUGHTEN
FORGIVENESS
FORLORNNESS
FORMULATION
FORNICATION
FORTHCOMING
FORTNIGHTLY
FORTUNATELY
FORTUNELOUD
FOTHERGILLA
FOULMOUTHED
FOUNDATIONS
FRAGMENTARY
FRANKFURTER
FRANKLINITE
FRANTICALLY
FRATERNALLY
FRAUDULENCE
FREEMASONRY
FREETHINKER
FRENCHWOMAN
FRENCHWOMEN
FRIGHTENING
FRIGHTFULLY
FRIVOLOUSLY
FRONTRUNNER
FROSTBITTEN
FRUITLESSLY
FRUSTRATING
FRUSTRATION
FULFILLMENT
FULLBLOODED
FULMINATION
FUNAMBULIST
FUNCTIONARY
FUNCTIONING
FUNDAMENTAL
FUNDRAISING
FURNISHINGS

FURTHERANCE
FURTHERMORE
FURTHERMOST
FURTHERSOME
FURTIVENESS
FUSTILARIAN
GABERLUNZIE
GALLIBAGGER
GALLIBEGGAR
GALLIGANTUS
GALLIMAUFRY
GALLOVIDIAN
GALLOWGLASS
GALLYBAGGER
GALLYBEGGAR
GAMETOPHYTE
GAMOGENESIS
GARNISHMENT
GARRULOUSLY
GASTRECTOMY
GASTRONOMIC
GATECRASHER
GEGENSCHEIN
GELSEMININE
GENEALOGIST
GENERALIZED
GENERICALLY
GENETICALLY
GENOUILLÈRE
GENTLEMANLY
GENTLEWOMAN
GENUFLEXION
GENUINENESS
GEOMETRICAL
GEOSYNCLINE
GERMINATION
GERONTOLOGY
GERRYMANDER
GESTATORIAL
GESTICULATE
GHASTLINESS
GIBBERELLIN
GIGGLESTICK
GIGGLESWICK
GIGGLEWATER
GILLYFLOWER
GINGERBREAD
GIRDLESTEAD
GLADWELLISE
GLASTONBURY
GLIMMERGOWK
GLOSSOLALIA
GNATHONICAL
GODDAUGHTER
GODFORSAKEN
GONFALONIER
GOODLOOKING
GOODNATURED
GORDONSTOUN
GRALLATORES
GRAMMALOGUE
GRAMMATICAL
GRANDFATHER
GRANDMASTER
GRANDMOTHER
GRAPHICALLY
GRASSHOPPER
GRAVEDIGGER
GRAVITATION
GREASEPAINT
GREENBOTTLE
GREENGROCER
GREENOCKITE
GREGARINIDA
GRENZGANGER
GROUNDSHEET
GROUNDSPEED
GROUNDSWELL
GUADALCANAL
GUBERNATION
GUESSTIMATE
GULLIBILITY
GUTTERSNIPE
GUTTURALISE
GYNAECOLOGY
HABERDASHER
HABILIMENTS
HAEMOGLOBIN
HAEMOPHILIA
HAEMORRHAGE
HAEMORRHOID
HAGIOGRAPHY
HAIRDRESSER
HAIRRAISING
HALBSTARKER
HALFBROTHER
HALFHEARTED
HALFHOLIDAY
HALLEFLINTA
HALLUCINATE
HAMMERCLOTH
HANDCRAFTED
HANDICAPPED
HANDICAPPER
HANDWRITING
HANDWRITTEN
HANGGLIDING
HAPHAZARDLY
HARDHITTING
HARDICANUTE
HARDPRESSED
HARDWORKING
HAREBRAINED
HARIOLATION
HARPSICHORD
HATCHETTITE
HAUGHTINESS
HEALTHINESS
HEARTBROKEN
HEARTLESSLY
HEAVYHANDED
HEAVYWEIGHT
HEBDOMADARY
HECKELPHONE
HELPFULNESS
HEMERALOPIA
HEMIANOPSIA
HEMOPHILIAC
HEMORRHOIDS
HEPATOSCOPY
HEPPLEWHITE
HERBIVOROUS
HERPETOLOGY
HERRINGBONE
HETEROSCIAN
HIBERNATING
HIBERNATION
HIDEOUSNESS
HIGHLIGHTER
HIGHPITCHED
HIGHPOWERED
HIGHPROFILE
HIGHQUALITY
HIGHRANKING
HILARIOUSLY
HINDERLANDS
HIPPOCAMPUS
HIPPOCRATES
HIPPOCRATIC
HISTOLOGIST
HISTORIATED
HISTRIONICS
HOBBLEDEHOY
HOGGISHNESS
HOHENLINDEN
HOLLANDAISE
HOLOTHURIAN
HOMEOPATHIC
HOMOEOPATHY
HOMOGENEITY
HOMOGENEOUS
HOMOGENIZED
HOMOTHERMAL
HOMOTHERMIC
HONEYCOMBED
HONEYMOONER
HONEYSUCKLE
HOOLIGANISM
HOOTANANNIE
HOOTENANNIE
HORNSWOGGLE
HORSERACING
HORSERADISH
HORSERIDING
HOSPITALITY
HOSPITALIZE
HOSPITALLER
HOSTILITIES
HOUSEHOLDER
HOUSEKEEPER
HOUSEMASTER
HUCKLEBERRY
HUCKSTERAGE
HUMGRUFFIAN
HUMILIATING
HUMILIATION
HUMMINGBIRD
HUNDREDFOLD
HURTLEBERRY
HUSBANDLAND
HYDROCARBON
HYDROMEDUSA
HYDROPHIDAE
HYDROPHOBIA
HYDROPHOBIC
HYDROPONICS
HYDROSTATIC
HYMNOLOGIST
HYOPLASTRON
HYPERMARKET
HYPERTROPHY
HYPHENATION
HYPOCORISMA
HYPOTENSION
HYPOTHECATE
HYPOTHERMIA
ICHTHYOLITE
ICHTHYORNIS
ICONOGRAPHY
ICONOSTASIS
IDENTICALLY
IDENTIFYING
IDEOLOGICAL
IDEOPRAXIST
IDIOTICALLY
IDOLIZATION
IDYLLICALLY
IGNOMINIOUS
IGNORANTINE
ILLMANNERED
ILLOGICALLY
ILLUMINATED
ILLUSIONARY
ILLUSIONIST
ILLUSTRATOR
ILLUSTRIOUS
ILLYWHACKER
IMAGINATION
IMAGINATIVE
IMMEDIATELY
IMMIGRATION
IMMORTALISE
IMMORTALITY
IMMORTALIZE
IMPARTIALLY
IMPASSIONED
IMPASSIVELY
IMPATIENTLY
IMPEACHMENT
IMPECUNIOUS
IMPEDIMENTA
IMPERIALISM
IMPERIALIST
IMPERIOUSLY
IMPERMANENT
IMPERMEABLE
IMPERSONATE
IMPERTINENT
IMPETUOSITY
IMPETUOUSLY
IMPIGNORATE
IMPLAUSIBLE
IMPLEMENTAL
IMPLICATION
IMPORTANTLY
IMPORTATION
IMPORTUNATE
IMPRACTICAL
IMPRECATION
IMPRECISION
IMPREGNABLE
IMPROPRIETY
IMPROVEMENT
IMPROVIDENT
IMPRUDENTLY
IMPULSIVELY
INADVERTENT
INADVISABLE
INALIENABLE
INATTENTION
INATTENTIVE
INAUTHENTIC
INCALESCENT
INCANTATION
INCAPSULATE
INCARCERATE
INCARNADINE
INCARNATION
INCESSANTLY
INCINERATOR
INCLINATION
INCOHERENCE
INCOMPETENT
INCOMPOSITE
INCONGRUITY
INCONGRUOUS
INCONSTANCY
INCONTINENT
INCORPORATE
INCORPOREAL
INCORRECTLY
INCREDULITY
INCREDULOUS
INCREMENTAL
INCRIMINATE
INDEFINABLE
INDENTATION
INDEPENDENT
INDEXLINKED
INDIARUBBER

INDIFFERENT
INDIGESTION
INDIGNANTLY
INDIGNATION
INDIVISIBLE
INDIVISIBLY
INDOMITABLE
INDUBITABLE
INDUBITABLY
INDULGENTLY
INDUSTRIOUS
INEBRIATION
INEFFECTIVE
INEFFECTUAL
INEFFICIENT
INELUCTABLE
INEQUITABLE
INESCAPABLE
INESSENTIAL
INESTIMABLE
INEXCITABLE
INEXCUSABLE
INEXCUSABLY
INEXPEDIENT
INEXPENSIVE
INFANGTHIEF
INFANTICIDE
INFANTRYMAN
INFATUATION
INFERIORITY
INFERTILITY
INFESTATION
INFILTRATOR
INFLAMMABLE
INFLUENTIAL
INFORMALITY
INFORMATICS
INFORMATION
INFORMATIVE
INFREQUENCY
INFURIATING
INGENIOUSLY
INGRATITUDE
INGREDIENTS
INHABITABLE
INHABITANTS
INHERITANCE
INJUDICIOUS
INNUMERABLE
INOCULATION
INOFFENSIVE
INOPERATIVE
INOPPORTUNE
INQUIRINGLY
INQUISITION
INQUISITIVE
INSCRIPTION
INSCRUTABLE
INSECTICIDE
INSECTIVORE
INSENSITIVE
INSEPARABLE
INSIDIOUSLY
INSINCERITY
INSINUATING
INSINUATION
INSISTENTLY
INSOUCIANCE
INSPIRATION
INSTABILITY
INSTALLMENT
INSTANTIATE
INSTIGATION
INSTINCTIVE
INSTITUTION
INSTRUCTION
INSTRUCTIVE
INSTRUMENTS
INSULTINGLY
INSUPERABLE
INTEGRATION
INTELLIGENT
INTEMPERATE
INTENSIVELY
INTENTIONAL
INTERACTION
INTERACTIVE
INTERCALARY
INTERCEPTOR
INTERCHANGE
INTERCOSTAL
INTERCOURSE
INTERESTING
INTERGLOSSA
INTERGROWTH
INTERLACING
INTERLEUKIN
INTERLINGUA
INTERMINGLE
INTERNECINE
INTERNUNCIO
INTERPOLATE
INTERPRETER
INTERREGNUM
INTERRELATE
INTERROGATE
INTERRUPTER
INTERSPERSE
INTERVENING
INTERVIEWEE
INTERVIEWER
INTOLERABLE
INTOLERABLY
INTOLERANCE
INTOXICATED
INTOXIMETER
INTRACTABLE
INTRAVENOUS
INTREPIDITY
INTRICATELY
INTROVERTED
INTUITIVELY
INVESTIGATE
INVESTITURE
INVIGILATOR
INVINCIBLES
INVOLUNTARY
INVOLVEMENT
IPECACUANHA
IRIDESCENCE
IRONMONGERS
IRONMONGERY
IRRADIATION
IRREDENTIST
IRREDUCIBLE
IRREFUTABLE
IRREGULARLY
IRRELEVANCE
IRRELIGIOUS
IRREPARABLE
IRREPARABLY
IRREVERENCE
IRREVOCABLE
ISOELECTRIC
ISOXSUPRINE
ISTIOPHORUS
ITHYPHALLIC
ITHYPHALLUS
JABBERWOCKY
JACQUEMINOT
JACTITATION
JAMAHIRIYAH
JERRYMANDER
JINRICKSHAW
JOSEPHINITE
JUDICIOUSLY
JUSTIFIABLE
JUSTIFIABLY
KALASHNIKOV
KAMELAUKION
KATABOTHRON
KATAVOTHRON
KETAVOTHRON
KIDDLEYWINK
KILIMANJARO
KILOCALORIE
KIMERIDGIAN
KINCHINMORT
KINDERSPIEL
KINDHEARTED
KINNIKINICK
KIRKPATRICK
KITCHENETTE
KLEPTOMANIA
KOMMERSBUCH
KOTABOTHRON
KRIEGSSPIEL
KULTURKREIS
KWASHIORKOR
LABORIOUSLY
LABORSAVING
LACONICALLY
LAMENTATION
LAMMERGEIER
LAMMERGEYER
LAMPLIGHTER
LAMPROPHYRE
LANDSKNECHT
LAPIDESCENT
LARYNGISMUS
LASERPICIUM
LATERIGRADE
LATERITIOUS
LATIFUNDIUM
LATROCINIUM
LAUNDERETTE
LAWBREAKING
LAWLESSNESS
LEADSWINGER
LEASEHOLDER
LEATHERBACK
LEATHERETTE
LEATHERHEAD
LEATHERNECK
LECTURESHIP
LEFTLUGGAGE
LEGERDEMAIN
LEGIONNAIRE
LEGISLATION
LEGISLATIVE
LEGISLATURE
LENGTHENING
LENGTHINESS
LENTIGINOSE
LEPIDOPTERA
LEPIDOSIREN
LETTERPRESS
LEVELHEADED
LIBERTARIAN
LICKSPITTLE
LIGHTHEADED
LIGHTWEIGHT
LILLIPUTIAN
LINDISFARNE
LINGUISTICS
LIQUIDAMBAR
LIQUIDATION
LITERALNESS
LITHOGRAPHY
LITTÉRATEUR
LIVINGSTONE
LOCORESTIVE
LOGARITHMIC
LOGGERHEADS
LOGODAEDALY
LOGOGRAPHER
LONGANIMITY
LONGAWAITED
LONGINQUITY
LONGLASTING
LONGRUNNING
LONGSIGHTED
LONGSLEEVED
LOUDSPEAKER
LOUISIANIAN
LUBRICATION
LUMINESCENT
LUXEMBURGER
LUXULYANITE
LUXURIANTLY
LUXURIOUSLY
LYCANTHROPE
LYCANTHROPY
LYCHNOSCOPE
MACADAMIZED
MACERANDUBA
MACHAIRODUS
MACHINATION
MACROBIOTIC
MAGISTERIAL
MAGISTRATES
MAGLEMOSIAN
MAGNANIMITY
MAGNANIMOUS
MAGNIFICENT
MAINTENANCE
MAISTERDOME
MAKEBELIEVE
MALADJUSTED
MALAKATOONE
MALAPROPISM
MALEDICTION
MALEFACTION
MALEVOLENCE
MALFEASANCE
MALFUNCTION
MALICIOUSLY
MALPRACTICE
MANCIPATION
MANEUVERING
MANGALSUTRA
MANIPULATOR
MANTELLETTA
MANTELPIECE
MANTELSHELF
MANUFACTURE
MANUMISSION
MAQUILADORA
MARCONIGRAM
MARGINALIST
MARGINALIZE
MARIONBERRY
MARIONETTES
MARIVAUDAGE
MARKETPLACE
MARLBOROUGH
MARSHMALLOW
MASCULINITY
MASKALLONGE
MASOCHISTIC

MASQUERADER
MASSIVENESS
MASTERFULLY
MASTERPIECE
MASTICATION
MATERIALISE
MATERIALISM
MATERIALIST
MATERIALIZE
MATHEMATICS
MATRIARCHAL
MATRICULATE
MATRIMONIAL
MAURETANIAN
MAURITANIAN
MEADOWSWEET
MEANDERINGS
MEANINGLESS
MEASURELESS
MEASUREMENT
MECKLENBURG
MEDIASTINUM
MEDICINALLY
MEDIUMSIZED
MEGALOMANIA
MEGALOMANIC
MEGALOPOLIS
MEGATHERIUM
MEKHITARIST
MELANCHOLIA
MELANCHOLIC
MELANOCHROI
MELLIFLUOUS
MELODIOUSLY
MEMORABILIA
MENDELEVIUM
MENDELSSOHN
MENSURATION
MENTHOLATED
MENTONNIÈRE
MEPROBAMATE
MERCHANDISE
MERCHANDIZE
MERCHANTMAN
MERCILESSLY
MERITORIOUS
MERRYMAKING
METACARPALS
METAGENESIS
METALWORKER
METAPHYSICS
METATARSALS
METEOROLOGY
METHODOLOGY
METRICATION
MICHURINISM
MICROGAMETE
MICROSCOPIC
MICTURITION
MIDDENSTEAD
MIDDLEMARCH
MIDDLESIZED
MILLIONAIRE
MILQUETOAST
MINESWEEPER
MINIATURIST
MINIATURIZE
MINISTERIAL
MINISTERING
MINNESINGER
MISALLIANCE
MISANTHROPE
MISANTHROPY
MISBEGOTTEN
MISBEHAVIOR
MISCARRIAGE
MISCHIEVOUS
MISCONSTRUE
MISDEMEANOR
MISERICORDE
MISERLINESS
MISIDENTIFY
MISSISSIPPI
MISSPELLING
MISTRUSTFUL
MOCKINGBIRD
MODELMOLEST
MODERNISTIC
MOISTURIZER
MOLESTATION
MOLLYCODDLE
MOMENTARILY
MONARCHICAL
MONCHIQUITE
MONEYLENDER
MONEYMAKING
MONOCHINOUS
MONOGRAMMED
MONONGAHELA
MONOPSONIST
MONOTHELITE
MONOTREMATA
MONSTROSITY
MONTESQUIEU
MONTGOLFIER
MONTMORENCY
MOONLIGHTER
MORGENSTERN
MOSSTROOPER
MOUNTAINEER
MOUNTAINOUS
MOXIBUSTION
MOZAMBIQUAN
MUDSLINGING
MULTIRACIAL
MULTISTOREY
MUNCHHAUSEN
MUNIFICENCE
MURMURATION
MUSCHELKALK
MUSKELLUNGE
MYCOLOGICAL
MYCOPHAGIST
MYXOMATOSIS
NAPHTHALENE
NARRAGANSET
NATIONALISM
NATIONALIST
NATIONALITY
NATIONALIZE
NATIONSTATE
NATURALNESS
NAUGHTINESS
NEANDERTHAL
NEARSIGHTED
NECESSARILY
NECESSITATE
NECESSITOUS
NECROMANCER
NEEDLEPOINT
NEEDLESTICK
NEEDLEWOMAN
NEGOTIATING
NEGOTIATION
NEIGHBORING
NEIGHBOURLY
NERVOUSNESS
NETHERLANDS
NETHERLINGS
NEUROLOGIST
NEUTRALISED
NEVERENDING
NEWSCASTING
NICKELODEON
NICKNACKERY
NIERSTEINER
NIGHTINGALE
NIGHTMARISH
NIKETHAMIDE
NIPFARTHING
NOISELESSLY
NOMENCLATOR
NONCHALANCE
NONDESCRIPT
NONETHELESS
NONEXISTENT
NONFEASANCE
NONSENSICAL
NORTHCLIFFE
NOSTRADAMUS
NOTHINGNESS
NOTICEBOARD
NOTORIOUSLY
NOTOTHERIUM
NOURISHMENT
NOVELETTISH
NUMBERPLATE
NUMERICALLY
NUMISMATICS
NUMISMATIST
NUTCRACKERS
NUTRITIONAL
NYMPHOMANIA
OARSMANSHIP
OBJECTIVELY
OBJECTIVITY
OBLITERATED
OBMUTESCENT
OBSERVATION
OBSERVATORY
OBSESSIVELY
OBSOLESCENT
OBSTETRICAL
OBSTINATELY
OBSTRICTION
OBSTRUCTION
OBSTRUCTIVE
OBTEMPERATE
OBVIOUSNESS
OCHLOCRATIC
OCTASTICHON
ODONTOBLAST
ODONTOPHORE
OFFENSIVELY
OFFHANDEDLY
OFFICIALDOM
OFFICIALESE
OFFICIOUSLY
OLIGOCHAETE
OMMATOPHORE
OMNIPOTENCE
OMNIPRESENT
OMNISCIENCE
ONEIRODYNIA
ONEIROMANCY
ONOMASTICON
ONTOLOGICAL
OPALESCENCE
OPERATIONAL
OPINIONATED
OPPIGNORATE
OPPORTUNELY
OPPORTUNISM
OPPORTUNIST
OPPORTUNITY
OPPROBRIOUS
OPTOMETRIST
ORCHESTRATE
ORCHESTRINA
ORCHESTRION
ORDERLINESS
ORGANICALLY
ORGANIZAION
ORIENTALIST
ORIENTATION
ORIGINALITY
ORIGINATING
ORIGINATION
ORNITHOLOGY
ORNITHOPTER
ORTHOCENTRE
ORTHOGRAPHY
ORTHOPAEDIC
OSCILLATION
OSTENTATION
OSTEOPATHIC
OSTEOPLASTY
OSTRACODERM
OSTREOPHAGE
OUAGADOUGOU
OUTDISTANCE
OUTMANEUVER
OUTPOURINGS
OUTSTANDING
OVERBALANCE
OVERBEARING
OVERCROWDED
OVEREXPOSED
OVERFISHING
OVERFLOWING
OVERHANGING
OVERLAPPING
OVERLEARNED
OVERMANNING
OVERPAYMENT
OVERSTUFFED
OVERTURNING
OVERWEENING
OVERWHELMED
OVERWROUGHT
OVERZEALOUS
OXODIZATION
OXYRHYNCHUS
PACIFICALLY
PAEDIATRICS
PAEDOTROPHY
PAINKILLING
PAINSTAKING
PALEOGRAPHY
PALEOLITHIC
PALESTINIAN
PAMPELMOOSE
PAMPELMOUSE
PAMPHLETEER
PANDEMONIUM
PANOMPHAEAN
PANTALETTES
PAPERWEIGHT
PARABLEPSIS
PARABOLANUS
PARACETAMOL
PARACHUTIST
PARACROSTIC
PARADOXICAL
PARALEIPSIS
PARAMASTOID
PARAMEDICAL
PARANEPHROS
PARATROOPER
PARATYPHOID

PARENTHESIS
PARISHIONER
PARLIPOMENA
PARONOMASIA
PARTICIPANT
PARTICIPATE
PARTICIPIAL
PARTNERSHIP
PARTURITION
PARVANIMITY
PASSACAGLIA
PASSIVENESS
PASTEURELLA
PASTOURELLE
PATERNALISM
PATERNOSTER
PATHOLOGIST
PATRIARCHAL
PATRONISING
PATRONIZING
PAWNBROKERS
PEACEKEEPER
PECULIARITY
PEDAGOGICAL
PEDESTRIANS
PEDETENTOUS
PEEVISHNESS
PELARGONIUM
PELOPONNESE
PENETRATING
PENETRATION
PENICILLATE
PENITENTIAL
PENNYFATHER
PENSIONABLE
PENSIVENESS
PENTATHLETE
PENTECONTER
PENTECOSTAL
PENTHESILEA
PENTONVILLE
PENULTIMATE
PERAMBULATE
PERCEFOREST
PERCEPTIBLE
PERCEPTIBLY
PERCHLORATE
PERCIPIENCE
PERCOLATION
PERDUELLION
PEREGRINATE
PERENNIALLY
PERESTROIKA
PERFORATION
PERFORMANCE
PERFUNCTORY
PERICARDIUM
PERIGORDIAN
PERIODONTIC
PERIPATETIC
PERIPHRASIS
PERISSOLOGY
PERISTALITH
PERISTALSIS
PERITONAEUM
PERITONITIS
PERLUSTRATE
PERMANENTLY
PERMISSIBLE
PERMUTATION
PERPETRATOR
PERPETUALLY
PERSECUTION
PERSEVERING
PERSISTENCE
PERSONALIST
PERSONALITY
PERSONALIZE
PERSONIFIED
PERSPECTIVE
PERSPICUITY
PERSPICUOUS
PERTINACITY
PERTINENTLY
PESSIMISTIC
PETITMAITRE
PETRODOLLAR
PETTICOATED
PETTIFOGGER
PHALANSTERY
PHARISAICAL
PHARYNGITIS
PHILANDERER
PHILATELIST
PHILIPPINES
PHILLIPSITE
PHILOCTETES
PHILOLOGIST
PHILOSOPHER
PHONETICIAN
PHONOFIDDLE
PHOTOCOPIER
PHOTOFINISH
PHOTOGRAPHY
PHOTOSPHERE
PHRASEOLOGY
PHTHIRIASIS
PHYSIOGNOMY
PICKELHAUBE
PICKYOUROWN
PICTURESQUE
PIEDMONTITE
PIERREPOINT
PINACOTHECA
PINNYWINKLE
PISCATORIAL
PISSASPHALT
PITCHBLENDE
PLAGIARISED
PLAGIOSTOMI
PLANETARIUM
PLANTAGENET
PLANTIGRADE
PLATERESQUE
PLATYRRHINE
PLAYFULNESS
PLEASURABLE
PLEBEIANISE
PLEISTOCENE
PLOUGHSHARE
POCOCURANTE
PODSNAPPERY
POINTLESSLY
POLICEWOMAN
POLIORCETIC
POLITICALLY
POLITICIANS
POLLENBRUSH
POLLINATION
POLTERGEIST
POLYMORPHIC
POLYSTYRENE
POLYTECHNIC
POLYTRICHUM
POMEGRANATE
POMPELMOOSE
POMPELMOUSE
PONDEROUSLY
PONTIFICATE
PORNOGRAPHY
PORTERHOUSE
PORTLANDIAN
PORTMANTEAU
PORTRAITIST
PORTRAITURE
POSSESSIONS
POSSIBILITY
POTAMOGETON
POTENTIALLY
PRACTICABLE
PRACTICALLY
PRECAUTIONS
PRECIPITATE
PRECIPITOUS
PRECONCEIVE
PREDECESSOR
PREDESTINED
PREDICAMENT
PREDICATIVE
PREDICTABLE
PREDICTABLY
PREDOMINANT
PREDOMINATE
PREEMINENCE
PREHISTORIC
PREJUDICIAL
PRELIBATION
PRELIMINARY
PREMATURELY
PREMEDITATE
PREMIERSHIP
PREMONITION
PREMONITORY
PREOCCUPIED
PREPARATION
PREPARATORY
PREPOLLENCE
PREPOSITION
PREROGATIVE
PRESENTABLE
PRESSURIZED
PRESTIGIOUS
PRESTISSIMO
PRESTONPANS
PRESTRESSED
PRESUMPTION
PRESUMPTIVE
PRETENSIONS
PRETENTIOUS
PRETERITION
PREVARICATE
PREVENTABLE
PRICKLINESS
PRIMIGENIAL
PRINCIPALLY
PRISCIANIST
PRIZEWINNER
PROBABILITY
PROBATIONER
PROCEEDINGS
PROCREATION
PROCRUSTEAN
PROCUREMENT
PRODIGALISE
PRODIGALITY
PROFESSEDLY
PROFICIENCY
PROFITEROLE
PROFUSENESS
PROGENITRIX
PROGNATHOUS
PROGRESSION
PROGRESSIVE
PROHIBITION
PROHIBITIVE
PROLEGOMENA
PROLETARIAN
PROLETARIAT
PROLIFERATE
PROLOCUTION
PROMINENTLY
PROMISCUITY
PROMISCUOUS
PROMOTIONAL
PROMPTITUDE
PROOFREADER
PROPAGATION
PROPHETICAL
PROPHYLAXIS
PROPINQUITY
PROPOSITION
PROPRIETARY
PROROGATION
PROSAICALLY
PROSECUTION
PROSELYTISM
PROSELYTIZE
PROSPECTIVE
PROSTHETICS
PROSTRATION
PROTAGONIST
PROTOCOCCUS
PROTONOTARY
PROTRACTING
PROTRACTION
PROTUBERANT
PROVISIONAL
PROVISIONER
PROVOCATION
PROVOCATIVE
PRZEWALSKIS
PSEUDOLOGIA
PSEUDOMORPH
PSITTACOSIS
PSYCHEDELIC
PSYCHIATRIC
PSYCHODELIC
PTERODACTYL
PTOCHOCRACY
PUBLICATION
PUBLISHABLE
PULCHRITUDE
PUNCHINELLO
PUNCTILIOUS
PUNCTUALITY
PUNCTUATION
PURITANICAL
PURPOSELESS
PURPRESTURE
PYTHONESQUE
QUADRENNIAL
QUADRENNIUM
QUADRUPLETS
QUALITATIVE
QUARRELLING
QUARRELSOME
QUARRINGTON
QUARTERBACK
QUARTERDECK
QUERULOUSLY
QUESTIONING
QUICKSILVER
QUINTUPLETS
RABELAISIAN
RADIOACTIVE
RADIOCARBON
RADIOGRAPHY
RADIOLOGIST
RAFFISHNESS
RALLENTANDO

RAMGUNSHOCH
RANGEFINDER
RAPSCALLION
RAPTUROUSLY
RASTAFARIAN
RATATOUILLE
RATIOCINATE
RATIONALITY
RATIONALIZE
RATTLESNAKE
RAUCOUSNESS
RAVISHINGLY
RAZZAMATAZZ
REACTIONARY
READABILITY
REALIGNMENT
REALIZATION
REALPOLITIK
REANIMATION
REAPPRAISAL
REASSURANCE
REBARBATIVE
RECANTATION
RECEPTIVITY
RECESSIONAL
RECIPROCATE
RECIPROCITY
RECLAMATION
RECOGNITION
RECONDITION
RECONNOITER
RECONNOITRE
RECONSTRUCT
RECOVERABLE
RECRIMINATE
RECRUITMENT
RECTANGULAR
RECTIFIABLE
RECTILINEAR
RECURRENTLY
REDOUBTABLE
REDUPLICATE
REFLEXOLOGY
REFOCILLATE
REFORMATION
REFORMATORY
REFRESHMENT
REFRIGERANT
REFRIGERATE
REFURBISHED
REGIMENTALS
REGISTERING
REGRETFULLY
REGRETTABLE
REGRETTABLY
REGURGITATE
REICHENBACH
REINCARNATE
REITERATION
RELEASEMENT
RELIABILITY
RELIGIOUSLY
RELUCTANTLY
REMEMBRANCE
REMINISCENT
REMONSTRATE
REMORSELESS
RENAISSANCE
REORIENTATE
REPETITIOUS
REPLACEABLE
REPLACEMENT
REPRESENTED
REPROACHFUL
REPUDIATION
REQUIREMENT
REQUISITION
RESEMBLANCE
RESENTFULLY
RESERVATION
RESIDENTIAL
RESIGNATION
RESISTIVITY
RESOURCEFUL
RESPECTABLE
RESPECTABLY
RESPIRATION
RESPIRATORY
RESPLENDANT
RESPLENDENT
RESPONSIBLE
RESPONSIBLY
RESPONSIONS
RESTATEMENT
RESTITUTION
RESTIVENESS
RESTORATION
RESTORATIVE
RESTRICTION
RESTRICTIVE
RESTRUCTURE
RESUSCITATE
RETALIATION
RETALIATORY
RETARDATION
RETINACULUM
RETINOSPORA
RETRACTABLE
RETRIBUTION
RETRIBUTIVE
RETRIEVABLE
RETROACTIVE
RETROROCKET
REVALUATION
REVELATIONS
REVENDICATE
REVERBERATE
REVERENTIAL
REVISIONISM
REVOLUTIONS
RHABDOMANCY
RHAPSODICAL
RHEUMATICKY
RHOPALOCERA
RIBONUCLEIC
RIDDLEMEREE
RIFACIMENTO
RIGHTANGLED
RIGHTEOUSLY
RIGHTHANDED
RIGHTHANDER
RIGHTWINGER
RINTHEREOUT
ROBESPIERRE
ROCKEFELLER
RODOMONTADE
ROGUISHNESS
ROMANTICISM
ROMANTICIZE
ROSICRUCIAN
ROTTENSTONE
RUDESHEIMER
RUDIMENTARY
RUMBUSTIOUS
RUMFRUCTION
RUMGUMPTION
SABBATARIAN
SACHERTORTE
SACRAMENTAL
SACRIFICIAL
SADDLEHORSE
SAGACIOUSLY
SAGITTARIUS
SAINTLINESS
SAINTPAULIA
SALACIOUSLY
SALESPERSON
SALPINGITIS
SALTIMBANCO
SALTIMBOCCA
SALVADORIAN
SALVOGUNNER
SANDERSWOOD
SAPONACEOUS
SAPROLEGNIA
SAPROPHYTIC
SARCENCHYME
SARCOPHAGUS
SATIRICALLY
SAUSAGEMEAT
SAVOURINESS
SAXOPHONIST
SCAFFOLDING
SCALPRIFORM
SCANDALIZED
SCANDANAVIA
SCANDINAVIA
SCARABAEOID
SCARBOROUGH
SCAREMONGER
SCATTERGOOD
SCATTERLING
SCEPTICALLY
SCEUOPHYLAX
SCHECKLATON
SCHISTOSOMA
SCHISTOSOME
SCHOLARSHIP
SCHOTTISCHE
SCHRECKLICH
SCHWARMEREI
SCIENTOLOGY
SCINTILLATE
SCIREFACIAS
SCITAMINEAE
SCOLECIFORM
SCOLOPENDRA
SCOPOLAMINE
SCOUTMASTER
SCREAMINGLY
SCREWDRIVER
SCRIMSHANDY
SCRIPTORIUM
SCRUFFINESS
SCRUMPTIOUS
SCULDUDDERY
SCULDUGGERY
SCULLABOGUE
SCUPPERNONG
SCUTTLEBUTT
SCYPHISTOMA
SEARCHLIGHT
SEASICKNESS
SECONDARILY
SECONDCLASS
SECRETARIAL
SECRETARIAT
SECRETIVELY
SEDIMENTARY
SEGREGATION
SEIGNIORAGE
SEISMOGRAPH
SELAGINELLA
SELECTIVELY
SELECTIVITY
SELFCONTROL
SELFDEFENCE
SELFEVIDENT
SELFIMPOSED
SELFISHNESS
SELFRESPECT
SELFSERVICE
SEMPITERNAL
SEMPITERNUM
SENNACHERIB
SENSATIONAL
SENSIBILITY
SENSITIVELY
SENSITIVITY
SENTENTIOUS
SENTIMENTAL
SEPIOSTAIRE
SEPTENARIUS
SEPTENTRION
SEPTICAEMIA
SEQUESTRATE
SERENDIPITY
SERICULTURE
SERIOUSNESS
SERVICEABLE
SESQUIOXIDE
SEVENTEENTH
SEVERALFOLD
SEXOLOGICAL
SHAFTESBURY
SHAKESPEARE
SHALLOWNESS
SHAMELESSLY
SHAPELINESS
SHAREHOLDER
SHEATHKNIFE
SHENANIGANS
SHEPHERDESS
SHINPLASTER
SHIPBUILDER
SHIPWRECKED
SHITTIMWOOD
SHOPLIFTING
SHORTCHANGE
SHORTCOMING
SHORTHANDED
SHOVELBOARD
SHOWERPROOF
SHOWJUMPING
SHOWMANSHIP
SHUNAMITISM
SHUTTLECOCK
SIGHTSCREEN
SIGHTSEEING
SIGNIFICANT
SILLIMANITE
SILVERSMITH
SINGAPOREAN
SINGLESTICK
SINGULARITY
SINISTRORSE
SKEPTICALLY
SKETCHINESS
SKIDBLADNIR
SKILLIGALEE
SKILLIGOLEE
SKIMMINGTON
SKULDUDDERY
SKULDUGGERY
SLEEPWALKER
SLENDERNESS
SLIGHTINGLY
SLUMBERWEAR
SLUMGULLION
SMALLHOLDER

SMITHEREENS
SMITHSONIAN
SMITHSONITE
SMOKESCREEN
SMORGASBORD
SMOULDERING
SNICKERSNEE
SNORKELLING
SOCIABILITY
SOCIOLOGIST
SOCKDALAGER
SOCKDOLAGER
SOCKDOLIGER
SOCKDOLOGER
SOLILOQUIZE
SOLIPSISTIC
SOROPTIMIST
SORROWFULLY
SOUNDLESSLY
SOUTHAMPTON
SOUTHWESTER
SOVEREIGNTY
SPACESAVING
SPANGCOCKLE
SPARROWHAWK
SPATTERDASH
SPATTERDOCK
SPECIALIZED
SPECTACULAR
SPECULATION
SPECULATIVE
SPEECHCRAFT
SPEEDOMETER
SPELLBINDER
SPENDTHRIFT
SPERMATOZOA
SPERMICIDAL
SPERMOPHILE
SPESSARTITE
SPHRAGISTIC
SPIFFLICATE
SPIRITUALLY
SPIROCHAETE
SPITSTICKER
SPLUTTERING
SPOKESWOMAN
SPONDULICKS
SPONDYLITIS
SPONSORSHIP
SPONTANEITY
SPONTANEOUS
SPORTSFIELD
SPORTSWOMAN
SPREADSHEET
SPRINGBOARD
SPRINGCLEAN
SPRINGHOUSE
SPRINGINESS
STADTHOLDER
STAGFLATION
STAIRCARPET
STAKEHOLDER
STALLHOLDER
STANDARDIZE
STANDOFFISH
STANDPATTER
STATELINESS
STATISTICAL
STEADFASTLY
STEAMROLLER
STEEPLEJACK
STEGANOGRAM
STEGANOPODE
STEINBERGER
STELLIONATE
STENOCHROME
STENOGRAPHY
STEPBROTHER
STEREOMETER
STEREOSCOPE
STEREOTYPED
STETHOSCOPE
STICKLEBACK
STIMULATION
STIPENDIARY
STIPULATION
STOCKBROKER
STOCKHAUSEN
STOCKHOLDER
STOCKJOBBER
STOCKTAKING
STOOLPIGEON
STOREKEEPER
STORYTELLER
STRADUARIUS
STRAITLACED
STRAMINEOUS
STRANDLOPER
STRANGENESS
STRANGEWAYS
STRANGULATE
STRAPHANGER
STRATEGICAL
STREAMLINED
STREETLIGHT
STRENUOUSLY
STRETCHABLE
STRETCHLESS
STRIKEBOUND
STRINGENTLY
STRINGYBARK
STROBOSCOPE
STRONGYLOID
STROPHILLUS
STRUTHIONES
STYLISHNESS
STYLIZATION
STYLOPODIUM
STYMPHALIAN
SUBCONTRACT
SUBDIVISION
SUBDOMINANT
SUBITANEOUS
SUBJUGATION
SUBJUNCTIVE
SUBLIMATION
SUBMERGENCE
SUBMULTIPLE
SUBORDINATE
SUBPANATION
SUBSERVIENT
SUBSISTENCE
SUBSTANDARD
SUBSTANTIAL
SUBSTANTIVE
SUBTRACTION
SUBTROPICAL
SUBUNGULATA
SUCCEDANEUM
SUDETENLAND
SUFFICIENCY
SUFFOCATING
SUFFOCATION
SUFFRAGETTE
SUGARCOATED
SUGGESTIBLE
SUITABILITY
SUMMERHOUSE
SUMPTUOUSLY
SUNDRENCHED
SUPERALTERN
SUPERCHARGE
SUPERCHERIE
SUPERFICIAL
SUPERFICIES
SUPERFLUITY
SUPERFLUOUS
SUPERIMPOSE
SUPERINTEND
SUPERIORITY
SUPERLATIVE
SUPERMARKET
SUPERSCRIBE
SUPERSEDEAS
SUPERSEDERE
SUPERTANKER
SUPERVISION
SUPERVISORY
SUPPEDANEUM
SUPPOSITION
SUPPOSITORY
SUPPRESSION
SUPPURATION
SURROUNDING
SURTARBRAND
SURTURBRAND
SURVEILLANT
SUSCEPTIBLE
SUSTAINABLE
SUSURRATION
SVARABHAKTI
SWALLOWABLE
SWITCHBOARD
SWITZERLAND
SWORDSWOMAN
SYCOPHANTIC
SYMMETRICAL
SYMPATHETIC
SYMPATHISER
SYMPATHIZER
SYMPLEGADES
SYMPOSIARCH
SYMPTOMATIC
SYNCHROMESH
SYNCHRONISE
SYNCHRONISM
SYNCHRONIZE
SYNCOPATION
SYNDICALISM
SYNDICATION
SYNTHESIZED
SYNTHESIZER
SYSTEMATIZE
TABERNACLES
TACHYCARDIA
TACHYGRAPHY
TACITURNITY
TAGLIATELLE
TANGIBILITY
TANTALIZING
TARATANTARA
TARRADIDDLE
TASTELESSLY
TATTERSALLS
TAUROBOLIUM
TAUTOCHRONE
TAXIDERMIST
TCHAIKOVSKY
TEASPOONFUL
TECHNICALLY
TECTIBRANCH
TEDIOUSNESS
TEENYBOPPER
TEETOTALLER
TEGUCICALPA
TÉLÉFÉRIQUE
TELEGRAPHER
TELEGRAPHIC
TELEKINESIS
TELEPHONIST
TELEPRINTER
TEMPERAMENT
TEMPERATURE
TEMPESTUOUS
TEMPORARILY
TENACIOUSLY
TENDENTIOUS
TENTATIVELY
TENTERHOOKS
TENUOUSNESS
TERMINATION
TERMINOLOGY
TERPSICHORE
TERREMOTIVE
TERRESTRIAL
TERRITORIAL
TESSARAGLOT
TESSELLATED
TESTIMONIAL
TETRADRACHM
TETRAHEDRON
THALIDOMIDE
THALLOPHYTE
THANATOPSIS
THANKLESSLY
THAUMATROPE
THEATERGOER
THEATREGOER
THEATRICALS
THENCEFORTH
THEOBROMINE
THEOLOGICAL
THEOPNEUSTY
THEORETICAL
THERAPEUTAE
THERAPEUTIC
THEREABOUTS
THERMOMETER
THERMOPYLAE
THESMOTHETE
THINGAMAJIG
THINGLINESS
THINGUMAJIG
THISTLEDOWN
THOROUGHPIN
THOUGHTLESS
THREATENING
THRIFTINESS
THROGMORTON
THUNDERBIRD
THUNDERBOLT
THUNDERCLAP
THUNDERHEAD
TICKTACKTOE
TIDDLEYWINK
TIGGYWINKLE
TIGHTFISTED
TIGHTLIPPED
TIMBROMANIA
TIMBROPHILY
TIMEKEEPING
TIMESHARING
TIRONENSIAN
TITILLATION
TOASTMASTER
TOBACCONIST
TOBOGGANING
TONSILLITIS
TOPLOFTICAL
TOPOGRAPHER

TORRIDONIAN
TORTICOLLIS
TORTICULLUS
TOSTICATION
TOTALIZATOR
TOURBILLION
TOWNSPEOPLE
TOXOPHILITE
TRACASSERIE
TRACHEOTOMY
TRACKLEMENT
TRADITIONAL
TRAFFICATOR
TRAGELAPHUS
TRANQUILITY
TRANSACTION
TRANSCEIVER
TRANSFERRED
TRANSFERRIN
TRANSFIGURE
TRANSFORMED
TRANSFORMER
TRANSFUSION
TRANSILIENT
TRANSLATION
TRANSLUCENT
TRANSMITTED
TRANSMITTER
TRANSPARENT
TRANSPONDER
TRANSPORTED
TRANSPORTER
TRANSURANIC
TREACHEROUS
TREACHETOUR
TREASONABLE
TREECREEPER
TRENCHERMAN
TREPIDATION
TREPONEMATA
TRESPASSING
TRIBULATION
TRICERATOPS
TRICHINELLA
TRICHINOSED
TRICHOPTERA
TRIMESTRIAL
TRINCOMALEE
TRINIDADIAN
TRINITARIAN
TRINOBANTES
TRIPTOLEMUS
TRITAGONIST
TRIUMVIRATE
TROMPELOEIL
TROPHOBLAST
TROPOSPHERE
TROUBLESOME
TROUBLESPOT
TRUCULENTLY
TRUSTEESHIP
TRUSTWORTHY
TRYPANOSOMA
TRYPANOSOME
TSCHERNOSEM
TURBELLARIA
TURRICULATE
TWELVEMONTH
TYPESETTING
TYPEWRITTEN
TYPOGRAPHER
TYPOGRAPHIC
TYROGLYPHID
TYRONENSIAN
ULOTRICHALE
ULTRAMARINE
ULTRAMODERN
ULTRAVIOLET
UNALTERABLE
UNAMBIGUOUS
UNANIMOUSLY
UNANNOUNCED
UNASSERTIVE
UNAUTHENTIC
UNAVAILABLE
UNAVOIDABLE
UNAVOIDABLY
UNBEFITTING
UNBLEMISHED
UNBREAKABLE
UNCASTRATED
UNCERTAINTY
UNCHRISTIAN
UNCIVILISED
UNCIVILIZED
UNCLEANNESS
UNCLUTTERED
UNCOMMITTED
UNCONCEALED
UNCONCERNED
UNCONFIRMED
UNCONNECTED
UNCONQUERED
UNCONSCIOUS
UNCONTESTED
UNCONVERTED
UNCONVINCED
UNCOUTHNESS
UNCRUSHABLE
UNDEMANDING
UNDERCHARGE
UNDERCOOKED
UNDERGROUND
UNDERGROWTH
UNDERHANDED
UNDERMANNED
UNDERSIGNED
UNDERSTATED
UNDERTAKING
UNDERVALUED
UNDERWEIGHT
UNDERWRITER
UNDESERVING
UNDESIRABLE
UNDEVELOPED
UNDIGNIFIED
UNDISCLOSED
UNDISGUISED
UNDISTURBED
UNDOUBTEDLY
UNDRINKABLE
UNEMOTIONAL
UNENDURABLE
UNENVELOPED
UNEQUIVOCAL
UNEXPLAINED
UNEXPRESSED
UNFAILINGLY
UNFAVORABLE
UNFLAPPABLE
UNFLINCHING
UNFORTUNATE
UNFULFILLED
UNFURNISHED
UNGETATABLE
UNGODLINESS
UNHAPPINESS
UNIFICATION
UNIMPORTANT
UNIMPRESSED
UNINHABITED
UNINHIBITED
UNINITIATED
UNIVERSALLY
UNJUSTIFIED
UNMITIGATED
UNMOTIVATED
UNNATURALLY
UNNECESSARY
UNOBSERVANT
UNOBTRUSIVE
UNPALATABLE
UNPATRIOTIC
UNPERTURBED
UNPRACTICAL
UNPRINTABLE
UNPROTECTED
UNPUBLISHED
UNQUALIFIED
UNREALISTIC
UNREASONING
UNREHEARSED
UNRELENTING
UNREMITTING
UNREPENTANT
UNRIGHTEOUS
UNSATISFIED
UNSATURATED
UNSCHEDULED
UNSHAKEABLE
UNSHELTERED
UNSHRINKING
UNSOLICITED
UNSPEAKABLE
UNSPECIFIED
UNSTOPPABLE
UNSUPPORTED
UNSURPASSED
UNSUSPECTED
UNSWEETENED
UNTHINKABLE
UNTOUCHABLE
UNTRAMELLED
UNUTTERABLE
UNVARNISHED
UNWARRANTED
UNWELCOMING
UNWHOLESOME
UNWITTINGLY
UPHOLSTERER
UPRIGHTNESS
USELESSNESS
UTILITARIAN
UTILIZATION
UTRICULARIA
VACCINATION
VACILLATING
VACILLATION
VACUOUSNESS
VALEDICTION
VALEDICTORY
VALLAMBROSA
VALLISNERIA
VARANGARIAN
VARIABILITY
VARIEGATION
VARIOLATION
VARSOVIENNE
VASOPRESSIN
VENDEMIAIRE
VENTILATION
VENTURESOME
VERBIGERATE
VERMICULITE
VERSATILITY
VERTIGINOUS
VESPERTINAL
VICARIOUSLY
VICHYSOISSE
VICIOUSNESS
VICISSITUDE
VIDEOCAMERA
VINAIGRETTE
VINBLASTINE
VINCRISTINE
VINDICATION
VIOLINCELLO
VIOLONCELLO
VISCOUNTESS
VITAMINIZED
VIVACIOUSLY
VIVISECTION
VOLCANOLOGY
VOLKSKAMMER
VOLUNTARILY
VOORTREKKER
VORACIOUSLY
VOTERIGGING
VULCANOLOGY
WAINSCOTING
WAKEFULNESS
WAPPENSCHAW
WAREHOUSING
WARMHEARTED
WASHERWOMAN
WASHLEATHER
WASTEBASKET
WATERCOLOUR
WATERCOURSE
WATEREDDOWN
WATERLOGGED
WATERMEADOW
WATERSKIING
WATERSPLASH
WAYWARDNESS
WEATHERCOCK
WEIGHBRIDGE
WELLADVISED
WELLBEHAVED
WELLDEFINED
WELLDRESSED
WELLFOUNDED
WELLINGTONS
WELLMEANING
WENSLEYDALE
WESTERNMOST
WESTMINSTER
WESTPHALIAN
WHEELBARROW
WHEELWRIGHT
WHEREABOUTS
WHEREWITHAL
WHIGMALEERY
WHISKERANDO
WHISTLESTOP
WHITEBOYISM
WHITECHAPEL
WHITECOLLAR
WHITEFRIARS
WHITETHROAT
WHITLEATHER
WHITTINGTON
WIDERANGING
WIENERWURST
WILBERFORCE
WILLINGNESS
WINDBREAKER
WINDCHEATER
WINDLESTRAW
WINDOWFRAME

WINDOWLEDGE
WINDSURFING
WINTERBERRY
WINTERGREEN
WISHTONWISH
WISTFULNESS
WITCHDOCTOR
WITENAGEMOT
WITHERSHINS
WITHHOLDING
WOMANLINESS
WONDERFULLY
WOODCARVING
WORKMANLIKE
WORKMANSHIP
WORKSTATION
WORLDFAMOUS
WORLDLINESS
WORRYTROUGH
WRONGHEADED
XENODOCHIUM
XEROTRIPSIS
XYLOGRAPHER
YELLOWPLUSH
YELLOWSTONE
ZOROASTRIAN
ZWISCHENZUG

11:2

BACCHANALIA
BACKBENCHER
BACKFIELDER
BACKPACKING
BACKSLIDING
BADDELEYITE
BADTEMPERED
BALISTRARIA
BALLBEARING
BANDEIRANTE
BANGLADESHI
BANNOCKBURN
BARBASTELLE
BARBITURATE
BARNSTORMER
BARTHOLOMEW
BARYCENTRIC
BASHFULNESS
BASKERVILLE
BATHYSPHERE
BATTLEDRESS
BATTLEFIELD
BATTLEFRONT
BATTLEMENTS
CABBALISTIC
CACOGASTRIC
CACOPHONOUS
CALCEOLARIA
CALCULATING
CALCULATION
CALEFACIENT
CALENDERING
CALIBRATION
CALIFORNIUM
CALLANETICS
CALLIGRAPHY
CALLISTEMON
CALLITRICHE
CALLOUSNESS
CAMALDOLITE
CAMARADERIE
CAMEROONIAN
CAMOUFLAGED
CAMPANOLOGY
CAMPESTRIAN
CAMPHORATED
CANDESCENCE
CANDIDATURE
CANDLELIGHT
CANDLESTICK
CANNIBALISM
CANNIBALIZE
CAPACITANCE
CAPACITATOR
CAPERNOITED
CAPERNOITIE
CAPRICCIOSO
CAPTIVATING
CAPTIVATION
CARABINIERE
CARAVANNING
CARBORUNDUM
CARBURETTOR
CARDIOGRAPH
CARDOPHAGUS
CAREFULNESS
CARMINATIVE
CARNAPTIOUS
CARNIVOROUS
CAROLINGIAN
CARRIAGEWAY
CARSICKNESS
CARTOGRAPHY
CASSITERITE
CASTELLATED
CATACAUSTIC
CATACHRESIS
CATACLYSMIC
CATALLACTIC
CATASTROPHE
CATCHPHRASE
CATEGORICAL
CATERPILLAR
CATHOLICISM
CAULIFLOWER
CAUSTICALLY
DACTYLOGRAM
DANGEROUSLY
DARDANELLES
EARNESTNESS
EARTHENWARE
EARTHSHAKER
EASTERNMOST
FABRICATION
FACETIOUSLY
FACTFINDING
FAIRWEATHER
FALLIBILITY
FAMILIARISE
FAMILIARITY
FAMILIARIZE
FANATICALLY
FANFARONADE
FARINACEOUS
FARRAGINOUS
FARREACHING
FARTHERMOST
FARTHINGALE
FASCINATING
FASCINATION
FASHIONABLE
FASHIONABLY
FATUOUSNESS
FAULTFINDER
FAULTLESSLY
FAUXBOURDON
FAVOURITISM
GABERLUNZIE
GALLIBAGGER
GALLIBEGGAR
GALLIGANTUS
GALLIMAUFRY
GALLOVIDIAN
GALLOWGLASS
GALLYBAGGER
GALLYBEGGAR
GAMETOPHYTE
GAMOGENESIS
GARNISHMENT
GARRULOUSLY
GASTRECTOMY
GASTRONOMIC
GATECRASHER
HABERDASHER
HABILIMENTS
HAEMOGLOBIN
HAEMOPHILIA
HAEMORRHAGE
HAEMORRHOID
HAGIOGRAPHY
HAIRDRESSER
HAIRRAISING
HALBSTARKER
HALFBROTHER
HALFHEARTED
HALFHOLIDAY
HALLEFLINTA
HALLUCINATE
HAMMERCLOTH
HANDCRAFTED
HANDICAPPED
HANDICAPPER
HANDWRITING
HANDWRITTEN
HANGGLIDING
HAPHAZARDLY
HARDHITTING
HARDICANUTE
HARDPRESSED
HARDWORKING
HAREBRAINED
HARIOLATION
HARPSICHORD
HATCHETTITE
HAUGHTINESS
JABBERWOCKY
JACQUEMINOT
JACTITATION
JAMAHIRIYAH
KALASHNIKOV
KAMELAUKION
KATABOTHRON
KATAVOTHRON
LABORIOUSLY
LABORSAVING
LACONICALLY
LAMENTATION
LAMMERGEIER
LAMMERGEYER
LAMPLIGHTER
LAMPROPHYRE
LANDSKNECHT
LAPIDESCENT
LARYNGISMUS
LASERPICIUM
LATERIGRADE
LATERITIOUS
LATIFUNDIUM
LATROCINIUM
LAUNDERETTE
LAWBREAKING
LAWLESSNESS
MACADAMIZED
MACERANDUBA
MACHAIRODUS
MACHINATION
MACROBIOTIC
MAGISTERIAL
MAGISTRATES
MAGLEMOSIAN
MAGNANIMITY
MAGNANIMOUS
MAGNIFICENT
MAINTENANCE
MAISTERDOME
MAKEBELIEVE
MALADJUSTED
MALAKATOONE
MALAPROPISM
MALEDICTION
MALEFACTION
MALEVOLENCE
MALFEASANCE
MALFUNCTION
MALICIOUSLY
MALPRACTICE
MANCIPATION
MANEUVERING
MANGALSUTRA
MANIPULATOR
MANTELLETTA
MANTELPIECE
MANTELSHELF
MANUFACTURE
MANUMISSION
MAQUILADORA
MARCONIGRAM
MARGINALIST
MARGINALIZE
MARIONBERRY
MARIONETTES
MARIVAUDAGE
MARKETPLACE
MARLBOROUGH
MARSHMALLOW
MASCULINITY
MASKALLONGE
MASOCHISTIC
MASQUERADER
MASSIVENESS
MASTERFULLY
MASTERPIECE
MASTICATION
MATERIALISE
MATERIALISM
MATERIALIST
MATERIALIZE
MATHEMATICS
MATRIARCHAL
MATRICULATE
MATRIMONIAL
MAURETANIAN
MAURITANIAN
NAPHTHALENE
NARRAGANSET
NATIONALISM
NATIONALIST
NATIONALITY
NATIONALIZE
NATIONSTATE
NATURALNESS
NAUGHTINESS
OARSMANSHIP
PACIFICALLY
PAEDIATRICS
PAEDOTROPHY
PAINKILLING
PAINSTAKING
PALEOGRAPHY
PALEOLITHIC

PALESTINIAN
PAMPELMOOSE
PAMPELMOUSE
PAMPHLETEER
PANDEMONIUM
PANOMPHAEAN
PANTALETTES
PAPERWEIGHT
PARABLEPSIS
PARABOLANUS
PARACETAMOL
PARACHUTIST
PARACROSTIC
PARADOXICAL
PARALEIPSIS
PARAMASTOID
PARAMEDICAL
PARANEPHROS
PARATROOPER
PARATYPHOID
PARENTHESIS
PARISHIONER
PARLIPOMENA
PARONOMASIA
PARTICIPANT
PARTICIPATE
PARTICIPIAL
PARTNERSHIP
PARTURITION
PARVANIMITY
PASSACAGLIA
PASSIVENESS
PASTEURELLA
PASTOURELLE
PATERNALISM
PATERNOSTER
PATHOLOGIST
PATRIARCHAL
PATRONISING
PATRONIZING
PAWNBROKERS
RABELAISIAN
RADIOACTIVE
RADIOCARBON
RADIOGRAPHY
RADIOLOGIST
RAFFISHNESS
RALLENTANDO
RAMGUNSHOCH
RANGEFINDER
RAPSCALLION
RAPTUROUSLY
RASTAFARIAN
RATATOUILLE
RATIOCINATE
RATIONALITY
RATIONALIZE
RATTLESNAKE
RAUCOUSNESS
RAVISHINGLY
RAZZAMATAZZ
SABBATARIAN
SACHERTORTE
SACRAMENTAL
SACRIFICIAL
SADDLEHORSE
SAGACIOUSLY
SAGITTARIUS
SAINTLINESS
SAINTPAULIA
SALACIOUSLY
SALESPERSON
SALPINGITIS
SALTIMBANCO
SALTIMBOCCA
SALVADORIAN
SALVOGUNNER
SANDERSWOOD
SAPONACEOUS
SAPROLEGNIA
SAPROPHYTIC
SARCENCHYME
SARCOPHAGUS
SATIRICALLY
SAUSAGEMEAT
SAVOURINESS
SAXOPHONIST
TABERNACLES
TACHYCARDIA
TACHYGRAPHY
TACITURNITY
TAGLIATELLE
TANGIBILITY
TANTALIZING
TARATANTARA
TARRADIDDLE
TASTELESSLY
TATTERSALLS
TAUROBOLIUM
TAUTOCHRONE
TAXIDERMIST
VACCINATION
VACILLATING
VACILLATION
VACUOUSNESS
VALEDICTION
VALEDICTORY
VALLAMBROSA
VALLISNERIA
VARANGARIAN
VARIABILITY
VARIEGATION
VARIOLATION
VARSOVIENNE
VASOPRESSIN
WAINSCOTING
WAKEFULNESS
WAPPENSCHAW
WAREHOUSING
WARMHEARTED
WASHERWOMAN
WASHLEATHER
WASTEBASKET
WATERCOLOUR
WATERCOURSE
WATEREDDOWN
WATERLOGGED
WATERMEADOW
WATERSKIING
WATERSPLASH
WAYWARDNESS
ABANDONMENT
ABBREVIATED
ABECEDARIAN
ABIOGENETIC
ABLACTATION
ABNORMALITY
ABOMINATION
ABORTIONIST
ABRACADABRA
ABRIDGEMENT
ABSENTEEISM
ABSTRACTION
OBJECTIVELY
OBJECTIVITY
OBLITERATED
OBMUTESCENT
OBSERVATION
OBSERVATORY
OBSESSIVELY
OBSOLESCENT
OBSTETRICAL
OBSTINATELY
OBSTRICTION
OBSTRUCTION
OBSTRUCTIVE
OBTEMPERATE
OBVIOUSNESS
ACADEMICIAN
ACATALECTIC
ACCELERATOR
ACCESSORIES
ACCIPITRINE
ACCLAMATION
ACCLIMATION
ACCLIMATISE
ACCLIMATIZE
ACCOMMODATE
ACCOMPANIST
ACCORDINGLY
ACCOUNTABLE
ACCOUNTANCY
ACCRESCENCE
ACCUMULATOR
ACHIEVEMENT
ACINACIFORM
ACKNOWLEDGE
ACOLOUTHITE
ACQUIESCENT
ACQUISITION
ACQUISITIVE
ACRIFLAVINE
ACRIMONIOUS
ACTUALITIES
ACUPUNCTURE
ECCALEOBION
ICHTHYOLITE
ICHTHYORNIS
ICONOGRAPHY
ICONOSTASIS
OCHLOCRATIC
OCTASTICHON
SCAFFOLDING
SCALPRIFORM
SCANDALIZED
SCANDANAVIA
SCANDINAVIA
SCARABAEOID
SCARBOROUGH
SCAREMONGER
SCATTERGOOD
SCATTERLING
SCEPTICALLY
SCEUOPHYLAX
SCHECKLATON
SCHISTOSOMA
SCHISTOSOME
SCHOLARSHIP
SCHOTTISCHE
SCHRECKLICH
SCHWARMEREI
SCIENTOLOGY
SCINTILLATE
SCIREFACIAS
SCITAMINEAE
SCOLECIFORM
SCOLOPENDRA
SCOPOLAMINE
SCOUTMASTER
SCREAMINGLY
SCREWDRIVER
SCRIMSHANDY
SCRIPTORIUM
SCRUFFINESS
SCRUMPTIOUS
SCULDUDDERY
SCULDUGGERY
SCULLABOGUE
SCUPPERNONG
SCUTTLEBUTT
SCYPHISTOMA
TCHAIKOVSKY
ADJOURNMENT
ADJUDICATOR
ADOLESCENCE
ADOPTIANISM
ADOPTIONISM
ADULLAMITES
ADULTERATED
ADUMBRATION
ADVANCEMENT
ADVENTURESS
ADVENTUROUS
ADVERBIALLY
ADVERTISING
EDIFICATION
EDUCATIONAL
IDENTICALLY
IDENTIFYING
IDEOLOGICAL
IDEOPRAXIST
IDIOTICALLY
IDOLIZATION
IDYLLICALLY
ODONTOBLAST
ODONTOPHORE
AERODYNAMIC
AERONAUTICS
AESCULAPIAN
AESCULAPIUS
BEACHCOMBER
BEASTLINESS
BEAUMONTAGE
BEAUTIFULLY
BEHAVIOURAL
BELEAGUERED
BELLEROPHON
BELLETTRIST
BELLIGERENT
BELLYTIMBER
BELORUSSIAN
BENEDICTINE
BENEDICTION
BENEFICIARY
BENEFICIATE
BENEVOLENCE
BEREAVEMENT
BERGSCHRUND
BESIEGEMENT
BESSARABIAN
BESTSELLING
BEWILDERING
CEASELESSLY
CELEBRATION
CENTENARIAN
CENTERPIECE
CENTREBOARD
CENTREPIECE
CENTRIFUGAL
CENTRIPETAL
CENTUMVIRUS
CENTURIATOR
CERARGYRITE
CEREBRATION
CEREMONIOUS
CERTIFIABLE
CERTIFICATE
CESAREWITCH
DEBILITATED
DECAPITATED

DECARBONIZE
DECEITFULLY
DECEPTIVELY
DECLAMATION
DECLAMATORY
DECLARATION
DECONSTRUCT
DECORATIONS
DECORTICATE
DECREPITATE
DECREPITUDE
DEERSTALKER
DEFENCELESS
DEFENSELESS
DEFENSIVELY
DEFERENTIAL
DEFOLIATION
DEFORMATION
DEGLUTINATE
DEGLUTITION
DEGRADATION
DEGRINGOLER
DEHORTATIVE
DEHYDRATION
DEIFICATION
DELECTATION
DELETERIOUS
DELICIOUSLY
DELICTATION
DELINEATION
DELINQUENCY
DELITESCENT
DELIVERANCE
DEMAGOGUERY
DEMARCATION
DEMIBASTION
DEMOGRAPHIC
DEMONOMANIA
DEMONSTRATE
DEMORALIZED
DEMOSTHENES
DEMOSTHENIC
DENDRACHATE
DENOMINATOR
DEPARTEMENT
DEPHLEGMATE
DEPORTATION
DEPREDATION
DEPRIVATION
DERANGEMENT
DERELICTION
DERMATOLOGY
DESCENDANTS
DESCRIPTION
DESCRIPTIVE
DESECRATION
DESEGREGATE
DESELECTION
DESERPIDINE
DESICCATION
DESIGNATION
DESPERATELY
DESPERATION
DESPONDENCY
DESTABILIZE
DESTINATION
DESTITUTION
DESTRUCTION
DESTRUCTIVE
DETERIORATE
DETERMINANT
DETERMINING
DETESTATION
DETRIMENTAL
DEUTERONOMY
DEUTSCHMARK
DEVALUATION
DEVASTATING
DEVASTATION
DEVELOPMENT
DEVIOUSNESS
DEVITRIFIED
FEASIBILITY
FEATURELESS
FEHMGERICHT
FERNITICKLE
FEROCIOUSLY
FERRONNIÈRE
FESTINATELY
FESTSCHRIFT
GEGENSCHEIN
GELSEMININE
GENEALOGIST
GENERALIZED
GENERICALLY
GENETICALLY
GENOUILLÈRE
GENTLEMANLY
GENTLEWOMAN
GENUFLEXION
GENUINENESS
GEOMETRICAL
GEOSYNCLINE
GERMINATION
GERONTOLOGY
GERRYMANDER
GESTATORIAL
GESTICULATE
HEALTHINESS
HEARTBROKEN
HEARTLESSLY
HEAVYHANDED
HEAVYWEIGHT
HEBDOMADARY
HECKELPHONE
HELPFULNESS
HEMERALOPIA
HEMIANOPSIA
HEMOPHILIAC
HEMORRHOIDS
HEPATOSCOPY
HEPPLEWHITE
HERBIVOROUS
HERPETOLOGY
HERRINGBONE
HETEROSCIAN
JERRYMANDER
KETAVOTHRON
LEADSWINGER
LEASEHOLDER
LEATHERBACK
LEATHERETTE
LEATHERHEAD
LEATHERNECK
LECTURESHIP
LEFTLUGGAGE
LEGERDEMAIN
LEGIONNAIRE
LEGISLATION
LEGISLATIVE
LEGISLATURE
LENGTHENING
LENGTHINESS
LENTIGINOSE
LEPIDOPTERA
LEPIDOSIREN
LETTERPRESS
LEVELHEADED
MEADOWSWEET
MEANDERINGS
MEANINGLESS
MEASURELESS
MEASUREMENT
MECKLENBURG
MEDIASTINUM
MEDICINALLY
MEDIUMSIZED
MEGALOMANIA
MEGALOMANIC
MEGALOPOLIS
MEGATHERIUM
MEKHITARIST
MELANCHOLIA
MELANCHOLIC
MELANOCHROI
MELLIFLUOUS
MELODIOUSLY
MEMORABILIA
MENDELEVIUM
MENDELSSOHN
MENSURATION
MENTHOLATED
MENTONNIÈRE
MEPROBAMATE
MERCHANDISE
MERCHANDIZE
MERCHANTMAN
MERCILESSLY
MERITORIOUS
MERRYMAKING
METACARPALS
METAGENESIS
METALWORKER
METAPHYSICS
METATARSALS
METEOROLOGY
METHODOLOGY
METRICATION
NEANDERTHAL
NEARSIGHTED
NECESSARILY
NECESSITATE
NECESSITOUS
NECROMANCER
NEEDLEPOINT
NEEDLESTICK
NEEDLEWOMAN
NEGOTIATING
NEGOTIATION
NEIGHBORING
NEIGHBOURLY
NERVOUSNESS
NETHERLANDS
NETHERLINGS
NEUROLOGIST
NEUTRALISED
NEVERENDING
NEWSCASTING
PEACEKEEPER
PECULIARITY
PEDAGOGICAL
PEDESTRIANS
PEDETENTOUS
PEEVISHNESS
PELARGONIUM
PELOPONNESE
PENETRATING
PENETRATION
PENICILLATE
PENITENTIAL
PENNYFATHER
PENSIONABLE
PENSIVENESS
PENTATHLETE
PENTECONTER
PENTECOSTAL
PENTHESILEA
PENTONVILLE
PENULTIMATE
PERAMBULATE
PERCEFOREST
PERCEPTIBLE
PERCEPTIBLY
PERCHLORATE
PERCIPIENCE
PERCOLATION
PERDUELLION
PEREGRINATE
PERENNIALLY
PERESTROIKA
PERFORATION
PERFORMANCE
PERFUNCTORY
PERICARDIUM
PERIGORDIAN
PERIODONTIC
PERIPATETIC
PERIPHRASIS
PERISSOLOGY
PERISTALITH
PERISTALSIS
PERITONAEUM
PERITONITIS
PERLUSTRATE
PERMANENTLY
PERMISSIBLE
PERMUTATION
PERPETRATOR
PERPETUALLY
PERSECUTION
PERSEVERING
PERSISTENCE
PERSONALIST
PERSONALITY
PERSONALIZE
PERSONIFIED
PERSPECTIVE
PERSPICUITY
PERSPICUOUS
PERTINACITY
PERTINENTLY
PESSIMISTIC
PETITMAITRE
PETRODOLLAR
PETTICOATED
PETTIFOGGER
REACTIONARY
READABILITY
REALIGNMENT
REALIZATION
REALPOLITIK
REANIMATION
REAPPRAISAL
REASSURANCE
REBARBATIVE
RECANTATION
RECEPTIVITY
RECESSIONAL
RECIPROCATE
RECIPROCITY
RECLAMATION
RECOGNITION
RECONDITION
RECONNOITER
RECONNOITRE
RECONSTRUCT
RECOVERABLE
RECRIMINATE
RECRUITMENT
RECTANGULAR

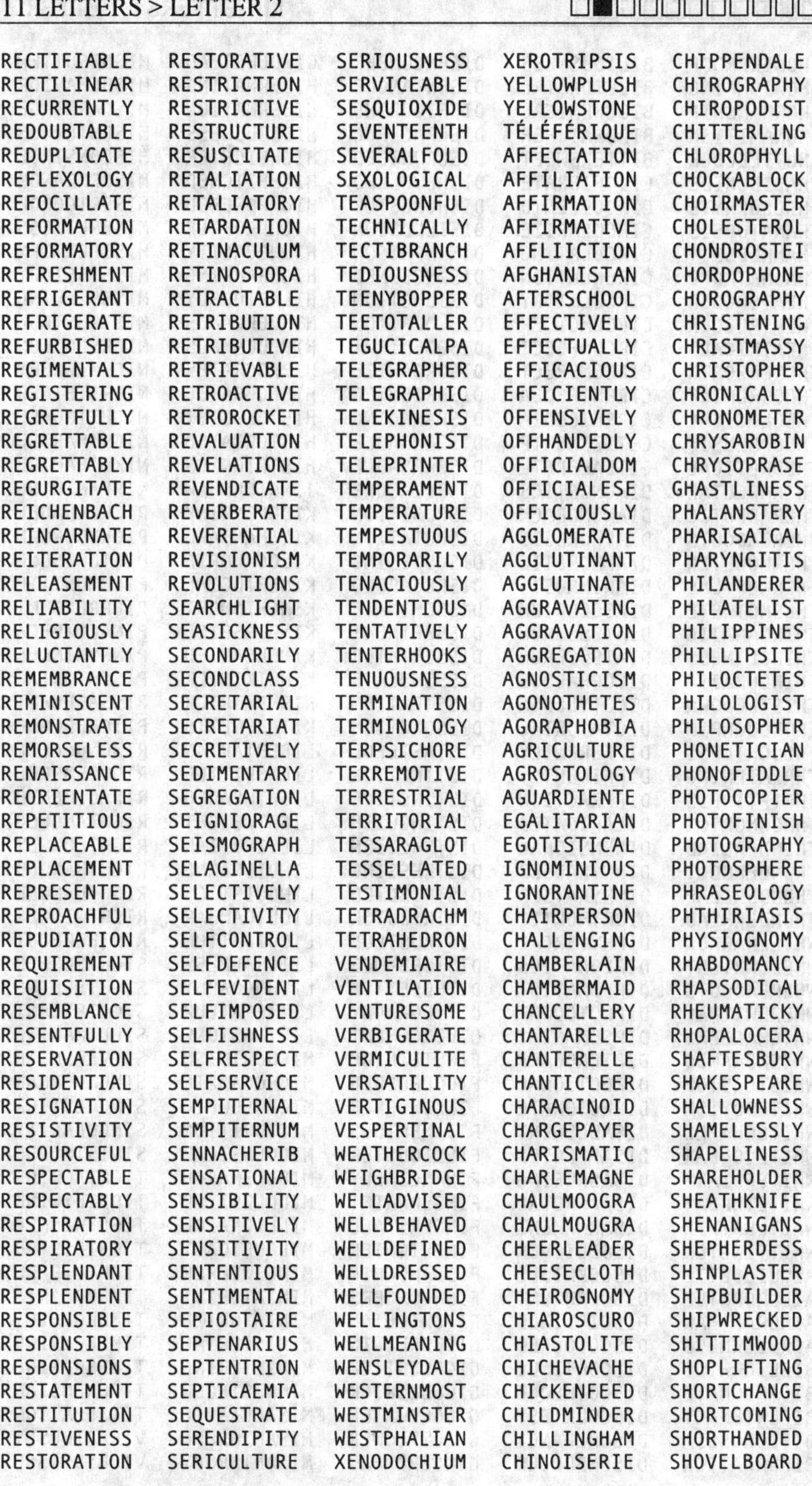

RECTIFIABLE
RECTILINEAR
RECURRENTLY
REDOUBTABLE
REDUPLICATE
REFLEXOLOGY
REFOCILLATE
REFORMATION
REFORMATORY
REFRESHMENT
REFRIGERANT
REFRIGERATE
REFURBISHED
REGIMENTALS
REGISTERING
REGRETFULLY
REGRETTABLE
REGRETTABLY
REGURGITATE
REICHENBACH
REINCARNATE
REITERATION
RELEASEMENT
RELIABILITY
RELIGIOUSLY
RELUCTANTLY
REMEMBRANCE
REMINISCENT
REMONSTRATE
REMORSELESS
RENAISSANCE
REORIENTATE
REPETITIOUS
REPLACEABLE
REPLACEMENT
REPRESENTED
REPROACHFUL
REPUDIATION
REQUIREMENT
REQUISITION
RESEMBLANCE
RESENTFULLY
RESERVATION
RESIDENTIAL
RESIGNATION
RESISTIVITY
RESOURCEFUL
RESPECTABLE
RESPECTABLY
RESPIRATION
RESPIRATORY
RESPLENDANT
RESPLENDENT
RESPONSIBLE
RESPONSIBLY
RESPONSIONS
RESTATEMENT
RESTITUTION
RESTIVENESS
RESTORATION
RESTORATIVE
RESTRICTION
RESTRICTIVE
RESTRUCTURE
RESUSCITATE
RETALIATION
RETALIATORY
RETARDATION
RETINACULUM
RETINOSPORA
RETRACTABLE
RETRIBUTION
RETRIBUTIVE
RETRIEVABLE
RETROACTIVE
RETROROCKET
REVALUATION
REVELATIONS
REVENDICATE
REVERBERATE
REVERENTIAL
REVISIONISM
REVOLUTIONS
SEARCHLIGHT
SEASICKNESS
SECONDARILY
SECONDCLASS
SECRETARIAL
SECRETARIAT
SECRETIVELY
SEDIMENTARY
SEGREGATION
SEIGNIORAGE
SEISMOGRAPH
SELAGINELLA
SELECTIVELY
SELECTIVITY
SELFCONTROL
SELFDEFENCE
SELFEVIDENT
SELFIMPOSED
SELFISHNESS
SELFRESPECT
SELFSERVICE
SEMPITERNAL
SEMPITERNUM
SENNACHERIB
SENSATIONAL
SENSIBILITY
SENSITIVELY
SENSITIVITY
SENTENTIOUS
SENTIMENTAL
SEPIOSTAIRE
SEPTENARIUS
SEPTENTRION
SEPTICAEMIA
SEQUESTRATE
SERENDIPITY
SERICULTURE
SERIOUSNESS
SERVICEABLE
SESQUIOXIDE
SEVENTEENTH
SEVERALFOLD
SEXOLOGICAL
TEASPOONFUL
TECHNICALLY
TECTIBRANCH
TEDIOUSNESS
TEENYBOPPER
TEETOTALLER
TEGUCICALPA
TELEGRAPHER
TELEGRAPHIC
TELEKINESIS
TELEPHONIST
TELEPRINTER
TEMPERAMENT
TEMPERATURE
TEMPESTUOUS
TEMPORARILY
TENACIOUSLY
TENDENTIOUS
TENTATIVELY
TENTERHOOKS
TENUOUSNESS
TERMINATION
TERMINOLOGY
TERPSICHORE
TERREMOTIVE
TERRESTRIAL
TERRITORIAL
TESSARAGLOT
TESSELLATED
TESTIMONIAL
TETRADRACHM
TETRAHEDRON
VENDEMIAIRE
VENTILATION
VENTURESOME
VERBIGERATE
VERMICULITE
VERSATILITY
VERTIGINOUS
VESPERTINAL
WEATHERCOCK
WEIGHBRIDGE
WELLADVISED
WELLBEHAVED
WELLDEFINED
WELLDRESSED
WELLFOUNDED
WELLINGTONS
WELLMEANING
WENSLEYDALE
WESTERNMOST
WESTMINSTER
WESTPHALIAN
XENODOCHIUM
XEROTRIPSIS
YELLOWPLUSH
YELLOWSTONE
TÉLÉFÉRIQUE
AFFECTATION
AFFILIATION
AFFIRMATION
AFFIRMATIVE
AFFLIICTION
AFGHANISTAN
AFTERSCHOOL
EFFECTIVELY
EFFECTUALLY
EFFICACIOUS
EFFICIENTLY
OFFENSIVELY
OFFHANDEDLY
OFFICIALDOM
OFFICIALESE
OFFICIOUSLY
AGGLOMERATE
AGGLUTINANT
AGGLUTINATE
AGGRAVATING
AGGRAVATION
AGGREGATION
AGNOSTICISM
AGONOTHETES
AGORAPHOBIA
AGRICULTURE
AGROSTOLOGY
AGUARDIENTE
EGALITARIAN
EGOTISTICAL
IGNOMINIOUS
IGNORANTINE
CHAIRPERSON
CHALLENGING
CHAMBERLAIN
CHAMBERMAID
CHANCELLERY
CHANTARELLE
CHANTERELLE
CHANTICLEER
CHARACINOID
CHARGEPAYER
CHARISMATIC
CHARLEMAGNE
CHAULMOOGRA
CHAULMOUGRA
CHEERLEADER
CHEESECLOTH
CHEIROGNOMY
CHIAROSCURO
CHIASTOLITE
CHICHEVACHE
CHICKENFEED
CHILDMINDER
CHILLINGHAM
CHINOISERIE
CHIPPENDALE
CHIROGRAPHY
CHIROPODIST
CHITTERLING
CHLOROPHYLL
CHOCKABLOCK
CHOIRMASTER
CHOLESTEROL
CHONDROSTEI
CHORDOPHONE
CHOROGRAPHY
CHRISTENING
CHRISTMASSY
CHRISTOPHER
CHRONICALLY
CHRONOMETER
CHRYSAROBIN
CHRYSOPRASE
GHASTLINESS
PHALANSTERY
PHARISAICAL
PHARYNGITIS
PHILANDERER
PHILATELIST
PHILIPPINES
PHILLIPSITE
PHILOCTETES
PHILOLOGIST
PHILOSOPHER
PHONETICIAN
PHONOFIDDLE
PHOTOCOPIER
PHOTOFINISH
PHOTOGRAPHY
PHOTOSPHERE
PHRASEOLOGY
PHTHIRIASIS
PHYSIOGNOMY
RHABDOMANCY
RHAPSODICAL
RHEUMATICKY
RHOPALOCERA
SHAFTESBURY
SHAKESPEARE
SHALLOWNESS
SHAMELESSLY
SHAPELINESS
SHAREHOLDER
SHEATHKNIFE
SHENANIGANS
SHEPHERDESS
SHINPLASTER
SHIPBUILDER
SHIPWRECKED
SHITTIMWOOD
SHOPLIFTING
SHORTCHANGE
SHORTCOMING
SHORTHANDED
SHOVELBOARD

SHOWERPROOF
SHOWJUMPING
SHOWMANSHIP
SHUNAMITISM
SHUTTLECOCK
THALIDOMIDE
THALLOPHYTE
THANATOPSIS
THANKLESSLY
THAUMATROPE
THEATERGOER
THEATREGOER
THEATRICALS
THENCEFORTH
THEOBROMINE
THEOLOGICAL
THEOPNEUSTY
THEORETICAL
THERAPEUTAE
THERAPEUTIC
THEREABOUTS
THERMOMETER
THERMOPYLAE
THESMOTHETE
THINGAMAJIG
THINGLINESS
THINGUMAJIG
THISTLEDOWN
THOROUGHPIN
THOUGHTLESS
THREATENING
THRIFTINESS
THROGMORTON
THUNDERBIRD
THUNDERBOLT
THUNDERCLAP
THUNDERHEAD
WHEELBARROW
WHEELWRIGHT
WHEREABOUTS
WHEREWITHAL
WHIGMALEERY
WHISKERANDO
WHISTLESTOP
WHITEBOYISM
WHITECHAPEL
WHITECOLLAR
WHITEFRIARS
WHITETHROAT
WHITLEATHER
WHITTINGTON
AIGUILLETTE
AILUROPHILE
AIRCRAFTMAN
AIRSICKNESS
BIBLIOPHILE
BICARBONATE
BICENTENARY
BIELORUSSIA
BIFURCATION
BILIOUSNESS
BILLIONAIRE
BIOCHEMICAL
BIRDWATCHER
BITTERSWEET
CILOFIBRATE
CINQUECENTO
CIRCULARIZE
CIRCULATING
CIRCULATION
CIRCULATORY
CIRCUMCISER
CIRCUMFLECT
CIRCUMSPECT
CIRRHIPEDEA
CIRRHIPEDIA
CITIZENSHIP
CITLALEPETL
DIAGNOSTICS
DIAMONDBACK
DIAPHORESIS
DIAPHORETIC
DIARTHROSIS
DIASCORDIUM
DIATESSARON
DIATESSERON
DICEPHALOUS
DICOTYLEDON
DICTATORIAL
DIFFERENTLY
DIFFIDENTLY
DIFFRACTION
DILAPIDATED
DIMENSIONAL
DINNYHAUSER
DINNYHAYSER
DIORTHORTIC
DIPHYCERCAL
DIPLOMATICS
DIPLOMATIST
DIPROTODONT
DIPSOMANIAC
DIPTEROCARP
DIRECTIONAL
DIRECTORATE
DISABLEMENT
DISAFFECTED
DISAGREEING
DISAPPROVAL
DISARMAMENT
DISBELIEVER
DISCERNIBLE
DISCERNMENT
DISCIPLINED
DISCOLOURED
DISCONTINUE
DISCOTHEQUE
DISCOURTESY
DISCREPANCY
DISEMBODIED
DISENCUMBER
DISENTANGLE
DISFIGURING
DISGRACEFUL
DISGRUNTLED
DISHEVELLED
DISHONESTLY
DISILLUSION
DISIMPRISON
DISINCLINED
DISJUNCTION
DISLOCATION
DISOBEDIENT
DISORGANIZE
DISORIENTED
DISPARAGING
DISPENSABLE
DISPERSABLE
DISPLEASURE
DISPOSITION
DISPUTATION
DISQUIETING
DISREGARDED
DISSEMINATE
DISSEPIMENT
DISSERTATOR
DISSIMULATE
DISSIPATION
DISSOLUTION
DISTASTEFUL
DISTINCTION
DISTINCTIVE
DISTINGUISH
DISTRACTION
DISTRESSING
DISTRIBUTED
DISTRIBUTOR
DISTRUSTFUL
DISTURBANCE
DITHELETISM
DITTOGRAPHY
DIVORCEMENT
EINSTEINIUM
FIDDLEDEDEE
FIELDWORKER
FILAMENTOUS
FILLIBUSTER
FINANCIALLY
FINGERPRINT
FINGERSTALL
FIRELIGHTER
FISHANDCHIP
FISHMONGERS
FITZWILLIAM
GIBBERELLIN
GIGGLESTICK
GIGGLESWICK
GIGGLEWATER
GILLYFLOWER
GINGERBREAD
GIRDLESTEAD
HIBERNATING
HIBERNATION
HIDEOUSNESS
HIGHLIGHTER
HIGHPITCHED
HIGHPOWERED
HIGHPROFILE
HIGHQUALITY
HIGHRANKING
HILARIOUSLY
HINDERLANDS
HIPPOCAMPUS
HIPPOCRATES
HIPPOCRATIC
HISTOLOGIST
HISTORIATED
HISTRIONICS
JINRICKSHAW
KIDDLEYWINK
KILIMANJARO
KILOCALORIE
KIMERIDGIAN
KINCHINMORT
KINDERSPIEL
KINDHEARTED
KINNIKINICK
KIRKPATRICK
KITCHENETTE
LIBERTARIAN
LICKSPITTLE
LIGHTHEADED
LIGHTWEIGHT
LILLIPUTIAN
LINDISFARNE
LINGUISTICS
LIQUIDAMBAR
LIQUIDATION
LITERALNESS
LITHOGRAPHY
LITTÉRATEUR
LIVINGSTONE
MICHURINISM
MICROGAMETE
MICROSCOPIC
MICTURITION
MIDDENSTEAD
MIDDLEMARCH
MIDDLESIZED
MILLIONAIRE
MILQUETOAST
MINESWEEPER
MINIATURIST
MINIATURIZE
MINISTERIAL
MINISTERING
MINNESINGER
MISALLIANCE
MISANTHROPE
MISANTHROPY
MISBEGOTTEN
MISBEHAVIOR
MISCARRIAGE
MISCHIEVOUS
MISCONSTRUE
MISDEMEANOR
MISERICORDE
MISERLINESS
MISIDENTIFY
MISSISSIPPI
MISSPELLING
MISTRUSTFUL
NICKELODEON
NICKNACKERY
NIERSTEINER
NIGHTINGALE
NIGHTMARISH
NIKETHAMIDE
NIPFARTHING
PICKELHAUBE
PICKYOUROWN
PICTURESQUE
PIEDMONTITE
PIERREPOINT
PINACOTHECA
PINNYWINKLE
PISCATORIAL
PISSASPHALT
PITCHBLENDE
RIBONUCLEIC
RIDDLEMEREE
RIFACIMENTO
RIGHTANGLED
RIGHTEOUSLY
RIGHTHANDED
RIGHTHANDER
RIGHTWINGER
RINTHEREOUT
SIGHTSCREEN
SIGHTSEEING
SIGNIFICANT
SILLIMANITE
SILVERSMITH
SINGAPOREAN
SINGLESTICK
SINGULARITY
SINISTRORSE
TICKTACKTOE
TIDDLEYWINK
TIGGYWINKLE
TIGHTFISTED
TIGHTLIPPED
TIMBROMANIA
TIMBROPHILY
TIMEKEEPING
TIMESHARING
TIRONENSIAN
TITILLATION
VICARIOUSLY
VICHYSOISSE

VICIOUSNESS
VICISSITUDE
VIDEOCAMERA
VINAIGRETTE
VINBLASTINE
VINCRISTINE
VINDICATION
VIOLINCELLO
VIOLONCELLO
VISCOUNTESS
VITAMINIZED
VIVACIOUSLY
VIVISECTION
WIDERANGING
WIENERWURST
WILBERFORCE
WILLINGNESS
WINDBREAKER
WINDCHEATER
WINDLESTRAW
WINDOWFRAME
WINDOWLEDGE
WINDSURFING
WINTERBERRY
WINTERGREEN
WISHTONWISH
WISTFULNESS
WITCHDOCTOR
WITENAGEMOT
WITHERSHINS
WITHHOLDING
EJACULATION
SKEPTICALLY
SKETCHINESS
SKIDBLADNIR
SKILLIGALEE
SKILLIGOLEE
SKIMMINGTON
SKULDUDDERY
SKULDUGGERY
ALBIGENSIAN
ALBUGINEOUS
ALCYONARIAN
ALEXANDRINE
ALEXANDRITE
ALIFANFARON
ALLEGORICAL
ALLELOMORPH
ALLEVIATION
ALPHABETIZE
ALTERCATION
ALTERNATELY
ALTERNATING
ALTERNATION
ALTERNATIVE
BLACKFELLOW
BLACKMAILER
BLADDERWORT
BLAMEWORTHY
BLANKURSINE
BLASPHEMOUS
BLESSEDNESS
BLOCKBUSTER
BLOODSPORTS
BLOODSTREAM
BLOODSUCKER
BLUNDERBORE
CLADOSPORUM
CLAIRSCHACH
CLAIRVOYANT
CLANDESTINE
CLANJAMFRAY
CLAPPERCLAW
CLARENCIEUX
CLEANLINESS
CLEANSHAVEN
CLIFFHANGER
CLIMACTERIC
CLIMATOLOGY
CLINOCHLORE
CLIOMETRICS
ELABORATELY
ELABORATION
ELASTOPLAST
ELECTRICIAN
ELECTRICITY
ELECTROCUTE
ELECTROLIER
ELECTROLYTE
ELECTRONICS
ELECTROTINT
ELEPHANTINE
ELEUTHERIAN
ELIGIBILITY
ELIMINATION
ELIZABETHAN
ELUCIDATION
FLABBERGAST
FLAMBOYANCE
FLAMBOYANTE
FLANNELETTE
FLAVOURSOME
FLEXIBILITY
FLICKERTAIL
FLIRTATIOUS
FLORILEGIUM
FLOURISHING
FLUCTUATING
FLUCTUATION
FLUORESCENT
GLADWELLISE
GLASTONBURY
GLIMMERGOWK
GLOSSOLALIA
ILLMANNERED
ILLOGICALLY
ILLUMINATED
ILLUSIONARY
ILLUSIONIST
ILLUSTRATOR
ILLUSTRIOUS
ILLYWHACKER
KLEPTOMANIA
OLIGOCHAETE
PLAGIARISED
PLAGIOSTOMI
PLANETARIUM
PLANTAGENET
PLANTIGRADE
PLATERESQUE
PLATYRRHINE
PLAYFULNESS
PLEASURABLE
PLEBEIANISE
PLEISTOCENE
PLOUGHSHARE
SLEEPWALKER
SLENDERNESS
SLIGHTINGLY
SLUMBERWEAR
SLUMGULLION
ULOTRICHALE
ULTRAMARINE
ULTRAMODERN
ULTRAVIOLET
AMBIVALENCE
AMELANCHIER
AMERCIAMENT
AMERICANISM
AMINOBUTENE
AMMOPHILOUS
AMONTILLADO
AMPHETAMINE
AMPHIBOLOGY
AMPHISBAENA
AMPHISBOENA
AMPLEXICAUL
EMBARKATION
EMBARRASSED
EMBELLISHED
EMBOÎTEMENT
EMBROCATION
EMMENAGOGUE
EMMENTHALER
EMOTIONALLY
EMPHYTEUSIS
EMPIECEMENT
EMPIRICUTIC
EMPLACEMENT
EMPOWERMENT
EMPTYHANDED
EMPYROMANCY
IMAGINATION
IMAGINATIVE
IMMEDIATELY
IMMIGRATION
IMMORTALISE
IMMORTALITY
IMMORTALIZE
IMPARTIALLY
IMPASSIONED
IMPASSIVELY
IMPATIENTLY
IMPEACHMENT
IMPECUNIOUS
IMPEDIMENTA
IMPERIALISM
IMPERIALIST
IMPERIOUSLY
IMPERMANENT
IMPERMEABLE
IMPERSONATE
IMPERTINENT
IMPETUOSITY
IMPETUOUSLY
IMPIGNORATE
IMPLAUSIBLE
IMPLEMENTAL
IMPLICATION
IMPORTANTLY
IMPORTATION
IMPORTUNATE
IMPRACTICAL
IMPRECATION
IMPRECISION
IMPREGNABLE
IMPROPRIETY
IMPROVEMENT
IMPROVIDENT
IMPRUDENTLY
IMPULSIVELY
OMMATOPHORE
OMNIPOTENCE
OMNIPRESENT
OMNISCIENCE
SMALLHOLDER
SMITHEREENS
SMITHSONIAN
SMITHSONITE
SMOKESCREEN
SMORGASBORD
SMOULDERING
ANACHRONISM
ANACOLUTHIA
ANACREONTIC
ANADIPLOSIS
ANAESTHESIA
ANAESTHETIC
ANAGNORISIS
ANAPHYLAXIS
ANAPLEROSIS
ANAPLEROTIC
ANASTOMOSIS
ANAXIMANDER
ANDROGENOUS
ANENCEPHALY
ANESTHETIST
ANESTHETIZE
ANFRACTUOUS
ANGELOLATRY
ANISOCERCAL
ANNABERGITE
ANNIVERSARY
ANONYMOUSLY
ANTECEDENCE
ANTECHAMBER
ANTEPENDIUM
ANTHESTERIA
ANTHOCYANIN
ANTHOLOGIZE
ANTHONOMOUS
ANTIBURGHER
ANTICYCLONE
ANTINEUTRON
ANTIPHRASIS
ANTIPYRETIC
ANTIQUARIAN
ANTIRRHINUM
ANTISTHENES
ANTISTROPHE
ANTONOMASIA
ENARTHROSIS
ENCAPSULATE
ENCEPHALOMA
ENCHANTMENT
ENCHANTRESS
ENCHIRIDION
ENCHONDROMA
ENCOURAGING
ENCROACHING
ENCUMBRANCE
ENDOCARDIUM
ENDORSEMENT
ENDOTHERMIC
ENFEOFFMENT
ENFORCEABLE
ENFORCEMENT
ENFOULDERED
ENFRANCHISE
ENGHALSKRUG
ENGINEERING
ENHANCEMENT
ENJAMBEMENT
ENKEPHALINE
ENLARGEMENT
ENLIGHTENED
ENNEAHEDRON
ENSLAVEMENT
ENTABLATURE
ENTABLEMENT
ENTERTAINER
ENTHRALLING
ENTITLEMENT
ENUMERATION
ENUNCIATION
ENVIRONMENT
GNATHONICAL
INADVERTENT
INADVISABLE
INALIENABLE

INATTENTION
INATTENTIVE
INAUTHENTIC
INCALESCENT
INCANTATION
INCAPSULATE
INCARCERATE
INCARNADINE
INCARNATION
INCESSANTLY
INCINERATOR
INCLINATION
INCOHERENCE
INCOMPETENT
INCOMPOSITE
INCONGRUITY
INCONGRUOUS
INCONSTANCY
INCONTINENT
INCORPORATE
INCORPOREAL
INCORRECTLY
INCREDULITY
INCREDULOUS
INCREMENTAL
INCRIMINATE
INDEFINABLE
INDENTATION
INDEPENDENT
INDEXLINKED
INDIARUBBER
INDIFFERENT
INDIGESTION
INDIGNANTLY
INDIGNATION
INDIVISIBLE
INDIVISIBLY
INDOMITABLE
INDUBITABLE
INDUBITABLY
INDULGENTLY
INDUSTRIOUS
INEBRIATION
INEFFECTIVE
INEFFECTUAL
INEFFICIENT
INELUCTABLE
INEQUITABLE
INESCAPABLE
INESSENTIAL
INESTIMABLE
INEXCITABLE
INEXCUSABLE
INEXCUSABLY
INEXPEDIENT
INEXPENSIVE
INFANGTHIEF
INFANTICIDE
INFANTRYMAN
INFATUATION
INFERIORITY
INFERTILITY
INFESTATION
INFILTRATOR
INFLAMMABLE
INFLUENTIAL
INFORMALITY
INFORMATICS
INFORMATION
INFORMATIVE
INFREQUENCY
INFURIATING
INGENIOUSLY
INGRATITUDE
INGREDIENTS
INHABITABLE
INHABITANTS
INHERITANCE
INJUDICIOUS
INNUMERABLE
INOCULATION
INOFFENSIVE
INOPERATIVE
INOPPORTUNE
INQUIRINGLY
INQUISITION
INQUISITIVE
INSCRIPTION
INSCRUTABLE
INSECTICIDE
INSECTIVORE
INSENSITIVE
INSEPARABLE
INSIDIOUSLY
INSINCERITY
INSINUATING
INSINUATION
INSISTENTLY
INSOUCIANCE
INSPIRATION
INSTABILITY
INSTALLMENT
INSTANTIATE
INSTIGATION
INSTINCTIVE
INSTITUTION
INSTRUCTION
INSTRUCTIVE
INSTRUMENTS
INSULTINGLY
INSUPERABLE
INTEGRATION
INTELLIGENT
INTEMPERATE
INTENSIVELY
INTENTIONAL
INTERACTION
INTERACTIVE
INTERCALARY
INTERCEPTOR
INTERCHANGE
INTERCOSTAL
INTERCOURSE
INTERESTING
INTERGLOSSA
INTERGROWTH
INTERLACING
INTERLEUKIN
INTERLINGUA
INTERMINGLE
INTERNECINE
INTERNUNCIO
INTERPOLATE
INTERPRETER
INTERREGNUM
INTERRELATE
INTERROGATE
INTERRUPTER
INTERSPERSE
INTERVENING
INTERVIEWEE
INTERVIEWER
INTOLERABLE
INTOLERABLY
INTOLERANCE
INTOXICATED
INTOXIMETER
INTRACTABLE
INTRAVENOUS
INTREPIDITY
INTRICATELY
INTROVERTED
INTUITIVELY
INVESTIGATE
INVESTITURE
INVIGILATOR
INVINCIBLES
INVOLUNTARY
INVOLVEMENT
ONEIRODYNIA
ONEIROMANCY
ONOMASTICON
ONTOLOGICAL
SNICKERSNEE
SNORKELLING
UNALTERABLE
UNAMBIGUOUS
UNANIMOUSLY
UNANNOUNCED
UNASSERTIVE
UNAUTHENTIC
UNAVAILABLE
UNAVOIDABLE
UNAVOIDABLY
UNBEFITTING
UNBLEMISHED
UNBREAKABLE
UNCASTRATED
UNCERTAINTY
UNCHRISTIAN
UNCIVILISED
UNCIVILIZED
UNCLEANNESS
UNCLUTTERED
UNCOMMITTED
UNCONCEALED
UNCONCERNED
UNCONFIRMED
UNCONNECTED
UNCONQUERED
UNCONSCIOUS
UNCONTESTED
UNCONVERTED
UNCONVINCED
UNCOUTHNESS
UNCRUSHABLE
UNDEMANDING
UNDERCHARGE
UNDERCOOKED
UNDERGROUND
UNDERGROWTH
UNDERHANDED
UNDERMANNED
UNDERSIGNED
UNDERSTATED
UNDERTAKING
UNDERVALUED
UNDERWEIGHT
UNDERWRITER
UNDESERVING
UNDESIRABLE
UNDEVELOPED
UNDIGNIFIED
UNDISCLOSED
UNDISGUISED
UNDISTURBED
UNDOUBTEDLY
UNDRINKABLE
UNEMOTIONAL
UNENDURABLE
UNENVELOPED
UNEQUIVOCAL
UNEXPLAINED
UNEXPRESSED
UNFAILINGLY
UNFAVORABLE
UNFLAPPABLE
UNFLINCHING
UNFORTUNATE
UNFULFILLED
UNFURNISHED
UNGETATABLE
UNGODLINESS
UNHAPPINESS
UNIFICATION
UNIMPORTANT
UNIMPRESSED
UNINHABITED
UNINHIBITED
UNINITIATED
UNIVERSALLY
UNJUSTIFIED
UNMITIGATED
UNMOTIVATED
UNNATURALLY
UNNECESSARY
UNOBSERVANT
UNOBTRUSIVE
UNPALATABLE
UNPATRIOTIC
UNPERTURBED
UNPRACTICAL
UNPRINTABLE
UNPROTECTED
UNPUBLISHED
UNQUALIFIED
UNREALISTIC
UNREASONING
UNREHEARSED
UNRELENTING
UNREMITTING
UNREPENTANT
UNRIGHTEOUS
UNSATISFIED
UNSATURATED
UNSCHEDULED
UNSHAKEABLE
UNSHELTERED
UNSHRINKING
UNSOLICITED
UNSPEAKABLE
UNSPECIFIED
UNSTOPPABLE
UNSUPPORTED
UNSURPASSED
UNSUSPECTED
UNSWEETENED
UNTHINKABLE
UNTOUCHABLE
UNTRAMELLED
UNUTTERABLE
UNVARNISHED
UNWARRANTED
UNWELCOMING
UNWHOLESOME
UNWITTINGLY
BODHISATTVA
BOMBARDMENT
BOOKBINDING
BOOKKEEPING
BOOKSELLERS
BORBORYGMUS
BOTANOMANCY
BOURGEOISIE
BOUTONNIERE
BOYSENBERRY
COACHFELLOW
COAGULATION
COALESCENCE
COBBLESTONE

COCKLESHELL
COEFFICIENT
COENOBITISM
COEXISTENCE
COGNOSCENTE
COGNOSCENTI
COHORTATIVE
COINCIDENCE
COLDBLOODED
COLEORRHIZA
COLLABORATE
COLLAPSIBLE
COLLECTANEA
COLLENCHYMA
COLLOCATION
COLONIALISM
COLONIALIST
COLOURBLIND
COLUMBARIUM
COMBINATION
COMBUSTIBLE
COMESTIBLES
COMEUPPANCE
COMFORTABLE
COMFORTABLY
COMFORTLESS
COMMANDMENT
COMMEMORATE
COMMENDABLE
COMMENDABLY
COMMENTATOR
COMMINATION
COMMISERATE
COMMONPLACE
COMMONSENSE
COMMUNICANT
COMMUNICATE
COMMUTATION
COMPARATIVE
COMPARTMENT
COMPENDIOUS
COMPETENTLY
COMPETITION
COMPETITIVE
COMPILATION
COMPILEMENT
COMPLACENCY
COMPLAISANT
COMPLICATED
COMPLIMENTS
COMPOSITION
COMPOTATION
COMPRIMARIO
COMPTROLLER
COMPUNCTION
COMPUTATION
COMPUTERIZE
COMRADESHIP
COMSTOCKERY
CONCEALMENT
CONCEIVABLE
CONCEIVABLY
CONCENTRATE
CONCEPTICLE
CONCILIATOR
CONCISENESS
CONCOMITANT
CONCORDANCE
CONCURRENCE
CONDITIONAL
CONDITIONER
CONDOLENCES
CONDOMINIUM
CONDOTTIERE
CONDOTTIORE
CONDUCTRESS
CONFABULATE
CONFARREATE
CONFEDERACY
CONFEDERATE
CONFIDENTLY
CONFINEMENT
CONFUTATION
CONGRESSMAN
CONJECTURAL
CONJUGATION
CONJUNCTION
CONJUNCTURE
CONNECTICUT
CONNOISSEUR
CONNOTATION
CONSCIOUSLY
CONSECUTIVE
CONSEQUENCE
CONSERVANCY
CONSIDERATE
CONSIDERING
CONSIGNMENT
CONSILIENCE
CONSISTENCE
CONSISTENCY
CONSOLATION
CONSOLIDATE
CONSPICUOUS
CONSPIRATOR
CONSTANTINE
CONSTELLATE
CONSTERNATE
CONSTIPATED
CONSTITUENT
CONSTRAINED
CONSTRICTED
CONSTRICTOR
CONSTRUCTOR
CONSTUPRATE
CONSULTANCY
CONSUMABLES
CONSUMERISM
CONSUMPTION
CONSUMPTIVE
CONTAINMENT
CONTAMINANT
CONTAMINATE
CONTEMPLANT
CONTEMPLATE
CONTENEMENT
CONTENTEDLY
CONTENTIOUS
CONTENTMENT
CONTINENTAL
CONTINGENCE
CONTINGENCY
CONTINUALLY
CONTINUANCE
CONTRACTION
CONTRACTUAL
CONTRAPTION
CONTRASTING
CONTRAYERVA
CONTRETEMPS
CONTRIBUTOR
CONTRIVANCE
CONTROVERSY
CONTUBERNAL
CONURBATION
CONVALLARIA
CONVENIENCE
CONVENTICLE
CONVERGENCE
CONVERTIBLE
CONVOCATION
CONVOLUTION
CONVOLVULUS
CONVULSIONS
COOPERATION
COOPERATIVE
COORDINATED
COORDINATES
COPPERPLATE
COPROPHAGAN
COPROSTEROL
CORDWAINERS
CORINTHIANS
CORNERSTONE
CORPORATION
CORRECTNESS
CORRELATION
CORROBORATE
CORRUGATION
CORRUPTIBLE
COTTONMOUTH
COULOMMIERS
COUNSELLING
COUNTENANCE
COUNTERFEIT
COUNTERFOIL
COUNTERFORT
COUNTERGLOW
COUNTERHAND
COUNTERMAND
COUNTERPANE
COUNTERPART
COUNTERSIGN
COUNTERSINK
COUNTRIFIED
COUNTRYSIDE
COURTEOUSLY
COURTLINESS
COXWAINLESS
DOCTRINAIRE
DOCUMENTARY
DODECASTYLE
DOLABRIFORM
DOMESTICATE
DOMESTICITY
DOMINEERING
DOUBLECHECK
DOUBLECROSS
DOUROUCOULI
DOWNHEARTED
DOWNTRODDEN
EOANTHROPUS
FOMENTATION
FOOLISHNESS
FOOTBALLING
FOOTWASHING
FORAMINIFER
FORBEARANCE
FORBIDDANCE
FORECASTING
FORECLOSURE
FOREFATHERS
FORESEEABLE
FORESHORTEN
FORESTATION
FORETHOUGHT
FOREWARNING
FORFOUGHTEN
FORGIVENESS
FORLORNNESS
FORMULATION
FORNICATION
FORTHCOMING
FORTNIGHTLY
FORTUNATELY
FORTUNELOUD
FOTHERGILLA
FOULMOUTHED
FOUNDATIONS
GODDAUGHTER
GODFORSAKEN
GONFALONIER
GOODLOOKING
GOODNATURED
GORDONSTOUN
HOBBLEDEHOY
HOGGISHNESS
HOHENLINDEN
HOLLANDAISE
HOLOTHURIAN
HOMEOPATHIC
HOMOEOPATHY
HOMOGENEITY
HOMOGENEOUS
HOMOGENIZED
HOMOTHERMAL
HOMOTHERMIC
HONEYCOMBED
HONEYMOONER
HONEYSUCKLE
HOOLIGANISM
HOOTANANNIE
HOOTENANNIE
HORNSWOGGLE
HORSERACING
HORSERADISH
HORSERIDING
HOSPITALITY
HOSPITALIZE
HOSPITALLER
HOSTILITIES
HOUSEHOLDER
HOUSEKEEPER
HOUSEMASTER
JOSEPHINITE
KOMMERSBUCH
KOTABOTHRON
LOCORESTIVE
LOGARITHMIC
LOGGERHEADS
LOGODAEDALY
LOGOGRAPHER
LONGANIMITY
LONGAWAITED
LONGINQUITY
LONGLASTING
LONGRUNNING
LONGSIGHTED
LONGSLEEVED
LOUDSPEAKER
LOUISIANIAN
MOCKINGBIRD
MODELMOLEST
MODERNISTIC
MOISTURIZER
MOLESTATION
MOLLYCODDLE
MOMENTARILY
MONARCHICAL
MONCHIQUITE
MONEYLENDER
MONEYMAKING
MONOCHINOUS
MONOGRAMMED
MONONGAHELA
MONOPSONIST
MONOTHELITE
MONOTREMATA
MONSTROSITY
MONTESQUIEU

MONTGOLFIER
MONTMORENCY
MOONLIGHTER
MORGENSTERN
MOSSTROOPER
MOUNTAINEER
MOUNTAINOUS
MOXIBUSTION
MOZAMBIQUAN
NOISELESSLY
NOMENCLATOR
NONCHALANCE
NONDESCRIPT
NONETHELESS
NONEXISTENT
NONFEASANCE
NONSENSICAL
NORTHCLIFFE
NOSTRADAMUS
NOTHINGNESS
NOTICEBOARD
NOTORIOUSLY
NOTOTHERIUM
NOURISHMENT
NOVELETTISH
POCOCURANTE
PODSNAPPERY
POINTLESSLY
POLICEWOMAN
POLIORCETIC
POLITICALLY
POLITICIANS
POLLENBRUSH
POLLINATION
POLTERGEIST
POLYMORPHIC
POLYSTYRENE
POLYTECHNIC
POLYTRICHUM
POMEGRANATE
POMPELMOOSE
POMPELMOUSE
PONDEROUSLY
PONTIFICATE
PORNOGRAPHY
PORTERHOUSE
PORTLANDIAN
PORTMANTEAU
PORTRAITIST
PORTRAITURE
POSSESSIONS
POSSIBILITY
POTAMOGETON
POTENTIALLY
ROBESPIERRE
ROCKEFELLER
RODOMONTADE
ROGUISHNESS
ROMANTICISM
ROMANTICIZE

ROSICRUCIAN
ROTTENSTONE
SOCIABILITY
SOCIOLOGIST
SOCKDALAGER
SOCKDOLAGER
SOCKDOLIGER
SOCKDOLOGER
SOLILOQUIZE
SOLIPSISTIC
SOROPTIMIST
SORROWFULLY
SOUNDLESSLY
SOUTHAMPTON
SOUTHWESTER
SOVEREIGNTY
TOASTMASTER
TOBACCONIST
TOBOGGANING
TONSILLITIS
TOPLOFTICAL
TOPOGRAPHER
TORRIDONIAN
TORTICOLLIS
TORTICULLUS
TOSTICATION
TOTALIZATOR
TOURBILLION
TOWNSPEOPLE
TOXOPHILITE
VOLCANOLOGY
VOLKSKAMMER
VOLUNTARILY
VOORTREKKER
VORACIOUSLY
VOTERIGGING
WOMANLINESS
WONDERFULLY
WOODCARVING
WORKMANLIKE
WORKMANSHIP
WORKSTATION
WORLDFAMOUS
WORLDLINESS
WORRYTROUGH
ZOROASTRIAN
APATOSAURUS
APHANIPTERA
APHRODISIAC
APLANOSPORE
APOCALYPTIC
APODYTERIUM
APOLLINARIS
APOLLONICON
APOMORPHINE
APONEUROSIS
APOPHYLLITE
APOSIOPESIS
APOSTROPHUS
APPALLINGLY

APPARATCHIK
APPEARANCES
APPEASEMENT
APPELLATION
APPELLATIVE
APPLICATION
APPOINTMENT
APPRECIABLE
APPRECIABLY
APPRENTICED
APPROACHING
APPROBATION
APPROPRIATE
APPROVINGLY
APPROXIMATE
APPURTENANT
EPAMINONDAS
EPANALEPSIS
EPICHEIREMA
EPIDIASCOPE
EPIGENESIST
EPINEPHRINE
EPITHYMETIC
EPOCHMAKING
IPECACUANHA
OPALESCENCE
OPERATIONAL
OPINIONATED
OPPIGNORATE
OPPORTUNELY
OPPORTUNISM
OPPORTUNIST
OPPORTUNITY
OPPROBRIOUS
OPTOMETRIST
SPACESAVING
SPANGCOCKLE
SPARROWHAWK
SPATTERDASH
SPATTERDOCK
SPECIALIZED
SPECTACULAR
SPECULATION
SPECULATIVE
SPEECHCRAFT
SPEEDOMETER
SPELLBINDER
SPENDTHRIFT
SPERMATOZOA
SPERMICIDAL
SPERMOPHILE
SPESSARTITE
SPHRAGISTIC
SPIFFLICATE
SPIRITUALLY
SPIROCHAETE
SPITSTICKER
SPLUTTERING
SPOKESWOMAN
SPONDULICKS

SPONDYLITIS
SPONSORSHIP
SPONTANEITY
SPONTANEOUS
SPORTSFIELD
SPORTSWOMAN
SPREADSHEET
SPRINGBOARD
SPRINGCLEAN
SPRINGHOUSE
SPRINGINESS
UPHOLSTERER
UPRIGHTNESS
EQUIDISTANT
EQUILATERAL
EQUILIBRIST
EQUILIBRIUM
EQUINOCTIAL
EQUIPOLLENT
EQUIVALENCE
EQUIVOCALLY
ARBITRAGEUR
ARBITRAMENT
ARBITRARILY
ARBITRATION
ARCHAEOLOGY
ARCHEGONIAL
ARCHEGONIUM
ARCHENTERON
ARCHILOCHUS
ARCHIPELAGO
ARGATHELIAN
ARGENTINIAN
ARISTOCRACY
ARQUEBUSIER
ARRANGEMENT
ARRHENOTOKY
ARRIVEDERCI
ARTHRAPODAL
ARTHRODESIS
ARTHROSPORE
ARTICULATED
ARTILLERIST
ARTIODACTYL
BRAGGADOCIO
BRANDENBURG
BRAZZAVILLE
BREADCRUMBS
BREADWINNER
BREASTPLATE
BREATHALYSE
BRILLIANTLY
BRISTLECONE
BRITTLENESS
BROADCASTER
BROADMINDED
BROBDINGNAG
BROTHERHOOD
BRUCELLOSIS
CRACKERJACK

CRACKHALTER
CRACOVIENNE
CRATERELLUS
CREDENTIALS
CREDIBILITY
CREDULOUSLY
CRÉMAILLÈRE
CREMATORIUM
CRENELLATED
CREPITATION
CREPUSCULAR
CRESCENTADE
CRESTFALLEN
CRIMINOLOGY
CRITHOMANCY
CRITICASTER
CROCIDOLITE
CROMWELLIAN
CROOKEDNESS
CROSSLEGGED
CRUCIFIXION
CRYSTALLINE
CRYSTALLISE
CRYSTALLIZE
DRACUNCULUS
DRAGGLETAIL
DRAGONNADES
DRASTICALLY
DRAUGHTSMAN
DREADLOCKED
DREADNOUGHT
DRESSMAKING
DRINKDRIVER
DRUNKENNESS
DRYCLEANERS
DRYCLEANING
ERADICATION
EREMACAUSIS
ERIODENDRON
ERRATICALLY
ERRONEOUSLY
ERYMANTHIAN
ERYTHROCYTE
FRAGMENTARY
FRANKFURTER
FRANKLINITE
FRANTICALLY
FRATERNALLY
FRAUDULENCE
FREEMASONRY
FREETHINKER
FRENCHWOMAN
FRENCHWOMEN
FRIGHTENING
FRIGHTFULLY
FRIVOLOUSLY
FRONTRUNNER
FROSTBITTEN
FRUITLESSLY
FRUSTRATING

FRUSTRATION
GRALLATORES
GRAMMALOGUE
GRAMMATICAL
GRANDFATHER
GRANDMASTER
GRANDMOTHER
GRAPHICALLY
GRASSHOPPER
GRAVEDIGGER
GRAVITATION
GREASEPAINT
GREENBOTTLE
GREENGROCER
GREENOCKITE
GREGARINIDA
GRENZGANGER
GROUNDSHEET
GROUNDSPEED
GROUNDSWELL
IRIDESCENCE
IRONMONGERS
IRONMONGERY
IRRADIATION
IRREDENTIST
IRREDUCIBLE
IRREFUTABLE
IRREGULARLY
IRRELEVANCE
IRRELIGIOUS
IRREPARABLE
IRREPARABLY
IRREVERENCE
IRREVOCABLE
KRIEGSSPIEL
ORCHESTRATE
ORCHESTRINA
ORCHESTRION
ORDERLINESS
ORGANICALLY
ORGANIZAION
ORIENTALIST
ORIENTATION
ORIGINALITY
ORIGINATING
ORIGINATION
ORNITHOLOGY
ORNITHOPTER
ORTHOCENTRE
ORTHOGRAPHY
ORTHOPAEDIC
PRACTICABLE
PRACTICALLY
PRECAUTIONS
PRECIPITATE
PRECIPITOUS
PRECONCEIVE
PREDECESSOR
PREDESTINED
PREDICAMENT
PREDICATIVE
PREDICTABLE
PREDICTABLY
PREDOMINANT
PREDOMINATE
PREEMINENCE
PREHISTORIC
PREJUDICIAL
PRELIBATION
PRELIMINARY
PREMATURELY
PREMEDITATE
PREMIERSHIP
PREMONITION
PREMONITORY
PREOCCUPIED
PREPARATION
PREPARATORY
PREPOLLENCE
PREPOSITION
PREROGATIVE
PRESENTABLE
PRESSURIZED
PRESTIGIOUS
PRESTISSIMO
PRESTONPANS
PRESTRESSED
PRESUMPTION
PRESUMPTIVE
PRETENSIONS
PRETENTIOUS
PRETERITION
PREVARICATE
PREVENTABLE
PRICKLINESS
PRIMIGENIAL
PRINCIPALLY
PRISCIANIST
PRIZEWINNER
PROBABILITY
PROBATIONER
PROCEEDINGS
PROCREATION
PROCRUSTEAN
PROCUREMENT
PRODIGALISE
PRODIGALITY
PROFESSEDLY
PROFICIENCY
PROFITEROLE
PROFUSENESS
PROGENITRIX
PROGNATHOUS
PROGRESSION
PROGRESSIVE
PROHIBITION
PROHIBITIVE
PROLEGOMENA
PROLETARIAN
PROLETARIAT
PROLIFERATE
PROLOCUTION
PROMINENTLY
PROMISCUITY
PROMISCUOUS
PROMOTIONAL
PROMPTITUDE
PROOFREADER
PROPAGATION
PROPHETICAL
PROPHYLAXIS
PROPINQUITY
PROPOSITION
PROPRIETARY
PROROGATION
PROSAICALLY
PROSECUTION
PROSELYTISM
PROSELYTIZE
PROSPECTIVE
PROSTHETICS
PROSTRATION
PROTAGONIST
PROTOCOCCUS
PROTONOTARY
PROTRACTING
PROTRACTION
PROTUBERANT
PROVISIONAL
PROVISIONER
PROVOCATION
PROVOCATIVE
PRZEWALSKIS
TRACASSERIE
TRACHEOTOMY
TRACKLEMENT
TRADITIONAL
TRAFFICATOR
TRAGELAPHUS
TRANQUILITY
TRANSACTION
TRANSCEIVER
TRANSFERRED
TRANSFERRIN
TRANSFIGURE
TRANSFORMED
TRANSFORMER
TRANSFUSION
TRANSILIENT
TRANSLATION
TRANSLUCENT
TRANSMITTED
TRANSMITTER
TRANSPARENT
TRANSPONDER
TRANSPORTED
TRANSPORTER
TRANSURANIC
TREACHEROUS
TREACHETOUR
TREASONABLE
TREECREEPER
TRENCHERMAN
TREPIDATION
TREPONEMATA
TRESPASSING
TRIBULATION
TRICERATOPS
TRICHINELLA
TRICHINOSED
TRICHOPTERA
TRIMESTRIAL
TRINCOMALEE
TRINIDADIAN
TRINITARIAN
TRINOBANTES
TRIPTOLEMUS
TRITAGONIST
TRIUMVIRATE
TROMPELOEIL
TROPHOBLAST
TROPOSPHERE
TROUBLESOME
TROUBLESPOT
TRUCULENTLY
TRUSTEESHIP
TRUSTWORTHY
TRYPANOSOMA
TRYPANOSOME
WRONGHEADED
ASCLEPIADES
ASPERGILLUM
ASPERGILLUS
ASPERSORIUM
ASPHETERISM
ASSASSINATE
ASSEMBLYMAN
ASSIDUOUSLY
ASSIGNATION
ASSIMILATED
ASSOCIATION
ASSYTHEMENT
ASTIGMATISM
ASTONISHING
ASTRINGENCY
ESCARMOUCHE
ESCHATOLOGY
ESCHERICHIA
ESPIEGLERIE
ESSENTIALLY
ESTABLISHED
ESTABLISHER
ESTRAMAZONE
ESTRANGHELO
ISOELECTRIC
ISOXSUPRINE
ISTIOPHORUS
OSCILLATION
OSTENTATION
OSTEOPATHIC
OSTEOPLASTY
OSTRACODERM
OSTREOPHAGE
PSEUDOLOGIA
PSEUDOMORPH
PSITTACOSIS
PSYCHEDELIC
PSYCHIATRIC
PSYCHODELIC
TSCHERNOSEM
USELESSNESS
ATHARVAVEDA
ATHERINIDAE
ATHERMANOUS
ATMOSPHERIC
ATRABILIOUS
ATROCIOUSLY
ATTENTIVELY
ATTENUATION
ATTESTATION
ATTRIBUTION
ATTRIBUTIVE
ETHNOGRAPHY
ETHNOLOGIST
ETYMOLOGIST
ITHYPHALLIC
ITHYPHALLUS
PTERODACTYL
PTOCHOCRACY
STADTHOLDER
STAGFLATION
STAIRCARPET
STAKEHOLDER
STALLHOLDER
STANDARDIZE
STANDOFFISH
STANDPATTER
STATELINESS
STATISTICAL
STEADFASTLY
STEAMROLLER
STEEPLEJACK
STEGANOGRAM
STEGANOPODE
STEINBERGER
STELLIONATE
STENOCHROME
STENOGRAPHY
STEPBROTHER
STEREOMETER
STEREOSCOPE
STEREOTYPED
STETHOSCOPE
STICKLEBACK
STIMULATION
STIPENDIARY
STIPULATION
STOCKBROKER
STOCKHAUSEN
STOCKHOLDER

STOCKJOBBER
STOCKTAKING
STOOLPIGEON
STOREKEEPER
STORYTELLER
STRADUARIUS
STRAITLACED
STRAMINEOUS
STRANDLOPER
STRANGENESS
STRANGEWAYS
STRANGULATE
STRAPHANGER
STRATEGICAL
STREAMLINED
STREETLIGHT
STRENUOUSLY
STRETCHABLE
STRETCHLESS
STRIKEBOUND
STRINGENTLY
STRINGYBARK
STROBOSCOPE
STRONGYLOID
STROPHILLUS
STRUTHIONES
STYLISHNESS
STYLIZATION
STYLOPODIUM
STYMPHALIAN
UTILITARIAN
UTILIZATION
UTRICULARIA
AUDACIOUSLY
AUDIOVISUAL
AUGUSTINIAN
AURIGNACIAN
AUXANOMETER
BULLFIGHTER
BUMBERSHOOT
BUPRESTIDAE
BUREAUCRACY
BURGOMASTER
BUSHWHACKER
BUSINESSMAN
CULMINATION
CULPABILITY
CULTIVATION
CULVERINEER
CURNAPTIOUS
CURTAILMENT
CUSTOMARILY
DUBIOUSNESS
DUMBFOUNDED
DUNIEWASSAL
DUPLICATING
DUPLICATION
DUSTWRAPPER
EUCALYPTOLE
EUCHARISTIC
EUPHEMISTIC
EURHYTHMICS
FULFILLMENT
FULLBLOODED
FULMINATION
FUNAMBULIST
FUNCTIONARY
FUNCTIONING
FUNDAMENTAL
FUNDRAISING
FURNISHINGS
FURTHERANCE
FURTHERMORE
FURTHERMOST
FURTHERSOME
FURTIVENESS
FUSTILARIAN
GUADALCANAL
GUBERNATION
GUESSTIMATE
GULLIBILITY
GUTTERSNIPE
GUTTURALISE
HUCKLEBERRY
HUCKSTERAGE
HUMGRUFFIAN
HUMILIATING
HUMILIATION
HUMMINGBIRD
HUNDREDFOLD
HURTLEBERRY
HUSBANDLAND
JUDICIOUSLY
JUSTIFIABLE
JUSTIFIABLY
KULTURKREIS
LUBRICATION
LUMINESCENT
LUXEMBURGER
LUXULYANITE
LUXURIANTLY
LUXURIOUSLY
MUDSLINGING
MULTIRACIAL
MULTISTOREY
MUNCHHAUSEN
MUNIFICENCE
MURMURATION
MUSCHELKALK
MUSKELLUNGE
NUMBERPLATE
NUMERICALLY
NUMISMATICS
NUMISMATIST
NUTCRACKERS
NUTRITIONAL
OUAGADOUGOU
OUTDISTANCE
OUTMANEUVER
OUTPOURINGS
OUTSTANDING
PUBLICATION
PUBLISHABLE
PULCHRITUDE
PUNCHINELLO
PUNCTILIOUS
PUNCTUALITY
PUNCTUATION
PURITANICAL
PURPOSELESS
PURPRESTURE
QUADRENNIAL
QUADRENNIUM
QUADRUPLETS
QUALITATIVE
QUARRELLING
QUARRELSOME
QUARRINGTON
QUARTERBACK
QUARTERDECK
QUERULOUSLY
QUESTIONING
QUICKSILVER
QUINTUPLETS
RUDESHEIMER
RUDIMENTARY
RUMBUSTIOUS
RUMFRUCTION
RUMGUMPTION
SUBCONTRACT
SUBDIVISION
SUBDOMINANT
SUBITANEOUS
SUBJUGATION
SUBJUNCTIVE
SUBLIMATION
SUBMERGENCE
SUBMULTIPLE
SUBORDINATE
SUBPANATION
SUBSERVIENT
SUBSISTENCE
SUBSTANDARD
SUBSTANTIAL
SUBSTANTIVE
SUBTRACTION
SUBTROPICAL
SUBUNGULATA
SUCCEDANEUM
SUDETENLAND
SUFFICIENCY
SUFFOCATING
SUFFOCATION
SUFFRAGETTE
SUGARCOATED
SUGGESTIBLE
SUITABILITY
SUMMERHOUSE
SUMPTUOUSLY
SUNDRENCHED
SUPERALTERN
SUPERCHARGE
SUPERCHERIE
SUPERFICIAL
SUPERFICIES
SUPERFLUITY
SUPERFLUOUS
SUPERIMPOSE
SUPERINTEND
SUPERIORITY
SUPERLATIVE
SUPERMARKET
SUPERSCRIBE
SUPERSEDEAS
SUPERSEDERE
SUPERTANKER
SUPERVISION
SUPERVISORY
SUPPEDANEUM
SUPPOSITION
SUPPOSITORY
SUPPRESSION
SUPPURATION
SURROUNDING
SURTARBRAND
SURTURBRAND
SURVEILLANT
SUSCEPTIBLE
SUSTAINABLE
SUSURRATION
TURBELLARIA
TURRICULATE
VULCANOLOGY
AVERRUNCATE
AVOIRDUPOIS
EVANGELICAL
EVAPORATION
EVASIVENESS
EVENTRATION
EVENTUALITY
EVERLASTING
EVISCERATED
OVERBALANCE
OVERBEARING
OVERCROWDED
OVEREXPOSED
OVERFISHING
OVERFLOWING
OVERHANGING
OVERLAPPING
OVERLEARNED
OVERMANNING
OVERPAYMENT
OVERSTUFFED
OVERTURNING
OVERWEENING
OVERWHELMED
OVERWROUGHT
OVERZEALOUS
SVARABHAKTI
AWKWARDNESS
KWASHIORKOR
SWALLOWABLE
SWITCHBOARD
SWITZERLAND
SWORDSWOMAN
TWELVEMONTH
ZWISCHENZUG
AXEROPHTHOL
EXAGGERATED
EXAMINATION
EXANTHEMATA
EXASPERATED
EXCEEDINGLY
EXCEPTIONAL
EXCESSIVELY
EXCLAMATION
EXCLUSIVELY
EXCRESCENCE
EXECUTIONER
EXHILARATED
EXHORTATION
EXONERATION
EXORBITANCE
EXOSKELETON
EXPECTANTLY
EXPECTATION
EXPECTORANT
EXPECTORATE
EXPEDITIOUS
EXPENDITURE
EXPERIENCED
EXPLANATION
EXPLANATORY
EXPLORATION
EXPLORATORY
EXPONENTIAL
EXPOSTULATE
EXPROPRIATE
EXPURGATION
EXQUISITELY
EXTEMPORISE
EXTEMPORIZE
EXTENSIVELY
EXTENUATING
EXTENUATION
EXTERMINATE
EXTORTIONER
EXTRADITION
EXTRAPOLATE
EXTRAVAGANT
EXTROGENOUS
EXTROVERTED
OXODIZATION
OXYRHYNCHUS
CYBERNETICS
CYCLOSTYLED
CYLINDRICAL
CYMOPHANOUS
DYAESTHESIA

DYSFUNCTION
DYSLOGISTIC
EYECATCHING
GYNAECOLOGY
HYDROCARBON
HYDROMEDUSA
HYDROPHIDAE
HYDROPHOBIA
HYDROPHOBIC
HYDROPONICS
HYDROSTATIC
HYMNOLOGIST
HYOPLASTRON
HYPERMARKET
HYPERTROPHY
HYPHENATION
HYPOCORISMA
HYPOTENSION
HYPOTHECATE
HYPOTHERMIA
LYCANTHROPE
LYCANTHROPY
LYCHNOSCOPE
MYCOLOGICAL
MYCOPHAGIST
MYXOMATOSIS
NYMPHOMANIA
PYTHONESQUE
SYCOPHANTIC
SYMMETRICAL
SYMPATHETIC
SYMPATHISER
SYMPATHIZER
SYMPLEGADES
SYMPOSIARCH
SYMPTOMATIC
SYNCHROMESH
SYNCHRONISE
SYNCHRONISM
SYNCHRONIZE
SYNCOPATION
SYNDICALISM
SYNDICATION
SYNTHESIZED
SYNTHESIZER
SYSTEMATIZE
TYPESETTING
TYPEWRITTEN
TYPOGRAPHER
TYPOGRAPHIC
TYROGLYPHID
TYRONENSIAN
XYLOGRAPHER
AZOTOBACTER

11:3

ABANDONMENT
ACADEMICIAN
ACATALECTIC
ANACHRONISM
ANACOLUTHIA
ANACREONTIC
ANADIPLOSIS
ANAESTHESIA
ANAESTHETIC
ANAGNORISIS
ANAPHYLAXIS
ANAPLEROSIS
ANAPLEROTIC
ANASTOMOSIS
ANAXIMANDER
APATOSAURUS
BEACHCOMBER
BEASTLINESS
BEAUMONTAGE
BEAUTIFULLY
BLACKFELLOW
BLACKMAILER
BLADDERWORT
BLAMEWORTHY
BLANKURSINE
BLASPHEMOUS
BRAGGADOCIO
BRANDENBURG
BRAZZAVILLE
CEASELESSLY
CHAIRPERSON
CHALLENGING
CHAMBERLAIN
CHAMBERMAID
CHANCELLERY
CHANTARELLE
CHANTERELLE
CHANTICLEER
CHARACINOID
CHARGEPAYER
CHARISMATIC
CHARLEMAGNE
CHAULMOOGRA
CHAULMOUGRA
CLADOSPORUM
CLAIRSCHACH
CLAIRVOYANT
CLANDESTINE
CLANJAMFRAY
CLAPPERCLAW
CLARENCIEUX
COACHFELLOW
COAGULATION
COALESCENCE
CRACKERJACK
CRACKHALTER
CRACOVIENNE
CRATERELLUS
DIAGNOSTICS
DIAMONDBACK
DIAPHORESIS
DIAPHORETIC
DIARTHROSIS
DIASCORDIUM
DIATESSARON
DIATESSERON
DRACUNCULUS
DRAGGLETAIL
DRAGONNADES
DRASTICALLY
DRAUGHTSMAN
DYAESTHESIA
EGALITARIAN
EJACULATION
ELABORATELY
ELABORATION
ELASTOPLAST
ENARTHROSIS
EOANTHROPUS
EPAMINONDAS
EPANALEPSIS
ERADICATION
EVANGELICAL
EVAPORATION
EVASIVENESS
EXAGGERATED
EXAMINATION
EXANTHEMATA
EXASPERATED
FEASIBILITY
FEATURELESS
FLABBERGAST
FLAMBOYANCE
FLAMBOYANTE
FLANNELETTE
FLAVOURSOME
FRAGMENTARY
FRANKFURTER
FRANKLINITE
FRANTICALLY
FRATERNALLY
FRAUDULENCE
GHASTLINESS
GLADWELLISE
GLASTONBURY
GNATHONICAL
GRALLATORES
GRAMMALOGUE
GRAMMATICAL
GRANDFATHER
GRANDMASTER
GRANDMOTHER
GRAPHICALLY
GRASSHOPPER
GRAVEDIGGER
GRAVITATION
GUADALCANAL
HEALTHINESS
HEARTBROKEN
HEARTLESSLY
HEAVYHANDED
HEAVYWEIGHT
IMAGINATION
IMAGINATIVE
INADVERTENT
INADVISABLE
INALIENABLE
INATTENTION
INATTENTIVE
INAUTHENTIC
KWASHIORKOR
LEADSWINGER
LEASEHOLDER
LEATHERBACK
LEATHERETTE
LEATHERHEAD
LEATHERNECK
MEADOWSWEET
MEANDERINGS
MEANINGLESS
MEASURELESS
MEASUREMENT
NEANDERTHAL
NEARSIGHTED
OPALESCENCE
OUAGADOUGOU
PEACEKEEPER
PHALANSTERY
PHARISAICAL
PHARYNGITIS
PLAGIARISED
PLAGIOSTOMI
PLANETARIUM
PLANTAGENET
PLANTIGRADE
PLATERESQUE
PLATYRRHINE
PLAYFULNESS
PRACTICABLE
PRACTICALLY
QUADRENNIAL
QUADRENNIUM
QUADRUPLETS
QUALITATIVE
QUARRELLING
QUARRELSOME
QUARRINGTON
QUARTERBACK
QUARTERDECK
REACTIONARY
READABILITY
REALIGNMENT
REALIZATION
REALPOLITIK
REANIMATION
REAPPRAISAL
REASSURANCE
RHABDOMANCY
RHAPSODICAL
SCAFFOLDING
SCALPRIFORM
SCANDALIZED
SCANDANAVIA
SCANDINAVIA
SCARABAEOID
SCARBOROUGH
SCAREMONGER
SCATTERGOOD
SCATTERLING
SEARCHLIGHT
SEASICKNESS
SHAFTESBURY
SHAKESPEARE
SHALLOWNESS
SHAMELESSLY
SHAPELINESS
SHAREHOLDER
SMALLHOLDER
SPACESAVING
SPANGCOCKLE
SPARROWHAWK
SPATTERDASH
SPATTERDOCK
STADTHOLDER
STAGFLATION
STAIRCARPET
STAKEHOLDER
STALLHOLDER
STANDARDIZE
STANDOFFISH
STANDPATTER
STATELINESS
STATISTICAL
SVARABHAKTI
SWALLOWABLE
TEASPOONFUL
THALIDOMIDE
THALLOPHYTE
THANATOPSIS
THANKLESSLY
THAUMATROPE
TOASTMASTER
TRACASSERIE
TRACHEOTOMY
TRACKLEMENT
TRADITIONAL
TRAFFICATOR
TRAGELAPHUS
TRANQUILITY
TRANSACTION
TRANSCEIVER
TRANSFERRED
TRANSFERRIN
TRANSFIGURE
TRANSFORMED
TRANSFORMER
TRANSFUSION
TRANSILIENT
TRANSLATION
TRANSLUCENT
TRANSMITTED
TRANSMITTER
TRANSPARENT

TRANSPONDER
TRANSPORTED
TRANSPORTER
TRANSURANIC
UNALTERABLE
UNAMBIGUOUS
UNANIMOUSLY
UNANNOUNCED
UNASSERTIVE
UNAUTHENTIC
UNAVAILABLE
UNAVOIDABLE
UNAVOIDABLY
WEATHERCOCK
ABBREVIATED
ALBIGENSIAN
ALBUGINEOUS
AMBIVALENCE
ARBITRAGEUR
ARBITRAMENT
ARBITRARILY
ARBITRATION
BIBLIOPHILE
CABBALISTIC
COBBLESTONE
CYBERNETICS
DEBILITATED
DUBIOUSNESS
EMBARKATION
EMBARRASSED
EMBELLISHED
EMBOÎTEMENT
EMBROCATION
FABRICATION
GABERLUNZIE
GIBBERELLIN
GUBERNATION
HABERDASHER
HABILIMENTS
HEBDOMADARY
HIBERNATING
HIBERNATION
HOBBLEDEHOY
JABBERWOCKY
LABORIOUSLY
LABORSAVING
LIBERTARIAN
LUBRICATION
PUBLICATION
PUBLISHABLE
RABELAISIAN
REBARBATIVE
RIBONUCLEIC
ROBESPIERRE
SABBATARIAN
SUBCONTRACT
SUBDIVISION
SUBDOMINANT
SUBITANEOUS
SUBJUGATION

SUBJUNCTIVE
SUBLIMATION
SUBMERGENCE
SUBMULTIPLE
SUBORDINATE
SUBPANATION
SUBSERVIENT
SUBSISTENCE
SUBSTANDARD
SUBSTANTIAL
SUBSTANTIVE
SUBTRACTION
SUBTROPICAL
SUBUNGULATA
TABERNACLES
TOBACCONIST
TOBOGGANING
UNBEFITTING
UNBLEMISHED
UNBREAKABLE
ACCELERATOR
ACCESSORIES
ACCIPITRINE
ACCLAMATION
ACCLIMATION
ACCLIMATISE
ACCLIMATIZE
ACCOMMODATE
ACCOMPANIST
ACCORDINGLY
ACCOUNTABLE
ACCOUNTANCY
ACCRESCENCE
ACCUMULATOR
ALCYONARIAN
ARCHAEOLOGY
ARCHEGONIAL
ARCHEGONIUM
ARCHENTERON
ARCHILOCHUS
ARCHIPELAGO
ASCLEPIADES
BACCHANALIA
BACKBENCHER
BACKFIELDER
BACKPACKING
BACKSLIDING
BICARBONATE
BICENTENARY
CACOGASTRIC
CACOPHONOUS
COCKLESHELL
CYCLOSTYLED
DACTYLOGRAM
DECAPITATED
DECARBONIZE
DECEITFULLY
DECEPTIVELY
DECLAMATION
DECLAMATORY

DECLARATION
DECONSTRUCT
DECORATIONS
DECORTICATE
DECREPITATE
DECREPITUDE
DICEPHALOUS
DICOTYLEDON
DICTATORIAL
DOCTRINAIRE
DOCUMENTARY
ECCALEOBION
ENCAPSULATE
ENCEPHALOMA
ENCHANTMENT
ENCHANTRESS
ENCHIRIDION
ENCHONDROMA
ENCOURAGING
ENCROACHING
ENCUMBRANCE
ESCARMOUCHE
ESCHATOLOGY
ESCHERICHIA
EUCALYPTOLE
EUCHARISTIC
EXCEEDINGLY
EXCEPTIONAL
EXCESSIVELY
EXCLAMATION
EXCLUSIVELY
EXCRESCENCE
FACETIOUSLY
FACTFINDING
HECKELPHONE
HUCKLEBERRY
HUCKSTERAGE
INCALESCENT
INCANTATION
INCAPSULATE
INCARCERATE
INCARNADINE
INCARNATION
INCESSANTLY
INCINERATOR
INCLINATION
INCOHERENCE
INCOMPETENT
INCOMPOSITE
INCONGRUITY
INCONGRUOUS
INCONSTANCY
INCONTINENT
INCORPORATE
INCORPOREAL
INCORRECTLY
INCREDULITY
INCREDULOUS
INCREMENTAL
INCRIMINATE

JACQUEMINOT
JACTITATION
LACONICALLY
LECTURESHIP
LICKSPITTLE
LOCORESTIVE
LYCANTHROPE
LYCANTHROPY
LYCHNOSCOPE
MACADAMIZED
MACERANDUBA
MACHAIRODUS
MACHINATION
MACROBIOTIC
MECKLENBURG
MICHURINISM
MICROGAMETE
MICROSCOPIC
MICTURITION
MOCKINGBIRD
MYCOLOGICAL
MYCOPHAGIST
NECESSARILY
NECESSITATE
NECESSITOUS
NECROMANCER
NICKELODEON
NICKNACKERY
ORCHESTRATE
ORCHESTRINA
ORCHESTRION
OSCILLATION
PACIFICALLY
PECULIARITY
PICKELHAUBE
PICKYOUROWN
PICTURESQUE
POCOCURANTE
RECANTATION
RECEPTIVITY
RECESSIONAL
RECIPROCATE
RECIPROCITY
RECLAMATION
RECOGNITION
RECONDITION
RECONNOITER
RECONNOITRE
RECONSTRUCT
RECOVERABLE
RECRIMINATE
RECRUITMENT
RECTANGULAR
RECTIFIABLE
RECTILINEAR
RECURRENTLY
ROCKEFELLER
SACHERTORTE
SACRAMENTAL
SACRIFICIAL

SECONDARILY
SECONDCLASS
SECRETARIAL
SECRETARIAT
SECRETIVELY
SOCIABILITY
SOCIOLOGIST
SOCKDALAGER
SOCKDOLAGER
SOCKDOLIGER
SOCKDOLOGER
SUCCEDANEUM
SYCOPHANTIC
TACHYCARDIA
TACHYGRAPHY
TACITURNITY
TECHNICALLY
TECTIBRANCH
TICKTACKTOE
TSCHERNOSEM
UNCASTRATED
UNCERTAINTY
UNCHRISTIAN
UNCIVILISED
UNCIVILIZED
UNCLEANNESS
UNCLUTTERED
UNCOMMITTED
UNCONCEALED
UNCONCERNED
UNCONFIRMED
UNCONNECTED
UNCONQUERED
UNCONSCIOUS
UNCONTESTED
UNCONVERTED
UNCONVINCED
UNCOUTHNESS
UNCRUSHABLE
VACCINATION
VACILLATING
VACILLATION
VACUOUSNESS
VICARIOUSLY
VICHYSOISSE
VICIOUSNESS
VICISSITUDE
ANDROGENOUS
AUDACIOUSLY
AUDIOVISUAL
BADDELEYITE
BADTEMPERED
BODHISATTVA
DODECASTYLE
ENDOCARDIUM
ENDORSEMENT
ENDOTHERMIC
FIDDLEDEDEE
GODDAUGHTER
GODFORSAKEN

HIDEOUSNESS
HYDROCARBON
HYDROMEDUSA
HYDROPHIDAE
HYDROPHOBIA
HYDROPHOBIC
HYDROPONICS
HYDROSTATIC
INDEFINABLE
INDENTATION
INDEPENDENT
INDEXLINKED
INDIARUBBER
INDIFFERENT
INDIGESTION
INDIGNANTLY
INDIGNATION
INDIVISIBLE
INDIVISIBLY
INDOMITABLE
INDUBITABLE
INDUBITABLY
INDULGENTLY
INDUSTRIOUS
JUDICIOUSLY
KIDDLEYWINK
MEDIASTINUM
MEDICINALLY
MEDIUMSIZED
MIDDENSTEAD
MIDDLEMARCH
MIDDLESIZED
MODELMOLEST
MODERNISTIC
MUDSLINGING
ORDERLINESS
PEDAGOGICAL
PEDESTRIANS
PEDETENTOUS
PODSNAPPERY
RADIOACTIVE
RADIOCARBON
RADIOGRAPHY
RADIOLOGIST
REDOUBTABLE
REDUPLICATE
RIDDLEMEREE
RODOMONTADE
RUDESHEIMER
RUDIMENTARY
SADDLEHORSE
SEDIMENTARY
SUDETENLAND
TEDIOUSNESS
TIDDLEYWINK
UNDEMANDING
UNDERCHARGE
UNDERCOOKED
UNDERGROUND
UNDERGROWTH
UNDERHANDED
UNDERMANNED
UNDERSIGNED
UNDERSTATED
UNDERTAKING
UNDERVALUED
UNDERWEIGHT
UNDERWRITER
UNDESERVING
UNDESIRABLE
UNDEVELOPED
UNDIGNIFIED
UNDISCLOSED
UNDISGUISED
UNDISTURBED
UNDOUBTEDLY
UNDRINKABLE
VIDEOCAMERA
WIDERANGING
ABECEDARIAN
ALEXANDRINE
ALEXANDRITE
AMELANCHIER
AMERCIAMENT
AMERICANISM
ANENCEPHALY
ANESTHETIST
ANESTHETIZE
AVERRUNCATE
AXEROPHTHOL
BIELORUSSIA
BLESSEDNESS
BREADCRUMBS
BREADWINNER
BREASTPLATE
BREATHALYSE
CHEERLEADER
CHEESECLOTH
CHEIROGNOMY
CLEANLINESS
CLEANSHAVEN
COEFFICIENT
COENOBITISM
COEXISTENCE
CREDENTIALS
CREDIBILITY
CREDULOUSLY
CREMATORIUM
CRENELLATED
CREPITATION
CREPUSCULAR
CRESCENTADE
CRESTFALLEN
DEERSTALKER
DREADLOCKED
DREADNOUGHT
DRESSMAKING
ELECTRICIAN
ELECTRICITY
ELECTROCUTE
ELECTROLIER
ELECTROLYTE
ELECTRONICS
ELECTROTINT
ELEPHANTINE
ELEUTHERIAN
EREMACAUSIS
EVENTRATION
EVENTUALITY
EVERLASTING
EXECUTIONER
EYECATCHING
FIELDWORKER
FLEXIBILITY
FREEMASONRY
FREETHINKER
FRENCHWOMAN
FRENCHWOMEN
GREASEPAINT
GREENBOTTLE
GREENGROCER
GREENOCKITE
GREGARINIDA
GRENZGANGER
GUESSTIMATE
HAEMOGLOBIN
HAEMOPHILIA
HAEMORRHAGE
HAEMORRHOID
IDENTICALLY
IDENTIFYING
IDEOLOGICAL
IDEOPRAXIST
INEBRIATION
INEFFECTIVE
INEFFECTUAL
INEFFICIENT
INELUCTABLE
INEQUITABLE
INESCAPABLE
INESSENTIAL
INESTIMABLE
INEXCITABLE
INEXCUSABLE
INEXCUSABLY
INEXPEDIENT
INEXPENSIVE
IPECACUANHA
KLEPTOMANIA
NEEDLEPOINT
NEEDLESTICK
NEEDLEWOMAN
NIERSTEINER
ONEIRODYNIA
ONEIROMANCY
OPERATIONAL
OVERBALANCE
OVERBEARING
OVERCROWDED
OVEREXPOSED
OVERFISHING
OVERFLOWING
OVERHANGING
OVERLAPPING
OVERLEARNED
OVERMANNING
OVERPAYMENT
OVERSTUFFED
OVERTURNING
OVERWEENING
OVERWHELMED
OVERWROUGHT
OVERZEALOUS
PAEDIATRICS
PAEDOTROPHY
PEEVISHNESS
PIEDMONTITE
PIERREPOINT
PLEASURABLE
PLEBEIANISE
PLEISTOCENE
PRECAUTIONS
PRECIPITATE
PRECIPITOUS
PRECONCEIVE
PREDECESSOR
PREDESTINED
PREDICAMENT
PREDICATIVE
PREDICTABLE
PREDICTABLY
PREDOMINANT
PREDOMINATE
PREEMINENCE
PREHISTORIC
PREJUDICIAL
PRELIBATION
PRELIMINARY
PREMATURELY
PREMEDITATE
PREMIERSHIP
PREMONITION
PREMONITORY
PREOCCUPIED
PREPARATION
PREPARATORY
PREPOLLENCE
PREPOSITION
PREROGATIVE
PRESENTABLE
PRESSURIZED
PRESTIGIOUS
PRESTISSIMO
PRESTONPANS
PRESTRESSED
PRESUMPTION
PRESUMPTIVE
PRETENSIONS
PRETENTIOUS
PRETERITION
PREVARICATE
PREVENTABLE
PSEUDOLOGIA
PSEUDOMORPH
PTERODACTYL
QUERULOUSLY
QUESTIONING
RHEUMATICKY
SCEPTICALLY
SCEUOPHYLAX
SHEATHKNIFE
SHENANIGANS
SHEPHERDESS
SKEPTICALLY
SKETCHINESS
SLEEPWALKER
SLENDERNESS
SPECIALIZED
SPECTACULAR
SPECULATION
SPECULATIVE
SPEECHCRAFT
SPEEDOMETER
SPELLBINDER
SPENDTHRIFT
SPERMATOZOA
SPERMICIDAL
SPERMOPHILE
SPESSARTITE
STEADFASTLY
STEAMROLLER
STEEPLEJACK
STEGANOGRAM
STEGANOPODE
STEINBERGER
STELLIONATE
STENOCHROME
STENOGRAPHY
STEPBROTHER
STEREOMETER
STEREOSCOPE
STEREOTYPED
STETHOSCOPE
TEENYBOPPER
TEETOTALLER
THEATERGOER
THEATREGOER
THEATRICALS
THENCEFORTH
THEOBROMINE
THEOLOGICAL
THEOPNEUSTY
THEORETICAL
THERAPEUTAE
THERAPEUTIC
THEREABOUTS
THERMOMETER
THERMOPYLAE
THESMOTHETE
TREACHEROUS

TREACHETOUR
TREASONABLE
TREECREEPER
TRENCHERMAN
TREPIDATION
TREPONEMATA
TRESPASSING
TWELVEMONTH
UNEMOTIONAL
UNENDURABLE
UNENVELOPED
UNEQUIVOCAL
UNEXPLAINED
UNEXPRESSED
USELESSNESS
WHEELBARROW
WHEELWRIGHT
WHEREABOUTS
WHEREWITHAL
WIENERWURST
CRÉMAILLÈRE
AFFECTATION
AFFILIATION
AFFIRMATION
AFFIRMATIVE
AFFLIICTION
ANFRACTUOUS
BIFURCATION
DEFENCELESS
DEFENSELESS
DEFENSIVELY
DEFERENTIAL
DEFOLIATION
DEFORMATION
DIFFERENTLY
DIFFIDENTLY
DIFFRACTION
EFFECTIVELY
EFFECTUALLY
EFFICACIOUS
EFFICIENTLY
ENFEOFFMENT
ENFORCEABLE
ENFORCEMENT
ENFOULDERED
ENFRANCHISE
INFANGTHIEF
INFANTICIDE
INFANTRYMAN
INFATUATION
INFERIORITY
INFERTILITY
INFESTATION
INFILTRATOR
INFLAMMABLE
INFLUENTIAL
INFORMALITY
INFORMATICS
INFORMATION
INFORMATIVE
INFREQUENCY
INFURIATING
LEFTLUGGAGE
OFFENSIVELY
OFFHANDEDLY
OFFICIALDOM
OFFICIALESE
OFFICIOUSLY
RAFFISHNESS
REFLEXOLOGY
REFOCILLATE
REFORMATION
REFORMATORY
REFRESHMENT
REFRIGERANT
REFRIGERATE
REFURBISHED
RIFACIMENTO
SUFFICIENCY
SUFFOCATING
SUFFOCATION
SUFFRAGETTE
UNFAILINGLY
UNFAVORABLE
UNFLAPPABLE
UNFLINCHING
UNFORTUNATE
UNFULFILLED
UNFURNISHED
AFGHANISTAN
AGGLOMERATE
AGGLUTINANT
AGGLUTINATE
AGGRAVATING
AGGRAVATION
AGGREGATION
AIGUILLETTE
ANGELOLATRY
ARGATHELIAN
ARGENTINIAN
AUGUSTINIAN
COGNOSCENTE
COGNOSCENTI
DEGLUTINATE
DEGLUTITION
DEGRADATION
DEGRINGOLER
ENGHALSKRUG
ENGINEERING
GEGENSCHEIN
GIGGLESTICK
GIGGLESWICK
GIGGLEWATER
HAGIOGRAPHY
HIGHLIGHTER
HIGHPITCHED
HIGHPOWERED
HIGHPROFILE
HIGHQUALITY
HIGHRANKING
HOGGISHNESS
INGENIOUSLY
INGRATITUDE
INGREDIENTS
LEGERDEMAIN
LEGIONNAIRE
LEGISLATION
LEGISLATIVE
LEGISLATURE
LIGHTHEADED
LIGHTWEIGHT
LOGARITHMIC
LOGGERHEADS
LOGODAEDALY
LOGOGRAPHER
MAGISTERIAL
MAGISTRATES
MAGLEMOSIAN
MAGNANIMITY
MAGNANIMOUS
MAGNIFICENT
MEGALOMANIA
MEGALOMANIC
MEGALOPOLIS
MEGATHERIUM
NEGOTIATING
NEGOTIATION
NIGHTINGALE
NIGHTMARISH
ORGANICALLY
ORGANIZAION
REGIMENTALS
REGISTERING
REGRETFULLY
REGRETTABLE
REGRETTABLY
REGURGITATE
RIGHTANGLED
RIGHTEOUSLY
RIGHTHANDED
RIGHTHANDER
RIGHTWINGER
ROGUISHNESS
SAGACIOUSLY
SAGITTARIUS
SEGREGATION
SIGHTSCREEN
SIGHTSEEING
SIGNIFICANT
SUGARCOATED
SUGGESTIBLE
TAGLIATELLE
TEGUCICALPA
TIGGYWINKLE
TIGHTFISTED
TIGHTLIPPED
UNGETATABLE
UNGODLINESS
ACHIEVEMENT
APHANIPTERA
APHRODISIAC
ATHARVAVEDA
ATHERINIDAE
ATHERMANOUS
BEHAVIOURAL
COHORTATIVE
DEHORTATIVE
DEHYDRATION
ENHANCEMENT
ETHNOGRAPHY
ETHNOLOGIST
EXHILARATED
EXHORTATION
FEHMGERICHT
HOHENLINDEN
ICHTHYOLITE
ICHTHYORNIS
INHABITABLE
INHABITANTS
INHERITANCE
ITHYPHALLIC
ITHYPHALLUS
OCHLOCRATIC
SCHECKLATON
SCHISTOSOMA
SCHISTOSOME
SCHOLARSHIP
SCHOTTISCHE
SCHRECKLICH
SCHWARMEREI
SPHRAGISTIC
TCHAIKOVSKY
UNHAPPINESS
UPHOLSTERER
ABIOGENETIC
ACINACIFORM
ALIFANFARON
AMINOBUTENE
ANISOCERCAL
ARISTOCRACY
BRILLIANTLY
BRISTLECONE
BRITTLENESS
CHIAROSCURO
CHIASTOLITE
CHICHEVACHE
CHICKENFEED
CHILDMINDER
CHILLINGHAM
CHINOISERIE
CHIPPENDALE
CHIROGRAPHY
CHIROPODIST
CHITTERLING
CLIFFHANGER
CLIMACTERIC
CLIMATOLOGY
CLINOCHLORE
CLIOMETRICS
COINCIDENCE
CRIMINOLOGY
CRITHOMANCY
CRITICASTER
DEIFICATION
DRINKDRIVER
EDIFICATION
ELIGIBILITY
ELIMINATION
ELIZABETHAN
EPICHEIREMA
EPIDIASCOPE
EPIGENESIST
EPINEPHRINE
EPITHYMETIC
ERIODENDRON
EVISCERATED
FAIRWEATHER
FLICKERTAIL
FLIRTATIOUS
FRIGHTENING
FRIGHTFULLY
FRIVOLOUSLY
GLIMMERGOWK
HAIRDRESSER
HAIRRAISING
IDIOTICALLY
IRIDESCENCE
KRIEGSSPIEL
MAINTENANCE
MAISTERDOME
MOISTURIZER
NEIGHBORING
NEIGHBOURLY
NOISELESSLY
OLIGOCHAETE
OPINIONATED
ORIENTALIST
ORIENTATION
ORIGINALITY
ORIGINATING
ORIGINATION
PAINKILLING
PAINSTAKING
PHILANDERER
PHILATELIST
PHILIPPINES
PHILLIPSITE
PHILOCTETES
PHILOLOGIST
PHILOSOPHER
POINTLESSLY
PRICKLINESS
PRIMIGENIAL
PRINCIPALLY
PRISCIANIST
PRIZEWINNER
PSITTACOSIS
QUICKSILVER
QUINTUPLETS
REICHENBACH

REINCARNATE
REITERATION
SAINTLINESS
SAINTPAULIA
SCIENTOLOGY
SCINTILLATE
SCIREFACIAS
SCITAMINEAE
SEIGNIORAGE
SEISMOGRAPH
SHINPLASTER
SHIPBUILDER
SHIPWRECKED
SHITTIMWOOD
SKIDBLADNIR
SKILLIGALEE
SKILLIGOLEE
SKIMMINGTON
SLIGHTINGLY
SMITHEREENS
SMITHSONIAN
SMITHSONITE
SNICKERSNEE
SPIFFLICATE
SPIRITUALLY
SPIROCHAETE
SPITSTICKER
STICKLEBACK
STIMULATION
STIPENDIARY
STIPULATION
SUITABILITY
SWITCHBOARD
SWITZERLAND
THINGAMAJIG
THINGLINESS
THINGUMAJIG
THISTLEDOWN
TRIBULATION
TRICERATOPS
TRICHINELLA
TRICHINOSED
TRICHOPTERA
TRIMESTRIAL
TRINCOMALEE
TRINIDADIAN
TRINITARIAN
TRINOBANTES
TRIPTOLEMUS
TRITAGONIST
TRIUMVIRATE
UNIFICATION
UNIMPORTANT
UNIMPRESSED
UNINHABITED
UNINHIBITED
UNINITIATED
UNIVERSALLY
UTILITARIAN
UTILIZATION
WAINSCOTING
WEIGHBRIDGE
WHIGMALEERY
WHISKERANDO
WHISTLESTOP
WHITEBOYISM
WHITECHAPEL
WHITECOLLAR
WHITEFRIARS
WHITETHROAT
WHITLEATHER
WHITTINGTON
ZWISCHENZUG
ADJOURNMENT
ADJUDICATOR
ENJAMBEMENT
INJUDICIOUS
OBJECTIVELY
OBJECTIVITY
UNJUSTIFIED
ACKNOWLEDGE
AWKWARDNESS
ENKEPHALINE
MAKEBELIEVE
MEKHITARIST
NIKETHAMIDE
WAKEFULNESS
ABLACTATION
AILUROPHILE
ALLEGORICAL
ALLELOMORPH
ALLEVIATION
APLANOSPORE
BALISTRARIA
BALLBEARING
BELEAGUERED
BELLEROPHON
BELLETTRIST
BELLIGERENT
BELLYTIMBER
BELORUSSIAN
BILIOUSNESS
BILLIONAIRE
BULLFIGHTER
CALCEOLARIA
CALCULATING
CALCULATION
CALEFACIENT
CALENDERING
CALIBRATION
CALIFORNIUM
CALLANETICS
CALLIGRAPHY
CALLISTEMON
CALLITRICHE
CALLOUSNESS
CELEBRATION
CHLOROPHYLL
CILOFIBRATE
COLDBLOODED
COLEORRHIZA
COLLABORATE
COLLAPSIBLE
COLLECTANEA
COLLENCHYMA
COLLOCATION
COLONIALISM
COLONIALIST
COLOURBLIND
COLUMBARIUM
CULMINATION
CULPABILITY
CULTIVATION
CULVERINEER
CYLINDRICAL
DELECTATION
DELETERIOUS
DELICIOUSLY
DELICTATION
DELINEATION
DELINQUENCY
DELITESCENT
DELIVERANCE
DILAPIDATED
DOLABRIFORM
ENLARGEMENT
ENLIGHTENED
FALLIBILITY
FILAMENTOUS
FILLIBUSTER
FULFILLMENT
FULLBLOODED
FULMINATION
GALLIBAGGER
GALLIBEGGAR
GALLIGANTUS
GALLIMAUFRY
GALLOVIDIAN
GALLOWGLASS
GALLYBAGGER
GALLYBEGGAR
GELSEMININE
GILLYFLOWER
GULLIBILITY
HALBSTARKER
HALFBROTHER
HALFHEARTED
HALFHOLIDAY
HALLEFLINTA
HALLUCINATE
HELPFULNESS
HILARIOUSLY
HOLLANDAISE
HOLOTHURIAN
ILLMANNERED
ILLOGICALLY
ILLUMINATED
ILLUSIONARY
ILLUSIONIST
ILLUSTRATOR
ILLUSTRIOUS
ILLYWHACKER
KALASHNIKOV
KILIMANJARO
KILOCALORIE
KULTURKREIS
LILLIPUTIAN
MALADJUSTED
MALAKATOONE
MALAPROPISM
MALEDICTION
MALEFACTION
MALEVOLENCE
MALFEASANCE
MALFUNCTION
MALICIOUSLY
MALPRACTICE
MELANCHOLIA
MELANCHOLIC
MELANOCHROI
MELLIFLUOUS
MELODIOUSLY
MILLIONAIRE
MILQUETOAST
MOLESTATION
MOLLYCODDLE
MULTIRACIAL
MULTISTOREY
OBLITERATED
PALEOGRAPHY
PALEOLITHIC
PALESTINIAN
PELARGONIUM
PELOPONNESE
POLICEWOMAN
POLIORCETIC
POLITICALLY
POLITICIANS
POLLENBRUSH
POLLINATION
POLTERGEIST
POLYMORPHIC
POLYSTYRENE
POLYTECHNIC
POLYTRICHUM
PULCHRITUDE
RALLENTANDO
RELEASEMENT
RELIABILITY
RELIGIOUSLY
RELUCTANTLY
SALACIOUSLY
SALESPERSON
SALPINGITIS
SALTIMBANCO
SALTIMBOCCA
SALVADORIAN
SALVOGUNNER
SELAGINELLA
SELECTIVELY
SELECTIVITY
SELFCONTROL
SELFDEFENCE
SELFEVIDENT
SELFIMPOSED
SELFISHNESS
SELFRESPECT
SELFSERVICE
SILLIMANITE
SILVERSMITH
SOLILOQUIZE
SOLIPSISTIC
SPLUTTERING
TÉLÉFÉRIQUE
TELEGRAPHER
TELEGRAPHIC
TELEKINESIS
TELEPHONIST
TELEPRINTER
VALEDICTION
VALEDICTORY
VALLAMBROSA
VALLISNERIA
VOLCANOLOGY
VOLKSKAMMER
VOLUNTARILY
VULCANOLOGY
WELLADVISED
WELLBEHAVED
WELLDEFINED
WELLDRESSED
WELLFOUNDED
WELLINGTONS
WELLMEANING
WILBERFORCE
WILLINGNESS
XYLOGRAPHER
YELLOWPLUSH
YELLOWSTONE
AMMOPHILOUS
ATMOSPHERIC
BOMBARDMENT
BUMBERSHOOT
CAMALDOLITE
CAMARADERIE
CAMEROONIAN
CAMOUFLAGED
CAMPANOLOGY
CAMPESTRIAN
CAMPHORATED
COMBINATION
COMBUSTIBLE
COMESTIBLES
COMEUPPANCE
COMFORTABLE
COMFORTABLY
COMFORTLESS
COMMANDMENT
COMMEMORATE
COMMENDABLE

COMMENDABLY
COMMENTATOR
COMMINATION
COMMISERATE
COMMONPLACE
COMMONSENSE
COMMUNICANT
COMMUNICATE
COMMUTATION
COMPARATIVE
COMPARTMENT
COMPENDIOUS
COMPETENTLY
COMPETITION
COMPETITIVE
COMPILATION
COMPILEMENT
COMPLACENCY
COMPLAISANT
COMPLICATED
COMPLIMENTS
COMPOSITION
COMPOTATION
COMPRIMARIO
COMPTROLLER
COMPUNCTION
COMPUTATION
COMPUTERIZE
COMRADESHIP
COMSTOCKERY
CYMOPHANOUS
DEMAGOGUERY
DEMARCATION
DEMIBASTION
DEMOGRAPHIC
DEMONOMANIA
DEMONSTRATE
DEMORALIZED
DEMOSTHENES
DEMOSTHENIC
DIMENSIONAL
DOMESTICATE
DOMESTICITY
DOMINEERING
DUMBFOUNDED
EMMENAGOGUE
EMMENTHALER
FAMILIARISE
FAMILIARITY
FAMILIARIZE
FOMENTATION
GAMETOPHYTE
GAMOGENESIS
HAMMERCLOTH
HEMERALOPIA
HEMIANOPSIA
HEMOPHILIAC
HEMORRHOIDS
HOMEOPATHIC
HOMOEOPATHY
HOMOGENEITY
HOMOGENEOUS
HOMOGENIZED
HOMOTHERMAL
HOMOTHERMIC
HUMGRUFFIAN
HUMILIATING
HUMILIATION
HUMMINGBIRD
HYMNOLOGIST
IMMEDIATELY
IMMIGRATION
IMMORTALISE
IMMORTALITY
IMMORTALIZE
JAMAHIRIYAH
KAMELAUKION
KIMERIDGIAN
KOMMERSBUCH
LAMENTATION
LAMMERGEIER
LAMMERGEYER
LAMPLIGHTER
LAMPROPHYRE
LUMINESCENT
MEMORABILIA
MOMENTARILY
NOMENCLATOR
NUMBERPLATE
NUMERICALLY
NUMISMATICS
NUMISMATIST
NYMPHOMANIA
OBMUTESCENT
OMMATOPHORE
PAMPELMOOSE
PAMPELMOUSE
PAMPHLETEER
POMEGRANATE
POMPELMOOSE
POMPELMOUSE
RAMGUNSHOCH
REMEMBRANCE
REMINISCENT
REMONSTRATE
REMORSELESS
ROMANTICISM
ROMANTICIZE
RUMBUSTIOUS
RUMFRUCTION
RUMGUMPTION
SEMPITERNAL
SEMPITERNUM
SUMMERHOUSE
SUMPTUOUSLY
SYMMETRICAL
SYMPATHETIC
SYMPATHISER
SYMPATHIZER
SYMPLEGADES
SYMPOSIARCH
SYMPTOMATIC
TEMPERAMENT
TEMPERATURE
TEMPESTUOUS
TEMPORARILY
TIMBROMANIA
TIMBROPHILY
TIMEKEEPING
TIMESHARING
UNMITIGATED
UNMOTIVATED
WOMANLINESS
ABNORMALITY
AGNOSTICISM
ANNABERGITE
ANNIVERSARY
BANDEIRANTE
BANGLADESHI
BANNOCKBURN
BENEDICTINE
BENEDICTION
BENEFICIARY
BENEFICIATE
BENEVOLENCE
CANDESCENCE
CANDIDATURE
CANDLELIGHT
CANDLESTICK
CANNIBALISM
CANNIBALIZE
CENTENARIAN
CENTERPIECE
CENTREBOARD
CENTREPIECE
CENTRIFUGAL
CENTRIPETAL
CENTUMVIRUS
CENTURIATOR
CINQUECENTO
CONCEALMENT
CONCEIVABLE
CONCEIVABLY
CONCENTRATE
CONCEPTICLE
CONCILIATOR
CONCISENESS
CONCOMITANT
CONCORDANCE
CONCURRENCE
CONDITIONAL
CONDITIONER
CONDOLENCES
CONDOMINIUM
CONDOTTIERE
CONDOTTIORE
CONDUCTRESS
CONFABULATE
CONFARREATE
CONFEDERACY
CONFEDERATE
CONFIDENTLY
CONFINEMENT
CONFUTATION
CONGRESSMAN
CONJECTURAL
CONJUGATION
CONJUNCTION
CONJUNCTURE
CONNECTICUT
CONNOISSEUR
CONNOTATION
CONSCIOUSLY
CONSECUTIVE
CONSEQUENCE
CONSERVANCY
CONSIDERATE
CONSIDERING
CONSIGNMENT
CONSILIENCE
CONSISTENCE
CONSISTENCY
CONSOLATION
CONSOLIDATE
CONSPICUOUS
CONSPIRATOR
CONSTANTINE
CONSTELLATE
CONSTERNATE
CONSTIPATED
CONSTITUENT
CONSTRAINED
CONSTRICTED
CONSTRICTOR
CONSTRUCTOR
CONSTUPRATE
CONSULTANCY
CONSUMABLES
CONSUMERISM
CONSUMPTION
CONSUMPTIVE
CONTAINMENT
CONTAMINANT
CONTAMINATE
CONTEMPLANT
CONTEMPLATE
CONTENEMENT
CONTENTEDLY
CONTENTIOUS
CONTENTMENT
CONTINENTAL
CONTINGENCE
CONTINGENCY
CONTINUALLY
CONTINUANCE
CONTRACTION
CONTRACTUAL
CONTRAPTION
CONTRASTING
CONTRAYERVA
CONTRETEMPS
CONTRIBUTOR
CONTRIVANCE
CONTROVERSY
CONTUBERNAL
CONURBATION
CONVALLARIA
CONVENIENCE
CONVENTICLE
CONVERGENCE
CONVERTIBLE
CONVOCATION
CONVOLUTION
CONVOLVULUS
CONVULSIONS
DANGEROUSLY
DENDRACHATE
DENOMINATOR
DINNYHAUSER
DINNYHAYSER
DUNIEWASSAL
EINSTEINIUM
ENNEAHEDRON
FANATICALLY
FANFARONADE
FINANCIALLY
FINGERPRINT
FINGERSTALL
FUNAMBULIST
FUNCTIONARY
FUNCTIONING
FUNDAMENTAL
FUNDRAISING
GENEALOGIST
GENERALIZED
GENERICALLY
GENETICALLY
GENOUILLÈRE
GENTLEMANLY
GENTLEWOMAN
GENUFLEXION
GENUINENESS
GINGERBREAD
GONFALONIER
GYNAECOLOGY
HANDCRAFTED
HANDICAPPED
HANDICAPPER
HANDWRITING
HANDWRITTEN
HANGGLIDING
HINDERLANDS
HONEYCOMBED
HONEYMOONER
HONEYSUCKLE
HUNDREDFOLD
IGNOMINIOUS
IGNORANTINE
INNUMERABLE
JINRICKSHAW

KINCHINMORT
KINDERSPIEL
KINDHEARTED
KINNIKINICK
LANDSKNECHT
LENGTHENING
LENGTHINESS
LENTIGINOSE
LINDISFARNE
LINGUISTICS
LONGANIMITY
LONGAWAITED
LONGINQUITY
LONGLASTING
LONGRUNNING
LONGSIGHTED
LONGSLEEVED
MANCIPATION
MANEUVERING
MANGALSUTRA
MANIPULATOR
MANTELLETTA
MANTELPIECE
MANTELSHELF
MANUFACTURE
MANUMISSION
MENDELEVIUM
MENDELSSOHN
MENSURATION
MENTHOLATED
MENTONNIÈRE
MINESWEEPER
MINIATURIST
MINIATURIZE
MINISTERIAL
MINISTERING
MINNESINGER
MONARCHICAL
MONCHIQUITE
MONEYLENDER
MONEYMAKING
MONOCHINOUS
MONOGRAMMED
MONONGAHELA
MONOPSONIST
MONOTHELITE
MONOTREMATA
MONSTROSITY
MONTESQUIEU
MONTGOLFIER
MONTMORENCY
MUNCHHAUSEN
MUNIFICENCE
NONCHALANCE
NONDESCRIPT
NONETHELESS
NONEXISTENT
NONFEASANCE
NONSENSICAL
OMNIPOTENCE
OMNIPRESENT
OMNISCIENCE
ORNITHOLOGY
ORNITHOPTER
PANDEMONIUM
PANOMPHAEAN
PANTALETTES
PENETRATING
PENETRATION
PENICILLATE
PENITENTIAL
PENNYFATHER
PENSIONABLE
PENSIVENESS
PENTATHLETE
PENTECONTER
PENTECOSTAL
PENTHESILEA
PENTONVILLE
PENULTIMATE
PINACOTHECA
PINNYWINKLE
PONDEROUSLY
PONTIFICATE
PUNCHINELLO
PUNCTILIOUS
PUNCTUALITY
PUNCTUATION
RANGEFINDER
RENAISSANCE
RINTHEREOUT
SANDERSWOOD
SENNACHERIB
SENSATIONAL
SENSIBILITY
SENSITIVELY
SENSITIVITY
SENTENTIOUS
SENTIMENTAL
SINGAPOREAN
SINGLESTICK
SINGULARITY
SINISTRORSE
SUNDRENCHED
SYNCHROMESH
SYNCHRONISE
SYNCHRONISM
SYNCHRONIZE
SYNCOPATION
SYNDICALISM
SYNDICATION
SYNTHESIZED
SYNTHESIZER
TANGIBILITY
TANTALIZING
TENACIOUSLY
TENDENTIOUS
TENTATIVELY
TENTERHOOKS
TENUOUSNESS
TONSILLITIS
UNNATURALLY
UNNECESSARY
VENDEMIAIRE
VENTILATION
VENTURESOME
VINAIGRETTE
VINBLASTINE
VINCRISTINE
VINDICATION
WENSLEYDALE
WINDBREAKER
WINDCHEATER
WINDLESTRAW
WINDOWFRAME
WINDOWLEDGE
WINDSURFING
WINTERBERRY
WINTERGREEN
WONDERFULLY
XENODOCHIUM
ABOMINATION
ABORTIONIST
ACOLOUTHITE
ADOLESCENCE
ADOPTIANISM
ADOPTIONISM
AGONOTHETES
AGORAPHOBIA
AMONTILLADO
ANONYMOUSLY
APOCALYPTIC
APODYTERIUM
APOLLINARIS
APOLLONICON
APOMORPHINE
APONEUROSIS
APOPHYLLITE
APOSIOPESIS
APOSTROPHUS
AVOIRDUPOIS
AZOTOBACTER
BIOCHEMICAL
BLOCKBUSTER
BLOODSPORTS
BLOODSTREAM
BLOODSUCKER
BOOKBINDING
BOOKKEEPING
BOOKSELLERS
BROADCASTER
BROADMINDED
BROBDINGNAG
BROTHERHOOD
CHOCKABLOCK
CHOIRMASTER
CHOLESTEROL
CHONDROSTEI
CHORDOPHONE
CHOROGRAPHY
COOPERATION
COOPERATIVE
COORDINATED
COORDINATES
CROCIDOLITE
CROMWELLIAN
CROOKEDNESS
CROSSLEGGED
DIORTHORTIC
EGOTISTICAL
EMOTIONALLY
EPOCHMAKING
EXONERATION
EXORBITANCE
EXOSKELETON
FLORILEGIUM
FLOURISHING
FOOLISHNESS
FOOTBALLING
FOOTWASHING
FRONTRUNNER
FROSTBITTEN
GEOMETRICAL
GEOSYNCLINE
GLOSSOLALIA
GOODLOOKING
GOODNATURED
GROUNDSHEET
GROUNDSPEED
GROUNDSWELL
HOOLIGANISM
HOOTANANNIE
HOOTENANNIE
HYOPLASTRON
ICONOGRAPHY
ICONOSTASIS
IDOLIZATION
INOCULATION
INOFFENSIVE
INOPERATIVE
INOPPORTUNE
IRONMONGERS
IRONMONGERY
ISOELECTRIC
ISOXSUPRINE
MOONLIGHTER
ODONTOBLAST
ODONTOPHORE
ONOMASTICON
OXODIZATION
PHONETICIAN
PHONOFIDDLE
PHOTOCOPIER
PHOTOFINISH
PHOTOGRAPHY
PHOTOSPHERE
PLOUGHSHARE
PROBABILITY
PROBATIONER
PROCEEDINGS
PROCREATION
PROCRUSTEAN
PROCUREMENT
PRODIGALISE
PRODIGALITY
PROFESSEDLY
PROFICIENCY
PROFITEROLE
PROFUSENESS
PROGENITRIX
PROGNATHOUS
PROGRESSION
PROGRESSIVE
PROHIBITION
PROHIBITIVE
PROLEGOMENA
PROLETARIAN
PROLETARIAT
PROLIFERATE
PROLOCUTION
PROMINENTLY
PROMISCUITY
PROMISCUOUS
PROMOTIONAL
PROMPTITUDE
PROOFREADER
PROPAGATION
PROPHETICAL
PROPHYLAXIS
PROPINQUITY
PROPOSITION
PROPRIETARY
PROROGATION
PROSAICALLY
PROSECUTION
PROSELYTISM
PROSELYTIZE
PROSPECTIVE
PROSTHETICS
PROSTRATION
PROTAGONIST
PROTOCOCCUS
PROTONOTARY
PROTRACTING
PROTRACTION
PROTUBERANT
PROVISIONAL
PROVISIONER
PROVOCATION
PROVOCATIVE
PTOCHOCRACY
REORIENTATE
RHOPALOCERA
SCOLECIFORM
SCOLOPENDRA
SCOPOLAMINE
SCOUTMASTER
SHOPLIFTING
SHORTCHANGE
SHORTCOMING

SHORTHANDED
SHOVELBOARD
SHOWERPROOF
SHOWJUMPING
SHOWMANSHIP
SMOKESCREEN
SMORGASBORD
SMOULDERING
SNORKELLING
SPOKESWOMAN
SPONDULICKS
SPONDYLITIS
SPONSORSHIP
SPONTANEITY
SPONTANEOUS
SPORTSFIELD
SPORTSWOMAN
STOCKBROKER
STOCKHAUSEN
STOCKHOLDER
STOCKJOBBER
STOCKTAKING
STOOLPIGEON
STOREKEEPER
STORYTELLER
SWORDSWOMAN
THOROUGHPIN
THOUGHTLESS
TROMPELOEIL
TROPHOBLAST
TROPOSPHERE
TROUBLESOME
TROUBLESPOT
ULOTRICHALE
UNOBSERVANT
UNOBTRUSIVE
VIOLINCELLO
VIOLONCELLO
VOORTREKKER
WOODCARVING
WRONGHEADED
ALPHABETIZE
AMPHETAMINE
AMPHIBOLOGY
AMPHISBAENA
AMPHISBOENA
AMPLEXICAUL
APPALLINGLY
APPARATCHIK
APPEARANCES
APPEASEMENT
APPELLATION
APPELLATIVE
APPLICATION
APPOINTMENT
APPRECIABLE
APPRECIABLY
APPRENTICED
APPROACHING
APPROBATION
APPROPRIATE
APPROVINGLY
APPROXIMATE
APPURTENANT
ASPERGILLUM
ASPERGILLUS
ASPERSORIUM
ASPHETERISM
BUPRESTIDAE
CAPACITANCE
CAPACITATOR
CAPERNOITED
CAPERNOITIE
CAPRICCIOSO
CAPTIVATING
CAPTIVATION
COPPERPLATE
COPROPHAGAN
COPROSTEROL
DEPARTEMENT
DEPHLEGMATE
DEPORTATION
DEPREDATION
DEPRIVATION
DIPHYCERCAL
DIPLOMATICS
DIPLOMATIST
DIPROTODONT
DIPSOMANIAC
DIPTEROCARP
DUPLICATING
DUPLICATION
EMPHYTEUSIS
EMPIECEMENT
EMPIRICUTIC
EMPLACEMENT
EMPOWERMENT
EMPTYHANDED
EMPYROMANCY
ESPIEGLERIE
EUPHEMISTIC
EXPECTANTLY
EXPECTATION
EXPECTORANT
EXPECTORATE
EXPEDITIOUS
EXPENDITURE
EXPERIENCED
EXPLANATION
EXPLANATORY
EXPLORATION
EXPLORATORY
EXPONENTIAL
EXPOSTULATE
EXPROPRIATE
EXPURGATION
HAPHAZARDLY
HEPATOSCOPY
HEPPLEWHITE
HIPPOCAMPUS
HIPPOCRATES
HIPPOCRATIC
HYPERMARKET
HYPERTROPHY
HYPHENATION
HYPOCORISMA
HYPOTENSION
HYPOTHECATE
HYPOTHERMIA
IMPARTIALLY
IMPASSIONED
IMPASSIVELY
IMPATIENTLY
IMPEACHMENT
IMPECUNIOUS
IMPEDIMENTA
IMPERIALISM
IMPERIALIST
IMPERIOUSLY
IMPERMANENT
IMPERMEABLE
IMPERSONATE
IMPERTINENT
IMPETUOSITY
IMPETUOUSLY
IMPIGNORATE
IMPLAUSIBLE
IMPLEMENTAL
IMPLICATION
IMPORTANTLY
IMPORTATION
IMPORTUNATE
IMPRACTICAL
IMPRECATION
IMPRECISION
IMPREGNABLE
IMPROPRIETY
IMPROVEMENT
IMPROVIDENT
IMPRUDENTLY
IMPULSIVELY
LAPIDESCENT
LEPIDOPTERA
LEPIDOSIREN
MEPROBAMATE
NAPHTHALENE
NIPFARTHING
OPPIGNORATE
OPPORTUNELY
OPPORTUNISM
OPPORTUNIST
OPPORTUNITY
OPPROBRIOUS
PAPERWEIGHT
RAPSCALLION
RAPTUROUSLY
REPETITIOUS
REPLACEABLE
REPLACEMENT
REPRESENTED
REPROACHFUL
REPUDIATION
SAPONACEOUS
SAPROLEGNIA
SAPROPHYTIC
SEPIOSTAIRE
SEPTENARIUS
SEPTENTRION
SEPTICAEMIA
SUPERALTERN
SUPERCHARGE
SUPERCHERIE
SUPERFICIAL
SUPERFICIES
SUPERFLUITY
SUPERFLUOUS
SUPERIMPOSE
SUPERINTEND
SUPERIORITY
SUPERLATIVE
SUPERMARKET
SUPERSCRIBE
SUPERSEDEAS
SUPERSEDERE
SUPERTANKER
SUPERVISION
SUPERVISORY
SUPPEDANEUM
SUPPOSITION
SUPPOSITORY
SUPPRESSION
SUPPURATION
TOPLOFTICAL
TOPOGRAPHER
TYPESETTING
TYPEWRITTEN
TYPOGRAPHER
TYPOGRAPHIC
UNPALATABLE
UNPATRIOTIC
UNPERTURBED
UNPRACTICAL
UNPRINTABLE
UNPROTECTED
UNPUBLISHED
WAPPENSCHAW
ACQUIESCENT
ACQUISITION
ACQUISITIVE
ARQUEBUSIER
EXQUISITELY
INQUIRINGLY
INQUISITION
INQUISITIVE
LIQUIDAMBAR
LIQUIDATION
MAQUILADORA
REQUIREMENT
REQUISITION
SEQUESTRATE
UNQUALIFIED
ABRACADABRA
ABRIDGEMENT
ACRIFLAVINE
ACRIMONIOUS
AERODYNAMIC
AERONAUTICS
AGRICULTURE
AGROSTOLOGY
AIRCRAFTMAN
AIRSICKNESS
ARRANGEMENT
ARRHENOTOKY
ARRIVEDERCI
ATRABILIOUS
ATROCIOUSLY
AURIGNACIAN
BARBASTELLE
BARBITURATE
BARNSTORMER
BARTHOLOMEW
BARYCENTRIC
BEREAVEMENT
BERGSCHRUND
BIRDWATCHER
BORBORYGMUS
BUREAUCRACY
BURGOMASTER
CARABINIERE
CARAVANNING
CARBORUNDUM
CARBURETTOR
CARDIOGRAPH
CARDOPHAGUS
CAREFULNESS
CARMINATIVE
CARNAPTIOUS
CARNIVOROUS
CAROLINGIAN
CARRIAGEWAY
CARSICKNESS
CARTOGRAPHY
CERARGYRITE
CEREBRATION
CEREMONIOUS
CERTIFIABLE
CERTIFICATE
CHRISTENING
CHRISTMASSY
CHRISTOPHER
CHRONICALLY
CHRONOMETER
CHRYSAROBIN
CHRYSOPRASE
CIRCULARIZE
CIRCULATING
CIRCULATION
CIRCULATORY
CIRCUMCISER
CIRCUMFLECT

CIRCUMSPECT
CIRRHIPEDEA
CIRRHIPEDIA
CORDWAINERS
CORINTHIANS
CORNERSTONE
CORPORATION
CORRECTNESS
CORRELATION
CORROBORATE
CORRUGATION
CORRUPTIBLE
CURNAPTIOUS
CURTAILMENT
DARDANELLES
DERANGEMENT
DERELICTION
DERMATOLOGY
DIRECTIONAL
DIRECTORATE
EARNESTNESS
EARTHENWARE
EARTHSHAKER
ERRATICALLY
ERRONEOUSLY
EURHYTHMICS
FARINACEOUS
FARRAGINOUS
FARREACHING
FARTHERMOST
FARTHINGALE
FERNITICKLE
FEROCIOUSLY
FERRONNIÈRE
FIRELIGHTER
FORAMINIFER
FORBEARANCE
FORBIDDANCE
FORECASTING
FORECLOSURE
FOREFATHERS
FORESEEABLE
FORESHORTEN
FORESTATION
FORETHOUGHT
FOREWARNING
FORFOUGHTEN
FORGIVENESS
FORLORNNESS
FORMULATION
FORNICATION
FORTHCOMING
FORTNIGHTLY
FORTUNATELY
FORTUNELOUD
FURNISHINGS
FURTHERANCE
FURTHERMORE
FURTHERMOST
FURTHERSOME
FURTIVENESS
GARNISHMENT
GARRULOUSLY
GERMINATION
GERONTOLOGY
GERRYMANDER
GIRDLESTEAD
GORDONSTOUN
HARDHITTING
HARDICANUTE
HARDPRESSED
HARDWORKING
HAREBRAINED
HARIOLATION
HARPSICHORD
HERBIVOROUS
HERPETOLOGY
HERRINGBONE
HORNSWOGGLE
HORSERACING
HORSERADISH
HORSERIDING
HURTLEBERRY
IRRADIATION
IRREDENTIST
IRREDUCIBLE
IRREFUTABLE
IRREGULARLY
IRRELEVANCE
IRRELIGIOUS
IRREPARABLE
IRREPARABLY
IRREVERENCE
IRREVOCABLE
JERRYMANDER
KIRKPATRICK
LARYNGISMUS
MARCONIGRAM
MARGINALIST
MARGINALIZE
MARIONBERRY
MARIONETTES
MARIVAUDAGE
MARKETPLACE
MARLBOROUGH
MARSHMALLOW
MERCHANDISE
MERCHANDIZE
MERCHANTMAN
MERCILESSLY
MERITORIOUS
MERRYMAKING
MORGENSTERN
MURMURATION
NARRAGANSET
NERVOUSNESS
NORTHCLIFFE
OARSMANSHIP
PARABLEPSIS
PARABOLANUS
PARACETAMOL
PARACHUTIST
PARACROSTIC
PARADOXICAL
PARALEIPSIS
PARAMASTOID
PARAMEDICAL
PARANEPHROS
PARATROOPER
PARATYPHOID
PARENTHESIS
PARISHIONER
PARLIPOMENA
PARONOMASIA
PARTICIPANT
PARTICIPATE
PARTICIPIAL
PARTNERSHIP
PARTURITION
PARVANIMITY
PERAMBULATE
PERCEFOREST
PERCEPTIBLE
PERCEPTIBLY
PERCHLORATE
PERCIPIENCE
PERCOLATION
PERDUELLION
PEREGRINATE
PERENNIALLY
PERESTROIKA
PERFORATION
PERFORMANCE
PERFUNCTORY
PERICARDIUM
PERIGORDIAN
PERIODONTIC
PERIPATETIC
PERIPHRASIS
PERISSOLOGY
PERISTALITH
PERISTALSIS
PERITONAEUM
PERITONITIS
PERLUSTRATE
PERMANENTLY
PERMISSIBLE
PERMUTATION
PERPETRATOR
PERPETUALLY
PERSECUTION
PERSEVERING
PERSISTENCE
PERSONALIST
PERSONALITY
PERSONALIZE
PERSONIFIED
PERSPECTIVE
PERSPICUITY
PERSPICUOUS
PERTINACITY
PERTINENTLY
PHRASEOLOGY
PORNOGRAPHY
PORTERHOUSE
PORTLANDIAN
PORTMANTEAU
PORTRAITIST
PORTRAITURE
PURITANICAL
PURPOSELESS
PURPRESTURE
SARCENCHYME
SARCOPHAGUS
SCREAMINGLY
SCREWDRIVER
SCRIMSHANDY
SCRIPTORIUM
SCRUFFINESS
SCRUMPTIOUS
SERENDIPITY
SERICULTURE
SERIOUSNESS
SERVICEABLE
SOROPTIMIST
SORROWFULLY
SPREADSHEET
SPRINGBOARD
SPRINGCLEAN
SPRINGHOUSE
SPRINGINESS
STRADUARIUS
STRAITLACED
STRAMINEOUS
STRANDLOPER
STRANGENESS
STRANGEWAYS
STRANGULATE
STRAPHANGER
STRATEGICAL
STREAMLINED
STREETLIGHT
STRENUOUSLY
STRETCHABLE
STRETCHLESS
STRIKEBOUND
STRINGENTLY
STRINGYBARK
STROBOSCOPE
STRONGYLOID
STROPHILLUS
STRUTHIONES
SURROUNDING
SURTARBRAND
SURTURBRAND
SURVEILLANT
TARATANTARA
TARRADIDDLE
TERMINATION
TERMINOLOGY
TERPSICHORE
TERREMOTIVE
TERRESTRIAL
TERRITORIAL
THREATENING
THRIFTINESS
THROGMORTON
TIRONENSIAN
TORRIDONIAN
TORTICOLLIS
TORTICULLUS
TURBELLARIA
TURRICULATE
TYROGLYPHID
TYRONENSIAN
UNREALISTIC
UNREASONING
UNREHEARSED
UNRELENTING
UNREMITTING
UNREPENTANT
UNRIGHTEOUS
UPRIGHTNESS
UTRICULARIA
VARANGARIAN
VARIABILITY
VARIEGATION
VARIOLATION
VARSOVIENNE
VERBIGERATE
VERMICULITE
VERSATILITY
VERTIGINOUS
VORACIOUSLY
WAREHOUSING
WARMHEARTED
WORKMANLIKE
WORKMANSHIP
WORKSTATION
WORLDFAMOUS
WORLDLINESS
WORRYTROUGH
XEROTRIPSIS
ZOROASTRIAN
ABSENTEEISM
ABSTRACTION
AESCULAPIAN
AESCULAPIUS
ASSASSINATE
ASSEMBLYMAN
ASSIDUOUSLY
ASSIGNATION
ASSIMILATED
ASSOCIATION
ASSYTHEMENT
BASHFULNESS
BASKERVILLE
BESIEGEMENT
BESSARABIAN
BESTSELLING

BUSHWHACKER
BUSINESSMAN
CASSITERITE
CASTELLATED
CESAREWITCH
CUSTOMARILY
DESCENDANTS
DESCRIPTION
DESCRIPTIVE
DESECRATION
DESEGREGATE
DESELECTION
DESERPIDINE
DESICCATION
DESIGNATION
DESPERATELY
DESPERATION
DESPONDENCY
DESTABILIZE
DESTINATION
DESTITUTION
DESTRUCTION
DESTRUCTIVE
DISABLEMENT
DISAFFECTED
DISAGREEING
DISAPPROVAL
DISARMAMENT
DISBELIEVER
DISCERNIBLE
DISCERNMENT
DISCIPLINED
DISCOLOURED
DISCONTINUE
DISCOTHEQUE
DISCOURTESY
DISCREPANCY
DISEMBODIED
DISENCUMBER
DISENTANGLE
DISFIGURING
DISGRACEFUL
DISGRUNTLED
DISHEVELLED
DISHONESTLY
DISILLUSION
DISIMPRISON
DISINCLINED
DISJUNCTION
DISLOCATION
DISOBEDIENT
DISORGANIZE
DISORIENTED
DISPARAGING
DISPENSABLE
DISPERSABLE
DISPLEASURE
DISPOSITION
DISPUTATION
DISQUIETING

DISREGARDED
DISSEMINATE
DISSEPIMENT
DISSERTATOR
DISSIMULATE
DISSIPATION
DISSOLUTION
DISTASTEFUL
DISTINCTION
DISTINCTIVE
DISTINGUISH
DISTRACTION
DISTRESSING
DISTRIBUTED
DISTRIBUTOR
DISTRUSTFUL
DISTURBANCE
DUSTWRAPPER
DYSFUNCTION
DYSLOGISTIC
EASTERNMOST
ENSLAVEMENT
ESSENTIALLY
FASCINATING
FASCINATION
FASHIONABLE
FASHIONABLY
FESTINATELY
FESTSCHRIFT
FISHANDCHIP
FISHMONGERS
FUSTILARIAN
GASTRECTOMY
GASTRONOMIC
GESTATORIAL
GESTICULATE
HISTOLOGIST
HISTORIATED
HISTRIONICS
HOSPITALITY
HOSPITALIZE
HOSPITALLER
HOSTILITIES
HUSBANDLAND
INSCRIPTION
INSCRUTABLE
INSECTICIDE
INSECTIVORE
INSENSITIVE
INSEPARABLE
INSIDIOUSLY
INSINCERITY
INSINUATING
INSINUATION
INSISTENTLY
INSOUCIANCE
INSPIRATION
INSTABILITY
INSTALLMENT
INSTANTIATE

INSTIGATION
INSTINCTIVE
INSTITUTION
INSTRUCTION
INSTRUCTIVE
INSTRUMENTS
INSULTINGLY
INSUPERABLE
JOSEPHINITE
JUSTIFIABLE
JUSTIFIABLY
LASERPICIUM
MASCULINITY
MASKALLONGE
MASOCHISTIC
MASQUERADER
MASSIVENESS
MASTERFULLY
MASTERPIECE
MASTICATION
MISALLIANCE
MISANTHROPE
MISANTHROPY
MISBEGOTTEN
MISBEHAVIOR
MISCARRIAGE
MISCHIEVOUS
MISCONSTRUE
MISDEMEANOR
MISERICORDE
MISERLINESS
MISIDENTIFY
MISSISSIPPI
MISSPELLING
MISTRUSTFUL
MOSSTROOPER
MUSCHELKALK
MUSKELLUNGE
NOSTRADAMUS
OBSERVATION
OBSERVATORY
OBSESSIVELY
OBSOLESCENT
OBSTETRICAL
OBSTINATELY
OBSTRICTION
OBSTRUCTION
OBSTRUCTIVE
PASSACAGLIA
PASSIVENESS
PASTEURELLA
PASTOURELLE
PESSIMISTIC
PISCATORIAL
PISSASPHALT
POSSESSIONS
POSSIBILITY
RASTAFARIAN
RESEMBLANCE
RESENTFULLY

RESERVATION
RESIDENTIAL
RESIGNATION
RESISTIVITY
RESOURCEFUL
RESPECTABLE
RESPECTABLY
RESPIRATION
RESPIRATORY
RESPLENDANT
RESPLENDENT
RESPONSIBLE
RESPONSIBLY
RESPONSIONS
RESTATEMENT
RESTITUTION
RESTIVENESS
RESTORATION
RESTORATIVE
RESTRICTION
RESTRICTIVE
RESTRUCTURE
RESUSCITATE
ROSICRUCIAN
SESQUIOXIDE
SUSCEPTIBLE
SUSTAINABLE
SUSURRATION
SYSTEMATIZE
TASTELESSLY
TESSARAGLOT
TESSELLATED
TESTIMONIAL
TOSTICATION
UNSATISFIED
UNSATURATED
UNSCHEDULED
UNSHAKEABLE
UNSHELTERED
UNSHRINKING
UNSOLICITED
UNSPEAKABLE
UNSPECIFIED
UNSTOPPABLE
UNSUPPORTED
UNSURPASSED
UNSUSPECTED
UNSWEETENED
VASOPRESSIN
VESPERTINAL
VISCOUNTESS
WASHERWOMAN
WASHLEATHER
WASTEBASKET
WESTERNMOST
WESTMINSTER
WESTPHALIAN
WISHTONWISH
WISTFULNESS
ACTUALITIES

AFTERSCHOOL
ALTERCATION
ALTERNATELY
ALTERNATING
ALTERNATION
ALTERNATIVE
ANTECEDENCE
ANTECHAMBER
ANTEPENDIUM
ANTHESTERIA
ANTHOCYANIN
ANTHOLOGIZE
ANTHONOMOUS
ANTIBURGHER
ANTICYCLONE
ANTINEUTRON
ANTIPHRASIS
ANTIPYRETIC
ANTIQUARIAN
ANTIRRHINUM
ANTISTHENES
ANTISTROPHE
ANTONOMASIA
ARTHRAPODAL
ARTHRODESIS
ARTHROSPORE
ARTICULATED
ARTILLERIST
ARTIODACTYL
ASTIGMATISM
ASTONISHING
ASTRINGENCY
ATTENTIVELY
ATTENUATION
ATTESTATION
ATTRIBUTION
ATTRIBUTIVE
BATHYSPHERE
BATTLEDRESS
BATTLEFIELD
BATTLEFRONT
BATTLEMENTS
BITTERSWEET
BOTANOMANCY
CATACAUSTIC
CATACHRESIS
CATACLYSMIC
CATALLACTIC
CATASTROPHE
CATCHPHRASE
CATEGORICAL
CATERPILLAR
CATHOLICISM
CITIZENSHIP
CITLALEPETL
COTTONMOUTH
DETERIORATE
DETERMINANT
DETERMINING
DETESTATION

DETRIMENTAL
DITHELETISM
DITTOGRAPHY
ENTABLATURE
ENTABLEMENT
ENTERTAINER
ENTHRALLING
ENTITLEMENT
ESTABLISHED
ESTABLISHER
ESTRAMAZONE
ESTRANGHELO
EXTEMPORISE
EXTEMPORIZE
EXTENSIVELY
EXTENUATING
EXTENUATION
EXTERMINATE
EXTORTIONER
EXTRADITION
EXTRAPOLATE
EXTRAVAGANT
EXTROGENOUS
EXTROVERTED
FATUOUSNESS
FITZWILLIAM
FOTHERGILLA
GATECRASHER
GUTTERSNIPE
GUTTURALISE
HATCHETTITE
HETEROSCIAN
INTEGRATION
INTELLIGENT
INTEMPERATE
INTENSIVELY
INTENTIONAL
INTERACTION
INTERACTIVE
INTERCALARY
INTERCEPTOR
INTERCHANGE
INTERCOSTAL
INTERCOURSE
INTERESTING
INTERGLOSSA
INTERGROWTH
INTERLACING
INTERLEUKIN
INTERLINGUA
INTERMINGLE
INTERNECINE
INTERNUNCIO
INTERPOLATE
INTERPRETER
INTERREGNUM
INTERRELATE
INTERROGATE
INTERRUPTER
INTERSPERSE
INTERVENING
INTERVIEWEE
INTERVIEWER
INTOLERABLE
INTOLERABLY
INTOLERANCE
INTOXICATED
INTOXIMETER
INTRACTABLE
INTRAVENOUS
INTREPIDITY
INTRICATELY
INTROVERTED
INTUITIVELY
ISTIOPHORUS
KATABOTHRON
KATAVOTHRON
KETAVOTHRON
KITCHENETTE
KOTABOTHRON
LATERIGRADE
LATERITIOUS
LATIFUNDIUM
LATROCINIUM
LETTERPRESS
LITERALNESS
LITHOGRAPHY
LITTÉRATEUR
MATERIALISE
MATERIALISM
MATERIALIST
MATERIALIZE
MATHEMATICS
MATRIARCHAL
MATRICULATE
MATRIMONIAL
METACARPALS
METAGENESIS
METALWORKER
METAPHYSICS
METATARSALS
METEOROLOGY
METHODOLOGY
METRICATION
NATIONALISM
NATIONALIST
NATIONALITY
NATIONALIZE
NATIONSTATE
NATURALNESS
NETHERLANDS
NETHERLINGS
NOTHINGNESS
NOTICEBOARD
NOTORIOUSLY
NOTOTHERIUM
NUTCRACKERS
NUTRITIONAL
OBTEMPERATE
OCTASTICHON
ONTOLOGICAL
OPTOMETRIST
ORTHOCENTRE
ORTHOGRAPHY
ORTHOPAEDIC
OSTENTATION
OSTEOPATHIC
OSTEOPLASTY
OSTRACODERM
OSTREOPHAGE
OUTDISTANCE
OUTMANEUVER
OUTPOURINGS
OUTSTANDING
PATERNALISM
PATERNOSTER
PATHOLOGIST
PATRIARCHAL
PATRONISING
PATRONIZING
PETITMAITRE
PETRODOLLAR
PETTICOATED
PETTIFOGGER
PHTHIRIASIS
PITCHBLENDE
POTAMOGETON
POTENTIALLY
PYTHONESQUE
RATATOUILLE
RATIOCINATE
RATIONALITY
RATIONALIZE
RATTLESNAKE
RETALIATION
RETALIATORY
RETARDATION
RETINACULUM
RETINOSPORA
RETRACTABLE
RETRIBUTION
RETRIBUTIVE
RETRIEVABLE
RETROACTIVE
RETROROCKET
ROTTENSTONE
SATIRICALLY
TATTERSALLS
TETRADRACHM
TETRAHEDRON
TITILLATION
TOTALIZATOR
ULTRAMARINE
ULTRAMODERN
ULTRAVIOLET
UNTHINKABLE
UNTOUCHABLE
UNTRAMELLED
VITAMINIZED
VOTERIGGING
WATERCOLOUR
WATERCOURSE
WATEREDDOWN
WATERLOGGED
WATERMEADOW
WATERSKIING
WATERSPLASH
WITCHDOCTOR
WITENAGEMOT
WITHERSHINS
WITHHOLDING
ACUPUNCTURE
ADULLAMITES
ADULTERATED
ADUMBRATION
AGUARDIENTE
BLUNDERBORE
BOURGEOISIE
BOUTONNIERE
BRUCELLOSIS
CAULIFLOWER
CAUSTICALLY
COULOMMIERS
COUNSELLING
COUNTENANCE
COUNTERFEIT
COUNTERFOIL
COUNTERFORT
COUNTERGLOW
COUNTERHAND
COUNTERMAND
COUNTERPANE
COUNTERPART
COUNTERSIGN
COUNTERSINK
COUNTRIFIED
COUNTRYSIDE
COURTEOUSLY
COURTLINESS
CRUCIFIXION
DEUTERONOMY
DEUTSCHMARK
DOUBLECHECK
DOUBLECROSS
DOUROUCOULI
DRUNKENNESS
EDUCATIONAL
ELUCIDATION
ENUMERATION
ENUNCIATION
EQUIDISTANT
EQUILATERAL
EQUILIBRIST
EQUILIBRIUM
EQUINOCTIAL
EQUIPOLLENT
EQUIVALENCE
EQUIVOCALLY
FAULTFINDER
FAULTLESSLY
FAUXBOURDON
FLUCTUATING
FLUCTUATION
FLUORESCENT
FOULMOUTHED
FOUNDATIONS
FRUITLESSLY
FRUSTRATING
FRUSTRATION
HAUGHTINESS
HOUSEHOLDER
HOUSEKEEPER
HOUSEMASTER
LAUNDERETTE
LOUDSPEAKER
LOUISIANIAN
MAURETANIAN
MAURITANIAN
MOUNTAINEER
MOUNTAINOUS
NAUGHTINESS
NEUROLOGIST
NEUTRALISED
NOURISHMENT
RAUCOUSNESS
SAUSAGEMEAT
SCULDUDDERY
SCULDUGGERY
SCULLABOGUE
SCUPPERNONG
SCUTTLEBUTT
SHUNAMITISM
SHUTTLECOCK
SKULDUDDERY
SKULDUGGERY
SLUMBERWEAR
SLUMGULLION
SOUNDLESSLY
SOUTHAMPTON
SOUTHWESTER
TAUROBOLIUM
TAUTOCHRONE
THUNDERBIRD
THUNDERBOLT
THUNDERCLAP
THUNDERHEAD
TOURBILLION
TRUCULENTLY
TRUSTEESHIP
TRUSTWORTHY
UNUTTERABLE
ADVANCEMENT
ADVENTURESS
ADVENTUROUS
ADVERBIALLY
ADVERTISING
DEVALUATION
DEVASTATING
DEVASTATION
DEVELOPMENT

DEVIOUSNESS
DEVITRIFIED
DIVORCEMENT
ENVIRONMENT
FAVOURITISM
INVESTIGATE
INVESTITURE
INVIGILATOR
INVINCIBLES
INVOLUNTARY
INVOLVEMENT
LEVELHEADED
LIVINGSTONE
NEVERENDING
NOVELETTISH
OBVIOUSNESS
RAVISHINGLY
REVALUATION
REVELATIONS
REVENDICATE
REVERBERATE
REVERENTIAL
REVISIONISM
REVOLUTIONS
SAVOURINESS
SEVENTEENTH
SEVERALFOLD
SOVEREIGNTY
UNVARNISHED
VIVACIOUSLY
VIVISECTION
BEWILDERING
DOWNHEARTED
DOWNTRODDEN
LAWBREAKING
LAWLESSNESS
NEWSCASTING
PAWNBROKERS
TOWNSPEOPLE
UNWARRANTED
UNWELCOMING
UNWHOLESOME
UNWITTINGLY
AUXANOMETER
COXWAINLESS
LUXEMBURGER
LUXULYANITE
LUXURIANTLY
LUXURIOUSLY
MOXIBUSTION
MYXOMATOSIS
SAXOPHONIST
SEXOLOGICAL
TAXIDERMIST
TOXOPHILITE
BOYSENBERRY
CRYSTALLINE
CRYSTALLISE
CRYSTALLIZE
DRYCLEANERS
DRYCLEANING
ERYMANTHIAN
ERYTHROCYTE
ETYMOLOGIST
IDYLLICALLY
OXYRHYNCHUS
PHYSIOGNOMY
PSYCHEDELIC
PSYCHIATRIC
PSYCHODELIC
SCYPHISTOMA
STYLISHNESS
STYLIZATION
STYLOPODIUM
STYMPHALIAN
TRYPANOSOMA
TRYPANOSOME
WAYWARDNESS
MOZAMBIQUAN
PRZEWALSKIS
RAZZAMATAZZ

11:4

ABLACTATION
ABRACADABRA
ADVANCEMENT
AGUARDIENTE
ANNABERGITE
APHANIPTERA
APLANOSPORE
APPALLINGLY
APPARATCHIK
ARGATHELIAN
ARRANGEMENT
ASSASSINATE
ATHARVAVEDA
ATRABILIOUS
AUDACIOUSLY
AUXANOMETER
BEHAVIOURAL
BICARBONATE
BOTANOMANCY
BREADCRUMBS
BREADWINNER
BREASTPLATE
BREATHALYSE
BROADCASTER
BROADMINDED
CAMALDOLITE
CAMARADERIE
CAPACITANCE
CAPACITATOR
CARABINIERE
CARAVANNING
CATACAUSTIC
CATACHRESIS
CATACLYSMIC
CATALLACTIC
CATASTROPHE
CERARGYRITE
CESAREWITCH
CHIAROSCURO
CHIASTOLITE
CLEANLINESS
CLEANSHAVEN
DECAPITATED
DECARBONIZE
DEMAGOGUERY
DEMARCATION
DEPARTEMENT
DERANGEMENT
DEVALUATION
DEVASTATING
DEVASTATION
DILAPIDATED
DISABLEMENT
DISAFFECTED
DISAGREEING
DISAPPROVAL
DISARMAMENT
DOLABRIFORM
DREADLOCKED
DREADNOUGHT
ECCALEOBION
EMBARKATION
EMBARRASSED
ENCAPSULATE
ENHANCEMENT
ENJAMBEMENT
ENLARGEMENT
ENTABLATURE
ENTABLEMENT
ERRATICALLY
ESCARMOUCHE
ESTABLISHED
ESTABLISHER
EUCALYPTOLE
FANATICALLY
FILAMENTOUS
FINANCIALLY
FORAMINIFER
FUNAMBULIST
GREASEPAINT
GYNAECOLOGY
HEPATOSCOPY
HILARIOUSLY
IMPARTIALLY
IMPASSIONED
IMPASSIVELY
IMPATIENTLY
INCALESCENT
INCANTATION
INCAPSULATE
INCARCERATE
INCARNADINE
INCARNATION
INFANGTHIEF
INFANTICIDE
INFANTRYMAN
INFATUATION
INHABITABLE
INHABITANTS
IRRADIATION
JAMAHIRIYAH
KALASHNIKOV
KATABOTHRON
KATAVOTHRON
KETAVOTHRON
KOTABOTHRON
LOGARITHMIC
LYCANTHROPE
LYCANTHROPY
MACADAMIZED
MALADJUSTED
MALAKATOONE
MALAPROPISM
MEGALOMANIA
MEGALOMANIC
MEGALOPOLIS
MEGATHERIUM
MELANCHOLIA
MELANCHOLIC
MELANOCHROI
METACARPALS
METAGENESIS
METALWORKER
METAPHYSICS
METATARSALS
MISALLIANCE
MISANTHROPE
MISANTHROPY
MONARCHICAL
MOZAMBIQUAN
OCTASTICHON
OMMATOPHORE
ORGANICALLY
ORGANIZAION
PARABLEPSIS
PARABOLANUS
PARACETAMOL
PARACHUTIST
PARACROSTIC
PARADOXICAL
PARALEIPSIS
PARAMASTOID
PARAMEDICAL
PARANEPHROS
PARATROOPER
PARATYPHOID
PEDAGOGICAL
PELARGONIUM
PERAMBULATE
PHRASEOLOGY
PINACOTHECA
PLEASURABLE
POTAMOGETON
RATATOUILLE
REBARBATIVE
RECANTATION
RENAISSANCE
RETALIATION
RETALIATORY
RETARDATION
REVALUATION
RIFACIMENTO
ROMANTICISM
ROMANTICIZE
SAGACIOUSLY
SALACIOUSLY
SELAGINELLA
SHEATHKNIFE
STEADFASTLY
STEAMROLLER
STRADUARIUS
STRAITLACED
STRAMINEOUS
STRANDLOPER
STRANGENESS
STRANGEWAYS
STRANGULATE
STRAPHANGER
STRATEGICAL
SUGARCOATED
TARATANTARA
TCHAIKOVSKY
TENACIOUSLY
THEATERGOER
THEATREGOER
THEATRICALS
TOBACCONIST
TOTALIZATOR
TREACHEROUS
TREACHETOUR
TREASONABLE
UNCASTRATED
UNFAILINGLY
UNFAVORABLE
UNHAPPINESS
UNNATURALLY
UNPALATABLE
UNPATRIOTIC
UNSATISFIED
UNSATURATED
UNVARNISHED
UNWARRANTED
VARANGARIAN
VICARIOUSLY
VINAIGRETTE
VITAMINIZED
VIVACIOUSLY
VORACIOUSLY
WOMANLINESS
BARBASTELLE
BARBITURATE
BOMBARDMENT
BORBORYGMUS
BROBDINGNAG
BUMBERSHOOT
CABBALISTIC

CARBORUNDUM
CARBURETTOR
COBBLESTONE
COMBINATION
COMBUSTIBLE
DISBELIEVER
DOUBLECHECK
DOUBLECROSS
DUMBFOUNDED
ELABORATELY
ELABORATION
FLABBERGAST
FORBEARANCE
FORBIDDANCE
GIBBERELLIN
HALBSTARKER
HERBIVOROUS
HOBBLEDEHOY
HUSBANDLAND
INEBRIATION
JABBERWOCKY
LAWBREAKING
MISBEGOTTEN
MISBEHAVIOR
NUMBERPLATE
PLEBEIANISE
PROBABILITY
PROBATIONER
RHABDOMANCY
RUMBUSTIOUS
SABBATARIAN
TIMBROMANIA
TIMBROPHILY
TRIBULATION
TURBELLARIA
UNOBSERVANT
UNOBTRUSIVE
VERBIGERATE
VINBLASTINE
WILBERFORCE
ABECEDARIAN
AESCULAPIAN
AESCULAPIUS
AIRCRAFTMAN
ANACHRONISM
ANACOLUTHIA
ANACREONTIC
APOCALYPTIC
BACCHANALIA
BEACHCOMBER
BIOCHEMICAL
BLACKFELLOW
BLACKMAILER
BLOCKBUSTER
BRUCELLOSIS
CALCEOLARIA
CALCULATING
CALCULATION
CATCHPHRASE
CHICHEVACHE
CHICKENFEED
CHOCKABLOCK
CIRCULARIZE
CIRCULATING
CIRCULATION
CIRCULATORY
CIRCUMCISER
CIRCUMFLECT
CIRCUMSPECT
COACHFELLOW
CONCEALMENT
CONCEIVABLE
CONCEIVABLY
CONCENTRATE
CONCEPTICLE
CONCILIATOR
CONCISENESS
CONCOMITANT
CONCORDANCE
CONCURRENCE
CRACKERJACK
CRACKHALTER
CRACOVIENNE
CROCIDOLITE
CRUCIFIXION
DESCENDANTS
DESCRIPTION
DESCRIPTIVE
DISCERNIBLE
DISCERNMENT
DISCIPLINED
DISCOLOURED
DISCONTINUE
DISCOTHEQUE
DISCOURTESY
DISCREPANCY
DRACUNCULUS
DRYCLEANERS
DRYCLEANING
EDUCATIONAL
EJACULATION
ELECTRICIAN
ELECTRICITY
ELECTROCUTE
ELECTROLIER
ELECTROLYTE
ELECTRONICS
ELECTROTINT
ELUCIDATION
EPICHEIREMA
EPOCHMAKING
EXECUTIONER
EYECATCHING
FASCINATING
FASCINATION
FLICKERTAIL
FLUCTUATING
FLUCTUATION
FUNCTIONARY
FUNCTIONING
HATCHETTITE
INOCULATION
INSCRIPTION
INSCRUTABLE
IPECACUANHA
KINCHINMORT
KITCHENETTE
MANCIPATION
MARCONIGRAM
MASCULINITY
MERCHANDISE
MERCHANDIZE
MERCHANTMAN
MERCILESSLY
MISCARRIAGE
MISCHIEVOUS
MISCONSTRUE
MONCHIQUITE
MUNCHHAUSEN
MUSCHELKALK
NONCHALANCE
NUTCRACKERS
PEACEKEEPER
PERCEFOREST
PERCEPTIBLE
PERCEPTIBLY
PERCHLORATE
PERCIPIENCE
PERCOLATION
PISCATORIAL
PITCHBLENDE
PRACTICABLE
PRACTICALLY
PRECAUTIONS
PRECIPITATE
PRECIPITOUS
PRECONCEIVE
PRICKLINESS
PROCEEDINGS
PROCREATION
PROCRUSTEAN
PROCUREMENT
PSYCHEDELIC
PSYCHIATRIC
PSYCHODELIC
PTOCHOCRACY
PULCHRITUDE
PUNCHINELLO
PUNCTILIOUS
PUNCTUALITY
PUNCTUATION
QUICKSILVER
RAUCOUSNESS
REACTIONARY
REICHENBACH
SARCENCHYME
SARCOPHAGUS
SNICKERSNEE
SPACESAVING
SPECIALIZED
SPECTACULAR
SPECULATION
SPECULATIVE
STICKLEBACK
STOCKBROKER
STOCKHAUSEN
STOCKHOLDER
STOCKJOBBER
STOCKTAKING
SUBCONTRACT
SUCCEDANEUM
SUSCEPTIBLE
SYNCHROMESH
SYNCHRONISE
SYNCHRONISM
SYNCHRONIZE
SYNCOPATION
TRACASSERIE
TRACHEOTOMY
TRACKLEMENT
TRICERATOPS
TRICHINELLA
TRICHINOSED
TRICHOPTERA
TRUCULENTLY
UNSCHEDULED
VACCINATION
VINCRISTINE
VISCOUNTESS
VOLCANOLOGY
VULCANOLOGY
WITCHDOCTOR
ACADEMICIAN
ANADIPLOSIS
APODYTERIUM
BADDELEYITE
BANDEIRANTE
BIRDWATCHER
BLADDERWORT
CANDESCENCE
CANDIDATURE
CANDLELIGHT
CANDLESTICK
CARDIOGRAPH
CARDOPHAGUS
CLADOSPORUM
COLDBLOODED
CONDITIONAL
CONDITIONER
CONDOLENCES
CONDOMINIUM
CONDOTTIERE
CONDOTTIORE
CONDUCTRESS
CORDWAINERS
CREDENTIALS
CREDIBILITY
CREDULOUSLY
DARDANELLES
DENDRACHATE
EPIDIASCOPE
ERADICATION
FIDDLEDEDEE
FUNDAMENTAL
FUNDRAISING
GIRDLESTEAD
GLADWELLISE
GODDAUGHTER
GOODLOOKING
GOODNATURED
GORDONSTOUN
GUADALCANAL
HANDCRAFTED
HANDICAPPED
HANDICAPPER
HANDWRITING
HANDWRITTEN
HARDHITTING
HARDICANUTE
HARDPRESSED
HARDWORKING
HEBDOMADARY
HINDERLANDS
HUNDREDFOLD
INADVERTENT
INADVISABLE
IRIDESCENCE
KIDDLEYWINK
KINDERSPIEL
KINDHEARTED
LANDSKNECHT
LEADSWINGER
LINDISFARNE
LOUDSPEAKER
MEADOWSWEET
MENDELEVIUM
MENDELSSOHN
MIDDENSTEAD
MIDDLEMARCH
MIDDLESIZED
MISDEMEANOR
NEEDLEPOINT
NEEDLESTICK
NEEDLEWOMAN
NONDESCRIPT
OUTDISTANCE
OXODIZATION
PAEDIATRICS
PAEDOTROPHY
PANDEMONIUM
PERDUELLION
PIEDMONTITE
PONDEROUSLY
PREDECESSOR
PREDESTINED
PREDICAMENT
PREDICATIVE
PREDICTABLE
PREDICTABLY
PREDOMINANT

PREDOMINATE
PRODIGALISE
PRODIGALITY
QUADRENNIAL
QUADRENNIUM
QUADRUPLETS
READABILITY
RIDDLEMEREE
SADDLEHORSE
SANDERSWOOD
SKIDBLADNIR
STADTHOLDER
SUBDIVISION
SUBDOMINANT
SUNDRENCHED
SYNDICALISM
SYNDICATION
TENDENTIOUS
TIDDLEYWINK
TRADITIONAL
VENDEMIAIRE
VINDICATION
WINDBREAKER
WINDCHEATER
WINDLESTRAW
WINDOWFRAME
WINDOWLEDGE
WINDSURFING
WONDERFULLY
WOODCARVING
ABSENTEEISM
ACCELERATOR
ACCESSORIES
ADVENTURESS
ADVENTUROUS
ADVERBIALLY
ADVERTISING
AFFECTATION
AFTERSCHOOL
ALLEGORICAL
ALLELOMORPH
ALLEVIATION
ALTERCATION
ALTERNATELY
ALTERNATING
ALTERNATION
ALTERNATIVE
ANAESTHESIA
ANAESTHETIC
ANGELOLATRY
ANTECEDENCE
ANTECHAMBER
ANTEPENDIUM
APPEARANCES
APPEASEMENT
APPELLATION
APPELLATIVE
ARGENTINIAN
ASPERGILLUM
ASPERGILLUS
ASPERSORIUM
ASSEMBLYMAN
ATHERINIDAE
ATHERMANOUS
ATTENTIVELY
ATTENUATION
ATTESTATION
BELEAGUERED
BENEDICTINE
BENEDICTION
BENEFICIARY
BENEFICIATE
BENEVOLENCE
BEREAVEMENT
BICENTENARY
BUREAUCRACY
CALEFACIENT
CALENDERING
CAMEROONIAN
CAPERNOITED
CAPERNOITIE
CAREFULNESS
CATEGORICAL
CATERPILLAR
CELEBRATION
CEREBRATION
CEREMONIOUS
CHEERLEADER
CHEESECLOTH
COLEORRHIZA
COMESTIBLES
COMEUPPANCE
CYBERNETICS
DECEITFULLY
DECEPTIVELY
DEFENCELESS
DEFENSELESS
DEFENSIVELY
DEFERENTIAL
DELECTATION
DELETERIOUS
DERELICTION
DESECRATION
DESEGREGATE
DESELECTION
DESERPIDINE
DETERIORATE
DETERMINANT
DETERMINING
DETESTATION
DEVELOPMENT
DICEPHALOUS
DIMENSIONAL
DIRECTIONAL
DIRECTORATE
DISEMBODIED
DISENCUMBER
DISENTANGLE
DODECASTYLE
DOMESTICATE
DOMESTICITY
DYAESTHESIA
EFFECTIVELY
EFFECTUALLY
EMBELLISHED
EMMENAGOGUE
EMMENTHALER
ENCEPHALOMA
ENFEOFFMENT
ENKEPHALINE
ENNEAHEDRON
ENTERTAINER
ESSENTIALLY
EXCEEDINGLY
EXCEPTIONAL
EXCESSIVELY
EXPECTANTLY
EXPECTATION
EXPECTORANT
EXPECTORATE
EXPEDITIOUS
EXPENDITURE
EXPERIENCED
EXTEMPORISE
EXTEMPORIZE
EXTENSIVELY
EXTENUATING
EXTENUATION
EXTERMINATE
FACETIOUSLY
FIRELIGHTER
FOMENTATION
FORECASTING
FORECLOSURE
FOREFATHERS
FORESEEABLE
FORESHORTEN
FORESTATION
FORETHOUGHT
FOREWARNING
FREEMASONRY
FREETHINKER
GABERLUNZIE
GAMETOPHYTE
GATECRASHER
GEGENSCHEIN
GENEALOGIST
GENERALIZED
GENERICALLY
GENETICALLY
GREENBOTTLE
GREENGROCER
GREENOCKITE
GUBERNATION
HABERDASHER
HAREBRAINED
HEMERALOPIA
HETEROSCIAN
HIBERNATING
HIBERNATION
HIDEOUSNESS
HOHENLINDEN
HOMEOPATHIC
HONEYCOMBED
HONEYMOONER
HONEYSUCKLE
HYPERMARKET
HYPERTROPHY
IMMEDIATELY
IMPEACHMENT
IMPECUNIOUS
IMPEDIMENTA
IMPERIALISM
IMPERIALIST
IMPERIOUSLY
IMPERMANENT
IMPERMEABLE
IMPERSONATE
IMPERTINENT
IMPETUOSITY
IMPETUOUSLY
INCESSANTLY
INDEFINABLE
INDENTATION
INDEPENDENT
INDEXLINKED
INFERIORITY
INFERTILITY
INFESTATION
INGENIOUSLY
INHERITANCE
INSECTICIDE
INSECTIVORE
INSENSITIVE
INSEPARABLE
INTEGRATION
INTELLIGENT
INTEMPERATE
INTENSIVELY
INTENTIONAL
INTERACTION
INTERACTIVE
INTERCALARY
INTERCEPTOR
INTERCHANGE
INTERCOSTAL
INTERCOURSE
INTERESTING
INTERGLOSSA
INTERGROWTH
INTERLACING
INTERLEUKIN
INTERLINGUA
INTERMINGLE
INTERNECINE
INTERNUNCIO
INTERPOLATE
INTERPRETER
INTERREGNUM
INTERRELATE
INTERROGATE
INTERRUPTER
INTERSPERSE
INTERVENING
INTERVIEWEE
INTERVIEWER
INVESTIGATE
INVESTITURE
IRREDENTIST
IRREDUCIBLE
IRREFUTABLE
IRREGULARLY
IRRELEVANCE
IRRELIGIOUS
IRREPARABLE
IRREPARABLY
IRREVERENCE
IRREVOCABLE
ISOELECTRIC
JOSEPHINITE
KAMELAUKION
KIMERIDGIAN
KRIEGSSPIEL
LAMENTATION
LASERPICIUM
LATERIGRADE
LATERITIOUS
LEGERDEMAIN
LEVELHEADED
LIBERTARIAN
LITERALNESS
LUXEMBURGER
MACERANDUBA
MAKEBELIEVE
MALEDICTION
MALEFACTION
MALEVOLENCE
MANEUVERING
MATERIALISE
MATERIALISM
MATERIALIST
MATERIALIZE
METEOROLOGY
MINESWEEPER
MISERICORDE
MISERLINESS
MODELMOLEST
MODERNISTIC
MOLESTATION
MOMENTARILY
MONEYLENDER
MONEYMAKING
NECESSARILY
NECESSITATE
NECESSITOUS
NEVERENDING
NIKETHAMIDE
NOMENCLATOR
NONETHELESS
NONEXISTENT

NOVELETTISH
NUMERICALLY
OBJECTIVELY
OBJECTIVITY
OBSERVATION
OBSERVATORY
OBSESSIVELY
OBTEMPERATE
OFFENSIVELY
ORDERLINESS
ORIENTALIST
ORIENTATION
OSTENTATION
OSTEOPATHIC
OSTEOPLASTY
PALEOGRAPHY
PALEOLITHIC
PALESTINIAN
PAPERWEIGHT
PARENTHESIS
PATERNALISM
PATERNOSTER
PEDESTRIANS
PEDETENTOUS
PENETRATING
PENETRATION
PEREGRINATE
PERENNIALLY
PERESTROIKA
POMEGRANATE
POTENTIALLY
PREEMINENCE
PRZEWALSKIS
RABELAISIAN
RECEPTIVITY
RECESSIONAL
RELEASEMENT
REMEMBRANCE
REPETITIOUS
RESEMBLANCE
RESENTFULLY
RESERVATION
REVELATIONS
REVENDICATE
REVERBERATE
REVERENTIAL
ROBESPIERRE
RUDESHEIMER
SALESPERSON
SCHECKLATON
SCIENTOLOGY
SCREAMINGLY
SCREWDRIVER
SELECTIVELY
SELECTIVITY
SERENDIPITY
SEVENTEENTH
SEVERALFOLD
SLEEPWALKER
SOVEREIGNTY

SPEECHCRAFT
SPEEDOMETER
SPREADSHEET
STEEPLEJACK
STREAMLINED
STREETLIGHT
STRENUOUSLY
STRETCHABLE
STRETCHLESS
SUDETENLAND
SUPERALTERN
SUPERCHARGE
SUPERCHERIE
SUPERFICIAL
SUPERFICIES
SUPERFLUITY
SUPERFLUOUS
SUPERIMPOSE
SUPERINTEND
SUPERIORITY
SUPERLATIVE
SUPERMARKET
SUPERSCRIBE
SUPERSEDEAS
SUPERSEDERE
SUPERTANKER
SUPERVISION
SUPERVISORY
TABERNACLES
TELEGRAPHER
TELEGRAPHIC
TELEKINESIS
TELEPHONIST
TELEPRINTER
THREATENING
TIMEKEEPING
TIMESHARING
TREECREEPER
TYPESETTING
TYPEWRITTEN
UNBEFITTING
UNCERTAINTY
UNDEMANDING
UNDERCHARGE
UNDERCOOKED
UNDERGROUND
UNDERGROWTH
UNDERHANDED
UNDERMANNED
UNDERSIGNED
UNDERSTATED
UNDERTAKING
UNDERVALUED
UNDERWEIGHT
UNDERWRITER
UNDESERVING
UNDESIRABLE
UNDEVELOPED
UNGETATABLE
UNNECESSARY

UNPERTURBED
UNREALISTIC
UNREASONING
UNREHEARSED
UNRELENTING
UNREMITTING
UNREPENTANT
UNWELCOMING
VALEDICTION
VALEDICTORY
VIDEOCAMERA
VOTERIGGING
WAKEFULNESS
WAREHOUSING
WATERCOLOUR
WATERCOURSE
WATEREDDOWN
WATERLOGGED
WATERMEADOW
WATERSKIING
WATERSPLASH
WHEELBARROW
WHEELWRIGHT
WIDERANGING
WITENAGEMOT
TÉLÉFÉRIQUE
ALIFANFARON
CLIFFHANGER
COEFFICIENT
COMFORTABLE
COMFORTABLY
COMFORTLESS
CONFABULATE
CONFARREATE
CONFEDERACY
CONFEDERATE
CONFIDENTLY
CONFINEMENT
CONFUTATION
DEIFICATION
DIFFERENTLY
DIFFIDENTLY
DIFFRACTION
DISFIGURING
DYSFUNCTION
EDIFICATION
FANFARONADE
FORFOUGHTEN
FULFILLMENT
GODFORSAKEN
GONFALONIER
HALFBROTHER
HALFHEARTED
HALFHOLIDAY
INEFFECTIVE
INEFFECTUAL
INEFFICIENT
INOFFENSIVE
MALFEASANCE
MALFUNCTION

NIPFARTHING
NONFEASANCE
PERFORATION
PERFORMANCE
PERFUNCTORY
PROFESSEDLY
PROFICIENCY
PROFITEROLE
PROFUSENESS
RAFFISHNESS
RUMFRUCTION
SCAFFOLDING
SELFCONTROL
SELFDEFENCE
SELFEVIDENT
SELFIMPOSED
SELFISHNESS
SELFRESPECT
SELFSERVICE
SHAFTESBURY
SPIFFLICATE
SUFFICIENCY
SUFFOCATING
SUFFOCATION
SUFFRAGETTE
TRAFFICATOR
UNIFICATION
ANAGNORISIS
BANGLADESHI
BERGSCHRUND
BRAGGADOCIO
BURGOMASTER
COAGULATION
CONGRESSMAN
DANGEROUSLY
DIAGNOSTICS
DISGRACEFUL
DISGRUNTLED
DRAGGLETAIL
DRAGONNADES
ELIGIBILITY
EPIGENESIST
EXAGGERATED
FINGERPRINT
FINGERSTALL
FORGIVENESS
FRAGMENTARY
FRIGHTENING
FRIGHTFULLY
GIGGLESTICK
GIGGLESWICK
GIGGLEWATER
GINGERBREAD
GREGARINIDA
HANGGLIDING
HAUGHTINESS
HOGGISHNESS
HUMGRUFFIAN
IMAGINATION
IMAGINATIVE

LENGTHENING
LENGTHINESS
LINGUISTICS
LOGGERHEADS
LONGANIMITY
LONGAWAITED
LONGINQUITY
LONGLASTING
LONGRUNNING
LONGSIGHTED
LONGSLEEVED
MANGALSUTRA
MARGINALIST
MARGINALIZE
MORGENSTERN
NAUGHTINESS
NEIGHBORING
NEIGHBOURLY
OLIGOCHAETE
ORIGINALITY
ORIGINATING
ORIGINATION
OUAGADOUGOU
PLAGIARISED
PLAGIOSTOMI
PROGENITRIX
PROGNATHOUS
PROGRESSION
PROGRESSIVE
RAMGUNSHOCH
RANGEFINDER
RUMGUMPTION
SEIGNIORAGE
SINGAPOREAN
SINGLESTICK
SINGULARITY
SLIGHTINGLY
STAGFLATION
STEGANOGRAM
STEGANOPODE
SUGGESTIBLE
TANGIBILITY
TIGGYWINKLE
TRAGELAPHUS
WEIGHBRIDGE
WHIGMALEERY
AFGHANISTAN
ALPHABETIZE
AMPHETAMINE
AMPHIBOLOGY
AMPHISBAENA
AMPHISBOENA
ANTHESTERIA
ANTHOCYANIN
ANTHOLOGIZE
ANTHONOMOUS
ARCHAEOLOGY
ARCHEGONIAL
ARCHEGONIUM
ARCHENTERON

ARCHILOCHUS
ARCHIPELAGO
ARRHENOTOKY
ARTHRAPODAL
ARTHRODESIS
ARTHROSPORE
ASPHETERISM
BASHFULNESS
BATHYSPHERE
BODHISATTVA
BUSHWHACKER
CATHOLICISM
DEPHLEGMATE
DIPHYCERCAL
DISHEVELLED
DISHONESTLY
DITHELETISM
EMPHYTEUSIS
ENCHANTMENT
ENCHANTRESS
ENCHIRIDION
ENCHONDROMA
ENGHALSKRUG
ENTHRALLING
ESCHATOLOGY
ESCHERICHIA
EUCHARISTIC
EUPHEMISTIC
EURHYTHMICS
FASHIONABLE
FASHIONABLY
FISHANDCHIP
FISHMONGERS
FOTHERGILLA
HAPHAZARDLY
HIGHLIGHTER
HIGHPITCHED
HIGHPOWERED
HIGHPROFILE
HIGHQUALITY
HIGHRANKING
HYPHENATION
LIGHTHEADED
LIGHTWEIGHT
LITHOGRAPHY
LYCHNOSCOPE
MACHAIRODUS
MACHINATION
MATHEMATICS
MEKHITARIST
METHODOLOGY
MICHURINISM
NAPHTHALENE
NETHERLANDS
NETHERLINGS
NIGHTINGALE
NIGHTMARISH
NOTHINGNESS
OFFHANDEDLY
ORCHESTRATE
ORCHESTRINA
ORCHESTRION
ORTHOCENTRE
ORTHOGRAPHY
ORTHOPAEDIC
PATHOLOGIST
PHTHIRIASIS
PREHISTORIC
PROHIBITION
PROHIBITIVE
PYTHONESQUE
RIGHTANGLED
RIGHTEOUSLY
RIGHTHANDED
RIGHTHANDER
RIGHTWINGER
SACHERTORTE
SIGHTSCREEN
SIGHTSEEING
TACHYCARDIA
TACHYGRAPHY
TECHNICALLY
TIGHTFISTED
TIGHTLIPPED
TSCHERNOSEM
UNCHRISTIAN
UNSHAKEABLE
UNSHELTERED
UNSHRINKING
UNTHINKABLE
UNWHOLESOME
VICHYSOISSE
WASHERWOMAN
WASHLEATHER
WISHTONWISH
WITHERSHINS
WITHHOLDING
ABRIDGEMENT
ACCIPITRINE
ACHIEVEMENT
ACRIFLAVINE
ACRIMONIOUS
AFFILIATION
AFFIRMATION
AFFIRMATIVE
AGRICULTURE
ALBIGENSIAN
AMBIVALENCE
ANNIVERSARY
ANTIBURGHER
ANTICYCLONE
ANTINEUTRON
ANTIPHRASIS
ANTIPYRETIC
ANTIQUARIAN
ANTIRRHINUM
ANTISTHENES
ANTISTROPHE
ARBITRAGEUR
ARBITRAMENT
ARBITRARILY
ARBITRATION
ARRIVEDERCI
ARTICULATED
ARTILLERIST
ARTIODACTYL
ASSIDUOUSLY
ASSIGNATION
ASSIMILATED
ASTIGMATISM
AUDIOVISUAL
AURIGNACIAN
AVOIRDUPOIS
BALISTRARIA
BESIEGEMENT
BEWILDERING
BILIOUSNESS
BUSINESSMAN
CALIBRATION
CALIFORNIUM
CHAIRPERSON
CHEIROGNOMY
CHOIRMASTER
CHRISTENING
CHRISTMASSY
CHRISTOPHER
CITIZENSHIP
CLAIRSCHACH
CLAIRVOYANT
CORINTHIANS
CYLINDRICAL
DEBILITATED
DELICIOUSLY
DELICTATION
DELINEATION
DELINQUENCY
DELITESCENT
DELIVERANCE
DEMIBASTION
DESICCATION
DESIGNATION
DEVIOUSNESS
DEVITRIFIED
DISILLUSION
DISIMPRISON
DISINCLINED
DOMINEERING
DUBIOUSNESS
DUNIEWASSAL
EFFICACIOUS
EFFICIENTLY
EMPIECEMENT
EMPIRICUTIC
ENGINEERING
ENLIGHTENED
ENTITLEMENT
ENVIRONMENT
EQUIDISTANT
EQUILATERAL
EQUILIBRIST
EQUILIBRIUM
EQUINOCTIAL
EQUIPOLLENT
EQUIVALENCE
EQUIVOCALLY
ESPIEGLERIE
EXHILARATED
FAMILIARISE
FAMILIARITY
FAMILIARIZE
FARINACEOUS
FRUITLESSLY
HABILIMENTS
HAGIOGRAPHY
HARIOLATION
HEMIANOPSIA
HUMILIATING
HUMILIATION
IMMIGRATION
IMPIGNORATE
INCINERATOR
INDIARUBBER
INDIFFERENT
INDIGESTION
INDIGNANTLY
INDIGNATION
INDIVISIBLE
INDIVISIBLY
INFILTRATOR
INSIDIOUSLY
INSINCERITY
INSINUATING
INSINUATION
INSISTENTLY
INVIGILATOR
INVINCIBLES
ISTIOPHORUS
JUDICIOUSLY
KILIMANJARO
LAPIDESCENT
LATIFUNDIUM
LEGIONNAIRE
LEGISLATION
LEGISLATIVE
LEGISLATURE
LEPIDOPTERA
LEPIDOSIREN
LIVINGSTONE
LOUISIANIAN
LUMINESCENT
MAGISTERIAL
MAGISTRATES
MALICIOUSLY
MANIPULATOR
MARIONBERRY
MARIONETTES
MARIVAUDAGE
MEDIASTINUM
MEDICINALLY
MEDIUMSIZED
MERITORIOUS
MINIATURIST
MINIATURIZE
MINISTERIAL
MINISTERING
MISIDENTIFY
MOXIBUSTION
MUNIFICENCE
NATIONALISM
NATIONALIST
NATIONALITY
NATIONALIZE
NATIONSTATE
NOTICEBOARD
NUMISMATICS
NUMISMATIST
OBLITERATED
OBVIOUSNESS
OFFICIALDOM
OFFICIALESE
OFFICIOUSLY
OMNIPOTENCE
OMNIPRESENT
OMNISCIENCE
ONEIRODYNIA
ONEIROMANCY
OPPIGNORATE
ORNITHOLOGY
ORNITHOPTER
OSCILLATION
PACIFICALLY
PARISHIONER
PENICILLATE
PENITENTIAL
PERICARDIUM
PERIGORDIAN
PERIODONTIC
PERIPATETIC
PERIPHRASIS
PERISSOLOGY
PERISTALITH
PERISTALSIS
PERITONAEUM
PERITONITIS
PETITMAITRE
PLEISTOCENE
POLICEWOMAN
POLIORCETIC
POLITICALLY
POLITICIANS
PURITANICAL
RADIOACTIVE
RADIOCARBON
RADIOGRAPHY
RADIOLOGIST
RATIOCINATE
RATIONALITY
RATIONALIZE
RAVISHINGLY
RECIPROCATE

RECIPROCITY
REGIMENTALS
REGISTERING
RELIABILITY
RELIGIOUSLY
REMINISCENT
RESIDENTIAL
RESIGNATION
RESISTIVITY
RETINACULUM
RETINOSPORA
REVISIONISM
ROSICRUCIAN
RUDIMENTARY
SAGITTARIUS
SATIRICALLY
SCHISTOSOMA
SCHISTOSOME
SCRIMSHANDY
SCRIPTORIUM
SEDIMENTARY
SEPIOSTAIRE
SERICULTURE
SERIOUSNESS
SINISTRORSE
SOCIABILITY
SOCIOLOGIST
SOLILOQUIZE
SOLIPSISTIC
SPRINGBOARD
SPRINGCLEAN
SPRINGHOUSE
SPRINGINESS
STAIRCARPET
STEINBERGER
STRIKEBOUND
STRINGENTLY
STRINGYBARK
SUBITANEOUS
TACITURNITY
TAXIDERMIST
TEDIOUSNESS
THRIFTINESS
TITILLATION
UNCIVILISED
UNCIVILIZED
UNDIGNIFIED
UNDISCLOSED
UNDISGUISED
UNDISTURBED
UNMITIGATED
UNRIGHTEOUS
UNWITTINGLY
UPRIGHTNESS
UTRICULARIA
VACILLATING
VACILLATION
VARIABILITY
VARIEGATION
VARIOLATION

VICIOUSNESS
VICISSITUDE
VIVISECTION
CONJECTURAL
CONJUGATION
CONJUNCTION
CONJUNCTURE
DISJUNCTION
PREJUDICIAL
SUBJUGATION
SUBJUNCTIVE
BACKBENCHER
BACKFIELDER
BACKPACKING
BACKSLIDING
BASKERVILLE
BOOKBINDING
BOOKKEEPING
BOOKSELLERS
COCKLESHELL
HECKELPHONE
HUCKLEBERRY
HUCKSTERAGE
KIRKPATRICK
LICKSPITTLE
MARKETPLACE
MASKALLONGE
MECKLENBURG
MOCKINGBIRD
MUSKELLUNGE
NICKELODEON
NICKNACKERY
PICKELHAUBE
PICKYOUROWN
ROCKEFELLER
SHAKESPEARE
SMOKESCREEN
SOCKDALAGER
SOCKDOLAGER
SOCKDOLIGER
SOCKDOLOGER
SPOKESWOMAN
STAKEHOLDER
TICKTACKTOE
VOLKSKAMMER
WORKMANLIKE
WORKMANSHIP
WORKSTATION
ACCLAMATION
ACCLIMATION
ACCLIMATISE
ACCLIMATIZE
ACOLOUTHITE
ADOLESCENCE
ADULLAMITES
ADULTERATED
AFFLIICTION
AGGLOMERATE
AGGLUTINANT
AGGLUTINATE

AMELANCHIER
AMPLEXICAUL
APOLLINARIS
APOLLONICON
APPLICATION
ASCLEPIADES
BALLBEARING
BELLEROPHON
BELLETTRIST
BELLIGERENT
BELLYTIMBER
BIBLIOPHILE
BIELORUSSIA
BILLIONAIRE
BRILLIANTLY
BULLFIGHTER
CALLANETICS
CALLIGRAPHY
CALLISTEMON
CALLITRICHE
CALLOUSNESS
CAULIFLOWER
CHALLENGING
CHILDMINDER
CHILLINGHAM
CHOLESTEROL
CITLALEPETL
COALESCENCE
COLLABORATE
COLLAPSIBLE
COLLECTANEA
COLLENCHYMA
COLLOCATION
COULOMMIERS
CYCLOSTYLED
DECLAMATION
DECLAMATORY
DECLARATION
DEGLUTINATE
DEGLUTITION
DIPLOMATICS
DIPLOMATIST
DISLOCATION
DUPLICATING
DUPLICATION
DYSLOGISTIC
EGALITARIAN
EMPLACEMENT
ENSLAVEMENT
EXCLAMATION
EXCLUSIVELY
EXPLANATION
EXPLANATORY
EXPLORATION
EXPLORATORY
FALLIBILITY
FAULTFINDER
FAULTLESSLY
FIELDWORKER
FILLIBUSTER

FOOLISHNESS
FORLORNNESS
FOULMOUTHED
FULLBLOODED
GALLIBAGGER
GALLIBEGGAR
GALLIGANTUS
GALLIMAUFRY
GALLOVIDIAN
GALLOWGLASS
GALLYBAGGER
GALLYBEGGAR
GILLYFLOWER
GRALLATORES
GULLIBILITY
HALLEFLINTA
HALLUCINATE
HEALTHINESS
HOLLANDAISE
HOOLIGANISM
IDOLIZATION
IDYLLICALLY
IMPLAUSIBLE
IMPLEMENTAL
IMPLICATION
INALIENABLE
INCLINATION
INELUCTABLE
INFLAMMABLE
INFLUENTIAL
LAWLESSNESS
LILLIPUTIAN
MAGLEMOSIAN
MARLBOROUGH
MELLIFLUOUS
MILLIONAIRE
MOLLYCODDLE
OCHLOCRATIC
OPALESCENCE
PARLIPOMENA
PERLUSTRATE
PHALANSTERY
PHILANDERER
PHILATELIST
PHILIPPINES
PHILLIPSITE
PHILOCTETES
PHILOLOGIST
PHILOSOPHER
POLLENBRUSH
POLLINATION
PRELIBATION
PRELIMINARY
PROLEGOMENA
PROLETARIAN
PROLETARIAT
PROLIFERATE
PROLOCUTION
PUBLICATION
PUBLISHABLE

QUALITATIVE
RALLENTANDO
REALIGNMENT
REALIZATION
REALPOLITIK
RECLAMATION
REFLEXOLOGY
REPLACEABLE
REPLACEMENT
SCALPRIFORM
SCOLECIFORM
SCOLOPENDRA
SCULDUDDERY
SCULDUGGERY
SCULLABOGUE
SHALLOWNESS
SILLIMANITE
SKILLIGALEE
SKILLIGOLEE
SKULDUDDERY
SKULDUGGERY
SMALLHOLDER
SPELLBINDER
STALLHOLDER
STELLIONATE
STYLISHNESS
STYLIZATION
STYLOPODIUM
SUBLIMATION
SWALLOWABLE
TAGLIATELLE
THALIDOMIDE
THALLOPHYTE
TOPLOFTICAL
TWELVEMONTH
UNALTERABLE
UNBLEMISHED
UNCLEANNESS
UNCLUTTERED
UNFLAPPABLE
UNFLINCHING
USELESSNESS
UTILITARIAN
UTILIZATION
VALLAMBROSA
VALLISNERIA
VIOLINCELLO
VIOLONCELLO
WELLADVISED
WELLBEHAVED
WELLDEFINED
WELLDRESSED
WELLFOUNDED
WELLINGTONS
WELLMEANING
WILLINGNESS
WORLDFAMOUS
WORLDLINESS
YELLOWPLUSH
YELLOWSTONE

ABOMINATION
ADUMBRATION
APOMORPHINE
BLAMEWORTHY
CARMINATIVE
CHAMBERLAIN
CHAMBERMAID
CLIMACTERIC
CLIMATOLOGY
COMMANDMENT
COMMEMORATE
COMMENDABLE
COMMENDABLY
COMMENTATOR
COMMINATION
COMMISERATE
COMMONPLACE
COMMONSENSE
COMMUNICANT
COMMUNICATE
COMMUTATION
CRÉMAILLÈRE
CREMATORIUM
CRIMINOLOGY
CROMWELLIAN
CULMINATION
DERMATOLOGY
DIAMONDBACK
ELIMINATION
ENUMERATION
EPAMINONDAS
EREMACAUSIS
ERYMANTHIAN
ETYMOLOGIST
EXAMINATION
FEHMGERICHT
FLAMBOYANCE
FLAMBOYANTE
FORMULATION
FULMINATION
GEOMETRICAL
GERMINATION
GLIMMERGOWK
GRAMMALOGUE
GRAMMATICAL
HAEMOGLOBIN
HAEMOPHILIA
HAEMORRHAGE
HAEMORRHOID
HAMMERCLOTH
HUMMINGBIRD
ILLMANNERED
KOMMERSBUCH
LAMMERGEIER
LAMMERGEYER
MURMURATION
ONOMASTICON
OUTMANEUVER
PERMANENTLY
PERMISSIBLE
PERMUTATION
PREMATURELY
PREMEDITATE
PREMIERSHIP
PREMONITION
PREMONITORY
PRIMIGENIAL
PROMINENTLY
PROMISCUITY
PROMISCUOUS
PROMOTIONAL
PROMPTITUDE
SHAMELESSLY
SKIMMINGTON
SLUMBERWEAR
SLUMGULLION
STIMULATION
STYMPHALIAN
SUBMERGENCE
SUBMULTIPLE
SUMMERHOUSE
SYMMETRICAL
TERMINATION
TERMINOLOGY
TRIMESTRIAL
TROMPELOEIL
UNAMBIGUOUS
UNEMOTIONAL
UNIMPORTANT
UNIMPRESSED
VERMICULITE
WARMHEARTED
ABANDONMENT
ACINACIFORM
ACKNOWLEDGE
AGONOTHETES
AMINOBUTENE
AMONTILLADO
ANENCEPHALY
ANONYMOUSLY
APONEUROSIS
BANNOCKBURN
BARNSTORMER
BLANKURSINE
BLUNDERBORE
BRANDENBURG
CANNIBALISM
CANNIBALIZE
CARNAPTIOUS
CARNIVOROUS
CHANCELLERY
CHANTARELLE
CHANTERELLE
CHANTICLEER
CHINOISERIE
CHONDROSTEI
CLANDESTINE
CLANJAMFRAY
CLINOCHLORE
COENOBITISM
COGNOSCENTE
COGNOSCENTI
COINCIDENCE
CONNECTICUT
CONNOISSEUR
CONNOTATION
CORNERSTONE
COUNSELLING
COUNTENANCE
COUNTERFEIT
COUNTERFOIL
COUNTERFORT
COUNTERGLOW
COUNTERHAND
COUNTERMAND
COUNTERPANE
COUNTERPART
COUNTERSIGN
COUNTERSINK
COUNTRIFIED
COUNTRYSIDE
CRENELLATED
CURNAPTIOUS
DINNYHAUSER
DINNYHAYSER
DOWNHEARTED
DOWNTRODDEN
DRINKDRIVER
DRUNKENNESS
EARNESTNESS
ENUNCIATION
EOANTHROPUS
EPANALEPSIS
EPINEPHRINE
ETHNOGRAPHY
ETHNOLOGIST
EVANGELICAL
EVENTRATION
EVENTUALITY
EXANTHEMATA
EXONERATION
FERNITICKLE
FLANNELETTE
FORNICATION
FOUNDATIONS
FRANKFURTER
FRANKLINITE
FRANTICALLY
FRENCHWOMAN
FRENCHWOMEN
FRONTRUNNER
FURNISHINGS
GARNISHMENT
GRANDFATHER
GRANDMASTER
GRANDMOTHER
GRENZGANGER
HORNSWOGGLE
HYMNOLOGIST
ICONOGRAPHY
ICONOSTASIS
IDENTICALLY
IDENTIFYING
IRONMONGERS
IRONMONGERY
KINNIKINICK
LAUNDERETTE
MAGNANIMITY
MAGNANIMOUS
MAGNIFICENT
MAINTENANCE
MEANDERINGS
MEANINGLESS
MINNESINGER
MOONLIGHTER
MOUNTAINEER
MOUNTAINOUS
NEANDERTHAL
ODONTOBLAST
ODONTOPHORE
OPINIONATED
PAINKILLING
PAINSTAKING
PAWNBROKERS
PENNYFATHER
PHONETICIAN
PHONOFIDDLE
PINNYWINKLE
PLANETARIUM
PLANTAGENET
PLANTIGRADE
POINTLESSLY
PORNOGRAPHY
PRINCIPALLY
QUINTUPLETS
REANIMATION
REINCARNATE
SAINTLINESS
SAINTPAULIA
SCANDALIZED
SCANDANAVIA
SCANDINAVIA
SCINTILLATE
SENNACHERIB
SHENANIGANS
SHINPLASTER
SHUNAMITISM
SIGNIFICANT
SLENDERNESS
SOUNDLESSLY
SPANGCOCKLE
SPENDTHRIFT
SPONDULICKS
SPONDYLITIS
SPONSORSHIP
SPONTANEITY
SPONTANEOUS
STANDARDIZE
STANDOFFISH
STANDPATTER
STENOCHROME
STENOGRAPHY
TEENYBOPPER
THANATOPSIS
THANKLESSLY
THENCEFORTH
THINGAMAJIG
THINGLINESS
THINGUMAJIG
THUNDERBIRD
THUNDERBOLT
THUNDERCLAP
THUNDERHEAD
TOWNSPEOPLE
TRANQUILITY
TRANSACTION
TRANSCEIVER
TRANSFERRED
TRANSFERRIN
TRANSFIGURE
TRANSFORMED
TRANSFORMER
TRANSFUSION
TRANSILIENT
TRANSLATION
TRANSLUCENT
TRANSMITTED
TRANSMITTER
TRANSPARENT
TRANSPONDER
TRANSPORTED
TRANSPORTER
TRANSURANIC
TRENCHERMAN
TRINCOMALEE
TRINIDADIAN
TRINITARIAN
TRINOBANTES
UNANIMOUSLY
UNANNOUNCED
UNENDURABLE
UNENVELOPED
UNINHABITED
UNINHIBITED
UNINITIATED
WAINSCOTING
WIENERWURST
WRONGHEADED
ABIOGENETIC
ABNORMALITY
ACCOMMODATE
ACCOMPANIST
ACCORDINGLY
ACCOUNTABLE
ACCOUNTANCY
ADJOURNMENT
AERODYNAMIC
AERONAUTICS
AGNOSTICISM
AGROSTOLOGY

AMMOPHILOUS
ANTONOMASIA
APPOINTMENT
ASSOCIATION
ASTONISHING
ATMOSPHERIC
ATROCIOUSLY
BELORUSSIAN
BLOODSPORTS
BLOODSTREAM
BLOODSUCKER
CACOGASTRIC
CACOPHONOUS
CAMOUFLAGED
CAROLINGIAN
CHLOROPHYLL
CHRONICALLY
CHRONOMETER
CILOFIBRATE
CLIOMETRICS
COHORTATIVE
COLONIALISM
COLONIALIST
COLOURBLIND
CROOKEDNESS
CYMOPHANOUS
DECONSTRUCT
DECORATIONS
DECORTICATE
DEFOLIATION
DEFORMATION
DEHORTATIVE
DEMOGRAPHIC
DEMONOMANIA
DEMONSTRATE
DEMORALIZED
DEMOSTHENES
DEMOSTHENIC
DENOMINATOR
DEPORTATION
DICOTYLEDON
DISOBEDIENT
DISORGANIZE
DISORIENTED
DIVORCEMENT
EMBOÎTEMENT
EMPOWERMENT
ENCOURAGING
ENDOCARDIUM
ENDORSEMENT
ENDOTHERMIC
ENFORCEABLE
ENFORCEMENT
ENFOULDERED
ERIODENDRON
ERRONEOUSLY
EXHORTATION
EXPONENTIAL
EXPOSTULATE
EXTORTIONER
FAVOURITISM
FEROCIOUSLY
FLUORESCENT
GAMOGENESIS
GENOUILLÈRE
GERONTOLOGY
HEMOPHILIAC
HEMORRHOIDS
HOLOTHURIAN
HOMOEOPATHY
HOMOGENEITY
HOMOGENEOUS
HOMOGENIZED
HOMOTHERMAL
HOMOTHERMIC
HYPOCORISMA
HYPOTENSION
HYPOTHECATE
HYPOTHERMIA
IDEOLOGICAL
IDEOPRAXIST
IDIOTICALLY
IGNOMINIOUS
IGNORANTINE
ILLOGICALLY
IMMORTALISE
IMMORTALITY
IMMORTALIZE
IMPORTANTLY
IMPORTATION
IMPORTUNATE
INCOHERENCE
INCOMPETENT
INCOMPOSITE
INCONGRUITY
INCONGRUOUS
INCONSTANCY
INCONTINENT
INCORPORATE
INCORPOREAL
INCORRECTLY
INDOMITABLE
INFORMALITY
INFORMATICS
INFORMATION
INFORMATIVE
INSOUCIANCE
INTOLERABLE
INTOLERABLY
INTOLERANCE
INTOXICATED
INTOXIMETER
INVOLUNTARY
INVOLVEMENT
KILOCALORIE
LABORIOUSLY
LABORSAVING
LACONICALLY
LOCORESTIVE
LOGODAEDALY
LOGOGRAPHER
MASOCHISTIC
MELODIOUSLY
MEMORABILIA
MONOCHINOUS
MONOGRAMMED
MONONGAHELA
MONOPSONIST
MONOTHELITE
MONOTREMATA
MYCOLOGICAL
MYCOPHAGIST
MYXOMATOSIS
NEGOTIATING
NEGOTIATION
NOTORIOUSLY
NOTOTHERIUM
OBSOLESCENT
ONTOLOGICAL
OPPORTUNELY
OPPORTUNISM
OPPORTUNIST
OPPORTUNITY
OPTOMETRIST
PANOMPHAEAN
PARONOMASIA
PELOPONNESE
POCOCURANTE
PREOCCUPIED
PROOFREADER
RECOGNITION
RECONDITION
RECONNOITER
RECONNOITRE
RECONSTRUCT
RECOVERABLE
REDOUBTABLE
REFOCILLATE
REFORMATION
REFORMATORY
REMONSTRATE
REMORSELESS
RESOURCEFUL
REVOLUTIONS
RIBONUCLEIC
RODOMONTADE
SAPONACEOUS
SAVOURINESS
SAXOPHONIST
SCHOLARSHIP
SCHOTTISCHE
SECONDARILY
SECONDCLASS
SEXOLOGICAL
SOROPTIMIST
STOOLPIGEON
STROBOSCOPE
STRONGYLOID
STROPHILLUS
SUBORDINATE
SYCOPHANTIC
THEOBROMINE
THEOLOGICAL
THEOPNEUSTY
THEORETICAL
THROGMORTON
TIRONENSIAN
TOBOGGANING
TOPOGRAPHER
TOXOPHILITE
TYPOGRAPHER
TYPOGRAPHIC
TYROGLYPHID
TYRONENSIAN
UNCOMMITTED
UNCONCEALED
UNCONCERNED
UNCONFIRMED
UNCONNECTED
UNCONQUERED
UNCONSCIOUS
UNCONTESTED
UNCONVERTED
UNCONVINCED
UNCOUTHNESS
UNDOUBTEDLY
UNFORTUNATE
UNGODLINESS
UNMOTIVATED
UNSOLICITED
UNTOUCHABLE
UPHOLSTERER
VASOPRESSIN
XENODOCHIUM
XEROTRIPSIS
XYLOGRAPHER
ZOROASTRIAN
ACUPUNCTURE
ADOPTIANISM
ADOPTIONISM
ANAPHYLAXIS
ANAPLEROSIS
ANAPLEROTIC
APOPHYLLITE
CAMPANOLOGY
CAMPESTRIAN
CAMPHORATED
CHIPPENDALE
CLAPPERCLAW
COMPARATIVE
COMPARTMENT
COMPENDIOUS
COMPETENTLY
COMPETITION
COMPETITIVE
COMPILATION
COMPILEMENT
COMPLACENCY
COMPLAISANT
COMPLICATED
COMPLIMENTS
COMPOSITION
COMPOTATION
COMPRIMARIO
COMPTROLLER
COMPUNCTION
COMPUTATION
COMPUTERIZE
COOPERATION
COOPERATIVE
COPPERPLATE
CORPORATION
CREPITATION
CREPUSCULAR
CULPABILITY
DESPERATELY
DESPERATION
DESPONDENCY
DIAPHORESIS
DIAPHORETIC
DISPARAGING
DISPENSABLE
DISPERSABLE
DISPLEASURE
DISPOSITION
DISPUTATION
ELEPHANTINE
EVAPORATION
GRAPHICALLY
HARPSICHORD
HELPFULNESS
HEPPLEWHITE
HERPETOLOGY
HIPPOCAMPUS
HIPPOCRATES
HIPPOCRATIC
HOSPITALITY
HOSPITALIZE
HOSPITALLER
HYOPLASTRON
INOPERATIVE
INOPPORTUNE
INSPIRATION
KLEPTOMANIA
LAMPLIGHTER
LAMPROPHYRE
MALPRACTICE
NYMPHOMANIA
OUTPOURINGS
PAMPELMOOSE
PAMPELMOUSE
PAMPHLETEER
PERPETRATOR
PERPETUALLY
POMPELMOOSE
POMPELMOUSE
PREPARATION
PREPARATORY
PREPOLLENCE
PREPOSITION

PROPAGATION
PROPHETICAL
PROPHYLAXIS
PROPINQUITY
PROPOSITION
PROPRIETARY
PURPOSELESS
PURPRESTURE
REAPPRAISAL
RESPECTABLE
RESPECTABLY
RESPIRATION
RESPIRATORY
RESPLENDANT
RESPLENDENT
RESPONSIBLE
RESPONSIBLY
RESPONSIONS
RHAPSODICAL
RHOPALOCERA
SALPINGITIS
SCEPTICALLY
SCOPOLAMINE
SCUPPERNONG
SCYPHISTOMA
SEMPITERNAL
SEMPITERNUM
SHAPELINESS
SHEPHERDESS
SHIPBUILDER
SHIPWRECKED
SHOPLIFTING
SKEPTICALLY
STEPBROTHER
STIPENDIARY
STIPULATION
SUBPANATION
SUMPTUOUSLY
SUPPEDANEUM
SUPPOSITION
SUPPOSITORY
SUPPRESSION
SUPPURATION
SYMPATHETIC
SYMPATHISER
SYMPATHIZER
SYMPLEGADES
SYMPOSIARCH
SYMPTOMATIC
TEMPERAMENT
TEMPERATURE
TEMPESTUOUS
TEMPORARILY
TERPSICHORE
TREPIDATION
TREPONEMATA
TRIPTOLEMUS
TROPHOBLAST
TROPOSPHERE
TRYPANOSOMA
TRYPANOSOME
UNSPEAKABLE
UNSPECIFIED
VESPERTINAL
WAPPENSCHAW
CINQUECENTO
DISQUIETING
INEQUITABLE
JACQUEMINOT
MASQUERADER
MILQUETOAST
SESQUIOXIDE
UNEQUIVOCAL
ABBREVIATED
ABORTIONIST
ACCRESCENCE
AGGRAVATING
AGGRAVATION
AGGREGATION
AGORAPHOBIA
AMERCIAMENT
AMERICANISM
ANDROGENOUS
ANFRACTUOUS
APHRODISIAC
APPRECIABLE
APPRECIABLY
APPRENTICED
APPROACHING
APPROBATION
APPROPRIATE
APPROVINGLY
APPROXIMATE
ASTRINGENCY
ATTRIBUTION
ATTRIBUTIVE
AVERRUNCATE
AXEROPHTHOL
BOURGEOISIE
BUPRESTIDAE
CAPRICCIOSO
CARRIAGEWAY
CHARACINOID
CHARGEPAYER
CHARISMATIC
CHARLEMAGNE
CHIROGRAPHY
CHIROPODIST
CHORDOPHONE
CHOROGRAPHY
CIRRHIPEDEA
CIRRHIPEDIA
CLARENCIEUX
COMRADESHIP
COORDINATED
COORDINATES
COPROPHAGAN
COPROSTEROL
CORRECTNESS
CORRELATION
CORROBORATE
CORRUGATION
CORRUPTIBLE
COURTEOUSLY
COURTLINESS
DECREPITATE
DECREPITUDE
DEERSTALKER
DEGRADATION
DEGRINGOLER
DEPREDATION
DEPRIVATION
DETRIMENTAL
DIARTHROSIS
DIORTHORTIC
DIPROTODONT
DISREGARDED
DOUROUCOULI
EMBROCATION
ENARTHROSIS
ENCROACHING
ENFRANCHISE
ESTRAMAZONE
ESTRANGHELO
EVERLASTING
EXCRESCENCE
EXORBITANCE
EXPROPRIATE
EXTRADITION
EXTRAPOLATE
EXTRAVAGANT
EXTROGENOUS
EXTROVERTED
FABRICATION
FAIRWEATHER
FARRAGINOUS
FARREACHING
FERRONNIÈRE
FLIRTATIOUS
FLORILEGIUM
GARRULOUSLY
GERRYMANDER
HAIRDRESSER
HAIRRAISING
HEARTBROKEN
HEARTLESSLY
HERRINGBONE
HYDROCARBON
HYDROMEDUSA
HYDROPHIDAE
HYDROPHOBIA
HYDROPHOBIC
HYDROPONICS
HYDROSTATIC
IMPRACTICAL
IMPRECATION
IMPRECISION
IMPREGNABLE
IMPROPRIETY
IMPROVEMENT
IMPROVIDENT
IMPRUDENTLY
INCREDULITY
INCREDULOUS
INCREMENTAL
INCRIMINATE
INFREQUENCY
INGRATITUDE
INGREDIENTS
INTRACTABLE
INTRAVENOUS
INTREPIDITY
INTRICATELY
INTROVERTED
JERRYMANDER
JINRICKSHAW
LATROCINIUM
LUBRICATION
MACROBIOTIC
MATRIARCHAL
MATRICULATE
MATRIMONIAL
MAURETANIAN
MAURITANIAN
MEPROBAMATE
MERRYMAKING
METRICATION
MICROGAMETE
MICROSCOPIC
NARRAGANSET
NEARSIGHTED
NECROMANCER
NEUROLOGIST
NIERSTEINER
NOURISHMENT
NUTRITIONAL
OPERATIONAL
OPPROBRIOUS
OSTRACODERM
OSTREOPHAGE
OVERBALANCE
OVERBEARING
OVERCROWDED
OVEREXPOSED
OVERFISHING
OVERFLOWING
OVERHANGING
OVERLAPPING
OVERLEARNED
OVERMANNING
OVERPAYMENT
OVERSTUFFED
OVERTURNING
OVERWEENING
OVERWHELMED
OVERWROUGHT
OVERZEALOUS
OXYRHYNCHUS
PATRIARCHAL
PATRONISING
PATRONIZING
PETRODOLLAR
PHARISAICAL
PHARYNGITIS
PIERREPOINT
PREROGATIVE
PROROGATION
PTERODACTYL
QUARRELLING
QUARRELSOME
QUARRINGTON
QUARTERBACK
QUARTERDECK
QUERULOUSLY
RECRIMINATE
RECRUITMENT
REFRESHMENT
REFRIGERANT
REFRIGERATE
REGRETFULLY
REGRETTABLE
REGRETTABLY
REORIENTATE
REPRESENTED
REPROACHFUL
RETRACTABLE
RETRIBUTION
RETRIBUTIVE
RETRIEVABLE
RETROACTIVE
RETROROCKET
SACRAMENTAL
SACRIFICIAL
SAPROLEGNIA
SAPROPHYTIC
SCARABAEOID
SCARBOROUGH
SCAREMONGER
SCHRECKLICH
SCIREFACIAS
SEARCHLIGHT
SECRETARIAL
SECRETARIAT
SECRETIVELY
SEGREGATION
SHAREHOLDER
SHORTCHANGE
SHORTCOMING
SHORTHANDED
SMORGASBORD
SNORKELLING
SORROWFULLY
SPARROWHAWK
SPERMATOZOA
SPERMICIDAL
SPERMOPHILE
SPHRAGISTIC
SPIRITUALLY
SPIROCHAETE
SPORTSFIELD

SPORTSWOMAN
STEREOMETER
STEREOSCOPE
STEREOTYPED
STOREKEEPER
STORYTELLER
SURROUNDING
SVARABHAKTI
SWORDSWOMAN
TARRADIDDLE
TAUROBOLIUM
TERREMOTIVE
TERRESTRIAL
TERRITORIAL
TETRADRACHM
TETRAHEDRON
THERAPEUTAE
THERAPEUTIC
THEREABOUTS
THERMOMETER
THERMOPYLAE
THOROUGHPIN
TORRIDONIAN
TOURBILLION
TURRICULATE
ULTRAMARINE
ULTRAMODERN
ULTRAVIOLET
UNBREAKABLE
UNCRUSHABLE
UNDRINKABLE
UNPRACTICAL
UNPRINTABLE
UNPROTECTED
UNTRAMELLED
VOORTREKKER
WHEREABOUTS
WHEREWITHAL
WORRYTROUGH
AIRSICKNESS
ANASTOMOSIS
ANESTHETIST
ANESTHETIZE
ANISOCERCAL
APOSIOPESIS
APOSTROPHUS
ARISTOCRACY
BEASTLINESS
BESSARABIAN
BLASPHEMOUS
BLESSEDNESS
BOYSENBERRY
BRISTLECONE
CARSICKNESS
CASSITERITE
CAUSTICALLY
CEASELESSLY
COMSTOCKERY
CONSCIOUSLY
CONSECUTIVE

CONSEQUENCE
CONSERVANCY
CONSIDERATE
CONSIDERING
CONSIGNMENT
CONSILIENCE
CONSISTENCE
CONSISTENCY
CONSOLATION
CONSOLIDATE
CONSPICUOUS
CONSPIRATOR
CONSTANTINE
CONSTELLATE
CONSTERNATE
CONSTIPATED
CONSTITUENT
CONSTRAINED
CONSTRICTED
CONSTRICTOR
CONSTRUCTOR
CONSTUPRATE
CONSULTANCY
CONSUMABLES
CONSUMERISM
CONSUMPTION
CONSUMPTIVE
CRESCENTADE
CRESTFALLEN
CROSSLEGGED
CRYSTALLINE
CRYSTALLISE
CRYSTALLIZE
DIASCORDIUM
DIPSOMANIAC
DISSEMINATE
DISSEPIMENT
DISSERTATOR
DISSIMULATE
DISSIPATION
DISSOLUTION
DRASTICALLY
DRESSMAKING
EINSTEINIUM
ELASTOPLAST
EVASIVENESS
EVISCERATED
EXASPERATED
EXOSKELETON
FEASIBILITY
FROSTBITTEN
FRUSTRATING
FRUSTRATION
GELSEMININE
GEOSYNCLINE
GHASTLINESS
GLASTONBURY
GLOSSOLALIA
GRASSHOPPER
GUESSTIMATE

HORSERACING
HORSERADISH
HORSERIDING
HOUSEHOLDER
HOUSEKEEPER
HOUSEMASTER
INESCAPABLE
INESSENTIAL
INESTIMABLE
KWASHIORKOR
LEASEHOLDER
MAISTERDOME
MARSHMALLOW
MASSIVENESS
MEASURELESS
MEASUREMENT
MENSURATION
MISSISSIPPI
MISSPELLING
MOISTURIZER
MONSTROSITY
MOSSTROOPER
MUDSLINGING
NEWSCASTING
NOISELESSLY
NONSENSICAL
OARSMANSHIP
OUTSTANDING
PASSACAGLIA
PASSIVENESS
PENSIONABLE
PENSIVENESS
PERSECUTION
PERSEVERING
PERSISTENCE
PERSONALIST
PERSONALITY
PERSONALIZE
PERSONIFIED
PERSPECTIVE
PERSPICUITY
PERSPICUOUS
PESSIMISTIC
PHYSIOGNOMY
PISSASPHALT
PODSNAPPERY
POSSESSIONS
POSSIBILITY
PRESENTABLE
PRESSURIZED
PRESTIGIOUS
PRESTISSIMO
PRESTONPANS
PRESTRESSED
PRESUMPTION
PRESUMPTIVE
PRISCIANIST
PROSAICALLY
PROSECUTION
PROSELYTISM

PROSELYTIZE
PROSPECTIVE
PROSTHETICS
PROSTRATION
QUESTIONING
RAPSCALLION
REASSURANCE
SAUSAGEMEAT
SEASICKNESS
SEISMOGRAPH
SENSATIONAL
SENSIBILITY
SENSITIVELY
SENSITIVITY
SPESSARTITE
SUBSERVIENT
SUBSISTENCE
SUBSTANDARD
SUBSTANTIAL
SUBSTANTIVE
TEASPOONFUL
TESSARAGLOT
TESSELLATED
THESMOTHETE
THISTLEDOWN
TOASTMASTER
TONSILLITIS
TRESPASSING
TRUSTEESHIP
TRUSTWORTHY
UNASSERTIVE
VARSOVIENNE
VERSATILITY
WENSLEYDALE
WHISKERANDO
WHISTLESTOP
ZWISCHENZUG
ABSTRACTION
ACATALECTIC
APATOSAURUS
AZOTOBACTER
BADTEMPERED
BARTHOLOMEW
BATTLEDRESS
BATTLEFIELD
BATTLEFRONT
BATTLEMENTS
BESTSELLING
BITTERSWEET
BOUTONNIERE
BRITTLENESS
BROTHERHOOD
CAPTIVATING
CAPTIVATION
CARTOGRAPHY
CASTELLATED
CENTENARIAN
CENTERPIECE
CENTREBOARD
CENTREPIECE

CENTRIFUGAL
CENTRIPETAL
CENTUMVIRUS
CENTURIATOR
CERTIFIABLE
CERTIFICATE
CHITTERLING
CONTAINMENT
CONTAMINANT
CONTAMINATE
CONTEMPLANT
CONTEMPLATE
CONTENEMENT
CONTENTEDLY
CONTENTIOUS
CONTENTMENT
CONTINENTAL
CONTINGENCE
CONTINGENCY
CONTINUALLY
CONTINUANCE
CONTRACTION
CONTRACTUAL
CONTRAPTION
CONTRASTING
CONTRAYERVA
CONTRETEMPS
CONTRIBUTOR
CONTRIVANCE
CONTROVERSY
CONTUBERNAL
COTTONMOUTH
CRATERELLUS
CRITHOMANCY
CRITICASTER
CULTIVATION
CURTAILMENT
CUSTOMARILY
DACTYLOGRAM
DESTABILIZE
DESTINATION
DESTITUTION
DESTRUCTION
DESTRUCTIVE
DEUTERONOMY
DEUTSCHMARK
DIATESSARON
DIATESSERON
DICTATORIAL
DIPTEROCARP
DISTASTEFUL
DISTINCTION
DISTINCTIVE
DISTINGUISH
DISTRACTION
DISTRESSING
DISTRIBUTED
DISTRIBUTOR
DISTRUSTFUL
DISTURBANCE

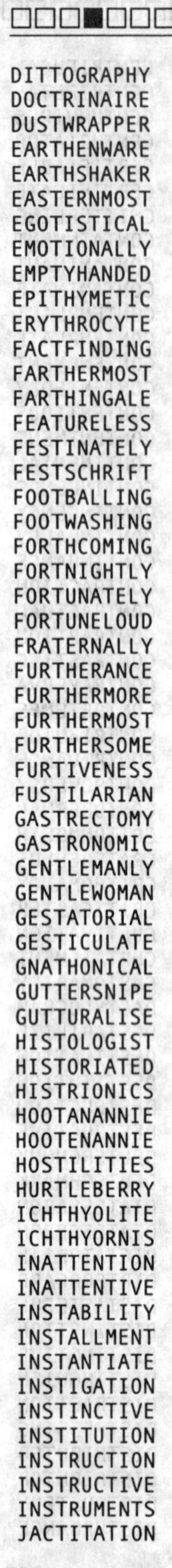

DITTOGRAPHY
DOCTRINAIRE
DUSTWRAPPER
EARTHENWARE
EARTHSHAKER
EASTERNMOST
EGOTISTICAL
EMOTIONALLY
EMPTYHANDED
EPITHYMETIC
ERYTHROCYTE
FACTFINDING
FARTHERMOST
FARTHINGALE
FEATURELESS
FESTINATELY
FESTSCHRIFT
FOOTBALLING
FOOTWASHING
FORTHCOMING
FORTNIGHTLY
FORTUNATELY
FORTUNELOUD
FRATERNALLY
FURTHERANCE
FURTHERMORE
FURTHERMOST
FURTHERSOME
FURTIVENESS
FUSTILARIAN
GASTRECTOMY
GASTRONOMIC
GENTLEMANLY
GENTLEWOMAN
GESTATORIAL
GESTICULATE
GNATHONICAL
GUTTERSNIPE
GUTTURALISE
HISTOLOGIST
HISTORIATED
HISTRIONICS
HOOTANANNIE
HOOTENANNIE
HOSTILITIES
HURTLEBERRY
ICHTHYOLITE
ICHTHYORNIS
INATTENTION
INATTENTIVE
INSTABILITY
INSTALLMENT
INSTANTIATE
INSTIGATION
INSTINCTIVE
INSTITUTION
INSTRUCTION
INSTRUCTIVE
INSTRUMENTS
JACTITATION

JUSTIFIABLE
JUSTIFIABLY
KULTURKREIS
LEATHERBACK
LEATHERETTE
LEATHERHEAD
LEATHERNECK
LECTURESHIP
LEFTLUGGAGE
LENTIGINOSE
LETTERPRESS
LITTÉRATEUR
MANTELLETTA
MANTELPIECE
MANTELSHELF
MASTERFULLY
MASTERPIECE
MASTICATION
MENTHOLATED
MENTONNIÈRE
MICTURITION
MISTRUSTFUL
MONTESQUIEU
MONTGOLFIER
MONTMORENCY
MULTIRACIAL
MULTISTOREY
NEUTRALISED
NORTHCLIFFE
NOSTRADAMUS
OBSTETRICAL
OBSTINATELY
OBSTRICTION
OBSTRUCTION
OBSTRUCTIVE
PANTALETTES
PARTICIPANT
PARTICIPATE
PARTICIPIAL
PARTNERSHIP
PARTURITION
PASTEURELLA
PASTOURELLE
PENTATHLETE
PENTECONTER
PENTECOSTAL
PENTHESILEA
PENTONVILLE
PERTINACITY
PERTINENTLY
PETTICOATED
PETTIFOGGER
PHOTOCOPIER
PHOTOFINISH
PHOTOGRAPHY
PHOTOSPHERE
PICTURESQUE
PLATERESQUE
PLATYRRHINE
POLTERGEIST

PONTIFICATE
PORTERHOUSE
PORTLANDIAN
PORTMANTEAU
PORTRAITIST
PORTRAITURE
PRETENSIONS
PRETENTIOUS
PRETERITION
PROTAGONIST
PROTOCOCCUS
PROTONOTARY
PROTRACTING
PROTRACTION
PROTUBERANT
PSITTACOSIS
RAPTUROUSLY
RASTAFARIAN
RATTLESNAKE
RECTANGULAR
RECTIFIABLE
RECTILINEAR
REITERATION
RESTATEMENT
RESTITUTION
RESTIVENESS
RESTORATION
RESTORATIVE
RESTRICTION
RESTRICTIVE
RESTRUCTURE
RINTHEREOUT
ROTTENSTONE
SALTIMBANCO
SALTIMBOCCA
SCATTERGOOD
SCATTERLING
SCITAMINEAE
SCUTTLEBUTT
SENTENTIOUS
SENTIMENTAL
SEPTENARIUS
SEPTENTRION
SEPTICAEMIA
SHITTIMWOOD
SHUTTLECOCK
SKETCHINESS
SMITHEREENS
SMITHSONIAN
SMITHSONITE
SOUTHAMPTON
SOUTHWESTER
SPATTERDASH
SPATTERDOCK
SPITSTICKER
STATELINESS
STATISTICAL
STETHOSCOPE
SUBTRACTION
SUBTROPICAL

SUITABILITY
SURTARBRAND
SURTURBRAND
SUSTAINABLE
SWITCHBOARD
SWITZERLAND
SYNTHESIZED
SYNTHESIZER
SYSTEMATIZE
TANTALIZING
TASTELESSLY
TATTERSALLS
TAUTOCHRONE
TECTIBRANCH
TEETOTALLER
TENTATIVELY
TENTERHOOKS
TESTIMONIAL
TORTICOLLIS
TORTICULLUS
TOSTICATION
TRITAGONIST
ULOTRICHALE
UNSTOPPABLE
UNUTTERABLE
VENTILATION
VENTURESOME
VERTIGINOUS
WASTEBASKET
WEATHERCOCK
WESTERNMOST
WESTMINSTER
WESTPHALIAN
WHITEBOYISM
WHITECHAPEL
WHITECOLLAR
WHITEFRIARS
WHITETHROAT
WHITLEATHER
WHITTINGTON
WINTERBERRY
WINTERGREEN
WISTFULNESS
ACCUMULATOR
ACQUIESCENT
ACQUISITION
ACQUISITIVE
ACTUALITIES
ADJUDICATOR
AIGUILLETTE
AILUROPHILE
ALBUGINEOUS
APPURTENANT
ARQUEBUSIER
AUGUSTINIAN
BEAUMONTAGE
BEAUTIFULLY
BIFURCATION
CHAULMOOGRA
CHAULMOUGRA

COLUMBARIUM
CONURBATION
DOCUMENTARY
DRAUGHTSMAN
ELEUTHERIAN
ENCUMBRANCE
EXPURGATION
EXQUISITELY
FATUOUSNESS
FLOURISHING
FRAUDULENCE
GENUFLEXION
GENUINENESS
GROUNDSHEET
GROUNDSPEED
GROUNDSWELL
ILLUMINATED
ILLUSIONARY
ILLUSIONIST
ILLUSTRATOR
ILLUSTRIOUS
IMPULSIVELY
INAUTHENTIC
INDUBITABLE
INDUBITABLY
INDULGENTLY
INDUSTRIOUS
INFURIATING
INJUDICIOUS
INNUMERABLE
INQUIRINGLY
INQUISITION
INQUISITIVE
INSULTINGLY
INSUPERABLE
INTUITIVELY
LIQUIDAMBAR
LIQUIDATION
LUXULYANITE
LUXURIANTLY
LUXURIOUSLY
MANUFACTURE
MANUMISSION
MAQUILADORA
NATURALNESS
OBMUTESCENT
PECULIARITY
PENULTIMATE
PLOUGHSHARE
PSEUDOLOGIA
PSEUDOMORPH
RECURRENTLY
REDUPLICATE
REFURBISHED
REGURGITATE
RELUCTANTLY
REPUDIATION
REQUIREMENT
REQUISITION
RESUSCITATE

RHEUMATICKY
ROGUISHNESS
SCEUOPHYLAX
SCOUTMASTER
SCRUFFINESS
SCRUMPTIOUS
SEQUESTRATE
SMOULDERING
SPLUTTERING
STRUTHIONES
SUBUNGULATA
SUSURRATION
TEGUCICALPA
TENUOUSNESS
THAUMATROPE
THOUGHTLESS
TRIUMVIRATE
TROUBLESOME
TROUBLESPOT
UNAUTHENTIC
UNFULFILLED
UNFURNISHED
UNJUSTIFIED
UNPUBLISHED
UNQUALIFIED
UNSUPPORTED
UNSURPASSED
UNSUSPECTED
VACUOUSNESS
VOLUNTARILY
CONVALLARIA
CONVENIENCE
CONVENTICLE
CONVERGENCE
CONVERTIBLE
CONVOCATION
CONVOLUTION
CONVOLVULUS
CONVULSIONS
CULVERINEER
FLAVOURSOME
FRIVOLOUSLY
GRAVEDIGGER
GRAVITATION
HEAVYHANDED
HEAVYWEIGHT
NERVOUSNESS
PARVANIMITY
PEEVISHNESS
PREVARICATE
PREVENTABLE
PROVISIONAL
PROVISIONER
PROVOCATION
PROVOCATIVE
SALVADORIAN
SALVOGUNNER
SERVICEABLE
SHOVELBOARD
SILVERSMITH
SURVEILLANT
UNAVAILABLE
UNAVOIDABLE
UNAVOIDABLY
UNIVERSALLY
AWKWARDNESS
COXWAINLESS
SCHWARMEREI
SHOWERPROOF
SHOWJUMPING
SHOWMANSHIP
UNSWEETENED
WAYWARDNESS
ALEXANDRINE
ALEXANDRITE
ANAXIMANDER
COEXISTENCE
FAUXBOURDON
FLEXIBILITY
INEXCITABLE
INEXCUSABLE
INEXCUSABLY
INEXPEDIENT
INEXPENSIVE
ISOXSUPRINE
UNEXPLAINED
UNEXPRESSED
ALCYONARIAN
ASSYTHEMENT
BARYCENTRIC
CHRYSAROBIN
CHRYSOPRASE
DEHYDRATION
EMPYROMANCY
ILLYWHACKER
ITHYPHALLIC
ITHYPHALLUS
LARYNGISMUS
PLAYFULNESS
POLYMORPHIC
POLYSTYRENE
POLYTECHNIC
POLYTRICHUM
BRAZZAVILLE
ELIZABETHAN
FITZWILLIAM
PRIZEWINNER
RAZZAMATAZZ

11:5

ACATALECTIC
ACCLAMATION
ACINACIFORM
ACTUALITIES
AFGHANISTAN
AGGRAVATING
AGGRAVATION
AGORAPHOBIA
ALEXANDRINE
ALEXANDRITE
ALIFANFARON
ALPHABETIZE
AMELANCHIER
ANFRACTUOUS
APOCALYPTIC
APPEARANCES
APPEASEMENT
ARCHAEOLOGY
AWKWARDNESS
BARBASTELLE
BELEAGUERED
BEREAVEMENT
BESSARABIAN
BOMBARDMENT
BUREAUCRACY
CABBALISTIC
CALLANETICS
CAMPANOLOGY
CARNAPTIOUS
CHARACINOID
CITLALEPETL
CLIMACTERIC
CLIMATOLOGY
COLLABORATE
COLLAPSIBLE
COMMANDMENT
COMPARATIVE
COMPARTMENT
COMRADESHIP
CONFABULATE
CONFARREATE
CONTAINMENT
CONTAMINANT
CONTAMINATE
CONVALLARIA
COXWAINLESS
CRÉMAILLÈRE
CREMATORIUM
CULPABILITY
CURNAPTIOUS
CURTAILMENT
DARDANELLES
DECLAMATION
DECLAMATORY
DECLARATION
DEGRADATION
DERMATOLOGY
DESTABILIZE
DICTATORIAL
DISPARAGING
DISTASTEFUL
EDUCATIONAL
ELIZABETHAN
EMPLACEMENT
ENCHANTMENT
ENCHANTRESS
ENFRANCHISE
ENGHALSKRUG
ENNEAHEDRON
ENSLAVEMENT
EPANALEPSIS
EREMACAUSIS
ERYMANTHIAN
ESCHATOLOGY
ESTRAMAZONE
ESTRANGHELO
EUCHARISTIC
EXCLAMATION
EXPLANATION
EXPLANATORY
EXTRADITION
EXTRAPOLATE
EXTRAVAGANT
EYECATCHING
FANFARONADE
FARRAGINOUS
FISHANDCHIP
FUNDAMENTAL
GENEALOGIST
GESTATORIAL
GODDAUGHTER
GONFALONIER
GREGARINIDA
GUADALCANAL
HAPHAZARDLY
HEMIANOPSIA
HOLLANDAISE
HOOTANANNIE
HUSBANDLAND
ILLMANNERED
IMPEACHMENT
IMPLAUSIBLE
IMPRACTICAL
INDIARUBBER
INFLAMMABLE
INGRATITUDE
INSTABILITY
INSTALLMENT
INSTANTIATE
INTRACTABLE
INTRAVENOUS
IPECACUANHA
LONGANIMITY
LONGAWAITED
MACHAIRODUS
MAGNANIMITY
MAGNANIMOUS
MANGALSUTRA
MASKALLONGE
MEDIASTINUM
MINIATURIST
MINIATURIZE
MISCARRIAGE
NARRAGANSET
NIPFARTHING
OFFHANDEDLY
ONOMASTICON
OPERATIONAL
OSTRACODERM
OUAGADOUGOU
OUTMANEUVER
PANTALETTES
PARVANIMITY
PASSACAGLIA
PENTATHLETE
PERMANENTLY
PHALANSTERY
PHILANDERER
PHILATELIST
PISCATORIAL
PISSASPHALT
PRECAUTIONS
PREMATURELY
PREPARATION
PREPARATORY
PREVARICATE
PROBABILITY
PROBATIONER
PROPAGATION
PROSAICALLY
PROTAGONIST
RASTAFARIAN
RAZZAMATAZZ
READABILITY
RECLAMATION
RECTANGULAR
RELEASEMENT
RELIABILITY
REPLACEABLE
REPLACEMENT
RESTATEMENT
RETRACTABLE
RHOPALOCERA
SABBATARIAN
SACRAMENTAL
SALVADORIAN
SAUSAGEMEAT
SCARABAEOID
SCHWARMEREI
SCITAMINEAE
SCREAMINGLY
SENNACHERIB
SENSATIONAL
SHENANIGANS
SHUNAMITISM
SINGAPOREAN
SOCIABILITY
SPHRAGISTIC
SPREADSHEET
STEGANOGRAM
STEGANOPODE
STREAMLINED
SUBPANATION
SUITABILITY
SURTARBRAND
SUSTAINABLE
SVARABHAKTI
SYMPATHETIC
SYMPATHISER

SYMPATHIZER
TANTALIZING
TARRADIDDLE
TENTATIVELY
TESSARAGLOT
TETRADRACHM
TETRAHEDRON
THANATOPSIS
THERAPEUTAE
THERAPEUTIC
THREATENING
TRACASSERIE
TRITAGONIST
TRYPANOSOMA
TRYPANOSOME
ULTRAMARINE
ULTRAMODERN
ULTRAVIOLET
UNAVAILABLE
UNFLAPPABLE
UNPRACTICAL
UNQUALIFIED
UNREALISTIC
UNREASONING
UNSHAKEABLE
UNTRAMELLED
VALLAMBROSA
VARIABILITY
VERSATILITY
VOLCANOLOGY
VULCANOLOGY
WAYWARDNESS
WELLADVISED
ZOROASTRIAN
ADUMBRATION
ANNABERGITE
ANTIBURGHER
ATRABILIOUS
BACKBENCHER
BALLBEARING
BOOKBINDING
CALIBRATION
CARABINIERE
CELEBRATION
CEREBRATION
CHAMBERLAIN
CHAMBERMAID
COLDBLOODED
DEMIBASTION
DISABLEMENT
DISOBEDIENT
DOLABRIFORM
ENTABLATURE
ENTABLEMENT
ESTABLISHED
ESTABLISHER
EXORBITANCE
FAUXBOURDON
FLABBERGAST
FLAMBOYANCE
FLAMBOYANTE
FOOTBALLING
FULLBLOODED
HALFBROTHER
HAREBRAINED
INDUBITABLE
INDUBITABLY
INHABITABLE
INHABITANTS
KATABOTHRON
KOTABOTHRON
MAKEBELIEVE
MARLBOROUGH
MOXIBUSTION
OVERBALANCE
OVERBEARING
PARABLEPSIS
PARABOLANUS
PAWNBROKERS
SCARBOROUGH
SHIPBUILDER
SKIDBLADNIR
SLUMBERWEAR
STEPBROTHER
STROBOSCOPE
THEOBROMINE
TOURBILLION
TROUBLESOME
TROUBLESPOT
UNAMBIGUOUS
UNPUBLISHED
WELLBEHAVED
WINDBREAKER
ABLACTATION
ABRACADABRA
AFFECTATION
AGRICULTURE
AMERCIAMENT
ANENCEPHALY
ANTECEDENCE
ANTECHAMBER
ANTICYCLONE
ARTICULATED
ASSOCIATION
ATROCIOUSLY
AUDACIOUSLY
BARYCENTRIC
CAPACITANCE
CAPACITATOR
CATACAUSTIC
CATACHRESIS
CATACLYSMIC
CHANCELLERY
COINCIDENCE
CONSCIOUSLY
CRESCENTADE
DELECTATION
DELICIOUSLY
DELICTATION
DESECRATION
DESICCATION
DIASCORDIUM
DIRECTIONAL
DIRECTORATE
DODECASTYLE
EFFECTIVELY
EFFECTUALLY
EFFICACIOUS
EFFICIENTLY
ENDOCARDIUM
ENUNCIATION
EVISCERATED
EXPECTANTLY
EXPECTATION
EXPECTORANT
EXPECTORATE
FEROCIOUSLY
FORECASTING
FORECLOSURE
FRENCHWOMAN
FRENCHWOMEN
GATECRASHER
HANDCRAFTED
HYPOCORISMA
IMPECUNIOUS
INESCAPABLE
INEXCITABLE
INEXCUSABLE
INEXCUSABLY
INSECTICIDE
INSECTIVORE
JUDICIOUSLY
KILOCALORIE
MALICIOUSLY
MASOCHISTIC
MEDICINALLY
METACARPALS
MONOCHINOUS
NEWSCASTING
NOTICEBOARD
OBJECTIVELY
OBJECTIVITY
OFFICIALDOM
OFFICIALESE
OFFICIOUSLY
OVERCROWDED
PARACETAMOL
PARACHUTIST
PARACROSTIC
PENICILLATE
PERICARDIUM
PINACOTHECA
POCOCURANTE
POLICEWOMAN
PREOCCUPIED
PRINCIPALLY
PRISCIANIST
RAPSCALLION
REFOCILLATE
REINCARNATE
RELUCTANTLY
RIFACIMENTO
ROSICRUCIAN
SAGACIOUSLY
SALACIOUSLY
SCHECKLATON
SEARCHLIGHT
SELECTIVELY
SELECTIVITY
SELFCONTROL
SERICULTURE
SKETCHINESS
SPEECHCRAFT
SWITCHBOARD
TEGUCICALPA
TENACIOUSLY
THENCEFORTH
TOBACCONIST
TREACHEROUS
TREACHETOUR
TREECREEPER
TRENCHERMAN
TRINCOMALEE
UNNECESSARY
UTRICULARIA
VIVACIOUSLY
VORACIOUSLY
WINDCHEATER
WOODCARVING
ZWISCHENZUG
ABANDONMENT
ABRIDGEMENT
ADJUDICATOR
AERODYNAMIC
ASSIDUOUSLY
BENEDICTINE
BENEDICTION
BLADDERWORT
BLOODSPORTS
BLOODSTREAM
BLOODSUCKER
BLUNDERBORE
BRANDENBURG
BREADCRUMBS
BREADWINNER
BROADCASTER
BROADMINDED
BROBDINGNAG
CHILDMINDER
CHONDROSTEI
CHORDOPHONE
CLANDESTINE
COORDINATED
COORDINATES
DEHYDRATION
DREADLOCKED
DREADNOUGHT
EQUIDISTANT
ERIODENDRON
EXPEDITIOUS
FIELDWORKER
FOUNDATIONS
FRAUDULENCE
GRANDFATHER
GRANDMASTER
GRANDMOTHER
HAIRDRESSER
IMMEDIATELY
IMPEDIMENTA
INJUDICIOUS
INSIDIOUSLY
IRRADIATION
IRREDENTIST
IRREDUCIBLE
LAPIDESCENT
LAUNDERETTE
LEPIDOPTERA
LEPIDOSIREN
LOGODAEDALY
MACADAMIZED
MALADJUSTED
MALEDICTION
MEANDERINGS
MELODIOUSLY
MISIDENTIFY
NEANDERTHAL
PARADOXICAL
PSEUDOLOGIA
PSEUDOMORPH
REPUDIATION
RESIDENTIAL
RHABDOMANCY
SCANDALIZED
SCANDANAVIA
SCANDINAVIA
SCULDUDDERY
SCULDUGGERY
SELFDEFENCE
SKULDUDDERY
SKULDUGGERY
SLENDERNESS
SOCKDALAGER
SOCKDOLAGER
SOCKDOLIGER
SOCKDOLOGER
SOUNDLESSLY
SPEEDOMETER
SPENDTHRIFT
SPONDULICKS
SPONDYLITIS
STANDARDIZE
STANDOFFISH
STANDPATTER
STEADFASTLY
STRADUARIUS
SWORDSWOMAN
TAXIDERMIST
THUNDERBIRD
THUNDERBOLT
THUNDERCLAP

THUNDERHEAD
UNENDURABLE
UNGODLINESS
VALEDICTION
VALEDICTORY
WELLDEFINED
WELLDRESSED
WORLDFAMOUS
WORLDLINESS
XENODOCHIUM
ABBREVIATED
ABECEDARIAN
ACADEMICIAN
ACCRESCENCE
ACHIEVEMENT
ADOLESCENCE
AGGREGATION
AMPHETAMINE
AMPLEXICAUL
ANTHESTERIA
APONEUROSIS
APPRECIABLE
APPRECIABLY
APPRENTICED
ARCHEGONIAL
ARCHEGONIUM
ARCHENTERON
ARQUEBUSIER
ARRHENOTOKY
ASCLEPIADES
ASPHETERISM
BADDELEYITE
BADTEMPERED
BANDEIRANTE
BASKERVILLE
BELLEROPHON
BELLETTRIST
BESIEGEMENT
BITTERSWEET
BLAMEWORTHY
BOYSENBERRY
BRUCELLOSIS
BUMBERSHOOT
BUPRESTIDAE
CALCEOLARIA
CAMPESTRIAN
CANDESCENCE
CASTELLATED
CEASELESSLY
CENTENARIAN
CENTERPIECE
CHOLESTEROL
CLARENCIEUX
COALESCENCE
COLLECTANEA
COLLENCHYMA
COMMEMORATE
COMMENDABLE
COMMENDABLY
COMMENTATOR
COMPENDIOUS
COMPETENTLY
COMPETITION
COMPETITIVE
CONCEALMENT
CONCEIVABLE
CONCEIVABLY
CONCENTRATE
CONCEPTICLE
CONFEDERACY
CONFEDERATE
CONJECTURAL
CONNECTICUT
CONSECUTIVE
CONSEQUENCE
CONSERVANCY
CONTEMPLANT
CONTEMPLATE
CONTENEMENT
CONTENTEDLY
CONTENTIOUS
CONTENTMENT
CONVENIENCE
CONVENTICLE
CONVERGENCE
CONVERTIBLE
COOPERATION
COOPERATIVE
COPPERPLATE
CORNERSTONE
CORRECTNESS
CORRELATION
CRATERELLUS
CREDENTIALS
CRENELLATED
CULVERINEER
DANGEROUSLY
DECREPITATE
DECREPITUDE
DEPREDATION
DESCENDANTS
DESPERATELY
DESPERATION
DEUTERONOMY
DIATESSARON
DIATESSERON
DIFFERENTLY
DIPTEROCARP
DISBELIEVER
DISCERNIBLE
DISCERNMENT
DISHEVELLED
DISPENSABLE
DISPERSABLE
DISREGARDED
DISSEMINATE
DISSEPIMENT
DISSERTATOR
DITHELETISM
DUNIEWASSAL
EARNESTNESS
EASTERNMOST
EMPIECEMENT
ENUMERATION
EPIGENESIST
EPINEPHRINE
ESCHERICHIA
ESPIEGLERIE
EUPHEMISTIC
EXCEEDINGLY
EXCRESCENCE
EXONERATION
FARREACHING
FINGERPRINT
FINGERSTALL
FORBEARANCE
FOTHERGILLA
FRATERNALLY
GELSEMININE
GEOMETRICAL
GIBBERELLIN
GINGERBREAD
GRAVEDIGGER
GUTTERSNIPE
GYNAECOLOGY
HALLEFLINTA
HAMMERCLOTH
HECKELPHONE
HERPETOLOGY
HINDERLANDS
HOMOEOPATHY
HOOTENANNIE
HORSERACING
HORSERADISH
HORSERIDING
HOUSEHOLDER
HOUSEKEEPER
HOUSEMASTER
HYPHENATION
IMPLEMENTAL
IMPRECATION
IMPRECISION
IMPREGNABLE
INCREDULITY
INCREDULOUS
INCREMENTAL
INFREQUENCY
INGREDIENTS
INOPERATIVE
INTREPIDITY
IRIDESCENCE
JABBERWOCKY
KINDERSPIEL
KOMMERSBUCH
LAMMERGEIER
LAMMERGEYER
LAWLESSNESS
LEASEHOLDER
LETTERPRESS
LOGGERHEADS
MAGLEMOSIAN
MALFEASANCE
MANTELLETTA
MANTELPIECE
MANTELSHELF
MARKETPLACE
MASTERFULLY
MASTERPIECE
MATHEMATICS
MAURETANIAN
MENDELEVIUM
MENDELSSOHN
MIDDENSTEAD
MINNESINGER
MISBEGOTTEN
MISBEHAVIOR
MISDEMEANOR
MONTESQUIEU
MORGENSTERN
MUSKELLUNGE
NETHERLANDS
NETHERLINGS
NICKELODEON
NOISELESSLY
NONDESCRIPT
NONFEASANCE
NONSENSICAL
NUMBERPLATE
OBSTETRICAL
OPALESCENCE
ORCHESTRATE
ORCHESTRINA
ORCHESTRION
OSTREOPHAGE
OVEREXPOSED
PAMPELMOOSE
PAMPELMOUSE
PANDEMONIUM
PASTEURELLA
PEACEKEEPER
PENTECONTER
PENTECOSTAL
PERCEFOREST
PERCEPTIBLE
PERCEPTIBLY
PERPETRATOR
PERPETUALLY
PERSECUTION
PERSEVERING
PHONETICIAN
PICKELHAUBE
PLANETARIUM
PLATERESQUE
PLEBEIANISE
POLLENBRUSH
POLTERGEIST
POMPELMOOSE
POMPELMOUSE
PONDEROUSLY
PORTERHOUSE
POSSESSIONS
PREDECESSOR
PREDESTINED
PREMEDITATE
PRESENTABLE
PRETENSIONS
PRETENTIOUS
PRETERITION
PREVENTABLE
PRIZEWINNER
PROCEEDINGS
PROFESSEDLY
PROGENITRIX
PROLEGOMENA
PROLETARIAN
PROLETARIAT
PROSECUTION
PROSELYTISM
PROSELYTIZE
RALLENTANDO
RANGEFINDER
REFLEXOLOGY
REFRESHMENT
REGRETFULLY
REGRETTABLE
REGRETTABLY
REITERATION
REPRESENTED
RESPECTABLE
RESPECTABLY
ROCKEFELLER
ROTTENSTONE
SACHERTORTE
SANDERSWOOD
SARCENCHYME
SCAREMONGER
SCHRECKLICH
SCIREFACIAS
SCOLECIFORM
SECRETARIAL
SECRETARIAT
SECRETIVELY
SEGREGATION
SELFEVIDENT
SENTENTIOUS
SEPTENARIUS
SEPTENTRION
SEQUESTRATE
SHAKESPEARE
SHAMELESSLY
SHAPELINESS
SHAREHOLDER
SHOVELBOARD
SHOWERPROOF
SILVERSMITH
SMOKESCREEN
SPACESAVING
SPOKESWOMAN
STAKEHOLDER
STATELINESS

STEREOMETER
STEREOSCOPE
STEREOTYPED
STIPENDIARY
STOREKEEPER
STREETLIGHT
SUBMERGENCE
SUBSERVIENT
SUCCEDANEUM
SUGGESTIBLE
SUMMERHOUSE
SUPPEDANEUM
SURVEILLANT
SUSCEPTIBLE
SYMMETRICAL
SYSTEMATIZE
TASTELESSLY
TATTERSALLS
TEMPERAMENT
TEMPERATURE
TEMPESTUOUS
TENDENTIOUS
TENTERHOOKS
TERREMOTIVE
TERRESTRIAL
TESSELLATED
THEREABOUTS
TRAGELAPHUS
TRICERATOPS
TRIMESTRIAL
TSCHERNOSEM
TURBELLARIA
UNBLEMISHED
UNBREAKABLE
UNCLEANNESS
UNIVERSALLY
UNSHELTERED
UNSPEAKABLE
UNSPECIFIED
UNSWEETENED
USELESSNESS
VARIEGATION
VENDEMIAIRE
VESPERTINAL
WAPPENSCHAW
WASHERWOMAN
WASTEBASKET
WESTERNMOST
WHEREABOUTS
WHEREWITHAL
WHITEBOYISM
WHITECHAPEL
WHITECOLLAR
WHITEFRIARS
WHITETHROAT
WIENERWURST
WILBERFORCE
WINTERBERRY
WINTERGREEN
WITHERSHINS
WONDERFULLY
LITTÉRATEUR
ACRIFLAVINE
BACKFIELDER
BASHFULNESS
BENEFICIARY
BENEFICIATE
BULLFIGHTER
CALEFACIENT
CALIFORNIUM
CAREFULNESS
CILOFIBRATE
CLIFFHANGER
COEFFICIENT
DISAFFECTED
DUMBFOUNDED
FACTFINDING
FOREFATHERS
GENUFLEXION
HELPFULNESS
INDEFINABLE
INDIFFERENT
INEFFECTIVE
INEFFECTUAL
INEFFICIENT
INOFFENSIVE
IRREFUTABLE
LATIFUNDIUM
MALEFACTION
MANUFACTURE
MUNIFICENCE
OVERFISHING
OVERFLOWING
PACIFICALLY
PLAYFULNESS
PROOFREADER
SCAFFOLDING
SCRUFFINESS
SPIFFLICATE
STAGFLATION
TÉLÉFÉRIQUE
THRIFTINESS
TRAFFICATOR
UNBEFITTING
WAKEFULNESS
WELLFOUNDED
WISTFULNESS
ABIOGENETIC
ALBIGENSIAN
ALBUGINEOUS
ALLEGORICAL
ASSIGNATION
ASTIGMATISM
AURIGNACIAN
BOURGEOISIE
BRAGGADOCIO
CACOGASTRIC
CATEGORICAL
CHARGEPAYER
DEMAGOGUERY
DEMOGRAPHIC
DESEGREGATE
DESIGNATION
DISAGREEING
DRAGGLETAIL
DRAUGHTSMAN
ENLIGHTENED
EVANGELICAL
EXAGGERATED
FEHMGERICHT
GAMOGENESIS
HANGGLIDING
HOMOGENEITY
HOMOGENEOUS
HOMOGENIZED
ILLOGICALLY
IMMIGRATION
IMPIGNORATE
INDIGESTION
INDIGNANTLY
INDIGNATION
INTEGRATION
INVIGILATOR
IRREGULARLY
KRIEGSSPIEL
LOGOGRAPHER
METAGENESIS
MONOGRAMMED
MONTGOLFIER
OPPIGNORATE
PEDAGOGICAL
PEREGRINATE
PERIGORDIAN
PLOUGHSHARE
POMEGRANATE
RECOGNITION
RELIGIOUSLY
RESIGNATION
SELAGINELLA
SLUMGULLION
SMORGASBORD
SPANGCOCKLE
TELEGRAPHER
TELEGRAPHIC
THINGAMAJIG
THINGLINESS
THINGUMAJIG
THOUGHTLESS
THROGMORTON
TOBOGGANING
TOPOGRAPHER
TYPOGRAPHER
TYPOGRAPHIC
TYROGLYPHID
UNDIGNIFIED
UNRIGHTEOUS
UPRIGHTNESS
WRONGHEADED
XYLOGRAPHER
ANACHRONISM
ANAPHYLAXIS
APOPHYLLITE
BACCHANALIA
BARTHOLOMEW
BEACHCOMBER
BIOCHEMICAL
BROTHERHOOD
CAMPHORATED
CATCHPHRASE
CHICHEVACHE
CIRRHIPEDEA
CIRRHIPEDIA
COACHFELLOW
CRITHOMANCY
DIAPHORESIS
DIAPHORETIC
DOWNHEARTED
EARTHENWARE
EARTHSHAKER
ELEPHANTINE
EPICHEIREMA
EPITHYMETIC
EPOCHMAKING
ERYTHROCYTE
FARTHERMOST
FARTHINGALE
FORTHCOMING
FRIGHTENING
FRIGHTFULLY
FURTHERANCE
FURTHERMORE
FURTHERMOST
FURTHERSOME
GNATHONICAL
GRAPHICALLY
HALFHEARTED
HALFHOLIDAY
HARDHITTING
HATCHETTITE
HAUGHTINESS
ICHTHYOLITE
ICHTHYORNIS
INCOHERENCE
JAMAHIRIYAH
KINCHINMORT
KINDHEARTED
KITCHENETTE
KWASHIORKOR
LEATHERBACK
LEATHERETTE
LEATHERHEAD
LEATHERNECK
MARSHMALLOW
MENTHOLATED
MERCHANDISE
MERCHANDIZE
MERCHANTMAN
MISCHIEVOUS
MONCHIQUITE
MUNCHHAUSEN
MUSCHELKALK
NAUGHTINESS
NEIGHBORING
NEIGHBOURLY
NONCHALANCE
NORTHCLIFFE
NYMPHOMANIA
OVERHANGING
OXYRHYNCHUS
PAMPHLETEER
PENTHESILEA
PERCHLORATE
PITCHBLENDE
PROPHETICAL
PROPHYLAXIS
PSYCHEDELIC
PSYCHIATRIC
PSYCHODELIC
PTOCHOCRACY
PULCHRITUDE
PUNCHINELLO
REICHENBACH
RINTHEREOUT
SCYPHISTOMA
SHEPHERDESS
SLIGHTINGLY
SMITHEREENS
SMITHSONIAN
SMITHSONITE
SOUTHAMPTON
SOUTHWESTER
STETHOSCOPE
SYNCHROMESH
SYNCHRONISE
SYNCHRONISM
SYNCHRONIZE
SYNTHESIZED
SYNTHESIZER
TRACHEOTOMY
TRICHINELLA
TRICHINOSED
TRICHOPTERA
TROPHOBLAST
UNINHABITED
UNINHIBITED
UNREHEARSED
UNSCHEDULED
WAREHOUSING
WARMHEARTED
WEATHERCOCK
WEIGHBRIDGE
WITCHDOCTOR
WITHHOLDING
ABOMINATION
ACCLIMATION
ACCLIMATISE
ACCLIMATIZE
ACQUIESCENT
ACQUISITION
ACQUISITIVE

AFFLIICTION
AIGUILLETTE
AIRSICKNESS
AMERICANISM
AMPHIBOLOGY
AMPHISBAENA
AMPHISBOENA
ANADIPLOSIS
ANAXIMANDER
APOSIOPESIS
APPLICATION
APPOINTMENT
ARCHILOCHUS
ARCHIPELAGO
ASTRINGENCY
ATTRIBUTION
ATTRIBUTIVE
BARBITURATE
BELLIGERENT
BIBLIOPHILE
BILLIONAIRE
BODHISATTVA
CALLIGRAPHY
CALLISTEMON
CALLITRICHE
CANDIDATURE
CANNIBALISM
CANNIBALIZE
CAPRICCIOSO
CAPTIVATING
CAPTIVATION
CARDIOGRAPH
CARMINATIVE
CARNIVOROUS
CARRIAGEWAY
CARSICKNESS
CASSITERITE
CAULIFLOWER
CERTIFIABLE
CERTIFICATE
CHARISMATIC
COEXISTENCE
COMBINATION
COMMINATION
COMMISERATE
COMPILATION
COMPILEMENT
CONCILIATOR
CONCISENESS
CONDITIONAL
CONDITIONER
CONFIDENTLY
CONFINEMENT
CONSIDERATE
CONSIDERING
CONSIGNMENT
CONSILIENCE
CONSISTENCE
CONSISTENCY
CONTINENTAL
CONTINGENCE
CONTINGENCY
CONTINUALLY
CONTINUANCE
CREDIBILITY
CREPITATION
CRIMINOLOGY
CRITICASTER
CROCIDOLITE
CRUCIFIXION
CULMINATION
CULTIVATION
DECEITFULLY
DEGRINGOLER
DEIFICATION
DEPRIVATION
DESTINATION
DESTITUTION
DETRIMENTAL
DIFFIDENTLY
DISCIPLINED
DISFIGURING
DISSIMULATE
DISSIPATION
DISTINCTION
DISTINCTIVE
DISTINGUISH
DUPLICATING
DUPLICATION
EDIFICATION
EGALITARIAN
EGOTISTICAL
ELIGIBILITY
ELIMINATION
ELUCIDATION
EMOTIONALLY
ENCHIRIDION
EPAMINONDAS
EPIDIASCOPE
ERADICATION
EVASIVENESS
EXAMINATION
EXQUISITELY
FABRICATION
FALLIBILITY
FASCINATING
FASCINATION
FASHIONABLE
FASHIONABLY
FEASIBILITY
FERNITICKLE
FESTINATELY
FILLIBUSTER
FLEXIBILITY
FLORILEGIUM
FOOLISHNESS
FORBIDDANCE
FORGIVENESS
FORNICATION
FULFILLMENT
FULMINATION
FURNISHINGS
FURTIVENESS
FUSTILARIAN
GALLIBAGGER
GALLIBEGGAR
GALLIGANTUS
GALLIMAUFRY
GARNISHMENT
GENUINENESS
GERMINATION
GESTICULATE
GRAVITATION
GULLIBILITY
HANDICAPPED
HANDICAPPER
HARDICANUTE
HERBIVOROUS
HERRINGBONE
HOGGISHNESS
HOOLIGANISM
HOSPITALITY
HOSPITALIZE
HOSPITALLER
HOSTILITIES
HUMMINGBIRD
IDOLIZATION
IMAGINATION
IMAGINATIVE
IMPLICATION
INALIENABLE
INCLINATION
INCRIMINATE
INQUIRINGLY
INQUISITION
INQUISITIVE
INSPIRATION
INSTIGATION
INSTINCTIVE
INSTITUTION
INTRICATELY
INTUITIVELY
JACTITATION
JINRICKSHAW
JUSTIFIABLE
JUSTIFIABLY
KINNIKINICK
LENTIGINOSE
LILLIPUTIAN
LINDISFARNE
LIQUIDAMBAR
LIQUIDATION
LONGINQUITY
LUBRICATION
MACHINATION
MAGNIFICENT
MANCIPATION
MAQUILADORA
MARGINALIST
MARGINALIZE
MASSIVENESS
MASTICATION
MATRIARCHAL
MATRICULATE
MATRIMONIAL
MAURITANIAN
MEANINGLESS
MEKHITARIST
MELLIFLUOUS
MERCILESSLY
METRICATION
MILLIONAIRE
MISSISSIPPI
MOCKINGBIRD
MULTIRACIAL
MULTISTOREY
NOTHINGNESS
NOURISHMENT
NUTRITIONAL
OBSTINATELY
OPINIONATED
ORIGINALITY
ORIGINATING
ORIGINATION
OUTDISTANCE
OXODIZATION
PAEDIATRICS
PARLIPOMENA
PARTICIPANT
PARTICIPATE
PARTICIPIAL
PASSIVENESS
PATRIARCHAL
PEEVISHNESS
PENSIONABLE
PENSIVENESS
PERCIPIENCE
PERMISSIBLE
PERSISTENCE
PERTINACITY
PERTINENTLY
PESSIMISTIC
PETTICOATED
PETTIFOGGER
PHARISAICAL
PHILIPPINES
PHTHIRIASIS
PHYSIOGNOMY
PLAGIARISED
PLAGIOSTOMI
POLLINATION
PONTIFICATE
POSSIBILITY
PRECIPITATE
PRECIPITOUS
PREDICAMENT
PREDICATIVE
PREDICTABLE
PREDICTABLY
PREHISTORIC
PRELIBATION
PRELIMINARY
PREMIERSHIP
PRIMIGENIAL
PRODIGALISE
PRODIGALITY
PROFICIENCY
PROFITEROLE
PROHIBITION
PROHIBITIVE
PROLIFERATE
PROMINENTLY
PROMISCUITY
PROMISCUOUS
PROPINQUITY
PROVISIONAL
PROVISIONER
PUBLICATION
PUBLISHABLE
QUALITATIVE
RAFFISHNESS
REALIGNMENT
REALIZATION
REANIMATION
RECRIMINATE
RECTIFIABLE
RECTILINEAR
REFRIGERANT
REFRIGERATE
RENAISSANCE
REORIENTATE
REQUIREMENT
REQUISITION
RESPIRATION
RESPIRATORY
RESTITUTION
RESTIVENESS
RETRIBUTION
RETRIBUTIVE
RETRIEVABLE
ROGUISHNESS
SACRIFICIAL
SALPINGITIS
SALTIMBANCO
SALTIMBOCCA
SEASICKNESS
SELFIMPOSED
SELFISHNESS
SEMPITERNAL
SEMPITERNUM
SENSIBILITY
SENSITIVELY
SENSITIVITY
SENTIMENTAL
SEPTICAEMIA
SERVICEABLE
SIGNIFICANT
SILLIMANITE
SPECIALIZED
SPIRITUALLY

STATISTICAL
STRAITLACED
STYLISHNESS
STYLIZATION
SUBDIVISION
SUBLIMATION
SUBSISTENCE
SUFFICIENCY
SYNDICALISM
SYNDICATION
TAGLIATELLE
TANGIBILITY
TCHAIKOVSKY
TECTIBRANCH
TERMINATION
TERMINOLOGY
TERRITORIAL
TESTIMONIAL
THALIDOMIDE
TONSILLITIS
TORRIDONIAN
TORTICOLLIS
TORTICULLUS
TOSTICATION
TRADITIONAL
TREPIDATION
TRINIDADIAN
TRINITARIAN
TURRICULATE
UNANIMOUSLY
UNDRINKABLE
UNFAILINGLY
UNFLINCHING
UNIFICATION
UNINITIATED
UNPRINTABLE
UNTHINKABLE
UTILITARIAN
UTILIZATION
VACCINATION
VALLISNERIA
VENTILATION
VERBIGERATE
VERMICULITE
VERTIGINOUS
VINAIGRETTE
VINDICATION
VIOLINCELLO
WELLINGTONS
WILLINGNESS
EMBOÎTEMENT
CLANJAMFRAY
SHOWJUMPING
BLACKFELLOW
BLACKMAILER
BLANKURSINE
BLOCKBUSTER
BOOKKEEPING
CHICKENFEED
CHOCKABLOCK
CRACKERJACK
CRACKHALTER
CROOKEDNESS
DRINKDRIVER
DRUNKENNESS
EXOSKELETON
FLICKERTAIL
FRANKFURTER
FRANKLINITE
MALAKATOONE
PAINKILLING
PRICKLINESS
QUICKSILVER
SNICKERSNEE
SNORKELLING
STICKLEBACK
STOCKBROKER
STOCKHAUSEN
STOCKHOLDER
STOCKJOBBER
STOCKTAKING
STRIKEBOUND
TELEKINESIS
THANKLESSLY
TIMEKEEPING
TRACKLEMENT
WHISKERANDO
ACCELERATOR
ADULLAMITES
AFFILIATION
ALLELOMORPH
ANAPLEROSIS
ANAPLEROTIC
ANGELOLATRY
APOLLINARIS
APOLLONICON
APPALLINGLY
APPELLATION
APPELLATIVE
ARTILLERIST
BANGLADESHI
BATTLEDRESS
BATTLEFIELD
BATTLEFRONT
BATTLEMENTS
BEWILDERING
BRILLIANTLY
CAMALDOLITE
CANDLELIGHT
CANDLESTICK
CAROLINGIAN
CATALLACTIC
CHALLENGING
CHARLEMAGNE
CHAULMOOGRA
CHAULMOUGRA
CHILLINGHAM
COBBLESTONE
COCKLESHELL
COMPLACENCY
COMPLAISANT
COMPLICATED
COMPLIMENTS
DEBILITATED
DEFOLIATION
DEPHLEGMATE
DERELICTION
DESELECTION
DEVALUATION
DEVELOPMENT
DISILLUSION
DISPLEASURE
DOUBLECHECK
DOUBLECROSS
DRYCLEANERS
DRYCLEANING
ECCALEOBION
EMBELLISHED
EQUILATERAL
EQUILIBRIST
EQUILIBRIUM
EUCALYPTOLE
EVERLASTING
EXHILARATED
FAMILIARISE
FAMILIARITY
FAMILIARIZE
FIDDLEDEDEE
FIRELIGHTER
GENTLEMANLY
GENTLEWOMAN
GIGGLESTICK
GIGGLESWICK
GIGGLEWATER
GIRDLESTEAD
GOODLOOKING
GRALLATORES
HABILIMENTS
HEPPLEWHITE
HIGHLIGHTER
HOBBLEDEHOY
HUCKLEBERRY
HUMILIATING
HUMILIATION
HURTLEBERRY
HYOPLASTRON
IDEOLOGICAL
IDYLLICALLY
IMPULSIVELY
INCALESCENT
INDULGENTLY
INFILTRATOR
INSULTINGLY
INTELLIGENT
INTOLERABLE
INTOLERABLY
INTOLERANCE
INVOLUNTARY
INVOLVEMENT
IRRELEVANCE
IRRELIGIOUS
ISOELECTRIC
KAMELAUKION
KIDDLEYWINK
LAMPLIGHTER
LEFTLUGGAGE
LEVELHEADED
LONGLASTING
LUXULYANITE
MECKLENBURG
MEGALOMANIA
MEGALOMANIC
MEGALOPOLIS
METALWORKER
MIDDLEMARCH
MIDDLESIZED
MISALLIANCE
MODELMOLEST
MOONLIGHTER
MUDSLINGING
MYCOLOGICAL
NEEDLEPOINT
NEEDLESTICK
NEEDLEWOMAN
NOVELETTISH
OBSOLESCENT
ONTOLOGICAL
OSCILLATION
OVERLAPPING
OVERLEARNED
PARALEIPSIS
PECULIARITY
PENULTIMATE
PHILLIPSITE
PORTLANDIAN
RABELAISIAN
RATTLESNAKE
RESPLENDANT
RESPLENDENT
RETALIATION
RETALIATORY
REVALUATION
REVELATIONS
REVOLUTIONS
RIDDLEMEREE
SADDLEHORSE
SCHOLARSHIP
SCULLABOGUE
SEXOLOGICAL
SHALLOWNESS
SHOPLIFTING
SINGLESTICK
SKILLIGALEE
SKILLIGOLEE
SMALLHOLDER
SMOULDERING
SOLILOQUIZE
SPELLBINDER
STALLHOLDER
STELLIONATE
STOOLPIGEON
SWALLOWABLE
SYMPLEGADES
THALLOPHYTE
THEOLOGICAL
TIDDLEYWINK
TITILLATION
TOTALIZATOR
UNFULFILLED
UNPALATABLE
UNRELENTING
UNSOLICITED
UNWELCOMING
UPHOLSTERER
VACILLATING
VACILLATION
VINBLASTINE
WASHLEATHER
WENSLEYDALE
WHEELBARROW
WHEELWRIGHT
WHITLEATHER
WINDLESTRAW
ACCOMMODATE
ACCOMPANIST
ACCUMULATOR
ACRIMONIOUS
ASSEMBLYMAN
ASSIMILATED
BEAUMONTAGE
CEREMONIOUS
CLIOMETRICS
COLUMBARIUM
DENOMINATOR
DISEMBODIED
DISIMPRISON
DOCUMENTARY
ENCUMBRANCE
ENJAMBEMENT
EXTEMPORISE
EXTEMPORIZE
FILAMENTOUS
FISHMONGERS
FORAMINIFER
FOULMOUTHED
FRAGMENTARY
FREEMASONRY
FUNAMBULIST
GLIMMERGOWK
GRAMMALOGUE
GRAMMATICAL
IGNOMINIOUS
ILLUMINATED
INCOMPETENT
INCOMPOSITE
INDOMITABLE
INNUMERABLE
INTEMPERATE
IRONMONGERS
IRONMONGERY

KILIMANJARO
LUXEMBURGER
MANUMISSION
MONTMORENCY
MOZAMBIQUAN
MYXOMATOSIS
OARSMANSHIP
OBTEMPERATE
OPTOMETRIST
OVERMANNING
PANOMPHAEAN
PARAMASTOID
PARAMEDICAL
PERAMBULATE
PIEDMONTITE
POLYMORPHIC
PORTMANTEAU
POTAMOGETON
PREEMINENCE
REGIMENTALS
REMEMBRANCE
RESEMBLANCE
RHEUMATICKY
RODOMONTADE
RUDIMENTARY
SCRIMSHANDY
SCRUMPTIOUS
SEDIMENTARY
SEISMOGRAPH
SHOWMANSHIP
SKIMMINGTON
SPERMATOZOA
SPERMICIDAL
SPERMOPHILE
STEAMROLLER
STRAMINEOUS
THAUMATROPE
THERMOMETER
THERMOPYLAE
THESMOTHETE
TRIUMVIRATE
UNCOMMITTED
UNDEMANDING
UNREMITTING
VITAMINIZED
WELLMEANING
WESTMINSTER
WHIGMALEERY
WORKMANLIKE
WORKMANSHIP
ABSENTEEISM
ADVANCEMENT
ADVENTURESS
ADVENTUROUS
AERONAUTICS
ANAGNORISIS
ANTINEUTRON
ANTONOMASIA
APHANIPTERA
APLANOSPORE
ARGENTINIAN
ARRANGEMENT
ASTONISHING
ATTENTIVELY
ATTENUATION
AUXANOMETER
BICENTENARY
BOTANOMANCY
BUSINESSMAN
CALENDERING
CHRONICALLY
CHRONOMETER
CLEANLINESS
CLEANSHAVEN
COLONIALISM
COLONIALIST
CORINTHIANS
CYLINDRICAL
DECONSTRUCT
DEFENCELESS
DEFENSELESS
DEFENSIVELY
DELINEATION
DELINQUENCY
DEMONOMANIA
DEMONSTRATE
DERANGEMENT
DIAGNOSTICS
DIMENSIONAL
DISENCUMBER
DISENTANGLE
DISINCLINED
DOMINEERING
EMMENAGOGUE
EMMENTHALER
ENGINEERING
ENHANCEMENT
EQUINOCTIAL
ERRONEOUSLY
ESSENTIALLY
EXPENDITURE
EXPONENTIAL
EXTENSIVELY
EXTENUATING
EXTENUATION
FARINACEOUS
FINANCIALLY
FLANNELETTE
FOMENTATION
FORTNIGHTLY
GEGENSCHEIN
GERONTOLOGY
GOODNATURED
GREENBOTTLE
GREENGROCER
GREENOCKITE
GROUNDSHEET
GROUNDSPEED
GROUNDSWELL
HOHENLINDEN
INCANTATION
INCINERATOR
INCONGRUITY
INCONGRUOUS
INCONSTANCY
INCONTINENT
INDENTATION
INFANGTHIEF
INFANTICIDE
INFANTRYMAN
INGENIOUSLY
INSENSITIVE
INSINCERITY
INSINUATING
INSINUATION
INTENSIVELY
INTENTIONAL
INVINCIBLES
LACONICALLY
LAMENTATION
LARYNGISMUS
LIVINGSTONE
LUMINESCENT
LYCANTHROPE
LYCANTHROPY
LYCHNOSCOPE
MELANCHOLIA
MELANCHOLIC
MELANOCHROI
MISANTHROPE
MISANTHROPY
MOMENTARILY
MONONGAHELA
NICKNACKERY
NOMENCLATOR
OFFENSIVELY
ORGANICALLY
ORGANIZAION
ORIENTALIST
ORIENTATION
OSTENTATION
PARANEPHROS
PARENTHESIS
PARONOMASIA
PARTNERSHIP
PERENNIALLY
PODSNAPPERY
POTENTIALLY
PROGNATHOUS
RECANTATION
RECONDITION
RECONNOITER
RECONNOITRE
RECONSTRUCT
REMINISCENT
REMONSTRATE
RESENTFULLY
RETINACULUM
RETINOSPORA
REVENDICATE
RIBONUCLEIC
ROMANTICISM
ROMANTICIZE
SAPONACEOUS
SCIENTOLOGY
SECONDARILY
SECONDCLASS
SEIGNIORAGE
SERENDIPITY
SEVENTEENTH
SPRINGBOARD
SPRINGCLEAN
SPRINGHOUSE
SPRINGINESS
STEINBERGER
STRANDLOPER
STRANGENESS
STRANGEWAYS
STRANGULATE
STRENUOUSLY
STRINGENTLY
STRINGYBARK
STRONGYLOID
SUBUNGULATA
TECHNICALLY
TIRONENSIAN
TYRONENSIAN
UNANNOUNCED
UNCONCEALED
UNCONCERNED
UNCONFIRMED
UNCONNECTED
UNCONQUERED
UNCONSCIOUS
UNCONTESTED
UNCONVERTED
UNCONVINCED
VARANGARIAN
VOLUNTARILY
WITENAGEMOT
WOMANLINESS
ACKNOWLEDGE
ACOLOUTHITE
AGGLOMERATE
AGONOTHETES
ALCYONARIAN
AMINOBUTENE
ANACOLUTHIA
ANDROGENOUS
ANISOCERCAL
ANTHOCYANIN
ANTHOLOGIZE
ANTHONOMOUS
APATOSAURUS
APHRODISIAC
APOMORPHINE
APPROACHING
APPROBATION
APPROPRIATE
APPROVINGLY
APPROXIMATE
ARTIODACTYL
AUDIOVISUAL
AXEROPHTHOL
AZOTOBACTER
BANNOCKBURN
BIELORUSSIA
BILIOUSNESS
BORBORYGMUS
BOUTONNIERE
BURGOMASTER
CALLOUSNESS
CARBORUNDUM
CARDOPHAGUS
CARTOGRAPHY
CATHOLICISM
CHINOISERIE
CHIROGRAPHY
CHIROPODIST
CHOROGRAPHY
CLADOSPORUM
CLINOCHLORE
COENOBITISM
COGNOSCENTE
COGNOSCENTI
COLEORRHIZA
COLLOCATION
COMFORTABLE
COMFORTABLY
COMFORTLESS
COMMONPLACE
COMMONSENSE
COMPOSITION
COMPOTATION
CONCOMITANT
CONCORDANCE
CONDOLENCES
CONDOMINIUM
CONDOTTIERE
CONDOTTIORE
CONNOISSEUR
CONNOTATION
CONSOLATION
CONSOLIDATE
CONVOCATION
CONVOLUTION
CONVOLVULUS
COPROPHAGAN
COPROSTEROL
CORPORATION
CORROBORATE
COTTONMOUTH
COULOMMIERS
CRACOVIENNE
CUSTOMARILY
CYCLOSTYLED
DESPONDENCY
DEVIOUSNESS
DIAMONDBACK
DIPLOMATICS

DIPLOMATIST
DIPROTODONT
DIPSOMANIAC
DISCOLOURED
DISCONTINUE
DISCOTHEQUE
DISCOURTESY
DISHONESTLY
DISLOCATION
DISPOSITION
DISSOLUTION
DITTOGRAPHY
DOUROUCOULI
DRAGONNADES
DUBIOUSNESS
DYSLOGISTIC
ELABORATELY
ELABORATION
EMBROCATION
ENCHONDROMA
ENCROACHING
ENFEOFFMENT
ETHNOGRAPHY
ETHNOLOGIST
ETYMOLOGIST
EVAPORATION
EXPLORATION
EXPLORATORY
EXPROPRIATE
EXTROGENOUS
EXTROVERTED
FATUOUSNESS
FERRONNIÈRE
FLAVOURSOME
FORFOUGHTEN
FORLORNNESS
FRIVOLOUSLY
GALLOVIDIAN
GALLOWGLASS
GODFORSAKEN
GORDONSTOUN
HAEMOGLOBIN
HAEMOPHILIA
HAEMORRHAGE
HAEMORRHOID
HAGIOGRAPHY
HARIOLATION
HEBDOMADARY
HIDEOUSNESS
HIPPOCAMPUS
HIPPOCRATES
HIPPOCRATIC
HISTOLOGIST
HISTORIATED
HOMEOPATHIC
HYDROCARBON
HYDROMEDUSA
HYDROPHIDAE
HYDROPHOBIA
HYDROPHOBIC
HYDROPONICS
HYDROSTATIC
HYMNOLOGIST
ICONOGRAPHY
ICONOSTASIS
IMPROPRIETY
IMPROVEMENT
IMPROVIDENT
INTROVERTED
ISTIOPHORUS
LATROCINIUM
LEGIONNAIRE
LITHOGRAPHY
MACROBIOTIC
MARCONIGRAM
MARIONBERRY
MARIONETTES
MEADOWSWEET
MENTONNIÈRE
MEPROBAMATE
METEOROLOGY
METHODOLOGY
MICROGAMETE
MICROSCOPIC
MISCONSTRUE
NATIONALISM
NATIONALIST
NATIONALITY
NATIONALIZE
NATIONSTATE
NECROMANCER
NERVOUSNESS
NEUROLOGIST
OBVIOUSNESS
OCHLOCRATIC
OLIGOCHAETE
OPPROBRIOUS
ORTHOCENTRE
ORTHOGRAPHY
ORTHOPAEDIC
OSTEOPATHIC
OSTEOPLASTY
OUTPOURINGS
PAEDOTROPHY
PALEOGRAPHY
PALEOLITHIC
PASTOURELLE
PATHOLOGIST
PATRONISING
PATRONIZING
PENTONVILLE
PERCOLATION
PERFORATION
PERFORMANCE
PERIODONTIC
PERSONALIST
PERSONALITY
PERSONALIZE
PERSONIFIED
PETRODOLLAR
PHILOCTETES
PHILOLOGIST
PHILOSOPHER
PHONOFIDDLE
PHOTOCOPIER
PHOTOFINISH
PHOTOGRAPHY
PHOTOSPHERE
POLIORCETIC
PORNOGRAPHY
PRECONCEIVE
PREDOMINANT
PREDOMINATE
PREMONITION
PREMONITORY
PREPOLLENCE
PREPOSITION
PREROGATIVE
PROLOCUTION
PROMOTIONAL
PROPOSITION
PROROGATION
PROTOCOCCUS
PROTONOTARY
PROVOCATION
PROVOCATIVE
PTERODACTYL
PURPOSELESS
PYTHONESQUE
RADIOACTIVE
RADIOCARBON
RADIOGRAPHY
RADIOLOGIST
RATIOCINATE
RATIONALITY
RATIONALIZE
RAUCOUSNESS
REPROACHFUL
RESPONSIBLE
RESPONSIBLY
RESPONSIONS
RESTORATION
RESTORATIVE
RETROACTIVE
RETROROCKET
SALVOGUNNER
SAPROLEGNIA
SAPROPHYTIC
SARCOPHAGUS
SCEUOPHYLAX
SCOLOPENDRA
SCOPOLAMINE
SEPIOSTAIRE
SERIOUSNESS
SOCIOLOGIST
SORROWFULLY
SPIROCHAETE
STENOCHROME
STENOGRAPHY
STYLOPODIUM
SUBCONTRACT
SUBDOMINANT
SUFFOCATING
SUFFOCATION
SUPPOSITION
SUPPOSITORY
SURROUNDING
SYMPOSIARCH
SYNCOPATION
TAUROBOLIUM
TAUTOCHRONE
TEDIOUSNESS
TEETOTALLER
TEMPORARILY
TENUOUSNESS
THOROUGHPIN
TOPLOFTICAL
TREPONEMATA
TRINOBANTES
TROPOSPHERE
UNAVOIDABLE
UNAVOIDABLY
UNEMOTIONAL
UNPROTECTED
UNSTOPPABLE
UNWHOLESOME
VACUOUSNESS
VARIOLATION
VARSOVIENNE
VICIOUSNESS
VIDEOCAMERA
VIOLONCELLO
VISCOUNTESS
WINDOWFRAME
WINDOWLEDGE
YELLOWPLUSH
YELLOWSTONE
ACCIPITRINE
AMMOPHILOUS
ANTEPENDIUM
ANTIPHRASIS
ANTIPYRETIC
BACKPACKING
BLASPHEMOUS
CACOPHONOUS
CHIPPENDALE
CLAPPERCLAW
CONSPICUOUS
CONSPIRATOR
CYMOPHANOUS
DECAPITATED
DECEPTIVELY
DICEPHALOUS
DILAPIDATED
DISAPPROVAL
ENCAPSULATE
ENCEPHALOMA
ENKEPHALINE
EQUIPOLLENT
EXASPERATED
EXCEPTIONAL
HARDPRESSED
HEMOPHILIAC
HIGHPITCHED
HIGHPOWERED
HIGHPROFILE
IDEOPRAXIST
INCAPSULATE
INDEPENDENT
INEXPEDIENT
INEXPENSIVE
INOPPORTUNE
INSEPARABLE
INSUPERABLE
IRREPARABLE
IRREPARABLY
ITHYPHALLIC
ITHYPHALLUS
JOSEPHINITE
KIRKPATRICK
MALAPROPISM
MANIPULATOR
METAPHYSICS
MISSPELLING
MONOPSONIST
MYCOPHAGIST
OMNIPOTENCE
OMNIPRESENT
OVERPAYMENT
PELOPONNESE
PERIPATETIC
PERIPHRASIS
PERSPECTIVE
PERSPICUITY
PERSPICUOUS
PROMPTITUDE
PROSPECTIVE
REALPOLITIK
REAPPRAISAL
RECEPTIVITY
RECIPROCATE
RECIPROCITY
REDUPLICATE
SAXOPHONIST
SCALPRIFORM
SCRIPTORIUM
SCUPPERNONG
SHINPLASTER
SLEEPWALKER
SOLIPSISTIC
SOROPTIMIST
STEEPLEJACK
STRAPHANGER
STROPHILLUS
STYMPHALIAN
SYCOPHANTIC
TEASPOONFUL
TELEPHONIST
TELEPRINTER
THEOPNEUSTY

TOXOPHILITE
TRESPASSING
TROMPELOEIL
UNEXPLAINED
UNEXPRESSED
UNHAPPINESS
UNIMPORTANT
UNIMPRESSED
UNREPENTANT
UNSUPPORTED
VASOPRESSIN
WESTPHALIAN
ANTIQUARIAN
HIGHQUALITY
TRANQUILITY
ABNORMALITY
ABSTRACTION
ACCORDINGLY
ADVERBIALLY
ADVERTISING
AFFIRMATION
AFFIRMATIVE
AFTERSCHOOL
AGUARDIENTE
AILUROPHILE
AIRCRAFTMAN
ALTERCATION
ALTERNATELY
ALTERNATING
ALTERNATION
ALTERNATIVE
ANACREONTIC
ANTIRRHINUM
APPARATCHIK
APPURTENANT
ARTHRAPODAL
ARTHRODESIS
ARTHROSPORE
ASPERGILLUM
ASPERGILLUS
ASPERSORIUM
ATHARVAVEDA
ATHERINIDAE
ATHERMANOUS
AVERRUNCATE
AVOIRDUPOIS
BELORUSSIAN
BICARBONATE
BIFURCATION
CAMARADERIE
CAMEROONIAN
CAPERNOITED
CAPERNOITIE
CATERPILLAR
CENTREBOARD
CENTREPIECE
CENTRIFUGAL
CENTRIPETAL
CERARGYRITE
CESAREWITCH
CHAIRPERSON
CHEERLEADER
CHEIROGNOMY
CHIAROSCURO
CHLOROPHYLL
CHOIRMASTER
CLAIRSCHACH
CLAIRVOYANT
COHORTATIVE
COMPRIMARIO
CONGRESSMAN
CONTRACTION
CONTRACTUAL
CONTRAPTION
CONTRASTING
CONTRAYERVA
CONTRETEMPS
CONTRIBUTOR
CONTRIVANCE
CONTROVERSY
CONURBATION
CYBERNETICS
DECARBONIZE
DECORATIONS
DECORTICATE
DEFERENTIAL
DEFORMATION
DEHORTATIVE
DEMARCATION
DEMORALIZED
DENDRACHATE
DEPARTEMENT
DEPORTATION
DESCRIPTION
DESCRIPTIVE
DESERPIDINE
DESTRUCTION
DESTRUCTIVE
DETERIORATE
DETERMINANT
DETERMINING
DIFFRACTION
DISARMAMENT
DISCREPANCY
DISGRACEFUL
DISGRUNTLED
DISORGANIZE
DISORIENTED
DISTRACTION
DISTRESSING
DISTRIBUTED
DISTRIBUTOR
DISTRUSTFUL
DIVORCEMENT
DOCTRINAIRE
EMBARKATION
EMBARRASSED
EMPIRICUTIC
EMPYROMANCY
ENDORSEMENT
ENFORCEABLE
ENFORCEMENT
ENLARGEMENT
ENTERTAINER
ENTHRALLING
ENVIRONMENT
ESCARMOUCHE
EXHORTATION
EXPERIENCED
EXPURGATION
EXTERMINATE
EXTORTIONER
FLOURISHING
FLUORESCENT
FUNDRAISING
GABERLUNZIE
GASTRECTOMY
GASTRONOMIC
GENERALIZED
GENERICALLY
GUBERNATION
HABERDASHER
HAIRRAISING
HEMERALOPIA
HEMORRHOIDS
HETEROSCIAN
HIBERNATING
HIBERNATION
HIGHRANKING
HILARIOUSLY
HISTRIONICS
HUMGRUFFIAN
HUNDREDFOLD
HYPERMARKET
HYPERTROPHY
IGNORANTINE
IMMORTALISE
IMMORTALITY
IMMORTALIZE
IMPARTIALLY
IMPERIALISM
IMPERIALIST
IMPERIOUSLY
IMPERMANENT
IMPERMEABLE
IMPERSONATE
IMPERTINENT
IMPORTANTLY
IMPORTATION
IMPORTUNATE
INCARCERATE
INCARNADINE
INCARNATION
INCORPORATE
INCORPOREAL
INCORRECTLY
INEBRIATION
INFERIORITY
INFERTILITY
INFORMALITY
INFORMATICS
INFORMATION
INFORMATIVE
INFURIATING
INHERITANCE
INSCRIPTION
INSCRUTABLE
INSTRUCTION
INSTRUCTIVE
INSTRUMENTS
INTERACTION
INTERACTIVE
INTERCALARY
INTERCEPTOR
INTERCHANGE
INTERCOSTAL
INTERCOURSE
INTERESTING
INTERGLOSSA
INTERGROWTH
INTERLACING
INTERLEUKIN
INTERLINGUA
INTERMINGLE
INTERNECINE
INTERNUNCIO
INTERPOLATE
INTERPRETER
INTERREGNUM
INTERRELATE
INTERROGATE
INTERRUPTER
INTERSPERSE
INTERVENING
INTERVIEWEE
INTERVIEWER
KIMERIDGIAN
LABORIOUSLY
LABORSAVING
LAMPROPHYRE
LASERPICIUM
LATERIGRADE
LATERITIOUS
LAWBREAKING
LEGERDEMAIN
LIBERTARIAN
LITERALNESS
LOCORESTIVE
LOGARITHMIC
LONGRUNNING
LUXURIANTLY
LUXURIOUSLY
MACERANDUBA
MALPRACTICE
MATERIALISE
MATERIALISM
MATERIALIST
MATERIALIZE
MEMORABILIA
MISERICORDE
MISERLINESS
MISTRUSTFUL
MODERNISTIC
MONARCHICAL
NATURALNESS
NEUTRALISED
NEVERENDING
NOSTRADAMUS
NOTORIOUSLY
NUMERICALLY
NUTCRACKERS
OBSERVATION
OBSERVATORY
OBSTRICTION
OBSTRUCTION
OBSTRUCTIVE
ONEIRODYNIA
ONEIROMANCY
OPPORTUNELY
OPPORTUNISM
OPPORTUNIST
OPPORTUNITY
ORDERLINESS
PAPERWEIGHT
PATERNALISM
PATERNOSTER
PELARGONIUM
PIERREPOINT
PORTRAITIST
PORTRAITURE
PROCREATION
PROCRUSTEAN
PROGRESSION
PROGRESSIVE
PROPRIETARY
PROTRACTING
PROTRACTION
PURPRESTURE
QUADRENNIAL
QUADRENNIUM
QUADRUPLETS
QUARRELLING
QUARRELSOME
QUARRINGTON
REBARBATIVE
RECURRENTLY
REFORMATION
REFORMATORY
REFURBISHED
REGURGITATE
REMORSELESS
RESERVATION
RESTRICTION
RESTRICTIVE
RESTRUCTURE
RETARDATION
REVERBERATE
REVERENTIAL
RUMFRUCTION
SATIRICALLY

SELFRESPECT
SEVERALFOLD
SOVEREIGNTY
SPARROWHAWK
STAIRCARPET
SUBORDINATE
SUBTRACTION
SUBTROPICAL
SUFFRAGETTE
SUGARCOATED
SUNDRENCHED
SUPERALTERN
SUPERCHARGE
SUPERCHERIE
SUPERFICIAL
SUPERFICIES
SUPERFLUITY
SUPERFLUOUS
SUPERIMPOSE
SUPERINTEND
SUPERIORITY
SUPERLATIVE
SUPERMARKET
SUPERSCRIBE
SUPERSEDEAS
SUPERSEDERE
SUPERTANKER
SUPERVISION
SUPERVISORY
SUPPRESSION
SUSURRATION
TABERNACLES
THEORETICAL
TIMBROMANIA
TIMBROPHILY
ULOTRICHALE
UNCERTAINTY
UNCHRISTIAN
UNDERCHARGE
UNDERCOOKED
UNDERGROUND
UNDERGROWTH
UNDERHANDED
UNDERMANNED
UNDERSIGNED
UNDERSTATED
UNDERTAKING
UNDERVALUED
UNDERWEIGHT
UNDERWRITER
UNFORTUNATE
UNFURNISHED
UNPERTURBED
UNSHRINKING
UNSURPASSED
UNVARNISHED
UNWARRANTED
VICARIOUSLY
VINCRISTINE
VOTERIGGING
WATERCOLOUR
WATERCOURSE
WATEREDDOWN
WATERLOGGED
WATERMEADOW
WATERSKIING
WATERSPLASH
WIDERANGING
ACCESSORIES
AGNOSTICISM
AGROSTOLOGY
ANAESTHESIA
ANAESTHETIC
ANTISTHENES
ANTISTROPHE
ASSASSINATE
ATMOSPHERIC
ATTESTATION
AUGUSTINIAN
BACKSLIDING
BALISTRARIA
BARNSTORMER
BERGSCHRUND
BESTSELLING
BLESSEDNESS
BOOKSELLERS
BREASTPLATE
CATASTROPHE
CHEESECLOTH
CHIASTOLITE
CHRISTENING
CHRISTMASSY
CHRISTOPHER
CHRYSAROBIN
CHRYSOPRASE
COMESTIBLES
COUNSELLING
CROSSLEGGED
DEERSTALKER
DEMOSTHENES
DEMOSTHENIC
DETESTATION
DEUTSCHMARK
DEVASTATING
DEVASTATION
DOMESTICATE
DOMESTICITY
DRESSMAKING
DYAESTHESIA
EXCESSIVELY
EXPOSTULATE
FESTSCHRIFT
FORESEEABLE
FORESHORTEN
FORESTATION
GLOSSOLALIA
GRASSHOPPER
GREASEPAINT
GUESSTIMATE
HALBSTARKER
HARPSICHORD
HORNSWOGGLE
HUCKSTERAGE
ILLUSIONARY
ILLUSIONIST
ILLUSTRATOR
ILLUSTRIOUS
IMPASSIONED
IMPASSIVELY
INCESSANTLY
INDUSTRIOUS
INESSENTIAL
INFESTATION
INSISTENTLY
INVESTIGATE
INVESTITURE
ISOXSUPRINE
KALASHNIKOV
LANDSKNECHT
LEADSWINGER
LEGISLATION
LEGISLATIVE
LEGISLATURE
LICKSPITTLE
LONGSIGHTED
LONGSLEEVED
LOUDSPEAKER
LOUISIANIAN
MAGISTERIAL
MAGISTRATES
MINESWEEPER
MINISTERIAL
MINISTERING
MOLESTATION
NEARSIGHTED
NECESSARILY
NECESSITATE
NECESSITOUS
NIERSTEINER
NUMISMATICS
NUMISMATIST
OBSESSIVELY
OCTASTICHON
OMNISCIENCE
OVERSTUFFED
PAINSTAKING
PALESTINIAN
PARISHIONER
PEDESTRIANS
PERESTROIKA
PERISSOLOGY
PERISTALITH
PERISTALSIS
PHRASEOLOGY
PLEASURABLE
PLEISTOCENE
POLYSTYRENE
PRESSURIZED
RAVISHINGLY
REASSURANCE
RECESSIONAL
REGISTERING
RESISTIVITY
RESUSCITATE
REVISIONISM
RHAPSODICAL
ROBESPIERRE
RUDESHEIMER
SALESPERSON
SCHISTOSOMA
SCHISTOSOME
SELFSERVICE
SINISTRORSE
SPESSARTITE
SPITSTICKER
SPONSORSHIP
TERPSICHORE
TIMESHARING
TOWNSPEOPLE
TRANSACTION
TRANSCEIVER
TRANSFERRED
TRANSFERRIN
TRANSFIGURE
TRANSFORMED
TRANSFORMER
TRANSFUSION
TRANSILIENT
TRANSLATION
TRANSLUCENT
TRANSMITTED
TRANSMITTER
TRANSPARENT
TRANSPONDER
TRANSPORTED
TRANSPORTER
TRANSURANIC
TREASONABLE
TYPESETTING
UNASSERTIVE
UNCASTRATED
UNDESERVING
UNDESIRABLE
UNDISCLOSED
UNDISGUISED
UNDISTURBED
UNJUSTIFIED
UNOBSERVANT
UNSUSPECTED
VICISSITUDE
VIVISECTION
VOLKSKAMMER
WAINSCOTING
WINDSURFING
WORKSTATION
ABORTIONIST
ADOPTIANISM
ADOPTIONISM
ADULTERATED
AMONTILLADO
ANASTOMOSIS
ANESTHETIST
ANESTHETIZE
APOSTROPHUS
ARBITRAGEUR
ARBITRAMENT
ARBITRARILY
ARBITRATION
ARGATHELIAN
ARISTOCRACY
ASSYTHEMENT
BEASTLINESS
BEAUTIFULLY
BREATHALYSE
BRISTLECONE
BRITTLENESS
CAUSTICALLY
CHANTARELLE
CHANTERELLE
CHANTICLEER
CHITTERLING
COMPTROLLER
COMSTOCKERY
CONSTANTINE
CONSTELLATE
CONSTERNATE
CONSTIPATED
CONSTITUENT
CONSTRAINED
CONSTRICTED
CONSTRICTOR
CONSTRUCTOR
CONSTUPRATE
COUNTENANCE
COUNTERFEIT
COUNTERFOIL
COUNTERFORT
COUNTERGLOW
COUNTERHAND
COUNTERMAND
COUNTERPANE
COUNTERPART
COUNTERSIGN
COUNTERSINK
COUNTRIFIED
COUNTRYSIDE
COURTEOUSLY
COURTLINESS
CRESTFALLEN
CRYSTALLINE
CRYSTALLISE
CRYSTALLIZE
DELETERIOUS
DELITESCENT
DEVITRIFIED
DIARTHROSIS
DICOTYLEDON
DIORTHORTIC
DOWNTRODDEN
DRASTICALLY

EINSTEINIUM
ELASTOPLAST
ELECTRICIAN
ELECTRICITY
ELECTROCUTE
ELECTROLIER
ELECTROLYTE
ELECTRONICS
ELECTROTINT
ELEUTHERIAN
ENARTHROSIS
ENDOTHERMIC
ENTITLEMENT
EOANTHROPUS
ERRATICALLY
EVENTRATION
EVENTUALITY
EXANTHEMATA
FACETIOUSLY
FANATICALLY
FAULTFINDER
FAULTLESSLY
FLIRTATIOUS
FLUCTUATING
FLUCTUATION
FORETHOUGHT
FRANTICALLY
FREETHINKER
FRONTRUNNER
FROSTBITTEN
FRUITLESSLY
FRUSTRATING
FRUSTRATION
FUNCTIONARY
FUNCTIONING
GAMETOPHYTE
GENETICALLY
GHASTLINESS
GLASTONBURY
HEALTHINESS
HEARTBROKEN
HEARTLESSLY
HEPATOSCOPY
HOLOTHURIAN
HOMOTHERMAL
HOMOTHERMIC
HYPOTENSION
HYPOTHECATE
HYPOTHERMIA
IDENTICALLY
IDENTIFYING
IDIOTICALLY
IMPATIENTLY
IMPETUOSITY
IMPETUOUSLY
INATTENTION
INATTENTIVE
INAUTHENTIC
INESTIMABLE
INFATUATION
KLEPTOMANIA
LENGTHENING
LENGTHINESS
LIGHTHEADED
LIGHTWEIGHT
MAINTENANCE
MAISTERDOME
MEGATHERIUM
MERITORIOUS
METATARSALS
MOISTURIZER
MONOTHELITE
MONOTREMATA
MONSTROSITY
MOSSTROOPER
MOUNTAINEER
MOUNTAINOUS
NAPHTHALENE
NEGOTIATING
NEGOTIATION
NIGHTINGALE
NIGHTMARISH
NIKETHAMIDE
NONETHELESS
NOTOTHERIUM
OBLITERATED
OBMUTESCENT
ODONTOBLAST
ODONTOPHORE
OMMATOPHORE
ORNITHOLOGY
ORNITHOPTER
OUTSTANDING
OVERTURNING
PARATROOPER
PARATYPHOID
PEDETENTOUS
PENETRATING
PENETRATION
PENITENTIAL
PERITONAEUM
PERITONITIS
PETITMAITRE
PLANTAGENET
PLANTIGRADE
POINTLESSLY
POLITICALLY
POLITICIANS
POLYTECHNIC
POLYTRICHUM
PRACTICABLE
PRACTICALLY
PRESTIGIOUS
PRESTISSIMO
PRESTONPANS
PRESTRESSED
PROSTHETICS
PROSTRATION
PSITTACOSIS
PUNCTILIOUS
PUNCTUALITY
PUNCTUATION
PURITANICAL
QUARTERBACK
QUARTERDECK
QUESTIONING
QUINTUPLETS
RATATOUILLE
REACTIONARY
REPETITIOUS
RIGHTANGLED
RIGHTEOUSLY
RIGHTHANDED
RIGHTHANDER
RIGHTWINGER
SAGITTARIUS
SAINTLINESS
SAINTPAULIA
SCATTERGOOD
SCATTERLING
SCEPTICALLY
SCHOTTISCHE
SCINTILLATE
SCOUTMASTER
SCUTTLEBUTT
SHAFTESBURY
SHEATHKNIFE
SHITTIMWOOD
SHORTCHANGE
SHORTCOMING
SHORTHANDED
SHUTTLECOCK
SIGHTSCREEN
SIGHTSEEING
SKEPTICALLY
SPATTERDASH
SPATTERDOCK
SPECTACULAR
SPLUTTERING
SPONTANEITY
SPONTANEOUS
SPORTSFIELD
SPORTSWOMAN
STADTHOLDER
STRATEGICAL
STRETCHABLE
STRETCHLESS
STRUTHIONES
SUBITANEOUS
SUBSTANDARD
SUBSTANTIAL
SUBSTANTIVE
SUDETENLAND
SUMPTUOUSLY
SYMPTOMATIC
TACITURNITY
TARATANTARA
THEATERGOER
THEATREGOER
THEATRICALS
THISTLEDOWN
TICKTACKTOE
TIGHTFISTED
TIGHTLIPPED
TOASTMASTER
TRIPTOLEMUS
TRUSTEESHIP
TRUSTWORTHY
UNALTERABLE
UNAUTHENTIC
UNGETATABLE
UNMITIGATED
UNMOTIVATED
UNNATURALLY
UNOBTRUSIVE
UNPATRIOTIC
UNSATISFIED
UNSATURATED
UNUTTERABLE
UNWITTINGLY
VOORTREKKER
WHISTLESTOP
WHITTINGTON
WISHTONWISH
XEROTRIPSIS
ACCOUNTABLE
ACCOUNTANCY
ACUPUNCTURE
ADJOURNMENT
AESCULAPIAN
AESCULAPIUS
AGGLUTINANT
AGGLUTINATE
CALCULATING
CALCULATION
CAMOUFLAGED
CARBURETTOR
CENTUMVIRUS
CENTURIATOR
CINQUECENTO
CIRCULARIZE
CIRCULATING
CIRCULATION
CIRCULATORY
CIRCUMCISER
CIRCUMFLECT
CIRCUMSPECT
COAGULATION
COLOURBLIND
COMBUSTIBLE
COMEUPPANCE
COMMUNICANT
COMMUNICATE
COMMUTATION
COMPUNCTION
COMPUTATION
COMPUTERIZE
CONCURRENCE
CONDUCTRESS
CONFUTATION
CONJUGATION
CONJUNCTION
CONJUNCTURE
CONSULTANCY
CONSUMABLES
CONSUMERISM
CONSUMPTION
CONSUMPTIVE
CONTUBERNAL
CONVULSIONS
CORRUGATION
CORRUPTIBLE
CREDULOUSLY
CREPUSCULAR
DEGLUTINATE
DEGLUTITION
DISJUNCTION
DISPUTATION
DISQUIETING
DISTURBANCE
DRACUNCULUS
DYSFUNCTION
EJACULATION
ENCOURAGING
ENFOULDERED
EXCLUSIVELY
EXECUTIONER
FAVOURITISM
FEATURELESS
FORMULATION
FORTUNATELY
FORTUNELOUD
GARRULOUSLY
GENOUILLÈRE
GUTTURALISE
HALLUCINATE
IMPRUDENTLY
INELUCTABLE
INEQUITABLE
INFLUENTIAL
INOCULATION
INSOUCIANCE
JACQUEMINOT
KULTURKREIS
LECTURESHIP
LINGUISTICS
MALFUNCTION
MANEUVERING
MASCULINITY
MASQUERADER
MEASURELESS
MEASUREMENT
MEDIUMSIZED
MENSURATION
MICHURINISM
MICTURITION
MILQUETOAST
MURMURATION
PARTURITION
PERDUELLION

PERFUNCTORY
PERLUSTRATE
PERMUTATION
PICTURESQUE
PREJUDICIAL
PRESUMPTION
PRESUMPTIVE
PROCUREMENT
PROFUSENESS
PROTUBERANT
QUERULOUSLY
RAMGUNSHOCH
RAPTUROUSLY
RECRUITMENT
REDOUBTABLE
RESOURCEFUL
RUMBUSTIOUS
RUMGUMPTION
SAVOURINESS
SESQUIOXIDE
SINGULARITY
SPECULATION
SPECULATIVE
STIMULATION
STIPULATION
SUBJUGATION
SUBJUNCTIVE
SUBMULTIPLE
SUPPURATION
SURTURBRAND
TRIBULATION
TRUCULENTLY
UNCLUTTERED
UNCOUTHNESS
UNCRUSHABLE
UNDOUBTEDLY
UNEQUIVOCAL
UNTOUCHABLE
VENTURESOME
ALLEVIATION
AMBIVALENCE
ANNIVERSARY
ARRIVEDERCI
BEHAVIOURAL
BENEVOLENCE
CARAVANNING
DELIVERANCE
EQUIVALENCE
EQUIVOCALLY
INADVERTENT
INADVISABLE
INDIVISIBLE
INDIVISIBLY
IRREVERENCE
IRREVOCABLE
KATAVOTHRON
KETAVOTHRON
MALEVOLENCE
MARIVAUDAGE
RECOVERABLE
TWELVEMONTH
UNCIVILISED
UNCIVILIZED
UNDEVELOPED
UNENVELOPED
UNFAVORABLE
BIRDWATCHER
BUSHWHACKER
CORDWAINERS
CROMWELLIAN
DUSTWRAPPER
EMPOWERMENT
FAIRWEATHER
FITZWILLIAM
FOOTWASHING
FOREWARNING
GLADWELLISE
HANDWRITING
HANDWRITTEN
HARDWORKING
ILLYWHACKER
OVERWEENING
OVERWHELMED
OVERWROUGHT
PRZEWALSKIS
SCREWDRIVER
SHIPWRECKED
TYPEWRITTEN
INDEXLINKED
INTOXICATED
INTOXIMETER
NONEXISTENT
ANONYMOUSLY
APODYTERIUM
BATHYSPHERE
BELLYTIMBER
DACTYLOGRAM
DINNYHAUSER
DINNYHAYSER
DIPHYCERCAL
EMPHYTEUSIS
EMPTYHANDED
EURHYTHMICS
GALLYBAGGER
GALLYBEGGAR
GEOSYNCLINE
GERRYMANDER
GILLYFLOWER
HEAVYHANDED
HEAVYWEIGHT
HONEYCOMBED
HONEYMOONER
HONEYSUCKLE
JERRYMANDER
MERRYMAKING
MOLLYCODDLE
MONEYLENDER
MONEYMAKING
PENNYFATHER
PHARYNGITIS
PICKYOUROWN
PINNYWINKLE
PLATYRRHINE
STORYTELLER
TACHYCARDIA
TACHYGRAPHY
TEENYBOPPER
TIGGYWINKLE
VICHYSOISSE
WORRYTROUGH
BRAZZAVILLE
CITIZENSHIP
GRENZGANGER
OVERZEALOUS
SWITZERLAND

11:6

ABRACADABRA
ABSTRACTION
ADULLAMITES
AERONAUTICS
AIRCRAFTMAN
AMBIVALENCE
APPARATCHIK
APPROACHING
ARTHRAPODAL
BACCHANALIA
BACKPACKING
BANGLADESHI
BIRDWATCHER
BRAGGADOCIO
BRAZZAVILLE
CACOGASTRIC
CALEFACIENT
CAMARADERIE
CARAVANNING
CARRIAGEWAY
CATACAUSTIC
CHANTARELLE
CHOCKABLOCK
CHRYSAROBIN
CLANJAMFRAY
COMPLACENCY
COMPLAISANT
CONCEALMENT
CONSTANTINE
CONTRACTION
CONTRACTUAL
CONTRAPTION
CONTRASTING
CONTRAYERVA
CORDWAINERS
CRYSTALLINE
CRYSTALLISE
CRYSTALLIZE
DECORATIONS
DEMIBASTION
DEMORALIZED
DENDRACHATE
DIFFRACTION
DISGRACEFUL
DISTRACTION
DODECASTYLE
EFFICACIOUS
ELEPHANTINE
EMMENAGOGUE
ENCROACHING
ENDOCARDIUM
ENTHRALLING
EPIDIASCOPE
EQUILATERAL
EQUIVALENCE
EVERLASTING
EXHILARATED
FARINACEOUS
FARREACHING
FLIRTATIOUS
FOOTBALLING
FOOTWASHING
FORBEARANCE
FORECASTING
FOREFATHERS
FOREWARNING
FOUNDATIONS
FREEMASONRY
FUNDRAISING
GENERALIZED
GOODNATURED
GRALLATORES
GRAMMALOGUE
GRAMMATICAL
HAIRRAISING
HEMERALOPIA
HIGHRANKING
HYOPLASTRON
IGNORANTINE
INESCAPABLE
INSEPARABLE
INTERACTION
INTERACTIVE
IRREPARABLE
IRREPARABLY
KAMELAUKION
KILIMANJARO
KILOCALORIE
KIRKPATRICK
LITERALNESS
LOGODAEDALY
LONGLASTING
MACADAMIZED
MACERANDUBA
MALAKATOONE
MALEFACTION
MALFEASANCE
MALPRACTICE
MANUFACTURE
MARIVAUDAGE
MATRIARCHAL
MEMORABILIA
MERCHANDISE
MERCHANDIZE
MERCHANTMAN
METACARPALS
METATARSALS
MOUNTAINEER
MOUNTAINOUS
MYXOMATOSIS
NATURALNESS
NEUTRALISED
NEWSCASTING
NICKNACKERY
NONCHALANCE
NONFEASANCE
NOSTRADAMUS
NUTCRACKERS
OARSMANSHIP
OUTSTANDING
OVERBALANCE
OVERHANGING
OVERLAPPING
OVERMANNING
OVERPAYMENT
PAEDIATRICS
PARAMASTOID
PATRIARCHAL
PERICARDIUM
PERIPATETIC
PLAGIARISED
PLANTAGENET
PODSNAPPERY
PORTLANDIAN
PORTMANTEAU
PORTRAITIST
PORTRAITURE
PROGNATHOUS
PROTRACTING
PROTRACTION
PRZEWALSKIS
PSITTACOSIS
PURITANICAL
RABELAISIAN
RADIOACTIVE
RAPSCALLION
REINCARNATE
REPROACHFUL
RETINACULUM
RETROACTIVE
REVELATIONS
RHEUMATICKY
RIGHTANGLED
SAPONACEOUS
SCANDALIZED
SCANDANAVIA
SCHOLARSHIP
SCULLABOGUE
SEVERALFOLD
SHOWMANSHIP
SMORGASBORD
SOCKDALAGER

SOUTHAMPTON
SPECIALIZED
SPECTACULAR
SPERMATOZOA
SPESSARTITE
SPONTANEITY
SPONTANEOUS
STANDARDIZE
SUBITANEOUS
SUBSTANDARD
SUBSTANTIAL
SUBSTANTIVE
SUBTRACTION
SUFFRAGETTE
SUPERALTERN
TAGLIATELLE
TARATANTARA
THAUMATROPE
THEREABOUTS
THINGAMAJIG
TICKTACKTOE
TRANSACTION
TRESPASSING
UNBREAKABLE
UNCLEANNESS
UNDEMANDING
UNGETATABLE
UNINHABITED
UNPALATABLE
UNSPEAKABLE
VINBLASTINE
WHEREABOUTS
WHIGMALEERY
WIDERANGING
WITENAGEMOT
WOODCARVING
WORKMANLIKE
WORKMANSHIP
ADVERBIALLY
ALPHABETIZE
AMINOBUTENE
AMPHIBOLOGY
APPROBATION
ARQUEBUSIER
ASSEMBLYMAN
ATTRIBUTION
ATTRIBUTIVE
AZOTOBACTER
BICARBONATE
BLOCKBUSTER
CANNIBALISM
CANNIBALIZE
COENOBITISM
COLLABORATE
COLUMBARIUM
CONFABULATE
CONTUBERNAL
CONURBATION
CORROBORATE
CREDIBILITY
CULPABILITY
DECARBONIZE
DESTABILIZE
DISEMBODIED
ELIGIBILITY
ELIZABETHAN
ENCUMBRANCE
ENJAMBEMENT
FALLIBILITY
FEASIBILITY
FILLIBUSTER
FLEXIBILITY
FROSTBITTEN
FUNAMBULIST
GALLIBAGGER
GALLIBEGGAR
GALLYBAGGER
GALLYBEGGAR
GREENBOTTLE
GULLIBILITY
HEARTBROKEN
INSTABILITY
LUXEMBURGER
MACROBIOTIC
MEPROBAMATE
MOZAMBIQUAN
NEIGHBORING
NEIGHBOURLY
OPPROBRIOUS
PERAMBULATE
PITCHBLENDE
POSSIBILITY
PRELIBATION
PROBABILITY
PROHIBITION
PROHIBITIVE
PROTUBERANT
READABILITY
REBARBATIVE
REDOUBTABLE
REFURBISHED
RELIABILITY
REMEMBRANCE
RESEMBLANCE
RETRIBUTION
RETRIBUTIVE
REVERBERATE
SCARABAEOID
SENSIBILITY
SOCIABILITY
SPELLBINDER
STEINBERGER
STOCKBROKER
SUITABILITY
SVARABHAKTI
TANGIBILITY
TAUROBOLIUM
TECTIBRANCH
TEENYBOPPER
TRINOBANTES
UNDOUBTEDLY
VARIABILITY
WASTEBASKET
WEIGHBRIDGE
WHEELBARROW
WHITEBOYISM
ACINACIFORM
ADVANCEMENT
AIRSICKNESS
ALTERCATION
AMERICANISM
ANFRACTUOUS
ANISOCERCAL
ANTHOCYANIN
APPLICATION
APPRECIABLE
APPRECIABLY
BANNOCKBURN
BEACHCOMBER
BERGSCHRUND
BIFURCATION
BREADCRUMBS
BROADCASTER
CAPRICCIOSO
CARSICKNESS
CHARACINOID
CLIMACTERIC
CLINOCHLORE
COLLECTANEA
COLLOCATION
CONDUCTRESS
CONJECTURAL
CONNECTICUT
CONSECUTIVE
CONVOCATION
CORRECTNESS
CRITICASTER
DEFENCELESS
DEIFICATION
DEMARCATION
DESICCATION
DEUTSCHMARK
DIPHYCERCAL
DISENCUMBER
DISINCLINED
DISLOCATION
DIVORCEMENT
DUPLICATING
DUPLICATION
EDIFICATION
EMBROCATION
EMPIECEMENT
EMPLACEMENT
ENFORCEABLE
ENFORCEMENT
ENHANCEMENT
ERADICATION
EREMACAUSIS
FABRICATION
FESTSCHRIFT
FINANCIALLY
FORNICATION
FORTHCOMING
GESTICULATE
GYNAECOLOGY
HALLUCINATE
HANDICAPPED
HANDICAPPER
HARDICANUTE
HIPPOCAMPUS
HIPPOCRATES
HIPPOCRATIC
HONEYCOMBED
HYDROCARBON
IMPEACHMENT
IMPLICATION
IMPRACTICAL
IMPRECATION
IMPRECISION
INCARCERATE
INELUCTABLE
INSINCERITY
INSOUCIANCE
INTERCALARY
INTERCEPTOR
INTERCHANGE
INTERCOSTAL
INTERCOURSE
INTRACTABLE
INTRICATELY
INVINCIBLES
IPECACUANHA
JINRICKSHAW
LATROCINIUM
LUBRICATION
MASTICATION
MATRICULATE
MELANCHOLIA
MELANCHOLIC
METRICATION
MOLLYCODDLE
MONARCHICAL
NOMENCLATOR
NORTHCLIFFE
OCHLOCRATIC
OLIGOCHAETE
OMNISCIENCE
ORTHOCENTRE
OSTRACODERM
PARTICIPANT
PARTICIPATE
PARTICIPIAL
PASSACAGLIA
PENTECONTER
PENTECOSTAL
PERSECUTION
PETTICOATED
PHILOCTETES
PHOTOCOPIER
PREDECESSOR
PREDICAMENT
PREDICATIVE
PREDICTABLE
PREDICTABLY
PREOCCUPIED
PROFICIENCY
PROLOCUTION
PROSECUTION
PROTOCOCCUS
PROVOCATION
PROVOCATIVE
PUBLICATION
RADIOCARBON
RATIOCINATE
REPLACEABLE
REPLACEMENT
RESPECTABLE
RESPECTABLY
RESUSCITATE
RETRACTABLE
SCHRECKLICH
SCOLECIFORM
SEASICKNESS
SENNACHERIB
SEPTICAEMIA
SERVICEABLE
SHORTCHANGE
SHORTCOMING
SPANGCOCKLE
SPIROCHAETE
STAIRCARPET
STENOCHROME
STRETCHABLE
STRETCHLESS
SUFFICIENCY
SUFFOCATING
SUFFOCATION
SUGARCOATED
SUPERCHARGE
SUPERCHERIE
SYNDICALISM
SYNDICATION
TACHYCARDIA
TAUTOCHRONE
TOBACCONIST
TORTICOLLIS
TORTICULLUS
TOSTICATION
TRANSCEIVER
TURRICULATE
UNCONCEALED
UNCONCERNED
UNDERCHARGE
UNDERCOOKED
UNDISCLOSED
UNIFICATION
UNPRACTICAL
UNSPECIFIED
UNTOUCHABLE
UNWELCOMING

VERMICULITE
VIDEOCAMERA
VINDICATION
WAINSCOTING
WATERCOLOUR
WATERCOURSE
WHITECHAPEL
WHITECOLLAR
ABECEDARIAN
ACCORDINGLY
AGUARDIENTE
APHRODISIAC
ARTIODACTYL
AVOIRDUPOIS
BEWILDERING
CALENDERING
CAMALDOLITE
CANDIDATURE
COMRADESHIP
CONFEDERACY
CONFEDERATE
CONFIDENTLY
CONSIDERATE
CONSIDERING
CROCIDOLITE
CYLINDRICAL
DEGRADATION
DEPREDATION
DIFFIDENTLY
DRINKDRIVER
ELUCIDATION
EXCEEDINGLY
EXPENDITURE
EXTRADITION
FORBIDDANCE
GRAVEDIGGER
GROUNDSHEET
GROUNDSPEED
GROUNDSWELL
HABERDASHER
IMPRUDENTLY
INCREDULITY
INCREDULOUS
INGREDIENTS
LEGERDEMAIN
LIQUIDAMBAR
LIQUIDATION
METHODOLOGY
OUAGADOUGOU
PERIODONTIC
PETRODOLLAR
PREJUDICIAL
PREMEDITATE
PTERODACTYL
RECONDITION
RETARDATION
REVENDICATE
SALVADORIAN
SCREWDRIVER
SECONDARILY
SECONDCLASS
SERENDIPITY
SMOULDERING
SPREADSHEET
STRANDLOPER
SUBORDINATE
SUCCEDANEUM
SUPPEDANEUM
TARRADIDDLE
TETRADRACHM
THALIDOMIDE
TORRIDONIAN
TREPIDATION
TRINIDADIAN
WELLADVISED
WITCHDOCTOR
ABIOGENETIC
ACCELERATOR
ACQUIESCENT
ADULTERATED
ALBIGENSIAN
ANACREONTIC
ANAPLEROSIS
ANAPLEROTIC
ANENCEPHALY
ANNABERGITE
ANNIVERSARY
ANTECEDENCE
ANTEPENDIUM
ANTINEUTRON
ARCHAEOLOGY
ARRIVEDERCI
BACKBENCHER
BALLBEARING
BARYCENTRIC
BATTLEDRESS
BATTLEFIELD
BATTLEFRONT
BATTLEMENTS
BESTSELLING
BIOCHEMICAL
BLADDERWORT
BLESSEDNESS
BLUNDERBORE
BOOKKEEPING
BOOKSELLERS
BOURGEOISIE
BRANDENBURG
BROTHERHOOD
BUSINESSMAN
CANDLELIGHT
CANDLESTICK
CENTREBOARD
CENTREPIECE
CESAREWITCH
CHALLENGING
CHAMBERLAIN
CHAMBERMAID
CHANCELLERY
CHANTERELLE
CHARGEPAYER
CHARLEMAGNE
CHEESECLOTH
CHICHEVACHE
CHICKENFEED
CHIPPENDALE
CHITTERLING
CINQUECENTO
CITIZENSHIP
CLANDESTINE
CLAPPERCLAW
CLIOMETRICS
COBBLESTONE
COCKLESHELL
CONGRESSMAN
CONSTELLATE
CONSTERNATE
CONTRETEMPS
COUNSELLING
COUNTENANCE
COUNTERFEIT
COUNTERFOIL
COUNTERFORT
COUNTERGLOW
COUNTERHAND
COUNTERMAND
COUNTERPANE
COUNTERPART
COUNTERSIGN
COUNTERSINK
COURTEOUSLY
CRACKERJACK
CRESCENTADE
CROMWELLIAN
CROOKEDNESS
DEFERENTIAL
DELETERIOUS
DELINEATION
DELITESCENT
DELIVERANCE
DEPHLEGMATE
DESELECTION
DISCREPANCY
DISOBEDIENT
DISPLEASURE
DISTRESSING
DOCUMENTARY
DOMINEERING
DOUBLECHECK
DOUBLECROSS
DOWNHEARTED
DRUNKENNESS
DRYCLEANERS
DRYCLEANING
EARTHENWARE
ECCALEOBION
EINSTEINIUM
EMPOWERMENT
ENGINEERING
EPICHEIREMA
ERIODENDRON
ERRONEOUSLY
EVANGELICAL
EVISCERATED
EXAGGERATED
EXASPERATED
EXOSKELETON
EXPONENTIAL
FAIRWEATHER
FARTHERMOST
FEHMGERICHT
FIDDLEDEDEE
FILAMENTOUS
FLABBERGAST
FLANNELETTE
FLICKERTAIL
FLUORESCENT
FORESEEABLE
FRAGMENTARY
FURTHERANCE
FURTHERMORE
FURTHERMOST
FURTHERSOME
GAMOGENESIS
GASTRECTOMY
GENTLEMANLY
GENTLEWOMAN
GIGGLESTICK
GIGGLESWICK
GIGGLEWATER
GIRDLESTEAD
GLADWELLISE
GLIMMERGOWK
GREASEPAINT
HALFHEARTED
HATCHETTITE
HEPPLEWHITE
HOBBLEDEHOY
HOMOGENEITY
HOMOGENEOUS
HOMOGENIZED
HUCKLEBERRY
HUNDREDFOLD
HURTLEBERRY
HYPOTENSION
INADVERTENT
INALIENABLE
INATTENTION
INATTENTIVE
INCALESCENT
INCINERATOR
INCOHERENCE
INDEPENDENT
INDIGESTION
INEFFECTIVE
INEFFECTUAL
INESSENTIAL
INEXPEDIENT
INEXPENSIVE
INFLUENTIAL
INNUMERABLE
INOFFENSIVE
INSUPERABLE
INTERESTING
INTOLERABLE
INTOLERABLY
INTOLERANCE
IRREDENTIST
IRRELEVANCE
IRREVERENCE
ISOELECTRIC
JACQUEMINOT
KIDDLEYWINK
KINDHEARTED
KITCHENETTE
LAPIDESCENT
LAUNDERETTE
LAWBREAKING
LEATHERBACK
LEATHERETTE
LEATHERHEAD
LEATHERNECK
LOCORESTIVE
LUMINESCENT
MAINTENANCE
MAISTERDOME
MAKEBELIEVE
MASQUERADER
MEANDERINGS
MECKLENBURG
METAGENESIS
MIDDLEMARCH
MIDDLESIZED
MILQUETOAST
MISIDENTIFY
MISSPELLING
MUSCHELKALK
NEANDERTHAL
NEEDLEPOINT
NEEDLESTICK
NEEDLEWOMAN
NEVERENDING
NOTICEBOARD
NOVELETTISH
OBLITERATED
OBMUTESCENT
OBSOLESCENT
OPTOMETRIST
OVERBEARING
OVERLEARNED
OVERWEENING
OVERZEALOUS
PARACETAMOL
PARALEIPSIS
PARAMEDICAL
PARANEPHROS
PARTNERSHIP
PEDETENTOUS
PENITENTIAL
PENTHESILEA

PERDUELLION
PERSPECTIVE
PHRASEOLOGY
PIERREPOINT
POLICEWOMAN
POLYTECHNIC
PREMIERSHIP
PROCEEDINGS
PROCREATION
PROGRESSION
PROGRESSIVE
PROPHETICAL
PROSPECTIVE
PSYCHEDELIC
PURPRESTURE
QUADRENNIAL
QUADRENNIUM
QUARRELLING
QUARRELSOME
QUARTERBACK
QUARTERDECK
RATTLESNAKE
RECOVERABLE
REGIMENTALS
REICHENBACH
REORIENTATE
RESIDENTIAL
RESPLENDANT
RESPLENDENT
RETRIEVABLE
REVERENTIAL
RIDDLEMEREE
RIGHTEOUSLY
RINTHEREOUT
RUDIMENTARY
SADDLEHORSE
SCATTERGOOD
SCATTERLING
SCUPPERNONG
SEDIMENTARY
SELFDEFENCE
SELFRESPECT
SELFSERVICE
SHAFTESBURY
SHEPHERDESS
SINGLESTICK
SLENDERNESS
SLUMBERWEAR
SMITHEREENS
SNICKERSNEE
SNORKELLING
SOVEREIGNTY
SPATTERDASH
SPATTERDOCK
STRATEGICAL
STRIKEBOUND
SUDETENLAND
SUNDRENCHED
SUPPRESSION
SWITZERLAND
SYMPLEGADES
SYNTHESIZED
SYNTHESIZER
TAXIDERMIST
THEATERGOER
THENCEFORTH
THEORETICAL
THUNDERBIRD
THUNDERBOLT
THUNDERCLAP
THUNDERHEAD
TIDDLEYWINK
TIMEKEEPING
TIRONENSIAN
TRACHEOTOMY
TROMPELOEIL
TRUSTEESHIP
TWELVEMONTH
TYPESETTING
TYRONENSIAN
UNALTERABLE
UNASSERTIVE
UNDESERVING
UNDEVELOPED
UNENVELOPED
UNNECESSARY
UNOBSERVANT
UNREHEARSED
UNRELENTING
UNREPENTANT
UNSCHEDULED
UNSWEETENED
UNUTTERABLE
VIVISECTION
WARMHEARTED
WASHLEATHER
WATEREDDOWN
WEATHERCOCK
WELLBEHAVED
WELLDEFINED
WELLMEANING
WENSLEYDALE
WHISKERANDO
WHITLEATHER
WINDLESTRAW
TÉLÉFÉRIQUE
BLACKFELLOW
CAMOUFLAGED
CAULIFLOWER
CERTIFIABLE
CERTIFICATE
COACHFELLOW
CRESTFALLEN
CRUCIFIXION
DISAFFECTED
ENFEOFFMENT
FAULTFINDER
FRANKFURTER
GILLYFLOWER
GRANDFATHER
HALLEFLINTA
INDIFFERENT
JUSTIFIABLE
JUSTIFIABLY
MAGNIFICENT
MELLIFLUOUS
PENNYFATHER
PERCEFOREST
PETTIFOGGER
PHONOFIDDLE
PHOTOFINISH
PONTIFICATE
PROLIFERATE
RANGEFINDER
RASTAFARIAN
RECTIFIABLE
ROCKEFELLER
SACRIFICIAL
SCIREFACIAS
SCRUFFINESS
SIGNIFICANT
STEADFASTLY
SUPERFICIAL
SUPERFICIES
SUPERFLUITY
SUPERFLUOUS
TIGHTFISTED
TOPLOFTICAL
TRANSFERRED
TRANSFERRIN
TRANSFIGURE
TRANSFORMED
TRANSFORMER
TRANSFUSION
UNCONFIRMED
UNFULFILLED
WHITEFRIARS
WORLDFAMOUS
ABRIDGEMENT
AGGREGATION
ANDROGENOUS
ARCHEGONIAL
ARCHEGONIUM
ARRANGEMENT
ASPERGILLUM
ASPERGILLUS
BELEAGUERED
BELLIGERENT
BESIEGEMENT
CALLIGRAPHY
CARTOGRAPHY
CERARGYRITE
CHIROGRAPHY
CHOROGRAPHY
CONJUGATION
CONSIGNMENT
CORRUGATION
DERANGEMENT
DISFIGURING
DISORGANIZE
DISREGARDED
DITTOGRAPHY
DYSLOGISTIC
ENLARGEMENT
ESPIEGLERIE
ETHNOGRAPHY
EXPURGATION
EXTROGENOUS
FARRAGINOUS
GALLIGANTUS
GREENGROCER
GRENZGANGER
HAEMOGLOBIN
HAGIOGRAPHY
HOOLIGANISM
ICONOGRAPHY
IMPREGNABLE
INCONGRUITY
INCONGRUOUS
INDULGENTLY
INFANGTHIEF
INSTIGATION
INTERGLOSSA
INTERGROWTH
LARYNGISMUS
LENTIGINOSE
LITHOGRAPHY
LIVINGSTONE
MICROGAMETE
MISBEGOTTEN
MONONGAHELA
NARRAGANSET
ORTHOGRAPHY
PALEOGRAPHY
PELARGONIUM
PHOTOGRAPHY
PORNOGRAPHY
PREROGATIVE
PRIMIGENIAL
PRODIGALISE
PRODIGALITY
PROLEGOMENA
PROPAGATION
PROROGATION
PROTAGONIST
RADIOGRAPHY
REALIGNMENT
REFRIGERANT
REFRIGERATE
REGURGITATE
SALVOGUNNER
SAUSAGEMEAT
SEGREGATION
SPHRAGISTIC
SPRINGBOARD
SPRINGCLEAN
SPRINGHOUSE
SPRINGINESS
STENOGRAPHY
STRANGENESS
STRANGEWAYS
STRANGULATE
STRINGENTLY
STRINGYBARK
STRONGYLOID
SUBJUGATION
SUBUNGULATA
TACHYGRAPHY
TOBOGGANING
TRITAGONIST
UNDERGROUND
UNDERGROWTH
UNDISGUISED
VARANGARIAN
VARIEGATION
VERBIGERATE
VERTIGINOUS
VINAIGRETTE
AMMOPHILOUS
ANESTHETIST
ANESTHETIZE
ANTECHAMBER
ANTIPHRASIS
ARGATHELIAN
ASSYTHEMENT
BLASPHEMOUS
BREATHALYSE
BUSHWHACKER
CACOPHONOUS
CATACHRESIS
CLIFFHANGER
CRACKHALTER
CYMOPHANOUS
DIARTHROSIS
DICEPHALOUS
DINNYHAUSER
DINNYHAYSER
DIORTHORTIC
DRAUGHTSMAN
ELEUTHERIAN
EMPTYHANDED
ENARTHROSIS
ENCEPHALOMA
ENDOTHERMIC
ENKEPHALINE
ENLIGHTENED
ENNEAHEDRON
EOANTHROPUS
EXANTHEMATA
FORESHORTEN
FORETHOUGHT
FREETHINKER
FRENCHWOMAN
FRENCHWOMEN
GRASSHOPPER
HEALTHINESS
HEAVYHANDED
HEMOPHILIAC
HOLOTHURIAN
HOMOTHERMAL

HOMOTHERMIC
HOUSEHOLDER
HYPOTHECATE
HYPOTHERMIA
ILLYWHACKER
INAUTHENTIC
ITHYPHALLIC
ITHYPHALLUS
JOSEPHINITE
KALASHNIKOV
LEASEHOLDER
LENGTHENING
LENGTHINESS
LEVELHEADED
LIGHTHEADED
MASOCHISTIC
MEGATHERIUM
METAPHYSICS
MISBEHAVIOR
MONOCHINOUS
MONOTHELITE
MUNCHHAUSEN
MYCOPHAGIST
NAPHTHALENE
NIKETHAMIDE
NONETHELESS
NOTOTHERIUM
ORNITHOLOGY
ORNITHOPTER
OVERWHELMED
PARACHUTIST
PARISHIONER
PERIPHRASIS
PLOUGHSHARE
PROSTHETICS
RAVISHINGLY
RIGHTHANDED
RIGHTHANDER
RUDESHEIMER
SAXOPHONIST
SEARCHLIGHT
SHAREHOLDER
SHEATHKNIFE
SHORTHANDED
SKETCHINESS
SMALLHOLDER
SPEECHCRAFT
STADTHOLDER
STAKEHOLDER
STALLHOLDER
STOCKHAUSEN
STOCKHOLDER
STRAPHANGER
STROPHILLUS
STRUTHIONES
STYMPHALIAN
SWITCHBOARD
SYCOPHANTIC
TELEPHONIST
TETRAHEDRON

THOUGHTLESS
TIMESHARING
TOXOPHILITE
TREACHEROUS
TREACHETOUR
TRENCHERMAN
UNAUTHENTIC
UNDERHANDED
UNRIGHTEOUS
UPRIGHTNESS
WESTPHALIAN
WINDCHEATER
WRONGHEADED
ZWISCHENZUG
ABORTIONIST
ACCIPITRINE
ADJUDICATOR
ADOPTIANISM
ADOPTIONISM
AFFILIATION
AFFLIICTION
ALBUGINEOUS
ALLEVIATION
AMERCIAMENT
AMONTILLADO
APHANIPTERA
APOLLINARIS
ASSIMILATED
ASSOCIATION
ASTONISHING
ATHERINIDAE
ATRABILIOUS
ATROCIOUSLY
AUDACIOUSLY
BACKFIELDER
BANDEIRANTE
BEAUTIFULLY
BEHAVIOURAL
BENEDICTINE
BENEDICTION
BENEFICIARY
BENEFICIATE
BOOKBINDING
BRILLIANTLY
BROBDINGNAG
BULLFIGHTER
CAPACITANCE
CAPACITATOR
CARABINIERE
CAROLINGIAN
CAUSTICALLY
CENTRIFUGAL
CENTRIPETAL
CHANTICLEER
CHILLINGHAM
CHINOISERIE
CHRONICALLY
CILOFIBRATE
CIRRHIPEDEA
CIRRHIPEDIA

COEFFICIENT
COINCIDENCE
COLONIALISM
COLONIALIST
COMPLICATED
COMPLIMENTS
COMPRIMARIO
CONCEIVABLE
CONCEIVABLY
CONNOISSEUR
CONSCIOUSLY
CONSPICUOUS
CONSPIRATOR
CONSTIPATED
CONSTITUENT
CONTAINMENT
CONTRIBUTOR
CONTRIVANCE
COORDINATED
COORDINATES
COXWAINLESS
CRÉMAILLÈRE
CURTAILMENT
DEBILITATED
DECAPITATED
DEFOLIATION
DELICIOUSLY
DENOMINATOR
DERELICTION
DESCRIPTION
DESCRIPTIVE
DETERIORATE
DILAPIDATED
DISORIENTED
DISQUIETING
DISTRIBUTED
DISTRIBUTOR
DOCTRINAIRE
DRASTICALLY
EFFICIENTLY
EMPIRICUTIC
ENUNCIATION
EQUIDISTANT
EQUILIBRIST
EQUILIBRIUM
ERRATICALLY
EXORBITANCE
EXPEDITIOUS
EXPERIENCED
FACETIOUSLY
FACTFINDING
FAMILIARISE
FAMILIARITY
FAMILIARIZE
FANATICALLY
FARTHINGALE
FEROCIOUSLY
FIRELIGHTER
FITZWILLIAM
FLOURISHING

FORAMINIFER
FORTNIGHTLY
FRANTICALLY
FUNCTIONARY
FUNCTIONING
GENERICALLY
GENETICALLY
GENOUILLÈRE
GRAPHICALLY
HABILIMENTS
HARDHITTING
HARPSICHORD
HIGHLIGHTER
HIGHPITCHED
HILARIOUSLY
HISTRIONICS
HUMILIATING
HUMILIATION
IDENTICALLY
IDENTIFYING
IDIOTICALLY
IDYLLICALLY
IGNOMINIOUS
ILLOGICALLY
ILLUMINATED
ILLUSIONARY
ILLUSIONIST
IMMEDIATELY
IMPATIENTLY
IMPEDIMENTA
IMPERIALISM
IMPERIALIST
IMPERIOUSLY
INADVISABLE
INDEFINABLE
INDIVISIBLE
INDIVISIBLY
INDOMITABLE
INDUBITABLE
INDUBITABLY
INEBRIATION
INEFFICIENT
INEQUITABLE
INESTIMABLE
INEXCITABLE
INFERIORITY
INFURIATING
INGENIOUSLY
INHABITABLE
INHABITANTS
INHERITANCE
INJUDICIOUS
INSCRIPTION
INSIDIOUSLY
INTOXICATED
INTOXIMETER
INVIGILATOR
IRRADIATION
IRRELIGIOUS
JAMAHIRIYAH

JUDICIOUSLY
KIMERIDGIAN
KINCHINMORT
KWASHIORKOR
LABORIOUSLY
LACONICALLY
LAMPLIGHTER
LATERIGRADE
LATERITIOUS
LINGUISTICS
LOGARITHMIC
LONGSIGHTED
LOUISIANIAN
LUXURIANTLY
LUXURIOUSLY
MACHAIRODUS
MALEDICTION
MALICIOUSLY
MANUMISSION
MATERIALISE
MATERIALISM
MATERIALIST
MATERIALIZE
MEDICINALLY
MELODIOUSLY
MISCHIEVOUS
MISERICORDE
MONCHIQUITE
MOONLIGHTER
MUDSLINGING
MUNIFICENCE
NEARSIGHTED
NEGOTIATING
NEGOTIATION
NIGHTINGALE
NONEXISTENT
NOTORIOUSLY
NUMERICALLY
OBSTRICTION
OFFICIALDOM
OFFICIALESE
OFFICIOUSLY
ORGANICALLY
ORGANIZAION
OVERFISHING
PACIFICALLY
PAINKILLING
PECULIARITY
PENICILLATE
PERSPICUITY
PERSPICUOUS
PHILLIPSITE
PLANTIGRADE
PLEBEIANISE
POLITICALLY
POLITICIANS
PRACTICABLE
PRACTICALLY
PREEMINENCE
PRESTIGIOUS

PRESTISSIMO
PRINCIPALLY
PRISCIANIST
PROPRIETARY
PROSAICALLY
PSYCHIATRIC
PUNCHINELLO
PUNCTILIOUS
QUARRINGTON
QUESTIONING
REACTIONARY
RECRUITMENT
REFOCILLATE
RELIGIOUSLY
REMINISCENT
REPETITIOUS
REPUDIATION
RESTRICTION
RESTRICTIVE
RETALIATION
RETALIATORY
REVISIONISM
RIFACIMENTO
SAGACIOUSLY
SALACIOUSLY
SATIRICALLY
SCANDINAVIA
SCEPTICALLY
SCINTILLATE
SCYPHISTOMA
SEIGNIORAGE
SELAGINELLA
SESQUIOXIDE
SHITTIMWOOD
SHOPLIFTING
SKEPTICALLY
SKILLIGALEE
SKILLIGOLEE
SKIMMINGTON
SPERMICIDAL
STELLIONATE
STRAMINEOUS
SUPERIMPOSE
SUPERINTEND
SUPERIORITY
SURVEILLANT
SUSTAINABLE
TECHNICALLY
TEGUCICALPA
TELEKINESIS
TENACIOUSLY
TERPSICHORE
TOTALIZATOR
TOURBILLION
TRAFFICATOR
TRANSILIENT
TRICHINELLA
TRICHINOSED
ULOTRICHALE
UNAMBIGUOUS
UNAVAILABLE
UNAVOIDABLE
UNAVOIDABLY
UNBEFITTING
UNCHRISTIAN
UNCIVILISED
UNCIVILIZED
UNDESIRABLE
UNEQUIVOCAL
UNINHIBITED
UNMITIGATED
UNMOTIVATED
UNREMITTING
UNSATISFIED
UNSHRINKING
UNSOLICITED
VALEDICTION
VALEDICTORY
VICARIOUSLY
VINCRISTINE
VITAMINIZED
VIVACIOUSLY
VORACIOUSLY
VOTERIGGING
WESTMINSTER
WHITTINGTON
MALADJUSTED
STOCKJOBBER
EMBARKATION
HOUSEKEEPER
KINNIKINICK
LANDSKNECHT
PEACEKEEPER
SCHECKLATON
STOREKEEPER
TCHAIKOVSKY
UNSHAKEABLE
VOLKSKAMMER
ACATALECTIC
ACRIFLAVINE
ACTUALITIES
AESCULAPIAN
AESCULAPIUS
AIGUILLETTE
ANACOLUTHIA
ANTHOLOGIZE
APOCALYPTIC
APPALLINGLY
APPELLATION
APPELLATIVE
ARCHILOCHUS
ARTILLERIST
BACKSLIDING
BADDELEYITE
BEASTLINESS
BRISTLECONE
BRITTLENESS
BRUCELLOSIS
CABBALISTIC
CALCULATING
CALCULATION
CASTELLATED
CATACLYSMIC
CATALLACTIC
CATHOLICISM
CEASELESSLY
CHEERLEADER
CIRCULARIZE
CIRCULATING
CIRCULATION
CIRCULATORY
CITLALEPETL
CLEANLINESS
COAGULATION
COLDBLOODED
COMPILATION
COMPILEMENT
CONCILIATOR
CONDOLENCES
CONSILIENCE
CONSOLATION
CONSOLIDATE
CONSULTANCY
CONVALLARIA
CONVOLUTION
CONVOLVULUS
CONVULSIONS
CORRELATION
COURTLINESS
CREDULOUSLY
CRENELLATED
CROSSLEGGED
DACTYLOGRAM
DISABLEMENT
DISBELIEVER
DISCOLOURED
DISILLUSION
DISSOLUTION
DITHELETISM
DRAGGLETAIL
DREADLOCKED
EJACULATION
EMBELLISHED
ENFOULDERED
ENGHALSKRUG
ENTABLATURE
ENTABLEMENT
ENTITLEMENT
EPANALEPSIS
ESTABLISHED
ESTABLISHER
ETHNOLOGIST
ETYMOLOGIST
FAULTLESSLY
FLORILEGIUM
FORECLOSURE
FORMULATION
FRANKLINITE
FRIVOLOUSLY
FRUITLESSLY
FULFILLMENT
FULLBLOODED
FUSTILARIAN
GABERLUNZIE
GARRULOUSLY
GENEALOGIST
GENUFLEXION
GHASTLINESS
GONFALONIER
GUADALCANAL
HANGGLIDING
HARIOLATION
HEARTLESSLY
HECKELPHONE
HISTOLOGIST
HOHENLINDEN
HOSTILITIES
HYMNOLOGIST
INDEXLINKED
INOCULATION
INSTALLMENT
INTELLIGENT
INTERLACING
INTERLEUKIN
INTERLINGUA
LEGISLATION
LEGISLATIVE
LEGISLATURE
LONGSLEEVED
MANGALSUTRA
MANTELLETTA
MANTELPIECE
MANTELSHELF
MAQUILADORA
MASCULINITY
MASKALLONGE
MENDELEVIUM
MENDELSSOHN
MERCILESSLY
MISALLIANCE
MISERLINESS
MONEYLENDER
MUSKELLUNGE
NEUROLOGIST
NICKELODEON
NOISELESSLY
ORDERLINESS
OSCILLATION
OVERFLOWING
PALEOLITHIC
PAMPELMOOSE
PAMPELMOUSE
PAMPHLETEER
PANTALETTES
PARABLEPSIS
PATHOLOGIST
PERCHLORATE
PERCOLATION
PHILOLOGIST
PICKELHAUBE
POINTLESSLY
POMPELMOOSE
POMPELMOUSE
PREPOLLENCE
PRICKLINESS
PROSELYTISM
PROSELYTIZE
QUERULOUSLY
RADIOLOGIST
RECTILINEAR
REDUPLICATE
RHOPALOCERA
SAINTLINESS
SAPROLEGNIA
SCOPOLAMINE
SCUTTLEBUTT
SHAMELESSLY
SHAPELINESS
SHINPLASTER
SHOVELBOARD
SHUTTLECOCK
SINGULARITY
SKIDBLADNIR
SOCIOLOGIST
SOUNDLESSLY
SPECULATION
SPECULATIVE
SPIFFLICATE
STAGFLATION
STATELINESS
STEEPLEJACK
STICKLEBACK
STIMULATION
STIPULATION
SUBMULTIPLE
SUPERLATIVE
TANTALIZING
TASTELESSLY
TESSELLATED
THANKLESSLY
THINGLINESS
THISTLEDOWN
TIGHTLIPPED
TITILLATION
TONSILLITIS
TRACKLEMENT
TRAGELAPHUS
TRANSLATION
TRANSLUCENT
TRIBULATION
TROUBLESOME
TROUBLESPOT
TRUCULENTLY
TURBELLARIA
TYROGLYPHID
UNEXPLAINED
UNFAILINGLY
UNGODLINESS
UNPUBLISHED
UNQUALIFIED

UNREALISTIC
UNSHELTERED
UNWHOLESOME
VACILLATING
VACILLATION
VARIOLATION
VENTILATION
WATERLOGGED
WHISTLESTOP
WOMANLINESS
WORLDLINESS
ABNORMALITY
ACADEMICIAN
ACCLAMATION
ACCLIMATION
ACCLIMATISE
ACCLIMATIZE
ACCOMMODATE
AFFIRMATION
AFFIRMATIVE
AGGLOMERATE
ANAXIMANDER
ANONYMOUSLY
ASTIGMATISM
ATHERMANOUS
BADTEMPERED
BLACKMAILER
BROADMINDED
BURGOMASTER
CENTUMVIRUS
CHAULMOOGRA
CHAULMOUGRA
CHILDMINDER
CHOIRMASTER
CIRCUMCISER
CIRCUMFLECT
CIRCUMSPECT
COMMEMORATE
CONCOMITANT
CONDOMINIUM
CONSUMABLES
CONSUMERISM
CONSUMPTION
CONSUMPTIVE
CONTAMINANT
CONTAMINATE
CONTEMPLANT
CONTEMPLATE
COULOMMIERS
CUSTOMARILY
DECLAMATION
DECLAMATORY
DEFORMATION
DETERMINANT
DETERMINING
DETRIMENTAL
DIPLOMATICS
DIPLOMATIST
DIPSOMANIAC
DISARMAMENT
DISSEMINATE
DISSIMULATE
DRESSMAKING
EPOCHMAKING
ESCARMOUCHE
ESTRAMAZONE
EUPHEMISTIC
EXCLAMATION
EXTERMINATE
FUNDAMENTAL
GALLIMAUFRY
GELSEMININE
GERRYMANDER
GRANDMASTER
GRANDMOTHER
HEBDOMADARY
HONEYMOONER
HOUSEMASTER
HYDROMEDUSA
HYPERMARKET
IMPERMANENT
IMPERMEABLE
IMPLEMENTAL
INCREMENTAL
INCRIMINATE
INFLAMMABLE
INFORMALITY
INFORMATICS
INFORMATION
INFORMATIVE
INTERMINGLE
JERRYMANDER
MAGLEMOSIAN
MARSHMALLOW
MATHEMATICS
MATRIMONIAL
MEDIUMSIZED
MERRYMAKING
MISDEMEANOR
MODELMOLEST
MONEYMAKING
NECROMANCER
NIGHTMARISH
NUMISMATICS
NUMISMATIST
PANDEMONIUM
PESSIMISTIC
PETITMAITRE
PREDOMINANT
PREDOMINATE
PRELIMINARY
PRESUMPTION
PRESUMPTIVE
RAZZAMATAZZ
REANIMATION
RECLAMATION
RECRIMINATE
REFORMATION
REFORMATORY
RUMGUMPTION
SACRAMENTAL
SALTIMBANCO
SALTIMBOCCA
SCAREMONGER
SCITAMINEAE
SCOUTMASTER
SCREAMINGLY
SELFIMPOSED
SENTIMENTAL
SHUNAMITISM
SILLIMANITE
STREAMLINED
SUBDOMINANT
SUBLIMATION
SUPERMARKET
SYSTEMATIZE
TERREMOTIVE
TESTIMONIAL
THROGMORTON
TOASTMASTER
TRANSMITTED
TRANSMITTER
ULTRAMARINE
ULTRAMODERN
UNANIMOUSLY
UNBLEMISHED
UNCOMMITTED
UNDERMANNED
UNTRAMELLED
VALLAMBROSA
VENDEMIAIRE
WATERMEADOW
ABOMINATION
ACCOUNTABLE
ACCOUNTANCY
ACUPUNCTURE
AFGHANISTAN
ALCYONARIAN
ALEXANDRINE
ALEXANDRITE
ALIFANFARON
ALTERNATELY
ALTERNATING
ALTERNATION
ALTERNATIVE
AMELANCHIER
ANTHONOMOUS
APPOINTMENT
APPRENTICED
ARCHENTERON
ARRHENOTOKY
ASSIGNATION
ASTRINGENCY
AURIGNACIAN
BOUTONNIERE
BOYSENBERRY
CALLANETICS
CAMPANOLOGY
CAPERNOITED
CAPERNOITIE
CARMINATIVE
CENTENARIAN
CLARENCIEUX
COLLENCHYMA
COMBINATION
COMMANDMENT
COMMENDABLE
COMMENDABLY
COMMENTATOR
COMMINATION
COMMONPLACE
COMMONSENSE
COMMUNICANT
COMMUNICATE
COMPENDIOUS
COMPUNCTION
CONCENTRATE
CONFINEMENT
CONJUNCTION
CONJUNCTURE
CONTENEMENT
CONTENTEDLY
CONTENTIOUS
CONTENTMENT
CONTINENTAL
CONTINGENCE
CONTINGENCY
CONTINUALLY
CONTINUANCE
CONVENIENCE
CONVENTICLE
COTTONMOUTH
CREDENTIALS
CRIMINOLOGY
CULMINATION
CYBERNETICS
DARDANELLES
DEGRINGOLER
DESCENDANTS
DESIGNATION
DESPONDENCY
DESTINATION
DIAMONDBACK
DISCONTINUE
DISHONESTLY
DISJUNCTION
DISPENSABLE
DISTINCTION
DISTINCTIVE
DISTINGUISH
DRACUNCULUS
DRAGONNADES
DREADNOUGHT
DYSFUNCTION
ELIMINATION
ENCHANTMENT
ENCHANTRESS
ENCHONDROMA
ENFRANCHISE
EPAMINONDAS
EPIGENESIST
ERYMANTHIAN
ESTRANGHELO
EXAMINATION
EXPLANATION
EXPLANATORY
FASCINATING
FASCINATION
FERRONNIÈRE
FESTINATELY
FISHANDCHIP
FORTUNATELY
FORTUNELOUD
FULMINATION
GENUINENESS
GEOSYNCLINE
GERMINATION
GORDONSTOUN
GUBERNATION
HEMIANOPSIA
HERRINGBONE
HIBERNATING
HIBERNATION
HOLLANDAISE
HOOTANANNIE
HOOTENANNIE
HUMMINGBIRD
HUSBANDLAND
HYPHENATION
ILLMANNERED
IMAGINATION
IMAGINATIVE
IMPIGNORATE
INCARNADINE
INCARNATION
INCLINATION
INDIGNANTLY
INDIGNATION
INSTANTIATE
INSTINCTIVE
INTERNECINE
INTERNUNCIO
LEGIONNAIRE
LONGANIMITY
LONGINQUITY
MACHINATION
MAGNANIMITY
MAGNANIMOUS
MALFUNCTION
MARCONIGRAM
MARGINALIST
MARGINALIZE
MARIONBERRY
MARIONETTES
MEANINGLESS
MENTONNIÈRE
MIDDENSTEAD
MISCONSTRUE
MOCKINGBIRD
MODERNISTIC

MORGENSTERN
NATIONALISM
NATIONALIST
NATIONALITY
NATIONALIZE
NATIONSTATE
NONSENSICAL
NOTHINGNESS
OBSTINATELY
OFFHANDEDLY
OPPIGNORATE
ORIGINALITY
ORIGINATING
ORIGINATION
OUTMANEUVER
PARVANIMITY
PATERNALISM
PATERNOSTER
PATRONISING
PATRONIZING
PENTONVILLE
PERENNIALLY
PERFUNCTORY
PERMANENTLY
PERSONALIST
PERSONALITY
PERSONALIZE
PERSONIFIED
PERTINACITY
PERTINENTLY
PHALANSTERY
PHARYNGITIS
PHILANDERER
POLLENBRUSH
POLLINATION
PRECONCEIVE
PREMONITION
PREMONITORY
PRESENTABLE
PRETENSIONS
PRETENTIOUS
PREVENTABLE
PROGENITRIX
PROMINENTLY
PROPINQUITY
PROTONOTARY
PYTHONESQUE
RALLENTANDO
RAMGUNSHOCH
RATIONALITY
RATIONALIZE
RECOGNITION
RECONNOITER
RECONNOITRE
RECTANGULAR
RESIGNATION
RESPONSIBLE
RESPONSIBLY
RESPONSIONS
ROTTENSTONE

SALPINGITIS
SARCENCHYME
SENTENTIOUS
SEPTENARIUS
SEPTENTRION
SHENANIGANS
STEGANOGRAM
STEGANOPODE
STIPENDIARY
SUBCONTRACT
SUBJUNCTIVE
SUBPANATION
TABERNACLES
TENDENTIOUS
TERMINATION
TERMINOLOGY
THEOPNEUSTY
TREPONEMATA
TRYPANOSOMA
TRYPANOSOME
UNCONNECTED
UNDIGNIFIED
UNDRINKABLE
UNFLINCHING
UNFURNISHED
UNPRINTABLE
UNTHINKABLE
UNVARNISHED
VACCINATION
VIOLINCELLO
VIOLONCELLO
VOLCANOLOGY
VULCANOLOGY
WAPPENSCHAW
WELLINGTONS
WILLINGNESS
ABANDONMENT
ACRIMONIOUS
AILUROPHILE
ALLEGORICAL
ALLELOMORPH
ANAGNORISIS
ANASTOMOSIS
ANGELOLATRY
ANTONOMASIA
APLANOSPORE
APOLLONICON
APOSIOPESIS
ARISTOCRACY
ARTHRODESIS
ARTHROSPORE
AUXANOMETER
BARTHOLOMEW
BEAUMONTAGE
BENEVOLENCE
BIBLIOPHILE
BILLIONAIRE
BOTANOMANCY
CALCEOLARIA
CALIFORNIUM

CAMEROONIAN
CAMPHORATED
CARDIOGRAPH
CATEGORICAL
CEREMONIOUS
CHEIROGNOMY
CHIAROSCURO
CHLOROPHYLL
CHORDOPHONE
CHRONOMETER
CHRYSOPRASE
COMSTOCKERY
CONTROVERSY
CRITHOMANCY
DEMAGOGUERY
DEMONOMANIA
DEVELOPMENT
DIAGNOSTICS
DIAPHORESIS
DIAPHORETIC
DIASCORDIUM
DUMBFOUNDED
ELASTOPLAST
EMOTIONALLY
EMPYROMANCY
ENVIRONMENT
EQUINOCTIAL
EQUIPOLLENT
EQUIVOCALLY
FASHIONABLE
FASHIONABLY
FAUXBOURDON
FISHMONGERS
FLAMBOYANCE
FLAMBOYANTE
FOULMOUTHED
GAMETOPHYTE
GASTRONOMIC
GLASTONBURY
GLOSSOLALIA
GNATHONICAL
GOODLOOKING
GREENOCKITE
HALFHOLIDAY
HARDWORKING
HEPATOSCOPY
HETEROSCIAN
HIGHPOWERED
HOMOEOPATHY
HYPOCORISMA
IDEOLOGICAL
INOPPORTUNE
IRONMONGERS
IRONMONGERY
IRREVOCABLE
KATABOTHRON
KATAVOTHRON
KETAVOTHRON
KLEPTOMANIA
KOTABOTHRON

LAMPROPHYRE
LEPIDOPTERA
LEPIDOSIREN
LYCHNOSCOPE
MALEVOLENCE
MARLBOROUGH
MEGALOMANIA
MEGALOMANIC
MEGALOPOLIS
MELANOCHROI
MENTHOLATED
MERITORIOUS
MILLIONAIRE
MONTGOLFIER
MONTMORENCY
MYCOLOGICAL
NYMPHOMANIA
ODONTOBLAST
ODONTOPHORE
OMMATOPHORE
OMNIPOTENCE
ONEIRODYNIA
ONEIROMANCY
ONTOLOGICAL
OPINIONATED
OSTREOPHAGE
PARABOLANUS
PARADOXICAL
PARONOMASIA
PEDAGOGICAL
PELOPONNESE
PENSIONABLE
PERIGORDIAN
PERITONAEUM
PERITONITIS
PHYSIOGNOMY
PICKYOUROWN
PIEDMONTITE
PINACOTHECA
PLAGIOSTOMI
POLYMORPHIC
POTAMOGETON
PRESTONPANS
PSEUDOLOGIA
PSEUDOMORPH
PSYCHODELIC
PTOCHOCRACY
RATATOUILLE
REALPOLITIK
RETINOSPORA
RHABDOMANCY
RHAPSODICAL
RODOMONTADE
SCAFFOLDING
SCARBOROUGH
SEISMOGRAPH
SELFCONTROL
SEXOLOGICAL
SHALLOWNESS
SOCKDOLAGER

SOCKDOLIGER
SOCKDOLOGER
SOLILOQUIZE
SPARROWHAWK
SPEEDOMETER
SPERMOPHILE
SPONSORSHIP
STANDOFFISH
STEREOMETER
STEREOSCOPE
STEREOTYPED
STETHOSCOPE
STROBOSCOPE
SUBTROPICAL
SWALLOWABLE
SYMPTOMATIC
TEASPOONFUL
THALLOPHYTE
THEOLOGICAL
THERMOMETER
THERMOPYLAE
THESMOTHETE
TIMBROMANIA
TIMBROPHILY
TREASONABLE
TRICHOPTERA
TRINCOMALEE
TRIPTOLEMUS
TROPHOBLAST
UNANNOUNCED
UNFAVORABLE
UNIMPORTANT
WAREHOUSING
WELLFOUNDED
WISHTONWISH
WITHHOLDING
XENODOCHIUM
ACCOMPANIST
AGORAPHOBIA
ANADIPLOSIS
APPROPRIATE
ARCHIPELAGO
ASCLEPIADES
ATMOSPHERIC
AXEROPHTHOL
CARDOPHAGUS
CARNAPTIOUS
CATCHPHRASE
CATERPILLAR
CHAIRPERSON
CHIROPODIST
COLLAPSIBLE
COMEUPPANCE
CONCEPTICLE
COPROPHAGAN
CORRUPTIBLE
CURNAPTIOUS
DECREPITATE
DECREPITUDE
DESERPIDINE

DISAPPROVAL
DISCIPLINED
DISIMPRISON
DISSEPIMENT
DISSIPATION
EPINEPHRINE
EXPROPRIATE
EXTEMPORISE
EXTEMPORIZE
EXTRAPOLATE
HAEMOPHILIA
HOMEOPATHIC
HYDROPHIDAE
HYDROPHOBIA
HYDROPHOBIC
HYDROPONICS
IMPROPRIETY
INCOMPETENT
INCOMPOSITE
INCORPORATE
INCORPOREAL
INTEMPERATE
INTERPOLATE
INTERPRETER
INTREPIDITY
ISTIOPHORUS
LASERPICIUM
LICKSPITTLE
LILLIPUTIAN
LOUDSPEAKER
MANCIPATION
OBTEMPERATE
ORTHOPAEDIC
OSTEOPATHIC
OSTEOPLASTY
PANOMPHAEAN
PARLIPOMENA
PERCEPTIBLE
PERCEPTIBLY
PERCIPIENCE
PHILIPPINES
PRECIPITATE
PRECIPITOUS
ROBESPIERRE
SAINTPAULIA
SALESPERSON
SAPROPHYTIC
SARCOPHAGUS
SCEUOPHYLAX
SCOLOPENDRA
SCRUMPTIOUS
SINGAPOREAN
STANDPATTER
STOOLPIGEON
STYLOPODIUM
SUSCEPTIBLE
SYNCOPATION
THERAPEUTAE
THERAPEUTIC
TOWNSPEOPLE
TRANSPARENT
TRANSPONDER
TRANSPORTED
TRANSPORTER
UNFLAPPABLE
UNHAPPINESS
UNSTOPPABLE
UNSUPPORTED
UNSURPASSED
UNSUSPECTED
CONSEQUENCE
DELINQUENCY
INFREQUENCY
UNCONQUERED
ADJOURNMENT
ADUMBRATION
ANACHRONISM
ANTIRRHINUM
APOMORPHINE
APOSTROPHUS
APPEARANCES
ARBITRAGEUR
ARBITRAMENT
ARBITRARILY
ARBITRATION
AWKWARDNESS
BASKERVILLE
BELLEROPHON
BESSARABIAN
BIELORUSSIA
BITTERSWEET
BOMBARDMENT
BORBORYGMUS
BUMBERSHOOT
CALIBRATION
CARBORUNDUM
CARBURETTOR
CELEBRATION
CENTERPIECE
CENTURIATOR
CEREBRATION
CHONDROSTEI
COLEORRHIZA
COLOURBLIND
COMFORTABLE
COMFORTABLY
COMFORTLESS
COMPARATIVE
COMPARTMENT
COMPTROLLER
CONCORDANCE
CONCURRENCE
CONFARREATE
CONSERVANCY
CONSTRAINED
CONSTRICTED
CONSTRICTOR
CONSTRUCTOR
CONVERGENCE
CONVERTIBLE
COOPERATION
COOPERATIVE
COPPERPLATE
CORNERSTONE
CORPORATION
COUNTRIFIED
COUNTRYSIDE
CRATERELLUS
CULVERINEER
DANGEROUSLY
DECLARATION
DEHYDRATION
DEMOGRAPHIC
DESECRATION
DESEGREGATE
DESPERATELY
DESPERATION
DEUTERONOMY
DEVITRIFIED
DIFFERENTLY
DIPTEROCARP
DISAGREEING
DISCERNIBLE
DISCERNMENT
DISPARAGING
DISPERSABLE
DISSERTATOR
DISTURBANCE
DOLABRIFORM
DOWNTRODDEN
DUSTWRAPPER
EASTERNMOST
ELABORATELY
ELABORATION
ELECTRICIAN
ELECTRICITY
ELECTROCUTE
ELECTROLIER
ELECTROLYTE
ELECTRONICS
ELECTROTINT
EMBARRASSED
ENCHIRIDION
ENCOURAGING
ENUMERATION
ERYTHROCYTE
ESCHERICHIA
EUCHARISTIC
EVAPORATION
EVENTRATION
EXONERATION
EXPLORATION
EXPLORATORY
FANFARONADE
FAVOURITISM
FEATURELESS
FINGERPRINT
FINGERSTALL
FORLORNNESS
FOTHERGILLA
FRATERNALLY
FRONTRUNNER
FRUSTRATING
FRUSTRATION
GATECRASHER
GIBBERELLIN
GINGERBREAD
GODFORSAKEN
GREGARINIDA
GUTTERSNIPE
GUTTURALISE
HAEMORRHAGE
HAEMORRHOID
HAIRDRESSER
HALFBROTHER
HAMMERCLOTH
HANDCRAFTED
HANDWRITING
HANDWRITTEN
HARDPRESSED
HAREBRAINED
HEMORRHOIDS
HIGHPROFILE
HINDERLANDS
HISTORIATED
HORSERACING
HORSERADISH
HORSERIDING
IDEOPRAXIST
IMMIGRATION
INCORRECTLY
INDIARUBBER
INOPERATIVE
INQUIRINGLY
INSPIRATION
INTEGRATION
INTERREGNUM
INTERRELATE
INTERROGATE
INTERRUPTER
JABBERWOCKY
KINDERSPIEL
KOMMERSBUCH
KULTURKREIS
LAMMERGEIER
LAMMERGEYER
LECTURESHIP
LETTERPRESS
LITTÉRATEUR
LOGGERHEADS
LOGOGRAPHER
MALAPROPISM
MASTERFULLY
MASTERPIECE
MEASURELESS
MEASUREMENT
MENSURATION
METEOROLOGY
MICHURINISM
MICTURITION
MISCARRIAGE
MONOGRAMMED
MONOTREMATA
MONSTROSITY
MOSSTROOPER
MULTIRACIAL
MURMURATION
NETHERLANDS
NETHERLINGS
NIPFARTHING
NUMBERPLATE
OMNIPRESENT
OVERCROWDED
OVERWROUGHT
PARACROSTIC
PARATROOPER
PARTURITION
PAWNBROKERS
PENETRATING
PENETRATION
PEREGRINATE
PERFORATION
PERFORMANCE
PHTHIRIASIS
PICTURESQUE
PLATERESQUE
PLATYRRHINE
POLIORCETIC
POLTERGEIST
POLYTRICHUM
POMEGRANATE
PONDEROUSLY
PORTERHOUSE
PREPARATION
PREPARATORY
PRESTRESSED
PRETERITION
PREVARICATE
PROCUREMENT
PROOFREADER
PROSTRATION
PULCHRITUDE
RAPTUROUSLY
REAPPRAISAL
RECIPROCATE
RECIPROCITY
RECURRENTLY
REITERATION
REQUIREMENT
RESOURCEFUL
RESPIRATION
RESPIRATORY
RESTORATION
RESTORATIVE
RETROROCKET
ROSICRUCIAN
SACHERTORTE
SANDERSWOOD
SAVOURINESS
SCALPRIFORM

SCHWARMEREI
SHIPWRECKED
SHOWERPROOF
SILVERSMITH
STEAMROLLER
STEPBROTHER
SUBMERGENCE
SUBSERVIENT
SUMMERHOUSE
SUPPURATION
SURTARBRAND
SURTURBRAND
SUSURRATION
SYNCHROMESH
SYNCHRONISE
SYNCHRONISM
SYNCHRONIZE
TATTERSALLS
TELEGRAPHER
TELEGRAPHIC
TELEPRINTER
TEMPERAMENT
TEMPERATURE
TEMPORARILY
TENTERHOOKS
TESSARAGLOT
THEATREGOER
THEATRICALS
THEOBROMINE
TOPOGRAPHER
TREECREEPER
TRICERATOPS
TSCHERNOSEM
TYPEWRITTEN
TYPOGRAPHER
TYPOGRAPHIC
UNEXPRESSED
UNIMPRESSED
UNIVERSALLY
UNOBTRUSIVE
UNPATRIOTIC
UNWARRANTED
VASOPRESSIN
VENTURESOME
VESPERTINAL
VOORTREKKER
WASHERWOMAN
WAYWARDNESS
WELLDRESSED
WESTERNMOST
WIENERWURST
WILBERFORCE
WINDBREAKER
WINTERBERRY
WINTERGREEN
WITHERSHINS
WONDERFULLY
XEROTRIPSIS
XYLOGRAPHER
ACCESSORIES
ACCRESCENCE
ACQUISITION
ACQUISITIVE
ADOLESCENCE
AFTERSCHOOL
AMPHISBAENA
AMPHISBOENA
ANTHESTERIA
APATOSAURUS
APPEASEMENT
ASPERSORIUM
ASSASSINATE
BARBASTELLE
BATHYSPHERE
BLOODSPORTS
BLOODSTREAM
BLOODSUCKER
BODHISATTVA
BUPRESTIDAE
CALLISTEMON
CAMPESTRIAN
CANDESCENCE
CHARISMATIC
CHOLESTEROL
CLADOSPORUM
CLAIRSCHACH
CLEANSHAVEN
COALESCENCE
COEXISTENCE
COGNOSCENTE
COGNOSCENTI
COMBUSTIBLE
COMMISERATE
COMPOSITION
CONCISENESS
CONSISTENCE
CONSISTENCY
COPROSTEROL
CREPUSCULAR
CYCLOSTYLED
DECONSTRUCT
DEFENSELESS
DEFENSIVELY
DEMONSTRATE
DIATESSARON
DIATESSERON
DIMENSIONAL
DISPOSITION
DISTASTEFUL
EARNESTNESS
EARTHSHAKER
EGOTISTICAL
ENCAPSULATE
ENDORSEMENT
EXCESSIVELY
EXCLUSIVELY
EXCRESCENCE
EXQUISITELY
EXTENSIVELY
FOOLISHNESS
FURNISHINGS
GARNISHMENT
GEGENSCHEIN
HOGGISHNESS
HONEYSUCKLE
HYDROSTATIC
ICONOSTASIS
IMPASSIONED
IMPASSIVELY
IMPERSONATE
IMPULSIVELY
INCAPSULATE
INCESSANTLY
INCONSTANCY
INQUISITION
INQUISITIVE
INSENSITIVE
INTENSIVELY
INTERSPERSE
IRIDESCENCE
KRIEGSSPIEL
LABORSAVING
LAWLESSNESS
LINDISFARNE
MEDIASTINUM
MICROSCOPIC
MINNESINGER
MISSISSIPPI
MONOPSONIST
MONTESQUIEU
MULTISTOREY
NECESSARILY
NECESSITATE
NECESSITOUS
NONDESCRIPT
NOURISHMENT
OBSESSIVELY
OFFENSIVELY
ONOMASTICON
OPALESCENCE
ORCHESTRATE
ORCHESTRINA
ORCHESTRION
OUTDISTANCE
PEEVISHNESS
PERISSOLOGY
PERLUSTRATE
PERMISSIBLE
PERSISTENCE
PHARISAICAL
PHILOSOPHER
PHOTOSPHERE
PISSASPHALT
POSSESSIONS
PREDESTINED
PREHISTORIC
PREPOSITION
PROFESSEDLY
PROFUSENESS
PROMISCUITY
PROMISCUOUS
PROPOSITION
PROVISIONAL
PROVISIONER
PUBLISHABLE
PURPOSELESS
QUICKSILVER
RAFFISHNESS
RECESSIONAL
RECONSTRUCT
REFRESHMENT
RELEASEMENT
REMONSTRATE
REMORSELESS
RENAISSANCE
REPRESENTED
REQUISITION
ROGUISHNESS
RUMBUSTIOUS
SCRIMSHANDY
SELFISHNESS
SEPIOSTAIRE
SEQUESTRATE
SHAKESPEARE
SIGHTSCREEN
SIGHTSEEING
SMITHSONIAN
SMITHSONITE
SMOKESCREEN
SOLIPSISTIC
SPACESAVING
SPOKESWOMAN
SPORTSFIELD
SPORTSWOMAN
STATISTICAL
STYLISHNESS
SUBSISTENCE
SUGGESTIBLE
SUPERSCRIBE
SUPERSEDEAS
SUPERSEDERE
SUPPOSITION
SUPPOSITORY
SWORDSWOMAN
SYMPOSIARCH
TEMPESTUOUS
TERRESTRIAL
TRACASSERIE
TRIMESTRIAL
TROPOSPHERE
UNCONSCIOUS
UNCRUSHABLE
UNDERSIGNED
UNDERSTATED
UNREASONING
UPHOLSTERER
USELESSNESS
VALLISNERIA
VICHYSOISSE
VICISSITUDE
WATERSKIING
WATERSPLASH
ZOROASTRIAN
ABLACTATION
ABSENTEEISM
ADVENTURESS
ADVENTUROUS
ADVERTISING
AFFECTATION
AGGLUTINANT
AGGLUTINATE
AGNOSTICISM
AGONOTHETES
AGROSTOLOGY
AMPHETAMINE
ANAESTHESIA
ANAESTHETIC
ANTISTHENES
ANTISTROPHE
APODYTERIUM
APPURTENANT
ARGENTINIAN
ASPHETERISM
ATTENTIVELY
ATTESTATION
AUGUSTINIAN
BALISTRARIA
BARBITURATE
BARNSTORMER
BELLETTRIST
BELLYTIMBER
BICENTENARY
BREASTPLATE
CALLITRICHE
CASSITERITE
CATASTROPHE
CHIASTOLITE
CHRISTENING
CHRISTMASSY
CHRISTOPHER
CLIMATOLOGY
COHORTATIVE
COMESTIBLES
COMMUTATION
COMPETENTLY
COMPETITION
COMPETITIVE
COMPOTATION
COMPUTATION
COMPUTERIZE
CONDITIONAL
CONDITIONER
CONDOTTIERE
CONDOTTIORE
CONFUTATION
CONNOTATION
CORINTHIANS
CREMATORIUM
CREPITATION
DECEITFULLY

DECEPTIVELY
DECORTICATE
DEERSTALKER
DEGLUTINATE
DEGLUTITION
DEHORTATIVE
DELECTATION
DELICTATION
DEMOSTHENES
DEMOSTHENIC
DEPARTEMENT
DEPORTATION
DERMATOLOGY
DESTITUTION
DETESTATION
DEVASTATING
DEVASTATION
DICTATORIAL
DIPROTODONT
DIRECTIONAL
DIRECTORATE
DISCOTHEQUE
DISENTANGLE
DISPUTATION
DOMESTICATE
DOMESTICITY
DYAESTHESIA
EDUCATIONAL
EFFECTIVELY
EFFECTUALLY
EGALITARIAN
EMBOÎTEMENT
EMMENTHALER
EMPHYTEUSIS
ENTERTAINER
ESCHATOLOGY
ESSENTIALLY
EURHYTHMICS
EXCEPTIONAL
EXECUTIONER
EXHORTATION
EXPECTANTLY
EXPECTATION
EXPECTORANT
EXPECTORATE
EXPOSTULATE
EXTORTIONER
EYECATCHING
FERNITICKLE
FOMENTATION
FORESTATION
FRIGHTENING
FRIGHTFULLY
GEOMETRICAL
GERONTOLOGY
GESTATORIAL
GRAVITATION
GUESSTIMATE
HALBSTARKER
HAUGHTINESS
HERPETOLOGY
HOSPITALITY
HOSPITALIZE
HOSPITALLER
HUCKSTERAGE
HYPERTROPHY
ILLUSTRATOR
ILLUSTRIOUS
IMMORTALISE
IMMORTALITY
IMMORTALIZE
IMPARTIALLY
IMPERTINENT
IMPORTANTLY
IMPORTATION
IMPORTUNATE
INCANTATION
INCONTINENT
INDENTATION
INDUSTRIOUS
INFANTICIDE
INFANTRYMAN
INFERTILITY
INFESTATION
INFILTRATOR
INGRATITUDE
INSECTICIDE
INSECTIVORE
INSISTENTLY
INSTITUTION
INSULTINGLY
INTENTIONAL
INTUITIVELY
INVESTIGATE
INVESTITURE
JACTITATION
LAMENTATION
LIBERTARIAN
LYCANTHROPE
LYCANTHROPY
MAGISTERIAL
MAGISTRATES
MARKETPLACE
MAURETANIAN
MAURITANIAN
MEKHITARIST
MINIATURIST
MINIATURIZE
MINISTERIAL
MINISTERING
MISANTHROPE
MISANTHROPY
MOLESTATION
MOMENTARILY
NAUGHTINESS
NIERSTEINER
NUTRITIONAL
OBJECTIVELY
OBJECTIVITY
OBSTETRICAL
OCTASTICHON
OPERATIONAL
OPPORTUNELY
OPPORTUNISM
OPPORTUNIST
OPPORTUNITY
ORIENTALIST
ORIENTATION
OSTENTATION
OVERSTUFFED
PAEDOTROPHY
PAINSTAKING
PALESTINIAN
PARENTHESIS
PEDESTRIANS
PENTATHLETE
PENULTIMATE
PERESTROIKA
PERISTALITH
PERISTALSIS
PERMUTATION
PERPETRATOR
PERPETUALLY
PHILATELIST
PHONETICIAN
PISCATORIAL
PLANETARIUM
PLEISTOCENE
POLYSTYRENE
POTENTIALLY
PREMATURELY
PROBATIONER
PROFITEROLE
PROLETARIAN
PROLETARIAT
PROMOTIONAL
PROMPTITUDE
QUALITATIVE
RECANTATION
RECEPTIVITY
REGISTERING
REGRETFULLY
REGRETTABLE
REGRETTABLY
RELUCTANTLY
RESENTFULLY
RESISTIVITY
RESTATEMENT
RESTITUTION
ROMANTICISM
ROMANTICIZE
SABBATARIAN
SAGITTARIUS
SCHISTOSOMA
SCHISTOSOME
SCHOTTISCHE
SCIENTOLOGY
SCRIPTORIUM
SECRETARIAL
SECRETARIAT
SECRETIVELY
SELECTIVELY
SELECTIVITY
SEMPITERNAL
SEMPITERNUM
SENSATIONAL
SENSITIVELY
SENSITIVITY
SEVENTEENTH
SINISTRORSE
SLIGHTINGLY
SOROPTIMIST
SPENDTHRIFT
SPIRITUALLY
SPITSTICKER
SPLUTTERING
STOCKTAKING
STORYTELLER
STRAITLACED
STREETLIGHT
SUPERTANKER
SYMMETRICAL
SYMPATHETIC
SYMPATHISER
SYMPATHIZER
TEETOTALLER
TENTATIVELY
TERRITORIAL
THANATOPSIS
THREATENING
THRIFTINESS
TRADITIONAL
TRINITARIAN
UNCASTRATED
UNCERTAINTY
UNCLUTTERED
UNCONTESTED
UNCOUTHNESS
UNDERTAKING
UNDISTURBED
UNEMOTIONAL
UNFORTUNATE
UNINITIATED
UNJUSTIFIED
UNPERTURBED
UNPROTECTED
UNWITTINGLY
UTILITARIAN
VERSATILITY
VOLUNTARILY
WHITETHROAT
WORKSTATION
WORRYTROUGH
ACCUMULATOR
ACOLOUTHITE
AGRICULTURE
ANTIBURGHER
ANTIQUARIAN
APONEUROSIS
ARTICULATED
ASSIDUOUSLY
ATTENUATION
AVERRUNCATE
BASHFULNESS
BELORUSSIAN
BILIOUSNESS
BLANKURSINE
BUREAUCRACY
CALLOUSNESS
CAREFULNESS
CONSTUPRATE
DESTRUCTION
DESTRUCTIVE
DEVALUATION
DEVIOUSNESS
DISCOURTESY
DISGRUNTLED
DISTRUSTFUL
DOUROUCOULI
DUBIOUSNESS
EVENTUALITY
EXTENUATING
EXTENUATION
FATUOUSNESS
FLAVOURSOME
FLUCTUATING
FLUCTUATION
FORFOUGHTEN
FRAUDULENCE
GODDAUGHTER
HELPFULNESS
HIDEOUSNESS
HIGHQUALITY
HUMGRUFFIAN
IMPECUNIOUS
IMPETUOSITY
IMPETUOUSLY
IMPLAUSIBLE
INEXCUSABLE
INEXCUSABLY
INFATUATION
INSCRUTABLE
INSINUATING
INSINUATION
INSTRUCTION
INSTRUCTIVE
INSTRUMENTS
INVOLUNTARY
IRREDUCIBLE
IRREFUTABLE
IRREGULARLY
ISOXSUPRINE
LATIFUNDIUM
LEFTLUGGAGE
LONGRUNNING
MANIPULATOR
MISTRUSTFUL
MOISTURIZER
MOXIBUSTION
NERVOUSNESS

OBSTRUCTION
OBSTRUCTIVE
OBVIOUSNESS
OUTPOURINGS
OVERTURNING
PASTEURELLA
PASTOURELLE
PLAYFULNESS
PLEASURABLE
POCOCURANTE
PRECAUTIONS
PRESSURIZED
PROCRUSTEAN
PUNCTUALITY
PUNCTUATION
QUADRUPLETS
QUINTUPLETS
RAUCOUSNESS
REASSURANCE
RESTRUCTURE
REVALUATION
REVOLUTIONS
RIBONUCLEIC
RUMFRUCTION
SCULDUDDERY
SCULDUGGERY
SERICULTURE
SERIOUSNESS
SHIPBUILDER
SHOWJUMPING
SKULDUDDERY
SKULDUGGERY
SLUMGULLION
SPONDULICKS
STRADUARIUS
STRENUOUSLY
SUMPTUOUSLY
SURROUNDING
TACITURNITY
TEDIOUSNESS
TENUOUSNESS
THINGUMAJIG
THOROUGHPIN
TRANQUILITY
TRANSURANIC
UNENDURABLE
UNNATURALLY
UNSATURATED
UTRICULARIA
VACUOUSNESS
VICIOUSNESS
VISCOUNTESS
WAKEFULNESS
WINDSURFING
WISTFULNESS
ABBREVIATED
ACHIEVEMENT
AGGRAVATING
AGGRAVATION
APPROVINGLY
ATHARVAVEDA
AUDIOVISUAL
BEREAVEMENT
CAPTIVATING
CAPTIVATION
CARNIVOROUS
CLAIRVOYANT
CRACOVIENNE
CULTIVATION
DEPRIVATION
DISHEVELLED
ENSLAVEMENT
EVASIVENESS
EXTRAVAGANT
EXTROVERTED
FORGIVENESS
FURTIVENESS
GALLOVIDIAN
HERBIVOROUS
IMPROVEMENT
IMPROVIDENT
INTERVENING
INTERVIEWEE
INTERVIEWER
INTRAVENOUS
INTROVERTED
INVOLVEMENT
MANEUVERING
MASSIVENESS
OBSERVATION
OBSERVATORY
PASSIVENESS
PENSIVENESS
PERSEVERING
RESERVATION
RESTIVENESS
SELFEVIDENT
SUBDIVISION
SUPERVISION
SUPERVISORY
TRIUMVIRATE
ULTRAVIOLET
UNCONVERTED
UNCONVINCED
UNDERVALUED
VARSOVIENNE
ACKNOWLEDGE
BLAMEWORTHY
BREADWINNER
DUNIEWASSAL
FIELDWORKER
GALLOWGLASS
HEAVYWEIGHT
HORNSWOGGLE
LEADSWINGER
LIGHTWEIGHT
LONGAWAITED
MEADOWSWEET
METALWORKER
MINESWEEPER
PAPERWEIGHT
PINNYWINKLE
PRIZEWINNER
RIGHTWINGER
SLEEPWALKER
SORROWFULLY
SOUTHWESTER
TIGGYWINKLE
TRUSTWORTHY
UNDERWEIGHT
UNDERWRITER
WHEELWRIGHT
WHEREWITHAL
WINDOWFRAME
WINDOWLEDGE
YELLOWPLUSH
YELLOWSTONE
AMPLEXICAUL
APPROXIMATE
OVEREXPOSED
REFLEXOLOGY
AERODYNAMIC
ANAPHYLAXIS
ANTICYCLONE
ANTIPYRETIC
APOPHYLLITE
DICOTYLEDON
EPITHYMETIC
EUCALYPTOLE
ICHTHYOLITE
ICHTHYORNIS
LUXULYANITE
OXYRHYNCHUS
PARATYPHOID
PROPHYLAXIS
SPONDYLITIS
HAPHAZARDLY
IDOLIZATION
OXODIZATION
REALIZATION
STYLIZATION
UTILIZATION

11:7

ABECEDARIAN
ABLACTATION
ABNORMALITY
ABOMINATION
ACCLAMATION
ACCLIMATION
ACCLIMATISE
ACCLIMATIZE
ACCOMPANIST
ACRIFLAVINE
ADOPTIANISM
ADUMBRATION
AESCULAPIAN
AESCULAPIUS
AFFECTATION
AFFILIATION
AFFIRMATION
AFFIRMATIVE
AGGRAVATING
AGGRAVATION
AGGREGATION
ALCYONARIAN
ALLEVIATION
ALTERCATION
ALTERNATELY
ALTERNATING
ALTERNATION
ALTERNATIVE
AMERCIAMENT
AMERICANISM
AMPHETAMINE
ANAXIMANDER
ANTECHAMBER
ANTIQUARIAN
APATOSAURUS
APPEARANCES
APPELLATION
APPELLATIVE
APPLICATION
APPROBATION
ARBITRAGEUR
ARBITRAMENT
ARBITRARILY
ARBITRATION
ARTIODACTYL
ASSIGNATION
ASSOCIATION
ASTIGMATISM
ATHARVAVEDA
ATHERMANOUS
ATTENUATION
ATTESTATION
AURIGNACIAN
AZOTOBACTER
BALLBEARING
BESSARABIAN
BIFURCATION
BLACKMAILER
BODHISATTVA
BREATHALYSE
BRILLIANTLY
BROADCASTER
BURGOMASTER
BUSHWHACKER
CALCULATING
CALCULATION
CALIBRATION
CANDIDATURE
CANNIBALISM
CANNIBALIZE
CAPTIVATING
CAPTIVATION
CARMINATIVE
CATALLACTIC
CELEBRATION
CENTENARIAN
CEREBRATION
CHOIRMASTER
CIRCULARIZE
CIRCULATING
CIRCULATION
CIRCULATORY
CLIFFHANGER
COAGULATION
COHORTATIVE
COLLOCATION
COLONIALISM
COLONIALIST
COLUMBARIUM
COMBINATION
COMMINATION
COMMUTATION
COMPARATIVE
COMPILATION
COMPOTATION
COMPUTATION
CONFUTATION
CONJUGATION
CONNOTATION
CONSOLATION
CONSTRAINED
CONSUMABLES
CONURBATION
CONVOCATION
COOPERATION
COOPERATIVE
CORPORATION
CORRELATION
CORRUGATION
CRACKHALTER
CREPITATION
CRESTFALLEN
CRITICASTER
CULMINATION
CULTIVATION
CUSTOMARILY
CYMOPHANOUS
DECLAMATION
DECLAMATORY
DECLARATION
DEERSTALKER
DEFOLIATION
DEFORMATION
DEGRADATION
DEHORTATIVE
DEHYDRATION
DEIFICATION
DELECTATION
DELICTATION
DELINEATION
DEMARCATION
DEMOGRAPHIC
DEPORTATION
DEPREDATION
DEPRIVATION

DESECRATION
DESICCATION
DESIGNATION
DESPERATELY
DESPERATION
DESTINATION
DETESTATION
DEVALUATION
DEVASTATING
DEVASTATION
DICEPHALOUS
DINNYHAUSER
DINNYHAYSER
DIPLOMATICS
DIPLOMATIST
DIPSOMANIAC
DISARMAMENT
DISENTANGLE
DISLOCATION
DISORGANIZE
DISPARAGING
DISPLEASURE
DISPUTATION
DISREGARDED
DISSIPATION
DOWNHEARTED
DRESSMAKING
DRYCLEANERS
DRYCLEANING
DUNIEWASSAL
DUPLICATING
DUPLICATION
DUSTWRAPPER
EDIFICATION
EGALITARIAN
EJACULATION
ELABORATELY
ELABORATION
ELIMINATION
ELUCIDATION
EMBARKATION
EMBARRASSED
EMBROCATION
EMPTYHANDED
ENCEPHALOMA
ENCOURAGING
ENKEPHALINE
ENTABLATURE
ENTERTAINER
ENUMERATION
ENUNCIATION
EPOCHMAKING
ERADICATION
EREMACAUSIS
ESTRAMAZONE
EVAPORATION
EVENTRATION
EVENTUALITY
EXAMINATION
EXCLAMATION
EXHORTATION
EXONERATION
EXPECTANTLY
EXPECTATION
EXPLANATION
EXPLANATORY
EXPLORATION
EXPLORATORY
EXPURGATION
EXTENUATING
EXTENUATION
EXTRAVAGANT
FABRICATION
FAIRWEATHER
FAMILIARISE
FAMILIARITY
FAMILIARIZE
FASCINATING
FASCINATION
FESTINATELY
FLUCTUATING
FLUCTUATION
FOMENTATION
FORESTATION
FORMULATION
FORNICATION
FORTUNATELY
FRUSTRATING
FRUSTRATION
FULMINATION
FUSTILARIAN
GALLIBAGGER
GALLIGANTUS
GALLIMAUFRY
GALLYBAGGER
GATECRASHER
GERMINATION
GERRYMANDER
GRANDFATHER
GRANDMASTER
GRAVITATION
GRENZGANGER
GUBERNATION
GUTTURALISE
HABERDASHER
HALBSTARKER
HALFHEARTED
HANDCRAFTED
HANDICAPPED
HANDICAPPER
HAPHAZARDLY
HARDICANUTE
HAREBRAINED
HARIOLATION
HEAVYHANDED
HEBDOMADARY
HIBERNATING
HIBERNATION
HIGHQUALITY
HIPPOCAMPUS
HOMEOPATHIC
HOOLIGANISM
HOOTANANNIE
HOOTENANNIE
HORSERACING
HORSERADISH
HOSPITALITY
HOSPITALIZE
HOSPITALLER
HOUSEMASTER
HUMILIATING
HUMILIATION
HYDROCARBON
HYPERMARKET
HYPHENATION
IDEOPRAXIST
IDOLIZATION
ILLYWHACKER
IMAGINATION
IMAGINATIVE
IMMEDIATELY
IMMIGRATION
IMMORTALISE
IMMORTALITY
IMMORTALIZE
IMPERIALISM
IMPERIALIST
IMPERMANENT
IMPLICATION
IMPORTANTLY
IMPORTATION
IMPRECATION
INCANTATION
INCARNADINE
INCARNATION
INCESSANTLY
INCLINATION
INDENTATION
INDIGNANTLY
INDIGNATION
INEBRIATION
INFATUATION
INFESTATION
INFORMALITY
INFORMATICS
INFORMATION
INFORMATIVE
INFURIATING
INOCULATION
INOPERATIVE
INSINUATING
INSINUATION
INSPIRATION
INSTIGATION
INTEGRATION
INTERCALARY
INTERLACING
INTRICATELY
IRRADIATION
ITHYPHALLIC
ITHYPHALLUS
JACTITATION
JERRYMANDER
KINDHEARTED
LABORSAVING
LAMENTATION
LAWBREAKING
LEGISLATION
LEGISLATIVE
LEGISLATURE
LIBERTARIAN
LIQUIDAMBAR
LIQUIDATION
LITTÉRATEUR
LOGOGRAPHER
LONGAWAITED
LOUISIANIAN
LUBRICATION
LUXULYANITE
LUXURIANTLY
MACHINATION
MANCIPATION
MAQUILADORA
MARGINALIST
MARGINALIZE
MARSHMALLOW
MASTICATION
MATERIALISE
MATERIALISM
MATERIALIST
MATERIALIZE
MATHEMATICS
MAURETANIAN
MAURITANIAN
MEKHITARIST
MENSURATION
MEPROBAMATE
MERRYMAKING
METRICATION
MICROGAMETE
MISBEHAVIOR
MOLESTATION
MOMENTARILY
MONEYMAKING
MONOGRAMMED
MONONGAHELA
MULTIRACIAL
MUNCHHAUSEN
MURMURATION
MYCOPHAGIST
NAPHTHALENE
NARRAGANSET
NATIONALISM
NATIONALIST
NATIONALITY
NATIONALIZE
NECESSARILY
NECROMANCER
NEGOTIATING
NEGOTIATION
NIGHTMARISH
NIKETHAMIDE
NUMISMATICS
NUMISMATIST
OBSERVATION
OBSERVATORY
OBSTINATELY
OFFICIALDOM
OFFICIALESE
ORIENTALIST
ORIENTATION
ORIGINALITY
ORIGINATING
ORIGINATION
ORTHOPAEDIC
OSCILLATION
OSTENTATION
OSTEOPATHIC
OVERBEARING
OVERLEARNED
OVERZEALOUS
OXODIZATION
PAINSTAKING
PASSACAGLIA
PATERNALISM
PECULIARITY
PENETRATING
PENETRATION
PENNYFATHER
PERCOLATION
PERFORATION
PERISTALITH
PERISTALSIS
PERMUTATION
PERSONALIST
PERSONALITY
PERSONALIZE
PERTINACITY
PETITMAITRE
PHARISAICAL
PLANETARIUM
PLEBEIANISE
POLLINATION
POMEGRANATE
PREDICAMENT
PREDICATIVE
PRELIBATION
PREPARATION
PREPARATORY
PREROGATIVE
PRISCIANIST
PROCREATION
PRODIGALISE
PRODIGALITY
PROLETARIAN
PROLETARIAT
PROPAGATION
PROROGATION
PROSTRATION
PROVOCATION

PROVOCATIVE
PSYCHIATRIC
PTERODACTYL
PUBLICATION
PUNCTUALITY
PUNCTUATION
QUALITATIVE
RADIOCARBON
RASTAFARIAN
RATIONALITY
RATIONALIZE
RAZZAMATAZZ
REALIZATION
REANIMATION
REAPPRAISAL
REBARBATIVE
RECANTATION
RECLAMATION
REFORMATION
REFORMATORY
REITERATION
RELUCTANTLY
REPUDIATION
RESERVATION
RESIGNATION
RESPIRATION
RESPIRATORY
RESTORATION
RESTORATIVE
RETALIATION
RETALIATORY
RETARDATION
REVALUATION
RIGHTHANDED
RIGHTHANDER
SABBATARIAN
SAGITTARIUS
SAINTPAULIA
SCARABAEOID
SCIREFACIAS
SCOPOLAMINE
SCOUTMASTER
SECONDARILY
SECRETARIAL
SECRETARIAT
SEGREGATION
SEPTENARIUS
SEPTICAEMIA
SHINPLASTER
SHORTHANDED
SILLIMANITE
SINGULARITY
SKIDBLADNIR
SLEEPWALKER
SPACESAVING
SPECULATION
SPECULATIVE
STAGFLATION
STAIRCARPET
STANDPATTER
STEADFASTLY
STIMULATION
STIPULATION
STOCKHAUSEN
STOCKTAKING
STRADUARIUS
STRAPHANGER
STYLIZATION
STYMPHALIAN
SUBJUGATION
SUBLIMATION
SUBPANATION
SUCCEDANEUM
SUFFOCATING
SUFFOCATION
SUPERLATIVE
SUPERMARKET
SUPERTANKER
SUPPEDANEUM
SUPPURATION
SUSURRATION
SYCOPHANTIC
SYNCOPATION
SYNDICALISM
SYNDICATION
SYSTEMATIZE
TABERNACLES
TACHYCARDIA
TEETOTALLER
TELEGRAPHER
TELEGRAPHIC
TEMPERAMENT
TEMPERATURE
TEMPORARILY
TERMINATION
TESSARAGLOT
TIMESHARING
TITILLATION
TOASTMASTER
TOBOGGANING
TOPOGRAPHER
TOSTICATION
TRAGELAPHUS
TRANSLATION
TRANSPARENT
TREPIDATION
TRIBULATION
TRICERATOPS
TRINIDADIAN
TRINITARIAN
TRINOBANTES
TYPOGRAPHER
TYPOGRAPHIC
ULTRAMARINE
UNCERTAINTY
UNDERHANDED
UNDERMANNED
UNDERTAKING
UNDERVALUED
UNEXPLAINED
UNIFICATION
UNREHEARSED
UNSURPASSED
UNWARRANTED
UTILITARIAN
UTILIZATION
VACCINATION
VACILLATING
VACILLATION
VARANGARIAN
VARIEGATION
VARIOLATION
VENTILATION
VIDEOCAMERA
VINDICATION
VOLKSKAMMER
VOLUNTARILY
WARMHEARTED
WASHLEATHER
WASTEBASKET
WELLMEANING
WESTPHALIAN
WHEELBARROW
WHITLEATHER
WORKSTATION
WORLDFAMOUS
XYLOGRAPHER
AMPHISBAENA
AMPHISBOENA
BOYSENBERRY
CENTREBOARD
CHOCKABLOCK
CILOFIBRATE
COLOURBLIND
CONTRIBUTOR
DISTRIBUTED
DISTRIBUTOR
DISTURBANCE
EQUILIBRIST
EQUILIBRIUM
GINGERBREAD
HUCKLEBERRY
HURTLEBERRY
MARIONBERRY
MEMORABILIA
NOTICEBOARD
ODONTOBLAST
POLLENBRUSH
SALTIMBANCO
SALTIMBOCCA
SCULLABOGUE
SHOVELBOARD
SPRINGBOARD
STRIKEBOUND
SURTARBRAND
SURTURBRAND
SWITCHBOARD
THEREABOUTS
TROPHOBLAST
UNINHABITED
UNINHIBITED
VALLAMBROSA
WHEREABOUTS
WINTERBERRY
ABSTRACTION
ACCRESCENCE
ACUPUNCTURE
ADJUDICATOR
ADOLESCENCE
AFFLIICTION
AFTERSCHOOL
AMELANCHIER
ANTICYCLONE
APPROACHING
ARISTOCRACY
BACKPACKING
BENEDICTINE
BENEDICTION
BENEFICIARY
BENEFICIATE
BUREAUCRACY
CALEFACIENT
CANDESCENCE
CAPRICCIOSO
CAUSTICALLY
CHANTICLEER
CHEESECLOTH
CHRONICALLY
CINQUECENTO
CIRCUMCISER
CLAIRSCHACH
CLARENCIEUX
COALESCENCE
COEFFICIENT
COGNOSCENTE
COGNOSCENTI
COLLENCHYMA
COMPLACENCY
COMPLICATED
COMPUNCTION
COMSTOCKERY
CONJUNCTION
CONJUNCTURE
CONSPICUOUS
CONTRACTION
CONTRACTUAL
CREPUSCULAR
DENDRACHATE
DERELICTION
DESELECTION
DESTRUCTION
DESTRUCTIVE
DIFFRACTION
DISGRACEFUL
DISJUNCTION
DISTINCTION
DISTINCTIVE
DISTRACTION
DOUBLECHECK
DOUBLECROSS
DOUROUCOULI
DRACUNCULUS
DRASTICALLY
DYSFUNCTION
EFFICACIOUS
EMPIRICUTIC
ENCROACHING
ENFRANCHISE
EQUINOCTIAL
EQUIVOCALLY
ERRATICALLY
EXCRESCENCE
EYECATCHING
FANATICALLY
FARINACEOUS
FARREACHING
FRANTICALLY
GASTRECTOMY
GEGENSCHEIN
GENERICALLY
GENETICALLY
GEOSYNCLINE
GRAPHICALLY
GREENOCKITE
GUADALCANAL
HAMMERCLOTH
HARPSICHORD
IDENTICALLY
IDIOTICALLY
IDYLLICALLY
ILLOGICALLY
INEFFECTIVE
INEFFECTUAL
INEFFICIENT
INJUDICIOUS
INSTINCTIVE
INSTRUCTION
INSTRUCTIVE
INTERACTION
INTERACTIVE
INTOXICATED
IRIDESCENCE
IRREDUCIBLE
IRREVOCABLE
ISOELECTRIC
LACONICALLY
MALEDICTION
MALEFACTION
MALFUNCTION
MALPRACTICE
MANUFACTURE
MELANOCHROI
MICROSCOPIC
MISERICORDE
MUNIFICENCE
NICKNACKERY
NONDESCRIPT
NUMERICALLY
NUTCRACKERS
OBSTRICTION

OBSTRUCTION
OBSTRUCTIVE
OPALESCENCE
ORGANICALLY
PACIFICALLY
PERFUNCTORY
PERSPECTIVE
PERSPICUITY
PERSPICUOUS
POLIORCETIC
POLITICALLY
POLITICIANS
POLYTECHNIC
PRACTICABLE
PRACTICALLY
PRECONCEIVE
PROMISCUITY
PROMISCUOUS
PROSAICALLY
PROSPECTIVE
PROTRACTING
PROTRACTION
PSITTACOSIS
PTOCHOCRACY
RADIOACTIVE
REPROACHFUL
RESOURCEFUL
RESTRICTION
RESTRICTIVE
RESTRUCTURE
RETINACULUM
RETROACTIVE
RIBONUCLEIC
RUMFRUCTION
SAPONACEOUS
SARCENCHYME
SATIRICALLY
SCEPTICALLY
SECONDCLASS
SIGHTSCREEN
SKEPTICALLY
SMOKESCREEN
SPECTACULAR
SPEECHCRAFT
SPERMICIDAL
SPRINGCLEAN
SUBJUNCTIVE
SUBTRACTION
SUPERSCRIBE
TECHNICALLY
TEGUCICALPA
TERPSICHORE
TICKTACKTOE
TRAFFICATOR
TRANSACTION
ULOTRICHALE
UNCONSCIOUS
UNFLINCHING
UNSOLICITED
VALEDICTION
VALEDICTORY
VIOLINCELLO
VIOLONCELLO
VIVISECTION
XENODOCHIUM
ABRACADABRA
ALEXANDRINE
ALEXANDRITE
ANTECEDENCE
ARRIVEDERCI
ARTHRODESIS
AWKWARDNESS
BANGLADESHI
BATTLEDRESS
BLESSEDNESS
BOMBARDMENT
BRAGGADOCIO
CAMARADERIE
COINCIDENCE
COMMANDMENT
COMMENDABLE
COMMENDABLY
COMPENDIOUS
CONCORDANCE
CROOKEDNESS
DESCENDANTS
DESPONDENCY
DIAMONDBACK
DILAPIDATED
DISOBEDIENT
ENCHONDROMA
ENFOULDERED
FIDDLEDEDEE
FISHANDCHIP
FORBIDDANCE
HOBBLEDEHOY
HOLLANDAISE
HUNDREDFOLD
HUSBANDLAND
INEXPEDIENT
KIMERIDGIAN
NOSTRADAMUS
OFFHANDEDLY
ONEIRODYNIA
PARAMEDICAL
PHILANDERER
PROCEEDINGS
PSYCHEDELIC
PSYCHODELIC
RHAPSODICAL
SCULDUDDERY
SKULDUDDERY
STIPENDIARY
UNAVOIDABLE
UNAVOIDABLY
UNSCHEDULED
WATEREDDOWN
WAYWARDNESS
ABRIDGEMENT
ABSENTEEISM
ACATALECTIC
ACHIEVEMENT
ADVANCEMENT
AGGLOMERATE
ALPHABETIZE
ANDROGENOUS
ANESTHETIST
ANESTHETIZE
ANISOCERCAL
APODYTERIUM
APPEASEMENT
APPURTENANT
ARCHIPELAGO
ARGATHELIAN
ARRANGEMENT
ARTILLERIST
ASPHETERISM
ASSYTHEMENT
BACKFIELDER
BADDELEYITE
BELLIGERENT
BEREAVEMENT
BESIEGEMENT
BEWILDERING
BICENTENARY
BLACKFELLOW
BLASPHEMOUS
BOOKKEEPING
BRISTLECONE
BRITTLENESS
CALENDERING
CALLANETICS
CARBURETTOR
CASSITERITE
CEASELESSLY
CHAIRPERSON
CHEERLEADER
CHRISTENING
CITLALEPETL
COACHFELLOW
COMMISERATE
COMPETENTLY
COMPILEMENT
COMPUTERIZE
COMRADESHIP
CONCISENESS
CONDOLENCES
CONFEDERACY
CONFEDERATE
CONFIDENTLY
CONFINEMENT
CONSIDERATE
CONSIDERING
CONSUMERISM
CONTENEMENT
CONTINENTAL
CONTUBERNAL
CRATERELLUS
CROSSLEGGED
CYBERNETICS
DARDANELLES
DEFENCELESS
DEFENSELESS
DEPARTEMENT
DERANGEMENT
DESEGREGATE
DETRIMENTAL
DIFFERENTLY
DIFFIDENTLY
DIPHYCERCAL
DISABLEMENT
DISAFFECTED
DISAGREEING
DISHEVELLED
DISHONESTLY
DISORIENTED
DISQUIETING
DITHELETISM
DIVORCEMENT
DOMINEERING
DRAGGLETAIL
EFFICIENTLY
ELEUTHERIAN
ELIZABETHAN
EMBOÎTEMENT
EMPHYTEUSIS
EMPIECEMENT
EMPLACEMENT
ENDORSEMENT
ENDOTHERMIC
ENFORCEABLE
ENFORCEMENT
ENGINEERING
ENHANCEMENT
ENJAMBEMENT
ENLARGEMENT
ENNEAHEDRON
ENSLAVEMENT
ENTABLEMENT
ENTITLEMENT
EPANALEPSIS
EPIGENESIST
EVASIVENESS
EXANTHEMATA
EXPERIENCED
EXTROGENOUS
EXTROVERTED
FAULTLESSLY
FEATURELESS
FLORILEGIUM
FORESEEABLE
FORGIVENESS
FORTUNELOUD
FRIGHTENING
FRUITLESSLY
FUNDAMENTAL
FURTIVENESS
GALLIBEGGAR
GALLYBEGGAR
GENUFLEXION
GENUINENESS
GIBBERELLIN
HAIRDRESSER
HARDPRESSED
HEARTLESSLY
HEAVYWEIGHT
HOMOTHERMAL
HOMOTHERMIC
HOUSEKEEPER
HUCKSTERAGE
HYDROMEDUSA
HYPOTHECATE
HYPOTHERMIA
IMPATIENTLY
IMPERMEABLE
IMPLEMENTAL
IMPROVEMENT
IMPRUDENTLY
INAUTHENTIC
INCARCERATE
INCOMPETENT
INCORRECTLY
INCREMENTAL
INDIFFERENT
INDULGENTLY
INSINCERITY
INSISTENTLY
INTEMPERATE
INTERCEPTOR
INTERLEUKIN
INTERNECINE
INTERREGNUM
INTERRELATE
INTERVENING
INTRAVENOUS
INTROVERTED
INVOLVEMENT
LECTURESHIP
LEGERDEMAIN
LENGTHENING
LEVELHEADED
LIGHTHEADED
LIGHTWEIGHT
LOGODAEDALY
LONGSLEEVED
LOUDSPEAKER
MAGISTERIAL
MANEUVERING
MARIONETTES
MASSIVENESS
MEASURELESS
MEASUREMENT
MEGATHERIUM
MENDELEVIUM
MERCILESSLY
MINESWEEPER
MINISTERIAL
MINISTERING
MISCHIEVOUS
MISDEMEANOR

MONEYLENDER
MONOTHELITE
MONOTREMATA
NIERSTEINER
NOISELESSLY
NONETHELESS
NOTOTHERIUM
OBTEMPERATE
OMNIPRESENT
ORTHOCENTRE
OUTMANEUVER
OVERWEENING
OVERWHELMED
PAMPHLETEER
PANTALETTES
PAPERWEIGHT
PARABLEPSIS
PASSIVENESS
PEACEKEEPER
PENSIVENESS
PERMANENTLY
PERSEVERING
PERTINENTLY
PHILATELIST
PICTURESQUE
PLATERESQUE
POINTLESSLY
PREDECESSOR
PRESTRESSED
PRIMIGENIAL
PROCUREMENT
PROFITEROLE
PROFUSENESS
PROLIFERATE
PROMINENTLY
PROOFREADER
PROPRIETARY
PROSTHETICS
PROTUBERANT
PURPOSELESS
PYTHONESQUE
RECURRENTLY
REFRIGERANT
REFRIGERATE
REGISTERING
RELEASEMENT
REMORSELESS
REPLACEABLE
REPLACEMENT
REPRESENTED
REQUIREMENT
RESTATEMENT
RESTIVENESS
REVERBERATE
ROCKEFELLER
RUDESHEIMER
SACRAMENTAL
SALESPERSON
SAPROLEGNIA
SAUSAGEMEAT

SCOLOPENDRA
SCUTTLEBUTT
SEMPITERNAL
SEMPITERNUM
SENTIMENTAL
SERVICEABLE
SEVENTEENTH
SHAMELESSLY
SHIPWRECKED
SHUTTLECOCK
SIGHTSEEING
SMOULDERING
SOUNDLESSLY
SOUTHWESTER
SPLUTTERING
STEEPLEJACK
STEINBERGER
STICKLEBACK
STOREKEEPER
STORYTELLER
STRANGENESS
STRANGEWAYS
STRINGENTLY
SUPERSEDEAS
SUPERSEDERE
TASTELESSLY
TETRAHEDRON
THANKLESSLY
THEATREGOER
THEOPNEUSTY
THERAPEUTAE
THERAPEUTIC
THISTLEDOWN
THREATENING
TIMEKEEPING
TOWNSPEOPLE
TRACKLEMENT
TRANSCEIVER
TRANSFERRED
TRANSFERRIN
TREACHEROUS
TREACHETOUR
TREECREEPER
TRENCHERMAN
TREPONEMATA
TROUBLESOME
TROUBLESPOT
TRUCULENTLY
TRUSTEESHIP
UNAUTHENTIC
UNCONCEALED
UNCONCERNED
UNCONNECTED
UNCONTESTED
UNCONVERTED
UNDERWEIGHT
UNEXPRESSED
UNIMPRESSED
UNPROTECTED
UNSHAKEABLE

UNSUSPECTED
UNTRAMELLED
UNWHOLESOME
VASOPRESSIN
VENTURESOME
VERBIGERATE
VOORTREKKER
WATERMEADOW
WELLDRESSED
WHISTLESTOP
WINDBREAKER
WINDCHEATER
WRONGHEADED
ZWISCHENZUG
AIRCRAFTMAN
ALIFANFARON
BATTLEFIELD
BATTLEFRONT
BEAUTIFULLY
CENTRIFUGAL
CIRCUMFLECT
DECEITFULLY
ENFEOFFMENT
FRIGHTFULLY
HUMGRUFFIAN
IDENTIFYING
LINDISFARNE
MASTERFULLY
REGRETFULLY
RESENTFULLY
SELFDEFENCE
SHOPLIFTING
SORROWFULLY
SPORTSFIELD
STANDOFFISH
THENCEFORTH
WELLDEFINED
WILBERFORCE
WINDOWFRAME
WONDERFULLY
ASTRINGENCY
BULLFIGHTER
CARDIOGRAPH
CARRIAGEWAY
CHEIROGNOMY
CONTINGENCE
CONTINGENCY
CONVERGENCE
DEGRINGOLER
DEMAGOGUERY
DEPHLEGMATE
DISTINGUISH
EMMENAGOGUE
ESTRANGHELO
FIRELIGHTER
FORFOUGHTEN
FORTNIGHTLY
FOTHERGILLA
GALLOWGLASS
GODDAUGHTER

HERRINGBONE
HIGHLIGHTER
HUMMINGBIRD
IDEOLOGICAL
IRRELIGIOUS
LAMMERGEIER
LAMMERGEYER
LAMPLIGHTER
LATERIGRADE
LEFTLUGGAGE
LONGSIGHTED
MEANINGLESS
MOCKINGBIRD
MOONLIGHTER
MYCOLOGICAL
NEARSIGHTED
NOTHINGNESS
ONTOLOGICAL
PEDAGOGICAL
PHARYNGITIS
PHYSIOGNOMY
PLANTAGENET
PLANTIGRADE
POLTERGEIST
POTAMOGETON
PRESTIGIOUS
RECTANGULAR
SALPINGITIS
SCULDUGGERY
SEISMOGRAPH
SEXOLOGICAL
SKILLIGALEE
SKILLIGOLEE
SKULDUGGERY
STRATEGICAL
SUBMERGENCE
SUFFRAGETTE
SYMPLEGADES
THEOLOGICAL
THOROUGHPIN
UNAMBIGUOUS
UNMITIGATED
VOTERIGGING
WELLINGTONS
WILLINGNESS
WINTERGREEN
WITENAGEMOT
AGONOTHETES
AGORAPHOBIA
ANAESTHESIA
ANAESTHETIC
ANTIRRHINUM
ANTISTHENES
ATMOSPHERIC
AXEROPHTHOL
BERGSCHRUND
CARDOPHAGUS
CATCHPHRASE
CLEANSHAVEN
CLINOCHLORE

COPROPHAGAN
CORINTHIANS
DEMOSTHENES
DEMOSTHENIC
DEUTSCHMARK
DISCOTHEQUE
DYAESTHESIA
EARTHSHAKER
EMMENTHALER
EPINEPHRINE
EURHYTHMICS
FESTSCHRIFT
FOOLISHNESS
FURNISHINGS
GARNISHMENT
HAEMOPHILIA
HEMORRHOIDS
HOGGISHNESS
HYDROPHIDAE
HYDROPHOBIA
HYDROPHOBIC
IMPEACHMENT
INTERCHANGE
ISTIOPHORUS
LOGGERHEADS
LYCANTHROPE
LYCANTHROPY
MELANCHOLIA
MELANCHOLIC
MISANTHROPE
MISANTHROPY
MONARCHICAL
NOURISHMENT
OLIGOCHAETE
PANOMPHAEAN
PARENTHESIS
PEEVISHNESS
PENTATHLETE
PICKELHAUBE
PORTERHOUSE
PUBLISHABLE
RAFFISHNESS
REFRESHMENT
ROGUISHNESS
SADDLEHORSE
SAPROPHYTIC
SARCOPHAGUS
SCEUOPHYLAX
SCRIMSHANDY
SELFISHNESS
SENNACHERIB
SHORTCHANGE
SPENDTHRIFT
SPIROCHAETE
SPRINGHOUSE
STENOCHROME
STRETCHABLE
STRETCHLESS
STYLISHNESS
SUMMERHOUSE

SUPERCHARGE
SUPERCHERIE
SVARABHAKTI
SYMPATHETIC
SYMPATHISER
SYMPATHIZER
TAUTOCHRONE
TENTERHOOKS
UNCOUTHNESS
UNCRUSHABLE
UNDERCHARGE
UNTOUCHABLE
WELLBEHAVED
WHITECHAPEL
WHITETHROAT
ABBREVIATED
ACADEMICIAN
ACCORDINGLY
ACINACIFORM
ACQUISITION
ACQUISITIVE
ACTUALITIES
ADVERBIALLY
ADVERTISING
AFGHANISTAN
AGGLUTINANT
AGGLUTINATE
AGNOSTICISM
AGUARDIENTE
AMMOPHILOUS
AMPLEXICAUL
APHRODISIAC
APPALLINGLY
APPRECIABLE
APPRECIABLY
APPROVINGLY
APPROXIMATE
ARGENTINIAN
ASCLEPIADES
ASPERGILLUM
ASPERGILLUS
ASSASSINATE
ATTENTIVELY
AUDIOVISUAL
AUGUSTINIAN
BACKSLIDING
BEASTLINESS
BELLYTIMBER
BREADWINNER
BROADMINDED
CABBALISTIC
CATERPILLAR
CATHOLICISM
CENTURIATOR
CERTIFIABLE
CERTIFICATE
CHARACINOID
CHILDMINDER
CLEANLINESS
COENOBITISM
COMESTIBLES
COMMUNICANT
COMMUNICATE
COMPETITION
COMPETITIVE
COMPLAISANT
COMPOSITION
CONCILIATOR
CONCOMITANT
CONDITIONAL
CONDITIONER
CONDOMINIUM
CONSILIENCE
CONSOLIDATE
CONSTRICTED
CONSTRICTOR
CONTAMINANT
CONTAMINATE
CONVENIENCE
CORDWAINERS
COUNTRIFIED
COURTLINESS
CRACOVIENNE
CREDIBILITY
CRUCIFIXION
CULPABILITY
CULVERINEER
DECEPTIVELY
DECORTICATE
DECREPITATE
DECREPITUDE
DEFENSIVELY
DEGLUTINATE
DEGLUTITION
DESERPIDINE
DESTABILIZE
DETERMINANT
DETERMINING
DEVITRIFIED
DIMENSIONAL
DIRECTIONAL
DISBELIEVER
DISPOSITION
DISSEMINATE
DISSEPIMENT
DOLABRIFORM
DOMESTICATE
DOMESTICITY
DYSLOGISTIC
EDUCATIONAL
EFFECTIVELY
EINSTEINIUM
ELECTRICIAN
ELECTRICITY
ELIGIBILITY
EMBELLISHED
ENCHIRIDION
EPICHEIREMA
ESCHERICHIA
ESSENTIALLY
ESTABLISHED
ESTABLISHER
EUCHARISTIC
EUPHEMISTIC
EXCEEDINGLY
EXCEPTIONAL
EXCESSIVELY
EXCLUSIVELY
EXECUTIONER
EXPENDITURE
EXQUISITELY
EXTENSIVELY
EXTERMINATE
EXTORTIONER
EXTRADITION
FALLIBILITY
FARRAGINOUS
FAULTFINDER
FAVOURITISM
FEASIBILITY
FERNITICKLE
FINANCIALLY
FLEXIBILITY
FRANKLINITE
FREETHINKER
FROSTBITTEN
FUNDRAISING
GALLOVIDIAN
GELSEMININE
GHASTLINESS
GRAVEDIGGER
GREGARINIDA
GUESSTIMATE
GULLIBILITY
HAIRRAISING
HALLUCINATE
HANDWRITING
HANDWRITTEN
HANGGLIDING
HAUGHTINESS
HEALTHINESS
HEMOPHILIAC
HISTORIATED
HOHENLINDEN
HORSERIDING
HOSTILITIES
IMPARTIALLY
IMPASSIONED
IMPASSIVELY
IMPERTINENT
IMPRECISION
IMPROVIDENT
IMPULSIVELY
INCONTINENT
INCRIMINATE
INDEXLINKED
INFANTICIDE
INFERTILITY
INGRATITUDE
INGREDIENTS
INQUIRINGLY
INQUISITION
INQUISITIVE
INSECTICIDE
INSECTIVORE
INSENSITIVE
INSOUCIANCE
INSTABILITY
INSULTINGLY
INTELLIGENT
INTENSIVELY
INTENTIONAL
INTERLINGUA
INTERMINGLE
INTERVIEWEE
INTERVIEWER
INTREPIDITY
INTUITIVELY
INVESTIGATE
INVESTITURE
INVINCIBLES
JOSEPHINITE
JUSTIFIABLE
JUSTIFIABLY
KINNIKINICK
LARYNGISMUS
LASERPICIUM
LATROCINIUM
LEADSWINGER
LENGTHINESS
LENTIGINOSE
LICKSPITTLE
LONGANIMITY
MACROBIOTIC
MAGNANIMITY
MAGNANIMOUS
MAGNIFICENT
MARCONIGRAM
MASCULINITY
MASOCHISTIC
MICHURINISM
MICTURITION
MINNESINGER
MISALLIANCE
MISERLINESS
MODERNISTIC
MONOCHINOUS
MOUNTAINEER
MOUNTAINOUS
MOZAMBIQUAN
NAUGHTINESS
NECESSITATE
NECESSITOUS
NUTRITIONAL
OBJECTIVELY
OBJECTIVITY
OBSESSIVELY
OCTASTICHON
OFFENSIVELY
OMNISCIENCE
OPERATIONAL
ORDERLINESS
PALEOLITHIC
PALESTINIAN
PARALEIPSIS
PARISHIONER
PARTICIPANT
PARTICIPATE
PARTICIPIAL
PARTURITION
PARVANIMITY
PATRONISING
PATRONIZING
PENULTIMATE
PERCIPIENCE
PEREGRINATE
PERENNIALLY
PERSONIFIED
PESSIMISTIC
PHONETICIAN
PHONOFIDDLE
PHOTOFINISH
PHTHIRIASIS
PINNYWINKLE
POLYTRICHUM
PONTIFICATE
PORTRAITIST
PORTRAITURE
POSSIBILITY
POTENTIALLY
PRECIPITATE
PRECIPITOUS
PREDOMINANT
PREDOMINATE
PREJUDICIAL
PRELIMINARY
PREMEDITATE
PREMONITION
PREMONITORY
PREPOSITION
PRETERITION
PREVARICATE
PRICKLINESS
PRIZEWINNER
PROBABILITY
PROBATIONER
PROFICIENCY
PROGENITRIX
PROHIBITION
PROHIBITIVE
PROMOTIONAL
PROMPTITUDE
PROPOSITION
PROVISIONAL
PROVISIONER
PULCHRITUDE
QUICKSILVER
RABELAISIAN
RANGEFINDER
RATIOCINATE

RAVISHINGLY
READABILITY
RECEPTIVITY
RECESSIONAL
RECOGNITION
RECONDITION
RECRIMINATE
RECTIFIABLE
RECTILINEAR
REDUPLICATE
REFURBISHED
REGURGITATE
RELIABILITY
REQUISITION
RESISTIVITY
RESUSCITATE
REVENDICATE
RIGHTWINGER
ROBESPIERRE
ROMANTICISM
ROMANTICIZE
SACRIFICIAL
SAINTLINESS
SAVOURINESS
SCALPRIFORM
SCHOTTISCHE
SCITAMINEAE
SCOLECIFORM
SCREAMINGLY
SCRUFFINESS
SECRETIVELY
SELECTIVELY
SELECTIVITY
SELFEVIDENT
SENSATIONAL
SENSIBILITY
SENSITIVELY
SENSITIVITY
SERENDIPITY
SHAPELINESS
SHENANIGANS
SHIPBUILDER
SHUNAMITISM
SIGNIFICANT
SKETCHINESS
SLIGHTINGLY
SOCIABILITY
SOLIPSISTIC
SOROPTIMIST
SOVEREIGNTY
SPELLBINDER
SPHRAGISTIC
SPIFFLICATE
SPITSTICKER
SPRINGINESS
STATELINESS
STOOLPIGEON
STROPHILLUS
STRUTHIONES
SUBDIVISION
SUBDOMINANT
SUBORDINATE
SUFFICIENCY
SUITABILITY
SUPERFICIAL
SUPERFICIES
SUPERVISION
SUPERVISORY
SUPPOSITION
SUPPOSITORY
SYMPOSIARCH
TANGIBILITY
TANTALIZING
TARRADIDDLE
TELEPRINTER
TENTATIVELY
THEATRICALS
THINGLINESS
THRIFTINESS
TIGGYWINKLE
TIGHTFISTED
TIGHTLIPPED
TOXOPHILITE
TRADITIONAL
TRANQUILITY
TRANSFIGURE
TRANSMITTED
TRANSMITTER
TRIUMVIRATE
TYPEWRITTEN
ULTRAVIOLET
UNBLEMISHED
UNCOMMITTED
UNCONFIRMED
UNCONVINCED
UNDERSIGNED
UNDIGNIFIED
UNEMOTIONAL
UNFAILINGLY
UNFULFILLED
UNFURNISHED
UNGODLINESS
UNHAPPINESS
UNINITIATED
UNJUSTIFIED
UNPATRIOTIC
UNPUBLISHED
UNQUALIFIED
UNREALISTIC
UNSPECIFIED
UNVARNISHED
UNWITTINGLY
VARIABILITY
VARSOVIENNE
VENDEMIAIRE
VERSATILITY
VERTIGINOUS
VICISSITUDE
WHEREWITHAL
WOMANLINESS
WORLDLINESS
XEROTRIPSIS
AIRSICKNESS
BANNOCKBURN
CARSICKNESS
JINRICKSHAW
KULTURKREIS
SCHRECKLICH
SEASICKNESS
SHEATHKNIFE
UNBREAKABLE
UNDRINKABLE
UNSPEAKABLE
UNTHINKABLE
WATERSKIING
ACCUMULATOR
ACKNOWLEDGE
AGRICULTURE
AIGUILLETTE
AMBIVALENCE
AMONTILLADO
ANADIPLOSIS
ANAPHYLAXIS
ANGELOLATRY
APOPHYLLITE
ARTICULATED
ASSEMBLYMAN
ASSIMILATED
ATRABILIOUS
BARTHOLOMEW
BASHFULNESS
BENEVOLENCE
BESTSELLING
BOOKSELLERS
BRUCELLOSIS
CALCEOLARIA
CAMOUFLAGED
CANDLELIGHT
CAREFULNESS
CASTELLATED
CAULIFLOWER
CHANCELLERY
CONCEALMENT
CONSTELLATE
CONVALLARIA
COUNSELLING
CRÉMAILLÈRE
CRENELLATED
CROMWELLIAN
CRYSTALLINE
CRYSTALLISE
CRYSTALLIZE
CURTAILMENT
DEMORALIZED
DICOTYLEDON
DISCIPLINED
DISINCLINED
ENTHRALLING
EQUIPOLLENT
EQUIVALENCE
ESPIEGLERIE
EVANGELICAL
EXOSKELETON
FITZWILLIAM
FLANNELETTE
FOOTBALLING
FRAUDULENCE
FULFILLMENT
GENERALIZED
GENOUILLÈRE
GILLYFLOWER
GLADWELLISE
GLOSSOLALIA
GRAMMALOGUE
HAEMOGLOBIN
HALFHOLIDAY
HALLEFLINTA
HELPFULNESS
HEMERALOPIA
HINDERLANDS
INSTALLMENT
INTERGLOSSA
INVIGILATOR
IRREGULARLY
KILOCALORIE
LITERALNESS
MAKEBELIEVE
MALEVOLENCE
MANIPULATOR
MANTELLETTA
MASKALLONGE
MELLIFLUOUS
MENTHOLATED
MISSPELLING
MONTGOLFIER
MUSCHELKALK
MUSKELLUNGE
NATURALNESS
NETHERLANDS
NETHERLINGS
NEUTRALISED
NOMENCLATOR
NONCHALANCE
NORTHCLIFFE
OSTEOPLASTY
OVERBALANCE
PAINKILLING
PARABOLANUS
PENICILLATE
PERDUELLION
PITCHBLENDE
PLAYFULNESS
PREPOLLENCE
PROPHYLAXIS
PRZEWALSKIS
PSEUDOLOGIA
PUNCTILIOUS
QUARRELLING
QUARRELSOME
RAPSCALLION
REALPOLITIK
REFOCILLATE
RESEMBLANCE
SCAFFOLDING
SCANDALIZED
SCHECKLATON
SCINTILLATE
SEARCHLIGHT
SERICULTURE
SEVERALFOLD
SLUMGULLION
SNORKELLING
SOCKDALAGER
SOCKDOLAGER
SOCKDOLIGER
SOCKDOLOGER
SPECIALIZED
SPONDULICKS
SPONDYLITIS
STRAITLACED
STRANDLOPER
STREAMLINED
STREETLIGHT
SUPERALTERN
SUPERFLUITY
SUPERFLUOUS
SURVEILLANT
TESSELLATED
TONSILLITIS
TOURBILLION
TRANSILIENT
TRIPTOLEMUS
TROMPELOEIL
TURBELLARIA
UNAVAILABLE
UNCIVILISED
UNCIVILIZED
UNDEVELOPED
UNDISCLOSED
UNENVELOPED
UTRICULARIA
WAKEFULNESS
WHIGMALEERY
WINDOWLEDGE
WISTFULNESS
WITHHOLDING
ADULLAMITES
ALLELOMORPH
ANASTOMOSIS
ANTONOMASIA
AUXANOMETER
BATTLEMENTS
BIOCHEMICAL
BOTANOMANCY
CHARISMATIC
CHARLEMAGNE
CHRISTMASSY
CHRONOMETER
CLANJAMFRAY
COMPLIMENTS

COMPRIMARIO
COTTONMOUTH
COULOMMIERS
CRITHOMANCY
DEMONOMANIA
EMPYROMANCY
EPITHYMETIC
GENTLEMANLY
HABILIMENTS
IMPEDIMENTA
INESTIMABLE
INFLAMMABLE
INSTRUMENTS
INTOXIMETER
JACQUEMINOT
KLEPTOMANIA
MACADAMIZED
MEGALOMANIA
MEGALOMANIC
MIDDLEMARCH
NYMPHOMANIA
ONEIROMANCY
PAMPELMOOSE
PAMPELMOUSE
PARONOMASIA
PERFORMANCE
POMPELMOOSE
POMPELMOUSE
PSEUDOMORPH
RHABDOMANCY
RIDDLEMEREE
RIFACIMENTO
SCHWARMEREI
SHITTIMWOOD
SHOWJUMPING
SOUTHAMPTON
SPEEDOMETER
STEREOMETER
SUPERIMPOSE
SYMPTOMATIC
THERMOMETER
THINGAMAJIG
THINGUMAJIG
TIMBROMANIA
TRINCOMALEE
TWELVEMONTH
ABANDONMENT
ABIOGENETIC
ACRIMONIOUS
ADJOURNMENT
AERODYNAMIC
ALBIGENSIAN
ALBUGINEOUS
ANTEPENDIUM
APOLLINARIS
APOLLONICON
ATHERINIDAE
AVERRUNCATE
BACCHANALIA
BACKBENCHER
BARYCENTRIC
BEAUMONTAGE
BILLIONAIRE
BOOKBINDING
BOUTONNIERE
BRANDENBURG
BROBDINGNAG
CARABINIERE
CARAVANNING
CAROLINGIAN
CEREMONIOUS
CHALLENGING
CHICKENFEED
CHILLINGHAM
CHIPPENDALE
CITIZENSHIP
CONSIGNMENT
CONSTANTINE
CONTAINMENT
COORDINATED
COORDINATES
COUNTENANCE
COXWAINLESS
CRESCENTADE
DEFERENTIAL
DENOMINATOR
DISCERNIBLE
DISCERNMENT
DISGRUNTLED
DOCTRINAIRE
DOCUMENTARY
DRAGONNADES
DRUNKENNESS
EARTHENWARE
EASTERNMOST
ELEPHANTINE
EMOTIONALLY
ENVIRONMENT
ERIODENDRON
EXPONENTIAL
FACTFINDING
FARTHINGALE
FASHIONABLE
FASHIONABLY
FERRONNIÈRE
FILAMENTOUS
FISHMONGERS
FORAMINIFER
FORLORNNESS
FRAGMENTARY
FRATERNALLY
GAMOGENESIS
GASTRONOMIC
GLASTONBURY
GNATHONICAL
HIGHRANKING
HOMOGENEITY
HOMOGENEOUS
HOMOGENIZED
HYPOTENSION
IGNOMINIOUS
IGNORANTINE
ILLMANNERED
ILLUMINATED
IMPECUNIOUS
IMPREGNABLE
INALIENABLE
INATTENTION
INATTENTIVE
INDEFINABLE
INDEPENDENT
INESSENTIAL
INEXPENSIVE
INFLUENTIAL
INOFFENSIVE
INVOLUNTARY
IRONMONGERS
IRONMONGERY
IRREDENTIST
KALASHNIKOV
KILIMANJARO
KINCHINMORT
KITCHENETTE
LANDSKNECHT
LATIFUNDIUM
LEGIONNAIRE
LONGRUNNING
MACERANDUBA
MAINTENANCE
MECKLENBURG
MEDICINALLY
MENTONNIÈRE
MERCHANDISE
MERCHANDIZE
MERCHANTMAN
METAGENESIS
MILLIONAIRE
MISIDENTIFY
MUDSLINGING
NEVERENDING
NIGHTINGALE
OARSMANSHIP
OPINIONATED
OUTSTANDING
OVERHANGING
OVERMANNING
OXYRHYNCHUS
PEDETENTOUS
PELOPONNESE
PENITENTIAL
PENSIONABLE
PERITONAEUM
PERITONITIS
PIEDMONTITE
PORTLANDIAN
PORTMANTEAU
PREEMINENCE
PRESTONPANS
PUNCHINELLO
PURITANICAL
QUADRENNIAL
QUADRENNIUM
QUARRINGTON
REALIGNMENT
REGIMENTALS
REICHENBACH
REORIENTATE
RESIDENTIAL
RESPLENDANT
RESPLENDENT
REVERENTIAL
RIGHTANGLED
RODOMONTADE
RUDIMENTARY
SCANDANAVIA
SCANDINAVIA
SEDIMENTARY
SELAGINELLA
SELFCONTROL
SHOWMANSHIP
SKIMMINGTON
SPONTANEITY
SPONTANEOUS
STRAMINEOUS
SUBITANEOUS
SUBSTANDARD
SUBSTANTIAL
SUBSTANTIVE
SUDETENLAND
SUNDRENCHED
SUPERINTEND
SURROUNDING
SUSTAINABLE
TARATANTARA
TELEKINESIS
TIRONENSIAN
TREASONABLE
TRICHINELLA
TRICHINOSED
TSCHERNOSEM
TYRONENSIAN
UNCLEANNESS
UNDEMANDING
UNRELENTING
UNREPENTANT
UNSHRINKING
VALLISNERIA
VISCOUNTESS
VITAMINIZED
WESTERNMOST
WESTMINSTER
WHITTINGTON
WIDERANGING
WISHTONWISH
WORKMANLIKE
WORKMANSHIP
ABORTIONIST
ACCESSORIES
ACCOMMODATE
ADOPTIONISM
AGROSTOLOGY
AMPHIBOLOGY
ANACHRONISM
ANACREONTIC
ANONYMOUSLY
ANTHOLOGIZE
ANTHONOMOUS
APOSTROPHUS
ARCHAEOLOGY
ARCHEGONIAL
ARCHEGONIUM
ARCHILOCHUS
ARRHENOTOKY
ASPERSORIUM
ASSIDUOUSLY
ATROCIOUSLY
AUDACIOUSLY
BARNSTORMER
BEACHCOMBER
BEHAVIOURAL
BELLEROPHON
BICARBONATE
BLAMEWORTHY
BOURGEOISIE
CACOPHONOUS
CAMALDOLITE
CAMEROONIAN
CAMPANOLOGY
CAPERNOITED
CAPERNOITIE
CARNIVOROUS
CHAULMOOGRA
CHAULMOUGRA
CHIASTOLITE
CHIROPODIST
CHONDROSTEI
CHRISTOPHER
CLAIRVOYANT
CLIMATOLOGY
COLDBLOODED
COLLABORATE
COMMEMORATE
COMPTROLLER
CONSCIOUSLY
CORROBORATE
COURTEOUSLY
CREDULOUSLY
CREMATORIUM
CRIMINOLOGY
CROCIDOLITE
DACTYLOGRAM
DANGEROUSLY
DECARBONIZE
DELICIOUSLY
DERMATOLOGY
DETERIORATE
DEUTERONOMY
DICTATORIAL
DIORTHORTIC
DIPROTODONT

DIPTEROCARP
DIRECTORATE
DISCOLOURED
DISEMBODIED
DOWNTRODDEN
DREADLOCKED
DREADNOUGHT
ECCALEOBION
ELECTROCUTE
ELECTROLIER
ELECTROLYTE
ELECTRONICS
ELECTROTINT
EPAMINONDAS
ERRONEOUSLY
ERYTHROCYTE
ESCARMOUCHE
ESCHATOLOGY
ETHNOLOGIST
ETYMOLOGIST
EXPECTORANT
EXPECTORATE
EXTEMPORISE
EXTEMPORIZE
EXTRAPOLATE
FACETIOUSLY
FANFARONADE
FEROCIOUSLY
FIELDWORKER
FORECLOSURE
FORESHORTEN
FORETHOUGHT
FORTHCOMING
FRIVOLOUSLY
FULLBLOODED
FUNCTIONARY
FUNCTIONING
GARRULOUSLY
GENEALOGIST
GERONTOLOGY
GESTATORIAL
GONFALONIER
GOODLOOKING
GRANDMOTHER
GRASSHOPPER
GREENBOTTLE
GYNAECOLOGY
HALFBROTHER
HEMIANOPSIA
HERBIVOROUS
HERPETOLOGY
HIGHPROFILE
HILARIOUSLY
HISTOLOGIST
HISTRIONICS
HONEYCOMBED
HONEYMOONER
HORNSWOGGLE
HOUSEHOLDER
HYDROPONICS
HYMNOLOGIST
ICHTHYOLITE
ICHTHYORNIS
ILLUSIONARY
ILLUSIONIST
IMPERIOUSLY
IMPERSONATE
IMPETUOSITY
IMPETUOUSLY
IMPIGNORATE
INCOMPOSITE
INCORPORATE
INCORPOREAL
INFERIORITY
INGENIOUSLY
INSIDIOUSLY
INTERCOSTAL
INTERCOURSE
INTERPOLATE
INTERROGATE
JUDICIOUSLY
KWASHIORKOR
LABORIOUSLY
LEASEHOLDER
LUXURIOUSLY
MAGLEMOSIAN
MALAPROPISM
MALICIOUSLY
MATRIMONIAL
MELODIOUSLY
METALWORKER
METEOROLOGY
METHODOLOGY
MISBEGOTTEN
MODELMOLEST
MOLLYCODDLE
MONOPSONIST
MONSTROSITY
MOSSTROOPER
NEIGHBORING
NEIGHBOURLY
NEUROLOGIST
NICKELODEON
NOTORIOUSLY
OFFICIOUSLY
OPPIGNORATE
ORNITHOLOGY
ORNITHOPTER
OSTRACODERM
OUAGADOUGOU
OVERCROWDED
OVERFLOWING
OVERWROUGHT
PANDEMONIUM
PARACROSTIC
PARATROOPER
PARLIPOMENA
PATERNOSTER
PATHOLOGIST
PAWNBROKERS
PELARGONIUM
PENTECONTER
PENTECOSTAL
PERCEFOREST
PERCHLORATE
PERIODONTIC
PERISSOLOGY
PETRODOLLAR
PETTICOATED
PETTIFOGGER
PHILOLOGIST
PHILOSOPHER
PHOTOCOPIER
PHRASEOLOGY
PISCATORIAL
PLEISTOCENE
PONDEROUSLY
PROLEGOMENA
PROTAGONIST
PROTOCOCCUS
PROTONOTARY
QUERULOUSLY
QUESTIONING
RADIOLOGIST
RAPTUROUSLY
REACTIONARY
RECIPROCATE
RECIPROCITY
RECONNOITER
RECONNOITRE
REFLEXOLOGY
RELIGIOUSLY
RETROROCKET
REVISIONISM
RHOPALOCERA
RIGHTEOUSLY
SAGACIOUSLY
SALACIOUSLY
SALVADORIAN
SAXOPHONIST
SCAREMONGER
SCHISTOSOMA
SCHISTOSOME
SCIENTOLOGY
SCRIPTORIUM
SEIGNIORAGE
SESQUIOXIDE
SHAREHOLDER
SHORTCOMING
SINGAPOREAN
SMALLHOLDER
SMITHSONIAN
SMITHSONITE
SOCIOLOGIST
SPANGCOCKLE
STADTHOLDER
STAKEHOLDER
STALLHOLDER
STEAMROLLER
STEGANOGRAM
STEGANOPODE
STELLIONATE
STEPBROTHER
STOCKHOLDER
STOCKJOBBER
STRENUOUSLY
STYLOPODIUM
SUGARCOATED
SUMPTUOUSLY
SUPERIORITY
SYNCHROMESH
SYNCHRONISE
SYNCHRONISM
SYNCHRONIZE
TAUROBOLIUM
TCHAIKOVSKY
TEASPOONFUL
TEENYBOPPER
TELEPHONIST
TENACIOUSLY
TERMINOLOGY
TERREMOTIVE
TERRITORIAL
TESTIMONIAL
THALIDOMIDE
THANATOPSIS
THEOBROMINE
THROGMORTON
TOBACCONIST
TORRIDONIAN
TORTICOLLIS
TRACHEOTOMY
TRANSFORMED
TRANSFORMER
TRANSPONDER
TRANSPORTED
TRANSPORTER
TRITAGONIST
TRUSTWORTHY
TRYPANOSOMA
TRYPANOSOME
ULTRAMODERN
UNANIMOUSLY
UNDERCOOKED
UNREASONING
UNSUPPORTED
UNWELCOMING
VICARIOUSLY
VICHYSOISSE
VIVACIOUSLY
VOLCANOLOGY
VORACIOUSLY
VULCANOLOGY
WAINSCOTING
WATERCOLOUR
WATERCOURSE
WATERLOGGED
WHITEBOYISM
WHITECOLLAR
WITCHDOCTOR
AILUROPHILE
ANENCEPHALY
APHANIPTERA
APOMORPHINE
APOSIOPESIS
ARTHRAPODAL
BADTEMPERED
BATHYSPHERE
BIBLIOPHILE
BLOODSPORTS
BREASTPLATE
CENTERPIECE
CENTREPIECE
CENTRIPETAL
CHARGEPAYER
CHLOROPHYLL
CHORDOPHONE
CHRYSOPRASE
CIRRHIPEDEA
CIRRHIPEDIA
CLADOSPORUM
COMEUPPANCE
COMMONPLACE
CONSTIPATED
CONSTUPRATE
CONSUMPTION
CONSUMPTIVE
CONTEMPLANT
CONTEMPLATE
CONTRAPTION
COPPERPLATE
DESCRIPTION
DESCRIPTIVE
DEVELOPMENT
DISCREPANCY
ELASTOPLAST
EUCALYPTOLE
FINGERPRINT
GAMETOPHYTE
GREASEPAINT
HECKELPHONE
HOMOEOPATHY
INESCAPABLE
INSCRIPTION
INTERSPERSE
ISOXSUPRINE
LAMPROPHYRE
LEPIDOPTERA
LETTERPRESS
MANTELPIECE
MARKETPLACE
MASTERPIECE
MEGALOPOLIS
NEEDLEPOINT
NUMBERPLATE
ODONTOPHORE
OMMATOPHORE
OSTREOPHAGE
OVEREXPOSED
OVERLAPPING

PARANEPHROS
PARATYPHOID
PHILIPPINES
PHILLIPSITE
PHOTOSPHERE
PIERREPOINT
PISSASPHALT
PODSNAPPERY
PRESUMPTION
PRESUMPTIVE
PRINCIPALLY
QUADRUPLETS
QUINTUPLETS
RUMGUMPTION
SELFIMPOSED
SHAKESPEARE
SHOWERPROOF
SPERMOPHILE
SUBTROPICAL
THALLOPHYTE
THERMOPYLAE
TIMBROPHILY
TRICHOPTERA
TROPOSPHERE
UNFLAPPABLE
UNSTOPPABLE
WATERSPLASH
YELLOWPLUSH
LONGINQUITY
MONCHIQUITE
MONTESQUIEU
PROPINQUITY
SOLILOQUIZE
ACCELERATOR
ADULTERATED
ALLEGORICAL
ANAGNORISIS
ANAPLEROSIS
ANAPLEROTIC
ANNABERGITE
ANNIVERSARY
ANTIBURGHER
ANTIPHRASIS
ANTIPYRETIC
ANTISTROPHE
APONEUROSIS
APPROPRIATE
BALISTRARIA
BANDEIRANTE
BLADDERWORT
BLANKURSINE
BLUNDERBORE
BREADCRUMBS
BROTHERHOOD
CALIFORNIUM
CALLIGRAPHY
CALLITRICHE
CAMPHORATED
CARTOGRAPHY
CATACHRESIS
CATASTROPHE
CATEGORICAL
CHAMBERLAIN
CHAMBERMAID
CHANTARELLE
CHANTERELLE
CHIROGRAPHY
CHITTERLING
CHOROGRAPHY
CHRYSAROBIN
CLAPPERCLAW
COLEORRHIZA
CONCURRENCE
CONFARREATE
CONSPIRATOR
CONSTERNATE
COUNTERFEIT
COUNTERFOIL
COUNTERFORT
COUNTERGLOW
COUNTERHAND
COUNTERMAND
COUNTERPANE
COUNTERPART
COUNTERSIGN
COUNTERSINK
CRACKERJACK
CYLINDRICAL
DELETERIOUS
DELIVERANCE
DIAPHORESIS
DIAPHORETIC
DIARTHROSIS
DIASCORDIUM
DISAPPROVAL
DISCOURTESY
DISIMPRISON
DITTOGRAPHY
DRINKDRIVER
EMPOWERMENT
ENARTHROSIS
ENCUMBRANCE
ENDOCARDIUM
EOANTHROPUS
ETHNOGRAPHY
EVISCERATED
EXAGGERATED
EXASPERATED
EXHILARATED
EXPROPRIATE
FARTHERMOST
FEHMGERICHT
FLABBERGAST
FLAVOURSOME
FLICKERTAIL
FORBEARANCE
FOREWARNING
FURTHERANCE
FURTHERMORE
FURTHERMOST
FURTHERSOME
GEOMETRICAL
GLIMMERGOWK
GREENGROCER
HAEMORRHAGE
HAEMORRHOID
HAGIOGRAPHY
HARDWORKING
HEARTBROKEN
HIPPOCRATES
HIPPOCRATIC
HYPERTROPHY
HYPOCORISMA
ICONOGRAPHY
ILLUSTRATOR
ILLUSTRIOUS
IMPROPRIETY
INADVERTENT
INCINERATOR
INCOHERENCE
INCONGRUITY
INCONGRUOUS
INDUSTRIOUS
INFANTRYMAN
INFILTRATOR
INNUMERABLE
INOPPORTUNE
INSEPARABLE
INSUPERABLE
INTERGROWTH
INTERPRETER
INTOLERABLE
INTOLERABLY
INTOLERANCE
IRREPARABLE
IRREPARABLY
IRREVERENCE
JAMAHIRIYAH
LAUNDERETTE
LEATHERBACK
LEATHERETTE
LEATHERHEAD
LEATHERNECK
LITHOGRAPHY
MACHAIRODUS
MAGISTRATES
MAISTERDOME
MARLBOROUGH
MASQUERADER
MATRIARCHAL
MEANDERINGS
MERITORIOUS
METACARPALS
METATARSALS
MISCARRIAGE
MOISTURIZER
MONTMORENCY
NEANDERTHAL
OBLITERATED
OBSTETRICAL
OCHLOCRATIC
OPPROBRIOUS
ORTHOGRAPHY
OUTPOURINGS
OVERTURNING
PAEDOTROPHY
PALEOGRAPHY
PARTNERSHIP
PASTEURELLA
PASTOURELLE
PATRIARCHAL
PEDESTRIANS
PERESTROIKA
PERICARDIUM
PERIGORDIAN
PERIPHRASIS
PERPETRATOR
PHOTOGRAPHY
PLAGIARISED
PLATYRRHINE
PLEASURABLE
POCOCURANTE
POLYMORPHIC
PORNOGRAPHY
PREMIERSHIP
PRESSURIZED
QUARTERBACK
QUARTERDECK
RADIOGRAPHY
REASSURANCE
RECOVERABLE
REINCARNATE
REMEMBRANCE
RINTHEREOUT
SCARBOROUGH
SCATTERGOOD
SCATTERLING
SCHOLARSHIP
SCREWDRIVER
SCUPPERNONG
SELFSERVICE
SHEPHERDESS
SINISTRORSE
SLENDERNESS
SLUMBERWEAR
SMITHEREENS
SNICKERSNEE
SPATTERDASH
SPATTERDOCK
SPESSARTITE
SPONSORSHIP
STANDARDIZE
STENOGRAPHY
STOCKBROKER
SWITZERLAND
SYMMETRICAL
TACHYGRAPHY
TACITURNITY
TAXIDERMIST
TECTIBRANCH
TÉLÉFÉRIQUE
TETRADRACHM
THEATERGOER
THUNDERBIRD
THUNDERBOLT
THUNDERCLAP
THUNDERHEAD
TRANSURANIC
UNALTERABLE
UNASSERTIVE
UNCASTRATED
UNDERGROUND
UNDERGROWTH
UNDERWRITER
UNDESERVING
UNDESIRABLE
UNENDURABLE
UNFAVORABLE
UNIMPORTANT
UNNATURALLY
UNOBSERVANT
UNSATURATED
UNUTTERABLE
VINAIGRETTE
WEATHERCOCK
WEIGHBRIDGE
WHEELWRIGHT
WHISKERANDO
WHITEFRIARS
WINDSURFING
WOODCARVING
WORRYTROUGH
ACQUIESCENT
APLANOSPORE
ARTHROSPORE
ASTONISHING
BELORUSSIAN
BILIOUSNESS
BITTERSWEET
BUMBERSHOOT
BUSINESSMAN
CACOGASTRIC
CALLOUSNESS
CANDLESTICK
CHIAROSCURO
CHINOISERIE
CIRCUMSPECT
CLANDESTINE
COBBLESTONE
COCKLESHELL
COLLAPSIBLE
COMMONSENSE
CONGRESSMAN
CONNOISSEUR
CONTRASTING
CONVULSIONS
CORNERSTONE
DELITESCENT
DEMIBASTION
DEVIOUSNESS

DIAGNOSTICS
DIATESSARON
DIATESSERON
DISPENSABLE
DISPERSABLE
DISTRESSING
DISTRUSTFUL
DODECASTYLE
DUBIOUSNESS
ENGHALSKRUG
EPIDIASCOPE
EQUIDISTANT
EVERLASTING
FATUOUSNESS
FINGERSTALL
FLOURISHING
FLUORESCENT
FOOTWASHING
FORECASTING
FREEMASONRY
GIGGLESTICK
GIGGLESWICK
GIRDLESTEAD
GODFORSAKEN
GORDONSTOUN
GROUNDSHEET
GROUNDSPEED
GROUNDSWELL
GUTTERSNIPE
HEPATOSCOPY
HETEROSCIAN
HIDEOUSNESS
HYOPLASTRON
IMPLAUSIBLE
INADVISABLE
INCALESCENT
INDIGESTION
INDIVISIBLE
INDIVISIBLY
INEXCUSABLE
INEXCUSABLY
INTERESTING
KINDERSPIEL
KOMMERSBUCH
KRIEGSSPIEL
LAPIDESCENT
LAWLESSNESS
LEPIDOSIREN
LINGUISTICS
LIVINGSTONE
LOCORESTIVE
LONGLASTING
LUMINESCENT
LYCHNOSCOPE
MALFEASANCE
MANGALSUTRA
MANTELSHELF
MANUMISSION
MEADOWSWEET
MEDIUMSIZED
MENDELSSOHN
MIDDENSTEAD
MIDDLESIZED
MISCONSTRUE
MISSISSIPPI
MISTRUSTFUL
MORGENSTERN
MOXIBUSTION
NATIONSTATE
NEEDLESTICK
NERVOUSNESS
NEWSCASTING
NONEXISTENT
NONFEASANCE
NONSENSICAL
OBMUTESCENT
OBSOLESCENT
OBVIOUSNESS
OVERFISHING
PARAMASTOID
PENTHESILEA
PERMISSIBLE
PHALANSTERY
PLAGIOSTOMI
PLOUGHSHARE
POSSESSIONS
PRESTISSIMO
PRETENSIONS
PROCRUSTEAN
PROFESSEDLY
PROGRESSION
PROGRESSIVE
PURPRESTURE
RAMGUNSHOCH
RATTLESNAKE
RAUCOUSNESS
REMINISCENT
RENAISSANCE
RESPONSIBLE
RESPONSIBLY
RESPONSIONS
RETINOSPORA
ROTTENSTONE
SANDERSWOOD
SCYPHISTOMA
SELFRESPECT
SERIOUSNESS
SHAFTESBURY
SILVERSMITH
SINGLESTICK
SMORGASBORD
SPREADSHEET
STEREOSCOPE
STETHOSCOPE
STROBOSCOPE
SUPPRESSION
SYNTHESIZED
SYNTHESIZER
TATTERSALLS
TEDIOUSNESS
TENUOUSNESS
TRACASSERIE
TRESPASSING
UNCHRISTIAN
UNIVERSALLY
UNNECESSARY
UNSATISFIED
USELESSNESS
VACUOUSNESS
VICIOUSNESS
VINBLASTINE
VINCRISTINE
WAPPENSCHAW
WINDLESTRAW
WITHERSHINS
YELLOWSTONE
ACCIPITRINE
ACCOUNTABLE
ACCOUNTANCY
ACOLOUTHITE
ANFRACTUOUS
ANTHESTERIA
APPARATCHIK
APPOINTMENT
APPRENTICED
ARCHENTERON
BARBASTELLE
BELLETTRIST
BIRDWATCHER
BLOODSTREAM
BUPRESTIDAE
CALLISTEMON
CAMPESTRIAN
CAPACITANCE
CAPACITATOR
CARNAPTIOUS
CHOLESTEROL
CLIMACTERIC
CLIOMETRICS
COEXISTENCE
COLLECTANEA
COMBUSTIBLE
COMFORTABLE
COMFORTABLY
COMFORTLESS
COMMENTATOR
COMPARTMENT
CONCENTRATE
CONCEPTICLE
CONDOTTIERE
CONDOTTIORE
CONDUCTRESS
CONJECTURAL
CONNECTICUT
CONSISTENCE
CONSISTENCY
CONSTITUENT
CONSULTANCY
CONTENTEDLY
CONTENTIOUS
CONTENTMENT
CONTRETEMPS
CONVENTICLE
CONVERTIBLE
COPROSTEROL
CORRECTNESS
CORRUPTIBLE
CREDENTIALS
CURNAPTIOUS
CYCLOSTYLED
DEBILITATED
DECAPITATED
DECONSTRUCT
DECORATIONS
DEMONSTRATE
DISCONTINUE
DISSERTATOR
DISTASTEFUL
DRAUGHTSMAN
EARNESTNESS
EGOTISTICAL
ENCHANTMENT
ENCHANTRESS
ENLIGHTENED
EQUILATERAL
ERYMANTHIAN
EXORBITANCE
EXPEDITIOUS
FLIRTATIOUS
FOREFATHERS
FOUNDATIONS
GOODNATURED
GRALLATORES
GRAMMATICAL
HARDHITTING
HATCHETTITE
HIGHPITCHED
HYDROSTATIC
ICONOSTASIS
IMPRACTICAL
INCONSTANCY
INDOMITABLE
INDUBITABLE
INDUBITABLY
INELUCTABLE
INEQUITABLE
INEXCITABLE
INFANGTHIEF
INHABITABLE
INHABITANTS
INHERITANCE
INSCRUTABLE
INSTANTIATE
INTRACTABLE
IRREFUTABLE
KATABOTHRON
KATAVOTHRON
KETAVOTHRON
KIRKPATRICK
KOTABOTHRON
LATERITIOUS
LOGARITHMIC
MALAKATOONE
MEDIASTINUM
MILQUETOAST
MULTISTOREY
MYXOMATOSIS
NIPFARTHING
NOVELETTISH
OMNIPOTENCE
ONOMASTICON
OPTOMETRIST
ORCHESTRATE
ORCHESTRINA
ORCHESTRION
OUTDISTANCE
PAEDIATRICS
PARACETAMOL
PERCEPTIBLE
PERCEPTIBLY
PERIPATETIC
PERLUSTRATE
PERSISTENCE
PHILOCTETES
PINACOTHECA
PRECAUTIONS
PREDESTINED
PREDICTABLE
PREDICTABLY
PREHISTORIC
PRESENTABLE
PRETENTIOUS
PREVENTABLE
PROGNATHOUS
PROPHETICAL
RALLENTANDO
RECONSTRUCT
RECRUITMENT
REDOUBTABLE
REGRETTABLE
REGRETTABLY
REMONSTRATE
REPETITIOUS
RESPECTABLE
RESPECTABLY
RETRACTABLE
REVELATIONS
REVOLUTIONS
RHEUMATICKY
RUMBUSTIOUS
SACHERTORTE
SCRUMPTIOUS
SENTENTIOUS
SEPIOSTAIRE
SEPTENTRION
SEQUESTRATE
SPERMATOZOA
STATISTICAL
STEREOTYPED
SUBCONTRACT

SUBMULTIPLE
SUBSISTENCE
SUGGESTIBLE
SUSCEPTIBLE
TAGLIATELLE
TEMPESTUOUS
TENDENTIOUS
TERRESTRIAL
THAUMATROPE
THEORETICAL
THESMOTHETE
THOUGHTLESS
TOPLOFTICAL
TRIMESTRIAL
TYPESETTING
UNBEFITTING
UNCLUTTERED
UNDERSTATED
UNDOUBTEDLY
UNGETATABLE
UNPALATABLE
UNPRACTICAL
UNPRINTABLE
UNREMITTING
UNRIGHTEOUS
UNSHELTERED
UNSWEETENED
UPHOLSTERER
UPRIGHTNESS
VESPERTINAL
ZOROASTRIAN
ADVENTURESS
ADVENTUROUS
AERONAUTICS
AMINOBUTENE
ANACOLUTHIA
ANTINEUTRON
ARQUEBUSIER
ATTRIBUTION
ATTRIBUTIVE
AVOIRDUPOIS
BARBITURATE
BELEAGUERED
BIELORUSSIA
BLOCKBUSTER
BLOODSUCKER
CARBORUNDUM
CATACAUSTIC
CONFABULATE
CONSECUTIVE
CONSEQUENCE
CONSTRUCTOR
CONTINUALLY
CONTINUANCE
CONVOLUTION
DELINQUENCY
DESTITUTION
DISENCUMBER
DISFIGURING
DISILLUSION
DISSIMULATE
DISSOLUTION
DUMBFOUNDED
EFFECTUALLY
ENCAPSULATE
EXPOSTULATE
FAUXBOURDON
FILLIBUSTER
FOULMOUTHED
FRANKFURTER
FRONTRUNNER
FUNAMBULIST
GABERLUNZIE
GESTICULATE
HOLOTHURIAN
HONEYSUCKLE
IMPORTUNATE
INCAPSULATE
INCREDULITY
INCREDULOUS
INDIARUBBER
INFREQUENCY
INSTITUTION
INTERNUNCIO
INTERRUPTER
IPECACUANHA
KAMELAUKION
LILLIPUTIAN
LUXEMBURGER
MALADJUSTED
MARIVAUDAGE
MATRICULATE
MINIATURIST
MINIATURIZE
OPPORTUNELY
OPPORTUNISM
OPPORTUNIST
OPPORTUNITY
OVERSTUFFED
PARACHUTIST
PERAMBULATE
PERPETUALLY
PERSECUTION
PICKYOUROWN
PREMATURELY
PREOCCUPIED
PROLOCUTION
PROSECUTION
RATATOUILLE
RESTITUTION
RETRIBUTION
RETRIBUTIVE
ROSICRUCIAN
SALVOGUNNER
SPIRITUALLY
STRANGULATE
SUBUNGULATA
TORTICULLUS
TRANSFUSION
TRANSLUCENT
TURRICULATE
UNANNOUNCED
UNCONQUERED
UNDISGUISED
UNDISTURBED
UNFORTUNATE
UNOBTRUSIVE
UNPERTURBED
VERMICULITE
WAREHOUSING
WELLFOUNDED
BASKERVILLE
BRAZZAVILLE
CENTUMVIRUS
CHICHEVACHE
CONCEIVABLE
CONCEIVABLY
CONSERVANCY
CONTRIVANCE
CONTROVERSY
CONVOLVULUS
IRRELEVANCE
PENTONVILLE
RETRIEVABLE
SUBSERVIENT
UNEQUIVOCAL
UNMOTIVATED
WELLADVISED
CESAREWITCH
FRENCHWOMAN
FRENCHWOMEN
GENTLEWOMAN
GIGGLEWATER
HEPPLEWHITE
HIGHPOWERED
JABBERWOCKY
NEEDLEWOMAN
POLICEWOMAN
SHALLOWNESS
SPARROWHAWK
SPOKESWOMAN
SPORTSWOMAN
SWALLOWABLE
SWORDSWOMAN
WASHERWOMAN
WIENERWURST
PARADOXICAL
ANTHOCYANIN
APOCALYPTIC
BORBORYGMUS
CATACLYSMIC
CERARGYRITE
CONTRAYERVA
COUNTRYSIDE
FLAMBOYANCE
FLAMBOYANTE
KIDDLEYWINK
METAPHYSICS
OVERPAYMENT
POLYSTYRENE
PROSELYTISM
PROSELYTIZE
STRINGYBARK
STRONGYLOID
TIDDLEYWINK
TYROGLYPHID
WENSLEYDALE
ORGANIZAION
TOTALIZATOR

11:8

ABBREVIATED
ABRACADABRA
ACCELERATOR
ACCOUNTABLE
ACCOUNTANCY
ACCUMULATOR
ADJUDICATOR
ADULTERATED
ADVERBIALLY
AERODYNAMIC
ALIFANFARON
AMPHISBAENA
ANAPHYLAXIS
ANGELOLATRY
ANTHOCYANIN
ANTIPHRASIS
ANTONOMASIA
APOLLINARIS
APPRECIABLE
APPRECIABLY
ARTICULATED
ASCLEPIADES
ASSIMILATED
BACCHANALIA
BALISTRARIA
BANDEIRANTE
BILLIONAIRE
BOTANOMANCY
CALCEOLARIA
CALLIGRAPHY
CAMOUFLAGED
CAMPHORATED
CAPACITANCE
CAPACITATOR
CARDOPHAGUS
CARTOGRAPHY
CASTELLATED
CAUSTICALLY
CENTURIATOR
CERTIFIABLE
CHARGEPAYER
CHARISMATIC
CHARLEMAGNE
CHEERLEADER
CHICHEVACHE
CHIROGRAPHY
CHOROGRAPHY
CHRISTMASSY
CHRONICALLY
CLEANSHAVEN
COLLECTANEA
COMEUPPANCE
COMFORTABLE
COMFORTABLY
COMMENDABLE
COMMENDABLY
COMMENTATOR
COMPLICATED
COMPRIMARIO
CONCEIVABLE
CONCEIVABLY
CONCILIATOR
CONCORDANCE
CONSERVANCY
CONSPIRATOR
CONSTIPATED
CONSULTANCY
CONTINUALLY
CONTINUANCE
CONTRIVANCE
CONVALLARIA
COORDINATED
COORDINATES
COPROPHAGAN
COUNTENANCE
CRENELLATED
CRITHOMANCY
DEBILITATED
DECAPITATED
DELIVERANCE
DEMONOMANIA
DENOMINATOR
DESCENDANTS
DIATESSARON
DILAPIDATED
DISCREPANCY
DISPENSABLE
DISPERSABLE
DISSERTATOR
DISTURBANCE
DITTOGRAPHY
DOCTRINAIRE
DRAGONNADES
DRASTICALLY
EARTHSHAKER
EFFECTUALLY
EMMENTHALER
EMOTIONALLY
EMPYROMANCY
ENCUMBRANCE
ENFORCEABLE
EQUIVOCALLY
ERRATICALLY
ESSENTIALLY
ETHNOGRAPHY
EVISCERATED
EXAGGERATED
EXASPERATED

EXHILARATED
EXORBITANCE
FANATICALLY
FASHIONABLE
FASHIONABLY
FINANCIALLY
FLAMBOYANCE
FLAMBOYANTE
FORBEARANCE
FORBIDDANCE
FORESEEABLE
FRANTICALLY
FRATERNALLY
FURTHERANCE
GENERICALLY
GENETICALLY
GENTLEMANLY
GIGGLEWATER
GLOSSOLALIA
GODFORSAKEN
GRAPHICALLY
GREASEPAINT
GUADALCANAL
HAGIOGRAPHY
HINDERLANDS
HIPPOCRATES
HIPPOCRATIC
HISTORIATED
HOLLANDAISE
HOMOEOPATHY
HYDROSTATIC
ICONOGRAPHY
ICONOSTASIS
IDENTICALLY
IDIOTICALLY
IDYLLICALLY
ILLOGICALLY
ILLUMINATED
ILLUSTRATOR
IMPARTIALLY
IMPERMEABLE
IMPREGNABLE
INADVISABLE
INALIENABLE
INCINERATOR
INCONSTANCY
INDEFINABLE
INDOMITABLE
INDUBITABLE
INDUBITABLY
INELUCTABLE
INEQUITABLE
INESCAPABLE
INESTIMABLE
INEXCITABLE
INEXCUSABLE
INEXCUSABLY
INFILTRATOR
INFLAMMABLE
INHABITABLE
INHABITANTS
INHERITANCE
INNUMERABLE
INSCRUTABLE
INSEPARABLE
INSOUCIANCE
INSUPERABLE
INTERCHANGE
INTOLERABLE
INTOLERABLY
INTOLERANCE
INTOXICATED
INTRACTABLE
INVIGILATOR
IPECACUANHA
IRREFUTABLE
IRREGULARLY
IRRELEVANCE
IRREPARABLE
IRREPARABLY
IRREVOCABLE
JUSTIFIABLE
JUSTIFIABLY
KLEPTOMANIA
LACONICALLY
LEGIONNAIRE
LEVELHEADED
LIGHTHEADED
LINDISFARNE
LITHOGRAPHY
LOUDSPEAKER
MAGISTRATES
MAINTENANCE
MALFEASANCE
MANIPULATOR
MASQUERADER
MEDICINALLY
MEGALOMANIA
MEGALOMANIC
MENTHOLATED
MIDDLEMARCH
MILLIONAIRE
MISALLIANCE
MISDEMEANOR
NETHERLANDS
NOMENCLATOR
NONCHALANCE
NONFEASANCE
NOSTRADAMUS
NUMERICALLY
NYMPHOMANIA
OBLITERATED
OCHLOCRATIC
OLIGOCHAETE
ONEIROMANCY
OPINIONATED
ORGANICALLY
ORGANIZAION
ORTHOGRAPHY
OSTEOPLASTY
OUTDISTANCE
OVERBALANCE
PACIFICALLY
PALEOGRAPHY
PANOMPHAEAN
PARABOLANUS
PARACETAMOL
PARONOMASIA
PENSIONABLE
PERENNIALLY
PERFORMANCE
PERIPHRASIS
PERITONAEUM
PERPETRATOR
PERPETUALLY
PETTICOATED
PHOTOGRAPHY
PHTHIRIASIS
PICKELHAUBE
PLEASURABLE
POCOCURANTE
POLITICALLY
PORNOGRAPHY
POTENTIALLY
PRACTICABLE
PRACTICALLY
PREDICTABLE
PREDICTABLY
PRESENTABLE
PREVENTABLE
PRINCIPALLY
PROOFREADER
PROPHYLAXIS
PROSAICALLY
PUBLISHABLE
RADIOGRAPHY
RALLENTANDO
REASSURANCE
RECOVERABLE
RECTIFIABLE
REDOUBTABLE
REGRETTABLE
REGRETTABLY
REMEMBRANCE
RENAISSANCE
REPLACEABLE
RESEMBLANCE
RESPECTABLE
RESPECTABLY
RETRACTABLE
RETRIEVABLE
RHABDOMANCY
SALTIMBANCO
SARCOPHAGUS
SATIRICALLY
SCANDANAVIA
SCANDINAVIA
SCEPTICALLY
SCHECKLATON
SCRIMSHANDY
SEPIOSTAIRE
SERVICEABLE
SHORTCHANGE
SKEPTICALLY
SKILLIGALEE
SOCKDALAGER
SOCKDOLAGER
SPIRITUALLY
SPIROCHAETE
STENOGRAPHY
STRAITLACED
STRETCHABLE
SUGARCOATED
SUPERCHARGE
SUSTAINABLE
SVARABHAKTI
SWALLOWABLE
SYMPLEGADES
SYMPOSIARCH
SYMPTOMATIC
TACHYGRAPHY
TATTERSALLS
TECHNICALLY
TECTIBRANCH
TEGUCICALPA
TESSELLATED
TETRADRACHM
THINGAMAJIG
THINGUMAJIG
TIMBROMANIA
TOTALIZATOR
TRAFFICATOR
TRANSURANIC
TREASONABLE
TRINCOMALEE
TURBELLARIA
UNALTERABLE
UNAVAILABLE
UNAVOIDABLE
UNAVOIDABLY
UNBREAKABLE
UNCASTRATED
UNCONCEALED
UNCRUSHABLE
UNDERCHARGE
UNDERSTATED
UNDESIRABLE
UNDRINKABLE
UNENDURABLE
UNFAVORABLE
UNFLAPPABLE
UNGETATABLE
UNINITIATED
UNIVERSALLY
UNMITIGATED
UNMOTIVATED
UNNATURALLY
UNPALATABLE
UNPRINTABLE
UNSATURATED
UNSHAKEABLE
UNSPEAKABLE
UNSTOPPABLE
UNTHINKABLE
UNTOUCHABLE
UNUTTERABLE
UTRICULARIA
VENDEMIAIRE
WATERMEADOW
WELLBEHAVED
WHISKERANDO
WHITECHAPEL
WINDBREAKER
WINDCHEATER
WRONGHEADED
BANNOCKBURN
BESSARABIAN
BLUNDERBORE
BRANDENBURG
COMESTIBLES
CONSUMABLES
DIAMONDBACK
ECCALEOBION
GLASTONBURY
HERRINGBONE
HUMMINGBIRD
INDIARUBBER
INVINCIBLES
KOMMERSBUCH
LEATHERBACK
MECKLENBURG
MOCKINGBIRD
QUARTERBACK
REICHENBACH
SCUTTLEBUTT
SHAFTESBURY
SMORGASBORD
STICKLEBACK
STOCKJOBBER
STRINGYBARK
THUNDERBIRD
THUNDERBOLT
ACADEMICIAN
ACATALECTIC
ACQUIESCENT
AGNOSTICISM
AMPLEXICAUL
APPARATCHIK
ARCHILOCHUS
ARTIODACTYL
AURIGNACIAN
AVERRUNCATE
AZOTOBACTER
BACKBENCHER
BIRDWATCHER
BLOODSUCKER
BRISTLECONE
BUSHWHACKER
CATALLACTIC
CATHOLICISM

CERTIFICATE
CHIAROSCURO
CLAPPERCLAW
COMMUNICANT
COMMUNICATE
CONSTRICTED
CONSTRICTOR
CONSTRUCTOR
DECORTICATE
DELITESCENT
DIPTEROCARP
DISAFFECTED
DOMESTICATE
DOMESTICITY
DREADLOCKED
ELECTRICIAN
ELECTRICITY
ELECTROCUTE
EPIDIASCOPE
ERYTHROCYTE
ESCHERICHIA
FERNITICKLE
FISHANDCHIP
FLUORESCENT
HEPATOSCOPY
HETEROSCIAN
HIGHPITCHED
HONEYSUCKLE
HORSERACING
HYPOTHECATE
ILLYWHACKER
INCALESCENT
INCORRECTLY
INFANTICIDE
INSECTICIDE
INTERLACING
INTERNECINE
LAPIDESCENT
LASERPICIUM
LUMINESCENT
LYCHNOSCOPE
MAGNIFICENT
MATRIARCHAL
MULTIRACIAL
OBMUTESCENT
OBSOLESCENT
OCTASTICHON
OXYRHYNCHUS
PATRIARCHAL
PERTINACITY
PHONETICIAN
PLEISTOCENE
POLYTRICHUM
PONTIFICATE
PREJUDICIAL
PREVARICATE
PROTOCOCCUS
PTERODACTYL
RECIPROCATE
RECIPROCITY
REDUPLICATE
REMINISCENT
RETROROCKET
REVENDICATE
RHOPALOCERA
ROMANTICISM
ROMANTICIZE
ROSICRUCIAN
SACRIFICIAL
SCIREFACIAS
SHIPWRECKED
SHUTTLECOCK
SIGNIFICANT
SPANGCOCKLE
SPIFFLICATE
SPITSTICKER
STEREOSCOPE
STETHOSCOPE
STROBOSCOPE
SUNDRENCHED
SUPERFICIAL
SUPERFICIES
TABERNACLES
THEATRICALS
THUNDERCLAP
TRANSLUCENT
UNCONNECTED
UNPROTECTED
UNSUSPECTED
WAPPENSCHAW
WEATHERCOCK
WITCHDOCTOR
ACCOMMODATE
ANTEPENDIUM
BACKSLIDING
BOOKBINDING
CHIPPENDALE
CHIROPODIST
CONSOLIDATE
DESERPIDINE
DIASCORDIUM
DIPROTODONT
DISEMBODIED
DOWNTRODDEN
ENCHIRIDION
ENDOCARDIUM
ENNEAHEDRON
ERIODENDRON
FACTFINDING
GALLOVIDIAN
HANGGLIDING
HEBDOMADARY
HORSERADISH
HORSERIDING
HYDROMEDUSA
IMPROVIDENT
INCARNADINE
INDEPENDENT
INTREPIDITY
LATIFUNDIUM
LOGODAEDALY
MACERANDUBA
MAISTERDOME
MAQUILADORA
MARIVAUDAGE
MERCHANDISE
MERCHANDIZE
MOLLYCODDLE
NEVERENDING
NICKELODEON
OSTRACODERM
OUTSTANDING
PERICARDIUM
PERIGORDIAN
PHONOFIDDLE
PORTLANDIAN
QUARTERDECK
RESPLENDANT
RESPLENDENT
SCAFFOLDING
SCULDUDDERY
SELFEVIDENT
SHEPHERDESS
SKIDBLADNIR
SKULDUDDERY
SPATTERDASH
SPATTERDOCK
STANDARDIZE
STYLOPODIUM
SUBSTANDARD
SUPERSEDEAS
SUPERSEDERE
SURROUNDING
TARRADIDDLE
TETRAHEDRON
THISTLEDOWN
TRINIDADIAN
ULTRAMODERN
UNDEMANDING
WATEREDDOWN
WENSLEYDALE
WITHHOLDING
ABIOGENETIC
ABSENTEEISM
ACCRESCENCE
ACKNOWLEDGE
ADOLESCENCE
AGONOTHETES
AGUARDIENTE
AIGUILLETTE
ALBUGINEOUS
AMBIVALENCE
ANAESTHESIA
ANAESTHETIC
ANTECEDENCE
ANTHESTERIA
ANTIPYRETIC
ANTISTHENES
APOSIOPESIS
ARCHENTERON
ARRIVEDERCI
ARTHRODESIS
ASTRINGENCY
ATMOSPHERIC
AUXANOMETER
BADTEMPERED
BANGLADESHI
BARBASTELLE
BATTLEMENTS
BELEAGUERED
BENEVOLENCE
BOYSENBERRY
CALLISTEMON
CAMARADERIE
CANDESCENCE
CARRIAGEWAY
CATACHRESIS
CENTRIPETAL
CHANTARELLE
CHANTERELLE
CHINOISERIE
CHOLESTEROL
CHRONOMETER
CINQUECENTO
CIRRHIPEDEA
CIRRHIPEDIA
CLIMACTERIC
COALESCENCE
COEXISTENCE
COGNOSCENTE
COGNOSCENTI
COINCIDENCE
COMMONSENSE
COMPLACENCY
COMPLIMENTS
CONCURRENCE
CONFARREATE
CONSEQUENCE
CONSILIENCE
CONSISTENCE
CONSISTENCY
CONTENTEDLY
CONTINGENCE
CONTINGENCY
CONTRAYERVA
CONTRETEMPS
CONTROVERSY
CONVENIENCE
CONVERGENCE
COPROSTEROL
CRACOVIENNE
DELINQUENCY
DEMOSTHENES
DEMOSTHENIC
DESPONDENCY
DIAPHORESIS
DIAPHORETIC
DIATESSERON
DICOTYLEDON
DISAGREEING
DISBELIEVER
DISCOTHEQUE
DISGRACEFUL
DISTASTEFUL
DYAESTHESIA
ENFOULDERED
ENLIGHTENED
EPITHYMETIC
EQUILATERAL
EQUIVALENCE
ESPIEGLERIE
EXCRESCENCE
EXOSKELETON
FARINACEOUS
FIDDLEDEDEE
FLANNELETTE
FRAUDULENCE
GAMOGENESIS
HABILIMENTS
HIGHPOWERED
HOBBLEDEHOY
HOMOGENEITY
HOMOGENEOUS
HOUSEKEEPER
HUCKLEBERRY
HURTLEBERRY
ILLMANNERED
IMPEDIMENTA
INCOHERENCE
INFREQUENCY
INGREDIENTS
INSTRUMENTS
INTERPRETER
INTERSPERSE
INTERVIEWEE
INTERVIEWER
INTOXIMETER
IRIDESCENCE
IRREVERENCE
KITCHENETTE
LAMMERGEIER
LAMMERGEYER
LANDSKNECHT
LAUNDERETTE
LEATHERETTE
LOGGERHEADS
LONGSLEEVED
MALEVOLENCE
MANTELLETTA
MARIONBERRY
METAGENESIS
MINESWEEPER
MONTMORENCY
MUNIFICENCE
OFFHANDEDLY
OMNIPOTENCE
OMNISCIENCE
OPALESCENCE
ORTHOPAEDIC
PARENTHESIS

PASTEURELLA
PASTOURELLE
PEACEKEEPER
PERCIPIENCE
PERIPATETIC
PERSISTENCE
PHILANDERER
PHILOCTETES
PITCHBLENDE
PLANTAGENET
POLIORCETIC
POLTERGEIST
POTAMOGETON
PRECONCEIVE
PREEMINENCE
PREPOLLENCE
PROFESSEDLY
PROFICIENCY
PSYCHEDELIC
PSYCHODELIC
PUNCHINELLO
RESOURCEFUL
RIDDLEMEREE
RIFACIMENTO
RINTHEREOUT
ROBESPIERRE
SAPONACEOUS
SCARABAEOID
SCHWARMEREI
SELAGINELLA
SELFDEFENCE
SENNACHERIB
SEPTICAEMIA
SEVENTEENTH
SHAKESPEARE
SIGHTSEEING
SMITHEREENS
SPEEDOMETER
SPONTANEITY
SPONTANEOUS
STEREOMETER
STOREKEEPER
STRAMINEOUS
SUBITANEOUS
SUBMERGENCE
SUBSISTENCE
SUFFICIENCY
SUFFRAGETTE
SUPERCHERIE
SYMPATHETIC
TAGLIATELLE
TELEKINESIS
THERMOMETER
TRACASSERIE
TREECREEPER
TRICHINELLA
TRIPTOLEMUS
UNCLUTTERED
UNCONQUERED
UNDOUBTEDLY
UNRIGHTEOUS
UNSHELTERED
UNSWEETENED
UPHOLSTERER
VALLISNERIA
VARSOVIENNE
VINAIGRETTE
VIOLINCELLO
VIOLONCELLO
WHIGMALEERY
WINDOWLEDGE
WINTERBERRY
WITENAGEMOT
ACINACIFORM
CHICKENFEED
CLANJAMFRAY
COUNTERFEIT
COUNTERFOIL
COUNTERFORT
COUNTRIFIED
DEVITRIFIED
DOLABRIFORM
HANDCRAFTED
HIGHPROFILE
HUMGRUFFIAN
HUNDREDFOLD
MONTGOLFIER
OVERSTUFFED
PERSONIFIED
SCALPRIFORM
SCOLECIFORM
SEVERALFOLD
STANDOFFISH
UNDIGNIFIED
UNJUSTIFIED
UNQUALIFIED
UNSATISFIED
UNSPECIFIED
WINDSURFING
ANNABERGITE
ANTHOLOGIZE
ANTIBURGHER
ARBITRAGEUR
BORBORYGMUS
BROBDINGNAG
CAROLINGIAN
CHALLENGING
CHILLINGHAM
COUNTERGLOW
CROSSLEGGED
DACTYLOGRAM
DESEGREGATE
DISPARAGING
ENCOURAGING
ETHNOLOGIST
ETYMOLOGIST
EXTRAVAGANT
FARTHINGALE
FISHMONGERS
FLABBERGAST
FLORILEGIUM
GALLIBAGGER
GALLIBEGGAR
GALLYBAGGER
GALLYBEGGAR
GENEALOGIST
GLIMMERGOWK
GRAVEDIGGER
HISTOLOGIST
HORNSWOGGLE
HYMNOLOGIST
INTELLIGENT
INTERREGNUM
INTERROGATE
INVESTIGATE
IRONMONGERS
IRONMONGERY
KIMERIDGIAN
LEFTLUGGAGE
MARCONIGRAM
MUDSLINGING
MYCOPHAGIST
NEUROLOGIST
NIGHTINGALE
OVERHANGING
PASSACAGLIA
PATHOLOGIST
PETTIFOGGER
PHILOLOGIST
QUARRINGTON
RADIOLOGIST
RIGHTANGLED
SAPROLEGNIA
SCATTERGOOD
SCULDUGGERY
SHENANIGANS
SKIMMINGTON
SKULDUGGERY
SOCIOLOGIST
SOVEREIGNTY
STEGANOGRAM
STOOLPIGEON
TESSARAGLOT
THEATERGOER
THEATREGOER
TRANSFIGURE
UNDERSIGNED
VOTERIGGING
WATERLOGGED
WHITTINGTON
WIDERANGING
ACOLOUTHITE
AFTERSCHOOL
AILUROPHILE
AMELANCHIER
ANENCEPHALY
APOMORPHINE
APPROACHING
ASTONISHING
BATHYSPHERE
BIBLIOPHILE
BROTHERHOOD
BULLFIGHTER
BUMBERSHOOT
CHLOROPHYLL
CHORDOPHONE
CLAIRSCHACH
COCKLESHELL
COLEORRHIZA
COLLENCHYMA
COUNTERHAND
DENDRACHATE
DOUBLECHECK
ENCROACHING
ENFRANCHISE
ERYMANTHIAN
ESTRANGHELO
EYECATCHING
FARREACHING
FIRELIGHTER
FLOURISHING
FOOTWASHING
FOREFATHERS
FORFOUGHTEN
FORTNIGHTLY
GAMETOPHYTE
GEGENSCHEIN
GODDAUGHTER
GROUNDSHEET
HAEMORRHAGE
HAEMORRHOID
HARPSICHORD
HECKELPHONE
HEPPLEWHITE
HIGHLIGHTER
INFANGTHIEF
KATABOTHRON
KATAVOTHRON
KETAVOTHRON
KOTABOTHRON
LAMPLIGHTER
LAMPROPHYRE
LEATHERHEAD
LOGARITHMIC
LONGSIGHTED
MANTELSHELF
MELANOCHROI
MONONGAHELA
MOONLIGHTER
NEARSIGHTED
NIPFARTHING
ODONTOPHORE
OMMATOPHORE
OSTREOPHAGE
OVERFISHING
PARANEPHROS
PARATYPHOID
PHOTOSPHERE
PINACOTHECA
PISSASPHALT
PLATYRRHINE
PLOUGHSHARE
POLYTECHNIC
PROGNATHOUS
RAMGUNSHOCH
REPROACHFUL
SARCENCHYME
SPARROWHAWK
SPERMOPHILE
SPREADSHEET
TERPSICHORE
THALLOPHYTE
THESMOTHETE
THOROUGHPIN
THUNDERHEAD
TIMBROPHILY
TROPOSPHERE
ULOTRICHALE
UNFLINCHING
WITHERSHINS
XENODOCHIUM
ACRIMONIOUS
ADULLAMITES
ALLEGORICAL
ANAGNORISIS
ANTIRRHINUM
APOLLONICON
APPRENTICED
APPROPRIATE
ATHERINIDAE
ATRABILIOUS
BASKERVILLE
BATTLEFIELD
BENEFICIARY
BENEFICIATE
BIOCHEMICAL
BLACKMAILER
BOURGEOISIE
BOUTONNIERE
BRAZZAVILLE
BUPRESTIDAE
CALEFACIENT
CALLITRICHE
CANDLELIGHT
CAPERNOITED
CAPERNOITIE
CAPRICCIOSO
CARABINIERE
CARNAPTIOUS
CATEGORICAL
CENTERPIECE
CENTREPIECE
CENTUMVIRUS
CEREMONIOUS
CESAREWITCH
CIRCUMCISER
CLARENCIEUX
COEFFICIENT
COLLAPSIBLE
COMBUSTIBLE

COMPENDIOUS
CONCEPTICLE
CONDOTTIERE
CONDOTTIORE
CONNECTICUT
CONSTRAINED
CONTENTIOUS
CONVENTICLE
CONVERTIBLE
CONVULSIONS
CORINTHIANS
CORRUPTIBLE
COULOMMIERS
CREDENTIALS
CURNAPTIOUS
CYLINDRICAL
DECORATIONS
DELETERIOUS
DEMORALIZED
DISCERNIBLE
DISCIPLINED
DISCONTINUE
DISIMPRISON
DISINCLINED
DISOBEDIENT
DRINKDRIVER
EFFICACIOUS
EGOTISTICAL
ENTERTAINER
EVANGELICAL
EXPEDITIOUS
EXPROPRIATE
FEHMGERICHT
FERRONNIÈRE
FLIRTATIOUS
FORAMINIFER
FOTHERGILLA
FOUNDATIONS
FURNISHINGS
GENERALIZED
GEOMETRICAL
GNATHONICAL
GRAMMATICAL
HAEMOPHILIA
HALFHOLIDAY
HALLEFLINTA
HAREBRAINED
HEAVYWEIGHT
HOMOGENIZED
HYDROPHIDAE
HYPOCORISMA
IDEOLOGICAL
IGNOMINIOUS
ILLUSTRIOUS
IMPECUNIOUS
IMPLAUSIBLE
IMPRACTICAL
IMPROPRIETY
INDIVISIBLE
INDIVISIBLY
INDUSTRIOUS
INEFFICIENT
INEXPEDIENT
INJUDICIOUS
INSTANTIATE
IRREDUCIBLE
IRRELIGIOUS
JACQUEMINOT
JAMAHIRIYAH
KALASHNIKOV
LATERITIOUS
LEPIDOSIREN
LIGHTWEIGHT
LONGAWAITED
MACADAMIZED
MAKEBELIEVE
MANTELPIECE
MASTERPIECE
MEANDERINGS
MEDIASTINUM
MEDIUMSIZED
MEMORABILIA
MENTONNIÈRE
MERITORIOUS
MIDDLESIZED
MISCARRIAGE
MISSISSIPPI
MOISTURIZER
MONARCHICAL
MYCOLOGICAL
NETHERLINGS
NEUTRALISED
NIERSTEINER
NONSENSICAL
NORTHCLIFFE
OBSTETRICAL
ONOMASTICON
ONTOLOGICAL
OPPROBRIOUS
OUTPOURINGS
PAPERWEIGHT
PARADOXICAL
PARAMEDICAL
PEDAGOGICAL
PEDESTRIANS
PENTHESILEA
PENTONVILLE
PERCEPTIBLE
PERCEPTIBLY
PERITONITIS
PERMISSIBLE
PETITMAITRE
PHARISAICAL
PHARYNGITIS
PHILIPPINES
PLAGIARISED
POLITICIANS
POSSESSIONS
PRECAUTIONS
PREDESTINED
PRESSURIZED
PRESTIGIOUS
PRETENSIONS
PRETENTIOUS
PROCEEDINGS
PROPHETICAL
PUNCTILIOUS
PURITANICAL
RATATOUILLE
REALPOLITIK
REAPPRAISAL
RECONNOITER
RECONNOITRE
REPETITIOUS
RESPONSIBLE
RESPONSIBLY
RESPONSIONS
REVELATIONS
REVOLUTIONS
RHAPSODICAL
RHEUMATICKY
RUDESHEIMER
RUMBUSTIOUS
SALPINGITIS
SCANDALIZED
SCREWDRIVER
SCRUMPTIOUS
SEARCHLIGHT
SENTENTIOUS
SEXOLOGICAL
SOCKDOLIGER
SPECIALIZED
SPERMICIDAL
SPONDULICKS
SPONDYLITIS
SPORTSFIELD
STATISTICAL
STIPENDIARY
STRATEGICAL
STREAMLINED
STREETLIGHT
SUBMULTIPLE
SUBSERVIENT
SUBTROPICAL
SUGGESTIBLE
SUSCEPTIBLE
SYMMETRICAL
SYMPATHISER
SYMPATHIZER
SYNTHESIZED
SYNTHESIZER
TÉLÉFÉRIQUE
TENDENTIOUS
THEOLOGICAL
THEORETICAL
TONSILLITIS
TOPLOFTICAL
TRANSCEIVER
TRANSILIENT
UNCERTAINTY
UNCIVILISED
UNCIVILIZED
UNCONSCIOUS
UNDERWEIGHT
UNDERWRITER
UNDISGUISED
UNEXPLAINED
UNINHABITED
UNINHIBITED
UNPRACTICAL
UNSOLICITED
VESPERTINAL
VICHYSOISSE
VITAMINIZED
WATERSKIING
WEIGHBRIDGE
WELLADVISED
WELLDEFINED
WHEELWRIGHT
WHITEFRIARS
CRACKERJACK
KILIMANJARO
STEEPLEJACK
BACKPACKING
COMSTOCKERY
DRESSMAKING
ENGHALSKRUG
EPOCHMAKING
GOODLOOKING
GREENOCKITE
HARDWORKING
HIGHRANKING
KAMELAUKION
LAWBREAKING
MERRYMAKING
MONEYMAKING
MUSCHELKALK
NICKNACKERY
NUTCRACKERS
PAINSTAKING
PAWNBROKERS
STOCKTAKING
TICKTACKTOE
UNDERTAKING
UNSHRINKING
VOORTREKKER
ABNORMALITY
AGROSTOLOGY
AMMOPHILOUS
AMONTILLADO
AMPHIBOLOGY
ANTICYCLONE
APOPHYLLITE
ARCHAEOLOGY
ARCHIPELAGO
ARGATHELIAN
ASPERGILLUM
ASPERGILLUS
BACKFIELDER
BESTSELLING
BLACKFELLOW
BOOKSELLERS
BREASTPLATE
BREATHALYSE
CAMALDOLITE
CAMPANOLOGY
CANNIBALISM
CANNIBALIZE
CATERPILLAR
CHAMBERLAIN
CHANCELLERY
CHANTICLEER
CHEESECLOTH
CHIASTOLITE
CHITTERLING
CHOCKABLOCK
CIRCUMFLECT
CLIMATOLOGY
CLINOCHLORE
COACHFELLOW
COLONIALISM
COLONIALIST
COLOURBLIND
COMFORTLESS
COMMONPLACE
COMPTROLLER
CONFABULATE
CONSTELLATE
CONTEMPLANT
CONTEMPLATE
COPPERPLATE
COUNSELLING
COXWAINLESS
CRACKHALTER
CRATERELLUS
CREDIBILITY
CRÉMAILLÈRE
CRESTFALLEN
CRIMINOLOGY
CROCIDOLITE
CROMWELLIAN
CRYSTALLINE
CRYSTALLISE
CRYSTALLIZE
CULPABILITY
DARDANELLES
DEERSTALKER
DEFENCELESS
DEFENSELESS
DERMATOLOGY
DESTABILIZE
DICEPHALOUS
DISHEVELLED
DISSIMULATE
ELASTOPLAST
ELECTROLIER
ELECTROLYTE
ELIGIBILITY
ENCAPSULATE
ENCEPHALOMA

ENKEPHALINE
ENTHRALLING
EQUIPOLLENT
ESCHATOLOGY
EVENTUALITY
EXPOSTULATE
EXTRAPOLATE
FALLIBILITY
FEASIBILITY
FEATURELESS
FITZWILLIAM
FLEXIBILITY
FOOTBALLING
FORTUNELOUD
FUNAMBULIST
GALLOWGLASS
GENOUILLÈRE
GEOSYNCLINE
GERONTOLOGY
GESTICULATE
GIBBERELLIN
GLADWELLISE
GULLIBILITY
GUTTURALISE
GYNAECOLOGY
HAMMERCLOTH
HEMOPHILIAC
HERPETOLOGY
HIGHQUALITY
HOSPITALITY
HOSPITALIZE
HOSPITALLER
HOUSEHOLDER
HUSBANDLAND
ICHTHYOLITE
IMMORTALISE
IMMORTALITY
IMMORTALIZE
IMPERIALISM
IMPERIALIST
INCAPSULATE
INCREDULITY
INCREDULOUS
INFERTILITY
INFORMALITY
INSTABILITY
INTERCALARY
INTERPOLATE
INTERRELATE
ITHYPHALLIC
ITHYPHALLUS
LEASEHOLDER
MARGINALIST
MARGINALIZE
MARKETPLACE
MARSHMALLOW
MATERIALISE
MATERIALISM
MATERIALIST
MATERIALIZE
MATRICULATE
MEANINGLESS
MEASURELESS
METEOROLOGY
METHODOLOGY
MISSPELLING
MODELMOLEST
MONOTHELITE
NAPHTHALENE
NATIONALISM
NATIONALIST
NATIONALITY
NATIONALIZE
NONETHELESS
NUMBERPLATE
ODONTOBLAST
OFFICIALDOM
OFFICIALESE
ORIENTALIST
ORIGINALITY
ORNITHOLOGY
OVERWHELMED
OVERZEALOUS
PAINKILLING
PATERNALISM
PENICILLATE
PENTATHLETE
PERAMBULATE
PERDUELLION
PERISSOLOGY
PERISTALITH
PERISTALSIS
PERSONALIST
PERSONALITY
PERSONALIZE
PETRODOLLAR
PHILATELIST
PHRASEOLOGY
POSSIBILITY
PROBABILITY
PRODIGALISE
PRODIGALITY
PUNCTUALITY
PURPOSELESS
QUADRUPLETS
QUARRELLING
QUICKSILVER
QUINTUPLETS
RAPSCALLION
RATIONALITY
RATIONALIZE
READABILITY
REFLEXOLOGY
REFOCILLATE
RELIABILITY
REMORSELESS
RIBONUCLEIC
ROCKEFELLER
SCATTERLING
SCHRECKLICH
SCIENTOLOGY
SCINTILLATE
SECONDCLASS
SENSIBILITY
SHAREHOLDER
SHIPBUILDER
SLEEPWALKER
SLUMGULLION
SMALLHOLDER
SNORKELLING
SOCIABILITY
SPRINGCLEAN
STADTHOLDER
STAKEHOLDER
STALLHOLDER
STEAMROLLER
STOCKHOLDER
STORYTELLER
STRANGULATE
STRETCHLESS
STRONGYLOID
STROPHILLUS
STYMPHALIAN
SUBUNGULATA
SUDETENLAND
SUITABILITY
SURVEILLANT
SWITZERLAND
SYNDICALISM
TANGIBILITY
TAUROBOLIUM
TEETOTALLER
TERMINOLOGY
THOUGHTLESS
TORTICOLLIS
TORTICULLUS
TOURBILLION
TOXOPHILITE
TRANQUILITY
TROPHOBLAST
TURRICULATE
UNDERVALUED
UNFULFILLED
UNTRAMELLED
VARIABILITY
VERMICULITE
VERSATILITY
VOLCANOLOGY
VULCANOLOGY
WATERCOLOUR
WATERSPLASH
WESTPHALIAN
WHITECOLLAR
WORKMANLIKE
YELLOWPLUSH
ABANDONMENT
ABRIDGEMENT
ACHIEVEMENT
ADJOURNMENT
ADVANCEMENT
AMERCIAMENT
AMPHETAMINE
ANTECHAMBER
ANTHONOMOUS
APPEASEMENT
APPOINTMENT
APPROXIMATE
ARBITRAMENT
ARRANGEMENT
ASSYTHEMENT
BEACHCOMBER
BELLYTIMBER
BEREAVEMENT
BESIEGEMENT
BLASPHEMOUS
BOMBARDMENT
CHAMBERMAID
COMMANDMENT
COMPARTMENT
COMPILEMENT
CONCEALMENT
CONFINEMENT
CONSIGNMENT
CONTAINMENT
CONTENEMENT
CONTENTMENT
COUNTERMAND
CURTAILMENT
DEPARTEMENT
DEPHLEGMATE
DERANGEMENT
DEUTSCHMARK
DEVELOPMENT
DISABLEMENT
DISARMAMENT
DISCERNMENT
DISENCUMBER
DISSEPIMENT
DIVORCEMENT
EASTERNMOST
EMBOÎTEMENT
EMPIECEMENT
EMPLACEMENT
EMPOWERMENT
ENCHANTMENT
ENDORSEMENT
ENFEOFFMENT
ENFORCEMENT
ENHANCEMENT
ENJAMBEMENT
ENLARGEMENT
ENSLAVEMENT
ENTABLEMENT
ENTITLEMENT
ENVIRONMENT
EURHYTHMICS
EXANTHEMATA
FARTHERMOST
FORTHCOMING
FULFILLMENT
FURTHERMORE
FURTHERMOST
GARNISHMENT
GUESSTIMATE
HIPPOCAMPUS
HONEYCOMBED
IMPEACHMENT
IMPROVEMENT
INSTALLMENT
INVOLVEMENT
KINCHINMORT
LEGERDEMAIN
LIQUIDAMBAR
LONGANIMITY
MAGNANIMITY
MAGNANIMOUS
MEASUREMENT
MEPROBAMATE
MICROGAMETE
MONOGRAMMED
MONOTREMATA
NIKETHAMIDE
NOURISHMENT
OVERPAYMENT
PARLIPOMENA
PARVANIMITY
PENULTIMATE
PREDICAMENT
PROCUREMENT
PROLEGOMENA
REALIGNMENT
RECRUITMENT
REFRESHMENT
RELEASEMENT
REPLACEMENT
REQUIREMENT
RESTATEMENT
SAUSAGEMEAT
SCOPOLAMINE
SHORTCOMING
SILVERSMITH
SOROPTIMIST
SYNCHROMESH
TAXIDERMIST
TEMPERAMENT
THALIDOMIDE
THEOBROMINE
TRACKLEMENT
TREPONEMATA
UNWELCOMING
VIDEOCAMERA
VOLKSKAMMER
WESTERNMOST
WORLDFAMOUS
ABORTIONIST
ACCOMPANIST
ACCORDINGLY
ADOPTIANISM
ADOPTIONISM
AGGLUTINANT

AGGLUTINATE
AIRSICKNESS
AMERICANISM
ANACHRONISM
ANACREONTIC
ANAXIMANDER
ANDROGENOUS
APPALLINGLY
APPEARANCES
APPROVINGLY
APPURTENANT
ARCHEGONIAL
ARCHEGONIUM
ARGENTINIAN
ASSASSINATE
ATHERMANOUS
AUGUSTINIAN
AWKWARDNESS
BASHFULNESS
BEASTLINESS
BICARBONATE
BICENTENARY
BILIOUSNESS
BLESSEDNESS
BREADWINNER
BRILLIANTLY
BRITTLENESS
BROADMINDED
CACOPHONOUS
CALIFORNIUM
CALLOUSNESS
CAMEROONIAN
CARAVANNING
CARBORUNDUM
CAREFULNESS
CARSICKNESS
CHARACINOID
CHEIROGNOMY
CHILDMINDER
CHRISTENING
CLEANLINESS
CLIFFHANGER
COMPETENTLY
CONCISENESS
CONDOLENCES
CONDOMINIUM
CONFIDENTLY
CONSTERNATE
CONTAMINANT
CONTAMINATE
CONTINENTAL
CORDWAINERS
CORRECTNESS
COURTLINESS
CROOKEDNESS
CULVERINEER
CYMOPHANOUS
DECARBONIZE
DEGLUTINATE
DETERMINANT
DETERMINING
DETRIMENTAL
DEUTERONOMY
DEVIOUSNESS
DIFFERENTLY
DIFFIDENTLY
DIPSOMANIAC
DISENTANGLE
DISORGANIZE
DISORIENTED
DISSEMINATE
DRUNKENNESS
DRYCLEANERS
DRYCLEANING
DUBIOUSNESS
DUMBFOUNDED
EARNESTNESS
EFFICIENTLY
EINSTEINIUM
ELECTRONICS
EMPTYHANDED
EPAMINONDAS
EVASIVENESS
EXCEEDINGLY
EXPECTANTLY
EXPERIENCED
EXTERMINATE
EXTROGENOUS
FANFARONADE
FARRAGINOUS
FATUOUSNESS
FAULTFINDER
FOOLISHNESS
FOREWARNING
FORGIVENESS
FORLORNNESS
FRANKLINITE
FREETHINKER
FRIGHTENING
FRONTRUNNER
FUNCTIONARY
FUNCTIONING
FUNDAMENTAL
FURTIVENESS
GABERLUNZIE
GALLIGANTUS
GELSEMININE
GENUINENESS
GERRYMANDER
GHASTLINESS
GONFALONIER
GREGARINIDA
GRENZGANGER
GUTTERSNIPE
HALLUCINATE
HARDICANUTE
HAUGHTINESS
HEALTHINESS
HEAVYHANDED
HELPFULNESS
HIDEOUSNESS
HISTRIONICS
HOGGISHNESS
HOHENLINDEN
HOOLIGANISM
HOOTANANNIE
HOOTENANNIE
HYDROPONICS
ILLUSIONARY
ILLUSIONIST
IMPATIENTLY
IMPERMANENT
IMPERSONATE
IMPERTINENT
IMPLEMENTAL
IMPORTANTLY
IMPORTUNATE
IMPRUDENTLY
INAUTHENTIC
INCESSANTLY
INCONTINENT
INCREMENTAL
INCRIMINATE
INDEXLINKED
INDIGNANTLY
INDULGENTLY
INQUIRINGLY
INSISTENTLY
INSULTINGLY
INTERLINGUA
INTERMINGLE
INTERNUNCIO
INTERVENING
INTRAVENOUS
JERRYMANDER
JOSEPHINITE
KINNIKINICK
LATROCINIUM
LAWLESSNESS
LEADSWINGER
LEATHERNECK
LENGTHENING
LENGTHINESS
LENTIGINOSE
LITERALNESS
LONGRUNNING
LOUISIANIAN
LUXULYANITE
LUXURIANTLY
MASCULINITY
MASSIVENESS
MATRIMONIAL
MAURETANIAN
MAURITANIAN
MICHURINISM
MINNESINGER
MISERLINESS
MONEYLENDER
MONOCHINOUS
MONOPSONIST
MOUNTAINEER
MOUNTAINOUS
NARRAGANSET
NATURALNESS
NAUGHTINESS
NECROMANCER
NERVOUSNESS
NOTHINGNESS
OBVIOUSNESS
OPPORTUNELY
OPPORTUNISM
OPPORTUNIST
OPPORTUNITY
ORDERLINESS
ORTHOCENTRE
OVERMANNING
OVERTURNING
OVERWEENING
PALESTINIAN
PANDEMONIUM
PASSIVENESS
PEEVISHNESS
PELARGONIUM
PELOPONNESE
PENSIVENESS
PENTECONTER
PEREGRINATE
PERIODONTIC
PERMANENTLY
PERTINENTLY
PHOTOFINISH
PHYSIOGNOMY
PINNYWINKLE
PLAYFULNESS
PLEBEIANISE
POMEGRANATE
PREDOMINANT
PREDOMINATE
PRELIMINARY
PRICKLINESS
PRIMIGENIAL
PRISCIANIST
PRIZEWINNER
PROFUSENESS
PROMINENTLY
PROTAGONIST
QUADRENNIAL
QUADRENNIUM
QUESTIONING
RAFFISHNESS
RANGEFINDER
RATIOCINATE
RATTLESNAKE
RAUCOUSNESS
RAVISHINGLY
REACTIONARY
RECRIMINATE
RECTILINEAR
RECURRENTLY
REINCARNATE
RELUCTANTLY
REPRESENTED
RESTIVENESS
REVISIONISM
RIGHTHANDED
RIGHTHANDER
RIGHTWINGER
ROGUISHNESS
SACRAMENTAL
SAINTLINESS
SALVOGUNNER
SAVOURINESS
SAXOPHONIST
SCAREMONGER
SCITAMINEAE
SCOLOPENDRA
SCREAMINGLY
SCRUFFINESS
SCUPPERNONG
SEASICKNESS
SELFISHNESS
SENTIMENTAL
SERIOUSNESS
SHALLOWNESS
SHAPELINESS
SHEATHKNIFE
SHORTHANDED
SILLIMANITE
SKETCHINESS
SLENDERNESS
SLIGHTINGLY
SMITHSONIAN
SMITHSONITE
SPELLBINDER
SPRINGINESS
STATELINESS
STELLIONATE
STRANGENESS
STRAPHANGER
STRINGENTLY
STYLISHNESS
SUBDOMINANT
SUBORDINATE
SUCCEDANEUM
SUPERTANKER
SUPPEDANEUM
SYCOPHANTIC
SYNCHRONISE
SYNCHRONISM
SYNCHRONIZE
TACITURNITY
TEASPOONFUL
TEDIOUSNESS
TELEPHONIST
TELEPRINTER
TENUOUSNESS
TESTIMONIAL
THINGLINESS
THREATENING
THRIFTINESS

TIGGYWINKLE
TOBACCONIST
TOBOGGANING
TORRIDONIAN
TRANSPONDER
TRINOBANTES
TRITAGONIST
TRUCULENTLY
UNANNOUNCED
UNAUTHENTIC
UNCLEANNESS
UNCONVINCED
UNCOUTHNESS
UNDERHANDED
UNDERMANNED
UNFAILINGLY
UNFORTUNATE
UNGODLINESS
UNHAPPINESS
UNREASONING
UNWARRANTED
UNWITTINGLY
UPRIGHTNESS
USELESSNESS
VACUOUSNESS
VERTIGINOUS
VICIOUSNESS
WAKEFULNESS
WAYWARDNESS
WELLFOUNDED
WELLMEANING
WILLINGNESS
WISTFULNESS
WOMANLINESS
WORLDLINESS
ZWISCHENZUG
AGORAPHOBIA
ALLELOMORPH
AMPHISBOENA
ANADIPLOSIS
ANAPLEROSIS
ANAPLEROTIC
ANASTOMOSIS
ANTISTROPHE
APONEUROSIS
ARTHRAPODAL
BARTHOLOMEW
BLOODSPORTS
BRAGGADOCIO
BRUCELLOSIS
CATASTROPHE
CAULIFLOWER
CENTREBOARD
CHAULMOOGRA
CHRYSAROBIN
CLADOSPORUM
COLDBLOODED
CONDITIONAL
CONDITIONER
COTTONMOUTH
DEGRINGOLER
DIARTHROSIS
DIMENSIONAL
DIRECTIONAL
DISAPPROVAL
DOUROUCOULI
EDUCATIONAL
EMMENAGOGUE
ENARTHROSIS
EOANTHROPUS
EXCEPTIONAL
EXECUTIONER
EXTORTIONER
FREEMASONRY
FRENCHWOMAN
FRENCHWOMEN
FULLBLOODED
GASTRONOMIC
GENTLEWOMAN
GILLYFLOWER
GRALLATORES
GRAMMALOGUE
GREENGROCER
HAEMOGLOBIN
HEARTBROKEN
HEMERALOPIA
HEMORRHOIDS
HONEYMOONER
HYDROPHOBIA
HYDROPHOBIC
HYPERTROPHY
IMPASSIONED
INTENTIONAL
INTERGLOSSA
INTERGROWTH
ISTIOPHORUS
JABBERWOCKY
KILOCALORIE
MACHAIRODUS
MACROBIOTIC
MALAKATOONE
MARLBOROUGH
MASKALLONGE
MEGALOPOLIS
MELANCHOLIA
MELANCHOLIC
MICROSCOPIC
MILQUETOAST
MISERICORDE
MOSSTROOPER
MULTISTOREY
MYXOMATOSIS
NEEDLEPOINT
NEEDLEWOMAN
NOTICEBOARD
NUTRITIONAL
OPERATIONAL
OVEREXPOSED
PAEDOTROPHY
PAMPELMOOSE
PAMPELMOUSE
PARATROOPER
PARISHIONER
PERESTROIKA
PIERREPOINT
POLICEWOMAN
POMPELMOOSE
POMPELMOUSE
PORTERHOUSE
PREHISTORIC
PROBATIONER
PROMOTIONAL
PROVISIONAL
PROVISIONER
PSEUDOLOGIA
PSEUDOMORPH
PSITTACOSIS
RECESSIONAL
SACHERTORTE
SADDLEHORSE
SALTIMBOCCA
SCARBOROUGH
SCULLABOGUE
SELFIMPOSED
SENSATIONAL
SHOVELBOARD
SINISTRORSE
SKILLIGOLEE
SOCKDOLOGER
SPERMATOZOA
SPOKESWOMAN
SPORTSWOMAN
SPRINGBOARD
SPRINGHOUSE
STOCKBROKER
STRANDLOPER
STRIKEBOUND
STRUTHIONES
SUMMERHOUSE
SWITCHBOARD
SWORDSWOMAN
TENTERHOOKS
THENCEFORTH
THEREABOUTS
TOWNSPEOPLE
TRADITIONAL
TRICHINOSED
TROMPELOEIL
TSCHERNOSEM
TWELVEMONTH
ULTRAVIOLET
UNDERCOOKED
UNDERGROUND
UNDERGROWTH
UNDEVELOPED
UNDISCLOSED
UNEMOTIONAL
UNENVELOPED
UNEQUIVOCAL
UNPATRIOTIC
WASHERWOMAN
WHEREABOUTS
WILBERFORCE
WORRYTROUGH
AESCULAPIAN
AESCULAPIUS
APLANOSPORE
APOCALYPTIC
APOSTROPHUS
ARTHROSPORE
AVOIRDUPOIS
BELLEROPHON
BOOKKEEPING
CHRISTOPHER
CIRCUMSPECT
CITLALEPETL
COUNTERPANE
COUNTERPART
DEMOGRAPHIC
DUSTWRAPPER
EPANALEPSIS
GRASSHOPPER
GROUNDSPEED
HANDICAPPED
HANDICAPPER
HEMIANOPSIA
INTERCEPTOR
INTERRUPTER
KINDERSPIEL
KRIEGSSPIEL
LOGOGRAPHER
MALAPROPISM
METACARPALS
ORNITHOPTER
OVERLAPPING
PARABLEPSIS
PARALEIPSIS
PARTICIPANT
PARTICIPATE
PARTICIPIAL
PHILOSOPHER
PHOTOCOPIER
PODSNAPPERY
POLYMORPHIC
PREOCCUPIED
PRESTONPANS
RETINOSPORA
SELFRESPECT
SERENDIPITY
SHOWJUMPING
SOUTHAMPTON
STEGANOPODE
SUPERIMPOSE
TEENYBOPPER
TELEGRAPHER
TELEGRAPHIC
THANATOPSIS
TIGHTLIPPED
TIMEKEEPING
TOPOGRAPHER
TRAGELAPHUS
TYPOGRAPHER
TYPOGRAPHIC
TYROGLYPHID
XEROTRIPSIS
XYLOGRAPHER
MOZAMBIQUAN
ABECEDARIAN
ACCESSORIES
ACCIPITRINE
ADVENTURESS
ADVENTUROUS
AGGLOMERATE
ALCYONARIAN
ALEXANDRINE
ALEXANDRITE
ANISOCERCAL
ANTIQUARIAN
APODYTERIUM
ARBITRARILY
ARISTOCRACY
ARTILLERIST
ASPERSORIUM
ASPHETERISM
BALLBEARING
BARBITURATE
BARNSTORMER
BATTLEDRESS
BATTLEFRONT
BELLETTRIST
BELLIGERENT
BERGSCHRUND
BEWILDERING
BLAMEWORTHY
BLOODSTREAM
BUREAUCRACY
CALENDERING
CAMPESTRIAN
CARDIOGRAPH
CARNIVOROUS
CASSITERITE
CATCHPHRASE
CENTENARIAN
CERARGYRITE
CHAIRPERSON
CHRYSOPRASE
CILOFIBRATE
CIRCULARIZE
CLIOMETRICS
COLLABORATE
COLUMBARIUM
COMMEMORATE
COMMISERATE
COMPUTERIZE
CONCENTRATE
CONDUCTRESS
CONFEDERACY
CONFEDERATE
CONSIDERATE
CONSIDERING

CONSTUPRATE
CONSUMERISM
CONTUBERNAL
CORROBORATE
CREMATORIUM
CUSTOMARILY
DECONSTRUCT
DEMONSTRATE
DETERIORATE
DICTATORIAL
DIORTHORTIC
DIPHYCERCAL
DIRECTORATE
DISFIGURING
DISREGARDED
DOMINEERING
DOUBLECROSS
DOWNHEARTED
EGALITARIAN
ELEUTHERIAN
ENCHANTRESS
ENCHONDROMA
ENDOTHERMIC
ENGINEERING
EPICHEIREMA
EPINEPHRINE
EQUILIBRIST
EQUILIBRIUM
EXPECTORANT
EXPECTORATE
EXTEMPORISE
EXTEMPORIZE
EXTROVERTED
FAMILIARISE
FAMILIARITY
FAMILIARIZE
FAUXBOURDON
FESTSCHRIFT
FIELDWORKER
FINGERPRINT
FORESHORTEN
FRANKFURTER
FUSTILARIAN
GESTATORIAL
GINGERBREAD
HALBSTARKER
HALFHEARTED
HAPHAZARDLY
HERBIVOROUS
HOLOTHURIAN
HOMOTHERMAL
HOMOTHERMIC
HUCKSTERAGE
HYDROCARBON
HYPERMARKET
HYPOTHERMIA
ICHTHYORNIS
IMPIGNORATE
INCARCERATE
INCORPORATE
INCORPOREAL
INDIFFERENT
INFERIORITY
INSINCERITY
INTEMPERATE
INTROVERTED
ISOXSUPRINE
KINDHEARTED
KIRKPATRICK
KULTURKREIS
KWASHIORKOR
LATERIGRADE
LETTERPRESS
LIBERTARIAN
LUXEMBURGER
LYCANTHROPE
LYCANTHROPY
MAGISTERIAL
MANEUVERING
MEGATHERIUM
MEKHITARIST
METALWORKER
MINIATURIST
MINIATURIZE
MINISTERIAL
MINISTERING
MISANTHROPE
MISANTHROPY
MOMENTARILY
NECESSARILY
NEIGHBORING
NIGHTMARISH
NONDESCRIPT
NOTOTHERIUM
OBTEMPERATE
OPPIGNORATE
OPTOMETRIST
ORCHESTRATE
ORCHESTRINA
ORCHESTRION
OVERBEARING
OVERLEARNED
PAEDIATRICS
PECULIARITY
PERCEFOREST
PERCHLORATE
PERLUSTRATE
PERSEVERING
PICKYOUROWN
PISCATORIAL
PLANETARIUM
PLANTIGRADE
POLLENBRUSH
POLYSTYRENE
PREMATURELY
PROFITEROLE
PROLETARIAN
PROLETARIAT
PROLIFERATE
PROTUBERANT
PTOCHOCRACY
RADIOCARBON
RASTAFARIAN
RECONSTRUCT
REFRIGERANT
REFRIGERATE
REGISTERING
REMONSTRATE
REVERBERATE
SABBATARIAN
SAGITTARIUS
SALESPERSON
SALVADORIAN
SCRIPTORIUM
SECONDARILY
SECRETARIAL
SECRETARIAT
SEIGNIORAGE
SEISMOGRAPH
SEMPITERNAL
SEMPITERNUM
SEPTENARIUS
SEPTENTRION
SEQUESTRATE
SHOWERPROOF
SIGHTSCREEN
SINGAPOREAN
SINGULARITY
SMOKESCREEN
SMOULDERING
SPEECHCRAFT
SPENDTHRIFT
SPLUTTERING
STAIRCARPET
STEINBERGER
STENOCHROME
STRADUARIUS
SUBCONTRACT
SUPERIORITY
SUPERMARKET
SUPERSCRIBE
SURTARBRAND
SURTURBRAND
TACHYCARDIA
TAUTOCHRONE
TEMPORARILY
TERRESTRIAL
TERRITORIAL
THAUMATROPE
THROGMORTON
TIMESHARING
TRANSFERRED
TRANSFERRIN
TRANSFORMED
TRANSFORMER
TRANSPARENT
TRANSPORTED
TRANSPORTER
TREACHEROUS
TRENCHERMAN
TRIMESTRIAL
TRINITARIAN
TRIUMVIRATE
TRUSTWORTHY
ULTRAMARINE
UNCONCERNED
UNCONFIRMED
UNCONVERTED
UNDISTURBED
UNPERTURBED
UNREHEARSED
UNSUPPORTED
UTILITARIAN
VALLAMBROSA
VARANGARIAN
VERBIGERATE
VOLUNTARILY
WARMHEARTED
WHEELBARROW
WHITETHROAT
WINDOWFRAME
WINTERGREEN
ZOROASTRIAN
ADVERTISING
AFGHANISTAN
ALBIGENSIAN
ANNIVERSARY
APHRODISIAC
ARQUEBUSIER
AUDIOVISUAL
BELORUSSIAN
BIELORUSSIA
BLANKURSINE
BLOCKBUSTER
BROADCASTER
BURGOMASTER
BUSINESSMAN
CABBALISTIC
CATACAUSTIC
CATACLYSMIC
CEASELESSLY
CHOIRMASTER
CHONDROSTEI
CITIZENSHIP
COMPLAISANT
COMRADESHIP
CONGRESSMAN
CONNOISSEUR
COUNTERSIGN
COUNTERSINK
COUNTRYSIDE
CRITICASTER
DISHONESTLY
DISILLUSION
DISPLEASURE
DISTRESSING
DRAUGHTSMAN
DUNIEWASSAL
DYSLOGISTIC
EMBARRASSED
EMBELLISHED
EPIGENESIST
ESTABLISHED
ESTABLISHER
EUCHARISTIC
EUPHEMISTIC
FAULTLESSLY
FILLIBUSTER
FLAVOURSOME
FORECLOSURE
FRUITLESSLY
FUNDRAISING
FURTHERSOME
GATECRASHER
GRANDMASTER
HABERDASHER
HAIRDRESSER
HAIRRAISING
HARDPRESSED
HEARTLESSLY
HOUSEMASTER
HYPOTENSION
IMPETUOSITY
IMPRECISION
INCOMPOSITE
INEXPENSIVE
INOFFENSIVE
INTERCOSTAL
JINRICKSHAW
LARYNGISMUS
LECTURESHIP
MAGLEMOSIAN
MALADJUSTED
MANUMISSION
MASOCHISTIC
MENDELSSOHN
MERCILESSLY
METAPHYSICS
METATARSALS
MODERNISTIC
MONSTROSITY
NOISELESSLY
OARSMANSHIP
OMNIPRESENT
PARACROSTIC
PARTNERSHIP
PATERNOSTER
PATRONISING
PENTECOSTAL
PESSIMISTIC
PHILLIPSITE
PICTURESQUE
PLATERESQUE
POINTLESSLY
PREDECESSOR
PREMIERSHIP
PRESTISSIMO
PRESTRESSED
PROGRESSION
PROGRESSIVE

PRZEWALSKIS
PYTHONESQUE
QUARRELSOME
RABELAISIAN
REFURBISHED
SCHISTOSOMA
SCHISTOSOME
SCHOLARSHIP
SCHOTTISCHE
SCOUTMASTER
SHAMELESSLY
SHINPLASTER
SHOWMANSHIP
SNICKERSNEE
SOLIPSISTIC
SOUNDLESSLY
SOUTHWESTER
SPHRAGISTIC
SPONSORSHIP
STEADFASTLY
SUBDIVISION
SUPERVISION
SUPERVISORY
SUPPRESSION
TASTELESSLY
THANKLESSLY
TIGHTFISTED
TIRONENSIAN
TOASTMASTER
TRANSFUSION
TRESPASSING
TROUBLESOME
TROUBLESPOT
TRUSTEESHIP
TRYPANOSOMA
TRYPANOSOME
TYRONENSIAN
UNBLEMISHED
UNCONTESTED
UNEXPRESSED
UNFURNISHED
UNIMPRESSED
UNNECESSARY
UNOBTRUSIVE
UNPUBLISHED
UNREALISTIC
UNSURPASSED
UNVARNISHED
UNWHOLESOME
VASOPRESSIN
VENTURESOME
WAREHOUSING
WASTEBASKET
WELLDRESSED
WESTMINSTER
WHISTLESTOP
WORKMANSHIP
ABLACTATION
ABOMINATION
ABSTRACTION
ACCLAMATION
ACCLIMATION
ACCLIMATISE
ACCLIMATIZE
ACQUISITION
ACQUISITIVE
ACTUALITIES
ACUPUNCTURE
ADUMBRATION
AERONAUTICS
AFFECTATION
AFFILIATION
AFFIRMATION
AFFIRMATIVE
AFFLIICTION
AGGRAVATING
AGGRAVATION
AGGREGATION
AGRICULTURE
AIRCRAFTMAN
ALLEVIATION
ALPHABETIZE
ALTERCATION
ALTERNATELY
ALTERNATING
ALTERNATION
ALTERNATIVE
AMINOBUTENE
ANACOLUTHIA
ANESTHETIST
ANESTHETIZE
ANTINEUTRON
APHANIPTERA
APPELLATION
APPELLATIVE
APPLICATION
APPROBATION
ARBITRATION
ARRHENOTOKY
ASSIGNATION
ASSOCIATION
ASTIGMATISM
ATTENUATION
ATTESTATION
ATTRIBUTION
ATTRIBUTIVE
AXEROPHTHOL
BARYCENTRIC
BEAUMONTAGE
BENEDICTINE
BENEDICTION
BIFURCATION
BODHISATTVA
CACOGASTRIC
CALCULATING
CALCULATION
CALIBRATION
CALLANETICS
CANDIDATURE
CANDLESTICK
CAPTIVATING
CAPTIVATION
CARBURETTOR
CARMINATIVE
CELEBRATION
CEREBRATION
CIRCULATING
CIRCULATION
CIRCULATORY
CLANDESTINE
COAGULATION
COBBLESTONE
COENOBITISM
COHORTATIVE
COLLOCATION
COMBINATION
COMMINATION
COMMUTATION
COMPARATIVE
COMPETITION
COMPETITIVE
COMPILATION
COMPOSITION
COMPOTATION
COMPUNCTION
COMPUTATION
CONCOMITANT
CONFUTATION
CONJUGATION
CONJUNCTION
CONJUNCTURE
CONNOTATION
CONSECUTIVE
CONSOLATION
CONSTANTINE
CONSUMPTION
CONSUMPTIVE
CONTRACTION
CONTRACTUAL
CONTRAPTION
CONTRASTING
CONURBATION
CONVOCATION
CONVOLUTION
COOPERATION
COOPERATIVE
CORNERSTONE
CORPORATION
CORRELATION
CORRUGATION
CREPITATION
CRESCENTADE
CULMINATION
CULTIVATION
CYBERNETICS
DECLAMATION
DECLAMATORY
DECLARATION
DECREPITATE
DECREPITUDE
DEFERENTIAL
DEFOLIATION
DEFORMATION
DEGLUTITION
DEGRADATION
DEHORTATIVE
DEHYDRATION
DEIFICATION
DELECTATION
DELICTATION
DELINEATION
DEMARCATION
DEMIBASTION
DEPORTATION
DEPREDATION
DEPRIVATION
DERELICTION
DESCRIPTION
DESCRIPTIVE
DESECRATION
DESELECTION
DESICCATION
DESIGNATION
DESPERATELY
DESPERATION
DESTINATION
DESTITUTION
DESTRUCTION
DESTRUCTIVE
DETESTATION
DEVALUATION
DEVASTATING
DEVASTATION
DIAGNOSTICS
DIFFRACTION
DIPLOMATICS
DIPLOMATIST
DISCOURTESY
DISGRUNTLED
DISJUNCTION
DISLOCATION
DISPOSITION
DISPUTATION
DISQUIETING
DISSIPATION
DISSOLUTION
DISTINCTION
DISTINCTIVE
DISTRACTION
DISTRUSTFUL
DITHELETISM
DOCUMENTARY
DODECASTYLE
DRAGGLETAIL
DUPLICATING
DUPLICATION
DYSFUNCTION
EDIFICATION
EJACULATION
ELABORATELY
ELABORATION
ELECTROTINT
ELEPHANTINE
ELIMINATION
ELIZABETHAN
ELUCIDATION
EMBARKATION
EMBROCATION
ENTABLATURE
ENUMERATION
ENUNCIATION
EQUIDISTANT
EQUINOCTIAL
ERADICATION
EUCALYPTOLE
EVAPORATION
EVENTRATION
EVERLASTING
EXAMINATION
EXCLAMATION
EXHORTATION
EXONERATION
EXPECTATION
EXPENDITURE
EXPLANATION
EXPLANATORY
EXPLORATION
EXPLORATORY
EXPONENTIAL
EXPURGATION
EXQUISITELY
EXTENUATING
EXTENUATION
EXTRADITION
FABRICATION
FAIRWEATHER
FASCINATING
FASCINATION
FAVOURITISM
FESTINATELY
FILAMENTOUS
FINGERSTALL
FLICKERTAIL
FLUCTUATING
FLUCTUATION
FOMENTATION
FORECASTING
FORESTATION
FORMULATION
FORNICATION
FORTUNATELY
FOULMOUTHED
FRAGMENTARY
FROSTBITTEN
FRUSTRATING
FRUSTRATION
FULMINATION
GASTRECTOMY
GERMINATION
GIGGLESTICK

GIRDLESTEAD
GORDONSTOUN
GRANDFATHER
GRANDMOTHER
GRAVITATION
GREENBOTTLE
GUBERNATION
HALFBROTHER
HANDWRITING
HANDWRITTEN
HARDHITTING
HARIOLATION
HATCHETTITE
HIBERNATING
HIBERNATION
HOMEOPATHIC
HOSTILITIES
HUMILIATING
HUMILIATION
HYOPLASTRON
HYPHENATION
IDOLIZATION
IGNORANTINE
IMAGINATION
IMAGINATIVE
IMMEDIATELY
IMMIGRATION
IMPLICATION
IMPORTATION
IMPRECATION
INADVERTENT
INATTENTION
INATTENTIVE
INCANTATION
INCARNATION
INCLINATION
INCOMPETENT
INDENTATION
INDIGESTION
INDIGNATION
INEBRIATION
INEFFECTIVE
INEFFECTUAL
INESSENTIAL
INFATUATION
INFESTATION
INFLUENTIAL
INFORMATICS
INFORMATION
INFORMATIVE
INFURIATING
INGRATITUDE
INOCULATION
INOPERATIVE
INOPPORTUNE
INQUISITION
INQUISITIVE
INSCRIPTION
INSENSITIVE
INSINUATING
INSINUATION
INSPIRATION
INSTIGATION
INSTINCTIVE
INSTITUTION
INSTRUCTION
INSTRUCTIVE
INTEGRATION
INTERACTION
INTERACTIVE
INTERESTING
INTRICATELY
INVESTITURE
INVOLUNTARY
IRRADIATION
IRREDENTIST
ISOELECTRIC
JACTITATION
LAMENTATION
LEGISLATION
LEGISLATIVE
LEGISLATURE
LEPIDOPTERA
LICKSPITTLE
LILLIPUTIAN
LINGUISTICS
LIQUIDATION
LITTÉRATEUR
LIVINGSTONE
LOCORESTIVE
LONGLASTING
LUBRICATION
MACHINATION
MALEDICTION
MALEFACTION
MALFUNCTION
MALPRACTICE
MANCIPATION
MANUFACTURE
MARIONETTES
MASTICATION
MATHEMATICS
MENSURATION
MERCHANTMAN
METRICATION
MICTURITION
MIDDENSTEAD
MISBEGOTTEN
MISCONSTRUE
MISIDENTIFY
MISTRUSTFUL
MOLESTATION
MORGENSTERN
MOXIBUSTION
MURMURATION
NATIONSTATE
NEANDERTHAL
NECESSITATE
NECESSITOUS
NEEDLESTICK
NEGOTIATING
NEGOTIATION
NEWSCASTING
NONEXISTENT
NOVELETTISH
NUMISMATICS
NUMISMATIST
OBSERVATION
OBSERVATORY
OBSTINATELY
OBSTRICTION
OBSTRUCTION
OBSTRUCTIVE
ORIENTATION
ORIGINATING
ORIGINATION
OSCILLATION
OSTENTATION
OSTEOPATHIC
OXODIZATION
PALEOLITHIC
PAMPHLETEER
PANTALETTES
PARACHUTIST
PARAMASTOID
PARTURITION
PEDETENTOUS
PENETRATING
PENETRATION
PENITENTIAL
PENNYFATHER
PERCOLATION
PERFORATION
PERFUNCTORY
PERMUTATION
PERSECUTION
PERSPECTIVE
PHALANSTERY
PIEDMONTITE
PLAGIOSTOMI
POLLINATION
PORTMANTEAU
PORTRAITIST
PORTRAITURE
PRECIPITATE
PRECIPITOUS
PREDICATIVE
PRELIBATION
PREMEDITATE
PREMONITION
PREMONITORY
PREPARATION
PREPARATORY
PREPOSITION
PREROGATIVE
PRESUMPTION
PRESUMPTIVE
PRETERITION
PROCREATION
PROCRUSTEAN
PROGENITRIX
PROHIBITION
PROHIBITIVE
PROLOCUTION
PROMPTITUDE
PROPAGATION
PROPOSITION
PROPRIETARY
PROROGATION
PROSECUTION
PROSELYTISM
PROSELYTIZE
PROSPECTIVE
PROSTHETICS
PROSTRATION
PROTONOTARY
PROTRACTING
PROTRACTION
PROVOCATION
PROVOCATIVE
PSYCHIATRIC
PUBLICATION
PULCHRITUDE
PUNCTUATION
PURPRESTURE
QUALITATIVE
RADIOACTIVE
RAZZAMATAZZ
REALIZATION
REANIMATION
REBARBATIVE
RECANTATION
RECLAMATION
RECOGNITION
RECONDITION
REFORMATION
REFORMATORY
REGIMENTALS
REGURGITATE
REITERATION
REORIENTATE
REPUDIATION
REQUISITION
RESERVATION
RESIDENTIAL
RESIGNATION
RESPIRATION
RESPIRATORY
RESTITUTION
RESTORATION
RESTORATIVE
RESTRICTION
RESTRICTIVE
RESTRUCTURE
RESUSCITATE
RETALIATION
RETALIATORY
RETARDATION
RETRIBUTION
RETRIBUTIVE
RETROACTIVE
REVALUATION
REVERENTIAL
RODOMONTADE
ROTTENSTONE
RUDIMENTARY
RUMFRUCTION
RUMGUMPTION
SCYPHISTOMA
SEDIMENTARY
SEGREGATION
SELFCONTROL
SERICULTURE
SHOPLIFTING
SHUNAMITISM
SINGLESTICK
SPECULATION
SPECULATIVE
SPESSARTITE
STAGFLATION
STANDPATTER
STEPBROTHER
STIMULATION
STIPULATION
STYLIZATION
SUBJUGATION
SUBJUNCTIVE
SUBLIMATION
SUBPANATION
SUBSTANTIAL
SUBSTANTIVE
SUBTRACTION
SUFFOCATING
SUFFOCATION
SUPERALTERN
SUPERINTEND
SUPERLATIVE
SUPPOSITION
SUPPOSITORY
SUPPURATION
SUSURRATION
SYNCOPATION
SYNDICATION
SYSTEMATIZE
TARATANTARA
TEMPERATURE
TERMINATION
TERREMOTIVE
TITILLATION
TOSTICATION
TRACHEOTOMY
TRANSACTION
TRANSLATION
TRANSMITTED
TRANSMITTER
TREACHETOUR
TREPIDATION
TRIBULATION
TRICERATOPS
TRICHOPTERA

TYPESETTING
TYPEWRITTEN
UNASSERTIVE
UNBEFITTING
UNCHRISTIAN
UNCOMMITTED
UNIFICATION
UNIMPORTANT
UNRELENTING
UNREMITTING
UNREPENTANT
UTILIZATION
VACCINATION
VACILLATING
VACILLATION
VALEDICTION
VALEDICTORY
VARIEGATION
VARIOLATION
VENTILATION
VICISSITUDE
VINBLASTINE
VINCRISTINE
VINDICATION
VISCOUNTESS
VIVISECTION
WAINSCOTING
WASHLEATHER
WELLINGTONS
WHEREWITHAL
WHITLEATHER
WINDLESTRAW
WORKSTATION
YELLOWSTONE
ANFRACTUOUS
ANONYMOUSLY
APATOSAURUS
ASSIDUOUSLY
ATROCIOUSLY
AUDACIOUSLY
BEAUTIFULLY
BEHAVIOURAL
BREADCRUMBS
CENTRIFUGAL
CHAULMOUGRA
CONJECTURAL
CONSCIOUSLY
CONSPICUOUS
CONSTITUENT
CONTRIBUTOR
CONVOLVULUS
COURTEOUSLY
CREDULOUSLY
CREPUSCULAR
DANGEROUSLY
DECEITFULLY
DELICIOUSLY
DEMAGOGUERY
DINNYHAUSER
DISCOLOURED
DISTINGUISH
DISTRIBUTED
DISTRIBUTOR
DRACUNCULUS
DREADNOUGHT
EMPHYTEUSIS
EMPIRICUTIC
EREMACAUSIS
ERRONEOUSLY
ESCARMOUCHE
FACETIOUSLY
FEROCIOUSLY
FORETHOUGHT
FRIGHTFULLY
FRIVOLOUSLY
GALLIMAUFRY
GARRULOUSLY
GOODNATURED
HILARIOUSLY
IMPERIOUSLY
IMPETUOUSLY
INCONGRUITY
INCONGRUOUS
INGENIOUSLY
INSIDIOUSLY
INTERCOURSE
INTERLEUKIN
JUDICIOUSLY
LABORIOUSLY
LONGINQUITY
LUXURIOUSLY
MALICIOUSLY
MANGALSUTRA
MASTERFULLY
MELLIFLUOUS
MELODIOUSLY
MONCHIQUITE
MONTESQUIEU
MUNCHHAUSEN
MUSKELLUNGE
NEIGHBOURLY
NOTORIOUSLY
OFFICIOUSLY
OUAGADOUGOU
OUTMANEUVER
OVERWROUGHT
PERSPICUITY
PERSPICUOUS
PONDEROUSLY
PROMISCUITY
PROMISCUOUS
PROPINQUITY
QUERULOUSLY
RAPTUROUSLY
RECTANGULAR
REGRETFULLY
RELIGIOUSLY
RESENTFULLY
RETINACULUM
RIGHTEOUSLY
SAGACIOUSLY
SAINTPAULIA
SALACIOUSLY
SOLILOQUIZE
SORROWFULLY
SPECTACULAR
STOCKHAUSEN
STRENUOUSLY
SUMPTUOUSLY
SUPERFLUITY
SUPERFLUOUS
TEMPESTUOUS
TENACIOUSLY
THEOPNEUSTY
THERAPEUTAE
THERAPEUTIC
UNAMBIGUOUS
UNANIMOUSLY
UNSCHEDULED
VICARIOUSLY
VIVACIOUSLY
VORACIOUSLY
WATERCOURSE
WIENERWURST
WONDERFULLY
ACRIFLAVINE
ATHARVAVEDA
ATTENTIVELY
DECEPTIVELY
DEFENSIVELY
EFFECTIVELY
EXCESSIVELY
EXCLUSIVELY
EXTENSIVELY
IMPASSIVELY
IMPULSIVELY
INSECTIVORE
INTENSIVELY
INTUITIVELY
LABORSAVING
MENDELEVIUM
MISBEHAVIOR
MISCHIEVOUS
OBJECTIVELY
OBJECTIVITY
OBSESSIVELY
OFFENSIVELY
RECEPTIVITY
RESISTIVITY
SECRETIVELY
SELECTIVELY
SELECTIVITY
SELFSERVICE
SENSITIVELY
SENSITIVITY
SPACESAVING
TCHAIKOVSKY
TENTATIVELY
UNDESERVING
UNOBSERVANT
WOODCARVING
BITTERSWEET
BLADDERWORT
EARTHENWARE
GIGGLESWICK
GROUNDSWELL
KIDDLEYWINK
MEADOWSWEET
OVERCROWDED
OVERFLOWING
SANDERSWOOD
SHITTIMWOOD
SLUMBERWEAR
STRANGEWAYS
TIDDLEYWINK
WISHTONWISH
CRUCIFIXION
GENUFLEXION
IDEOPRAXIST
SESQUIOXIDE
ASSEMBLYMAN
BADDELEYITE
CLAIRVOYANT
CYCLOSTYLED
DINNYHAYSER
IDENTIFYING
INFANTRYMAN
ONEIRODYNIA
SAPROPHYTIC
SCEUOPHYLAX
STEREOTYPED
THERMOPYLAE
WHITEBOYISM
ESTRAMAZONE
PATRONIZING
TANTALIZING

11:9

ACCOMMODATE
AGGLOMERATE
AGGLUTINANT
AGGLUTINATE
AMONTILLADO
AMPLEXICAUL
ANENCEPHALY
ANNIVERSARY
APPROPRIATE
APPROXIMATE
APPURTENANT
ARCHIPELAGO
ARISTOCRACY
ASSASSINATE
AVERRUNCATE
BARBITURATE
BEAUMONTAGE
BENEFICIARY
BENEFICIATE
BICARBONATE
BICENTENARY
BREASTPLATE
BUREAUCRACY
CARDIOGRAPH
CATCHPHRASE
CENTREBOARD
CERTIFICATE
CHAMBERLAIN
CHAMBERMAID
CHIPPENDALE
CHRYSOPRASE
CILOFIBRATE
CLAIRSCHACH
CLAIRVOYANT
COLLABORATE
COMMEMORATE
COMMISERATE
COMMONPLACE
COMMUNICANT
COMMUNICATE
COMPLAISANT
CONCENTRATE
CONCOMITANT
CONFABULATE
CONFARREATE
CONFEDERACY
CONFEDERATE
CONSIDERATE
CONSOLIDATE
CONSTELLATE
CONSTERNATE
CONSTUPRATE
CONTAMINANT
CONTAMINATE
CONTEMPLANT
CONTEMPLATE
COPPERPLATE
CORINTHIANS
CORROBORATE
COUNTERHAND
COUNTERMAND
COUNTERPANE
COUNTERPART
CRACKERJACK
CREDENTIALS
CRESCENTADE
DECORTICATE
DECREPITATE
DEGLUTINATE
DEMONSTRATE
DENDRACHATE
DEPHLEGMATE
DESEGREGATE
DETERIORATE
DETERMINANT
DEUTSCHMARK
DIAMONDBACK
DIPTEROCARP
DIRECTORATE
DISSEMINATE
DISSIMULATE

DOCUMENTARY
DOMESTICATE
DRAGGLETAIL
EARTHENWARE
ELASTOPLAST
ENCAPSULATE
EQUIDISTANT
EXANTHEMATA
EXPECTORANT
EXPECTORATE
EXPOSTULATE
EXPROPRIATE
EXTERMINATE
EXTRAPOLATE
EXTRAVAGANT
FANFARONADE
FARTHINGALE
FINGERSTALL
FLABBERGAST
FLICKERTAIL
FRAGMENTARY
FUNCTIONARY
GALLOWGLASS
GESTICULATE
GUESSTIMATE
HAEMORRHAGE
HALLUCINATE
HEBDOMADARY
HUCKSTERAGE
HUSBANDLAND
HYPOTHECATE
ILLUSIONARY
IMPERSONATE
IMPIGNORATE
IMPORTUNATE
INCAPSULATE
INCARCERATE
INCORPORATE
INCRIMINATE
INSTANTIATE
INTEMPERATE
INTERCALARY
INTERPOLATE
INTERRELATE
INTERROGATE
INVESTIGATE
INVOLUNTARY
KILIMANJARO
LATERIGRADE
LEATHERBACK
LEFTLUGGAGE
LEGERDEMAIN
LOGGERHEADS
LOGODAEDALY
MARIVAUDAGE
MARKETPLACE
MATRICULATE
MEPROBAMATE
METACARPALS
METATARSALS
MILQUETOAST
MISCARRIAGE
MONOTREMATA
MUSCHELKALK
NATIONSTATE
NECESSITATE
NIGHTINGALE
NOTICEBOARD
NUMBERPLATE
OBTEMPERATE
ODONTOBLAST
OPPIGNORATE
ORCHESTRATE
OSTREOPHAGE
PARTICIPANT
PARTICIPATE
PEDESTRIANS
PENICILLATE
PENULTIMATE
PERAMBULATE
PERCHLORATE
PEREGRINATE
PERLUSTRATE
PISSASPHALT
PLANTIGRADE
PLOUGHSHARE
POLITICIANS
POMEGRANATE
PONTIFICATE
PRECIPITATE
PREDOMINANT
PREDOMINATE
PRELIMINARY
PREMEDITATE
PRESTONPANS
PREVARICATE
PROLIFERATE
PROPRIETARY
PROTONOTARY
PROTUBERANT
PTOCHOCRACY
QUARTERBACK
RATIOCINATE
RATTLESNAKE
RAZZAMATAZZ
REACTIONARY
RECIPROCATE
RECRIMINATE
REDUPLICATE
REFOCILLATE
REFRIGERANT
REFRIGERATE
REGIMENTALS
REGURGITATE
REICHENBACH
REINCARNATE
REMONSTRATE
REORIENTATE
RESPLENDANT
RESUSCITATE
REVENDICATE
REVERBERATE
RODOMONTADE
RUDIMENTARY
SCINTILLATE
SECONDCLASS
SEDIMENTARY
SEIGNIORAGE
SEISMOGRAPH
SEQUESTRATE
SHAKESPEARE
SHENANIGANS
SHOVELBOARD
SIGNIFICANT
SPARROWHAWK
SPATTERDASH
SPEECHCRAFT
SPIFFLICATE
SPRINGBOARD
STEEPLEJACK
STELLIONATE
STICKLEBACK
STIPENDIARY
STRANGEWAYS
STRANGULATE
STRINGYBARK
SUBCONTRACT
SUBDOMINANT
SUBORDINATE
SUBSTANDARD
SUBUNGULATA
SUDETENLAND
SURTARBRAND
SURTURBRAND
SURVEILLANT
SWITCHBOARD
SWITZERLAND
TARATANTARA
THEATRICALS
TREPONEMATA
TRIUMVIRATE
TROPHOBLAST
TURRICULATE
ULOTRICHALE
UNFORTUNATE
UNIMPORTANT
UNNECESSARY
UNOBSERVANT
UNREPENTANT
VERBIGERATE
WATERSPLASH
WENSLEYDALE
WHITEFRIARS
WINDOWFRAME
ABRACADABRA
ACCOUNTABLE
AGORAPHOBIA
ANTECHAMBER
APPRECIABLE
APPRECIABLY
BEACHCOMBER
BELLYTIMBER
CERTIFIABLE
CHRYSAROBIN
COLLAPSIBLE
COMBUSTIBLE
COMFORTABLE
COMFORTABLY
COMMENDABLE
COMMENDABLY
CONCEIVABLE
CONCEIVABLY
CONVERTIBLE
CORRUPTIBLE
DISCERNIBLE
DISENCUMBER
DISPENSABLE
DISPERSABLE
ENFORCEABLE
FASHIONABLE
FASHIONABLY
FORESEEABLE
HAEMOGLOBIN
HONEYCOMBED
HYDROCARBON
HYDROPHOBIA
HYDROPHOBIC
IMPERMEABLE
IMPLAUSIBLE
IMPREGNABLE
INADVISABLE
INALIENABLE
INDEFINABLE
INDIARUBBER
INDIVISIBLE
INDIVISIBLY
INDOMITABLE
INDUBITABLE
INDUBITABLY
INELUCTABLE
INEQUITABLE
INESCAPABLE
INESTIMABLE
INEXCITABLE
INEXCUSABLE
INEXCUSABLY
INFLAMMABLE
INHABITABLE
INNUMERABLE
INSCRUTABLE
INSEPARABLE
INSUPERABLE
INTOLERABLE
INTOLERABLY
INTRACTABLE
IRREDUCIBLE
IRREFUTABLE
IRREPARABLE
IRREPARABLY
IRREVOCABLE
JUSTIFIABLE
JUSTIFIABLY
LIQUIDAMBAR
PENSIONABLE
PERCEPTIBLE
PERCEPTIBLY
PERMISSIBLE
PLEASURABLE
PRACTICABLE
PREDICTABLE
PREDICTABLY
PRESENTABLE
PREVENTABLE
PUBLISHABLE
RADIOCARBON
RECOVERABLE
RECTIFIABLE
REDOUBTABLE
REGRETTABLE
REGRETTABLY
REPLACEABLE
RESPECTABLE
RESPECTABLY
RESPONSIBLE
RESPONSIBLY
RETRACTABLE
RETRIEVABLE
SERVICEABLE
STOCKJOBBER
STRETCHABLE
SUGGESTIBLE
SUSCEPTIBLE
SUSTAINABLE
SWALLOWABLE
TREASONABLE
UNALTERABLE
UNAVAILABLE
UNAVOIDABLE
UNAVOIDABLY
UNBREAKABLE
UNCRUSHABLE
UNDESIRABLE
UNDISTURBED
UNDRINKABLE
UNENDURABLE
UNFAVORABLE
UNFLAPPABLE
UNGETATABLE
UNPALATABLE
UNPERTURBED
UNPRINTABLE
UNSHAKEABLE
UNSPEAKABLE
UNSTOPPABLE
UNTHINKABLE
UNTOUCHABLE
UNUTTERABLE
ALLEGORICAL
ANISOCERCAL
APOLLONICON

APPEARANCES
APPRENTICED
BIOCHEMICAL
BRAGGADOCIO
CALLITRICHE
CATEGORICAL
CHICHEVACHE
CONCEPTICLE
CONDOLENCES
CONNECTICUT
CONVENTICLE
CYLINDRICAL
DIPHYCERCAL
EGOTISTICAL
ESCARMOUCHE
EVANGELICAL
EXPERIENCED
FEHMGERICHT
GEOMETRICAL
GNATHONICAL
GRAMMATICAL
GREENGROCER
IDEOLOGICAL
IMPRACTICAL
INTERNUNCIO
JABBERWOCKY
LANDSKNECHT
MONARCHICAL
MYCOLOGICAL
NECROMANCER
NONSENSICAL
OBSTETRICAL
ONOMASTICON
ONTOLOGICAL
PARADOXICAL
PARAMEDICAL
PEDAGOGICAL
PHARISAICAL
PROPHETICAL
PROTOCOCCUS
PURITANICAL
RHAPSODICAL
RHEUMATICKY
SALTIMBOCCA
SCHOTTISCHE
SEXOLOGICAL
SPONDULICKS
STATISTICAL
STRAITLACED
STRATEGICAL
SUBTROPICAL
SYMMETRICAL
TETRADRACHM
THEOLOGICAL
THEORETICAL
TOPLOFTICAL
UNANNOUNCED
UNCONVINCED
UNEQUIVOCAL
UNPRACTICAL
ACKNOWLEDGE
ANAXIMANDER
ARTHRAPODAL
ASCLEPIADES
ATHERINIDAE
BACKFIELDER
BROADMINDED
BUPRESTIDAE
CARBORUNDUM
CHEERLEADER
CHILDMINDER
CIRRHIPEDEA
CIRRHIPEDIA
COLDBLOODED
CONTENTEDLY
DICOTYLEDON
DISREGARDED
DOWNTRODDEN
DRAGONNADES
DUMBFOUNDED
EMPTYHANDED
EPAMINONDAS
FAULTFINDER
FAUXBOURDON
FIDDLEDEDEE
FULLBLOODED
GERRYMANDER
HALFHOLIDAY
HAPHAZARDLY
HEAVYHANDED
HOHENLINDEN
HOUSEHOLDER
HYDROPHIDAE
JERRYMANDER
LEASEHOLDER
LEVELHEADED
LIGHTHEADED
MACHAIRODUS
MASQUERADER
MOLLYCODDLE
MONEYLENDER
OFFHANDEDLY
OFFICIALDOM
ORTHOPAEDIC
OVERCROWDED
PHONOFIDDLE
PROFESSEDLY
PROOFREADER
RANGEFINDER
RIGHTHANDED
RIGHTHANDER
SCOLOPENDRA
SHAREHOLDER
SHIPBUILDER
SHORTHANDED
SMALLHOLDER
SPELLBINDER
SPERMICIDAL
STADTHOLDER
STAKEHOLDER
STALLHOLDER
STOCKHOLDER
SYMPLEGADES
TACHYCARDIA
TARRADIDDLE
TRANSPONDER
UNDERHANDED
UNDOUBTEDLY
WATERMEADOW
WEIGHBRIDGE
WELLFOUNDED
WINDOWLEDGE
WRONGHEADED
ABANDONMENT
ABRIDGEMENT
ACHIEVEMENT
ACQUIESCENT
ADJOURNMENT
ADVANCEMENT
ADVENTURESS
AIRSICKNESS
ALTERNATELY
AMERCIAMENT
AMINOBUTENE
AMPHISBAENA
AMPHISBOENA
APHANIPTERA
APPEASEMENT
APPOINTMENT
ARBITRAGEUR
ARBITRAMENT
ARRANGEMENT
ASSYTHEMENT
ATHARVAVEDA
ATTENTIVELY
AWKWARDNESS
BASHFULNESS
BATHYSPHERE
BATTLEDRESS
BATTLEFIELD
BEASTLINESS
BELLIGERENT
BEREAVEMENT
BESIEGEMENT
BILIOUSNESS
BITTERSWEET
BLESSEDNESS
BLOODSTREAM
BOMBARDMENT
BOOKSELLERS
BOUTONNIERE
BRITTLENESS
CALEFACIENT
CALLOUSNESS
CARABINIERE
CAREFULNESS
CARSICKNESS
CENTERPIECE
CENTREPIECE
CHANCELLERY
CHANTICLEER
CHICKENFEED
CIRCUMFLECT
CIRCUMSPECT
CITLALEPETL
CLARENCIEUX
CLEANLINESS
COCKLESHELL
COEFFICIENT
COMFORTLESS
COMMANDMENT
COMPARTMENT
COMPILEMENT
COMSTOCKERY
CONCEALMENT
CONCISENESS
CONDOTTIERE
CONDUCTRESS
CONFINEMENT
CONNOISSEUR
CONSIGNMENT
CONSTITUENT
CONTAINMENT
CONTENEMENT
CONTENTMENT
CORDWAINERS
CORRECTNESS
COULOMMIERS
COUNTERFEIT
COURTLINESS
COXWAINLESS
CROOKEDNESS
CULVERINEER
CURTAILMENT
DECEPTIVELY
DEFENCELESS
DEFENSELESS
DEFENSIVELY
DELITESCENT
DEMAGOGUERY
DEPARTEMENT
DERANGEMENT
DESPERATELY
DEVELOPMENT
DEVIOUSNESS
DISABLEMENT
DISARMAMENT
DISCERNMENT
DISCOURTESY
DISOBEDIENT
DISSEPIMENT
DIVORCEMENT
DOUBLECHECK
DRUNKENNESS
DRYCLEANERS
DUBIOUSNESS
EARNESTNESS
EFFECTIVELY
ELABORATELY
EMBOÎTEMENT
EMPIECEMENT
EMPLACEMENT
EMPOWERMENT
ENCHANTMENT
ENCHANTRESS
ENDORSEMENT
ENFEOFFMENT
ENFORCEMENT
ENHANCEMENT
ENJAMBEMENT
ENLARGEMENT
ENSLAVEMENT
ENTABLEMENT
ENTITLEMENT
ENVIRONMENT
EPICHEIREMA
EQUIPOLLENT
ESTRANGHELO
EVASIVENESS
EXCESSIVELY
EXCLUSIVELY
EXQUISITELY
EXTENSIVELY
FATUOUSNESS
FEATURELESS
FESTINATELY
FISHMONGERS
FLUORESCENT
FOOLISHNESS
FOREFATHERS
FORGIVENESS
FORLORNNESS
FORTUNATELY
FULFILLMENT
FURTIVENESS
GARNISHMENT
GEGENSCHEIN
GENUINENESS
GHASTLINESS
GINGERBREAD
GIRDLESTEAD
GROUNDSHEET
GROUNDSPEED
GROUNDSWELL
HAUGHTINESS
HEALTHINESS
HELPFULNESS
HIDEOUSNESS
HOGGISHNESS
IMMEDIATELY
IMPASSIVELY
IMPEACHMENT
IMPERMANENT
IMPERTINENT
IMPROPRIETY
IMPROVEMENT
IMPROVIDENT
IMPULSIVELY
INADVERTENT
INCALESCENT

INCOMPETENT
INCONTINENT
INCORPOREAL
INDEPENDENT
INDIFFERENT
INEFFICIENT
INEXPEDIENT
INSTALLMENT
INTELLIGENT
INTENSIVELY
INTRICATELY
INTUITIVELY
INVOLVEMENT
IRONMONGERS
IRONMONGERY
KULTURKREIS
LAPIDESCENT
LAWLESSNESS
LEATHERHEAD
LEATHERNECK
LENGTHINESS
LEPIDOPTERA
LETTERPRESS
LITERALNESS
LITTÉRATEUR
LUMINESCENT
MAGNIFICENT
MAKEBELIEVE
MANTELPIECE
MANTELSHELF
MASSIVENESS
MASTERPIECE
MEADOWSWEET
MEANINGLESS
MEASURELESS
MEASUREMENT
MICROGAMETE
MIDDENSTEAD
MISERLINESS
MODELMOLEST
MONONGAHELA
MORGENSTERN
MOUNTAINEER
NAPHTHALENE
NATURALNESS
NAUGHTINESS
NERVOUSNESS
NICKELODEON
NICKNACKERY
NONETHELESS
NONEXISTENT
NOTHINGNESS
NOURISHMENT
NUTCRACKERS
OBJECTIVELY
OBMUTESCENT
OBSESSIVELY
OBSOLESCENT
OBSTINATELY
OBVIOUSNESS
OFFENSIVELY
OFFICIALESE
OLIGOCHAETE
OMNIPRESENT
OPPORTUNELY
ORDERLINESS
OSTRACODERM
OVERPAYMENT
PAMPHLETEER
PANOMPHAEAN
PARLIPOMENA
PASSIVENESS
PAWNBROKERS
PEEVISHNESS
PELOPONNESE
PENSIVENESS
PENTATHLETE
PERCEFOREST
PERITONAEUM
PHALANSTERY
PHOTOSPHERE
PINACOTHECA
PLAYFULNESS
PLEISTOCENE
PODSNAPPERY
POLYSTYRENE
PORTMANTEAU
PREDICAMENT
PREMATURELY
PRICKLINESS
PROCRUSTEAN
PROCUREMENT
PROFUSENESS
PROLEGOMENA
PURPOSELESS
QUADRUPLETS
QUARTERDECK
QUINTUPLETS
RAFFISHNESS
RAUCOUSNESS
REALIGNMENT
RECRUITMENT
RECTILINEAR
REFRESHMENT
RELEASEMENT
REMINISCENT
REMORSELESS
REPLACEMENT
REQUIREMENT
RESPLENDENT
RESTATEMENT
RESTIVENESS
RHOPALOCERA
RIBONUCLEIC
ROGUISHNESS
SAINTLINESS
SAUSAGEMEAT
SAVOURINESS
SCITAMINEAE
SCRUFFINESS
SCULDUDDERY
SCULDUGGERY
SEASICKNESS
SECRETIVELY
SELECTIVELY
SELFEVIDENT
SELFISHNESS
SELFRESPECT
SENSITIVELY
SERIOUSNESS
SHALLOWNESS
SHAPELINESS
SHEPHERDESS
SIGHTSCREEN
SINGAPOREAN
SKETCHINESS
SKULDUDDERY
SKULDUGGERY
SLENDERNESS
SLUMBERWEAR
SMITHEREENS
SMOKESCREEN
SPIROCHAETE
SPORTSFIELD
SPREADSHEET
SPRINGCLEAN
SPRINGINESS
STATELINESS
STOOLPIGEON
STRANGENESS
STRETCHLESS
STYLISHNESS
SUBSERVIENT
SUCCEDANEUM
SUPERALTERN
SUPERINTEND
SUPERSEDEAS
SUPERSEDERE
SUPPEDANEUM
SYNCHROMESH
TEDIOUSNESS
TEMPERAMENT
TENTATIVELY
TENUOUSNESS
THESMOTHETE
THINGLINESS
THOUGHTLESS
THRIFTINESS
THUNDERHEAD
TRACKLEMENT
TRANSILIENT
TRANSLUCENT
TRANSPARENT
TRICHOPTERA
TROMPELOEIL
TROPOSPHERE
ULTRAMODERN
UNCLEANNESS
UNCOUTHNESS
UNGODLINESS
UNHAPPINESS
UPRIGHTNESS
USELESSNESS
VACUOUSNESS
VICIOUSNESS
VIDEOCAMERA
VISCOUNTESS
WAKEFULNESS
WAYWARDNESS
WHIGMALEERY
WILLINGNESS
WINTERGREEN
WISTFULNESS
WOMANLINESS
WORLDLINESS
CRÉMAILLÈRE
FERRONNIÈRE
GENOUILLÈRE
MENTONNIÈRE
DISGRACEFUL
DISTASTEFUL
DISTRUSTFUL
FORAMINIFER
GALLIMAUFRY
MISTRUSTFUL
NORTHCLIFFE
OVERSTUFFED
REPROACHFUL
RESOURCEFUL
TEASPOONFUL
ACCORDINGLY
APPALLINGLY
APPROVINGLY
CAMOUFLAGED
CANDLELIGHT
CARDOPHAGUS
CENTRIFUGAL
CHARLEMAGNE
CHAULMOOGRA
CHAULMOUGRA
CLIFFHANGER
COPROPHAGAN
CROSSLEGGED
DISENTANGLE
DREADNOUGHT
EMMENAGOGUE
EXCEEDINGLY
FORETHOUGHT
GALLIBAGGER
GALLIBEGGAR
GALLYBAGGER
GALLYBEGGAR
GRAMMALOGUE
GRAVEDIGGER
GRENZGANGER
HEAVYWEIGHT
HORNSWOGGLE
INQUIRINGLY
INSULTINGLY
INTERLINGUA
INTERMINGLE
LEADSWINGER
LIGHTWEIGHT
LUXEMBURGER
MINNESINGER
OUAGADOUGOU
OVERWROUGHT
PAPERWEIGHT
PETTIFOGGER
PSEUDOLOGIA
RAVISHINGLY
RIGHTWINGER
SARCOPHAGUS
SCAREMONGER
SCREAMINGLY
SCULLABOGUE
SEARCHLIGHT
SLIGHTINGLY
SOCKDALAGER
SOCKDOLAGER
SOCKDOLIGER
SOCKDOLOGER
STEINBERGER
STRAPHANGER
STREETLIGHT
UNDERWEIGHT
UNFAILINGLY
UNWITTINGLY
WATERLOGGED
WHEELWRIGHT
ANACOLUTHIA
ANTIBURGHER
APOSTROPHUS
APPARATCHIK
ARCHILOCHUS
AXEROPHTHOL
BACKBENCHER
BELLEROPHON
BIRDWATCHER
CHILLINGHAM
CHRISTOPHER
CITIZENSHIP
COMRADESHIP
DEMOGRAPHIC
ELIZABETHAN
EMBELLISHED
ESCHERICHIA
ESTABLISHED
ESTABLISHER
FAIRWEATHER
FISHANDCHIP
FOULMOUTHED
GATECRASHER
GRANDFATHER
GRANDMOTHER
HABERDASHER
HALFBROTHER
HIGHPITCHED
HOBBLEDEHOY
HOMEOPATHIC

JINRICKSHAW
LECTURESHIP
LOGOGRAPHER
MATRIARCHAL
NEANDERTHAL
OARSMANSHIP
OCTASTICHON
OSTEOPATHIC
OXYRHYNCHUS
PALEOLITHIC
PARTNERSHIP
PATRIARCHAL
PENNYFATHER
PHILOSOPHER
POLYMORPHIC
POLYTRICHUM
PREMIERSHIP
REFURBISHED
SCHOLARSHIP
SHOWMANSHIP
SPONSORSHIP
STEPBROTHER
SUNDRENCHED
TELEGRAPHER
TELEGRAPHIC
TOPOGRAPHER
TRAGELAPHUS
TRUSTEESHIP
TYPOGRAPHER
TYPOGRAPHIC
TYROGLYPHID
UNBLEMISHED
UNFURNISHED
UNPUBLISHED
UNVARNISHED
WAPPENSCHAW
WASHLEATHER
WHEREWITHAL
WHITLEATHER
WORKMANSHIP
XYLOGRAPHER
ABECEDARIAN
ABLACTATION
ABNORMALITY
ABOMINATION
ABORTIONIST
ABSENTEEISM
ABSTRACTION
ACADEMICIAN
ACCESSORIES
ACCIPITRINE
ACCLAMATION
ACCLIMATION
ACCLIMATISE
ACCLIMATIZE
ACCOMPANIST
ACOLOUTHITE
ACQUISITION
ACQUISITIVE
ACRIFLAVINE
ACTUALITIES
ADOPTIANISM
ADOPTIONISM
ADUMBRATION
ADVERTISING
AERONAUTICS
AESCULAPIAN
AESCULAPIUS
AFFECTATION
AFFILIATION
AFFIRMATION
AFFIRMATIVE
AFFLIICTION
AGGRAVATING
AGGRAVATION
AGGREGATION
AGNOSTICISM
AILUROPHILE
ALBIGENSIAN
ALCYONARIAN
ALEXANDRINE
ALEXANDRITE
ALLEVIATION
ALPHABETIZE
ALTERCATION
ALTERNATING
ALTERNATION
ALTERNATIVE
AMELANCHIER
AMERICANISM
AMPHETAMINE
ANACHRONISM
ANESTHETIST
ANESTHETIZE
ANNABERGITE
ANTEPENDIUM
ANTHOLOGIZE
ANTIQUARIAN
APHRODISIAC
APODYTERIUM
APOMORPHINE
APOPHYLLITE
APPELLATION
APPELLATIVE
APPLICATION
APPROACHING
APPROBATION
ARBITRARILY
ARBITRATION
ARCHEGONIAL
ARCHEGONIUM
ARGATHELIAN
ARGENTINIAN
ARQUEBUSIER
ARTILLERIST
ASPERSORIUM
ASPHETERISM
ASSIGNATION
ASSOCIATION
ASTIGMATISM
ASTONISHING
ATTENUATION
ATTESTATION
ATTRIBUTION
ATTRIBUTIVE
AUGUSTINIAN
AURIGNACIAN
BACKPACKING
BACKSLIDING
BADDELEYITE
BALLBEARING
BELLETTRIST
BELORUSSIAN
BENEDICTINE
BENEDICTION
BESSARABIAN
BESTSELLING
BEWILDERING
BIBLIOPHILE
BIFURCATION
BILLIONAIRE
BLANKURSINE
BOOKBINDING
BOOKKEEPING
CALCULATING
CALCULATION
CALENDERING
CALIBRATION
CALIFORNIUM
CALLANETICS
CAMALDOLITE
CAMEROONIAN
CAMPESTRIAN
CANDLESTICK
CANNIBALISM
CANNIBALIZE
CAPTIVATING
CAPTIVATION
CARAVANNING
CARMINATIVE
CAROLINGIAN
CASSITERITE
CATHOLICISM
CELEBRATION
CENTENARIAN
CERARGYRITE
CEREBRATION
CHALLENGING
CHIASTOLITE
CHIROPODIST
CHITTERLING
CHRISTENING
CIRCULARIZE
CIRCULATING
CIRCULATION
CLANDESTINE
CLIOMETRICS
COAGULATION
COENOBITISM
COHORTATIVE
COLEORRHIZA
COLLOCATION
COLONIALISM
COLONIALIST
COLOURBLIND
COLUMBARIUM
COMBINATION
COMMINATION
COMMUTATION
COMPARATIVE
COMPETITION
COMPETITIVE
COMPILATION
COMPOSITION
COMPOTATION
COMPUNCTION
COMPUTATION
COMPUTERIZE
CONDOMINIUM
CONFUTATION
CONJUGATION
CONJUNCTION
CONNOTATION
CONSECUTIVE
CONSIDERING
CONSOLATION
CONSTANTINE
CONSUMERISM
CONSUMPTION
CONSUMPTIVE
CONTRACTION
CONTRAPTION
CONTRASTING
CONURBATION
CONVOCATION
CONVOLUTION
COOPERATION
COOPERATIVE
CORPORATION
CORRELATION
CORRUGATION
COUNSELLING
COUNTERSIGN
COUNTERSINK
COUNTRIFIED
COUNTRYSIDE
CREDIBILITY
CREMATORIUM
CREPITATION
CROCIDOLITE
CROMWELLIAN
CRUCIFIXION
CRYSTALLINE
CRYSTALLISE
CRYSTALLIZE
CULMINATION
CULPABILITY
CULTIVATION
CUSTOMARILY
CYBERNETICS
DECARBONIZE
DECLAMATION
DECLARATION
DEFERENTIAL
DEFOLIATION
DEFORMATION
DEGLUTITION
DEGRADATION
DEHORTATIVE
DEHYDRATION
DEIFICATION
DELECTATION
DELICTATION
DELINEATION
DEMARCATION
DEMIBASTION
DEPORTATION
DEPREDATION
DEPRIVATION
DERELICTION
DESCRIPTION
DESCRIPTIVE
DESECRATION
DESELECTION
DESERPIDINE
DESICCATION
DESIGNATION
DESPERATION
DESTABILIZE
DESTINATION
DESTITUTION
DESTRUCTION
DESTRUCTIVE
DETERMINING
DETESTATION
DEVALUATION
DEVASTATING
DEVASTATION
DEVITRIFIED
DIAGNOSTICS
DIASCORDIUM
DICTATORIAL
DIFFRACTION
DIPLOMATICS
DIPLOMATIST
DIPSOMANIAC
DISAGREEING
DISEMBODIED
DISFIGURING
DISILLUSION
DISJUNCTION
DISLOCATION
DISORGANIZE
DISPARAGING
DISPOSITION
DISPUTATION
DISQUIETING
DISSIPATION
DISSOLUTION
DISTINCTION

DISTINCTIVE
DISTINGUISH
DISTRACTION
DISTRESSING
DITHELETISM
DOCTRINAIRE
DOMESTICITY
DOMINEERING
DRESSMAKING
DRYCLEANING
DUPLICATING
DUPLICATION
DYSFUNCTION
ECCALEOBION
EDIFICATION
EGALITARIAN
EINSTEINIUM
EJACULATION
ELABORATION
ELECTRICIAN
ELECTRICITY
ELECTROLIER
ELECTRONICS
ELECTROTINT
ELEPHANTINE
ELEUTHERIAN
ELIGIBILITY
ELIMINATION
ELUCIDATION
EMBARKATION
EMBROCATION
ENCHIRIDION
ENCOURAGING
ENCROACHING
ENDOCARDIUM
ENFRANCHISE
ENGINEERING
ENKEPHALINE
ENTHRALLING
ENUMERATION
ENUNCIATION
EPIGENESIST
EPINEPHRINE
EPOCHMAKING
EQUILIBRIST
EQUILIBRIUM
EQUINOCTIAL
ERADICATION
ERYMANTHIAN
ETHNOLOGIST
ETYMOLOGIST
EURHYTHMICS
EVAPORATION
EVENTRATION
EVENTUALITY
EVERLASTING
EXAMINATION
EXCLAMATION
EXHORTATION
EXONERATION
EXPECTATION
EXPLANATION
EXPLORATION
EXPONENTIAL
EXPURGATION
EXTEMPORISE
EXTEMPORIZE
EXTENUATING
EXTENUATION
EXTRADITION
EYECATCHING
FABRICATION
FACTFINDING
FALLIBILITY
FAMILIARISE
FAMILIARITY
FAMILIARIZE
FARREACHING
FASCINATING
FASCINATION
FAVOURITISM
FEASIBILITY
FESTSCHRIFT
FINGERPRINT
FITZWILLIAM
FLEXIBILITY
FLORILEGIUM
FLOURISHING
FLUCTUATING
FLUCTUATION
FOMENTATION
FOOTBALLING
FOOTWASHING
FORECASTING
FORESTATION
FOREWARNING
FORMULATION
FORNICATION
FORTHCOMING
FRANKLINITE
FRIGHTENING
FRUSTRATING
FRUSTRATION
FULMINATION
FUNAMBULIST
FUNCTIONING
FUNDRAISING
FUSTILARIAN
GALLOVIDIAN
GELSEMININE
GENEALOGIST
GENUFLEXION
GEOSYNCLINE
GERMINATION
GESTATORIAL
GIGGLESTICK
GIGGLESWICK
GLADWELLISE
GONFALONIER
GOODLOOKING
GRAVITATION
GREASEPAINT
GREENOCKITE
GREGARINIDA
GUBERNATION
GULLIBILITY
GUTTERSNIPE
GUTTURALISE
HAIRRAISING
HANDWRITING
HANGGLIDING
HARDHITTING
HARDWORKING
HARIOLATION
HATCHETTITE
HEMOPHILIAC
HEMORRHOIDS
HEPPLEWHITE
HETEROSCIAN
HIBERNATING
HIBERNATION
HIGHPROFILE
HIGHQUALITY
HIGHRANKING
HISTOLOGIST
HISTRIONICS
HOLLANDAISE
HOLOTHURIAN
HOMOGENEITY
HOOLIGANISM
HORSERACING
HORSERADISH
HORSERIDING
HOSPITALITY
HOSPITALIZE
HOSTILITIES
HUMGRUFFIAN
HUMILIATING
HUMILIATION
HUMMINGBIRD
HYDROPONICS
HYMNOLOGIST
HYPHENATION
HYPOTENSION
ICHTHYOLITE
IDENTIFYING
IDEOPRAXIST
IDOLIZATION
IGNORANTINE
ILLUSIONIST
IMAGINATION
IMAGINATIVE
IMMIGRATION
IMMORTALISE
IMMORTALITY
IMMORTALIZE
IMPERIALISM
IMPERIALIST
IMPETUOSITY
IMPLICATION
IMPORTATION
IMPRECATION
IMPRECISION
INATTENTION
INATTENTIVE
INCANTATION
INCARNADINE
INCARNATION
INCLINATION
INCOMPOSITE
INCONGRUITY
INCREDULITY
INDENTATION
INDIGESTION
INDIGNATION
INEBRIATION
INEFFECTIVE
INESSENTIAL
INEXPENSIVE
INFANGTHIEF
INFANTICIDE
INFATUATION
INFERIORITY
INFERTILITY
INFESTATION
INFLUENTIAL
INFORMALITY
INFORMATICS
INFORMATION
INFORMATIVE
INFURIATING
INOCULATION
INOFFENSIVE
INOPERATIVE
INQUISITION
INQUISITIVE
INSCRIPTION
INSECTICIDE
INSENSITIVE
INSINCERITY
INSINUATING
INSINUATION
INSPIRATION
INSTABILITY
INSTIGATION
INSTINCTIVE
INSTITUTION
INSTRUCTION
INSTRUCTIVE
INTEGRATION
INTERACTION
INTERACTIVE
INTERESTING
INTERLACING
INTERNECINE
INTERVENING
INTREPIDITY
IRRADIATION
IRREDENTIST
ISOXSUPRINE
JACTITATION
JOSEPHINITE
KAMELAUKION
KIDDLEYWINK
KIMERIDGIAN
KINDERSPIEL
KINNIKINICK
KIRKPATRICK
KRIEGSSPIEL
LABORSAVING
LAMENTATION
LAMMERGEIER
LASERPICIUM
LATIFUNDIUM
LATROCINIUM
LAWBREAKING
LEGIONNAIRE
LEGISLATION
LEGISLATIVE
LENGTHENING
LIBERTARIAN
LILLIPUTIAN
LINGUISTICS
LIQUIDATION
LOCORESTIVE
LONGANIMITY
LONGINQUITY
LONGLASTING
LONGRUNNING
LOUISIANIAN
LUBRICATION
LUXULYANITE
MACHINATION
MAGISTERIAL
MAGLEMOSIAN
MAGNANIMITY
MALAPROPISM
MALEDICTION
MALEFACTION
MALFUNCTION
MALPRACTICE
MANCIPATION
MANEUVERING
MANUMISSION
MARGINALIST
MARGINALIZE
MASCULINITY
MASTICATION
MATERIALISE
MATERIALISM
MATERIALIST
MATERIALIZE
MATHEMATICS
MATRIMONIAL
MAURETANIAN
MAURITANIAN
MEGATHERIUM
MEKHITARIST
MENDELEVIUM
MENSURATION

MERCHANDISE
MERCHANDIZE
MERRYMAKING
METAPHYSICS
METRICATION
MICHURINISM
MICTURITION
MILLIONAIRE
MINIATURIST
MINIATURIZE
MINISTERIAL
MINISTERING
MISBEHAVIOR
MISIDENTIFY
MISSPELLING
MOCKINGBIRD
MOLESTATION
MOMENTARILY
MONCHIQUITE
MONEYMAKING
MONOPSONIST
MONOTHELITE
MONSTROSITY
MONTESQUIEU
MONTGOLFIER
MOXIBUSTION
MUDSLINGING
MULTIRACIAL
MURMURATION
MYCOPHAGIST
NATIONALISM
NATIONALIST
NATIONALITY
NATIONALIZE
NECESSARILY
NEEDLEPOINT
NEEDLESTICK
NEGOTIATING
NEGOTIATION
NEIGHBORING
NEUROLOGIST
NEVERENDING
NEWSCASTING
NIGHTMARISH
NIKETHAMIDE
NIPFARTHING
NONDESCRIPT
NOTOTHERIUM
NOVELETTISH
NUMISMATICS
NUMISMATIST
OBJECTIVITY
OBSERVATION
OBSTRICTION
OBSTRUCTION
OBSTRUCTIVE
OPPORTUNISM
OPPORTUNIST
OPPORTUNITY
OPTOMETRIST
ORCHESTRINA
ORCHESTRION
ORGANIZAION
ORIENTALIST
ORIENTATION
ORIGINALITY
ORIGINATING
ORIGINATION
OSCILLATION
OSTENTATION
OUTSTANDING
OVERBEARING
OVERFISHING
OVERFLOWING
OVERHANGING
OVERLAPPING
OVERMANNING
OVERTURNING
OVERWEENING
OXODIZATION
PAEDIATRICS
PAINKILLING
PAINSTAKING
PALESTINIAN
PANDEMONIUM
PARACHUTIST
PARTICIPIAL
PARTURITION
PARVANIMITY
PATERNALISM
PATHOLOGIST
PATRONISING
PATRONIZING
PECULIARITY
PELARGONIUM
PENETRATING
PENETRATION
PENITENTIAL
PERCOLATION
PERDUELLION
PERESTROIKA
PERFORATION
PERICARDIUM
PERIGORDIAN
PERISTALITH
PERMUTATION
PERSECUTION
PERSEVERING
PERSONALIST
PERSONALITY
PERSONALIZE
PERSONIFIED
PERSPECTIVE
PERSPICUITY
PERTINACITY
PHILATELIST
PHILLIPSITE
PHILOLOGIST
PHONETICIAN
PHOTOCOPIER
PHOTOFINISH
PIEDMONTITE
PIERREPOINT
PISCATORIAL
PLANETARIUM
PLATYRRHINE
PLEBEIANISE
POLLINATION
POLTERGEIST
PORTLANDIAN
PORTRAITIST
POSSIBILITY
PRECONCEIVE
PREDICATIVE
PREJUDICIAL
PRELIBATION
PREMONITION
PREOCCUPIED
PREPARATION
PREPOSITION
PREROGATIVE
PRESTISSIMO
PRESUMPTION
PRESUMPTIVE
PRETERITION
PRIMIGENIAL
PRISCIANIST
PROBABILITY
PROCREATION
PRODIGALISE
PRODIGALITY
PROGRESSION
PROGRESSIVE
PROHIBITION
PROHIBITIVE
PROLETARIAN
PROLETARIAT
PROLOCUTION
PROMISCUITY
PROPAGATION
PROPINQUITY
PROPOSITION
PROROGATION
PROSECUTION
PROSELYTISM
PROSELYTIZE
PROSPECTIVE
PROSTHETICS
PROSTRATION
PROTAGONIST
PROTRACTING
PROTRACTION
PROVOCATION
PROVOCATIVE
PUBLICATION
PUNCTUALITY
PUNCTUATION
QUADRENNIAL
QUADRENNIUM
QUALITATIVE
QUARRELLING
QUESTIONING
RABELAISIAN
RADIOACTIVE
RADIOLOGIST
RAPSCALLION
RASTAFARIAN
RATIONALITY
RATIONALIZE
READABILITY
REALIZATION
REANIMATION
REBARBATIVE
RECANTATION
RECEPTIVITY
RECIPROCITY
RECLAMATION
RECOGNITION
RECONDITION
REFORMATION
REGISTERING
REITERATION
RELIABILITY
REPUDIATION
REQUISITION
RESERVATION
RESIDENTIAL
RESIGNATION
RESISTIVITY
RESPIRATION
RESTITUTION
RESTORATION
RESTORATIVE
RESTRICTION
RESTRICTIVE
RETALIATION
RETARDATION
RETRIBUTION
RETRIBUTIVE
RETROACTIVE
REVALUATION
REVERENTIAL
REVISIONISM
ROMANTICISM
ROMANTICIZE
ROSICRUCIAN
RUMFRUCTION
RUMGUMPTION
SABBATARIAN
SACRIFICIAL
SAGITTARIUS
SALVADORIAN
SAXOPHONIST
SCAFFOLDING
SCATTERLING
SCHRECKLICH
SCIREFACIAS
SCOPOLAMINE
SCRIPTORIUM
SECONDARILY
SECRETARIAL
SECRETARIAT
SEGREGATION
SELECTIVITY
SELFSERVICE
SENSIBILITY
SENSITIVITY
SEPIOSTAIRE
SEPTENARIUS
SEPTENTRION
SERENDIPITY
SESQUIOXIDE
SHEATHKNIFE
SHOPLIFTING
SHORTCOMING
SHOWJUMPING
SHUNAMITISM
SIGHTSEEING
SILLIMANITE
SILVERSMITH
SINGLESTICK
SINGULARITY
SLUMGULLION
SMITHSONIAN
SMITHSONITE
SMOULDERING
SNORKELLING
SOCIABILITY
SOCIOLOGIST
SOLILOQUIZE
SOROPTIMIST
SPACESAVING
SPECULATION
SPECULATIVE
SPENDTHRIFT
SPERMOPHILE
SPESSARTITE
SPLUTTERING
SPONTANEITY
STAGFLATION
STANDARDIZE
STANDOFFISH
STIMULATION
STIPULATION
STOCKTAKING
STRADUARIUS
STYLIZATION
STYLOPODIUM
STYMPHALIAN
SUBDIVISION
SUBJUGATION
SUBJUNCTIVE
SUBLIMATION
SUBPANATION
SUBSTANTIAL
SUBSTANTIVE
SUBTRACTION
SUFFOCATING
SUFFOCATION
SUITABILITY

SUPERFICIAL
SUPERFICIES
SUPERFLUITY
SUPERIORITY
SUPERLATIVE
SUPERSCRIBE
SUPERVISION
SUPPOSITION
SUPPRESSION
SUPPURATION
SURROUNDING
SUSURRATION
SYNCHRONISE
SYNCHRONISM
SYNCHRONIZE
SYNCOPATION
SYNDICALISM
SYNDICATION
SYSTEMATIZE
TACITURNITY
TANGIBILITY
TANTALIZING
TAUROBOLIUM
TAXIDERMIST
TELEPHONIST
TEMPORARILY
TERMINATION
TERREMOTIVE
TERRESTRIAL
TERRITORIAL
TESTIMONIAL
THALIDOMIDE
THEOBROMINE
THREATENING
THUNDERBIRD
TIDDLEYWINK
TIMBROPHILY
TIMEKEEPING
TIMESHARING
TIRONENSIAN
TITILLATION
TOBACCONIST
TOBOGGANING
TORRIDONIAN
TOSTICATION
TOURBILLION
TOXOPHILITE
TRANQUILITY
TRANSACTION
TRANSFUSION
TRANSLATION
TREPIDATION
TRESPASSING
TRIBULATION
TRIMESTRIAL
TRINIDADIAN
TRINITARIAN
TRITAGONIST
TYPESETTING
TYRONENSIAN
ULTRAMARINE
UNASSERTIVE
UNBEFITTING
UNCHRISTIAN
UNDEMANDING
UNDERTAKING
UNDESERVING
UNDIGNIFIED
UNFLINCHING
UNIFICATION
UNJUSTIFIED
UNOBTRUSIVE
UNQUALIFIED
UNREASONING
UNRELENTING
UNREMITTING
UNSATISFIED
UNSHRINKING
UNSPECIFIED
UNWELCOMING
UTILITARIAN
UTILIZATION
VACCINATION
VACILLATING
VACILLATION
VALEDICTION
VARANGARIAN
VARIABILITY
VARIEGATION
VARIOLATION
VENDEMIAIRE
VENTILATION
VERMICULITE
VERSATILITY
VINBLASTINE
VINCRISTINE
VINDICATION
VIVISECTION
VOLUNTARILY
VOTERIGGING
WAINSCOTING
WAREHOUSING
WATERSKIING
WELLMEANING
WESTPHALIAN
WHITEBOYISM
WIDERANGING
WINDSURFING
WISHTONWISH
WITHERSHINS
WITHHOLDING
WOODCARVING
WORKMANLIKE
WORKSTATION
XENODOCHIUM
ZOROASTRIAN
THINGAMAJIG
THINGUMAJIG
BLOODSUCKER
BUSHWHACKER
DEERSTALKER
DREADLOCKED
EARTHSHAKER
FERNITICKLE
FIELDWORKER
FREETHINKER
GODFORSAKEN
HALBSTARKER
HEARTBROKEN
HONEYSUCKLE
HYPERMARKET
ILLYWHACKER
INDEXLINKED
INTERLEUKIN
KALASHNIKOV
KWASHIORKOR
LOUDSPEAKER
METALWORKER
PINNYWINKLE
PRZEWALSKIS
RETROROCKET
SHIPWRECKED
SLEEPWALKER
SPANGCOCKLE
SPITSTICKER
STOCKBROKER
SUPERMARKET
SUPERTANKER
SVARABHAKTI
TIGGYWINKLE
UNDERCOOKED
VOORTREKKER
WASTEBASKET
WINDBREAKER
ADVERBIALLY
ASPERGILLUM
ASPERGILLUS
BACCHANALIA
BARBASTELLE
BASKERVILLE
BEAUTIFULLY
BLACKFELLOW
BLACKMAILER
BRAZZAVILLE
CATERPILLAR
CAUSTICALLY
CHANTARELLE
CHANTERELLE
CHRONICALLY
CLAPPERCLAW
COACHFELLOW
COMESTIBLES
COMPTROLLER
CONSUMABLES
CONTINUALLY
CONVOLVULUS
COUNTERGLOW
CRATERELLUS
CREPUSCULAR
CRESTFALLEN
CYCLOSTYLED
DARDANELLES
DECEITFULLY
DEGRINGOLER
DISGRUNTLED
DISHEVELLED
DRACUNCULUS
DRASTICALLY
EFFECTUALLY
EMMENTHALER
EMOTIONALLY
EQUIVOCALLY
ERRATICALLY
ESSENTIALLY
FANATICALLY
FINANCIALLY
FOTHERGILLA
FRANTICALLY
FRATERNALLY
FRIGHTFULLY
GENERICALLY
GENETICALLY
GIBBERELLIN
GLOSSOLALIA
GRAPHICALLY
HAEMOPHILIA
HOSPITALLER
IDENTICALLY
IDIOTICALLY
IDYLLICALLY
ILLOGICALLY
IMPARTIALLY
INVINCIBLES
ITHYPHALLIC
ITHYPHALLUS
LACONICALLY
MARSHMALLOW
MASTERFULLY
MEDICINALLY
MEGALOPOLIS
MELANCHOLIA
MELANCHOLIC
MEMORABILIA
NUMERICALLY
ORGANICALLY
PACIFICALLY
PASSACAGLIA
PASTEURELLA
PASTOURELLE
PENTHESILEA
PENTONVILLE
PERENNIALLY
PERPETUALLY
PETRODOLLAR
POLITICALLY
POTENTIALLY
PRACTICALLY
PRINCIPALLY
PROSAICALLY
PSYCHEDELIC
PSYCHODELIC
PUNCHINELLO
RATATOUILLE
RECTANGULAR
REGRETFULLY
RESENTFULLY
RETINACULUM
RIGHTANGLED
ROCKEFELLER
SAINTPAULIA
SATIRICALLY
SCEPTICALLY
SCEUOPHYLAX
SELAGINELLA
SKEPTICALLY
SKILLIGALEE
SKILLIGOLEE
SORROWFULLY
SPECTACULAR
SPIRITUALLY
STEAMROLLER
STORYTELLER
STROPHILLUS
TABERNACLES
TAGLIATELLE
TATTERSALLS
TECHNICALLY
TEETOTALLER
TEGUCICALPA
TESSARAGLOT
THERMOPYLAE
THUNDERCLAP
TORTICOLLIS
TORTICULLUS
TRICHINELLA
TRINCOMALEE
ULTRAVIOLET
UNCONCEALED
UNFULFILLED
UNIVERSALLY
UNNATURALLY
UNSCHEDULED
UNTRAMELLED
VIOLINCELLO
VIOLONCELLO
WHITECOLLAR
WONDERFULLY
AERODYNAMIC
AIRCRAFTMAN
ASSEMBLYMAN
BARNSTORMER
BARTHOLOMEW
BORBORYGMUS
BREADCRUMBS
BUSINESSMAN
CALLISTEMON
CATACLYSMIC
CONGRESSMAN
CONTRETEMPS
DRAUGHTSMAN

ENDOTHERMIC
FRENCHWOMAN
FRENCHWOMEN
GASTRONOMIC
GENTLEWOMAN
HOMOTHERMAL
HOMOTHERMIC
HYPOTHERMIA
INFANTRYMAN
LARYNGISMUS
LOGARITHMIC
MERCHANTMAN
MONOGRAMMED
NEEDLEWOMAN
NOSTRADAMUS
OVERWHELMED
PARACETAMOL
POLICEWOMAN
RUDESHEIMER
SEPTICAEMIA
SPOKESWOMAN
SPORTSWOMAN
SWORDSWOMAN
TRANSFORMED
TRANSFORMER
TRENCHERMAN
TRIPTOLEMUS
UNCONFIRMED
VOLKSKAMMER
WASHERWOMAN
WITENAGEMOT
ACCOUNTANCY
ACCRESCENCE
ADOLESCENCE
AGUARDIENTE
AMBIVALENCE
ANTECEDENCE
ANTHOCYANIN
ANTIRRHINUM
ANTISTHENES
ASTRINGENCY
BANDEIRANTE
BATTLEMENTS
BENEVOLENCE
BOTANOMANCY
BREADWINNER
BROBDINGNAG
CANDESCENCE
CAPACITANCE
CINQUECENTO
COALESCENCE
COEXISTENCE
COGNOSCENTE
COGNOSCENTI
COINCIDENCE
COLLECTANEA
COMEUPPANCE
COMMONSENSE
COMPLACENCY
COMPLIMENTS
CONCORDANCE
CONCURRENCE
CONDITIONAL
CONDITIONER
CONSEQUENCE
CONSERVANCY
CONSILIENCE
CONSISTENCE
CONSISTENCY
CONSTRAINED
CONSULTANCY
CONTINGENCE
CONTINGENCY
CONTINUANCE
CONTRIVANCE
CONTUBERNAL
CONVENIENCE
CONVERGENCE
COUNTENANCE
CRACOVIENNE
CRITHOMANCY
DELINQUENCY
DELIVERANCE
DEMONOMANIA
DEMOSTHENES
DEMOSTHENIC
DESCENDANTS
DESPONDENCY
DIMENSIONAL
DIRECTIONAL
DISCIPLINED
DISCONTINUE
DISCREPANCY
DISINCLINED
DISTURBANCE
EDUCATIONAL
EMPYROMANCY
ENCUMBRANCE
ENLIGHTENED
ENTERTAINER
EQUIVALENCE
EXCEPTIONAL
EXCRESCENCE
EXECUTIONER
EXORBITANCE
EXTORTIONER
FLAMBOYANCE
FLAMBOYANTE
FORBEARANCE
FORBIDDANCE
FRAUDULENCE
FREEMASONRY
FRONTRUNNER
FURNISHINGS
FURTHERANCE
GENTLEMANLY
GUADALCANAL
HABILIMENTS
HALLEFLINTA
HAREBRAINED
HINDERLANDS
HONEYMOONER
HOOTANANNIE
HOOTENANNIE
ICHTHYORNIS
IMPASSIONED
IMPEDIMENTA
INCOHERENCE
INCONSTANCY
INFREQUENCY
INGREDIENTS
INHABITANTS
INHERITANCE
INSOUCIANCE
INSTRUMENTS
INTENTIONAL
INTERCHANGE
INTERREGNUM
INTOLERANCE
IPECACUANHA
IRIDESCENCE
IRRELEVANCE
IRREVERENCE
JACQUEMINOT
KLEPTOMANIA
MAINTENANCE
MALEVOLENCE
MALFEASANCE
MASKALLONGE
MEANDERINGS
MEDIASTINUM
MEGALOMANIA
MEGALOMANIC
MISALLIANCE
MISDEMEANOR
MONTMORENCY
MUNIFICENCE
MUSKELLUNGE
NETHERLANDS
NETHERLINGS
NIERSTEINER
NONCHALANCE
NONFEASANCE
NUTRITIONAL
NYMPHOMANIA
OMNIPOTENCE
OMNISCIENCE
ONEIRODYNIA
ONEIROMANCY
OPALESCENCE
OPERATIONAL
OUTDISTANCE
OUTPOURINGS
OVERBALANCE
OVERLEARNED
PARABOLANUS
PARISHIONER
PERCIPIENCE
PERFORMANCE
PERSISTENCE
PHILIPPINES
PITCHBLENDE
PLANTAGENET
POCOCURANTE
POLYTECHNIC
PREDESTINED
PREEMINENCE
PREPOLLENCE
PRIZEWINNER
PROBATIONER
PROCEEDINGS
PROFICIENCY
PROMOTIONAL
PROVISIONAL
PROVISIONER
RALLENTANDO
REASSURANCE
RECESSIONAL
REMEMBRANCE
RENAISSANCE
RESEMBLANCE
RHABDOMANCY
RIFACIMENTO
SALTIMBANCO
SALVOGUNNER
SAPROLEGNIA
SCRIMSHANDY
SELFDEFENCE
SEMPITERNAL
SEMPITERNUM
SENSATIONAL
SEVENTEENTH
SHORTCHANGE
SKIDBLADNIR
SNICKERSNEE
SOVEREIGNTY
STREAMLINED
STRUTHIONES
SUBMERGENCE
SUBSISTENCE
SUFFICIENCY
TECTIBRANCH
TIMBROMANIA
TRADITIONAL
TRANSURANIC
TWELVEMONTH
UNCERTAINTY
UNCONCERNED
UNDERMANNED
UNDERSIGNED
UNEMOTIONAL
UNEXPLAINED
UNSWEETENED
VARSOVIENNE
VESPERTINAL
WELLDEFINED
WHISKERANDO
ACINACIFORM
ACRIMONIOUS
ADVENTUROUS
AFTERSCHOOL
AGROSTOLOGY
ALBUGINEOUS
AMMOPHILOUS
AMPHIBOLOGY
ANDROGENOUS
ANFRACTUOUS
ANTHONOMOUS
ANTICYCLONE
APLANOSPORE
ARCHAEOLOGY
ARRHENOTOKY
ARTHROSPORE
ATHERMANOUS
ATRABILIOUS
AVOIRDUPOIS
BATTLEFRONT
BLADDERWORT
BLASPHEMOUS
BLUNDERBORE
BRISTLECONE
BROTHERHOOD
BUMBERSHOOT
CACOPHONOUS
CAMPANOLOGY
CAPRICCIOSO
CARNAPTIOUS
CARNIVOROUS
CEREMONIOUS
CHARACINOID
CHEESECLOTH
CHEIROGNOMY
CHOCKABLOCK
CHORDOPHONE
CIRCULATORY
CLIMATOLOGY
CLINOCHLORE
COBBLESTONE
COMPENDIOUS
CONDOTTIORE
CONSPICUOUS
CONTENTIOUS
CONVULSIONS
CORNERSTONE
COUNTERFOIL
COUNTERFORT
CRIMINOLOGY
CURNAPTIOUS
CYMOPHANOUS
DECLAMATORY
DECORATIONS
DELETERIOUS
DERMATOLOGY
DEUTERONOMY
DICEPHALOUS
DIPROTODONT
DOLABRIFORM
DOUBLECROSS
EASTERNMOST
EFFICACIOUS

ENCEPHALOMA
ENCHONDROMA
EPIDIASCOPE
ESCHATOLOGY
ESTRAMAZONE
EUCALYPTOLE
EXPEDITIOUS
EXPLANATORY
EXPLORATORY
EXTROGENOUS
FARINACEOUS
FARRAGINOUS
FARTHERMOST
FILAMENTOUS
FLAVOURSOME
FLIRTATIOUS
FORTUNELOUD
FOUNDATIONS
FURTHERMORE
FURTHERMOST
FURTHERSOME
GASTRECTOMY
GERONTOLOGY
GLIMMERGOWK
GORDONSTOUN
GYNAECOLOGY
HAEMORRHOID
HAMMERCLOTH
HARPSICHORD
HECKELPHONE
HEPATOSCOPY
HERBIVOROUS
HERPETOLOGY
HERRINGBONE
HOMOGENEOUS
HUNDREDFOLD
IGNOMINIOUS
ILLUSTRIOUS
IMPECUNIOUS
INCONGRUOUS
INCREDULOUS
INDUSTRIOUS
INJUDICIOUS
INSECTIVORE
INTRAVENOUS
IRRELIGIOUS
KINCHINMORT
LATERITIOUS
LENTIGINOSE
LIVINGSTONE
LYCANTHROPE
LYCANTHROPY
LYCHNOSCOPE
MAGNANIMOUS
MAISTERDOME
MALAKATOONE
MAQUILADORA
MELLIFLUOUS
MENDELSSOHN
MERITORIOUS
METEOROLOGY
METHODOLOGY
MISANTHROPE
MISANTHROPY
MISCHIEVOUS
MONOCHINOUS
MOUNTAINOUS
NECESSITOUS
OBSERVATORY
ODONTOPHORE
OMMATOPHORE
OPPROBRIOUS
ORNITHOLOGY
OVERZEALOUS
PAMPELMOOSE
PARAMASTOID
PARATYPHOID
PEDETENTOUS
PERFUNCTORY
PERISSOLOGY
PERSPICUOUS
PHRASEOLOGY
PHYSIOGNOMY
PICKYOUROWN
PLAGIOSTOMI
POMPELMOOSE
POSSESSIONS
PRECAUTIONS
PRECIPITOUS
PREMONITORY
PREPARATORY
PRESTIGIOUS
PRETENSIONS
PRETENTIOUS
PROFITEROLE
PROGNATHOUS
PROMISCUOUS
PUNCTILIOUS
QUARRELSOME
RAMGUNSHOCH
REFLEXOLOGY
REFORMATORY
REPETITIOUS
RESPIRATORY
RESPONSIONS
RETALIATORY
RETINOSPORA
REVELATIONS
REVOLUTIONS
RINTHEREOUT
ROTTENSTONE
RUMBUSTIOUS
SANDERSWOOD
SAPONACEOUS
SCALPRIFORM
SCARABAEOID
SCATTERGOOD
SCHISTOSOMA
SCHISTOSOME
SCIENTOLOGY
SCOLECIFORM
SCRUMPTIOUS
SCUPPERNONG
SCYPHISTOMA
SENTENTIOUS
SEVERALFOLD
SHITTIMWOOD
SHOWERPROOF
SHUTTLECOCK
SMORGASBORD
SPATTERDOCK
SPONTANEOUS
STEGANOPODE
STENOCHROME
STEREOSCOPE
STETHOSCOPE
STRAMINEOUS
STROBOSCOPE
STRONGYLOID
SUBITANEOUS
SUPERFLUOUS
SUPERIMPOSE
SUPERVISORY
SUPPOSITORY
TAUTOCHRONE
TEMPESTUOUS
TENDENTIOUS
TENTERHOOKS
TERMINOLOGY
TERPSICHORE
THAUMATROPE
THEATERGOER
THEATREGOER
THISTLEDOWN
THUNDERBOLT
TRACHEOTOMY
TREACHEROUS
TREACHETOUR
TRICERATOPS
TROUBLESOME
TRYPANOSOMA
TRYPANOSOME
UNAMBIGUOUS
UNCONSCIOUS
UNRIGHTEOUS
UNWHOLESOME
VALEDICTORY
VALLAMBROSA
VENTURESOME
VERTIGINOUS
VOLCANOLOGY
VULCANOLOGY
WATERCOLOUR
WATEREDDOWN
WEATHERCOCK
WELLINGTONS
WESTERNMOST
WHITETHROAT
WORLDFAMOUS
YELLOWSTONE
ANTISTROPHE
CALLIGRAPHY
CARTOGRAPHY
CATASTROPHE
CHIROGRAPHY
CHOROGRAPHY
DITTOGRAPHY
DUSTWRAPPER
EOANTHROPUS
ETHNOGRAPHY
GRASSHOPPER
HAGIOGRAPHY
HANDICAPPED
HANDICAPPER
HEMERALOPIA
HIPPOCAMPUS
HOUSEKEEPER
HYPERTROPHY
ICONOGRAPHY
LITHOGRAPHY
MICROSCOPIC
MINESWEEPER
MISSISSIPPI
MOSSTROOPER
ORTHOGRAPHY
PAEDOTROPHY
PALEOGRAPHY
PARATROOPER
PEACEKEEPER
PHOTOGRAPHY
PORNOGRAPHY
RADIOGRAPHY
STAIRCARPET
STENOGRAPHY
STEREOTYPED
STOREKEEPER
STRANDLOPER
SUBMULTIPLE
TACHYGRAPHY
TEENYBOPPER
THOROUGHPIN
TIGHTLIPPED
TOWNSPEOPLE
TREECREEPER
TROUBLESPOT
UNDEVELOPED
UNENVELOPED
WHITECHAPEL
DISCOTHEQUE
PICTURESQUE
PLATERESQUE
PYTHONESQUE
TÉLÉFÉRIQUE
ALIFANFARON
ALLELOMORPH
ANTHESTERIA
ANTINEUTRON
APATOSAURUS
APOLLINARIS
ARCHENTERON
ARRIVEDERCI
ATMOSPHERIC
BADTEMPERED
BALISTRARIA
BARYCENTRIC
BEHAVIOURAL
BELEAGUERED
BLOODSPORTS
BOYSENBERRY
CACOGASTRIC
CALCEOLARIA
CAMARADERIE
CENTUMVIRUS
CHINOISERIE
CHOLESTEROL
CLADOSPORUM
CLANJAMFRAY
CLIMACTERIC
COMPRIMARIO
CONJECTURAL
CONTRAYERVA
CONTROVERSY
CONVALLARIA
COPROSTEROL
DACTYLOGRAM
DIATESSARON
DIATESSERON
DISCOLOURED
ENFOULDERED
ENGHALSKRUG
ENNEAHEDRON
EQUILATERAL
ERIODENDRON
ESPIEGLERIE
GOODNATURED
GRALLATORES
HIGHPOWERED
HUCKLEBERRY
HURTLEBERRY
HYOPLASTRON
ILLMANNERED
INTERCOURSE
INTERSPERSE
IRREGULARLY
ISOELECTRIC
ISTIOPHORUS
KATABOTHRON
KATAVOTHRON
KETAVOTHRON
KILOCALORIE
KOTABOTHRON
LEPIDOSIREN
LINDISFARNE
MARCONIGRAM
MARIONBERRY
MELANOCHROI
MIDDLEMARCH
MISCONSTRUE
MISERICORDE
MULTISTOREY

NEIGHBOURLY
PARANEPHROS
PHILANDERER
PREHISTORIC
PROGENITRIX
PSEUDOMORPH
PSYCHIATRIC
RIDDLEMEREE
ROBESPIERRE
SACHERTORTE
SADDLEHORSE
SCHWARMEREI
SELFCONTROL
SENNACHERIB
SINISTRORSE
STEGANOGRAM
SUPERCHARGE
SUPERCHERIE
SYMPOSIARCH
TETRAHEDRON
THENCEFORTH
TRACASSERIE
TRANSFERRED
TRANSFERRIN
TURBELLARIA
UNCLUTTERED
UNCONQUERED
UNDERCHARGE
UNSHELTERED
UPHOLSTERER
UTRICULARIA
VALLISNERIA
WATERCOURSE
WHEELBARROW
WIENERWURST
WILBERFORCE
WINDLESTRAW
WINTERBERRY
ANADIPLOSIS
ANAESTHESIA
ANAGNORISIS
ANAPLEROSIS
ANASTOMOSIS
ANONYMOUSLY
ANTIPHRASIS
ANTONOMASIA
APONEUROSIS
APOSIOPESIS
ARTHRODESIS
ASSIDUOUSLY
ATROCIOUSLY
AUDACIOUSLY
BANGLADESHI
BIELORUSSIA
BOURGEOISIE
BRUCELLOSIS
CATACHRESIS
CEASELESSLY
CHAIRPERSON
CHRISTMASSY
CIRCUMCISER
CONSCIOUSLY
COURTEOUSLY
CREDULOUSLY
DANGEROUSLY
DELICIOUSLY
DIAPHORESIS
DIARTHROSIS
DINNYHAUSER
DINNYHAYSER
DISIMPRISON
DUNIEWASSAL
DYAESTHESIA
EMBARRASSED
EMPHYTEUSIS
ENARTHROSIS
EPANALEPSIS
EREMACAUSIS
ERRONEOUSLY
FACETIOUSLY
FAULTLESSLY
FEROCIOUSLY
FRIVOLOUSLY
FRUITLESSLY
GAMOGENESIS
GARRULOUSLY
HAIRDRESSER
HARDPRESSED
HEARTLESSLY
HEMIANOPSIA
HILARIOUSLY
HYPOCORISMA
ICONOSTASIS
IMPERIOUSLY
IMPETUOUSLY
INGENIOUSLY
INSIDIOUSLY
INTERGLOSSA
JUDICIOUSLY
LABORIOUSLY
LUXURIOUSLY
MALICIOUSLY
MELODIOUSLY
MERCILESSLY
METAGENESIS
MUNCHHAUSEN
MYXOMATOSIS
NARRAGANSET
NEUTRALISED
NOISELESSLY
NOTORIOUSLY
OFFICIOUSLY
OSTEOPLASTY
OVEREXPOSED
PARABLEPSIS
PARALEIPSIS
PARENTHESIS
PARONOMASIA
PERIPHRASIS
PERISTALSIS
PHTHIRIASIS
PLAGIARISED
POINTLESSLY
PONDEROUSLY
PREDECESSOR
PRESTRESSED
PSITTACOSIS
QUERULOUSLY
RAPTUROUSLY
REAPPRAISAL
RELIGIOUSLY
RIGHTEOUSLY
SAGACIOUSLY
SALACIOUSLY
SALESPERSON
SELFIMPOSED
SHAMELESSLY
SOUNDLESSLY
STOCKHAUSEN
STRENUOUSLY
SUMPTUOUSLY
SYMPATHISER
TASTELESSLY
TCHAIKOVSKY
TELEKINESIS
TENACIOUSLY
THANATOPSIS
THANKLESSLY
THEOPNEUSTY
TRICHINOSED
TSCHERNOSEM
UNANIMOUSLY
UNCIVILISED
UNDISCLOSED
UNDISGUISED
UNEXPRESSED
UNIMPRESSED
UNREHEARSED
UNSURPASSED
VASOPRESSIN
VICARIOUSLY
VICHYSOISSE
VIVACIOUSLY
VORACIOUSLY
WELLADVISED
WELLDRESSED
XEROTRIPSIS
ABBREVIATED
ABIOGENETIC
ACATALECTIC
ACCELERATOR
ACCUMULATOR
ADJUDICATOR
ADULLAMITES
ADULTERATED
AFGHANISTAN
AGONOTHETES
AIGUILLETTE
ANACREONTIC
ANAESTHETIC
ANAPLEROTIC
ANGELOLATRY
ANTIPYRETIC
APOCALYPTIC
ARTICULATED
ARTIODACTYL
ASSIMILATED
AUXANOMETER
AZOTOBACTER
BLAMEWORTHY
BLOCKBUSTER
BODHISATTVA
BRILLIANTLY
BROADCASTER
BULLFIGHTER
BURGOMASTER
CABBALISTIC
CAMPHORATED
CAPACITATOR
CAPERNOITED
CAPERNOITIE
CARBURETTOR
CASTELLATED
CATACAUSTIC
CATALLACTIC
CENTRIPETAL
CENTURIATOR
CESAREWITCH
CHARISMATIC
CHOIRMASTER
CHONDROSTEI
CHRONOMETER
COMMENTATOR
COMPETENTLY
COMPLICATED
CONCILIATOR
CONFIDENTLY
CONSPIRATOR
CONSTIPATED
CONSTRICTED
CONSTRICTOR
CONSTRUCTOR
CONTINENTAL
CONTRIBUTOR
COORDINATED
COORDINATES
CRACKHALTER
CRENELLATED
CRITICASTER
DEBILITATED
DECAPITATED
DENOMINATOR
DETRIMENTAL
DIAPHORETIC
DIFFERENTLY
DIFFIDENTLY
DILAPIDATED
DIORTHORTIC
DISAFFECTED
DISHONESTLY
DISORIENTED
DISSERTATOR
DISTRIBUTED
DISTRIBUTOR
DOWNHEARTED
DYSLOGISTIC
EFFICIENTLY
EMPIRICUTIC
EPITHYMETIC
EUCHARISTIC
EUPHEMISTIC
EVISCERATED
EXAGGERATED
EXASPERATED
EXHILARATED
EXOSKELETON
EXPECTANTLY
EXTROVERTED
FILLIBUSTER
FIRELIGHTER
FLANNELETTE
FORESHORTEN
FORFOUGHTEN
FORTNIGHTLY
FRANKFURTER
FROSTBITTEN
FUNDAMENTAL
GALLIGANTUS
GIGGLEWATER
GODDAUGHTER
GRANDMASTER
GREENBOTTLE
HALFHEARTED
HANDCRAFTED
HANDWRITTEN
HIGHLIGHTER
HIPPOCRATES
HIPPOCRATIC
HISTORIATED
HOMOEOPATHY
HOUSEMASTER
HYDROSTATIC
ILLUMINATED
ILLUSTRATOR
IMPATIENTLY
IMPLEMENTAL
IMPORTANTLY
IMPRUDENTLY
INAUTHENTIC
INCESSANTLY
INCINERATOR
INCORRECTLY
INCREMENTAL
INDIGNANTLY
INDULGENTLY
INFILTRATOR
INSISTENTLY
INTERCEPTOR
INTERCOSTAL
INTERPRETER

INTERRUPTER
INTOXICATED
INTOXIMETER
INTROVERTED
INVIGILATOR
KINDHEARTED
KITCHENETTE
LAMPLIGHTER
LAUNDERETTE
LEATHERETTE
LICKSPITTLE
LONGAWAITED
LONGSIGHTED
LUXURIANTLY
MACROBIOTIC
MAGISTRATES
MALADJUSTED
MANGALSUTRA
MANIPULATOR
MANTELLETTA
MARIONETTES
MASOCHISTIC
MENTHOLATED
MISBEGOTTEN
MODERNISTIC
MOONLIGHTER
NEARSIGHTED
NOMENCLATOR
OBLITERATED
OCHLOCRATIC
OPINIONATED
ORNITHOPTER
ORTHOCENTRE
PANTALETTES
PARACROSTIC
PATERNOSTER
PENTECONTER
PENTECOSTAL
PERIODONTIC
PERIPATETIC
PERITONITIS
PERMANENTLY
PERPETRATOR
PERTINENTLY
PESSIMISTIC
PETITMAITRE
PETTICOATED
PHARYNGITIS
PHILOCTETES
POLIORCETIC
POTAMOGETON
PROMINENTLY
PTERODACTYL
QUARRINGTON
REALPOLITIK
RECONNOITER
RECONNOITRE
RECURRENTLY
RELUCTANTLY
REPRESENTED
SACRAMENTAL
SALPINGITIS
SAPROPHYTIC
SCHECKLATON
SCOUTMASTER
SENTIMENTAL
SHINPLASTER
SKIMMINGTON
SOLIPSISTIC
SOUTHAMPTON
SOUTHWESTER
SPEEDOMETER
SPHRAGISTIC
SPONDYLITIS
STANDPATTER
STEADFASTLY
STEREOMETER
STRINGENTLY
SUFFRAGETTE
SUGARCOATED
SYCOPHANTIC
SYMPATHETIC
SYMPTOMATIC
TELEPRINTER
TESSELLATED
THERAPEUTAE
THERAPEUTIC
THERMOMETER
THROGMORTON
TICKTACKTOE
TIGHTFISTED
TOASTMASTER
TONSILLITIS
TOTALIZATOR
TRAFFICATOR
TRANSMITTED
TRANSMITTER
TRANSPORTED
TRANSPORTER
TRINOBANTES
TRUCULENTLY
TRUSTWORTHY
TYPEWRITTEN
UNAUTHENTIC
UNCASTRATED
UNCOMMITTED
UNCONNECTED
UNCONTESTED
UNCONVERTED
UNDERSTATED
UNDERWRITER
UNINHABITED
UNINHIBITED
UNINITIATED
UNMITIGATED
UNMOTIVATED
UNPATRIOTIC
UNPROTECTED
UNREALISTIC
UNSATURATED
UNSOLICITED
UNSUPPORTED
UNSUSPECTED
UNWARRANTED
VINAIGRETTE
WARMHEARTED
WESTMINSTER
WHISTLESTOP
WHITTINGTON
WINDCHEATER
WITCHDOCTOR
ACUPUNCTURE
AGRICULTURE
AUDIOVISUAL
BANNOCKBURN
BERGSCHRUND
BRANDENBURG
CANDIDATURE
CHIAROSCURO
CONJUNCTURE
CONTRACTUAL
COTTONMOUTH
DECONSTRUCT
DECREPITUDE
DISPLEASURE
DOUROUCOULI
ELECTROCUTE
ENTABLATURE
EXPENDITURE
FORECLOSURE
GLASTONBURY
HARDICANUTE
HYDROMEDUSA
INEFFECTUAL
INGRATITUDE
INOPPORTUNE
INVESTITURE
KOMMERSBUCH
LEGISLATURE
MACERANDUBA
MANUFACTURE
MARLBOROUGH
MECKLENBURG
MOZAMBIQUAN
PAMPELMOUSE
PICKELHAUBE
POLLENBRUSH
POMPELMOUSE
PORTERHOUSE
PORTRAITURE
PROMPTITUDE
PULCHRITUDE
PURPRESTURE
RECONSTRUCT
RESTRUCTURE
SCARBOROUGH
SCUTTLEBUTT
SERICULTURE
SHAFTESBURY
SPRINGHOUSE
STRIKEBOUND
SUMMERHOUSE
TEMPERATURE
THEREABOUTS
TRANSFIGURE
UNDERGROUND
UNDERVALUED
VICISSITUDE
WHEREABOUTS
WORRYTROUGH
YELLOWPLUSH
CLEANSHAVEN
DISAPPROVAL
DISBELIEVER
DRINKDRIVER
LONGSLEEVED
OUTMANEUVER
QUICKSILVER
SCANDANAVIA
SCANDINAVIA
SCREWDRIVER
TRANSCEIVER
WELLBEHAVED
CARRIAGEWAY
CAULIFLOWER
GILLYFLOWER
INTERGROWTH
INTERVIEWEE
INTERVIEWER
UNDERGROWTH
ANAPHYLAXIS
PROPHYLAXIS
BREATHALYSE
CHARGEPAYER
CHLOROPHYLL
COLLENCHYMA
DODECASTYLE
ELECTROLYTE
ERYTHROCYTE
GAMETOPHYTE
JAMAHIRIYAH
LAMMERGEYER
LAMPROPHYRE
SARCENCHYME
THALLOPHYTE
DEMORALIZED
GABERLUNZIE
GENERALIZED
HOMOGENIZED
MACADAMIZED
MEDIUMSIZED
MIDDLESIZED
MOISTURIZER
PRESSURIZED
SCANDALIZED
SPECIALIZED
SPERMATOZOA
SYMPATHIZER
SYNTHESIZED
SYNTHESIZER
UNCIVILIZED
VITAMINIZED
ZWISCHENZUG

11:10

ABECEDARIAN
ACADEMICIAN
AESCULAPIAN
AFGHANISTAN
AIRCRAFTMAN
ALBIGENSIAN
ALCYONARIAN
ALLEGORICAL
ANISOCERCAL
ANTIQUARIAN
APHRODISIAC
ARCHEGONIAL
ARGATHELIAN
ARGENTINIAN
ARTHRAPODAL
ASSEMBLYMAN
ATHERINIDAE
AUDIOVISUAL
AUGUSTINIAN
AURIGNACIAN
BEHAVIOURAL
BELORUSSIAN
BESSARABIAN
BIOCHEMICAL
BLOODSTREAM
BROBDINGNAG
BUPRESTIDAE
BUSINESSMAN
CAMEROONIAN
CAMPESTRIAN
CAROLINGIAN
CARRIAGEWAY
CATEGORICAL
CATERPILLAR
CENTENARIAN
CENTRIFUGAL
CENTRIPETAL
CHILLINGHAM
CLANJAMFRAY
CLAPPERCLAW
CONDITIONAL
CONGRESSMAN
CONJECTURAL
CONTINENTAL
CONTRACTUAL
CONTUBERNAL
COPROPHAGAN
CREPUSCULAR
CROMWELLIAN
CYLINDRICAL
DACTYLOGRAM
DEFERENTIAL
DETRIMENTAL
DICTATORIAL

DIMENSIONAL
DIPHYCERCAL
DIPSOMANIAC
DIRECTIONAL
DISAPPROVAL
DRAUGHTSMAN
DUNIEWASSAL
EDUCATIONAL
EGALITARIAN
EGOTISTICAL
ELECTRICIAN
ELEUTHERIAN
ELIZABETHAN
EPAMINONDAS
EQUILATERAL
EQUINOCTIAL
ERYMANTHIAN
EVANGELICAL
EXCEPTIONAL
EXPONENTIAL
FITZWILLIAM
FRENCHWOMAN
FUNDAMENTAL
FUSTILARIAN
GALLIBEGGAR
GALLOVIDIAN
GALLYBEGGAR
GENTLEWOMAN
GEOMETRICAL
GESTATORIAL
GINGERBREAD
GIRDLESTEAD
GNATHONICAL
GRAMMATICAL
GUADALCANAL
HALFHOLIDAY
HEMOPHILIAC
HETEROSCIAN
HOLOTHURIAN
HOMOTHERMAL
HUMGRUFFIAN
HYDROPHIDAE
IDEOLOGICAL
IMPLEMENTAL
IMPRACTICAL
INCORPOREAL
INCREMENTAL
INEFFECTUAL
INESSENTIAL
INFANTRYMAN
INFLUENTIAL
INTENTIONAL
INTERCOSTAL
JAMAHIRIYAH
JINRICKSHAW
KIMERIDGIAN
LEATHERHEAD
LIBERTARIAN
LILLIPUTIAN
LIQUIDAMBAR

LOUISIANIAN
MAGISTERIAL
MAGLEMOSIAN
MARCONIGRAM
MATRIARCHAL
MATRIMONIAL
MAURETANIAN
MAURITANIAN
MERCHANTMAN
MIDDENSTEAD
MINISTERIAL
MONARCHICAL
MOZAMBIQUAN
MULTIRACIAL
MYCOLOGICAL
NEANDERTHAL
NEEDLEWOMAN
NONSENSICAL
NUTRITIONAL
OBSTETRICAL
ONTOLOGICAL
OPERATIONAL
PALESTINIAN
PANOMPHAEAN
PARADOXICAL
PARAMEDICAL
PARTICIPIAL
PATRIARCHAL
PEDAGOGICAL
PENITENTIAL
PENTECOSTAL
PERIGORDIAN
PETRODOLLAR
PHARISAICAL
PHONETICIAN
PISCATORIAL
POLICEWOMAN
PORTLANDIAN
PORTMANTEAU
PREJUDICIAL
PRIMIGENIAL
PROCRUSTEAN
PROLETARIAN
PROLETARIAT
PROMOTIONAL
PROPHETICAL
PROVISIONAL
PURITANICAL
QUADRENNIAL
RABELAISIAN
RASTAFARIAN
REAPPRAISAL
RECESSIONAL
RECTANGULAR
RECTILINEAR
RESIDENTIAL
REVERENTIAL
RHAPSODICAL
ROSICRUCIAN
SABBATARIAN

SACRAMENTAL
SACRIFICIAL
SALVADORIAN
SAUSAGEMEAT
SCEUOPHYLAX
SCIREFACIAS
SCITAMINEAE
SECRETARIAL
SECRETARIAT
SEMPITERNAL
SENSATIONAL
SENTIMENTAL
SEXOLOGICAL
SINGAPOREAN
SLUMBERWEAR
SMITHSONIAN
SPECTACULAR
SPERMICIDAL
SPOKESWOMAN
SPORTSWOMAN
SPRINGCLEAN
STATISTICAL
STEGANOGRAM
STRATEGICAL
STYMPHALIAN
SUBSTANTIAL
SUBTROPICAL
SUPERFICIAL
SUPERSEDEAS
SWORDSWOMAN
SYMMETRICAL
TERRESTRIAL
TERRITORIAL
TESTIMONIAL
THEOLOGICAL
THEORETICAL
THERAPEUTAE
THERMOPYLAE
THUNDERCLAP
THUNDERHEAD
TIRONENSIAN
TOPLOFTICAL
TORRIDONIAN
TRADITIONAL
TRENCHERMAN
TRIMESTRIAL
TRINIDADIAN
TRINITARIAN
TYRONENSIAN
UNCHRISTIAN
UNEMOTIONAL
UNEQUIVOCAL
UNPRACTICAL
UTILITARIAN
VARANGARIAN
VESPERTINAL
WAPPENSCHAW
WASHERWOMAN
WESTPHALIAN
WHEREWITHAL

WHITECOLLAR
WHITETHROAT
WINDLESTRAW
ZOROASTRIAN
BREADCRUMBS
MACERANDUBA
PICKELHAUBE
SUPERSCRIBE
ACCOUNTANCY
ACCRESCENCE
ADOLESCENCE
AERONAUTICS
AMBIVALENCE
ANTECEDENCE
ARISTOCRACY
ARRIVEDERCI
ASTRINGENCY
BENEVOLENCE
BOTANOMANCY
BUREAUCRACY
CALLANETICS
CANDESCENCE
CANDLESTICK
CAPACITANCE
CENTERPIECE
CENTREPIECE
CESAREWITCH
CHOCKABLOCK
CIRCUMFLECT
CIRCUMSPECT
CLAIRSCHACH
CLIOMETRICS
COALESCENCE
COEXISTENCE
COINCIDENCE
COMEUPPANCE
COMMONPLACE
COMPLACENCY
CONCORDANCE
CONCURRENCE
CONFEDERACY
CONSEQUENCE
CONSERVANCY
CONSILIENCE
CONSISTENCE
CONSISTENCY
CONSULTANCY
CONTINGENCE
CONTINGENCY
CONTINUANCE
CONTRIVANCE
CONVENIENCE
CONVERGENCE
COUNTENANCE
CRACKERJACK
CRITHOMANCY
CYBERNETICS
DECONSTRUCT
DELINQUENCY
DELIVERANCE

DESPONDENCY
DIAGNOSTICS
DIAMONDBACK
DIPLOMATICS
DISCREPANCY
DISTURBANCE
DOUBLECHECK
ELECTRONICS
EMPYROMANCY
ENCUMBRANCE
EQUIVALENCE
EURHYTHMICS
EXCRESCENCE
EXORBITANCE
FLAMBOYANCE
FORBEARANCE
FORBIDDANCE
FRAUDULENCE
FURTHERANCE
GIGGLESTICK
GIGGLESWICK
HISTRIONICS
HYDROPONICS
INCOHERENCE
INCONSTANCY
INFORMATICS
INFREQUENCY
INHERITANCE
INSOUCIANCE
INTOLERANCE
IRIDESCENCE
IRRELEVANCE
IRREVERENCE
KINNIKINICK
KIRKPATRICK
KOMMERSBUCH
LEATHERBACK
LEATHERNECK
LINGUISTICS
MAINTENANCE
MALEVOLENCE
MALFEASANCE
MALPRACTICE
MANTELPIECE
MARKETPLACE
MASTERPIECE
MATHEMATICS
METAPHYSICS
MIDDLEMARCH
MISALLIANCE
MONTMORENCY
MUNIFICENCE
NEEDLESTICK
NONCHALANCE
NONFEASANCE
NUMISMATICS
OMNIPOTENCE
OMNISCIENCE
ONEIROMANCY
OPALESCENCE

OUTDISTANCE
OVERBALANCE
PAEDIATRICS
PERCIPIENCE
PERFORMANCE
PERSISTENCE
PINACOTHECA
PREEMINENCE
PREPOLLENCE
PROFICIENCY
PROSTHETICS
PTOCHOCRACY
QUARTERBACK
QUARTERDECK
RAMGUNSHOCH
REASSURANCE
RECONSTRUCT
REICHENBACH
REMEMBRANCE
RENAISSANCE
RESEMBLANCE
RHABDOMANCY
SALTIMBANCO
SALTIMBOCCA
SCHRECKLICH
SELFDEFENCE
SELFRESPECT
SELFSERVICE
SHUTTLECOCK
SINGLESTICK
SPATTERDOCK
STEEPLEJACK
STICKLEBACK
SUBCONTRACT
SUBMERGENCE
SUBSISTENCE
SUFFICIENCY
SYMPOSIARCH
TECTIBRANCH
WEATHERCOCK
WILBERFORCE
AMONTILLADO
ATHARVAVEDA
COUNTRYSIDE
CRESCENTADE
DECREPITUDE
FANFARONADE
GREGARINIDA
HEMORRHOIDS
HINDERLANDS
INFANTICIDE
INGRATITUDE
INSECTICIDE
LATERIGRADE
LOGGERHEADS
MISERICORDE
NETHERLANDS
NIKETHAMIDE
PITCHBLENDE
PLANTIGRADE
PROMPTITUDE
PULCHRITUDE
RALLENTANDO
RODOMONTADE
SCRIMSHANDY
SESQUIOXIDE
STEGANOPODE
THALIDOMIDE
VICISSITUDE
WHISKERANDO
ABBREVIATED
ACCESSORIES
ACTUALITIES
ADULLAMITES
ADULTERATED
AGONOTHETES
AMELANCHIER
ANAXIMANDER
ANTECHAMBER
ANTIBURGHER
ANTISTHENES
APPEARANCES
APPRENTICED
ARQUEBUSIER
ARTICULATED
ASCLEPIADES
ASSIMILATED
AUXANOMETER
AZOTOBACTER
BACKBENCHER
BACKFIELDER
BADTEMPERED
BARNSTORMER
BARTHOLOMEW
BEACHCOMBER
BELEAGUERED
BELLYTIMBER
BIRDWATCHER
BITTERSWEET
BLACKMAILER
BLOCKBUSTER
BLOODSUCKER
BREADWINNER
BROADCASTER
BROADMINDED
BULLFIGHTER
BURGOMASTER
BUSHWHACKER
CAMOUFLAGED
CAMPHORATED
CAPERNOITED
CASTELLATED
CAULIFLOWER
CHANTICLEER
CHARGEPAYER
CHEERLEADER
CHICKENFEED
CHILDMINDER
CHOIRMASTER
CHONDROSTEI
CHRISTOPHER
CHRONOMETER
CIRCUMCISER
CIRRHIPEDEA
CLEANSHAVEN
CLIFFHANGER
COLDBLOODED
COLLECTANEA
COMESTIBLES
COMPLICATED
COMPTROLLER
CONDITIONER
CONDOLENCES
CONSTIPATED
CONSTRAINED
CONSTRICTED
CONSUMABLES
COORDINATED
COORDINATES
COUNTRIFIED
CRACKHALTER
CRENELLATED
CRESTFALLEN
CRITICASTER
CROSSLEGGED
CULVERINEER
CYCLOSTYLED
DARDANELLES
DEBILITATED
DECAPITATED
DEERSTALKER
DEGRINGOLER
DEMORALIZED
DEMOSTHENES
DEVITRIFIED
DILAPIDATED
DINNYHAUSER
DINNYHAYSER
DISAFFECTED
DISBELIEVER
DISCIPLINED
DISCOLOURED
DISEMBODIED
DISENCUMBER
DISGRUNTLED
DISHEVELLED
DISINCLINED
DISORIENTED
DISREGARDED
DISTRIBUTED
DOWNHEARTED
DOWNTRODDEN
DRAGONNADES
DREADLOCKED
DRINKDRIVER
DUMBFOUNDED
DUSTWRAPPER
EARTHSHAKER
ELECTROLIER
EMBARRASSED
EMBELLISHED
EMMENTHALER
EMPTYHANDED
ENFOULDERED
ENLIGHTENED
ENTERTAINER
ESTABLISHED
ESTABLISHER
EVISCERATED
EXAGGERATED
EXASPERATED
EXECUTIONER
EXHILARATED
EXPERIENCED
EXTORTIONER
EXTROVERTED
FAIRWEATHER
FAULTFINDER
FIDDLEDEDEE
FIELDWORKER
FILLIBUSTER
FIRELIGHTER
FORAMINIFER
FORESHORTEN
FORFOUGHTEN
FOULMOUTHED
FRANKFURTER
FREETHINKER
FRENCHWOMEN
FRONTRUNNER
FROSTBITTEN
FULLBLOODED
GALLIBAGGER
GALLYBAGGER
GATECRASHER
GENERALIZED
GERRYMANDER
GIGGLEWATER
GILLYFLOWER
GODDAUGHTER
GODFORSAKEN
GONFALONIER
GOODNATURED
GRALLATORES
GRANDFATHER
GRANDMASTER
GRANDMOTHER
GRASSHOPPER
GRAVEDIGGER
GREENGROCER
GRENZGANGER
GROUNDSHEET
GROUNDSPEED
HABERDASHER
HAIRDRESSER
HALBSTARKER
HALFBROTHER
HALFHEARTED
HANDCRAFTED
HANDICAPPED
HANDICAPPER
HANDWRITTEN
HARDPRESSED
HAREBRAINED
HEARTBROKEN
HEAVYHANDED
HIGHLIGHTER
HIGHPITCHED
HIGHPOWERED
HIPPOCRATES
HISTORIATED
HOHENLINDEN
HOMOGENIZED
HONEYCOMBED
HONEYMOONER
HOSPITALLER
HOSTILITIES
HOUSEHOLDER
HOUSEKEEPER
HOUSEMASTER
HYPERMARKET
ILLMANNERED
ILLUMINATED
ILLYWHACKER
IMPASSIONED
INDEXLINKED
INDIARUBBER
INFANGTHIEF
INTERPRETER
INTERRUPTER
INTERVIEWEE
INTERVIEWER
INTOXICATED
INTOXIMETER
INTROVERTED
INVINCIBLES
JERRYMANDER
KINDERSPIEL
KINDHEARTED
KRIEGSSPIEL
LAMMERGEIER
LAMMERGEYER
LAMPLIGHTER
LEADSWINGER
LEASEHOLDER
LEPIDOSIREN
LEVELHEADED
LIGHTHEADED
LOGOGRAPHER
LONGAWAITED
LONGSIGHTED
LONGSLEEVED
LOUDSPEAKER
LUXEMBURGER
MACADAMIZED
MAGISTRATES
MALADJUSTED
MARIONETTES
MASQUERADER
MEADOWSWEET

MEDIUMSIZED
MENTHOLATED
METALWORKER
MIDDLESIZED
MINESWEEPER
MINNESINGER
MISBEGOTTEN
MOISTURIZER
MONEYLENDER
MONOGRAMMED
MONTESQUIEU
MONTGOLFIER
MOONLIGHTER
MOSSTROOPER
MOUNTAINEER
MULTISTOREY
MUNCHHAUSEN
NARRAGANSET
NEARSIGHTED
NECROMANCER
NEUTRALISED
NIERSTEINER
OBLITERATED
OPINIONATED
ORNITHOPTER
OUTMANEUVER
OVERCROWDED
OVEREXPOSED
OVERLEARNED
OVERSTUFFED
OVERWHELMED
PAMPHLETEER
PANTALETTES
PARATROOPER
PARISHIONER
PATERNOSTER
PEACEKEEPER
PENNYFATHER
PENTECONTER
PENTHESILEA
PERSONIFIED
PETTICOATED
PETTIFOGGER
PHILANDERER
PHILIPPINES
PHILOCTETES
PHILOSOPHER
PHOTOCOPIER
PLAGIARISED
PLANTAGENET
PREDESTINED
PREOCCUPIED
PRESSURIZED
PRESTRESSED
PRIZEWINNER
PROBATIONER
PROOFREADER
PROVISIONER
QUICKSILVER
RANGEFINDER
RECONNOITER
REFURBISHED
REPRESENTED
RETROROCKET
RIDDLEMEREE
RIGHTANGLED
RIGHTHANDED
RIGHTHANDER
RIGHTWINGER
ROCKEFELLER
RUDESHEIMER
SALVOGUNNER
SCANDALIZED
SCAREMONGER
SCHWARMEREI
SCOUTMASTER
SCREWDRIVER
SELFIMPOSED
SHAREHOLDER
SHINPLASTER
SHIPBUILDER
SHIPWRECKED
SHORTHANDED
SIGHTSCREEN
SKILLIGALEE
SKILLIGOLEE
SLEEPWALKER
SMALLHOLDER
SMOKESCREEN
SNICKERSNEE
SOCKDALAGER
SOCKDOLAGER
SOCKDOLIGER
SOCKDOLOGER
SOUTHWESTER
SPECIALIZED
SPEEDOMETER
SPELLBINDER
SPITSTICKER
SPREADSHEET
STADTHOLDER
STAIRCARPET
STAKEHOLDER
STALLHOLDER
STANDPATTER
STEAMROLLER
STEINBERGER
STEPBROTHER
STEREOMETER
STEREOTYPED
STOCKBROKER
STOCKHAUSEN
STOCKHOLDER
STOCKJOBBER
STOREKEEPER
STORYTELLER
STRAITLACED
STRANDLOPER
STRAPHANGER
STREAMLINED
STRUTHIONES
SUGARCOATED
SUNDRENCHED
SUPERFICIES
SUPERMARKET
SUPERTANKER
SYMPATHISER
SYMPATHIZER
SYMPLEGADES
SYNTHESIZED
SYNTHESIZER
TABERNACLES
TEENYBOPPER
TEETOTALLER
TELEGRAPHER
TELEPRINTER
TESSELLATED
THEATERGOER
THEATREGOER
THERMOMETER
TIGHTFISTED
TIGHTLIPPED
TOASTMASTER
TOPOGRAPHER
TRANSCEIVER
TRANSFERRED
TRANSFORMED
TRANSFORMER
TRANSMITTED
TRANSMITTER
TRANSPONDER
TRANSPORTED
TRANSPORTER
TREECREEPER
TRICHINOSED
TRINCOMALEE
TRINOBANTES
TSCHERNOSEM
TYPEWRITTEN
TYPOGRAPHER
ULTRAVIOLET
UNANNOUNCED
UNBLEMISHED
UNCASTRATED
UNCIVILISED
UNCIVILIZED
UNCLUTTERED
UNCOMMITTED
UNCONCEALED
UNCONCERNED
UNCONFIRMED
UNCONNECTED
UNCONQUERED
UNCONTESTED
UNCONVERTED
UNCONVINCED
UNDERCOOKED
UNDERHANDED
UNDERMANNED
UNDERSIGNED
UNDERSTATED
UNDERVALUED
UNDERWRITER
UNDEVELOPED
UNDIGNIFIED
UNDISCLOSED
UNDISGUISED
UNDISTURBED
UNENVELOPED
UNEXPLAINED
UNEXPRESSED
UNFULFILLED
UNFURNISHED
UNIMPRESSED
UNINHABITED
UNINHIBITED
UNINITIATED
UNJUSTIFIED
UNMITIGATED
UNMOTIVATED
UNPERTURBED
UNPROTECTED
UNPUBLISHED
UNQUALIFIED
UNREHEARSED
UNSATISFIED
UNSATURATED
UNSCHEDULED
UNSHELTERED
UNSOLICITED
UNSPECIFIED
UNSUPPORTED
UNSURPASSED
UNSUSPECTED
UNSWEETENED
UNTRAMELLED
UNVARNISHED
UNWARRANTED
UPHOLSTERER
VITAMINIZED
VOLKSKAMMER
VOORTREKKER
WARMHEARTED
WASHLEATHER
WASTEBASKET
WATERLOGGED
WELLADVISED
WELLBEHAVED
WELLDEFINED
WELLDRESSED
WELLFOUNDED
WESTMINSTER
WHITECHAPEL
WHITLEATHER
WINDBREAKER
WINDCHEATER
WINTERGREEN
WRONGHEADED
XYLOGRAPHER
FESTSCHRIFT
MISIDENTIFY
NORTHCLIFFE
SHEATHKNIFE
SPEECHCRAFT
SPENDTHRIFT
ACKNOWLEDGE
AGROSTOLOGY
AMPHIBOLOGY
ARCHAEOLOGY
ARCHIPELAGO
BEAUMONTAGE
CAMPANOLOGY
CLIMATOLOGY
COUNTERSIGN
CRIMINOLOGY
DERMATOLOGY
ESCHATOLOGY
FURNISHINGS
GERONTOLOGY
GYNAECOLOGY
HAEMORRHAGE
HERPETOLOGY
HUCKSTERAGE
INTERCHANGE
LEFTLUGGAGE
MARIVAUDAGE
MARLBOROUGH
MASKALLONGE
MEANDERINGS
METEOROLOGY
METHODOLOGY
MISCARRIAGE
MUSKELLUNGE
NETHERLINGS
ORNITHOLOGY
OSTREOPHAGE
OUTPOURINGS
PERISSOLOGY
PHRASEOLOGY
PROCEEDINGS
REFLEXOLOGY
SCARBOROUGH
SCIENTOLOGY
SEIGNIORAGE
SHORTCHANGE
SUPERCHARGE
TERMINOLOGY
UNDERCHARGE
VOLCANOLOGY
VULCANOLOGY
WEIGHBRIDGE
WINDOWLEDGE
WORRYTROUGH
ANTISTROPHE
BANGLADESHI
BLAMEWORTHY
CALLIGRAPHY
CALLITRICHE
CANDLELIGHT
CARTOGRAPHY

CATASTROPHE
CHICHEVACHE
CHIROGRAPHY
CHOROGRAPHY
DITTOGRAPHY
DREADNOUGHT
ESCARMOUCHE
ETHNOGRAPHY
FEHMGERICHT
FORETHOUGHT
HAGIOGRAPHY
HEAVYWEIGHT
HOMOEOPATHY
HYPERTROPHY
ICONOGRAPHY
IPECACUANHA
LANDSKNECHT
LIGHTWEIGHT
LITHOGRAPHY
MENDELSSOHN
ORTHOGRAPHY
OVERWROUGHT
PAEDOTROPHY
PALEOGRAPHY
PAPERWEIGHT
PHOTOGRAPHY
PORNOGRAPHY
RADIOGRAPHY
SCHOTTISCHE
SEARCHLIGHT
STENOGRAPHY
STREETLIGHT
TACHYGRAPHY
TETRADRACHM
TRUSTWORTHY
UNDERWEIGHT
WHEELWRIGHT
ABIOGENETIC
ACATALECTIC
AERODYNAMIC
AGORAPHOBIA
ANACOLUTHIA
ANACREONTIC
ANADIPLOSIS
ANAESTHESIA
ANAESTHETIC
ANAGNORISIS
ANAPHYLAXIS
ANAPLEROSIS
ANAPLEROTIC
ANASTOMOSIS
ANTHESTERIA
ANTHOCYANIN
ANTIPHRASIS
ANTIPYRETIC
ANTONOMASIA
APOCALYPTIC
APOLLINARIS
APONEUROSIS
APOSIOPESIS

APPARATCHIK
ARTHRODESIS
ATMOSPHERIC
AVOIRDUPOIS
BACCHANALIA
BALISTRARIA
BARYCENTRIC
BIELORUSSIA
BOURGEOISIE
BRAGGADOCIO
BRUCELLOSIS
CABBALISTIC
CACOGASTRIC
CALCEOLARIA
CAMARADERIE
CAPERNOITIE
CATACAUSTIC
CATACHRESIS
CATACLYSMIC
CATALLACTIC
CHAMBERLAIN
CHAMBERMAID
CHARACINOID
CHARISMATIC
CHINOISERIE
CHRYSAROBIN
CIRRHIPEDIA
CITIZENSHIP
CLIMACTERIC
COMPRIMARIO
COMRADESHIP
CONVALLARIA
COUNTERFEIT
COUNTERFOIL
DEMOGRAPHIC
DEMONOMANIA
DEMOSTHENIC
DIAPHORESIS
DIAPHORETIC
DIARTHROSIS
DIORTHORTIC
DRAGGLETAIL
DYAESTHESIA
DYSLOGISTIC
EMPHYTEUSIS
EMPIRICUTIC
ENARTHROSIS
ENDOTHERMIC
EPANALEPSIS
EPITHYMETIC
EREMACAUSIS
ESCHERICHIA
ESPIEGLERIE
EUCHARISTIC
EUPHEMISTIC
FISHANDCHIP
FLICKERTAIL
GABERLUNZIE
GAMOGENESIS
GASTRONOMIC

GEGENSCHEIN
GIBBERELLIN
GLOSSOLALIA
HAEMOGLOBIN
HAEMOPHILIA
HAEMORRHOID
HEMERALOPIA
HEMIANOPSIA
HIPPOCRATIC
HOMEOPATHIC
HOMOTHERMIC
HOOTANANNIE
HOOTENANNIE
HYDROPHOBIA
HYDROPHOBIC
HYDROSTATIC
HYPOTHERMIA
ICHTHYORNIS
ICONOSTASIS
INAUTHENTIC
INTERLEUKIN
INTERNUNCIO
ISOELECTRIC
ITHYPHALLIC
KILOCALORIE
KLEPTOMANIA
KULTURKREIS
LECTURESHIP
LEGERDEMAIN
LOGARITHMIC
MACROBIOTIC
MASOCHISTIC
MEGALOMANIA
MEGALOMANIC
MEGALOPOLIS
MELANCHOLIA
MELANCHOLIC
MEMORABILIA
METAGENESIS
MICROSCOPIC
MODERNISTIC
MYXOMATOSIS
NYMPHOMANIA
OARSMANSHIP
OCHLOCRATIC
ONEIRODYNIA
ORTHOPAEDIC
OSTEOPATHIC
PALEOLITHIC
PARABLEPSIS
PARACROSTIC
PARALEIPSIS
PARAMASTOID
PARATYPHOID
PARENTHESIS
PARONOMASIA
PARTNERSHIP
PASSACAGLIA
PERIODONTIC
PERIPATETIC

PERIPHRASIS
PERISTALSIS
PERITONITIS
PESSIMISTIC
PHARYNGITIS
PHTHIRIASIS
POLIORCETIC
POLYMORPHIC
POLYTECHNIC
PREHISTORIC
PREMIERSHIP
PROGENITRIX
PROPHYLAXIS
PRZEWALSKIS
PSEUDOLOGIA
PSITTACOSIS
PSYCHEDELIC
PSYCHIATRIC
PSYCHODELIC
REALPOLITIK
RIBONUCLEIC
SAINTPAULIA
SALPINGITIS
SAPROLEGNIA
SAPROPHYTIC
SCANDANAVIA
SCANDINAVIA
SCARABAEOID
SCHOLARSHIP
SENNACHERIB
SEPTICAEMIA
SHOWMANSHIP
SKIDBLADNIR
SOLIPSISTIC
SPHRAGISTIC
SPONDYLITIS
SPONSORSHIP
STRONGYLOID
SUPERCHERIE
SYCOPHANTIC
SYMPATHETIC
SYMPTOMATIC
TACHYCARDIA
TELEGRAPHIC
TELEKINESIS
THANATOPSIS
THERAPEUTIC
THINGAMAJIG
THINGUMAJIG
THOROUGHPIN
TIMBROMANIA
TONSILLITIS
TORTICOLLIS
TRACASSERIE
TRANSFERRIN
TRANSURANIC
TROMPELOEIL
TRUSTEESHIP
TURBELLARIA
TYPOGRAPHIC

TYROGLYPHID
UNAUTHENTIC
UNPATRIOTIC
UNREALISTIC
UTRICULARIA
VALLISNERIA
VASOPRESSIN
WORKMANSHIP
XEROTRIPSIS
ARRHENOTOKY
JABBERWOCKY
PERESTROIKA
RATTLESNAKE
RHEUMATICKY
SPONDULICKS
TCHAIKOVSKY
TENTERHOOKS
WORKMANLIKE
ACCORDINGLY
ACCOUNTABLE
ADVERBIALLY
AILUROPHILE
ALTERNATELY
ANENCEPHALY
ANONYMOUSLY
APPALLINGLY
APPRECIABLE
APPRECIABLY
APPROVINGLY
ARBITRARILY
ASSIDUOUSLY
ATROCIOUSLY
ATTENTIVELY
AUDACIOUSLY
BARBASTELLE
BASKERVILLE
BATTLEFIELD
BEAUTIFULLY
BIBLIOPHILE
BRAZZAVILLE
BRILLIANTLY
CAUSTICALLY
CEASELESSLY
CERTIFIABLE
CHANTARELLE
CHANTERELLE
CHIPPENDALE
CHLOROPHYLL
CHRONICALLY
COCKLESHELL
COLLAPSIBLE
COMBUSTIBLE
COMFORTABLE
COMFORTABLY
COMMENDABLE
COMMENDABLY
COMPETENTLY
CONCEIVABLE
CONCEIVABLY
CONCEPTICLE

CONFIDENTLY
CONSCIOUSLY
CONTENTEDLY
CONTINUALLY
CONVENTICLE
CONVERTIBLE
CORRUPTIBLE
COURTEOUSLY
CREDENTIALS
CREDULOUSLY
CUSTOMARILY
DANGEROUSLY
DECEITFULLY
DECEPTIVELY
DEFENSIVELY
DELICIOUSLY
DESPERATELY
DIFFERENTLY
DIFFIDENTLY
DISCERNIBLE
DISENTANGLE
DISHONESTLY
DISPENSABLE
DISPERSABLE
DODECASTYLE
DOUROUCOULI
DRASTICALLY
EFFECTIVELY
EFFECTUALLY
EFFICIENTLY
ELABORATELY
EMOTIONALLY
ENFORCEABLE
EQUIVOCALLY
ERRATICALLY
ERRONEOUSLY
ESSENTIALLY
ESTRANGHELO
EUCALYPTOLE
EXCEEDINGLY
EXCESSIVELY
EXCLUSIVELY
EXPECTANTLY
EXQUISITELY
EXTENSIVELY
FACETIOUSLY
FANATICALLY
FARTHINGALE
FASHIONABLE
FASHIONABLY
FAULTLESSLY
FERNITICKLE
FEROCIOUSLY
FESTINATELY
FINANCIALLY
FINGERSTALL
FORESEEABLE
FORTNIGHTLY
FORTUNATELY
FOTHERGILLA
FRANTICALLY
FRATERNALLY
FRIGHTFULLY
FRIVOLOUSLY
FRUITLESSLY
GARRULOUSLY
GENERICALLY
GENETICALLY
GENTLEMANLY
GRAPHICALLY
GREENBOTTLE
GROUNDSWELL
HAPHAZARDLY
HEARTLESSLY
HIGHPROFILE
HILARIOUSLY
HONEYSUCKLE
HORNSWOGGLE
HUNDREDFOLD
IDENTICALLY
IDIOTICALLY
IDYLLICALLY
ILLOGICALLY
IMMEDIATELY
IMPARTIALLY
IMPASSIVELY
IMPATIENTLY
IMPERIOUSLY
IMPERMEABLE
IMPETUOUSLY
IMPLAUSIBLE
IMPORTANTLY
IMPREGNABLE
IMPRUDENTLY
IMPULSIVELY
INADVISABLE
INALIENABLE
INCESSANTLY
INCORRECTLY
INDEFINABLE
INDIGNANTLY
INDIVISIBLE
INDIVISIBLY
INDOMITABLE
INDUBITABLE
INDUBITABLY
INDULGENTLY
INELUCTABLE
INEQUITABLE
INESCAPABLE
INESTIMABLE
INEXCITABLE
INEXCUSABLE
INEXCUSABLY
INFLAMMABLE
INGENIOUSLY
INHABITABLE
INNUMERABLE
INQUIRINGLY
INSCRUTABLE
INSEPARABLE
INSIDIOUSLY
INSISTENTLY
INSULTINGLY
INSUPERABLE
INTENSIVELY
INTERMINGLE
INTOLERABLE
INTOLERABLY
INTRACTABLE
INTRICATELY
INTUITIVELY
IRREDUCIBLE
IRREFUTABLE
IRREGULARLY
IRREPARABLE
IRREPARABLY
IRREVOCABLE
JUDICIOUSLY
JUSTIFIABLE
JUSTIFIABLY
LABORIOUSLY
LACONICALLY
LICKSPITTLE
LOGODAEDALY
LUXURIANTLY
LUXURIOUSLY
MALICIOUSLY
MANTELSHELF
MASTERFULLY
MEDICINALLY
MELODIOUSLY
MERCILESSLY
METACARPALS
METATARSALS
MOLLYCODDLE
MOMENTARILY
MONONGAHELA
MUSCHELKALK
NECESSARILY
NEIGHBOURLY
NIGHTINGALE
NOISELESSLY
NOTORIOUSLY
NUMERICALLY
OBJECTIVELY
OBSESSIVELY
OBSTINATELY
OFFENSIVELY
OFFHANDEDLY
OFFICIOUSLY
OPPORTUNELY
ORGANICALLY
PACIFICALLY
PASTEURELLA
PASTOURELLE
PENSIONABLE
PENTONVILLE
PERCEPTIBLE
PERCEPTIBLY
PERENNIALLY
PERMANENTLY
PERMISSIBLE
PERPETUALLY
PERTINENTLY
PHONOFIDDLE
PINNYWINKLE
PISSASPHALT
PLEASURABLE
POINTLESSLY
POLITICALLY
PONDEROUSLY
POTENTIALLY
PRACTICABLE
PRACTICALLY
PREDICTABLE
PREDICTABLY
PREMATURELY
PRESENTABLE
PREVENTABLE
PRINCIPALLY
PROFESSEDLY
PROFITEROLE
PROMINENTLY
PROSAICALLY
PUBLISHABLE
PUNCHINELLO
QUERULOUSLY
RAPTUROUSLY
RATATOUILLE
RAVISHINGLY
RECOVERABLE
RECTIFIABLE
RECURRENTLY
REDOUBTABLE
REGIMENTALS
REGRETFULLY
REGRETTABLE
REGRETTABLY
RELIGIOUSLY
RELUCTANTLY
REPLACEABLE
RESENTFULLY
RESPECTABLE
RESPECTABLY
RESPONSIBLE
RESPONSIBLY
RETRACTABLE
RETRIEVABLE
RIGHTEOUSLY
SAGACIOUSLY
SALACIOUSLY
SATIRICALLY
SCEPTICALLY
SCREAMINGLY
SECONDARILY
SECRETIVELY
SELAGINELLA
SELECTIVELY
SENSITIVELY
SERVICEABLE
SEVERALFOLD
SHAMELESSLY
SKEPTICALLY
SLIGHTINGLY
SORROWFULLY
SOUNDLESSLY
SPANGCOCKLE
SPERMOPHILE
SPIRITUALLY
SPORTSFIELD
STEADFASTLY
STRENUOUSLY
STRETCHABLE
STRINGENTLY
SUBMULTIPLE
SUGGESTIBLE
SUMPTUOUSLY
SUSCEPTIBLE
SUSTAINABLE
SWALLOWABLE
TAGLIATELLE
TARRADIDDLE
TASTELESSLY
TATTERSALLS
TECHNICALLY
TEMPORARILY
TENACIOUSLY
TENTATIVELY
THANKLESSLY
THEATRICALS
THUNDERBOLT
TIGGYWINKLE
TIMBROPHILY
TOWNSPEOPLE
TREASONABLE
TRICHINELLA
TRUCULENTLY
ULOTRICHALE
UNALTERABLE
UNANIMOUSLY
UNAVAILABLE
UNAVOIDABLE
UNAVOIDABLY
UNBREAKABLE
UNCRUSHABLE
UNDESIRABLE
UNDOUBTEDLY
UNDRINKABLE
UNENDURABLE
UNFAILINGLY
UNFAVORABLE
UNFLAPPABLE
UNGETATABLE
UNIVERSALLY
UNNATURALLY
UNPALATABLE
UNPRINTABLE
UNSHAKEABLE
UNSPEAKABLE

UNSTOPPABLE
UNTHINKABLE
UNTOUCHABLE
UNUTTERABLE
UNWITTINGLY
VICARIOUSLY
VIOLINCELLO
VIOLONCELLO
VIVACIOUSLY
VOLUNTARILY
VORACIOUSLY
WENSLEYDALE
WONDERFULLY
CHEIROGNOMY
COLLENCHYMA
DEUTERONOMY
ENCEPHALOMA
ENCHONDROMA
EPICHEIREMA
FLAVOURSOME
FURTHERSOME
GASTRECTOMY
HYPOCORISMA
MAISTERDOME
PHYSIOGNOMY
PLAGIOSTOMI
PRESTISSIMO
QUARRELSOME
SARCENCHYME
SCHISTOSOMA
SCHISTOSOME
SCYPHISTOMA
STENOCHROME
TRACHEOTOMY
TROUBLESOME
TRYPANOSOMA
TRYPANOSOME
UNWHOLESOME
VENTURESOME
WINDOWFRAME
ABANDONMENT
ABRIDGEMENT
ACCIPITRINE
ACHIEVEMENT
ACQUIESCENT
ACRIFLAVINE
ADJOURNMENT
ADVANCEMENT
ADVERTISING
AGGLUTINANT
AGGRAVATING
ALEXANDRINE
ALTERNATING
AMERCIAMENT
AMINOBUTENE
AMPHETAMINE
AMPHISBAENA
AMPHISBOENA
ANTICYCLONE
APOMORPHINE
APPEASEMENT
APPOINTMENT
APPROACHING
APPURTENANT
ARBITRAMENT
ARRANGEMENT
ASSYTHEMENT
ASTONISHING
BACKPACKING
BACKSLIDING
BALLBEARING
BATTLEFRONT
BELLIGERENT
BENEDICTINE
BEREAVEMENT
BERGSCHRUND
BESIEGEMENT
BESTSELLING
BEWILDERING
BLANKURSINE
BOMBARDMENT
BOOKBINDING
BOOKKEEPING
BRISTLECONE
CALCULATING
CALEFACIENT
CALENDERING
CAPTIVATING
CARAVANNING
CHALLENGING
CHARLEMAGNE
CHITTERLING
CHORDOPHONE
CHRISTENING
CIRCULATING
CLAIRVOYANT
CLANDESTINE
COBBLESTONE
COEFFICIENT
COLOURBLIND
COMMANDMENT
COMMUNICANT
COMPARTMENT
COMPILEMENT
COMPLAISANT
CONCEALMENT
CONCOMITANT
CONFINEMENT
CONSIDERING
CONSIGNMENT
CONSTANTINE
CONSTITUENT
CONTAINMENT
CONTAMINANT
CONTEMPLANT
CONTENEMENT
CONTENTMENT
CONTRASTING
CONVULSIONS
CORINTHIANS
CORNERSTONE
COUNSELLING
COUNTERHAND
COUNTERMAND
COUNTERPANE
COUNTERSINK
CRACOVIENNE
CRYSTALLINE
CURTAILMENT
DECORATIONS
DELITESCENT
DEPARTEMENT
DERANGEMENT
DESERPIDINE
DETERMINANT
DETERMINING
DEVASTATING
DEVELOPMENT
DIPROTODONT
DISABLEMENT
DISAGREEING
DISARMAMENT
DISCERNMENT
DISFIGURING
DISOBEDIENT
DISPARAGING
DISQUIETING
DISSEPIMENT
DISTRESSING
DIVORCEMENT
DOMINEERING
DRESSMAKING
DRYCLEANING
DUPLICATING
ELECTROTINT
ELEPHANTINE
EMBOÎTEMENT
EMPIECEMENT
EMPLACEMENT
EMPOWERMENT
ENCHANTMENT
ENCOURAGING
ENCROACHING
ENDORSEMENT
ENFEOFFMENT
ENFORCEMENT
ENGINEERING
ENHANCEMENT
ENJAMBEMENT
ENKEPHALINE
ENLARGEMENT
ENSLAVEMENT
ENTABLEMENT
ENTHRALLING
ENTITLEMENT
ENVIRONMENT
EPINEPHRINE
EPOCHMAKING
EQUIDISTANT
EQUIPOLLENT
ESTRAMAZONE
EVERLASTING
EXPECTORANT
EXTENUATING
EXTRAVAGANT
EYECATCHING
FACTFINDING
FARREACHING
FASCINATING
FINGERPRINT
FLOURISHING
FLUCTUATING
FLUORESCENT
FOOTBALLING
FOOTWASHING
FORECASTING
FOREWARNING
FORTHCOMING
FOUNDATIONS
FRIGHTENING
FRUSTRATING
FULFILLMENT
FUNCTIONING
FUNDRAISING
GARNISHMENT
GELSEMININE
GEOSYNCLINE
GOODLOOKING
GREASEPAINT
HAIRRAISING
HANDWRITING
HANGGLIDING
HARDHITTING
HARDWORKING
HECKELPHONE
HERRINGBONE
HIBERNATING
HIGHRANKING
HORSERACING
HORSERIDING
HUMILIATING
HUSBANDLAND
IDENTIFYING
IGNORANTINE
IMPEACHMENT
IMPERMANENT
IMPERTINENT
IMPROVEMENT
IMPROVIDENT
INADVERTENT
INCALESCENT
INCARNADINE
INCOMPETENT
INCONTINENT
INDEPENDENT
INDIFFERENT
INEFFICIENT
INEXPEDIENT
INFURIATING
INOPPORTUNE
INSINUATING
INSTALLMENT
INTELLIGENT
INTERESTING
INTERLACING
INTERNECINE
INTERVENING
INVOLVEMENT
ISOXSUPRINE
KIDDLEYWINK
LABORSAVING
LAPIDESCENT
LAWBREAKING
LENGTHENING
LINDISFARNE
LIVINGSTONE
LONGLASTING
LONGRUNNING
LUMINESCENT
MAGNIFICENT
MALAKATOONE
MANEUVERING
MEASUREMENT
MERRYMAKING
MINISTERING
MISSPELLING
MONEYMAKING
MUDSLINGING
NAPHTHALENE
NEEDLEPOINT
NEGOTIATING
NEIGHBORING
NEVERENDING
NEWSCASTING
NIPFARTHING
NONEXISTENT
NOURISHMENT
OBMUTESCENT
OBSOLESCENT
OMNIPRESENT
ORCHESTRINA
ORIGINATING
OUTSTANDING
OVERBEARING
OVERFISHING
OVERFLOWING
OVERHANGING
OVERLAPPING
OVERMANNING
OVERPAYMENT
OVERTURNING
OVERWEENING
PAINKILLING
PAINSTAKING
PARLIPOMENA
PARTICIPANT
PATRONISING
PATRONIZING
PEDESTRIANS
PENETRATING

PERSEVERING
PIERREPOINT
PLATYRRHINE
PLEISTOCENE
POLITICIANS
POLYSTYRENE
POSSESSIONS
PRECAUTIONS
PREDICAMENT
PREDOMINANT
PRESTONPANS
PRETENSIONS
PROCUREMENT
PROLEGOMENA
PROTRACTING
PROTUBERANT
QUARRELLING
QUESTIONING
REALIGNMENT
RECRUITMENT
REFRESHMENT
REFRIGERANT
REGISTERING
RELEASEMENT
REMINISCENT
REPLACEMENT
REQUIREMENT
RESPLENDANT
RESPLENDENT
RESPONSIONS
RESTATEMENT
REVELATIONS
REVOLUTIONS
ROTTENSTONE
SCAFFOLDING
SCATTERLING
SCOPOLAMINE
SCUPPERNONG
SELFEVIDENT
SHENANIGANS
SHOPLIFTING
SHORTCOMING
SHOWJUMPING
SIGHTSEEING
SIGNIFICANT
SMITHEREENS
SMOULDERING
SNORKELLING
SPACESAVING
SPLUTTERING
STOCKTAKING
STRIKEBOUND
SUBDOMINANT
SUBSERVIENT
SUDETENLAND
SUFFOCATING
SUPERINTEND
SURROUNDING
SURTARBRAND
SURTURBRAND
SURVEILLANT
SWITZERLAND
TANTALIZING
TAUTOCHRONE
TEMPERAMENT
THEOBROMINE
THREATENING
TIDDLEYWINK
TIMEKEEPING
TIMESHARING
TOBOGGANING
TRACKLEMENT
TRANSILIENT
TRANSLUCENT
TRANSPARENT
TRESPASSING
TYPESETTING
ULTRAMARINE
UNBEFITTING
UNDEMANDING
UNDERGROUND
UNDERTAKING
UNDESERVING
UNFLINCHING
UNIMPORTANT
UNOBSERVANT
UNREASONING
UNRELENTING
UNREMITTING
UNREPENTANT
UNSHRINKING
UNWELCOMING
VACILLATING
VARSOVIENNE
VINBLASTINE
VINCRISTINE
VOTERIGGING
WAINSCOTING
WAREHOUSING
WATERSKIING
WELLINGTONS
WELLMEANING
WIDERANGING
WINDSURFING
WITHERSHINS
WITHHOLDING
WOODCARVING
YELLOWSTONE
ABLACTATION
ABOMINATION
ABSTRACTION
ACCELERATOR
ACCLAMATION
ACCLIMATION
ACCUMULATOR
ACQUISITION
ADJUDICATOR
ADUMBRATION
AFFECTATION
AFFILIATION
AFFIRMATION
AFFLIICTION
AFTERSCHOOL
AGGRAVATION
AGGREGATION
ALIFANFARON
ALLEVIATION
ALTERCATION
ALTERNATION
ANTINEUTRON
APOLLONICON
APPELLATION
APPLICATION
APPROBATION
ARBITRATION
ARCHENTERON
ASSIGNATION
ASSOCIATION
ATTENUATION
ATTESTATION
ATTRIBUTION
AXEROPHTHOL
BELLEROPHON
BENEDICTION
BIFURCATION
BLACKFELLOW
BROTHERHOOD
BUMBERSHOOT
CALCULATION
CALIBRATION
CALLISTEMON
CAPACITATOR
CAPTIVATION
CARBURETTOR
CELEBRATION
CENTURIATOR
CEREBRATION
CHAIRPERSON
CHOLESTEROL
CIRCULATION
COACHFELLOW
COAGULATION
COLLOCATION
COMBINATION
COMMENTATOR
COMMINATION
COMMUTATION
COMPETITION
COMPILATION
COMPOSITION
COMPOTATION
COMPUNCTION
COMPUTATION
CONCILIATOR
CONFUTATION
CONJUGATION
CONJUNCTION
CONNOTATION
CONSOLATION
CONSPIRATOR
CONSTRICTOR
CONSTRUCTOR
CONSUMPTION
CONTRACTION
CONTRAPTION
CONTRIBUTOR
CONURBATION
CONVOCATION
CONVOLUTION
COOPERATION
COPROSTEROL
CORPORATION
CORRELATION
CORRUGATION
COUNTERGLOW
CREPITATION
CRUCIFIXION
CULMINATION
CULTIVATION
DECLAMATION
DECLARATION
DEFOLIATION
DEFORMATION
DEGLUTITION
DEGRADATION
DEHYDRATION
DEIFICATION
DELECTATION
DELICTATION
DELINEATION
DEMARCATION
DEMIBASTION
DENOMINATOR
DEPORTATION
DEPREDATION
DEPRIVATION
DERELICTION
DESCRIPTION
DESECRATION
DESELECTION
DESICCATION
DESIGNATION
DESPERATION
DESTINATION
DESTITUTION
DESTRUCTION
DETESTATION
DEVALUATION
DEVASTATION
DIATESSARON
DIATESSERON
DICOTYLEDON
DIFFRACTION
DISILLUSION
DISIMPRISON
DISJUNCTION
DISLOCATION
DISPOSITION
DISPUTATION
DISSERTATOR
DISSIPATION
DISSOLUTION
DISTINCTION
DISTRACTION
DISTRIBUTOR
DUPLICATION
DYSFUNCTION
ECCALEOBION
EDIFICATION
EJACULATION
ELABORATION
ELIMINATION
ELUCIDATION
EMBARKATION
EMBROCATION
ENCHIRIDION
ENNEAHEDRON
ENUMERATION
ENUNCIATION
ERADICATION
ERIODENDRON
EVAPORATION
EVENTRATION
EXAMINATION
EXCLAMATION
EXHORTATION
EXONERATION
EXOSKELETON
EXPECTATION
EXPLANATION
EXPLORATION
EXPURGATION
EXTENUATION
EXTRADITION
FABRICATION
FASCINATION
FAUXBOURDON
FLUCTUATION
FOMENTATION
FORESTATION
FORMULATION
FORNICATION
FRUSTRATION
FULMINATION
GENUFLEXION
GERMINATION
GRAVITATION
GUBERNATION
HARIOLATION
HIBERNATION
HOBBLEDEHOY
HUMILIATION
HYDROCARBON
HYOPLASTRON
HYPHENATION
HYPOTENSION
IDOLIZATION
ILLUSTRATOR
IMAGINATION
IMMIGRATION

IMPLICATION
IMPORTATION
IMPRECATION
IMPRECISION
INATTENTION
INCANTATION
INCARNATION
INCINERATOR
INCLINATION
INDENTATION
INDIGESTION
INDIGNATION
INEBRIATION
INFATUATION
INFESTATION
INFILTRATOR
INFORMATION
INOCULATION
INQUISITION
INSCRIPTION
INSINUATION
INSPIRATION
INSTIGATION
INSTITUTION
INSTRUCTION
INTEGRATION
INTERACTION
INTERCEPTOR
INVIGILATOR
IRRADIATION
JACQUEMINOT
JACTITATION
KALASHNIKOV
KAMELAUKION
KATABOTHRON
KATAVOTHRON
KETAVOTHRON
KOTABOTHRON
KWASHIORKOR
LAMENTATION
LEGISLATION
LIQUIDATION
LUBRICATION
MACHINATION
MALEDICTION
MALEFACTION
MALFUNCTION
MANCIPATION
MANIPULATOR
MANUMISSION
MARSHMALLOW
MASTICATION
MELANOCHROI
MENSURATION
METRICATION
MICTURITION
MISBEHAVIOR
MISDEMEANOR
MOLESTATION
MOXIBUSTION
MURMURATION
NEGOTIATION
NICKELODEON
NOMENCLATOR
OBSERVATION
OBSTRICTION
OBSTRUCTION
OCTASTICHON
OFFICIALDOM
ONOMASTICON
ORCHESTRION
ORGANIZAION
ORIENTATION
ORIGINATION
OSCILLATION
OSTENTATION
OUAGADOUGOU
OXODIZATION
PARACETAMOL
PARANEPHROS
PARTURITION
PENETRATION
PERCOLATION
PERDUELLION
PERFORATION
PERMUTATION
PERPETRATOR
PERSECUTION
POLLINATION
POTAMOGETON
PREDECESSOR
PRELIBATION
PREMONITION
PREPARATION
PREPOSITION
PRESUMPTION
PRETERITION
PROCREATION
PROGRESSION
PROHIBITION
PROLOCUTION
PROPAGATION
PROPOSITION
PROROGATION
PROSECUTION
PROSTRATION
PROTRACTION
PROVOCATION
PUBLICATION
PUNCTUATION
QUARRINGTON
RADIOCARBON
RAPSCALLION
REALIZATION
REANIMATION
RECANTATION
RECLAMATION
RECOGNITION
RECONDITION
REFORMATION
REITERATION
REPUDIATION
REQUISITION
RESERVATION
RESIGNATION
RESPIRATION
RESTITUTION
RESTORATION
RESTRICTION
RETALIATION
RETARDATION
RETRIBUTION
REVALUATION
RUMFRUCTION
RUMGUMPTION
SALESPERSON
SANDERSWOOD
SCATTERGOOD
SCHECKLATON
SEGREGATION
SELFCONTROL
SEPTENTRION
SHITTIMWOOD
SHOWERPROOF
SKIMMINGTON
SLUMGULLION
SOUTHAMPTON
SPECULATION
SPERMATOZOA
STAGFLATION
STIMULATION
STIPULATION
STOOLPIGEON
STYLIZATION
SUBDIVISION
SUBJUGATION
SUBLIMATION
SUBPANATION
SUBTRACTION
SUFFOCATION
SUPERVISION
SUPPOSITION
SUPPRESSION
SUPPURATION
SUSURRATION
SYNCOPATION
SYNDICATION
TERMINATION
TESSARAGLOT
TETRAHEDRON
THROGMORTON
TICKTACKTOE
TITILLATION
TOSTICATION
TOTALIZATOR
TOURBILLION
TRAFFICATOR
TRANSACTION
TRANSFUSION
TRANSLATION
TREPIDATION
TRIBULATION
TROUBLESPOT
UNIFICATION
UTILIZATION
VACCINATION
VACILLATION
VALEDICTION
VARIEGATION
VARIOLATION
VENTILATION
VINDICATION
VIVISECTION
WATERMEADOW
WHEELBARROW
WHISTLESTOP
WHITTINGTON
WITCHDOCTOR
WITENAGEMOT
WORKSTATION
ALLELOMORPH
CARDIOGRAPH
CONTRETEMPS
EPIDIASCOPE
GUTTERSNIPE
HEPATOSCOPY
LYCANTHROPE
LYCANTHROPY
LYCHNOSCOPE
MISANTHROPE
MISANTHROPY
MISSISSIPPI
NONDESCRIPT
PSEUDOMORPH
SEISMOGRAPH
STEREOSCOPE
STETHOSCOPE
STROBOSCOPE
TEGUCICALPA
THAUMATROPE
TRICERATOPS
ABRACADABRA
ACINACIFORM
ACUPUNCTURE
AGRICULTURE
ANGELOLATRY
ANNIVERSARY
APHANIPTERA
APLANOSPORE
ARTHROSPORE
BANNOCKBURN
BATHYSPHERE
BENEFICIARY
BICENTENARY
BILLIONAIRE
BLADDERWORT
BLUNDERBORE
BOOKSELLERS
BOUTONNIERE
BOYSENBERRY
BRANDENBURG
CANDIDATURE
CARABINIERE
CENTREBOARD
CHANCELLERY
CHAULMOOGRA
CHAULMOUGRA
CHIAROSCURO
CIRCULATORY
CLINOCHLORE
COMSTOCKERY
CONDOTTIERE
CONDOTTIORE
CONJUNCTURE
CORDWAINERS
COULOMMIERS
COUNTERFORT
COUNTERPART
CRÉMAILLÈRE
DECLAMATORY
DEMAGOGUERY
DEUTSCHMARK
DIPTEROCARP
DISPLEASURE
DOCTRINAIRE
DOCUMENTARY
DOLABRIFORM
DRYCLEANERS
EARTHENWARE
ENTABLATURE
EXPENDITURE
EXPLANATORY
EXPLORATORY
FERRONNIÈRE
FISHMONGERS
FORECLOSURE
FOREFATHERS
FRAGMENTARY
FREEMASONRY
FUNCTIONARY
FURTHERMORE
GALLIMAUFRY
GENOUILLÈRE
GLASTONBURY
HARPSICHORD
HEBDOMADARY
HUCKLEBERRY
HUMMINGBIRD
HURTLEBERRY
ILLUSIONARY
INSECTIVORE
INTERCALARY
INVESTITURE
INVOLUNTARY
IRONMONGERS
IRONMONGERY
KILIMANJARO
KINCHINMORT
LAMPROPHYRE
LEGIONNAIRE

LEGISLATURE
LEPIDOPTERA
MANGALSUTRA
MANUFACTURE
MAQUILADORA
MARIONBERRY
MECKLENBURG
MENTONNIÈRE
MILLIONAIRE
MOCKINGBIRD
MORGENSTERN
NICKNACKERY
NOTICEBOARD
NUTCRACKERS
OBSERVATORY
ODONTOPHORE
OMMATOPHORE
ORTHOCENTRE
OSTRACODERM
PAWNBROKERS
PERFUNCTORY
PETITMAITRE
PHALANSTERY
PHOTOSPHERE
PLOUGHSHARE
PODSNAPPERY
PORTRAITURE
PRELIMINARY
PREMONITORY
PREPARATORY
PROPRIETARY
PROTONOTARY
PURPRESTURE
REACTIONARY
RECONNOITRE
REFORMATORY
RESPIRATORY
RESTRUCTURE
RETALIATORY
RETINOSPORA
RHOPALOCERA
ROBESPIERRE
RUDIMENTARY
SCALPRIFORM
SCOLECIFORM
SCOLOPENDRA
SCULDUDDERY
SCULDUGGERY
SEDIMENTARY
SEPIOSTAIRE
SERICULTURE
SHAFTESBURY
SHAKESPEARE
SHOVELBOARD
SKULDUDDERY
SKULDUGGERY
SMORGASBORD
SPRINGBOARD
STIPENDIARY
STRINGYBARK
SUBSTANDARD
SUPERALTERN
SUPERSEDERE
SUPERVISORY
SUPPOSITORY
SWITCHBOARD
TARATANTARA
TEMPERATURE
TERPSICHORE
THUNDERBIRD
TRANSFIGURE
TRICHOPTERA
TROPOSPHERE
ULTRAMODERN
UNNECESSARY
VALEDICTORY
VENDEMIAIRE
VIDEOCAMERA
WHIGMALEERY
WHITEFRIARS
WINTERBERRY
ABORTIONIST
ABSENTEEISM
ACCLIMATISE
ACCOMPANIST
ADOPTIANISM
ADOPTIONISM
ADVENTURESS
AGNOSTICISM
AIRSICKNESS
AMERICANISM
ANACHRONISM
ANESTHETIST
ARTILLERIST
ASPHETERISM
ASTIGMATISM
AWKWARDNESS
BASHFULNESS
BATTLEDRESS
BEASTLINESS
BELLETTRIST
BILIOUSNESS
BLESSEDNESS
BREATHALYSE
BRITTLENESS
CALLOUSNESS
CANNIBALISM
CAPRICCIOSO
CAREFULNESS
CARSICKNESS
CATCHPHRASE
CATHOLICISM
CHIROPODIST
CHRISTMASSY
CHRYSOPRASE
CLEANLINESS
COENOBITISM
COLONIALISM
COLONIALIST
COMFORTLESS
COMMONSENSE
CONCISENESS
CONDUCTRESS
CONSUMERISM
CONTROVERSY
CORRECTNESS
COURTLINESS
COXWAINLESS
CROOKEDNESS
CRYSTALLISE
DEFENCELESS
DEFENSELESS
DEVIOUSNESS
DIPLOMATIST
DISCOURTESY
DISTINGUISH
DITHELETISM
DOUBLECROSS
DRUNKENNESS
DUBIOUSNESS
EARNESTNESS
EASTERNMOST
ELASTOPLAST
ENCHANTRESS
ENFRANCHISE
EPIGENESIST
EQUILIBRIST
ETHNOLOGIST
ETYMOLOGIST
EVASIVENESS
EXTEMPORISE
FAMILIARISE
FARTHERMOST
FATUOUSNESS
FAVOURITISM
FEATURELESS
FLABBERGAST
FOOLISHNESS
FORGIVENESS
FORLORNNESS
FUNAMBULIST
FURTHERMOST
FURTIVENESS
GALLOWGLASS
GENEALOGIST
GENUINENESS
GHASTLINESS
GLADWELLISE
GUTTURALISE
HAUGHTINESS
HEALTHINESS
HELPFULNESS
HIDEOUSNESS
HISTOLOGIST
HOGGISHNESS
HOLLANDAISE
HOOLIGANISM
HORSERADISH
HYDROMEDUSA
HYMNOLOGIST
IDEOPRAXIST
ILLUSIONIST
IMMORTALISE
IMPERIALISM
IMPERIALIST
INTERCOURSE
INTERGLOSSA
INTERSPERSE
IRREDENTIST
LAWLESSNESS
LENGTHINESS
LENTIGINOSE
LETTERPRESS
LITERALNESS
MALAPROPISM
MARGINALIST
MASSIVENESS
MATERIALISE
MATERIALISM
MATERIALIST
MEANINGLESS
MEASURELESS
MEKHITARIST
MERCHANDISE
MICHURINISM
MILQUETOAST
MINIATURIST
MISERLINESS
MODELMOLEST
MONOPSONIST
MYCOPHAGIST
NATIONALISM
NATIONALIST
NATURALNESS
NAUGHTINESS
NERVOUSNESS
NEUROLOGIST
NIGHTMARISH
NONETHELESS
NOTHINGNESS
NOVELETTISH
NUMISMATIST
OBVIOUSNESS
ODONTOBLAST
OFFICIALESE
OPPORTUNISM
OPPORTUNIST
OPTOMETRIST
ORDERLINESS
ORIENTALIST
PAMPELMOOSE
PAMPELMOUSE
PARACHUTIST
PASSIVENESS
PATERNALISM
PATHOLOGIST
PEEVISHNESS
PELOPONNESE
PENSIVENESS
PERCEFOREST
PERSONALIST
PHILATELIST
PHILOLOGIST
PHOTOFINISH
PLAYFULNESS
PLEBEIANISE
POLLENBRUSH
POLTERGEIST
POMPELMOOSE
POMPELMOUSE
PORTERHOUSE
PORTRAITIST
PRICKLINESS
PRISCIANIST
PRODIGALISE
PROFUSENESS
PROSELYTISM
PROTAGONIST
PURPOSELESS
RADIOLOGIST
RAFFISHNESS
RAUCOUSNESS
REMORSELESS
RESTIVENESS
REVISIONISM
ROGUISHNESS
ROMANTICISM
SADDLEHORSE
SAINTLINESS
SAVOURINESS
SAXOPHONIST
SCRUFFINESS
SEASICKNESS
SECONDCLASS
SELFISHNESS
SERIOUSNESS
SHALLOWNESS
SHAPELINESS
SHEPHERDESS
SHUNAMITISM
SINISTRORSE
SKETCHINESS
SLENDERNESS
SOCIOLOGIST
SOROPTIMIST
SPATTERDASH
SPRINGHOUSE
SPRINGINESS
STANDOFFISH
STATELINESS
STRANGENESS
STRETCHLESS
STYLISHNESS
SUMMERHOUSE
SUPERIMPOSE
SYNCHROMESH
SYNCHRONISE
SYNCHRONISM
SYNDICALISM
TAXIDERMIST

TEDIOUSNESS
TELEPHONIST
TENUOUSNESS
THINGLINESS
THOUGHTLESS
THRIFTINESS
TOBACCONIST
TRITAGONIST
TROPHOBLAST
UNCLEANNESS
UNCOUTHNESS
UNGODLINESS
UNHAPPINESS
UPRIGHTNESS
USELESSNESS
VACUOUSNESS
VALLAMBROSA
VICHYSOISSE
VICIOUSNESS
VISCOUNTESS
WAKEFULNESS
WATERCOURSE
WATERSPLASH
WAYWARDNESS
WESTERNMOST
WHITEBOYISM
WIENERWURST
WILLINGNESS
WISHTONWISH
WISTFULNESS
WOMANLINESS
WORLDLINESS
YELLOWPLUSH
ABNORMALITY
ACCOMMODATE
ACOLOUTHITE
AGGLOMERATE
AGGLUTINATE
AGUARDIENTE
AIGUILLETTE
ALEXANDRITE
ANNABERGITE
APOPHYLLITE
APPROPRIATE
APPROXIMATE
ASSASSINATE
AVERRUNCATE
BADDELEYITE
BANDEIRANTE
BARBITURATE
BATTLEMENTS
BENEFICIATE
BICARBONATE
BLOODSPORTS
BREASTPLATE
CAMALDOLITE
CASSITERITE
CERARGYRITE
CERTIFICATE
CHEESECLOTH
CHIASTOLITE
CILOFIBRATE
CINQUECENTO
CITLALEPETL
COGNOSCENTE
COGNOSCENTI
COLLABORATE
COMMEMORATE
COMMISERATE
COMMUNICATE
COMPLIMENTS
CONCENTRATE
CONFABULATE
CONFARREATE
CONFEDERATE
CONSIDERATE
CONSOLIDATE
CONSTELLATE
CONSTERNATE
CONSTUPRATE
CONTAMINATE
CONTEMPLATE
COPPERPLATE
CORROBORATE
COTTONMOUTH
CREDIBILITY
CROCIDOLITE
CULPABILITY
DECORTICATE
DECREPITATE
DEGLUTINATE
DEMONSTRATE
DENDRACHATE
DEPHLEGMATE
DESCENDANTS
DESEGREGATE
DETERIORATE
DIRECTORATE
DISSEMINATE
DISSIMULATE
DOMESTICATE
DOMESTICITY
ELECTRICITY
ELECTROCUTE
ELECTROLYTE
ELIGIBILITY
ENCAPSULATE
ERYTHROCYTE
EVENTUALITY
EXANTHEMATA
EXPECTORATE
EXPOSTULATE
EXPROPRIATE
EXTERMINATE
EXTRAPOLATE
FALLIBILITY
FAMILIARITY
FEASIBILITY
FLAMBOYANTE
FLANNELETTE
FLEXIBILITY
FRANKLINITE
GAMETOPHYTE
GESTICULATE
GREENOCKITE
GUESSTIMATE
GULLIBILITY
HABILIMENTS
HALLEFLINTA
HALLUCINATE
HAMMERCLOTH
HARDICANUTE
HATCHETTITE
HEPPLEWHITE
HIGHQUALITY
HOMOGENEITY
HOSPITALITY
HYPOTHECATE
ICHTHYOLITE
IMMORTALITY
IMPEDIMENTA
IMPERSONATE
IMPETUOSITY
IMPIGNORATE
IMPORTUNATE
IMPROPRIETY
INCAPSULATE
INCARCERATE
INCOMPOSITE
INCONGRUITY
INCORPORATE
INCREDULITY
INCRIMINATE
INFERIORITY
INFERTILITY
INFORMALITY
INGREDIENTS
INHABITANTS
INSINCERITY
INSTABILITY
INSTANTIATE
INSTRUMENTS
INTEMPERATE
INTERGROWTH
INTERPOLATE
INTERRELATE
INTERROGATE
INTREPIDITY
INVESTIGATE
JOSEPHINITE
KITCHENETTE
LAUNDERETTE
LEATHERETTE
LONGANIMITY
LONGINQUITY
LUXULYANITE
MAGNANIMITY
MANTELLETTA
MASCULINITY
MATRICULATE
MEPROBAMATE
MICROGAMETE
MONCHIQUITE
MONOTHELITE
MONOTREMATA
MONSTROSITY
NATIONALITY
NATIONSTATE
NECESSITATE
NUMBERPLATE
OBJECTIVITY
OBTEMPERATE
OLIGOCHAETE
OPPIGNORATE
OPPORTUNITY
ORCHESTRATE
ORIGINALITY
OSTEOPLASTY
PARTICIPATE
PARVANIMITY
PECULIARITY
PENICILLATE
PENTATHLETE
PENULTIMATE
PERAMBULATE
PERCHLORATE
PEREGRINATE
PERISTALITH
PERLUSTRATE
PERSONALITY
PERSPICUITY
PERTINACITY
PHILLIPSITE
PIEDMONTITE
POCOCURANTE
POMEGRANATE
PONTIFICATE
POSSIBILITY
PRECIPITATE
PREDOMINATE
PREMEDITATE
PREVARICATE
PROBABILITY
PRODIGALITY
PROLIFERATE
PROMISCUITY
PROPINQUITY
PUNCTUALITY
QUADRUPLETS
QUINTUPLETS
RATIOCINATE
RATIONALITY
READABILITY
RECEPTIVITY
RECIPROCATE
RECIPROCITY
RECRIMINATE
REDUPLICATE
REFOCILLATE
REFRIGERATE
REGURGITATE
REINCARNATE
RELIABILITY
REMONSTRATE
REORIENTATE
RESISTIVITY
RESUSCITATE
REVENDICATE
REVERBERATE
RIFACIMENTO
SACHERTORTE
SCINTILLATE
SCUTTLEBUTT
SELECTIVITY
SENSIBILITY
SENSITIVITY
SEQUESTRATE
SERENDIPITY
SEVENTEENTH
SILLIMANITE
SILVERSMITH
SINGULARITY
SMITHSONITE
SOCIABILITY
SOVEREIGNTY
SPESSARTITE
SPIFFLICATE
SPIROCHAETE
SPONTANEITY
STELLIONATE
STRANGULATE
SUBORDINATE
SUBUNGULATA
SUFFRAGETTE
SUITABILITY
SUPERFLUITY
SUPERIORITY
SVARABHAKTI
TACITURNITY
TANGIBILITY
THALLOPHYTE
THENCEFORTH
THEOPNEUSTY
THEREABOUTS
THESMOTHETE
TOXOPHILITE
TRANQUILITY
TREPONEMATA
TRIUMVIRATE
TURRICULATE
TWELVEMONTH
UNCERTAINTY
UNDERGROWTH
UNFORTUNATE
VARIABILITY
VERBIGERATE
VERMICULITE
VERSATILITY
VINAIGRETTE
WHEREABOUTS

ACRIMONIOUS
ADVENTUROUS
AESCULAPIUS
ALBUGINEOUS
AMMOPHILOUS
AMPLEXICAUL
ANDROGENOUS
ANFRACTUOUS
ANTEPENDIUM
ANTHONOMOUS
ANTIRRHINUM
APATOSAURUS
APODYTERIUM
APOSTROPHUS
ARBITRAGEUR
ARCHEGONIUM
ARCHILOCHUS
ASPERGILLUM
ASPERGILLUS
ASPERSORIUM
ATHERMANOUS
ATRABILIOUS
BLASPHEMOUS
BORBORYGMUS
CACOPHONOUS
CALIFORNIUM
CARBORUNDUM
CARDOPHAGUS
CARNAPTIOUS
CARNIVOROUS
CENTUMVIRUS
CEREMONIOUS
CLADOSPORUM
CLARENCIEUX
COLUMBARIUM
COMPENDIOUS
CONDOMINIUM
CONNECTICUT
CONNOISSEUR
CONSPICUOUS
CONTENTIOUS
CONVOLVULUS
CRATERELLUS
CREMATORIUM
CURNAPTIOUS
CYMOPHANOUS
DELETERIOUS
DIASCORDIUM
DICEPHALOUS
DISCONTINUE
DISCOTHEQUE
DISGRACEFUL
DISTASTEFUL
DISTRUSTFUL
DRACUNCULUS
EFFICACIOUS
EINSTEINIUM
EMMENAGOGUE
ENDOCARDIUM
ENGHALSKRUG
EOANTHROPUS
EQUILIBRIUM
EXPEDITIOUS
EXTROGENOUS
FARINACEOUS
FARRAGINOUS
FILAMENTOUS
FLIRTATIOUS
FLORILEGIUM
FORTUNELOUD
GALLIGANTUS
GORDONSTOUN
GRAMMALOGUE
HERBIVOROUS
HIPPOCAMPUS
HOMOGENEOUS
IGNOMINIOUS
ILLUSTRIOUS
IMPECUNIOUS
INCONGRUOUS
INCREDULOUS
INDUSTRIOUS
INJUDICIOUS
INTERLINGUA
INTERREGNUM
INTRAVENOUS
IRRELIGIOUS
ISTIOPHORUS
ITHYPHALLUS
LARYNGISMUS
LASERPICIUM
LATERITIOUS
LATIFUNDIUM
LATROCINIUM
LITTÉRATEUR
MACHAIRODUS
MAGNANIMOUS
MEDIASTINUM
MEGATHERIUM
MELLIFLUOUS
MENDELEVIUM
MERITORIOUS
MISCHIEVOUS
MISCONSTRUE
MISTRUSTFUL
MONOCHINOUS
MOUNTAINOUS
NECESSITOUS
NOSTRADAMUS
NOTOTHERIUM
OPPROBRIOUS
OVERZEALOUS
OXYRHYNCHUS
PANDEMONIUM
PARABOLANUS
PEDETENTOUS
PELARGONIUM
PERICARDIUM
PERITONAEUM
PERSPICUOUS
PICTURESQUE
PLANETARIUM
PLATERESQUE
POLYTRICHUM
PRECIPITOUS
PRESTIGIOUS
PRETENTIOUS
PROGNATHOUS
PROMISCUOUS
PROTOCOCCUS
PUNCTILIOUS
PYTHONESQUE
QUADRENNIUM
REPETITIOUS
REPROACHFUL
RESOURCEFUL
RETINACULUM
RINTHEREOUT
RUMBUSTIOUS
SAGITTARIUS
SAPONACEOUS
SARCOPHAGUS
SCRIPTORIUM
SCRUMPTIOUS
SCULLABOGUE
SEMPITERNUM
SENTENTIOUS
SEPTENARIUS
SPONTANEOUS
STRADUARIUS
STRAMINEOUS
STROPHILLUS
STYLOPODIUM
SUBITANEOUS
SUCCEDANEUM
SUPERFLUOUS
SUPPEDANEUM
TAUROBOLIUM
TEASPOONFUL
TÉLÉFÉRIQUE
TEMPESTUOUS
TENDENTIOUS
TORTICULLUS
TRAGELAPHUS
TREACHEROUS
TREACHETOUR
TRIPTOLEMUS
UNAMBIGUOUS
UNCONSCIOUS
UNRIGHTEOUS
VERTIGINOUS
WATERCOLOUR
WORLDFAMOUS
XENODOCHIUM
ZWISCHENZUG
ACQUISITIVE
AFFIRMATIVE
ALTERNATIVE
APPELLATIVE
ATTRIBUTIVE
BODHISATTVA
CARMINATIVE
COHORTATIVE
COMPARATIVE
COMPETITIVE
CONSECUTIVE
CONSUMPTIVE
CONTRAYERVA
COOPERATIVE
DEHORTATIVE
DESCRIPTIVE
DESTRUCTIVE
DISTINCTIVE
IMAGINATIVE
INATTENTIVE
INEFFECTIVE
INEXPENSIVE
INFORMATIVE
INOFFENSIVE
INOPERATIVE
INQUISITIVE
INSENSITIVE
INSTINCTIVE
INSTRUCTIVE
INTERACTIVE
LEGISLATIVE
LOCORESTIVE
MAKEBELIEVE
OBSTRUCTIVE
PERSPECTIVE
PRECONCEIVE
PREDICATIVE
PREROGATIVE
PRESUMPTIVE
PROGRESSIVE
PROHIBITIVE
PROSPECTIVE
PROVOCATIVE
QUALITATIVE
RADIOACTIVE
REBARBATIVE
RESTORATIVE
RESTRICTIVE
RETRIBUTIVE
RETROACTIVE
SPECULATIVE
SUBJUNCTIVE
SUBSTANTIVE
SUPERLATIVE
TERREMOTIVE
UNASSERTIVE
UNOBTRUSIVE
GLIMMERGOWK
PICKYOUROWN
SPARROWHAWK
THISTLEDOWN
WATEREDDOWN
ARTIODACTYL
PTERODACTYL
STRANGEWAYS
ACCLIMATIZE
ALPHABETIZE
ANESTHETIZE
ANTHOLOGIZE
CANNIBALIZE
CIRCULARIZE
COLEORRHIZA
COMPUTERIZE
CRYSTALLIZE
DECARBONIZE
DESTABILIZE
DISORGANIZE
EXTEMPORIZE
FAMILIARIZE
HOSPITALIZE
IMMORTALIZE
MARGINALIZE
MATERIALIZE
MERCHANDIZE
MINIATURIZE
NATIONALIZE
PERSONALIZE
PROSELYTIZE
RATIONALIZE
RAZZAMATAZZ
ROMANTICIZE
SOLILOQUIZE
STANDARDIZE
SYNCHRONIZE
SYSTEMATIZE

11:11

ABRACADABRA
AGORAPHOBIA
AMPHISBAENA
AMPHISBOENA
ANACOLUTHIA
ANAESTHESIA
ANTHESTERIA
ANTONOMASIA
APHANIPTERA
ATHARVAVEDA
BACCHANALIA
BALISTRARIA
BIELORUSSIA
BODHISATTVA
CALCEOLARIA
CHAULMOOGRA
CHAULMOUGRA
CIRRHIPEDEA
CIRRHIPEDIA
COLEORRHIZA
COLLECTANEA
COLLENCHYMA
CONTRAYERVA
CONVALLARIA
DEMONOMANIA
DYAESTHESIA
ENCEPHALOMA

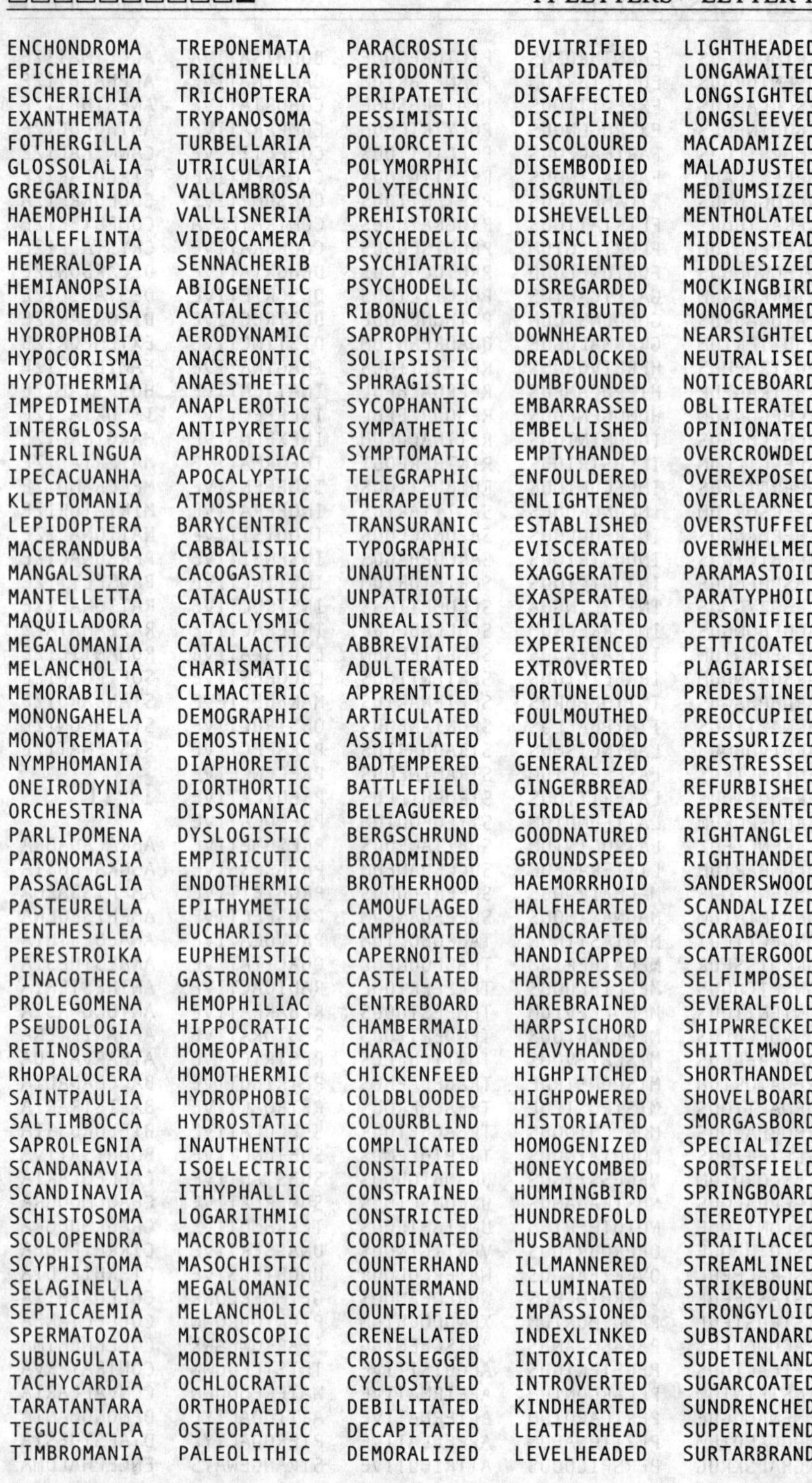

ENCHONDROMA
EPICHEIREMA
ESCHERICHIA
EXANTHEMATA
FOTHERGILLA
GLOSSOLALIA
GREGARINIDA
HAEMOPHILIA
HALLEFLINTA
HEMERALOPIA
HEMIANOPSIA
HYDROMEDUSA
HYDROPHOBIA
HYPOCORISMA
HYPOTHERMIA
IMPEDIMENTA
INTERGLOSSA
INTERLINGUA
IPECACUANHA
KLEPTOMANIA
LEPIDOPTERA
MACERANDUBA
MANGALSUTRA
MANTELLETTA
MAQUILADORA
MEGALOMANIA
MELANCHOLIA
MEMORABILIA
MONONGAHELA
MONOTREMATA
NYMPHOMANIA
ONEIRODYNIA
ORCHESTRINA
PARLIPOMENA
PARONOMASIA
PASSACAGLIA
PASTEURELLA
PENTHESILEA
PERESTROIKA
PINACOTHECA
PROLEGOMENA
PSEUDOLOGIA
RETINOSPORA
RHOPALOCERA
SAINTPAULIA
SALTIMBOCCA
SAPROLEGNIA
SCANDANAVIA
SCANDINAVIA
SCHISTOSOMA
SCOLOPENDRA
SCYPHISTOMA
SELAGINELLA
SEPTICAEMIA
SPERMATOZOA
SUBUNGULATA
TACHYCARDIA
TARATANTARA
TEGUCICALPA
TIMBROMANIA
TREPONEMATA
TRICHINELLA
TRICHOPTERA
TRYPANOSOMA
TURBELLARIA
UTRICULARIA
VALLAMBROSA
VALLISNERIA
VIDEOCAMERA
SENNACHERIB
ABIOGENETIC
ACATALECTIC
AERODYNAMIC
ANACREONTIC
ANAESTHETIC
ANAPLEROTIC
ANTIPYRETIC
APHRODISIAC
APOCALYPTIC
ATMOSPHERIC
BARYCENTRIC
CABBALISTIC
CACOGASTRIC
CATACAUSTIC
CATACLYSMIC
CATALLACTIC
CHARISMATIC
CLIMACTERIC
DEMOGRAPHIC
DEMOSTHENIC
DIAPHORETIC
DIORTHORTIC
DIPSOMANIAC
DYSLOGISTIC
EMPIRICUTIC
ENDOTHERMIC
EPITHYMETIC
EUCHARISTIC
EUPHEMISTIC
GASTRONOMIC
HEMOPHILIAC
HIPPOCRATIC
HOMEOPATHIC
HOMOTHERMIC
HYDROPHOBIC
HYDROSTATIC
INAUTHENTIC
ISOELECTRIC
ITHYPHALLIC
LOGARITHMIC
MACROBIOTIC
MASOCHISTIC
MEGALOMANIC
MELANCHOLIC
MICROSCOPIC
MODERNISTIC
OCHLOCRATIC
ORTHOPAEDIC
OSTEOPATHIC
PALEOLITHIC
PARACROSTIC
PERIODONTIC
PERIPATETIC
PESSIMISTIC
POLIORCETIC
POLYMORPHIC
POLYTECHNIC
PREHISTORIC
PSYCHEDELIC
PSYCHIATRIC
PSYCHODELIC
RIBONUCLEIC
SAPROPHYTIC
SOLIPSISTIC
SPHRAGISTIC
SYCOPHANTIC
SYMPATHETIC
SYMPTOMATIC
TELEGRAPHIC
THERAPEUTIC
TRANSURANIC
TYPOGRAPHIC
UNAUTHENTIC
UNPATRIOTIC
UNREALISTIC
ABBREVIATED
ADULTERATED
APPRENTICED
ARTICULATED
ASSIMILATED
BADTEMPERED
BATTLEFIELD
BELEAGUERED
BERGSCHRUND
BROADMINDED
BROTHERHOOD
CAMOUFLAGED
CAMPHORATED
CAPERNOITED
CASTELLATED
CENTREBOARD
CHAMBERMAID
CHARACINOID
CHICKENFEED
COLDBLOODED
COLOURBLIND
COMPLICATED
CONSTIPATED
CONSTRAINED
CONSTRICTED
COORDINATED
COUNTERHAND
COUNTERMAND
COUNTRIFIED
CRENELLATED
CROSSLEGGED
CYCLOSTYLED
DEBILITATED
DECAPITATED
DEMORALIZED
DEVITRIFIED
DILAPIDATED
DISAFFECTED
DISCIPLINED
DISCOLOURED
DISEMBODIED
DISGRUNTLED
DISHEVELLED
DISINCLINED
DISORIENTED
DISREGARDED
DISTRIBUTED
DOWNHEARTED
DREADLOCKED
DUMBFOUNDED
EMBARRASSED
EMBELLISHED
EMPTYHANDED
ENFOULDERED
ENLIGHTENED
ESTABLISHED
EVISCERATED
EXAGGERATED
EXASPERATED
EXHILARATED
EXPERIENCED
EXTROVERTED
FORTUNELOUD
FOULMOUTHED
FULLBLOODED
GENERALIZED
GINGERBREAD
GIRDLESTEAD
GOODNATURED
GROUNDSPEED
HAEMORRHOID
HALFHEARTED
HANDCRAFTED
HANDICAPPED
HARDPRESSED
HAREBRAINED
HARPSICHORD
HEAVYHANDED
HIGHPITCHED
HIGHPOWERED
HISTORIATED
HOMOGENIZED
HONEYCOMBED
HUMMINGBIRD
HUNDREDFOLD
HUSBANDLAND
ILLMANNERED
ILLUMINATED
IMPASSIONED
INDEXLINKED
INTOXICATED
INTROVERTED
KINDHEARTED
LEATHERHEAD
LEVELHEADED
LIGHTHEADED
LONGAWAITED
LONGSIGHTED
LONGSLEEVED
MACADAMIZED
MALADJUSTED
MEDIUMSIZED
MENTHOLATED
MIDDENSTEAD
MIDDLESIZED
MOCKINGBIRD
MONOGRAMMED
NEARSIGHTED
NEUTRALISED
NOTICEBOARD
OBLITERATED
OPINIONATED
OVERCROWDED
OVEREXPOSED
OVERLEARNED
OVERSTUFFED
OVERWHELMED
PARAMASTOID
PARATYPHOID
PERSONIFIED
PETTICOATED
PLAGIARISED
PREDESTINED
PREOCCUPIED
PRESSURIZED
PRESTRESSED
REFURBISHED
REPRESENTED
RIGHTANGLED
RIGHTHANDED
SANDERSWOOD
SCANDALIZED
SCARABAEOID
SCATTERGOOD
SELFIMPOSED
SEVERALFOLD
SHIPWRECKED
SHITTIMWOOD
SHORTHANDED
SHOVELBOARD
SMORGASBORD
SPECIALIZED
SPORTSFIELD
SPRINGBOARD
STEREOTYPED
STRAITLACED
STREAMLINED
STRIKEBOUND
STRONGYLOID
SUBSTANDARD
SUDETENLAND
SUGARCOATED
SUNDRENCHED
SUPERINTEND
SURTARBRAND

SURTURBRAND
SWITCHBOARD
SWITZERLAND
SYNTHESIZED
TESSELLATED
THUNDERBIRD
THUNDERHEAD
TIGHTFISTED
TIGHTLIPPED
TRANSFERRED
TRANSFORMED
TRANSMITTED
TRANSPORTED
TRICHINOSED
TYROGLYPHID
UNANNOUNCED
UNBLEMISHED
UNCASTRATED
UNCIVILISED
UNCIVILIZED
UNCLUTTERED
UNCOMMITTED
UNCONCEALED
UNCONCERNED
UNCONFIRMED
UNCONNECTED
UNCONQUERED
UNCONTESTED
UNCONVERTED
UNCONVINCED
UNDERCOOKED
UNDERGROUND
UNDERHANDED
UNDERMANNED
UNDERSIGNED
UNDERSTATED
UNDERVALUED
UNDEVELOPED
UNDIGNIFIED
UNDISCLOSED
UNDISGUISED
UNDISTURBED
UNENVELOPED
UNEXPLAINED
UNEXPRESSED
UNFULFILLED
UNFURNISHED
UNIMPRESSED
UNINHABITED
UNINHIBITED
UNINITIATED
UNJUSTIFIED
UNMITIGATED
UNMOTIVATED
UNPERTURBED
UNPROTECTED
UNPUBLISHED
UNQUALIFIED
UNREHEARSED
UNSATISFIED

UNSATURATED
UNSCHEDULED
UNSHELTERED
UNSOLICITED
UNSPECIFIED
UNSUPPORTED
UNSURPASSED
UNSUSPECTED
UNSWEETENED
UNTRAMELLED
UNVARNISHED
UNWARRANTED
VITAMINIZED
WARMHEARTED
WATERLOGGED
WELLADVISED
WELLBEHAVED
WELLDEFINED
WELLDRESSED
WELLFOUNDED
WRONGHEADED
ACCIPITRINE
ACCLIMATISE
ACCLIMATIZE
ACCOMMODATE
ACCOUNTABLE
ACCRESCENCE
ACKNOWLEDGE
ACOLOUTHITE
ACQUISITIVE
ACRIFLAVINE
ACUPUNCTURE
ADOLESCENCE
AFFIRMATIVE
AGGLOMERATE
AGGLUTINATE
AGRICULTURE
AGUARDIENTE
AIGUILLETTE
AILUROPHILE
ALEXANDRINE
ALEXANDRITE
ALPHABETIZE
ALTERNATIVE
AMBIVALENCE
AMINOBUTENE
AMPHETAMINE
ANESTHETIZE
ANNABERGITE
ANTECEDENCE
ANTHOLOGIZE
ANTICYCLONE
ANTISTROPHE
APLANOSPORE
APOMORPHINE
APOPHYLLITE
APPELLATIVE
APPRECIABLE
APPROPRIATE
APPROXIMATE

ARTHROSPORE
ASSASSINATE
ATHERINIDAE
ATTRIBUTIVE
AVERRUNCATE
BADDELEYITE
BANDEIRANTE
BARBASTELLE
BARBITURATE
BASKERVILLE
BATHYSPHERE
BEAUMONTAGE
BENEDICTINE
BENEFICIATE
BENEVOLENCE
BIBLIOPHILE
BICARBONATE
BILLIONAIRE
BLANKURSINE
BLUNDERBORE
BOURGEOISIE
BOUTONNIERE
BRAZZAVILLE
BREASTPLATE
BREATHALYSE
BRISTLECONE
BUPRESTIDAE
CALLITRICHE
CAMALDOLITE
CAMARADERIE
CANDESCENCE
CANDIDATURE
CANNIBALIZE
CAPACITANCE
CAPERNOITIE
CARABINIERE
CARMINATIVE
CASSITERITE
CATASTROPHE
CATCHPHRASE
CENTERPIECE
CENTREPIECE
CERARGYRITE
CERTIFIABLE
CERTIFICATE
CHANTARELLE
CHANTERELLE
CHARLEMAGNE
CHIASTOLITE
CHICHEVACHE
CHINOISERIE
CHIPPENDALE
CHORDOPHONE
CHRYSOPRASE
CILOFIBRATE
CIRCULARIZE
CLANDESTINE
CLINOCHLORE
COALESCENCE
COBBLESTONE

COEXISTENCE
COGNOSCENTE
COHORTATIVE
COINCIDENCE
COLLABORATE
COLLAPSIBLE
COMBUSTIBLE
COMEUPPANCE
COMFORTABLE
COMMEMORATE
COMMENDABLE
COMMISERATE
COMMONPLACE
COMMONSENSE
COMMUNICATE
COMPARATIVE
COMPETITIVE
COMPUTERIZE
CONCEIVABLE
CONCENTRATE
CONCEPTICLE
CONCORDANCE
CONCURRENCE
CONDOTTIERE
CONDOTTIORE
CONFABULATE
CONFARREATE
CONFEDERATE
CONJUNCTURE
CONSECUTIVE
CONSEQUENCE
CONSIDERATE
CONSILIENCE
CONSISTENCE
CONSOLIDATE
CONSTANTINE
CONSTELLATE
CONSTERNATE
CONSTUPRATE
CONSUMPTIVE
CONTAMINATE
CONTEMPLATE
CONTINGENCE
CONTINUANCE
CONTRIVANCE
CONVENIENCE
CONVENTICLE
CONVERGENCE
CONVERTIBLE
COOPERATIVE
COPPERPLATE
CORNERSTONE
CORROBORATE
CORRUPTIBLE
COUNTENANCE
COUNTERPANE
COUNTRYSIDE
CRACOVIENNE
CRÉMAILLÈRE
CRESCENTADE

CROCIDOLITE
CRYSTALLINE
CRYSTALLISE
CRYSTALLIZE
DECARBONIZE
DECORTICATE
DECREPITATE
DECREPITUDE
DEGLUTINATE
DEHORTATIVE
DELIVERANCE
DEMONSTRATE
DENDRACHATE
DEPHLEGMATE
DESCRIPTIVE
DESEGREGATE
DESERPIDINE
DESTABILIZE
DESTRUCTIVE
DETERIORATE
DIRECTORATE
DISCERNIBLE
DISCONTINUE
DISCOTHEQUE
DISENTANGLE
DISORGANIZE
DISPENSABLE
DISPERSABLE
DISPLEASURE
DISSEMINATE
DISSIMULATE
DISTINCTIVE
DISTURBANCE
DOCTRINAIRE
DODECASTYLE
DOMESTICATE
EARTHENWARE
ELECTROCUTE
ELECTROLYTE
ELEPHANTINE
EMMENAGOGUE
ENCAPSULATE
ENCUMBRANCE
ENFORCEABLE
ENFRANCHISE
ENKEPHALINE
ENTABLATURE
EPIDIASCOPE
EPINEPHRINE
EQUIVALENCE
ERYTHROCYTE
ESCARMOUCHE
ESPIEGLERIE
ESTRAMAZONE
EUCALYPTOLE
EXCRESCENCE
EXORBITANCE
EXPECTORATE
EXPENDITURE
EXPOSTULATE

EXPROPRIATE
EXTEMPORISE
EXTEMPORIZE
EXTERMINATE
EXTRAPOLATE
FAMILIARISE
FAMILIARIZE
FANFARONADE
FARTHINGALE
FASHIONABLE
FERNITICKLE
FERRONNIÈRE
FIDDLEDEDEE
FLAMBOYANCE
FLAMBOYANTE
FLANNELETTE
FLAVOURSOME
FORBEARANCE
FORBIDDANCE
FORECLOSURE
FORESEEABLE
FRANKLINITE
FRAUDULENCE
FURTHERANCE
FURTHERMORE
FURTHERSOME
GABERLUNZIE
GAMETOPHYTE
GELSEMININE
GENOUILLÈRE
GEOSYNCLINE
GESTICULATE
GLADWELLISE
GRAMMALOGUE
GREENBOTTLE
GREENOCKITE
GUESSTIMATE
GUTTERSNIPE
GUTTURALISE
HAEMORRHAGE
HALLUCINATE
HARDICANUTE
HATCHETTITE
HECKELPHONE
HEPPLEWHITE
HERRINGBONE
HIGHPROFILE
HOLLANDAISE
HONEYSUCKLE
HOOTANANNIE
HOOTENANNIE
HORNSWOGGLE
HOSPITALIZE
HUCKSTERAGE
HYDROPHIDAE
HYPOTHECATE
ICHTHYOLITE
IGNORANTINE
IMAGINATIVE
IMMORTALISE
IMMORTALIZE
IMPERMEABLE
IMPERSONATE
IMPIGNORATE
IMPLAUSIBLE
IMPORTUNATE
IMPREGNABLE
INADVISABLE
INALIENABLE
INATTENTIVE
INCAPSULATE
INCARCERATE
INCARNADINE
INCOHERENCE
INCOMPOSITE
INCORPORATE
INCRIMINATE
INDEFINABLE
INDIVISIBLE
INDOMITABLE
INDUBITABLE
INEFFECTIVE
INELUCTABLE
INEQUITABLE
INESCAPABLE
INESTIMABLE
INEXCITABLE
INEXCUSABLE
INEXPENSIVE
INFANTICIDE
INFLAMMABLE
INFORMATIVE
INGRATITUDE
INHABITABLE
INHERITANCE
INNUMERABLE
INOFFENSIVE
INOPERATIVE
INOPPORTUNE
INQUISITIVE
INSCRUTABLE
INSECTICIDE
INSECTIVORE
INSENSITIVE
INSEPARABLE
INSOUCIANCE
INSTANTIATE
INSTINCTIVE
INSTRUCTIVE
INSUPERABLE
INTEMPERATE
INTERACTIVE
INTERCHANGE
INTERCOURSE
INTERMINGLE
INTERNECINE
INTERPOLATE
INTERRELATE
INTERROGATE
INTERSPERSE
INTERVIEWEE
INTOLERABLE
INTOLERANCE
INTRACTABLE
INVESTIGATE
INVESTITURE
IRIDESCENCE
IRREDUCIBLE
IRREFUTABLE
IRRELEVANCE
IRREPARABLE
IRREVERENCE
IRREVOCABLE
ISOXSUPRINE
JOSEPHINITE
JUSTIFIABLE
KILOCALORIE
KITCHENETTE
LAMPROPHYRE
LATERIGRADE
LAUNDERETTE
LEATHERETTE
LEFTLUGGAGE
LEGIONNAIRE
LEGISLATIVE
LEGISLATURE
LENTIGINOSE
LICKSPITTLE
LINDISFARNE
LIVINGSTONE
LOCORESTIVE
LUXULYANITE
LYCANTHROPE
LYCHNOSCOPE
MAINTENANCE
MAISTERDOME
MAKEBELIEVE
MALAKATOONE
MALEVOLENCE
MALFEASANCE
MALPRACTICE
MANTELPIECE
MANUFACTURE
MARGINALIZE
MARIVAUDAGE
MARKETPLACE
MASKALLONGE
MASTERPIECE
MATERIALISE
MATERIALIZE
MATRICULATE
MENTONNIÈRE
MEPROBAMATE
MERCHANDISE
MERCHANDIZE
MICROGAMETE
MILLIONAIRE
MINIATURIZE
MISALLIANCE
MISANTHROPE
MISCARRIAGE
MISCONSTRUE
MISERICORDE
MOLLYCODDLE
MONCHIQUITE
MONOTHELITE
MUNIFICENCE
MUSKELLUNGE
NAPHTHALENE
NATIONALIZE
NATIONSTATE
NECESSITATE
NIGHTINGALE
NIKETHAMIDE
NONCHALANCE
NONFEASANCE
NORTHCLIFFE
NUMBERPLATE
OBSTRUCTIVE
OBTEMPERATE
ODONTOPHORE
OFFICIALESE
OLIGOCHAETE
OMMATOPHORE
OMNIPOTENCE
OMNISCIENCE
OPALESCENCE
OPPIGNORATE
ORCHESTRATE
ORTHOCENTRE
OSTREOPHAGE
OUTDISTANCE
OVERBALANCE
PAMPELMOOSE
PAMPELMOUSE
PARTICIPATE
PASTOURELLE
PELOPONNESE
PENICILLATE
PENSIONABLE
PENTATHLETE
PENTONVILLE
PENULTIMATE
PERAMBULATE
PERCEPTIBLE
PERCHLORATE
PERCIPIENCE
PEREGRINATE
PERFORMANCE
PERLUSTRATE
PERMISSIBLE
PERSISTENCE
PERSONALIZE
PERSPECTIVE
PETITMAITRE
PHILLIPSITE
PHONOFIDDLE
PHOTOSPHERE
PICKELHAUBE
PICTURESQUE
PIEDMONTITE
PINNYWINKLE
PITCHBLENDE
PLANTIGRADE
PLATERESQUE
PLATYRRHINE
PLEASURABLE
PLEBEIANISE
PLEISTOCENE
PLOUGHSHARE
POCOCURANTE
POLYSTYRENE
POMEGRANATE
POMPELMOOSE
POMPELMOUSE
PONTIFICATE
PORTERHOUSE
PORTRAITURE
PRACTICABLE
PRECIPITATE
PRECONCEIVE
PREDICATIVE
PREDICTABLE
PREDOMINATE
PREEMINENCE
PREMEDITATE
PREPOLLENCE
PREROGATIVE
PRESENTABLE
PRESUMPTIVE
PREVARICATE
PREVENTABLE
PRODIGALISE
PROFITEROLE
PROGRESSIVE
PROHIBITIVE
PROLIFERATE
PROMPTITUDE
PROSELYTIZE
PROSPECTIVE
PROVOCATIVE
PUBLISHABLE
PULCHRITUDE
PURPRESTURE
PYTHONESQUE
QUALITATIVE
QUARRELSOME
RADIOACTIVE
RATATOUILLE
RATIOCINATE
RATIONALIZE
RATTLESNAKE
REASSURANCE
REBARBATIVE
RECIPROCATE
RECONNOITRE
RECOVERABLE
RECRIMINATE
RECTIFIABLE
REDOUBTABLE

REDUPLICATE
REFOCILLATE
REFRIGERATE
REGRETTABLE
REGURGITATE
REINCARNATE
REMEMBRANCE
REMONSTRATE
RENAISSANCE
REORIENTATE
REPLACEABLE
RESEMBLANCE
RESPECTABLE
RESPONSIBLE
RESTORATIVE
RESTRICTIVE
RESTRUCTURE
RESUSCITATE
RETRACTABLE
RETRIBUTIVE
RETRIEVABLE
RETROACTIVE
REVENDICATE
REVERBERATE
RIDDLEMEREE
ROBESPIERRE
RODOMONTADE
ROMANTICIZE
ROTTENSTONE
SACHERTORTE
SADDLEHORSE
SARCENCHYME
SCHISTOSOME
SCHOTTISCHE
SCINTILLATE
SCITAMINEAE
SCOPOLAMINE
SCULLABOGUE
SEIGNIORAGE
SELFDEFENCE
SELFSERVICE
SEPIOSTAIRE
SEQUESTRATE
SERICULTURE
SERVICEABLE
SESQUIOXIDE
SHAKESPEARE
SHEATHKNIFE
SHORTCHANGE
SILLIMANITE
SINISTRORSE
SKILLIGALEE
SKILLIGOLEE
SMITHSONITE
SNICKERSNEE
SOLILOQUIZE
SPANGCOCKLE
SPECULATIVE
SPERMOPHILE
SPESSARTITE
SPIFFLICATE
SPIROCHAETE
SPRINGHOUSE
STANDARDIZE
STEGANOPODE
STELLIONATE
STENOCHROME
STEREOSCOPE
STETHOSCOPE
STRANGULATE
STRETCHABLE
STROBOSCOPE
SUBJUNCTIVE
SUBMERGENCE
SUBMULTIPLE
SUBORDINATE
SUBSISTENCE
SUBSTANTIVE
SUFFRAGETTE
SUGGESTIBLE
SUMMERHOUSE
SUPERCHARGE
SUPERCHERIE
SUPERIMPOSE
SUPERLATIVE
SUPERSCRIBE
SUPERSEDERE
SUSCEPTIBLE
SUSTAINABLE
SWALLOWABLE
SYNCHRONISE
SYNCHRONIZE
SYSTEMATIZE
TAGLIATELLE
TARRADIDDLE
TAUTOCHRONE
TÉLÉFÉRIQUE
TEMPERATURE
TERPSICHORE
TERREMOTIVE
THALIDOMIDE
THALLOPHYTE
THAUMATROPE
THEOBROMINE
THERAPEUTAE
THERMOPYLAE
THESMOTHETE
TICKTACKTOE
TIGGYWINKLE
TOWNSPEOPLE
TOXOPHILITE
TRACASSERIE
TRANSFIGURE
TREASONABLE
TRINCOMALEE
TRIUMVIRATE
TROPOSPHERE
TROUBLESOME
TRYPANOSOME
TURRICULATE
ULOTRICHALE
ULTRAMARINE
UNALTERABLE
UNASSERTIVE
UNAVAILABLE
UNAVOIDABLE
UNBREAKABLE
UNCRUSHABLE
UNDERCHARGE
UNDESIRABLE
UNDRINKABLE
UNENDURABLE
UNFAVORABLE
UNFLAPPABLE
UNFORTUNATE
UNGETATABLE
UNOBTRUSIVE
UNPALATABLE
UNPRINTABLE
UNSHAKEABLE
UNSPEAKABLE
UNSTOPPABLE
UNTHINKABLE
UNTOUCHABLE
UNUTTERABLE
UNWHOLESOME
VARSOVIENNE
VENDEMIAIRE
VENTURESOME
VERBIGERATE
VERMICULITE
VICHYSOISSE
VICISSITUDE
VINAIGRETTE
VINBLASTINE
VINCRISTINE
WATERCOURSE
WEIGHBRIDGE
WENSLEYDALE
WILBERFORCE
WINDOWFRAME
WINDOWLEDGE
WORKMANLIKE
YELLOWSTONE
INFANGTHIEF
MANTELSHELF
SHOWERPROOF
ADVERTISING
AGGRAVATING
ALTERNATING
APPROACHING
ASTONISHING
BACKPACKING
BACKSLIDING
BALLBEARING
BESTSELLING
BEWILDERING
BOOKBINDING
BOOKKEEPING
BRANDENBURG
BROBDINGNAG
CALCULATING
CALENDERING
CAPTIVATING
CARAVANNING
CHALLENGING
CHITTERLING
CHRISTENING
CIRCULATING
CONSIDERING
CONTRASTING
COUNSELLING
DETERMINING
DEVASTATING
DISAGREEING
DISFIGURING
DISPARAGING
DISQUIETING
DISTRESSING
DOMINEERING
DRESSMAKING
DRYCLEANING
DUPLICATING
ENCOURAGING
ENCROACHING
ENGHALSKRUG
ENGINEERING
ENTHRALLING
EPOCHMAKING
EVERLASTING
EXTENUATING
EYECATCHING
FACTFINDING
FARREACHING
FASCINATING
FLOURISHING
FLUCTUATING
FOOTBALLING
FOOTWASHING
FORECASTING
FOREWARNING
FORTHCOMING
FRIGHTENING
FRUSTRATING
FUNCTIONING
FUNDRAISING
GOODLOOKING
HAIRRAISING
HANDWRITING
HANGGLIDING
HARDHITTING
HARDWORKING
HIBERNATING
HIGHRANKING
HORSERACING
HORSERIDING
HUMILIATING
IDENTIFYING
INFURIATING
INSINUATING
INTERESTING
INTERLACING
INTERVENING
LABORSAVING
LAWBREAKING
LENGTHENING
LONGLASTING
LONGRUNNING
MANEUVERING
MECKLENBURG
MERRYMAKING
MINISTERING
MISSPELLING
MONEYMAKING
MUDSLINGING
NEGOTIATING
NEIGHBORING
NEVERENDING
NEWSCASTING
NIPFARTHING
ORIGINATING
OUTSTANDING
OVERBEARING
OVERFISHING
OVERFLOWING
OVERHANGING
OVERLAPPING
OVERMANNING
OVERTURNING
OVERWEENING
PAINKILLING
PAINSTAKING
PATRONISING
PATRONIZING
PENETRATING
PERSEVERING
PROTRACTING
QUARRELLING
QUESTIONING
REGISTERING
SCAFFOLDING
SCATTERLING
SCUPPERNONG
SHOPLIFTING
SHORTCOMING
SHOWJUMPING
SIGHTSEEING
SMOULDERING
SNORKELLING
SPACESAVING
SPLUTTERING
STOCKTAKING
SUFFOCATING
SURROUNDING
TANTALIZING
THINGAMAJIG
THINGUMAJIG
THREATENING
TIMEKEEPING
TIMESHARING

TOBOGGANING
TRESPASSING
TYPESETTING
UNBEFITTING
UNDEMANDING
UNDERTAKING
UNDESERVING
UNFLINCHING
UNREASONING
UNRELENTING
UNREMITTING
UNSHRINKING
UNWELCOMING
VACILLATING
VOTERIGGING
WAINSCOTING
WAREHOUSING
WATERSKIING
WELLMEANING
WIDERANGING
WINDSURFING
WITHHOLDING
WOODCARVING
ZWISCHENZUG
ALLELOMORPH
CARDIOGRAPH
CESAREWITCH
CHEESECLOTH
CLAIRSCHACH
COTTONMOUTH
DISTINGUISH
HAMMERCLOTH
HORSERADISH
INTERGROWTH
JAMAHIRIYAH
KOMMERSBUCH
MARLBOROUGH
MIDDLEMARCH
NIGHTMARISH
NOVELETTISH
PERISTALITH
PHOTOFINISH
POLLENBRUSH
PSEUDOMORPH
RAMGUNSHOCH
REICHENBACH
SCARBOROUGH
SCHRECKLICH
SEISMOGRAPH
SEVENTEENTH
SILVERSMITH
SPATTERDASH
STANDOFFISH
SYMPOSIARCH
SYNCHROMESH
TECTIBRANCH
THENCEFORTH
TWELVEMONTH
UNDERGROWTH
WATERSPLASH
WISHTONWISH
WORRYTROUGH
YELLOWPLUSH
ARRIVEDERCI
BANGLADESHI
CHONDROSTEI
COGNOSCENTI
DOUROUCOULI
MELANOCHROI
MISSISSIPPI
PLAGIOSTOMI
SCHWARMEREI
SVARABHAKTI
APPARATCHIK
CANDLESTICK
CHOCKABLOCK
COUNTERSINK
CRACKERJACK
DEUTSCHMARK
DIAMONDBACK
DOUBLECHECK
GIGGLESTICK
GIGGLESWICK
GLIMMERGOWK
KIDDLEYWINK
KINNIKINICK
KIRKPATRICK
LEATHERBACK
LEATHERNECK
MUSCHELKALK
NEEDLESTICK
QUARTERBACK
QUARTERDECK
REALPOLITIK
SHUTTLECOCK
SINGLESTICK
SPARROWHAWK
SPATTERDOCK
STEEPLEJACK
STICKLEBACK
STRINGYBARK
TIDDLEYWINK
WEATHERCOCK
AFTERSCHOOL
ALLEGORICAL
AMPLEXICAUL
ANISOCERCAL
ARCHEGONIAL
ARTHRAPODAL
ARTIODACTYL
AUDIOVISUAL
AXEROPHTHOL
BEHAVIOURAL
BIOCHEMICAL
CATEGORICAL
CENTRIFUGAL
CENTRIPETAL
CHLOROPHYLL
CHOLESTEROL
CITLALEPETL
COCKLESHELL
CONDITIONAL
CONJECTURAL
CONTINENTAL
CONTRACTUAL
CONTUBERNAL
COPROSTEROL
COUNTERFOIL
CYLINDRICAL
DEFERENTIAL
DETRIMENTAL
DICTATORIAL
DIMENSIONAL
DIPHYCERCAL
DIRECTIONAL
DISAPPROVAL
DISGRACEFUL
DISTASTEFUL
DISTRUSTFUL
DRAGGLETAIL
DUNIEWASSAL
EDUCATIONAL
EGOTISTICAL
EQUILATERAL
EQUINOCTIAL
EVANGELICAL
EXCEPTIONAL
EXPONENTIAL
FINGERSTALL
FLICKERTAIL
FUNDAMENTAL
GEOMETRICAL
GESTATORIAL
GNATHONICAL
GRAMMATICAL
GROUNDSWELL
GUADALCANAL
HOMOTHERMAL
IDEOLOGICAL
IMPLEMENTAL
IMPRACTICAL
INCORPOREAL
INCREMENTAL
INEFFECTUAL
INESSENTIAL
INFLUENTIAL
INTENTIONAL
INTERCOSTAL
KINDERSPIEL
KRIEGSSPIEL
MAGISTERIAL
MATRIARCHAL
MATRIMONIAL
MINISTERIAL
MISTRUSTFUL
MONARCHICAL
MULTIRACIAL
MYCOLOGICAL
NEANDERTHAL
NONSENSICAL
NUTRITIONAL
OBSTETRICAL
ONTOLOGICAL
OPERATIONAL
PARACETAMOL
PARADOXICAL
PARAMEDICAL
PARTICIPIAL
PATRIARCHAL
PEDAGOGICAL
PENITENTIAL
PENTECOSTAL
PHARISAICAL
PISCATORIAL
PREJUDICIAL
PRIMIGENIAL
PROMOTIONAL
PROPHETICAL
PROVISIONAL
PTERODACTYL
PURITANICAL
QUADRENNIAL
REAPPRAISAL
RECESSIONAL
REPROACHFUL
RESIDENTIAL
RESOURCEFUL
REVERENTIAL
RHAPSODICAL
SACRAMENTAL
SACRIFICIAL
SECRETARIAL
SELFCONTROL
SEMPITERNAL
SENSATIONAL
SENTIMENTAL
SEXOLOGICAL
SPERMICIDAL
STATISTICAL
STRATEGICAL
SUBSTANTIAL
SUBTROPICAL
SUPERFICIAL
SYMMETRICAL
TEASPOONFUL
TERRESTRIAL
TERRITORIAL
TESTIMONIAL
THEOLOGICAL
THEORETICAL
TOPLOFTICAL
TRADITIONAL
TRIMESTRIAL
TROMPELOEIL
UNEMOTIONAL
UNEQUIVOCAL
UNPRACTICAL
VESPERTINAL
WHEREWITHAL
WHITECHAPEL
ABSENTEEISM
ACINACIFORM
ADOPTIANISM
ADOPTIONISM
AGNOSTICISM
AMERICANISM
ANACHRONISM
ANTEPENDIUM
ANTIRRHINUM
APODYTERIUM
ARCHEGONIUM
ASPERGILLUM
ASPERSORIUM
ASPHETERISM
ASTIGMATISM
BLOODSTREAM
CALIFORNIUM
CANNIBALISM
CARBORUNDUM
CATHOLICISM
CHILLINGHAM
CLADOSPORUM
COENOBITISM
COLONIALISM
COLUMBARIUM
CONDOMINIUM
CONSUMERISM
CREMATORIUM
DACTYLOGRAM
DIASCORDIUM
DITHELETISM
DOLABRIFORM
EINSTEINIUM
ENDOCARDIUM
EQUILIBRIUM
FAVOURITISM
FITZWILLIAM
FLORILEGIUM
HOOLIGANISM
IMPERIALISM
INTERREGNUM
LASERPICIUM
LATIFUNDIUM
LATROCINIUM
MALAPROPISM
MARCONIGRAM
MATERIALISM
MEDIASTINUM
MEGATHERIUM
MENDELEVIUM
MICHURINISM
NATIONALISM
NOTOTHERIUM
OFFICIALDOM
OPPORTUNISM
OSTRACODERM
PANDEMONIUM
PATERNALISM
PELARGONIUM
PERICARDIUM

PERITONAEUM
PLANETARIUM
POLYTRICHUM
PROSELYTISM
QUADRENNIUM
RETINACULUM
REVISIONISM
ROMANTICISM
SCALPRIFORM
SCOLECIFORM
SCRIPTORIUM
SEMPITERNUM
SHUNAMITISM
STEGANOGRAM
STYLOPODIUM
SUCCEDANEUM
SUPPEDANEUM
SYNCHRONISM
SYNDICALISM
TAUROBOLIUM
TETRADRACHM
TSCHERNOSEM
WHITEBOYISM
XENODOCHIUM
ABECEDARIAN
ABLACTATION
ABOMINATION
ABSTRACTION
ACADEMICIAN
ACCLAMATION
ACCLIMATION
ACQUISITION
ADUMBRATION
AESCULAPIAN
AFFECTATION
AFFILIATION
AFFIRMATION
AFFLIICTION
AFGHANISTAN
AGGRAVATION
AGGREGATION
AIRCRAFTMAN
ALBIGENSIAN
ALCYONARIAN
ALIFANFARON
ALLEVIATION
ALTERCATION
ALTERNATION
ANTHOCYANIN
ANTINEUTRON
ANTIQUARIAN
APOLLONICON
APPELLATION
APPLICATION
APPROBATION
ARBITRATION
ARCHENTERON
ARGATHELIAN
ARGENTINIAN
ASSEMBLYMAN
ASSIGNATION
ASSOCIATION
ATTENUATION
ATTESTATION
ATTRIBUTION
AUGUSTINIAN
AURIGNACIAN
BANNOCKBURN
BELLEROPHON
BELORUSSIAN
BENEDICTION
BESSARABIAN
BIFURCATION
BUSINESSMAN
CALCULATION
CALIBRATION
CALLISTEMON
CAMEROONIAN
CAMPESTRIAN
CAPTIVATION
CAROLINGIAN
CELEBRATION
CENTENARIAN
CEREBRATION
CHAIRPERSON
CHAMBERLAIN
CHRYSAROBIN
CIRCULATION
CLEANSHAVEN
COAGULATION
COLLOCATION
COMBINATION
COMMINATION
COMMUTATION
COMPETITION
COMPILATION
COMPOSITION
COMPOTATION
COMPUNCTION
COMPUTATION
CONFUTATION
CONGRESSMAN
CONJUGATION
CONJUNCTION
CONNOTATION
CONSOLATION
CONSUMPTION
CONTRACTION
CONTRAPTION
CONURBATION
CONVOCATION
CONVOLUTION
COOPERATION
COPROPHAGAN
CORPORATION
CORRELATION
CORRUGATION
COUNTERSIGN
CREPITATION
CRESTFALLEN
CROMWELLIAN
CRUCIFIXION
CULMINATION
CULTIVATION
DECLAMATION
DECLARATION
DEFOLIATION
DEFORMATION
DEGLUTITION
DEGRADATION
DEHYDRATION
DEIFICATION
DELECTATION
DELICTATION
DELINEATION
DEMARCATION
DEMIBASTION
DEPORTATION
DEPREDATION
DEPRIVATION
DERELICTION
DESCRIPTION
DESECRATION
DESELECTION
DESICCATION
DESIGNATION
DESPERATION
DESTINATION
DESTITUTION
DESTRUCTION
DETESTATION
DEVALUATION
DEVASTATION
DIATESSARON
DIATESSERON
DICOTYLEDON
DIFFRACTION
DISILLUSION
DISIMPRISON
DISJUNCTION
DISLOCATION
DISPOSITION
DISPUTATION
DISSIPATION
DISSOLUTION
DISTINCTION
DISTRACTION
DOWNTRODDEN
DRAUGHTSMAN
DUPLICATION
DYSFUNCTION
ECCALEOBION
EDIFICATION
EGALITARIAN
EJACULATION
ELABORATION
ELECTRICIAN
ELEUTHERIAN
ELIMINATION
ELIZABETHAN
ELUCIDATION
EMBARKATION
EMBROCATION
ENCHIRIDION
ENNEAHEDRON
ENUMERATION
ENUNCIATION
ERADICATION
ERIODENDRON
ERYMANTHIAN
EVAPORATION
EVENTRATION
EXAMINATION
EXCLAMATION
EXHORTATION
EXONERATION
EXOSKELETON
EXPECTATION
EXPLANATION
EXPLORATION
EXPURGATION
EXTENUATION
EXTRADITION
FABRICATION
FASCINATION
FAUXBOURDON
FLUCTUATION
FOMENTATION
FORESHORTEN
FORESTATION
FORFOUGHTEN
FORMULATION
FORNICATION
FRENCHWOMAN
FRENCHWOMEN
FROSTBITTEN
FRUSTRATION
FULMINATION
FUSTILARIAN
GALLOVIDIAN
GEGENSCHEIN
GENTLEWOMAN
GENUFLEXION
GERMINATION
GIBBERELLIN
GODFORSAKEN
GORDONSTOUN
GRAVITATION
GUBERNATION
HAEMOGLOBIN
HANDWRITTEN
HARIOLATION
HEARTBROKEN
HETEROSCIAN
HIBERNATION
HOHENLINDEN
HOLOTHURIAN
HUMGRUFFIAN
HUMILIATION
HYDROCARBON
HYOPLASTRON
HYPHENATION
HYPOTENSION
IDOLIZATION
IMAGINATION
IMMIGRATION
IMPLICATION
IMPORTATION
IMPRECATION
IMPRECISION
INATTENTION
INCANTATION
INCARNATION
INCLINATION
INDENTATION
INDIGESTION
INDIGNATION
INEBRIATION
INFANTRYMAN
INFATUATION
INFESTATION
INFORMATION
INOCULATION
INQUISITION
INSCRIPTION
INSINUATION
INSPIRATION
INSTIGATION
INSTITUTION
INSTRUCTION
INTEGRATION
INTERACTION
INTERLEUKIN
IRRADIATION
JACTITATION
KAMELAUKION
KATABOTHRON
KATAVOTHRON
KETAVOTHRON
KIMERIDGIAN
KOTABOTHRON
LAMENTATION
LEGERDEMAIN
LEGISLATION
LEPIDOSIREN
LIBERTARIAN
LILLIPUTIAN
LIQUIDATION
LOUISIANIAN
LUBRICATION
MACHINATION
MAGLEMOSIAN
MALEDICTION
MALEFACTION
MALFUNCTION
MANCIPATION
MANUMISSION
MASTICATION
MAURETANIAN
MAURITANIAN

MENDELSSOHN
MENSURATION
MERCHANTMAN
METRICATION
MICTURITION
MISBEGOTTEN
MOLESTATION
MORGENSTERN
MOXIBUSTION
MOZAMBIQUAN
MUNCHHAUSEN
MURMURATION
NEEDLEWOMAN
NEGOTIATION
NICKELODEON
OBSERVATION
OBSTRICTION
OBSTRUCTION
OCTASTICHON
ONOMASTICON
ORCHESTRION
ORGANIZAION
ORIENTATION
ORIGINATION
OSCILLATION
OSTENTATION
OXODIZATION
PALESTINIAN
PANOMPHAEAN
PARTURITION
PENETRATION
PERCOLATION
PERDUELLION
PERFORATION
PERIGORDIAN
PERMUTATION
PERSECUTION
PHONETICIAN
PICKYOUROWN
POLICEWOMAN
POLLINATION
PORTLANDIAN
POTAMOGETON
PRELIBATION
PREMONITION
PREPARATION
PREPOSITION
PRESUMPTION
PRETERITION
PROCREATION
PROCRUSTEAN
PROGRESSION
PROHIBITION
PROLETARIAN
PROLOCUTION
PROPAGATION
PROPOSITION
PROROGATION
PROSECUTION
PROSTRATION
PROTRACTION
PROVOCATION
PUBLICATION
PUNCTUATION
QUARRINGTON
RABELAISIAN
RADIOCARBON
RAPSCALLION
RASTAFARIAN
REALIZATION
REANIMATION
RECANTATION
RECLAMATION
RECOGNITION
RECONDITION
REFORMATION
REITERATION
REPUDIATION
REQUISITION
RESERVATION
RESIGNATION
RESPIRATION
RESTITUTION
RESTORATION
RESTRICTION
RETALIATION
RETARDATION
RETRIBUTION
REVALUATION
ROSICRUCIAN
RUMFRUCTION
RUMGUMPTION
SABBATARIAN
SALESPERSON
SALVADORIAN
SCHECKLATON
SEGREGATION
SEPTENTRION
SIGHTSCREEN
SINGAPOREAN
SKIMMINGTON
SLUMGULLION
SMITHSONIAN
SMOKESCREEN
SOUTHAMPTON
SPECULATION
SPOKESWOMAN
SPORTSWOMAN
SPRINGCLEAN
STAGFLATION
STIMULATION
STIPULATION
STOCKHAUSEN
STOOLPIGEON
STYLIZATION
STYMPHALIAN
SUBDIVISION
SUBJUGATION
SUBLIMATION
SUBPANATION
SUBTRACTION
SUFFOCATION
SUPERALTERN
SUPERVISION
SUPPOSITION
SUPPRESSION
SUPPURATION
SUSURRATION
SWORDSWOMAN
SYNCOPATION
SYNDICATION
TERMINATION
TETRAHEDRON
THISTLEDOWN
THOROUGHPIN
THROGMORTON
TIRONENSIAN
TITILLATION
TORRIDONIAN
TOSTICATION
TOURBILLION
TRANSACTION
TRANSFERRIN
TRANSFUSION
TRANSLATION
TRENCHERMAN
TREPIDATION
TRIBULATION
TRINIDADIAN
TRINITARIAN
TYPEWRITTEN
TYRONENSIAN
ULTRAMODERN
UNCHRISTIAN
UNIFICATION
UTILITARIAN
UTILIZATION
VACCINATION
VACILLATION
VALEDICTION
VARANGARIAN
VARIEGATION
VARIOLATION
VASOPRESSIN
VENTILATION
VINDICATION
VIVISECTION
WASHERWOMAN
WATEREDDOWN
WESTPHALIAN
WHITTINGTON
WINTERGREEN
WORKSTATION
ZOROASTRIAN
AMONTILLADO
ARCHIPELAGO
BRAGGADOCIO
CAPRICCIOSO
CHIAROSCURO
CINQUECENTO
COMPRIMARIO
ESTRANGHELO
INTERNUNCIO
KILIMANJARO
PRESTISSIMO
PUNCHINELLO
RALLENTANDO
RIFACIMENTO
SALTIMBANCO
VIOLINCELLO
VIOLONCELLO
WHISKERANDO
CITIZENSHIP
COMRADESHIP
DIPTEROCARP
FISHANDCHIP
LECTURESHIP
OARSMANSHIP
PARTNERSHIP
PREMIERSHIP
SCHOLARSHIP
SHOWMANSHIP
SPONSORSHIP
THUNDERCLAP
TRUSTEESHIP
WHISTLESTOP
WORKMANSHIP
ACCELERATOR
ACCUMULATOR
ADJUDICATOR
AMELANCHIER
ANAXIMANDER
ANTECHAMBER
ANTIBURGHER
ARBITRAGEUR
ARQUEBUSIER
AUXANOMETER
AZOTOBACTER
BACKBENCHER
BACKFIELDER
BARNSTORMER
BEACHCOMBER
BELLYTIMBER
BIRDWATCHER
BLACKMAILER
BLOCKBUSTER
BLOODSUCKER
BREADWINNER
BROADCASTER
BULLFIGHTER
BURGOMASTER
BUSHWHACKER
CAPACITATOR
CARBURETTOR
CATERPILLAR
CAULIFLOWER
CENTURIATOR
CHANTICLEER
CHARGEPAYER
CHEERLEADER
CHILDMINDER
CHOIRMASTER
CHRISTOPHER
CHRONOMETER
CIRCUMCISER
CLIFFHANGER
COMMENTATOR
COMPTROLLER
CONCILIATOR
CONDITIONER
CONNOISSEUR
CONSPIRATOR
CONSTRICTOR
CONSTRUCTOR
CONTRIBUTOR
CRACKHALTER
CREPUSCULAR
CRITICASTER
CULVERINEER
DEERSTALKER
DEGRINGOLER
DENOMINATOR
DINNYHAUSER
DINNYHAYSER
DISBELIEVER
DISENCUMBER
DISSERTATOR
DISTRIBUTOR
DRINKDRIVER
DUSTWRAPPER
EARTHSHAKER
ELECTROLIER
EMMENTHALER
ENTERTAINER
ESTABLISHER
EXECUTIONER
EXTORTIONER
FAIRWEATHER
FAULTFINDER
FIELDWORKER
FILLIBUSTER
FIRELIGHTER
FORAMINIFER
FRANKFURTER
FREETHINKER
FRONTRUNNER
GALLIBAGGER
GALLIBEGGAR
GALLYBAGGER
GALLYBEGGAR
GATECRASHER
GERRYMANDER
GIGGLEWATER
GILLYFLOWER
GODDAUGHTER
GONFALONIER
GRANDFATHER
GRANDMASTER
GRANDMOTHER
GRASSHOPPER

GRAVEDIGGER
GREENGROCER
GRENZGANGER
HABERDASHER
HAIRDRESSER
HALBSTARKER
HALFBROTHER
HANDICAPPER
HIGHLIGHTER
HONEYMOONER
HOSPITALLER
HOUSEHOLDER
HOUSEKEEPER
HOUSEMASTER
ILLUSTRATOR
ILLYWHACKER
INCINERATOR
INDIARUBBER
INFILTRATOR
INTERCEPTOR
INTERPRETER
INTERRUPTER
INTERVIEWER
INTOXIMETER
INVIGILATOR
JERRYMANDER
KWASHIORKOR
LAMMERGEIER
LAMMERGEYER
LAMPLIGHTER
LEADSWINGER
LEASEHOLDER
LIQUIDAMBAR
LITTÉRATEUR
LOGOGRAPHER
LOUDSPEAKER
LUXEMBURGER
MANIPULATOR
MASQUERADER
METALWORKER
MINESWEEPER
MINNESINGER
MISBEHAVIOR
MISDEMEANOR
MOISTURIZER
MONEYLENDER
MONTGOLFIER
MOONLIGHTER
MOSSTROOPER
MOUNTAINEER
NECROMANCER
NIERSTEINER
NOMENCLATOR
ORNITHOPTER
OUTMANEUVER
PAMPHLETEER
PARATROOPER
PARISHIONER
PATERNOSTER
PEACEKEEPER
PENNYFATHER
PENTECONTER
PERPETRATOR
PETRODOLLAR
PETTIFOGGER
PHILANDERER
PHILOSOPHER
PHOTOCOPIER
PREDECESSOR
PRIZEWINNER
PROBATIONER
PROOFREADER
PROVISIONER
QUICKSILVER
RANGEFINDER
RECONNOITER
RECTANGULAR
RECTILINEAR
RIGHTHANDER
RIGHTWINGER
ROCKEFELLER
RUDESHEIMER
SALVOGUNNER
SCAREMONGER
SCOUTMASTER
SCREWDRIVER
SHAREHOLDER
SHINPLASTER
SHIPBUILDER
SKIDBLADNIR
SLEEPWALKER
SLUMBERWEAR
SMALLHOLDER
SOCKDALAGER
SOCKDOLAGER
SOCKDOLIGER
SOCKDOLOGER
SOUTHWESTER
SPECTACULAR
SPEEDOMETER
SPELLBINDER
SPITSTICKER
STADTHOLDER
STAKEHOLDER
STALLHOLDER
STANDPATTER
STEAMROLLER
STEINBERGER
STEPBROTHER
STEREOMETER
STOCKBROKER
STOCKHOLDER
STOCKJOBBER
STOREKEEPER
STORYTELLER
STRANDLOPER
STRAPHANGER
SUPERTANKER
SYMPATHISER
SYMPATHIZER
SYNTHESIZER
TEENYBOPPER
TEETOTALLER
TELEGRAPHER
TELEPRINTER
THEATERGOER
THEATREGOER
THERMOMETER
TOASTMASTER
TOPOGRAPHER
TOTALIZATOR
TRAFFICATOR
TRANSCEIVER
TRANSFORMER
TRANSMITTER
TRANSPONDER
TRANSPORTER
TREACHETOUR
TREECREEPER
TYPOGRAPHER
UNDERWRITER
UPHOLSTERER
VOLKSKAMMER
VOORTREKKER
WASHLEATHER
WATERCOLOUR
WESTMINSTER
WHITECOLLAR
WHITLEATHER
WINDBREAKER
WINDCHEATER
WITCHDOCTOR
XYLOGRAPHER
ACCESSORIES
ACRIMONIOUS
ACTUALITIES
ADULLAMITES
ADVENTURESS
ADVENTUROUS
AERONAUTICS
AESCULAPIUS
AGONOTHETES
AIRSICKNESS
ALBUGINEOUS
AMMOPHILOUS
ANADIPLOSIS
ANAGNORISIS
ANAPHYLAXIS
ANAPLEROSIS
ANASTOMOSIS
ANDROGENOUS
ANFRACTUOUS
ANTHONOMOUS
ANTIPHRASIS
ANTISTHENES
APATOSAURUS
APOLLINARIS
APONEUROSIS
APOSIOPESIS
APOSTROPHUS
APPEARANCES
ARCHILOCHUS
ARTHRODESIS
ASCLEPIADES
ASPERGILLUS
ATHERMANOUS
ATRABILIOUS
AVOIRDUPOIS
AWKWARDNESS
BASHFULNESS
BATTLEDRESS
BATTLEMENTS
BEASTLINESS
BILIOUSNESS
BLASPHEMOUS
BLESSEDNESS
BLOODSPORTS
BOOKSELLERS
BORBORYGMUS
BREADCRUMBS
BRITTLENESS
BRUCELLOSIS
CACOPHONOUS
CALLANETICS
CALLOUSNESS
CARDOPHAGUS
CAREFULNESS
CARNAPTIOUS
CARNIVOROUS
CARSICKNESS
CATACHRESIS
CENTUMVIRUS
CEREMONIOUS
CLEANLINESS
CLIOMETRICS
COMESTIBLES
COMFORTLESS
COMPENDIOUS
COMPLIMENTS
CONCISENESS
CONDOLENCES
CONDUCTRESS
CONSPICUOUS
CONSUMABLES
CONTENTIOUS
CONTRETEMPS
CONVOLVULUS
CONVULSIONS
COORDINATES
CORDWAINERS
CORINTHIANS
CORRECTNESS
COULOMMIERS
COURTLINESS
COXWAINLESS
CRATERELLUS
CREDENTIALS
CROOKEDNESS
CURNAPTIOUS
CYBERNETICS
CYMOPHANOUS
DARDANELLES
DECORATIONS
DEFENCELESS
DEFENSELESS
DELETERIOUS
DEMOSTHENES
DESCENDANTS
DEVIOUSNESS
DIAGNOSTICS
DIAPHORESIS
DIARTHROSIS
DICEPHALOUS
DIPLOMATICS
DOUBLECROSS
DRACUNCULUS
DRAGONNADES
DRUNKENNESS
DRYCLEANERS
DUBIOUSNESS
EARNESTNESS
EFFICACIOUS
ELECTRONICS
EMPHYTEUSIS
ENARTHROSIS
ENCHANTRESS
EOANTHROPUS
EPAMINONDAS
EPANALEPSIS
EREMACAUSIS
EURHYTHMICS
EVASIVENESS
EXPEDITIOUS
EXTROGENOUS
FARINACEOUS
FARRAGINOUS
FATUOUSNESS
FEATURELESS
FILAMENTOUS
FISHMONGERS
FLIRTATIOUS
FOOLISHNESS
FOREFATHERS
FORGIVENESS
FORLORNNESS
FOUNDATIONS
FURNISHINGS
FURTIVENESS
GALLIGANTUS
GALLOWGLASS
GAMOGENESIS
GENUINENESS
GHASTLINESS
GRALLATORES
HABILIMENTS
HAUGHTINESS
HEALTHINESS
HELPFULNESS
HEMORRHOIDS
HERBIVOROUS

HIDEOUSNESS
HINDERLANDS
HIPPOCAMPUS
HIPPOCRATES
HISTRIONICS
HOGGISHNESS
HOMOGENEOUS
HOSTILITIES
HYDROPONICS
ICHTHYORNIS
ICONOSTASIS
IGNOMINIOUS
ILLUSTRIOUS
IMPECUNIOUS
INCONGRUOUS
INCREDULOUS
INDUSTRIOUS
INFORMATICS
INGREDIENTS
INHABITANTS
INJUDICIOUS
INSTRUMENTS
INTRAVENOUS
INVINCIBLES
IRONMONGERS
IRRELIGIOUS
ISTIOPHORUS
ITHYPHALLUS
KULTURKREIS
LARYNGISMUS
LATERITIOUS
LAWLESSNESS
LENGTHINESS
LETTERPRESS
LINGUISTICS
LITERALNESS
LOGGERHEADS
MACHAIRODUS
MAGISTRATES
MAGNANIMOUS
MARIONETTES
MASSIVENESS
MATHEMATICS
MEANDERINGS
MEANINGLESS
MEASURELESS
MEGALOPOLIS
MELLIFLUOUS
MERITORIOUS
METACARPALS
METAGENESIS
METAPHYSICS
METATARSALS
MISCHIEVOUS
MISERLINESS
MONOCHINOUS
MOUNTAINOUS
MYXOMATOSIS
NATURALNESS
NAUGHTINESS
NECESSITOUS
NERVOUSNESS
NETHERLANDS
NETHERLINGS
NONETHELESS
NOSTRADAMUS
NOTHINGNESS
NUMISMATICS
NUTCRACKERS
OBVIOUSNESS
OPPROBRIOUS
ORDERLINESS
OUTPOURINGS
OVERZEALOUS
OXYRHYNCHUS
PAEDIATRICS
PANTALETTES
PARABLEPSIS
PARABOLANUS
PARALEIPSIS
PARANEPHROS
PARENTHESIS
PASSIVENESS
PAWNBROKERS
PEDESTRIANS
PEDETENTOUS
PEEVISHNESS
PENSIVENESS
PERIPHRASIS
PERISTALSIS
PERITONITIS
PERSPICUOUS
PHARYNGITIS
PHILIPPINES
PHILOCTETES
PHTHIRIASIS
PLAYFULNESS
POLITICIANS
POSSESSIONS
PRECAUTIONS
PRECIPITOUS
PRESTIGIOUS
PRESTONPANS
PRETENSIONS
PRETENTIOUS
PRICKLINESS
PROCEEDINGS
PROFUSENESS
PROGNATHOUS
PROMISCUOUS
PROPHYLAXIS
PROSTHETICS
PROTOCOCCUS
PRZEWALSKIS
PSITTACOSIS
PUNCTILIOUS
PURPOSELESS
QUADRUPLETS
QUINTUPLETS
RAFFISHNESS
RAUCOUSNESS
REGIMENTALS
REMORSELESS
REPETITIOUS
RESPONSIONS
RESTIVENESS
REVELATIONS
REVOLUTIONS
ROGUISHNESS
RUMBUSTIOUS
SAGITTARIUS
SAINTLINESS
SALPINGITIS
SAPONACEOUS
SARCOPHAGUS
SAVOURINESS
SCIREFACIAS
SCRUFFINESS
SCRUMPTIOUS
SEASICKNESS
SECONDCLASS
SELFISHNESS
SENTENTIOUS
SEPTENARIUS
SERIOUSNESS
SHALLOWNESS
SHAPELINESS
SHENANIGANS
SHEPHERDESS
SKETCHINESS
SLENDERNESS
SMITHEREENS
SPONDULICKS
SPONDYLITIS
SPONTANEOUS
SPRINGINESS
STATELINESS
STRADUARIUS
STRAMINEOUS
STRANGENESS
STRANGEWAYS
STRETCHLESS
STROPHILLUS
STRUTHIONES
STYLISHNESS
SUBITANEOUS
SUPERFICIES
SUPERFLUOUS
SUPERSEDEAS
SYMPLEGADES
TABERNACLES
TATTERSALLS
TEDIOUSNESS
TELEKINESIS
TEMPESTUOUS
TENDENTIOUS
TENTERHOOKS
TENUOUSNESS
THANATOPSIS
THEATRICALS
THEREABOUTS
THINGLINESS
THOUGHTLESS
THRIFTINESS
TONSILLITIS
TORTICOLLIS
TORTICULLUS
TRAGELAPHUS
TREACHEROUS
TRICERATOPS
TRINOBANTES
TRIPTOLEMUS
UNAMBIGUOUS
UNCLEANNESS
UNCONSCIOUS
UNCOUTHNESS
UNGODLINESS
UNHAPPINESS
UNRIGHTEOUS
UPRIGHTNESS
USELESSNESS
VACUOUSNESS
VERTIGINOUS
VICIOUSNESS
VISCOUNTESS
WAKEFULNESS
WAYWARDNESS
WELLINGTONS
WHEREABOUTS
WHITEFRIARS
WILLINGNESS
WISTFULNESS
WITHERSHINS
WOMANLINESS
WORLDFAMOUS
WORLDLINESS
XEROTRIPSIS
ABANDONMENT
ABORTIONIST
ABRIDGEMENT
ACCOMPANIST
ACHIEVEMENT
ACQUIESCENT
ADJOURNMENT
ADVANCEMENT
AGGLUTINANT
AMERCIAMENT
ANESTHETIST
APPEASEMENT
APPOINTMENT
APPURTENANT
ARBITRAMENT
ARRANGEMENT
ARTILLERIST
ASSYTHEMENT
BATTLEFRONT
BELLETTRIST
BELLIGERENT
BEREAVEMENT
BESIEGEMENT
BITTERSWEET
BLADDERWORT
BOMBARDMENT
BUMBERSHOOT
CALEFACIENT
CANDLELIGHT
CHIROPODIST
CIRCUMFLECT
CIRCUMSPECT
CLAIRVOYANT
COEFFICIENT
COLONIALIST
COMMANDMENT
COMMUNICANT
COMPARTMENT
COMPILEMENT
COMPLAISANT
CONCEALMENT
CONCOMITANT
CONFINEMENT
CONNECTICUT
CONSIGNMENT
CONSTITUENT
CONTAINMENT
CONTAMINANT
CONTEMPLANT
CONTENEMENT
CONTENTMENT
COUNTERFEIT
COUNTERFORT
COUNTERPART
CURTAILMENT
DECONSTRUCT
DELITESCENT
DEPARTEMENT
DERANGEMENT
DETERMINANT
DEVELOPMENT
DIPLOMATIST
DIPROTODONT
DISABLEMENT
DISARMAMENT
DISCERNMENT
DISOBEDIENT
DISSEPIMENT
DIVORCEMENT
DREADNOUGHT
EASTERNMOST
ELASTOPLAST
ELECTROTINT
EMBOÎTEMENT
EMPIECEMENT
EMPLACEMENT
EMPOWERMENT
ENCHANTMENT
ENDORSEMENT
ENFEOFFMENT
ENFORCEMENT
ENHANCEMENT
ENJAMBEMENT

ENLARGEMENT
ENSLAVEMENT
ENTABLEMENT
ENTITLEMENT
ENVIRONMENT
EPIGENESIST
EQUIDISTANT
EQUILIBRIST
EQUIPOLLENT
ETHNOLOGIST
ETYMOLOGIST
EXPECTORANT
EXTRAVAGANT
FARTHERMOST
FEHMGERICHT
FESTSCHRIFT
FINGERPRINT
FLABBERGAST
FLUORESCENT
FORETHOUGHT
FULFILLMENT
FUNAMBULIST
FURTHERMOST
GARNISHMENT
GENEALOGIST
GREASEPAINT
GROUNDSHEET
HEAVYWEIGHT
HISTOLOGIST
HYMNOLOGIST
HYPERMARKET
IDEOPRAXIST
ILLUSIONIST
IMPEACHMENT
IMPERIALIST
IMPERMANENT
IMPERTINENT
IMPROVEMENT
IMPROVIDENT
INADVERTENT
INCALESCENT
INCOMPETENT
INCONTINENT
INDEPENDENT
INDIFFERENT
INEFFICIENT
INEXPEDIENT
INSTALLMENT
INTELLIGENT
INVOLVEMENT
IRREDENTIST
JACQUEMINOT
KINCHINMORT
LANDSKNECHT
LAPIDESCENT
LIGHTWEIGHT
LUMINESCENT
MAGNIFICENT
MARGINALIST
MATERIALIST

MEADOWSWEET
MEASUREMENT
MEKHITARIST
MILQUETOAST
MINIATURIST
MODELMOLEST
MONOPSONIST
MYCOPHAGIST
NARRAGANSET
NATIONALIST
NEEDLEPOINT
NEUROLOGIST
NONDESCRIPT
NONEXISTENT
NOURISHMENT
NUMISMATIST
OBMUTESCENT
OBSOLESCENT
ODONTOBLAST
OMNIPRESENT
OPPORTUNIST
OPTOMETRIST
ORIENTALIST
OVERPAYMENT
OVERWROUGHT
PAPERWEIGHT
PARACHUTIST
PARTICIPANT
PATHOLOGIST
PERCEFOREST
PERSONALIST
PHILATELIST
PHILOLOGIST
PIERREPOINT
PISSASPHALT
PLANTAGENET
POLTERGEIST
PORTRAITIST
PREDICAMENT
PREDOMINANT
PRISCIANIST
PROCUREMENT
PROLETARIAT
PROTAGONIST
PROTUBERANT
RADIOLOGIST
REALIGNMENT
RECONSTRUCT
RECRUITMENT
REFRESHMENT
REFRIGERANT
RELEASEMENT
REMINISCENT
REPLACEMENT
REQUIREMENT
RESPLENDANT
RESPLENDENT
RESTATEMENT
RETROROCKET
RINTHEREOUT

SAUSAGEMEAT
SAXOPHONIST
SCUTTLEBUTT
SEARCHLIGHT
SECRETARIAT
SELFEVIDENT
SELFRESPECT
SIGNIFICANT
SOCIOLOGIST
SOROPTIMIST
SPEECHCRAFT
SPENDTHRIFT
SPREADSHEET
STAIRCARPET
STREETLIGHT
SUBCONTRACT
SUBDOMINANT
SUBSERVIENT
SUPERMARKET
SURVEILLANT
TAXIDERMIST
TELEPHONIST
TEMPERAMENT
TESSARAGLOT
THUNDERBOLT
TOBACCONIST
TRACKLEMENT
TRANSILIENT
TRANSLUCENT
TRANSPARENT
TRITAGONIST
TROPHOBLAST
TROUBLESPOT
ULTRAVIOLET
UNDERWEIGHT
UNIMPORTANT
UNOBSERVANT
UNREPENTANT
WASTEBASKET
WESTERNMOST
WHEELWRIGHT
WHITETHROAT
WIENERWURST
WITENAGEMOT
MONTESQUIEU
OUAGADOUGOU
PORTMANTEAU
KALASHNIKOV
BARTHOLOMEW
BLACKFELLOW
CLAPPERCLAW
COACHFELLOW
COUNTERGLOW
JINRICKSHAW
MARSHMALLOW
WAPPENSCHAW
WATERMEADOW
WHEELBARROW
WINDLESTRAW
CLARENCIEUX

PROGENITRIX
SCEUOPHYLAX
ABNORMALITY
ACCORDINGLY
ACCOUNTANCY
ADVERBIALLY
AGROSTOLOGY
ALTERNATELY
AMPHIBOLOGY
ANENCEPHALY
ANGELOLATRY
ANNIVERSARY
ANONYMOUSLY
APPALLINGLY
APPRECIABLY
APPROVINGLY
ARBITRARILY
ARCHAEOLOGY
ARISTOCRACY
ARRHENOTOKY
ASSIDUOUSLY
ASTRINGENCY
ATROCIOUSLY
ATTENTIVELY
AUDACIOUSLY
BEAUTIFULLY
BENEFICIARY
BICENTENARY
BLAMEWORTHY
BOTANOMANCY
BOYSENBERRY
BRILLIANTLY
BUREAUCRACY
CALLIGRAPHY
CAMPANOLOGY
CARRIAGEWAY
CARTOGRAPHY
CAUSTICALLY
CEASELESSLY
CHANCELLERY
CHEIROGNOMY
CHIROGRAPHY
CHOROGRAPHY
CHRISTMASSY
CHRONICALLY
CIRCULATORY
CLANJAMFRAY
CLIMATOLOGY
COMFORTABLY
COMMENDABLY
COMPETENTLY
COMPLACENCY
COMSTOCKERY
CONCEIVABLY
CONFEDERACY
CONFIDENTLY
CONSCIOUSLY
CONSERVANCY
CONSISTENCY
CONSULTANCY

CONTENTEDLY
CONTINGENCY
CONTINUALLY
CONTROVERSY
COURTEOUSLY
CREDIBILITY
CREDULOUSLY
CRIMINOLOGY
CRITHOMANCY
CULPABILITY
CUSTOMARILY
DANGEROUSLY
DECEITFULLY
DECEPTIVELY
DECLAMATORY
DEFENSIVELY
DELICIOUSLY
DELINQUENCY
DEMAGOGUERY
DERMATOLOGY
DESPERATELY
DESPONDENCY
DEUTERONOMY
DIFFERENTLY
DIFFIDENTLY
DISCOURTESY
DISCREPANCY
DISHONESTLY
DITTOGRAPHY
DOCUMENTARY
DOMESTICITY
DRASTICALLY
EFFECTIVELY
EFFECTUALLY
EFFICIENTLY
ELABORATELY
ELECTRICITY
ELIGIBILITY
EMOTIONALLY
EMPYROMANCY
EQUIVOCALLY
ERRATICALLY
ERRONEOUSLY
ESCHATOLOGY
ESSENTIALLY
ETHNOGRAPHY
EVENTUALITY
EXCEEDINGLY
EXCESSIVELY
EXCLUSIVELY
EXPECTANTLY
EXPLANATORY
EXPLORATORY
EXQUISITELY
EXTENSIVELY
FACETIOUSLY
FALLIBILITY
FAMILIARITY
FANATICALLY
FASHIONABLY

FAULTLESSLY
FEASIBILITY
FEROCIOUSLY
FESTINATELY
FINANCIALLY
FLEXIBILITY
FORTNIGHTLY
FORTUNATELY
FRAGMENTARY
FRANTICALLY
FRATERNALLY
FREEMASONRY
FRIGHTFULLY
FRIVOLOUSLY
FRUITLESSLY
FUNCTIONARY
GALLIMAUFRY
GARRULOUSLY
GASTRECTOMY
GENERICALLY
GENETICALLY
GENTLEMANLY
GERONTOLOGY
GLASTONBURY
GRAPHICALLY
GULLIBILITY
GYNAECOLOGY
HAGIOGRAPHY
HALFHOLIDAY
HAPHAZARDLY
HEARTLESSLY
HEBDOMADARY
HEPATOSCOPY
HERPETOLOGY
HIGHQUALITY
HILARIOUSLY
HOBBLEDEHOY
HOMOEOPATHY
HOMOGENEITY
HOSPITALITY
HUCKLEBERRY
HURTLEBERRY
HYPERTROPHY
ICONOGRAPHY
IDENTICALLY
IDIOTICALLY
IDYLLICALLY
ILLOGICALLY
ILLUSIONARY
IMMEDIATELY
IMMORTALITY
IMPARTIALLY
IMPASSIVELY
IMPATIENTLY
IMPERIOUSLY
IMPETUOSITY
IMPETUOUSLY
IMPORTANTLY
IMPROPRIETY
IMPRUDENTLY
IMPULSIVELY
INCESSANTLY
INCONGRUITY
INCONSTANCY
INCORRECTLY
INCREDULITY
INDIGNANTLY
INDIVISIBLY
INDUBITABLY
INDULGENTLY
INEXCUSABLY
INFERIORITY
INFERTILITY
INFORMALITY
INFREQUENCY
INGENIOUSLY
INQUIRINGLY
INSIDIOUSLY
INSINCERITY
INSISTENTLY
INSTABILITY
INSULTINGLY
INTENSIVELY
INTERCALARY
INTOLERABLY
INTREPIDITY
INTRICATELY
INTUITIVELY
INVOLUNTARY
IRONMONGERY
IRREGULARLY
IRREPARABLY
JABBERWOCKY
JUDICIOUSLY
JUSTIFIABLY
LABORIOUSLY
LACONICALLY
LITHOGRAPHY
LOGODAEDALY
LONGANIMITY
LONGINQUITY
LUXURIANTLY
LUXURIOUSLY
LYCANTHROPY
MAGNANIMITY
MALICIOUSLY
MARIONBERRY
MASCULINITY
MASTERFULLY
MEDICINALLY
MELODIOUSLY
MERCILESSLY
METEOROLOGY
METHODOLOGY
MISANTHROPY
MISIDENTIFY
MOMENTARILY
MONSTROSITY
MONTMORENCY
MULTISTOREY
NATIONALITY
NECESSARILY
NEIGHBOURLY
NICKNACKERY
NOISELESSLY
NOTORIOUSLY
NUMERICALLY
OBJECTIVELY
OBJECTIVITY
OBSERVATORY
OBSESSIVELY
OBSTINATELY
OFFENSIVELY
OFFHANDEDLY
OFFICIOUSLY
ONEIROMANCY
OPPORTUNELY
OPPORTUNITY
ORGANICALLY
ORIGINALITY
ORNITHOLOGY
ORTHOGRAPHY
OSTEOPLASTY
PACIFICALLY
PAEDOTROPHY
PALEOGRAPHY
PARVANIMITY
PECULIARITY
PERCEPTIBLY
PERENNIALLY
PERFUNCTORY
PERISSOLOGY
PERMANENTLY
PERPETUALLY
PERSONALITY
PERSPICUITY
PERTINACITY
PERTINENTLY
PHALANSTERY
PHOTOGRAPHY
PHRASEOLOGY
PHYSIOGNOMY
PODSNAPPERY
POINTLESSLY
POLITICALLY
PONDEROUSLY
PORNOGRAPHY
POSSIBILITY
POTENTIALLY
PRACTICALLY
PREDICTABLY
PRELIMINARY
PREMATURELY
PREMONITORY
PREPARATORY
PRINCIPALLY
PROBABILITY
PRODIGALITY
PROFESSEDLY
PROFICIENCY
PROMINENTLY
PROMISCUITY
PROPINQUITY
PROPRIETARY
PROSAICALLY
PROTONOTARY
PTOCHOCRACY
PUNCTUALITY
QUERULOUSLY
RADIOGRAPHY
RAPTUROUSLY
RATIONALITY
RAVISHINGLY
REACTIONARY
READABILITY
RECEPTIVITY
RECIPROCITY
RECURRENTLY
REFLEXOLOGY
REFORMATORY
REGRETFULLY
REGRETTABLY
RELIABILITY
RELIGIOUSLY
RELUCTANTLY
RESENTFULLY
RESISTIVITY
RESPECTABLY
RESPIRATORY
RESPONSIBLY
RETALIATORY
RHABDOMANCY
RHEUMATICKY
RIGHTEOUSLY
RUDIMENTARY
SAGACIOUSLY
SALACIOUSLY
SATIRICALLY
SCEPTICALLY
SCIENTOLOGY
SCREAMINGLY
SCRIMSHANDY
SCULDUDDERY
SCULDUGGERY
SECONDARILY
SECRETIVELY
SEDIMENTARY
SELECTIVELY
SELECTIVITY
SENSIBILITY
SENSITIVELY
SENSITIVITY
SERENDIPITY
SHAFTESBURY
SHAMELESSLY
SINGULARITY
SKEPTICALLY
SKULDUDDERY
SKULDUGGERY
SLIGHTINGLY
SOCIABILITY
SORROWFULLY
SOUNDLESSLY
SOVEREIGNTY
SPIRITUALLY
SPONTANEITY
STEADFASTLY
STENOGRAPHY
STIPENDIARY
STRENUOUSLY
STRINGENTLY
SUFFICIENCY
SUITABILITY
SUMPTUOUSLY
SUPERFLUITY
SUPERIORITY
SUPERVISORY
SUPPOSITORY
TACHYGRAPHY
TACITURNITY
TANGIBILITY
TASTELESSLY
TCHAIKOVSKY
TECHNICALLY
TEMPORARILY
TENACIOUSLY
TENTATIVELY
TERMINOLOGY
THANKLESSLY
THEOPNEUSTY
TIMBROPHILY
TRACHEOTOMY
TRANQUILITY
TRUCULENTLY
TRUSTWORTHY
UNANIMOUSLY
UNAVOIDABLY
UNCERTAINTY
UNDOUBTEDLY
UNFAILINGLY
UNIVERSALLY
UNNATURALLY
UNNECESSARY
UNWITTINGLY
VALEDICTORY
VARIABILITY
VERSATILITY
VICARIOUSLY
VIVACIOUSLY
VOLCANOLOGY
VOLUNTARILY
VORACIOUSLY
VULCANOLOGY
WHIGMALEERY
WINTERBERRY
WONDERFULLY
RAZZAMATAZZ

12:1

ABBREVIATION
ABOLITIONIST
ABSQUATULATE
ACADEMICALLY
ACCELERATION
ACCENTUATION
ACCIDENTALLY
ACCOMPANYING
ACCOMPLISHED
ACCORDIONIST
ACCOUCHEMENT
ACCOUTREMENT
ACCUMULATION
ACHLAMYDEOUS
ACKNOWLEDGED
ACQUAINTANCE
ACQUIESCENCE
ADAPTABILITY
ADDITIONALLY
ADJECTIVALLY
ADJUDICATION
ADMINISTRATE
ADMONISHMENT
ADSCITITIOUS
ADULTERATION
ADVANTAGEOUS
ADVANTAGIOUS
ADVENTITIOUS
ADVISABILITY
AECIDIOSPORE
AERODYNAMICS
AERONAUTICAL
AETHRIOSCOPE
AFFECTIONATE
AFORETHOUGHT
AFTEREFFECTS
AFTERTHOUGHT
AGALMATOLITE
AGAMOGENETIC
AGATHODAIMON
AGGRESSIVELY
AGRIBUSINESS
AGRICULTURAL
AIRCRAFTSMAN
ALEXIPHARMIC
ALIMENTATIVE
ALLITERATION
ALPHABETICAL
ALPHANUMERIC
AMALGAMATION
AMARANTACEAE
AMBASSADRESS
AMBIDEXTROUS
AMBULANCEMAN
AMELIORATION
AMPHISBAENIC
AMPHISTOMOUS
AMPHITHEATER
AMPHITHEATRE
ANAESTHETISE
ANAESTHETIST
ANAESTHETIZE
ANAMORPHOSIS
ANDOUILLETTE
ANDROSTERONE
ANECATHARSIS
ANEMOPHILOUS
ANNIHILATION
ANNOUNCEMENT
ANNUNCIATION
ANTAGONISTIC
ANTANANARIVO
ANTEDILUVIAN
ANTEMERIDIAN
ANTHELMINTIC
ANTHROPOLOGY
ANTIBACCHIUS
ANTIBARBARUS
ANTICIPATION
ANTICIPATORY
ANTILEGOMENA
ANTIMACASSAR
ANTIMETABOLE
ANTIMNEMONIC
ANTINEUTRINO
ANTIPARTICLE
ANTIRACHITIC
ANTISTROPHON
ANTITHROMBIN
ANTONINIANUS
APFELSTRUDEL
APLANOGAMETE
APOLLINARIAN
APOSTROPHISE
APPENDECTOMY
APPENDICITIS
APPOGGIATURA
APPRECIATION
APPRECIATIVE
APPREHENSION
APPREHENSIVE
APPROACHABLE
APPURTENANCE
ARBORESCENCE
ARCHILOCHIAN
ARCHIPELAGOS
ARCHITECTURE
ARFVEDSONITE
ARISTOCRATIC
ARISTOLOCHIA
ARISTOPHANES
ARISTOTELEAN
ARITHMETICAL
AROMATHERAPY
ARSENOPYRITE
ARTHROPLASTY
ARTICULATION
ARTIFICIALLY
ARTILLERYMAN
ARTIODACTYLA
ARTISTICALLY
ASPARAGINASE
ASPHYXIATION
ASSIMILATION
ASSUEFACTION
ASTONISHMENT
ASTROLOGICAL
ASTRONOMICAL
ASTROPHYSICS
ASYMMETRICAL
ATHEROMATOUS
ATMOSPHERICS
ATTRACTIVELY
ATTRIBUTABLE
AUGMENTATION
AUSCULTATION
AUSPICIOUSLY
AUSTRALASIAN
AUSTRONESIAN
AUTHENTICATE
AUTHENTICITY
AVAILABILITY
AWARDWINNING
AWAYABSOLUTE
AWEINSPIRING
AYUNTAMIENTO
BABINGTONITE
BACCHANALIAN
BACKBREAKING
BACKWARDNESS
BACKWOODSMAN
BACTERIOLOGY
BACTERIOSTAT
BAIRNSFATHER
BAMBOCCIADES
BANANALANDER
BANDERSNATCH
BANTAMWEIGHT
BARBERMONGER
BARNSTORMING
BARRANQUILLA
BATTLEGROUND
BEACONSFIELD
BEAUMARCHAIS
BEAUMONTAGUE
BEAUMONTIQUE
BEHAVIOURISM
BELLIGERENCY
BENEFACTRESS
BENEVOLENTLY
BERTHOLLETIA
BERTILLONAGE
BESSERWISSER
BETHLEHEMITE
BEWILDERMENT
BIBLIOGRAPHY
BIBLIOPEGIST
BICAMERALISM
BICENTENNIAL
BIELORUSSIAN
BILLINGSGATE
BIOCHEMISTRY
BIODIVERSITY
BIOGRAPHICAL
BIRDWATCHING
BLABBERMOUTH
BLACKCURRANT
BLANDISHMENT
BLEFUSCUDIAN
BLENNORRHOEA
BLETHERSKATE
BLOODSTAINED
BLOODTHIRSTY
BLUESTOCKING
BOISTEROUSLY
BOOBYTRAPPED
BOONDOGGLING
BOUGAINVILLE
BOULEVARDIER
BRACHYCEPHAL
BRAINWASHING
BRANCHIOPODA
BREAKTHROUGH
BREASTPLOUGH
BREASTSUMMER
BREATHALYSER
BREATHLESSLY
BREATHTAKING
BRICKFIELDER
BRILLIANTINE
BROADCASTING
BRONTOSAURUS
BUCKLEBEGGAR
BUNKOSTEERER
BUREAUCRATIC
BUSINESSLIKE
BUTTERSCOTCH
BYELORUSSIAN
CABINETMAKER
CALCEAMENTUM
CALLIGRAPHIC
CALLISTHENES
CALUMNIATION
CAMIKNICKERS
CAMPANULARIA
CAMPODEIFORM
CANCELLATION
CANONIZATION
CANTANKEROUS
CANTILEVERED
CAPERCAILLIE
CAPERCAILZIE
CAPITULATION
CARAVANSERAI
CARBOHYDRATE
CARCINOGENIC
CARDINDEXING

CARDIOLOGIST
CARELESSNESS
CARICATURIST
CARLOVINGIAN
CARPETBAGGER
CARRIWITCHET
CARTHAGINIAN
CARTOGRAPHER
CARTOGRAPHIC
CASSITERIDES
CASTERBRIDGE
CATADIOPTRIC
CATAPHYSICAL
CATASTROPHIC
CATHETOMETER
CAUTIOUSNESS
CEREBROTONIC
CEREMONIALLY
CHAIRMANSHIP
CHALICOTHERE
CHAMPIONSHIP
CHARACTERIZE
CHARTERHOUSE
CHASTISEMENT
CHAUVINISTIC
CHEERFULNESS
CHEESEBURGER
CHEESEMONGER
CHEESEPARING
CHEMOTHERAPY
CHESTERFIELD
CHILDBEARING
CHILDISHNESS
CHIROPRACTIC
CHIROPRACTOR
CHITTERLINGS
CHLORINATION
CHONDRIOSOME
CHOREOGRAPHY
CHORIZONTIST
CHREMATISTIC
CHRESTOMATHY
CHRISTIANITY
CHURCHWARDEN
CHURLISHNESS
CIRCASSIENNE
CIRCUMCISION
CIRCUMGYRATE
CIRCUMSCRIBE
CIRCUMSTANCE
CIVILISATION
CIVILIZATION
CLAIRVOYANCE
CLAIRVOYANCY
CLAMJAMPHRIE
CLANNISHNESS
CLAPPERBOARD
CLARINETTIST
CLASSIFIABLE
CLAUDICATION

CLAVICEMBALO
CLEARSIGHTED
CLEISTOGAMIC
COCCIDIOSTAT
CODIFICATION
COHABITATION
COINCIDENTAL
COLDSHOULDER
COLLABORATOR
COLLECTIVELY
COLLECTORATE
COLLOQUIALLY
COLLUCTATION
COLLYWOBBLES
COLONIZATION
COLOQUINTIDA
COMBINATIONS
COMMANDMENTS
COMMENCEMENT
COMMENDATION
COMMENDATORY
COMMENSURATE
COMMERCIALLY
COMMISSARIAT
COMMISSIONED
COMMISSIONER
COMMONWEALTH
COMMUNICABLE
COMPANIONWAY
COMPELLATION
COMPENSATION
COMPENSATORY
COMPLACENTLY
COMPLETENESS
COMPLICATION
COMPROMISING
COMPURGATION
CONCENTRATED
CONCILIATION
CONCILIATORY
CONCLUSIVELY
CONCURRENTLY
CONDEMNATION
CONDENSATION
CONDUCTIVITY
CONFECTIONER
CONFESSIONAL
CONFIDENTIAL
CONFIRMATION
CONFIRMATORY
CONFISCATION
CONGENITALLY
CONGLOMERATE
CONGRATULATE
CONGREGATION
CONQUISTADOR
CONSCRIPTION
CONSECRATION
CONSEQUENCES
CONSEQUENTLY

CONSERVATION
CONSERVATISM
CONSERVATIVE
CONSERVATORY
CONSIDERABLE
CONSIDERABLY
CONSISTENTLY
CONSOLIDATED
CONSOLIDATOR
CONSPECTUITY
CONSTABULARY
CONSTIPATION
CONSTITUENCY
CONSTITUENTS
CONSTITUTION
CONSTRICTION
CONSTRUCTION
CONSTRUCTIVE
CONSULTATION
CONSULTATIVE
CONSUMMATION
CONTABESCENT
CONTAMINATED
CONTEMPORARY
CONTEMPTIBLE
CONTEMPTUOUS
CONTERMINOUS
CONTIGNATION
CONTINUATION
CONTINUOUSLY
CONTRAPPOSTO
CONTRAPUNTAL
CONTRARINESS
CONTRIBUTION
CONTRIBUTORY
CONTRITURATE
CONTROLLABLE
CONTUMACIOUS
CONVALESCENT
CONVALESCING
CONVENIENCES
CONVENIENTLY
CONVENTIONAL
CONVERSATION
CONVEYANCING
CONVINCINGLY
CONVIVIALITY
COORDINATION
COSCINOMANCY
COSMOPOLITAN
COSTERMONGER
COUNTERBLAST
COUNTERCLAIM
COUNTERMARCH
COUNTERPOINT
COUNTERPOISE
COURAGEOUSLY
COURTMARTIAL
COVETOUSNESS
CRASHLANDING

CRASSAMENTUM
CREATIVENESS
CREMAILLIÈRE
CRISTOBALITE
CROSSBENCHER
CROSSCOUNTRY
CROSSEXAMINE
CROSSSECTION
CRYPTOGRAPHY
CURMUDGEONLY
CYMOTRICHOUS
DAGUERROTYPE
DARLINGTONIA
DEAMBULATORY
DEASPIRATION
DEBILITATING
DECAPITATION
DECELERATION
DECENTRALISE
DECENTRALIZE
DECIPHERABLE
DECIPHERMENT
DECONGESTANT
DECORATIVELY
DEFLATIONARY
DEGENERATION
DEHUMIDIFIER
DELIBERATELY
DELIBERATION
DELICATESSEN
DEMILITARIZE
DEMIMONDAINE
DEMONSTRABLE
DEMONSTRABLY
DEMONSTRATOR
DENDROLOGIST
DENOMINATION
DENUNCIATION
DEPARTMENTAL
DEPOPULATION
DEPRECIATION
DEPRECIATORY
DEREGULATION
DERESTRICTED
DESIRABILITY
DESSERTSPOON
DEUTEROSCOPY
DIAGRAMMATIC
DIALECTICIAN
DICTATORSHIP
DIENCEPHALON
DIFFERENTIAL
DILAPIDATION
DILATORINESS
DIPLOGENESIS
DIPRIONIDIAN
DIRECTORSHIP
DISACCHARIDE
DISADVANTAGE
DISAGREEABLE

DISAGREEMENT
DISAPPEARING
DISAPPOINTED
DISASTROUSLY
DISCIPLINARY
DISCOMEDUSAE
DISCOMFITURE
DISCOMYCETES
DISCONCERTED
DISCONNECTED
DISCONSOLATE
DISCONTENTED
DISCOURAGING
DISCOURTEOUS
DISCRIMINATE
DISDAINFULLY
DISEMBARRASS
DISENCHANTED
DISFRANCHISE
DISHONORABLE
DISHONORABLY
DISINCENTIVE
DISINFECTANT
DISINGENUOUS
DISINTEGRATE
DISOBEDIENCE
DISORGANIZED
DISORIENTATE
DISPENSATION
DISPLACEMENT
DISPOSSESSED
DISQUISITION
DISREPECTFUL
DISREPUTABLE
DISSATISFIED
DISSERTATION
DISSOCIATION
DISTILLATION
DISTINCTNESS
DISTRIBUTION
DISTRIBUTIVE
DIVERTICULUM
DIVERTIMENTO
DOGMATICALLY
DOLPHINARIUM
DOMESTICATED
DONNERWETTER
DORSIVENTRAL
DOUBLEDECKER
DOUBLEGLAZED
DRAMATICALLY
DRAMATURGIST
DRESSINGDOWN
DRINKDRIVING
DUNNIEWASSAL
DYSTELEOLOGY
EAVESDROPPER
ECCENTRICITY
ECCLESIASTES
ECCLESIASTIC
ECONOMICALLY
ECSTATICALLY
EDUCATIONIST
EFFERVESCENT
EFFORTLESSLY
EGYPTOLOGIST
ELASMOBRANCH
ELECTRICALLY
ELECTROLYSIS
ELECTROPLATE
ELECTROTONUS
ELEEMOSYNARY
EMANCIPATION
EMASCULATION
EMBARRASSING
EMBEZZLEMENT
EMBROIDERESS
EMPHATICALLY
ENANTIOMORPH
ENANTIOPATHY
ENCHEIRIDION
ENCIRCLEMENT
ENCROACHMENT
ENCYCLOPEDIA
ENCYCLOPEDIC
ENERGYSAVING
ENGLISHWOMAN
ENGLISHWOMEN
ENHYPOSTASIA
ENTANGLEMENT
ENTEROMORPHA
ENTEROPNEUST
ENTERPRISING
ENTERTAINING
ENTHUSIASTIC
ENTOMOLOGIST
ENTOMOSTRACA
ENTOPLASTRON
ENTREATINGLY
ENTRENCHMENT
ENTREPRENEUR
EPACRIDACEAE
EPANORTHOSIS
EPENCEPHALON
EPIDEICTICAL
EPIGRAMMATIC
EPIPHENOMENA
EPISCOPALIAN
EPISTEMOLOGY
EPISTOLATERS
EPITHALAMION
EPITHALAMIUM
EQUIVOCATION
EQUIVOCATORY
ERATOSTHENES
ERYTHROMYCIN
ESCAPOLOGIST
ESPAGNOLETTE
ESSENTIALITY
ESTHETICALLY
ESTRANGEMENT
ETEPIMELETIC
ETHEROMANIAC
ETHNOLOGICAL
ETYMOLOGICAL
ETYMOLOGICON
EULENSPIEGEL
EVENHANDEDLY
EVENTEMPERED
EVOLUTIONARY
EXACERBATION
EXAGGERATION
EXASPERATING
EXASPERATION
EXCHANGEABLE
EXCITABILITY
EXCRUCIATING
EXCRUCIATION
EXHAUSTIVELY
EXHIBITIONER
EXHILARATING
EXHILARATION
EXPERIMENTAL
EXPLOITATION
EXSERVICEMAN
EXSUFFLICATE
EXTENSIONIST
EXTINGUISHER
EXTORTIONATE
EXTRADITABLE
EXTRAVAGANCE
EXTRAVAGANZA
FAINTHEARTED
FAITHFULNESS
FARTHINGLAND
FASTIDIOUSLY
FEARLESSNESS
FEATHERBRAIN
FEHMGERICHTE
FELDSPATHOID
FERMENTATION
FIDDLESTICKS
FIGURATIVELY
FINALIZATION
FIRSTFOOTING
FLAGELLATION
FLAMBOYANTLY
FLITTERMOUSE
FLORICULTURE
FLUORESCENCE
FLUORIDATION
FOOTSLOGGING
FORCEFULNESS
FORMALDEHYDE
FORTUITOUSLY
FOTHERINGHAY
FRACTIONALLY
FRANKALMOIGN
FRANKENSTEIN
FRANKINCENSE
FRAUENDIENST
FREIGHTLINER
FRIENDLINESS
FRONTIERSMAN
FRONTISPIECE
FRUITFULNESS
FRUMENTATION
FULMINATIONS
FUNCTIONALLY
FUNCTIONLESS
FUNDAMENTALS
FUSTILLIRIAN
GAINSBOROUGH
GALLIGASKINS
GALLINACEOUS
GALLIVANTING
GALVANOMETER
GAMESMANSHIP
GASTARBEITER
GASTROSOPHER
GENEALOGICAL
GENETHLIACON
GENTLETAMPER
GEOGRAPHICAL
GEOLOGICALLY
GEOMETRICIAN
GEOPHYSICIST
GERIATRICIAN
GERONTOCRACY
GESELLSCHAFT
GIBRALTARIAN
GIGANTOMACHY
GLADIATORIAL
GLOBETROTTER
GLOCKENSPIEL
GLUBBDUBDRIB
GLYNDEBOURNE
GOBBLEDEGOOK
GOBBLEDYGOOK
GONADOTROPIN
GONDWANALAND
GOOSEPIMPLES
GOVERNMENTAL
GRACEFULNESS
GRACIOUSNESS
GRANDISONIAN
GRANDMONTINE
GRANDPARENTS
GRAPHOLOGIST
GRASSWIDOWER
GRATEFULNESS
GREENGROCERS
GREENGROCERY
GRISEOFULVIN
GROSSULARITE
GUARDIANSHIP
GUILDENSTERN
GYMNOSOPHIST
GYNECOLOGIST
HABERDASHERS

HABERDASHERY
HAEMATEMESIS
HAEMOPHILIAC
HAEMORRHOIDS
HAIRDRESSERS
HAIRDRESSING
HAIRSPLITTER
HALLANSHAKER
HALLUCINOGEN
HAMARTHRITIS
HAMBLETONIAN
HAMMERHEADED
HANDKERCHIEF
HAPPENSTANCE
HAPPYGOLUCKY
HARMONIOUSLY
HARNESSMAKER
HARUMFRODITE
HEADMISTRESS
HEADQUARTERS
HEARTSTRINGS
HEARTWARMING
HELIOGABALUS
HELLGRAMMITE
HELPLESSNESS
HEMICHORDATA
HENCEFORWARD
HEPHTHEMIMER
HEREDITAMENT
HERMENEUTICS
HERMENEUTIST
HERMETICALLY
HEROICOMICAL
HETEROCLITIC
HETEROCONTAE
HETEROPHORIA
HETEROPLASIA
HETEROSEXUAL
HETEROSOMATA
HIERARCHICAL
HIEROGLYPHIC
HIEROGRAMMAT
HIEROPHANTIC
HIGHFALUTING
HILDEBRANDIC
HINDQUARTERS
HIPPOCRATISE
HIPPOCREPIAN
HIPPOPOTAMUS
HISTIOPHORUS
HISTORICALLY
HOBBIDIDANCE
HOLIDAYMAKER
HOMESICKNESS
HOMOEOPATHIC
HOMOTHERMOUS
HOPELESSNESS
HORIZONTALLY
HORRIFICALLY
HORSEMANSHIP
HORTICULTURE
HOUSEBREAKER
HOUSEKEEPING
HOUSETOHOUSE
HOUSEWARMING
HUDIBRASTICS
HUMANITARIAN
HUMANIZATION
HYDROCHLORIC
HYDROGRAPHER
HYDROQUINONE
HYDROTHERAPY
HYGIENICALLY
HYMNOGRAPHER
HYPERBOLICAL
HYPERPYRETIC
HYPERSARCOMA
HYPERTENSION
HYPNOTHERAPY
HYPNOTICALLY
HYPOCHONDRIA
HYPOCRITICAL
HYPOTHECATOR
HYPOTHETICAL
HYSTERECTOMY
HYSTERICALLY
IAMBOGRAPHER
ICHTHYOCOLLA
ICHTHYOPSIDA
ICONOCLASTIC
IDEALIZATION
IDENTIFIABLE
IDIOSYNCRASY
IDIOTHERMOUS
ILLEGIBILITY
ILLEGITIMACY
ILLEGITIMATE
ILLOGICALITY
ILLUMINATING
ILLUMINATION
ILLUSTRATION
ILLUSTRATIVE
IMMACULATELY
IMMEASURABLE
IMMEASURABLY
IMMODERATELY
IMMODERATION
IMMUNIZATION
IMMUNOLOGIST
IMMUTABILITY
IMPARTIALITY
IMPENETRABLE
IMPERFECTION
IMPERISHABLE
IMPERSONALLY
IMPERSONATOR
IMPERTINENCE
IMPLANTATION
IMPOLITENESS
IMPOVERISHED
IMPREGNATION
IMPRESSIVELY
IMPRISONMENT
IMPROVIDENCE
INACCESSIBLE
INACCURATELY
INADEQUATELY
INADMISSIBLE
INADVERTENCE
INAPPLICABLE
INARTICULATE
INAUGURATION
INAUSPICIOUS
INCALCULABLE
INCANDESCENT
INCAPABILITY
INCAPACITATE
INCAUTIOUSLY
INCIDENTALLY
INCINERATION
INCOHERENTLY
INCOMPARABLE
INCOMPARABLY
INCOMPATIBLE
INCOMPETENCE
INCOMPLETELY
INCONCLUSIVE
INCONSEQUENT
INCONSISTENT
INCONSOLABLE
INCONTINENCE
INCONVENIENT
INCORPORATED
INCORRIGIBLE
INCORRIGIBLY
INCREASINGLY
INCRUSTATION
INCUNABULIST
INDEBTEDNESS
INDECLINABLE
INDEFENSIBLE
INDEFINITELY
INDEPENDENCE
INDIFFERENCE
INDIGESTIBLE
INDISCRETION
INDISPUTABLE
INDISPUTABLY
INDISSOLUBLE
INDISTINCTLY
INDIVIDUALLY
INDOCTRINATE
INDUSTRIALLY
INEFFICIENCY
INERADICABLE
INESCUTCHEON
INEXACTITUDE
INEXPERIENCE
INEXPLICABLE
INEXPLICABLY
INEXTRICABLE
INEXTRICABLY
INFELICITOUS
INFILTRATION
INFLAMMATION
INFLAMMATORY
INFLATIONARY
INFORMIDABLE
INFREQUENTLY
INFRINGEMENT
INGRATIATING
INHARMONIOUS
INHOSPITABLE
INNATTENTIVE
INNOMINABLES
INORDINATELY
INSALUBRIOUS
INSEMINATION
INSOLUBILITY
INSPECTORATE
INSTALLATION
INSTAURATION
INSTRUCTIONS
INSTRUCTRESS
INSTRUMENTAL
INSUFFERABLE
INSUFFERABLY
INSUFFICIENT
INSURRECTION
INTELLECTUAL
INTELLIGENCE
INTELLIGIBLE
INTEMPERANCE
INTENERATION
INTERCEPTION
INTERCESSION
INTERCHANGED
INTERFERENCE
INTERJECTION
INTERLOCUTOR
INTERMEDIARY
INTERMEDIATE
INTERMINABLE
INTERMINABLY
INTERMISSION
INTERMITTENT
INTERPRETING
INTERRELATED
INTERROGATOR
INTERRUPTION
INTERSECTION
INTERSPERSED
INTERSTELLAR
INTERVENTION
INTIMIDATING
INTIMIDATION
INTOXICATING
INTOXICATION
INTRANSIGENT
INTRANSITIVE

INTRAUTERINE
INTRODUCTION
INTRODUCTORY
INVALIDATION
INVERTEBRATE
INVESTIGATOR
INVIGORATING
INVIGORATION
INVISIBILITY
INVULNERABLE
IRASCIBILITY
IRRATIONALLY
IRREDEEMABLE
IRREGULARITY
IRRESISTIBLE
IRRESOLUTELY
IRRESOLUTION
IRRESOLVABLE
IRRESPECTIVE
IRREVERENTLY
IRREVERSIBLE
IRRITABILITY
ISHMAELITISH
ISOBILATERAL
ISOLATIONISM
ISOLATIONIST
JENNYSPINNER
JOURNALISTIC
JURISDICTION
KALEIDOSCOPE
KALISTOCRACY
KATHAREVOUSA
KATZENJAMMER
KERAUNOGRAPH
KILLIKINNICK
KINAESTHETIC
KINDERGARTEN
KIRSCHWASSER
KLEPTOMANIAC
KLETTERSCHUE
KLIPSPRINGER
LABANOTATION
LABOURSAVING
LABYRINTHINE
LALLAPALOOZA
LAMELLICORNE
LAMENTATIONS
LAMPADEDROMY
LANCASTERIAN
LANGUEDOCIAN
LASCIVIOUSLY
LATIROSTRATE
LAUREATESHIP
LEGALIZATION
LEGIONNAIRES
LEGITIMATELY
LEIOTRICHOUS
LEPIDOMELANE
LEXICOGRAPHY
LICKTRENCHER
LIFELESSNESS
LIGHTHEARTED
LILLIBULLERO
LILLIBURLERO
LINCOLNSHIRE
LIQUEFACTION
LISTLESSNESS
LITHOGRAPHIC
LITHOLATROUS
LIVERPUDLIAN
LONGDISTANCE
LONGITUDINAL
LONGSHOREMAN
LONGSTANDING
LOXODROMICAL
LUGUBRIOUSLY
LUMINESCENCE
LUMINISCENCE
LUXEMBOURGER
LUXULLIANITE
LYMANTRIIDAE
MACABERESQUE
MACHAIRODONT
MACMILLANITE
MACROPODIDAE
MADEMOISELLE
MAGNETICALLY
MAGNIFICENCE
MAGNILOQUENT
MAJESTICALLY
MALACOSTRACA
MALFORMATION
MALLEABILITY
MALLOPHAGOUS
MALNUTRITION
MALPRACTICES
MALTREATMENT
MANGELWURZEL
MANIPULATION
MANIPULATIVE
MANOEUVRABLE
MANSLAUGHTER
MANUFACTURER
MARCOBRUNNER
MARCONIGRAPH
MARKSMANSHIP
MARLINESPIKE
MARRIAGEABLE
MARSEILLAISE
MASSERANDUBA
MASSPRODUCED
MASTERSTROKE
MASTIGOPHORA
MASTURBATION
MATHEMATICAL
MEANINGFULLY
MECHANICALLY
MECHITHARIST
MELODRAMATIC
MENSTRUATION
MERETRICIOUS
MERISTEMATIC
MERITRICIOUS
MERRYTHOUGHT
MERVEILLEUSE
MESOTHELIOMA
METAGNATHOUS
METALLOPHONE
METALLURGIST
METAMORPHISM
METAMORPHOSE
METAPHORICAL
METAPHYSICAL
METHODICALLY
METICULOUSLY
METROPOLITAN
MICHELANGELO
MICROCLIMATE
MIDDLEWEIGHT
MILITARISTIC
MINDBOGGLING
MINDFULLNESS
MINERALOGIST
MINICOMPUTER
MINISTRATION
MIRACULOUSLY
MISADVENTURE
MISANTHROPIC
MISAPPREHEND
MISBEHAVIOUR
MISCALCULATE
MISDELIVERED
MISDEMEANOUR
MISINTERPRET
MISPLACEMENT
MISPRONOUNCE
MISQUOTATION
MISREPRESENT
MISSTATEMENT
MISTREATMENT
MITRAILLEUSE
MNEMOTECHNIC
MOBILIZATION
MODIFICATION
MOISTURIZING
MONOSYLLABIC
MONOSYLLABLE
MONOTONOUSLY
MONTESSORIAN
MOONLIGHTING
MOSBOLLETJIE
MOTORCYCLIST
MOUSQUETAIRE
MOUTHBROODER
MUCILAGINOUS
MUDDLEHEADED
MUGGLETONIAN
MULLIGATAWNY
MULTICOLORED
MULTIFARIOUS
MULTILATERAL
MULTIPLICITY
MUNICIPALITY
MUSICOLOGIST
MUTESSARIFAT
MYRINGOSCOPE
MYSTERIOUSLY
MYTHOLOGICAL
NARCISSISTIC
NATURALISTIC
NAVIGABILITY
NEIGHBORHOOD
NEIGHBOURING
NEOCLASSICAL
NEOPLATONISM
NEPENTHACEAE
NEPHELOMETER
NEUROLOGICAL
NEUROTICALLY
NEVERTHELESS
NEWFOUNDLAND
NEWSPAPERMAN
NIGHTCLOTHES
NOCONFIDENCE
NOMENCLATURE
NONAGENARIAN
NONALCOHOLIC
NONCHALANTLY
NONCOMMITTAL
NONEXISTENCE
NONRESIDENCE
NONRESISTANT
NORTHEASTERN
NORTHERNMOST
NORTHWESTERN
NOTIFICATION
NUTRITIONIST
NYCHTHEMERON
NYMPHOMANIAC
OBEDIENTIARY
OBLITERATION
OBSEQUIOUSLY
OBSERVANTINE
OBSOLESCENCE
OBSOLETENESS
OBSTETRICIAN
OBSTREPEROUS
OCCASIONALLY
OCCUPATIONAL
OCEANOGRAPHY
OCTASTROPHIC
OCTOGENARIAN
OLDFASHIONED
ONCORHYNCHUS
ONEIROCRITIC
ONOMATOPOEIA
ONOMATOPOEIC
OPHIOGLOSSUM
OPINIONATIVE
OPISTHOGRAPH

OPPRESSIVELY
OREOPITHECUS
OREOPITHEOUS
ORGANISATION
ORGANIZATION
ORIENTEERING
ORNITHOGALUM
ORTHODONTICS
ORTHOGENESIS
ORTHOPAEDICS
ORTHOPAEDIST
ORTHORHOMBIC
ORTHOTONESIS
OSCILLOSCOPE
OSSIFICATION
OSTENTATIOUS
OSTEOMALACIA
OSTEOPOROSIS
OTHERWORLDLY
OUTBUILDINGS
OUTMANOEUVRE
OUTRAGEOUSLY
OUTSTRETCHED
OVERCROWDING
OVERDRESSING
OVERESTIMATE
OVEREXERTION
OVERPOWERING
OVERSCUTCHED
OVERSTRAINED
OVERWHELMING
OXYACETYLENE
PACIFICATION
PAINLESSNESS
PALEONTOLOGY
PALINGENESIA
PALINGENESIS
PALPITATIONS
PALUDAMENTUM
PANAESTHESIA
PANATHENAEAN
PANCHATANTRA
PANCHROMATIC
PANDAEMONIUM
PANDANACEOUS
PANPHARMACON
PANTECHNICON
PANTISOCRACY
PANTOPHAGOUS
PAPILIONIDAE
PARACENTESIS
PARALIPOMENA
PARAMILITARY
PARANTHELIUM
PARSIMONIOUS
PARTICOLORED
PARTICULARLY
PARTISANSHIP
PASSEMEASURE
PASSEPARTOUT
PASSIONATELY
PASSIONFRUIT
PATHETICALLY
PATHOLOGICAL
PEACEFULNESS
PEACEKEEPING
PECTORILOQUY
PEDANTICALLY
PEDIATRICIAN
PEDICELLARIA
PENALIZATION
PENITENTIARY
PENNSYLVANIA
PERADVENTURE
PERAMBULATOR
PERCEPTIVELY
PERCEPTIVITY
PEREMPTORILY
PERGAMENEOUS
PERICARDITIS
PERIODICALLY
PERIOSTRACUM
PERIPHRASTIC
PERISTERONIC
PERMANGANATE
PERMEABILITY
PERNOCTATION
PERPETRATION
PERSEVERANCE
PERSISTENTLY
PERSONALIZED
PERSPICACITY
PERSPIRATION
PERSUASIVELY
PERSULPHURIC
PERTINACIOUS
PERTURBATION
PERVERSENESS
PERVICACIOUS
PESTILENTIAL
PETRIFACTION
PETTIFOGGERS
PETTIFOGGERY
PETTIFOGGING
PHARMACOLOGY
PHENOMENALLY
PHILANTHROPY
PHILHARMONIC
PHILISTINISM
PHILODENDRON
PHILOLOGICAL
PHILOSOPHIZE
PHLEBOTOMIST
PHONETICALLY
PHOSPHORENCE
PHOSPHORESCE
PHOTOGLYPHIC
PHOTOGRAPHER
PHOTOGRAPHIC
PHOTOGRAVURE
PHRONTISTERY
PHYCOXANTHIN
PHYSIOLOGIST
PHYTOBENTHOS
PHYTONADIONE
PIGMENTATION
PINNIEWINKLE
PISCICULTURE
PITTERPATTER
PLACENTIFORM
PLAINCLOTHES
PLASTERSTONE
PLAUSIBILITY
PLECTOGNATHI
PLEIOCHASIUM
POINTILLISME
POLARIZATION
POLICYMAKING
POLYETHYLENE
POLYSYLLABIC
POLYSYLLABLE
POLYSYNDETON
POLYURETHANE
POPOCATEPETL
PORNOGRAPHIC
POSSESSIVELY
POSTGRADUATE
POSTHUMOUSLY
POSTLIMINARY
POSTMISTRESS
POSTPONEMENT
POSTPRANDIAL
POTAMOLOGIST
POTENTIALITY
POTICHOMANIA
POWERSHARING
PRACTICALITY
PRACTICIONER
PRACTITIONER
PRAISEWORTHY
PRALLTRILLER
PRASEODYMIUM
PRAXINOSCOPE
PRECARIOUSLY
PRECOCIOUSLY
PRECONDITION
PREDESTINATE
PREDETERMINE
PREDILECTION
PREDOMINANCE
PREFERENTIAL
PREGUSTATION
PREHISTORIAN
PREMAXILLARY
PREMONSTRANT
PREPAREDNESS
PREPONDERANT
PREPONDERATE
PREPONDERENT
PREPOSSESSED
PREPOSTEROUS
PREREQUISITE
PRESBYTERIAN
PRESCRIPTION
PRESCRIPTIVE
PRESENTATION
PRESENTIMENT
PRESERVATION
PRESERVATIVE
PRESIDENTIAL
PRESTRICTION
PRESUMPTUOUS
PREVARICATOR
PREVENTATIVE
PRIGGISHNESS
PRINCIPALITY
PRIZEFIGHTER
PRIZEWINNING
PROBATIONARY
PROCESSIONAL
PROCLAMATION
PRODIGIOUSLY
PRODUCTIVITY
PROFESSIONAL
PROFESSORIAL
PROFICIENTLY
PROFITEERING
PROGESTERONE
PROGRAMMABLE
PROGYMNASIUM
PROLEGOMENON
PROLETARIATE
PROLIFICALLY
PROLONGATION
PROMULGATION
PROPAGANDISM
PROPAGANDIST
PROPHYLACTIC
PROPITIATION
PROPITIATORY
PROPITIOUSLY
PROPORTIONAL
PROPRIETRESS
PROSCRIPTION
PROSOPOPOEIA
PROSTITUTION
PROTACTINIUM
PROTECTIVELY
PROTECTORATE
PROTESTATION
PROTHALAMION
PROTHALAMIUM
PROTOPLASMAL
PROTOPLASMIC
PROTUBERANCE
PROVERBIALLY
PROVIDENTIAL
PSEPHOLOGIST
PSEUDONYMOUS
PSIPHENOMENA

PSYCHIATRIST
PSYCHOLOGIST
PSYCHOPATHIC
PTERIDOPHYTE
PTERODACTYLE
PUGNACIOUSLY
PUMPERNICKEL
PURIFICATION
PURPOSEBUILT
PURPOSEFULLY
PUTREFACTION
PYROTECHNICS
PYTHONOMORPH
QUADRAGESIMA
QUADRAPHONIC
QUANTIFIABLE
QUANTITATIVE
QUARTERFINAL
QUARTERLIGHT
QUARTERSTAFF
QUESTIONABLE
QUINQUENNIAL
QUINTESSENCE
QUIXOTICALLY
RACKETEERING
RADIOGRAPHER
RADIOISOTOPE
RADIOTHERAPY
RAMBUNCTIOUS
RAMIFICATION
RATIFICATION
READJUSTMENT
REAPPEARANCE
RECALCITRANT
RECAPITULATE
RECEIVERSHIP
RECEPTIONIST
RECHARGEABLE
RECIPROCALLY
RECKLESSNESS
RECOGNIZABLE
RECOGNIZANCE
RECOLLECTION
RECONSTITUTE
RECORDPLAYER
RECREATIONAL
RECRUDESCENT
RECUPERATION
RECUPERATIVE
REDEMPTIONER
REDEPLOYMENT
REDINTEGRATE
REDISCOVERED
REDISTRIBUTE
REFLATIONARY
REFRIGERATED
REFRIGERATOR
REGENERATION
REGISTRATION
REHABILITATE
REINVIGORATE
REJUVENATION
RELATIONSHIP
RELENTLESSLY
REMEMBRANCER
REMINISCENCE
REMONSTRANCE
REMUNERATION
REMUNERATIVE
RENOUNCEMENT
RENUNCIATION
REPATRIATION
REPERCUSSION
REPOSSESSION
REPROCESSING
REPRODUCTION
REPRODUCTIVE
RESETTLEMENT
RESIPISCENCE
RESPECTFULLY
RESPECTIVELY
RESPONDENTIA
RESTAURATEUR
RESTLESSNESS
RESURRECTION
RESUSCITATED
RETARDEDNESS
RETICULATION
RETRENCHMENT
REVERSIONARY
RHADAMANTHUS
RHAMPHOTHECA
RHINORRHOEAL
RHIPIDOPTERA
RHODODENDRON
RHYTHMICALLY
RHYTIDECTOMY
RIDICULOUSLY
RISORGIMENTO
RODOMONTADER
ROLLERBLADER
ROLLERBLADES
ROMANTICALLY
RONCESVALLES
ROOMINGHOUSE
RUTHLESSNESS
SACRILEGIOUS
SADISTICALLY
SALESMANSHIP
SALTATORIOUS
SALVATIONIST
SARDANAPALUS
SARDONICALLY
SARRUSOPHONE
SARSAPARILLA
SATISFACTION
SATISFACTORY
SAUROGNATHAE
SCANDALOUSLY
SCANDINAVIAN
SCAPULIMANCY
SCATTERBRAIN
SCATTERMOUCH
SCHEHERAZADE
SCHILLERSPAR
SCHINDYLESIS
SCHIZOMYCETE
SCHNEIDERIAN
SCHOOLMASTER
SCHOPENHAUER
SCINTILLATOR
SCLERENCHYMA
SCLERODERMIA
SCOPOPHILIAC
SCREENWRITER
SCRIMSHANDER
SCRIMSHANKER
SCRIPTWRITER
SCRUPULOUSLY
SCURRILOUSLY
SECESSIONIST
SECRETARIATE
SECTARIANISM
SEGMENTATION
SELFADHESIVE
SELFCATERING
SELFEMPLOYED
SELFINTEREST
SELFPORTRAIT
SEMANTICALLY
SEMICIRCULAR
SEMIDETACHED
SEMIPRECIOUS
SEPTEMBRISER
SEPTUAGESIMA
SEQUENTIALLY
SEQUESTRATOR
SERASKIERATE
SERVICEWOMAN
SESQUIALTERA
SESQUITERTIA
SEXAGENARIAN
SHAMEFACEDLY
SHAREHOLDING
SHARPSHOOTER
SHEEPISHNESS
SHILLYSHALLY
SHIPBUILDING
SHIRTSLEEVES
SHIRTWAISTER
SHORTCIRCUIT
SHORTCOMINGS
SHORTSIGHTED
SHORTSLEEVED
SHORTSTAFFED
SHOSTAKOVICH
SHUFFLEBOARD
SIDEWHISKERS
SIGNIFICANCE
SILVERHAIRED
SIMULTANEOUS
SINANTHROPUS
SINGLEDECKER
SINGLEHANDED
SINGLEMINDED
SIPHONOPHORA
SIPHONOSTELE
SIPUNCULACEA
SITTLICHKEIT
SIVAPITHECUS
SKUTTERUDITE
SLEEPWALKING
SLOCKDOLAGER
SLOCKDOLIGER
SLOCKDOLOGER
SLOVENLINESS
SLUBBERINGLY
SMALLHOLDING
SNOBBISHNESS
SNOWBOARDING
SOCIOLOGICAL
SOLICITATION
SOLICITOUSLY
SOMATOPLEURE
SOMNAMBULISM
SOMNAMBULIST
SOPHISTICATE
SOUTHCOTTIAN
SOUTHEASTERN
SOUTHERNMOST
SOUTHERNWOOD
SOUTHWESTERN
SPACIOUSNESS
SPATANGOIDEA
SPECIFICALLY
SPECIOUSNESS
SPECKTIONEER
SPECTROSCOPE
SPELEOLOGIST
SPELLCHECKER
SPERMATOCYTE
SPHACELATION
SPHAIRISTIKE
SPIEGELEISEN
SPINECHILLER
SPINSTERHOOD
SPIRITUALISM
SPIRITUALIST
SPIRITUALITY
SPITEFULNESS
SPLENOMEGALY
SPOKESPERSON
SPORADICALLY
SPORTSGROUND
SPREADEAGLED
SPURIOUSNESS
SPURTLEBLADE
STAGGERINGLY
STAKHANOVITE
STANISLAVSKI

STATISTICIAN
STEALTHINESS
STEEPLECHASE
STEGOPHOLIST
STELLENBOSCH
STENOGRAPHER
STENTORPHONE
STEPDAUGHTER
STEREOPHONIC
STEREOPTICON
STEREOSCOPIC
STEREOTYPING
STERNUTATION
STERNWHEELER
STILBOESTROL
STOCKBREEDER
STOCKINGETTE
STONECHATTER
STORMTROOPER
STRADIVARIUS
STRAIGHTAWAY
STRAIGHTEDGE
STRAIGHTNESS
STRAITJACKET
STRANGLEHOLD
STRANGLEWEED
STRATOSPHERE
STREPITATION
STREPSIPTERA
STREPTOMYCIN
STREPTONEURA
STRIDULATION
STRIGIFORMES
STRINGCOURSE
STROMATOLITE
STRONGMINDED
STROPHANTHUS
STRUCTURALLY
STUBBORNNESS
STUDIOUSNESS
STUPEFACTION
SUBARRHATION
SUBCOMMITTEE
SUBCONSCIOUS
SUBCONTINENT
SUBCUTANEOUS
SUBHASTATION
SUBJECTIVELY
SUBJECTIVITY
SUBLAPSARIAN
SUBMISSIVELY
SUBSCRIPTION
SUBSEQUENTLY
SUBSERVIENCE
SUBSIDIARITY
SUBSTANTIATE
SUBSTITUTION
SUBSTRUCTURE
SUBTERRANEAN
SUCCESSFULLY
SUCCESSIVELY
SUCCUSSATION
SUFFICIENTLY
SUGGESTIVELY
SULPHONAMIDE
SUPERANNUATE
SUPERCHARGED
SUPERCHARGER
SUPERCILIARY
SUPERCILIOUS
SUPERHIGHWAY
SUPERNACULUM
SUPERNATURAL
SUPERSTITION
SUPPLICATION
SURMOUNTABLE
SURPRISINGLY
SURREALISTIC
SURROUNDINGS
SURVEILLANCE
SUSPICIOUSLY
SWASHBUCKLER
SWIZZLESTICK
SYMBOLICALLY
SYNADELPHITE
SYNTAGMATITE
TACTLESSNESS
TAGLIACOTIAN
TAMARICACEAE
TAPERECORDER
TAPSALTEERIE
TAPSLETEERIE
TARAMASALATA
TAUTOLOGICAL
TECHNICALITY
TECHNOLOGIST
TEETERTOTTER
TELEASTHETIC
TELEGRAPHESE
TELEGRAPHIST
TELEOSAURIAN
TELEUTOSPORE
TERCENTENARY
TERGIVERSATE
TERRIFICALLY
TERRITORIALS
TESTAMENTARY
TESTOSTERONE
TETRACYCLINE
TETRAHEDRITE
TETRODOTOXIN
THANKFULNESS
THANKSGIVING
THAUMATURGIC
THAUMATURGUS
THEATRICALLY
THEOPHYLLINE
THEORETICIAN
THERAPEUTICS
THEREAGAINST
THERMOSTATIC
THESMOPHORIA
THESSALONIAN
THICKSKINNED
THIGMOTROPIC
THIRDBOROUGH
THOROUGHBRED
THOROUGHFARE
THOROUGHNESS
THOUGHTFULLY
THREADNEEDLE
THREEQUARTER
THUNDERCLOUD
THUNDERFLASH
THUNDERSTORM
THYSANOPTERA
TIGHTFITTING
TIMELESSNESS
TITANOSAURUS
TOBACCONISTS
TOGETHERNESS
TORRICELLIAN
TOTALITARIAN
TOXICOLOGIST
TRABECULATED
TRACTABILITY
TRADESCANTIA
TRADESPEOPLE
TRALATICIOUS
TRALATITIOUS
TRANQUILIZER
TRANQUILLISE
TRANQUILLITY
TRANQUILLIZE
TRANSACTIONS
TRANSCENDENT
TRANSFERABLE
TRANSFERENCE
TRANSGRESSOR
TRANSITIONAL
TRANSLATABLE
TRANSLUCENCE
TRANSMIGRATE
TRANSMISSION
TRANSMOGRIFY
TRANSOCEANIC
TRANSPARENCY
TRANSPONTINE
TRANSVESTISM
TRANSVESTITE
TREMENDOUSLY
TRICHOLOGIST
TRICHOPHYTON
TRIGONOMETRY
TRIUMPHANTLY
TROCHELMINTH
TROCHOSPHERE
TROPHALLAXIS
TROUBLEMAKER
TRUTHFULNESS
TUBERCULOSIS
TURACOVERDIN
TURBOCHARGER
UINTATHERIUM
ULOTRICHALES
ULTRAMONTANE
UMBRADARLING
UNACCEPTABLE
UNACCUSTOMED
UNACQUAINTED
UNANSWERABLE
UNAPPARELLED
UNAPPETIZING
UNATTAINABLE
UNATTRACTIVE
UNAUTHORISED
UNAUTHORIZED
UNBELIEVABLE
UNBELIEVABLY
UNCHALLENGED
UNCHANGEABLE
UNCHARITABLE
UNCHARITABLY
UNCLASSIFIED
UNCONSIDERED
UNCONTROLLED
UNCONVERSANT
UNCONVINCING
UNCTUOUSNESS
UNCULTIVATED
UNDEMOCRATIC
UNDERACHIEVE
UNDERCLOTHES
UNDERCURRENT
UNDEREXPOSED
UNDERGARMENT
UNDERPINNING
UNDERSKINKER
UNDERSTAFFED
UNDERWRITTEN
UNDESERVEDLY
UNDETECTABLE
UNDETERMINED
UNDIMINISHED
UNDISCHARGED
UNECONOMICAL
UNEMPLOYMENT
UNEXPECTEDLY
UNEXPURGATED
UNFATHOMABLE
UNFAVOURABLE
UNFREQUENTED
UNIDENTIFIED
UNILATERALLY
UNIMAGINABLE
UNIMPORTANCE
UNINTERESTED
UNIVERSALIST
UNMANAGEABLE
UNMISTAKABLE

UNNEIGHBORLY
UNOBSTRUCTED
UNOBTAINABLE
UNOFFICIALLY
UNOPPRESSIVE
UNPARALLELED
UNPARDONABLE
UNPOPULARITY
UNPREJUDICED
UNPRETENDING
UNPRINCIPLED
UNPRODUCTIVE
UNPROFITABLE
UNREASONABLE
UNRECOGNISED
UNRECOGNIZED
UNRESERVEDLY
UNRESPONSIVE
UNRESTRAINED
UNRESTRICTED
UNRETURNABLE
UNSATISFYING
UNSCIENTIFIC
UNSCRUPULOUS
UNSEASONABLE
UNSUCCESSFUL
UNSURPRISING
UNSUSPECTING
UNUTTERABLES
UPROARIOUSLY
URBANIZATION
URTRICULARIA
USERFRIENDLY
VAINGLORIOUS
VALENCIENNES
VAPORIZATION
VARICOLOURED
VEHMGERICHTE
VENEPUNCTURE
VENGEFULNESS
VENTRIPOTENT
VERIFICATION
VERUMONTANUM
VETERINARIAN
VIBRATIUNCLE
VILIFICATION
VILLEGIATURA
VINDICTIVELY
VITUPERATION
VITUPERATIVE
VOCIFERATION
VOCIFEROUSLY
VOLUPTUOUSLY
WALLYDRAIGLE
WAREHOUSEMAN
WASHINGTONIA
WATCHFULNESS
WATERCARRIER
WEATHERPROOF
WEIGHTLIFTER
WELLBALANCED
WELLINFORMED
WELLINGTONIA
WELTERWEIGHT
WHIGMALEERIE
WHIMSICALITY
WHIPPOORWILL
WHOLEHEARTED
WICKETKEEPER
WILLIEWAUGHT
WILTSHIREMAN
WINTERHALTER
WOLLASTONITE
WOLSTENHOLME
WOODBURYTYPE
WRETCHEDNESS
XANTHOPTERIN
YELLOWHAMMER
YORKSHIREMAN
YOUTHFULNESS
ZALAMBDODONT
ZARATHUSTRIC

12:2

BABINGTONITE
BACCHANALIAN
BACKBREAKING
BACKWARDNESS
BACKWOODSMAN
BACTERIOLOGY
BACTERIOSTAT
BAIRNSFATHER
BAMBOCCIADES
BANANALANDER
BANDERSNATCH
BANTAMWEIGHT
BARBERMONGER
BARNSTORMING
BARRANQUILLA
BATTLEGROUND
CABINETMAKER
CALCEAMENTUM
CALLIGRAPHIC
CALLISTHENES
CALUMNIATION
CAMIKNICKERS
CAMPANULARIA
CAMPODEIFORM
CANCELLATION
CANONIZATION
CANTANKEROUS
CANTILEVERED
CAPERCAILLIE
CAPERCAILZIE
CAPITULATION
CARAVANSERAI
CARBOHYDRATE
CARCINOGENIC
CARDINDEXING
CARDIOLOGIST
CARELESSNESS
CARICATURIST
CARLOVINGIAN
CARPETBAGGER
CARRIWITCHET
CARTHAGINIAN
CARTOGRAPHER
CARTOGRAPHIC
CASSITERIDES
CASTERBRIDGE
CATADIOPTRIC
CATAPHYSICAL
CATASTROPHIC
CATHETOMETER
CAUTIOUSNESS
DAGUERROTYPE
DARLINGTONIA
EAVESDROPPER
FAINTHEARTED
FAITHFULNESS
FARTHINGLAND
FASTIDIOUSLY
GAINSBOROUGH
GALLIGASKINS
GALLINACEOUS
GALLIVANTING
GALVANOMETER
GAMESMANSHIP
GASTARBEITER
GASTROSOPHER
HABERDASHERS
HABERDASHERY
HAEMATEMESIS
HAEMOPHILIAC
HAEMORRHOIDS
HAIRDRESSERS
HAIRDRESSING
HAIRSPLITTER
HALLANSHAKER
HALLUCINOGEN
HAMARTHRITIS
HAMBLETONIAN
HAMMERHEADED
HANDKERCHIEF
HAPPENSTANCE
HAPPYGOLUCKY
HARMONIOUSLY
HARNESSMAKER
HARUMFRODITE
IAMBOGRAPHER
KALEIDOSCOPE
KALISTOCRACY
KATHAREVOUSA
KATZENJAMMER
LABANOTATION
LABOURSAVING
LABYRINTHINE
LALLAPALOOZA
LAMELLICORNE
LAMENTATIONS
LAMPADEDROMY
LANCASTERIAN
LANGUEDOCIAN
LASCIVIOUSLY
LATIROSTRATE
LAUREATESHIP
MACABERESQUE
MACHAIRODONT
MACMILLANITE
MACROPODIDAE
MADEMOISELLE
MAGNETICALLY
MAGNIFICENCE
MAGNILOQUENT
MAJESTICALLY
MALACOSTRACA
MALFORMATION
MALLEABILITY
MALLOPHAGOUS
MALNUTRITION
MALPRACTICES
MALTREATMENT
MANGELWURZEL
MANIPULATION
MANIPULATIVE
MANOEUVRABLE
MANSLAUGHTER
MANUFACTURER
MARCOBRUNNER
MARCONIGRAPH
MARKSMANSHIP
MARLINESPIKE
MARRIAGEABLE
MARSEILLAISE
MASSERANDUBA
MASSPRODUCED
MASTERSTROKE
MASTIGOPHORA
MASTURBATION
MATHEMATICAL
NARCISSISTIC
NATURALISTIC
NAVIGABILITY
PACIFICATION
PAINLESSNESS
PALEONTOLOGY
PALINGENESIA
PALINGENESIS
PALPITATIONS
PALUDAMENTUM
PANAESTHESIA
PANATHENAEAN
PANCHATANTRA
PANCHROMATIC
PANDAEMONIUM
PANDANACEOUS
PANPHARMACON
PANTECHNICON
PANTISOCRACY

PANTOPHAGOUS
PAPILIONIDAE
PARACENTESIS
PARALIPOMENA
PARAMILITARY
PARANTHELIUM
PARSIMONIOUS
PARTICOLORED
PARTICULARLY
PARTISANSHIP
PASSEMEASURE
PASSEPARTOUT
PASSIONATELY
PASSIONFRUIT
PATHETICALLY
PATHOLOGICAL
RACKETEERING
RADIOGRAPHER
RADIOISOTOPE
RADIOTHERAPY
RAMBUNCTIOUS
RAMIFICATION
RATIFICATION
SACRILEGIOUS
SADISTICALLY
SALESMANSHIP
SALTATORIOUS
SALVATIONIST
SARDANAPALUS
SARDONICALLY
SARRUSOPHONE
SARSAPARILLA
SATISFACTION
SATISFACTORY
SAUROGNATHAE
TACTLESSNESS
TAGLIACOTIAN
TAMARICACEAE
TAPERECORDER
TAPSALTEERIE
TAPSLETEERIE
TARAMASALATA
TAUTOLOGICAL
VAINGLORIOUS
VALENCIENNES
VAPORIZATION
VARICOLOURED
WALLYDRAIGLE
WAREHOUSEMAN
WASHINGTONIA
WATCHFULNESS
WATERCARRIER
XANTHOPTERIN
ZALAMBDODONT
ZARATHUSTRIC
ABBREVIATION
ABOLITIONIST
ABSQUATULATE
OBEDIENTIARY
OBLITERATION
OBSEQUIOUSLY
OBSERVANTINE
OBSOLESCENCE
OBSOLETENESS
OBSTETRICIAN
OBSTREPEROUS
ACADEMICALLY
ACCELERATION
ACCENTUATION
ACCIDENTALLY
ACCOMPANYING
ACCOMPLISHED
ACCORDIONIST
ACCOUCHEMENT
ACCOUTREMENT
ACCUMULATION
ACHLAMYDEOUS
ACKNOWLEDGED
ACQUAINTANCE
ACQUIESCENCE
ECCENTRICITY
ECCLESIASTES
ECCLESIASTIC
ECONOMICALLY
ECSTATICALLY
ICHTHYOCOLLA
ICHTHYOPSIDA
ICONOCLASTIC
OCCASIONALLY
OCCUPATIONAL
OCEANOGRAPHY
OCTASTROPHIC
OCTOGENARIAN
SCANDALOUSLY
SCANDINAVIAN
SCAPULIMANCY
SCATTERBRAIN
SCATTERMOUCH
SCHEHERAZADE
SCHILLERSPAR
SCHINDYLESIS
SCHIZOMYCETE
SCHNEIDERIAN
SCHOOLMASTER
SCHOPENHAUER
SCINTILLATOR
SCLERENCHYMA
SCLERODERMIA
SCOPOPHILIAC
SCREENWRITER
SCRIMSHANDER
SCRIMSHANKER
SCRIPTWRITER
SCRUPULOUSLY
SCURRILOUSLY
ADAPTABILITY
ADDITIONALLY
ADJECTIVALLY
ADJUDICATION
ADMINISTRATE
ADMONISHMENT
ADSCITITIOUS
ADULTERATION
ADVANTAGEOUS
ADVANTAGIOUS
ADVENTITIOUS
ADVISABILITY
EDUCATIONIST
IDEALIZATION
IDENTIFIABLE
IDIOSYNCRASY
IDIOTHERMOUS
AECIDIOSPORE
AERODYNAMICS
AERONAUTICAL
AETHRIOSCOPE
BEACONSFIELD
BEAUMARCHAIS
BEAUMONTAGUE
BEAUMONTIQUE
BEHAVIOURISM
BELLIGERENCY
BENEFACTRESS
BENEVOLENTLY
BERTHOLLETIA
BERTILLONAGE
BESSERWISSER
BETHLEHEMITE
BEWILDERMENT
CEREBROTONIC
CEREMONIALLY
DEAMBULATORY
DEASPIRATION
DEBILITATING
DECAPITATION
DECELERATION
DECENTRALISE
DECENTRALIZE
DECIPHERABLE
DECIPHERMENT
DECONGESTANT
DECORATIVELY
DEFLATIONARY
DEGENERATION
DEHUMIDIFIER
DELIBERATELY
DELIBERATION
DELICATESSEN
DEMILITARIZE
DEMIMONDAINE
DEMONSTRABLE
DEMONSTRABLY
DEMONSTRATOR
DENDROLOGIST
DENOMINATION
DENUNCIATION
DEPARTMENTAL
DEPOPULATION
DEPRECIATION
DEPRECIATORY
DEREGULATION
DERESTRICTED
DESIRABILITY
DESSERTSPOON
DEUTEROSCOPY
FEARLESSNESS
FEATHERBRAIN
FEHMGERICHTE
FELDSPATHOID
FERMENTATION
GENEALOGICAL
GENETHLIACON
GENTLETAMPER
GEOGRAPHICAL
GEOLOGICALLY
GEOMETRICIAN
GEOPHYSICIST
GERIATRICIAN
GERONTOCRACY
GESELLSCHAFT
HEADMISTRESS
HEADQUARTERS
HEARTSTRINGS
HEARTWARMING
HELIOGABALUS
HELLGRAMMITE
HELPLESSNESS
HEMICHORDATA
HENCEFORWARD
HEPHTHEMIMER
HEREDITAMENT
HERMENEUTICS
HERMENEUTIST
HERMETICALLY
HEROICOMICAL
HETEROCLITIC
HETEROCONTAE
HETEROPHORIA
HETEROPLASIA
HETEROSEXUAL
HETEROSOMATA
JENNYSPINNER
KERAUNOGRAPH
LEGALIZATION
LEGIONNAIRES
LEGITIMATELY
LEIOTRICHOUS
LEPIDOMELANE
LEXICOGRAPHY
MEANINGFULLY
MECHANICALLY
MECHITHARIST
MELODRAMATIC
MENSTRUATION
MERETRICIOUS
MERISTEMATIC
MERITRICIOUS
MERRYTHOUGHT
MERVEILLEUSE
MESOTHELIOMA

METAGNATHOUS
METALLOPHONE
METALLURGIST
METAMORPHISM
METAMORPHOSE
METAPHORICAL
METAPHYSICAL
METHODICALLY
METICULOUSLY
METROPOLITAN
NEIGHBORHOOD
NEIGHBOURING
NEOCLASSICAL
NEOPLATONISM
NEPENTHACEAE
NEPHELOMETER
NEUROLOGICAL
NEUROTICALLY
NEVERTHELESS
NEWFOUNDLAND
NEWSPAPERMAN
PEACEFULNESS
PEACEKEEPING
PECTORILOQUY
PEDANTICALLY
PEDIATRICIAN
PEDICELLARIA
PENALIZATION
PENITENTIARY
PENNSYLVANIA
PERADVENTURE
PERAMBULATOR
PERCEPTIVELY
PERCEPTIVITY
PEREMPTORILY
PERGAMENEOUS
PERICARDITIS
PERIODICALLY
PERIOSTRACUM
PERIPHRASTIC
PERISTERONIC
PERMANGANATE
PERMEABILITY
PERNOCTATION
PERPETRATION
PERSEVERANCE
PERSISTENTLY
PERSONALIZED
PERSPICACITY
PERSPIRATION
PERSUASIVELY
PERSULPHURIC
PERTINACIOUS
PERTURBATION
PERVERSENESS
PERVICACIOUS
PESTILENTIAL
PETRIFACTION
PETTIFOGGERS
PETTIFOGGERY
PETTIFOGGING
READJUSTMENT
REAPPEARANCE
RECALCITRANT
RECAPITULATE
RECEIVERSHIP
RECEPTIONIST
RECHARGEABLE
RECIPROCALLY
RECKLESSNESS
RECOGNIZABLE
RECOGNIZANCE
RECOLLECTION
RECONSTITUTE
RECORDPLAYER
RECREATIONAL
RECRUDESCENT
RECUPERATION
RECUPERATIVE
REDEMPTIONER
REDEPLOYMENT
REDINTEGRATE
REDISCOVERED
REDISTRIBUTE
REFLATIONARY
REFRIGERATED
REFRIGERATOR
REGENERATION
REGISTRATION
REHABILITATE
REINVIGORATE
REJUVENATION
RELATIONSHIP
RELENTLESSLY
REMEMBRANCER
REMINISCENCE
REMONSTRANCE
REMUNERATION
REMUNERATIVE
RENOUNCEMENT
RENUNCIATION
REPATRIATION
REPERCUSSION
REPOSSESSION
REPROCESSING
REPRODUCTION
REPRODUCTIVE
RESETTLEMENT
RESIPISCENCE
RESPECTFULLY
RESPECTIVELY
RESPONDENTIA
RESTAURATEUR
RESTLESSNESS
RESURRECTION
RESUSCITATED
RETARDEDNESS
RETICULATION
RETRENCHMENT
REVERSIONARY
SECESSIONIST
SECRETARIATE
SECTARIANISM
SEGMENTATION
SELFADHESIVE
SELFCATERING
SELFEMPLOYED
SELFINTEREST
SELFPORTRAIT
SEMANTICALLY
SEMICIRCULAR
SEMIDETACHED
SEMIPRECIOUS
SEPTEMBRISER
SEPTUAGESIMA
SEQUENTIALLY
SEQUESTRATOR
SERASKIERATE
SERVICEWOMAN
SESQUIALTERA
SESQUITERTIA
SEXAGENARIAN
TECHNICALITY
TECHNOLOGIST
TEETERTOTTER
TELEASTHETIC
TELEGRAPHESE
TELEGRAPHIST
TELEOSAURIAN
TELEUTOSPORE
TERCENTENARY
TERGIVERSATE
TERRIFICALLY
TERRITORIALS
TESTAMENTARY
TESTOSTERONE
TETRACYCLINE
TETRAHEDRITE
TETRODOTOXIN
VEHMGERICHTE
VENEPUNCTURE
VENGEFULNESS
VENTRIPOTENT
VERIFICATION
VERUMONTANUM
VETERINARIAN
WEATHERPROOF
WEIGHTLIFTER
WELLBALANCED
WELLINFORMED
WELLINGTONIA
WELTERWEIGHT
YELLOWHAMMER
AFFECTIONATE
AFORETHOUGHT
AFTEREFFECTS
AFTERTHOUGHT
EFFERVESCENT
EFFORTLESSLY
AGALMATOLITE
AGAMOGENETIC
AGATHODAIMON
AGGRESSIVELY
AGRIBUSINESS
AGRICULTURAL
EGYPTOLOGIST
CHAIRMANSHIP
CHALICOTHERE
CHAMPIONSHIP
CHARACTERIZE
CHARTERHOUSE
CHASTISEMENT
CHAUVINISTIC
CHEERFULNESS
CHEESEBURGER
CHEESEMONGER
CHEESEPARING
CHEMOTHERAPY
CHESTERFIELD
CHILDBEARING
CHILDISHNESS
CHIROPRACTIC
CHIROPRACTOR
CHITTERLINGS
CHLORINATION
CHONDRIOSOME
CHOREOGRAPHY
CHORIZONTIST
CHREMATISTIC
CHRESTOMATHY
CHRISTIANITY
CHURCHWARDEN
CHURLISHNESS
PHARMACOLOGY
PHENOMENALLY
PHILANTHROPY
PHILHARMONIC
PHILISTINISM
PHILODENDRON
PHILOLOGICAL
PHILOSOPHIZE
PHLEBOTOMIST
PHONETICALLY
PHOSPHORENCE
PHOSPHORESCE
PHOTOGLYPHIC
PHOTOGRAPHER
PHOTOGRAPHIC
PHOTOGRAVURE
PHRONTISTERY
PHYCOXANTHIN
PHYSIOLOGIST
PHYTOBENTHOS
PHYTONADIONE
RHADAMANTHUS
RHAMPHOTHECA
RHINORRHOEAL
RHIPIDOPTERA
RHODODENDRON
RHYTHMICALLY

RHYTIDECTOMY
SHAMEFACEDLY
SHAREHOLDING
SHARPSHOOTER
SHEEPISHNESS
SHILLYSHALLY
SHIPBUILDING
SHIRTSLEEVES
SHIRTWAISTER
SHORTCIRCUIT
SHORTCOMINGS
SHORTSIGHTED
SHORTSLEEVED
SHORTSTAFFED
SHOSTAKOVICH
SHUFFLEBOARD
THANKFULNESS
THANKSGIVING
THAUMATURGIC
THAUMATURGUS
THEATRICALLY
THEOPHYLLINE
THEORETICIAN
THERAPEUTICS
THEREAGAINST
THERMOSTATIC
THESMOPHORIA
THESSALONIAN
THICKSKINNED
THIGMOTROPIC
THIRDBOROUGH
THOROUGHBRED
THOROUGHFARE
THOROUGHNESS
THOUGHTFULLY
THREADNEEDLE
THREEQUARTER
THUNDERCLOUD
THUNDERFLASH
THUNDERSTORM
THYSANOPTERA
WHIGMALEERIE
WHIMSICALITY
WHIPPOORWILL
WHOLEHEARTED
AIRCRAFTSMAN
BIBLIOGRAPHY
BIBLIOPEGIST
BICAMERALISM
BICENTENNIAL
BIELORUSSIAN
BILLINGSGATE
BIOCHEMISTRY
BIODIVERSITY
BIOGRAPHICAL
BIRDWATCHING
CIRCASSIENNE
CIRCUMCISION
CIRCUMGYRATE
CIRCUMSCRIBE
CIRCUMSTANCE
CIVILISATION
CIVILIZATION
DIAGRAMMATIC
DIALECTICIAN
DICTATORSHIP
DIENCEPHALON
DIFFERENTIAL
DILAPIDATION
DILATORINESS
DIPLOGENESIS
DIPRIONIDIAN
DIRECTORSHIP
DISACCHARIDE
DISADVANTAGE
DISAGREEABLE
DISAGREEMENT
DISAPPEARING
DISAPPOINTED
DISASTROUSLY
DISCIPLINARY
DISCOMEDUSAE
DISCOMFITURE
DISCOMYCETES
DISCONCERTED
DISCONNECTED
DISCONSOLATE
DISCONTENTED
DISCOURAGING
DISCOURTEOUS
DISCRIMINATE
DISDAINFULLY
DISEMBARRASS
DISENCHANTED
DISFRANCHISE
DISHONORABLE
DISHONORABLY
DISINCENTIVE
DISINFECTANT
DISINGENUOUS
DISINTEGRATE
DISOBEDIENCE
DISORGANIZED
DISORIENTATE
DISPENSATION
DISPLACEMENT
DISPOSSESSED
DISQUISITION
DISREPECTFUL
DISREPUTABLE
DISSATISFIED
DISSERTATION
DISSOCIATION
DISTILLATION
DISTINCTNESS
DISTRIBUTION
DISTRIBUTIVE
DIVERTICULUM
DIVERTIMENTO
FIDDLESTICKS
FIGURATIVELY
FINALIZATION
FIRSTFOOTING
GIBRALTARIAN
GIGANTOMACHY
HIERARCHICAL
HIEROGLYPHIC
HIEROGRAMMAT
HIEROPHANTIC
HIGHFALUTING
HILDEBRANDIC
HINDQUARTERS
HIPPOCRATISE
HIPPOCREPIAN
HIPPOPOTAMUS
HISTIOPHORUS
HISTORICALLY
KILLIKINNICK
KINAESTHETIC
KINDERGARTEN
KIRSCHWASSER
LICKTRENCHER
LIFELESSNESS
LIGHTHEARTED
LILLIBULLERO
LILLIBURLERO
LINCOLNSHIRE
LIQUEFACTION
LISTLESSNESS
LITHOGRAPHIC
LITHOLATROUS
LIVERPUDLIAN
MICHELANGELO
MICROCLIMATE
MIDDLEWEIGHT
MILITARISTIC
MINDBOGGLING
MINDFULLNESS
MINERALOGIST
MINICOMPUTER
MINISTRATION
MIRACULOUSLY
MISADVENTURE
MISANTHROPIC
MISAPPREHEND
MISBEHAVIOUR
MISCALCULATE
MISDELIVERED
MISDEMEANOUR
MISINTERPRET
MISPLACEMENT
MISPRONOUNCE
MISQUOTATION
MISREPRESENT
MISSTATEMENT
MISTREATMENT
MITRAILLEUSE
NIGHTCLOTHES
PIGMENTATION
PINNIEWINKLE
PISCICULTURE
PITTERPATTER
RIDICULOUSLY
RISORGIMENTO
SIDEWHISKERS
SIGNIFICANCE
SILVERHAIRED
SIMULTANEOUS
SINANTHROPUS
SINGLEDECKER
SINGLEHANDED
SINGLEMINDED
SIPHONOPHORA
SIPHONOSTELE
SIPUNCULACEA
SITTLICHKEIT
SIVAPITHECUS
TIGHTFITTING
TIMELESSNESS
TITANOSAURUS
UINTATHERIUM
VIBRATIUNCLE
VILIFICATION
VILLEGIATURA
VINDICTIVELY
VITUPERATION
VITUPERATIVE
WICKETKEEPER
WILLIEWAUGHT
WILTSHIREMAN
WINTERHALTER
SKUTTERUDITE
ALEXIPHARMIC
ALIMENTATIVE
ALLITERATION
ALPHABETICAL
ALPHANUMERIC
BLABBERMOUTH
BLACKCURRANT
BLANDISHMENT
BLEFUSCUDIAN
BLENNORRHOEA
BLETHERSKATE
BLOODSTAINED
BLOODTHIRSTY
BLUESTOCKING
CLAIRVOYANCE
CLAIRVOYANCY
CLAMJAMPHRIE
CLANNISHNESS
CLAPPERBOARD
CLARINETTIST
CLASSIFIABLE
CLAUDICATION
CLAVICEMBALO
CLEARSIGHTED
CLEISTOGAMIC
ELASMOBRANCH
ELECTRICALLY
ELECTROLYSIS

ELECTROPLATE
ELECTROTONUS
ELEEMOSYNARY
FLAGELLATION
FLAMBOYANTLY
FLITTERMOUSE
FLORICULTURE
FLUORESCENCE
FLUORIDATION
GLADIATORIAL
GLOBETROTTER
GLOCKENSPIEL
GLUBBDUBDRIB
GLYNDEBOURNE
ILLEGIBILITY
ILLEGITIMACY
ILLEGITIMATE
ILLOGICALITY
ILLUMINATING
ILLUMINATION
ILLUSTRATION
ILLUSTRATIVE
KLEPTOMANIAC
KLETTERSCHUE
KLIPSPRINGER
OLDFASHIONED
PLACENTIFORM
PLAINCLOTHES
PLASTERSTONE
PLAUSIBILITY
PLECTOGNATHI
PLEIOCHASIUM
SLEEPWALKING
SLOCKDOLAGER
SLOCKDOLIGER
SLOCKDOLOGER
SLOVENLINESS
SLUBBERINGLY
ULOTRICHALES
ULTRAMONTANE
AMALGAMATION
AMARANTACEAE
AMBASSADRESS
AMBIDEXTROUS
AMBULANCEMAN
AMELIORATION
AMPHISBAENIC
AMPHISTOMOUS
AMPHITHEATER
AMPHITHEATRE
EMANCIPATION
EMASCULATION
EMBARRASSING
EMBEZZLEMENT
EMBROIDERESS
EMPHATICALLY
IMMACULATELY
IMMEASURABLE
IMMEASURABLY
IMMODERATELY

IMMODERATION
IMMUNIZATION
IMMUNOLOGIST
IMMUTABILITY
IMPARTIALITY
IMPENETRABLE
IMPERFECTION
IMPERISHABLE
IMPERSONALLY
IMPERSONATOR
IMPERTINENCE
IMPLANTATION
IMPOLITENESS
IMPOVERISHED
IMPREGNATION
IMPRESSIVELY
IMPRISONMENT
IMPROVIDENCE
SMALLHOLDING
UMBRADARLING
ANAESTHETISE
ANAESTHETIST
ANAESTHETIZE
ANAMORPHOSIS
ANDOUILLETTE
ANDROSTERONE
ANECATHARSIS
ANEMOPHILOUS
ANNIHILATION
ANNOUNCEMENT
ANNUNCIATION
ANTAGONISTIC
ANTANANARIVO
ANTEDILUVIAN
ANTEMERIDIAN
ANTHELMINTIC
ANTHROPOLOGY
ANTIBACCHIUS
ANTIBARBARUS
ANTICIPATION
ANTICIPATORY
ANTILEGOMENA
ANTIMACASSAR
ANTIMETABOLE
ANTIMNEMONIC
ANTINEUTRINO
ANTIPARTICLE
ANTIRACHITIC
ANTISTROPHON
ANTITHROMBIN
ANTONINIANUS
ENANTIOMORPH
ENANTIOPATHY
ENCHEIRIDION
ENCIRCLEMENT
ENCROACHMENT
ENCYCLOPEDIA
ENCYCLOPEDIC
ENERGYSAVING
ENGLISHWOMAN

ENGLISHWOMEN
ENHYPOSTASIA
ENTANGLEMENT
ENTEROMORPHA
ENTEROPNEUST
ENTERPRISING
ENTERTAINING
ENTHUSIASTIC
ENTOMOLOGIST
ENTOMOSTRACA
ENTOPLASTRON
ENTREATINGLY
ENTRENCHMENT
ENTREPRENEUR
INACCESSIBLE
INACCURATELY
INADEQUATELY
INADMISSIBLE
INADVERTENCE
INAPPLICABLE
INARTICULATE
INAUGURATION
INAUSPICIOUS
INCALCULABLE
INCANDESCENT
INCAPABILITY
INCAPACITATE
INCAUTIOUSLY
INCIDENTALLY
INCINERATION
INCOHERENTLY
INCOMPARABLE
INCOMPARABLY
INCOMPATIBLE
INCOMPETENCE
INCOMPLETELY
INCONCLUSIVE
INCONSEQUENT
INCONSISTENT
INCONSOLABLE
INCONTINENCE
INCONVENIENT
INCORPORATED
INCORRIGIBLE
INCORRIGIBLY
INCREASINGLY
INCRUSTATION
INCUNABULIST
INDEBTEDNESS
INDECLINABLE
INDEFENSIBLE
INDEFINITELY
INDEPENDENCE
INDIFFERENCE
INDIGESTIBLE
INDISCRETION
INDISPUTABLE
INDISPUTABLY
INDISSOLUBLE
INDISTINCTLY

INDIVIDUALLY
INDOCTRINATE
INDUSTRIALLY
INEFFICIENCY
INERADICABLE
INESCUTCHEON
INEXACTITUDE
INEXPERIENCE
INEXPLICABLE
INEXPLICABLY
INEXTRICABLE
INEXTRICABLY
INFELICITOUS
INFILTRATION
INFLAMMATION
INFLAMMATORY
INFLATIONARY
INFORMIDABLE
INFREQUENTLY
INFRINGEMENT
INGRATIATING
INHARMONIOUS
INHOSPITABLE
INNATTENTIVE
INNOMINABLES
INORDINATELY
INSALUBRIOUS
INSEMINATION
INSOLUBILITY
INSPECTORATE
INSTALLATION
INSTAURATION
INSTRUCTIONS
INSTRUCTRESS
INSTRUMENTAL
INSUFFERABLE
INSUFFERABLY
INSUFFICIENT
INSURRECTION
INTELLECTUAL
INTELLIGENCE
INTELLIGIBLE
INTEMPERANCE
INTENERATION
INTERCEPTION
INTERCESSION
INTERCHANGED
INTERFERENCE
INTERJECTION
INTERLOCUTOR
INTERMEDIARY
INTERMEDIATE
INTERMINABLE
INTERMINABLY
INTERMISSION
INTERMITTENT
INTERPRETING
INTERRELATED
INTERROGATOR
INTERRUPTION

INTERSECTION
INTERSPERSED
INTERSTELLAR
INTERVENTION
INTIMIDATING
INTIMIDATION
INTOXICATING
INTOXICATION
INTRANSIGENT
INTRANSITIVE
INTRAUTERINE
INTRODUCTION
INTRODUCTORY
INVALIDATION
INVERTEBRATE
INVESTIGATOR
INVIGORATING
INVIGORATION
INVISIBILITY
INVULNERABLE
MNEMOTECHNIC
ONCORHYNCHUS
ONEIROCRITIC
ONOMATOPOEIA
ONOMATOPOEIC
SNOBBISHNESS
SNOWBOARDING
UNACCEPTABLE
UNACCUSTOMED
UNACQUAINTED
UNANSWERABLE
UNAPPARELLED
UNAPPETIZING
UNATTAINABLE
UNATTRACTIVE
UNAUTHORISED
UNAUTHORIZED
UNBELIEVABLE
UNBELIEVABLY
UNCHALLENGED
UNCHANGEABLE
UNCHARITABLE
UNCHARITABLY
UNCLASSIFIED
UNCONSIDERED
UNCONTROLLED
UNCONVERSANT
UNCONVINCING
UNCTUOUSNESS
UNCULTIVATED
UNDEMOCRATIC
UNDERACHIEVE
UNDERCLOTHES
UNDERCURRENT
UNDEREXPOSED
UNDERGARMENT
UNDERPINNING
UNDERSKINKER
UNDERSTAFFED
UNDERWRITTEN

UNDESERVEDLY
UNDETECTABLE
UNDETERMINED
UNDIMINISHED
UNDISCHARGED
UNECONOMICAL
UNEMPLOYMENT
UNEXPECTEDLY
UNEXPURGATED
UNFATHOMABLE
UNFAVOURABLE
UNFREQUENTED
UNIDENTIFIED
UNILATERALLY
UNIMAGINABLE
UNIMPORTANCE
UNINTERESTED
UNIVERSALIST
UNMANAGEABLE
UNMISTAKABLE
UNNEIGHBORLY
UNOBSTRUCTED
UNOBTAINABLE
UNOFFICIALLY
UNOPPRESSIVE
UNPARALLELED
UNPARDONABLE
UNPOPULARITY
UNPREJUDICED
UNPRETENDING
UNPRINCIPLED
UNPRODUCTIVE
UNPROFITABLE
UNREASONABLE
UNRECOGNISED
UNRECOGNIZED
UNRESERVEDLY
UNRESPONSIVE
UNRESTRAINED
UNRESTRICTED
UNRETURNABLE
UNSATISFYING
UNSCIENTIFIC
UNSCRUPULOUS
UNSEASONABLE
UNSUCCESSFUL
UNSURPRISING
UNSUSPECTING
UNUTTERABLES
BOISTEROUSLY
BOOBYTRAPPED
BOONDOGGLING
BOUGAINVILLE
BOULEVARDIER
COCCIDIOSTAT
CODIFICATION
COHABITATION
COINCIDENTAL
COLDSHOULDER
COLLABORATOR

COLLECTIVELY
COLLECTORATE
COLLOQUIALLY
COLLUCTATION
COLLYWOBBLES
COLONIZATION
COLOQUINTIDA
COMBINATIONS
COMMANDMENTS
COMMENCEMENT
COMMENDATION
COMMENDATORY
COMMENSURATE
COMMERCIALLY
COMMISSARIAT
COMMISSIONED
COMMISSIONER
COMMONWEALTH
COMMUNICABLE
COMPANIONWAY
COMPELLATION
COMPENSATION
COMPENSATORY
COMPLACENTLY
COMPLETENESS
COMPLICATION
COMPROMISING
COMPURGATION
CONCENTRATED
CONCILIATION
CONCILIATORY
CONCLUSIVELY
CONCURRENTLY
CONDEMNATION
CONDENSATION
CONDUCTIVITY
CONFECTIONER
CONFESSIONAL
CONFIDENTIAL
CONFIRMATION
CONFIRMATORY
CONFISCATION
CONGENITALLY
CONGLOMERATE
CONGRATULATE
CONGREGATION
CONQUISTADOR
CONSCRIPTION
CONSECRATION
CONSEQUENCES
CONSEQUENTLY
CONSERVATION
CONSERVATISM
CONSERVATIVE
CONSERVATORY
CONSIDERABLE
CONSIDERABLY
CONSISTENTLY
CONSOLIDATED
CONSOLIDATOR

CONSPECTUITY
CONSTABULARY
CONSTIPATION
CONSTITUENCY
CONSTITUENTS
CONSTITUTION
CONSTRICTION
CONSTRUCTION
CONSTRUCTIVE
CONSULTATION
CONSULTATIVE
CONSUMMATION
CONTABESCENT
CONTAMINATED
CONTEMPORARY
CONTEMPTIBLE
CONTEMPTUOUS
CONTERMINOUS
CONTIGNATION
CONTINUATION
CONTINUOUSLY
CONTRAPPOSTO
CONTRAPUNTAL
CONTRARINESS
CONTRIBUTION
CONTRIBUTORY
CONTRITURATE
CONTROLLABLE
CONTUMACIOUS
CONVALESCENT
CONVALESCING
CONVENIENCES
CONVENIENTLY
CONVENTIONAL
CONVERSATION
CONVEYANCING
CONVINCINGLY
CONVIVIALITY
COORDINATION
COSCINOMANCY
COSMOPOLITAN
COSTERMONGER
COUNTERBLAST
COUNTERCLAIM
COUNTERMARCH
COUNTERPOINT
COUNTERPOISE
COURAGEOUSLY
COURTMARTIAL
COVETOUSNESS
DOGMATICALLY
DOLPHINARIUM
DOMESTICATED
DONNERWETTER
DORSIVENTRAL
DOUBLEDECKER
DOUBLEGLAZED
FOOTSLOGGING
FORCEFULNESS
FORMALDEHYDE

FORTUITOUSLY
FOTHERINGHAY
GOBBLEDEGOOK
GOBBLEDYGOOK
GONADOTROPIN
GONDWANALAND
GOOSEPIMPLES
GOVERNMENTAL
HOBBIDIDANCE
HOLIDAYMAKER
HOMESICKNESS
HOMOEOPATHIC
HOMOTHERMOUS
HOPELESSNESS
HORIZONTALLY
HORRIFICALLY
HORSEMANSHIP
HORTICULTURE
HOUSEBREAKER
HOUSEKEEPING
HOUSETOHOUSE
HOUSEWARMING
JOURNALISTIC
LONGDISTANCE
LONGITUDINAL
LONGSHOREMAN
LONGSTANDING
LOXODROMICAL
MOBILIZATION
MODIFICATION
MOISTURIZING
MONOSYLLABIC
MONOSYLLABLE
MONOTONOUSLY
MONTESSORIAN
MOONLIGHTING
MOSBOLLETJIE
MOTORCYCLIST
MOUSQUETAIRE
MOUTHBROODER
NOCONFIDENCE
NOMENCLATURE
NONAGENARIAN
NONALCOHOLIC
NONCHALANTLY
NONCOMMITTAL
NONEXISTENCE
NONRESIDENCE
NONRESISTANT
NORTHEASTERN
NORTHERNMOST
NORTHWESTERN
NOTIFICATION
POINTILLISME
POLARIZATION
POLICYMAKING
POLYETHYLENE
POLYSYLLABIC
POLYSYLLABLE
POLYSYNDETON
POLYURETHANE
POPOCATEPETL
PORNOGRAPHIC
POSSESSIVELY
POSTGRADUATE
POSTHUMOUSLY
POSTLIMINARY
POSTMISTRESS
POSTPONEMENT
POSTPRANDIAL
POTAMOLOGIST
POTENTIALITY
POTICHOMANIA
POWERSHARING
RODOMONTADER
ROLLERBLADER
ROLLERBLADES
ROMANTICALLY
RONCESVALLES
ROOMINGHOUSE
SOCIOLOGICAL
SOLICITATION
SOLICITOUSLY
SOMATOPLEURE
SOMNAMBULISM
SOMNAMBULIST
SOPHISTICATE
SOUTHCOTTIAN
SOUTHEASTERN
SOUTHERNMOST
SOUTHERNWOOD
SOUTHWESTERN
TOBACCONISTS
TOGETHERNESS
TORRICELLIAN
TOTALITARIAN
TOXICOLOGIST
VOCIFERATION
VOCIFEROUSLY
VOLUPTUOUSLY
WOLLASTONITE
WOLSTENHOLME
WOODBURYTYPE
YORKSHIREMAN
YOUTHFULNESS
APFELSTRUDEL
APLANOGAMETE
APOLLINARIAN
APOSTROPHISE
APPENDECTOMY
APPENDICITIS
APPOGGIATURA
APPRECIATION
APPRECIATIVE
APPREHENSION
APPREHENSIVE
APPROACHABLE
APPURTENANCE
EPACRIDACEAE
EPANORTHOSIS
EPENCEPHALON
EPIDEICTICAL
EPIGRAMMATIC
EPIPHENOMENA
EPISCOPALIAN
EPISTEMOLOGY
EPISTOLATERS
EPITHALAMION
EPITHALAMIUM
OPHIOGLOSSUM
OPINIONATIVE
OPISTHOGRAPH
OPPRESSIVELY
SPACIOUSNESS
SPATANGOIDEA
SPECIFICALLY
SPECIOUSNESS
SPECKTIONEER
SPECTROSCOPE
SPELEOLOGIST
SPELLCHECKER
SPERMATOCYTE
SPHACELATION
SPHAIRISTIKE
SPIEGELEISEN
SPINECHILLER
SPINSTERHOOD
SPIRITUALISM
SPIRITUALIST
SPIRITUALITY
SPITEFULNESS
SPLENOMEGALY
SPOKESPERSON
SPORADICALLY
SPORTSGROUND
SPREADEAGLED
SPURIOUSNESS
SPURTLEBLADE
UPROARIOUSLY
EQUIVOCATION
EQUIVOCATORY
ARBORESCENCE
ARCHILOCHIAN
ARCHIPELAGOS
ARCHITECTURE
ARFVEDSONITE
ARISTOCRATIC
ARISTOLOCHIA
ARISTOPHANES
ARISTOTELEAN
ARITHMETICAL
AROMATHERAPY
ARSENOPYRITE
ARTHROPLASTY
ARTICULATION
ARTIFICIALLY
ARTILLERYMAN
ARTIODACTYLA
ARTISTICALLY
BRACHYCEPHAL
BRAINWASHING
BRANCHIOPODA
BREAKTHROUGH
BREASTPLOUGH
BREASTSUMMER
BREATHALYSER
BREATHLESSLY
BREATHTAKING
BRICKFIELDER
BRILLIANTINE
BROADCASTING
BRONTOSAURUS
CRASHLANDING
CRASSAMENTUM
CREATIVENESS
CREMAILLIÈRE
CRISTOBALITE
CROSSBENCHER
CROSSCOUNTRY
CROSSEXAMINE
CROSSSECTION
CRYPTOGRAPHY
DRAMATICALLY
DRAMATURGIST
DRESSINGDOWN
DRINKDRIVING
ERATOSTHENES
ERYTHROMYCIN
FRACTIONALLY
FRANKALMOIGN
FRANKENSTEIN
FRANKINCENSE
FRAUENDIENST
FREIGHTLINER
FRIENDLINESS
FRONTIERSMAN
FRONTISPIECE
FRUITFULNESS
FRUMENTATION
GRACEFULNESS
GRACIOUSNESS
GRANDISONIAN
GRANDMONTINE
GRANDPARENTS
GRAPHOLOGIST
GRASSWIDOWER
GRATEFULNESS
GREENGROCERS
GREENGROCERY
GRISEOFULVIN
GROSSULARITE
IRASCIBILITY
IRRATIONALLY
IRREDEEMABLE
IRREGULARITY
IRRESISTIBLE
IRRESOLUTELY
IRRESOLUTION
IRRESOLVABLE
IRRESPECTIVE

IRREVERENTLY
IRREVERSIBLE
IRRITABILITY
OREOPITHECUS
OREOPITHEOUS
ORGANISATION
ORGANIZATION
ORIENTEERING
ORNITHOGALUM
ORTHODONTICS
ORTHOGENESIS
ORTHOPAEDICS
ORTHOPAEDIST
ORTHORHOMBIC
ORTHOTONESIS
PRACTICALITY
PRACTICIONER
PRACTITIONER
PRAISEWORTHY
PRALLTRILLER
PRASEODYMIUM
PRAXINOSCOPE
PRECARIOUSLY
PRECOCIOUSLY
PRECONDITION
PREDESTINATE
PREDETERMINE
PREDILECTION
PREDOMINANCE
PREFERENTIAL
PREGUSTATION
PREHISTORIAN
PREMAXILLARY
PREMONSTRANT
PREPAREDNESS
PREPONDERANT
PREPONDERATE
PREPONDERENT
PREPOSSESSED
PREPOSTEROUS
PREREQUISITE
PRESBYTERIAN
PRESCRIPTION
PRESCRIPTIVE
PRESENTATION
PRESENTIMENT
PRESERVATION
PRESERVATIVE
PRESIDENTIAL
PRESTRICTION
PRESUMPTUOUS
PREVARICATOR
PREVENTATIVE
PRIGGISHNESS
PRINCIPALITY
PRIZEFIGHTER
PRIZEWINNING
PROBATIONARY
PROCESSIONAL
PROCLAMATION
PRODIGIOUSLY
PRODUCTIVITY
PROFESSIONAL
PROFESSORIAL
PROFICIENTLY
PROFITEERING
PROGESTERONE
PROGRAMMABLE
PROGYMNASIUM
PROLEGOMENON
PROLETARIATE
PROLIFICALLY
PROLONGATION
PROMULGATION
PROPAGANDISM
PROPAGANDIST
PROPHYLACTIC
PROPITIATION
PROPITIATORY
PROPITIOUSLY
PROPORTIONAL
PROPRIETRESS
PROSCRIPTION
PROSOPOPOEIA
PROSTITUTION
PROTACTINIUM
PROTECTIVELY
PROTECTORATE
PROTESTATION
PROTHALAMION
PROTHALAMIUM
PROTOPLASMAL
PROTOPLASMIC
PROTUBERANCE
PROVERBIALLY
PROVIDENTIAL
TRABECULATED
TRACTABILITY
TRADESCANTIA
TRADESPEOPLE
TRALATICIOUS
TRALATITIOUS
TRANQUILIZER
TRANQUILLISE
TRANQUILLITY
TRANQUILLIZE
TRANSACTIONS
TRANSCENDENT
TRANSFERABLE
TRANSFERENCE
TRANSGRESSOR
TRANSITIONAL
TRANSLATABLE
TRANSLUCENCE
TRANSMIGRATE
TRANSMISSION
TRANSMOGRIFY
TRANSOCEANIC
TRANSPARENCY
TRANSPONTINE
TRANSVESTISM
TRANSVESTITE
TREMENDOUSLY
TRICHOLOGIST
TRICHOPHYTON
TRIGONOMETRY
TRIUMPHANTLY
TROCHELMINTH
TROCHOSPHERE
TROPHALLAXIS
TROUBLEMAKER
TRUTHFULNESS
URBANIZATION
URTRICULARIA
WRETCHEDNESS
ASPARAGINASE
ASPHYXIATION
ASSIMILATION
ASSUEFACTION
ASTONISHMENT
ASTROLOGICAL
ASTRONOMICAL
ASTROPHYSICS
ASYMMETRICAL
ESCAPOLOGIST
ESPAGNOLETTE
ESSENTIALITY
ESTHETICALLY
ESTRANGEMENT
ISHMAELITISH
ISOBILATERAL
ISOLATIONISM
ISOLATIONIST
OSCILLOSCOPE
OSSIFICATION
OSTENTATIOUS
OSTEOMALACIA
OSTEOPOROSIS
PSEPHOLOGIST
PSEUDONYMOUS
PSIPHENOMENA
PSYCHIATRIST
PSYCHOLOGIST
PSYCHOPATHIC
USERFRIENDLY
ATHEROMATOUS
ATMOSPHERICS
ATTRACTIVELY
ATTRIBUTABLE
ETEPIMELETIC
ETHEROMANIAC
ETHNOLOGICAL
ETYMOLOGICAL
ETYMOLOGICON
OTHERWORLDLY
PTERIDOPHYTE
PTERODACTYLE
STAGGERINGLY
STAKHANOVITE
STANISLAVSKI
STATISTICIAN
STEALTHINESS
STEEPLECHASE
STEGOPHOLIST
STELLENBOSCH
STENOGRAPHER
STENTORPHONE
STEPDAUGHTER
STEREOPHONIC
STEREOPTICON
STEREOSCOPIC
STEREOTYPING
STERNUTATION
STERNWHEELER
STILBOESTROL
STOCKBREEDER
STOCKINGETTE
STONECHATTER
STORMTROOPER
STRADIVARIUS
STRAIGHTAWAY
STRAIGHTEDGE
STRAIGHTNESS
STRAITJACKET
STRANGLEHOLD
STRANGLEWEED
STRATOSPHERE
STREPITATION
STREPSIPTERA
STREPTOMYCIN
STREPTONEURA
STRIDULATION
STRIGIFORMES
STRINGCOURSE
STROMATOLITE
STRONGMINDED
STROPHANTHUS
STRUCTURALLY
STUBBORNNESS
STUDIOUSNESS
STUPEFACTION
AUGMENTATION
AUSCULTATION
AUSPICIOUSLY
AUSTRALASIAN
AUSTRONESIAN
AUTHENTICATE
AUTHENTICITY
BUCKLEBEGGAR
BUNKOSTEERER
BUREAUCRATIC
BUSINESSLIKE
BUTTERSCOTCH
CURMUDGEONLY
DUNNIEWASSAL
EULENSPIEGEL
FULMINATIONS
FUNCTIONALLY
FUNCTIONLESS
FUNDAMENTALS

FUSTILLIRIAN
GUARDIANSHIP
GUILDENSTERN
HUDIBRASTICS
HUMANITARIAN
HUMANIZATION
JURISDICTION
LUGUBRIOUSLY
LUMINESCENCE
LUMINISCENCE
LUXEMBOURGER
LUXULLIANITE
MUCILAGINOUS
MUDDLEHEADED
MUGGLETONIAN
MULLIGATAWNY
MULTICOLORED
MULTIFARIOUS
MULTILATERAL
MULTIPLICITY
MUNICIPALITY
MUSICOLOGIST
MUTESSARIFAT
NUTRITIONIST
OUTBUILDINGS
OUTMANOEUVRE
OUTRAGEOUSLY
OUTSTRETCHED
PUGNACIOUSLY
PUMPERNICKEL
PURIFICATION
PURPOSEBUILT
PURPOSEFULLY
PUTREFACTION
QUADRAGESIMA
QUADRAPHONIC
QUANTIFIABLE
QUANTITATIVE
QUARTERFINAL
QUARTERLIGHT
QUARTERSTAFF
QUESTIONABLE
QUINQUENNIAL
QUINTESSENCE
QUIXOTICALLY
RUTHLESSNESS
SUBARRHATION
SUBCOMMITTEE
SUBCONSCIOUS
SUBCONTINENT
SUBCUTANEOUS
SUBHASTATION
SUBJECTIVELY
SUBJECTIVITY
SUBLAPSARIAN
SUBMISSIVELY
SUBSCRIPTION
SUBSEQUENTLY
SUBSERVIENCE
SUBSIDIARITY
SUBSTANTIATE
SUBSTITUTION
SUBSTRUCTURE
SUBTERRANEAN
SUCCESSFULLY
SUCCESSIVELY
SUCCUSSATION
SUFFICIENTLY
SUGGESTIVELY
SULPHONAMIDE
SUPERANNUATE
SUPERCHARGED
SUPERCHARGER
SUPERCILIARY
SUPERCILIOUS
SUPERHIGHWAY
SUPERNACULUM
SUPERNATURAL
SUPERSTITION
SUPPLICATION
SURMOUNTABLE
SURPRISINGLY
SURREALISTIC
SURROUNDINGS
SURVEILLANCE
SUSPICIOUSLY
TUBERCULOSIS
TURACOVERDIN
TURBOCHARGER
AVAILABILITY
EVENHANDEDLY
EVENTEMPERED
EVOLUTIONARY
OVERCROWDING
OVERDRESSING
OVERESTIMATE
OVEREXERTION
OVERPOWERING
OVERSCUTCHED
OVERSTRAINED
OVERWHELMING
AWARDWINNING
AWAYABSOLUTE
AWEINSPIRING
SWASHBUCKLER
SWIZZLESTICK
EXACERBATION
EXAGGERATION
EXASPERATING
EXASPERATION
EXCHANGEABLE
EXCITABILITY
EXCRUCIATING
EXCRUCIATION
EXHAUSTIVELY
EXHIBITIONER
EXHILARATING
EXHILARATION
EXPERIMENTAL
EXPLOITATION
EXSERVICEMAN
EXSUFFLICATE
EXTENSIONIST
EXTINGUISHER
EXTORTIONATE
EXTRADITABLE
EXTRAVAGANCE
EXTRAVAGANZA
OXYACETYLENE
AYUNTAMIENTO
BYELORUSSIAN
CYMOTRICHOUS
DYSTELEOLOGY
GYMNOSOPHIST
GYNECOLOGIST
HYDROCHLORIC
HYDROGRAPHER
HYDROQUINONE
HYDROTHERAPY
HYGIENICALLY
HYMNOGRAPHER
HYPERBOLICAL
HYPERPYRETIC
HYPERSARCOMA
HYPERTENSION
HYPNOTHERAPY
HYPNOTICALLY
HYPOCHONDRIA
HYPOCRITICAL
HYPOTHECATOR
HYPOTHETICAL
HYSTERECTOMY
HYSTERICALLY
LYMANTRIIDAE
MYRINGOSCOPE
MYSTERIOUSLY
MYTHOLOGICAL
NYCHTHEMERON
NYMPHOMANIAC
PYROTECHNICS
PYTHONOMORPH
SYMBOLICALLY
SYNADELPHITE
SYNTAGMATITE

12:3

ACADEMICALLY
ADAPTABILITY
AGALMATOLITE
AGAMOGENETIC
AGATHODAIMON
AMALGAMATION
AMARANTACEAE
ANAESTHETISE
ANAESTHETIST
ANAESTHETIZE
ANAMORPHOSIS
AVAILABILITY
AWARDWINNING
AWAYABSOLUTE
BEACONSFIELD
BEAUMARCHAIS
BEAUMONTAGUE
BEAUMONTIQUE
BLABBERMOUTH
BLACKCURRANT
BLANDISHMENT
BRACHYCEPHAL
BRAINWASHING
BRANCHIOPODA
CHAIRMANSHIP
CHALICOTHERE
CHAMPIONSHIP
CHARACTERIZE
CHARTERHOUSE
CHASTISEMENT
CHAUVINISTIC
CLAIRVOYANCE
CLAIRVOYANCY
CLAMJAMPHRIE
CLANNISHNESS
CLAPPERBOARD
CLARINETTIST
CLASSIFIABLE
CLAUDICATION
CLAVICEMBALO
CRASHLANDING
CRASSAMENTUM
DEAMBULATORY
DEASPIRATION
DIAGRAMMATIC
DIALECTICIAN
DRAMATICALLY
DRAMATURGIST
ELASMOBRANCH
EMANCIPATION
EMASCULATION
ENANTIOMORPH
ENANTIOPATHY
EPACRIDACEAE
EPANORTHOSIS
ERATOSTHENES
EXACERBATION
EXAGGERATION
EXASPERATING
EXASPERATION
FEARLESSNESS
FEATHERBRAIN
FLAGELLATION
FLAMBOYANTLY
FRACTIONALLY
FRANKALMOIGN
FRANKENSTEIN
FRANKINCENSE
FRAUENDIENST
GLADIATORIAL
GRACEFULNESS
GRACIOUSNESS
GRANDISONIAN

GRANDMONTINE
GRANDPARENTS
GRAPHOLOGIST
GRASSWIDOWER
GRATEFULNESS
GUARDIANSHIP
HEADMISTRESS
HEADQUARTERS
HEARTSTRINGS
HEARTWARMING
INACCESSIBLE
INACCURATELY
INADEQUATELY
INADMISSIBLE
INADVERTENCE
INAPPLICABLE
INARTICULATE
INAUGURATION
INAUSPICIOUS
IRASCIBILITY
MEANINGFULLY
PEACEFULNESS
PEACEKEEPING
PHARMACOLOGY
PLACENTIFORM
PLAINCLOTHES
PLASTERSTONE
PLAUSIBILITY
PRACTICALITY
PRACTICIONER
PRACTITIONER
PRAISEWORTHY
PRALLTRILLER
PRASEODYMIUM
PRAXINOSCOPE
QUADRAGESIMA
QUADRAPHONIC
QUANTIFIABLE
QUANTITATIVE
QUARTERFINAL
QUARTERLIGHT
QUARTERSTAFF
READJUSTMENT
REAPPEARANCE
RHADAMANTHUS
RHAMPHOTHECA
SCANDALOUSLY
SCANDINAVIAN
SCAPULIMANCY
SCATTERBRAIN
SCATTERMOUCH
SHAMEFACEDLY
SHAREHOLDING
SHARPSHOOTER
SMALLHOLDING
SPACIOUSNESS
SPATANGOIDEA
STAGGERINGLY
STAKHANOVITE
STANISLAVSKI
STATISTICIAN
SWASHBUCKLER
THANKFULNESS
THANKSGIVING
THAUMATURGIC
THAUMATURGUS
TRABECULATED
TRACTABILITY
TRADESCANTIA
TRADESPEOPLE
TRALATICIOUS
TRALATITIOUS
TRANQUILIZER
TRANQUILLISE
TRANQUILLITY
TRANQUILLIZE
TRANSACTIONS
TRANSCENDENT
TRANSFERABLE
TRANSFERENCE
TRANSGRESSOR
TRANSITIONAL
TRANSLATABLE
TRANSLUCENCE
TRANSMIGRATE
TRANSMISSION
TRANSMOGRIFY
TRANSOCEANIC
TRANSPARENCY
TRANSPONTINE
TRANSVESTISM
TRANSVESTITE
UNACCEPTABLE
UNACCUSTOMED
UNACQUAINTED
UNANSWERABLE
UNAPPARELLED
UNAPPETIZING
UNATTAINABLE
UNATTRACTIVE
UNAUTHORISED
UNAUTHORIZED
WEATHERPROOF
ABBREVIATION
AMBASSADRESS
AMBIDEXTROUS
AMBULANCEMAN
ARBORESCENCE
BABINGTONITE
BIBLIOGRAPHY
BIBLIOPEGIST
CABINETMAKER
DEBILITATING
EMBARRASSING
EMBEZZLEMENT
EMBROIDERESS
GIBRALTARIAN
GOBBLEDEGOOK
GOBBLEDYGOOK
HABERDASHERS
HABERDASHERY
HOBBIDIDANCE
LABANOTATION
LABOURSAVING
LABYRINTHINE
MOBILIZATION
SUBARRHATION
SUBCOMMITTEE
SUBCONSCIOUS
SUBCONTINENT
SUBCUTANEOUS
SUBHASTATION
SUBJECTIVELY
SUBJECTIVITY
SUBLAPSARIAN
SUBMISSIVELY
SUBSCRIPTION
SUBSEQUENTLY
SUBSERVIENCE
SUBSIDIARITY
SUBSTANTIATE
SUBSTITUTION
SUBSTRUCTURE
SUBTERRANEAN
TOBACCONISTS
TUBERCULOSIS
UMBRADARLING
UNBELIEVABLE
UNBELIEVABLY
URBANIZATION
VIBRATIUNCLE
ACCELERATION
ACCENTUATION
ACCIDENTALLY
ACCOMPANYING
ACCOMPLISHED
ACCORDIONIST
ACCOUCHEMENT
ACCOUTREMENT
ACCUMULATION
AECIDIOSPORE
ARCHILOCHIAN
ARCHIPELAGOS
ARCHITECTURE
BACCHANALIAN
BACKBREAKING
BACKWARDNESS
BACKWOODSMAN
BACTERIOLOGY
BACTERIOSTAT
BICAMERALISM
BICENTENNIAL
BUCKLEBEGGAR
COCCIDIOSTAT
DECAPITATION
DECELERATION
DECENTRALISE
DECENTRALIZE
DECIPHERABLE
DECIPHERMENT
DECONGESTANT
DECORATIVELY
DICTATORSHIP
ECCENTRICITY
ECCLESIASTES
ECCLESIASTIC
ENCHEIRIDION
ENCIRCLEMENT
ENCROACHMENT
ENCYCLOPEDIA
ENCYCLOPEDIC
ESCAPOLOGIST
EXCHANGEABLE
EXCITABILITY
EXCRUCIATING
EXCRUCIATION
INCALCULABLE
INCANDESCENT
INCAPABILITY
INCAPACITATE
INCAUTIOUSLY
INCIDENTALLY
INCINERATION
INCOHERENTLY
INCOMPARABLE
INCOMPARABLY
INCOMPATIBLE
INCOMPETENCE
INCOMPLETELY
INCONCLUSIVE
INCONSEQUENT
INCONSISTENT
INCONSOLABLE
INCONTINENCE
INCONVENIENT
INCORPORATED
INCORRIGIBLE
INCORRIGIBLY
INCREASINGLY
INCRUSTATION
INCUNABULIST
LICKTRENCHER
MACABERESQUE
MACHAIRODONT
MACMILLANITE
MACROPODIDAE
MECHANICALLY
MECHITHARIST
MICHELANGELO
MICROCLIMATE
MUCILAGINOUS
NOCONFIDENCE
NYCHTHEMERON
OCCASIONALLY
OCCUPATIONAL
ONCORHYNCHUS
OSCILLOSCOPE
PACIFICATION
PECTORILOQUY
RACKETEERING

RECALCITRANT
RECAPITULATE
RECEIVERSHIP
RECEPTIONIST
RECHARGEABLE
RECIPROCALLY
RECKLESSNESS
RECOGNIZABLE
RECOGNIZANCE
RECOLLECTION
RECONSTITUTE
RECORDPLAYER
RECREATIONAL
RECRUDESCENT
RECUPERATION
RECUPERATIVE
SACRILEGIOUS
SECESSIONIST
SECRETARIATE
SECTARIANISM
SOCIOLOGICAL
SUCCESSFULLY
SUCCESSIVELY
SUCCUSSATION
TACTLESSNESS
TECHNICALITY
TECHNOLOGIST
UNCHALLENGED
UNCHANGEABLE
UNCHARITABLE
UNCHARITABLY
UNCLASSIFIED
UNCONSIDERED
UNCONTROLLED
UNCONVERSANT
UNCONVINCING
UNCTUOUSNESS
UNCULTIVATED
VOCIFERATION
VOCIFEROUSLY
WICKETKEEPER
ADDITIONALLY
ANDOUILLETTE
ANDROSTERONE
CODIFICATION
FIDDLESTICKS
HUDIBRASTICS
HYDROCHLORIC
HYDROGRAPHER
HYDROQUINONE
HYDROTHERAPY
INDEBTEDNESS
INDECLINABLE
INDEFENSIBLE
INDEFINITELY
INDEPENDENCE
INDIFFERENCE
INDIGESTIBLE
INDISCRETION
INDISPUTABLE
INDISPUTABLY
INDISSOLUBLE
INDISTINCTLY
INDIVIDUALLY
INDOCTRINATE
INDUSTRIALLY
MADEMOISELLE
MIDDLEWEIGHT
MODIFICATION
MUDDLEHEADED
OLDFASHIONED
PEDANTICALLY
PEDIATRICIAN
PEDICELLARIA
RADIOGRAPHER
RADIOISOTOPE
RADIOTHERAPY
REDEMPTIONER
REDEPLOYMENT
REDINTEGRATE
REDISCOVERED
REDISTRIBUTE
RIDICULOUSLY
RODOMONTADER
SADISTICALLY
SIDEWHISKERS
UNDEMOCRATIC
UNDERACHIEVE
UNDERCLOTHES
UNDERCURRENT
UNDEREXPOSED
UNDERGARMENT
UNDERPINNING
UNDERSKINKER
UNDERSTAFFED
UNDERWRITTEN
UNDESERVEDLY
UNDETECTABLE
UNDETERMINED
UNDIMINISHED
UNDISCHARGED
ALEXIPHARMIC
AMELIORATION
ANECATHARSIS
ANEMOPHILOUS
AWEINSPIRING
BIELORUSSIAN
BLEFUSCUDIAN
BLENNORRHOEA
BLETHERSKATE
BREAKTHROUGH
BREASTPLOUGH
BREASTSUMMER
BREATHALYSER
BREATHLESSLY
BREATHTAKING
BYELORUSSIAN
CHEERFULNESS
CHEESEBURGER
CHEESEMONGER
CHEESEPARING
CHEMOTHERAPY
CHESTERFIELD
CLEARSIGHTED
CLEISTOGAMIC
CREATIVENESS
CREMAILLIÈRE
DIENCEPHALON
DRESSINGDOWN
ELECTRICALLY
ELECTROLYSIS
ELECTROPLATE
ELECTROTONUS
ELEEMOSYNARY
ENERGYSAVING
EPENCEPHALON
ETEPIMELETIC
EVENHANDEDLY
EVENTEMPERED
FREIGHTLINER
GREENGROCERS
GREENGROCERY
HAEMATEMESIS
HAEMOPHILIAC
HAEMORRHOIDS
HIERARCHICAL
HIEROGLYPHIC
HIEROGRAMMAT
HIEROPHANTIC
IDEALIZATION
IDENTIFIABLE
INEFFICIENCY
INERADICABLE
INESCUTCHEON
INEXACTITUDE
INEXPERIENCE
INEXPLICABLE
INEXPLICABLY
INEXTRICABLE
INEXTRICABLY
KLEPTOMANIAC
KLETTERSCHUE
MNEMOTECHNIC
OBEDIENTIARY
OCEANOGRAPHY
ONEIROCRITIC
OREOPITHECUS
OREOPITHEOUS
OVERCROWDING
OVERDRESSING
OVERESTIMATE
OVEREXERTION
OVERPOWERING
OVERSCUTCHED
OVERSTRAINED
OVERWHELMING
PHENOMENALLY
PLECTOGNATHI
PLEIOCHASIUM
PRECARIOUSLY
PRECOCIOUSLY
PRECONDITION
PREDESTINATE
PREDETERMINE
PREDILECTION
PREDOMINANCE
PREFERENTIAL
PREGUSTATION
PREHISTORIAN
PREMAXILLARY
PREMONSTRANT
PREPAREDNESS
PREPONDERANT
PREPONDERATE
PREPONDERENT
PREPOSSESSED
PREPOSTEROUS
PREREQUISITE
PRESBYTERIAN
PRESCRIPTION
PRESCRIPTIVE
PRESENTATION
PRESENTIMENT
PRESERVATION
PRESERVATIVE
PRESIDENTIAL
PRESTRICTION
PRESUMPTUOUS
PREVARICATOR
PREVENTATIVE
PSEPHOLOGIST
PSEUDONYMOUS
PTERIDOPHYTE
PTERODACTYLE
QUESTIONABLE
SHEEPISHNESS
SLEEPWALKING
SPECIFICALLY
SPECIOUSNESS
SPECKTIONEER
SPECTROSCOPE
SPELEOLOGIST
SPELLCHECKER
SPERMATOCYTE
STEALTHINESS
STEEPLECHASE
STEGOPHOLIST
STELLENBOSCH
STENOGRAPHER
STENTORPHONE
STEPDAUGHTER
STEREOPHONIC
STEREOPTICON
STEREOSCOPIC
STEREOTYPING
STERNUTATION
STERNWHEELER
TEETERTOTTER
THEATRICALLY
THEOPHYLLINE

THEORETICIAN
THERAPEUTICS
THEREAGAINST
THERMOSTATIC
THESMOPHORIA
THESSALONIAN
TREMENDOUSLY
UNECONOMICAL
UNEMPLOYMENT
UNEXPECTEDLY
UNEXPURGATED
USERFRIENDLY
WRETCHEDNESS
AFFECTIONATE
APFELSTRUDEL
ARFVEDSONITE
DEFLATIONARY
DIFFERENTIAL
EFFERVESCENT
EFFORTLESSLY
INFELICITOUS
INFILTRATION
INFLAMMATION
INFLAMMATORY
INFLATIONARY
INFORMIDABLE
INFREQUENTLY
INFRINGEMENT
LIFELESSNESS
REFLATIONARY
REFRIGERATED
REFRIGERATOR
SUFFICIENTLY
UNFATHOMABLE
UNFAVOURABLE
UNFREQUENTED
AGGRESSIVELY
AUGMENTATION
DAGUERROTYPE
DEGENERATION
DOGMATICALLY
ENGLISHWOMAN
ENGLISHWOMEN
FIGURATIVELY
GIGANTOMACHY
HIGHFALUTING
HYGIENICALLY
INGRATIATING
LEGALIZATION
LEGIONNAIRES
LEGITIMATELY
LIGHTHEARTED
LUGUBRIOUSLY
MAGNETICALLY
MAGNIFICENCE
MAGNILOQUENT
MUGGLETONIAN
NIGHTCLOTHES
ORGANISATION
ORGANIZATION
PIGMENTATION
PUGNACIOUSLY
REGENERATION
REGISTRATION
SEGMENTATION
SIGNIFICANCE
SUGGESTIVELY
TAGLIACOTIAN
TIGHTFITTING
TOGETHERNESS
ACHLAMYDEOUS
ATHEROMATOUS
BEHAVIOURISM
COHABITATION
DEHUMIDIFIER
ENHYPOSTASIA
ETHEROMANIAC
ETHNOLOGICAL
EXHAUSTIVELY
EXHIBITIONER
EXHILARATING
EXHILARATION
FEHMGERICHTE
ICHTHYOCOLLA
ICHTHYOPSIDA
INHARMONIOUS
INHOSPITABLE
ISHMAELITISH
OPHIOGLOSSUM
OTHERWORLDLY
REHABILITATE
SCHEHERAZADE
SCHILLERSPAR
SCHINDYLESIS
SCHIZOMYCETE
SCHNEIDERIAN
SCHOOLMASTER
SCHOPENHAUER
SPHACELATION
SPHAIRISTIKE
VEHMGERICHTE
ALIMENTATIVE
ARISTOCRATIC
ARISTOLOCHIA
ARISTOPHANES
ARISTOTELEAN
ARITHMETICAL
BAIRNSFATHER
BOISTEROUSLY
BRICKFIELDER
BRILLIANTINE
CHILDBEARING
CHILDISHNESS
CHIROPRACTIC
CHIROPRACTOR
CHITTERLINGS
COINCIDENTAL
CRISTOBALITE
DRINKDRIVING
EPIDEICTICAL
EPIGRAMMATIC
EPIPHENOMENA
EPISCOPALIAN
EPISTEMOLOGY
EPISTOLATERS
EPITHALAMION
EPITHALAMIUM
FAINTHEARTED
FAITHFULNESS
FLITTERMOUSE
FRIENDLINESS
GAINSBOROUGH
GRISEOFULVIN
GUILDENSTERN
HAIRDRESSERS
HAIRDRESSING
HAIRSPLITTER
IDIOSYNCRASY
IDIOTHERMOUS
KLIPSPRINGER
LEIOTRICHOUS
MOISTURIZING
NEIGHBORHOOD
NEIGHBOURING
OPINIONATIVE
OPISTHOGRAPH
ORIENTEERING
PAINLESSNESS
PHILANTHROPY
PHILHARMONIC
PHILISTINISM
PHILODENDRON
PHILOLOGICAL
PHILOSOPHIZE
POINTILLISME
PRIGGISHNESS
PRINCIPALITY
PRIZEFIGHTER
PRIZEWINNING
PSIPHENOMENA
QUINQUENNIAL
QUINTESSENCE
QUIXOTICALLY
REINVIGORATE
RHINORRHOEAL
RHIPIDOPTERA
SCINTILLATOR
SHILLYSHALLY
SHIPBUILDING
SHIRTSLEEVES
SHIRTWAISTER
SPIEGELEISEN
SPINECHILLER
SPINSTERHOOD
SPIRITUALISM
SPIRITUALIST
SPIRITUALITY
SPITEFULNESS
STILBOESTROL
SWIZZLESTICK
THICKSKINNED
THIGMOTROPIC
THIRDBOROUGH
TRICHOLOGIST
TRICHOPHYTON
TRIGONOMETRY
TRIUMPHANTLY
UNIDENTIFIED
UNILATERALLY
UNIMAGINABLE
UNIMPORTANCE
UNINTERESTED
UNIVERSALIST
VAINGLORIOUS
WEIGHTLIFTER
WHIGMALEERIE
WHIMSICALITY
WHIPPOORWILL
ADJECTIVALLY
ADJUDICATION
MAJESTICALLY
REJUVENATION
ACKNOWLEDGED
ALLITERATION
APLANOGAMETE
BELLIGERENCY
BILLINGSGATE
CALCEAMENTUM
CALLIGRAPHIC
CALLISTHENES
CALUMNIATION
CHLORINATION
COLDSHOULDER
COLLABORATOR
COLLECTIVELY
COLLECTORATE
COLLOQUIALLY
COLLUCTATION
COLLYWOBBLES
COLONIZATION
COLOQUINTIDA
DELIBERATELY
DELIBERATION
DELICATESSEN
DILAPIDATION
DILATORINESS
DOLPHINARIUM
EULENSPIEGEL
FELDSPATHOID
FULMINATIONS
GALLIGASKINS
GALLINACEOUS
GALLIVANTING
GALVANOMETER
HALLANSHAKER
HALLUCINOGEN
HELIOGABALUS
HELLGRAMMITE
HELPLESSNESS
HILDEBRANDIC

HOLIDAYMAKER
ILLEGIBILITY
ILLEGITIMACY
ILLEGITIMATE
ILLOGICALITY
ILLUMINATING
ILLUMINATION
ILLUSTRATION
ILLUSTRATIVE
KALEIDOSCOPE
KALISTOCRACY
KILLIKINNICK
LALLAPALOOZA
LILLIBULLERO
LILLIBURLERO
MALACOSTRACA
MALFORMATION
MALLEABILITY
MALLOPHAGOUS
MALNUTRITION
MALPRACTICES
MALTREATMENT
MELODRAMATIC
MILITARISTIC
MULLIGATAWNY
MULTICOLORED
MULTIFARIOUS
MULTILATERAL
MULTIPLICITY
OBLITERATION
PALEONTOLOGY
PALINGENESIA
PALINGENESIS
PALPITATIONS
PALUDAMENTUM
PHLEBOTOMIST
POLARIZATION
POLICYMAKING
POLYETHYLENE
POLYSYLLABIC
POLYSYLLABLE
POLYSYNDETON
POLYURETHANE
RELATIONSHIP
RELENTLESSLY
ROLLERBLADER
ROLLERBLADES
SALESMANSHIP
SALTATORIOUS
SALVATIONIST
SCLERENCHYMA
SCLERODERMIA
SELFADHESIVE
SELFCATERING
SELFEMPLOYED
SELFINTEREST
SELFPORTRAIT
SILVERHAIRED
SOLICITATION
SOLICITOUSLY

SPLENOMEGALY
SULPHONAMIDE
TELEASTHETIC
TELEGRAPHESE
TELEGRAPHIST
TELEOSAURIAN
TELEUTOSPORE
VALENCIENNES
VILIFICATION
VILLEGIATURA
VOLUPTUOUSLY
WALLYDRAIGLE
WELLBALANCED
WELLINFORMED
WELLINGTONIA
WELTERWEIGHT
WILLIEWAUGHT
WILTSHIREMAN
WOLLASTONITE
WOLSTENHOLME
YELLOWHAMMER
ZALAMBDODONT
ADMINISTRATE
ADMONISHMENT
ATMOSPHERICS
BAMBOCCIADES
CAMIKNICKERS
CAMPANULARIA
CAMPODEIFORM
COMBINATIONS
COMMANDMENTS
COMMENCEMENT
COMMENDATION
COMMENDATORY
COMMENSURATE
COMMERCIALLY
COMMISSARIAT
COMMISSIONED
COMMISSIONER
COMMONWEALTH
COMMUNICABLE
COMPANIONWAY
COMPELLATION
COMPENSATION
COMPENSATORY
COMPLACENTLY
COMPLETENESS
COMPLICATION
COMPROMISING
COMPURGATION
CYMOTRICHOUS
DEMILITARIZE
DEMIMONDAINE
DEMONSTRABLE
DEMONSTRABLY
DEMONSTRATOR
DOMESTICATED
GAMESMANSHIP
GYMNOSOPHIST
HAMARTHRITIS

HAMBLETONIAN
HAMMERHEADED
HEMICHORDATA
HOMESICKNESS
HOMOEOPATHIC
HOMOTHERMOUS
HUMANITARIAN
HUMANIZATION
HYMNOGRAPHER
IAMBOGRAPHER
IMMACULATELY
IMMEASURABLE
IMMEASURABLY
IMMODERATELY
IMMODERATION
IMMUNIZATION
IMMUNOLOGIST
IMMUTABILITY
LAMELLICORNE
LAMENTATIONS
LAMPADEDROMY
LUMINESCENCE
LUMINISCENCE
LYMANTRIIDAE
NOMENCLATURE
NYMPHOMANIAC
PUMPERNICKEL
RAMBUNCTIOUS
RAMIFICATION
REMEMBRANCER
REMINISCENCE
REMONSTRANCE
REMUNERATION
REMUNERATIVE
ROMANTICALLY
SEMANTICALLY
SEMICIRCULAR
SEMIDETACHED
SEMIPRECIOUS
SIMULTANEOUS
SOMATOPLEURE
SOMNAMBULISM
SOMNAMBULIST
SYMBOLICALLY
TAMARICACEAE
TIMELESSNESS
UNMANAGEABLE
UNMISTAKABLE
ANNIHILATION
ANNOUNCEMENT
ANNUNCIATION
BANANALANDER
BANDERSNATCH
BANTAMWEIGHT
BENEFACTRESS
BENEVOLENTLY
BUNKOSTEERER
CANCELLATION
CANONIZATION
CANTANKEROUS

CANTILEVERED
CONCENTRATED
CONCILIATION
CONCILIATORY
CONCLUSIVELY
CONCURRENTLY
CONDEMNATION
CONDENSATION
CONDUCTIVITY
CONFECTIONER
CONFESSIONAL
CONFIDENTIAL
CONFIRMATION
CONFIRMATORY
CONFISCATION
CONGENITALLY
CONGLOMERATE
CONGRATULATE
CONGREGATION
CONQUISTADOR
CONSCRIPTION
CONSECRATION
CONSEQUENCES
CONSEQUENTLY
CONSERVATION
CONSERVATISM
CONSERVATIVE
CONSERVATORY
CONSIDERABLE
CONSIDERABLY
CONSISTENTLY
CONSOLIDATED
CONSOLIDATOR
CONSPECTUITY
CONSTABULARY
CONSTIPATION
CONSTITUENCY
CONSTITUENTS
CONSTITUTION
CONSTRICTION
CONSTRUCTION
CONSTRUCTIVE
CONSULTATION
CONSULTATIVE
CONSUMMATION
CONTABESCENT
CONTAMINATED
CONTEMPORARY
CONTEMPTIBLE
CONTEMPTUOUS
CONTERMINOUS
CONTIGNATION
CONTINUATION
CONTINUOUSLY
CONTRAPPOSTO
CONTRAPUNTAL
CONTRARINESS
CONTRIBUTION
CONTRIBUTORY
CONTRITURATE

CONTROLLABLE
CONTUMACIOUS
CONVALESCENT
CONVALESCING
CONVENIENCES
CONVENIENTLY
CONVENTIONAL
CONVERSATION
CONVEYANCING
CONVINCINGLY
CONVIVIALITY
DENDROLOGIST
DENOMINATION
DENUNCIATION
DONNERWETTER
DUNNIEWASSAL
FINALIZATION
FUNCTIONALLY
FUNCTIONLESS
FUNDAMENTALS
GENEALOGICAL
GENETHLIACON
GENTLETAMPER
GONADOTROPIN
GONDWANALAND
GYNECOLOGIST
HANDKERCHIEF
HENCEFORWARD
HINDQUARTERS
INNATTENTIVE
INNOMINABLES
JENNYSPINNER
KINAESTHETIC
KINDERGARTEN
LANCASTERIAN
LANGUEDOCIAN
LINCOLNSHIRE
LONGDISTANCE
LONGITUDINAL
LONGSHOREMAN
LONGSTANDING
MANGELWURZEL
MANIPULATION
MANIPULATIVE
MANOEUVRABLE
MANSLAUGHTER
MANUFACTURER
MENSTRUATION
MINDBOGGLING
MINDFULLNESS
MINERALOGIST
MINICOMPUTER
MINISTRATION
MONOSYLLABIC
MONOSYLLABLE
MONOTONOUSLY
MONTESSORIAN
MUNICIPALITY
NONAGENARIAN
NONALCOHOLIC
NONCHALANTLY
NONCOMMITTAL
NONEXISTENCE
NONRESIDENCE
NONRESISTANT
ORNITHOGALUM
PANAESTHESIA
PANATHENAEAN
PANCHATANTRA
PANCHROMATIC
PANDAEMONIUM
PANDANACEOUS
PANPHARMACON
PANTECHNICON
PANTISOCRACY
PANTOPHAGOUS
PENALIZATION
PENITENTIARY
PENNSYLVANIA
PINNIEWINKLE
RENOUNCEMENT
RENUNCIATION
RONCESVALLES
SINANTHROPUS
SINGLEDECKER
SINGLEHANDED
SINGLEMINDED
SYNADELPHITE
SYNTAGMATITE
UINTATHERIUM
UNNEIGHBORLY
VENEPUNCTURE
VENGEFULNESS
VENTRIPOTENT
VINDICTIVELY
WINTERHALTER
XANTHOPTERIN
ABOLITIONIST
AFORETHOUGHT
APOLLINARIAN
APOSTROPHISE
AROMATHERAPY
BIOCHEMISTRY
BIODIVERSITY
BIOGRAPHICAL
BLOODSTAINED
BLOODTHIRSTY
BOOBYTRAPPED
BOONDOGGLING
BROADCASTING
BRONTOSAURUS
CHONDRIOSOME
CHOREOGRAPHY
CHORIZONTIST
COORDINATION
CROSSBENCHER
CROSSCOUNTRY
CROSSEXAMINE
CROSSSECTION
ECONOMICALLY
EVOLUTIONARY
FLORICULTURE
FOOTSLOGGING
FRONTIERSMAN
FRONTISPIECE
GEOGRAPHICAL
GEOLOGICALLY
GEOMETRICIAN
GEOPHYSICIST
GLOBETROTTER
GLOCKENSPIEL
GOOSEPIMPLES
GROSSULARITE
ICONOCLASTIC
INORDINATELY
ISOBILATERAL
ISOLATIONISM
ISOLATIONIST
MOONLIGHTING
NEOCLASSICAL
NEOPLATONISM
ONOMATOPOEIA
ONOMATOPOEIC
PHONETICALLY
PHOSPHORENCE
PHOSPHORESCE
PHOTOGLYPHIC
PHOTOGRAPHER
PHOTOGRAPHIC
PHOTOGRAVURE
PROBATIONARY
PROCESSIONAL
PROCLAMATION
PRODIGIOUSLY
PRODUCTIVITY
PROFESSIONAL
PROFESSORIAL
PROFICIENTLY
PROFITEERING
PROGESTERONE
PROGRAMMABLE
PROGYMNASIUM
PROLEGOMENON
PROLETARIATE
PROLIFICALLY
PROLONGATION
PROMULGATION
PROPAGANDISM
PROPAGANDIST
PROPHYLACTIC
PROPITIATION
PROPITIATORY
PROPITIOUSLY
PROPORTIONAL
PROPRIETRESS
PROSCRIPTION
PROSOPOPOEIA
PROSTITUTION
PROTACTINIUM
PROTECTIVELY
PROTECTORATE
PROTESTATION
PROTHALAMION
PROTHALAMIUM
PROTOPLASMAL
PROTOPLASMIC
PROTUBERANCE
PROVERBIALLY
PROVIDENTIAL
RHODODENDRON
ROOMINGHOUSE
SCOPOPHILIAC
SHORTCIRCUIT
SHORTCOMINGS
SHORTSIGHTED
SHORTSLEEVED
SHORTSTAFFED
SHOSTAKOVICH
SLOCKDOLAGER
SLOCKDOLIGER
SLOCKDOLOGER
SLOVENLINESS
SNOBBISHNESS
SNOWBOARDING
SPOKESPERSON
SPORADICALLY
SPORTSGROUND
STOCKBREEDER
STOCKINGETTE
STONECHATTER
STORMTROOPER
THOROUGHBRED
THOROUGHFARE
THOROUGHNESS
THOUGHTFULLY
TROCHELMINTH
TROCHOSPHERE
TROPHALLAXIS
TROUBLEMAKER
ULOTRICHALES
UNOBSTRUCTED
UNOBTAINABLE
UNOFFICIALLY
UNOPPRESSIVE
WHOLEHEARTED
WOODBURYTYPE
ALPHABETICAL
ALPHANUMERIC
AMPHISBAENIC
AMPHISTOMOUS
AMPHITHEATER
AMPHITHEATRE
APPENDECTOMY
APPENDICITIS
APPOGGIATURA
APPRECIATION
APPRECIATIVE
APPREHENSION
APPREHENSIVE
APPROACHABLE

APPURTENANCE
ASPARAGINASE
ASPHYXIATION
CAPERCAILLIE
CAPERCAILZIE
CAPITULATION
DEPARTMENTAL
DEPOPULATION
DEPRECIATION
DEPRECIATORY
DIPLOGENESIS
DIPRIONIDIAN
EMPHATICALLY
ESPAGNOLETTE
EXPERIMENTAL
EXPLOITATION
HAPPENSTANCE
HAPPYGOLUCKY
HEPHTHEMIMER
HIPPOCRATISE
HIPPOCREPIAN
HIPPOPOTAMUS
HOPELESSNESS
HYPERBOLICAL
HYPERPYRETIC
HYPERSARCOMA
HYPERTENSION
HYPNOTHERAPY
HYPNOTICALLY
HYPOCHONDRIA
HYPOCRITICAL
HYPOTHECATOR
HYPOTHETICAL
IMPARTIALITY
IMPENETRABLE
IMPERFECTION
IMPERISHABLE
IMPERSONALLY
IMPERSONATOR
IMPERTINENCE
IMPLANTATION
IMPOLITENESS
IMPOVERISHED
IMPREGNATION
IMPRESSIVELY
IMPRISONMENT
IMPROVIDENCE
LEPIDOMELANE
NEPENTHACEAE
NEPHELOMETER
OPPRESSIVELY
PAPILIONIDAE
POPOCATEPETL
REPATRIATION
REPERCUSSION
REPOSSESSION
REPROCESSING
REPRODUCTION
REPRODUCTIVE
SEPTEMBRISER
SEPTUAGESIMA
SIPHONOPHORA
SIPHONOSTELE
SIPUNCULACEA
SOPHISTICATE
SUPERANNUATE
SUPERCHARGED
SUPERCHARGER
SUPERCILIARY
SUPERCILIOUS
SUPERHIGHWAY
SUPERNACULUM
SUPERNATURAL
SUPERSTITION
SUPPLICATION
TAPERECORDER
TAPSALTEERIE
TAPSLETEERIE
UNPARALLELED
UNPARDONABLE
UNPOPULARITY
UNPREJUDICED
UNPRETENDING
UNPRINCIPLED
UNPRODUCTIVE
UNPROFITABLE
VAPORIZATION
ACQUAINTANCE
ACQUIESCENCE
LIQUEFACTION
SEQUENTIALLY
SEQUESTRATOR
AERODYNAMICS
AERONAUTICAL
AGRIBUSINESS
AGRICULTURAL
AIRCRAFTSMAN
BARBERMONGER
BARNSTORMING
BARRANQUILLA
BERTHOLLETIA
BERTILLONAGE
BIRDWATCHING
BUREAUCRATIC
CARAVANSERAI
CARBOHYDRATE
CARCINOGENIC
CARDINDEXING
CARDIOLOGIST
CARELESSNESS
CARICATURIST
CARLOVINGIAN
CARPETBAGGER
CARRIWITCHET
CARTHAGINIAN
CARTOGRAPHER
CARTOGRAPHIC
CEREBROTONIC
CEREMONIALLY
CHREMATISTIC
CHRESTOMATHY
CHRISTIANITY
CIRCASSIENNE
CIRCUMCISION
CIRCUMGYRATE
CIRCUMSCRIBE
CIRCUMSTANCE
CURMUDGEONLY
DARLINGTONIA
DEREGULATION
DERESTRICTED
DIRECTORSHIP
DORSIVENTRAL
FARTHINGLAND
FERMENTATION
FIRSTFOOTING
FORCEFULNESS
FORMALDEHYDE
FORTUITOUSLY
GERIATRICIAN
GERONTOCRACY
HARMONIOUSLY
HARNESSMAKER
HARUMFRODITE
HEREDITAMENT
HERMENEUTICS
HERMENEUTIST
HERMETICALLY
HEROICOMICAL
HORIZONTALLY
HORRIFICALLY
HORSEMANSHIP
HORTICULTURE
IRRATIONALLY
IRREDEEMABLE
IRREGULARITY
IRRESISTIBLE
IRRESOLUTELY
IRRESOLUTION
IRRESOLVABLE
IRRESPECTIVE
IRREVERENTLY
IRREVERSIBLE
IRRITABILITY
JURISDICTION
KERAUNOGRAPH
KIRSCHWASSER
MARCOBRUNNER
MARCONIGRAPH
MARKSMANSHIP
MARLINESPIKE
MARRIAGEABLE
MARSEILLAISE
MERETRICIOUS
MERISTEMATIC
MERITRICIOUS
MERRYTHOUGHT
MERVEILLEUSE
MIRACULOUSLY
MYRINGOSCOPE
NARCISSISTIC
NORTHEASTERN
NORTHERNMOST
NORTHWESTERN
PARACENTESIS
PARALIPOMENA
PARAMILITARY
PARANTHELIUM
PARSIMONIOUS
PARTICOLORED
PARTICULARLY
PARTISANSHIP
PERADVENTURE
PERAMBULATOR
PERCEPTIVELY
PERCEPTIVITY
PEREMPTORILY
PERGAMENEOUS
PERICARDITIS
PERIODICALLY
PERIOSTRACUM
PERIPHRASTIC
PERISTERONIC
PERMANGANATE
PERMEABILITY
PERNOCTATION
PERPETRATION
PERSEVERANCE
PERSISTENTLY
PERSONALIZED
PERSPICACITY
PERSPIRATION
PERSUASIVELY
PERSULPHURIC
PERTINACIOUS
PERTURBATION
PERVERSENESS
PERVICACIOUS
PHRONTISTERY
PORNOGRAPHIC
PURIFICATION
PURPOSEBUILT
PURPOSEFULLY
PYROTECHNICS
SARDANAPALUS
SARDONICALLY
SARRUSOPHONE
SARSAPARILLA
SCREENWRITER
SCRIMSHANDER
SCRIMSHANKER
SCRIPTWRITER
SCRUPULOUSLY
SERASKIERATE
SERVICEWOMAN
SPREADEAGLED
STRADIVARIUS
STRAIGHTAWAY
STRAIGHTEDGE
STRAIGHTNESS

STRAITJACKET
STRANGLEHOLD
STRANGLEWEED
STRATOSPHERE
STREPITATION
STREPSIPTERA
STREPTOMYCIN
STREPTONEURA
STRIDULATION
STRIGIFORMES
STRINGCOURSE
STROMATOLITE
STRONGMINDED
STROPHANTHUS
STRUCTURALLY
SURMOUNTABLE
SURPRISINGLY
SURREALISTIC
SURROUNDINGS
SURVEILLANCE
TARAMASALATA
TERCENTENARY
TERGIVERSATE
TERRIFICALLY
TERRITORIALS
THREADNEEDLE
THREEQUARTER
TORRICELLIAN
TURACOVERDIN
TURBOCHARGER
UNREASONABLE
UNRECOGNISED
UNRECOGNIZED
UNRESERVEDLY
UNRESPONSIVE
UNRESTRAINED
UNRESTRICTED
UNRETURNABLE
UPROARIOUSLY
VARICOLOURED
VERIFICATION
VERUMONTANUM
WAREHOUSEMAN
YORKSHIREMAN
ZARATHUSTRIC
ABSQUATULATE
ADSCITITIOUS
ARSENOPYRITE
ASSIMILATION
ASSUEFACTION
AUSCULTATION
AUSPICIOUSLY
AUSTRALASIAN
AUSTRONESIAN
BESSERWISSER
BUSINESSLIKE
CASSITERIDES
CASTERBRIDGE
COSCINOMANCY
COSMOPOLITAN
COSTERMONGER
DESIRABILITY
DESSERTSPOON
DISACCHARIDE
DISADVANTAGE
DISAGREEABLE
DISAGREEMENT
DISAPPEARING
DISAPPOINTED
DISASTROUSLY
DISCIPLINARY
DISCOMEDUSAE
DISCOMFITURE
DISCOMYCETES
DISCONCERTED
DISCONNECTED
DISCONSOLATE
DISCONTENTED
DISCOURAGING
DISCOURTEOUS
DISCRIMINATE
DISDAINFULLY
DISEMBARRASS
DISENCHANTED
DISFRANCHISE
DISHONORABLE
DISHONORABLY
DISINCENTIVE
DISINFECTANT
DISINGENUOUS
DISINTEGRATE
DISOBEDIENCE
DISORGANIZED
DISORIENTATE
DISPENSATION
DISPLACEMENT
DISPOSSESSED
DISQUISITION
DISREPECTFUL
DISREPUTABLE
DISSATISFIED
DISSERTATION
DISSOCIATION
DISTILLATION
DISTINCTNESS
DISTRIBUTION
DISTRIBUTIVE
DYSTELEOLOGY
ECSTATICALLY
ESSENTIALITY
EXSERVICEMAN
EXSUFFLICATE
FASTIDIOUSLY
FUSTILLIRIAN
GASTARBEITER
GASTROSOPHER
GESELLSCHAFT
HISTIOPHORUS
HISTORICALLY
HYSTERECTOMY
HYSTERICALLY
INSALUBRIOUS
INSEMINATION
INSOLUBILITY
INSPECTORATE
INSTALLATION
INSTAURATION
INSTRUCTIONS
INSTRUCTRESS
INSTRUMENTAL
INSUFFERABLE
INSUFFERABLY
INSUFFICIENT
INSURRECTION
LASCIVIOUSLY
LISTLESSNESS
MASSERANDUBA
MASSPRODUCED
MASTERSTROKE
MASTIGOPHORA
MASTURBATION
MESOTHELIOMA
MISADVENTURE
MISANTHROPIC
MISAPPREHEND
MISBEHAVIOUR
MISCALCULATE
MISDELIVERED
MISDEMEANOUR
MISINTERPRET
MISPLACEMENT
MISPRONOUNCE
MISQUOTATION
MISREPRESENT
MISSTATEMENT
MISTREATMENT
MOSBOLLETJIE
MUSICOLOGIST
MYSTERIOUSLY
OBSEQUIOUSLY
OBSERVANTINE
OBSOLESCENCE
OBSOLETENESS
OBSTETRICIAN
OBSTREPEROUS
OSSIFICATION
PASSEMEASURE
PASSEPARTOUT
PASSIONATELY
PASSIONFRUIT
PESTILENTIAL
PISCICULTURE
POSSESSIVELY
POSTGRADUATE
POSTHUMOUSLY
POSTLIMINARY
POSTMISTRESS
POSTPONEMENT
POSTPRANDIAL
RESETTLEMENT
RESIPISCENCE
RESPECTFULLY
RESPECTIVELY
RESPONDENTIA
RESTAURATEUR
RESTLESSNESS
RESURRECTION
RESUSCITATED
RISORGIMENTO
SESQUIALTERA
SESQUITERTIA
SUSPICIOUSLY
TESTAMENTARY
TESTOSTERONE
UNSATISFYING
UNSCIENTIFIC
UNSCRUPULOUS
UNSEASONABLE
UNSUCCESSFUL
UNSURPRISING
UNSUSPECTING
WASHINGTONIA
AETHRIOSCOPE
AFTEREFFECTS
AFTERTHOUGHT
ANTAGONISTIC
ANTANANARIVO
ANTEDILUVIAN
ANTEMERIDIAN
ANTHELMINTIC
ANTHROPOLOGY
ANTIBACCHIUS
ANTIBARBARUS
ANTICIPATION
ANTICIPATORY
ANTILEGOMENA
ANTIMACASSAR
ANTIMETABOLE
ANTIMNEMONIC
ANTINEUTRINO
ANTIPARTICLE
ANTIRACHITIC
ANTISTROPHON
ANTITHROMBIN
ANTONINIANUS
ARTHROPLASTY
ARTICULATION
ARTIFICIALLY
ARTILLERYMAN
ARTIODACTYLA
ARTISTICALLY
ASTONISHMENT
ASTROLOGICAL
ASTRONOMICAL
ASTROPHYSICS
ATTRACTIVELY
ATTRIBUTABLE
AUTHENTICATE
AUTHENTICITY
BATTLEGROUND

BETHLEHEMITE
BUTTERSCOTCH
CATADIOPTRIC
CATAPHYSICAL
CATASTROPHIC
CATHETOMETER
ENTANGLEMENT
ENTEROMORPHA
ENTEROPNEUST
ENTERPRISING
ENTERTAINING
ENTHUSIASTIC
ENTOMOLOGIST
ENTOMOSTRACA
ENTOPLASTRON
ENTREATINGLY
ENTRENCHMENT
ENTREPRENEUR
ESTHETICALLY
ESTRANGEMENT
EXTENSIONIST
EXTINGUISHER
EXTORTIONATE
EXTRADITABLE
EXTRAVAGANCE
EXTRAVAGANZA
FOTHERINGHAY
HETEROCLITIC
HETEROCONTAE
HETEROPHORIA
HETEROPLASIA
HETEROSEXUAL
HETEROSOMATA
INTELLECTUAL
INTELLIGENCE
INTELLIGIBLE
INTEMPERANCE
INTENERATION
INTERCEPTION
INTERCESSION
INTERCHANGED
INTERFERENCE
INTERJECTION
INTERLOCUTOR
INTERMEDIARY
INTERMEDIATE
INTERMINABLE
INTERMINABLY
INTERMISSION
INTERMITTENT
INTERPRETING
INTERRELATED
INTERROGATOR
INTERRUPTION
INTERSECTION
INTERSPERSED
INTERSTELLAR
INTERVENTION
INTIMIDATING
INTIMIDATION
INTOXICATING
INTOXICATION
INTRANSIGENT
INTRANSITIVE
INTRAUTERINE
INTRODUCTION
INTRODUCTORY
KATHAREVOUSA
KATZENJAMMER
LATIROSTRATE
LITHOGRAPHIC
LITHOLATROUS
MATHEMATICAL
METAGNATHOUS
METALLOPHONE
METALLURGIST
METAMORPHISM
METAMORPHOSE
METAPHORICAL
METAPHYSICAL
METHODICALLY
METICULOUSLY
METROPOLITAN
MITRAILLEUSE
MOTORCYCLIST
MUTESSARIFAT
MYTHOLOGICAL
NATURALISTIC
NOTIFICATION
NUTRITIONIST
OCTASTROPHIC
OCTOGENARIAN
ORTHODONTICS
ORTHOGENESIS
ORTHOPAEDICS
ORTHOPAEDIST
ORTHORHOMBIC
ORTHOTONESIS
OSTENTATIOUS
OSTEOMALACIA
OSTEOPOROSIS
OUTBUILDINGS
OUTMANOEUVRE
OUTRAGEOUSLY
OUTSTRETCHED
PATHETICALLY
PATHOLOGICAL
PETRIFACTION
PETTIFOGGERS
PETTIFOGGERY
PETTIFOGGING
PITTERPATTER
POTAMOLOGIST
POTENTIALITY
POTICHOMANIA
PUTREFACTION
PYTHONOMORPH
RATIFICATION
RETARDEDNESS
RETICULATION
RETRENCHMENT
RUTHLESSNESS
SATISFACTION
SATISFACTORY
SITTLICHKEIT
TETRACYCLINE
TETRAHEDRITE
TETRODOTOXIN
TITANOSAURUS
TOTALITARIAN
ULTRAMONTANE
URTRICULARIA
VETERINARIAN
VITUPERATION
VITUPERATIVE
WATCHFULNESS
WATERCARRIER
ADULTERATION
AYUNTAMIENTO
BLUESTOCKING
BOUGAINVILLE
BOULEVARDIER
CAUTIOUSNESS
CHURCHWARDEN
CHURLISHNESS
COUNTERBLAST
COUNTERCLAIM
COUNTERMARCH
COUNTERPOINT
COUNTERPOISE
COURAGEOUSLY
COURTMARTIAL
DEUTEROSCOPY
DOUBLEDECKER
DOUBLEGLAZED
EDUCATIONIST
EQUIVOCATION
EQUIVOCATORY
FLUORESCENCE
FLUORIDATION
FRUITFULNESS
FRUMENTATION
GLUBBDUBDRIB
HOUSEBREAKER
HOUSEKEEPING
HOUSETOHOUSE
HOUSEWARMING
JOURNALISTIC
LAUREATESHIP
MOUSQUETAIRE
MOUTHBROODER
NEUROLOGICAL
NEUROTICALLY
SAUROGNATHAE
SCURRILOUSLY
SHUFFLEBOARD
SKUTTERUDITE
SLUBBERINGLY
SOUTHCOTTIAN
SOUTHEASTERN
SOUTHERNMOST
SOUTHERNWOOD
SOUTHWESTERN
SPURIOUSNESS
SPURTLEBLADE
STUBBORNNESS
STUDIOUSNESS
STUPEFACTION
TAUTOLOGICAL
THUNDERCLOUD
THUNDERFLASH
THUNDERSTORM
TRUTHFULNESS
UNUTTERABLES
YOUTHFULNESS
ADVANTAGEOUS
ADVANTAGIOUS
ADVENTITIOUS
ADVISABILITY
CIVILISATION
CIVILIZATION
COVETOUSNESS
DIVERTICULUM
DIVERTIMENTO
EAVESDROPPER
GOVERNMENTAL
INVALIDATION
INVERTEBRATE
INVESTIGATOR
INVIGORATING
INVIGORATION
INVISIBILITY
INVULNERABLE
LIVERPUDLIAN
NAVIGABILITY
NEVERTHELESS
REVERSIONARY
SIVAPITHECUS
BEWILDERMENT
NEWFOUNDLAND
NEWSPAPERMAN
POWERSHARING
LEXICOGRAPHY
LOXODROMICAL
LUXEMBOURGER
LUXULLIANITE
SEXAGENARIAN
TOXICOLOGIST
ASYMMETRICAL
CRYPTOGRAPHY
EGYPTOLOGIST
ERYTHROMYCIN
ETYMOLOGICAL
ETYMOLOGICON
GLYNDEBOURNE
OXYACETYLENE
PHYCOXANTHIN
PHYSIOLOGIST
PHYTOBENTHOS
PHYTONADIONE

PSYCHIATRIST
PSYCHOLOGIST
PSYCHOPATHIC
RHYTHMICALLY
RHYTIDECTOMY
THYSANOPTERA

12:4

ADVANTAGEOUS
ADVANTAGIOUS
AMBASSADRESS
ANTAGONISTIC
ANTANANARIVO
APLANOGAMETE
ASPARAGINASE
BANANALANDER
BEHAVIOURISM
BICAMERALISM
BREAKTHROUGH
BREASTPLOUGH
BREASTSUMMER
BREATHALYSER
BREATHLESSLY
BREATHTAKING
BROADCASTING
CARAVANSERAI
CATADIOPTRIC
CATAPHYSICAL
CATASTROPHIC
CLEARSIGHTED
COHABITATION
CREATIVENESS
DECAPITATION
DEPARTMENTAL
DILAPIDATION
DILATORINESS
DISACCHARIDE
DISADVANTAGE
DISAGREEABLE
DISAGREEMENT
DISAPPEARING
DISAPPOINTED
DISASTROUSLY
EMBARRASSING
ENTANGLEMENT
ESCAPOLOGIST
ESPAGNOLETTE
EXHAUSTIVELY
FINALIZATION
GIGANTOMACHY
GONADOTROPIN
HAMARTHRITIS
HUMANITARIAN
HUMANIZATION
IDEALIZATION
IMMACULATELY
IMPARTIALITY
INCALCULABLE
INCANDESCENT
INCAPABILITY
INCAPACITATE
INCAUTIOUSLY
INHARMONIOUS
INNATTENTIVE
INSALUBRIOUS
INVALIDATION
IRRATIONALLY
KERAUNOGRAPH
KINAESTHETIC
LABANOTATION
LEGALIZATION
LYMANTRIIDAE
MACABERESQUE
MALACOSTRACA
METAGNATHOUS
METALLOPHONE
METALLURGIST
METAMORPHISM
METAMORPHOSE
METAPHORICAL
METAPHYSICAL
MIRACULOUSLY
MISADVENTURE
MISANTHROPIC
MISAPPREHEND
NONAGENARIAN
NONALCOHOLIC
OCCASIONALLY
OCEANOGRAPHY
OCTASTROPHIC
ORGANISATION
ORGANIZATION
OXYACETYLENE
PANAESTHESIA
PANATHENAEAN
PARACENTESIS
PARALIPOMENA
PARAMILITARY
PARANTHELIUM
PEDANTICALLY
PENALIZATION
PERADVENTURE
PERAMBULATOR
POLARIZATION
POTAMOLOGIST
RECALCITRANT
RECAPITULATE
REHABILITATE
RELATIONSHIP
REPATRIATION
RETARDEDNESS
ROMANTICALLY
SEMANTICALLY
SERASKIERATE
SEXAGENARIAN
SINANTHROPUS
SIVAPITHECUS
SOMATOPLEURE
SPHACELATION
SPHAIRISTIKE
STEALTHINESS
STRADIVARIUS
STRAIGHTAWAY
STRAIGHTEDGE
STRAIGHTNESS
STRAITJACKET
STRANGLEHOLD
STRANGLEWEED
STRATOSPHERE
SUBARRHATION
SYNADELPHITE
TAMARICACEAE
TARAMASALATA
THEATRICALLY
TITANOSAURUS
TOBACCONISTS
TOTALITARIAN
TURACOVERDIN
UNFATHOMABLE
UNFAVOURABLE
UNMANAGEABLE
UNPARALLELED
UNPARDONABLE
UNSATISFYING
URBANIZATION
ZALAMBDODONT
ZARATHUSTRIC
BAMBOCCIADES
BARBERMONGER
BLABBERMOUTH
BOOBYTRAPPED
CARBOHYDRATE
COMBINATIONS
DOUBLEDECKER
DOUBLEGLAZED
GLOBETROTTER
GLUBBDUBDRIB
GOBBLEDEGOOK
GOBBLEDYGOOK
HAMBLETONIAN
HOBBIDIDANCE
IAMBOGRAPHER
ISOBILATERAL
MISBEHAVIOUR
MOSBOLLETJIE
OUTBUILDINGS
PROBATIONARY
RAMBUNCTIOUS
SLUBBERINGLY
SNOBBISHNESS
STUBBORNNESS
SYMBOLICALLY
TRABECULATED
TURBOCHARGER
UNOBSTRUCTED
UNOBTAINABLE
ADSCITITIOUS
AIRCRAFTSMAN
ANECATHARSIS
AUSCULTATION
BACCHANALIAN
BEACONSFIELD
BIOCHEMISTRY
BLACKCURRANT
BRACHYCEPHAL
BRICKFIELDER
CALCEAMENTUM
CANCELLATION
CARCINOGENIC
CIRCASSIENNE
CIRCUMCISION
CIRCUMGYRATE
CIRCUMSCRIBE
CIRCUMSTANCE
COCCIDIOSTAT
CONCENTRATED
CONCILIATION
CONCILIATORY
CONCLUSIVELY
CONCURRENTLY
COSCINOMANCY
DISCIPLINARY
DISCOMEDUSAE
DISCOMFITURE
DISCOMYCETES
DISCONCERTED
DISCONNECTED
DISCONSOLATE
DISCONTENTED
DISCOURAGING
DISCOURTEOUS
DISCRIMINATE
EDUCATIONIST
ELECTRICALLY
ELECTROLYSIS
ELECTROPLATE
ELECTROTONUS
EPACRIDACEAE
EXACERBATION
FORCEFULNESS
FRACTIONALLY
FUNCTIONALLY
FUNCTIONLESS
GLOCKENSPIEL
GRACEFULNESS
GRACIOUSNESS
HENCEFORWARD
INACCESSIBLE
INACCURATELY
LANCASTERIAN
LASCIVIOUSLY
LINCOLNSHIRE
MARCOBRUNNER
MARCONIGRAPH
MISCALCULATE
NARCISSISTIC
NEOCLASSICAL
NONCHALANTLY
NONCOMMITTAL

PANCHATANTRA
PANCHROMATIC
PEACEFULNESS
PEACEKEEPING
PERCEPTIVELY
PERCEPTIVITY
PHYCOXANTHIN
PISCICULTURE
PLACENTIFORM
PLECTOGNATHI
PRACTICALITY
PRACTICIONER
PRACTITIONER
PRECARIOUSLY
PRECOCIOUSLY
PRECONDITION
PROCESSIONAL
PROCLAMATION
PSYCHIATRIST
PSYCHOLOGIST
PSYCHOPATHIC
RONCESVALLES
SLOCKDOLAGER
SLOCKDOLIGER
SLOCKDOLOGER
SPACIOUSNESS
SPECIFICALLY
SPECIOUSNESS
SPECKTIONEER
SPECTROSCOPE
STOCKBREEDER
STOCKINGETTE
SUBCOMMITTEE
SUBCONSCIOUS
SUBCONTINENT
SUBCUTANEOUS
SUCCESSFULLY
SUCCESSIVELY
SUCCUSSATION
TERCENTENARY
THICKSKINNED
TRACTABILITY
TRICHOLOGIST
TRICHOPHYTON
TROCHELMINTH
TROCHOSPHERE
UNACCEPTABLE
UNACCUSTOMED
UNACQUAINTED
UNECONOMICAL
UNSCIENTIFIC
UNSCRUPULOUS
WATCHFULNESS
ACADEMICALLY
BANDERSNATCH
BIODIVERSITY
BIRDWATCHING
CARDINDEXING
CARDIOLOGIST
COLDSHOULDER

CONDEMNATION
CONDENSATION
CONDUCTIVITY
DENDROLOGIST
DISDAINFULLY
EPIDEICTICAL
FELDSPATHOID
FIDDLESTICKS
FUNDAMENTALS
GLADIATORIAL
GONDWANALAND
HANDKERCHIEF
HEADMISTRESS
HEADQUARTERS
HILDEBRANDIC
HINDQUARTERS
INADEQUATELY
INADMISSIBLE
INADVERTENCE
KINDERGARTEN
MIDDLEWEIGHT
MINDBOGGLING
MINDFULLNESS
MISDELIVERED
MISDEMEANOUR
MUDDLEHEADED
OBEDIENTIARY
PANDAEMONIUM
PANDANACEOUS
PREDESTINATE
PREDETERMINE
PREDILECTION
PREDOMINANCE
PRODIGIOUSLY
PRODUCTIVITY
QUADRAGESIMA
QUADRAPHONIC
READJUSTMENT
RHADAMANTHUS
RHODODENDRON
SARDANAPALUS
SARDONICALLY
STUDIOUSNESS
TRADESCANTIA
TRADESPEOPLE
UNIDENTIFIED
VINDICTIVELY
WOODBURYTYPE
ACCELERATION
ACCENTUATION
ADJECTIVALLY
ADVENTITIOUS
AFFECTIONATE
AFTEREFFECTS
AFTERTHOUGHT
ANAESTHETISE
ANAESTHETIST
ANAESTHETIZE
ANTEDILUVIAN
ANTEMERIDIAN

APFELSTRUDEL
APPENDECTOMY
APPENDICITIS
ARSENOPYRITE
ATHEROMATOUS
BENEFACTRESS
BENEVOLENTLY
BICENTENNIAL
BLUESTOCKING
BUREAUCRATIC
CAPERCAILLIE
CAPERCAILZIE
CARELESSNESS
CEREBROTONIC
CEREMONIALLY
CHEERFULNESS
CHEESEBURGER
CHEESEMONGER
CHEESEPARING
CHREMATISTIC
CHRESTOMATHY
COVETOUSNESS
DECELERATION
DECENTRALISE
DECENTRALIZE
DEGENERATION
DEREGULATION
DERESTRICTED
DIRECTORSHIP
DISEMBARRASS
DISENCHANTED
DIVERTICULUM
DIVERTIMENTO
DOMESTICATED
EAVESDROPPER
ECCENTRICITY
EFFERVESCENT
ELEEMOSYNARY
EMBEZZLEMENT
ENTEROMORPHA
ENTEROPNEUST
ENTERPRISING
ENTERTAINING
ESSENTIALITY
ETHEROMANIAC
EULENSPIEGEL
EXPERIMENTAL
EXSERVICEMAN
EXTENSIONIST
FRIENDLINESS
GAMESMANSHIP
GENEALOGICAL
GENETHLIACON
GESELLSCHAFT
GOVERNMENTAL
GREENGROCERS
GREENGROCERY
GYNECOLOGIST
HABERDASHERS
HABERDASHERY

HEREDITAMENT
HETEROCLITIC
HETEROCONTAE
HETEROPHORIA
HETEROPLASIA
HETEROSEXUAL
HETEROSOMATA
HOMESICKNESS
HOPELESSNESS
HYPERBOLICAL
HYPERPYRETIC
HYPERSARCOMA
HYPERTENSION
ILLEGIBILITY
ILLEGITIMACY
ILLEGITIMATE
IMMEASURABLE
IMMEASURABLY
IMPENETRABLE
IMPERFECTION
IMPERISHABLE
IMPERSONALLY
IMPERSONATOR
IMPERTINENCE
INDEBTEDNESS
INDECLINABLE
INDEFENSIBLE
INDEFINITELY
INDEPENDENCE
INFELICITOUS
INSEMINATION
INTELLECTUAL
INTELLIGENCE
INTELLIGIBLE
INTEMPERANCE
INTENERATION
INTERCEPTION
INTERCESSION
INTERCHANGED
INTERFERENCE
INTERJECTION
INTERLOCUTOR
INTERMEDIARY
INTERMEDIATE
INTERMINABLE
INTERMINABLY
INTERMISSION
INTERMITTENT
INTERPRETING
INTERRELATED
INTERROGATOR
INTERRUPTION
INTERSECTION
INTERSPERSED
INTERSTELLAR
INTERVENTION
INVERTEBRATE
INVESTIGATOR
IRREDEEMABLE
IRREGULARITY

IRRESISTIBLE
IRRESOLUTELY
IRRESOLUTION
IRRESOLVABLE
IRRESPECTIVE
IRREVERENTLY
IRREVERSIBLE
KALEIDOSCOPE
LAMELLICORNE
LAMENTATIONS
LIFELESSNESS
LIVERPUDLIAN
LUXEMBOURGER
MADEMOISELLE
MAJESTICALLY
MERETRICIOUS
MINERALOGIST
MUTESSARIFAT
NEPENTHACEAE
NEVERTHELESS
NOMENCLATURE
NONEXISTENCE
OBSEQUIOUSLY
OBSERVANTINE
ORIENTEERING
OSTENTATIOUS
OSTEOMALACIA
OSTEOPOROSIS
OTHERWORLDLY
PALEONTOLOGY
PEREMPTORILY
PHLEBOTOMIST
POTENTIALITY
POWERSHARING
RECEIVERSHIP
RECEPTIONIST
REDEMPTIONER
REDEPLOYMENT
REGENERATION
RELENTLESSLY
REMEMBRANCER
REPERCUSSION
RESETTLEMENT
REVERSIONARY
SALESMANSHIP
SCHEHERAZADE
SCLERENCHYMA
SCLERODERMIA
SCREENWRITER
SECESSIONIST
SHEEPISHNESS
SIDEWHISKERS
SLEEPWALKING
SPIEGELEISEN
SPLENOMEGALY
SPREADEAGLED
STEEPLECHASE
STREPITATION
STREPSIPTERA
STREPTOMYCIN
STREPTONEURA
SUPERANNUATE
SUPERCHARGED
SUPERCHARGER
SUPERCILIARY
SUPERCILIOUS
SUPERHIGHWAY
SUPERNACULUM
SUPERNATURAL
SUPERSTITION
TAPERECORDER
TELEASTHETIC
TELEGRAPHESE
TELEGRAPHIST
TELEOSAURIAN
TELEUTOSPORE
THREADNEEDLE
THREEQUARTER
TIMELESSNESS
TOGETHERNESS
TUBERCULOSIS
UNBELIEVABLE
UNBELIEVABLY
UNDEMOCRATIC
UNDERACHIEVE
UNDERCLOTHES
UNDERCURRENT
UNDEREXPOSED
UNDERGARMENT
UNDERPINNING
UNDERSKINKER
UNDERSTAFFED
UNDERWRITTEN
UNDESERVEDLY
UNDETECTABLE
UNDETERMINED
UNNEIGHBORLY
UNREASONABLE
UNRECOGNISED
UNRECOGNIZED
UNRESERVEDLY
UNRESPONSIVE
UNRESTRAINED
UNRESTRICTED
UNRETURNABLE
UNSEASONABLE
VALENCIENNES
VENEPUNCTURE
VETERINARIAN
WAREHOUSEMAN
WATERCARRIER
BLEFUSCUDIAN
CONFECTIONER
CONFESSIONAL
CONFIDENTIAL
CONFIRMATION
CONFIRMATORY
CONFISCATION
DIFFERENTIAL
DISFRANCHISE
INEFFICIENCY
MALFORMATION
NEWFOUNDLAND
OLDFASHIONED
PREFERENTIAL
PROFESSIONAL
PROFESSORIAL
PROFICIENTLY
PROFITEERING
SELFADHESIVE
SELFCATERING
SELFEMPLOYED
SELFINTEREST
SELFPORTRAIT
SHUFFLEBOARD
SUFFICIENTLY
UNOFFICIALLY
BIOGRAPHICAL
BOUGAINVILLE
CONGENITALLY
CONGLOMERATE
CONGRATULATE
CONGREGATION
DIAGRAMMATIC
EPIGRAMMATIC
EXAGGERATION
FLAGELLATION
GEOGRAPHICAL
LANGUEDOCIAN
LONGDISTANCE
LONGITUDINAL
LONGSHOREMAN
LONGSTANDING
MANGELWURZEL
MUGGLETONIAN
NEIGHBORHOOD
NEIGHBOURING
PERGAMENEOUS
PREGUSTATION
PRIGGISHNESS
PROGESTERONE
PROGRAMMABLE
PROGYMNASIUM
SINGLEDECKER
SINGLEHANDED
SINGLEMINDED
STAGGERINGLY
STEGOPHOLIST
SUGGESTIVELY
TERGIVERSATE
THIGMOTROPIC
TRIGONOMETRY
VENGEFULNESS
WEIGHTLIFTER
WHIGMALEERIE
AETHRIOSCOPE
ALPHABETICAL
ALPHANUMERIC
AMPHISBAENIC
AMPHISTOMOUS
AMPHITHEATER
AMPHITHEATRE
ANTHELMINTIC
ANTHROPOLOGY
ARCHILOCHIAN
ARCHIPELAGOS
ARCHITECTURE
ARTHROPLASTY
ASPHYXIATION
AUTHENTICATE
AUTHENTICITY
BETHLEHEMITE
CATHETOMETER
DISHONORABLE
DISHONORABLY
EMPHATICALLY
ENCHEIRIDION
ENTHUSIASTIC
ESTHETICALLY
EXCHANGEABLE
FOTHERINGHAY
HEPHTHEMIMER
HIGHFALUTING
KATHAREVOUSA
LIGHTHEARTED
LITHOGRAPHIC
LITHOLATROUS
MACHAIRODONT
MATHEMATICAL
MECHANICALLY
MECHITHARIST
METHODICALLY
MICHELANGELO
MYTHOLOGICAL
NEPHELOMETER
NIGHTCLOTHES
NYCHTHEMERON
ORTHODONTICS
ORTHOGENESIS
ORTHOPAEDICS
ORTHOPAEDIST
ORTHORHOMBIC
ORTHOTONESIS
PATHETICALLY
PATHOLOGICAL
PREHISTORIAN
PYTHONOMORPH
RECHARGEABLE
RUTHLESSNESS
SIPHONOPHORA
SIPHONOSTELE
SOPHISTICATE
SUBHASTATION
TECHNICALITY
TECHNOLOGIST
TIGHTFITTING
UNCHALLENGED
UNCHANGEABLE
UNCHARITABLE
UNCHARITABLY

WASHINGTONIA
ACCIDENTALLY
ADDITIONALLY
ADMINISTRATE
ADVISABILITY
AECIDIOSPORE
AGRIBUSINESS
AGRICULTURAL
ALLITERATION
AMBIDEXTROUS
ANNIHILATION
ANTIBACCHIUS
ANTIBARBARUS
ANTICIPATION
ANTICIPATORY
ANTILEGOMENA
ANTIMACASSAR
ANTIMETABOLE
ANTIMNEMONIC
ANTINEUTRINO
ANTIPARTICLE
ANTIRACHITIC
ANTISTROPHON
ANTITHROMBIN
ARTICULATION
ARTIFICIALLY
ARTILLERYMAN
ARTIODACTYLA
ARTISTICALLY
ASSIMILATION
AVAILABILITY
AWEINSPIRING
BABINGTONITE
BEWILDERMENT
BRAINWASHING
BUSINESSLIKE
CABINETMAKER
CAMIKNICKERS
CAPITULATION
CARICATURIST
CHAIRMANSHIP
CHRISTIANITY
CIVILISATION
CIVILIZATION
CLAIRVOYANCE
CLAIRVOYANCY
CLEISTOGAMIC
CODIFICATION
DEBILITATING
DECIPHERABLE
DECIPHERMENT
DELIBERATELY
DELIBERATION
DELICATESSEN
DEMILITARIZE
DEMIMONDAINE
DESIRABILITY
DISINCENTIVE
DISINFECTANT
DISINGENUOUS

DISINTEGRATE
ENCIRCLEMENT
EQUIVOCATION
EQUIVOCATORY
EXCITABILITY
EXHIBITIONER
EXHILARATING
EXHILARATION
EXTINGUISHER
FREIGHTLINER
FRUITFULNESS
GERIATRICIAN
HELIOGABALUS
HEMICHORDATA
HOLIDAYMAKER
HORIZONTALLY
HUDIBRASTICS
HYGIENICALLY
INCIDENTALLY
INCINERATION
INDIFFERENCE
INDIGESTIBLE
INDISCRETION
INDISPUTABLE
INDISPUTABLY
INDISSOLUBLE
INDISTINCTLY
INDIVIDUALLY
INFILTRATION
INTIMIDATING
INTIMIDATION
INVIGORATING
INVIGORATION
INVISIBILITY
IRRITABILITY
JURISDICTION
KALISTOCRACY
LATIROSTRATE
LEGIONNAIRES
LEGITIMATELY
LEPIDOMELANE
LEXICOGRAPHY
LUMINESCENCE
LUMINISCENCE
MANIPULATION
MANIPULATIVE
MERISTEMATIC
MERITRICIOUS
METICULOUSLY
MILITARISTIC
MINICOMPUTER
MINISTRATION
MISINTERPRET
MOBILIZATION
MODIFICATION
MUCILAGINOUS
MUNICIPALITY
MUSICOLOGIST
MYRINGOSCOPE
NAVIGABILITY

NOTIFICATION
OBLITERATION
ONEIROCRITIC
OPHIOGLOSSUM
ORNITHOGALUM
OSCILLOSCOPE
OSSIFICATION
PACIFICATION
PALINGENESIA
PALINGENESIS
PAPILIONIDAE
PEDIATRICIAN
PEDICELLARIA
PENITENTIARY
PERICARDITIS
PERIODICALLY
PERIOSTRACUM
PERIPHRASTIC
PERISTERONIC
PLAINCLOTHES
PLEIOCHASIUM
POLICYMAKING
POTICHOMANIA
PRAISEWORTHY
PURIFICATION
RADIOGRAPHER
RADIOISOTOPE
RADIOTHERAPY
RAMIFICATION
RATIFICATION
RECIPROCALLY
REDINTEGRATE
REDISCOVERED
REDISTRIBUTE
REGISTRATION
REMINISCENCE
RESIPISCENCE
RETICULATION
RIDICULOUSLY
SADISTICALLY
SATISFACTION
SATISFACTORY
SCHILLERSPAR
SCHINDYLESIS
SCHIZOMYCETE
SCRIMSHANDER
SCRIMSHANKER
SCRIPTWRITER
SEMICIRCULAR
SEMIDETACHED
SEMIPRECIOUS
SOCIOLOGICAL
SOLICITATION
SOLICITOUSLY
STRIDULATION
STRIGIFORMES
STRINGCOURSE
TOXICOLOGIST
UNDIMINISHED
UNDISCHARGED

UNMISTAKABLE
VARICOLOURED
VERIFICATION
VILIFICATION
VOCIFERATION
VOCIFEROUSLY
SUBJECTIVELY
SUBJECTIVITY
BACKBREAKING
BACKWARDNESS
BACKWOODSMAN
BUCKLEBEGGAR
BUNKOSTEERER
LICKTRENCHER
MARKSMANSHIP
RACKETEERING
RECKLESSNESS
SPOKESPERSON
STAKHANOVITE
WICKETKEEPER
YORKSHIREMAN
ABOLITIONIST
ACHLAMYDEOUS
ADULTERATION
AGALMATOLITE
AMALGAMATION
AMELIORATION
APOLLINARIAN
BELLIGERENCY
BIBLIOGRAPHY
BIBLIOPEGIST
BIELORUSSIAN
BILLINGSGATE
BOULEVARDIER
BRILLIANTINE
BYELORUSSIAN
CALLIGRAPHIC
CALLISTHENES
CARLOVINGIAN
CHALICOTHERE
CHILDBEARING
CHILDISHNESS
COLLABORATOR
COLLECTIVELY
COLLECTORATE
COLLOQUIALLY
COLLUCTATION
COLLYWOBBLES
DARLINGTONIA
DEFLATIONARY
DIALECTICIAN
DIPLOGENESIS
ECCLESIASTES
ECCLESIASTIC
ENGLISHWOMAN
ENGLISHWOMEN
EVOLUTIONARY
EXPLOITATION
GALLIGASKINS
GALLINACEOUS

GALLIVANTING
GEOLOGICALLY
GUILDENSTERN
HALLANSHAKER
HALLUCINOGEN
HELLGRAMMITE
IMPLANTATION
INFLAMMATION
INFLAMMATORY
INFLATIONARY
ISOLATIONISM
ISOLATIONIST
KILLIKINNICK
LALLAPALOOZA
LILLIBULLERO
LILLIBURLERO
MALLEABILITY
MALLOPHAGOUS
MARLINESPIKE
MULLIGATAWNY
PHILANTHROPY
PHILHARMONIC
PHILISTINISM
PHILODENDRON
PHILOLOGICAL
PHILOSOPHIZE
PRALLTRILLER
PROLEGOMENON
PROLETARIATE
PROLIFICALLY
PROLONGATION
REFLATIONARY
ROLLERBLADER
ROLLERBLADES
SHILLYSHALLY
SMALLHOLDING
SPELEOLOGIST
SPELLCHECKER
STELLENBOSCH
STILBOESTROL
SUBLAPSARIAN
TAGLIACOTIAN
TRALATICIOUS
TRALATITIOUS
UNCLASSIFIED
UNILATERALLY
VILLEGIATURA
WALLYDRAIGLE
WELLBALANCED
WELLINFORMED
WELLINGTONIA
WHOLEHEARTED
WILLIEWAUGHT
WOLLASTONITE
YELLOWHAMMER
AGAMOGENETIC
ALIMENTATIVE
ANAMORPHOSIS
ANEMOPHILOUS
AROMATHERAPY
ASYMMETRICAL
AUGMENTATION
CHAMPIONSHIP
CHEMOTHERAPY
CLAMJAMPHRIE
COMMANDMENTS
COMMENCEMENT
COMMENDATION
COMMENDATORY
COMMENSURATE
COMMERCIALLY
COMMISSARIAT
COMMISSIONED
COMMISSIONER
COMMONWEALTH
COMMUNICABLE
COSMOPOLITAN
CREMAILLIÈRE
CURMUDGEONLY
DEAMBULATORY
DOGMATICALLY
DRAMATICALLY
DRAMATURGIST
ETYMOLOGICAL
ETYMOLOGICON
FEHMGERICHTE
FERMENTATION
FLAMBOYANTLY
FORMALDEHYDE
FRUMENTATION
FULMINATIONS
GEOMETRICIAN
HAEMATEMESIS
HAEMOPHILIAC
HAEMORRHOIDS
HAMMERHEADED
HARMONIOUSLY
HERMENEUTICS
HERMENEUTIST
HERMETICALLY
ISHMAELITISH
MACMILLANITE
MNEMOTECHNIC
ONOMATOPOEIA
ONOMATOPOEIC
OUTMANOEUVRE
PERMANGANATE
PERMEABILITY
PIGMENTATION
PREMAXILLARY
PREMONSTRANT
PROMULGATION
RHAMPHOTHECA
ROOMINGHOUSE
SEGMENTATION
SHAMEFACEDLY
SUBMISSIVELY
SURMOUNTABLE
TREMENDOUSLY
UNEMPLOYMENT
UNIMAGINABLE
UNIMPORTANCE
VEHMGERICHTE
WHIMSICALITY
ACKNOWLEDGED
AYUNTAMIENTO
BARNSTORMING
BLANDISHMENT
BLENNORRHOEA
BOONDOGGLING
BRANCHIOPODA
BRONTOSAURUS
CHONDRIOSOME
CLANNISHNESS
COINCIDENTAL
COUNTERBLAST
COUNTERCLAIM
COUNTERMARCH
COUNTERPOINT
COUNTERPOISE
DIENCEPHALON
DONNERWETTER
DRINKDRIVING
DUNNIEWASSAL
ECONOMICALLY
EMANCIPATION
ENANTIOMORPH
ENANTIOPATHY
EPANORTHOSIS
EPENCEPHALON
ETHNOLOGICAL
EVENHANDEDLY
EVENTEMPERED
FAINTHEARTED
FRANKALMOIGN
FRANKENSTEIN
FRANKINCENSE
FRONTIERSMAN
FRONTISPIECE
GAINSBOROUGH
GLYNDEBOURNE
GRANDISONIAN
GRANDMONTINE
GRANDPARENTS
GYMNOSOPHIST
HARNESSMAKER
HYMNOGRAPHER
HYPNOTHERAPY
HYPNOTICALLY
ICONOCLASTIC
IDENTIFIABLE
JENNYSPINNER
MAGNETICALLY
MAGNIFICENCE
MAGNILOQUENT
MALNUTRITION
MEANINGFULLY
MOONLIGHTING
OPINIONATIVE
PAINLESSNESS
PENNSYLVANIA
PERNOCTATION
PHENOMENALLY
PHONETICALLY
PINNIEWINKLE
POINTILLISME
PORNOGRAPHIC
PRINCIPALITY
PUGNACIOUSLY
QUANTIFIABLE
QUANTITATIVE
QUINQUENNIAL
QUINTESSENCE
REINVIGORATE
RHINORRHOEAL
SCANDALOUSLY
SCANDINAVIAN
SCHNEIDERIAN
SCINTILLATOR
SIGNIFICANCE
SOMNAMBULISM
SOMNAMBULIST
SPINECHILLER
SPINSTERHOOD
STANISLAVSKI
STENOGRAPHER
STENTORPHONE
STONECHATTER
THANKFULNESS
THANKSGIVING
THUNDERCLOUD
THUNDERFLASH
THUNDERSTORM
TRANQUILIZER
TRANQUILLISE
TRANQUILLITY
TRANQUILLIZE
TRANSACTIONS
TRANSCENDENT
TRANSFERABLE
TRANSFERENCE
TRANSGRESSOR
TRANSITIONAL
TRANSLATABLE
TRANSLUCENCE
TRANSMIGRATE
TRANSMISSION
TRANSMOGRIFY
TRANSOCEANIC
TRANSPARENCY
TRANSPONTINE
TRANSVESTISM
TRANSVESTITE
UNANSWERABLE
UNINTERESTED
VAINGLORIOUS
ACCOMPANYING
ACCOMPLISHED
ACCORDIONIST
ACCOUCHEMENT

ACCOUTREMENT
ADMONISHMENT
AERODYNAMICS
AERONAUTICAL
ANDOUILLETTE
ANNOUNCEMENT
ANTONINIANUS
APPOGGIATURA
ARBORESCENCE
ASTONISHMENT
ATMOSPHERICS
BLOODSTAINED
BLOODTHIRSTY
CANONIZATION
CHLORINATION
COLONIZATION
COLOQUINTIDA
CYMOTRICHOUS
DECONGESTANT
DECORATIVELY
DEMONSTRABLE
DEMONSTRABLY
DEMONSTRATOR
DENOMINATION
DEPOPULATION
DISOBEDIENCE
DISORGANIZED
DISORIENTATE
EFFORTLESSLY
ENTOMOLOGIST
ENTOMOSTRACA
ENTOPLASTRON
EXTORTIONATE
FLUORESCENCE
FLUORIDATION
GERONTOCRACY
HEROICOMICAL
HOMOEOPATHIC
HOMOTHERMOUS
HYPOCHONDRIA
HYPOCRITICAL
HYPOTHECATOR
HYPOTHETICAL
IDIOSYNCRASY
IDIOTHERMOUS
ILLOGICALITY
IMMODERATELY
IMMODERATION
IMPOLITENESS
IMPOVERISHED
INCOHERENTLY
INCOMPARABLE
INCOMPARABLY
INCOMPATIBLE
INCOMPETENCE
INCOMPLETELY
INCONCLUSIVE
INCONSEQUENT
INCONSISTENT
INCONSOLABLE
INCONTINENCE
INCONVENIENT
INCORPORATED
INCORRIGIBLE
INCORRIGIBLY
INDOCTRINATE
INFORMIDABLE
INHOSPITABLE
INNOMINABLES
INSOLUBILITY
INTOXICATING
INTOXICATION
LABOURSAVING
LEIOTRICHOUS
LOXODROMICAL
MANOEUVRABLE
MELODRAMATIC
MESOTHELIOMA
MONOSYLLABIC
MONOSYLLABLE
MONOTONOUSLY
MOTORCYCLIST
NOCONFIDENCE
OBSOLESCENCE
OBSOLETENESS
OCTOGENARIAN
ONCORHYNCHUS
OREOPITHECUS
OREOPITHEOUS
PHRONTISTERY
POPOCATEPETL
PYROTECHNICS
RECOGNIZABLE
RECOGNIZANCE
RECOLLECTION
RECONSTITUTE
RECORDPLAYER
REMONSTRANCE
RENOUNCEMENT
REPOSSESSION
RISORGIMENTO
RODOMONTADER
SCHOOLMASTER
SCHOPENHAUER
STROMATOLITE
STRONGMINDED
STROPHANTHUS
THEOPHYLLINE
THEORETICIAN
UNCONSIDERED
UNCONTROLLED
UNCONVERSANT
UNCONVINCING
UNPOPULARITY
UPROARIOUSLY
VAPORIZATION
ADAPTABILITY
AUSPICIOUSLY
CAMPANULARIA
CAMPODEIFORM
CARPETBAGGER
CLAPPERBOARD
COMPANIONWAY
COMPELLATION
COMPENSATION
COMPENSATORY
COMPLACENTLY
COMPLETENESS
COMPLICATION
COMPROMISING
COMPURGATION
CRYPTOGRAPHY
DISPENSATION
DISPLACEMENT
DISPOSSESSED
DOLPHINARIUM
EGYPTOLOGIST
EPIPHENOMENA
ETEPIMELETIC
GEOPHYSICIST
GRAPHOLOGIST
HAPPENSTANCE
HAPPYGOLUCKY
HELPLESSNESS
HIPPOCRATISE
HIPPOCREPIAN
HIPPOPOTAMUS
INAPPLICABLE
INSPECTORATE
KLEPTOMANIAC
KLIPSPRINGER
LAMPADEDROMY
MALPRACTICES
MISPLACEMENT
MISPRONOUNCE
NEOPLATONISM
NYMPHOMANIAC
PALPITATIONS
PANPHARMACON
PERPETRATION
PREPAREDNESS
PREPONDERANT
PREPONDERATE
PREPONDERENT
PREPOSSESSED
PREPOSTEROUS
PROPAGANDISM
PROPAGANDIST
PROPHYLACTIC
PROPITIATION
PROPITIATORY
PROPITIOUSLY
PROPORTIONAL
PROPRIETRESS
PSEPHOLOGIST
PSIPHENOMENA
PUMPERNICKEL
PURPOSEBUILT
PURPOSEFULLY
REAPPEARANCE
RESPECTFULLY
RESPECTIVELY
RESPONDENTIA
RHIPIDOPTERA
SCAPULIMANCY
SCOPOPHILIAC
SHIPBUILDING
STEPDAUGHTER
STUPEFACTION
SULPHONAMIDE
SUPPLICATION
SURPRISINGLY
SUSPICIOUSLY
TROPHALLAXIS
UNAPPARELLED
UNAPPETIZING
UNOPPRESSIVE
WHIPPOORWILL
ABSQUATULATE
CONQUISTADOR
DISQUISITION
MISQUOTATION
SESQUIALTERA
SESQUITERTIA
ABBREVIATION
AFORETHOUGHT
AGGRESSIVELY
AMARANTACEAE
ANDROSTERONE
APPRECIATION
APPRECIATIVE
APPREHENSION
APPREHENSIVE
APPROACHABLE
ASTROLOGICAL
ASTRONOMICAL
ASTROPHYSICS
ATTRACTIVELY
ATTRIBUTABLE
AWARDWINNING
BAIRNSFATHER
BARRANQUILLA
CARRIWITCHET
CHARACTERIZE
CHARTERHOUSE
CHIROPRACTIC
CHIROPRACTOR
CHOREOGRAPHY
CHORIZONTIST
CHURCHWARDEN
CHURLISHNESS
CLARINETTIST
COORDINATION
COURAGEOUSLY
COURTMARTIAL
DEPRECIATION
DEPRECIATORY
DIPRIONIDIAN
DISREPECTFUL
DISREPUTABLE

EMBROIDERESS
ENCROACHMENT
ENERGYSAVING
ENTREATINGLY
ENTRENCHMENT
ENTREPRENEUR
ESTRANGEMENT
EXCRUCIATING
EXCRUCIATION
EXTRADITABLE
EXTRAVAGANCE
EXTRAVAGANZA
FEARLESSNESS
FLORICULTURE
GIBRALTARIAN
GUARDIANSHIP
HAIRDRESSERS
HAIRDRESSING
HAIRSPLITTER
HEARTSTRINGS
HEARTWARMING
HIERARCHICAL
HIEROGLYPHIC
HIEROGRAMMAT
HIEROPHANTIC
HORRIFICALLY
HYDROCHLORIC
HYDROGRAPHER
HYDROQUINONE
HYDROTHERAPY
IMPREGNATION
IMPRESSIVELY
IMPRISONMENT
IMPROVIDENCE
INARTICULATE
INCREASINGLY
INCRUSTATION
INERADICABLE
INFREQUENTLY
INFRINGEMENT
INGRATIATING
INORDINATELY
INTRANSIGENT
INTRANSITIVE
INTRAUTERINE
INTRODUCTION
INTRODUCTORY
JOURNALISTIC
LAUREATESHIP
MACROPODIDAE
MARRIAGEABLE
MERRYTHOUGHT
METROPOLITAN
MICROCLIMATE
MISREPRESENT
MITRAILLEUSE
NEUROLOGICAL
NEUROTICALLY
NONRESIDENCE
NONRESISTANT
NUTRITIONIST
OPPRESSIVELY
OUTRAGEOUSLY
OVERCROWDING
OVERDRESSING
OVERESTIMATE
OVEREXERTION
OVERPOWERING
OVERSCUTCHED
OVERSTRAINED
OVERWHELMING
PETRIFACTION
PHARMACOLOGY
PREREQUISITE
PTERIDOPHYTE
PTERODACTYLE
PUTREFACTION
QUARTERFINAL
QUARTERLIGHT
QUARTERSTAFF
RECREATIONAL
RECRUDESCENT
REFRIGERATED
REFRIGERATOR
REPROCESSING
REPRODUCTION
REPRODUCTIVE
RETRENCHMENT
SACRILEGIOUS
SARRUSOPHONE
SAUROGNATHAE
SCURRILOUSLY
SECRETARIATE
SHAREHOLDING
SHARPSHOOTER
SHIRTSLEEVES
SHIRTWAISTER
SHORTCIRCUIT
SHORTCOMINGS
SHORTSIGHTED
SHORTSLEEVED
SHORTSTAFFED
SPERMATOCYTE
SPIRITUALISM
SPIRITUALIST
SPIRITUALITY
SPORADICALLY
SPORTSGROUND
SPURIOUSNESS
SPURTLEBLADE
STEREOPHONIC
STEREOPTICON
STEREOSCOPIC
STEREOTYPING
STERNUTATION
STERNWHEELER
STORMTROOPER
SURREALISTIC
SURROUNDINGS
TERRIFICALLY
TERRITORIALS
TETRACYCLINE
TETRAHEDRITE
TETRODOTOXIN
THERAPEUTICS
THEREAGAINST
THERMOSTATIC
THIRDBOROUGH
THOROUGHBRED
THOROUGHFARE
THOROUGHNESS
TORRICELLIAN
ULTRAMONTANE
UMBRADARLING
UNFREQUENTED
UNPREJUDICED
UNPRETENDING
UNPRINCIPLED
UNPRODUCTIVE
UNPROFITABLE
URTRICULARIA
USERFRIENDLY
VIBRATIUNCLE
APOSTROPHISE
ARISTOCRATIC
ARISTOLOCHIA
ARISTOPHANES
ARISTOTELEAN
BESSERWISSER
BOISTEROUSLY
CASSITERIDES
CHASTISEMENT
CHESTERFIELD
CLASSIFIABLE
CONSCRIPTION
CONSECRATION
CONSEQUENCES
CONSEQUENTLY
CONSERVATION
CONSERVATISM
CONSERVATIVE
CONSERVATORY
CONSIDERABLE
CONSIDERABLY
CONSISTENTLY
CONSOLIDATED
CONSOLIDATOR
CONSPECTUITY
CONSTABULARY
CONSTIPATION
CONSTITUENCY
CONSTITUENTS
CONSTITUTION
CONSTRICTION
CONSTRUCTION
CONSTRUCTIVE
CONSULTATION
CONSULTATIVE
CONSUMMATION
CRASHLANDING
CRASSAMENTUM
CRISTOBALITE
CROSSBENCHER
CROSSCOUNTRY
CROSSEXAMINE
CROSSSECTION
DEASPIRATION
DESSERTSPOON
DISSATISFIED
DISSERTATION
DISSOCIATION
DORSIVENTRAL
DRESSINGDOWN
ELASMOBRANCH
EMASCULATION
EPISCOPALIAN
EPISTEMOLOGY
EPISTOLATERS
EXASPERATING
EXASPERATION
FIRSTFOOTING
GOOSEPIMPLES
GRASSWIDOWER
GRISEOFULVIN
GROSSULARITE
HORSEMANSHIP
HOUSEBREAKER
HOUSEKEEPING
HOUSETOHOUSE
HOUSEWARMING
INESCUTCHEON
IRASCIBILITY
KIRSCHWASSER
MANSLAUGHTER
MARSEILLAISE
MASSERANDUBA
MASSPRODUCED
MENSTRUATION
MISSTATEMENT
MOISTURIZING
MOUSQUETAIRE
NEWSPAPERMAN
OPISTHOGRAPH
OUTSTRETCHED
PARSIMONIOUS
PASSEMEASURE
PASSEPARTOUT
PASSIONATELY
PASSIONFRUIT
PERSEVERANCE
PERSISTENTLY
PERSONALIZED
PERSPICACITY
PERSPIRATION
PERSUASIVELY
PERSULPHURIC
PHOSPHORENCE
PHOSPHORESCE
PHYSIOLOGIST
PLASTERSTONE

POSSESSIVELY
PRASEODYMIUM
PRESBYTERIAN
PRESCRIPTION
PRESCRIPTIVE
PRESENTATION
PRESENTIMENT
PRESERVATION
PRESERVATIVE
PRESIDENTIAL
PRESTRICTION
PRESUMPTUOUS
PROSCRIPTION
PROSOPOPOEIA
PROSTITUTION
QUESTIONABLE
SARSAPARILLA
SHOSTAKOVICH
SUBSCRIPTION
SUBSEQUENTLY
SUBSERVIENCE
SUBSIDIARITY
SUBSTANTIATE
SUBSTITUTION
SUBSTRUCTURE
SWASHBUCKLER
TAPSALTEERIE
TAPSLETEERIE
THESMOPHORIA
THESSALONIAN
THYSANOPTERA
WOLSTENHOLME
AGATHODAIMON
ARITHMETICAL
AUSTRALASIAN
AUSTRONESIAN
BACTERIOLOGY
BACTERIOSTAT
BANTAMWEIGHT
BATTLEGROUND
BERTHOLLETIA
BERTILLONAGE
BLETHERSKATE
BUTTERSCOTCH
CANTANKEROUS
CANTILEVERED
CARTHAGINIAN
CARTOGRAPHER
CARTOGRAPHIC
CASTERBRIDGE
CAUTIOUSNESS
CHITTERLINGS
CONTABESCENT
CONTAMINATED
CONTEMPORARY
CONTEMPTIBLE
CONTEMPTUOUS
CONTERMINOUS
CONTIGNATION
CONTINUATION
CONTINUOUSLY
CONTRAPPOSTO
CONTRAPUNTAL
CONTRARINESS
CONTRIBUTION
CONTRIBUTORY
CONTRITURATE
CONTROLLABLE
CONTUMACIOUS
COSTERMONGER
DEUTEROSCOPY
DICTATORSHIP
DISTILLATION
DISTINCTNESS
DISTRIBUTION
DISTRIBUTIVE
DYSTELEOLOGY
ECSTATICALLY
EPITHALAMION
EPITHALAMIUM
ERATOSTHENES
ERYTHROMYCIN
FAITHFULNESS
FARTHINGLAND
FASTIDIOUSLY
FEATHERBRAIN
FLITTERMOUSE
FOOTSLOGGING
FORTUITOUSLY
FUSTILLIRIAN
GASTARBEITER
GASTROSOPHER
GENTLETAMPER
GRATEFULNESS
HISTIOPHORUS
HISTORICALLY
HORTICULTURE
HYSTERECTOMY
HYSTERICALLY
ICHTHYOCOLLA
ICHTHYOPSIDA
INSTALLATION
INSTAURATION
INSTRUCTIONS
INSTRUCTRESS
INSTRUMENTAL
KLETTERSCHUE
LISTLESSNESS
MALTREATMENT
MASTERSTROKE
MASTIGOPHORA
MASTURBATION
MISTREATMENT
MONTESSORIAN
MOUTHBROODER
MULTICOLORED
MULTIFARIOUS
MULTILATERAL
MULTIPLICITY
MYSTERIOUSLY
NORTHEASTERN
NORTHERNMOST
NORTHWESTERN
OBSTETRICIAN
OBSTREPEROUS
PANTECHNICON
PANTISOCRACY
PANTOPHAGOUS
PARTICOLORED
PARTICULARLY
PARTISANSHIP
PECTORILOQUY
PERTINACIOUS
PERTURBATION
PESTILENTIAL
PETTIFOGGERS
PETTIFOGGERY
PETTIFOGGING
PHOTOGLYPHIC
PHOTOGRAPHER
PHOTOGRAPHIC
PHOTOGRAVURE
PHYTOBENTHOS
PHYTONADIONE
PITTERPATTER
POSTGRADUATE
POSTHUMOUSLY
POSTLIMINARY
POSTMISTRESS
POSTPONEMENT
POSTPRANDIAL
PROTACTINIUM
PROTECTIVELY
PROTECTORATE
PROTESTATION
PROTHALAMION
PROTHALAMIUM
PROTOPLASMAL
PROTOPLASMIC
PROTUBERANCE
RESTAURATEUR
RESTLESSNESS
RHYTHMICALLY
RHYTIDECTOMY
SALTATORIOUS
SCATTERBRAIN
SCATTERMOUCH
SECTARIANISM
SEPTEMBRISER
SEPTUAGESIMA
SITTLICHKEIT
SKUTTERUDITE
SOUTHCOTTIAN
SOUTHEASTERN
SOUTHERNMOST
SOUTHERNWOOD
SOUTHWESTERN
SPATANGOIDEA
SPITEFULNESS
STATISTICIAN
SUBTERRANEAN
SYNTAGMATITE
TACTLESSNESS
TAUTOLOGICAL
TEETERTOTTER
TESTAMENTARY
TESTOSTERONE
TRUTHFULNESS
UINTATHERIUM
ULOTRICHALES
UNATTAINABLE
UNATTRACTIVE
UNCTUOUSNESS
UNUTTERABLES
VENTRIPOTENT
WEATHERPROOF
WELTERWEIGHT
WILTSHIREMAN
WINTERHALTER
WRETCHEDNESS
XANTHOPTERIN
YOUTHFULNESS
ACCUMULATION
ACQUAINTANCE
ACQUIESCENCE
ADJUDICATION
AMBULANCEMAN
ANNUNCIATION
APPURTENANCE
ASSUEFACTION
BEAUMARCHAIS
BEAUMONTAGUE
BEAUMONTIQUE
CALUMNIATION
CHAUVINISTIC
CLAUDICATION
DAGUERROTYPE
DEHUMIDIFIER
DENUNCIATION
EXSUFFLICATE
FIGURATIVELY
FRAUENDIENST
HARUMFRODITE
ILLUMINATING
ILLUMINATION
ILLUSTRATION
ILLUSTRATIVE
IMMUNIZATION
IMMUNOLOGIST
IMMUTABILITY
INAUGURATION
INAUSPICIOUS
INCUNABULIST
INDUSTRIALLY
INSUFFERABLE
INSUFFERABLY
INSUFFICIENT
INSURRECTION
INVULNERABLE
LIQUEFACTION

LUGUBRIOUSLY
LUXULLIANITE
MANUFACTURER
NATURALISTIC
OCCUPATIONAL
PALUDAMENTUM
PLAUSIBILITY
PSEUDONYMOUS
RECUPERATION
RECUPERATIVE
REJUVENATION
REMUNERATION
REMUNERATIVE
RENUNCIATION
RESURRECTION
RESUSCITATED
SCRUPULOUSLY
SEQUENTIALLY
SEQUESTRATOR
SIMULTANEOUS
SIPUNCULACEA
STRUCTURALLY
THAUMATURGIC
THAUMATURGUS
THOUGHTFULLY
TRIUMPHANTLY
TROUBLEMAKER
UNAUTHORISED
UNAUTHORIZED
UNCULTIVATED
UNSUCCESSFUL
UNSURPRISING
UNSUSPECTING
VERUMONTANUM
VITUPERATION
VITUPERATIVE
VOLUPTUOUSLY
ARFVEDSONITE
CLAVICEMBALO
CONVALESCENT
CONVALESCING
CONVENIENCES
CONVENIENTLY
CONVENTIONAL
CONVERSATION
CONVEYANCING
CONVINCINGLY
CONVIVIALITY
GALVANOMETER
MERVEILLEUSE
PERVERSENESS
PERVICACIOUS
PREVARICATOR
PREVENTATIVE
PROVERBIALLY
PROVIDENTIAL
SALVATIONIST
SERVICEWOMAN
SILVERHAIRED
SLOVENLINESS
SURVEILLANCE
UNIVERSALIST
SNOWBOARDING
ALEXIPHARMIC
INEXACTITUDE
INEXPERIENCE
INEXPLICABLE
INEXPLICABLY
INEXTRICABLE
INEXTRICABLY
PRAXINOSCOPE
QUIXOTICALLY
UNEXPECTEDLY
UNEXPURGATED
AWAYABSOLUTE
ENCYCLOPEDIA
ENCYCLOPEDIC
ENHYPOSTASIA
LABYRINTHINE
POLYETHYLENE
POLYSYLLABIC
POLYSYLLABLE
POLYSYNDETON
POLYURETHANE
KATZENJAMMER
PRIZEFIGHTER
PRIZEWINNING
SWIZZLESTICK

12:5

ACHLAMYDEOUS
ACQUAINTANCE
ALPHABETICAL
ALPHANUMERIC
AMARANTACEAE
ANECATHARSIS
AROMATHERAPY
ATTRACTIVELY
AWAYABSOLUTE
BANTAMWEIGHT
BARRANQUILLA
BOUGAINVILLE
BUREAUCRATIC
CAMPANULARIA
CANTANKEROUS
CHARACTERIZE
CIRCASSIENNE
COLLABORATOR
COMMANDMENTS
COMPANIONWAY
CONTABESCENT
CONTAMINATED
CONVALESCENT
CONVALESCING
COURAGEOUSLY
CREMAILLIÈRE
DEFLATIONARY
DICTATORSHIP
DISDAINFULLY
DISSATISFIED
DOGMATICALLY
DRAMATICALLY
DRAMATURGIST
ECSTATICALLY
EDUCATIONIST
EMPHATICALLY
ESTRANGEMENT
EXCHANGEABLE
EXTRADITABLE
EXTRAVAGANCE
EXTRAVAGANZA
FORMALDEHYDE
FUNDAMENTALS
GALVANOMETER
GASTARBEITER
GENEALOGICAL
GERIATRICIAN
GIBRALTARIAN
HAEMATEMESIS
HALLANSHAKER
HIERARCHICAL
IMMEASURABLE
IMMEASURABLY
IMPLANTATION
INERADICABLE
INEXACTITUDE
INFLAMMATION
INFLAMMATORY
INFLATIONARY
INGRATIATING
INSTALLATION
INSTAURATION
INTRANSIGENT
INTRANSITIVE
INTRAUTERINE
ISHMAELITISH
ISOLATIONISM
ISOLATIONIST
KATHAREVOUSA
LALLAPALOOZA
LAMPADEDROMY
LANCASTERIAN
MACHAIRODONT
MECHANICALLY
MISCALCULATE
MITRAILLEUSE
OLDFASHIONED
ONOMATOPOEIA
ONOMATOPOEIC
OUTMANOEUVRE
OUTRAGEOUSLY
PANDAEMONIUM
PANDANACEOUS
PEDIATRICIAN
PERGAMENEOUS
PERMANGANATE
PHILANTHROPY
PRECARIOUSLY
PREMAXILLARY
PREPAREDNESS
PREVARICATOR
PROBATIONARY
PROPAGANDISM
PROPAGANDIST
PROTACTINIUM
PUGNACIOUSLY
RECHARGEABLE
REFLATIONARY
RESTAURATEUR
RHADAMANTHUS
SALTATORIOUS
SALVATIONIST
SARDANAPALUS
SARSAPARILLA
SECTARIANISM
SELFADHESIVE
SOMNAMBULISM
SOMNAMBULIST
SPATANGOIDEA
SPORADICALLY
SPREADEAGLED
SUBHASTATION
SUBLAPSARIAN
SYNTAGMATITE
TAPSALTEERIE
TELEASTHETIC
TESTAMENTARY
TETRACYCLINE
TETRAHEDRITE
THERAPEUTICS
THREADNEEDLE
THYSANOPTERA
TRALATICIOUS
TRALATITIOUS
UINTATHERIUM
ULTRAMONTANE
UMBRADARLING
UNCHALLENGED
UNCHANGEABLE
UNCHARITABLE
UNCHARITABLY
UNCLASSIFIED
UNILATERALLY
UNIMAGINABLE
UNREASONABLE
UNSEASONABLE
UPROARIOUSLY
VIBRATIUNCLE
WOLLASTONITE
AGRIBUSINESS
ANTIBACCHIUS
ANTIBARBARUS
BACKBREAKING
BLABBERMOUTH
CEREBROTONIC
COHABITATION
DEAMBULATORY
DELIBERATELY
DELIBERATION

DISOBEDIENCE
EXHIBITIONER
FLAMBOYANTLY
GLUBBDUBDRIB
HUDIBRASTICS
INDEBTEDNESS
LUGUBRIOUSLY
MACABERESQUE
MINDBOGGLING
PHLEBOTOMIST
PRESBYTERIAN
REHABILITATE
SHIPBUILDING
SLUBBERINGLY
SNOBBISHNESS
SNOWBOARDING
STILBOESTROL
STUBBORNNESS
TROUBLEMAKER
WELLBALANCED
WOODBURYTYPE
ADJECTIVALLY
AFFECTIONATE
AGRICULTURAL
ANTICIPATION
ANTICIPATORY
ARTICULATION
BRANCHIOPODA
CARICATURIST
CHURCHWARDEN
COINCIDENTAL
CONSCRIPTION
DELICATESSEN
DIENCEPHALON
DIRECTORSHIP
DISACCHARIDE
EMANCIPATION
EMASCULATION
ENCYCLOPEDIA
ENCYCLOPEDIC
EPENCEPHALON
EPISCOPALIAN
GYNECOLOGIST
HEMICHORDATA
HYPOCHONDRIA
HYPOCRITICAL
IMMACULATELY
INACCESSIBLE
INACCURATELY
INDECLINABLE
INDOCTRINATE
INESCUTCHEON
IRASCIBILITY
KIRSCHWASSER
LEXICOGRAPHY
MALACOSTRACA
METICULOUSLY
MINICOMPUTER
MIRACULOUSLY
MUNICIPALITY
MUSICOLOGIST
OVERCROWDING
OXYACETYLENE
PARACENTESIS
PEDICELLARIA
PERICARDITIS
POLICYMAKING
POPOCATEPETL
POTICHOMANIA
PRESCRIPTION
PRESCRIPTIVE
PRINCIPALITY
PROSCRIPTION
RETICULATION
RIDICULOUSLY
SELFCATERING
SEMICIRCULAR
SOLICITATION
SOLICITOUSLY
SPHACELATION
STRUCTURALLY
SUBSCRIPTION
TOBACCONISTS
TOXICOLOGIST
TURACOVERDIN
UNACCEPTABLE
UNACCUSTOMED
UNRECOGNISED
UNRECOGNIZED
UNSUCCESSFUL
VARICOLOURED
WRETCHEDNESS
ACCIDENTALLY
ADJUDICATION
AECIDIOSPORE
AERODYNAMICS
AMBIDEXTROUS
ANTEDILUVIAN
AWARDWINNING
BLANDISHMENT
BLOODSTAINED
BLOODTHIRSTY
BOONDOGGLING
BROADCASTING
CATADIOPTRIC
CHILDBEARING
CHILDISHNESS
CHONDRIOSOME
CLAUDICATION
COORDINATION
DISADVANTAGE
GLYNDEBOURNE
GONADOTROPIN
GRANDISONIAN
GRANDMONTINE
GRANDPARENTS
GUARDIANSHIP
GUILDENSTERN
HAIRDRESSERS
HAIRDRESSING
HEREDITAMENT
HOLIDAYMAKER
IMMODERATELY
IMMODERATION
INCIDENTALLY
INORDINATELY
IRREDEEMABLE
LEPIDOMELANE
LONGDISTANCE
LOXODROMICAL
MELODRAMATIC
MISADVENTURE
OVERDRESSING
PALUDAMENTUM
PERADVENTURE
PSEUDONYMOUS
SCANDALOUSLY
SCANDINAVIAN
SEMIDETACHED
STEPDAUGHTER
STRADIVARIUS
STRIDULATION
SYNADELPHITE
THIRDBOROUGH
THUNDERCLOUD
THUNDERFLASH
THUNDERSTORM
ABBREVIATION
ACADEMICALLY
AFORETHOUGHT
AGGRESSIVELY
ALIMENTATIVE
ANTHELMINTIC
APPRECIATION
APPRECIATIVE
APPREHENSION
APPREHENSIVE
ARFVEDSONITE
ASSUEFACTION
AUGMENTATION
AUTHENTICATE
AUTHENTICITY
BACTERIOLOGY
BACTERIOSTAT
BANDERSNATCH
BARBERMONGER
BESSERWISSER
BOULEVARDIER
BUTTERSCOTCH
CALCEAMENTUM
CANCELLATION
CARPETBAGGER
CASTERBRIDGE
CATHETOMETER
CHOREOGRAPHY
COLLECTIVELY
COLLECTORATE
COMMENCEMENT
COMMENDATION
COMMENDATORY
COMMENSURATE
COMMERCIALLY
COMPELLATION
COMPENSATION
COMPENSATORY
CONCENTRATED
CONDEMNATION
CONDENSATION
CONFECTIONER
CONFESSIONAL
CONGENITALLY
CONSECRATION
CONSEQUENCES
CONSEQUENTLY
CONSERVATION
CONSERVATISM
CONSERVATIVE
CONSERVATORY
CONTEMPORARY
CONTEMPTIBLE
CONTEMPTUOUS
CONTERMINOUS
CONVENIENCES
CONVENIENTLY
CONVENTIONAL
CONVERSATION
CONVEYANCING
COSTERMONGER
DAGUERROTYPE
DEPRECIATION
DEPRECIATORY
DESSERTSPOON
DEUTEROSCOPY
DIALECTICIAN
DIFFERENTIAL
DISPENSATION
DISREPECTFUL
DISREPUTABLE
DISSERTATION
DONNERWETTER
DYSTELEOLOGY
ECCLESIASTES
ECCLESIASTIC
ENCHEIRIDION
ENTREATINGLY
ENTRENCHMENT
ENTREPRENEUR
EPIDEICTICAL
ESTHETICALLY
EXACERBATION
FERMENTATION
FLAGELLATION
FORCEFULNESS
FOTHERINGHAY
FRAUENDIENST
FRUMENTATION
GEOMETRICIAN
GLOBETROTTER
GOOSEPIMPLES
GRACEFULNESS

GRATEFULNESS
GRISEOFULVIN
HAMMERHEADED
HAPPENSTANCE
HARNESSMAKER
HENCEFORWARD
HERMENEUTICS
HERMENEUTIST
HERMETICALLY
HILDEBRANDIC
HOMOEOPATHIC
HORSEMANSHIP
HOUSEBREAKER
HOUSEKEEPING
HOUSETOHOUSE
HOUSEWARMING
HYGIENICALLY
HYSTERECTOMY
HYSTERICALLY
IMPREGNATION
IMPRESSIVELY
INADEQUATELY
INCREASINGLY
INFREQUENTLY
INSPECTORATE
KATZENJAMMER
KINAESTHETIC
KINDERGARTEN
LAUREATESHIP
LIQUEFACTION
MAGNETICALLY
MALLEABILITY
MANGELWURZEL
MANOEUVRABLE
MARSEILLAISE
MASSERANDUBA
MASTERSTROKE
MATHEMATICAL
MERVEILLEUSE
MICHELANGELO
MISBEHAVIOUR
MISDELIVERED
MISDEMEANOUR
MISREPRESENT
MONTESSORIAN
MYSTERIOUSLY
NEPHELOMETER
NONRESIDENCE
NONRESISTANT
OBSTETRICIAN
OPPRESSIVELY
OVERESTIMATE
OVEREXERTION
PANAESTHESIA
PANTECHNICON
PASSEMEASURE
PASSEPARTOUT
PATHETICALLY
PEACEFULNESS
PEACEKEEPING
PERCEPTIVELY
PERCEPTIVITY
PERMEABILITY
PERPETRATION
PERSEVERANCE
PERVERSENESS
PHONETICALLY
PIGMENTATION
PITTERPATTER
PLACENTIFORM
POLYETHYLENE
POSSESSIVELY
PRASEODYMIUM
PREDESTINATE
PREDETERMINE
PREFERENTIAL
PREREQUISITE
PRESENTATION
PRESENTIMENT
PRESERVATION
PRESERVATIVE
PREVENTATIVE
PRIZEFIGHTER
PRIZEWINNING
PROCESSIONAL
PROFESSIONAL
PROFESSORIAL
PROGESTERONE
PROLEGOMENON
PROLETARIATE
PROTECTIVELY
PROTECTORATE
PROTESTATION
PROVERBIALLY
PUMPERNICKEL
PUTREFACTION
RACKETEERING
RECREATIONAL
RESPECTFULLY
RESPECTIVELY
RETRENCHMENT
ROLLERBLADER
ROLLERBLADES
RONCESVALLES
SCHNEIDERIAN
SCREENWRITER
SECRETARIATE
SEGMENTATION
SELFEMPLOYED
SEPTEMBRISER
SEQUENTIALLY
SEQUESTRATOR
SHAMEFACEDLY
SHAREHOLDING
SILVERHAIRED
SLOVENLINESS
SPELEOLOGIST
SPINECHILLER
SPITEFULNESS
SPOKESPERSON
STEREOPHONIC
STEREOPTICON
STEREOSCOPIC
STEREOTYPING
STONECHATTER
STUPEFACTION
SUBJECTIVELY
SUBJECTIVITY
SUBSEQUENTLY
SUBSERVIENCE
SUBTERRANEAN
SUCCESSFULLY
SUCCESSIVELY
SUGGESTIVELY
SURREALISTIC
SURVEILLANCE
TEETERTOTTER
TERCENTENARY
THEREAGAINST
THREEQUARTER
TRABECULATED
TRADESCANTIA
TRADESPEOPLE
TREMENDOUSLY
UNFREQUENTED
UNIDENTIFIED
UNIVERSALIST
UNPREJUDICED
UNPRETENDING
VENGEFULNESS
VILLEGIATURA
WELTERWEIGHT
WHOLEHEARTED
WICKETKEEPER
WINTERHALTER
ARTIFICIALLY
BENEFACTRESS
CODIFICATION
EXSUFFLICATE
HIGHFALUTING
INDEFENSIBLE
INDEFINITELY
INDIFFERENCE
INEFFICIENCY
INSUFFERABLE
INSUFFERABLY
INSUFFICIENT
MANUFACTURER
MINDFULLNESS
MODIFICATION
NOTIFICATION
OSSIFICATION
PACIFICATION
PURIFICATION
RAMIFICATION
RATIFICATION
SHUFFLEBOARD
UNOFFICIALLY
USERFRIENDLY
VERIFICATION
VILIFICATION
VOCIFERATION
VOCIFEROUSLY
AMALGAMATION
ANTAGONISTIC
APPOGGIATURA
DEREGULATION
DISAGREEABLE
DISAGREEMENT
ENERGYSAVING
ESPAGNOLETTE
EXAGGERATION
FEHMGERICHTE
FREIGHTLINER
HELLGRAMMITE
ILLEGIBILITY
ILLEGITIMACY
ILLEGITIMATE
ILLOGICALITY
INAUGURATION
INDIGESTIBLE
INVIGORATING
INVIGORATION
IRREGULARITY
METAGNATHOUS
NAVIGABILITY
NONAGENARIAN
OCTOGENARIAN
POSTGRADUATE
PRIGGISHNESS
RECOGNIZABLE
RECOGNIZANCE
SEXAGENARIAN
SPIEGELEISEN
STAGGERINGLY
STRIGIFORMES
TELEGRAPHESE
TELEGRAPHIST
THOUGHTFULLY
VAINGLORIOUS
VEHMGERICHTE
AGATHODAIMON
ANNIHILATION
ARITHMETICAL
BACCHANALIAN
BERTHOLLETIA
BIOCHEMISTRY
BLETHERSKATE
BRACHYCEPHAL
CARTHAGINIAN
CRASHLANDING
DOLPHINARIUM
EPIPHENOMENA
EPITHALAMION
EPITHALAMIUM
ERYTHROMYCIN
EVENHANDEDLY
FAITHFULNESS
FARTHINGLAND
FEATHERBRAIN

GEOPHYSICIST
GRAPHOLOGIST
ICHTHYOCOLLA
ICHTHYOPSIDA
INCOHERENTLY
MOUTHBROODER
NEIGHBORHOOD
NEIGHBOURING
NONCHALANTLY
NORTHEASTERN
NORTHERNMOST
NORTHWESTERN
NYMPHOMANIAC
PANCHATANTRA
PANCHROMATIC
PANPHARMACON
PHILHARMONIC
POSTHUMOUSLY
PROPHYLACTIC
PROTHALAMION
PROTHALAMIUM
PSEPHOLOGIST
PSIPHENOMENA
PSYCHIATRIST
PSYCHOLOGIST
PSYCHOPATHIC
RHYTHMICALLY
SCHEHERAZADE
SOUTHCOTTIAN
SOUTHEASTERN
SOUTHERNMOST
SOUTHERNWOOD
SOUTHWESTERN
STAKHANOVITE
SULPHONAMIDE
SWASHBUCKLER
TRICHOLOGIST
TRICHOPHYTON
TROCHELMINTH
TROCHOSPHERE
TROPHALLAXIS
TRUTHFULNESS
WAREHOUSEMAN
WATCHFULNESS
WEATHERPROOF
WEIGHTLIFTER
XANTHOPTERIN
YOUTHFULNESS
ABOLITIONIST
ACQUIESCENCE
ADSCITITIOUS
ALEXIPHARMIC
AMELIORATION
AMPHISBAENIC
AMPHISTOMOUS
AMPHITHEATER
AMPHITHEATRE
ARCHILOCHIAN
ARCHIPELAGOS
ARCHITECTURE
ATTRIBUTABLE
AUSPICIOUSLY
BELLIGERENCY
BERTILLONAGE
BIBLIOGRAPHY
BIBLIOPEGIST
BILLINGSGATE
BIODIVERSITY
CALLIGRAPHIC
CALLISTHENES
CANTILEVERED
CARCINOGENIC
CARDINDEXING
CARDIOLOGIST
CARRIWITCHET
CASSITERIDES
CAUTIOUSNESS
CHALICOTHERE
CHORIZONTIST
CLARINETTIST
CLAVICEMBALO
COCCIDIOSTAT
COMBINATIONS
COMMISSARIAT
COMMISSIONED
COMMISSIONER
CONCILIATION
CONCILIATORY
CONFIDENTIAL
CONFIRMATION
CONFIRMATORY
CONFISCATION
CONSIDERABLE
CONSIDERABLY
CONSISTENTLY
CONTIGNATION
CONTINUATION
CONTINUOUSLY
CONVINCINGLY
CONVIVIALITY
COSCINOMANCY
DARLINGTONIA
DIPRIONIDIAN
DISCIPLINARY
DISTILLATION
DISTINCTNESS
DORSIVENTRAL
DUNNIEWASSAL
ENGLISHWOMAN
ENGLISHWOMEN
ETEPIMELETIC
FASTIDIOUSLY
FLORICULTURE
FULMINATIONS
FUSTILLIRIAN
GALLIGASKINS
GALLINACEOUS
GALLIVANTING
GLADIATORIAL
GRACIOUSNESS
HEROICOMICAL
HISTIOPHORUS
HOBBIDIDANCE
HORRIFICALLY
HORTICULTURE
IMPRISONMENT
INFRINGEMENT
ISOBILATERAL
KALEIDOSCOPE
KILLIKINNICK
LASCIVIOUSLY
LILLIBULLERO
LILLIBURLERO
LONGITUDINAL
MACMILLANITE
MAGNIFICENCE
MAGNILOQUENT
MARLINESPIKE
MARRIAGEABLE
MASTIGOPHORA
MEANINGFULLY
MECHITHARIST
MULLIGATAWNY
MULTICOLORED
MULTIFARIOUS
MULTILATERAL
MULTIPLICITY
NARCISSISTIC
NUTRITIONIST
OBEDIENTIARY
OPINIONATIVE
PALPITATIONS
PANTISOCRACY
PARSIMONIOUS
PARTICOLORED
PARTICULARLY
PARTISANSHIP
PASSIONATELY
PASSIONFRUIT
PERSISTENTLY
PERTINACIOUS
PERVICACIOUS
PESTILENTIAL
PETRIFACTION
PETTIFOGGERS
PETTIFOGGERY
PETTIFOGGING
PHILISTINISM
PHYSIOLOGIST
PINNIEWINKLE
PISCICULTURE
PRAXINOSCOPE
PREDILECTION
PREHISTORIAN
PRESIDENTIAL
PRODIGIOUSLY
PROFICIENTLY
PROFITEERING
PROLIFICALLY
PROPITIATION
PROPITIATORY
PROPITIOUSLY
PROVIDENTIAL
PTERIDOPHYTE
RECEIVERSHIP
REFRIGERATED
REFRIGERATOR
RHIPIDOPTERA
RHYTIDECTOMY
ROOMINGHOUSE
SACRILEGIOUS
SELFINTEREST
SERVICEWOMAN
SIGNIFICANCE
SOPHISTICATE
SPACIOUSNESS
SPECIFICALLY
SPECIOUSNESS
SPHAIRISTIKE
SPIRITUALISM
SPIRITUALIST
SPIRITUALITY
SPURIOUSNESS
STANISLAVSKI
STATISTICIAN
STRAIGHTAWAY
STRAIGHTEDGE
STRAIGHTNESS
STRAITJACKET
STUDIOUSNESS
SUBMISSIVELY
SUBSIDIARITY
SUFFICIENTLY
SUSPICIOUSLY
TAGLIACOTIAN
TERGIVERSATE
TERRIFICALLY
TERRITORIALS
TORRICELLIAN
UNNEIGHBORLY
UNPRINCIPLED
UNSCIENTIFIC
URTRICULARIA
VINDICTIVELY
WASHINGTONIA
WELLINFORMED
WELLINGTONIA
WILLIEWAUGHT
CLAMJAMPHRIE
READJUSTMENT
BLACKCURRANT
BREAKTHROUGH
BRICKFIELDER
CAMIKNICKERS
DRINKDRIVING
FRANKALMOIGN
FRANKENSTEIN
FRANKINCENSE
GLOCKENSPIEL
HANDKERCHIEF

SLOCKDOLAGER
SLOCKDOLIGER
SLOCKDOLOGER
SPECKTIONEER
STOCKBREEDER
STOCKINGETTE
THANKFULNESS
THANKSGIVING
THICKSKINNED
ACCELERATION
AMBULANCEMAN
ANTILEGOMENA
APFELSTRUDEL
APOLLINARIAN
ARTILLERYMAN
AVAILABILITY
BATTLEGROUND
BETHLEHEMITE
BEWILDERMENT
BRILLIANTINE
BUCKLEBEGGAR
CARELESSNESS
CHURLISHNESS
CIVILISATION
CIVILIZATION
COMPLACENTLY
COMPLETENESS
COMPLICATION
CONCLUSIVELY
CONGLOMERATE
DEBILITATING
DECELERATION
DEMILITARIZE
DISPLACEMENT
DOUBLEDECKER
DOUBLEGLAZED
EXHILARATING
EXHILARATION
FEARLESSNESS
FIDDLESTICKS
FINALIZATION
GENTLETAMPER
GESELLSCHAFT
GOBBLEDEGOOK
GOBBLEDYGOOK
HAMBLETONIAN
HELPLESSNESS
HOPELESSNESS
IDEALIZATION
IMPOLITENESS
INCALCULABLE
INFELICITOUS
INFILTRATION
INSALUBRIOUS
INSOLUBILITY
INTELLECTUAL
INTELLIGENCE
INTELLIGIBLE
INVALIDATION
INVULNERABLE
LAMELLICORNE
LEGALIZATION
LIFELESSNESS
LISTLESSNESS
LUXULLIANITE
MANSLAUGHTER
METALLOPHONE
METALLURGIST
MIDDLEWEIGHT
MISPLACEMENT
MOBILIZATION
MOONLIGHTING
MUCILAGINOUS
MUDDLEHEADED
MUGGLETONIAN
NEOCLASSICAL
NEOPLATONISM
NONALCOHOLIC
OBSOLESCENCE
OBSOLETENESS
OSCILLOSCOPE
PAINLESSNESS
PAPILIONIDAE
PARALIPOMENA
PENALIZATION
POSTLIMINARY
PRALLTRILLER
PROCLAMATION
RECALCITRANT
RECKLESSNESS
RECOLLECTION
RESTLESSNESS
RUTHLESSNESS
SCHILLERSPAR
SHILLYSHALLY
SIMULTANEOUS
SINGLEDECKER
SINGLEHANDED
SINGLEMINDED
SITTLICHKEIT
SMALLHOLDING
SPELLCHECKER
STEALTHINESS
STELLENBOSCH
SUPPLICATION
TACTLESSNESS
TAPSLETEERIE
TIMELESSNESS
TOTALITARIAN
UNBELIEVABLE
UNBELIEVABLY
UNCULTIVATED
ACCOMPANYING
ACCOMPLISHED
ACCUMULATION
AGALMATOLITE
ANTEMERIDIAN
ANTIMACASSAR
ANTIMETABOLE
ANTIMNEMONIC
ASSIMILATION
ASYMMETRICAL
BEAUMARCHAIS
BEAUMONTAGUE
BEAUMONTIQUE
BICAMERALISM
CALUMNIATION
CEREMONIALLY
CHREMATISTIC
DEHUMIDIFIER
DEMIMONDAINE
DENOMINATION
DISEMBARRASS
ELASMOBRANCH
ELEEMOSYNARY
ENTOMOLOGIST
ENTOMOSTRACA
HARUMFRODITE
HEADMISTRESS
ILLUMINATING
ILLUMINATION
INADMISSIBLE
INCOMPARABLE
INCOMPARABLY
INCOMPATIBLE
INCOMPETENCE
INCOMPLETELY
INNOMINABLES
INSEMINATION
INTEMPERANCE
INTIMIDATING
INTIMIDATION
LUXEMBOURGER
MADEMOISELLE
METAMORPHISM
METAMORPHOSE
PARAMILITARY
PERAMBULATOR
PEREMPTORILY
PHARMACOLOGY
POSTMISTRESS
POTAMOLOGIST
REDEMPTIONER
REMEMBRANCER
RODOMONTADER
SCRIMSHANDER
SCRIMSHANKER
SPERMATOCYTE
STORMTROOPER
STROMATOLITE
TARAMASALATA
THAUMATURGIC
THAUMATURGUS
THERMOSTATIC
THESMOPHORIA
THIGMOTROPIC
TRIUMPHANTLY
UNDEMOCRATIC
UNDIMINISHED
VERUMONTANUM
WHIGMALEERIE
ZALAMBDODONT
ACCENTUATION
ADMINISTRATE
ADMONISHMENT
ADVANTAGEOUS
ADVANTAGIOUS
ADVENTITIOUS
AERONAUTICAL
ANNUNCIATION
ANTANANARIVO
ANTINEUTRINO
ANTONINIANUS
APLANOGAMETE
APPENDECTOMY
APPENDICITIS
ARSENOPYRITE
ASTONISHMENT
AWEINSPIRING
BABINGTONITE
BAIRNSFATHER
BANANALANDER
BICENTENNIAL
BLENNORRHOEA
BRAINWASHING
BUSINESSLIKE
CABINETMAKER
CANONIZATION
CLANNISHNESS
COLONIZATION
DECENTRALISE
DECENTRALIZE
DECONGESTANT
DEGENERATION
DEMONSTRABLE
DEMONSTRABLY
DEMONSTRATOR
DENUNCIATION
DISENCHANTED
DISINCENTIVE
DISINFECTANT
DISINGENUOUS
DISINTEGRATE
ECCENTRICITY
ENTANGLEMENT
ESSENTIALITY
EULENSPIEGEL
EXTENSIONIST
EXTINGUISHER
FRIENDLINESS
GERONTOCRACY
GIGANTOMACHY
GREENGROCERS
GREENGROCERY
HUMANITARIAN
HUMANIZATION
IMMUNIZATION
IMMUNOLOGIST
IMPENETRABLE
INCANDESCENT

INCINERATION
INCONCLUSIVE
INCONSEQUENT
INCONSISTENT
INCONSOLABLE
INCONTINENCE
INCONVENIENT
INCUNABULIST
INTENERATION
JOURNALISTIC
LABANOTATION
LAMENTATIONS
LUMINESCENCE
LUMINISCENCE
LYMANTRIIDAE
MISANTHROPIC
MISINTERPRET
MYRINGOSCOPE
NEPENTHACEAE
NOCONFIDENCE
NOMENCLATURE
OCEANOGRAPHY
ORGANISATION
ORGANIZATION
ORIENTEERING
OSTENTATIOUS
PALINGENESIA
PALINGENESIS
PARANTHELIUM
PEDANTICALLY
PHRONTISTERY
PLAINCLOTHES
POTENTIALITY
RECONSTITUTE
REDINTEGRATE
REGENERATION
RELENTLESSLY
REMINISCENCE
REMONSTRANCE
REMUNERATION
REMUNERATIVE
RENUNCIATION
ROMANTICALLY
SCHINDYLESIS
SEMANTICALLY
SINANTHROPUS
SIPUNCULACEA
SPLENOMEGALY
STERNUTATION
STERNWHEELER
STRANGLEHOLD
STRANGLEWEED
STRINGCOURSE
STRONGMINDED
TECHNICALITY
TECHNOLOGIST
TITANOSAURUS
UNCONSIDERED
UNCONTROLLED
UNCONVERSANT
UNCONVINCING
UNMANAGEABLE
URBANIZATION
VALENCIENNES
ACKNOWLEDGED
AGAMOGENETIC
ANAMORPHOSIS
ANDROSTERONE
ANEMOPHILOUS
APPROACHABLE
ARTIODACTYLA
ASTROLOGICAL
ASTRONOMICAL
ASTROPHYSICS
BAMBOCCIADES
BEACONSFIELD
BIELORUSSIAN
BUNKOSTEERER
BYELORUSSIAN
CAMPODEIFORM
CARBOHYDRATE
CARLOVINGIAN
CARTOGRAPHER
CARTOGRAPHIC
CHEMOTHERAPY
CHIROPRACTIC
CHIROPRACTOR
COLLOQUIALLY
COMMONWEALTH
CONSOLIDATED
CONSOLIDATOR
COSMOPOLITAN
DIPLOGENESIS
DISCOMEDUSAE
DISCOMFITURE
DISCOMYCETES
DISCONCERTED
DISCONNECTED
DISCONSOLATE
DISCONTENTED
DISCOURAGING
DISCOURTEOUS
DISHONORABLE
DISHONORABLY
DISPOSSESSED
DISSOCIATION
ECONOMICALLY
EMBROIDERESS
ENCROACHMENT
EPANORTHOSIS
ERATOSTHENES
ETHNOLOGICAL
ETYMOLOGICAL
ETYMOLOGICON
EXPLOITATION
GEOLOGICALLY
GYMNOSOPHIST
HAEMOPHILIAC
HAEMORRHOIDS
HARMONIOUSLY
HELIOGABALUS
HIEROGLYPHIC
HIEROGRAMMAT
HIEROPHANTIC
HIPPOCRATISE
HIPPOCREPIAN
HIPPOPOTAMUS
HISTORICALLY
HYDROCHLORIC
HYDROGRAPHER
HYDROQUINONE
HYDROTHERAPY
HYMNOGRAPHER
HYPNOTHERAPY
HYPNOTICALLY
IAMBOGRAPHER
ICONOCLASTIC
IMPROVIDENCE
INTRODUCTION
INTRODUCTORY
LEGIONNAIRES
LINCOLNSHIRE
LITHOGRAPHIC
LITHOLATROUS
MACROPODIDAE
MALFORMATION
MALLOPHAGOUS
MARCOBRUNNER
MARCONIGRAPH
METHODICALLY
METROPOLITAN
MICROCLIMATE
MNEMOTECHNIC
MOSBOLLETJIE
MYTHOLOGICAL
NEUROLOGICAL
NEUROTICALLY
NEWFOUNDLAND
NONCOMMITTAL
OPHIOGLOSSUM
ORTHODONTICS
ORTHOGENESIS
ORTHOPAEDICS
ORTHOPAEDIST
ORTHORHOMBIC
ORTHOTONESIS
OSTEOMALACIA
OSTEOPOROSIS
PALEONTOLOGY
PANTOPHAGOUS
PATHOLOGICAL
PECTORILOQUY
PERIODICALLY
PERIOSTRACUM
PERNOCTATION
PERSONALIZED
PHENOMENALLY
PHILODENDRON
PHILOLOGICAL
PHILOSOPHIZE
PHOTOGLYPHIC
PHOTOGRAPHER
PHOTOGRAPHIC
PHOTOGRAVURE
PHYCOXANTHIN
PHYTOBENTHOS
PHYTONADIONE
PLEIOCHASIUM
PORNOGRAPHIC
PRECOCIOUSLY
PRECONDITION
PREDOMINANCE
PREMONSTRANT
PREPONDERANT
PREPONDERATE
PREPONDERENT
PREPOSSESSED
PREPOSTEROUS
PROLONGATION
PROPORTIONAL
PROSOPOPOEIA
PROTOPLASMAL
PROTOPLASMIC
PTERODACTYLE
PURPOSEBUILT
PURPOSEFULLY
PYTHONOMORPH
QUIXOTICALLY
RADIOGRAPHER
RADIOISOTOPE
RADIOTHERAPY
REPROCESSING
REPRODUCTION
REPRODUCTIVE
RESPONDENTIA
RHINORRHOEAL
RHODODENDRON
SARDONICALLY
SAUROGNATHAE
SCHOOLMASTER
SCOPOPHILIAC
SIPHONOPHORA
SIPHONOSTELE
SOCIOLOGICAL
STEGOPHOLIST
STENOGRAPHER
SUBCOMMITTEE
SUBCONSCIOUS
SUBCONTINENT
SURMOUNTABLE
SURROUNDINGS
SYMBOLICALLY
TAUTOLOGICAL
TELEOSAURIAN
TESTOSTERONE
TETRODOTOXIN
THOROUGHBRED
THOROUGHFARE
THOROUGHNESS
TRIGONOMETRY

TURBOCHARGER
UNECONOMICAL
UNPRODUCTIVE
UNPROFITABLE
YELLOWHAMMER
ANTIPARTICLE
CATAPHYSICAL
CHAMPIONSHIP
CLAPPERBOARD
CONSPECTUITY
DEASPIRATION
DECAPITATION
DECIPHERABLE
DECIPHERMENT
DEPOPULATION
DILAPIDATION
DISAPPEARING
DISAPPOINTED
ENHYPOSTASIA
ENTOPLASTRON
ESCAPOLOGIST
EXASPERATING
EXASPERATION
INAPPLICABLE
INCAPABILITY
INCAPACITATE
INDEPENDENCE
INEXPERIENCE
INEXPLICABLE
INEXPLICABLY
MANIPULATION
MANIPULATIVE
MASSPRODUCED
METAPHORICAL
METAPHYSICAL
MISAPPREHEND
NEWSPAPERMAN
OCCUPATIONAL
OREOPITHECUS
OREOPITHEOUS
OVERPOWERING
PERIPHRASTIC
PERSPICACITY
PERSPIRATION
PHOSPHORENCE
PHOSPHORESCE
POSTPONEMENT
POSTPRANDIAL
REAPPEARANCE
RECAPITULATE
RECEPTIONIST
RECIPROCALLY
RECUPERATION
RECUPERATIVE
REDEPLOYMENT
RESIPISCENCE
RHAMPHOTHECA
SCHOPENHAUER
SCRIPTWRITER
SCRUPULOUSLY
SELFPORTRAIT
SEMIPRECIOUS
SHARPSHOOTER
SHEEPISHNESS
SIVAPITHECUS
SLEEPWALKING
STEEPLECHASE
STREPITATION
STREPSIPTERA
STREPTOMYCIN
STREPTONEURA
STROPHANTHUS
THEOPHYLLINE
UNAPPARELLED
UNAPPETIZING
UNEMPLOYMENT
UNEXPECTEDLY
UNEXPURGATED
UNIMPORTANCE
UNOPPRESSIVE
UNPOPULARITY
VENEPUNCTURE
VITUPERATION
VITUPERATIVE
VOLUPTUOUSLY
WHIPPOORWILL
COLOQUINTIDA
HEADQUARTERS
HINDQUARTERS
MOUSQUETAIRE
OBSEQUIOUSLY
QUINQUENNIAL
TRANQUILIZER
TRANQUILLISE
TRANQUILLITY
TRANQUILLIZE
UNACQUAINTED
ACCORDIONIST
AETHRIOSCOPE
AFTEREFFECTS
AFTERTHOUGHT
AIRCRAFTSMAN
ANTHROPOLOGY
ANTIRACHITIC
APPURTENANCE
ARBORESCENCE
ARTHROPLASTY
ASPARAGINASE
ATHEROMATOUS
AUSTRALASIAN
AUSTRONESIAN
BIOGRAPHICAL
CAPERCAILLIE
CAPERCAILZIE
CHAIRMANSHIP
CHEERFULNESS
CHLORINATION
CLAIRVOYANCE
CLAIRVOYANCY
CLEARSIGHTED
COMPROMISING
CONGRATULATE
CONGREGATION
CONTRAPPOSTO
CONTRAPUNTAL
CONTRARINESS
CONTRIBUTION
CONTRIBUTORY
CONTRITURATE
CONTROLLABLE
DECORATIVELY
DENDROLOGIST
DEPARTMENTAL
DESIRABILITY
DIAGRAMMATIC
DISCRIMINATE
DISFRANCHISE
DISORGANIZED
DISORIENTATE
DISTRIBUTION
DISTRIBUTIVE
DIVERTICULUM
DIVERTIMENTO
EFFERVESCENT
EFFORTLESSLY
EMBARRASSING
ENCIRCLEMENT
ENTEROMORPHA
ENTEROPNEUST
ENTERPRISING
ENTERTAINING
EPACRIDACEAE
EPIGRAMMATIC
ETHEROMANIAC
EXPERIMENTAL
EXSERVICEMAN
EXTORTIONATE
FIGURATIVELY
FLUORESCENCE
FLUORIDATION
GASTROSOPHER
GEOGRAPHICAL
GOVERNMENTAL
HABERDASHERS
HABERDASHERY
HAMARTHRITIS
HETEROCLITIC
HETEROCONTAE
HETEROPHORIA
HETEROPLASIA
HETEROSEXUAL
HETEROSOMATA
HYPERBOLICAL
HYPERPYRETIC
HYPERSARCOMA
HYPERTENSION
IMPARTIALITY
IMPERFECTION
IMPERISHABLE
IMPERSONALLY
IMPERSONATOR
IMPERTINENCE
INCORPORATED
INCORRIGIBLE
INCORRIGIBLY
INFORMIDABLE
INHARMONIOUS
INSTRUCTIONS
INSTRUCTRESS
INSTRUMENTAL
INSURRECTION
INTERCEPTION
INTERCESSION
INTERCHANGED
INTERFERENCE
INTERJECTION
INTERLOCUTOR
INTERMEDIARY
INTERMEDIATE
INTERMINABLE
INTERMINABLY
INTERMISSION
INTERMITTENT
INTERPRETING
INTERRELATED
INTERROGATOR
INTERRUPTION
INTERSECTION
INTERSPERSED
INTERSTELLAR
INTERVENTION
INVERTEBRATE
LABYRINTHINE
LATIROSTRATE
LIVERPUDLIAN
MALPRACTICES
MALTREATMENT
MINERALOGIST
MISPRONOUNCE
MISTREATMENT
MOTORCYCLIST
NATURALISTIC
NEVERTHELESS
OBSERVANTINE
OBSTREPEROUS
ONCORHYNCHUS
ONEIROCRITIC
OTHERWORLDLY
POLARIZATION
POWERSHARING
PROGRAMMABLE
PROPRIETRESS
QUADRAGESIMA
QUADRAPHONIC
RECORDPLAYER
REPERCUSSION
RESURRECTION
RETARDEDNESS
REVERSIONARY
RISORGIMENTO

SCLERENCHYMA
SCLERODERMIA
SCURRILOUSLY
SUBARRHATION
SUPERANNUATE
SUPERCHARGED
SUPERCHARGER
SUPERCILIARY
SUPERCILIOUS
SUPERHIGHWAY
SUPERNACULUM
SUPERNATURAL
SUPERSTITION
SURPRISINGLY
TAMARICACEAE
TAPERECORDER
THEORETICIAN
TUBERCULOSIS
ULOTRICHALES
UNDERACHIEVE
UNDERCLOTHES
UNDERCURRENT
UNDEREXPOSED
UNDERGARMENT
UNDERPINNING
UNDERSKINKER
UNDERSTAFFED
UNDERWRITTEN
UNPARALLELED
UNPARDONABLE
UNSCRUPULOUS
UNSURPRISING
VAPORIZATION
VENTRIPOTENT
VETERINARIAN
WATERCARRIER
ADVISABILITY
AMBASSADRESS
ANAESTHETISE
ANAESTHETIST
ANAESTHETIZE
ANTISTROPHON
ARTISTICALLY
ATMOSPHERICS
BARNSTORMING
BLUESTOCKING
BREASTPLOUGH
BREASTSUMMER
CATASTROPHIC
CHEESEBURGER
CHEESEMONGER
CHEESEPARING
CHRESTOMATHY
CHRISTIANITY
CLASSIFIABLE
CLEISTOGAMIC
COLDSHOULDER
CRASSAMENTUM
CROSSBENCHER
CROSSCOUNTRY

CROSSEXAMINE
CROSSSECTION
DERESTRICTED
DISASTROUSLY
DOMESTICATED
DRESSINGDOWN
EAVESDROPPER
FELDSPATHOID
FOOTSLOGGING
GAINSBOROUGH
GAMESMANSHIP
GRASSWIDOWER
GROSSULARITE
HAIRSPLITTER
HOMESICKNESS
IDIOSYNCRASY
ILLUSTRATION
ILLUSTRATIVE
INAUSPICIOUS
INDISCRETION
INDISPUTABLE
INDISPUTABLY
INDISSOLUBLE
INDISTINCTLY
INDUSTRIALLY
INHOSPITABLE
INVESTIGATOR
INVISIBILITY
IRRESISTIBLE
IRRESOLUTELY
IRRESOLUTION
IRRESOLVABLE
IRRESPECTIVE
JURISDICTION
KALISTOCRACY
KLIPSPRINGER
LONGSHOREMAN
LONGSTANDING
MAJESTICALLY
MARKSMANSHIP
MERISTEMATIC
MINISTRATION
MONOSYLLABIC
MONOSYLLABLE
MUTESSARIFAT
OCCASIONALLY
OCTASTROPHIC
OVERSCUTCHED
OVERSTRAINED
PENNSYLVANIA
PERISTERONIC
PLAUSIBILITY
POLYSYLLABIC
POLYSYLLABLE
POLYSYNDETON
PRAISEWORTHY
REDISCOVERED
REDISTRIBUTE
REGISTRATION
REPOSSESSION

RESUSCITATED
SADISTICALLY
SALESMANSHIP
SATISFACTION
SATISFACTORY
SECESSIONIST
SERASKIERATE
SPINSTERHOOD
THESSALONIAN
TRANSACTIONS
TRANSCENDENT
TRANSFERABLE
TRANSFERENCE
TRANSGRESSOR
TRANSITIONAL
TRANSLATABLE
TRANSLUCENCE
TRANSMIGRATE
TRANSMISSION
TRANSMOGRIFY
TRANSOCEANIC
TRANSPARENCY
TRANSPONTINE
TRANSVESTISM
TRANSVESTITE
UNANSWERABLE
UNDESERVEDLY
UNDISCHARGED
UNMISTAKABLE
UNOBSTRUCTED
UNRESERVEDLY
UNRESPONSIVE
UNRESTRAINED
UNRESTRICTED
UNSUSPECTING
WHIMSICALITY
WILTSHIREMAN
YORKSHIREMAN
ADAPTABILITY
ADDITIONALLY
ADULTERATION
ALLITERATION
ANTITHROMBIN
APOSTROPHISE
ARISTOCRATIC
ARISTOLOCHIA
ARISTOPHANES
ARISTOTELEAN
AYUNTAMIENTO
BOISTEROUSLY
BREATHALYSER
BREATHLESSLY
BREATHTAKING
BRONTOSAURUS
CAPITULATION
CHARTERHOUSE
CHASTISEMENT
CHESTERFIELD
CHITTERLINGS
CONSTABULARY

CONSTIPATION
CONSTITUENCY
CONSTITUENTS
CONSTITUTION
CONSTRICTION
CONSTRUCTION
CONSTRUCTIVE
COUNTERBLAST
COUNTERCLAIM
COUNTERMARCH
COUNTERPOINT
COUNTERPOISE
COURTMARTIAL
COVETOUSNESS
CREATIVENESS
CRISTOBALITE
CRYPTOGRAPHY
CYMOTRICHOUS
DILATORINESS
EGYPTOLOGIST
ELECTRICALLY
ELECTROLYSIS
ELECTROPLATE
ELECTROTONUS
ENANTIOMORPH
ENANTIOPATHY
EPISTEMOLOGY
EPISTOLATERS
EVENTEMPERED
EXCITABILITY
FAINTHEARTED
FIRSTFOOTING
FLITTERMOUSE
FRACTIONALLY
FRONTIERSMAN
FRONTISPIECE
FRUITFULNESS
FUNCTIONALLY
FUNCTIONLESS
GENETHLIACON
HEARTSTRINGS
HEARTWARMING
HEPHTHEMIMER
HOMOTHERMOUS
HYPOTHECATOR
HYPOTHETICAL
IDENTIFIABLE
IDIOTHERMOUS
IMMUTABILITY
INARTICULATE
INEXTRICABLE
INEXTRICABLY
INNATTENTIVE
IRRATIONALLY
IRRITABILITY
KLEPTOMANIAC
KLETTERSCHUE
LEGITIMATELY
LEIOTRICHOUS
LICKTRENCHER

LIGHTHEARTED
MENSTRUATION
MERETRICIOUS
MERITRICIOUS
MESOTHELIOMA
MILITARISTIC
MISSTATEMENT
MOISTURIZING
MONOTONOUSLY
NIGHTCLOTHES
NYCHTHEMERON
OBLITERATION
OPISTHOGRAPH
ORNITHOGALUM
OUTSTRETCHED
PANATHENAEAN
PENITENTIARY
PLASTERSTONE
PLECTOGNATHI
POINTILLISME
PRACTICALITY
PRACTICIONER
PRACTITIONER
PRESTRICTION
PROSTITUTION
PYROTECHNICS
QUANTIFIABLE
QUANTITATIVE
QUARTERFINAL
QUARTERLIGHT
QUARTERSTAFF
QUESTIONABLE
QUINTESSENCE
RELATIONSHIP
REPATRIATION
RESETTLEMENT
SCATTERBRAIN
SCATTERMOUCH
SCINTILLATOR
SHIRTSLEEVES
SHIRTWAISTER
SHORTCIRCUIT
SHORTCOMINGS
SHORTSIGHTED
SHORTSLEEVED
SHORTSTAFFED
SHOSTAKOVICH
SKUTTERUDITE
SOMATOPLEURE
SPECTROSCOPE
SPORTSGROUND
SPURTLEBLADE
STENTORPHONE
STRATOSPHERE
SUBSTANTIATE
SUBSTITUTION
SUBSTRUCTURE
THEATRICALLY
TIGHTFITTING
TOGETHERNESS

TRACTABILITY
UNATTAINABLE
UNATTRACTIVE
UNAUTHORISED
UNAUTHORIZED
UNDETECTABLE
UNDETERMINED
UNFATHOMABLE
UNINTERESTED
UNOBTAINABLE
UNRETURNABLE
UNSATISFYING
UNUTTERABLES
WOLSTENHOLME
ZARATHUSTRIC
ABSQUATULATE
ACCOUCHEMENT
ACCOUTREMENT
ANDOUILLETTE
ANNOUNCEMENT
AUSCULTATION
BLEFUSCUDIAN
CIRCUMCISION
CIRCUMGYRATE
CIRCUMSCRIBE
CIRCUMSTANCE
COLLUCTATION
COMMUNICABLE
COMPURGATION
CONCURRENTLY
CONDUCTIVITY
CONQUISTADOR
CONSULTATION
CONSULTATIVE
CONSUMMATION
CONTUMACIOUS
CURMUDGEONLY
DISQUISITION
ENTHUSIASTIC
EVOLUTIONARY
EXCRUCIATING
EXCRUCIATION
EXHAUSTIVELY
FORTUITOUSLY
HALLUCINOGEN
INCAUTIOUSLY
INCRUSTATION
KERAUNOGRAPH
LABOURSAVING
LANGUEDOCIAN
MALNUTRITION
MASTURBATION
MISQUOTATION
OUTBUILDINGS
PERSUASIVELY
PERSULPHURIC
PERTURBATION
POLYURETHANE
PREGUSTATION
PRESUMPTUOUS

PRODUCTIVITY
PROMULGATION
PROTUBERANCE
RAMBUNCTIOUS
RECRUDESCENT
RENOUNCEMENT
SARRUSOPHONE
SCAPULIMANCY
SEPTUAGESIMA
SESQUIALTERA
SESQUITERTIA
SUBCUTANEOUS
SUCCUSSATION
TELEUTOSPORE
UNCTUOUSNESS
BEHAVIOURISM
BENEVOLENTLY
CARAVANSERAI
CHAUVINISTIC
EQUIVOCATION
EQUIVOCATORY
IMPOVERISHED
INADVERTENCE
INDIVIDUALLY
IRREVERENTLY
IRREVERSIBLE
REINVIGORATE
REJUVENATION
UNFAVOURABLE
BACKWARDNESS
BACKWOODSMAN
BIRDWATCHING
GONDWANALAND
OVERWHELMING
SIDEWHISKERS
INTOXICATING
INTOXICATION
NONEXISTENCE
ASPHYXIATION
BOOBYTRAPPED
COLLYWOBBLES
HAPPYGOLUCKY
JENNYSPINNER
MERRYTHOUGHT
PROGYMNASIUM
WALLYDRAIGLE
EMBEZZLEMENT
HORIZONTALLY
SCHIZOMYCETE
SWIZZLESTICK

12:6

ABSQUATULATE
ADAPTABILITY
ADVISABILITY
AERONAUTICAL
AGALMATOLITE
AIRCRAFTSMAN
AMALGAMATION

AMBULANCEMAN
ANTANANARIVO
ANTIBACCHIUS
ANTIBARBARUS
ANTIMACASSAR
ANTIPARTICLE
ANTIRACHITIC
APPROACHABLE
ASPARAGINASE
AUSTRALASIAN
AVAILABILITY
AYUNTAMIENTO
BACCHANALIAN
BACKWARDNESS
BANANALANDER
BEAUMARCHAIS
BENEFACTRESS
BIOGRAPHICAL
BIRDWATCHING
CALCEAMENTUM
CARAVANSERAI
CARICATURIST
CARTHAGINIAN
CHREMATISTIC
CLAMJAMPHRIE
COMPLACENTLY
CONGRATULATE
CONSTABULARY
CONTRAPPOSTO
CONTRAPUNTAL
CONTRARINESS
CRASSAMENTUM
DECORATIVELY
DELICATESSEN
DESIRABILITY
DIAGRAMMATIC
DISFRANCHISE
DISPLACEMENT
ENCROACHMENT
ENTREATINGLY
EPIGRAMMATIC
EPITHALAMION
EPITHALAMIUM
EVENHANDEDLY
EXCITABILITY
EXHILARATING
EXHILARATION
FIGURATIVELY
FRANKALMOIGN
GEOGRAPHICAL
GLADIATORIAL
GONDWANALAND
HIGHFALUTING
HOLIDAYMAKER
IMMUTABILITY
INCAPABILITY
INCAPACITATE
INCREASINGLY
INCUNABULIST
IRRITABILITY

JOURNALISTIC
LAUREATESHIP
MALLEABILITY
MALPRACTICES
MANSLAUGHTER
MANUFACTURER
MARRIAGEABLE
MILITARISTIC
MINERALOGIST
MISPLACEMENT
MISSTATEMENT
MUCILAGINOUS
NATURALISTIC
NAVIGABILITY
NEOCLASSICAL
NEOPLATONISM
NEWSPAPERMAN
NONCHALANTLY
OCCUPATIONAL
PALUDAMENTUM
PANCHATANTRA
PANPHARMACON
PERICARDITIS
PERMEABILITY
PERSUASIVELY
PHARMACOLOGY
PHILHARMONIC
POPOCATEPETL
PROCLAMATION
PROGRAMMABLE
PROTHALAMION
PROTHALAMIUM
QUADRAGESIMA
QUADRAPHONIC
RECREATIONAL
SCANDALOUSLY
SELFCATERING
SEPTUAGESIMA
SHOSTAKOVICH
SPERMATOCYTE
STAKHANOVITE
STEPDAUGHTER
STROMATOLITE
SUBSTANTIATE
SUPERANNUATE
SURREALISTIC
TAGLIACOTIAN
TARAMASALATA
THAUMATURGIC
THAUMATURGUS
THEREAGAINST
THESSALONIAN
TRACTABILITY
TRANSACTIONS
TROPHALLAXIS
UNAPPARELLED
UNATTAINABLE
UNDERACHIEVE
UNMANAGEABLE
UNOBTAINABLE
UNPARALLELED
WELLBALANCED
WHIGMALEERIE
ALPHABETICAL
ATTRIBUTABLE
AWAYABSOLUTE
CHILDBEARING
COLLABORATOR
CONTABESCENT
CROSSBENCHER
DISEMBARRASS
GAINSBOROUGH
HILDEBRANDIC
HOUSEBREAKER
HYPERBOLICAL
LILLIBULLERO
LILLIBURLERO
LUXEMBOURGER
MARCOBRUNNER
MOUTHBROODER
NEIGHBORHOOD
NEIGHBOURING
PERAMBULATOR
PHYTOBENTHOS
PROTUBERANCE
REMEMBRANCER
STOCKBREEDER
SWASHBUCKLER
THIRDBOROUGH
ZALAMBDODONT
ACCOUCHEMENT
ANNUNCIATION
APPRECIATION
APPRECIATIVE
ATTRACTIVELY
AUSPICIOUSLY
BAMBOCCIADES
BLACKCURRANT
BROADCASTING
CAPERCAILLIE
CAPERCAILZIE
CHALICOTHERE
CHARACTERIZE
CLAVICEMBALO
COLLECTIVELY
COLLECTORATE
COLLUCTATION
CONDUCTIVITY
CONFECTIONER
CONSECRATION
CROSSCOUNTRY
DENUNCIATION
DEPRECIATION
DEPRECIATORY
DIALECTICIAN
DISACCHARIDE
DISENCHANTED
DISINCENTIVE
DISSOCIATION
ENCIRCLEMENT
EXCRUCIATING
EXCRUCIATION
FLORICULTURE
HALLUCINOGEN
HEROICOMICAL
HIPPOCRATISE
HIPPOCREPIAN
HORTICULTURE
HYDROCHLORIC
ICONOCLASTIC
INCALCULABLE
INCONCLUSIVE
INDISCRETION
INEXACTITUDE
INSPECTORATE
INTERCEPTION
INTERCESSION
INTERCHANGED
MICROCLIMATE
MOTORCYCLIST
MULTICOLORED
NIGHTCLOTHES
NOMENCLATURE
NONALCOHOLIC
OVERSCUTCHED
PANTECHNICON
PARTICOLORED
PARTICULARLY
PERNOCTATION
PERVICACIOUS
PISCICULTURE
PLAINCLOTHES
PLEIOCHASIUM
PRECOCIOUSLY
PRODUCTIVITY
PROFICIENTLY
PROTACTINIUM
PROTECTIVELY
PROTECTORATE
PUGNACIOUSLY
RECALCITRANT
REDISCOVERED
RENUNCIATION
REPERCUSSION
REPROCESSING
RESPECTFULLY
RESPECTIVELY
RESUSCITATED
SERVICEWOMAN
SHORTCIRCUIT
SHORTCOMINGS
SIPUNCULACEA
SOUTHCOTTIAN
SPELLCHECKER
SPINECHILLER
STONECHATTER
SUBJECTIVELY
SUBJECTIVITY
SUFFICIENTLY
SUPERCHARGED
SUPERCHARGER
SUPERCILIARY
SUPERCILIOUS
SUSPICIOUSLY
TETRACYCLINE
TOBACCONISTS
TORRICELLIAN
TRABECULATED
TRANSCENDENT
TUBERCULOSIS
TURBOCHARGER
UNDERCLOTHES
UNDERCURRENT
UNDISCHARGED
UNSUCCESSFUL
URTRICULARIA
VALENCIENNES
VINDICTIVELY
WATERCARRIER
ACCORDIONIST
APPENDECTOMY
APPENDICITIS
ARFVEDSONITE
ARTIODACTYLA
BEWILDERMENT
CAMPODEIFORM
COCCIDIOSTAT
CONFIDENTIAL
CONSIDERABLE
CONSIDERABLY
CURMUDGEONLY
DRINKDRIVING
EAVESDROPPER
EXTRADITABLE
FASTIDIOUSLY
FRIENDLINESS
GLUBBDUBDRIB
HABERDASHERS
HABERDASHERY
HOBBIDIDANCE
INCANDESCENT
INERADICABLE
INTRODUCTION
INTRODUCTORY
JURISDICTION
KALEIDOSCOPE
LAMPADEDROMY
METHODICALLY
ORTHODONTICS
PERIODICALLY
PHILODENDRON
PRESIDENTIAL
PROVIDENTIAL
PTERIDOPHYTE
PTERODACTYLE
RECORDPLAYER
RECRUDESCENT
REPRODUCTION
REPRODUCTIVE
RETARDEDNESS

RHIPIDOPTERA
RHODODENDRON
RHYTIDECTOMY
SCHINDYLESIS
SELFADHESIVE
SLOCKDOLAGER
SLOCKDOLIGER
SLOCKDOLOGER
SPORADICALLY
SPREADEAGLED
SUBSIDIARITY
TETRODOTOXIN
THREADNEEDLE
UMBRADARLING
UNPARDONABLE
UNPRODUCTIVE
WALLYDRAIGLE
ACCELERATION
ACCIDENTALLY
ACQUIESCENCE
ADULTERATION
AFTEREFFECTS
ALLITERATION
AMBIDEXTROUS
ANTEMERIDIAN
ANTILEGOMENA
ANTIMETABOLE
ANTINEUTRINO
ARBORESCENCE
ASYMMETRICAL
BATTLEGROUND
BETHLEHEMITE
BICAMERALISM
BIOCHEMISTRY
BLABBERMOUTH
BLETHERSKATE
BOISTEROUSLY
BUCKLEBEGGAR
BUSINESSLIKE
CABINETMAKER
CARELESSNESS
CHARTERHOUSE
CHEESEBURGER
CHEESEMONGER
CHEESEPARING
CHESTERFIELD
CHITTERLINGS
CLAPPERBOARD
COMPLETENESS
CONGREGATION
CONSPECTUITY
COUNTERBLAST
COUNTERCLAIM
COUNTERMARCH
COUNTERPOINT
COUNTERPOISE
CROSSEXAMINE
DECELERATION
DEGENERATION
DELIBERATELY
DELIBERATION
DIENCEPHALON
DISOBEDIENCE
DOUBLEDECKER
DOUBLEGLAZED
DUNNIEWASSAL
EPENCEPHALON
EPIPHENOMENA
EPISTEMOLOGY
EVENTEMPERED
EXAGGERATION
EXASPERATING
EXASPERATION
FEARLESSNESS
FEATHERBRAIN
FEHMGERICHTE
FIDDLESTICKS
FLITTERMOUSE
FLUORESCENCE
FRANKENSTEIN
GENTLETAMPER
GLOCKENSPIEL
GLYNDEBOURNE
GOBBLEDEGOOK
GOBBLEDYGOOK
GUILDENSTERN
HAMBLETONIAN
HANDKERCHIEF
HELPLESSNESS
HOPELESSNESS
IMMODERATELY
IMMODERATION
IMPENETRABLE
IMPOVERISHED
INACCESSIBLE
INADVERTENCE
INCIDENTALLY
INCINERATION
INCOHERENTLY
INDEFENSIBLE
INDEPENDENCE
INDIGESTIBLE
INEXPERIENCE
INTENERATION
IRREDEEMABLE
IRREVERENTLY
IRREVERSIBLE
ISHMAELITISH
KLETTERSCHUE
LANGUEDOCIAN
LIFELESSNESS
LISTLESSNESS
LUMINESCENCE
MACABERESQUE
MALTREATMENT
MIDDLEWEIGHT
MISTREATMENT
MUDDLEHEADED
MUGGLETONIAN
NONAGENARIAN
NORTHEASTERN
NORTHERNMOST
OBEDIENTIARY
OBLITERATION
OBSOLESCENCE
OBSOLETENESS
OBSTREPEROUS
OCTOGENARIAN
OXYACETYLENE
PAINLESSNESS
PANDAEMONIUM
PARACENTESIS
PEDICELLARIA
PENITENTIARY
PINNIEWINKLE
PLASTERSTONE
PRAISEWORTHY
PSIPHENOMENA
PYROTECHNICS
QUARTERFINAL
QUARTERLIGHT
QUARTERSTAFF
QUINTESSENCE
REAPPEARANCE
RECKLESSNESS
RECUPERATION
RECUPERATIVE
REGENERATION
REJUVENATION
REMUNERATION
REMUNERATIVE
RESTLESSNESS
RUTHLESSNESS
SCATTERBRAIN
SCATTERMOUCH
SCHEHERAZADE
SCHOPENHAUER
SCLERENCHYMA
SEMIDETACHED
SEXAGENARIAN
SINGLEDECKER
SINGLEHANDED
SINGLEMINDED
SKUTTERUDITE
SLUBBERINGLY
SOUTHEASTERN
SOUTHERNMOST
SOUTHERNWOOD
SPHACELATION
SPIEGELEISEN
STAGGERINGLY
STELLENBOSCH
SYNADELPHITE
TACTLESSNESS
TAPERECORDER
TAPSLETEERIE
THEORETICIAN
THUNDERCLOUD
THUNDERFLASH
THUNDERSTORM
TIMELESSNESS
TROCHELMINTH
UNACCEPTABLE
UNAPPETIZING
UNDEREXPOSED
UNDESERVEDLY
UNDETECTABLE
UNDETERMINED
UNEXPECTEDLY
UNINTERESTED
UNRESERVEDLY
UNSCIENTIFIC
UNUTTERABLES
VEHMGERICHTE
VITUPERATION
VITUPERATIVE
VOCIFERATION
VOCIFEROUSLY
WEATHERPROOF
WILLIEWAUGHT
WOLSTENHOLME
ASSUEFACTION
BRICKFIELDER
CHEERFULNESS
DISINFECTANT
EXSUFFLICATE
FAITHFULNESS
FIRSTFOOTING
FORCEFULNESS
FRUITFULNESS
GRACEFULNESS
GRATEFULNESS
HARUMFRODITE
HENCEFORWARD
HORRIFICALLY
IMPERFECTION
INDIFFERENCE
INSUFFERABLE
INSUFFERABLY
INSUFFICIENT
INTERFERENCE
LIQUEFACTION
MAGNIFICENCE
MULTIFARIOUS
NOCONFIDENCE
PEACEFULNESS
PETRIFACTION
PETTIFOGGERS
PETTIFOGGERY
PETTIFOGGING
PRIZEFIGHTER
PROLIFICALLY
PUTREFACTION
SATISFACTION
SATISFACTORY
SHAMEFACEDLY
SIGNIFICANCE
SPECIFICALLY
SPITEFULNESS
STUPEFACTION

TERRIFICALLY
THANKFULNESS
TIGHTFITTING
TRANSFERABLE
TRANSFERENCE
TRUTHFULNESS
UNPROFITABLE
VENGEFULNESS
WATCHFULNESS
YOUTHFULNESS
AGAMOGENETIC
APPOGGIATURA
BABINGTONITE
BELLIGERENCY
CALLIGRAPHIC
CARTOGRAPHER
CARTOGRAPHIC
CONTIGNATION
COURAGEOUSLY
DECONGESTANT
DIPLOGENESIS
DISINGENUOUS
DISORGANIZED
ENTANGLEMENT
EXTINGUISHER
GALLIGASKINS
GEOLOGICALLY
GREENGROCERS
GREENGROCERY
HAPPYGOLUCKY
HELIOGABALUS
HIEROGLYPHIC
HIEROGRAMMAT
HYDROGRAPHER
HYMNOGRAPHER
IAMBOGRAPHER
IMPREGNATION
LITHOGRAPHIC
MASTIGOPHORA
MULLIGATAWNY
MYRINGOSCOPE
OPHIOGLOSSUM
ORTHOGENESIS
OUTRAGEOUSLY
PALINGENESIA
PALINGENESIS
PHOTOGLYPHIC
PHOTOGRAPHER
PHOTOGRAPHIC
PHOTOGRAVURE
PORNOGRAPHIC
PRODIGIOUSLY
PROLEGOMENON
PROPAGANDISM
PROPAGANDIST
RADIOGRAPHER
REFRIGERATED
REFRIGERATOR
RISORGIMENTO
SAUROGNATHAE
STENOGRAPHER
STRAIGHTAWAY
STRAIGHTEDGE
STRAIGHTNESS
STRANGLEHOLD
STRANGLEWEED
STRINGCOURSE
STRONGMINDED
SYNTAGMATITE
TRANSGRESSOR
UNDERGARMENT
UNIMAGINABLE
UNNEIGHBORLY
VILLEGIATURA
ANTITHROMBIN
APPREHENSION
APPREHENSIVE
BRANCHIOPODA
BREATHALYSER
BREATHLESSLY
BREATHTAKING
CARBOHYDRATE
CATAPHYSICAL
CHURCHWARDEN
COLDSHOULDER
DECIPHERABLE
DECIPHERMENT
FAINTHEARTED
FREIGHTLINER
GENETHLIACON
HEMICHORDATA
HEPHTHEMIMER
HOMOTHERMOUS
HYPOCHONDRIA
HYPOTHECATOR
HYPOTHETICAL
IDIOTHERMOUS
KIRSCHWASSER
LIGHTHEARTED
LONGSHOREMAN
MESOTHELIOMA
METAPHORICAL
METAPHYSICAL
MISBEHAVIOUR
NYCHTHEMERON
ONCORHYNCHUS
OPISTHOGRAPH
ORNITHOGALUM
OVERWHELMING
PANATHENAEAN
PERIPHRASTIC
PHOSPHORENCE
PHOSPHORESCE
POTICHOMANIA
RHAMPHOTHECA
SHAREHOLDING
SIDEWHISKERS
SMALLHOLDING
STROPHANTHUS
SUPERHIGHWAY
TETRAHEDRITE
THEOPHYLLINE
THOUGHTFULLY
TOGETHERNESS
UNAUTHORISED
UNAUTHORIZED
UNFATHOMABLE
WHOLEHEARTED
WILTSHIREMAN
WRETCHEDNESS
YORKSHIREMAN
ZARATHUSTRIC
ACQUAINTANCE
ADDITIONALLY
ADJUDICATION
ADMINISTRATE
ADMONISHMENT
AECIDIOSPORE
AETHRIOSCOPE
ANDOUILLETTE
ANNIHILATION
ANTEDILUVIAN
ANTICIPATION
ANTICIPATORY
ANTONINIANUS
APOLLINARIAN
ARTIFICIALLY
ASSIMILATION
ASTONISHMENT
BEHAVIOURISM
BLANDISHMENT
BOUGAINVILLE
BRILLIANTINE
CANONIZATION
CATADIOPTRIC
CHAMPIONSHIP
CHASTISEMENT
CHAUVINISTIC
CHILDISHNESS
CHLORINATION
CHURLISHNESS
CIVILISATION
CIVILIZATION
CLANNISHNESS
CLASSIFIABLE
CLAUDICATION
CODIFICATION
COHABITATION
COINCIDENTAL
COLONIZATION
COMPLICATION
CONQUISTADOR
CONSTIPATION
CONSTITUENCY
CONSTITUENTS
CONSTITUTION
CONTRIBUTION
CONTRIBUTORY
CONTRITURATE
COORDINATION
CREATIVENESS
CREMAILLIÈRE
DEASPIRATION
DEBILITATING
DECAPITATION
DEHUMIDIFIER
DEMILITARIZE
DENOMINATION
DILAPIDATION
DISCRIMINATE
DISDAINFULLY
DISORIENTATE
DISQUISITION
DISTRIBUTION
DISTRIBUTIVE
DOLPHINARIUM
DRESSINGDOWN
EMANCIPATION
EMBROIDERESS
ENANTIOMORPH
ENANTIOPATHY
ENCHEIRIDION
EPACRIDACEAE
EPIDEICTICAL
EXHIBITIONER
EXPERIMENTAL
EXPLOITATION
FARTHINGLAND
FINALIZATION
FLUORIDATION
FORTUITOUSLY
FRACTIONALLY
FRANKINCENSE
FRONTIERSMAN
FRONTISPIECE
FUNCTIONALLY
FUNCTIONLESS
GRANDISONIAN
GUARDIANSHIP
HEADMISTRESS
HEREDITAMENT
HOMESICKNESS
HUMANITARIAN
HUMANIZATION
IDEALIZATION
IDENTIFIABLE
ILLEGIBILITY
ILLEGITIMACY
ILLEGITIMATE
ILLOGICALITY
ILLUMINATING
ILLUMINATION
IMMUNIZATION
IMPERISHABLE
IMPOLITENESS
INADMISSIBLE
INARTICULATE
INDEFINITELY
INDIVIDUALLY
INEFFICIENCY

INFELICITOUS
INNOMINABLES
INORDINATELY
INSEMINATION
INTIMIDATING
INTIMIDATION
INTOXICATING
INTOXICATION
INVALIDATION
INVISIBILITY
IRASCIBILITY
IRRATIONALLY
IRRESISTIBLE
LABYRINTHINE
LEGALIZATION
LEGITIMATELY
LONGDISTANCE
LUMINISCENCE
MACHAIRODONT
MARSEILLAISE
MERVEILLEUSE
MITRAILLEUSE
MOBILIZATION
MODIFICATION
MOONLIGHTING
MUNICIPALITY
NONEXISTENCE
NOTIFICATION
OCCASIONALLY
OREOPITHECUS
OREOPITHEOUS
ORGANISATION
ORGANIZATION
OSSIFICATION
OUTBUILDINGS
PACIFICATION
PAPILIONIDAE
PARALIPOMENA
PARAMILITARY
PENALIZATION
PERSPICACITY
PERSPIRATION
PLAUSIBILITY
POINTILLISME
POLARIZATION
POSTLIMINARY
POSTMISTRESS
PRACTICALITY
PRACTICIONER
PRACTITIONER
PRIGGISHNESS
PRINCIPALITY
PROPRIETRESS
PROSTITUTION
PSYCHIATRIST
PURIFICATION
QUANTIFIABLE
QUANTITATIVE
QUESTIONABLE
RADIOISOTOPE
RAMIFICATION
RATIFICATION
RECAPITULATE
REHABILITATE
REINVIGORATE
RELATIONSHIP
REMINISCENCE
RESIPISCENCE
SCANDINAVIAN
SCHNEIDERIAN
SCINTILLATOR
SCURRILOUSLY
SEMICIRCULAR
SESQUIALTERA
SESQUITERTIA
SHEEPISHNESS
SITTLICHKEIT
SIVAPITHECUS
SNOBBISHNESS
SOLICITATION
SOLICITOUSLY
STOCKINGETTE
STRADIVARIUS
STREPITATION
STRIGIFORMES
SUBSTITUTION
SUPPLICATION
SURPRISINGLY
SURVEILLANCE
TAMARICACEAE
TECHNICALITY
TOTALITARIAN
TRANSITIONAL
ULOTRICHALES
UNBELIEVABLE
UNBELIEVABLY
UNDIMINISHED
UNOFFICIALLY
UNSATISFYING
URBANIZATION
VAPORIZATION
VENTRIPOTENT
VERIFICATION
VETERINARIAN
VILIFICATION
WHIMSICALITY
INTERJECTION
UNPREJUDICED
HOUSEKEEPING
KILLIKINNICK
PEACEKEEPING
SERASKIERATE
ANTHELMINTIC
ARCHILOCHIAN
ARTILLERYMAN
ASTROLOGICAL
AUSCULTATION
BERTILLONAGE
CANCELLATION
CANTILEVERED
COMPELLATION
CONCILIATION
CONCILIATORY
CONSOLIDATED
CONSOLIDATOR
CONSULTATION
CONSULTATIVE
CONVALESCENT
CONVALESCING
CRASHLANDING
DISTILLATION
DYSTELEOLOGY
ENCYCLOPEDIA
ENCYCLOPEDIC
ENTOPLASTRON
ETHNOLOGICAL
ETYMOLOGICAL
ETYMOLOGICON
FLAGELLATION
FOOTSLOGGING
FORMALDEHYDE
FUSTILLIRIAN
GENEALOGICAL
GESELLSCHAFT
GIBRALTARIAN
INAPPLICABLE
INDECLINABLE
INEXPLICABLE
INEXPLICABLY
INSTALLATION
INTELLECTUAL
INTELLIGENCE
INTELLIGIBLE
INTERLOCUTOR
ISOBILATERAL
LAMELLICORNE
LINCOLNSHIRE
LITHOLATROUS
LUXULLIANITE
MACMILLANITE
MAGNILOQUENT
MANGELWURZEL
METALLOPHONE
METALLURGIST
MICHELANGELO
MISCALCULATE
MISDELIVERED
MOSBOLLETJIE
MULTILATERAL
MYTHOLOGICAL
NEPHELOMETER
NEUROLOGICAL
OSCILLOSCOPE
PATHOLOGICAL
PERSULPHURIC
PESTILENTIAL
PHILOLOGICAL
PREDILECTION
PROMULGATION
RECOLLECTION
REDEPLOYMENT
SACRILEGIOUS
SCAPULIMANCY
SCHILLERSPAR
SCHOOLMASTER
SHUFFLEBOARD
SOCIOLOGICAL
SPURTLEBLADE
STEEPLECHASE
SWIZZLESTICK
SYMBOLICALLY
TAPSALTEERIE
TAUTOLOGICAL
TRANSLATABLE
TRANSLUCENCE
TROUBLEMAKER
UNCHALLENGED
UNEMPLOYMENT
VAINGLORIOUS
ACADEMICALLY
ACHLAMYDEOUS
ARITHMETICAL
BANTAMWEIGHT
CHAIRMANSHIP
CIRCUMCISION
CIRCUMGYRATE
CIRCUMSCRIBE
CIRCUMSTANCE
CONDEMNATION
CONSUMMATION
CONTAMINATED
CONTEMPORARY
CONTEMPTIBLE
CONTEMPTUOUS
CONTUMACIOUS
COURTMARTIAL
DISCOMEDUSAE
DISCOMFITURE
DISCOMYCETES
ECONOMICALLY
ETEPIMELETIC
FUNDAMENTALS
GAMESMANSHIP
GRANDMONTINE
HORSEMANSHIP
INFLAMMATION
INFLAMMATORY
INFORMIDABLE
INHARMONIOUS
INTERMEDIARY
INTERMEDIATE
INTERMINABLE
INTERMINABLY
INTERMISSION
INTERMITTENT
MARKSMANSHIP
MATHEMATICAL
MISDEMEANOUR
NONCOMMITTAL
OSTEOMALACIA

PARSIMONIOUS
PASSEMEASURE
PERGAMENEOUS
PHENOMENALLY
PREDOMINANCE
PRESUMPTUOUS
PROGYMNASIUM
RHADAMANTHUS
RHYTHMICALLY
SALESMANSHIP
SELFEMPLOYED
SEPTEMBRISER
SOMNAMBULISM
SOMNAMBULIST
SUBCOMMITTEE
TESTAMENTARY
TRANSMIGRATE
TRANSMISSION
TRANSMOGRIFY
ULTRAMONTANE
ALIMENTATIVE
ALPHANUMERIC
AMARANTACEAE
ANNOUNCEMENT
ANTIMNEMONIC
ASTRONOMICAL
AUGMENTATION
AUTHENTICATE
AUTHENTICITY
BARRANQUILLA
BEACONSFIELD
BILLINGSGATE
CALUMNIATION
CAMIKNICKERS
CAMPANULARIA
CANTANKEROUS
CARCINOGENIC
CARDINDEXING
CLARINETTIST
COMBINATIONS
COMMANDMENTS
COMMENCEMENT
COMMENDATION
COMMENDATORY
COMMENSURATE
COMMONWEALTH
COMMUNICABLE
COMPANIONWAY
COMPENSATION
COMPENSATORY
CONCENTRATED
CONDENSATION
CONGENITALLY
CONTINUATION
CONTINUOUSLY
CONVENIENCES
CONVENIENTLY
CONVENTIONAL
CONVINCINGLY
COSCINOMANCY

DARLINGTONIA
DISCONCERTED
DISCONNECTED
DISCONSOLATE
DISCONTENTED
DISHONORABLE
DISHONORABLY
DISPENSATION
DISTINCTNESS
ENTRENCHMENT
ESPAGNOLETTE
ESTRANGEMENT
EXCHANGEABLE
FERMENTATION
FRAUENDIENST
FRUMENTATION
FULMINATIONS
GALLINACEOUS
GALVANOMETER
GOVERNMENTAL
HALLANSHAKER
HAPPENSTANCE
HARMONIOUSLY
HERMENEUTICS
HERMENEUTIST
HYGIENICALLY
IMPLANTATION
INFRINGEMENT
INTRANSIGENT
INTRANSITIVE
INVULNERABLE
KATZENJAMMER
KERAUNOGRAPH
LEGIONNAIRES
MARCONIGRAPH
MARLINESPIKE
MEANINGFULLY
MECHANICALLY
METAGNATHOUS
OUTMANOEUVRE
PALEONTOLOGY
PANDANACEOUS
PERMANGANATE
PERSONALIZED
PERTINACIOUS
PHILANTHROPY
PHYTONADIONE
PIGMENTATION
PLACENTIFORM
PRAXINOSCOPE
PRECONDITION
PREMONSTRANT
PREPONDERANT
PREPONDERATE
PREPONDERENT
PRESENTATION
PRESENTIMENT
PREVENTATIVE
PROLONGATION
PYTHONOMORPH

RAMBUNCTIOUS
RECOGNIZABLE
RECOGNIZANCE
RENOUNCEMENT
RESPONDENTIA
RETRENCHMENT
ROOMINGHOUSE
SARDANAPALUS
SARDONICALLY
SCREENWRITER
SEGMENTATION
SELFINTEREST
SEQUENTIALLY
SIPHONOPHORA
SIPHONOSTELE
SLOVENLINESS
SPATANGOIDEA
SUBCONSCIOUS
SUBCONTINENT
SUPERNACULUM
SUPERNATURAL
TERCENTENARY
THYSANOPTERA
TREMENDOUSLY
TRIGONOMETRY
UNCHANGEABLE
UNECONOMICAL
UNIDENTIFIED
UNPRINCIPLED
WASHINGTONIA
WELLINFORMED
WELLINGTONIA
AGATHODAIMON
AMELIORATION
ANTAGONISTIC
ANTHROPOLOGY
APLANOGAMETE
ARISTOCRATIC
ARISTOLOCHIA
ARISTOPHANES
ARISTOTELEAN
ARSENOPYRITE
ARTHROPLASTY
ATHEROMATOUS
AUSTRONESIAN
BACKWOODSMAN
BEAUMONTAGUE
BEAUMONTIQUE
BENEVOLENTLY
BERTHOLLETIA
BIBLIOGRAPHY
BIBLIOPEGIST
BLENNORRHOEA
BOONDOGGLING
BRONTOSAURUS
CARDIOLOGIST
CAUTIOUSNESS
CEREMONIALLY
CHOREOGRAPHY
COMPROMISING

CONGLOMERATE
CONTROLLABLE
COVETOUSNESS
CRISTOBALITE
CRYPTOGRAPHY
DEMIMONDAINE
DENDROLOGIST
DILATORINESS
DIPRIONIDIAN
EGYPTOLOGIST
ELASMOBRANCH
ELEEMOSYNARY
ENHYPOSTASIA
ENTEROMORPHA
ENTEROPNEUST
ENTOMOLOGIST
ENTOMOSTRACA
EPISCOPALIAN
EPISTOLATERS
EQUIVOCATION
EQUIVOCATORY
ESCAPOLOGIST
ETHEROMANIAC
FLAMBOYANTLY
GASTROSOPHER
GONADOTROPIN
GRACIOUSNESS
GRAPHOLOGIST
GRISEOFULVIN
GYNECOLOGIST
HETEROCLITIC
HETEROCONTAE
HETEROPHORIA
HETEROPLASIA
HETEROSEXUAL
HETEROSOMATA
HISTIOPHORUS
HOMOEOPATHIC
HORIZONTALLY
IMMUNOLOGIST
INVIGORATING
INVIGORATION
IRRESOLUTELY
IRRESOLUTION
IRRESOLVABLE
KLEPTOMANIAC
LABANOTATION
LATIROSTRATE
LEPIDOMELANE
LEXICOGRAPHY
MADEMOISELLE
MALACOSTRACA
METAMORPHISM
METAMORPHOSE
MINDBOGGLING
MINICOMPUTER
MISPRONOUNCE
MISQUOTATION
MONOTONOUSLY
MUSICOLOGIST

NYMPHOMANIAC
OCEANOGRAPHY
ONEIROCRITIC
OPINIONATIVE
OVERPOWERING
PASSIONATELY
PASSIONFRUIT
PHLEBOTOMIST
PHYSIOLOGIST
PLECTOGNATHI
POSTPONEMENT
POTAMOLOGIST
PRASEODYMIUM
PSEPHOLOGIST
PSEUDONYMOUS
PSYCHOLOGIST
PSYCHOPATHIC
RODOMONTADER
SCHIZOMYCETE
SCLERODERMIA
SELFPORTRAIT
SNOWBOARDING
SOMATOPLEURE
SPACIOUSNESS
SPECIOUSNESS
SPELEOLOGIST
SPLENOMEGALY
SPURIOUSNESS
STENTORPHONE
STEREOPHONIC
STEREOPTICON
STEREOSCOPIC
STEREOTYPING
STILBOESTROL
STRATOSPHERE
STUBBORNNESS
STUDIOUSNESS
SULPHONAMIDE
TECHNOLOGIST
THERMOSTATIC
THESMOPHORIA
THIGMOTROPIC
TITANOSAURUS
TOXICOLOGIST
TRANSOCEANIC
TRICHOLOGIST
TRICHOPHYTON
TROCHOSPHERE
TURACOVERDIN
UNCTUOUSNESS
UNDEMOCRATIC
UNFAVOURABLE
UNIMPORTANCE
UNRECOGNISED
UNRECOGNIZED
VARICOLOURED
VERUMONTANUM
WAREHOUSEMAN
WHIPPOORWILL
XANTHOPTERIN

ACCOMPANYING
ACCOMPLISHED
ALEXIPHARMIC
ANEMOPHILOUS
ARCHIPELAGOS
ASTROPHYSICS
ATMOSPHERICS
CHIROPRACTIC
CHIROPRACTOR
COSMOPOLITAN
DISAPPEARING
DISAPPOINTED
DISCIPLINARY
DISREPECTFUL
DISREPUTABLE
ENTERPRISING
ENTREPRENEUR
FELDSPATHOID
GOOSEPIMPLES
GRANDPARENTS
HAEMOPHILIAC
HAIRSPLITTER
HIEROPHANTIC
HIPPOPOTAMUS
HYPERPYRETIC
INAUSPICIOUS
INCOMPARABLE
INCOMPARABLY
INCOMPATIBLE
INCOMPETENCE
INCOMPLETELY
INCORPORATED
INDISPUTABLE
INDISPUTABLY
INHOSPITABLE
INTEMPERANCE
INTERPRETING
IRRESPECTIVE
KLIPSPRINGER
LALLAPALOOZA
LIVERPUDLIAN
MACROPODIDAE
MALLOPHAGOUS
METROPOLITAN
MISAPPREHEND
MISREPRESENT
MULTIPLICITY
ORTHOPAEDICS
ORTHOPAEDIST
OSTEOPOROSIS
PANTOPHAGOUS
PASSEPARTOUT
PERCEPTIVELY
PERCEPTIVITY
PEREMPTORILY
PROSOPOPOEIA
PROTOPLASMAL
PROTOPLASMIC
REDEMPTIONER
SARSAPARILLA

SCOPOPHILIAC
STEGOPHOLIST
SUBLAPSARIAN
THERAPEUTICS
TRANSPARENCY
TRANSPONTINE
TRIUMPHANTLY
UNDERPINNING
UNRESPONSIVE
UNSURPRISING
UNSUSPECTING
COLLOQUIALLY
CONSEQUENCES
CONSEQUENTLY
HYDROQUINONE
INADEQUATELY
INFREQUENTLY
PREREQUISITE
SUBSEQUENTLY
THREEQUARTER
UNFREQUENTED
ANAMORPHOSIS
APOSTROPHISE
BACKBREAKING
BACTERIOLOGY
BACTERIOSTAT
BANDERSNATCH
BARBERMONGER
BESSERWISSER
BIELORUSSIAN
BUTTERSCOTCH
BYELORUSSIAN
CASTERBRIDGE
CEREBROTONIC
CHONDRIOSOME
COMMERCIALLY
COMPURGATION
CONCURRENTLY
CONFIRMATION
CONFIRMATORY
CONSCRIPTION
CONSERVATION
CONSERVATISM
CONSERVATIVE
CONSERVATORY
CONSTRICTION
CONSTRUCTION
CONSTRUCTIVE
CONTERMINOUS
CONVERSATION
COSTERMONGER
CYMOTRICHOUS
DAGUERROTYPE
DESSERTSPOON
DEUTEROSCOPY
DIFFERENTIAL
DISAGREEABLE
DISAGREEMENT
DISSERTATION
DONNERWETTER

ELECTRICALLY
ELECTROLYSIS
ELECTROPLATE
ELECTROTONUS
EMBARRASSING
EPANORTHOSIS
ERYTHROMYCIN
EXACERBATION
FOTHERINGHAY
GASTARBEITER
HAEMORRHOIDS
HAIRDRESSERS
HAIRDRESSING
HAMMERHEADED
HELLGRAMMITE
HIERARCHICAL
HISTORICALLY
HUDIBRASTICS
HYPOCRITICAL
HYSTERECTOMY
HYSTERICALLY
INCORRIGIBLE
INCORRIGIBLY
INEXTRICABLE
INEXTRICABLY
INSURRECTION
INTERRELATED
INTERROGATOR
INTERRUPTION
KATHAREVOUSA
KINDERGARTEN
LABOURSAVING
LEIOTRICHOUS
LICKTRENCHER
LOXODROMICAL
LUGUBRIOUSLY
MALFORMATION
MASSERANDUBA
MASSPRODUCED
MASTERSTROKE
MASTURBATION
MELODRAMATIC
MENSTRUATION
MERETRICIOUS
MERITRICIOUS
MYSTERIOUSLY
ORTHORHOMBIC
OUTSTRETCHED
OVERCROWDING
OVERDRESSING
PANCHROMATIC
PECTORILOQUY
PERTURBATION
PERVERSENESS
PITTERPATTER
POLYURETHANE
POSTGRADUATE
POSTPRANDIAL
PRECARIOUSLY
PREFERENTIAL

PREPAREDNESS
PRESCRIPTION
PRESCRIPTIVE
PRESERVATION
PRESERVATIVE
PRESTRICTION
PREVARICATOR
PROPORTIONAL
PROSCRIPTION
PROVERBIALLY
PUMPERNICKEL
RECHARGEABLE
RECIPROCALLY
REPATRIATION
RESURRECTION
RHINORRHOEAL
ROLLERBLADER
ROLLERBLADES
SECTARIANISM
SEMIPRECIOUS
SILVERHAIRED
SPECTROSCOPE
SPHAIRISTIKE
SUBARRHATION
SUBSCRIPTION
SUBSERVIENCE
SUBSTRUCTURE
SUBTERRANEAN
TEETERTOTTER
TELEGRAPHESE
TELEGRAPHIST
THEATRICALLY
UNATTRACTIVE
UNCHARITABLE
UNCHARITABLY
UNIVERSALIST
UNOPPRESSIVE
UPROARIOUSLY
USERFRIENDLY
WELTERWEIGHT
WINTERHALTER
AGGRESSIVELY
AMBASSADRESS
AMPHISBAENIC
AMPHISTOMOUS
ANDROSTERONE
APFELSTRUDEL
AWEINSPIRING
BAIRNSFATHER
BLEFUSCUDIAN
BLOODSTAINED
BUNKOSTEERER
CALLISTHENES
CIRCASSIENNE
CLEARSIGHTED
COMMISSARIAT
COMMISSIONED
COMMISSIONER
CONFESSIONAL
CONFISCATION
CONSISTENTLY
CROSSSECTION
DEMONSTRABLE
DEMONSTRABLY
DEMONSTRATOR
DISPOSSESSED
ECCLESIASTES
ECCLESIASTIC
ENGLISHWOMAN
ENGLISHWOMEN
ENTHUSIASTIC
ERATOSTHENES
EULENSPIEGEL
EXHAUSTIVELY
EXTENSIONIST
GYMNOSOPHIST
HARNESSMAKER
HEARTSTRINGS
HYPERSARCOMA
IMMEASURABLE
IMMEASURABLY
IMPERSONALLY
IMPERSONATOR
IMPRESSIVELY
IMPRISONMENT
INCONSEQUENT
INCONSISTENT
INCONSOLABLE
INCRUSTATION
INDISSOLUBLE
INTERSECTION
INTERSPERSED
INTERSTELLAR
JENNYSPINNER
KINAESTHETIC
LANCASTERIAN
MONTESSORIAN
MUTESSARIFAT
NARCISSISTIC
NONRESIDENCE
NONRESISTANT
OLDFASHIONED
OPPRESSIVELY
OVERESTIMATE
PANAESTHESIA
PANTISOCRACY
PARTISANSHIP
PERIOSTRACUM
PERSISTENTLY
PHILISTINISM
PHILOSOPHIZE
POSSESSIVELY
POWERSHARING
PREDESTINATE
PREGUSTATION
PREHISTORIAN
PREPOSSESSED
PREPOSTEROUS
PROCESSIONAL
PROFESSIONAL
PROFESSORIAL
PROGESTERONE
PROTESTATION
PURPOSEBUILT
PURPOSEFULLY
RECONSTITUTE
REMONSTRANCE
REPOSSESSION
REVERSIONARY
RONCESVALLES
SARRUSOPHONE
SCRIMSHANDER
SCRIMSHANKER
SECESSIONIST
SEQUESTRATOR
SHARPSHOOTER
SHIRTSLEEVES
SHORTSIGHTED
SHORTSLEEVED
SHORTSTAFFED
SOPHISTICATE
SPOKESPERSON
SPORTSGROUND
STANISLAVSKI
STATISTICIAN
STREPSIPTERA
SUBHASTATION
SUBMISSIVELY
SUCCESSFULLY
SUCCESSIVELY
SUCCUSSATION
SUGGESTIVELY
SUPERSTITION
TELEASTHETIC
TELEOSAURIAN
TESTOSTERONE
THANKSGIVING
THICKSKINNED
TRADESCANTIA
TRADESPEOPLE
UNCLASSIFIED
UNCONSIDERED
UNDERSKINKER
UNDERSTAFFED
UNREASONABLE
UNSEASONABLE
WOLLASTONITE
ABOLITIONIST
ACCENTUATION
ACCOUTREMENT
ADJECTIVALLY
ADSCITITIOUS
ADVANTAGEOUS
ADVANTAGIOUS
ADVENTITIOUS
AFFECTIONATE
AFORETHOUGHT
AFTERTHOUGHT
AMPHITHEATER
AMPHITHEATRE
ANAESTHETISE
ANAESTHETIST
ANAESTHETIZE
ANECATHARSIS
ANTISTROPHON
APPURTENANCE
ARCHITECTURE
AROMATHERAPY
ARTISTICALLY
BARNSTORMING
BICENTENNIAL
BLOODTHIRSTY
BLUESTOCKING
BOOBYTRAPPED
BREAKTHROUGH
BREASTPLOUGH
BREASTSUMMER
CARPETBAGGER
CASSITERIDES
CATASTROPHIC
CATHETOMETER
CHEMOTHERAPY
CHRESTOMATHY
CHRISTIANITY
CLEISTOGAMIC
DECENTRALISE
DECENTRALIZE
DEFLATIONARY
DEPARTMENTAL
DERESTRICTED
DICTATORSHIP
DIRECTORSHIP
DISASTROUSLY
DISINTEGRATE
DISSATISFIED
DIVERTICULUM
DIVERTIMENTO
DOGMATICALLY
DOMESTICATED
DRAMATICALLY
DRAMATURGIST
ECCENTRICITY
ECSTATICALLY
EDUCATIONIST
EFFORTLESSLY
EMPHATICALLY
ENTERTAINING
ESSENTIALITY
ESTHETICALLY
EVOLUTIONARY
EXTORTIONATE
GEOMETRICIAN
GERIATRICIAN
GERONTOCRACY
GIGANTOMACHY
GLOBETROTTER
HAEMATEMESIS
HAMARTHRITIS
HERMETICALLY
HOUSETOHOUSE

HYDROTHERAPY
HYPERTENSION
HYPNOTHERAPY
HYPNOTICALLY
ILLUSTRATION
ILLUSTRATIVE
IMPARTIALITY
IMPERTINENCE
INCAUTIOUSLY
INCONTINENCE
INDEBTEDNESS
INDISTINCTLY
INDOCTRINATE
INDUSTRIALLY
INFILTRATION
INFLATIONARY
INGRATIATING
INNATTENTIVE
INVERTEBRATE
INVESTIGATOR
ISOLATIONISM
ISOLATIONIST
KALISTOCRACY
LAMENTATIONS
LONGITUDINAL
LONGSTANDING
LYMANTRIIDAE
MAGNETICALLY
MAJESTICALLY
MALNUTRITION
MECHITHARIST
MERISTEMATIC
MERRYTHOUGHT
MINISTRATION
MISANTHROPIC
MISINTERPRET
MNEMOTECHNIC
NEPENTHACEAE
NEUROTICALLY
NEVERTHELESS
NUTRITIONIST
OBSTETRICIAN
OCTASTROPHIC
ONOMATOPOEIA
ONOMATOPOEIC
ORIENTEERING
ORTHOTONESIS
OSTENTATIOUS
OVERSTRAINED
PALPITATIONS
PARANTHELIUM
PATHETICALLY
PEDANTICALLY
PEDIATRICIAN
PERISTERONIC
PERPETRATION
PHONETICALLY
PHRONTISTERY
POLYETHYLENE
POTENTIALITY
PRALLTRILLER
PREDETERMINE
PROBATIONARY
PROFITEERING
PROLETARIATE
PROPITIATION
PROPITIATORY
PROPITIOUSLY
QUIXOTICALLY
RACKETEERING
RADIOTHERAPY
RECEPTIONIST
REDINTEGRATE
REDISTRIBUTE
REFLATIONARY
REGISTRATION
RELENTLESSLY
RESETTLEMENT
ROMANTICALLY
SADISTICALLY
SALTATORIOUS
SALVATIONIST
SCRIPTWRITER
SECRETARIATE
SEMANTICALLY
SIMULTANEOUS
SINANTHROPUS
SPECKTIONEER
SPINSTERHOOD
SPIRITUALISM
SPIRITUALIST
SPIRITUALITY
STEALTHINESS
STORMTROOPER
STRAITJACKET
STREPTOMYCIN
STREPTONEURA
STRUCTURALLY
SUBCUTANEOUS
TELEUTOSPORE
TERRITORIALS
TRALATICIOUS
TRALATITIOUS
UINTATHERIUM
UNCONTROLLED
UNCULTIVATED
UNILATERALLY
UNMISTAKABLE
UNOBSTRUCTED
UNPRETENDING
UNRESTRAINED
UNRESTRICTED
VIBRATIUNCLE
VOLUPTUOUSLY
WEIGHTLIFTER
WICKETKEEPER
ACCUMULATION
AGRIBUSINESS
AGRICULTURAL
ARTICULATION
BUREAUCRATIC
CAPITULATION
COLOQUINTIDA
CONCLUSIVELY
DEAMBULATORY
DEPOPULATION
DEREGULATION
DISCOURAGING
DISCOURTEOUS
EMASCULATION
GROSSULARITE
HEADQUARTERS
HINDQUARTERS
IMMACULATELY
INACCURATELY
INAUGURATION
INESCUTCHEON
INSALUBRIOUS
INSOLUBILITY
INSTAURATION
INSTRUCTIONS
INSTRUCTRESS
INSTRUMENTAL
INTRAUTERINE
IRREGULARITY
MANIPULATION
MANIPULATIVE
MANOEUVRABLE
METICULOUSLY
MINDFULLNESS
MIRACULOUSLY
MOISTURIZING
MOUSQUETAIRE
NEWFOUNDLAND
OBSEQUIOUSLY
POSTHUMOUSLY
QUINQUENNIAL
READJUSTMENT
RESTAURATEUR
RETICULATION
RIDICULOUSLY
SCRUPULOUSLY
SHIPBUILDING
STERNUTATION
STRIDULATION
SURMOUNTABLE
SURROUNDINGS
THOROUGHBRED
THOROUGHFARE
THOROUGHNESS
TRANQUILIZER
TRANQUILLISE
TRANQUILLITY
TRANQUILLIZE
UNACCUSTOMED
UNACQUAINTED
UNEXPURGATED
UNPOPULARITY
UNRETURNABLE
UNSCRUPULOUS
VENEPUNCTURE
WOODBURYTYPE
ABBREVIATION
BIODIVERSITY
BOULEVARDIER
CARLOVINGIAN
CLAIRVOYANCE
CLAIRVOYANCY
CONVIVIALITY
DISADVANTAGE
DORSIVENTRAL
EFFERVESCENT
EXSERVICEMAN
EXTRAVAGANCE
EXTRAVAGANZA
GALLIVANTING
IMPROVIDENCE
INCONVENIENT
INTERVENTION
LASCIVIOUSLY
MISADVENTURE
OBSERVANTINE
PERADVENTURE
PERSEVERANCE
RECEIVERSHIP
TERGIVERSATE
TRANSVESTISM
TRANSVESTITE
UNCONVERSANT
UNCONVINCING
ACKNOWLEDGED
AWARDWINNING
BRAINWASHING
CARRIWITCHET
COLLYWOBBLES
GRASSWIDOWER
HEARTWARMING
HOUSEWARMING
NORTHWESTERN
OTHERWORLDLY
PRIZEWINNING
SHIRTWAISTER
SLEEPWALKING
SOUTHWESTERN
STERNWHEELER
UNANSWERABLE
UNDERWRITTEN
YELLOWHAMMER
ASPHYXIATION
OVEREXERTION
PHYCOXANTHIN
PREMAXILLARY
AERODYNAMICS
BRACHYCEPHAL
CONVEYANCING
ENERGYSAVING
GEOPHYSICIST
ICHTHYOCOLLA
ICHTHYOPSIDA
IDIOSYNCRASY

MONOSYLLABIC
MONOSYLLABLE
PENNSYLVANIA
POLICYMAKING
POLYSYLLABIC
POLYSYLLABLE
POLYSYNDETON
PRESBYTERIAN
PROPHYLACTIC
SHILLYSHALLY
CHORIZONTIST
EMBEZZLEMENT

12:7

ACCOMPANYING
ADVANTAGEOUS
ADVANTAGIOUS
AMBASSADRESS
ARTIODACTYLA
ASSUEFACTION
BOULEVARDIER
BRAINWASHING
BREATHALYSER
BRILLIANTINE
BROADCASTING
CAPERCAILLIE
CAPERCAILZIE
CHAIRMANSHIP
COMBINATIONS
CONTUMACIOUS
CONVEYANCING
COURTMARTIAL
CRASHLANDING
DISADVANTAGE
DISEMBARRASS
DISORGANIZED
EMBARRASSING
ENTERTAINING
ENTOPLASTRON
EXTRAVAGANCE
EXTRAVAGANZA
FELDSPATHOID
FULMINATIONS
GALLIGASKINS
GALLINACEOUS
GALLIVANTING
GAMESMANSHIP
GRANDPARENTS
GUARDIANSHIP
HABERDASHERS
HABERDASHERY
HEADQUARTERS
HEARTWARMING
HELIOGABALUS
HELLGRAMMITE
HINDQUARTERS
HORSEMANSHIP
HOUSEWARMING
HUDIBRASTICS
HYPERSARCOMA
INCOMPARABLE
INCOMPARABLY
INCOMPATIBLE
ISOBILATERAL
LALLAPALOOZA
LAMENTATIONS
LIQUEFACTION
LITHOLATROUS
LONGSTANDING
MALTREATMENT
MARKSMANSHIP
MASSERANDUBA
MATHEMATICAL
MELODRAMATIC
METAGNATHOUS
MICHELANGELO
MISBEHAVIOUR
MISTREATMENT
MULLIGATAWNY
MULTIFARIOUS
MULTILATERAL
MUTESSARIFAT
NORTHEASTERN
OBSERVANTINE
ORTHOPAEDICS
ORTHOPAEDIST
OSTENTATIOUS
OSTEOMALACIA
PALPITATIONS
PANDANACEOUS
PARTISANSHIP
PASSEPARTOUT
PERSONALIZED
PERTINACIOUS
PERVICACIOUS
PETRIFACTION
PHYCOXANTHIN
PHYTONADIONE
POSTGRADUATE
POSTPRANDIAL
PROLETARIATE
PROPAGANDISM
PROPAGANDIST
PSYCHIATRIST
PTERODACTYLE
PUTREFACTION
REAPPEARANCE
RHADAMANTHUS
SALESMANSHIP
SARDANAPALUS
SARSAPARILLA
SATISFACTION
SATISFACTORY
SECRETARIATE
SESQUIALTERA
SHAMEFACEDLY
SHIRTWAISTER
SIMULTANEOUS
SLEEPWALKING
SNOWBOARDING
SOUTHEASTERN
STROPHANTHUS
STUPEFACTION
SUBCUTANEOUS
SUPERNACULUM
SUPERNATURAL
TELEGRAPHESE
TELEGRAPHIST
TELEOSAURIAN
TRANSLATABLE
TRANSPARENCY
UMBRADARLING
UNACQUAINTED
UNATTRACTIVE
UNDERGARMENT
UNMISTAKABLE
WATERCARRIER
ADAPTABILITY
ADVISABILITY
AMPHISBAENIC
AVAILABILITY
BUCKLEBEGGAR
CARPETBAGGER
CASTERBRIDGE
CHEESEBURGER
CONSTABULARY
CONTRIBUTION
CONTRIBUTORY
CRISTOBALITE
DESIRABILITY
DISTRIBUTION
DISTRIBUTIVE
ELASMOBRANCH
EXACERBATION
EXCITABILITY
GASTARBEITER
GLYNDEBOURNE
ILLEGIBILITY
IMMUTABILITY
INCAPABILITY
INCUNABULIST
INSALUBRIOUS
INSOLUBILITY
INVISIBILITY
IRASCIBILITY
IRRITABILITY
MALLEABILITY
MASTURBATION
NAVIGABILITY
PERMEABILITY
PERTURBATION
PLAUSIBILITY
PROVERBIALLY
ROLLERBLADER
ROLLERBLADES
SEPTEMBRISER
SOMNAMBULISM
SOMNAMBULIST
TRACTABILITY
ADJUDICATION
ANNOUNCEMENT
ANTIBACCHIUS
ANTIMACASSAR
ANTIRACHITIC
APPROACHABLE
ARISTOCRATIC
ARTIFICIALLY
BAMBOCCIADES
BENEFACTRESS
BLEFUSCUDIAN
BRACHYCEPHAL
BUREAUCRATIC
CIRCUMCISION
CLAUDICATION
CODIFICATION
COMMENCEMENT
COMMERCIALLY
COMPLACENTLY
COMPLICATION
CONFISCATION
CONSPECTUITY
CONVINCINGLY
DISCONCERTED
DISPLACEMENT
DISTINCTNESS
ENCROACHMENT
ENTRENCHMENT
EPIDEICTICAL
EQUIVOCATION
EQUIVOCATORY
HETEROCLITIC
HETEROCONTAE
HIERARCHICAL
HOMESICKNESS
ILLOGICALITY
INARTICULATE
INCAPACITATE
INEFFICIENCY
INFELICITOUS
INSTRUCTIONS
INSTRUCTRESS
INTOXICATING
INTOXICATION
MALPRACTICES
MANUFACTURER
MISCALCULATE
MISPLACEMENT
MODIFICATION
NOTIFICATION
ONEIROCRITIC
OSSIFICATION
PACIFICATION
PERSPICACITY
PHARMACOLOGY
PRACTICALITY
PRACTICIONER
PURIFICATION
PYROTECHNICS
RAMBUNCTIOUS

RAMIFICATION
RATIFICATION
RENOUNCEMENT
RETRENCHMENT
SITTLICHKEIT
STRINGCOURSE
SUPPLICATION
TAGLIACOTIAN
TAMARICACEAE
TAPERECORDER
TECHNICALITY
TRADESCANTIA
TRANSACTIONS
TRANSOCEANIC
ULOTRICHALES
UNDEMOCRATIC
UNDERACHIEVE
UNDETECTABLE
UNEXPECTEDLY
UNOFFICIALLY
UNPRINCIPLED
VERIFICATION
VILIFICATION
WHIMSICALITY
AGATHODAIMON
CARDINDEXING
COINCIDENTAL
COMMANDMENTS
COMMENDATION
COMMENDATORY
DEHUMIDIFIER
DILAPIDATION
DISOBEDIENCE
DOUBLEDECKER
EMBROIDERESS
EPACRIDACEAE
FLUORIDATION
FORMALDEHYDE
FRAUENDIENST
GOBBLEDEGOOK
GOBBLEDYGOOK
INDIVIDUALLY
INTIMIDATING
INTIMIDATION
INVALIDATION
LANGUEDOCIAN
PRASEODYMIUM
PRECONDITION
PREPONDERANT
PREPONDERATE
PREPONDERENT
RESPONDENTIA
SCHNEIDERIAN
SCLERODERMIA
SINGLEDECKER
TREMENDOUSLY
ZALAMBDODONT
AGAMOGENETIC
ALPHABETICAL
ANTIMNEMONIC
APPENDECTOMY
APPREHENSION
APPREHENSIVE
APPURTENANCE
ARCHIPELAGOS
ARCHITECTURE
ARITHMETICAL
ARTILLERYMAN
BACKBREAKING
BELLIGERENCY
BEWILDERMENT
BICENTENNIAL
BIODIVERSITY
CAMPODEIFORM
CANTILEVERED
CASSITERIDES
CHILDBEARING
CLARINETTIST
CLAVICEMBALO
CONFIDENTIAL
CONSIDERABLE
CONSIDERABLY
CONTABESCENT
CONVALESCENT
CONVALESCING
COURAGEOUSLY
CROSSBENCHER
CROSSSECTION
DECIPHERABLE
DECIPHERMENT
DECONGESTANT
DIFFERENTIAL
DIPLOGENESIS
DISAGREEABLE
DISAGREEMENT
DISAPPEARING
DISCOMEDUSAE
DISINCENTIVE
DISINFECTANT
DISINGENUOUS
DISINTEGRATE
DISORIENTATE
DISREPECTFUL
DORSIVENTRAL
DYSTELEOLOGY
EFFERVESCENT
ETEPIMELETIC
FAINTHEARTED
FRONTIERSMAN
FUNDAMENTALS
HAEMATEMESIS
HAIRDRESSERS
HAIRDRESSING
HEPHTHEMIMER
HERMENEUTICS
HERMENEUTIST
HOMOTHERMOUS
HOUSEKEEPING
HYPERTENSION
HYPOTHECATOR
HYPOTHETICAL
HYSTERECTOMY
IDIOTHERMOUS
IMPERFECTION
INCANDESCENT
INCOMPETENCE
INCONSEQUENT
INCONVENIENT
INDEBTEDNESS
INDIFFERENCE
INNATTENTIVE
INSUFFERABLE
INSUFFERABLY
INSURRECTION
INTELLECTUAL
INTEMPERANCE
INTERCEPTION
INTERCESSION
INTERFERENCE
INTERJECTION
INTERMEDIARY
INTERMEDIATE
INTERRELATED
INTERSECTION
INTERVENTION
INVERTEBRATE
INVULNERABLE
IRREDEEMABLE
IRRESPECTIVE
KATHAREVOUSA
LAMPADEDROMY
LICKTRENCHER
LIGHTHEARTED
MARLINESPIKE
MERISTEMATIC
MESOTHELIOMA
MISADVENTURE
MISDEMEANOUR
MISINTERPRET
MNEMOTECHNIC
MOUSQUETAIRE
NORTHWESTERN
NYCHTHEMERON
ORIENTEERING
ORTHOGENESIS
OUTRAGEOUSLY
OUTSTRETCHED
OVERDRESSING
OVEREXERTION
OVERWHELMING
PALINGENESIA
PALINGENESIS
PANATHENAEAN
PASSEMEASURE
PEACEKEEPING
PERADVENTURE
PERGAMENEOUS
PERISTERONIC
PERSEVERANCE
PESTILENTIAL
PHENOMENALLY
PHILODENDRON
PHYTOBENTHOS
POLYURETHANE
PREDETERMINE
PREDILECTION
PREFERENTIAL
PREPAREDNESS
PRESIDENTIAL
PROFITEERING
PROPRIETRESS
PROTUBERANCE
PROVIDENTIAL
PURPOSEBUILT
PURPOSEFULLY
QUINQUENNIAL
RACKETEERING
RECEIVERSHIP
RECOLLECTION
RECRUDESCENT
REDINTEGRATE
REFRIGERATED
REFRIGERATOR
REPOSSESSION
REPROCESSING
RESURRECTION
RETARDEDNESS
RHODODENDRON
RHYTIDECTOMY
SACRILEGIOUS
SCHILLERSPAR
SEMIPRECIOUS
SERVICEWOMAN
SHUFFLEBOARD
SOUTHWESTERN
SPINSTERHOOD
SPREADEAGLED
SPURTLEBLADE
STEEPLECHASE
STILBOESTROL
SWIZZLESTICK
TERGIVERSATE
TESTAMENTARY
TETRAHEDRITE
THERAPEUTICS
TOGETHERNESS
TORRICELLIAN
TRANSCENDENT
TRANSFERABLE
TRANSFERENCE
TRANSVESTISM
TRANSVESTITE
TROUBLEMAKER
UNANSWERABLE
UNBELIEVABLE
UNBELIEVABLY
UNCONVERSANT
UNILATERALLY
UNOPPRESSIVE
UNPRETENDING

UNSUCCESSFUL
UNSUSPECTING
WHOLEHEARTED
WRETCHEDNESS
AFTEREFFECTS
AIRCRAFTSMAN
BAIRNSFATHER
CLASSIFIABLE
DISCOMFITURE
GRISEOFULVIN
IDENTIFIABLE
QUANTIFIABLE
STRIGIFORMES
WELLINFORMED
ANTILEGOMENA
APLANOGAMETE
ASPARAGINASE
BATTLEGROUND
BIBLIOGRAPHY
BILLINGSGATE
BOONDOGGLING
CARTHAGINIAN
CHOREOGRAPHY
CIRCUMGYRATE
COMPURGATION
CONGREGATION
CRYPTOGRAPHY
CURMUDGEONLY
DARLINGTONIA
DOUBLEGLAZED
ESTRANGEMENT
EXCHANGEABLE
INFRINGEMENT
KINDERGARTEN
LEXICOGRAPHY
MARRIAGEABLE
MEANINGFULLY
MINDBOGGLING
MOONLIGHTING
MUCILAGINOUS
OCEANOGRAPHY
PERMANGANATE
PLECTOGNATHI
PROLONGATION
PROMULGATION
QUADRAGESIMA
RECHARGEABLE
REINVIGORATE
ROOMINGHOUSE
SEPTUAGESIMA
SPATANGOIDEA
SPORTSGROUND
THANKSGIVING
THEREAGAINST
THOROUGHBRED
THOROUGHFARE
THOROUGHNESS
UNCHANGEABLE
UNMANAGEABLE
UNRECOGNISED

UNRECOGNIZED
WASHINGTONIA
WELLINGTONIA
ACCOUCHEMENT
AFORETHOUGHT
AFTERTHOUGHT
ALEXIPHARMIC
AMPHITHEATER
AMPHITHEATRE
ANAESTHETISE
ANAESTHETIST
ANAESTHETIZE
ANECATHARSIS
ANEMOPHILOUS
AROMATHERAPY
ASTROPHYSICS
ATMOSPHERICS
BETHLEHEMITE
BLOODTHIRSTY
BREAKTHROUGH
CHEMOTHERAPY
DISACCHARIDE
DISENCHANTED
ENGLISHWOMAN
ENGLISHWOMEN
HAEMOPHILIAC
HAMARTHRITIS
HAMMERHEADED
HIEROPHANTIC
HYDROCHLORIC
HYDROTHERAPY
HYPNOTHERAPY
INTERCHANGED
MALLOPHAGOUS
MECHITHARIST
MERRYTHOUGHT
MISANTHROPIC
MUDDLEHEADED
NEPENTHACEAE
NEVERTHELESS
OLDFASHIONED
ORTHORHOMBIC
PANTECHNICON
PANTOPHAGOUS
PARANTHELIUM
PLEIOCHASIUM
POLYETHYLENE
POWERSHARING
RADIOTHERAPY
SCOPOPHILIAC
SCRIMSHANDER
SCRIMSHANKER
SELFADHESIVE
SHARPSHOOTER
SILVERHAIRED
SINANTHROPUS
SINGLEHANDED
SPELLCHECKER
SPINECHILLER
STEALTHINESS

STEGOPHOLIST
STERNWHEELER
STONECHATTER
STRAIGHTAWAY
STRAIGHTEDGE
STRAIGHTNESS
SUBARRHATION
SUPERCHARGED
SUPERCHARGER
TRIUMPHANTLY
TURBOCHARGER
UINTATHERIUM
UNDISCHARGED
UNNEIGHBORLY
WINTERHALTER
YELLOWHAMMER
ABBREVIATION
ABOLITIONIST
ACADEMICALLY
ACCORDIONIST
ADJECTIVALLY
ADSCITITIOUS
ADVENTITIOUS
AFFECTIONATE
ANNUNCIATION
APPENDICITIS
APPOGGIATURA
APPRECIATION
APPRECIATIVE
ARTISTICALLY
ASPHYXIATION
AUSPICIOUSLY
AWARDWINNING
BACTERIOLOGY
BACTERIOSTAT
BRANCHIOPODA
BRICKFIELDER
CALUMNIATION
CAMIKNICKERS
CARLOVINGIAN
CARRIWITCHET
CHONDRIOSOME
CHRISTIANITY
CLEARSIGHTED
COCCIDIOSTAT
COLOQUINTIDA
COMMUNICABLE
COMPANIONWAY
CONCILIATION
CONCILIATORY
CONGENITALLY
CONSCRIPTION
CONSOLIDATED
CONSOLIDATOR
CONSTRICTION
CONTAMINATED
CONVENIENCES
CONVENIENTLY
CONVIVIALITY
CYMOTRICHOUS

DEFLATIONARY
DENUNCIATION
DEPRECIATION
DEPRECIATORY
DISSATISFIED
DISSOCIATION
DIVERTICULUM
DIVERTIMENTO
DOGMATICALLY
DOMESTICATED
DRAMATICALLY
ECCLESIASTES
ECCLESIASTIC
ECONOMICALLY
ECSTATICALLY
EDUCATIONIST
ELECTRICALLY
EMPHATICALLY
ENTHUSIASTIC
ESSENTIALITY
ESTHETICALLY
EVOLUTIONARY
EXCRUCIATING
EXCRUCIATION
EXSERVICEMAN
EXTENSIONIST
EXTORTIONATE
EXTRADITABLE
FASTIDIOUSLY
FOTHERINGHAY
GEOLOGICALLY
GOOSEPIMPLES
GRASSWIDOWER
HALLUCINOGEN
HARMONIOUSLY
HERMETICALLY
HISTORICALLY
HOBBIDIDANCE
HORRIFICALLY
HYGIENICALLY
HYPNOTICALLY
HYPOCRITICAL
HYSTERICALLY
IMPARTIALITY
IMPERTINENCE
IMPROVIDENCE
INAPPLICABLE
INAUSPICIOUS
INCAUTIOUSLY
INCONSISTENT
INCONTINENCE
INCORRIGIBLE
INCORRIGIBLY
INDECLINABLE
INDISTINCTLY
INERADICABLE
INEXPLICABLE
INEXPLICABLY
INEXTRICABLE
INEXTRICABLY

INFLATIONARY
INFORMIDABLE
INGRATIATING
INHOSPITABLE
INSUFFICIENT
INTELLIGENCE
INTELLIGIBLE
INTERMINABLE
INTERMINABLY
INTERMISSION
INTERMITTENT
INVESTIGATOR
ISOLATIONISM
ISOLATIONIST
JURISDICTION
KILLIKINNICK
LAMELLICORNE
LASCIVIOUSLY
LEIOTRICHOUS
LUGUBRIOUSLY
LUXULLIANITE
MADEMOISELLE
MAGNETICALLY
MAGNIFICENCE
MAJESTICALLY
MARCONIGRAPH
MECHANICALLY
MERETRICIOUS
MERITRICIOUS
METHODICALLY
MISDELIVERED
MYSTERIOUSLY
NEUROTICALLY
NOCONFIDENCE
NONRESIDENCE
NONRESISTANT
NUTRITIONIST
OBSEQUIOUSLY
PATHETICALLY
PECTORILOQUY
PEDANTICALLY
PERIODICALLY
PHONETICALLY
PHRONTISTERY
POTENTIALITY
PRECARIOUSLY
PRECOCIOUSLY
PREDOMINANCE
PREMAXILLARY
PRESCRIPTION
PRESCRIPTIVE
PRESTRICTION
PREVARICATOR
PRIZEFIGHTER
PRIZEWINNING
PROBATIONARY
PRODIGIOUSLY
PROFICIENTLY
PROLIFICALLY
PROPITIATION
PROPITIATORY
PROPITIOUSLY
PROSCRIPTION
PUGNACIOUSLY
QUIXOTICALLY
RECALCITRANT
RECEPTIONIST
RECOGNIZABLE
RECOGNIZANCE
REFLATIONARY
RENUNCIATION
REPATRIATION
RESUSCITATED
REVERSIONARY
RHYTHMICALLY
RISORGIMENTO
ROMANTICALLY
SADISTICALLY
SALVATIONIST
SARDONICALLY
SCAPULIMANCY
SECESSIONIST
SECTARIANISM
SEMANTICALLY
SERASKIERATE
SHIPBUILDING
SHORTCIRCUIT
SHORTSIGHTED
SIDEWHISKERS
SIGNIFICANCE
SPECIFICALLY
SPECKTIONEER
SPHAIRISTIKE
SPORADICALLY
STREPSIPTERA
SUBSCRIPTION
SUBSIDIARITY
SUFFICIENTLY
SUPERCILIARY
SUPERCILIOUS
SUPERHIGHWAY
SUSPICIOUSLY
SYMBOLICALLY
TERRIFICALLY
THEATRICALLY
TIGHTFITTING
TRALATICIOUS
TRALATITIOUS
TRANQUILIZER
TRANQUILLISE
TRANQUILLITY
TRANQUILLIZE
TRANSMIGRATE
TRANSMISSION
UNATTAINABLE
UNCHARITABLE
UNCHARITABLY
UNCONSIDERED
UNCONVINCING
UNCULTIVATED
UNDERPINNING
UNIMAGINABLE
UNOBTAINABLE
UNPROFITABLE
UPROARIOUSLY
USERFRIENDLY
VALENCIENNES
VIBRATIUNCLE
VILLEGIATURA
WILTSHIREMAN
YORKSHIREMAN
KATZENJAMMER
STRAITJACKET
CANTANKEROUS
SHOSTAKOVICH
THICKSKINNED
UNDERSKINKER
WICKETKEEPER
ACCOMPLISHED
ACCUMULATION
ACKNOWLEDGED
AGRICULTURAL
ANDOUILLETTE
ANNIHILATION
ANTEDILUVIAN
ARISTOLOCHIA
ARTICULATION
ASSIMILATION
AUSTRALASIAN
BANANALANDER
BENEVOLENTLY
BERTHOLLETIA
BERTILLONAGE
BREATHLESSLY
CANCELLATION
CAPITULATION
CARDIOLOGIST
COMPELLATION
CONTROLLABLE
CREMAILLIÈRE
DEAMBULATORY
DENDROLOGIST
DEPOPULATION
DEREGULATION
DISCIPLINARY
DISTILLATION
EFFORTLESSLY
EGYPTOLOGIST
EMASCULATION
EMBEZZLEMENT
ENCIRCLEMENT
ENTANGLEMENT
ENTOMOLOGIST
EPISTOLATERS
EPITHALAMION
EPITHALAMIUM
ESCAPOLOGIST
EXSUFFLICATE
FLAGELLATION
FRANKALMOIGN
FRIENDLINESS
FUSTILLIRIAN
GENETHLIACON
GRAPHOLOGIST
GROSSULARITE
GYNECOLOGIST
HAIRSPLITTER
HIEROGLYPHIC
HIGHFALUTING
ICONOCLASTIC
IMMACULATELY
IMMUNOLOGIST
INCOMPLETELY
INCONCLUSIVE
INSTALLATION
IRREGULARITY
IRRESOLUTELY
IRRESOLUTION
IRRESOLVABLE
ISHMAELITISH
JOURNALISTIC
MACMILLANITE
MANIPULATION
MANIPULATIVE
MARSEILLAISE
MERVEILLEUSE
METICULOUSLY
MICROCLIMATE
MINDFULLNESS
MINERALOGIST
MIRACULOUSLY
MITRAILLEUSE
MONOSYLLABIC
MONOSYLLABLE
MOSBOLLETJIE
MULTIPLICITY
MUSICOLOGIST
NATURALISTIC
NIGHTCLOTHES
NOMENCLATURE
NONCHALANTLY
OPHIOGLOSSUM
OUTBUILDINGS
PARAMILITARY
PEDICELLARIA
PENNSYLVANIA
PHOTOGLYPHIC
PHYSIOLOGIST
PLAINCLOTHES
POINTILLISME
POLYSYLLABIC
POLYSYLLABLE
POTAMOLOGIST
PROPHYLACTIC
PROTHALAMION
PROTHALAMIUM
PROTOPLASMAL
PROTOPLASMIC
PSEPHOLOGIST
PSYCHOLOGIST

REHABILITATE
RELENTLESSLY
RESETTLEMENT
RETICULATION
RIDICULOUSLY
SCANDALOUSLY
SCINTILLATOR
SCRUPULOUSLY
SCURRILOUSLY
SHIRTSLEEVES
SHORTSLEEVED
SLOVENLINESS
SPELEOLOGIST
SPHACELATION
SPIEGELEISEN
STANISLAVSKI
STRANGLEHOLD
STRANGLEWEED
STRIDULATION
SURREALISTIC
SURVEILLANCE
SYNADELPHITE
TECHNOLOGIST
THESSALONIAN
TOXICOLOGIST
TRICHOLOGIST
TROCHELMINTH
TROPHALLAXIS
UNCHALLENGED
UNDERCLOTHES
UNPARALLELED
UNPOPULARITY
VARICOLOURED
WEIGHTLIFTER
WELLBALANCED
WHIGMALEERIE
AMALGAMATION
ANTHELMINTIC
ATHEROMATOUS
AYUNTAMIENTO
BARBERMONGER
BIOCHEMISTRY
CALCEAMENTUM
CHEESEMONGER
CLAMJAMPHRIE
COMPROMISING
CONFIRMATION
CONFIRMATORY
CONGLOMERATE
CONSUMMATION
CONTERMINOUS
COSTERMONGER
CRASSAMENTUM
DEPARTMENTAL
DIAGRAMMATIC
DISCRIMINATE
ENTEROMORPHA
EPIGRAMMATIC
EPISTEMOLOGY
ETHEROMANIAC

EVENTEMPERED
EXPERIMENTAL
GOVERNMENTAL
INFLAMMATION
INFLAMMATORY
INSTRUMENTAL
KLEPTOMANIAC
LEGITIMATELY
LEPIDOMELANE
MALFORMATION
MINICOMPUTER
NONCOMMITTAL
NYMPHOMANIAC
PALUDAMENTUM
PANDAEMONIUM
POLICYMAKING
POSTHUMOUSLY
POSTLIMINARY
PROCLAMATION
PROGRAMMABLE
SCHIZOMYCETE
SCHOOLMASTER
SINGLEMINDED
SPLENOMEGALY
STRONGMINDED
SUBCOMMITTEE
SYNTAGMATITE
ACCIDENTALLY
ACQUAINTANCE
AERODYNAMICS
AMBULANCEMAN
ANTAGONISTIC
ANTANANARIVO
ANTONINIANUS
APOLLINARIAN
AUSTRONESIAN
BACCHANALIAN
BEAUMONTAGUE
BEAUMONTIQUE
BOUGAINVILLE
CARAVANSERAI
CEREMONIALLY
CHAUVINISTIC
CHLORINATION
CONDEMNATION
CONTIGNATION
COORDINATION
DEMIMONDAINE
DENOMINATION
DIPRIONIDIAN
DISCONNECTED
DISDAINFULLY
DISFRANCHISE
DOLPHINARIUM
DRESSINGDOWN
EPIPHENOMENA
EVENHANDEDLY
FARTHINGLAND
FRANKENSTEIN
FRANKINCENSE

GLOCKENSPIEL
GONDWANALAND
GUILDENSTERN
HORIZONTALLY
IDIOSYNCRASY
ILLUMINATING
ILLUMINATION
IMPREGNATION
INCIDENTALLY
INDEFENSIBLE
INDEFINITELY
INDEPENDENCE
INNOMINABLES
INORDINATELY
INSEMINATION
LABYRINTHINE
LEGIONNAIRES
LINCOLNSHIRE
MISPRONOUNCE
MONOTONOUSLY
NEWFOUNDLAND
NONAGENARIAN
OBEDIENTIARY
OCTOGENARIAN
OPINIONATIVE
PARACENTESIS
PASSIONATELY
PASSIONFRUIT
PENITENTIARY
POLYSYNDETON
POSTPONEMENT
PROGYMNASIUM
PSEUDONYMOUS
PSIPHENOMENA
PUMPERNICKEL
REJUVENATION
RODOMONTADER
SAUROGNATHAE
SCANDINAVIAN
SCHOPENHAUER
SCLERENCHYMA
SEXAGENARIAN
STAKHANOVITE
STELLENBOSCH
STOCKINGETTE
SUBSTANTIATE
SULPHONAMIDE
SUPERANNUATE
SURMOUNTABLE
SURROUNDINGS
THREADNEEDLE
UNDIMINISHED
UNSCIENTIFIC
VENEPUNCTURE
VERUMONTANUM
VETERINARIAN
WOLSTENHOLME
ADDITIONALLY
AECIDIOSPORE
AETHRIOSCOPE

APOSTROPHISE
ARCHILOCHIAN
ASTROLOGICAL
ASTRONOMICAL
BACKWOODSMAN
BARNSTORMING
BEHAVIOURISM
BLUESTOCKING
CARCINOGENIC
CATADIOPTRIC
CATHETOMETER
CEREBROTONIC
CHALICOTHERE
CHAMPIONSHIP
CHORIZONTIST
CHRESTOMATHY
CLAIRVOYANCE
CLAIRVOYANCY
CLEISTOGAMIC
COLDSHOULDER
COLLABORATOR
COLLYWOBBLES
COSCINOMANCY
COSMOPOLITAN
CROSSCOUNTRY
DEUTEROSCOPY
DICTATORSHIP
DIRECTORSHIP
DISAPPOINTED
DISHONORABLE
DISHONORABLY
ELECTROLYSIS
ELECTROPLATE
ELECTROTONUS
ENANTIOMORPH
ENANTIOPATHY
ENCYCLOPEDIA
ENCYCLOPEDIC
ERYTHROMYCIN
ESPAGNOLETTE
ETHNOLOGICAL
ETYMOLOGICAL
ETYMOLOGICON
FIRSTFOOTING
FOOTSLOGGING
FRACTIONALLY
FUNCTIONALLY
FUNCTIONLESS
GAINSBOROUGH
GALVANOMETER
GENEALOGICAL
GERONTOCRACY
GIGANTOMACHY
GRANDMONTINE
GYMNOSOPHIST
HAPPYGOLUCKY
HEMICHORDATA
HENCEFORWARD
HEROICOMICAL
HIPPOPOTAMUS

HOUSETOHOUSE
HYPERBOLICAL
HYPOCHONDRIA
ICHTHYOCOLLA
ICHTHYOPSIDA
IMPERSONALLY
IMPERSONATOR
IMPRISONMENT
INCONSOLABLE
INCORPORATED
INDISSOLUBLE
INHARMONIOUS
INTERLOCUTOR
INTERROGATOR
IRRATIONALLY
KALEIDOSCOPE
KALISTOCRACY
KERAUNOGRAPH
LONGSHOREMAN
LOXODROMICAL
LUXEMBOURGER
MACROPODIDAE
MAGNILOQUENT
MASSPRODUCED
MASTIGOPHORA
METALLOPHONE
METAPHORICAL
METROPOLITAN
MULTICOLORED
MYRINGOSCOPE
MYTHOLOGICAL
NEIGHBORHOOD
NEIGHBOURING
NEPHELOMETER
NEUROLOGICAL
NONALCOHOLIC
OCCASIONALLY
ONOMATOPOEIA
ONOMATOPOEIC
OPISTHOGRAPH
ORNITHOGALUM
ORTHODONTICS
ORTHOTONESIS
OSCILLOSCOPE
OSTEOPOROSIS
OTHERWORLDLY
OUTMANOEUVRE
OVERCROWDING
PANCHROMATIC
PANTISOCRACY
PAPILIONIDAE
PARSIMONIOUS
PARTICOLORED
PATHOLOGICAL
PETTIFOGGERS
PETTIFOGGERY
PETTIFOGGING
PHILOLOGICAL
PHILOSOPHIZE
PHOSPHORENCE

PHOSPHORESCE
POTICHOMANIA
PRAXINOSCOPE
PROLEGOMENON
PROSOPOPOEIA
PTERIDOPHYTE
PYTHONOMORPH
QUESTIONABLE
RECIPROCALLY
REDEPLOYMENT
REDISCOVERED
RELATIONSHIP
RHAMPHOTHECA
RHIPIDOPTERA
SALTATORIOUS
SARRUSOPHONE
SHAREHOLDING
SHORTCOMINGS
SIPHONOPHORA
SIPHONOSTELE
SLOCKDOLAGER
SLOCKDOLIGER
SLOCKDOLOGER
SMALLHOLDING
SOCIOLOGICAL
SOUTHCOTTIAN
SPECTROSCOPE
STREPTOMYCIN
STREPTONEURA
TAUTOLOGICAL
TELEUTOSPORE
TERRITORIALS
TETRODOTOXIN
THIRDBOROUGH
THYSANOPTERA
TOBACCONISTS
TRANSMOGRIFY
TRANSPONTINE
TRIGONOMETRY
ULTRAMONTANE
UNAUTHORISED
UNAUTHORIZED
UNECONOMICAL
UNEMPLOYMENT
UNFATHOMABLE
UNPARDONABLE
UNREASONABLE
UNRESPONSIVE
UNSEASONABLE
VAINGLORIOUS
WHIPPOORWILL
ANAMORPHOSIS
ANTHROPOLOGY
ANTICIPATION
ANTICIPATORY
ARISTOPHANES
ARSENOPYRITE
ARTHROPLASTY
AWEINSPIRING
BIBLIOPEGIST

BIOGRAPHICAL
BREASTPLOUGH
CHEESEPARING
CONSTIPATION
CONTEMPORARY
CONTEMPTIBLE
CONTEMPTUOUS
CONTRAPPOSTO
CONTRAPUNTAL
DIENCEPHALON
EMANCIPATION
ENTEROPNEUST
EPENCEPHALON
EPISCOPALIAN
EULENSPIEGEL
GEOGRAPHICAL
HETEROPHORIA
HETEROPLASIA
HISTIOPHORUS
HOMOEOPATHIC
INTERSPERSED
JENNYSPINNER
MUNICIPALITY
NEWSPAPERMAN
OBSTREPEROUS
PARALIPOMENA
PERSULPHURIC
PITTERPATTER
PRESUMPTUOUS
PRINCIPALITY
PSYCHOPATHIC
QUADRAPHONIC
RECORDPLAYER
SELFEMPLOYED
SOMATOPLEURE
SPOKESPERSON
STEREOPHONIC
STEREOPTICON
THESMOPHORIA
TRADESPEOPLE
TRICHOPHYTON
UNACCEPTABLE
UNSCRUPULOUS
VENTRIPOTENT
XANTHOPTERIN
BARRANQUILLA
ACCELERATION
ACCOUTREMENT
ADULTERATION
ALLITERATION
AMELIORATION
ANTEMERIDIAN
ANTIBARBARUS
ANTIPARTICLE
ANTISTROPHON
ANTITHROMBIN
BACKWARDNESS
BEAUMARCHAIS
BICAMERALISM
BLABBERMOUTH

BLENNORRHOEA
BLETHERSKATE
BOISTEROUSLY
BOOBYTRAPPED
CALLIGRAPHIC
CARTOGRAPHER
CARTOGRAPHIC
CATASTROPHIC
CHARTERHOUSE
CHESTERFIELD
CHIROPRACTIC
CHIROPRACTOR
CHITTERLINGS
CLAPPERBOARD
CONCURRENTLY
CONSECRATION
CONTRARINESS
COUNTERBLAST
COUNTERCLAIM
COUNTERMARCH
COUNTERPOINT
COUNTERPOISE
DAGUERROTYPE
DEASPIRATION
DECELERATION
DECENTRALISE
DECENTRALIZE
DEGENERATION
DELIBERATELY
DELIBERATION
DERESTRICTED
DILATORINESS
DISASTROUSLY
DISCOURAGING
DISCOURTEOUS
DRINKDRIVING
EAVESDROPPER
ECCENTRICITY
ENCHEIRIDION
ENTERPRISING
ENTREPRENEUR
EXAGGERATION
EXASPERATING
EXASPERATION
EXHILARATING
EXHILARATION
FEATHERBRAIN
FEHMGERICHTE
FLITTERMOUSE
GEOMETRICIAN
GERIATRICIAN
GLOBETROTTER
GREENGROCERS
GREENGROCERY
HAEMORRHOIDS
HANDKERCHIEF
HARUMFRODITE
HIEROGRAMMAT
HILDEBRANDIC
HIPPOCRATISE

HIPPOCREPIAN
HOUSEBREAKER
HYDROGRAPHER
HYMNOGRAPHER
IAMBOGRAPHER
ILLUSTRATION
ILLUSTRATIVE
IMMODERATELY
IMMODERATION
IMPOVERISHED
INACCURATELY
INADVERTENCE
INAUGURATION
INCINERATION
INCOHERENTLY
INDISCRETION
INDOCTRINATE
INDUSTRIALLY
INEXPERIENCE
INFILTRATION
INSTAURATION
INTENERATION
INTERPRETING
INVIGORATING
INVIGORATION
IRREVERENTLY
IRREVERSIBLE
KLETTERSCHUE
KLIPSPRINGER
LITHOGRAPHIC
LYMANTRIIDAE
MACABERESQUE
MACHAIRODONT
MALNUTRITION
MARCOBRUNNER
METAMORPHISM
METAMORPHOSE
MILITARISTIC
MINISTRATION
MISAPPREHEND
MISREPRESENT
MOISTURIZING
MOUTHBROODER
NORTHERNMOST
OBLITERATION
OBSTETRICIAN
OCTASTROPHIC
OVERSTRAINED
PANPHARMACON
PEDIATRICIAN
PERICARDITIS
PERIPHRASTIC
PERPETRATION
PERSPIRATION
PHILHARMONIC
PHOTOGRAPHER
PHOTOGRAPHIC
PHOTOGRAVURE
PLASTERSTONE
PORNOGRAPHIC
PRALLTRILLER
QUARTERFINAL
QUARTERLIGHT
QUARTERSTAFF
RADIOGRAPHER
RECUPERATION
RECUPERATIVE
REDISTRIBUTE
REGENERATION
REGISTRATION
REMEMBRANCER
REMUNERATION
REMUNERATIVE
RESTAURATEUR
RHINORRHOEAL
SCATTERBRAIN
SCATTERMOUCH
SCHEHERAZADE
SELFPORTRAIT
SEMICIRCULAR
SKUTTERUDITE
SLUBBERINGLY
SOUTHERNMOST
SOUTHERNWOOD
STAGGERINGLY
STENOGRAPHER
STENTORPHONE
STOCKBREEDER
STORMTROOPER
STUBBORNNESS
SUBTERRANEAN
THUNDERCLOUD
THUNDERFLASH
THUNDERSTORM
TRANSGRESSOR
UNAPPARELLED
UNCONTROLLED
UNDERWRITTEN
UNDESERVEDLY
UNDETERMINED
UNEXPURGATED
UNIMPORTANCE
UNINTERESTED
UNOBSTRUCTED
UNRESERVEDLY
UNRESTRAINED
UNRESTRICTED
UNRETURNABLE
UNSURPRISING
UNUTTERABLES
VEHMGERICHTE
VITUPERATION
VITUPERATIVE
VOCIFERATION
VOCIFEROUSLY
WALLYDRAIGLE
WEATHERPROOF
WOODBURYTYPE
ACQUIESCENCE
ADMINISTRATE
ADMONISHMENT
AGGRESSIVELY
AGRIBUSINESS
ARBORESCENCE
ARFVEDSONITE
ASTONISHMENT
AWAYABSOLUTE
BANDERSNATCH
BEACONSFIELD
BLANDISHMENT
BREASTSUMMER
BRONTOSAURUS
BUSINESSLIKE
BUTTERSCOTCH
CARELESSNESS
CHASTISEMENT
CHILDISHNESS
CHURLISHNESS
CIRCASSIENNE
CIRCUMSCRIBE
CIRCUMSTANCE
CIVILISATION
CLANNISHNESS
COMMENSURATE
COMMISSARIAT
COMMISSIONED
COMMISSIONER
COMPENSATION
COMPENSATORY
CONCLUSIVELY
CONDENSATION
CONFESSIONAL
CONQUISTADOR
CONVERSATION
DISCONSOLATE
DISPENSATION
DISPOSSESSED
DISQUISITION
ELEEMOSYNARY
ENERGYSAVING
ENHYPOSTASIA
ENTOMOSTRACA
FEARLESSNESS
FIDDLESTICKS
FLUORESCENCE
FRONTISPIECE
GASTROSOPHER
GEOPHYSICIST
GESELLSCHAFT
GRANDISONIAN
HALLANSHAKER
HAPPENSTANCE
HARNESSMAKER
HEADMISTRESS
HELPLESSNESS
HETEROSEXUAL
HETEROSOMATA
HOPELESSNESS
IMPERISHABLE
IMPRESSIVELY
INACCESSIBLE
INADMISSIBLE
INCREASINGLY
INDIGESTIBLE
INTRANSIGENT
INTRANSITIVE
IRRESISTIBLE
LABOURSAVING
LATIROSTRATE
LIFELESSNESS
LISTLESSNESS
LONGDISTANCE
LUMINESCENCE
LUMINISCENCE
MALACOSTRACA
MASTERSTROKE
MONTESSORIAN
NARCISSISTIC
NEOCLASSICAL
NONEXISTENCE
OBSOLESCENCE
OPPRESSIVELY
ORGANISATION
PAINLESSNESS
PERSUASIVELY
PERVERSENESS
POSSESSIVELY
POSTMISTRESS
PREMONSTRANT
PREPOSSESSED
PRIGGISHNESS
PROCESSIONAL
PROFESSIONAL
PROFESSORIAL
QUINTESSENCE
RADIOISOTOPE
READJUSTMENT
RECKLESSNESS
REMINISCENCE
RESIPISCENCE
RESTLESSNESS
RUTHLESSNESS
SHEEPISHNESS
SHILLYSHALLY
SNOBBISHNESS
STEREOSCOPIC
STRATOSPHERE
SUBCONSCIOUS
SUBLAPSARIAN
SUBMISSIVELY
SUCCESSFULLY
SUCCESSIVELY
SUCCUSSATION
SURPRISINGLY
TACTLESSNESS
TARAMASALATA
THERMOSTATIC
TIMELESSNESS
TITANOSAURUS
TROCHOSPHERE

UNACCUSTOMED
UNCLASSIFIED
UNIVERSALIST
UNSATISFYING
ABSQUATULATE
AGALMATOLITE
ALIMENTATIVE
AMARANTACEAE
AMPHISTOMOUS
ANDROSTERONE
ANTIMETABOLE
APFELSTRUDEL
ARISTOTELEAN
ASYMMETRICAL
ATTRACTIVELY
AUGMENTATION
AUSCULTATION
AUTHENTICATE
AUTHENTICITY
BABINGTONITE
BIRDWATCHING
BLOODSTAINED
BREATHTAKING
BUNKOSTEERER
CABINETMAKER
CALLISTHENES
CARICATURIST
CHARACTERIZE
CHREMATISTIC
COHABITATION
COLLECTIVELY
COLLECTORATE
COLLUCTATION
COMPLETENESS
CONCENTRATED
CONDUCTIVITY
CONFECTIONER
CONGRATULATE
CONSISTENTLY
CONSTITUENCY
CONSTITUENTS
CONSTITUTION
CONSULTATION
CONSULTATIVE
CONTRITURATE
CONVENTIONAL
DEBILITATING
DECAPITATION
DECORATIVELY
DELICATESSEN
DEMILITARIZE
DEMONSTRABLE
DEMONSTRABLY
DEMONSTRATOR
DESSERTSPOON
DIALECTICIAN
DISCONTENTED
DISSERTATION
ENTREATINGLY
EPANORTHOSIS
ERATOSTHENES
EXHAUSTIVELY
EXHIBITIONER
EXPLOITATION
FERMENTATION
FIGURATIVELY
FORTUITOUSLY
FREIGHTLINER
FRUMENTATION
GENTLETAMPER
GIBRALTARIAN
GLADIATORIAL
GONADOTROPIN
HAMBLETONIAN
HEARTSTRINGS
HEREDITAMENT
HUMANITARIAN
ILLEGITIMACY
ILLEGITIMATE
IMPENETRABLE
IMPLANTATION
IMPOLITENESS
INCRUSTATION
INESCUTCHEON
INEXACTITUDE
INSPECTORATE
INTERSTELLAR
INTRAUTERINE
KINAESTHETIC
LABANOTATION
LANCASTERIAN
LAUREATESHIP
MISQUOTATION
MISSTATEMENT
MUGGLETONIAN
NEOPLATONISM
OBSOLETENESS
OCCUPATIONAL
OREOPITHECUS
OREOPITHEOUS
OVERESTIMATE
OXYACETYLENE
PALEONTOLOGY
PANAESTHESIA
PANCHATANTRA
PERCEPTIVELY
PERCEPTIVITY
PEREMPTORILY
PERIOSTRACUM
PERNOCTATION
PERSISTENTLY
PHILANTHROPY
PHILISTINISM
PHLEBOTOMIST
PIGMENTATION
PLACENTIFORM
POPOCATEPETL
PRACTITIONER
PREDESTINATE
PREGUSTATION
PREHISTORIAN
PREPOSTEROUS
PRESBYTERIAN
PRESENTATION
PRESENTIMENT
PREVENTATIVE
PRODUCTIVITY
PROGESTERONE
PROPORTIONAL
PROSTITUTION
PROTACTINIUM
PROTECTIVELY
PROTECTORATE
PROTESTATION
QUANTITATIVE
RECAPITULATE
RECONSTITUTE
RECREATIONAL
REDEMPTIONER
REMONSTRANCE
RESPECTFULLY
RESPECTIVELY
SEGMENTATION
SELFCATERING
SELFINTEREST
SEMIDETACHED
SEQUENTIALLY
SEQUESTRATOR
SESQUITERTIA
SHORTSTAFFED
SIVAPITHECUS
SOLICITATION
SOLICITOUSLY
SOPHISTICATE
SPERMATOCYTE
STATISTICIAN
STEREOTYPING
STERNUTATION
STREPITATION
STROMATOLITE
SUBCONTINENT
SUBHASTATION
SUBJECTIVELY
SUBJECTIVITY
SUBSTITUTION
SUGGESTIVELY
SUPERSTITION
TAPSALTEERIE
TAPSLETEERIE
TEETERTOTTER
TELEASTHETIC
TERCENTENARY
TESTOSTERONE
THAUMATURGIC
THAUMATURGUS
THEORETICIAN
THIGMOTROPIC
THOUGHTFULLY
TOTALITARIAN
TRANSITIONAL
UNAPPETIZING
UNDERSTAFFED
UNIDENTIFIED
VINDICTIVELY
WOLLASTONITE
ACCENTUATION
AERONAUTICAL
ALPHANUMERIC
ANTINEUTRINO
ATTRIBUTABLE
BIELORUSSIAN
BLACKCURRANT
BYELORUSSIAN
CAMPANULARIA
CAUTIOUSNESS
CHEERFULNESS
COLLOQUIALLY
CONSEQUENCES
CONSEQUENTLY
CONSTRUCTION
CONSTRUCTIVE
CONTINUATION
CONTINUOUSLY
COVETOUSNESS
DISREPUTABLE
DRAMATURGIST
EXTINGUISHER
FAITHFULNESS
FLORICULTURE
FORCEFULNESS
FRUITFULNESS
GLUBBDUBDRIB
GRACEFULNESS
GRACIOUSNESS
GRATEFULNESS
HORTICULTURE
HYDROQUINONE
IMMEASURABLE
IMMEASURABLY
INADEQUATELY
INCALCULABLE
INDISPUTABLE
INDISPUTABLY
INFREQUENTLY
INTERRUPTION
INTRODUCTION
INTRODUCTORY
LILLIBULLERO
LILLIBURLERO
LIVERPUDLIAN
LONGITUDINAL
MANSLAUGHTER
MENSTRUATION
METALLURGIST
OVERSCUTCHED
PARTICULARLY
PEACEFULNESS
PERAMBULATOR
PISCICULTURE
PREREQUISITE

REPERCUSSION
REPRODUCTION
REPRODUCTIVE
SIPUNCULACEA
SPACIOUSNESS
SPECIOUSNESS
SPIRITUALISM
SPIRITUALIST
SPIRITUALITY
SPITEFULNESS
SPURIOUSNESS
STEPDAUGHTER
STRUCTURALLY
STUDIOUSNESS
SUBSEQUENTLY
SUBSTRUCTURE
SWASHBUCKLER
THANKFULNESS
THREEQUARTER
TRABECULATED
TRANSLUCENCE
TRUTHFULNESS
TUBERCULOSIS
UNCTUOUSNESS
UNDERCURRENT
UNFAVOURABLE
UNFREQUENTED
UNPREJUDICED
UNPRODUCTIVE
URTRICULARIA
VENGEFULNESS
VOLUPTUOUSLY
WAREHOUSEMAN
WATCHFULNESS
YOUTHFULNESS
ZARATHUSTRIC
CONSERVATION
CONSERVATISM
CONSERVATIVE
CONSERVATORY
CREATIVENESS
MANOEUVRABLE
PRESERVATION
PRESERVATIVE
RONCESVALLES
STRADIVARIUS
SUBSERVIENCE
TURACOVERDIN
BANTAMWEIGHT
BESSERWISSER
CHURCHWARDEN
COMMONWEALTH
DONNERWETTER
DUNNIEWASSAL
KIRSCHWASSER
MANGELWURZEL
MIDDLEWEIGHT
OVERPOWERING
PINNIEWINKLE
PRAISEWORTHY
SCREENWRITER
SCRIPTWRITER
WELTERWEIGHT
WILLIEWAUGHT
AMBIDEXTROUS
CROSSEXAMINE
UNDEREXPOSED
ACHLAMYDEOUS
CARBOHYDRATE
CATAPHYSICAL
DISCOMYCETES
FLAMBOYANTLY
HOLIDAYMAKER
HYPERPYRETIC
METAPHYSICAL
MOTORCYCLIST
ONCORHYNCHUS
SCHINDYLESIS
TETRACYCLINE
THEOPHYLLINE
CANONIZATION
CIVILIZATION
COLONIZATION
FINALIZATION
HUMANIZATION
IDEALIZATION
IMMUNIZATION
LEGALIZATION
MOBILIZATION
ORGANIZATION
PENALIZATION
POLARIZATION
URBANIZATION
VAPORIZATION

12:8

ABBREVIATION
ACCELERATION
ACCENTUATION
ACCUMULATION
ADJUDICATION
ADULTERATION
AERODYNAMICS
AGATHODAIMON
ALEXIPHARMIC
ALIMENTATIVE
ALLITERATION
AMALGAMATION
AMARANTACEAE
AMELIORATION
AMPHISBAENIC
ANECATHARSIS
ANNIHILATION
ANNUNCIATION
ANTANANARIVO
ANTICIPATION
ANTICIPATORY
ANTIMACASSAR
ANTIMETABOLE
APLANOGAMETE
APOLLINARIAN
APPOGGIATURA
APPRECIATION
APPRECIATIVE
ARTICULATION
ASPHYXIATION
ASSIMILATION
ATHEROMATOUS
AUGMENTATION
AUSCULTATION
AUSTRALASIAN
BACCHANALIAN
BACKBREAKING
BAIRNSFATHER
BANANALANDER
BICAMERALISM
BLOODSTAINED
BOOBYTRAPPED
BREATHTAKING
BRONTOSAURUS
CALLIGRAPHIC
CALUMNIATION
CANCELLATION
CANONIZATION
CAPITULATION
CARPETBAGGER
CARTOGRAPHER
CARTOGRAPHIC
CHEESEPARING
CHILDBEARING
CHIROPRACTIC
CHIROPRACTOR
CHLORINATION
CHRISTIANITY
CHURCHWARDEN
CIVILISATION
CIVILIZATION
CLAUDICATION
CODIFICATION
COHABITATION
COLLUCTATION
COLONIZATION
COMMENDATION
COMMENDATORY
COMMISSARIAT
COMPELLATION
COMPENSATION
COMPENSATORY
COMPLICATION
COMPURGATION
CONCILIATION
CONCILIATORY
CONDEMNATION
CONDENSATION
CONFIRMATION
CONFIRMATORY
CONFISCATION
CONGREGATION
CONSECRATION
CONSERVATION
CONSERVATISM
CONSERVATIVE
CONSERVATORY
CONSTIPATION
CONSULTATION
CONSULTATIVE
CONSUMMATION
CONTIGNATION
CONTINUATION
CONVERSATION
CONVIVIALITY
COORDINATION
CRISTOBALITE
CROSSEXAMINE
DEAMBULATORY
DEASPIRATION
DEBILITATING
DECAPITATION
DECELERATION
DECENTRALISE
DECENTRALIZE
DEGENERATION
DELIBERATELY
DELIBERATION
DEMILITARIZE
DENOMINATION
DENUNCIATION
DEPOPULATION
DEPRECIATION
DEPRECIATORY
DEREGULATION
DILAPIDATION
DISACCHARIDE
DISAPPEARING
DISCOURAGING
DISENCHANTED
DISPENSATION
DISSERTATION
DISSOCIATION
DISTILLATION
DOLPHINARIUM
DUNNIEWASSAL
ECCLESIASTES
ECCLESIASTIC
EMANCIPATION
EMASCULATION
ENERGYSAVING
ENTHUSIASTIC
EPACRIDACEAE
EPISCOPALIAN
EPISTOLATERS
EPITHALAMION
EPITHALAMIUM
EQUIVOCATION
EQUIVOCATORY
ESSENTIALITY
ETHEROMANIAC
EXACERBATION
EXAGGERATION

EXASPERATING
EXASPERATION
EXCRUCIATING
EXCRUCIATION
EXHILARATING
EXHILARATION
EXPLOITATION
FAINTHEARTED
FERMENTATION
FINALIZATION
FLAGELLATION
FLAMBOYANTLY
FLUORIDATION
FRUMENTATION
GENTLETAMPER
GIBRALTARIAN
GONDWANALAND
GROSSULARITE
HEREDITAMENT
HIEROGRAMMAT
HIEROPHANTIC
HILDEBRANDIC
HIPPOCRATISE
HOMOEOPATHIC
HUMANITARIAN
HUMANIZATION
HYDROGRAPHER
HYMNOGRAPHER
IAMBOGRAPHER
ICONOCLASTIC
IDEALIZATION
ILLOGICALITY
ILLUMINATING
ILLUMINATION
ILLUSTRATION
ILLUSTRATIVE
IMMACULATELY
IMMODERATELY
IMMODERATION
IMMUNIZATION
IMPARTIALITY
IMPLANTATION
IMPREGNATION
INACCURATELY
INADEQUATELY
INAUGURATION
INCINERATION
INCRUSTATION
INFILTRATION
INFLAMMATION
INFLAMMATORY
INGRATIATING
INNOMINABLES
INORDINATELY
INSEMINATION
INSTALLATION
INSTAURATION
INTENERATION
INTERCHANGED
INTIMIDATING
INTIMIDATION
INTOXICATING
INTOXICATION
INVALIDATION
INVIGORATING
INVIGORATION
IRREGULARITY
KATZENJAMMER
KINDERGARTEN
KIRSCHWASSER
KLEPTOMANIAC
LABANOTATION
LABOURSAVING
LEGALIZATION
LEGIONNAIRES
LEGITIMATELY
LIGHTHEARTED
LITHOGRAPHIC
LUXULLIANITE
MACMILLANITE
MALFORMATION
MALLOPHAGOUS
MANIPULATION
MANIPULATIVE
MASTURBATION
MECHITHARIST
MENSTRUATION
MINISTRATION
MISDEMEANOUR
MISQUOTATION
MOBILIZATION
MODIFICATION
MUNICIPALITY
NEPENTHACEAE
NOMENCLATURE
NONAGENARIAN
NONCHALANTLY
NOTIFICATION
NYMPHOMANIAC
OBLITERATION
OCTOGENARIAN
OPINIONATIVE
ORGANISATION
ORGANIZATION
OSSIFICATION
OVERSTRAINED
PACIFICATION
PANCHATANTRA
PANTOPHAGOUS
PASSEMEASURE
PASSIONATELY
PENALIZATION
PERIPHRASTIC
PERMANGANATE
PERNOCTATION
PERPETRATION
PERSPICACITY
PERSPIRATION
PERTURBATION
PHOTOGRAPHER
PHOTOGRAPHIC
PHOTOGRAVURE
PIGMENTATION
PITTERPATTER
PLEIOCHASIUM
POLARIZATION
POLICYMAKING
PORNOGRAPHIC
POTENTIALITY
POWERSHARING
PRACTICALITY
PREGUSTATION
PRESENTATION
PRESERVATION
PRESERVATIVE
PREVENTATIVE
PRINCIPALITY
PROCLAMATION
PROGYMNASIUM
PROLONGATION
PROMULGATION
PROPHYLACTIC
PROPITIATION
PROPITIATORY
PROTESTATION
PROTHALAMION
PROTHALAMIUM
PROTOPLASMAL
PROTOPLASMIC
PSYCHOPATHIC
PURIFICATION
QUANTITATIVE
RADIOGRAPHER
RAMIFICATION
RATIFICATION
RECUPERATION
RECUPERATIVE
REGENERATION
REGISTRATION
REJUVENATION
REMEMBRANCER
REMUNERATION
REMUNERATIVE
RENUNCIATION
REPATRIATION
RESTAURATEUR
RETICULATION
RONCESVALLES
SAUROGNATHAE
SCANDINAVIAN
SCHEHERAZADE
SCHOOLMASTER
SCRIMSHANDER
SCRIMSHANKER
SECTARIANISM
SEGMENTATION
SEMIDETACHED
SEXAGENARIAN
SHORTSTAFFED
SILVERHAIRED
SINGLEHANDED
SOLICITATION
SPHACELATION
SPIRITUALISM
SPIRITUALIST
SPIRITUALITY
SPREADEAGLED
STANISLAVSKI
STENOGRAPHER
STERNUTATION
STONECHATTER
STRADIVARIUS
STRAITJACKET
STREPITATION
STRIDULATION
SUBARRHATION
SUBHASTATION
SUBLAPSARIAN
SUBSIDIARITY
SUBTERRANEAN
SUCCUSSATION
SULPHONAMIDE
SUPERCHARGED
SUPERCHARGER
SUPPLICATION
SYNTAGMATITE
TAMARICACEAE
TARAMASALATA
TECHNICALITY
THEREAGAINST
THREEQUARTER
TITANOSAURUS
TOTALITARIAN
TRADESCANTIA
TRIUMPHANTLY
TURBOCHARGER
UNDERSTAFFED
UNDISCHARGED
UNIVERSALIST
UNPOPULARITY
UNRESTRAINED
UNUTTERABLES
URBANIZATION
VAPORIZATION
VERIFICATION
VETERINARIAN
VILIFICATION
VILLEGIATURA
VITUPERATION
VITUPERATIVE
VOCIFERATION
WALLYDRAIGLE
WELLBALANCED
WHIMSICALITY
WHOLEHEARTED
WILLIEWAUGHT
WINTERHALTER
YELLOWHAMMER
ANTIBARBARUS
CLAPPERBOARD

COLLYWOBBLES
COUNTERBLAST
FEATHERBRAIN
GLUBBDUBDRIB
HELIOGABALUS
INVERTEBRATE
PURPOSEBUILT
SCATTERBRAIN
SHUFFLEBOARD
SPURTLEBLADE
STELLENBOSCH
UNNEIGHBORLY
ACADEMICALLY
ACQUIESCENCE
AMBULANCEMAN
ANTIBACCHIUS
APPENDECTOMY
APPENDICITIS
ARBORESCENCE
ARCHILOCHIAN
ARCHITECTURE
ARTIODACTYLA
ARTISTICALLY
ASSUEFACTION
BEAUMARCHAIS
BIRDWATCHING
BLUESTOCKING
BUTTERSCOTCH
CAMIKNICKERS
CIRCUMSCRIBE
COMMUNICABLE
CONSTRICTION
CONSTRUCTION
CONSTRUCTIVE
CONTUMACIOUS
COUNTERCLAIM
CROSSSECTION
CYMOTRICHOUS
DISCOMYCETES
DISFRANCHISE
DISINFECTANT
DISREPECTFUL
DIVERTICULUM
DOGMATICALLY
DOMESTICATED
DRAMATICALLY
ECONOMICALLY
ECSTATICALLY
ELECTRICALLY
EMPHATICALLY
ESTHETICALLY
EXSERVICEMAN
FLUORESCENCE
FRANKINCENSE
GALLINACEOUS
GEOLOGICALLY
GERONTOCRACY
GESELLSCHAFT
HANDKERCHIEF
HERMETICALLY
HISTORICALLY
HORRIFICALLY
HYGIENICALLY
HYPNOTICALLY
HYPOTHECATOR
HYSTERECTOMY
HYSTERICALLY
ICHTHYOCOLLA
IDIOSYNCRASY
IMPERFECTION
INAPPLICABLE
INAUSPICIOUS
INERADICABLE
INESCUTCHEON
INEXPLICABLE
INEXPLICABLY
INEXTRICABLE
INEXTRICABLY
INSUFFICIENT
INSURRECTION
INTELLECTUAL
INTERJECTION
INTERLOCUTOR
INTERSECTION
INTRODUCTION
INTRODUCTORY
IRRESPECTIVE
JURISDICTION
KALISTOCRACY
LAMELLICORNE
LEIOTRICHOUS
LIQUEFACTION
LUMINESCENCE
LUMINISCENCE
MAGNETICALLY
MAGNIFICENCE
MAJESTICALLY
MECHANICALLY
MERETRICIOUS
MERITRICIOUS
METHODICALLY
MNEMOTECHNIC
MOTORCYCLIST
NEUROTICALLY
OBSOLESCENCE
PANDANACEOUS
PANTISOCRACY
PATHETICALLY
PEDANTICALLY
PERIODICALLY
PERTINACIOUS
PERVICACIOUS
PETRIFACTION
PHONETICALLY
PREDILECTION
PRESTRICTION
PREVARICATOR
PROLIFICALLY
PTERODACTYLE
PUTREFACTION
QUIXOTICALLY
RECIPROCALLY
RECOLLECTION
REMINISCENCE
REPRODUCTION
REPRODUCTIVE
RESIPISCENCE
RESURRECTION
RHYTHMICALLY
RHYTIDECTOMY
ROMANTICALLY
SADISTICALLY
SARDONICALLY
SATISFACTION
SATISFACTORY
SCLERENCHYMA
SEMANTICALLY
SEMICIRCULAR
SEMIPRECIOUS
SHAMEFACEDLY
SIGNIFICANCE
SPECIFICALLY
SPORADICALLY
STEEPLECHASE
STEREOSCOPIC
STUPEFACTION
SUBCONSCIOUS
SUBSTRUCTURE
SUPERNACULUM
SWASHBUCKLER
SYMBOLICALLY
TERRIFICALLY
TETRACYCLINE
THEATRICALLY
THUNDERCLOUD
TRALATICIOUS
TRANSLUCENCE
UNATTRACTIVE
UNPRODUCTIVE
UNSUSPECTING
VENEPUNCTURE
ACHLAMYDEOUS
AMBASSADRESS
BACKWARDNESS
BACKWOODSMAN
CARBOHYDRATE
CONSOLIDATED
CONSOLIDATOR
DEMIMONDAINE
DISCOMEDUSAE
EVENHANDEDLY
GRASSWIDOWER
HOBBIDIDANCE
IMPROVIDENCE
INDEBTEDNESS
INDEPENDENCE
INFORMIDABLE
INTERMEDIARY
INTERMEDIATE
LAMPADEDROMY
LIVERPUDLIAN
LONGITUDINAL
MACROPODIDAE
MASSPRODUCED
NEWFOUNDLAND
NOCONFIDENCE
NONRESIDENCE
OUTBUILDINGS
PERICARDITIS
PHYTONADIONE
POLYSYNDETON
POSTGRADUATE
PREPAREDNESS
RETARDEDNESS
SURROUNDINGS
TETRAHEDRITE
UNCONSIDERED
UNPREJUDICED
WRETCHEDNESS
ACCOUCHEMENT
ACCOUTREMENT
ACKNOWLEDGED
AMPHITHEATER
AMPHITHEATRE
ANAESTHETISE
ANAESTHETIST
ANAESTHETIZE
ANDROSTERONE
ANNOUNCEMENT
ARISTOTELEAN
AROMATHERAPY
ATMOSPHERICS
AUSTRONESIAN
BANTAMWEIGHT
BENEVOLENTLY
BETHLEHEMITE
BIBLIOPEGIST
BRACHYCEPHAL
BREATHLESSLY
BRICKFIELDER
BUCKLEBEGGAR
BUNKOSTEERER
CALCEAMENTUM
CANTANKEROUS
CARDINDEXING
CHARACTERIZE
CHASTISEMENT
CHEMOTHERAPY
COINCIDENTAL
COMMENCEMENT
COMMONWEALTH
COMPLACENTLY
COMPLETENESS
CONCURRENTLY
CONGLOMERATE
CONSEQUENCES
CONSEQUENTLY
CONSISTENTLY
CONVENIENCES
CONVENIENTLY

CRASSAMENTUM
CREATIVENESS
CURMUDGEONLY
DELICATESSEN
DEPARTMENTAL
DISAGREEABLE
DISAGREEMENT
DISCONCERTED
DISCONNECTED
DISCONTENTED
DISPLACEMENT
DISPOSSESSED
DONNERWETTER
DOUBLEDECKER
EFFORTLESSLY
EMBEZZLEMENT
EMBROIDERESS
ENCIRCLEMENT
ENTANGLEMENT
ENTREPRENEUR
ESTRANGEMENT
EXCHANGEABLE
EXPERIMENTAL
FORMALDEHYDE
GASTARBEITER
GOBBLEDEGOOK
GOVERNMENTAL
HAMMERHEADED
HETEROSEXUAL
HIPPOCREPIAN
HOUSEBREAKER
HOUSEKEEPING
HYDROTHERAPY
HYPNOTHERAPY
IMPOLITENESS
INCOHERENTLY
INCOMPLETELY
INDISCRETION
INFREQUENTLY
INFRINGEMENT
INSTRUMENTAL
INTERPRETING
INTERSPERSED
INTERSTELLAR
INTRAUTERINE
IRREVERENTLY
LANCASTERIAN
LAUREATESHIP
LEPIDOMELANE
MACABERESQUE
MARRIAGEABLE
MIDDLEWEIGHT
MISAPPREHEND
MISPLACEMENT
MISREPRESENT
MISSTATEMENT
MOSBOLLETJIE
MUDDLEHEADED
NEVERTHELESS
NEWSPAPERMAN
OBSOLETENESS
OBSTREPEROUS
ORIENTEERING
ORTHOPAEDICS
ORTHOPAEDIST
OUTMANOEUVRE
OVERPOWERING
PALUDAMENTUM
PARANTHELIUM
PEACEKEEPING
PERSISTENTLY
PERVERSENESS
POPOCATEPETL
POSTPONEMENT
PREPONDERANT
PREPONDERATE
PREPONDERENT
PREPOSSESSED
PREPOSTEROUS
PRESBYTERIAN
PROFICIENTLY
PROFITEERING
PROGESTERONE
QUADRAGESIMA
RACKETEERING
RADIOTHERAPY
RECHARGEABLE
RELENTLESSLY
RENOUNCEMENT
RESETTLEMENT
RESPONDENTIA
SCHNEIDERIAN
SCLERODERMIA
SELFADHESIVE
SELFCATERING
SELFINTEREST
SEPTUAGESIMA
SERASKIERATE
SESQUITERTIA
SHIRTSLEEVES
SHORTSLEEVED
SINGLEDECKER
SPELLCHECKER
SPIEGELEISEN
SPLENOMEGALY
SPOKESPERSON
STERNWHEELER
STOCKBREEDER
STRANGLEHOLD
STRANGLEWEED
SUBSEQUENTLY
SUFFICIENTLY
TAPSALTEERIE
TAPSLETEERIE
TERCENTENARY
TESTOSTERONE
THREADNEEDLE
TRADESPEOPLE
TRANSGRESSOR
TRANSOCEANIC
TURACOVERDIN
UINTATHERIUM
UNAPPARELLED
UNCHALLENGED
UNCHANGEABLE
UNFREQUENTED
UNINTERESTED
UNMANAGEABLE
USERFRIENDLY
VALENCIENNES
WELTERWEIGHT
WHIGMALEERIE
WICKETKEEPER
AFTEREFFECTS
BEACONSFIELD
CHESTERFIELD
DISDAINFULLY
MEANINGFULLY
PASSIONFRUIT
PURPOSEFULLY
QUARTERFINAL
RESPECTFULLY
SUCCESSFULLY
THOUGHTFULLY
THUNDERFLASH
UNSATISFYING
ADVANTAGEOUS
ADVANTAGIOUS
ASTROLOGICAL
BOONDOGGLING
CARCINOGENIC
CLEARSIGHTED
CLEISTOGAMIC
DISINTEGRATE
DRESSINGDOWN
ETHNOLOGICAL
ETYMOLOGICAL
ETYMOLOGICON
EXTRAVAGANCE
EXTRAVAGANZA
FARTHINGLAND
FOOTSLOGGING
GENEALOGICAL
INCORRIGIBLE
INCORRIGIBLY
INTELLIGENCE
INTELLIGIBLE
INTERROGATOR
INVESTIGATOR
KERAUNOGRAPH
MANSLAUGHTER
MARCONIGRAPH
MINDBOGGLING
MYTHOLOGICAL
NEUROLOGICAL
OPISTHOGRAPH
ORNITHOGALUM
PATHOLOGICAL
PETTIFOGGERS
PETTIFOGGERY
PETTIFOGGING
PHILOLOGICAL
PRIZEFIGHTER
REDINTEGRATE
SACRILEGIOUS
SHORTSIGHTED
SOCIOLOGICAL
STEPDAUGHTER
STOCKINGETTE
SUPERHIGHWAY
TAUTOLOGICAL
TRANSMIGRATE
TRANSMOGRIFY
UNEXPURGATED
ADMONISHMENT
ANAMORPHOSIS
ANTIRACHITIC
APPROACHABLE
ARISTOPHANES
ASTONISHMENT
BIOGRAPHICAL
BLANDISHMENT
CALLISTHENES
CHARTERHOUSE
CHILDISHNESS
CHURLISHNESS
CLANNISHNESS
DIENCEPHALON
ENCROACHMENT
ENTRENCHMENT
EPANORTHOSIS
EPENCEPHALON
ERATOSTHENES
GEOGRAPHICAL
HAEMORRHOIDS
HALLANSHAKER
HETEROPHORIA
HIERARCHICAL
HISTIOPHORUS
HOUSETOHOUSE
IMPERISHABLE
KINAESTHETIC
MOONLIGHTING
NONALCOHOLIC
OREOPITHECUS
OREOPITHEOUS
PANAESTHESIA
PERSULPHURIC
PHILANTHROPY
PRIGGISHNESS
PYROTECHNICS
QUADRAPHONIC
RETRENCHMENT
RHINORRHOEAL
ROOMINGHOUSE
SCHOPENHAUER
SHEEPISHNESS
SHILLYSHALLY
SITTLICHKEIT
SIVAPITHECUS

SNOBBISHNESS
STEREOPHONIC
TELEASTHETIC
THESMOPHORIA
THOROUGHBRED
THOROUGHFARE
THOROUGHNESS
TRICHOPHYTON
ULOTRICHALES
UNDERACHIEVE
WOLSTENHOLME
ACCOMPLISHED
ADAPTABILITY
ADVISABILITY
AGGRESSIVELY
AGRIBUSINESS
ANEMOPHILOUS
ANTAGONISTIC
ANTEMERIDIAN
ANTHELMINTIC
ANTONINIANUS
ARTIFICIALLY
ASPARAGINASE
ATTRACTIVELY
AUTHENTICATE
AUTHENTICITY
AVAILABILITY
AWEINSPIRING
AYUNTAMIENTO
BAMBOCCIADES
BESSERWISSER
BIOCHEMISTRY
BLOODTHIRSTY
CAMPODEIFORM
CAPERCAILLIE
CAPERCAILZIE
CARTHAGINIAN
CEREMONIALLY
CHAUVINISTIC
CHREMATISTIC
CIRCASSIENNE
CIRCUMCISION
CLASSIFIABLE
COLLECTIVELY
COLLOQUIALLY
COMMERCIALLY
COMMISSIONED
COMMISSIONER
COMPROMISING
CONCLUSIVELY
CONDUCTIVITY
CONFECTIONER
CONFESSIONAL
CONTERMINOUS
CONTRARINESS
CONVENTIONAL
CONVINCINGLY
DECORATIVELY
DEHUMIDIFIER
DERESTRICTED
DESIRABILITY
DIALECTICIAN
DILATORINESS
DIPRIONIDIAN
DISAPPOINTED
DISCIPLINARY
DISCOMFITURE
DISCRIMINATE
DISOBEDIENCE
DISQUISITION
DRINKDRIVING
ECCENTRICITY
ENCHEIRIDION
ENTERPRISING
ENTERTAINING
ENTREATINGLY
EULENSPIEGEL
EXCITABILITY
EXHAUSTIVELY
EXHIBITIONER
EXSUFFLICATE
EXTINGUISHER
FEHMGERICHTE
FIGURATIVELY
FRAUENDIENST
FRIENDLINESS
FUSTILLIRIAN
GENETHLIACON
GEOMETRICIAN
GEOPHYSICIST
GERIATRICIAN
HAEMOPHILIAC
HAIRSPLITTER
HYDROQUINONE
IDENTIFIABLE
ILLEGIBILITY
ILLEGITIMACY
ILLEGITIMATE
IMMUTABILITY
IMPOVERISHED
IMPRESSIVELY
INCAPABILITY
INCAPACITATE
INCREASINGLY
INDEFINITELY
INDOCTRINATE
INDUSTRIALLY
INEFFICIENCY
INEXACTITUDE
INEXPERIENCE
INFELICITOUS
INSOLUBILITY
INTRANSIGENT
INTRANSITIVE
INVISIBILITY
IRASCIBILITY
IRRITABILITY
ISHMAELITISH
JENNYSPINNER
JOURNALISTIC
KLIPSPRINGER
LYMANTRIIDAE
MALLEABILITY
MALNUTRITION
MICROCLIMATE
MILITARISTIC
MOISTURIZING
MUCILAGINOUS
MULTIPLICITY
NARCISSISTIC
NATURALISTIC
NAVIGABILITY
NONCOMMITTAL
OBSTETRICIAN
OCCUPATIONAL
OLDFASHIONED
OPPRESSIVELY
OVERESTIMATE
PARAMILITARY
PEDIATRICIAN
PERCEPTIVELY
PERCEPTIVITY
PERMEABILITY
PERSUASIVELY
PHILISTINISM
PINNIEWINKLE
PLACENTIFORM
PLAUSIBILITY
POSSESSIVELY
POSTLIMINARY
PRACTICIONER
PRACTITIONER
PRALLTRILLER
PRECONDITION
PREDESTINATE
PREREQUISITE
PRESENTIMENT
PROCESSIONAL
PRODUCTIVITY
PROFESSIONAL
PROPORTIONAL
PROTACTINIUM
PROTECTIVELY
PROVERBIALLY
PUMPERNICKEL
QUANTIFIABLE
RECONSTITUTE
RECREATIONAL
REDEMPTIONER
REDISTRIBUTE
REHABILITATE
RESPECTIVELY
SCOPOPHILIAC
SEQUENTIALLY
SHIRTWAISTER
SINGLEMINDED
SLOVENLINESS
SLUBBERINGLY
SOPHISTICATE
SPINECHILLER
STAGGERINGLY
STATISTICIAN
STEALTHINESS
STRONGMINDED
SUBCOMMITTEE
SUBCONTINENT
SUBJECTIVELY
SUBJECTIVITY
SUBMISSIVELY
SUBSERVIENCE
SUCCESSIVELY
SUGGESTIVELY
SUPERSTITION
SURPRISINGLY
SURREALISTIC
THANKSGIVING
THEORETICIAN
THICKSKINNED
TRACTABILITY
TRANSITIONAL
UNACQUAINTED
UNAPPETIZING
UNCLASSIFIED
UNDERSKINKER
UNDERWRITTEN
UNDIMINISHED
UNIDENTIFIED
UNOFFICIALLY
UNPRINCIPLED
UNRESTRICTED
UNSURPRISING
VEHMGERICHTE
VINDICTIVELY
WEIGHTLIFTER
HOMESICKNESS
UNMISTAKABLE
ANDOUILLETTE
ARCHIPELAGOS
ARTHROPLASTY
BERTHOLLETIA
BREASTPLOUGH
BREATHALYSER
CAMPANULARIA
CHEERFULNESS
CHITTERLINGS
CONTROLLABLE
COSMOPOLITAN
CREMAILLIÈRE
DOUBLEGLAZED
ELECTROLYSIS
ESPAGNOLETTE
ETEPIMELETIC
FAITHFULNESS
FLORICULTURE
FORCEFULNESS
FREIGHTLINER
FRUITFULNESS
GRACEFULNESS
GRATEFULNESS
HAPPYGOLUCKY

HETEROCLITIC
HETEROPLASIA
HORTICULTURE
HYDROCHLORIC
HYPERBOLICAL
INCALCULABLE
INCONSOLABLE
INDISSOLUBLE
INTERRELATED
LALLAPALOOZA
LILLIBULLERO
MARSEILLAISE
MERVEILLEUSE
MESOTHELIOMA
METROPOLITAN
MINDFULLNESS
MITRAILLEUSE
MONOSYLLABIC
MONOSYLLABLE
MULTICOLORED
OSTEOMALACIA
OVERWHELMING
PARTICOLORED
PARTICULARLY
PEACEFULNESS
PECTORILOQUY
PEDICELLARIA
PERAMBULATOR
PERSONALIZED
PISCICULTURE
POINTILLISME
POLYSYLLABIC
POLYSYLLABLE
PREMAXILLARY
QUARTERLIGHT
RECORDPLAYER
ROLLERBLADER
ROLLERBLADES
SCHINDYLESIS
SCINTILLATOR
SELFEMPLOYED
SESQUIALTERA
SHAREHOLDING
SHIPBUILDING
SIPUNCULACEA
SLEEPWALKING
SLOCKDOLAGER
SLOCKDOLIGER
SLOCKDOLOGER
SMALLHOLDING
SOMATOPLEURE
SPITEFULNESS
SUPERCILIARY
SUPERCILIOUS
SURVEILLANCE
THANKFULNESS
THEOPHYLLINE
TORRICELLIAN
TRABECULATED
TRANQUILIZER

TRANQUILLISE
TRANQUILLITY
TRANQUILLIZE
TROPHALLAXIS
TRUTHFULNESS
TUBERCULOSIS
UNPARALLELED
URTRICULARIA
VENGEFULNESS
WATCHFULNESS
YOUTHFULNESS
ALPHANUMERIC
ANTIMNEMONIC
ASTRONOMICAL
BLABBERMOUTH
CABINETMAKER
CATHETOMETER
CHRESTOMATHY
CLAVICEMBALO
COMMANDMENTS
COSCINOMANCY
COUNTERMARCH
DIAGRAMMATIC
DIVERTIMENTO
ENANTIOMORPH
EPIGRAMMATIC
ERYTHROMYCIN
FLITTERMOUSE
FRANKALMOIGN
GALVANOMETER
GIGANTOMACHY
GOOSEPIMPLES
HAEMATEMESIS
HARNESSMAKER
HELLGRAMMITE
HEPHTHEMIMER
HEROICOMICAL
HOLIDAYMAKER
IRREDEEMABLE
LOXODROMICAL
MELODRAMATIC
MERISTEMATIC
NEPHELOMETER
NYCHTHEMERON
PANCHROMATIC
PANPHARMACON
PHILHARMONIC
POTICHOMANIA
PROGRAMMABLE
PROLEGOMENON
PYTHONOMORPH
RISORGIMENTO
SCAPULIMANCY
SCATTERMOUCH
SHORTCOMINGS
STREPTOMYCIN
TRIGONOMETRY
TROCHELMINTH
TROUBLEMAKER
UNDETERMINED

UNECONOMICAL
UNFATHOMABLE
ACCOMPANYING
ADDITIONALLY
AGAMOGENETIC
APPREHENSION
APPREHENSIVE
APPURTENANCE
AWARDWINNING
BANDERSNATCH
BICENTENNIAL
BRILLIANTINE
CARLOVINGIAN
CHAIRMANSHIP
CHAMPIONSHIP
CHORIZONTIST
COLOQUINTIDA
CONFIDENTIAL
CONTAMINATED
CONVEYANCING
CRASHLANDING
CROSSBENCHER
DIFFERENTIAL
DIPLOGENESIS
DISADVANTAGE
DISINCENTIVE
DISINGENUOUS
DISORGANIZED
DISORIENTATE
DORSIVENTRAL
ENTEROPNEUST
FOTHERINGHAY
FRACTIONALLY
FUNCTIONALLY
FUNCTIONLESS
FUNDAMENTALS
GALLIVANTING
GAMESMANSHIP
GRANDMONTINE
GUARDIANSHIP
HALLUCINOGEN
HORSEMANSHIP
HYPERTENSION
HYPOCHONDRIA
IMPERSONALLY
IMPERSONATOR
IMPERTINENCE
IMPRISONMENT
INCONTINENCE
INCONVENIENT
INDECLINABLE
INDISTINCTLY
INHARMONIOUS
INNATTENTIVE
INTERMINABLE
INTERMINABLY
INTERVENTION
IRRATIONALLY
KILLIKINNICK
LICKTRENCHER

LONGSTANDING
MARKSMANSHIP
MASSERANDUBA
MICHELANGELO
MISADVENTURE
NORTHERNMOST
OBSERVANTINE
OCCASIONALLY
ONCORHYNCHUS
ORTHODONTICS
ORTHOGENESIS
ORTHOTONESIS
PALINGENESIA
PALINGENESIS
PANATHENAEAN
PANTECHNICON
PAPILIONIDAE
PARSIMONIOUS
PARTISANSHIP
PERADVENTURE
PERGAMENEOUS
PESTILENTIAL
PHENOMENALLY
PHILODENDRON
PHYCOXANTHIN
PHYTOBENTHOS
PLECTOGNATHI
POSTPRANDIAL
PREDOMINANCE
PREFERENTIAL
PRESIDENTIAL
PRIZEWINNING
PROPAGANDISM
PROPAGANDIST
PROVIDENTIAL
QUESTIONABLE
QUINQUENNIAL
RELATIONSHIP
RHADAMANTHUS
RHODODENDRON
SALESMANSHIP
SIMULTANEOUS
SOUTHERNMOST
SOUTHERNWOOD
STREPTONEURA
STROPHANTHUS
STUBBORNNESS
SUBCUTANEOUS
SUPERANNUATE
TESTAMENTARY
TOBACCONISTS
TRANSCENDENT
TRANSPONTINE
ULTRAMONTANE
UNATTAINABLE
UNCONVINCING
UNDERPINNING
UNIMAGINABLE
UNOBTAINABLE
UNPARDONABLE

UNPRETENDING
UNREASONABLE
UNRECOGNISED
UNRECOGNIZED
UNRESPONSIVE
UNRETURNABLE
UNSEASONABLE
ABOLITIONIST
ACCORDIONIST
AFFECTIONATE
AFORETHOUGHT
AFTERTHOUGHT
AGALMATOLITE
AMPHISTOMOUS
ANTHROPOLOGY
ANTILEGOMENA
ANTISTROPHON
ANTITHROMBIN
ARFVEDSONITE
ARISTOLOCHIA
AUSPICIOUSLY
AWAYABSOLUTE
BABINGTONITE
BACTERIOLOGY
BACTERIOSTAT
BARBERMONGER
BERTILLONAGE
BOISTEROUSLY
BRANCHIOPODA
CARDIOLOGIST
CATASTROPHIC
CHEESEMONGER
CHONDRIOSOME
COCCIDIOSTAT
COLLECTORATE
COMPANIONWAY
CONTEMPORARY
CONTINUOUSLY
COSTERMONGER
COURAGEOUSLY
DAGUERROTYPE
DEFLATIONARY
DENDROLOGIST
DISASTROUSLY
DISCONSOLATE
DYSTELEOLOGY
EAVESDROPPER
EDUCATIONIST
EGYPTOLOGIST
ENTEROMORPHA
ENTOMOLOGIST
EPIPHENOMENA
EPISTEMOLOGY
ESCAPOLOGIST
EVOLUTIONARY
EXTENSIONIST
EXTORTIONATE
FASTIDIOUSLY
FIRSTFOOTING
FORTUITOUSLY
GASTROSOPHER
GLADIATORIAL
GLOBETROTTER
GLYNDEBOURNE
GRANDISONIAN
GRAPHOLOGIST
GREENGROCERS
GREENGROCERY
GYNECOLOGIST
HAMBLETONIAN
HARMONIOUSLY
HARUMFRODITE
HETEROCONTAE
HETEROSOMATA
IMMUNOLOGIST
INCAUTIOUSLY
INFLATIONARY
INSPECTORATE
ISOLATIONISM
ISOLATIONIST
LANGUEDOCIAN
LASCIVIOUSLY
LUGUBRIOUSLY
MACHAIRODONT
MERRYTHOUGHT
METICULOUSLY
MINERALOGIST
MIRACULOUSLY
MISPRONOUNCE
MONOTONOUSLY
MONTESSORIAN
MOUTHBROODER
MUGGLETONIAN
MUSICOLOGIST
MYSTERIOUSLY
NEOPLATONISM
NIGHTCLOTHES
NUTRITIONIST
OBSEQUIOUSLY
OCTASTROPHIC
OPHIOGLOSSUM
ORTHORHOMBIC
OUTRAGEOUSLY
PALEONTOLOGY
PANDAEMONIUM
PARALIPOMENA
PEREMPTORILY
PHARMACOLOGY
PHLEBOTOMIST
PHYSIOLOGIST
PLAINCLOTHES
POSTHUMOUSLY
POTAMOLOGIST
PRAISEWORTHY
PRECARIOUSLY
PRECOCIOUSLY
PREHISTORIAN
PROBATIONARY
PRODIGIOUSLY
PROFESSORIAL
PROPITIOUSLY
PROTECTORATE
PSEPHOLOGIST
PSIPHENOMENA
PSYCHOLOGIST
PUGNACIOUSLY
RADIOISOTOPE
RECEPTIONIST
REFLATIONARY
REINVIGORATE
REVERSIONARY
RIDICULOUSLY
SALVATIONIST
SCANDALOUSLY
SCRUPULOUSLY
SCURRILOUSLY
SECESSIONIST
SHARPSHOOTER
SHOSTAKOVICH
SOLICITOUSLY
SPATANGOIDEA
SPECKTIONEER
SPELEOLOGIST
SPERMATOCYTE
STAKHANOVITE
STEGOPHOLIST
STORMTROOPER
STRIGIFORMES
STRINGCOURSE
STROMATOLITE
SUSPICIOUSLY
TAGLIACOTIAN
TAPERECORDER
TECHNOLOGIST
TEETERTOTTER
THESSALONIAN
TOXICOLOGIST
TREMENDOUSLY
TRICHOLOGIST
UNCONTROLLED
UNDERCLOTHES
UPROARIOUSLY
VARICOLOURED
VENTRIPOTENT
VOCIFEROUSLY
VOLUPTUOUSLY
WELLINFORMED
WOLLASTONITE
ZALAMBDODONT
APOSTROPHISE
CATADIOPTRIC
CLAMJAMPHRIE
CONSCRIPTION
CONTRAPPOSTO
COUNTERPOINT
COUNTERPOISE
ELECTROPLATE
ENANTIOPATHY
ENCYCLOPEDIA
ENCYCLOPEDIC
EVENTEMPERED
FRONTISPIECE
GYMNOSOPHIST
ICHTHYOPSIDA
INTERCEPTION
INTERRUPTION
MASTIGOPHORA
METALLOPHONE
METAMORPHISM
METAMORPHOSE
MINICOMPUTER
ONOMATOPOEIA
ONOMATOPOEIC
PHILOSOPHIZE
PRESCRIPTION
PRESCRIPTIVE
PROSCRIPTION
PROSOPOPOEIA
PTERIDOPHYTE
RHIPIDOPTERA
SARDANAPALUS
SARRUSOPHONE
SIPHONOPHORA
STENTORPHONE
STRATOSPHERE
STREPSIPTERA
SUBSCRIPTION
SYNADELPHITE
TELEGRAPHESE
TELEGRAPHIST
THYSANOPTERA
TROCHOSPHERE
UNDEREXPOSED
WEATHERPROOF
INCONSEQUENT
MAGNILOQUENT
APFELSTRUDEL
ARISTOCRATIC
ARTILLERYMAN
ASYMMETRICAL
BARNSTORMING
BATTLEGROUND
BELLIGERENCY
BEWILDERMENT
BIBLIOGRAPHY
BIODIVERSITY
BLACKCURRANT
BLENNORRHOEA
BOULEVARDIER
BREAKTHROUGH
BUREAUCRATIC
CASSITERIDES
CASTERBRIDGE
CHOREOGRAPHY
COLLABORATOR
CONCENTRATED
CONSIDERABLE
CONSIDERABLY
COURTMARTIAL
CRYPTOGRAPHY

DECIPHERABLE
DECIPHERMENT
DEMONSTRABLE
DEMONSTRABLY
DEMONSTRATOR
DICTATORSHIP
DIRECTORSHIP
DISEMBARRASS
DISHONORABLE
DISHONORABLY
DRAMATURGIST
ELASMOBRANCH
FRONTIERSMAN
GAINSBOROUGH
GONADOTROPIN
GRANDPARENTS
HAMARTHRITIS
HEADQUARTERS
HEARTSTRINGS
HEARTWARMING
HEMICHORDATA
HENCEFORWARD
HINDQUARTERS
HOMOTHERMOUS
HOUSEWARMING
HYPERPYRETIC
HYPERSARCOMA
IDIOTHERMOUS
IMMEASURABLE
IMMEASURABLY
IMPENETRABLE
INCOMPARABLE
INCOMPARABLY
INCORPORATED
INDIFFERENCE
INSALUBRIOUS
INSUFFERABLE
INSUFFERABLY
INTEMPERANCE
INTERFERENCE
INVULNERABLE
LEXICOGRAPHY
LILLIBURLERO
LONGSHOREMAN
MANOEUVRABLE
METALLURGIST
METAPHORICAL
MISANTHROPIC
MISINTERPRET
MULTIFARIOUS
MUTESSARIFAT
NEIGHBORHOOD
OCEANOGRAPHY
ONEIROCRITIC
OSTEOPOROSIS
OTHERWORLDLY
OVEREXERTION
PASSEPARTOUT
PERIOSTRACUM
PERISTERONIC
PERSEVERANCE
PHOSPHORENCE
PHOSPHORESCE
PREDETERMINE
PROLETARIATE
PROTUBERANCE
REAPPEARANCE
RECEIVERSHIP
REFRIGERATED
REFRIGERATOR
REMONSTRANCE
SALTATORIOUS
SARSAPARILLA
SCHILLERSPAR
SCREENWRITER
SCRIPTWRITER
SECRETARIATE
SEPTEMBRISER
SEQUESTRATOR
SHORTCIRCUIT
SINANTHROPUS
SNOWBOARDING
SPINSTERHOOD
SPORTSGROUND
STRUCTURALLY
TERGIVERSATE
TERRITORIALS
THIGMOTROPIC
THIRDBOROUGH
TOGETHERNESS
TRANSFERABLE
TRANSFERENCE
TRANSPARENCY
UMBRADARLING
UNANSWERABLE
UNAUTHORISED
UNAUTHORIZED
UNCONVERSANT
UNDEMOCRATIC
UNDERCURRENT
UNDERGARMENT
UNFAVOURABLE
UNILATERALLY
VAINGLORIOUS
WATERCARRIER
WHIPPOORWILL
WILTSHIREMAN
YORKSHIREMAN
AECIDIOSPORE
AETHRIOSCOPE
BIELORUSSIAN
BILLINGSGATE
BLETHERSKATE
BRAINWASHING
BROADCASTING
BUSINESSLIKE
BYELORUSSIAN
CARAVANSERAI
CARELESSNESS
CATAPHYSICAL
CAUTIOUSNESS
CONTABESCENT
CONVALESCENT
CONVALESCING
COVETOUSNESS
DECONGESTANT
DESSERTSPOON
DEUTEROSCOPY
DISSATISFIED
EFFERVESCENT
EMBARRASSING
ENTOPLASTRON
FEARLESSNESS
FRANKENSTEIN
GALLIGASKINS
GLOCKENSPIEL
GRACIOUSNESS
GUILDENSTERN
HABERDASHERS
HABERDASHERY
HAIRDRESSERS
HAIRDRESSING
HELPLESSNESS
HOPELESSNESS
HUDIBRASTICS
INACCESSIBLE
INADMISSIBLE
INCANDESCENT
INCONSISTENT
INDEFENSIBLE
INTERCESSION
INTERMISSION
IRREVERSIBLE
KALEIDOSCOPE
KLETTERSCHUE
LIFELESSNESS
LINCOLNSHIRE
LISTLESSNESS
MADEMOISELLE
MARLINESPIKE
METAPHYSICAL
MYRINGOSCOPE
NEOCLASSICAL
NONRESISTANT
NORTHEASTERN
NORTHWESTERN
OSCILLOSCOPE
OVERDRESSING
PAINLESSNESS
PHRONTISTERY
PLASTERSTONE
PRAXINOSCOPE
QUARTERSTAFF
QUINTESSENCE
RECKLESSNESS
RECRUDESCENT
REPERCUSSION
REPOSSESSION
REPROCESSING
RESTLESSNESS
RUTHLESSNESS
SIDEWHISKERS
SIPHONOSTELE
SOUTHEASTERN
SOUTHWESTERN
SPACIOUSNESS
SPECIOUSNESS
SPECTROSCOPE
SPHAIRISTIKE
SPURIOUSNESS
STILBOESTROL
STUDIOUSNESS
SWIZZLESTICK
TACTLESSNESS
TELEUTOSPORE
THUNDERSTORM
TIMELESSNESS
TRANSMISSION
TRANSVESTISM
TRANSVESTITE
UNCTUOUSNESS
UNOPPRESSIVE
UNSUCCESSFUL
WAREHOUSEMAN
ZARATHUSTRIC
ACCIDENTALLY
ACQUAINTANCE
ADMINISTRATE
ADSCITITIOUS
ADVENTITIOUS
AERONAUTICAL
AGRICULTURAL
AIRCRAFTSMAN
ALPHABETICAL
AMBIDEXTROUS
ANTINEUTRINO
ANTIPARTICLE
ARITHMETICAL
ATTRIBUTABLE
BEAUMONTAGUE
BEAUMONTIQUE
BENEFACTRESS
CARRIWITCHET
CEREBROTONIC
CHALICOTHERE
CIRCUMSTANCE
CLARINETTIST
COMBINATIONS
CONGENITALLY
CONQUISTADOR
CONSPECTUITY
CONTEMPTIBLE
CONTEMPTUOUS
DARLINGTONIA
DISCOURTEOUS
DISREPUTABLE
DISTINCTNESS
ELECTROTONUS
ENHYPOSTASIA
ENTOMOSTRACA

EPIDEICTICAL
EXTRADITABLE
FELDSPATHOID
FIDDLESTICKS
FULMINATIONS
HAPPENSTANCE
HEADMISTRESS
HIPPOPOTAMUS
HORIZONTALLY
HYPOCRITICAL
HYPOTHETICAL
INADVERTENCE
INCIDENTALLY
INCOMPATIBLE
INCOMPETENCE
INDIGESTIBLE
INDISPUTABLE
INDISPUTABLY
INHOSPITABLE
INSTRUCTIONS
INSTRUCTRESS
INTERMITTENT
IRRESISTIBLE
ISOBILATERAL
LABYRINTHINE
LAMENTATIONS
LATIROSTRATE
LITHOLATROUS
LONGDISTANCE
MALACOSTRACA
MALPRACTICES
MALTREATMENT
MANUFACTURER
MASTERSTROKE
MATHEMATICAL
METAGNATHOUS
MISTREATMENT
MOUSQUETAIRE
MULLIGATAWNY
MULTILATERAL
NONEXISTENCE
OBEDIENTIARY
OSTENTATIOUS
OUTSTRETCHED
OVERSCUTCHED
PALPITATIONS
PARACENTESIS
PENITENTIARY
POLYURETHANE
POSTMISTRESS
PREMONSTRANT
PRESUMPTUOUS
PROPRIETRESS
PSYCHIATRIST
RAMBUNCTIOUS
READJUSTMENT
RECALCITRANT
RESUSCITATED
RHAMPHOTHECA
RODOMONTADER
SELFPORTRAIT
SOUTHCOTTIAN
STEREOPTICON
STRAIGHTAWAY
STRAIGHTEDGE
STRAIGHTNESS
SUBSTANTIATE
SUPERNATURAL
SURMOUNTABLE
TETRODOTOXIN
THERMOSTATIC
TIGHTFITTING
TRALATITIOUS
TRANSACTIONS
TRANSLATABLE
UNACCEPTABLE
UNACCUSTOMED
UNCHARITABLE
UNCHARITABLY
UNDETECTABLE
UNEXPECTEDLY
UNIMPORTANCE
UNPROFITABLE
UNSCIENTIFIC
VERUMONTANUM
WASHINGTONIA
WELLINGTONIA
XANTHOPTERIN
ABSQUATULATE
ANTEDILUVIAN
BARRANQUILLA
BEHAVIOURISM
BLEFUSCUDIAN
BREASTSUMMER
CARICATURIST
CHEESEBURGER
COLDSHOULDER
COMMENSURATE
CONGRATULATE
CONSTABULARY
CONSTITUENCY
CONSTITUENTS
CONSTITUTION
CONTRAPUNTAL
CONTRIBUTION
CONTRIBUTORY
CONTRITURATE
CROSSCOUNTRY
DISTRIBUTION
DISTRIBUTIVE
GRISEOFULVIN
HERMENEUTICS
HERMENEUTIST
HIGHFALUTING
INARTICULATE
INCONCLUSIVE
INCUNABULIST
INDIVIDUALLY
IRRESOLUTELY
IRRESOLUTION
LUXEMBOURGER
MANGELWURZEL
MARCOBRUNNER
MISCALCULATE
NEIGHBOURING
PROSTITUTION
RECAPITULATE
SKUTTERUDITE
SOMNAMBULISM
SOMNAMBULIST
SUBSTITUTION
TELEOSAURIAN
THAUMATURGIC
THAUMATURGUS
THERAPEUTICS
UNOBSTRUCTED
UNSCRUPULOUS
VIBRATIUNCLE
ADJECTIVALLY
BOUGAINVILLE
CANTILEVERED
IRRESOLVABLE
KATHAREVOUSA
MISBEHAVIOUR
MISDELIVERED
PENNSYLVANIA
REDISCOVERED
UNBELIEVABLE
UNBELIEVABLY
UNCULTIVATED
UNDESERVEDLY
UNRESERVEDLY
ENGLISHWOMAN
ENGLISHWOMEN
OVERCROWDING
SERVICEWOMAN
ARSENOPYRITE
ASTROPHYSICS
CIRCUMGYRATE
CLAIRVOYANCE
CLAIRVOYANCY
ELEEMOSYNARY
GOBBLEDYGOOK
HIEROGLYPHIC
OXYACETYLENE
PHOTOGLYPHIC
POLYETHYLENE
PRASEODYMIUM
PSEUDONYMOUS
REDEPLOYMENT
SCHIZOMYCETE
STEREOTYPING
UNEMPLOYMENT
WOODBURYTYPE
RECOGNIZABLE
RECOGNIZANCE

12:9

ACADEMICALLY
ACCIDENTALLY
ACQUAINTANCE
ADDITIONALLY
ADJECTIVALLY
AMPHITHEATER
AMPHITHEATRE
ANTIBARBARUS
ANTONINIANUS
APPROACHABLE
APPURTENANCE
ARCHIPELAGOS
ARISTOCRATIC
ARISTOPHANES
ARTHROPLASTY
ARTIFICIALLY
ARTISTICALLY
ATTRIBUTABLE
BAMBOCCIADES
BANDERSNATCH
BEAUMONTAGUE
BIBLIOGRAPHY
BUREAUCRATIC
CABINETMAKER
CAMPANULARIA
CEREMONIALLY
CHOREOGRAPHY
CHRESTOMATHY
CIRCUMSTANCE
CLAIRVOYANCE
CLAIRVOYANCY
CLASSIFIABLE
CLEISTOGAMIC
COLLABORATOR
COLLOQUIALLY
COMMERCIALLY
COMMONWEALTH
COMMUNICABLE
CONCENTRATED
CONGENITALLY
CONQUISTADOR
CONSIDERABLE
CONSIDERABLY
CONSOLIDATED
CONSOLIDATOR
CONTAMINATED
CONTROLLABLE
COSCINOMANCY
COUNTERMARCH
CRYPTOGRAPHY
DECIPHERABLE
DEMIMONDAINE
DEMONSTRABLE
DEMONSTRABLY
DEMONSTRATOR
DIAGRAMMATIC
DIENCEPHALON

DISAGREEABLE
DISHONORABLE
DISHONORABLY
DISREPUTABLE
DOGMATICALLY
DOMESTICATED
DOUBLEGLAZED
DRAMATICALLY
ECONOMICALLY
ECSTATICALLY
ELASMOBRANCH
ELECTRICALLY
EMPHATICALLY
ENANTIOPATHY
ENHYPOSTASIA
EPENCEPHALON
EPIGRAMMATIC
ESTHETICALLY
EXCHANGEABLE
EXTRADITABLE
EXTRAVAGANCE
EXTRAVAGANZA
FRACTIONALLY
FUNCTIONALLY
GENETHLIACON
GEOLOGICALLY
GIGANTOMACHY
HALLANSHAKER
HAMMERHEADED
HAPPENSTANCE
HARNESSMAKER
HELIOGABALUS
HERMETICALLY
HETEROPLASIA
HIPPOPOTAMUS
HISTORICALLY
HOBBIDIDANCE
HOLIDAYMAKER
HORIZONTALLY
HORRIFICALLY
HOUSEBREAKER
HYGIENICALLY
HYPNOTICALLY
HYPOTHECATOR
HYSTERICALLY
IDENTIFIABLE
IMMEASURABLE
IMMEASURABLY
IMPENETRABLE
IMPERISHABLE
IMPERSONALLY
IMPERSONATOR
INAPPLICABLE
INCALCULABLE
INCIDENTALLY
INCOMPARABLE
INCOMPARABLY
INCONSOLABLE
INCORPORATED
INDECLINABLE
INDISPUTABLE
INDISPUTABLY
INDIVIDUALLY
INDUSTRIALLY
INERADICABLE
INEXPLICABLE
INEXPLICABLY
INEXTRICABLE
INEXTRICABLY
INFORMIDABLE
INHOSPITABLE
INSUFFERABLE
INSUFFERABLY
INTEMPERANCE
INTERMINABLE
INTERMINABLY
INTERRELATED
INTERROGATOR
INVESTIGATOR
INVULNERABLE
IRRATIONALLY
IRREDEEMABLE
IRRESOLVABLE
LEXICOGRAPHY
LONGDISTANCE
MAGNETICALLY
MAJESTICALLY
MANOEUVRABLE
MARRIAGEABLE
MARSEILLAISE
MECHANICALLY
MELODRAMATIC
MERISTEMATIC
METHODICALLY
MONOSYLLABIC
MONOSYLLABLE
MOUSQUETAIRE
MUDDLEHEADED
MULLIGATAWNY
NEUROTICALLY
OCCASIONALLY
OCEANOGRAPHY
ORNITHOGALUM
OSTEOMALACIA
PANATHENAEAN
PANCHROMATIC
PANPHARMACON
PARTICULARLY
PATHETICALLY
PEDANTICALLY
PEDICELLARIA
PENNSYLVANIA
PERAMBULATOR
PERIODICALLY
PERIOSTRACUM
PERSEVERANCE
PHENOMENALLY
PHONETICALLY
PLECTOGNATHI
POLYSYLLABIC
POLYSYLLABLE
POTICHOMANIA
PREDOMINANCE
PREVARICATOR
PROGRAMMABLE
PROLIFICALLY
PROTUBERANCE
PROVERBIALLY
QUANTIFIABLE
QUESTIONABLE
QUIXOTICALLY
REAPPEARANCE
RECHARGEABLE
RECIPROCALLY
RECOGNIZABLE
RECOGNIZANCE
RECORDPLAYER
REFRIGERATED
REFRIGERATOR
REMONSTRANCE
RESUSCITATED
RHYTHMICALLY
RODOMONTADER
ROLLERBLADER
ROLLERBLADES
ROMANTICALLY
SADISTICALLY
SARDANAPALUS
SARDONICALLY
SCAPULIMANCY
SCHOPENHAUER
SCINTILLATOR
SEMANTICALLY
SEQUENTIALLY
SEQUESTRATOR
SHILLYSHALLY
SIGNIFICANCE
SIPUNCULACEA
SLOCKDOLAGER
SPECIFICALLY
SPORADICALLY
STRAIGHTAWAY
STRUCTURALLY
SURMOUNTABLE
SURVEILLANCE
SYMBOLICALLY
TERRIFICALLY
THEATRICALLY
THERMOSTATIC
TRABECULATED
TRANSFERABLE
TRANSLATABLE
TRANSOCEANIC
TROPHALLAXIS
TROUBLEMAKER
ULOTRICHALES
UNACCEPTABLE
UNANSWERABLE
UNATTAINABLE
UNBELIEVABLE
UNBELIEVABLY
UNCHANGEABLE
UNCHARITABLE
UNCHARITABLY
UNCULTIVATED
UNDEMOCRATIC
UNDETECTABLE
UNEXPURGATED
UNFATHOMABLE
UNFAVOURABLE
UNILATERALLY
UNIMAGINABLE
UNIMPORTANCE
UNMANAGEABLE
UNMISTAKABLE
UNOBTAINABLE
UNOFFICIALLY
UNPARDONABLE
UNPROFITABLE
UNREASONABLE
UNRETURNABLE
UNSEASONABLE
URTRICULARIA
VERUMONTANUM
ANTIMETABOLE
CLAVICEMBALO
COLLYWOBBLES
INNOMINABLES
REDISTRIBUTE
THOROUGHBRED
UNUTTERABLES
AETHRIOSCOPE
AMARANTACEAE
ARISTOLOCHIA
AUTHENTICATE
AUTHENTICITY
CARRIWITCHET
CHIROPRACTIC
CHIROPRACTOR
CONTABESCENT
CONVALESCENT
CONVALESCING
CONVEYANCING
CROSSBENCHER
DERESTRICTED
DEUTEROSCOPY
DIALECTICIAN
DISCONNECTED
DOUBLEDECKER
ECCENTRICITY
EFFERVESCENT
EPACRIDACEAE
EXSUFFLICATE
FEHMGERICHTE
GEOMETRICIAN
GEOPHYSICIST
GERIATRICIAN
GREENGROCERS
GREENGROCERY
HYPERSARCOMA

INCANDESCENT
INDISTINCTLY
KALEIDOSCOPE
KLETTERSCHUE
LANGUEDOCIAN
LICKTRENCHER
MULTIPLICITY
MYRINGOSCOPE
NEPENTHACEAE
OBSTETRICIAN
ONCORHYNCHUS
OSCILLOSCOPE
OUTSTRETCHED
OVERSCUTCHED
PEDIATRICIAN
PERSPICACITY
PRAXINOSCOPE
PROPHYLACTIC
PUMPERNICKEL
RECRUDESCENT
SCHIZOMYCETE
SEMIDETACHED
SHORTCIRCUIT
SINGLEDECKER
SOPHISTICATE
SPECTROSCOPE
SPELLCHECKER
SPERMATOCYTE
STATISTICIAN
STRAITJACKET
TAMARICACEAE
THEORETICIAN
UNCONVINCING
UNOBSTRUCTED
UNRESTRICTED
VEHMGERICHTE
ACKNOWLEDGED
ANTEMERIDIAN
BLEFUSCUDIAN
BOULEVARDIER
CRASHLANDING
DIPRIONIDIAN
DRESSINGDOWN
ENCHEIRIDION
GLUBBDUBDRIB
HARUMFRODITE
HEMICHORDATA
HYPOCHONDRIA
LONGSTANDING
MACHAIRODONT
MASSERANDUBA
ORTHOPAEDICS
ORTHOPAEDIST
OVERCROWDING
PHILODENDRON
POSTPRANDIAL
PROPAGANDISM
PROPAGANDIST
RHODODENDRON
SHAREHOLDING
SHIPBUILDING
SKUTTERUDITE
SMALLHOLDING
SNOWBOARDING
TRANSCENDENT
UNPRETENDING
ZALAMBDODONT
ACHLAMYDEOUS
ACQUIESCENCE
ADVANTAGEOUS
AFTEREFFECTS
AGAMOGENETIC
ALPHANUMERIC
AMBULANCEMAN
AMPHISBAENIC
ANDOUILLETTE
ARBORESCENCE
AYUNTAMIENTO
BELLIGERENCY
BERTHOLLETIA
BUNKOSTEERER
CALLISTHENES
CANTILEVERED
CARAVANSERAI
CARCINOGENIC
CATHETOMETER
CIRCASSIENNE
COMMANDMENTS
CONSTITUENCY
CONSTITUENTS
DIPLOGENESIS
DISCOMYCETES
DISCOURTEOUS
DISOBEDIENCE
DIVERTIMENTO
ENCYCLOPEDIA
ENCYCLOPEDIC
ENTEROPNEUST
ERATOSTHENES
ESPAGNOLETTE
ETEPIMELETIC
EULENSPIEGEL
EVENHANDEDLY
EVENTEMPERED
EXSERVICEMAN
FLUORESCENCE
FRANKINCENSE
FRAUENDIENST
GALLINACEOUS
GALVANOMETER
GRANDPARENTS
HAEMATEMESIS
HYPERPYRETIC
IMPERTINENCE
IMPROVIDENCE
INADVERTENCE
INCOMPETENCE
INCONTINENCE
INDEPENDENCE
INDIFFERENCE
INEFFICIENCY
INEXPERIENCE
INTELLIGENCE
INTERFERENCE
ISOBILATERAL
KINAESTHETIC
LONGSHOREMAN
LUMINESCENCE
LUMINISCENCE
MADEMOISELLE
MAGNIFICENCE
MERVEILLEUSE
MISDELIVERED
MITRAILLEUSE
MULTILATERAL
NEPHELOMETER
NOCONFIDENCE
NONEXISTENCE
NONRESIDENCE
NYCHTHEMERON
OBSOLESCENCE
OREOPITHECUS
OREOPITHEOUS
ORTHOGENESIS
ORTHOTONESIS
PALINGENESIA
PALINGENESIS
PANAESTHESIA
PANDANACEOUS
PARACENTESIS
PERGAMENEOUS
PHOSPHORENCE
PHOSPHORESCE
POLYSYNDETON
PROLEGOMENON
QUINTESSENCE
REDISCOVERED
REMINISCENCE
RESIPISCENCE
RISORGIMENTO
SCHINDYLESIS
SHAMEFACEDLY
SHIRTSLEEVES
SHORTSLEEVED
SIMULTANEOUS
SIVAPITHECUS
SOMATOPLEURE
STERNWHEELER
STOCKBREEDER
STOCKINGETTE
STRAIGHTEDGE
STREPTONEURA
SUBCUTANEOUS
SUBSERVIENCE
TAPSALTEERIE
TAPSLETEERIE
TELEASTHETIC
THREADNEEDLE
TRANSFERENCE
TRANSLUCENCE
TRANSPARENCY
TRIGONOMETRY
UNCONSIDERED
UNDESERVEDLY
UNEXPECTEDLY
UNPARALLELED
UNRESERVEDLY
WAREHOUSEMAN
WHIGMALEERIE
WICKETKEEPER
WILTSHIREMAN
XANTHOPTERIN
YORKSHIREMAN
CAMPODEIFORM
DEHUMIDIFIER
DISSATISFIED
PLACENTIFORM
SHORTSTAFFED
THOROUGHFARE
UNCLASSIFIED
UNDERSTAFFED
UNIDENTIFIED
WEIGHTLIFTER
BIBLIOPEGIST
BILLINGSGATE
BUCKLEBEGGAR
CARDIOLOGIST
CARLOVINGIAN
CARPETBAGGER
DENDROLOGIST
DISCOURAGING
DRAMATURGIST
EGYPTOLOGIST
ENTOMOLOGIST
ESCAPOLOGIST
FOOTSLOGGING
FOTHERINGHAY
GOBBLEDEGOOK
GOBBLEDYGOOK
GRAPHOLOGIST
GYNECOLOGIST
IMMUNOLOGIST
INTRANSIGENT
MALLOPHAGOUS
METALLURGIST
MICHELANGELO
MINERALOGIST
MUSICOLOGIST
PANTOPHAGOUS
PETTIFOGGERS
PETTIFOGGERY
PETTIFOGGING
PHYSIOLOGIST
POTAMOLOGIST
PSEPHOLOGIST
PSYCHOLOGIST
SPELEOLOGIST
SPLENOMEGALY
SPREADEAGLED
TECHNOLOGIST

TOXICOLOGIST
TRICHOLOGIST
ANTIBACCHIUS
APOSTROPHISE
ARCHILOCHIAN
BEAUMARCHAIS
BIRDWATCHING
BLENNORRHOEA
BRAINWASHING
CHALICOTHERE
CLAMJAMPHRIE
CLEARSIGHTED
CYMOTRICHOUS
DISFRANCHISE
FELDSPATHOID
FORMALDEHYDE
GESELLSCHAFT
GYMNOSOPHIST
HABERDASHERS
HABERDASHERY
HANDKERCHIEF
INESCUTCHEON
LABYRINTHINE
LEIOTRICHOUS
LINCOLNSHIRE
MANSLAUGHTER
MASTIGOPHORA
METAGNATHOUS
METALLOPHONE
METAMORPHISM
METAMORPHOSE
MISAPPREHEND
MNEMOTECHNIC
NEIGHBORHOOD
PHILOSOPHIZE
POLYURETHANE
PRIZEFIGHTER
PTERIDOPHYTE
RHAMPHOTHECA
SARRUSOPHONE
SCLERENCHYMA
SHORTSIGHTED
SIPHONOPHORA
SPINSTERHOOD
STEEPLECHASE
STENTORPHONE
STEPDAUGHTER
STRANGLEHOLD
STRATOSPHERE
SUPERHIGHWAY
SYNADELPHITE
TELEGRAPHESE
TELEGRAPHIST
TROCHOSPHERE
ADSCITITIOUS
ADVANTAGIOUS
ADVENTITIOUS
AERONAUTICAL
AGATHODAIMON
ALPHABETICAL
ANTIPARTICLE
ANTIRACHITIC
APPENDICITIS
ARITHMETICAL
ASTROLOGICAL
ASTRONOMICAL
ASYMMETRICAL
BANTAMWEIGHT
BARRANQUILLA
BEACONSFIELD
BEAUMONTIQUE
BIOGRAPHICAL
BLOODSTAINED
BOUGAINVILLE
CASSITERIDES
CASTERBRIDGE
CATAPHYSICAL
CHESTERFIELD
CHITTERLINGS
COMBINATIONS
CONTEMPTIBLE
CONTUMACIOUS
COSMOPOLITAN
CREMAILLIÈRE
DISORGANIZED
EPIDEICTICAL
ETHNOLOGICAL
ETYMOLOGICAL
ETYMOLOGICON
FIDDLESTICKS
FREIGHTLINER
FRONTISPIECE
FULMINATIONS
GASTARBEITER
GENEALOGICAL
GEOGRAPHICAL
HAMARTHRITIS
HEARTSTRINGS
HEPHTHEMIMER
HEROICOMICAL
HETEROCLITIC
HIERARCHICAL
HYPERBOLICAL
HYPOCRITICAL
HYPOTHETICAL
INACCESSIBLE
INADMISSIBLE
INAUSPICIOUS
INCOMPATIBLE
INCONVENIENT
INCORRIGIBLE
INCORRIGIBLY
INDEFENSIBLE
INDIGESTIBLE
INHARMONIOUS
INSALUBRIOUS
INSTRUCTIONS
INSUFFICIENT
INTELLIGIBLE
INTERMEDIARY
INTERMEDIATE
IRRESISTIBLE
IRREVERSIBLE
LAMENTATIONS
LEGIONNAIRES
LONGITUDINAL
LOXODROMICAL
LYMANTRIIDAE
MACROPODIDAE
MALPRACTICES
MATHEMATICAL
MERETRICIOUS
MERITRICIOUS
MESOTHELIOMA
METAPHORICAL
METAPHYSICAL
METROPOLITAN
MIDDLEWEIGHT
MISBEHAVIOUR
MULTIFARIOUS
MUTESSARIFAT
MYTHOLOGICAL
NEOCLASSICAL
NEUROLOGICAL
OBEDIENTIARY
ONEIROCRITIC
OSTENTATIOUS
OUTBUILDINGS
OVERSTRAINED
PALPITATIONS
PANTECHNICON
PAPILIONIDAE
PARSIMONIOUS
PATHOLOGICAL
PENITENTIARY
PERICARDITIS
PERSONALIZED
PERTINACIOUS
PERVICACIOUS
PHILOLOGICAL
PHYTONADIONE
POINTILLISME
PROLETARIATE
QUARTERFINAL
QUARTERLIGHT
RAMBUNCTIOUS
SACRILEGIOUS
SALTATORIOUS
SARSAPARILLA
SCREENWRITER
SCRIPTWRITER
SECRETARIATE
SEMIPRECIOUS
SEPTEMBRISER
SHORTCOMINGS
SILVERHAIRED
SLOCKDOLIGER
SOCIOLOGICAL
SPATANGOIDEA
SPIEGELEISEN
STEREOPTICON
SUBCONSCIOUS
SUBSTANTIATE
SUPERCILIARY
SUPERCILIOUS
SURROUNDINGS
TAUTOLOGICAL
TERRITORIALS
THEREAGAINST
TOBACCONISTS
TRALATICIOUS
TRALATITIOUS
TRANQUILIZER
TRANSACTIONS
TROCHELMINTH
UNAUTHORISED
UNAUTHORIZED
UNDERACHIEVE
UNDETERMINED
UNECONOMICAL
UNPREJUDICED
UNRECOGNISED
UNRECOGNIZED
UNRESTRAINED
UNSCIENTIFIC
VAINGLORIOUS
WALLYDRAIGLE
WELTERWEIGHT
BACKBREAKING
BLETHERSKATE
BLUESTOCKING
BREATHTAKING
CAMIKNICKERS
GALLIGASKINS
POLICYMAKING
SIDEWHISKERS
SITTLICHKEIT
SLEEPWALKING
SWASHBUCKLER
ABSQUATULATE
ADAPTABILITY
ADVISABILITY
AGALMATOLITE
ANEMOPHILOUS
ANTHROPOLOGY
ARISTOTELEAN
AVAILABILITY
AWAYABSOLUTE
BACCHANALIAN
BACTERIOLOGY
BICAMERALISM
BOONDOGGLING
BRICKFIELDER
BUSINESSLIKE
CAPERCAILLIE
CAPERCAILZIE
COLDSHOULDER
CONGRATULATE
CONSTABULARY
CONVIVIALITY

COUNTERBLAST
COUNTERCLAIM
CRISTOBALITE
DECENTRALISE
DECENTRALIZE
DESIRABILITY
DISCONSOLATE
DYSTELEOLOGY
ELECTROPLATE
EPISCOPALIAN
EPISTEMOLOGY
ESSENTIALITY
EXCITABILITY
FARTHINGLAND
FUNCTIONLESS
GONDWANALAND
GRISEOFULVIN
HAEMOPHILIAC
ILLEGIBILITY
ILLOGICALITY
IMMUTABILITY
IMPARTIALITY
INARTICULATE
INCAPABILITY
INCUNABULIST
INSOLUBILITY
INTERSTELLAR
INVISIBILITY
IRASCIBILITY
IRRITABILITY
LEPIDOMELANE
LILLIBULLERO
LILLIBURLERO
LIVERPUDLIAN
MALLEABILITY
MINDBOGGLING
MISCALCULATE
MOTORCYCLIST
MUNICIPALITY
NAVIGABILITY
NEVERTHELESS
NEWFOUNDLAND
OTHERWORLDLY
OXYACETYLENE
PALEONTOLOGY
PARANTHELIUM
PERMEABILITY
PHARMACOLOGY
PLAUSIBILITY
POLYETHYLENE
POTENTIALITY
PRACTICALITY
PRALLTRILLER
PREMAXILLARY
PRINCIPALITY
RECAPITULATE
RONCESVALLES
SCOPOPHILIAC
SOMNAMBULISM
SOMNAMBULIST
SPINECHILLER
SPIRITUALISM
SPIRITUALIST
SPIRITUALITY
SPURTLEBLADE
STEGOPHOLIST
STROMATOLITE
TARAMASALATA
TECHNICALITY
TETRACYCLINE
THEOPHYLLINE
THUNDERCLOUD
THUNDERFLASH
TORRICELLIAN
TRACTABILITY
TRANQUILLISE
TRANQUILLITY
TRANQUILLIZE
UMBRADARLING
UNAPPARELLED
UNCONTROLLED
UNIVERSALIST
UNSCRUPULOUS
WHIMSICALITY
WINTERHALTER
ACCOUCHEMENT
ACCOUTREMENT
ADMONISHMENT
AERODYNAMICS
AMPHISTOMOUS
ANNOUNCEMENT
ANTILEGOMENA
ANTITHROMBIN
APLANOGAMETE
ASTONISHMENT
BARNSTORMING
BETHLEHEMITE
BEWILDERMENT
BLANDISHMENT
BREASTSUMMER
CHASTISEMENT
COMMENCEMENT
CROSSEXAMINE
DECIPHERMENT
DISAGREEMENT
DISPLACEMENT
EMBEZZLEMENT
ENCIRCLEMENT
ENCROACHMENT
ENTANGLEMENT
ENTRENCHMENT
EPIPHENOMENA
EPITHALAMION
EPITHALAMIUM
ESTRANGEMENT
GENTLETAMPER
HEARTWARMING
HELLGRAMMITE
HEREDITAMENT
HETEROSOMATA
HIEROGRAMMAT
HOMOTHERMOUS
HOUSEWARMING
IDIOTHERMOUS
ILLEGITIMACY
ILLEGITIMATE
IMPRISONMENT
INFRINGEMENT
KATZENJAMMER
MALTREATMENT
MICROCLIMATE
MISPLACEMENT
MISSTATEMENT
MISTREATMENT
NORTHERNMOST
ORTHORHOMBIC
OVERESTIMATE
OVERWHELMING
PARALIPOMENA
PHLEBOTOMIST
POSTPONEMENT
PRASEODYMIUM
PREDETERMINE
PRESENTIMENT
PROTHALAMION
PROTHALAMIUM
PSEUDONYMOUS
PSIPHENOMENA
READJUSTMENT
REDEPLOYMENT
RENOUNCEMENT
RESETTLEMENT
RETRENCHMENT
SOUTHERNMOST
SULPHONAMIDE
UNDERGARMENT
UNEMPLOYMENT
YELLOWHAMMER
ABOLITIONIST
ACCORDIONIST
AFFECTIONATE
AGRIBUSINESS
ANTHELMINTIC
ARFVEDSONITE
ASPARAGINASE
AWARDWINNING
BABINGTONITE
BACKWARDNESS
BANANALANDER
BARBERMONGER
BENEVOLENTLY
BERTILLONAGE
BICENTENNIAL
CALCEAMENTUM
CARELESSNESS
CARTHAGINIAN
CAUTIOUSNESS
CHEERFULNESS
CHEESEMONGER
CHILDISHNESS
CHRISTIANITY
CHURLISHNESS
CLANNISHNESS
COINCIDENTAL
COMPANIONWAY
COMPLACENTLY
COMPLETENESS
CONCURRENTLY
CONSEQUENCES
CONSEQUENTLY
CONSISTENTLY
CONTERMINOUS
CONTRAPUNTAL
CONTRARINESS
CONVENIENCES
CONVENIENTLY
CONVINCINGLY
COSTERMONGER
COVETOUSNESS
CRASSAMENTUM
CREATIVENESS
CROSSCOUNTRY
DEFLATIONARY
DEPARTMENTAL
DILATORINESS
DISAPPOINTED
DISCIPLINARY
DISCONTENTED
DISCRIMINATE
DISENCHANTED
DISTINCTNESS
EDUCATIONIST
ELEEMOSYNARY
ENTERTAINING
ENTREATINGLY
ENTREPRENEUR
ETHEROMANIAC
EVOLUTIONARY
EXPERIMENTAL
EXTENSIONIST
EXTORTIONATE
FAITHFULNESS
FEARLESSNESS
FLAMBOYANTLY
FORCEFULNESS
FRIENDLINESS
FRUITFULNESS
GOVERNMENTAL
GRACEFULNESS
GRACIOUSNESS
GRANDISONIAN
GRATEFULNESS
HAMBLETONIAN
HELPLESSNESS
HETEROCONTAE
HIEROPHANTIC
HILDEBRANDIC
HOMESICKNESS
HOPELESSNESS
HYDROQUINONE

IMPOLITENESS
INCOHERENTLY
INCREASINGLY
INDEBTEDNESS
INDOCTRINATE
INFLATIONARY
INFREQUENTLY
INSTRUMENTAL
INTERCHANGED
IRREVERENTLY
ISOLATIONISM
ISOLATIONIST
JENNYSPINNER
KILLIKINNICK
KLEPTOMANIAC
KLIPSPRINGER
LIFELESSNESS
LISTLESSNESS
LUXULLIANITE
MACMILLANITE
MARCOBRUNNER
MINDFULLNESS
MISDEMEANOUR
MUCILAGINOUS
MUGGLETONIAN
NEOPLATONISM
NONCHALANTLY
NUTRITIONIST
NYMPHOMANIAC
OBSOLETENESS
PAINLESSNESS
PALUDAMENTUM
PANCHATANTRA
PANDAEMONIUM
PEACEFULNESS
PERMANGANATE
PERSISTENTLY
PERVERSENESS
PHILISTINISM
PINNIEWINKLE
POSTLIMINARY
PREDESTINATE
PREPAREDNESS
PRIGGISHNESS
PRIZEWINNING
PROBATIONARY
PROFICIENTLY
PROTACTINIUM
PYROTECHNICS
QUINQUENNIAL
RECEPTIONIST
RECKLESSNESS
REFLATIONARY
REMEMBRANCER
RESPONDENTIA
RESTLESSNESS
RETARDEDNESS
REVERSIONARY
RUTHLESSNESS
SALVATIONIST

SCRIMSHANDER
SCRIMSHANKER
SECESSIONIST
SECTARIANISM
SHEEPISHNESS
SINGLEHANDED
SINGLEMINDED
SLOVENLINESS
SLUBBERINGLY
SNOBBISHNESS
SPACIOUSNESS
SPECIOUSNESS
SPECKTIONEER
SPITEFULNESS
SPURIOUSNESS
STAGGERINGLY
STEALTHINESS
STRAIGHTNESS
STRONGMINDED
STUBBORNNESS
STUDIOUSNESS
SUBCONTINENT
SUBSEQUENTLY
SUBTERRANEAN
SUFFICIENTLY
SURPRISINGLY
TACTLESSNESS
TERCENTENARY
THANKFULNESS
THESSALONIAN
THICKSKINNED
THOROUGHNESS
TIMELESSNESS
TOGETHERNESS
TRADESCANTIA
TRIUMPHANTLY
TRUTHFULNESS
UNACQUAINTED
UNCHALLENGED
UNCTUOUSNESS
UNDERPINNING
UNDERSKINKER
UNFREQUENTED
USERFRIENDLY
VALENCIENNES
VENGEFULNESS
VIBRATIUNCLE
WATCHFULNESS
WELLBALANCED
WOLLASTONITE
WRETCHEDNESS
YOUTHFULNESS
ANAMORPHOSIS
ANTIMNEMONIC
BATTLEGROUND
BLABBERMOUTH
BREAKTHROUGH
BREASTPLOUGH
BUTTERSCOTCH
CEREBROTONIC

CHARTERHOUSE
CLAPPERBOARD
COMMISSIONED
COMMISSIONER
CONFECTIONER
CONFESSIONAL
CONTRAPPOSTO
CONVENTIONAL
COUNTERPOINT
COUNTERPOISE
CURMUDGEONLY
DARLINGTONIA
ELECTROTONUS
ENANTIOMORPH
ENGLISHWOMAN
ENGLISHWOMEN
EPANORTHOSIS
EXHIBITIONER
FLITTERMOUSE
FRANKALMOIGN
GAINSBOROUGH
GONADOTROPIN
GRASSWIDOWER
HAEMORRHOIDS
HALLUCINOGEN
HETEROPHORIA
HISTIOPHORUS
HOUSETOHOUSE
HYDROCHLORIC
ICHTHYOCOLLA
KATHAREVOUSA
LALLAPALOOZA
LAMELLICORNE
MISANTHROPIC
MOUTHBROODER
MULTICOLORED
NONALCOHOLIC
OCCUPATIONAL
OLDFASHIONED
ONOMATOPOEIA
ONOMATOPOEIC
OSTEOPOROSIS
PARTICOLORED
PECTORILOQUY
PERISTERONIC
PHILHARMONIC
PRACTICIONER
PRACTITIONER
PROCESSIONAL
PROFESSIONAL
PROPORTIONAL
PROSOPOPOEIA
PYTHONOMORPH
QUADRAPHONIC
RECREATIONAL
REDEMPTIONER
RHINORRHOEAL
ROOMINGHOUSE
SCATTERMOUCH
SELFEMPLOYED

SERVICEWOMAN
SHARPSHOOTER
SHUFFLEBOARD
SINANTHROPUS
SLOCKDOLOGER
SPORTSGROUND
STELLENBOSCH
STEREOPHONIC
STEREOSCOPIC
STORMTROOPER
TETRODOTOXIN
THESMOPHORIA
THIGMOTROPIC
THIRDBOROUGH
TRADESPEOPLE
TRANSITIONAL
TUBERCULOSIS
UNACCUSTOMED
UNDEREXPOSED
UNNEIGHBORLY
WASHINGTONIA
WELLINGTONIA
WOLSTENHOLME
AECIDIOSPORE
ANTISTROPHON
BOOBYTRAPPED
BRACHYCEPHAL
BRANCHIOPODA
CALLIGRAPHIC
CARTOGRAPHER
CARTOGRAPHIC
CATASTROPHIC
DESSERTSPOON
EAVESDROPPER
GASTROSOPHER
GLOCKENSPIEL
GOOSEPIMPLES
HIEROGLYPHIC
HIPPOCREPIAN
HOUSEKEEPING
HYDROGRAPHER
HYMNOGRAPHER
IAMBOGRAPHER
LITHOGRAPHIC
MARLINESPIKE
MISINTERPRET
OCTASTROPHIC
PEACEKEEPING
PHOTOGLYPHIC
PHOTOGRAPHER
PHOTOGRAPHIC
POPOCATEPETL
PORNOGRAPHIC
RADIOGRAPHER
STENOGRAPHER
STEREOTYPING
TELEUTOSPORE
UNPRINCIPLED
ADMINISTRATE
ALEXIPHARMIC

AMBASSADRESS
AMBIDEXTROUS
ANDROSTERONE
ANECATHARSIS
ANTANANARIVO
ANTINEUTRINO
APOLLINARIAN
AROMATHERAPY
ARSENOPYRITE
ATMOSPHERICS
AWEINSPIRING
BEHAVIOURISM
BENEFACTRESS
BLACKCURRANT
BLOODTHIRSTY
CANTANKEROUS
CARBOHYDRATE
CARICATURIST
CHARACTERIZE
CHEESEBURGER
CHEESEPARING
CHEMOTHERAPY
CHILDBEARING
CHURCHWARDEN
CIRCUMGYRATE
CIRCUMSCRIBE
COLLECTORATE
COMMENSURATE
COMMISSARIAT
CONGLOMERATE
CONTEMPORARY
CONTRITURATE
DEMILITARIZE
DISACCHARIDE
DISAPPEARING
DISCONCERTED
DISEMBARRASS
DISINTEGRATE
DOLPHINARIUM
EMBROIDERESS
ENTEROMORPHA
ENTOMOSTRACA
FAINTHEARTED
FEATHERBRAIN
FUSTILLIRIAN
GERONTOCRACY
GIBRALTARIAN
GLADIATORIAL
GROSSULARITE
HEADMISTRESS
HUMANITARIAN
HYDROTHERAPY
HYPNOTHERAPY
IDIOSYNCRASY
INSPECTORATE
INSTRUCTRESS
INTERSPERSED
INTRAUTERINE
INVERTEBRATE
IRREGULARITY
KALISTOCRACY
KERAUNOGRAPH
KINDERGARTEN
LAMPADEDROMY
LANCASTERIAN
LATIROSTRATE
LIGHTHEARTED
LITHOLATROUS
LUXEMBOURGER
MALACOSTRACA
MANGELWURZEL
MARCONIGRAPH
MASTERSTROKE
MECHITHARIST
MONTESSORIAN
NEIGHBOURING
NEWSPAPERMAN
NONAGENARIAN
OBSTREPEROUS
OCTOGENARIAN
OPISTHOGRAPH
ORIENTEERING
OVERPOWERING
PANTISOCRACY
PASSIONFRUIT
PEREMPTORILY
PHILANTHROPY
POSTMISTRESS
POWERSHARING
PRAISEWORTHY
PREHISTORIAN
PREMONSTRANT
PREPONDERANT
PREPONDERATE
PREPONDERENT
PREPOSTEROUS
PRESBYTERIAN
PROFESSORIAL
PROFITEERING
PROGESTERONE
PROPRIETRESS
PROTECTORATE
PSYCHIATRIST
RACKETEERING
RADIOTHERAPY
RECALCITRANT
REDINTEGRATE
REINVIGORATE
SCATTERBRAIN
SCHNEIDERIAN
SCLERODERMIA
SELFCATERING
SELFINTEREST
SELFPORTRAIT
SERASKIERATE
SESQUITERTIA
SEXAGENARIAN
SPOKESPERSON
STRADIVARIUS
STRIGIFORMES
SUBLAPSARIAN
SUBSIDIARITY
SUPERCHARGED
SUPERCHARGER
TAPERECORDER
TELEOSAURIAN
TESTOSTERONE
TETRAHEDRITE
THAUMATURGIC
THAUMATURGUS
THREEQUARTER
TOTALITARIAN
TRANSMIGRATE
TRANSMOGRIFY
TURACOVERDIN
TURBOCHARGER
UINTATHERIUM
UNDERCURRENT
UNDISCHARGED
UNPOPULARITY
VETERINARIAN
WATERCARRIER
WEATHERPROOF
WELLINFORMED
WHOLEHEARTED
ACCOMPLISHED
AIRCRAFTSMAN
ANTAGONISTIC
ANTIMACASSAR
APPREHENSION
APPREHENSIVE
ASTROPHYSICS
AUSTRALASIAN
AUSTRONESIAN
BACKWOODSMAN
BACTERIOSTAT
BESSERWISSER
BIELORUSSIAN
BIOCHEMISTRY
BIODIVERSITY
BREATHLESSLY
BYELORUSSIAN
CHAIRMANSHIP
CHAMPIONSHIP
CHAUVINISTIC
CHONDRIOSOME
CHREMATISTIC
CIRCUMCISION
COCCIDIOSTAT
COMPROMISING
DELICATESSEN
DICTATORSHIP
DIRECTORSHIP
DISPOSSESSED
DUNNIEWASSAL
ECCLESIASTES
ECCLESIASTIC
EFFORTLESSLY
EMBARRASSING
ENTERPRISING
ENTHUSIASTIC
EXTINGUISHER
FRONTIERSMAN
GAMESMANSHIP
GUARDIANSHIP
HAIRDRESSERS
HAIRDRESSING
HORSEMANSHIP
HYPERTENSION
ICHTHYOPSIDA
ICONOCLASTIC
IMPOVERISHED
INCONCLUSIVE
INTERCESSION
INTERMISSION
JOURNALISTIC
KIRSCHWASSER
LAUREATESHIP
MACABERESQUE
MARKSMANSHIP
MILITARISTIC
MISREPRESENT
NARCISSISTIC
NATURALISTIC
OPHIOGLOSSUM
OVERDRESSING
PARTISANSHIP
PASSEMEASURE
PERIPHRASTIC
PLEIOCHASIUM
PREPOSSESSED
PREREQUISITE
PROGYMNASIUM
PROTOPLASMAL
PROTOPLASMIC
QUADRAGESIMA
RECEIVERSHIP
RELATIONSHIP
RELENTLESSLY
REPERCUSSION
REPOSSESSION
REPROCESSING
SALESMANSHIP
SCHILLERSPAR
SCHOOLMASTER
SELFADHESIVE
SEPTUAGESIMA
SHIRTWAISTER
SURREALISTIC
TERGIVERSATE
TRANSGRESSOR
TRANSMISSION
UNCONVERSANT
UNDIMINISHED
UNINTERESTED
UNOPPRESSIVE
UNRESPONSIVE
UNSUCCESSFUL
UNSURPRISING
ABBREVIATION

ACCELERATION
ACCENTUATION
ACCUMULATION
ADJUDICATION
ADULTERATION
ALIMENTATIVE
ALLITERATION
AMALGAMATION
AMELIORATION
ANAESTHETISE
ANAESTHETIST
ANAESTHETIZE
ANNIHILATION
ANNUNCIATION
ANTICIPATION
ANTICIPATORY
APPENDECTOMY
APPOGGIATURA
APPRECIATION
APPRECIATIVE
ARCHITECTURE
ARTICULATION
ARTIODACTYLA
ASPHYXIATION
ASSIMILATION
ASSUEFACTION
ATHEROMATOUS
AUGMENTATION
AUSCULTATION
BAIRNSFATHER
BRILLIANTINE
BROADCASTING
CALUMNIATION
CANCELLATION
CANONIZATION
CAPITULATION
CATADIOPTRIC
CHLORINATION
CHORIZONTIST
CIVILISATION
CIVILIZATION
CLARINETTIST
CLAUDICATION
CODIFICATION
COHABITATION
COLLUCTATION
COLONIZATION
COLOQUINTIDA
COMMENDATION
COMMENDATORY
COMPELLATION
COMPENSATION
COMPENSATORY
COMPLICATION
COMPURGATION
CONCILIATION
CONCILIATORY
CONDEMNATION
CONDENSATION
CONFIDENTIAL
CONFIRMATION
CONFIRMATORY
CONFISCATION
CONGREGATION
CONSCRIPTION
CONSECRATION
CONSERVATION
CONSERVATISM
CONSERVATIVE
CONSERVATORY
CONSTIPATION
CONSTITUTION
CONSTRICTION
CONSTRUCTION
CONSTRUCTIVE
CONSULTATION
CONSULTATIVE
CONSUMMATION
CONTIGNATION
CONTINUATION
CONTRIBUTION
CONTRIBUTORY
CONVERSATION
COORDINATION
COURTMARTIAL
CROSSSECTION
DAGUERROTYPE
DEAMBULATORY
DEASPIRATION
DEBILITATING
DECAPITATION
DECELERATION
DECONGESTANT
DEGENERATION
DELIBERATELY
DELIBERATION
DENOMINATION
DENUNCIATION
DEPOPULATION
DEPRECIATION
DEPRECIATORY
DEREGULATION
DIFFERENTIAL
DILAPIDATION
DISADVANTAGE
DISCOMFITURE
DISINCENTIVE
DISINFECTANT
DISORIENTATE
DISPENSATION
DISQUISITION
DISREPECTFUL
DISSERTATION
DISSOCIATION
DISTILLATION
DISTRIBUTION
DISTRIBUTIVE
DONNERWETTER
DORSIVENTRAL
EMANCIPATION
EMASCULATION
ENTOPLASTRON
EPISTOLATERS
EQUIVOCATION
EQUIVOCATORY
EXACERBATION
EXAGGERATION
EXASPERATING
EXASPERATION
EXCRUCIATING
EXCRUCIATION
EXHILARATING
EXHILARATION
EXPLOITATION
FERMENTATION
FINALIZATION
FIRSTFOOTING
FLAGELLATION
FLORICULTURE
FLUORIDATION
FRANKENSTEIN
FRUMENTATION
FUNDAMENTALS
GALLIVANTING
GLOBETROTTER
GRANDMONTINE
GUILDENSTERN
HAIRSPLITTER
HEADQUARTERS
HERMENEUTICS
HERMENEUTIST
HIGHFALUTING
HINDQUARTERS
HIPPOCRATISE
HOMOEOPATHIC
HORTICULTURE
HUDIBRASTICS
HUMANIZATION
HYSTERECTOMY
IDEALIZATION
ILLUMINATING
ILLUMINATION
ILLUSTRATION
ILLUSTRATIVE
IMMACULATELY
IMMODERATELY
IMMODERATION
IMMUNIZATION
IMPERFECTION
IMPLANTATION
IMPREGNATION
INACCURATELY
INADEQUATELY
INAUGURATION
INCAPACITATE
INCINERATION
INCOMPLETELY
INCONSISTENT
INCRUSTATION
INDEFINITELY
INDISCRETION
INEXACTITUDE
INFELICITOUS
INFILTRATION
INFLAMMATION
INFLAMMATORY
INGRATIATING
INNATTENTIVE
INORDINATELY
INSEMINATION
INSTALLATION
INSTAURATION
INSURRECTION
INTELLECTUAL
INTENERATION
INTERCEPTION
INTERJECTION
INTERMITTENT
INTERPRETING
INTERRUPTION
INTERSECTION
INTERVENTION
INTIMIDATING
INTIMIDATION
INTOXICATING
INTOXICATION
INTRANSITIVE
INTRODUCTION
INTRODUCTORY
INVALIDATION
INVIGORATING
INVIGORATION
IRRESOLUTELY
IRRESOLUTION
IRRESPECTIVE
ISHMAELITISH
JURISDICTION
LABANOTATION
LEGALIZATION
LEGITIMATELY
LIQUEFACTION
MALFORMATION
MALNUTRITION
MANIPULATION
MANIPULATIVE
MASTURBATION
MENSTRUATION
MINISTRATION
MISADVENTURE
MISQUOTATION
MOBILIZATION
MODIFICATION
MOONLIGHTING
MOSBOLLETJIE
NIGHTCLOTHES
NOMENCLATURE
NONCOMMITTAL
NONRESISTANT
NORTHEASTERN
NORTHWESTERN

NOTIFICATION
OBLITERATION
OBSERVANTINE
OPINIONATIVE
ORGANISATION
ORGANIZATION
ORTHODONTICS
OSSIFICATION
OVEREXERTION
PACIFICATION
PARAMILITARY
PASSEPARTOUT
PASSIONATELY
PENALIZATION
PERADVENTURE
PERNOCTATION
PERPETRATION
PERSPIRATION
PERTURBATION
PESTILENTIAL
PETRIFACTION
PHRONTISTERY
PHYCOXANTHIN
PHYTOBENTHOS
PIGMENTATION
PISCICULTURE
PITTERPATTER
PLAINCLOTHES
PLASTERSTONE
POLARIZATION
PRECONDITION
PREDILECTION
PREFERENTIAL
PREGUSTATION
PRESCRIPTION
PRESCRIPTIVE
PRESENTATION
PRESERVATION
PRESERVATIVE
PRESIDENTIAL
PRESTRICTION
PREVENTATIVE
PROCLAMATION
PROLONGATION
PROMULGATION
PROPITIATION
PROPITIATORY
PROSCRIPTION
PROSTITUTION
PROTESTATION
PROVIDENTIAL
PSYCHOPATHIC
PTERODACTYLE
PURIFICATION
PUTREFACTION
QUANTITATIVE
QUARTERSTAFF
RADIOISOTOPE
RAMIFICATION
RATIFICATION
RECOLLECTION
RECONSTITUTE
RECUPERATION
RECUPERATIVE
REGENERATION
REGISTRATION
REHABILITATE
REJUVENATION
REMUNERATION
REMUNERATIVE
RENUNCIATION
REPATRIATION
REPRODUCTION
REPRODUCTIVE
RESTAURATEUR
RESURRECTION
RETICULATION
RHADAMANTHUS
RHIPIDOPTERA
RHYTIDECTOMY
SATISFACTION
SATISFACTORY
SAUROGNATHAE
SEGMENTATION
SESQUIALTERA
SIPHONOSTELE
SOLICITATION
SOUTHCOTTIAN
SOUTHEASTERN
SOUTHWESTERN
SPHACELATION
SPHAIRISTIKE
STERNUTATION
STILBOESTROL
STONECHATTER
STREPITATION
STREPSIPTERA
STRIDULATION
STROPHANTHUS
STUPEFACTION
SUBARRHATION
SUBCOMMITTEE
SUBHASTATION
SUBSCRIPTION
SUBSTITUTION
SUBSTRUCTURE
SUCCUSSATION
SUPERSTITION
SUPPLICATION
SWIZZLESTICK
SYNTAGMATITE
TAGLIACOTIAN
TEETERTOTTER
TESTAMENTARY
THERAPEUTICS
THUNDERSTORM
THYSANOPTERA
TIGHTFITTING
TRANSPONTINE
TRANSVESTISM
TRANSVESTITE
ULTRAMONTANE
UNATTRACTIVE
UNDERCLOTHES
UNDERWRITTEN
UNPRODUCTIVE
UNSUSPECTING
URBANIZATION
VAPORIZATION
VENEPUNCTURE
VENTRIPOTENT
VERIFICATION
VILIFICATION
VILLEGIATURA
VITUPERATION
VITUPERATIVE
VOCIFERATION
WOODBURYTYPE
ZARATHUSTRIC
AFORETHOUGHT
AFTERTHOUGHT
AGRICULTURAL
APFELSTRUDEL
AUSPICIOUSLY
BOISTEROUSLY
BRONTOSAURUS
CONSPECTUITY
CONTEMPTUOUS
CONTINUOUSLY
COURAGEOUSLY
DISASTROUSLY
DISCOMEDUSAE
DISDAINFULLY
DISINGENUOUS
DIVERTICULUM
FASTIDIOUSLY
FORTUITOUSLY
GLYNDEBOURNE
HAPPYGOLUCKY
HARMONIOUSLY
INCAUTIOUSLY
INCONSEQUENT
INDISSOLUBLE
INTERLOCUTOR
LASCIVIOUSLY
LUGUBRIOUSLY
MAGNILOQUENT
MANUFACTURER
MASSPRODUCED
MEANINGFULLY
MERRYTHOUGHT
METICULOUSLY
MINICOMPUTER
MIRACULOUSLY
MISPRONOUNCE
MONOTONOUSLY
MYSTERIOUSLY
OBSEQUIOUSLY
OUTMANOEUVRE
OUTRAGEOUSLY
PERSULPHURIC
POSTGRADUATE
POSTHUMOUSLY
PRECARIOUSLY
PRECOCIOUSLY
PRESUMPTUOUS
PRODIGIOUSLY
PROPITIOUSLY
PUGNACIOUSLY
PURPOSEBUILT
PURPOSEFULLY
RESPECTFULLY
RIDICULOUSLY
SCANDALOUSLY
SCRUPULOUSLY
SCURRILOUSLY
SEMICIRCULAR
SOLICITOUSLY
STRINGCOURSE
SUCCESSFULLY
SUPERANNUATE
SUPERNACULUM
SUPERNATURAL
SUSPICIOUSLY
THOUGHTFULLY
TITANOSAURUS
TREMENDOUSLY
UPROARIOUSLY
VARICOLOURED
VOCIFEROUSLY
VOLUPTUOUSLY
WILLIEWAUGHT
AGGRESSIVELY
ANTEDILUVIAN
ATTRACTIVELY
COLLECTIVELY
CONCLUSIVELY
CONDUCTIVITY
DECORATIVELY
DRINKDRIVING
ENERGYSAVING
EXHAUSTIVELY
FIGURATIVELY
IMPRESSIVELY
LABOURSAVING
OPPRESSIVELY
PERCEPTIVELY
PERCEPTIVITY
PERSUASIVELY
PHOTOGRAVURE
POSSESSIVELY
PRODUCTIVITY
PROTECTIVELY
RESPECTIVELY
SCANDINAVIAN
SHOSTAKOVICH
STAKHANOVITE
STANISLAVSKI
SUBJECTIVELY
SUBJECTIVITY

SUBMISSIVELY
SUCCESSIVELY
SUGGESTIVELY
THANKSGIVING
VINDICTIVELY
HENCEFORWARD
SOUTHERNWOOD
STRANGLEWEED
WHIPPOORWILL
CARDINDEXING
HETEROSEXUAL
ACCOMPANYING
ARTILLERYMAN
BREATHALYSER
ELECTROLYSIS
ERYTHROMYCIN
STREPTOMYCIN
TRICHOPHYTON
UNSATISFYING
MOISTURIZING
SCHEHERAZADE
UNAPPETIZING

12:10

ABSQUATULATE
ADMINISTRATE
AFFECTIONATE
AROMATHERAPY
ASPARAGINASE
AUTHENTICATE
BEAUMARCHAIS
BERTILLONAGE
BILLINGSGATE
BLACKCURRANT
BLETHERSKATE
CARBOHYDRATE
CHEMOTHERAPY
CIRCUMGYRATE
CLAPPERBOARD
CLAVICEMBALO
COLLECTORATE
COMMENSURATE
CONGLOMERATE
CONGRATULATE
CONSTABULARY
CONTEMPORARY
CONTRITURATE
COUNTERBLAST
COUNTERCLAIM
DECONGESTANT
DEFLATIONARY
DISADVANTAGE
DISCIPLINARY
DISCONSOLATE
DISCRIMINATE
DISEMBARRASS
DISINFECTANT
DISINTEGRATE
DISORIENTATE
ELECTROPLATE
ELEEMOSYNARY
ENTOMOSTRACA
EVOLUTIONARY
EXSUFFLICATE
EXTORTIONATE
FARTHINGLAND
FEATHERBRAIN
FUNDAMENTALS
GERONTOCRACY
GESELLSCHAFT
GONDWANALAND
HEMICHORDATA
HENCEFORWARD
HETEROSOMATA
HYDROTHERAPY
HYPNOTHERAPY
IDIOSYNCRASY
ILLEGITIMACY
ILLEGITIMATE
INARTICULATE
INCAPACITATE
INDOCTRINATE
INFLATIONARY
INSPECTORATE
INTERMEDIARY
INTERMEDIATE
INVERTEBRATE
KALISTOCRACY
KERAUNOGRAPH
LATIROSTRATE
LEPIDOMELANE
MALACOSTRACA
MARCONIGRAPH
MICROCLIMATE
MISCALCULATE
NEWFOUNDLAND
NONRESISTANT
OBEDIENTIARY
OPISTHOGRAPH
OVERESTIMATE
PANTISOCRACY
PARAMILITARY
PENITENTIARY
PERMANGANATE
POLYURETHANE
POSTGRADUATE
POSTLIMINARY
PREDESTINATE
PREMAXILLARY
PREMONSTRANT
PREPONDERANT
PREPONDERATE
PROBATIONARY
PROLETARIATE
PROTECTORATE
QUARTERSTAFF
RADIOTHERAPY
RECALCITRANT
RECAPITULATE
REDINTEGRATE
REFLATIONARY
REHABILITATE
REINVIGORATE
REVERSIONARY
SCATTERBRAIN
SCHEHERAZADE
SECRETARIATE
SELFPORTRAIT
SERASKIERATE
SHUFFLEBOARD
SOPHISTICATE
SPLENOMEGALY
SPURTLEBLADE
STEEPLECHASE
SUBSTANTIATE
SUPERANNUATE
SUPERCILIARY
TARAMASALATA
TERCENTENARY
TERGIVERSATE
TERRITORIALS
TESTAMENTARY
THOROUGHFARE
THUNDERFLASH
TRANSMIGRATE
ULTRAMONTANE
UNCONVERSANT
ANTITHROMBIN
APPROACHABLE
ATTRIBUTABLE
CLASSIFIABLE
COMMUNICABLE
CONSIDERABLE
CONSIDERABLY
CONTEMPTIBLE
CONTROLLABLE
DECIPHERABLE
DEMONSTRABLE
DEMONSTRABLY
DISAGREEABLE
DISHONORABLE
DISHONORABLY
DISREPUTABLE
EXCHANGEABLE
EXTRADITABLE
IDENTIFIABLE
IMMEASURABLE
IMMEASURABLY
IMPENETRABLE
IMPERISHABLE
INACCESSIBLE
INADMISSIBLE
INAPPLICABLE
INCALCULABLE
INCOMPARABLE
INCOMPARABLY
INCOMPATIBLE
INCONSOLABLE
INCORRIGIBLE
INCORRIGIBLY
INDECLINABLE
INDEFENSIBLE
INDIGESTIBLE
INDISPUTABLE
INDISPUTABLY
INDISSOLUBLE
INERADICABLE
INEXPLICABLE
INEXPLICABLY
INEXTRICABLE
INEXTRICABLY
INFORMIDABLE
INHOSPITABLE
INSUFFERABLE
INSUFFERABLY
INTELLIGIBLE
INTERMINABLE
INTERMINABLY
INVULNERABLE
IRREDEEMABLE
IRRESISTIBLE
IRRESOLVABLE
IRREVERSIBLE
MANOEUVRABLE
MARRIAGEABLE
MONOSYLLABIC
MONOSYLLABLE
ORTHORHOMBIC
POLYSYLLABIC
POLYSYLLABLE
PROGRAMMABLE
QUANTIFIABLE
QUESTIONABLE
RECHARGEABLE
RECOGNIZABLE
SURMOUNTABLE
TRANSFERABLE
TRANSLATABLE
UNACCEPTABLE
UNANSWERABLE
UNATTAINABLE
UNBELIEVABLE
UNBELIEVABLY
UNCHANGEABLE
UNCHARITABLE
UNCHARITABLY
UNDETECTABLE
UNFATHOMABLE
UNFAVOURABLE
UNIMAGINABLE
UNMANAGEABLE
UNMISTAKABLE
UNOBTAINABLE
UNPARDONABLE
UNPROFITABLE
UNREASONABLE
UNRETURNABLE
UNSEASONABLE
AERONAUTICAL

AFTEREFFECTS
ALPHABETICAL
ANTIPARTICLE
ARITHMETICAL
ASTROLOGICAL
ASTRONOMICAL
ASYMMETRICAL
BIOGRAPHICAL
CATAPHYSICAL
CONSEQUENCES
CONVENIENCES
EPIDEICTICAL
ERYTHROMYCIN
ETHNOLOGICAL
ETYMOLOGICAL
ETYMOLOGICON
FIDDLESTICKS
GENEALOGICAL
GENETHLIACON
GEOGRAPHICAL
GIGANTOMACHY
HAPPYGOLUCKY
HEROICOMICAL
HIERARCHICAL
HYPERBOLICAL
HYPOCRITICAL
HYPOTHETICAL
LOXODROMICAL
MALPRACTICES
MASSPRODUCED
MATHEMATICAL
METAPHORICAL
METAPHYSICAL
MYTHOLOGICAL
NEOCLASSICAL
NEUROLOGICAL
OREOPITHECUS
OSTEOMALACIA
PANPHARMACON
PANTECHNICON
PATHOLOGICAL
PERIOSTRACUM
PHILOLOGICAL
REMEMBRANCER
SIPUNCULACEA
SIVAPITHECUS
SOCIOLOGICAL
STEREOPTICON
STREPTOMYCIN
TAUTOLOGICAL
UNECONOMICAL
UNPREJUDICED
VIBRATIUNCLE
WELLBALANCED
APFELSTRUDEL
BAMBOCCIADES
BANANALANDER
BRICKFIELDER
CASSITERIDES
CASTERBRIDGE
CHURCHWARDEN
COLDSHOULDER
CONQUISTADOR
ENCYCLOPEDIA
ENCYCLOPEDIC
EVENHANDEDLY
HAMMERHEADED
HILDEBRANDIC
LYMANTRIIDAE
MACROPODIDAE
MOUTHBROODER
MUDDLEHEADED
OTHERWORLDLY
PAPILIONIDAE
RODOMONTADER
ROLLERBLADER
ROLLERBLADES
SCRIMSHANDER
SHAMEFACEDLY
SINGLEHANDED
SINGLEMINDED
SPATANGOIDEA
STOCKBREEDER
STRAIGHTEDGE
STRONGMINDED
TAPERECORDER
THREADNEEDLE
TURACOVERDIN
UNDESERVEDLY
UNEXPECTEDLY
UNRESERVEDLY
USERFRIENDLY
ACCOUCHEMENT
ACCOUTREMENT
ADMONISHMENT
AGGRESSIVELY
AGRIBUSINESS
AMARANTACEAE
AMBASSADRESS
ANNOUNCEMENT
ANTILEGOMENA
APLANOGAMETE
ARISTOTELEAN
ASTONISHMENT
ATTRACTIVELY
BACKWARDNESS
BEACONSFIELD
BENEFACTRESS
BEWILDERMENT
BLANDISHMENT
CAMIKNICKERS
CARELESSNESS
CAUTIOUSNESS
CHALICOTHERE
CHASTISEMENT
CHEERFULNESS
CHESTERFIELD
CHILDISHNESS
CHURLISHNESS
CLANNISHNESS
COLLECTIVELY
COMMENCEMENT
COMPLETENESS
CONCLUSIVELY
CONTABESCENT
CONTRARINESS
CONVALESCENT
COVETOUSNESS
CREATIVENESS
DECIPHERMENT
DECORATIVELY
DELIBERATELY
DILATORINESS
DISAGREEMENT
DISPLACEMENT
DISTINCTNESS
EFFERVESCENT
EMBEZZLEMENT
EMBROIDERESS
ENCIRCLEMENT
ENCROACHMENT
ENTANGLEMENT
ENTRENCHMENT
ENTREPRENEUR
EPACRIDACEAE
EPIPHENOMENA
EPISTOLATERS
ESTRANGEMENT
EXHAUSTIVELY
FAITHFULNESS
FEARLESSNESS
FIGURATIVELY
FORCEFULNESS
FRANKENSTEIN
FRIENDLINESS
FRONTISPIECE
FRUITFULNESS
FUNCTIONLESS
GRACEFULNESS
GRACIOUSNESS
GRATEFULNESS
GREENGROCERS
GREENGROCERY
GUILDENSTERN
HABERDASHERS
HABERDASHERY
HAIRDRESSERS
HEADMISTRESS
HEADQUARTERS
HELPLESSNESS
HEREDITAMENT
HINDQUARTERS
HOMESICKNESS
HOPELESSNESS
IMMACULATELY
IMMODERATELY
IMPOLITENESS
IMPRESSIVELY
IMPRISONMENT
INACCURATELY
INADEQUATELY
INCANDESCENT
INCOMPLETELY
INCONSEQUENT
INCONSISTENT
INCONVENIENT
INDEBTEDNESS
INDEFINITELY
INESCUTCHEON
INFRINGEMENT
INORDINATELY
INSTRUCTRESS
INSUFFICIENT
INTERMITTENT
INTRANSIGENT
IRRESOLUTELY
LEGITIMATELY
LIFELESSNESS
LILLIBULLERO
LILLIBURLERO
LISTLESSNESS
MAGNILOQUENT
MALTREATMENT
MICHELANGELO
MINDFULLNESS
MISAPPREHEND
MISPLACEMENT
MISREPRESENT
MISSTATEMENT
MISTREATMENT
NEPENTHACEAE
NEVERTHELESS
NORTHEASTERN
NORTHWESTERN
OBSOLETENESS
ONOMATOPOEIA
ONOMATOPOEIC
OPPRESSIVELY
OXYACETYLENE
PAINLESSNESS
PANATHENAEAN
PARALIPOMENA
PASSIONATELY
PEACEFULNESS
PERCEPTIVELY
PERSUASIVELY
PERVERSENESS
PETTIFOGGERS
PETTIFOGGERY
PHRONTISTERY
POLYETHYLENE
POPOCATEPETL
POSSESSIVELY
POSTMISTRESS
POSTPONEMENT
PREPAREDNESS
PREPONDERENT
PRESENTIMENT
PRIGGISHNESS
PROPRIETRESS

PROSOPOPOEIA
PROTECTIVELY
PSIPHENOMENA
READJUSTMENT
RECKLESSNESS
RECRUDESCENT
REDEPLOYMENT
RENOUNCEMENT
RESETTLEMENT
RESPECTIVELY
RESTAURATEUR
RESTLESSNESS
RETARDEDNESS
RETRENCHMENT
RHAMPHOTHECA
RHINORRHOEAL
RHIPIDOPTERA
RUTHLESSNESS
SCHIZOMYCETE
SELFINTEREST
SESQUIALTERA
SHEEPISHNESS
SIDEWHISKERS
SIPHONOSTELE
SITTLICHKEIT
SLOVENLINESS
SNOBBISHNESS
SOUTHEASTERN
SOUTHWESTERN
SPACIOUSNESS
SPECIOUSNESS
SPECKTIONEER
SPITEFULNESS
SPURIOUSNESS
STEALTHINESS
STRAIGHTNESS
STRANGLEWEED
STRATOSPHERE
STREPSIPTERA
STUBBORNNESS
STUDIOUSNESS
SUBCONTINENT
SUBJECTIVELY
SUBMISSIVELY
SUBTERRANEAN
SUCCESSIVELY
SUGGESTIVELY
TACTLESSNESS
TAMARICACEAE
TELEGRAPHESE
THANKFULNESS
THOROUGHNESS
THYSANOPTERA
TIMELESSNESS
TOGETHERNESS
TRANSCENDENT
TROCHOSPHERE
TRUTHFULNESS
UNCTUOUSNESS
UNDERACHIEVE
UNDERCURRENT
UNDERGARMENT
UNEMPLOYMENT
VENGEFULNESS
VENTRIPOTENT
VINDICTIVELY
WATCHFULNESS
WRETCHEDNESS
YOUTHFULNESS
CREMAILLIÈRE
DISREPECTFUL
MUTESSARIFAT
SHORTSTAFFED
UNDERSTAFFED
UNSCIENTIFIC
UNSUCCESSFUL
ACKNOWLEDGED
AFORETHOUGHT
AFTERTHOUGHT
ARCHIPELAGOS
BANTAMWEIGHT
BARBERMONGER
BEAUMONTAGUE
BUCKLEBEGGAR
CARPETBAGGER
CHEESEBURGER
CHEESEMONGER
CONVINCINGLY
COSTERMONGER
ENTREATINGLY
EULENSPIEGEL
HALLUCINOGEN
INCREASINGLY
INTERCHANGED
KLIPSPRINGER
LUXEMBOURGER
MERRYTHOUGHT
MIDDLEWEIGHT
QUARTERLIGHT
SLOCKDOLAGER
SLOCKDOLIGER
SLOCKDOLOGER
SLUBBERINGLY
STAGGERINGLY
SUPERCHARGED
SUPERCHARGER
SURPRISINGLY
THAUMATURGIC
THAUMATURGUS
TURBOCHARGER
UNCHALLENGED
UNDISCHARGED
WALLYDRAIGLE
WELTERWEIGHT
WILLIEWAUGHT
ACCOMPLISHED
ANTISTROPHON
ARISTOLOCHIA
BAIRNSFATHER
BRACHYCEPHAL
CALLIGRAPHIC
CARRIWITCHET
CARTOGRAPHER
CARTOGRAPHIC
CATASTROPHIC
CHAIRMANSHIP
CHAMPIONSHIP
CROSSBENCHER
DICTATORSHIP
DIRECTORSHIP
EXTINGUISHER
FEHMGERICHTE
FOTHERINGHAY
GAMESMANSHIP
GASTROSOPHER
GUARDIANSHIP
HIEROGLYPHIC
HOMOEOPATHIC
HORSEMANSHIP
HYDROGRAPHER
HYMNOGRAPHER
IAMBOGRAPHER
IMPOVERISHED
KLETTERSCHUE
LAUREATESHIP
LICKTRENCHER
LITHOGRAPHIC
MARKSMANSHIP
NIGHTCLOTHES
OCTASTROPHIC
ONCORHYNCHUS
OUTSTRETCHED
OVERSCUTCHED
PARTISANSHIP
PHOTOGLYPHIC
PHOTOGRAPHER
PHOTOGRAPHIC
PHYCOXANTHIN
PHYTOBENTHOS
PLAINCLOTHES
PORNOGRAPHIC
PSYCHOPATHIC
RADIOGRAPHER
RECEIVERSHIP
RELATIONSHIP
RHADAMANTHUS
SALESMANSHIP
SAUROGNATHAE
SEMIDETACHED
STENOGRAPHER
STROPHANTHUS
UNDERCLOTHES
UNDIMINISHED
VEHMGERICHTE
ABBREVIATION
ABOLITIONIST
ACCELERATION
ACCENTUATION
ACCOMPANYING
ACCORDIONIST
ACCUMULATION
ADAPTABILITY
ADJUDICATION
ADULTERATION
ADVISABILITY
AERODYNAMICS
AGALMATOLITE
ALIMENTATIVE
ALLITERATION
AMALGAMATION
AMELIORATION
ANAESTHETISE
ANAESTHETIST
ANAESTHETIZE
ANNIHILATION
ANNUNCIATION
ANTANANARIVO
ANTEDILUVIAN
ANTEMERIDIAN
ANTIBACCHIUS
ANTICIPATION
ANTINEUTRINO
APOLLINARIAN
APOSTROPHISE
APPRECIATION
APPRECIATIVE
APPREHENSION
APPREHENSIVE
ARCHILOCHIAN
ARFVEDSONITE
ARSENOPYRITE
ARTICULATION
ASPHYXIATION
ASSIMILATION
ASSUEFACTION
ASTROPHYSICS
ATMOSPHERICS
AUGMENTATION
AUSCULTATION
AUSTRALASIAN
AUSTRONESIAN
AUTHENTICITY
AVAILABILITY
AWARDWINNING
AWEINSPIRING
BABINGTONITE
BACCHANALIAN
BACKBREAKING
BARNSTORMING
BEHAVIOURISM
BETHLEHEMITE
BIBLIOPEGIST
BICAMERALISM
BICENTENNIAL
BIELORUSSIAN
BIODIVERSITY
BIRDWATCHING
BLEFUSCUDIAN
BLUESTOCKING
BOONDOGGLING

BOULEVARDIER
BRAINWASHING
BREATHTAKING
BRILLIANTINE
BROADCASTING
BUSINESSLIKE
BYELORUSSIAN
CALUMNIATION
CANCELLATION
CANONIZATION
CAPITULATION
CARDINDEXING
CARDIOLOGIST
CARICATURIST
CARLOVINGIAN
CARTHAGINIAN
CHARACTERIZE
CHEESEPARING
CHILDBEARING
CHLORINATION
CHORIZONTIST
CHRISTIANITY
CIRCUMCISION
CIRCUMSCRIBE
CIVILISATION
CIVILIZATION
CLARINETTIST
CLAUDICATION
CODIFICATION
COHABITATION
COLLUCTATION
COLONIZATION
COLOQUINTIDA
COMMENDATION
COMMISSARIAT
COMPELLATION
COMPENSATION
COMPLICATION
COMPROMISING
COMPURGATION
CONCILIATION
CONDEMNATION
CONDENSATION
CONDUCTIVITY
CONFIDENTIAL
CONFIRMATION
CONFISCATION
CONGREGATION
CONSCRIPTION
CONSECRATION
CONSERVATION
CONSERVATISM
CONSERVATIVE
CONSPECTUITY
CONSTIPATION
CONSTITUTION
CONSTRICTION
CONSTRUCTION
CONSTRUCTIVE
CONSULTATION
CONSULTATIVE
CONSUMMATION
CONTIGNATION
CONTINUATION
CONTRIBUTION
CONVALESCING
CONVERSATION
CONVEYANCING
CONVIVIALITY
COORDINATION
COUNTERPOINT
COUNTERPOISE
COURTMARTIAL
CRASHLANDING
CRISTOBALITE
CROSSEXAMINE
CROSSSECTION
DEASPIRATION
DEBILITATING
DECAPITATION
DECELERATION
DECENTRALISE
DECENTRALIZE
DEGENERATION
DEHUMIDIFIER
DELIBERATION
DEMILITARIZE
DEMIMONDAINE
DENDROLOGIST
DENOMINATION
DENUNCIATION
DEPOPULATION
DEPRECIATION
DEREGULATION
DESIRABILITY
DIALECTICIAN
DIFFERENTIAL
DILAPIDATION
DIPRIONIDIAN
DISACCHARIDE
DISAPPEARING
DISCOURAGING
DISFRANCHISE
DISINCENTIVE
DISPENSATION
DISQUISITION
DISSATISFIED
DISSERTATION
DISSOCIATION
DISTILLATION
DISTRIBUTION
DISTRIBUTIVE
DOLPHINARIUM
DRAMATURGIST
DRINKDRIVING
ECCENTRICITY
EDUCATIONIST
EGYPTOLOGIST
EMANCIPATION
EMASCULATION
EMBARRASSING
ENCHEIRIDION
ENERGYSAVING
ENTERPRISING
ENTERTAINING
ENTOMOLOGIST
EPISCOPALIAN
EPITHALAMION
EPITHALAMIUM
EQUIVOCATION
ESCAPOLOGIST
ESSENTIALITY
ETHEROMANIAC
EXACERBATION
EXAGGERATION
EXASPERATING
EXASPERATION
EXCITABILITY
EXCRUCIATING
EXCRUCIATION
EXHILARATING
EXHILARATION
EXPLOITATION
EXTENSIONIST
FERMENTATION
FINALIZATION
FIRSTFOOTING
FLAGELLATION
FLUORIDATION
FOOTSLOGGING
FRANKALMOIGN
FRUMENTATION
FUSTILLIRIAN
GALLIGASKINS
GALLIVANTING
GEOMETRICIAN
GEOPHYSICIST
GERIATRICIAN
GIBRALTARIAN
GLADIATORIAL
GLOCKENSPIEL
GRANDISONIAN
GRANDMONTINE
GRAPHOLOGIST
GROSSULARITE
GYMNOSOPHIST
GYNECOLOGIST
HAEMOPHILIAC
HAEMORRHOIDS
HAIRDRESSING
HAMBLETONIAN
HANDKERCHIEF
HARUMFRODITE
HEARTWARMING
HELLGRAMMITE
HERMENEUTICS
HERMENEUTIST
HIGHFALUTING
HIPPOCRATISE
HIPPOCREPIAN
HOUSEKEEPING
HOUSEWARMING
HUDIBRASTICS
HUMANITARIAN
HUMANIZATION
HYPERTENSION
ICHTHYOPSIDA
IDEALIZATION
ILLEGIBILITY
ILLOGICALITY
ILLUMINATING
ILLUMINATION
ILLUSTRATION
ILLUSTRATIVE
IMMODERATION
IMMUNIZATION
IMMUNOLOGIST
IMMUTABILITY
IMPARTIALITY
IMPERFECTION
IMPLANTATION
IMPREGNATION
INAUGURATION
INCAPABILITY
INCINERATION
INCONCLUSIVE
INCRUSTATION
INCUNABULIST
INDISCRETION
INFILTRATION
INFLAMMATION
INGRATIATING
INNATTENTIVE
INSEMINATION
INSOLUBILITY
INSTALLATION
INSTAURATION
INSURRECTION
INTENERATION
INTERCEPTION
INTERCESSION
INTERJECTION
INTERMISSION
INTERPRETING
INTERRUPTION
INTERSECTION
INTERVENTION
INTIMIDATING
INTIMIDATION
INTOXICATING
INTOXICATION
INTRANSITIVE
INTRAUTERINE
INTRODUCTION
INVALIDATION
INVIGORATING
INVIGORATION
INVISIBILITY
IRASCIBILITY
IRREGULARITY

IRRESOLUTION
IRRESPECTIVE
IRRITABILITY
ISHMAELITISH
ISOLATIONISM
ISOLATIONIST
JURISDICTION
KILLIKINNICK
KLEPTOMANIAC
LABANOTATION
LABOURSAVING
LABYRINTHINE
LANCASTERIAN
LANGUEDOCIAN
LEGALIZATION
LINCOLNSHIRE
LIQUEFACTION
LIVERPUDLIAN
LONGSTANDING
LUXULLIANITE
MACMILLANITE
MALFORMATION
MALLEABILITY
MALNUTRITION
MANIPULATION
MANIPULATIVE
MARLINESPIKE
MARSEILLAISE
MASTURBATION
MECHITHARIST
MENSTRUATION
METALLURGIST
METAMORPHISM
MINDBOGGLING
MINERALOGIST
MINISTRATION
MISQUOTATION
MOBILIZATION
MODIFICATION
MOISTURIZING
MONTESSORIAN
MOONLIGHTING
MOTORCYCLIST
MOUSQUETAIRE
MUGGLETONIAN
MULTIPLICITY
MUNICIPALITY
MUSICOLOGIST
NAVIGABILITY
NEIGHBOURING
NEOPLATONISM
NONAGENARIAN
NOTIFICATION
NUTRITIONIST
NYMPHOMANIAC
OBLITERATION
OBSERVANTINE
OBSTETRICIAN
OCTOGENARIAN
OPINIONATIVE
ORGANISATION
ORGANIZATION
ORIENTEERING
ORTHODONTICS
ORTHOPAEDICS
ORTHOPAEDIST
OSSIFICATION
OVERCROWDING
OVERDRESSING
OVEREXERTION
OVERPOWERING
OVERWHELMING
PACIFICATION
PANDAEMONIUM
PARANTHELIUM
PEACEKEEPING
PEDIATRICIAN
PENALIZATION
PERCEPTIVITY
PEREMPTORILY
PERMEABILITY
PERNOCTATION
PERPETRATION
PERSPICACITY
PERSPIRATION
PERTURBATION
PESTILENTIAL
PETRIFACTION
PETTIFOGGING
PHILISTINISM
PHILOSOPHIZE
PHLEBOTOMIST
PHYSIOLOGIST
PIGMENTATION
PLAUSIBILITY
PLEIOCHASIUM
POLARIZATION
POLICYMAKING
POSTPRANDIAL
POTAMOLOGIST
POTENTIALITY
POWERSHARING
PRACTICALITY
PRASEODYMIUM
PRECONDITION
PREDETERMINE
PREDILECTION
PREFERENTIAL
PREGUSTATION
PREHISTORIAN
PREREQUISITE
PRESBYTERIAN
PRESCRIPTION
PRESCRIPTIVE
PRESENTATION
PRESERVATION
PRESERVATIVE
PRESIDENTIAL
PRESTRICTION
PREVENTATIVE
PRINCIPALITY
PRIZEWINNING
PROCLAMATION
PRODUCTIVITY
PROFESSORIAL
PROFITEERING
PROGYMNASIUM
PROLONGATION
PROMULGATION
PROPAGANDISM
PROPAGANDIST
PROPITIATION
PROSCRIPTION
PROSTITUTION
PROTACTINIUM
PROTESTATION
PROTHALAMION
PROTHALAMIUM
PROVIDENTIAL
PSEPHOLOGIST
PSYCHIATRIST
PSYCHOLOGIST
PURIFICATION
PURPOSEBUILT
PUTREFACTION
PYROTECHNICS
QUADRAGESIMA
QUANTITATIVE
QUINQUENNIAL
RACKETEERING
RAMIFICATION
RATIFICATION
RECEPTIONIST
RECOLLECTION
RECUPERATION
RECUPERATIVE
REGENERATION
REGISTRATION
REJUVENATION
REMUNERATION
REMUNERATIVE
RENUNCIATION
REPATRIATION
REPERCUSSION
REPOSSESSION
REPROCESSING
REPRODUCTION
REPRODUCTIVE
RESURRECTION
RETICULATION
SALVATIONIST
SATISFACTION
SCANDINAVIAN
SCHNEIDERIAN
SCOPOPHILIAC
SECESSIONIST
SECTARIANISM
SEGMENTATION
SELFADHESIVE
SELFCATERING
SEPTUAGESIMA
SEXAGENARIAN
SHAREHOLDING
SHIPBUILDING
SHOSTAKOVICH
SKUTTERUDITE
SLEEPWALKING
SMALLHOLDING
SNOWBOARDING
SOLICITATION
SOMNAMBULISM
SOMNAMBULIST
SOUTHCOTTIAN
SPELEOLOGIST
SPHACELATION
SPHAIRISTIKE
SPIRITUALISM
SPIRITUALIST
SPIRITUALITY
STAKHANOVITE
STATISTICIAN
STEGOPHOLIST
STEREOTYPING
STERNUTATION
STRADIVARIUS
STREPITATION
STRIDULATION
STROMATOLITE
STUPEFACTION
SUBARRHATION
SUBHASTATION
SUBJECTIVITY
SUBLAPSARIAN
SUBSCRIPTION
SUBSIDIARITY
SUBSTITUTION
SUCCUSSATION
SULPHONAMIDE
SUPERSTITION
SUPPLICATION
SWIZZLESTICK
SYNADELPHITE
SYNTAGMATITE
TAGLIACOTIAN
TECHNICALITY
TECHNOLOGIST
TELEGRAPHIST
TELEOSAURIAN
TETRACYCLINE
TETRAHEDRITE
THANKSGIVING
THEOPHYLLINE
THEORETICIAN
THERAPEUTICS
THESSALONIAN
TIGHTFITTING
TORRICELLIAN
TOTALITARIAN
TOXICOLOGIST
TRACTABILITY

TRANQUILLISE
TRANQUILLITY
TRANQUILLIZE
TRANSMISSION
TRANSMOGRIFY
TRANSPONTINE
TRANSVESTISM
TRANSVESTITE
TRICHOLOGIST
UINTATHERIUM
UMBRADARLING
UNAPPETIZING
UNATTRACTIVE
UNCLASSIFIED
UNCONVINCING
UNDERPINNING
UNIDENTIFIED
UNIVERSALIST
UNOPPRESSIVE
UNPOPULARITY
UNPRETENDING
UNPRODUCTIVE
UNRESPONSIVE
UNSATISFYING
UNSURPRISING
UNSUSPECTING
URBANIZATION
VAPORIZATION
VERIFICATION
VETERINARIAN
VILIFICATION
VITUPERATION
VITUPERATIVE
VOCIFERATION
WATERCARRIER
WHIMSICALITY
WHIPPOORWILL
WOLLASTONITE
MOSBOLLETJIE
CABINETMAKER
DOUBLEDECKER
HALLANSHAKER
HARNESSMAKER
HOLIDAYMAKER
HOUSEBREAKER
PINNIEWINKLE
PUMPERNICKEL
SCRIMSHANKER
SINGLEDECKER
SPELLCHECKER
STRAITJACKET
TROUBLEMAKER
UNDERSKINKER
ACADEMICALLY
ACCIDENTALLY
ADDITIONALLY
ADJECTIVALLY
ARTIFICIALLY
ARTISTICALLY
BARRANQUILLA

BOUGAINVILLE
CAPERCAILLIE
CEREMONIALLY
COLLOQUIALLY
COLLYWOBBLES
COMMERCIALLY
COMMONWEALTH
CONGENITALLY
DIENCEPHALON
DISDAINFULLY
DIVERTICULUM
DOGMATICALLY
DRAMATICALLY
ECONOMICALLY
ECSTATICALLY
ELECTRICALLY
EMPHATICALLY
EPENCEPHALON
ESTHETICALLY
FRACTIONALLY
FUNCTIONALLY
GEOLOGICALLY
GOOSEPIMPLES
HELIOGABALUS
HERMETICALLY
HISTORICALLY
HORIZONTALLY
HORRIFICALLY
HYGIENICALLY
HYPNOTICALLY
HYSTERICALLY
ICHTHYOCOLLA
IMPERSONALLY
INCIDENTALLY
INDIVIDUALLY
INDUSTRIALLY
INNOMINABLES
INTERSTELLAR
IRRATIONALLY
MADEMOISELLE
MAGNETICALLY
MAJESTICALLY
MEANINGFULLY
MECHANICALLY
METHODICALLY
NEUROTICALLY
NONALCOHOLIC
OCCASIONALLY
ORNITHOGALUM
PATHETICALLY
PEDANTICALLY
PERIODICALLY
PHENOMENALLY
PHONETICALLY
PRALLTRILLER
PROLIFICALLY
PROVERBIALLY
PURPOSEFULLY
QUIXOTICALLY
RECIPROCALLY

RESPECTFULLY
RHYTHMICALLY
ROMANTICALLY
RONCESVALLES
SADISTICALLY
SARDANAPALUS
SARDONICALLY
SARSAPARILLA
SEMANTICALLY
SEMICIRCULAR
SEQUENTIALLY
SHILLYSHALLY
SPECIFICALLY
SPINECHILLER
SPORADICALLY
SPREADEAGLED
STERNWHEELER
STRUCTURALLY
SUCCESSFULLY
SUPERNACULUM
SWASHBUCKLER
SYMBOLICALLY
TERRIFICALLY
THEATRICALLY
THOUGHTFULLY
ULOTRICHALES
UNAPPARELLED
UNCONTROLLED
UNILATERALLY
UNOFFICIALLY
UNPARALLELED
UNPRINCIPLED
UNUTTERABLES
WOLSTENHOLME
AGATHODAIMON
AIRCRAFTSMAN
ALEXIPHARMIC
AMBULANCEMAN
ARTILLERYMAN
BACKWOODSMAN
BREASTSUMMER
CLEISTOGAMIC
ENGLISHWOMAN
ENGLISHWOMEN
EXSERVICEMAN
FRONTIERSMAN
HEPHTHEMIMER
HIEROGRAMMAT
HIPPOPOTAMUS
KATZENJAMMER
LONGSHOREMAN
NEWSPAPERMAN
PROTOPLASMAL
PROTOPLASMIC
SCLERODERMIA
SERVICEWOMAN
STRIGIFORMES
UNACCUSTOMED
WAREHOUSEMAN
WELLINFORMED

WILTSHIREMAN
YELLOWHAMMER
YORKSHIREMAN
ACQUAINTANCE
ACQUIESCENCE
AMPHISBAENIC
ANTIMNEMONIC
ANTONINIANUS
APPURTENANCE
ARBORESCENCE
ARISTOPHANES
AYUNTAMIENTO
BELLIGERENCY
BLOODSTAINED
CALLISTHENES
CARCINOGENIC
CEREBROTONIC
CHITTERLINGS
CIRCASSIENNE
CIRCUMSTANCE
CLAIRVOYANCE
CLAIRVOYANCY
COMMANDMENTS
COMMISSIONED
COMMISSIONER
CONFECTIONER
CONFESSIONAL
CONSTITUENCY
CONSTITUENTS
CONVENTIONAL
COSCINOMANCY
CURMUDGEONLY
DARLINGTONIA
DISOBEDIENCE
DIVERTIMENTO
ELASMOBRANCH
ELECTROTONUS
ERATOSTHENES
EXHIBITIONER
EXTRAVAGANCE
EXTRAVAGANZA
FLUORESCENCE
FRANKINCENSE
FRAUENDIENST
FREIGHTLINER
GRANDPARENTS
HAPPENSTANCE
HEARTSTRINGS
HOBBIDIDANCE
IMPERTINENCE
IMPROVIDENCE
INADVERTENCE
INCOMPETENCE
INCONTINENCE
INDEPENDENCE
INDIFFERENCE
INEFFICIENCY
INEXPERIENCE
INTELLIGENCE
INTEMPERANCE

INTERFERENCE
JENNYSPINNER
LONGDISTANCE
LONGITUDINAL
LUMINESCENCE
LUMINISCENCE
MAGNIFICENCE
MARCOBRUNNER
MISPRONOUNCE
MNEMOTECHNIC
NOCONFIDENCE
NONEXISTENCE
NONRESIDENCE
OBSOLESCENCE
OCCUPATIONAL
OLDFASHIONED
OUTBUILDINGS
OVERSTRAINED
PENNSYLVANIA
PERISTERONIC
PERSEVERANCE
PHILHARMONIC
PHOSPHORENCE
POTICHOMANIA
PRACTICIONER
PRACTITIONER
PREDOMINANCE
PROCESSIONAL
PROFESSIONAL
PROLEGOMENON
PROPORTIONAL
PROTUBERANCE
QUADRAPHONIC
QUARTERFINAL
QUINTESSENCE
REAPPEARANCE
RECOGNIZANCE
RECREATIONAL
REDEMPTIONER
REMINISCENCE
REMONSTRANCE
RESIPISCENCE
RISORGIMENTO
SCAPULIMANCY
SHORTCOMINGS
SIGNIFICANCE
STEREOPHONIC
SUBSERVIENCE
SURROUNDINGS
SURVEILLANCE
THEREAGAINST
THICKSKINNED
TRANSFERENCE
TRANSITIONAL
TRANSLUCENCE
TRANSOCEANIC
TRANSPARENCY
TROCHELMINTH
UNDETERMINED
UNIMPORTANCE
UNRESTRAINED
VALENCIENNES
VERUMONTANUM
WASHINGTONIA
WELLINGTONIA
ACHLAMYDEOUS
ADSCITITIOUS
ADVANTAGEOUS
ADVANTAGIOUS
ADVENTITIOUS
AECIDIOSPORE
AETHRIOSCOPE
AMBIDEXTROUS
AMPHISTOMOUS
ANDROSTERONE
ANEMOPHILOUS
ANTHROPOLOGY
ANTICIPATORY
ANTIMETABOLE
APPENDECTOMY
ATHEROMATOUS
BACTERIOLOGY
BLENNORRHOEA
BRANCHIOPODA
CAMPODEIFORM
CANTANKEROUS
CHONDRIOSOME
COMBINATIONS
COMMENDATORY
COMPENSATORY
CONCILIATORY
CONFIRMATORY
CONSERVATORY
CONTEMPTUOUS
CONTERMINOUS
CONTRIBUTORY
CONTUMACIOUS
CYMOTRICHOUS
DEAMBULATORY
DEPRECIATORY
DESSERTSPOON
DEUTEROSCOPY
DISCOURTEOUS
DISINGENUOUS
DRESSINGDOWN
DYSTELEOLOGY
EPISTEMOLOGY
EQUIVOCATORY
FELDSPATHOID
FULMINATIONS
GALLINACEOUS
GOBBLEDEGOOK
GOBBLEDYGOOK
HOMOTHERMOUS
HYDROQUINONE
HYPERSARCOMA
HYSTERECTOMY
IDIOTHERMOUS
INAUSPICIOUS
INFELICITOUS
INFLAMMATORY
INHARMONIOUS
INSALUBRIOUS
INSTRUCTIONS
INTRODUCTORY
KALEIDOSCOPE
LALLAPALOOZA
LAMENTATIONS
LAMPADEDROMY
LEIOTRICHOUS
LITHOLATROUS
MACHAIRODONT
MALLOPHAGOUS
MASTERSTROKE
MASTIGOPHORA
MERETRICIOUS
MERITRICIOUS
MESOTHELIOMA
METAGNATHOUS
METALLOPHONE
METAMORPHOSE
MISBEHAVIOUR
MISDEMEANOUR
MUCILAGINOUS
MULTIFARIOUS
MYRINGOSCOPE
NEIGHBORHOOD
NORTHERNMOST
OBSTREPEROUS
OREOPITHEOUS
OSCILLOSCOPE
OSTENTATIOUS
PALEONTOLOGY
PALPITATIONS
PANDANACEOUS
PANTOPHAGOUS
PARSIMONIOUS
PASSEPARTOUT
PERGAMENEOUS
PERTINACIOUS
PERVICACIOUS
PHARMACOLOGY
PHILANTHROPY
PHYTONADIONE
PLACENTIFORM
PLASTERSTONE
PRAXINOSCOPE
PREPOSTEROUS
PRESUMPTUOUS
PROGESTERONE
PROPITIATORY
PSEUDONYMOUS
RADIOISOTOPE
RAMBUNCTIOUS
RHYTIDECTOMY
SACRILEGIOUS
SALTATORIOUS
SARRUSOPHONE
SATISFACTORY
SEMIPRECIOUS
SIMULTANEOUS
SIPHONOPHORA
SOUTHERNMOST
SOUTHERNWOOD
SPECTROSCOPE
SPINSTERHOOD
STENTORPHONE
STRANGLEHOLD
SUBCONSCIOUS
SUBCUTANEOUS
SUPERCILIOUS
TELEUTOSPORE
TESTOSTERONE
THUNDERCLOUD
THUNDERSTORM
TRALATICIOUS
TRALATITIOUS
TRANSACTIONS
UNSCRUPULOUS
VAINGLORIOUS
WEATHERPROOF
ZALAMBDODONT
BIBLIOGRAPHY
BOOBYTRAPPED
CHOREOGRAPHY
CRYPTOGRAPHY
EAVESDROPPER
ENTEROMORPHA
GENTLETAMPER
GONADOTROPIN
LEXICOGRAPHY
MISANTHROPIC
OCEANOGRAPHY
SCHILLERSPAR
SINANTHROPUS
STEREOSCOPIC
STORMTROOPER
THIGMOTROPIC
TRADESPEOPLE
WICKETKEEPER
BEAUMONTIQUE
MACABERESQUE
PECTORILOQUY
AGRICULTURAL
ALPHANUMERIC
ANTIBARBARUS
BRONTOSAURUS
BUNKOSTEERER
CAMPANULARIA
CANTILEVERED
CARAVANSERAI
CATADIOPTRIC
CLAMJAMPHRIE
COUNTERMARCH
DORSIVENTRAL
ENANTIOMORPH
ENTOPLASTRON
EVENTEMPERED
GLUBBDUBDRIB
GLYNDEBOURNE

HETEROPHORIA
HISTIOPHORUS
HYDROCHLORIC
HYPOCHONDRIA
ISOBILATERAL
LAMELLICORNE
LEGIONNAIRES
MANUFACTURER
MISDELIVERED
MISINTERPRET
MULTICOLORED
MULTILATERAL
NYCHTHEMERON
PARTICOLORED
PARTICULARLY
PEDICELLARIA
PERSULPHURIC
PHILODENDRON
PYTHONOMORPH
REDISCOVERED
RHODODENDRON
SILVERHAIRED
STILBOESTROL
STRINGCOURSE
SUPERNATURAL
TAPSALTEERIE
TAPSLETEERIE
THESMOPHORIA
THOROUGHBRED
TITANOSAURUS
UNCONSIDERED
UNNEIGHBORLY
URTRICULARIA
VARICOLOURED
WHIGMALEERIE
XANTHOPTERIN
ZARATHUSTRIC
ANAMORPHOSIS
ANECATHARSIS
ANTIMACASSAR
ARTHROPLASTY
AUSPICIOUSLY
BESSERWISSER
BLOODTHIRSTY
BOISTEROUSLY
BREATHALYSER
BREATHLESSLY
CONTINUOUSLY
CONTRAPPOSTO
COURAGEOUSLY
DELICATESSEN
DIPLOGENESIS
DISASTROUSLY
DISCOMEDUSAE
DISPOSSESSED
DUNNIEWASSAL
EFFORTLESSLY
ELECTROLYSIS
ENHYPOSTASIA
EPANORTHOSIS

FASTIDIOUSLY
FORTUITOUSLY
HAEMATEMESIS
HARMONIOUSLY
HETEROPLASIA
INCAUTIOUSLY
INTERSPERSED
KIRSCHWASSER
LASCIVIOUSLY
LUGUBRIOUSLY
METICULOUSLY
MIRACULOUSLY
MONOTONOUSLY
MYSTERIOUSLY
OBSEQUIOUSLY
OPHIOGLOSSUM
ORTHOGENESIS
ORTHOTONESIS
OSTEOPOROSIS
OUTRAGEOUSLY
PALINGENESIA
PALINGENESIS
PANAESTHESIA
PARACENTESIS
PHOSPHORESCE
POINTILLISME
POSTHUMOUSLY
PRECARIOUSLY
PRECOCIOUSLY
PREPOSSESSED
PRODIGIOUSLY
PROPITIOUSLY
PUGNACIOUSLY
RELENTLESSLY
RIDICULOUSLY
SCANDALOUSLY
SCHINDYLESIS
SCRUPULOUSLY
SCURRILOUSLY
SEPTEMBRISER
SOLICITOUSLY
SPIEGELEISEN
SPOKESPERSON
STANISLAVSKI
STELLENBOSCH
SUSPICIOUSLY
TOBACCONISTS
TRANSGRESSOR
TREMENDOUSLY
TUBERCULOSIS
UNAUTHORISED
UNDEREXPOSED
UNRECOGNISED
UPROARIOUSLY
VOCIFEROUSLY
VOLUPTUOUSLY
AGAMOGENETIC
AMPHITHEATER
AMPHITHEATRE
ANDOUILLETTE

ANTAGONISTIC
ANTHELMINTIC
ANTIRACHITIC
APPENDICITIS
ARISTOCRATIC
BACTERIOSTAT
BANDERSNATCH
BENEVOLENTLY
BERTHOLLETIA
BIOCHEMISTRY
BUREAUCRATIC
BUTTERSCOTCH
CALCEAMENTUM
CATHETOMETER
CHAUVINISTIC
CHIROPRACTIC
CHIROPRACTOR
CHREMATISTIC
CHRESTOMATHY
CLEARSIGHTED
COCCIDIOSTAT
COINCIDENTAL
COLLABORATOR
COMPLACENTLY
CONCENTRATED
CONCURRENTLY
CONSEQUENTLY
CONSISTENTLY
CONSOLIDATED
CONSOLIDATOR
CONTAMINATED
CONTRAPUNTAL
CONVENIENTLY
COSMOPOLITAN
CRASSAMENTUM
CROSSCOUNTRY
DEMONSTRATOR
DEPARTMENTAL
DERESTRICTED
DIAGRAMMATIC
DISAPPOINTED
DISCOMYCETES
DISCONCERTED
DISCONNECTED
DISCONTENTED
DISENCHANTED
DOMESTICATED
DONNERWETTER
ECCLESIASTES
ECCLESIASTIC
ENANTIOPATHY
ENTHUSIASTIC
EPIGRAMMATIC
ESPAGNOLETTE
ETEPIMELETIC
EXPERIMENTAL
FAINTHEARTED
FLAMBOYANTLY
GALVANOMETER
GASTARBEITER

GLOBETROTTER
GOVERNMENTAL
HAIRSPLITTER
HAMARTHRITIS
HETEROCLITIC
HETEROCONTAE
HIEROPHANTIC
HYPERPYRETIC
HYPOTHECATOR
ICONOCLASTIC
IMPERSONATOR
INCOHERENTLY
INCORPORATED
INDISTINCTLY
INFREQUENTLY
INSTRUMENTAL
INTERLOCUTOR
INTERRELATED
INTERROGATOR
INVESTIGATOR
IRREVERENTLY
JOURNALISTIC
KINAESTHETIC
KINDERGARTEN
LIGHTHEARTED
MANSLAUGHTER
MELODRAMATIC
MERISTEMATIC
METROPOLITAN
MILITARISTIC
MINICOMPUTER
NARCISSISTIC
NATURALISTIC
NEPHELOMETER
NONCHALANTLY
NONCOMMITTAL
ONEIROCRITIC
PALUDAMENTUM
PANCHATANTRA
PANCHROMATIC
PERAMBULATOR
PERICARDITIS
PERIPHRASTIC
PERSISTENTLY
PITTERPATTER
PLECTOGNATHI
POLYSYNDETON
PRAISEWORTHY
PREVARICATOR
PRIZEFIGHTER
PROFICIENTLY
PROPHYLACTIC
REFRIGERATED
REFRIGERATOR
RESPONDENTIA
RESUSCITATED
SCHOOLMASTER
SCINTILLATOR
SCREENWRITER
SCRIPTWRITER

SEQUESTRATOR
SESQUITERTIA
SHARPSHOOTER
SHIRTWAISTER
SHORTSIGHTED
STEPDAUGHTER
STOCKINGETTE
STONECHATTER
SUBCOMMITTEE
SUBSEQUENTLY
SUFFICIENTLY
SURREALISTIC
TEETERTOTTER
TELEASTHETIC
THERMOSTATIC
THREEQUARTER
TRABECULATED
TRADESCANTIA
TRICHOPHYTON
TRIGONOMETRY
TRIUMPHANTLY
UNACQUAINTED
UNCULTIVATED
UNDEMOCRATIC
UNDERWRITTEN
UNEXPURGATED
UNFREQUENTED
UNINTERESTED
UNOBSTRUCTED
UNRESTRICTED
WEIGHTLIFTER
WHOLEHEARTED
WINTERHALTER
APPOGGIATURA
ARCHITECTURE
AWAYABSOLUTE
BATTLEGROUND
BLABBERMOUTH
BREAKTHROUGH
BREASTPLOUGH
CHARTERHOUSE
DISCOMFITURE
ENTEROPNEUST
FLITTERMOUSE
FLORICULTURE
GAINSBOROUGH
HETEROSEXUAL
HORTICULTURE
HOUSETOHOUSE
INEXACTITUDE
INTELLECTUAL
KATHAREVOUSA
MASSERANDUBA
MERVEILLEUSE
MISADVENTURE
MITRAILLEUSE
NOMENCLATURE
PASSEMEASURE
PASSIONFRUIT
PERADVENTURE
PHOTOGRAVURE
PISCICULTURE
RECONSTITUTE
REDISTRIBUTE
ROOMINGHOUSE
SCATTERMOUCH
SCHOPENHAUER
SHORTCIRCUIT
SOMATOPLEURE
SPORTSGROUND
STREPTONEURA
SUBSTRUCTURE
THIRDBOROUGH
VENEPUNCTURE
VILLEGIATURA
GRISEOFULVIN
OUTMANOEUVRE
SHIRTSLEEVES
SHORTSLEEVED
COMPANIONWAY
GRASSWIDOWER
MULLIGATAWNY
STRAIGHTAWAY
SUPERHIGHWAY
TETRODOTOXIN
TROPHALLAXIS
ARTIODACTYLA
DAGUERROTYPE
FORMALDEHYDE
PTERIDOPHYTE
PTERODACTYLE
RECORDPLAYER
SCLERENCHYMA
SELFEMPLOYED
SPERMATOCYTE
WOODBURYTYPE
CAPERCAILZIE
DISORGANIZED
DOUBLEGLAZED
MANGELWURZEL
PERSONALIZED
TRANQUILIZER
UNAUTHORIZED
UNRECOGNIZED

12:11

AERONAUTICAL
AGRICULTURAL
AIRCRAFTSMAN
ALPHABETICAL
AMARANTACEAE
AMBULANCEMAN
ANTEDILUVIAN
ANTEMERIDIAN
ANTIMACASSAR
APOLLINARIAN
ARCHILOCHIAN
ARISTOTELEAN
ARITHMETICAL
ARTILLERYMAN
ASTROLOGICAL
ASTRONOMICAL
ASYMMETRICAL
AUSTRALASIAN
AUSTRONESIAN
BACCHANALIAN
BACKWOODSMAN
BACTERIOSTAT
BICENTENNIAL
BIELORUSSIAN
BIOGRAPHICAL
BLEFUSCUDIAN
BRACHYCEPHAL
BUCKLEBEGGAR
BYELORUSSIAN
CARAVANSERAI
CARLOVINGIAN
CARTHAGINIAN
CATAPHYSICAL
COCCIDIOSTAT
COINCIDENTAL
COMMISSARIAT
COMPANIONWAY
CONFESSIONAL
CONFIDENTIAL
CONTRAPUNTAL
CONVENTIONAL
COSMOPOLITAN
COURTMARTIAL
DEPARTMENTAL
DIALECTICIAN
DIFFERENTIAL
DIPRIONIDIAN
DISCOMEDUSAE
DORSIVENTRAL
DUNNIEWASSAL
ENGLISHWOMAN
EPACRIDACEAE
EPIDEICTICAL
EPISCOPALIAN
ETHEROMANIAC
ETHNOLOGICAL
ETYMOLOGICAL
EXPERIMENTAL
EXSERVICEMAN
FOTHERINGHAY
FRONTIERSMAN
FUSTILLIRIAN
GENEALOGICAL
GEOGRAPHICAL
GEOMETRICIAN
GERIATRICIAN
GIBRALTARIAN
GLADIATORIAL
GOVERNMENTAL
GRANDISONIAN
HAEMOPHILIAC
HAMBLETONIAN
HEROICOMICAL
HETEROCONTAE
HETEROSEXUAL
HIERARCHICAL
HIEROGRAMMAT
HIPPOCREPIAN
HUMANITARIAN
HYPERBOLICAL
HYPOCRITICAL
HYPOTHETICAL
INSTRUMENTAL
INTELLECTUAL
INTERSTELLAR
ISOBILATERAL
KLEPTOMANIAC
LANCASTERIAN
LANGUEDOCIAN
LIVERPUDLIAN
LONGITUDINAL
LONGSHOREMAN
LOXODROMICAL
LYMANTRIIDAE
MACROPODIDAE
MATHEMATICAL
METAPHORICAL
METAPHYSICAL
METROPOLITAN
MONTESSORIAN
MUGGLETONIAN
MULTILATERAL
MUTESSARIFAT
MYTHOLOGICAL
NEOCLASSICAL
NEPENTHACEAE
NEUROLOGICAL
NEWSPAPERMAN
NONAGENARIAN
NONCOMMITTAL
NYMPHOMANIAC
OBSTETRICIAN
OCCUPATIONAL
OCTOGENARIAN
PANATHENAEAN
PAPILIONIDAE
PATHOLOGICAL
PEDIATRICIAN
PESTILENTIAL
PHILOLOGICAL
POSTPRANDIAL
PREFERENTIAL
PREHISTORIAN
PRESBYTERIAN
PRESIDENTIAL
PROCESSIONAL
PROFESSIONAL
PROFESSORIAL
PROPORTIONAL
PROTOPLASMAL
PROVIDENTIAL
QUARTERFINAL
QUINQUENNIAL

RECREATIONAL
RHINORRHOEAL
SAUROGNATHAE
SCANDINAVIAN
SCHILLERSPAR
SCHNEIDERIAN
SCOPOPHILIAC
SEMICIRCULAR
SERVICEWOMAN
SEXAGENARIAN
SOCIOLOGICAL
SOUTHCOTTIAN
STATISTICIAN
STRAIGHTAWAY
SUBLAPSARIAN
SUBTERRANEAN
SUPERHIGHWAY
SUPERNATURAL
TAGLIACOTIAN
TAMARICACEAE
TAUTOLOGICAL
TELEOSAURIAN
THEORETICIAN
THESSALONIAN
TORRICELLIAN
TOTALITARIAN
TRANSITIONAL
UNECONOMICAL
VETERINARIAN
WAREHOUSEMAN
WILTSHIREMAN
YORKSHIREMAN
CIRCUMSCRIBE
MASSERANDUBA
ACQUAINTANCE
ACQUIESCENCE
AERODYNAMICS
APPURTENANCE
ARBORESCENCE
ASTROPHYSICS
ATMOSPHERICS
BANDERSNATCH
BELLIGERENCY
BUTTERSCOTCH
CIRCUMSTANCE
CLAIRVOYANCE
CLAIRVOYANCY
CONSTITUENCY
COSCINOMANCY
COUNTERMARCH
DISOBEDIENCE
ELASMOBRANCH
ENTOMOSTRACA
EXTRAVAGANCE
FLUORESCENCE
FRONTISPIECE
GERONTOCRACY
HAPPENSTANCE
HERMENEUTICS
HOBBIDIDANCE
HUDIBRASTICS
ILLEGITIMACY
IMPERTINENCE
IMPROVIDENCE
INADVERTENCE
INCOMPETENCE
INCONTINENCE
INDEPENDENCE
INDIFFERENCE
INEFFICIENCY
INEXPERIENCE
INTELLIGENCE
INTEMPERANCE
INTERFERENCE
KALISTOCRACY
KILLIKINNICK
LONGDISTANCE
LUMINESCENCE
LUMINISCENCE
MAGNIFICENCE
MALACOSTRACA
MISPRONOUNCE
NOCONFIDENCE
NONEXISTENCE
NONRESIDENCE
OBSOLESCENCE
ORTHODONTICS
ORTHOPAEDICS
PANTISOCRACY
PERSEVERANCE
PHOSPHORENCE
PHOSPHORESCE
PREDOMINANCE
PROTUBERANCE
PYROTECHNICS
QUINTESSENCE
REAPPEARANCE
RECOGNIZANCE
REMINISCENCE
REMONSTRANCE
RESIPISCENCE
RHAMPHOTHECA
SCAPULIMANCY
SCATTERMOUCH
SHOSTAKOVICH
SIGNIFICANCE
STELLENBOSCH
SUBSERVIENCE
SURVEILLANCE
SWIZZLESTICK
THERAPEUTICS
TRANSFERENCE
TRANSLUCENCE
TRANSPARENCY
UNIMPORTANCE
BRANCHIOPODA
COLOQUINTIDA
DISACCHARIDE
FORMALDEHYDE
HAEMORRHOIDS
ICHTHYOPSIDA
INEXACTITUDE
SCHEHERAZADE
SPURTLEBLADE
SULPHONAMIDE
ACCOMPLISHED
ACKNOWLEDGED
AMPHITHEATER
APFELSTRUDEL
ARISTOPHANES
BAIRNSFATHER
BAMBOCCIADES
BANANALANDER
BARBERMONGER
BESSERWISSER
BLENNORRHOEA
BLOODSTAINED
BOOBYTRAPPED
BOULEVARDIER
BREASTSUMMER
BREATHALYSER
BRICKFIELDER
BUNKOSTEERER
CABINETMAKER
CALLISTHENES
CANTILEVERED
CARPETBAGGER
CARRIWITCHET
CARTOGRAPHER
CASSITERIDES
CATHETOMETER
CHEESEBURGER
CHEESEMONGER
CHURCHWARDEN
CLEARSIGHTED
COLDSHOULDER
COLLYWOBBLES
COMMISSIONED
COMMISSIONER
CONCENTRATED
CONFECTIONER
CONSEQUENCES
CONSOLIDATED
CONTAMINATED
CONVENIENCES
COSTERMONGER
CROSSBENCHER
DEHUMIDIFIER
DELICATESSEN
DERESTRICTED
DISAPPOINTED
DISCOMYCETES
DISCONCERTED
DISCONNECTED
DISCONTENTED
DISENCHANTED
DISORGANIZED
DISPOSSESSED
DISSATISFIED
DOMESTICATED
DONNERWETTER
DOUBLEDECKER
DOUBLEGLAZED
EAVESDROPPER
ECCLESIASTES
ENGLISHWOMEN
ERATOSTHENES
EULENSPIEGEL
EVENTEMPERED
EXHIBITIONER
EXTINGUISHER
FAINTHEARTED
FREIGHTLINER
GALVANOMETER
GASTARBEITER
GASTROSOPHER
GENTLETAMPER
GLOBETROTTER
GLOCKENSPIEL
GOOSEPIMPLES
GRASSWIDOWER
HAIRSPLITTER
HALLANSHAKER
HALLUCINOGEN
HAMMERHEADED
HANDKERCHIEF
HARNESSMAKER
HEPHTHEMIMER
HOLIDAYMAKER
HOUSEBREAKER
HYDROGRAPHER
HYMNOGRAPHER
IAMBOGRAPHER
IMPOVERISHED
INCORPORATED
INNOMINABLES
INTERCHANGED
INTERRELATED
INTERSPERSED
JENNYSPINNER
KATZENJAMMER
KINDERGARTEN
KIRSCHWASSER
KLIPSPRINGER
LEGIONNAIRES
LICKTRENCHER
LIGHTHEARTED
LUXEMBOURGER
MALPRACTICES
MANGELWURZEL
MANSLAUGHTER
MANUFACTURER
MARCOBRUNNER
MASSPRODUCED
MINICOMPUTER
MISDELIVERED
MISINTERPRET
MOUTHBROODER
MUDDLEHEADED
MULTICOLORED

NEPHELOMETER
NIGHTCLOTHES
OLDFASHIONED
OUTSTRETCHED
OVERSCUTCHED
OVERSTRAINED
PARTICOLORED
PERSONALIZED
PHOTOGRAPHER
PITTERPATTER
PLAINCLOTHES
PRACTICIONER
PRACTITIONER
PRALLTRILLER
PREPOSSESSED
PRIZEFIGHTER
PUMPERNICKEL
RADIOGRAPHER
RECORDPLAYER
REDEMPTIONER
REDISCOVERED
REFRIGERATED
REMEMBRANCER
RESUSCITATED
RODOMONTADER
ROLLERBLADER
ROLLERBLADES
RONCESVALLES
SCHOOLMASTER
SCHOPENHAUER
SCREENWRITER
SCRIMSHANDER
SCRIMSHANKER
SCRIPTWRITER
SELFEMPLOYED
SEMIDETACHED
SEPTEMBRISER
SHARPSHOOTER
SHIRTSLEEVES
SHIRTWAISTER
SHORTSIGHTED
SHORTSLEEVED
SHORTSTAFFED
SILVERHAIRED
SINGLEDECKER
SINGLEHANDED
SINGLEMINDED
SIPUNCULACEA
SLOCKDOLAGER
SLOCKDOLIGER
SLOCKDOLOGER
SPATANGOIDEA
SPECKTIONEER
SPELLCHECKER
SPIEGELEISEN
SPINECHILLER
SPREADEAGLED
STENOGRAPHER
STEPDAUGHTER
STERNWHEELER
STOCKBREEDER
STONECHATTER
STORMTROOPER
STRAITJACKET
STRANGLEWEED
STRIGIFORMES
STRONGMINDED
SUBCOMMITTEE
SUPERCHARGED
SUPERCHARGER
SWASHBUCKLER
TAPERECORDER
TEETERTOTTER
THICKSKINNED
THOROUGHBRED
THREEQUARTER
TRABECULATED
TRANQUILIZER
TROUBLEMAKER
TURBOCHARGER
ULOTRICHALES
UNACCUSTOMED
UNACQUAINTED
UNAPPARELLED
UNAUTHORISED
UNAUTHORIZED
UNCHALLENGED
UNCLASSIFIED
UNCONSIDERED
UNCONTROLLED
UNCULTIVATED
UNDERCLOTHES
UNDEREXPOSED
UNDERSKINKER
UNDERSTAFFED
UNDERWRITTEN
UNDETERMINED
UNDIMINISHED
UNDISCHARGED
UNEXPURGATED
UNFREQUENTED
UNIDENTIFIED
UNINTERESTED
UNOBSTRUCTED
UNPARALLELED
UNPREJUDICED
UNPRINCIPLED
UNRECOGNISED
UNRECOGNIZED
UNRESTRAINED
UNRESTRICTED
UNUTTERABLES
VALENCIENNES
VARICOLOURED
WATERCARRIER
WEIGHTLIFTER
WELLBALANCED
WELLINFORMED
WHOLEHEARTED
WICKETKEEPER
WINTERHALTER
YELLOWHAMMER
GESELLSCHAFT
QUARTERSTAFF
TRANSMOGRIFY
ANTHROPOLOGY
BACTERIOLOGY
BERTILLONAGE
BREAKTHROUGH
BREASTPLOUGH
CASTERBRIDGE
CHITTERLINGS
DISADVANTAGE
DYSTELEOLOGY
EPISTEMOLOGY
FRANKALMOIGN
GAINSBOROUGH
HEARTSTRINGS
OUTBUILDINGS
PALEONTOLOGY
PHARMACOLOGY
SHORTCOMINGS
STRAIGHTEDGE
SURROUNDINGS
THIRDBOROUGH
AFORETHOUGHT
AFTERTHOUGHT
BANTAMWEIGHT
BIBLIOGRAPHY
CHOREOGRAPHY
CHRESTOMATHY
CRYPTOGRAPHY
ENANTIOPATHY
ENTEROMORPHA
GIGANTOMACHY
LEXICOGRAPHY
MERRYTHOUGHT
MIDDLEWEIGHT
OCEANOGRAPHY
PLECTOGNATHI
PRAISEWORTHY
QUARTERLIGHT
WELTERWEIGHT
WILLIEWAUGHT
AGAMOGENETIC
ALEXIPHARMIC
ALPHANUMERIC
AMPHISBAENIC
ANAMORPHOSIS
ANECATHARSIS
ANTAGONISTIC
ANTHELMINTIC
ANTIMNEMONIC
ANTIRACHITIC
ANTITHROMBIN
APPENDICITIS
ARISTOCRATIC
ARISTOLOCHIA
BEAUMARCHAIS
BERTHOLLETIA
BUREAUCRATIC
CALLIGRAPHIC
CAMPANULARIA
CAPERCAILLIE
CAPERCAILZIE
CARCINOGENIC
CARTOGRAPHIC
CATADIOPTRIC
CATASTROPHIC
CEREBROTONIC
CHAIRMANSHIP
CHAMPIONSHIP
CHAUVINISTIC
CHIROPRACTIC
CHREMATISTIC
CLAMJAMPHRIE
CLEISTOGAMIC
COUNTERCLAIM
DARLINGTONIA
DIAGRAMMATIC
DICTATORSHIP
DIPLOGENESIS
DIRECTORSHIP
ECCLESIASTIC
ELECTROLYSIS
ENCYCLOPEDIA
ENCYCLOPEDIC
ENHYPOSTASIA
ENTHUSIASTIC
EPANORTHOSIS
EPIGRAMMATIC
ERYTHROMYCIN
ETEPIMELETIC
FEATHERBRAIN
FELDSPATHOID
FRANKENSTEIN
GAMESMANSHIP
GLUBBDUBDRIB
GONADOTROPIN
GRISEOFULVIN
GUARDIANSHIP
HAEMATEMESIS
HAMARTHRITIS
HETEROCLITIC
HETEROPHORIA
HETEROPLASIA
HIEROGLYPHIC
HIEROPHANTIC
HILDEBRANDIC
HOMOEOPATHIC
HORSEMANSHIP
HYDROCHLORIC
HYPERPYRETIC
HYPOCHONDRIA
ICONOCLASTIC
JOURNALISTIC
KINAESTHETIC
LAUREATESHIP
LITHOGRAPHIC
MARKSMANSHIP

MELODRAMATIC
MERISTEMATIC
MILITARISTIC
MISANTHROPIC
MNEMOTECHNIC
MONOSYLLABIC
MOSBOLLETJIE
NARCISSISTIC
NATURALISTIC
NONALCOHOLIC
OCTASTROPHIC
ONEIROCRITIC
ONOMATOPOEIA
ONOMATOPOEIC
ORTHOGENESIS
ORTHORHOMBIC
ORTHOTONESIS
OSTEOMALACIA
OSTEOPOROSIS
PALINGENESIA
PALINGENESIS
PANAESTHESIA
PANCHROMATIC
PARACENTESIS
PARTISANSHIP
PASSIONFRUIT
PEDICELLARIA
PENNSYLVANIA
PERICARDITIS
PERIPHRASTIC
PERISTERONIC
PERSULPHURIC
PHILHARMONIC
PHOTOGLYPHIC
PHOTOGRAPHIC
PHYCOXANTHIN
POLYSYLLABIC
PORNOGRAPHIC
POTICHOMANIA
PROPHYLACTIC
PROSOPOPOEIA
PROTOPLASMIC
PSYCHOPATHIC
QUADRAPHONIC
RECEIVERSHIP
RELATIONSHIP
RESPONDENTIA
SALESMANSHIP
SCATTERBRAIN
SCHINDYLESIS
SCLERODERMIA
SELFPORTRAIT
SESQUITERTIA
SHORTCIRCUIT
SITTLICHKEIT
STEREOPHONIC
STEREOSCOPIC
STREPTOMYCIN
SURREALISTIC
TAPSALTEERIE
TAPSLETEERIE
TELEASTHETIC
TETRODOTOXIN
THAUMATURGIC
THERMOSTATIC
THESMOPHORIA
THIGMOTROPIC
TRADESCANTIA
TRANSOCEANIC
TROPHALLAXIS
TUBERCULOSIS
TURACOVERDIN
UNDEMOCRATIC
UNSCIENTIFIC
URTRICULARIA
WASHINGTONIA
WELLINGTONIA
WHIGMALEERIE
XANTHOPTERIN
ZARATHUSTRIC
BUSINESSLIKE
FIDDLESTICKS
HAPPYGOLUCKY
MARLINESPIKE
MASTERSTROKE
SPHAIRISTIKE
STANISLAVSKI
ACADEMICALLY
ACCIDENTALLY
ADDITIONALLY
ADJECTIVALLY
AGGRESSIVELY
ANTIMETABOLE
ANTIPARTICLE
APPROACHABLE
ARTIFICIALLY
ARTIODACTYLA
ARTISTICALLY
ATTRACTIVELY
ATTRIBUTABLE
AUSPICIOUSLY
BARRANQUILLA
BEACONSFIELD
BENEVOLENTLY
BOISTEROUSLY
BOUGAINVILLE
BREATHLESSLY
CEREMONIALLY
CHESTERFIELD
CLASSIFIABLE
CLAVICEMBALO
COLLECTIVELY
COLLOQUIALLY
COMMERCIALLY
COMMUNICABLE
COMPLACENTLY
CONCLUSIVELY
CONCURRENTLY
CONGENITALLY
CONSEQUENTLY
CONSIDERABLE
CONSIDERABLY
CONSISTENTLY
CONTEMPTIBLE
CONTINUOUSLY
CONTROLLABLE
CONVENIENTLY
CONVINCINGLY
COURAGEOUSLY
CURMUDGEONLY
DECIPHERABLE
DECORATIVELY
DELIBERATELY
DEMONSTRABLE
DEMONSTRABLY
DISAGREEABLE
DISASTROUSLY
DISDAINFULLY
DISHONORABLE
DISHONORABLY
DISREPUTABLE
DOGMATICALLY
DRAMATICALLY
ECONOMICALLY
ECSTATICALLY
EFFORTLESSLY
ELECTRICALLY
EMPHATICALLY
ENTREATINGLY
ESTHETICALLY
EVENHANDEDLY
EXCHANGEABLE
EXHAUSTIVELY
EXTRADITABLE
FASTIDIOUSLY
FIGURATIVELY
FLAMBOYANTLY
FORTUITOUSLY
FRACTIONALLY
FUNCTIONALLY
FUNDAMENTALS
GEOLOGICALLY
HARMONIOUSLY
HERMETICALLY
HISTORICALLY
HORIZONTALLY
HORRIFICALLY
HYGIENICALLY
HYPNOTICALLY
HYSTERICALLY
ICHTHYOCOLLA
IDENTIFIABLE
IMMACULATELY
IMMEASURABLE
IMMEASURABLY
IMMODERATELY
IMPENETRABLE
IMPERISHABLE
IMPERSONALLY
IMPRESSIVELY
INACCESSIBLE
INACCURATELY
INADEQUATELY
INADMISSIBLE
INAPPLICABLE
INCALCULABLE
INCAUTIOUSLY
INCIDENTALLY
INCOHERENTLY
INCOMPARABLE
INCOMPARABLY
INCOMPATIBLE
INCOMPLETELY
INCONSOLABLE
INCORRIGIBLE
INCORRIGIBLY
INCREASINGLY
INDECLINABLE
INDEFENSIBLE
INDEFINITELY
INDIGESTIBLE
INDISPUTABLE
INDISPUTABLY
INDISSOLUBLE
INDISTINCTLY
INDIVIDUALLY
INDUSTRIALLY
INERADICABLE
INEXPLICABLE
INEXPLICABLY
INEXTRICABLE
INEXTRICABLY
INFORMIDABLE
INFREQUENTLY
INHOSPITABLE
INORDINATELY
INSUFFERABLE
INSUFFERABLY
INTELLIGIBLE
INTERMINABLE
INTERMINABLY
INVULNERABLE
IRRATIONALLY
IRREDEEMABLE
IRRESISTIBLE
IRRESOLUTELY
IRRESOLVABLE
IRREVERENTLY
IRREVERSIBLE
LASCIVIOUSLY
LEGITIMATELY
LUGUBRIOUSLY
MADEMOISELLE
MAGNETICALLY
MAJESTICALLY
MANOEUVRABLE
MARRIAGEABLE
MEANINGFULLY
MECHANICALLY
METHODICALLY

METICULOUSLY
MICHELANGELO
MIRACULOUSLY
MONOSYLLABLE
MONOTONOUSLY
MYSTERIOUSLY
NEUROTICALLY
NONCHALANTLY
OBSEQUIOUSLY
OCCASIONALLY
OPPRESSIVELY
OTHERWORLDLY
OUTRAGEOUSLY
PARTICULARLY
PASSIONATELY
PATHETICALLY
PEDANTICALLY
PERCEPTIVELY
PEREMPTORILY
PERIODICALLY
PERSISTENTLY
PERSUASIVELY
PHENOMENALLY
PHONETICALLY
PINNIEWINKLE
POLYSYLLABLE
POSSESSIVELY
POSTHUMOUSLY
PRECARIOUSLY
PRECOCIOUSLY
PRODIGIOUSLY
PROFICIENTLY
PROGRAMMABLE
PROLIFICALLY
PROPITIOUSLY
PROTECTIVELY
PROVERBIALLY
PTERODACTYLE
PUGNACIOUSLY
PURPOSEBUILT
PURPOSEFULLY
QUANTIFIABLE
QUESTIONABLE
QUIXOTICALLY
RECHARGEABLE
RECIPROCALLY
RECOGNIZABLE
RELENTLESSLY
RESPECTFULLY
RESPECTIVELY
RHYTHMICALLY
RIDICULOUSLY
ROMANTICALLY
SADISTICALLY
SARDONICALLY
SARSAPARILLA
SCANDALOUSLY
SCRUPULOUSLY
SCURRILOUSLY
SEMANTICALLY

SEQUENTIALLY
SHAMEFACEDLY
SHILLYSHALLY
SIPHONOSTELE
SLUBBERINGLY
SOLICITOUSLY
SPECIFICALLY
SPLENOMEGALY
SPORADICALLY
STAGGERINGLY
STRANGLEHOLD
STRUCTURALLY
SUBJECTIVELY
SUBMISSIVELY
SUBSEQUENTLY
SUCCESSFULLY
SUCCESSIVELY
SUFFICIENTLY
SUGGESTIVELY
SURMOUNTABLE
SURPRISINGLY
SUSPICIOUSLY
SYMBOLICALLY
TERRIFICALLY
TERRITORIALS
THEATRICALLY
THOUGHTFULLY
THREADNEEDLE
TRADESPEOPLE
TRANSFERABLE
TRANSLATABLE
TREMENDOUSLY
TRIUMPHANTLY
UNACCEPTABLE
UNANSWERABLE
UNATTAINABLE
UNBELIEVABLE
UNBELIEVABLY
UNCHANGEABLE
UNCHARITABLE
UNCHARITABLY
UNDESERVEDLY
UNDETECTABLE
UNEXPECTEDLY
UNFATHOMABLE
UNFAVOURABLE
UNILATERALLY
UNIMAGINABLE
UNMANAGEABLE
UNMISTAKABLE
UNNEIGHBORLY
UNOBTAINABLE
UNOFFICIALLY
UNPARDONABLE
UNPROFITABLE
UNREASONABLE
UNRESERVEDLY
UNRETURNABLE
UNSEASONABLE
UPROARIOUSLY

USERFRIENDLY
VIBRATIUNCLE
VINDICTIVELY
VOCIFEROUSLY
VOLUPTUOUSLY
WALLYDRAIGLE
WHIPPOORWILL
APPENDECTOMY
CHONDRIOSOME
HYPERSARCOMA
HYSTERECTOMY
LAMPADEDROMY
MESOTHELIOMA
POINTILLISME
QUADRAGESIMA
RHYTIDECTOMY
SCLERENCHYMA
SEPTUAGESIMA
WOLSTENHOLME
ACCOMPANYING
ACCOUCHEMENT
ACCOUTREMENT
ADMONISHMENT
ANDROSTERONE
ANNOUNCEMENT
ANTILEGOMENA
ANTINEUTRINO
ASTONISHMENT
AWARDWINNING
AWEINSPIRING
BACKBREAKING
BARNSTORMING
BATTLEGROUND
BEWILDERMENT
BIRDWATCHING
BLACKCURRANT
BLANDISHMENT
BLUESTOCKING
BOONDOGGLING
BRAINWASHING
BREATHTAKING
BRILLIANTINE
BROADCASTING
CARDINDEXING
CHASTISEMENT
CHEESEPARING
CHILDBEARING
CIRCASSIENNE
COMBINATIONS
COMMENCEMENT
COMPROMISING
CONTABESCENT
CONVALESCENT
CONVALESCING
CONVEYANCING
COUNTERPOINT
CRASHLANDING
CROSSEXAMINE
DEBILITATING
DECIPHERMENT

DECONGESTANT
DEMIMONDAINE
DISAGREEMENT
DISAPPEARING
DISCOURAGING
DISINFECTANT
DISPLACEMENT
DRINKDRIVING
EFFERVESCENT
EMBARRASSING
EMBEZZLEMENT
ENCIRCLEMENT
ENCROACHMENT
ENERGYSAVING
ENTANGLEMENT
ENTERPRISING
ENTERTAINING
ENTRENCHMENT
EPIPHENOMENA
ESTRANGEMENT
EXASPERATING
EXCRUCIATING
EXHILARATING
FARTHINGLAND
FIRSTFOOTING
FOOTSLOGGING
FULMINATIONS
GALLIGASKINS
GALLIVANTING
GLYNDEBOURNE
GONDWANALAND
GRANDMONTINE
HAIRDRESSING
HEARTWARMING
HEREDITAMENT
HIGHFALUTING
HOUSEKEEPING
HOUSEWARMING
HYDROQUINONE
ILLUMINATING
IMPRISONMENT
INCANDESCENT
INCONSEQUENT
INCONSISTENT
INCONVENIENT
INFRINGEMENT
INGRATIATING
INSTRUCTIONS
INSUFFICIENT
INTERMITTENT
INTERPRETING
INTIMIDATING
INTOXICATING
INTRANSIGENT
INTRAUTERINE
INVIGORATING
LABOURSAVING
LABYRINTHINE
LAMELLICORNE
LAMENTATIONS

LEPIDOMELANE
LONGSTANDING
MACHAIRODONT
MAGNILOQUENT
MALTREATMENT
METALLOPHONE
MINDBOGGLING
MISAPPREHEND
MISPLACEMENT
MISREPRESENT
MISSTATEMENT
MISTREATMENT
MOISTURIZING
MOONLIGHTING
MULLIGATAWNY
NEIGHBOURING
NEWFOUNDLAND
NONRESISTANT
OBSERVANTINE
ORIENTEERING
OVERCROWDING
OVERDRESSING
OVERPOWERING
OVERWHELMING
OXYACETYLENE
PALPITATIONS
PARALIPOMENA
PEACEKEEPING
PETTIFOGGING
PHYTONADIONE
PLASTERSTONE
POLICYMAKING
POLYETHYLENE
POLYURETHANE
POSTPONEMENT
POWERSHARING
PREDETERMINE
PREMONSTRANT
PREPONDERANT
PREPONDERENT
PRESENTIMENT
PRIZEWINNING
PROFITEERING
PROGESTERONE
PSIPHENOMENA
RACKETEERING
READJUSTMENT
RECALCITRANT
RECRUDESCENT
REDEPLOYMENT
RENOUNCEMENT
REPROCESSING
RESETTLEMENT
RETRENCHMENT
SARRUSOPHONE
SELFCATERING
SHAREHOLDING
SHIPBUILDING
SLEEPWALKING
SMALLHOLDING

SNOWBOARDING
SPORTSGROUND
STENTORPHONE
STEREOTYPING
SUBCONTINENT
TESTOSTERONE
TETRACYCLINE
THANKSGIVING
THEOPHYLLINE
TIGHTFITTING
TRANSACTIONS
TRANSCENDENT
TRANSPONTINE
ULTRAMONTANE
UMBRADARLING
UNAPPETIZING
UNCONVERSANT
UNCONVINCING
UNDERCURRENT
UNDERGARMENT
UNDERPINNING
UNEMPLOYMENT
UNPRETENDING
UNSATISFYING
UNSURPRISING
UNSUSPECTING
VENTRIPOTENT
ZALAMBDODONT
ABBREVIATION
ACCELERATION
ACCENTUATION
ACCUMULATION
ADJUDICATION
ADULTERATION
AGATHODAIMON
ALLITERATION
AMALGAMATION
AMELIORATION
ANNIHILATION
ANNUNCIATION
ANTICIPATION
ANTISTROPHON
APPRECIATION
APPREHENSION
ARCHIPELAGOS
ARTICULATION
ASPHYXIATION
ASSIMILATION
ASSUEFACTION
AUGMENTATION
AUSCULTATION
CALUMNIATION
CANCELLATION
CANONIZATION
CAPITULATION
CHIROPRACTOR
CHLORINATION
CIRCUMCISION
CIVILISATION
CIVILIZATION

CLAUDICATION
CODIFICATION
COHABITATION
COLLABORATOR
COLLUCTATION
COLONIZATION
COMMENDATION
COMPELLATION
COMPENSATION
COMPLICATION
COMPURGATION
CONCILIATION
CONDEMNATION
CONDENSATION
CONFIRMATION
CONFISCATION
CONGREGATION
CONQUISTADOR
CONSCRIPTION
CONSECRATION
CONSERVATION
CONSOLIDATOR
CONSTIPATION
CONSTITUTION
CONSTRICTION
CONSTRUCTION
CONSULTATION
CONSUMMATION
CONTIGNATION
CONTINUATION
CONTRIBUTION
CONVERSATION
COORDINATION
CROSSSECTION
DEASPIRATION
DECAPITATION
DECELERATION
DEGENERATION
DELIBERATION
DEMONSTRATOR
DENOMINATION
DENUNCIATION
DEPOPULATION
DEPRECIATION
DEREGULATION
DESSERTSPOON
DIENCEPHALON
DILAPIDATION
DISPENSATION
DISQUISITION
DISSERTATION
DISSOCIATION
DISTILLATION
DISTRIBUTION
EMANCIPATION
EMASCULATION
ENCHEIRIDION
ENTOPLASTRON
EPENCEPHALON
EPITHALAMION

EQUIVOCATION
ETYMOLOGICON
EXACERBATION
EXAGGERATION
EXASPERATION
EXCRUCIATION
EXHILARATION
EXPLOITATION
FERMENTATION
FINALIZATION
FLAGELLATION
FLUORIDATION
FRUMENTATION
GENETHLIACON
GOBBLEDEGOOK
GOBBLEDYGOOK
HUMANIZATION
HYPERTENSION
HYPOTHECATOR
IDEALIZATION
ILLUMINATION
ILLUSTRATION
IMMODERATION
IMMUNIZATION
IMPERFECTION
IMPERSONATOR
IMPLANTATION
IMPREGNATION
INAUGURATION
INCINERATION
INCRUSTATION
INDISCRETION
INESCUTCHEON
INFILTRATION
INFLAMMATION
INSEMINATION
INSTALLATION
INSTAURATION
INSURRECTION
INTENERATION
INTERCEPTION
INTERCESSION
INTERJECTION
INTERLOCUTOR
INTERMISSION
INTERROGATOR
INTERRUPTION
INTERSECTION
INTERVENTION
INTIMIDATION
INTOXICATION
INTRODUCTION
INVALIDATION
INVESTIGATOR
INVIGORATION
IRRESOLUTION
JURISDICTION
LABANOTATION
LEGALIZATION
LIQUEFACTION

MALFORMATION
MALNUTRITION
MANIPULATION
MASTURBATION
MENSTRUATION
MINISTRATION
MISQUOTATION
MOBILIZATION
MODIFICATION
NEIGHBORHOOD
NOTIFICATION
NYCHTHEMERON
OBLITERATION
ORGANISATION
ORGANIZATION
OSSIFICATION
OVEREXERTION
PACIFICATION
PANPHARMACON
PANTECHNICON
PENALIZATION
PERAMBULATOR
PERNOCTATION
PERPETRATION
PERSPIRATION
PERTURBATION
PETRIFACTION
PHILODENDRON
PHYTOBENTHOS
PIGMENTATION
POLARIZATION
POLYSYNDETON
PRECONDITION
PREDILECTION
PREGUSTATION
PRESCRIPTION
PRESENTATION
PRESERVATION
PRESTRICTION
PREVARICATOR
PROCLAMATION
PROLEGOMENON
PROLONGATION
PROMULGATION
PROPITIATION
PROSCRIPTION
PROSTITUTION
PROTESTATION
PROTHALAMION
PURIFICATION
PUTREFACTION
RAMIFICATION
RATIFICATION
RECOLLECTION
RECUPERATION
REFRIGERATOR
REGENERATION
REGISTRATION
REJUVENATION
REMUNERATION

RENUNCIATION
REPATRIATION
REPERCUSSION
REPOSSESSION
REPRODUCTION
RESURRECTION
RETICULATION
RHODODENDRON
SATISFACTION
SCINTILLATOR
SEGMENTATION
SEQUESTRATOR
SOLICITATION
SOUTHERNWOOD
SPHACELATION
SPINSTERHOOD
SPOKESPERSON
STEREOPTICON
STERNUTATION
STILBOESTROL
STREPITATION
STRIDULATION
STUPEFACTION
SUBARRHATION
SUBHASTATION
SUBSCRIPTION
SUBSTITUTION
SUCCUSSATION
SUPERSTITION
SUPPLICATION
TRANSGRESSOR
TRANSMISSION
TRICHOPHYTON
URBANIZATION
VAPORIZATION
VERIFICATION
VILIFICATION
VITUPERATION
VOCIFERATION
WEATHERPROOF
AETHRIOSCOPE
AROMATHERAPY
CHEMOTHERAPY
DAGUERROTYPE
DEUTEROSCOPY
ENANTIOMORPH
HYDROTHERAPY
HYPNOTHERAPY
KALEIDOSCOPE
KERAUNOGRAPH
MARCONIGRAPH
MYRINGOSCOPE
OPISTHOGRAPH
OSCILLOSCOPE
PHILANTHROPY
PRAXINOSCOPE
PYTHONOMORPH
RADIOISOTOPE
RADIOTHERAPY
SPECTROSCOPE

WOODBURYTYPE
AECIDIOSPORE
AMPHITHEATRE
ANTICIPATORY
APPOGGIATURA
ARCHITECTURE
BIOCHEMISTRY
CAMIKNICKERS
CAMPODEIFORM
CHALICOTHERE
CLAPPERBOARD
COMMENDATORY
COMPENSATORY
CONCILIATORY
CONFIRMATORY
CONSERVATORY
CONSTABULARY
CONTEMPORARY
CONTRIBUTORY
CREMAILLIÈRE
CROSSCOUNTRY
DEAMBULATORY
DEFLATIONARY
DEPRECIATORY
DISCIPLINARY
DISCOMFITURE
ELEEMOSYNARY
EPISTOLATERS
EQUIVOCATORY
EVOLUTIONARY
FLORICULTURE
GREENGROCERS
GREENGROCERY
GUILDENSTERN
HABERDASHERS
HABERDASHERY
HAIRDRESSERS
HEADQUARTERS
HENCEFORWARD
HINDQUARTERS
HORTICULTURE
INFLAMMATORY
INFLATIONARY
INTERMEDIARY
INTRODUCTORY
LILLIBULLERO
LILLIBURLERO
LINCOLNSHIRE
MASTIGOPHORA
MISADVENTURE
MOUSQUETAIRE
NOMENCLATURE
NORTHEASTERN
NORTHWESTERN
OBEDIENTIARY
OUTMANOEUVRE
PANCHATANTRA
PARAMILITARY
PASSEMEASURE
PENITENTIARY

PERADVENTURE
PETTIFOGGERS
PETTIFOGGERY
PHOTOGRAVURE
PHRONTISTERY
PISCICULTURE
PLACENTIFORM
POSTLIMINARY
PREMAXILLARY
PROBATIONARY
PROPITIATORY
REFLATIONARY
REVERSIONARY
RHIPIDOPTERA
SATISFACTORY
SESQUIALTERA
SHUFFLEBOARD
SIDEWHISKERS
SIPHONOPHORA
SOMATOPLEURE
SOUTHEASTERN
SOUTHWESTERN
STRATOSPHERE
STREPSIPTERA
STREPTONEURA
SUBSTRUCTURE
SUPERCILIARY
TELEUTOSPORE
TERCENTENARY
TESTAMENTARY
THOROUGHFARE
THUNDERSTORM
THYSANOPTERA
TRIGONOMETRY
TROCHOSPHERE
VENEPUNCTURE
VILLEGIATURA
ABOLITIONIST
ACCORDIONIST
AGRIBUSINESS
AMBASSADRESS
ANAESTHETISE
ANAESTHETIST
APOSTROPHISE
ASPARAGINASE
BACKWARDNESS
BEHAVIOURISM
BENEFACTRESS
BIBLIOPEGIST
BICAMERALISM
CARDIOLOGIST
CARELESSNESS
CARICATURIST
CAUTIOUSNESS
CHARTERHOUSE
CHEERFULNESS
CHILDISHNESS
CHORIZONTIST
CHURLISHNESS
CLANNISHNESS

CLARINETTIST
COMPLETENESS
CONSERVATISM
CONTRARINESS
COUNTERBLAST
COUNTERPOISE
COVETOUSNESS
CREATIVENESS
DECENTRALISE
DENDROLOGIST
DILATORINESS
DISEMBARRASS
DISFRANCHISE
DISTINCTNESS
DRAMATURGIST
EDUCATIONIST
EGYPTOLOGIST
EMBROIDERESS
ENTEROPNEUST
ENTOMOLOGIST
ESCAPOLOGIST
EXTENSIONIST
FAITHFULNESS
FEARLESSNESS
FLITTERMOUSE
FORCEFULNESS
FRANKINCENSE
FRAUENDIENST
FRIENDLINESS
FRUITFULNESS
FUNCTIONLESS
GEOPHYSICIST
GRACEFULNESS
GRACIOUSNESS
GRAPHOLOGIST
GRATEFULNESS
GYMNOSOPHIST
GYNECOLOGIST
HEADMISTRESS
HELPLESSNESS
HERMENEUTIST
HIPPOCRATISE
HOMESICKNESS
HOPELESSNESS
HOUSETOHOUSE
IDIOSYNCRASY
IMMUNOLOGIST
IMPOLITENESS
INCUNABULIST
INDEBTEDNESS
INSTRUCTRESS
ISHMAELITISH
ISOLATIONISM
ISOLATIONIST
KATHAREVOUSA
LIFELESSNESS
LISTLESSNESS
MARSEILLAISE
MECHITHARIST
MERVEILLEUSE
METALLURGIST
METAMORPHISM
METAMORPHOSE
MINDFULLNESS
MINERALOGIST
MITRAILLEUSE
MOTORCYCLIST
MUSICOLOGIST
NEOPLATONISM
NEVERTHELESS
NORTHERNMOST
NUTRITIONIST
OBSOLETENESS
ORTHOPAEDIST
PAINLESSNESS
PEACEFULNESS
PERVERSENESS
PHILISTINISM
PHLEBOTOMIST
PHYSIOLOGIST
POSTMISTRESS
POTAMOLOGIST
PREPAREDNESS
PRIGGISHNESS
PROPAGANDISM
PROPAGANDIST
PROPRIETRESS
PSEPHOLOGIST
PSYCHIATRIST
PSYCHOLOGIST
RECEPTIONIST
RECKLESSNESS
RESTLESSNESS
RETARDEDNESS
ROOMINGHOUSE
RUTHLESSNESS
SALVATIONIST
SECESSIONIST
SECTARIANISM
SELFINTEREST
SHEEPISHNESS
SLOVENLINESS
SNOBBISHNESS
SOMNAMBULISM
SOMNAMBULIST
SOUTHERNMOST
SPACIOUSNESS
SPECIOUSNESS
SPELEOLOGIST
SPIRITUALISM
SPIRITUALIST
SPITEFULNESS
SPURIOUSNESS
STEALTHINESS
STEEPLECHASE
STEGOPHOLIST
STRAIGHTNESS
STRINGCOURSE
STUBBORNNESS
STUDIOUSNESS
TACTLESSNESS
TECHNOLOGIST
TELEGRAPHESE
TELEGRAPHIST
THANKFULNESS
THEREAGAINST
THOROUGHNESS
THUNDERFLASH
TIMELESSNESS
TOGETHERNESS
TOXICOLOGIST
TRANQUILLISE
TRANSVESTISM
TRICHOLOGIST
TRUTHFULNESS
UNCTUOUSNESS
UNIVERSALIST
VENGEFULNESS
WATCHFULNESS
WRETCHEDNESS
YOUTHFULNESS
ABSQUATULATE
ADAPTABILITY
ADMINISTRATE
ADVISABILITY
AFFECTIONATE
AFTEREFFECTS
AGALMATOLITE
ANDOUILLETTE
APLANOGAMETE
ARFVEDSONITE
ARSENOPYRITE
ARTHROPLASTY
AUTHENTICATE
AUTHENTICITY
AVAILABILITY
AWAYABSOLUTE
AYUNTAMIENTO
BABINGTONITE
BETHLEHEMITE
BILLINGSGATE
BIODIVERSITY
BLABBERMOUTH
BLETHERSKATE
BLOODTHIRSTY
CARBOHYDRATE
CHRISTIANITY
CIRCUMGYRATE
COLLECTORATE
COMMANDMENTS
COMMENSURATE
COMMONWEALTH
CONDUCTIVITY
CONGLOMERATE
CONGRATULATE
CONSPECTUITY
CONSTITUENTS
CONTRAPPOSTO
CONTRITURATE
CONVIVIALITY
CRISTOBALITE
DESIRABILITY
DISCONSOLATE
DISCRIMINATE
DISINTEGRATE
DISORIENTATE
DIVERTIMENTO
ECCENTRICITY
ELECTROPLATE
ESPAGNOLETTE
ESSENTIALITY
EXCITABILITY
EXSUFFLICATE
EXTORTIONATE
FEHMGERICHTE
GRANDPARENTS
GROSSULARITE
HARUMFRODITE
HELLGRAMMITE
HEMICHORDATA
HETEROSOMATA
ILLEGIBILITY
ILLEGITIMATE
ILLOGICALITY
IMMUTABILITY
IMPARTIALITY
INARTICULATE
INCAPABILITY
INCAPACITATE
INDOCTRINATE
INSOLUBILITY
INSPECTORATE
INTERMEDIATE
INVERTEBRATE
INVISIBILITY
IRASCIBILITY
IRREGULARITY
IRRITABILITY
LATIROSTRATE
LUXULLIANITE
MACMILLANITE
MALLEABILITY
MICROCLIMATE
MISCALCULATE
MULTIPLICITY
MUNICIPALITY
NAVIGABILITY
OVERESTIMATE
PERCEPTIVITY
PERMANGANATE
PERMEABILITY
PERSPICACITY
PLAUSIBILITY
POPOCATEPETL
POSTGRADUATE
POTENTIALITY
PRACTICALITY
PREDESTINATE
PREPONDERATE
PREREQUISITE

PRINCIPALITY
PRODUCTIVITY
PROLETARIATE
PROTECTORATE
PTERIDOPHYTE
RECAPITULATE
RECONSTITUTE
REDINTEGRATE
REDISTRIBUTE
REHABILITATE
REINVIGORATE
RISORGIMENTO
SCHIZOMYCETE
SECRETARIATE
SERASKIERATE
SKUTTERUDITE
SOPHISTICATE
SPERMATOCYTE
SPIRITUALITY
STAKHANOVITE
STOCKINGETTE
STROMATOLITE
SUBJECTIVITY
SUBSIDIARITY
SUBSTANTIATE
SUPERANNUATE
SYNADELPHITE
SYNTAGMATITE
TARAMASALATA
TECHNICALITY
TERGIVERSATE
TETRAHEDRITE
TOBACCONISTS
TRACTABILITY
TRANQUILLITY
TRANSMIGRATE
TRANSVESTITE
TROCHELMINTH
UNPOPULARITY
VEHMGERICHTE
WHIMSICALITY
WOLLASTONITE
ACHLAMYDEOUS
ADSCITITIOUS
ADVANTAGEOUS
ADVANTAGIOUS
ADVENTITIOUS
AMBIDEXTROUS
AMPHISTOMOUS
ANEMOPHILOUS
ANTIBACCHIUS
ANTIBARBARUS
ANTONINIANUS
ATHEROMATOUS
BEAUMONTAGUE
BEAUMONTIQUE
BRONTOSAURUS
CALCEAMENTUM
CANTANKEROUS
CONTEMPTUOUS
CONTERMINOUS
CONTUMACIOUS
CRASSAMENTUM
CYMOTRICHOUS
DISCOURTEOUS
DISINGENUOUS
DISREPECTFUL
DIVERTICULUM
DOLPHINARIUM
ELECTROTONUS
ENTREPRENEUR
EPITHALAMIUM
GALLINACEOUS
HELIOGABALUS
HIPPOPOTAMUS
HISTIOPHORUS
HOMOTHERMOUS
IDIOTHERMOUS
INAUSPICIOUS
INFELICITOUS
INHARMONIOUS
INSALUBRIOUS
KLETTERSCHUE
LEIOTRICHOUS
LITHOLATROUS
MACABERESQUE
MALLOPHAGOUS
MERETRICIOUS
MERITRICIOUS
METAGNATHOUS
MISBEHAVIOUR
MISDEMEANOUR
MUCILAGINOUS
MULTIFARIOUS
OBSTREPEROUS
ONCORHYNCHUS
OPHIOGLOSSUM
OREOPITHECUS
OREOPITHEOUS
ORNITHOGALUM
OSTENTATIOUS
PALUDAMENTUM
PANDAEMONIUM
PANDANACEOUS
PANTOPHAGOUS
PARANTHELIUM
PARSIMONIOUS
PASSEPARTOUT
PECTORILOQUY
PERGAMENEOUS
PERIOSTRACUM
PERTINACIOUS
PERVICACIOUS
PLEIOCHASIUM
PRASEODYMIUM
PREPOSTEROUS
PRESUMPTUOUS
PROGYMNASIUM
PROTACTINIUM
PROTHALAMIUM
PSEUDONYMOUS
RAMBUNCTIOUS
RESTAURATEUR
RHADAMANTHUS
SACRILEGIOUS
SALTATORIOUS
SARDANAPALUS
SEMIPRECIOUS
SIMULTANEOUS
SINANTHROPUS
SIVAPITHECUS
STRADIVARIUS
STROPHANTHUS
SUBCONSCIOUS
SUBCUTANEOUS
SUPERCILIOUS
SUPERNACULUM
THAUMATURGUS
THUNDERCLOUD
TITANOSAURUS
TRALATICIOUS
TRALATITIOUS
UINTATHERIUM
UNSCRUPULOUS
UNSUCCESSFUL
VAINGLORIOUS
VERUMONTANUM
ALIMENTATIVE
ANTANANARIVO
APPRECIATIVE
APPREHENSIVE
CONSERVATIVE
CONSTRUCTIVE
CONSULTATIVE
DISINCENTIVE
DISTRIBUTIVE
ILLUSTRATIVE
INCONCLUSIVE
INNATTENTIVE
INTRANSITIVE
IRRESPECTIVE
MANIPULATIVE
OPINIONATIVE
PRESCRIPTIVE
PRESERVATIVE
PREVENTATIVE
QUANTITATIVE
RECUPERATIVE
REMUNERATIVE
REPRODUCTIVE
SELFADHESIVE
UNATTRACTIVE
UNDERACHIEVE
UNOPPRESSIVE
UNPRODUCTIVE
UNRESPONSIVE
VITUPERATIVE
DRESSINGDOWN
ANAESTHETIZE
CHARACTERIZE
DECENTRALIZE
DEMILITARIZE
EXTRAVAGANZA
LALLAPALOOZA
PHILOSOPHIZE
TRANQUILLIZE

12:12

ANTILEGOMENA
APPOGGIATURA
ARISTOLOCHIA
ARTIODACTYLA
BARRANQUILLA
BERTHOLLETIA
BLENNORRHOEA
BRANCHIOPODA
CAMPANULARIA
COLOQUINTIDA
DARLINGTONIA
ENCYCLOPEDIA
ENHYPOSTASIA
ENTEROMORPHA
ENTOMOSTRACA
EPIPHENOMENA
EXTRAVAGANZA
HEMICHORDATA
HETEROPHORIA
HETEROPLASIA
HETEROSOMATA
HYPERSARCOMA
HYPOCHONDRIA
ICHTHYOCOLLA
ICHTHYOPSIDA
KATHAREVOUSA
LALLAPALOOZA
MALACOSTRACA
MASSERANDUBA
MASTIGOPHORA
MESOTHELIOMA
ONOMATOPOEIA
OSTEOMALACIA
PALINGENESIA
PANAESTHESIA
PANCHATANTRA
PARALIPOMENA
PEDICELLARIA
PENNSYLVANIA
POTICHOMANIA
PROSOPOPOEIA
PSIPHENOMENA
QUADRAGESIMA
RESPONDENTIA
RHAMPHOTHECA
RHIPIDOPTERA
SARSAPARILLA
SCLERENCHYMA
SCLERODERMIA
SEPTUAGESIMA
SESQUIALTERA

SESQUITERTIA
SIPHONOPHORA
SIPUNCULACEA
SPATANGOIDEA
STREPSIPTERA
STREPTONEURA
TARAMASALATA
THESMOPHORIA
THYSANOPTERA
TRADESCANTIA
URTRICULARIA
VILLEGIATURA
WASHINGTONIA
WELLINGTONIA
GLUBBDUBDRIB
AGAMOGENETIC
ALEXIPHARMIC
ALPHANUMERIC
AMPHISBAENIC
ANTAGONISTIC
ANTHELMINTIC
ANTIMNEMONIC
ANTIRACHITIC
ARISTOCRATIC
BUREAUCRATIC
CALLIGRAPHIC
CARCINOGENIC
CARTOGRAPHIC
CATADIOPTRIC
CATASTROPHIC
CEREBROTONIC
CHAUVINISTIC
CHIROPRACTIC
CHREMATISTIC
CLEISTOGAMIC
DIAGRAMMATIC
ECCLESIASTIC
ENCYCLOPEDIC
ENTHUSIASTIC
EPIGRAMMATIC
ETEPIMELETIC
ETHEROMANIAC
HAEMOPHILIAC
HETEROCLITIC
HIEROGLYPHIC
HIEROPHANTIC
HILDEBRANDIC
HOMOEOPATHIC
HYDROCHLORIC
HYPERPYRETIC
ICONOCLASTIC
JOURNALISTIC
KINAESTHETIC
KLEPTOMANIAC
LITHOGRAPHIC
MELODRAMATIC
MERISTEMATIC
MILITARISTIC
MISANTHROPIC
MNEMOTECHNIC

MONOSYLLABIC
NARCISSISTIC
NATURALISTIC
NONALCOHOLIC
NYMPHOMANIAC
OCTASTROPHIC
ONEIROCRITIC
ONOMATOPOEIC
ORTHORHOMBIC
PANCHROMATIC
PERIPHRASTIC
PERISTERONIC
PERSULPHURIC
PHILHARMONIC
PHOTOGLYPHIC
PHOTOGRAPHIC
POLYSYLLABIC
PORNOGRAPHIC
PROPHYLACTIC
PROTOPLASMIC
PSYCHOPATHIC
QUADRAPHONIC
SCOPOPHILIAC
STEREOPHONIC
STEREOSCOPIC
SURREALISTIC
TELEASTHETIC
THAUMATURGIC
THERMOSTATIC
THIGMOTROPIC
TRANSOCEANIC
UNDEMOCRATIC
UNSCIENTIFIC
ZARATHUSTRIC
ACCOMPLISHED
ACKNOWLEDGED
BATTLEGROUND
BEACONSFIELD
BLOODSTAINED
BOOBYTRAPPED
CANTILEVERED
CHESTERFIELD
CLAPPERBOARD
CLEARSIGHTED
COMMISSIONED
CONCENTRATED
CONSOLIDATED
CONTAMINATED
DERESTRICTED
DISAPPOINTED
DISCONCERTED
DISCONNECTED
DISCONTENTED
DISENCHANTED
DISORGANIZED
DISPOSSESSED
DISSATISFIED
DOMESTICATED
DOUBLEGLAZED
EVENTEMPERED

FAINTHEARTED
FARTHINGLAND
FELDSPATHOID
GONDWANALAND
HAMMERHEADED
HENCEFORWARD
IMPOVERISHED
INCORPORATED
INTERCHANGED
INTERRELATED
INTERSPERSED
LIGHTHEARTED
MASSPRODUCED
MISAPPREHEND
MISDELIVERED
MUDDLEHEADED
MULTICOLORED
NEIGHBORHOOD
NEWFOUNDLAND
OLDFASHIONED
OUTSTRETCHED
OVERSCUTCHED
OVERSTRAINED
PARTICOLORED
PERSONALIZED
PREPOSSESSED
REDISCOVERED
REFRIGERATED
RESUSCITATED
SELFEMPLOYED
SEMIDETACHED
SHORTSIGHTED
SHORTSLEEVED
SHORTSTAFFED
SHUFFLEBOARD
SILVERHAIRED
SINGLEHANDED
SINGLEMINDED
SOUTHERNWOOD
SPINSTERHOOD
SPORTSGROUND
SPREADEAGLED
STRANGLEHOLD
STRANGLEWEED
STRONGMINDED
SUPERCHARGED
THICKSKINNED
THOROUGHBRED
THUNDERCLOUD
TRABECULATED
UNACCUSTOMED
UNACQUAINTED
UNAPPARELLED
UNAUTHORISED
UNAUTHORIZED
UNCHALLENGED
UNCLASSIFIED
UNCONSIDERED
UNCONTROLLED
UNCULTIVATED

UNDEREXPOSED
UNDERSTAFFED
UNDETERMINED
UNDIMINISHED
UNDISCHARGED
UNEXPURGATED
UNFREQUENTED
UNIDENTIFIED
UNINTERESTED
UNOBSTRUCTED
UNPARALLELED
UNPREJUDICED
UNPRINCIPLED
UNRECOGNISED
UNRECOGNIZED
UNRESTRAINED
UNRESTRICTED
VARICOLOURED
WELLBALANCED
WELLINFORMED
WHOLEHEARTED
ABSQUATULATE
ACQUAINTANCE
ACQUIESCENCE
ADMINISTRATE
AECIDIOSPORE
AETHRIOSCOPE
AFFECTIONATE
AGALMATOLITE
ALIMENTATIVE
AMARANTACEAE
AMPHITHEATRE
ANAESTHETISE
ANAESTHETIZE
ANDOUILLETTE
ANDROSTERONE
ANTIMETABOLE
ANTIPARTICLE
APLANOGAMETE
APOSTROPHISE
APPRECIATIVE
APPREHENSIVE
APPROACHABLE
APPURTENANCE
ARBORESCENCE
ARCHITECTURE
ARFVEDSONITE
ARSENOPYRITE
ASPARAGINASE
ATTRIBUTABLE
AUTHENTICATE
AWAYABSOLUTE
BABINGTONITE
BEAUMONTAGUE
BEAUMONTIQUE
BERTILLONAGE
BETHLEHEMITE
BILLINGSGATE
BLETHERSKATE
BOUGAINVILLE

BRILLIANTINE
BUSINESSLIKE
CAPERCAILLIE
CAPERCAILZIE
CARBOHYDRATE
CASTERBRIDGE
CHALICOTHERE
CHARACTERIZE
CHARTERHOUSE
CHONDRIOSOME
CIRCASSIENNE
CIRCUMGYRATE
CIRCUMSCRIBE
CIRCUMSTANCE
CLAIRVOYANCE
CLAMJAMPHRIE
CLASSIFIABLE
COLLECTORATE
COMMENSURATE
COMMUNICABLE
CONGLOMERATE
CONGRATULATE
CONSERVATIVE
CONSIDERABLE
CONSTRUCTIVE
CONSULTATIVE
CONTEMPTIBLE
CONTRITURATE
CONTROLLABLE
COUNTERPOISE
CREMAILLIÈRE
CRISTOBALITE
CROSSEXAMINE
DAGUERROTYPE
DECENTRALISE
DECENTRALIZE
DECIPHERABLE
DEMILITARIZE
DEMIMONDAINE
DEMONSTRABLE
DISACCHARIDE
DISADVANTAGE
DISAGREEABLE
DISCOMEDUSAE
DISCOMFITURE
DISCONSOLATE
DISCRIMINATE
DISFRANCHISE
DISHONORABLE
DISINCENTIVE
DISINTEGRATE
DISOBEDIENCE
DISORIENTATE
DISREPUTABLE
DISTRIBUTIVE
ELECTROPLATE
EPACRIDACEAE
ESPAGNOLETTE
EXCHANGEABLE
EXSUFFLICATE
EXTORTIONATE
EXTRADITABLE
EXTRAVAGANCE
FEHMGERICHTE
FLITTERMOUSE
FLORICULTURE
FLUORESCENCE
FORMALDEHYDE
FRANKINCENSE
FRONTISPIECE
GLYNDEBOURNE
GRANDMONTINE
GROSSULARITE
HAPPENSTANCE
HARUMFRODITE
HELLGRAMMITE
HETEROCONTAE
HIPPOCRATISE
HOBBIDIDANCE
HORTICULTURE
HOUSETOHOUSE
HYDROQUINONE
IDENTIFIABLE
ILLEGITIMATE
ILLUSTRATIVE
IMMEASURABLE
IMPENETRABLE
IMPERISHABLE
IMPERTINENCE
IMPROVIDENCE
INACCESSIBLE
INADMISSIBLE
INADVERTENCE
INAPPLICABLE
INARTICULATE
INCALCULABLE
INCAPACITATE
INCOMPARABLE
INCOMPATIBLE
INCOMPETENCE
INCONCLUSIVE
INCONSOLABLE
INCONTINENCE
INCORRIGIBLE
INDECLINABLE
INDEFENSIBLE
INDEPENDENCE
INDIFFERENCE
INDIGESTIBLE
INDISPUTABLE
INDISSOLUBLE
INDOCTRINATE
INERADICABLE
INEXACTITUDE
INEXPERIENCE
INEXPLICABLE
INEXTRICABLE
INFORMIDABLE
INHOSPITABLE
INNATTENTIVE
INSPECTORATE
INSUFFERABLE
INTELLIGENCE
INTELLIGIBLE
INTEMPERANCE
INTERFERENCE
INTERMEDIATE
INTERMINABLE
INTRANSITIVE
INTRAUTERINE
INVERTEBRATE
INVULNERABLE
IRREDEEMABLE
IRRESISTIBLE
IRRESOLVABLE
IRRESPECTIVE
IRREVERSIBLE
KALEIDOSCOPE
KLETTERSCHUE
LABYRINTHINE
LAMELLICORNE
LATIROSTRATE
LEPIDOMELANE
LINCOLNSHIRE
LONGDISTANCE
LUMINESCENCE
LUMINISCENCE
LUXULLIANITE
LYMANTRIIDAE
MACABERESQUE
MACMILLANITE
MACROPODIDAE
MADEMOISELLE
MAGNIFICENCE
MANIPULATIVE
MANOEUVRABLE
MARLINESPIKE
MARRIAGEABLE
MARSEILLAISE
MASTERSTROKE
MERVEILLEUSE
METALLOPHONE
METAMORPHOSE
MICROCLIMATE
MISADVENTURE
MISCALCULATE
MISPRONOUNCE
MITRAILLEUSE
MONOSYLLABLE
MOSBOLLETJIE
MOUSQUETAIRE
MYRINGOSCOPE
NEPENTHACEAE
NOCONFIDENCE
NOMENCLATURE
NONEXISTENCE
NONRESIDENCE
OBSERVANTINE
OBSOLESCENCE
OPINIONATIVE
OSCILLOSCOPE
OUTMANOEUVRE
OVERESTIMATE
OXYACETYLENE
PAPILIONIDAE
PASSEMEASURE
PERADVENTURE
PERMANGANATE
PERSEVERANCE
PHILOSOPHIZE
PHOSPHORENCE
PHOSPHORESCE
PHOTOGRAVURE
PHYTONADIONE
PINNIEWINKLE
PISCICULTURE
PLASTERSTONE
POINTILLISME
POLYETHYLENE
POLYSYLLABLE
POLYURETHANE
POSTGRADUATE
PRAXINOSCOPE
PREDESTINATE
PREDETERMINE
PREDOMINANCE
PREPONDERATE
PREREQUISITE
PRESCRIPTIVE
PRESERVATIVE
PREVENTATIVE
PROGESTERONE
PROGRAMMABLE
PROLETARIATE
PROTECTORATE
PROTUBERANCE
PTERIDOPHYTE
PTERODACTYLE
QUANTIFIABLE
QUANTITATIVE
QUESTIONABLE
QUINTESSENCE
RADIOISOTOPE
REAPPEARANCE
RECAPITULATE
RECHARGEABLE
RECOGNIZABLE
RECOGNIZANCE
RECONSTITUTE
RECUPERATIVE
REDINTEGRATE
REDISTRIBUTE
REHABILITATE
REINVIGORATE
REMINISCENCE
REMONSTRANCE
REMUNERATIVE
REPRODUCTIVE
RESIPISCENCE
ROOMINGHOUSE

SARRUSOPHONE
SAUROGNATHAE
SCHEHERAZADE
SCHIZOMYCETE
SECRETARIATE
SELFADHESIVE
SERASKIERATE
SIGNIFICANCE
SIPHONOSTELE
SKUTTERUDITE
SOMATOPLEURE
SOPHISTICATE
SPECTROSCOPE
SPERMATOCYTE
SPHAIRISTIKE
SPURTLEBLADE
STAKHANOVITE
STEEPLECHASE
STENTORPHONE
STOCKINGETTE
STRAIGHTEDGE
STRATOSPHERE
STRINGCOURSE
STROMATOLITE
SUBCOMMITTEE
SUBSERVIENCE
SUBSTANTIATE
SUBSTRUCTURE
SULPHONAMIDE
SUPERANNUATE
SURMOUNTABLE
SURVEILLANCE
SYNADELPHITE
SYNTAGMATITE
TAMARICACEAE
TAPSALTEERIE
TAPSLETEERIE
TELEGRAPHESE
TELEUTOSPORE
TERGIVERSATE
TESTOSTERONE
TETRACYCLINE
TETRAHEDRITE
THEOPHYLLINE
THOROUGHFARE
THREADNEEDLE
TRADESPEOPLE
TRANQUILLISE
TRANQUILLIZE
TRANSFERABLE
TRANSFERENCE
TRANSLATABLE
TRANSLUCENCE
TRANSMIGRATE
TRANSPONTINE
TRANSVESTITE
TROCHOSPHERE
ULTRAMONTANE
UNACCEPTABLE
UNANSWERABLE
UNATTAINABLE
UNATTRACTIVE
UNBELIEVABLE
UNCHANGEABLE
UNCHARITABLE
UNDERACHIEVE
UNDETECTABLE
UNFATHOMABLE
UNFAVOURABLE
UNIMAGINABLE
UNIMPORTANCE
UNMANAGEABLE
UNMISTAKABLE
UNOBTAINABLE
UNOPPRESSIVE
UNPARDONABLE
UNPRODUCTIVE
UNPROFITABLE
UNREASONABLE
UNRESPONSIVE
UNRETURNABLE
UNSEASONABLE
VEHMGERICHTE
VENEPUNCTURE
VIBRATIUNCLE
VITUPERATIVE
WALLYDRAIGLE
WHIGMALEERIE
WOLLASTONITE
WOLSTENHOLME
WOODBURYTYPE
HANDKERCHIEF
QUARTERSTAFF
WEATHERPROOF
ACCOMPANYING
AWARDWINNING
AWEINSPIRING
BACKBREAKING
BARNSTORMING
BIRDWATCHING
BLUESTOCKING
BOONDOGGLING
BRAINWASHING
BREATHTAKING
BROADCASTING
CARDINDEXING
CHEESEPARING
CHILDBEARING
COMPROMISING
CONVALESCING
CONVEYANCING
CRASHLANDING
DEBILITATING
DISAPPEARING
DISCOURAGING
DRINKDRIVING
EMBARRASSING
ENERGYSAVING
ENTERPRISING
ENTERTAINING
EXASPERATING
EXCRUCIATING
EXHILARATING
FIRSTFOOTING
FOOTSLOGGING
GALLIVANTING
HAIRDRESSING
HEARTWARMING
HIGHFALUTING
HOUSEKEEPING
HOUSEWARMING
ILLUMINATING
INGRATIATING
INTERPRETING
INTIMIDATING
INTOXICATING
INVIGORATING
LABOURSAVING
LONGSTANDING
MINDBOGGLING
MOISTURIZING
MOONLIGHTING
NEIGHBOURING
ORIENTEERING
OVERCROWDING
OVERDRESSING
OVERPOWERING
OVERWHELMING
PEACEKEEPING
PETTIFOGGING
POLICYMAKING
POWERSHARING
PRIZEWINNING
PROFITEERING
RACKETEERING
REPROCESSING
SELFCATERING
SHAREHOLDING
SHIPBUILDING
SLEEPWALKING
SMALLHOLDING
SNOWBOARDING
STEREOTYPING
THANKSGIVING
TIGHTFITTING
UMBRADARLING
UNAPPETIZING
UNCONVINCING
UNDERPINNING
UNPRETENDING
UNSATISFYING
UNSURPRISING
UNSUSPECTING
BANDERSNATCH
BLABBERMOUTH
BREAKTHROUGH
BREASTPLOUGH
BUTTERSCOTCH
COMMONWEALTH
COUNTERMARCH
ELASMOBRANCH
ENANTIOMORPH
GAINSBOROUGH
ISHMAELITISH
KERAUNOGRAPH
MARCONIGRAPH
OPISTHOGRAPH
PYTHONOMORPH
SCATTERMOUCH
SHOSTAKOVICH
STELLENBOSCH
THIRDBOROUGH
THUNDERFLASH
TROCHELMINTH
CARAVANSERAI
PLECTOGNATHI
STANISLAVSKI
GOBBLEDEGOOK
GOBBLEDYGOOK
KILLIKINNICK
SWIZZLESTICK
AERONAUTICAL
AGRICULTURAL
ALPHABETICAL
APFELSTRUDEL
ARITHMETICAL
ASTROLOGICAL
ASTRONOMICAL
ASYMMETRICAL
BICENTENNIAL
BIOGRAPHICAL
BRACHYCEPHAL
CATAPHYSICAL
COINCIDENTAL
CONFESSIONAL
CONFIDENTIAL
CONTRAPUNTAL
CONVENTIONAL
COURTMARTIAL
DEPARTMENTAL
DIFFERENTIAL
DISREPECTFUL
DORSIVENTRAL
DUNNIEWASSAL
EPIDEICTICAL
ETHNOLOGICAL
ETYMOLOGICAL
EULENSPIEGEL
EXPERIMENTAL
GENEALOGICAL
GEOGRAPHICAL
GLADIATORIAL
GLOCKENSPIEL
GOVERNMENTAL
HEROICOMICAL
HETEROSEXUAL
HIERARCHICAL
HYPERBOLICAL
HYPOCRITICAL
HYPOTHETICAL

INSTRUMENTAL
INTELLECTUAL
ISOBILATERAL
LONGITUDINAL
LOXODROMICAL
MANGELWURZEL
MATHEMATICAL
METAPHORICAL
METAPHYSICAL
MULTILATERAL
MYTHOLOGICAL
NEOCLASSICAL
NEUROLOGICAL
NONCOMMITTAL
OCCUPATIONAL
PATHOLOGICAL
PESTILENTIAL
PHILOLOGICAL
POPOCATEPETL
POSTPRANDIAL
PREFERENTIAL
PRESIDENTIAL
PROCESSIONAL
PROFESSIONAL
PROFESSORIAL
PROPORTIONAL
PROTOPLASMAL
PROVIDENTIAL
PUMPERNICKEL
QUARTERFINAL
QUINQUENNIAL
RECREATIONAL
RHINORRHOEAL
SOCIOLOGICAL
STILBOESTROL
SUPERNATURAL
TAUTOLOGICAL
TRANSITIONAL
UNECONOMICAL
UNSUCCESSFUL
WHIPPOORWILL
BEHAVIOURISM
BICAMERALISM
CALCEAMENTUM
CAMPODEIFORM
CONSERVATISM
COUNTERCLAIM
CRASSAMENTUM
DIVERTICULUM
DOLPHINARIUM
EPITHALAMIUM
ISOLATIONISM
METAMORPHISM
NEOPLATONISM
OPHIOGLOSSUM
ORNITHOGALUM
PALUDAMENTUM
PANDAEMONIUM
PARANTHELIUM
PERIOSTRACUM
PHILISTINISM
PLACENTIFORM
PLEIOCHASIUM
PRASEODYMIUM
PROGYMNASIUM
PROPAGANDISM
PROTACTINIUM
PROTHALAMIUM
SECTARIANISM
SOMNAMBULISM
SPIRITUALISM
SUPERNACULUM
THUNDERSTORM
TRANSVESTISM
UINTATHERIUM
VERUMONTANUM
ABBREVIATION
ACCELERATION
ACCENTUATION
ACCUMULATION
ADJUDICATION
ADULTERATION
AGATHODAIMON
AIRCRAFTSMAN
ALLITERATION
AMALGAMATION
AMBULANCEMAN
AMELIORATION
ANNIHILATION
ANNUNCIATION
ANTEDILUVIAN
ANTEMERIDIAN
ANTICIPATION
ANTISTROPHON
ANTITHROMBIN
APOLLINARIAN
APPRECIATION
APPREHENSION
ARCHILOCHIAN
ARISTOTELEAN
ARTICULATION
ARTILLERYMAN
ASPHYXIATION
ASSIMILATION
ASSUEFACTION
AUGMENTATION
AUSCULTATION
AUSTRALASIAN
AUSTRONESIAN
BACCHANALIAN
BACKWOODSMAN
BIELORUSSIAN
BLEFUSCUDIAN
BYELORUSSIAN
CALUMNIATION
CANCELLATION
CANONIZATION
CAPITULATION
CARLOVINGIAN
CARTHAGINIAN
CHLORINATION
CHURCHWARDEN
CIRCUMCISION
CIVILISATION
CIVILIZATION
CLAUDICATION
CODIFICATION
COHABITATION
COLLUCTATION
COLONIZATION
COMMENDATION
COMPELLATION
COMPENSATION
COMPLICATION
COMPURGATION
CONCILIATION
CONDEMNATION
CONDENSATION
CONFIRMATION
CONFISCATION
CONGREGATION
CONSCRIPTION
CONSECRATION
CONSERVATION
CONSTIPATION
CONSTITUTION
CONSTRICTION
CONSTRUCTION
CONSULTATION
CONSUMMATION
CONTIGNATION
CONTINUATION
CONTRIBUTION
CONVERSATION
COORDINATION
COSMOPOLITAN
CROSSSECTION
DEASPIRATION
DECAPITATION
DECELERATION
DEGENERATION
DELIBERATION
DELICATESSEN
DENOMINATION
DENUNCIATION
DEPOPULATION
DEPRECIATION
DEREGULATION
DESSERTSPOON
DIALECTICIAN
DIENCEPHALON
DILAPIDATION
DIPRIONIDIAN
DISPENSATION
DISQUISITION
DISSERTATION
DISSOCIATION
DISTILLATION
DISTRIBUTION
DRESSINGDOWN
EMANCIPATION
EMASCULATION
ENCHEIRIDION
ENGLISHWOMAN
ENGLISHWOMEN
ENTOPLASTRON
EPENCEPHALON
EPISCOPALIAN
EPITHALAMION
EQUIVOCATION
ERYTHROMYCIN
ETYMOLOGICON
EXACERBATION
EXAGGERATION
EXASPERATION
EXCRUCIATION
EXHILARATION
EXPLOITATION
EXSERVICEMAN
FEATHERBRAIN
FERMENTATION
FINALIZATION
FLAGELLATION
FLUORIDATION
FRANKALMOIGN
FRANKENSTEIN
FRONTIERSMAN
FRUMENTATION
FUSTILLIRIAN
GENETHLIACON
GEOMETRICIAN
GERIATRICIAN
GIBRALTARIAN
GONADOTROPIN
GRANDISONIAN
GRISEOFULVIN
GUILDENSTERN
HALLUCINOGEN
HAMBLETONIAN
HIPPOCREPIAN
HUMANITARIAN
HUMANIZATION
HYPERTENSION
IDEALIZATION
ILLUMINATION
ILLUSTRATION
IMMODERATION
IMMUNIZATION
IMPERFECTION
IMPLANTATION
IMPREGNATION
INAUGURATION
INCINERATION
INCRUSTATION
INDISCRETION
INESCUTCHEON
INFILTRATION
INFLAMMATION
INSEMINATION
INSTALLATION

INSTAURATION
INSURRECTION
INTENERATION
INTERCEPTION
INTERCESSION
INTERJECTION
INTERMISSION
INTERRUPTION
INTERSECTION
INTERVENTION
INTIMIDATION
INTOXICATION
INTRODUCTION
INVALIDATION
INVIGORATION
IRRESOLUTION
JURISDICTION
KINDERGARTEN
LABANOTATION
LANCASTERIAN
LANGUEDOCIAN
LEGALIZATION
LIQUEFACTION
LIVERPUDLIAN
LONGSHOREMAN
MALFORMATION
MALNUTRITION
MANIPULATION
MASTURBATION
MENSTRUATION
METROPOLITAN
MINISTRATION
MISQUOTATION
MOBILIZATION
MODIFICATION
MONTESSORIAN
MUGGLETONIAN
NEWSPAPERMAN
NONAGENARIAN
NORTHEASTERN
NORTHWESTERN
NOTIFICATION
NYCHTHEMERON
OBLITERATION
OBSTETRICIAN
OCTOGENARIAN
ORGANISATION
ORGANIZATION
OSSIFICATION
OVEREXERTION
PACIFICATION
PANATHENAEAN
PANPHARMACON
PANTECHNICON
PEDIATRICIAN
PENALIZATION
PERNOCTATION
PERPETRATION
PERSPIRATION
PERTURBATION
PETRIFACTION
PHILODENDRON
PHYCOXANTHIN
PIGMENTATION
POLARIZATION
POLYSYNDETON
PRECONDITION
PREDILECTION
PREGUSTATION
PREHISTORIAN
PRESBYTERIAN
PRESCRIPTION
PRESENTATION
PRESERVATION
PRESTRICTION
PROCLAMATION
PROLEGOMENON
PROLONGATION
PROMULGATION
PROPITIATION
PROSCRIPTION
PROSTITUTION
PROTESTATION
PROTHALAMION
PURIFICATION
PUTREFACTION
RAMIFICATION
RATIFICATION
RECOLLECTION
RECUPERATION
REGENERATION
REGISTRATION
REJUVENATION
REMUNERATION
RENUNCIATION
REPATRIATION
REPERCUSSION
REPOSSESSION
REPRODUCTION
RESURRECTION
RETICULATION
RHODODENDRON
SATISFACTION
SCANDINAVIAN
SCATTERBRAIN
SCHNEIDERIAN
SEGMENTATION
SERVICEWOMAN
SEXAGENARIAN
SOLICITATION
SOUTHCOTTIAN
SOUTHEASTERN
SOUTHWESTERN
SPHACELATION
SPIEGELEISEN
SPOKESPERSON
STATISTICIAN
STEREOPTICON
STERNUTATION
STREPITATION
STREPTOMYCIN
STRIDULATION
STUPEFACTION
SUBARRHATION
SUBHASTATION
SUBLAPSARIAN
SUBSCRIPTION
SUBSTITUTION
SUBTERRANEAN
SUCCUSSATION
SUPERSTITION
SUPPLICATION
TAGLIACOTIAN
TELEOSAURIAN
TETRODOTOXIN
THEORETICIAN
THESSALONIAN
TORRICELLIAN
TOTALITARIAN
TRANSMISSION
TRICHOPHYTON
TURACOVERDIN
UNDERWRITTEN
URBANIZATION
VAPORIZATION
VERIFICATION
VETERINARIAN
VILIFICATION
VITUPERATION
VOCIFERATION
WAREHOUSEMAN
WILTSHIREMAN
XANTHOPTERIN
YORKSHIREMAN
ANTANANARIVO
ANTINEUTRINO
AYUNTAMIENTO
CLAVICEMBALO
CONTRAPPOSTO
DIVERTIMENTO
LILLIBULLERO
LILLIBURLERO
MICHELANGELO
RISORGIMENTO
CHAIRMANSHIP
CHAMPIONSHIP
DICTATORSHIP
DIRECTORSHIP
GAMESMANSHIP
GUARDIANSHIP
HORSEMANSHIP
LAUREATESHIP
MARKSMANSHIP
PARTISANSHIP
RECEIVERSHIP
RELATIONSHIP
SALESMANSHIP
AMPHITHEATER
ANTIMACASSAR
BAIRNSFATHER
BANANALANDER
BARBERMONGER
BESSERWISSER
BOULEVARDIER
BREASTSUMMER
BREATHALYSER
BRICKFIELDER
BUCKLEBEGGAR
BUNKOSTEERER
CABINETMAKER
CARPETBAGGER
CARTOGRAPHER
CATHETOMETER
CHEESEBURGER
CHEESEMONGER
CHIROPRACTOR
COLDSHOULDER
COLLABORATOR
COMMISSIONER
CONFECTIONER
CONQUISTADOR
CONSOLIDATOR
COSTERMONGER
CROSSBENCHER
DEHUMIDIFIER
DEMONSTRATOR
DONNERWETTER
DOUBLEDECKER
EAVESDROPPER
ENTREPRENEUR
EXHIBITIONER
EXTINGUISHER
FREIGHTLINER
GALVANOMETER
GASTARBEITER
GASTROSOPHER
GENTLETAMPER
GLOBETROTTER
GRASSWIDOWER
HAIRSPLITTER
HALLANSHAKER
HARNESSMAKER
HEPHTHEMIMER
HOLIDAYMAKER
HOUSEBREAKER
HYDROGRAPHER
HYMNOGRAPHER
HYPOTHECATOR
IAMBOGRAPHER
IMPERSONATOR
INTERLOCUTOR
INTERROGATOR
INTERSTELLAR
INVESTIGATOR
JENNYSPINNER
KATZENJAMMER
KIRSCHWASSER
KLIPSPRINGER
LICKTRENCHER
LUXEMBOURGER

MANSLAUGHTER
MANUFACTURER
MARCOBRUNNER
MINICOMPUTER
MISBEHAVIOUR
MISDEMEANOUR
MOUTHBROODER
NEPHELOMETER
PERAMBULATOR
PHOTOGRAPHER
PITTERPATTER
PRACTICIONER
PRACTITIONER
PRALLTRILLER
PREVARICATOR
PRIZEFIGHTER
RADIOGRAPHER
RECORDPLAYER
REDEMPTIONER
REFRIGERATOR
REMEMBRANCER
RESTAURATEUR
RODOMONTADER
ROLLERBLADER
SCHILLERSPAR
SCHOOLMASTER
SCHOPENHAUER
SCINTILLATOR
SCREENWRITER
SCRIMSHANDER
SCRIMSHANKER
SCRIPTWRITER
SEMICIRCULAR
SEPTEMBRISER
SEQUESTRATOR
SHARPSHOOTER
SHIRTWAISTER
SINGLEDECKER
SLOCKDOLAGER
SLOCKDOLIGER
SLOCKDOLOGER
SPECKTIONEER
SPELLCHECKER
SPINECHILLER
STENOGRAPHER
STEPDAUGHTER
STERNWHEELER
STOCKBREEDER
STONECHATTER
STORMTROOPER
SUPERCHARGER
SWASHBUCKLER
TAPERECORDER
TEETERTOTTER
THREEQUARTER
TRANQUILIZER
TRANSGRESSOR
TROUBLEMAKER
TURBOCHARGER
UNDERSKINKER
WATERCARRIER
WEIGHTLIFTER
WICKETKEEPER
WINTERHALTER
YELLOWHAMMER
ACHLAMYDEOUS
ADSCITITIOUS
ADVANTAGEOUS
ADVANTAGIOUS
ADVENTITIOUS
AERODYNAMICS
AFTEREFFECTS
AGRIBUSINESS
AMBASSADRESS
AMBIDEXTROUS
AMPHISTOMOUS
ANAMORPHOSIS
ANECATHARSIS
ANEMOPHILOUS
ANTIBACCHIUS
ANTIBARBARUS
ANTONINIANUS
APPENDICITIS
ARCHIPELAGOS
ARISTOPHANES
ASTROPHYSICS
ATHEROMATOUS
ATMOSPHERICS
BACKWARDNESS
BAMBOCCIADES
BEAUMARCHAIS
BENEFACTRESS
BRONTOSAURUS
CALLISTHENES
CAMIKNICKERS
CANTANKEROUS
CARELESSNESS
CASSITERIDES
CAUTIOUSNESS
CHEERFULNESS
CHILDISHNESS
CHITTERLINGS
CHURLISHNESS
CLANNISHNESS
COLLYWOBBLES
COMBINATIONS
COMMANDMENTS
COMPLETENESS
CONSEQUENCES
CONSTITUENTS
CONTEMPTUOUS
CONTERMINOUS
CONTRARINESS
CONTUMACIOUS
CONVENIENCES
COVETOUSNESS
CREATIVENESS
CYMOTRICHOUS
DILATORINESS
DIPLOGENESIS
DISCOMYCETES
DISCOURTEOUS
DISEMBARRASS
DISINGENUOUS
DISTINCTNESS
ECCLESIASTES
ELECTROLYSIS
ELECTROTONUS
EMBROIDERESS
EPANORTHOSIS
EPISTOLATERS
ERATOSTHENES
FAITHFULNESS
FEARLESSNESS
FIDDLESTICKS
FORCEFULNESS
FRIENDLINESS
FRUITFULNESS
FULMINATIONS
FUNCTIONLESS
FUNDAMENTALS
GALLIGASKINS
GALLINACEOUS
GOOSEPIMPLES
GRACEFULNESS
GRACIOUSNESS
GRANDPARENTS
GRATEFULNESS
GREENGROCERS
HABERDASHERS
HAEMATEMESIS
HAEMORRHOIDS
HAIRDRESSERS
HAMARTHRITIS
HEADMISTRESS
HEADQUARTERS
HEARTSTRINGS
HELIOGABALUS
HELPLESSNESS
HERMENEUTICS
HINDQUARTERS
HIPPOPOTAMUS
HISTIOPHORUS
HOMESICKNESS
HOMOTHERMOUS
HOPELESSNESS
HUDIBRASTICS
IDIOTHERMOUS
IMPOLITENESS
INAUSPICIOUS
INDEBTEDNESS
INFELICITOUS
INHARMONIOUS
INNOMINABLES
INSALUBRIOUS
INSTRUCTIONS
INSTRUCTRESS
LAMENTATIONS
LEGIONNAIRES
LEIOTRICHOUS
LIFELESSNESS
LISTLESSNESS
LITHOLATROUS
MALLOPHAGOUS
MALPRACTICES
MERETRICIOUS
MERITRICIOUS
METAGNATHOUS
MINDFULLNESS
MUCILAGINOUS
MULTIFARIOUS
NEVERTHELESS
NIGHTCLOTHES
OBSOLETENESS
OBSTREPEROUS
ONCORHYNCHUS
OREOPITHECUS
OREOPITHEOUS
ORTHODONTICS
ORTHOGENESIS
ORTHOPAEDICS
ORTHOTONESIS
OSTENTATIOUS
OSTEOPOROSIS
OUTBUILDINGS
PAINLESSNESS
PALINGENESIS
PALPITATIONS
PANDANACEOUS
PANTOPHAGOUS
PARACENTESIS
PARSIMONIOUS
PEACEFULNESS
PERGAMENEOUS
PERICARDITIS
PERTINACIOUS
PERVERSENESS
PERVICACIOUS
PETTIFOGGERS
PHYTOBENTHOS
PLAINCLOTHES
POSTMISTRESS
PREPAREDNESS
PREPOSTEROUS
PRESUMPTUOUS
PRIGGISHNESS
PROPRIETRESS
PSEUDONYMOUS
PYROTECHNICS
RAMBUNCTIOUS
RECKLESSNESS
RESTLESSNESS
RETARDEDNESS
RHADAMANTHUS
ROLLERBLADES
RONCESVALLES
RUTHLESSNESS
SACRILEGIOUS
SALTATORIOUS
SARDANAPALUS

SCHINDYLESIS
SEMIPRECIOUS
SHEEPISHNESS
SHIRTSLEEVES
SHORTCOMINGS
SIDEWHISKERS
SIMULTANEOUS
SINANTHROPUS
SIVAPITHECUS
SLOVENLINESS
SNOBBISHNESS
SPACIOUSNESS
SPECIOUSNESS
SPITEFULNESS
SPURIOUSNESS
STEALTHINESS
STRADIVARIUS
STRAIGHTNESS
STRIGIFORMES
STROPHANTHUS
STUBBORNNESS
STUDIOUSNESS
SUBCONSCIOUS
SUBCUTANEOUS
SUPERCILIOUS
SURROUNDINGS
TACTLESSNESS
TERRITORIALS
THANKFULNESS
THAUMATURGUS
THERAPEUTICS
THOROUGHNESS
TIMELESSNESS
TITANOSAURUS
TOBACCONISTS
TOGETHERNESS
TRALATICIOUS
TRALATITIOUS
TRANSACTIONS
TROPHALLAXIS
TRUTHFULNESS
TUBERCULOSIS
ULOTRICHALES
UNCTUOUSNESS
UNDERCLOTHES
UNSCRUPULOUS
UNUTTERABLES
VAINGLORIOUS
VALENCIENNES
VENGEFULNESS
WATCHFULNESS
WRETCHEDNESS
YOUTHFULNESS
ABOLITIONIST
ACCORDIONIST
ACCOUCHEMENT
ACCOUTREMENT
ADMONISHMENT
AFORETHOUGHT
AFTERTHOUGHT

ANAESTHETIST
ANNOUNCEMENT
ASTONISHMENT
BACTERIOSTAT
BANTAMWEIGHT
BEWILDERMENT
BIBLIOPEGIST
BLACKCURRANT
BLANDISHMENT
CARDIOLOGIST
CARICATURIST
CARRIWITCHET
CHASTISEMENT
CHORIZONTIST
CLARINETTIST
COCCIDIOSTAT
COMMENCEMENT
COMMISSARIAT
CONTABESCENT
CONVALESCENT
COUNTERBLAST
COUNTERPOINT
DECIPHERMENT
DECONGESTANT
DENDROLOGIST
DISAGREEMENT
DISINFECTANT
DISPLACEMENT
DRAMATURGIST
EDUCATIONIST
EFFERVESCENT
EGYPTOLOGIST
EMBEZZLEMENT
ENCIRCLEMENT
ENCROACHMENT
ENTANGLEMENT
ENTEROPNEUST
ENTOMOLOGIST
ENTRENCHMENT
ESCAPOLOGIST
ESTRANGEMENT
EXTENSIONIST
FRAUENDIENST
GEOPHYSICIST
GESELLSCHAFT
GRAPHOLOGIST
GYMNOSOPHIST
GYNECOLOGIST
HEREDITAMENT
HERMENEUTIST
HIEROGRAMMAT
IMMUNOLOGIST
IMPRISONMENT
INCANDESCENT
INCONSEQUENT
INCONSISTENT
INCONVENIENT
INCUNABULIST
INFRINGEMENT
INSUFFICIENT

INTERMITTENT
INTRANSIGENT
ISOLATIONIST
MACHAIRODONT
MAGNILOQUENT
MALTREATMENT
MECHITHARIST
MERRYTHOUGHT
METALLURGIST
MIDDLEWEIGHT
MINERALOGIST
MISINTERPRET
MISPLACEMENT
MISREPRESENT
MISSTATEMENT
MISTREATMENT
MOTORCYCLIST
MUSICOLOGIST
MUTESSARIFAT
NONRESISTANT
NORTHERNMOST
NUTRITIONIST
ORTHOPAEDIST
PASSEPARTOUT
PASSIONFRUIT
PHLEBOTOMIST
PHYSIOLOGIST
POSTPONEMENT
POTAMOLOGIST
PREMONSTRANT
PREPONDERANT
PREPONDERENT
PRESENTIMENT
PROPAGANDIST
PSEPHOLOGIST
PSYCHIATRIST
PSYCHOLOGIST
PURPOSEBUILT
QUARTERLIGHT
READJUSTMENT
RECALCITRANT
RECEPTIONIST
RECRUDESCENT
REDEPLOYMENT
RENOUNCEMENT
RESETTLEMENT
RETRENCHMENT
SALVATIONIST
SECESSIONIST
SELFINTEREST
SELFPORTRAIT
SHORTCIRCUIT
SITTLICHKEIT
SOMNAMBULIST
SOUTHERNMOST
SPELEOLOGIST
SPIRITUALIST
STEGOPHOLIST
STRAITJACKET
SUBCONTINENT

TECHNOLOGIST
TELEGRAPHIST
THEREAGAINST
TOXICOLOGIST
TRANSCENDENT
TRICHOLOGIST
UNCONVERSANT
UNDERCURRENT
UNDERGARMENT
UNEMPLOYMENT
UNIVERSALIST
VENTRIPOTENT
WELTERWEIGHT
WILLIEWAUGHT
ZALAMBDODONT
ACADEMICALLY
ACCIDENTALLY
ADAPTABILITY
ADDITIONALLY
ADJECTIVALLY
ADVISABILITY
AGGRESSIVELY
ANTHROPOLOGY
ANTICIPATORY
APPENDECTOMY
AROMATHERAPY
ARTHROPLASTY
ARTIFICIALLY
ARTISTICALLY
ATTRACTIVELY
AUSPICIOUSLY
AUTHENTICITY
AVAILABILITY
BACTERIOLOGY
BELLIGERENCY
BENEVOLENTLY
BIBLIOGRAPHY
BIOCHEMISTRY
BIODIVERSITY
BLOODTHIRSTY
BOISTEROUSLY
BREATHLESSLY
CEREMONIALLY
CHEMOTHERAPY
CHOREOGRAPHY
CHRESTOMATHY
CHRISTIANITY
CLAIRVOYANCY
COLLECTIVELY
COLLOQUIALLY
COMMENDATORY
COMMERCIALLY
COMPANIONWAY
COMPENSATORY
COMPLACENTLY
CONCILIATORY
CONCLUSIVELY
CONCURRENTLY
CONDUCTIVITY
CONFIRMATORY

CONGENITALLY
CONSEQUENTLY
CONSERVATORY
CONSIDERABLY
CONSISTENTLY
CONSPECTUITY
CONSTABULARY
CONSTITUENCY
CONTEMPORARY
CONTINUOUSLY
CONTRIBUTORY
CONVENIENTLY
CONVINCINGLY
CONVIVIALITY
COSCINOMANCY
COURAGEOUSLY
CROSSCOUNTRY
CRYPTOGRAPHY
CURMUDGEONLY
DEAMBULATORY
DECORATIVELY
DEFLATIONARY
DELIBERATELY
DEMONSTRABLY
DEPRECIATORY
DESIRABILITY
DEUTEROSCOPY
DISASTROUSLY
DISCIPLINARY
DISDAINFULLY
DISHONORABLY
DOGMATICALLY
DRAMATICALLY
DYSTELEOLOGY
ECCENTRICITY
ECONOMICALLY
ECSTATICALLY
EFFORTLESSLY
ELECTRICALLY
ELEEMOSYNARY
EMPHATICALLY
ENANTIOPATHY
ENTREATINGLY
EPISTEMOLOGY
EQUIVOCATORY
ESSENTIALITY
ESTHETICALLY
EVENHANDEDLY
EVOLUTIONARY
EXCITABILITY
EXHAUSTIVELY
FASTIDIOUSLY
FIGURATIVELY
FLAMBOYANTLY
FORTUITOUSLY
FOTHERINGHAY
FRACTIONALLY
FUNCTIONALLY
GEOLOGICALLY
GERONTOCRACY

GIGANTOMACHY
GREENGROCERY
HABERDASHERY
HAPPYGOLUCKY
HARMONIOUSLY
HERMETICALLY
HISTORICALLY
HORIZONTALLY
HORRIFICALLY
HYDROTHERAPY
HYGIENICALLY
HYPNOTHERAPY
HYPNOTICALLY
HYSTERECTOMY
HYSTERICALLY
IDIOSYNCRASY
ILLEGIBILITY
ILLEGITIMACY
ILLOGICALITY
IMMACULATELY
IMMEASURABLY
IMMODERATELY
IMMUTABILITY
IMPARTIALITY
IMPERSONALLY
IMPRESSIVELY
INACCURATELY
INADEQUATELY
INCAPABILITY
INCAUTIOUSLY
INCIDENTALLY
INCOHERENTLY
INCOMPARABLY
INCOMPLETELY
INCORRIGIBLY
INCREASINGLY
INDEFINITELY
INDISPUTABLY
INDISTINCTLY
INDIVIDUALLY
INDUSTRIALLY
INEFFICIENCY
INEXPLICABLY
INEXTRICABLY
INFLAMMATORY
INFLATIONARY
INFREQUENTLY
INORDINATELY
INSOLUBILITY
INSUFFERABLY
INTERMEDIARY
INTERMINABLY
INTRODUCTORY
INVISIBILITY
IRASCIBILITY
IRRATIONALLY
IRREGULARITY
IRRESOLUTELY
IRREVERENTLY
IRRITABILITY

KALISTOCRACY
LAMPADEDROMY
LASCIVIOUSLY
LEGITIMATELY
LEXICOGRAPHY
LUGUBRIOUSLY
MAGNETICALLY
MAJESTICALLY
MALLEABILITY
MEANINGFULLY
MECHANICALLY
METHODICALLY
METICULOUSLY
MIRACULOUSLY
MONOTONOUSLY
MULLIGATAWNY
MULTIPLICITY
MUNICIPALITY
MYSTERIOUSLY
NAVIGABILITY
NEUROTICALLY
NONCHALANTLY
OBEDIENTIARY
OBSEQUIOUSLY
OCCASIONALLY
OCEANOGRAPHY
OPPRESSIVELY
OTHERWORLDLY
OUTRAGEOUSLY
PALEONTOLOGY
PANTISOCRACY
PARAMILITARY
PARTICULARLY
PASSIONATELY
PATHETICALLY
PECTORILOQUY
PEDANTICALLY
PENITENTIARY
PERCEPTIVELY
PERCEPTIVITY
PEREMPTORILY
PERIODICALLY
PERMEABILITY
PERSISTENTLY
PERSPICACITY
PERSUASIVELY
PETTIFOGGERY
PHARMACOLOGY
PHENOMENALLY
PHILANTHROPY
PHONETICALLY
PHRONTISTERY
PLAUSIBILITY
POSSESSIVELY
POSTHUMOUSLY
POSTLIMINARY
POTENTIALITY
PRACTICALITY
PRAISEWORTHY
PRECARIOUSLY

PRECOCIOUSLY
PREMAXILLARY
PRINCIPALITY
PROBATIONARY
PRODIGIOUSLY
PRODUCTIVITY
PROFICIENTLY
PROLIFICALLY
PROPITIATORY
PROPITIOUSLY
PROTECTIVELY
PROVERBIALLY
PUGNACIOUSLY
PURPOSEFULLY
QUIXOTICALLY
RADIOTHERAPY
RECIPROCALLY
REFLATIONARY
RELENTLESSLY
RESPECTFULLY
RESPECTIVELY
REVERSIONARY
RHYTHMICALLY
RHYTIDECTOMY
RIDICULOUSLY
ROMANTICALLY
SADISTICALLY
SARDONICALLY
SATISFACTORY
SCANDALOUSLY
SCAPULIMANCY
SCRUPULOUSLY
SCURRILOUSLY
SEMANTICALLY
SEQUENTIALLY
SHAMEFACEDLY
SHILLYSHALLY
SLUBBERINGLY
SOLICITOUSLY
SPECIFICALLY
SPIRITUALITY
SPLENOMEGALY
SPORADICALLY
STAGGERINGLY
STRAIGHTAWAY
STRUCTURALLY
SUBJECTIVELY
SUBJECTIVITY
SUBMISSIVELY
SUBSEQUENTLY
SUBSIDIARITY
SUCCESSFULLY
SUCCESSIVELY
SUFFICIENTLY
SUGGESTIVELY
SUPERCILIARY
SUPERHIGHWAY
SURPRISINGLY
SUSPICIOUSLY
SYMBOLICALLY

TECHNICALITY
TERCENTENARY
TERRIFICALLY
TESTAMENTARY
THEATRICALLY
THOUGHTFULLY
TRACTABILITY
TRANQUILLITY
TRANSMOGRIFY
TRANSPARENCY
TREMENDOUSLY
TRIGONOMETRY
TRIUMPHANTLY
UNBELIEVABLY
UNCHARITABLY
UNDESERVEDLY
UNEXPECTEDLY
UNILATERALLY
UNNEIGHBORLY
UNOFFICIALLY
UNPOPULARITY
UNRESERVEDLY
UPROARIOUSLY
USERFRIENDLY
VINDICTIVELY
VOCIFEROUSLY
VOLUPTUOUSLY
WHIMSICALITY

13:1

ACCEPTABILITY
ACCEPTILATION
ACCESSIBILITY
ACCOMMODATING
ACCOMMODATION
ACCOMPANIMENT
ACCOUTREMENTS
ACRYLONITRILE
ACUPUNCTURIST
ADMINISTRATOR
ADVENTUROUSLY
ADVERTISEMENT
AESTHETICALLY
AFFENPINSCHER
AFFIRMATIVELY
AFFORESTATION
AFFREIGHTMENT
AGGIORNAMENTO
AGGLOMERATION
AIRCRAFTWOMAN
AIRWORTHINESS
ALPHABETARIAN
ALTERNATIVELY
AMPHIGASTRIUM
AMPLIFICATION
ANACHRONISTIC
ANIMADVERSION
ANTHELMINTHIC
ANTICLOCKWISE
ANTICOAGULANT
ANTIGROPELOES
ANTIHISTAMINE
ANYTHINGARIAN
APOCATASTASIS
APPORTIONMENT
APPROPINQUATE
APPROPRIATION
APPROXIMATELY
APPROXIMATION
AQUIFOLIACEAE
ARCHAEOLOGIST
ARCHAEOPTERYX
ARCHIMANDRITE
ARCHITECTURAL
ARGUMENTATIVE
ARISTROCRATIC
ARITHMETICIAN
ARMOURPLATING
ARTIFICIALITY
ARUNDINACEOUS
ASCERTAINABLE
ASSASSINATION
ASTONISHINGLY
ATTENTIVENESS
AUTHORISATION
AUTHORITARIAN
AUTHORITATIVE
AUTHORIZATION
AUTOBIOGRAPHY
AUTOCEPHALOUS
AUTOMATICALLY
BACCALAUREATE
BEATIFICATION
BIBLIOGRAPHER
BIBLIOPHAGIST
BILDUNGSROMAN
BIODEGRADABLE
BIOTECHNOLOGY
BLANDISHMENTS
BLOODCURDLING
BOUGAINVILLEA
BOUILLABAISSE
BOUSTROPHEDON
BRACHIOSAURUS
BREASTFEEDING
BROKENHEARTED
BUNGEEJUMPING
BUSINESSWOMAN
BUTTERFINGERS
CALLISTHENICS
CARBONIFEROUS
CARTILAGINOUS
CATEGORICALLY
CAUTERIZATION
CEREMONIOUSLY
CERTIFICATION
CHANGEABILITY
CHARACTERISED
CHARACTERLESS
CHATEAUBRIAND
CHEESEMONGERS
CHINKERINCHEE
CHOREOGRAPHER
CHRISTMASTIME
CHRONOLOGICAL
CHRYSANTHEMUM
CIRCUMAMBIENT
CIRCUMFERENCE
CIRCUMSTANCES
CIRCUMVENTION
CLAIRAUDIENCE
CLARIFICATION
CLISHMACLAVER
CLOSEDCIRCUIT
COEDUCATIONAL
COLLABORATION
COLLABORATIVE
COLLIESHANGIE
COLLOQUIALISM
COMMEMORATION
COMMEMORATIVE
COMMENSURABLE
COMMERCIALIZE
COMMISERATION
COMMUNICATION
COMMUNICATIVE
COMPANIONABLE
COMPANIONSHIP
COMPARABILITY
COMPARATIVELY
COMPASSIONATE
COMPATIBILITY
COMPLEMENTARY
COMPLIMENTARY
COMPREHENSION
COMPREHENSIVE
COMRADEINARMS
CONCATENATION
CONCENTRATION
CONCEPTIONIST
CONCEPTUALIZE
CONCESSIONARY
CONCUPISCENCE
CONDESCENDING
CONDESCENSION
CONDITIONALLY
CONFARREATION
CONFECTIONERS
CONFECTIONERY
CONFEDERATION
CONFIGURATION
CONFLAGRATION
CONFRONTATION
CONGRESSIONAL
CONGRESSWOMAN
CONSANGUINITY
CONSCIENTIOUS
CONSCIOUSNESS
CONSECTANEOUS
CONSECUTIVELY
CONSEQUENTIAL
CONSERVATOIRE
CONSIDERATELY
CONSIDERATION
CONSOLIDATION
CONSPICUOUSLY
CONSPURCATION
CONSTELLATION
CONSTERNATION
CONTAMINATION
CONTEMPLATION
CONTEMPLATIVE
CONTENTEDNESS
CONTINUATIONS
CONTORTIONIST
CONTRABASSOON
CONTRACEPTION
CONTRACEPTIVE
CONTRADICTION
CONTRADICTORY
CONTRAFAGOTTO
CONTRAVENTION
CONTRIBUTIONS
CONTROVERSIAL
CONVALESCENCE
CONVERSAZIONE
CORRESPONDENT
CORRESPONDING
CORROBORATION
CORROBORATORY
COSTEFFECTIVE
COUNTERACTING
COUNTERATTACK
COUNTERCHARGE
COUNTERFEITER
COUNTRYPEOPLE
CRAFTSMANSHIP
CREDULOUSNESS
CRIMINOLOGIST
CROSSQUESTION
DAGUERREOTYPE
DEATHLESSNESS
DECAFFEINATED
DECOMPOSITION
DECOMPRESSION
DECONTAMINATE
DECRIMINALIZE
DEFENSIBILITY
DEFERVESCENCE
DEFIBRILLATOR
DEFORESTATION

DEIPNOSOPHIST
DEMILITARIZED
DEMONSTRATION
DEMONSTRATIVE
DENATIONALIZE
DEPENDABILITY
DERMATOLOGIST
DESEGREGATION
DÉSOBLIGEANTE
DETERIORATION
DETERMINATION
DEVELOPMENTAL
DIACATHOLICON
DIAMETRICALLY
DIFFARREATION
DIFFERENTIATE
DISADVANTAGED
DISAPPEARANCE
DISAPPOINTING
DISCOLORATION
DISCONCERTING
DISCONNECTION
DISCONTINUITY
DISCONTINUOUS
DISCREDITABLE
DISCREDITABLY
DISCRETIONARY
DISENGAGEMENT
DISESTIMATION
DISFIGUREMENT
DISGRACEFULLY
DISHEARTENING
DISHONOURABLE
DISHONOURABLY
DISILLUSIONED
DISINTERESTED
DISPARAGEMENT
DISPASSIONATE
DISPROPORTION
DISRESPECTFUL
DISSEMINATION
DISSIMILARITY
DISSIMULATION
DISTINGUISHED
DOCUMENTATION
DOUBLEGLAZING
DRAMATIZATION
DRYOPITHECINE
ECCENTRICALLY
EFFECTIVENESS
EFFERVESCENCE
EFFLORESCENCE
ELECTROCUTION
ELECTROMAGNET
ELECTROMOTIVE
ELEPHANTIASIS
EMBARRASSMENT
EMBELLISHMENT
ENCEPHALOCELE
ENCOURAGEMENT
ENCYCLOPAEDIA
ENCYCLOPAEDIC
ENERGETICALLY
ENLIGHTENMENT
ENTEROPNEUSTA
ENTERTAINMENT
ENTOMOLOGICAL
ENVIRONMENTAL
EPANADIPLOSIS
EPHEMEROPTERA
EPIPHENOMENON
EPITRACHELION
EQUIPONDERATE
ESCHSCHOLTZIA
ESTABLISHMENT
EXCEPTIONABLE
EXCEPTIONALLY
EXCOMMUNICATE
EXHIBITIONIST
EXPANSIVENESS
EXPEDITIONARY
EXPEDITIOUSLY
EXPOSTULATION
EXPROPRIATION
EXTERMINATION
EXTRAORDINARY
EXTRAPOLATION
EXTRAVAGANTLY
FACETIOUSNESS
FALSIFICATION
FANTASTICALLY
FEATHERWEIGHT
FERROCONCRETE
FERTILISATION
FERTILIZATION
FLABBERGASTED
FONTAINEBLEAU
FOREKNOWLEDGE
FORGETFULNESS
FORMALIZATION
FORTIFICATION
FORTUNETELLER
FOSSILIZATION
FOSTERPARENTS
FRACTIOUSNESS
FRAGMENTATION
FRANKALMOIGNE
FRIGHTENINGLY
FRIGHTFULNESS
FRIVOLOUSNESS
FUERTEVENTURA
FUNDAMENTALLY
GALVANIZATION
GARRULOUSNESS
GASTROCNEMIUS
GENERALISSIMO
GEOMETRICALLY
GESTICULATION
GLOBETROTTING
GLORIFICATION
GLOSSOGRAPHER
GLUMDALCLITCH
GOODRIGHTEOUS
GRAMMATICALLY
GRANDDAUGHTER
GRANDILOQUENT
GRANDPARENTAL
GRATIFICATION
GRAVITATIONAL
GRIEFSTRICKEN
GUILTLESSNESS
GYNAECOLOGIST
GYNANDROMORPH
GYNECOLOGICAL
HALLUCINATION
HALLUCINATORY
HAMMERKLAVIER
HAMMERTHROWER
HARMONIZATION
HEARTBREAKING
HEMISPHERICAL
HERMAPHRODITE
HETERAUXESISM
HETEROGENEOUS
HIEROGLYPHICS
HOMOSEXUALITY
HORRIPILATION
HORSEFEATHERS
HORTICULTURAL
HOUSEBREAKING
HUNDREDWEIGHT
HYBRIDIZATION
HYDRAULICALLY
HYDROELECTRIC
HYPERCRITICAL
HYPERSTHENITE
HYPOCHONDRIAC
IDIORRHYTHMIC
IDIOSYNCRATIC
IGNOMINIOUSLY
ILLUMINATIONS
IMAGINATIVELY
IMPERCEPTIBLE
IMPERCEPTIBLY
IMPERIALISTIC
IMPERSONATING
IMPERSONATION
IMPERTINENTLY
IMPERTURBABLE
IMPERTURBABLY
IMPONDERABLES
IMPOSSIBILITY
IMPRACTICABLE
IMPRESSIONISM
IMPRESSIONIST
IMPROBABILITY
IMPROVIDENTLY
IMPROVISATION
IMPULSIVENESS
INADVERTENTLY
INAPPROPRIATE
INCANDESCENCE
INCARCERATION
INCOMBUSTIBLE
INCOMMUNICADO
INCOMPETENTLY
INCONCEIVABLE
INCONSIDERATE
INCONSISTENCY
INCONSPICUOUS
INCONTESTABLE
INCONVENIENCE
INCORPORATION
INCORRUPTIBLE
INCREDULOUSLY
INCRIMINATING
INCRIMINATORY
INDEFATIGABLE
INDEFATIGABLY
INDEPENDENTLY
INDESCRIBABLE
INDESCRIBABLY
INDETERMINATE
INDIFFERENTLY
INDISPENSABLE
INDISPOSITION
INDIVIDUALISM
INDIVIDUALIST
INDIVIDUALITY
INDUSTRIALIST
INDUSTRIALIZE
INDUSTRIOUSLY
INEFFICIENTLY
INEVITABILITY
INEXHAUSTIBLE
INEXPERIENCED
INEXPRESSIBLE
INFALLIBILITY
INFINITESIMAL
INFLEXIBILITY
INFLORESCENCE
INGENUOUSNESS
INQUISITIVELY
INSECTIVOROUS
INSENSITIVITY
INSIDIOUSNESS
INSIGNIFICANT
INSPIRATIONAL
INSTANTANEOUS
INSTINCTIVELY
INSTITUTIONAL
INSTRUCTIONAL
INSUBORDINATE
INSUBSTANTIAL
INSUFFICIENCY
INSUPPORTABLE
INTELLIGENTLY
INTENTIONALLY
INTERCALATION
INTERESTINGLY

INTERMARRIAGE
INTERNATIONAL
INTERPERSONAL
INTERPOLATION
INTERROGATION
INTERROGATIVE
INTRANSIGENCE
INTRINSICALLY
INTROSPECTION
INTROSPECTIVE
INVENTIVENESS
INVESTIGATION
INVESTIGATIVE
INVINCIBILITY
INVIOLABILITY
INVOLUNTARILY
IRRECOVERABLE
IRREPLACEABLE
IRREPRESSIBLE
IRRESPONSIBLE
IRRESPONSIBLY
IRRETRIEVABLE
IRRETRIEVABLY
ISOGEOTHERMAL
JIGGERYPOKERY
JOLLIFICATION
JURISPRUDENCE
JUSTIFICATION
JUXTAPOSITION
KALEIDOSCOPIC
KANGCHENJUNGA
KAPPELMEISTER
KIDDERMINSTER
KNICKERBOCKER
KNICKKNACKERY
KNOWLEDGEABLE
LACKADAISICAL
LAEVOROTATORY
LAMPADEPHORIA
LEATHERJACKET
LECTISTERNIUM
LEISURELINESS
LEPIDOPTERIST
LEPTOCEPHALUS
LEXICOGRAPHER
LIBRARIANSHIP
LIEBFRAUMILCH
LIECHTENSTEIN
LIGHTFINGERED
LISSOTRICHOUS
LONGSUFFERING
LUXURIOUSNESS
LYCANTHROPIST
MACHIAVELLIAN
MACHICOLATION
MADETOMEASURE
MAGISTERIALLY
MAGNANIMOUSLY
MAGNIFICATION
MAGNIFICENTLY
MAGNILOQUENCE
MALADJUSTMENT
MALLEMAROKING
MANIFESTATION
MANUFACTURING
MASSACHUSETTS
MASTIGOPHORAN
MATERIALISTIC
MATHEMATICIAN
MATRICULATION
MAURIKIGUSARI
MECHANIZATION
MEDITERRANEAN
MEISTERSINGER
MERCHANDIZING
MERCILESSNESS
MESSERSCHMITT
METAGRABOLISE
METAGROBOLISE
METAMORPHOSIS
METAPHYSICIAN
METEOROLOGIST
MICROCOMPUTER
MICROORGANISM
MIDDLEBREAKER
MISANTHROPIST
MISCEGENATION
MISCELLANEOUS
MISCHIEVOUSLY
MISCONCEPTION
MISMANAGEMENT
MISUNDERSTAND
MISUNDERSTOOD
MOCKTECHNICAL
MODERNIZATION
MOLLIFICATION
MONOCOTYLEDON
MONONUCLEOSIS
MONOTHALAMOUS
MORPHOLOGICAL
MORTIFICATION
MOUTHWATERING
MULTICOLOURED
MULTINATIONAL
MULTINUCLEATE
MULTITUDINOUS
MYSTIFICATION
NATIONALISTIC
NEANDERTHALER
NEIGHBOURHOOD
NEMATHELMINTH
NERVELESSNESS
NIGHTWATCHMAN
NONCONFORMIST
NONCONFORMITY
NONRESISTANCE
NONSUFFICIENT
NORMALIZATION
NOSTALGICALLY
NULLIFICATION
OBJECTIONABLE
OBJECTIVENESS
OFFENSIVENESS
OFFICIOUSNESS
OPHTHALMOLOGY
OPPORTUNISTIC
OPPORTUNITIES
ORCHESTRATION
ORNAMENTATION
ORNITHOLOGIST
OUTRECUIDANCE
OUTSTANDINGLY
OVEREMPHASIZE
OVERSTATEMENT
OWNEROCCUPIER
OYSTERCATCHER
PAEDIATRICIAN
PAINSTAKINGLY
PALAEONTOLOGY
PANDICULATION
PANHARMONICON
PAPAPRELATIST
PARADOXICALLY
PARALLELOGRAM
PARANTHROPOUS
PARAPHERNALIA
PARENTHETICAL
PARLIAMENTARY
PARTHOGENESIS
PARTICIPATION
PARTICIPATORY
PARTICOLOURED
PARTICULARISE
PARTICULARITY
PARTICULARIZE
PASSCHENDAELE
PASSEMENTERIE
PASSIONFLOWER
PATERFAMILIAS
PATERNALISTIC
PATRIOTICALLY
PELOPONNESIAN
PENETRABILITY
PERAMBULATION
PEREGRINATION
PERFECTIONIST
PERFUNCTORILY
PERPENDICULAR
PERSONALITIES
PERSPICACIOUS
PERVASIVENESS
PETRIFICATION
PETROCHEMICAL
PHARMACOPOEIA
PHILADELPHIAN
PHILANTHROPIC
PHILOSOPHICAL
PHOTOCHEMICAL
PHOTOELECTRIC
PHYSHARMONICA
PHYSIOGNOMIST
PHYSIOLOGICAL
PHYSIOTHERAPY
PLATOCEPHALUS
PNEUMATICALLY
POLIOMYELITIS
POLLICITATION
POTENTIOMETER
PRAGMATICALLY
PRECAUTIONARY
PRECIPITATELY
PRECIPITATION
PRECONCEPTION
PREDOMINANTLY
PREFABRICATED
PRELIMINARIES
PREMEDITATION
PREOCCUPATION
PREPONDERANCE
PREPOSSESSING
PREPOSSESSION
PREPROGRAMMED
PRESERVATIVES
PRESSURELOCAL
PRETERNATURAL
PREVARICATION
PRIMOGENITURE
PRIVATIZATION
PROBLEMATICAL
PROCLEUSMATIC
PROCRASTINATE
PROFECTITIOUS
PROFESSORSHIP
PROFITABILITY
PROGNOSTICATE
PROGRESSIVELY
PROJECTIONIST
PROLIFERATION
PROMISCUOUSLY
PRONOUNCEMENT
PRONUNCIATION
PROPHETICALLY
PROPORTIONATE
PROPRIETORIAL
PROSOPOGRAPHY
PROTECTIONISM
PROTECTIONIST
PROTESTANTISM
PROTONOTARIAT
PROVINCIALISM
PROVISIONALLY
PROVOCATIVELY
PSYCHOANALYSE
PSYCHOANALYST
PSYCHOLOGICAL
PSYCHOSOMATIC
PSYCHOTHERAPY
PULVERIZATION
PUNCTILIOUSLY
PUSILLANIMITY

PUSILLANIMOUS
PYROTECHNICAL
QUADRAGESIMAL
QUADRILATERAL
QUADRUPLICATE
QUALIFICATION
QUARTERMASTER
QUARTODECIMAN
QUERULOUSNESS
QUESTIONNAIRE
QUINQUAGESIMA
RADIOACTIVITY
RAMIFICATIONS
RAPPROCHEMENT
RATIONALALITY
REALISTICALLY
REARRANGEMENT
RECALCITRANCE
RECEPTIVENESS
RECITATIONIST
RECRIMINATION
RECRIMINATORY
RECRUDESCENCE
RECTIFICATION
REDEMPTIONIST
REDEVELOPMENT
REFRIGERATION
REFRIGERATORS
REFURBISHMENT
REGIMENTATION
REGURGITATION
REIMBURSEMENT
REINCARNATION
REINFORCEMENT
REINSTATEMENT
REMINISCENCES
REMORSELESSLY
RENSSELAERITE
REPERCUSSIONS
REPLENISHMENT
REPREHENSIBLE
REPREHENSIBLY
REPROACHFULLY
REPROGRAPHICS
REPUBLICANISM
RESOURCEFULLY
RESUSCITATION
RETROGRESSION
RETROSPECTIVE
REUNIFICATION
REVERBERATION
REVOLUTIONARY
REVOLUTIONIZE
RHADAMANTHINE
RHYPAROGRAPHY
RIGHTEOUSNESS
ROLLERBLADING
ROLLERCOASTER
ROUNDTHEWORLD
RUTHERFORDIUM

SACCHAROMYCES
SALACIOUSNESS
SANCTIMONIOUS
SARCASTICALLY
SCANDALMONGER
SCHADENFREUDE
SCHEMATICALLY
SCHIZOPHRENIA
SCHIZOPHRENIC
SCHOLARLINESS
SCHOOLTEACHER
SCHUTZSTAFFEL
SCINTILLATING
SCINTILLATION
SECRETIVENESS
SEDIMENTATION
SEISMOLOGICAL
SELFADDRESSED
SELFCONFESSED
SELFCONFIDENT
SELFCONSCIOUS
SELFCONTAINED
SELFGOVERNING
SEMBLANCECORD
SEMICONDUCTOR
SENSATIONALLY
SENSELESSNESS
SENSITIVENESS
SENTENTIOUSLY
SENTIMENTALLY
SEPTENTRIONES
SEQUESTRATION
SERVILEMENTAL
SHAPELESSNESS
SHOULDERBLADE
SHRINKWRAPPED
SIGNIFICANTLY
SIGNIFICATION
SIPUNCULOIDEA
SLEEPLESSNESS
SNOWBLINDNESS
SOCIOECONOMIC
SOLEMNIZATION
SOMATOTROPHIN
SOPHISTICATED
SOUTHEASTERLY
SOUTHWESTERLY
SPASMODICALLY
SPECIFICATION
SPECTACULARLY
SPECTROGRAPHY
SPELEOLOGICAL
SPINDLESHANKS
SPINECHILLING
SPITESPLENDID
SPONTANEOUSLY
SPORTSMANLIKE
SPORTSMANSHIP
SPRIGHTLINESS
SQUEAMISHNESS

STABILIZATION
STAPHYLINIDAE
STATESMANLIKE
STATESMANSHIP
STATIONMASTER
STATISTICALLY
STEADFASTNESS
STEEPLECHASER
STEPPINGSTONE
STERCORACEOUS
STERILIZATION
STOCKBREEDING
STRANGULATION
STRATEGICALLY
STRENUOUSNESS
STREPTOCOCCUS
STRIKEBREAKER
STYLISTICALLY
SUBCONTRACTOR
SUBJECTMATTER
SUBLIEUTENANT
SUBORDINATION
SUBSERVIENTLY
SUBSTANTIALLY
SUOVETAURILIA
SUPERABUNDANT
SUPERANNUATED
SUPERFICIALLY
SUPERFLUOUSLY
SUPERLATIVELY
SUPERNUMERARY
SUPERORDINATE
SUPERSTITIOUS
SUPPLEMENTARY
SUPRANATIONAL
SURREPTITIOUS
SUSPERCOLLATE
SWASHBUCKLING
SWEDENBORGIAN
SWEETSMELLING
SWOLLENHEADED
SYMPIESOMETER
SYNTACTICALLY
SYNTHETICALLY
TABLESPOONFUL
TALKATIVENESS
TANTALIZINGLY
TAPERECORDING
TECHNOLOGICAL
TEMPERAMENTAL
TENDERHEARTED
TETRASYLLABIC
THANKLESSNESS
THAUMATURGICS
THAUMATURGIST
THEATRICALITY
THEOLOGICALLY
THEORETICALLY
THERMONUCLEAR
THERMOPLASTIC

THOROUGHBRACE
THOROUGHGOING
THOUGHTLESSLY
THREATENINGLY
THUNDERSTRUCK
THYROIDECTOMY
TINTINNABULUM
TONGUEINCHEEK
TONGUETWISTER
TONSILLECTOMY
TOPOGRAPHICAL
TORTOISESHELL
TRACTARIANISM
TRADITIONALLY
TRANQUILLISER
TRANQUILLIZER
TRANSATLANTIC
TRANSCRIPTION
TRANSGRESSION
TRANSISTORIZE
TRANSLITERATE
TRANSMUTATION
TRANSPARENTLY
TRANSPIRATION
TRANSPORTABLE
TRANSPOSITION
TRAUMATICALLY
TREACHEROUSLY
TRIANGULATION
TRICHOSANTHIN
TYPOGRAPHICAL
UMBELLIFEROUS
UNACCOMPANIED
UNACCOUNTABLE
UNACCOUNTABLY
UNADULTERATED
UNANTICIPATED
UNCEREMONIOUS
UNCOMFORTABLE
UNCOMFORTABLY
UNCOMMUNICATE
UNCOMPLICATED
UNCONDITIONAL
UNCONQUERABLE
UNCONSCIOUSLY
UNCOOPERATIVE
UNCOORDINATED
UNDERACHIEVER
UNDERCARRIAGE
UNDERCLOTHING
UNDERESTIMATE
UNDERGRADUATE
UNDERSTANDING
UNDERSTRAPPER
UNDISCIPLINED
UNEMBARRASSED
UNENLIGHTENED
UNESTABLISHED
UNEXCEPTIONAL
UNEXPERIENCED

UNFASHIONABLE
UNFLINCHINGLY
UNFORESEEABLE
UNFORGETTABLE
UNFORTUNATELY
UNGENTLEMANLY
UNGRAMMATICAL
UNIMAGINATIVE
UNIMPEACHABLE
UNIMPRESSIBLE
UNINHABITABLE
UNINTELLIGENT
UNINTENTIONAL
UNINTERESTING
UNINTERRUPTED
UNMENTIONABLE
UNNECESSARILY
UNPARTITIONED
UNPRECEDENTED
UNPREDICTABLE
UNPRETENTIOUS
UNPROGRESSIVE
UNQUESTIONING
UNSERVICEABLE
UNSUBSTANTIAL
UNSYMMETRICAL
UNSYMPATHETIC
UNTRUSTWORTHY
UNWILLINGNESS
UPTOTHEMINUTE
VEGETARIANISM
VENTRILOQUISM
VENTRILOQUIST
VERCINGETORIX
VERSIFICATION
VICEPRESIDENT
VICTIMIZATION
VIDEOCASSETTE
VIDEORECORDER
VITRIFICATION
VIVACIOUSNESS
VORACIOUSNESS
VULCANIZATION
VULGARIZATION
VULNERABILITY
WEATHERBEATEN
WEIGHTLIFTING
WHOLESOMENESS
WITWATERSRAND
XIPHIPLASTRON

13:2

BACCALAUREATE
CALLISTHENICS
CARBONIFEROUS
CARTILAGINOUS
CATEGORICALLY
CAUTERIZATION
DAGUERREOTYPE
FACETIOUSNESS
FALSIFICATION
FANTASTICALLY
GALVANIZATION
GARRULOUSNESS
GASTROCNEMIUS
HALLUCINATION
HALLUCINATORY
HAMMERKLAVIER
HAMMERTHROWER
HARMONIZATION
KALEIDOSCOPIC
KANGCHENJUNGA
KAPPELMEISTER
LACKADAISICAL
LAEVOROTATORY
LAMPADEPHORIA
MACHIAVELLIAN
MACHICOLATION
MADETOMEASURE
MAGISTERIALLY
MAGNANIMOUSLY
MAGNIFICATION
MAGNIFICENTLY
MAGNILOQUENCE
MALADJUSTMENT
MALLEMAROKING
MANIFESTATION
MANUFACTURING
MASSACHUSETTS
MASTIGOPHORAN
MATERIALISTIC
MATHEMATICIAN
MATRICULATION
MAURIKIGUSARI
NATIONALISTIC
PAEDIATRICIAN
PAINSTAKINGLY
PALAEONTOLOGY
PANDICULATION
PANHARMONICON
PAPAPRELATIST
PARADOXICALLY
PARALLELOGRAM
PARANTHROPOUS
PARAPHERNALIA
PARENTHETICAL
PARLIAMENTARY
PARTHOGENESIS
PARTICIPATION
PARTICIPATORY
PARTICOLOURED
PARTICULARISE
PARTICULARITY
PARTICULARIZE
PASSCHENDAELE
PASSEMENTERIE
PASSIONFLOWER
PATERFAMILIAS
PATERNALISTIC
PATRIOTICALLY
RADIOACTIVITY
RAMIFICATIONS
RAPPROCHEMENT
RATIONALALITY
SACCHAROMYCES
SALACIOUSNESS
SANCTIMONIOUS
SARCASTICALLY
TABLESPOONFUL
TALKATIVENESS
TANTALIZINGLY
TAPERECORDING
OBJECTIONABLE
OBJECTIVENESS
ACCEPTABILITY
ACCEPTILATION
ACCESSIBILITY
ACCOMMODATING
ACCOMMODATION
ACCOMPANIMENT
ACCOUTREMENTS
ACRYLONITRILE
ACUPUNCTURIST
ECCENTRICALLY
SCANDALMONGER
SCHADENFREUDE
SCHEMATICALLY
SCHIZOPHRENIA
SCHIZOPHRENIC
SCHOLARLINESS
SCHOOLTEACHER
SCHUTZSTAFFEL
SCINTILLATING
SCINTILLATION
ADMINISTRATOR
ADVENTUROUSLY
ADVERTISEMENT
IDIORRHYTHMIC
IDIOSYNCRATIC
AESTHETICALLY
BEATIFICATION
CEREMONIOUSLY
CERTIFICATION
DEATHLESSNESS
DECAFFEINATED
DECOMPOSITION
DECOMPRESSION
DECONTAMINATE
DECRIMINALIZE
DEFENSIBILITY
DEFERVESCENCE
DEFIBRILLATOR
DEFORESTATION
DEIPNOSOPHIST
DEMILITARIZED
DEMONSTRATION
DEMONSTRATIVE
DENATIONALIZE
DEPENDABILITY
DERMATOLOGIST
DESEGREGATION
DETERIORATION
DETERMINATION
DEVELOPMENTAL
FEATHERWEIGHT
FERROCONCRETE
FERTILISATION
FERTILIZATION
GENERALISSIMO
GEOMETRICALLY
GESTICULATION
HEARTBREAKING
HEMISPHERICAL
HERMAPHRODITE
HETERAUXESISM
HETEROGENEOUS
LEATHERJACKET
LECTISTERNIUM
LEISURELINESS
LEPIDOPTERIST
LEPTOCEPHALUS
LEXICOGRAPHER
MECHANIZATION
MEDITERRANEAN
MEISTERSINGER
MERCHANDIZING
MERCILESSNESS
MESSERSCHMITT
METAGRABOLISE
METAGROBOLISE
METAMORPHOSIS
METAPHYSICIAN
METEOROLOGIST
NEANDERTHALER
NEIGHBOURHOOD
NEMATHELMINTH
NERVELESSNESS
PELOPONNESIAN
PENETRABILITY
PERAMBULATION
PEREGRINATION
PERFECTIONIST
PERFUNCTORILY
PERPENDICULAR
PERSONALITIES
PERSPICACIOUS
PERVASIVENESS
PETRIFICATION
PETROCHEMICAL
REALISTICALLY
REARRANGEMENT
RECALCITRANCE
RECEPTIVENESS
RECITATIONIST
RECRIMINATION
RECRIMINATORY
RECRUDESCENCE
RECTIFICATION

REDEMPTIONIST
REDEVELOPMENT
REFRIGERATION
REFRIGERATORS
REFURBISHMENT
REGIMENTATION
REGURGITATION
REIMBURSEMENT
REINCARNATION
REINFORCEMENT
REINSTATEMENT
REMINISCENCES
REMORSELESSLY
RENSSELAERITE
REPERCUSSIONS
REPLENISHMENT
REPREHENSIBLE
REPREHENSIBLY
REPROACHFULLY
REPROGRAPHICS
REPUBLICANISM
RESOURCEFULLY
RESUSCITATION
RETROGRESSION
RETROSPECTIVE
REUNIFICATION
REVERBERATION
REVOLUTIONARY
REVOLUTIONIZE
SECRETIVENESS
SEDIMENTATION
SEISMOLOGICAL
SELFADDRESSED
SELFCONFESSED
SELFCONFIDENT
SELFCONSCIOUS
SELFCONTAINED
SELFGOVERNING
SEMBLANCECORD
SEMICONDUCTOR
SENSATIONALLY
SENSELESSNESS
SENSITIVENESS
SENTENTIOUSLY
SENTIMENTALLY
SEPTENTRIONES
SEQUESTRATION
SERVILEMENTAL
TECHNOLOGICAL
TEMPERAMENTAL
TENDERHEARTED
TETRASYLLABIC
VEGETARIANISM
VENTRILOQUISM
VENTRILOQUIST
VERCINGETORIX
VERSIFICATION
WEATHERBEATEN
WEIGHTLIFTING
DÉSOBLIGEANTE
AFFENPINSCHER
AFFIRMATIVELY
AFFORESTATION
AFFREIGHTMENT
EFFECTIVENESS
EFFERVESCENCE
EFFLORESCENCE
OFFENSIVENESS
OFFICIOUSNESS
AGGIORNAMENTO
AGGLOMERATION
IGNOMINIOUSLY
CHANGEABILITY
CHARACTERISED
CHARACTERLESS
CHATEAUBRIAND
CHEESEMONGERS
CHINKERINCHEE
CHOREOGRAPHER
CHRISTMASTIME
CHRONOLOGICAL
CHRYSANTHEMUM
PHARMACOPOEIA
PHILADELPHIAN
PHILANTHROPIC
PHILOSOPHICAL
PHOTOCHEMICAL
PHOTOELECTRIC
PHYSHARMONICA
PHYSIOGNOMIST
PHYSIOLOGICAL
PHYSIOTHERAPY
RHADAMANTHINE
RHYPAROGRAPHY
SHAPELESSNESS
SHOULDERBLADE
SHRINKWRAPPED
THANKLESSNESS
THAUMATURGICS
THAUMATURGIST
THEATRICALITY
THEOLOGICALLY
THEORETICALLY
THERMONUCLEAR
THERMOPLASTIC
THOROUGHBRACE
THOROUGHGOING
THOUGHTLESSLY
THREATENINGLY
THUNDERSTRUCK
THYROIDECTOMY
WHOLESOMENESS
AIRCRAFTWOMAN
AIRWORTHINESS
BIBLIOGRAPHER
BIBLIOPHAGIST
BILDUNGSROMAN
BIODEGRADABLE
BIOTECHNOLOGY
CIRCUMAMBIENT
CIRCUMFERENCE
CIRCUMSTANCES
CIRCUMVENTION
DIACATHOLICON
DIAMETRICALLY
DIFFARREATION
DIFFERENTIATE
DISADVANTAGED
DISAPPEARANCE
DISAPPOINTING
DISCOLORATION
DISCONCERTING
DISCONNECTION
DISCONTINUITY
DISCONTINUOUS
DISCREDITABLE
DISCREDITABLY
DISCRETIONARY
DISENGAGEMENT
DISESTIMATION
DISFIGUREMENT
DISGRACEFULLY
DISHEARTENING
DISHONOURABLE
DISHONOURABLY
DISILLUSIONED
DISINTERESTED
DISPARAGEMENT
DISPASSIONATE
DISPROPORTION
DISRESPECTFUL
DISSEMINATION
DISSIMILARITY
DISSIMULATION
DISTINGUISHED
HIEROGLYPHICS
JIGGERYPOKERY
KIDDERMINSTER
LIBRARIANSHIP
LIEBFRAUMILCH
LIECHTENSTEIN
LIGHTFINGERED
LISSOTRICHOUS
MICROCOMPUTER
MICROORGANISM
MIDDLEBREAKER
MISANTHROPIST
MISCEGENATION
MISCELLANEOUS
MISCHIEVOUSLY
MISCONCEPTION
MISMANAGEMENT
MISUNDERSTAND
MISUNDERSTOOD
NIGHTWATCHMAN
RIGHTEOUSNESS
SIGNIFICANTLY
SIGNIFICATION
SIPUNCULOIDEA
TINTINNABULUM
VICEPRESIDENT
VICTIMIZATION
VIDEOCASSETTE
VIDEORECORDER
VITRIFICATION
VIVACIOUSNESS
WITWATERSRAND
XIPHIPLASTRON
ALPHABETARIAN
ALTERNATIVELY
BLANDISHMENTS
BLOODCURDLING
CLAIRAUDIENCE
CLARIFICATION
CLISHMACLAVER
CLOSEDCIRCUIT
ELECTROCUTION
ELECTROMAGNET
ELECTROMOTIVE
ELEPHANTIASIS
FLABBERGASTED
GLOBETROTTING
GLORIFICATION
GLOSSOGRAPHER
GLUMDALCLITCH
ILLUMINATIONS
PLATOCEPHALUS
SLEEPLESSNESS
AMPHIGASTRIUM
AMPLIFICATION
EMBARRASSMENT
EMBELLISHMENT
IMAGINATIVELY
IMPERCEPTIBLE
IMPERCEPTIBLY
IMPERIALISTIC
IMPERSONATING
IMPERSONATION
IMPERTINENTLY
IMPERTURBABLE
IMPERTURBABLY
IMPONDERABLES
IMPOSSIBILITY
IMPRACTICABLE
IMPRESSIONISM
IMPRESSIONIST
IMPROBABILITY
IMPROVIDENTLY
IMPROVISATION
IMPULSIVENESS
UMBELLIFEROUS
ANACHRONISTIC
ANIMADVERSION
ANTHELMINTHIC
ANTICLOCKWISE
ANTICOAGULANT
ANTIGROPELOES
ANTIHISTAMINE
ANYTHINGARIAN
ENCEPHALOCELE

ENCOURAGEMENT
ENCYCLOPAEDIA
ENCYCLOPAEDIC
ENERGETICALLY
ENLIGHTENMENT
ENTEROPNEUSTA
ENTERTAINMENT
ENTOMOLOGICAL
ENVIRONMENTAL
INADVERTENTLY
INAPPROPRIATE
INCANDESCENCE
INCARCERATION
INCOMBUSTIBLE
INCOMMUNICADO
INCOMPETENTLY
INCONCEIVABLE
INCONSIDERATE
INCONSISTENCY
INCONSPICUOUS
INCONTESTABLE
INCONVENIENCE
INCORPORATION
INCORRUPTIBLE
INCREDULOUSLY
INCRIMINATING
INCRIMINATORY
INDEFATIGABLE
INDEFATIGABLY
INDEPENDENTLY
INDESCRIBABLE
INDESCRIBABLY
INDETERMINATE
INDIFFERENTLY
INDISPENSABLE
INDISPOSITION
INDIVIDUALISM
INDIVIDUALIST
INDIVIDUALITY
INDUSTRIALIST
INDUSTRIALIZE
INDUSTRIOUSLY
INEFFICIENTLY
INEVITABILITY
INEXHAUSTIBLE
INEXPERIENCED
INEXPRESSIBLE
INFALLIBILITY
INFINITESIMAL
INFLEXIBILITY
INFLORESCENCE
INGENUOUSNESS
INQUISITIVELY
INSECTIVOROUS
INSENSITIVITY
INSIDIOUSNESS
INSIGNIFICANT
INSPIRATIONAL
INSTANTANEOUS
INSTINCTIVELY
INSTITUTIONAL
INSTRUCTIONAL
INSUBORDINATE
INSUBSTANTIAL
INSUFFICIENCY
INSUPPORTABLE
INTELLIGENTLY
INTENTIONALLY
INTERCALATION
INTERESTINGLY
INTERMARRIAGE
INTERNATIONAL
INTERPERSONAL
INTERPOLATION
INTERROGATION
INTERROGATIVE
INTRANSIGENCE
INTRINSICALLY
INTROSPECTION
INTROSPECTIVE
INVENTIVENESS
INVESTIGATION
INVESTIGATIVE
INVINCIBILITY
INVIOLABILITY
INVOLUNTARILY
KNICKERBOCKER
KNICKKNACKERY
KNOWLEDGEABLE
PNEUMATICALLY
SNOWBLINDNESS
UNACCOMPANIED
UNACCOUNTABLE
UNACCOUNTABLY
UNADULTERATED
UNANTICIPATED
UNCEREMONIOUS
UNCOMFORTABLE
UNCOMFORTABLY
UNCOMMUNICATE
UNCOMPLICATED
UNCONDITIONAL
UNCONQUERABLE
UNCONSCIOUSLY
UNCOOPERATIVE
UNCOORDINATED
UNDERACHIEVER
UNDERCARRIAGE
UNDERCLOTHING
UNDERESTIMATE
UNDERGRADUATE
UNDERSTANDING
UNDERSTRAPPER
UNDISCIPLINED
UNEMBARRASSED
UNENLIGHTENED
UNESTABLISHED
UNEXCEPTIONAL
UNEXPERIENCED
UNFASHIONABLE
UNFLINCHINGLY
UNFORESEEABLE
UNFORGETTABLE
UNFORTUNATELY
UNGENTLEMANLY
UNGRAMMATICAL
UNIMAGINATIVE
UNIMPEACHABLE
UNIMPRESSIBLE
UNINHABITABLE
UNINTELLIGENT
UNINTENTIONAL
UNINTERESTING
UNINTERRUPTED
UNMENTIONABLE
UNNECESSARILY
UNPARTITIONED
UNPRECEDENTED
UNPREDICTABLE
UNPRETENTIOUS
UNPROGRESSIVE
UNQUESTIONING
UNSERVICEABLE
UNSUBSTANTIAL
UNSYMMETRICAL
UNSYMPATHETIC
UNTRUSTWORTHY
UNWILLINGNESS
BOUGAINVILLEA
BOUILLABAISSE
BOUSTROPHEDON
COEDUCATIONAL
COLLABORATION
COLLABORATIVE
COLLIESHANGIE
COLLOQUIALISM
COMMEMORATION
COMMEMORATIVE
COMMENSURABLE
COMMERCIALIZE
COMMISERATION
COMMUNICATION
COMMUNICATIVE
COMPANIONABLE
COMPANIONSHIP
COMPARABILITY
COMPARATIVELY
COMPASSIONATE
COMPATIBILITY
COMPLEMENTARY
COMPLIMENTARY
COMPREHENSION
COMPREHENSIVE
COMRADEINARMS
CONCATENATION
CONCENTRATION
CONCEPTIONIST
CONCEPTUALIZE
CONCESSIONARY
CONCUPISCENCE
CONDESCENDING
CONDESCENSION
CONDITIONALLY
CONFARREATION
CONFECTIONERS
CONFECTIONERY
CONFEDERATION
CONFIGURATION
CONFLAGRATION
CONFRONTATION
CONGRESSIONAL
CONGRESSWOMAN
CONSANGUINITY
CONSCIENTIOUS
CONSCIOUSNESS
CONSECTANEOUS
CONSECUTIVELY
CONSEQUENTIAL
CONSERVATOIRE
CONSIDERATELY
CONSIDERATION
CONSOLIDATION
CONSPICUOUSLY
CONSPURCATION
CONSTELLATION
CONSTERNATION
CONTAMINATION
CONTEMPLATION
CONTEMPLATIVE
CONTENTEDNESS
CONTINUATIONS
CONTORTIONIST
CONTRABASSOON
CONTRACEPTION
CONTRACEPTIVE
CONTRADICTION
CONTRADICTORY
CONTRAFAGOTTO
CONTRAVENTION
CONTRIBUTIONS
CONTROVERSIAL
CONVALESCENCE
CONVERSAZIONE
CORRESPONDENT
CORRESPONDING
CORROBORATION
CORROBORATORY
COSTEFFECTIVE
COUNTERACTING
COUNTERATTACK
COUNTERCHARGE
COUNTERFEITER
COUNTRYPEOPLE
DOCUMENTATION
DOUBLEGLAZING
FONTAINEBLEAU
FOREKNOWLEDGE
FORGETFULNESS
FORMALIZATION
FORTIFICATION

FORTUNETELLER
FOSSILIZATION
FOSTERPARENTS
GOODRIGHTEOUS
HOMOSEXUALITY
HORRIPILATION
HORSEFEATHERS
HORTICULTURAL
HOUSEBREAKING
JOLLIFICATION
LONGSUFFERING
MOCKTECHNICAL
MODERNIZATION
MOLLIFICATION
MONOCOTYLEDON
MONONUCLEOSIS
MONOTHALAMOUS
MORPHOLOGICAL
MORTIFICATION
MOUTHWATERING
NONCONFORMIST
NONCONFORMITY
NONRESISTANCE
NONSUFFICIENT
NORMALIZATION
NOSTALGICALLY
POLIOMYELITIS
POLLICITATION
POTENTIOMETER
ROLLERBLADING
ROLLERCOASTER
ROUNDTHEWORLD
SOCIOECONOMIC
SOLEMNIZATION
SOMATOTROPHIN
SOPHISTICATED
SOUTHEASTERLY
SOUTHWESTERLY
TONGUEINCHEEK
TONGUETWISTER
TONSILLECTOMY
TOPOGRAPHICAL
TORTOISESHELL
VORACIOUSNESS
APOCATASTASIS
APPORTIONMENT
APPROPINQUATE
APPROPRIATION
APPROXIMATELY
APPROXIMATION
EPANADIPLOSIS
EPHEMEROPTERA
EPIPHENOMENON
EPITRACHELION
OPHTHALMOLOGY
OPPORTUNISTIC
OPPORTUNITIES
SPASMODICALLY
SPECIFICATION
SPECTACULARLY
SPECTROGRAPHY
SPELEOLOGICAL
SPINDLESHANKS
SPINECHILLING
SPITESPLENDID
SPONTANEOUSLY
SPORTSMANLIKE
SPORTSMANSHIP
SPRIGHTLINESS
UPTOTHEMINUTE
AQUIFOLIACEAE
EQUIPONDERATE
SQUEAMISHNESS
ARCHAEOLOGIST
ARCHAEOPTERYX
ARCHIMANDRITE
ARCHITECTURAL
ARGUMENTATIVE
ARISTROCRATIC
ARITHMETICIAN
ARMOURPLATING
ARTIFICIALITY
ARUNDINACEOUS
BRACHIOSAURUS
BREASTFEEDING
BROKENHEARTED
CRAFTSMANSHIP
CREDULOUSNESS
CRIMINOLOGIST
CROSSQUESTION
DRAMATIZATION
DRYOPITHECINE
FRACTIOUSNESS
FRAGMENTATION
FRANKALMOIGNE
FRIGHTENINGLY
FRIGHTFULNESS
FRIVOLOUSNESS
GRAMMATICALLY
GRANDDAUGHTER
GRANDILOQUENT
GRANDPARENTAL
GRATIFICATION
GRAVITATIONAL
GRIEFSTRICKEN
IRRECOVERABLE
IRREPLACEABLE
IRREPRESSIBLE
IRRESPONSIBLE
IRRESPONSIBLY
IRRETRIEVABLE
IRRETRIEVABLY
ORCHESTRATION
ORNAMENTATION
ORNITHOLOGIST
PRAGMATICALLY
PRECAUTIONARY
PRECIPITATELY
PRECIPITATION
PRECONCEPTION
PREDOMINANTLY
PREFABRICATED
PRELIMINARIES
PREMEDITATION
PREOCCUPATION
PREPONDERANCE
PREPOSSESSING
PREPOSSESSION
PREPROGRAMMED
PRESERVATIVES
PRESSURELOCAL
PRETERNATURAL
PREVARICATION
PRIMOGENITURE
PRIVATIZATION
PROBLEMATICAL
PROCLEUSMATIC
PROCRASTINATE
PROFECTITIOUS
PROFESSORSHIP
PROFITABILITY
PROGNOSTICATE
PROGRESSIVELY
PROJECTIONIST
PROLIFERATION
PROMISCUOUSLY
PRONOUNCEMENT
PRONUNCIATION
PROPHETICALLY
PROPORTIONATE
PROPRIETORIAL
PROSOPOGRAPHY
PROTECTIONISM
PROTECTIONIST
PROTESTANTISM
PROTONOTARIAT
PROVINCIALISM
PROVISIONALLY
PROVOCATIVELY
TRACTARIANISM
TRADITIONALLY
TRANQUILLISER
TRANQUILLIZER
TRANSATLANTIC
TRANSCRIPTION
TRANSGRESSION
TRANSISTORIZE
TRANSLITERATE
TRANSMUTATION
TRANSPARENTLY
TRANSPIRATION
TRANSPORTABLE
TRANSPOSITION
TRAUMATICALLY
TREACHEROUSLY
TRIANGULATION
TRICHOSANTHIN
ASCERTAINABLE
ASSASSINATION
ASTONISHINGLY
ESCHSCHOLTZIA
ESTABLISHMENT
ISOGEOTHERMAL
PSYCHOANALYSE
PSYCHOANALYST
PSYCHOLOGICAL
PSYCHOSOMATIC
PSYCHOTHERAPY
ATTENTIVENESS
STABILIZATION
STAPHYLINIDAE
STATESMANLIKE
STATESMANSHIP
STATIONMASTER
STATISTICALLY
STEADFASTNESS
STEEPLECHASER
STEPPINGSTONE
STERCORACEOUS
STERILIZATION
STOCKBREEDING
STRANGULATION
STRATEGICALLY
STRENUOUSNESS
STREPTOCOCCUS
STRIKEBREAKER
STYLISTICALLY
AUTHORISATION
AUTHORITARIAN
AUTHORITATIVE
AUTHORIZATION
AUTOBIOGRAPHY
AUTOCEPHALOUS
AUTOMATICALLY
BUNGEEJUMPING
BUSINESSWOMAN
BUTTERFINGERS
FUERTEVENTURA
FUNDAMENTALLY
GUILTLESSNESS
HUNDREDWEIGHT
JURISPRUDENCE
JUSTIFICATION
JUXTAPOSITION
LUXURIOUSNESS
MULTICOLOURED
MULTINATIONAL
MULTINUCLEATE
MULTITUDINOUS
NULLIFICATION
OUTRECUIDANCE
OUTSTANDINGLY
PULVERIZATION
PUNCTILIOUSLY
PUSILLANIMITY
PUSILLANIMOUS
QUADRAGESIMAL
QUADRILATERAL
QUADRUPLICATE
QUALIFICATION

QUARTERMASTER
QUARTODECIMAN
QUERULOUSNESS
QUESTIONNAIRE
QUINQUAGESIMA
RUTHERFORDIUM
SUBCONTRACTOR
SUBJECTMATTER
SUBLIEUTENANT
SUBORDINATION
SUBSERVIENTLY
SUBSTANTIALLY
SUOVETAURILIA
SUPERABUNDANT
SUPERANNUATED
SUPERFICIALLY
SUPERFLUOUSLY
SUPERLATIVELY
SUPERNUMERARY
SUPERORDINATE
SUPERSTITIOUS
SUPPLEMENTARY
SUPRANATIONAL
SURREPTITIOUS
SUSPERCOLLATE
VULCANIZATION
VULGARIZATION
VULNERABILITY
OVEREMPHASIZE
OVERSTATEMENT
OWNEROCCUPIER
SWASHBUCKLING
SWEDENBORGIAN
SWEETSMELLING
SWOLLENHEADED
EXCEPTIONABLE
EXCEPTIONALLY
EXCOMMUNICATE
EXHIBITIONIST
EXPANSIVENESS
EXPEDITIONARY
EXPEDITIOUSLY
EXPOSTULATION
EXPROPRIATION
EXTERMINATION
EXTRAORDINARY
EXTRAPOLATION
EXTRAVAGANTLY
GYNAECOLOGIST
GYNANDROMORPH
GYNECOLOGICAL
HYBRIDIZATION
HYDRAULICALLY
HYDROELECTRIC
HYPERCRITICAL
HYPERSTHENITE
HYPOCHONDRIAC
LYCANTHROPIST
MYSTIFICATION
OYSTERCATCHER
PYROTECHNICAL
SYMPIESOMETER
SYNTACTICALLY
SYNTHETICALLY
TYPOGRAPHICAL

13:3

ANACHRONISTIC
BEATIFICATION
BLANDISHMENTS
BRACHIOSAURUS
CHANGEABILITY
CHARACTERISED
CHARACTERLESS
CHATEAUBRIAND
CLAIRAUDIENCE
CLARIFICATION
CRAFTSMANSHIP
DEATHLESSNESS
DIACATHOLICON
DIAMETRICALLY
DRAMATIZATION
EPANADIPLOSIS
FEATHERWEIGHT
FLABBERGASTED
FRACTIOUSNESS
FRAGMENTATION
FRANKALMOIGNE
GRAMMATICALLY
GRANDDAUGHTER
GRANDILOQUENT
GRANDPARENTAL
GRATIFICATION
GRAVITATIONAL
HEARTBREAKING
IMAGINATIVELY
INADVERTENTLY
INAPPROPRIATE
LEATHERJACKET
NEANDERTHALER
PHARMACOPOEIA
PLATOCEPHALUS
PRAGMATICALLY
QUADRAGESIMAL
QUADRILATERAL
QUADRUPLICATE
QUALIFICATION
QUARTERMASTER
QUARTODECIMAN
REALISTICALLY
REARRANGEMENT
RHADAMANTHINE
SCANDALMONGER
SHAPELESSNESS
SPASMODICALLY
STABILIZATION
STAPHYLINIDAE
STATESMANLIKE
STATESMANSHIP
STATIONMASTER
STATISTICALLY
SWASHBUCKLING
THANKLESSNESS
THAUMATURGICS
THAUMATURGIST
TRACTARIANISM
TRADITIONALLY
TRANQUILLISER
TRANQUILLIZER
TRANSATLANTIC
TRANSCRIPTION
TRANSGRESSION
TRANSISTORIZE
TRANSLITERATE
TRANSMUTATION
TRANSPARENTLY
TRANSPIRATION
TRANSPORTABLE
TRANSPOSITION
TRAUMATICALLY
UNACCOMPANIED
UNACCOUNTABLE
UNACCOUNTABLY
UNADULTERATED
UNANTICIPATED
WEATHERBEATEN
BIBLIOGRAPHER
BIBLIOPHAGIST
EMBARRASSMENT
EMBELLISHMENT
HYBRIDIZATION
LIBRARIANSHIP
SUBCONTRACTOR
SUBJECTMATTER
SUBLIEUTENANT
SUBORDINATION
SUBSERVIENTLY
SUBSTANTIALLY
TABLESPOONFUL
UMBELLIFEROUS
ACCEPTABILITY
ACCEPTILATION
ACCESSIBILITY
ACCOMMODATING
ACCOMMODATION
ACCOMPANIMENT
ACCOUTREMENTS
ARCHAEOLOGIST
ARCHAEOPTERYX
ARCHIMANDRITE
ARCHITECTURAL
ASCERTAINABLE
BACCALAUREATE
DECAFFEINATED
DECOMPOSITION
DECOMPRESSION
DECONTAMINATE
DECRIMINALIZE
DOCUMENTATION
ECCENTRICALLY
ENCEPHALOCELE
ENCOURAGEMENT
ENCYCLOPAEDIA
ENCYCLOPAEDIC
ESCHSCHOLTZIA
EXCEPTIONABLE
EXCEPTIONALLY
EXCOMMUNICATE
FACETIOUSNESS
INCANDESCENCE
INCARCERATION
INCOMBUSTIBLE
INCOMMUNICADO
INCOMPETENTLY
INCONCEIVABLE
INCONSIDERATE
INCONSISTENCY
INCONSPICUOUS
INCONTESTABLE
INCONVENIENCE
INCORPORATION
INCORRUPTIBLE
INCREDULOUSLY
INCRIMINATING
INCRIMINATORY
LACKADAISICAL
LECTISTERNIUM
LYCANTHROPIST
MACHIAVELLIAN
MACHICOLATION
MECHANIZATION
MICROCOMPUTER
MICROORGANISM
MOCKTECHNICAL
ORCHESTRATION
RECALCITRANCE
RECEPTIVENESS
RECITATIONIST
RECRIMINATION
RECRIMINATORY
RECRUDESCENCE
RECTIFICATION
SACCHAROMYCES
SECRETIVENESS
SOCIOECONOMIC
TECHNOLOGICAL
UNCEREMONIOUS
UNCOMFORTABLE
UNCOMFORTABLY
UNCOMMUNICATE
UNCOMPLICATED
UNCONDITIONAL
UNCONQUERABLE
UNCONSCIOUSLY
UNCOOPERATIVE
UNCOORDINATED
VICEPRESIDENT
VICTIMIZATION
HYDRAULICALLY

HYDROELECTRIC
INDEFATIGABLE
INDEFATIGABLY
INDEPENDENTLY
INDESCRIBABLE
INDESCRIBABLY
INDETERMINATE
INDIFFERENTLY
INDISPENSABLE
INDISPOSITION
INDIVIDUALISM
INDIVIDUALIST
INDIVIDUALITY
INDUSTRIALIST
INDUSTRIALIZE
INDUSTRIOUSLY
KIDDERMINSTER
MADETOMEASURE
MEDITERRANEAN
MIDDLEBREAKER
MODERNIZATION
RADIOACTIVITY
REDEMPTIONIST
REDEVELOPMENT
SEDIMENTATION
UNDERACHIEVER
UNDERCARRIAGE
UNDERCLOTHING
UNDERESTIMATE
UNDERGRADUATE
UNDERSTANDING
UNDERSTRAPPER
UNDISCIPLINED
VIDEOCASSETTE
VIDEORECORDER
BREASTFEEDING
CHEESEMONGERS
COEDUCATIONAL
CREDULOUSNESS
ELECTROCUTION
ELECTROMAGNET
ELECTROMOTIVE
ELEPHANTIASIS
ENERGETICALLY
FUERTEVENTURA
HIEROGLYPHICS
INEFFICIENTLY
INEVITABILITY
INEXHAUSTIBLE
INEXPERIENCED
INEXPRESSIBLE
LAEVOROTATORY
LIEBFRAUMILCH
LIECHTENSTEIN
OVEREMPHASIZE
OVERSTATEMENT
PAEDIATRICIAN
PNEUMATICALLY
PRECAUTIONARY
PRECIPITATELY
PRECIPITATION
PRECONCEPTION
PREDOMINANTLY
PREFABRICATED
PRELIMINARIES
PREMEDITATION
PREOCCUPATION
PREPONDERANCE
PREPOSSESSING
PREPOSSESSION
PREPROGRAMMED
PRESERVATIVES
PRESSURELOCAL
PRETERNATURAL
PREVARICATION
QUERULOUSNESS
QUESTIONNAIRE
SLEEPLESSNESS
SPECIFICATION
SPECTACULARLY
SPECTROGRAPHY
SPELEOLOGICAL
STEADFASTNESS
STEEPLECHASER
STEPPINGSTONE
STERCORACEOUS
STERILIZATION
SWEDENBORGIAN
SWEETSMELLING
THEATRICALITY
THEOLOGICALLY
THEORETICALLY
THERMONUCLEAR
THERMOPLASTIC
TREACHEROUSLY
UNEMBARRASSED
UNENLIGHTENED
UNESTABLISHED
UNEXCEPTIONAL
UNEXPERIENCED
AFFENPINSCHER
AFFIRMATIVELY
AFFORESTATION
AFFREIGHTMENT
DEFENSIBILITY
DEFERVESCENCE
DEFIBRILLATOR
DEFORESTATION
DIFFARREATION
DIFFERENTIATE
EFFECTIVENESS
EFFERVESCENCE
EFFLORESCENCE
INFALLIBILITY
INFINITESIMAL
INFLEXIBILITY
INFLORESCENCE
OFFENSIVENESS
OFFICIOUSNESS
REFRIGERATION
REFRIGERATORS
REFURBISHMENT
UNFASHIONABLE
UNFLINCHINGLY
UNFORESEEABLE
UNFORGETTABLE
UNFORTUNATELY
AGGIORNAMENTO
AGGLOMERATION
ARGUMENTATIVE
DAGUERREOTYPE
INGENUOUSNESS
JIGGERYPOKERY
LIGHTFINGERED
MAGISTERIALLY
MAGNANIMOUSLY
MAGNIFICATION
MAGNIFICENTLY
MAGNILOQUENCE
NIGHTWATCHMAN
REGIMENTATION
REGURGITATION
RIGHTEOUSNESS
SIGNIFICANTLY
SIGNIFICATION
UNGENTLEMANLY
UNGRAMMATICAL
VEGETARIANISM
EPHEMEROPTERA
EXHIBITIONIST
OPHTHALMOLOGY
SCHADENFREUDE
SCHEMATICALLY
SCHIZOPHRENIA
SCHIZOPHRENIC
SCHOLARLINESS
SCHOOLTEACHER
SCHUTZSTAFFEL
ANIMADVERSION
ARISTROCRATIC
ARITHMETICIAN
CHINKERINCHEE
CLISHMACLAVER
CRIMINOLOGIST
DEIPNOSOPHIST
EPIPHENOMENON
EPITRACHELION
FRIGHTENINGLY
FRIGHTFULNESS
FRIVOLOUSNESS
GRIEFSTRICKEN
GUILTLESSNESS
IDIORRHYTHMIC
IDIOSYNCRATIC
KNICKERBOCKER
KNICKKNACKERY
LEISURELINESS
MEISTERSINGER
NEIGHBOURHOOD
PAINSTAKINGLY
PHILADELPHIAN
PHILANTHROPIC
PHILOSOPHICAL
PRIMOGENITURE
PRIVATIZATION
QUINQUAGESIMA
REIMBURSEMENT
REINCARNATION
REINFORCEMENT
REINSTATEMENT
SCINTILLATING
SCINTILLATION
SEISMOLOGICAL
SPINDLESHANKS
SPINECHILLING
SPITESPLENDID
TRIANGULATION
TRICHOSANTHIN
UNIMAGINATIVE
UNIMPEACHABLE
UNIMPRESSIBLE
UNINHABITABLE
UNINTELLIGENT
UNINTENTIONAL
UNINTERESTING
UNINTERRUPTED
WEIGHTLIFTING
OBJECTIONABLE
OBJECTIVENESS
BILDUNGSROMAN
CALLISTHENICS
COLLABORATION
COLLABORATIVE
COLLIESHANGIE
COLLOQUIALISM
ENLIGHTENMENT
FALSIFICATION
GALVANIZATION
HALLUCINATION
HALLUCINATORY
ILLUMINATIONS
JOLLIFICATION
KALEIDOSCOPIC
MALADJUSTMENT
MALLEMAROKING
MOLLIFICATION
MULTICOLOURED
MULTINATIONAL
MULTINUCLEATE
MULTITUDINOUS
NULLIFICATION
PALAEONTOLOGY
PELOPONNESIAN
POLIOMYELITIS
POLLICITATION
PULVERIZATION
ROLLERBLADING
ROLLERCOASTER
SALACIOUSNESS
SELFADDRESSED

SELFCONFESSED
SELFCONFIDENT
SELFCONSCIOUS
SELFCONTAINED
SELFGOVERNING
SOLEMNIZATION
TALKATIVENESS
VULCANIZATION
VULGARIZATION
VULNERABILITY
ADMINISTRATOR
ARMOURPLATING
COMMEMORATION
COMMEMORATIVE
COMMENSURABLE
COMMERCIALIZE
COMMISERATION
COMMUNICATION
COMMUNICATIVE
COMPANIONABLE
COMPANIONSHIP
COMPARABILITY
COMPARATIVELY
COMPASSIONATE
COMPATIBILITY
COMPLEMENTARY
COMPLIMENTARY
COMPREHENSION
COMPREHENSIVE
COMRADEINARMS
DEMILITARIZED
DEMONSTRATION
DEMONSTRATIVE
HAMMERKLAVIER
HAMMERTHROWER
HEMISPHERICAL
HOMOSEXUALITY
LAMPADEPHORIA
NEMATHELMINTH
RAMIFICATIONS
REMINISCENCES
REMORSELESSLY
SEMBLANCECORD
SEMICONDUCTOR
SOMATOTROPHIN
SYMPIESOMETER
TEMPERAMENTAL
UNMENTIONABLE
BUNGEEJUMPING
CONCATENATION
CONCENTRATION
CONCEPTIONIST
CONCEPTUALIZE
CONCESSIONARY
CONCUPISCENCE
CONDESCENDING
CONDESCENSION
CONDITIONALLY
CONFARREATION
CONFECTIONERS
CONFECTIONERY
CONFEDERATION
CONFIGURATION
CONFLAGRATION
CONFRONTATION
CONGRESSIONAL
CONGRESSWOMAN
CONSANGUINITY
CONSCIENTIOUS
CONSCIOUSNESS
CONSECTANEOUS
CONSECUTIVELY
CONSEQUENTIAL
CONSERVATOIRE
CONSIDERATELY
CONSIDERATION
CONSOLIDATION
CONSPICUOUSLY
CONSPURCATION
CONSTELLATION
CONSTERNATION
CONTAMINATION
CONTEMPLATION
CONTEMPLATIVE
CONTENTEDNESS
CONTINUATIONS
CONTORTIONIST
CONTRABASSOON
CONTRACEPTION
CONTRACEPTIVE
CONTRADICTION
CONTRADICTORY
CONTRAFAGOTTO
CONTRAVENTION
CONTRIBUTIONS
CONTROVERSIAL
CONVALESCENCE
CONVERSAZIONE
DENATIONALIZE
FANTASTICALLY
FONTAINEBLEAU
FUNDAMENTALLY
GENERALISSIMO
GYNAECOLOGIST
GYNANDROMORPH
GYNECOLOGICAL
HUNDREDWEIGHT
IGNOMINIOUSLY
KANGCHENJUNGA
LONGSUFFERING
MANIFESTATION
MANUFACTURING
MONOCOTYLEDON
MONONUCLEOSIS
MONOTHALAMOUS
NONCONFORMIST
NONCONFORMITY
NONRESISTANCE
NONSUFFICIENT
ORNAMENTATION
ORNITHOLOGIST
OWNEROCCUPIER
PANDICULATION
PANHARMONICON
PENETRABILITY
PUNCTILIOUSLY
RENSSELAERITE
SANCTIMONIOUS
SENSATIONALLY
SENSELESSNESS
SENSITIVENESS
SENTENTIOUSLY
SENTIMENTALLY
SYNTACTICALLY
SYNTHETICALLY
TANTALIZINGLY
TENDERHEARTED
TINTINNABULUM
TONGUEINCHEEK
TONGUETWISTER
TONSILLECTOMY
UNNECESSARILY
VENTRILOQUISM
VENTRILOQUIST
APOCATASTASIS
BIODEGRADABLE
BIOTECHNOLOGY
BLOODCURDLING
BROKENHEARTED
CHOREOGRAPHER
CLOSEDCIRCUIT
CROSSQUESTION
GEOMETRICALLY
GLOBETROTTING
GLORIFICATION
GLOSSOGRAPHER
GOODRIGHTEOUS
ISOGEOTHERMAL
KNOWLEDGEABLE
PHOTOCHEMICAL
PHOTOELECTRIC
PROBLEMATICAL
PROCLEUSMATIC
PROCRASTINATE
PROFECTITIOUS
PROFESSORSHIP
PROFITABILITY
PROGNOSTICATE
PROGRESSIVELY
PROJECTIONIST
PROLIFERATION
PROMISCUOUSLY
PRONOUNCEMENT
PRONUNCIATION
PROPHETICALLY
PROPORTIONATE
PROPRIETORIAL
PROSOPOGRAPHY
PROTECTIONISM
PROTECTIONIST
PROTESTANTISM
PROTONOTARIAT
PROVINCIALISM
PROVISIONALLY
PROVOCATIVELY
SHOULDERBLADE
SNOWBLINDNESS
SPONTANEOUSLY
SPORTSMANLIKE
SPORTSMANSHIP
STOCKBREEDING
SUOVETAURILIA
SWOLLENHEADED
THOROUGHBRACE
THOROUGHGOING
THOUGHTLESSLY
WHOLESOMENESS
ALPHABETARIAN
AMPHIGASTRIUM
AMPLIFICATION
APPORTIONMENT
APPROPINQUATE
APPROPRIATION
APPROXIMATELY
APPROXIMATION
DEPENDABILITY
EXPANSIVENESS
EXPEDITIONARY
EXPEDITIOUSLY
EXPOSTULATION
EXPROPRIATION
HYPERCRITICAL
HYPERSTHENITE
HYPOCHONDRIAC
IMPERCEPTIBLE
IMPERCEPTIBLY
IMPERIALISTIC
IMPERSONATING
IMPERSONATION
IMPERTINENTLY
IMPERTURBABLE
IMPERTURBABLY
IMPONDERABLES
IMPOSSIBILITY
IMPRACTICABLE
IMPRESSIONISM
IMPRESSIONIST
IMPROBABILITY
IMPROVIDENTLY
IMPROVISATION
IMPULSIVENESS
KAPPELMEISTER
LEPIDOPTERIST
LEPTOCEPHALUS
OPPORTUNISTIC
OPPORTUNITIES
PAPAPRELATIST
RAPPROCHEMENT
REPERCUSSIONS
REPLENISHMENT

REPREHENSIBLE
REPREHENSIBLY
REPROACHFULLY
REPROGRAPHICS
REPUBLICANISM
SEPTENTRIONES
SIPUNCULOIDEA
SOPHISTICATED
SUPERABUNDANT
SUPERANNUATED
SUPERFICIALLY
SUPERFLUOUSLY
SUPERLATIVELY
SUPERNUMERARY
SUPERORDINATE
SUPERSTITIOUS
SUPPLEMENTARY
SUPRANATIONAL
TAPERECORDING
TOPOGRAPHICAL
TYPOGRAPHICAL
UNPARTITIONED
UNPRECEDENTED
UNPREDICTABLE
UNPRETENTIOUS
UNPROGRESSIVE
XIPHIPLASTRON
INQUISITIVELY
SEQUESTRATION
UNQUESTIONING
ACRYLONITRILE
AIRCRAFTWOMAN
AIRWORTHINESS
CARBONIFEROUS
CARTILAGINOUS
CEREMONIOUSLY
CERTIFICATION
CHRISTMASTIME
CHRONOLOGICAL
CHRYSANTHEMUM
CIRCUMAMBIENT
CIRCUMFERENCE
CIRCUMSTANCES
CIRCUMVENTION
CORRESPONDENT
CORRESPONDING
CORROBORATION
CORROBORATORY
DERMATOLOGIST
FERROCONCRETE
FERTILISATION
FERTILIZATION
FOREKNOWLEDGE
FORGETFULNESS
FORMALIZATION
FORTIFICATION
FORTUNETELLER
GARRULOUSNESS
HARMONIZATION
HERMAPHRODITE

HORRIPILATION
HORSEFEATHERS
HORTICULTURAL
IRRECOVERABLE
IRREPLACEABLE
IRREPRESSIBLE
IRRESPONSIBLE
IRRESPONSIBLY
IRRETRIEVABLE
IRRETRIEVABLY
JURISPRUDENCE
MERCHANDIZING
MERCILESSNESS
MORPHOLOGICAL
MORTIFICATION
NERVELESSNESS
NORMALIZATION
PARADOXICALLY
PARALLELOGRAM
PARANTHROPOUS
PARAPHERNALIA
PARENTHETICAL
PARLIAMENTARY
PARTHOGENESIS
PARTICIPATION
PARTICIPATORY
PARTICOLOURED
PARTICULARISE
PARTICULARITY
PARTICULARIZE
PERAMBULATION
PEREGRINATION
PERFECTIONIST
PERFUNCTORILY
PERPENDICULAR
PERSONALITIES
PERSPICACIOUS
PERVASIVENESS
PYROTECHNICAL
SARCASTICALLY
SERVILEMENTAL
SHRINKWRAPPED
SPRIGHTLINESS
STRANGULATION
STRATEGICALLY
STRENUOUSNESS
STREPTOCOCCUS
STRIKEBREAKER
SURREPTITIOUS
THREATENINGLY
TORTOISESHELL
VERCINGETORIX
VERSIFICATION
VORACIOUSNESS
AESTHETICALLY
ASSASSINATION
BUSINESSWOMAN
COSTEFFECTIVE
DESEGREGATION
DÉSOBLIGEANTE

DISADVANTAGED
DISAPPEARANCE
DISAPPOINTING
DISCOLORATION
DISCONCERTING
DISCONNECTION
DISCONTINUITY
DISCONTINUOUS
DISCREDITABLE
DISCREDITABLY
DISCRETIONARY
DISENGAGEMENT
DISESTIMATION
DISFIGUREMENT
DISGRACEFULLY
DISHEARTENING
DISHONOURABLE
DISHONOURABLY
DISILLUSIONED
DISINTERESTED
DISPARAGEMENT
DISPASSIONATE
DISPROPORTION
DISRESPECTFUL
DISSEMINATION
DISSIMILARITY
DISSIMULATION
DISTINGUISHED
FOSSILIZATION
FOSTERPARENTS
GASTROCNEMIUS
GESTICULATION
INSECTIVOROUS
INSENSITIVITY
INSIDIOUSNESS
INSIGNIFICANT
INSPIRATIONAL
INSTANTANEOUS
INSTINCTIVELY
INSTITUTIONAL
INSTRUCTIONAL
INSUBORDINATE
INSUBSTANTIAL
INSUFFICIENCY
INSUPPORTABLE
JUSTIFICATION
LISSOTRICHOUS
MASSACHUSETTS
MASTIGOPHORAN
MESSERSCHMITT
MISANTHROPIST
MISCEGENATION
MISCELLANEOUS
MISCHIEVOUSLY
MISCONCEPTION
MISMANAGEMENT
MISUNDERSTAND
MISUNDERSTOOD
MYSTIFICATION
NOSTALGICALLY

OYSTERCATCHER
PASSCHENDAELE
PASSEMENTERIE
PASSIONFLOWER
PUSILLANIMITY
PUSILLANIMOUS
RESOURCEFULLY
RESUSCITATION
SUSPERCOLLATE
UNSERVICEABLE
UNSUBSTANTIAL
UNSYMMETRICAL
UNSYMPATHETIC
ALTERNATIVELY
ANTHELMINTHIC
ANTICLOCKWISE
ANTICOAGULANT
ANTIGROPELOES
ANTIHISTAMINE
ARTIFICIALITY
ASTONISHINGLY
ATTENTIVENESS
AUTHORISATION
AUTHORITARIAN
AUTHORITATIVE
AUTHORIZATION
AUTOBIOGRAPHY
AUTOCEPHALOUS
AUTOMATICALLY
BUTTERFINGERS
CATEGORICALLY
DETERIORATION
DETERMINATION
ENTEROPNEUSTA
ENTERTAINMENT
ENTOMOLOGICAL
ESTABLISHMENT
EXTERMINATION
EXTRAORDINARY
EXTRAPOLATION
EXTRAVAGANTLY
HETERAUXESISM
HETEROGENEOUS
INTELLIGENTLY
INTENTIONALLY
INTERCALATION
INTERESTINGLY
INTERMARRIAGE
INTERNATIONAL
INTERPERSONAL
INTERPOLATION
INTERROGATION
INTERROGATIVE
INTRANSIGENCE
INTRINSICALLY
INTROSPECTION
INTROSPECTIVE
MATERIALISTIC
MATHEMATICIAN
MATRICULATION

METAGRABOLISE
METAGROBOLISE
METAMORPHOSIS
METAPHYSICIAN
METEOROLOGIST
NATIONALISTIC
OUTRECUIDANCE
OUTSTANDINGLY
PATERFAMILIAS
PATERNALISTIC
PATRIOTICALLY
PETRIFICATION
PETROCHEMICAL
POTENTIOMETER
RATIONALALITY
RETROGRESSION
RETROSPECTIVE
RUTHERFORDIUM
TETRASYLLABIC
UNTRUSTWORTHY
UPTOTHEMINUTE
VITRIFICATION
WITWATERSRAND
ACUPUNCTURIST
AQUIFOLIACEAE
ARUNDINACEOUS
BOUGAINVILLEA
BOUILLABAISSE
BOUSTROPHEDON
CAUTERIZATION
COUNTERACTING
COUNTERATTACK
COUNTERCHARGE
COUNTERFEITER
COUNTRYPEOPLE
DOUBLEGLAZING
EQUIPONDERATE
GLUMDALCLITCH
HOUSEBREAKING
MAURIKIGUSARI
MOUTHWATERING
REUNIFICATION
ROUNDTHEWORLD
SOUTHEASTERLY
SOUTHWESTERLY
SQUEAMISHNESS
THUNDERSTRUCK
ADVENTUROUSLY
ADVERTISEMENT
DEVELOPMENTAL
ENVIRONMENTAL
INVENTIVENESS
INVESTIGATION
INVESTIGATIVE
INVINCIBILITY
INVIOLABILITY
INVOLUNTARILY
REVERBERATION
REVOLUTIONARY
REVOLUTIONIZE

VIVACIOUSNESS
UNWILLINGNESS
JUXTAPOSITION
LEXICOGRAPHER
LUXURIOUSNESS
ANYTHINGARIAN
DRYOPITHECINE
PHYSHARMONICA
PHYSIOGNOMIST
PHYSIOLOGICAL
PHYSIOTHERAPY
PSYCHOANALYSE
PSYCHOANALYST
PSYCHOLOGICAL
PSYCHOSOMATIC
PSYCHOTHERAPY
RHYPAROGRAPHY
STYLISTICALLY
THYROIDECTOMY

13:4

ASSASSINATION
BREASTFEEDING
DECAFFEINATED
DENATIONALIZE
DISADVANTAGED
DISAPPEARANCE
DISAPPOINTING
EMBARRASSMENT
ESTABLISHMENT
EXPANSIVENESS
GYNAECOLOGIST
GYNANDROMORPH
INCANDESCENCE
INCARCERATION
INFALLIBILITY
LYCANTHROPIST
MALADJUSTMENT
METAGRABOLISE
METAGROBOLISE
METAMORPHOSIS
METAPHYSICIAN
MISANTHROPIST
NEMATHELMINTH
ORNAMENTATION
PALAEONTOLOGY
PAPAPRELATIST
PARADOXICALLY
PARALLELOGRAM
PARANTHROPOUS
PARAPHERNALIA
PERAMBULATION
RECALCITRANCE
SALACIOUSNESS
SCHADENFREUDE
SOMATOTROPHIN
STEADFASTNESS
STRANGULATION
STRATEGICALLY

THEATRICALITY
TREACHEROUSLY
TRIANGULATION
UNFASHIONABLE
UNPARTITIONED
VIVACIOUSNESS
VORACIOUSNESS
CARBONIFEROUS
DOUBLEGLAZING
FLABBERGASTED
GLOBETROTTING
LIEBFRAUMILCH
PROBLEMATICAL
SEMBLANCECORD
STABILIZATION
AIRCRAFTWOMAN
ANACHRONISTIC
APOCATASTASIS
BACCALAUREATE
BRACHIOSAURUS
CIRCUMAMBIENT
CIRCUMFERENCE
CIRCUMSTANCES
CIRCUMVENTION
CONCATENATION
CONCENTRATION
CONCEPTIONIST
CONCEPTUALIZE
CONCESSIONARY
CONCUPISCENCE
DIACATHOLICON
DISCOLORATION
DISCONCERTING
DISCONNECTION
DISCONTINUITY
DISCONTINUOUS
DISCREDITABLE
DISCREDITABLY
DISCRETIONARY
ELECTROCUTION
ELECTROMAGNET
ELECTROMOTIVE
FRACTIOUSNESS
KNICKERBOCKER
KNICKKNACKERY
LIECHTENSTEIN
MERCHANDIZING
MERCILESSNESS
MISCEGENATION
MISCELLANEOUS
MISCHIEVOUSLY
MISCONCEPTION
NONCONFORMIST
NONCONFORMITY
PRECAUTIONARY
PRECIPITATELY
PRECIPITATION
PRECONCEPTION
PROCLEUSMATIC
PROCRASTINATE

PSYCHOANALYSE
PSYCHOANALYST
PSYCHOLOGICAL
PSYCHOSOMATIC
PSYCHOTHERAPY
PUNCTILIOUSLY
SACCHAROMYCES
SANCTIMONIOUS
SARCASTICALLY
SPECIFICATION
SPECTACULARLY
SPECTROGRAPHY
STOCKBREEDING
SUBCONTRACTOR
TRACTARIANISM
TRICHOSANTHIN
UNACCOMPANIED
UNACCOUNTABLE
UNACCOUNTABLY
VERCINGETORIX
VULCANIZATION
BILDUNGSROMAN
BIODEGRADABLE
COEDUCATIONAL
CONDESCENDING
CONDESCENSION
CONDITIONALLY
CREDULOUSNESS
FUNDAMENTALLY
GOODRIGHTEOUS
HUNDREDWEIGHT
INADVERTENTLY
KIDDERMINSTER
MIDDLEBREAKER
PAEDIATRICIAN
PANDICULATION
PREDOMINANTLY
QUADRAGESIMAL
QUADRILATERAL
QUADRUPLICATE
RHADAMANTHINE
SWEDENBORGIAN
TENDERHEARTED
TRADITIONALLY
UNADULTERATED
ACCEPTABILITY
ACCEPTILATION
ACCESSIBILITY
ADVENTUROUSLY
ADVERTISEMENT
AFFENPINSCHER
ALTERNATIVELY
ASCERTAINABLE
ATTENTIVENESS
CATEGORICALLY
CEREMONIOUSLY
CHEESEMONGERS
DEFENSIBILITY
DEFERVESCENCE
DEPENDABILITY

DESEGREGATION
DETERIORATION
DETERMINATION
DEVELOPMENTAL
DISENGAGEMENT
DISESTIMATION
ECCENTRICALLY
EFFECTIVENESS
EFFERVESCENCE
EMBELLISHMENT
ENCEPHALOCELE
ENTEROPNEUSTA
ENTERTAINMENT
EPHEMEROPTERA
EXCEPTIONABLE
EXCEPTIONALLY
EXPEDITIONARY
EXPEDITIOUSLY
EXTERMINATION
FACETIOUSNESS
FOREKNOWLEDGE
GENERALISSIMO
GRIEFSTRICKEN
GYNECOLOGICAL
HETERAUXESISM
HETEROGENEOUS
HYPERCRITICAL
HYPERSTHENITE
IMPERCEPTIBLE
IMPERCEPTIBLY
IMPERIALISTIC
IMPERSONATING
IMPERSONATION
IMPERTINENTLY
IMPERTURBABLE
IMPERTURBABLY
INDEFATIGABLE
INDEFATIGABLY
INDEPENDENTLY
INDESCRIBABLE
INDESCRIBABLY
INDETERMINATE
INGENUOUSNESS
INSECTIVOROUS
INSENSITIVITY
INTELLIGENTLY
INTENTIONALLY
INTERCALATION
INTERESTINGLY
INTERMARRIAGE
INTERNATIONAL
INTERPERSONAL
INTERPOLATION
INTERROGATION
INTERROGATIVE
INVENTIVENESS
INVESTIGATION
INVESTIGATIVE
IRRECOVERABLE
IRREPLACEABLE
IRREPRESSIBLE
IRRESPONSIBLE
IRRESPONSIBLY
IRRETRIEVABLE
IRRETRIEVABLY
KALEIDOSCOPIC
MADETOMEASURE
MATERIALISTIC
METEOROLOGIST
MODERNIZATION
OBJECTIONABLE
OBJECTIVENESS
OFFENSIVENESS
OWNEROCCUPIER
PARENTHETICAL
PATERFAMILIAS
PATERNALISTIC
PENETRABILITY
PEREGRINATION
POTENTIOMETER
RECEPTIVENESS
REDEMPTIONIST
REDEVELOPMENT
REPERCUSSIONS
REVERBERATION
SCHEMATICALLY
SLEEPLESSNESS
SOLEMNIZATION
SQUEAMISHNESS
STEEPLECHASER
STRENUOUSNESS
STREPTOCOCCUS
SUPERABUNDANT
SUPERANNUATED
SUPERFICIALLY
SUPERFLUOUSLY
SUPERLATIVELY
SUPERNUMERARY
SUPERORDINATE
SUPERSTITIOUS
SWEETSMELLING
TAPERECORDING
THREATENINGLY
UMBELLIFEROUS
UNCEREMONIOUS
UNDERACHIEVER
UNDERCARRIAGE
UNDERCLOTHING
UNDERESTIMATE
UNDERGRADUATE
UNDERSTANDING
UNDERSTRAPPER
UNGENTLEMANLY
UNMENTIONABLE
UNNECESSARILY
UNSERVICEABLE
VEGETARIANISM
VICEPRESIDENT
VIDEOCASSETTE
VIDEORECORDER
CONFARREATION
CONFECTIONERS
CONFECTIONERY
CONFEDERATION
CONFIGURATION
CONFLAGRATION
CONFRONTATION
CRAFTSMANSHIP
DIFFARREATION
DIFFERENTIATE
DISFIGUREMENT
INEFFICIENTLY
PERFECTIONIST
PERFUNCTORILY
PREFABRICATED
PROFECTITIOUS
PROFESSORSHIP
PROFITABILITY
SELFADDRESSED
SELFCONFESSED
SELFCONFIDENT
SELFCONSCIOUS
SELFCONTAINED
SELFGOVERNING
BOUGAINVILLEA
BUNGEEJUMPING
CONGRESSIONAL
CONGRESSWOMAN
DISGRACEFULLY
FORGETFULNESS
FRAGMENTATION
FRIGHTENINGLY
FRIGHTFULNESS
IMAGINATIVELY
ISOGEOTHERMAL
JIGGERYPOKERY
KANGCHENJUNGA
LONGSUFFERING
NEIGHBOURHOOD
PRAGMATICALLY
PROGNOSTICATE
PROGRESSIVELY
TONGUEINCHEEK
TONGUETWISTER
VULGARIZATION
WEIGHTLIFTING
ALPHABETARIAN
AMPHIGASTRIUM
ANTHELMINTHIC
ARCHAEOLOGIST
ARCHAEOPTERYX
ARCHIMANDRITE
ARCHITECTURAL
AUTHORISATION
AUTHORITARIAN
AUTHORITATIVE
AUTHORIZATION
DISHEARTENING
DISHONOURABLE
DISHONOURABLY
ESCHSCHOLTZIA
LIGHTFINGERED
MACHIAVELLIAN
MACHICOLATION
MATHEMATICIAN
MECHANIZATION
NIGHTWATCHMAN
ORCHESTRATION
PANHARMONICON
RIGHTEOUSNESS
RUTHERFORDIUM
SOPHISTICATED
TECHNOLOGICAL
XIPHIPLASTRON
ADMINISTRATOR
AFFIRMATIVELY
AGGIORNAMENTO
ANTICLOCKWISE
ANTICOAGULANT
ANTIGROPELOES
ANTIHISTAMINE
AQUIFOLIACEAE
ARTIFICIALITY
BOUILLABAISSE
BUSINESSWOMAN
CHRISTMASTIME
CLAIRAUDIENCE
DEFIBRILLATOR
DEMILITARIZED
DISILLUSIONED
DISINTERESTED
ENLIGHTENMENT
ENVIRONMENTAL
EQUIPONDERATE
EXHIBITIONIST
HEMISPHERICAL
INDIFFERENTLY
INDISPENSABLE
INDISPOSITION
INDIVIDUALISM
INDIVIDUALIST
INDIVIDUALITY
INFINITESIMAL
INSIDIOUSNESS
INSIGNIFICANT
INVINCIBILITY
INVIOLABILITY
JURISPRUDENCE
LEPIDOPTERIST
LEXICOGRAPHER
MAGISTERIALLY
MANIFESTATION
MEDITERRANEAN
NATIONALISTIC
OFFICIOUSNESS
ORNITHOLOGIST
POLIOMYELITIS
PUSILLANIMITY
PUSILLANIMOUS
RADIOACTIVITY

RAMIFICATIONS
RATIONALALITY
RECITATIONIST
REGIMENTATION
REMINISCENCES
SCHIZOPHRENIA
SCHIZOPHRENIC
SEDIMENTATION
SEMICONDUCTOR
SHRINKWRAPPED
SOCIOECONOMIC
SPRIGHTLINESS
STRIKEBREAKER
UNDISCIPLINED
UNWILLINGNESS
PROJECTIONIST
SUBJECTMATTER
BROKENHEARTED
LACKADAISICAL
MOCKTECHNICAL
TALKATIVENESS
AGGLOMERATION
AMPLIFICATION
BIBLIOGRAPHER
BIBLIOPHAGIST
CALLISTHENICS
COLLABORATION
COLLABORATIVE
COLLIESHANGIE
COLLOQUIALISM
EFFLORESCENCE
GUILTLESSNESS
HALLUCINATION
HALLUCINATORY
INFLEXIBILITY
INFLORESCENCE
JOLLIFICATION
MALLEMAROKING
MOLLIFICATION
NULLIFICATION
PARLIAMENTARY
PHILADELPHIAN
PHILANTHROPIC
PHILOSOPHICAL
POLLICITATION
PRELIMINARIES
PROLIFERATION
QUALIFICATION
REALISTICALLY
REPLENISHMENT
ROLLERBLADING
ROLLERCOASTER
SPELEOLOGICAL
STYLISTICALLY
SUBLIEUTENANT
SWOLLENHEADED
TABLESPOONFUL
UNFLINCHINGLY
WHOLESOMENESS
ANIMADVERSION
COMMEMORATION
COMMEMORATIVE
COMMENSURABLE
COMMERCIALIZE
COMMISERATION
COMMUNICATION
COMMUNICATIVE
CRIMINOLOGIST
DERMATOLOGIST
DIAMETRICALLY
DRAMATIZATION
FORMALIZATION
GEOMETRICALLY
GLUMDALCLITCH
GRAMMATICALLY
HAMMERKLAVIER
HAMMERTHROWER
HARMONIZATION
HERMAPHRODITE
MISMANAGEMENT
NORMALIZATION
PREMEDITATION
PRIMOGENITURE
PROMISCUOUSLY
REIMBURSEMENT
UNEMBARRASSED
UNIMAGINATIVE
UNIMPEACHABLE
UNIMPRESSIBLE
ARUNDINACEOUS
BLANDISHMENTS
CHANGEABILITY
CHINKERINCHEE
COUNTERACTING
COUNTERATTACK
COUNTERCHARGE
COUNTERFEITER
COUNTRYPEOPLE
EPANADIPLOSIS
FRANKALMOIGNE
GRANDDAUGHTER
GRANDILOQUENT
GRANDPARENTAL
MAGNANIMOUSLY
MAGNIFICATION
MAGNIFICENTLY
MAGNILOQUENCE
NEANDERTHALER
PAINSTAKINGLY
PRONOUNCEMENT
PRONUNCIATION
QUINQUAGESIMA
REINCARNATION
REINFORCEMENT
REINSTATEMENT
REUNIFICATION
ROUNDTHEWORLD
SCANDALMONGER
SCINTILLATING
SCINTILLATION
SIGNIFICANTLY
SIGNIFICATION
SPINDLESHANKS
SPINECHILLING
SPONTANEOUSLY
THANKLESSNESS
THUNDERSTRUCK
TRANQUILLISER
TRANQUILLIZER
TRANSATLANTIC
TRANSCRIPTION
TRANSGRESSION
TRANSISTORIZE
TRANSLITERATE
TRANSMUTATION
TRANSPARENTLY
TRANSPIRATION
TRANSPORTABLE
TRANSPOSITION
UNANTICIPATED
UNENLIGHTENED
UNINHABITABLE
UNINTELLIGENT
UNINTENTIONAL
UNINTERESTING
UNINTERRUPTED
VULNERABILITY
ACCOMMODATING
ACCOMMODATION
ACCOMPANIMENT
ACCOUTREMENTS
AFFORESTATION
APPORTIONMENT
ARMOURPLATING
ASTONISHINGLY
AUTOBIOGRAPHY
AUTOCEPHALOUS
AUTOMATICALLY
BLOODCURDLING
CHRONOLOGICAL
DECOMPOSITION
DECOMPRESSION
DECONTAMINATE
DEFORESTATION
DEMONSTRATION
DEMONSTRATIVE
DÉSOBLIGEANTE
DRYOPITHECINE
ENCOURAGEMENT
ENTOMOLOGICAL
EXCOMMUNICATE
EXPOSTULATION
HOMOSEXUALITY
HYPOCHONDRIAC
IDIORRHYTHMIC
IDIOSYNCRATIC
IGNOMINIOUSLY
IMPONDERABLES
IMPOSSIBILITY
INCOMBUSTIBLE
INCOMMUNICADO
INCOMPETENTLY
INCONCEIVABLE
INCONSIDERATE
INCONSISTENCY
INCONSPICUOUS
INCONTESTABLE
INCONVENIENCE
INCORPORATION
INCORRUPTIBLE
INVOLUNTARILY
MONOCOTYLEDON
MONONUCLEOSIS
MONOTHALAMOUS
OPPORTUNISTIC
OPPORTUNITIES
PELOPONNESIAN
PREOCCUPATION
PYROTECHNICAL
REMORSELESSLY
RESOURCEFULLY
REVOLUTIONARY
REVOLUTIONIZE
SCHOLARLINESS
SCHOOLTEACHER
SUBORDINATION
THEOLOGICALLY
THEORETICALLY
TOPOGRAPHICAL
TYPOGRAPHICAL
UNCOMFORTABLE
UNCOMFORTABLY
UNCOMMUNICATE
UNCOMPLICATED
UNCONDITIONAL
UNCONQUERABLE
UNCONSCIOUSLY
UNCOOPERATIVE
UNCOORDINATED
UNFORESEEABLE
UNFORGETTABLE
UNFORTUNATELY
UPTOTHEMINUTE
ACUPUNCTURIST
COMPANIONABLE
COMPANIONSHIP
COMPARABILITY
COMPARATIVELY
COMPASSIONATE
COMPATIBILITY
COMPLEMENTARY
COMPLIMENTARY
COMPREHENSION
COMPREHENSIVE
DEIPNOSOPHIST
DISPARAGEMENT
DISPASSIONATE
DISPROPORTION
ELEPHANTIASIS
EPIPHENOMENON

INAPPROPRIATE
INSPIRATIONAL
KAPPELMEISTER
LAMPADEPHORIA
MORPHOLOGICAL
PERPENDICULAR
PREPONDERANCE
PREPOSSESSING
PREPOSSESSION
PREPROGRAMMED
PROPHETICALLY
PROPORTIONATE
PROPRIETORIAL
RAPPROCHEMENT
RHYPAROGRAPHY
SHAPELESSNESS
STAPHYLINIDAE
STEPPINGSTONE
SUPPLEMENTARY
SUSPERCOLLATE
SYMPIESOMETER
TEMPERAMENTAL
AFFREIGHTMENT
APPROPINQUATE
APPROPRIATION
APPROXIMATELY
APPROXIMATION
CHARACTERISED
CHARACTERLESS
CHOREOGRAPHER
CLARIFICATION
COMRADEINARMS
CORRESPONDENT
CORRESPONDING
CORROBORATION
CORROBORATORY
DECRIMINALIZE
DISRESPECTFUL
ENERGETICALLY
EXPROPRIATION
EXTRAORDINARY
EXTRAPOLATION
EXTRAVAGANTLY
FERROCONCRETE
FUERTEVENTURA
GARRULOUSNESS
GLORIFICATION
HEARTBREAKING
HIEROGLYPHICS
HORRIPILATION
HYBRIDIZATION
HYDRAULICALLY
HYDROELECTRIC
IMPRACTICABLE
IMPRESSIONISM
IMPRESSIONIST
IMPROBABILITY
IMPROVIDENTLY
IMPROVISATION
INCREDULOUSLY
INCRIMINATING
INCRIMINATORY
INTRANSIGENCE
INTRINSICALLY
INTROSPECTION
INTROSPECTIVE
LIBRARIANSHIP
MATRICULATION
MAURIKIGUSARI
MICROCOMPUTER
MICROORGANISM
NONRESISTANCE
OUTRECUIDANCE
OVEREMPHASIZE
OVERSTATEMENT
PATRIOTICALLY
PETRIFICATION
PETROCHEMICAL
PHARMACOPOEIA
QUARTERMASTER
QUARTODECIMAN
QUERULOUSNESS
REARRANGEMENT
RECRIMINATION
RECRIMINATORY
RECRUDESCENCE
REFRIGERATION
REFRIGERATORS
REPREHENSIBLE
REPREHENSIBLY
REPROACHFULLY
REPROGRAPHICS
RETROGRESSION
RETROSPECTIVE
SECRETIVENESS
SPORTSMANLIKE
SPORTSMANSHIP
STERCORACEOUS
STERILIZATION
SUPRANATIONAL
SURREPTITIOUS
TETRASYLLABIC
THERMONUCLEAR
THERMOPLASTIC
THOROUGHBRACE
THOROUGHGOING
THYROIDECTOMY
UNGRAMMATICAL
UNPRECEDENTED
UNPREDICTABLE
UNPRETENTIOUS
UNPROGRESSIVE
UNTRUSTWORTHY
VITRIFICATION
ARISTROCRATIC
BOUSTROPHEDON
CLISHMACLAVER
CLOSEDCIRCUIT
CONSANGUINITY
CONSCIENTIOUS
CONSCIOUSNESS
CONSECTANEOUS
CONSECUTIVELY
CONSEQUENTIAL
CONSERVATOIRE
CONSIDERATELY
CONSIDERATION
CONSOLIDATION
CONSPICUOUSLY
CONSPURCATION
CONSTELLATION
CONSTERNATION
CROSSQUESTION
DISSEMINATION
DISSIMILARITY
DISSIMULATION
FALSIFICATION
FOSSILIZATION
GLOSSOGRAPHER
HORSEFEATHERS
HOUSEBREAKING
LEISURELINESS
LISSOTRICHOUS
MASSACHUSETTS
MEISTERSINGER
MESSERSCHMITT
NONSUFFICIENT
OUTSTANDINGLY
PASSCHENDAELE
PASSEMENTERIE
PASSIONFLOWER
PERSONALITIES
PERSPICACIOUS
PHYSHARMONICA
PHYSIOGNOMIST
PHYSIOLOGICAL
PHYSIOTHERAPY
PRESERVATIVES
PRESSURELOCAL
PROSOPOGRAPHY
QUESTIONNAIRE
RENSSELAERITE
SEISMOLOGICAL
SENSATIONALLY
SENSELESSNESS
SENSITIVENESS
SPASMODICALLY
SUBSERVIENTLY
SUBSTANTIALLY
SWASHBUCKLING
TONSILLECTOMY
UNESTABLISHED
VERSIFICATION
AESTHETICALLY
ANYTHINGARIAN
ARITHMETICIAN
BEATIFICATION
BIOTECHNOLOGY
BUTTERFINGERS
CARTILAGINOUS
CAUTERIZATION
CERTIFICATION
CHATEAUBRIAND
CONTAMINATION
CONTEMPLATION
CONTEMPLATIVE
CONTENTEDNESS
CONTINUATIONS
CONTORTIONIST
CONTRABASSOON
CONTRACEPTION
CONTRACEPTIVE
CONTRADICTION
CONTRADICTORY
CONTRAFAGOTTO
CONTRAVENTION
CONTRIBUTIONS
CONTROVERSIAL
COSTEFFECTIVE
DEATHLESSNESS
DISTINGUISHED
EPITRACHELION
FANTASTICALLY
FEATHERWEIGHT
FERTILISATION
FERTILIZATION
FONTAINEBLEAU
FORTIFICATION
FORTUNETELLER
FOSTERPARENTS
GASTROCNEMIUS
GESTICULATION
GRATIFICATION
HORTICULTURAL
INSTANTANEOUS
INSTINCTIVELY
INSTITUTIONAL
INSTRUCTIONAL
JUSTIFICATION
JUXTAPOSITION
LEATHERJACKET
LECTISTERNIUM
LEPTOCEPHALUS
MASTIGOPHORAN
MORTIFICATION
MOUTHWATERING
MULTICOLOURED
MULTINATIONAL
MULTINUCLEATE
MULTITUDINOUS
MYSTIFICATION
NOSTALGICALLY
OPHTHALMOLOGY
OYSTERCATCHER
PARTHOGENESIS
PARTICIPATION
PARTICIPATORY
PARTICOLOURED
PARTICULARISE
PARTICULARITY

PARTICULARIZE
PHOTOCHEMICAL
PHOTOELECTRIC
PLATOCEPHALUS
PRETERNATURAL
PROTECTIONISM
PROTECTIONIST
PROTESTANTISM
PROTONOTARIAT
RECTIFICATION
SENTENTIOUSLY
SENTIMENTALLY
SEPTENTRIONES
SOUTHEASTERLY
SOUTHWESTERLY
SPITESPLENDID
STATESMANLIKE
STATESMANSHIP
STATIONMASTER
STATISTICALLY
SYNTACTICALLY
SYNTHETICALLY
TANTALIZINGLY
TINTINNABULUM
TORTOISESHELL
VENTRILOQUISM
VENTRILOQUIST
VICTIMIZATION
WEATHERBEATEN
ARGUMENTATIVE
DAGUERREOTYPE
DOCUMENTATION
ILLUMINATIONS
IMPULSIVENESS
INDUSTRIALIST
INDUSTRIALIZE
INDUSTRIOUSLY
INQUISITIVELY
INSUBORDINATE
INSUBSTANTIAL
INSUFFICIENCY
INSUPPORTABLE
LUXURIOUSNESS
MANUFACTURING
MISUNDERSTAND
MISUNDERSTOOD
PNEUMATICALLY
REFURBISHMENT
REGURGITATION
REPUBLICANISM
RESUSCITATION
SCHUTZSTAFFEL
SEQUESTRATION
SHOULDERBLADE
SIPUNCULOIDEA
THAUMATURGICS
THAUMATURGIST
THOUGHTLESSLY
TRAUMATICALLY
UNQUESTIONING

UNSUBSTANTIAL
CONVALESCENCE
CONVERSAZIONE
FRIVOLOUSNESS
GALVANIZATION
GRAVITATIONAL
INEVITABILITY
LAEVOROTATORY
NERVELESSNESS
PERVASIVENESS
PREVARICATION
PRIVATIZATION
PROVINCIALISM
PROVISIONALLY
PROVOCATIVELY
PULVERIZATION
SERVILEMENTAL
SUOVETAURILIA
AIRWORTHINESS
KNOWLEDGEABLE
SNOWBLINDNESS
WITWATERSRAND
INEXHAUSTIBLE
INEXPERIENCED
INEXPRESSIBLE
UNEXCEPTIONAL
UNEXPERIENCED
ACRYLONITRILE
CHRYSANTHEMUM
ENCYCLOPAEDIA
ENCYCLOPAEDIC
UNSYMMETRICAL
UNSYMPATHETIC

13:5

ALPHABETARIAN
ANIMADVERSION
APOCATASTASIS
ARCHAEOLOGIST
ARCHAEOPTERYX
BACCALAUREATE
BOUGAINVILLEA
CHARACTERISED
CHARACTERLESS
COLLABORATION
COLLABORATIVE
COMPANIONABLE
COMPANIONSHIP
COMPARABILITY
COMPARATIVELY
COMPASSIONATE
COMPATIBILITY
COMRADEINARMS
CONCATENATION
CONFARREATION
CONSANGUINITY
CONTAMINATION
CONVALESCENCE

DERMATOLOGIST
DIACATHOLICON
DIFFARREATION
DISPARAGEMENT
DISPASSIONATE
DRAMATIZATION
EPANADIPLOSIS
EXTRAORDINARY
EXTRAPOLATION
EXTRAVAGANTLY
FANTASTICALLY
FONTAINEBLEAU
FORMALIZATION
FUNDAMENTALLY
GALVANIZATION
HERMAPHRODITE
HYDRAULICALLY
IMPRACTICABLE
INSTANTANEOUS
INTRANSIGENCE
JUXTAPOSITION
LACKADAISICAL
LAMPADEPHORIA
LIBRARIANSHIP
MAGNANIMOUSLY
MASSACHUSETTS
MECHANIZATION
MISMANAGEMENT
NORMALIZATION
NOSTALGICALLY
PANHARMONICON
PERVASIVENESS
PHILADELPHIAN
PHILANTHROPIC
PRECAUTIONARY
PREFABRICATED
PREVARICATION
PRIVATIZATION
RHADAMANTHINE
RHYPAROGRAPHY
SARCASTICALLY
SELFADDRESSED
SENSATIONALLY
SQUEAMISHNESS
SUPRANATIONAL
SYNTACTICALLY
TALKATIVENESS
TANTALIZINGLY
TETRASYLLABIC
THREATENINGLY
UNGRAMMATICAL
UNIMAGINATIVE
VULCANIZATION
VULGARIZATION
WITWATERSRAND
AUTOBIOGRAPHY
DEFIBRILLATOR
DÉSOBLIGEANTE
ESTABLISHMENT
EXHIBITIONIST

FLABBERGASTED
INSUBORDINATE
INSUBSTANTIAL
REIMBURSEMENT
REPUBLICANISM
SNOWBLINDNESS
UNEMBARRASSED
UNSUBSTANTIAL
ANTICLOCKWISE
ANTICOAGULANT
AUTOCEPHALOUS
CONSCIENTIOUS
CONSCIOUSNESS
EFFECTIVENESS
ENCYCLOPAEDIA
ENCYCLOPAEDIC
GYNECOLOGICAL
HYPOCHONDRIAC
INSECTIVOROUS
IRRECOVERABLE
KANGCHENJUNGA
LEXICOGRAPHER
MONOCOTYLEDON
OBJECTIONABLE
OBJECTIVENESS
OFFICIOUSNESS
PASSCHENDAELE
PREOCCUPATION
REINCARNATION
SALACIOUSNESS
SELFCONFESSED
SELFCONFIDENT
SELFCONSCIOUS
SELFCONTAINED
SEMICONDUCTOR
STERCORACEOUS
TREACHEROUSLY
UNACCOMPANIED
UNACCOUNTABLE
UNACCOUNTABLY
UNEXCEPTIONAL
UNNECESSARILY
VIVACIOUSNESS
VORACIOUSNESS
ARUNDINACEOUS
BLANDISHMENTS
BLOODCURDLING
DISADVANTAGED
EXPEDITIONARY
EXPEDITIOUSLY
GLUMDALCLITCH
GRANDDAUGHTER
GRANDILOQUENT
GRANDPARENTAL
INSIDIOUSNESS
LEPIDOPTERIST
MALADJUSTMENT
NEANDERTHALER
PARADOXICALLY
ROUNDTHEWORLD

SCANDALMONGER
SCHADENFREUDE
SPINDLESHANKS
STEADFASTNESS
THUNDERSTRUCK
AFFREIGHTMENT
ANTHELMINTHIC
BIODEGRADABLE
BIOTECHNOLOGY
BROKENHEARTED
BUNGEEJUMPING
BUTTERFINGERS
CAUTERIZATION
CHATEAUBRIAND
CHOREOGRAPHER
CLOSEDCIRCUIT
COMMEMORATION
COMMEMORATIVE
COMMENSURABLE
COMMERCIALIZE
CONCENTRATION
CONCEPTIONIST
CONCEPTUALIZE
CONCESSIONARY
CONDESCENDING
CONDESCENSION
CONFECTIONERS
CONFECTIONERY
CONFEDERATION
CONSECTANEOUS
CONSECUTIVELY
CONSEQUENTIAL
CONSERVATOIRE
CONTEMPLATION
CONTEMPLATIVE
CONTENTEDNESS
CONVERSAZIONE
CORRESPONDENT
CORRESPONDING
COSTEFFECTIVE
DAGUERREOTYPE
DIAMETRICALLY
DIFFERENTIATE
DISHEARTENING
DISRESPECTFUL
DISSEMINATION
FORGETFULNESS
FOSTERPARENTS
GEOMETRICALLY
GLOBETROTTING
GYNAECOLOGIST
HAMMERKLAVIER
HAMMERTHROWER
HORSEFEATHERS
HOUSEBREAKING
IMPRESSIONISM
IMPRESSIONIST
INCREDULOUSLY
INFLEXIBILITY
ISOGEOTHERMAL
JIGGERYPOKERY
KAPPELMEISTER
KIDDERMINSTER
MALLEMAROKING
MATHEMATICIAN
MESSERSCHMITT
MISCEGENATION
MISCELLANEOUS
NERVELESSNESS
NONRESISTANCE
ORCHESTRATION
OUTRECUIDANCE
OVEREMPHASIZE
OYSTERCATCHER
PALAEONTOLOGY
PASSEMENTERIE
PERFECTIONIST
PERPENDICULAR
PREMEDITATION
PRESERVATIVES
PRETERNATURAL
PROFECTITIOUS
PROFESSORSHIP
PROJECTIONIST
PROTECTIONISM
PROTECTIONIST
PROTESTANTISM
PULVERIZATION
REPLENISHMENT
REPREHENSIBLE
REPREHENSIBLY
ROLLERBLADING
ROLLERCOASTER
RUTHERFORDIUM
SECRETIVENESS
SENSELESSNESS
SENTENTIOUSLY
SEPTENTRIONES
SEQUESTRATION
SHAPELESSNESS
SPELEOLOGICAL
SPINECHILLING
SPITESPLENDID
STATESMANLIKE
STATESMANSHIP
SUBJECTMATTER
SUBSERVIENTLY
SUOVETAURILIA
SURREPTITIOUS
SUSPERCOLLATE
SWEDENBORGIAN
TABLESPOONFUL
TEMPERAMENTAL
TENDERHEARTED
UNPRECEDENTED
UNPREDICTABLE
UNPRETENTIOUS
UNQUESTIONING
VULNERABILITY
WHOLESOMENESS
AQUIFOLIACEAE
ARTIFICIALITY
DECAFFEINATED
GRIEFSTRICKEN
INDEFATIGABLE
INDEFATIGABLY
INDIFFERENTLY
INEFFICIENTLY
INSUFFICIENCY
LIEBFRAUMILCH
MANIFESTATION
MANUFACTURING
RAMIFICATIONS
REINFORCEMENT
ANTIGROPELOES
CATEGORICALLY
CHANGEABILITY
DESEGREGATION
ENERGETICALLY
ENLIGHTENMENT
INSIGNIFICANT
METAGRABOLISE
METAGROBOLISE
PEREGRINATION
SELFGOVERNING
SPRIGHTLINESS
THOUGHTLESSLY
TOPOGRAPHICAL
TYPOGRAPHICAL
AESTHETICALLY
ANACHRONISTIC
ANTIHISTAMINE
ANYTHINGARIAN
ARITHMETICIAN
BRACHIOSAURUS
CLISHMACLAVER
DEATHLESSNESS
ELEPHANTIASIS
EPIPHENOMENON
FEATHERWEIGHT
FRIGHTENINGLY
FRIGHTFULNESS
INEXHAUSTIBLE
LEATHERJACKET
LIECHTENSTEIN
MERCHANDIZING
MISCHIEVOUSLY
MORPHOLOGICAL
MOUTHWATERING
NEIGHBOURHOOD
OPHTHALMOLOGY
PARTHOGENESIS
PHYSHARMONICA
PROPHETICALLY
PSYCHOANALYSE
PSYCHOANALYST
PSYCHOLOGICAL
PSYCHOSOMATIC
PSYCHOTHERAPY
SACCHAROMYCES
SOUTHEASTERLY
SOUTHWESTERLY
STAPHYLINIDAE
SWASHBUCKLING
SYNTHETICALLY
TRICHOSANTHIN
UNINHABITABLE
WEATHERBEATEN
WEIGHTLIFTING
AMPHIGASTRIUM
AMPLIFICATION
ARCHIMANDRITE
ARCHITECTURAL
BEATIFICATION
BIBLIOGRAPHER
BIBLIOPHAGIST
CALLISTHENICS
CARTILAGINOUS
CERTIFICATION
CLARIFICATION
COLLIESHANGIE
COMMISERATION
CONDITIONALLY
CONFIGURATION
CONSIDERATELY
CONSIDERATION
CONTINUATIONS
CRIMINOLOGIST
DECRIMINALIZE
DISFIGUREMENT
DISSIMILARITY
DISSIMULATION
DISTINGUISHED
FALSIFICATION
FERTILISATION
FERTILIZATION
FORTIFICATION
FOSSILIZATION
GESTICULATION
GLORIFICATION
GRATIFICATION
GRAVITATIONAL
HORRIPILATION
HORTICULTURAL
HYBRIDIZATION
IMAGINATIVELY
INCRIMINATING
INCRIMINATORY
INEVITABILITY
INQUISITIVELY
INSPIRATIONAL
INSTINCTIVELY
INSTITUTIONAL
INTRINSICALLY
JOLLIFICATION
JUSTIFICATION
KALEIDOSCOPIC
LECTISTERNIUM
MACHIAVELLIAN
MACHICOLATION

MAGNIFICATION
MAGNIFICENTLY
MAGNILOQUENCE
MASTIGOPHORAN
MATRICULATION
MAURIKIGUSARI
MERCILESSNESS
MOLLIFICATION
MORTIFICATION
MULTICOLOURED
MULTINATIONAL
MULTINUCLEATE
MULTITUDINOUS
MYSTIFICATION
NULLIFICATION
PAEDIATRICIAN
PANDICULATION
PARLIAMENTARY
PARTICIPATION
PARTICIPATORY
PARTICOLOURED
PARTICULARISE
PARTICULARITY
PARTICULARIZE
PASSIONFLOWER
PATRIOTICALLY
PETRIFICATION
PHYSIOGNOMIST
PHYSIOLOGICAL
PHYSIOTHERAPY
POLLICITATION
PRECIPITATELY
PRECIPITATION
PRELIMINARIES
PROFITABILITY
PROLIFERATION
PROMISCUOUSLY
PROVINCIALISM
PROVISIONALLY
QUALIFICATION
REALISTICALLY
RECRIMINATION
RECRIMINATORY
RECTIFICATION
REFRIGERATION
REFRIGERATORS
REUNIFICATION
SENSITIVENESS
SENTIMENTALLY
SERVILEMENTAL
SIGNIFICANTLY
SIGNIFICATION
SOPHISTICATED
SPECIFICATION
STABILIZATION
STATIONMASTER
STATISTICALLY
STERILIZATION
STYLISTICALLY
SUBLIEUTENANT

SYMPIESOMETER
TINTINNABULUM
TONSILLECTOMY
TRADITIONALLY
UNFLINCHINGLY
VERCINGETORIX
VERSIFICATION
VICTIMIZATION
VITRIFICATION
XIPHIPLASTRON
CHINKERINCHEE
FOREKNOWLEDGE
FRANKALMOIGNE
KNICKERBOCKER
KNICKKNACKERY
STOCKBREEDING
STRIKEBREAKER
THANKLESSNESS
ACRYLONITRILE
BOUILLABAISSE
COMPLEMENTARY
COMPLIMENTARY
CONFLAGRATION
DEMILITARIZED
DEVELOPMENTAL
DISILLUSIONED
DOUBLEGLAZING
EMBELLISHMENT
IMPULSIVENESS
INFALLIBILITY
INTELLIGENTLY
INVOLUNTARILY
KNOWLEDGEABLE
MIDDLEBREAKER
PARALLELOGRAM
PROBLEMATICAL
PROCLEUSMATIC
PUSILLANIMITY
PUSILLANIMOUS
RECALCITRANCE
REVOLUTIONARY
REVOLUTIONIZE
SCHOLARLINESS
SEMBLANCECORD
SHOULDERBLADE
SUPPLEMENTARY
SWOLLENHEADED
THEOLOGICALLY
UMBELLIFEROUS
UNENLIGHTENED
UNWILLINGNESS
ACCOMMODATING
ACCOMMODATION
ACCOMPANIMENT
ARGUMENTATIVE
AUTOMATICALLY
CEREMONIOUSLY
DECOMPOSITION
DECOMPRESSION
DOCUMENTATION

ENTOMOLOGICAL
EPHEMEROPTERA
EXCOMMUNICATE
FRAGMENTATION
GRAMMATICALLY
IGNOMINIOUSLY
ILLUMINATIONS
INCOMBUSTIBLE
INCOMMUNICADO
INCOMPETENTLY
METAMORPHOSIS
ORNAMENTATION
PERAMBULATION
PHARMACOPOEIA
PNEUMATICALLY
PRAGMATICALLY
REDEMPTIONIST
REGIMENTATION
SCHEMATICALLY
SEDIMENTATION
SEISMOLOGICAL
SOLEMNIZATION
SPASMODICALLY
THAUMATURGICS
THAUMATURGIST
THERMONUCLEAR
THERMOPLASTIC
TRAUMATICALLY
UNCOMFORTABLE
UNCOMFORTABLY
UNCOMMUNICATE
UNCOMPLICATED
UNSYMMETRICAL
UNSYMPATHETIC
ADMINISTRATOR
ADVENTUROUSLY
AFFENPINSCHER
ASTONISHINGLY
ATTENTIVENESS
BUSINESSWOMAN
CHRONOLOGICAL
DECONTAMINATE
DEFENSIBILITY
DEIPNOSOPHIST
DEMONSTRATION
DEMONSTRATIVE
DEPENDABILITY
DISENGAGEMENT
DISINTERESTED
ECCENTRICALLY
EXPANSIVENESS
GYNANDROMORPH
IMPONDERABLES
INCANDESCENCE
INCONCEIVABLE
INCONSIDERATE
INCONSISTENCY
INCONSPICUOUS
INCONTESTABLE
INCONVENIENCE

INFINITESIMAL
INGENUOUSNESS
INSENSITIVITY
INTENTIONALLY
INVENTIVENESS
INVINCIBILITY
LYCANTHROPIST
MISANTHROPIST
MISUNDERSTAND
MISUNDERSTOOD
MONONUCLEOSIS
OFFENSIVENESS
PARANTHROPOUS
PARENTHETICAL
POTENTIOMETER
PROGNOSTICATE
REMINISCENCES
SHRINKWRAPPED
SIPUNCULOIDEA
STRANGULATION
STRENUOUSNESS
TECHNOLOGICAL
TRIANGULATION
UNCONDITIONAL
UNCONQUERABLE
UNCONSCIOUSLY
UNGENTLEMANLY
UNMENTIONABLE
AGGIORNAMENTO
AGGLOMERATION
AIRWORTHINESS
APPROPINQUATE
APPROPRIATION
APPROXIMATELY
APPROXIMATION
AUTHORISATION
AUTHORITARIAN
AUTHORITATIVE
AUTHORIZATION
CARBONIFEROUS
COLLOQUIALISM
CONSOLIDATION
CONTORTIONIST
CORROBORATION
CORROBORATORY
DISCOLORATION
DISCONCERTING
DISCONNECTION
DISCONTINUITY
DISCONTINUOUS
DISHONOURABLE
DISHONOURABLY
EFFLORESCENCE
EXPROPRIATION
FERROCONCRETE
FRIVOLOUSNESS
HARMONIZATION
HIEROGLYPHICS
HYDROELECTRIC
IMPROBABILITY

IMPROVIDENTLY
IMPROVISATION
INFLORESCENCE
INTROSPECTION
INTROSPECTIVE
INVIOLABILITY
LAEVOROTATORY
LEPTOCEPHALUS
LISSOTRICHOUS
METEOROLOGIST
MICROCOMPUTER
MICROORGANISM
MISCONCEPTION
NATIONALISTIC
NONCONFORMIST
NONCONFORMITY
PERSONALITIES
PETROCHEMICAL
PHILOSOPHICAL
PHOTOCHEMICAL
PHOTOELECTRIC
PLATOCEPHALUS
POLIOMYELITIS
PRECONCEPTION
PREDOMINANTLY
PREPONDERANCE
PREPOSSESSING
PREPOSSESSION
PRIMOGENITURE
PRONOUNCEMENT
PROPORTIONATE
PROSOPOGRAPHY
PROTONOTARIAT
PROVOCATIVELY
RADIOACTIVITY
RATIONALALITY
REPROACHFULLY
REPROGRAPHICS
RETROGRESSION
RETROSPECTIVE
SCHOOLTEACHER
SOCIOECONOMIC
SUBCONTRACTOR
THOROUGHBRACE
THOROUGHGOING
THYROIDECTOMY
TORTOISESHELL
UNCOOPERATIVE
UNCOORDINATED
UNPROGRESSIVE
VIDEOCASSETTE
VIDEORECORDER
ACCEPTABILITY
ACCEPTILATION
CONSPICUOUSLY
CONSPURCATION
DISAPPEARANCE
DISAPPOINTING
DRYOPITHECINE
ENCEPHALOCELE

EQUIPONDERATE
EXCEPTIONABLE
EXCEPTIONALLY
INAPPROPRIATE
INDEPENDENTLY
INEXPERIENCED
INEXPRESSIBLE
INSUPPORTABLE
IRREPLACEABLE
IRREPRESSIBLE
METAPHYSICIAN
PAPAPRELATIST
PARAPHERNALIA
PELOPONNESIAN
PERSPICACIOUS
RECEPTIVENESS
SLEEPLESSNESS
STEEPLECHASER
STEPPINGSTONE
STREPTOCOCCUS
UNEXPERIENCED
UNIMPEACHABLE
UNIMPRESSIBLE
VICEPRESIDENT
QUINQUAGESIMA
TRANQUILLISER
TRANQUILLIZER
ADVERTISEMENT
AFFIRMATIVELY
AFFORESTATION
AIRCRAFTWOMAN
ALTERNATIVELY
APPORTIONMENT
ASCERTAINABLE
CLAIRAUDIENCE
COMPREHENSION
COMPREHENSIVE
CONFRONTATION
CONGRESSIONAL
CONGRESSWOMAN
CONTRABASSOON
CONTRACEPTION
CONTRACEPTIVE
CONTRADICTION
CONTRADICTORY
CONTRAFAGOTTO
CONTRAVENTION
CONTRIBUTIONS
CONTROVERSIAL
DEFERVESCENCE
DEFORESTATION
DETERIORATION
DETERMINATION
DISCREDITABLE
DISCREDITABLY
DISCRETIONARY
DISGRACEFULLY
DISPROPORTION
EFFERVESCENCE
EMBARRASSMENT

ENTEROPNEUSTA
ENTERTAINMENT
ENVIRONMENTAL
EPITRACHELION
EXTERMINATION
GASTROCNEMIUS
GENERALISSIMO
GOODRIGHTEOUS
HETERAUXESISM
HETEROGENEOUS
HUNDREDWEIGHT
HYPERCRITICAL
HYPERSTHENITE
IDIORRHYTHMIC
IMPERCEPTIBLE
IMPERCEPTIBLY
IMPERIALISTIC
IMPERSONATING
IMPERSONATION
IMPERTINENTLY
IMPERTURBABLE
IMPERTURBABLY
INCARCERATION
INCORPORATION
INCORRUPTIBLE
INSTRUCTIONAL
INTERCALATION
INTERESTINGLY
INTERMARRIAGE
INTERNATIONAL
INTERPERSONAL
INTERPOLATION
INTERROGATION
INTERROGATIVE
LUXURIOUSNESS
MATERIALISTIC
MODERNIZATION
OPPORTUNISTIC
OPPORTUNITIES
OWNEROCCUPIER
PATERFAMILIAS
PATERNALISTIC
PREPROGRAMMED
PROCRASTINATE
PROGRESSIVELY
PROPRIETORIAL
QUADRAGESIMAL
QUADRILATERAL
QUADRUPLICATE
RAPPROCHEMENT
REARRANGEMENT
REFURBISHMENT
REGURGITATION
REMORSELESSLY
REPERCUSSIONS
REVERBERATION
SUBORDINATION
SUPERABUNDANT
SUPERANNUATED
SUPERFICIALLY

SUPERFLUOUSLY
SUPERLATIVELY
SUPERNUMERARY
SUPERORDINATE
SUPERSTITIOUS
TAPERECORDING
THEORETICALLY
UNCEREMONIOUS
UNDERACHIEVER
UNDERCARRIAGE
UNDERCLOTHING
UNDERESTIMATE
UNDERGRADUATE
UNDERSTANDING
UNDERSTRAPPER
UNFORESEEABLE
UNFORGETTABLE
UNFORTUNATELY
UNPARTITIONED
UNSERVICEABLE
VENTRILOQUISM
VENTRILOQUIST
ACCESSIBILITY
ASSASSINATION
BREASTFEEDING
CHEESEMONGERS
CHRISTMASTIME
CHRYSANTHEMUM
CROSSQUESTION
DISESTIMATION
ESCHSCHOLTZIA
EXPOSTULATION
GLOSSOGRAPHER
HEMISPHERICAL
HOMOSEXUALITY
IDIOSYNCRATIC
IMPOSSIBILITY
INDESCRIBABLE
INDESCRIBABLY
INDISPENSABLE
INDISPOSITION
INDUSTRIALIST
INDUSTRIALIZE
INDUSTRIOUSLY
INVESTIGATION
INVESTIGATIVE
IRRESPONSIBLE
IRRESPONSIBLY
JURISPRUDENCE
LONGSUFFERING
MAGISTERIALLY
OVERSTATEMENT
PAINSTAKINGLY
PRESSURELOCAL
REINSTATEMENT
RENSSELAERITE
RESUSCITATION
TRANSATLANTIC
TRANSCRIPTION
TRANSGRESSION

TRANSISTORIZE
TRANSLITERATE
TRANSMUTATION
TRANSPARENTLY
TRANSPIRATION
TRANSPORTABLE
TRANSPOSITION
UNDISCIPLINED
UNFASHIONABLE
ARISTROCRATIC
BOUSTROPHEDON
CONSTELLATION
CONSTERNATION
COUNTERACTING
COUNTERATTACK
COUNTERCHARGE
COUNTERFEITER
COUNTRYPEOPLE
CRAFTSMANSHIP
DENATIONALIZE
ELECTROCUTION
ELECTROMAGNET
ELECTROMOTIVE
FACETIOUSNESS
FRACTIOUSNESS
FUERTEVENTURA
GUILTLESSNESS
HEARTBREAKING
INDETERMINATE
IRRETRIEVABLE
IRRETRIEVABLY
LIGHTFINGERED
MADETOMEASURE
MEDITERRANEAN
MEISTERSINGER
MOCKTECHNICAL
MONOTHALAMOUS
NEMATHELMINTH
NIGHTWATCHMAN
ORNITHOLOGIST
OUTSTANDINGLY
PENETRABILITY
PUNCTILIOUSLY
PYROTECHNICAL
QUARTERMASTER
QUARTODECIMAN
QUESTIONNAIRE
RECITATIONIST
RIGHTEOUSNESS
SANCTIMONIOUS
SCHUTZSTAFFEL
SCINTILLATING
SCINTILLATION
SOMATOTROPHIN
SPECTACULARLY
SPECTROGRAPHY
SPONTANEOUSLY
SPORTSMANLIKE
SPORTSMANSHIP
STRATEGICALLY

SUBSTANTIALLY
SWEETSMELLING
THEATRICALITY
TRACTARIANISM
UNANTICIPATED
UNESTABLISHED
UNINTELLIGENT
UNINTENTIONAL
UNINTERESTING
UNINTERRUPTED
UPTOTHEMINUTE
VEGETARIANISM
ACCOUTREMENTS
ACUPUNCTURIST
ARMOURPLATING
BILDUNGSROMAN
CIRCUMAMBIENT
CIRCUMFERENCE
CIRCUMSTANCES
CIRCUMVENTION
COEDUCATIONAL
COMMUNICATION
COMMUNICATIVE
CONCUPISCENCE
CREDULOUSNESS
ENCOURAGEMENT
FORTUNETELLER
GARRULOUSNESS
HALLUCINATION
HALLUCINATORY
LEISURELINESS
NONSUFFICIENT
PERFUNCTORILY
PRONUNCIATION
QUERULOUSNESS
RECRUDESCENCE
RESOURCEFULLY
TONGUEINCHEEK
TONGUETWISTER
UNADULTERATED
UNTRUSTWORTHY
INADVERTENTLY
INDIVIDUALISM
INDIVIDUALIST
INDIVIDUALITY
REDEVELOPMENT
SCHIZOPHRENIA
SCHIZOPHRENIC

13:6

AIRCRAFTWOMAN
AUTOMATICALLY
CHATEAUBRIAND
CHRYSANTHEMUM
CLAIRAUDIENCE
CONFLAGRATION
CONTRABASSOON
CONTRACEPTION
CONTRACEPTIVE

CONTRADICTION
CONTRADICTORY
CONTRAFAGOTTO
CONTRAVENTION
DISGRACEFULLY
DISHEARTENING
ELEPHANTIASIS
EPITRACHELION
FRANKALMOIGNE
GENERALISSIMO
GLUMDALCLITCH
GRAMMATICALLY
HETERAUXESISM
INDEFATIGABLE
INDEFATIGABLY
INEXHAUSTIBLE
MACHIAVELLIAN
MANUFACTURING
MERCHANDIZING
OPHTHALMOLOGY
OUTSTANDINGLY
PAEDIATRICIAN
PARLIAMENTARY
PHARMACOPOEIA
PHYSHARMONICA
PNEUMATICALLY
PRAGMATICALLY
PROCRASTINATE
QUADRAGESIMAL
RADIOACTIVITY
REARRANGEMENT
RECITATIONIST
REINCARNATION
REPROACHFULLY
SACCHAROMYCES
SCANDALMONGER
SCHEMATICALLY
SCHOLARLINESS
SEMBLANCECORD
SPECTACULARLY
SPONTANEOUSLY
SUBSTANTIALLY
SUPERABUNDANT
SUPERANNUATED
THAUMATURGICS
THAUMATURGIST
TRACTARIANISM
TRANSATLANTIC
TRAUMATICALLY
UNDERACHIEVER
UNEMBARRASSED
UNESTABLISHED
UNINHABITABLE
VEGETARIANISM
ALPHABETARIAN
COLLABORATION
COLLABORATIVE
CORROBORATION
CORROBORATORY
HEARTBREAKING

HOUSEBREAKING
IMPROBABILITY
INCOMBUSTIBLE
NEIGHBOURHOOD
PERAMBULATION
PREFABRICATED
REFURBISHMENT
REVERBERATION
STOCKBREEDING
SWASHBUCKLING
BIOTECHNOLOGY
BLOODCURDLING
CHARACTERISED
CHARACTERLESS
COEDUCATIONAL
CONFECTIONERS
CONFECTIONERY
CONSECTANEOUS
CONSECUTIVELY
ESCHSCHOLTZIA
FERROCONCRETE
GESTICULATION
GYNAECOLOGIST
HALLUCINATION
HALLUCINATORY
HORTICULTURAL
HYPERCRITICAL
IMPERCEPTIBLE
IMPERCEPTIBLY
IMPRACTICABLE
INCARCERATION
INCONCEIVABLE
INDESCRIBABLE
INDESCRIBABLY
INTERCALATION
INVINCIBILITY
LEPTOCEPHALUS
MACHICOLATION
MASSACHUSETTS
MATRICULATION
MICROCOMPUTER
MULTICOLOURED
OUTRECUIDANCE
PANDICULATION
PARTICIPATION
PARTICIPATORY
PARTICOLOURED
PARTICULARISE
PARTICULARITY
PARTICULARIZE
PERFECTIONIST
PETROCHEMICAL
PHOTOCHEMICAL
PLATOCEPHALUS
POLLICITATION
PREOCCUPATION
PROFECTITIOUS
PROJECTIONIST
PROTECTIONISM
PROTECTIONIST

PROVOCATIVELY
RECALCITRANCE
REPERCUSSIONS
RESUSCITATION
SIPUNCULOIDEA
SPINECHILLING
SUBJECTMATTER
SYNTACTICALLY
TRANSCRIPTION
UNDERCARRIAGE
UNDERCLOTHING
UNDISCIPLINED
UNPRECEDENTED
VIDEOCASSETTE
ANIMADVERSION
CLOSEDCIRCUIT
COMRADEINARMS
CONFEDERATION
CONSIDERATELY
CONSIDERATION
DEPENDABILITY
EPANADIPLOSIS
GRANDDAUGHTER
GYNANDROMORPH
HYBRIDIZATION
IMPONDERABLES
INCANDESCENCE
INCREDULOUSLY
KALEIDOSCOPIC
LACKADAISICAL
LAMPADEPHORIA
MISUNDERSTAND
MISUNDERSTOOD
PHILADELPHIAN
PREMEDITATION
RECRUDESCENCE
SELFADDRESSED
SHOULDERBLADE
SUBORDINATION
UNCONDITIONAL
UNPREDICTABLE
AESTHETICALLY
AFFORESTATION
ARCHAEOLOGIST
ARCHAEOPTERYX
ARGUMENTATIVE
AUTOCEPHALOUS
BUNGEEJUMPING
BUSINESSWOMAN
CHANGEABILITY
CHEESEMONGERS
CHINKERINCHEE
COLLIESHANGIE
COMPLEMENTARY
COMPREHENSION
COMPREHENSIVE
CONGRESSIONAL
CONGRESSWOMAN
CONSTELLATION
CONSTERNATION

COUNTERACTING
COUNTERATTACK
COUNTERCHARGE
COUNTERFEITER
DEFORESTATION
DISCREDITABLE
DISCREDITABLY
DISCRETIONARY
DOCUMENTATION
DOUBLEGLAZING
ENERGETICALLY
EPHEMEROPTERA
EPIPHENOMENON
FEATHERWEIGHT
FLABBERGASTED
FRAGMENTATION
FUERTEVENTURA
HOMOSEXUALITY
HUNDREDWEIGHT
HYDROELECTRIC
INADVERTENTLY
INDEPENDENTLY
INDETERMINATE
INEXPERIENCED
INTERESTINGLY
KNICKERBOCKER
KNOWLEDGEABLE
LEATHERJACKET
MANIFESTATION
MEDITERRANEAN
MEISTERSINGER
MIDDLEBREAKER
MOCKTECHNICAL
NEANDERTHALER
ORNAMENTATION
PHOTOELECTRIC
PROBLEMATICAL
PROCLEUSMATIC
PROGRESSIVELY
PROPHETICALLY
PYROTECHNICAL
QUARTERMASTER
REDEVELOPMENT
REGIMENTATION
RENSSELAERITE
RIGHTEOUSNESS
SCHADENFREUDE
SEDIMENTATION
SOCIOECONOMIC
SOUTHEASTERLY
STRATEGICALLY
STRIKEBREAKER
SUBLIEUTENANT
SUPPLEMENTARY
SWOLLENHEADED
SYMPIESOMETER
SYNTHETICALLY
TAPERECORDING
THEORETICALLY
THUNDERSTRUCK

TONGUEINCHEEK
TONGUETWISTER
UNCEREMONIOUS
UNDERESTIMATE
UNEXCEPTIONAL
UNEXPERIENCED
UNFORESEEABLE
UNIMPEACHABLE
UNINTELLIGENT
UNINTENTIONAL
UNINTERESTING
UNINTERRUPTED
UNNECESSARILY
WEATHERBEATEN
AMPLIFICATION
BEATIFICATION
CERTIFICATION
CLARIFICATION
COSTEFFECTIVE
DECAFFEINATED
FALSIFICATION
FORTIFICATION
GLORIFICATION
GRATIFICATION
HORSEFEATHERS
INDIFFERENTLY
INSUFFICIENCY
JOLLIFICATION
JUSTIFICATION
LIGHTFINGERED
MAGNIFICATION
MAGNIFICENTLY
MOLLIFICATION
MORTIFICATION
MYSTIFICATION
NONSUFFICIENT
NULLIFICATION
PATERFAMILIAS
PETRIFICATION
PROLIFERATION
QUALIFICATION
RECTIFICATION
REUNIFICATION
SIGNIFICANTLY
SIGNIFICATION
SPECIFICATION
STEADFASTNESS
SUPERFICIALLY
SUPERFLUOUSLY
UNCOMFORTABLE
UNCOMFORTABLY
VERSIFICATION
VITRIFICATION
AMPHIGASTRIUM
BIODEGRADABLE
CONFIGURATION
DISENGAGEMENT
DISFIGUREMENT
HIEROGLYPHICS
MASTIGOPHORAN

MISCEGENATION
PRIMOGENITURE
REFRIGERATION
REFRIGERATORS
REGURGITATION
REPROGRAPHICS
RETROGRESSION
STRANGULATION
TRANSGRESSION
TRIANGULATION
UNDERGRADUATE
UNFORGETTABLE
UNIMAGINATIVE
UNPROGRESSIVE
ENCEPHALOCELE
ENLIGHTENMENT
HYPOCHONDRIAC
KANGCHENJUNGA
METAPHYSICIAN
MONOTHALAMOUS
NEMATHELMINTH
ORNITHOLOGIST
PARAPHERNALIA
PASSCHENDAELE
REPREHENSIBLE
REPREHENSIBLY
SPRIGHTLINESS
THOUGHTLESSLY
TREACHEROUSLY
UNFASHIONABLE
UPTOTHEMINUTE
ADMINISTRATOR
AFFREIGHTMENT
ANTIHISTAMINE
ANYTHINGARIAN
ARTIFICIALITY
ARUNDINACEOUS
ASTONISHINGLY
AUTOBIOGRAPHY
BLANDISHMENTS
BOUGAINVILLEA
BRACHIOSAURUS
COMPLIMENTARY
CONSCIENTIOUS
CONSCIOUSNESS
CONSPICUOUSLY
CONTRIBUTIONS
DEMILITARIZED
DENATIONALIZE
DETERIORATION
DRYOPITHECINE
EXHIBITIONIST
EXPEDITIONARY
EXPEDITIOUSLY
FACETIOUSNESS
FONTAINEBLEAU
FRACTIOUSNESS
GOODRIGHTEOUS
GRANDILOQUENT
IGNOMINIOUSLY

ILLUMINATIONS
IMPERIALISTIC
INDIVIDUALISM
INDIVIDUALIST
INDIVIDUALITY
INEFFICIENTLY
INFINITESIMAL
INSIDIOUSNESS
LUXURIOUSNESS
MATERIALISTIC
MISCHIEVOUSLY
OFFICIOUSNESS
PERSPICACIOUS
PROPRIETORIAL
PUNCTILIOUSLY
QUADRILATERAL
QUESTIONNAIRE
RAMIFICATIONS
REMINISCENCES
SALACIOUSNESS
SANCTIMONIOUS
SCINTILLATING
SCINTILLATION
STEPPINGSTONE
THYROIDECTOMY
TORTOISESHELL
TRANSISTORIZE
UNANTICIPATED
UNENLIGHTENED
VENTRILOQUISM
VENTRILOQUIST
VIVACIOUSNESS
VORACIOUSNESS
MALADJUSTMENT
KNICKKNACKERY
MAURIKIGUSARI
SHRINKWRAPPED
ANTHELMINTHIC
ANTICLOCKWISE
BACCALAUREATE
BOUILLABAISSE
CARTILAGINOUS
CONSOLIDATION
CONVALESCENCE
CREDULOUSNESS
DEATHLESSNESS
DÉSOBLIGEANTE
DISCOLORATION
DISILLUSIONED
EMBELLISHMENT
ENCYCLOPAEDIA
ENCYCLOPAEDIC
ESTABLISHMENT
FERTILISATION
FERTILIZATION
FORMALIZATION
FOSSILIZATION
FRIVOLOUSNESS
GARRULOUSNESS
GUILTLESSNESS
INFALLIBILITY
INTELLIGENTLY
INVIOLABILITY
IRREPLACEABLE
KAPPELMEISTER
MAGNILOQUENCE
MERCILESSNESS
MISCELLANEOUS
NERVELESSNESS
NORMALIZATION
NOSTALGICALLY
PARALLELOGRAM
PUSILLANIMITY
PUSILLANIMOUS
QUERULOUSNESS
REPUBLICANISM
SCHOOLTEACHER
SENSELESSNESS
SERVILEMENTAL
SHAPELESSNESS
SLEEPLESSNESS
SNOWBLINDNESS
SPINDLESHANKS
STABILIZATION
STEEPLECHASER
STERILIZATION
SUPERLATIVELY
TANTALIZINGLY
THANKLESSNESS
TONSILLECTOMY
TRANSLITERATE
UMBELLIFEROUS
UNADULTERATED
UNWILLINGNESS
ACCOMMODATING
ACCOMMODATION
AFFIRMATIVELY
AGGLOMERATION
ARCHIMANDRITE
ARITHMETICIAN
CIRCUMAMBIENT
CIRCUMFERENCE
CIRCUMSTANCES
CIRCUMVENTION
CLISHMACLAVER
COMMEMORATION
COMMEMORATIVE
CONTAMINATION
CONTEMPLATION
CONTEMPLATIVE
DECRIMINALIZE
DETERMINATION
DISSEMINATION
DISSIMILARITY
DISSIMULATION
EXCOMMUNICATE
EXTERMINATION
FUNDAMENTALLY
INCOMMUNICADO
INCRIMINATING
INCRIMINATORY
INTERMARRIAGE
MALLEMAROKING
MATHEMATICIAN
OVEREMPHASIZE
PASSEMENTERIE
POLIOMYELITIS
PREDOMINANTLY
PRELIMINARIES
RECRIMINATION
RECRIMINATORY
RHADAMANTHINE
SENTIMENTALLY
SQUEAMISHNESS
TRANSMUTATION
UNCOMMUNICATE
UNGRAMMATICAL
UNSYMMETRICAL
VICTIMIZATION
ACUPUNCTURIST
ALTERNATIVELY
BILDUNGSROMAN
BROKENHEARTED
CARBONIFEROUS
COMMENSURABLE
COMMUNICATION
COMMUNICATIVE
COMPANIONABLE
COMPANIONSHIP
CONCENTRATION
CONSANGUINITY
CONTENTEDNESS
CONTINUATIONS
CRIMINOLOGIST
DISCONCERTING
DISCONNECTION
DISCONTINUITY
DISCONTINUOUS
DISHONOURABLE
DISHONOURABLY
DISTINGUISHED
FOREKNOWLEDGE
FORTUNETELLER
GALVANIZATION
HARMONIZATION
IMAGINATIVELY
INSIGNIFICANT
INSTANTANEOUS
INSTINCTIVELY
INTERNATIONAL
INTRANSIGENCE
INTRINSICALLY
MAGNANIMOUSLY
MECHANIZATION
MISCONCEPTION
MISMANAGEMENT
MODERNIZATION
MULTINATIONAL
MULTINUCLEATE
NATIONALISTIC
NONCONFORMIST
NONCONFORMITY
PATERNALISTIC
PERFUNCTORILY
PERPENDICULAR
PERSONALITIES
PHILANTHROPIC
PRECONCEPTION
PREPONDERANCE
PRONUNCIATION
PROTONOTARIAT
PROVINCIALISM
RATIONALALITY
REPLENISHMENT
SENTENTIOUSLY
SEPTENTRIONES
SOLEMNIZATION
SUBCONTRACTOR
SUPERNUMERARY
SUPRANATIONAL
SWEDENBORGIAN
TINTINNABULUM
UNFLINCHINGLY
VERCINGETORIX
VULCANIZATION
ACRYLONITRILE
ANTICOAGULANT
AQUIFOLIACEAE
BIBLIOGRAPHER
BIBLIOPHAGIST
CATEGORICALLY
CEREMONIOUSLY
CHOREOGRAPHER
CHRONOLOGICAL
CONFRONTATION
CONTROVERSIAL
DEIPNOSOPHIST
DEVELOPMENTAL
DISPROPORTION
ENTEROPNEUSTA
ENTOMOLOGICAL
ENVIRONMENTAL
EQUIPONDERATE
EXTRAORDINARY
GASTROCNEMIUS
GLOSSOGRAPHER
GYNECOLOGICAL
HETEROGENEOUS
INSUBORDINATE
IRRECOVERABLE
ISOGEOTHERMAL
LEPIDOPTERIST
LEXICOGRAPHER
MADETOMEASURE
METAMORPHOSIS
MICROORGANISM
MONOCOTYLEDON
MORPHOLOGICAL
OWNEROCCUPIER
PALAEONTOLOGY

PARADOXICALLY
PARTHOGENESIS
PASSIONFLOWER
PATRIOTICALLY
PELOPONNESIAN
PHYSIOGNOMIST
PHYSIOLOGICAL
PHYSIOTHERAPY
PREPROGRAMMED
PROGNOSTICATE
PSYCHOANALYSE
PSYCHOANALYST
PSYCHOLOGICAL
PSYCHOSOMATIC
PSYCHOTHERAPY
QUARTODECIMAN
RAPPROCHEMENT
REINFORCEMENT
SCHIZOPHRENIA
SCHIZOPHRENIC
SEISMOLOGICAL
SELFCONFESSED
SELFCONFIDENT
SELFCONSCIOUS
SELFCONTAINED
SELFGOVERNING
SEMICONDUCTOR
SOMATOTROPHIN
SPASMODICALLY
SPELEOLOGICAL
STATIONMASTER
STERCORACEOUS
SUPERORDINATE
TECHNOLOGICAL
THEOLOGICALLY
THERMONUCLEAR
THERMOPLASTIC
TRICHOSANTHIN
UNACCOMPANIED
UNACCOUNTABLE
UNACCOUNTABLY
ACCOMPANIMENT
AFFENPINSCHER
APPROPINQUATE
APPROPRIATION
CONCEPTIONIST
CONCEPTUALIZE
CONCUPISCENCE
DECOMPOSITION
DECOMPRESSION
DISAPPEARANCE
DISAPPOINTING
EXPROPRIATION
EXTRAPOLATION
GRANDPARENTAL
HEMISPHERICAL
HERMAPHRODITE
HORRIPILATION
INCOMPETENTLY
INCORPORATION

INDISPENSABLE
INDISPOSITION
INSUPPORTABLE
INTERPERSONAL
INTERPOLATION
IRRESPONSIBLE
IRRESPONSIBLY
JURISPRUDENCE
JUXTAPOSITION
PRECIPITATELY
PRECIPITATION
PROSOPOGRAPHY
REDEMPTIONIST
SURREPTITIOUS
TRANSPARENTLY
TRANSPIRATION
TRANSPORTABLE
TRANSPOSITION
UNCOMPLICATED
UNCOOPERATIVE
UNSYMPATHETIC
XIPHIPLASTRON
COLLOQUIALISM
CONSEQUENTIAL
CROSSQUESTION
UNCONQUERABLE
AGGIORNAMENTO
AIRWORTHINESS
ANACHRONISTIC
ANTIGROPELOES
ARISTROCRATIC
ARMOURPLATING
AUTHORISATION
AUTHORITARIAN
AUTHORITATIVE
AUTHORIZATION
BOUSTROPHEDON
BUTTERFINGERS
CAUTERIZATION
COMMERCIALIZE
COMPARABILITY
COMPARATIVELY
CONFARREATION
CONSERVATOIRE
CONTORTIONIST
CONVERSAZIONE
COUNTRYPEOPLE
DAGUERREOTYPE
DEFIBRILLATOR
DESEGREGATION
DIFFARREATION
DIFFERENTIATE
DISPARAGEMENT
EFFLORESCENCE
ELECTROCUTION
ELECTROMAGNET
ELECTROMOTIVE
EMBARRASSMENT
ENCOURAGEMENT
FOSTERPARENTS

HAMMERKLAVIER
HAMMERTHROWER
IDIORRHYTHMIC
INAPPROPRIATE
INCORRUPTIBLE
INEXPRESSIBLE
INFLORESCENCE
INSPIRATIONAL
INTERROGATION
INTERROGATIVE
IRREPRESSIBLE
IRRETRIEVABLE
IRRETRIEVABLY
JIGGERYPOKERY
KIDDERMINSTER
LAEVOROTATORY
LEISURELINESS
LIBRARIANSHIP
LIEBFRAUMILCH
MESSERSCHMITT
METAGRABOLISE
METAGROBOLISE
METEOROLOGIST
OYSTERCATCHER
PANHARMONICON
PAPAPRELATIST
PENETRABILITY
PEREGRINATION
PRESERVATIVES
PRETERNATURAL
PREVARICATION
PROPORTIONATE
PULVERIZATION
RESOURCEFULLY
RHYPAROGRAPHY
ROLLERBLADING
ROLLERCOASTER
RUTHERFORDIUM
SPECTROGRAPHY
SUBSERVIENTLY
SUSPERCOLLATE
TEMPERAMENTAL
TENDERHEARTED
THEATRICALITY
TOPOGRAPHICAL
TYPOGRAPHICAL
UNCOORDINATED
UNIMPRESSIBLE
VICEPRESIDENT
VIDEORECORDER
VULGARIZATION
VULNERABILITY
ACCESSIBILITY
ASSASSINATION
CALLISTHENICS
COMMISERATION
COMPASSIONATE
CONCESSIONARY
CONDESCENDING
CONDESCENSION

CORRESPONDENT
CORRESPONDING
CRAFTSMANSHIP
DEFENSIBILITY
DEMONSTRATION
DEMONSTRATIVE
DISPASSIONATE
DISRESPECTFUL
EXPANSIVENESS
FANTASTICALLY
GRIEFSTRICKEN
HYPERSTHENITE
IMPERSONATING
IMPERSONATION
IMPOSSIBILITY
IMPRESSIONISM
IMPRESSIONIST
IMPULSIVENESS
INCONSIDERATE
INCONSISTENCY
INCONSPICUOUS
INQUISITIVELY
INSENSITIVITY
INSUBSTANTIAL
INTROSPECTION
INTROSPECTIVE
LECTISTERNIUM
NONRESISTANCE
OFFENSIVENESS
ORCHESTRATION
PERVASIVENESS
PHILOSOPHICAL
PREPOSSESSING
PREPOSSESSION
PROFESSORSHIP
PROMISCUOUSLY
PROTESTANTISM
PROVISIONALLY
REALISTICALLY
REMORSELESSLY
RETROSPECTIVE
SARCASTICALLY
SEQUESTRATION
SOPHISTICATED
SPITESPLENDID
SPORTSMANLIKE
SPORTSMANSHIP
STATESMANLIKE
STATESMANSHIP
STATISTICALLY
STYLISTICALLY
SUPERSTITIOUS
SWEETSMELLING
TABLESPOONFUL
TETRASYLLABIC
UNCONSCIOUSLY
UNDERSTANDING
UNDERSTRAPPER
UNQUESTIONING
UNSUBSTANTIAL

UNTRUSTWORTHY
WHOLESOMENESS
ACCEPTABILITY
ACCEPTILATION
ACCOUTREMENTS
ADVENTUROUSLY
ADVERTISEMENT
APOCATASTASIS
APPORTIONMENT
ARCHITECTURAL
ASCERTAINABLE
ATTENTIVENESS
BREASTFEEDING
CHRISTMASTIME
COMPATIBILITY
CONCATENATION
CONDITIONALLY
DECONTAMINATE
DERMATOLOGIST
DIACATHOLICON
DIAMETRICALLY
DISESTIMATION
DISINTERESTED
DRAMATIZATION
ECCENTRICALLY
EFFECTIVENESS
ENTERTAINMENT
EXCEPTIONABLE
EXCEPTIONALLY
EXPOSTULATION
FORGETFULNESS
FRIGHTENINGLY
FRIGHTFULNESS
GEOMETRICALLY
GLOBETROTTING
GRAVITATIONAL
IMPERTINENTLY
IMPERTURBABLE
IMPERTURBABLY
INCONTESTABLE
INDUSTRIALIST
INDUSTRIALIZE
INDUSTRIOUSLY
INEVITABILITY
INSECTIVOROUS
INSTITUTIONAL
INTENTIONALLY
INVENTIVENESS
INVESTIGATION
INVESTIGATIVE
LIECHTENSTEIN
LISSOTRICHOUS
LYCANTHROPIST
MAGISTERIALLY
MISANTHROPIST
MULTITUDINOUS
OBJECTIONABLE
OBJECTIVENESS
OPPORTUNISTIC
OPPORTUNITIES
OVERSTATEMENT
PAINSTAKINGLY
PARANTHROPOUS
PARENTHETICAL
POTENTIOMETER
PRIVATIZATION
PROFITABILITY
RECEPTIVENESS
REINSTATEMENT
ROUNDTHEWORLD
SECRETIVENESS
SENSATIONALLY
SENSITIVENESS
STREPTOCOCCUS
SUOVETAURILIA
TALKATIVENESS
THREATENINGLY
TRADITIONALLY
UNFORTUNATELY
UNGENTLEMANLY
UNMENTIONABLE
UNPARTITIONED
UNPRETENTIOUS
WEIGHTLIFTING
WITWATERSRAND
CONSPURCATION
HYDRAULICALLY
INGENUOUSNESS
INSTRUCTIONAL
INVOLUNTARILY
LONGSUFFERING
MONONUCLEOSIS
PRECAUTIONARY
PRESSURELOCAL
PRONOUNCEMENT
QUADRUPLICATE
QUINQUAGESIMA
REIMBURSEMENT
REVOLUTIONARY
REVOLUTIONIZE
STRENUOUSNESS
THOROUGHBRACE
THOROUGHGOING
TRANQUILLISER
TRANQUILLIZER
DEFERVESCENCE
DISADVANTAGED
EFFERVESCENCE
EXTRAVAGANTLY
IMPROVIDENTLY
IMPROVISATION
INCONVENIENCE
UNSERVICEABLE
MOUTHWATERING
NIGHTWATCHMAN
SOUTHWESTERLY
APPROXIMATELY
APPROXIMATION
INFLEXIBILITY
IDIOSYNCRATIC
STAPHYLINIDAE
SCHUTZSTAFFEL

13:7

ACCEPTABILITY
ACCOMPANIMENT
AFFIRMATIVELY
ALTERNATIVELY
AMPHIGASTRIUM
ANTICOAGULANT
APOCATASTASIS
ARCHIMANDRITE
ASCERTAINABLE
BACCALAUREATE
BOUILLABAISSE
CARTILAGINOUS
CHANGEABILITY
CIRCUMAMBIENT
CLISHMACLAVER
COEDUCATIONAL
COMPARABILITY
COMPARATIVELY
DECONTAMINATE
DEPENDABILITY
DISADVANTAGED
DISENGAGEMENT
DISPARAGEMENT
EMBARRASSMENT
ENCEPHALOCELE
ENCOURAGEMENT
ENTERTAINMENT
EXTRAVAGANTLY
GRANDDAUGHTER
GRANDPARENTAL
GRAVITATIONAL
IMAGINATIVELY
IMPERIALISTIC
IMPROBABILITY
INEVITABILITY
INSPIRATIONAL
INTERCALATION
INTERMARRIAGE
INTERNATIONAL
INVIOLABILITY
IRREPLACEABLE
LACKADAISICAL
LIEBFRAUMILCH
MALLEMAROKING
MATERIALISTIC
MATHEMATICIAN
METAGRABOLISE
MISMANAGEMENT
MONOTHALAMOUS
MOUTHWATERING
MULTINATIONAL
NATIONALISTIC
NIGHTWATCHMAN
OVERSTATEMENT
PAINSTAKINGLY
PATERFAMILIAS
PATERNALISTIC
PENETRABILITY
PERSONALITIES
PROFITABILITY
PROVOCATIVELY
PSYCHOANALYSE
PSYCHOANALYST
PUSILLANIMITY
PUSILLANIMOUS
QUINQUAGESIMA
RATIONALALITY
REINSTATEMENT
RHADAMANTHINE
SOUTHEASTERLY
STEADFASTNESS
SUOVETAURILIA
SUPERLATIVELY
SUPRANATIONAL
TEMPERAMENTAL
TOPOGRAPHICAL
TRANSPARENTLY
TYPOGRAPHICAL
UNDERCARRIAGE
UNIMPEACHABLE
UNSYMPATHETIC
VIDEOCASSETTE
VULNERABILITY
CONTRABASSOON
CONTRIBUTIONS
MIDDLEBREAKER
ROLLERBLADING
STRIKEBREAKER
SUPERABUNDANT
SWEDENBORGIAN
UNESTABLISHED
UNINHABITABLE
ACUPUNCTURIST
ARTIFICIALITY
CLOSEDCIRCUIT
COMMERCIALIZE
CONDESCENDING
CONDESCENSION
CONSPICUOUSLY
CONTRACEPTION
CONTRACEPTIVE
DISCONCERTING
DISGRACEFULLY
EPITRACHELION
GASTROCNEMIUS
INEFFICIENTLY
INSTINCTIVELY
INSTRUCTIONAL
MANUFACTURING
MISCONCEPTION
MOCKTECHNICAL
MONONUCLEOSIS
OWNEROCCUPIER
OYSTERCATCHER
PERFUNCTORILY

PERSPICACIOUS
PHARMACOPOEIA
PRECONCEPTION
PROMISCUOUSLY
PRONUNCIATION
PROVINCIALISM
PYROTECHNICAL
RADIOACTIVITY
RAMIFICATIONS
RAPPROCHEMENT
REPROACHFULLY
RESOURCEFULLY
ROLLERCOASTER
SOCIOECONOMIC
SPECTACULARLY
SUSPERCOLLATE
TAPERECORDING
UNANTICIPATED
UNCONSCIOUSLY
UNDERACHIEVER
UNFLINCHINGLY
CONTRADICTION
CONTRADICTORY
DISCREDITABLE
DISCREDITABLY
HUNDREDWEIGHT
INDIVIDUALISM
INDIVIDUALIST
INDIVIDUALITY
KNOWLEDGEABLE
PERPENDICULAR
PREPONDERANCE
QUARTODECIMAN
SELFADDRESSED
SPASMODICALLY
THYROIDECTOMY
UNCOORDINATED
AGGLOMERATION
ALPHABETARIAN
ARCHITECTURAL
ARITHMETICIAN
COMMISERATION
COMRADEINARMS
CONCATENATION
CONFEDERATION
CONSCIENTIOUS
CONSIDERATELY
CONSIDERATION
CONVALESCENCE
DEATHLESSNESS
DECAFFEINATED
DEFERVESCENCE
DESEGREGATION
DIFFERENTIATE
DISAPPEARANCE
DISINTERESTED
EFFERVESCENCE
EFFLORESCENCE
FORTUNETELLER
FRIGHTENINGLY
FUNDAMENTALLY
GUILTLESSNESS
HORSEFEATHERS
IMPERCEPTIBLE
IMPERCEPTIBLY
IMPONDERABLES
INCANDESCENCE
INCARCERATION
INCOMPETENTLY
INCONCEIVABLE
INCONTESTABLE
INCONVENIENCE
INDIFFERENTLY
INDISPENSABLE
INEXPRESSIBLE
INFLORESCENCE
INTERPERSONAL
IRREPRESSIBLE
KANGCHENJUNGA
LAMPADEPHORIA
LEISURELINESS
LEPTOCEPHALUS
LIECHTENSTEIN
MAGISTERIALLY
MERCILESSNESS
MISCEGENATION
MISCHIEVOUSLY
MISUNDERSTAND
MISUNDERSTOOD
NEMATHELMINTH
NERVELESSNESS
PAPAPRELATIST
PARALLELOGRAM
PARAPHERNALIA
PASSCHENDAELE
PASSEMENTERIE
PHILADELPHIAN
PLATOCEPHALUS
PRIMOGENITURE
PROLIFERATION
PROPRIETORIAL
RECRUDESCENCE
REFRIGERATION
REFRIGERATORS
REMORSELESSLY
REPREHENSIBLE
REPREHENSIBLY
REVERBERATION
SENSELESSNESS
SENTIMENTALLY
SERVILEMENTAL
SHAPELESSNESS
SHOULDERBLADE
SLEEPLESSNESS
SOUTHWESTERLY
SPINDLESHANKS
STEEPLECHASER
THANKLESSNESS
THREATENINGLY
TREACHEROUSLY
UNCOOPERATIVE
UNFORGETTABLE
UNIMPRESSIBLE
UNPRECEDENTED
UNPRETENTIOUS
UNSYMMETRICAL
UPTOTHEMINUTE
VICEPRESIDENT
VIDEORECORDER
WITWATERSRAND
AIRCRAFTWOMAN
BREASTFEEDING
BUTTERFINGERS
CIRCUMFERENCE
CONTRAFAGOTTO
COSTEFFECTIVE
FORGETFULNESS
FRIGHTFULNESS
LONGSUFFERING
NONCONFORMIST
NONCONFORMITY
NONSUFFICIENT
RUTHERFORDIUM
AFFREIGHTMENT
BIBLIOGRAPHER
BILDUNGSROMAN
CHOREOGRAPHER
CONFLAGRATION
CONSANGUINITY
DISTINGUISHED
DOUBLEGLAZING
GLOSSOGRAPHER
GOODRIGHTEOUS
HETEROGENEOUS
LEXICOGRAPHER
NOSTALGICALLY
PARTHOGENESIS
PHYSIOGNOMIST
PREPROGRAMMED
QUADRAGESIMAL
STRATEGICALLY
THEOLOGICALLY
THOROUGHBRACE
THOROUGHGOING
UNENLIGHTENED
VERCINGETORIX
BIOTECHNOLOGY
BROKENHEARTED
COMPREHENSION
COMPREHENSIVE
DIACATHOLICON
ESCHSCHOLTZIA
HEMISPHERICAL
HERMAPHRODITE
IDIORRHYTHMIC
LYCANTHROPIST
MASSACHUSETTS
MISANTHROPIST
PARANTHROPOUS
PARENTHETICAL
PETROCHEMICAL
PHOTOCHEMICAL
ROUNDTHEWORLD
SPINECHILLING
TENDERHEARTED
ACCEPTILATION
ACCESSIBILITY
ADVERTISEMENT
AFFENPINSCHER
AMPLIFICATION
APPORTIONMENT
APPROPINQUATE
APPROXIMATELY
APPROXIMATION
ASSASSINATION
ATTENTIVENESS
AUTHORISATION
AUTHORITARIAN
AUTHORITATIVE
AUTHORIZATION
BEATIFICATION
CARBONIFEROUS
CAUTERIZATION
CERTIFICATION
CLARIFICATION
COMMUNICATION
COMMUNICATIVE
COMPANIONABLE
COMPANIONSHIP
COMPATIBILITY
CONCUPISCENCE
CONDITIONALLY
CONSOLIDATION
CONTAMINATION
DECRIMINALIZE
DEFENSIBILITY
DEFIBRILLATOR
DÉSOBLIGEANTE
DETERMINATION
DISESTIMATION
DISSEMINATION
DISSIMILARITY
DRAMATIZATION
EFFECTIVENESS
EMBELLISHMENT
EPANADIPLOSIS
ESTABLISHMENT
EXCEPTIONABLE
EXCEPTIONALLY
EXPANSIVENESS
EXTERMINATION
FALSIFICATION
FERTILISATION
FERTILIZATION
FORMALIZATION
FORTIFICATION
FOSSILIZATION
GALVANIZATION
GLORIFICATION
GRATIFICATION

HALLUCINATION
HALLUCINATORY
HARMONIZATION
HORRIPILATION
HYBRIDIZATION
IMPERTINENTLY
IMPOSSIBILITY
IMPROVIDENTLY
IMPROVISATION
IMPULSIVENESS
INCONSIDERATE
INCONSISTENCY
INCRIMINATING
INCRIMINATORY
INFALLIBILITY
INFLEXIBILITY
INQUISITIVELY
INSECTIVOROUS
INSENSITIVITY
INSIGNIFICANT
INSUFFICIENCY
INTELLIGENTLY
INTENTIONALLY
INVENTIVENESS
INVESTIGATION
INVESTIGATIVE
INVINCIBILITY
IRRETRIEVABLE
IRRETRIEVABLY
JOLLIFICATION
JUSTIFICATION
LIBRARIANSHIP
LIGHTFINGERED
MAGNANIMOUSLY
MAGNIFICATION
MAGNIFICENTLY
MAURIKIGUSARI
MECHANIZATION
MODERNIZATION
MOLLIFICATION
MORTIFICATION
MYSTIFICATION
NONRESISTANCE
NORMALIZATION
NULLIFICATION
OBJECTIONABLE
OBJECTIVENESS
OFFENSIVENESS
PARTICIPATION
PARTICIPATORY
PEREGRINATION
PERVASIVENESS
PETRIFICATION
POLLICITATION
POTENTIOMETER
PRECIPITATELY
PRECIPITATION
PREDOMINANTLY
PRELIMINARIES
PREMEDITATION
PREVARICATION
PRIVATIZATION
PROVISIONALLY
PULVERIZATION
QUALIFICATION
RECALCITRANCE
RECEPTIVENESS
RECRIMINATION
RECRIMINATORY
RECTIFICATION
REFURBISHMENT
REGURGITATION
REPLENISHMENT
REPUBLICANISM
RESUSCITATION
REUNIFICATION
SECRETIVENESS
SENSATIONALLY
SENSITIVENESS
SIGNIFICANTLY
SIGNIFICATION
SNOWBLINDNESS
SOLEMNIZATION
SPECIFICATION
SQUEAMISHNESS
STABILIZATION
STERILIZATION
SUBORDINATION
SUPERFICIALLY
TALKATIVENESS
TANTALIZINGLY
THEATRICALITY
TONGUEINCHEEK
TRADITIONALLY
TRANQUILLISER
TRANQUILLIZER
TRANSLITERATE
TRANSPIRATION
UMBELLIFEROUS
UNCONDITIONAL
UNDISCIPLINED
UNFASHIONABLE
UNIMAGINATIVE
UNMENTIONABLE
UNPARTITIONED
UNPREDICTABLE
UNSERVICEABLE
UNWILLINGNESS
VERSIFICATION
VICTIMIZATION
VITRIFICATION
VULCANIZATION
VULGARIZATION
BUNGEEJUMPING
HAMMERKLAVIER
AQUIFOLIACEAE
CHRONOLOGICAL
CONSTELLATION
ENTOMOLOGICAL
FRANKALMOIGNE
GENERALISSIMO
GLUMDALCLITCH
GRANDILOQUENT
GYNECOLOGICAL
HIEROGLYPHICS
HYDRAULICALLY
HYDROELECTRIC
MISCELLANEOUS
MORPHOLOGICAL
OPHTHALMOLOGY
PHOTOELECTRIC
PHYSIOLOGICAL
PSYCHOLOGICAL
PUNCTILIOUSLY
QUADRILATERAL
REDEVELOPMENT
RENSSELAERITE
SCANDALMONGER
SCINTILLATING
SCINTILLATION
SEISMOLOGICAL
SPELEOLOGICAL
STAPHYLINIDAE
SUPERFLUOUSLY
TECHNOLOGICAL
TONSILLECTOMY
UNCOMPLICATED
UNDERCLOTHING
UNGENTLEMANLY
UNINTELLIGENT
VENTRILOQUISM
VENTRILOQUIST
WEIGHTLIFTING
XIPHIPLASTRON
ANTHELMINTHIC
CHEESEMONGERS
CHRISTMASTIME
COMPLEMENTARY
COMPLIMENTARY
CRAFTSMANSHIP
KAPPELMEISTER
KIDDERMINSTER
MADETOMEASURE
PANHARMONICON
PARLIAMENTARY
PROBLEMATICAL
SANCTIMONIOUS
SPORTSMANLIKE
SPORTSMANSHIP
STATESMANLIKE
STATESMANSHIP
SUPPLEMENTARY
SWEETSMELLING
UNACCOMPANIED
UNCEREMONIOUS
UNGRAMMATICAL
ACRYLONITRILE
AGGIORNAMENTO
ANYTHINGARIAN
ARGUMENTATIVE
ARUNDINACEOUS
BOUGAINVILLEA
CEREMONIOUSLY
CHRYSANTHEMUM
CONFRONTATION
DISCONNECTION
DOCUMENTATION
ELEPHANTIASIS
ENVIRONMENTAL
EPIPHENOMENON
EQUIPONDERATE
FONTAINEBLEAU
FRAGMENTATION
IDIOSYNCRATIC
IGNOMINIOUSLY
ILLUMINATIONS
INDEPENDENTLY
INVOLUNTARILY
KNICKKNACKERY
MERCHANDIZING
ORNAMENTATION
OUTSTANDINGLY
PALAEONTOLOGY
PASSIONFLOWER
PELOPONNESIAN
PRETERNATURAL
PRONOUNCEMENT
REARRANGEMENT
REGIMENTATION
SCHADENFREUDE
SEDIMENTATION
SELFCONFESSED
SELFCONFIDENT
SELFCONSCIOUS
SELFCONTAINED
SEMBLANCECORD
SEMICONDUCTOR
SPONTANEOUSLY
STATIONMASTER
STEPPINGSTONE
SUBSTANTIALLY
SUPERANNUATED
SWOLLENHEADED
THERMONUCLEAR
TINTINNABULUM
UNINTENTIONAL
ACCOMMODATING
ACCOMMODATION
ANACHRONISTIC
ANTICLOCKWISE
ANTIGROPELOES
ARCHAEOLOGIST
ARCHAEOPTERYX
ARISTROCRATIC
AUTOBIOGRAPHY
BOUSTROPHEDON
BRACHIOSAURUS
COLLABORATION
COLLABORATIVE
COMMEMORATION

COMMEMORATIVE
CONSCIOUSNESS
CORROBORATION
CORROBORATORY
CREDULOUSNESS
CRIMINOLOGIST
DECOMPOSITION
DENATIONALIZE
DERMATOLOGIST
DETERIORATION
DISAPPOINTING
DISCOLORATION
DISHONOURABLE
DISHONOURABLY
ELECTROCUTION
ELECTROMAGNET
ELECTROMOTIVE
ENCYCLOPAEDIA
ENCYCLOPAEDIC
EXTRAPOLATION
FACETIOUSNESS
FERROCONCRETE
FOREKNOWLEDGE
FRACTIOUSNESS
FRIVOLOUSNESS
GARRULOUSNESS
GYNAECOLOGIST
HYPOCHONDRIAC
IMPERSONATING
IMPERSONATION
INAPPROPRIATE
INCORPORATION
INDISPOSITION
INGENUOUSNESS
INSIDIOUSNESS
INSUPPORTABLE
INTERPOLATION
INTERROGATION
INTERROGATIVE
IRRESPONSIBLE
IRRESPONSIBLY
JUXTAPOSITION
KALEIDOSCOPIC
LAEVOROTATORY
LUXURIOUSNESS
MACHICOLATION
MAGNILOQUENCE
MASTIGOPHORAN
METAGROBOLISE
METEOROLOGIST
MICROCOMPUTER
MULTICOLOURED
NEIGHBOURHOOD
OFFICIOUSNESS
ORNITHOLOGIST
PARTICOLOURED
PHILOSOPHICAL
PROSOPOGRAPHY
PROTONOTARIAT
QUERULOUSNESS
QUESTIONNAIRE
RHYPAROGRAPHY
RIGHTEOUSNESS
SALACIOUSNESS
SPECTROGRAPHY
STRENUOUSNESS
STREPTOCOCCUS
TRANSPORTABLE
TRANSPOSITION
UNCOMFORTABLE
UNCOMFORTABLY
VIVACIOUSNESS
VORACIOUSNESS
WHOLESOMENESS
ARMOURPLATING
AUTOCEPHALOUS
BIBLIOPHAGIST
CONTEMPLATION
CONTEMPLATIVE
CORRESPONDENT
CORRESPONDING
DEVELOPMENTAL
DISPROPORTION
DISRESPECTFUL
ENTEROPNEUSTA
FOSTERPARENTS
INCONSPICUOUS
INTROSPECTION
INTROSPECTIVE
LEPIDOPTERIST
OVEREMPHASIZE
QUADRUPLICATE
RETROSPECTIVE
SCHIZOPHRENIA
SCHIZOPHRENIC
SPITESPLENDID
TABLESPOONFUL
THERMOPLASTIC
UNEXCEPTIONAL
ACCOUTREMENTS
APPROPRIATION
BIODEGRADABLE
CATEGORICALLY
CHINKERINCHEE
CONFARREATION
CONSPURCATION
CONSTERNATION
COUNTERACTING
COUNTERATTACK
COUNTERCHARGE
COUNTERFEITER
DAGUERREOTYPE
DECOMPRESSION
DIAMETRICALLY
DIFFARREATION
DISHEARTENING
ECCENTRICALLY
EPHEMEROPTERA
EXPROPRIATION
EXTRAORDINARY
FEATHERWEIGHT
FLABBERGASTED
GEOMETRICALLY
GLOBETROTTING
GYNANDROMORPH
HEARTBREAKING
HOUSEBREAKING
HYPERCRITICAL
INADVERTENTLY
INDESCRIBABLE
INDESCRIBABLY
INDETERMINATE
INDUSTRIALIST
INDUSTRIALIZE
INDUSTRIOUSLY
INEXPERIENCED
INSUBORDINATE
JURISPRUDENCE
KNICKERBOCKER
LEATHERJACKET
LISSOTRICHOUS
MEDITERRANEAN
MEISTERSINGER
METAMORPHOSIS
MICROORGANISM
NEANDERTHALER
PHYSHARMONICA
PREFABRICATED
PRESSURELOCAL
QUARTERMASTER
REIMBURSEMENT
REINCARNATION
REINFORCEMENT
REPROGRAPHICS
RETROGRESSION
SACCHAROMYCES
SCHOLARLINESS
STERCORACEOUS
STOCKBREEDING
SUPERORDINATE
THUNDERSTRUCK
TRACTARIANISM
TRANSCRIPTION
TRANSGRESSION
UNDERGRADUATE
UNEMBARRASSED
UNEXPERIENCED
UNINTERESTING
UNINTERRUPTED
UNPROGRESSIVE
VEGETARIANISM
WEATHERBEATEN
ADMINISTRATOR
AFFORESTATION
ANTIHISTAMINE
ASTONISHINGLY
BLANDISHMENTS
BUSINESSWOMAN
CIRCUMSTANCES
COLLIESHANGIE
COMMENSURABLE
COMPASSIONATE
CONCESSIONARY
CONGRESSIONAL
CONGRESSWOMAN
CONVERSAZIONE
DEFORESTATION
DEIPNOSOPHIST
DISPASSIONATE
IMPRESSIONISM
IMPRESSIONIST
INTERESTINGLY
INTRANSIGENCE
INTRINSICALLY
MANIFESTATION
MESSERSCHMITT
PREPOSSESSING
PREPOSSESSION
PROCRASTINATE
PROFESSORSHIP
PROGNOSTICATE
PROGRESSIVELY
PSYCHOSOMATIC
REMINISCENCES
SCHUTZSTAFFEL
SYMPIESOMETER
TORTOISESHELL
TRANSISTORIZE
TRICHOSANTHIN
UNDERESTIMATE
UNFORESEEABLE
UNNECESSARILY
AESTHETICALLY
AIRWORTHINESS
AUTOMATICALLY
CALLISTHENICS
CHARACTERISED
CHARACTERLESS
CONCENTRATION
CONCEPTIONIST
CONCEPTUALIZE
CONFECTIONERS
CONFECTIONERY
CONSECTANEOUS
CONTENTEDNESS
CONTORTIONIST
DEMILITARIZED
DEMONSTRATION
DEMONSTRATIVE
DISCONTINUITY
DISCONTINUOUS
DISCRETIONARY
DRYOPITHECINE
ENERGETICALLY
ENLIGHTENMENT
EXHIBITIONIST
EXPEDITIONARY
EXPEDITIOUSLY
FANTASTICALLY
GRAMMATICALLY

GRIEFSTRICKEN
HAMMERTHROWER
HYPERSTHENITE
IMPRACTICABLE
INDEFATIGABLE
INDEFATIGABLY
INFINITESIMAL
INSTANTANEOUS
INSUBSTANTIAL
ISOGEOTHERMAL
LECTISTERNIUM
MONOCOTYLEDON
ORCHESTRATION
PAEDIATRICIAN
PATRIOTICALLY
PERFECTIONIST
PHILANTHROPIC
PHYSIOTHERAPY
PNEUMATICALLY
PRAGMATICALLY
PRECAUTIONARY
PROFECTITIOUS
PROJECTIONIST
PROPHETICALLY
PROPORTIONATE
PROTECTIONISM
PROTECTIONIST
PROTESTANTISM
PSYCHOTHERAPY
REALISTICALLY
RECITATIONIST
REDEMPTIONIST
REVOLUTIONARY
REVOLUTIONIZE
SARCASTICALLY
SCHEMATICALLY
SCHOOLTEACHER
SENTENTIOUSLY
SEPTENTRIONES
SEQUESTRATION
SOMATOTROPHIN
SOPHISTICATED
SPRIGHTLINESS
STATISTICALLY
STYLISTICALLY
SUBCONTRACTOR
SUBJECTMATTER
SUPERSTITIOUS
SURREPTITIOUS
SYNTACTICALLY
SYNTHETICALLY
THAUMATURGICS
THAUMATURGIST
THEORETICALLY
THOUGHTLESSLY
TONGUETWISTER
TRANSATLANTIC
TRAUMATICALLY
UNADULTERATED
UNDERSTANDING
UNDERSTRAPPER
UNQUESTIONING
UNSUBSTANTIAL
UNTRUSTWORTHY
ADVENTUROUSLY
BLOODCURDLING
CHATEAUBRIAND
CLAIRAUDIENCE
COLLOQUIALISM
CONFIGURATION
CONSECUTIVELY
CONSEQUENTIAL
CONTINUATIONS
CROSSQUESTION
DISFIGUREMENT
DISILLUSIONED
DISSIMULATION
EXCOMMUNICATE
EXPOSTULATION
GESTICULATION
HETERAUXESISM
HORTICULTURAL
IMPERTURBABLE
IMPERTURBABLY
INCOMBUSTIBLE
INCOMMUNICADO
INCORRUPTIBLE
INCREDULOUSLY
INEXHAUSTIBLE
INSTITUTIONAL
MALADJUSTMENT
MATRICULATION
MULTINUCLEATE
MULTITUDINOUS
OPPORTUNISTIC
OPPORTUNITIES
OUTRECUIDANCE
PANDICULATION
PARTICULARISE
PARTICULARITY
PARTICULARIZE
PERAMBULATION
PREOCCUPATION
PROCLEUSMATIC
REPERCUSSIONS
SIPUNCULOIDEA
STRANGULATION
SUBLIEUTENANT
SUPERNUMERARY
SWASHBUCKLING
TRANSMUTATION
TRIANGULATION
UNACCOUNTABLE
UNACCOUNTABLY
UNCOMMUNICATE
UNCONQUERABLE
UNFORTUNATELY
ANIMADVERSION
CIRCUMVENTION
CONSERVATOIRE
CONTRAVENTION
CONTROVERSIAL
FUERTEVENTURA
IRRECOVERABLE
MACHIAVELLIAN
PRESERVATIVES
SELFGOVERNING
SUBSERVIENTLY
SHRINKWRAPPED
HOMOSEXUALITY
PARADOXICALLY
COUNTRYPEOPLE
JIGGERYPOKERY
METAPHYSICIAN
POLIOMYELITIS
TETRASYLLABIC

13:8

AGGIORNAMENTO
ARUNDINACEOUS
BIODEGRADABLE
CHRISTMASTIME
CONSECTANEOUS
CONSERVATOIRE
CONTINUATIONS
CONTRABASSOON
CONTRAFAGOTTO
CONVERSAZIONE
COUNTERACTING
COUNTERATTACK
CRAFTSMANSHIP
DEMILITARIZED
DISAPPEARANCE
FOSTERPARENTS
HORSEFEATHERS
ILLUMINATIONS
INSTANTANEOUS
INSUBSTANTIAL
KNICKKNACKERY
LIBRARIANSHIP
MISCELLANEOUS
OYSTERCATCHER
PERSPICACIOUS
PRESERVATIVES
PRETERNATURAL
PROBLEMATICAL
PROTESTANTISM
QUADRILATERAL
RAMIFICATIONS
RENSSELAERITE
REPROGRAPHICS
SPORTSMANLIKE
SPORTSMANSHIP
STATESMANLIKE
STATESMANSHIP
STERCORACEOUS
TINTINNABULUM
TRICHOSANTHIN
UNDERGRADUATE
UNDERSTANDING
UNGRAMMATICAL
UNSUBSTANTIAL
XIPHIPLASTRON
ACCEPTABILITY
ACCESSIBILITY
BOUILLABAISSE
CHANGEABILITY
CHATEAUBRIAND
COMPARABILITY
COMPATIBILITY
DEFENSIBILITY
DEPENDABILITY
IMPOSSIBILITY
IMPROBABILITY
INEVITABILITY
INFALLIBILITY
INFLEXIBILITY
INVINCIBILITY
INVIOLABILITY
KNICKERBOCKER
METAGRABOLISE
METAGROBOLISE
PENETRABILITY
PROFITABILITY
VULNERABILITY
WEATHERBEATEN
AMPLIFICATION
ANTICLOCKWISE
ARCHITECTURAL
ARISTROCRATIC
BEATIFICATION
CERTIFICATION
CLARIFICATION
CLISHMACLAVER
COMMUNICATION
COMMUNICATIVE
CONSPURCATION
COUNTERCHARGE
ELECTROCUTION
FALSIFICATION
FORTIFICATION
GLORIFICATION
GLUMDALCLITCH
GRATIFICATION
IDIOSYNCRATIC
INSUFFICIENCY
IRREPLACEABLE
JOLLIFICATION
JUSTIFICATION
MAGNIFICATION
MAGNIFICENTLY
MESSERSCHMITT
MOLLIFICATION
MORTIFICATION
MULTINUCLEATE
MYSTIFICATION
NULLIFICATION
OWNEROCCUPIER
PETRIFICATION

PREVARICATION
PRONOUNCEMENT
QUALIFICATION
RECTIFICATION
REINFORCEMENT
REMINISCENCES
REPUBLICANISM
REUNIFICATION
SEMBLANCECORD
SIGNIFICANTLY
SIGNIFICATION
SPECIFICATION
STEEPLECHASER
STREPTOCOCCUS
SUPERFICIALLY
SWASHBUCKLING
THEATRICALITY
UNIMPEACHABLE
UNPREDICTABLE
UNSERVICEABLE
VERSIFICATION
VIDEORECORDER
VITRIFICATION
ACCOMMODATING
ACCOMMODATION
CLAIRAUDIENCE
CONSOLIDATION
EQUIPONDERATE
EXTRAORDINARY
IMPROVIDENTLY
INCONSIDERATE
INDEPENDENTLY
INSUBORDINATE
MERCHANDIZING
MULTITUDINOUS
OUTSTANDINGLY
SEMICONDUCTOR
SUPERORDINATE
UNPRECEDENTED
ACCOUTREMENTS
ANIMADVERSION
BREASTFEEDING
BROKENHEARTED
CHARACTERISED
CHARACTERLESS
CIRCUMFERENCE
CIRCUMVENTION
COMPLEMENTARY
COMPLIMENTARY
COMPREHENSION
COMPREHENSIVE
CONDESCENDING
CONDESCENSION
CONFARREATION
CONSEQUENTIAL
CONTENTEDNESS
CONTRACEPTION
CONTRACEPTIVE
CONTRAVENTION
CONTROVERSIAL
COSTEFFECTIVE
CROSSQUESTION
DAGUERREOTYPE
DECOMPRESSION
DIFFARREATION
DISCONCERTING
DISCONNECTION
DISGRACEFULLY
DISRESPECTFUL
ENLIGHTENMENT
FONTAINEBLEAU
FUERTEVENTURA
HEARTBREAKING
HEMISPHERICAL
HETEROGENEOUS
HOUSEBREAKING
HYDROELECTRIC
INFINITESIMAL
INTROSPECTION
INTROSPECTIVE
IRRECOVERABLE
IRRETRIEVABLE
IRRETRIEVABLY
KAPPELMEISTER
LECTISTERNIUM
MACHIAVELLIAN
MADETOMEASURE
MISCONCEPTION
PARENTHETICAL
PARLIAMENTARY
PARTHOGENESIS
PETROCHEMICAL
PHOTOCHEMICAL
PHOTOELECTRIC
POLIOMYELITIS
PRECONCEPTION
PREPONDERANCE
PREPOSSESSING
PREPOSSESSION
PRESSURELOCAL
QUADRAGESIMAL
QUARTODECIMAN
RESOURCEFULLY
RETROGRESSION
RETROSPECTIVE
ROUNDTHEWORLD
SCHOOLTEACHER
SELFGOVERNING
SPONTANEOUSLY
STOCKBREEDING
SUPPLEMENTARY
SWEETSMELLING
TENDERHEARTED
THYROIDECTOMY
TONSILLECTOMY
TORTOISESHELL
TRANSGRESSION
UNADULTERATED
UNCONQUERABLE
UNFORESEEABLE
UNGENTLEMANLY
UNINTERESTING
UNPROGRESSIVE
VERCINGETORIX
CARBONIFEROUS
COUNTERFEITER
INSIGNIFICANT
LONGSUFFERING
PASSIONFLOWER
SCHADENFREUDE
SELFCONFESSED
SELFCONFIDENT
UMBELLIFEROUS
ANTICOAGULANT
ANYTHINGARIAN
AUTOBIOGRAPHY
CARTILAGINOUS
DESEGREGATION
DÉSOBLIGEANTE
DISENGAGEMENT
DISPARAGEMENT
ENCOURAGEMENT
EXTRAVAGANTLY
FLABBERGASTED
INTELLIGENTLY
INTERROGATION
INTERROGATIVE
INVESTIGATION
INVESTIGATIVE
KNOWLEDGEABLE
MAURIKIGUSARI
MICROORGANISM
MISMANAGEMENT
PROSOPOGRAPHY
QUINQUAGESIMA
REARRANGEMENT
RHYPAROGRAPHY
SPECTROGRAPHY
STEPPINGSTONE
AFFREIGHTMENT
AIRWORTHINESS
ASTONISHINGLY
AUTOCEPHALOUS
BIBLIOPHAGIST
BLANDISHMENTS
CALLISTHENICS
COLLIESHANGIE
DRYOPITHECINE
EPITRACHELION
GOODRIGHTEOUS
HAMMERTHROWER
HYPERSTHENITE
ISOGEOTHERMAL
MOCKTECHNICAL
OVEREMPHASIZE
PHILANTHROPIC
PHYSIOTHERAPY
PSYCHOTHERAPY
PYROTECHNICAL
RAPPROCHEMENT
REPROACHFULLY
SCHIZOPHRENIA
SCHIZOPHRENIC
SWOLLENHEADED
THOROUGHBRACE
THOROUGHGOING
UNDERACHIEVER
UNENLIGHTENED
UNFLINCHINGLY
ACRYLONITRILE
AESTHETICALLY
ANTHELMINTHIC
APPROPRIATION
AQUIFOLIACEAE
ARTIFICIALITY
ASCERTAINABLE
AUTOMATICALLY
BUTTERFINGERS
CATEGORICALLY
CEREMONIOUSLY
CHINKERINCHEE
CLOSEDCIRCUIT
COLLOQUIALISM
COMMERCIALIZE
COMPASSIONATE
COMRADEINARMS
CONCEPTIONIST
CONCESSIONARY
CONFECTIONERS
CONFECTIONERY
CONTORTIONIST
CONTRADICTION
CONTRADICTORY
DECAFFEINATED
DIAMETRICALLY
DISAPPOINTING
DISCONTINUITY
DISCONTINUOUS
DISCREDITABLE
DISCREDITABLY
DISCRETIONARY
DISPASSIONATE
ECCENTRICALLY
ENERGETICALLY
ENTERTAINMENT
EXHIBITIONIST
EXPEDITIONARY
EXPEDITIOUSLY
EXPROPRIATION
FANTASTICALLY
GENERALISSIMO
GEOMETRICALLY
GRAMMATICALLY
HYDRAULICALLY
HYPERCRITICAL
IGNOMINIOUSLY
IMPRACTICABLE
IMPRESSIONISM
IMPRESSIONIST
INCONCEIVABLE

INCONSPICUOUS
INDEFATIGABLE
INDEFATIGABLY
INDESCRIBABLE
INDESCRIBABLY
INDUSTRIALIST
INDUSTRIALIZE
INDUSTRIOUSLY
INEFFICIENTLY
INEXPERIENCED
INTRANSIGENCE
INTRINSICALLY
KIDDERMINSTER
LACKADAISICAL
LISSOTRICHOUS
NONSUFFICIENT
NOSTALGICALLY
OUTRECUIDANCE
PARADOXICALLY
PATRIOTICALLY
PERFECTIONIST
PERPENDICULAR
PNEUMATICALLY
PRAGMATICALLY
PRECAUTIONARY
PREFABRICATED
PROFECTITIOUS
PROJECTIONIST
PRONUNCIATION
PROPHETICALLY
PROPORTIONATE
PROTECTIONISM
PROTECTIONIST
PROVINCIALISM
PUNCTILIOUSLY
REALISTICALLY
RECITATIONIST
REDEMPTIONIST
REVOLUTIONARY
REVOLUTIONIZE
SARCASTICALLY
SCHEMATICALLY
SENTENTIOUSLY
SOPHISTICATED
SPASMODICALLY
SPINECHILLING
STAPHYLINIDAE
STATISTICALLY
STRATEGICALLY
STYLISTICALLY
SUBSERVIENTLY
SUPERSTITIOUS
SURREPTITIOUS
SYNTACTICALLY
SYNTHETICALLY
THEOLOGICALLY
THEORETICALLY
TRACTARIANISM
TRANSCRIPTION
TRAUMATICALLY

UNANTICIPATED
UNCOMPLICATED
UNCONSCIOUSLY
UNCOORDINATED
UNEXPERIENCED
UNINHABITABLE
UNQUESTIONING
VEGETARIANISM
WEIGHTLIFTING
LEATHERJACKET
PAINSTAKINGLY
ACCEPTILATION
ARCHAEOLOGIST
ARMOURPLATING
CONSTELLATION
CONTEMPLATION
CONTEMPLATIVE
CRIMINOLOGIST
DEFIBRILLATOR
DERMATOLOGIST
DISSIMILARITY
DISSIMULATION
DOUBLEGLAZING
ENCEPHALOCELE
EXPOSTULATION
EXTRAPOLATION
GESTICULATION
GYNAECOLOGIST
HAMMERKLAVIER
HORRIPILATION
HORTICULTURAL
IMPERIALISTIC
INCREDULOUSLY
INTERCALATION
INTERPOLATION
LEISURELINESS
MACHICOLATION
MATERIALISTIC
MATRICULATION
METEOROLOGIST
MONONUCLEOSIS
MONOTHALAMOUS
MULTICOLOURED
NATIONALISTIC
NEMATHELMINTH
ORNITHOLOGIST
PANDICULATION
PAPAPRELATIST
PARALLELOGRAM
PARTICOLOURED
PARTICULARISE
PARTICULARITY
PARTICULARIZE
PATERNALISTIC
PERAMBULATION
PERSONALITIES
PHILADELPHIAN
QUADRUPLICATE
RATIONALALITY
REMORSELESSLY

ROLLERBLADING
SCHOLARLINESS
SCINTILLATING
SCINTILLATION
SIPUNCULOIDEA
SPITESPLENDID
SPRIGHTLINESS
STRANGULATION
TETRASYLLABIC
THERMOPLASTIC
THOUGHTLESSLY
TRANQUILLISER
TRANQUILLIZER
TRANSATLANTIC
TRIANGULATION
UNESTABLISHED
UNINTELLIGENT
APPROXIMATELY
APPROXIMATION
CIRCUMAMBIENT
DECONTAMINATE
DEVELOPMENTAL
DISESTIMATION
ELECTROMAGNET
ELECTROMOTIVE
ENVIRONMENTAL
FRANKALMOIGNE
INDETERMINATE
MAGNANIMOUSLY
MICROCOMPUTER
OPHTHALMOLOGY
PATERFAMILIAS
PHYSHARMONICA
QUARTERMASTER
SCANDALMONGER
SERVILEMENTAL
STATIONMASTER
SUBJECTMATTER
SUPERNUMERARY
TEMPERAMENTAL
UPTOTHEMINUTE
WHOLESOMENESS
ACCOMPANIMENT
AFFENPINSCHER
ANACHRONISTIC
APPROPINQUATE
ARCHIMANDRITE
ASSASSINATION
BIOTECHNOLOGY
CONCATENATION
CONSCIENTIOUS
CONSTERNATION
CONTAMINATION
DECRIMINALIZE
DENATIONALIZE
DETERMINATION
DIFFERENTIATE
DISADVANTAGED
DISSEMINATION
ENTEROPNEUSTA

EXCOMMUNICATE
EXTERMINATION
FERROCONCRETE
FRIGHTENINGLY
FUNDAMENTALLY
GASTROCNEMIUS
HALLUCINATION
HALLUCINATORY
HYPOCHONDRIAC
IMPERSONATING
IMPERSONATION
IMPERTINENTLY
INCOMMUNICADO
INCONVENIENCE
INCRIMINATING
INCRIMINATORY
INDISPENSABLE
IRRESPONSIBLE
IRRESPONSIBLY
KANGCHENJUNGA
LIECHTENSTEIN
LIGHTFINGERED
MISCEGENATION
OPPORTUNISTIC
OPPORTUNITIES
PASSCHENDAELE
PASSEMENTERIE
PELOPONNESIAN
PEREGRINATION
PHYSIOGNOMIST
PREDOMINANTLY
PRELIMINARIES
PRIMOGENITURE
PSYCHOANALYSE
PSYCHOANALYST
PUSILLANIMITY
PUSILLANIMOUS
QUESTIONNAIRE
RECRIMINATION
RECRIMINATORY
REINCARNATION
REPREHENSIBLE
REPREHENSIBLY
RHADAMANTHINE
SENTIMENTALLY
SNOWBLINDNESS
SUBORDINATION
SUPERANNUATED
THREATENINGLY
TONGUEINCHEEK
UNACCOUNTABLE
UNACCOUNTABLY
UNCOMMUNICATE
UNFORTUNATELY
UNIMAGINATIVE
UNPRETENTIOUS
UNWILLINGNESS
APPORTIONMENT
CHEESEMONGERS
CHRONOLOGICAL

COMPANIONABLE
COMPANIONSHIP
CONDITIONALLY
CORRESPONDENT
CORRESPONDING
DEIPNOSOPHIST
DIACATHOLICON
DISPROPORTION
ENTOMOLOGICAL
EPHEMEROPTERA
EPIPHENOMENON
ESCHSCHOLTZIA
EXCEPTIONABLE
EXCEPTIONALLY
GLOBETROTTING
GRANDILOQUENT
GYNANDROMORPH
GYNECOLOGICAL
INTENTIONALLY
MORPHOLOGICAL
NONCONFORMIST
NONCONFORMITY
OBJECTIONABLE
PANHARMONICON
PHARMACOPOEIA
PHYSIOLOGICAL
POTENTIOMETER
PROFESSORSHIP
PROVISIONALLY
PSYCHOLOGICAL
PSYCHOSOMATIC
REDEVELOPMENT
ROLLERCOASTER
RUTHERFORDIUM
SACCHAROMYCES
SANCTIMONIOUS
SEISMOLOGICAL
SENSATIONALLY
SOCIOECONOMIC
SPELEOLOGICAL
SUSPERCOLLATE
SWEDENBORGIAN
SYMPIESOMETER
TABLESPOONFUL
TAPERECORDING
TECHNOLOGICAL
TRADITIONALLY
UNCEREMONIOUS
UNDERCLOTHING
UNFASHIONABLE
UNMENTIONABLE
VENTRILOQUISM
VENTRILOQUIST
ANTIGROPELOES
ARCHAEOPTERYX
BOUSTROPHEDON
COUNTRYPEOPLE
ENCYCLOPAEDIA
ENCYCLOPAEDIC
EPANADIPLOSIS
IMPERCEPTIBLE
IMPERCEPTIBLY
INAPPROPRIATE
INCORRUPTIBLE
JIGGERYPOKERY
LAMPADEPHORIA
LEPTOCEPHALUS
MASTIGOPHORAN
METAMORPHOSIS
PARTICIPATION
PARTICIPATORY
PHILOSOPHICAL
PLATOCEPHALUS
PREOCCUPATION
TOPOGRAPHICAL
TYPOGRAPHICAL
UNACCOMPANIED
UNDISCIPLINED
MAGNILOQUENCE
ADVENTUROUSLY
AGGLOMERATION
BIBLIOGRAPHER
BLOODCURDLING
CHOREOGRAPHER
COLLABORATION
COLLABORATIVE
COMMEMORATION
COMMEMORATIVE
COMMISERATION
CONCENTRATION
CONFEDERATION
CONFIGURATION
CONFLAGRATION
CONSIDERATELY
CONSIDERATION
CORROBORATION
CORROBORATORY
DEMONSTRATION
DEMONSTRATIVE
DETERIORATION
DISCOLORATION
DISFIGUREMENT
DISINTERESTED
GLOSSOGRAPHER
GRANDPARENTAL
GRIEFSTRICKEN
HERMAPHRODITE
IMPERTURBABLE
IMPERTURBABLY
IMPONDERABLES
INCARCERATION
INCORPORATION
INDIFFERENTLY
INSUPPORTABLE
INTERMARRIAGE
INTERPERSONAL
LEXICOGRAPHER
LYCANTHROPIST
MAGISTERIALLY
MALLEMAROKING
MEDITERRANEAN
MIDDLEBREAKER
MISANTHROPIST
MISUNDERSTAND
MISUNDERSTOOD
ORCHESTRATION
PAEDIATRICIAN
PARANTHROPOUS
PARAPHERNALIA
PREPROGRAMMED
PROLIFERATION
REFRIGERATION
REFRIGERATORS
REVERBERATION
SELFADDRESSED
SEPTENTRIONES
SEQUESTRATION
SHOULDERBLADE
SHRINKWRAPPED
SOMATOTROPHIN
STRIKEBREAKER
SUBCONTRACTOR
TRANSPARENTLY
TRANSPIRATION
TRANSPORTABLE
TREACHEROUSLY
UNCOMFORTABLE
UNCOMFORTABLY
UNCOOPERATIVE
UNDERCARRIAGE
UNDERSTRAPPER
UNEMBARRASSED
UNINTERRUPTED
WITWATERSRAND
ADVERTISEMENT
AMPHIGASTRIUM
APOCATASTASIS
AUTHORISATION
BILDUNGSROMAN
BRACHIOSAURUS
BUSINESSWOMAN
CONCUPISCENCE
CONGRESSIONAL
CONGRESSWOMAN
CONVALESCENCE
DEATHLESSNESS
DECOMPOSITION
DEFERVESCENCE
DISILLUSIONED
EFFERVESCENCE
EFFLORESCENCE
EMBARRASSMENT
EMBELLISHMENT
ESTABLISHMENT
FERTILISATION
GUILTLESSNESS
IMPROVISATION
INCANDESCENCE
INCOMBUSTIBLE
INCONSISTENCY
INCONTESTABLE
INDISPOSITION
INEXHAUSTIBLE
INEXPRESSIBLE
INFLORESCENCE
IRREPRESSIBLE
JUXTAPOSITION
KALEIDOSCOPIC
MALADJUSTMENT
MEISTERSINGER
MERCILESSNESS
METAPHYSICIAN
NERVELESSNESS
NONRESISTANCE
PROCLEUSMATIC
PROGRESSIVELY
RECRUDESCENCE
REFURBISHMENT
REIMBURSEMENT
REPERCUSSIONS
REPLENISHMENT
SELFCONSCIOUS
SENSELESSNESS
SHAPELESSNESS
SLEEPLESSNESS
SOUTHEASTERLY
SOUTHWESTERLY
SPINDLESHANKS
SQUEAMISHNESS
STEADFASTNESS
THANKLESSNESS
THUNDERSTRUCK
TRANSPOSITION
UNIMPRESSIBLE
UNNECESSARILY
VICEPRESIDENT
VIDEOCASSETTE
ACUPUNCTURIST
ADMINISTRATOR
AFFIRMATIVELY
AFFORESTATION
AIRCRAFTWOMAN
ALPHABETARIAN
ALTERNATIVELY
ANTIHISTAMINE
ARGUMENTATIVE
ARITHMETICIAN
AUTHORITARIAN
AUTHORITATIVE
CHRYSANTHEMUM
CIRCUMSTANCES
COEDUCATIONAL
COMPARATIVELY
CONFRONTATION
CONSECUTIVELY
DEFORESTATION
DISHEARTENING
DOCUMENTATION
ELEPHANTIASIS
FORTUNETELLER

FRAGMENTATION
GRAVITATIONAL
IMAGINATIVELY
INADVERTENTLY
INCOMPETENTLY
INQUISITIVELY
INSENSITIVITY
INSPIRATIONAL
INSTINCTIVELY
INSTITUTIONAL
INSTRUCTIONAL
INTERESTINGLY
INTERNATIONAL
INVOLUNTARILY
LAEVOROTATORY
LEPIDOPTERIST
MANIFESTATION
MANUFACTURING
MATHEMATICIAN
MOUTHWATERING
MULTINATIONAL
NEANDERTHALER
NIGHTWATCHMAN
ORNAMENTATION
OVERSTATEMENT
PALAEONTOLOGY
PERFUNCTORILY
POLLICITATION
PRECIPITATELY
PRECIPITATION
PREMEDITATION
PROCRASTINATE
PROGNOSTICATE
PROPRIETORIAL
PROTONOTARIAT
PROVOCATIVELY
RADIOACTIVITY
RECALCITRANCE
REGIMENTATION
REGURGITATION
REINSTATEMENT
RESUSCITATION
SCHUTZSTAFFEL
SEDIMENTATION
SELFCONTAINED
SUBLIEUTENANT
SUBSTANTIALLY
SUPERLATIVELY
SUPRANATIONAL
TRANSISTORIZE
TRANSLITERATE
TRANSMUTATION
UNCONDITIONAL
UNDERESTIMATE
UNEXCEPTIONAL
UNFORGETTABLE
UNINTENTIONAL
UNPARTITIONED
UNSYMMETRICAL
UNSYMPATHETIC
BACCALAUREATE
BUNGEEJUMPING
COMMENSURABLE
CONCEPTUALIZE
CONSANGUINITY
CONSCIOUSNESS
CONSPICUOUSLY
CONTRIBUTIONS
CREDULOUSNESS
DISHONOURABLE
DISHONOURABLY
DISTINGUISHED
FACETIOUSNESS
FORGETFULNESS
FRACTIOUSNESS
FRIGHTFULNESS
FRIVOLOUSNESS
GARRULOUSNESS
GRANDDAUGHTER
HOMOSEXUALITY
INDIVIDUALISM
INDIVIDUALIST
INDIVIDUALITY
INGENUOUSNESS
INSIDIOUSNESS
JURISPRUDENCE
LIEBFRAUMILCH
LUXURIOUSNESS
MASSACHUSETTS
NEIGHBOURHOOD
OFFICIOUSNESS
PROMISCUOUSLY
QUERULOUSNESS
RIGHTEOUSNESS
SALACIOUSNESS
SPECTACULARLY
STRENUOUSNESS
SUOVETAURILIA
SUPERABUNDANT
SUPERFLUOUSLY
THAUMATURGICS
THAUMATURGIST
THERMONUCLEAR
VIVACIOUSNESS
VORACIOUSNESS
ATTENTIVENESS
BOUGAINVILLEA
EFFECTIVENESS
EXPANSIVENESS
IMPULSIVENESS
INSECTIVOROUS
INVENTIVENESS
MISCHIEVOUSLY
OBJECTIVENESS
OFFENSIVENESS
PERVASIVENESS
RECEPTIVENESS
SECRETIVENESS
SENSITIVENESS
TALKATIVENESS
FEATHERWEIGHT
FOREKNOWLEDGE
HUNDREDWEIGHT
TONGUETWISTER
UNTRUSTWORTHY
HETERAUXESISM
HIEROGLYPHICS
IDIORRHYTHMIC
MONOCOTYLEDON
AUTHORIZATION
CAUTERIZATION
DRAMATIZATION
FERTILIZATION
FORMALIZATION
FOSSILIZATION
GALVANIZATION
HARMONIZATION
HYBRIDIZATION
MECHANIZATION
MODERNIZATION
NORMALIZATION
PRIVATIZATION
PULVERIZATION
SOLEMNIZATION
STABILIZATION
STERILIZATION
TANTALIZINGLY
VICTIMIZATION
VULCANIZATION
VULGARIZATION

13:9

ACCEPTILATION
ACCOMMODATING
ACCOMMODATION
AFFORESTATION
AGGLOMERATION
ALPHABETARIAN
AMPLIFICATION
ANTIHISTAMINE
ANYTHINGARIAN
APPROPRIATION
APPROXIMATELY
APPROXIMATION
AQUIFOLIACEAE
ARGUMENTATIVE
ARMOURPLATING
ARTIFICIALITY
ASSASSINATION
AUTHORISATION
AUTHORITARIAN
AUTHORITATIVE
AUTHORIZATION
AUTOCEPHALOUS
BEATIFICATION
BIBLIOGRAPHER
BIBLIOPHAGIST
BOUILLABAISSE
BRACHIOSAURUS
BROKENHEARTED
CAUTERIZATION
CERTIFICATION
CHOREOGRAPHER
CIRCUMSTANCES
CLARIFICATION
COLLABORATION
COLLABORATIVE
COLLIESHANGIE
COLLOQUIALISM
COMMEMORATION
COMMEMORATIVE
COMMERCIALIZE
COMMISERATION
COMMUNICATION
COMMUNICATIVE
CONCATENATION
CONCENTRATION
CONCEPTUALIZE
CONFARREATION
CONFEDERATION
CONFIGURATION
CONFLAGRATION
CONFRONTATION
CONSIDERATELY
CONSIDERATION
CONSOLIDATION
CONSPURCATION
CONSTELLATION
CONSTERNATION
CONTAMINATION
CONTEMPLATION
CONTEMPLATIVE
CORROBORATION
CORROBORATORY
DECRIMINALIZE
DEFORESTATION
DEMONSTRATION
DEMONSTRATIVE
DENATIONALIZE
DESEGREGATION
DETERIORATION
DETERMINATION
DIFFARREATION
DISCOLORATION
DISESTIMATION
DISSEMINATION
DISSIMILARITY
DISSIMULATION
DOCUMENTATION
DOUBLEGLAZING
DRAMATIZATION
ELECTROMAGNET
ENCYCLOPAEDIA
ENCYCLOPAEDIC
EXPOSTULATION
EXPROPRIATION
EXTERMINATION
EXTRAPOLATION
EXTRAVAGANTLY

FALSIFICATION
FERTILISATION
FERTILIZATION
FLABBERGASTED
FORMALIZATION
FORTIFICATION
FOSSILIZATION
FRAGMENTATION
GALVANIZATION
GESTICULATION
GLORIFICATION
GLOSSOGRAPHER
GRATIFICATION
HALLUCINATION
HALLUCINATORY
HAMMERKLAVIER
HARMONIZATION
HEARTBREAKING
HOMOSEXUALITY
HORRIPILATION
HOUSEBREAKING
HYBRIDIZATION
IMPERSONATING
IMPERSONATION
IMPONDERABLES
IMPROVISATION
INCARCERATION
INCORPORATION
INCRIMINATING
INCRIMINATORY
INDIVIDUALISM
INDIVIDUALIST
INDIVIDUALITY
INDUSTRIALIST
INDUSTRIALIZE
INTERCALATION
INTERPOLATION
INTERROGATION
INTERROGATIVE
INVESTIGATION
INVESTIGATIVE
INVOLUNTARILY
JOLLIFICATION
JUSTIFICATION
LAEVOROTATORY
LEATHERJACKET
LEXICOGRAPHER
MACHICOLATION
MADETOMEASURE
MAGNIFICATION
MANIFESTATION
MATRICULATION
MECHANIZATION
MEDITERRANEAN
MICROORGANISM
MISCEGENATION
MODERNIZATION
MOLLIFICATION
MONOTHALAMOUS
MORTIFICATION
MYSTIFICATION
NORMALIZATION
NULLIFICATION
ORCHESTRATION
ORNAMENTATION
OVEREMPHASIZE
PANDICULATION
PAPAPRELATIST
PARTICIPATION
PARTICIPATORY
PARTICULARISE
PARTICULARITY
PARTICULARIZE
PERAMBULATION
PEREGRINATION
PETRIFICATION
POLLICITATION
PRECIPITATELY
PRECIPITATION
PREDOMINANTLY
PRELIMINARIES
PREMEDITATION
PREOCCUPATION
PREPROGRAMMED
PREVARICATION
PRIVATIZATION
PROLIFERATION
PRONUNCIATION
PROTONOTARIAT
PROVINCIALISM
PSYCHOANALYSE
PSYCHOANALYST
PULVERIZATION
QUALIFICATION
QUARTERMASTER
RATIONALALITY
RECRIMINATION
RECRIMINATORY
RECTIFICATION
REFRIGERATION
REFRIGERATORS
REGIMENTATION
REGURGITATION
REINCARNATION
REPUBLICANISM
RESUSCITATION
REUNIFICATION
REVERBERATION
ROLLERBLADING
ROLLERCOASTER
SCHOOLTEACHER
SCHUTZSTAFFEL
SCINTILLATING
SCINTILLATION
SEDIMENTATION
SELFCONTAINED
SEQUESTRATION
SHRINKWRAPPED
SIGNIFICANTLY
SIGNIFICATION
SOLEMNIZATION
SPECIFICATION
STABILIZATION
STATIONMASTER
STERILIZATION
STRANGULATION
SUBCONTRACTOR
SUBJECTMATTER
SUBORDINATION
TENDERHEARTED
THEATRICALITY
THERMOPLASTIC
TRACTARIANISM
TRANSATLANTIC
TRANSMUTATION
TRANSPIRATION
TRIANGULATION
UNACCOMPANIED
UNCOOPERATIVE
UNDERSTRAPPER
UNEMBARRASSED
UNFORTUNATELY
UNIMAGINATIVE
UNNECESSARILY
VEGETARIANISM
VERSIFICATION
VICTIMIZATION
VITRIFICATION
VULCANIZATION
VULGARIZATION
CIRCUMAMBIENT
FONTAINEBLEAU
IMPERTURBABLE
IMPERTURBABLY
INDESCRIBABLE
INDESCRIBABLY
SHOULDERBLADE
THOROUGHBRACE
TINTINNABULUM
AESTHETICALLY
ARUNDINACEOUS
AUTOMATICALLY
CATEGORICALLY
CONCUPISCENCE
CONTRADICTION
CONTRADICTORY
CONVALESCENCE
COSTEFFECTIVE
COUNTERACTING
DEFERVESCENCE
DIAMETRICALLY
DISCONNECTION
DISRESPECTFUL
ECCENTRICALLY
EFFERVESCENCE
EFFLORESCENCE
ENERGETICALLY
FANTASTICALLY
FERROCONCRETE
GEOMETRICALLY
GRAMMATICALLY
HYDRAULICALLY
HYDROELECTRIC
IMPRACTICABLE
INCANDESCENCE
INCONSPICUOUS
INFLORESCENCE
INTRINSICALLY
INTROSPECTION
INTROSPECTIVE
KALEIDOSCOPIC
KNICKKNACKERY
LISSOTRICHOUS
NIGHTWATCHMAN
NONSUFFICIENT
NOSTALGICALLY
PARADOXICALLY
PATRIOTICALLY
PERPENDICULAR
PERSPICACIOUS
PHOTOELECTRIC
PNEUMATICALLY
PRAGMATICALLY
PREFABRICATED
PROPHETICALLY
QUARTODECIMAN
REALISTICALLY
RECRUDESCENCE
RETROSPECTIVE
SARCASTICALLY
SCHEMATICALLY
SELFCONSCIOUS
SOPHISTICATED
SPASMODICALLY
STATISTICALLY
STERCORACEOUS
STRATEGICALLY
STYLISTICALLY
SYNTACTICALLY
SYNTHETICALLY
THEOLOGICALLY
THEORETICALLY
THERMONUCLEAR
THYROIDECTOMY
TONGUEINCHEEK
TONSILLECTOMY
TRAUMATICALLY
UNCOMPLICATED
ARCHIMANDRITE
BIODEGRADABLE
BLOODCURDLING
CONTENTEDNESS
HYPOCHONDRIAC
JURISPRUDENCE
OUTRECUIDANCE
PASSCHENDAELE
SNOWBLINDNESS
UNDERGRADUATE
ADVERTISEMENT
ANTIGROPELOES

ATTENTIVENESS
BREASTFEEDING
CALLISTHENICS
CARBONIFEROUS
COUNTERFEITER
COUNTRYPEOPLE
DÉSOBLIGEANTE
DEVELOPMENTAL
DISENGAGEMENT
DISFIGUREMENT
DISHEARTENING
DISINTERESTED
DISPARAGEMENT
DRYOPITHECINE
EFFECTIVENESS
ENCOURAGEMENT
ENTEROPNEUSTA
ENVIRONMENTAL
EPITRACHELION
EQUIPONDERATE
EXPANSIVENESS
FEATHERWEIGHT
FORTUNETELLER
GASTROCNEMIUS
GRANDPARENTAL
HETERAUXESISM
HUNDREDWEIGHT
HYPERSTHENITE
IMPERTINENTLY
IMPROVIDENTLY
IMPULSIVENESS
INADVERTENTLY
INCOMPETENTLY
INCONSIDERATE
INDEPENDENTLY
INDIFFERENTLY
INEFFICIENTLY
INEXPERIENCED
INTELLIGENTLY
INVENTIVENESS
IRREPLACEABLE
ISOGEOTHERMAL
KNOWLEDGEABLE
LEPIDOPTERIST
LONGSUFFERING
MAGNIFICENTLY
MIDDLEBREAKER
MISMANAGEMENT
MONONUCLEOSIS
MOUTHWATERING
OBJECTIVENESS
OFFENSIVENESS
OVERSTATEMENT
PELOPONNESIAN
PERVASIVENESS
PHYSIOTHERAPY
PRONOUNCEMENT
PSYCHOTHERAPY
QUINQUAGESIMA
RAPPROCHEMENT

REARRANGEMENT
RECEPTIVENESS
REIMBURSEMENT
REINFORCEMENT
REINSTATEMENT
REMINISCENCES
REMORSELESSLY
RENSSELAERITE
SECRETIVENESS
SELFADDRESSED
SELFCONFESSED
SEMBLANCECORD
SENSITIVENESS
SERVILEMENTAL
SPITESPLENDID
STOCKBREEDING
STRIKEBREAKER
SUBLIEUTENANT
SUBSERVIENTLY
SUPERNUMERARY
SWOLLENHEADED
TALKATIVENESS
TEMPERAMENTAL
THOUGHTLESSLY
TRANSLITERATE
TRANSPARENTLY
UMBELLIFEROUS
UNEXPERIENCED
UNFORESEEABLE
UNPRECEDENTED
UNSERVICEABLE
WEATHERBEATEN
WHOLESOMENESS
DISGRACEFULLY
REPROACHFULLY
RESOURCEFULLY
WEIGHTLIFTING
CHRONOLOGICAL
CONTRAFAGOTTO
ENTOMOLOGICAL
GRANDDAUGHTER
GYNECOLOGICAL
INDEFATIGABLE
INDEFATIGABLY
INTRANSIGENCE
LIGHTFINGERED
MORPHOLOGICAL
PHYSIOLOGICAL
PSYCHOLOGICAL
SEISMOLOGICAL
SPELEOLOGICAL
TECHNOLOGICAL
THOROUGHGOING
UNWILLINGNESS
BOUSTROPHEDON
CHRYSANTHEMUM
COUNTERCHARGE
EMBELLISHMENT
ESTABLISHMENT
LAMPADEPHORIA

LEPTOCEPHALUS
MASTIGOPHORAN
MESSERSCHMITT
METAMORPHOSIS
NEANDERTHALER
PHILOSOPHICAL
PLATOCEPHALUS
REFURBISHMENT
REPLENISHMENT
SPINDLESHANKS
SQUEAMISHNESS
STEEPLECHASER
TOPOGRAPHICAL
TYPOGRAPHICAL
UNIMPEACHABLE
UNSYMPATHETIC
ACCEPTABILITY
ACCESSIBILITY
ACCOMPANIMENT
AFFIRMATIVELY
AIRWORTHINESS
ALTERNATIVELY
ANACHRONISTIC
ARITHMETICIAN
ASTONISHINGLY
BOUGAINVILLEA
CARTILAGINOUS
CHANGEABILITY
CLAIRAUDIENCE
COEDUCATIONAL
COMPARABILITY
COMPARATIVELY
COMPATIBILITY
CONGRESSIONAL
CONSANGUINITY
CONSECUTIVELY
DECOMPOSITION
DECONTAMINATE
DEFENSIBILITY
DEPENDABILITY
DISILLUSIONED
DISTINGUISHED
ELEPHANTIASIS
EXCOMMUNICATE
EXTRAORDINARY
FRIGHTENINGLY
GRAVITATIONAL
GRIEFSTRICKEN
IMAGINATIVELY
IMPERIALISTIC
IMPOSSIBILITY
IMPROBABILITY
INCOMMUNICADO
INCONVENIENCE
INDETERMINATE
INDISPOSITION
INEVITABILITY
INFALLIBILITY
INFLEXIBILITY
INQUISITIVELY

INSENSITIVITY
INSIGNIFICANT
INSPIRATIONAL
INSTINCTIVELY
INSTITUTIONAL
INSTRUCTIONAL
INSUBORDINATE
INSUFFICIENCY
INTERESTINGLY
INTERNATIONAL
INVINCIBILITY
INVIOLABILITY
JUXTAPOSITION
KAPPELMEISTER
LEISURELINESS
MAGISTERIALLY
MATERIALISTIC
MATHEMATICIAN
MEISTERSINGER
MERCHANDIZING
METAPHYSICIAN
MULTINATIONAL
MULTITUDINOUS
NATIONALISTIC
OPPORTUNISTIC
OPPORTUNITIES
OUTSTANDINGLY
PAEDIATRICIAN
PAINSTAKINGLY
PATERFAMILIAS
PATERNALISTIC
PENETRABILITY
PERSONALITIES
PRIMOGENITURE
PROCRASTINATE
PROFITABILITY
PROGNOSTICATE
PROGRESSIVELY
PROVOCATIVELY
PUSILLANIMITY
PUSILLANIMOUS
QUADRUPLICATE
RADIOACTIVITY
SCHOLARLINESS
SELFCONFIDENT
SEPTENTRIONES
SPRIGHTLINESS
SUBSTANTIALLY
SUPERFICIALLY
SUPERLATIVELY
SUPERORDINATE
SUPRANATIONAL
TANTALIZINGLY
THREATENINGLY
TONGUETWISTER
TRANSPOSITION
UNCOMMUNICATE
UNCONDITIONAL
UNDERACHIEVER
UNDERESTIMATE

UNESTABLISHED
UNEXCEPTIONAL
UNFLINCHINGLY
UNINTELLIGENT
UNINTENTIONAL
UNPARTITIONED
UPTOTHEMINUTE
VICEPRESIDENT
VULNERABILITY
KANGCHENJUNGA
ANTICLOCKWISE
SWASHBUCKLING
CLISHMACLAVER
DEFIBRILLATOR
DIACATHOLICON
EPANADIPLOSIS
ESCHSCHOLTZIA
FOREKNOWLEDGE
FORGETFULNESS
FRIGHTFULNESS
GLUMDALCLITCH
MACHIAVELLIAN
MONOCOTYLEDON
MULTINUCLEATE
PASSIONFLOWER
POLIOMYELITIS
PRESSURELOCAL
SPECTACULARLY
SPINECHILLING
SUSPERCOLLATE
SWEETSMELLING
TETRASYLLABIC
TRANQUILLISER
TRANQUILLIZER
UNDISCIPLINED
ACCOUTREMENTS
AGGIORNAMENTO
BLANDISHMENTS
BUNGEEJUMPING
EPIPHENOMENON
GYNANDROMORPH
LIEBFRAUMILCH
NEMATHELMINTH
PETROCHEMICAL
PHOTOCHEMICAL
POTENTIOMETER
PROCLEUSMATIC
PSYCHOSOMATIC
SACCHAROMYCES
SYMPIESOMETER
UNGENTLEMANLY
ANTHELMINTHIC
APPORTIONMENT
ASCERTAINABLE
BUTTERFINGERS
CHEESEMONGERS
CHINKERINCHEE
CIRCUMVENTION
COMPANIONABLE
COMPANIONSHIP
COMPLEMENTARY
COMPLIMENTARY
COMPREHENSION
COMPREHENSIVE
COMRADEINARMS
CONDESCENDING
CONDESCENSION
CONDITIONALLY
CONSECTANEOUS
CONSEQUENTIAL
CONTRAVENTION
CORRESPONDENT
CORRESPONDING
CRAFTSMANSHIP
DECAFFEINATED
DISAPPOINTING
DISCONTINUITY
DISCONTINUOUS
ENLIGHTENMENT
ENTERTAINMENT
EXCEPTIONABLE
EXCEPTIONALLY
FUERTEVENTURA
HETEROGENEOUS
INSTANTANEOUS
INSUBSTANTIAL
INTENTIONALLY
KIDDERMINSTER
LIBRARIANSHIP
MISCELLANEOUS
MOCKTECHNICAL
OBJECTIONABLE
PANHARMONICON
PARAPHERNALIA
PARLIAMENTARY
PARTHOGENESIS
PROTESTANTISM
PROVISIONALLY
PYROTECHNICAL
QUESTIONNAIRE
SANCTIMONIOUS
SENSATIONALLY
SOCIOECONOMIC
SPORTSMANLIKE
SPORTSMANSHIP
STAPHYLINIDAE
STATESMANLIKE
STATESMANSHIP
SUPERABUNDANT
SUPPLEMENTARY
TRADITIONALLY
TRICHOSANTHIN
UNCEREMONIOUS
UNCOORDINATED
UNDERSTANDING
UNFASHIONABLE
UNMENTIONABLE
UNSUBSTANTIAL
ADVENTUROUSLY
ARCHAEOLOGIST
BIOTECHNOLOGY
CEREMONIOUSLY
COMPASSIONATE
CONCEPTIONIST
CONCESSIONARY
CONFECTIONERS
CONFECTIONERY
CONSPICUOUSLY
CONTORTIONIST
CRIMINOLOGIST
DAGUERREOTYPE
DERMATOLOGIST
DISCRETIONARY
DISPASSIONATE
ELECTROMOTIVE
ENCEPHALOCELE
EXHIBITIONIST
EXPEDITIONARY
EXPEDITIOUSLY
FRANKALMOIGNE
GYNAECOLOGIST
HERMAPHRODITE
IGNOMINIOUSLY
IMPRESSIONISM
IMPRESSIONIST
INCREDULOUSLY
INDUSTRIOUSLY
INSECTIVOROUS
JIGGERYPOKERY
KNICKERBOCKER
LYCANTHROPIST
MAGNANIMOUSLY
MALLEMAROKING
METAGRABOLISE
METAGROBOLISE
METEOROLOGIST
MISANTHROPIST
MISCHIEVOUSLY
MULTICOLOURED
OPHTHALMOLOGY
ORNITHOLOGIST
PALAEONTOLOGY
PARALLELOGRAM
PARANTHROPOUS
PARTICOLOURED
PERFECTIONIST
PERFUNCTORILY
PHYSHARMONICA
PHYSIOGNOMIST
PRECAUTIONARY
PROJECTIONIST
PROMISCUOUSLY
PROPORTIONATE
PROPRIETORIAL
PROTECTIONISM
PROTECTIONIST
PUNCTILIOUSLY
RECITATIONIST
REDEMPTIONIST
REVOLUTIONARY
REVOLUTIONIZE
SCANDALMONGER
SENTENTIOUSLY
SIPUNCULOIDEA
SOMATOTROPHIN
SPONTANEOUSLY
STREPTOCOCCUS
SUPERFLUOUSLY
TABLESPOONFUL
TRANSISTORIZE
TREACHEROUSLY
UNCONSCIOUSLY
UNQUESTIONING
UNTRUSTWORTHY
VIDEORECORDER
CONTRACEPTION
CONTRACEPTIVE
DEIPNOSOPHIST
EPHEMEROPTERA
HIEROGLYPHICS
MICROCOMPUTER
MISCONCEPTION
PHARMACOPOEIA
PHILADELPHIAN
PRECONCEPTION
REDEVELOPMENT
REPROGRAPHICS
TRANSCRIPTION
UNANTICIPATED
APPROPINQUATE
GRANDILOQUENT
VENTRILOQUISM
VENTRILOQUIST
ADMINISTRATOR
ANIMADVERSION
ARISTROCRATIC
AUTOBIOGRAPHY
BACCALAUREATE
BILDUNGSROMAN
CHARACTERISED
CHARACTERLESS
CHATEAUBRIAND
CIRCUMFERENCE
CLOSEDCIRCUIT
COMMENSURABLE
CONTROVERSIAL
DEMILITARIZED
DISAPPEARANCE
DISCONCERTING
DISHONOURABLE
DISHONOURABLY
DISPROPORTION
FOSTERPARENTS
HAMMERTHROWER
HEMISPHERICAL
IDIOSYNCRATIC
INAPPROPRIATE
INTERMARRIAGE
IRRECOVERABLE
LECTISTERNIUM

NEIGHBOURHOOD
NONCONFORMIST
NONCONFORMITY
PHILANTHROPIC
PREPONDERANCE
PROFESSORSHIP
PROSOPOGRAPHY
RECALCITRANCE
RHYPAROGRAPHY
RUTHERFORDIUM
SCHADENFREUDE
SCHIZOPHRENIA
SCHIZOPHRENIC
SELFGOVERNING
SPECTROGRAPHY
SUOVETAURILIA
SWEDENBORGIAN
TAPERECORDING
THAUMATURGICS
THAUMATURGIST
UNADULTERATED
UNCONQUERABLE
UNDERCARRIAGE
UNSYMMETRICAL
AFFENPINSCHER
CHRISTMASTIME
CONSCIOUSNESS
CONTRABASSOON
CREDULOUSNESS
CROSSQUESTION
DEATHLESSNESS
DECOMPRESSION
EMBARRASSMENT
FACETIOUSNESS
FRACTIOUSNESS
FRIVOLOUSNESS
GARRULOUSNESS
GENERALISSIMO
GUILTLESSNESS
INDISPENSABLE
INEXPRESSIBLE
INFINITESIMAL
INGENUOUSNESS
INSIDIOUSNESS
INTERPERSONAL
IRREPRESSIBLE
IRRESPONSIBLE
IRRESPONSIBLY
LACKADAISICAL
LIECHTENSTEIN
LUXURIOUSNESS
MASSACHUSETTS
MERCILESSNESS
MISUNDERSTAND
MISUNDERSTOOD
NERVELESSNESS
OFFICIOUSNESS
PREPOSSESSING
PREPOSSESSION
QUADRAGESIMAL
QUERULOUSNESS
REPERCUSSIONS
REPREHENSIBLE
REPREHENSIBLY
RETROGRESSION
RIGHTEOUSNESS
SALACIOUSNESS
SENSELESSNESS
SHAPELESSNESS
SLEEPLESSNESS
STEPPINGSTONE
STRENUOUSNESS
THANKLESSNESS
TORTOISESHELL
TRANSGRESSION
UNIMPRESSIBLE
UNINTERESTING
UNPROGRESSIVE
VIDEOCASSETTE
VIVACIOUSNESS
VORACIOUSNESS
WITWATERSRAND
XIPHIPLASTRON
ACRYLONITRILE
AFFREIGHTMENT
AMPHIGASTRIUM
APOCATASTASIS
ARCHAEOPTERYX
ARCHITECTURAL
CONSCIENTIOUS
CONSERVATOIRE
CONTINUATIONS
CONTRIBUTIONS
COUNTERATTACK
DIFFERENTIATE
DISADVANTAGED
DISCREDITABLE
DISCREDITABLY
FUNDAMENTALLY
GLOBETROTTING
GOODRIGHTEOUS
HORSEFEATHERS
HORTICULTURAL
HYPERCRITICAL
IDIORRHYTHMIC
ILLUMINATIONS
IMPERCEPTIBLE
IMPERCEPTIBLY
INCOMBUSTIBLE
INCONSISTENCY
INCONTESTABLE
INCORRUPTIBLE
INEXHAUSTIBLE
INSUPPORTABLE
MALADJUSTMENT
NONRESISTANCE
OYSTERCATCHER
PARENTHETICAL
PASSEMENTERIE
PRESERVATIVES
PRETERNATURAL
PROBLEMATICAL
PROFECTITIOUS
QUADRILATERAL
RAMIFICATIONS
RHADAMANTHINE
SENTIMENTALLY
SOUTHEASTERLY
SOUTHWESTERLY
STEADFASTNESS
SUPERSTITIOUS
SURREPTITIOUS
THUNDERSTRUCK
TRANSPORTABLE
UNACCOUNTABLE
UNACCOUNTABLY
UNCOMFORTABLE
UNCOMFORTABLY
UNDERCLOTHING
UNENLIGHTENED
UNFORGETTABLE
UNGRAMMATICAL
UNINHABITABLE
UNPREDICTABLE
UNPRETENTIOUS
VERCINGETORIX
ACUPUNCTURIST
ANTICOAGULANT
ELECTROCUTION
MAGNILOQUENCE
MANUFACTURING
MAURIKIGUSARI
OWNEROCCUPIER
SEMICONDUCTOR
SUPERANNUATED
UNINTERRUPTED
INCONCEIVABLE
IRRETRIEVABLE
IRRETRIEVABLY
AIRCRAFTWOMAN
BUSINESSWOMAN
CONGRESSWOMAN
ROUNDTHEWORLD
CONVERSAZIONE

13:10

ADMINISTRATOR
AESTHETICALLY
APOCATASTASIS
ARISTROCRATIC
ASCERTAINABLE
AUTOBIOGRAPHY
AUTOMATICALLY
BIODEGRADABLE
CATEGORICALLY
CLISHMACLAVER
COMMENSURABLE
COMPANIONABLE
COMRADEINARMS
CONDITIONALLY
COUNTERCHARGE
DECAFFEINATED
DEFIBRILLATOR
DÉSOBLIGEANTE
DIAMETRICALLY
DISADVANTAGED
DISAPPEARANCE
DISCREDITABLE
DISCREDITABLY
DISHONOURABLE
DISHONOURABLY
ECCENTRICALLY
ELEPHANTIASIS
ENERGETICALLY
EXCEPTIONABLE
EXCEPTIONALLY
FANTASTICALLY
FUNDAMENTALLY
GEOMETRICALLY
GRAMMATICALLY
HYDRAULICALLY
IDIOSYNCRATIC
IMPERTURBABLE
IMPERTURBABLY
IMPRACTICABLE
INCONCEIVABLE
INCONTESTABLE
INDEFATIGABLE
INDEFATIGABLY
INDESCRIBABLE
INDESCRIBABLY
INDISPENSABLE
INSUPPORTABLE
INTENTIONALLY
INTRINSICALLY
IRRECOVERABLE
IRREPLACEABLE
IRRETRIEVABLE
IRRETRIEVABLY
KNOWLEDGEABLE
LEPTOCEPHALUS
MAGISTERIALLY
MIDDLEBREAKER
NEANDERTHALER
NONRESISTANCE
NOSTALGICALLY
OBJECTIONABLE
OUTRECUIDANCE
PARADOXICALLY
PARAPHERNALIA
PASSCHENDAELE
PATRIOTICALLY
PLATOCEPHALUS
PNEUMATICALLY
PRAGMATICALLY
PREFABRICATED
PREPONDERANCE
PROCLEUSMATIC
PROPHETICALLY

PROSOPOGRAPHY
PROVISIONALLY
PSYCHOSOMATIC
QUESTIONNAIRE
REALISTICALLY
RECALCITRANCE
RHYPAROGRAPHY
SARCASTICALLY
SCHEMATICALLY
SENSATIONALLY
SENTIMENTALLY
SOPHISTICATED
SPASMODICALLY
SPECTACULARLY
SPECTROGRAPHY
SPINDLESHANKS
STATISTICALLY
STEEPLECHASER
STRATEGICALLY
STRIKEBREAKER
STYLISTICALLY
SUBSTANTIALLY
SUPERANNUATED
SUPERFICIALLY
SWOLLENHEADED
SYNTACTICALLY
SYNTHETICALLY
TETRASYLLABIC
THEOLOGICALLY
THEORETICALLY
TRADITIONALLY
TRANSPORTABLE
TRAUMATICALLY
UNACCOUNTABLE
UNACCOUNTABLY
UNADULTERATED
UNANTICIPATED
UNCOMFORTABLE
UNCOMFORTABLY
UNCOMPLICATED
UNCONQUERABLE
UNCOORDINATED
UNFASHIONABLE
UNFORESEEABLE
UNFORGETTABLE
UNGENTLEMANLY
UNIMPEACHABLE
UNINHABITABLE
UNMENTIONABLE
UNPREDICTABLE
UNSERVICEABLE
WEATHERBEATEN
IMPONDERABLES
AFFENPINSCHER
AQUIFOLIACEAE
ARITHMETICIAN
CHINKERINCHEE
CLOSEDCIRCUIT
DRYOPITHECINE
ENCEPHALOCELE

EXCOMMUNICATE
GRIEFSTRICKEN
INCOMMUNICADO
INSIGNIFICANT
KNICKERBOCKER
LEATHERJACKET
MATHEMATICIAN
METAPHYSICIAN
OYSTERCATCHER
PAEDIATRICIAN
PROGNOSTICATE
QUADRUPLICATE
SCHOOLTEACHER
SEMBLANCECORD
SEMICONDUCTOR
STREPTOCOCCUS
SUBCONTRACTOR
UNCOMMUNICATE
BREASTFEEDING
CONDESCENDING
CORRESPONDENT
CORRESPONDING
HERMAPHRODITE
ROLLERBLADING
RUTHERFORDIUM
SELFCONFIDENT
STOCKBREEDING
SUPERABUNDANT
TAPERECORDING
UNDERSTANDING
VICEPRESIDENT
ACCOUTREMENTS
AGGIORNAMENTO
ARCHAEOPTERYX
ARUNDINACEOUS
BACCALAUREATE
BLANDISHMENTS
BOUSTROPHEDON
CHRYSANTHEMUM
CIRCUMFERENCE
CLAIRAUDIENCE
CONCUPISCENCE
CONSECTANEOUS
CONVALESCENCE
DEFERVESCENCE
EFFERVESCENCE
EFFLORESCENCE
ENCYCLOPAEDIA
ENCYCLOPAEDIC
EPIPHENOMENON
FOREKNOWLEDGE
FOSTERPARENTS
GOODRIGHTEOUS
HETEROGENEOUS
INCANDESCENCE
INCONSISTENCY
INCONVENIENCE
INFLORESCENCE
INSTANTANEOUS
INSUFFICIENCY

INTRANSIGENCE
JURISPRUDENCE
LIGHTFINGERED
MAGNILOQUENCE
MASSACHUSETTS
MISCELLANEOUS
MONOCOTYLEDON
MULTINUCLEATE
PARTHOGENESIS
PASSEMENTERIE
POTENTIOMETER
QUADRILATERAL
RECRUDESCENCE
SCHADENFREUDE
SCHIZOPHRENIA
SCHIZOPHRENIC
SOUTHEASTERLY
SOUTHWESTERLY
STERCORACEOUS
SYMPIESOMETER
UNDERACHIEVER
UNENLIGHTENED
UNSYMPATHETIC
VIDEOCASSETTE
SCHUTZSTAFFEL
ARCHAEOLOGIST
BIBLIOPHAGIST
BUTTERFINGERS
CHEESEMONGERS
CRIMINOLOGIST
DERMATOLOGIST
ELECTROMAGNET
GYNAECOLOGIST
METEOROLOGIST
ORNITHOLOGIST
PARALLELOGRAM
SWEDENBORGIAN
THAUMATURGICS
THAUMATURGIST
UNINTELLIGENT
DEIPNOSOPHIST
GRANDDAUGHTER
HIEROGLYPHICS
HORSEFEATHERS
IDIORRHYTHMIC
LISSOTRICHOUS
NEIGHBOURHOOD
NIGHTWATCHMAN
PHILADELPHIAN
REPROGRAPHICS
RHADAMANTHINE
TONGUEINCHEEK
TORTOISESHELL
UNDERCLOTHING
BOUILLABAISSE
CHARACTERISED
CHATEAUBRIAND
CHRONOLOGICAL
CIRCUMAMBIENT
CONSCIENTIOUS

CONTINUATIONS
CONTRIBUTIONS
CONVERSAZIONE
COUNTERFEITER
DEMILITARIZED
DIACATHOLICON
DIFFERENTIATE
ENTOMOLOGICAL
FEATHERWEIGHT
FRANKALMOIGNE
GLUMDALCLITCH
GYNECOLOGICAL
HEMISPHERICAL
HUNDREDWEIGHT
HYPERCRITICAL
ILLUMINATIONS
IMPERCEPTIBLE
IMPERCEPTIBLY
INAPPROPRIATE
INCOMBUSTIBLE
INCORRUPTIBLE
INEXHAUSTIBLE
INEXPRESSIBLE
INFINITESIMAL
INTERMARRIAGE
IRREPRESSIBLE
IRRESPONSIBLE
IRRESPONSIBLY
LACKADAISICAL
LIEBFRAUMILCH
MOCKTECHNICAL
MORPHOLOGICAL
NEMATHELMINTH
NONSUFFICIENT
PANHARMONICON
PARENTHETICAL
PERSPICACIOUS
PETROCHEMICAL
PHILOSOPHICAL
PHOTOCHEMICAL
PHYSIOLOGICAL
POLIOMYELITIS
PRESERVATIVES
PROBLEMATICAL
PROFECTITIOUS
PSYCHOLOGICAL
PYROTECHNICAL
QUADRAGESIMAL
QUARTODECIMAN
RAMIFICATIONS
REPERCUSSIONS
REPREHENSIBLE
REPREHENSIBLY
SANCTIMONIOUS
SEISMOLOGICAL
SELFCONSCIOUS
SELFCONTAINED
SIPUNCULOIDEA
SPELEOLOGICAL
STAPHYLINIDAE

SUOVETAURILIA
SUPERSTITIOUS
SURREPTITIOUS
TECHNOLOGICAL
TOPOGRAPHICAL
TRANQUILLISER
TRANQUILLIZER
TYPOGRAPHICAL
UNCEREMONIOUS
UNDERCARRIAGE
UNDISCIPLINED
UNGRAMMATICAL
UNIMPRESSIBLE
UNPRETENTIOUS
UNSYMMETRICAL
HEARTBREAKING
HOUSEBREAKING
JIGGERYPOKERY
KNICKKNACKERY
MALLEMAROKING
ACCEPTABILITY
ACCESSIBILITY
ANTICOAGULANT
ANTIGROPELOES
ARTIFICIALITY
AUTOCEPHALOUS
BIOTECHNOLOGY
BLOODCURDLING
BOUGAINVILLEA
CHANGEABILITY
CHARACTERLESS
COLLOQUIALISM
COMMERCIALIZE
COMPARABILITY
COMPATIBILITY
CONCEPTUALIZE
DECRIMINALIZE
DEFENSIBILITY
DENATIONALIZE
DEPENDABILITY
EPITRACHELION
FONTAINEBLEAU
FORTUNETELLER
HOMOSEXUALITY
IMPOSSIBILITY
IMPROBABILITY
INDIVIDUALISM
INDIVIDUALIST
INDIVIDUALITY
INDUSTRIALIST
INDUSTRIALIZE
INEVITABILITY
INFALLIBILITY
INFLEXIBILITY
INVINCIBILITY
INVIOLABILITY
MACHIAVELLIAN
METAGRABOLISE
METAGROBOLISE
OPHTHALMOLOGY
PALAEONTOLOGY
PATERFAMILIAS
PENETRABILITY
PROFITABILITY
PROVINCIALISM
PSYCHOANALYSE
PSYCHOANALYST
RATIONALALITY
SHOULDERBLADE
SPINECHILLING
SPORTSMANLIKE
STATESMANLIKE
SUSPERCOLLATE
SWASHBUCKLING
SWEETSMELLING
THEATRICALITY
THERMONUCLEAR
VULNERABILITY
ACCOMPANIMENT
ADVERTISEMENT
AFFREIGHTMENT
ANTIHISTAMINE
APPORTIONMENT
DISENGAGEMENT
DISFIGUREMENT
DISPARAGEMENT
EMBARRASSMENT
EMBELLISHMENT
ENCOURAGEMENT
ENLIGHTENMENT
ENTERTAINMENT
ESTABLISHMENT
GASTROCNEMIUS
MALADJUSTMENT
MESSERSCHMITT
MISMANAGEMENT
MONOTHALAMOUS
NONCONFORMIST
NONCONFORMITY
OVERSTATEMENT
PHYSIOGNOMIST
PREPROGRAMMED
PRONOUNCEMENT
PUSILLANIMITY
PUSILLANIMOUS
RAPPROCHEMENT
REARRANGEMENT
REDEVELOPMENT
REFURBISHMENT
REIMBURSEMENT
REINFORCEMENT
REINSTATEMENT
REPLENISHMENT
UNDERESTIMATE
AIRWORTHINESS
ASTONISHINGLY
ATTENTIVENESS
CALLISTHENICS
CARTILAGINOUS
CIRCUMSTANCES
COLLIESHANGIE
COMPASSIONATE
CONCEPTIONIST
CONCESSIONARY
CONFECTIONERS
CONFECTIONERY
CONSANGUINITY
CONSCIOUSNESS
CONTENTEDNESS
CONTORTIONIST
CREDULOUSNESS
DEATHLESSNESS
DECONTAMINATE
DEVELOPMENTAL
DISCRETIONARY
DISHEARTENING
DISPASSIONATE
EFFECTIVENESS
ENVIRONMENTAL
EXHIBITIONIST
EXPANSIVENESS
EXPEDITIONARY
EXTRAORDINARY
EXTRAVAGANTLY
FACETIOUSNESS
FORGETFULNESS
FRACTIOUSNESS
FRIGHTENINGLY
FRIGHTFULNESS
FRIVOLOUSNESS
GARRULOUSNESS
GRANDPARENTAL
GUILTLESSNESS
HYPERSTHENITE
IMPERTINENTLY
IMPRESSIONISM
IMPRESSIONIST
IMPROVIDENTLY
IMPULSIVENESS
INADVERTENTLY
INCOMPETENTLY
INDEPENDENTLY
INDETERMINATE
INDIFFERENTLY
INEFFICIENTLY
INEXPERIENCED
INGENUOUSNESS
INSIDIOUSNESS
INSUBORDINATE
INTELLIGENTLY
INTERESTINGLY
INVENTIVENESS
LECTISTERNIUM
LEISURELINESS
LUXURIOUSNESS
MAGNIFICENTLY
MEDITERRANEAN
MEISTERSINGER
MERCILESSNESS
MICROORGANISM
MULTITUDINOUS
NERVELESSNESS
OBJECTIVENESS
OFFENSIVENESS
OFFICIOUSNESS
OUTSTANDINGLY
PAINSTAKINGLY
PERFECTIONIST
PERVASIVENESS
PHYSHARMONICA
PRECAUTIONARY
PREDOMINANTLY
PROCRASTINATE
PROJECTIONIST
PROPORTIONATE
PROTECTIONISM
PROTECTIONIST
QUERULOUSNESS
RECEPTIVENESS
RECITATIONIST
REDEMPTIONIST
REMINISCENCES
REPUBLICANISM
REVOLUTIONARY
REVOLUTIONIZE
RIGHTEOUSNESS
SALACIOUSNESS
SCANDALMONGER
SCHOLARLINESS
SECRETIVENESS
SELFGOVERNING
SENSELESSNESS
SENSITIVENESS
SERVILEMENTAL
SHAPELESSNESS
SIGNIFICANTLY
SLEEPLESSNESS
SNOWBLINDNESS
SPITESPLENDID
SPRIGHTLINESS
SQUEAMISHNESS
STEADFASTNESS
STRENUOUSNESS
SUBLIEUTENANT
SUBSERVIENTLY
SUPERORDINATE
TABLESPOONFUL
TALKATIVENESS
TANTALIZINGLY
TEMPERAMENTAL
THANKLESSNESS
THREATENINGLY
TRACTARIANISM
TRANSATLANTIC
TRANSPARENTLY
UNACCOMPANIED
UNEXPERIENCED
UNFLINCHINGLY
UNPRECEDENTED
UNQUESTIONING

UNWILLINGNESS
UPTOTHEMINUTE
VEGETARIANISM
VIVACIOUSNESS
VORACIOUSNESS
WHOLESOMENESS
AIRCRAFTWOMAN
BILDUNGSROMAN
BUSINESSWOMAN
COEDUCATIONAL
CONGRESSIONAL
CONGRESSWOMAN
CONSERVATOIRE
CONTRAFAGOTTO
COUNTRYPEOPLE
DISILLUSIONED
EPANADIPLOSIS
GRAVITATIONAL
GYNANDROMORPH
HAMMERTHROWER
INSPIRATIONAL
INSTITUTIONAL
INSTRUCTIONAL
INTERNATIONAL
INTERPERSONAL
KALEIDOSCOPIC
LAMPADEPHORIA
MASTIGOPHORAN
METAMORPHOSIS
MONONUCLEOSIS
MULTINATIONAL
PASSIONFLOWER
PHARMACOPOEIA
PHILANTHROPIC
PRESSURELOCAL
ROUNDTHEWORLD
SEPTENTRIONES
SOCIOECONOMIC
SUPRANATIONAL
THOROUGHGOING
UNCONDITIONAL
UNEXCEPTIONAL
UNINTENTIONAL
UNPARTITIONED
VERCINGETORIX
BIBLIOGRAPHER
BUNGEEJUMPING
CHOREOGRAPHER
GLOSSOGRAPHER
LEXICOGRAPHER
LYCANTHROPIST
MISANTHROPIST
OWNEROCCUPIER
PARANTHROPOUS
SHRINKWRAPPED
SOMATOTROPHIN
UNDERSTRAPPER
UNINTERRUPTED
ACRYLONITRILE
ACUPUNCTURIST

ALPHABETARIAN
AMPHIGASTRIUM
ANYTHINGARIAN
ARCHIMANDRITE
AUTHORITARIAN
BROKENHEARTED
CARBONIFEROUS
DISSIMILARITY
EQUIPONDERATE
FERROCONCRETE
HYPOCHONDRIAC
INCONSIDERATE
INSECTIVOROUS
INVOLUNTARILY
ISOGEOTHERMAL
LEPIDOPTERIST
LONGSUFFERING
MANUFACTURING
MOUTHWATERING
PARTICULARISE
PARTICULARITY
PARTICULARIZE
PERFUNCTORILY
PHYSIOTHERAPY
PRELIMINARIES
PROPRIETORIAL
PROTONOTARIAT
PSYCHOTHERAPY
RENSSELAERITE
SUPERNUMERARY
TENDERHEARTED
THOROUGHBRACE
THUNDERSTRUCK
TRANSISTORIZE
TRANSLITERATE
UMBELLIFEROUS
UNNECESSARILY
UNTRUSTWORTHY
VIDEORECORDER
WITWATERSRAND
ANACHRONISTIC
ANIMADVERSION
COMPANIONSHIP
COMPREHENSION
COMPREHENSIVE
CONDESCENSION
CONTRABASSOON
CONTROVERSIAL
CRAFTSMANSHIP
DECOMPRESSION
DISINTERESTED
DISTINGUISHED
FLABBERGASTED
GENERALISSIMO
HETERAUXESISM
IMPERIALISTIC
KAPPELMEISTER
KIDDERMINSTER
LIBRARIANSHIP
MADETOMEASURE

MATERIALISTIC
MAURIKIGUSARI
NATIONALISTIC
OPPORTUNISTIC
OVEREMPHASIZE
PATERNALISTIC
PELOPONNESIAN
PREPOSSESSING
PREPOSSESSION
PROFESSORSHIP
QUARTERMASTER
QUINQUAGESIMA
REMORSELESSLY
RETROGRESSION
ROLLERCOASTER
SELFADDRESSED
SELFCONFESSED
SPORTSMANSHIP
STATESMANSHIP
STATIONMASTER
THERMOPLASTIC
THOUGHTLESSLY
TONGUETWISTER
TRANSGRESSION
UNEMBARRASSED
UNESTABLISHED
UNPROGRESSIVE
ACCEPTILATION
ACCOMMODATING
ACCOMMODATION
AFFORESTATION
AGGLOMERATION
AMPLIFICATION
ANTHELMINTHIC
APPROPRIATION
APPROXIMATELY
APPROXIMATION
ARGUMENTATIVE
ARMOURPLATING
ASSASSINATION
AUTHORISATION
AUTHORITATIVE
AUTHORIZATION
BEATIFICATION
CAUTERIZATION
CERTIFICATION
CHRISTMASTIME
CIRCUMVENTION
CLARIFICATION
COLLABORATION
COLLABORATIVE
COMMEMORATION
COMMEMORATIVE
COMMISERATION
COMMUNICATION
COMMUNICATIVE
COMPLEMENTARY
COMPLIMENTARY
CONCATENATION
CONCENTRATION

CONFARREATION
CONFEDERATION
CONFIGURATION
CONFLAGRATION
CONFRONTATION
CONSEQUENTIAL
CONSIDERATELY
CONSIDERATION
CONSOLIDATION
CONSPURCATION
CONSTELLATION
CONSTERNATION
CONTAMINATION
CONTEMPLATION
CONTEMPLATIVE
CONTRACEPTION
CONTRACEPTIVE
CONTRADICTION
CONTRADICTORY
CONTRAVENTION
CORROBORATION
CORROBORATORY
COSTEFFECTIVE
COUNTERACTING
COUNTERATTACK
CROSSQUESTION
DAGUERREOTYPE
DECOMPOSITION
DEFORESTATION
DEMONSTRATION
DEMONSTRATIVE
DESEGREGATION
DETERIORATION
DETERMINATION
DIFFARREATION
DISAPPOINTING
DISCOLORATION
DISCONCERTING
DISCONNECTION
DISESTIMATION
DISPROPORTION
DISRESPECTFUL
DISSEMINATION
DISSIMULATION
DOCUMENTATION
DRAMATIZATION
ELECTROCUTION
ELECTROMOTIVE
EPHEMEROPTERA
ESCHSCHOLTZIA
EXPOSTULATION
EXPROPRIATION
EXTERMINATION
EXTRAPOLATION
FALSIFICATION
FERTILISATION
FERTILIZATION
FORMALIZATION
FORTIFICATION
FOSSILIZATION

FRAGMENTATION
FUERTEVENTURA
GALVANIZATION
GESTICULATION
GLOBETROTTING
GLORIFICATION
GRATIFICATION
HALLUCINATION
HALLUCINATORY
HARMONIZATION
HORRIPILATION
HYBRIDIZATION
HYDROELECTRIC
IMPERSONATING
IMPERSONATION
IMPROVISATION
INCARCERATION
INCORPORATION
INCRIMINATING
INCRIMINATORY
INDISPOSITION
INSUBSTANTIAL
INTERCALATION
INTERPOLATION
INTERROGATION
INTERROGATIVE
INTROSPECTION
INTROSPECTIVE
INVESTIGATION
INVESTIGATIVE
JOLLIFICATION
JUSTIFICATION
JUXTAPOSITION
LAEVOROTATORY
LIECHTENSTEIN
MACHICOLATION
MAGNIFICATION
MANIFESTATION
MATRICULATION
MECHANIZATION
MISCEGENATION
MISCONCEPTION
MISUNDERSTAND
MISUNDERSTOOD
MODERNIZATION
MOLLIFICATION
MORTIFICATION
MYSTIFICATION
NORMALIZATION
NULLIFICATION
OPPORTUNITIES
ORCHESTRATION
ORNAMENTATION
PANDICULATION
PAPAPRELATIST
PARLIAMENTARY
PARTICIPATION
PARTICIPATORY
PERAMBULATION
PEREGRINATION
PERSONALITIES
PETRIFICATION
PHOTOELECTRIC
POLLICITATION
PRECIPITATELY
PRECIPITATION
PRECONCEPTION
PREMEDITATION
PREOCCUPATION
PREVARICATION
PRIMOGENITURE
PRIVATIZATION
PROLIFERATION
PRONUNCIATION
PROTESTANTISM
PULVERIZATION
QUALIFICATION
RECRIMINATION
RECRIMINATORY
RECTIFICATION
REFRIGERATION
REFRIGERATORS
REGIMENTATION
REGURGITATION
REINCARNATION
RESUSCITATION
RETROSPECTIVE
REUNIFICATION
REVERBERATION
SCINTILLATING
SCINTILLATION
SEDIMENTATION
SEQUESTRATION
SIGNIFICATION
SOLEMNIZATION
SPECIFICATION
STABILIZATION
STEPPINGSTONE
STERILIZATION
STRANGULATION
SUBJECTMATTER
SUBORDINATION
SUPPLEMENTARY
THYROIDECTOMY
TONSILLECTOMY
TRANSCRIPTION
TRANSMUTATION
TRANSPIRATION
TRANSPOSITION
TRIANGULATION
TRICHOSANTHIN
UNCOOPERATIVE
UNFORTUNATELY
UNIMAGINATIVE
UNINTERESTING
UNSUBSTANTIAL
VERSIFICATION
VICTIMIZATION
VITRIFICATION
VULCANIZATION
VULGARIZATION
WEIGHTLIFTING
XIPHIPLASTRON
ADVENTUROUSLY
APPROPINQUATE
ARCHITECTURAL
BRACHIOSAURUS
CEREMONIOUSLY
CONSPICUOUSLY
DISCONTINUITY
DISCONTINUOUS
DISGRACEFULLY
ENTEROPNEUSTA
EXPEDITIOUSLY
GRANDILOQUENT
HORTICULTURAL
IGNOMINIOUSLY
INCONSPICUOUS
INCREDULOUSLY
INDUSTRIOUSLY
KANGCHENJUNGA
MAGNANIMOUSLY
MICROCOMPUTER
MISCHIEVOUSLY
MULTICOLOURED
PARTICOLOURED
PERPENDICULAR
PRETERNATURAL
PROMISCUOUSLY
PUNCTILIOUSLY
REPROACHFULLY
RESOURCEFULLY
SENTENTIOUSLY
SPONTANEOUSLY
SUPERFLUOUSLY
TINTINNABULUM
TREACHEROUSLY
UNCONSCIOUSLY
UNDERGRADUATE
VENTRILOQUISM
VENTRILOQUIST
AFFIRMATIVELY
ALTERNATIVELY
COMPARATIVELY
CONSECUTIVELY
HAMMERKLAVIER
IMAGINATIVELY
INQUISITIVELY
INSENSITIVITY
INSTINCTIVELY
PROGRESSIVELY
PROVOCATIVELY
RADIOACTIVITY
SUPERLATIVELY
ANTICLOCKWISE
SACCHAROMYCES
DOUBLEGLAZING
MERCHANDIZING

13:11

ANTICOAGULANT
APPROPINQUATE
BACCALAUREATE
CHATEAUBRIAND
COMPASSIONATE
COMPLEMENTARY
COMPLIMENTARY
CONCESSIONARY
COUNTERATTACK
DECONTAMINATE
DIFFERENTIATE
DISCRETIONARY
DISPASSIONATE
EQUIPONDERATE
EXCOMMUNICATE
EXPEDITIONARY
EXTRAORDINARY
INAPPROPRIATE
INCOMMUNICADO
INCONSIDERATE
INDETERMINATE
INSIGNIFICANT
INSUBORDINATE
INTERMARRIAGE
MAURIKIGUSARI
MISUNDERSTAND
MULTINUCLEATE
PARLIAMENTARY
PHYSIOTHERAPY
PRECAUTIONARY
PROCRASTINATE
PROGNOSTICATE
PROPORTIONATE
PSYCHOTHERAPY
QUADRUPLICATE
REVOLUTIONARY
SHOULDERBLADE
SUBLIEUTENANT
SUPERABUNDANT
SUPERNUMERARY
SUPERORDINATE
SUPPLEMENTARY
SUSPERCOLLATE
THOROUGHBRACE
TRANSLITERATE
UNCOMMUNICATE
UNDERCARRIAGE
UNDERESTIMATE
UNDERGRADUATE
WITWATERSRAND
ASCERTAINABLE
BIODEGRADABLE
COMMENSURABLE
COMPANIONABLE
DISCREDITABLE
DISCREDITABLY
DISHONOURABLE
DISHONOURABLY

EXCEPTIONABLE
IMPERCEPTIBLE
IMPERCEPTIBLY
IMPERTURBABLE
IMPERTURBABLY
IMPRACTICABLE
INCOMBUSTIBLE
INCONCEIVABLE
INCONTESTABLE
INCORRUPTIBLE
INDEFATIGABLE
INDEFATIGABLY
INDESCRIBABLE
INDESCRIBABLY
INDISPENSABLE
INEXHAUSTIBLE
INEXPRESSIBLE
INSUPPORTABLE
IRRECOVERABLE
IRREPLACEABLE
IRREPRESSIBLE
IRRESPONSIBLE
IRRESPONSIBLY
IRRETRIEVABLE
IRRETRIEVABLY
KNOWLEDGEABLE
OBJECTIONABLE
REPREHENSIBLE
REPREHENSIBLY
TETRASYLLABIC
TRANSPORTABLE
UNACCOUNTABLE
UNACCOUNTABLY
UNCOMFORTABLE
UNCOMFORTABLY
UNCONQUERABLE
UNFASHIONABLE
UNFORESEEABLE
UNFORGETTABLE
UNIMPEACHABLE
UNIMPRESSIBLE
UNINHABITABLE
UNMENTIONABLE
UNPREDICTABLE
UNSERVICEABLE
CHRONOLOGICAL
CIRCUMSTANCES
DIACATHOLICON
ENTOMOLOGICAL
GYNECOLOGICAL
HEMISPHERICAL
HYPERCRITICAL
INEXPERIENCED
LACKADAISICAL
MOCKTECHNICAL
MORPHOLOGICAL
PANHARMONICON
PARENTHETICAL
PETROCHEMICAL
PHILOSOPHICAL

PHOTOCHEMICAL
PHYSIOLOGICAL
PRESSURELOCAL
PROBLEMATICAL
PSYCHOLOGICAL
PYROTECHNICAL
REMINISCENCES
SACCHAROMYCES
SEISMOLOGICAL
SPELEOLOGICAL
STREPTOCOCCUS
TECHNOLOGICAL
TOPOGRAPHICAL
TYPOGRAPHICAL
UNEXPERIENCED
UNGRAMMATICAL
UNSYMMETRICAL
BOUSTROPHEDON
ENCYCLOPAEDIA
ENCYCLOPAEDIC
FOREKNOWLEDGE
MONOCOTYLEDON
SIPUNCULOIDEA
SPITESPLENDID
STAPHYLINIDAE
SWOLLENHEADED
VIDEORECORDER
ACCOMPANIMENT
ADVERTISEMENT
AFFIRMATIVELY
AFFREIGHTMENT
AIRWORTHINESS
ALTERNATIVELY
APPORTIONMENT
APPROXIMATELY
AQUIFOLIACEAE
ATTENTIVENESS
BUTTERFINGERS
CHARACTERLESS
CHEESEMONGERS
CIRCUMAMBIENT
COMPARATIVELY
CONFECTIONERS
CONFECTIONERY
CONSCIOUSNESS
CONSECUTIVELY
CONSIDERATELY
CONTENTEDNESS
CORRESPONDENT
CREDULOUSNESS
DEATHLESSNESS
DISENGAGEMENT
DISFIGUREMENT
DISPARAGEMENT
EFFECTIVENESS
EMBARRASSMENT
EMBELLISHMENT
ENCEPHALOCELE
ENCOURAGEMENT
ENLIGHTENMENT

ENTERTAINMENT
EPHEMEROPTERA
ESTABLISHMENT
EXPANSIVENESS
FACETIOUSNESS
FERROCONCRETE
FONTAINEBLEAU
FORGETFULNESS
FRACTIOUSNESS
FRIGHTFULNESS
FRIVOLOUSNESS
GARRULOUSNESS
GRANDILOQUENT
GUILTLESSNESS
HORSEFEATHERS
IMAGINATIVELY
IMPULSIVENESS
INGENUOUSNESS
INQUISITIVELY
INSIDIOUSNESS
INSTINCTIVELY
INVENTIVENESS
JIGGERYPOKERY
KNICKKNACKERY
LEISURELINESS
LIECHTENSTEIN
LUXURIOUSNESS
MALADJUSTMENT
MEDITERRANEAN
MERCILESSNESS
MISMANAGEMENT
NERVELESSNESS
NONSUFFICIENT
OBJECTIVENESS
OFFENSIVENESS
OFFICIOUSNESS
OVERSTATEMENT
PASSCHENDAELE
PERVASIVENESS
PHARMACOPOEIA
PRECIPITATELY
PROGRESSIVELY
PRONOUNCEMENT
PROVOCATIVELY
QUERULOUSNESS
RAPPROCHEMENT
REARRANGEMENT
RECEPTIVENESS
REDEVELOPMENT
REFURBISHMENT
REIMBURSEMENT
REINFORCEMENT
REINSTATEMENT
REPLENISHMENT
RIGHTEOUSNESS
SALACIOUSNESS
SCHOLARLINESS
SECRETIVENESS
SELFCONFIDENT
SENSELESSNESS

SENSITIVENESS
SHAPELESSNESS
SLEEPLESSNESS
SNOWBLINDNESS
SPRIGHTLINESS
SQUEAMISHNESS
STEADFASTNESS
STRENUOUSNESS
SUPERLATIVELY
TALKATIVENESS
THANKLESSNESS
THERMONUCLEAR
TONGUEINCHEEK
TORTOISESHELL
UNFORTUNATELY
UNINTELLIGENT
UNWILLINGNESS
VICEPRESIDENT
VIVACIOUSNESS
VORACIOUSNESS
WHOLESOMENESS
DISRESPECTFUL
SCHUTZSTAFFEL
TABLESPOONFUL
ASTONISHINGLY
COLLIESHANGIE
DISADVANTAGED
FEATHERWEIGHT
FRANKALMOIGNE
FRIGHTENINGLY
HUNDREDWEIGHT
INTERESTINGLY
MEISTERSINGER
OUTSTANDINGLY
PAINSTAKINGLY
SCANDALMONGER
TANTALIZINGLY
THREATENINGLY
UNFLINCHINGLY
AFFENPINSCHER
ANTHELMINTHIC
BIBLIOGRAPHER
CHINKERINCHEE
CHOREOGRAPHER
COMPANIONSHIP
CRAFTSMANSHIP
DISTINGUISHED
GLOSSOGRAPHER
LEXICOGRAPHER
LIBRARIANSHIP
OYSTERCATCHER
PROFESSORSHIP
SCHOOLTEACHER
SOMATOTROPHIN
SPORTSMANSHIP
STATESMANSHIP
TRICHOSANTHIN
UNESTABLISHED
ACCEPTABILITY
ACCEPTILATION

ACCESSIBILITY
ACCOMMODATING
ACCOMMODATION
ACRYLONITRILE
ACUPUNCTURIST
AFFORESTATION
AGGLOMERATION
ALPHABETARIAN
AMPHIGASTRIUM
AMPLIFICATION
ANIMADVERSION
ANTICLOCKWISE
ANTIHISTAMINE
ANYTHINGARIAN
APPROPRIATION
APPROXIMATION
ARCHAEOLOGIST
ARCHIMANDRITE
ARGUMENTATIVE
ARITHMETICIAN
ARMOURPLATING
ARTIFICIALITY
ASSASSINATION
AUTHORISATION
AUTHORITARIAN
AUTHORITATIVE
AUTHORIZATION
BEATIFICATION
BIBLIOPHAGIST
BLOODCURDLING
BREASTFEEDING
BUNGEEJUMPING
CALLISTHENICS
CAUTERIZATION
CERTIFICATION
CHANGEABILITY
CHRISTMASTIME
CIRCUMVENTION
CLARIFICATION
COLLABORATION
COLLABORATIVE
COLLOQUIALISM
COMMEMORATION
COMMEMORATIVE
COMMERCIALIZE
COMMISERATION
COMMUNICATION
COMMUNICATIVE
COMPARABILITY
COMPATIBILITY
COMPREHENSION
COMPREHENSIVE
CONCATENATION
CONCENTRATION
CONCEPTIONIST
CONCEPTUALIZE
CONDESCENDING
CONDESCENSION
CONFARREATION
CONFEDERATION
CONFIGURATION
CONFLAGRATION
CONFRONTATION
CONSANGUINITY
CONSEQUENTIAL
CONSERVATOIRE
CONSIDERATION
CONSOLIDATION
CONSPURCATION
CONSTELLATION
CONSTERNATION
CONTAMINATION
CONTEMPLATION
CONTEMPLATIVE
CONTORTIONIST
CONTRACEPTION
CONTRACEPTIVE
CONTRADICTION
CONTRAVENTION
CONTROVERSIAL
CORRESPONDING
CORROBORATION
COSTEFFECTIVE
COUNTERACTING
CRIMINOLOGIST
CROSSQUESTION
DECOMPOSITION
DECOMPRESSION
DECRIMINALIZE
DEFENSIBILITY
DEFORESTATION
DEIPNOSOPHIST
DEMONSTRATION
DEMONSTRATIVE
DENATIONALIZE
DEPENDABILITY
DERMATOLOGIST
DESEGREGATION
DETERIORATION
DETERMINATION
DIFFARREATION
DISAPPOINTING
DISCOLORATION
DISCONCERTING
DISCONNECTION
DISCONTINUITY
DISESTIMATION
DISHEARTENING
DISPROPORTION
DISSEMINATION
DISSIMILARITY
DISSIMULATION
DOCUMENTATION
DOUBLEGLAZING
DRAMATIZATION
DRYOPITHECINE
ELECTROCUTION
ELECTROMOTIVE
EPITRACHELION
EXHIBITIONIST
EXPOSTULATION
EXPROPRIATION
EXTERMINATION
EXTRAPOLATION
FALSIFICATION
FERTILISATION
FERTILIZATION
FORMALIZATION
FORTIFICATION
FOSSILIZATION
FRAGMENTATION
GALVANIZATION
GASTROCNEMIUS
GENERALISSIMO
GESTICULATION
GLOBETROTTING
GLORIFICATION
GRATIFICATION
GYNAECOLOGIST
HALLUCINATION
HAMMERKLAVIER
HARMONIZATION
HEARTBREAKING
HERMAPHRODITE
HETERAUXESISM
HIEROGLYPHICS
HOMOSEXUALITY
HORRIPILATION
HOUSEBREAKING
HYBRIDIZATION
HYPERSTHENITE
HYPOCHONDRIAC
IMPERSONATING
IMPERSONATION
IMPOSSIBILITY
IMPRESSIONISM
IMPRESSIONIST
IMPROBABILITY
IMPROVISATION
INCARCERATION
INCORPORATION
INCRIMINATING
INDISPOSITION
INDIVIDUALISM
INDIVIDUALIST
INDIVIDUALITY
INDUSTRIALIST
INDUSTRIALIZE
INEVITABILITY
INFALLIBILITY
INFLEXIBILITY
INSENSITIVITY
INSUBSTANTIAL
INTERCALATION
INTERPOLATION
INTERROGATION
INTERROGATIVE
INTROSPECTION
INTROSPECTIVE
INVESTIGATION
INVESTIGATIVE
INVINCIBILITY
INVIOLABILITY
INVOLUNTARILY
JOLLIFICATION
JUSTIFICATION
JUXTAPOSITION
LECTISTERNIUM
LEPIDOPTERIST
LONGSUFFERING
LYCANTHROPIST
MACHIAVELLIAN
MACHICOLATION
MAGNIFICATION
MALLEMAROKING
MANIFESTATION
MANUFACTURING
MATHEMATICIAN
MATRICULATION
MECHANIZATION
MERCHANDIZING
MESSERSCHMITT
METAGRABOLISE
METAGROBOLISE
METAPHYSICIAN
METEOROLOGIST
MICROORGANISM
MISANTHROPIST
MISCEGENATION
MISCONCEPTION
MODERNIZATION
MOLLIFICATION
MORTIFICATION
MOUTHWATERING
MYSTIFICATION
NONCONFORMIST
NONCONFORMITY
NORMALIZATION
NULLIFICATION
OPPORTUNITIES
ORCHESTRATION
ORNAMENTATION
ORNITHOLOGIST
OVEREMPHASIZE
OWNEROCCUPIER
PAEDIATRICIAN
PANDICULATION
PAPAPRELATIST
PARTICIPATION
PARTICULARISE
PARTICULARITY
PARTICULARIZE
PATERFAMILIAS
PELOPONNESIAN
PENETRABILITY
PERAMBULATION
PEREGRINATION
PERFECTIONIST
PERFUNCTORILY
PERSONALITIES

PETRIFICATION
PHILADELPHIAN
PHYSHARMONICA
PHYSIOGNOMIST
POLLICITATION
PRECIPITATION
PRECONCEPTION
PRELIMINARIES
PREMEDITATION
PREOCCUPATION
PREPOSSESSING
PREPOSSESSION
PREVARICATION
PRIVATIZATION
PROFITABILITY
PROJECTIONIST
PROLIFERATION
PRONUNCIATION
PROPRIETORIAL
PROTECTIONISM
PROTECTIONIST
PROTESTANTISM
PROTONOTARIAT
PROVINCIALISM
PULVERIZATION
PUSILLANIMITY
QUALIFICATION
QUESTIONNAIRE
QUINQUAGESIMA
RADIOACTIVITY
RATIONALALITY
RECITATIONIST
RECRIMINATION
RECTIFICATION
REDEMPTIONIST
REFRIGERATION
REGIMENTATION
REGURGITATION
REINCARNATION
RENSSELAERITE
REPROGRAPHICS
REPUBLICANISM
RESUSCITATION
RETROGRESSION
RETROSPECTIVE
REUNIFICATION
REVERBERATION
REVOLUTIONIZE
RHADAMANTHINE
ROLLERBLADING
RUTHERFORDIUM
SCINTILLATING
SCINTILLATION
SEDIMENTATION
SELFGOVERNING
SEQUESTRATION
SIGNIFICATION
SOLEMNIZATION
SPECIFICATION
SPINECHILLING
SPORTSMANLIKE
STABILIZATION
STATESMANLIKE
STERILIZATION
STOCKBREEDING
STRANGULATION
SUBORDINATION
SWASHBUCKLING
SWEDENBORGIAN
SWEETSMELLING
TAPERECORDING
THAUMATURGICS
THAUMATURGIST
THEATRICALITY
THOROUGHGOING
TRACTARIANISM
TRANSCRIPTION
TRANSGRESSION
TRANSISTORIZE
TRANSMUTATION
TRANSPIRATION
TRANSPOSITION
TRIANGULATION
UNACCOMPANIED
UNCOOPERATIVE
UNDERCLOTHING
UNDERSTANDING
UNIMAGINATIVE
UNINTERESTING
UNNECESSARILY
UNPROGRESSIVE
UNQUESTIONING
UNSUBSTANTIAL
VEGETARIANISM
VENTRILOQUISM
VENTRILOQUIST
VERSIFICATION
VICTIMIZATION
VITRIFICATION
VULCANIZATION
VULGARIZATION
VULNERABILITY
WEIGHTLIFTING
GRIEFSTRICKEN
KNICKERBOCKER
LEATHERJACKET
MIDDLEBREAKER
STRIKEBREAKER
AESTHETICALLY
AUTOMATICALLY
BOUGAINVILLEA
CATEGORICALLY
CONDITIONALLY
DIAMETRICALLY
DISGRACEFULLY
ECCENTRICALLY
ENERGETICALLY
EXCEPTIONALLY
FANTASTICALLY
FORTUNETELLER
FUNDAMENTALLY
GEOMETRICALLY
GRAMMATICALLY
HYDRAULICALLY
IMPONDERABLES
INTENTIONALLY
INTRINSICALLY
LEPTOCEPHALUS
LIEBFRAUMILCH
MAGISTERIALLY
NEANDERTHALER
NOSTALGICALLY
PARADOXICALLY
PARAPHERNALIA
PATRIOTICALLY
PERPENDICULAR
PLATOCEPHALUS
PNEUMATICALLY
PRAGMATICALLY
PROPHETICALLY
PROVISIONALLY
REALISTICALLY
REPROACHFULLY
RESOURCEFULLY
SARCASTICALLY
SCHEMATICALLY
SENSATIONALLY
SENTIMENTALLY
SPASMODICALLY
STATISTICALLY
STRATEGICALLY
STYLISTICALLY
SUBSTANTIALLY
SUOVETAURILIA
SUPERFICIALLY
SYNTACTICALLY
SYNTHETICALLY
THEOLOGICALLY
THEORETICALLY
TINTINNABULUM
TRADITIONALLY
TRAUMATICALLY
AIRCRAFTWOMAN
BILDUNGSROMAN
BUSINESSWOMAN
CHRYSANTHEMUM
CONGRESSWOMAN
IDIORRHYTHMIC
INFINITESIMAL
ISOGEOTHERMAL
NIGHTWATCHMAN
PREPROGRAMMED
QUADRAGESIMAL
QUARTODECIMAN
SOCIOECONOMIC
ACCOUTREMENTS
AGGIORNAMENTO
BLANDISHMENTS
CIRCUMFERENCE
CLAIRAUDIENCE
COEDUCATIONAL
CONCUPISCENCE
CONGRESSIONAL
CONVALESCENCE
DEFERVESCENCE
DÉSOBLIGEANTE
DISAPPEARANCE
DISILLUSIONED
EFFERVESCENCE
EFFLORESCENCE
ELECTROMAGNET
EPIPHENOMENON
FOSTERPARENTS
GRAVITATIONAL
INCANDESCENCE
INCONSISTENCY
INCONVENIENCE
INFLORESCENCE
INSPIRATIONAL
INSTITUTIONAL
INSTRUCTIONAL
INSUFFICIENCY
INTERNATIONAL
INTERPERSONAL
INTRANSIGENCE
JURISPRUDENCE
KANGCHENJUNGA
MAGNILOQUENCE
MULTINATIONAL
NEMATHELMINTH
NONRESISTANCE
OUTRECUIDANCE
PREPONDERANCE
RECALCITRANCE
RECRUDESCENCE
SCHIZOPHRENIA
SCHIZOPHRENIC
SELFCONTAINED
SEPTENTRIONES
SPINDLESHANKS
SUPRANATIONAL
UNCONDITIONAL
UNDISCIPLINED
UNENLIGHTENED
UNEXCEPTIONAL
UNGENTLEMANLY
UNINTENTIONAL
UNPARTITIONED
ANTIGROPELOES
ARUNDINACEOUS
AUTOCEPHALOUS
BIOTECHNOLOGY
CARBONIFEROUS
CARTILAGINOUS
CONSCIENTIOUS
CONSECTANEOUS
CONTINUATIONS
CONTRABASSOON
CONTRADICTORY
CONTRIBUTIONS

CONVERSAZIONE
CORROBORATORY
DISCONTINUOUS
GOODRIGHTEOUS
HALLUCINATORY
HETEROGENEOUS
ILLUMINATIONS
INCONSPICUOUS
INCRIMINATORY
INSECTIVOROUS
INSTANTANEOUS
LAEVOROTATORY
LISSOTRICHOUS
MISCELLANEOUS
MISUNDERSTOOD
MONOTHALAMOUS
MULTITUDINOUS
NEIGHBOURHOOD
OPHTHALMOLOGY
PALAEONTOLOGY
PARANTHROPOUS
PARTICIPATORY
PERSPICACIOUS
PROFECTITIOUS
PUSILLANIMOUS
RAMIFICATIONS
RECRIMINATORY
REFRIGERATORS
REPERCUSSIONS
SANCTIMONIOUS
SELFCONSCIOUS
SEMBLANCECORD
STEPPINGSTONE
STERCORACEOUS
SUPERSTITIOUS
SURREPTITIOUS
THYROIDECTOMY
TONSILLECTOMY
UMBELLIFEROUS
UNCEREMONIOUS
UNPRETENTIOUS
AUTOBIOGRAPHY
COUNTRYPEOPLE
KALEIDOSCOPIC
PHILANTHROPIC
PROSOPOGRAPHY
RHYPAROGRAPHY
SHRINKWRAPPED
SPECTROGRAPHY
UNDERSTRAPPER
ARCHAEOPTERYX
ARCHITECTURAL
BRACHIOSAURUS
COMRADEINARMS
COUNTERCHARGE
GYNANDROMORPH
HORTICULTURAL
HYDROELECTRIC
LAMPADEPHORIA
LIGHTFINGERED
MASTIGOPHORAN
MULTICOLOURED
PARALLELOGRAM
PARTICOLOURED
PASSEMENTERIE
PHOTOELECTRIC
PRETERNATURAL
QUADRILATERAL
ROUNDTHEWORLD
SOUTHEASTERLY
SOUTHWESTERLY
SPECTACULARLY
VERCINGETORIX
XIPHIPLASTRON
ADVENTUROUSLY
APOCATASTASIS
BOUILLABAISSE
CEREMONIOUSLY
CHARACTERISED
CONSPICUOUSLY
ELEPHANTIASIS
ENTEROPNEUSTA
EPANADIPLOSIS
EXPEDITIOUSLY
IGNOMINIOUSLY
INCREDULOUSLY
INDUSTRIOUSLY
MAGNANIMOUSLY
METAMORPHOSIS
MISCHIEVOUSLY
MONONUCLEOSIS
PARTHOGENESIS
PROMISCUOUSLY
PUNCTILIOUSLY
REMORSELESSLY
SELFADDRESSED
SELFCONFESSED
SENTENTIOUSLY
SPONTANEOUSLY
STEEPLECHASER
SUPERFLUOUSLY
THOUGHTLESSLY
TRANQUILLISER
TREACHEROUSLY
UNCONSCIOUSLY
UNEMBARRASSED
ADMINISTRATOR
ANACHRONISTIC
ARISTROCRATIC
BROKENHEARTED
CONTRAFAGOTTO
COUNTERFEITER
DECAFFEINATED
DEFIBRILLATOR
DEVELOPMENTAL
DISINTERESTED
ENVIRONMENTAL
EXTRAVAGANTLY
FLABBERGASTED
GLUMDALCLITCH
GRANDDAUGHTER
GRANDPARENTAL
IDIOSYNCRATIC
IMPERIALISTIC
IMPERTINENTLY
IMPROVIDENTLY
INADVERTENTLY
INCOMPETENTLY
INDEPENDENTLY
INDIFFERENTLY
INEFFICIENTLY
INTELLIGENTLY
KAPPELMEISTER
KIDDERMINSTER
MAGNIFICENTLY
MASSACHUSETTS
MATERIALISTIC
MICROCOMPUTER
NATIONALISTIC
OPPORTUNISTIC
PATERNALISTIC
POLIOMYELITIS
POTENTIOMETER
PREDOMINANTLY
PREFABRICATED
PROCLEUSMATIC
PSYCHOSOMATIC
QUARTERMASTER
ROLLERCOASTER
SEMICONDUCTOR
SERVILEMENTAL
SIGNIFICANTLY
SOPHISTICATED
STATIONMASTER
SUBCONTRACTOR
SUBJECTMATTER
SUBSERVIENTLY
SUPERANNUATED
SYMPIESOMETER
TEMPERAMENTAL
TENDERHEARTED
THERMOPLASTIC
TONGUETWISTER
TRANSATLANTIC
TRANSPARENTLY
UNADULTERATED
UNANTICIPATED
UNCOMPLICATED
UNCOORDINATED
UNINTERRUPTED
UNPRECEDENTED
UNSYMPATHETIC
UNTRUSTWORTHY
VIDEOCASSETTE
WEATHERBEATEN
CLOSEDCIRCUIT
FUERTEVENTURA
MADETOMEASURE
PRIMOGENITURE
SCHADENFREUDE
THUNDERSTRUCK
UPTOTHEMINUTE
CLISHMACLAVER
PRESERVATIVES
UNDERACHIEVER
HAMMERTHROWER
PASSIONFLOWER
DAGUERREOTYPE
PSYCHOANALYSE
PSYCHOANALYST
DEMILITARIZED
ESCHSCHOLTZIA
TRANQUILLIZER

13:12

AIRCRAFTWOMAN
ALPHABETARIAN
ANYTHINGARIAN
AQUIFOLIACEAE
ARCHITECTURAL
ARITHMETICIAN
AUTHORITARIAN
BILDUNGSROMAN
BUSINESSWOMAN
CHRONOLOGICAL
COEDUCATIONAL
CONGRESSIONAL
CONGRESSWOMAN
CONSEQUENTIAL
CONTROVERSIAL
DEVELOPMENTAL
ENTOMOLOGICAL
ENVIRONMENTAL
FONTAINEBLEAU
GRANDPARENTAL
GRAVITATIONAL
GYNECOLOGICAL
HEMISPHERICAL
HORTICULTURAL
HYPERCRITICAL
HYPOCHONDRIAC
INFINITESIMAL
INSPIRATIONAL
INSTITUTIONAL
INSTRUCTIONAL
INSUBSTANTIAL
INTERNATIONAL
INTERPERSONAL
ISOGEOTHERMAL
LACKADAISICAL
MACHIAVELLIAN
MASTIGOPHORAN
MATHEMATICIAN
MEDITERRANEAN
METAPHYSICIAN
MOCKTECHNICAL
MORPHOLOGICAL
MULTINATIONAL
NIGHTWATCHMAN

PAEDIATRICIAN
PARALLELOGRAM
PARENTHETICAL
PATERFAMILIAS
PELOPONNESIAN
PERPENDICULAR
PETROCHEMICAL
PHILADELPHIAN
PHILOSOPHICAL
PHOTOCHEMICAL
PHYSIOLOGICAL
PRESSURELOCAL
PRETERNATURAL
PROBLEMATICAL
PROPRIETORIAL
PROTONOTARIAT
PSYCHOLOGICAL
PYROTECHNICAL
QUADRAGESIMAL
QUADRILATERAL
QUARTODECIMAN
SEISMOLOGICAL
SERVILEMENTAL
SPELEOLOGICAL
STAPHYLINIDAE
SUPRANATIONAL
SWEDENBORGIAN
TECHNOLOGICAL
TEMPERAMENTAL
THERMONUCLEAR
TOPOGRAPHICAL
TYPOGRAPHICAL
UNCONDITIONAL
UNEXCEPTIONAL
UNGRAMMATICAL
UNINTENTIONAL
UNSUBSTANTIAL
UNSYMMETRICAL
CALLISTHENICS
CIRCUMFERENCE
CLAIRAUDIENCE
CONCUPISCENCE
CONVALESCENCE
COUNTERATTACK
DEFERVESCENCE
DISAPPEARANCE
EFFERVESCENCE
EFFLORESCENCE
GLUMDALCLITCH
HIEROGLYPHICS
INCANDESCENCE
INCONSISTENCY
INCONVENIENCE
INFLORESCENCE
INSUFFICIENCY
INTRANSIGENCE
JURISPRUDENCE
LIEBFRAUMILCH
MAGNILOQUENCE
NONRESISTANCE

OUTRECUIDANCE
PHYSHARMONICA
PREPONDERANCE
RECALCITRANCE
RECRUDESCENCE
REPROGRAPHICS
THAUMATURGICS
THOROUGHBRACE
THUNDERSTRUCK
INCOMMUNICADO
SCHADENFREUDE
SHOULDERBLADE
AFFENPINSCHER
ANTIGROPELOES
BIBLIOGRAPHER
BOUGAINVILLEA
BROKENHEARTED
CHARACTERISED
CHINKERINCHEE
CHOREOGRAPHER
CIRCUMSTANCES
CLISHMACLAVER
COUNTERFEITER
DECAFFEINATED
DEMILITARIZED
DISADVANTAGED
DISILLUSIONED
DISINTERESTED
DISTINGUISHED
ELECTROMAGNET
FLABBERGASTED
FORTUNETELLER
GLOSSOGRAPHER
GRANDDAUGHTER
GRIEFSTRICKEN
HAMMERKLAVIER
HAMMERTHROWER
IMPONDERABLES
INEXPERIENCED
KAPPELMEISTER
KIDDERMINSTER
KNICKERBOCKER
LEATHERJACKET
LEXICOGRAPHER
LIGHTFINGERED
MEISTERSINGER
MICROCOMPUTER
MIDDLEBREAKER
MULTICOLOURED
NEANDERTHALER
OPPORTUNITIES
OWNEROCCUPIER
OYSTERCATCHER
PARTICOLOURED
PASSIONFLOWER
PERSONALITIES
POTENTIOMETER
PREFABRICATED
PRELIMINARIES
PREPROGRAMMED

PRESERVATIVES
QUARTERMASTER
REMINISCENCES
ROLLERCOASTER
SACCHAROMYCES
SCANDALMONGER
SCHOOLTEACHER
SCHUTZSTAFFEL
SELFADDRESSED
SELFCONFESSED
SELFCONTAINED
SEPTENTRIONES
SHRINKWRAPPED
SIPUNCULOIDEA
SOPHISTICATED
STATIONMASTER
STEEPLECHASER
STRIKEBREAKER
SUBJECTMATTER
SUPERANNUATED
SWOLLENHEADED
SYMPIESOMETER
TENDERHEARTED
TONGUEINCHEEK
TONGUETWISTER
TRANQUILLISER
TRANQUILLIZER
UNACCOMPANIED
UNADULTERATED
UNANTICIPATED
UNCOMPLICATED
UNCOORDINATED
UNDERACHIEVER
UNDERSTRAPPER
UNDISCIPLINED
UNEMBARRASSED
UNENLIGHTENED
UNESTABLISHED
UNEXPERIENCED
UNINTERRUPTED
UNPARTITIONED
UNPRECEDENTED
VIDEORECORDER
WEATHERBEATEN
BIOTECHNOLOGY
COUNTERCHARGE
FOREKNOWLEDGE
INTERMARRIAGE
KANGCHENJUNGA
OPHTHALMOLOGY
PALAEONTOLOGY
UNDERCARRIAGE
AUTOBIOGRAPHY
FEATHERWEIGHT
HUNDREDWEIGHT
PROSOPOGRAPHY
RHYPAROGRAPHY
SPECTROGRAPHY
UNTRUSTWORTHY
ANACHRONISTIC

ANTHELMINTHIC
APOCATASTASIS
ARISTROCRATIC
CLOSEDCIRCUIT
COLLIESHANGIE
COMPANIONSHIP
CRAFTSMANSHIP
ELEPHANTIASIS
ENCYCLOPAEDIA
ENCYCLOPAEDIC
EPANADIPLOSIS
ESCHSCHOLTZIA
HYDROELECTRIC
IDIORRHYTHMIC
IDIOSYNCRATIC
IMPERIALISTIC
KALEIDOSCOPIC
LAMPADEPHORIA
LIBRARIANSHIP
LIECHTENSTEIN
MATERIALISTIC
METAMORPHOSIS
MONONUCLEOSIS
NATIONALISTIC
OPPORTUNISTIC
PARAPHERNALIA
PARTHOGENESIS
PASSEMENTERIE
PATERNALISTIC
PHARMACOPOEIA
PHILANTHROPIC
PHOTOELECTRIC
POLIOMYELITIS
PROCLEUSMATIC
PROFESSORSHIP
PSYCHOSOMATIC
SCHIZOPHRENIA
SCHIZOPHRENIC
SOCIOECONOMIC
SOMATOTROPHIN
SPITESPLENDID
SPORTSMANSHIP
STATESMANSHIP
SUOVETAURILIA
TETRASYLLABIC
THERMOPLASTIC
TRANSATLANTIC
TRICHOSANTHIN
UNSYMPATHETIC
VERCINGETORIX
SPINDLESHANKS
SPORTSMANLIKE
STATESMANLIKE
ACRYLONITRILE
ADVENTUROUSLY
AESTHETICALLY
AFFIRMATIVELY
ALTERNATIVELY
APPROXIMATELY
ASCERTAINABLE

ASTONISHINGLY
AUTOMATICALLY
BIODEGRADABLE
CATEGORICALLY
CEREMONIOUSLY
COMMENSURABLE
COMPANIONABLE
COMPARATIVELY
CONDITIONALLY
CONSECUTIVELY
CONSIDERATELY
CONSPICUOUSLY
COUNTRYPEOPLE
DIAMETRICALLY
DISCREDITABLE
DISCREDITABLY
DISGRACEFULLY
DISHONOURABLE
DISHONOURABLY
ECCENTRICALLY
ENCEPHALOCELE
ENERGETICALLY
EXCEPTIONABLE
EXCEPTIONALLY
EXPEDITIOUSLY
EXTRAVAGANTLY
FANTASTICALLY
FRIGHTENINGLY
FUNDAMENTALLY
GEOMETRICALLY
GRAMMATICALLY
HYDRAULICALLY
IGNOMINIOUSLY
IMAGINATIVELY
IMPERCEPTIBLE
IMPERCEPTIBLY
IMPERTINENTLY
IMPERTURBABLE
IMPERTURBABLY
IMPRACTICABLE
IMPROVIDENTLY
INADVERTENTLY
INCOMBUSTIBLE
INCOMPETENTLY
INCONCEIVABLE
INCONTESTABLE
INCORRUPTIBLE
INCREDULOUSLY
INDEFATIGABLE
INDEFATIGABLY
INDEPENDENTLY
INDESCRIBABLE
INDESCRIBABLY
INDIFFERENTLY
INDISPENSABLE
INDUSTRIOUSLY
INEFFICIENTLY
INEXHAUSTIBLE
INEXPRESSIBLE
INQUISITIVELY
INSTINCTIVELY
INSUPPORTABLE
INTELLIGENTLY
INTENTIONALLY
INTERESTINGLY
INTRINSICALLY
INVOLUNTARILY
IRRECOVERABLE
IRREPLACEABLE
IRREPRESSIBLE
IRRESPONSIBLE
IRRESPONSIBLY
IRRETRIEVABLE
IRRETRIEVABLY
KNOWLEDGEABLE
MAGISTERIALLY
MAGNANIMOUSLY
MAGNIFICENTLY
MISCHIEVOUSLY
NOSTALGICALLY
OBJECTIONABLE
OUTSTANDINGLY
PAINSTAKINGLY
PARADOXICALLY
PASSCHENDAELE
PATRIOTICALLY
PERFUNCTORILY
PNEUMATICALLY
PRAGMATICALLY
PRECIPITATELY
PREDOMINANTLY
PROGRESSIVELY
PROMISCUOUSLY
PROPHETICALLY
PROVISIONALLY
PROVOCATIVELY
PUNCTILIOUSLY
REALISTICALLY
REMORSELESSLY
REPREHENSIBLE
REPREHENSIBLY
REPROACHFULLY
RESOURCEFULLY
ROUNDTHEWORLD
SARCASTICALLY
SCHEMATICALLY
SENSATIONALLY
SENTENTIOUSLY
SENTIMENTALLY
SIGNIFICANTLY
SOUTHEASTERLY
SOUTHWESTERLY
SPASMODICALLY
SPECTACULARLY
SPONTANEOUSLY
STATISTICALLY
STRATEGICALLY
STYLISTICALLY
SUBSERVIENTLY
SUBSTANTIALLY
SUPERFICIALLY
SUPERFLUOUSLY
SUPERLATIVELY
SYNTACTICALLY
SYNTHETICALLY
TANTALIZINGLY
THEOLOGICALLY
THEORETICALLY
THOUGHTLESSLY
THREATENINGLY
TORTOISESHELL
TRADITIONALLY
TRANSPARENTLY
TRANSPORTABLE
TRAUMATICALLY
TREACHEROUSLY
UNACCOUNTABLE
UNACCOUNTABLY
UNCOMFORTABLE
UNCOMFORTABLY
UNCONQUERABLE
UNCONSCIOUSLY
UNFASHIONABLE
UNFLINCHINGLY
UNFORESEEABLE
UNFORGETTABLE
UNFORTUNATELY
UNGENTLEMANLY
UNIMPEACHABLE
UNIMPRESSIBLE
UNINHABITABLE
UNMENTIONABLE
UNNECESSARILY
UNPREDICTABLE
UNSERVICEABLE
CHRISTMASTIME
COMRADEINARMS
GENERALISSIMO
QUINQUAGESIMA
THYROIDECTOMY
TONSILLECTOMY
ACCOMMODATING
ACCOMPANIMENT
ADVERTISEMENT
AFFREIGHTMENT
ANTICOAGULANT
ANTIHISTAMINE
APPORTIONMENT
ARMOURPLATING
BLOODCURDLING
BREASTFEEDING
BUNGEEJUMPING
CHATEAUBRIAND
CIRCUMAMBIENT
CONDESCENDING
CONTINUATIONS
CONTRIBUTIONS
CONVERSAZIONE
CORRESPONDENT
CORRESPONDING
COUNTERACTING
DISAPPOINTING
DISCONCERTING
DISENGAGEMENT
DISFIGUREMENT
DISHEARTENING
DISPARAGEMENT
DOUBLEGLAZING
DRYOPITHECINE
EMBARRASSMENT
EMBELLISHMENT
ENCOURAGEMENT
ENLIGHTENMENT
ENTERTAINMENT
ESTABLISHMENT
FRANKALMOIGNE
GLOBETROTTING
GRANDILOQUENT
HEARTBREAKING
HOUSEBREAKING
ILLUMINATIONS
IMPERSONATING
INCRIMINATING
INSIGNIFICANT
LONGSUFFERING
MALADJUSTMENT
MALLEMAROKING
MANUFACTURING
MERCHANDIZING
MISMANAGEMENT
MISUNDERSTAND
MOUTHWATERING
NONSUFFICIENT
OVERSTATEMENT
PREPOSSESSING
PRONOUNCEMENT
RAMIFICATIONS
RAPPROCHEMENT
REARRANGEMENT
REDEVELOPMENT
REFURBISHMENT
REIMBURSEMENT
REINFORCEMENT
REINSTATEMENT
REPERCUSSIONS
REPLENISHMENT
RHADAMANTHINE
ROLLERBLADING
SCINTILLATING
SELFCONFIDENT
SELFGOVERNING
SPINECHILLING
STEPPINGSTONE
STOCKBREEDING
SUBLIEUTENANT
SUPERABUNDANT
SWASHBUCKLING
SWEETSMELLING
TAPERECORDING
THOROUGHGOING

UNDERCLOTHING
UNDERSTANDING
UNINTELLIGENT
UNINTERESTING
UNQUESTIONING
VICEPRESIDENT
WEIGHTLIFTING
WITWATERSRAND
ACCEPTILATION
ACCOMMODATION
ADMINISTRATOR
AFFORESTATION
AGGLOMERATION
AMPLIFICATION
ANIMADVERSION
APPROPRIATION
APPROXIMATION
ASSASSINATION
AUTHORISATION
AUTHORIZATION
BEATIFICATION
BOUSTROPHEDON
CAUTERIZATION
CERTIFICATION
CIRCUMVENTION
CLARIFICATION
COLLABORATION
COMMEMORATION
COMMISERATION
COMMUNICATION
COMPREHENSION
CONCATENATION
CONCENTRATION
CONDESCENSION
CONFARREATION
CONFEDERATION
CONFIGURATION
CONFLAGRATION
CONFRONTATION
CONSIDERATION
CONSOLIDATION
CONSPURCATION
CONSTELLATION
CONSTERNATION
CONTAMINATION
CONTEMPLATION
CONTRABASSOON
CONTRACEPTION
CONTRADICTION
CONTRAVENTION
CORROBORATION
CROSSQUESTION
DECOMPOSITION
DECOMPRESSION
DEFIBRILLATOR
DEFORESTATION
DEMONSTRATION
DESEGREGATION
DETERIORATION
DETERMINATION
DIACATHOLICON
DIFFARREATION
DISCOLORATION
DISCONNECTION
DISESTIMATION
DISPROPORTION
DISSEMINATION
DISSIMULATION
DOCUMENTATION
DRAMATIZATION
ELECTROCUTION
EPIPHENOMENON
EPITRACHELION
EXPOSTULATION
EXPROPRIATION
EXTERMINATION
EXTRAPOLATION
FALSIFICATION
FERTILISATION
FERTILIZATION
FORMALIZATION
FORTIFICATION
FOSSILIZATION
FRAGMENTATION
GALVANIZATION
GESTICULATION
GLORIFICATION
GRATIFICATION
HALLUCINATION
HARMONIZATION
HORRIPILATION
HYBRIDIZATION
IMPERSONATION
IMPROVISATION
INCARCERATION
INCORPORATION
INDISPOSITION
INTERCALATION
INTERPOLATION
INTERROGATION
INTROSPECTION
INVESTIGATION
JOLLIFICATION
JUSTIFICATION
JUXTAPOSITION
MACHICOLATION
MAGNIFICATION
MANIFESTATION
MATRICULATION
MECHANIZATION
MISCEGENATION
MISCONCEPTION
MISUNDERSTOOD
MODERNIZATION
MOLLIFICATION
MONOCOTYLEDON
MORTIFICATION
MYSTIFICATION
NEIGHBOURHOOD
NORMALIZATION
NULLIFICATION
ORCHESTRATION
ORNAMENTATION
PANDICULATION
PANHARMONICON
PARTICIPATION
PERAMBULATION
PEREGRINATION
PETRIFICATION
POLLICITATION
PRECIPITATION
PRECONCEPTION
PREMEDITATION
PREOCCUPATION
PREPOSSESSION
PREVARICATION
PRIVATIZATION
PROLIFERATION
PRONUNCIATION
PULVERIZATION
QUALIFICATION
RECRIMINATION
RECTIFICATION
REFRIGERATION
REGIMENTATION
REGURGITATION
REINCARNATION
RESUSCITATION
RETROGRESSION
REUNIFICATION
REVERBERATION
SCINTILLATION
SEDIMENTATION
SEMICONDUCTOR
SEQUESTRATION
SIGNIFICATION
SOLEMNIZATION
SPECIFICATION
STABILIZATION
STERILIZATION
STRANGULATION
SUBCONTRACTOR
SUBORDINATION
TRANSCRIPTION
TRANSGRESSION
TRANSMUTATION
TRANSPIRATION
TRANSPOSITION
TRIANGULATION
VERSIFICATION
VICTIMIZATION
VITRIFICATION
VULCANIZATION
VULGARIZATION
XIPHIPLASTRON
DAGUERREOTYPE
GYNANDROMORPH
PHYSIOTHERAPY
PSYCHOTHERAPY
BUTTERFINGERS
CHEESEMONGERS
COMPLEMENTARY
COMPLIMENTARY
CONCESSIONARY
CONFECTIONERS
CONFECTIONERY
CONSERVATOIRE
CONTRADICTORY
CORROBORATORY
DISCRETIONARY
EPHEMEROPTERA
EXPEDITIONARY
EXTRAORDINARY
FUERTEVENTURA
HALLUCINATORY
HORSEFEATHERS
INCRIMINATORY
JIGGERYPOKERY
KNICKKNACKERY
LAEVOROTATORY
MADETOMEASURE
MAURIKIGUSARI
PARLIAMENTARY
PARTICIPATORY
PRECAUTIONARY
PRIMOGENITURE
QUESTIONNAIRE
RECRIMINATORY
REFRIGERATORS
REVOLUTIONARY
SEMBLANCECORD
SUPERNUMERARY
SUPPLEMENTARY
ACUPUNCTURIST
AIRWORTHINESS
ANTICLOCKWISE
ARCHAEOLOGIST
ATTENTIVENESS
BIBLIOPHAGIST
BOUILLABAISSE
CHARACTERLESS
COLLOQUIALISM
CONCEPTIONIST
CONSCIOUSNESS
CONTENTEDNESS
CONTORTIONIST
CREDULOUSNESS
CRIMINOLOGIST
DEATHLESSNESS
DEIPNOSOPHIST
DERMATOLOGIST
EFFECTIVENESS
EXHIBITIONIST
EXPANSIVENESS
FACETIOUSNESS
FORGETFULNESS
FRACTIOUSNESS
FRIGHTFULNESS
FRIVOLOUSNESS
GARRULOUSNESS

GUILTLESSNESS
GYNAECOLOGIST
HETERAUXESISM
IMPRESSIONISM
IMPRESSIONIST
IMPULSIVENESS
INDIVIDUALISM
INDIVIDUALIST
INDUSTRIALIST
INGENUOUSNESS
INSIDIOUSNESS
INVENTIVENESS
LEISURELINESS
LEPIDOPTERIST
LUXURIOUSNESS
LYCANTHROPIST
MERCILESSNESS
METAGRABOLISE
METAGROBOLISE
METEOROLOGIST
MICROORGANISM
MISANTHROPIST
NERVELESSNESS
NONCONFORMIST
OBJECTIVENESS
OFFENSIVENESS
OFFICIOUSNESS
ORNITHOLOGIST
PAPAPRELATIST
PARTICULARISE
PERFECTIONIST
PERVASIVENESS
PHYSIOGNOMIST
PROJECTIONIST
PROTECTIONISM
PROTECTIONIST
PROTESTANTISM
PROVINCIALISM
PSYCHOANALYSE
PSYCHOANALYST
QUERULOUSNESS
RECEPTIVENESS
RECITATIONIST
REDEMPTIONIST
REPUBLICANISM
RIGHTEOUSNESS
SALACIOUSNESS
SCHOLARLINESS
SECRETIVENESS
SENSELESSNESS
SENSITIVENESS
SHAPELESSNESS
SLEEPLESSNESS
SNOWBLINDNESS
SPRIGHTLINESS
SQUEAMISHNESS
STEADFASTNESS
STRENUOUSNESS
TALKATIVENESS
THANKLESSNESS
THAUMATURGIST
TRACTARIANISM
UNWILLINGNESS
VEGETARIANISM
VENTRILOQUISM
VENTRILOQUIST
VIVACIOUSNESS
VORACIOUSNESS
WHOLESOMENESS
ACCEPTABILITY
ACCESSIBILITY
ACCOUTREMENTS
AGGIORNAMENTO
APPROPINQUATE
ARCHIMANDRITE
ARTIFICIALITY
BACCALAUREATE
BLANDISHMENTS
CHANGEABILITY
COMPARABILITY
COMPASSIONATE
COMPATIBILITY
CONSANGUINITY
CONTRAFAGOTTO
DECONTAMINATE
DEFENSIBILITY
DEPENDABILITY
DÉSOBLIGEANTE
DIFFERENTIATE
DISCONTINUITY
DISPASSIONATE
DISSIMILARITY
ENTEROPNEUSTA
EQUIPONDERATE
EXCOMMUNICATE
FERROCONCRETE
FOSTERPARENTS
HERMAPHRODITE
HOMOSEXUALITY
HYPERSTHENITE
IMPOSSIBILITY
IMPROBABILITY
INAPPROPRIATE
INCONSIDERATE
INDETERMINATE
INDIVIDUALITY
INEVITABILITY
INFALLIBILITY
INFLEXIBILITY
INSENSITIVITY
INSUBORDINATE
INVINCIBILITY
INVIOLABILITY
MASSACHUSETTS
MESSERSCHMITT
MULTINUCLEATE
NEMATHELMINTH
NONCONFORMITY
PARTICULARITY
PENETRABILITY
PROCRASTINATE
PROFITABILITY
PROGNOSTICATE
PROPORTIONATE
PUSILLANIMITY
QUADRUPLICATE
RADIOACTIVITY
RATIONALALITY
RENSSELAERITE
SUPERORDINATE
SUSPERCOLLATE
THEATRICALITY
TRANSLITERATE
UNCOMMUNICATE
UNDERESTIMATE
UNDERGRADUATE
UPTOTHEMINUTE
VIDEOCASSETTE
VULNERABILITY
AMPHIGASTRIUM
ARUNDINACEOUS
AUTOCEPHALOUS
BRACHIOSAURUS
CARBONIFEROUS
CARTILAGINOUS
CHRYSANTHEMUM
CONSCIENTIOUS
CONSECTANEOUS
DISCONTINUOUS
DISRESPECTFUL
GASTROCNEMIUS
GOODRIGHTEOUS
HETEROGENEOUS
INCONSPICUOUS
INSECTIVOROUS
INSTANTANEOUS
LECTISTERNIUM
LEPTOCEPHALUS
LISSOTRICHOUS
MISCELLANEOUS
MONOTHALAMOUS
MULTITUDINOUS
PARANTHROPOUS
PERSPICACIOUS
PLATOCEPHALUS
PROFECTITIOUS
PUSILLANIMOUS
RUTHERFORDIUM
SANCTIMONIOUS
SELFCONSCIOUS
STERCORACEOUS
STREPTOCOCCUS
SUPERSTITIOUS
SURREPTITIOUS
TABLESPOONFUL
TINTINNABULUM
UMBELLIFEROUS
UNCEREMONIOUS
UNPRETENTIOUS
ARGUMENTATIVE
AUTHORITATIVE
COLLABORATIVE
COMMEMORATIVE
COMMUNICATIVE
COMPREHENSIVE
CONTEMPLATIVE
CONTRACEPTIVE
COSTEFFECTIVE
DEMONSTRATIVE
ELECTROMOTIVE
INTERROGATIVE
INTROSPECTIVE
INVESTIGATIVE
RETROSPECTIVE
UNCOOPERATIVE
UNIMAGINATIVE
UNPROGRESSIVE
ARCHAEOPTERYX
COMMERCIALIZE
CONCEPTUALIZE
DECRIMINALIZE
DENATIONALIZE
INDUSTRIALIZE
OVEREMPHASIZE
PARTICULARIZE
REVOLUTIONIZE
TRANSISTORIZE

13:13

BOUGAINVILLEA
ENCYCLOPAEDIA
ENTEROPNEUSTA
EPHEMEROPTERA
ESCHSCHOLTZIA
FUERTEVENTURA
KANGCHENJUNGA
LAMPADEPHORIA
PARAPHERNALIA
PHARMACOPOEIA
PHYSHARMONICA
QUINQUAGESIMA
SCHIZOPHRENIA
SIPUNCULOIDEA
SUOVETAURILIA
ANACHRONISTIC
ANTHELMINTHIC
ARISTROCRATIC
ENCYCLOPAEDIC
HYDROELECTRIC
HYPOCHONDRIAC
IDIORRHYTHMIC
IDIOSYNCRATIC
IMPERIALISTIC
KALEIDOSCOPIC
MATERIALISTIC
NATIONALISTIC
OPPORTUNISTIC
PATERNALISTIC
PHILANTHROPIC

PHOTOELECTRIC
PROCLEUSMATIC
PSYCHOSOMATIC
SCHIZOPHRENIC
SOCIOECONOMIC
TETRASYLLABIC
THERMOPLASTIC
TRANSATLANTIC
UNSYMPATHETIC
BROKENHEARTED
CHARACTERISED
CHATEAUBRIAND
DECAFFEINATED
DEMILITARIZED
DISADVANTAGED
DISILLUSIONED
DISINTERESTED
DISTINGUISHED
FLABBERGASTED
INEXPERIENCED
LIGHTFINGERED
MISUNDERSTAND
MISUNDERSTOOD
MULTICOLOURED
NEIGHBOURHOOD
PARTICOLOURED
PREFABRICATED
PREPROGRAMMED
ROUNDTHEWORLD
SELFADDRESSED
SELFCONFESSED
SELFCONTAINED
SEMBLANCECORD
SHRINKWRAPPED
SOPHISTICATED
SPITESPLENDID
SUPERANNUATED
SWOLLENHEADED
TENDERHEARTED
UNACCOMPANIED
UNADULTERATED
UNANTICIPATED
UNCOMPLICATED
UNCOORDINATED
UNDISCIPLINED
UNEMBARRASSED
UNENLIGHTENED
UNESTABLISHED
UNEXPERIENCED
UNINTERRUPTED
UNPARTITIONED
UNPRECEDENTED
WITWATERSRAND
ACRYLONITRILE
ANTICLOCKWISE
ANTIHISTAMINE
APPROPINQUATE
AQUIFOLIACEAE
ARCHIMANDRITE
ARGUMENTATIVE
ASCERTAINABLE
AUTHORITATIVE
BACCALAUREATE
BIODEGRADABLE
BOUILLABAISSE
CHINKERINCHEE
CHRISTMASTIME
CIRCUMFERENCE
CLAIRAUDIENCE
COLLABORATIVE
COLLIESHANGIE
COMMEMORATIVE
COMMENSURABLE
COMMERCIALIZE
COMMUNICATIVE
COMPANIONABLE
COMPASSIONATE
COMPREHENSIVE
CONCEPTUALIZE
CONCUPISCENCE
CONSERVATOIRE
CONTEMPLATIVE
CONTRACEPTIVE
CONVALESCENCE
CONVERSAZIONE
COSTEFFECTIVE
COUNTERCHARGE
COUNTRYPEOPLE
DAGUERREOTYPE
DECONTAMINATE
DECRIMINALIZE
DEFERVESCENCE
DEMONSTRATIVE
DENATIONALIZE
DÉSOBLIGEANTE
DIFFERENTIATE
DISAPPEARANCE
DISCREDITABLE
DISHONOURABLE
DISPASSIONATE
DRYOPITHECINE
EFFERVESCENCE
EFFLORESCENCE
ELECTROMOTIVE
ENCEPHALOCELE
EQUIPONDERATE
EXCEPTIONABLE
EXCOMMUNICATE
FERROCONCRETE
FOREKNOWLEDGE
FRANKALMOIGNE
HERMAPHRODITE
HYPERSTHENITE
IMPERCEPTIBLE
IMPERTURBABLE
IMPRACTICABLE
INAPPROPRIATE
INCANDESCENCE
INCOMBUSTIBLE
INCONCEIVABLE
INCONSIDERATE
INCONTESTABLE
INCONVENIENCE
INCORRUPTIBLE
INDEFATIGABLE
INDESCRIBABLE
INDETERMINATE
INDISPENSABLE
INDUSTRIALIZE
INEXHAUSTIBLE
INEXPRESSIBLE
INFLORESCENCE
INSUBORDINATE
INSUPPORTABLE
INTERMARRIAGE
INTERROGATIVE
INTRANSIGENCE
INTROSPECTIVE
INVESTIGATIVE
IRRECOVERABLE
IRREPLACEABLE
IRREPRESSIBLE
IRRESPONSIBLE
IRRETRIEVABLE
JURISPRUDENCE
KNOWLEDGEABLE
MADETOMEASURE
MAGNILOQUENCE
METAGRABOLISE
METAGROBOLISE
MULTINUCLEATE
NONRESISTANCE
OBJECTIONABLE
OUTRECUIDANCE
OVEREMPHASIZE
PARTICULARISE
PARTICULARIZE
PASSCHENDAELE
PASSEMENTERIE
PREPONDERANCE
PRIMOGENITURE
PROCRASTINATE
PROGNOSTICATE
PROPORTIONATE
PSYCHOANALYSE
QUADRUPLICATE
QUESTIONNAIRE
RECALCITRANCE
RECRUDESCENCE
RENSSELAERITE
REPREHENSIBLE
RETROSPECTIVE
REVOLUTIONIZE
RHADAMANTHINE
SCHADENFREUDE
SHOULDERBLADE
SPORTSMANLIKE
STAPHYLINIDAE
STATESMANLIKE
STEPPINGSTONE
SUPERORDINATE
SUSPERCOLLATE
THOROUGHBRACE
TRANSISTORIZE
TRANSLITERATE
TRANSPORTABLE
UNACCOUNTABLE
UNCOMFORTABLE
UNCOMMUNICATE
UNCONQUERABLE
UNCOOPERATIVE
UNDERCARRIAGE
UNDERESTIMATE
UNDERGRADUATE
UNFASHIONABLE
UNFORESEEABLE
UNFORGETTABLE
UNIMAGINATIVE
UNIMPEACHABLE
UNIMPRESSIBLE
UNINHABITABLE
UNMENTIONABLE
UNPREDICTABLE
UNPROGRESSIVE
UNSERVICEABLE
UPTOTHEMINUTE
VIDEOCASSETTE
ACCOMMODATING
ARMOURPLATING
BLOODCURDLING
BREASTFEEDING
BUNGEEJUMPING
CONDESCENDING
CORRESPONDING
COUNTERACTING
DISAPPOINTING
DISCONCERTING
DISHEARTENING
DOUBLEGLAZING
GLOBETROTTING
HEARTBREAKING
HOUSEBREAKING
IMPERSONATING
INCRIMINATING
LONGSUFFERING
MALLEMAROKING
MANUFACTURING
MERCHANDIZING
MOUTHWATERING
PREPOSSESSING
ROLLERBLADING
SCINTILLATING
SELFGOVERNING
SPINECHILLING
STOCKBREEDING
SWASHBUCKLING
SWEETSMELLING
TAPERECORDING
THOROUGHGOING
UNDERCLOTHING

UNDERSTANDING
UNINTERESTING
UNQUESTIONING
WEIGHTLIFTING
GLUMDALCLITCH
GYNANDROMORPH
LIEBFRAUMILCH
NEMATHELMINTH
MAURIKIGUSARI
COUNTERATTACK
THUNDERSTRUCK
TONGUEINCHEEK
ARCHITECTURAL
CHRONOLOGICAL
COEDUCATIONAL
CONGRESSIONAL
CONSEQUENTIAL
CONTROVERSIAL
DEVELOPMENTAL
DISRESPECTFUL
ENTOMOLOGICAL
ENVIRONMENTAL
GRANDPARENTAL
GRAVITATIONAL
GYNECOLOGICAL
HEMISPHERICAL
HORTICULTURAL
HYPERCRITICAL
INFINITESIMAL
INSPIRATIONAL
INSTITUTIONAL
INSTRUCTIONAL
INSUBSTANTIAL
INTERNATIONAL
INTERPERSONAL
ISOGEOTHERMAL
LACKADAISICAL
MOCKTECHNICAL
MORPHOLOGICAL
MULTINATIONAL
PARENTHETICAL
PETROCHEMICAL
PHILOSOPHICAL
PHOTOCHEMICAL
PHYSIOLOGICAL
PRESSURELOCAL
PRETERNATURAL
PROBLEMATICAL
PROPRIETORIAL
PSYCHOLOGICAL
PYROTECHNICAL
QUADRAGESIMAL
QUADRILATERAL
SCHUTZSTAFFEL
SEISMOLOGICAL
SERVILEMENTAL
SPELEOLOGICAL
SUPRANATIONAL
TABLESPOONFUL
TECHNOLOGICAL

TEMPERAMENTAL
TOPOGRAPHICAL
TORTOISESHELL
TYPOGRAPHICAL
UNCONDITIONAL
UNEXCEPTIONAL
UNGRAMMATICAL
UNINTENTIONAL
UNSUBSTANTIAL
UNSYMMETRICAL
AMPHIGASTRIUM
CHRYSANTHEMUM
COLLOQUIALISM
HETERAUXESISM
IMPRESSIONISM
INDIVIDUALISM
LECTISTERNIUM
MICROORGANISM
PARALLELOGRAM
PROTECTIONISM
PROTESTANTISM
PROVINCIALISM
REPUBLICANISM
RUTHERFORDIUM
TINTINNABULUM
TRACTARIANISM
VEGETARIANISM
VENTRILOQUISM
ACCEPTILATION
ACCOMMODATION
AFFORESTATION
AGGLOMERATION
AIRCRAFTWOMAN
ALPHABETARIAN
AMPLIFICATION
ANIMADVERSION
ANYTHINGARIAN
APPROPRIATION
APPROXIMATION
ARITHMETICIAN
ASSASSINATION
AUTHORISATION
AUTHORITARIAN
AUTHORIZATION
BEATIFICATION
BILDUNGSROMAN
BOUSTROPHEDON
BUSINESSWOMAN
CAUTERIZATION
CERTIFICATION
CIRCUMVENTION
CLARIFICATION
COLLABORATION
COMMEMORATION
COMMISERATION
COMMUNICATION
COMPREHENSION
CONCATENATION
CONCENTRATION
CONDESCENSION

CONFARREATION
CONFEDERATION
CONFIGURATION
CONFLAGRATION
CONFRONTATION
CONGRESSWOMAN
CONSIDERATION
CONSOLIDATION
CONSPURCATION
CONSTELLATION
CONSTERNATION
CONTAMINATION
CONTEMPLATION
CONTRABASSOON
CONTRACEPTION
CONTRADICTION
CONTRAVENTION
CORROBORATION
CROSSQUESTION
DECOMPOSITION
DECOMPRESSION
DEFORESTATION
DEMONSTRATION
DESEGREGATION
DETERIORATION
DETERMINATION
DIACATHOLICON
DIFFARREATION
DISCOLORATION
DISCONNECTION
DISESTIMATION
DISPROPORTION
DISSEMINATION
DISSIMULATION
DOCUMENTATION
DRAMATIZATION
ELECTROCUTION
EPIPHENOMENON
EPITRACHELION
EXPOSTULATION
EXPROPRIATION
EXTERMINATION
EXTRAPOLATION
FALSIFICATION
FERTILISATION
FERTILIZATION
FORMALIZATION
FORTIFICATION
FOSSILIZATION
FRAGMENTATION
GALVANIZATION
GESTICULATION
GLORIFICATION
GRATIFICATION
GRIEFSTRICKEN
HALLUCINATION
HARMONIZATION
HORRIPILATION
HYBRIDIZATION
IMPERSONATION

IMPROVISATION
INCARCERATION
INCORPORATION
INDISPOSITION
INTERCALATION
INTERPOLATION
INTERROGATION
INTROSPECTION
INVESTIGATION
JOLLIFICATION
JUSTIFICATION
JUXTAPOSITION
LIECHTENSTEIN
MACHIAVELLIAN
MACHICOLATION
MAGNIFICATION
MANIFESTATION
MASTIGOPHORAN
MATHEMATICIAN
MATRICULATION
MECHANIZATION
MEDITERRANEAN
METAPHYSICIAN
MISCEGENATION
MISCONCEPTION
MODERNIZATION
MOLLIFICATION
MONOCOTYLEDON
MORTIFICATION
MYSTIFICATION
NIGHTWATCHMAN
NORMALIZATION
NULLIFICATION
ORCHESTRATION
ORNAMENTATION
PAEDIATRICIAN
PANDICULATION
PANHARMONICON
PARTICIPATION
PELOPONNESIAN
PERAMBULATION
PEREGRINATION
PETRIFICATION
PHILADELPHIAN
POLLICITATION
PRECIPITATION
PRECONCEPTION
PREMEDITATION
PREOCCUPATION
PREPOSSESSION
PREVARICATION
PRIVATIZATION
PROLIFERATION
PRONUNCIATION
PULVERIZATION
QUALIFICATION
QUARTODECIMAN
RECRIMINATION
RECTIFICATION
REFRIGERATION

REGIMENTATION
REGURGITATION
REINCARNATION
RESUSCITATION
RETROGRESSION
REUNIFICATION
REVERBERATION
SCINTILLATION
SEDIMENTATION
SEQUESTRATION
SIGNIFICATION
SOLEMNIZATION
SOMATOTROPHIN
SPECIFICATION
STABILIZATION
STERILIZATION
STRANGULATION
SUBORDINATION
SWEDENBORGIAN
TRANSCRIPTION
TRANSGRESSION
TRANSMUTATION
TRANSPIRATION
TRANSPOSITION
TRIANGULATION
TRICHOSANTHIN
VERSIFICATION
VICTIMIZATION
VITRIFICATION
VULCANIZATION
VULGARIZATION
WEATHERBEATEN
XIPHIPLASTRON
AGGIORNAMENTO
CONTRAFAGOTTO
GENERALISSIMO
INCOMMUNICADO
COMPANIONSHIP
CRAFTSMANSHIP
LIBRARIANSHIP
PROFESSORSHIP
SPORTSMANSHIP
STATESMANSHIP
ADMINISTRATOR
AFFENPINSCHER
BIBLIOGRAPHER
CHOREOGRAPHER
CLISHMACLAVER
COUNTERFEITER
DEFIBRILLATOR
FORTUNETELLER
GLOSSOGRAPHER
GRANDDAUGHTER
HAMMERKLAVIER
HAMMERTHROWER
KAPPELMEISTER
KIDDERMINSTER
KNICKERBOCKER
LEXICOGRAPHER
MEISTERSINGER

MICROCOMPUTER
MIDDLEBREAKER
NEANDERTHALER
OWNEROCCUPIER
OYSTERCATCHER
PASSIONFLOWER
PERPENDICULAR
POTENTIOMETER
QUARTERMASTER
ROLLERCOASTER
SCANDALMONGER
SCHOOLTEACHER
SEMICONDUCTOR
STATIONMASTER
STEEPLECHASER
STRIKEBREAKER
SUBCONTRACTOR
SUBJECTMATTER
SYMPIESOMETER
THERMONUCLEAR
TONGUETWISTER
TRANQUILLISER
TRANQUILLIZER
UNDERACHIEVER
UNDERSTRAPPER
VIDEORECORDER
ACCOUTREMENTS
AIRWORTHINESS
ANTIGROPELOES
APOCATASTASIS
ARUNDINACEOUS
ATTENTIVENESS
AUTOCEPHALOUS
BLANDISHMENTS
BRACHIOSAURUS
BUTTERFINGERS
CALLISTHENICS
CARBONIFEROUS
CARTILAGINOUS
CHARACTERLESS
CHEESEMONGERS
CIRCUMSTANCES
COMRADEINARMS
CONFECTIONERS
CONSCIENTIOUS
CONSCIOUSNESS
CONSECTANEOUS
CONTENTEDNESS
CONTINUATIONS
CONTRIBUTIONS
CREDULOUSNESS
DEATHLESSNESS
DISCONTINUOUS
EFFECTIVENESS
ELEPHANTIASIS
EPANADIPLOSIS
EXPANSIVENESS
FACETIOUSNESS
FORGETFULNESS
FOSTERPARENTS

FRACTIOUSNESS
FRIGHTFULNESS
FRIVOLOUSNESS
GARRULOUSNESS
GASTROCNEMIUS
GOODRIGHTEOUS
GUILTLESSNESS
HETEROGENEOUS
HIEROGLYPHICS
HORSEFEATHERS
ILLUMINATIONS
IMPONDERABLES
IMPULSIVENESS
INCONSPICUOUS
INGENUOUSNESS
INSECTIVOROUS
INSIDIOUSNESS
INSTANTANEOUS
INVENTIVENESS
LEISURELINESS
LEPTOCEPHALUS
LISSOTRICHOUS
LUXURIOUSNESS
MASSACHUSETTS
MERCILESSNESS
METAMORPHOSIS
MISCELLANEOUS
MONONUCLEOSIS
MONOTHALAMOUS
MULTITUDINOUS
NERVELESSNESS
OBJECTIVENESS
OFFENSIVENESS
OFFICIOUSNESS
OPPORTUNITIES
PARANTHROPOUS
PARTHOGENESIS
PATERFAMILIAS
PERSONALITIES
PERSPICACIOUS
PERVASIVENESS
PLATOCEPHALUS
POLIOMYELITIS
PRELIMINARIES
PRESERVATIVES
PROFECTITIOUS
PUSILLANIMOUS
QUERULOUSNESS
RAMIFICATIONS
RECEPTIVENESS
REFRIGERATORS
REMINISCENCES
REPERCUSSIONS
REPROGRAPHICS
RIGHTEOUSNESS
SACCHAROMYCES
SALACIOUSNESS
SANCTIMONIOUS
SCHOLARLINESS
SECRETIVENESS

SELFCONSCIOUS
SENSELESSNESS
SENSITIVENESS
SEPTENTRIONES
SHAPELESSNESS
SLEEPLESSNESS
SNOWBLINDNESS
SPINDLESHANKS
SPRIGHTLINESS
SQUEAMISHNESS
STEADFASTNESS
STERCORACEOUS
STRENUOUSNESS
STREPTOCOCCUS
SUPERSTITIOUS
SURREPTITIOUS
TALKATIVENESS
THANKLESSNESS
THAUMATURGICS
UMBELLIFEROUS
UNCEREMONIOUS
UNPRETENTIOUS
UNWILLINGNESS
VIVACIOUSNESS
VORACIOUSNESS
WHOLESOMENESS
ACCOMPANIMENT
ACUPUNCTURIST
ADVERTISEMENT
AFFREIGHTMENT
ANTICOAGULANT
APPORTIONMENT
ARCHAEOLOGIST
BIBLIOPHAGIST
CIRCUMAMBIENT
CLOSEDCIRCUIT
CONCEPTIONIST
CONTORTIONIST
CORRESPONDENT
CRIMINOLOGIST
DEIPNOSOPHIST
DERMATOLOGIST
DISENGAGEMENT
DISFIGUREMENT
DISPARAGEMENT
ELECTROMAGNET
EMBARRASSMENT
EMBELLISHMENT
ENCOURAGEMENT
ENLIGHTENMENT
ENTERTAINMENT
ESTABLISHMENT
EXHIBITIONIST
FEATHERWEIGHT
GRANDILOQUENT
GYNAECOLOGIST
HUNDREDWEIGHT
IMPRESSIONIST
INDIVIDUALIST
INDUSTRIALIST

INSIGNIFICANT
LEATHERJACKET
LEPIDOPTERIST
LYCANTHROPIST
MALADJUSTMENT
MESSERSCHMITT
METEOROLOGIST
MISANTHROPIST
MISMANAGEMENT
NONCONFORMIST
NONSUFFICIENT
ORNITHOLOGIST
OVERSTATEMENT
PAPAPRELATIST
PERFECTIONIST
PHYSIOGNOMIST
PROJECTIONIST
PRONOUNCEMENT
PROTECTIONIST
PROTONOTARIAT
PSYCHOANALYST
RAPPROCHEMENT
REARRANGEMENT
RECITATIONIST
REDEMPTIONIST
REDEVELOPMENT
REFURBISHMENT
REIMBURSEMENT
REINFORCEMENT
REINSTATEMENT
REPLENISHMENT
SELFCONFIDENT
SUBLIEUTENANT
SUPERABUNDANT
THAUMATURGIST
UNINTELLIGENT
VENTRILOQUIST
VICEPRESIDENT
FONTAINEBLEAU
ARCHAEOPTERYX
VERCINGETORIX
ACCEPTABILITY
ACCESSIBILITY
ADVENTUROUSLY
AESTHETICALLY
AFFIRMATIVELY
ALTERNATIVELY
APPROXIMATELY
ARTIFICIALITY
ASTONISHINGLY
AUTOBIOGRAPHY
AUTOMATICALLY
BIOTECHNOLOGY
CATEGORICALLY
CEREMONIOUSLY
CHANGEABILITY

COMPARABILITY
COMPARATIVELY
COMPATIBILITY
COMPLEMENTARY
COMPLIMENTARY
CONCESSIONARY
CONDITIONALLY
CONFECTIONERY
CONSANGUINITY
CONSECUTIVELY
CONSIDERATELY
CONSPICUOUSLY
CONTRADICTORY
CORROBORATORY
DEFENSIBILITY
DEPENDABILITY
DIAMETRICALLY
DISCONTINUITY
DISCREDITABLY
DISCRETIONARY
DISGRACEFULLY
DISHONOURABLY
DISSIMILARITY
ECCENTRICALLY
ENERGETICALLY
EXCEPTIONALLY
EXPEDITIONARY
EXPEDITIOUSLY
EXTRAORDINARY
EXTRAVAGANTLY
FANTASTICALLY
FRIGHTENINGLY
FUNDAMENTALLY
GEOMETRICALLY
GRAMMATICALLY
HALLUCINATORY
HOMOSEXUALITY
HYDRAULICALLY
IGNOMINIOUSLY
IMAGINATIVELY
IMPERCEPTIBLY
IMPERTINENTLY
IMPERTURBABLY
IMPOSSIBILITY
IMPROBABILITY
IMPROVIDENTLY
INADVERTENTLY
INCOMPETENTLY
INCONSISTENCY
INCREDULOUSLY
INCRIMINATORY
INDEFATIGABLY
INDEPENDENTLY
INDESCRIBABLY
INDIFFERENTLY
INDIVIDUALITY

INDUSTRIOUSLY
INEFFICIENTLY
INEVITABILITY
INFALLIBILITY
INFLEXIBILITY
INQUISITIVELY
INSENSITIVITY
INSTINCTIVELY
INSUFFICIENCY
INTELLIGENTLY
INTENTIONALLY
INTERESTINGLY
INTRINSICALLY
INVINCIBILITY
INVIOLABILITY
INVOLUNTARILY
IRRESPONSIBLY
IRRETRIEVABLY
JIGGERYPOKERY
KNICKKNACKERY
LAEVOROTATORY
MAGISTERIALLY
MAGNANIMOUSLY
MAGNIFICENTLY
MISCHIEVOUSLY
NONCONFORMITY
NOSTALGICALLY
OPHTHALMOLOGY
OUTSTANDINGLY
PAINSTAKINGLY
PALAEONTOLOGY
PARADOXICALLY
PARLIAMENTARY
PARTICIPATORY
PARTICULARITY
PATRIOTICALLY
PENETRABILITY
PERFUNCTORILY
PHYSIOTHERAPY
PNEUMATICALLY
PRAGMATICALLY
PRECAUTIONARY
PRECIPITATELY
PREDOMINANTLY
PROFITABILITY
PROGRESSIVELY
PROMISCUOUSLY
PROPHETICALLY
PROSOPOGRAPHY
PROVISIONALLY
PROVOCATIVELY
PSYCHOTHERAPY
PUNCTILIOUSLY
PUSILLANIMITY
RADIOACTIVITY
RATIONALALITY

REALISTICALLY
RECRIMINATORY
REMORSELESSLY
REPREHENSIBLY
REPROACHFULLY
RESOURCEFULLY
REVOLUTIONARY
RHYPAROGRAPHY
SARCASTICALLY
SCHEMATICALLY
SENSATIONALLY
SENTENTIOUSLY
SENTIMENTALLY
SIGNIFICANTLY
SOUTHEASTERLY
SOUTHWESTERLY
SPASMODICALLY
SPECTACULARLY
SPECTROGRAPHY
SPONTANEOUSLY
STATISTICALLY
STRATEGICALLY
STYLISTICALLY
SUBSERVIENTLY
SUBSTANTIALLY
SUPERFICIALLY
SUPERFLUOUSLY
SUPERLATIVELY
SUPERNUMERARY
SUPPLEMENTARY
SYNTACTICALLY
SYNTHETICALLY
TANTALIZINGLY
THEATRICALITY
THEOLOGICALLY
THEORETICALLY
THOUGHTLESSLY
THREATENINGLY
THYROIDECTOMY
TONSILLECTOMY
TRADITIONALLY
TRANSPARENTLY
TRAUMATICALLY
TREACHEROUSLY
UNACCOUNTABLY
UNCOMFORTABLY
UNCONSCIOUSLY
UNFLINCHINGLY
UNFORTUNATELY
UNGENTLEMANLY
UNNECESSARILY
UNTRUSTWORTHY
VULNERABILITY

14:1

ABSTEMIOUSNESS
ACCOMPLISHMENT
ACCOUNTABILITY
ACHONDROPLASIA
ACKNOWLEDGMENT
ADMINISTRATION
ADMINISTRATIVE
AFFECTIONATELY
AFOREMENTIONED
AGGRANDISEMENT
AGGRESSIVENESS
AIRCONDITIONED
AIRCONDITIONER
AIRCRAFTSWOMAN
ALLOIOSTROPHUS
ALPHABETICALLY
ANTHROPOLOGIST
ANTHROPOPHAGUS
ANTIDEPRESSANT
ANTILYMPHOCYTE
ANTIMETATHESIS
ANTIMONARCHIST
ANTIODONTALGIC
ANTIPERSPIRANT
APOLOGETICALLY
APPREHENSIVELY
APPRENTICESHIP
APPROVECOMMENT
ARCHAEOLOGICAL
ARCHGENETHLIAC
ARRONDISSEMENT
ASTROGEOLOGIST
ASTRONOMICALLY
AUTHENTICATION
AUTOCRATICALLY
AUTOSUGGESTION
BACTERIOLOGIST
BALUCHITHERIUM
BATTERYPOWERED
BIOENGINEERING
BOISTEROUSNESS
BREATHLESSNESS
BROBDINGNAGIAN
CAPITALIZATION
CAPRICIOUSNESS
CARDIOVASCULAR
CASTRAMETATION
CENTRALIZATION
CHARACTERISTIC
CHINCHERINCHEE
CINEMATOGRAPHY
CIRCUMLOCUTION
CIRCUMNAVIGATE
CIRCUMSCISSILE
CIRCUMSTANTIAL
CLASSIFICATION
CLAUSTROPHOBIA
CLAUSTROPHOBIC
COINCIDENTALLY
COMMISSIONAIRE
COMPREHENSIBLE
CONFIDENTIALLY
CONGLOMERATION
CONGRATULATION
CONGRATULATORY
CONJUNCTIVITIS
CONSERVATIVELY
CONSPIRATORIAL
CONSTANTINOPLE
CONSTITUTIONAL
CONSTRUCTIVELY
CONSTRUCTIVISM
CONTESSERATION
CONTROVERTIBLE
CONVENTIONALLY
CONVERSATIONAL
CONVERTIBILITY
CORRESPONDENCE
CORRUPTIBILITY
COUNTERBALANCE
COUNTERMEASURE
CREEPYCRAWLIES
CROSSREFERENCE
CRYPTAESTHETIC
CRYSTALLOMANCY
CZECHOSLOVAKIA
DECISIONMAKING
DEMOBILIZATION
DEMOCRATICALLY
DEMORALIZATION
DENOMINATIONAL
DERMATOLOGICAL
DESISTABSTRACT
DIPLOMATICALLY
DISAPPOINTMENT
DISAPPROBATION
DISAPPROVINGLY
DISCIPLINARIAN
DISCOLOURATION
DISCOMBOBERATE
DISCOMBOBULATE
DISCONSOLATELY
DISCONTENTMENT
DISCOUNTENANCE
DISCOURAGEMENT
DISCOURTEOUSLY
DISCRIMINATING
DISCRIMINATION
DISCRIMINATORY
DISEMBARKATION
DISENCHANTMENT
DISENFRANCHISE
DISINCLINATION
DISINFORMATION
DISINTEGRATION
DISORIENTATION
DISTINGUISHING
DIVERTISSEMENT
ECCLESIASTICAL
EDUCATIONALIST
EGALITARIANISM
ELECTIONEERING
ELECTRONICALLY
EMBELLISHMENTS
ENCEPHALOPATHY
ESTABLISHVERSE
EXISTENTIALISM
EXISTENTIALIST
EXPERIMENTALLY
EXPRESSIONLESS
FASTIDIOUSNESS
FORTUNETELLING
FRATERNIZATION
FRUCTIFICATION
FUNDAMENTALISM
FUNDAMENTALIST
GENERALIZATION
GENTRIFICATION
GEOGRAPHICALLY
GRANDILOQUENCE
GYNAECOLOGICAL
HALLUCINATIONS
HALLUCINOGENIC
HEARTSEARCHING
HIEROSOLYMITAN
HOMOGENIZATION
HORTICULTURIST
HYPERSENSITIVE
HYPOTHETICALLY
IDENTIFICATION
ILLEGITIMATELY
IMMOBILIZATION
IMPERMEABILITY
IMPLEMENTATION
IMPOVERISHMENT
IMPREGNABILITY
IMPRESSIONABLE
INCONCLUSIVELY
INCONSIDERABLE
INCONVENIENTLY
INDECIPHERABLE
INDESTRUCTIBLE
INDETERMINABLE
INDISCRIMINATE
INDOCTRINATION
INEXPRESSIBLES
INFRALAPSARIAN
INFRASTRUCTURE
INSIGNIFICANCE
INSUFFICIENTLY
INSURMOUNTABLE
INTELLECTUALLY
INTELLIGENTSIA
INTERCONNECTED
INTERFEROMETER
INTERMITTENTLY
INTERNATIONALE
INTERPELLATION
INTERPLANETARY
INTERPRETATION
INTERPRETATIVE
IRRECONCILABLE
IRREPROACHABLE
JOHANNISBERGER
KNICKERBOCKERS
KNIPPERDOLLING
KNOTENSCHIEFER
LASCIVIOUSNESS
LIBERALIZATION
LICENTIOUSNESS
LIGHTSENSITIVE
LONGITUDINALLY
LOQUACIOUSNESS
MACROECONOMICS
MALAPPROPRIATE
MATHEMATICALLY
MEPHISTOPHELES
METAMORPHOSING
METAPHORICALLY
METEMPSYCHOSIS
METEOROLOGICAL
METICULOUSNESS
MICROPROCESSOR
MISAPPLICATION
MISAPPROPRIATE
MISCALCULATION
MONOPOLIZATION
MOUNTAINEERING
MULTIPLICATION
NATURALIZATION
NEBUCHADNEZZAR
NETHERSTOCKING
NEUTRALIZATION
NIBELUNGENLIED
NITROGLYCERINE
OBSEQUIOUSNESS
ONCHOCERCIASIS
OPPRESSIVENESS
OPTIMISTICALLY
ORGANIZATIONAL
ORNITHOLOGICAL
ORTHOGRAPHICAL
OSTENTATIOUSLY
OSTEOARTHRITIS
OVERPRODUCTION
OVERSUBSCRIBED
PARALEIPOMENON
PARAPSYCHOLOGY
PARSIMONIOUSLY
PASTEURIZATION
PERCEPTIVENESS
PEREGRINATIONS
PERMISSIVENESS
PERSUASIVENESS
PHANTASMAGORIA
PHARMACEUTICAL
PHARMACOLOGIST

PHENOBARBITONE
PHILANTHROPIST
PHLEGMATICALLY
PHOSPHORESCENT
PHOTOSYNTHESIS
POLYMERIZATION
POPULARIZATION
PORPHYROGENITE
POSSESSINHUMAN
PRACTICABILITY
PRECOCIOUSNESS
PREDESTINATION
PREDISPOSITION
PREFABRICATION
PRESSURIZATION
PRESUMPTUOUSLY
PRESUPPOSITION
PRODUCTIVENESS
PROFESSIONALLY
PROHIBITIONIST
PRONUNCIAMENTO
PROPORTIONALLY
PROVIDENTIALLY
PSYCHOANALYSIS
PURPOSEFULNESS
QUALIFICATIONS
QUINTESSENTIAL
RADIOTELEPHONE
RECAPITULATION
RECOMMENDATION
RECONCILIATION
RECONNAISSANCE
RECONSTITUTION
RECONSTRUCTION
RECORDBREAKING
REGULARIZATION
REHABILITATION
RELINQUISHMENT
REORGANIZATION
REPRESENTATION
REPRESENTATIVE
RESPECTABILITY
RESPONSIBILITY
RESPONSIVENESS
RIDICULOUSNESS
ROADWORTHINESS
SANCTIFICATION
SANSCULOTTERIE
SATISFACTORILY
SCAREMONGERING
SCATTERBRAINED
SCHOOLCHILDREN
SCHOOLMISTRESS
SCIENTIFICALLY
SCRUPULOUSNESS
SCURRILOUSNESS
SELFASSESSMENT
SELFCONFIDENCE
SELFGOVERNMENT
SELFRESPECTING
SELFSUFFICIENT
SENTIMENTALITY
SEPTUAGENARIAN
SESQUIPEDALIAN
SESQUIPEDALION
SEXCENTENARIAN
SHRINKWRAPPING
SIMPLIFICATION
SIMULTANEOUSLY
SINGLEBREASTED
SINGLEMINDEDLY
SLAUGHTERHOUSE
SOLIDIFICATION
SOPHISTICATION
SPECIALIZATION
STAPHYLOCOCCUS
STEGANOGRAPHIC
STRAIGHTFOWARD
STRATIFICATION
STULTIFICATION
SUBCONSCIOUSLY
SUBMISSIVENESS
SUBSTANTIATION
SULPHANILAMIDE
SUPERABUNDANCE
SUPERANNUATION
SUPERCILIOUSLY
SUPEREROGATION
SUPERFICIALITY
SUPERINTENDENT
SUPERNATURALLY
SUPERPHOSPHATE
SUPERSCRIPTION
SUPERSTRUCTURE
SUSCEPTIBILITY
SYSTEMATICALLY
TATTERDEMALION
TELETYPEWRITER
TERMINOLOGICAL
THERMODYNAMICS
THOUGHTFULNESS
THREEHALFPENCE
TINTINNABULATE
TRADITIONALIST
TRANSCENDENTAL
TRANSFORMATION
TRANSMIGRATION
TRANSPORTATION
TRICHOPHYTOSIS
TROUBLESHOOTER
ULTRACREPIDATE
UNAPPROACHABLE
UNATTRIBUTABLE
UNCOMPROMISING
UNCONSCIONABLE
UNCONTROLLABLE
UNCONVENTIONAL
UNCORROBORATED
UNDERDEVELOPED
UNDERMENTIONED
UNDERNOURISHED
UNDERSECRETARY
UNDERSTANDABLE
UNDERSTANDABLY
UNDERSTATEMENT
UNDESIRABILITY
UNENTHUSIASTIC
UNINTELLIGIBLE
UNMENTIONABLES
UNPLEASANTNESS
UNPREMEDITATED
UNPREPAREDNESS
UNPROFESSIONAL
UNQUESTIONABLE
UNQUESTIONABLY
UNRECOGNIZABLE
UNSATISFACTORY
UNSKILLFULNESS
VALETUDINARIAN
VERISIMILITUDE
VINDICTIVENESS
WEIGHTLESSNESS
WESTERNIZATION
WHIPPERSNAPPER
WHOLEHEARTEDLY

14:2

BACTERIOLOGIST
BALUCHITHERIUM
BATTERYPOWERED
CAPITALIZATION
CAPRICIOUSNESS
CARDIOVASCULAR
CASTRAMETATION
FASTIDIOUSNESS
HALLUCINATIONS
HALLUCINOGENIC
LASCIVIOUSNESS
MACROECONOMICS
MALAPPROPRIATE
MATHEMATICALLY
NATURALIZATION
PARALEIPOMENON
PARAPSYCHOLOGY
PARSIMONIOUSLY
PASTEURIZATION
RADIOTELEPHONE
SANCTIFICATION
SANSCULOTTERIE
SATISFACTORILY
TATTERDEMALION
VALETUDINARIAN
ABSTEMIOUSNESS
OBSEQUIOUSNESS
ACCOMPLISHMENT
ACCOUNTABILITY
ACHONDROPLASIA
ACKNOWLEDGMENT
ECCLESIASTICAL
SCAREMONGERING
SCATTERBRAINED
SCHOOLCHILDREN
SCHOOLMISTRESS
SCIENTIFICALLY
SCRUPULOUSNESS
SCURRILOUSNESS
ADMINISTRATION
ADMINISTRATIVE
EDUCATIONALIST
IDENTIFICATION
CENTRALIZATION
DECISIONMAKING
DEMOBILIZATION
DEMOCRATICALLY
DEMORALIZATION
DENOMINATIONAL
DERMATOLOGICAL
DESISTABSTRACT
GENERALIZATION
GENTRIFICATION
GEOGRAPHICALLY
HEARTSEARCHING
MEPHISTOPHELES
METAMORPHOSING
METAPHORICALLY
METEMPSYCHOSIS
METEOROLOGICAL
METICULOUSNESS
NEBUCHADNEZZAR
NETHERSTOCKING
NEUTRALIZATION
PERCEPTIVENESS
PEREGRINATIONS
PERMISSIVENESS
PERSUASIVENESS
RECAPITULATION
RECOMMENDATION
RECONCILIATION
RECONNAISSANCE
RECONSTITUTION
RECONSTRUCTION
RECORDBREAKING
REGULARIZATION
REHABILITATION
RELINQUISHMENT
REORGANIZATION
REPRESENTATION
REPRESENTATIVE
RESPECTABILITY
RESPONSIBILITY
RESPONSIVENESS
SELFASSESSMENT
SELFCONFIDENCE
SELFGOVERNMENT
SELFRESPECTING
SELFSUFFICIENT
SENTIMENTALITY
SEPTUAGENARIAN

SESQUIPEDALIAN
SESQUIPEDALION
SEXCENTENARIAN
TELETYPEWRITER
TERMINOLOGICAL
VERISIMILITUDE
WEIGHTLESSNESS
WESTERNIZATION
AFFECTIONATELY
AFOREMENTIONED
AGGRANDISEMENT
AGGRESSIVENESS
EGALITARIANISM
CHARACTERISTIC
CHINCHERINCHEE
PHANTASMAGORIA
PHARMACEUTICAL
PHARMACOLOGIST
PHENOBARBITONE
PHILANTHROPIST
PHLEGMATICALLY
PHOSPHORESCENT
PHOTOSYNTHESIS
SHRINKWRAPPING
THERMODYNAMICS
THOUGHTFULNESS
THREEHALFPENCE
WHIPPERSNAPPER
WHOLEHEARTEDLY
AIRCONDITIONED
AIRCONDITIONER
AIRCRAFTSWOMAN
BIOENGINEERING
CINEMATOGRAPHY
CIRCUMLOCUTION
CIRCUMNAVIGATE
CIRCUMSCISSILE
CIRCUMSTANTIAL
DIPLOMATICALLY
DISAPPOINTMENT
DISAPPROBATION
DISAPPROVINGLY
DISCIPLINARIAN
DISCOLOURATION
DISCOMBOBERATE
DISCOMBOBULATE
DISCONSOLATELY
DISCONTENTMENT
DISCOUNTENANCE
DISCOURAGEMENT
DISCOURTEOUSLY
DISCRIMINATING
DISCRIMINATION
DISCRIMINATORY
DISEMBARKATION
DISENCHANTMENT
DISENFRANCHISE
DISINCLINATION
DISINFORMATION
DISINTEGRATION
DISORIENTATION
DISTINGUISHING
DIVERTISSEMENT
HIEROSOLYMITAN
LIBERALIZATION
LICENTIOUSNESS
LIGHTSENSITIVE
MICROPROCESSOR
MISAPPLICATION
MISAPPROPRIATE
MISCALCULATION
NIBELUNGENLIED
NITROGLYCERINE
RIDICULOUSNESS
SIMPLIFICATION
SIMULTANEOUSLY
SINGLEBREASTED
SINGLEMINDEDLY
TINTINNABULATE
VINDICTIVENESS
ALLOIOSTROPHUS
ALPHABETICALLY
CLASSIFICATION
CLAUSTROPHOBIA
CLAUSTROPHOBIC
ELECTIONEERING
ELECTRONICALLY
ILLEGITIMATELY
SLAUGHTERHOUSE
ULTRACREPIDATE
EMBELLISHMENTS
IMMOBILIZATION
IMPERMEABILITY
IMPLEMENTATION
IMPOVERISHMENT
IMPREGNABILITY
IMPRESSIONABLE
ANTHROPOLOGIST
ANTHROPOPHAGUS
ANTIDEPRESSANT
ANTILYMPHOCYTE
ANTIMETATHESIS
ANTIMONARCHIST
ANTIODONTALGIC
ANTIPERSPIRANT
ENCEPHALOPATHY
INCONCLUSIVELY
INCONSIDERABLE
INCONVENIENTLY
INDECIPHERABLE
INDESTRUCTIBLE
INDETERMINABLE
INDISCRIMINATE
INDOCTRINATION
INEXPRESSIBLES
INFRALAPSARIAN
INFRASTRUCTURE
INSIGNIFICANCE
INSUFFICIENTLY
INSURMOUNTABLE
INTELLECTUALLY
INTELLIGENTSIA
INTERCONNECTED
INTERFEROMETER
INTERMITTENTLY
INTERNATIONALE
INTERPELLATION
INTERPLANETARY
INTERPRETATION
INTERPRETATIVE
KNICKERBOCKERS
KNIPPERDOLLING
KNOTENSCHIEFER
ONCHOCERCIASIS
UNAPPROACHABLE
UNATTRIBUTABLE
UNCOMPROMISING
UNCONSCIONABLE
UNCONTROLLABLE
UNCONVENTIONAL
UNCORROBORATED
UNDERDEVELOPED
UNDERMENTIONED
UNDERNOURISHED
UNDERSECRETARY
UNDERSTANDABLE
UNDERSTANDABLY
UNDERSTATEMENT
UNDESIRABILITY
UNENTHUSIASTIC
UNINTELLIGIBLE
UNMENTIONABLES
UNPLEASANTNESS
UNPREMEDITATED
UNPREPAREDNESS
UNPROFESSIONAL
UNQUESTIONABLE
UNQUESTIONABLY
UNRECOGNIZABLE
UNSATISFACTORY
UNSKILLFULNESS
BOISTEROUSNESS
COINCIDENTALLY
COMMISSIONAIRE
COMPREHENSIBLE
CONFIDENTIALLY
CONGLOMERATION
CONGRATULATION
CONGRATULATORY
CONJUNCTIVITIS
CONSERVATIVELY
CONSPIRATORIAL
CONSTANTINOPLE
CONSTITUTIONAL
CONSTRUCTIVELY
CONSTRUCTIVISM
CONTESSERATION
CONTROVERTIBLE
CONVENTIONALLY
CONVERSATIONAL
CONVERTIBILITY
CORRESPONDENCE
CORRUPTIBILITY
COUNTERBALANCE
COUNTERMEASURE
FORTUNETELLING
HOMOGENIZATION
HORTICULTURIST
JOHANNISBERGER
LONGITUDINALLY
LOQUACIOUSNESS
MONOPOLIZATION
MOUNTAINEERING
POLYMERIZATION
POPULARIZATION
PORPHYROGENITE
POSSESSINHUMAN
ROADWORTHINESS
SOLIDIFICATION
SOPHISTICATION
APOLOGETICALLY
APPREHENSIVELY
APPRENTICESHIP
APPROVECOMMENT
OPPRESSIVENESS
OPTIMISTICALLY
SPECIALIZATION
ARCHAEOLOGICAL
ARCHGENETHLIAC
ARRONDISSEMENT
BREATHLESSNESS
BROBDINGNAGIAN
CREEPYCRAWLIES
CROSSREFERENCE
CRYPTAESTHETIC
CRYSTALLOMANCY
FRATERNIZATION
FRUCTIFICATION
GRANDILOQUENCE
IRRECONCILABLE
IRREPROACHABLE
ORGANIZATIONAL
ORNITHOLOGICAL
ORTHOGRAPHICAL
PRACTICABILITY
PRECOCIOUSNESS
PREDESTINATION
PREDISPOSITION
PREFABRICATION
PRESSURIZATION
PRESUMPTUOUSLY
PRESUPPOSITION
PRODUCTIVENESS
PROFESSIONALLY
PROHIBITIONIST
PRONUNCIAMENTO
PROPORTIONALLY
PROVIDENTIALLY
TRADITIONALIST
TRANSCENDENTAL

TRANSFORMATION
TRANSMIGRATION
TRANSPORTATION
TRICHOPHYTOSIS
TROUBLESHOOTER
ASTROGEOLOGIST
ASTRONOMICALLY
ESTABLISHVERSE
OSTENTATIOUSLY
OSTEOARTHRITIS
PSYCHOANALYSIS
STAPHYLOCOCCUS
STEGANOGRAPHIC
STRAIGHTFOWARD
STRATIFICATION
STULTIFICATION
AUTHENTICATION
AUTOCRATICALLY
AUTOSUGGESTION
FUNDAMENTALISM
FUNDAMENTALIST
MULTIPLICATION
PURPOSEFULNESS
QUALIFICATIONS
QUINTESSENTIAL
SUBCONSCIOUSLY
SUBMISSIVENESS
SUBSTANTIATION
SULPHANILAMIDE
SUPERABUNDANCE
SUPERANNUATION
SUPERCILIOUSLY
SUPEREROGATION
SUPERFICIALITY
SUPERINTENDENT
SUPERNATURALLY
SUPERPHOSPHATE
SUPERSCRIPTION
SUPERSTRUCTURE
SUSCEPTIBILITY
OVERPRODUCTION
OVERSUBSCRIBED
EXISTENTIALISM
EXISTENTIALIST
EXPERIMENTALLY
EXPRESSIONLESS
GYNAECOLOGICAL
HYPERSENSITIVE
HYPOTHETICALLY
SYSTEMATICALLY
CZECHOSLOVAKIA

14:3

CHARACTERISTIC
CLASSIFICATION
CLAUSTROPHOBIA
CLAUSTROPHOBIC
EGALITARIANISM

FRATERNIZATION
GRANDILOQUENCE
HEARTSEARCHING
PHANTASMAGORIA
PHARMACEUTICAL
PHARMACOLOGIST
PRACTICABILITY
QUALIFICATIONS
ROADWORTHINESS
SCAREMONGERING
SCATTERBRAINED
SLAUGHTERHOUSE
STAPHYLOCOCCUS
TRADITIONALIST
TRANSCENDENTAL
TRANSFORMATION
TRANSMIGRATION
TRANSPORTATION
UNAPPROACHABLE
UNATTRIBUTABLE
EMBELLISHMENTS
LIBERALIZATION
NEBUCHADNEZZAR
NIBELUNGENLIED
SUBCONSCIOUSLY
SUBMISSIVENESS
SUBSTANTIATION
ACCOMPLISHMENT
ACCOUNTABILITY
ARCHAEOLOGICAL
ARCHGENETHLIAC
BACTERIOLOGIST
DECISIONMAKING
ECCLESIASTICAL
ENCEPHALOPATHY
INCONCLUSIVELY
INCONSIDERABLE
INCONVENIENTLY
LICENTIOUSNESS
MACROECONOMICS
MICROPROCESSOR
ONCHOCERCIASIS
RECAPITULATION
RECOMMENDATION
RECONCILIATION
RECONNAISSANCE
RECONSTITUTION
RECONSTRUCTION
RECORDBREAKING
UNCOMPROMISING
UNCONSCIONABLE
UNCONTROLLABLE
UNCONVENTIONAL
UNCORROBORATED
INDECIPHERABLE
INDESTRUCTIBLE
INDETERMINABLE
INDISCRIMINATE
INDOCTRINATION
RADIOTELEPHONE

RIDICULOUSNESS
UNDERDEVELOPED
UNDERMENTIONED
UNDERNOURISHED
UNDERSECRETARY
UNDERSTANDABLE
UNDERSTANDABLY
UNDERSTATEMENT
UNDESIRABILITY
BREATHLESSNESS
CREEPYCRAWLIES
CZECHOSLOVAKIA
ELECTIONEERING
ELECTRONICALLY
HIEROSOLYMITAN
IDENTIFICATION
INEXPRESSIBLES
OVERPRODUCTION
OVERSUBSCRIBED
PHENOBARBITONE
PRECOCIOUSNESS
PREDESTINATION
PREDISPOSITION
PREFABRICATION
PRESSURIZATION
PRESUMPTUOUSLY
PRESUPPOSITION
SPECIALIZATION
STEGANOGRAPHIC
THERMODYNAMICS
UNENTHUSIASTIC
AFFECTIONATELY
INFRALAPSARIAN
INFRASTRUCTURE
AGGRANDISEMENT
AGGRESSIVENESS
LIGHTSENSITIVE
ORGANIZATIONAL
REGULARIZATION
ACHONDROPLASIA
JOHANNISBERGER
REHABILITATION
SCHOOLCHILDREN
SCHOOLMISTRESS
BOISTEROUSNESS
CHINCHERINCHEE
COINCIDENTALLY
EXISTENTIALISM
EXISTENTIALIST
KNICKERBOCKERS
KNIPPERDOLLING
PHILANTHROPIST
QUINTESSENTIAL
SCIENTIFICALLY
TRICHOPHYTOSIS
UNINTELLIGIBLE
WEIGHTLESSNESS
WHIPPERSNAPPER
ACKNOWLEDGMENT
ALLOIOSTROPHUS

BALUCHITHERIUM
HALLUCINATIONS
HALLUCINOGENIC
ILLEGITIMATELY
MALAPPROPRIATE
MULTIPLICATION
PHLEGMATICALLY
POLYMERIZATION
RELINQUISHMENT
SELFASSESSMENT
SELFCONFIDENCE
SELFGOVERNMENT
SELFRESPECTING
SELFSUFFICIENT
SOLIDIFICATION
SULPHANILAMIDE
TELETYPEWRITER
VALETUDINARIAN
ADMINISTRATION
ADMINISTRATIVE
COMMISSIONAIRE
COMPREHENSIBLE
DEMOBILIZATION
DEMOCRATICALLY
DEMORALIZATION
HOMOGENIZATION
IMMOBILIZATION
SIMPLIFICATION
SIMULTANEOUSLY
UNMENTIONABLES
CENTRALIZATION
CINEMATOGRAPHY
CONFIDENTIALLY
CONGLOMERATION
CONGRATULATION
CONGRATULATORY
CONJUNCTIVITIS
CONSERVATIVELY
CONSPIRATORIAL
CONSTANTINOPLE
CONSTITUTIONAL
CONSTRUCTIVELY
CONSTRUCTIVISM
CONTESSERATION
CONTROVERTIBLE
CONVENTIONALLY
CONVERSATIONAL
CONVERTIBILITY
DENOMINATIONAL
FUNDAMENTALISM
FUNDAMENTALIST
GENERALIZATION
GENTRIFICATION
GYNAECOLOGICAL
LONGITUDINALLY
MONOPOLIZATION
ORNITHOLOGICAL
SANCTIFICATION
SANSCULOTTERIE
SENTIMENTALITY

SINGLEBREASTED
SINGLEMINDEDLY
TINTINNABULATE
VINDICTIVENESS
AFOREMENTIONED
APOLOGETICALLY
BIOENGINEERING
BROBDINGNAGIAN
CROSSREFERENCE
GEOGRAPHICALLY
KNOTENSCHIEFER
PHOSPHORESCENT
PHOTOSYNTHESIS
PRODUCTIVENESS
PROFESSIONALLY
PROHIBITIONIST
PRONUNCIAMENTO
PROPORTIONALLY
PROVIDENTIALLY
REORGANIZATION
THOUGHTFULNESS
TROUBLESHOOTER
WHOLEHEARTEDLY
ALPHABETICALLY
APPREHENSIVELY
APPRENTICESHIP
APPROVECOMMENT
CAPITALIZATION
CAPRICIOUSNESS
DIPLOMATICALLY
EXPERIMENTALLY
EXPRESSIONLESS
HYPERSENSITIVE
HYPOTHETICALLY
IMPERMEABILITY
IMPLEMENTATION
IMPOVERISHMENT
IMPREGNABILITY
IMPRESSIONABLE
MEPHISTOPHELES
OPPRESSIVENESS
POPULARIZATION
REPRESENTATION
REPRESENTATIVE
SEPTUAGENARIAN
SOPHISTICATION
SUPERABUNDANCE
SUPERANNUATION
SUPERCILIOUSLY
SUPEREROGATION
SUPERFICIALITY
SUPERINTENDENT
SUPERNATURALLY
SUPERPHOSPHATE
SUPERSCRIPTION
SUPERSTRUCTURE
UNPLEASANTNESS
UNPREMEDITATED
UNPREPAREDNESS
UNPROFESSIONAL
LOQUACIOUSNESS
UNQUESTIONABLE
UNQUESTIONABLY
AIRCONDITIONED
AIRCONDITIONER
AIRCRAFTSWOMAN
ARRONDISSEMENT
CARDIOVASCULAR
CIRCUMLOCUTION
CIRCUMNAVIGATE
CIRCUMSCISSILE
CIRCUMSTANTIAL
CORRESPONDENCE
CORRUPTIBILITY
DERMATOLOGICAL
FORTUNETELLING
HORTICULTURIST
IRRECONCILABLE
IRREPROACHABLE
PARALEIPOMENON
PARAPSYCHOLOGY
PARSIMONIOUSLY
PERCEPTIVENESS
PEREGRINATIONS
PERMISSIVENESS
PERSUASIVENESS
PORPHYROGENITE
PURPOSEFULNESS
SCRUPULOUSNESS
SHRINKWRAPPING
STRAIGHTFOWARD
STRATIFICATION
TERMINOLOGICAL
THREEHALFPENCE
UNRECOGNIZABLE
VERISIMILITUDE
ABSTEMIOUSNESS
CASTRAMETATION
DESISTABSTRACT
DISAPPOINTMENT
DISAPPROBATION
DISAPPROVINGLY
DISCIPLINARIAN
DISCOLOURATION
DISCOMBOBERATE
DISCOMBOBULATE
DISCONSOLATELY
DISCONTENTMENT
DISCOUNTENANCE
DISCOURAGEMENT
DISCOURTEOUSLY
DISCRIMINATING
DISCRIMINATION
DISCRIMINATORY
DISEMBARKATION
DISENCHANTMENT
DISENFRANCHISE
DISINCLINATION
DISINFORMATION
DISINTEGRATION
DISORIENTATION
DISTINGUISHING
FASTIDIOUSNESS
INSIGNIFICANCE
INSUFFICIENTLY
INSURMOUNTABLE
LASCIVIOUSNESS
MISAPPLICATION
MISAPPROPRIATE
MISCALCULATION
OBSEQUIOUSNESS
PASTEURIZATION
POSSESSINHUMAN
RESPECTABILITY
RESPONSIBILITY
RESPONSIVENESS
SESQUIPEDALIAN
SESQUIPEDALION
SUSCEPTIBILITY
SYSTEMATICALLY
UNSATISFACTORY
UNSKILLFULNESS
WESTERNIZATION
ANTHROPOLOGIST
ANTHROPOPHAGUS
ANTIDEPRESSANT
ANTILYMPHOCYTE
ANTIMETATHESIS
ANTIMONARCHIST
ANTIODONTALGIC
ANTIPERSPIRANT
ASTROGEOLOGIST
ASTRONOMICALLY
AUTHENTICATION
AUTOCRATICALLY
AUTOSUGGESTION
BATTERYPOWERED
ESTABLISHVERSE
INTELLECTUALLY
INTELLIGENTSIA
INTERCONNECTED
INTERFEROMETER
INTERMITTENTLY
INTERNATIONALE
INTERPELLATION
INTERPLANETARY
INTERPRETATION
INTERPRETATIVE
MATHEMATICALLY
METAMORPHOSING
METAPHORICALLY
METEMPSYCHOSIS
METEOROLOGICAL
METICULOUSNESS
NATURALIZATION
NETHERSTOCKING
NITROGLYCERINE
OPTIMISTICALLY
ORTHOGRAPHICAL
OSTENTATIOUSLY
OSTEOARTHRITIS
SATISFACTORILY
TATTERDEMALION
ULTRACREPIDATE
COUNTERBALANCE
COUNTERMEASURE
EDUCATIONALIST
FRUCTIFICATION
MOUNTAINEERING
NEUTRALIZATION
SCURRILOUSNESS
STULTIFICATION
DIVERTISSEMENT
SEXCENTENARIAN
CRYPTAESTHETIC
CRYSTALLOMANCY
PSYCHOANALYSIS

14:4

BREATHLESSNESS
DISAPPOINTMENT
DISAPPROBATION
DISAPPROVINGLY
ESTABLISHVERSE
GYNAECOLOGICAL
JOHANNISBERGER
MALAPPROPRIATE
METAMORPHOSING
METAPHORICALLY
MISAPPLICATION
MISAPPROPRIATE
ORGANIZATIONAL
PARALEIPOMENON
PARAPSYCHOLOGY
RECAPITULATION
REHABILITATION
STRAIGHTFOWARD
STRATIFICATION
UNSATISFACTORY
BROBDINGNAGIAN
AIRCONDITIONED
AIRCONDITIONER
AIRCRAFTSWOMAN
CIRCUMLOCUTION
CIRCUMNAVIGATE
CIRCUMSCISSILE
CIRCUMSTANTIAL
CZECHOSLOVAKIA
DISCIPLINARIAN
DISCOLOURATION
DISCOMBOBERATE
DISCOMBOBULATE
DISCONSOLATELY
DISCONTENTMENT
DISCOUNTENANCE
DISCOURAGEMENT
DISCOURTEOUSLY
DISCRIMINATING
DISCRIMINATION

DISCRIMINATORY
EDUCATIONALIST
ELECTIONEERING
ELECTRONICALLY
FRUCTIFICATION
KNICKERBOCKERS
LASCIVIOUSNESS
MISCALCULATION
PERCEPTIVENESS
PRACTICABILITY
PRECOCIOUSNESS
PSYCHOANALYSIS
SANCTIFICATION
SEXCENTENARIAN
SPECIALIZATION
SUBCONSCIOUSLY
SUSCEPTIBILITY
TRICHOPHYTOSIS
CARDIOVASCULAR
FUNDAMENTALISM
FUNDAMENTALIST
PREDESTINATION
PREDISPOSITION
PRODUCTIVENESS
ROADWORTHINESS
TRADITIONALIST
VINDICTIVENESS
AFFECTIONATELY
BIOENGINEERING
CINEMATOGRAPHY
CREEPYCRAWLIES
DISEMBARKATION
DISENCHANTMENT
DISENFRANCHISE
DIVERTISSEMENT
EMBELLISHMENTS
ENCEPHALOPATHY
EXPERIMENTALLY
GENERALIZATION
HYPERSENSITIVE
ILLEGITIMATELY
IMPERMEABILITY
INDECIPHERABLE
INDESTRUCTIBLE
INDETERMINABLE
INTELLECTUALLY
INTELLIGENTSIA
INTERCONNECTED
INTERFEROMETER
INTERMITTENTLY
INTERNATIONALE
INTERPELLATION
INTERPLANETARY
INTERPRETATION
INTERPRETATIVE
IRRECONCILABLE
IRREPROACHABLE
LIBERALIZATION
LICENTIOUSNESS
METEMPSYCHOSIS

METEOROLOGICAL
NIBELUNGENLIED
OBSEQUIOUSNESS
OSTENTATIOUSLY
OSTEOARTHRITIS
PEREGRINATIONS
PHLEGMATICALLY
SCIENTIFICALLY
SUPERABUNDANCE
SUPERANNUATION
SUPERCILIOUSLY
SUPEREROGATION
SUPERFICIALITY
SUPERINTENDENT
SUPERNATURALLY
SUPERPHOSPHATE
SUPERSCRIPTION
SUPERSTRUCTURE
TELETYPEWRITER
THREEHALFPENCE
UNDERDEVELOPED
UNDERMENTIONED
UNDERNOURISHED
UNDERSECRETARY
UNDERSTANDABLE
UNDERSTANDABLY
UNDERSTATEMENT
UNDESIRABILITY
UNMENTIONABLES
UNRECOGNIZABLE
VALETUDINARIAN
CONFIDENTIALLY
PREFABRICATION
PROFESSIONALLY
SELFASSESSMENT
SELFCONFIDENCE
SELFGOVERNMENT
SELFRESPECTING
SELFSUFFICIENT
CONGLOMERATION
CONGRATULATION
CONGRATULATORY
GEOGRAPHICALLY
LONGITUDINALLY
SINGLEBREASTED
SINGLEMINDEDLY
STEGANOGRAPHIC
WEIGHTLESSNESS
ALPHABETICALLY
ANTHROPOLOGIST
ANTHROPOPHAGUS
ARCHAEOLOGICAL
ARCHGENETHLIAC
AUTHENTICATION
LIGHTSENSITIVE
MATHEMATICALLY
MEPHISTOPHELES
NETHERSTOCKING
ONCHOCERCIASIS
ORTHOGRAPHICAL

PROHIBITIONIST
SOPHISTICATION
ADMINISTRATION
ADMINISTRATIVE
ANTIDEPRESSANT
ANTILYMPHOCYTE
ANTIMETATHESIS
ANTIMONARCHIST
ANTIODONTALGIC
ANTIPERSPIRANT
CAPITALIZATION
DECISIONMAKING
DESISTABSTRACT
DISINCLINATION
DISINFORMATION
DISINTEGRATION
INDISCRIMINATE
INSIGNIFICANCE
METICULOUSNESS
OPTIMISTICALLY
ORNITHOLOGICAL
RADIOTELEPHONE
RELINQUISHMENT
RIDICULOUSNESS
SATISFACTORILY
SHRINKWRAPPING
SOLIDIFICATION
VERISIMILITUDE
CONJUNCTIVITIS
UNSKILLFULNESS
APOLOGETICALLY
DIPLOMATICALLY
ECCLESIASTICAL
EGALITARIANISM
HALLUCINATIONS
HALLUCINOGENIC
IMPLEMENTATION
PHILANTHROPIST
QUALIFICATIONS
STULTIFICATION
UNPLEASANTNESS
WHOLEHEARTEDLY
COMMISSIONAIRE
DERMATOLOGICAL
PERMISSIVENESS
SUBMISSIVENESS
TERMINOLOGICAL
ACKNOWLEDGMENT
CHINCHERINCHEE
COINCIDENTALLY
COUNTERBALANCE
COUNTERMEASURE
GRANDILOQUENCE
IDENTIFICATION
MOUNTAINEERING
PHANTASMAGORIA
PHENOBARBITONE
PRONUNCIAMENTO
QUINTESSENTIAL
TRANSCENDENTAL

TRANSFORMATION
TRANSMIGRATION
TRANSPORTATION
UNENTHUSIASTIC
UNINTELLIGIBLE
ACCOMPLISHMENT
ACCOUNTABILITY
ACHONDROPLASIA
ALLOIOSTROPHUS
ARRONDISSEMENT
AUTOCRATICALLY
AUTOSUGGESTION
DEMOBILIZATION
DEMOCRATICALLY
DEMORALIZATION
DENOMINATIONAL
DISORIENTATION
HOMOGENIZATION
HYPOTHETICALLY
IMMOBILIZATION
IMPOVERISHMENT
INCONCLUSIVELY
INCONSIDERABLE
INCONVENIENTLY
INDOCTRINATION
MONOPOLIZATION
RECOMMENDATION
RECONCILIATION
RECONNAISSANCE
RECONSTITUTION
RECONSTRUCTION
RECORDBREAKING
SCHOOLCHILDREN
SCHOOLMISTRESS
UNCOMPROMISING
UNCONSCIONABLE
UNCONTROLLABLE
UNCONVENTIONAL
UNCORROBORATED
COMPREHENSIBLE
CRYPTAESTHETIC
KNIPPERDOLLING
PORPHYROGENITE
PROPORTIONALLY
PURPOSEFULNESS
RESPECTABILITY
RESPONSIBILITY
RESPONSIVENESS
SIMPLIFICATION
STAPHYLOCOCCUS
SULPHANILAMIDE
UNAPPROACHABLE
WHIPPERSNAPPER
SESQUIPEDALIAN
SESQUIPEDALION
AFOREMENTIONED
AGGRANDISEMENT
AGGRESSIVENESS
APPREHENSIVELY
APPRENTICESHIP

APPROVECOMMENT
ASTROGEOLOGIST
ASTRONOMICALLY
CAPRICIOUSNESS
CHARACTERISTIC
CORRESPONDENCE
CORRUPTIBILITY
EXPRESSIONLESS
HEARTSEARCHING
HIEROSOLYMITAN
IMPREGNABILITY
IMPRESSIONABLE
INFRALAPSARIAN
INFRASTRUCTURE
MACROECONOMICS
MICROPROCESSOR
NITROGLYCERINE
OPPRESSIVENESS
OVERPRODUCTION
OVERSUBSCRIBED
PHARMACEUTICAL
PHARMACOLOGIST
REORGANIZATION
REPRESENTATION
REPRESENTATIVE
SCAREMONGERING
SCURRILOUSNESS
THERMODYNAMICS
ULTRACREPIDATE
UNPREMEDITATED
UNPREPAREDNESS
UNPROFESSIONAL
BOISTEROUSNESS
CLASSIFICATION
CONSERVATIVELY
CONSPIRATORIAL
CONSTANTINOPLE
CONSTITUTIONAL
CONSTRUCTIVELY
CONSTRUCTIVISM
CROSSREFERENCE
CRYSTALLOMANCY
EXISTENTIALISM
EXISTENTIALIST
PARSIMONIOUSLY
PERSUASIVENESS
PHOSPHORESCENT
POSSESSINHUMAN
PRESSURIZATION
PRESUMPTUOUSLY
PRESUPPOSITION
SANSCULOTTERIE
SUBSTANTIATION
ABSTEMIOUSNESS
BACTERIOLOGIST
BATTERYPOWERED
CASTRAMETATION
CENTRALIZATION
CONTESSERATION
CONTROVERTIBLE

DISTINGUISHING
FASTIDIOUSNESS
FORTUNETELLING
FRATERNIZATION
GENTRIFICATION
HORTICULTURIST
KNOTENSCHIEFER
MULTIPLICATION
NEUTRALIZATION
PASTEURIZATION
PHOTOSYNTHESIS
SCATTERBRAINED
SENTIMENTALITY
SEPTUAGENARIAN
SYSTEMATICALLY
TATTERDEMALION
TINTINNABULATE
UNATTRIBUTABLE
WESTERNIZATION
BALUCHITHERIUM
CLAUSTROPHOBIA
CLAUSTROPHOBIC
INSUFFICIENTLY
INSURMOUNTABLE
LOQUACIOUSNESS
NATURALIZATION
NEBUCHADNEZZAR
POPULARIZATION
REGULARIZATION
SCRUPULOUSNESS
SIMULTANEOUSLY
SLAUGHTERHOUSE
THOUGHTFULNESS
TROUBLESHOOTER
UNQUESTIONABLE
UNQUESTIONABLY
CONVENTIONALLY
CONVERSATIONAL
CONVERTIBILITY
PROVIDENTIALLY
INEXPRESSIBLES
POLYMERIZATION

14:5

AGGRANDISEMENT
ALPHABETICALLY
ARCHAEOLOGICAL
CHARACTERISTIC
DERMATOLOGICAL
EDUCATIONALIST
FUNDAMENTALISM
FUNDAMENTALIST
INFRALAPSARIAN
INFRASTRUCTURE
LOQUACIOUSNESS
MISCALCULATION
PHILANTHROPIST
PREFABRICATION

SELFASSESSMENT
STEGANOGRAPHIC
ULTRACREPIDATE
DEMOBILIZATION
ESTABLISHVERSE
IMMOBILIZATION
REHABILITATION
TROUBLESHOOTER
AFFECTIONATELY
AUTOCRATICALLY
BALUCHITHERIUM
CHINCHERINCHEE
COINCIDENTALLY
DEMOCRATICALLY
INDECIPHERABLE
INDOCTRINATION
IRRECONCILABLE
METICULOUSNESS
NEBUCHADNEZZAR
RIDICULOUSNESS
SANSCULOTTERIE
SELFCONFIDENCE
UNRECOGNIZABLE
ANTIDEPRESSANT
BROBDINGNAGIAN
GRANDILOQUENCE
SOLIDIFICATION
ABSTEMIOUSNESS
AFOREMENTIONED
AGGRESSIVENESS
APPREHENSIVELY
APPRENTICESHIP
AUTHENTICATION
BACTERIOLOGIST
BATTERYPOWERED
CONSERVATIVELY
CONTESSERATION
CONVENTIONALLY
CONVERSATIONAL
CONVERTIBILITY
CORRESPONDENCE
ECCLESIASTICAL
EXPRESSIONLESS
FRATERNIZATION
GYNAECOLOGICAL
IMPLEMENTATION
IMPREGNABILITY
IMPRESSIONABLE
KNOTENSCHIEFER
MATHEMATICALLY
NETHERSTOCKING
OPPRESSIVENESS
PASTEURIZATION
PERCEPTIVENESS
POSSESSINHUMAN
PREDESTINATION
PROFESSIONALLY
REPRESENTATION
REPRESENTATIVE
RESPECTABILITY

SCAREMONGERING
SEXCENTENARIAN
SUSCEPTIBILITY
SYSTEMATICALLY
TATTERDEMALION
THREEHALFPENCE
UNPLEASANTNESS
UNPREMEDITATED
UNPREPAREDNESS
UNQUESTIONABLE
UNQUESTIONABLY
WESTERNIZATION
WHOLEHEARTEDLY
INSUFFICIENTLY
ARCHGENETHLIAC
HOMOGENIZATION
ILLEGITIMATELY
INSIGNIFICANCE
PEREGRINATIONS
PHLEGMATICALLY
REORGANIZATION
SELFGOVERNMENT
SLAUGHTERHOUSE
THOUGHTFULNESS
CZECHOSLOVAKIA
PORPHYROGENITE
PSYCHOANALYSIS
STAPHYLOCOCCUS
SULPHANILAMIDE
TRICHOPHYTOSIS
WEIGHTLESSNESS
ALLOIOSTROPHUS
CAPRICIOUSNESS
CARDIOVASCULAR
COMMISSIONAIRE
CONFIDENTIALLY
DISCIPLINARIAN
DISTINGUISHING
EGALITARIANISM
FASTIDIOUSNESS
HORTICULTURIST
LASCIVIOUSNESS
LONGITUDINALLY
MEPHISTOPHELES
MULTIPLICATION
PARSIMONIOUSLY
PERMISSIVENESS
PREDISPOSITION
PROHIBITIONIST
PROVIDENTIALLY
QUALIFICATIONS
SENTIMENTALITY
SOPHISTICATION
SPECIALIZATION
STRAIGHTFOWARD
SUBMISSIVENESS
TERMINOLOGICAL
TINTINNABULATE
TRADITIONALIST
UNSKILLFULNESS

VINDICTIVENESS
KNICKERBOCKERS
ANTILYMPHOCYTE
CONGLOMERATION
EMBELLISHMENTS
INTELLECTUALLY
INTELLIGENTSIA
NIBELUNGENLIED
PARALEIPOMENON
POPULARIZATION
REGULARIZATION
SIMPLIFICATION
SIMULTANEOUSLY
SINGLEBREASTED
SINGLEMINDEDLY
ACCOMPLISHMENT
ANTIMETATHESIS
ANTIMONARCHIST
CINEMATOGRAPHY
DENOMINATIONAL
DISEMBARKATION
METAMORPHOSING
METEMPSYCHOSIS
OPTIMISTICALLY
PHARMACEUTICAL
PHARMACOLOGIST
POLYMERIZATION
RECOMMENDATION
THERMODYNAMICS
UNCOMPROMISING
ACHONDROPLASIA
ADMINISTRATION
ADMINISTRATIVE
ARRONDISSEMENT
BIOENGINEERING
DISENCHANTMENT
DISENFRANCHISE
DISINCLINATION
DISINFORMATION
DISINTEGRATION
INCONCLUSIVELY
INCONSIDERABLE
INCONVENIENTLY
JOHANNISBERGER
LICENTIOUSNESS
ORGANIZATIONAL
OSTENTATIOUSLY
RECONCILIATION
RECONNAISSANCE
RECONSTITUTION
RECONSTRUCTION
RELINQUISHMENT
SCIENTIFICALLY
SHRINKWRAPPING
UNCONSCIONABLE
UNCONTROLLABLE
UNCONVENTIONAL
UNMENTIONABLES
ACKNOWLEDGMENT
AIRCONDITIONED
AIRCONDITIONER
ANTIODONTALGIC
APOLOGETICALLY
APPROVECOMMENT
ASTROGEOLOGIST
ASTRONOMICALLY
DIPLOMATICALLY
DISCOLOURATION
DISCOMBOBERATE
DISCOMBOBULATE
DISCONSOLATELY
DISCONTENTMENT
DISCOUNTENANCE
DISCOURAGEMENT
DISCOURTEOUSLY
HIEROSOLYMITAN
MACROECONOMICS
METEOROLOGICAL
MICROPROCESSOR
NITROGLYCERINE
ONCHOCERCIASIS
ORTHOGRAPHICAL
OSTEOARTHRITIS
PHENOBARBITONE
PHOTOSYNTHESIS
PRECOCIOUSNESS
PROPORTIONALLY
PURPOSEFULNESS
RADIOTELEPHONE
RESPONSIBILITY
RESPONSIVENESS
SCHOOLCHILDREN
SCHOOLMISTRESS
SUBCONSCIOUSLY
UNPROFESSIONAL
ANTIPERSPIRANT
CONSPIRATORIAL
CREEPYCRAWLIES
DISAPPOINTMENT
DISAPPROBATION
DISAPPROVINGLY
ENCEPHALOPATHY
INEXPRESSIBLES
IRREPROACHABLE
KNIPPERDOLLING
MALAPPROPRIATE
METAPHORICALLY
MISAPPLICATION
MISAPPROPRIATE
MONOPOLIZATION
OVERPRODUCTION
PARAPSYCHOLOGY
PHOSPHORESCENT
RECAPITULATION
SCRUPULOUSNESS
UNAPPROACHABLE
WHIPPERSNAPPER
OBSEQUIOUSNESS
AIRCRAFTSWOMAN
ANTHROPOLOGIST
ANTHROPOPHAGUS
CASTRAMETATION
CENTRALIZATION
COMPREHENSIBLE
CONGRATULATION
CONGRATULATORY
CONTROVERTIBLE
DEMORALIZATION
DISCRIMINATING
DISCRIMINATION
DISCRIMINATORY
DISORIENTATION
DIVERTISSEMENT
EXPERIMENTALLY
GENERALIZATION
GENTRIFICATION
GEOGRAPHICALLY
HYPERSENSITIVE
IMPERMEABILITY
INSURMOUNTABLE
INTERCONNECTED
INTERFEROMETER
INTERMITTENTLY
INTERNATIONALE
INTERPELLATION
INTERPLANETARY
INTERPRETATION
INTERPRETATIVE
LIBERALIZATION
NATURALIZATION
NEUTRALIZATION
RECORDBREAKING
SCURRILOUSNESS
SELFRESPECTING
SUPERABUNDANCE
SUPERANNUATION
SUPERCILIOUSLY
SUPEREROGATION
SUPERFICIALITY
SUPERINTENDENT
SUPERNATURALLY
SUPERPHOSPHATE
SUPERSCRIPTION
SUPERSTRUCTURE
UNCORROBORATED
UNDERDEVELOPED
UNDERMENTIONED
UNDERNOURISHED
UNDERSECRETARY
UNDERSTANDABLE
UNDERSTANDABLY
UNDERSTATEMENT
AUTOSUGGESTION
CLASSIFICATION
CLAUSTROPHOBIA
CLAUSTROPHOBIC
CROSSREFERENCE
DECISIONMAKING
DESISTABSTRACT
INDESTRUCTIBLE
INDISCRIMINATE
OVERSUBSCRIBED
PRESSURIZATION
SATISFACTORILY
SELFSUFFICIENT
TRANSCENDENTAL
TRANSFORMATION
TRANSMIGRATION
TRANSPORTATION
UNDESIRABILITY
VERISIMILITUDE
BOISTEROUSNESS
BREATHLESSNESS
CAPITALIZATION
CONSTANTINOPLE
CONSTITUTIONAL
CONSTRUCTIVELY
CONSTRUCTIVISM
COUNTERBALANCE
COUNTERMEASURE
CRYPTAESTHETIC
CRYSTALLOMANCY
ELECTIONEERING
ELECTRONICALLY
EXISTENTIALISM
EXISTENTIALIST
FRUCTIFICATION
HEARTSEARCHING
HYPOTHETICALLY
IDENTIFICATION
INDETERMINABLE
LIGHTSENSITIVE
MOUNTAINEERING
ORNITHOLOGICAL
PHANTASMAGORIA
PRACTICABILITY
QUINTESSENTIAL
SANCTIFICATION
SCATTERBRAINED
STRATIFICATION
STULTIFICATION
SUBSTANTIATION
TELETYPEWRITER
UNATTRIBUTABLE
UNENTHUSIASTIC
UNINTELLIGIBLE
UNSATISFACTORY
VALETUDINARIAN
ACCOUNTABILITY
CIRCUMLOCUTION
CIRCUMNAVIGATE
CIRCUMSCISSILE
CIRCUMSTANTIAL
CONJUNCTIVITIS
CORRUPTIBILITY
FORTUNETELLING
HALLUCINATIONS
HALLUCINOGENIC
PERSUASIVENESS
PRESUMPTUOUSLY

PRESUPPOSITION
PRODUCTIVENESS
PRONUNCIAMENTO
SEPTUAGENARIAN
SESQUIPEDALIAN
SESQUIPEDALION
IMPOVERISHMENT
ROADWORTHINESS

14:6

AIRCRAFTSWOMAN
CAPITALIZATION
CASTRAMETATION
CENTRALIZATION
CINEMATOGRAPHY
CONGRATULATION
CONGRATULATORY
CONSTANTINOPLE
CRYPTAESTHETIC
CRYSTALLOMANCY
DEMORALIZATION
GENERALIZATION
GEOGRAPHICALLY
LIBERALIZATION
MOUNTAINEERING
NATURALIZATION
NEUTRALIZATION
OSTEOARTHRITIS
PERSUASIVENESS
PHANTASMAGORIA
PHARMACEUTICAL
PHARMACOLOGIST
POPULARIZATION
REGULARIZATION
REORGANIZATION
SEPTUAGENARIAN
SPECIALIZATION
SUBSTANTIATION
SULPHANILAMIDE
SUPERABUNDANCE
SUPERANNUATION
UNPLEASANTNESS
ALPHABETICALLY
DISEMBARKATION
PHENOBARBITONE
PREFABRICATION
PROHIBITIONIST
CAPRICIOUSNESS
CHARACTERISTIC
DISENCHANTMENT
DISINCLINATION
GYNAECOLOGICAL
HALLUCINATIONS
HALLUCINOGENIC
HORTICULTURIST
INCONCLUSIVELY
INDISCRIMINATE
INTERCONNECTED
LOQUACIOUSNESS
ONCHOCERCIASIS
PRECOCIOUSNESS
PRODUCTIVENESS
RECONCILIATION
RESPECTABILITY
SUPERCILIOUSLY
TRANSCENDENTAL
ULTRACREPIDATE
VINDICTIVENESS
ACHONDROPLASIA
ANTIODONTALGIC
ARRONDISSEMENT
CONFIDENTIALLY
FASTIDIOUSNESS
PROVIDENTIALLY
RECORDBREAKING
UNDERDEVELOPED
ANTIDEPRESSANT
ANTIMETATHESIS
ANTIPERSPIRANT
ARCHAEOLOGICAL
ARCHGENETHLIAC
BOISTEROUSNESS
COMPREHENSIBLE
COUNTERBALANCE
COUNTERMEASURE
EXISTENTIALISM
EXISTENTIALIST
HOMOGENIZATION
IMPOVERISHMENT
INDETERMINABLE
KNICKERBOCKERS
KNIPPERDOLLING
MACROECONOMICS
PARALEIPOMENON
POLYMERIZATION
QUINTESSENTIAL
SCATTERBRAINED
SELFRESPECTING
SINGLEBREASTED
SINGLEMINDEDLY
SUPEREROGATION
UNINTELLIGIBLE
WHIPPERSNAPPER
DISENFRANCHISE
DISINFORMATION
INSUFFICIENTLY
INTERFEROMETER
QUALIFICATIONS
SATISFACTORILY
SUPERFICIALITY
TRANSFORMATION
UNPROFESSIONAL
APOLOGETICALLY
ASTROGEOLOGIST
BIOENGINEERING
IMPREGNABILITY
NITROGLYCERINE
ORTHOGRAPHICAL
STRAIGHTFOWARD
APPREHENSIVELY
BALUCHITHERIUM
BREATHLESSNESS
CHINCHERINCHEE
ENCEPHALOPATHY
HYPOTHETICALLY
METAPHORICALLY
NEBUCHADNEZZAR
ORNITHOLOGICAL
PHOSPHORESCENT
SLAUGHTERHOUSE
THOUGHTFULNESS
THREEHALFPENCE
UNENTHUSIASTIC
WHOLEHEARTEDLY
ADMINISTRATION
ADMINISTRATIVE
BROBDINGNAGIAN
CLASSIFICATION
COINCIDENTALLY
CONSPIRATORIAL
CONSTITUTIONAL
DECISIONMAKING
DEMOBILIZATION
DENOMINATIONAL
DISCRIMINATING
DISCRIMINATION
DISCRIMINATORY
DISORIENTATION
ELECTIONEERING
EXPERIMENTALLY
FRUCTIFICATION
GENTRIFICATION
GRANDILOQUENCE
IDENTIFICATION
ILLEGITIMATELY
IMMOBILIZATION
INDECIPHERABLE
OPTIMISTICALLY
ORGANIZATIONAL
PRACTICABILITY
RECAPITULATION
REHABILITATION
SANCTIFICATION
SCURRILOUSNESS
SESQUIPEDALIAN
SESQUIPEDALION
SIMPLIFICATION
SOLIDIFICATION
STRATIFICATION
STULTIFICATION
SUPERINTENDENT
UNDESIRABILITY
UNSATISFACTORY
VERISIMILITUDE
SHRINKWRAPPING
DISCOLOURATION
EMBELLISHMENTS
ESTABLISHVERSE
INFRALAPSARIAN
INTELLECTUALLY
INTELLIGENTSIA
MISCALCULATION
SCHOOLCHILDREN
SCHOOLMISTRESS
TROUBLESHOOTER
UNSKILLFULNESS
ABSTEMIOUSNESS
AFOREMENTIONED
CIRCUMLOCUTION
CIRCUMNAVIGATE
CIRCUMSCISSILE
CIRCUMSTANTIAL
DIPLOMATICALLY
DISCOMBOBERATE
DISCOMBOBULATE
FUNDAMENTALISM
FUNDAMENTALIST
IMPERMEABILITY
IMPLEMENTATION
INSURMOUNTABLE
INTERMITTENTLY
MATHEMATICALLY
PARSIMONIOUSLY
PHLEGMATICALLY
PRESUMPTUOUSLY
RECOMMENDATION
SCAREMONGERING
SENTIMENTALITY
SYSTEMATICALLY
TRANSMIGRATION
UNDERMENTIONED
UNPREMEDITATED
ACCOUNTABILITY
AGGRANDISEMENT
AIRCONDITIONED
AIRCONDITIONER
APPRENTICESHIP
ASTRONOMICALLY
AUTHENTICATION
CONJUNCTIVITIS
CONVENTIONALLY
DISCONSOLATELY
DISCONTENTMENT
DISTINGUISHING
FORTUNETELLING
INSIGNIFICANCE
INTERNATIONALE
JOHANNISBERGER
KNOTENSCHIEFER
PHILANTHROPIST
PRONUNCIAMENTO
RECONNAISSANCE
RESPONSIBILITY
RESPONSIVENESS
SEXCENTENARIAN
STEGANOGRAPHIC
SUBCONSCIOUSLY
SUPERNATURALLY

TERMINOLOGICAL
TINTINNABULATE
UNDERNOURISHED
ALLOIOSTROPHUS
ANTHROPOLOGIST
ANTHROPOPHAGUS
ANTIMONARCHIST
CARDIOVASCULAR
CONGLOMERATION
CONTROVERTIBLE
CZECHOSLOVAKIA
IRRECONCILABLE
METAMORPHOSING
MONOPOLIZATION
PSYCHOANALYSIS
ROADWORTHINESS
SELFCONFIDENCE
SELFGOVERNMENT
THERMODYNAMICS
TRICHOPHYTOSIS
UNRECOGNIZABLE
ACCOMPLISHMENT
CORRUPTIBILITY
DISAPPOINTMENT
DISAPPROBATION
DISAPPROVINGLY
DISCIPLINARIAN
INTERPELLATION
INTERPLANETARY
INTERPRETATION
INTERPRETATIVE
MALAPPROPRIATE
METEMPSYCHOSIS
MICROPROCESSOR
MISAPPLICATION
MISAPPROPRIATE
MULTIPLICATION
PERCEPTIVENESS
PRESUPPOSITION
SUPERPHOSPHATE
SUSCEPTIBILITY
TRANSPORTATION
UNCOMPROMISING
UNPREPAREDNESS
RELINQUISHMENT
AUTOCRATICALLY
BACTERIOLOGIST
BATTERYPOWERED
CONSERVATIVELY
CONSTRUCTIVELY
CONSTRUCTIVISM
CONVERSATIONAL
CONVERTIBILITY
CROSSREFERENCE
DEMOCRATICALLY
ELECTRONICALLY
FRATERNIZATION
INEXPRESSIBLES
IRREPROACHABLE
METEOROLOGICAL

NETHERSTOCKING
OVERPRODUCTION
PEREGRINATIONS
PROPORTIONALLY
TATTERDEMALION
UNAPPROACHABLE
UNATTRIBUTABLE
UNCORROBORATED
WESTERNIZATION
AGGRESSIVENESS
COMMISSIONAIRE
CONTESSERATION
CORRESPONDENCE
ECCLESIASTICAL
EXPRESSIONLESS
HEARTSEARCHING
HIEROSOLYMITAN
HYPERSENSITIVE
IMPRESSIONABLE
INCONSIDERABLE
INFRASTRUCTURE
LIGHTSENSITIVE
MEPHISTOPHELES
OPPRESSIVENESS
PARAPSYCHOLOGY
PERMISSIVENESS
PHOTOSYNTHESIS
POSSESSINHUMAN
PREDESTINATION
PREDISPOSITION
PROFESSIONALLY
PURPOSEFULNESS
RECONSTITUTION
RECONSTRUCTION
REPRESENTATION
REPRESENTATIVE
SELFASSESSMENT
SOPHISTICATION
SUBMISSIVENESS
SUPERSCRIPTION
SUPERSTRUCTURE
UNCONSCIONABLE
UNDERSECRETARY
UNDERSTANDABLE
UNDERSTANDABLY
UNDERSTATEMENT
UNQUESTIONABLE
UNQUESTIONABLY
AFFECTIONATELY
CLAUSTROPHOBIA
CLAUSTROPHOBIC
DERMATOLOGICAL
DESISTABSTRACT
DISINTEGRATION
DIVERTISSEMENT
EDUCATIONALIST
EGALITARIANISM
INDESTRUCTIBLE
INDOCTRINATION
LICENTIOUSNESS

LONGITUDINALLY
OSTENTATIOUSLY
RADIOTELEPHONE
SCIENTIFICALLY
SIMULTANEOUSLY
TRADITIONALIST
UNCONTROLLABLE
UNMENTIONABLES
WEIGHTLESSNESS
AUTOSUGGESTION
DISCOUNTENANCE
DISCOURAGEMENT
DISCOURTEOUSLY
METICULOUSNESS
NIBELUNGENLIED
OBSEQUIOUSNESS
OVERSUBSCRIBED
PASTEURIZATION
PRESSURIZATION
RIDICULOUSNESS
SANSCULOTTERIE
SCRUPULOUSNESS
SELFSUFFICIENT
VALETUDINARIAN
APPROVECOMMENT
INCONVENIENTLY
LASCIVIOUSNESS
UNCONVENTIONAL
ACKNOWLEDGMENT
ANTILYMPHOCYTE
CREEPYCRAWLIES
PORPHYROGENITE
STAPHYLOCOCCUS
TELETYPEWRITER

14:7

AUTOCRATICALLY
DEMOCRATICALLY
DESISTABSTRACT
DIPLOMATICALLY
DISEMBARKATION
EGALITARIANISM
ENCEPHALOPATHY
INFRALAPSARIAN
INTERNATIONALE
MATHEMATICALLY
NEBUCHADNEZZAR
OSTENTATIOUSLY
PHENOBARBITONE
PHLEGMATICALLY
PSYCHOANALYSIS
RECONNAISSANCE
SATISFACTORILY
SIMULTANEOUSLY
SUPERNATURALLY
SYSTEMATICALLY
THREEHALFPENCE
UNPREPAREDNESS

DISCOMBOBERATE
DISCOMBOBULATE
OVERSUBSCRIBED
RECORDBREAKING
SINGLEBREASTED
SUPERABUNDANCE
CONJUNCTIVITIS
CREEPYCRAWLIES
MACROECONOMICS
MISCALCULATION
PHARMACEUTICAL
PHARMACOLOGIST
PRACTICABILITY
PRONUNCIAMENTO
SCHOOLCHILDREN
SUPERSCRIPTION
UNCONSCIONABLE
AGGRANDISEMENT
AIRCONDITIONED
AIRCONDITIONER
COINCIDENTALLY
TATTERDEMALION
THERMODYNAMICS
VALETUDINARIAN
AFOREMENTIONED
ALPHABETICALLY
APOLOGETICALLY
APPREHENSIVELY
APPROVECOMMENT
ASTROGEOLOGIST
CHINCHERINCHEE
CONFIDENTIALLY
CROSSREFERENCE
CRYPTAESTHETIC
DISINTEGRATION
DISORIENTATION
FORTUNETELLING
FUNDAMENTALISM
FUNDAMENTALIST
HEARTSEARCHING
HYPERSENSITIVE
HYPOTHETICALLY
IMPERMEABILITY
IMPLEMENTATION
INCONVENIENTLY
INEXPRESSIBLES
INTELLECTUALLY
INTERFEROMETER
INTERPELLATION
LIGHTSENSITIVE
ONCHOCERCIASIS
PROVIDENTIALLY
PURPOSEFULNESS
RADIOTELEPHONE
RECOMMENDATION
REPRESENTATION
REPRESENTATIVE
SENTIMENTALITY
TRANSCENDENTAL
TROUBLESHOOTER

UNCONVENTIONAL
UNDERDEVELOPED
UNDERMENTIONED
UNDERSECRETARY
UNPREMEDITATED
UNPROFESSIONAL
WHOLEHEARTEDLY
AIRCRAFTSWOMAN
CLASSIFICATION
FRUCTIFICATION
GENTRIFICATION
IDENTIFICATION
SANCTIFICATION
SELFSUFFICIENT
SIMPLIFICATION
SOLIDIFICATION
STRATIFICATION
STULTIFICATION
AUTOSUGGESTION
DISTINGUISHING
SEPTUAGENARIAN
UNRECOGNIZABLE
COMPREHENSIBLE
DISENCHANTMENT
STRAIGHTFOWARD
SUPERPHOSPHATE
ABSTEMIOUSNESS
AFFECTIONATELY
ARRONDISSEMENT
BACTERIOLOGIST
BALUCHITHERIUM
BIOENGINEERING
CAPRICIOUSNESS
DIVERTISSEMENT
ECCLESIASTICAL
EDUCATIONALIST
EMBELLISHMENTS
ESTABLISHVERSE
FASTIDIOUSNESS
HALLUCINATIONS
HALLUCINOGENIC
INCONSIDERABLE
INSIGNIFICANCE
INSUFFICIENTLY
INTELLIGENTSIA
INTERMITTENTLY
JOHANNISBERGER
LASCIVIOUSNESS
LICENTIOUSNESS
LOQUACIOUSNESS
MOUNTAINEERING
OBSEQUIOUSNESS
PARALEIPOMENON
PEREGRINATIONS
PRECOCIOUSNESS
PROHIBITIONIST
QUALIFICATIONS
RECONCILIATION
SCIENTIFICALLY
SUPERCILIOUSLY

SUPERFICIALITY
TRADITIONALIST
TRANSMIGRATION
UNATTRIBUTABLE
UNMENTIONABLES
ACCOMPLISHMENT
ACKNOWLEDGMENT
BREATHLESSNESS
CAPITALIZATION
CENTRALIZATION
CIRCUMLOCUTION
CRYSTALLOMANCY
DEMOBILIZATION
DEMORALIZATION
DISCIPLINARIAN
DISINCLINATION
GENERALIZATION
GRANDILOQUENCE
IMMOBILIZATION
INCONCLUSIVELY
INTERPLANETARY
LIBERALIZATION
METICULOUSNESS
MISAPPLICATION
MONOPOLIZATION
MULTIPLICATION
NATURALIZATION
NEUTRALIZATION
NITROGLYCERINE
REHABILITATION
RIDICULOUSNESS
SANSCULOTTERIE
SCRUPULOUSNESS
SCURRILOUSNESS
SPECIALIZATION
STAPHYLOCOCCUS
UNINTELLIGIBLE
UNSKILLFULNESS
WEIGHTLESSNESS
ANTILYMPHOCYTE
CASTRAMETATION
CONGLOMERATION
DISCRIMINATING
DISCRIMINATION
DISCRIMINATORY
EXPERIMENTALLY
SCHOOLMISTRESS
SINGLEMINDEDLY
VERISIMILITUDE
ANTIMONARCHIST
ARCHGENETHLIAC
BROBDINGNAGIAN
CIRCUMNAVIGATE
CONSTANTINOPLE
DENOMINATIONAL
DISCOUNTENANCE
EXISTENTIALISM
EXISTENTIALIST
FRATERNIZATION
HOMOGENIZATION

IMPREGNABILITY
IRRECONCILABLE
NIBELUNGENLIED
REORGANIZATION
SELFCONFIDENCE
SUBSTANTIATION
SULPHANILAMIDE
SUPERANNUATION
SUPERINTENDENT
TINTINNABULATE
WESTERNIZATION
ANTIODONTALGIC
ARCHAEOLOGICAL
ASTRONOMICALLY
DECISIONMAKING
DERMATOLOGICAL
DISAPPOINTMENT
DISCOLOURATION
DISINFORMATION
ELECTIONEERING
ELECTRONICALLY
GYNAECOLOGICAL
HIEROSOLYMITAN
INSURMOUNTABLE
INTERCONNECTED
IRREPROACHABLE
METAPHORICALLY
METEOROLOGICAL
ORNITHOLOGICAL
OVERPRODUCTION
PARSIMONIOUSLY
PHOSPHORESCENT
SCAREMONGERING
STEGANOGRAPHIC
TERMINOLOGICAL
TRANSFORMATION
TRANSPORTATION
UNAPPROACHABLE
UNCORROBORATED
UNDERNOURISHED
ANTHROPOLOGIST
ANTHROPOPHAGUS
ANTIDEPRESSANT
CORRESPONDENCE
GEOGRAPHICALLY
INDECIPHERABLE
PREDISPOSITION
PRESUMPTUOUSLY
PRESUPPOSITION
SESQUIPEDALIAN
SESQUIPEDALION
TELETYPEWRITER
TRICHOPHYTOSIS
ACHONDROPLASIA
ANTIPERSPIRANT
BOISTEROUSNESS
CLAUSTROPHOBIA
CLAUSTROPHOBIC
CONSPIRATORIAL
COUNTERBALANCE

COUNTERMEASURE
DISAPPROBATION
DISAPPROVINGLY
DISCOURAGEMENT
DISCOURTEOUSLY
DISENFRANCHISE
IMPOVERISHMENT
INDESTRUCTIBLE
INDETERMINABLE
INDISCRIMINATE
INDOCTRINATION
INTERPRETATION
INTERPRETATIVE
KNICKERBOCKERS
KNIPPERDOLLING
MALAPPROPRIATE
METAMORPHOSING
MICROPROCESSOR
MISAPPROPRIATE
ORTHOGRAPHICAL
OSTEOARTHRITIS
PASTEURIZATION
POLYMERIZATION
POPULARIZATION
PORPHYROGENITE
PREFABRICATION
PRESSURIZATION
REGULARIZATION
ROADWORTHINESS
SCATTERBRAINED
SUPEREROGATION
ULTRACREPIDATE
UNCOMPROMISING
UNCONTROLLABLE
UNDESIRABILITY
WHIPPERSNAPPER
ADMINISTRATION
ADMINISTRATIVE
AGGRESSIVENESS
ALLOIOSTROPHUS
CIRCUMSCISSILE
CIRCUMSTANTIAL
COMMISSIONAIRE
CONTESSERATION
CONVERSATIONAL
CZECHOSLOVAKIA
DISCONSOLATELY
EXPRESSIONLESS
IMPRESSIONABLE
KNOTENSCHIEFER
METEMPSYCHOSIS
NETHERSTOCKING
OPPRESSIVENESS
OPTIMISTICALLY
PERMISSIVENESS
PERSUASIVENESS
PHANTASMAGORIA
POSSESSINHUMAN
PROFESSIONALLY
QUINTESSENTIAL

RESPONSIBILITY
RESPONSIVENESS
SELFASSESSMENT
SELFRESPECTING
SUBCONSCIOUSLY
SUBMISSIVENESS
UNPLEASANTNESS
UNSATISFACTORY
ACCOUNTABILITY
ANTIMETATHESIS
APPRENTICESHIP
AUTHENTICATION
CHARACTERISTIC
CINEMATOGRAPHY
CONGRATULATION
CONGRATULATORY
CONSTITUTIONAL
CONVENTIONALLY
CONVERTIBILITY
CORRUPTIBILITY
DISCONTENTMENT
ILLEGITIMATELY
INFRASTRUCTURE
MEPHISTOPHELES
PERCEPTIVENESS
PHILANTHROPIST
PREDESTINATION
PRODUCTIVENESS
PROPORTIONALLY
RECAPITULATION
RECONSTITUTION
RECONSTRUCTION
RESPECTABILITY
SEXCENTENARIAN
SLAUGHTERHOUSE
SOPHISTICATION
SUPERSTRUCTURE
SUSCEPTIBILITY
THOUGHTFULNESS
UNDERSTANDABLE
UNDERSTANDABLY
UNDERSTATEMENT
UNQUESTIONABLE
UNQUESTIONABLY
VINDICTIVENESS
CONSTRUCTIVELY
CONSTRUCTIVISM
HORTICULTURIST
LONGITUDINALLY
RELINQUISHMENT
UNENTHUSIASTIC
CARDIOVASCULAR
CONSERVATIVELY
CONTROVERTIBLE
SELFGOVERNMENT
SHRINKWRAPPING
BATTERYPOWERED
PARAPSYCHOLOGY
PHOTOSYNTHESIS
ORGANIZATIONAL

14:8

ACCOUNTABILITY
ANTIMETATHESIS
ANTIMONARCHIST
CARDIOVASCULAR
CIRCUMNAVIGATE
CONSERVATIVELY
CONSPIRATORIAL
CONVERSATIONAL
DENOMINATIONAL
DISCOURAGEMENT
DISENCHANTMENT
DISENFRANCHISE
ECCLESIASTICAL
HEARTSEARCHING
IMPERMEABILITY
IMPREGNABILITY
INTERPLANETARY
IRREPROACHABLE
ORGANIZATIONAL
ORTHOGRAPHICAL
PRACTICABILITY
RESPECTABILITY
TINTINNABULATE
UNAPPROACHABLE
UNDERSTANDABLE
UNDERSTANDABLY
UNDERSTATEMENT
UNDESIRABILITY
UNPLEASANTNESS
WHOLEHEARTEDLY
COUNTERBALANCE
DESISTABSTRACT
KNICKERBOCKERS
SCATTERBRAINED
UNATTRIBUTABLE
UNCORROBORATED
APPROVECOMMENT
CIRCUMSCISSILE
CONSTRUCTIVELY
CONSTRUCTIVISM
INSUFFICIENTLY
INTELLECTUALLY
IRRECONCILABLE
KNOTENSCHIEFER
PARAPSYCHOLOGY
QUALIFICATIONS
SATISFACTORILY
SUBCONSCIOUSLY
SUPERFICIALITY
UNDERSECRETARY
INCONSIDERABLE
KNIPPERDOLLING
LONGITUDINALLY
NEBUCHADNEZZAR
OVERPRODUCTION
UNPREMEDITATED
ACKNOWLEDGMENT

ARCHGENETHLIAC
BREATHLESSNESS
CASTRAMETATION
CHARACTERISTIC
COINCIDENTALLY
COMPREHENSIBLE
CONGLOMERATION
CONTESSERATION
CONTROVERTIBLE
DISCONTENTMENT
EXPERIMENTALLY
INTERPRETATION
INTERPRETATIVE
PHARMACEUTICAL
SELFASSESSMENT
SELFGOVERNMENT
SEPTUAGENARIAN
SESQUIPEDALIAN
SESQUIPEDALION
SEXCENTENARIAN
SLAUGHTERHOUSE
TATTERDEMALION
TELETYPEWRITER
ULTRACREPIDATE
WEIGHTLESSNESS
CROSSREFERENCE
INSIGNIFICANCE
PURPOSEFULNESS
SCIENTIFICALLY
SELFCONFIDENCE
SELFSUFFICIENT
THOUGHTFULNESS
UNSATISFACTORY
UNSKILLFULNESS
AUTOSUGGESTION
BROBDINGNAGIAN
DISINTEGRATION
INTELLIGENTSIA
NIBELUNGENLIED
STEGANOGRAPHIC
TRANSMIGRATION
GEOGRAPHICALLY
INDECIPHERABLE
PHILANTHROPIST
SCHOOLCHILDREN
TRICHOPHYTOSIS
ACCOMPLISHMENT
AGGRANDISEMENT
AGGRESSIVENESS
AIRCONDITIONED
AIRCONDITIONER
APPRENTICESHIP
AUTHENTICATION
CAPITALIZATION
CENTRALIZATION
CLASSIFICATION
COMMISSIONAIRE
CONVENTIONALLY
CONVERTIBILITY
CORRUPTIBILITY

DEMOBILIZATION
DEMORALIZATION
DISAPPOINTMENT
DISCIPLINARIAN
DISCRIMINATING
DISCRIMINATION
DISCRIMINATORY
DISINCLINATION
EXPRESSIONLESS
FRATERNIZATION
FRUCTIFICATION
GENERALIZATION
GENTRIFICATION
HOMOGENIZATION
IDENTIFICATION
ILLEGITIMATELY
IMMOBILIZATION
IMPOVERISHMENT
IMPRESSIONABLE
INDISCRIMINATE
INDOCTRINATION
LIBERALIZATION
MISAPPLICATION
MONOPOLIZATION
MULTIPLICATION
NATURALIZATION
NEUTRALIZATION
OPPRESSIVENESS
PASTEURIZATION
PERCEPTIVENESS
PERMISSIVENESS
PERSUASIVENESS
POLYMERIZATION
POPULARIZATION
POSSESSINHUMAN
PREDESTINATION
PREFABRICATION
PRESSURIZATION
PRODUCTIVENESS
PROFESSIONALLY
PRONUNCIAMENTO
PROPORTIONALLY
RECONNAISSANCE
RECONSTITUTION
REGULARIZATION
REHABILITATION
RELINQUISHMENT
REORGANIZATION
RESPONSIBILITY
RESPONSIVENESS
SANCTIFICATION
SCHOOLMISTRESS
SIMPLIFICATION
SINGLEMINDEDLY
SOLIDIFICATION
SOPHISTICATION
SPECIALIZATION
STRATIFICATION
STULTIFICATION
SUBMISSIVENESS

SULPHANILAMIDE
SUSCEPTIBILITY
UNCONSCIONABLE
UNQUESTIONABLE
UNQUESTIONABLY
VALETUDINARIAN
VERISIMILITUDE
VINDICTIVENESS
WESTERNIZATION
ARCHAEOLOGICAL
CRYSTALLOMANCY
CZECHOSLOVAKIA
DERMATOLOGICAL
ENCEPHALOPATHY
GYNAECOLOGICAL
HIEROSOLYMITAN
HORTICULTURIST
INTERPELLATION
METEOROLOGICAL
ORNITHOLOGICAL
RADIOTELEPHONE
RECONCILIATION
SUPERCILIOUSLY
TERMINOLOGICAL
THREEHALFPENCE
UNINTELLIGIBLE
ASTRONOMICALLY
COUNTERMEASURE
INDETERMINABLE
PHANTASMAGORIA
AFOREMENTIONED
ANTIODONTALGIC
APPREHENSIVELY
BIOENGINEERING
CONFIDENTIALLY
DECISIONMAKING
DISORIENTATION
ELECTIONEERING
ELECTRONICALLY
FUNDAMENTALISM
FUNDAMENTALIST
HALLUCINATIONS
HALLUCINOGENIC
HYPERSENSITIVE
IMPLEMENTATION
INCONVENIENTLY
INTERCONNECTED
LIGHTSENSITIVE
MOUNTAINEERING
PARSIMONIOUSLY
PEREGRINATIONS
PHOTOSYNTHESIS
PROVIDENTIALLY
PSYCHOANALYSIS
RECOMMENDATION
REPRESENTATION
REPRESENTATIVE
SCAREMONGERING
SENTIMENTALITY
SIMULTANEOUSLY

SUPERANNUATION
TRANSCENDENTAL
UNCONVENTIONAL
UNDERMENTIONED
UNRECOGNIZABLE
ABSTEMIOUSNESS
ACHONDROPLASIA
AFFECTIONATELY
ANTHROPOLOGIST
ANTHROPOPHAGUS
ASTROGEOLOGIST
BACTERIOLOGIST
BOISTEROUSNESS
CAPRICIOUSNESS
CINEMATOGRAPHY
CIRCUMLOCUTION
CLAUSTROPHOBIA
CLAUSTROPHOBIC
CORRESPONDENCE
DISAPPROBATION
DISAPPROVINGLY
DISCOMBOBERATE
DISCOMBOBULATE
DISCONSOLATELY
EDUCATIONALIST
FASTIDIOUSNESS
GRANDILOQUENCE
LASCIVIOUSNESS
LICENTIOUSNESS
LOQUACIOUSNESS
MACROECONOMICS
MALAPPROPRIATE
MEPHISTOPHELES
METICULOUSNESS
MICROPROCESSOR
MISAPPROPRIATE
OBSEQUIOUSNESS
PHARMACOLOGIST
PORPHYROGENITE
PRECOCIOUSNESS
PREDISPOSITION
PRESUPPOSITION
RIDICULOUSNESS
SANSCULOTTERIE
SCRUPULOUSNESS
SCURRILOUSNESS
STAPHYLOCOCCUS
SUPEREROGATION
SUPERPHOSPHATE
TRADITIONALIST
UNCOMPROMISING
UNCONTROLLABLE
UNMENTIONABLES
ANTILYMPHOCYTE
BATTERYPOWERED
INFRALAPSARIAN
METAMORPHOSING
PARALEIPOMENON
SELFRESPECTING
ANTIDEPRESSANT

CHINCHERINCHEE
CREEPYCRAWLIES
DISEMBARKATION
DISINFORMATION
EGALITARIANISM
INFRASTRUCTURE
INTERFEROMETER
METAPHORICALLY
ONCHOCERCIASIS
PHENOBARBITONE
PHOSPHORESCENT
RECONSTRUCTION
RECORDBREAKING
SHRINKWRAPPING
SINGLEBREASTED
SUPERSCRIPTION
SUPERSTRUCTURE
TRANSFORMATION
TRANSPORTATION
UNPREPAREDNESS
ANTIPERSPIRANT
ARRONDISSEMENT
CRYPTAESTHETIC
DIVERTISSEMENT
EMBELLISHMENTS
ESTABLISHVERSE
INEXPRESSIBLES
JOHANNISBERGER
OVERSUBSCRIBED
QUINTESSENTIAL
TROUBLESHOOTER
UNENTHUSIASTIC
UNPROFESSIONAL
WHIPPERSNAPPER
ADMINISTRATION
ADMINISTRATIVE
AIRCRAFTSWOMAN
ALLOIOSTROPHUS
ALPHABETICALLY
APOLOGETICALLY
AUTOCRATICALLY
BALUCHITHERIUM
CIRCUMSTANTIAL
CONJUNCTIVITIS
CONSTANTINOPLE
DEMOCRATICALLY
DIPLOMATICALLY
DISCOUNTENANCE
DISCOURTEOUSLY
EXISTENTIALISM
EXISTENTIALIST
FORTUNETELLING
HYPOTHETICALLY
INTERMITTENTLY
INTERNATIONALE
MATHEMATICALLY
NETHERSTOCKING
OPTIMISTICALLY
OSTENTATIOUSLY
OSTEOARTHRITIS

PHLEGMATICALLY
PRESUMPTUOUSLY
PROHIBITIONIST
ROADWORTHINESS
STRAIGHTFOWARD
SUBSTANTIATION
SUPERINTENDENT
SUPERNATURALLY
SYSTEMATICALLY
CONGRATULATION
CONGRATULATORY
CONSTITUTIONAL
DISCOLOURATION
DISTINGUISHING
INCONCLUSIVELY
INDESTRUCTIBLE
INSURMOUNTABLE
MISCALCULATION
RECAPITULATION
SUPERABUNDANCE
UNDERNOURISHED
UNDERDEVELOPED
METEMPSYCHOSIS
NITROGLYCERINE
THERMODYNAMICS

14:9

CIRCUMSTANTIAL
COUNTERBALANCE
CREEPYCRAWLIES
HALLUCINATIONS
PEREGRINATIONS
PHANTASMAGORIA
PRONUNCIAMENTO
PSYCHOANALYSIS
QUALIFICATIONS
SHRINKWRAPPING
UNSATISFACTORY
ACCOUNTABILITY
CONVERTIBILITY
CORRUPTIBILITY
DISAPPROBATION
DISCOMBOBERATE
DISCOMBOBULATE
IMPERMEABILITY
IMPREGNABILITY
JOHANNISBERGER
PHENOBARBITONE
PRACTICABILITY
RESPECTABILITY
RESPONSIBILITY
SUSCEPTIBILITY
TINTINNABULATE
UNDESIRABILITY
APPRENTICESHIP
AUTHENTICATION
CIRCUMLOCUTION
CLASSIFICATION

FRUCTIFICATION
GENTRIFICATION
IDENTIFICATION
INDESTRUCTIBLE
IRREPROACHABLE
METEMPSYCHOSIS
MICROPROCESSOR
MISAPPLICATION
MULTIPLICATION
NITROGLYCERINE
ONCHOCERCIASIS
OVERSUBSCRIBED
PREFABRICATION
SANCTIFICATION
SIMPLIFICATION
SOLIDIFICATION
SOPHISTICATION
STAPHYLOCOCCUS
STRATIFICATION
STULTIFICATION
UNAPPROACHABLE
ACKNOWLEDGMENT
RECOMMENDATION
SESQUIPEDALIAN
SESQUIPEDALION
TRANSCENDENTAL
ANTIDEPRESSANT
AUTOSUGGESTION
BIOENGINEERING
COUNTERMEASURE
CROSSREFERENCE
DISCOUNTENANCE
DISCOURTEOUSLY
ELECTIONEERING
FORTUNETELLING
INCONSIDERABLE
INDECIPHERABLE
INTELLIGENTSIA
MOUNTAINEERING
NIBELUNGENLIED
PHOSPHORESCENT
QUINTESSENTIAL
RADIOTELEPHONE
RECORDBREAKING
SELFRESPECTING
SIMULTANEOUSLY
SINGLEBREASTED
SUPERINTENDENT
UNDERDEVELOPED
UNPREPAREDNESS
STRAIGHTFOWARD
THREEHALFPENCE
CINEMATOGRAPHY
DISCOURAGEMENT
PORPHYROGENITE
SCAREMONGERING
SUPEREROGATION
ANTILYMPHOCYTE
BALUCHITHERIUM
EMBELLISHMENTS

ESTABLISHVERSE
KNOTENSCHIEFER
METAMORPHOSING
OSTEOARTHRITIS
PARAPSYCHOLOGY
ROADWORTHINESS
TROUBLESHOOTER
ALPHABETICALLY
APOLOGETICALLY
ASTRONOMICALLY
AUTOCRATICALLY
CHINCHERINCHEE
CIRCUMSCISSILE
CONJUNCTIVITIS
CONSTANTINOPLE
DEMOCRATICALLY
DIPLOMATICALLY
DISTINGUISHING
EGALITARIANISM
ELECTRONICALLY
EXISTENTIALISM
EXISTENTIALIST
GEOGRAPHICALLY
HYPOTHETICALLY
INCONVENIENTLY
INDETERMINABLE
INSIGNIFICANCE
INSUFFICIENTLY
INTERNATIONALE
IRRECONCILABLE
LONGITUDINALLY
MATHEMATICALLY
METAPHORICALLY
OPTIMISTICALLY
OSTENTATIOUSLY
PARSIMONIOUSLY
PHLEGMATICALLY
PROHIBITIONIST
RECONCILIATION
SCHOOLCHILDREN
SCIENTIFICALLY
SELFCONFIDENCE
SELFSUFFICIENT
SUBCONSCIOUSLY
SUBSTANTIATION
SUPERCILIOUSLY
SUPERFICIALITY
SUPERSCRIPTION
SYSTEMATICALLY
UNENTHUSIASTIC
UNINTELLIGIBLE
UNPREMEDITATED
UNRECOGNIZABLE
DISEMBARKATION
ANTHROPOLOGIST
ASTROGEOLOGIST
BACTERIOLOGIST
CONGRATULATION
CONGRATULATORY
DISCONSOLATELY

INTERPELLATION
MISCALCULATION
PHARMACOLOGIST
RECAPITULATION
SULPHANILAMIDE
UNCONTROLLABLE
VERISIMILITUDE
DECISIONMAKING
DISINFORMATION
ILLEGITIMATELY
INDISCRIMINATE
TATTERDEMALION
TRANSFORMATION
UNCOMPROMISING
AFFECTIONATELY
BROBDINGNAGIAN
COINCIDENTALLY
COMPREHENSIBLE
CORRESPONDENCE
DISAPPOINTMENT
DISCIPLINARIAN
DISCONTENTMENT
DISCRIMINATING
DISCRIMINATION
DISCRIMINATORY
DISENCHANTMENT
DISENFRANCHISE
DISINCLINATION
EDUCATIONALIST
EXPERIMENTALLY
INDOCTRINATION
INSURMOUNTABLE
INTERCONNECTED
INTERPLANETARY
MACROECONOMICS
NEBUCHADNEZZAR
POSSESSINHUMAN
PREDESTINATION
SEPTUAGENARIAN
SEXCENTENARIAN
SINGLEMINDEDLY
SUPERABUNDANCE
THERMODYNAMICS
TRADITIONALIST
UNDERSTANDABLE
UNDERSTANDABLY
UNMENTIONABLES
UNPLEASANTNESS
VALETUDINARIAN
WHIPPERSNAPPER
APPROVECOMMENT
ARCHAEOLOGICAL
BATTERYPOWERED
COMMISSIONAIRE
CONVENTIONALLY
CRYSTALLOMANCY
CZECHOSLOVAKIA
DERMATOLOGICAL
ENCEPHALOPATHY
EXPRESSIONLESS

GYNAECOLOGICAL
HALLUCINOGENIC
IMPRESSIONABLE
INTERFEROMETER
KNICKERBOCKERS
KNIPPERDOLLING
METEOROLOGICAL
NETHERSTOCKING
ORNITHOLOGICAL
PARALEIPOMENON
PROFESSIONALLY
PROPORTIONALLY
TERMINOLOGICAL
UNCONSCIONABLE
UNCORROBORATED
UNQUESTIONABLE
UNQUESTIONABLY
ACHONDROPLASIA
ANTHROPOPHAGUS
ANTIPERSPIRANT
CLAUSTROPHOBIA
CLAUSTROPHOBIC
MALAPPROPRIATE
MEPHISTOPHELES
MISAPPROPRIATE
ORTHOGRAPHICAL
ULTRACREPIDATE
GRANDILOQUENCE
ADMINISTRATION
ADMINISTRATIVE
ALLOIOSTROPHUS
ANTIMONARCHIST
CHARACTERISTIC
CONGLOMERATION
CONTESSERATION
CONTROVERTIBLE
DISCOLOURATION
DISINTEGRATION
HEARTSEARCHING
PHILANTHROPIST
SCATTERBRAINED
SELFGOVERNMENT
SLAUGHTERHOUSE
STEGANOGRAPHIC
TRANSMIGRATION
UNDERNOURISHED
UNDERSECRETARY
WHOLEHEARTEDLY
ACCOMPLISHMENT
AGGRANDISEMENT
AIRCRAFTSWOMAN
APPREHENSIVELY
ARRONDISSEMENT
BREATHLESSNESS
CARDIOVASCULAR
DESISTABSTRACT
DIVERTISSEMENT
ECCLESIASTICAL
HYPERSENSITIVE
IMPOVERISHMENT

INCONCLUSIVELY
INEXPRESSIBLES
INFRALAPSARIAN
LIGHTSENSITIVE
PREDISPOSITION
PRESUPPOSITION
RECONNAISSANCE
RELINQUISHMENT
SCHOOLMISTRESS
SELFASSESSMENT
SUPERPHOSPHATE
UNPROFESSIONAL
WEIGHTLESSNESS
AFOREMENTIONED
AIRCONDITIONED
AIRCONDITIONER
ANTIMETATHESIS
ANTIODONTALGIC
ARCHGENETHLIAC
CASTRAMETATION
CONFIDENTIALLY
CONSERVATIVELY
CONSPIRATORIAL
CONSTITUTIONAL
CONSTRUCTIVELY
CONSTRUCTIVISM
CONVERSATIONAL
CRYPTAESTHETIC
DENOMINATIONAL
DISORIENTATION
FUNDAMENTALISM
FUNDAMENTALIST
HORTICULTURIST
IMPLEMENTATION
INTELLECTUALLY
INTERMITTENTLY
INTERPRETATION
INTERPRETATIVE
ORGANIZATIONAL
PHOTOSYNTHESIS
PROVIDENTIALLY
RECONSTITUTION
REHABILITATION
REPRESENTATION
REPRESENTATIVE
SANSCULOTTERIE
SATISFACTORILY
SENTIMENTALITY
TRANSPORTATION
UNCONVENTIONAL
UNDERMENTIONED
UNDERSTATEMENT
ABSTEMIOUSNESS
BOISTEROUSNESS
CAPRICIOUSNESS
FASTIDIOUSNESS
INFRASTRUCTURE
LASCIVIOUSNESS
LICENTIOUSNESS
LOQUACIOUSNESS
METICULOUSNESS
OBSEQUIOUSNESS
OVERPRODUCTION
PHARMACEUTICAL
PRECOCIOUSNESS
PRESUMPTUOUSLY
PURPOSEFULNESS
RECONSTRUCTION
RIDICULOUSNESS
SCRUPULOUSNESS
SCURRILOUSNESS
SUPERANNUATION
SUPERNATURALLY
SUPERSTRUCTURE
THOUGHTFULNESS
UNATTRIBUTABLE
UNSKILLFULNESS
AGGRESSIVENESS
CIRCUMNAVIGATE
DISAPPROVINGLY
OPPRESSIVENESS
PERCEPTIVENESS
PERMISSIVENESS
PERSUASIVENESS
PRODUCTIVENESS
RESPONSIVENESS
SUBMISSIVENESS
VINDICTIVENESS
TELETYPEWRITER
HIEROSOLYMITAN
TRICHOPHYTOSIS
CAPITALIZATION
CENTRALIZATION
DEMOBILIZATION
DEMORALIZATION
FRATERNIZATION
GENERALIZATION
HOMOGENIZATION
IMMOBILIZATION
LIBERALIZATION
MONOPOLIZATION
NATURALIZATION
NEUTRALIZATION
PASTEURIZATION
POLYMERIZATION
POPULARIZATION
PRESSURIZATION
REGULARIZATION
REORGANIZATION
SPECIALIZATION
WESTERNIZATION

14:10

ADMINISTRATION
ADMINISTRATIVE
AFFECTIONATELY
ANTIODONTALGIC
AUTHENTICATION
BROBDINGNAGIAN
CAPITALIZATION
CASTRAMETATION
CENTRALIZATION
CLASSIFICATION
CONGLOMERATION
CONGRATULATION
CONGRATULATORY
CONTESSERATION
COUNTERMEASURE
DECISIONMAKING
DEMOBILIZATION
DEMORALIZATION
DISAPPROBATION
DISCIPLINARIAN
DISCOLOURATION
DISCONSOLATELY
DISCRIMINATING
DISCRIMINATION
DISCRIMINATORY
DISEMBARKATION
DISINCLINATION
DISINFORMATION
DISINTEGRATION
DISORIENTATION
EDUCATIONALIST
EGALITARIANISM
EXISTENTIALISM
EXISTENTIALIST
FRATERNIZATION
FRUCTIFICATION
FUNDAMENTALISM
FUNDAMENTALIST
GENERALIZATION
GENTRIFICATION
HOMOGENIZATION
IDENTIFICATION
ILLEGITIMATELY
IMMOBILIZATION
IMPLEMENTATION
INDOCTRINATION
INFRALAPSARIAN
INTERPELLATION
INTERPRETATION
INTERPRETATIVE
LIBERALIZATION
MISAPPLICATION
MISCALCULATION
MONOPOLIZATION
MULTIPLICATION
NATURALIZATION
NEUTRALIZATION
PASTEURIZATION
POLYMERIZATION
POPULARIZATION
PREDESTINATION
PREFABRICATION
PRESSURIZATION
RECAPITULATION
RECOMMENDATION
RECONCILIATION
RECORDBREAKING
REGULARIZATION
REHABILITATION
REORGANIZATION
REPRESENTATION
REPRESENTATIVE
SANCTIFICATION
SCATTERBRAINED
SENTIMENTALITY
SEPTUAGENARIAN
SESQUIPEDALIAN
SESQUIPEDALION
SEXCENTENARIAN
SIMPLIFICATION
SINGLEBREASTED
SOLIDIFICATION
SOPHISTICATION
SPECIALIZATION
STEGANOGRAPHIC
STRATIFICATION
STULTIFICATION
SUBSTANTIATION
SULPHANILAMIDE
SUPERANNUATION
SUPEREROGATION
SUPERFICIALITY
TATTERDEMALION
THERMODYNAMICS
TRADITIONALIST
TRANSFORMATION
TRANSMIGRATION
TRANSPORTATION
UNENTHUSIASTIC
UNMENTIONABLES
VALETUDINARIAN
WESTERNIZATION
WHIPPERSNAPPER
ALPHABETICALLY
ANTIMONARCHIST
APOLOGETICALLY
ASTRONOMICALLY
AUTOCRATICALLY
CARDIOVASCULAR
DEMOCRATICALLY
DIPLOMATICALLY
DISENFRANCHISE
ELECTRONICALLY
GEOGRAPHICALLY
HEARTSEARCHING
HYPOTHETICALLY
INFRASTRUCTURE
INSIGNIFICANCE
KNICKERBOCKERS
MATHEMATICALLY
METAPHORICALLY
NETHERSTOCKING
OPTIMISTICALLY
OVERPRODUCTION
PHLEGMATICALLY

RECONSTRUCTION
SCIENTIFICALLY
SELFRESPECTING
SELFSUFFICIENT
SUPERSTRUCTURE
SYSTEMATICALLY
UNSATISFACTORY
CORRESPONDENCE
SELFCONFIDENCE
SINGLEMINDEDLY
SUPERABUNDANCE
UNDERSTANDABLE
UNDERSTANDABLY
UNPREPAREDNESS
AGGRANDISEMENT
AGGRESSIVENESS
APPRENTICESHIP
ARRONDISSEMENT
BALUCHITHERIUM
BIOENGINEERING
DISCOMBOBERATE
DISCOURAGEMENT
DIVERTISSEMENT
ELECTIONEERING
INCONVENIENTLY
INSUFFICIENTLY
INTERCONNECTED
INTERMITTENTLY
INTERPLANETARY
JOHANNISBERGER
MICROPROCESSOR
MOUNTAINEERING
NEBUCHADNEZZAR
NITROGLYCERINE
OPPRESSIVENESS
PERCEPTIVENESS
PERMISSIVENESS
PERSUASIVENESS
PORPHYROGENITE
PRODUCTIVENESS
RESPONSIVENESS
SCAREMONGERING
SUBMISSIVENESS
TRANSCENDENTAL
UNDERSECRETARY
UNDERSTATEMENT
VINDICTIVENESS
ACKNOWLEDGMENT
ARCHAEOLOGICAL
DERMATOLOGICAL
GYNAECOLOGICAL
HALLUCINOGENIC
METEOROLOGICAL
ORNITHOLOGICAL
PHANTASMAGORIA
TERMINOLOGICAL
UNINTELLIGIBLE
ACCOMPLISHMENT
ANTHROPOPHAGUS
ANTIMETATHESIS

ARCHGENETHLIAC
CLAUSTROPHOBIA
CLAUSTROPHOBIC
CRYPTAESTHETIC
IMPOVERISHMENT
IRREPROACHABLE
MEPHISTOPHELES
METEMPSYCHOSIS
ORTHOGRAPHICAL
PHOTOSYNTHESIS
POSSESSINHUMAN
RELINQUISHMENT
SLAUGHTERHOUSE
UNAPPROACHABLE
ACCOUNTABILITY
AFOREMENTIONED
AIRCONDITIONED
AIRCONDITIONER
ANTIPERSPIRANT
APPREHENSIVELY
CHARACTERISTIC
CIRCUMNAVIGATE
CONFIDENTIALLY
CONSERVATIVELY
CONSTITUTIONAL
CONSTRUCTIVELY
CONSTRUCTIVISM
CONVERSATIONAL
CONVERTIBILITY
CORRUPTIBILITY
DENOMINATIONAL
DISAPPROVINGLY
HYPERSENSITIVE
IMPERMEABILITY
IMPREGNABILITY
INCONCLUSIVELY
INDISCRIMINATE
INEXPRESSIBLES
KNOTENSCHIEFER
LIGHTSENSITIVE
ONCHOCERCIASIS
ORGANIZATIONAL
PHENOBARBITONE
PRACTICABILITY
PREDISPOSITION
PRESUPPOSITION
PROVIDENTIALLY
RESPECTABILITY
RESPONSIBILITY
ROADWORTHINESS
SUSCEPTIBILITY
ULTRACREPIDATE
UNCOMPROMISING
UNCONVENTIONAL
UNDERMENTIONED
UNDERNOURISHED
UNDESIRABILITY
UNPROFESSIONAL
VERISIMILITUDE
ACHONDROPLASIA

COUNTERBALANCE
FORTUNETELLING
IRRECONCILABLE
KNIPPERDOLLING
PSYCHOANALYSIS
PURPOSEFULNESS
SCHOOLCHILDREN
THOUGHTFULNESS
UNCONTROLLABLE
UNDERDEVELOPED
UNSKILLFULNESS
APPROVECOMMENT
CRYSTALLOMANCY
EMBELLISHMENTS
HIEROSOLYMITAN
INTERFEROMETER
PARALEIPOMENON
PRONUNCIAMENTO
CHINCHERINCHEE
CIRCUMSTANTIAL
COMMISSIONAIRE
CONSTANTINOPLE
CONVENTIONALLY
DISCOUNTENANCE
EXPRESSIONLESS
IMPRESSIONABLE
INDETERMINABLE
INTELLIGENTSIA
LONGITUDINALLY
NIBELUNGENLIED
PROFESSIONALLY
PROPORTIONALLY
QUINTESSENTIAL
SELFGOVERNMENT
SUPERINTENDENT
UNCONSCIONABLE
UNQUESTIONABLE
UNQUESTIONABLY
ALLOIOSTROPHUS
ANTHROPOLOGIST
ANTILYMPHOCYTE
ASTROGEOLOGIST
BACTERIOLOGIST
CONSPIRATORIAL
DISCOURTEOUSLY
INTERNATIONALE
MACROECONOMICS
METAMORPHOSING
OSTENTATIOUSLY
PARAPSYCHOLOGY
PARSIMONIOUSLY
PHARMACOLOGIST
PHILANTHROPIST
PRESUMPTUOUSLY
PROHIBITIONIST
SATISFACTORILY
SIMULTANEOUSLY
STAPHYLOCOCCUS
STRAIGHTFOWARD
SUBCONSCIOUSLY

SUPERCILIOUSLY
TROUBLESHOOTER
ENCEPHALOPATHY
RADIOTELEPHONE
SHRINKWRAPPING
SUPERPHOSPHATE
SUPERSCRIPTION
THREEHALFPENCE
CINEMATOGRAPHY
CROSSREFERENCE
INCONSIDERABLE
INDECIPHERABLE
MALAPPROPRIATE
MISAPPROPRIATE
OSTEOARTHRITIS
OVERSUBSCRIBED
SUPERNATURALLY
TELETYPEWRITER
UNCORROBORATED
ABSTEMIOUSNESS
ANTIDEPRESSANT
AUTOSUGGESTION
BOISTEROUSNESS
BREATHLESSNESS
CAPRICIOUSNESS
CIRCUMSCISSILE
COMPREHENSIBLE
DISTINGUISHING
FASTIDIOUSNESS
LASCIVIOUSNESS
LICENTIOUSNESS
LOQUACIOUSNESS
METICULOUSNESS
OBSEQUIOUSNESS
PHOSPHORESCENT
PRECOCIOUSNESS
RECONNAISSANCE
RIDICULOUSNESS
SCRUPULOUSNESS
SCURRILOUSNESS
SELFASSESSMENT
WEIGHTLESSNESS
COINCIDENTALLY
CONTROVERTIBLE
DESISTABSTRACT
DISAPPOINTMENT
DISCONTENTMENT
DISENCHANTMENT
ECCLESIASTICAL
EXPERIMENTALLY
HALLUCINATIONS
INDESTRUCTIBLE
INSURMOUNTABLE
PEREGRINATIONS
PHARMACEUTICAL
QUALIFICATIONS
SANSCULOTTERIE
SCHOOLMISTRESS
TRICHOPHYTOSIS
UNATTRIBUTABLE

UNPLEASANTNESS
UNPREMEDITATED
WHOLEHEARTEDLY
CIRCUMLOCUTION
DISCOMBOBULATE
GRANDILOQUENCE
HORTICULTURIST
INTELLECTUALLY
RECONSTITUTION
TINTINNABULATE
CONJUNCTIVITIS
CZECHOSLOVAKIA
ESTABLISHVERSE
AIRCRAFTSWOMAN
BATTERYPOWERED
CREEPYCRAWLIES
UNRECOGNIZABLE

14:11

ACHONDROPLASIA
ALPHABETICALLY
ANTHROPOPHAGUS
APOLOGETICALLY
ASTRONOMICALLY
AUTOCRATICALLY
CINEMATOGRAPHY
COINCIDENTALLY
COMMISSIONAIRE
CONFIDENTIALLY
CONVENTIONALLY
COUNTERBALANCE
CRYSTALLOMANCY
CZECHOSLOVAKIA
DEMOCRATICALLY
DIPLOMATICALLY
DISCOUNTENANCE
ELECTRONICALLY
ENCEPHALOPATHY
EXPERIMENTALLY
GEOGRAPHICALLY
HYPOTHETICALLY
IMPRESSIONABLE
INCONSIDERABLE
INDECIPHERABLE
INDETERMINABLE
INSIGNIFICANCE
INSURMOUNTABLE
INTELLECTUALLY
IRRECONCILABLE
IRREPROACHABLE
LONGITUDINALLY
MATHEMATICALLY
METAPHORICALLY
ONCHOCERCIASIS
OPTIMISTICALLY
PHLEGMATICALLY
PROFESSIONALLY
PROPORTIONALLY
PROVIDENTIALLY
RECONNAISSANCE
SCIENTIFICALLY
SUPERABUNDANCE
SUPERNATURALLY
SYSTEMATICALLY
UNAPPROACHABLE
UNATTRIBUTABLE
UNCONSCIONABLE
UNCONTROLLABLE
UNCORROBORATED
UNDERSTANDABLE
UNDERSTANDABLY
UNPREMEDITATED
UNQUESTIONABLE
UNQUESTIONABLY
UNRECOGNIZABLE
INEXPRESSIBLES
UNMENTIONABLES
ANTILYMPHOCYTE
CHINCHERINCHEE
INTERCONNECTED
PHOSPHORESCENT
STAPHYLOCOCCUS
SCHOOLCHILDREN
SUPERINTENDENT
ULTRACREPIDATE
ANTIMETATHESIS
BATTERYPOWERED
CORRESPONDENCE
CROSSREFERENCE
CRYPTAESTHETIC
EMBELLISHMENTS
ESTABLISHVERSE
GRANDILOQUENCE
HALLUCINOGENIC
INTERFEROMETER
KNOTENSCHIEFER
MEPHISTOPHELES
PARALEIPOMENON
PHOTOSYNTHESIS
PRONUNCIAMENTO
SANSCULOTTERIE
SELFCONFIDENCE
SINGLEMINDEDLY
THREEHALFPENCE
WHOLEHEARTEDLY
ANTHROPOLOGIST
ASTROGEOLOGIST
BACTERIOLOGIST
BROBDINGNAGIAN
CIRCUMNAVIGATE
PHARMACOLOGIST
ANTIMONARCHIST
DISENFRANCHISE
DISTINGUISHING
HEARTSEARCHING
RADIOTELEPHONE
SUPERPHOSPHATE
ARCHAEOLOGICAL
COMPREHENSIBLE
CONJUNCTIVITIS
CONTROVERTIBLE
DERMATOLOGICAL
ECCLESIASTICAL
GYNAECOLOGICAL
HALLUCINATIONS
HIEROSOLYMITAN
INDESTRUCTIBLE
MALAPPROPRIATE
METEOROLOGICAL
MISAPPROPRIATE
ORNITHOLOGICAL
ORTHOGRAPHICAL
OSTEOARTHRITIS
OVERSUBSCRIBED
PEREGRINATIONS
PHARMACEUTICAL
QUALIFICATIONS
SCATTERBRAINED
SELFSUFFICIENT
TELETYPEWRITER
TERMINOLOGICAL
UNINTELLIGIBLE
DECISIONMAKING
KNICKERBOCKERS
NETHERSTOCKING
RECORDBREAKING
ACCOUNTABILITY
ANTIODONTALGIC
ARCHGENETHLIAC
CONVERTIBILITY
CORRUPTIBILITY
CREEPYCRAWLIES
DISCOMBOBULATE
EDUCATIONALIST
EXISTENTIALISM
EXISTENTIALIST
EXPRESSIONLESS
FORTUNETELLING
FUNDAMENTALISM
FUNDAMENTALIST
IMPERMEABILITY
IMPREGNABILITY
KNIPPERDOLLING
NIBELUNGENLIED
PARAPSYCHOLOGY
PRACTICABILITY
RESPECTABILITY
RESPONSIBILITY
SENTIMENTALITY
SESQUIPEDALIAN
SESQUIPEDALION
SUPERFICIALITY
SUSCEPTIBILITY
TATTERDEMALION
TINTINNABULATE
TRADITIONALIST
UNDESIRABILITY
ACCOMPLISHMENT
ACKNOWLEDGMENT
AGGRANDISEMENT
APPROVECOMMENT
ARRONDISSEMENT
DISAPPOINTMENT
DISCONTENTMENT
DISCOURAGEMENT
DISENCHANTMENT
DIVERTISSEMENT
IMPOVERISHMENT
MACROECONOMICS
RELINQUISHMENT
SELFASSESSMENT
SELFGOVERNMENT
SULPHANILAMIDE
THERMODYNAMICS
UNDERSTATEMENT
ABSTEMIOUSNESS
AGGRESSIVENESS
BOISTEROUSNESS
BREATHLESSNESS
CAPRICIOUSNESS
DISAPPROVINGLY
EGALITARIANISM
FASTIDIOUSNESS
INCONVENIENTLY
INDISCRIMINATE
INSUFFICIENTLY
INTERMITTENTLY
INTERNATIONALE
LASCIVIOUSNESS
LICENTIOUSNESS
LOQUACIOUSNESS
METICULOUSNESS
OBSEQUIOUSNESS
OPPRESSIVENESS
PERCEPTIVENESS
PERMISSIVENESS
PERSUASIVENESS
PORPHYROGENITE
PRECOCIOUSNESS
PRODUCTIVENESS
PROHIBITIONIST
PURPOSEFULNESS
RESPONSIVENESS
RIDICULOUSNESS
ROADWORTHINESS
SCRUPULOUSNESS
SCURRILOUSNESS
SUBMISSIVENESS
THOUGHTFULNESS
TRANSCENDENTAL
UNPLEASANTNESS
UNPREPAREDNESS
UNSKILLFULNESS
VINDICTIVENESS
WEIGHTLESSNESS
AFOREMENTIONED
AIRCONDITIONED
AIRCONDITIONER

AIRCRAFTSWOMAN
CLAUSTROPHOBIA
CLAUSTROPHOBIC
CONSTANTINOPLE
CONSTITUTIONAL
CONVERSATIONAL
DENOMINATIONAL
METEMPSYCHOSIS
ORGANIZATIONAL
PHANTASMAGORIA
SLAUGHTERHOUSE
TRICHOPHYTOSIS
TROUBLESHOOTER
UNCONVENTIONAL
UNDERDEVELOPED
UNDERMENTIONED
UNPROFESSIONAL
ALLOIOSTROPHUS
PHILANTHROPIST
SHRINKWRAPPING
STEGANOGRAPHIC
WHIPPERSNAPPER
ANTIPERSPIRANT
BALUCHITHERIUM
BIOENGINEERING
CONSPIRATORIAL
DESISTABSTRACT
DISCIPLINARIAN
DISCOMBOBERATE
ELECTIONEERING
HORTICULTURIST
INFRALAPSARIAN
JOHANNISBERGER
MOUNTAINEERING
NITROGLYCERINE
SATISFACTORILY
SCAREMONGERING
SCHOOLMISTRESS
SEPTUAGENARIAN
SEXCENTENARIAN
VALETUDINARIAN
ANTIDEPRESSANT
APPRENTICESHIP
CHARACTERISTIC
CIRCUMSCISSILE
COUNTERMEASURE
METAMORPHOSING
MICROPROCESSOR
SINGLEBREASTED
UNCOMPROMISING
UNDERNOURISHED
UNENTHUSIASTIC
ADMINISTRATION
ADMINISTRATIVE
AFFECTIONATELY
AUTHENTICATION
AUTOSUGGESTION
CAPITALIZATION
CASTRAMETATION
CENTRALIZATION

CIRCUMLOCUTION
CIRCUMSTANTIAL
CLASSIFICATION
CONGLOMERATION
CONGRATULATION
CONGRATULATORY
CONTESSERATION
DEMOBILIZATION
DEMORALIZATION
DISAPPROBATION
DISCOLOURATION
DISCONSOLATELY
DISCRIMINATING
DISCRIMINATION
DISCRIMINATORY
DISEMBARKATION
DISINCLINATION
DISINFORMATION
DISINTEGRATION
DISORIENTATION
FRATERNIZATION
FRUCTIFICATION
GENERALIZATION
GENTRIFICATION
HOMOGENIZATION
HYPERSENSITIVE
IDENTIFICATION
ILLEGITIMATELY
IMMOBILIZATION
IMPLEMENTATION
INDOCTRINATION
INFRASTRUCTURE
INTELLIGENTSIA
INTERPELLATION
INTERPLANETARY
INTERPRETATION
INTERPRETATIVE
LIBERALIZATION
LIGHTSENSITIVE
MISAPPLICATION
MISCALCULATION
MONOPOLIZATION
MULTIPLICATION
NATURALIZATION
NEUTRALIZATION
OVERPRODUCTION
PASTEURIZATION
PHENOBARBITONE
POLYMERIZATION
POPULARIZATION
PREDESTINATION
PREDISPOSITION
PREFABRICATION
PRESSURIZATION
PRESUPPOSITION
QUINTESSENTIAL
RECAPITULATION
RECOMMENDATION
RECONCILIATION
RECONSTITUTION

RECONSTRUCTION
REGULARIZATION
REHABILITATION
REORGANIZATION
REPRESENTATION
REPRESENTATIVE
SANCTIFICATION
SELFRESPECTING
SIMPLIFICATION
SOLIDIFICATION
SOPHISTICATION
SPECIALIZATION
STRATIFICATION
STULTIFICATION
SUBSTANTIATION
SUPERANNUATION
SUPEREROGATION
SUPERSCRIPTION
SUPERSTRUCTURE
TRANSFORMATION
TRANSMIGRATION
TRANSPORTATION
UNDERSECRETARY
UNSATISFACTORY
VERISIMILITUDE
WESTERNIZATION
CARDIOVASCULAR
DISCOURTEOUSLY
OSTENTATIOUSLY
PARSIMONIOUSLY
POSSESSINHUMAN
PRESUMPTUOUSLY
SIMULTANEOUSLY
SUBCONSCIOUSLY
SUPERCILIOUSLY
APPREHENSIVELY
CONSERVATIVELY
CONSTRUCTIVELY
CONSTRUCTIVISM
INCONCLUSIVELY
STRAIGHTFOWARD
PSYCHOANALYSIS
NEBUCHADNEZZAR

14:12

ANTIDEPRESSANT
ANTIPERSPIRANT
CIRCUMNAVIGATE
DESISTABSTRACT
DISCOMBOBERATE
DISCOMBOBULATE
INDISCRIMINATE
INTERNATIONALE
INTERPLANETARY
MALAPPROPRIATE
MISAPPROPRIATE
STRAIGHTFOWARD
SUPERPHOSPHATE

TINTINNABULATE
ULTRACREPIDATE
UNDERSECRETARY
CLAUSTROPHOBIA
CLAUSTROPHOBIC
COMPREHENSIBLE
CONTROVERTIBLE
IMPRESSIONABLE
INCONSIDERABLE
INDECIPHERABLE
INDESTRUCTIBLE
INDETERMINABLE
INSURMOUNTABLE
IRRECONCILABLE
IRREPROACHABLE
OVERSUBSCRIBED
UNAPPROACHABLE
UNATTRIBUTABLE
UNCONSCIONABLE
UNCONTROLLABLE
UNDERSTANDABLE
UNDERSTANDABLY
UNINTELLIGIBLE
UNQUESTIONABLE
UNQUESTIONABLY
UNRECOGNIZABLE
ARCHAEOLOGICAL
DERMATOLOGICAL
ECCLESIASTICAL
GYNAECOLOGICAL
METEOROLOGICAL
ORNITHOLOGICAL
ORTHOGRAPHICAL
PHARMACEUTICAL
STAPHYLOCOCCUS
TERMINOLOGICAL
SINGLEMINDEDLY
WHOLEHEARTEDLY
ABSTEMIOUSNESS
ACCOMPLISHMENT
ACKNOWLEDGMENT
AFFECTIONATELY
AGGRANDISEMENT
AGGRESSIVENESS
APPREHENSIVELY
APPROVECOMMENT
ARRONDISSEMENT
BOISTEROUSNESS
BREATHLESSNESS
CAPRICIOUSNESS
CONSERVATIVELY
CONSTRUCTIVELY
DISAPPOINTMENT
DISCONSOLATELY
DISCONTENTMENT
DISCOURAGEMENT
DISENCHANTMENT
DIVERTISSEMENT
EXPRESSIONLESS
FASTIDIOUSNESS

ILLEGITIMATELY
IMPOVERISHMENT
INCONCLUSIVELY
KNICKERBOCKERS
LASCIVIOUSNESS
LICENTIOUSNESS
LOQUACIOUSNESS
METICULOUSNESS
OBSEQUIOUSNESS
OPPRESSIVENESS
PERCEPTIVENESS
PERMISSIVENESS
PERSUASIVENESS
PHOSPHORESCENT
PRECOCIOUSNESS
PRODUCTIVENESS
PURPOSEFULNESS
RELINQUISHMENT
RESPONSIVENESS
RIDICULOUSNESS
ROADWORTHINESS
SCHOOLMISTRESS
SCRUPULOUSNESS
SCURRILOUSNESS
SELFASSESSMENT
SELFGOVERNMENT
SELFSUFFICIENT
SUBMISSIVENESS
SUPERINTENDENT
THOUGHTFULNESS
UNDERSTATEMENT
UNPLEASANTNESS
UNPREPAREDNESS
UNSKILLFULNESS
VINDICTIVENESS
WEIGHTLESSNESS
KNOTENSCHIEFER
ANTHROPOPHAGUS
ANTIODONTALGIC
DISAPPROVINGLY
JOHANNISBERGER
ALLOIOSTROPHUS
APPRENTICESHIP
CHINCHERINCHEE
STEGANOGRAPHIC
UNDERNOURISHED
ACCOUNTABILITY
ADMINISTRATION
ADMINISTRATIVE
ANTHROPOLOGIST
ANTIMONARCHIST
ARCHGENETHLIAC
ASTROGEOLOGIST
AUTHENTICATION
AUTOSUGGESTION
BACTERIOLOGIST
BALUCHITHERIUM
BIOENGINEERING
BROBDINGNAGIAN
CAPITALIZATION
CASTRAMETATION
CENTRALIZATION
CIRCUMLOCUTION
CIRCUMSCISSILE
CIRCUMSTANTIAL
CLASSIFICATION
COMMISSIONAIRE
CONGLOMERATION
CONGRATULATION
CONSPIRATORIAL
CONSTRUCTIVISM
CONTESSERATION
CONVERTIBILITY
CORRUPTIBILITY
CREEPYCRAWLIES
DECISIONMAKING
DEMOBILIZATION
DEMORALIZATION
DISAPPROBATION
DISCIPLINARIAN
DISCOLOURATION
DISCRIMINATING
DISCRIMINATION
DISEMBARKATION
DISENFRANCHISE
DISINCLINATION
DISINFORMATION
DISINTEGRATION
DISORIENTATION
DISTINGUISHING
EDUCATIONALIST
EGALITARIANISM
ELECTIONEERING
EXISTENTIALISM
EXISTENTIALIST
FORTUNETELLING
FRATERNIZATION
FRUCTIFICATION
FUNDAMENTALISM
FUNDAMENTALIST
GENERALIZATION
GENTRIFICATION
HEARTSEARCHING
HOMOGENIZATION
HORTICULTURIST
HYPERSENSITIVE
IDENTIFICATION
IMMOBILIZATION
IMPERMEABILITY
IMPLEMENTATION
IMPREGNABILITY
INDOCTRINATION
INFRALAPSARIAN
INTERPELLATION
INTERPRETATION
INTERPRETATIVE
KNIPPERDOLLING
LIBERALIZATION
LIGHTSENSITIVE
MACROECONOMICS
METAMORPHOSING
MISAPPLICATION
MISCALCULATION
MONOPOLIZATION
MOUNTAINEERING
MULTIPLICATION
NATURALIZATION
NETHERSTOCKING
NEUTRALIZATION
NIBELUNGENLIED
NITROGLYCERINE
OVERPRODUCTION
PASTEURIZATION
PHARMACOLOGIST
PHILANTHROPIST
POLYMERIZATION
POPULARIZATION
PORPHYROGENITE
PRACTICABILITY
PREDESTINATION
PREDISPOSITION
PREFABRICATION
PRESSURIZATION
PRESUPPOSITION
PROHIBITIONIST
QUINTESSENTIAL
RECAPITULATION
RECOMMENDATION
RECONCILIATION
RECONSTITUTION
RECONSTRUCTION
RECORDBREAKING
REGULARIZATION
REHABILITATION
REORGANIZATION
REPRESENTATION
REPRESENTATIVE
RESPECTABILITY
RESPONSIBILITY
SANCTIFICATION
SATISFACTORILY
SCAREMONGERING
SELFRESPECTING
SENTIMENTALITY
SEPTUAGENARIAN
SESQUIPEDALIAN
SESQUIPEDALION
SEXCENTENARIAN
SHRINKWRAPPING
SIMPLIFICATION
SOLIDIFICATION
SOPHISTICATION
SPECIALIZATION
STRATIFICATION
STULTIFICATION
SUBSTANTIATION
SULPHANILAMIDE
SUPERANNUATION
SUPEREROGATION
SUPERFICIALITY
SUPERSCRIPTION
SUSCEPTIBILITY
TATTERDEMALION
THERMODYNAMICS
TRADITIONALIST
TRANSFORMATION
TRANSMIGRATION
TRANSPORTATION
UNCOMPROMISING
UNDESIRABILITY
VALETUDINARIAN
WESTERNIZATION
CZECHOSLOVAKIA
ALPHABETICALLY
APOLOGETICALLY
ASTRONOMICALLY
AUTOCRATICALLY
CARDIOVASCULAR
COINCIDENTALLY
CONFIDENTIALLY
CONVENTIONALLY
DEMOCRATICALLY
DIPLOMATICALLY
ELECTRONICALLY
EXPERIMENTALLY
GEOGRAPHICALLY
HYPOTHETICALLY
INEXPRESSIBLES
INTELLECTUALLY
LONGITUDINALLY
MATHEMATICALLY
MEPHISTOPHELES
METAPHORICALLY
OPTIMISTICALLY
PHLEGMATICALLY
PROFESSIONALLY
PROPORTIONALLY
PROVIDENTIALLY
SCIENTIFICALLY
SUPERNATURALLY
SYSTEMATICALLY
UNMENTIONABLES
AIRCRAFTSWOMAN
POSSESSINHUMAN
AFOREMENTIONED
AIRCONDITIONED
AIRCONDITIONER
CONSTITUTIONAL
CONVERSATIONAL
CORRESPONDENCE
COUNTERBALANCE
CROSSREFERENCE
CRYSTALLOMANCY
DENOMINATIONAL
DISCOUNTENANCE
EMBELLISHMENTS
GRANDILOQUENCE
HALLUCINOGENIC
INSIGNIFICANCE
ORGANIZATIONAL

PARALEIPOMENON
PRONUNCIAMENTO
RECONNAISSANCE
SCATTERBRAINED
SELFCONFIDENCE
SUPERABUNDANCE
THREEHALFPENCE
UNCONVENTIONAL
UNDERMENTIONED
UNPROFESSIONAL
CONGRATULATORY
DISCRIMINATORY
HALLUCINATIONS
PARAPSYCHOLOGY
PEREGRINATIONS
PHENOBARBITONE
QUALIFICATIONS
RADIOTELEPHONE
UNSATISFACTORY
CINEMATOGRAPHY
CONSTANTINOPLE
UNDERDEVELOPED
WHIPPERSNAPPER
BATTERYPOWERED
ESTABLISHVERSE
PHANTASMAGORIA
SANSCULOTTERIE
SCHOOLCHILDREN
ACHONDROPLASIA
ANTIMETATHESIS
DISCOURTEOUSLY
INTELLIGENTSIA
METEMPSYCHOSIS
MICROPROCESSOR
ONCHOCERCIASIS
OSTENTATIOUSLY
PARSIMONIOUSLY
PHOTOSYNTHESIS
PRESUMPTUOUSLY
PSYCHOANALYSIS
SIMULTANEOUSLY
SUBCONSCIOUSLY
SUPERCILIOUSLY
TRICHOPHYTOSIS
CHARACTERISTIC
CONJUNCTIVITIS
CRYPTAESTHETIC
ENCEPHALOPATHY
HIEROSOLYMITAN
INCONVENIENTLY
INSUFFICIENTLY
INTERCONNECTED
INTERFEROMETER
INTERMITTENTLY
OSTEOARTHRITIS
SINGLEBREASTED
TELETYPEWRITER
TRANSCENDENTAL
TROUBLESHOOTER
UNCORROBORATED

UNENTHUSIASTIC
UNPREMEDITATED
COUNTERMEASURE
INFRASTRUCTURE
SLAUGHTERHOUSE
SUPERSTRUCTURE
VERISIMILITUDE
ANTILYMPHOCYTE
NEBUCHADNEZZAR

14:13

AIRCRAFTSWOMAN
ARCHAEOLOGICAL
ARCHGENETHLIAC
BROBDINGNAGIAN
CARDIOVASCULAR
CIRCUMSTANTIAL
CONSPIRATORIAL
CONSTITUTIONAL
CONVERSATIONAL
DENOMINATIONAL
DERMATOLOGICAL
DISCIPLINARIAN
ECCLESIASTICAL
GYNAECOLOGICAL
HIEROSOLYMITAN
INFRALAPSARIAN
METEOROLOGICAL
NEBUCHADNEZZAR
ORGANIZATIONAL
ORNITHOLOGICAL
ORTHOGRAPHICAL
PHARMACEUTICAL
POSSESSINHUMAN
QUINTESSENTIAL
SEPTUAGENARIAN
SESQUIPEDALIAN
SEXCENTENARIAN
TERMINOLOGICAL
TRANSCENDENTAL
UNCONVENTIONAL
UNPROFESSIONAL
VALETUDINARIAN
CORRESPONDENCE
COUNTERBALANCE
CROSSREFERENCE
CRYSTALLOMANCY
DESISTABSTRACT
DISCOUNTENANCE
GRANDILOQUENCE
INSIGNIFICANCE
MACROECONOMICS
RECONNAISSANCE
SELFCONFIDENCE
SUPERABUNDANCE
THERMODYNAMICS
THREEHALFPENCE
SULPHANILAMIDE

VERISIMILITUDE
AFOREMENTIONED
AIRCONDITIONED
AIRCONDITIONER
BATTERYPOWERED
CHINCHERINCHEE
CREEPYCRAWLIES
INEXPRESSIBLES
INTERCONNECTED
INTERFEROMETER
JOHANNISBERGER
KNOTENSCHIEFER
MEPHISTOPHELES
NIBELUNGENLIED
OVERSUBSCRIBED
SCATTERBRAINED
SCHOOLCHILDREN
SINGLEBREASTED
TELETYPEWRITER
TROUBLESHOOTER
UNCORROBORATED
UNDERDEVELOPED
UNDERMENTIONED
UNDERNOURISHED
UNMENTIONABLES
UNPREMEDITATED
WHIPPERSNAPPER
PARAPSYCHOLOGY
CINEMATOGRAPHY
ENCEPHALOPATHY
ACHONDROPLASIA
ANTIMETATHESIS
ANTIODONTALGIC
APPRENTICESHIP
CHARACTERISTIC
CLAUSTROPHOBIA
CLAUSTROPHOBIC
CONJUNCTIVITIS
CRYPTAESTHETIC
CZECHOSLOVAKIA
HALLUCINOGENIC
INTELLIGENTSIA
METEMPSYCHOSIS
ONCHOCERCIASIS
OSTEOARTHRITIS
PHANTASMAGORIA
PHOTOSYNTHESIS
PSYCHOANALYSIS
SANSCULOTTERIE
STEGANOGRAPHIC
TRICHOPHYTOSIS
UNENTHUSIASTIC
AFFECTIONATELY
ALPHABETICALLY
APOLOGETICALLY
APPREHENSIVELY
ASTRONOMICALLY
AUTOCRATICALLY
CIRCUMSCISSILE
COINCIDENTALLY

COMPREHENSIBLE
CONFIDENTIALLY
CONSERVATIVELY
CONSTANTINOPLE
CONSTRUCTIVELY
CONTROVERTIBLE
CONVENTIONALLY
DEMOCRATICALLY
DIPLOMATICALLY
DISAPPROVINGLY
DISCONSOLATELY
DISCOURTEOUSLY
ELECTRONICALLY
EXPERIMENTALLY
GEOGRAPHICALLY
HYPOTHETICALLY
ILLEGITIMATELY
IMPRESSIONABLE
INCONCLUSIVELY
INCONSIDERABLE
INCONVENIENTLY
INDECIPHERABLE
INDESTRUCTIBLE
INDETERMINABLE
INSUFFICIENTLY
INSURMOUNTABLE
INTELLECTUALLY
INTERMITTENTLY
INTERNATIONALE
IRRECONCILABLE
IRREPROACHABLE
LONGITUDINALLY
MATHEMATICALLY
METAPHORICALLY
OPTIMISTICALLY
OSTENTATIOUSLY
PARSIMONIOUSLY
PHLEGMATICALLY
PRESUMPTUOUSLY
PROFESSIONALLY
PROPORTIONALLY
PROVIDENTIALLY
SATISFACTORILY
SCIENTIFICALLY
SIMULTANEOUSLY
SINGLEMINDEDLY
SUBCONSCIOUSLY
SUPERCILIOUSLY
SUPERNATURALLY
SYSTEMATICALLY
UNAPPROACHABLE
UNATTRIBUTABLE
UNCONSCIONABLE
UNCONTROLLABLE
UNDERSTANDABLE
UNDERSTANDABLY
UNINTELLIGIBLE
UNQUESTIONABLE
UNQUESTIONABLY
UNRECOGNIZABLE

WHOLEHEARTEDLY
ACCOMPLISHMENT
ACKNOWLEDGMENT
AGGRANDISEMENT
ANTIDEPRESSANT
ANTIPERSPIRANT
APPROVECOMMENT
ARRONDISSEMENT
BIOENGINEERING
DECISIONMAKING
DISAPPOINTMENT
DISCONTENTMENT
DISCOURAGEMENT
DISCRIMINATING
DISENCHANTMENT
DISTINGUISHING
DIVERTISSEMENT
ELECTIONEERING
FORTUNETELLING
HALLUCINATIONS
HEARTSEARCHING
IMPOVERISHMENT
KNIPPERDOLLING
METAMORPHOSING
MOUNTAINEERING
NETHERSTOCKING
NITROGLYCERINE
PEREGRINATIONS
PHENOBARBITONE
PHOSPHORESCENT
QUALIFICATIONS
RADIOTELEPHONE
RECORDBREAKING
RELINQUISHMENT
SCAREMONGERING
SELFASSESSMENT
SELFGOVERNMENT
SELFRESPECTING
SELFSUFFICIENT
SHRINKWRAPPING
SUPERINTENDENT
UNCOMPROMISING
UNDERSTATEMENT
ADMINISTRATION
AUTHENTICATION
AUTOSUGGESTION
CAPITALIZATION
CASTRAMETATION
CENTRALIZATION
CIRCUMLOCUTION
CLASSIFICATION
CONGLOMERATION
CONGRATULATION
CONTESSERATION
DEMOBILIZATION
DEMORALIZATION
DISAPPROBATION
DISCOLOURATION
DISCRIMINATION
DISEMBARKATION
DISINCLINATION
DISINFORMATION
DISINTEGRATION
DISORIENTATION
FRATERNIZATION
FRUCTIFICATION
GENERALIZATION
GENTRIFICATION
HOMOGENIZATION
IDENTIFICATION
IMMOBILIZATION
IMPLEMENTATION
INDOCTRINATION
INTERPELLATION
INTERPRETATION
LIBERALIZATION
MICROPROCESSOR
MISAPPLICATION
MISCALCULATION
MONOPOLIZATION
MULTIPLICATION
NATURALIZATION
NEUTRALIZATION
OVERPRODUCTION
PARALEIPOMENON
PASTEURIZATION
POLYMERIZATION
POPULARIZATION
PREDESTINATION
PREDISPOSITION
PREFABRICATION
PRESSURIZATION
PRESUPPOSITION
RECAPITULATION
RECOMMENDATION
RECONCILIATION
RECONSTITUTION
RECONSTRUCTION
REGULARIZATION
REHABILITATION
REORGANIZATION
REPRESENTATION
SANCTIFICATION
SESQUIPEDALION
SIMPLIFICATION
SOLIDIFICATION
SOPHISTICATION
SPECIALIZATION
STRATIFICATION
STULTIFICATION
SUBSTANTIATION
SUPERANNUATION
SUPEREROGATION
SUPERSCRIPTION
TATTERDEMALION
TRANSFORMATION
TRANSMIGRATION
TRANSPORTATION
WESTERNIZATION
COMMISSIONAIRE
CONGRATULATORY
COUNTERMEASURE
DISCRIMINATORY
INFRASTRUCTURE
INTERPLANETARY
KNICKERBOCKERS
STRAIGHTFOWARD
SUPERSTRUCTURE
UNDERSECRETARY
UNSATISFACTORY
ABSTEMIOUSNESS
AGGRESSIVENESS
ANTHROPOLOGIST
ANTIMONARCHIST
ASTROGEOLOGIST
BACTERIOLOGIST
BOISTEROUSNESS
BREATHLESSNESS
CAPRICIOUSNESS
CONSTRUCTIVISM
DISENFRANCHISE
EDUCATIONALIST
EGALITARIANISM
ESTABLISHVERSE
EXISTENTIALISM
EXISTENTIALIST
EXPRESSIONLESS
FASTIDIOUSNESS
FUNDAMENTALISM
FUNDAMENTALIST
HORTICULTURIST
LASCIVIOUSNESS
LICENTIOUSNESS
LOQUACIOUSNESS
METICULOUSNESS
OBSEQUIOUSNESS
OPPRESSIVENESS
PERCEPTIVENESS
PERMISSIVENESS
PERSUASIVENESS
PHARMACOLOGIST
PHILANTHROPIST
PRECOCIOUSNESS
PRODUCTIVENESS
PROHIBITIONIST
PURPOSEFULNESS
RESPONSIVENESS
RIDICULOUSNESS
ROADWORTHINESS
SCHOOLMISTRESS
SCRUPULOUSNESS
SCURRILOUSNESS
SLAUGHTERHOUSE
SUBMISSIVENESS
THOUGHTFULNESS
TRADITIONALIST
UNPLEASANTNESS
UNPREPAREDNESS
UNSKILLFULNESS
VINDICTIVENESS
WEIGHTLESSNESS
ACCOUNTABILITY
ANTILYMPHOCYTE
CIRCUMNAVIGATE
CONVERTIBILITY
CORRUPTIBILITY
DISCOMBOBERATE
DISCOMBOBULATE
EMBELLISHMENTS
IMPERMEABILITY
IMPREGNABILITY
INDISCRIMINATE
MALAPPROPRIATE
MISAPPROPRIATE
PORPHYROGENITE
PRACTICABILITY
PRONUNCIAMENTO
RESPECTABILITY
RESPONSIBILITY
SENTIMENTALITY
SUPERFICIALITY
SUPERPHOSPHATE
SUSCEPTIBILITY
TINTINNABULATE
ULTRACREPIDATE
UNDESIRABILITY
ALLOIOSTROPHUS
ANTHROPOPHAGUS
BALUCHITHERIUM
STAPHYLOCOCCUS
ADMINISTRATIVE
HYPERSENSITIVE
INTERPRETATIVE
LIGHTSENSITIVE
REPRESENTATIVE

14:14

ACHONDROPLASIA
CLAUSTROPHOBIA
CZECHOSLOVAKIA
INTELLIGENTSIA
PHANTASMAGORIA
ANTIODONTALGIC
ARCHGENETHLIAC
CHARACTERISTIC
CLAUSTROPHOBIC
CRYPTAESTHETIC
HALLUCINOGENIC
STEGANOGRAPHIC
UNENTHUSIASTIC
AFOREMENTIONED
AIRCONDITIONED
BATTERYPOWERED
INTERCONNECTED
NIBELUNGENLIED
OVERSUBSCRIBED
SCATTERBRAINED
SINGLEBREASTED

STRAIGHTFOWARD
UNCORROBORATED
UNDERDEVELOPED
UNDERMENTIONED
UNDERNOURISHED
UNPREMEDITATED
ADMINISTRATIVE
ANTILYMPHOCYTE
CHINCHERINCHEE
CIRCUMNAVIGATE
CIRCUMSCISSILE
COMMISSIONAIRE
COMPREHENSIBLE
CONSTANTINOPLE
CONTROVERTIBLE
CORRESPONDENCE
COUNTERBALANCE
COUNTERMEASURE
CROSSREFERENCE
DISCOMBOBERATE
DISCOMBOBULATE
DISCOUNTENANCE
DISENFRANCHISE
ESTABLISHVERSE
GRANDILOQUENCE
HYPERSENSITIVE
IMPRESSIONABLE
INCONSIDERABLE
INDECIPHERABLE
INDESTRUCTIBLE
INDETERMINABLE
INDISCRIMINATE
INFRASTRUCTURE
INSIGNIFICANCE
INSURMOUNTABLE
INTERNATIONALE
INTERPRETATIVE
IRRECONCILABLE
IRREPROACHABLE
LIGHTSENSITIVE
MALAPPROPRIATE
MISAPPROPRIATE
NITROGLYCERINE
PHENOBARBITONE
PORPHYROGENITE
RADIOTELEPHONE
RECONNAISSANCE
REPRESENTATIVE
SANSCULOTTERIE
SELFCONFIDENCE
SLAUGHTERHOUSE
SULPHANILAMIDE
SUPERABUNDANCE
SUPERPHOSPHATE
SUPERSTRUCTURE
THREEHALFPENCE
TINTINNABULATE
ULTRACREPIDATE
UNAPPROACHABLE
UNATTRIBUTABLE

UNCONSCIONABLE
UNCONTROLLABLE
UNDERSTANDABLE
UNINTELLIGIBLE
UNQUESTIONABLE
UNRECOGNIZABLE
VERISIMILITUDE
BIOENGINEERING
DECISIONMAKING
DISCRIMINATING
DISTINGUISHING
ELECTIONEERING
FORTUNETELLING
HEARTSEARCHING
KNIPPERDOLLING
METAMORPHOSING
MOUNTAINEERING
NETHERSTOCKING
RECORDBREAKING
SCAREMONGERING
SELFRESPECTING
SHRINKWRAPPING
UNCOMPROMISING
ARCHAEOLOGICAL
CIRCUMSTANTIAL
CONSPIRATORIAL
CONSTITUTIONAL
CONVERSATIONAL
DENOMINATIONAL
DERMATOLOGICAL
ECCLESIASTICAL
GYNAECOLOGICAL
METEOROLOGICAL
ORGANIZATIONAL
ORNITHOLOGICAL
ORTHOGRAPHICAL
PHARMACEUTICAL
QUINTESSENTIAL
TERMINOLOGICAL
TRANSCENDENTAL
UNCONVENTIONAL
UNPROFESSIONAL
BALUCHITHERIUM
CONSTRUCTIVISM
EGALITARIANISM
EXISTENTIALISM
FUNDAMENTALISM
ADMINISTRATION
AIRCRAFTSWOMAN
AUTHENTICATION
AUTOSUGGESTION
BROBDINGNAGIAN
CAPITALIZATION
CASTRAMETATION
CENTRALIZATION
CIRCUMLOCUTION
CLASSIFICATION
CONGLOMERATION
CONGRATULATION
CONTESSERATION

DEMOBILIZATION
DEMORALIZATION
DISAPPROBATION
DISCIPLINARIAN
DISCOLOURATION
DISCRIMINATION
DISEMBARKATION
DISINCLINATION
DISINFORMATION
DISINTEGRATION
DISORIENTATION
FRATERNIZATION
FRUCTIFICATION
GENERALIZATION
GENTRIFICATION
HIEROSOLYMITAN
HOMOGENIZATION
IDENTIFICATION
IMMOBILIZATION
IMPLEMENTATION
INDOCTRINATION
INFRALAPSARIAN
INTERPELLATION
INTERPRETATION
LIBERALIZATION
MISAPPLICATION
MISCALCULATION
MONOPOLIZATION
MULTIPLICATION
NATURALIZATION
NEUTRALIZATION
OVERPRODUCTION
PARALEIPOMENON
PASTEURIZATION
POLYMERIZATION
POPULARIZATION
POSSESSINHUMAN
PREDESTINATION
PREDISPOSITION
PREFABRICATION
PRESSURIZATION
PRESUPPOSITION
RECAPITULATION
RECOMMENDATION
RECONCILIATION
RECONSTITUTION
RECONSTRUCTION
REGULARIZATION
REHABILITATION
REORGANIZATION
REPRESENTATION
SANCTIFICATION
SCHOOLCHILDREN
SEPTUAGENARIAN
SESQUIPEDALIAN
SESQUIPEDALION
SEXCENTENARIAN
SIMPLIFICATION
SOLIDIFICATION
SOPHISTICATION

SPECIALIZATION
STRATIFICATION
STULTIFICATION
SUBSTANTIATION
SUPERANNUATION
SUPEREROGATION
SUPERSCRIPTION
TATTERDEMALION
TRANSFORMATION
TRANSMIGRATION
TRANSPORTATION
VALETUDINARIAN
WESTERNIZATION
PRONUNCIAMENTO
APPRENTICESHIP
AIRCONDITIONER
CARDIOVASCULAR
INTERFEROMETER
JOHANNISBERGER
KNOTENSCHIEFER
MICROPROCESSOR
NEBUCHADNEZZAR
TELETYPEWRITER
TROUBLESHOOTER
WHIPPERSNAPPER
ABSTEMIOUSNESS
AGGRESSIVENESS
ALLOIOSTROPHUS
ANTHROPOPHAGUS
ANTIMETATHESIS
BOISTEROUSNESS
BREATHLESSNESS
CAPRICIOUSNESS
CONJUNCTIVITIS
CREEPYCRAWLIES
EMBELLISHMENTS
EXPRESSIONLESS
FASTIDIOUSNESS
HALLUCINATIONS
INEXPRESSIBLES
KNICKERBOCKERS
LASCIVIOUSNESS
LICENTIOUSNESS
LOQUACIOUSNESS
MACROECONOMICS
MEPHISTOPHELES
METEMPSYCHOSIS
METICULOUSNESS
OBSEQUIOUSNESS
ONCHOCERCIASIS
OPPRESSIVENESS
OSTEOARTHRITIS
PERCEPTIVENESS
PEREGRINATIONS
PERMISSIVENESS
PERSUASIVENESS
PHOTOSYNTHESIS
PRECOCIOUSNESS
PRODUCTIVENESS
PSYCHOANALYSIS

PURPOSEFULNESS
QUALIFICATIONS
RESPONSIVENESS
RIDICULOUSNESS
ROADWORTHINESS
SCHOOLMISTRESS
SCRUPULOUSNESS
SCURRILOUSNESS
STAPHYLOCOCCUS
SUBMISSIVENESS
THERMODYNAMICS
THOUGHTFULNESS
TRICHOPHYTOSIS
UNMENTIONABLES
UNPLEASANTNESS
UNPREPAREDNESS
UNSKILLFULNESS
VINDICTIVENESS
WEIGHTLESSNESS
ACCOMPLISHMENT
ACKNOWLEDGMENT
AGGRANDISEMENT
ANTHROPOLOGIST
ANTIDEPRESSANT
ANTIMONARCHIST
ANTIPERSPIRANT
APPROVECOMMENT
ARRONDISSEMENT
ASTROGEOLOGIST
BACTERIOLOGIST
DESISTABSTRACT

DISAPPOINTMENT
DISCONTENTMENT
DISCOURAGEMENT
DISENCHANTMENT
DIVERTISSEMENT
EDUCATIONALIST
EXISTENTIALIST
FUNDAMENTALIST
HORTICULTURIST
IMPOVERISHMENT
PHARMACOLOGIST
PHILANTHROPIST
PHOSPHORESCENT
PROHIBITIONIST
RELINQUISHMENT
SELFASSESSMENT
SELFGOVERNMENT
SELFSUFFICIENT
SUPERINTENDENT
TRADITIONALIST
UNDERSTATEMENT
ACCOUNTABILITY
AFFECTIONATELY
ALPHABETICALLY
APOLOGETICALLY
APPREHENSIVELY
ASTRONOMICALLY
AUTOCRATICALLY
CINEMATOGRAPHY
COINCIDENTALLY
CONFIDENTIALLY

CONGRATULATORY
CONSERVATIVELY
CONSTRUCTIVELY
CONVENTIONALLY
CONVERTIBILITY
CORRUPTIBILITY
CRYSTALLOMANCY
DEMOCRATICALLY
DIPLOMATICALLY
DISAPPROVINGLY
DISCONSOLATELY
DISCOURTEOUSLY
DISCRIMINATORY
ELECTRONICALLY
ENCEPHALOPATHY
EXPERIMENTALLY
GEOGRAPHICALLY
HYPOTHETICALLY
ILLEGITIMATELY
IMPERMEABILITY
IMPREGNABILITY
INCONCLUSIVELY
INCONVENIENTLY
INSUFFICIENTLY
INTELLECTUALLY
INTERMITTENTLY
INTERPLANETARY
LONGITUDINALLY
MATHEMATICALLY
METAPHORICALLY
OPTIMISTICALLY

OSTENTATIOUSLY
PARAPSYCHOLOGY
PARSIMONIOUSLY
PHLEGMATICALLY
PRACTICABILITY
PRESUMPTUOUSLY
PROFESSIONALLY
PROPORTIONALLY
PROVIDENTIALLY
RESPECTABILITY
RESPONSIBILITY
SATISFACTORILY
SCIENTIFICALLY
SENTIMENTALITY
SIMULTANEOUSLY
SINGLEMINDEDLY
SUBCONSCIOUSLY
SUPERCILIOUSLY
SUPERFICIALITY
SUPERNATURALLY
SUSCEPTIBILITY
SYSTEMATICALLY
UNDERSECRETARY
UNDERSTANDABLY
UNDESIRABILITY
UNQUESTIONABLY
UNSATISFACTORY
WHOLEHEARTEDLY

15:1

ACCLIMATIZATION
ACKNOWLEDGEMENT
ACQUISITIVENESS
ADVENTUROUSNESS
AGRICULTURALIST
AIRCONDITIONING
ALLOTRIOMORPHIC
ANTHROPOLOGICAL
ANTHROPOMORPHIC
ATTORNEYGENERAL
AUTHORITATIVELY
BACKWARDLOOKING
BACTERIOLOGICAL
BATTERYOPERATED
BIBLIOGRAPHICAL
CHARACTERISTICS
CHRISTADELPHIAN
CHRONOLOGICALLY
CHURRIGUERESQUE
CINEMATOGRAPHIC
CIRCUMSCRIPTION
CIRCUMSTANTIATE
COINSTANTANEOUS
COMPASSIONATELY
COMPUTERIZATION
CONFIDENTIALITY
CONFRONTATIONAL
CONGRATULATIONS
CONSCIENTIOUSLY
CONSERVATIONIST
CONTEMPORANEOUS
CONTRAVALLATION
CORRESPONDINGLY
CRYSTALLIZATION
CRYSTALLOGRAPHY
DECONTAMINATION
DESERTIFICATION
DESTRUCTIVENESS
DIFFERENTIATION
DISADVANTAGEOUS
DISILLUSIONMENT
DISPASSIONATELY
DISSATISFACTION
DISTINGUISHABLE
DIVERSIFICATION
DRAUGHTSMANSHIP
ELECTRIFICATION
ELECTROMAGNETIC
ENTREPRENEURIAL
EUPHEMISTICALLY
EXCOMMUNICATION
EXPERIMENTATION
EXTRAORDINARILY
FAMILIARIZATION
FLIBBERTIGIBBET
GASTROENTERITIS
GLEICHSCHALTUNG
GOTTERDAMMERUNG
GOVERNORGENERAL
HOSPITALIZATION
ICHTHYODUROLITE
IMPENETRABILITY
IMPRESSIONISTIC
INCOMPATIBILITY
INCOMPHEHENSION
INCONSEQUENTIAL
INCONSIDERATELY
INCONSPICUOUSLY
INDEMNIFICATION
INDIVIDUALISTIC
INQUISITIVENESS
INSTANTANEOUSLY
INSTRUMENTALIST
INSTRUMENTATION
INSUBORDINATION
INTELLIGIBILITY
INTENSIFICATION
INTERCHANGEABLE
INTERNATIONALLY
INTERVENTIONIST
LEATHERSTOCKING
LIFETHREATENING
LONGSIGHTEDNESS
LOPHOBRANCHIATE
MALPRACTITIONER
MANOEUVRABILITY
MISAPPREHENSION
MISCHIEVOUSNESS
MISCONSTRUCTION
MISINTELLIGENCE
NATIONALIZATION
NONCOMMISSIONED
NONGOVERNMENTAL
NONPROFESSIONAL
NONPROFITMAKING
NOTHINGARIANISM
NOTWITHSTANDING
OMNIDIRECTIONAL
ONYCHOCRYPTOSIS
OPHTHALMOLOGIST
ORNITHORHYNCHUS
OVERSENTIMENTAL
PALAEONTOLOGIST
PARLIAMENTARIAN
PERPENDICULARLY
PERSONIFICATION
PESSIMISTICALLY
PHARMACOLOGICAL
PHILOSOPHICALLY
PHOSPHORESCENCE
PHYSIOTHERAPIST
PLENIPOTENTIARY
POLYUNSATURATED
PRESTIDIGITATOR
PRETENTIOUSNESS
PROCRASTINATING
PROCRASTINATION
PROFESSIONALISM
PROGNOSTICATION
PROPORTIONATELY
PROSELYTIZATION
PSYCHOLOGICALLY
PSYCHOTHERAPIST
PUNCTILIOUSNESS
RATIONALIZATION
REPRESENTATIVES
RESOURCEFULNESS
RHYNCHOBDELLIDA
RUMPELSTILTSKIN
SACRAMENTMYSTIC
SANCTIMONIOUSLY
SCAPHOCEPHALATE
SCHOOLMASTERING
SELFEXPLANATORY
SELFSUFFICIENCY
STANDARDIZATION
STANDOFFISHNESS
STILPNOSIDERITE
STRAIGHTFORWARD
STREPHOSYMBOLIA
SUBLAPSARIANISM
SURREPTITIOUSLY
SYMPATHETICALLY
SYNCHRONIZATION
TECHNOLOGICALLY
TEMPERAMENTALLY
THERAPEUTICALLY
THOUGHTLESSNESS
THUNDERSTRICKEN
TOTALITARIANISM
TRANSFIGURATION
TRANSLITERATION
TRIGONOMETRICAL
TRINITROTOLUENE
TRUSTWORTHINESS
UNCEREMONIOUSLY
UNCOMMUNICATIVE
UNCOMPANIONABLE
UNCOMPLIMENTARY
UNCOMPREHENDING
UNCONDITIONALLY
UNCONSCIOUSNESS
UNDEMONSTRATIVE
UNDERPRIVILEGED
UNDISTINGUISHED
UNEXCEPTIONABLE
UNPARLIAMENTARY
UNPREPOSSESSING
UNPRONOUNCEABLE
UNRIGHTEOUSNESS
UNSOPHISTICATED
WELLESTABLISHED

15:2

BACKWARDLOOKING
BACTERIOLOGICAL
BATTERYOPERATED
FAMILIARIZATION
GASTROENTERITIS
MALPRACTITIONER
MANOEUVRABILITY
NATIONALIZATION
PALAEONTOLOGIST
PARLIAMENTARIAN
RATIONALIZATION
SACRAMENTMYSTIC
SANCTIMONIOUSLY
ACCLIMATIZATION
ACKNOWLEDGEMENT
ACQUISITIVENESS
ICHTHYODUROLITE
SCAPHOCEPHALATE
SCHOOLMASTERING
ADVENTUROUSNESS
DECONTAMINATION
DESERTIFICATION
DESTRUCTIVENESS
LEATHERSTOCKING
PERPENDICULARLY
PERSONIFICATION
PESSIMISTICALLY
REPRESENTATIVES
RESOURCEFULNESS
SELFEXPLANATORY
SELFSUFFICIENCY
TECHNOLOGICALLY
TEMPERAMENTALLY
WELLESTABLISHED
AGRICULTURALIST
CHARACTERISTICS
CHRISTADELPHIAN
CHRONOLOGICALLY
CHURRIGUERESQUE
PHARMACOLOGICAL
PHILOSOPHICALLY
PHOSPHORESCENCE
PHYSIOTHERAPIST
RHYNCHOBDELLIDA
THERAPEUTICALLY
THOUGHTLESSNESS
THUNDERSTRICKEN
AIRCONDITIONING
BIBLIOGRAPHICAL
CINEMATOGRAPHIC
CIRCUMSCRIPTION
CIRCUMSTANTIATE
DIFFERENTIATION
DISADVANTAGEOUS
DISILLUSIONMENT
DISPASSIONATELY
DISSATISFACTION

DISTINGUISHABLE
DIVERSIFICATION
LIFETHREATENING
MISAPPREHENSION
MISCHIEVOUSNESS
MISCONSTRUCTION
MISINTELLIGENCE
ALLOTRIOMORPHIC
ELECTRIFICATION
ELECTROMAGNETIC
FLIBBERTIGIBBET
GLEICHSCHALTUNG
PLENIPOTENTIARY
IMPENETRABILITY
IMPRESSIONISTIC
OMNIDIRECTIONAL
ANTHROPOLOGICAL
ANTHROPOMORPHIC
ENTREPRENEURIAL
INCOMPATIBILITY
INCOMPHEHENSION
INCONSEQUENTIAL
INCONSIDERATELY
INCONSPICUOUSLY
INDEMNIFICATION
INDIVIDUALISTIC
INQUISITIVENESS
INSTANTANEOUSLY
INSTRUMENTALIST
INSTRUMENTATION
INSUBORDINATION
INTELLIGIBILITY
INTENSIFICATION
INTERCHANGEABLE
INTERNATIONALLY
INTERVENTIONIST
ONYCHOCRYPTOSIS
UNCEREMONIOUSLY
UNCOMMUNICATIVE
UNCOMPANIONABLE
UNCOMPLIMENTARY
UNCOMPREHENDING
UNCONDITIONALLY
UNCONSCIOUSNESS
UNDEMONSTRATIVE
UNDERPRIVILEGED
UNDISTINGUISHED
UNEXCEPTIONABLE
UNPARLIAMENTARY
UNPREPOSSESSING
UNPRONOUNCEABLE
UNRIGHTEOUSNESS
UNSOPHISTICATED
COINSTANTANEOUS
COMPASSIONATELY
COMPUTERIZATION
CONFIDENTIALITY
CONFRONTATIONAL
CONGRATULATIONS
CONSCIENTIOUSLY

CONSERVATIONIST
CONTEMPORANEOUS
CONTRAVALLATION
CORRESPONDINGLY
GOTTERDAMMERUNG
GOVERNORGENERAL
HOSPITALIZATION
LONGSIGHTEDNESS
LOPHOBRANCHIATE
NONCOMMISSIONED
NONGOVERNMENTAL
NONPROFESSIONAL
NONPROFITMAKING
NOTHINGARIANISM
NOTWITHSTANDING
POLYUNSATURATED
TOTALITARIANISM
OPHTHALMOLOGIST
CRYSTALLIZATION
CRYSTALLOGRAPHY
DRAUGHTSMANSHIP
ORNITHORHYNCHUS
PRESTIDIGITATOR
PRETENTIOUSNESS
PROCRASTINATING
PROCRASTINATION
PROFESSIONALISM
PROGNOSTICATION
PROPORTIONATELY
PROSELYTIZATION
TRANSFIGURATION
TRANSLITERATION
TRIGONOMETRICAL
TRINITROTOLUENE
TRUSTWORTHINESS
PSYCHOLOGICALLY
PSYCHOTHERAPIST
ATTORNEYGENERAL
STANDARDIZATION
STANDOFFISHNESS
STILPNOSIDERITE
STRAIGHTFORWARD
STREPHOSYMBOLIA
AUTHORITATIVELY
EUPHEMISTICALLY
PUNCTILIOUSNESS
RUMPELSTILTSKIN
SUBLAPSARIANISM
SURREPTITIOUSLY
OVERSENTIMENTAL
EXCOMMUNICATION
EXPERIMENTATION
EXTRAORDINARILY
SYMPATHETICALLY
SYNCHRONIZATION

15:3

CHARACTERISTICS
DRAUGHTSMANSHIP
LEATHERSTOCKING
PHARMACOLOGICAL
SCAPHOCEPHALATE
STANDARDIZATION
STANDOFFISHNESS
TRANSFIGURATION
TRANSLITERATION
BIBLIOGRAPHICAL
SUBLAPSARIANISM
ACCLIMATIZATION
BACKWARDLOOKING
BACTERIOLOGICAL
DECONTAMINATION
EXCOMMUNICATION
INCOMPATIBILITY
INCOMPHEHENSION
INCONSEQUENTIAL
INCONSIDERATELY
INCONSPICUOUSLY
SACRAMENTMYSTIC
TECHNOLOGICALLY
UNCEREMONIOUSLY
UNCOMMUNICATIVE
UNCOMPANIONABLE
UNCOMPLIMENTARY
UNCOMPREHENDING
UNCONDITIONALLY
UNCONSCIOUSNESS
INDEMNIFICATION
INDIVIDUALISTIC
UNDEMONSTRATIVE
UNDERPRIVILEGED
UNDISTINGUISHED
ELECTRIFICATION
ELECTROMAGNETIC
GLEICHSCHALTUNG
OVERSENTIMENTAL
PLENIPOTENTIARY
PRESTIDIGITATOR
PRETENTIOUSNESS
THERAPEUTICALLY
UNEXCEPTIONABLE
DIFFERENTIATION
LIFETHREATENING
ICHTHYODUROLITE
OPHTHALMOLOGIST
SCHOOLMASTERING
COINSTANTANEOUS
FLIBBERTIGIBBET
PHILOSOPHICALLY
STILPNOSIDERITE
TRIGONOMETRICAL
TRINITROTOLUENE
ACKNOWLEDGEMENT
ALLOTRIOMORPHIC

MALPRACTITIONER
PALAEONTOLOGIST
POLYUNSATURATED
SELFEXPLANATORY
SELFSUFFICIENCY
WELLESTABLISHED
COMPASSIONATELY
COMPUTERIZATION
FAMILIARIZATION
RUMPELSTILTSKIN
SYMPATHETICALLY
TEMPERAMENTALLY
CINEMATOGRAPHIC
CONFIDENTIALITY
CONFRONTATIONAL
CONGRATULATIONS
CONSCIENTIOUSLY
CONSERVATIONIST
CONTEMPORANEOUS
CONTRAVALLATION
LONGSIGHTEDNESS
MANOEUVRABILITY
NONCOMMISSIONED
NONGOVERNMENTAL
NONPROFESSIONAL
NONPROFITMAKING
OMNIDIRECTIONAL
ORNITHORHYNCHUS
PUNCTILIOUSNESS
SANCTIMONIOUSLY
SYNCHRONIZATION
PHOSPHORESCENCE
PROCRASTINATING
PROCRASTINATION
PROFESSIONALISM
PROGNOSTICATION
PROPORTIONATELY
PROSELYTIZATION
THOUGHTLESSNESS
EUPHEMISTICALLY
EXPERIMENTATION
IMPENETRABILITY
IMPRESSIONISTIC
LOPHOBRANCHIATE
REPRESENTATIVES
UNPARLIAMENTARY
UNPREPOSSESSING
UNPRONOUNCEABLE
ACQUISITIVENESS
INQUISITIVENESS
AGRICULTURALIST
AIRCONDITIONING
CHRISTADELPHIAN
CHRONOLOGICALLY
CIRCUMSCRIPTION
CIRCUMSTANTIATE
CORRESPONDINGLY
PARLIAMENTARIAN
PERPENDICULARLY
PERSONIFICATION

STRAIGHTFORWARD
STREPHOSYMBOLIA
SURREPTITIOUSLY
UNRIGHTEOUSNESS
DESERTIFICATION
DESTRUCTIVENESS
DISADVANTAGEOUS
DISILLUSIONMENT
DISPASSIONATELY
DISSATISFACTION
DISTINGUISHABLE
GASTROENTERITIS
HOSPITALIZATION
INSTANTANEOUSLY
INSTRUMENTALIST
INSTRUMENTATION
INSUBORDINATION
MISAPPREHENSION
MISCHIEVOUSNESS
MISCONSTRUCTION
MISINTELLIGENCE
PESSIMISTICALLY
RESOURCEFULNESS
UNSOPHISTICATED
ANTHROPOLOGICAL
ANTHROPOMORPHIC
ATTORNEYGENERAL
AUTHORITATIVELY
BATTERYOPERATED
ENTREPRENEURIAL
EXTRAORDINARILY
GOTTERDAMMERUNG
INTELLIGIBILITY
INTENSIFICATION
INTERCHANGEABLE
INTERNATIONALLY
INTERVENTIONIST
NATIONALIZATION
NOTHINGARIANISM
NOTWITHSTANDING
RATIONALIZATION
TOTALITARIANISM
CHURRIGUERESQUE
THUNDERSTRICKEN
TRUSTWORTHINESS
ADVENTUROUSNESS
DIVERSIFICATION
GOVERNORGENERAL
CRYSTALLIZATION
CRYSTALLOGRAPHY
ONYCHOCRYPTOSIS
PHYSIOTHERAPIST
PSYCHOLOGICALLY
PSYCHOTHERAPIST
RHYNCHOBDELLIDA

15:4

DISADVANTAGEOUS
MISAPPREHENSION
PALAEONTOLOGIST
STRAIGHTFORWARD
TOTALITARIANISM
UNPARLIAMENTARY
FLIBBERTIGIBBET
AIRCONDITIONING
CIRCUMSCRIPTION
CIRCUMSTANTIATE
ELECTRIFICATION
ELECTROMAGNETIC
MISCHIEVOUSNESS
MISCONSTRUCTION
NONCOMMISSIONED
ONYCHOCRYPTOSIS
PROCRASTINATING
PROCRASTINATION
PSYCHOLOGICALLY
PSYCHOTHERAPIST
PUNCTILIOUSNESS
SANCTIMONIOUSLY
SYNCHRONIZATION
ADVENTUROUSNESS
CINEMATOGRAPHIC
DESERTIFICATION
DIVERSIFICATION
EXPERIMENTATION
GOVERNORGENERAL
IMPENETRABILITY
INDEMNIFICATION
INTELLIGIBILITY
INTENSIFICATION
INTERCHANGEABLE
INTERNATIONALLY
INTERVENTIONIST
LIFETHREATENING
STREPHOSYMBOLIA
UNCEREMONIOUSLY
UNDEMONSTRATIVE
UNDERPRIVILEGED
CONFIDENTIALITY
CONFRONTATIONAL
DIFFERENTIATION
PROFESSIONALISM
SELFEXPLANATORY
SELFSUFFICIENCY
CONGRATULATIONS
LONGSIGHTEDNESS
NONGOVERNMENTAL
PROGNOSTICATION
TRIGONOMETRICAL
ANTHROPOLOGICAL
ANTHROPOMORPHIC
AUTHORITATIVELY
EUPHEMISTICALLY
LOPHOBRANCHIATE

NOTHINGARIANISM
TECHNOLOGICALLY
AGRICULTURALIST
CHRISTADELPHIAN
DISILLUSIONMENT
FAMILIARIZATION
GLEICHSCHALTUNG
INDIVIDUALISTIC
MISINTELLIGENCE
NATIONALIZATION
OMNIDIRECTIONAL
ORNITHORHYNCHUS
RATIONALIZATION
UNDISTINGUISHED
UNRIGHTEOUSNESS
BACKWARDLOOKING
ACCLIMATIZATION
BIBLIOGRAPHICAL
PARLIAMENTARIAN
PHILOSOPHICALLY
STILPNOSIDERITE
SUBLAPSARIANISM
WELLESTABLISHED
ACKNOWLEDGEMENT
COINSTANTANEOUS
PLENIPOTENTIARY
RHYNCHOBDELLIDA
STANDARDIZATION
STANDOFFISHNESS
THUNDERSTRICKEN
TRANSFIGURATION
TRANSLITERATION
TRINITROTOLUENE
ALLOTRIOMORPHIC
ATTORNEYGENERAL
CHRONOLOGICALLY
DECONTAMINATION
EXCOMMUNICATION
INCOMPATIBILITY
INCOMPHEHENSION
INCONSEQUENTIAL
INCONSIDERATELY
INCONSPICUOUSLY
MANOEUVRABILITY
RESOURCEFULNESS
SCHOOLMASTERING
UNCOMMUNICATIVE
UNCOMPANIONABLE
UNCOMPLIMENTARY
UNCOMPREHENDING
UNCONDITIONALLY
UNCONSCIOUSNESS
UNSOPHISTICATED
COMPASSIONATELY
COMPUTERIZATION
DISPASSIONATELY
HOSPITALIZATION
MALPRACTITIONER
NONPROFESSIONAL
NONPROFITMAKING

PERPENDICULARLY
PROPORTIONATELY
RUMPELSTILTSKIN
SCAPHOCEPHALATE
SYMPATHETICALLY
TEMPERAMENTALLY
CHARACTERISTICS
CHURRIGUERESQUE
CORRESPONDINGLY
ENTREPRENEURIAL
EXTRAORDINARILY
IMPRESSIONISTIC
OVERSENTIMENTAL
PHARMACOLOGICAL
REPRESENTATIVES
SACRAMENTMYSTIC
SURREPTITIOUSLY
THERAPEUTICALLY
UNPREPOSSESSING
UNPRONOUNCEABLE
CONSCIENTIOUSLY
CONSERVATIONIST
CRYSTALLIZATION
CRYSTALLOGRAPHY
DISSATISFACTION
PERSONIFICATION
PESSIMISTICALLY
PHOSPHORESCENCE
PHYSIOTHERAPIST
PRESTIDIGITATOR
PROSELYTIZATION
TRUSTWORTHINESS
BACTERIOLOGICAL
BATTERYOPERATED
CONTEMPORANEOUS
CONTRAVALLATION
DESTRUCTIVENESS
DISTINGUISHABLE
GASTROENTERITIS
GOTTERDAMMERUNG
ICHTHYODUROLITE
INSTANTANEOUSLY
INSTRUMENTALIST
INSTRUMENTATION
LEATHERSTOCKING
OPHTHALMOLOGIST
PRETENTIOUSNESS
ACQUISITIVENESS
DRAUGHTSMANSHIP
INQUISITIVENESS
INSUBORDINATION
THOUGHTLESSNESS
NOTWITHSTANDING
UNEXCEPTIONABLE
POLYUNSATURATED

15:5

CHARACTERISTICS
COMPASSIONATELY
DISPASSIONATELY
DISSATISFACTION
EXTRAORDINARILY
INSTANTANEOUSLY
SACRAMENTMYSTIC
SUBLAPSARIANISM
SYMPATHETICALLY
THERAPEUTICALLY
FLIBBERTIGIBBET
INSUBORDINATION
AGRICULTURALIST
CONSCIENTIOUSLY
GLEICHSCHALTUNG
RHYNCHOBDELLIDA
UNEXCEPTIONABLE
DISADVANTAGEOUS
OMNIDIRECTIONAL
STANDARDIZATION
STANDOFFISHNESS
THUNDERSTRICKEN
BACTERIOLOGICAL
BATTERYOPERATED
CONSERVATIONIST
CONTEMPORANEOUS
CORRESPONDINGLY
DIFFERENTIATION
ENTREPRENEURIAL
EUPHEMISTICALLY
GOTTERDAMMERUNG
IMPRESSIONISTIC
MANOEUVRABILITY
PALAEONTOLOGIST
PERPENDICULARLY
PRETENTIOUSNESS
PROFESSIONALISM
PROSELYTIZATION
REPRESENTATIVES
RUMPELSTILTSKIN
SELFEXPLANATORY
SURREPTITIOUSLY
TEMPERAMENTALLY
UNPREPOSSESSING
WELLESTABLISHED
DRAUGHTSMANSHIP
THOUGHTLESSNESS
UNRIGHTEOUSNESS
ICHTHYODUROLITE
LEATHERSTOCKING
MISCHIEVOUSNESS
ONYCHOCRYPTOSIS
OPHTHALMOLOGIST
PSYCHOLOGICALLY
PSYCHOTHERAPIST
SCAPHOCEPHALATE
SYNCHRONIZATION
ACCLIMATIZATION
ACQUISITIVENESS
BIBLIOGRAPHICAL
CONFIDENTIALITY
DISTINGUISHABLE
HOSPITALIZATION
INQUISITIVENESS
NOTHINGARIANISM
NOTWITHSTANDING
PARLIAMENTARIAN
PESSIMISTICALLY
PHYSIOTHERAPIST
PLENIPOTENTIARY
STRAIGHTFORWARD
TRINITROTOLUENE
DISILLUSIONMENT
FAMILIARIZATION
INTELLIGIBILITY
TOTALITARIANISM
CINEMATOGRAPHIC
EXCOMMUNICATION
INCOMPATIBILITY
INCOMPHEHENSION
INDEMNIFICATION
PHARMACOLOGICAL
UNCOMMUNICATIVE
UNCOMPANIONABLE
UNCOMPLIMENTARY
UNCOMPREHENDING
UNDEMONSTRATIVE
ADVENTUROUSNESS
CHRONOLOGICALLY
DECONTAMINATION
IMPENETRABILITY
INCONSEQUENTIAL
INCONSIDERATELY
INCONSPICUOUSLY
INTENSIFICATION
MISINTELLIGENCE
PROGNOSTICATION
TECHNOLOGICALLY
UNCONDITIONALLY
UNCONSCIOUSNESS
ACKNOWLEDGEMENT
AIRCONDITIONING
AUTHORITATIVELY
LOPHOBRANCHIATE
MISCONSTRUCTION
NATIONALIZATION
NONCOMMISSIONED
NONGOVERNMENTAL
PERSONIFICATION
PHILOSOPHICALLY
PROPORTIONATELY
RATIONALIZATION
SCHOOLMASTERING
TRIGONOMETRICAL
UNPRONOUNCEABLE
MISAPPREHENSION
PHOSPHORESCENCE
STILPNOSIDERITE
STREPHOSYMBOLIA
UNSOPHISTICATED
ANTHROPOLOGICAL
ANTHROPOMORPHIC
ATTORNEYGENERAL
CHURRIGUERESQUE
CONFRONTATIONAL
CONGRATULATIONS
CONTRAVALLATION
DESERTIFICATION
DESTRUCTIVENESS
DIVERSIFICATION
EXPERIMENTATION
GASTROENTERITIS
GOVERNORGENERAL
INSTRUMENTALIST
INSTRUMENTATION
INTERCHANGEABLE
INTERNATIONALLY
INTERVENTIONIST
MALPRACTITIONER
NONPROFESSIONAL
NONPROFITMAKING
PROCRASTINATING
PROCRASTINATION
UNCEREMONIOUSLY
UNDERPRIVILEGED
UNPARLIAMENTARY
CHRISTADELPHIAN
COINSTANTANEOUS
LONGSIGHTEDNESS
OVERSENTIMENTAL
SELFSUFFICIENCY
TRANSFIGURATION
TRANSLITERATION
UNDISTINGUISHED
ALLOTRIOMORPHIC
CRYSTALLIZATION
CRYSTALLOGRAPHY
ELECTRIFICATION
ELECTROMAGNETIC
LIFETHREATENING
ORNITHORHYNCHUS
PRESTIDIGITATOR
PUNCTILIOUSNESS
SANCTIMONIOUSLY
TRUSTWORTHINESS
CIRCUMSCRIPTION
CIRCUMSTANTIATE
COMPUTERIZATION
POLYUNSATURATED
RESOURCEFULNESS
INDIVIDUALISTIC
BACKWARDLOOKING

15:6

BACKWARDLOOKING
CINEMATOGRAPHIC
CONGRATULATIONS
CONTRAVALLATION
CRYSTALLIZATION
CRYSTALLOGRAPHY
MALPRACTITIONER
OPHTHALMOLOGIST
PARLIAMENTARIAN
PHARMACOLOGICAL
PROCRASTINATING
PROCRASTINATION
STANDARDIZATION
LOPHOBRANCHIATE
CHARACTERISTICS
INTERCHANGEABLE
CONFIDENTIALITY
UNCONDITIONALLY
FLIBBERTIGIBBET
IMPENETRABILITY
LEATHERSTOCKING
OVERSENTIMENTAL
THUNDERSTRICKEN
UNCEREMONIOUSLY
UNEXCEPTIONABLE
TRANSFIGURATION
STRAIGHTFORWARD
DRAUGHTSMANSHIP
GLEICHSCHALTUNG
LIFETHREATENING
ORNITHORHYNCHUS
PHOSPHORESCENCE
RHYNCHOBDELLIDA
STREPHOSYMBOLIA
THOUGHTLESSNESS
UNRIGHTEOUSNESS
UNSOPHISTICATED
CHURRIGUERESQUE
CONSCIENTIOUSLY
EXPERIMENTATION
FAMILIARIZATION
INDIVIDUALISTIC
LONGSIGHTEDNESS
MISCHIEVOUSNESS
OMNIDIRECTIONAL
PRESTIDIGITATOR
PUNCTILIOUSNESS
SANCTIMONIOUSLY
TOTALITARIANISM
DISILLUSIONMENT
INTELLIGIBILITY
PROSELYTIZATION
RUMPELSTILTSKIN
SCHOOLMASTERING
TRANSLITERATION
UNPARLIAMENTARY
ACCLIMATIZATION

CIRCUMSCRIPTION
CIRCUMSTANTIATE
CONTEMPORANEOUS
EUPHEMISTICALLY
EXCOMMUNICATION
NONCOMMISSIONED
PESSIMISTICALLY
SACRAMENTMYSTIC
UNCOMMUNICATIVE
AIRCONDITIONING
ATTORNEYGENERAL
DISTINGUISHABLE
GOVERNORGENERAL
INDEMNIFICATION
INSTANTANEOUSLY
INTERNATIONALLY
MISCONSTRUCTION
NATIONALIZATION
NOTHINGARIANISM
PERPENDICULARLY
PERSONIFICATION
POLYUNSATURATED
PRETENTIOUSNESS
RATIONALIZATION
STILPNOSIDERITE
TRIGONOMETRICAL
UNPRONOUNCEABLE
ANTHROPOLOGICAL
ANTHROPOMORPHIC
BIBLIOGRAPHICAL
CHRONOLOGICALLY
CONFRONTATIONAL
EXTRAORDINARILY
GASTROENTERITIS
INSUBORDINATION
NONPROFESSIONAL
NONPROFITMAKING
ONYCHOCRYPTOSIS
PALAEONTOLOGIST
PHYSIOTHERAPIST
PROGNOSTICATION
PSYCHOLOGICALLY
PSYCHOTHERAPIST
SCAPHOCEPHALATE
STANDOFFISHNESS
TECHNOLOGICALLY
UNDEMONSTRATIVE
ENTREPRENEURIAL
INCOMPATIBILITY
INCOMPHEHENSION
MISAPPREHENSION
PLENIPOTENTIARY
SUBLAPSARIANISM
SURREPTITIOUSLY
THERAPEUTICALLY
UNCOMPANIONABLE
UNCOMPLIMENTARY
UNCOMPREHENDING
UNDERPRIVILEGED
UNPREPOSSESSING

ALLOTRIOMORPHIC
AUTHORITATIVELY
BACTERIOLOGICAL
BATTERYOPERATED
CONSERVATIONIST
DIFFERENTIATION
ELECTRIFICATION
ELECTROMAGNETIC
GOTTERDAMMERUNG
PROPORTIONATELY
RESOURCEFULNESS
SYNCHRONIZATION
TEMPERAMENTALLY
ACQUISITIVENESS
COMPASSIONATELY
CORRESPONDINGLY
DISPASSIONATELY
DIVERSIFICATION
IMPRESSIONISTIC
INCONSEQUENTIAL
INCONSIDERATELY
INCONSPICUOUSLY
INQUISITIVENESS
INTENSIFICATION
PHILOSOPHICALLY
PROFESSIONALISM
REPRESENTATIVES
UNCONSCIOUSNESS
WELLESTABLISHED
ADVENTUROUSNESS
CHRISTADELPHIAN
COINSTANTANEOUS
COMPUTERIZATION
DECONTAMINATION
DESERTIFICATION
DISSATISFACTION
HOSPITALIZATION
MISINTELLIGENCE
NOTWITHSTANDING
SYMPATHETICALLY
TRINITROTOLUENE
UNDISTINGUISHED
AGRICULTURALIST
DESTRUCTIVENESS
INSTRUMENTALIST
INSTRUMENTATION
MANOEUVRABILITY
SELFSUFFICIENCY
DISADVANTAGEOUS
INTERVENTIONIST
NONGOVERNMENTAL
ACKNOWLEDGEMENT
TRUSTWORTHINESS
SELFEXPLANATORY
ICHTHYODUROLITE

15:7

ACCLIMATIZATION
CHRISTADELPHIAN
COINSTANTANEOUS
DECONTAMINATION
DISADVANTAGEOUS
FAMILIARIZATION
HOSPITALIZATION
INCOMPATIBILITY
INTERNATIONALLY
NATIONALIZATION
RATIONALIZATION
TEMPERAMENTALLY
UNCOMPANIONABLE
DESTRUCTIVENESS
MALPRACTITIONER
ONYCHOCRYPTOSIS
PHARMACOLOGICAL
RESOURCEFULNESS
SCAPHOCEPHALATE
UNCONSCIOUSNESS
AIRCONDITIONING
GOTTERDAMMERUNG
INDIVIDUALISTIC
PERPENDICULARLY
PRESTIDIGITATOR
ATTORNEYGENERAL
COMPUTERIZATION
CONFIDENTIALITY
CONSCIENTIOUSLY
DIFFERENTIATION
GASTROENTERITIS
INCONSEQUENTIAL
INTERVENTIONIST
MISCHIEVOUSNESS
MISINTELLIGENCE
NONGOVERNMENTAL
REPRESENTATIVES
SACRAMENTMYSTIC
THERAPEUTICALLY
NONPROFESSIONAL
NONPROFITMAKING
SELFSUFFICIENCY
STANDOFFISHNESS
BIBLIOGRAPHICAL
CHURRIGUERESQUE
DISTINGUISHABLE
LONGSIGHTEDNESS
NOTHINGARIANISM
INCOMPHEHENSION
INTERCHANGEABLE
NOTWITHSTANDING
STRAIGHTFORWARD
SYMPATHETICALLY
ACQUISITIVENESS
ALLOTRIOMORPHIC
AUTHORITATIVELY
BACTERIOLOGICAL

DESERTIFICATION
DISSATISFACTION
DIVERSIFICATION
ELECTRIFICATION
EUPHEMISTICALLY
INCONSIDERATELY
INDEMNIFICATION
INQUISITIVENESS
INTELLIGIBILITY
INTENSIFICATION
PERSONIFICATION
PESSIMISTICALLY
TRANSFIGURATION
TRANSLITERATION
UNCONDITIONALLY
UNDISTINGUISHED
UNPARLIAMENTARY
UNSOPHISTICATED
ACKNOWLEDGEMENT
AGRICULTURALIST
CHRONOLOGICALLY
CRYSTALLIZATION
CRYSTALLOGRAPHY
OPHTHALMOLOGIST
PSYCHOLOGICALLY
PUNCTILIOUSNESS
TECHNOLOGICALLY
UNCOMPLIMENTARY
EXPERIMENTATION
INSTRUMENTALIST
INSTRUMENTATION
NONCOMMISSIONED
PARLIAMENTARIAN
SANCTIMONIOUSLY
SCHOOLMASTERING
UNCEREMONIOUSLY
CONFRONTATIONAL
OVERSENTIMENTAL
PALAEONTOLOGIST
UNDEMONSTRATIVE
ELECTROMAGNETIC
GOVERNORGENERAL
ICHTHYODUROLITE
ORNITHORHYNCHUS
PHILOSOPHICALLY
PHOSPHORESCENCE
PLENIPOTENTIARY
RHYNCHOBDELLIDA
STILPNOSIDERITE
STREPHOSYMBOLIA
SYNCHRONIZATION
TRIGONOMETRICAL
TRUSTWORTHINESS
UNPREPOSSESSING
UNPRONOUNCEABLE
ANTHROPOLOGICAL
ANTHROPOMORPHIC
CONTEMPORANEOUS
CORRESPONDINGLY
INCONSPICUOUSLY

15:8

SELFEXPLANATORY
UNEXCEPTIONABLE
BACKWARDLOOKING
ENTREPRENEURIAL
EXTRAORDINARILY
FLIBBERTIGIBBET
INSUBORDINATION
LEATHERSTOCKING
LIFETHREATENING
LOPHOBRANCHIATE
MISAPPREHENSION
OMNIDIRECTIONAL
STANDARDIZATION
THUNDERSTRICKEN
TRINITROTOLUENE
UNCOMPREHENDING
UNDERPRIVILEGED
CIRCUMSCRIPTION
CIRCUMSTANTIATE
COMPASSIONATELY
DISPASSIONATELY
GLEICHSCHALTUNG
IMPRESSIONISTIC
MISCONSTRUCTION
POLYUNSATURATED
PROCRASTINATING
PROCRASTINATION
PROFESSIONALISM
PROGNOSTICATION
RUMPELSTILTSKIN
SUBLAPSARIANISM
CHARACTERISTICS
CINEMATOGRAPHIC
CONGRATULATIONS
DRAUGHTSMANSHIP
IMPENETRABILITY
INSTANTANEOUSLY
PHYSIOTHERAPIST
PRETENTIOUSNESS
PROPORTIONATELY
PSYCHOTHERAPIST
SURREPTITIOUSLY
THOUGHTLESSNESS
TOTALITARIANISM
UNRIGHTEOUSNESS
WELLESTABLISHED
ADVENTUROUSNESS
DISILLUSIONMENT
EXCOMMUNICATION
UNCOMMUNICATIVE
CONSERVATIONIST
CONTRAVALLATION
MANOEUVRABILITY
BATTERYOPERATED
PROSELYTIZATION

CONSERVATIONIST
CONTRAVALLATION
GOTTERDAMMERUNG
INSTANTANEOUSLY
INTERCHANGEABLE
LOPHOBRANCHIATE
NOTHINGARIANISM
POLYUNSATURATED
SCHOOLMASTERING
SUBLAPSARIANISM
TOTALITARIANISM
UNPARLIAMENTARY
WELLESTABLISHED
RHYNCHOBDELLIDA
CIRCUMSCRIPTION
GLEICHSCHALTUNG
BACKWARDLOOKING
CHRISTADELPHIAN
EXTRAORDINARILY
ICHTHYODUROLITE
INCONSIDERATELY
INSUBORDINATION
STANDARDIZATION
ACKNOWLEDGEMENT
CHARACTERISTICS
ENTREPRENEURIAL
EXPERIMENTATION
INCOMPHEHENSION
INSTRUMENTALIST
INSTRUMENTATION
LIFETHREATENING
MISAPPREHENSION
NONPROFESSIONAL
OMNIDIRECTIONAL
PARLIAMENTARIAN
RESOURCEFULNESS
SCAPHOCEPHALATE
SYMPATHETICALLY
UNCOMPREHENDING
UNRIGHTEOUSNESS
DESERTIFICATION
DIVERSIFICATION
ELECTRIFICATION
INDEMNIFICATION
INTENSIFICATION
PERSONIFICATION
SELFSUFFICIENCY
STANDOFFISHNESS
INTELLIGIBILITY
TRANSFIGURATION
LONGSIGHTEDNESS
PHYSIOTHERAPIST
PSYCHOTHERAPIST
AIRCONDITIONING
COMPASSIONATELY
DISPASSIONATELY
IMPRESSIONISTIC

INCONSPICUOUSLY
NONCOMMISSIONED
NONPROFITMAKING
PERPENDICULARLY
PRESTIDIGITATOR
PRETENTIOUSNESS
PROFESSIONALISM
PROPORTIONATELY
PUNCTILIOUSNESS
SURREPTITIOUSLY
UNCOMPLIMENTARY
UNCONSCIOUSNESS
UNDERPRIVILEGED
CRYSTALLIZATION
CRYSTALLOGRAPHY
HOSPITALIZATION
MISINTELLIGENCE
NATIONALIZATION
RATIONALIZATION
SELFEXPLANATORY
THOUGHTLESSNESS
DECONTAMINATION
ELECTROMAGNETIC
OPHTHALMOLOGIST
TEMPERAMENTALLY
TRIGONOMETRICAL
COINSTANTANEOUS
CONFIDENTIALITY
CONSCIENTIOUSLY
DIFFERENTIATION
DISADVANTAGEOUS
EXCOMMUNICATION
GASTROENTERITIS
INTERVENTIONIST
REPRESENTATIVES
SACRAMENTMYSTIC
SYNCHRONIZATION
UNCOMMUNICATIVE
UNCOMPANIONABLE
UNDISTINGUISHED
ALLOTRIOMORPHIC
ANTHROPOLOGICAL
ANTHROPOMORPHIC
BACTERIOLOGICAL
BATTERYOPERATED
CHRONOLOGICALLY
CINEMATOGRAPHIC
CONTEMPORANEOUS
CORRESPONDINGLY
PHARMACOLOGICAL
PSYCHOLOGICALLY
SANCTIMONIOUSLY
TECHNOLOGICALLY
TRINITROTOLUENE
UNCEREMONIOUSLY
PHILOSOPHICALLY
INCONSEQUENTIAL
ADVENTUROUSNESS
BIBLIOGRAPHICAL
COMPUTERIZATION

FAMILIARIZATION
GOVERNORGENERAL
IMPENETRABILITY
MANOEUVRABILITY
NONGOVERNMENTAL
ONYCHOCRYPTOSIS
ORNITHORHYNCHUS
PHOSPHORESCENCE
TRUSTWORTHINESS
DISILLUSIONMENT
DISSATISFACTION
DRAUGHTSMANSHIP
EUPHEMISTICALLY
LEATHERSTOCKING
NOTWITHSTANDING
PESSIMISTICALLY
STILPNOSIDERITE
STREPHOSYMBOLIA
THUNDERSTRICKEN
UNDEMONSTRATIVE
UNPREPOSSESSING
UNSOPHISTICATED
ACCLIMATIZATION
ACQUISITIVENESS
AGRICULTURALIST
AUTHORITATIVELY
CIRCUMSTANTIATE
CONFRONTATIONAL
DESTRUCTIVENESS
FLIBBERTIGIBBET
INCOMPATIBILITY
INQUISITIVENESS
INTERNATIONALLY
MALPRACTITIONER
MISCONSTRUCTION
OVERSENTIMENTAL
PALAEONTOLOGIST
PLENIPOTENTIARY
PROCRASTINATING
PROCRASTINATION
PROGNOSTICATION
PROSELYTIZATION
RUMPELSTILTSKIN
STRAIGHTFORWARD
TRANSLITERATION
UNCONDITIONALLY
UNEXCEPTIONABLE
CHURRIGUERESQUE
CONGRATULATIONS
DISTINGUISHABLE
INDIVIDUALISTIC
THERAPEUTICALLY
UNPRONOUNCEABLE
MISCHIEVOUSNESS
ATTORNEYGENERAL

15:9

AUTHORITATIVELY
BIBLIOGRAPHICAL
CIRCUMSTANTIATE
CONFRONTATIONAL
ELECTROMAGNETIC
IMPENETRABILITY
INDIVIDUALISTIC
LIFETHREATENING
MANOEUVRABILITY
SELFEXPLANATORY
WELLESTABLISHED
INCONSPICUOUSLY
OMNIDIRECTIONAL
PERPENDICULARLY
ACKNOWLEDGEMENT
RHYNCHOBDELLIDA
CHRISTADELPHIAN
CHURRIGUERESQUE
INCONSIDERATELY
PHOSPHORESCENCE
PHYSIOTHERAPIST
PLENIPOTENTIARY
PSYCHOTHERAPIST
TEMPERAMENTALLY
THOUGHTLESSNESS
TRANSLITERATION
TRIGONOMETRICAL
DISSATISFACTION
RESOURCEFULNESS
STRAIGHTFORWARD
ATTORNEYGENERAL
CHRONOLOGICALLY
CINEMATOGRAPHIC
GOVERNORGENERAL
·PRESTIDIGITATOR
PSYCHOLOGICALLY
TECHNOLOGICALLY
UNDISTINGUISHED
GLEICHSCHALTUNG
INCOMPHEHENSION
MISAPPREHENSION
ORNITHORHYNCHUS
PHILOSOPHICALLY
UNCOMPREHENDING
ACCLIMATIZATION
ACQUISITIVENESS
COMPUTERIZATION
CRYSTALLIZATION
DECONTAMINATION
DESERTIFICATION
DESTRUCTIVENESS
DISILLUSIONMENT
DISTINGUISHABLE
DIVERSIFICATION
ELECTRIFICATION
EXCOMMUNICATION
EXTRAORDINARILY
FAMILIARIZATION
FLIBBERTIGIBBET
HOSPITALIZATION
INCOMPATIBILITY
INDEMNIFICATION
INQUISITIVENESS
INSUBORDINATION
INTELLIGIBILITY
INTENSIFICATION
INTERNATIONALLY
MALPRACTITIONER
NATIONALIZATION
OVERSENTIMENTAL
PERSONIFICATION
PROCRASTINATING
PROCRASTINATION
PROGNOSTICATION
PROSELYTIZATION
RATIONALIZATION
RUMPELSTILTSKIN
SELFSUFFICIENCY
STANDARDIZATION
STANDOFFISHNESS
STILPNOSIDERITE
SYNCHRONIZATION
UNCOMMUNICATIVE
UNCOMPANIONABLE
UNCONDITIONALLY
UNEXCEPTIONABLE
ANTHROPOLOGICAL
BACKWARDLOOKING
BACTERIOLOGICAL
CONGRATULATIONS
CONTRAVALLATION
MISINTELLIGENCE
PHARMACOLOGICAL
ALLOTRIOMORPHIC
ANTHROPOMORPHIC
DRAUGHTSMANSHIP
GOTTERDAMMERUNG
UNCOMPLIMENTARY
UNPARLIAMENTARY
CORRESPONDINGLY
ENTREPRENEURIAL
EXPERIMENTATION
INSTANTANEOUSLY
INSTRUMENTALIST
INSTRUMENTATION
INTERCHANGEABLE
LOPHOBRANCHIATE
NONGOVERNMENTAL
PARLIAMENTARIAN
SANCTIMONIOUSLY
UNCEREMONIOUSLY
UNPRONOUNCEABLE
ADVENTUROUSNESS
COMPASSIONATELY
CRYSTALLOGRAPHY
DISPASSIONATELY
IMPRESSIONISTIC
MISCHIEVOUSNESS
OPHTHALMOLOGIST
PALAEONTOLOGIST
PRETENTIOUSNESS
PROFESSIONALISM
PROPORTIONATELY
PUNCTILIOUSNESS
UNCONSCIOUSNESS
UNRIGHTEOUSNESS
BATTERYOPERATED
SCAPHOCEPHALATE
CHARACTERISTICS
CIRCUMSCRIPTION
CONTEMPORANEOUS
MISCONSTRUCTION
NOTHINGARIANISM
SUBLAPSARIANISM
TOTALITARIANISM
NONCOMMISSIONED
NONPROFESSIONAL
SCHOOLMASTERING
UNPREPOSSESSING
AIRCONDITIONING
COINSTANTANEOUS
CONFIDENTIALITY
CONSCIENTIOUSLY
CONSERVATIONIST
DIFFERENTIATION
DISADVANTAGEOUS
EUPHEMISTICALLY
GASTROENTERITIS
INTERVENTIONIST
LEATHERSTOCKING
LONGSIGHTEDNESS
NONPROFITMAKING
NOTWITHSTANDING
PESSIMISTICALLY
POLYUNSATURATED
REPRESENTATIVES
SACRAMENTMYSTIC
SURREPTITIOUSLY
SYMPATHETICALLY
THERAPEUTICALLY
THUNDERSTRICKEN
TRINITROTOLUENE
TRUSTWORTHINESS
UNDEMONSTRATIVE
UNSOPHISTICATED
AGRICULTURALIST
ICHTHYODUROLITE
INCONSEQUENTIAL
TRANSFIGURATION
UNDERPRIVILEGED
ONYCHOCRYPTOSIS
STREPHOSYMBOLIA

15:10

COINSTANTANEOUS
CONGRATULATIONS
CONTEMPORANEOUS
DISADVANTAGEOUS
DISSATISFACTION
DRAUGHTSMANSHIP
GLEICHSCHALTUNG
NOTWITHSTANDING
REPRESENTATIVES
IMPENETRABILITY
INCOMPATIBILITY
INTELLIGIBILITY
MANOEUVRABILITY
DESERTIFICATION
DIVERSIFICATION
ELECTRIFICATION
EXCOMMUNICATION
INDEMNIFICATION
INTENSIFICATION
LOPHOBRANCHIATE
PERSONIFICATION
PROGNOSTICATION
SELFSUFFICIENCY
UNCOMMUNICATIVE
UNPRONOUNCEABLE
CORRESPONDINGLY
STILPNOSIDERITE
ATTORNEYGENERAL
BATTERYOPERATED
ENTREPRENEURIAL
GASTROENTERITIS
GOVERNORGENERAL
INCOMPHEHENSION
INCONSEQUENTIAL
INSTANTANEOUSLY
LONGSIGHTEDNESS
MISAPPREHENSION
RHYNCHOBDELLIDA
UNCOMPLIMENTARY
UNCOMPREHENDING
UNPARLIAMENTARY
UNPREPOSSESSING
ACKNOWLEDGEMENT
CRYSTALLOGRAPHY
ELECTROMAGNETIC
FLIBBERTIGIBBET
INTERCHANGEABLE
SCAPHOCEPHALATE
TRUSTWORTHINESS
AIRCONDITIONING
CHARACTERISTICS
CHRONOLOGICALLY
CIRCUMSCRIPTION
CONFIDENTIALITY
CONSCIENTIOUSLY
CONSERVATIONIST
DIFFERENTIATION

EUPHEMISTICALLY
INTERVENTIONIST
MISINTELLIGENCE
NOTHINGARIANISM
PESSIMISTICALLY
PHILOSOPHICALLY
PRESTIDIGITATOR
PSYCHOLOGICALLY
SANCTIMONIOUSLY
SUBLAPSARIANISM
SURREPTITIOUSLY
SYMPATHETICALLY
TECHNOLOGICALLY
THERAPEUTICALLY
TOTALITARIANISM
UNCEREMONIOUSLY
UNDERPRIVILEGED
UNSOPHISTICATED
CHRISTADELPHIAN
CONTRAVALLATION
INDIVIDUALISTIC
OPHTHALMOLOGIST
PALAEONTOLOGIST
RUMPELSTILTSKIN
WELLESTABLISHED
GOTTERDAMMERUNG
NONGOVERNMENTAL
NONPROFITMAKING
OVERSENTIMENTAL
SACRAMENTMYSTIC
STREPHOSYMBOLIA
CIRCUMSTANTIATE
COMPASSIONATELY
DECONTAMINATION
DISPASSIONATELY
EXTRAORDINARILY
IMPRESSIONISTIC
INSUBORDINATION
PLENIPOTENTIARY
PROCRASTINATING
PROCRASTINATION
PROFESSIONALISM
PROPORTIONATELY
SELFEXPLANATORY
TEMPERAMENTALLY
ALLOTRIOMORPHIC
ANTHROPOLOGICAL
ANTHROPOMORPHIC
BACKWARDLOOKING
BACTERIOLOGICAL
DISILLUSIONMENT
INTERNATIONALLY
LEATHERSTOCKING
PHARMACOLOGICAL
STRAIGHTFORWARD
TRINITROTOLUENE
UNCOMPANIONABLE
UNCONDITIONALLY
UNEXCEPTIONABLE
BIBLIOGRAPHICAL

ONYCHOCRYPTOSIS
AGRICULTURALIST
CHURRIGUERESQUE
CINEMATOGRAPHIC
ICHTHYODUROLITE
INCONSIDERATELY
PHYSIOTHERAPIST
PSYCHOTHERAPIST
THUNDERSTRICKEN
TRANSFIGURATION
TRANSLITERATION
UNDEMONSTRATIVE
DISTINGUISHABLE
NONCOMMISSIONED
NONPROFESSIONAL
PHOSPHORESCENCE
STANDOFFISHNESS
THOUGHTLESSNESS
AUTHORITATIVELY
CONFRONTATIONAL
EXPERIMENTATION
INSTRUMENTALIST
INSTRUMENTATION
LIFETHREATENING
MALPRACTITIONER
OMNIDIRECTIONAL
PARLIAMENTARIAN
SCHOOLMASTERING
TRIGONOMETRICAL
ADVENTUROUSNESS
INCONSPICUOUSLY
MISCHIEVOUSNESS
MISCONSTRUCTION
PERPENDICULARLY
POLYUNSATURATED
PRETENTIOUSNESS
PUNCTILIOUSNESS
RESOURCEFULNESS
UNCONSCIOUSNESS
UNDISTINGUISHED
UNRIGHTEOUSNESS
ACQUISITIVENESS
DESTRUCTIVENESS
INQUISITIVENESS
ORNITHORHYNCHUS
ACCLIMATIZATION
COMPUTERIZATION
CRYSTALLIZATION
FAMILIARIZATION
HOSPITALIZATION
NATIONALIZATION
PROSELYTIZATION
RATIONALIZATION
STANDARDIZATION
SYNCHRONIZATION

15:11

ACCLIMATIZATION
AGRICULTURALIST
CINEMATOGRAPHIC
COMPASSIONATELY
COMPUTERIZATION
CONFIDENTIALITY
CONTRAVALLATION
CRYSTALLIZATION
DECONTAMINATION
DESERTIFICATION
DIFFERENTIATION
DISPASSIONATELY
DIVERSIFICATION
ELECTRIFICATION
EXCOMMUNICATION
EXPERIMENTATION
EXTRAORDINARILY
FAMILIARIZATION
HOSPITALIZATION
INCONSIDERATELY
INDEMNIFICATION
INSTRUMENTALIST
INSTRUMENTATION
INSUBORDINATION
INTENSIFICATION
NATIONALIZATION
NONPROFITMAKING
NOTHINGARIANISM
PARLIAMENTARIAN
PERSONIFICATION
PHYSIOTHERAPIST
PROCRASTINATING
PROCRASTINATION
PROFESSIONALISM
PROGNOSTICATION
PROPORTIONATELY
PROSELYTIZATION
PSYCHOTHERAPIST
RATIONALIZATION
SCAPHOCEPHALATE
SELFEXPLANATORY
STANDARDIZATION
SUBLAPSARIANISM
SYNCHRONIZATION
TOTALITARIANISM
TRANSFIGURATION
TRANSLITERATION
UNCOMMUNICATIVE
UNDEMONSTRATIVE
STREPHOSYMBOLIA
CHRONOLOGICALLY
DISSATISFACTION
EUPHEMISTICALLY
LEATHERSTOCKING
MISCONSTRUCTION
PESSIMISTICALLY
PHILOSOPHICALLY

PHOSPHORESCENCE
PSYCHOLOGICALLY
SYMPATHETICALLY
TECHNOLOGICALLY
THERAPEUTICALLY
UNSOPHISTICATED
LONGSIGHTEDNESS
ACKNOWLEDGEMENT
ACQUISITIVENESS
CHURRIGUERESQUE
DESTRUCTIVENESS
GOTTERDAMMERUNG
INQUISITIVENESS
INTERCHANGEABLE
LIFETHREATENING
NONGOVERNMENTAL
OVERSENTIMENTAL
SCHOOLMASTERING
STILPNOSIDERITE
UNPRONOUNCEABLE
ANTHROPOLOGICAL
BACTERIOLOGICAL
DISADVANTAGEOUS
MISINTELLIGENCE
PHARMACOLOGICAL
BIBLIOGRAPHICAL
DISTINGUISHABLE
LOPHOBRANCHIATE
STANDOFFISHNESS
AUTHORITATIVELY
CONFRONTATIONAL
CORRESPONDINGLY
FLIBBERTIGIBBET
IMPENETRABILITY
IMPRESSIONISTIC
INCOMPATIBILITY
INDIVIDUALISTIC
INTELLIGIBILITY
MALPRACTITIONER
MANOEUVRABILITY
NONCOMMISSIONED
NONPROFESSIONAL
OMNIDIRECTIONAL
SELFSUFFICIENCY
THUNDERSTRICKEN
TRUSTWORTHINESS
UNDISTINGUISHED
WELLESTABLISHED
GLEICHSCHALTUNG
PERPENDICULARLY
RESOURCEFULNESS
RHYNCHOBDELLIDA
TRINITROTOLUENE
UNDERPRIVILEGED
ATTORNEYGENERAL
COINSTANTANEOUS
CONTEMPORANEOUS
DISILLUSIONMENT
DRAUGHTSMANSHIP
ELECTROMAGNETIC

GOVERNORGENERAL
INCOMPHEHENSION
INCONSEQUENTIAL
INTERNATIONALLY
MISAPPREHENSION
NOTWITHSTANDING
ORNITHORHYNCHUS
UNCOMPANIONABLE
UNCOMPLIMENTARY
UNCOMPREHENDING
UNCONDITIONALLY
UNEXCEPTIONABLE
UNPARLIAMENTARY
AIRCONDITIONING
BACKWARDLOOKING
CONSCIENTIOUSLY
CONSERVATIONIST
ICHTHYODUROLITE
INCONSPICUOUSLY
INSTANTANEOUSLY
INTERVENTIONIST
OPHTHALMOLOGIST
PALAEONTOLOGIST
SANCTIMONIOUSLY
SURREPTITIOUSLY
UNCEREMONIOUSLY
CHRISTADELPHIAN
CIRCUMSCRIPTION
ALLOTRIOMORPHIC
ANTHROPOMORPHIC
BATTERYOPERATED
CRYSTALLOGRAPHY
GASTROENTERITIS
POLYUNSATURATED
STRAIGHTFORWARD
TRIGONOMETRICAL
ADVENTUROUSNESS
CHARACTERISTICS
MISCHIEVOUSNESS
PRETENTIOUSNESS
PUNCTILIOUSNESS
THOUGHTLESSNESS
UNCONSCIOUSNESS
UNPREPOSSESSING
UNRIGHTEOUSNESS
CIRCUMSTANTIATE
CONGRATULATIONS
ONYCHOCRYPTOSIS
PLENIPOTENTIARY
PRESTIDIGITATOR
REPRESENTATIVES
RUMPELSTILTSKIN
TEMPERAMENTALLY
ENTREPRENEURIAL
SACRAMENTMYSTIC

15:12

BATTERYOPERATED
CHRONOLOGICALLY
CRYSTALLOGRAPHY
DISTINGUISHABLE
EUPHEMISTICALLY
INTERCHANGEABLE
INTERNATIONALLY
PERPENDICULARLY
PESSIMISTICALLY
PHILOSOPHICALLY
POLYUNSATURATED
PRESTIDIGITATOR
PSYCHOLOGICALLY
SYMPATHETICALLY
TECHNOLOGICALLY
TEMPERAMENTALLY
THERAPEUTICALLY
UNCOMPANIONABLE
UNCONDITIONALLY
UNEXCEPTIONABLE
UNPRONOUNCEABLE
UNSOPHISTICATED
FLIBBERTIGIBBET
ORNITHORHYNCHUS
THUNDERSTRICKEN
NOTWITHSTANDING
UNCOMPREHENDING
ATTORNEYGENERAL
COINSTANTANEOUS
CONTEMPORANEOUS
DISADVANTAGEOUS
ELECTROMAGNETIC
GOVERNORGENERAL
MISINTELLIGENCE
PHOSPHORESCENCE
SELFSUFFICIENCY
UNDERPRIVILEGED
OPHTHALMOLOGIST
PALAEONTOLOGIST
CHRISTADELPHIAN
ANTHROPOLOGICAL
BACTERIOLOGICAL
BIBLIOGRAPHICAL
CIRCUMSTANTIATE
CONGRATULATIONS
GASTROENTERITIS
LOPHOBRANCHIATE
PHARMACOLOGICAL
PLENIPOTENTIARY
REPRESENTATIVES
TRIGONOMETRICAL
BACKWARDLOOKING
LEATHERSTOCKING
NONPROFITMAKING
AGRICULTURALIST
CONFIDENTIALITY
ICHTHYODUROLITE

IMPENETRABILITY
INCOMPATIBILITY
INSTRUMENTALIST
INTELLIGIBILITY
MANOEUVRABILITY
PROFESSIONALISM
RHYNCHOBDELLIDA
SCAPHOCEPHALATE
ACKNOWLEDGEMENT
DISILLUSIONMENT
ACQUISITIVENESS
ADVENTUROUSNESS
AIRCONDITIONING
CONSERVATIONIST
CORRESPONDINGLY
DESTRUCTIVENESS
INQUISITIVENESS
INTERVENTIONIST
LIFETHREATENING
LONGSIGHTEDNESS
MISCHIEVOUSNESS
NONGOVERNMENTAL
NOTHINGARIANISM
OVERSENTIMENTAL
PRETENTIOUSNESS
PUNCTILIOUSNESS
RESOURCEFULNESS
STANDOFFISHNESS
SUBLAPSARIANISM
THOUGHTLESSNESS
TOTALITARIANISM
TRUSTWORTHINESS
UNCONSCIOUSNESS
UNRIGHTEOUSNESS
CONFRONTATIONAL
MALPRACTITIONER
NONCOMMISSIONED
NONPROFESSIONAL
OMNIDIRECTIONAL
ONYCHOCRYPTOSIS
STREPHOSYMBOLIA
ALLOTRIOMORPHIC
ANTHROPOMORPHIC
CINEMATOGRAPHIC
PHYSIOTHERAPIST
PSYCHOTHERAPIST
ENTREPRENEURIAL
EXTRAORDINARILY
GOTTERDAMMERUNG
PARLIAMENTARIAN
SCHOOLMASTERING
STILPNOSIDERITE
CHURRIGUERESQUE
DRAUGHTSMANSHIP
IMPRESSIONISTIC
INCOMPHEHENSION
INDIVIDUALISTIC
MISAPPREHENSION
RUMPELSTILTSKIN
SACRAMENTMYSTIC

UNDISTINGUISHED
UNPREPOSSESSING
WELLESTABLISHED
ACCLIMATIZATION
CHARACTERISTICS
CIRCUMSCRIPTION
COMPASSIONATELY
COMPUTERIZATION
CONTRAVALLATION
CRYSTALLIZATION
DECONTAMINATION
DESERTIFICATION
DIFFERENTIATION
DISPASSIONATELY
DISSATISFACTION
DIVERSIFICATION
ELECTRIFICATION
EXCOMMUNICATION
EXPERIMENTATION
FAMILIARIZATION
GLEICHSCHALTUNG
HOSPITALIZATION
INCONSEQUENTIAL
INCONSIDERATELY
INDEMNIFICATION
INSTRUMENTATION
INSUBORDINATION
INTENSIFICATION
MISCONSTRUCTION
NATIONALIZATION
PERSONIFICATION
PROCRASTINATING
PROCRASTINATION
PROGNOSTICATION
PROPORTIONATELY
PROSELYTIZATION
RATIONALIZATION
SELFEXPLANATORY
STANDARDIZATION
SYNCHRONIZATION
TRANSFIGURATION
TRANSLITERATION
UNCOMMUNICATIVE
UNCOMPLIMENTARY
UNDEMONSTRATIVE
UNPARLIAMENTARY
CONSCIENTIOUSLY
INCONSPICUOUSLY
INSTANTANEOUSLY
SANCTIMONIOUSLY
SURREPTITIOUSLY
TRINITROTOLUENE
UNCEREMONIOUSLY
AUTHORITATIVELY
STRAIGHTFORWARD

15:13

CIRCUMSTANTIATE
LOPHOBRANCHIATE
PLENIPOTENTIARY
SCAPHOCEPHALATE
STRAIGHTFORWARD
UNCOMPLIMENTARY
UNPARLIAMENTARY
DISTINGUISHABLE
FLIBBERTIGIBBET
INTERCHANGEABLE
UNCOMPANIONABLE
UNEXCEPTIONABLE
UNPRONOUNCEABLE
ANTHROPOLOGICAL
BACTERIOLOGICAL
BIBLIOGRAPHICAL
PHARMACOLOGICAL
TRIGONOMETRICAL
ACKNOWLEDGEMENT
ACQUISITIVENESS
ADVENTUROUSNESS
AUTHORITATIVELY
COMPASSIONATELY
DESTRUCTIVENESS
DISILLUSIONMENT
DISPASSIONATELY
INCONSIDERATELY
INQUISITIVENESS
LONGSIGHTEDNESS
MISCHIEVOUSNESS
PRETENTIOUSNESS
PROPORTIONATELY
PUNCTILIOUSNESS
RESOURCEFULNESS
STANDOFFISHNESS
THOUGHTLESSNESS
TRINITROTOLUENE
TRUSTWORTHINESS
UNCONSCIOUSNESS
UNRIGHTEOUSNESS
CORRESPONDINGLY
UNDERPRIVILEGED
ALLOTRIOMORPHIC
ANTHROPOMORPHIC
CINEMATOGRAPHIC
DRAUGHTSMANSHIP
ORNITHORHYNCHUS
UNDISTINGUISHED
WELLESTABLISHED
ACCLIMATIZATION
AGRICULTURALIST
AIRCONDITIONING
BACKWARDLOOKING
CHARACTERISTICS
CHRISTADELPHIAN
CIRCUMSCRIPTION
COMPUTERIZATION
CONFIDENTIALITY
CONSERVATIONIST
CONTRAVALLATION
CRYSTALLIZATION
DECONTAMINATION
DESERTIFICATION
DIFFERENTIATION
DISSATISFACTION
DIVERSIFICATION
ELECTRIFICATION
ENTREPRENEURIAL
EXCOMMUNICATION
EXPERIMENTATION
EXTRAORDINARILY
FAMILIARIZATION
HOSPITALIZATION
ICHTHYODUROLITE
IMPENETRABILITY
INCOMPATIBILITY
INCOMPHEHENSION
INCONSEQUENTIAL
INDEMNIFICATION
INSTRUMENTALIST
INSTRUMENTATION
INSUBORDINATION
INTELLIGIBILITY
INTENSIFICATION
INTERVENTIONIST
LEATHERSTOCKING
LIFETHREATENING
MANOEUVRABILITY
MISAPPREHENSION
MISCONSTRUCTION
NATIONALIZATION
NONPROFITMAKING
NOTHINGARIANISM
NOTWITHSTANDING
OPHTHALMOLOGIST
PALAEONTOLOGIST
PARLIAMENTARIAN
PERSONIFICATION
PHYSIOTHERAPIST
PROCRASTINATING
PROCRASTINATION
PROFESSIONALISM
PROGNOSTICATION
PROSELYTIZATION
PSYCHOTHERAPIST
RATIONALIZATION
RHYNCHOBDELLIDA
SCHOOLMASTERING
STANDARDIZATION
STILPNOSIDERITE
SUBLAPSARIANISM
SYNCHRONIZATION
TOTALITARIANISM
TRANSFIGURATION
TRANSLITERATION
UNCOMMUNICATIVE
UNCOMPREHENDING
UNDEMONSTRATIVE
UNPREPOSSESSING
RUMPELSTILTSKIN
THUNDERSTRICKEN
CHRONOLOGICALLY
EUPHEMISTICALLY
INTERNATIONALLY
PESSIMISTICALLY
PHILOSOPHICALLY
PSYCHOLOGICALLY
STREPHOSYMBOLIA
SYMPATHETICALLY
TECHNOLOGICALLY
TEMPERAMENTALLY
THERAPEUTICALLY
UNCONDITIONALLY
CONFRONTATIONAL
MALPRACTITIONER
MISINTELLIGENCE
NONCOMMISSIONED
NONPROFESSIONAL
OMNIDIRECTIONAL
PHOSPHORESCENCE
SELFSUFFICIENCY
COINSTANTANEOUS
CONGRATULATIONS
CONTEMPORANEOUS
DISADVANTAGEOUS
SELFEXPLANATORY
CRYSTALLOGRAPHY
CHURRIGUERESQUE
ATTORNEYGENERAL
GOVERNORGENERAL
PERPENDICULARLY
CONSCIENTIOUSLY
INCONSPICUOUSLY
INSTANTANEOUSLY
ONYCHOCRYPTOSIS
SANCTIMONIOUSLY
SURREPTITIOUSLY
UNCEREMONIOUSLY
BATTERYOPERATED
ELECTROMAGNETIC
GASTROENTERITIS
IMPRESSIONISTIC
INDIVIDUALISTIC
NONGOVERNMENTAL
OVERSENTIMENTAL
POLYUNSATURATED
PRESTIDIGITATOR
SACRAMENTMYSTIC
UNSOPHISTICATED
GLEICHSCHALTUNG
GOTTERDAMMERUNG
REPRESENTATIVES

15:14

ANTHROPOLOGICAL
ATTORNEYGENERAL
BACTERIOLOGICAL
BIBLIOGRAPHICAL
CHRISTADELPHIAN
CONFRONTATIONAL
ENTREPRENEURIAL
GOVERNORGENERAL
INCONSEQUENTIAL
NONGOVERNMENTAL
NONPROFESSIONAL
OMNIDIRECTIONAL
OVERSENTIMENTAL
PARLIAMENTARIAN
PHARMACOLOGICAL
TRIGONOMETRICAL
CHARACTERISTICS
MISINTELLIGENCE
PHOSPHORESCENCE
SELFSUFFICIENCY
RHYNCHOBDELLIDA
BATTERYOPERATED
FLIBBERTIGIBBET
MALPRACTITIONER
NONCOMMISSIONED
POLYUNSATURATED
REPRESENTATIVES
THUNDERSTRICKEN
UNDERPRIVILEGED
UNDISTINGUISHED
UNSOPHISTICATED
WELLESTABLISHED
CRYSTALLOGRAPHY
ALLOTRIOMORPHIC
ANTHROPOMORPHIC
CINEMATOGRAPHIC
DRAUGHTSMANSHIP
ELECTROMAGNETIC
GASTROENTERITIS
IMPRESSIONISTIC
INDIVIDUALISTIC
ONYCHOCRYPTOSIS
RUMPELSTILTSKIN
SACRAMENTMYSTIC
STREPHOSYMBOLIA
AUTHORITATIVELY
CHRONOLOGICALLY
COMPASSIONATELY
CONSCIENTIOUSLY
CORRESPONDINGLY
DISPASSIONATELY
DISTINGUISHABLE
EUPHEMISTICALLY
EXTRAORDINARILY
INCONSIDERATELY
INCONSPICUOUSLY
INSTANTANEOUSLY

INTERCHANGEABLE
INTERNATIONALLY
PERPENDICULARLY
PESSIMISTICALLY
PHILOSOPHICALLY
PROPORTIONATELY
PSYCHOLOGICALLY
SANCTIMONIOUSLY
SURREPTITIOUSLY
SYMPATHETICALLY
TECHNOLOGICALLY
TEMPERAMENTALLY
THERAPEUTICALLY
UNCEREMONIOUSLY
UNCOMPANIONABLE
UNCONDITIONALLY
UNEXCEPTIONABLE
UNPRONOUNCEABLE
ACKNOWLEDGEMENT
AIRCONDITIONING
BACKWARDLOOKING
CONGRATULATIONS
DISILLUSIONMENT
GLEICHSCHALTUNG
GOTTERDAMMERUNG
LEATHERSTOCKING
LIFETHREATENING
NONPROFITMAKING
NOTWITHSTANDING
PROCRASTINATING
SCHOOLMASTERING
TRINITROTOLUENE
UNCOMPREHENDING
UNPREPOSSESSING
ACCLIMATIZATION
CIRCUMSCRIPTION
COMPUTERIZATION
CONTRAVALLATION
CRYSTALLIZATION
DECONTAMINATION
DESERTIFICATION
DIFFERENTIATION
DISSATISFACTION
DIVERSIFICATION
ELECTRIFICATION
EXCOMMUNICATION
EXPERIMENTATION
FAMILIARIZATION
HOSPITALIZATION
INCOMPHEHENSION
INDEMNIFICATION
INSTRUMENTATION
INSUBORDINATION
INTENSIFICATION
MISAPPREHENSION
MISCONSTRUCTION
NATIONALIZATION
PERSONIFICATION
PRESTIDIGITATOR
PROCRASTINATION

PROGNOSTICATION
PROSELYTIZATION
RATIONALIZATION
STANDARDIZATION
SYNCHRONIZATION
TRANSFIGURATION
TRANSLITERATION
PLENIPOTENTIARY
SELFEXPLANATORY
STRAIGHTFORWARD
UNCOMPLIMENTARY
UNPARLIAMENTARY
ACQUISITIVENESS
ADVENTUROUSNESS
AGRICULTURALIST
CONSERVATIONIST
DESTRUCTIVENESS
INQUISITIVENESS
INSTRUMENTALIST
INTERVENTIONIST
LONGSIGHTEDNESS
MISCHIEVOUSNESS
NOTHINGARIANISM
OPHTHALMOLOGIST
PALAEONTOLOGIST
PHYSIOTHERAPIST
PRETENTIOUSNESS
PROFESSIONALISM
PSYCHOTHERAPIST
PUNCTILIOUSNESS
RESOURCEFULNESS
STANDOFFISHNESS
SUBLAPSARIANISM
THOUGHTLESSNESS
TOTALITARIANISM
TRUSTWORTHINESS
UNCONSCIOUSNESS
UNRIGHTEOUSNESS
CIRCUMSTANTIATE
CONFIDENTIALITY
ICHTHYODUROLITE
IMPENETRABILITY
INCOMPATIBILITY
INTELLIGIBILITY
LOPHOBRANCHIATE
MANOEUVRABILITY
SCAPHOCEPHALATE
STILPNOSIDERITE
CHURRIGUERESQUE
COINSTANTANEOUS
CONTEMPORANEOUS
DISADVANTAGEOUS
ORNITHORHYNCHUS
UNCOMMUNICATIVE
UNDEMONSTRATIVE

15:15

RHYNCHOBDELLIDA
STREPHOSYMBOLIA
ALLOTRIOMORPHIC
ANTHROPOMORPHIC
CINEMATOGRAPHIC
ELECTROMAGNETIC
IMPRESSIONISTIC
INDIVIDUALISTIC
SACRAMENTMYSTIC
BATTERYOPERATED
NONCOMMISSIONED
POLYUNSATURATED
STRAIGHTFORWARD
UNDERPRIVILEGED
UNDISTINGUISHED
UNSOPHISTICATED
WELLESTABLISHED
CHURRIGUERESQUE
CIRCUMSTANTIATE
DISTINGUISHABLE
ICHTHYODUROLITE
INTERCHANGEABLE
LOPHOBRANCHIATE
MISINTELLIGENCE
PHOSPHORESCENCE
SCAPHOCEPHALATE
STILPNOSIDERITE
TRINITROTOLUENE
UNCOMMUNICATIVE
UNCOMPANIONABLE
UNDEMONSTRATIVE
UNEXCEPTIONABLE
UNPRONOUNCEABLE
AIRCONDITIONING
BACKWARDLOOKING
GLEICHSCHALTUNG
GOTTERDAMMERUNG
LEATHERSTOCKING
LIFETHREATENING
NONPROFITMAKING
NOTWITHSTANDING
PROCRASTINATING
SCHOOLMASTERING
UNCOMPREHENDING
UNPREPOSSESSING
ANTHROPOLOGICAL
ATTORNEYGENERAL
BACTERIOLOGICAL
BIBLIOGRAPHICAL
CONFRONTATIONAL
ENTREPRENEURIAL
GOVERNORGENERAL
INCONSEQUENTIAL
NONGOVERNMENTAL
NONPROFESSIONAL
OMNIDIRECTIONAL
OVERSENTIMENTAL

PHARMACOLOGICAL
TRIGONOMETRICAL
NOTHINGARIANISM
PROFESSIONALISM
SUBLAPSARIANISM
TOTALITARIANISM
ACCLIMATIZATION
CHRISTADELPHIAN
CIRCUMSCRIPTION
COMPUTERIZATION
CONTRAVALLATION
CRYSTALLIZATION
DECONTAMINATION
DESERTIFICATION
DIFFERENTIATION
DISSATISFACTION
DIVERSIFICATION
ELECTRIFICATION
EXCOMMUNICATION
EXPERIMENTATION
FAMILIARIZATION
HOSPITALIZATION
INCOMPHEHENSION
INDEMNIFICATION
INSTRUMENTATION
INSUBORDINATION
INTENSIFICATION
MISAPPREHENSION
MISCONSTRUCTION
NATIONALIZATION
PARLIAMENTARIAN
PERSONIFICATION
PROCRASTINATION
PROGNOSTICATION
PROSELYTIZATION
RATIONALIZATION
RUMPELSTILTSKIN
STANDARDIZATION
SYNCHRONIZATION
THUNDERSTRICKEN
TRANSFIGURATION
TRANSLITERATION
DRAUGHTSMANSHIP
MALPRACTITIONER
PRESTIDIGITATOR
ACQUISITIVENESS
ADVENTUROUSNESS
CHARACTERISTICS
COINSTANTANEOUS
CONGRATULATIONS
CONTEMPORANEOUS
DESTRUCTIVENESS
DISADVANTAGEOUS
GASTROENTERITIS
INQUISITIVENESS
LONGSIGHTEDNESS
MISCHIEVOUSNESS
ONYCHOCRYPTOSIS
ORNITHORHYNCHUS
PRETENTIOUSNESS

PUNCTILIOUSNESS
REPRESENTATIVES
RESOURCEFULNESS
STANDOFFISHNESS
THOUGHTLESSNESS
TRUSTWORTHINESS
UNCONSCIOUSNESS
UNRIGHTEOUSNESS
ACKNOWLEDGEMENT
AGRICULTURALIST
CONSERVATIONIST
DISILLUSIONMENT
FLIBBERTIGIBBET
INSTRUMENTALIST
INTERVENTIONIST
OPHTHALMOLOGIST
PALAEONTOLOGIST
PHYSIOTHERAPIST
PSYCHOTHERAPIST
AUTHORITATIVELY
CHRONOLOGICALLY
COMPASSIONATELY
CONFIDENTIALITY
CONSCIENTIOUSLY
CORRESPONDINGLY
CRYSTALLOGRAPHY
DISPASSIONATELY
EUPHEMISTICALLY
EXTRAORDINARILY
IMPENETRABILITY
INCOMPATIBILITY
INCONSIDERATELY
INCONSPICUOUSLY
INSTANTANEOUSLY
INTELLIGIBILITY
INTERNATIONALLY
MANOEUVRABILITY
PERPENDICULARLY
PESSIMISTICALLY
PHILOSOPHICALLY
PLENIPOTENTIARY
PROPORTIONATELY
PSYCHOLOGICALLY
SANCTIMONIOUSLY
SELFEXPLANATORY
SELFSUFFICIENCY
SURREPTITIOUSLY
SYMPATHETICALLY
TECHNOLOGICALLY
TEMPERAMENTALLY
THERAPEUTICALLY
UNCEREMONIOUSLY
UNCOMPLIMENTARY
UNCONDITIONALLY
UNPARLIAMENTARY

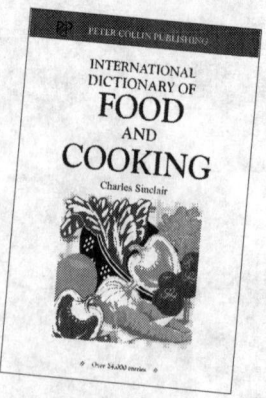